THE RYRIE STUDY BIBLE

NEW AMERICAN STANDARD TRANSLATION

With introductions, annotations, outlines, marginal references, harmony of the Gospels, synopsis of Bible doctrine, index of Scripture, index to notes, concordance, maps and timeline charts, and many other helps

CHARLES CALDWELL RYRIE, Th.D., Ph.D.

Professor of Systematic Theology
Dallas Theological Seminary

MOODY PRESS

CHICAGO

©1976, 1978 by
THE MOODY BIBLE INSTITUTE
OF CHICAGO

The Scripture text of the New American Standard Bible and marginal references are sed by permission of The Lockman Foundation, a corporation not for profit, La Habra, Cibrnia, ©1960, 1962, 1963, 1968, 1971, 1972, 1973, 1975, 1977. All rights reserved.

Library of Congress Cataloging in Publication Data

Bible. English. New American standard. 1978.
The Ryrie study Bible.

I. Ryrie, Charles Caldwell.   II. Title.
BS195.N35   1978   220.5'204   76-20615

ISBN 0-8024-7471-3 Cloth
ISBN 0-8024-7425-X Cloth (red letter)
ISBN 0-8024-7491-8 Brown Bonded Leather
ISBN 0-8024-7426-8 Brown Bonded Leather (red letter)
ISBN 0-8024-7492-6 Burgundy Bonded Leather
ISBN 0-8024-7427-6 Burgundy Bonded Leather (red letter)
ISBN 0-8024-7472-1 Black Leather
ISBN 0-8024-7473-X Blue Leather
ISBN 0-8024-7474-8 Brown Leather
ISBN 0-8024-7476-4 Black Cowhide
ISBN 0-8024-7477-2 Blue Cowhide
ISBN 0-8024-7478-0 Brown Cowhide
ISBN 0-8024-7428-4 Brown Cowhide (red letter)
ISBN 0-8024-7480-2 Blue Cowhide Deluxe
ISBN 0-8024-7481-0 Burgundy Cowhide Deluxe
ISBN 0-8024-7482-9 Brown Cowhide Deluxe
ISBN 0-8024-7487-X Burgundy Morocco
ISBN 0-8024-7488-8 Blue Morocco
ISBN 0-8024-7429-2 Blue Morocco (red letter)
ISBN 0-8024-7485-3 Blue Pinseal
ISBN 0-8024-7495-0 Blue Cowhide Indexed
ISBN 0-8024-7493-4 Blue Cowhide Deluxe Indexed
ISBN 0-8024-7494-2 Burgundy Cowhide Deluxe Indexed

Designer: Ernst Reichl
Cover Design: Ray Lahikainen

Printed in the United States of America

CONTENTS

THE INSPIRATION OF THE BIBLE
1955

UNDERSTANDING THE BIBLE
1959

HOW WE GOT OUR BIBLE
1961

THE MEANING AND BLESSINGS OF SALVATION
1963

BETWEEN THE TESTAMENTS
1967

ARCHAEOLOGY AND THE BIBLE
1970

THE MIRACLES OF JESUS
1973

THE PARABLES OF JESUS
1974

TABLES OF WEIGHTS, MEASURES AND COINS
1975

THROUGH THE BIBLE IN A YEAR
1977

TOPICAL INDEX OF SCRIPTURE
1979

INDEX TO THE PRINCIPAL SUBJECTS
IN THE NOTES
1991

CONCORDANCE
1999

MAPS AND TIMELINE CHARTS

TO THE READER

The Bible is the greatest of all books; to study it is the noblest of all pursuits; to understand it, the highest of all goals. The *Ryrie Study Bible* is especially designed to help you achieve that goal.

Every time you read this Bible, whether carefully or casually, be sure to look at the notes at the bottom of the page. These are designed to illuminate and help you understand the verses you are reading. The notes provide a variety of helps: some furnish historical or archaeological background; others translate or interpret the text more clearly; some define words and doctrines; and many refer you to other passages which relate to the same subject.

When you wish to study a book of the Bible more systematically, you will want to read the Introduction to that book, which will give you information about the author, background, and contents. A unique feature of this Bible is the outline of each book printed at the end of each Introduction and also interspersed throughout the text. You can readily see as you are reading through a book exactly where you are in the development of the ideas of that book by simply referring to the complete outline in the Introduction.

The Introductions will help lead you into the messages of the books; the outlines will help you see the development of the messages; and the notes will help shed light on the messages.

In addition, you will find at the back of the Bible an index of the principal subjects treated in the notes, a synopsis of Bible doctrine, and a concordance. There is also a Harmony of the Gospels for use when you want to locate the several accounts of an event in the Gospels. Finally, the maps and timelines will enable you to see where and when biblical events took place.

Useful as helps can be, the most important thing is to read the Bible itself. This is God's Word to you. I pray that these notes will serve to make it clearer and more personally meaningful.

CHARLES CALDWELL RYRIE, Th.D., Ph.D.

HOW TO USE THIS STUDY BIBLE

Congratulations! You are obviously serious about studying Scripture, since you invested in this study Bible. How can you get the most out of your investment?

First, you must use it. The most important and often the most difficult step in Bible study is simply opening the book to read it. Where should you read first? That is not a question with a universal answer, for each person's likes and needs are different. If you have never seriously studied the Bible, you might feel more comfortable reading first one of the shorter books of the New Testament, such as 1 Thessalonians, Philippians, or 1 John. If you want to start with a Gospel, read Mark's fast-moving account of the life of Christ. If you like action, try Acts. If you are studying a particular book in a Bible class or if your pastor is preaching through a book, use that as a basis for your own in-depth study. Whatever book you choose, read it in its entirety first, then do some detailed study in it before starting another one. Hit-or-miss reading usually misses more than it hits!

Second, read and study wisely. The Bible is God's message to us; therefore, read to understand what He is clearly saying, not to discover some supposed hidden meaning.

To do this, you need (1) to understand the meaning of the words you are reading. Some are explained in the notes of this study Bible. Others you may have to look up in an English dictionary, which is one of the most important tools to have within reach when you study the Bible. For still other words, you may want to consult a good Bible dictionary. But do not go on until you understand what you have already read. Take the meaning of the words in their normal, natural, and usual sense. That is the way we speak, the way we read other literature, and the way God intended His word to be read and understood.

You need also (2) to grasp the main point of each paragraph or section. You are using a well-outlined Bible, so notice what the headings in the outline tell you about the contents of each section. Summarize the main points in your own words and write those summaries in the margin or above or below the printed outlines. As you proceed through a book, look back frequently to the entire outline at the beginning of the book in order to check your bearings.

You want also (3) to correlate the teaching of the particular section you are studying with other parts of Scripture. For example, the note on Matthew 1:19 mentions the subject of divorce without developing it. So you would be wise to look in the index of subjects in the back and read the notes on the references listed there on divorce. Sometimes a note will tell you where a particular word is used elsewhere in the New Testament (there is such a note on 1 Thessalonians 4:11). If so, take time to look up those other references and write in the margin enough to remind you of the substance of those references. The next time you read that verse, your eye will see those reminders, and you will not have to look up the references again.

Of course, you want (4) to hear God speak to *you* through what you are studying. But do not be tempted to see "deeper" meanings or try to discover hidden ideas that no one else has ever seen! Do not invent some "message" that is not in the text in order to justify an idea you have or course of action you want to take. In the plain meaning of the text there is ample material for the Holy Spirit to use to speak to you and meet your individual needs. Further, the more you study, the greater reservoir of Bible truth you build up from which the Spirit can draw to correct, encourage, and guide you.

Here are some additional ideas for using this study Bible:

1. Write in the margins the meanings of words you look up, so the next time you read the passage you will not have to look them up again.
2. Write a summary word or phrase of the contents of sections.
3. Write a key word or phrase that conveys a principal idea in that chapter. If you memorize those words, you will be able to think your way through an entire book. For instance, you might write "genealogy of Christ" for Matthew 1; "wise men" for chapter 2; and "John the Baptist" for chapter 3.
4. Do not underline or circle a word or phrase simply because at the time it seemed to say something to you. Write the *reason* you underlined it in the margin. For instance, if you underline *save* in Matthew 1:21, note that it is connected with the meaning of "Jesus," as explained in the note on Matthew 1:1.
5. Indicate relevant cross references not listed in the printed helps, and jot down a word or two to remind you what the cross reference says. For example, in connection with the marginal references on Matthew 1:21 you may write "virgin birth" by Luke 1:31, "circumcision" by Luke 2:21, "Lamb of God" by John 1:29, and "Son of David" by Acts 13:23.
6. Use the margins to preserve, in condensed form, any good idea you hear or read.
7. Briefly note personal applications of texts in the margin. Later, as you read those texts again, you will be reminded of commitments you made to the Lord.

I wrote the study helps in this Bible to meet a variety of needs of many people, and within a limited space. It is my prayer that, over the years, these notes, along with those you add, will make this Bible the most useful and valuable one you own.

C. C. R.

The grass withers, the flower fades, but the word of our God stands forever.
(Isaiah 40:8)

FOREWORD

The New American Standard Bible has been produced with the conviction that the words of Scripture as originally penned in the Hebrew and Greek were inspired by God. Since they are the eternal Word of God, the Holy Scriptures speak with fresh power to each generation, to give wisdom that leads to salvation, that men may serve Christ to the glory of God.

The Editorial Board had a twofold purpose in making this translation: to adhere as closely as possible to the original languages of the Holy Scriptures, and to make the translation in a fluent and readable style according to current English usage.

PREFACE TO THE NEW AMERICAN STANDARD BIBLE

In the history of English Bible translations, the King James Version is the most prestigious. This time-honored version of 1611, itself a revision of the Bishops' Bible of 1568, became the basis for the English Revised Version appearing in 1881 (New Testament) and 1885 (Old Testament). The American counterpart of this last work was published in 1901 as the American Standard Version. Recognizing the values of the American Standard Version, the Lockman Foundation felt an urgency to update it by incorporating recent discoveries of Hebrew and Greek textual sources and by rendering it into more current English. Therefore, in 1959 a new translation project was launched, based on the ASV. The result is the New American Standard Bible.

The American Standard Version (1901) has been highly regarded for its scholarship and accuracy. A product of both British and American scholarship, it has frequently been used as a standard for other translations. It is still recognized as a valuable tool for study of the Scriptures. The New American Standard Bible has sought to preserve these and other lasting values of the ASV.

Furthermore, in the preparation of this work numerous other translations have been consulted along with the linguistic tools and literature of biblical scholarship. Decisions about English renderings were made by consensus of a team composed of educators and pastors. Subsequently, review and evaluation by other Hebrew and Greek scholars outside the Editorial Board were sought and carefully considered.

The Editorial Board has continued to function since publication of the complete Bible in 1971. Minor revisions and refinements, recommended over the last five years, are presented in this edition.

PRINCIPLES OF TRANSLATION

Modern English Usage: The attempt has been made to render the grammar and terminology in contemporary English. When it was felt that the word-for-word literalness was unacceptable to the modern reader, a change was made in the direction of a more current English idiom.

Hebrew Text: In the present translation the latest edition of Rudolph Kittel's *Biblia Hebraica* has been employed together with the most recent light from lexicography, cognate languages, and the Dead Sea Scrolls.

Hebrew Tenses: Consecution of tenses in Hebrew remains a puzzling factor in translation. The translators have been guided by the requirements of a literal translation, the sequence of tenses, and the immediate and broad contexts.

The Proper Name of God in the Old Testament: In the Scriptures, the name of God is most significant and understandably so. It is inconceivable to think of spiritual matters without a proper designation for the Supreme Deity. Thus the most common name for deity is God, a translation of the Hebrew *Elohim.* The normal word for Master is Lord, a rendering of *Adonai.* There is yet another name which is particularly assigned to God as His special or proper name, that is, the four letters YHWH (Exodus 3:14 and Isaiah 42:8). This name has not been pronounced by the Jews because of reverence for the great sacredness of the divine name. Therefore, it was consistently pronounced and translated LORD. The only exception to this translation of YHWH is when it occurs in immediate proximity to the word Lord, that is, *Adonai.* In that case it is regularly translated GOD in order to avoid confusion.

It is known that for many years YHWH has been transliterated as Yahweh, however no complete certainty attaches to this pronunciation.

Greek Text: Consideration was given to the latest available manuscripts with a view to determining the best Greek text. In most instances the 23rd edition of the Nestle Greek New Testament was followed.

Greek Tenses: A careful distinction has been made in the treatment of the Greek aorist tense (usually translated as the English past, "He did") and the Greek imperfect tense (rendered either as English past progressive, "He was doing"; or, if inceptive, as "He *began* to do" or "He started to do"; or else if customary past, as "He used to do"). "Began" is italicized if it renders an imperfect tense, in order to distinguish it from the Greek verb for "begin."

On the other hand, not all aorists have been rendered as English pasts ("He did"), for some of them are clearly to be rendered as English perfects ("He has done"), or even as past perfects ("He had done"), judging from the context in which they occur. Such aorists have been rendered as perfects or past perfects in this translation.

As for the distinction between aorist and present imperatives, the translators have usually rendered these imperatives in the customary manner, rather than attempting any such fine distinction as "Begin to do!" (for the aorist imperative), or, "Continually do!" (for the present imperative).

As for sequence of tenses, the translators took care to follow English rules rather than Greek in translating Greek presents, imperfects and aorists. Thus, where English says, "We knew that he was doing," Greek puts it, "We knew that he does"; similarly, "We knew that he had done" is the Greek, "We knew that he did." Likewise, the English, "When he had come, they met him," is represented in Greek by: "When he came, they met him." In all cases a consistent transfer has been made from the Greek tense in the subordinate clause to the appropriate tense in English.

In the rendering of negative questions introduced by the particle **mē** (which always expects the answer, "No") the wording has been altered from a mere, "Will he not do this?" to a more accurate, "He will not do this, will he?"

Editorial Board
THE LOCKMAN FOUNDATION

EXPLANATION OF GENERAL FORMAT
OF THE NEW AMERICAN STANDARD BIBLE

Cross References are placed in the outside columns of the page and are listed under verse numbers to which they refer. Superior letters refer to cross references. Cross references in italics are parallel passages.

Paragraphs are designated by bold face numbers or letters.

Quotation Marks are used in the text in accordance with modern English usage.

"Thou," "Thee" and *"Thy"* are not used in this translation except in the language of prayer when addressing Deity.

Personal Pronouns are capitalized when pertaining to Deity.

Italics are used in the text to indicate words which are not found in the original Hebrew or Greek but implied by it.

Small Caps in the New Testament are used in the text to indicate Old Testament quotations or obvious allusions to Old Testament texts. Variations of Old Testament wording are found in New Testament citations depending on whether the New Testament writer translated from a Hebrew text, used existing Greek or Aramaic translations, or paraphrased the material. It should be noted that modern rules for the indication of direct quotation were not used in biblical times thus allowing freedom for omissions or insertions without specific indication of these.

Asterisk—In regard to the use in Greek of the historical present, the translators recognized that in some contexts the present tense seems more unexpected and unjustified to the English reader than a past tense would have been. But Greek authors frequently used the present tense for the sake of heightened vividness, thereby transporting their readers in imagination to the actual scene at the time of occurrence. However, the translators felt that it would be wise to change these historical presents to English past tenses. Therefore verbs marked with an asterisk (*) represent historical presents in the Greek which have been translated with an English past tense in order to conform to modern usage.

ABBREVIATIONS AND SPECIAL MARKINGS

A.D.	*Anno Domini* (in the year of our Lord)
B.C.	Before Christ
cf.	*confer* (compare)
chap(s).	chapter(s)
e.g.	*exempli gratia* (for example)
f., ff.	following verse or verses
i.e.	*id est* (that is)
Lit.	A literal translation, literally
LXX	The Septuagint (Greek translation of the Old Testament)
ms., mss.	manuscript, manuscripts
N.T.	New Testament
O.T.	Old Testament
p., pp.	page, pages
ref(s).	reference(s)
v., vv.	verse, verses
[ ]	Brackets in the text are around words probably not in the original writings.
★	A five-pointed star preceding a verse or verses in the marginal notes indicates that this passage is treated in the footnotes.

THE NAMES AND ORDER OF THE BOOKS OF THE BIBLE

Old Testament

New Testament

The Old Testament
Annotated

INTRODUCTION TO THE OLD TESTAMENT

The Bible is a Book of books, sixty-six of them, divided into two testaments, or covenants. The designations *Old Testament* and *New Testament,* though not commonly used until the end of the second century, focus on the two great covenants God made with His people: the Mosaic Covenant (Exod. 24:8; 2 Kings 23:2) and the New Covenant (Matt. 26:28).

The Old Testament mainly records God's dealings with the people of Israel on the basis of the covenant He made with them through Moses on Mt. Sinai. Earlier parts of the Old Testament tell of the creation of man, the Flood, the call of Abraham, and the delimiting of the people of Israel through the line of Isaac and Jacob.

After the account of the establishing of the Mosaic covenant, the Old Testament records the history of God's relationship with Israel: their wilderness wanderings, their incomplete conquest of the land of Canaan; their life under judges and kings, including the division of the nation into northern and southern kingdoms; the many prophetic warnings of impending captivity; the captivities; and the return of Judah to Palestine. Throughout the Old Testament there extends a line of prophecies concerning a coming Deliverer-Saviour, the Messiah, and the institution of a new covenant. The fulfillment of these prophecies is the story of the New Testament.

THE DIVISION OF THE BOOKS OF THE OLD TESTAMENT

Probably the earliest division of the Old Testament was into two parts (see Matt. 5:18): the Law (Genesis—Deuteronomy) and the Prophets (Joshua—Malachi). A threefold division also developed (see Luke 24:44): the Law (Genesis—Deuteronomy), the Prophets (Joshua, Judges, Samuel, Kings, Isaiah, Jeremiah, Ezekiel, the twelve minor prophets), and the Writings (the remaining books). Our English Old Testament is divided as follows: the Law (Genesis—Deuteronomy), History (Joshua—Esther), Poetry (Job—Song of Solomon), and the Prophets (Isaiah—Malachi). The content of the English and Hebrew Old Testaments is identical, though the arrangement of the books differs.

THE ORDER OF EVENTS IN THE BOOKS OF THE OLD TESTAMENT

The arrangement of the books of the Old Testament does not follow the chronological order in which the recorded events occurred. The following listing shows which books cover approximately the same periods of time.

Genesis	Job
Exodus	Leviticus
Numbers	Deuteronomy
Joshua	
Judges	Ruth
1 Samuel	
2 Samuel	Psalms

1 Kings	1 Chronicles, Song of Solomon, Proverbs, Ecclesiastes
2 Kings	2 Chronicles, Obadiah, Joel, Jonah, Amos, Hosea, Micah, Isaiah, Nahum, Zephaniah, Habakkuk, Jeremiah, Lamentations
Daniel	Ezekiel
Ezra	Esther, Haggai, Zechariah
Nehemiah	Malachi

The Collecting of the Books of the Old Testament

The collecting and recognition of the books of the Old Testament took considerable time. Some believe the process was finished by the time of Ezra, in the fifth century B.C. References by Josephus (ca. A.D. 95) and in 2 Esdras 14 (ca. A.D. 100) indicate that the Hebrew scriptures then contained the same thirty-nine books as our Old Testament. The records of the teaching-house at Jamnia (A.D. 70–100) seem to reflect the same canon.

Most significant, however, is the statement of the Lord (Luke 11:51) in which He delimited the extent of the canonical books of the Old Testament when He accused the scribes of being guilty of slaying all the prophets God had sent Israel from the time of Abel to the time of Zechariah. Abel's death is recorded in Genesis; Zechariah's in 2 Chronicles 24:20-21, which is the last book in the Hebrew Bible (rather than Malachi, as in our English Bibles). Jesus was saying that the Jews' guilt was recorded from the beginning to the end of the Hebrew scriptures. He excluded all of the Apocrypha, all of which was in existence at that time.

Between the Testaments

During the four hundred years between the close of the Old Testament revelation and the coming of Christ, several important events occurred. (1) The Greeks under Alexander the Great and his successors ruled the world for a time. (2) Under the Maccabees, the Jews revolted and attempted to break away from the rule of the Greeks. (3) The Roman empire succeeded the Greek and ruled the known world when Christ was born. (4) The Jewish synagogue, the Sanhedrin, and sects such as the Pharisees and Sadducees developed. All of these events and developments set the stage for the birth and ministry of Jesus Christ and for the birth and early growth of His Church.

INTRODUCTION TO
THE BOOK OF GENESIS

AUTHOR: Moses   DATE: 1450-1410 B.C.

Title *The English word* genesis *comes, by way of Latin, from the Greek title to this book. In Hebrew, the book was named from its first word, which means "in the beginning." Genesis means "origin" and thus is an apt title for a book that reveals the origins of all human history.*

Authorship *Genesis is the first book of a larger work, the first five books of the O.T., called the Pentateuch, the authorship of which has traditionally been ascribed to Moses. This is supported by the following considerations: (1) the Pentateuch itself affirms Moses as its author (Exod. 17:14; 24:4, 7; 34:27; Num. 33:1-2; Deut. 31:9); (2) other O.T. books testify to the Mosaic authorship of the Pentateuch (Josh. 1:7-8; 8:32, 34; 22:5; 1 Kings 2:3; 2 Kings 14:6; 21:8; Ezra 6:18; Dan. 9:11-13; Mal. 4:4); (3) the N.T. affirms the same (Matt. 19:8; Mark 12:26; John 5:46-47; 7:19; Rom. 10:5); (4) eyewitness details point to a participant being the author, not an editor who lived centuries later (Exod. 15:27; Num. 2:1-31; 11:7-8); (5) the author's information about Egyptian names, words, customs, and geography would have been difficult for an author or editor to have obtained in Canaan centuries after Moses' time (Gen. 13:10; 16:1-3; 33:18; 41:43; cf. Acts 7:22).*

The critical view of the authorship of the Pentateuch has passed through several stages. At first, Genesis was divided into two documents on the basis of the use of the two different names for God: Elohim and Yahweh. About 1875, Julius Wellhausen argued for four documents from which the entire Pentateuch was compiled. These were: J, written about 850 B.C. by an unknown writer in Judah; E, written about 750 B.C. by an unknown writer in the Northern Kingdom of Israel; D, composed by the high priest at the time of the revival under King Josiah in 621 B.C.; and P, composed from the time of Ezekiel to Ezra. Archaeological discoveries, however, many since World War I, have demonstrated the historical accuracy of the Pentateuch and have brought to light customs practiced in the second millennium B.C. that were not practiced in the first millennium B.C. How, then, would an author have known of these customs (e.g., the double portion going to the oldest son, the sale of a birthright, the validity of an oral will; cf. Gen. 48:17-20) unless he had lived during that earlier period?

Undoubtedly, Moses had both oral and written records of early history, which he used under the guidance of the Holy Spirit to write about events that antedated his own life. Naturally, someone else must have written the account of his death (Deut. 34).

Contents *Genesis is a real life history of individual people, a fact which is emphasized by the ten sections (following the prologue, 1:1-2:3) that usually begin "these are the records of the generations of" (6:9; 10:1; 11:10; 11:27; 25:12; 25:19; 36:1; 37:2; cf. 2:4; 5:1). This thrust provides a natural unity to the book (cf. Luke 3:23-38).*

Genesis is a book about the beginning of many things: the world, man, sin, civilization, the nations, and Israel.

Genesis also contains important theological themes: the doctrine of the living, personal God; the doctrine of man made in the image of God, then of sinful man; the anticipation of a Redeemer (3:15); and the covenant promises made to the nation Israel (12:1-3; 15:18-21).

Genesis is a book unique among all Near Eastern literature and foundational to all the other books of the Bible.

OUTLINE OF GENESIS

I. **The Creation of the World, 1:1-2:25**
A. The Beginning of Creation, 1:1-2
B. The Days of Creation, 1:3-2:3
C. The Beginnings of Man and Woman, 2:4-25
II. **The Sin of Man, 3:1-24**
A. The Temptation, 3:1-7
B. The Judgments, 3:8-24
III. **The Beginnings of Civilization, 4:1-5:32**
A. Cain and his Descendants, 4:1-24

B. Seth, 4:25-26
C. Adam to Noah, 5:1-32
IV. **The History of Noah, 6:1-9:29**
A. The Causes of the Flood, 6:1-13
B. The Course of the Flood, 6:14-8:19
C. The Events after the Flood, 8:20-9:29
V. **The Descendants of Noah, and the Tower of Babel, 10:1-11:26**
A. The Sons of Japheth, 10:1-5
B. The Sons of Ham, 10:6-20

THE BOOK OF GENESIS

I THE CREATION OF THE WORLD, 1:1–2:25

A The Beginning of Creation, 1:1–2

★ 1 aPs. 102:25; Is. 40:21; John 1:1, 2; Heb. 1:10 bPs. 90:2; Acts 17:24; Rom. 1:20; Heb. 11:3 cJob 38:4; Is. 42:5; 45:18; Rev. 4:11

1 ᵃIn the beginning ᵇGod ᶜcreated the heavens and the earth.

★ 2 aJer. 4:23 bJob 38:9 cPs. 104:30 dDeut. 32:11

2 And the earth was ᵃformless and void, and ᵇdarkness was over the surface of the deep; and ᶜthe Spirit of God ᵈwas moving over the surface of the waters.

B The Days of Creation, 1:3–2:3

★ 3 aPs. 33:6, 9; 2 Cor. 4:6

3 Then ᵃGod said, "Let there be light"; and there was light.

★ 4 aPs. 145:9, 10 bIs. 45:7

4 And God saw that the light was ᵃgood; and God ᵇseparated the light from the darkness.

★ 5 aPs. 74:16 bPs. 65:8

5 And ᵃGod called the light day, and the darkness He called night. And ᵇthere was evening and there was morning, one day.

★ 6 aIs. 40:22; Jer. 10:12; 2 Pet. 3:5

6 Then God said, "Let there be an ᵃexpanse in the midst of the

---

1:1 *In the beginning*, not of eternity, but of the creation of the world as described in this chapter. This marks the first break in the past endless eternity. *God.* Lit., *Elohim*, a generic term for deity as well as a proper name for the true God. It is used of pagan gods (Gen. 31:30; Exod. 12:12), angels (Psalm 8:5), men (Psalm 82:6), and judges (Exod. 21:6), though most frequently of the true God. Its basic meaning is strong one, mighty leader, supreme Deity. The form of the word is plural, indicating plentitude of power and majesty and allowing for the N.T. revelation of the triunity of the Godhead. Cf. note on Gen. 2:4. *created.* Heb., *bara*, used also in verses 21 and 27. The word itself does not preclude the use of preexisting material (Isa. 65:18), though none is mentioned or implied here (cf. other occurrences in Psalm 51:10; Isa. 65:17; Amos 4:13). *Bara* means essentially the same as *asa*, "to do or make" (used in Gen. 1:25 and also of the entire creative activity in Exod. 20:11 and Neh. 9:6). A third word for God's creative activity, *yasar* ("formed"), occurs in Gen. 2:7. *the heavens and the earth.* I.e., the universe.

1:2 *the earth was formless and void.* Some understand a "gap" of an indeterminate period of time between verses 1 and 2, and translate "became" rather than "was." While the Hebrew word may mean "became" (as in Gen. 19:26), the construction of the clause does not support a consecutive statement describing something that happened subsequent to verse 1 ("and") but rather describing something included in verse 1 ("but"). In other words, the initial creation was formless and empty, a condition soon remedied (see note on Isa. 45:18).

The phrase means that at this point in God's creative activity the earth was yet unfashioned and uninhabited. *the deep.* Not a reference to the mythological Babylonian monster Tiamat, as has been alleged, but simply "waters." *was moving.* I.e., hovered in the sense of protecting and participating in the creative work (the same Hebrew word is used in Deut. 32:11).

1:3 *light.* Not the sun (which was created on the fourth day, v. 16), but some fixed light source outside the earth. In reference to that light, the rotating earth passed through a day-night cycle.

1:4 *God separated.* The first of three separations. Here, light from darkness; then sky from water (v. 7); and finally, the land from the seas (v. 9). Only when this spatial separation was complete did God pronounce everything good (v. 10).

1:5 *And there was evening and there was morning, one day.* Better, "day one." Later Jewish reckoning began the day with eventide (Lev. 23:32). This may be the reason for the order here, or it may simply mean that one day-night cycle was completed. Since daytime closes at evening and the night ends with the morning, the phrase indicates that the first day and night had been completed. Evening and morning cannot be construed to mean an age, but only a day; everywhere in the Pentateuch the word *day*, when used (as here) with a numerical adjective, means a solar day (now calibrated as 24 hours).

1:6 *an expanse.* From a verb meaning "to beat out and spread out"; i.e., the open expanse of the heavens, which appeared as a vast canopy or tent above the earth.

waters, and let it separate the waters from the waters."

★ 7 a Job 38:8-11 b Ps. 148:4

7 And God made the expanse, and separated ᵃthe waters which were below the expanse from the waters ᵇwhich were above the expanse; and it was so.

8 And God called the expanse heaven. And there was evening and there was morning, a second day.

9 a Ps. 104:6-9; Jer. 5:22; 2 Pet. 3:5 b Ps. 24:1, 2; 95:5

9 Then God said, "ᵃLet the waters below the heavens be gathered into one place, and let ᵇthe dry land appear"; and it was so.

★10 a Ps. 33:7; 95:5; 146:6

10 And God called the dry land earth, and the ᵃgathering of the waters He called seas; and God saw that it was good.

★11 a Ps. 65:9-13; 104:14; Heb. 6:7

11 Then God said, "Let the earth sprout ᵃvegetation, plants yielding seed, and fruit trees bearing fruit after their kind, with seed in them, on the earth"; and it was so.

12 And the earth brought forth vegetation, plants yielding seed after their kind, and trees bearing fruit, with seed in them, after their kind; and God saw that it was good.

13 And there was evening and there was morning, a third day.

★14-19

14 a Ps. 74:16; 136:7 b Ps. 19:1; 150:1 c Jer. 10:2 d Ps. 104:19

14 Then God said, "Let there be ᵃlights in the ᵇexpanse of the heavens to separate the day from the night, and let them be for ᶜsigns, and for ᵈseasons, and for days and years;

15 and let them be for lights in the expanse of the heavens to give light on the earth"; and it was so.

16 a Ps. 136:8, 9 b Job 38:7; Ps. 8:3; Is. 40:26

16 And God made the two great lights, the ᵃgreater light to govern the day, and the lesser light to govern the night; He made ᵇthe stars also.

17 a Jer. 33:20, 25

17 ᵃAnd God placed them in the expanse of the heavens to give light on the earth,

18 a Jer. 31:35

18 and to ᵃgovern the day and the night, and to separate the light from the darkness; and God saw that it was good.

19 And there was evening and there was morning, a fourth day.

20 Then God said, "Let the waters teem with swarms of living creatures, and let birds fly above the earth in the open expanse of the heavens."

★21 a Ps. 104:25-28

21 And God created ᵃthe great sea monsters, and every living creature that moves, with which the waters swarmed after their kind, and every winged bird after its kind; and God saw that it was good.

22 And God blessed them, saying, "Be fruitful and multiply, and fill the waters in the seas, and let birds multiply on the earth."

23 And there was evening and there was morning, a fifth day.

★24 a Gen. 2:19; 6:20; 7:14; 8:19

24 ᵃThen God said, "Let the earth bring forth living creatures after their kind: cattle and creeping things and beasts of the earth after their kind"; and it was so.

1:7 *the waters which were above the expanse.* Apparently God suspended a vast body of water in vapor form over the earth, making a canopy that caused conditions on the earth to resemble those inside a greenhouse. This may account for the longevity of human life (Gen. 5) and for the tremendous amount of water involved in the worldwide flood (Gen. 6-9).

1:10 *God called.* The act of naming this and other parts of the creation was, in the Semitic world, an evidence of lordship (cf. 2 Kings 23:34). Note the significance of this in Gen. 2:19.

1:11 *after their kind.* There are fixed boundaries beyond which reproductive variations cannot go, but it is impossible to know whether "kind" is to be equated with families, genera, or some other category of biological classification.

1:14-19 The light source of the first day was replaced by the sun and moon. Their purposes were to distinguish day and night, to be signs (by which men get their bearings, as well as signs of judgment, Matt. 24:29), to mark off the seasons, and to give light to the earth.

1:21 *good.* I.e., beautiful and in perfect ecological balance.

1:24 *cattle.* I.e., large, domesticated quadrupeds. *creeping things.* I.e., creatures that move on the earth or close to it, having no legs or, at best, only short ones (e.g., worms, insects, and reptiles).

25 *a*Gen. 7:21, 22; Jer. 27:5

25 And God made the *a*beasts of the earth after their kind, and the cattle after their kind, and everything that creeps on the ground after its kind; and God saw that it was good.

★**26** *a*Gen. 3:22; 11:7 *b*Gen. 5:1; 9:6; 1 Cor. 11:7; Eph. 4:24; James 3:9 *c*Ps. 8:6-8

26 Then God said, "Let *a*Us make *b*man in Our image, according to Our likeness; and let them *c*rule over the fish of the sea and over the birds of the sky and over the cattle and over all the earth, and over every creeping thing that creeps on the earth."

★**27** *a*Gen. 5:1f.; 1 Cor. 11:7; Eph. 4:24; Col. 3:10 *b*Matt. 19:4; Mark 10:6

27 And God created man *a*in His own image, in the image of God He created him; *b*male and female He created them.

★**28** *a*Gen. 9:1, 7; Lev. 26:9; Ps. 127:3, 5

28 And God blessed them; and God said to them, "*a*Be fruitful and multiply, and fill the earth, and subdue it; and rule over the fish of the sea and over the birds of the sky, and over every living thing that moves on the earth."

★**29** *a*Ps. 104:14; 136:25

29 Then God said, "Behold, *a*I have given you every plant yielding seed that is on the surface of all the earth, and every tree which has fruit yielding seed; it shall be food for you;

30 *a*Ps. 145:15, 16; 147:9

30 and *a*to every beast of the earth and to every bird of the sky and to every thing that moves on the earth which has life, *I have given* every green plant for food"; and it was so.

31 And God saw all that He had made, and behold, it was very *a*good. And there was evening and there was morning, the sixth day.

31 *a*Ps. 104:24, 28; 119:68; 1 Tim. 4:4

2 Thus the heavens and the earth were completed, and all *a*their hosts.

★**1** *a*Deut. 4:19; 17:3

2 And by *a*the seventh day God completed His work which He had done; and *b*He rested on the seventh day from all His work which He had done.

★**2** *a*Ex. 20:8-11; 31:17 *b*Heb. 4:4, 10

3 Then God blessed the seventh day and sanctified it, because in it He rested from all His work which God had created and made.

C The Beginnings of Man and Woman, 2:4-25

4 *a*This is the account of the heavens and the earth when they were created, in *b*the day that the LORD God made earth and heaven.

★**4** *a*Job 38:4-11 *b*Gen. 1:3-31

5 *a*Now no shrub of the field was yet in the earth, and no plant of the field had yet sprouted, *b*for

★**5** *a*Gen. 1:11 *b*Ps. 65:9, 10; Jer. 10:12, 13

1:26 *Us . . . Our.* Plurals of majesty. *image . . . likeness.* Interchangeable terms (5:3) indicating that man was created in a natural and moral likeness to God. When he sinned, he lost the moral likeness, which was his sinlessness, but the natural likeness of intellect, emotions, and will he still retains (cf. Gen. 9:6; James 3:9).

1:27 *man.* The word is used generically here, then amplified by the phrase *male and female* (although Eve's physical formation is not detailed until 2:18-23).

1:28 *fill.* The word cannot be used to support the idea of a refilling of the earth after destruction of an earlier civilization, as some theories hold.

1:29 Man was not given meat to eat until after the Flood (Gen. 9:3).

2:1 *their hosts.* In Neh. 9:6, the same Hebrew word depicts "stars"; and in 1 Kings 22:19, it refers to angels. Here, it probably means simply all the things that God created.

2:2 *He rested.* I.e., He ceased or desisted from His work. No weariness is implied. The Hebrew word is *sabbath*, the name of the day which later was given to Israel as a time of cessation from normal activities (Exod. 16:29; 20:10-11; Deut. 5:15; Jer. 17:21; Amos 8:5).

2:4 *in the day.* The creation week is not specified as a single day by this phrase; rather, without the article "the," it means "at the time." *the LORD.* Lit., *YHWH* (probably pronounced "Yahweh"), the most significant name for God in the O.T. It has a twofold meaning: the active, self-existent One (since the word is connected with the verb meaning "to be," Exod. 3:14); and Israel's Redeemer (Exod. 6:6). The name occurs 6,823 times in the O.T. and is especially associated with God's holiness (Lev. 11:44-45), His hatred of sin (Gen. 6:3-7), and His gracious provision of redemption (Isa. 53:1, 5, 6, 10).

2:5 This sentence may begin at verse 4b, "At the time the LORD God made the earth and the heavens, then no shrub of the field was as yet in the earth . . ." The kind of plants referred to here are those requiring cultivation, which (though green plants appeared the third day, 1:11-12) did not grow until after there was a man to take care of them.

the LORD God had not sent rain upon the earth; and there was no man to cultivate the ground.

★ 6　　6 But a mist used to rise from the earth and water the whole surface of the ground.

★ 7 aGen.
3:19 b1 Cor.
15:45

7 Then the LORD God formed man of adust from the ground, and breathed into his nostrils the breath of life; and bman became a living being.

★ 8 aGen.
13:10; Is.
51:3; Ezek.
28:13

8 And the LORD God planted a agarden toward the east, in Eden; and there He placed the man whom He had formed.

★ 9 aEzek.
47:12 bGen.
3:22; Rev.
2:7; 22:2, 14

9 And out of the ground the LORD God caused to grow aevery tree that is pleasing to the sight and good for food; bthe tree of life also in the midst of the garden, and the tree of the knowledge of good and evil.

10 aPs. 46:4

10 Now a ariver flowed out of Eden to water the garden; and from there it divided and became four rivers.

★11 aGen.
25:18

11 The name of the first is Pishon; it flows around the whole land of aHavilah, where there is gold.

★12

12 And the gold of that land is good; the bdellium and the onyx stone are there.

13 And the name of the second river is Gihon; it flows around the whole land of Cush.

14 aDan.
10:4 bGen.
15:18

14 And the name of the third river is aTigris; it flows east of Assyria. And the fourth river is the bEuphrates.

15 Then the LORD God took the man and put him into the garden of Eden to cultivate it and keep it.

16 And the LORD God acommanded the man, saying, "From any tree of the garden you may eat freely;

16 aGen.
3:2, 3

17 but from the tree of the knowledge of good and evil you shall not eat, for in the day that you eat from it ayou shall surely die."

17 aDeut.
30:15, 19,
20; Rom.
6:23; 1 Tim.
5:6; James
1:15

18 Then the LORD God said, "It is not good for the man to be alone; aI will make him a helper suitable for him."

★18 a1 Cor.
11:9

19 And aout of the ground the LORD God formed every beast of the field and every bird of the sky, and bbrought them to the man to see what he would call them; and whatever the man called a living creature, that was its name.

19 aGen.
1:24 bGen.
1:26

20 And the man gave names to all the cattle, and to the birds of the sky, and to every beast of the field, but for Adam there was not found aa helper suitable for him.

★20 aGen.
2:18

21 So the LORD God caused a adeep sleep to fall upon the man, and he slept; then He took one of his ribs, and closed up the flesh at that place.

★21 aGen.
15:12

22 And the LORD God fashioned into a woman athe rib which He had taken from the man, and brought her to the man.

22 a1 Cor.
11:8, 9

23 And the man said, "aThis is now bone of my bones,

★23 aGen.
29:14; Eph.
5:28, 29

2:6 *a mist.* Probably caused by daily evaporation and condensation, which occurred because of the change in temperature between daytime and nighttime; cf. note on 1:7.

2:7 Man's body was formed from small particles of the earth (the Hebrew words for man and earth are similar, cf. 1 Cor. 15:47), but his life came from the breath of God. *a living being.* I.e., a living person. The phrase is also used of animals (Gen. 1:21, 24). Man is distinguished from animals by being created in the image of God.

2:8 *toward the east, in Eden.* Apparently somewhere in Mesopotamia (modern Iraq), since two of the four rivers in its vicinity are the well-known Tigris and Euphrates, verse 14. *Eden* means "delight."

2:9 *the tree of life . . . and the tree of the knowledge of good and evil* were two actual trees to which God gave special significance.

2:11 The exact locations are not certain.

2:12 *bdellium.* A precious gum resin. *onyx.* A nontransparent variety of agate.

2:18 *a helper suitable.* I.e., to him, his counterpart (cf. 1 Cor. 11:9).

2:20 *gave names.* See note on 1:10.

2:21 *ribs.* Though elsewhere the Hebrew word means "side," here it means "rib" (and doubtless includes the surrounding flesh, cf. v. 23).

2:23 *Woman.* Heb., *ishshah,* similar to *ish* (man), reflecting the fact that woman was derived from man (though the word itself may come from a root meaning "to be soft").

And flesh of my flesh;
She shall be called
Woman,
Because she was taken
out of Man."

★24 aMatt.
19:5; Mark
10:7, 8;
1 Cor. 6:16;
Eph. 5:31

24 ªFor this cause a man shall leave his father and his mother, and shall cleave to his wife; and they shall become one flesh.

25 aGen.
3:7, 10, 11

25 ªAnd the man and his wife were both naked and were not ashamed.

II THE SIN OF MAN, 3:1-24
A The Temptation, 3:1-7

★ 1 a2 Cor.
11:3; Rev.
12:9; 20:2

3 Now ªthe serpent was more crafty than any beast of the field which the Lord God had made. And he said to the woman, "Indeed, has God said, 'You shall not eat from any tree of the garden'?"

2 aGen.
2:16, 17

2 And the woman said to the serpent, "ªFrom the fruit of the trees of the garden we may eat;

3 but from the fruit of the tree which is in the middle of the garden, God has said, 'You shall not eat from it or touch it, lest you die.'"

4 aJohn
8:44; 2 Cor.
11:3

4 ªAnd the serpent said to the woman, "You surely shall not die!

5 aIs.
14:14; Ezek.
28:2; 12-17

5 "For God knows that in the day you eat from it your eyes will be opened, and ªyou will be like God, knowing good and evil."

★ 6 aRom.
5:12-19;
1 Tim. 2:14;
James 1:14,
15; 1 John
2:16

6 ªWhen the woman saw that the tree was good for food, and that it was a delight to the eyes, and that the tree was desirable to make one wise, she took from its fruit and ate; and she gave also to her husband with her, and he ate.

7 Then the eyes of both of them were opened, and they ªknew that they were naked; and they sewed fig leaves together and made themselves loin coverings.

★ 7 aIs.
47:3; Lam.
1:8

B The Judgments, 3:8-24

8 And they heard the sound of ªthe Lord God walking in the garden in the cool of the day, ᵇand the man and his wife hid themselves from the presence of the Lord God among the trees of the garden.

★ 8 aGen.
18:33; Lev.
26:12; Deut.
23:14 bJob
31:33; Ps.
139:1-12;
Hos. 10:8;
Amos 9:3;
Rev. 6:15-17

9 Then the Lord God called to the man, and said to him, "ªWhere are you?"

9 aGen.
4:9; 18:9

10 And he said, "ªI heard the sound of Thee in the garden, and I was afraid because I was naked; so I hid myself."

10 aEx.
20:18, 19;
Deut. 5:25

11 And He said, "Who told you that you were naked? Have you eaten from the tree of which I commanded you not to eat?"

12 ªAnd the man said, "The woman whom Thou gavest to be with me, she gave me from the tree, and I ate."

12 aJob
31:33; Prov.
28:13

13 Then the Lord God said to the woman, "What is this you have done?" And the woman said,

13 a2 Cor.
11:3; 1 Tim.
2:14

2:24 This verse emphasizes the complete identification of the two personalities in marriage. The passage tells us that God instituted marriage and that it is to be monogamous, heterosexual, and the complete union of the two persons. Jesus added that it is to be permanent (cf. Mark 10:7-9).

3:1 the serpent. Apparently a beautiful creature, in its uncursed state, that Satan used in the temptation. more crafty. I.e., clever, not in a degrading sense at this point. he said. Satan spoke through the serpent. Perhaps Eve did not realize animals could not speak; at any rate, she was not alarmed. from any tree of the garden. The question was designed to suggest that God was not good and fair since He restricted the eating of the fruit of one of the trees.

3:6 The three areas of Eve's self-deception are in the same categories of temptation as those found in 1 John 2:16. Eve was deceived; Adam ate knowingly (cf. 1 Tim. 2:14). Their sin was more than merely eating forbidden fruit; it was disobeying the revealed word of God, believing the lie of Satan, and placing their own wills above God's. Sin, with all its dreadful consequences, now entered the human race and the world in general (see note on Rom. 5:12).

3:7 A keen sense of guilt immediately followed the act of sinning.

3:8 hid themselves. Their intimate fellowship with God was broken.

"ªThe serpent deceived me, and I ate."

★14 ªDeut.
28:15-20 ᵇIs.
65:25; Mic.
7:17

14 And the LORD God said to the serpent,

"ªBecause you have done this,
Cursed are you more than all cattle,
And more than every beast of the field;
On your belly shall you go,
And ᵇdust shall you eat
All the days of your life;

★15 ªRev.
12:17 ᵇRom.
16:20

15 And I will put ªenmity
Between you and the woman,
And between your seed and her seed;
ᵇHe shall bruise you on the head,
And you shall bruise him on the heel."

★16 ªJohn
16:21; 1 Tim.
2:15 ᵇ1 Cor.
14:34

16 To the woman He said,
"I will greatly multiply
Your pain in childbirth,
In pain you shall ªbring forth children;
Yet your desire shall be for your husband,
And ᵇhe shall rule over you."

★17-19

17 ªGen.
5:29; Rom.
8:20-22;
Heb. 6:8
ᵇJob 5:7;
14:1; Eccl.
2:23

17 Then to Adam He said,
"Because you have listened to the voice of your wife, and have eaten from the tree about which I commanded you, saying, 'You shall not eat from it';
ªCursed is the ground because of you;

ᵇIn toil you shall eat of it
All the days of your life.

18 "Both thorns and thistles
it shall grow for you;
And you shall eat the plants of the field;

19 By the sweat of your face
You shall eat bread,
Till you ªreturn to the ground,
Because ᵇfrom it you were taken;
For you are dust,
And to dust you shall return."

19 ªPs. 90:3;
104:29; Eccl.
12:7 ᵇGen.
2:7

20 Now the man called his wife's name ªEve, because she was the mother of all *the* living.

★20 ª2 Cor.
11:3; 1 Tim.
2:13

21 And the LORD God made garments of skin for Adam and his wife, and clothed them.

★21

22 Then the LORD God said, "Behold, the man has become like one of ªUs, knowing good and evil; and now, lest he stretch out his hand, and take also from ᵇthe tree of life, and eat, and live forever"—

★22-24

22 ªGen.
1:26 ᵇGen.
2:9; Rev.
22:14

23 therefore the LORD God sent him out from the garden of Eden, to cultivate the ground from which he was taken.

24 So ªHe drove the man out; and at the ᵇeast of the garden of Eden He stationed the ᶜcherubim, and the flaming sword which turned every direction, to guard the way to ᵈthe tree of life.

24 ªEzek.
31:11 ᵇGen.
2:8 ᶜEx.
25:18-22; Ps.
104:4; Ezek.
10:1-20;
Heb. 1:7
ᵈGen. 2:9

3:14 The entire animal kingdom was affected by man's fall (cf. Jer. 12:4; Rom. 8:20), but the serpent's very form and movements were altered and he was humbled (*dust shall you eat* is a symbol of humiliation, not an item of diet, cf. Mic. 7:17; Isa. 65:25).

3:15 *between your seed* (the spiritual descendants of Satan, cf. John 8:44; Eph. 2:2) *and her seed* (those who are in the family of God). *He.* An individual from among the woman's seed, namely, Christ, will deal a death blow to Satan's *head* at the cross, while Satan (*you*) would *bruise* Christ's *heel* (cause Him to suffer).

3:16 Women were condemned to suffer in childbearing. See note on 1 Tim. 2:15. At the same time, the wife would have a deep attraction to her husband, perhaps to compensate for the sorrow of childbirth. *he shall rule over you.* See Eph. 5:23.

3:17-19 Man is condemned to exhausting labor, in order to make a living, because of a curse on the ground (Adam worked before his fall).

3:20 *Eve* = life or life-producer.

3:21 The *garments of skin* were God's provision for restoring Adam's and Eve's fellowship with Himself and imply slaying of an animal in order to provide them.

3:22-24 Driving Adam and Eve from the garden was both a punishment and an act of mercy, lest they should eat of the tree of life and live forever in a state of death and alienation. *cherubim.* See notes on Ezek. 1:5 and Rev. 4:6.

III THE BEGINNINGS OF CIVILIZATION,
4:1–5:32
A Cain and his Descendants, 4:1–24

★ 1 **4** Now the man had relations with his wife Eve, and she conceived and gave birth to Cain, and she said, "I have gotten a manchild with *the help of* the LORD."

★ 2 *a*Luke 11:50, 51 *b*Gen. 46:32; 47:3

2 And again, she gave birth to his brother Abel. And *a*Abel was *b*a keeper of flocks, but Cain was a tiller of the ground.

★ 3 3 So it came about in the course of time that Cain brought an offering to the LORD of the fruit of the ground.

★ 4 *a*Heb. 11:4 *b*1 Sam. 15:22

4 And *a*Abel, on his part also brought of the firstlings of his flock and of their fat portions. And *b*the LORD had regard for Abel and for his offering;

5 *a*1 Sam. 16:7 *b*Is. 3:9; Jude 11

5 but *a*for Cain and for his offering He had no regard. So *b*Cain became very angry and his countenance fell.

6 *a*Jon. 4:4

6 Then the LORD said to Cain, "*a*Why are you angry? And why has your countenance fallen?

★ 7 *a*Jer. 3:12; Mic. 7:18 *b*Num. 32:23 *c*Job 11:14, 15; Rom. 6:12, 16

7 "*a*If you do well, will not *your countenance* be lifted up? *b*And if you do not do well, sin is crouching at the door; and its desire is for you, *c*but you must master it."

★ 8 *a*Matt. 23:35; Luke 11:51; 1 John 3:12-15; Jude 11

8 And Cain told Abel his brother. And it came about when they were in the field, that Cain rose up against Abel his brother and *a*killed him.

9 *a*Gen. 3:9

9 Then the LORD said to Cain, "*a*Where is Abel your brother?" And he said, "I do not know. Am I my brother's keeper?"

★10 *a*Num. 35:33; Deut. 21:1-9; Heb. 12:24; Rev. 6:9, 10

10 And He said, "What have you done? *a*The voice of your brother's blood is crying to Me from the ground.

11 *a*Gen. 3:14; Deut. 28:15-20; Gal. 3:10

11 "And now *a*you are cursed from the ground, which has opened its mouth to receive your brother's blood from your hand.

12 *a*Deut. 28:15-24; Joel 1:10-20 *b*Lev. 26:17, 36

12 "*a*When you cultivate the ground, it shall no longer yield its strength to you; *b*you shall be a vagrant and a wanderer on the earth."

13 And Cain said to the LORD, "My punishment is too great to bear!

14 *a*Gen. 3:24; Jer. 52:3 *b*Deut. 28:64-67 *c*Num. 35:19

14 "Behold, Thou hast *a*driven me this day from the face of the ground; and from Thy face I shall be hidden; and *b*I shall be a vagrant and a wanderer on the earth, and it will come about that *c*whoever finds me will kill me."

★15 *a*Gen. 4:24 *b*Ezek. 9:4, 6

15 So the LORD said to him, "Therefore whoever kills Cain, vengeance will be taken on him *a*sevenfold." And the LORD *b*appointed a sign for Cain, lest anyone finding him should slay him.

★16 *a*2 Kin. 24:20; Jer. 23:39; 52:3

16 Then Cain went out from the presence *a*of the LORD, and settled in the land of Nod, east of Eden.

★17 17 And Cain had relations

4:1 *had relations.* Lit., knew; a common euphemism for sexual relations. In Hebrew, *Cain* (*qayin*) and *I have gotten* (*qaniti*) represent a play on words. The meaning of Cain is probably "spear."

4:2 *Abel* means "breath" or "vanity," reflecting perhaps Eve's understanding of the import of the curse (Rom. 8:20).

4:3 *of the fruit of the ground.* A bloodless offering was perfectly appropriate (cf. Lev. 2:1, 4, 14, 15); it was Cain's attitude of unbelief that displeased God.

4:4 See Heb. 11:4.

4:7 Cain is promised restored fellowship if he does well; but if not, the effects of *sin* are ready to pounce (*is crouching*) on him.

4:8 See 1 John 3:12.

4:10 *your brother's blood is crying to Me.* I.e.,

for vengeance.

4:15 *And the LORD appointed a sign for Cain.* Not some kind of mark on Cain, but a sign to reassure him of God's gracious protection of his life.

4:16 *Nod* means "wandering," "exile." It was an area *east of Eden.*

4:17 *his wife.* Obviously a daughter of Adam (cf. 5:4). She may have been Cain's sister, niece, or even grand-niece. Since Adam's and Eve's genetic systems had no mutant genes in them, such a marriage would not be dangerous as it is today. *Enoch* means "consecration" or "initiation," a new beginning for Cain. *city.* Lit., a permanent settlement, perhaps an attempt on Cain's part to neutralize God's curse on him (v. 12). This was not necessarily the first city or settlement.

with his wife and she conceived, and gave birth to Enoch; and he built a city, and called the name of the city Enoch, after the name of his son.

18 Now to Enoch was born Irad; and Irad became the father of Mehujael; and Mehujael became the father of Methushael; and Methushael became the father of Lamech.

★19 *a*Gen.
2:24

19 And Lamech took to himself *a*two wives: the name of the one was Adah, and the name of the other, Zillah.

20 And Adah gave birth to Jabal; he was the father of those who dwell in tents and *have* livestock.

21 And his brother's name was Jubal; he was the father of all those who play the lyre and pipe.

22 As for Zillah, she also gave birth to Tubal-cain, the forger of all implements of bronze and iron; and the sister of Tubal-cain was Naamah.

★23-24

23 *a*Ex.
20:13; Lev.
19:18; Deut.
32:35; Ps.
94:1

23 And Lamech said to his wives,

"Adah and Zillah,
Listen to my voice,
You wives of Lamech,
Give heed to my speech,
*a*For I have killed a man
for wounding me;
And a boy for striking
me;

24 *a*Gen.
4:15

24 If Cain is avenged *a*sevenfold,
Then Lamech seventy-sevenfold."

B Seth, 4:25-26

25 And *a*Adam had relations with his wife again; and she gave birth to a son, and named him Seth, for, *she said,* "God has appointed me another offspring in place of Abel; *b*for Cain killed him."

★25 *a*Gen.
5:3 *b*Gen.
4:8

26 And to Seth, to him also *a*a son was born; and he called his name Enosh. Then *men* began *b*to call upon the name of the LORD.

26 *a*Luke
3:38 *b*Gen.
12:8; 26:25;
1 Kin. 18:24;
Ps. 116:17;
Joel 2:32;
Zeph. 3:9;
1 Cor. 1:2

C Adam to Noah, 5:1-32

5 This is the book of the generations of Adam. In the day when God created man, He made him *a*in the likeness of God.

★1 *a*Gen.
1:26, 27;
Eph. 4:24;
Col. 3:10

2 He created them *a*male and female, and He *b*blessed them and named them Man in the day when they were created.

2 *a*Matt.
19:4; Mark
10:6 *b*Gen.
1:28

3 When Adam had lived one hundred and thirty years, he became the father of *a son* in his own likeness, according to his image, and named him Seth.

★3

4 Then the days of Adam after he became the father of Seth were eight hundred years, and he had *other* sons and daughters.

5 So all the days that Adam lived were nine hundred and thirty years, and he died.

6 And Seth lived one hundred and five years, and became the father of Enosh.

4:19 This bigamy was the first recorded violation of God's pattern of monogamy.

4:23-24 Lamech had killed someone who tried to kill him; now he was boasting that if anyone should try to avenge the murder, he would take care of himself *seventy-sevenfold,* without any help from God, such as Cain received.

4:25 *Seth* means "the appointed one," the substitute (for slain Abel).

5:1 *This is the book . . .* Cf. 2:4; 6:9; 10:1; 11:10, 27; 25:12, 19; 36:1; 37:2 for other occurrences of this phrase. The word *book* may indicate the written source that Moses used in composing Genesis. *In the day.* Better, at the time; cf. 2:4.

5:3 *his own likeness.* Now sinful, in contrast to

1:26. Each reference to a patriarch gives four details: (1) his name, (2) his age at the birth of his first son, (3) the length of his remaining life, and (4) his age at death. There are variations in the cases of Adam (v. 3), Enoch (vv. 22, 24), and Lamech (vv. 28-29). The longevity of the patriarchs (averaging 912 years, not including Enoch who did not die) may have been due to the canopy (see note on 1:7), which was not dispersed until the Flood, or simply to the fact that it took some time for the effects of sin to shorten man's life span. If there are no gaps in this chronology, then 1,656 years elapsed between creation and the Flood. It is possible, however, that the genealogy is selective, resulting in gaps in the list and pushing the date of creation farther back.

7 Then Seth lived eight hundred and seven years after he became the father of Enosh, and he had *other* sons and daughters.

8 So all the days of Seth were nine hundred and twelve years, and he died.

9 And Enosh lived ninety years, and became the father of Kenan.

10 Then Enosh lived eight hundred and fifteen years after he became the father of Kenan, and he had *other* sons and daughters.

11 So all the days of Enosh were nine hundred and five years, and he died.

12 And Kenan lived seventy years, and became the father of Mahalalel.

13 Then Kenan lived eight hundred and forty years after he became the father of Mahalalel, and he had *other* sons and daughters.

14 So all the days of Kenan were nine hundred and ten years, and he died.

15 And Mahalalel lived sixty-five years, and became the father of Jared.

16 Then Mahalalel lived eight hundred and thirty years after he became the father of Jared, and he had *other* sons and daughters.

17 So all the days of Mahalalel were eight hundred and ninety-five years, and he died.

18 And Jared lived one hundred and sixty-two years, and became the father of Enoch.

19 Then Jared lived eight hundred years after he became the father of Enoch, and he had *other* sons and daughters.

20 So all the days of Jared were nine hundred and sixty-two years, and he died.

21 And Enoch lived sixty-five years, and became the father of Methuselah.

22 Then Enoch ªwalked with God three hundred years after he became the father of Methuselah, and he had *other* sons and daughters.

23 So all the days of Enoch were three hundred and sixty-five years.

24 And ªEnoch walked with God; and he was not, for God ᵇtook him.

25 And Methuselah lived one hundred and eighty-seven years, and became the father of Lamech.

26 Then Methuselah lived seven hundred and eighty-two years after he became the father of Lamech, and he had *other* sons and daughters.

27 So all the days of Methuselah were nine hundred and sixty-nine years, and he died.

28 And Lamech lived one hundred and eighty-two years, and became the father of a son.

29 Now he called his name Noah, saying, "This one shall give us rest from our work and from the toil of our hands *arising from* ªthe ground which the LORD has cursed."

30 Then Lamech lived five hundred and ninety-five years after he became the father of Noah, and he had *other* sons and daughters.

31 So all the days of Lamech were seven hundred and seventy-seven years, and he died.

32 And Noah was ªfive hundred years old, and Noah became the father of Shem, Ham, and Japheth.

IV THE HISTORY OF NOAH, 6:1–9:29
A The Causes of the Flood,
6:1–13

6 Now it came about, when ★1 men began to multiply on the

★22-24

22 ªGen. 6:9; 17:1; 24:40; 48:15; Mic. 6:8; Mal. 2:6; 1 Thess. 2:12

24 ª2 Kin. 2:11; Jude 14 ᵇ2 Kin. 2:10; Ps. 49:15; 73:24; Heb. 11:5

★29 ªGen. 3:17-19; 4:11

32 ªGen. 7:6

5:22-24 Enoch is an exception to the dismal refrain ("and he died") of this chapter. He *walked* (lit., walked about, i.e., lived) *with God,* and instead of letting him die, *God took him* (the same Hebrew word is used for the translation of Elijah, 2 Kings 2:3, 5; cf. Heb. 11:5). In other words, Enoch went directly to heaven without dying. See also note on Jude 14.

5:29 *shall give us rest.* I.e., by preserving a remnant in the ark. Christ would eventually come and give ultimate victory over the curse.

6:1 The earth's population grew rapidly with the longevity of men.

face of the land, and daughters were born to them,

★ 2   2   that the sons of God saw that the daughters of men were beautiful; and they took wives for themselves, whomever they chose.

★ 3 ªGal.
5:16, 17;
1 Pet. 3:20   3   Then the LORD said, "ªMy Spirit shall not strive with man
ᵇPs. 78:39   forever, ᵇbecause he also is flesh; nevertheless his days shall be one hundred and twenty years."

★ 4 ªNum.
13:33   4   The ªNephilim were on the earth in those days, and also afterward, when the sons of God came in to the daughters of men, and they bore *children* to them. Those were the mighty men who *were* of old, men of renown.

5 ªGen.
8:21; Ps.
14:1-3; Prov.
6:18; Matt.
15:19; Rom.
1:28-32   5   Then the LORD saw that the wickedness of man was great on the earth, and that ªevery intent of the thoughts of his heart was only evil continually.

★ 6 ªGen.
6:7; Jer.
18:7-10 ᵇIs.
63:10; Eph.
4:30   6   And ªthe LORD was sorry that He had made man on the earth, and He was ᵇgrieved in His heart.

7 ªDeut.
28:63; 29:20
ᵇGen. 6:6;
Amos 7:3, 6   7   And the LORD said, "ªI will blot out man whom I have created from the face of the land, from man to animals to creeping things and to birds of the sky; for ᵇI am sorry that I have made them."

★ 8 ªMatt.
24:37; Luke
17:26; 1 Pet.
3:20 ᵇGen.
19:19; Ex.
33:17; Luke
1:30   8   But ªNoah ᵇfound favor in the eyes of the LORD.

9   These are *the records of* the generations of Noah. Noah was a ªrighteous man, ᵇblameless in his time; Noah ᶜwalked with God.

10   And Noah became the father of three sons: Shem, Ham, and Japheth.

11   Now the earth was ªcorrupt in the sight of God, and the earth was ᵇfilled with violence.

12   And God looked on the earth, and behold, it was corrupt; for ªall flesh had corrupted their way upon the earth.

13   Then God said to Noah, "ªThe end of all flesh has come before Me; for the earth is filled with violence because of them; and behold, I am about to destroy them with the earth.

B   The Course of the Flood, 6:14–8:19

14   "Make for yourself an ark of gopher wood; you shall make the ark with rooms, and shall cover it inside and out with pitch.

15   "And this is how you shall make it: the length of the ark three hundred cubits, its breadth fifty cubits, and its height thirty cubits.

★ 9 ªPs.
37:39; 2 Pet.
2:5 ᵇGen.
17:1; Deut.
18:13; Job
1:1 ᶜGen.
5:24

11 ªDeut.
31:29; Judg.
2:19 ᵇEzek.
8:17

12 ªPs.
14:1-3

13 ªIs. 34:1-
4; Ezek. 7:2,
3; Amos 8:2;
1 Pet. 4:7

★14

★15

6:2 *the sons of God.* Possibly the godly line of Seth, or ungodly kings and kinglets of that day, or, more likely, a group of fallen angels who, because of this unique sin, were confined (see notes on 2 Pet. 2:4 and Jude 6). The phrase "sons of God" is used in the O.T. almost exclusively of angels (Job 1:6; 2:1; 38:7). *took wives for themselves.* Angels do not procreate after their kind (Mark 12:25), but if these were angels, they did on this unique occasion cohabit with human women to produce human offspring.

6:3 *My Spirit shall not strive with man forever.* Two interpretations are possible. (1) The reference is to the Holy Spirit striving in the sense of judging or executing judgment on mankind for its sinfulness. (2) The human spirit that God placed in human beings would not always abide; i.e., mankind was doomed to death. Man was given 120 years after this warning before the judgment of the Flood.

6:4 *Nephilim.* From a root meaning "to fall"; i.e., to fall upon others because they were men of strength (only other use of this Hebrew word is in Num. 13:33). Evidently they were in the

earth before the marriages of Gen. 6:2, and were not the offspring of those marriages from which came the *mighty men* (military men) and *men of renown* (of wealth or power).

6:6 *it repented the LORD.* Better, the Lord was sorry (not that God changed His mind).

6:8 *favor.* Or grace. Heb., *chen*, from a root meaning "to bend or stoop," thus condescending or unmerited favor of a superior person to an inferior one. It is sometimes used redemptively (Jer. 31:2; Zech. 12:10). This is its first occurrence. Cf. the note on lovingkindness at Hos. 2:19.

6:9 *righteous . . . blameless.* I.e., mature or well-rounded, though not sinless.

6:14 *gopher wood.* Probably cypress or cedar.

6:15 Although we do not know the exact length of the cubit at this time, later it was about 18 inches (see note on 2 Chron. 32:30), making the ark 450 feet long, 75 feet broad, and 45 feet high, with a displacement of about 20,000 tons and gross tonnage of about 14,000 tons. Its carrying capacity equaled that of 522 standard railroad stock cars (each of which can hold 240 sheep). Only 188 cars would be re-

*16

16 "You shall make a window for the ark, and finish it to a cubit from the top; and set the door of the ark in the side of it; you shall make it with lower, second, and third decks.

17 *a*2 Pet. 2:5

17 "And behold, *a*I, even I am bringing the flood of water upon the earth, to destroy all flesh in which is the breath of life, from under heaven; everything that is on the earth shall perish.

18 *a*Gen. 9:9-16; 17:7 *b*Gen. 7:7

18 "But I will establish *a*My covenant with you; and *b*you shall enter the ark—you and your sons and your wife, and your sons' wives with you.

19 *a*Gen. 7:2, 14, 15

19 "*a*And of every living thing of all flesh, you shall bring two of every *kind* into the ark, to keep *them* alive with you; they shall be male and female.

20 *a*Gen. 7:3

20 "*a*Of the birds after their kind, and of the animals after their kind, of every creeping thing of the ground after its kind, two of every *kind* shall come to you to keep *them* alive.

21 *a*Gen. 1:29, 30

21 "And as for you, take for yourself some of all *a*food which is edible, and gather *it* to yourself; and it shall be for food for you and for them."

22 *a*Gen. 7:5; Heb. 11:7

22 *a*Thus Noah did; according to all that God had commanded him, so he did.

1 *a*Gen. 6:9

7 Then the LORD said to Noah, "Enter the ark, you and all your household; for you *alone* I have seen *to be* *a*righteous before Me in this time.

★ 2 *a*Lev. 11:1-31; Deut. 14:3-20

2 "You shall take with you of every *a*clean animal by sevens, a male and his female; and of the animals that are not clean two, a male and his female;

3 also of the birds of the sky, by sevens, male and female, to keep offspring alive on the face of all the earth.

4 "For after *a*seven more days, I will send rain on the earth *b*forty days and forty nights; and I will blot out from the face of the land *c*every living thing that I have made."

★ 4 *a*Gen. 7:10 *b*Gen. 7:12, 17 *c*Gen. 6:7, 13

5 *a*And Noah did according to all that the LORD had commanded him.

5 *a*Gen. 6:22

6 Now Noah was *a*six hundred years old when the flood of water came upon the earth.

6 *a*Gen. 5:32

7 Then *a*Noah and his sons and his wife and his sons' wives with him entered the ark because of the water of the flood.

7 *a*Gen. 6:18; 7:13; Matt. 24:38f.; Luke 17:27

8 *a*Of clean animals and animals that are not clean and birds and everything that creeps on the ground,

8 *a*Gen. 6:19, 20; 7:2, 3

9 there went into the ark to Noah by twos, male and female, as God had commanded Noah.

10 And it came about after *a*the seven days, that the water of the flood came upon the earth.

10 *a*Gen. 7:4

11 In the *a*six hundredth year of Noah's life, in the second month, on the seventeenth day of the month, on the same day all *b*the fountains of the great deep burst open, and the floodgates of the sky were opened.

★11 *a*Gen. 7:6 *b*Gen. 8:2

12 And *a*the rain fell upon the earth for forty days and forty nights.

12 *a*Gen. 7:4, 17

13 On the very same day *a*Noah and Shem and Ham and Japheth, the sons of Noah, and Noah's wife and the three wives of his sons with them, entered the ark,

13 *a*Gen. 6:18; 7:7

14 they and every beast after its kind, and all the cattle after

---

quired to hold 45,000 sheep-sized animals, leaving three trains of 104 cars each for food, Noah's family, and "range" for the animals. Today it is estimated that there are 17,600 species of animals, making 45,000 a likely approximation of the number Noah might have taken into the ark.

6:16 *a window.* A space for light and air, measuring a cubit in height and running like a gallery around the top edge of the ark.

7:2 *clean . . . not clean.* Here the distinction had to do with sacrifice (cf. 8:20); later, with eating (Lev. 11; Deut. 14). *by sevens.* Lit., seven seven, which may mean seven pairs of the clean animals, or it may indicate three pairs plus one extra.

7:4 The duration of the rain assumes a vast store of moisture suspended above the earth (see note on 1:7).

7:11 *the fountains of the great deep.* I.e., subterranean waters, as well as rain, contributed to the Flood.

their kind, and every creeping thing that creeps on the earth after its kind, and every bird after its kind, all sorts of birds.

15 aGen. 6:19; 7:9
15 So they went into the ark to Noah, ^aby twos of all flesh in which was the breath of life.

16 And those that entered, male and female of all flesh, entered as God had commanded him; and the LORD closed it behind him.

17 aGen. 7:4
17 Then the flood came upon the earth for ^aforty days; and the water increased and lifted up the ark, so that it rose above the earth.

18 And the water prevailed and increased greatly upon the earth; and the ark floated on the surface of the water.

★19
19 And the water prevailed more and more upon the earth, so that all the high mountains everywhere under the heavens were covered.

20 aGen. 8:4
20 The water prevailed fifteen cubits higher, ^aand the mountains were covered.

21 aGen. 6:7, 13, 17; 7:4
21 ^aAnd all flesh that moved on the earth perished, birds and cattle and beasts and every swarming thing that swarms upon the earth, and all mankind;

22 aGen. 2:7
22 of all that was on the dry land, all ^ain whose nostrils was the breath of the spirit of life, died.

23 aMatt. 24:38, 39; Luke 17:26, 27; Heb. 11:7; 1 Pet. 3:20; 2 Pet. 2:5
23 Thus He blotted out every living thing that was upon the face of the land, from man to animals to creeping things and to birds of the sky, and they were blotted out from the earth; and only ^aNoah was left, together with those that were with him in the ark.

★24 aGen. 8:3
24 ^aAnd the water prevailed upon the earth one hundred and fifty days.

1 aGen. 19:29; Ex. 2:24; 1 Sam. 1:19; Ps. 105:42 bEx. 14:21; 15:10; Job 12:15; Ps. 29:10; Is. 44:27; Nah. 1:4
8 But ^aGod remembered Noah and all the beasts and all the cattle that were with him in the ark; and ^bGod caused a wind to pass over the earth, and the water subsided.

2 aGen. 7:11 bGen. 7:4, 12
2 Also ^athe fountains of the deep and the floodgates of the sky were closed, and ^bthe rain from the sky was restrained;

★3 aGen. 7:24
3 and the water receded steadily from the earth, and at the end ^aof one hundred and fifty days the water decreased.

★4 aGen. 7:20
4 And in the seventh month, on the seventeenth day of the month, ^athe ark rested upon the mountains of Ararat.

5 And the water decreased steadily until the tenth month; in the tenth month, on the first day of the month, the tops of the mountains became visible.

6 aGen. 6:16
6 Then it came about at the end of forty days, that Noah opened the ^awindow of the ark which he had made;

★7
7 and he sent out a raven, and it flew here and there until the water was dried up from the earth.

★8-9
8 Then he sent out a dove from him, to see if the water was abated from the face of the land;

9 but the dove found no resting place for the sole of her foot, so she returned to him into the ark; for the water was on the surface of all the earth. Then he put out his hand and took her,

---

7:19 *under the heavens.* Better, under all the heavens. The phrase indicates a universal flood rather than a local one. The promise of 9:11, 15 confirms this. There are over 270 flood stories from all parts of the world. See also 2 Pet. 2:5; 3:6; Matt. 24:37–39.

7:24 The waters reached their highest point after 150 days (which period included the 40 days of constant rain, v. 12).

8:3 *one hundred and fifty days.* The same period referred to in 7:24.

8:4 Today Mt. Ararat rises about 17,000 feet above sea level, though the reference here is to the *mountains of Ararat,* which indicates a range of mountains, not necessarily a particular peak. The ark rested on land 74 days after the end of the 150 days (cf. 7:11).

8:7 The *raven,* a scavenger, would have no trouble finding food and no qualms about perching on any slimy surface, so it apparently did not return to the ark.

8:8-9 The *dove* would not alight in unclean places, so returned to the ark.

and brought her into the ark to himself.

10 So he waited yet another seven days; and again he sent out the dove from the ark.

11 And the dove came to him toward evening; and behold, in her beak was a freshly picked olive leaf. So Noah knew that the water was abated from the earth.

12 Then he waited yet another seven days, and sent out ᵃthe dove; but she did not return to him again.

13 Now it came about in the ᵃsix hundred and first year, in the first *month,* on the first of the month, the water was dried up from the earth. Then Noah removed the covering of the ark, and looked, and behold, the surface of the ground was dried up.

14 And in the second month, on the twenty-seventh day of the month, the earth was dry.

15 Then God spoke to Noah, saying,

16 "Go out of the ark, you and your wife and your sons and your sons' wives with you.

17 "Bring out with you every living thing of all flesh that is with you, birds and animals and every creeping thing that creeps on the earth, that they may ᵃbreed abundantly on the earth, and be fruitful and multiply on the earth."

18 So Noah went out, and his sons and his wife and his sons' wives with him.

19 Every beast, every creeping thing, and every bird, everything that moves on the earth, went out by their families from the ark.

C The Events after the Flood, 8:20–9:29

20 Then Noah built ᵃan altar to the LORD, and took of every ᵇclean animal and of every clean bird and offered ᶜburnt offerings on the altar.

21 And the LORD ᵃsmelled the soothing aroma; and the LORD said to Himself, "I will never again ᵇcurse the ground on account of man, for ᶜthe intent of man's heart is evil from his youth; ᵈand I will never again destroy every living thing, as I have done.

22 "While the earth remains,

Seedtime and harvest,
And cold and heat,
And ᵃsummer and winter,
And ᵇday and night
Shall not cease."

9 And God blessed Noah and his sons and said to them, "ᵃBe fruitful and multiply, and fill the earth.

2 "And the fear of you and the terror of you shall be on every beast of the earth and on every bird of the sky; with everything that creeps on the ground, and all the fish of the sea, into your hand they are given.

3 "Every moving thing that is alive shall be food for you; I give all to you, ᵃas *I gave* the green plant.

4 "Only you shall not eat flesh with its life, *that is,* ᵃits blood.

5 "And surely I will require ᵃyour lifeblood; ᵇfrom every beast I will require it. And from *every*

Marginal references

12 ᵃJer. 48:28
13 ᵃGen. 7:6
★14
★17 ᵃGen. 1:22, 28
20 ᵃGen. 12:7, 8; 13:18; 22:9 ᵇGen. 7:2; Lev. 11:1-47 ᶜGen. 22:2; Ex. 10:25
★21 ᵃEx. 29:18, 25 ᵇGen. 3:17; 6:7, 13, 17; Is. 54:9 ᶜGen. 6:5; Ps. 51:5; Jer. 17:9; Rom. 1:21; 3:23; ᵈGen. 9:11, 15
22 ᵃPs. 74:17 ᵇJer. 33:20, 25
1 ᵃGen. 1:28; 9:7
★ 2-4
3 ᵃGen. 1:29
4 ᵃLev. 7:26f.; 17:10-16; 19:26; Deut. 12:16, 23; 15:23; 1 Sam. 14:34; Acts 15:20, 29
★ 5-6
5 ᵃEx. 20:13; 21:12 ᵇEx. 21:28, 29

8:14 Noah and his family were in the ark 371 days (53 weeks).

8:17 *the earth,* radically affected by the Flood, confronted Noah with a more hostile environment. Longevity was decreased, habitable land areas reduced, oceans made more extensive, the crust of the earth made unstable and subject to seismic activity, and the land laid barren.

8:21 *And the LORD smelled the soothing aroma.* Lit., a smell of satisfaction. God was pleased

with Noah's offerings.

9:2-4 *Fear* and *terror* now supplant the previous harmony between man and animals. God now sanctions an animal diet for man, as long as it is not eaten with blood (cf. Lev. 17:10).

9:5-6 Homicide (which in a sense is always fratricide, v. 5) demands a punishment that matches the crime. The justification for capital punishment, here established, is the nobility of human life, which is made *in the image of God.*

man, from every man's brother I will require the life of man.

6 "ᵃWhoever sheds man's blood,
By man his blood shall be shed,
For ᵇin the image of God He made man.

7 "And as for you, ᵃbe fruitful and multiply; Populate the earth abundantly and multiply in it."

8 Then God spoke to Noah and to his sons with him, saying,

9 "Now behold, ᵃI Myself do establish My covenant with you, and with your descendants after you;

10 and with every living creature that is with you, the birds, the cattle, and every beast of the earth with you; of all that comes out of the ark, even every beast of the earth.

11 "And I establish My covenant with you; and all flesh shall ᵃnever again be cut off by the water of the flood, ᵇneither shall there again be a flood to destroy the earth."

12 And God said, "This is ᵃthe sign of the covenant which I am making between Me and you and every living creature that is with you, for all successive generations;

13 I set My ᵃbow in the cloud, and it shall be for a sign of a covenant between Me and the earth.

14 "And it shall come about, when I bring a cloud over the earth, that the bow shall be seen in the cloud,

15 and ᵃI will remember My covenant, which is between Me and you and every living creature of all flesh; and ᵇnever again shall the water become a flood to destroy all flesh.

16 "When the bow is in the cloud, then I will look upon it, to remember the ᵃeverlasting covenant between God and every living creature of all flesh that is on the earth."

17 And God said to Noah, "This is the sign of the covenant which I have established between Me and all flesh that is on the earth."

18 Now the sons of Noah who came out of the ark were Shem and Ham and Japheth; and ᵃHam was the father of Canaan.

19 These three *were* the sons of Noah; and ᵃfrom these the whole earth was populated.

20 Then Noah began farming and planted a vineyard.

21 And he drank of the wine and ᵃbecame drunk, and uncovered himself inside his tent.

22 And Ham, the father of Canaan, ᵃsaw the nakedness of his father, and told his two brothers outside.

23 But Shem and Japheth took a garment and laid it upon both their shoulders and walked backward and covered the nakedness of their father; and their faces were turned away, so that they did not see their father's nakedness.

24 When Noah awoke from his wine, he knew what his youngest son had done to him.

25 So he said,
"ᵃCursed be Canaan;

Side references (left column):

6 ᵃEx. 21:12-14; Lev. 24:17; Num. 35:33; Matt. 26:52
ᵇGen. 1:26, 27

7 ᵃGen. 9:1

9 ᵃGen. 6:18

11 ᵃGen. 8:21 ᵇIs. 54:9

12 ᵃGen. 9:13, 17; 17:11

★13 ᵃEzek. 1:28

15 ᵃLev. 26:42, 45; Deut. 7:9; Ezek. 16:60
ᵇGen. 9:11

Side references (right column):

16 ᵃGen. 17:13, 19; 2 Sam. 23:5

18 ᵃGen. 9:25-27; 10:6

19 ᵃGen. 9:1, 7; 10:32; 1 Chr. 1:4

★21 ᵃProv. 20:1

★22 ᵃHab. 2:15

★25 ᵃDeut. 27:16 ᵇJosh. 9:23

9:13 *My bow.* Likely a new phenomenon due to the changed atmospheric and cloud conditions after the Flood. It serves as the sign of God's covenant never again to send a universally destructive flood.

9:21 Though this is the first use of the word *wine* in the Bible, it was not the first occasion of drinking (Matt. 24:38), so Noah must have known the effects of drinking. Probably Noah's becoming warm from the wine caused him to uncover himself.

9:22 *Ham . . . saw.* Lit., gazed with satisfaction. By contrast, Shem and Japheth showed respect for their father (v. 23).

9:25 *Cursed be Canaan.* Whether Canaan was personally involved with his father Ham's sin we do not know (he might have seen Noah's condition first and then told his father). But Ham is punished for his dishonor to his father by having a son who would bring dishonor to him. The curse is not on the Hamites, but on the Canaanites, the inhabitants of Palestine who were first subjected by Joshua and later by Solomon (cf. 1 Kings 9:20-21). The Canaanites long ago became extinct; the curse, therefore, cannot be applied to anyone today.

*26 aGen.
14:20; 24:27

ᵇA servant of servants
He shall be to his broth-
ers."

26 He also said,
"ᵃBlessed be the Lᴏʀᴅ,
The God of Shem;
And let Canaan be his
servant.

*27 aGen.
10:2-5; Is.
66:19

27 "ᵃMay God enlarge Ja-
pheth,
And let him dwell in the
tents of Shem;
And let Canaan be his
servant."

28 And Noah lived three
hundred and fifty years after the
flood.

29 So all the days of Noah
were nine hundred and fifty
years, and he died.

V THE DESCENDANTS OF NOAH,
AND THE TOWER OF BABEL,
10:1–11:26

A The Sons of Japheth, 10:1-5

* 1

10 Now these are the records of the generations of Shem, Ham, and Japheth, the sons of Noah; and sons were born to them after the flood.

* 2-5
2 a1 Chr.
1:5-7 bEzek.
38:2, 6
c2 Kin. 17:6
dIs. 66:19
eEzek. 38:2

2 ᵃThe sons of Japheth were ᵇGomer and Magog and ᶜMadai and ᵈJavan and Tubal and ᵉMe-shech and Tiras.

3 aJer.
51:27 bEzek.
27:14

3 And the sons of Gomer were ᵃAshkenaz and Riphath and ᵇTogarmah.

4 aEzek.
27:12, 25

4 And the sons of Javan were Elishah and ᵃTarshish, Kit-tim and Dodanim.

5 From these the coastlands of the nations were separated into their lands, every one according

to his language, according to their families, into their nations.

B The Sons of Ham, 10:6-20

* 6-20
6 a1 Chr.
1:8-10

6 ᵃAnd the sons of Ham were Cush and Mizraim and Put and Canaan.

7 aIs. 43:3
bEzek. 27:22
cEzek.
27:15, 20

7 And the sons of Cush were ᵃSeba and Havilah and Sabtah and ᵇRaamah and Sabteca; and the sons of Raamah were ᵇSheba and ᶜDedan.

8 Now Cush became the fa-ther of Nimrod; he became a mighty one on the earth.

9 He was a mighty hunter before the Lᴏʀᴅ; therefore it is said, "Like Nimrod a mighty hunter before the Lᴏʀᴅ."

*10-11
10 aGen.
11:9 bGen.
11:2; 14:1

10 And the beginning of his kingdom was ᵃBabel and Erech and Accad and Calneh, in the land of ᵇShinar.

11 aMic. 5:6

11 From that land he went forth ᵃinto Assyria, and built Nineveh and Rehoboth-Ir and Calah,

12 and Resen between Nine-veh and Calah; that is the great city.

13 aJer. 46:9

13 And Mizraim became the father of ᵃLudim and Anamim and Lehabim and Naphtuhim

14 a1 Chr.
1:12

14 and ᵃPathrusim and Caslu-him (from which came the Philis-tines) and Caphtorim.

15 a1 Chr.
1:13; Jer.
47:4 bGen.
23:3

15 And Canaan became the father of ᵃSidon, his first-born, and ᵇHeth

16 aGen.
15:19-21

16 and ᵃthe Jebusite and the Amorite and the Girgashite

17 and the Hivite and the Ar-kite and the Sinite

9:26 Yahweh will be Shem's God and Shem's blessing. (Jews are of Semitic—from "Shem"—descent.)

9:27 The descendants of *Japheth* (which means "enlargement") would spread throughout the earth and prosper. *dwell in the tents of Shem* means that spiritual blessings will come to the Japhethites through the God of the Semites.

10:1 All the people of the world since the Flood have descended from the three sons of Noah (cf. Acts 17:26).

10:2-5 These verses list the descendants of Ja-pheth, who settled in an area that stretched

across Eurasia from the Black and Caspian Seas to Spain. Concerning *Gomer,* see note on Ezek. 38:5-6. Concerning *Magog,* see note on Ezek. 38:2. Concerning *Tarshish,* see note on Jonah 1:3.

10:6-20 These verses detail Ham's descendants, who went to Africa and later spread west along the Mediterranean coast of N. Africa.

10:10-11 Nimrod's activities centered first in *Shinar* (Babylonia) and included building the tower of Babel, described in 11:1-9; then he went to Assyria (cf. Mic. 5:6).

18 and the Arvadite and the Zemarite and the Hamathite; and afterward the families of the Canaanite were spread abroad.

19 And ^athe territory of the Canaanite extended from Sidon as you go toward Gerar, as far as Gaza; as you go toward ^bSodom and Gomorrah and Admah and Zeboiim, as far as Lasha.

20 These are the sons of Ham, according to their families, according to their languages, by their lands, by their nations.

C   The Sons of Shem, 10:21-32

21 And also to Shem, the father of all the children of Eber, *and* the older brother of Japheth, children were born.

22 ^aThe sons of Shem *were* ^bElam and Asshur and ^cArpachshad and ^dLud and Aram.

23 And the sons of Aram *were* ^aUz and Hul and Gether and Mash.

24 And Arpachshad became the father of ^aShelah; and Shelah became the father of Eber.

25 And ^atwo sons were born to Eber; the name of the one *was* Peleg, for in his days the earth was divided; and his brother's name *was* Joktan.

26 And Joktan became the father of Almodad and Sheleph and Hazarmaveth and Jerah

27 and Hadoram and Uzal and Diklah

28 and Obal and Abimael and Sheba

29 and Ophir and Havilah and Jobab; all these were the sons of Joktan.

30 Now their settlement extended from Mesha as you go toward Sephar, the hill country of the east.

31 These are the sons of Shem, according to their families, according to their languages, by their lands, according to their nations.

32 These are the families of the sons of Noah, according to their genealogies, by their nations; and ^aout of these the nations were separated on the earth after the flood.

D   The Tower of Babel, 11:1-9

11 Now the whole earth used the same language and the same words.

2 And it came about as they journeyed east, that they found a plain in the land ^aof Shinar and settled there.

3 And they said to one another, "Come, let us make bricks and burn *them* thoroughly." And they used brick for stone, and they used ^atar for mortar.

4 And they said, "Come, let us build for ourselves a city, and a tower whose top ^a*will reach* into heaven, and let us make for ourselves ^ba name; lest we ^cbe scattered abroad over the face of the whole earth."

5 ^aAnd the LORD came down to see the city and the tower which the sons of men had built.

6 And the LORD said, "Behold, they are one people, and they all have ^athe same language. And this is what they began to do, and now nothing which they purpose to do will be impossible for them.

7 "Come, ^alet Us go down and there ^bconfuse their lan-

Marginal references

19 ^aNum. 34:2-12 ^bGen. 14:2, 3

★21-32

22 ^a1 Chr. 1:17 ^bGen. 14:1, 9 ^cGen. 11:10 ^dIs. 66:19

23 ^aJob 1:1; Jer. 25:20

24 ^aGen. 11:12; Luke 3:35

25 ^a1 Chr. 1:19

32 ^aGen. 9:19

★ 1

2 ^aGen. 10:10; 14:1; Dan. 1:2

3 ^aGen. 14:10

★ 4 ^aDeut. 1:28; 9:1; Ps. 107:26 ^bGen. 6:4; 2 Sam. 8:13 ^cDeut. 4:27

5 ^aGen. 18:21; Ex. 3:8; 19:11, 18, 20

6 ^aGen. 11:1

★ 7 ^aGen. 1:26 ^bGen. 42:23; Ex. 4:11; Deut. 28:49; Is. 33:19; Jer. 5:15

10:21-32 These verses describe the descendants of Shem, who occupied the area N. of the Persian Gulf. The dividing in the days of *Peleg* (v. 25) apparently refers to the scattering of 11:9.
11:1 The unbridgeable gap between animal sounds and human language, as well as the statement of this verse that originally all men spoke the same language, are inexplicable by the theory of evolution.
11:4 *a city, and a tower* were built in order to prevent people from scattering through the earth, in direct defiance of God's command (9:1). This *tower*, unlike ziggurats, which were built for the purpose of worshiping a deity, served these people as a rallying point and symbol of their fame.
11:7 By confusing language, God established the parent languages of the earth from which other languages and dialects developed (today, a total of more than 3,000). The result of this confusion was the scattering of mankind.

guage, that they may not understand one another's speech."

8 aGen.
11:4; Ps.
92:9; Luke
1:51

8 So the LORD ªscattered them abroad from there over the face of the whole earth; and they stopped building the city.

★ 9 aGen.
10:10

9 Therefore its name was called ªBabel, because there the LORD confused the language of the whole earth; and from there the LORD scattered them abroad over the face of the whole earth.

E The Descendants of Shem,
11:10–26

★10-26

10 aGen.
10:22-25

10 ªThese are the records of the generations of Shem. Shem was one hundred years old, and became the father of Arpachshad two years after the flood;

11 and Shem lived five hundred years after he became the father of Arpachshad, and he had other sons and daughters.

12 And Arpachshad lived thirty-five years, and became the father of Shelah;

13 and Arpachshad lived four hundred and three years after he became the father of Shelah, and he had other sons and daughters.

14 And Shelah lived thirty years, and became the father of Eber;

15 and Shelah lived four hundred and three years after he became the father of Eber, and he had other sons and daughters.

16 And Eber lived thirty-four years, and became the father of Peleg;

17 and Eber lived four hundred and thirty years after he became the father of Peleg, and he had other sons and daughters.

18 And Peleg lived thirty years, and became the father of Reu;

19 and Peleg lived two hundred and nine years after he became the father of Reu, and he had other sons and daughters.

20 And Reu lived thirty-two years, and became the father of Serug;

21 and Reu lived two hundred and seven years after he became the father of Serug, and he had other sons and daughters.

22 And Serug lived thirty years, and became the father of Nahor;

23 and Serug lived two hundred years after he became the father of Nahor, and he had other sons and daughters.

24 And Nahor lived twenty-nine years, and became the father of ªTerah;

24 aJosh.
24:2

25 and Nahor lived one hundred and nineteen years after he became the father of Terah, and he had other sons and daughters.

26 And Terah lived seventy years, and became ªthe father of Abram, Nahor and Haran.

26 aJosh.
24:2

VI THE HISTORY OF ABRAHAM,
11:27–25:11
A The Family of Abram,
11:27–32

27 Now these are the records of the generations of Terah. Terah became the father of Abram, Nahor and Haran; and ªHaran became the father of ᵇLot.

★27 aGen.
11:31; 12:4
bGen. 13:10;
14:12; 19:1,
29

28 And Haran died in the presence of his father Terah in the land of his birth, in ªUr of the Chaldeans.

★28 aGen.
11:31

11:9 *Babel.* Linked by a play on words with a Hebrew verb meaning "to confuse," though the Babylonians preferred to use the meaning that was more acceptable to them: "gate of God."

11:10-26 This selective list of ten generations is recorded for the purpose of tracing the ancestry of Abraham.

11:27 *Abram* means "exalted father," the progenitor of God's chosen people. Later (17:5) his name was changed to Abraham, which means

"father of a great number." He was born in 2165 B.C. Though we are told little about Terah, Abraham's father, Josh. 24:2 states that he worshiped heathen gods.

11:28 *Ur of the Chaldeans.* A wealthy, populous, and sophisticated pagan center of southern Mesopotamia (220 miles SE. of Baghdad). Its most prosperous and literate era was during the time of Abraham. A great ziggurat was built there, and Abraham must have seen it.

29 And Abram and [a]Nahor took wives for themselves. The name of Abram's wife was [b]Sarai; and the name of Nahor's wife was [c]Milcah, the daughter of Haran, the father of Milcah and Iscah.

30 And [a]Sarai was barren; she had no child.

31 And Terah took Abram his son, and Lot the son of Haran, his grandson, and Sarai his daughter-in-law, his son Abram's wife; and they went out together from [a]Ur of the Chaldeans in order to enter the land of Canaan; and they went as far as Haran, and settled there.

32 And the days of Terah were two hundred and five years; and Terah died in Haran.

B The Call of Abram, 12:1-20

12 Now [a]the Lord said to Abram,

"Go forth from your country,
And from your relatives
And from your father's house,
To the land which I will show you;

2 And [a]I will make you a great nation,
And [b]I will bless you,
And make your name great;

And so [c]you shall be a blessing;

3 And [a]I will bless those who bless you,
And the one who curses you I will curse.
[b]And in you all the families of the earth shall be blessed."

4 So Abram went forth as the Lord had spoken to him; and [a]Lot went with him. Now Abram was seventy-five years old when he departed from Haran.

5 And Abram took Sarai his wife and Lot his nephew, and all their [a]possessions which they had accumulated, and [b]the persons which they had acquired in Haran, and they set out for the land of Canaan; [c]thus they came to the land of Canaan.

6 And Abram passed through the land as far as the site of [a]Shechem, to the oak of Moreh. Now the Canaanite was then in the land.

7 And the Lord [a]appeared to Abram and said, "[b]To your descendants I will give this land." So he built [c]an altar there to the Lord who had appeared to him.

8 Then he proceeded from there to the mountain on the east of Bethel, and pitched his tent, with [a]Bethel on the west and Ai on the east; and there he built an altar to the Lord and [b]called upon the name of the Lord.

Marginal references

29 [a]Gen. 24:10 [b]Gen. 17:15; 20:12 [c]Gen. 22:20, 23; 24:15

30 [a]Gen. 16:1

★31 [a]Gen. 15:7; Neh. 9:7; Acts 7:4

★1 [a]Gen. 15:7; Acts 7:3; Heb. 11:8

★2 [a]Gen. 17:4-6; 18:18; 46:3; Deut. 26:5 [b]Gen. 22:17 [c]Zech. 8:13

★3 [a]Gen. 24:35; 27:29; Num. 24:9 [b]Gen. 22:18; 26:4; 28:14; Acts 3:25; Gal. 3:8

4 [a]Gen. 11:27, 31

★5 [a]Gen. 13:6 [b]Gen. 14:14; Lev. 22:11 [c]Gen. 11:31; Heb. 11:8

★6 [a]Gen. 35:4; Deut. 11:30

7 [a]Gen. 17:1; 18:1 [b]Gen. 13:15; 15:18; Deut. 34:4; Ps. 105: 9-12; Acts 7:5; Gal. 3:16 [c]Gen. 13:4, 18; 22:9

★8 [a]Josh. 8:9, 12 [b]Gen. 4:26; 21:33

11:31 God called Abraham while he was in Ur (Acts 7:2-3). Only two routes to *Canaan* were available: one across the Arabian desert (impossible for transporting large herds), and the other along the Euphrates to *Haran*, in Syria, then down to Canaan.

12:1 *To the land.* I.e., Canaan. Abraham was still in Haran when this call, originally given to him in Ur (Acts 7:2), was reiterated.

12:2 *a great nation.* When God made this promise, Abraham had no son. The reference is to the Jewish nation, i.e., the descendants of Abraham through Isaac and Jacob. *I will bless you, And make your name great.* This promise was fulfilled in Abraham's temporal blessings (13:2; 24:35), spiritual blessings (21:22), and fame (23:6; Isa. 41:8). *so you shall be a blessing.* Lit., be a blessing, a certain consequence

of God's blessing upon Abraham.

12:3 *bless . . . curse.* Abraham's relation to God was so close that to bless or curse him was, in effect, to bless or curse God (see examples in 20:2-18; 21:22-34; 23:1-20). *in you all the families of the earth shall be blessed.* This promise was fulfilled in the coming of Abraham's seed, Christ (Gal. 3:8, 16).

12:5 *their possessions.* I.e., goods, herds, and flocks. *the persons which they had acquired.* I.e., his retinue, which was increased during his stay in Haran.

12:6 *Shechem, to the oak of Moreh.* Between Mt. Ebal and Mt. Gerizim, near present-day Nablus. The promised land was then occupied by *the Canaanite.*

12:8 *Bethel . . . Ai.* 20 miles further S. of Shechem.

9 And Abram journeyed on, continuing toward ᵃthe Negev.

★ 9 ᵃGen.
13:1, 3; 20:1;
24:62

10 Now there was ᵃa famine in the land; so Abram went down to Egypt to sojourn there, for the famine was ᵇsevere in the land.

★10 ᵃGen.
26:1 ᵇGen.
43:1

11 And it came about when he came near to Egypt, that he said to Sarai his wife, "See now, I know that you are a ᵃbeautiful woman;

★11 ᵃGen.
26:7; 29:17

12 ᵃand it will come about when the Egyptians see you, that they will say, 'This is his wife'; and they will kill me, but they will let you live.

★12 ᵃGen.
20:11

13 "Please say that you are ᵃmy sister so that it may go well with me because of you, and that ᵇI may live on account of you."

★13 ᵃGen.
20:2, 5, 12;
26:7 ᵇJer.
38:17, 20

14 And it came about when Abram came into Egypt, the Egyptians saw that the woman was very beautiful.

15 And Pharaoh's officials saw her and praised her to Pharaoh; and ᵃthe woman was taken into Pharaoh's house.

15 ᵃGen.
20:2

16 Therefore ᵃhe treated Abram well for her sake; and ᵇgave him sheep and oxen and donkeys and male and female servants and female donkeys and camels.

16 ᵃGen.
20:14 ᵇGen.
13:2

17 But the LORD ᵃstruck Pharaoh and his house with great plagues because of Sarai, Abram's wife.

★17 ᵃGen.
20:18; 1 Chr.
16:21; Ps.
105:14

18 Then Pharaoh called Abram and said, "ᵃWhat is this you have done to me? Why did you not tell me that she was your wife?

18 ᵃGen.
20:9, 10;
26:10

19 "Why did you say, 'She is my sister,' so that I took her for my wife? Now then, here is your wife, take her and go."

20 And Pharaoh commanded his men concerning him; and they escorted him away, with his wife and all that belonged to him.

C The Separation of Abram and Lot, 13:1-18

13 So Abram went up from Egypt to ᵃthe Negev, he and his wife and all that belonged to him; and Lot with him.

1 ᵃGen.
12:9

2 Now Abram was ᵃvery rich in livestock, in silver and in gold.

2 ᵃGen.
24:35

3 And he went on his journeys from the Negev as far as Bethel, to the place where his tent had been at the beginning, ᵃbetween Bethel and Ai,

3 ᵃGen.
12:8

4 to the place of the ᵃaltar, which he had made there formerly; and there Abram called on the name of the LORD.

4 ᵃGen.
12:7, 8

5 Now ᵃLot, who went with Abram, also had flocks and herds and tents.

★ 5-7

5 ᵃGen.
12:5

6 And ᵃthe land could not sustain them while dwelling together; ᵇfor their possessions were so great that they were not able to remain together.

6 ᵃGen.
36:7 ᵇGen.
12:5; 16;
13:2

7 ᵃAnd there was strife between the herdsmen of Abram's livestock and the herdsmen of Lot's livestock. Now ᵇthe Canaanite and the Perizzite were dwelling then in the land.

7 ᵃGen.
26:20 ᵇGen.
12:6; 15:20,
21

8 ᵃThen Abram said to Lot, "Please let there be no strife

★ 8-9
8 ᵃProv.
15:18, 20:3

12:9 *toward the Negev.* Archaeological evidence of settlements in this area at this time supports the biblical record, which places the patriarch's residence there in the same period.

12:10 *a famine.* Not uncommon in Palestine. Note other major famines in 26:1 and 41:56.

12:11 *a beautiful woman.* Though *Sarai* was 65, she doubtless was in her prime, since the life span of the patriarchs was about twice that of people today. Sarah was 127 when she died, and Abraham was 175 when he died.

12:12 *they will kill me.* The Egyptians respected marriage, so they would feel compelled to kill Abraham before taking his wife into Pharaoh's harem.

12:13 *my sister.* A half-truth (and thus a lie),

since Sarah was Abraham's half-sister (20:12).

12:17 *with great plagues.* What these were is not stated, though they were perhaps an illness that kept Pharaoh from defiling Sarah. Abraham certainly did not deserve such mercy from God!

13:5-7 Increase in possessions created a shortage of available grazing *land* and caused *strife* between Lot's shepherds and Abraham's. *Perizzite.* One of the Canaanite tribes (cf. 34:30; Deut. 7:1-4; Judg. 1:1-7; 3:5-6; 1 Kings 9:20-21; Ezra 9:1).

13:8-9 *Please . . . Please.* Notice the courtesy and magnanimity exhibited by Abraham, who was Lot's senior.

between you and me, nor between my herdsmen and your herdsmen, for we are brothers.

9 "Is not the whole land before you? Please separate from me: if *to* the left, then I will go to the right; or if *to* the right, then I will go to the left."

★**10** ᵃGen. 19:17-29; Deut. 34:3 ᵇGen. 19:24 ᶜGen. 2:8, 10 ᵈGen. 47:6 ᵉGen. 14:2, 8; 19:22; Deut. 34:3

10 And Lot lifted up his eyes and saw all the ᵃvalley of the Jordan, that it was well watered everywhere—*this was* before the Lord ᵇdestroyed Sodom and Gomorrah—like ᶜthe garden of the Lord, ᵈlike the land of Egypt as you go to ᵉZoar.

11 So Lot chose for himself all the valley of the Jordan; and Lot journeyed eastward. Thus they separated from each other.

12 ᵃGen. 14:2; 19:24, 25, 29

12 Abram settled in the land of Canaan, while Lot settled in ᵃthe cities of the valley, and moved his tents as far as Sodom.

13 ᵃGen. 18:20; Ezek. 16:49 ᵇNum. 39:9; Num. 32:23; 2 Pet. 2:7, 8

13 Now ᵃthe men of Sodom were wicked exceedingly and ᵇsinners against the Lord.

14 And the Lord said to Abram, after Lot had separated from him, "ᵃNow lift up your eyes and look from the place where you are, ᵇnorthward and southward and eastward and westward;

★**14-17**

14 ᵃDeut. 3:27; 34:1-4; Is. 49:18 ᵇGen. 28:14

15 ᵃGen. 12:7 ᵇGen. 13:17; 15:7; 17:8; 2 Chr. 20:7; Acts 7:5

15 ᵃfor all the land which you see, ᵇI will give it to you and to your descendants forever.

16 "And I will make your descendants ᵃas the dust of the earth; so that if anyone can number the dust of the earth, then your descendants can also be numbered.

16 ᵃGen. 16:10; 28:14; Num. 23:10

17 "Arise, ᵃwalk about the land through its length and breadth; for ᵇI will give it to you."

17 ᵃNum. 13:17-24 ᵇGen. 13:15

18 Then Abram moved his tent and came and dwelt by the ᵃoaks of Mamre, which are in Hebron, and there he built ᵇan altar to the Lord.

★**18** ᵃGen. 14:13 ᵇGen. 8:20; 12:7, 8

D   The Deliverance of Lot by Abram, 14:1-24

14 And it came about in the days of Amraphel king of ᵃShinar, Arioch king of Ellasar, Chedorlaomer king of ᵇElam, and Tidal king of Goiim,

★**1** ᵃGen. 10:10; 11:2 ᵇGen. 10:22; Is. 11:11; Dan. 8:2

2 *that* they made war with Bera king of Sodom, and with Birsha king of Gomorrah, Shinab king of ᵃAdmah, and Shemeber king of ᵇZeboiim, and the king of Bela (that is, ᶜZoar).

★**2** ᵃGen. 10:19 ᵇDeut. 29:23 ᶜGen. 13:10; 19:22

3 All these came as allies to ᵃthe valley of Siddim (that is, ᵇthe Salt Sea).

★**3** ᵃGen. 14:8, 10 ᵇNum. 34:12; Deut. 3:17; Josh. 3:16

4 Twelve years they had served Chedorlaomer, but the thirteenth year they rebelled.

13:10 *the valley of the Jordan . . . well watered.* Irrigation systems were in use long before Lot's time. Lot's greed to inhabit the Jordan valley with its lush vegetation exposed him to the wickedness of Sodom (vv. 12-13; 19:1-25). *Zoar.* A town located at the S. end of the Dead Sea. See also 14:8; 19:20-23.

13:14-17 After separation from Lot, Abraham received a reaffirmation of God's promise to give the land of Canaan to him and his *descendants forever* (v. 15).

13:18 *moved his tent.* Lit., he tented, or kept moving his tent along, staking his claim to the land God promised. Then he settled by *the oaks of Mamre* (named for a noted man of that time, 14:13) at Hebron, 22 miles S. of Jerusalem.

14:1 Though some have dismissed this chapter as being an historical impossibility, archaeological discoveries have demonstrated the existence of a flourishing civilization in Palestine

between the 21st and 19th centuries B.C. and of the savage destruction of the cities at the end of that period. *Amraphel.* Not to be identified with Hammurabi, who lived later. *Shinar.* Babylonia. *Ellasar.* Its identity is uncertain, perhaps a town between Carchemish and Haran in N. Mesopotamia. *Elam.* The area that was later Persia. *king of Goiim.* Or king of nations. Uncertain, but likely means *Tidal* ruled over a nomadic people who had not yet formed a kingdom.

14:2 *Admah . . . Zeboiim.* Towns in the Dead Sea basin (cf. Hos. 11:8).

14:3 *the valley of Siddim.* Likely the land S. of the tongue-shaped peninsula that juts out from the E. bank of the Dead Sea. It may have actually joined the western shore (near Masada) in Abraham's time, causing the southern area of the Dead Sea to be dry land. Geological evidence shows a cataclysmic upheaval in that region in the time of Abraham.

★ 5-7

5 *a*Deut.
3:11, 13
*b*Deut. 1:4;
Josh. 9:10
*c*Num. 32:37

6 *a*Gen.
36:20; Deut.
2:12, 22
*b*Gen. 21:21;
Num. 10:12

7 *a*Num.
13:26
*b*2 Chr. 20:2

8 *a*Gen.
14:3

10 *a*Gen.
14:17, 21, 22
*b*Gen. 19:17

5 And in the fourteenth year Chedorlaomer and the kings that were with him, came and defeated the *a*Rephaim in *b*Ashteroth-karnaim and the Zuzim in Ham and the Emim in *c*Shaveh-kiriathaim,

6 and the *a*Horites in their Mount Seir, as far as *b*El-paran, which is by the wilderness.

7 Then they turned back and came to En-mishpat (that is, *a*Kadesh), and conquered all the country of the Amalekites, and also the Amorites, who lived in *b*Hazazon-tamar.

8 And the king of Sodom and the king of Gomorrah and the king of Admah and the king of Zeboiim and the king of Bela (that is, Zoar) came out; and they arrayed for battle against them in *a*the valley of Siddim,

9 against Chedorlaomer king of Elam and Tidal king of Goiim and Amraphel king of Shinar and Arioch king of Ellasar—four kings against five.

10 Now the valley of Siddim was full of tar pits; and *a*the kings of Sodom and Gomorrah fled, and they fell into them. But those who survived fled to the *b*hill country.

11 Then they took all the goods of Sodom and Gomorrah and all their food supply, and departed.

12 And they also took Lot, *a*Abram's nephew, and his possessions and departed, *b*for he was living in Sodom.

13 Then a fugitive came and told Abram the *a*Hebrew. Now he was living by the *b*oaks of Mamre the Amorite, brother of Eshcol and brother of Aner, and these were *c*allies with Abram.

14 And when Abram heard that *a*his relative had been taken captive, he led out his trained men, *b*born in his house, three hundred and eighteen, and went in pursuit as far as *c*Dan.

15 And *a*he divided his forces against them by night, he and his servants, and defeated them, and pursued them as far as Hobah, which is north of *b*Damascus.

16 And he *a*brought back all the goods, and also brought back *b*his relative Lot with his possessions, and also the women, and the people.

17 Then after his return from the defeat of Chedorlaomer and the kings who were with him, *a*the king of Sodom went out to meet him at the valley of Shaveh (that is, *b*the King's Valley).

12 *a*Gen.
11:27 *b*Gen.
13:12

★13 *a*Gen.
40:15; Ex.
3:18 *b*Gen.
13:18; 14:24
*c*Gen. 21:27,
32

★14 *a*Gen.
14:12 *b*Gen.
12:5; 15:3;
17:27; Eccl.
2:7 *c*Deut.
34:1; Judg.
18:29; 1 Kin.
15:20

★15 *a*Judg.
7:16 *b*Gen.
15:2

16 *a*1 Sam.
30:8, 18, 19
*b*Gen. 14:12,
14

★17 *a*Gen.
14:10
*b*2 Sam.
18:18

14:5-7 *the Rephaim* lived on both sides of the Jordan River. *the Zuzim* lived S. of the Rephaim and E. of the Jordan. *the Emim* were giants who lived in the land of Moab. *the Horites* lived in *Mount Seir*, SW. of the Dead Sea, a land later inhabited by the Edomites. *the country of the Amalekites* was between the Negev (the desert area of southern Judah) and Sinai. The Amalekites did not exist in Abraham's time (see 36:12), but the territory is described this way in order to identify it clearly for Moses' readers. *the Amorites* were scattered throughout Palestine. The route of the invasion was NW. through the Negev, circling back on the allies in the valley of Siddim.
14:13 Abraham was the first person to be referred to as a *Hebrew*, an ethnic designation that his descendants derived from him. The word comes from the name of his ancestor, Eber (11:10-14). It also had a wider use as a general designation for nomadic people like Abraham, who would have been considered a migrant by the Canaanites, since he came from Ur and Haran.
14:14 *he led out his trained men.* Lit., he unsheathed his armed retainers. *born in his house.* Thus more dependable for this important mission that took them on a long and difficult journey north to Dan.
14:15 *Hobah.* The site is uncertain, though it was N. of Damascus.
14:17 *the valley of Shaveh.* One of the valleys surrounding Jerusalem, possibly the Kidron (see also 2 Sam. 18:18).

★18 aHeb.
7:1-10 bPs.
104:15 cPs.
110:4; Heb.
5:6, 10

18 And aMelchizedek king of Salem brought out bbread and wine; now he was a cpriest of God Most High.

19 aGen.
14:22

19 And he blessed him and said,

"Blessed be Abram of
    God Most High,
aPossessor of heaven
    and earth;

★20 aHeb.
7:4

20 And blessed be God
    Most High,
Who has delivered your
    enemies into your
    hand."

aAnd he gave him a tenth of all.

★21-24

21 And the king of Sodom said to Abram, "Give the people to me and take the goods for yourself."

22 aGen.
14:19 bPs.
24:1

22 And Abram said to the king of Sodom, "I have sworn to the Lord aGod Most High, bpossessor of heaven and earth,

23 a2 Kin.
5:16

23 that aI will not take a thread or a sandal thong or anything that is yours, lest you should say, 'I have made Abram rich.'

24 aGen.
14:13

24 "I will take nothing except what the young men have eaten, and the share of the men who went with me, aAner, Eshcol, and Mamre; let them take their share."

E The Covenant with Abram, 15:1-21

15 After these things athe word of the Lord came to Abram in a vision, saying,
"bDo not fear, Abram,
I am ca shield to you;
Your dreward shall be
    very great."

2 And Abram said, "O Lord God, what wilt Thou give me, since I am childless, and the heir of my house is Eliezer of Damascus?"

3 And Abram said, "Since Thou hast given no offspring to me, one aborn in my house is my heir."

4 Then behold, the word of the Lord came to him, saying, "This man will not be your heir; abut one who shall come forth from your own body, he shall be your heir."

5 And He took him outside and said, "Now look toward the heavens, and acount the stars, if you are able to count them." And

★ 1 aGen.
15:4; 46:2;
1 Sam. 15:10
bGen. 21:17;
26:24; Is.
41:10 cDeut.
33:29 dNum.
18:20; Ps.
58:11

★ 2

3 aGen.
14:14

4 aGal.
4:28

★ 5 aGen.
22:17; 26:4;
Deut. 1:10
bEx. 32:13;
Rom. 4:18;
Heb. 11:12

14:18 *Melchizedek king of Salem.* An historical person, king of Jerusalem (cf. Psalm 76:2), who typified Christ (see Psalm 110:4; notes on Heb. 7). His name means "king of righteousness." *bread and wine.* Rations for the troops, in appreciation of Abraham's laudable victory. *God Most High.* Heb., *El Elyon,* emphasizing God's strength and sovereignty. Evidently a group of people who knew the true Creator-God lived in Jerusalem under the king-priest Melchizedek. The Tell Mardikh tablets (c. 2300 B.C.) contain the name Jerusalem and hundreds of other place and personal names like Hazor, Megiddo, Gaza, Abram, Israel.

14:20 *he* (Abraham) *gave him* (Melchizedek) *a tenth of all* (the spoils of the battle, see Heb. 7:4). The gift was an expression of gratitude to God for victory and to God's priest for sanctuary at Salem.

14:21-24 Abraham refused to take anything from the *king of Sodom,* lest he become obligated to him. By this Abraham demonstrated his total allegiance to the Lord (Yahweh) and rejected any attempt by the king of Sodom to assume the role of overlord and make Abraham his vassal. Abraham took only food for his men and gave his allies liberty to accept the spoils due them.

15:1 *Do not fear.* Perhaps Abraham feared that the kings of the east might initiate some punitive military action against him because of his rescue of Lot. *Your reward shall be very great.* Better, I am your very great reward.

15:2 *Lord God.* Heb., *Adonai Yahweh.* Adonai means "master, lord, sovereign" and is equivalent to the Greek *kurios.* For Yahweh, see note on 2:4. Abraham did not doubt God's promise or power to fulfill His covenant with him, though 10 years had passed without progeny. In referring to *Eliezer* (born in Abraham's house, v. 3), Abraham is suggesting to the Lord that he be permitted to adopt Eliezer as his heir. Tablets that have been discovered show that it was customary for wealthy, childless couples to adopt a servant and make him their heir. But God assured Abraham he would have his own son (v. 4).

15:5 *the stars.* Cf. 22:17; 26:4; Exod. 32:13.

He said to him, "[b]So shall your descendants be."

★ 6 [a]Rom. 4:3, 20-22; Gal. 3:6; James 2:23

6 [a]Then he believed in the LORD; and He reckoned it to him as righteousness.

7 [a]Gen. 11:31 [b]Gen. 13:15, 17

7 And He said to him, "I am the LORD who brought you out of [a]Ur of the Chaldeans, to [b]give you this land to possess it."

8 [a]Judg. 6:36-40; Luke 1:18

8 And he said, "O Lord GOD, [a]how may I know that I shall possess it?"

9 So He said to him, "Bring Me a three year old heifer, and a three year old female goat, and a three year old ram, and a turtledove, and a young pigeon."

★10 [a]Gen. 15:17 [b]Lev. 1:17

10 Then he brought all these to Him and [a]cut them in two, and laid each half opposite the other; but he [b]did not cut the birds.

11 And the birds of prey came down upon the carcasses, and Abram drove them away.

★12 [a]Gen. 2:21; 28:11; Job 33:15

12 Now when the sun was going down, [a]a deep sleep fell upon Abram; and behold, terror *and* great darkness fell upon him.

★13-16

13 [a]Acts 7:6, 17 [b]Ex. 1:11; Deut. 5:15 [c]Ex. 12:40; Gal. 3:17

13 And God said to Abram, "Know for certain that [a]your descendants will be strangers in a land that is not theirs, where [b]they will be enslaved and oppressed [c]four hundred years.

14 [a]Ex. 12:32-38

14 "But I will also judge the nation whom they will serve; and afterward they will come out [a]with many possessions.

15 [a]Gen. 25:8; 47:30

15 "And as for you, [a]you shall go to your fathers in peace; you

shall be buried at a good old age.

16 "Then in [a]the fourth generation they shall return here, for [b]the iniquity of the Amorite is not yet complete."

16 [a]Gen. 15:13 [b]Lev. 18:24-28

17 And it came about when the sun had set, that it was very dark, and behold, *there appeared* a smoking oven and a flaming torch which [a]passed between these pieces.

★17 [a]Jer. 34:18, 19

18 On that day the LORD made a covenant with Abram, saying,

★18-21

"[a]To your descendants I have given this land,
From [b]the river of Egypt as far as the great river, the river Euphrates:

18 [a]Gen. 17:8; Josh. 21:43; Acts 7:5 [b]Ex. 23:31; Num. 34:1-15; Deut. 1:7, 8

19 [a]the Kenite and the Kenizzite and the Kadmonite

19 [a]Ex. 3:17; 23:28; Josh. 24:11; Neh. 9:8

20 and the Hittite and the Perizzite and the Rephaim

21 and the Amorite and the Canaanite and the Girgashite and the Jebusite."

F   The Birth of Ishmael, 16:1-16

16 Now [a]Sarai, Abram's wife had borne him no *children*, and she had [b]an Egyptian maid whose name was Hagar.

1 [a]Gen. 11:30 [b]Gen. 12:16

2 So Sarai said to Abram, "Now behold, the LORD has prevented me from bearing *children*. [a]Please go in to my maid; perhaps

★ 2-3

2 [a]Gen. 30:3, 4, 9, 10

15:6 *believed.* From the Heb. verb *aman* ("to confirm, affirm"), an "amen" to God's promise of verse 5, such as vassals gave in covenant ceremonies. *reckoned . . . as righteousness.* A judicial verdict whereby God said of Abraham, "Not guilty!" See also Rom. 4:3.

15:10 *cut them in two.* The idea is this: may the same be done to the one who breaks this covenant. See Jer. 34:18-19.

15:12 The *great darkness* was designed to underscore the severity of the prediction of Egyptian bondage (v. 13).

15:13-16 *a land that is not theirs.* A prophecy of the Israelites' sojourn in Egypt, which was not the land promised to them. The sojourn would last 400 years (= the 430 years of Exod. 12:40 rounded off). The people would be delivered *with many possessions* (Exod. 12:34-36) in the *fourth generation*, a generation at that time

being about 100 years. *the iniquity of the Amorite.* Meaning here all the Canaanite tribes in Palestine whose sins God would tolerate until the Israelites would come out of Egypt under Moses and conquer Palestine under Joshua, destroying the Canaanites.

15:17 By passing alone between the pieces of the animals, God (whose presence was evident by the fire and smoke, cf. Exod. 13:21) swore fidelity to His promises and placed the obligation for their fulfillment on Himself alone.

15:18-21 The boundaries of the promised land are now given for the first time. *the river of Egypt.* I.e., the Nile. This promise has not yet been fulfilled, but will be when Christ returns (see note on 1 Kings 4:21).

16:2-3 This suggestion was in accord with the practice of the day, as attested in legal codes and marriage contracts of that time.

I shall obtain children through her." And Abram listened to the voice of Sarai.

3 And after Abram had lived ᵃten years in the land of Canaan, Abram's wife Sarai took Hagar the Egyptian, her maid, and gave her to her husband Abram as his wife.

4 And he went in to Hagar, and she conceived; and when she saw that she had conceived, her mistress was despised in her sight.

5 And Sarai said to Abram, "ᵃMay the wrong done me be upon you. I gave my maid into your arms; but when she saw that she had conceived, I was despised in her sight. ᵇMay the LORD judge between you and me."

6 But Abram said to Sarai, "Behold, your maid is in your power; do to her what is good in your sight." So Sarai treated her harshly, and ᵃshe fled from her presence.

7 Now ᵃthe angel of the LORD found her by a spring of water in the wilderness, by the spring on the way to ᵇShur.

8 And he said, "Hagar, Sarai's maid, ᵃwhere have you come from and where are you going?" And she said, "I am fleeing from the presence of my mistress Sarai."

9 Then the angel of the LORD said to her, "Return to your mistress, and submit yourself to her authority."

10 Moreover, the ᵃangel of the LORD said to her, "ᵇI will greatly multiply your descendants so that they shall be too many to count."

11 The angel of the LORD said to her further,
"Behold, you are with child,
And you shall bear a son;
And you shall call his name Ishmael,
Because ᵃthe LORD has given heed to your affliction.

12 "And he will be a ᵃwild donkey of a man,
His hand *will be* against everyone,
And everyone's hand *will be* against him;
And he will live ᵇto the east of all his brothers."

13 Then she called the name of the LORD who spoke to her, "Thou art a God who sees"; for she said, "ᵃHave I even remained alive here after seeing Him?"

14 Therefore the well was called Beer-lahai-roi; behold, it is between ᵃKadesh and Bered.

15 So Hagar bore Abram a son; and Abram called the name of his son, whom Hagar bore, Ishmael.

16 And Abram was ᵃeighty-six years old when Hagar bore Ishmael to him.

---

3 ᵃGen. 12:4
★ 4-6
5 ᵃJer. 51:35 ᵇGen. 31:53; Ex. 5:21
6 ᵃGen. 16:9
★ 7 ᵃGen. 21:17, 18; 22:11, 15; 31:11 ᵇGen. 20:1; 25:18
8 ᵃGen. 3:9; 1 Kin. 19:9, 13
★10 ᵃGen. 22:15-18 ᵇGen. 17:20
★11 ᵃEx. 2:23, 24; 3:7, 9
★12 ᵃJob 24:5; 39:5-8 ᵇGen. 25:18
13 ᵃGen. 32:30; Ps. 139:1-12
★14 ᵃGen. 14:7
16 ᵃGen. 12:4; 16:3

16:4–6 After Hagar conceived, Sarah apparently reduced her to her former status as a slave and she was no longer Abraham's concubine. This was Sarah's legal right, though we may sympathize with Hagar's plight.

16:7 *the way to Shur.* Somewhere on the road from Beersheba to Egypt, Egypt being Hagar's homeland.

16:10 *the angel of the LORD.* A theophany, a self-manifestation of God. He here speaks as God, identifies Himself with God, and claims to exercise the prerogatives of God (see Gen. 16:7-14; 21:17-21; 22:11-18; 31:11, 13; Exod. 3:2; Judg. 2:1-4; 5:23; 6:11-24; 13:3-22; 2 Sam. 24:16; Zech. 1:12; 3:1; 12:8). Since the angel of the Lord ceases to appear after the incarnation, it is often inferred that the angel in the O.T. is a preincarnate appearance of the Second Per-

son of the Trinity.

16:11 *Ishmael* means "God hears." Many Arabs claim him as their forefather and thus Palestine as their land (cf. Gen. 17:20 and 25:12-18).

16:12 *a wild donkey of a man.* The epithet was one of praise since the almost untameable onager (wild ass) was an admired and valuable animal. The last phrase of the verse may mean that Ishmael's descendants would live to the east of Abraham's other descendants, or it may mean they would live in defiance of Abraham's other descendants. The hostility between Arabs and Jews is well-known.

16:14 *Beer-lahai-roi* means "a well of the Living One who sees me." The exact location is unknown, though possibly it was SW. of Beersheba.

G The Circumcision of
Abraham, 17:1-27

★ 1 *a*Gen.
12:7; 18:1
*b*Gen. 28:3;
35:11 *c*Gen.
6:9; Deut.
18:13

17 Now when Abram was ninety-nine years old, *a*the LORD appeared to Abram and said to him,

"I am God *b*Almighty;
Walk before Me, and be
*c*blameless.

2 *a*Gen.
15:18 *b*Gen.
13:16; 15:5

2 "And I will establish My
*a*covenant   between
Me and you,
And I will *b*multiply you
exceedingly."

3 *a*Gen.
17:17; 18:2

3 And Abram *a*fell on his face, and God talked with him, saying,

4 *a*Gen.
35:11; 48:19

4 "As for Me, behold, My
covenant is with you,
And you shall be the fa-
ther of a *a*multitude of
nations.

★ 5 *a*Neh.
9:7 *b*Rom.
4:17

5 "No longer shall your
name be called A-
bram,
But *a*your name shall be
Abraham;
For *b*I will make you the
father of a multitude
of nations.

6 *a*Gen.
17:16; 35:11
★ 7-8
7 *a*Gen.
17:13, 19;
Ps. 105:9,
10; Luke
1:55 *b*Gen.
26:24; Lev.
11:45; 26:12,
45; Heb.
11:16 *c*Gen.
28:13; Gal.
3:16
8 *a*Gen.
12:7; 13:15,
17; Acts 7:5
*b*Ex. 6:7;
29:45; Lev.
26:12; Deut.
29:13; Rev.
21:7

6 "And I will make you ex-
ceedingly fruitful, and I will make nations of you, and *a*kings shall come forth from you.

7 "And I will establish My covenant between Me and you and your descendants after you throughout their generations for an *a*everlasting covenant, *b*to be God to you and *c*to your descend-ants after you.

8 "And *a*I will give to you and to your descendants after you, the land of your sojournings, all the land of Canaan, for an everlasting possession; and *b*I will be their God."

9 God said further to Abra-ham, "Now as for you, *a*you shall keep My covenant, you and your descendants after you throughout their generations.

10 "*a*This is My covenant, which you shall keep, between Me and you and your descend-ants after you: every male among you shall be circumcised.

11 "And *a*you shall be circum-cised in the flesh of your foreskin; and it shall be the sign of the cov-enant between Me and you.

12 "And every male among you who is *a*eight days old shall be circumcised throughout your generations, a *servant* who is born in the house or who is bought with money from any foreigner, who is not of your descendants.

13 "A *servant* who is born in your house or *a*who is bought with your money shall surely be circumcised; thus shall My cov-enant be in your flesh for an ever-lasting covenant.

14 "But an uncircumcised male who is not circumcised in the flesh of his foreskin, that person shall be *a*cut off from his people; he has broken My covenant."

15 Then God said to Abra-ham, "As for Sarai your wife, you shall not call her name Sarai, but Sarah *shall be* her name.

16 "And I will bless her, and indeed I will give you *a*a son by her. Then I will bless her, and she shall be *a mother of* nations;

★ 9-14

9 *a*Ex. 19:5

10 *a*John
7:22; Acts
7:8; Rom.
4:11

11 *a*Ex.
12:48; Deut.
10:16; Acts
7:8; Rom.
4:11

12 *a*Lev.
12:3

13 *a*Ex.
12:44

14 *a*Ex.
4:24-26

★15

16 *a*Gen.
18:10 *b*Gen.
17:6; 36:31

17:1 Thirteen years had passed since the birth of Ishmael. *God Almighty.* Heb., *El Shaddai.* Shaddai is derived from a related word that means "mountain," thus picturing God as the overpowering, almighty One, standing on a mountain.

17:5 *Abraham.* See note on 11:27.

17:7-8 The covenant is *everlasting* and includes possession of the *land of Canaan* (and more, see 15:18).

17:9-14 Abraham's part in the covenant-making process was circumcision, a rite practiced ear-lier and by other peoples. God here makes it a sign of this covenant (see Rom. 4:11). For a Hebrew to refuse circumcision was to excise himself from the covenant community, Gen. 17:14.

17:15 Sarah's name change was less important than Abraham's. *Sarai* means "my princess" and *Sarah* means "princess." Perhaps the sig-nificance lay only in marking the occasion.

*kings of peoples shall come from her."

★17 ªGen. 17:3; 18:12; 21:6 bGen. 21:7
17 Then Abraham ªfell on his face and laughed, and said in his heart, "Will a child be born to a man one hundred years old? And *will Sarah, who is ninety years old, bear a child?"
18 And Abraham said to God, "Oh that Ishmael might live before Thee!"

★19 ªGen. 17:16; 18:10; 21:2 bGen. 26:2-5
19 But God said, "No, but Sarah your wife shall bear you ªa son, and you shall call his name Isaac; and *I will establish My covenant with him for an everlasting covenant for his descendants after him.

★20 ªGen. 16:10 bGen. 25:12-16 cGen. 21:18
20 "And as for Ishmael, I have heard you; behold, I will bless him, and ªwill make him fruitful, and will multiply him exceedingly. *He shall become the father of twelve princes, and I will make him a cgreat nation.

★21 ªGen. 17:19; 18:10, 14 bGen. 21:2
21 "But My covenant I will establish with ªIsaac, whom *Sarah will bear to you at this season next year."

22 ªGen. 18:33; 35:13
22 And when He finished talking with him, ªGod went up from Abraham.

23 ªGen. 14:14 bGen. 17:9-11
23 Then Abraham took Ishmael his son, and all the servants who were ªborn in his house and all who were bought with his money, every male among the men of Abraham's household, and circumcised the flesh of their foreskin in the very same day, *as God had said to him.

24 ªRom. 4:11
24 Now Abraham was ninety-nine years old when ªhe was circumcised in the flesh of his foreskin.

25 ªGen. 16:16
25 And ªIshmael his son was thirteen years old when he was circumcised in the flesh of his foreskin.
26 In the very same day Abraham was circumcised, and Ishmael his son.

27 ªGen. 14:14
27 And all the men of his household, who were ªborn in the house or bought with money from a foreigner, were circumcised with him.

H   The Destruction of Sodom and Gomorrah, 18:1-19:38

★ 1 ªGen. 12:7; 17:1 bGen. 13:18; 14:13
18 Now ªthe Lord appeared to him by the *oaks of Mamre, while he was sitting at the tent door in the heat of the day.

★ 2 ªGen. 18:16, 22; 32:24; Josh. 5:13; Judg. 13:6-11; Heb. 13:2
2 And when he lifted up his eyes and looked, behold, three ªmen were standing opposite him; and when he saw them, he ran from the tent door to meet them, and bowed himself to the earth,

★ 3
3 and said, "My lord, if now I have found favor in your sight, please do not pass your servant by.

★ 4-8

4 ªGen. 19:2; 24:32; 43:24
4 "Please let a little water be brought and ªwash your feet, and rest yourselves under the tree;

5 ªJudg. 6:18, 19; 13:15, 16
5 and I will ªbring a piece of bread, that you may refresh yourselves; after that you may go on, since you have visited your servant." And they said, "So do, as you have said."
6 So Abraham hurried into the tent to Sarah, and said, "Quickly, prepare three measures of fine flour, knead it, and make bread cakes."

17:17 Some feel that Abraham laughed for joy, but verse 18 indicates it was an expression of doubt as he struggled to match his faith to his circumstances.
17:19 Isaac means "he laughs." God specifically designated him, not Ishmael, as heir of the covenant.
17:20 See 25:12-16.
17:21 Legally, the natural son became the heir, even though born after the son of a slave-wife.
18:1 Mamre. See note on 13:18. the tent door. Abraham's stay in Palestine was characterized by tents (cf. 12:8; 13:3) and altars (cf. 12:7, 8; 13:4, 18; 26:25) rather than by palaces and temples.
18:2 three men. One was the Lord, Yahweh (v. 1), the other two, angels (cf. 19:1).
18:3 My lord. Abraham probably did not immediately recognize his visitor as Yahweh. (Cf. Manoah's similar experience in Judg. 13:15-23.)
18:4-8 Abraham offered typical oriental courtesies to his guests. The details of these verses (e.g., they ate) show this was no vision or dream.

7 Abraham also ran to the herd, and took a tender and choice calf, and gave *it* to the servant; and he hurried to prepare it. **8** And he took curds and milk and the calf which he had prepared, and placed *it* before them; and he was standing by them under the tree as they ate. **9** Then they said to him, "Where is Sarah your wife?" And he said, "Behold, in the tent."

10 *a*Gen. 21:2; Rom. 9:9

10 And he said, "*a*I will surely return to you at this time next year; and behold, Sarah your wife shall have a son." And Sarah was listening at the tent door, which was behind him.

11 *a*Gen. 17:17; Rom. 4:19 *b*Heb. 11:11

11 Now *a*Abraham and Sarah were old, advanced in age; Sarah was *b*past childbearing.

*12 *a*Gen. 17:17; Luke 1:18 *b*1 Pet. 3:6

12 And Sarah laughed to herself, saying, "*a*After I have become old, shall I have pleasure, my *b*lord being old also?"

*13

13 And the LORD said to Abraham, "Why did Sarah laugh, saying, 'Shall I indeed bear *a child*, when I am *so* old?'

14 *a*Jer. 32:17, 27; Zech. 8:6; Matt. 19:26; Luke 1:37; Rom. 4:21 *b*Gen. 17:21; 18:10

14 "*a*Is anything too difficult for the LORD? At the *b*appointed time I will return to you, at this time next year, and Sarah shall have a son."

15 Sarah denied *it* however, saying, "I did not laugh"; for she was afraid. And He said, "No, but you did laugh."

16 *a*Gen. 18:2, 22; 19:1

16 Then *a*the men rose up from there, and looked down toward Sodom; and Abraham was walking with them to send them off.

*17 *a*Gen. 18:22, 26, 33; Amos 3:7 *b*Gen. 18:21; 19:24

17 And *a*the LORD said, "Shall I hide from Abraham *b*what I am about to do,

18 *a*Gen. 12:3; 22:18; Acts 3:25; Gal. 3:8

18 since Abraham will surely become a great and mighty nation, and in him *a*all the nations of the earth will be blessed?

19 *a*Neh. 9:7; Amos 3:2 *b*Deut. 6:6, 7 *c*Gen. 17:9 *d*Gen. 12:2, 3

19 "For I have *a*chosen him, in order that he may *b*command his children and his household after him to *c*keep the way of the LORD by doing righteousness and justice; in order that the LORD may bring upon Abraham *d*what He has spoken about him."

*20 *a*Gen. 19:13; Ezek. 16:49, 50

20 And the LORD said, "*a*The outcry of Sodom and Gomorrah is indeed great, and their sin is exceedingly grave.

*21 *a*Gen. 11:5; Ex. 3:8; Ps. 14:2

21 "I will *a*go down now, and see if they have done entirely according to its outcry, which has come to Me; and if not, I will know."

22 *a*Gen. 18:16; 19:1 *b*Gen. 18:1, 17

22 Then *a*the men turned away from there and went toward Sodom, while Abraham was still standing before *b*the LORD.

*23 *a*Ex. 23:7; Num. 16:22; 2 Sam. 24:17; Ps. 11:4-7

23 And Abraham came near and said, "*a*Wilt Thou indeed sweep away the righteous with the wicked?

*24

24 "Suppose there are fifty righteous within the city; wilt Thou indeed sweep *it* away and not spare the place for the sake of the fifty righteous who are in it?

25 *a*Deut. 1:16, 17; 32:4; Job 8:3, 20; Ps. 58:11; 94:2; Is. 3:10, 11; Rom. 3:5, 6

25 "Far be it from Thee to do such a thing, to slay the righteous with the wicked, so that the righteous and the wicked are *treated* alike. Far be it from Thee! Shall not *a*the Judge of all the earth deal justly?"

26 *a*Jer. 5:1

26 So the LORD said, "*a*If I find in Sodom fifty righteous within

---

18:12 *Sarah laughed* inwardly, either because she did not know of the promise of 17:19 or because she was unconvinced it would be fulfilled.

18:13 One of the three men (see v. 2) was now clearly identified as Yahweh, who knew Sarah's thoughts.

18:17 This section (through v. 33) gives the basis for Abraham's being called the friend of God (2 Chron. 20:7; Isa. 41:8; James 2:23).

18:20 *The outcry of Sodom and Gomorrah*. The terrible sins of Sodom and Gomorrah "cried out to heaven" for punishment (cf. 4:10).

18:21 Of course the omniscient God was fully aware of what was happening in Sodom, but His justice moved Him to demonstrate that He was in full possession of the facts. Actually, only the two angels went to Sodom (see v. 22).

18:23 Notice again Abraham's concern for other people (cf. 13:8-9).

18:24 *fifty righteous*. Lot was one of them (see 2 Pet. 2:7), though Abraham obviously assumed there were others as well. He was not merely haggling with God, who has no pleasure in the death of the wicked (cf. Ezek. 33:11).

the city, then I will spare the whole place on their account."

27 **27** And Abraham answered and said, "Now behold, I have ventured to speak to the Lord, although I am *but* ᵃdust and ashes.

27 ᵃGen. 3:19; Job 30:19; 42:6

28 "Suppose the fifty righteous are lacking five, wilt Thou destroy the whole city because of five?" And He said, "I will not destroy *it* if I find forty-five there."

29 And he spoke to Him yet again and said, "Suppose forty are found there?" And He said, "I will not do *it* on account of the forty."

30 Then he said, "Oh may the Lord not be angry, and I shall speak; suppose thirty are found there?" And He said, "I will not do *it* if I find thirty there."

31 And he said, "Now behold, I have ventured to speak to the Lord; suppose twenty are found there?" And He said, "I will not destroy *it* on account of the twenty."

32 **32** Then he said, "ᵃOh may the Lord not be angry, and I shall speak only this once; suppose ten are found there?" And He said, "I will not destroy *it* on account of the ten."

★*32* ᵃJudg. 6:39

33 **33** And as soon as He had finished speaking to Abraham ᵃthe Lᴏʀᴅ departed; and Abraham returned to his place.

33 ᵃGen. 17:22; 35:13

19 Now the ᵃtwo angels came to Sodom in the evening as Lot was sitting in the gate of Sodom. When ᵇLot saw *them,* he rose to meet them and bowed down *with his* face to the ground.

★ *1* ᵃGen. 18:2, 22
ᵇGen. 18:2-5

2 And he said, "Now behold, my lords, please turn aside into your servant's house, and spend the night, and wash your feet;

then you may rise early and go on your way." They said however, "No, but we shall spend the night in the square."

3 Yet he urged them strongly, so they turned aside to him and entered his house; ᵃand he prepared a feast for them, and baked unleavened bread, and they ate.

★ *3* ᵃGen. 18:6-8

4 Before they lay down, ᵃthe men of the city, the men of Sodom, surrounded the house, both young and old, all the people from every quarter;

4 ᵃGen. 13:13; 18:20

5 and they called to Lot and said to him, "ᵃWhere are the men who came to you tonight? Bring them out to us that we may have relations with them."

★ *5* ᵃLev. 18:22; Judg. 19:22

6 But Lot went out to them at the doorway, and shut the door behind him,

7 and said, "Please, my brothers, do not act wickedly.

8 "Now behold, ᵃI have two daughters who have not had relations with man; please let me bring them out to you, and do to them whatever you like; only do nothing to these men, inasmuch as they have come under the shelter of my roof."

★ *8* ᵃJudg. 19:24

9 But they said, "Stand aside." Furthermore, they said, "This one came in as an alien, and already ᵃhe is acting like a judge; now we will treat you worse than them." So they pressed hard against Lot and came near to break the door.

9 ᵃEx. 2:14

10 But ᵃthe men reached out their hands and brought Lot into the house with them, and shut the door.

10 ᵃGen. 19:1

18:32 Not even *ten* righteous people could be found in Sodom (cf. 19:14), so the city had to be destroyed.
19:1 *the two angels.* I.e., the same two who visited Abraham, see 18:22. *the gate of Sodom* was the center of public activity. Lot's being there may indicate he was a judge in the city (see 19:9). He greeted the angels with the customary sign of respect of bowing.
19:3 Lot insisted that the visitors come into his house, since he knew the danger they would

face if they stayed all night outside.
19:5 *that we may have relations with them.* I.e., have homosexual relations. God's attitude toward this sin is seen in the destruction of Sodom and in Lev. 18:22, 29; 20:13; Rom. 1:26; 1 Cor. 6:9; 1 Tim. 1:10.
19:8 Lot's offering his daughters is explained (though not justified) by the demands of hospitality, which obligated a host to protect his guests at all cost.

*11 aDeut.
28:28, 29;
2 Kin. 6:18;
Acts 13:11

11 And ªthey struck the men who were at the doorway of the house with blindness, both small and great, so that they wearied *themselves trying* to find the doorway.

12 Then the men said to Lot, "Whom else have you here? A son-in-law, and your sons, and your daughters, and whomever you have in the city, bring *them* out of the place;

13 aGen.
18:20 bLev.
26:30-33;
Deut. 4:26;
28:45; 1 Chr.
21:15

13 for we are about to destroy this place, because ªtheir outcry has become so great before the LORD that ᵇthe LORD has sent us to destroy it."

*14 aNum.
16:21, 45;
Rev. 18:4
bJer. 43:1, 2

14 And Lot went out and spoke to his sons-in-law, who were to marry his daughters, and said, "Up, ªget out of this place, for the LORD will destroy the city." ᵇBut he appeared to his sons-in-law to be jesting.

15 And when morning dawned, the angels urged Lot, saying, "Up, take your wife and your two daughters, who are here, lest you be swept away in the punishment of the city."

*16 aDeut.
5:15; 6:21;
7:8; 2 Pet.
2:7 bEx.
34:7; Ps.
32:10; 33:18,
19

16 But he hesitated. So the men ªseized his hand and the hand of his wife and the hands of his daughters, for ᵇthe compassion of the LORD *was* upon him; and they brought him out, and put him outside the city.

17 aJer. 48:6
bGen. 19:26
cGen. 13:10
dGen. 14:10

17 And it came about when they had brought them outside, that one said, "ªEscape for your life! ᵇDo not look behind you, and do not stay anywhere in the ᶜvalley; escape to ᵈthe mountains, lest you be swept away."

18 But Lot said to them, "Oh no, my lords!

19 "Now behold, your servant has found favor in your sight, and you have magnified your lovingkindness, which you have shown me by saving my life; but I cannot escape to the mountains, lest the disaster overtake me and I die;

20 now behold, this town is near *enough* to flee to, and it is small. Please, let me escape there (is it not small?) that my life may be saved."

*20

21 And he said to him, "Behold, I grant you this request also, not to overthrow the town of which you have spoken.

22 "Hurry, escape there, for I cannot do anything until you arrive there." Therefore the name of the town was called ªZoar.

22 aGen.
13:10; 14:2

23 The sun had risen over the earth when Lot came to Zoar.

24 Then the LORD ªrained on Sodom and Gomorrah brimstone and fire from the LORD out of heaven,

*24 aDeut.
29:23; Ps.
11:6; Is.
13:19; Ezek.
16:49, 50;
Luke 17:29;
Jude 7

25 and ªHe overthrew those cities, and all the valley, and all the inhabitants of the cities, and what grew on the ground.

25 aDeut.
29:23; Ps.
107:34; Is.
13:19; Lam.
4:6; 2 Pet.
2:6

26 But his wife, from behind him, ªlooked *back;* and she became a pillar of salt.

*26 aGen.
19:17; Luke
17:32

27 Now Abraham arose early in the morning *and went* to ªthe place where he had stood before the LORD;

27 aGen.
18:22

28 and he looked down toward Sodom and Gomorrah, and toward all the land of the valley, and he saw, and behold, ªthe

28 aRev. 9:2;
18:9

19:11 *blindness.* The Hebrew word (found only here and in 2 Kings 6:18) has the idea of loss or distortion of vision resulting in mental confusion and bewilderment.

19:14 Lot's *sons-in-law,* having rejected his warning, apparently perished (cf. v. 16).

19:16 God's mercy overcame Lot's procrastination.

19:20 *this town.* Bela (see 14:2), afterward called Zoar, means "tiny place."

19:24 *brimstone and fire.* Deposits of sulphur

(brimstone) and asphalt (cf. 14:10) have been found in this area. Possibly an earthquake occurred and lightning ignited the gases that were released, causing a rain of fire and smoke.

19:26 Lot's wife, who was trailing *behind him* with her heart still in Sodom, *looked back,* died, and possibly was enveloped by blowing *salt,* which formed a "pillar" around her body. This event was used by Jesus as a warning to others not to look back (Luke 17:21-33).

smoke of the land ascended like the smoke of a furnace.

★29 *a*Deut. 7:8; 9:5, 27 *b*2 Pet. 2:7

29 Thus it came about, when God destroyed the cities of the valley, that *a*God remembered Abraham, and *b*sent Lot out of the midst of the overthrow, when He overthrew the cities in which Lot lived.

★30 *a*Gen. 19:17, 19

30 And Lot went up from Zoar, and *a*stayed in the mountains, and his two daughters with him; for he was afraid to stay in Zoar; and he stayed in a cave, he and his two daughters.

★31-38

31 Then the first-born said to the younger, "Our father is old, and there is not a man on earth to *a*come in to us after the manner of the earth.

31 *a*Gen. 16:2, 4; 38:8; Deut. 25:5

32 *a*Luke 21:34

32 "Come, *a*let us make our father drink wine, and let us lie with him, that we may preserve our family through our father."

33 So they made their father drink wine that night, and the first-born went in and lay with her father; and he did not know when she lay down or when she arose.

34 And it came about on the morrow, that the first-born said to the younger, "Behold, I lay last night with my father; let us make him drink wine tonight also; then you go in and lie with him, that we may preserve our family through our father."

35 So they made their father drink wine that night also, and the younger arose and lay with

him; and he did not know when she lay down or when she arose.

36 Thus both the daughters of Lot were with child by their father.

37 And the first-born bore a son, and called his name *a*Moab; he is the father of the Moabites to this day.

37 *a*Deut. 2:9

38 And as for the younger, she also bore a son, and called his name Ben-ammi; he is the father of the sons of *a*Ammon to this day.

38 *a*Deut. 2:19

I Abraham and Abimelech, 20:1-18

20 Now Abraham journeyed from *a*there toward the land of *b*the Negev, and settled between Kadesh and Shur; then he sojourned in *c*Gerar.

★ 1 *a*Gen. 18:1 *b*Gen. 12:9 *c*Gen. 26:1, 6

2 And Abraham said of Sarah his wife, "*a*She is my sister." So *b*Abimelech king of Gerar sent and took Sarah.

★ 2 *a*Gen. 12:11-13; 20:12; 26:7 *b*Gen. 12:15

3 *a*But God came to Abimelech in a dream of the night, and said to him, "Behold, *b*you are a dead man because of the woman whom you have taken, for she is married."

3 *a*Gen. 12:17, 18 *b*Gen. 20:7

4 Now Abimelech had not come near her; and he said, "Lord, *a*wilt Thou slay a nation, even *though* blameless?

4 *a*Gen. 18:23-25

5 "Did he not himself say to me, 'She is my sister'? And she *a*herself said, 'He is my brother.' In *b*the integrity of my heart and

5 *a*Gen. 20:13 *b*1 Kin. 9:4; Ps. 7:8; 26:6

19:29 The *overthrow* of Sodom and Gomorrah is used as a warning on several occasions in both the Old and New Testaments (see Deut. 29:23; Isa. 1:9-10; Jer. 49:18; Amos 4:11; Matt. 10:15; 11:23-24; Rom. 9:29; 2 Pet. 2:6; Jude 7; Rev. 11:8).

19:30 *he was afraid to stay in Zoar.* Possibly because the people thought Lot was somehow responsible for the destruction of Sodom or because Lot feared further seismic disturbances.

19:31-38 The Sodom-tainted, virgin (v. 8) daughters of Lot (he had other, married daughters who perished, v. 14), fearing they would die childless, shamelessly committed incest with their father, using wine to make

him insensible to their action. The babies thus conceived were named *Moab* (meaning "from the father"; see note on Amos 2:1), from whom the Moabites came, and *Ben-ammi* (meaning "son of my people"; i.e., his father and mother were of the same family), from whom the Ammonites came (see note on Amos 1:13). The Moabites lived E. of the Dead Sea (cf. Num. 21:13), while the Ammonites lived to the NE. of it (cf. Deut. 2:37).

20:1 *Gerar.* About 10 miles S. of Gaza.

20:2 Abraham had practiced the same deception before (12:13). Like Pharaoh, *Abimelech* took many unmarried women into his harem. Sarah was now 90.

the innocence of my hands I have done this."

6 *a* 1 Sam. 25:26, 34

6 Then God said to him in the dream, "Yes, I know that in the integrity of your heart you have done this, and I also *a*kept you from sinning against Me; therefore I did not let you touch her.

★ **7** *a* 1 Sam. 7:5; 2 Kin. 5:11; Job 42:8

7 "Now therefore, restore the man's wife, for *a*he is a prophet, and he will pray for you, and you will live. But if you do not restore *her,* know that you shall surely die, you and all who are yours."

8 So Abimelech arose early in the morning and called all his servants and told all these things in their hearing; and the men were greatly frightened.

9 *a* Gen. 12:18 *b* Gen. 39:9

9 *a*Then Abimelech called Abraham and said to him, "What have you done to us? And how have I sinned against you, that you have brought on me and on my kingdom *b*a great sin? You have done to me things that ought not to be done."

10 And Abimelech said to Abraham, "What have you encountered, that you have done this thing?"

11 *a* Neh. 5:15; Prov. 16:6 *b* Gen. 12:12; 26:7

11 And Abraham said, "Because I thought, surely there is no *a*fear of God in this place; and *b*they will kill me because of my wife.

12 "Besides, she actually is my sister, the daughter of my father, but not the daughter of my mother, and she became my wife;

13 *a* Gen. 12:1-9 *b* Gen. 12:13; 20:5

13 and it came about, when *a*God caused me to wander from my father's house, that I said to her, 'This is the kindness which you will show to me: everywhere we go, *b*say of me, "He is my brother." ' "

14 *a*Abimelech then took sheep and oxen and male and female servants, and gave them to Abraham, and restored his wife Sarah to him.

14 *a* Gen. 12:16

15 And Abimelech said, "*a*Behold, my land is before you; settle wherever you please."

15 *a* Gen. 13:9; 34:10; 47:6

16 And to Sarah he said, "Behold, I have given your *a*brother a thousand pieces of silver; behold, it is your vindication before all who are with you, and before all men you are cleared."

★**16** *a* Gen. 20:5

17 And *a*Abraham prayed to God; and God healed Abimelech and his wife and his maids, so that they bore *children.*

17 *a* Num. 12:13; 21:7; James 5:16

18 *a*For the LORD had closed fast all the wombs of the household of Abimelech because of Sarah, Abraham's wife.

18 *a* Gen. 12:17

J The Birth of Isaac, 21:1-34

21 *a*Then the LORD took note of Sarah as He had said, and the LORD did for Sarah as He had promised.

1 *a* Gen. 17:16, 21; 18:10, 14; Gal. 4:23

2 *a*So Sarah conceived and bore a son to Abraham in his old age, at *b*the appointed time of which God had spoken to him.

2 *a* Acts 7:8; Gal. 4:22; Heb. 11:11 *b* Gen. 17:21; 18:10, 14

3 And Abraham called the name of his son who was born to him, whom Sarah bore to him, *a*Isaac.

★ **3** *a* Gen. 17:19, 21

4 Then Abraham circumcised his son Isaac when he was *a*eight days old, as God had commanded him.

★ **4** *a* Gen. 17:12; Acts 7:8

5 Now Abraham was *a*one hundred years old when his son Isaac was born to him.

5 *a* Gen. 17:17

6 And Sarah said, "God has made *a*laughter for me; everyone who hears will laugh with me."

★ **6** *a* Gen. 18:13; Ps. 126:2; Is. 54:1

20:7 *a prophet.* This is the first occurrence of the Hebrew word *nabi,* meaning "to proclaim, declare, speak as an intermediary," here used to emphasize the official character of Abraham's intercession. Normally it refers to someone who declares a message on behalf of a superior. The superior is usually, though not always, God (cf. Exod. 7:1). Abraham's intercession saved Abimelech's life and removed the barrenness of his household (Gen. 20:7,

17-18).

20:16 *it is your vindication.* Abimelech's large gift of *a thousand pieces of silver* (30 pieces was the price of a slave), proof of his high esteem for Abraham and Sarah, would serve to stop any scoffing on the part of her household.

21:3 *Isaac* means "he laughs" (see note on 17:19).

21:4 On circumcision, see note on 17:9-14.

21:6 This is the laughter of rejoicing.

★ **7** ᵃGen.
18:11, 13

7 And she said, "ᵃWho would have said to Abraham that Sarah would nurse children? Yet I have borne him a son in his old age."

★ **8**

8 And the child grew and was weaned, and Abraham made a great feast on the day that Isaac was weaned.

★ **9** ᵃGen.
16:1, 4, 15
ᵇGal. 4:29

9 Now Sarah saw ᵃthe son of Hagar the Egyptian, whom she had borne to Abraham, ᵇmocking.

★**10** ᵃGal.
4:30

10 Therefore she said to Abraham, "ᵃDrive out this maid and her son, for the son of this maid shall not be an heir with my son Isaac."

11 ᵃGen.
17:18

11 ᵃAnd the matter distressed Abraham greatly because of his son.

12 ᵃRom.
9:7; Heb.
11:18

12 But God said to Abraham, "Do not be distressed because of the lad and your maid; whatever Sarah tells you, listen to her, for ᵃthrough Isaac your descendants shall be named.

★**13** ᵃGen.
16:10; 21:18;
25:12-18

13 "And of ᵃthe son of the maid I will make a nation also, because he is your descendant."

14 So Abraham rose early in the morning, and took bread and a skin of water, and gave *them* to Hagar, putting *them* on her shoulder, and *gave her* the boy, and sent her away. And she departed, and wandered about in the wilderness of Beersheba.

15 And the water in the skin was used up, and she left the boy under one of the bushes.

16 ᵃJer.
6:26; Amos
8:10

16 Then she went and sat down opposite him, about a bowshot away, for she said, "Do not let me see the boy die." And she sat opposite him, and ᵃlifted up her voice and wept.

17 And God ᵃheard the lad crying; and the angel of God called to Hagar from heaven, and said to her, "What is the matter with you, Hagar? ᵇDo not fear, for God has heard the voice of the lad where he is.

17 ᵃEx. 3:7;
Deut. 26:7;
Ps. 6:8
ᵇGen. 26:24

18 "Arise, lift up the lad, and hold him by the hand; ᵃfor I will make a great nation of him."

★**18** ᵃGen.
16:10; 21:13;
25:12-16

19 Then God ᵃopened her eyes and she saw ᵇa well of water; and she went and filled the skin with water, and gave the lad a drink.

19 ᵃNum.
22:31; 2 Kin.
6:17 ᵇGen.
16:7, 14

20 And ᵃGod was with the lad, and he grew; and he lived in the wilderness, and became an archer.

20 ᵃGen.
28:15; 39:2,
3, 21

21 And ᵃhe lived in the wilderness of Paran; and his mother took a wife for him from the land of Egypt.

★**21** ᵃGen.
25:18

22 Now it came about at that time, that ᵃAbimelech and Phicol, the commander of his army, spoke to Abraham, saying, "ᵇGod is with you in all that you do;

★**22** ᵃGen.
20:2, 14;
26:26 ᵇGen.
26:28; Is.
8:10

23 now therefore, ᵃswear to me here by God that you will not deal falsely with me, or with my offspring, or with my posterity; but according to the kindness that I have shown to you, you shall show to me, and to the land in which you have sojourned."

23 ᵃJosh.
2:12; 1 Sam.
24:21

24 And Abraham said, "I swear it."

25 But Abraham complained to Abimelech because of the well of water which the servants of Abimelech ᵃhad seized.

★**25-26**

25 ᵃGen.
26:15, 18,
20-22

26 And Abimelech said, "I do not know who has done this

21:7 Sarah's body was not only rejuvenated to bear a child but also to nurse him.

21:8 *Isaac was weaned* in his second or third year, as was customary.

21:9 *mocking.* From the same Hebrew root as *Isaac,* though in an intensive form. The word is also used in 19:14 and 39:14-17. In Isaac, Ishmael saw all his hopes for an inheritance shattered.

21:10 See Gal. 4:22-31.

21:13 See notes on 16:11 and 16:12.

21:18 This promise assured Hagar that Ishmael

would survive.

21:21 *the wilderness of Paran.* The NE. part of the Sinai peninsula.

21:22 *Abimelech* (see also 20:2), though militarily and politically superior, recognized God's protection of Abraham and desired an amicable relationship with him.

21:25-26 Abraham took advantage of the cordial relationship to mention the subject of a well that, unknown to Abimelech, had been seized by his servants.

thing; neither did you tell me, nor did I hear of it until today."

★27 ᵃGen. 26:31

27 And Abraham took sheep and oxen, and gave them to Abimelech; and ᵃthe two of them made a covenant.

★28

28 Then Abraham set seven ewe lambs of the flock by themselves.

29 And Abimelech said to Abraham, "What do these seven ewe lambs mean, which you have set by themselves?"

30 ᵃGen. 31:48

30 And he said, "You shall take these seven ewe lambs from my hand in order that it may be a ᵃwitness to me, that I dug this well."

★31 ᵃGen. 21:14; 26:33

31 Therefore he called that place ᵃBeersheba; because there the two of them took an oath.

★32

32 So they made a covenant at Beersheba; and Abimelech and Phicol, the commander of his army, arose and returned to the land of the Philistines.

★33 ᵃGen. 12:8 ᵇEx. 15:18; Deut. 32:40; Ps. 90:2; 93:2; Is. 40:28; Jer. 10:10; Hab. 1:12; Heb. 13:8

33 And *Abraham* planted a tamarisk tree at Beersheba, and there ᵃhe called on the name of the Lᴏʀᴅ, the ᵇEverlasting God.

34 ᵃGen. 22:19

34 And Abraham sojourned ᵃin the land of the Philistines for many days.

K The Offering of Isaac, 22:1-24

★ 1 ᵃDeut. 8:2, 16; Heb. 11:17; James 1:12-14 ᵇGen. 22:11

22 Now it came about after these things, that ᵃGod tested Abraham, and said to him, "ᵇAbraham!" And he said, "Here I am."

★ 2 ᵃGen. 22:12, 16; John 3:16; 1 John 4:9 ᵇ2 Chr. 3:1 ᶜGen. 8:20

2 And He said, "Take now ᵃyour son, your only son, whom you love, Isaac, and go to the land of ᵇMoriah; and offer him there as a ᶜburnt offering on one of the mountains of which I will tell you."

3 So Abraham rose early in the morning and saddled his donkey, and took two of his young men with him and Isaac his son; and he split wood for the burnt offering, and arose and went to the place of which God had told him.

4 On the third day Abraham raised his eyes and saw the place from a distance.

★ 5

5 And Abraham said to his young men, "Stay here with the donkey, and I and the lad will go yonder; and we will worship and return to you."

6 ᵃJohn 19:17

6 And Abraham took the wood of the burnt offering and ᵃlaid it on Isaac his son, and he took in his hand the fire and the knife. So the two of them walked on together.

★ 7-8

7 ᵃEx. 29:38-42; John 1:29, 36; Rev. 13:8

7 And Isaac spoke to Abraham his father and said, "My father!" And he said, "Here I am, my son." And he said, "Behold, the fire and the wood, but where is the ᵃlamb for the burnt offering?"

21:27 These animals were used in ratifying the covenant (cf. 15:9-10 and note on 15:10).

21:28 These animals were a special gift of friendship, not usually given in ratifying a covenant (see Abimelech's question in v. 29).

21:31 *Beersheba* means "well of the seven, or of the oath."

21:32 It is alleged that the mention of the *Philistines* is an anachronism since they supposedly did not appear in Palestine until after 1190 B.C. However, there is evidence of expansion of Aegean trade during the period of Abraham, and the Philistines mentioned here likely were peaceful traders who settled on the SW. coast of Palestine.

21:33 *the Everlasting God.* Heb., *El Olam*, from an original form meaning "the God of Eternity."

22:1 *God tested Abraham.* God does not tempt anyone with evil (see note on James 1:13), but in certain instances He does test, try, or prove us, as in this case with Abraham.

22:2 Human sacrifice was practiced (though not by the godly) in O.T. times, and Abraham would have been acquainted with it in Mesopotamia. God's intention here was to see if Abraham loved Him more than he loved Isaac, and to try Abraham's faith in His promise concerning descendants. *Moriah* was a general area that included the hills on which Solomon later built his Temple in Jerusalem (see 2 Chron. 3:1). The journey was about 50 miles.

22:5 *we will worship and return to you.* Abraham's confidence that Isaac would return with him from the place of sacrifice stemmed from his explicit belief in resurrection (cf. Heb. 11:17-19).

22:7-8 Isaac's confidence in Abraham and Abraham's consideration for Isaac are striking.

8 And Abraham said, "God will provide for Himself the lamb for the burnt offering, my son." So the two of them walked on together.

9 Then they came to ᵃthe place of which God had told him; and Abraham built ᵇthe altar there, and arranged the wood, and bound his son Isaac, and ᶜlaid him on the altar on top of the wood.

10 And Abraham stretched out his hand, and took the knife to slay his son.

11 But ᵃthe angel of the LORD called to him from heaven, and said, "Abraham, Abraham!" And he said, "Here I am."

12 And he said, "Do not stretch out your hand against the lad, and do nothing to him; for now ᵃI know that you fear God, since you have not withheld ᵇyour son, your only son, from Me."

13 Then Abraham raised his eyes and looked, and behold, behind *him* a ram caught in the thicket by his horns; and Abraham went and took the ram, and offered him up for a burnt offering in the place of his son.

14 And Abraham called the name of that place The LORD Will Provide, as it is said to this day, "In the mount of the LORD ᵃit will be provided."

15 Then the angel of the LORD called to Abraham a second time from heaven,

16 and said, "ᵃBy Myself I have sworn, declares the LORD, because you have done this thing, and have not withheld your son, your only son,

17 indeed I will greatly bless you, and I will greatly ᵃmultiply your seed as the stars of the heavens, and as ᵇthe sand which is on the seashore; and ᶜyour seed shall possess the gate of their enemies.

18 "And ᵃin your seed all the nations of the earth shall be blessed, because you have ᵇobeyed My voice."

19 ᵃSo Abraham returned to his young men, and they arose and went together to Beersheba; and Abraham lived at Beersheba.

20 Now it came about after these things, that it was told Abraham, saying, "Behold, ᵃMilcah also has borne children to your brother Nahor:

21 Uz his first-born and Buz his brother and Kemuel the father of Aram

22 and Chesed and Hazo and Pildash and Jidlaph and Bethuel."

23 And Bethuel became the father of ᵃRebekah: these eight Milcah bore to Nahor, Abraham's brother.

24 And his concubine, whose name was Reumah, also bore Tebah and Gaham and Tahash and Maacah.

L The Death and Burial of Sarah, 23:1-20

23 Now Sarah lived one hundred and twenty-seven years; *these were* the years of the life of Sarah.

2 And Sarah died in ᵃKiriath-arba (that is, Hebron) in the land of Canaan; and Abraham went in to mourn for Sarah and to weep for her.

Cross-references

9 ᵃGen. 22:2 ᵇGen. 12:7, 8; 13:18 ᶜHeb. 11:17-19; James 2:21

★11 ᵃGen. 16:7-11; 21:17, 18

★12 ᵃJames 2:21, 22 ᵇGen. 22:2, 16

★13

★14 ᵃGen. 22:8

★16-18

16 ᵃPs. 105:9; Luke 1:73; Heb. 6:13, 14

17 ᵃGen. 15:5; 26:4; Jer. 33:22; Heb. 11:12 ᵇGen. 32:12 ᶜGen. 24:60

18 ᵃGen. 12:3; 18:18; Acts 3:25; Gal. 3:8, 16 ᵇGen. 18:19; 22:3, 10; 26:5

19 ᵃGen. 22:5

20 ᵃGen. 11:29

★23 ᵃGen. 24:15

2 ᵃJosh. 14:15; 15:13; 21:11

22:11 *the angel of the LORD.* See note on 16:10.
22:12 God was now certain that Abraham feared (reverenced) Him more than anyone else since he was willing to offer Him his son.
22:13 The ram offered as a substitute for Isaac illustrates the substitutionary sacrifice of the Lamb of God (cf. John 1:29).
22:14 *The LORD Will Provide.* Heb., *Yahweh yireh,* meaning "the Lord will see to it."
22:16-18 God assures Abraham again that His covenant with him would be fulfilled. *and as*

the sand which is on the seashore. Cf. 13:16 and 15:5. About 3,000 stars can be counted with the naked eye, but the comparison of Abraham's seed to dust and sand increases the number almost immeasurably. *your seed shall possess the gate of their enemies.* This anticipates the conquest of Canaan under Joshua.
22:23 *Bethuel* and *Rebekah.* Abraham's nephew and grandniece. Rebekah later became Isaac's wife, see 24:15, 67.

3 Then Abraham rose from before his dead, and spoke to the ᵃsons of Heth, saying,

4 "I am ᵃa stranger and a sojourner among you; ᵇgive me a ᶜburial site among you, that I may bury my dead out of my sight."

5 And the sons of Heth answered Abraham, saying to him,

6 "Hear us, my lord, you are a ᵃmighty prince among us; bury your dead in the choicest of our graves; none of us will refuse you his grave for burying your dead."

7 So Abraham rose and bowed to the people of the land, the sons of Heth.

8 And he spoke with them, saying, "If it is your wish *for me* to bury my dead out of my sight, hear me, and approach ᵃEphron the son of Zohar for me,

9 that he may give me the cave of Machpelah which he owns, which is at the end of his field; for the full price let him give it to me in your presence for a burial site."

10 Now Ephron was sitting among the sons of Heth; and Ephron the Hittite answered Abraham in the hearing of the sons of Heth; *even* ᵃof all who went in at the gate of his city, saying,

11 "No, my lord, hear me; ᵃI give you the field, and I give you the cave that is in it. In the presence of the sons of my people I give it to you; bury your dead."

12 And Abraham bowed before the people of the land.

13 And he spoke to Ephron in the hearing of the people of the land, saying, "If you will only please listen to me; I will give the price of the field, accept *it* from me, that I may bury my dead there."

14 Then Ephron answered Abraham, saying to him,

15 "My lord, listen to me; a piece of land worth four hundred ᵃshekels of silver, what is that between me and you? So bury your dead."

16 And Abraham listened to Ephron; and Abraham ᵃweighed out for Ephron the silver which he had named in the hearing of the sons of Heth, four hundred shekels of silver, commercial standard.

17 So ᵃEphron's field, which was in Machpelah, which faced Mamre, the field and cave which was in it, and all the trees which were in the field, that were within all the confines of its border, were deeded over

18 to Abraham for a possession ᵃin the presence of the sons of Heth, before all who went in at the gate of his city.

19 And after this, Abraham buried Sarah his wife in the cave of the field at Machpelah facing Mamre (that is, Hebron) in the land of Canaan.

20 So the field, and the cave that is in it, were ᵃdeeded over to Abraham for a burial site by the sons of Heth.

23:3 *the sons of Heth* were Hittites (cf. v. 10), descendants of Ham and Canaan (cf. 10:15). The name also refers to a Hattian people of Asia Minor, some of whom may have penetrated southern Palestine for commercial reasons. By the time the Hittites became a great empire (Josh 1:4), Indo-Europeans had established themselves as the ruling class and ruling dynasty among them.

23:9 *that he may give me.* Better, sell me. Abraham wanted to buy only the *cave of Machpelah,* but Ephron wished also to sell him the *field* in which it was located. Hittite law required Ephron to be responsible for dues on the entire property if he sold Abraham only the cave, but not if he sold him the entire parcel.

23:15 *four hundred shekels of silver.* At this time a shekel was a weight (perhaps ½ oz.). The field sold for a high price for those days.

23:19 Not only *Sarah,* but Abraham, Isaac, Rebekah, Leah, and Jacob were buried there (see 25:9; 49:31; 50:13). The site of the cave has been identified with two caves, one above the other, beneath the great mosque in the center of modern Hebron.

M The Marriage of Isaac,
24:1-67

1 aGen.
18:11 bGen.
12:2; 13:2;
24:35; Gal.
3:9

24 Now aAbraham was old, advanced in age; and the LORD had bblessed Abraham in every way.

★ **2** aGen.
39:4-6 bGen.
24:9; 47:29

2 And Abraham said to his servant, the oldest of his household, who had acharge of all that he owned, "bPlease place your hand under my thigh,

★ **3** aGen.
14:19, 22
bDeut. 7:3;
2 Cor. 6:14-
17 cGen.
10:15-19,
26:34, 35;
28:1, 8

3 and I will make you swear by the LORD, athe God of heaven and the God of earth, that you bshall not take a wife for my son from the daughters of cthe Canaanites, among whom I live,

★ **4-9**

4 aGen.
12:1; Heb.
11:15

4 but you shall go to amy country and to my relatives, and take a wife for my son Isaac."

5 And the servant said to him, "Suppose the woman will not be willing to follow me to this land; should I take your son back to the land from where you came?"

6 aGen.
24:8

6 Then Abraham said to him, "aBeware lest you take my son back there!

7 aGen.
24:3 bGen.
12:7; 13:15;
15:18; Ex.
32:13 cGen.
16:7; 21:17;
22:11; Ex.
23:20, 23

7 "aThe LORD, the God of heaven, who took me from my father's house and from the land of my birth, and who spoke to me, and who swore to me, saying, 'bTo your descendants I will give this land,' He will send cHis angel before you, and you will take a wife for my son from there.

8 aJosh.
2:17-20
bGen. 24:6

8 "But if the woman is not willing to follow you, then you will abe free from this my oath; bonly do not take my son back there."

9 aGen.
24:2

9 So the servant aplaced his hand under the thigh of Abraham his master, and swore to him concerning this matter.

★**10** aGen.
24:22, 53
bGen. 11:31,
32

10 Then the servant took ten camels from the camels of his master, and set out with a variety of agood things of his master's in his hand; and he arose, and went to Mesopotamia, to bthe city of Nahor.

11 aGen.
24:42 bEx.
2:16; 1 Sam.
9:11

11 And he made the camels kneel down outside the city by athe well of water at evening time, bthe time when women go out to draw water.

12 aGen.
24:27, 42,
48; 26:24;
Ex. 3:6, 15
bGen. 27:20

12 And he said, "aO LORD, the God of my master Abraham, please bgrant me success today, and show lovingkindness to my master Abraham.

13 aGen.
24:43

13 "Behold, aI am standing by the spring, and the daughters of the men of the city are coming out to draw water;

★**14**

14 now may it be that the girl to whom I say, 'Please let down your jar so that I may drink,' and who answers, 'Drink, and I will water your camels also';—may she *be the one* whom Thou hast appointed for Thy servant Isaac; and by this I shall know that Thou hast shown lovingkindness to my master."

15 aGen.
24:45 bGen.
22:20, 23
cGen. 11:29

15 And it came about abefore he had finished speaking, that behold, bRebekah who was born to Bethuel the son of cMilcah, the wife of Abraham's brother Nahor, came out with her jar on her shoulder.

16 aGen.
12:11; 26:7;
29:17

16 And the girl was avery beautiful, a virgin, and no man had had relations with her; and she went down to the spring and filled her jar, and came up.

24:2 Abraham's oldest *servant* was doubtless Eliezer (cf. 15:2). *thigh* (cf. 47:29) is a euphemism for the procreative organ. This act either symbolized that the yet unborn children would avenge any violation of the oath, or solemnized the oath in the name of the God who gave circumcision as the sign of His covenant.

24:3 *the daughters of the Canaanites* did not know the true God and therefore would not be suitable for Isaac. Abraham was now about 140. Isaac was 40 when he married Rebekah (see 25:20).

24:4-9 The journey back to Mesopotamia was over 500 miles, and the servant was forbidden to allow Isaac to accompany him, even with the likelihood that a prospective bride would not wish to make the long trip to Palestine to meet Isaac.

24:10 *the city of Nahor* was in the vicinity of Haran (see also 11:31; 22:20; 27:43).

24:14 Notice how specific the servant's prayer was (cf. James 4:2). To water ten camels (Gen. 24:10) involved considerable hard work.

17 [a] John 4:7

17 Then the servant ran to meet her, and said, "[a]Please let me drink a little water from your jar."

18 [a] Gen. 24:14, 46

18 And [a]she said, "Drink, my lord"; and she quickly lowered her jar to her hand, and gave him a drink.

19 [a] Gen. 24:14

19 Now when she had finished giving him a drink, [a]she said, "I will draw also for your camels until they have finished drinking."

20 So she quickly emptied her jar into the trough, and ran back to the well to draw, and she drew for all his camels.

21 [a] Gen. 24:12-14, 27, 52

21 [a]Meanwhile, the man was gazing at her in silence, to know whether the LORD had made his journey successful or not.

★22 [a] Gen. 24:47; Ex. 32:2, 3

22 Then it came about, when the camels had finished drinking, that the man took a [a]gold ring weighing a half-shekel and two bracelets for her wrists weighing ten shekels in gold,

23 and said, "Whose daughter are you? Please tell me, is there room for us to lodge in your father's house?"

24 [a] Gen. 24:15

24 And she said to him, "[a]I am the daughter of Bethuel, the son of Milcah, whom she bore to Nahor."

25 Again she said to him, "We have plenty of both straw and feed, and room to lodge in."

26 [a] Gen. 24:48, 52; Ex. 4:31

26 Then the man [a]bowed low and worshiped the LORD.

27 [a] Gen. 24:12, 42, 48; Ex. 18:10; Ruth 4:14; 1 Sam. 25:32; 2 Sam. 18:28; Luke 1:68 [b] Gen. 32:10; Ps. 98:3 [c] Gen. 24:21, 48

27 And he said, "[a]Blessed be the LORD, the God of my master Abraham, who has not forsaken [b]His lovingkindness and His truth toward my master; as for me, [c]the LORD has guided me in the way to the house of my master's brothers."

28 [a] Gen. 29:12

28 Then [a]the girl ran and told her mother's household about these things.

29 [a] Gen. 29:5, 13

29 Now Rebekah had a brother whose name was [a]Laban; and Laban ran outside to the man at the spring.

30 And it came about that when he saw the ring, and the bracelets on his sister's wrists, and when he heard the words of Rebekah his sister, saying, "This is what the man said to me," he went to the man; and behold, he was standing by the camels at the spring.

31 [a] Gen. 29:13 [b] Gen. 26:29; Ruth 3:10; Ps. 115:15 [c] Gen. 18:3-5; 19:2, 3

31 And he said, "[a]Come in, [b]blessed of the LORD! Why do you stand outside since [c]I have prepared the house, and a place for the camels?"

32 [a] Gen. 43:24; Judg. 19:21

32 So the man entered the house. Then [a]Laban unloaded the camels, and he gave straw and feed to the camels, and water to wash his feet and the feet of the men who were with him.

33 But when *food* was set before him to eat, he said, "I will not eat until I have told my business." And he said, "Speak on."

34 [a] Gen. 24:2

34 So he said, "I am [a]Abraham's servant.

35 [a] Gen. 24:1 [b] Gen. 13:2

35 "And the LORD has greatly [a]blessed my master, so that he has become rich; and He has given him [b]flocks and herds, and silver and gold, and servants and maids, and camels and donkeys.

36 [a] Gen. 21:1-7 [b] Gen. 25:5

36 "Now [a]Sarah my master's wife bore a son to my master in her old age; and [b]he has given him all that he has.

37 [a] Gen. 24:2-4

37 "[a]And my master made me swear, saying, 'You shall not take a wife for my son from the daughters of the Canaanites, in whose land I live;

38 but you shall go to my father's house, and to my relatives, and take a wife for my son.'

39 [a] Gen. 24:5

39 "[a]And I said to my master, 'Suppose the woman does not follow me.'

40 [a] Gen. 24:7 [b] Gen. 5:22, 24; 17:1 [c] Ex. 23:20

40 "And he said to me, '[a]The LORD, before whom I have [b]walked, will send [c]His angel with you to make your journey successful, and you will take a wife for my son from my relatives, and from my father's house;

41 [a] Gen. 24:8

41 [a]then you will be free from my oath, when you come to my

---

24:22 *shekels.* See note on 23:15.

relatives; and if they do not give her to you, you will be free from my oath.'

42 ^aGen. 24:11, 12 ^bNeh. 1:11

42 "So ^aI came today to the spring, and said, 'O Lᴏʀᴅ, the God of my master Abraham, if now Thou wilt make my journey on which I go ^bsuccessful;

43 ^aGen. 24:13 ^bGen. 24:14

43 behold, ^aI am standing by the spring, and may it be that the maiden who comes out to draw, and to whom I say, "^bPlease let me drink a little water from your jar";

44 and she will say to me, "You drink, and I will draw for your camels also"; let her be the woman whom the Lᴏʀᴅ has appointed for my master's son.'

45 ^a1 Sam. 1:13 ^bGen. 24:15 ^cGen. 24:17

45 "Before I had finished ^aspeaking in my heart, behold, ^bRebekah came out with her jar on her shoulder, and went down to the spring and drew; and ^cI said to her, 'Please let me drink.'

46 ^aGen. 24:18, 19

46 "And she quickly lowered her jar from her *shoulder*, and said, '^aDrink, and I will water your camels also'; so I drank, and she watered the camels also.

47 ^aGen. 24:23, 24 ^bEzek. 16:11, 12

47 "^aThen I asked her, and said, 'Whose daughter are you?' And she said, 'The daughter of Bethuel, Nahor's son, whom Milcah bore to him'; and I put the ^bring on her nose, and the bracelets on her wrists.

48 ^aGen. 24:26, 52 ^bGen. 24:27; Ps. 32:8; 48:14; Is. 48:17

48 "And I ^abowed low and worshiped the Lᴏʀᴅ, and blessed the Lᴏʀᴅ, the God of my master Abraham, ^bwho had guided me in the right way to take the daughter of my master's kinsman for his son.

49 ^aGen. 47:29; Josh. 2:14

49 "So now if you are going to ^adeal kindly and truly with my master, tell me; and if not, let me know, that I may turn to the right hand or the left."

50 ^aPs. 118:23; Mark 12:11 ^bGen. 31:24, 29

50 Then Laban and Bethuel answered and said, "^aThe matter comes from the Lᴏʀᴅ; ^bso we cannot speak to you bad or good.

51 "Behold, Rebekah is before you, take *her* and go, and let her be the wife of your master's son, as the Lᴏʀᴅ has spoken."

52 ^aGen. 24:26, 48

52 And it came about when Abraham's servant heard their words, that he ^abowed himself to the ground before the Lᴏʀᴅ.

★53 ^aGen. 24:10, 22; Ex. 3:22; 11:2; 12:35

53 And the servant brought out ^aarticles of silver and articles of gold, and garments, and gave them to Rebekah; he also gave precious things to her brother and to her mother.

54 ^aGen. 24:56, 59; 30:25

54 Then he and the men who were with him ate and drank and spent the night. When they arose in the morning, he said, "^aSend me away to my master."

★55-57

55 ^aJudg. 19:4

55 But her brother and her mother said, "^aLet the girl stay with us *a few* days, say ten; afterward she may go."

56 ^aGen. 24:40

56 And he said to them, "Do not delay me, since ^athe Lᴏʀᴅ has prospered my way. Send me away that I may go to my master."

57 And they said, "We will call the girl and consult her wishes."

58 Then they called Rebekah and said to her, "Will you go with this man?" And she said, "I will go."

59 ^aGen. 35:8

59 Thus they sent away their sister Rebekah and ^aher nurse with Abraham's servant and his men.

60 ^aGen. 17:16 ^bGen. 22:17

60 And they blessed Rebekah and said to her,

"May you, our sister,
^aBecome thousands of
  ten thousands,
And may ^byour descendants possess
The gate of those who
  hate them."

24:53 These gifts to the bride-to-be and her family constituted a kind of dowry, assuring the financial competence of the groom.

24:55-57 Rebekah's family wanted time to become accustomed to the thought of her leav-ing, but the servant, reminding them that God had clearly led, wanted no prolonged parting. In the end, the decision was made by Rebekah.

61 Then Rebekah arose with her maids, and they mounted the camels and followed the man. So the servant took Rebekah and departed.

*62 *aGen. 16:14; 25:11 bGen. 20:1*

62 Now Isaac had come from going to *aBeer-lahai-roi; for he was living in *bthe Negev.

*63 *aJosh. 1:8; Ps. 1:2; 77:12; 119:15, 27, 48; 143:5; 145:5 bGen. 18:2*

63 And Isaac went out *ato meditate in the field toward evening; and *bhe lifted up his eyes and looked, and behold, camels were coming.

64 And Rebekah lifted up her eyes, and when she saw Isaac she dismounted from the camel.

★65

65 And she said to the servant, "Who is that man walking in the field to meet us?" And the servant said, "He is my master." Then she took her veil and covered herself.

66 And the servant told Isaac all the things that he had done.

*67 *aGen. 25:20 bGen. 29:18 cGen. 23:1, 2*

67 Then Isaac brought her into his mother Sarah's tent, and *ahe took Rebekah, and she became his wife; and *bhe loved her; thus Isaac was comforted after *chis mother's death.

N   The Death of Abraham,
25:1-11

★1

25 Now Abraham took another wife, whose name was Keturah.

★2-4

*2 *a1 Chr. 1:32, 33*

2 And *ashe bore to him Zimran and Jokshan and Medan and Midian and Ishbak and Shuah.

3 And Jokshan became the father of Sheba and Dedan. And the sons of Dedan were Asshurim and Letushim and Leummim.

4 And the sons of Midian *were* Ephah and Epher and Hanoch and Abida and Eldaah. All these *were* the sons of Keturah.

*5 *aGen. 24:35, 36*

5 *aNow Abraham gave all that he had to Isaac;

*★6 *aGen. 21:14*

6 but to the sons of his concubines, Abraham gave gifts while he was still living, and *asent them away from his son Isaac eastward, to the land of the east.

*7 *aGen. 12:4*

7 And these are all the years of Abraham's life that he lived, *aone hundred and seventy-five years.

*★8 *aGen. 15:15; 47:8, 9 bGen. 25:17; 35:29; 49:29, 33*

8 And Abraham breathed his last and died *ain a ripe old age, an old man and satisfied *with life;* and he was *bgathered to his people.

*★9 *aGen. 23:17, 18; 49:29, 30; 50:13*

9 Then his sons Isaac and Ishmael buried him in *athe cave of Machpelah, in the field of Ephron the son of Zohar the Hittite, facing Mamre,

*★10 *aGen. 23:3-16*

10 *athe field which Abraham purchased from the sons of Heth; there Abraham was buried with Sarah his wife.

*★11 *aGen. 12:2, 3; 22:17; 26:3 bGen. 16:14; 24:62*

11 And it came about after the death of Abraham, that *aGod blessed his son Isaac; and Isaac lived by *bBeer-lahai-roi.

VII   THE DESCENDANTS OF ISHMAEL, 25:12-18

★12-16

*12 *aGen. 16:15*

12 Now these are *the records of* the generations of *aIshmael, Abraham's son, whom Hagar the Egyptian, Sarah's maid, bore to Abraham;

24:62 *Beer-lahai-roi.* See note on 16:14.

24:65 The *veil,* a sign of modesty and respect, was large enough to wrap around both face and body.

25:1 *Keturah* was a concubine (cf. v. 6; 1 Chron. 1:32), suggesting to some that Abraham may have married her while Sarah was still living.

25:2-4 Many of these names have been identified with various Arab tribes, fulfilling God's promise to Abraham that he would be the father of many nations (see 17:4).

25:6 Though Abraham provided for all his children by giving them *gifts* (probably starter flocks and herds), he dismissed them and

made Isaac his principal heir.

25:8 *was gathered to his people.* An indication that those who had died were regarded as people still existing. This is an early testimony to belief in life after death.

25:9 The presence of Ishmael at Abraham's funeral shows a reconciliation between him and Isaac.

25:10 See notes on 23:9, 15, 19.

25:11 *Beer-lahai-roi.* See note on 16:14.

25:12-16 This list of Ishmael's descendants shows the fulfillment of the promise of 17:20. They settled in the general regions of central and north central Arabia.

13 *a*1 Chr. 1:29-31

13 and these are the names of *a*the sons of Ishmael, by their names, in the order of their birth: Nebaioth, the first-born of Ishmael, and Kedar and Adbeel and Mibsam

14 and Mishma and Dumah and Massa,

15 Hadad and Tema, Jetur, Naphish and Kedemah.

16 *a*Gen. 17:20

16 These are the sons of Ishmael and these are their names, by their villages, and by their camps; *a*twelve princes according to their tribes.

17 *a*Gen. 16:16 *b*Gen. 25:8; 49:33

17 And these are the years of the life of Ishmael, *a*one hundred and thirty-seven years; and he breathed his last and died, and was *b*gathered to his people.

★**18** *a*1 Sam. 15:7 *b*Gen. 20:1 *c*Gen. 16:12

18 And they settled from *a*Havilah to *b*Shur which is east of Egypt as one goes toward Assyria; *c*he settled in defiance of all his relatives.

VIII   THE HISTORY OF ISAAC AND HIS SONS, 25:19–36:43

A   The Birth of Jacob and Esau, and Selling of Esau's Birthright, 25:19–34

19 *a*Matt. 1:2

19 Now these are *the records of* *a*the generations of Isaac, Abraham's son: Abraham became the father of Isaac;

★**20** *a*Gen. 24:15, 29, 67 *b*Gen. 22:23 *c*Gen. 24:29

20 and Isaac was forty years old when he took *a*Rebekah, the *b*daughter of Bethuel the Aramean of Paddan-aram, the *c*sister of Laban the Aramean, to be his wife.

21 *a*1 Sam. 1:17; 1 Chr. 5:20; 2 Chr. 33:13; Ezra 8:23; Ps. 127:3 *b*Rom. 9:10

21 And Isaac prayed to the LORD on behalf of his wife, because she was barren; and *a*the LORD answered him and Rebekah his wife *b*conceived.

★**22-23**

22 *a*1 Sam. 9:9; 10:22

22 But the children struggled together within her; and she said, "If it is so, why then am I *this* way?" So she went to *a*inquire of the LORD.

23 *a*Gen. 17:4-6, 16; Num. 20:14; Deut. 2:4, 8 *b*Gen. 27:29 *c*Gen. 27:40; Mal. 1:2, 3; Rom. 9:12

23 And the LORD said to her,
  "*a*Two nations are in your
    womb;
    *b*And two peoples shall
      be separated from
      your body;
  And one people shall be
    stronger than the other;
  And *c*the older shall
    serve the younger."

24 When her days to be delivered were fulfilled, behold, there were twins in her womb.

★**25** *a*Gen. 27:11

25 Now the first came forth red, *a*all over like a hairy garment; and they named him Esau.

★**26** *a*Hos. 12:3 *b*Gen. 27:36 *c*Gen. 25:20

26 And afterward his brother came forth with *a*his hand holding on to Esau's heel, so *b*his name was called Jacob; and Isaac was *c*sixty years old when she gave birth to them.

★**27** *a*Heb. 11:9

27 When the boys grew up, Esau became a skillful hunter, a man of the field; but Jacob was a peaceful man, *a*living in tents.

28 *a*Gen. 27:19 *b*Gen. 27:6-10

28 Now Isaac loved Esau, because he had *a*a taste for game; *b*but Rebekah loved Jacob.

★**29** *a*2 Kin. 4:38

29 And when Jacob had cooked *a*stew, Esau came in from the field and he was famished;

25:18 *Havilah* was located in central Arabia N. of modern Yemen. *Shur*. See note on 16:7. *he settled in defiance of all his relatives.* Better, he settled to the east of all his brethren.

25:20 *Paddan-aram* was also called Mesopotamia (cf. 24:10) and lay E. of Palestine. Its chief city was Haran.

25:22-23 The struggle within Rebekah's womb foreshadowed the struggle between the two peoples (the Edomites and the Israelites) of which Esau and Jacob were the progenitors. Further, the *younger* would occupy the preeminent place that normally went to the first-born. See also Hos. 12:3; Rom. 9:10-13.

25:25 *red* anticipates the play on the meaning of Esau's other name, Edom, which means "red," (cf. v. 30). *hairy* was a Hebrew pun on the name Esau.

25:26 *Jacob* means "heel catcher," "trickster," or "supplanter" (cf. 27:36).

25:27 The only other *hunter*, in addition to Esau, mentioned in the Bible is Nimrod (see 10:9). Notice the other description of Esau in Heb. 12:16. Jacob is described as *peaceful*, i.e., amiable, pious, cultured.

25:29 *cooked stew*. I.e., boiled a thick soup of red lentils.

30 and Esau said to Jacob, "Please let me have a swallow of that red stuff there, for I am famished." Therefore his name was called Edom.

★31 *a*Deut. 21:16, 17; 1 Chr. 5:1, 2

31 But Jacob said, "First sell me your *a*birthright."

32 And Esau said, "Behold, I am about to die; so of what *use* then is the birthright to me?"

33 *a*Heb. 12:16

33 And Jacob said, "First swear to me"; so he swore to him, and *a*sold his birthright to Jacob.

34 Then Jacob gave Esau bread and lentil stew; and he ate and drank, and rose and went on his way. Thus Esau despised his birthright.

B Isaac and Abimelech, 26:1-35

★ 1 *a*Gen. 12:10 *b*Gen. 20:1, 2

26 Now there was *a*a famine in the land, besides the previous famine that had occurred in the days of Abraham. So Isaac went to Gerar, to *b*Abimelech king of the Philistines.

2 *a*Gen. 12:7; 17:1; 18:1 *b*Gen. 12:1

2 And the LORD *a*appeared to him and said, "Do not go down to Egypt; *b*stay in the land of which I shall tell you.

3 *a*Gen. 26:24; 28:15; 31:3 *b*Gen. 12:2 *c*Gen. 12:7; 13:15; 15:18 *d*Gen. 22:16-18; Ps. 105:9

3 "Sojourn in this land and *a*I will be with you and *b*bless you, for *c*to you and to your descendants I will give all these lands, and I will establish *d*the oath which I swore to your father Abraham.

4 *a*Gen. 15:5; 22:17; Ex. 32:13 *b*Gen. 22:18; Gal. 3:8

4 "And *a*I will multiply your descendants as the stars of heaven, and will give your descendants all these lands; and *b*by your descendants all the nations of the earth shall be blessed;

★ 5 *a*Gen. 22:16

5 because Abraham *a*obeyed Me and kept My charge, My commandments, My statutes and My laws."

6 So Isaac lived in Gerar.

7 When the men of the place asked about his wife, he said, "*a*She is my sister," for he was *b*afraid to say, "my wife," *thinking*, "the men of the place might kill me on account of Rebekah, for she is *c*beautiful."

7 *a*Gen. 12:13; 20:2, 12 *b*Prov. 29:25 *c*Gen. 12:11; 24:16; 29:17

8 And it came about, when he had been there a long time, that Abimelech king of the Philistines looked out through a window, and saw, and behold, Isaac was caressing his wife Rebekah.

9 Then Abimelech called Isaac and said, "Behold, certainly she is your wife! How then did you say, 'She is my sister'?" And Isaac said to him, "Because I said, 'Lest I die on account of her.'"

10 And *a*Abimelech said, "What is this you have done to us? One of the people might easily have lain with your wife, and you would have brought guilt upon us."

10 *a*Gen. 20:9

11 So Abimelech charged all the people, saying, "He who *a*touches this man or his wife shall surely be put to death."

11 *a*Ps. 105:15

12 Now Isaac sowed in that land, and reaped in the same year a hundredfold. And *a*the LORD blessed him,

12 *a*Gen. 24:1; 26:3; Job 42:12; Prov. 10:22

13 and the man *a*became rich, and continued to grow richer until he became very wealthy;

13 *a*Prov. 10:22

14 for *a*he had possessions of flocks and herds and a great household, so that the Philistines envied him.

14 *a*Gen. 24:35; 25:5

15 Now *a*all the wells which his father's servants had dug in the days of Abraham his father,

★15 *a*Gen. 21:25, 30

25:31 The *birthright* of the eldest son gave him precedence over his brothers (cf. 43:33) and assured him a double share of his father's inheritance (cf. Deut. 21:17). It could be forfeited by committing a serious sin (cf. 1 Chron. 5:1) and it could be bartered, as in this instance. The agreement was solemnized by an oath (Gen. 25:33).

26:1 *famine . . . in the days of Abraham.* See 12:10. On *Gerar,* see note on 20:1. *Abimelech* is a dynastic title, such as pharaoh. Since this occurred 97 years later, the Abimelech mentioned here was probably not the same as the ruler of chapter 20.

26:5 Though the covenant made with Abraham was initiated by God's unconditional grace, God delighted to acknowledge the worthiness of Abraham (as also in 22:16) and to confirm the covenant to Isaac.

26:15 The Philistines, who at this point in history were limited in number and power, began to fill up the wells which were essential to Isaac's continued prosperity, and he acceded to their request that he leave their territory.

the Philistines stopped up by filling them with earth.

16 ^aEx. 1:9   **16** Then Abimelech said to Isaac, "Go away from us, for you are ^atoo powerful for us."

17 And Isaac departed from there and camped in the valley of Gerar, and settled there.

18 Then Isaac dug again the wells of water which had been dug in the days of his father Abraham, for the Philistines had stopped them up after the death of Abraham; and he gave them the same names which his father had given them.

19 But when Isaac's servants dug in the valley and found there a well of flowing water,

★**20** ^aGen. 21:25   **20** the herdsmen of Gerar ^aquarreled with the herdsmen of Isaac, saying, "The water is ours!" So he named the well Esek, because they contended with him.

★**21**   **21** Then they dug another well, and they quarreled over it too, so he named it Sitnah.

★**22** ^aPs. 4:1; Is. 54:2, 3 ^bGen. 17:6; Ex. 1:7   **22** And he moved away from there and dug another well, and they did not quarrel over it; so he named it Rehoboth, for he said, "^aAt last the Lord has made room for us, and we shall be ^bfruitful in the land."

23 ^aGen. 22:19   **23** Then he went up from there to ^aBeersheba.

★**24-25**   **24** And the Lord ^aappeared to him the same night and said,

24 ^aGen. 26:2 ^bGen. 17:7, 8; 24:12; Ex. 3:6; Acts 7:32 ^cGen. 15:1 ^dGen. 22:17; 26:3, 4

"^bI am the God of your father Abraham;
^cDo not fear, for I am with you.
I ^dwill bless you, and multiply your descendants,
For the sake of My servant Abraham."

25 ^aGen. 12:7, 8; 13:4, 18; Ps. 116:17   **25** So he built an ^aaltar there, and called upon the name of the Lord, and pitched his tent there;

and there Isaac's servants dug a well.

26 Then ^aAbimelech came to him from Gerar with his adviser Ahuzzath, and Phicol the commander of his army.

27 And Isaac said to them, "^aWhy have you come to me, since you hate me, and have sent me away from you?"

28 And they said, "We see plainly ^athat the Lord has been with you; so we said, 'Let there now be an oath between us, even between you and us, and let us make a covenant with you,

29 that you will do us no harm, just as we have not touched you and have done to you nothing but good, and have sent you away in peace. You are now the ^ablessed of the Lord.'"

30 Then ^ahe made them a feast, and they ate and drank.

31 And in the morning they arose early and ^aexchanged oaths; then Isaac sent them away and they departed from him in peace.

32 Now it came about on the same day, that Isaac's servants came in and told him about the well which they had dug, and said to him, "We have found water."

33 So he called it Shibah; therefore the name of the city is ^aBeersheba to this day.

34 And when Esau was forty years old ^ahe married Judith the daughter of Beeri the Hittite, and Basemath the daughter of Elon the Hittite;

35 and ^athey brought grief to Isaac and Rebekah.

★**26-31**
26 ^aGen. 21:22
27 ^aJudg. 11:7
28 ^aGen. 21:22, 23
29 ^aGen. 24:31; Ps. 115:15
30 ^aGen. 19:3
31 ^aGen. 21:31
★**33** ^aGen. 21:31
★**34** ^aGen. 28:8; 36:2
35 ^aGen. 27:46

C   The Blessing of Jacob by Deception, 27:1-46

1 ^aGen. 48:10; 1 Sam. 3:2 ^bGen. 25:25, 33, 34

27 Now it came about, when Isaac was old, and ^ahis

26:20 *Esek* means "contention."
26:21 *Sitnah* means "enmity."
26:22 *Rehoboth* means "plenty of room."
26:24-25 The appearance of the Lord, confirming again the Abrahamic covenant, called for the building of an altar and worship of the Lord.
26:26-31 Abimelech, fearing possible reprisals

from Isaac (see vv. 15-16), sought and received an agreement from Isaac to live in peace (see also 21:22-32).
26:33 *Shibah.* See note on 21:31. The meaning "oath" is emphasized here.
26:34 Esau married two heathen women, additional evidence of his spiritual dullness.

eyes were too dim to see, that he called his [b]older son Esau and said to him, "My son." And he said to him, "Here I am."

★ 2 [a]Gen. 47:29

2   [a]And Isaac said, "Behold now, I am old and I do not know the day of my death.

3 [a]Gen. 25:28

3 "Now then, please take your gear, your quiver and your bow, and go out to the field and [a]hunt game for me;

★ 4 [a]Gen. 27:19, 25, 31; 48:9, 15, 16; Deut. 33:1; Heb. 11:20

4   and prepare a savory dish for me such as I love, and bring it to me that I may eat, so that [a]my soul may bless you before I die."

5   And Rebekah was listening while Isaac spoke to his son Esau. So when Esau went to the field to hunt for game to bring home,

★ 6-10

6 [a]Gen. 25:28

6   [a]Rebekah said to her son Jacob, "Behold, I heard your father speak to your brother Esau, saying,

7 'Bring me some game and prepare a savory dish for me, that I may eat, and bless you in the presence of the LORD before my death.'

8 [a]Gen. 27:13, 43

8 "Now therefore, my son, [a]listen to me as I command you.

9 "Go now to the flock and bring me two choice kids from there, that I may prepare them as a savory dish for your father, such as he loves.

10 "Then you shall bring it to your father, that he may eat, so that he may bless you before his death."

★11-17

11 [a]Gen. 25:25

11   And Jacob answered his mother Rebekah, "Behold, Esau my brother is a [a]hairy man and I am a smooth man.

12 [a]Gen. 27:21, 22

12   "[a]Perhaps my father will feel me, then I shall be as a de-

ceiver in his sight; and I shall bring upon myself a curse and not a blessing."

13 [a]Gen. 27:8

13   But his mother said to him, "Your curse be on me, my son; only [a]obey my voice, and go, get them for me."

14   So he went and got them, and brought them to his mother; and his mother made savory food such as his father loved.

15 [a]Gen. 27:27

15   Then Rebekah took the best [a]garments of Esau her elder son, which were with her in the house, and put them on Jacob her younger son.

16   And she put the skins of the kids on his hands and on the smooth part of his neck.

17   She also gave the savory food and the bread, which she had made, to her son Jacob.

★18-29

18   Then he came to his father and said, "My father." And he said, "Here I am. Who are you, my son?"

19 [a]Gen. 27:31 [b]Gen. 27:4

19   And Jacob said to his father, "I am Esau your first-born; I have done as you told me. [a]Get up, please, sit and eat of my game, that [b]you may bless me."

20 [a]Gen. 24:12

20   And Isaac said to his son, "How is it that you have it so quickly, my son?" And he said, "[a]Because the LORD your God caused it to happen to me."

21 [a]Gen. 27:12

21   Then Isaac said to Jacob, "Please come close, that [a]I may feel you, my son, whether you are really my son Esau or not."

22   So Jacob came close to Isaac his father, and he felt him and said, "The voice is the voice of Jacob, but the hands are the hands of Esau."

23 [a]Gen. 27:16

23   And he did not recognize him, because his hands were

27:2 I am old. Isaac was 137 at this time, but he lived 43 more years (cf. 35:28).

27:4 Isaac still favored Esau (cf. 25:28), apparently ignoring the facts that he had bartered his birthright (25:34) and married heathen women (26:34).

27:6-10 Like (deceitful) mother, like son.

27:11-17 Rebekah answered all of Jacob's objections to the scheme by offering to take any curse that might follow if Isaac discovered the deception, of dressing Jacob in Esau's clothes

and placing hairy goatskins on Jacob's hands and neck, and of skillfully preparing a substitute meal.

27:18-29 Jacob had to resort to lying (vv. 19, 24), and Isaac allowed his senses of touch (v. 22), taste (v. 25), and smell (v. 27) to overrule what he heard (v. 22). The blessing included both benediction (v. 28) and prediction (v. 29). Be master of your brothers meant that Jacob would be head of the household (cf. 25:23). Cursed . . . blessed echoes 12:3.

ahairy like his brother Esau's hands; so he blessed him.

24 And he said, "Are you really my son Esau?" And he said, "I am."

25 So he said, "Bring it to me, and I will eat of my son's game, that aI may bless you." And he brought it to him, and he ate; he also brought him wine and he drank.

26 Then his father Isaac said to him, "Please come close and kiss me, my son."

27 So he came close and kissed him; and when he smelled the smell of his garments, he ablessed him and said,

"See, bthe smell of my son
Is like the smell of a field cwhich the LORD has blessed;

28   Now may aGod give you of the dew of heaven,
And of the bfatness of the earth,
And an abundance of grain and new wine;

29   aMay peoples serve you,
And nations bow down to you;
bBe master of your brothers,
cAnd may your mother's sons bow down to you.
dCursed be those who curse you,
And blessed be those who bless you."

30 Now it came about, as soon as Isaac had finished blessing Jacob, and Jacob had hardly gone out from the presence of Isaac his father, that Esau his brother came in from his hunting.

31 Then he also made savory food, and brought it to his father; and he said to his father, "aLet my father arise, and eat of his son's game, that byou may bless me."

32 And Isaac his father said to him, "aWho are you?" And he said, "I am your son, byour first-born, Esau."

33 Then Isaac trembled violently, and said, "aWho was he then that hunted game and brought it to me, so that I ate of all of it before you came, and blessed him? bYes, and he shall be blessed."

34 When Esau heard the words of his father, ahe cried out with an exceedingly great and bitter cry, and said to his father, "Bless me, even me also, O my father!"

35 And he said, "aYour brother came deceitfully, and has taken away your blessing."

36 Then he said, "Is he not rightly named aJacob, for he has supplanted me these two times? He took away my birthright, and behold, now he has taken away my blessing." And he said, "Have you not reserved a blessing for me?"

37 But Isaac answered and said to Esau, "Behold, I have made him ayour master, and all his relatives I have given to him as servants; and with grain and new wine I have sustained him. Now as for you then, what can I do, my son?"

38 And Esau said to his father, "Do you have only one blessing, my father? Bless me, even me also, O my father." So Esau lifted his voice and awept.

39 Then aIsaac his father answered and said to him,

"Behold, baway from the fertility of the earth shall be your dwelling,
And away from the dew of heaven from above.

40   "And by your sword you shall live,
And your brother ayou shall serve;

Side references (left column):

25 aGen. 27:4

27 aHeb. 11:20 bSong 4:11 cPs. 65:10

28 aGen. 27:39; Deut. 33:13, 28; Prov. 3:20; Zech. 8:12 bNum. 18:12

29 aGen. 25:23; Is. 45:14; 49:7, 23; 60:12, 14 bGen. 9:26, 27; 27:37 cGen. 37:7, 10 dGen. 12:3; Num. 24:9

31 aGen. 27:19 bGen. 27:4

Side references (right column):

32 aGen. 27:18 bGen. 25:33, 34

★33 aGen. 27:35 bGen. 25:23; 28:3, 4; Num. 23:20

34 aHeb. 12:17

35 aGen. 27:19

★36 aGen. 25:26, 32-34

37 aGen. 27:28, 29

38 aHeb. 12:17

★39 aHeb. 11:20 bGen. 27:28; Deut. 33:13, 28

40 aGen. 25:23; 27:29 b2 Kin. 8:20-22

27:33 *he shall be blessed.* Isaac realized that his blessing had been given in irreversible legal form.
27:36 *Jacob.* See 25:26

27:39 *away from the fertility of the earth shall be your dwelling.* Esau's descendants (the Edomites) would occupy a territory less fertile than Canaan (cf. Mal. 1:3).

But it shall come about
bwhen you become
restless,
That you shall break his
yoke from your
neck."

41 So Esau abore a grudge against Jacob because of the blessing with which his father had blessed him; and Esau said to himself, "bThe days of mourning for my father are near; then I will kill my brother Jacob."

42 Now when the words of her elder son Esau were reported to Rebekah, she sent and called her younger son Jacob, and said to him, "Behold your brother Esau is consoling himself concerning you, by planning to kill you.

43 "Now therefore, my son, aobey my voice, and arise, flee to bHaran, to my brother cLaban!

44 "And stay with him aa few days, until your brother's fury subsides,

45 until your brother's anger against you subsides, and he forgets awhat you did to him. Then I shall send and get you from there. Why should I be bereaved of you both in one day?"

46 And Rebekah said to Isaac, "I am tired of living because of athe daughters of Heth; bif Jacob takes a wife from the daughters of Heth, like these, from the daughters of the land, what good will my life be to me?"

**D Jacob's Flight to
Mesopotamia,
28:1-9**

28 So Isaac called Jacob and ablessed him and charged

him, and said to him, "bYou shall not take a wife from the daughters of Canaan.

2 "Arise, go to Paddan-aram, to the house of aBethuel your mother's father; and from there take to yourself a wife from the daughters of Laban your mother's brother.

3 "And may aGod Almighty bbless you and cmake you fruitful and dmultiply you, that you may become a ecompany of peoples.

4 "May He also give you the ablessing of Abraham, to you and to your descendants with you; that you may bpossess the land of your csojournings, which God gave to Abraham."

5 Then aIsaac sent Jacob away, and he went to Paddan-aram to Laban, son of Bethuel the Aramean, the brother of Rebekah, the mother of Jacob and Esau.

6 Now Esau saw that Isaac had blessed Jacob and sent him away to Paddan-aram, to take to himself a wife from there, and that when he blessed him he charged him, saying, "aYou shall not take a wife from the daughters of Canaan,"

7 and that Jacob had obeyed his father and his mother and had gone to Paddan-aram.

8 So Esau saw that athe daughters of Canaan displeased his father Isaac;

9 and Esau went to Ishmael, and married, abesides the wives that he had, Mahalath the daughter of Ishmael, Abraham's son, the sister of Nebaioth.

Cross references (left margin):

41 aGen. 32:3-11; 37:4, 8
bGen. 50:2-4, 10

43 aGen. 27:8, 13
bGen. 11:31
cGen. 24:29

44 aGen. 31:41

★45 aGen. 27:12, 19, 35

★46 aGen. 26:34, 35; 28:8 bGen. 24:3

1 aGen. 27:33 bGen. 24:3, 4

Cross references (right margin):

★ 2 aGen. 25:20

★ 3 aGen. 17:1; 35:11; 48:3 bGen. 22:17 cGen. 17:6, 20 dGen. 17:2; 26:4, 24 eGen. 35:11; 48:4

★ 4 aGen. 12:2; 22:17 bGen. 15:7, 8; 17:8 c1-Chr. 29:15; Ps. 39:12

5 aGen. 27:43

6 aGen. 28:1

8 aGen. 24:3; 26:34, 35; 27:46.

★ 9 aGen. 26:34; 36:2

27:45 Why should I be bereaved of you both in one day? The meaning is this: if Esau should kill Jacob, then the nearest elder relative would be obliged to avenge the murder and kill Esau. In that way, Rebekah would lose both sons.

27:46 Again Rebekah deceived Isaac, this time in getting him to agree to send Jacob away. She never saw her son again.

28:2 Paddan-aram. See note on 25:20.

28:3 God Almighty. Heb., El Shaddai. See note on 17:1.

28:4 The land promised to Abraham (cf. 15:18-21) was now guaranteed to Jacob and his descendants.

28:9 to Ishmael. I.e., to Ishmael's family. Ishmael himself had died 14 years earlier. Note that Esau did not put away his heathen wives when he married into Ishmael's family.

E Jacob's Dream at Bethel,
28:10-22

10 aGen.
26:23 bGen.
12:4, 5;
27:43
10 Then Jacob departed from aBeersheba and went toward bHaran.

11 aGen.
28:19
11 And he came to a acertain place and spent the night there, because the sun had set; and he took one of the stones of the place and put it under his head, and lay down in that place.

★12 aGen.
41:1; Num.
12:6 bJohn
1:51
12 And ahe had a dream, and behold, a ladder was set on the earth with its top reaching to heaven; and behold, bthe angels of God were ascending and descending on it.

★13-15

13 aGen.
35:1; Amos
7:7 bGen.
26:3, 24
cGen. 13:15;
17; 26:3
dGen. 12:7;
15:18
13 And behold, athe LORD stood above it and said, "I am the LORD, bthe God of your father Abraham and the God of Isaac; the land on which you lie, I will give it cto you and to dyour descendants.

14 aGen.
13:16; 22:17
bGen. 13:14,
15 cGen.
12:3; 18:18;
22:18; 26:4
14 "Your descendants shall also be like athe dust of the earth, and you shall spread out bto the west and to the east and to the north and to the south; and cin you and in your descendants shall all the families of the earth be blessed.

15 aGen.
26:3, 24;
31:3 bNum.
6:24; Ps.
121:5, 7, 8
cGen. 48:21;
Deut. 30:3
dNum.
23:19; Deut.
7:9, 31:6, 8
15 "And behold, aI am with you, and bwill keep you wherever you go, and cwill bring you back to this land; for dI will not leave you until I have done what I have promised you."

16 a1 Kin.
3:15; Jer.
31:26 bEx.
3:4-6; Josh.
5:13-15; Ps.
139:7-12
16 Then Jacob aawoke from his sleep and said, "bSurely the LORD is in this place, and I did not know it."

17 aPs.
68:35
17 And he was afraid and said, "aHow awesome is this place! This is none other than the house of God, and this is the gate of heaven."

18 So Jacob rose early in the morning, and took athe stone that he had put under his head and set it up as a pillar, and poured oil on its top.

★18 aGen.
28:11; 35:14

19 And he called the name of that place aBethel; however, previously the name of the city had been bLuz.

★19 aJudg.
1:23 bGen.
35:6; 48:3

20 Then Jacob amade a vow, saying, "bIf God will be with me and will keep me on this journey that I take, and will give me cfood to eat and garments to wear,

20 aGen.
31:13; Judg.
11:30;
2 Sam. 15:8
bGen. 28:15
c1 Tim. 6:8

21 and aI return to my father's house in safety, bthen the LORD will be my God.

21 aJudg.
11:31 bDeut.
26:17

22 "And this stone, which I have set up as a pillar, awill be God's house; and bof all that Thou dost give me I will surely give a tenth to Thee."

★22 aGen.
35:7 bLev.
27:30; Deut.
14:22

F Jacob and the Daughters of Laban, 29:1-30:43
1 Jacob meets Rachel, 29:1-14

29 Then Jacob went on his journey, and came to the land of athe sons of the east.

★ 1 aJudg.
6:3, 33

2 And he looked, and saw aa well in the field, and behold, three flocks of sheep were lying there beside it, for from that well they watered the flocks. Now the stone on the mouth of the well was large.

2 aGen.
24:10, 11;
Ex. 2:15, 16

3 When all the flocks were gathered there, they would then roll the stone from the mouth of the well, and water the sheep, and put the stone back in its place on the mouth of the well.

4 And Jacob said to them, "My brothers, where are you from?" And they said, "We are from aHaran."

4 aGen.
28:10

28:12 *a ladder.* More like a stairway.
28:13-15 After identifying Himself as the *God of Abraham* and *Isaac,* God confirmed to Jacob the Abrahamic covenant and added the promise of His presence with Jacob, wherever Jacob would go.
28:18 *poured oil.* An act that consecrated the altar.

28:19 *Bethel* means "house of God" and became the name of nearby Luz.
28:22 Giving a *tenth,* or tithe, was common among Semitic peoples and was an act that acknowledged the superiority of the one to whom it was paid (cf. 14:20).
29:1 *the land of the sons of the east.* In the vicinity of Haran.

★ 5 aGen.
24.24, 29

5 And he said to them, "Do you know Laban the ason of Nahor?" And they said, "We know him."

6 aEx. 2.16

6 And he said to them, "Is it well with him?" And they said, "It is well, and behold, aRachel his daughter is coming with the sheep."

★ 7-8

7 And he said, "Behold, it is still high day; it is not time for the livestock to be gathered. Water the sheep, and go, pasture them."

8 But they said, "We cannot, until all the flocks are gathered, and they roll the stone from the mouth of the well; then we water the sheep."

★ 9

9 While he was still speaking with them, Rachel came with her father's sheep, for she was a shepherdess.

10 And it came about, when Jacob saw Rachel the daughter of Laban his mother's brother, and the sheep of Laban his mother's brother, that Jacob went up, and rolled the stone from the mouth of the well, and watered the flock of Laban his mother's brother.

★11 aGen.
33.4

11 Then Jacob akissed Rachel, and lifted his voice and wept.

12 aGen.
28.5 bGen.
24.28

12 And Jacob told Rachel that he was a arelative of her father and that he was Rebekah's son, and bshe ran and told her father.

13 aGen.
24.29-31
bGen. 33.4

13 So it came about, when aLaban heard the news of Jacob his sister's son, that he ran to meet him, and bembraced him and kissed him, and brought him to his house. Then he related to Laban all these things.

★14 aGen.
2.23; Judg.
9.2; 2 Sam.
5.1; 19.12,
13

14 And Laban said to him, "Surely you are amy bone and my

flesh." And he stayed with him a month.

2   Jacob marries Leah and Rachel, 29:15–30

15 aGen.
31.41

15 Then Laban said to Jacob, "Because you are my relative, should you therefore serve me for nothing? Tell me, what shall ayour wages be?"

16 Now Laban had two daughters; the name of the older was Leah, and the name of the younger was Rachel.

★17 aGen.
12.11, 14;
26.7

17 And Leah's eyes were weak, but Rachel was abeautiful of form and face.

18 aGen.
24.67 bHos.
12.12

18 Now Jacob aloved Rachel, so he said, "bI will serve you seven years for your younger daughter Rachel."

19 And Laban said, "It is better that I give her to you than that I should give her to another man; stay with me."

20 aSong
8.7

20 So Jacob served seven years for Rachel and they seemed to him but a few days abecause of his love for her.

★21 aJudg.
15.1

21 Then Jacob said to Laban, "Give me my wife, for my time is completed, that I may ago in to her."

22 And Laban gathered all the men of the place, and made a feast.

23 Now it came about in the evening that he took his daughter Leah, and brought her to him; and Jacob went in to her.

24 Laban also gave his maid Zilpah to his daughter Leah as a maid.

★25 aGen.
12.18; 20.9;
26.10
b1 Sam.
28.12

25 So it came about in the morning that, behold, it was Leah!

29:5 *the son of Nahor.* Laban was actually his grandson (see 24:15, 29), though it was not unusual to use "son" in such references.

29:7-8 Jacob was apparently trying to get the men to leave before Rachel (cf. v. 6) arrived.

29:9 *she was a shepherdess.* Shepherdesses were not unusual, and were sometimes necessary, as in this case, since Laban had no sons.

29:11 Jacob *kissed* Rachel, a proper greeting for cousins, and *wept* for joy at finding his relatives.

29:14 *my bone and my flesh* may indicate that

Laban adopted Jacob as a son. The phrase is found in ancient adoption rituals. However, Laban reduced Jacob to the status of a servant.

29:17 *Leah's eyes were weak.* Either her eyes were visually weak or they lacked luster, which was a great defect among people who admired sparkling eyes.

29:21 *that I may go in to her.* I.e., that I may marry her.

29:25 Jacob, the deceiver, reaped deception (cf. Gal. 6:7).

And he said to Laban, "ªWhat is this you have done to me? Was it not for Rachel that I served with you? Why then have you ᵇdeceived me?"

26 But Laban said, "It is not the practice in our place, to marry off the younger before the firstborn.

★27 ªGen. 31:41

27 "Complete the week of this one, and we will give you the other also for the service which ªyou shall serve with me for another seven years."

28 And Jacob did so and completed her week, and he gave him his daughter Rachel as his wife.

★29

29 Laban also gave his maid Bilhah to his daughter Rachel as her maid.

★30 ªGen. 29:17, 18 ᵇGen. 31:41

30 So Jacob went in to Rachel also, and indeed ªhe loved Rachel more than Leah, and he served with Laban for ᵇanother seven years.

3 Jacob begets children, 29:31–30:24

31 Now the LORD saw that Leah was unloved, and He opened her womb, but Rachel was barren.

★32 ªGen. 16:11; 31:42; Ex. 3:7; 4:31; Deut. 26:7; Ps. 25:18

32 And Leah conceived and bore a son and named him Reuben, for she said, "Because the LORD has ªseen my affliction; surely now my husband will love me."

★33 ªDeut. 21:15

33 Then she conceived again and bore a son and said, "ªBecause the LORD has heard that I am unloved, He has therefore giv-

en me this *son* also." So she named him Simeon.

34 And she conceived again and bore a son and said, "Now this time my husband will become attached to me, because I have borne him three sons." Therefore he was named ªLevi.

★34 ªGen. 49:5

35 And she conceived again and bore a son and said, "This time I will praise the LORD." Therefore she named him ªJudah. Then she stopped bearing.

★35 ªGen. 49:8; Matt. 1:2

30 Now when Rachel saw that ªshe bore Jacob no children, she became jealous of her sister; and she said to Jacob, "ᵇGive me children, or else I die."

1 ªGen. 29:31 ᵇ1 Sam. 1:5, 6

2 Then Jacob's anger burned against Rachel, and he said, "Am I in the place of God, who has ªwithheld from you the fruit of the womb?"

2 ªGen. 20:18; 29:31

3 And she said, "ªHere is my maid Bilhah, go in to her, that she may ᵇbear on my knees, that ᶜthrough her I too may have children."

★ 3-4

3 ªGen. 16:2 ᵇGen. 50:23; Job 3:12 ᶜGen. 16:2

4 So ªshe gave him her maid Bilhah as a wife, and Jacob went in to her.

4 ªGen. 16:3, 4

5 And Bilhah conceived and bore a son.

6 Then Rachel said, "God has ªvindicated me, and has indeed heard my voice and has given me a son." Therefore she named him Dan.

★ 6 ªPs. 35:24; 43:1; Lam. 3:59

7 And Rachel's maid Bilhah conceived again and bore Jacob a second son.

8 So Rachel said, "With mighty wrestlings I have wrestled with my sister, *and* I have indeed

★ 8

29:27 *Complete the week.* A week of festivities for the bride and groom.

29:29 It was customary to give a maid as a wedding gift to a daughter (cf. v. 24).

29:30 Jacob received Rachel as his second wife after Leah's wedding week was over and before he served the second seven years.

29:32 *Reuben* means "look, a son."

29:33 *Simeon* means "hearing." The baby came because God heard Leah's prayer.

29:34 *Levi* means "attachment" and expressed Leah's confidence that bearing Jacob three healthy sons would assure his attachment to

her.

29:35 *Judah* means "praise."

30:3-4 As Sarah had given her maid Hagar to Abraham many years earlier, so Rachel gave her maid Bilhah to Jacob to bear children on her behalf. Jacob should have followed his father's example (cf. 25:21) instead of his grandfather's. *on my knees.* Rachel would place any children born to her maid on her knees as a sign acknowledging them as her own.

30:6 *Dan* means "justice," signifying that God had vindicated or intervened for Rachel.

30:8 *Naphtali* means "wrestling."

prevailed." And she named him Naphtali.

★ 9   **9** When Leah saw that she had stopped bearing, she took her maid Zilpah and gave her to Jacob as a wife.

10 And Leah's maid Zilpah bore Jacob a son.

★11   **11** Then Leah said, "How fortunate!" So she named him Gad.

12 And Leah's maid Zilpah bore Jacob a second son.

★13 ªLuke 1:48   **13** Then Leah said, "Happy am I! For women ªwill call me happy." So she named him Asher.

★14-18   **14** Now in the days of wheat harvest Reuben went and found 14 ªSong 7:13 ªmandrakes in the field, and brought them to his mother Leah. Then Rachel said to Leah, "Please give me some of your son's mandrakes."

15 But she said to her, "Is it a small matter for you to take my husband? And would you take my son's mandrakes also?" So Rachel said, "Therefore he may lie with you tonight in return for your son's mandrakes."

16 When Jacob came in from the field in the evening, then Leah went out to meet him and said, "You must come in to me, for I have surely hired you with my son's mandrakes." So he lay with her that night.

17 And God gave heed to Leah, and she conceived and bore Jacob a fifth son.

18 Then Leah said, "God has given me my wages, because I gave my maid to my husband." So she named him Issachar.

19 And Leah conceived again and bore a sixth son to Jacob.

★20   **20** Then Leah said, "God has endowed me with a good gift;

now my husband will dwell with me, because I have borne him six sons." So she named him Zebulun.

★21   **21** And afterward she bore a daughter and named her Dinah.

★22-24   **22** Then ªGod remembered 22 ª1 Sam. 1:19, 20 Rachel, and God gave heed to her bGen. 29:31 and bopened her womb.

23 ªIs. 4:1; Luke 1:25   **23** So she conceived and bore a son and said, "God has ªtaken away my reproach."

24 ªGen. 35:17   **24** And she named him Joseph, saying, "ªMay the LORD give me another son."

4 Jacob bargains with Laban,
30:25-43

25 ªGen. 24:54, 56   **25** Now it came about when Rachel had borne Joseph, that Jacob said to Laban, "ªSend me away, that I may go to my own place and to my own country.

26 ªGen. 29:18, 20, 27; Hos. 12:12   **26** "Give *me* my wives and my children ªfor whom I have served you, and let me depart; for you yourself know my service which I have rendered you."

27 ªGen. 26:24; 39:3, 5; Is. 61:9   **27** But Laban said to him, "If now it pleases you, *stay with me;* I have divined ªthat the LORD has blessed me on your account."

★28 ªGen. 29:15; 31:7, 41   **28** And he continued, "ªName me your wages, and I will give it."

29 ªGen. 31:6   **29** But he said to him, "ªYou yourself know how I have served you and how your cattle have fared with me.

30 "For you had little before I came, and it has increased to a multitude; and the LORD has blessed you wherever I turned. But now, when shall I provide for my own household also?"

30:9 Leah, who was no longer bearing children, resorted to Rachel's strategy of concubinage.
30:11 *Gad* means "luck" or "fortune."
30:13 *Asher* means "happy."
30:14-18 *mandrakes.* An herb of the belladonna family, considered to be aphrodisiac. Bickering and shameless bargaining characterized this bigamous household. *Issachar* means "reward," apparently indicating some faith on Leah's part.

30:20 *Zebulun* means "dwelling."
30:21 The mention of *Dinah*, one of Jacob's daughters (cf. 37:35; 46:7, 15), prepares the reader for the tragedy of chapter 34.
30:22-24 Rachel's conception was from God, not from the mandrakes. *Joseph* means either "may the Lord add" or "He has taken away." Perhaps there is deliberate ambiguity.
30:28 How generous of Laban, in light of 31:7!

★31-33   **31** So he said, "What shall I give you?" And Jacob said, "You shall not give me anything. If you will do this *one* thing for me, I will again pasture *and* keep your flock:

32 *a*Gen. 31:8   **32** let me pass through your entire flock today, removing from there every *a*speckled and spotted sheep, and every black one among the lambs, and the spotted and speckled among the goats; and *such* shall be my wages.

33 "So my honesty will answer for me later, when you come concerning my wages. Every one that is not speckled and spotted among the goats and black among the lambs, *if found* with me, will be considered stolen."

★34-36   **34** And Laban said, "Good, let it be according to your word."

35 So he removed on that day the striped and spotted male goats and all the speckled and spotted female goats, every one with white in it, and all the black ones among the sheep, and gave them into the care of his sons.

36 And he put *a distance of* three days' journey between himself and Jacob, and Jacob fed the rest of Laban's flocks.

★37-43   **37** Then Jacob took fresh rods of poplar and almond and plane trees, and peeled white stripes in them, exposing the white which *was* in the rods.

38 And he set the rods which he had peeled in front of the flocks in the gutters, *even* in the watering troughs, where the flocks came to drink; and they mated when they came to drink.

39 So the flocks mated by the rods, and the flocks brought forth striped, speckled, and spotted.

40 And Jacob separated the lambs, and made the flocks face toward the striped and all the black in the flock of Laban; and he put his own herds apart, and did not put them with Laban's flock.

41 Moreover, it came about whenever the stronger of the flock were mating, that Jacob would place the rods in the sight of the flock in the gutters, so that they might mate by the rods;

42 but when the flock was feeble, he did not put *them* in; so the feebler were Laban's and the stronger Jacob's.

43 So *a*the man became exceedingly prosperous, and had large flocks and female and male servants and camels and donkeys.   **43** *a*Gen. 12:16; 13:2; 24:35; 26:13, 14; 30:30

G   Jacob's Return to Canaan, 31:1–33:20

1   His separation from Laban, 31:1-55

31 Now Jacob heard the words of Laban's sons, saying, "Jacob has taken away all that was our father's, and from what belonged to our father he has made all this wealth."   **★ 1-16**

2 And Jacob saw the attitude of Laban, and behold, it was not *friendly* toward him as formerly.

30:31-33 Jacob agreed to take care of Laban's flocks if he could keep as his wages the off-colored and spotted animals that would be born.

30:34-36 Laban, true to character and acting in a manner not entirely foreign to the basic laws of heredity, separated the off-colored animals so as to reduce further Jacob's chances of acquiring a large herd. However, those animals not visibly spotted had latent genes that would produce spotted offspring.

30:37-43 Jacob placed partially stripped branches from certain trees in the watering troughs to stimulate the animals to reproductive activity. The Hebrew word for *mated* in verse 38 comes from a root which means "to be hot," i.e., to be in heat. Jacob, an experienced shepherd, also practiced selective breeding (vv. 40-42). Yet he attributed his prosperity to the intervention of God (cf. 31:7, 9).

31:1-16 Because Laban became openly hostile to Jacob, God told him to return to Canaan. Jacob's wives, who secretly met with him in the *field* (v. 4), agreed that this was the best plan. Whether they were convinced that this was God's leading or merely the only way to insure receiving any inheritance for themselves and their children (cf. v. 16) is hard to know. The reference in verse 13 is to 28:16-22.

3 *a*Gen.
32:9 *b*Gen.
28:15

3 Then the LORD said to Jacob, "*a*Return to the land of your fathers and to your relatives, and *b*I will be with you."

4 So Jacob sent and called Rachel and Leah to his flock in the field,

5 *a*Gen.
31:2 *b*Gen.
21:22; 28:13,
15; 31:29,
42, 53; Is.
41:10; Heb.
13:5

5 and said to them, "*a*I see your father's attitude, that it is not *friendly* toward me as formerly, but *b*the God of my father has been with me.

6 *a*Gen.
30:29

6 "And *a*you know that I have served your father with all my strength.

7 *a*Gen.
29:25 *b*Gen.
31:41 *c*Gen.
15:1; 31:29

7 "Yet your father has *a*cheated me and *b*changed my wages ten times; however, *c*God did not allow him to hurt me.

8 *a*Gen.
30:32

8 "If *a*he spoke thus, 'The speckled shall be your wages,' then all the flock brought forth speckled; and if he spoke thus, 'The striped shall be your wages,' then all the flock brought forth striped.

9 *a*Gen.
31:1, 16

9 "Thus God has *a*taken away your father's livestock and given *them* to me.

10 "And it came about at the time when the flock were mating that I lifted up my eyes and saw in a dream, and behold, the male goats which were mating *were* striped, speckled, and mottled.

11 *a*Gen.
16:7-11;
22:11, 15;
31:13; 48:16

11 "Then *a*the angel of God said to me in the dream, 'Jacob,' and I said, 'Here I am.'

12 *a*Ex. 3:7

12 "And he said, 'Lift up, now, your eyes and see *that* all the male goats which are mating are striped, speckled, and mottled; for *a*I have seen all that Laban has been doing to you.

13 *a*Gen.
28:13, 19
*b*Gen. 28:18,
20 *c*Gen.
28:15; 32:9

13 'I am *a*the God *of* Bethel, where you *b*anointed a pillar, where you made a vow to Me; now arise, leave this land, and *c*return to the land of your birth.' "

14 And Rachel and Leah answered and said to him, "Do we still have any portion or inheritance in our father's house?

15 *a*Gen.
29:20, 23, 27

15 "Are we not reckoned by him as foreigners? For *a*he has sold us, and has also entirely consumed our purchase price.

16 "Surely all the wealth which God has taken away from our father belongs to us and our children; now then, do whatever God has said to you."

17 Then Jacob arose and put his children and his wives upon camels;

18 *a*Gen.
35:27

18 and he drove away all his livestock and all his property which he had gathered, his acquired livestock which he had gathered in Paddan-aram, *a*to go to the land of Canaan to his father Isaac.

★19 *a*Gen.
31:30, 34;
35:2; Judg.
17:5; 1 Sam.
19:13; Hos.
3:4

19 When Laban had gone to shear his flock, then Rachel stole the *a*household idols that were her father's.

20 And Jacob deceived Laban the Aramean, by not telling him that he was fleeing.

21 *a*Gen.
37:25

21 So he fled with all that he had; and he arose and crossed the *Euphrates* River, and set his face toward the hill country of *a*Gilead.

22 When it was told Laban on the third day that Jacob had fled,

23 then he took his kinsmen with him, and pursued him *a distance of* seven days' journey; and he overtook him in the hill country of Gilead.

24 *a*Gen.
20:3; 31:29
*b*Gen. 20:3,
6; 31:11
*c*Gen. 24:50;
31:7, 29

24 And *a*God came to Laban the Aramean in a *b*dream of the night, and said to him, "*c*Be careful that you do not speak to Jacob either good or bad."

25 And Laban caught up with Jacob. Now Jacob had pitched his tent in the hill country, and Laban

---

31:19 The *household idols* (Heb., *teraphim*), which Rachel stole and hid in her saddle (v. 34) and which Laban diligently searched for, were small figurines have been made as to why Rachel felt it necessary to have them: (1) They were supposed to guarantee fertility. (2) They guar-

anteed Jacob's right to Laban's estate when he died (though this claim may have been weakened because Laban had not voluntarily given them). (3) They were still in some sense Rachel's gods on which she depended for religious or divination purposes.

with his kinsmen camped in the hill country of Gilead.

26 Then Laban said to Jacob, "What have you done by deceiving me and carrying away my daughters like captives of the sword?

27 "Why did you flee secretly and deceive me, and did not tell me, so that I might have sent you away with joy and with songs, with *a*timbrel and with *b*lyre;

28 and did not allow me *a*to kiss my sons and my daughters? Now you have done foolishly.

29 "It is in my power to do you harm, but *a*the God of your father spoke to me last night, saying, '*b*Be careful not to speak either good or bad to Jacob.'

30 "And now you have indeed gone away because you longed greatly for your father's house; *but* why did you steal *a*my gods?"

31 Then Jacob answered and said to Laban, "Because I was afraid, for I said, 'Lest you would take your daughters from me by force.'

32 "*a*The one with whom you find your gods shall not live; in the presence of our kinsmen point out what is yours among my belongings and take *it* for yourself." For Jacob did not know that Rachel had stolen them.

33 So Laban went into Jacob's tent, and into Leah's tent, and into the tent of the two maids, but he did not find *them*. Then he went out of Leah's tent and entered Rachel's tent.

34 Now Rachel had taken the household idols and put them in the camel's saddle, and she sat on them. And Laban felt through all the tent, but did not find *them*.

35 And she said to her father, "Let not my lord be angry that I cannot *a*rise before you, for the manner of women is upon me."

So he searched, but did not find the *b*household idols.

36 Then Jacob became angry and contended with Laban; and Jacob answered and said to Laban, "What is my transgression? What is my sin, that you have hotly pursued me?

37 "Though you have felt through all my goods, what have you found of all your household goods? Set *it* here before my kinsmen and your kinsmen, that they may decide between us two.

38 "These twenty years I *have been* with you; your ewes and your female goats have not miscarried, nor have I eaten the rams of your flocks.

39 "That which was torn *of beasts* I did not bring to you; I bore the loss of it myself. You required it of my hand *whether* stolen by day or stolen by night.

40 "*Thus* I was: by day the heat consumed me, and the frost by night, and my sleep fled from my eyes.

41 "These twenty years I have been in your house; *a*I served you fourteen years for your two daughters, and six years for your flock, and you *b*changed my wages ten times.

42 "If *a*the God of my father, the God of Abraham, and the fear of Isaac, had not been for me, surely now you would have sent me away empty-handed. *b*God has seen my affliction and the toil of my hands, so He *c*rendered judgment last night."

43 Then Laban answered and said to Jacob, "The daughters are my daughters, and the children are my children, and *a*the flocks are my flocks, and all that you see is mine. But what can I do this day to these my daughters or to their children whom they have borne?

Margin references

27 *a*Ex. 15:20 *b*Gen. 4:21

28 *a*Gen. 31:55

★29 *a*Gen. 31:5, 24, 42, 53 *b*Gen. 31:24

30 *a*Gen. 31:19; Josh. 24:2; Judg. 18:24

32 *a*Gen. 44:9

★35 *a*Lev. 19:32 *b*Gen. 31:19

41 *a*Gen. 29:27, 30 *b*Gen. 31:7

42 *a*Gen. 31:5, 29, 53 *b*Gen. 29:32; Ex. 3:7 *c*Gen. 31:24, 29

43 *a*Gen. 31:1

31:29 *either good or bad.* This warning probably refers to Laban's speaking to Jacob about returning to Haran or about any claims Laban may have thought he had to Jacob's possessions or family.

31:35 It was customary for children, regardless of age, to stand in the presence of their parents (cf. Lev. 19:32; 1 Kings 2:19), but Rachel claimed to be menstruating.

★44-55

44 aGen. 21:27, 32; 26:28 bJosh. 24:27

45 aGen. 28:18; Josh. 24:26, 27

47 aJosh. 22:34

48 aJosh. 24:27

49 aJudg. 11:29; 1 Sam. 7:5, 6

50 aJer. 29:23; 42:5

53 aGen. 28:13 bGen. 16:5 cGen. 31:42

54 aEx. 18:12

★55 aGen. 31:28, 43

44 "So now come, let us ªmake a covenant, you and I, and ᵇlet it be a witness between you and me."

45 Then Jacob took ªa stone and set it up *as* a pillar.

46 And Jacob said to his kinsmen, "Gather stones." So they took stones and made a heap, and they ate there by the heap.

47 Now Laban ªcalled it Jegarsahadutha, but Jacob called it Galeed.

48 And Laban said, "ªThis heap is a witness between you and me this day." Therefore it was named Galeed;

49 and ªMizpah, for he said, "May the Lᴏʀᴅ watch between you and me when we are absent one from the other.

50 "If you mistreat my daughters, or if you take wives besides my daughters, *although* no man is with us, see, ªGod is witness between you and me."

51 And Laban said to Jacob, "Behold this heap and behold the pillar which I have set between you and me.

52 "This heap is a witness, and the pillar is a witness, that I will not pass by this heap to you for harm, and you will not pass by this heap and this pillar to me, for harm.

53 "ªThe God of Abraham and the God of Nahor, the God of their father, ᵇjudge between us." So Jacob swore by ᶜthe fear of his father Isaac.

54 Then Jacob ªoffered a sacrifice on the mountain, and called his kinsmen to the meal; and they ate the meal and spent the night on the mountain.

55 And early in the morning Laban arose, and ªkissed his sons

and his daughters and blessed them. Then Laban departed and returned to his place.

2 *His reconciliation with Esau,* 32:1–33:20

32 Now as Jacob went on his way, ªthe angels of God met him.

2 And Jacob said when he saw them, "This is God's camp." So he named that place ªMahanaim.

3 Then Jacob ªsent messengers before him to his brother Esau in the land of ᵇSeir, the country of ᶜEdom.

4 He also commanded them saying, "Thus you shall say to my lord Esau: 'Thus says your servant Jacob, "I have sojourned with Laban, and ªstayed until now;

5 and ªI have oxen and donkeys *and* flocks and male and female servants; and I have sent to tell my lord, ᵇthat I may find favor in your sight." ' "

6 And the messengers returned to Jacob, saying, "We came to your brother Esau, and furthermore ªhe is coming to meet you, and four hundred men are with him."

7 Then Jacob was ªgreatly afraid and distressed; and he divided the people who were with him, and the flocks and the herds and the camels, into two companies;

8 for he said, "If Esau comes to the one company and attacks it, then the company which is left will escape."

9 And Jacob said, "O ªGod of my father Abraham and God of my father Isaac, O Lᴏʀᴅ, who didst say to me, 'ᵇReturn to your

1 a2 Kin. 6:16, 17; Ps. 34:7

★ 2 aJosh. 21:38; 2 Sam. 2:8

3 aGen. 27:41, 42; 32:7, 11 bGen. 14:6; 33:14 cGen. 25:30; 36:8, 9

4 aGen. 31:41

5 aGen. 30:43 bGen. 33:8

★ 6-7

6 aGen. 33:1

7 aGen. 32:11

9 aGen. 28:13; 31:42 bGen. 28:15; 31:3, 13

31:44-55 Laban and Jacob made a mutual non-aggression pact. Its features included God as witness (vv. 49, 53), the pillar and cairn (*heap*) as boundary markers (v. 52), and a covenant meal to seal the arrangement (v. 54). Suspicion permeated the entire arrangement (e.g., v. 50). *Jegarsahadutha* and *Galeed* (v. 47) both mean "heap of witness," the former being Aramaic and the latter, Hebrew. *Mizpah* (v. 49) means "watchtower."

31:55 *Laban* disappears from the narrative at this point, and there is no further recorded contact between Jacob's family and his relatives in Mesopotamia.

32:2 *Mahanaim* means "double camp," referring to the angel's and Jacob's companies.

32:6-7 Jacob remembered Esau's threat (27:41-42) and had reason to be frightened, not knowing his brother's intentions. Jacob's prayer (32:9-12) shows humility of spirit.

country and to your relatives, and I will prosper you,'

10 ^aGen. 24:27

10 I am unworthy ^aof all the lovingkindness and of all the faithfulness which Thou hast shown to Thy servant; for with my staff *only* I crossed this Jordan, and now I have become two companies.

11 ^aPs. 59:1, 2 ^bGen. 27:41, 42; 33:4 ^cHos. 10:14

11 "^aDeliver me, I pray, ^bfrom the hand of my brother, from the hand of Esau; for I fear him, lest he come and attack me, the ^cmothers with the children.

12 ^aGen. 28:14 ^bGen. 22:17

12 "For Thou didst say, '^aI will surely prosper you, and ^bmake your descendants as the sand of the sea, which cannot be numbered for multitude.'"

13 ^aGen. 43:11

13 So he spent the night there. Then he selected from what he had with him a ^apresent for his brother Esau:

14 two hundred female goats and twenty male goats, two hundred ewes and twenty rams,

15 thirty milking camels and their colts, forty cows and ten bulls, twenty female donkeys and ten male donkeys.

16 And he delivered *them* into the hand of his servants, every drove by itself, and said to his servants, "Pass on before me, and put a space between droves."

17 And he commanded the one in front, saying, "When my brother Esau meets you and asks you, saying, 'To whom do you belong, and where are you going, and to whom do these *animals* in front of you belong?'

18 then you shall say, 'These belong to your servant Jacob; it is a present sent to my lord Esau.

And behold, he also is behind us.'"

19 Then he commanded also the second and the third, and all those who followed the droves, saying, "After this manner you shall speak to Esau when you find him;

    ★19

20 and you shall say, 'Behold, your servant Jacob also is behind us.'" For he said, "I will appease him with the present that goes before me. Then afterward I will see his face; perhaps he will accept me."

21 So the present passed on before him, while he himself spent that night in the camp.

22 Now he arose that same night and took his two wives and his two maids and his eleven children, and crossed the ford of the ^aJabbok.

    ★**22** ^aDeut. 3:16; Josh. 12:2

23 And he took them and sent them across the stream. And he sent across whatever he had.

24 Then Jacob was left alone, and a man ^awrestled with him until daybreak.

    ★**24** ^aHos. 12:3, 4

25 And when he saw that he had not prevailed against him, he touched the socket of his thigh; so the socket of Jacob's thigh was dislocated while he wrestled with him.

    ★**25-28**

26 Then he said, "Let me go, for the dawn is breaking." But he said, "^aI will not let you go unless you bless me."

    26 ^aHos. 12:4

27 So he said to him, "What is your name?" And he said, "Jacob."

28 And ^ahe said, "Your name shall no longer be Jacob, but Israel; for you have striven with God and with men and have prevailed."

    28 ^aGen. 35:10; 1 Kin. 18:31

32:19 *droves* = herds.
32:22 The *Jabbok* is a tributary of the Jordan, flowing into it about 24 miles N. of the Dead Sea. The name is related to the Hebrew word for "wrestled" (see v. 24).
32:24 The *man* who wrestled Jacob is called an angel in Hosea 12:4 and was evidently the preincarnate Christ. Jacob's wrestling involved agonizing prayer (Hos. 12:4).
32:25-28 God allowed Himself to be overcome

by Jacob, though He crippled him (whether temporarily or for the rest of his life is not stated). His limp, however, was proof that this was no mere dream. The Lord wanted to depart before daylight lest Jacob see Him (cf. Exod. 33:20), but Jacob insisted on being blessed first. So God changed his name from *Jacob* (see note on 25:26) to *Israel* which means "he fights or persists with God" (in prevailing prayer).

★29 aJudg.
13:17, 18

29 Then aJacob asked him and said, "Please tell me your name." But he said, "Why is it that you ask my name?" And he blessed him there.

★30 aGen.
16:13; Ex.
24:10, 11;
33:20; Num.
12:8; Judg.
6:22; 13:22

30 So Jacob named the place Peniel, for he said, "aI have seen God face to face, yet my life has been preserved."

31 aJudg.
8:8

31 Now the sun rose upon him just as he crossed over aPenuel, and he was limping on his thigh.

★32

32 Therefore, to this day the sons of Israel do not eat the sinew of the hip which is on the socket of the thigh, because he touched the socket of Jacob's thigh in the sinew of the hip.

1 aGen.
32:6

33 Then Jacob lifted his eyes and looked, and behold, aEsau was coming, and four hundred men with him. So he divided the children among Leah and Rachel and the two maids.

2 And he put the maids and their children in front, and Leah and her children next, and Rachel and Joseph last.

★ 3 aGen.
42:6, 43:26

3 But he himself passed on ahead of them and abowed down to the ground seven times, until he came near to his brother.

4 aGen.
45:14, 15

4 Then Esau ran to meet him and embraced him, and afell on his neck and kissed him, and they wept.

5 aGen.
48:9; Ps.
127:3; Is.
8:18

5 And he lifted his eyes and saw the women and the children, and said, "Who are these with you?" So he said, "aThe children whom God has graciously given your servant."

6 Then the maids came near with their children, and they bowed down.

7 And Leah likewise came near with her children, and they bowed down; and afterward Joseph came near with Rachel, and they bowed down.

8 And he said, "What do you mean by aall this company which I have met?" And he said, "bTo find favor in the sight of my lord."

★ 8 aGen.
32:13-16
bGen. 32:5

9 But Esau said, "aI have plenty, my brother; let what you have be your own."

9 aGen.
27:39, 40

10 And Jacob said, "No, please, if now I have found favor in your sight, then take my present from my hand, for I see your face as one sees the face of God, and you have received me favorably.

11 "Please take my agift which has been brought to you, bbecause God has dealt graciously with me, and because I have plenty." Thus he urged him and he took it.

11 a1 Sam.
25:27 bGen.
30:43

12 Then Esau said, "Let us take our journey and go, and I will go before you."

★12

13 But he said to him, "My lord knows that the children are frail and that the flocks and herds which are nursing are a care to me. And if they are driven hard one day, all the flocks will die.

14 "Please let my lord pass on before his servant; and I will proceed at my leisure, according to the pace of the cattle that are before me and according to the pace of the children, until I come to my lord at aSeir."

14 aGen.
32:3

15 And Esau said, "Please let me leave with you some of the people who are with me." But he said, "What need is there? aLet me find favor in the sight of my lord."

15 aRuth
2:13

16 So Esau returned that day on his way to Seir.

32:29 Jacob's question had already been answered in the name bestowed on him, since the *el* in Israel means "god."

32:30 *Peniel* means "the face of God."

32:32 Though the practice is not forbidden in Scripture, Jews have traditionally avoided eating the sciatic nerve (*sinew*) of the hind quarter of animals.

33:3 *bowed . . . seven times.* A widely attested sign of homage, fit for a king. Jacob was taking no chances!

33:8 *company.* Lit., host, referring to the large present of animals Jacob offered Esau (cf. 32:13–18).

33:12 *before.* Better, near or alongside. Esau's suggestion that they travel together as well as his further offer to send a guard with Jacob (v. 15) are both refused.

★17 aJosh.
13:27; Judg.
8:5, 14; Ps.
60:6

17 And Jacob journeyed to aSuccoth; and built for himself a house, and made booths for his livestock, therefore the place is named Succoth.

★18 aGen.
12:6; Josh.
24:1; Judg.
9:1 bGen.
25:20; 28:2

18 Now Jacob came safely to the city of aShechem, which is in the land of Canaan, when he came from bPaddan-aram, and camped before the city.

19 aJosh.
24:32; John
4:5

19 And ahe bought the piece of land where he had pitched his tent from the hand of the sons of Hamor, Shechem's father, for one hundred pieces of money.

★20

20 Then he erected there an altar, and called it El-Elohe-Israel.

H   Jacob's Later Life, 34:1–36:43
1   The massacre at Shechem, 34:1–31

1 aGen.
30:21

34 Now aDinah the daughter of Leah, whom she had borne to Jacob, went out to visit the daughters of the land.

2 aGen.
34:30

2 And when Shechem the son of Hamor athe Hivite, the prince of the land, saw her, he took her and lay with her by force.

★ 3

3 And he was deeply attracted to Dinah the daughter of Jacob, and he loved the girl and spoke tenderly to her.

4 aJudg.
14:2

4 So Shechem aspoke to his father Hamor, saying, "Get me this young girl for a wife."

5 Now Jacob heard that he had defiled Dinah his daughter; but his sons were with his livestock in the field, so Jacob kept silent until they came in.

★ 6

6 Then Hamor the father of Shechem went out to Jacob to speak with him.

7 aDeut.
22:20-30;
Judg. 20:6;
2 Sam. 13:12

7 Now the sons of Jacob came in from the field when they heard *it;* and the men were grieved, and they were very angry because he had done a adisgraceful thing in Israel by lying with Jacob's daughter, for such a thing ought not to be done.

8 But Hamor spoke with them, saying, "The soul of my son Shechem longs for your daughter; please give her to him in marriage.

9 "And intermarry with us; give your daughters to us, and take our daughters for yourselves.

10 "Thus you shall live with us, and athe land shall be *open* before you; live and btrade in it, and cacquire property in it."

10 aGen.
13:9; 20:15
bGen. 42:34
cGen. 47:27

11 Shechem also said to her father and to her brothers, "If I find favor in your sight, then I will give whatever you say to me.

12 "Ask me ever so much bridal payment and gift, and I will give according as you say to me; but give me the girl in marriage."

13 But Jacob's sons answered Shechem and his father Hamor, with deceit, and spoke to them, because he had defiled Dinah their sister.

14 And they said to them, "We cannot do this thing, to give our sister to aone who is uncircumcised, for that would be a disgrace to us.

14 aGen.
17:14

15 "Only on this *condition* will we consent to you: if you will become like us, in that every male of you be circumcised,

16 then we will give our daughters to you, and we will take your daughters for ourselves, and we will live with you and become one people.

17 "But if you will not listen to us to be circumcised, then we will take our daughter and go."

33:17 *Succoth* means "booths." It was E. of the Jordan and just N. of the Jabbok (see note on 32:22).

33:18 As much as 10 years' time may have been spent in Succoth before Jacob went to Shechem, an important city in Canaan, near present-day Nablus (see note on 12:6).

33:20 *El-Elohe-Israel* means "a Mighty God is the God of Israel."

34:3 Even after defiling Dinah (who was about 14 or 15 at this time), Shechem wished to marry her.

34:6 The father, *Hamor,* approached Jacob in order to arrange the marriage between Dinah and Shechem. Hamor's further proposal of intermarriage of the two groups was accepted on the condition that his family be circumcised (v. 15).

18 Now their words seemed reasonable to Hamor and Shechem, Hamor's son.

19 And the young man did not delay to do the thing, because he was delighted with Jacob's daughter. Now he was more respected than all the household of his father.

★20 aRuth 4:1; 2 Sam. 15:2   **20** So Hamor and his son Shechem came to the agate of their city, and spoke to the men of their city, saying,

21 "These men are friendly with us; therefore let them live in the land and trade in it, for behold, the land is large enough for them. Let us take their daughters in marriage, and give our daughters to them.

22 "Only on this *condition* will the men consent to us to live with us, to become one people: that every male among us be circumcised as they are circumcised.

23 "Will not their livestock and their property and all their animals be ours? Only let us consent to them, and they will live with us."

24 aGen. 23:10   **24** And aall who went out of the gate of his city listened to Hamor and to his son Shechem, and every male was circumcised, all who went out of the gate of his city.

★25-29
25 aGen. 49:5-7   **25** Now it came about on the third day, when they were in pain, that two of Jacob's sons, aSimeon and Levi, Dinah's brothers, each took his sword and came upon the city unawares, and killed every male.

26 And they killed Hamor and his son Shechem with the edge of the sword, and took Di-

nah from Shechem's house, and went forth.

27 Jacob's sons came upon the slain and looted the city, because they had defiled their sister.

28 They took their flocks and their herds and their donkeys, and that which was in the city and that which was in the field;

29 and they captured and looted all their wealth and all their little ones and their wives, even all that *was* in the houses.

30 Then Jacob said to Simeon and Levi, "You have abrought trouble on me, by bmaking me odious among the inhabitants of the land, among cthe Canaanites and the Perizzites; and dmy men being few in number, they will gather together against me and attack me and I shall be destroyed, I and my household."

31 But they said, "Should he treat our sister as a harlot?"

★30-31
30 aJosh. 7:25 bEx. 5:21; 1 Sam. 13:4; 2 Sam. 10:6 cGen. 13:7; 34:2 dGen. 46:26, 27; Deut. 4:27; 1 Chr. 16:19; Ps. 105:12

2   The renewal of the covenant at Bethel, 35:1-15

35 Then God said to Jacob, "Arise, go up to aBethel, and live there; and make an altar there to bGod, who appeared to you cwhen you fled from your brother Esau."

★ 1 aGen. 28:19 bGen. 28:13 cGen. 27:43

2 So Jacob said to his ahousehold and to all who were with him, "Put away bthe foreign gods which are among you, and cpurify yourselves, and change your garments;

★ 2-4
2 aGen. 18:19; Josh. 24:15 bGen. 31:19, 30, 34 cEx. 19:10, 14

3 and let us arise and go up to Bethel; and I will make aan altar there to God, bwho answered me in the day of my distress, and chas been with me wherever I have gone."

3 aGen. 28:20-22 bPs. 107:6 cGen. 28:15; 31:3, 42

34:20 The *gate* of the city was the center of public activity (cf. 19:1). Here Hamor and Shechem persuaded the others to be circumcised.
34:25-29 *on the third day,* at the height of incapacitation, *Simeon and Levi* waged a two-man war of revenge, killing all the men of Shechem, including Hamor and Shechem, rescuing Dinah, and taking as spoil the women and wealth of the city.
34:30-31 Jacob was suddenly concerned about what this massacre would mean to the peace

and security of his family when other groups learned about it. But his objections were apparently silenced by his sons' question (v. 31).
35:1 *Bethel* was the place where God confirmed the Abrahamic covenant to Jacob (see 28:10-19). It was about 15 miles S. of Shechem.
35:2-4 Jacob called for a purging of all remnants of heathen practices, including idols, Rachel's teraphim (cf. 31:19), and earrings, which must have been used as amulets or cultic tokens.

4 So they gave to Jacob all the foreign gods which they had, and the rings which were in their ears; and Jacob hid them under the oak which was near Shechem.

★ **5** *a*Ex. 15:16; 23:27; Deut. 2:25

5 As they journeyed, there was *a*a great terror upon the cities which were around them, and they did not pursue the sons of Jacob.

6 *a*Gen. 28:19; 48:3

6 So Jacob came to *a*Luz (that is, Bethel), which is in the land of Canaan, he and all the people who were with him.

★ **7** *a*Gen. 35:3

7 And *a*he built an altar there, and called the place El-bethel, because there God had revealed Himself to him, when he fled from his brother.

★ **8** *a*Gen. 24:59

8 Now *a*Deborah, Rebekah's nurse, died, and she was buried below Bethel under the oak; it was named Allon-bacuth.

9 *a*Gen. 32:29

9 Then God appeared to Jacob again when he came from Paddan-aram, and He *a*blessed him.

★**10** *a*Gen. 17:5; 32:28

10 And *a*God said to him,
"Your name is Jacob;
You shall no longer be
called Jacob,
But Israel shall be your
name."
Thus He called him Israel.

★**11** *a*Gen. 17:1; 28:3; Ex. 6:3
*b*Gen. 9:1, 7
*c*Gen. 48:4
*d*Gen. 17:6, 16; 36:31

11 God also said to him,
"I am *a*God Almighty;
*b*Be fruitful and multiply;
A nation and a *c*company of nations shall
come from you,
And *d*kings shall come
forth from you.

12 *a*Gen. 12:7; 13:15; 26:3, 4; 28:13; Ex. 32:13

12 "And *a*the land which I
gave to Abraham and
Isaac,

I will give it to you,
And I will give the land
to your descendants
after you."

13 *a*Gen. 17:22; 18:33

13 Then *a*God went up from him in the place where He had spoken with him.

★**14** *a*Gen. 28:18, 19; 31:45

14 And Jacob set up *a*a pillar in the place where He had spoken with him, a pillar of stone, and he poured out a libation on it; he also poured oil on it.

15 *a*Gen. 28:19

15 So Jacob named the place where God had spoken with him, *a*Bethel.

3 The deaths of Rachel and Isaac, 35:16–29

★**16-18**

16 *a*Gen. 35:19; 48:7; Ruth 4:11; Mic. 5:2

16 Then they journeyed from Bethel; and when there was still some distance to go to *a*Ephrath, Rachel began to give birth and she suffered severe labor.

17 *a*Gen. 30:24

17 And it came about when she was in severe labor that the midwife said to her, "Do not fear, for now *a*you have *another* son."

18 And it came about as her soul was departing (for she died), that she named him Ben-oni; but his father called him Benjamin.

19 *a*Gen. 48:7 *b*Ruth 1:2; 4:11; Mic. 5:2

19 So *a*Rachel died and was buried on the way to *b*Ephrath (that is, Bethlehem).

20 *a*1 Sam. 10:2

20 And Jacob set up a pillar over her grave; that is the *a*pillar of Rachel's grave to this day.

★**21** *a*Mic. 4:8

21 Then Israel journeyed on and pitched his tent beyond the *a*tower of Eder.

★**22** *a*Gen. 49:4; 1 Chr. 5:1

22 And it came about while Israel was dwelling in that land, that *a*Reuben went and lay with Bilhah his father's concubine; and Israel heard *of it.*

35:5 God restrained the Canaanites from avenging the Shechemites.

35:7 *El-bethel* means "God of Bethel." See note on 28:19.

35:8 *Allon-bacuth* means "oak of weeping."

35:10 On the significance of the name *Israel*, see note on 32:25–28.

35:11 *God Almighty.* Heb., *El Shaddai.* See note on 17:1.

35:14 *a pillar of stone.* A customary covenant witness. A *libation* consisted of wine poured

on the pillar (cf. Num. 15:5, 7).

35:16-18 *Ephrath* is the ancient name of Bethlehem, where Rachel gave birth to *Benjamin.* Benjamin means "son of the right hand," son of honor or good fortune. *Ben-oni* means "son of my sorrow or misfortune."

35:21 *the tower of Eder* was a watchtower (for shepherds) between Bethlehem and Hebron.

35:22 Israel did not forget this shameful act (see 49:4).

Now there were twelve sons of Jacob—

23 [a]the sons of Leah: Reuben, Jacob's first-born, then Simeon and Levi and Judah and Issachar and Zebulun;

24 [a]the sons of Rachel: Joseph and Benjamin;

25 and [a]the sons of Bilhah, Rachel's maid: Dan and Naphtali;

26 and [a]the sons of Zilpah, Leah's maid: Gad and Asher. These are the sons of Jacob who were born to him in Paddan-aram.

27 And Jacob came to his father Isaac at [a]Mamre of [b]Kiriath-arba (that is, Hebron), where Abraham and Isaac had sojourned.

28 Now the days of Isaac were [a]one hundred and eighty years.

29 And Isaac breathed his last and died, and was [a]gathered to his people, an [b]old man of ripe age; and [c]his sons Esau and Jacob buried him.

4 The descendants of Esau, 36:1-43

36 Now these are the records of the generations of [a]Esau (that is, Edom).

2 Esau [a]took his wives from the daughters of Canaan: Adah the daughter of Elon the Hittite, and [b]Oholibamah the daughter of Anah and the [c]granddaughter of Zibeon the Hivite;

3 also Basemath, Ishmael's daughter, the sister of Nebaioth.

4 And Adah bore [a]Eliphaz to Esau, and Basemath bore Reuel,

5 and Oholibamah bore Jeush and Jalam and Korah. These are the sons of Esau who were born to him in the land of Canaan.

6 [a]Then Esau took his wives and his sons and his daughters and all his household, and his livestock and all his cattle and all his goods which he had acquired in the land of Canaan, and went to another land away from his brother Jacob.

7 [a]For their property had become too great for them to live together, and the [b]land where they [c]sojourned could not sustain them because of their livestock.

8 So Esau lived in the hill country of [a]Seir; Esau is [b]Edom.

9 These then are the records of the generations of Esau the father of the Edomites in the hill country of Seir.

10 These are the names of Esau's sons: Eliphaz the son of Esau's wife Adah, Reuel the son of Esau's wife Basemath.

11 And the sons of Eliphaz were Teman, Omar, Zepho and Gatam and Kenaz.

12 And Timna was a concubine of Esau's son Eliphaz and she bore [a]Amalek to Eliphaz. These are the sons of Esau's wife Adah.

13 And these are the sons of Reuel: Nahath and Zerah, Shammah and Mizzah. These were the sons of Esau's wife Basemath.

14 And these were the sons of Esau's wife Oholibamah, the daughter of Anah and the granddaughter of Zibeon: she bore to Esau, Jeush and Jalam and Korah.

15 These are the chiefs of the sons of Esau. The sons of Eliphaz, the first-born of Esau, are chief Teman, chief Omar, chief Zepho, chief Kenaz,

16 chief Korah, chief Gatam, chief Amalek. These are the chiefs descended from Eliphaz in the land of Edom; these are the sons of Adah.

17 And these are the sons of Reuel, Esau's son: chief Nahath, chief Zerah, chief Shammah, chief Mizzah. These are the chiefs descended from Reuel in the land

---

23 [a]Gen. 29:31-35; 30:18-20; 46:8; Ex. 1:1-4

24 [a]Gen. 30:22-24; 35:18

25 [a]Gen. 30:5-8

26 [a]Gen. 30:10-13

★27 [a]Gen. 13:18; 18:1; 23:19 [b]Josh. 14:15

28 [a]Gen. 25:26

29 [a]Gen. 25:8; 49:33 [b]Gen. 15:15 [c]Gen. 25:9

★ 1ff.

1 [a]Gen. 25:30

2 [a]Gen. 28:9 [b]Gen. 36:25 [c]Gen. 36:24

4 [a]1 Chr. 1:35

6 [a]Gen. 12:5

7 [a]Gen. 13:6 [b]Gen. 17:8; Heb. 11:9 [c]1 Chr. 29:15; Ps. 39:12

8 [a]Gen. 32:3 [b]Gen. 36:1, 19

12 [a]Ex. 17:8-16; Num. 24:20; Deut. 25:17-19; 1 Sam. 15:2, 3

35:27 *Mamre.* See note on 13:18. There Jacob witnessed the death of his father Isaac, who was 180 years old.

36:1ff. This chapter lists the wives of Esau (vv. 1-3), the sons of Esau (vv. 4-5), the enormous wealth of Esau (vv. 6-8; on *Edom* see the Introduction to Obadiah), and the descendants of Esau and Seir the Horite, whose families intermarried (vv. 9-42).

of Edom; these are the sons of Esau's wife Basemath.

18 And these are the sons of Esau's wife Oholibamah: chief Jeush, chief Jalam, chief Korah. These are the chiefs descended from Esau's wife Oholibamah, the daughter of Anah.

19 These are the sons of Esau (that is, Edom), and these are their chiefs.

20 These are the sons of Seir the Horite, the inhabitants of the land: Lotan and Shobal and Zibeon and Anah,

21 and Dishon and Ezer and Dishan. These are the chiefs descended from the Horites, the sons of Seir in the land of Edom.

22 And the sons of Lotan were Hori and Hemam; and Lotan's sister was Timna.

23 And these are the sons of Shobal: Alvan and Manahath and Ebal, Shepho and Onam.

24 And these are the sons of Zibeon: Aiah and Anah—he is the Anah who found the hot springs in the wilderness when he was pasturing the donkeys of his father Zibeon.

25 And these are the children of Anah: Dishon, and Oholibamah, the daughter of Anah.

26 And these are the sons of aDishon: Hemdan and Eshban and Ithran and Cheran.

27 These are the sons of Ezer: Bilhan and Zaavan and Akan.

28 These are the sons of Dishan: Uz and Aran.

29 These are the chiefs descended from the Horites: chief Lotan, chief Shobal, chief Zibeon, chief Anah,

30 chief Dishon, chief Ezer, chief Dishan. These are the chiefs descended from the Horites, according to their various chiefs in the land of Seir.

31 Now these are the kings who reigned in the land of Edom before any aking reigned over the sons of Israel.

32 aBela the son of Beor reigned in Edom, and the name of his city was Dinhabah.

33 Then Bela died, and Jobab the son of Zerah of Bozrah became king in his place.

34 Then Jobab died, and Husham of the land of the Temanites became king in his place.

35 Then Husham died, and Hadad the son of Bedad, who defeated Midian in the field of Moab, became king in his place; and the name of his city was Avith.

36 Then Hadad died, and Samlah of Masrekah became king in his place.

37 Then Samlah died, and Shaul of Rehoboth on the *Euphrates* River became king in his place.

38 Then Shaul died, and Baal-hanan the son of Achbor became king in his place.

39 Then Baal-hanan the son of Achbor died, and Hadar became king in his place; and the name of his city was Pau; and his wife's name was Mehetabel, the daughter of Matred, daughter of Mezahab.

40 Now these are the names of the chiefs descended from Esau, according to their families *and* their localities, by their names: chief Timna, chief Alvah, chief Jetheth,

41 chief Oholibamah, chief Elah, chief Pinon,

42 chief Kenaz, chief Teman, chief Mibzar,

43 chief Magdiel, chief Iram. These are the chiefs of Edom (that is, Esau, the father of the Edomites), according to their habitations in the land of their possession.

IX THE HISTORY OF JOSEPH, 37:1–50:26

A Joseph Sold into Slavery, 37:1–36

37 Now Jacob lived in athe land where his father had sojourned, in the land of Canaan.

Margin references:

20 aGen. 14:6; Deut. 2:12, 22; 1 Chr. 1:38-42

26 a1 Chr. 1:41

31 aGen. 17:6, 16; 35:11; 1 Chr. 1:43

32 a1 Chr. 1:43

1 aGen. 17:8; 28:4

★ 2 aGen.
41:46 bGen.
35:25, 26
cI Sam.
2:22-24

2   These are *the records of*
the generations of Jacob.

Joseph, when ªseventeen years
of age, was pasturing the flock
with his brothers while he was
still a youth, along with ᵇthe sons
of Bilhah and the sons of Zilpah,
his father's wives. And Joseph
brought back a ᶜbad report about
them to their father.

★ 3 aGen.
44:20 bGen.
37:23, 32

3   Now Israel loved Joseph
more than all his sons, because he
was ªthe son of his old age; and
he made him a ᵇvaricolored tunic.

4 aGen.
27:41;
1 Sam. 17:28

4   And his brothers saw that
their father loved him more than
all his brothers; and *so* they
ªhated him and could not speak
to him on friendly terms.

5 aGen.
28:12; 31:10,
11, 24

5   Then Joseph ªhad a dream,
and when he told it to his brothers, they hated him even more.

★ 6-8

6   And he said to them,
"Please listen to this dream which
I have had;

7 aGen.
42:6, 9;
43:26; 44:14

7   for behold, we were binding sheaves in the field, and lo,
my sheaf rose up and also stood
erect; and behold, your sheaves
gathered around and ªbowed
down to my sheaf."

8 aGen.
49:26; Deut.
33:16

8   Then his brothers said to
him, "ªAre you actually going to
reign over us? Or are you really
going to rule over us?" So they
hated him even more for his
dreams and for his words.

★ 9-11

9   Now he had still another
dream, and related it to his brothers, and said, "Lo, I have had still
another dream; and behold, the
sun and the moon and eleven
stars were bowing down to me."

10 aGen.
27:29

10   And he related *it* to his father and to his brothers; and his
father rebuked him and said to

him, "What is this dream that
you have had? Shall I and your
mother and ªyour brothers actually come to bow ourselves down
before you to the ground?"

11   And ªhis brothers were
jealous of him, but his father
ᵇkept the saying *in mind.*

11 aActs 7:9
bDan. 7:28;
Luke 2:19,
51

12   Then his brothers went to
pasture their father's flock in Shechem.

13   And Israel said to Joseph,
"Are not your brothers pasturing
the flock in ªShechem? Come, and
I will send you to them." And he
said to him, "I will go."

13 aGen.
33:18-20

14   Then he said to him, "Go
now and see about the welfare of
your brothers and the welfare of
the flock; and bring word back to
me." So he sent him from the valley of ªHebron, and he came to
Shechem.

14 aGen.
13:18; 23:2,
19; 35:27;
Josh. 14:14,
15; Judg.
1:10

15   And a man found him, and
behold, he was wandering in the
field; and the man asked him,
"What are you looking for?"

16   And he said, "I am looking
for my brothers; please tell me
where they are pasturing *the
flock.*"

17   Then the man said, "They
have moved from here; for I
heard *them* say, 'Let us go to ªDo-
than.'" So Joseph went after his
brothers and found them at Dothan.

★17 a2 Kin.
6:13

18   When they saw him from
a distance and before he came
close to them, they ªplotted
against him to put him to death.

18 aPs.
31:13; 37:12,
32; Mark
14:1; John
11:53; Acts
23:12

19   And they said to one another, "Here comes this dreamer!

20   "Now then, come and let us
kill him and throw him into one
of the pits; and ªwe will say, 'A

20 aGen.
37:32, 33

37:2 The events of this chapter took place some
years prior to Isaac's death, while Jacob and
his family were living near Hebron (35:27; cf.
37:14).

37:3 *a varicolored tunic.* The words have been
understood as meaning a varicolored coat (tunic), a long-sleeved coat, or an ornamented
coat. In any case, its special appearance indicated Joseph's favored position in his father's
eyes.

37:6-8 The meaning of Joseph's dream was ob-

vious to his brothers. However, there was no
need for him to have told them and thus incur
their anger.

37:9-11 Joseph's second dream included the
added detail that he would some day be supreme over his parents (represented in the
dream by *the sun and the moon*).

37:17 *Dothan* is about 20 miles N. of Shechem.
Archaeologists have confirmed that the site
was occupied in the time of Jacob.

wild beast devoured him.' Then let us see what will become of his dreams!"

★21-22

21 aGen. 42:22

21 But aReuben heard *this* and rescued him out of their hands and said, "Let us not take his life."

22 Reuben further said to them, "Shed no blood. Throw him into this pit that is in the wilderness, but do not lay hands on him"—that he might rescue him out of their hands, to restore him to his father.

23 So it came about, when Joseph reached his brothers, that they stripped Joseph of his tunic, the varicolored tunic that was on him;

24 and they took him and threw him into the pit. Now the pit was empty, without any water in it.

★25 aGen. 16:11, 12; 37:28; 39:1 bGen. 43:11 cJer. 8:22; 46:11

25 Then they sat down to eat a meal. And as they raised their eyes and looked, behold, a caravan of aIshmaelites was coming from Gilead, with their camels bearing baromatic gum and cbalm and myrrh, on their way to bring *them* down to Egypt.

26 aGen. 37:20

26 And Judah said to his brothers, "What profit is it for us to kill our brother and acover up his blood?

27 aGen. 42:21

27 "aCome and let us sell him to the Ishmaelites and not lay our hands on him; for he is our brother, our *own* flesh." And his brothers listened *to him.*

★28 aGen. 37:25; Judg. 6:1-3; 8:22, 24 bGen. 45:4, 5; Ps. 105:17; Acts 7:9 cGen. 39:1

28 Then some aMidianite traders passed by, so they pulled *him* up and lifted Joseph out of

the pit, and bsold him to the Ishmaelites for twenty *shekels* of silver. Thus cthey brought Joseph into Egypt.

29 Now Reuben returned to the pit, and behold, Joseph was not in the pit; so he atore his garments.

★29 aGen. 37:34; 44:13

30 And he returned to his brothers and said, "aThe boy is not *there;* as for me, where am I to go?"

30 aGen. 42:13, 36

31 So athey took Joseph's tunic, and slaughtered a male goat, and dipped the tunic in the blood;

31 aGen. 37:3, 23

32 and they sent the varicolored tunic and brought it to their father and said, "We found this; please examine *it* to *see* whether it is your son's tunic or not."

33 Then he examined it and said, "It is my son's tunic. aA wild beast has devoured him; bJoseph has surely been torn to pieces!"

33 aGen. 37:20 bGen. 44:28

34 So Jacob atore his clothes, and put sackcloth on his loins, and mourned for his son many days.

★34 aGen. 37:29

35 Then all his sons and all his daughters arose to comfort him, but he refused to be comforted. And he said, "Surely I will ago down to Sheol in mourning for my son." So his father wept for him.

★35 aGen. 25:8; 35:29; 42:38; 44:29, 31

36 Meanwhile, the Midianites asold him in Egypt to Potiphar, Pharaoh's officer, the captain of the bodyguard.

36 aGen. 39:1

B Judah and Tamar, 38:1-30

38 And it came about at that time, that Judah departed

★ 1 aJosh. 15:35; 1 Sam. 22:1

37:21-22 As the eldest, Reuben felt some responsibility to try to save Joseph. The *pit* was like a cistern.

37:25 Their dastardly act did not affect their appetites, so great was their hatred for their brother. The *Ishmaelites* and the *Midianites* (v. 28) were both descendants of Abraham (cf. 16:15; 25:2). *Gilead* is the mountainous area E. of the Jordan.

37:28 The price of a mature slave was later set at 30 pieces of silver (Exod. 21:32; but see Lev. 27:5).

37:29 Reuben, absent at the time of the sale, discovered that he was too late to rescue Joseph

(v. 22).

37:34 *sackcloth.* A coarse, loose cloth (like burlap), worn as a sign of mourning.

37:35 *Sheol.* Used 65 times in the O.T., Sheol often means the grave where the body is placed at death (cf. Num. 16:30, 33; Psalm 16:10). It can also refer to the place of departed spirits, of both the righteous (as here) and the wicked (cf. Prov. 9:18).

38:1 *Adullamite.* Person from Adullam, a town about 15 miles NW. of Hebron. There Judah married a Canaanite (v. 2), and there his firstborn was slain by the Lord for acting wickedly (v. 7).

from his brothers, and visited a certain ªAdullamite, whose name was Hirah.

2 And Judah saw there a daughter of a certain Canaanite whose name was ªShua; and he took her and went in to her.

3 So she conceived and bore a son and he named him ªEr.

4 Then she conceived again and bore a son and named him ªOnan.

5 And she bore still another son and named him ªShelah; and it was at Chezib that she bore him.

6 Now Judah took a wife for Er his first-born, and her name *was* Tamar.

7 But ªEr, Judah's first-born, was evil in the sight of the LORD, so the LORD took his life.

8 Then Judah said to Onan, "ªGo in to your brother's wife, and perform your duty as a brother-in-law to her, and raise up offspring for your brother."

9 And Onan knew that the ªoffspring would not be his; so it came about that when he went in to his brother's wife, he wasted his seed on the ground, in order not to give offspring to his brother.

10 But what he did was displeasing in the sight of the LORD; so He ªtook his life also.

11 Then Judah said to his daughter-in-law Tamar, "ªRemain a widow in your father's house until my son Shelah grows up"; for he thought, "*I am afraid* that he too may die like his brothers." So Tamar went and lived in her father's house.

12 Now after a considerable time Shua's daughter, the wife of Judah, died; and when the time of mourning was ended, Judah went up to his sheepshearers at ªTim-nah, he and his friend Hirah the Adullamite.

13 And it was told to Tamar, "Behold, your father-in-law is going up to ªTimnah to shear his sheep."

14 So she removed her widow's garments and ªcovered *herself* with a veil, and wrapped herself, and sat in the gateway of Enaim, which is on the road to Timnah; for she saw that Shelah had grown up, and ᵇshe had not been given to him as a wife.

15 When Judah saw her, he thought she *was* a harlot, for she had covered her face.

16 So he turned aside to her by the road, and said, "Here now, let me come in to you"; for he did not know that she was his daughter-in-law. And she said, "What will you give me, that you may come in to me?"

17 He said, therefore, "I will send you a kid from the flock." She said, moreover, "Will you give a pledge until you send *it*?"

18 And he said, "What pledge shall I give you?" And she said, "ªYour seal and your cord, and your staff that is in your hand." So he gave *them* to her, and went in to her, and she conceived by him.

19 Then she arose and departed, and removed her veil and put on her widow's garments.

20 When Judah sent the kid by his friend the Adullamite, to receive the pledge from the woman's hand, he did not find her.

21 And he asked the men of her place, saying, "Where is the temple prostitute who was by the road at Enaim?" But they said, "There has been no temple prostitute here."

22 So he returned to Judah, and said, "I did not find her; and furthermore, the men of the place

---

2 ª1 Chr. 2:3

3 ªGen. 46:12; Num. 26:19

4 ªGen. 46:12

5 ªNum. 26:20

7 ªGen. 46:12; Num. 26:19; 1 Chr. 2:3

★ **8-9**

8 ªDeut. 25:5, 6; Matt. 22:24

9 ªDeut. 25:6

10 ªGen. 46:12; Num. 26:19

11 ªRuth 1:12, 13

12 ªJosh. 15:10, 57

13 ªJosh. 15:10, 57; Judg. 14:1

14 ªGen. 24:65 ᵇGen. 38:11, 26

★ **18** ªGen. 38:25; 41:42

38:8-9 Levirate marriage (the marriage of a widow to the brother of her deceased husband) was widely practiced and later incorporated into the Law of Moses (see note on Deut. 25:5-10). Onan's refusal to perform this duty stemmed from his desire to have the inheritance of the firstborn for himself (normally it would have gone to Tamar's child, even though fathered by Onan).

38:18 Tamar asked for and received, as pledge of later payment for her services, Judah's *seal*, worn on a *cord* around his neck, and his *staff*.

said, 'There has been no temple prostitute here.' "

23 Then Judah said, "Let her keep them, lest we become a laughingstock. After all, I sent this kid, but you did not find her."

24 *a*Lev. 21:9

24 Now it was about three months later that Judah was informed, "Your daughter-in-law Tamar has played the harlot, and behold, she is also with child by harlotry." Then Judah said, "Bring her out and *a*let her be burned!"

25 *a*Gen. 37:32

25 It was while she was being brought out that she sent to her father-in-law, saying, "I am with child by the man to whom these things belong." And she said, "*a*Please examine and see, whose signet ring and cords and staff are these?"

★26 *a*1 Sam. 24:17 *b*Gen. 38:14

26 And Judah recognized *them*, and said, "*a*She is more righteous than I, inasmuch as *b*I did not give her to my son Shelah." And he did not have relations with her again.

27 *a*Gen. 25:24-26

27 And it came about at the time she was giving birth, that behold, there were *a*twins in her womb.

★28-30

28 Moreover, it took place while she was giving birth, one put out a hand, and the midwife took and tied a scarlet *thread* on his hand, saying, "This one came out first."

29 *a*Gen. 46:12; Ruth 4:12

29 But it came about as he drew back his hand, that behold, his brother came out. Then she said, "What a breach you have made for yourself!" So he was named *a*Perez.

30 *a*1 Chr. 2:4

30 And afterward his brother came out who had the scarlet *thread* on his hand; and he was named *a*Zerah.

C Joseph in Potiphar's House,
39:1-23

★ 1 *a*Gen. 37:25, 28, 36; Ps. 105:17

39 Now Joseph had been taken down to Egypt; and Potiphar, an Egyptian officer of Pharaoh, the captain of the bodyguard, bought him from the *a*Ishmaelites, who had taken him down there.

2 *a*Gen. 39:3, 21, 23; Acts 7:9

2 And *a*the LORD was with Joseph, so he became a successful man. And he was in the house of his master, the Egyptian.

3 *a*Gen. 21:22; 26:28 *b*Ps. 1:3

3 Now his master *a*saw that the LORD was with him and *how* the LORD *b*caused all that he did to prosper in his hand.

★ 4 *a*Gen. 18:3; 19:19 *b*Gen. 24:2; 39:8, 22

4 So Joseph *a*found favor in his sight, and became his personal servant; and he made him overseer over his house, and *b*all that he owned he put in his charge.

5 *a*Gen. 30:27 *b*Deut. 28:3, 4, 11

5 And it came about that from the time he made him overseer in his house, and over all that he owned, the LORD *a*blessed the Egyptian's house on account of Joseph; thus *b*the LORD's blessing was upon all that he owned, in the house and in the field.

6 *a*Gen. 29:17; 1 Sam. 16:12

6 So he left everything he owned in Joseph's charge; and with him *there* he did not concern himself with anything except the food which he ate. Now Joseph was *a*handsome in form and appearance.

7 *a*Prov. 7:15-20 *b*2 Sam. 13:11

7 And it came about after these events *a*that his master's wife looked with desire at Joseph, and she said, "*b*Lie with me."

8 *a*Prov. 6:23, 24

8 But *a*he refused and said to his master's wife, "Behold, with me *here*, my master does not concern himself with anything in the house, and he has put all that he owns in my charge.

38:26 Judah was wrong on two counts: refusing to give Tamar his son for her husband, and committing adultery with her.

38:28-30 Although *Zerah's* hand appeared first, *Perez* (meaning "breach" or "forging through") was actually born first and is listed in the genealogy of Christ (Matt. 1:3).

39:1 *Potiphar* was commanding officer of Pharaoh's *bodyguard. officer.* Lit., eunuch, though

not so here, where the term signifies a prominent court official. Though the reigning Pharaoh is not named, probably he was Sesostris III, who reigned 1878-1843 B.C. (see 1 Kings 6:1 and Exod. 12:40, which place Joseph's entrance into Egypt about 1875).

39:4 In the 13 or so years since arriving in Egypt, Joseph had risen to the place of comptroller, in charge of all the affairs of Potiphar.

9 aGen. 41:40 bGen. 20:6; 42:18; 2 Sam. 12:13; Ps. 51:4

9 "aThere is no one greater in this house than I, and he has withheld nothing from me except you, because you are his wife. How then could I do this great evil, and bsin against God?"

10 And it came about as she spoke to Joseph day after day, that he did not listen to her to lie beside her, or be with her.

11 Now it happened one day that he went into the house to do his work, and none of the men of the household was there inside.

12 And she caught him by his garment, saying, "Lie with me!" And he left his garment in her hand and fled, and went outside.

13 When she saw that he had left his garment in her hand, and had fled outside,

14 she called to the men of her household, and said to them, "See, he has brought in a Hebrew to us to make sport of us; he came in to me to lie with me, and I screamed.

★15

15 "And it came about when he heard that I raised my voice and screamed, that he left his garment beside me and fled, and went outside."

16 So she left his garment beside her until his master came home.

17 aEx. 23:1; Prov. 26:28

17 Then she aspoke to him with these words, "The Hebrew slave, whom you brought to us, came in to me to make sport of me;

18 and it happened as I raised my voice and screamed, that he left his garment beside me and fled outside."

19 aProv. 6:34

19 Now it came about when his master heard the words of his wife, which she spoke to him, saying, "This is what your slave did to me," that ahis anger burned.

★20 aGen. 40:3; Ps. 105:18

20 So Joseph's master took him and aput him into the jail, the place where the king's prisoners were confined; and he was there in the jail.

21 But athe LORD was with Joseph and extended kindness to him, and bgave him favor in the sight of the chief jailer.

21 aGen. 39:2; Ps. 105:19; Acts 7:9 bEx. 3:21; 11:3; 12:36

22 And the chief jailer acommitted to Joseph's charge all the prisoners who were in the jail; so that whatever was done there, he was responsible for it.

22 aGen. 39:4; 40:3, 4

23 aThe chief jailer did not supervise anything under Joseph's charge because bthe LORD was with him; and whatever he did, cthe LORD made to prosper.

23 aGen. 39:3, 8 bGen. 39:2, 3 cGen. 39:3

D Joseph Interprets the Dreams of the Butler and the Baker, 40:1-23

40 Then it came about after these things athe cupbearer and the baker for the king of Egypt offended their lord, the king of Egypt.

★ 1 aGen. 40:11, 13; Neh. 1:11

2 And Pharaoh was afurious with his two officials, the chief cupbearer and the chief baker.

2 aProv. 16:14

3 So he put them in confinement in the house of the acaptain of the bodyguard, in the jail, the same place where Joseph was imprisoned.

3 aGen. 39:1, 20

4 And the captain of the bodyguard put Joseph in charge of them, and he took care of them; and they were in confinement for some time.

5 Then the cupbearer and the baker for the king of Egypt, who were confined in jail, both had a dream the same night, each man with his own dream and each dream with its own interpretation.

6 When Joseph came to them in the morning and

39:15 This was the second time a *garment* of Joseph's was used to perpetrate a lie about him (cf. 37:33).

39:20 For added details of Joseph's imprisonment see Psalm 105:17-18.

40:1 *cupbearer.* An official who served drink to the king. He and the *baker* had to be trustworthy individuals, not involved in the frequent court intrigues.

observed them, behold, they were dejected.

7 aNeh. 2:2

7 And he asked Pharaoh's officials who were with him in confinement in his master's house, "aWhy are your faces so sad today?"

8 aGen. 41:15 bGen. 41:16; Dan. 2:27, 28

8 Then they said to him, "aWe have had a dream and there is no one to interpret it." Then Joseph said to them, "bDo not interpretations belong to God? Tell *it* to me, please."

9 So the chief cupbearer told his dream to Joseph, and said to him, "In my dream, behold, *there was* a vine in front of me;

10 and on the vine *were* three branches. And as it was budding, its blossoms came out, *and* its clusters produced ripe grapes.

11 "Now Pharaoh's cup was in my hand; so I took the grapes and squeezed them into Pharaoh's cup, and I put the cup into Pharaoh's hand."

12 aDan. 2:36; 4:18, 19

12 Then Joseph said to him, "This is the ainterpretation of it: the three branches are three days;

13 within three more days Pharaoh will lift up your head and restore you to your office; and you will put Pharaoh's cup into his hand according to your former custom when you were his cupbearer.

14 aJosh. 2:12; 1 Sam. 20:14; 1 Kin. 2:7

14 "Only keep me in mind when it goes well with you, and please ado me a kindness by mentioning me to Pharaoh, and get me out of this house.

15 aGen. 37:26-28

15 "For aI was in fact kidnapped from the land of the Hebrews, and even here I have done nothing that they should have put me into the dungeon."

16 When the chief baker saw that he had interpreted favorably, he said to Joseph, "I also *saw in* my dream, and behold, *there were* three baskets of white bread on my head;

17 and in the top basket *there were* some of all sorts of baked food for Pharaoh, and the birds were eating them out of the basket on my head."

18 Then Joseph answered and said, "This is its interpretation: the three baskets are three days;

19 within three more days Pharaoh will lift up your head from you and will hang you on a tree; and the birds will eat your flesh off you."

20 aMatt. 14:6 b2 Kin. 25:27; Jer. 52:31

20 Thus it came about on the third day, *which was* aPharaoh's birthday, that he made a feast for all his servants; band he lifted up the head of the chief cupbearer and the head of the chief baker among his servants.

21 aGen. 40:13

21 And he restored the chief cupbearer to his office, and ahe put the cup into Pharaoh's hand;

22 aGen. 40:19; Esth. 7:10

22 but ahe hanged the chief baker, just as Joseph had interpreted to them.

23 aJob 19:14; Ps. 31:12; Eccl. 9:15

23 Yet the chief cupbearer did not remember Joseph, but aforgot him.

E   Joseph Interprets Pharaoh's Dream, 41:1-57

41 Now it happened at the end of two full years that Pharaoh had a dream, and behold, he was standing by the Nile.

2 aJob 8:11; Is. 19:6, 7

2 And lo, from the Nile there came up seven cows, sleek and fat; and they grazed in the amarsh grass.

3 Then behold, seven other cows came up after them from the Nile, ugly and gaunt, and they stood by the *other* cows on the bank of the Nile.

4 And the ugly and gaunt cows ate up the seven sleek and fat cows. Then Pharaoh awoke.

5 And he fell asleep and dreamed a second time; and behold, seven ears of grain came up on a single stalk, plump and good.

6 Then behold, seven ears, thin and scorched by the east wind, sprouted up after them.

7 And the thin ears swallowed up the seven plump and full ears. Then Pharaoh awoke, and behold, *it was* a dream.

8 aDan. 2:1, 3 bEx. 7:11, 22; Dan. 1:20; 2:2 cMatt. 2:1 dDan. 2:27; 4:7

8 Now it came about in the morning that ahis spirit was troubled, so he sent and called for all the [b]magicians of Egypt, and all its [c]wise men. And Pharaoh told them his dreams, but [d]there was no one who could interpret them to Pharaoh.

9 Then the chief cupbearer spoke to Pharaoh, saying, "I would make mention today of [a]my *own* offenses.

10 "Pharaoh was [a]furious with his servants, and [b]he put me in confinement in the house of the captain of the bodyguard, *both* me and the chief baker.

11 "And [a]we had a dream on the same night, he and I; each of us dreamed according to the interpretation of his *own* dream.

12 "Now a Hebrew youth *was* with us there, a [a]servant of the captain of the bodyguard, and we related *them* to him, and [b]he interpreted our dreams for us. To each one he interpreted according to his *own* dream.

13 "And it came about that just [a]as he interpreted for us, so it happened; he restored me in my office, but he hanged him."

14 Then Pharaoh sent and [a]called for Joseph, and they [b]hurriedly brought him out of the dungeon; and when he had shaved himself and changed his clothes, he came to Pharaoh.

15 And Pharaoh said to Joseph, "I have had a dream, [a]but no one can interpret it; and [b]I have heard it said about you, that when you hear a dream you can interpret it."

16 Joseph then answered Pharaoh, saying, "[a]It is not in me; [b]God will give Pharaoh a favorable answer."

17 So Pharaoh spoke to Joseph, "In my dream, behold, I was standing on the bank of the Nile;

18 and behold, seven cows, fat and sleek came up out of the Nile; and they grazed in the marsh grass.

19 "And lo, seven other cows

came up after them, poor and very ugly and gaunt, such as I had never seen for ugliness in all the land of Egypt;

20 and the lean and ugly cows ate up the first seven fat cows.

21 "Yet when they had devoured them, it could not be detected that they had devoured them; for they were just as ugly as before. Then I awoke.

22 "I saw also in my dream, and behold, seven ears, full and good, came up on a single stalk;

23 and lo, seven ears, withered, thin, *and* scorched by the east wind, sprouted up after them;

24 and the thin ears swallowed the seven good ears. Then [a]I told it to the magicians, but there was no one who could explain it to me."

25 Now Joseph said to Pharaoh, "Pharaoh's dreams are one and the same; [a]God has told to Pharaoh what He is about to do.

26 "The seven good cows are seven years; and the seven good ears are seven years; the dreams are one *and* the same.

27 "And the seven lean and ugly cows that came up after them are seven years, and the seven thin ears scorched by the east wind [a]shall be seven years of famine.

28 "It is as I have spoken to Pharaoh: [a]God has shown to Pharaoh what He is about to do.

29 "Behold, [a]seven years of great abundance are coming in all the land of Egypt;

30 and after them [a]seven years of famine will come, and all the abundance will be forgotten in the land of Egypt; and the famine will ravage the land.

31 "So the abundance will be unknown in the land because of that subsequent famine; for it *will be* very severe.

32 "Now as for the repeating of the dream to Pharaoh twice, *it means* that [a]the matter is

---

9 [a]Gen. 40:14, 23

10 [a]Gen. 40:2, 3; [b]Gen. 39:20

11 [a]Gen. 40:5

12 [a]Gen. 37:36 [b]Gen. 40:12

13 [a]Gen. 40:21, 22

★**14** [a]Ps. 105:20 [b]Dan. 2:25

15 [a]Gen. 41:8 [b]Dan. 5:16

16 [a]Dan. 2:30; Zech. 4:6; Acts 3:12; 2 Cor. 3:5 [b]Gen. 40:8; 41:25, 28, 32; Deut. 29:29; Dan. 2:22, 28, 47

24 [a]Is. 8:19; Dan. 4:7

25 [a]Gen. 41:28, 32; Dan. 2:28, 29, 45

27 [a]2 Kin. 8:1

28 [a]Gen. 41:25, 32

29 [a]Gen. 41:47

30 [a]Gen. 41:54, 56; 47:13; Ps. 105:16

★**32** [a]Gen. 41:25, 28

41:14 Egyptians were clean-shaven, so it was important that Joseph appear that way in the presence of Pharaoh.

41:32 The meaning is this: the events are certain and coming soon.

determined by God, and God will quickly bring it about.

★33-36

33 "And now let Pharaoh look for a man [a]discerning and wise, and set him over the land of Egypt.

33 [a]Gen. 41:39

34 "Let Pharaoh take action to appoint overseers in charge of the land, and let him exact a fifth *of the produce* of the land of Egypt in the seven years of abundance.

35 [a]Gen. 41:48

35 "Then let them [a]gather all the food of these good years that are coming, and store up the grain for food in the cities under Pharaoh's authority, and let them guard *it*.

36 "And let the food become as a reserve for the land for the seven years of famine which will occur in the land of Egypt, so that the land may not perish during the famine."

★37-38

37 Now the proposal seemed good to Pharaoh and to all his servants.

38 [a]Job 32:8; Dan. 4:8, 9, 18; 5:11, 14

38 Then Pharaoh said to his servants, "Can we find a man like this, [a]in whom is a divine spirit?"

39 [a]Gen. 41:33

39 So Pharaoh said to Joseph, "Since God has informed you of all this, there is no one so [a]discerning and wise as you are.

★40-44

40 [a]Ps. 105:21; Acts 7:10

40 "[a]You shall be over my house, and according to your command all my people shall do homage; only in the throne I will be greater than you."

41 [a]Gen. 42:6; Ps. 105:21; Dan. 6:3; Acts 7:10

41 And Pharaoh said to Joseph, "See I have set you [a]over all the land of Egypt."

42 [a]Esth. 3:10; 8:2
[b]Dan. 5:7, 16, 29

42 Then Pharaoh [a]took off his signet ring from his hand, and put it on Joseph's hand, and clothed him in garments of fine linen, and [b]put the gold necklace around his neck.

43 And he had him ride in his second chariot; and they proclaimed before him, "Bow the knee!" And he set him over all the land of Egypt.

44 [a]Ps. 105:22

44 Moreover, Pharaoh said to Joseph, "*Though* I am Pharaoh, yet [a]without your permission no one shall raise his hand or foot in all the land of Egypt."

45 [a]Jer. 43:13; Ezek. 30:17

★45

45 Then Pharaoh named Joseph Zaphenath-paneah; and he gave him Asenath, the daughter of Potiphera priest of [a]On, as his wife. And Joseph went forth over the land of Egypt.

46 [a]Gen. 37:2

★46

46 Now Joseph was [a]thirty years old when he stood before Pharaoh, king of Egypt. And Joseph went out from the presence of Pharaoh, and went through all the land of Egypt.

47 And during the seven years of plenty the land brought forth abundantly.

48 So he gathered all the food of *these* seven years which occurred in the land of Egypt, and placed the food in the cities; he placed in every city the food from its own surrounding fields.

49 Thus Joseph stored up grain in great abundance like the sand of the sea, until he stopped measuring *it*, for it was beyond measure.

50 [a]Gen. 48:5

50 Now before the year of famine came, [a]two sons were born to Joseph, whom Asenath, the daughter of Potiphera priest of On, bore to him.

★51

51 And Joseph named the first-born Manasseh, "For," *he said,* "God has made me forget all my trouble and all my father's household."

41:33-36 Joseph not only interpreted the meaning of the dreams but also advised Pharaoh how to plan for the years of famine.

41:37-38 Pharaoh and his courtiers were convinced of Joseph's supernatural insight (cf. Dan. 5:11).

41:40-44 As prime minister, second only to Pharaoh, Joseph was invested with the honors of that office and given Pharaoh's *signet ring*, which gave him authority to sign documents and transact business in Pharaoh's name.

41:45 In order to "Egyptianize" Joseph, Pharaoh gave him an Egyptian name and an Egyptian wife. The meaning of his Egyptian name is uncertain. *Asenath* means "she belongs to Neith" (a goddess of the Egyptians). *On* is the city of Heliopolis, a center for the worship of the sun god, Ra.

41:46 Since Joseph was 17 when he arrived in Egypt (37:2), it follows that he had spent 13 years in slavery.

41:51 *Manasseh* means "one who causes to forget" (e.g., Joseph's trials in Egypt).

★52 ªGen.
17:6; 28:3;
49:22

54 ªGen.
41:30; Ps.
105:16; Acts
7:11

55 ªJohn 2:5

57 ªGen.
12:10

★ 1 ªActs
7:12

2 ªActs
7:12 ᵇGen.
43:8; Ps.
33:18, 19

★ 4 ªGen.
35:24 ᵇGen.
42:38

5 ªGen.
12:10; 26:1;
41:57; Acts
7:11

52 And he named the second Ephraim, "For," he said, "ªGod has made me fruitful in the land of my affliction."

53 When the seven years of plenty which had been in the land of Egypt came to an end,

54 and ªthe seven years of famine began to come, just as Joseph had said, then there was famine in all the lands; but in all the land of Egypt there was bread.

55 So when all the land of Egypt was famished, the people cried out to Pharaoh for bread; and Pharaoh said to all the Egyptians, "Go to Joseph; ªwhatever he says to you, you shall do."

56 When the famine was spread over all the face of the earth, then Joseph opened all the storehouses, and sold to the Egyptians; and the famine was severe in the land of Egypt.

57 And the people of all the earth came to Egypt to buy grain from Joseph, because ªthe famine was severe in all the earth.

F Joseph's Brothers in Egypt,
42:1–45:28

1 The first visit of his ten brothers, 42:1–38

42 Now ªJacob saw that there was grain in Egypt, and Jacob said to his sons, "Why are you staring at one another?"

2 And he said, "Behold, ªI have heard that there is grain in Egypt; go down there and buy some for us from that place, ᵇso that we may live and not die."

3 Then ten brothers of Joseph went down to buy grain from Egypt.

4 But Jacob did not send Joseph's brother ªBenjamin with his brothers, for he said, "ᵇI am afraid that harm may befall him."

5 So the sons of Israel came to buy grain among those who were coming, ªfor the famine was in the land of Canaan also.

6 Now ªJoseph was the ruler over the land; he was the one who sold to all the people of the land. And Joseph's brothers came and ᵇbowed down to him with their faces to the ground.

7 When Joseph saw his brothers he recognized them, but he disguised himself to them and ªspoke to them harshly. And he said to them, "Where have you come from?" And they said, "From the land of Canaan, to buy food."

8 But Joseph had recognized his brothers, although ªthey did not recognize him.

9 And Joseph ªremembered the dreams which he had about them, and said to them, "You are spies; you have come to look at the undefended parts of our land."

10 Then they said to him, "No, ªmy lord, but your servants have come to buy food.

11 "We are all sons of one man; we are ªhonest men, your servants are not spies."

12 Yet he said to them, "No, but you have come to look at the undefended parts of our land!"

13 But they said, "Your servants are twelve brothers in all, the sons of one man in the land of Canaan; and behold, the youngest is with ªour father today, and ᵇone is no more."

14 And Joseph said to them, "It is as I said to you, you are spies;

15 by this you will be tested: ªby the life of Pharaoh, you shall not go from this place unless your youngest brother comes here!

16 "Send one of you that he may get your brother, while you remain confined, that your words may be tested, whether there is ªtruth in you. But if not, by the

★ 6 ªGen.
41:41, 55
ᵇGen. 37:7-
10; 41:43; Is.
60:14

7 ªGen.
42:30

8 ªGen.
37:2; 41:46

9 ªGen.
37:6-9

10 ªGen.
37:8

11 ªGen.
42:16, 19,
31, 34

13 ªGen.
43:7 ᵇGen.
37:30; 42:32;
44:20

★15 ª1 Sam.
17:55

16 ªGen.
42:11

41:52 Ephraim means "fruitful."
42:1 Jacob's sons sat around looking at each other helplessly instead of trying to find grain to eat.
42:4 Benjamin, as the only other son of Rachel, had taken Joseph's place in his father's affection.
42:6 See 37:7-8.
42:15 Joseph wanted to be certain that his brothers had not killed Benjamin, as they had tried to kill him.

life of Pharaoh, surely you are spies."

^{17 aGen. 40:4, 7}

17 So he put them all together in ^aprison for three days.

^{18 aGen. 39:9; Lev. 25:43; Neh. 5:15}

18 Now Joseph said to them on the third day, "Do this and live, for ^aI fear God:

19 if you are honest men, let one of your brothers be confined in your prison; but as for *the rest of* you, go, carry grain for the famine of your households,

^{20 aGen. 42:34; 43:5; 44:23}

20 and ^abring your youngest brother to me, so your words may be verified, and you will not die." And they did so.

^{★21 aGen. 37:26-28; 45:3; Hos. 5:15}

21 Then they said to one another, "^aTruly we are guilty concerning our brother, because we saw the distress of his soul when he pleaded with us, yet we would not listen; therefore this distress has come upon us."

^{22 aGen. 37:21, 22 bGen. 9:5, 6; 1 Kin. 2:32; 2 Chr. 24:22; Ps. 9:12}

22 And Reuben answered them, saying, "^aDid I not tell you, 'Do not sin against the boy'; and you would not listen? ^bNow comes the reckoning for his blood."

23 They did not know, however, that Joseph understood, for there was an interpreter between them.

^{24 aGen. 43:30; 45:14, 15 bGen. 43:14, 23}

24 And he turned away from them and ^awept. But when he returned to them and spoke to them, he ^btook Simeon from them and bound him before their eyes.

^{25 aGen. 44:1; Rom. 12:17, 20, 21; 1 Pet. 3:9}

25 ^aThen Joseph gave orders to fill their bags with grain and to restore every man's money in his sack, and to give them provisions for the journey. And thus it was done for them.

26 So they loaded their donkeys with their grain, and departed from there.

^{27 aGen. 43:21, 22}

27 And as one *of them* opened his sack to give his donkey fodder at the lodging place, he saw his ^amoney; and behold, it was in the mouth of his sack.

^{28 aGen. 43:23}

28 Then he said to his brothers, "My money has been returned, and behold, it is even in my sack." And their hearts sank, and they *turned* trembling to one another, saying, "^aWhat is this that God has done to us?"

29 When they came to their father Jacob in the land of Canaan, they told him all that had happened to them, saying,

^{30 aGen. 42:7}

30 "The man, the lord of the land, ^aspoke harshly with us, and took us for spies of the country.

^{31 aGen. 42:11}

31 "But we said to him, 'We are ^ahonest men; we are not spies.

32 'We are twelve brothers, sons of our father; one is no more, and the youngest is with our father today in the land of Canaan.'

^{33 aGen. 42:19, 20}

33 "And the man, the lord of the land, said to us, '^aBy this I shall know that you are honest men: leave one of your brothers with me and take *grain for* the famine of your households, and go.

^{34 aGen. 34:10}

34 'But bring your youngest brother to me that I may know that you are not spies, but honest men. I will give your brother to you, and you may ^atrade in the land.' "

^{35 aGen. 43:12, 15, 21}

35 Now it came about as they were emptying their sacks, that behold, ^aevery man's bundle of money *was* in his sack; and when they and their father saw their bundles of money, they were dismayed.

^{36 aGen. 43:14}

36 And their father Jacob said to them, "You have ^abereaved me of my children: Joseph is no more, and Simeon is no more, and you would take Benjamin; all these things are against me."

37 Then Reuben spoke to his father, saying, "You may put my two sons to death if I do not bring him *back* to you; put him in my care, and I will return him to you."

^{38 aGen. 37:33, 34; 42:13; 44:27, 28 bGen. 42:4 cGen. 37:35; 44:29, 31}

38 But Jacob said, "My son shall not go down with you; for his ^abrother is dead, and he alone is left. ^bIf harm should befall him on the journey you are taking, then you will ^cbring my gray hair down to Sheol in sorrow."

42:21 This confession of sin was probably what Joseph was trying to elicit all along.

2 The second visit of his eleven brothers,
43:1–44:34

1 *a*Gen. 12:10; 26:1; 41:56, 57

43 *a*Now the famine was severe in the land.

2 So it came about when they had finished eating the grain which they had brought from Egypt, that their father said to them, "Go back, buy us a little food."

3 *a*Gen. 43:5; 44:23

3 Judah spoke to him, however, saying, "*a*The man solemnly warned us, 'You shall not see my face unless your brother is with you.'

4 "If you send our brother with us, we will go down and buy you food.

5 "But if you do not send *him*, we will not go down; for the man said to us, 'You shall not see my face unless your brother is with you.' "

6 Then Israel said, "Why did you treat me so badly by telling the man whether you still had *another* brother?"

7 *a*Gen. 42:13; 43:27

7 But they said, "The man questioned particularly about us and our relatives, saying, '*a*Is your father still alive? Have you *another* brother?' So we answered his questions. Could we possibly know that he would say, 'Bring your brother down'?"

8 *a*Gen. 42:2

8 And Judah said to his father Israel, "Send the lad with me, and we will arise and go, *a*that we may live and not die, we as well as you and our little ones.

9 *a*Gen. 42:37; 44:32; Philem. 18, 19

9 "*a*I myself will be surety for him; you may hold me responsible for him. If I do not bring him *back* to you and set him before you, then let me bear the blame before you forever.

10 "For if we had not delayed, surely by now we could have returned twice."

11 Then their father Israel said to them, "If *it must be* so, then do this: take some of the best products of the land in your bags, and carry down to the man *a*as a present, a little *b*balm and a little honey, aromatic gum and myrrh, pistachio nuts and almonds.

★**11** *a*Gen. 32:20; 43:25, 26 *b*Gen. 37:25; Jer. 8:22; Ezek. 27:17

12 "And take double *the* money in your hand, and take back in your hand *a*the money that was returned in the mouth of your sacks; perhaps it was a mistake.

12 *a*Gen. 42:25, 35; 43:21, 22

13 "Take your brother also, and arise, return to the man;

14 and may *a*God Almighty *b*grant you compassion in the sight of the man, that he may release to you *c*your other brother and Benjamin. And as for me, *d*if I am bereaved of my children, I am bereaved."

★**14** *a*Gen. 17:1; 28:3; 35:11 *b*Ps. 106:46 *c*Gen. 42:24 *d*Gen. 42:36

15 So the men took *a*this present, and they took double *the* money in their hand, and Benjamin; then they arose and went down to Egypt and stood before Joseph.

★**15** *a*Gen. 43:11

16 When Joseph saw Benjamin with them, he said to his *a*house steward, "Bring the men into the house, and slay *an animal* and make ready; for the men are to dine with me at noon."

16 *a*Gen. 44:1

17 So the man did as Joseph said, and brought the men to Joseph's house.

18 Now the men were afraid, because they were brought to Joseph's house; and they said, "*It is* because of the money that was returned in our sacks the first time that we are being brought in, that he may seek occasion against us and fall upon us, and take us for slaves with our donkeys."

19 So they came near to Joseph's house steward, and spoke to him at the entrance of the house,

---

43:11 The present consisted of things not produced in Egypt (see 37:25). The *honey* was not bee's honey but a thick syrup boiled down from fresh grape juice.

43:14 *God Almighty.* Heb., *El Shaddai.* See note on 17:1.

43:15 *double the money.* This was in order to pay for the original purchase of grain (cf. 42:28) as well as the later one.

20 and said, "Oh, my lord, we indeed came down the first time to buy food,

21 and it came about when we came to the lodging place, that we opened our sacks, and behold, ªeach man's money was in the mouth of his sack, our money in full. So ᵇwe have brought it back in our hand.

22 "We have also brought down other money in our hand to buy food; we do not know who put our money in our sacks."

23 And he said, "Be at ease, do not be afraid. ªYour God and the God of your father has given you treasure in your sacks; I had your money." Then ᵇhe brought Simeon out to them.

24 Then the man brought the men into Joseph's house and ªgave them water, and they ᵇwashed their feet; and he gave their donkeys fodder.

25 So they prepared ªthe present for Joseph's coming at noon; for they had heard that they were to eat a meal there.

26 When Joseph came home, they brought into the house to him the present which was in their hand and ªbowed to the ground before him.

27 Then he asked them about their welfare, and said, "ªIs your old father well, of whom you spoke? Is he still alive?"

28 And they said, "Your servant our father is well; he is still alive." ªAnd they bowed down in homage.

29 As he lifted his eyes and saw his brother Benjamin, his mother's son, he said, "Is this ªyour youngest brother, of whom you spoke to me?" And he said, "ᵇMay God be gracious to you, my son."

30 And Joseph hurried *out* for ªhe was deeply stirred over his brother, and he sought *a place* to weep; and he entered his chamber and ᵇwept there.

31 Then he washed his face, and came out; and he ªcontrolled himself and said, "Serve the meal."

32 So they served him by himself, and them by themselves, and the Egyptians, who ate with him, by themselves; because the Egyptians could not eat bread with the Hebrews, for that is ªloathsome to the Egyptians.

33 Now they were seated before him, ªthe first-born according to his birthright and the youngest according to his youth, and the men looked at one another in astonishment.

34 And he took portions to them from his own table; ªbut Benjamin's portion was five times as much as any of theirs. So they feasted and drank freely with him.

44 ªThen he commanded his house steward, saying, "Fill the men's sacks with food, as much as they can carry, and put each man's money in the mouth of his sack.

2 "And put my cup, the silver cup, in the mouth of the sack of the youngest, and his money for the grain." And he did as Joseph had told *him*.

3 As soon as it was light, the men were sent away, they with their donkeys.

4 They had *just* gone out of ªthe city, *and* were not far off, when Joseph said to his house steward, "Up, follow the men; and when you overtake them, say to them, 'Why have you repaid evil for good?

5 'Is not this the one from which my lord drinks, and which he indeed uses for ªdivination?

43:32 The Egyptians would not eat with the Hebrews, and Joseph did not violate this custom (cf. 46:34).

43:34 Joseph's deliberate favoring of Benjamin was another test to see if his brothers would be resentful.

44:5 It is unlikely that Joseph used divination; rather, this statement (made in order to attach special significance to the cup) was part of the situation Joseph contrived in order to test his brothers. Would they seize on this opportunity to get rid of Benjamin, or had their hearts indeed been changed so that they would stand with him?

Marginal references:

21 ªGen. 42:27, 35; ᵇGen. 43:12, 15
23 ªGen. 42:28 ᵇGen. 42:24
24 ªGen. 18:4; 19:2; 24:32 ᵇLuke 7:44; John 13:5; 1 Tim. 5:10
25 ªGen. 43:11, 15
26 ªGen. 37:7, 10
27 ªGen. 43:7; 45:3
28 ªGen. 37:7, 10
29 ªGen. 42:13 ᵇNum. 6:25; Ps. 67:1
30 ª1 Kin. 3:26 ᵇGen. 42:24; 45:2, 14, 15; 46:29
31 ªGen. 45:1
★32 ªGen. 46:34; Ex. 8:26
33 ªGen. 42:7
★34 ªGen. 35:24; 45:22
1 ªGen. 42:25
4 ªGen. 44:13
★5 ªGen. 30:27; 44:15; Lev. 19:26; Deut. 18:10-14

You have done wrong in doing this.' "

6 So he overtook them and spoke these words to them.

7 And they said to him, "Why does my lord speak such words as these? Far be it from your servants to do such a thing.

8 "Behold, [a]the money which we found in the mouth of our sacks we have brought back to you from the land of Canaan. How then could we steal silver or gold from your lord's house?

9 "[a]With whomever of your servants it is found, let him die, and we also will be my lord's [b]slaves."

10 So he said, "Now let it also be according to your words; he with whom it is found shall be my slave, and *the rest of* you shall be innocent."

11 Then they hurried, each man lowered his sack to the ground, and each man opened his sack.

12 And he searched, beginning with the oldest and ending with the youngest, and [a]the cup was found in Benjamin's sack.

13 Then they [a]tore their clothes, and when each man loaded his donkey, they returned to [b]the city.

14 When Judah and his brothers came to Joseph's house, he was still there, and [a]they fell to the ground before him.

15 And Joseph said to them, "What is this deed that you have done? Do you not know that such a man as I can indeed practice [a]divination?"

16 So Judah said, "What can we say to my lord? What can we speak? And how can we justify ourselves? God has found out the iniquity of your servants; behold, we are my lord's [a]slaves, both we and the one in whose possession the cup has been found."

17 But he said, "Far be it from me to do this. The man in whose possession the cup has been found, he shall be my slave; but as for you, go up in peace to your father."

18 Then Judah approached him, and said, "Oh my lord, may your servant please speak a word in my lord's ears, and [a]do not be angry with your servant; for [b]you are equal to Pharaoh.

19 "[a]My lord asked his servants, saying, 'Have you a father or a brother?'

20 "And we said to my lord, 'We have an old father and [a]a little child of *his* old age. Now [b]his brother is dead, so he alone is left of his mother, and his father loves him.'

21 "Then you said to your servants, '[a]Bring him down to me, that I may set my eyes on him.'

22 "But we said to my lord, 'The lad cannot leave his father, for if he should leave his father, his father would die.'

23 "You said to your servants, however, '[a]Unless your youngest brother comes down with you, you shall not see my face again.'

24 "Thus it came about when we went up to your servant my father, we told him the words of my lord.

25 "And [a]our father said, 'Go back, buy us a little food.'

26 "But we said, 'We cannot go down. If our youngest brother is with us, then we will go down; for we cannot see the man's face unless our youngest brother is with us.'

27 "And your servant my father said to us, 'You know that [a]my wife bore me two sons;

28 and the one went out from me, and [a]I said, "Surely he is torn in pieces," and I have not seen him since.

29 'And if you take this one also from me, and harm befalls him, you will [a]bring my gray hair down to Sheol in sorrow.'

30 "Now, therefore, when I come to your servant my father, and the lad is not with us, since [a]his life is bound up in the lad's life,

---

8 [a]Gen. 43:21

9 [a]Gen. 31:32 [b]Gen. 44:16

12 [a]Gen. 44:2

13 [a]Gen. 37:29, 34; Num. 14:6; 2 Sam. 1:11 [b]Gen. 44:4

14 [a]Gen. 37:7, 10

15 [a]Gen. 44:5

16 [a]Gen. 44:9

★17

18 [a]Gen. 18:30, 32; Ex. 32:22 [b]Gen. 37:7, 8; 41:40-44

19 [a]Gen. 43:7

20 [a]Gen. 37:3; 43:8; 44:30 [b]Gen. 37:33; 42:13, 38

21 [a]Gen. 42:15, 20

23 [a]Gen. 43:3, 5

25 [a]Gen. 43:2

27 [a]Gen. 46:19

28 [a]Gen. 37:31-35

29 [a]Gen. 42:38; 44:31

30 [a]1 Sam. 18:1

44:17 Joseph puts them to one final test by offering to release all but Benjamin.

31 aGen.
44:29

31 it will come about when he sees that the lad is not *with us*, that he will die. Thus your servants will abring the gray hair of your servant our father down to Sheol in sorrow.

32 aGen.
43:9

32 "For your servant abecame surety for the lad to my father, saying, 'If I do not bring him *back* to you, then let me bear the blame before my father forever.'

★**33**

33 "Now, therefore, please let your servant remain instead of the lad a slave to my lord, and let the lad go up with his brothers.

34 "For how shall I go up to my father if the lad is not with me, lest I see the evil that would overtake my father?"

3 Joseph's revelation of his identity, 45:1-28

1 aActs
7:13

45 Then Joseph could not control himself before all those who stood by him, and he cried, "Have everyone go out from me." So there was no man with him awhen Joseph made himself known to his brothers.

2 aGen.
45:14, 15;
46:29

2 And ahe wept so loudly that the Egyptians heard *it*, and the household of Pharaoh heard of it.

★ **3** aActs
7:13 bGen.
43:27 cGen.
37:20-28;
42:21, 22

3 Then Joseph said to his brothers, "aI am Joseph! bIs my father still alive?" But his brothers could not answer him, for cthey were dismayed at his presence.

4 aGen.
37:28

4 Then Joseph said to his brothers, "Please come closer to me." And they came closer. And he said, "I am your brother Joseph, whom you asold into Egypt.

★ **5-8**

5 aGen.
37:28 bGen.
45:7, 8;
50:20; Ps.
105:17

5 "And now do not be grieved or angry with yourselves, because ayou sold me here; for bGod sent me before you to preserve life.

6 aGen.
37:2; 41:46,
53

6 "For the famine *has been* in the land athese two years, and there are still five years in which there will be neither plowing nor harvesting.

7 aGen.
45:5

7 "And aGod sent me before you to preserve for you a remnant in the earth, and to keep you alive by a great deliverance.

8 aJudg
17:10

8 "Now, therefore, it was not you who sent me here, but God; and He has made me a afather to Pharaoh and lord of all his household and ruler over all the land of Egypt.

9 aActs
7:14

9 "Hurry and go up to my father, and asay to him, 'Thus says your son Joseph, "God has made me lord of all Egypt; come down to me, do not delay.

★**10** aGen.
46:28, 34;
47:1

10 "And you shall live in the land of aGoshen, and you shall be near me, you and your children and your children's children and your flocks and your herds and all that you have.

11 aGen.
47:12

11 "There I will also aprovide for you, for there are still five years of famine *to come*, lest you and your household and all that you have be impoverished." '

12 "And behold, your eyes see, and the eyes of my brother Benjamin *see*, that it is my mouth which is speaking to you.

13 aActs
7:14

13 "Now you must tell my father of all my splendor in Egypt, and all that you have seen; and you must hurry and abring my father down here."

14 aGen.
45:2

14 Then he fell on his brother Benjamin's neck and awept; and Benjamin wept on his neck.

15 And he kissed all his brothers and wept on them, and afterward his brothers talked with him.

16 aActs
7:13

16 Now when athe news was heard in Pharaoh's house that Jo-

44:33 Judah's eloquent plea is climaxed by his offer to take Benjamin's punishment on himself—a beautiful illustration of what Judah's illustrious descendant, Jesus, actually did at Calvary.

45:3 *they were dismayed.* I.e., terrified, trembling. This uneasiness remained with the brothers for years (cf. 50:15).

45:5-8 Joseph gave clear testimony to God's providential overruling in his life. Note verse 8: *not you . . . but God.* Joseph was a *father to Pharaoh* in the sense of being his adviser.

45:10 The *land of Goshen* was the eastern section of the Nile delta. It was a fertile area, the main valley of it extending about 40 miles.

seph's brothers had come, it pleased Pharaoh and his servants.

17 Then Pharaoh said to Joseph, "Say to your brothers, 'Do this: load your beasts and go to the land of Canaan,

18 and take your father and your households and come to me, and ªI will give you the best of the land of Egypt and you shall eat the fat of the land.'

19 "Now you are ordered, 'Do this: take ªwagons from the land of Egypt for your little ones and for your wives, and bring your father and come.

20 'And do not concern yourselves with your goods, for the best of all the land of Egypt is yours.'"

21 Then the sons of Israel did so; and Joseph gave them ªwagons according to the command of Pharaoh, and gave them provisions for the journey.

22 To each of them he gave ªchanges of garments, but to Benjamin he gave three hundred *pieces of* silver and ᵇfive changes of garments.

23 And to his father he sent as follows: ten donkeys loaded with the best things of Egypt, and ten female donkeys loaded with grain and bread and sustenance for his father on the journey.

24 So he sent his brothers away, and as they departed, he said to them, "Do not quarrel on the journey."

25 Then they went up from Egypt, and came to the land of Canaan to their father Jacob.

26 And they told him, saying, "Joseph is still alive, and indeed he is ruler over all the land of Egypt." But he was stunned, for ªhe did not believe them.

27 When they told him all the words of Joseph that he had spoken to them, and when he saw the ªwagons that Joseph had sent to carry him, the spirit of their father Jacob revived.

28 Then Israel said, "It is enough; my son Joseph is still alive. I will go and see him before I die."

G Joseph's Family in Egypt,
46:1–47:31

46 So Israel set out with all that he had, and came to ªBeersheba, and offered sacrifices to the ᵇGod of his father Isaac.

2 And ªGod spoke to Israel in visions of the night and said, "ᵇJacob, Jacob." And he said, "Here I am."

3 And He said, "ªI am God, the God of your father; do not be afraid to go down to Egypt, for I will ᵇmake you a great nation there.

4 "ªI will go down with you to Egypt, and ᵇI will also surely bring you up again; and ᶜJoseph will close your eyes."

5 Then Jacob arose from Beersheba; and the sons of Israel carried their father Jacob and their little ones and their wives, in the ªwagons which Pharaoh had sent to carry him.

6 And they took their livestock and their property, which they had acquired in the land of Canaan, and ªcame to Egypt, Jacob and all his descendants with him:

7 his sons and his grandsons with him, his daughters and his granddaughters, and all his descendants he brought with him to Egypt.

8 Now these are the ªnames of the sons of Israel, Jacob and his sons, who went to Egypt: Reuben, Jacob's first-born.

9 And the sons of Reuben: Hanoch and Pallu and Hezron and Carmi.

10 And the ªsons of Simeon: Jemuel and Jamin and Ohad and Jachin and Zohar and Shaul the son of a Canaanite woman.

---

18 ªGen. 27:28

19 ªGen. 45:21, 27; 46:5, Num. 7:3-8

21 ªGen. 45:19

22 ª2 Kin. 5:5 ᵇGen. 43:34

26 ªGen. 37:31-35

27 ªGen. 45:19

1 ªGen. 21:31; 28:10 ᵇGen. 26:24; 28:13; 31:42

★ 2-4

2 ªGen. 15:1; Num. 12:6; Job 33:14, 15 ᵇGen. 22:11; 31:11

3 ªGen. 17:1; 28:13 ᵇGen. 12:2; Ex. 1:9; Deut. 26:5

4 ªGen. 28:15; 48:21 ᵇGen. 50:24; Ex. 3:8 ᶜGen. 50:1

5 ªGen. 45:21

6 ªDeut. 26:5; Josh. 24:4; Ps. 105:23; Is. 52:4; Acts 7:15

8 ªEx. 1:1-4, Num. 26:4, 5; 1 Chr. 2:1ff.

10 ªEx. 6:15

46:2-4 God assured Jacob that he was doing the right thing to go to Egypt. It was in Egypt that the Lord would prosper their growth from a tribal clan into a great nation (cf. Exod. 1:7). *Joseph will close your eyes.* I.e., in death.

11 And the sons of Levi: Gershon, Kohath, and Merari.

12 *a*1 Chr. 2:5

12 And the sons of Judah: Er and Onan and Shelah and Perez and Zerah (but Er and Onan died in the land of Canaan). And the *a*sons of Perez were Hezron and Hamul.

13 And the sons of Issachar: Tola and Puvvah and Iob and Shimron.

14 And the sons of Zebulun: Sered and Elon and Jahleel.

15 These are the sons of Leah, whom she bore to Jacob in Paddan-aram, with his daughter Dinah; all his sons and his daughters *numbered* thirty-three.

16 *a*Num. 26:15-18

16 The *a*sons of Gad: Ziphion and Haggi, Shuni and Ezbon, Eri and Arodi and Areli.

17 *a*1 Chr. 7:30 *b*1 Chr. 7:31

17 And the *a*sons of Asher: Imnah and Ishvah and Ishvi and Beriah and their sister Serah. And the *b*sons of Beriah: Heber and Malchiel.

18 These are the sons of Zilpah, whom Laban gave to his daughter Leah; and she bore to Jacob these sixteen persons.

19 The sons of Jacob's wife Rachel: Joseph and Benjamin.

20 *a*Gen. 41:50-52

20 *a*Now to Joseph in the land of Egypt were born Manasseh and Ephraim, whom Asenath, the daughter of Potiphera, priest of On, bore to him.

21 *a*1 Chr. 7:6

21 And the *a*sons of Benjamin: Bela and Becher and Ashbel, Gera and Naaman, Ehi and Rosh, Muppim and Huppim and Ard.

22 These are the sons of Rachel, who were born to Jacob; *there were* fourteen persons in all.

23 And the sons of Dan: Hushim.

24 And the sons of Naphtali: Jahzeel and Guni and Jezer and Shillem.

25 *a*Gen. 30:5, 7 *b*Gen. 29:29

25 These are the *a*sons of Bilhah, whom *b*Laban gave to his daughter Rachel, and she bore these to Jacob; *there were* seven persons in all.

26 *a*Ex. 1:5

26 *a*All the persons belonging to Jacob, who came to Egypt, his direct descendants, not including the wives of Jacob's sons, *were* sixty-six persons in all,

★27 *a*Ex. 1:5; Deut. 10:22; Acts 7:14

27 and the sons of Joseph, who were born to him in Egypt were two; *a*all the persons of the house of Jacob, who came to Egypt, *were* seventy.

28 *a*Gen. 45:10

28 Now he sent Judah before him to Joseph, to point out *the way* before him to *a*Goshen; and they came into the land of Goshen.

29 *a*Gen. 45:14, 15

29 And Joseph prepared his chariot and went up to Goshen to meet his father Israel; as soon as he appeared before him, he fell on his neck and *a*wept on his neck a long time.

30 Then Israel said to Joseph, "Now let me die, since I have seen your face, that you are still alive."

31 *a*Gen. 47:1

31 And Joseph said to his brothers and to his father's household, "*a*I will go up and tell Pharaoh, and will say to him, 'My brothers and my father's household, who *were* in the land of Canaan, have come to me;

32 and the men are shepherds, for they have been keepers of livestock; and they have brought their flocks and their herds and all that they have.'

33 *a*Gen. 47:2, 3

33 "And it shall come about when Pharaoh calls you and says, '*a*What is your occupation?'

★34 *a*Gen. 13:7, 8; 26:20, 37:2 18; 47:6, 11 *b*Gen. 45:10 *c*Gen. 43:32; Ex. 8:26

34 that you shall say, 'Your servants have been *a*keepers of livestock from our youth even until now, both we and our fathers,' that you may live in the land of *b*Goshen; for every shepherd is *c*loathsome to the Egyptians."

46:27 The total of 70 included the 66 mentioned in v. 26, plus Jacob, Joseph, and Joseph's two sons (see also Exod. 1:5; Deut. 10:22). See note on Acts 7:14. However, the total number, including wives of Jacob's sons and grandsons and husbands of his daughters and grand-daughters (not listed), would have been greater than 70.

46:34 Joseph counseled his family to de-emphasize their sheepherding (which the Egyptians despised) and stress their tending of cattle.

47 Then ^aJoseph went in and told Pharaoh, and said, "My father and my brothers and their flocks and their herds and all that they have, have come out of the land of Canaan; and behold, they are in the land of ^bGoshen."

2 And he took five men from among his brothers, and ^apresented them to Pharaoh.

3 Then Pharaoh said to his brothers, "^aWhat is your occupation?" So they said to Pharaoh, "Your servants are ^bshepherds, both we and our fathers."

4 And they said to Pharaoh, "^aWe have come to sojourn in the land, for there is no pasture for your servants' flocks, for ^bthe famine is severe in the land of Canaan. Now, therefore, please let your servants ^clive in the land of Goshen."

5 Then Pharaoh said to Joseph, "Your father and your brothers have come to you.

6 "The land of Egypt is at your disposal; settle your father and your brothers in ^athe best of the land, let them live in the land of Goshen; and if you know any ^bcapable men among them, then put them in charge of my livestock."

7 Then Joseph brought his father Jacob and presented him to Pharaoh; and Jacob ^ablessed Pharaoh.

8 And Pharaoh said to Jacob, "How many years have you lived?"

9 So Jacob said to Pharaoh, "The ^ayears of my sojourning are one hundred and thirty; few and unpleasant have been the years of my life, nor have they attained ^bthe years that my fathers lived

during the days of their sojourning."

10 And Jacob ^ablessed Pharaoh, and went out from his presence.

11 So Joseph settled his father and his brothers, and gave them a possession in the land of Egypt, in ^athe best of the land, in the land of ^bRameses, as Pharaoh had ordered.

12 And Joseph ^aprovided his father and his brothers and all his father's household with food, according to their little ones.

13 Now there was no food in all the land, because the famine was very severe, so that ^athe land of Egypt and the land of Canaan languished because of the famine.

14 And ^aJoseph gathered all the money that was found in the land of Egypt and in the land of Canaan for the grain which they bought, and Joseph brought the money into Pharaoh's house.

15 And when the money was all spent in the land of Egypt and in the land of Canaan, all the Egyptians came to Joseph and said, "Give us food, for ^awhy should we die in your presence? For *our* money is gone."

16 Then Joseph said, "Give up your livestock, and I will give you *food* for your livestock, since *your* money is gone."

17 So they brought their livestock to Joseph, and Joseph gave them food in exchange for the horses and the flocks and the herds and the donkeys; and he fed them with food in exchange for all their livestock that year.

18 And when that year was ended, they came to him the next year and said to him, "We will

Margin references (left column)

1 ^aGen. 46:31 ^bGen. 45:10; 46:28

2 ^aActs 7:13

3 ^aGen. 46:33 ^bGen. 46:34

★ 4 ^aGen. 15:13; Deut. 26:5; Ps. 105:23 ^bGen. 43:1; Acts 7:11 ^cGen. 46:34

6 ^aGen. 45:10, 18; 47:11 ^bEx. 18:21, 25; 1 Kin. 11:28; Prov. 22:29

7 ^aGen. 47:10; 2 Sam. 14:22; 1 Kin. 8:66

★ 9 ^aHeb. 11:9, 13 ^bGen. 25:7; 35:28

Margin references (right column)

10 ^aGen. 47:7

★11 ^aGen. 47:6, 27 ^bEx. 1:11; 12:37

12 ^aGen. 45:11

★13-26

13 ^aGen. 41:30; Acts 7:11

14 ^aGen. 41:56

15 ^aGen. 47:19

47:4 Their answer was straightforward and tempered with the assurance that they only desired to *sojourn*, not settle, in Goshen while the famine lasted.

47:9 Jacob, who was 130 when he appeared before Pharaoh and 147 when he died (v. 28), did not attain the longevity of Abraham (175) or of Isaac (180).

47:11 *the land of Rameses.* A later designation for Goshen used by Moses (or added by a later

scribe) in order to aid in locating the area involved (cf. Exod. 1:11).

47:13-26 As the famine became more severe and the people ran out of money, Joseph permitted grain to be exchanged for their animals and finally for their other property. Soon Pharaoh owned all the land except that of the priests (v. 22), though the people tilled it and kept four-fifths of its produce.

not hide from my lord that our money is all spent, and the cattle are my lord's. There is nothing left for my lord except our bodies and our lands.

19 "Why should we die before your eyes, both we and our land? Buy us and our land for food, and we and our land will be slaves to Pharaoh. So give us seed, that we may live and not die, and that the land may not be desolate."

20 So Joseph bought all the land of Egypt for Pharaoh, for every Egyptian sold his field, because the famine was severe upon them. Thus the land became Pharaoh's.

21 And as for the people, he removed them to the cities from one end of Egypt's border to the other.

22 Only the land of the priests he did not buy, for the priests had an allotment from Pharaoh, and they lived off the allotment which Pharaoh gave them. Therefore, they did not sell their land.

23 Then Joseph said to the people, "Behold, I have today bought you and your land for Pharaoh; now, *here* is seed for you, and you may sow the land.

24 "And at the harvest you shall give a ªfifth to Pharaoh, and four-fifths shall be your own for seed of the field and for your food and for those of your households and as food for your little ones."

25 So they said, "You have saved our lives! Let us find favor in the sight of my lord, and we will be Pharaoh's slaves."

26 And Joseph made it a statute concerning the land of Egypt *valid* to this day, that Pharaoh should have the fifth; ªonly the land of the priests did not become Pharaoh's.

27 Now Israel lived in the land of Egypt, in Goshen, and they ªacquired property in it and ᵇwere fruitful and became very numerous.

28 And Jacob lived in the land of Egypt ªseventeen years; so the length of Jacob's life was one hundred and forty-seven years.

29 When ªthe time for Israel to die drew near, he called his son Joseph and said to him, "Please, if I have found favor in your sight, ᵇplace now your hand under my thigh and ᶜdeal with me in kindness and faithfulness. Please do not bury me in Egypt,

30 but when I ªlie down with my fathers, you shall carry me out of Egypt and bury me in ᵇtheir burial place." And he said, "I will do as you have said."

31 And he said, "ªSwear to me." So he swore to him. Then ᵇIsrael bowed *in worship* at the head of the bed.

H   The Blessing of Joseph's Sons, 48:1-22

48 Now it came about after these things that Joseph was told, "Behold, your father is sick." So he took his two sons ªManasseh and Ephraim with him.

2 When it was told to Jacob, "Behold, your son Joseph has come to you," Israel collected his strength and sat up in the bed.

3 Then Jacob said to Joseph, "ªGod Almighty appeared to me at ᵇLuz in the land of Canaan and blessed me,

4 and He said to me, 'Behold, I will make you fruitful and numerous, and I will make you a company of peoples, and will give this land to your descendants after you for ªan everlasting possession.'

5 "And now your two sons, who were born to you in the land

Marginal references

24 ªGen. 41:34
26 ªGen. 47:22
27 ªGen. 47:11 ᵇGen. 17:6; 26:4; 35:11; Ex. 1:7; Deut. 26:5; Acts 7:17
28 ªGen. 47:9
★29 ªDeut. 31:14; 1 Kin. 2:1 ᵇGen. 24:2 ᶜGen. 24:49
30 ªGen. 15:15; Deut. 31:16 ᵇGen. 23:17-20; 25:9, 10; 35:29; 49:29-32; 50:5, 13; Acts 7:15, 16
31 ªGen. 21:23, 24; 24:3; 31:53; 50:25 ᵇ1 Kin. 1:47
1 ªGen. 41:51, 52; Josh. 14:4
3 ªGen. 28:13f.; 35:9-12 ᵇGen. 28:19; 35:6
4 ªGen. 17:8
★ 5 ªGen. 41:50-52; 48:1; 46:20; Josh. 14:4 ᵇ1 Chr. 5:1, 2

47:29 *under my thigh.* See note on 24:2.
48:5 Jacob, by adopting Joseph's two sons, *Ephraim and Manasseh,* as his own sons (*shall be mine*) and thus elevating them to a position equal with his other sons, insured that Joseph's descendants would receive a double inheritance. Apparently at this time Jacob transferred the rights of the firstborn from Reuben to Joseph, the firstborn of his beloved Rachel (cf. vv. 15-16; 1 Chron. 5:1).

of Egypt before I came to you in Egypt, are mine; ^aEphraim and Manasseh shall be mine, as ^bReuben and Simeon are.

6 "But your offspring that have been born after them shall be yours; they shall be called by the names of their brothers in their inheritance.

7 "Now as for me, when I came from ^aPaddan, ^bRachel died, to my sorrow, in the land of Canaan on the journey, when there was still some distance to go to Ephrath; and I buried her there on the way to Ephrath (that is, Bethlehem)."

8 When Israel ^asaw Joseph's sons, he said, "Who are these?"

9 And Joseph said to his father, "^aThey are my sons, whom God has given me here." So he said, "Bring them to me, please, that ^bI may bless them."

10 Now ^athe eyes of Israel were *so* dim from age *that* he could not see. Then Joseph brought them close to him, and he ^bkissed them and embraced them.

11 And Israel said to Joseph, "I never expected to see your face, and behold, God has let me see your children as well."

12 Then Joseph took them from his knees, and ^abowed with his face to the ground.

13 And Joseph took them both, Ephraim with his right hand toward Israel's left, and Manasseh with his left hand toward Israel's right, and brought them close to him.

14 But Israel stretched out his right hand and laid it on the head of Ephraim, who was the younger, and his left hand on Manasseh's head, crossing his hands, al-

though ^aManasseh was the first-born.

15 And he blessed Joseph, and said,

"^aThe God before whom my fathers Abraham and Isaac walked,
^bThe God who has been my shepherd all my life to this day,

16 ^aThe angel who has redeemed me from all evil,
^bBless the lads;
And may my name live on in them,
And the names of my fathers Abraham and Isaac;
And ^cmay they grow into a multitude in the midst of the earth."

17 When Joseph saw that his father ^alaid his right hand on Ephraim's head, it displeased him; and he grasped his father's hand to remove it from Ephraim's head to Manasseh's head.

18 And Joseph said to his father, "Not so, my father, for this one is the first-born. Place your right hand on his head."

19 But his father refused and said, "I know, my son, I know; he also shall become a people and he also shall be great. However, his younger brother shall be greater than he, and ^ahis descendants shall become a multitude of nations."

20 And ^ahe blessed them that day, saying,

"By you Israel shall pronounce blessing, saying,
'May God make you like Ephraim and Manasseh!' "

Cross references

7 ^aGen. 33:18 ^bGen. 35:19, 20
8 ^aGen. 48:10
9 ^aGen. 33:5 ^bGen. 27:4
10 ^aGen. 27:1 ^bGen. 27:27
12 ^aGen. 42:6
★14 ^aGen. 41:51, 52
★15-16
15 ^aGen. 17:1 ^bGen. 49:24
16 ^aGen. 22:11, 15-18; 28:13-15; 31:11 ^bHeb. 11:21 ^cGen. 28:14; 46:3
17 ^aGen. 48:14
19 ^aGen. 28:14; 46:3
20 ^aHeb. 11:21

48:14 Again God bypassed the older son (Manasseh) in favor of the younger (Ephraim), just as was done in the cases of choosing Isaac over Ishmael, Jacob over Esau, and Joseph over Reuben. After the division of the kingdom in the days of Jeroboam, the tribe of Ephraim (as predicted in v. 19) did become dominant in the north, and its name was equated with Israel (see Isa. 7:2; Hos. 4:17; 13:1).

48:15-16 Here is the first reference in the Bible to God as shepherd. *The angel.* See note on 16:10. *redeemed.* Heb., *goel,* first used here in the Bible, means "to save" or "to be a savior or deliverer." See also Exod. 6:6 and Isa. 59:20, which speak of God as redeeming His people, and Lev. 27:13 and Ruth 4:4, which speak of human beings as redeeming property or rights.

Thus he put Ephraim before Manasseh.

21 Then Israel said to Joseph, "Behold, I am about to die, but *a*God will be with you, and *b*bring you back to the land of your fathers.

21 aGen. 26:3 bGen. 28:15; 46:4; 50:24

22 "And I give you one portion more than your brothers, *a*which I took from the hand of the Amorite with my sword and my bow."

★22 aJosh. 24:32; John 4:5

I   Jacob's Blessing of his Sons,
49:1–27

★1 aNum. 24:14

49 Then Jacob summoned his sons and said, "Assemble yourselves that I may tell you what shall befall you *a*in the days to come.

2 "Gather together and hear, O sons of Jacob; And *a*listen to Israel your father.

2 aPs. 34:11

3 "Reuben, you are my first-born; My might and *a*the beginning of my strength, Preeminent in dignity and preeminent in power.

★3-4

3 aDeut. 21:17; Ps. 78:51; 105:36

4 "Uncontrolled as water, you shall not have preeminence, *a*Because you went up to your father's bed; Then you defiled *it*—he went up to my couch.

4 aGen. 35:22; Deut. 27:20; 1 Chr. 5:1

5 "*a*Simeon and Levi are brothers; Their swords are implements of violence.

★5-7

5 aGen. 34:25-30

6 "*a*Let my soul not enter into their council; Let not my glory be united with their assembly; Because in their anger they slew men, And in their self-will they lamed oxen.

6 aPs. 64:2

7 "Cursed be their anger, for it is fierce; And their wrath, for it is cruel. *a*I will disperse them in Jacob, And scatter them in Israel.

7 aJosh. 19:1, 9; 21:1-42

8 "Judah, your brothers shall praise you;

★8-12

8 aGen. 27:29; 1 Chr. 5:2

48:22 *one portion.* A particular tract of ground conquered by Jacob (perhaps the same one referred to in John 4:5).

49:1 *in the days to come* refers to Israel's future in dual perspective: the period of their occupation of Canaan, and the time of the coming of Messiah. Sometimes the expression refers to Israel at the end of the Tribulation period (Deut. 4:30; Ezek. 38:16), sometimes to the history of Gentile nations (Dan. 2:28), and sometimes to the present church age in its entirety (Heb. 1:2) or at its conclusion (2 Tim. 3:1; James 5:3). Jacob's pronouncements in Gen. 49 included both prophecy (v. 1) and blessing (v. 28).

49:3-4 Reuben, the firstborn, forfeited his place of preeminence because of his fornication with Bilhah (35:22). Jacob predicted instability and ineffectiveness. *Uncontrolled as water* means literally "a boiling over of water," a vivid illustration of instability. No prophet, judge, or hero came from this tribe (Judg. 5:15-16; 1 Chron. 5:1).

49:5-7 *Simeon and Levi* are condemned for their cruelty and hot-tempered anger in the slaying of the Shechemites (34:25). In 49:6, Jacob disassociates himself from their motives and actions. *they lamed oxen.* I.e., cut the leg tendons, a wanton act of destruction. *I will*

disperse . . . And scatter. Simeon was given an inheritance within the inheritance of Judah (Josh. 19:1; see also 1 Chron. 4:39–43). The Levites had no inheritance of their own, only cities scattered throughout the land (Josh. 21:1-3). The Levites redeemed themselves by opposing the idolatry connected with the golden calf (Exod. 32:26), and they became the priestly tribe.

49:8-12 *Judah* (meaning "praise") would become the leader among the tribes, strong as a young lion that has eaten his prey and secure as a mature lion whom no one would dare to rouse (v. 9). This prediction did not begin to be fulfilled until the time of King David, some 640 years after Jacob's prophecy. *Shiloh* probably means "the one who brings (or, 'until he comes into that which belongs to') peace," referring to Messiah who would be of the tribe of Judah (Rev. 5:5). At His second coming, Messiah will receive international acknowledgment. Verses 11-12 describe the millennial prosperity, with vines so plentiful no one will hesitate to tie an ass to them (even though asses are herbivorous animals), with wine abundant as water, and with healthy people (*dull from wine* may possibly mean "brighter and more sparkling than wine").

Your hand shall be on
the neck of your en-
emies;
ªYour father's sons shall
bow down to you.

9 **9** ªEzek.
19:5-7; Mic.
5:8 ᵇNum.
24:9

9 "Judah is a ªlion's whelp;
From the prey, my son,
you have gone up.
ᵇHe couches, he lies
down as a lion,
And as a lion, who dares
rouse him up?

10 ªNum.
24:17; Ps.
60:7; 108:8
ᵇPs. 2:6-9;
72:8-11; Is.
42:1, 4; 49:6

10 "ªThe scepter shall not
depart from Judah,
Nor the ruler's staff
from between his feet,
Until Shiloh comes,
And ᵇto him *shall be* the
obedience of the peo-
ples.

11 ªDeut.
8:7, 8; 2 Kin.
18:32 ᵇIs.
63:2

11 "ªHe ties *his* foal to the
vine,
And his donkey's colt to
the choice vine;
ᵇHe washes his gar-
ments in wine,
And his robes in the
blood of grapes.

12 "His eyes are dull from
wine,
And his teeth white
from milk.

★**13** ªDeut.
33:18, 19

13 "ªZebulun shall dwell at
the seashore;
And he *shall be* a haven
for ships,
And his flank *shall be*
toward Sidon.

★**14-15**

14 ªJudg.
5:16; Ps.
68:13

14 "Issachar is a strong donkey,
ªLying down between
the sheepfolds.

15 "When he saw that a
resting place was good
And that the land was
pleasant,
He bowed his shoulder
to bear *burdens*,
And became a slave at
forced labor.

16 "ªDan shall ᵇjudge his
people,
As one of the tribes of
Israel.

★**16-18**

16 ªDeut.
33:22; Judg.
18:26, 27
ᵇGen. 30:6

17 "Dan shall be a serpent in
the way,
A horned snake in the
path,
That bites the horse's
heels,
So that his rider falls
backward.

18 "ªFor Thy salvation I
wait, O LORD.

18 ªEx. 15:2;
Ps. 25:5;
40:1-3;
119:166,
174; Is. 25:9;
Mic. 7:7

19 "ªAs for Gad, raiders
shall raid him,
But he shall raid *at* their
heels.

★**19** ªDeut.
33:20

20 "ªAs for ᵇAsher, his food
shall be rich,
And he shall yield royal
dainties.

★**20** ªDeut.
33:24, 25
ᵇGen. 30:13

21 "ªNaphtali is a doe let
loose,
He gives beautiful
words.

★**21** ªDeut.
33:23

22 "ªJoseph is a fruitful
bough,
A fruitful bough by a
spring;
Its branches run over a
wall.

★**22-26**

22 ªDeut.
33:13-17

49:13 *at the seashore.* Lit., toward the sea; i.e.,
Zebulun would have contact with sea merchants (Josh. 19:10-16).

49:14-15 *Issachar* would be strong, but docile
and lazy; *between the sheepfolds* (or, bowing
down beneath a double burden) may mean
that he will be situated between sheepkeeping
peoples or that he will be very strong.

49:16-18 Samson, a Danite (cf. Judg. 13:2ff.),
judged Israel for 20 years. But the Danites also
introduced idolatry into Israel on an official
basis (Judg. 18:30-31). This may be the reason
Dan is omitted from the tribes in Rev. 7:4-8
(see note there).

49:19 *Gad*, when settled E. of the Jordan, would
be vulnerable to attack and therefore need
strong warriors (1 Chron. 5:18; 12:8).

49:20 *Asher* was given the rich seacoast area N.
of Mount Carmel (Josh. 19:24-31).

49:21 *Naphtali* is described as a *doe*, known for
its swiftness, and as eloquent of speech (Judg.
4:6, 15; 5:1-31).

49:22-26 The blessing of *Joseph* is the most eloquent of all. Verses 23-24 are a brief biography of Joseph. Joshua, Deborah, and Samuel
were from the tribe of Ephraim, and Gideon
and Jephthah, from the tribe of Manasseh.

23 "The archers bitterly attacked him,
And shot *at him* and harassed him;

24 But his ᵃbow remained firm,
And ᵇhis arms were agile,
From the hands of the ᶜMighty One of Jacob
(From there is ᵈthe Shepherd, ᵉthe Stone of Israel),

25 From ᵃthe God of your father who helps you,
And ᵇby the Almighty who blesses you
With ᶜblessings of heaven above,
Blessings of the deep that lies beneath,
Blessings of the breasts and of the womb.

26 "The blessings of your father
Have surpassed the blessings of my ancestors
Up to the utmost bound of ᵃthe everlasting hills;
May they be on the head of Joseph,
And on the crown of the head of the one distinguished among his brothers.

★**27** **27** "Benjamin is a ravenous wolf;
In the morning he devours the prey,
And in the evening he divides the spoil."

J   Jacob's Death and Burial,
49:28–50:14

28 All these are the twelve tribes of Israel, and this is what their father said to them when he blessed them. He blessed them, every one with the blessing appropriate to him.

29 Then he charged them and said to them, "I am about to be ᵃgathered to my people; ᵇbury me with my fathers in the cave that is in ᶜthe field of Ephron the Hittite,

30 in the ᵃcave that is in the field of Machpelah, which is before Mamre, in the land of Canaan, which Abraham bought along with the field from Ephron the Hittite for a burial site.

31 "There they buried ᵃAbraham and his wife ᵇSarah, there they buried ᶜIsaac and his wife Rebekah, and there I buried Leah—

32 the field and the cave that is in it, purchased from the sons of Heth."

33 When Jacob finished charging his sons, he drew his feet into the bed and ᵃbreathed his last, and was ᵇgathered to his people.

50 Then Joseph fell on his father's face, and wept over him and kissed him.

2 And Joseph commanded his servants the physicians to embalm his father. So the physicians ᵃembalmed Israel.

3 Now forty days were required for it, for such is the period required for embalming. And the Egyptians ᵃwept for him seventy days.

4 And when the days of mourning for him were past, Joseph spoke to the household of Pharaoh, saying, "If now I have found favor in your sight, please speak to Pharaoh, saying,

5 'ᵃMy father made me swear, saying, "Behold, I am about to die; in my grave ᵇwhich I dug for myself in the land of Ca-

---

Cross references

24 ᵃJob 29:20 ᵇPs. 18:34; 73:23; Is. 41:10 ᶜPs. 132:2, 5; Is. 1:24; 49:26 ᵈPs. 23:1; 80:1 ᵉPs. 118:22; Is. 28:16; 1 Pet. 2:6-8

25 ᵃGen. 28:13; 32:9 ᵇGen. 28:3; 48:3 ᶜGen. 27:28

26 ᵃDeut. 33:15, 16

★**29** ᵃGen. 25:8 ᵇGen. 47:30 ᶜGen. 23:16-20; 50:13

30 ᵃGen. 23:3-20

31 ᵃGen. 25:9 ᵇGen. 23:19 ᶜGen. 35:29

33 ᵃGen. 25:8; Acts 7:15 ᵇGen. 49:29

2 ᵃGen. 50:26; 2 Chr. 16:14; Matt. 26:12; Mark 16:1; John 19:39, 40

★ 3 ᵃGen. 50:10; Num. 20:29; Deut. 34:8

5 ᵃGen. 47:29-31 ᵇ2 Chr. 16:14; Is. 22:16; Matt. 27:60

49:27 It is predicted that *Benjamin* would be like a ravenous wolf, successful in war, but also cruel (cf. Judg. 20). King Saul and the apostle Paul were Benjamites (see 1 Sam. 9:1-2; Rom. 11:1).

49:29 The phrase *gathered to my people* reflects Jacob's belief that his people, though dead, still existed. *the cave.* See note on 23:9.

50:3 *forty days* were required for embalming, an elaborate process during which the body was mummified by removing most of the vital organs, dehydrating the body, and wrapping it tightly.

naan, there you shall bury me." Now therefore, please let me go up and bury my father; then I will return.' "

6 And Pharaoh said, "Go up and bury your father, as he made you swear."

7 So Joseph went up to bury his father, and with him went up all the servants of Pharaoh, the elders of his household and all the elders of the land of Egypt,

8 and all the household of Joseph and his brothers and his father's household; they left only their little ones and their flocks and their herds in the land of Goshen.

9 There also went up with him both chariots and horsemen; and it was a very great company.

★10-11

10 *a*Acts 8:2   **10** When they came to the threshing floor of Atad, which is beyond the Jordan, they *a*lamented there with a very great and sorrowful lamentation; and he observed seven days mourning for his father.

11 Now when the inhabitants of the land, the Canaanites, saw the mourning at the threshing floor of Atad, they said, "This is a grievous mourning for the Egyptians." Therefore it was named Abel-mizraim, which is beyond the Jordan.

12 And thus his sons did for him as he had charged them;

13 *a*Gen. 23:16-20; Acts 7:16   **13** for his sons carried him to the land of Canaan, and buried him in *a*the cave of the field of Machpelah before Mamre, which Abraham had bought along with the field for a burial site from Ephron the Hittite.

14 And after he had buried his father, Joseph returned to Egypt, he and his brothers, and all who had gone up with him to bury his father.

K The Last Days of Joseph, 50:15-26

15 When Joseph's brothers saw that their father was dead, they said, "*a*What if Joseph should bear a grudge against us and pay us back in full for all the wrong which we did to him!"

15 *a*Gen. 37:28; 42:21, 22

16 So they sent a message to Joseph, saying, "Your father charged before he died, saying,

17 'Thus you shall say to Joseph, "Please forgive, I beg you, the transgression of your brothers and their sin, for they did you wrong." ' And now, please forgive the transgression of the servants of the God of your father." And Joseph wept when they spoke to him.

18 Then his brothers also came and *a*fell down before him and said, "Behold, we are your servants."

18 *a*Gen. 37:8-10; 41:43

19 But Joseph said to them, "Do not be afraid, for am I in God's place?

20 "And as for you, *a*you meant evil against me, *but* God meant it for good in order to bring about this present result, to preserve many people alive.

★20 *a*Gen. 37:26, 27; 45:5, 7

21 "So therefore, do not be afraid; *a*I will provide for you and your little ones." So he comforted them and spoke kindly to them.

21 *a*Gen. 45:11; 47:12

22 Now Joseph stayed in Egypt, he and his father's household, and Joseph lived one hundred and ten years.

23 And Joseph saw the third generation of Ephraim's sons; also the sons of Machir, the son of Manasseh, were *a*born on Joseph's knees.

23 *a*Gen. 30:3

24 And Joseph said to his brothers, "*a*I am about to die, but God will surely take care of you, and bring you up from this land

24 *a*Gen. 48:21; Ex. 3:16, 17; Heb. 11:22 *b*Gen. 13:15, 17; 15:7, 8, 18 *c*Gen. 26:3 *d*Gen. 28:13; 35:12

50:10-11 At *the threshing floor of Atad,* E. of the Jordan and N. of the Dead Sea, a formal seven-day period of mourning was carried out. Since the Egyptians who accompanied the large funeral procession joined in the mourn-

ing, the place was called *Abel-mizraim,* which means "mourning of Egypt."

50:20 Another clear statement of the overruling providence of God (cf. 45:5-8).

to the land which He promised on oath to [b]Abraham, to [c]Isaac and to [d]Jacob."

25 Then Joseph made the sons of Israel swear, saying, "God will surely take care of you, and

[a]you shall carry my bones up from here."

26 So Joseph died at the age of one hundred and ten years; and he was [a]embalmed and placed in a coffin in Egypt.

★25 [a]Gen.
47:29, 30;
Ex. 13:19;
Josh. 24:32;
Heb. 11:22

★26 [a]Gen.
50:2

50:25 Joseph believed that eventually his descendants would move back to Canaan and he wanted them to take his body with them,

which they did (cf. Exod. 13:19 and Josh. 24:32).
50:26 The *coffin* was a mummy case.

INTRODUCTION TO
THE BOOK OF EXODUS

AUTHOR: Moses   DATE: 1450-1410 B.C.

Title *The Hebrew title of the book is taken from the first verse, "these are the names of." The English title comes from the title in the Septuagint (a Greek translation). The Exodus ("way out") is the principal theme of the book (cf. 19:1).*

Authorship *Since the time of Joshua, the book has been attributed to Moses (Josh. 8:31-35; cf. Exod. 20:25), a conclusion affirmed by Jesus Christ (cf. Mark 12:26). Evidences from the book itself lead to the conclusion that the author was a highly educated man, who had been a long-time resident of Egypt and was an eyewitness of the Exodus. He was acquainted with the crop sequence in Lower Egypt (Exod. 9:31-32); his descriptions accurately conform to known conditions (Exod. 2:3, 12); and he includes details suitable only to an eyewitness account (e.g., Exod. 15:27).*

Date of the Exodus *Two principal views exist concerning the date of the Exodus: c. 1445-1440 B.C. during the reign of Amenhotep II (1450-1425), or c. 1290 B.C., during the reign of Raamses II (1299-1232). Scriptural evidence for the earlier date includes the statement of 1 Kings 6:1 that the Exodus occurred 480 years before the fourth year of Solomon's reign, thus placing it c. 1445. Further, in Judg. 11:26, Jephthah (c. 1100 B.C.) declared that Israel had possessed the land of Palestine for 300 years, which would date the Exodus c. 1400 B.C.*
Objections to this earlier date include the following: (1) The Exodus could not have taken place until after 1300 because the city of Raamses was named after the pharaoh who was ruling at that time, and Raamses did not rule until 1299. However, if the Exodus was about 1290 and Moses was 80 at that time, and since the city was built before Moses' birth, the Exodus could not have been as late as 1290 since there is no room for the 80 years of Moses' life between 1299 and 1290. (2) It is said that the presence of strong opposition to the Israelites from the Edomites (Num. 20:20-21) was impossible before 1300 since the area of southern Transjordan was unoccupied from 1900-1300. Yet excavations in that area have uncovered objects and pottery dating as early as 1600. (3) It is claimed that Hazor did not fall to the Israelites until 1300 B.C. However, Scripture states that it fell twice: first in the days of Joshua (Josh. 11:10-11) and later in the time of Deborah and Barak (Judg. 4:2, 23-24). Further, there is evidence in one area of the excavated city of a destruction around 1400. (4) The destruction of Lachish (Josh. 10:32) and Debir (Josh. 10:38-39) is said to have occurred 1230-1200 B.C., indicating a late date for the Exodus. But the book of Joshua does not claim that these cities were completely destroyed by Joshua (as Jericho was). Further, since the Stele of Pharaoh Merneptah represents the Hebrews as settled in Canaan when Merneptah's armies attacked them about 1230, the Exodus had to be somewhat earlier than 1290.
Thus there is no compelling reason not to accept the earlier date, particularly in view of scriptural evidence.

Contents *The theme of the book is deliverance from Egypt, in fulfillment of the promise of Gen. 15:13-14. The book records the birth of the nation Israel, the giving of the Law, and the origin of ritual worship. The revelation of God is paramount throughout the book. He is the one who controls history (Exod. 1); He revealed Himself in a new name (3:14); He is the sovereign of the covenant relationship (19:5); He is the faithful redeemer (6:6; 15:13); He is a judge of His own people (4:14; 20:5; 32:27-28) and of His foes (chaps. 7-12); He is the transcendent one (33:20) who nevertheless lived among His people (29:45). Favorite passages include the birth and protection of Moses (chap. 2), the call of Moses (3:14; 5:1), the crossing of the Red Sea (chap. 14), the manna story (chap. 16), the Ten Commandments (chap. 20), the tabernacle (chaps. 25-27), and the golden calf (chap. 32).*

OUTLINE OF EXODUS

I. **Israel in Egypt: Subjection, 1:1-12:36**
  A. God Chooses Moses, 1:1-4:31
   1. The oppression of Israel, 1:1-22
   2. The preparation of Moses, 2:1-25
    a. Moses' first forty years, 2:1-10
    b. Moses' second forty years, 2:11-25

  3. The call of Moses, 3:1-4:31
    a. God's revelation of Himself, 3:1-22
    b. Moses' objections, 4:1-17
    c. Moses' response to God's call, 4:18-31
  B. God Sends Moses to Pharaoh, 5:1-7:13

THE BOOK OF EXODUS

I ISRAEL IN EGYPT: SUBJECTION,
1:1-12:36

A God Chooses Moses,
1:1-4:31

1 The oppression of Israel,
1:1-22

★ 1-7

1 aGen.
46:8-27

1 Now these are the ᵃnames of the sons of Israel who came to Egypt with Jacob; they came each one with his household:

2 Reuben, Simeon, Levi and Judah;

3 Issachar, Zebulun and Benjamin;

4 Dan and Naphtali, Gad and Asher.

5 aGen.
46:26, 27;
Deut. 10:22

5 And all the persons who came from the loins of Jacob were ᵃseventy in number, but Joseph was *already* in Egypt.

6 aGen.
50:26

6 And ᵃJoseph died, and all his brothers and all that generation.

★ 7 aGen.
12:2; 28:3;
35:11; 46:3;
47:27; 48:4;
Deut. 26:5;
Ps. 105:24;
Acts 7:17

7 But the sons of Israel ᵃwere fruitful and increased greatly, and multiplied, and became exceedingly mighty, so that the land was filled with them.

★ 8 aActs
7:18, 19

8 Now a new ᵃking arose over Egypt, who did not know Joseph.

9 aPs.
105:24, 25

9 And ᵃhe said to his people, "Behold, the people of the sons of Israel are more and mightier than we.

10 aActs
7:19

10 "Come, let us ᵃdeal wisely with them, lest they multiply and in the event of war, they also join themselves to those who hate us, and fight against us, and depart from the land."

★11 aGen.
15:13; Ex.
3:7; 5:6 bEx.
1:14; 2:11;
5:4-9; 6:6f.
c1 Kin. 9:19;
2 Chr. 8:4
dGen. 47:11

11 So they appointed ᵃtaskmasters over them to afflict them with ᵇhard labor. And they built for Pharaoh ᶜstorage cities, Pithom and ᵈRaamses.

12 aEx. 1:7

12 But the more they afflicted them, ᵃthe more they multiplied and the more they spread out, so that they were in dread of the sons of Israel.

13 aGen.
15:13; Deut.
4:20

13 And the Egyptians compelled the sons of Israel ᵃto labor rigorously;

14 aEx. 2:23;
6:9; Num.
20:15; Acts
7:19

14 and they made ᵃtheir lives bitter with hard labor in mortar and bricks and at *all kinds* of labor in the field, all their labors which they rigorously imposed on them.

★15

15 Then the king of Egypt spoke to the Hebrew midwives, one of whom was named Shiphrah, and the other was named Puah;

★16 aActs
7:19

16 and he said, "When you are helping the Hebrew women to give birth and see *them* upon the birthstool, ᵃif it is a son, then you shall put him to death; but if it is a daughter, then she shall live."

17 aEx. 1:21;
Prov. 16:6
bActs 4:18-
20; 5:29

17 But the midwives ᵃfeared God, and ᵇdid not do as the king of Egypt had commanded them, but let the boys live.

18 So the king of Egypt called for the midwives, and said to

1:1-7 These verses repeat information given in Genesis (35:22-26; 46:27) and serve to link the two books. On *seventy* (v. 5) see note on Gen. 46:27.

1:7 The census at Sinai (Num. 1) showed 603,000 males 20 years and older. If they represented about one-fourth of the total population, then the Israelites numbered some 2,000,000 people. An annual growth rate of 5% would · increase population from 100 to 2,000,000 in only 215 years (see Gen. 46:27; Exod. 12:41).

1:8 The *new king* was either Amenhotep I (c. 1546-1525) or Thutmoses I (c. 1525-1508).

1:11 The Israelites were organized into large labor gangs under Egyptian *taskmasters*. The Hebrew word for *afflict* is the same one used in the prophecy of this event in Gen. 15:13. The *storage cities* housed weapons and supplies to be used in case of attack.

1:15 These were doubtless the chief midwives, not the only ones.

1:16 The *birthstool* (lit., two stones) was a pair of bricks or stones on which the women crouched in childbirth. Female children were allowed to live because they could be married to Egyptians and assimilated into the culture.

them, "Why have you done this thing, and let the boys live?"

★19   **19**   And the midwives said to Pharaoh, "Because the Hebrew women are not as the Egyptian women; for they are vigorous, and they give birth before the midwife can get to them."

20 aProv.
11:18; Eccl.
8:12; Heb.
6:10 bEx.
1:12; Is. 3:10

20   So ªGod was good to the midwives, and ᵇthe people multiplied, and became very mighty.

★21 aEx.
1:17 b1 Sam.
2:35; 2 Sam.
7:11, 27;
1 Kin. 2:24;
11:38

21   And it came about because the midwives ªfeared God, that He ᵇestablished households for them.

22 aActs
7:19 bGen.
41:1

22   Then Pharaoh commanded all his people, saying, "ªEvery son who is born you are to cast into ᵇthe Nile, and every daughter you are to keep alive."

2   The preparation of Moses, 2:1–25

a   Moses' first forty years, 2:1–10

★ 1 aEx.
6:16, 18, 20

2 Now a man from ªthe house of Levi went and married a daughter of Levi.

2 aActs
7:20; Heb.
11:23

2   And the woman conceived and bore a son; and when she saw that he was ªbeautiful, she hid him for three months.

★ 3 aIs.
18:2 bIs.
19:6

3   But when she could hide him no longer, she got him a ªwicker basket and covered it over with tar and pitch. Then she put the child in it, and set it among the ᵇreeds by the bank of the Nile.

4 aEx.
15:20; Num.
26:59

4   And ªhis sister stood at a distance to find out what would happen to him.

5 aEx. 7:15;
8:20

5   Then the daughter of Pharaoh came down ªto bathe at the Nile, with her maidens walking alongside the Nile; and she saw

the basket among the reeds and sent her maid, and she brought it *to her.*

6   When she opened *it,* she saw the child, and behold, *the* boy was crying. And she had pity on him and said, "This is one of the Hebrews' children."

7   Then his sister said to Pharaoh's daughter, "Shall I go and call a nurse for you from the Hebrew women, that she may nurse the child for you?"

8   And Pharaoh's daughter said to her, "Go *ahead.*" So the girl went and called the child's mother.

9   Then Pharaoh's daughter said to her, "Take this child away and nurse him for me and I shall give *you* your wages." So the woman took the child and nursed him.

★10 aActs
7:21

10   And the child grew, and she brought him to Pharaoh's daughter, and ªhe became her son. And she named him Moses, and said, "Because I drew him out of the water."

b   Moses' second forty years, 2:11–25

★11 aActs
7:23; Heb.
11:24-26
bEx. 1:11;
5:4, 5; 6:6, 7
cActs 7:24

11   Now it came about in those days, ªwhen Moses had grown up, that he went out to his brethren and looked on their ᵇhard labors; and ᶜhe saw an Egyptian beating a Hebrew, one of his brethren.

★12 aActs
7:24, 25

12   So he looked this way and that, and when he saw there was no one *around,* he ªstruck down the Egyptian and hid him in the sand.

13 aActs
7:26-28

13   And he went out ªthe next day, and behold, two Hebrews were fighting with each other; and

---

1:19 This may be a true statement; but even if it was a lie, the midwives are not commended for lying, but for refusing to kill. The pharaoh had resorted to male infanticide.

1:21 *households.* I.e., families.

2:1 The *man* was Amram (cf. 6:20), a grandson of Levi. His wife was Jochebed.

2:3 *a wicker basket.* Better, a papyrus basket. The Hebrew word for "basket" is the same as that for "ark" in Gen. 6. *the reeds.* Probably

papyrus plants.

2:10 *he became her son.* I.e., a member of the royal household. This likely occurred after Moses was weaned, at 2 or 3 years of age. *Moses* means "one who draws out."

2:11 Moses was 40 at this time (cf. Acts 7:23).

2:12 By this act of avenging the death of a fellow Hebrew, Moses cast his lot with his own people. But the act also showed he was not yet prepared to become their leader.

he said to the offender, "Why are you striking your companion?"

14 But he said, "*a*Who made you a prince or a judge over us? Are you intending to kill me, as you killed the Egyptian?" Then Moses was afraid, and said, "Surely the matter has become known."

15 When Pharaoh heard of this matter, he tried to kill Moses. But *a*Moses fled from the presence of Pharaoh and settled in the land of Midian; and he sat down *b*by a well.

16 Now *a*the priest of Midian had seven daughters; and *b*they came to draw water, and filled the troughs to water their father's flock.

17 Then the shepherds came and drove them away, but *a*Moses stood up and helped them, and watered their flock.

18 When they came to *a*Reuel their father, he said, "Why have you come *back* so soon today?"

19 So they said, "An Egyptian delivered us from the hand of the shepherds; and what is more, he even drew the water for us and watered the flock."

20 And he said to his daughters, "Where is he then? Why is it that you have left the man behind? Invite him to have something to eat."

21 *a*And Moses was willing to dwell with the man, and he gave his daughter *b*Zipporah to Moses.

22 Then she gave birth to *a*a son, and he named him Gershom, for he said, "I have been *b*a sojourner in a foreign land."

23 Now it came about in *the course of* those many days that the king of Egypt died. And the sons of Israel *a*sighed because of the bondage, and they cried out; and *b*their cry for help because of *their* bondage rose up to God.

24 So *a*God heard their groaning; and God remembered *b*His covenant with Abraham, Isaac, and Jacob.

25 And *a*God saw the sons of Israel, and God took notice *of them.*

3   The call of Moses, 3:1–4:31

a   God's revelation of Himself,
                                3:1–22

3 Now Moses was pasturing the flock of *a*Jethro his father-in-law, the priest of Midian; and he led the flock to the west side of the wilderness, and came to *b*Horeb, the *c*mountain of God.

2 And *a*the angel of the LORD appeared to him in a blazing fire from the midst of a *b*bush; and he looked, and behold, the bush was burning with fire, yet the bush was not consumed.

3 So Moses said, "*a*I must turn aside now, and see this marvelous sight, why the bush is not burned up."

4 When the LORD saw that he turned aside to look, *a*God called to him from the midst of the bush, and said, "Moses, Moses!" And he said, "Here I am."

5 Then He said, "Do not come near here; *a*remove your sandals from your feet, for the place on which you are standing is holy ground."

Margin references

14 *a*Gen. 19:9; Acts 7:27, 28

★15 *a*Acts 7:29; Heb. 11:27 *b*Gen. 24:11; 29:2

16 *a*Ex. 3:1; 18:12 *b*Gen. 24:11, 13, 19; 29:9, 10; 1 Sam. 9:11

17 *a*Gen. 29:3, 10

★18 *a*Ex. 3:1; Num. 10:29

★21 *a*Acts 7:29 *b*Ex. 4:25; 18:2
★22 *a*Ex. 4:20; 18:3, 4; *b*Gen. 23:4; Lev. 25:23; Acts 7:29; Heb. 11:13, 14
★23 *a*Ex. 6:5, 9 *b*Ex. 3:7, 9; Deut. 26:7; James 5:4

24 *a*Ex. 6:5; Acts 7:34 *b*Gen. 15:13f.; 22:16-18; 26:2-5; 28:13-15; Ps. 105:8, 42

25 *a*Ex. 3:7; 4:31; Acts 7:34

★ 1 *a*Ex. 2:18; 4:18; 18:12; Num. 10:29 *b*Ex. 3:12; 17:6; 33:6; 1 Kin. 19:8 *c*Ex. 4:27; 18:5; 24:13

★ 2 *a*Gen. 16:7-11; 21:17; 22:11, 15; Ex. 3:4-11, 16; Judg. 13:13-21; Acts 7:30 *b*Deut. 33:16; Mark 12:26; Luke 20:37; Acts 7:30
3 *a*Acts 7:31

4 *a*Ex. 4:5

★ 5 *a*Josh. 5:15; Acts 7:33

2:15 *the land of Midian.* An area E. of the Gulf of Aqaba or on the Sinai Peninsula, inhabited by the nomadic sons of Abraham by Keturah (cf. Gen. 25:2).
2:18 *Reuel.* Also called Jethro, see 3:1; 18:1. He may have been a priest of the true God at this time; later it becomes clear that he knew the true God (cf. 18:10-11).
2:21 *Zipporah* means "warbler."
2:22 *Gershom* means "a stranger here." A second son, Eliezer, is mentioned in 18:4.
2:23 The *king* would be Thutmose III (1482–1450), the predecessor to the pharaoh of the Exodus, Amenhotep II.
3:1 *Horeb* was another name for Mt. Sinai (cf. Deut. 5:2), traditionally located in the SW. part of the Sinai Peninsula.
3:2 *the angel of the LORD* was the Lord Himself (cf. v. 4; see note on Gen. 16:10). *the bush was burning with fire.* Moses saw a bush actually burning, but not consumed. Other explanations (like a bush with brilliant berries or leaves) do not do justice to the text.
3:5 *remove your sandals.* A sign of respect toward a superior. Slaves characteristically went barefooted (cf. Luke 15:22).

6 aGen.
28:13; Ex.
3:16; 4:5;
Matt. 22:32;
Mark 12:26;
Luke 20:37
bActs 7:32
cJudg.
13:22; Rev.
1:17

7 aEx. 2:25;
Neh. 9:9; Ps.
106:44; Is.
63:9; Acts
7:34

★ **8** aGen.
15:13-16;
46:4; 50:24,
25; Ex. 6:6-8;
12:51 bEx.
3:17; 13:5;
Num. 13:27;
Deut. 1:25;
8:7-9; Jer.
11:5; Ezek.
20:6 cGen.
15:19-21;
Josh. 24:11

9 aEx. 2:23

10 aGen.
15:13, 14;
Ex. 12:40,
41; Mic. 6:4;
Acts 7:6, 7

★**11** aEx.
4:10; 6:12;
1 Sam. 18:18

12 aGen.
31:3; Ex.
4:12, 15;
33:14-16;
Deut. 31:23;
Josh. 1:5; Is.
43:2 bEx.
19:1 cEx.
19:2, 3; Acts
7:7

6 He said also, "aI am the God of your father, the God of Abraham, the God of Isaac, and the God of Jacob." bThen Moses hid his face, for he was cafraid to look at God.

7 And the LORD said, "I have surely aseen the affliction of My people who are in Egypt, and have given heed to their cry because of their taskmasters, for I am aware of their sufferings.

8 "So I have come down ato deliver them from the power of the Egyptians, and to bring them up from that land to a bgood and spacious land, to a land flowing with milk and honey, to the place of cthe Canaanite and the Hittite and the Amorite and the Perizzite and the Hivite and the Jebusite.

9 "And now, behold, athe cry of the sons of Israel has come to Me; furthermore, I have seen the oppression with which the Egyptians are oppressing them.

10 "Therefore, come now, and I will send you to Pharaoh, aso that you may bring My people, the sons of Israel, out of Egypt."

11 But Moses said to God, "aWho am I, that I should go to Pharaoh, and that I should bring the sons of Israel out of Egypt?"

12 And He said, "Certainly aI will be with you, and this shall be the sign to you that it is I who have sent you: bwhen you have brought the people out of Egypt, cyou shall worship God at this mountain."

13 Then Moses said to God, "Behold, I am going to the sons of Israel, and I shall say to them, 'The God of your fathers has sent me to you.' Now they may say to me, 'What is His name?' What shall I say to them?"

14 And God said to Moses, "aI AM WHO I AM"; and He said, "Thus you shall say to the sons of Israel, 'I AM has sent me to you.' "

15 And God, furthermore, said to Moses, "Thus you shall say to the sons of Israel, 'aThe LORD, the God of your fathers, the God of Abraham, the God of Isaac, and the God of Jacob, has sent me to you.' This is My name forever, and this is My bmemorial-name to all generations.

16 "Go and agather the elders of Israel together, and say to them, 'bThe LORD, the God of your fathers, the God of Abraham, Isaac and Jacob, has appeared to me, saying, "cI am indeed concerned about you and what has been done to you in Egypt.

17 "So aI said, I will bring you up out of the affliction of Egypt to the land of bthe Canaanite and the Hittite and the Amorite and the Perizzite and the Hivite and the Jebusite, to a land cflowing with milk and honey." '

18 "And athey will pay heed to what you say; and byou with the elders of Israel will come to the king of Egypt, and you will say to him, 'The LORD, the God of the Hebrews, has met with us. So now, please, let us go a cthree days' journey into the wilderness, that we may sacrifice to the LORD our God.'

19 "But I know that the king of Egypt awill not permit you to go, bexcept under compulsion.

★**14** aEx.
6:3; John
8:24, 28, 58;
Heb. 13:8;
Rev. 1:8; 4:8

★**15** aEx.
3:6, 13 bPs.
30:4; 97:12;
102:12;
135:13; Hos.
12:5

16 aEx. 4:29
bGen. 28:13;
48:15; Ex.
3:2, 6; 4:5
cEx. 4:31;
Ps. 33:18f.

17 aGen.
15:13-21;
46:4; 50:24,
25 bJosh.
24:11 cEx.
3:8

★**18** aEx.
4:31 bEx.
5:1 cEx. 5:3;
8:27

19 aEx. 5:2
bEx. 6:1

3:8 This deliverance was first promised to Abraham (Gen. 13:15). The *milk* came mostly from sheep and goats.

3:11 Five times Moses tried to excuse himself from God's call (see also v. 13; 4:1, 10, 13). God assured Moses that He would be present during the deliverance and that the nation would one day worship God at that very mountain (v. 12).

3:14 *I AM WHO I AM.* The inner meaning of *Yahweh*—"I am the One who is"—emphasizes God's dynamic and active self-existence.

See also note on Gen. 2:4.

3:15 *The* LORD (Heb., *Yahweh*) was not pronounced in later years by pious Jews for fear of violating the command in Exod. 20:7. Instead, they substituted the word *Adonai* (Lord) whenever *Yahweh* occurred. The use of large and small capital letters (LORD) in the Bible text indicates the Hebrew word is Yahweh (or Jehovah).

3:18 *three days' journey.* A considerable distance was necessary in order to avoid Egyptian interference.

20 *Ex. 6:1;
7:4, 5; 9:15;
13:3, 9, 14
*Ex. 7:3;
15:11; Deut.
6:22; Neh.
9:10; Ps.
105:27;
135:9; Jer.
32:20; Acts
7:36 *Ex.
11:1; 12:31-
33
21 *Ex. 11:3;
12:36; 1 Kin.
8:50; Ps.
105:37f.;
106:46; Prov.
16:7
★22 *Gen.
15:14; Ex.
11:2; 12:35
*Ezek. 39:10

20 "So I will stretch out *My hand, and strike Egypt with all My *miracles which I shall do in the midst of it; and *after that he will let you go.

21 "And I will grant this people *favor in the sight of the Egyptians; and it shall be that when you go, you will not go empty-handed.

22 "But every woman *shall ask of her neighbor and the woman who lives in her house, articles of silver and articles of gold, and clothing; and you will put them on your sons and daughters. Thus you will *plunder the Egyptians."

b Moses' objections, 4:1-17

1 *Ex. 3:18;
6:30 *Ex.
3:15, 16

4 Then Moses answered and said, "What if they will not believe me, or *listen to what I say? For they may say, '*The LORD has not appeared to you.'"

★ 2 *Ex.
4:17, 20

2 And the LORD said to him, "What is that in your hand?" And he said, "*A staff."

3 *Ex.
7:10-12

3 Then He said, "Throw it on the ground." So he threw it on the ground, and *it became a serpent; and Moses fled from it.

4 But the LORD said to Moses, "Stretch out your hand and grasp *it by its tail"—so he stretched out his hand and caught it, and it became a staff in his hand—

5 *Ex. 4:31;
19:9 *Gen.
28:13; 48:15;
Ex. 3:6, 15

5 "that *they may believe that *the LORD, the God of their fathers, the God of Abraham, the God of Isaac, and the God of Jacob, has appeared to you."

6 *Num.
12:10; 2 Kin.
5:27

6 And the LORD furthermore said to him, "Now put your hand into your bosom." So he put his hand into his bosom, and when he took it out, behold, his hand was *leprous like snow.

7 Then He said, "Put your hand into your bosom again." So he put his hand into his bosom again; and when he took it out of his bosom, behold, *it was restored like *the rest of* his flesh.

8 "And it shall come about that if they will not believe you or heed the witness of the first sign, they may believe the witness of the last sign.

9 "But it shall be that if they will not believe even these two signs or heed what you say, then you shall take some water from the Nile and pour it on the dry ground; and the water which you take from the Nile *will become blood on the dry ground."

10 Then Moses said to the LORD, "Please, Lord, *I have never been eloquent, neither recently nor in time past, nor since Thou hast spoken to Thy servant; for I am slow of speech and slow of tongue."

11 And the LORD said to him, "Who has made man's mouth? Or *who makes *him* dumb or deaf, or seeing or blind? Is it not I, the LORD?

12 "Now then go, and *I, even I, will be with your mouth, and *teach you what you are to say."

13 But he said, "Please, Lord, now send *the message* by whomever Thou wilt."

14 Then the anger of the LORD burned against Moses, and He said, "Is there not your brother Aaron the Levite? I know that he speaks fluently. And moreover, behold, *he is coming out to meet you; when he sees you, he will be glad in his heart.

15 "And you are to speak to him and *put the words in his mouth; and I, even I, will be with your mouth and his mouth, and I will teach you what you are to do.

7 *Num.
12:13-15;
Deut. 32:39;
2 Kin. 5:14;
Matt. 8:3;
Luke 17:12-
14

9 *Ex. 7:19,
20

★10 *Ex.
3:11; 4:1;
6:12; Jer. 1:6

11 *Ps. 94:9;
146:8; Matt.
11:5; Luke
1:20, 64

12 *Ex. 4:15,
16; Deut.
18:18; Is.
50:4; Jer. 1:9
*Matt. 10:19,
20; Mark
13:11; Luke
12:11, 12;
21:14, 15

★13

★14 *Ex.
4:27

15 *Ex. 4:12,
30; 7:11.;
Num. 23:5,
12, 16; Deut.
18:18; Is.
51:16; 59:21;
Jer. 1:9

3:22 *ask of her neighbor.* To make partial compensation for their years of slavery and to fulfill the prophecy of Gen. 15:14.

4:2 *A staff.* A shepherd's crook.

4:10 Moses pleaded his lack of eloquence (*slow* means heavy; i.e., not of quick retort), a trait necessary in approaching Pharaoh, but hardly

a legitimate excuse, since Moses had been trained in Pharaoh's court for 40 years! Cf. Acts 7:22-23.

4:13 The phrase means "send some other person."

4:14 Because Moses now demonstrated a lack of obedience, God became angry.

★16 aEx.
7:1, 2
16 "Moreover, ^ahe shall speak for you to the people; and it shall come about that he shall be as a mouth for you, and you shall be as God to him.

17 aEx. 4:2,
20; 17:9
bEx. 7:9-20;
14:16.
17 "And you shall take in your hand ^athis staff, ^bwith which you shall perform the signs."

*c Moses' response to God's call,
4:18-31*

18 aEx. 2:21;
3:1
18 Then Moses departed and returned to Jethro ^ahis father-in-law, and said to him, "Please, let me go, that I may return to my brethren who are in Egypt, and see if they are still alive." And Jethro said to Moses, "Go in peace."

★19 aEx.
2:15, 23
19 Now the LORD said to Moses in Midian, "Go back to Egypt, for ^aall the men who were seeking your life are dead."

20 aEx. 18:3,
4; Acts 7:29
bEx. 4:17;
17:9; Num.
20:8, 9, 11
★21 aEx.
3:20; 11:9,
10 bEx. 7:3,
13; 9:12, 35;
10:1, 20, 27;
14:4, 8; Deut.
2:30; Josh.
11:20;
1 Sam. 6:6;
Is. 63:17;
John 12:40;
Rom. 9:18
20 So Moses took his wife and his ^asons and mounted them on a donkey, and he returned to the land of Egypt. Moses also took the ^bstaff of God in his hand.
21 And the LORD said to Moses, "When you go back to Egypt see that you perform before Pharaoh all ^athe wonders which I have put in your power; but ^bI will harden his heart so that he will not let the people go.

★22 aIs.
63:16; 64:8;
Jer. 31:9;
Hos. 11:1;
Rom. 9:4
23 aEx. 5:1;
6:11; 7:16
bEx. 11:5;
12:29; Ps.
105:36;
135:8;
136:10
★24-26
24 aNum.
22:22
22 "Then you shall say to Pharaoh, 'Thus says the LORD, "^aIsrael is My son, My first-born.
23 "So I said to you, 'Let My son go, that he may serve Me'; but you have refused to let him go. Behold, ^bI will kill your son, your first-born." ' "
24 Now it came about at the lodging place on the way that the LORD met him and ^asought to put him to death.

25 aGen.
17:14; Josh.
5:2, 3
25 Then Zipporah took ^aa flint and cut off her son's foreskin and threw *it* at Moses' feet, and she said, "You are indeed a bridegroom of blood to me."
26 So He let him alone. At that time she said, "*You are a bridegroom of blood*"—because of the circumcision.

27 aEx. 4:14
bEx. 3:1;
18:5; 24:13
27 ^aNow the LORD said to Aaron, "Go to meet Moses in the wilderness." So he went and met him at the ^bmountain of God, and he kissed him.

28 aEx.
4:15f. bEx.
4:8f.
28 And ^aMoses told Aaron all the words of the LORD with which He had sent him, and ^ball the signs that He had commanded him *to do.*

29 aEx. 3:16
29 Then Moses and Aaron went and ^aassembled all the elders of the sons of Israel;

30 aEx. 4:15,
16 bEx.
4:1-9
30 and ^aAaron spoke all the words which the LORD had spoken to Moses. He then performed the ^bsigns in the sight of the people.

31 aEx. 3:18,
4:8f.; 19:9
bGen. 50:24;
Ex. 3:16
cGen. 24:26;
Ex. 12:27;
1 Chr. 29:20
31 So ^athe people believed; and when they heard that the LORD ^bwas concerned about the sons of Israel and that He had seen their affliction, then ^cthey bowed low and worshiped.

B God Sends Moses to Pharaoh, 5:1-7:13

*1 First encounter with Pharaoh,
5:1-7:7*

1 aEx. 3:18
bEx. 4:23;
6:11; 7:16
5 And afterward Moses and Aaron came and said to Pharaoh, "^aThus says the LORD, God of Israel, '^bLet My people go

---

4:16 See 7:1-2.
4:19 See 2:15.
4:21 Ten times it is said that Pharaoh hardened his own heart (7:13, 14, 22; 8:15, 19, 32; 9:7, 34, 35; 13:15), and ten times that God hardened Pharaoh's heart (4:21; 7:3; 9:12; 10:1, 20, 27; 11:10; 14:4, 8, 17). Paul uses this as an example of the inscrutable will of God and of His mercy toward men (Rom. 9:14-18). Seven times Pharaoh hardened his own heart before God first hardened it, though the prediction that God would do it preceded all.
4:22 *My first-born.* I.e., special, even sacred.

4:24-26 Moses had apparently put off circumcising his son, in violation of God's express command (see Gen. 17:10) and perhaps at the insistence of Zipporah. He had to learn that disobeying God and incurring His wrath were more serious than anything that could befall him from the wrath of Pharaoh. The Lord *sought to put him to death,* and Zipporah performed the circumcision to save Moses' life. Then *He let him alone;* i.e., God healed him. It was probably at this time that Moses sent his family back to Jethro (cf. 18:2-3).

that they may celebrate a feast to Me in the wilderness.'"

★ 2 *a*2 Kin.
18:35; 2 Chr.
32:14; Job
21:15 *b*Ex.
3:19

2 But Pharaoh said, "*a*Who is the LORD that I should obey His voice to let Israel go? I do not know the LORD, and besides, *b*I will not let Israel go."

3 *a*Ex. 3:18

3 Then they said, "*a*The God of the Hebrews has met with us. Please, let us go a three days' journey into the wilderness that we may sacrifice to the LORD our God, lest He fall upon us with pestilence or with the sword."

4 *a*Ex. 1:11;
2:11; 6:5-7

4 But the king of Egypt said to them, "Moses and Aaron, why do you draw the people away from their work? Get *back* to your *a*labors!"

5 *a*Ex.
1:7, 9

5 Again Pharaoh said, "Look, *a*the people of the land are now many, and you would have them cease from their labors!"

★ 6 *a*Ex.
1:11; 3:7;
5:10, 13, 14
*b*Ex. 5:10,
14, 15, 19

6 So the same day Pharaoh commanded *a*the taskmasters over the people and their *b*foremen, saying,

★ 7-9

7 "You are no longer to give the people straw to make brick as previously; let them go and gather straw for themselves.

8 *a*Ex. 5:17

8 "But the quota of bricks which they were making previously, you shall impose on them; you are not to reduce any of it. Because they are *a*lazy, therefore they cry out, 'Let us go and sacrifice to our God.'

9 "Let the labor be heavier on the men, and let them work at it that they may pay no attention to false words."

10 *a*Ex. 1:11;
3:7; 5:6

10 So *a*the taskmasters of the people and their foremen went out and spoke to the people, saying, "Thus says Pharaoh, 'I am not going to give you *any* straw.

11 'You go *and* get straw for yourselves wherever you can find

it; but none of your labor will be reduced.'"

12 So the people scattered through all the land of Egypt to gather stubble for straw.

13 And the taskmasters pressed them, saying, "Complete your work quota, *your* daily amount, just as when you had straw."

★14 *a*Ex. 5:6
*b*Is. 10:24

14 Moreover, *a*the foremen of the sons of Israel, whom Pharaoh's taskmasters had set over them, *b*were beaten and were asked, "Why have you not completed your required amount either yesterday or today in making brick as previously?"

15 Then the foremen of the sons of Israel came and cried out to Pharaoh, saying, "Why do you deal this way with your servants?

16 "There is no straw given to your servants, yet they keep saying to us, 'Make bricks!' And behold, your servants are being beaten; but it is the fault of your *own* people."

17 *a*Ex. 5:8

17 But he said, "You are *a*lazy, *very* lazy; therefore you say, 'Let us go *and* sacrifice to the LORD.'

18 "So go now *and* work; for you shall be given no straw, yet you must deliver the quota of bricks."

19 And the foremen of the sons of Israel saw that they were in trouble because they were told, "You must not reduce *your* daily amount of bricks."

20 When they left Pharaoh's presence, they met Moses and Aaron as they were waiting for them.

21 *a*Ex.
14:11; 15:24;
16:2 *b*Gen.
16:5; 31:53
*c*Gen. 34:30;
1 Sam. 13:4;
27:12;
2 Sam. 10:6;
1 Chr. 19:6

21 And *a*they said to them, "*b*May the LORD look upon you and judge *you,* for you have *c*made us odious in Pharaoh's

---

5:2 In Egypt the king was generally considered a god, and he refused to acknowledge Yahweh.
5:6 *their foremen.* Lit., scribes; perhaps timekeepers. They were evidently Hebrews, not Egyptians like the *taskmasters,* because of the beating they received (see vv. 14-15).
5:7-9 Pharaoh greatly increased the work involved in making bricks by requiring the He-

brews to gather the *straw* themselves, from fields that were undoubtedly some distance from where the *bricks* were made. Mixing straw with the clay greatly increased the strength of the bricks.
5:14 By beating the Hebrew officers, Pharaoh succeeded in setting them against Moses and Aaron (cf. v. 21).

sight and in the sight of his servants, to put a sword in their hand to kill us."

22 Then Moses returned to the Lord and said, "[a]O Lord, why hast Thou brought harm to this people? Why didst Thou ever send me?

23 "Ever since I came to Pharaoh to speak in Thy name, he has done harm to this people; [a]and Thou hast not delivered Thy people at all."

6 Then the Lord said to Moses, "Now you shall see what I will do to Pharaoh; for [a]under compulsion he shall let them go, and under compulsion he shall drive them out of his land."

2 God spoke further to Moses and said to him, "I am [a]the Lord;

3 and I appeared to Abraham, Isaac, and Jacob, as [a]God Almighty, but by [b]My name, Lord, I did not make Myself known to them.

4 "And I also established [a]My covenant with them, to give them the land of Canaan, the land in which they sojourned.

5 "And furthermore I have [a]heard the groaning of the sons of Israel, because the Egyptians are holding them in bondage; and I have remembered My covenant.

6 "Say, therefore, to the sons of Israel, '[a]I am the Lord, and [b]I will bring you out from under the burdens of the Egyptians, and I will deliver you from their bondage. I will also [c]redeem you with [d]an outstretched arm and with great judgments.

7 'Then I will take you [a]for My people, and [b]I will be your God; and [c]you shall know that I am the Lord your God, who brought you out from under the burdens of the Egyptians.

8 'And I will bring you to the land which [a]I swore to give to Abraham, Isaac, and Jacob, and [b]I will give it to you for a possession; [c]I am the Lord.'"

9 So Moses spoke thus to the sons of Israel, but they did not listen to Moses on [a]account of their despondency and cruel bondage.

10 Now the Lord spoke to Moses, saying,

11 "[a]Go, tell Pharaoh king of Egypt to let the sons of Israel go out of his land."

12 But Moses spoke before the Lord, saying, "Behold, the sons of Israel have not listened to me; [a]how then will Pharaoh listen to me, for I am [b]unskilled in speech?"

13 Then the Lord spoke to Moses and to Aaron, and gave them a charge to the sons of Israel and to Pharaoh king of Egypt, to bring the sons of Israel out of the land of Egypt.

14 These are the heads of their fathers' households. [a]The sons of Reuben, Israel's first-born: Hanoch and Pallu, Hezron and Carmi; these are the families of Reuben.

15 And the [a]sons of Simeon: Jemuel and Jamin and Ohad and Jachin and Zohar and Shaul the son of a Canaanite woman; these are the families of Simeon.

16 And these are the names of [a]the sons of Levi according to their generations: Gershon and Kohath and Merari; and the length of Levi's life was one hundred and thirty-seven years.

17 [a]The sons of Gershon: Libni and Shimei, according to their families.

Margin cross-references (left column):

22 [a]Num. 11:11; Jer. 4:10

23 [a]Ex. 3:8

1 [a]Ex. 3:19, 20; 7:4, 5; 11:1; 12:31, 33, 39; 13:3

2 [a]Ex. 3:14, 15

★ 3 [a]Gen. 17:1; 35:11; 48:3 [b]Ps. 68:4; 83:18; Is. 52:6; Jer. 16:21; Ezek. 37:6, 13

★ 4 [a]Gen. 12:7; 15:18; 17:4, 7; 26:3, 4; 28:4, 13

5 [a]Ex. 2:24

★ 6 [a]Ex. 13:3, 14; 20:2; Deut. 6:12 [b]Ex. 3:17; 7:4; 12:51; 16:6; 18:1; Deut. 26:8; Ps. 136:11 [c]Ex. 15:13; Deut. 7:8; 1 Chr. 17:21; Neh. 1:10 [d]Deut. 4:34; 5:15; 26:8; Ps. 136:11f.

7 [a]Ex. 19:5; Deut. 4:20; 7:6; 2 Sam. 7:24 [b]Gen. 17:7f.; Ex. 29:45f.; Lev. 11:45; 26:12; 13, 45; Deut. 29:13 [c]Ex. 16:12; Is. 41:20; 49:23; 26; 60:16

Margin cross-references (right column):

8 [a]Gen. 15:18; 26:3; Num. 14:30; Neh. 9:15; Ezek. 20:5, 6 [b]Josh. 24:13; Ps. 136:21, 22 [c]Ex. 6:6

9 [a]Ex. 2:23

11 [a]Ex. 4:22, 23

12 [a]Ex. 4:1, 10; 6:30 [b]Jer. 1:6

★14-27

14 [a]Gen. 46:9; Num. 26:5-11; 1 Chr. 5:3

15 [a]Gen. 46:10; 1 Chr. 4:24

16 [a]Gen. 46:11; Num. 3:17; 26:57f.; 1 Chr. 6:1, 16-19

17 [a]Num. 3:18-20; 1 Chr. 6:17-19

6:3 God Almighty. Heb., El Shaddai, the strong or powerful God. See note on Gen. 17:1. The name Yahweh was known to the patriarchs (Gen. 13:4), but its significance as the One who would redeem Israel from Egyptian bondage was not known until this time.

6:4 See Gen. 13:15; 17:8.

6:6 I will also redeem. Lit., I will be a kinsman-redeemer (Heb., goel). See note on Gen. 48:15-16. The word suggests a close, personal relationship between redeemer and redeemed.

6:14-27 The genealogy is inserted in order to identify the lineage of Moses and Aaron and to position them as the ones freshly appointed to the present task of deliverance (cf. v. 29).

18 aNum.
3:19; 1 Chr.
6:2, 18

18 And athe sons of Kohath: Amram and Izhar and Hebron and Uzziel; and the length of Kohath's life was one hundred and thirty-three years.

19 aNum.
3:20; 1 Chr.
6:19; 23:21

19 And athe sons of Merari: Mahli and Mushi. These are the families of the Levites according to their generations.

20 aEx. 2:1,
2; Num.
26:59

20 And aAmram married his father's sister Jochebed, and she bore him Aaron and Moses; and the length of Amram's life was one hundred and thirty-seven years.

21 aNum.
16:1; 1 Chr.
6:37, 38

21 And athe sons of Izhar: Korah and Nepheg and Zichri.

22 aLev.
10:4; Num.
3:30

22 aAnd the sons of Uzziel: Mishael and Elzaphan and Sithri.

23 aRuth
4:19, 20;
1 Chr. 2:10
bNum. 1:7;
2:3 cLev.
10:1; Num.
3:2; 26:60;
1 Chr. 6:3;
24:1

23 And Aaron married Elisheba, the daughter of aAmminadab, the sister of bNahshon, and she bore him cNadab and Abihu, Eleazar and Ithamar.

24 aNum.
26:11; 1 Chr.
6:22, 23, 37

24 And the asons of Korah: Assir and Elkanah and Abiasaph; these are the families of the Korahites.

25 aJosh.
24:33 bNum.
25:7-13;
Josh. 24:33;
Ps. 106:30

25 And Aaron's son aEleazar married one of the daughters of Putiel, and she bore him bPhinehas. These are the heads of the fathers' *households* of the Levites according to their families.

26 aEx. 3:10;
6:13 bEx.
7:4; 12:17,
51

26 It was *the same* Aaron and Moses to whom the LORD said, "aBring out the sons of Israel from the land of Egypt according to their bhosts."

27 aEx. 5:1

27 They were the ones awho spoke to Pharaoh king of Egypt about bringing out the sons of Israel from Egypt; it was *the same* Moses and Aaron.

28 Now it came about on the day when the LORD spoke to Moses in the land of Egypt,

29 aEx. 6:2,
6, 8 bEx.
6:11; 7:2

29 that the LORD spoke to Moses, saying, "aI am the LORD; bspeak to Pharaoh king of Egypt all that I speak to you."

30 aEx. 4:10;
6:12; Jer. 1:6

30 But Moses said before the LORD, "Behold, I am aunskilled in speech; how then will Pharaoh listen to me?"

1 aEx. 4:16

7 Then the LORD said to Moses, "aSee, I make you *as* God to Pharaoh, and your brother Aaron shall be your prophet.

2 aEx. 4:15

2 "You shall speak all that I command you, and your brother aAaron shall speak to Pharaoh that he let the sons of Israel go out of his land.

★ 3 aEx.
4:21 bEx.
11:9; Acts
7:36

3 "But aI will harden Pharaoh's heart that I may bmultiply My signs and My wonders in the land of Egypt.

★ 4 aEx.
3:19, 20;
7:13, 16, 22;
8:15, 19;
9:12; 11:9
bEx. 12:51;
13:3, 9 cEx.
6:6

4 "When aPharaoh will not listen to you, then I will lay My hand on Egypt, and bbring out My hosts, My people the sons of Israel, from the land of Egypt by cgreat judgments.

5 aEx. 7:17;
8:19, 22;
10:7; 14:4,
18, 25 bEx.
3:20

5 "And athe Egyptians shall know that I am the LORD, when I bstretch out My hand on Egypt and bring out the sons of Israel from their midst."

6 aGen.
6:22; 7:5; Ex.
7:2

6 So Moses and Aaron did *it;* aas the LORD commanded them, thus they did.

7 aDeut.
29:5; 31:2;
34:7; Acts
7:23, 30

7 And Moses was aeighty years old and Aaron eighty-three, when they spoke to Pharaoh.

2 *Second encounter with Pharaoh, 7:8–13*

8 Now the LORD spoke to Moses and Aaron, saying,

9 aIs. 7:11;
John 2:18;
6:30 bEx.
4:2, 17

9 "When Pharaoh speaks to you, saying, 'aWork a miracle,' then you shall say to Aaron, 'bTake your staff and throw *it* down before Pharaoh, *that* it may become a serpent.'"

10 aEx. 4:3;
7:9

10 So Moses and Aaron came to Pharaoh, and thus they did just as the LORD had commanded; and Aaron threw his staff down before Pharaoh and his servants, and it abecame a serpent.

*11-12
11 aDan.
2:2; 4:6; 5:7
bGen. 41:8;
Ex. 7:22;
Dan. 2:2;
2 Tim. 3:8
cEx. 7:22;
8:7, 18;
2 Tim. 3:9;
Rev. 13:13,
14

11 Then Pharaoh also acalled for *the* wise men and *the*

7:3 See note on 4:21.
7:4 *My hosts.* Lit., my armies; i.e., equipped and organized like an army (cf. 13:18).
7:11-12 Some think the Egyptian *magicians* accomplished this feat through sleight of hand,

or through demonic power, or by using snakes that they charmed into a rigid position to appear as rods. The names of the sorcerers were Jannes and Jambres (cf. 2 Tim. 3:8).

sorcerers, and they also, the ᵇmagicians of Egypt, did the same with ᶜtheir secret arts.

12 For each one threw down his staff and they turned into serpents. But Aaron's staff swallowed up their staffs.

13 ^aEx. 4:21; 7:3, 22; 8:15, 19, 32; 9:7, 12, 34, 35; 10:1, 20, 27

13 Yet ᵃPharaoh's heart was hardened, and he did not listen to them, as the LORD had said.

C God Authenticates Moses by the Plagues, 7:14-12:36

1 First plague: blood, 7:14-25

14 Then the LORD said to Moses, "Pharaoh's heart is stubborn; he refuses to let the people go.

15 ^aEx. 2:5; 8:20 ^bEx. 4:2, 3; 7:10

15 "Go to Pharaoh in the morning as ᵃhe is going out to the water, and station yourself to meet him on the bank of the Nile; and you shall take in your hand ᵇthe staff that was turned into a serpent.

16 ^aEx. 3:13, 18; 4:22; 5:1 ^bEx. 4:23; 5:1, 3

16 "ᵃAnd you will say to him, 'The LORD, the God of the Hebrews, sent me to you, saying, "ᵇLet My people go, that they may serve Me in the wilderness. But behold, you have not listened until now."

★17 ^aEx. 5:2; 7:5; 10:2; Ps. 9:16; Ezek. 25:17 ^bEx. 4:9; 7:20; Rev. 11:6; 16:4, 6

17 'Thus says the LORD, "ᵃBy this you shall know that I am the LORD: behold, I will strike the water that is in the Nile with the staff that is in my hand, and ᵇit shall be turned to blood.

18 ^aEx. 7:21 ^bEx. 7:24

18 "And ᵃthe fish that are in the Nile will die, and the Nile will become foul; and the Egyptians will ᵇfind difficulty in drinking water from the Nile." ' "

★19 ^aEx. 8:5, 6, 16; 9:22; 10:12; 21; 14:21, 26

19 Then the LORD said to Moses, "Say to Aaron, 'Take your staff and ᵃstretch out your hand over the waters of Egypt, over their rivers, over their streams, and over their pools, and over all their reservoirs of water, that they may become blood; and there shall be blood throughout all the land of Egypt, both in vessels of wood and in vessels of stone.' "

20 ^aEx. 17:5 ^bPs. 78:44; 105:29

20 So Moses and Aaron did even as the LORD had commanded. And he lifted up ᵃthe staff and struck the water that was in the Nile, in the sight of Pharaoh and in the sight of his servants, and ᵇall the water that was in the Nile was turned to blood.

21 And the fish that were in the Nile died, and the Nile became foul, so that the Egyptians could not drink water from the Nile. And the blood was through all the land of Egypt.

★22 ^aEx. 7:11; 8:7

22 ᵃBut the magicians of Egypt did the same with their secret arts; and Pharaoh's heart was hardened, and he did not listen to them, as the LORD had said.

23 Then Pharaoh turned and went into his house with no concern even for this.

24 So all the Egyptians dug around the Nile for water to drink, for they could not drink of the water of the Nile.

25 And seven days passed after the LORD had struck the Nile.

2 Second plague: frogs, 8:1-15

1 ^aEx. 3:18; 4:23; 5:1, 3

8 Then the LORD said to Moses, "Go to Pharaoh and say to him, 'Thus says the LORD, "ᵃLet My people go, that they may serve Me.

2 "But if you refuse to let them go, behold, I will smite your whole territory with frogs.

3 ^aPs. 105:30

3 "And the Nile will ᵃswarm with frogs, which will come up

7:17 The reflection of the setting sun on the river might give the water a red appearance temporarily, but would not cause the fish to die and the water to become unusable. Nor would red silting, not uncommon to the Nile, do this. This was a supernatural judgment. The water was turned to *blood* in terms of appearance (taste, smell, and texture).

7:19 The tributaries of the Nile were also affected.

7:22 Evidently the *magicians* turned small quantities of water (obtained in the way described in v. 24) into blood, and this satisfied Pharaoh. It would have been more helpful had they been able to change the bloody water back to good water!

and go into your house and into your bedroom and on your bed, and into the houses of your servants and on your people, and into your ovens and into your kneading bowls.

4 "So the frogs will come up on you and your people and all your servants." '"

5 *a*Ex. 7:19 **5** Then the LORD said to Moses, "Say to Aaron, '*a*Stretch out your hand with your staff over the rivers, over the streams and over the pools, and make frogs come up on the land of Egypt.'"

★ 6 *a*Ps. 78:45; 105:30 **6** So Aaron stretched out his hand over the waters of Egypt, and the *a*frogs came up and covered the land of Egypt.

★ 7 *a*Ex. 7:11, 22 **7** *a*And the magicians did the same with their secret arts, making frogs come up on the land of Egypt.

8 *a*Ex. 8:25; 9:27; 10:16 *b*Ex. 8:28; 9:28; 10:17; Num. 21:7; 1 Kin. 13:6 *c*Ex. 8:15, 29, 32 **8** Then Pharaoh *a*called for Moses and Aaron and said, "*b*Entreat the LORD that He remove the frogs from me and from my people; and *c*I will let the people go, that they may sacrifice to the LORD."

9 And Moses said to Pharaoh, "The honor is yours to tell me: when shall I entreat for you and your servants and your people, that the frogs be destroyed from you and your houses, *that* they may be left only in the Nile?"

10 *a*Ex. 9:14; Deut. 4:35, 39; 33:26; 2 Sam. 7:22; 1 Chr. 17:20; Ps. 86:8; Is. 46:9; Jer. 10:6, 7 **10** Then he said, "Tomorrow." So he said, "*May it be* according to your word, that you may know that there is *a*no one like the LORD our God.

11 *a*Ex. 8:13 **11** "And the *a*frogs will depart from you and your houses and your servants and your people; they will be left only in the Nile."

12 Then Moses and Aaron went out from Pharaoh, and *a*Moses cried to the LORD concerning the frogs which He had inflicted upon Pharaoh. 12 *a*Ex. 8:30; 9:33; 10:18

13 And the LORD did according to the word of Moses, and the frogs died out of the houses, the courts, and the fields.

14 So they piled them in heaps, and the land became foul.

15 But when Pharaoh saw that there was relief, he hardened his heart and *a*did not listen to them, as the LORD had said. ★15 *a*Ex. 7:4

3 Third plague: lice, 8:16-19

16 Then the LORD said to Moses, "Say to Aaron, 'Stretch out your staff and strike the dust of the earth, that it may become gnats through all the land of Egypt.'" ★16

17 And they did so; and Aaron stretched out his hand with his staff, and struck the dust of the earth, and there were gnats on man and beast. All the dust of the earth became *a*gnats through all the land of Egypt. 17 *a*Ps. 105:31

18 And the magicians tried with their secret arts to bring forth gnats, but *a*they could not; so there were gnats on man and beast. ★18-19

18 *a*Ex. 7:11, 12; 8:7; 9:11

19 Then the magicians said to Pharaoh, "*a*This is the finger of God." But Pharaoh's heart was hardened, and he did not listen to them, as the LORD had said. 19 *a*Ex. 7:5; 10:7; Ps. 8:3; Luke 11:20

4 Fourth plague: flies, 8:20-32

20 Now the LORD said to Moses, "*a*Rise early in the morning and present yourself before Pharaoh, as *b*he comes out to the 20 *a*Ex. 7:15; 9:13 *b*Ex. 2:5; 7:15 *c*Ex. 3:18; 4:23; 5:1, 3; 8:1

8:6 *frogs*. These regularly appeared in abundance after the Nile receded in mid-December and were a symbol of fertility. This second plague used these creatures, sacred to the Egyptians, and made them heinous to the people, whose land and homes were overrun by them.

8:7 Again the *magicians* were no help. They only increased the number of frogs!

8:15 Temporary afflictions usually do not change the heart.

8:16 *gnats*. The exact meaning is uncertain. They were perhaps gnats, sand fleas, or mosquitoes.

8:18-19 For the first time, the *magicians* admitted their impotence and acknowledged the power of God (*finger of God* refers to His power or Spirit; see Exod. 31:18; Deut. 9:10; Psalm 8:3; and Luke 11:20 compared with Matt. 12:28).

water, and say to him, 'Thus says the Lord, "cLet My people go, that they may serve Me.

★21 21 "For if you will not let My people go, behold, I will send swarms of insects on you and on your servants and on your people and into your houses; and the houses of the Egyptians shall be full of swarms of insects, and also the ground on which they *dwell.*

★22 aEx. 9:4,
6, 24; 10:23;
11:7 bEx.
9:29, 19:5;
20:11
22 "aBut on that day I will set apart the land of Goshen, where My people are living, so that no swarms of insects will be there, in order that you may know that bI, the Lord, am in the midst of the land.

23 "And I will put a division between My people and your people. Tomorrow this sign shall occur." ' "

24 aPs.
78:45;
105:31
24 Then the Lord did so. And there came great swarms of insects into the house of Pharaoh and the houses of his servants and the land was alaid waste because of the swarms of insects in all the land of Egypt.

★25-26

25 aEx. 8:8;
9:27; 10:16
bEx. 9:28;
10:8, 24;
12:31
25 And Pharaoh acalled for Moses and Aaron and said, "bGo, sacrifice to your God within the land."

26 aGen.
43:32; 46:34;
Deut. 7:25f.
26 But Moses said, "It is not right to do so, for we shall sacrifice to the Lord our God what is aan abomination to the Egyptians. If we sacrifice what is an abomination to the Egyptians before their eyes, will they not then stone us?

27 aEx. 3:18;
5:3
27 "We must go a athree days' journey into the wilderness and sacrifice to the Lord our God as He commands us."

28 aEx. 8:8,
15, 29, 32
bEx. 8:8;
9:28; 1 Kin.
13:6
28 And Pharaoh said, "aI will let you go, that you may sacrifice

to the Lord your God in the wilderness; only you shall not go very far away. bMake supplication for me."

29 Then Moses said, "Behold, I am going out from you, and I shall make supplication to the Lord that the swarms of insects may depart from Pharaoh, from his servants, and from his people tomorrow; only do not let Pharaoh adeal deceitfully again in not letting the people go to sacrifice to the Lord."

29 aEx. 8:8,
15

30 So aMoses went out from Pharaoh and made supplication to the Lord.

30 aEx. 8:12

31 And the Lord did as Moses asked, and removed the swarms of insects from Pharaoh, from his servants and from his people; not one remained.

32 But Pharaoh hardened his heart this time also, and ahe did not let the people go.

32 aEx. 4:21;
8:8, 15

5 Fifth plague: disease on the beasts, 9:1-7

9 Then the Lord said to Moses, "Go to Pharaoh and speak to him, 'Thus says the Lord, the God of the Hebrews, "aLet My people go, that they may serve Me.

1 aEx. 4:23;
8:1

2 "For aif you refuse to let *them* go, and continue to hold them,

2 aEx. 8:2

3 behold, athe hand of the Lord will come *with* a very severe pestilence on your livestock which are in the field, on the horses, on the donkeys, on the camels, on the herds, and on the flocks.

★ 3 aEx.
7:4; 1 Sam.
5:6; Ps.
39:10; Acts
13:11

4 "aBut the Lord will make a distinction between the livestock of Israel and the livestock of Egypt, so that bnothing will die of

4 aEx. 8:22
bEx. 9:6

8:21 *swarms of insects.* A mixture of irritating insects.

8:22 *Goshen* (see note on Gen. 45:10), where the Israelites lived, was exempt from the plague.

8:25-26 Moses rejected Pharaoh's compromise offer to sacrifice *within the land.* To have used cows or sheep in sacrifice (an *abomination* to the Egyptians, who considered some animals sacred, cf. Gen. 46:34) would have incited rioting.

9:3 *a very severe pestilence.* The word is sometimes used of pestilence in general (cf. 5:3; 9:15), though here of an animal plague. Apparently it was highly infectious and fatal. *Horses* were a comparatively recent and highly prized importation into Egypt. The death of all these various animals would have affected transportation, agriculture, and worship (since cattle were sacred).

all that belongs to the sons of Israel.'''

5 And the LORD set a definite time, saying, "Tomorrow the LORD will do this thing in the land."

6 So the LORD did this thing on the morrow, and ªall the livestock of Egypt died; ᵇbut of the livestock of the sons of Israel, not one died.

7 And Pharaoh sent, and behold, there was not even one of the livestock of Israel dead. But ªthe heart of Pharaoh was hardened, and he did not let the people go.

6 Sixth plague: boils on man and beast, 9:8-12

8 Then the LORD said to Moses and Aaron, "Take for yourselves handfuls of soot from a kiln, and let Moses throw it toward the sky in the sight of Pharaoh.

9 "And it will become fine dust over all the land of Egypt, and will become ªboils breaking out with sores on man and beast through all the land of Egypt."

10 So they took soot from a kiln, and stood before Pharaoh; and Moses threw it toward the sky, and it became boils breaking out with sores on man and beast.

11 ªAnd the magicians could not stand before Moses because of the boils, for the boils were on the magicians as well as on all the Egyptians.

12 And ªthe LORD hardened Pharaoh's heart, and he did not listen to them, just as the LORD had spoken to Moses.

7 Seventh plague: hail, 9:13-35

13 Then the LORD said to Moses, "ªRise up early in the morning and stand before Pharaoh and say to him, 'Thus says the LORD, the God of the He-

brews, "ᵇLet My people go, that they may serve Me.

14 "For this time I will send all My plagues on you and your servants and your people, so that ªyou may know that there is no one like Me in all the earth.

15 "For *if by* now I had put forth My hand and struck you and your people with pestilence, you would then have been cut off from the earth.

16 "But, indeed, ªfor this cause I have allowed you to remain, in order to show you My power, and in order to proclaim My name through all the earth.

17 "Still you exalt yourself against My people by not letting them go.

18 "Behold, about this time tomorrow, ªI will send a very heavy hail, such as has not been *seen* in Egypt from the day it was founded until now.

19 "Now therefore send, bring ªyour livestock and whatever you have in the field to safety. ᵇEvery man and beast that is found in the field and is not brought home, when the hail comes down on them, will die."'"

20 ªThe one among the servants of Pharaoh who feared the word of the LORD made his servants and his livestock flee into the houses;

21 but he who paid no regard to the word of the LORD left his servants and his livestock in the field.

22 Now the LORD said to Moses, "Stretch out your hand toward the sky, that ªhail may fall on all the land of Egypt, on man and on beast and on every plant of the field, throughout the land of Egypt."

23 And Moses stretched out his staff toward the sky, and the LORD sent thunder and ªhail, and fire ran down to the earth. And the LORD rained hail on the land of Egypt.

---

6 ªEx. 9:19, 20, 25; Ps. 78:48 ᵇEx. 9:4

7 ªEx. 7:14; 8:32

★ **9** ªDeut. 28:27; Rev. 16:2

11 ªEx. 8:18

12 ªEx. 4:21; 10:1, 20; 14:8; Josh. 11:20; John 12:40

13 ªEx. 8:20 ᵇEx. 4:23

14 ªEx. 8:10; Deut. 3:24; 2 Sam. 7:22; 1 Chr. 17:20; Ps. 86:8; Is. 45:5-8; 46:9; Jer. 10:6, 7

16 ªProv. 16:4; Rom. 9:17

18 ªEx. 9:23, 24

19 ªEx. 9:6 ᵇEx. 9:25

20 ªProv. 13:13

22 ªRev. 16:21

★ **23** ªGen. 19:24; Josh. 10:11; Ps. 18:13; 78:47; 105:32; Is. 30:30; Ezek. 38:22; Rev. 8:7

9:9 *boils . . . sores.* I.e., inflamations and eruptions of the skin.

9:23 Hailstorms are a rarity in Egypt, a fact that heightened the effect of the miracle.

24 So there was hail, and fire flashing continually in the midst of the hail, very severe, such as had not been in all the land of Egypt since it became a nation.

25 *a*Ex. 9:19; Ps. 78:47, 48; 105:32, 33

25 And *a*the hail struck all that was in the field through all the land of Egypt, both man and beast; the hail also struck every plant of the field and shattered every tree of the field.

26 *a*Ex. 8:22, 9:4, 6; 11:7

26 *a*Only in the land of Goshen, where the sons of Israel *were*, there was no hail.

27 *a*Ex. 8:8
*b*Ex. 10:16, 17; 2 Chr. 12:6; Ps. 129:4; 145:17; Lam. 1:18

27 Then Pharaoh *a*sent for Moses and Aaron, and said to them, "*b*I have sinned this time; the LORD is the righteous one, and I and my people are the wicked ones.

28 *a*Ex. 8:8, 28; 10:17
*b*Ex. 8:25; 10:8, 24

28 "*a*Make supplication to the LORD, for there has been enough of God's thunder and hail; and *b*I will let you go, and you shall stay no longer."

29 *a*1 Kin. 8:22, 38; Ps. 143:6; Is. 1:15 *b*Ex. 8:22; 19:5; 20:11; Ps. 24:1; 1 Cor. 10:26

29 And Moses said to him, "As soon as I go out of the city, I will *a*spread out my hands to the LORD; the thunder will cease, and there will be hail no longer, that you may know that *b*the earth is the LORD's.

30 *a*Ex. 8:29
*b*Is. 26:10

30 "*a*But as for you and your servants, I know that *b*you do not yet fear the LORD God."

★31 *a*Ruth 1:22; 2:23

31 (Now the flax and the *a*barley were ruined, for the barley was in the ear and the flax was in bud.

★32

32 But the wheat and the spelt were not ruined, for they *ripen* late.)

33 *a*Ex. 8:12; 9:29

33 *a*So Moses went out of the city from Pharaoh, and spread out his hands to the LORD; and the thunder and the hail ceased, and rain no longer poured on the earth.

34 But when Pharaoh saw that the rain and the hail and the thunder had ceased, he sinned again and hardened his heart, he and his servants.

35 *a*Ex. 4:21

35 And Pharaoh's heart was hardened, and he did not let the sons of Israel go, just as the *a*LORD had spoken through Moses.

8   *Eighth plague: locusts,*
10:1-20

10 Then the LORD said to Moses, "Go to Pharaoh, for *a*I have hardened his heart and the heart of his servants, that I may perform these signs of Mine among them,

1 *a*Ex. 4:21; 7:13; Josh. 11:20; John 12:40; Rom. 9:18

2 and *a*that you may tell in the hearing of your son, and of your grandson, how I made a mockery of the Egyptians, and how I performed My signs among them; *b*that you may know that I am the LORD."

2 *a*Ex. 12:26, 27; 13:8, 14, 15; Deut. 4:9; Ps. 44:1; 78:5; Joel 1:3 *b*Ex. 7:5, 17

3 And Moses and Aaron went to Pharaoh and said to him, "Thus says the LORD, the God of the Hebrews, 'How long will you refuse to *a*humble yourself before Me? *b*Let My people go, that they may serve Me.

3 *a*1 Kin. 21:29; 2 Chr. 34:27; James 4:10; 1 Pet. 5:6 *b*Ex. 4:23

4 'For if you refuse to let My people go, behold, tomorrow I will bring locusts into your territory.

5 'And they shall cover the surface of the land, so that no one shall be able to see the land. *a*They shall also eat the rest of what has escaped—what is left to you from the hail—and they shall eat every tree which sprouts for you out of the field.

5 *a*Joel 1:4; 2:25

6 'Then *a*your houses shall be filled, and the houses of all your servants and the houses of all the Egyptians, *something* which neither your fathers nor your grandfathers have seen, from the day that they came upon the earth until this day.'" And he

6 *a*Ex. 8:3, 21

9:31 That *barley* was ripe and the *flax* in blossom indicates the plague of hail was in January. Also, from January to April, cattle were usually outdoors (cf. vv. 20–21).

9:32 The *wheat* and *spelt* (an inferior kind of wheat) were not harmed at this time because they ripen a month or so later (but see 10:5).

turned and went out from Pharaoh.

★ 7-10

7 aEx. 7:5;
8:19; 12:33
bEx. 23:33;
Josh. 23:13;
1 Sam.
18:21; Eccl.
7:26

7 And aPharaoh's servants said to him, "How long will this man be ba snare to us? Let the men go, that they may serve the Lord their God. Do you not realize that Egypt is destroyed?"

8 aEx. 8:8
bEx. 8:25

8 So Moses and Aaron awere brought back to Pharaoh, and he said to them, "bGo, serve the Lord your God! Who are the ones that are going?"

9 aEx.
12:37, 38
bEx. 10:26

9 And Moses said, "aWe shall go with our young and our old; with our sons and our daughters, bwith our flocks and our herds we will go, for we must hold a feast to the Lord."

10 Then he said to them, "Thus may the Lord be with you, if ever I let you and your little ones go! Take heed, for evil is in your mind.

11 aEx.
10:28

11 "Not so! Go now, the men among you, and serve the Lord, for that is what you desire." So athey were driven out from Pharaoh's presence.

12 aEx. 7:19
bEx. 10:5,
15

12 Then the Lord said to Moses, "aStretch out your hand over the land of Egypt for the locusts, that they may come up on the land of Egypt, and beat every plant of the land, even all that the hail has left."

13 aPs.
78:46;
105:34

13 So Moses stretched out his staff over the land of Egypt, and the Lord directed an east wind on the land all that day and all that night; and when it was morning, the east wind brought the alocusts.

★14-15
14 aDeut.
28:38; Ps.
78:46;
105:34; Joel
1:4, 7; 2:1-
11; Rev. 9:3

14 And athe locusts came up over all the land of Egypt and settled in all the territory of Egypt; they were very numerous. There had never been so many locusts,

nor would there be so many again.

15 aEx. 10:5;
Ps. 105:34f.

15 For they covered the surface of the whole land, so that the land was darkened; and they aate every plant of the land and all the fruit of the trees that the hail had left. Thus nothing green was left on tree or plant of the field through all the land of Egypt.

16 aEx. 8:8
bEx. 9:27

16 Then Pharaoh hurriedly acalled for Moses and Aaron, and he said, "bI have sinned against the Lord your God and against you.

17 aEx. 8:8,
28; 9:28;
1 Kin. 13:6

17 "Now therefore, please forgive my sin only this once, and amake supplication to the Lord your God, that He would only remove this death from me."

18 aEx. 8:30

18 And ahe went out from Pharaoh and made supplication to the Lord.

19 So the Lord shifted the wind to a very strong west wind which took up the locusts and drove them into the Red Sea; not one locust was left in all the territory of Egypt.

20 aEx. 4:21;
11:10

20 But athe Lord hardened Pharaoh's heart, and he did not let the sons of Israel go.

9 Ninth plague: darkness, 10:21-29

★21 aEx.
9:22 bDeut.
28:29

21 Then the Lord said to Moses, "aStretch out your hand toward the sky, that there may be darkness over the land of Egypt, even a darkness bwhich may be felt."

22 aPs.
105:28; Rev.
16:10

22 So Moses stretched out his hand toward the sky, and there was athick darkness in all the land of Egypt for three days.

23 aEx. 8:22

23 They did not see one another, nor did anyone rise from his place for three days, abut all

---

10:7-10 In response to the pleas of his servants, Pharaoh offered Moses another compromise. He would let the men go, but not their families or children, charging Moses with wanting to do *evil* by depriving him of such a large number of workers.

10:14-15 *locusts.* One of the most destructive of creatures. A swarm may have an average density of 130,000,000 locusts per square mile.

They can denude hundreds of square miles quickly, bringing horror, despair, and terrible economic consequences to the inhabitants.

10:21 *a darkness which may be felt.* Possibly a combination of a violent sandstorm and supernatural darkness. This was an especially significant judgment on Egypt, for the sun god Ra was one of her chief deities.

the sons of Israel had light in their dwellings.

24 Then Pharaoh [a]called to Moses, and said, "Go, serve the LORD; only let your flocks and your herds be detained. Even [b]your little ones may go with you."

25 But Moses said, "You must also let us have sacrifices and burnt offerings, that we may sacrifice *them* to the LORD our God.

26 "[a]Therefore, our livestock, too, will go with us; not a hoof will be left behind, for we shall take some of them to serve the LORD our God. And until we arrive there, we ourselves do not know with what we shall serve the LORD."

27 But [a]the LORD hardened Pharaoh's heart, and he was not willing to let them go.

28 Then Pharaoh said to him, "[a]Get away from me! Beware, do not see my face again, for in the day you see my face you shall die!"

29 And Moses said, "You are right; [a]I shall never see your face again!"

10   Tenth plague: death,
          11:1–12:36

a   The plague announced,
          11:1-10

11 Now the LORD said to Moses, "One more plague I will bring on Pharaoh and on Egypt; [a]after that he will let you go from here. When he lets you go, he will surely drive you out from here completely.

2 "Speak now in the hearing of the people that [a]each man ask from his neighbor and each woman from her neighbor for articles of silver and articles of gold."

3 [a]And the LORD gave the people favor in the sight of the Egyptians. [b]Furthermore, the man Moses *himself* was greatly esteemed in the land of Egypt, *both* in the sight of Pharaoh's servants and in the sight of the people.

4 And Moses said, "Thus says the LORD, 'About [a]midnight I am going out into the midst of Egypt,

5 and [a]all the first-born in the land of Egypt shall die, from the first-born of the Pharaoh who sits on his throne, even to the first-born of the slave girl who is behind the millstones; all the first-born of the cattle as well.

6 'Moreover, there shall be [a]a great cry in all the land of Egypt, such as there has not been *before* and such as shall never be again.

7 '[a]But against any of the sons of Israel a dog shall not *even* bark, whether against man or beast, that you may understand how the LORD makes a distinction between Egypt and Israel.'

8 "And [a]all these your servants will come down to me and bow themselves before me, saying, 'Go out, you and all the people who follow you,' and after that I will go out." [b]And he went out from Pharaoh in hot anger.

9 Then the LORD said to Moses, "[a]Pharaoh will not listen to you, so [b]that My wonders will be multiplied in the land of Egypt."

10 And [a]Moses and Aaron performed all these wonders before Pharaoh; yet [b]the LORD hardened Pharaoh's heart, and he did not let the sons of Israel go out of his land.

10:24 This was the fourth compromise Pharaoh offered Moses (see 8:25; 8:28; 10:11), and it, too, was unacceptable (10:25-26).
11:2 *ask.* See note on 3:22. Verse 3 explains at least one reason why the Egyptians complied: the miracles Moses had performed gave him esteem in their sight.
11:7 *a dog shall not even bark.* A proverbial saying meaning that no one would offer the least resistance when Israel left Egypt (cf. Josh. 10:21).

Marginal references:

★24 [a]Ex. 8:8, 25 [b]Ex. 10:10
26 [a]Ex. 10:9
27 [a]Ex. 4:21; 10:20; 14:4, 8
28 [a]Ex. 10:11
29 [a]Ex. 11:8; Heb. 11:27
1 [a]Ex. 12:31, 33, 39
★ 2 [a]Ex. 3:22; 12:35, 36
3 [a]Ex. 3:21; 12:36; Ps. 106:46 [b]Deut. 34:10-12
4 [a]Ex. 12:29
5 [a]Ex. 12:12, 29; Ps. 78:51; 105:36; 135:8; 136:10
6 [a]Ex. 12:30
★ 7 [a]Ex. 8:22; Josh. 10:21
8 [a]Ex. 12:31-33 [b]Heb. 11:27
9 [a]Ex. 7:4 [b]Ex. 7:3
10 [a]Ex. 4:21 [b]Ex. 7:3; 9:12; 10:20, 27; Josh. 11:20; Is. 63:17; John 12:40

b The Passover instituted,
12:1-36

12 Now the LORD said to Moses and Aaron in the land of Egypt,

★ 2 *a*Ex. 13:4; 23:15; 34:18; Deut. 16:1

2 "*a*This month shall be the beginning of months for you; it is to be the first month of the year to you.

★ 3

3 "Speak to all the congregation of Israel, saying, 'On the tenth of this month they are each one to take a lamb for themselves, according to their fathers' households, a lamb for each household.

4 'Now if the household is too small for a lamb, then he and his neighbor nearest to his house are to take one according to the number of persons *in them;* according to what each man should eat, you are to divide the lamb.

5 *a*Lev. 22:18-21; 23:12; Heb. 9:14; 1 Pet. 1:19

5 'Your lamb shall be *a*an unblemished male a year old; you may take it from the sheep or from the goats.

★ 6 *a*Ex. 12:14, 17; Lev. 23:5; Num. 9:1-3, 11; 28:16 *b*Ex. 16:12; Deut. 16:4, 6

6 'And you shall keep it until the *a*fourteenth day of the same month, then the whole assembly of the congregation of Israel is to kill it *b*at twilight.

7 *a*Ex. 12:22

7 '*a*Moreover, they shall take some of the blood and put it on the two doorposts and on the lintel of the houses in which they eat it.

8 *a*Ex. 34:25; Num. 9:12 *b*Deut. 16:7 *c*Deut. 16:3, 4; 1 Cor. 5:8 *d*Num. 9:11

8 'And they shall eat the flesh *a*that *same* night, *b*roasted with fire, and they shall eat it with *c*unleavened bread *d*and bitter herbs.

9 'Do not eat any of it raw or boiled at all with water, but rather *a*roasted with fire, *both* its head and its legs along with *b*its entrails.

9 *a*Ex. 12:8 *b*Ex. 29:13, 17, 22

10 '*a*And you shall not leave any of it over until morning, but whatever is left of it until morning, you shall burn with fire.

10 *a*Ex. 16:19; 23:18; 34:25

11 'Now you shall eat it in this manner: *with* your loins girded, your sandals on your feet, and your staff in your hand; and you shall eat it in haste—it is *a*the LORD's Passover.

★11 *a*Ex. 12:13, 21, 27, 43

12 'For *a*I will go through the land of Egypt on that night, and will strike down all the first-born in the land of Egypt, both man and beast; and *b*against all the gods of Egypt I will execute judgments—*c*I am the LORD.

12 *a*Ex. 11:4, 5 *b*Num. 33:4; Ps. 82:1 *c*Ex. 6:2

13 'And *a*the blood shall be a sign for you on the houses where you live; and when I see the blood I will pass over you, and no plague will befall you to destroy *you* when I strike the land of Egypt.

13 *a*Heb. 11:28

14 'Now *a*this day will be *b*a memorial to you, and you shall celebrate it *as* a feast to the LORD; throughout your generations you are to celebrate it *as* *c*a permanent ordinance.

14 *a*Ex. 12:6; Lev. 23:4, 5; 2 Kin. 23:21 *b*Ex. 13:9 *c*Ex. 12:17, 24; 13:10

12:2 *the first month of the year.* This month was called by its Canaanite name Abib (cf. 13:4), meaning "ear" (because the grain was in the ear), though it was later called by the Babylonian name Nisan (cf. Neh. 2:1). Correlated with the Western calendar, the Hebrew religious calendar is as follows:

Nisan (Abib)   = March-April
Iyyar (Ziv)   = April-May
Sivan   = May-June
Tammuz   = June-July
Ab   = July-August
Elul   = August-September
Tishri (Ethanim) = September-October
Marchesvan (Bul) = October-November
Chislev   = November-December
Tebeth   = December-January

Shebat   = January-February
Adar   = February-March

12:3 *a lamb* may refer to either a young sheep or goat.

12:6 *at twilight.* Lit., between the evenings. Some understand this to mean between sunset and nightfall (about 6-7 p.m.); others, between the sun's decline and sunset (about 3-5 p.m.).

12:11 *the LORD's Passover.* This event serves as a beautiful illustration of the redemption Christ accomplished at Calvary (cf. John 1:29; 1 Cor. 5:7). (1) The offering was to be without blemish (Exod. 12:5; cf. 1 Pet. 1:19). (2) The lamb had to be killed (Exod. 12:6; cf. John 12:24, 27). (3) The blood had to be applied (Exod. 12:7; cf. Heb. 9:22).

★15-20
15 *a*Ex. 13:6, 7; 23:15; 34:18; Lev. 23:6; Num. 28:17; Deut. 16:3, 8
*b*Gen. 17:14; Ex. 12:19; Num. 9:13
16 *a*Lev. 23:7, 8; Num. 28:18, 25

15 '*a*Seven days you shall eat unleavened bread, but on the first day you shall remove leaven from your houses; for whoever eats anything leavened from the first day until the seventh day, *b*that person shall be cut off from Israel.

16 'And *a*on the first day you shall have a holy assembly, and *another* holy assembly on the seventh day; no work at all shall be done on them, except what must be eaten by every person, that alone may be prepared by you.

17 *a*Deut. 16:3-8 *b*Ex. 12:41 *c*Ex. 12:14; 13:3, 10

17 'You shall also observe *a*the *Feast of* Unleavened Bread, for on this *b*very day I brought your hosts out of the land of Egypt; therefore you shall observe this day throughout your generations as *c*a permanent ordinance.

18 *a*Ex. 12:2; Lev. 23:5-8; Num. 28:16-25

18 '*a*In the first *month*, on the fourteenth day of the month at evening, you shall eat unleavened bread, until the twenty-first day of the month at evening.

19 *a*Ex. 12:15; 23:15; 34:18 *b*Num. 9:13

19 '*a*Seven days there shall be no leaven found in your houses; for whoever eats what is leavened, that *b*person shall be cut off from the congregation of Israel, whether *he is* an alien or a native of the land.

20 'You shall not eat anything leavened; in all your dwellings you shall eat unleavened bread.' "

21 *a*Num. 9:4; Heb. 11:28 *b*Ex. 12:3 *c*Ex. 12:11

21 Then *a*Moses called for all the elders of Israel, and said to them, "Go and *b*take for yourselves lambs according to your families, and slay *c*the Passover *lamb*.

★22 *a*Ex. 12:7

22 "*a*And you shall take a bunch of hyssop and dip it in the blood which is in the basin, and apply some of the blood that is in the basin to the lintel and the two doorposts; and none of you shall go outside the door of his house until morning.

23 "For *a*the LORD will pass through to smite the Egyptians; and when He sees the blood on the lintel and on the two doorposts, the LORD will pass over the door and will *b*not allow the *c*destroyer to come in to your houses to smite *you*.

23 *a*Ex. 11:4; 12:12, 13 *b*Rev. 7:3; 9:4 *c*1 Cor. 10:10; Heb. 11:28

24 "And *a*you shall observe this event as an ordinance for you and your children forever.

24 *a*Ex. 12:14, 17; 13:5, 10

25 "And it will come about when you enter the land which the LORD will give you, as He has promised, that you shall observe this rite.

26 "*a*And it will come about when your children will say to you, 'What does this rite mean to you?'

26 *a*Ex. 10:2; 13:8, 14, 15; Deut. 32:7; Josh. 4:6; Ps. 78:6

27 that you shall say, 'It is a Passover sacrifice to *a*the LORD who passed over the houses of the sons of Israel in Egypt when He smote the Egyptians, but spared our homes.' " *b*And the people bowed low and worshiped.

27 *a*Ex. 12:11 *b*Ex. 4:31

28 Then the sons of Israel went and did *so;* just as the LORD had commanded Moses and Aaron, so they did.

29 Now it came about at *a*midnight that *b*the LORD struck all *c*the first-born in the land of Egypt, from the first-born of Pharaoh who sat on his throne to the first-born of the captive who was in the dungeon, and all the first-born of *d*cattle.

★29 *a*Ex. 11:4, 5 *b*Num. 8:17; 33:4; Ps. 135:8; 136:10 *c*Ex. 4:23; Ps. 78:51; 105:36 *d*Ex. 9:6

30 And Pharaoh arose in the night, he and all his servants and

★30-32
30 *a*Ex. 11:6

12:15-20 The *Feast of Unleavened Bread* began on the evening of Passover (vv. 6, 18) and lasted for seven days. On the first day, homes were to be completely cleared of leaven (a symbol of corruption and evil, cf. Lev. 2:11; 1 Cor. 5:7-8), and a *holy assembly* was to be called (Exod. 12:16). The week was concluded with another convocation. See also Lev. 23:6-8.
12:22 *hyssop.* A common plant of the mint family. Because of its stiff branches and hairy leaves, it served well for sprinkling. In addi-

tion to the Passover, it was also used in the purifying of lepers (Lev. 14:2-7), the cleansing of a plague (Lev. 14:49-52), and the sacrificing of the red heifer (Num. 19:2-6). *lintel.* The horizontal piece above the door.
12:29 *the first-born of Pharaoh.* We know Thutmose IV succeeded Amenhotep II, the Pharaoh of the Exodus, but Thutmose IV was not his firstborn.
12:30-32 Though Pharaoh manufactured rationalizations for the other plagues, he could not reason away the trauma of the death of his

all the Egyptians; and there was [a]a great cry in Egypt, for there was no home where there was not someone dead.

31 aEx. 8:8
bEx. 8:25
31 Then [a]he called for Moses and Aaron at night and said, "Rise up, [b]get out from among my people, both you and the sons of Israel; and go, worship the LORD, as you have said.

32 aEx. 10:9, 26
32 "Take [a]both your flocks and your herds, as you have said, and go, and bless me also."

33 aEx. 10:7; 11:1; 12:39; Ps. 105:38
33 And [a]the Egyptians urged the people, to send them out of the land in haste, for they said, "We shall all be dead."

34 aEx. 12:39
34 So the people took [a]their dough before it was leavened, with their kneading bowls bound up in the clothes on their shoulders.

35 aEx. 3:21, 22; 11:2, 3; Ps. 105:37
35 [a]Now the sons of Israel had done according to the word of Moses, for they had requested from the Egyptians articles of silver and articles of gold, and clothing;

36 aEx. 3:22
36 and the LORD had given the people favor in the sight of the Egyptians, so that they let them have their request. Thus they [a]plundered the Egyptians.

II ISRAEL'S JOURNEY TO SINAI: EMANCIPATION, 12:37–18:27
A The Departure from Egypt, 12:37–51

★37 aNum. 33:3, 5
bGen. 47:11
cEx. 38:26; Num. 1:46; 2:32; 11:21; 26:51
37 Now the [a]sons of Israel journeyed from [b]Rameses to Succoth, about [c]six hundred thousand men on foot, aside from children.

38 And a [a]mixed multitude also went up with them, along with flocks and herds, a [b]very large number of livestock.

★38 aNum. 11:4 bEx. 17:3; Num. 20:19; 32:1; Deut. 3:19

39 And they baked the dough which they had brought out of Egypt into cakes of unleavened bread. For it had not become leavened, since they were [a]driven out of Egypt and could not delay, nor had they prepared any provisions for themselves.

39 aEx. 6:1; 11:1; 12:31-33

40 Now the time that the sons of Israel lived in Egypt was [a]four hundred and thirty years.

★40 aGen. 15:13, 16; Acts 7:6; Gal. 3:17

41 And it came about at the end of four hundred and thirty years, to [a]the very day, that [b]all the hosts of the LORD went out from the land of Egypt.

41 aEx. 12:17 bEx. 3:8, 10; 6:6

42 [a]It is a night to be observed for the LORD for having brought them out from the land of Egypt; this night is for the LORD, to be observed by all the sons of Israel throughout their generations.

42 aEx. 13:10; 34:18; Deut. 16:1

43 And the LORD said to Moses and Aaron, "This is the ordinance of [a]the Passover: no [b]foreigner is to eat of it;

43 aEx. 12:11; Num. 9:14 bEx. 12:48

44 but every man's [a]slave purchased with money, after you have circumcised him, then he may eat of it.

44 aGen. 17:12, 13; Lev. 22:11

45 "[a]A sojourner or a hired servant shall not eat of it.

45 aLev. 22:10

46 "It is to be eaten in a single house; you are not to bring forth any of the flesh outside of the house, [a]nor are you to break any bone of it.

★46 aNum. 9:12; Ps. 34:20; John 19:33, 36

47 "[a]All the congregation of Israel are to celebrate this.

47 aEx. 12:6; Num. 9:13, 14

---

own son. He called for *Moses and Aaron* that night and gave them permission to go, this time without insisting on any concessions. Indeed, Pharaoh, who was thought to be divine, asked Moses to bless him.

12:37 The total number was likely around 2,000,000 (see note on 1:7).

12:38 The *mixed multitude* included other Semites (see note on Gen. 9:26) who had settled in the Nile delta region, and some Egyptians. They later became a source of trouble to Moses (cf. Num. 11:4–6).

12:40 The 430 years may be the total number of years spent in bondage in Egypt, thus approxi-

mately equivalent to the 400 years of Gen. 15:13 and Acts 7:6. Or it may be that the years of bondage were 400, and the 430-year figure, used here and in Gal. 3:17, refers to the time between the last confirmation of the Abrahamic covenant and the giving of the Mosaic law. (See also Acts 13:19, where 450 years is the approximate time from the beginning of Egyptian bondage until after the conquest of Palestine, including the 40 years of wilderness wandering.)

12:46 On the prohibition against breaking a bone, cf. John 19:36.

48 *a*Num.
9:14

48 "But *a*if a stranger sojourns with you, and celebrates the Passover to the Lord, let all his males be circumcised, and then let him come near to celebrate it; and he shall be like a native of the land. But no uncircumcised person may eat of it.

49 *a*Lev.
24:22; Num.
15:15, 16, 29

49 "*a*The same law shall apply to the native as to the stranger who sojourns among you."

50 Then all the sons of Israel did *so;* they did just as the Lord had commanded Moses and Aaron.

51 *a*Ex.
12:41 *b*Ex.
6:26

51 And it came about on that same day that *a*the Lord brought the sons of Israel out of the land of Egypt *b*by their hosts.

B The Dedication of the First-born, 13:1-16

13 Then the Lord spoke to Moses, saying,

★ **2** *a*Ex.
13:12, 13,
15; 22:29;
Lev. 27:26;
Num. 3:13;
8:16f.; 18:15;
Deut. 15:19;
Luke 2:23

2 "*a*Sanctify to Me every firstborn, the first offspring of every womb among the sons of Israel, both of man and beast; it belongs to Me."

3 *a*Ex.
12:42; Deut.
16:3 *b*Ex.
3:20; 6:1
*c*Ex. 12:19

3 And Moses said to the people, "*a*Remember this day in which you went out from Egypt, from the house of slavery; for *b*by a powerful hand the Lord brought you out from this place. *c*And nothing leavened shall be eaten.

4 *a*Ex. 12:2;
23:15; 34:18;
Deut. 16:1

4 "On this day in the *a*month of Abib, you are about to go forth.

5 *a*Ex. 3:8,
17; Josh.
24:11 *b*Ex.
6:8 *c*Ex.
12:25

5 "And it shall be when the Lord *a*brings you to the land of the Canaanite, the Hittite, the Amorite, the Hivite and the Jebusite, which *b*He swore to your fathers to give you, a land flowing with milk and honey, *c*that you shall observe this rite in this month.

6 *a*Ex.
12:15-20

6 "For *a*seven days you shall eat unleavened bread, and on the seventh day there shall be a feast to the Lord.

7 *a*Ex.
12:19

7 "Unleavened bread shall be eaten throughout the seven days; and *a*nothing leavened shall be seen among you, nor shall any leaven be seen among you in all your borders.

8 *a*Ex. 10:2;
12:26f.;
13:14; Ps.
44:1

8 "*a*And you shall tell your son on that day, saying, 'It is because of what the Lord did for me when I came out of Egypt.'

★ **9** *a*Ex.
12:14; 13:16;
Num. 15:39;
Deut. 6:8;
11:18 *b*Ex.
13:3

9 "And *a*it shall serve as a sign to you on your hand, and as a reminder on your forehead, that the law of the Lord may be in your mouth; for with *b*a powerful hand the Lord brought you out of Egypt.

10 *a*Ex.
12:24, 25;
13:5

10 "Therefore, you shall *a*keep this ordinance at its appointed time from year to year.

11 *a*Ex. 13:5
*b*Gen. 15:18;
17:8; 28:15;
Ps. 105:42-
45

11 "Now it shall come about when *a*the Lord brings you to the land of the Canaanite, as *b*He swore to you and to your fathers, and gives it to you,

12 *a*Ex. 13:1,
2; 22:29;
34:19; Lev.
27:26; Num.
18:15; Ezek.
44:30; Luke
2:23

12 that *a*you shall devote to the Lord the first offspring of every womb, and the first offspring of every beast that you own; the males belong to the Lord.

★**13** *a*Ex.
34:20; Num.
18:15 *b*Num.
3:46

13 "But *a*every first offspring of a donkey you shall redeem with a lamb, but if you do not redeem *it,* then you shall break its neck; and *b*every first-born of man among your sons you shall redeem.

14 *a*Ex. 10:2;
12:26, 27;
13:8; Deut.
6:20; Josh.
4:6, 21 *b*Ex.
13:3, 9

14 "*a*And it shall be when your son asks you in time to come, saying, 'What is this?' then you shall say to him, '*b*With a powerful hand the Lord brought us out of Egypt, from the house of slavery.

15 *a*Ex.
12:29

15 'And it came about, when Pharaoh was stubborn about letting us go, that the *a*Lord killed

---

13:2 *Sanctify.* I.e., consider all the firstborn males of both man and beast as belonging to God (cf. vv. 12-13).

13:9 On the basis of this verse coupled with Deut. 6:8 and 11:18, some Jews still wear phylacteries (little leather pouches containing short sections of the Law, bound on the forehead and on the left arm above the elbow). For a detailed description of this practice and its abuse, see note on Matt. 23:5.

13:13 The *donkey* was an unclean animal (Lev. 11:2-7), and so could not be sacrificed to God. It either had to be killed or have a lamb used as a substitute sacrifice for it (so also for other unclean animals, cf. Num. 18:15). The word *redeem* means "to buy back for a price."

every first-born in the land of Egypt, both the first-born of man and the first-born of beast. Therefore, I sacrifice to the LORD the males, the first offspring of every womb, but every first-born of my sons I redeem.'

★16 [a]Ex. 13:9; Deut. 6:8

16 "So [a]it shall serve as a sign on your hand, and as phylacteries on your forehead, for with a powerful hand the LORD brought us out of Egypt."

C The Direction of the Cloud and Fire, 13:17-22

★17 [a]Ex. 14:11, 12; Num. 14:1-4; Deut. 17:16

17 Now it came about when Pharaoh had let the people go, that God did not lead them by the way of the land of the Philistines, even though it was near; for God said, "[a]Lest the people change their minds when they see war, and they return to Egypt."

★18 [a]Josh. 1:14; 4:12, 13

18 Hence God led the people around by the way of the wilderness to the Red Sea; and the sons of Israel went up [a]in martial array from the land of Egypt.

★19 [a]Gen. 50:24, 25; Josh. 24:32; Acts 7:15, 16

20 [a]Ex. 12:37; Num. 33:6

19 And Moses took [a]the bones of Joseph with him, for he had made the sons of Israel solemnly swear, saying, "God shall surely take care of you; and you shall carry my bones from here with you."

★21-22
21 [a]Ex. 14:19, 24; 33:9, 10; Num. 9:15; 14:14; Deut. 1:33; Neh. 9:12; Ps. 78:14; 99:7; 105:39; Is. 4:5; 1 Cor. 10:1

20 Then they set out from [a]Succoth and camped in Etham on the edge of the wilderness.

21 And [a]the LORD was going before them in a pillar of cloud by day to lead them on the way, and in a pillar of fire by night to give them light, that they might travel by day and by night.

22 [a]Neh. 9:19

22 He [a]did not take away the pillar of cloud by day, nor the pillar of fire by night, from before the people.

D The Drying Up of the Red Sea, 14:1-22

14 Now the LORD spoke to Moses, saying,

★ 2 [a]Num. 33:7 [b]Jer. 44:1

2 "Tell the sons of Israel to turn back and camp before [a]Pi-hahiroth, between [b]Migdol and the sea; you shall camp in front of Baal-zephon, opposite it, by the sea.

3 "For Pharaoh will say of the sons of Israel, 'They are wandering aimlessly in the land; the wilderness has shut them in.'

4 [a]Ex. 4:21; 7:3; 14:17 [b]Ex. 14:23 [c]Ex. 7:5; 14:25

4 "Thus [a]I will harden Pharaoh's heart, and [b]he will chase after them; and I will be honored through Pharaoh and all his army, and [c]the Egyptians will know that I am the LORD." And they did so.

5 When the king of Egypt was told that the people had fled, Pharaoh and his servants had a change of heart toward the people, and they said, "What is this we have done, that we have let Israel go from serving us?"

6 So he made his chariot ready and took his people with him;

13:16 *phylacteries.* From a word meaning "prayers" or "prayer cases." See note on v. 9.
13:17 God did not allow the people to take the direct route along the Mediterranean coast to Palestine (which would have been a journey of only a few weeks). This route was heavily guarded by Egyptian troops but, more significantly, the Israelites had a divine appointment to keep at Mt. Sinai (see 3:12).
13:18 The place of the crossing of the *Red Sea* was likely the northern extension of the Gulf of Suez, S. of the modern port of Suez. While the phrase literally means "Sea of Reeds," the reference is to the Red Sea, not simply to a marshy land (see also Num. 14:25; Acts 7:36; Heb. 11:29). *in martial array.* Organized and

equipped for the march. Not necessarily armed, but not in disarray as fleeing fugitives would be (cf. 7:4).
13:19 See Gen. 50:25 and Josh. 24:32.
13:21-22 The *pillar* of *cloud* and of *fire* guided the people through the wilderness and assured them of God's presence. It also protected them from the Egyptians (cf. 14:19-20).
14:2 The location of these places is uncertain, but the route of march was changed from southeasterly (which, if continued, would have brought the Israelites in conflict with the Egyptian border guards) to southwesterly (which put the Red Sea between them and Canaan).

7 and he took six hundred select chariots, and all the *other* chariots of Egypt with officers over all of them.

★ **8** *a*Ex. 14:4 *b*Num. 33:3; Acts 13:17

8 And *a*the LORD hardened the heart of Pharaoh, king of Egypt, and he chased after the sons of Israel as the sons of Israel were going out *b*boldly.

9 *a*Ex. 15:9; Josh. 24:6 *b*Ex. 14:2

9 Then *a*the Egyptians chased after them *with* all the horses *and* chariots of Pharaoh, his horsemen and his army, and they overtook them camping by the sea, *b*beside Pi-hahiroth, in front of Baal-zephon.

10 *a*Josh. 24:7; Neh. 9:9; Ps. 34:17; 107:6

10 And as Pharaoh drew near, the sons of Israel looked, and behold, the Egyptians were marching after them, and they became very frightened; *a*so the sons of Israel cried out to the LORD.

★**11** *a*Ex. 5:21; 15:24; 16:2; Ps. 106:7, 8

11 Then *a*they said to Moses, "Is it because there were no graves in Egypt that you have taken us away to die in the wilderness? Why have you dealt with us in this way, bringing us out of Egypt?

★**12** *a*Ex. 6:9

12 "*a*Is this not the word that we spoke to you in Egypt, saying, 'Leave us alone that we may serve the Egyptians'? For it would have been better for us to serve the Egyptians than to die in the wilderness."

★**13** *a*Gen. 15:1; 46:3; Ex. 20:20; 2 Chr. 20:15, 17; Is. 41:10, 13, 14 *b*Ex. 14:30; 15:2

13 But Moses said to the people, "*a*Do not fear! Stand by and see *b*the salvation of the LORD which He will accomplish for you today; for the Egyptians whom you have seen today, you will never see them again forever.

14 *a*Ex. 14:25; 15:3; Deut. 1:30; 3:22; Josh. 23:3; 2 Chr. 20:29; Neh. 4:20 *b*Is. 30:15

14 "*a*The LORD will fight for you while *b*you keep silent."

15 Then the LORD said to Moses, "Why are you crying out to Me? Tell the sons of Israel to go forward.

16 "And as for you, lift up *a*your staff and stretch out your hand over the sea and divide it, and the sons of Israel shall go through the midst of the sea on dry land.

16 *a*Ex. 4:17, 20; 7:19; 14:21, 26; 17:5, 6, 9; Num. 20:8, 9, 11; Is. 10:26

17 "And as for Me, behold, *a*I will harden the hearts of the Egyptians so that they will go in after them; and I will be honored through Pharaoh and all his army, through his chariots and his horsemen.

17 *a*Ex. 14:4, 8

18 "*a*Then the Egyptians will know that I am the LORD, when I am honored through Pharaoh, through his chariots and his horsemen."

18 *a*Ex. 14:25

19 And *a*the angel of God, who had been going before the camp of Israel, moved and went behind them; and the pillar of cloud moved from before them and stood behind them.

★**19-22**

19 *a*Ex. 13:21, 22

20 So it came between the camp of Egypt and the camp of Israel; and there was the cloud along with the darkness, yet it gave light at night. Thus the one did not come near the other all night.

21 *a*Then Moses stretched out his hand over the sea; and the LORD swept the sea *back* by a strong east wind all night, and turned the sea into *b*dry land, so *c*the waters were divided.

21 *a*Ex. 7:19; 14:16 *b*Ps. 66:6; 106:9; 136:13, 14 *c*Ex. 15:8; Josh. 3:16; 4:23; Neh. 9:11; Ps. 74:13; 78:13; 114:3, 5; Is. 63:12, 13

22 *a*And the sons of Israel went through the midst of the sea on the dry land, and *b*the waters *were like* a wall to them on their right hand and on their left.

22 *a*Ex. 15:19; Josh. 3:17; 4:22; Neh. 9:11; Ps. 66:6; 78:13; Heb. 11:29 *b*Ex. 14:29; 15:8

E The Destruction of the Pursuing Egyptians, 14:23-31

23 Then *a*the Egyptians took up the pursuit, and all Pharaoh's horses, his chariots and his horse-

23 *a*Ex. 14:4, 17

14:8 *boldly.* Lit., with a high hand; i.e., confidently and in defiance of Pharaoh (cf. note on Num. 15:30).

14:11 *no graves.* The people spoke with bitter sarcasm, in view of the abnormal preoccupation of the Egyptians with tombs!

14:12 Cf. 5:21.

14:13 *Stand by.* Better, stand firm.

14:19-22 *the angel of God.* See note on Gen. 16:10. By moving behind the Israelites, the cloud protected them from the Egyptians, while the *strong east wind* (the prevailing wind is north to south) parted the water and dried the land underneath.

men went in after them into the midst of the sea.

★24 aEx. 13:21

24 And it came about at the morning watch, that athe LORD looked down on the army of the Egyptians through the pillar of fire and cloud and brought the army of the Egyptians into confusion.

★25 aEx. 14:4, 14, 18

25 And He caused their chariot wheels to swerve, and He made them drive with difficulty; so the Egyptians said, "Let us flee from Israel, afor the LORD is fighting for them against the Egyptians."

26 aEx. 14:16

26 Then the LORD said to Moses, "aStretch out your hand over the sea so that the waters may come back over the Egyptians, over their chariots and their horsemen."

27 aJosh. 4:18 bEx. 15:1, 7; Deut. 11:4; Neh. 9:11; Ps. 78:53; Heb. 11:29

27 So Moses stretched out his hand over the sea, and athe sea returned to its normal state at daybreak, while the Egyptians were fleeing right into it; then the LORD boverthrew the Egyptians in the midst of the sea.

28 aPs. 78:53; 106:11

28 And the waters returned and covered the chariots and the horsemen, even Pharaoh's entire army that had gone into the sea after them; anot even one of them remained.

29 aEx. 14:22; Ps. 66:6; Is. 11:15

29 But the sons of Israel walked on adry land through the midst of the sea, and the waters *were like* a wall to them on their right hand and on their left.

30 aEx. 14:13; Ps. 106:8, 10; Is. 63:8, 11 bPs. 58:10; 59:10

30 aThus the LORD saved Israel that day from the hand of the Egyptians, and Israel bsaw the Egyptians dead on the seashore.

31 aEx. 4:31; 19:9; Ps. 106:12; John 2:11; 11:45

31 And when Israel saw the great power which the LORD had used against the Egyptians, the people feared the LORD, and athey believed in the LORD and in His servant Moses.

F   The Deliverance Sung by Moses and the People, 15:1-21

★ 1-21

15 aThen Moses and the sons of Israel sang this song to the LORD, and said,

1 aPs. 106:12; Rev. 15:3 bIs. 12:5; 42:10- 12 cJer. 51:21

"bI will sing to the LORD, for He is highly exalted;
cThe horse and its rider He has hurled into the sea.

2 aPs. 18:1, 2; Is. 12:2; Hab. 3:18f. bPs. 48:14 cEx. 3:6, 15, 16 d2 Sam. 22:47; Ps. 99:5; Is. 25:1

2 "aThe LORD is my strength and song,
And He has become my salvation;
bThis is my God, and I will praise Him;
cMy father's God, and I will dextol Him.

3 aEx. 14:14; Rev. 19:11 bEx. 3:15; 6:2, 3, 7, 8; Ps. 24:8; 83:18

3 "aThe LORD is a warrior;
bThe LORD is His name.

4 aEx. 14:6, 7, 17, 28

4 "aPharaoh's chariots and his army He has cast into the sea;
And the choicest of his officers are drowned in the Red Sea.

5 aEx. 15:10; Neh. 9:11

5 "The deeps cover them;
aThey went down into the depths like a stone.

6 aEx. 3:20; 6:1 bPs. 118:15, 16

6 "aThy right hand, O LORD, is majestic in power,
bThy right hand, O LORD, shatters the enemy.

7 aEx. 14:27 bPs. 78:49, 50 cDeut. 4:24; Is. 5:24; Heb. 12:29

7 "And in the greatness of Thine excellence Thou adost overthrow those who rise up against Thee;
bThou dost send forth Thy burning anger, *and* it cconsumes them as chaff.

14:24 *the morning watch.* From 2 a.m. to dawn.
14:25 *caused their chariot wheels to swerve.* Apparently the meaning is that God caused their wheels to be clogged with the sand and mud, though it may mean the wheels were broken off.

15:1-21 This beautiful song of Moses and the people exalts the greatness of God, exhibited in His victory over the Egyptians.

8 *a*Ex.
14:22, 29;
Job 4:9 *b*Ps.
78:13

8 "*a*And at the blast of Thy
nostrils the waters
were piled up,
*b*The flowing waters
stood up like a heap;
The deeps were con-
gealed in the heart of
the sea.

9 *a*Ex. 14:5,
8, 9 *b*Judg.
5:30; Is.
53:12; Luke
11:22

9 "*a*The enemy said, 'I will
pursue, I will over-
take, I will *b*divide the
spoil;
My desire shall be grati-
fied against them;
I will draw out my
sword, my hand shall
destroy them.'

10 *a*Ex.
14:27, 28
*b*Ex. 15:5

10 "*a*Thou didst blow with
Thy wind, the sea
covered them;
*b*They sank like lead in
the mighty waters.

11 *a*Ex. 8:10;
9:14; Deut.
3:24; 2 Sam.
7:22; 1 Kin.
8:23; Ps.
71:19; 86:8;
Mic. 7:18
*b*Is. 6:3; Rev.
4:8 *c*Ps.
22:23 *d*Ps.
72:18; 136:4

11 "*a*Who is like Thee
among the gods, O
Lord?
Who is like Thee, *b*ma-
jestic in holiness,
*c*Awesome in praises,
*d*working wonders?

12 *a*Ex. 15:6

12 "*a*Thou didst stretch out
Thy right hand,
The earth swallowed
them.

★13 *a*Neh.
9:12; Ps.
77:20 *b*Ex.
15:16; Ps.
77:15 *c*Ex.
15:17; Ps.
78:54

13 "In Thy lovingkindness
Thou hast *a*led the
people whom Thou
hast *b*redeemed;
In Thy strength Thou
hast guided *them* *c*to
Thy holy habitation.

★14 *a*Deut.
2:25; Hab.
3:7

14 "*a*The peoples have
heard, they tremble;
Anguish has gripped the
inhabitants of Philis-
tia.

15 *a*Gen.
36:15, 40
*b*Num. 22:3,
4 *c*Josh. 2:9,
11, 24; 5:1

15 "Then the *a*chiefs of
Edom were dismayed;
*b*The leaders of Moab,
trembling grips them;
*c*All the inhabitants of
Canaan have melted
away.

16 "*a*Terror and dread fall
upon them;
*b*By the greatness of
Thine arm they are
motionless as stone;
Until Thy people pass
over, O Lord,
Until the people pass
over whom Thou
*c*hast purchased.

16 *a*Ex.
23:27; Deut.
2:25; Josh.
2:9 *b*Ex.
15:5, 6 *c*Ex.
15:13; Ps.
74:2; Is.
43:1; Jer.
31:11; Titus
2:14; 2 Pet.
2:1

17 "*a*Thou wilt bring them
and *b*plant them in
*c*the mountain of
Thine inheritance,
*d*The place, O Lord,
which Thou hast
made for Thy dwell-
ing,
*e*The sanctuary, O Lord,
which Thy hands
have established.

17 *a*Ex.
23:20; 32:34
*b*Ps. 44:2;
80:8, 15 *c*Ps.
2:6; 78:54,
68 *d*Ps.
68:16; 76:2;
132:13, 14
*e*Ps. 78:69

18 "*a*The Lord shall reign
forever and ever."

18 *a*Ps.
10:16; 29:10;
Is. 57:15

19 *a*For the horses of Pharaoh
with his chariots and his horsemen went into the sea, and the
Lord brought back the waters of
the sea on them; but the sons of
Israel walked on *b*dry land
through the midst of the sea.

19 *a*Ex.
14:23, 28
*b*Ex. 14:22,
29

20 And *a*Miriam the prophetess, Aaron's sister, took the *b*timbrel in her hand, and all the
women went out after her with
timbrels and with *c*dancing.

★20-21

20 *a*Ex. 2:4;
Num. 26:59;
1 Chr. 6:3;
Mic. 6:4
*b*Judg.
11:34;
1 Sam. 18:6;
1 Chr. 15:16;
Ps. 68:25;
81:2; 149:3;
Jer. 31:4
*c*Judg.
11:34; 21:21;
1 Sam. 18:6;
Ps. 30:11;
150:4

21 And Miriam answered
them,

"*a*Sing to the Lord, for He
is highly exalted;
The horse and his rider
He has hurled into the
sea."

21 *a*Ex. 15:1

G The Dissatisfaction of the People, 15:22–17:7

1 The complaint about bitter water, 15:22–27

22 *a*Then Moses led Israel
from the Red Sea, and they went
out into *b*the wilderness of *c*Shur;

★22 *a*Ps.
77:20; 78:52,
53 *b*Num.
33:8 *c*Gen.
16:7; 20:1;
25:18

15:13 *lovingkindness.* Heb., *hesed.* See note on
Hos. 2:19.
15:14 *Philistia.* I.e., Palestine.
15:20-21 *Miriam* and a chorus of *women,* dancing and using *timbrels* (similar to tambou-

rines), repeated verse 21b as a refrain, perhaps
at various intervals during the song.
15:22 *the wilderness of Shur.* The entire desert
region between Egypt and Palestine.

and they went three days in the wilderness and found no water.

★23 aNum. 33:8; Ruth 1:20

23 And when they came to aMarah, they could not drink the waters of Marah, for they were bitter; therefore it was named Marah.

24 aEx. 14:11; 16:2; Ps. 106:13

24 So the people agrumbled at Moses, saying, "What shall we drink?"

25 aEx. 14:10 bEzek. 47:7, 8 cJosh. 24:25 dEx. 16:4; Deut. 8:2, 16; Judg. 2:22; 3:1, 4; Ps. 66:10

25 Then he acried out to the LORD, and the LORD showed him ba tree; and he threw it into the waters, and the waters became sweet. There He cmade for them a statute and regulation, and there He dtested them.

★26 aEx. 19:5, 6; Deut. 7:12 bEx. 20:2-17 cDeut. 7:15; 28:58, 60 dEx. 23:25; Deut. 32:39; Ps. 41:3, 4; 103:3; 147:3

26 And He said, "aIf you will give earnest heed to the voice of the LORD your God, and do what is right in His sight, and give ear bto His commandments, and keep all His statutes, cI will put none of the diseases on you which I have put on the Egyptians; for I, dthe LORD, am your healer."

★27 aNum. 33:9

27 Then they came to aElim where there were twelve springs of water and seventy date palms, and they camped there beside the waters.

2 The complaint about hunger: the manna, 16:1-36

★ 1 aNum. 33:10, 11; Ezek. 30:15 bEx. 12:6, 51; 19:1

16 Then they set out from Elim, and all the congregation of the sons of Israel came to the wilderness of aSin, which is between Elim and Sinai, on bthe fifteenth day of the second month after their departure from the land of Egypt.

2 aEx. 14:11; 15:24; Ps. 106:25; 1 Cor. 10:10

2 And the whole congregation of the sons of Israel agrumbled against Moses and Aaron in the wilderness.

★ 3 aEx. 17:3; Num. 14:2, 3; 20:3; Lam. 4:9 bNum. 11:4, 5

3 And the sons of Israel said to them, "aWould that we had died by the LORD's hand in the land of Egypt, bwhen we sat by the pots of meat, when we ate bread to the full; for you have brought us out into this wilderness to kill this whole assembly with hunger."

4 Then the LORD said to Moses, "Behold, aI will rain bread from heaven for you; and the people shall go out and gather a day's portion every day, that I may btest them, whether or not they will walk in My instruction.

4 aNeh. 9:15; Ps. 78:23-25; 105:40; John 6:31; 1 Cor. 10:3 bEx. 15:25; Deut. 8:2, 16

5 "And it will come about aon the sixth day, when they prepare what they bring in, it will be twice as much as they gather daily."

5 aEx. 16:22

6 So Moses and Aaron said to all the sons of Israel, "At evening ayou will know that the LORD has brought you out of the land of Egypt;

6 aEx. 6:7

7 and in the morning you will see athe glory of the LORD, for bHe hears your grumblings against the LORD; and cwhat are we, that you grumble against us?"

7 aEx. 16:10, 12; Is. 35:2; 40:5; John 11:4, 40 bNum. 14:27; 17:5 cNum. 16:11

8 And Moses said, "This will happen when the LORD gives you meat to eat in the evening, and bread to the full in the morning; for the LORD hears your grumblings which you grumble against Him. And what are we? Your grumblings are anot against us but against the LORD."

8 a1 Sam. 8:7; Luke 10:16; Rom. 13:2; 1 Thess. 4:8

9 Then Moses said to Aaron, "Say to all the congregation of the sons of Israel, 'aCome near before the LORD, for He has heard your grumblings.'"

9 aNum. 16:16

10 And it came about as Aaron spoke to the whole congregation of the sons of Israel, that they looked toward the wilderness, and behold, athe glory of the LORD appeared in the cloud.

10 aEx. 13:21; 16:7; Num. 16:19; 1 Kin. 8:10f.

11 And the LORD spoke to Moses, saying,

12 "aI have heard the grumblings of the sons of Israel; speak to them, saying, 'At twilight you shall eat meat, and in the morning you shall be filled with bread; and

12 aEx. 16:8; Num. 14:27 bEx. 6:7; 16:7; 1 Kin. 20:28; Joel 3:17

15:23 *Marah.* Traditionally located about 47 miles SE. of the modern town of Suez.

15:26 *diseases* refers to the plagues, particularly the plague that turned the water to blood, making it unusable.

15:27 *Elim,* meaning "trees," was about 7 miles S. of Marah.

16:1 They had left Egypt one month before.

16:3 The Israelites were accustomed to a good diet in Egypt (cf. Num. 11:5).

★13 *a*Num.
11:31; Ps.
78:27-29;
105:40
*b*Num. 11:9

*b*you shall know that I am the Lord your God.'"

13 So it came about at evening that *a*the quails came up and covered the camp, and in the morning *b*there was a layer of dew around the camp.

14 *a*Num.
11:7-9 *b*Ex.
16:31; Neh.
9:15; Ps.
78:24;
105:40

14 *a*When the layer of dew evaporated, behold, on the surface of the wilderness *b*there was a fine flake-like thing, fine as the frost on the ground.

★15 *a*Ex.
16:4; Neh.
9:15; Ps.
78:24; John
6:31; 1 Cor.
10:3

15 When the sons of Israel saw *it*, they said to one another, "What is it?" For they did not know what it was. And Moses said to them, "*a*It is the bread which the Lord has given you to eat.

★16 *a*Ex.
16:32, 36

16 "This is what the Lord has commanded, 'Gather of it every man as much as he should eat; you shall take *a*an omer apiece according to the number of persons each of you has in his tent.'"

17 And the sons of Israel did so, and *some* gathered much and *some* little.

★18 *a*2 Cor.
8:15

18 When they measured it with an omer, *a*he who had gathered much had no excess, and he who had gathered little had no lack; every man gathered as much as he should eat.

19 *a*Ex.
12:10; 16:23;
23:18

19 And Moses said to them, "*a*Let no man leave any of it until morning."

20 But they did not listen to Moses, and some left part of it until morning, and it bred worms and became foul; and Moses was angry with them.

21 And they gathered it morning by morning, every man as much as he should eat; but when the sun grew hot, it would melt.

22 *a*Now it came about on the sixth day they gathered twice as much bread, two omers for each one. When all the *b*leaders of the congregation came and told Moses,

22 *a*Ex. 16:5
*b*Ex. 34:31

23 then he said to them, "This is what the Lord meant: *a*Tomorrow is a sabbath observance, a holy sabbath to the Lord. Bake what you will bake and boil what you will boil, and *b*all that is left over put aside to be kept until morning."

★23 *a*Gen.
2:3; Ex. 20:8-
11; 23:12;
31:15; 35:2;
Lev. 23:3;
Neh. 9:13, 14
*b*Ex. 16:19

24 So they put it aside until morning, as Moses had ordered, and *a*it did not become foul, nor was there any worm in it.

24 *a*Ex.
16:20

25 And Moses said, "Eat it today, for today is a sabbath to the Lord; today you will not find it in the field.

26 "*a*Six days you shall gather it, but on the seventh day, *the* sabbath, there will be none."

26 *a*Ex. 20:9,
10

27 And it came about on the seventh day that some of the people went out to gather, but they found none.

28 Then the Lord said to Moses, "*a*How long do you refuse to keep My commandments and My instructions?

28 *a*2 Kin.
17:14; Ps.
78:10;
106:13

29 "See, the Lord has given you the sabbath; therefore He gives you bread for two days on the sixth day. Remain every man in his place; let no man go out of his place on the seventh day."

30 So the people rested on the seventh day.

31 And the house of *a*Israel named it manna, and it was like *b*coriander seed, white; and its taste was like wafers with honey.

31 *a*Num.
11:7-9; Deut.
8:3, 16 *b*Ex.
16:14

32 Then Moses said, "This is what the Lord has commanded, 'Let an omerful of it be kept

---

16:13 *quails.* Short-winged, bullet-headed little birds that are easily caught when exhausted from flight and were considered a delicacy. On a later occasion God used them to bring a plague on the people (Num. 11:31-34).

16:15 *What is it?* The Hebrew (*manna*) means "what?"—as if to say, "the what's its name." This food is further described in verse 31, Num. 11:7-9, Psalm 78:24-25, and Psalm 105:40.

16:16 *an omer.* Perhaps about 2 quarts, though it is uncertain as to what exact measure an omer represented at this time.

16:18 The meaning is that they pooled the manna collected so that each had an omer.

16:23 The seventh day was here set aside as a holy day to the Lord. At Sinai it became a part of the Law and a sign of God's covenant relationship with His people (cf. 20:8-11; 31:12-17).

throughout your generations, that they may see the bread that I fed you in the wilderness, when I brought you out of the land of Egypt.'"

33 aHeb. 9:4; Rev. 2:17

33 And Moses said to Aaron, "aTake a jar and put an omerful of manna in it, and place it before the LORD, to be kept throughout your generations."

★**34** aEx. 25:16, 21; 27:21; 40:20; Num. 17:10

34 As the LORD commanded Moses, so Aaron placed it before athe Testimony, to be kept.

35 aDeut. 8:2f.; Josh. 5:12; Neh. 9:20, 21

35 aAnd the sons of Israel ate the manna forty years, until they came to an inhabited land; they ate the manna until they came to the border of the land of Canaan.

36 aEx. 16:16

36 (Now aan omer is a tenth of an ephah.)

3 The complaint about lack of water, 17:1-7

★ 1 aEx. 16:1; Num. 33:12 bEx. 19:2; Num. 33:14

17 Then all the congregation of the sons of Israel journeyed by stages from the wilderness of aSin, according to the command of the LORD, and camped at bRephidim, and there was no water for the people to drink.

★ 2 aEx. 14:11; Num. 20:2, 3, 13 bEx. 16:8 cDeut. 6:16; Ps. 78:18, 41; Matt. 4:7; 1 Cor. 10:9

2 Therefore the people aquarreled with Moses and said, "Give us water that we may drink." And Moses said to them, "bWhy do you quarrel with me? cWhy do you test the LORD?"

3 aEx. 16:2, 3 bEx. 12:38

3 But the people thirsted there for water; and they agrumbled against Moses and said, "Why, now, have you brought us up from Egypt, to kill us and our children and bour livestock with thirst?"

4 aNum. 14:10; 1 Sam. 30:6

4 So Moses cried out to the LORD, saying, "What shall I do to

this people? A alittle more and they will stone me."

5 aEx. 3:16, 18 bEx. 7:20

5 Then the LORD said to Moses, "Pass before the people and take with you some of athe elders of Israel; and take in your hand your staff with which byou struck the Nile, and go.

★ 6 aEx. 3:1 bNum. 20:10, 11; Deut. 8:15; Neh. 9:15; Ps. 78:15; 105:41; 114:8, 1 Cor. 10:4

6 "Behold, I will stand before you there on the rock at aHoreb; and byou shall strike the rock, and water will come out of it, that the people may drink." And Moses did so in the sight of the elders of Israel.

7 aDeut. 6:16, 9:22; Ps. 95:8 bNum. 20:13, 24; 27:14; Ps. 81:7 cNum. 14:22; Deut. 33:8

7 And he named the place aMassah and bMeribah because of the quarrel of the sons of Israel, and because they ctested the LORD, saying, "Is the LORD among us, or not?"

H The Defeat of Amalek, 17:8-16

★ 8 aGen. 36:12; Num. 24:20; Deut. 25:17-19; 1 Sam. 15:2 bEx. 17:1

8 Then aAmalek came and fought against Israel at bRephidim.

★ 9 aEx. 24:13 bEx. 4:20

9 So Moses said to aJoshua, "Choose men for us, and go out, fight against Amalek. Tomorrow I will station myself on the top of the hill with bthe staff of God in my hand."

★10 aEx. 24:14, 31:2

10 And Joshua did as Moses told him, and fought against Amalek; and Moses, Aaron, and aHur went up to the top of the hill.

11 So it came about when Moses held his hand up, that Israel prevailed, and when he let his hand down, Amalek prevailed.

12 aIs. 35:3

12 But Moses' hands were heavy. Then they took a stone and put it under him, and he sat

---

16:34 the Testimony refers to the two tables of the Law, which, along with manna and Aaron's rod that budded, were deposited in the Ark of the Covenant (cf. Heb. 9:4).

17:1 Stops were made at Dophkah and Ahush before reaching Rephidim (see Num. 33:11-14).

17:2 quarreled. This explains why the place was called Meribah (v. 7), which means "argument" or "strife." test. The root behind the word Massah (v. 7).

17:6 Horeb. See note on 3:1.

17:8 The tribe of Amalek, descendants of Esau's grandson (cf. Gen. 36:12), attacked Israel from the rear, assaulting the stragglers (see Deut. 25:17-18).

17:9 This is the first mention of Joshua, who was about 45 at this time.

17:10 Hur, who tradition says was married to Miriam, Moses' sister, is mentioned only here and in 24:14.

on it; and Aaron and Hur ªsupported his hands, one on one side and one on the other. Thus his hands were steady until the sun set.

13 So Joshua overwhelmed Amalek and his people with the edge of the sword.

14 Then the LORD said to Moses, "ªWrite this in a book as a memorial, and recite it to Joshua, that ᵇI will utterly blot out the memory of Amalek from under heaven."

15 And Moses built an ªaltar, and named it ᵇThe LORD is My Banner;

16 and he said, "ªThe LORD has sworn; the LORD will have war against Amalek from generation to generation."

I   The Division of Responsibility,
18:1–27

18 Now ªJethro, the priest of Midian, Moses' father-in-law, heard of all that God had done for Moses and for Israel His people, how the LORD had brought Israel out of Egypt.

2 And Jethro, Moses' father-in-law, took Moses' wife ªZipporah, after he had sent her away,

3 and her ªtwo sons, of whom one was named Gershom, for he said, "I have been ᵇa sojourner in a foreign land."

4 And the other was named ªEliezer, for he said, "ᵇThe God of my father was my help, and delivered me from the sword of Pharaoh."

5 Then Jethro, Moses' father-in-law, came with his sons and his wife to Moses in the wilderness where he was camped, at ªthe mount of God.

6 And he sent word to Moses, "I, your father-in-law Jethro, am coming to you with your wife and her two sons with her."

7 Then Moses went out to meet his father-in-law, and ªhe bowed down and ᵇkissed him; and they ᶜasked each other of their welfare, and went into the tent.

8 And Moses told his father-in-law all that the LORD had done to Pharaoh and to the Egyptians ªfor Israel's sake, all the ᵇhardship that had befallen them on the journey, and how ᶜthe LORD had delivered them.

9 And Jethro rejoiced over all ªthe goodness which the LORD had done to Israel, in delivering them from the hand of the Egyptians.

10 So Jethro said, "ªBlessed be the LORD who delivered you from the hand of the Egyptians and from the hand of Pharaoh, *and* who delivered the people from under the hand of the Egyptians.

11 "Now I know that ªthe LORD is greater than all the gods; indeed, ᵇit was proven when they dealt proudly against the people."

12 ªThen Jethro, Moses' father-in-law, took a burnt offering and sacrifices for God, and Aaron came with all the elders of Israel to eat a meal with Moses' father-in-law before God.

13 And it came about the next day that Moses sat to judge the people, and the people stood about Moses from the morning until the evening.

Margin references

★14 ªEx. 24:4; 34:27; Num. 33:2 ᵇDeut. 25:19; 1 Sam. 15:3

★15 ªEx. 24:4 ᵇGen. 22:14; Judg. 6:24

16 ªGen. 22:16

1 ªEx. 2:16; 18; 3:1

★ 2-3
2 ªEx. 2:21; 4:25
3 ªEx. 2:22; 4:20; Acts 7:29 ᵇEx. 2:22

★ 4 ª1 Chr. 23:15, 17 ᵇGen. 49:25

★ 5 ªEx. 3:1, 12; 4:27; 24:13

7 ªGen. 43:26, 28 ᵇGen. 29:13; Ex. 4:27 ᶜGen. 43:27; 2 Sam. 11:7

8 ªEx. 4:23; 7:4, 5 ᵇNum. 20:14; Neh. 9:32 ᶜEx. 15:6, 16

9 ªIs. 63:7-14

10 ªGen. 14:20; 2 Sam. 18:28; 1 Kin. 8:56; Ps. 68:19, 20

★11-12
11 ªEx. 12:12; 15:11; 2 Chr. 2:5; Ps. 95:3; 97:9; 135:5 ᵇLuke 1:51

12 ªGen. 31:54; Ex. 24:5

★13-27

Footnotes

17:14 A judgment on *Amalek* occurred in Saul's time (cf. 1 Sam. 15). See also Num. 14:45 and note on Esther 3:1.

17:15 *The LORD is My Banner.* Heb., *Yahweh-nissi.*

18:2-3 See note on 4:24. On *Gershom*, see note on 2:22.

18:4 *Eliezer* means "my God is help." This is the only mention of Moses' second son.

18:5 *the mount of God.* Sinai, where the Law was shortly to be given.

18:11-12 The events of the Exodus confirmed Jethro's previous faith in the true God, and as a consequence he offered *sacrifices.*

18:13-27 Seeing Moses bogged down in adjudicating civil cases, Jethro recommended choosing others who were morally qualified to do this job (v. 21). However, the actual implementation of this suggestion was not until after the giving of the Law (Deut. 1:5-15).

14 Now when Moses' father-in-law saw all that he was doing for the people, he said, "What is this thing that you are doing for the people? Why do you alone sit *as judge* and all the people stand about you from morning until evening?"

15 And Moses said to his father-in-law, "Because the people come to me ^ato inquire of God.

16 "When they have a ^adispute, it comes to me, and I judge between a man and his neighbor, and make known the statutes of God and His laws."

17 And Moses' father-in-law said to him, "The thing that you are doing is not good.

18 "^aYou will surely wear out, both yourself and these people who are with you, for the task is too heavy for you; ^byou cannot do it alone.

19 "Now listen to me: I shall give you counsel, and God be with you. You be the people's representative before God, and you ^abring the disputes to God,

20 ^athen teach them the statutes and the laws, and make known to them ^bthe way in which they are to walk, and the work they are to do.

21 "Furthermore, you shall select out of all the people ^aable men ^bwho fear God, men of truth, those who ^chate dishonest gain; and you shall place *these* over them, *as* leaders of thousands, of hundreds, of fifties and of tens.

22 "And let them judge the people at all times; and let it be ^athat every major dispute they will bring to you, but every minor dispute they themselves will judge. So it will be easier for you,

and ^bthey will bear *the burden* with you.

23 "If you do this thing and God *so* commands you, then you will be able to endure, and all these people also will go to their place in peace."

24 So Moses listened to his father-in-law, and did all that he had said.

25 And Moses chose ^aable men out of all Israel, and made them heads over the people, leaders of thousands, of hundreds, of fifties and of tens.

26 And they judged the people at all times; ^athe difficult dispute they would bring to Moses, but every minor dispute they themselves would judge.

27 Then Moses ^abade his father-in-law farewell, and he went his way into his own land.

III ISRAEL AT SINAI: REVELATION, 19:1-40:38

A The Giving of the Law, 19:1-24:18

1 *The covenant proposed and accepted,* 19:1-25

19 ^aIn the third month after the sons of Israel had gone out of the land of Egypt, on that very day they came into the wilderness of ^bSinai.

2 When they set out from ^aRephidim, they came to the wilderness of Sinai, and camped in the wilderness; and there Israel camped in front of ^bthe mountain.

3 And Moses went up to God, and ^athe LORD called to him

Marginal references (left column):
15 ^aNum. 9:6, 8; 27:5; Deut. 17:8-13
16 ^aEx. 24:14
18 ^aNum. 11:14, 17; Deut. 1:12 ^bDeut. 1:9
19 ^aNum. 27:5
20 ^aDeut. 1:18; 4:1, 5; 5:1 ^bPs. 143:8
21 ^aEx. 18:25; Deut. 1:13, 15; 2 Chr. 19:5-10; Ps. 15:1-5; Acts 6:3 ^bGen. 42:18; 2 Sam. 23:3 ^cDeut. 16:19
22 ^aDeut. 1:17, 18 ^bNum. 11:17

Marginal references (right column):
25 ^aEx. 18:21; Deut. 1:15
26 ^aEx. 18:22
27 ^aNum. 10:29, 30
★ 1 ^aEx. 12:6, 51; 16:1 ^bDeut. 1:6; 4:10, 15; 5:2
2 ^aEx. 17:1; Num. 33:15 ^bEx. 3:1, 12; 18:5
★ 3 ^aEx. 3:4

19:1 *In the third month* after the Israelites left Egypt; i.e., May-June (see note on 12:2). Mt. *Sinai* is usually identified as Jebel Musa, a 7,500-foot peak at the S. end of the "V" formed by the gulfs of Suez and Aqaba. At the foot of this peak is a plain 2½ miles long by ½ mile wide in which the people could easily have camped for the more than 11 months they were there.

19:3 The rest of this book, plus Leviticus and the first ten chapters of Numbers contain the

block of teaching known as the Mosaic Law. It was given in the form of a contemporary suzerainty treaty, a treaty between a powerful king and his vassals. A typical treaty contained a preamble (v. 3), historical introduction (with emphasis on the benevolence of the king, v. 4), specific obligations of the vassals, witnesses to the treaty, and a list of the consequences of keeping or breaking the treaty (i.e., blessings and curses).

from the mountain, saying, "Thus you shall say to the house of Jacob and tell the sons of Israel:

4 [a]You yourselves have seen what I did to the Egyptians, and *how* I bore you on [b]eagles' wings, and brought you to Myself.

5 'Now then, [a]if you will indeed obey My voice and [b]keep My covenant, then you shall be [c]My own possession among all the peoples, for [d]all the earth is Mine;

6 and you shall be to Me [a]a kingdom of priests and [b]a holy nation.' These are the words that you shall speak to the sons of Israel."

7 [a]So Moses came and called the elders of the people, and set before them all these words which the LORD had commanded him.

8 [a]And all the people answered together and said, "All that the LORD has spoken we will do!" And Moses brought back the words of the people to the LORD.

9 And the LORD said to Moses, "Behold, I shall come to you in [a]a thick cloud, in order that the [b]people may hear when I speak with you, and may also believe in you forever." Then Moses told the words of the people to the LORD.

10 The LORD also said to Moses, "Go to the people and [a]consecrate them today and tomorrow, and let them [b]wash their garments;

11 and let them be ready for the third day, for on [a]the third day the LORD will come down on Mount Sinai in the sight of all the people.

12 "And you shall set bounds for the people all around, saying, 'Beware that you do not go up on the mountain or touch the border of it; [a]whoever touches the mountain shall surely be put to death.

13 'No hand shall touch him, but [a]he shall surely be stoned or shot through; whether beast or man, he shall not live.' When the ram's horn sounds a long blast, they shall come up to [b]the mountain."

14 So Moses went down from the mountain to the people and consecrated the people, and they washed their garments.

15 And he said to the people, "Be ready for the third day; do not go near a woman."

16 [a]So it came about on the third day, when it was morning, that there were thunder and lightning flashes and a thick cloud upon the mountain and a very loud trumpet sound, so that all the people who *were* in the camp trembled.

17 And Moses brought the people out of the camp to meet God, and they stood at the foot of the mountain.

18 [a]Now Mount Sinai *was* all in smoke because the LORD descended upon it [b]in fire; and its smoke ascended like [c]the smoke of a furnace, and [d]the whole mountain quaked violently.

19 When the sound of the trumpet grew louder and louder, Moses spoke and [a]God answered him with thunder.

20 [a]And the LORD came down on Mount Sinai, to the top of the mountain; and the LORD called Moses to the top of the mountain, and Moses went up.

21 Then the LORD spoke to Moses, "Go down, warn the people, lest [a]they break through to the LORD to gaze, and many of them perish.

22 "And also let the [a]priests who come near to the LORD consecrate themselves, lest the LORD break out against them."

---

4 [a]Deut. 29:2 [b]Deut. 32:11; Rev. 12:14

★ **5-6**

5 [a]Ex. 15:26; Deut. 5:2f. [b]Ps. 78:10 [c]Deut. 4:20; 7:6; 14:2; 26:18; Ps. 135:4; Titus 2:14; 1 Pet. 2:9 [d]Ex. 9:29; Deut. 10:14; Job 41:11; Ps. 50:12; 1 Cor. 10:26

6 [a]1 Pet. 2:5, 9; Rev. 1:6; 5:10 [b]Deut. 7:6; 14:21; 26:19; Is. 62:12

7 [a]Ex. 4:29, 30

8 [a]Ex. 4:31; 24:3, 7; Deut. 5:27; 26:17

9 [a]Ex. 19:16; 24:15, 16; Deut. 4:11; Ps. 99:7 [b]Deut. 4:12, 36

★ **10-15**

10 [a]Lev. 11:44, 45 [b]Gen. 35:2; Lev. 15:5; Num. 8:7, 21; 19:19; Rev. 22:14

11 [a]Ex. 19:16

12 [a]Heb. 12:20

13 [a]Heb. 12:20 [b]Ex. 19:17

16 [a]Heb. 12:18, 19, 21

18 [a]Deut. 4:11; Ps. 104:32; 144:5 [b]Ex. 3:2; 24:17; Deut. 5:4; 2 Chr. 7:1-3; Heb. 12:18 [c]Gen. 15:17; 19:28 [d]Judg. 5:5; Ps. 68:7, 8; Jer. 4:24

19 [a]Ps. 81:7

20 [a]Neh. 9:13

21 [a]Ex. 3:5; 1 Sam. 6:19

22 [a]Ex. 19:24; 24:5; Lev. 10:3; 21:6-8

19:5-6 The relationship specified in the covenant was that of Israel's being God's *possession* (lit., a special treasure), a kingdom whose citizens were all *priests* with access to God, and a *holy nation*, separated from all other nations and devoted only to God.

19:10-15 Three things had to be done to prepare for God's appearance: cleansing of body and clothes (v. 10), confining the people to camp by placing barriers around the mountain (vv. 12-13; cf. v. 21), and abstaining from sexual relations (v. 15).

23 *a*Ex. 19:12

23 And Moses said to the LORD, "The people cannot come up to Mount Sinai, for Thou didst warn us, saying, '*a*Set bounds about the mountain and consecrate it.'"

24 *a*Ex. 24:1, 9, 12 *b*Ex. 19:22

24 Then the LORD said to him, "Go down and come up *again*, *a*you and Aaron with you; but do not let the *b*priests and the people break through to come up to the LORD, lest He break forth upon them."

25 So Moses went down to the people and told them.

★ 2 *a*Lev. 26:1; Deut. 5:6; Ps. 81:10 *b*Ex. 13:3; 15:13, 16; Deut. 7:8
★ 3 *a*Deut. 6:14; 2 Kin. 17:35; Jer. 25:6; 35:15 *b*Ex. 15:11; 20:23
★ 4-6
4 *a*Lev. 19:4; 26:1; Deut. 4:15-19; 27:15
5 *a*Ex. 23:24; Josh. 23:7; 2 Kin. 17:35 *b*Ex. 34:14; Deut. 4:24; Josh. 24:19; Nah. 1:2 *c*Ex. 34:6, 7; Num. 14:18, 33; Deut. 5:9, 10; 1 Kin. 21:29; Jer. 32:18

2   The Ten Commandments,
20:1-26

20 Then God spoke all these words, saying,

2 "*a*I am the LORD your God, *b*who brought you out of the land of Egypt, out of the house of slavery.

3 "*a*You shall have no other *b*gods before Me.

4 "*a*You shall not make for yourself an idol, or any likeness of what is in heaven above or on the earth beneath or in the water under the earth.

5 "*a*You shall not worship them or serve them; for I, the LORD your God, am a *b*jealous

God, *c*visiting the iniquity of the fathers on the children, on the third and the fourth generations of those who hate Me,

6 but showing lovingkindness to *a*thousands, to those who love Me and keep My commandments.

7 "*a*You shall not take the name of the LORD your God in vain, for the LORD will not leave him unpunished who takes His name in vain.

8 "Remember *a*the sabbath day, to keep it holy.

9 "*a*Six days you shall labor and do all your work,

10 but the seventh day is a sabbath of the LORD your God; *in it* *a*you shall not do any work, you or your son or your daughter, your male or your female servant or your cattle or your sojourner who stays with you.

11 "*a*For in six days the LORD made the heavens and the earth, the sea and all that is in them, and rested on the seventh day; therefore the LORD blessed the sabbath day and made it holy.

12 "*a*Honor your father and your mother, that your *b*days may be prolonged in the land which the LORD your God gives you.

13 "*a*You shall not murder.

6 *a*Deut. 7:9
★ 7 *a*Lev. 19:12; Deut. 6:13; 10:20
★ 8-11
8 *a*Ex. 23:12; 31:13-16; Lev. 26:2; Deut. 5:12
9 *a*Ex. 34:21; 35:2, 3; Lev. 23:3; Deut. 5:13; Luke 13:14
10 *a*Neh. 13:16-19
11 *a*Gen. 2:2, 3; Ex. 31:17
★12 *a*Lev. 19:3; Deut. 27:16; Matt. 15:4; 19:19; Mark 7:10; 10:19; Luke 18:20; Eph. 6:2 *b*Deut. 5:16, 33; 6:2; 11:8, 9; Jer. 35:7
★13 *a*Gen. 9:6; Ex. 21:12; Lev. 24:17; Matt. 5:21; 19:18; Mark 10:19; Luke 18:20; Rom. 13:9; James 2:11

20:2 This is the beginning of the "Ten Words" of the Law (cf. 34:28) that were written on two stone tablets (cf. 31:18). The Jews regard verse 2 as the first commandment and verses 3-6 as the second. Roman Catholics also group verses 3-6, but regard them as the first commandment; then they divide verse 17 into two commandments in order to have a total of ten. Most Protestants consider verse 3 to be the first commandment; verses 4-6, the second; and verse 17 the tenth.

20:3 *before Me.* Lit., in My sight; i.e., either in addition to Me or in opposition to Me. God will not share His worship with another.

20:4-6 *idol.* A figure of wood or stone that is an object of worship (cf. Deut. 5:7-9). Thus, the artistry employed in the tabernacle (cf. Exod. 25:17-22; 1 Kings 6:23-26) did not violate this commandment. Verse 5 states the cumulative effects of sin (but responsibility is always on the individual; see note on Ezek. 18:2). *lovingkindness. Heb., hesed,* refers to God's steadfast covenant love.

20:7 Prohibition against false swearing (cf. Lev. 19:12) and frivolous use of God's name. The use of an oath of affirmation was not forbidden (cf. Deut. 6:13).

20:8-11 The *sabbath* served as a holy day and a day of rest for both man and animals, commemorating God's rest after the work of creation (see notes on Gen. 2:2 and Exod. 16:23). Other instructions for the Sabbath are found in Exod. 35:3; Lev. 25; Num. 15:32-36; Deut. 5:13-15. This is the only one of the Ten Commandments not repeated after the day of Pentecost. The Church made Sunday her day of worship (Acts 20:7), commemorating the resurrection of Christ.

20:12 Proper order in the family becomes the basis for a solid social structure (cf. Deut. 21:18-21; Eph. 6:1-4).

20:13 *murder.* The law differentiated accidental killing from deliberate murder and required capital punishment for the latter (21:12-14) as well as for numerous other offences (21:15-17, 29, etc.).

*14 aLev.
20:10; Deut.
5:18; Matt.
5:27; 19:18;
Rom. 13:9

15 aEx.
21:16; Lev.
19:11, 13;
Matt. 19:18;
Rom. 13:9

16 aEx. 23:1,
7; Deut. 5:20;
Matt. 19:18
bLev. 19:18

*17 aDeut.
5:21; Rom.
7:7; 13:9;
Eph. 5:3, 5
bProv. 6:29;
Matt. 5:28

18 aEx.
19:16, 18;
Heb. 12:18,
19

19 aDeut.
5:5, 23-27;
Gal. 3:19;
Heb. 12:19

*20 aEx.
14:13; Is.
41:10, 13
bEx. 15:25;
Deut. 13:3
cDeut. 4:10;
6:24; Prov.
3:7; 16:6; Is.
8:13

21 aEx.
19:16; Deut.
5:22

22 aDeut.
4:36; 5:24,
26; Neh. 9:13

23 aEx. 20:3
bEx. 32:1, 2,
4; Deut.
29:17

*24-26

24 aEx.
20:25; 27:1-8
bEx. 10:25;
18:12 cEx.
24:5; Lev.
1:2 dDeut.
12:5; 16:6,
11; 26:2;
2 Chr. 6:6
eDeut. 12:5;
26:2

14 "^aYou shall not commit adultery.

15 "^aYou shall not steal.

16 "^aYou shall not bear false witness against your ^bneighbor.

17 "^aYou shall not covet your neighbor's house; ^byou shall not covet your neighbor's wife or his male servant or his female servant or his ox or his donkey or anything that belongs to your neighbor."

18 ^aAnd all the people perceived the thunder and the lightning flashes and the sound of the trumpet and the mountain smoking; and when the people saw *it*, they trembled and stood at a distance.

19 ^aThen they said to Moses, "Speak to us yourself and we will listen; but let not God speak to us, lest we die."

20 And Moses said to the people, "^aDo not be afraid; for God has come in order ^bto test you, and in order that ^cthe fear of Him may remain with you, so that you may not sin."

21 So the people stood at a distance, while Moses approached ^athe thick cloud where God *was*.

22 Then the LORD said to Moses, "Thus you shall say to the sons of Israel, 'You yourselves have seen that ^aI have spoken to you from heaven.

23 '^aYou shall not make *other* gods besides Me; ^bgods of silver or gods of gold, you shall not make for yourselves.

24 'You shall make ^aan altar of earth for Me, and you shall sacrifice on it your ^bburnt offerings and your ^cpeace offerings, ^dyour sheep and your oxen; in every place ^ewhere I cause My name to be remembered, I will come to you and bless you.

25 'And if you make an altar of stone for Me, ^ayou shall not build it of cut stones, for if you wield your tool on it, you will profane it.

26 'And you shall not go up by steps to My altar, that ^ayour nakedness may not be exposed on it.'

3 Laws concerning slaves, 21:1-11

21 "Now these are the ^aordinances which you are to set before them.

2 "If you buy ^aa Hebrew slave, he shall serve for six years; but on the seventh he shall go out as a free man without payment.

3 "If he comes alone, he shall go out alone; if he is the husband of a wife, then his wife shall go out with him.

4 "If his master gives him a wife, and she bears him sons or daughters, the wife and her children shall belong to her master, and he shall go out alone.

5 "But ^aif the slave plainly says, 'I love my master, my wife and my children; I will not go out as a free man,'

6 then his master shall bring him to God, then he shall bring him to the door or the doorpost. And his master shall pierce his ear with an awl; and he shall serve him permanently.

7 "^aAnd if a man sells his daughter as a female slave, she is not to go free ^bas the male slaves do.

25 aDeut.
27:5, 6;
Josh. 8:31

26 aEx.
28:42, 43

* 1-6
1 aEx. 24:3,
4; Deut. 4:14;
6:1

2 aLev.
25:39-43;
Deut. 15:12-
18; Jer.
34:14

5 aDeut.
15:16, 17

* 7-11
7 aNeh. 5:5
bEx. 21:2, 3

20:14 The commandment against adultery applies to both husband and wife (cf. Lev. 20:10; Heb. 13:4).

20:17 The other commandments basically concern actions; this one deals with thoughts. Sin usually originates from a wrong desire (cf. James 1:13-15).

20:20 God's purpose was to *test* the faithfulness of the people to Him.

20:24-26 An acceptable altar had to be made of earth or natural (unhewn) stone, and without steps (to prevent indecent exposure while climbing up to the altar).

21:1-6 The laws regarding Hebrew slaves (for foreign slaves, see Lev. 25:44-46). A person was sold into slavery usually to pay a debt (cf. Lev. 25:39; Amos 2:6; 8:6), but he was to be treated as a hired laborer and offered his release after 6 years. *awl.* Similar to an ice pick.

21:7-11 A slave girl could expect to be married to her master or his son, or be purchased by her relatives, or be supported. She could never be sold to a foreigner.

8 "If she is displeasing in the eyes of her master who designated her for himself, then he shall let her be redeemed. He does not have authority to sell her to a foreign people because of his unfairness to her.

9 "And if he designates her for his son, he shall deal with her according to the custom of daughters.

10 a1 Cor. 7:3, 5

10 "If he takes to himself another woman, he may not reduce her food, her clothing, or ªher conjugal rights.

11 "And if he will not do these three *things* for her, then she shall go out for nothing, without *payment of* money.

4 Laws concerning personal injury, 21:12-36

12 aGen. 9:6; Lev. 24:17; Num. 35:30; Matt. 26:52

★13 aNum. 35:10-34; Deut. 19:1-13; Josh. 20:1-9 b1 Sam. 24:4, 10, 18

★14 aDeut. 19:11, 12; 1 Kin. 2:28-34

12 "ªHe who strikes a man so that he dies shall surely be put to death.

13 "ªBut if he did not lie in wait *for him,* but bGod let *him* fall into his hand, then I will appoint you a place to which he may flee.

14 "ªIf, however, a man acts presumptuously toward his neighbor, so as to kill him craftily, you are to take him *even* from My altar, that he may die.

15 "And he who strikes his father or his mother shall surely be put to death.

16 aDeut. 24:7

16 "ªAnd he who kidnaps a man, whether he sells him or he is found in his possession, shall surely be put to death.

17 aLev. 20:9; Prov. 20:20; Matt. 15:4; Mark 7:10

17 "ªAnd he who curses his father or his mother shall surely be put to death.

18 "And if men have a quarrel and one strikes the other with a stone or with *his* fist, and he does not die but remains in bed;

19 if he gets up and walks around outside on his staff, then he who struck him shall go un-

punished; he shall only pay for his loss of time, and shall take care of him until he is completely healed.

20 "And if a man strikes his male or female slave with a rod and he dies at his hand, he shall be punished.

21 aLev. 25:44-46

21 "If, however, he survives a day or two, no vengeance shall be taken; ªfor he is his property.

★22 aEx. 21:30; Deut. 22:18, 19

22 "And *if* men struggle with each other and strike a woman with child so that she has a miscarriage, yet there is no *further* injury, he shall surely be fined as the woman's husband may demand of him; and he shall ªpay as the judges *decide.*

23 aLev. 24:19; Deut. 19:21

23 "But if there is *any further* injury, ªthen you shall appoint *as a penalty* life for life,

24 aLev. 24:20; Deut. 19:21; Matt. 5:38

24 ªeye for eye, tooth for tooth, hand for hand, foot for foot,

25 burn for burn, wound for wound, bruise for bruise.

26 "And if a man strikes the eye of his male or female slave, and destroys it, he shall let him go free on account of his eye.

27 "And if he knocks out a tooth of his male or female slave, he shall let him go free on account of his tooth.

28 aGen. 9:5; Ex. 21:32

28 "And if an ox gores a man or a woman to death, ªthe ox shall surely be stoned and its flesh shall not be eaten; but the owner of the ox shall go unpunished.

29 "If, however, an ox was previously in the habit of goring, and its owner has been warned, yet he does not confine it, and it kills a man or a woman, the ox shall be stoned and its owner also shall be put to death.

30 "If a ransom is demanded of him, then he shall give for the redemption of his life whatever is demanded of him.

21:13 In the case of unpremeditated murder, the murderer could flee to a place of refuge (cf. Num. 35:11) to escape the avenging relatives of the dead person.

21:14 Even the altar would not avail as a place of

safety in intentional murder.

21:22 *she has a miscarriage.* Better, her fruit comes out (alive, not dead). In this case a fine was levied. If the baby died, then the law of retaliation applied.

31 "Whether it gores a son or a daughter, it shall be done to him according to the same rule.

32 "If the ox gores a male or female slave, the owner shall give his *or her* master [a]thirty shekels of silver, and the ox shall be stoned.

33 "And if a man opens a pit, or digs a pit and does not cover it over, and an ox or a donkey falls into it,

34 the owner of the pit shall make restitution; he shall give money to its owner, and the dead *animal* shall become his.

35 "And if one man's ox hurts another's so that it dies, then they shall sell the live ox and divide its price equally; and also they shall divide the dead *ox.*

36 "Or *if* it is known that the ox was previously in the habit of goring, yet its owner has not confined it, he shall surely pay ox for ox, and the dead *animal* shall become his.

5 Laws concerning theft, 22:1-4

22 "If a man steals an ox or a sheep, and slaughters it or sells it, he shall pay five oxen for the ox and [a]four sheep for the sheep.

2 "If the [a]thief is caught while breaking in, and is struck so that he dies, there will be no bloodguiltiness on his account.

3 "*But* if the sun has risen on him, there will be bloodguiltiness on his account. He shall surely make restitution; if he owns nothing, then he shall be [a]sold for his theft.

4 "If what he stole is actually found alive in his possession, whether an ox or a donkey or a sheep, [a]he shall pay double.

6 Laws concerning property damage, 22:5-6

5 "If a man lets a field or vineyard be grazed *bare* and lets his animal loose so that it grazes in another man's field, he shall make restitution from the best of his own field and the best of his own vineyard.

6 "If a fire breaks out and spreads to thorn bushes, so that stacked grain or the standing grain or the field *itself* is consumed, he who started the fire shall surely make restitution.

7 Laws concerning dishonesty, 22:7-15

7 "[a]If a man gives his neighbor money or goods to keep *for him,* and it is stolen from the man's house, if the thief is caught, he shall pay double.

8 "If the thief is not caught, then the owner of the house shall appear before [a]the judges, *to* determine whether he laid his hands on his neighbor's property.

9 "For every breach of trust, *whether it is* for ox, for donkey, for sheep, for clothing, *or* for any lost thing about which one says, 'This is it,' the case of both parties shall come before [a]the judges; he whom the judges condemn shall pay double to his neighbor.

10 "If a man gives his neighbor a donkey, an ox, a sheep, or any animal to keep *for him,* and it dies or is hurt or is driven away while no one is looking,

11 an [a]oath before the LORD shall be made by the two of them, that he has not laid hands on his neighbor's property; and its owner shall accept *it,* and he shall not make restitution.

★32 [a]Zech. 11:12; Matt. 26:15; 27:3, 9

1 [a]2 Sam. 12:6; Luke 19:8

★ 2-3

2 [a]Matt. 6:19; 24:43; 1 Pet. 4:15

3 [a]Matt. 18:25

4 [a]Ex. 22:7

★ 7-13

7 [a]Lev. 6:1-7

8 [a]Ex. 22:9; Deut. 17:8, 9; 19:17

9 [a]Ex. 22:8, 28; Deut. 25:1

11 [a]Heb. 6:16

21:32 *thirty shekels of silver.* The redemption price for a slave (see also Zech. 11:12; Matt. 26:15).

22:2-3 The meaning is this: killing a thief who was digging through a wall after dark was justifiable homicide, but to do so in daylight subjected the householder to revenge by the thief's next of kin.

22:7-13 These laws covered cases of destruction or theft of property deposited with someone for safekeeping while the owner was away.

12 "But if it is actually stolen from him, he shall make restitution to its owner.

13 "If it is all torn to pieces, let him bring it as evidence; he shall not make restitution for what has been torn to pieces.

★14-15 **14** "And if a man borrows *anything* from his neighbor, and it is injured or dies while its owner is not with it, he shall make full restitution.

15 "If its owner is with it, he shall not make restitution; if it is hired, it came for its hire.

8 Laws concerning immorality,
22:16-17

16 ªDeut. 22:28, 29
17 ªGen. 34:12; 1 Sam. 18:25
★18 ªLev. 19:31; 20:6, 27; Deut. 18:10, 11; 1 Sam. 28:3; Jer. 27:9, 10
19 ªLev. 18:23; 20:15, 16; Deut. 27:21
20 ªEx. 32:8; 34:15; Lev. 17:7; Num. 25:2; Deut. 17:2, 3, 5; 1 Kin. 18:40; 2 Kin. 10:25
21 ªEx. 23:9; Lev. 19:33, 34; 25:35; Deut. 1:16; 10:19; 27:19; Zech. 7:10
★22-24
22 ªDeut. 24:17, 18; Prov. 23:10, 11; Jer. 7:6, 7
23 ªDeut. 15:9; Job 35:9; Luke 18:7 ᵇDeut. 10:18; Job 34:28; Ps. 10:14, 17, 18; 18:6; 68:5; James 5:4

16 "ªAnd if a man seduces a virgin who is not engaged, and lies with her, he must pay a dowry for her *to be* his wife.

17 "If her father absolutely refuses to give her to him, he shall pay money equal to the ªdowry for virgins.

9 Laws concerning civil and religious obligations,
22:18-23:9

18 "You shall not allow a ªsorceress to live.

19 "ªWhoever lies with an animal shall surely be put to death.

20 "ªHe who sacrifices to any god, other than to the LORD alone, shall be utterly destroyed.

21 "And ªyou shall not wrong a stranger or oppress him, for you were strangers in the land of Egypt.

22 "ªYou shall not afflict any widow or orphan.

23 "If you afflict him at all, *and* ªif he does cry out to Me, ᵇI will surely hear his cry;

24 and My anger will be kindled, and I will kill you with the sword; ªand your wives shall become widows and your children fatherless.

25 "ªIf you lend money to My people, to the poor among you, you are not to act as a creditor to him; you shall not charge him ᵇinterest.

26 "If you ever take your neighbor's cloak ªas a pledge, you are to return it to him before the sun sets,

27 for that is his only covering; it is his cloak for his body. What else shall he sleep in? And it shall come about that ªwhen he cries out to Me, I will hear *him*, for ᵇI am gracious.

28 "You shall not ªcurse God, ᵇnor curse a ruler of your people.

29 "ªYou shall not delay *the offering from* your harvest and your vintage. ᵇThe first-born of your sons you shall give to Me.

30 "ªYou shall do the same with your oxen *and* with your sheep. It shall be with its mother seven days; ᵇon the eighth day you shall give it to Me.

31 "ªAnd you shall be holy men to Me, therefore ᵇyou shall not eat *any* flesh torn to pieces in the field; you shall throw it to the dogs.

23 "ªYou shall not bear a false report; do not join your hand with a wicked man to be a ᵇmalicious witness.

2 "You shall not follow a multitude in doing evil, nor shall you testify in a dispute so as to turn aside after a multitude in order to ªpervert *justice*;

3 ªnor shall you be partial to a poor man in his dispute.

24 ªPs. 109:2, 9
★25-27
25 ªLev. 25:35-37; Deut. 15:7-11 ᵇDeut. 23:19, 20; Neh. 5:7; Ps. 15:5; Ezek. 18:8
26 ªDeut. 24:6, 10-13; Job 24:3; Prov. 20:16; Amos 2:8
27 ªEx. 22:23 ᵇEx. 34:6
28 ªLev. 24:15, 16 ᵇEccl. 10:20; Acts 23:5
★29-30
29 ªEx. 23:16, 19; Deut. 26:2-11; Prov. 3:9 ᵇEx. 13:2, 12
30 ªDeut. 15:19; Lev. 22:27 ᵇGen. 17:12; Lev. 12:3
31 ªEx. 19:6; Lev. 11:44; 19:2 ᵇLev. 7:24; 17:15; Ezek. 4:14
1 ªEx. 20:16; Lev. 19:11; Deut. 5:20; Ps. 101:5; Prov. 10:18 ᵇDeut. 19:16-21; Ps. 35:11; Prov. 19:5; Acts 6:11
2 ªDeut. 16:19; 24:17
★ 3 ªEx. 23:6; Lev. 19:15; Deut. 1:17; 16:19

22:14-15 The borrower took all the risks unless the owner of the property remained with the property.

22:18 *sorceress.* A woman who claimed to have superhuman powers by means of spells, magic, or knowledge that came from evil spirits (cf. 1 Sam. 28:9).

22:22-24 Many laws concerned the protection of widows (see also Deut. 14:29; 16:11; 14;

24:19-21; 26:12-13).

22:25-27 Money was to be lent to the poor (and to all fellow-Israelites, cf. Deut. 23:20) without interest (see also Luke 6:34-35). *pledge.* See note on Amos 2:8.

22:29-30 Firstborn children were redeemed with money (cf. Num. 3:46-48); firstborn animals were sacrificed.

23:3 It is unjust to favor a *poor man.*

4 *a*Deut. 22:1-4

4 "*a*If you meet your enemy's ox or his donkey wandering away, you shall surely return it to him.

5 *a*Deut. 22:4

5 "*a*If you see the donkey of one who hates you lying *helpless* under its load, you shall refrain from leaving it to him, you shall surely release *it* with him.

6 *a*Ex. 23:2, 3; Lev. 19:15

6 "*a*You shall not pervert the justice *due* to your needy *brother* in his dispute.

7 *a*Ex. 20:16; Ps. 119:29; Eph. 4:25 *b*Ex. 20:13; Deut. 27:25 *c*Ex. 34:7; Deut. 25:1; Rom. 1:18

7 "*a*Keep far from a false charge, and *b*do not kill the innocent or the righteous, for *c*I will not acquit the guilty.

8 *a*Deut. 10:17; 16:19; Prov. 15:27; 17:8, 23; Is. 5:22, 23

8 "*a*And you shall not take a bribe, for a bribe blinds the clear-sighted and subverts the cause of the just.

9 *a*Ex. 22:21; Lev. 19:33f.; Deut. 24:17f.; 27:19

9 "*a*And you shall not oppress a stranger, since you yourselves know the feelings of a stranger, for you *also* were strangers in the land of Egypt.

10 Laws concerning the Sabbaths and feasts, 23:10-19

★10-11

10 *a*Lev. 25:1-7

10 "*a*And you shall sow your land for six years and gather in its yield,

11 but *on* the seventh year you shall let it rest and lie fallow, so that the needy of your people may eat; and whatever they leave the beast of the field may eat. You are to do the same with your vineyard *and* your olive grove.

12 *a*Ex. 20:8-11; 31:15; 34:21; 35:2, 3; Lev. 23:3; Deut. 5:13f.

12 "*a*Six days you are to do your work, but on the seventh day you shall cease *from labor* in order that your ox and your donkey may rest, and the son of your female slave, as well as your stranger, may refresh themselves.

13 *a*Deut. 4:9, 23; 1 Tim. 4:16 *b*Josh. 23:7; Ps. 16:4; Hos. 2:17

13 "Now *a*concerning everything which I have said to you, be on your guard; and *b*do not mention the name of other gods, nor let *them* be heard from your mouth.

14 "*a*Three times a year you shall celebrate a feast to Me.

★14-17

14 *a*Ex. 23:17; 34:22-24; Deut. 16:16

15 "You shall observe *a*the Feast of Unleavened Bread; for seven days you are to eat unleavened bread, as I commanded you, at the appointed time in the *b*month Abib, for in it you came out of Egypt. And *c*none shall appear before Me empty-handed.

15 *a*Ex. 12:14-20; Lev. 23:6-8; Num. 28:16-25 *b*Ex. 12:2; 13:4 *c*Ex. 22:29; 34:20

16 "Also *you shall observe* *a*the Feast of the Harvest *of the* first fruits of your labors *from* what you sow in the field; also the Feast of the Ingathering at the end of the year *b*when you gather in *the fruit of* your labors from the field.

16 *a*Ex. 34:22; Lev. 23:10; Num. 28:26 *b*Lev. 23:39

17 "*a*Three times a year all your males shall appear before the Lord God.

17 *a*Ex. 23:14; 34:23; Deut. 16:16

18 "*a*You shall not offer the blood of My sacrifice with leavened bread; *b*nor is the fat of My feast to remain overnight until morning.

★18-19

18 *a*Ex. 34:25; Lev. 2:11 *b*Ex. 12:10; Lev. 7:15; Deut. 16:4

19 "You shall bring *a*the choice first fruits of your soil into the house of the Lord your God. *b*You are not to boil a kid in the milk of its mother.

19 *a*Ex. 22:29; 34:26; Deut. 26:2, 10; Neh. 10:35; Prov. 3:9 *b*Deut. 14:21

11 Laws relating to conquest, 23:20-33

20 "Behold, I am going to send *a*an angel before you to guard you along the way, and *b*to bring you into the place which I have prepared.

★20 *a*Ex. 3:2; 14:19; 23:23; 32:34; 33:2 *b*Ex. 15:16, 17

21 "Be on your guard before him and obey his voice; *a*do not be rebellious toward him, for he will not pardon your transgression, since *b*My name is in him.

21 *a*Deut. 9:7; Ps. 78:40, 56 *b*Ex. 3:14; 6:3; 34:5-7

22 "But if you will truly obey his voice and do all that I say,

22 *a*Gen. 12:3; Num. 24:9; Deut. 30:7

23:10-11 God promised His people that the harvest of the sixth year would be sufficient to carry them over to the eighth year (see Lev. 25:20-23).

23:14-17 Attendance at the tabernacle was required of all men for three festivals each year: *Unleavened Bread* (see note on 12:15), *Harvest* or Pentecost (see Lev. 23:15-21), and *Ingather-*ing or Booths (see Lev. 23:33-36).

23:18-19 Leaven was a symbol of corruption and evil (cf. Matt. 16:6). Boiling a kid in its mother's milk was a common Canaanite ritual involving magic spells.

23:20 *angel.* Most likely the Angel of the Lord, the Lord Himself, though He was represented by His leaders, Moses and, later, Joshua.

then [a]I will be an enemy to your enemies and an adversary to your adversaries.

23 "[a]For My angel will go before you and bring you in to *the* land of the Amorites, the Hittites, the Perizzites, the Canaanites, the Hivites and the Jebusites; and I will completely destroy them.

24 "[a]You shall not worship their gods, nor serve them, nor do according to their deeds; [b]but you shall utterly overthrow them, and break their [c]*sacred* pillars in pieces.

25 "[a]But you shall serve the LORD your God, and He will bless your bread and your water; and [b]I will remove sickness from your midst.

26 "There shall be no one miscarrying or [a]barren in your land; [b]I will fulfill the number of your days.

27 "I will [a]send My terror ahead of you, and [b]throw into confusion all the people among whom you come, and I will [c]make all your enemies turn *their* backs to you.

28 "And I will send [a]hornets ahead of you, that they may [b]drive out the Hivites, the Canaanites, and the Hittites before you.

29 "[a]I will not drive them out before you in a single year, that the land may not become desolate, and the beasts of the field become too numerous for you.

30 "I will drive them out before you [a]little by little, until you become fruitful and take possession of the land.

31 "[a]And I will fix your boundary from the Red Sea to the sea of the Philistines, and from the wilderness to the River *Euphrates;* [b]for I will deliver the inhabitants

of the land into your hand, and you will [c]drive them out before you.

32 "[a]You shall make no covenant with them [b]or with their gods.

33 "[a]They shall not live in your land, lest they make you sin against Me; for *if* you serve their gods, [b]it will surely be a snare to you."

12 The covenant ratified,
24:1-8

24 Then He said to Moses, "[a]Come up to the LORD, you and Aaron, [b]Nadab and Abihu and [c]seventy of the elders of Israel, and you shall worship at a distance.

2 "Moses alone, however, shall come near to the LORD, but they shall not come near, nor shall the people come up with him."

3 Then Moses came and recounted to the people all the words of the LORD and all the ordinances; and all the people answered with one voice, and said, "[a]All the words which the LORD has spoken we will do!"

4 And [a]Moses wrote down all the words of the LORD. Then he arose early in the morning, and built an [b]altar at the foot of the mountain with twelve pillars for the twelve tribes of Israel.

5 And he sent young men of the sons of Israel, [a]and they offered burnt offerings and sacrificed young bulls as peace offerings to the LORD.

6 And [a]Moses took half of the blood and put *it* in basins, and the *other* half of the blood he sprinkled on the altar.

Cross references (left margin):

23 [a]Ex. 23:20; Josh. 24:8, 11

24 [a]Ex. 20:5; 23:13, 33; Deut. 12:30f. [b]Num. 33:52; Deut. 7:5; 12:3; 2 Kin. 18:4 [c]Ex. 34:13; Lev. 26:1; 2 Kin. 3:2

25 [a]Lev. 26:3-13; Deut. 6:13; 10:12; 28:1-14; Josh. 22:5; 1 Sam. 12:20; Matt. 4:10 [b]Ex. 15:26; Deut. 7:15

26 [a]Deut. 7:14 [b]Deut. 4:40; Job 5:26

27 [a]Gen. 35:5; Ex. 15:16; Deut. 2:25; Josh. 2:9 [b]Deut. 7:23 [c]Ps. 18:40; 21:12

★**28** [a]Deut. 7:20; Josh. 24:12 [b]Ex. 33:2; 34:11

29 [a]Deut. 7:22

30 [a]Deut. 7:22

★**31** [a]Gen. 15:18; Deut. 1:7, 8; 11:24 [b]Deut. 2:36; Josh. 21:44 [c]Josh. 24:12, 18

Cross references (right margin):

32 [a]Ex. 34:12; Deut. 7:2 [b]Ex. 23:13, 24

33 [a]Deut. 7:1-5, 16 [b]Ex. 34:12; Deut. 12:30; Josh. 23:13; Judg. 2:3; Ps. 106:36

★ **1** [a]Ex. 19:24 [b]Ex. 6:23; 28:1; Lev. 10:1, 2 [c]Num. 11:16

★ **3-8**

3 [a]Ex. 19:8; 24:7; Deut. 5:27

4 [a]Ex. 17:14; 34:27; Deut. 31:9 [b]Ex. 17:15

5 [a]Ex. 18:12

6 [a]Heb. 9:18

23:28 *hornets.* May be actual hornets or may represent the Egyptian army that raided Canaan regularly, weakening her before the Israelites came.

23:31 *Red Sea.* See note on 13:18. *sea of the Philistines.* The Mediterranean.

24:1 *Nadab and Abihu* were the oldest sons of Aaron (see 6:23) and died under God's judg-

ment (see Lev. 10).

24:3-8 The covenant was publicly ratified, written down, and ratified again. Various forms of ritual ratification included blood sacrifice (as here), passing through the pieces of the slaughtered sacrifice (cf. Gen. 15:10, 17), partaking of a meal (cf. Gen. 31:54), and eating salt together (cf. Num. 18:19).

7 aEx. 24:4;
Heb. 9:19
bEx. 24:3

7 Then he took athe book of the covenant and read *it* in the hearing of the people; and they said, "bAll that the LORD has spoken we will do, and we will be obedient!"

8 aHeb.
9:19, 20
bZech. 9:11;
Matt. 26:28;
Mark 14:24;
Luke 22:20;
1 Cor. 11:25;
Heb. 13:20

8 So aMoses took the blood and sprinkled *it* on the people, and said, "Behold bthe blood of the covenant, which the LORD has made with you in accordance with all these words."

13 The LORD's glory revealed,
24:9–18

9 aEx. 24:1

9 Then Moses went up with Aaron, aNadab and Abihu, and seventy of the elders of Israel,

★10-11
10 aEx.
24:11; Num.
12:8; Is. 6:5;
John 1:18;
6:46 bEzek.
1:26; 10:1;
Rev. 4:3

10 and athey saw the God of Israel; and under His feet bthere appeared to be a pavement of sapphire, as clear as the sky itself.

11 aGen.
16:13; 32:30;
Ex. 24:10

11 Yet He did not stretch out His hand against the nobles of the sons of Israel; and athey beheld God, and they ate and drank.

12 aEx.
31:18; 32:15;
Deut. 5:22

12 Now the LORD said to Moses, "Come up to Me on the mountain and remain there, and aI will give you the stone tablets with the law and the commandment which I have written for their instruction."

13 aEx.
17:9-14;
33:11 bEx.
3:1

13 So Moses arose with aJoshua his servant, and Moses went up to bthe mountain of God.

14 aGen.
22:5 bEx.
17:10, 12

14 But to the elders he said, "aWait here for us until we return to you. And behold, bAaron and Hur are with you; whoever has a legal matter, let him approach them."

15 aEx. 19:9

15 Then Moses went up to the mountain, and athe cloud covered the mountain.

16 aEx.
16:10; Num.
14:10 bPs.
99:7

16 And athe glory of the LORD rested on Mount Sinai, and the cloud covered it for six days; and on the seventh day He bcalled to Moses from the midst of the cloud.

17 aEx. 3:2;
Ezek. 1:28
bDeut. 4:24;
9:3; Heb.
12:29

17 aAnd to the eyes of the sons of Israel the appearance of the glory of the LORD was like a bconsuming fire on the mountain top.

18 aEx.
34:28; Deut.
9:9; 10:10

18 And Moses entered the midst of the cloud as he went up to the mountain; and Moses was on the mountain aforty days and forty nights.

B The Institution of the Tabernacle,
25:1–31:18
1 The materials, 25:1–9

★ 1-7
★ 1

25 Then the LORD spoke to Moses, saying,

2 aEx.
35:4-9 bEx.
35:21; 1 Chr.
29:3, 5, 9;
Ezra 2:68;
2 Cor. 8:11,
12; 9:7

2 "aTell the sons of Israel to raise a contribution for Me; bfrom every man whose heart moves him you shall raise My contribution.

3 "And this is the contribution which you are to raise from them: gold, silver and bronze,

4 aEx. 28:5,
6, 8

4 ablue, purple and scarlet *material,* fine linen, goat *hair,*

5 rams' skins dyed red, porpoise skins, acacia wood,

6 aEx.
27:20 bEx.
30:23f.

6 aoil for lighting, bspices for the anointing oil and for the fragrant incense,

7 aEx. 28:4,
6-14 bEx.
28:4, 15-30
★ 8 aEx.
36:1-5 bEx.
29:45, 46;
Num. 5:3;
Deut. 12:11;
1 Kin. 6:13;
2 Cor. 6:16;
Rev. 21:3

7 onyx stones and setting stones, for the aephod and for the bbreastpiece.

8 "And let them aconstruct a sanctuary for Me, bthat I may dwell among them.

24:10-11 We are not told the form in which God manifested Himself, but rather than being consumed, the people feasted in the glory of His beauty (see note on John 1:18).

25:1-7 The materials for the tabernacle came from voluntary contributions of the people, who gave more than enough (see 36:5-7). *bronze.* An alloy of copper and tin. *porpoise skins.* Skins of a seallike marine animal. *acacia.* A hard and durable desert wood, especially suitable for the framework and furniture of the tabernacle.

25:1 Fifty chapters in the Bible report instruc-

tions concerning the tabernacle: 13 in Exodus, 18 in Leviticus, 13 in Numbers, 2 in Deuteronomy, and 4 in Hebrews. It served as the place where God met with His people (cf. 25:8; 29:45), and it prefigured the perfect approach to God through the blood of Jesus Christ, who "tabernacled" among men (cf. John 1:14; Heb. 10:19-20).

25:8 *sanctuary.* Lit., holy place. Also called the tabernacle (v. 9, from a word meaning "to settle down, abide"); the tent (26:36); the tent of meeting (29:42); and the tent of the testimony (Num. 17:7).

9 *Ex.
25:40; 26:30;
Acts 7:44;
Heb. 8:2, 5

9 "*According to all that I am going to show you, *as the pattern of the tabernacle and the pattern of all its furniture, just so you shall construct *it.

2 The ark and mercy seat, 25:10-22

★10-16

10 *Ex.
37:1-9; Deut.
10:3; Heb.
9:4

10 "*And they shall construct an ark of acacia wood two and a half cubits long, and one and a half cubits wide, and one and a half cubits high.

11 *Heb. 9:4

11 "And you shall *overlay it with pure gold, inside and out you shall overlay it, and you shall make a gold molding around it.

12 "And you shall cast four gold rings for it, and fasten them on its four feet, and two rings shall be on one side of it and two rings on the other side of it.

13 "And you shall make poles of acacia wood and overlay them with gold.

14 "And you shall put the poles into the rings on the sides of the ark, to carry the ark with them.

15 *1 Kin.
8:8

15 "The *poles shall remain in the rings of the ark; they shall not be removed from it.

16 *Ex.
40:20; Deut.
10:2; 31:26;
1 Kin. 8:9;
Heb. 9:4

16 "And you shall *put into the ark the testimony which I shall give you.

★17 *Ex.
37:6

17 "And you shall *make a mercy seat of pure gold, two and a half cubits long and one and a half cubits wide.

★18

18 "And you shall make two cherubim of gold, make them of hammered work at the two ends of the mercy seat.

19 "And make one cherub at one end and one cherub at the other end; you shall make the cherubim *of one piece* with the mercy seat at its two ends.

20 *1 Kin.
8:7; 1 Chr.
28:18; Heb.
9:5

20 "And *the cherubim shall have *their* wings spread upward, covering the mercy seat with their wings and facing one another; the faces of the cherubim are to be *turned* toward the mercy seat.

21 *Ex.
26:34; 40:20.
*Ex. 25:16

21 "And *you shall put the mercy seat on top of the ark, and *in the ark you shall put the testimony which I shall give to you.

22 *Ex.
29:42, 43;
30:6, 36;
Lev. 16:2;
Num. 17:4
*Num. 7:89;
1 Sam. 4:4;
2 Sam. 6:2;
2 Kin. 19:15;
Ps. 80:1; Is.
37:16

22 "And *there I will meet with you; and from above the mercy seat, from *between the two cherubim which are upon the ark of the testimony, I will speak to you about all that I will give you in commandment for the sons of Israel.

3 The table for the bread, 25:23-30

★23-30

23 *Ex.
37:10-16

23 "*And you shall make a table of acacia wood, two cubits long and one cubit wide and one and a half cubits high.

24 *Ex.
25:11

24 "And you shall overlay it with pure gold and make a gold *border around it.

25 "And you shall make for it a rim of a handbreadth around *it;* and you shall make a gold border for the rim around it.

26 "And you shall make four gold rings for it and put rings on the four corners which are on its four feet.

27 "The rings shall be close to the rim as holders for the poles to carry the table.

28 "And you shall make the poles of acacia wood and overlay them with gold, so that with them the table may be carried.

29 *Ex.
37:16; Num.
4:7

29 "And you shall make its *dishes and its pans and its jars and its bowls, with which to pour libations; you shall make them of pure gold.

25:10-16 The *ark* was a coffer or box measuring about 3'9" x 2'3" x 2'3" that served to hold the tables of the Law (or *the testimony,* v. 16), a pot of manna, and Aaron's rod (Heb. 9:4).

25:17 *a mercy seat.* Lit., a covering. It was not only the lid for the Ark, but also the place where sins were covered, thus the place of propitiation.

25:18 *cherubim.* See notes on Ezek. 1:5 and Rev.

4:6.

25:23-30 The table, measuring about 3' x 1½', held the *bread of the Presence* (12 flat cakes arranged in two piles, see Lev. 24:6) and certain utensils (see Exod. 25:29). Bread of the Presence means bread laid before God, in His presence. Each of the 12 tribes was equally dear to Him, and He was the one who met their needs (see also John 6:32-35).

30 ^aEx.
39:36; 40:23;
Lev. 24:5-9

30 "And you shall set ^athe bread of the Presence on the table before Me at all times.

4 *The lampstand,* 25:31-40

★31-40

31 ^aEx.
37:17-24;
1 Kin. 7:49;
Zech. 4:2

31 "^aThen you shall make a lampstand of pure gold. The lampstand *and* its base and its shaft are to be made of hammered work; its cups, its bulbs and its flowers shall be *of one piece* with it.

32 ^aEx.
37:18

32 "And ^asix branches shall go out from its sides; three branches of the lampstand from its one side, and three branches of the lampstand from its other side.

33 ^aEx.
37:19

33 "^aThree cups *shall be* shaped like almond *blossoms* in the one branch, a bulb and a flower, and three cups shaped like almond *blossoms* in the other branch, a bulb and a flower—so for six branches going out from the lampstand;

34 ^aEx.
37:20

34 and ^ain the lampstand four cups shaped like almond *blossoms,* its bulbs and its flowers.

35 ^aEx.
37:21

35 "^aAnd a bulb shall be under the *first* pair of branches *coming* out of it, and a bulb under the *second* pair of branches *coming* out of it, and a bulb under the *third* pair of branches *coming* out of it, for the six branches coming out of the lampstand.

36 ^aEx.
37:22

36 "^aTheir bulbs and their branches *shall be of one piece* with it; all of it shall be one piece of hammered work of pure gold.

37 ^aNum.
8:2

37 "Then you shall make its lamps seven *in number;* and ^athey shall mount its lamps so as to shed light on the space in front of it.

38 "And its snuffers and their trays *shall be* of pure gold.

39 "It shall be made from a talent of pure gold, with all these utensils.

40 ^aHeb. 8:5
^bEx. 25:9;
26:30; Num.
8:4; Acts
7:44

40 "And ^asee that you make them ^bafter the pattern for them, which was shown to you on the mountain.

5 *The curtains,* 26:1-14

★1-6

1 ^aEx.
36:8-19

26 "^aMoreover you shall make the tabernacle with ten curtains of fine twisted linen and blue and purple and scarlet *material;* you shall make them with cherubim, the work of a skillful workman.

2 "The length of each curtain shall be twenty-eight cubits, and the width of each curtain four cubits; all the curtains shall have the same measurements.

3 "Five curtains shall be joined to one another; and *the other* five curtains *shall be* joined to one another.

4 "And you shall make loops of blue on the edge of the outermost curtain in the *first* set, and likewise you shall make *them* on the edge of the curtain that is outermost in the second set.

5 "You shall make fifty loops in the one curtain, and you shall make fifty loops on the edge of the curtain that is in the second set; the loops shall be opposite each other.

6 "And you shall make fifty clasps of gold, and join the curtains to one another with the clasps, that the tabernacle may be a unit.

★ 7-13

7 ^aEx.
36:14

7 "Then ^ayou shall make curtains of goats' *hair* for a tent over the tabernacle; you shall make eleven curtains in all.

8 "The length of each curtain *shall be* thirty cubits, and the width of each curtain four cubits; the eleven curtains shall have the same measurements.

25:31-40 The gold *lampstand* was an upright shaft, from each side of which three branches extended. A representation of the lampstand and the table of shewbread (from the second Temple) survives on the Arch of Titus in Rome. The lampstand provided light for the ministering priests and typified Christ, the Light of the world. A *bulb* was some sort of knob that supported the ornamental flowers. A *talent* weighed from 58-80 pounds (see also note on Matt. 18:24).

26:1-6 *curtains.* The inside curtains that covered the wooden framework of the tabernacle itself.

26:7-13 *curtains.* These curtains covered the inner linen curtains.

9 "And you shall join five curtains by themselves, and the *other* six curtains by themselves, and you shall double over the sixth curtain at the front of the tent.

10 "And you shall make fifty loops on the edge of the curtain that is outermost in the *first* set, and fifty loops on the edge of the curtain *that is outermost in* the second set.

11 "And you shall make fifty clasps of bronze, and you shall put the clasps into the loops and join the tent together, that it may be a unit.

12 "And the overlapping part that is left over in the curtains of the tent, the half curtain that is left over, shall lap over the back of the tabernacle.

13 "And the cubit on one side and the cubit on the other, of what is left over in the length of the curtains of the tent, shall lap over the sides of the tabernacle on one side and on the other, to cover it.

★14 *a*Ex. 36:19 **14** "And *a*you shall make a covering for the tent of rams' skins dyed red, and a covering of porpoise skins above.

6 The boards, 26:15-30

★15-30
15 *a*Ex. 36:20-34 **15** "Then you shall make *a*the boards for the tabernacle of acacia wood, standing upright.

16 "Ten cubits *shall be* the length of each board, and one and a half cubits the width of each board.

17 "There *shall be* two tenons for each board, fitted to one another; thus you shall do for all the boards of the tabernacle.

18 "And you shall make the boards for the tabernacle: twenty boards for the south side.

19 "And you shall make forty *a*sockets of silver under the twenty boards, two sockets under one board for its two tenons and two sockets under another board for its two tenons;

19 *a*Ex. 38:27

20 and for the second side of the tabernacle, on the north side, twenty boards,

21 and their forty sockets of silver; two sockets under one board and two sockets under another board.

22 "And for the rear of the tabernacle, to the west, you shall make six boards.

23 "And you shall make two boards for the corners of the tabernacle at the rear.

24 "And they shall be double beneath, and together they shall be complete to its top to the first ring; thus it shall be with both of them: they shall form the two corners.

25 "And there shall be eight boards with their sockets of silver, sixteen sockets; two sockets under one board and two sockets under another board.

26 "Then you shall make *a*bars of acacia wood, five for the boards of one side of the tabernacle,

26 *a*Ex. 36:31

27 and five bars for the boards of the other side of the tabernacle, and five bars for the boards of the side of the tabernacle for the rear *side* to the west.

28 "And the middle bar in the center of the boards shall pass through from end to end.

29 "And you shall overlay the boards with gold and make their rings of gold *as* holders for the bars; and you shall overlay the bars with gold.

30 "Then you shall erect the tabernacle *a*according to its plan which you have been shown in the mountain.

30 *a*Ex. 25:9, 40; Acts 7:44; Heb. 8:5

26:14 Two additional coverings were provided. Some feel these were used as a kind of wrapper when the tabernacle was being moved.
26:15-30 The walls of the tabernacle were apparently not solid, but of a trellislike construction that allowed the beauty of the linen curtains to be visible from the inside.

7 The veils, 26:31-37

★31-35

31 a**ᵃEx.**
36:35, 36;
2 Chr. 3:14;
Matt. 27:51;
Heb. 9:3

31 "And you shall make ᵃa veil of blue and purple and scarlet *material* and fine twisted linen; it shall be made with cherubim, the work of a skillful workman.

32 "And you shall hang it on four pillars of acacia overlaid with gold, their hooks *also being of* gold, on four sockets of silver.

33 ᵃEx.
25:16; 40:21
ᵇHeb. 9:2f.

33 "And you shall hang up the veil under the clasps, and shall bring in ᵃthe ark of the testimony there within the veil; and the veil shall serve for you as a partition ᵇbetween the holy place and the holy of holies.

34 ᵃEx.
25:21; 40:20;
Lev. 16:2

34 "And ᵃyou shall put the mercy seat on the ark of the testimony in the holy of holies.

35 ᵃEx.
40:22 ᵇEx.
40:24

35 "And ᵃyou shall set the table outside the veil, and the ᵇlampstand opposite the table on the side of the tabernacle toward the south; and you shall put the table on the north side.

★36-37

36 ᵃEx.
36:37

36 "And ᵃyou shall make a screen for the doorway of the tent of blue and purple and scarlet *material* and fine twisted linen, the work of a weaver.

37 ᵃEx.
36:38

37 "And ᵃyou shall make five pillars of acacia for the screen, and overlay them with gold, their hooks *also being of* gold; and you shall cast five sockets of bronze for them.

8 The brass altar, 27:1-8

★ 1-8

1 ᵃEx.
38:1-7

27 "And you shall make ᵃthe altar of acacia wood, five cubits long and five cubits wide; the altar shall be square, and its height shall be three cubits.

2 "And you shall make ᵃits horns on its four corners; its horns shall be of one piece with it, and you shall overlay it with bronze.

2 ᵃPs.
118:27

3 "And you shall make its pails for removing its ashes, and its shovels and its basins and its forks and its firepans; you shall make all its utensils of bronze.

4 "And you shall make for it a grating of network of bronze, and on the net you shall make four bronze rings at its four corners.

5 "And you shall put it beneath, under the ledge of the altar, that the net may reach halfway up the altar.

6 "And you shall make poles for the altar, poles of acacia wood, and overlay them with bronze.

7 "And its poles shall be inserted into the rings, so that the poles shall be on the two sides of the altar ᵃwhen it is carried.

7 ᵃNum.
4:15

8 "You shall make it hollow with planks; ᵃas it was shown to you in the mountain, so they shall make *it*.

8 ᵃEx.
25:40; 26:30;
Acts 7:44;
Heb. 8:5

9 The court, 27:9-19

9 "And you shall make ᵃthe court of the tabernacle. On the south side *there shall be* hangings for the court of fine twisted linen one hundred cubits long for one side;

★ 9-19

9 ᵃEx.
38:9-20

10 and its pillars *shall be* twenty, with their twenty sockets of bronze; the hooks of the pillars and their bands *shall be* of silver.

11 "And likewise for the north side in length *there shall be* hang-

---

26:31-35 The inner *veil* separated the Holy Place (which contained the Altar of Incense, the lampstand, and the table for the bread) from the Holy of Holies (which contained the Ark and the Mercy Seat). Josephus reported that the veil was 4 inches thick, was renewed every year, and that horses tied to each side could not pull it apart. It barred all but the High Priest from the presence of God, but when it was torn in two at the death of Jesus of Nazareth (see Mark 15:38), access to God was made available to all who come through Him (cf. Heb. 10:19-22).

26:36-37 The outer veil hanging at the E. end of the Holy Place functioned as a door to the tent.

27:1-8 *the altar* was made of wood covered with bronze (to make it lightweight for transporting and yet fireproof). The sacrifices were made on it. *horns.* Used to bind the sacrificial animals to the altar (cf. Psalm 118:27).

27:9-19 The *court* of the tabernacle measured 150' x 75' and was screened with linen curtains 7½' high. The tabernacle itself took up only about one-fifteenth of this area.

ings one hundred *cubits* long, and its twenty pillars with their twenty sockets of bronze; the hooks of the pillars and their bands *shall be* of silver.

12 "And *for* the width of the court on the west side *shall be* hangings of fifty cubits *with* their ten pillars and their ten sockets.

13 "And the width of the court on the east side *shall be* fifty cubits.

14 "The hangings for the *one* side *of the gate shall be* fifteen cubits *with* their three pillars and their three sockets.

15 "And for the other side *shall be* hangings of fifteen cubits *with* their three pillars and their three sockets.

16 "And for the gate of the court there *shall be* a screen of twenty cubits, of blue and purple and scarlet *material* and fine twisted linen, the work of a weaver, *with* their four pillars and their four sockets.

17 "All the pillars around the court shall be furnished with silver bands *with* their hooks of silver and their sockets of bronze.

18 "The length of the court *shall be* one hundred cubits, and the width fifty throughout, and the height five cubits of fine twisted linen, and their sockets of bronze.

19 "All the utensils of the tabernacle *used* in all its service, and all its pegs, and all the pegs of the court, *shall be* of bronze.

10   The oil, 27:20–21

20 "And you shall charge the sons of Israel, that they bring you *a* clear oil of beaten olives for the light, to make a lamp burn continually.

21 "In the *a* tent of meeting, outside *b* the veil which is before

the testimony, *c* Aaron and his sons shall keep it in order from evening to morning before the LORD; *it shall be* a perpetual *d* statute throughout their generations for the sons of Israel.

11   The priests' garments, 28:1–43

28 "Then *a* bring near to yourself Aaron your brother, and his sons with him, from among the sons of Israel, to minister as priest to Me—Aaron, *b* Nadab and Abihu, Eleazar and Ithamar, Aaron's sons.

2 "And you shall make *a* holy garments for Aaron your brother, for glory and for beauty.

3 "And you shall speak to all the *a* skillful persons *b* whom I have endowed with the spirit of wisdom, that they make Aaron's garments to consecrate him, that he may minister as priest to Me.

4 "And these are the garments which they shall make: a *a* breastpiece and an ephod and a robe and a tunic of checkered work, a turban and a sash; and they shall make holy garments for Aaron your brother and his sons, that he may minister as priest to Me.

5 "And they shall take *a* the gold and the blue and the purple and the scarlet *material* and the fine linen.

6 "They shall also make *a* the ephod of gold, of blue and purple *and* scarlet *material* and fine twisted linen, the work of the skillful workman.

7 "It shall have two shoulder pieces joined to its two ends, that it may be joined.

8 "And the skillfully woven band, which is on it, shall be like its workmanship, of the same material: of gold, of blue and purple

*20 *a*Ex. 35:8, 28; Lev. 24:1-4
21 *a*Ex. 25:22; 29:42; 30:36 *b*Ex. 26:31, 33 *c*Ex. 30:8; 1 Sam. 3:3; 2 Chr. 13:11 *d*Ex. 28:43; 29:9; Lev. 3:17; 16:34; Num. 18:23; 19:21; 1 Sam. 30:25

1 *a*Num. 18:7; Ps. 99:6; Heb. 5:1, 4 *b*Ex. 24:1, 9

★ 2 *a*Ex. 29:5, 29; 31:10; 39:1-31; Lev. 8:7-9, 30

3 *a*Ex. 31:6; 35:25, 31-35; 36:1 *b*Ex. 31:3; Is. 11:2; 1 Cor. 12:7-11; Eph. 1:17

4 *a*Ex. 28:15-43

5 *a*Ex. 25:3

★ 6-14

6 *a*Ex. 39:2-7; Lev. 8:7

27:20 The *oil* obtained from olives that were *beaten* rather than crushed would be of finer quality, burning more brightly and with less smoke.
28:2 *holy* means "separated" (for divine use).
28:6–14 The *ephod* was a beautiful, two-piece,

sleeveless garment, held to the body by a *skillfully woven band* (v. 8) and joined at the shoulders by straps. On the straps were placed *two onyx stones* (possibly emeralds), with the names of six tribes on each stone.

and scarlet *material* and fine twisted linen.

9 "And you shall take two onyx stones and engrave on them the names of the sons of Israel,

10 six of their names on the one stone, and the names of the remaining six on the other stone, according to their birth.

11 "As a jeweler engraves a signet, you shall engrave the two stones according to the names of the sons of Israel; you shall set them in filigree *settings* of gold.

12 "And you shall put the two stones on the shoulder pieces of the ephod, *as* stones of memorial for the sons of Israel, and Aaron shall *a*bear their names before the LORD on his two shoulders *b*for a memorial.

13 "*a*And you shall make filigree *settings* of gold,

14 and two chains of pure gold; you shall make them of twisted cordage work, and you shall put the corded chains on the filigree *settings*.

15 "And *a*you shall make a breastpiece of judgment, the work of a skillful workman; like the work of the ephod you shall make it: of gold, of blue and purple and scarlet *material* and fine twisted linen you shall make it.

16 "It shall be square *and* folded double, a span in length and a span in width.

17 "And you shall mount on it four rows of stones; the first row *shall be* a row of ruby, topaz and emerald;

18 and the second row a turquoise, a sapphire and a diamond;

19 and the third row a jacinth, an agate and an amethyst;

20 and the fourth row a beryl and an onyx and a jasper; they shall be set in gold filigree.

21 "And the stones shall be according to the names of the sons of Israel: twelve, according to their names; they shall be *like* the engravings of a seal, each *a*according to his name for the twelve tribes.

22 "And you shall make on the breastpiece chains of twisted cordage work in pure gold.

23 "And you shall make on the breastpiece two rings of gold, and shall put the two rings on the two ends of the breastpiece.

24 "And you shall put the two cords of gold on the two rings at the ends of the breastpiece.

25 "And you shall put the *oth*er two ends of the two cords on the two filigree *settings,* and put them on the shoulder pieces of the ephod, at the front of it.

26 "And you shall make two rings of gold and shall place them on the two ends of the breastpiece, on the edge of it, which is toward the inner side of the ephod.

27 "And you shall make two rings of gold and put them on the bottom of the two shoulder pieces of the ephod, on the front of it close to the place where it is joined, above the skillfully woven band of the ephod.

28 "And they shall bind the breastpiece by its rings to the rings of the ephod with a blue cord, that it may be on the skillfully woven band of the ephod, and that the breastpiece may not come loose from the ephod.

29 "And Aaron shall carry the names of the sons of Israel in the breastpiece of judgment over his heart when he enters the holy place, for a memorial before the LORD continually.

30 "And *a*you shall put in the breastpiece of judgment the *b*Urim and the Thummim, and they shall be over Aaron's heart when he goes in before the LORD;

28:15–29 *breastpiece of judgment.* A square piece of beautiful material, folded in half and open at the top like a pouch, and placed over the front of the ephod. It was adorned with 12 precious stones (in four rows), on which were engraved the names of the 12 tribes.

28:30 *Urim* and *Thummim.* Possibly two precious stones, which were put inside the pouch. They may have been used, like lots, to determine God's will. See also Lev. 8:8; Num. 27:21; Deut. 33:8; 1 Sam. 28:6; Ezra 2:63; Neh. 7:65.

---

12 *a*Ex. 28:29; 39:6f. *b*Ex. 39:7; Lev. 24:7; Num. 31:54; Josh. 4:7; 1 Cor. 11:24f.

13 *a*Ex. 39:16-18

★15-29

15 *a*Ex. 39:8-21

21 *a*Rev. 7:4-8; 21:12

★30 *a*Lev. 8:8 *b*Num. 27:21; Deut. 33:8; Ezra 2:63; Neh. 7:65

and Aaron shall carry the judgment of the sons of Israel over his heart before the LORD continually.

★31-35

31 "ᵃAnd you shall make the robe of the ephod all of blue.

32 "And there shall be an opening at its top in the middle of it; around its opening there shall be a binding of woven work, as *it were* the opening of a coat of mail, that it may not be torn.

33 "And you shall make on its hem pomegranates of blue and purple and scarlet *material,* all around on its hem, and bells of gold between them all around:

34 a golden bell and a pomegranate, a golden bell and a pomegranate, all around on the hem of the robe.

35 "And it shall be on Aaron when he ministers; and its tinkling may be heard when he enters and leaves the holy place before the LORD, that he may not die.

★36-38

36 "You shall also make ᵃa plate of pure gold and shall engrave on it, like the engravings of a seal, 'ᵇHoly to the LORD.'

37 "And you shall fasten it on a blue cord, and it shall be on the turban; it shall be at the front of the turban.

38 "And it shall be on Aaron's forehead, and Aaron shall ᵃtake away the iniquity of the holy things which the sons of Israel consecrate, with regard to all their holy gifts; and it shall always be on his forehead, that ᵇthey may be accepted before the LORD.

39 "And you shall weave ᵃthe tunic of checkered work of fine linen, and shall make a turban of fine linen, and you shall make a sash, the work of a weaver.

40 "And for Aaron's sons you shall make ᵃtunics; you shall also make sashes for them, and you shall make ᵇcaps for them, for glory and for beauty.

41 "And you shall put them on Aaron your brother and on his sons with him; and you shall ᵃanoint them and ordain them and consecrate them, that they may serve Me as priests.

42 "And you shall make for them ᵃlinen breeches to cover *their* bare flesh; they shall reach from the loins even to the thighs.

43 "And they shall be on Aaron and on his sons when they enter the tent of meeting, or ᵃwhen they approach the altar to minister in the holy place, so that they do not incur guilt and die. ᵇIt *shall be* a statute forever to him and to his descendants after him.

12 The priests' consecration, 29:1-46

29 "ᵃNow this is what you shall do to them to consecrate them to minister as priests to Me: take one young bull and two rams without blemish,

2 and ᵃunleavened bread and unleavened cakes mixed with oil, and unleavened wafers spread with oil; you shall make them of fine wheat flour.

3 "And you shall put them in one basket, and present them in the basket along with the bull and the two rams.

4 "Then ᵃyou shall bring Aaron and his sons to the doorway of the tent of meeting, and wash them with water.

5 "And you shall take the garments, and put on Aaron the ᵃtunic and ᵇthe robe of the ephod

Marginal references

31 ᵃEx. 39:22-26

36 ᵃEx. 39:30, 31; Lev. 8:9 ᵇZech. 14:20

38 ᵃLev. 10:17; 22:16; Num. 18:1 ᵇLev. 1:4; 22:27; 23:11; Is. 56:7

39 ᵃEx. 39:27-29

40 ᵃEx. 28:4; 39:27, 41 ᵇEx. 29:9; 39:28; Lev. 8:13; Ezek. 44:18

41 ᵃEx. 29:7, 9; 30:30; 40:15; Lev. 8:1-36; 10:7

42 ᵃEx. 39:28; Lev. 6:10; 16:4; Ezek. 44:18

43 ᵃEx. 20:26 ᵇEx. 27:21

★ 1-37

1 ᵃLev. 8:1-34

2 ᵃLev. 2:4; 6:19-23

4 ᵃEx. 40:12; Lev. 8:6

5 ᵃEx. 28:39; Lev. 8:7 ᵇEx. 28:31 ᶜEx. 28:6 ᵈEx. 28:15 ᵉEx. 28:8

28:31-35 *robe of the ephod.* A violet-colored robe worn under the ephod. It reached a little below the knees and had bells on its hem. When the High Priest made an offering in the Holy Place, where he was not visible to the people, the bells enabled them to know he was still alive.

28:36-38 On the *turban* was a gold plate with *Holy to the LORD* engraved on it. The High Priest's official holiness enabled him to present the imperfect offerings (*holy things*) to God acceptably (v. 38).

29:1-37 These verses describe the installation of the priests, which included washing (v. 4), anointing (v. 7), clothing (vv. 8-9), and offering sacrifices (vv. 10-28). The priests' ears (symbolizing obedience to God, cf. Exod. 21:6), thumbs and toes (symbolizing work for God) were specially dedicated to God (29:20). The ceremonies lasted seven days (v. 35).

and ᶜthe ephod and ᵈthe breast-piece, and gird him with the skill-fully ᵉwoven band of the ephod;

6 and you shall set the ᵃtur-ban on his head, and put ᵇthe holy crown on the turban.

7 "Then you shall take ᵃthe anointing oil, and pour it on his head and anoint him.

8 "And you shall bring his sons and put ᵃtunics on them.

9 "And you shall gird them with ᵃsashes, Aaron and his sons, and bind caps on them; and they shall have ᵇthe priesthood by a perpetual statute. So you shall ᶜordain Aaron and his sons.

10 "Then you shall bring the bull before the tent of meeting, and Aaron and his sons shall ᵃlay their hands on the head of the bull.

11 "And you shall slaughter the bull before the LORD at the doorway of the tent of meeting.

12 "And you shall ᵃtake some of the blood of the bull and put it on ᵇthe horns of the altar with your finger; and you shall pour out all the blood at the base of the altar.

13 "And you shall ᵃtake all the fat that covers the entrails and the lobe of the liver, and the two kid-neys and the fat that is on them, and offer them up in smoke on the altar.

14 "But ᵃthe flesh of the bull and its hide and its refuse, you shall burn with fire outside the camp; it is a sin offering.

15 "ᵃYou shall also take the one ram, and Aaron and his sons shall lay their hands on the head of the ram;

16 and you shall slaughter the ram and shall take its blood and sprinkle it around on the altar.

17 "Then you shall cut the ram into its pieces, and wash its en-trails and its legs, and put them with its pieces and its head.

18 "And you shall offer up in smoke the whole ram on the altar; it is a burnt offering to the LORD: ᵃit is a soothing aroma, an offer-ing by fire to the LORD.

19 "Then ᵃyou shall take the other ram, and Aaron and his

sons shall lay their hands on the head of the ram.

20 "And you shall slaughter the ram, and take some of its blood and put it on the lobe of Aaron's right ear and on the lobes of his sons' right ears and on the thumbs of their right hands and on the big toes of their right feet, and sprinkle the rest of the blood around on the altar.

21 "Then you shall take some of the blood that is on the altar and some of the ᵃanointing oil, and sprinkle it on Aaron and on his garments, and on his sons and on his sons' garments with him; so he and his garments shall be consecrated, as well as his sons and his sons' garments with him.

22 "You shall also take the fat from the ram and the fat tail, and the fat that covers the entrails and the lobe of the liver, and the two kidneys and the fat that is on them and the right thigh (for it is a ram of ordination),

23 and one cake of bread and ᵃone cake of bread mixed with oil and one wafer from the basket of unleavened bread which is set be-fore the LORD;

24 and you shall put all these in the hands of Aaron and in the hands of his sons, and shall wave them as a wave offering before the LORD.

25 "And ᵃyou shall take them from their hands, and offer them up in smoke on the altar on the burnt offering for a soothing aro-ma before the LORD; it is an offer-ing by fire to the LORD.

26 "Then you shall take ᵃthe breast of Aaron's ram of ordina-tion, and wave it as a wave offer-ing before the LORD; and it shall be your portion.

27 "And you shall consecrate the breast of the wave offering and the thigh of the heave offer-ing which was waved and which was offered from the ram of ordi-nation, from the one which was for Aaron and from the one which was for his sons.

28 "And it shall be for Aaron and his sons as their portion for-

6 ᵃEx. 28:4, 39 ᵇEx. 28:36, 37; Lev. 8:9

7 ᵃEx. 30:25; Lev. 8:12; 21:10; Num. 35:25; Ps. 133:2
8 ᵃEx. 28:39, 40; Lev. 8:13
9 ᵃEx. 28:40 ᵇEx. 40:15; Num. 3:10; 18:7; 25:13; Deut. 18:5 ᶜEx. 28:41; Lev. 8:1-36

10 ᵃLev. 1:4; 8:14

12 ᵃLev. 8:15 ᵇEx. 27:2; 30:2

13 ᵃLev. 3:3, 4

14 ᵃLev. 4:11, 12, 21; Heb. 13:11

15 ᵃLev. 8:18

18 ᵃGen. 8:21; Ex. 29:25

19 ᵃLev. 8:22f.

21 ᵃEx. 30:25, 31; Lev. 8:30

23 ᵃLev. 8:26

25 ᵃLev. 8:28

26 ᵃLev. 7:31, 34; 8:29

ever from the sons of Israel, for it is a heave offering; and it shall be a heave offering from the sons of Israel from the sacrifices of their peace offerings, *even* their heave offering to the LORD.

29 a Num. 20:26, 28

29 "And *a*the holy garments of Aaron shall be for his sons after him, that in them they may be anointed and ordained.

30 "For seven days the one of his sons who is priest in his stead shall put them on when he enters the tent of meeting to minister in the holy place.

31 a Lev. 8:31

31 "And you shall take the ram of ordination and *a*boil its flesh in a holy place.

32 "And Aaron and his sons shall eat the flesh of the ram, and the bread that is in the basket, at the doorway of the tent of meeting.

33 a Lev. 10:14 **b**Lev. 22:10, 13

33 "Thus *a*they shall eat those things by which atonement was made at their ordination *and* consecration; but a *b*layman shall not eat *them,* because they are holy.

34 a Ex. 12:10; 23:18; 34:25; Lev. 8:32

34 "And *a*if any of the flesh of ordination or any of the bread remains until morning, then you shall burn the remainder with fire; it shall not be eaten, because it is holy.

35 a Lev. 8:33

35 "And thus you shall do to Aaron and to his sons, according to all that I have commanded you; you shall ordain them through *a*seven days.

36 a Heb. 10:11 **b**Ex. 40:10

36 "And *a*each day you shall offer a bull as a sin offering for atonement, and you shall purify the altar when you make atonement for it; and *b*you shall anoint it to consecrate it.

37 a Ex. 30:28f.

37 "For seven days you shall make atonement for the altar and consecrate it; then *a*the altar shall be most holy, *and* whatever touches the altar shall be holy.

★38–41
38 a Num. 28:3-31; 29:6-38

38 "Now *a*this is what you shall offer on the altar: two one

year old lambs each day, continuously.

39 a Ezek. 46:13-15

39 "The *a*one lamb you shall offer in the morning, and the other lamb you shall offer at twilight;

40 and there *shall be* one-tenth *of an ephah* of fine flour mixed with one-fourth of a hin of beaten oil, and one-fourth of a hin of wine for a libation with one lamb.

41 "And the other lamb you shall offer at twilight, and shall offer with it the same grain offering as the morning and the same libation, for a soothing aroma, an offering by fire to the LORD.

42 a Ex. 25:22; Num. 17:4

42 "It shall be a continual burnt offering throughout your generations at the doorway of the tent of meeting before the LORD, *a*where I will meet with you, to speak to you there.

43 "And I will meet there with the sons of Israel, and it shall be consecrated by My glory.

44 "And I will consecrate the tent of meeting and the altar; I will also consecrate Aaron and his sons to minister as priests to Me.

45 a Ex. 25:8; Lev. 26:12; Num. 5:3; Deut. 12:11; Zech. 2:10; 2 Cor. 6:16; Rev. 21:3

45 "And *a*I will dwell among the sons of Israel and will be their God.

46 a Ex. 20:2

46 "And they shall know that *a*I am the LORD their God who brought them out of the land of Egypt, that I might dwell among them; I am the LORD their God.

13 The altar of incense, 30:1-10

★ 1-10
1 a Ex. 37:25-29

30 "Moreover, you shall make *a*an altar as a place for burning incense; you shall make it of acacia wood.

2 "Its length *shall be* a cubit, and its width a cubit, it shall be square, and its height *shall be* two cubits; its horns *shall be* of one piece with it.

3 "And you shall overlay it with pure gold, its top and its

29:38–41 These verses contain the law of the continual daily sacrifices (see also Acts 3:1). *twilight* (v. 39). See note on 12:6.
30:1–10 The *altar* of *incense* stood before the curtain that shut off the Holy of Holies (see

note on Heb. 9:4). Incense was burned on it morning and evening when the priest tended to the lamp. Exod. 30:34-38 describes the composition of the incense.

sides all around, and its horns; and you shall make a gold molding all around for it.

4 "And you shall make two gold rings for it under its molding; you shall make *them* on its two side walls—on opposite sides—and they shall be holders for poles with which to carry it.

5 "And you shall make the poles of acacia wood and overlay them with gold.

6 aEx. 25:21f.

6 "And you shall put this altar in front of the veil that is near the ark of the testimony, in front of the amercy seat that is over *the ark of* the testimony, where I will meet with you.

7 "And Aaron shall burn fragrant incense on it; he shall burn it every morning when he trims the lamps.

8 "And when Aaron trims the lamps at twilight, he shall burn incense. *There shall be* perpetual incense before the LORD throughout your generations.

9 "You shall not offer any strange incense on this altar, or burnt offering or meal offering; and you shall not pour out a libation on it.

10 aLev. 16:18

10 "And Aaron shall amake atonement on its horns once a year; he shall make atonement on it with the blood of the sin offering of atonement once a year throughout your generations. It is most holy to the LORD."

14 The atonement money, 30:11-16

★11-16

11 The LORD also spoke to Moses, saying,

12 aEx. 38:25, 26; Num. 1:2; 26:2 bNum. 31:50

12 "When you take aa census of the sons of Israel to number them, then each one of them shall give ba ransom for himself to the LORD, when you number them, that there may be no plague among them when you number them.

13 aLev. 27:25, Num. 3:47; Ezek. 45:12

13 "This is what everyone who is numbered shall give: half a shekel according to the shekel of the sanctuary (athe shekel is twenty gerahs), half a shekel as a contribution to the LORD.

14 "Everyone who is numbered, from twenty years old and over, shall give the contribution to the LORD.

15 "The rich shall not pay more, and the poor shall not pay less than the half shekel, when you give the contribution to the LORD to make atonement for yourselves.

16 "And you shall take the atonement money from the sons of Israel, and shall give it for the service of the tent of meeting, that it may be a memorial for the sons of Israel before the LORD, to make atonement for yourselves."

15 The laver, 30:17-21

★17-21

17 And the LORD spoke to Moses, saying,

18 aEx. 38:8 bEx. 40:30

18 "You shall also make aa laver of bronze, with its base of bronze, for washing; and you shall bput it between the tent of meeting and the altar, and you shall put water in it.

19 aEx. 40:31f.; Is. 52:11

19 "And Aaron and his sons shall awash their hands and their feet from it;

20 when they enter the tent of meeting, they shall wash with water, that they may not die; or when they approach the altar to minister, by offering up in smoke a fire *sacrifice* to the LORD.

21 aEx. 28:43

21 "So they shall wash their hands and their feet, that they may not die; and ait shall be a perpetual statute for them, for Aaron and his descendants throughout their generations."

30:11-16 Every male 20 years and older was required to pay a *ransom* on being formally enrolled among God's people. A shekel weighed about 224 grains, or one-half ounce. The silver collected was used in making the sockets, hooks, and rods (see 38:25-28). See also Neh. 10:32 and Matt. 17:24-27 regarding this same tax.

30:17-21 The bronze *laver*, made from mirrors (cf. 38:8), stood between the altar of burnt offering and the door of the tabernacle and was used for the ritual cleansing of the priests.

16 The anointing oil, 30:22-33

★22-33

22 Moreover, the LORD spoke to Moses, saying,

23 "Take also for yourself the finest of spices: of flowing myrrh five hundred *shekels*, and of fragrant cinnamon half as much, two hundred and fifty, and of fragrant cane two hundred and fifty,

24 and of cassia five hundred, according to the shekel of the sanctuary, and of olive oil a hin.

25 _{25 aEx. 37:29; 40:9; Lev. 8:10} "And you shall make of these a holy anointing oil, a perfume mixture, the work of a perfumer; it shall be ªa holy anointing oil.

26 _{26 aEx. 40:9; Lev. 8:10; Num. 7:1} "And with it ªyou shall anoint the tent of meeting and the ark of the testimony,

27 and the table and all its utensils, and the lampstand and its utensils, and the altar of incense,

28 and the altar of burnt offering and all its utensils, and the laver and its stand.

29 "You shall also consecrate them, that they may be most holy; whatever touches them shall be holy.

30 _{30 aEx. 29:7; Lev. 8:12} "ªAnd you shall anoint Aaron and his sons, and consecrate them, that they may minister as priests to Me.

31 "And you shall speak to the sons of Israel, saying, 'This shall be a holy anointing oil to Me throughout your generations.

32 _{32 aEx. 30:25, 37} 'It shall not be poured on anyone's body, nor shall you make *any* like it, in the same proportions; ªit is holy, *and* it shall be holy to you.

33 _{33 aEx. 30:38 bGen. 17:14; Ex. 12:15; Lev. 7:20f.} 'ªWhoever shall mix *any* like it, or whoever puts any of it on a layman, ᵇshall be cut off from his people.' "

17 The incense, 30:34-38

34 Then the LORD said to Moses, "Take for yourself spices, stacte and onycha and galbanum, spices with pure frankincense; there shall be an equal part of each.

35 "And with it you shall make incense, a perfume, the work of a perfumer, salted, pure, *and* holy.

36 _{36 aEx. 29:42} "And you shall beat some of it very fine, and put part of it before the testimony in the tent of meeting, ªwhere I shall meet with you; it shall be most holy to you.

37 _{37 aEx. 30:32} "And the incense which you shall make, ªyou shall not make in the same proportions for yourselves; it shall be holy to you for the LORD.

38 _{38 aEx. 30:33} "ªWhoever shall make *any* like it, to use as perfume, shall be cut off from his people."

18 The builders, 31:1-11

31 _{1 aEx. 35:30-36:1} ªNow the LORD spoke to Moses, saying,

2 _{2 a1 Chr. 2:20} "See, I have called by name Bezalel, the ªson of Uri, the son of Hur, of the tribe of Judah.

3 _{★ 3 aEx. 35:31; 1 Kin. 7:14; 1 Cor. 12:4-8} "And I have ªfilled him with the Spirit of God in wisdom, in understanding, in knowledge, and in all *kinds of* craftsmanship,

4 to make artistic designs for work in gold, in silver, and in bronze,

5 and in the cutting of stones for settings, and in the carving of wood, that he may work in all *kinds of* craftsmanship.

6 _{6 aEx. 35:34} "And behold, I Myself have appointed with him ªOholiab, the son of Ahisamach, of the tribe of Dan; and in the hearts of all who

---

30:22-33 *holy anointing oil.* This highly perfumed oil (v. 25) was to be used exclusively (vv. 32-35) for the prescribed consecrations of the tabernacle and its furnishings (vv. 26-29)

and of the priests (v. 30)

31:3 God empowered these craftsmen with the Holy Spirit (see also Judg. 6:34 and 1 Sam. 10:10).

are skillful I have put skill, that they may make all that I have commanded you:

7 ^athe tent of meeting, and ^bthe ark of testimony, and ^cthe mercy seat upon it, and all the furniture of the tent,

8 ^athe table also and its utensils, and the ^bpure *gold* lampstand with all its utensils, and ^cthe altar of incense,

9 ^athe altar of burnt offering also with all its utensils, and ^bthe laver and its stand,

10 the ^awoven garments as well, and the holy garments for Aaron the priest, and the garments of his sons, *with which* to carry on their priesthood;

11 ^athe anointing oil also, and the ^bfragrant incense for the holy place, they are to make *them* according to all that I have commanded you."

19 The sign of the Sabbath, 31:12–18

12 And the LORD spoke to Moses, saying,

13 "But as for you, speak to the sons of Israel, saying, '^aYou shall surely observe My sabbaths; for *this* is ^ba sign between Me and you throughout your generations, that you may know that I am the LORD who sanctifies you.

14 'Therefore you are to observe the sabbath, for it is holy to you. ^aEveryone who profanes it shall surely be put to death; for whoever does any work on it, that person shall be cut off from among his people.

15 '^aFor six days work may be done, but on the seventh day there is a ^bsabbath of complete rest, holy to the LORD; ^cwhoever

does any work on the sabbath day shall surely be put to death.

16 'So the sons of Israel shall observe the sabbath, to celebrate the sabbath throughout their generations as a perpetual covenant.'

17 "^aIt is a sign between Me and the sons of Israel forever; ^bfor in six days the LORD made heaven and earth, but on the seventh day He ceased *from labor*, and was refreshed."

18 And when He had finished speaking with him upon Mount Sinai, He gave Moses ^athe two tablets of the testimony, tablets of stone, ^bwritten by the finger of God.

C The Breaking of the Law, 32:1–34:35

1 The sin of the people: the golden calf, 32:1–10

32 Now when the people saw that Moses ^adelayed to come down from the mountain, the people assembled about Aaron, and said to him, "Come, ^bmake us a god who will go before us; as for ^cthis Moses, the man who brought us up from the land of Egypt, we do not know what has become of him."

2 And Aaron said to them, "^aTear off the gold rings which are in the ears of your wives, your sons, and your daughters, and bring *them* to me."

3 Then all the people tore off the gold rings which were in their ears, and brought *them* to Aaron.

4 And he took *this* from their hand, and fashioned it with a graving tool, and made it into a ^amolten calf; and they said, "This is your god, O Israel, who

Marginal references (left column):

7 ^aEx. 36:8-38 ^bEx. 37:1-5 ^cEx. 37:6-9

8 ^aEx. 37:10-16 ^bEx. 37:17-24; Lev. 24:4 ^cEx. 37:25-29

9 ^aEx. 38:1-7 ^bEx. 38:8

10 ^aEx. 39:1

11 ^aEx. 30:23-32 ^bEx. 30:34-38

★12-17

13 ^aEx. 20:8 ^bEx. 31:17; Ezek. 20:12, 20

14 ^aEx. 31:15; 35:2; Num. 15:32, 35; John 7:23

15 ^aEx. 20:9-11; 23:12; 34:21; 35:2; Lev. 23:3; Deut. 5:12-14 ^bGen. 2:2; Ex. 16:23; 20:8; 35:2, 3 ^cEx. 31:14

Marginal references (right column):

17 ^aEx. 31:13; Ezek. 20:12 ^bGen. 1:31; 2:2, 3; Ex. 20:11

★18 ^aEx. 24:12; 34:29; Deut. 4:13; 5:22; 9:10f. ^bEx. 32:15, 16; 34:1, 28; Deut. 9:10

★ 1 ^aEx. 24:18; Deut. 9:11, 12 ^bActs 7:40 ^cEx. 14:11

★ 2 ^aEx. 35:22

★ 4 ^aDeut. 9:16; Neh. 9:18; Ps. 106:19; Acts 7:41

31:12-17 The Sabbath was made a *sign* of God's unique relationship with Israel as His own people. The importance of this sign is seen in the insistence of later prophets that Sabbath-keeping was an indication of the spiritual condition of the people (Jer. 17:19-27; Ezek. 20:12-24). See note on Exod. 20:8-11.

31:18 Fulfillment of the promise of 24:12. *the finger of God.* See note on 8:18-19.

32:1 *Moses delayed.* He had been on the mountain 40 days (24:18).

32:2 *rings.* Presumably part of the booty taken from Egypt (12:36). Because of this occasion (32:2-4), the people were prohibited from wearing ornaments (33:4-6).

32:4 *calf.* Better, young bull. This particular idolatry was a throwback to life in Egypt (see note on 8:25).

brought you up from the land of Egypt."

5 Now when Aaron saw *this,* he built an altar before it; and Aaron made a proclamation and said, "Tomorrow *shall be* a feast to the LORD."

★ 6 aActs 7:41 b1 Cor. 10:7 cEx. 32:17-19; Num. 25:2

6 So the next day they rose early and aoffered burnt offerings, and brought peace offerings; and bthe people sat down to eat and to drink, and rose up cto play.

7 aEx. 32:4, 11; Deut. 9:12 bGen. 6:11f.

7 Then the LORD spoke to Moses, "Go down at once, for your people, whom ayou brought up from the land of Egypt, have bcorrupted *themselves.*

8 aEx. 20:3, 4, 23 bEx. 22:20; 34:15; Deut. 32:17 c1 Kin. 12:28

8 "They have quickly turned aside from the way which I commanded them. aThey have made for themselves a molten calf, and have worshiped it, and bhave sacrificed to it, and said, 'cThis is your god, O Israel, who brought you up from the land of Egypt!' "

★ 9 aNum. 14:11-20 bEx. 33:3, 5; 34:9; Is. 48:4; Acts 7:51

9 aAnd the LORD said to Moses, "I have seen this people, and behold, they are ban obstinate people.

10 aDeut. 9:14 bNum. 14:12

10 "Now then alet Me alone, that My anger may burn against them, and that I may destroy them; and bI will make of you a great nation."

2 The intercession and wrath of Moses, 32:11-35

★11-13

11 aDeut. 9:18, 26

11 Then aMoses entreated the LORD his God, and said, "O LORD, why doth Thine anger burn against Thy people whom Thou hast brought out from the land of Egypt with great power and with a mighty hand?

12 aNum. 14:13-19; Deut. 9:28; Josh. 7:9

12 "Why should athe Egyptians speak, saying, 'With evil *intent* He brought them out to kill

them in the mountains and to destroy them from the face of the earth'? Turn from Thy burning anger and change Thy mind about *doing* harm to Thy people.

13 "Remember Abraham, Isaac, and Israel, Thy servants to whom Thou didst aswear by Thyself, and didst say to them, 'I will bmultiply your descendants as the stars of the heavens, and call this land of which I have spoken I will give to your descendants, and they shall inherit *it* forever.' "

13 aGen. 22:16-18; Heb. 6:13 bGen. 15:5; 26:4 cGen. 12:7; 13:15; 15:18; 17:8; 35:12; Ex. 13:5, 11; 33:1

14 aSo the LORD changed His mind about the harm which He said He would do to His people.

★14 aPs. 106:45

15 aThen Moses turned and went down from the mountain with the two tablets of the testimony in his hand, btablets which were written on both sides; they were written on one *side* and the other.

15 aDeut. 9:15 bEx. 31:18

16 And the tablets were God's work, and the writing was God's writing engraved on the tablets.

17 Now when Joshua heard the sound of the people as they shouted, he said to Moses, "There is a sound of war in the camp."

18 But he said,
"It is not the sound of the cry of triumph,
Nor is it the sound of the cry of defeat;
But the sound of singing I hear."

19 And it came about, as soon as Moses came near the camp, that ahe saw the calf and *the* dancing; and Moses' anger burned, and bhe threw the tablets from his hands and shattered them at the foot of the mountain.

★19 aEx. 32:6; Deut. 9:16 bDeut. 9:17

20 aAnd he took the calf which they had made and burned *it* with fire, and ground it to

★20 aDeut. 9:21

32:6 *to play.* The word suggests sex play (it is the same Hebrew word as is used in Gen. 26:8). In light of the drinking and possible nakedness (Exod. 32:25, KJV; 1 Cor. 10:8), the scene likely became a drunken sex orgy.

32:9 *obstinate.* Lit., stiffnecked, like an ox or horse that will not respond to the reins.

32:11-13 Moses' appeal for mercy was based on three things: God Himself had chosen Israel (v. 11); God's name must be vindicated (v. 12);

God had made promises in the Abrahamic covenant that could not be fulfilled if Israel were destroyed (v. 13).

32:14 *changed His mind.* Better, was sorry.

32:19 The breaking of the *tablets* of the Law vividly symbolized the breach of the covenant.

32:20 *burned it.* The bull either stood on a wooden pedestal or was built on a wooden frame.

powder, and scattered it over the surface of the water, and made the sons of Israel drink *it*.

★21-24   **21**   Then Moses said to Aaron, "What did this people do to you, that you have brought *such* great sin upon them?"

22 *a*Deut. 9:24   **22**   And Aaron said, "Do not let the anger of my lord burn; you know the people yourself, *a*that they are prone to evil.

23 *a*Ex. 32:1-4   **23**   "For *a*they said to me, 'Make a god for us who will go before us; for this Moses, the man who brought us up from the land of Egypt, we do not know what has become of him.'

24 *a*Ex. 32:4   **24**   "And I said to them, 'Whoever has any gold, let them tear it off.' So they gave *it* to me, and *a*I threw it into the fire, and out came this calf."

25 *a*1 Kin. 12:28-30; 14:16   **25**   Now when Moses saw that the people were out of control— for Aaron had *a*let them get out of control to be a derision among their enemies—

26   then Moses stood in the gate of the camp, and said, "Whoever is for the LORD, *come* to me!" And all the sons of Levi gathered together to him.

★27   **27**   And he said to them, "Thus says the LORD, the God of Israel, 'Every man *of you* put his sword upon his thigh, and go back and forth from gate to gate in the camp, and kill every man his brother, and every man his friend, and every man his neighbor.'"

28 *a*Num. 25:7-13; Deut. 33:9   **28**   So *a*the sons of Levi did as Moses instructed, and about three thousand men of the people fell that day.

29   Then Moses said, "Dedicate yourselves today to the LORD—for every man has been against his son and against his brother—in order that He may bestow a blessing upon you today."

30   And it came about on the next day that Moses said to the people, "*a*You yourselves have committed a great sin; and now I am going up to the LORD, perhaps I can *b*make atonement for your sin."

30 *a*1 Sam. 12:20, 23 *b*Num. 25:13

31   Then Moses returned to the LORD, and said, "Alas, this people has committed a great sin, and they have made a *a*god of gold for themselves.

31 *a*Ex. 20:23

32   "But now, if Thou wilt, forgive their sin—and if not, please blot me out from Thy *a*book which Thou hast written!"

★32 *a*Ps. 69:28; Is. 4:3; Dan. 12:1; Mal. 3:16, 17; Phil. 4:3; Rev. 3:5; 21:27

33   And the LORD said to Moses, "Whoever has sinned against Me, *a*I will blot him out of My book.

33 *a*Ex. 17:14; Deut. 29:20; Ps. 9:5; Rev. 3:5

34   "But go now, lead the people *a*where I told you. Behold, *b*My angel shall go before you; nevertheless *c*in the day when I punish, *d*I will punish them for their sin."

34 *a*Ex. 3:17 *b*Ex. 23:20 *c*Deut. 32:35; Rom. 2:5, 6 *d*Ps. 99:8

35   *a*Then the LORD smote the people, because of *b*what they did with the calf which Aaron had made.

35 *a*Ex. 32:28 *b*Ex. 32:4, 24

3   *The repentance of the people,* 33:1-11

33   Then the LORD spoke to Moses, "Depart, go up from here, you and the people whom you have brought up from the land of Egypt, to the land of which *a*I swore to Abraham, *b*Isaac, and *c*Jacob, saying, '*d*To your descendants I will give it.'

1 *a*Ex. 32:13 *b*Gen. 26:1-3 *c*Gen. 28:10 *d*Gen. 12:7

2   "And I will send *a*an angel before you and *b*I will drive out the Canaanite, the Amorite, the Hittite, the Perizzite, the Hivite and the Jebusite.

2 *a*Ex. 32:34 *b*Ex. 23:27-31; Josh. 24:11

3   "*Go up* to a land *a*flowing with milk and honey; for I will not go up in your midst, because you are *b*an obstinate people, lest *c*I destroy you on the way."

3 *a*Ex. 3:8, 17 *b*Ex. 32:9; 33:5 *c*Ex. 32:10

32:21-24 Deut. 9:20 indicates how deserving of blame Aaron was.

32:27 *his brother.* I.e., his fellow Israelite. This whole incident is used as a warning in 1 Cor. 10:7.

32:32 *book.* A register of the physically living. To be blotted out meant to experience an untimely death. By contrast, the New Testament book of life (Rev. 13:8, etc.) is the register of those who have eternal life.

★ 4 aNum.
14:1, 39

4 When the people heard this sad word, athey went into mourning, and none of them put on his ornaments.

5 aEx. 33:3

5 For the LORD had said to Moses, "Say to the sons of Israel, 'You are aan obstinate people; should I go up in your midst for one moment, I would destroy you. Now therefore, put off your ornaments from you, that I may know what I will do with you.'"

6 So the sons of Israel stripped themselves of their ornaments from Mount Horeb onward.

★ 7 aEx.
18:7, 12-16
bEx. 29:42f.

7 Now Moses used to take athe tent and pitch it outside the camp, a good distance from the camp, and he called it the tent of meeting. And it came about, that beveryone who sought the LORD would go out to the tent of meeting which was outside the camp.

8 And it came about, whenever Moses went out to the tent, that all the people would arise and stand, each at the entrance of his tent, and gaze after Moses until he entered the tent.

9 aEx.
13:21 bPs.
99:7

9 And it came about, whenever Moses entered the tent, athe pillar of cloud would descend and stand at the entrance of the tent; band the LORD would speak with Moses.

10 When all the people saw the pillar of cloud standing at the entrance of the tent, all the people would arise and worship, each at the entrance of his tent.

11 aNum.
12:8; Deut.
34:10 bEx.
24:13

11 Thus athe LORD used to speak to Moses face to face, just as a man speaks to his friend. When Moses returned to the camp, bhis servant Joshua, the son of Nun, a young man, would not depart from the tent.

4 *The prayer of Moses,*
33:12-23

12 aEx. 3:10;
32:34 bEx.
33:2 cEx.
33:17

12 Then Moses said to the LORD, "See, Thou dost say to me, 'aBring up this people!' But Thou Thyself hast not let me know bwhom Thou wilt send with me. cMoreover, Thou hast said, 'I have known you by name, and you have also found favor in My sight.'

13 aPs. 25:4;
27:11; 51:13;
86:11;
119:33 bEx.
3:7, 10; 5:1;
32:12, 14;
Deut. 9:26,
29

13 "Now therefore, I pray Thee, if I have found favor in Thy sight, alet me know Thy ways, that I may know Thee, so that I may find favor in Thy sight. bConsider too, that this nation is Thy people."

14 aDeut.
4:37; Is. 63:9
bDeut.
12:10; 25:19;
Josh. 21:44;
22:4

14 And He said, "aMy presence shall go *with you,* and bI will give you rest."

15 aPs. 80:3,
7, 19

15 Then he said to Him, "aIf Thy presence does not go *with us,* do not lead us up from here.

16 aLev.
20:24, 26

16 "For how then can it be known that I have found favor in Thy sight, I and Thy people? Is it not by Thy going with us, so that awe, I and Thy people, may be distinguished from all the *other* people who are upon the face of the earth?"

17 aEx.
33:12

17 And the LORD said to Moses, "I will also do this thing of which you have spoken; afor you have found favor in My sight, and I have known you by name."

★18-23

18 aEx.
33:20-23

18 aThen Moses said, "I pray Thee, show me Thy glory!"

19 aEx. 34:6,
7 bRom.
9:15

19 And He said, "aI Myself will make all My goodness pass before you, and will proclaim the name of the LORD before you; and bI will be gracious to whom I will be gracious, and will show compassion on whom I will show compassion."

33:4 *this sad word.* I.e., that an angel, not God Himself, would lead them to the promised land. Moses successfully appealed this decision in verses 12-17.

33:7 *tent.* The tabernacle was not yet constructed.

33:18-23 Moses' request for a vision of God was granted, though not fully and with great precautions. Cf. note on John 1:18.

20 *a*Is. 6:5;
1 Tim. 6:16

20 But He said, "You cannot see My face, *a*for no man can see Me and live!"

21 *a*Ps. 18:2,
46; 27:5;
61:2; 62:7

21 Then the LORD said, "Behold, there is a place by Me, and *a*you shall stand *there* on the rock;

22 *a*Ps. 91:1,
4; Is. 49:2;
51:16

22 and it will come about, while My glory is passing by, that I will put you in the cleft of the rock and *a*cover you with My hand until I have passed by.

23 *a*Ex.
33:20; John
1:18

23 "Then I will take My hand away and you shall see My back, but *a*My face shall not be seen."

5 The covenant renewed,
34:1-35

1 *a*Ex.
24:12; 31:18;
32:16, 19
*b*Deut.
10:2, 4

34 Now the LORD said to Moses, "Cut out for yourself *a*two stone tablets like the former ones, and *b*I will write on the tablets the words that were on the former tablets which you shattered.

2 *a*Ex.
19:11, 18, 20

2 "So be ready by morning, and come up in the morning to *a*Mount Sinai, and present yourself there to Me on the top of the mountain.

3 *a*Ex.
19:12, 13

3 "And *a*no man is to come up with you, nor let any man be seen anywhere on the mountain; even the flocks and the herds may not graze in front of that mountain."

4 *a*Ex. 34:1

4 So he cut out *a*two stone tablets like the former ones, and Moses rose up early in the morning and went up to Mount Sinai, as the LORD had commanded him, and he took two stone tablets in his hand.

5 *a*Ex. 19:9;
33:9

5 And *a*the LORD descended in the cloud and stood there with him as he called upon the name of the LORD.

6 *a*Num.
14:18; Deut.
4:31; Neh.
9:17; Ps.
86:15; 103:8;
108:4; 145:8;
Joel 2:13;
Rom. 2:4

6 Then the LORD passed by in front of him and proclaimed, "The LORD, the LORD God, *a*compassionate and gracious, slow to anger, and abounding in loving-kindness and truth;

7 *a*Ex. 20:5,
6; Deut. 5:10;
7:9; Ps.
103:3; 130:3,
4; 1 John 1:9
*b*Ex. 23:7;
Deut. 7:10;
Job 10:14;
Nah. 1:3
*c*Deut. 5:9

7 who *a*keeps lovingkindness for thousands, who forgives iniquity, transgression and sin; yet He *b*will by no means leave *the guilty* unpunished, *c*visiting the iniquity of fathers on the children and on the grandchildren to the third and fourth generations."

8 *a*Ex. 4:31

8 And Moses made haste *a*to bow low toward the earth and worship.

9 *a*Ex.
33:13 *b*Ex.
32:9 *c*Ex.
34:7 *d*Deut.
4:20; 9:26,
29; 32:9; Ps.
33:12

9 And he said, "*a*If now I have found favor in Thy sight, O Lord, I pray, let the Lord go along in our midst, even though *b*the people are so obstinate; and do Thou *c*pardon our iniquity and our sin, and *d*take us as Thine own possession."

★10 *a*Ex.
34:27, 28;
Deut. 5:2
*b*Deut. 4:32;
Ps. 72:18;
136:4

10 Then God said, "Behold, *a*I am going to make a covenant. Before all your people *b*I will perform miracles which have not been produced in all the earth, nor among any of the nations; and all the people among whom you live will see the working of the LORD, for it is a fearful thing that I am going to perform with you.

11 *a*Ex. 33:2

11 "Be sure to observe what I am commanding you this day: behold, *a*I am going to drive out the Amorite before you, and the Canaanite, the Hittite, the Perizzite, the Hivite and the Jebusite.

★12-17

12 *a*Ex.
23:32, 33

12 "*a*Watch yourself that you make no covenant with the inhabitants of the land into which you are going, lest it become a snare in your midst.

13 *a*Ex.
23:24; Deut.
12:3 *b*Deut.
16:21; Judg.
6:25, 26;
2 Kin. 18:4;
2 Chr. 34:3f.

13 "*a*But *rather,* you are to tear down their altars and smash their *sacred* pillars and cut down their *b*Asherim

14 *a*Ex. 20:3,
5; Deut. 4:24

14 —for *a*you shall not worship any other god, for the LORD, whose name is Jealous, is a jealous God—

34:10 *a fearful thing.* Better, something of which men will stand in awe.

34:12-17 The people were warned against making any agreements with the Canaanites, against participating in their idolatrous practices, and against intermarriage. *Asherim* (v. 13). Wooden symbols of Asherah, the foremost deity of the Canaanites and mother of Baal.

15 lest you make a covenant with the inhabitants of the land and they play the harlot with their gods, and ªsacrifice to their gods, and someone ᵇinvite you to eat of his sacrifice;

16 and ªyou take some of his daughters for your sons, and his daughters play the harlot with their gods, and cause your sons *also* to play the harlot with their gods.

17 "ªYou shall make for yourself no molten gods.

18 "You shall observe ªthe Feast of Unleavened Bread. For ᵇseven days you are to eat unleavened bread, as I commanded you, at the appointed time in the ᶜmonth of Abib, for in the month of Abib you came out of Egypt.

19 "ªThe first offspring from every womb belongs to Me, and all your male livestock, the first offspring from cattle and sheep.

20 "ªAnd you shall redeem with a lamb the first offspring from a donkey; and if you do not redeem *it,* then you shall break its neck. You shall redeem ᵇall the first-born of your sons. And ᶜnone shall appear before Me empty-handed.

21 "You shall work ªsix days, but on the seventh day you shall rest; *even* during plowing time and harvest you shall rest.

22 "And you shall celebrate ªthe Feast of Weeks, *that is,* the first fruits of the wheat harvest, and the Feast of Ingathering at the turn of the year.

23 "ªThree times a year all your males are to appear before the Lord Goᴅ, the God of Israel.

24 "For I will ªdrive out nations before you and enlarge your borders, and no man shall covet your land when you go up three times a year to appear before the Lorᴅ your God.

25 "ªYou shall not offer the blood of My sacrifice with leavened bread, ᵇnor is the sacrifice of the Feast of the Passover to be left over until morning.

26 "You shall bring ªthe very first of the first fruits of your soil into the house of the Lorᴅ your God. You shall not boil a kid in its mother's milk."

27 Then the Lorᴅ said to Moses, "ªWrite down these words, for in accordance with these words I have made ᵇa covenant with you and with Israel."

28 So he was there with the Lorᴅ ªforty days and forty nights; he did not eat bread or drink water. And ᵇhe wrote on the tablets the words of the covenant, ᶜthe Ten Commandments.

29 And it came about when Moses was coming down from Mount Sinai (and the ªtwo tablets of the testimony *were* in Moses' hand as he was coming down from the mountain), that Moses did not know that ᵇthe skin of his face shone because of his speaking with Him.

30 So when Aaron and all the sons of Israel saw Moses, behold, the skin of his face shone, and ªthey were afraid to come near him.

31 Then Moses called to them, and Aaron and all the rulers in the congregation returned to him; and Moses spoke to them.

32 And afterward all the sons of Israel came near, and he commanded them *to do* everything that the Lorᴅ had spoken to him on Mount Sinai.

33 When Moses had finished speaking with them, ªhe put a veil over his face.

34 But whenever Moses went in before the Lorᴅ to speak with Him, ªhe would take off the veil until he came out; and whenever

---

15 ªEx. 22:20; 32:8 ᵇNum. 25:1, 2; Deut. 32:37, 38

16 ªDeut. 7:3; Josh. 23:12, 13; 1 Kin. 11:1-4

17 ªEx. 20:4, 23; Lev. 19:4; Deut. 5:8

★**18** ªEx. 12:17; Lev. 23:6; Num. 28:16f. ᵇEx. 12:15, 16 ᶜEx. 12:2; 13:4

19 ªEx. 13:2; 22:29f.

★**20** ªEx. 13:13 ᵇEx. 13:15; Num. 3:45 ᶜEx. 22:29; 23:15; Deut. 16:16

★**21** ªEx. 20:9f.; 23:12; 31:15; 35:2; Lev. 23:3; Deut. 5:13f.

22 ªEx. 23:16; Num. 28:26

★**23** ªEx. 23:14-17

24 ªEx. 33:2; Ps. 78:55

★**25-26**

25 ªEx. 23:18 ᵇEx. 12:10

26 ªEx. 23:19; Deut. 26:2

27 ªEx. 17:14; 24:4 ᵇEx. 34:10

28 ªEx. 24:18 ᵇEx. 31:18; 34:1 ᶜDeut. 4:13; 10:4

29 ªEx. 32:15 ᵇMatt. 17:2; 2 Cor. 3:7

30 ª2 Cor. 3:7

★**33** ª2 Cor. 3:13

34 ª2 Cor. 3:16

34:18 *the Feast of Unleavened Bread.* See note on 12:15.
34:20 See note on 13:13.
34:21 This was a far-reaching command in an agricultural community.
34:23 This regulation was designed to help

maintain the unity of the covenant people (see also note on 23:14).
34:25-26 See note on 23:18.
34:33 *a veil.* See note on 2 Cor. 3:13 for Paul's use of this.

he came out and spoke to the sons of Israel what he had been commanded,

35 a2 Cor. 3:13

35 a the sons of Israel would see the face of Moses, that the skin of Moses' face shone. So Moses would replace the veil over his face until he went in to speak with Him.

D The Construction of the Tabernacle, 35:1–40:38

1 The instructions to the people, 35:1–36:7

1 aEx. 34:32

35 Then Moses assembled all the congregation of the sons of Israel, and said to them, "a These are the things that the LORD has commanded *you* to do.

2 aEx. 20:9, 10; 23:12; 31:15; 34:21; Lev. 23:3; Deut. 5:13f. bEx. 16:23 cNum. 15:32-36

2 "a For six days work may be done, but on the seventh day you shall have a holy *day*, b a sabbath of complete rest to the LORD; c whoever does any work on it shall be put to death.

3 aEx. 12:16; 16:23

3 "a You shall not kindle a fire in any of your dwellings on the sabbath day."

4 And Moses spoke to all the congregation of the sons of Israel, saying, "This is the thing which the LORD has commanded, saying,

★ **5** aEx. 25:1-9

5 'a Take from among you a contribution to the LORD; whoever is of a willing heart, let him bring it as the LORD's contribution: gold, silver, and bronze,

6 and blue, purple and scarlet *material,* fine linen, goats' *hair,*

7 and rams' skins dyed red, and porpoise skins, and acacia wood,

8 and oil for lighting, and spices for the anointing oil, and for the fragrant incense,

9 and onyx stones and setting stones, for the ephod and for the breastpiece.

10 aEx. 31:6

10 'And a let every skillful man among you come, and make all that the LORD has commanded:

11 the a tabernacle, its tent and its covering, its hooks and its boards, its bars, its pillars, and its sockets;

11 aEx. 26:1-30

12 the a ark and its poles, the mercy seat, and the curtain of the screen;

12 aEx. 25:10-22

13 the a table and its poles, and all its utensils, and the bread of the Presence;

13 aEx. 25:23-30

14 the a lampstand also for the light and its utensils and its lamps and the oil for the light;

14 aEx. 25:31ff.

15 and the a altar of incense and its poles, and the b anointing oil and the c fragrant incense, and the screen for the doorway at the entrance of the tabernacle;

15 aEx. 30:1-6 bEx. 30:25 cEx. 30:34-38

16 a the altar of burnt offering with its bronze grating, its poles, and all its utensils, the basin and its stand;

16 aEx. 27:1-8

17 a the hangings of the court, its pillars and its sockets, and the screen for the gate of the court;

17 aEx. 27:9-18

18 the pegs of the tabernacle and the pegs of the court and their cords;

19 the a woven garments, for ministering in the holy place, the holy garments for Aaron the priest, and the garments of his sons, to minister as priests.' "

19 aEx. 31:10; 39:1

20 Then all the congregation of the sons of Israel departed from Moses' presence.

21 And a everyone whose heart stirred him and everyone whose spirit moved him came *and* brought the LORD's contribution for the work of the tent of meeting and for all its service and for the holy garments.

21 aEx. 25:2; 35:5, 22, 26, 29; 36:2

22 Then all whose hearts moved them, both men and women, came *and* brought brooches and earrings and signet rings and bracelets, all articles of gold; so *did* every man who presented an offering of gold to the LORD.

23 And every man, who had in his possession blue and purple and scarlet *material* and fine linen and goats' *hair* and rams' skins

---

35:5 All were invited to contribute materials for the tabernacle, but only from *a willing heart*

(cf. 2 Cor. 9:7).

dyed red and porpoise skins, brought them.

24 Everyone who could make a contribution of silver and bronze brought the LORD's contribution; and every man, who had in his possession acacia wood for any work of the service, brought it.

25 And all the skilled women spun with their hands, and brought what they had spun, *in* blue and purple *and* scarlet material and *in* fine linen.

26 And all the women whose heart stirred with a skill spun the goats' hair.

27 And the rulers brought the onyx stones and the stones for setting for the ephod and for the breastpiece;

28 and *a*the spice and the oil for the light and for the anointing oil and for the fragrant incense.

29 The Israelites, all the men and women, whose heart moved them to bring *material* for all the work, which the LORD had commanded through Moses to be done, brought a *a*freewill offering to the LORD.

30 *a*Then Moses said to the sons of Israel, "See, the LORD has called by name Bezalel the son of Uri, the son of Hur, of the tribe of Judah.

31 "And He has filled him with the Spirit of God, in wisdom, in understanding and in knowledge and in all craftsmanship;

32 to make designs for working in gold and in silver and in bronze,

33 and in the cutting of stones for settings, and in the carving of wood, so as to perform in every inventive work.

34 "He also has put in his heart to teach, both he and *a*Oholiab, the son of Ahisamach, of the tribe of Dan.

35 "*a*He has filled them with skill to perform every work of an engraver and of a designer and of an embroiderer, in blue and in purple *and* in scarlet *material,* and in fine linen, and of a weaver, as performers of every work and makers of designs.

36 "Now Bezalel and Oholiab, and every skillful person in whom the LORD has put skill and understanding to know how to perform all the work in the construction of the sanctuary, shall perform in accordance with all that the LORD has commanded."

2 Then Moses called Bezalel and Oholiab and every skillful person in whom the LORD had put skill, *a*everyone whose heart stirred him, to come to the work to perform it.

3 And they received from Moses all the contributions which the sons of Israel had brought to perform the work in the construction of the sanctuary. And they still *continued* bringing to him freewill offerings every morning.

4 And all the skillful men who were performing all the work of the sanctuary came, each from the work which he was performing,

5 and they said to Moses, "*a*The people are bringing much more than enough for the construction work which the LORD commanded *us* to perform."

6 So Moses issued a command, and a proclamation was circulated throughout the camp, saying, "Let neither man nor woman any longer perform work for the contributions of the sanctuary." Thus the people were restrained from bringing *any more.*

7 *a*For the material they had was sufficient and more than enough for all the work, to perform it.

2 The curtains made, 36:8-19

8 *a*And all the skillful men among those who were performing the work made the tabernacle with ten curtains; of fine twisted

Marginal references:

28 *a*Ex. 30:23ff.

29 *a*Ex. 35:21; 1 Chr. 29:9

30 *a*Ex. 31:1-6

34 *a*Ex. 31:6

35 *a*Ex. 31:3, 6; 35:31; 1 Kin. 7:14

2 *a*Ex. 35:21, 26

5 *a*2 Chr. 24:14; 31:6-10

7 *a*1 Kin. 8:64

★8-38

8 *a*Ex. 26:1-14

36:8-38 This section repeats the instructions of 26:1-37.

linen and blue and purple and scarlet *material,* with cherubim, the work of a skillful workman, Bezalel made them.

9 The length of each curtain was twenty-eight cubits, and the width of each curtain four cubits; all the curtains had the same measurements.

10 And he joined five curtains to one another, and *the other* five curtains he joined to one another.

11 And he made loops of blue on the edge of the outermost curtain in the first set; he did likewise on the edge of the curtain that was outermost in the second set.

12 *a*Ex. 26:5   12 He made *a*fifty loops in the one curtain and he made fifty loops on the edge of the curtain that was in the second set; the loops were opposite each other.

13 *a*Ex. 26:6   13 And he made *a*fifty clasps of gold, and joined the curtains to one another with the clasps, so the tabernacle was a unit.

14 *a*Ex. 26:7-14   14 Then *a*he made curtains of goats' *hair* for a tent over the tabernacle; he made eleven curtains in all.

15 The length of each curtain was thirty cubits, and four cubits the width of each curtain; the eleven curtains had the same measurements.

16 And he joined five curtains by themselves, and *the other* six curtains by themselves.

17 Moreover, he made fifty loops on the edge of the curtain that was outermost in the *first* set, and he made fifty loops on the edge of the curtain *that was outermost in* the second set.

18 And he made fifty clasps of bronze to join the tent together, that it might be a unit.

19 And he made a covering for the tent of rams' skins dyed red, and a covering of porpoise skins above.

3 The boards made, 36:20-34

20 *a*Ex. 26:15-29   20 *a*Then he made the boards for the tabernacle of acacia wood, standing upright.

21 Ten cubits was the length of each board, and one and a half cubits the width of each board.

22 There were two tenons for each board, fitted to one another; thus he did for all the boards of the tabernacle.

23 And he made the boards for the tabernacle: twenty boards for the south side;

24 and he made forty sockets of silver under the twenty boards; two sockets under one board for its two tenons and two sockets under another board for its two tenons.

25 Then for the second side of the tabernacle, on the north side, he made twenty boards,

26 and their forty sockets of silver; two sockets under one board and two sockets under another board.

27 And for the rear of the tabernacle, to the west, he made six boards.

28 And he made two boards for the corners of the tabernacle at the rear.

29 And they were double beneath, and together they were complete to its top to the first ring; thus he did with both of them for the two corners.

30 And there were eight boards with their sockets of silver, sixteen sockets, two under every board.

31 *a*Ex. 26:26-29   31 Then he made *a*bars of acacia wood, five for the boards of one side of the tabernacle,

32 and five bars for the boards of the other side of the tabernacle, and five bars for the boards of the tabernacle for the rear *side* to the west.

33 And he made the middle bar to pass through in the center of the boards from end to end.

34 And he overlaid the boards with gold and made their rings of gold *as* holders for the bars, and overlaid the bars with gold.

4 The veil made, 36:35-38

35 *a*Ex. 26:31-37   35 *a*Moreover, he made the veil of blue and purple and scarlet

material, and fine twisted linen; he made it with cherubim, the work of a skillful workman.

36 And he made four pillars of acacia for it, and overlaid them with gold, with their hooks of gold; and he cast four sockets of silver for them.

37 And he made a [a]screen for the doorway of the tent, of blue and purple and scarlet material, and fine twisted linen, the work of a weaver;

38 and he made its [a]five pillars with their hooks, and he overlaid their tops and their bands with gold; but their five sockets were of bronze.

5 The ark made, 37:1-9

37 [a]Now Bezalel made the ark of acacia wood; its length was two and a half cubits, and its width one and a half cubits, and its height one and a half cubits;

2 and he overlaid it with pure gold inside and out, and made a gold molding for it all around.

3 And he cast four rings of gold for it on its four feet; even two rings on one side of it, and two rings on the other side of it.

4 And he made poles of acacia wood and overlaid them with gold.

5 And he put the poles into the rings on the sides of the ark, to carry it.

6 And he made a mercy seat of pure gold, two and a half cubits long, and one and a half cubits wide.

7 And he made two cherubim of gold; he made them of hammered work, at the two ends of the mercy seat;

8 one cherub at the one end, and one cherub at the other end; he made the cherubim of one piece with the mercy seat at the two ends.

9 And the cherubim had their wings spread upward, covering the mercy seat with their wings, with their faces toward each other; the faces of the cherubim were toward the mercy seat.

6 The table made, 37:10-16

10 [a]Then he made the table of acacia wood, two cubits long and a cubit wide and one and a half cubits high.

11 And he overlaid it with pure gold, and made a gold molding for it all around.

12 And he made a rim for it of a handbreadth all around, and made a gold molding for its rim all around.

13 And he cast four gold rings for it and put the rings on the four corners that were on its four feet.

14 Close by the rim were the rings, the holders for the poles to carry the table.

15 And he made the poles of acacia wood and overlaid them with gold, to carry the table.

16 And he made the utensils which were on the table, its dishes and its pans and its bowls and its jars, with which to pour out libations, of pure gold.

7 The lampstand made, 37:17-24

17 [a]Then he made the lampstand of pure gold. He made the lampstand of hammered work, its base and its shaft; its cups, its bulbs and its flowers were of one piece with it.

18 And there were six branches going out of its sides; three branches of the lampstand from the one side of it, and three branches of the lampstand from the other side of it;

19 three cups shaped like almond blossoms, a bulb and a flower in one branch, and three cups shaped like almond

---

37 [a]Ex. 26:36

38 [a]Ex. 26:37

★ **1** [a]Ex. 25:10-20

10 [a]Ex. 25:23-29

★**17** [a]Ex. 25:31-39

37:1 Though Moses had the Ark made (Deut. 10:3), *Bezalel* did the actual work.

37:17 *bulbs.* See note on 25:31.

blossoms, a bulb and a flower in the other branch—so for the six branches going out of the lampstand.

20 And in the lampstand there were four cups shaped like almond blossoms, its bulbs and its flowers;

21 and a bulb was under the first pair of branches coming out of it, and a bulb under the second pair of branches coming out of it, and a bulb under the third pair of branches coming out of it, for the six branches coming out of the lampstand.

22 Their bulbs and their branches were of one piece with it; the whole of it was a single hammered work of pure gold.

23 And he made its seven lamps with its snuffers and its trays of pure gold.

24 He made it and all its utensils from a talent of pure gold.

8 The altar of incense made, 37:25-29

25 aEx. 30:1-5

25 aThen he made the altar of incense of acacia wood: a cubit long and a cubit wide, square, and two cubits high; its horns were of one piece with it.

26 And he overlaid it with pure gold, its top and its sides all around, and its horns; and he made a gold molding for it all around.

27 And he made two golden rings for it under its molding, on its two sides—on opposite sides—as holders for poles with which to carry it.

28 And he made the poles of acacia wood and overlaid them with gold.

29 aEx. 30:23-25, 34, 35

29 aAnd he made the holy anointing oil and the pure, fragrant incense of spices, the work of a perfumer.

9 The brass altar made, 38:1-7

1 aEx. 27:1-8

38 aThen he made the altar of burnt offering of acacia wood, five cubits long, and five cubits wide, square, and three cubits high.

2 And he made its horns on its four corners, its horns being of one piece with it, and he overlaid it with bronze.

3 And he made all the utensils of the altar, the pails and the shovels and the basins, the flesh hooks and the firepans; he made all its utensils of bronze.

4 And he made for the altar a grating of bronze network beneath, under its ledge, reaching halfway up.

5 And he cast four rings on the four ends of the bronze grating as holders for the poles.

6 And he made the poles of acacia wood and overlaid them with bronze.

7 And he inserted the poles into the rings on the sides of the altar, with which to carry it. He made it hollow with planks.

10 The laver made, 38:8

★ 8 aEx. 30:18

8 aMoreover, he made the laver of bronze with its base of bronze, from the mirrors of the serving women who served at the doorway of the tent of meeting.

11 The court made, 38:9-20

9 aEx. 27:9-19

9 aThen he made the court: for the south side the hangings of the court were of fine twisted linen, one hundred cubits;

10 their twenty pillars, and their twenty sockets, made of bronze; the hooks of the pillars and their bands were of silver.

11 And for the north side there were one hundred cubits; their twenty pillars and their

---

38:8 What these serving women did is not stated. Perhaps they served by singing or by cleaning the temporary tent (cf. note on 33:7).

twenty sockets *were* of bronze, the hooks of the pillars and their bands *were* of silver.

12   And for the west side *there were* hangings of fifty cubits *with* their ten pillars and their ten sockets; the hooks of the pillars and their bands *were* of silver.

13   And for the east side fifty cubits.

14   The hangings for the *one* side *of the gate were* fifteen cubits, *with* their three pillars and their three sockets;

15   and so for the other side. On both sides of the gate of the court *were* hangings of fifteen cubits, *with* their three pillars and their three sockets.

16   All the hangings of the court all around *were* of fine twisted linen.

17   And the sockets for the pillars *were* of bronze, the hooks of the pillars and their bands, of silver; and the overlaying of their tops, of silver, and all the pillars of the court were furnished with silver bands.

18   And the screen of the gate of the court was the work of the weaver, of blue and purple and scarlet *material*, and fine twisted linen. And the length was twenty cubits and the height was five cubits, corresponding to the hangings of the court.

19   And their four pillars and their four sockets *were* of bronze; their hooks *were* of silver, and the overlaying of their tops and their bands *were* of silver.

20   And all the pegs of the tabernacle and of the court all around *were* of bronze.

12   The materials used,
38:21-31

21   This is the number of *the things for* the tabernacle, the tabernacle of the testimony, as they were numbered according to the command of Moses, for the ser-

vice of the Levites, by the hand of Ithamar, the son of Aaron the priest.

22   Now ªBezalel, the son of Uri the son of Hur, of the tribe of Judah, made all that the Lord had commanded Moses.

23   And with him was ªOholiab, the son of Ahisamach, of the tribe of Dan, an engraver and a skillful workman and a weaver in blue and in purple and in scarlet *material*, and fine linen.

24   All the gold that was used for the work, in all the work of the sanctuary, even the gold of the wave offering, was 29 talents and 730 shekels, according to ªthe shekel of the sanctuary.

25   ªAnd the silver of those of the congregation who were numbered was 100 talents and 1,775 shekels, according to the shekel of the sanctuary;

26   ªa beka a head (*that is,* half a shekel according to the shekel of the sanctuary), for each one who passed over to those who were numbered, from twenty years old and upward, for ᵇ603,550 men.

27   And the hundred talents of silver were for casting the sockets of the sanctuary and the sockets of the veil; one hundred sockets for the hundred talents, a talent for a socket.

28   And of the 1,775 *shekels,* he made hooks for the pillars and overlaid their tops and made bands for them.

29   And the bronze of the wave offering was 70 talents, and 2,400 shekels.

30   And with it he made the sockets to the doorway of the tent of meeting, and the bronze altar and its bronze grating, and all the utensils of the altar,

31   and the sockets of the court all around and the sockets of the gate of the court, and all

22 ªEx. 31:2

23 ªEx. 31:6

★24 ªEx. 30:13; Lev. 27:25; Num. 3:47; 18:16

★25 ªEx. 30:11-16

26 ªEx. 30:13, 15 ᵇEx. 12:37; Num. 1:46; 26:51

★29

31

38:24 There was possibly 2,800 pounds of gold!
38:25 This amounted to perhaps 9,600 pounds of silver.
38:29 Possibly some 6,700 pounds of bronze.

Though we do not know the value of these metals in those days, the expenditure was enormous and demonstrated the peoples' dedication to God.

the pegs of the tabernacle and all the pegs of the court all around.

13 The garments for Aaron made, 39:1-31

39 Moreover, from the ᵃblue and purple and scarlet *material,* they made finely ᵇwoven garments for ministering in the holy place, as well as the holy garments which were for Aaron, just as the Lᴏʀᴅ had commanded Moses.

1 ᵃEx. 35:23, ᵇEx. 31:10; 35:19

2 ᵃEx. 28:6-12

2 ᵃAnd he made the ephod of gold, *and* of blue and purple and scarlet *material,* and fine twisted linen.

3 Then they hammered out gold sheets and cut *them* into threads to be woven in *with* the blue and the purple and the scarlet *material,* and the fine linen, the work of a skillful workman.

4 They made attaching shoulder pieces for the ephod; it was attached at its two *upper* ends.

5 And the skillfully woven band which was on it was like its workmanship, of the same material: of gold *and* of blue and purple and scarlet *material,* and fine twisted linen, just as the Lᴏʀᴅ had commanded Moses.

6 ᵃEx. 28:9-11

6 And ᵃthey made the onyx stones, set in gold filigree *settings;* they were engraved *like* the engravings of a signet, according to the names of the sons of Israel.

7 ᵃEx. 28:12

7 And ᵃhe placed them on the shoulder pieces of the ephod, *as* memorial stones for the sons of Israel, just as the Lᴏʀᴅ had commanded Moses.

8 ᵃEx. 28:15-28

8 ᵃAnd he made the breastpiece, the work of a skillful workman, like the workmanship of the ephod: of gold *and* of blue and purple and scarlet *material* and fine twisted linen.

9 It was square; they made the breastpiece folded double, a span long and a span wide when folded double.

10 And they mounted four rows of stones on it. The first row

was a row of ruby, topaz, and emerald;

11 and the second row, a turquoise, a sapphire and a diamond;

12 and the third row, a jacinth, an agate, and an amethyst;

13 and the fourth row, a beryl, an onyx, and a jasper. They were set in gold filigree *settings* when they were mounted.

14 And the stones were corresponding to the names of the sons of Israel; they were twelve, corresponding to their names, *engraved with* the engravings of a signet, each with its name for the twelve tribes.

15 And they made on the breastpiece chains like cords, of twisted cordage work in pure gold.

16 And they made two gold filigree *settings* and two gold rings, and put the two rings on the two ends of the breastpiece.

17 Then they put the two gold cords in the two rings at the ends of the breastpiece.

18 And they put the *other* two ends of the two cords on the two filigree *settings,* and put them on the shoulder pieces of the ephod at the front of it.

19 And they made two gold rings and placed *them* on the two ends of the breastpiece, on its inner edge which was next to the ephod.

20 Furthermore, they made two gold rings and placed them on the bottom of the two shoulder pieces of the ephod, on the front of it, close to the place where it joined, above the woven band of the ephod.

21 And they bound the breastpiece by its rings to the rings of the ephod with a blue cord, that it might be on the woven band of the ephod, and that the breastpiece might not come loose from the ephod, just as the Lᴏʀᴅ had commanded Moses.

22 ᵃEx. 28:31, 34

22 ᵃThen he made the robe of the ephod of woven work, all of blue;

★23 *a*Ex. 28:32

23 *a*and the opening of the robe was *at the top* in the center, as the opening of a coat of mail, with a binding all around its opening, that it might not be torn.

24 And they made pomegranates of blue and purple and scarlet *material and* twisted *linen* on the hem of the robe.

25 They also made bells of pure gold, and put the bells between the pomegranates all around on the hem of the robe,

26 alternating a bell and a pomegranate all around on the hem of the robe, for the service, just as the LORD had commanded Moses.

27 *a*Ex. 28:39, 40, 42

27 *a*And they made the tunics of finely woven linen for Aaron and his sons,

28 and the turban of fine linen, and the decorated caps of fine linen, and the linen breeches of fine twisted linen,

29 and the sash of fine twisted linen, and blue and purple and scarlet *material,* the work of the weaver, just as the LORD had commanded Moses.

30 *a*Ex. 28:36, 37

30 *a*And they made the plate of the holy crown of pure gold, and inscribed it like the engravings of a signet, "Holy to the LORD."

31 And they fastened a blue cord to it, to fasten it on the turban above, just as the LORD had commanded Moses.

14 The work inspected by Moses, 39:32–43

32 Thus all the work of the tabernacle of the tent of meeting was completed; and the sons of Israel did according to all that the LORD had commanded Moses; so they did.

★33-43

33 And they brought the tabernacle to Moses, the tent and all its furnishings: its clasps, its boards, its bars, and its pillars and its sockets;

34 and the covering of rams' skins dyed red, and the covering of porpoise skins, and the screening veil;

35 the ark of the testimony and its poles and the mercy seat;

36 the table, all its utensils, and the bread of the Presence;

37 the pure *gold* lampstand, with its arrangement of lamps and all its utensils, and the oil for the light;

38 and the gold altar, and the anointing oil and the fragrant incense, and the veil for the doorway of the tent;

39 the bronze altar and its bronze grating, its poles and all its utensils, the laver and its stand;

40 the hangings for the court, its pillars and its sockets, the screen for the gate of the court, its cords and its pegs and all the equipment for the service of the tabernacle, for the tent of meeting;

41 the woven garments for ministering in the holy place and the holy garments for Aaron the priest and the garments of his sons, to minister as priests.

42 So the sons of Israel did all the work according to all that the LORD had commanded Moses.

43 And Moses examined all the work and behold, they had done it; just as the LORD had commanded, this they had done. So Moses *a*blessed them.

43 *a*Lev. 9:22, 23; Num. 6:23-26

15 The tabernacle erected, 40:1–33

40 Then the LORD spoke to Moses, saying,

2 "*a*On the first day of the first month you shall set up the tabernacle of the tent of meeting.

2 *a*Ex. 19:1; 40:17; Num. 1:1

3 "And *a*you shall place the ark of the testimony there, and you shall screen the ark with the veil.

3 *a*Ex. 26:33; 40:21; Num. 4:5

4 "And you shall *a*bring in the table and *b*arrange what

4 *a*Ex. 26:35; 40:22 *b*Ex. 25:30; 40:23 *c*Ex. 40:24f.

39:23 The robe had a hole in the neck like a *coat of mail.*

39:33-43 Moses inspected the work and, seeing that it had been done as God had commanded, he blessed the people.

belongs on it; and you shall ^cbring in the lampstand and mount its lamps.

5 ^aEx. 40:26
5 "Moreover, you shall ^aset the gold altar of incense before the ark of the testimony, and set up the veil for the doorway to the tabernacle.

6 "And you shall set the altar of burnt offering in front of the doorway of the tabernacle of the tent of meeting.

7 ^aEx. 30:18, 40:30
7 "And you shall ^aset the laver between the tent of meeting and the altar, and put water in it.

8 "And you shall set up the court all around and hang up the veil for the gateway of the court.

9 ^aEx. 30:26; Lev. 8:10
9 "Then you shall take the anointing oil and ^aanoint the tabernacle and all that is in it, and shall consecrate it and all its furnishings; and it shall be holy.

10 ^aEx. 29:37
10 "And you shall anoint the altar of burnt offering and all its utensils, and consecrate the altar; and ^athe altar shall be most holy.

11 "And you shall anoint the laver and its stand, and consecrate it.

12 ^aLev. 8:1-6
12 "Then you shall ^abring Aaron and his sons to the doorway of the tent of meeting and wash them with water.

13 ^aEx. 28:41; Lev. 8:13
13 "And ^ayou shall put the holy garments on Aaron and anoint him and consecrate him, that he may minister as a priest to Me.

14 "And you shall bring his sons and put tunics on them;

15 ^aEx. 29:9; Num. 25:13
15 and you shall anoint them even as you have anointed their father, that they may minister as priests to Me; and their anointing shall qualify them for a ^aperpetual priesthood throughout their generations."

16 Thus Moses did; according to all that the LORD had commanded him, so he did.

★17 ^aEx. 40:2
17 Now it came about ^ain the first month of the second year, on the first day of the month, that the tabernacle was erected.

18 And Moses erected the tabernacle and laid its sockets, and set up its boards, and inserted its bars and erected its pillars.

19 And he spread the tent over the tabernacle and put the covering of the tent on top of it, just as the LORD had commanded Moses.

20 ^aEx. 25:16; Deut. 10:5; 1 Kin. 8:9; 2 Chr. 5:10; Heb. 9:4
20 Then he took ^athe testimony and put it into the ark, and attached the poles to the ark, and put the mercy seat on top of the ark.

21 ^aEx. 26:33
21 And he brought the ark into the tabernacle, and ^aset up a veil for the screen, and screened off the ark of the testimony, just as the LORD had commanded Moses.

22 ^aEx. 26:35
22 Then he ^aput the table in the tent of meeting, on the north side of the tabernacle, outside the veil.

23 ^aEx. 25:30; Lev. 24:5, 6
23 And he set the arrangement of ^abread in order on it before the LORD, just as the LORD had commanded Moses.

24 Then he placed the lampstand in the tent of meeting, opposite the table, on the south side of the tabernacle.

25 ^aEx. 25:37; 40:4
25 And he ^alighted the lamps before the LORD, just as the LORD had commanded Moses.

26 ^aEx. 30:6; 40:5
26 Then he ^aplaced the gold altar in the tent of meeting in front of the veil;

27 ^aEx. 30:7
27 and he ^aburned fragrant incense on it, just as the LORD had commanded Moses.

28 Then he set up the veil for the doorway of the tabernacle.

29 ^aEx. 40:6; ^bEx. 29:38-42
29 And he ^aset the altar of burnt offering before the doorway of the tabernacle of the tent of meeting, and ^boffered on it the burnt offering and the meal offering, just as the LORD had commanded Moses.

30 And he placed the laver between the tent of meeting and

40:17 The tabernacle was set up one year after the Exodus from Egypt (cf. 12:2) and nine months after Israel's arrival at Sinai (cf. 19:1).

the altar, and put water in it for washing.

31 a Ex. 30:19, 20

31 ^aAnd from it Moses and Aaron and his sons washed their hands and their feet.

32 When they entered the tent of meeting, and when they approached the altar, they washed, just as the LORD had commanded Moses.

33 a Ex. 27:9-18; 40:8

33 And he ^aerected the court all around the tabernacle and the altar, and hung up the veil for the gateway of the court. Thus Moses finished the work.

16   The tabernacle indwelt by the LORD Himself,
                              40:34-38

★34-38

34 a Num. 9:15-23
b 1 Kin. 8:11; Ezek. 43:41; Rev. 15:8

34 ^aThen the cloud covered the tent of meeting, and the ^bglory of the LORD filled the tabernacle.

35 And Moses ^awas not able to enter the tent of meeting because the cloud had settled on it, and the glory of the LORD filled the tabernacle.

35 a 1 Kin. 8:11; 2 Chr. 5:13, 14

36 And throughout all their journeys ^awhenever the cloud was taken up from over the tabernacle, the sons of Israel would set out;

36 a Num. 9:17; Neh. 9:19

37 but ^aif the cloud was not taken up, then they did not set out until the day when it was taken up,

37 a Num. 9:19-22

38 For throughout all their journeys, ^athe cloud of the LORD was on the tabernacle by day, and there was fire in it by night, in the sight of all the house of Israel.

38 a Ex. 13:21; Num. 9:12, 15; Ps. 78:14; Is. 4:5

40:34-38 The cloud of God's glory and presence showed His approval of the completed tabernacle and led the people by day and by night through the desert (see also 33:9).

INTRODUCTION TO
THE BOOK OF LEVITICUS

AUTHOR: Moses   DATE: 1450–1410 B.C.

Title *The English title of this book, derived from the Greek translation of the Old Testament (the Septuagint), means "pertaining to the Levites." Though the book is a manual for the priests (who were from the tribe of Levi), many of its laws concern all the Israelites. The Hebrew title ("and He called," from the first word of the book) emphasizes the theme of God's call to holiness (cf. 11:45).*

Authorship *About 56 times within the book it is said that the Lord spoke these words to Moses, who either wrote them down himself or had them written down (cf. 4:1; 6:1; 8:1; 11:1; 12:1). Jesus Christ also attested to the book's Mosaic authorship (Mark 1:44, cf. Lev. 13:49).*

Key Words and Themes *The language of sacrifice pervades the book, with the word "sacrifice" occurring about 42 times. "Priest" is found about 189 times, "blood" about 86 times, "holy" about 87 times, and "atonement" about 45 times. The regulations emphasize holiness of body as well as of spirit. The New Testament refers to Leviticus about 90 times.*

Historical Setting *The book of Exodus concludes with the erection of the tabernacle, which was constructed according to the pattern God gave to Moses. How was Israel to use the tabernacle? The instructions in Leviticus answer that question, and were given to Moses during the month and 20 days between the setting up of the tabernacle (Exod. 40:17) and the departure of the people from Sinai (Num. 10:11).*

Contents *The book may be viewed in three complementary ways. It is a book about the holiness of God and His requirements for fellowship with Himself. Thus, it is also a book that reveals the sinfulness of man. And it may be viewed as a book about atonement, the provision of access to God for sinful man.*

OUTLINE OF LEVITICUS

I. The Way to God: Sacrifice, 1:1–10:20
A. Through the Offerings, 1:1–7:38
  1. The burnt offering, 1:1–17
  2. The grain offering, 2:1–16
  3. The peace offering, 3:1–17
  4. The sin offering, 4:1–5:13
  5. The trespass offering, 5:14–6:7
  6. Added instructions concerning the offerings, 6:8–7:38
    a. The burnt offering, 6:8–13
    b. The grain offering, 6:14–23
    c. The sin offering, 6:24–30
    d. The trespass offering, 7:1–10
    e. The peace offering, 7:11–38
B. Through the Priests, 8:1–10:20
  1. The consecration to priestly service, 8:1–36
  2. The inauguration of priestly service, 9:1–24
  3. The sacrilege of priestly service: Nadab and Abihu, 10:1–20
II. The Walk with God: Sanctification, 11:1–27:34
A. Laws Concerning Purity, 11:1–15:33
  1. In relation to food, 11:1–47

  2. In relation to childbirth, 12:1–8
  3. In relation to leprosy, 13:1–14:57
    a. Classifications of leprosy, 13:1–59
    b. Cleansing for leprosy, 14:1–57
  4. In relation to the body, 15:1–33
B. Law of the Day of Atonement, 16:1–34
  1. Preparations, 16:1–4
  2. Offerings, 16:5–28
  3. Instructions, 16:29–34
C. Laws Concerning Sacrificing, 17:1–16
D. Laws Concerning Standards for the People, 18:1–20:27
  1. Concerning sexual relationships, 18:1–30
  2. Concerning daily life, 19:1–37
  3. Concerning heinous offenses, 20:1–27
E. Laws Concerning Standards for the Priests, 21:1–22:16
F. Laws Concerning Offerings, 22:17–33
G. Laws Concerning Festivals, 23:1–44
  1. The Sabbath, 23:1–3
  2. The Passover and Unleavened Bread, 23:4–8
  3. First fruits, 23:9–14
  4. Pentecost, 23:15–22
  5. Trumpets, 23:23–25

6. The Day of Atonement, 23:26-32
7. Tabernacles, 23:33-44
H. Laws Concerning the Oil, Bread, and
   Blasphemy, 24:1-23
I. Laws Concerning the Sabbatical Year,
   25:1-7

J. Laws Concerning the Year of Jubilee,
   25:8-55
K. Laws Concerning Obedience, 26:1-46
L. Laws Concerning Vows and Tithes,
   27:1-34

THE BOOK OF LEVITICUS

I THE WAY TO GOD: SACRIFICE,
1:1-10:20

A Through the Offerings,
1:1-7:38

1 The burnt offering, 1:1-17

★ **1** aEx.
19:3; 25:22;
Num. 7:89

1 Then athe Lord called to Moses and spoke to him from the tent of meeting, saying,

★ **2** aMark
7:11 bLev.
22:18f.

2 "Speak to the sons of Israel and say to them, 'When any man of you brings an aoffering to the Lord, you shall bring your offering of animals from bthe herd or the flock.

★ **3** aLev.
6:8-13 bEx.
12:5; Lev.
22:20-24;
Deut. 15:21;
17:1 cLev.
17:8, 9; Deut.
12:5, 6, 11

3 'If his offering is a aburnt offering from the herd, he shall offer it, a male bwithout defect; he shall offer it cat the doorway of the tent of meeting, that he may be accepted before the Lord.

★ **4** aEx.
29:10, 15,
19; Lev. 3:2,
8 bEx.
29:33; Lev.
4:20, 26, 31;
2 Chr. 29:23,
24

4 'aAnd he shall lay his hand on the head of the burnt offering, that it may be accepted for him to make batonement on his behalf.

5 aEx.
29:11, 16, 20
bLev. 17:11
cLev. 1:11;
3:2, 8, 13;
Heb. 12:24;
1 Pet. 1:2

5 'And ahe shall slay the young bull before the Lord; and Aaron's sons, the priests, shall offer up bthe blood and csprinkle the blood around on the altar that is at the doorway of the tent of meeting.

6 'aHe shall then skin the burnt offering and cut it into its pieces.

6 aLev. 7:8

7 'aAnd the sons of Aaron the priest shall put fire on the altar and arrange wood on the fire.

7 aLev. 6:8-13

8 'Then Aaron's sons, the priests, shall arrange the pieces, the head, and the asuet over the wood which is on the fire that is on the altar.

8 aLev.
1:12; 3:3, 4;
8:20

9 'Its aentrails, however, and its legs he shall wash with water. And bthe priest shall offer up in smoke all of it on the altar for a burnt offering, an offering by fire of ca soothing aroma to the Lord.

★ **9** aEx.
12:9 bNum.
15:8-10;
28:11-14
cGen. 8:21;
Ex. 29:18,
25; Lev.
1:13; Num.
15:3; Eph.
5:2

10 'But if his offering is from the flock, of the sheep or of the goats, for a burnt offering, he shall offer it a amale without defect.

★**10** aEx.
12:5; Lev.
1:3; Ezek.
43:22; 1 Pet.
1:19

11 'And ahe shall slay it on the side of the altar northward before the Lord, and Aaron's sons, the priests, shall sprinkle its blood around on the altar.

11 aEx. 24:6;
Lev. 1:5;
8:19; 9:12

12 'He shall then cut it into its pieces with its head and its asuet, and the priest shall arrange them on the wood which is on the fire that is on the altar.

12 aLev.
3:3, 4

1:1 *Then* connects the instructions of this book with the closing of Exodus (40:34-38); i.e., He who filled the tent with His glory now *called* to Moses.

1:2 An *offering* is that by which a man draws near to God (the root means "draw near"). Five offerings are mentioned in chapters 1-7 (not counting the peace offering in 7:32 and the drink offering, libation, in 23:13).

1:3 The *burnt* offering (lit., "ascent," since all of the offering, except the blood, was burned and ascended in smoke) symbolized the offerer's voluntary presentation to God. It typified the Lord Jesus' offering of Himself unto death (cf.

Heb. 10:5-7). The Christian should similarly offer himself as a sacrifice to God (Rom. 12:1-2).

1:4 The offerer's laying or pressing his hand on the head of the sacrifice symbolized his complete identification with the animal as his substitute.

1:9 *a soothing aroma*. I.e., the sacrifice smelled good to God and pleased Him.

1:10 Not only could a bull be used (v. 5), but also an unblemished sheep or goat and, in cases of extreme poverty, even a bird (cf. v. 14). See note on Luke 2:24.

13 aNum.
15:4-7;
28:11-14

13 'The entrails, however, and the legs he shall wash with water. And ªthe priest shall offer all of it, and offer it up in smoke on the altar; it is a burnt offering, an offering by fire of a soothing aroma to the Lord.

14 aGen.
15:9; Lev.
5:7, 11; 12:8;
Luke 2:24

14 'But if his offering to the Lord is a burnt offering of birds, then he shall bring his offering from the ªturtledoves or from young pigeons.

15 aLev. 5:9

15 'And the priest shall bring it to the altar and wring off its head, and offer it up in smoke on the altar; and its blood is to be drained out ªon the side of the altar.

16 aLev.
6:10

16 'He shall also take away its crop with its feathers, and cast it beside the altar eastward, to the place of the ªashes.

17 aGen.
15:10; Lev.
5:8 bLev.
9:13

17 'Then he shall tear it by its wings, *but* ªshall not sever *it*. And the priest shall offer it up in smoke on the altar on the wood which is on the fire; ᵇit is a burnt offering, an offering by fire of a soothing aroma to the Lord.

2   The grain offering, 2:1-16

★ 1 aLev.
6:14-18;
Num. 15:4

2 'Now when anyone presents a ªgrain offering as an offering to the Lord, his offering shall be of fine flour, and he shall pour oil on it and put frankincense on it.

2 aLev.
5:12; 6:15
bLev. 2:9,
16; 5:12;
24:7; Acts
10:4

2 'He shall then bring it to Aaron's sons, the priests; and shall take from it ªhis handful of its fine flour and of its oil with all of its frankincense. And the priest shall offer *it* up in smoke *as* its ᵇmemorial portion on the altar, an offering by fire of a soothing aroma to the Lord.

3 aLev.
2:10; 6:16
bLev. 10:12,
13

3 'And ªthe remainder of the grain offering belongs to ᵇAaron and his sons: a thing most holy, of the offerings to the Lord by fire.

4 'Now when you bring an offering of a grain offering baked in an oven, *it shall be* ªunleavened cakes of fine flour mixed with oil, or unleavened wafers spread with oil.

4 aEx. 29:2

5 'And if your offering is a grain offering *made* ªon the griddle, *it shall be* of fine flour, unleavened, mixed with oil;

5 aLev.
6:21; 7:9

6 you shall break it into bits, and pour oil on it; it is a grain offering.

7 'Now if your offering is a grain offering *made* ªin a pan, it shall be made of fine flour with oil.

7 aLev. 7:9

8 'When you bring in the grain offering which is made of these things to the Lord, it shall be presented to the priest and he shall bring it to the altar.

9 'The priest then shall take up from the grain offering ªits memorial portion, and shall offer *it* up in smoke on the altar *as* an offering by fire of a soothing aroma to the Lord.

9 aLev. 2:2,
16; 5:12

10 'And ªthe remainder of the grain offering belongs to Aaron and his sons: a thing most holy, of the offerings to the Lord by fire.

10 aLev. 2:3;
6:16

11 'ªNo grain offering, which you bring to the Lord, shall be made with leaven, for you shall not offer up in smoke any leaven or any honey as an ᵇoffering by fire to the Lord.

★11 aEx.
23:18; 34:25;
Lev. 6:16, 17
bEx. 29:25;
Lev. 1:13

12 'ªAs an offering of first fruits, you shall bring them to the Lord, but they shall not ascend for a soothing aroma on the altar.

12 aEx.
34:22; Lev.
7:13; 23:10,
17, 18

13 'Every grain offering of yours, moreover, you shall season with salt, so that ªthe salt of the covenant of your God shall not be lacking from your grain offering; with all your offerings you shall offer salt.

★13 aNum.
18:19; 2 Chr.
13:5; Ezek.
43:24

14 'Also if you bring a grain offering of early ripened things to

14 aLev.
23:14

2:1 The *grain offering* of fine flour, baked goods (vv. 4, 5, 7), or grain in the ear (v. 14) reminded the people that God gave them their basic food and that they in turn owed Him their lives as a gift or tribute (which is the meaning behind the Hebrew word for this offering). It

also prefigured the perfect life of Jesus Christ.
2:11 *leaven* and *honey* were excluded since they both ferment; but they could be used in the offering of first fruits (v. 12; 23:17).
2:13 *salt* stands for permanence and incorruption (cf. Num. 18:19; 2 Chron. 13:5).

the LORD, you shall bring [a]fresh heads of grain roasted in the fire, grits of new growth, for the grain offering of your early ripened things.

15 'You shall then put oil on it and lay incense on it; it is a grain offering.

16 aLev. 2:2

16 'And the priest shall offer up in smoke [a]its memorial portion, part of its grits and its oil with all its incense as an offering by fire to the LORD.

3 The peace offering, 3:1-17

★ 1 aLev.
7:11-34; 17:5
bLev. 1:3;
22:20-24

3 'Now if his offering is a [a]sacrifice of peace offerings, if he is going to offer out of the herd, whether male or female, he shall offer it [b]without defect before the LORD.

2 aLev. 1:4
bEx. 29:11,
16, 20

2 '[a]And he shall lay his hand on the head of his offering and [b]slay it at the doorway of the tent of meeting, and Aaron's sons, the priests, shall sprinkle the blood around on the altar.

★ 3-5

3 'And from the sacrifice of the peace offerings, he shall present an offering by fire to the LORD, the fat that covers the entrails and all the fat that is on the entrails,

4 and the two kidneys with the fat that is on them, which is on the loins, and the lobe of the liver, which he shall remove with the kidneys.

5 aLev.
7:28-34 bEx.
29:38-42;
Num. 28:3-
10 cNum.
15:8-10;
28:12-14

5 'Then [a]Aaron's sons shall offer it up in smoke on the altar [b]on the burnt offering, which is on the wood that is on the fire; [c]it is an offering by fire of a soothing aroma to the LORD.

6 aLev. 3:1;
22:20-24

6 'But if his offering for a sacrifice of peace offerings to the LORD is from the flock, he shall of-

fer it, male or female, [a]without defect.

7 'If he is going to offer [a]a lamb for his offering, then he shall offer it [b]before the LORD,

7 aNum.
15:4, 5; 28:4-
8 bLev. 17:8,
9; 1 Kin. 8:62

8 and [a]he shall lay his hand on the head of his offering, and [b]slay it before the tent of meeting; and Aaron's sons shall [c]sprinkle its blood around on the altar.

8 aLev. 1:4
bLev. 3:2
cLev. 1:5

9 'And from the [a]sacrifice of peace offerings he shall bring as an offering by fire to the LORD, its fat, the entire fat tail which he shall remove close to the backbone, and the fat that covers the entrails and all the fat that is on the entrails,

9 aLev.
17:5; Num.
7:88; 1 Sam.
10:8; 2 Sam.
6:17; 1 Kin.
3:15; 8:63,
64; 1 Chr.
16:1

10 and the two kidneys with the fat that is on them, which is on the loins, and the lobe of the liver, which he shall remove [a]with the kidneys.

10 aLev. 3:4,
15

11 'Then the priest shall offer it up in smoke [a]on the altar, as [b]food, an offering by fire to the LORD.

11 aLev. 3:5
bLev. 3:16;
21:6, 8, 17,
22

12 'Moreover, if his offering is [a]a goat, then he shall offer it before the LORD,

12 aNum.
15:6-11

13 and he shall lay his hand on its head and slay it before the tent of meeting; and the sons of Aaron shall sprinkle its blood around on the altar.

14 'And from it he shall present his offering as an offering by fire to the LORD, the fat that covers the entrails and all the fat that is on the entrails,

15 and the two kidneys with the fat that is on them, which is on the loins, and the lobe of the liver, which he shall remove [a]with the kidneys.

15 aLev. 3:4;
7:4

16 'And the priest shall offer them up in smoke on the altar as food, an offering by fire for a soothing aroma; [a]all fat is the LORD's.

16 aLev.
7:23-25

3:1 The *peace offerings* (lit., a sacrifice of concord or happiness) was the only offering in which the offerer shared by eating a portion of the sacrifice (7:15). Thus, it illustrated fellowship between God and man (as well as between man and man) on the basis of blood sacrifice. The animal could be an unblemished

male or female ox (3:1), lamb, or goat (vv. 7, 12).
3:3-5 The *fat* in the abdominal cavity, the *kidneys,* the *lobe* (membrane) on the *liver,* and the fat tail in the case of a lamb, were placed on the altar of burnt offering and burned.

★17 ᵃLev.
6:18, 22;
7:34, 36;
10:9, 15;
16:29, 17:7;
23:14, 21;
24:3 ᵇLev.
7:26; 17:10-
16

17 'It is a ᵃperpetual statute throughout your generations in all your dwellings: you shall not eat any fat ᵇor any blood.' "

4   The sin offering, 4:1–5:13

4 Then the LORD spoke to Moses, saying,

★ 2 ᵃLev.
4:22, 27;
5:15-18;
22:14 ᵇLev.
4:13

2 "Speak to the sons of Israel, saying, 'If a person sins ᵃunintentionally in any of the things which the LORD has ᵇcommanded not to be done, and commits any of them,

★ 3-12

3 ᵃif the anointed priest sins

3 ᵃLev.
4:14, 23, 28

so as to bring guilt on the people, then let him offer to the LORD a bull without defect as a sin offering for the sin he has committed.

4 ᵃLev. 1:4;
4:15; Num.
8:12

4 'And he shall bring the bull to the doorway of the tent of meeting before the LORD, and ᵃhe shall lay his hand on the head of the bull, and slay the bull before the LORD.

5 ᵃLev. 4:3,
17

5 'Then the ᵃanointed priest is to take some of the blood of the bull and bring it to the tent of meeting,

6 ᵃEx.
40:21, 26

6 and the priest shall dip his finger in the blood, and sprinkle some of the blood seven times before the LORD, in front of ᵃthe veil of the sanctuary.

7 ᵃLev.
4:18, 25, 30,
34; 8:15; 9:9;
16:18

7 'The priest shall also put some of the blood on the horns of ᵃthe altar of fragrant incense which is before the LORD in the tent of meeting; and all the blood of the bull he shall pour out at the base of the altar of burnt offering which is at the doorway of the tent of meeting.

8 ᵃLev.
3:3, 4

8 'ᵃAnd he shall remove from it all the fat of the bull of the sin offering: the fat that covers the entrails, and all the fat which is on the entrails,

9 and the two kidneys with the fat that is on them, which is on the loins, and the lobe of the liver, which he shall remove ᵃwith the kidneys

9 ᵃLev. 3:4

10 (just as it is removed from the ox of the sacrifice of peace offerings), and the priest is to offer them up in smoke on the altar of burnt offering.

11 'But ᵃthe hide of the bull and all its flesh with its head and its legs and its entrails and its refuse,

11 ᵃLev.
9:11; Num.
19:5

12 that is, all *the rest of* the bull, he is to bring out to ᵃa clean place outside the camp where the ashes are poured out, and burn it on wood with fire; where the ashes are poured out it shall be burned.

12 ᵃLev.
4:21; 6:10,
11, 16:27

13 'ᵃNow if the whole congregation of Israel commits error, and the matter escapes the notice of the assembly, and they commit any of the things which the LORD has commanded not to be done, and they become guilty;

★13-21

13 ᵃNum.
15:24-26

14 ᵃwhen the sin which they have committed becomes known, then the assembly shall offer ᵇa bull of the herd for a sin offering, and bring it before the tent of meeting.

14 ᵃLev. 4:3
ᵇLev. 4:3,
23, 28

15 'Then ᵃthe elders of the congregation shall lay their hands on the head of the bull before the LORD, and the bull shall be slain ᵇbefore the LORD.

15 ᵃLev.
8:14, 18, 22;
Num. 8:10,
12 ᵇLev. 1:3

16 'Then the anointed priest is to bring some of the blood of the bull to the tent of meeting;

17 and ᵃthe priest shall dip his finger in the blood, and sprinkle *it* seven times before the LORD, in front of the veil.

17 ᵃLev. 4:6

18 'And he shall put some of the blood on the horns of ᵃthe al-

18 ᵃLev. 4:7,
25, 30, 34

3:17 No mention is made of a peace offering of birds since they would not provide enough food for a meal. The poor would have to share in the peace offerings brought by others.

4:2 The sin offering (4:1–5:13) was to be brought in cases of sins done *unintentionally*; i.e., known sins committed out of weakness or waywardness, in contrast to sins of presumption done in defiance of God's laws (see note

on Num. 15:30). Some examples are listed in 5:1-4. The sacrifice of Jesus Christ was the full and final sin offering (2 Cor. 5:21).

4:3-12 The priest's sin offering was a young bull. Note that the carcass was burned outside the camp (v. 12; cf. Heb. 13:10-13).

4:13-21 A young bull also provided the sin offering for the whole congregation.

tar which is before the LORD in the tent of meeting; and all the blood he shall pour out at the base of the altar of burnt offering which is at the doorway of the tent of meeting.

19 aLev. 4:8

19 'aAnd he shall remove all its fat from it and offer it up in smoke on the altar.

20 aLev. 4:8, 21 bNum. 15:25, 28

20 'He shall also do with the bull just as he did with athe bull of the sin offering; thus he shall do with it. So bthe priest shall make atonement for them, and they shall be forgiven.

21 aLev. 4:13f.; 16:15-17; Num. 15:24-26

21 'Then he is to bring out the bull to a place outside the camp, and burn it as he burned the first bull; it is athe sin offering for the assembly.

★22-26

22 aNum. 31:13; 32:2 bLev. 4:2, 27

22 'When aa leader bsins and unintentionally does any one of all the things which the LORD God has commanded not to be done, and he becomes guilty,

23 aLev. 4:3 bLev. 4:3, 14, 28 cLev. 4:28

23 'aif his sin which he has committed is made known to him, he shall bring for his offering a bgoat, ca male without defect.

24 'And he shall lay his hand on the head of the male goat, and slay it in the place where they slay the burnt offering before the LORD; it is a sin offering.

25 aLev. 4:7, 18, 30, 34

25 'Then the priest is to take some of the blood of the sin offering with his finger, and put it on athe horns of the altar of burnt offering; and the rest of its blood he shall pour out at the base of the altar of burnt offering.

26 aLev. 4:19 bLev. 4:20, 31; 5:10, 13, 16, 18; 6:7

26 'aAnd all its fat he shall offer up in smoke on the altar as in the case of the fat of the sacrifice of peace offerings. Thus bthe priest shall make atonement for him in regard to his sin, and he shall be forgiven.

★27-35

27 aLev. 4:2; Num. 15:27

27 'Now if anyone of the common people sins aunintentionally in doing any of the things which

the LORD has commanded not to be done, and becomes guilty,

28 aLev. 4:3 bLev. 4:3, 14, 23, 32 cLev. 4:23

28 'aif his sin, which he has committed is made known to him, then he shall bring for his offering a bgoat, a cfemale without defect, for his sin which he has committed.

29 aLev. 1:4; 4:4, 24 bLev. 1:5, 11

29 'And ahe shall lay his hand on the head of the sin offering, and bslay the sin offering at the place of the burnt offering.

30 aLev. 4:7, 18, 25, 34 bLev. 4:7

30 'And the priest shall take some of its blood with his finger and put it on the horns of athe altar of burnt offering; and ball the rest of its blood he shall pour out at the base of the altar.

31 aLev. 4:8 bGen. 8:21; Ex. 29:18; Lev. 1:9, 13; 2:2, 9, 12

31 'aThen he shall remove all its fat, just as the fat was removed from the sacrifice of peace offerings; and the priest shall offer it up in smoke on the altar for ba soothing aroma to the LORD. Thus the priest shall make atonement for him, and he shall be forgiven.

32 aLev. 4:28

32 'But if he brings aa lamb as his offering for a sin offering, he shall bring it, a female without defect.

33 aLev. 1:4, 5 bLev. 4:29

33 'And ahe shall lay his hand on the head of the sin offering, and slay it for a sin offering bin the place where they slay the burnt offering.

34 aLev. 4:7, 18, 25, 30 bLev. 4:7

34 'And the priest is to take some of the blood of the sin offering with his finger and put it on the horns of athe altar of burnt offering; and ball the rest of its blood he shall pour out at the base of the altar.

35 aLev. 4:26, 31 bLev. 4:20

35 'Then he shall remove aall its fat, just as the fat of the lamb is removed from the sacrifice of the peace offerings, and the priest shall offer them up in smoke on the altar, on the offerings by fire to the LORD. Thus bthe priest shall make atonement for him in regard to his sin which he has committed, and he shall be forgiven.

4:22–26 If a ruler sinned, he had to bring a male goat, whose blood was put on the horns of the altar of burnt offering and poured out at its base, rather than being taken into the tent as in the other cases.

4:27–35 An ordinary person could bring as a sin

offering an unblemished female goat (v. 28) or lamb (v. 32) or, in cases of poverty, two doves or two pigeons (5:7). In extreme cases, one could offer a small portion of fine flour (5:11; see note on Heb. 9:22).

★ 1-4

1 aProv. 29:24; Jer. 23:10

5 'Now if a person sins, after he hears a public aadjuration *to testify*, when he *is* a witness, whether he has seen or *otherwise* known, if he does not tell *it*, then he will bear his guilt.

2 aLev. 11:8, 11, 24-40; Num. 19:11-16; Deut. 14:8

2 'Or if a person touches aany unclean thing, whether a carcass of an unclean beast, or the carcass of unclean cattle, or a carcass of unclean swarming things, though it is hidden from him, and he is unclean, then he will be guilty.

3 'Or if he touches human uncleanness, of whatever *sort* his uncleanness *may* be with which he becomes unclean, and it is hidden from him, and then he comes to know *it*, he will be guilty.

4 aNum. 30:6, 8; Ps. 106:33

4 'Or if a person aswears thoughtlessly with his lips to do evil or to do good, in whatever matter a man may speak thoughtlessly with an oath, and it is hidden from him, and then he comes to know *it*, he will be guilty in one of these.

5 aLev. 16:21; 26:40; Num. 5:7; Prov. 28:13

5 'So it shall be when he becomes guilty in one of these, that he shall aconfess that in which he has sinned.

6 aLev. 4:28, 32

6 'He shall also bring his guilt offering to the Lord for his sin which he has committed, aa female from the flock, a lamb or a goat as a sin offering. So the priest shall make atonement on his behalf for his sin.

7 aLev. 12:6, 8; 14:22, 30, 31

7 'But if he cannot afford a lamb, then he shall bring to the Lord his guilt offering for that in which he has sinned, two turtledoves or two young pigeons, aone for a sin offering and the other for a burnt offering.

8 aLev. 1:17

8 'And he shall bring them to the priest, who shall offer first that which is for the sin offering and shall nip its head at the front of its neck, but he ashall not sever it.

9 aLev. 1:15 bLev. 4:7, 18

9 'He shall also sprinkle some of the blood of the sin offering aon the side of the altar, while the rest of the blood shall be drained out bat the base of the altar: it is a sin offering.

10 aLev. 1:14-17 bLev. 4:20, 26; 5:13, 16

10 'The second he shall then prepare as a burnt offering aaccording to the ordinance. bSo the priest shall make atonement on his behalf for his sin which he has committed, and it shall be forgiven him.

11 aLev. 14:21-32; 27:8 bLev. 2:1, 2

11 'But aif his means are insufficient for two turtledoves or two young pigeons, then for his offering for that which he has sinned, he shall bring the tenth of an ephah of fine flour for a sin offering; bhe shall not put oil on it or place incense on it, for it is a sin offering.

12 'And he shall bring it to the priest, and the priest shall take his handful of it as its memorial portion and offer *it* up in smoke on the altar, with the offerings of the Lord by fire: it is a sin offering.

13 aLev. 5:4, 5 bLev. 2:3

13 'So the priest shall make atonement for him concerning his sin which he has committed from aone of these, and it shall be forgiven him; then bthe rest shall become the priest's, like the grain offering.' "

5 The trespass offering,
5:14-6:7

14 Then the Lord spoke to Moses, saying,

★15-16

15 aNum. 5:5-8 bLev. 4:2; 22:14 cLev. 7:1-10 dLev. 6:6 eEx. 30:13

15 "aIf a person acts unfaithfully and sins bunintentionally against the Lord's holy things, then he shall bring his cguilt offering to the Lord: da ram without defect from the flock, according to your valuation in silver by shek-

---

5:1-4 Three examples of sins requiring a sin offering are given. The first is that of withholding evidence when called upon to testify: *a public adjuration to testify*, i.e.; a summons to testify. Verses 2-3 give the case of accidental ceremonial defilement by contact with an unclean animal or man. The third example is that of being unable to fulfill a rash vow (v. 4).

5:15-16 *the Lord's holy things.* E.g., neglecting to pay a tithe, eating parts of the sacrifice that belonged to the priests, failing to redeem the firstborn. Not only did restitution have to be made, but a penalty had to be paid equal to a fifth part of the value.

els, in *terms of* the *e*shekel of the sanctuary, for a guilt offering.

16 "*a*And he shall make restitution for that which he has sinned against the holy thing, and shall add to it a fifth part of it, and give it to the priest. *b*The priest shall then make atonement for him with the ram of the guilt offering, and it shall be forgiven him.

17 "Now if a person sins and does any of the things which the LORD has commanded not to be done, *a*though he was unaware, still he is guilty, and shall bear his punishment.

18 "He is then to bring to the priest *a*a ram without defect from the flock, according to your valuation, for a guilt offering. So the priest shall make atonement for him concerning his error in which he sinned *b*unintentionally and did not know *it*, and it shall be forgiven him.

19 "It is a guilt offering; he was certainly guilty before the LORD."

6 Then the LORD spoke to Moses, saying,

2 "*a*When a person sins and acts unfaithfully against the LORD, and deceives his companion in regard to a deposit or a security entrusted *to him*, or through robbery, or *if* he has extorted from his companion,

3 or *a*has found what was lost and lied about it and sworn falsely, so that he sins in regard to any one of the things a man may do;

4 then it shall be, when he sins and becomes guilty, that he shall *a*restore what he took by robbery, or what he got by extortion, or the deposit which was entrusted to him, or the lost thing which he found,

5 or anything about which he swore falsely; *a*he shall make restitution for it in full, and add to

it one-fifth more. *b*He shall give it to the one to whom it belongs on the day *he presents* his guilt offering.

6 "Then he shall bring to the priest his guilt offering to the LORD, *a*a ram without defect from the flock, according to your valuation, for a guilt offering,

7 and *a*the priest shall make atonement for him before the LORD; and he shall be forgiven for any one of the things which he may have done to incur guilt."

6 Added instructions concerning the offerings, 6:8–7:38

a The burnt offering, 6:8–13

8 Then the LORD spoke to Moses, saying,

9 "Command Aaron and his sons, saying, 'This is *a*the law for the burnt offering: the burnt offering itself *shall remain* on the hearth on the altar all night until the morning, and *b*the fire on the altar is to be kept burning on it.

10 'And the priest is to put on *a*his linen robe, and he shall put on undergarments next to his flesh; and he shall take up the ashes *to* which the fire reduces the burnt offering on the altar, and place them beside the altar.

11 'Then he shall take off his garments and put on other garments, and carry the ashes outside the camp to a clean place.

12 'And the fire on the altar shall be kept burning on it. It shall not go out, but the priest shall burn wood on it every morning; and he shall lay out the burnt offering on it, and offer up in smoke the fat portions of the peace offerings *a*on it.

13 'Fire shall be kept burning continually on the altar; it is not to go out.

Marginal references (left column):
16 *a*Lev. 6:5; 22:14; Num. 5:7, 8 *b*Lev. 7:2-7
★17-18
17 *a*Lev. 4:2; 5:19
18 *a*Lev. 5:15 *b*Lev. 5:17
★ 1-7
2 *a*Ex. 22:7-15
3 *a*Ex. 23:4; Deut. 22:1-4
4 *a*Lev. 24:18, 21
5 *a*Lev. 5:16 *b*Num. 5:8

Marginal references (right column):
6 *a*Lev. 5:15
7 *a*Lev. 7:2-5
★ 8-13
9 *a*Ex. 29:38-42; Num. 28:3-10 *b*Lev. 6:12, 13
10 *a*Ex. 28:39, 42; 39:27, 28
12 *a*Lev. 3:5

5:17-18 When a man suspected that he may have used something holy for himself, he could bring a trespass offering in order to cover his possible guilt.

6:1-7 Examples of fraud, involving robbery, extortion, a deposit of money, or something found but unreported. Restitution included a 20% (or double tithe) penalty.

6:8-13 Additional details concerning the burnt offering of chapter 1.

b The grain offering, 6:14-23

★14-18

14 'Now this is the law of the grain offering: the sons of Aaron shall present it before the Lord in front of the altar.

15 *a*Lev.
2:2, 9

15 '*a*Then one *of them* shall lift up from it a handful of the fine flour of the grain offering, with its oil and all the incense that is on the grain offering, and he shall offer *it* up in smoke on the altar, a soothing aroma, as its memorial offering to the Lord.

16 *a*Lev. 2:3;
10:12-14;
Ezek. 44:29

16 '*a*And what is left of it Aaron and his sons are to eat. It shall be eaten as unleavened cakes in a holy place; they are to eat it in the court of the tent of meeting.

17 *a*Lev.
2:11 *b*Ex.
40:10; Lev.
6:25, 26, 29,
30; Num.
18:9 *c*Lev.
7:7; 10:16-18

17 '*a*It shall not be baked with leaven. I have given it as their share from My offerings by fire; *b*it is most holy, like the sin offering and *c*the guilt offering.

18 *a*Lev.
6:29; 7:6;
Num. 18:10;
1 Cor. 9:13
*b*Lev. 6:27

18 '*a*Every male among the sons of Aaron may eat it; it is a permanent ordinance throughout your generations, from the offerings by fire to the Lord. *b*Whoever touches them shall become consecrated.' ''

★19-23

19 Then the Lord spoke to Moses, saying,

20 *a*Lev.
5:11 *b*Num.
4:16

20 "This is the offering which Aaron and his sons are to present to the Lord on the day when he is anointed; the tenth of an *a*ephah of fine flour as *b*a regular grain offering, half of it in the morning and half of it in the evening.

21 *a*Lev. 2:5

21 "It shall be prepared with oil on a *a*griddle. When it is *well* stirred, you shall bring it. You shall present the grain offering in baked pieces as a soothing aroma to the Lord.

22 "And the anointed priest who will be in his place among his sons shall offer it. By a permanent ordinance it shall be entirely offered up in smoke to the Lord.

23 "So every grain offering of the priest shall be burned entirely. It shall not be eaten."

c The sin offering, 6:24-30

24 Then the Lord spoke to Moses, saying,

★24-30

25 "Speak to Aaron and to his sons, saying, 'This is the law of the sin offering: *a*in the place where the burnt offering is slain the sin offering shall be slain before the Lord; it is most holy.

25 *a*Lev.
1:11

26 '*a*The priest who offers it for sin shall eat it. It shall be eaten in a holy place, in the court of the tent of meeting.

26 *a*Lev.
6:29

27 '*a*Anyone who touches its flesh shall become consecrated; and when any of its blood splashes on a garment, in a holy place you shall wash what was splashed on.

27 *a*Lev.
7:19

28 'Also *a*the earthenware vessel in which it was boiled shall be broken; and if it was boiled in a bronze vessel, then it shall be scoured and rinsed in water.

28 *a*Lev.
11:33; 15:12

29 '*a*Every male among the priests may eat of it; *b*it is most holy.

29 *a*Lev.
6:18 *b*Lev.
6:17, 25

30 'But no sin offering *a*of which any of the blood is brought into the tent of meeting to make atonement *b*in the holy place shall be eaten; *c*it shall be burned with fire.

30 *a*Lev. 4:1-
21 *b*Lev. 4:7,
18 *c*Lev.
4:11, 12, 21

d The trespass offering, 7:1-10

7 'Now this is the law of the *a*guilt offering; it is most holy.

1 *a*Lev.
5:14-6:7

2 'In *a*the place where they are to slay the burnt offering they are to slay the guilt offering, and he shall sprinkle its blood around on the altar.

★ 2 *a*Lev.
1:11

3 'Then he shall offer from it all its fat: the *a*fat tail and the fat that covers the entrails,

3 *a*Lev. 3:9

6:14-18 Facts concerning the priests' portion of the meal offering.
6:19-23 A perpetual (morning and evening, like the burnt offering) meal offering for the priests, which, because it was for the priests,

could not be eaten but had to be burned.
6:24-30 Details about the eating of the sin offering by the priest who offered it.
7:2 *In the place.* I.e., on the N. side of the altar of burnt offering (cf. 1:11).

4 aLev. 3:4 **4** and the two kidneys with the fat that is on them, which is on the loins, and the lobe on the liver he shall remove ªwith the kidneys.

5 'And the priest shall offer them up in smoke on the altar as an offering by fire to the LORD; it is a guilt offering.

6 aLev. 6:18, 29; Num. 18:9 **6** 'ªEvery male among the priests may eat of it. It shall be eaten in a holy place; it is most holy.

★ 7 aLev. 6:25, 26, 30 b1 Cor. 9:13; 10:18 **7** 'The guilt offering is like the ªsin offering, there is one law for them; the ᵇpriest who makes atonement with it shall have it.

8 'Also the priest who presents any man's burnt offering, that priest shall have for himself the skin of the burnt offering which he has presented.

9 aLev. 2:5 **9** 'Likewise, every grain offering that is baked in the oven, and everything prepared in a pan or on a ªgriddle, shall belong to the priest who presents it.

10 'And every grain offering mixed with oil, or dry, shall belong to all the sons of Aaron, to all alike.

e The peace offering, 7:11–38

★11-36 **11** 'Now this is the law of the ªsacrifice of peace offerings which shall be presented to the LORD.

11 aLev. 3:1

★12-17 **12** 'If he offers it by way of ªthanksgiving, then along with the sacrifice of thanksgiving he shall offer ᵇunleavened cakes mixed with oil, and unleavened wafers spread with oil, and cakes of well stirred fine flour mixed with oil.

12 aLev. 7:15 bLev. 2:4; Num. 6:15

13 aLev. 2:12; 23:17, 18; Amos 4:5 **13** 'With the sacrifice of his peace offerings for thanksgiving,

he shall present his offering with cakes of ªleavened bread.

14 'And of this he shall present one of every offering as a contribution to the LORD; ªit shall belong to the priest who sprinkles the blood of the peace offerings.

14 aNum. 18:8, 11, 19

15 'ªNow as for the flesh of the sacrifice of his thanksgiving peace offerings, it shall be eaten on the day of his offering; he shall not leave any of it over until morning.

15 aLev. 22:29, 30

16 'But if the sacrifice of his offering is a ªvotive or a freewill offering, it shall be eaten on the day that he offers his sacrifice; and on the next day what is left of it may be eaten;

16 aLev. 19:5-8

17 ªbut what is left over from the flesh of the sacrifice on the third day shall be burned with fire.

17 aEx. 12:10

18 'So if any of the flesh of the sacrifice of his peace offerings should ever be eaten on the third day, he who offers it shall not be accepted, and it shall not be reckoned to his benefit. It shall be an ªoffensive thing, and the person who eats of it shall bear his own iniquity.

18 aLev. 19:7; Prov. 15:8

19 'Also the flesh that touches anything unclean shall not be eaten; it shall be burned with fire. As for other flesh, anyone who is clean may eat such flesh.

★19-21

20 'ªBut the person who eats the flesh of the sacrifice of peace offerings which belong to the LORD, in his uncleanness, that person ᵇshall be cut off from his people.

20 aLev. 22:3-7; Num. 19:13 bLev. 7:25

21 'ªAnd when anyone touches anything unclean, whether human uncleanness, or an unclean animal, or any

21 aLev. 5:2, 3

7:7 *there is one law for them.* I.e., whatever had not been differentiated between the sin and trespass offerings applied to both.
7:11–36 Details concerning peace offerings.
7:12–17 The peace offering could be brought (1) as an act of thanksgiving (vv. 12–15) for deliverance, answers to prayer, healing, etc., (2) in connection with a vow (votive offering) relative to a past or future favor (vv. 16–17), or (3) purely as a freewill, voluntary act (vv. 16–17).

The thanksgiving peace offering had to be eaten the same day it was offered; the vow or voluntary offerings might be eaten that day and the day following, but not left till the third day.
7:19–21 Matters of *uncleanness* are also discussed in chapters 11–16. To be *cut off* was to be excluded from the practices and protection of the ordinances of Israel, a kind of excommunication.

unclean detestable thing, and eats of the flesh of the sacrifice of peace offerings which belong to the LORD, that person shall be cut off from his people.' "

★22-27

22 Then the LORD spoke to Moses, saying,

23 aLev. 3:17

23 "Speak to the sons of Israel, saying, 'You shall not eat aany fat *from* an ox, a sheep, or a goat.

24 aEx. 22:31; Lev. 17:15; 22:8

24 'Also the fat of *an animal* which dies, and the fat of an animal atorn *by beasts*, may be put to any other use, but you must certainly not eat it.

25 'For whoever eats the fat of the animal from which an offering by fire is offered to the LORD, even the person who eats shall be cut off from his people.

26 aGen. 9:4; Lev. 17:10-16; 19:26; Deut. 12:23; 1 Sam. 14:33; Acts 15:20

26 'aAnd you are not to eat any blood, either of bird or animal, in any of your dwellings.

27 'Any person who eats any blood, even that person shall be cut off from his people.' "

28 Then the LORD spoke to Moses, saying,

29 aLev. 3:1

29 "Speak to the sons of Israel, saying, 'He who offers athe sacrifice of his peace offerings to the LORD shall bring his offering to the LORD from the sacrifice of his peace offerings.

★30-31

30 aEx. 29:26, 27; Lev. 8:29; Num. 6:20

30 'His own hands are to bring offerings by fire to the LORD. He shall bring the fat with the breast, that the abreast may be presented as a wave offering before the LORD.

31 aNum. 18:11; Deut. 18:3

31 'And the priest shall offer up the fat in smoke on the altar; but athe breast shall belong to Aaron and his sons.

★32 aEx. 29:27; Lev. 7:34; 9:21; Num. 6:20

32 'And you shall give athe right thigh to the priest as a contribution from the sacrifices of your peace offerings.

33 'The one among the sons of Aaron who offers the blood of the peace offerings and the fat, the right thigh shall be his as *his* portion.

34 'For I have taken athe breast of the wave offering and the thigh of the contribution from the sons of Israel from the sacrifices of their peace offerings, and have given them to Aaron the priest and to his sons as *their* due forever from the sons of Israel.

34 aEx. 29:27; Lev. 10:14, 15; Num. 18:18

35 'This is that which is consecrated to Aaron and that awhich is consecrated to his sons from the offerings by fire to the LORD, in that day when he presented them to serve as priests to the LORD.

35 aNum. 18:8

36 'These the LORD had commanded to be given them from the sons of Israel in the day that He aanointed them. It is *their* due forever throughout their generations.' "

36 aEx. 40:13-15; Lev. 8:12, 30

37 This is the law of the burnt offering, the grain offering and the sin offering and the guilt offering and athe ordination offering and the sacrifice of peace offerings,

37 aEx. 29:22-34; Lev. 8:22, 23

38 awhich the LORD commanded Moses at Mount Sinai in the day that He commanded the sons of Israel to present their offerings to the LORD in the wilderness of Sinai.

38 aLev. 1:1; 26:46; 27:34; Deut. 4:5

B   Through the Priests,
8:1-10:20

1   *The consecration to priestly*
***service*, 8:1-36**

8 Then the LORD spoke to Moses, saying, -

★1ff.

2 "aTake Aaron and his sons with him, and the bgarments and

2 aEx. 28:1 bLev. 6:10 cEx. 30:25

7:22-27 The fat of sacrificial animals was the Lord's portion, and blood was not to be eaten under any circumstances.

7:30-31 In a *wave offering*, the breast of the animal was waved or moved back and forth, toward and away from the altar, as a symbol of presenting the offering to God and of His returning it to the priest.

7:32 The *contribution* (or heave offering) consisted of heaving the right shoulder of the animal up and down, symbolically setting it aside as a contribution to God for the use of the priests.

8:1ff. Moses was now to carry out the instructions given in Exod. 28-29 for the consecration of the priests. The elaborate ritual was performed in the presence of all the people (cf. v. 3).

cthe anointing oil and the bull of the sin offering, and the two rams and the basket of unleavened bread;

3 and assemble all the congregation at the doorway of the tent of meeting."

4 So Moses did just as the LORD commanded him. When the congregation was assembled at the doorway of the tent of meeting,

5 Moses said to the congregation, "This is the thing which the LORD has commanded to do."

6 Then aMoses had Aaron and his sons come near, and bwashed them with water.

7 And he aput the tunic on him and girded him with the sash, and clothed him with the robe, and put the ephod on him; and he girded him with the artistic band of the ephod, with which he tied it to him.

8 He then placed the breastpiece on him, and in the breastpiece he put athe Urim and the Thummim.

9 He also placed the turban on his head, and on the turban, at its front, he placed athe golden plate, the holy crown, just as the LORD had commanded Moses.

10 Moses then took athe anointing oil and anointed the tabernacle and all that was in it, and consecrated them.

11 And he sprinkled some of it on the altar seven times and anointed the altar and all its utensils, and the basin and its stand, to aconsecrate them.

12 Then he poured some of the aanointing oil on Aaron's head and anointed him, to consecrate him.

13 aNext Moses had Aaron's sons come near and clothed them with tunics, and girded them with sashes, and bound caps on them,

just as the LORD had commanded Moses.

14 Then he brought athe bull of the sin offering, and Aaron and his sons laid their hands on the head of the bull of the sin offering.

15 Next Moses slaughtered it and took the blood and with his finger aput some of it around on the horns of the altar, and purified the altar. Then he poured out the rest of the blood at the base of the altar and consecrated it, to make atonement for it.

16 He also atook all the fat that was on the entrails and the lobe of the liver, and the two kidneys and their fat; and Moses offered it up in smoke on the altar.

17 aBut the bull and its hide and its flesh and its refuse, he burned in the fire outside the camp, just as the LORD had commanded Moses.

18 Then he presented athe ram of the burnt offering, and Aaron and his sons laid their hands on the head of the ram.

19 And Moses slaughtered it and sprinkled the blood around on the altar.

20 When he had cut the ram into its pieces, Moses aoffered up the head and the pieces and the suet in smoke.

21 After he had washed the entrails and the legs with water, Moses aoffered up the whole ram in smoke on the altar. It was a burnt offering for a soothing aroma; it was an offering by fire to the LORD, just as the LORD had commanded Moses.

22 Then he presented the second ram, athe ram of ordination; and Aaron and his sons laid their hands on the head of the ram.

Cross references (margin):

6 aEx. 29:4-6 bEx. 30:19, 20; Ps. 26:6; 1 Cor. 6:11; Eph. 5:26

7 aEx. 28:4

★ 8 aEx. 28:30; Num. 27:21; Deut. 33:8; 1 Sam. 2:6; Ezra 2:63; Neh. 7:65

9 aEx. 28:36

★10-12

10 aEx. 30:26-29; Lev. 8:2

11 aEx. 29:36, 37; 30:29

12 aEx. 29:7; 30:30; Lev. 21:10, 12; Ps. 133:2

13 aEx. 29:8, 9

★14 aEx. 29:10; Lev. 4:4; Ps. 66:15; Ezek. 43:19

15 aEx. 29:12; Lev. 4:7; Ezek. 43:20

16 aEx. 29:13

17 aEx. 29:14; Lev. 4:11, 12

★18 aEx. 29:15; Lev. 8:2

20 aLev. 1:8

21 aEx. 29:18

★22 aEx. 29:31; Lev. 8:2

8:8 the Urim and the Thummim. See note on Exod. 28:30.

8:10-12 See note on Exod. 30:32. On the anointing of Aaron, see Psalm 133:2.

8:14 Moses first offered a sin offering on behalf of Aaron and his sons (the laying of their hands on the animal indicated their identification with it).

8:18 Moses next offered a burnt offering.

8:22 The final major offering was that of ordination, not mentioned elsewhere, though similar to the peace offering. The Hebrew name for it literally means "fillings" and signified the investing of Aaron and his sons with their office.

★23 aEx.
29:20, 21

23 And Moses slaughtered *it* and took some of its blood and aput it on the lobe of Aaron's right ear, and on the thumb of his right hand, and on the big toe of his right foot.

24 aHeb.
9:18-22

24 He also had Aaron's sons come near; and Moses put some of the blood on the lobe of their right ear, and on the thumb of their right hand, and on the big toe of their right foot. Moses then asprinkled *the rest of* the blood around on the altar.

25 And he took the fat, and the fat tail, and all the fat that was on the entrails, and the lobe of the liver and the two kidneys and their fat and the right thigh.

26 aEx.
29:23

26 And afrom the basket of unleavened bread that was before the LORD, he took one unleavened cake and one cake of bread *mixed with* oil and one wafer, and placed *them* on the portions of fat and on the right thigh.

★27-29

27 aEx.
29:24

27 He then aput all *these* on the hands of Aaron and on the hands of his sons, and presented them as a wave offering before the LORD.

28 aEx.
29:25 bGen.
8:21

28 Then Moses atook them from their hands and offered them up in smoke on the altar with the burnt offering. They were an ordination offering for ba soothing aroma; it was an offering by fire to the LORD.

29 aLev.
7:31-34 bEx.
29:26; Ps.
99:6

29 Moses also took athe breast and presented it for a wave offering before the LORD; it was bMoses' portion of the ram of ordination, just as the LORD had commanded Moses.

30 aEx.
29:21

30 So Moses atook some of the anointing oil and some of the blood which was on the altar, and sprinkled it on Aaron, on his garments, on his sons, and on the garments of his sons with him; and he consecrated Aaron, his garments, and his sons, and the garments of his sons with him.

31 Then Moses said to Aaron and to his sons, "aBoil the flesh at the doorway of the tent of meeting, and eat it there together with the bread which is in the basket of the ordination offering, just as I commanded, bsaying, 'Aaron and his sons shall eat it.'

31 aEx.
29:31 bEx.
29:32

32 "And athe remainder of the flesh and of the bread you shall burn in the fire.

32 aEx.
29:34

33 "aAnd you shall not go outside the doorway of the tent of meeting for seven days, until the day that the period of your ordination is fulfilled; for he will ordain you through seven days.

★33 aEx.
29:35

34 "The LORD has commanded to do as has been done this day, to make atonement on your behalf.

35 "At the doorway of the tent of meeting, moreover, you shall remain day and night for seven days, and akeep the charge of the LORD, that you may not die, for so I have been commanded."

35 aNum.
3:7; 9:19;
Deut. 11:1;
1 Kin. 2:3;
Ezek. 48:11

36 Thus Aaron and his sons did all the things which the LORD had commanded through Moses.

2 The inauguration of priestly service, 9:1-24

9 Now it came about aon the eighth day that Moses called Aaron and his sons and the elders of Israel;

★ 1-21

1 aEzek.
43:27

2 and he said to Aaron, "aTake for yourself a calf, a bull, for a sin offering and a ram for a burnt offering, *both* without defect, and offer *them* before the LORD.

2 aEzek.
29:1; Lev.
4:3

8:23 See note on Exod. 29:1-37.

8:27-29 In this instance, the *wave offering* could not be eaten by Aaron and his sons because it was made on their behalf.

8:33 The same offerings were repeated daily for seven days while Aaron and his sons remained in the court of the tabernacle.

9:1-21 Aaron first offered a sin offering and a burnt offering for himself (vv. 8-14), then he offered a sin, a burnt, a grain, and a peace offering for the people (vv. 15-18). These symbolized (in order) atonement, dedication, sustenance, and communion. *offered it for sin* (v. 15). Lit., *he sinned it*; i.e., he made it sin (cf. 2 Cor. 5:21).

3 "Then to the sons of Israel you shall speak, saying, 'Take a male goat for a sin offering, and a calf and a lamb, both one year old, without defect, for a burnt offering,

4 and an ox and a ram for peace offerings, to sacrifice before the LORD, and a grain offering mixed with oil; for today ᵃthe LORD shall appear to you.'"

5 So they took what Moses had commanded to the front of the tent of meeting, and the whole congregation came near and stood before the LORD.

6 And Moses said, "This is the thing which the LORD has commanded you to do, that ᵃthe glory of the LORD may appear to you."

7 Moses then said to Aaron, "Come near to the altar and ᵃoffer your sin offering and your burnt offering, that you may make atonement for yourself and for the people; then make the offering for the people, that you may make atonement for them, just as the LORD has commanded."

8 ᵃSo Aaron came near to the altar and slaughtered the calf of the sin offering which was for himself.

9 ᵃAnd Aaron's sons presented the blood to him; and he dipped his finger in the blood, and ᵇput some on the horns of the altar, and poured out the rest of the blood at the base of the altar.

10 The fat and the kidneys and the lobe of the liver of the sin offering, he then offered up in smoke on the altar just as the LORD had commanded Moses.

11 ᵃThe flesh and the skin, however, he burned with fire outside the camp.

12 Then he slaughtered the burnt offering; and Aaron's sons handed the blood to him and he sprinkled it around on the altar.

13 And they handed the burnt offering to him in pieces with the head, and he offered

them up in smoke on the altar.

14 He also washed the entrails and the legs, and offered them up in smoke with the burnt offering on the altar.

15 Then he presented the people's offering, and took the ᵃgoat of the sin offering which was for the people, and slaughtered it and offered it for sin, like the first.

16 He also presented the burnt offering, and offered it according to ᵃthe ordinance.

17 Next he presented ᵃthe grain offering, and filled his hand with some of it and offered it up in smoke on the altar, ᵇbesides the burnt offering of the morning.

18 Then ᵃhe slaughtered the ox and the ram, the sacrifice of peace offerings which was for the people; and Aaron's sons handed the blood to him and he sprinkled it around on the altar.

19 As for the portions of fat from the ox and from the ram, the fat tail, and the fat ᵃcovering, and the kidneys and the lobe of the liver,

20 they now placed the portions of fat on the breasts; and he offered them up in smoke on the altar.

21 But ᵃthe breasts and the right thigh Aaron presented as a wave offering before the LORD, just as Moses had commanded.

22 Then Aaron lifted up his hands toward the people and ᵃblessed them, and he stepped down after making the sin offering and the burnt offering and the peace offerings.

23 And Moses and Aaron went into the tent of meeting. When they came out and blessed the people, ᵃthe glory of the LORD appeared to all the people.

24 ᵃThen fire came out from before the LORD and consumed the burnt offering and the portions of fat on the altar; and when all the people saw it, they shouted and fell on their faces.

Cross references (margin):

4 ᵃEx. 29:43

6 ᵃEx. 24:16; Lev. 9:23

7 ᵃHeb. 5:3; 7:27

8 ᵃLev. 4:1-12

9 ᵃLev. 9:12, 18 ᵇLev. 4:7

11 ᵃLev. 4:11, 12; 8:17

15 ᵃLev. 4:27-31

16 ᵃLev. 1:1-13

17 ᵃLev. 2:1-3 ᵇLev. 3:5

18 ᵃLev. 3:1-11

19 ᵃLev. 3:9

21 ᵃEx. 29:26, 27; Lev. 7:30-34

22 ᵃNum. 6:22-26; Deut. 21:5; Luke 24:50

23 ᵃLev. 9:6; Num. 16:19

★24 ᵃ1 Kin. 18:38, 39; 2 Chr. 7:1

9:24 This may have been the start of the *fire* that was to burn continually (6:12-13).

3 The sacrilege of priestly service: Nadab and Abihu, 10:1-20

★ 1 *a*Ex.
24:1, 9; Num.
3:2; 26:61
*b*Lev. 16:12

10 Now *a*Nadab and Abihu, the sons of Aaron, took their respective *b*firepans, and after putting fire in them, placed incense on it and offered strange fire before the LORD, which He had not commanded them.

★ 2 *a*Num.
3:4; 16:35;
26:61

2 *a*And fire came out from the presence of the LORD and consumed them, and they died before the LORD.

★ 3 *a*Ex.
19:22; Lev.
21:6 *b*Ex.
30:30; Ezek.
38:16 *c*Ex.
14:4, 17; Is.
49:3; Ezek.
28:22

3 Then Moses said to Aaron, "It is what the LORD spoke, saying,
'By those who *a*come near
Me I *b*will be treated
as holy,
And before all the people I
will *c*be honored.'"
So Aaron, therefore, kept silent.

4 *a*Ex. 6:22

4 Moses called also to *a*Mishael and Elzaphan, the sons of Aaron's uncle Uzziel, and said to them, "Come forward, carry your relatives away from the front of the sanctuary to the outside of the camp."

5 *a*Ex. 29:5;
Lev. 8:13

5 So they came forward and carried them still in their *a*tunics to the outside of the camp, as Moses had said.

★ 6 *a*Lev.
21:1-5, 10-12
*b*Num. 1:53;
16:22, 46;
18:5; Josh.
7:1; 22:18,
20; 2 Sam.
24:1

6 Then Moses said to Aaron and to his sons Eleazar and Ithamar, "*a*Do not uncover your heads nor tear your clothes, so that you may not die, and that He may not *b*become wrathful against all the congregation. But your kinsmen, the whole house of Israel, shall bewail the burning which the LORD has brought about.

7 "You shall not even go out from the doorway of the tent of meeting, lest you die; for *a*the LORD's anointing oil is upon you." So they did according to the word of Moses.

7 *a*Ex.
28:41; Lev.
21:12

8 The LORD then spoke to Aaron, saying,

9 "*a*Do not drink wine or strong drink, neither you nor your sons with you, when you come into the tent of meeting, so that you may not die—it is a perpetual statute throughout your generations—

★ 9-11
9 *a*Prov.
20:1; 31:5;
Is. 28:7;
Ezek. 44:21;
Hos. 4:11;
Luke 1:15;
Eph. 5:18;
1 Tim. 3:3;
Titus 1:7

10 and *a*so as to make a distinction between the holy and the profane, and between the unclean and the clean,

10 *a*Lev.
11:47; 20:25;
Ezek. 22:26

11 and *a*so as to teach the sons of Israel all the statutes which the LORD has spoken to them through Moses."

11 *a*Deut.
17:10, 11;
33:10

12 Then Moses spoke to Aaron, and to his surviving sons, *a*Eleazar and Ithamar, "*b*Take the grain offering that is left over from the LORD's offerings by fire and eat it unleavened beside the altar, for it is most holy.

12 *a*Ex. 6:23;
Num. 3:2
*b*Lev. 6:14-
18

13 "You shall eat it, moreover, in a holy place, because it is your due and your sons' due out of the LORD's offerings by fire; for thus I have been commanded.

14 "*a*The breast of the wave offering, however, and the thigh of the offering you may eat in a clean place; you and your sons and your daughters with you; for they have been given as your due and your sons' due out of the sacrifices of the peace offerings of the sons of Israel.

14 *a*Lev.
7:30-34;
Num. 18:11

15 "*a*The thigh offered by lifting up and the breast offered by

15 *a*Lev.
7:34

10:1 *strange fire.* Nadab and Abihu apparently used coals of fire that were not taken from the brazen altar as prescribed (see 6:12-13; 16:12). It seems, too, that they offered incense other than at the morning or evening sacrifice (cf. Exod. 30:7-8). Some feel that they were drunk, since a prohibition against drinking immediately follows their punishment (Lev. 10:9).

10:2 The fire that killed them came from the cloud of glory that rested over the Mercy Seat. Though it killed them, it did not consume their clothes or bodies (v. 5).

10:3 *I will be treated as holy.* Any disobedience of God's commands detracted from His glory.

10:6 *Do not uncover your heads.* Lit., let not the hair of your heads hang loose. This and tearing the clothes were signs of mourning (cf. 2 Sam. 15:30) but were forbidden to a ministering priest (Lev. 21:10).

10:9-11 The priests were warned against using *wine* and *strong drink* (from a word meaning "to inebriate"), in order that their faculties not be dulled when performing the rituals (v. 10) and teaching the people (v. 11; cf. Ezek. 44:23).

waving, they shall bring along with the offerings by fire of the portions of fat, to present as a wave offering before the Lord; so it shall be a thing perpetually due you and your sons with you, just as the Lord has commanded."

★16-20

16 aLev. 9:3, 15

16 But Moses searched carefully for the agoat of the sin offering, and behold, it had been burned up! So he was angry with Aaron's surviving sons Eleazar and Ithamar, saying,

17 aLev. 6:24-30 bEx. 28:38; Lev. 22:16; Num. 18:1

17 "Why adid you not eat the sin offering at the holy place? For it is most holy, and He gave it to you to bear away bthe guilt of the congregation, to make atonement for them before the Lord.

18 aLev. 6:30 bLev. 6:26

18 "Behold, asince its blood had not been brought inside, into the sanctuary, you should certainly have beaten it in the sanctuary, just as I commanded."

19 aLev. 9:8, 12

19 But Aaron spoke to Moses, "Behold, this very day they apresented their sin offering and their burnt offering before the Lord. When things like these happened to me, if I had eaten a sin offering today, would it have been good in the sight of the Lord?"

20 And when Moses heard that, it seemed good in his sight.

II THE WALK WITH GOD: SANCTIFICATION,
11:1-27:34
A Laws Concerning Purity,
11:1-15:33
1 In relation to food, 11:1-47

★ 1

11 The Lord spoke again to Moses and to Aaron, saying to them,

2 aDeut. 14:3-21

2 "Speak to the sons of Israel, saying, 'aThese are the creatures which you may eat from all the animals that are on the earth.

★ 3

3 'Whatever divides a hoof, thus making split hoofs, and chews the cud, among the animals, that you may eat.

4 aActs 10:14

4 'Nevertheless, ayou are not to eat of these, among those which chew the cud, or among those which divide the hoof: the camel, for though it chews cud, it does not divide the hoof, it is unclean to you.

★ 5

5 'Likewise, the rock badger, for though it chews cud, it does not divide the hoof, it is unclean to you;

6 the rabbit also, for though it chews cud, it does not divide the hoof, it is unclean to you;

7 and the pig, for though it divides the hoof, thus making a split hoof, it does not chew cud, it is unclean to you.

8 'You shall not eat of their flesh nor touch their carcasses; they are unclean to you.

★ 9-12

9 aDeut. 14:9

9 'aThese you may eat, whatever is in the water: all that have fins and scales, those in the water, in the seas or in the rivers, you may eat.

10 aDeut. 14:10

10 'aBut whatever is in the seas and in the rivers, that do not have fins and scales among all the teeming life of the water, and among all the living creatures that are in the water, they are detestable things to you,

11 and they shall be abhorrent to you; you may not eat of their flesh, and their carcasses you shall detest.

10:16-20 When Moses asked why the sin offering had not been eaten (cf. 6:26), Aaron replied that, because of the death of his two sons, he and his remaining sons had felt unworthy. Moses accepted the explanation.
11:1 In this section (through chapter 15), the word "unclean" occurs more than 100 times. Even though the emphasis is on ceremonial, rather than ethical, uncleanness was sin. Those laws served (1) to reflect the holiness of God, (2) to keep Israel distinct from the idolatrous practices of the nations around them, and (3) to help maintain physical health.

11:3 The regulation concerning quadrupeds (animals that have divided hooves and chew the cud) is stated in verse 3 and then illustrated with four animals that do not meet the qualifications. *split hoofs.* I.e., divided all the way through (cf. Deut. 14:6).
11:5 *rock badger.* A rodent. The fact that its jaws (as well as those of the rabbit, v. 6) are in constant motion gives it the appearance of chewing the cud.
11:9-12 Only fish that have both fins and scales could be eaten (cf. Deut. 14:9-10). This ruled out eels, shellfish, lobsters, crabs, oysters, etc.

12 'Whatever in the water does not have fins and scales is abhorrent to you.

★13-19

13 aDeut. 14:12-19

13 'These, moreover, ᵃyou shall detest among the birds; they are abhorrent, not to be eaten: the eagle and the vulture and the buzzard,

14 and the kite and the falcon in its kind,

15 every raven in its kind,

16 and the ostrich and the owl and the sea gull and the hawk in its kind,

17 and the little owl and the cormorant and the great owl,

18 and the white owl and the pelican and the carrion vulture,

19 and the stork, the heron in its kinds, and the hoopoe, and the bat.

★20-23

20 'All the winged insects that walk on *all* fours are detestable to you.

21 'Yet these you may eat among all the winged insects which walk on *all* fours: those which have above their feet jointed legs with which to jump on the earth.

22 'These of them you may eat: the locust in its kinds, and the devastating locust in its kinds, and the cricket in its kinds, and the grasshopper in its kinds.

23 'But all other winged insects which are four-footed are detestable to you.

★24-40

24 'By these, moreover, you will be made unclean: whoever touches their carcasses becomes unclean until evening,

25 aLev. 11:40

25 and ᵃwhoever picks up any of their carcasses shall wash his clothes and be unclean until evening.

26 'Concerning all the animals which divide the hoof, but do not make a split *hoof*, or which do not chew cud, they are unclean to you: whoever touches them becomes unclean.

27 'Also whatever walks on its paws, among all the creatures that walk on *all* fours, are unclean to you; whoever touches their carcasses becomes unclean until evening,

28 and the one who picks up their carcasses shall wash his clothes and be unclean until evening; they are unclean to you.

29 'Now these are to you the unclean among the swarming things which swarm on the earth: the mole, and the mouse, and the great lizard in its kinds,

30 and the gecko, and the crocodile, and the lizard, and the sand reptile, and the chameleon.

31 'These are to you the unclean among all the swarming things; whoever touches them when they are dead becomes unclean until evening.

32 aLev. 15:12

32 'Also anything on which one of them may fall when they are dead, becomes unclean, including any wooden article, or clothing, or a skin, or a sack—any article of which use is made—ᵃit shall be put in the water and be unclean until evening, then it becomes clean.

33 aLev. 6:28; 15:12

33 'As for any ᵃearthenware vessel into which one of them may fall, whatever is in it becomes unclean and you shall break the vessel.

34 'Any of the food which may be eaten, on which water comes, shall become unclean; and any liquid which may be drunk in every vessel shall become unclean.

35 'Everything, moreover, on which part of their carcass may fall becomes unclean; an oven or a stove shall be smashed; they are unclean and shall continue as unclean to you.

36 'Nevertheless a spring or a cistern collecting water shall be

---

11:13-19 Twenty unclean birds are specifically named. *kite.* A medium-size bird of prey. *cormorant.* A large, black, gooselike bird. *hoopoe.* A beautiful bird with colored plumage. **11:20-23** Insects that crawl like quadrupeds

were banned—except those with long jumping legs of the locust family.
11:24-40 Any person or thing that touched the *carcass* of an unclean animal would be unclean until washed.

clean, though the one who touches their carcass shall be unclean.

37 'And if a part of their carcass falls on any seed for sowing which is to be sown, it is clean.

38 'Though if water is put on the seed, and a part of their carcass falls on it, it is unclean to you.

39 'Also if one of the animals dies which you have for food, the one who touches its carcass becomes unclean until evening.

40 '[a]He too, who eats some of its carcass shall wash his clothes and be unclean until evening; and the one who picks up its carcass shall wash his clothes and be unclean until evening.

41 '[a]Now every swarming thing that swarms on the earth is detestable, not to be eaten.

42 'Whatever crawls on its belly, and whatever walks on *all* fours, whatever has many feet, in respect to every swarming thing that swarms on the earth, you shall not eat them, for they are detestable.

43 '[a]Do not render yourselves detestable through any of the swarming things that swarm; and you shall not make yourselves unclean with them so that you become unclean.

44 'For [a]I am the LORD your God. Consecrate yourselves therefore, and [b]be holy; for I am holy. And you shall not make yourselves unclean with any of the swarming things that swarm on the earth.

45 '[a]For I am the LORD, who brought you up from the land of Egypt, to be your God; thus [b]you shall be holy for I am holy.' "

46 This is the law regarding the animal, and the bird, and every living thing that moves in the waters, and everything that swarms on the earth,

47 [a]to make a distinction between the unclean and the clean, and between the edible creature and the creature which is not to be eaten.

2 In relation to childbirth, 12:1-8

12 Then the LORD spoke to Moses, saying,

2 "Speak to the sons of Israel, saying, 'When a woman gives birth and bears a male *child*, then she shall be unclean for seven days, [a]as in the days of her menstruation she shall be unclean.

3 'And on [a]the eighth day the flesh of his foreskin shall be circumcised.

4 'Then she shall remain in the blood of *her* purification for thirty-three days; she shall not touch any consecrated thing, nor enter the sanctuary, until the days of her purification are completed.

5 'But if she bears a female *child*, then she shall be unclean for two weeks, as in her menstruation; and she shall remain in the blood of *her* purification for sixty-six days.

6 'And [a]when the days of her purification are completed, for a son or for a daughter, she shall bring to the priest at the doorway of the tent of meeting, a one year old lamb for a burnt offering, and a young pigeon or a turtledove [b]for a sin offering.

7 'Then he shall offer it before the LORD and make atonement for her; and she shall be cleansed from the flow of her blood. This is the law for her who bears *a child, whether* a male or a female.

8 'But if she cannot afford a lamb, then she shall take [a]two turtledoves or two young pigeons, [b]the one for a burnt offering and the other for a sin offering; and

---

Marginal references (left column):

40 [a]Lev. 17:15; 22:8; Deut. 14:21; Ezek. 44:31

41 [a]Lev. 11:29

43 [a]Lev. 20:25

44 [a]Ex. 6:7; 16:12; 23:25; Is. 43:3; 51:15 [b]Lev. 19:2; 1 Pet. 1:16

45 [a]Ex. 6:7; 20:2; Lev. 22:33; 25:38; 26:45 [b]Lev. 19:2; 1 Pet. 1:16

Marginal references (right column):

47 [a]Lev. 10:10; Ezek. 22:26; 44:23

★ 1-8

2 [a]Lev. 15:19; 18:19

3 [a]Gen. 17:12; Luke 1:59; 2:21

6 [a]Luke 2:22 [b]Lev. 5:7

8 [a]Luke 2:22-24 [b]Lev. 5:7; [c]Lev. 4:26

12:1-8 The birth of a child, though a happy occasion, was a reminder that sin is transmitted to each person. Thus, the mother was banned from performing religious duties for 40 days (in the case of a baby boy) or 80 days (in the case of a baby girl). After this time she had to bring a burnt offering and a sin offering (cf. Luke 2:24).

the ^cpriest shall make atonement for her, and she shall be clean.' "

3   In relation to leprosy,
13:1–14:57

a   Classifications of leprosy,
13:1–59

13 Then the LORD spoke to Moses and to Aaron, saying,

★ **2** ^aDeut. 24:8

2 "When a man has on the skin of his body a swelling or a scab or a bright spot, and it becomes an infection of leprosy on the skin of his body, ^athen he shall be brought to Aaron the priest, or to one of his sons the priests.

3 "And the priest shall look at the mark on the skin of the body, and if the hair in the infection has turned white and the infection appears to be deeper than the skin of his body, it is an infection of leprosy; when the priest has looked at him, he shall pronounce him unclean.

4 "But if the bright spot is white on the skin of his body, and it does not appear to be deeper than the skin, and the hair on it has not turned white, then the priest shall isolate *him who has* the infection for seven days.

5 "And the priest shall look at him on the seventh day, and if in his eyes the infection has not changed, *and* the infection has not spread on the skin, then the priest shall isolate him for seven more days.

6 ^aLev. 11:25; 14:8

6 "And the priest shall look at him again on the seventh day; and if the infection has faded, and the mark has not spread on the skin, then the priest shall pronounce him clean; it is *only* a scab. And he shall ^awash his clothes and be clean.

7 "But if the scab spreads farther on the skin, after he has shown himself to the priest for his cleansing, he shall appear again to the priest.

8 "And the priest shall look, and if the scab has spread on the skin, then the priest shall pronounce him unclean; it is leprosy.

9 "When the infection of leprosy is on a man, then he shall be brought to the priest.

10 "The priest shall then look, and if there is a ^awhite swelling in the skin, and it has turned the hair white, and there is quick raw flesh in the swelling,

10 ^aNum. 12:10; 2 Kin. 5:27; 2 Chr. 26:19, 20

11 it is a chronic leprosy on the skin of his body, and the priest shall pronounce him unclean; he shall not isolate him, for he is unclean.

12 "And if the leprosy breaks out farther on the skin, and the leprosy covers all the skin of *him who has* the infection from his head even to his feet, as far as the priest can see,

13 then the priest shall look, and behold, *if* the leprosy has covered all his body, he shall pronounce clean *him who has* the infection; it has all turned white *and* he is clean.

14 "But whenever raw flesh appears on him, he shall be unclean.

15 "And the priest shall look at the raw flesh, and he shall pronounce him unclean; the raw flesh is unclean, it is leprosy.

16 "Or if the raw flesh turns again and is changed to white, then he shall ^acome to the priest,

16 ^aLuke 5:12-14

17 and the priest shall look at him, and behold, *if* the infection has turned to white, then the

---

13:2 *leprosy.* From a root that means "to strike," referring to a scaly condition of the skin or of inanimate objects, or to a disease that was sometimes serious. Though the word includes modern leprosy (Hansen's disease), in humans it referred to many other kinds of skin eruptions as well. The symptoms described in vv. 2, 6, 10, 18, 30, and 39 are not sufficient to diagnose precisely the various skin conditions referred to. Isolation and observation were required in all suspected cases. Though the leper is always described in Scripture as ceremonially unclean rather than sinful, the fact that leprosy was a "stroke" from God, something loathsome to which stigma and taboo were attached, strongly suggests that it may have served as an illustration of sin (cf. Isa. 1:6; Psalm 51:7).

priest shall pronounce clean *him who has* the infection; he is clean.

18 "And when the body has a boil on its skin, and it is healed,

19 and in the place of the boil there is a white swelling or a reddish-white, bright spot, then it shall be shown to the priest;

20 and the priest shall look, and behold, *if* it appears to be lower than the skin, and the hair on it has turned white, then the priest shall pronounce him unclean; it is the infection of leprosy, it has broken out in the boil.

21 "But if the priest looks at it, and behold, there are no white hairs in it and it is not lower than the skin and is faded, then the priest shall isolate him for seven days;

22 and if it spreads farther on the skin, then the priest shall pronounce him unclean; it is an infection.

23 "But if the bright spot remains in its place, and does not spread, it is *only* the scar of the boil; and the priest shall pronounce him clean.

24 "Or if the body sustains in its skin a burn by fire, and the raw *flesh* of the burn becomes a bright spot, reddish-white, or white,

^{25 ᵃEx. 4:6;}
^{Num. 12:10;}
^{2 Kin. 5:27}

25 then the priest shall look at it. And if the hair in the bright spot has ᵃturned white, and it appears to be deeper than the skin, it is leprosy; it has broken out in the burn. Therefore, the priest shall pronounce him unclean; it is an infection of leprosy.

26 "But if the priest looks at it, and indeed, there is no white hair in the bright spot, and it is no deeper than the skin, but is dim, then the priest shall isolate him for seven days;

27 and the priest shall look at him on the seventh day. If it spreads farther in the skin, then the priest shall pronounce him unclean; it is an infection of leprosy.

28 "But if the bright spot remains in its place, and has not spread in the skin, but is dim, it is the swelling from the burn; and the priest shall pronounce him clean, for it is *only* the scar of the burn.

29 "Now if a man or woman has an infection on the head or on the beard,

30 then the priest shall look at the infection, and if it appears to be deeper than the skin, and there is thin yellowish hair in it, then the priest shall pronounce him unclean; it is a scale, it is leprosy of the head or of the beard.

31 "But if the priest looks at the infection of the scale, and indeed, it appears to be no deeper than the skin, and there is no black hair in it, then the priest shall isolate *the person* with the scaly infection for seven days.

32 "And on the seventh day the priest shall look at the infection, and if the scale has not spread, and no yellowish hair has grown in it, and the appearance of the scale is no deeper than the skin,

33 then he shall shave himself, but he shall not shave the scale; and the priest shall isolate *the person* with the scale seven more days.

34 "Then on the seventh day the priest shall look at the scale, and if the scale has not spread in the skin, and it appears to be no deeper than the skin, the priest shall pronounce him clean; and he shall wash his clothes and be clean.

35 "But if the scale spreads farther in the skin after his cleansing,

36 then the priest shall look at him, and if the scale has spread in the skin, the priest need not seek for the yellowish hair; he is unclean.

37 "If in his sight the scale has remained, however, and black hair has grown in it, the scale has healed, he is clean; and the priest shall pronounce him clean.

38 "And when a man or a woman has bright spots on the skin of the body, *even* white bright spots,

39 then the priest shall look, and if the bright spots on the skin of their bodies are a faint white, it is eczema that has broken out on the skin; he is clean.

40 a2 Kin. 2:23; Is. 15:2; Amos 8:10

40 "Now if a man loses the hair of his head, he is ᵃbald; he is clean.

41 "And if his head becomes bald at the front and sides, he is bald on the forehead; he is clean.

42 "But if on the bald head or the bald forehead, there occurs a reddish-white infection, it is leprosy breaking out on his bald head or on his bald forehead.

43 aLev. 10:10; Ezek. 22:26

43 "Then ᵃthe priest shall look at him; and if the swelling of the infection is reddish-white on his bald head or on his bald forehead, like the appearance of leprosy in the skin of the body,

44 he is a leprous man, he is unclean. The priest shall surely pronounce him unclean; his infection is on his head.

★45-46

45 aLev. 10:6 bEzek. 24:17, 22; Mic. 3:7 cLam. 4:15

45 "As for the leper who has the infection, his clothes shall be torn, and ᵃthe hair of his head shall be uncovered, and he shall ᵇcover his mustache and cry, 'ᶜUnclean! Unclean!'

46 aNum. 5:1-4; 12:14

46 "He shall remain unclean all the days during which he has the infection; he is unclean. He shall live alone; his dwelling shall be ᵃoutside the camp.

★47-59

47 "When a garment has a mark of leprosy in it, whether it is a wool garment or a linen garment,

48 whether in warp or woof, of linen or of wool, whether in leather or in any article made of leather,

49 if the mark is greenish or reddish in the garment or in the leather, or in the warp or in the woof, or in any article of leather, it is a leprous mark and shall be shown to the priest.

50 "Then ᵃthe priest shall look at the mark, and shall quarantine the article with the mark for seven days.

50 aEzek. 44:23

51 "He shall then look at the mark on the seventh day; if the mark has spread in the garment, whether in the warp or in the woof, or in the leather, whatever the purpose for which the leather is used, the mark is a leprous malignancy, it is unclean.

52 "So he shall burn the garment, whether the warp or the woof, in wool or in linen, or any article of leather in which the mark occurs, for it is a leprous malignancy; it shall be burned in the fire.

53 "But if the priest shall look, and indeed, the mark has not spread in the garment, either in the warp or in the woof, or in any article of leather,

54 then the priest shall order them to wash the thing in which the mark occurs, and he shall quarantine it for seven more days.

55 "After the article with the mark has been washed, the priest shall again look, and if the mark has not changed its appearance, even though the mark has not spread, it is unclean; you shall burn it in the fire, whether an eating away has produced bareness on the top or on the front of it.

56 "Then if the priest shall look, and if the mark has faded after it has been washed, then he shall tear it out of the garment or out of the leather, whether from the warp or from the woof;

57 and if it appears again in the garment, whether in the warp or in the woof, or in any article of leather, it is an outbreak; the article with the mark shall be burned in the fire.

13:45-46 The plight of the leper was pitiable: he exhibited signs of mourning by tearing his *clothes*, having his *head uncovered* (better, hair disheveled), and covering his *mustache* (by throwing the skirt of his garment over it); he warned people of his approach by crying *"Unclean"*; and he lived outside the city.

13:47-59 These verses deal with "leprosy" in garments (probably some kind of mildew). Sometimes it might be *a malignancy*; i.e., it made holes in the garment (v. 51). The problem was to be solved by washing the garment, cutting out the affected part, or burning the garment.

58 "And the garment, whether the warp or the woof, or any article of leather from which the mark has departed when you washed it, it shall then be washed a second time and shall be clean."

59 This is the law for the mark of leprosy in a garment of wool or linen, whether in the warp or in the woof, or in any article of leather, for pronouncing it clean or unclean.

b Cleansing for leprosy,
14:1-57

★ 1-32

14 Then the LORD spoke to Moses, saying,

2 "This shall be the law of the leper in the day of his cleansing. ªNow he shall be brought to the priest,

3 and the priest shall go ªout to the outside of the camp. Thus the priest shall look, and if the infection of leprosy has been healed in the leper,

4 then the priest shall give orders to take two live clean birds and ªcedar wood and a scarlet string and hyssop for the one who is to be cleansed.

5 "The priest shall also give orders to slay the one bird in an earthenware vessel over running water.

6 "As for the live bird, he shall take it, together with ªthe cedar wood and the scarlet string and the ᵇhyssop, and shall dip them and the live bird in the blood of the bird that was slain over the running water.

7 "ªHe shall then sprinkle seven times the one who is to be cleansed from the leprosy, and shall pronounce him clean, and shall let the live bird go free over the open field.

8 "ªThe one to be cleansed shall then wash his clothes and shave off all his hair, and bathe in water and ᵇbe clean. Now afterward, he may enter the camp, but he ᶜshall stay outside his tent for seven days.

9 "And it will be on the seventh day that he shall shave off all his hair: he shall shave his head and his beard and his eyebrows, even all his hair. He shall then wash his clothes and bathe his body in water and ªbe clean.

10 "Now on the eighth day he is to take two male lambs without defect, and a yearling ewe lamb without defect, and three-tenths *of an ephah* of fine flour mixed with oil for a grain offering, and one ªlog of oil;

11 and the priest who pronounces him clean shall present the man to be cleansed and the aforesaid before the LORD at the doorway of the tent of meeting.

12 "Then the priest shall take the one male lamb and bring it for a ªguilt offering, with the ᵇlog of oil, and present them as a ᶜwave offering before the LORD.

13 "Next he shall slaughter the male lamb in ªthe place where they slaughter the sin offering and the burnt offering, at the place of the sanctuary—for the guilt offering, ᵇlike the sin offering, belongs to the priest; it is most holy.

14 "The priest shall then take some of the blood of the ªguilt offering, and the priest shall put *it* on ᵇthe lobe of the right ear of the one to be cleansed, and on the thumb of his right hand, and on the big toe of his right foot.

15 "The priest shall also take some of the ªlog of oil, and pour *it* into his left palm;

16 the priest shall then dip his right-hand finger into the oil that is in his left palm, and with his finger sprinkle some of the oil seven times before the LORD.

17 "And of the remaining oil which is in his palm, the priest shall put some on the right ear

---

Cross-references (margin):

2 ªMatt. 8:4; Mark 1:44; Luke 5:14; 17:14

3 ªLev. 13:46

4 ªLev. 14:6, 49, 51, 52; Num. 19:6

6 ªLev. 14:4 ᵇPs. 51:7

7 ªEzek. 36:25

8 ªLev. 11:25; 13:6; Num. 8:7 ᵇLev. 14:9, 20 ᶜNum. 5:2, 3; 12:14, 15; 2 Chr. 26:21

9 ªLev. 14:8, 20

10 ªLev. 14:12, 15, 21, 24

12 ªLev. 5:6, 18; 6:6; 14:19 ᵇLev. 14:10 ᶜEx. 29:22-24, 26

13 ªEx. 29:11; Lev. 1:11; 4:24 ᵇLev. 6:24-30; 7:7

14 ªLev. 14:19 ᵇEx. 29:20; Lev. 8:23, 24

15 ªLev. 14:10

14:1-32 The elaborate ritual of cleansing for a leper involved two birds, one killed as a symbol of purification and the other released as a symbol of the man's newfound freedom (vv. 4-7); shaving and washing (vv. 8-9); and the offering of trespass, sin, burnt, and grain offerings (vv. 12, 13, 21).

lobe of the one to be cleansed, and on the thumb of his right hand, and on the big toe of his right foot, on the blood of the guilt offering;

18 while the rest of the oil that is in the priest's palm, he shall put on the head of the one to be cleansed. So the priest shall make ᵃatonement on his behalf before the LORD.

18 ᵃLev. 4:26; Num. 15:28; Heb. 2:17

19 "The priest shall next offer the ᵃsin offering and make atonement for the one to be cleansed from his uncleanness. Then afterward, he shall slaughter the burnt offering.

19 ᵃLev. 14:12

20 "And the priest shall offer up the burnt offering and the grain offering on the altar. Thus the priest shall make atonement for him, and ᵃhe shall be clean.

20 ᵃLev. 14:8, 9

21 "ᵃBut if he is poor, and his means are insufficient, then he is to take one male lamb for a ᵇguilt offering as a wave offering to make atonement for him, and one-tenth *of an ephah* of fine flour mixed with oil for a grain offering, and a ᶜlog of oil,

21 ᵃLev. 5:11; 12:8; 27:8 ᵇLev. 14:22 ᶜLev. 14:10

22 and two turtledoves or two young pigeons which are within his means, ᵃthe one shall be a ᵇsin offering and the other a burnt offering.

22 ᵃLev. 5:7 ᵇLev. 14:21, 24, 25

23 "ᵃThen the eighth day he shall bring them for his cleansing to the priest, at the doorway of the tent of meeting, before the LORD.

23 ᵃLev. 14:10, 11

24 "And the priest shall take the lamb of the guilt offering, and ᵃthe log of oil, and the priest shall offer them for a wave offering before the LORD.

24 ᵃLev. 14:10

25 "Next he shall slaughter the lamb of the guilt offering; and the priest is to take some of the blood of the guilt offering and put *it* on ᵃthe lobe of the right ear of the one to be cleansed and on the thumb of his right hand, and on the big toe of his right foot.

25 ᵃLev. 14:14

26 "The priest shall also pour some of the oil into his left palm;

27 and with his right-hand finger the priest shall sprinkle some of the oil that is in his left palm seven times before the LORD.

28 "The priest shall then put some of the oil that is in his palm on the lobe of the right ear of the one to be cleansed, and on the thumb of his right hand, and on the big toe of his right foot, on the place of the blood of the guilt offering.

29 "Moreover, the rest of the oil that is in the priest's palm he shall put on the head of the one to be cleansed, to make atonement on his behalf before the LORD.

30 "He shall then offer one of the turtledoves or young pigeons, which are within his means.

31 "*He shall offer* what he can afford, ᵃthe one for a sin offering, and the other for a burnt offering, together with the grain offering. So the priest shall make atonement before the LORD on behalf of the one to be cleansed.

31 ᵃLev. 5:7

32 "This is the law *for him* in whom there is an infection of leprosy, whose means are limited for his cleansing."

33 The LORD further spoke to Moses and to Aaron, saying,

34 "ᵃWhen you enter the land of Canaan, which I give you for a possession, and I put a mark of leprosy on a house in the land of your possession,

★**34** ᵃGen. 17:8; Num. 32:22; Deut. 7:1; 32:49

35 then the one who owns the house shall come and tell the priest, saying, '*Something* like ᵃa mark *of leprosy* has become visible to me in the house.'

35 ᵃPs. 91:10

36 "The priest shall then order that they empty the house before the priest goes in to look at the mark, so that everything in the house need not become unclean; and afterward the priest shall go in to look at the house.

14:34 The "leprosy" in a *house* may have been a kind of mold or rot.

37 "So he shall look at the mark, and if the mark on the walls of the house has greenish or reddish depressions, and appears deeper than the surface;

38 then the priest shall come out of the house, to the doorway, and quarantine the house for seven days.

39 "And the priest shall return on the seventh day and make an inspection. If the mark has indeed spread in the walls of the house,

40 then the priest shall order them to tear out the stones with the mark in them and throw them away at an unclean place outside the city.

41 "And he shall have the house scraped all around inside, and they shall dump the plaster that they scrape off at an unclean place outside the city.

42 "Then they shall take other stones and replace *those* stones; and he shall take other plaster and replaster the house.

43 "If, however, the mark breaks out again in the house, after he has torn out the stones and scraped the house, and after it has been replastered,

44 then the priest shall come in and make an inspection. If he sees that the mark has indeed spread in the house, it is ᵃa malignant mark in the house; it is unclean.

45 "He shall therefore tear down the house, its stones, and its timbers, and all the plaster of the house, and he shall take *them* outside the city to an ᵃunclean place.

46 "Moreover, whoever goes into the house during the time that he has quarantined it, becomes ᵃunclean until evening.

47 "Likewise, whoever lies down in the house shall wash his clothes, and whoever eats in the house shall wash his clothes.

48 "If, on the other hand, the priest comes in and makes an inspection, and the mark has not indeed spread in the house after the house has been replastered, then the priest shall pronounce the house clean because the mark has not reappeared.

49 "To cleanse the house then, he shall take ᵃtwo birds and cedar wood and a scarlet string and hyssop,

50 and he shall slaughter the one bird in an earthenware vessel over running water.

51 "Then he shall take the cedar wood and the ᵃhyssop and the scarlet string, with the live bird, and dip them in the blood of the slain bird, as well as in the running water, and sprinkle the house seven times.

52 "He shall thus cleanse the house with the blood of the bird and with the running water, along with the live bird and with the cedar wood and with the hyssop and with the scarlet string.

53 "However, he shall let the live bird go free outside the city into the open field. So he shall make atonement for the house, and it shall be clean."

54 This is the law for any mark of leprosy—even for a ᵃscale,

55 and for the ᵃleprous garment or house,

56 and ᵃfor a swelling, and for a scab, and for a bright spot—

57 to teach when they are unclean, and when they are clean. This is the law of leprosy.

4 In relation to the body, 15:1-33

15 The LORD also spoke to Moses and to Aaron, saying,

2 "Speak to the sons of Israel, and say to them, 'ᵃWhen any man has a discharge from his body, his discharge is unclean.

---

44 ᵃLev. 13:51

45 ᵃLev. 14:41

46 ᵃNum. 19:7, 10, 21, 22

★49-53

49 ᵃLev. 14:4

51 ᵃ1 Kin. 4:33; Ps. 51:7

54 ᵃLev. 13:30

55 ᵃLev. 13:47-52

56 ᵃLev. 13:2

★ 2-15

2 ᵃLev. 22:4; Num. 5:2; 2 Sam. 3:29

14:49-53 The ritual of cleansing a house was the same as that for the first stage of cleansing a leprous person (cf. vv. 4-7).
15:2-15 These verses describe a diseased condition of the male sexual organs. After he became well, the man had to offer a sin and a burnt offering (v. 15).

3 'This, moreover, shall be his uncleanness in his discharge: it is his uncleanness whether his body allows its discharge to flow, or whether his body obstructs its discharge.

4 'Every bed on which the person with the discharge lies becomes unclean, and everything on which he sits becomes unclean.

5 'Anyone, moreover, who touches his bed shall wash his clothes and bathe in water and be unclean until evening;

6 and whoever sits on the thing on which the man with the discharge has been sitting, shall wash his clothes and bathe in water and be unclean until evening.

7 'Also whoever touches the person with the discharge shall wash his clothes and bathe in water and be unclean until evening.

8 'Or if the man with the discharge spits on one who is clean, he too shall wash his clothes and bathe in water and be unclean until evening.

9 'And every saddle on which the person with the discharge rides becomes unclean.

10 'Whoever then touches any of the things which were under him shall be unclean until evening, and he who carries them shall wash his clothes and bathe in water and be unclean until evening.

11 'Likewise, whomever the one with the discharge touches without having rinsed his hands in water shall wash his clothes and bathe in water and be unclean until evening.

12 'However, an ªearthenware vessel which the person with the discharge touches shall be broken, and every wooden vessel shall be rinsed in water.

13 'Now when the man with the discharge becomes cleansed from his discharge, then he ªshall count off for himself seven days for his cleansing; he shall then

wash his clothes and bathe his body in running water and shall become clean.

14 'Then on the eighth day he shall take for himself ªtwo turtle-doves or two young pigeons, and come before the LORD to the doorway of the tent of meeting, and give them to the priest;

15 and the priest shall offer them, ªone for a sin offering, and the other for a burnt offering. So ᵇthe priest shall make atonement on his behalf before the LORD because of his discharge.

16 'ªNow if a man has a seminal emission, he shall bathe all his body in water and be unclean until evening.

17 'As for any garment or any leather on which there is seminal emission, it shall be washed with water and be unclean until evening.

18 'If a man lies with a woman so that there is a seminal emission, they shall both bathe in water and be ªunclean until evening.

19 'ªWhen a woman has a discharge, if her discharge in her body is blood, she shall continue in her menstrual impurity for seven days; and whoever touches her shall be unclean until evening.

20 'Everything also on which she lies during her menstrual impurity shall be unclean, and everything on which she sits shall be unclean.

21 'And anyone who touches her bed shall wash his clothes and bathe in water and be unclean until evening.

22 'And whoever touches any thing on which she sits shall wash his clothes and bathe in water and be unclean until evening.

23 'Whether it be on the bed or on the thing on which she is sitting, when he touches it, he shall be unclean until evening.

24 'ªAnd if a man actually lies with her, so that her menstrual

12 ªLev. 6:28; 11:33

13 ªLev. 8:33; 14:8

14 ªLev. 14:22, 23

15 ªLev. 5:7; 14:31 ᵇLev. 14:19, 31

★16-18

16 ªLev. 22:4; Deut. 23:10, 11

18 ª1 Sam. 21:4

★19-24

19 ªLev. 12:2

24 ªLev. 18:19; 20:18

15:16-18 These verses refer to natural secretion for which no offerings had to be made.
15:19-24 These verses concern the natural menstrual discharge of a woman for which no offerings were required.

impurity is on him, he shall be unclean seven days, and every bed on which he lies shall be unclean.

★25-30

25 *a*Matt. 9:20; Mark 5:25; Luke 8:43

25 '*a*Now if a woman has a discharge of her blood many days, not at the period of her menstrual impurity, or if she has a discharge beyond that period, all the days of her impure discharge she shall continue as though in her menstrual impurity; she is unclean.

26 'Any bed on which she lies all the days of her discharge shall be to her like her bed at menstruation; and every thing on which she sits shall be unclean, like her uncleanness at that time.

27 'Likewise, whoever touches them shall be unclean and shall wash his clothes and bathe in water and be unclean until evening.

28 'When she becomes clean from her discharge, she shall count off for herself seven days; and afterward she shall be clean.

29 'Then on the eighth day she shall take for herself two turtledoves or two young pigeons, and bring them in to the priest, to the doorway of the tent of meeting.

30 *a*Lev. 5:7

30 'And the priest shall offer the *a*one for a sin offering and the other for a burnt offering. So the priest shall make atonement on her behalf before the LORD because of her impure discharge.'

31 *a*Lev. 20:3; Num. 19:13, 20; Ezek. 5:11; 36:17

31 "Thus you shall keep the sons of Israel separated from their uncleanness, lest they die in their uncleanness by their *a*defiling My tabernacle that is among them."

32 This is the law for the one

with a discharge, and for the man who has a seminal emission so that he is unclean by it,

33 and for the woman who is ill because of menstrual impurity, and for the one who has a discharge, whether a male or a female, or a man who lies with an unclean woman.

B Law of the Day of Atonement, 16:1-34

1 *Preparations,* 16:1-4

★ 1 *a*Lev. 10:1, 2

16 Now the LORD spoke to Moses after *a*the death of the two sons of Aaron, when they had approached the presence of the LORD and died.

★ 2 *a*Ex. 30:10; Heb. 6:19; 9:7, 25 *b*Ex. 25:21, 22; 40:34; 1 Kin. 8:10-12

2 And the LORD said to Moses, "Tell your brother Aaron that he shall not enter *a*at any time into the holy place inside the veil, before the mercy seat which is on the ark, lest he die; for *b*I will appear in the cloud over the mercy seat.

★ 3 *a*Lev. 4:1-12; 16:6; Heb. 9:7

3 "Aaron shall enter the holy place with this: with a bull for a *a*sin offering and a ram for a burnt offering.

4 *a*Ex. 28:39, 42 *b*Ex. 30:20; Lev. 16:24; Heb. 10:22

4 "He shall put on the *a*holy linen tunic, and the linen undergarments shall be next to his body, and he shall be girded with the linen sash, and attired with the linen turban (these are holy garments). Then he shall *b*bathe his body in water and put them on.

2 *Offerings,* 16:5-28

★ 5-10 5 *a*Lev. 4:13-21; 2 Chr. 29:21; Ezek. 45:22

5 "And he shall take from the congregation of the sons of Israel

---

15:25-30 These verses deal with a kind of discharge not connected with a woman's menstrual period. A sin and a burnt offering were required.

16:1 The Day of Atonement, described in this chapter, was the most important of all the ordinances given to Israel because on that day atonement was made for all the sins of the entire congregation (vv. 16, 21, 30, 33), as well as for the sanctuary (vv. 16, 33). It took place on the tenth day of the seventh month (Tishri, v. 29), and fasting was required from the evening of the ninth day to the evening of the

tenth day (see also note on Matt. 9:14).

16:2 *the holy place.* I.e., the Holy of Holies, inside the veil (cf. Heb. 9:7).

16:3 First, Aaron, the high priest, brought a sin offering for himself and the other priests.

16:5-10 Next, the high priest presented two goats as a sin offering for the people. One was slain, and the other was sent *into the wilderness. scapegoat* (v. 10). Lit., Azazel, a combination of the words for "goat" and "depart." The live goat was the removing goat, symbolizing the removal of Israel's sins.

^atwo male goats for a sin offering and one ram for a burnt offering.

6 aHeb. 5:3

6 "Then ^aAaron shall offer the bull for the sin offering which is for himself, that he may make atonement for himself and for his household.

7 "And he shall take the two goats and present them before the Lord at the doorway of the tent of meeting.

8 "And Aaron shall cast lots for the two goats, one lot for the Lord and the other lot for the scapegoat.

9 "Then Aaron shall offer the goat on which the lot for the Lord fell, and make it a sin offering.

10 aIs. 53:4-10; Rom. 3:25; 1 John 2:2

10 "But the goat on which the lot for the scapegoat fell, shall be presented alive before the Lord, to make ^aatonement upon it, to send it into the wilderness as the scapegoat.

11 aHeb. 7:27; 9:7 bLev. 16:33

11 "Then Aaron shall offer the bull of the sin offering ^awhich is for himself, and make atonement for himself and ^bfor his household, and he shall slaughter the bull of the sin offering which is for himself.

12 aLev. 10:1; Num. 16:18 bEx. 30:34-38

12 "And he shall take a ^afire-pan full of coals of fire from upon the altar before the Lord, and two handfuls of finely ground ^bsweet incense, and bring *it* inside the veil.

13 aEx. 25:21 bEx. 28:43; Lev. 22:9; Num. 4:15, 20

13 "And he shall put the incense on the fire before the Lord, that the cloud of incense may cover the ^amercy seat that is on *the ark of* the testimony, ^blest he die.

14 aHeb. 9:25 bLev. 4:6, 17

14 "Moreover, ^ahe shall take some of the blood of the bull and sprinkle *it* ^bwith his finger on the mercy seat on the east *side*; also in front of the mercy seat he shall sprinkle some of the blood with his finger seven times.

15 aHeb. 7:27; 9:7, 12

15 "Then he shall slaughter the goat of the sin offering ^awhich

is for the people, and bring its blood inside the veil, and do with its blood as he did with the blood of the bull, and sprinkle it on the mercy seat and in front of the mercy seat.

16 "And ^ahe shall make atonement for the holy place, because of the impurities of the sons of Israel, and because of their transgressions, in regard to all their sins; and thus he shall do for the tent of meeting which abides with them in the midst of their impurities.

★16-19

16 aEx. 29:36, 37; 30:10; Heb. 2:17

17 "When he goes in to make atonement in the holy place, no one shall be in the tent of meeting until he comes out, that he may make atonement for himself and for his household and for all the assembly of Israel.

18 "Then he shall go out to the altar that is before the Lord and make atonement for it, and shall take some of the blood of the bull and of the blood of the goat, and ^aput it on the horns of the altar on all sides.

18 aLev. 4:25; Ezek. 43:20, 22

19 "And ^awith his finger he shall sprinkle some of the blood on it seven times, and cleanse it, and from the impurities of the sons of Israel consecrate it.

19 aLev. 16:14; Ezek. 43:20

20 "When he finishes atoning for the holy place, and the tent of meeting and the altar, he shall offer the live goat.

21 "Then Aaron shall lay both of his hands on the head of the live goat, and ^aconfess over it all the iniquities of the sons of Israel, and all their transgressions in regard to all their sins; and he shall lay them on the head of the goat and send *it* away into the wilderness by the hand of a man who *stands* in readiness.

21 aLev. 5:5

22 "And the goat shall bear on itself all their iniquities to a solitary land; and he shall release the goat in the wilderness.

16:16-19 The *holy* of Holies and the *altar* of burnt offering also had to be cleansed because the tabernacle was in the midst of sinful people (cf. v. 16).

★23-28

23 aLev.
16:4; Ezek.
42:14; 44:19

23 "Then Aaron shall come into the tent of meeting, and take off ªthe linen garments which he put on when he went into the holy place, and shall leave them there.

24 aLev.
16:4 bEx.
28:40, 41

24 "And ªhe shall bathe his body with water in a holy place and put on ᵇhis clothes, and come forth and offer his burnt offering and the burnt offering of the people, and make atonement for himself and for the people.

25 "Then he shall offer up in smoke the fat of the sin offering on the altar.

26 aLev.
11:25, 40

26 "And the one who released the goat as the scapegoat ªshall wash his clothes and bathe his body with water; then afterward he shall come into the camp.

27 aLev.
6:30; Heb.
13:11

27 "But the bull of the sin offering and the goat of the sin offering, ªwhose blood was brought in to make atonement in the holy place, shall be taken outside the camp, and they shall burn their hides, their flesh, and their refuse in the fire.

28 aNum.
19:8

28 "Then the ªone who burns them shall wash his clothes and bathe his body with water, then afterward he shall come into the camp.

3 Instructions, 16:29-34

29 aLev.
23:27; Num.
29:7 bEx.
31:14, 15

29 "And *this* shall be a permanent statute for you: ªin the seventh month, on the tenth day of the month, you shall humble your souls, and not ᵇdo any work, whether the native, or the alien who sojourns among you;

30 aPs. 51:2;
Jer. 33:8;
Eph. 5:26

30 for it is on this day that atonement shall be made for you to ªcleanse you; you shall be clean from all your sins before the Lord.

31 aLev.
23:32; Ezra
8:21; Is.
58:3, 5; Dan.
10:12

31 "It is to be a sabbath of solemn rest for you, that you may ªhumble your souls; it is a permanent statute.

32 aLev.
16:4

32 "So the priest who is anointed and ordained to serve as priest in his father's place shall make atonement: he shall thus put on ªthe linen garments, the holy garments,

33 aLev.
16:11

33 and make atonement for the holy sanctuary; and he shall make atonement for the tent of meeting and for the altar. He shall also make atonement for ªthe priests and for all the people of the assembly.

34 aLev.
23:31 bHeb.
9:7

34 "Now you shall have this as a ªpermanent statute, to ᵇmake atonement for the sons of Israel for all their sins once every year." And just as the Lord had commanded Moses, *so* he did.

C Laws Concerning Sacrificing, 17:1-16

★ 1-7

17 Then the Lord spoke to Moses, saying,

2 "Speak to Aaron and to his sons, and to all the sons of Israel, and say to them, 'This is what the Lord has commanded, saying,

3 "Any man from the house of Israel who slaughters an ox, or a lamb, or a goat in the camp, or who slaughters it outside the camp,

4 aDeut.
12:5-21

4 and ªhas not brought it to the doorway of the tent of meeting to present *it* as an offering to the Lord before the tabernacle of the Lord, bloodguiltiness is to be reckoned to that man. He has shed blood and that man shall be cut off from among his people.

16:23-28 Finally Aaron, dressed again in the regular garb of the High Priest, offered his own and the people's burnt offerings (on the altar of burnt offering in the outer court), burned the fat of the sin offering on that altar, and saw that the remains of the animals used in the sin offering were carried outside the camp and burned.

17:1-7 Any animal killed for food was to be brought to the tabernacle, where the blood and fat became a peace offering (vv. 5-6); then the meat could be eaten. No hardship would be imposed on the people because meat was not part of the usual diet except during festivals. The command was designed to keep them from offering the blood of animals (slaughtered for food) to *goat demons* (i.e., goat-like demons), popular pagan idols of that day.

5 "The reason is so that the sons of Israel may bring their sacrifices which they were sacrificing in the open field, that they may bring them in to the LORD, at the doorway of the tent of meeting to the priest, and sacrifice them as sacrifices of peace offerings to the LORD.

6 "And the priest shall sprinkle the blood on the altar of the LORD at the doorway of the tent of meeting, and ᵃoffer up the fat in smoke as a soothing aroma to the LORD.

7 "And ᵃthey shall no longer sacrifice their sacrifices to the goat demons with which they play the harlot. This shall be a permanent statute to them throughout their generations."'

8 "Then you shall say to them, 'Any man from the house of Israel, or from the aliens who sojourn among them, who offers a burnt offering or sacrifice,

9 and ᵃdoes not bring it to the doorway of the tent of meeting to offer it to the LORD, that man also shall be cut off from his people.

10 'ᵃAnd any man from the house of Israel, or from the aliens who sojourn among them, who eats any blood, ᵇI will set My face against that person who eats blood, and will cut him off from among his people.

11 'For ᵃthe life of the flesh is in the blood, and I have given it to you on the altar to make atonement for your souls; for ᵇit is the blood by reason of the life that makes atonement.'

12 "Therefore I said to the sons of Israel, 'No person among you may eat blood, nor may any alien who sojourns among you eat blood.'

13 "So when any man from the sons of Israel, or from the aliens who sojourn among them, in hunting catches a beast or a bird which may be eaten, ᵃhe shall pour out its blood and cover it with earth.

14 'ᵃFor as for the life of all flesh, its blood is identified with its life. Therefore I said to the sons of Israel, 'You are not to eat the blood of any flesh, for the life of all flesh is its blood; whoever eats it shall be cut off.'

15 'ᵃAnd when any person eats an animal which dies, or is torn by beasts, whether he is a native or an alien, he shall wash his clothes and bathe in water, and remain unclean until evening; then he will become clean.

16 "But if he does not wash them or bathe his body, then ᵃhe shall bear his guilt."

D   Laws Concerning Standards for the People, 18:1–20:27

1   Concerning sexual relationships, 18:1–30

18 Then the LORD spoke to Moses, saying,

2 "Speak to the sons of Israel and say to them, 'ᵃI am the LORD your God.

3 'You shall not do what is ᵃdone in the land of Egypt where you lived, nor are you to do what is ᵇdone in the land of Canaan where I am bringing you; you shall not walk in their statutes.

4 'You are to perform My judgments and keep My statutes, to live in accord with them; ᵃI am the LORD your God.

5 'So you shall keep My statutes and My judgments, ᵃby

Marginal references

6 ᵃNum. 18:17

7 ᵃEx. 22:20; 32:8; 34:15; Deut. 32:17; 2 Chr. 11:15; Ps. 106:37f.; 1 Cor. 10:20

★ 8-9

9 ᵃEx. 20:24; Lev. 17:4

10 ᵃGen. 9:4; Lev. 3:17; 7:26, 27; Deut. 12:16, 23-25; 1 Sam. 14:33 ᵇLev. 20:3, 6; Jer. 44:11

★11 ᵃGen. 9:4; Lev. 17:14 ᵇHeb. 9:22

★13 ᵃDeut. 12:16

14 ᵃGen. 9:4; Lev. 17:11

★15-16

15 ᵃEx. 22:31; Lev. 7:24; 22:8; Deut. 14:21

16 ᵃNum. 19:20

2 ᵃEx. 6:7; Lev. 11:44; Ezek. 20:5

★ 3 ᵃEzek. 20:7, 8 ᵇLev. 18:24-30; 20:23

4 ᵃLev. 18:2

5 ᵃNeh. 9:29; Ezek. 18:9; 20:11; Luke 10:28; Rom. 10:5; Gal. 3:12

17:8-9 Animals used for sacrifices either by Israelites or by strangers also had to be brought to the tabernacle.

17:11 Two reasons are given for the command not to eat blood: the life of the body is derived from it, and it is the means by which atonement for sins is made (see also Gen. 9:4).

17:13 Not even the blood of edible game was to be eaten.

17:15-16 If someone happened to eat an animal that died naturally or was killed by other animals, he was ceremonially unclean.

18:3 The standards of God's people were not to be dictated by the practices of Egypt or Canaan but by the Lord Himself.

which a man may live if he does them; I am the LORD.

★ 6 **6** 'None of you shall approach any blood relative of his to uncover nakedness; I am the LORD.

7 aLev.
20:11; Deut.
27:20; Ezek.
22:10

7 'aYou shall not uncover the nakedness of your father, that is, the nakedness of your mother. She is your mother; you are not to uncover her nakedness.

★ 8 aLev.
20:11; Deut.
22:30; 27:20;
1 Cor. 5:1

8 'aYou shall not uncover the nakedness of your father's wife; it is your father's nakedness.

★ 9 aLev.
18:11; 20:17;
Deut. 27:22

9 'aThe nakedness of your sister, *either* your father's daughter or your mother's daughter, whether born at home or born outside, their nakedness you shall not uncover.

10 The nakedness of your son's daughter or your daughter's daughter, their nakedness you shall not uncover; for their nakedness is yours.

11 The nakedness of your father's wife's daughter, born to your father, she is your sister, you shall not uncover her nakedness.

12 aLev.
20:19

12 'aYou shall not uncover the nakedness of your father's sister; she is your father's blood relative.

13 'You shall not uncover the nakedness of your mother's sister, for she is your mother's blood relative.

14 aLev.
20:20

14 'aYou shall not uncover the nakedness of your father's brother; you shall not approach his wife, she is your aunt.

15 aLev.
20:12

15 'aYou shall not uncover the nakedness of your daughter-in-law; she is your son's wife, you shall not uncover her nakedness.

★16 aLev.
20:21

16 'aYou shall not uncover the nakedness of your brother's wife; it is your brother's nakedness.

17 aLev.
20:14

17 'aYou shall not uncover the nakedness of a woman and of her daughter, nor shall you take her son's daughter or her daughter's daughter, to uncover her nakedness; they are blood relatives. It is lewdness.

18 'And you shall not marry a woman in addition to her sister as a rival while she is alive, to uncover her nakedness.

★18

19 'aAlso you shall not approach a woman to uncover her nakedness during her bmenstrual impurity.

19 aLev.
15:24; 20:18
bLev. 12:2

20 'aAnd you shall not have intercourse with your neighbor's wife, to be defiled with her.

20 aLev.
20:10; Prov.
6:29; Matt.
5:27, 28;
1 Cor. 6:9;
Heb. 13:4

21 'Neither shall you give any of your offspring ato offer them to Molech, nor shall you bprofane the name of your God; I am the LORD.

★21 aLev.
20:2-5; Deut.
12:31 bLev.
19:12; 20:3;
21:6; Ezek.
36:20; Mal.
1:12

22 'aYou shall not lie with a male as one lies with a female; it is an abomination.

★22 aLev.
20:13; Deut.
23:18 mg.;
Rom. 1:27

23 'aAlso you shall not have intercourse with any animal to be defiled with it, nor shall any woman stand before an animal to mate with it; it is a perversion.

23 aEx.
22:19; Lev.
20:15, 16;
Deut. 27:21

24 'Do not defile yourselves by any of these things; for by all these athe nations which I am casting out before you have become defiled.

24 aLev.
18:3; Deut.
18:12

25 'For the land has become defiled, atherefore I have visited its punishment upon it, so the land bhas spewed out its inhabitants.

25 aLev.
20:23; Deut.
9:5; 18:12
bLev. 18:28;
20:22

26 'But as for you, you are to keep My statutes and My judgments, and shall not do any of these abominations, *neither* the native, nor the alien who sojourns among you

27 (for the men of the land who have been before you have done all these abominations, and the land has become defiled);

18:6 *to uncover nakedness.* I.e., to have sexual intercourse in the incestuous relationships listed in verses 6-18.
18:8 *your father's wife.* I.e., stepmother.
18:9 The reference is to a half sister and a stepsister.
18:16 If there were no children, the man was obliged to marry his brother's wife (see note

on Deut. 25:5).
18:18 Polygamous marriage to living sisters is forbidden.
18:21 Dedications to *Molech,* an Ammonite deity, sometimes involved human sacrifice (cf. 2 Kings 23:10; Jer. 32:35).
18:22 Homosexuality is clearly forbidden (as also in 1 Cor. 6:9).

28 so that the land may not spew you out, should you defile it, as it has spewed out the nation which has been before you.

29 'For whoever does any of these abominations, those persons who do *so* shall be cut off from among their people.

30 'Thus you are to keep ^aMy charge, that you do not practice any of the abominable customs which have been practiced before you, so as not to defile yourselves with them; ^bI am the LORD your God.' "

2 Concerning daily life,
19:1-37

19 Then the LORD spoke to Moses, saying,

2 "Speak to all the congregation of the sons of Israel and say to them, '^aYou shall be holy, for I the LORD your God am holy.

3 'Every one of you ^ashall reverence his mother and his father, and you shall keep ^bMy sabbaths; ^cI am the LORD your God.

4 'Do not turn to ^aidols or make for yourselves molten ^bgods; I am the LORD your God.

5 'Now when you offer a sacrifice of peace offerings to the LORD, you shall offer it so that you may be accepted.

6 'It shall be eaten the same day you offer *it*, and the next day; but what remains until the third day shall be burned with fire.

7 'So if it is eaten at all on the third day, it is an offense; it will not be accepted.

8 'And everyone who eats it will bear his iniquity, for he has profaned the holy thing of the LORD; and that person shall be cut off from his people.

9 '^aNow when you reap the harvest of your land, you shall not reap to the very corners of

your field, neither shall you gather the gleanings of your harvest.

10 'Nor shall you glean your vineyard, nor shall you gather the fallen fruit of your vineyard; you shall leave them for the needy and for the stranger. I am the LORD your God.

11 '^aYou shall not steal, nor deal falsely, ^bnor lie to one another.

12 '^aAnd you shall not swear falsely by My name, so as to ^bprofane the name of your God; I am the LORD.

13 '^aYou shall not oppress your neighbor, nor rob *him.* ^bThe wages of a hired man are not to remain with you all night until morning.

14 'You shall not curse a deaf man, nor ^aplace a stumbling block before the blind, but you shall revere your God; I am the LORD.

15 '^aYou shall do no injustice in judgment; you shall not be partial to the poor nor defer to the great, but you are to judge your neighbor fairly.

16 'You shall not go about as ^aa slanderer among your people, and you are not to act against the ^blife of your neighbor; I am the LORD.

17 'You ^ashall not hate your fellow countryman in your heart; you ^bmay surely reprove your neighbor, but shall not incur sin because of him.

18 '^aYou shall not take vengeance, ^bnor bear any grudge against the sons of your people, but ^cyou shall love your neighbor as yourself; I am the LORD.

19 'You are to keep My statutes. You shall not breed together two kinds of your cattle; ^ayou shall not sow your field with two

Cross references (margin)
30 ^aLev. 22:9; Deut. 11:1 ^bLev. 18:2

2 ^aEx. 19:6; Lev. 11:44; 20:7, 26; Eph. 1:4; 1 Pet. 1:16

★ 3-4

3 ^aEx. 20:12; 31:13; Deut. 5:16 ^bEx. 20:8 ^cLev. 11:44

4 ^aLev. 26:1; Ps. 96:5; 115:4-7 ^bEx. 20:23; 34:17

★ 5

★ 9-10
9 ^aLev. 23:22; Deut. 24:20-22

11 ^aEx. 20:15, 16 ^bJer. 9:3-5; Eph. 4:25

12 ^aEx. 20:7; Deut. 5:11; Matt. 5:33 ^bLev. 18:21

13 ^aEx. 22:7-15, 21-27 ^bDeut. 24:15; James 5:4

14 ^aDeut. 27:18

15 ^aEx. 23:3, 6; Deut. 1:17; 10:17; 16:19

★16 ^aPs. 15:3; Jer. 6:28; 9:4; Ezek. 22:9 ^bEx. 23:7; Deut. 27:25

17 ^a1 John 2:9, 11; 3:15 ^bMatt. 18:15; Luke 17:3

★18 ^aDeut. 32:35; Rom. 12:19; Heb. 10:30 ^bPs. 103:9 ^cMatt. 19:19; Mark 12:31; Luke 10:27; Rom. 13:9; Gal. 5:14; James 2:8

19 ^aDeut. 22:9, 11

19:3-4 Three of the Ten Commandments are reiterated here as being particularly important (concerning parents, sabbaths, and idolatry).
19:5 *peace offerings.* See note on 7:12.
19:9-10 See also Deut. 24:19-22 and Ruth 2:2 (where Ruth benefited from this provision).
19:16 Doing anything by slander or silence that

would endanger the life of one's neighbor is forbidden.
19:18 Jesus Christ designated the last part of this verse as the second greatest commandment. Observe its use in Matt. 22:39; Mark 12:31, 33; Rom. 13:9; Gal. 5:14; James 2:8.

kinds of seed, nor wear a garment upon you of two kinds of material mixed together.

20 a Deut. 22:23-27

20 '*a*Now if a man lies carnally with a woman who is a slave acquired for *another* man, but who has in no way been redeemed, nor given her freedom, there shall be punishment; they shall not, *however,* be put to death, because she was not free.

21 a Lev. 6:1-7

21 'And he shall bring his guilt offering to the LORD to the doorway of the tent of meeting, *a*a ram for a guilt offering.

22 'The priest shall also make atonement for him with the ram of the guilt offering before the LORD for his sin which he has committed, and the sin which he has committed shall be forgiven him.

★23-25

23 'And when you enter the land and plant all kinds of trees for food, then you shall count their fruit as forbidden. Three years it shall be forbidden to you; *it* shall not be eaten.

24 'But in the fourth year all its fruit shall be holy, an offering of praise to the LORD.

25 'And in the fifth year you are to eat of its fruit, that its yield may increase for you; I am the LORD your God.

26 a Gen. 9:4; Lev. 7:26f.; 17:10; Deut. 12:16, 23 b Deut. 18:10; 2 Kin. 17:17

26 'You shall not eat *anything* *a*with the blood, nor practice *b*divination or soothsaying.

★27 a Lev. 21:5; Deut. 14:1

27 '*a*You shall not round off the side-growth of your heads, nor harm the edges of your beard.

★28

28 'You shall not make any cuts in your body for the dead, nor make any tattoo marks on yourselves: I am the LORD.

29 a Lev. 21:9; Deut. 22:21; 23:17, 18

29 '*a*Do not profane your daughter by making her a harlot, so that the land may not fall to

harlotry, and the land become full of lewdness.

30 'You shall *a*keep My sabbaths and *b*revere My sanctuary; I am the LORD.

30 a Lev. 19:3 b Lev. 26:2

31 'Do not turn to *a*mediums or spiritists; do not seek them out to be defiled by them. I am the LORD your God.

★31 a Lev. 20:6, 27; Deut. 18:11; 1 Sam. 28:3; Is. 8:19

32 '*a*You shall rise up before the grayheaded, and honor the aged, and you shall revere your God; I am the LORD.

★32 a Prov. 23:22; Lam. 5:12; 1 Tim. 5:1

33 '*a*When a stranger resides with you in your land, you shall not do him wrong.

33 a Ex. 22:21; Deut. 24:17, 18

34 'The stranger who resides with you shall be to you as the native among you, and *a*you shall love him as yourself; for you were aliens in the land of Egypt: I am the LORD your God.

34 a Lev. 19:18

35 '*a*You shall do no wrong in judgment, in measurement of weight, or capacity.

35 a Deut. 25:13-16; Ezek. 45:10

36 'You shall have *a*just balances, just weights, a just ephah, and a just hin: I am the LORD your God, who brought you out from the land of Egypt.

36 a Deut. 25:13-15; Prov. 20:10

37 'You shall thus observe all My statutes, and all My ordinances, and do them: I am the LORD.'"

●

3   *Concerning heinous offenses,* 20:1-27

20 Then the LORD spoke to Moses, saying,

2 "You shall also say to the sons of Israel, 'Any man from the sons of Israel or from the aliens sojourning in Israel, *a*who gives any of his offspring to Molech, shall surely be put to death; *b*the people of the land shall stone him with stones.

★ 2 a Lev. 18:21 b Lev. 20:27; 24:14-23; Num. 15:35, 36; Deut. 21:21

19:23-25 When they came to Canaan, they were not to eat fruit from the fruit trees for the first four years (the first three years, it was considered unclean; the fourth, it was dedicated to the Lord).

19:27 This prohibits shaving around the temples and ears, leaving only a crown of hair on the top of the head, as well as mutilating the beard—practices of the heathen (cf. Jer. 9:26;

25:23; Ezek. 5:1).

19:28 Both cutting and tattooing the body were done by the heathen.

19:31 Using a medium or spiritist showed lack of faith in God.

19:32 I.e., show respect for the aged.

20:2 *Molech.* See note on 18:21. Offering children or infants to the idol was to be punished by stoning.

3 aLev.
15:31 bLev.
18:21

3 'I will also set My face against that man and will cut him off from among his people, because he has given some of his offspring to Molech, aso as to defile My sanctuary and bto profane My holy name.

4 'If the people of the land, however, should ever disregard that man when he gives any of his offspring to Molech, so as not to put him to death,

5 then I Myself will set My face against that man and against his family; and I will cut off from among their people both him and all those who play the harlot after him, by playing the harlot after Molech.

6 aLev.
19:31

6 'As for the person who turns to amediums and to spiritists, to play the harlot after them, I will also set My face against that person and will cut him off from among his people.

7 aEph.
1:4; 1 Pet.
1:16

7 'You shall consecrate yourselves therefore and abe holy, for I am the LORD your God.

8 aEx.
31:13

8 'And ayou shall keep My statutes and practice them; I am the LORD who sanctifies you.

★ **9** aEx.
21:17; Deut.
27:16

9 'aIf there is anyone who curses his father or his mother, he shall surely be put to death; he has cursed his father or his mother, his bloodguiltiness is upon him.

10 aEx.
20:14; Lev.
18:20; Deut.
5:18

10 'aIf there is a man who commits adultery with another man's wife, one who commits adultery with his friend's wife, the adulterer and the adulteress shall surely be put to death.

11 aLev.
18:7, 8; Deut.
27:20

11 'aIf there is a man who lies with his father's wife, he has uncovered his father's nakedness; both of them shall surely be put to death, their bloodguiltiness is upon him.

12 aLev.
18:15

12 'aIf there is a man who lies with his daughter-in-law, both of them shall surely be put to death; they have committed incest, their bloodguiltiness is upon them.

13 aLev.
18:22

13 'aIf there is a man who lies with a male as those who lie with a woman, both of them have committed a detestable act; they shall surely be put to death. Their bloodguiltiness is upon them.

14 aLev.
18:17; Deut.
27:23

14 'aIf there is a man who marries a woman and her mother, it is immorality; both he and they shall be burned with fire, that there may be no immorality in your midst.

15 aLev.
18:23; Deut.
27:21

15 'aIf there is a man who lies with an animal, he shall surely be put to death; you shall also kill the animal.

16 'If there is a woman who approaches any animal to mate with it, you shall kill the woman and the animal; they shall surely be put to death. Their bloodguiltiness is upon them.

17 aLev.
18:9; Deut.
27:22

17 'aIf there is a man who takes his sister, his father's daughter or his mother's daughter, so that he sees her nakedness and she sees his nakedness, it is a disgrace; and they shall be cut off in the sight of the sons of their people. He has uncovered his sister's nakedness; he bears his guilt.

18 aLev.
15:24; 18:19

18 'aIf there is a man who lies with a menstruous woman and uncovers her nakedness, he has laid bare her flow, and she has exposed the flow of her blood; thus both of them shall be cut off from among their people.

19 aLev.
18:12, 13

19 'aYou shall also not uncover the nakedness of your mother's sister or of your father's sister, for such a one has made naked his blood relative; they shall bear their guilt.

20 aLev.
18:14

20 'aIf there is a man who lies with his uncle's wife he has uncovered his uncle's nakedness; they shall bear their sin. They shall die childless.

21 aLev.
18:16

21 'aIf there is a man who takes his brother's wife, it is abhorrent; he has uncovered his brother's nakedness. They shall be childless.

20:9 *his bloodguiltiness is upon him.* I.e., he brought it upon himself to be killed.

22 'You are therefore to keep all My statutes and all My ordinances and do them, so that the land to which I am bringing you to live will not ^aspew you out.

★**23** 'Moreover, you shall not follow ^athe customs of the nation which I shall drive out before you, for they did all these things, and ^btherefore I have abhorred them.

24 'Hence I have said to you, "^aYou are to possess their land, and I Myself will give it to you to possess it, a land flowing with milk and honey." I am the LORD your God, who has ^bseparated you from the peoples.

25 '^aYou are therefore to make a distinction between the clean animal and the unclean, and between the unclean bird and the clean; and you shall not make yourselves detestable by animal or by bird or by anything that creeps on the ground, which I have separated for you as unclean.

26 'Thus you are to be holy to Me, for I the LORD am holy; and I ^ahave set you apart from the peoples to be Mine.

27 'Now a man or a woman ^awho is a medium or a spiritist shall surely be put to death. They shall be stoned with stones, their bloodguiltiness is upon them.' "

E Laws Concerning Standards for the Priests, 21:1–22:16

★ **1-4**

21 Then the LORD said to Moses, "Speak to the priests, the sons of Aaron, and say to them, '^aNo one shall defile himself for a *dead* person among his people,

2 ^aexcept for his relatives who are nearest to him, his mother and his father and his son and his daughter and his brother,

3 also for his virgin sister, who is near to him because she has had no husband; for her he may defile himself.

4 'He shall not defile himself as a relative by marriage among his people, and so profane himself.

5 '^aThey shall not make any baldness on their heads, ^bnor shave off the edges of their beards, ^cnor make any cuts in their flesh.

6 'They shall be holy to their God and ^anot profane the name of their God, for they present the offerings by fire to the LORD, ^bthe bread of their God; so they shall be holy.

7 '^aThey shall not take a woman who is profaned by harlotry, nor shall they take a woman divorced from her husband; for he is holy to his God.

8 'You shall consecrate him, therefore, for he offers ^athe bread of your God; he shall be holy to you; for I the LORD, who sanctifies you, am holy.

9 '^aAlso the daughter of any priest, if she profanes herself by harlotry, she profanes her father; she shall be burned with fire.

10 'And the priest who is the highest among his brothers, on whose head the anointing oil has been poured, and who has been consecrated to wear the garments, ^ashall not uncover his head, nor tear his clothes;

11 ^anor shall he approach any dead person, nor defile himself *even* for his father or his mother;

12 ^anor shall he go out of the sanctuary, nor profane the sanctuary of his God; for ^bthe consecration of the anointing oil of his God is on him: I am the LORD.

Cross references (margin):

22 ^aLev. 18:28

★23 ^aLev. 18:3 ^bLev. 18:25

24 ^aEx. 13:5; 33:1-3 ^bEx. 33:16; Lev. 20:26

25 ^aLev. 10:10; 11:1-47; Deut. 14:3-21

26 ^aLev. 20:24

27 ^aLev. 19:31

★ 1-4

1 ^aLev. 19:28; Ezek. 44:25

2 ^aLev. 21:11

★ 5 ^aDeut. 14:1; Ezek. 44:20 ^bLev. 19:27 ^cDeut. 14:1

6 ^aLev. 18:21 ^bLev. 3:11

7 ^aLev. 21:13, 14

8 ^aLev. 21:6

9 ^aGen. 38:24; Lev. 19:29

★10-12

10 ^aLev. 10:6

11 ^aLev. 19:28; Num. 19:14

12 ^aLev. 10:7 ^bEx. 29:6, 7

20:23 The heinous sins described in this chapter were practiced by the Canaanites.

21:1-4 These special restrictions on *priests* prohibited their touching the dead (by preparing or carrying a body, touching the grave, or coming into a tent or house where a dead body lay) except in the cases of the relatives listed in these verses (cf. Num. 19:11, 14).

Verse 4 is unclear and may mean that a priest may not defile himself even for a chief (important) person, or that he may not defile himself for his wife.

21:5 See notes on 19:27 and 19:28.

21:10-12 The High Priest could not show the customary signs of mourning or even leave the sanctuary in order to participate in mourning.

★13-15

13 'And he shall take a wife in her virginity.

14 aLev.
21:7; Ezek.
44:22

14 'aA widow, or a divorced woman, or one who is profaned by harlotry, these he may not take; but rather he is to marry a virgin of his own people;

15 that he may not profane his offspring among his people: for I am the LORD who sanctifies him.'"

16 Then the LORD spoke to Moses, saying,

17 aLev.
21:6

17 "Speak to Aaron, saying, 'No man of your offspring throughout their generations who has a defect shall approach to offer the abread of his God.

18 aLev.
22:19-25

18 'aFor no one who has a defect shall approach: a blind man, or a lame man, or he who has a adisfigured *face*, or any deformed *limb*,

19 or a man who has a broken foot or broken hand,

20 aDeut.
23:1; Is.
56:3-5

20 or a hunchback or a dwarf, or one *who has a* defect in his eye or eczema or scabs or acrushed testicles.

21 aLev.
21:6

21 'No man among the descendants of Aaron the priest, who has a defect, is to come near to offer the LORD's offerings by fire; *since* he has a defect, he shall not come near to offer athe bread of his God.

★22-23

22 a1 Cor.
9:13

22 'He may eat athe bread of his God, *both* of the most holy and of the holy,

23 only he shall not go in to the veil or come near the altar because he has a defect, that he may not profane My sanctuaries. For I am the LORD who sanctifies them.'"

24 So Moses spoke to Aaron and to his sons and to all the sons of Israel.

22 Then the LORD spoke to Moses, saying,

★ 1-9

2 "Tell Aaron and his sons to be careful with the holy *gifts* of the sons of Israel, which they dedicate to Me, so as not to profane My holy name; I am the LORD.

3 "Say to them, 'aIf any man among all your descendants throughout your generations approaches the holy *gifts* which the sons of Israel dedicate to the LORD, while he has an uncleanness, that person shall be cut off from before Me. I am the LORD.

3 aLev.
7:20, 21;
Num. 19:13

4 'aNo man, of the descendants of Aaron, who is a leper or who has a discharge, may eat of the holy *gifts* until he is clean. bAnd if one touches anything made unclean by a corpse or if ca man has a seminal emission,

4 aLev.
14:1-32
bLev. 11:24-
28, 39, 40
cLev. 15:16,
17

5 or aif a man touches any teeming things, by which he is made unclean, or any man by whom he is made unclean, whatever his uncleanness;

5 aLev.
11:23-28

6 a person who touches any such shall be unclean until evening, and shall not eat of the holy *gifts*, unless he has bathed his body in water.

7 'But when the sun sets, he shall be clean, and afterward he shall eat of the holy *gifts*, for ait is his food.

7 aNum.
18:11

8 'He shall not eat aan animal which dies or is torn *by beasts*, becoming unclean by it; I am the LORD.

8 aLev.
7:24; 11:39,
40; 17:15

9 'They shall therefore keep aMy charge, so that bthey may not bear sin because of it, and die thereby because they profane it; I am the LORD who sanctifies them.

9 aLev.
18:30 bEx.
28:43; Lev.
22:16; Num.
18:22

★10-13

10 'aNo layman, however, is to eat the holy *gift*; a sojourner

10 aEx.
29:33; Lev.
22:13; Num.
3:10

21:13-15 The High Priest could only marry a virgin Israelite; otherwise, he would render his children unfit for service (v. 15).

21:22-23 Priests with the physical defects listed in verses 18-20 could still eat the portions of the sacrifices given to the priests, though they could not perform priestly ministries.

22:1-9 Priests were liable to the same uncleanness as others (either in their own persons or by contact with others who were unclean) and could not minister as long as they were unclean.

22:10-13 A *layman* (not of the priestly tribe), a *sojourner*, or a *hired man* (even if they were a part of the priest's household) could not eat his portion of the sacrifices; but a slave and a childless widow who returned home could.

with the priest or a hired man shall not eat of the holy *gift*.

11 a Gen. 17:13; Ex. 12:44

11 'a But if a priest buys a slave as *his* property with his money, that one may eat of it, and those who are born in his house may eat of his food.

12 'And if a priest's daughter is married to a layman, she shall not eat of the offering of the *gifts*.

13 a Lev. 22:10

13 'But if a priest's daughter becomes a widow or divorced, and has no child and returns to her father's house as in her youth, she shall eat of her father's food; a but no layman shall eat of it.

14 a Lev. 5:15, 16

14 'But if a man eats a holy *gift* unintentionally, then he shall add to it a fifth of it and shall give the holy *gift* to the priest.

15 a Num. 18:32

15 'And a they shall not profane the holy *gifts* of the sons of Israel which they offer to the LORD,

16 a Lev. 22:9; 10:17

16 and *so* cause them a to bear punishment for guilt by eating their holy *gifts*; for I am the LORD who sanctifies them.' "

F Laws Concerning Offerings, 22:17-33

17 Then the LORD spoke to Moses, saying,

18 a Num. 15:14

18 "Speak to Aaron and to his sons and to all the sons of Israel, and say to them, 'a Any man of the house of Israel or of the aliens in Israel who presents his offering, whether it is any of their votive or any of their freewill offerings, which they present to the LORD for a burnt offering—

19 a Lev. 21:18-21; Deut. 15:21

19 a for you to be accepted—*it must be* a male without defect from the cattle, the sheep, or the goats.

20 a Deut. 15:21; 17:1; Mal. 1:8, 14; Heb. 9:14; 1 Pet. 1:19

20 'a Whatever has a defect, you shall not offer, for it will not be accepted for you.

21 a Num. 15:3, 8

21 'And when a man offers a sacrifice of peace offerings to the LORD a to fulfill a special vow, or for a freewill offering, of the herd or of the flock, it must be perfect to be accepted; there shall be no defect in it.

22 'Those *that are* blind or fractured or maimed or having a running sore or eczema or scabs, you shall not offer to the LORD, nor make of them an offering by fire on the altar to the LORD.

23 'In respect to an ox or a lamb which has an overgrown or stunted *member*, you may present it for a freewill offering, but for a vow it shall not be accepted.

24 a Lev. 21:20

24 'Also a anything *with its* testicles bruised or crushed or torn or cut, you shall not offer to the LORD, or sacrifice in your land,

25 a Lev. 21:22

25 nor shall you accept any such from the hand of a foreigner for offering a as the food of your God; for their corruption is in them, they have a defect, they shall not be accepted for you.' "

26 Then the LORD spoke to Moses, saying,

27 a Ex. 22:30

27 "When an ox or a sheep or a goat is born, it shall remain a seven days with its mother, and from the eighth day on it shall be accepted as a sacrifice of an offering by fire to the LORD.

28 a Deut. 22:6, 7

28 "a But, *whether* it is an ox or a sheep, you shall not kill *both* it and its young in one day.

29 a Lev. 7:12

29 "And when you sacrifice a a sacrifice of thanksgiving to the LORD, you shall sacrifice it so that you may be accepted.

30 "It shall be eaten on the same day, you shall leave none of it until morning: I am the LORD.

31 a Lev. 19:37; Num. 15:40; Deut. 4:40

31 "a So you shall keep My commandments, and do them: I am the LORD.

32 "And you shall not profane My holy name, but I will be sanctified among the sons of Israel: I am the LORD who sanctifies you,

33 a Lev. 11:45

33 a who brought you out from the land of Egypt, to be your God: I am the LORD."

G Laws Concerning Festivals, 23:1-44

1 The Sabbath, 23:1-3

23 The LORD spoke again to Moses, saying,

★ 2 aLev.
23:4, 37, 44;
Num. 29:39
bLev. 23:21

2 "Speak to the sons of Israel, and say to them, 'aThe Lord's appointed times which you shall bproclaim as holy convocations— My appointed times are these:

★ 3 aEx.
20:9, 10;
23:12; 31:13-
17; 35:2, 3;
Lev. 19:3;
Deut. 5:13,
14

3 'aFor six days work may be done; but on the seventh day there is a sabbath of complete rest, a holy convocation. You shall not do any work; it is a sabbath to the Lord in all your dwellings.

2 The Passover and Unleavened Bread, 23:4-8

4 aEx.
23:14; Lev.
23:2

4 'These are the aappointed times of the Lord, holy convocations which you shall proclaim at the times appointed for them.

★ 5 aEx.
12:18, 19;
Num. 28:16-
25; Deut.
16:1; Josh.
5:10.

5 'aIn the first month, on the fourteenth day of the month at twilight is the Lord's Passover.

6 Then on the fifteenth day of the same month there is the aFeast of Unleavened Bread to the Lord; for seven days you shall eat unleavened bread.

★ 6 aEx.
12:14-20;
23:15; 34:18;
Deut. 16:3-8

★ 7 aLev.
23:8, 21, 25,
35, 36

7 'On the first day you shall have a holy convocation; you shall anot do any laborious work.

★ 8

8 'But for seven days you shall present an offering by fire to the Lord. On the seventh day is a holy convocation; you shall not do any laborious work.' "

3 First fruits, 23:9-14

9 Then the Lord spoke to Moses, saying,

10 "Speak to the sons of Israel, and say to them, 'When you enter the land which I am going to give to you and areap its harvest, then you shall bring in the sheaf of the first fruits of your harvest to the priest.

★10-14

10 aEx.
23:19; 34:26

11 'And he shall wave the sheaf before the Lord for you to be accepted; on the day after the sabbath the priest shall wave it.

12 'Now on the day when you wave the sheaf, you shall offer a male lamb one year old without defect for a burnt offering to the Lord.

13 'Its agrain offering shall then be two-tenths of an ephah of fine flour mixed with oil, an offering by fire to the Lord for a soothing aroma, with its libation, a fourth of a hin of wine.

13 aLev.
6:20

14 'Until this same day, until you have brought in the offering of your God, ayou shall eat neither bread nor roasted grain nor new growth. It is to be a perpetual statute throughout your generations in all your dwelling places.

14 aEx.
34:26; Num.
15:20, 21

4 Pentecost, 23:15-22

15 'aYou shall also count for yourselves from the day after the sabbath, from the day when you brought in the sheaf of the wave offering; there shall be seven complete sabbaths.

★15-23

15 aNum.
28:26-31;
Deut. 16:9-
12

16 'You shall count fifty days to the day after the seventh sab-

16 aNum.
28:26

23:2 *holy convocations.* I.e., meetings for holy purposes.

23:3 *sabbath.* See notes on Gen. 2:2 and Exod. 20:8.

23:5 *Passover.* See note on Exod. 12:11.

23:6 *the Feast of Unleavened Bread.* See note on Exod. 12:15.

23:7 *laborious work.* Defined in a later period as building, weaving, reaping, threshing, grinding, etc.

23:8 Num. 28:19-23 lists details of these offerings.

23:10-14 The feast of *first fruits* involved presenting to the Lord a *sheaf* (lit., an omer, about two quarts; see note on Exod. 16:16) of the barley harvest on the second day of the Feast of Unleavened Bread (16th of Nisan). This was accompanied by burnt, grain, and drink offerings (cf. Exod. 29:40). The *libation* (cf. Exod.

29:41), consisting of about two pints of unmixed wine, was poured on the grain offering as a symbol of joy. First fruits symbolized the consecration of the entire harvest to God and was an earnest, or pledge, of the full harvest yet to be gathered (see notes on 1 Cor. 15:20; James 1:18; Rev. 14:4, as well as other N.T. uses in Rom. 8:23; 11:16; 1 Cor. 16:15).

23:15-23 *fifty days* (the meaning of the Greek word "Pentecost") after first fruits, two loaves of bread were offered for the people, along with burnt, grain, drink, sin, and peace offerings. The loaves, made with *leaven*, typified the formation of the Church on the day of Pentecost. The Church, the Body of Christ, is composed of sinners (leaven typifies sin; see note on Exod. 12:15-20) who are saved by the grace of God (see also 2:11).

bath; then you shall present a ᵃnew grain offering to the LORD.

17 'You shall bring in from your dwelling places two *loaves* of bread for a wave offering, made of two-tenths *of an ephah*; they shall be of a fine flour, baked ᵃwith leaven as first fruits to the LORD.

18 'Along with the bread, you shall present seven one year old male lambs without defect, and a bull of the herd, and two rams; they are to be a burnt offering to the LORD, with their grain offering and their libations, an offering by fire of a soothing aroma to the LORD.

19 'You shall also offer ᵃone male goat for a sin offering and two male lambs one year old for a sacrifice of peace offerings.

20 'The priest shall then wave them with the bread of the first fruits for a wave offering with two lambs before the LORD; they are to be holy to the LORD for the priest.

21 'On this same day you shall ᵃmake a proclamation as well; you are to have a holy convocation. You shall do no laborious ᵇwork. It is to be a perpetual statute in all your dwelling places throughout your generations.

22 'ᵃWhen you reap the harvest of your land, moreover, you shall not reap to the very corners of your field, nor gather the gleaning of your harvest; you are to leave them for the needy and the alien. I am the LORD your God.' "

5 Trumpets, 23:23-25

23 Again the LORD spoke to Moses, saying,

24 "Speak to the sons of Israel, saying, 'ᵃIn the seventh month on the first of the month, you shall have a rest, a ᵇreminder by blowing *of trumpets*, a holy convocation.

25 'You shall ᵃnot do any laborious work, but you shall present an offering by fire to the LORD.' "

6 The Day of Atonement, 23:26-32

26 And the LORD spoke to Moses, saying,

27 "On exactly ᵃthe tenth day of this seventh month is ᵇthe day of atonement; it shall be a holy convocation for you, and you shall humble your souls and present an offering by fire to the LORD.

28 "Neither shall you do any work on this same day, for it is a ᵃday of atonement, ᵇto make atonement on your behalf before the LORD your God.

29 "If there is any person who will not humble himself on this same day, ᵃhe shall be cut off from his people.

30 "As for any person who does any work on this same day, that person I will destroy from among his people.

31 "You shall do no work at all. It is to be a perpetual statute throughout your generations in all your dwelling places.

32 "It is to be a sabbath of complete rest to you, and you shall humble your souls; on the ninth of the month at evening, from evening until evening you shall keep your sabbath."

7 Tabernacles, 23:33-44

33 Again the LORD spoke to Moses, saying,

Marginal references:

17 ᵃLev. 2:12; 7:13

19 ᵃLev. 4:23; Num. 28:30

21 ᵃLev. 23:2, 4 ᵇLev. 23:7

22 ᵃLev. 19:9, 10; Deut. 24:19; Ruth 2:15f.

★24 ᵃNum. 29:1 ᵇNum. 10:9, 10

25 ᵃLev. 23:21

★27 ᵃLev. 16:29; 25:9; Num. 29:7 ᵇEx. 30:10; Lev. 16:30; 23:28; Num. 29:7-11

28 ᵃLev. 23:27 ᵇLev. 16:34

29 ᵃGen. 17:14; Lev. 13:46; Num. 5:2

23:24 Three festivals occurred in the *seventh month* (Tishri, Sept.-Oct.): those of *trumpets*, Atonement, and Tabernacles. The blowing of a trumpet (the shofar, or ram's horn) on the first day signaled the beginning of the civil new year, Rosh Hashanah (see also Num. 29:1-6).

23:27 *the day of atonement.* See the notes on chapter 16.

★34-43

34 aNum.
29:12 bLev.
23:42, 43;
Deut. 16:13,
16; Ezra 3:4;
Neh. 8:14;
Zech. 14:16;
John 7:2

34 "Speak to the sons of Israel, saying, 'On ᵃthe fifteenth of this seventh month is the ᵇFeast of Booths for seven days to the Lᴏʀᴅ.

35 'On the first day is a holy convocation; you shall do ᵃno laborious work of any kind.

35 aLev.
23:25

36 'ᵃFor seven days you shall present an offering by fire to the Lᴏʀᴅ. On ᵇthe eighth day you shall have a holy convocation and present an offering by fire to the Lᴏʀᴅ; it is an assembly. You shall do no laborious work.

36 aNum.
29:12-34
bNum.
29:35-38

37 aLev.
23:2 bNum.
28:1-29:38

37 'These are ᵃthe appointed times of the Lᴏʀᴅ which you shall proclaim as holy convocations, to present offerings by fire to the Lᴏʀᴅ—burnt offerings and grain offerings, sacrifices and libations, ᵇ*each* day's matter on its own day—

38 besides *those of* the sabbaths of the Lᴏʀᴅ, and besides your gifts, and besides all your votive and freewill offerings, which you give to the Lᴏʀᴅ.

39 aEx.
23:16

39 'On exactly the fifteenth day of the seventh month, ᵃwhen you have gathered in the crops of the land, you shall celebrate the feast of the Lᴏʀᴅ for seven days, with a rest on the first day and a rest on the eighth day.

40 'Now on the first day you shall take for yourselves the foliage of beautiful trees, palm branches and boughs of leafy trees and willows of the brook; and you shall rejoice before the Lᴏʀᴅ your God for seven days.

41 'You shall thus celebrate it *as* a feast to the Lᴏʀᴅ for seven days in the year. It *shall be* a perpetual statute throughout your generations; you shall celebrate it in the seventh month.

42 'You shall live ᵃin booths for seven days; all the native-born in Israel shall live in booths,

42 aLev.
23:34

43 so that ᵃyour generations may know that I had the sons of Israel live in booths when I brought them out from the land of Egypt. I am the Lᴏʀᴅ your God.'"

43 aDeut.
31:13; Ps.
78:5f.

44 So Moses declared to the sons of Israel ᵃthe appointed times of the Lᴏʀᴅ.

44 aLev.
23:37

H Laws Concerning the Oil, Bread, and Blasphemy, 24:1-23

24 Then the Lᴏʀᴅ spoke to Moses, saying,

2 "Command the sons of Israel that they bring to you ᵃclear oil from beaten olives for the light, to make a lamp burn continually.

★ 2 aEx.
27:20, 21

3 "Outside the veil of testimony in the tent of meeting, Aaron shall keep it in order from evening to morning before the Lᴏʀᴅ continually; *it shall be* a perpetual statute throughout your generations.

4 "He shall keep the lamps in order on the ᵃpure *gold* lampstand before the Lᴏʀᴅ continually.

4 aEx.
25:31; 31:8;
37:17

5 "ᵃThen you shall take fine flour and bake twelve cakes with it; two-tenths *of an ephah* shall be *in* each cake.

★ 5 aEx.
25:30; 39:36;
40:23

6 "And you shall set them *in* two rows, six *to* a row, on the ᵃpure *gold* table before the Lᴏʀᴅ.

6 aEx.
25:24; 1 Kin.
7:48

7 "And you shall put pure frankincense on each row, that it may be ᵃa memorial portion for the bread, *even* an offering by fire to the Lᴏʀᴅ.

★ 7 aLev.
2:2, 9, 16

23:34-43 The last festival was that of *Booths,* which was seven days in length and concluded with a holy convocation (v. 36). During that week, the people lived in booths or huts made of boughs (cf. Neh. 8:14-18), commemorating God's provision for them in bringing them out of Egypt and through the wilderness (Lev. 23:43). The sacrifices offered during this time amounted to 189 animals (cf. Num. 29:12-38). It also celebrated the autumn harvest of fruits and olives (cf. Exod. 23:16) and, according to Zech. 14:16, it will be celebrated during the Millennium.

24:2 *oil* for the lampstand. See Exod. 27:20.

24:5 Each *cake* contained about 4 quarts of flour (see note on 23:13).

24:7 The *frankincense* was likely placed in bowls beside the cakes rather than being baked with them.

8 *a*Matt. 12:5 *b*Ex. 25:30; Num. 4:7; 2 Chr. 2:4

8 "*a*Every sabbath day he shall set it in order before the LORD *b*continually; it is an everlasting covenant for the sons of Israel.

9 *a*Matt. 12:4; Mark 2:26; Luke 6:4

9 "*a*And it shall be for Aaron and his sons, and they shall eat it in a holy place; for it is most holy to him from the LORD's offerings by fire, *his* portion forever."

★**10-16**

10 Now the son of an Israelite woman, whose father was an Egyptian, went out among the sons of Israel; and the Israelite woman's son and a man of Israel struggled with each other in the camp.

11 *a*Ex. 3:15; 22:28; Job 2:5, 9; Is. 8:21

11 And the son of the Israelite woman blasphemed the *a*Name and cursed. So they brought him to Moses. (Now his mother's name was Shelomith, the daughter of Dibri, of the tribe of Dan.)

12 *a*Ex. 18:15; Num. 15:34

12 And they put him in custody so that *a*the command of the LORD might be made clear to them.

13 Then the LORD spoke to Moses, saying,

14 *a*Deut. 13:9; 17:7 *b*Lev. 20:2, 27; Deut. 21:21

14 "Bring the one who has cursed outside the camp, and let all who heard him *a*lay their hands on his head; then *b*let all the congregation stone him.

15 *a*Ex. 22:28

15 "And you shall speak to the sons of Israel, saying, '*a*If anyone curses his God, then he shall bear his sin.

16 *a*1 Kin. 21:10; Matt. 12:31; Mark 3:28f.

16 'Moreover, the one who *a*blasphemes the name of the LORD shall surely be put to death; all the congregation shall certainly stone him. The alien as well as the native, when he blasphemes the Name, shall be put to death.

17 *a*Gen. 9:6; Ex. 21:12; Num. 35:30, 31; Deut. 27:24

17 '*a*And if a man takes the life of any human being, he shall surely be put to death.

18 'And *a*the one who takes the life of an animal shall make it good, life for life.

18 *a*Lev. 24:21

19 'And if a man injures his neighbor, just as he has done, so it shall be done to him:

20 *a*fracture for fracture, *b*eye for eye, tooth for tooth; just as he has injured a man, so it shall be inflicted on him.

★**20** *a*Ex. 21:23; Deut. 19:21 *b*Matt. 5:38

21 'Thus the one who kills an animal shall make it good, but *a*the one who kills a man shall be put to death.

21 *a*Lev. 24:17

22 'There shall be *a*one standard for you; it shall be for the stranger as well as the native, for I am the LORD your God.'"

22 *a*Ex. 12:49; Num. 9:14; 15:15, 16, 29

23 Then Moses spoke to the sons of Israel, and they brought the one who had cursed outside the camp and stoned him with stones. Thus the sons of Israel did, just as the LORD had commanded Moses.

I Laws Concerning the Sabbatical Year,
25:1-7

25 The LORD then spoke to Moses at Mount Sinai, saying,

2 "Speak to the sons of Israel, and say to them, 'When you come into the land which I shall give you, then the land shall have a sabbath to the LORD.

★ **2-7**

3 '*a*Six years you shall sow your field, and six years you shall prune your vineyard and gather in its crop,

3 *a*Ex. 23:10, 11

4 but during *a*the seventh year the land shall have a sabbath rest, a sabbath to the LORD; you shall not sow your field nor prune your vineyard.

4 *a*Lev. 25:20

24:10-16 This blasphemer apparently was one of the "mixed multitude" of Exod. 12:38. By laying their hands on him, the people transferred to him whatever guilt might have accrued to the community. *shall bear his sin* (Lev. 24:15). The sinner bears full personal responsibility.

24:20 The law of retaliation, *lex talionis*, pro-

vided for exact justice, not revenge, and concerned public justice, not private vengeance (see note on Matt. 5:38).

25:2-7 Every seventh year the land was to have a sabbath, a rest. Whatever grew during that year was freely available to all alike (vv. 6-7). It was also a time of special instruction in the Law of God (cf. Deut. 31:10-13).

5 'Your harvest's aftergrowth you shall not reap, and your grapes of untrimmed vines you shall not gather; the land shall have a sabbatical year.

6 '*ª*And all of you shall have the sabbath *products* of the land for food; yourself, and your male and female slaves, and your hired man and your foreign resident, those who live as aliens with you.

7 'Even your cattle and the animals that are in your land shall have all its crops to eat.

J Laws Concerning the Year of Jubilee, 25:8-55

8 'You are also to count off seven sabbaths of years for yourself, seven times seven years, so that you have the time of the seven sabbaths of years, *namely,* forty-nine years.

9 'You shall then sound a ram's horn abroad on *ª*the tenth day of the seventh month; on the day of atonement you shall sound a horn all through your land.

10 'You shall thus consecrate the fiftieth year and *ª*proclaim a release through the land to all its inhabitants. It shall be a jubilee for you, and *b*each of you shall return to his own property, and each of you shall return to his family.

11 'You shall have the fiftieth year as a jubilee; you shall not sow, nor reap its aftergrowth, nor gather in *from* its untrimmed vines.

12 'For it is a jubilee; it shall be holy to you. You shall eat its crops out of the field.

13 '*ª*On this year of jubilee each of you shall return to his own property.

14 'If you make a sale, moreover, to your friend, or buy from your friend's hand, *ª*you shall not wrong one another.

15 'Corresponding to the number of years after the jubilee, you shall buy from your friend; he is to sell to you according to the number of years of crops.

16 '*ª*In proportion to the extent of the years you shall increase its price, and in proportion to the fewness of the years, you shall diminish its price; for *it is* a number of crops he is selling to you.

17 'So *ª*you shall not wrong one another, but you shall fear your God; for I am the LORD your God.

18 'You shall thus observe My statutes, and keep My judgments, so as to carry them out, that *ª*you may live securely on the land.

19 'Then the land will yield its produce, so that you can eat your fill and live securely on it.

20 'But if you say, "*ª*What are we going to eat on the seventh year if we do not sow or gather in our crops?"

21 then *ª*I will so order My blessing for you in the sixth year that it will bring forth the crop for three years.

22 'When you are sowing the eighth year, you can still eat *ª*old things from the crop, eating *the old* until the ninth year when its crop comes in.

23 'The land, moreover, shall not be sold permanently, for *ª*the land is Mine; for *b*you are *but* aliens and sojourners with Me.

24 'Thus for every piece of your property, you are to provide for the redemption of the land.

25 '*ª*If a fellow countryman of

Marginal references

6 *ª*Lev. 25:20, 21
★ 8-12
9 *ª*Lev. 23:27
10 *ª*Jer. 34:8, 15, 17 *b*Lev. 25:13, 28, 54
★13-17
13 *ª*Lev. 25:10; 27:24
14 *ª*Lev. 25:17
16 *ª*Lev. 25:27, 51, 52
17 *ª*Lev. 25:14; Prov. 14:31; 22:22; Jer. 7:5, 6; 1 Thess. 4:6
18 *ª*Lev. 26:5; Deut. 12:10; Jer. 23:6
20 *ª*Lev. 25:4
★21-22
21 *ª*Deut. 28:8
22 *ª*Lev. 26:10
23 *ª*Ex. 19:5 *b*Gen. 23:4; 1 Chr. 29:15; Ps. 39:12; Heb. 11:13; 1 Pet. 2:11
★25-28
25 *ª*Ruth 2:20; 4:4, 6

25:8-12 Every *fiftieth year* was a year of *jubilee,* during which there was to be no sowing or reaping, and during which all land was returned to its original owner and slaves to their families.

25:13-17 Buying and selling land was to be carried on equitably, with due regard to how near the year of jubilee was, when the land would have to be returned to its original owner.

25:21-22 God promised that the crops of the sixth year would be sufficient to sustain the people during the sabbatical year which followed and the year of jubilee.

25:25-28 An Israelite who was forced to sell his land could have it redeemed by a near relative, or buy it back himself (with due regard for the number of crops remaining until the year of jubilee), or wait until jubilee when it would be restored to him.

yours becomes so poor he has to sell part of his property, then his nearest kinsman is to come and buy back what his relative has sold.

26 'Or in case a man has no kinsman, but so recovers his means as to find sufficient for its redemption,

27 ªLev. 25:16

27 ªthen he shall calculate the years since its sale and refund the balance to the man to whom he sold it, and so return to his property.

28 ªLev. 25:10, 13

28 'But if he has not found sufficient means to get it back for himself, then what he has sold shall remain in the hands of its purchaser until the year of jubilee; but at the jubilee it shall revert, that ªhe may return to his property.

★29-33

29 'Likewise, if a man sells a dwelling house in a walled city, then his redemption right remains valid until a full year from its sale; his right of redemption lasts a full year.

30 'But if it is not bought back for him within the space of a full year, then the house that is in the walled city passes permanently to its purchaser throughout his generations; it does not revert in the jubilee.

31 'The houses of the villages, however, which have no surrounding wall shall be considered as open fields; they have redemption rights and revert in the jubilee.

32 ªNum. 35:1-8; Josh. 21:2

32 'As for ªcities of the Levites, the Levites have a permanent right of redemption for the houses of the cities which are their possession.

33 'What, therefore, belongs to the Levites may be redeemed and a house sale in the city of this possession reverts in the jubilee, for the houses of the Levites are

their possession among the sons of Israel.

34 ªNum. 35:2-5

34 'ªBut pasture fields of their cities shall not be sold, for that is their perpetual possession.

★35-46

35 ªDeut. 15:7-11; 24:14, 15

35 'ªNow in case a countryman of yours becomes poor and his means with regard to you falter, then you are to sustain him, like a stranger or a sojourner, that he may live with you.

36 ªEx. 22:25; Deut. 23:19, 20

36 'ªDo not take usurious interest from him, but revere your God, that your countryman may live with you.

37 'You shall not give him your silver at interest, nor your food for gain.

38 ªLev. 11:45 ᵇGen. 17:7

38 'ªI am the LORD your God, who brought you out of the land of Egypt to give you the land of Canaan and ᵇto be your God.

39 ªEx. 21:2-6; Deut. 15:12-18; 1 Kin. 9:22

39 'ªAnd if a countryman of yours becomes so poor with regard to you that he sells himself to you, you shall not subject him to a slave's service.

40 ªEx. 21:2

40 'He shall be with you as a hired man, as ªif he were a sojourner with you, until the year of jubilee.

41 'He shall then go out from you, he and his sons with him, and shall go back to his family, that he may return to the property of his forefathers.

42 'For they are My servants whom I brought out from the land of Egypt; they are not to be sold in a slave sale.

43 ªEx. 1:13, 14; Lev. 25:46, 53; Ezek. 34:4; Col. 4:1

43 'ªYou shall not rule over him with severity, but are to revere your God.

44 'As for your male and female slaves whom you may have—you may acquire male and female slaves from the pagan nations that are around you.

45 'Then, too, it is out of the sons of the sojourners who live as aliens among you that you may gain acquisition, and out of their

---

25:29-33 A house within a city, if sold and not repurchased within a year, became the permanent possession of the buyer (with the exception stated in v. 33).

25:35-46 Poor Israelites were to be assisted in

every way and without usury (interest; cf. Exod. 22:25). If one sold himself to a fellow Israelite, he was to be treated as a hired person rather than a slave. Slave labor came only from the heathen nations (cf. Lev. 25:44).

families who are with you, whom they will have produced in your land; they also may become your possession.

46 'You may even bequeath them to your sons after you, to receive as a possession; you can use them as permanent slaves. *But in respect to your countrymen, the sons of Israel, you shall not rule with severity over one another.

47 'Now if the means of a stranger or of a sojourner with you becomes sufficient, and a countryman of yours becomes so poor with regard to him as to sell himself to a stranger who is sojourning with you, or to the descendants of a stranger's family,

48 then he shall have redemption right after he has been sold. One of his brothers may redeem him,

49 or his uncle, or his uncle's son, may redeem him, or one of his blood relatives from his family may redeem him; or *if he prospers, he may redeem himself.

50 'He then with his purchaser shall calculate from the year when he sold himself to him up to the year of jubilee; and the price of his sale shall correspond to the number of years. *It is* like the days of a hired man *that* he shall be with him.

51 'If there are still many years, *he shall refund part of his purchase price in proportion to them for his own redemption;

52 and if few years remain until the year of jubilee, he shall so calculate with him. In proportion to his years he is to refund *the amount for* his redemption.

53 'Like a man hired year by year he shall be with him; *he shall not rule over him with severity in your sight.

54 'Even if he is not redeemed by these *means*, *he shall still go out in the year of jubilee, he and his sons with him.

55 'For the sons of Israel are My servants; they are My servants whom I brought out from the land of Egypt. I am the LORD your God.

K Laws Concerning Obedience, 26:1–46

26 'You shall not make for yourselves *idols, nor shall you set up for yourselves *an image or *a *sacred* pillar, nor shall you place a *figured stone in your land to bow down to it; for I am the LORD your God.

2 '*You shall keep My sabbaths and reverence My sanctuary; I am the LORD.

3 '*If you walk in My statutes and keep My commandments so as to carry them out,

4 then *I shall give you rains in their season, so that the land will yield its produce and the trees of the field will bear their fruit.

5 '*Indeed, your threshing will last for you until grape gathering, and grape gathering will last until sowing time. You will thus eat your food to the full and *live securely in your land.

6 '*I shall also grant peace in the land, so that *you may lie down with no one making *you* tremble. *I shall also eliminate harmful beasts from the land, and *no sword will pass through your land.

7 'But you will chase your enemies, and they will fall before you by the sword;

8 *five of you will chase a hundred, and a hundred of you will chase ten thousand, and your enemies will fall before you by the sword.

Cross references (margin):

46 *aLev. 25:43

★47-55

49 *aLev. 25:26, 27

51 *aLev. 25:16

53 *aLev. 25:43

54 *aLev. 25:10, 13, 28

★ 1 *aLev. 19:4; Deut. 5:8 *bEx. 20:4; Deut. 16:21f. *cEx. 23:24 *dNum. ·33:52

2 *aLev. 19:30

3 *aDeut. 7:12-26; 11:13; 28:1-14

4 *aDeut. 11:14

★ 5 *aDeut. 11:15; Joel 2:19, 26; Amos 9:13 *bLev. 25:18, 19; Ezek. 34:25

6 *aPs. 29:11; 85:8; 147:14 *bZeph. 3:13 *cLev. 26:22 *dLev. 26:25

8 *aDeut. 32:30

25:47-55 If an Israelite sold himself to a foreigner, he could be redeemed by a near relative, by himself, or automatically during the year of jubilee.

26:1 *idols.* Lit., nonentities. *image.* A carved or cast idol.
26:5 The *threshing* (begun in March) would continue until *grape gathering* (in July).

9 aGen.
17:6; 22:17;
48:4 bGen.
17:7

9 'So I will turn toward you and amake you fruitful and multiply you, and I will bconfirm My covenant with you.

★10 aLev.
25:22

10 'aAnd you will eat the old supply and clear out the old because of the new.

11 aEx. 25:8;
29:45, 46;
Ezek. 37:26

11 'aMoreover, I will make My dwelling among you, and My soul will not reject you.

12 aGen.
3:8; Deut.
23:14; 2 Cor.
6:16

12 'aI will also walk among you and be your God, and you shall be My people.

13 aEx. 20:2
bEzek. 34:27

13 'aI am the LORD your God, who brought you out of the land of Egypt so that you should not be their slaves, and bI broke the bars of your yoke and made you walk erect.

14 aDeut.
28:15-68;
Josh. 23:15

14 'aBut if you do not obey Me and do not carry out all these commandments,

15 aLev.
26:11; 2 Kin.
17:15 bLev.
26:9

15 if, instead, you areject My statutes, and if your soul abhors My ordinances so as not to carry out all My commandments, and so bbreak My covenant,

★16 aDeut.
28:22; Ps.
78:33
b1 Sam.
2:33; Ezek.
24:23; 33:10
cJudg. 6:3-6;
Job 31:8

16 I, in turn, will do this to you: I will appoint over you a asudden terror, consumption and fever that shall waste away the eyes and cause the bsoul to pine away; also, cyou shall sow your seed uselessly, for your enemies shall eat it up.

17 aPs.
106:41 bLev.
26:36, 37;
Ps. 53:5;
Prov. 28:1

17 'And I will set My face against you so that you shall be struck down before your enemies; and athose who hate you shall rule over you, and byou shall flee when no one is pursuing you.

18 aLev.
26:21, 24, 28

18 'If also after these things, you do not obey Me, then I will punish you aseven times more for your sins.

★19 aIs.
28:1-3; Ezek.
24:21

19 'And I will also abreak down your pride of power; I will also make your sky like iron and your earth like bronze.

20 aPs.
127:1; Is.
17:10, 11;
49:4; Jer.
12:13

20 'And ayour strength shall be spent uselessly, for your land shall not yield its produce and the trees of the land shall not yield their fruit.

21 'If then, you aact with hostility against Me and are unwilling to obey Me, I will increase the plague on you bseven times according to your sins.

21 aLev.
26:23, 27, 40
bLev. 26:18

22 'And aI will let loose among you the beasts of the field, which shall bereave you of your children and destroy your cattle and reduce your number so that byour roads lie deserted.

22 a2 Kin.
17:25 bJudg.
5:6

23 'aAnd if by these things you are not turned to Me, but act with hostility against Me,

23 aLev.
26:21; Jer.
5:3

24 then I will aact with hostility against you; and I, even I, will strike you bseven times for your sins.

24 aLev.
26:28, 41
bLev. 26:21

25 'I will also bring upon you a sword which will execute avengeance for the covenant; and when you gather together into your cities, I will send bpestilence among you, so that you shall be delivered into enemy hands.

★25 aJer.
50:28; 51:11
bNum. 14:12

26 'aWhen I break your staff of bread, ten women will bake your bread in one oven, and they will bring back your bread in rationed amounts, so that you will bbeat and not be satisfied.

★26 aIs. 3:1;
Ezek. 4:16,
17; 5:16
bMic. 6:14

27 'Yet if in spite of this, you do not obey Me, but act with hostility against Me,

28 then aI will act with wrathful hostility against you; and I, even I, will punish you seven times for your sins.

28 aLev.
26:24, 41; Is.
59:18

29 'Further, ayou shall eat the flesh of your sons and the flesh of your daughters you shall eat.

29 a2 Kin.
6:29

30 'I then awill destroy your high places, and cut down your bincense altars, and heap your remains on the remains of your idols; for My soul shall abhor you.

30 a2 Kin.
23:20; Ezek.
6:3, 6; Amos
7:9 b2 Chr.
34:4, 7; Is.
27:9

26:10 *because of the new.* I.e., because of the new crop, the old would have to be cleared out, so plentiful would be the harvests.
26:16 *consumption* = tuberculosis.
26:19 *sky like iron.* I.e., no rain. *earth like bronze.* I.e., no crops.
26:25 *execute vengeance for the covenant* (better, *avenge my covenant*). I.e., avenge the breaking of God's covenant (with the punishments described in these verses).
26:26 So scarce would bread be that *one oven* would suffice to bake the bread for ten families.

31 *a*Neh.
2:3; Jer.
44:2, 6, 22
*b*Is. 63:18;
Lam. 2:7
*c*Amos 5:21

32 *a*Jer.
9:11; 12:11;
25:11; 33:10
*b*Jer. 18:16;
19:8

★33-35

33 *a*Deut.
4:27; 28:64;
Ps. 44:11;
106:27; Jer.
31:10; Ezek.
12:15; 20:23;
Zech. 7:14

34 *a*Lev.
26:43; 2 Chr.
36:21

36 *a*Is.
30:17; Lam.
1:3, 6; 4:19;
Ezek. 21:7

37 *a*Jer.
6:21; Nah.
3:3

38 *a*Deut.
4:26

39 *a*Ezek.
4:17; 33:10

40 *a*Jer.
3:12-15;
14:20; Hos.
5:15

31 'I will lay *a*waste your cities as well, and will make your *b*sanctuaries desolate; and I will not *c*smell your soothing aromas.

32 'And I will make *a*the land desolate *b*so that your enemies who settle in it shall be appalled over it.

33 'You, however, I *a*will scatter among the nations and will draw out a sword after you, as your land becomes desolate and your cities become waste.

34 '*a*Then the land will enjoy its sabbaths all the days of the desolation, while you are in your enemies' land; then the land will rest and enjoy its sabbaths.

35 'All the days of *its* desolation it will observe the rest which it did not observe on your sabbaths, while you were living on it.

36 'As for those of you who may be left, I will also bring *a*weakness into their hearts in the lands of their enemies. And the sound of a driven leaf will chase them and even when no one is pursuing, they will flee as though from the sword, and they will fall.

37 '*a*They will therefore stumble over each other as if *running* from the sword, although no one is pursuing; and you will have *no strength* to stand up before your enemies.

38 'But *a*you will perish among the nations, and your enemies' land will consume you.

39 '*a*So those of you who may be left will rot away because of their iniquity in the lands of your enemies; and also because of the iniquities of their forefathers they will rot away with them.

40 '*a*If they confess their iniquity and the iniquity of their forefathers, in their unfaithfulness which they committed against Me, and also in their acting with hostility against Me—

41 I also was acting with hostility against them, to bring them into the land of their enemies— *a*or if their uncircumcised heart becomes humbled so that *b*they then make amends for their iniquity,

42 then I will remember *a*My covenant with Jacob, and I will remember also *b*My covenant with Isaac; and *c*My covenant with Abraham as well, and I will remember the land.

43 '*a*For the land shall be abandoned by them, and shall make up for its sabbaths while it is made desolate without them. They, meanwhile, shall be making amends for their iniquity, because they rejected My ordinances and their *b*soul abhorred My statutes.

44 'Yet in spite of this, when they are in the land of their enemies, I will not reject them, nor will I so *a*abhor them as *b*to destroy them, *c*breaking My covenant with them; for I am the LORD their God.

45 'But I will remember for them the *a*covenant with their ancestors, whom I brought out of the land of Egypt in the sight of the nations, that *b*I might be their God. I am the LORD.' ''

46 *a*These are the statutes and ordinances and laws which the LORD established between Himself and the sons of Israel through Moses at Mount Sinai.

41 *a*Jer. 4:4;
9:25, 26;
Ezek. 44:7,
9; Acts 7:51
*b*Ezek. 20:43

42 *a*Gen.
28:13-15;
35:11, 12
*b*Gen. 26:2-5
*c*Gen. 22:15-18

43 *a*Lev.
26:34 *b*Lev.
26:11

44 *a*Lev.
26:11 *b*Deut.
4:31; Jer.
30:11 *c*Jer.
33:20-26

45 *a*Ex. 6:6-8 *b*Gen. 17:7

46 *a*Lev.
7:38; 27:34;
Deut. 4:5;
29:1

L Laws Concerning Vows and Tithes, 27:1-34

27 Again, the LORD spoke to Moses, saying,

2 "Speak to the sons of Israel, and say to them, '*a*When a man makes a difficult vow, he *shall be valued* according to your valu-

★ 2 *a*Num.
6:2; Deut.
23:21-23

26:33-35 The exile of the people to Assyria and Babylonia is here predicted (cf. 2 Chron. 36:21).

27:2 *a difficult vow.* I.e., a special vow by which an individual consecrated to the Lord himself or his family (vv. 3-8), his animals (vv. 9-13),

his house (vv. 14-15), or his fields (vv. 16-25). Instead of actually transferring ownership, the individual could substitute a just sum of money (except when a clean animal was vowed to the Lord, in which case it could not be redeemed; vv. 9-10).

ation of persons belonging to the LORD.

★ 3-7

3 aEx. 30:13; Lev. 27:25; Num. 3:47; 18:16

3 'If your valuation is of the male from twenty years even to sixty years old, then your valuation shall be fifty shekels of silver, after athe shekel of the sanctuary.

4 'Or if it is a female, then your valuation shall be thirty shekels.

5 'And if it be from five years even to twenty years old then your valuation for the male shall be twenty shekels, and for the female ten shekels.

6 aNum. 18:16

6 'But if *they are* from a month even up to five years old, then your valuation shall be afive shekels of silver for the male, and for the female your valuation shall be three shekels of silver.

7 'And if *they are* from sixty years old and upward, if it is a male, then your valuation shall be fifteen shekels, and for the female ten shekels.

8 aLev. 5:11; 14:21-24

8 'But if he is poorer than your valuation, then he shall be placed before the priest, and the priest shall value him; aaccording to the means of the one who vowed, the priest shall value him.

9 'Now if it is an animal of the kind which men can present as an offering to the LORD, any such that one gives to the LORD shall be holy.

10 aLev. 27:33

10 'aHe shall not replace it or exchange it, a good for a bad, or a bad for a good; or if he does exchange animal for animal, then both it and its substitute shall become holy.

11 'If, however, it is any unclean animal of the kind which men do not present as an offering to the LORD, then he shall place the animal before the priest.

12 'And the priest shall value it as either good or bad; as you, the priest, value it, so it shall be.

★13

13 'But if he should ever *wish to* redeem it, then he shall add one-fifth of it to your valuation.

14 'Now if a man consecrates his house as holy to the LORD, then the priest shall value it as either good or bad; as the priest values it, so it shall stand.

★15

15 'Yet if the one who consecrates it should *wish to* redeem his house, then he shall add one-fifth of your valuation price to it, so that it may be his.

★16-25

16 'Again, if a man consecrates to the LORD part of the fields of his own property, then your valuation shall be proportionate to the seed needed for it: a homer of barley seed at fifty shekels of silver.

17 'If he consecrates his field as of the year of jubilee, according to your valuation it shall stand.

18 'If he consecrates his field after the jubilee, however, then the priest shall calculate the price for him proportionate to the years that are left until the year of jubilee; and it shall be deducted from your valuation.

19 'And if the one who consecrates it should ever wish to redeem the field, then he shall add one-fifth of your valuation price to it, so that it may pass to him.

20 'Yet if he will not redeem the field, but has sold the field to another man, it may no longer be redeemed;

21 aNum. 18:14; Ezek. 44:29

21 and when it reverts in the jubilee, the field shall be holy to the LORD, like a field set apart; ait shall be for the priest as his property.

22 'Or if he consecrates to the LORD a field which he has bought,

---

27:3-7 The estimation of the worth of a man or woman dedicated to the Lord was evidently based on his or her worth as a worker for a given number of years.

27:13 Unclean animals could be redeemed (and thus kept by the owner) if the value plus 20% was paid.

27:15 Houses also could be given to the Lord, yet retained, by giving the equivalent value

plus 20%.

27:16-25 Redemption of a field was more complicated. The owner could redeem it by adding 20% to its value in relation to the approaching year of jubilee. If he failed to redeem it or sold it surreptitiously after having devoted it to the Lord, it became the property of the priests at the year of jubilee.

which is not a part of the field of his own property,

23 then the priest shall calculate for him the amount of your valuation up to the year of jubilee; and he shall on that day give your valuation as holy to the LORD.

24 'In the year of jubilee the field shall return to the one from whom he bought it, to whom the possession of the land belongs.

25 'Every valuation of yours, moreover, shall be after ªthe shekel of the sanctuary. The shekel shall be twenty gerahs.

26 'ªHowever, a first-born among animals, which as a first-born belongs to the LORD, no man may consecrate it; whether ox or sheep, it is the LORD's.

27 'But if *it is* among the unclean animals, then he shall redeem it according to your valuation, and add to it one-fifth of it; and if it is not redeemed, then it shall be sold according to your valuation.

28 'Nevertheless, ªanything which a man sets apart to the LORD out of all that he has, of man or animal or of the fields of his own property, shall not be sold or redeemed. Anything devoted to destruction is most holy to the LORD.

29 'No one who may have been set apart among men shall be ransomed; he shall surely be put to death.

30 'Thus ªall the tithe of the land, of the seed of the land or of the fruit of the tree, is the LORD's; it is holy to the LORD.

31 'If, therefore, a man wishes to redeem part of his tithe, he shall add to it one-fifth of it.

32 'And for every tenth part of herd or flock, whatever ªpasses under the rod, the tenth one shall be holy to the LORD.

33 'ªHe is not to be concerned whether *it is* good or bad, nor shall he exchange it; or if he does exchange it, then both it and its substitute shall become holy. It shall not be redeemed.' "

34 ªThese are the commandments which the LORD commanded Moses for the sons of Israel at Mount Sinai.

---

25 ªEx. 30:13; Lev. 27:3; Num. 3:47, 18:16

★26-27

26 ªEx. 13:2

★28-29

28 ªNum. 18:14; Josh. 6:17-19

★30-33

30 ªGen. 28:22; 2 Chr. 31:5; Neh. 13:12

32 ªJer. 33:13; Ezek. 20:37

33 ªLev. 27:10

34 ªLev. 26:46; Deut. 4:5

27:26-27 The *first-born* among animals already belonged to the Lord, and so could not be dedicated (Exod. 13:2, 12).

27:28-29 In certain instances, a person could be placed under a ban, in which case he was to be put to death (an example is found in Josh. 7). No redemption was possible in such cases.

27:30-33 One-tenth of the increase of the land, trees, herds, and flocks had to be given to the Lord as His tithe. Part of the tithe could be substituted for with money (plus the usual 20% additional), except in the case of animals. For a discussion of the various tithes see notes on Mal. 3:8, and Gen. 14:20; 28:22. *passes under the rod.* Refers to the custom of making the animals pass by in single file and marking each tenth one with a rod dipped in a colored substance.

INTRODUCTION TO
THE BOOK OF NUMBERS

AUTHOR: Moses   DATE: 1450-1410 B.C.

Title *Appropriately, the Hebrew title of the book, taken from the first verse, means "in the wilderness of," since most of the book records the history of the Israelites in their forty years of wandering in the wilderness. The Septuagint, the Greek translation of the Old Testament, entitles the book Arithmoi (Numbers) because of the prominence of census figures (chaps. 1-3, 26).*

Historical Setting *The account covers the period between Israel's departure from Egypt and her arrival in Canaan. Exactly one year after they fled from Egypt, the Israelites were gathered at Mt. Sinai to receive instructions concerning the Law and the tabernacle (as recorded in the book of Leviticus). Numbers continues the historical narrative one month after the close of the last chapter of Exodus (cf. Exod. 40:2 and Num. 1:1). The book covers the winding 39 years' journey from Sinai to Kadesh-barnea, through various places in the wilderness, and finally to the plains of Moab across the Jordan River from Jericho.*

Theme *The principal lesson of Numbers is that God's people must walk by faith, trusting His promises, if they are to move forward. In reinforcing this theme, the book recounts the unbelief and discontent of the people in general (11:1) and of Miriam and Aaron (12:1), the refusal at Kadesh-barnea to enter the promised land (14:2), Moses' own failure (20:12), and the idolatrous worship (25:3). Yet, in spite of repeated failure, the Israelites' covenant-keeping God miraculously supported them during those years of rebellion and wandering and finally brought them to the promised land.*
The New Testament uses several of the events in Numbers to remind believers of the seriousness of sin (compare John 3:14 and Num. 21:9; 1 Cor. 10:5-11 and Num. 14:29-35, 16:41-50, 20:1-13; 2 Pet. 2:15-16, Rev. 2:14 and Num. 22-24; Jude 11 and Num. 16, 27:3). The lessons should not be lost on us.

OUTLINE OF NUMBERS

I. **Israel Preparing at Sinai, 1:1-10:10**
   A. The Census of the People, 1:1-4:49
      1. The population of the tribes, 1:1-54
      2. The position of the tribes in camp and on march, 2:1-34
      3. The place of the Levites, 3:1-4:49
   B. The Sanctification of the People, 5:1-10:10
      1. By separation from defiling things, 5:1-31
      2. By taking a Nazirite vow, 6:1-27
      3. By the offerings of the princes, 7:1-89
      4. By the setting apart of the Levites, 8:1-26
      5. By observing the first annual Passover, 9:1-14
      6. By being led by God, 9:15-10:10
II. **Israel Marching to Kadesh-barnea, 10:11-12:16**
   A. The March Begun, 10:11-36
   B. The Murmurings Begun, 11:1-12:16
      1. The murmuring of the people (the 70 elders and the quails), 11:1-35
      2. The murmuring of Miriam and Aaron (the leprosy of Miriam), 12:1-16
III. **Israel at Kadesh-barnea, 13:1-20:13**
   A. The Defiance of God, 13:1-14:45
      1. The reconnaissance and report of the spies, 13:1-33

   2. The reaction and judgment of the people, 14:1-45
   B. The Discipline from God, 15:1-20:13
      1. Miscellaneous laws concerning offerings, Sabbath-breaking, and garment fringes, 15:1-41
      2. The rebellion of Korah, 16:1-50
      3. Validation of the Aaronic priesthood: Aaron's rod that budded, 17:1-13
      4. The duties and support of the Levites, 18:1-32
      5. The red heifer sacrifice, 19:1-22
      6. The sin of Moses, 20:1-13
IV. **Israel Marching to Moab, 20:14-21:35**
   A. The Defiance of Edom, 20:14-22
   B. The Death of Aaron, 20:23-29
   C. The Defeat of Arad, 21:1-3
   D. The Discipline of Israel: the Bronze Serpent, 21:4-9
   E. The Defeat of Sihon and Og, 21:10-35
V. **Israel on the Plains of Moab, 22:1-36:13**
   A. Balak Propositions Balaam to Curse Israel, 22:1-41
   B. Balaam Blesses Israel, 23:1-24:25
   C. Israel Worships Baal of Peor, 25:1-18
   D. The New Generation Numbered, 26:1-65
   E. The People Instructed, 27:1-30:16
      1. The laws of inheritance, 27:1-11

THE BOOK OF NUMBERS

I ISRAEL PREPARING AT SINAI, 1:1-10:10

A The Census of the People, 1:1-4:49

1 The population of the tribes, 1:1-54

★ 1-2
1 Then the LORD spoke to Moses in the wilderness of Sinai, in the tent of meeting, on ᵃthe first of the second month, in the second year after they had come out of the land of Egypt, saying,

2 "ᵃTake a census of all the congregation of the sons of Israel, by their families, by their fathers' households, according to the number of names, every male, head by head

★ 3 **3** from ᵃtwenty years old and upward, whoever *is able to* go out to war in Israel, you and Aaron shall number them by their armies.

4 "With you, moreover, there shall be a man of each tribe, ᵃeach one head of his father's household.

5 "These then are the names of the men who shall stand with you: ᵃof Reuben, Elizur the son of Shedeur;

6 of Simeon, Shelumiel the son of Zurishaddai;

7 of Judah, ᵃNahshon the son of Amminadab;

8 of Issachar, Nethanel the son of Zuar;

9 of Zebulun, Eliab the son of Helon;

10 of the sons of Joseph: of E-phraim, Elishama the son of Ammihud; of Manasseh, Gamaliel the son of Pedahzur;

11 of Benjamin, Abidan the son of Gideoni;

12 of Dan, Ahiezer the son of Ammishaddai;

13 of Asher, Pagiel the son of Ochran;

14 of Gad, Eliasaph the son of ᵃDeuel;

15 of Naphtali, Ahira the son of Enan.

16 "These are they who were ᵃcalled of the congregation, the leaders of their fathers' tribes; they were the ᵇheads of divisions of Israel."

17 So Moses and Aaron took these men who had been designated by name,

18 and they assembled all the congregation together on the ᵃfirst of the second month. Then they registered by ᵇancestry in their families, by their fathers' households, according to the number of names, from twenty years old and upward, head by head,

19 just as ᵃthe LORD had commanded Moses. So he numbered them in the wilderness of Sinai.

20 ᵃNow the sons of Reuben, Israel's first-born, their genealogical registration by their families, by their fathers' households, according to the number of names, head by head, every male from twenty years old and upward,

---

Marginal references:
1 ᵃEx. 40:2, 17
2 ᵃEx. 12:37; 38:25, 26; Num. 26:2
3 ᵃEx. 30:14; 38:26
4 ᵃEx. 18:21, 25; Num. 1:16; Deut. 1:15
5 ᵃGen. 24:32; Ex. 1:2; Deut. 33:6; Rev. 7:5
7 ᵃRuth 4:20; 1 Chr. 2:10; Luke 3:32
14 ᵃNum. 2:14
16 ᵃEx. 18:21; Num. 7:2; 16:2; 26:9 ᵇEx. 18:25
18 ᵃNum. 1:1 ᵇEzra 2:59; Heb. 7:3
19 ᵃ2 Sam. 24:1
20 ᵃNum. 26:5-7

1:1-2 *the first of the second month.* This census was taken one month after the tabernacle was set up (cf. Exod. 40:2, 17).

1:3 *able to go out to war.* A phrase that occurs 14 times in the book. The census obviously had a military purpose.

whoever *was able to* go out to war,

21 their numbered men, of the tribe of Reuben, *were* 46,500.

22 [a]Of the sons of Simeon, their genealogical registration by their families, by their fathers' households, their numbered men, according to the number of names, head by head, every male from twenty years old and upward, [b]whoever *was able to* go out to war,

23 their numbered men, of the tribe of Simeon, *were* 59,300.

24 [a]Of the sons of Gad, their genealogical registration by their families, by their fathers' households, according to the number of names, from twenty years old and upward, whoever *was able to* go out to war,

25 their numbered men, of the tribe of Gad, *were* 45,650.

26 [a]Of the sons of Judah, their genealogical registration by their families, by their fathers' households, according to the number of names, from twenty years old and upward, whoever *was able to* go out to war,

27 their numbered men, of the tribe of Judah, *were* 74,600.

28 [a]Of the sons of Issachar, their genealogical registration by their families, by their fathers' households, according to the number of names, from twenty years old and upward, whoever *was able to* go out to war,

29 their numbered men, of the tribe of Issachar, *were* 54,400.

30 [a]Of the sons of Zebulun, their genealogical registration by their families, by their fathers' households, according to the number of names, from twenty years old and upward, whoever *was able to* go out to war,

31 their numbered men, of the tribe of Zebulun, *were* 57,400.

32 [a]Of the sons of Joseph, *namely*, of the sons of Ephraim, their genealogical registration by their families, by their fathers' households, according to the number of names, from twenty years old and upward, whoever *was able to* go out to war,

33 their numbered men, of the tribe of Ephraim, *were* 40,500.

34 [a]Of the sons of Manasseh, their genealogical registration by their families, by their fathers' households, according to the number of names, from twenty years old and upward, whoever *was able to* go out to war,

35 their numbered men, of the tribe of Manasseh, *were* 32,200.

36 [a]Of the sons of Benjamin, their genealogical registration by their families, by their fathers' households, according to the number of names, from twenty years old and upward, whoever *was able to* go out to war,

37 their numbered men, of the tribe of Benjamin, *were* 35,400.

38 [a]Of the sons of Dan, their genealogical registration by their families, by their fathers' households, according to the number of names, from twenty years old and upward, whoever *was able to* go out to war,

39 their numbered men, of the tribe of Dan, *were* 62,700.

40 [a]Of the sons of Asher, their genealogical registration by their families, by their fathers' households, according to the number of names, from twenty years old and upward, whoever *was able to* go out to war,

41 their numbered men, of the tribe of Asher, *were* 41,500.

42 [a]Of the sons of Naphtali, their genealogical registration by their families, by their fathers' households, according to the number of names, from twenty years old and upward, whoever *was able to* go out to war,

43 their numbered men, of the tribe of Naphtali, *were* 53,400.

44 These are the ones who were numbered, whom Moses and Aaron numbered, with the leaders of Israel, twelve men, each of whom was of his father's household.

45 So all the numbered men of the sons of Israel by their fathers' households, from twenty

---

22 [a]Num. 26:12-14; [b]Ps. 144:1

24 [a]Gen. 30:11; Num. 26:15-18; Josh. 4:12; Jer. 49:1

26 [a]Gen. 29:35; Num. 26:19-22; 2 Sam. 24:9; Ps. 78:68; Matt. 1:2

28 [a]Num. 26:23-25

30 [a]Num. 26:26, 27

32 [a]Num. 26:35-37; Deut. 33:13-17; Jer. 7:15; Obad. 19

34 [a]Num. 26:28-34

36 [a]Gen. 49:27; Num. 26:38-41; 2 Chr. 17:17; Rev. 7:8

38 [a]Gen. 30:6; 46:23; Num. 2:25; 26:42, 43

40 [a]Num. 26:44-47

42 [a]Num. 26:48-50

years old and upward, whoever *was able to* go out to war in Israel,

★46 *a*Ex. 12:37; 38:26; Num. 2:32; 26:51

46 even all the numbered men were *a*603,550.

★47 *a*Num. 2:33; 3:14-39; 4:49; 26:57-64

47 *a*The Levites, however, were not numbered among them by their fathers' tribe.

48 For the Lord had spoken to Moses, saying,

49 *a*Num. 26:62

49 "Only the tribe of Levi *a*you shall not number, nor shall you take their census among the sons of Israel.

50 *a*Ex. 38:21; Num. 3:6-8, 25-37; 4:15, 25-27, 31, 32

50 "But you shall *a*appoint the Levites over the tabernacle of the testimony, and over all its furnishings and over all that belongs to it. They shall carry the tabernacle and all its furnishings, and they shall take care of it; they shall also camp around the tabernacle.

51 *a*Num. 4:1-33 *b*Num. 3:10, 38; 4:15, 19, 20

51 "*a*So when the tabernacle is to set out, the Levites shall take it down; and when the tabernacle encamps, the Levites shall set it up. But *b*the layman who comes near shall be put to death.

52 *a*Num. 2:2, 34

52 "*a*And the sons of Israel shall camp, each man by his own camp, and each man by his own standard, according to their armies.

★53 *a*Num. 3:23, 29, 35, 38 *b*Lev. 10:6; Num. 16:46; 18:5 *c*Num. 8:24; 18:2-4; 1 Chr. 23:32

53 "*a*But the Levites shall camp around the tabernacle of the testimony, that there may be *b*no wrath on the congregation of the sons of Israel. *c*So the Levites shall keep charge of the tabernacle of the testimony."

54 Thus the sons of Israel did; according to all which the Lord had commanded Moses, so they did.

2   The position of the tribes in camp and on march, 2:1-34

2 *a*Num. 1:52; 24:2

2 Now the Lord spoke to Moses and to Aaron, saying, **2** "*a*The sons of Israel shall camp, each by his own standard, with the banners of their fathers' households; they shall camp around the tent of meeting at a distance.

3 *a*Num. 1:7; 10:14; Ruth 4:20; 1 Chr. 2:10; Luke 3:32, 33

3 "Now those who camp on the east side toward the sunrise *shall be* of the standard of the camp of Judah, by their armies, and the leader of the sons of Judah: *a*Nahshon the son of Amminadab,

4 and his army, even their numbered men, 74,600.

5 *a*Num. 1:8; 7:18, 23

5 "And those who camp next to him *shall be* the tribe of Issachar, and the leader of the sons of Issachar: *a*Nethanel the son of Zuar,

6 and his army, even their numbered men, 54,400.

7 *a*Num. 1:9

7 "Then *comes* the tribe of Zebulun, and the leader of the sons of Zebulun: *a*Eliab the son of Helon,

8 and his army, even his numbered men, 57,400.

9 *a*Num. 10:14

9 "The total of the numbered men of the camp of Judah: 186,400, by their armies. *a*They shall set out first.

10 *a*Num. 1:5

10 "On the south side *shall be* the standard of the camp of Reuben by their armies, and the leader of the sons of Reuben: *a*Elizur the son of Shedeur,

11 and his army, even their numbered men, 46,500.

12 *a*Num. 1:6

12 "And those who camp next to him *shall be* the tribe of Simeon, and the leader of the sons of Simeon: *a*Shelumiel the son of Zurishaddai,

13 and his army, even their numbered men, 59,300.

14 *a*Num. 1:14; 7:42

14 "Then *comes* the tribe of Gad, and the leader of the sons of Gad: *a*Eliasaph the son of Deuel,

15 and his army, even their numbered men, 45,650.

16 *a*Num. 10:18

16 "The total of the numbered men of the camp of Reuben:

1:46 This number, 603,550, was the number of those qualified for the army, making the total population of the nation somewhere between 2 and 3 million.
1:47 The nonmilitary tribe of Levi had a separate census and did not receive a tribal allotment of land.
1:53 The Levites, charged with tending the tabernacle, pitched their tents around it to protect it from any desecration (3:10, 38).

151,450 by their armies. And [a]they shall set out second.

★17 [a]Num. 1:53

17 "[a]Then the tent of meeting shall set out with the camp of the Levites in the midst of the camps; just as they camp, so they shall set out, every man in his place, by their standards.

18 [a]Gen. 48:14-20; Jer. 31:9, 18- **20** [b]Num. 1:10

18 "On the west side shall be the standard of the camp of [a]E-phraim by their armies, and the leader of the sons of Ephraim shall be [b]Elishama the son of Am-mihud,

19 and his army, even their numbered men, 40,500.

20 [a]Num. 1:10

20 "And next to him shall be the tribe of Manasseh, and the leader of the sons of Manasseh: [a]Gamaliel the son of Pedahzur,

21 and his army, even their numbered men, 32,200.

22 [a]Ps. 68:27 [b]Num. 1:11

22 "Then comes the tribe of [a]Benjamin, and the leader of the sons of Benjamin: [b]Abidan the son of Gideoni,

23 and his army, even their numbered men, 35,400.

24 [a]Num. 10:22

24 "The total of the numbered men of the camp of Ephraim: 108,100, by their armies. And [a]they shall set out third.

25 [a]Num. 1:12

25 "On the north side shall be the standard of the camp of Dan by their armies, and the leader of the sons of Dan: [a]Ahiezer the son of Ammishaddai,

26 and his army, even their numbered men, 62,700.

27 [a]Num. 1:13

27 "And those who camp next to him shall be the tribe of Asher, and the leader of the sons of Asher: [a]Pagiel the son of Ochran,

28 and his army, even their numbered men, 41,500.

29 [a]Gen. 30:8 [b]Num. 1:15

29 "Then comes the tribe of [a]Naphtali, and the leader of the sons of Naphtali: [b]Ahira the son of Enan,

30 and his army, even their numbered men, 53,400.

31 "The total of the numbered men of the camp of Dan, was 157,600. [a]They shall set out last by their standards."

31 [a]Num. 10:25

32 These are the numbered men of the sons of Israel by their fathers' households; the total of the numbered men of the camps by their armies, [a]603,550.

32 [a]Ex. 38:26; Num. 1:46

33 [a]The Levites, however, were not numbered among the sons of Israel, just as the LORD had commanded Moses.

33 [a]Num. 1:47; 26:57-62

34 Thus the sons of Israel did; according to all that the LORD commanded Moses, so they camped by their standards, and so they set out, every one by his family, according to his father's household.

★34

3 The place of the Levites, 3:1-4:49

3 [a]Now these are the records of the generations of Aaron and Moses at the time when the LORD spoke with Moses on Mount Sinai.

1 [a]Ex. 6:20-27

2 [a]These then are the names of the sons of Aaron: Nadab the first-born, and Abihu, Eleazar and Ithamar.

2 [a]Ex. 6:23; Num. 26:60

3 These are the names of the sons of Aaron, the [a]anointed priests, whom he ordained to serve as priests.

3 [a]Ex. 28:41

4 [a]But Nadab and Abihu died before the LORD when they offered strange fire before the LORD in the wilderness of Sinai; and they had no children. So Eleazar and Ithamar served as priests in the lifetime of their father Aaron.

★ 4 [a]Lev. 10:1, 2; Num. 26:61

5 Then the LORD spoke to Moses, saying,

6 "[a]Bring the tribe of Levi near and set them before Aaron the priest, that they may serve him.

6 [a]Num. 8:6-22; 18:1-7; Deut. 10:8

2:17 Half the tribes (those on the east—Judah, Issachar, Zebulun—and on the south—Reuben, Simeon, Gad) marched ahead of the tabernacle and the Levites, and half (those on the west—Ephraim, Manasseh, Benjamin—and north—Dan, Asher, Naphtali) marched behind.

2:34 The obedience of the people at this point is in marked contrast to subsequent events recorded in the book.

3:4 Nadab and Abihu died. See Lev. 10:1-2.

7 aNum. 1:50
9 aNum. 18:6
10 aEx. 29:9 bNum. 1:51
★12 aNum. 3:45; 8:14 bEx. 13:2
★13 aEx. 13:2; Lev. 27:26; Neh. 10:36
14 aEx. 19:1
15 aNum. 1:47
17 aEx. 6:16-22
18 aEx. 6:17

7 "And they shall perform the duties for him and for the whole congregation before the tent of meeting, to do the ªservice of the tabernacle.

8 "They shall also keep all the furnishings of the tent of meeting, along with the duties of the sons of Israel, to do the service of the tabernacle.

9 "You shall thus ªgive the Levites to Aaron and to his sons; they are wholly given to him from among the sons of Israel.

10 "So you shall appoint Aaron and his sons that ªthey may keep their priesthood, but ᵇthe layman who comes near shall be put to death."

11 Again the LORD spoke to Moses, saying,

12 "Now, behold, I ªhave taken the Levites from among the sons of Israel instead of every ᵇfirst-born, the first issue of the womb among the sons of Israel. So the Levites shall be Mine.

13 "For ªall the first-born are Mine; on the day that I struck down all the first-born in the land of Egypt, I sanctified to Myself all the first-born in Israel, from man to beast. They shall be Mine; I am the LORD."

14 Then the LORD spoke to Moses ªin the wilderness of Sinai, saying,

15 "ªNumber the sons of Levi by their fathers' households, by their families; every male from a month old and upward you shall number."

16 So Moses numbered them according to the word of the LORD, just as he had been commanded.

17 ªThese then are the sons of Levi by their names: Gershon and Kohath and Merari.

18 And these are the names of the ªsons of Gershon by their families: Libni and Shimei;

19 and the sons of Kohath by their families: Amram and Izhar, Hebron and Uzziel;

20 and the sons of Merari by their families: Mahli and Mushi. These are the families of the Levites according to their fathers' households.

21 Of Gershon *was* the family of the Libnites and the family of the Shimeites; these *were* the families of the Gershonites.

22 Their numbered men, in the numbering of every male from a month old and upward, *even* their numbered men *were* 7,500.

23 The families of the Gershonites were to camp behind the tabernacle westward,

24 and the leader of the fathers' households of the Gershonites *was* Eliasaph the son of Lael.

25 Now ªthe duties of the sons of Gershon in the tent of meeting *involved* the tabernacle and ᵇthe tent, its covering, and ᶜthe screen for the doorway of the tent of meeting,

26 and ªthe hangings of the court, and ᵇthe screen for the doorway of the court, which is around the tabernacle and the altar, and its cords, according to all the service concerning them.

27 And of Kohath *was* the family of the Amramites and the family of the Izharites and the family of the Hebronites and the family of the Uzzielites; these were the families of the Kohathites.

28 In the numbering of every male from a month old and upward, *there were* 8,600, performing the duties of the sanctuary.

29 The families of the sons of Kohath were to camp on the southward side of the tabernacle,

30 and the leader of the fathers' households of the Kohathite families was Elizaphan the son of Uzziel.

25 aNum. 4:24-26 bEx. 26:1, 7, 14 cEx. 26:36
26 aEx. 27:9, 12, 14, 15 bEx. 27:16
★28

3:12 *Levites ....instead of every first-born.* The tribe of Levi was used in the service of God in place of the firstborn from among all the tribes. *instead of* indicates substitution, as in Gen. 22:13 (see also note on Matt. 20:28).

3:13 See Exod. 13:2.

3:28 The addition of one Hebrew letter would change 8,600 to 8,300 and bring the figures in verses 22, 28, and 34 into agreement with the total in verse 39.

31 *a*Num.
4:15 *b*Ex.
25:10-22
*c*Ex. 25:23-
28 *d*Ex.
25:31-40
*e*Ex. 27:1, 2;
30:1-5

31 Now *a*their duties *involved* *b*the ark, *c*the table, *d*the lampstand, *e*the altars, and the utensils of the sanctuary with which they minister, and the screen, and all the service concerning them;

32 and Eleazar the son of Aaron the priest *was* the chief of the leaders of Levi, *and had* the oversight of those who perform the duties of the sanctuary.

33 Of Merari *was* the family of the Mahlites and the family of the Mushites; these *were* the families of Merari.

34 Their numbered men in the numbering of every male from a month old and upward, *were* 6,200.

35 *a*Num.
1:53; 2:25

35 And the leader of the fathers' households of the families of Merari *was* Zuriel the son of Abihail. They *were* to *a*camp on the northward side of the tabernacle.

36 Now the appointed duties of the sons of Merari *involved* the frames of the tabernacle, its bars, its pillars, its sockets, all its equipment, and the service concerning them,

37 and the pillars around the court with their sockets and their pegs and their cords.

38 *a*Num.
1:53; 2:3
*b*Num. 1:51

38 Now those who were to *a*camp before the tabernacle eastward, before the tent of meeting toward the sunrise, are Moses and Aaron and his sons, performing the duties of the sanctuary for the obligation of the sons of Israel; but *b*the layman coming near was to be put to death.

39 *a*Num.
3:43; 4:48;
26:62

39 All the numbered men of the Levites, whom Moses and Aaron numbered at the command of the Lord by their families, every male from a month old and upward, *were* *a*22,000.

40 *a*Num.
3:15

40 Then the Lord said to Moses, "*a*Number every first-born male of the sons of Israel from a month old and upward, and make a list of their names.

41 "And you *a*shall take the Levites for Me; I am the Lord, instead of all the first-born among the sons of Israel, and the cattle of the Levites instead of all the first-born among the cattle of the sons of Israel."

41 *a*Num.
3:12, 45

42 So Moses numbered all the first-born among the sons of Israel, just as the Lord had commanded him;

43 and all the first-born males by the number of names from a month old and upward, for their numbered men were *a*22,273.

★43 *a*Num.
3:39

44 Then the Lord spoke to Moses, saying,

45 "*a*Take the Levites instead of all the first-born among the sons of Israel and the cattle of the Levites. And the Levites shall be Mine; I am the Lord.

45 *a*Num.
3:12

46 "*a*And for the ransom of the 273 of the first-born of the sons of Israel who are in excess beyond the Levites,

46 *a*Ex.
13:13, 15;
Num. 18:15,
16

47 you shall take *a*five shekels apiece, per head; you shall take *them* in *b*terms of the shekel of the sanctuary (*c*the shekel is twenty gerahs),

★47 *a*Lev.
27:6; Num.
18:16 *b*Ex.
30:13 *c*Lev.
27:25; Ezek.
45:12

48 and give the money, the ransom of those who are in excess among them, to Aaron and to his sons."

49 So Moses took the ransom money from those who were in excess, beyond those ransomed by the Levites;

50 from the first-born of the sons of Israel he took the money in terms of the shekel of the sanctuary, 1,365.

51 Then Moses gave the ransom money to Aaron and to his sons, at the command of the Lord, just as the Lord had commanded Moses.

3:43 The number of *first-born males* (22,273) seems small in comparison with the total number of men over age 20 (603,550; cf. 1:46). The figure likely includes only those born since the Exodus, when the requirement to sanctify the firstborn was given (cf. Exod. 13:1-2).

3:47 The difference between the 22,273 firstborn (v. 43) and the 22,000 Levites (v. 39) was to be compensated for by paying *five shekels* for each of the 273 firstborn not matched by a Levite.

4 Then the LORD spoke to Moses and to Aaron, saying,

2 "Take a census of the descendants of Kohath from among the sons of Levi, by their families, by their fathers' households,

3 from ^athirty years and upward, even to fifty years old, all who enter the service to do the work in the tent of meeting.

4 "This is the work of the descendants of Kohath in the tent of meeting, *concerning* the most holy things.

5 "When the camp sets out, Aaron and his sons shall go in and they shall take down ^athe veil of the screen and cover the ^bark of the testimony with it;

6 and they shall lay a ^acovering of porpoise skin on it, and shall spread over *it* a cloth of pure blue, and shall insert its poles.

7 "Over the table of the bread of the Presence they shall also spread a cloth of blue and put on it the dishes and the pans and the sacrificial bowls and the jars for the libation, and ^athe continual bread shall be on it.

8 "And they shall spread over them a cloth of scarlet *material*, and cover the same with a covering of porpoise skin, and they shall insert its poles.

9 "Then they shall take a blue cloth and cover the ^alampstand for the light, ^balong with its lamps and its snuffers, and its trays and all its oil vessels, by which they serve it;

10 and they shall put it and all its utensils in a covering of porpoise skin, and shall put it on the carrying bars.

11 "And over the golden altar they shall spread a blue cloth and cover it with a covering of por-

poise skin, and shall insert its poles;

12 and they shall take all the utensils of service, with which they serve in the sanctuary, and put them in a blue cloth and cover them with a covering of porpoise skin, and put them on the carrying bars.

13 "Then they shall take away the ashes from the ^aaltar, and spread a purple cloth over it.

14 "They shall also put on it all its utensils by which they serve in connection with it: the firepans, the forks and shovels and the basins, all the utensils of the altar; and they shall spread a cover of porpoise skin over it and insert its poles.

15 "And when Aaron and his sons have finished covering the holy *objects* and all the furnishings of the sanctuary, when the camp is to set out, after that the sons of Kohath shall come to carry *them,* so that they may not touch the holy *objects* ^aand die. These are the things in the tent of meeting which the sons of Kohath are to carry.

16 "And the responsibility of Eleazar the son of Aaron the priest is ^athe oil for the light and the ^bfragrant incense and ^cthe continual grain offering and ^dthe anointing oil—the responsibility of all the tabernacle and of all that is in it, with the sanctuary and its furnishings."

17 Then the LORD spoke to Moses and to Aaron, saying,

18 "Do not let the tribe of the families of the Kohathites be cut off from among the Levites.

19 "But do this to them that they may live and ^anot die when

Margin references

★ 3 ^aNum. 4:23, 30, 35; 8:24; 1 Chr. 23:3, 24, 27; Ezra 3:8

★ 5 ^aEx. 40:5; Lev. 16:2; 2 Chr. 3:14; Matt. 27:51; Heb. 9:3 ^bEx. 25:10-16

★6 ^aNum. 4:25

7 ^aEx. 25:30; Lev. 24:5-9

9 ^aEx. 25:31 ^bEx. 25:37, 38

13 ^aEx. 27:1-8

15 ^aNum. 1:51; 4:19, 20; 2 Sam. 6:6, 7

★16 ^aLev. 24:1-3 ^bEx. 30:34-38 ^cLev. 6:20 ^dEx. 30:22-33

19 ^aNum. 4:15

4:3 *thirty years.* In 8:24, the age for entering service is given as 25. Possibly there was a five-year apprenticeship before a Levite was fully and officially prepared. *the service.* From the same Hebrew word used of military service in 1:3, suggesting that the work of the Levites for the Lord was as carefully organized as a militia.

4:5 *the veil of the screen.* I.e., the veil that sepa-

rated the Holy Place from the Holy of Holies (see note on Exod. 26:31).

4:6 The *blue* covering over the Ark was not covered with anything else (as were the other articles in the tabernacle), thus making it clearly visible to all during marches.

4:16 *Eleazar* (one of Aaron's sons, Lev. 10:6) had charge of the oil (Exod. 30:23-25).

they approach the most holy *objects:* Aaron and his sons shall go in and assign each of them to his work and to his load;

20 but ªthey shall not go in to see the holy *objects* even for a moment, lest they die."

21 Then the LORD spoke to Moses, saying,

22 "Take a census of the sons of Gershon also, by their fathers' households, by their families;

23 from ªthirty years and upward to fifty years old, you shall number them; all who enter to perform the service to do the work in the tent of meeting.

24 "This is the service of the families of the Gershonites, in serving and in carrying:

25 they shall carry ªthe curtains of the tabernacle and the tent of meeting *with* its covering and *ᵇ*the covering of porpoise skin that is on top of it, and the screen for the doorway of the tent of meeting,

26 and ªthe hangings of the court, and the screen for the doorway of the gate of the court which is around the tabernacle and the altar, and their cords and all the equipment for their service; and all that is to be done, they shall perform.

27 "All the service of the sons of the Gershonites, in all their loads and in all their work, shall be *performed* at the command of Aaron and his sons; and you shall assign to them as a duty all their loads.

28 "This is the service of the families of the sons of the Gershonites in the tent of meeting, and their duties *shall be* under the direction of Ithamar the son of Aaron the priest.

29 "*As for* the sons of Merari, you shall number them by their families, by their fathers' households;

30 from ªthirty years and upward even to fifty years old, you shall number them, everyone who enters the service to do the work of the tent of meeting.

31 "Now this is the duty of their loads, for all their service in

the tent of meeting: the boards of the tabernacle and its bars and its pillars and its sockets,

32 and the pillars around the court and their sockets and their pegs and their cords, with all their equipment and with all their service; and you shall assign *each man* by name the items he is to carry.

33 "This is the service of the families of the sons of Merari, according to all their service in the tent of meeting, under the direction of Ithamar the son of Aaron the priest."

34 So Moses and Aaron and the leaders of the congregation numbered the sons of the Kohathites by their families, and by their fathers' households,

35 from ªthirty years and upward even to fifty years old, everyone who entered the service for work in the tent of meeting.

36 And their numbered men by their families were 2,750.

37 These are the numbered men of the Kohathite families, everyone who was serving in the tent of meeting, whom Moses and Aaron numbered according to the commandment of the LORD through Moses.

38 And the numbered men of the sons of Gershon by their families, and by their fathers' households,

39 from thirty years and upward even to fifty years old, everyone who entered the service for work in the tent of meeting.

40 And their numbered men by their families, by their fathers' households, were 2,630.

41 These are the numbered men of the families of the sons of Gershon, everyone who was serving in the tent of meeting, whom Moses and Aaron numbered according to the commandment of the LORD.

42 And the numbered men of the families of the sons of Merari by their families, by their fathers' households,

43 from ªthirty years and upward even to fifty years old,

---

20 ªEx. 19:21; 1 Sam. 6:19

23 ªNum. 4:3; 1 Chr. 23:3, 24, 27

25 ªEx. 40:19 ᵇEx. 26:14; Num. 4:6

26 ªEx. 38:9

30 ªNum. 4:3; 8:24-26

35 ª1 Chr. 23:24

43 ªNum. 8:24-26

everyone who entered the service for work in the tent of meeting.

44 And their numbered men by their families were 3,200.

45 These are the numbered men of the families of the sons of Merari, whom Moses and Aaron numbered according to the commandment of the Lord through Moses.

46 All the numbered men of the Levites, whom Moses and Aaron and the leaders of Israel numbered, by their families and by their fathers' households,

47 from thirty years and upward even to fifty years old, everyone who could enter to do the work of service and the work of carrying in the tent of meeting.

48 And their numbered men were ᵃ8,580.

49 According to the commandment of the Lord through Moses, they ᵃwere numbered, everyone by his serving or carrying; thus these were his numbered men, just as the Lord had commanded Moses.

B The Sanctification of the People, 5:1–10:10

1 By separation from defiling things, 5:1–31

5 Then the Lord spoke to Moses, saying,

2 "Command the sons of Israel that they ᵃsend away from the camp every leper and everyone having a ᵇdischarge and everyone who is ᶜunclean because of a *dead* person.

3 "You shall send away both male and female; you shall send them outside the camp so that they will not defile their camp where I dwell ᵃin their midst."

4 And the sons of Israel did so and sent them outside the camp; just as the Lord had spoken to Moses, thus the sons of Israel did.

5 Then the Lord spoke to Moses, saying,

6 "Speak to the sons of Israel, 'ᵃWhen a man or woman commits any of the sins of mankind, acting unfaithfully against the Lord, and that person is guilty,

7 then he shall ᵃconfess his sins which he has committed, and he ᵇshall make restitution in full for his wrong, and add to it one-fifth of it, and give *it* to him whom he has wronged.

8 'But if the man has no relative to whom restitution may be made for the wrong, the restitution which is made for the wrong *must go* to the Lord for the priest, besides the ram of atonement, by which atonement is made for him.

9 'ᵃAlso every contribution pertaining to all the holy *gifts* of the sons of Israel, which they offer to the priest, shall be his.

10 'So every man's holy *gifts* shall be his; whatever any man gives to the priest, it ᵃbecomes his.' "

11 Then the Lord spoke to Moses, saying,

12 "Speak to the sons of Israel, and say to them, 'If any man's wife ᵃgoes astray and is unfaithful to him,

---

Marginal references:

★48 ᵃNum. 3:39

49 ᵃNum. 1:47

★2 ᵃLev. 13:8, 46; Num. 12:10, 14, 15 ᵇLev. 15:2 ᶜLev. 21:1; Num. 9:6-10; 19:11
3 ᵃLev. 26:12; Num. 35:34

★6-8
6 ᵃLev. 5:14-6:7

7 ᵃLev. 5:5; 26:40, 41; Josh. 7:19 ᵇLev. 6:4, 5

9 ᵃLev. 7:32, 34; 10:14, 15

10 ᵃLev. 10:13

★11-31

12 ᵃNum. 5:19-21, 29

4:48 Only 8,580 of the 22,000 Levites (3:39) were eligible for service in the tabernacle.

5:2 Chapters 5 and 6 show the need for the now organized nation to be pure. *leper.* See note on Lev. 13:2. *a discharge.* See note on Lev. 15:25. Regarding defilement because of touching a *dead* body, see 19:11.

5:6-8 See note on Lev. 6:1. If there were no living relative to whom restitution could be made, the compensation was to be paid to the priest, along with a *ram* (see Lev. 5:16). Whatever the priest received in this way was his alone (Num. 5:10).

5:11-31 These verses describe the "law of jeal-ousy," whereby a woman suspected of marital unfaithfulness had to be brought to the priest for trial *before the Lord* (v. 16), who alone could reveal the truth of the matter. The ritual of verse 23 symbolically transferred the written words of the curse to the water. Verse 27 may indicate a miscarriage (*waste away* literally means "fall"; see Job 3:16, where a similar Hebrew word refers to untimely birth). The practice here prescribed, apparently used only in the wilderness, prevented jealousy and suspicion from corrupting family and community life. God must have miraculously controlled the results whenever this test was used.

13 and a man has [a]intercourse with her and it is hidden from the eyes of her husband and she is undetected, although she has defiled herself, and there is no witness against her and she has not been caught in the act,

14 if a spirit of [a]jealousy comes over him and he is jealous of his wife when she has defiled herself, or if a spirit of jealousy comes over him and he is jealous of his wife when she has not defiled herself,

15 the man shall then bring his wife to the priest, and shall bring *as* an offering for her one-tenth of an ephah of barley meal; he shall not pour oil on it, nor put frankincense on it, for it is a grain offering of jealousy, a grain offering of memorial, [a]a reminder of iniquity.

16 Then the priest shall bring her near and have her stand before the LORD,

17 and the priest shall take holy water in an earthenware vessel; and he shall take some of the dust that is on the floor of the tabernacle and put *it* into the water.

18 The priest shall then have the woman stand before the LORD and let *the hair of* the woman's head go loose, and place the grain offering of memorial in her hands, which is the grain offering of jealousy, and in the hand of the priest is to be the water of bitterness that brings a curse.

19 'And the priest shall have her take an oath and shall say to the woman, "If no man has lain with you and if you have not [a]gone astray into uncleanness, *being* under *the authority of* your husband, be immune to this water of bitterness that brings a curse;

20 if you, however, have [a]gone astray, *being* under *the authority of* your husband, and if you have defiled yourself and a man other than your husband has had intercourse with you"

21 (then the priest shall have the woman [a]swear with the oath of the curse, and the priest shall say to the woman), "the LORD make you a curse and an oath among your people by the LORD's making your thigh waste away and your abdomen swell;

22 and this water that brings a curse shall go into your stomach, and make your abdomen swell and your thigh waste away." And the woman [a]shall say, "Amen. Amen."

23 'The priest shall then write these curses on a scroll, and he shall wash them off into the water of bitterness.

24 'Then he shall make the woman drink the water of bitterness that brings a curse, so that the water which brings a curse will go into her and *cause* bitterness.

25 'And the priest shall take the grain offering of jealousy from the woman's hand, and he shall wave the grain offering before the LORD and bring it to the altar;

26 and [a]the priest shall take a handful of the grain offering as its memorial offering and offer *it* up in smoke on the altar, and afterward he shall make the woman drink the water.

27 'When he has made her drink the water, then it shall come about, if she has defiled herself and has been unfaithful to her husband, that the water which brings a curse shall go into her and *cause* bitterness, and her abdomen will swell and her thigh will waste away, and the woman will become [a]a curse among her people.

28 'But if the woman has not defiled herself and is clean, she will then be free and conceive children.

29 'This is the law of jealousy: when a wife, *being* under *the authority of* her husband, [a]goes astray and defiles herself,

30 or when a spirit of jealousy comes over a man and he is jealous of his wife, he shall then make the woman stand before the LORD, and the priest shall apply all this law to her.

Marginal references:

13 [a]Lev. 18:20; 20:10

14 [a]Prov. 6:34; Song 8:6

15 [a]1 Kin. 17:18; Ezek. 29:16

19 [a]Num. 5:12

20 [a]Num. 5:12

21 [a]Josh. 6:26; 1 Sam. 14:24; Neh. 10:29

22 [a]Deut. 27:15

26 [a]Lev. 2:2, 9

27 [a]Jer. 29:18; 42:18; 44:12

29 [a]Num. 5:12

31 aLev.
20:17
31 'Moreover, the man shall be free from guilt, but that woman shall ^abear her guilt.' "

2 By taking a Nazirite vow,
6:1–27

★ 1-8
6 Again the LORD spoke to Moses, saying,

2 aJudg.
13:5; 16:17;
Amos 2:11,
12
2 "Speak to the sons of Israel, and say to them, 'When a man or woman makes a special vow, the vow of ^aa Nazirite, to dedicate himself to the LORD,

3 aLuke
1:15
3 he shall ^aabstain from wine and strong drink; he shall drink no vinegar, whether made from wine or strong drink, neither shall he drink any grape juice, nor eat fresh or dried grapes.

4 'All the days of his separation he shall not eat anything that is produced by the grape vine, from the seeds even to the skin.

5 a1 Sam.
1:11
5 'All the days of his vow of separation ^ano razor shall pass over his head. He shall be holy until the days are fulfilled for which he separated himself to the LORD; he shall let the locks of hair on his head grow long.

6 aLev.
21:1-3; Num.
19:11-22
6 '^aAll the days of his separation to the LORD he shall not go near to a dead person.

7 aNum.
9:6
7 'He ^ashall not make himself unclean for his father or for his mother, for his brother or for his sister, when they die, because his separation to God is on his head.

8 'All the days of his separation he is holy to the LORD.

9 aLev.
14:8, 9
bNum. 6:18
9 'But if a man dies very suddenly beside him and he defiles his dedicated head of hair, then ^ahe shall shave his head on the day when he becomes clean; ^bhe shall shave it on the seventh day.

10 aLev. 5:7;
14:22
10 'Then on the eighth day he shall bring ^atwo turtledoves or two young pigeons to the priest, to the doorway of the tent of meeting.

11 aLev. 5:7
11 'And the priest shall offer ^aone for a sin offering and the other for a burnt offering, and make atonement for him concerning his sin because of the dead person. And that same day he shall consecrate his head,

12 and shall dedicate to the LORD his days as a Nazirite, and shall bring a male lamb a year old for a guilt offering; but the former days shall be void because his separation was defiled.

★13-21
13 aActs
21:26
13 'Now this is the law of the Nazirite ^awhen the days of his separation are fulfilled, he shall bring the offering to the doorway of the tent of meeting.

14 aLev.
14:10; Num.
15:27
14 'And he shall present his offering to the LORD: one male lamb a year old without defect for a burnt offering and one ^aewe-lamb a year old without defect for a sin offering and one ram without defect for a peace offering,

15 aEx. 29:2;
Lev. 2:4
bNum.
15:1-7
15 and a basket of ^aunleavened cakes of fine flour mixed with oil and unleavened wafers spread with oil, along with ^btheir grain offering and their libations.

16 'Then the priest shall present them before the LORD and shall offer his sin offering and his burnt offering.

17 'He shall also offer the ram for a sacrifice of peace offerings to the LORD, together with the basket of unleavened cakes; the priest shall likewise offer its grain offering and its libation.

6:1-8 A Nazirite (from a verb meaning "to separate or abstain") was a layperson of either sex who was bound by a vow of consecration to God's service for a specific period of time or in some cases for life (see note on Lev. 27:2 on vows). He could drink no fruit of the vine (vv. 3–4), could not cut his hair (v. 5), and could not defile himself by going near a dead person (vv. 6–7). These outward signs served as a public testimony of his dedication to God. Examples of Nazirites were Samson, Judg. 13; Samuel, 1 Sam. 1:9-11; John the Baptist, Luke 1:15, 80; and Paul, Acts 18:18.

6:13-21 When the period of a temporary vow terminated, the Nazirite had to offer peace, grain, drink, sin, and burnt offerings and shave his head and burn the hair (see also note on Acts 21:24).

18 aNum.
6:9; Acts
21:23, 24

18 'aThe Nazirite shall then shave his dedicated head *of hair* at the doorway of the tent of meeting, and take the dedicated hair of his head and put *it* on the fire which is under the sacrifice of peace offerings.

19 aLev.
7:28-34

19 'aAnd the priest shall take the ram's shoulder *when it has been* boiled, and one unleavened cake out of the basket, and one unleavened wafer, and shall put *them* on the hands of the Nazirite after he has shaved his dedicated *hair.*

20 aEccl. 9:7

20 'Then the priest shall wave them for a wave offering before the Lord. It is holy for the priest, together with the breast offered by waving and the thigh offered by lifting up; and aafterward the Nazirite may drink wine.'

21 "This is the law of the Nazirite who vows his offering to the Lord according to his separation, in addition to what *else* he can afford; according to his vow which he takes, so he shall do according to the law of his separation."

22 Then the Lord spoke to Moses, saying,

23 a1 Chr.
23:13

23 "Speak to Aaron and to his sons, saying, 'Thus ayou shall bless the sons of Israel. You shall say to them:

24 aDeut.
28:3-6; Ps.
28:9 b1 Sam.
2:9; Ps. 17:8

24   The Lord abless you,
            and bkeep you;

★25 aPs.
80:3, 7, 19
bPs. 86:16

25   The Lord amake His
            face shine on you,
            And bbe gracious to you;

★26 aPs.
4:6; 44:3
bPs. 29:11;
37:37

26   The Lord alift up His
            countenance on you,
            And bgive you peace.'

27 a2 Sam.
7:23; 2 Chr.
7:14

27 "So they shall ainvoke My name on the sons of Israel, and I then will bless them."

3 By the offerings of the princes, 7:1-89

7 Now it came about on athe day that Moses had finished setting up the tabernacle, he banointed it and consecrated it with all its furnishings and the altar and all its utensils; he anointed them and consecrated them also.

1 aEx.
40:17 bEx.
40:9-11;
Num. 7:10,
84, 88

2 Then athe leaders of Israel, the heads of their fathers' households, bmade an offering (they were the leaders of the tribes; they were the ones who were over the numbered men).

2 aNum.
1:5-16
b2 Chr. 35:8

3 When they brought their offering before the Lord, six acovered carts and twelve oxen, a cart for *every* two of the leaders and an ox for each one, then they presented them before the tabernacle.

★ 3-9

3 aIs. 66:20

4 Then the Lord spoke to Moses, saying,

5 "Accept *these things* from them, that they may be used in the service of the tent of meeting, and you shall give them to the Levites, *to* each man according to his service."

6 So Moses took the carts and the oxen, and gave them to the Levites.

7 Two carts and four oxen he gave to the sons of Gershon, according to atheir service,

7 aNum.
4:24-26

8 and four carts and eight oxen he gave to the sons of Merari, according to atheir service, under the direction of Ithamar the son of Aaron the priest.

8 aNum.
4:31, 32

9 But he did not give *any* to the sons of Kohath because theirs *was* athe service of the holy

9 aNum.
4:5-15

6:25 *make His face shine.* I.e., be happy toward them.
6:26 *lift up His countenance.* I.e., in recognition and approval, so as to give them *peace*, or total well-being.
7:3-9 The *six covered carts and twelve oxen*

were given to the sons of Gershon (cf. 4:24-26) and Merari (cf. 4:31-33) to use in transporting the tabernacle. The Kohathites received none since they carried the holy furniture on their shoulders.

objects, which they carried on the shoulder.

★10-88

10 aNum. 7:1; 2 Chr. 7:9

10 And the leaders offered the dedication *offering* for the altar when ªit was anointed, so the leaders offered their offering before the altar.

11 Then the LORD said to Moses, "Let them present their offering, one leader each day, for the dedication of the altar."

12 Now the one who presented his offering on the first day *was* Nahshon the son of Amminadab, of the tribe of Judah;

13 aEx. 25:29; 37:16 bNum. 3:47

13 and his offering *was* one silver ªdish whose weight *was* one hundred and thirty *shekels,* one silver bowl of seventy shekels, ᵇaccording to the shekel of the sanctuary, both of them full of fine flour mixed with oil for a grain offering;

14 one gold pan of ten *shekels,* full of incense;

15 one bull, one ram, one male lamb one year old, for a burnt offering;

16 aLev. 4:23

16 ªone male goat for a sin offering;

17 aLuke 3:32, 33

17 and for the sacrifice of peace offerings, two oxen, five rams, five male goats, five male lambs one year old. This *was* the offering of ªNahshon the son of Amminadab.

18 On the second day Nethanel the son of Zuar, leader of Issachar, presented *an offering;*

19 he presented as his offering one silver dish whose weight *was* one hundred and thirty *shekels,* one silver bowl of seventy shekels, according to the shekel of the sanctuary, both of them full of fine flour mixed with oil for a grain offering;

20 one gold pan of ten *shekels,* full of incense;

21 one bull, one ram, one male lamb one year old, for a burnt offering;

22 one male goat for a sin offering;

23 aLev. 7:11-13

23 and for the sacrifice of ªpeace offerings, two oxen, five rams, five male goats, five male lambs one year old. This *was* the offering of Nethanel the son of Zuar.

24 On the third day *it was* Eliab the son of Helon, leader of the sons of Zebulun;

25 his offering *was* one silver dish whose weight *was* one hundred and thirty *shekels,* one silver bowl of seventy shekels, according to the shekel of the sanctuary, both of them full of fine flour mixed with oil for a grain offering;

26 one gold pan of ten *shekels,* full of incense;

27 aIs. 53:7; John 1:29; 1 Pet. 1:19

27 one young bull, one ram, one ªmale lamb one year old, for a burnt offering;

28 one male goat for a sin offering;

29 and for the sacrifice of peace offerings, two oxen, five rams, five male goats, five male lambs one year old. This *was* the offering of Eliab the son of Helon.

30 On the fourth day *it was* Elizur the son of Shedeur, leader of the sons of Reuben;

31 his offering *was* one silver dish whose weight *was* one hundred and thirty *shekels,* one silver bowl of seventy shekels, according to the shekel of the sanctuary, both of them full of fine flour mixed with oil for a grain offering;

32 one gold pan of ten *shekels,* full of incense;

33 aHeb. 9:28

33 one bull, one ram, one ªmale lamb one year old, for a burnt offering;

7:10-88 On twelve successive days, a different prince brought similar gifts and offerings for the dedication of the altar. The almost monotonous repetition of their generosity suggests God's delight with their gifts and intensifies the example they left for succeeding generations. Each brought a *silver dish* (plate) weighing 130 shekels (about 65 oz.), a *silver bowl* weighing 70 shekels (about 35 oz.), and a *gold pan* (a small vessel shaped like the palm of the hand) weighing ten shekels (about 5 oz.). In addition, each brought a burnt, a sin, and a peace offering. Verses 84-88 give a total of these gifts and offerings.

34 one male goat for a sin offering;

35 and for the sacrifice of peace offerings, two oxen, five rams, five male goats, five male lambs one year old. This *was* the offering of Elizur the son of Shedeur.

36 On the fifth day *it was* Shelumiel the son of Zurishaddai, leader of the children of Simeon;

37 his offering *was* one silver dish whose weight *was* one hundred and thirty *shekels,* one silver bowl of seventy shekels, according to the shekel of the sanctuary, both of them full of fine flour mixed with oil for a grain offering;

38 one gold pan of ten *shekels,* full of incense;

39 one bull, one ram, one male lamb one year old, for a burnt offering;

40 one male goat for a sin offering;

41 and for the sacrifice of peace offerings, two oxen, five rams, five male goats, five male lambs one year old. This *was* the offering of Shelumiel the son of Zurishaddai.

42 On the sixth day *it was* ᵃEliasaph the son of Deuel, leader of the sons of Gad;

43 his offering *was* one silver dish whose weight *was* one hundred and thirty *shekels,* one silver bowl of seventy shekels, according to the shekel of the sanctuary, both of them full of ᵃfine flour mixed with oil for a grain offering;

44 one gold pan of ten *shekels,* full of incense;

45 ᵃone bull, one ram, one male lamb one year old, for a burnt offering;

46 one male goat for a sin offering;

47 and for the sacrifice of peace offerings, two oxen, five rams, five male goats, five male lambs one year old. This *was* the offering of Eliasaph the son of Deuel.

48 On the seventh day *it was* ᵃElishama the son of Ammihud, leader of the sons of Ephraim;

49 his offering *was* one silver dish whose weight *was* one hundred and thirty *shekels,* one silver bowl of seventy shekels, according to the shekel of the sanctuary, both of them full of fine flour mixed with oil for a grain offering;

50 one gold pan of ten *shekels,* full of ᵃincense;

51 ᵃone bull, one ram, one male lamb one year old, for a burnt offering;

52 one male goat for a sin offering;

53 and for the sacrifice of peace offerings, two oxen, five rams, five male goats, five male lambs one year old. This *was* the offering of Elishama the son of Ammihud.

54 On the eighth day *it was* ᵃGamaliel the son of Pedahzur, leader of the sons of Manasseh;

55 his offering *was* one silver dish whose weight *was* one hundred and thirty *shekels,* one silver bowl of seventy shekels, according to the shekel of the sanctuary, both of them full of fine flour mixed with oil for a grain offering;

56 one gold pan of ten *shekels,* full of ᵃincense;

57 one bull, one ram, one ᵃmale lamb one year old, for a burnt offering;

58 one male goat for a sin offering;

59 and for the ᵃsacrifice of peace offerings, two oxen, five rams, five male goats, five male lambs one year old. This *was* the offering of Gamaliel the son of Pedahzur.

60 On the ninth day *it was* ᵃAbidan the son of Gideoni, leader of the sons of Benjamin;

61 his offering *was* one silver dish whose weight *was* one hundred and thirty *shekels,* one silver bowl of seventy shekels, according to the shekel of the sanctuary, both of them full of fine flour mixed with oil for a grain offering;

62 one gold pan of ten *shekels,* full of ᵃincense;

---

42 ᵃNum. 1:14; 10:20

43 ᵃLev. 2:5; 14:10

45 ᵃPs. 50:8-14; Is. 1:11

48 ᵃNum. 1:10; 2:18; 1 Chr. 7:26

50 ᵃDeut. 33:10; Ezek. 8:11; Luke 1:10

51 ᵃMic. 6:6-8

54 ᵃNum. 2:20

56 ᵃEx. 30:7

57 ᵃEx. 12:5; Acts 8:32; Rev. 5:6

59 ᵃLev. 3:1-17

60 ᵃNum. 1:11; 2:22

62 ᵃRev. 5:8; 8:3, 4

63 one bull, one ram, one male lamb one year old, for a burnt offering;

64 *a*2 Cor. 5:21

64 one male goat for a *a*sin offering;

65 *a*Col. 1:20

65 and for the sacrifice of *a*peace offerings, two oxen, five rams, five male goats, five male lambs one year old. This *was* the offering of Abidan the son of Gideoni.

66 *a*Num. 1:12; 2:25

66 On the tenth day *it was* *a*Ahiezer the son of Ammishaddai, leader of the sons of Dan;

67 *a*Ex. 30:13; Lev. 27:25

67 his offering *was* one silver dish whose weight *was* one hundred and thirty *shekels,* one silver bowl of seventy shekels, according to the *a*shekel of the sanctuary, both of them full of fine flour mixed with oil for a grain offering;

68 *a*Ps. 141:2

68 one gold pan of ten *shekels,* full of *a*incense;

69 one bull, one ram, one male lamb one year old, for a burnt offering;

70 one male goat for a sin offering;

71 and for the sacrifice of peace offerings, two oxen, five rams, five male goats, five male lambs one year old. This *was* the offering of Ahiezer the son of Ammishaddai.

72 *a*Num. 1:13; 2:27

72 On the eleventh day *it was* *a*Pagiel the son of Ochran, leader of the sons of Asher;

73 his offering *was* one silver dish whose weight *was* one hundred and thirty *shekels,* one silver bowl of seventy shekels, according to the shekel of the sanctuary, both of them full of fine flour mixed with oil for a grain offering;

74 *a*Mal. 1:11

74 one gold pan of ten *shekels,* full of *a*incense;

75 one bull, one ram, one male lamb one year old, for a burnt offering;

76 one male goat for a sin offering;

77 and for the sacrifice of peace offerings, two oxen, five rams, five male goats, five male lambs one year old. This *was* the offering of Pagiel the son of Ochran.

78 On the twelfth day *it was* *a*Ahira the son of Enan, leader of the sons of Naphtali;

78 *a*Num. 1:15; 2:29

79 his offering *was* one *a*silver dish whose weight *was* one hundred and thirty *shekels,* one silver bowl of seventy shekels, according to the shekel of the sanctuary, both of them full of fine flour mixed with oil for a grain offering;

79 *a*Ezra 1:9, 10; Dan. 5:2

80 one gold pan of ten *shekels,* full of incense;

81 one bull, one ram, one male lamb one year old, for a burnt offering;

82 one male goat for a sin offering;

83 and for the sacrifice of peace offerings, two oxen, five rams, five male goats, five male lambs one year old. This *was* the offering of Ahira the son of Enan.

84 This *was* *a*the dedication offering for the altar from the leaders of Israel when *b*it was anointed: twelve silver dishes, twelve silver bowls, twelve gold pans,

84 *a*Num. 7:10 *b*Num. 7:1

85 each silver dish *weighing* one hundred and thirty *shekels* and each bowl seventy; all the silver of the utensils *was* 2,400 *shekels,* according to the shekel of the sanctuary;

86 the twelve gold pans, full of incense, *weighing* ten *shekels* apiece, according to the *a*shekel of the sanctuary, all the gold of the pans 120 *shekels;*

86 *a*Ex. 30:13

87 all the oxen for the burnt offering twelve bulls, *all* the rams twelve, the male lambs one year old with their grain offering twelve, and the male goats for a sin offering twelve;

88 and all the oxen for the sacrifice of peace offerings 24 bulls, *all* the rams 60, the male goats 60, the male lambs one year old 60. *a*This *was* the dedication offering for the altar after it was anointed.

88 *a*Num. 7:1, 10

89 Now when *a*Moses went into the tent of meeting to speak with Him, he heard the voice speaking to him from above *b*the mercy seat that was on the ark of

89 *a*Ex. 40:34, 35 *b*Ex. 25:21, 22 *c*Ps. 80:1; 99:1

the testimony, from ^cbetween the two cherubim, so He spoke to him.

4 By the setting apart of the Levites, 8:1-26

★ 1-4   8 Then the LORD spoke to Moses, saying,

2 ^aEx. 25:37; Lev. 24:2, 4   2 "Speak to Aaron and say to him, 'When you mount the lamps, the seven lamps will ^agive light in the front of the lampstand.'"

3 Aaron therefore did so; he mounted its lamps at the front of the lampstand, just as the LORD had commanded Moses.

4 ^aEx. 25:31-40 ^bEx. 25:9, 31-40; 26:30; 37:17-24   4 ^aNow this was the workmanship of the lampstand, hammered work of gold; from its base to its flowers, it was hammered work; ^baccording to the pattern which the LORD had showed Moses, so he made the lampstand.

★ 5-22   5 Again the LORD spoke to Moses, saying,

6 ^aIs. 52:11   6 "Take the Levites from among the sons of Israel and ^acleanse them.

7 ^aNum. 19:9, 13, 20 ^bLev. 14:8, 9 ^cNum. 8:21   7 "And thus you shall do to them, for their cleansing: *sprinkle* purifying ^awater on them, and let them ^buse a razor over their whole body, and ^cwash their clothes, and they shall be clean.

8 ^aLev. 2:1; Num. 15:8-10   8 "Then let them take a bull with ^aits grain offering, fine flour mixed with oil; and a second bull you shall take for a sin offering.

9 ^aEx. 29:4; 40:12 ^bLev. 8:3   9 "So ^ayou shall present the Levites before the tent of meeting. ^bYou shall also assemble the whole congregation of the sons of Israel,

10 ^aLev. 1:4   10 and present the Levites before the LORD; and the sons of Israel ^ashall lay their hands on the Levites.

11 "Aaron then shall present the Levites before the LORD as a ^awave offering from the sons of Israel, that they may qualify to perform the service of the LORD.

11 ^aLev. 7:30, 34

12 "Now ^athe Levites shall lay their hands on the heads of the bulls; then offer the one for a sin offering and the other for a burnt offering to the LORD, to make atonement for the Levites.

12 ^aEx. 29:10

13 "And you shall have the Levites stand before Aaron and before his sons so as to present them as a wave offering to the LORD.

14 "Thus you shall separate the Levites from among the sons of Israel, and ^athe Levites shall be Mine.

14 ^aNum. 3:12; 16:9

15 "Then after that the Levites may go in to serve the tent of meeting. But you shall cleanse them and ^apresent them as a wave offering;

15 ^aEx. 29:24

16 for they are ^awholly given to Me from among the sons of Israel. I have taken them for Myself ^binstead of every first issue of the womb, the first-born of all the sons of Israel.

16 ^aNum. 3:9 ^bEx. 13:2; Num. 3:12, 45

17 "For ^aevery first-born among the sons of Israel is Mine, among the men and among the animals; on the day that I struck down all the first-born in the land of Egypt I sanctified them for Myself.

17 ^aEx. 13:2, 12, 13, 15; Luke 2:23

18 "But I have taken the Levites instead of every first-born among the sons of Israel.

19 "And ^aI have given the Levites as a gift to Aaron and to his sons from among the sons of Israel, to perform the service of the sons of Israel at the tent of meeting, and to make atonement on behalf of the sons of Israel, that there may be no ^bplague among

19 ^aNum. 3:9 ^bNum. 1:53; 16:46

8:1-4 Instructions for setting up the lamps on the lampstand (see note on Exod. 25:31).

8:5-22 Instructions for the cleansing of the priests, in preparation for their service. They were to be sprinkled with *water* and were to shave all the hair off their bodies (v. 7). They were then to bring burnt, grain, and sin offer-

ings (vv. 8, 12). Next, representatives of the people laid their hands on the Levites, since the Levites were substitutes for the firstborn (vv. 10, 17-18). Finally, Aaron offered the Levites to the Lord (vv. 11, 13). *purified* (v. 21) literally means "de-sinned" (so as to be ceremonially clean).

the sons of Israel by their coming near to the sanctuary."

20 Thus did Moses and Aaron and all the congregation of the sons of Israel to the Levites; according to all that the LORD had commanded Moses concerning the Levites, so the sons of Israel did to them.

21 aNum.
8:7

21 aThe Levites, too, purified themselves from sin and washed their clothes; and Aaron presented them as a wave offering before the LORD. Aaron also made atonement for them to cleanse them.

22 Then after that the Levites went in to perform their service in the tent of meeting before Aaron and before his sons; just as the LORD had commanded Moses concerning the Levites, so they did to them.

23 Now the LORD spoke to Moses, saying,

★24 aNum.
4:3; 1 Chr.
23:3, 24, 27

24 "This is what *applies* to the Levites: from atwenty-five years old and upward they shall enter to perform service in the work of the tent of meeting.

25 "But at the age of fifty years they shall retire from service in the work and not work any more.

26 aNum.
1:53

26 "They may, however, assist their brothers in the tent of meeting, ato keep an obligation; but they *themselves* shall do no work. Thus you shall deal with the Levites concerning their obligations."

5 By observing the first annual Passover, 9:1-14

1 aEx. 40:2,
17; Num. 1:1

9 Thus the LORD spoke to Moses in the wilderness of Sinai, in athe first month of the

★ 2 aEx
12:6; Lev.
23:5; Deut.
16:1, 2

second year after they had come out of the land of Egypt, saying,

2 "Now, let the sons of Israel observe the Passover at aits appointed time.

3 "On the fourteenth day of this month, at twilight, you shall observe it at its appointed time; you shall observe it according to all its statutes and according to all its ordinances."

4 So Moses told the sons of Israel to observe the Passover.

5 aJosh.
5:10 bEx.
12:1-13

5 And athey observed the Passover in the first *month,* on the fourteenth day of the month, at twilight, in the wilderness of Sinai; baccording to all that the LORD had commanded Moses, so the sons of Israel did.

★ 6-7

6 aNum.
5:2; 19:11-22
bEx. 18:15;
Num. 27:2

6 But there were *some* men who were aunclean because of *the* dead person, so that they could not observe Passover on that day; so bthey came before Moses and Aaron on that day.

7 And those men said to him, "*Though* we are unclean because of *the* dead person, why are we restrained from presenting the offering of the LORD at its appointed time among the sons of Israel?"

8 aEx.
18:15; Ps.
85:8

8 Moses therefore said to them, "aWait, and I will listen to what the LORD will command concerning you."

9 Then the LORD spoke to Moses, saying,

★10-11

10 "Speak to the sons of Israel, saying, 'If any one of you or of your generations becomes unclean because of a *dead* person, or is on a distant journey, he may, however, observe the Passover to the LORD.

11 a2 Chr.
30:2, 15
bEx. 12:8

11 'In the second month on the afourteenth day at twilight, they shall observe it; they bshall eat it with unleavened bread and bitter herbs.

12 aEx.
12:10 bEx.
12:46; John
19:36

12 'They ashall leave none of it until morning, bnor break a bone of it; according to all the

---

8:24 See note on 4:3.

9:2 *Passover.* See notes on Exod. 12.

9:6-7 A new problem confronted Moses, namely, what to do with those who wanted to observe the Passover but had been excluded from its regularly scheduled observance because of defilement by reason of touching a corpse.

9:10-11 Any who were defiled or on a *journey* at the regular time for Passover could observe a supplementary Passover one month later.

statute of the Passover they shall observe it.

13 aGen. 17:14; Ex. 12:15, 47
bNum. 5:31

13 '^aBut the man who is clean and is not on a journey, and yet neglects to observe the Passover, that person shall then be cut off from his people, for he did not present the offering of the LORD at its appointed time. That man ^bshall bear his sin.

14 aEx. 12:48 bEx. 12:49; Lev. 24:22; Num. 15:15, 16, 29

14 '^aAnd if an alien sojourns among you and observes the Passover to the LORD, according to the statute of the Passover and according to its ordinance, so he shall do; you shall have ^bone statute, both for the alien and for the native of the land.' "

6 By being led by God,
9:15–10:10

★15 aEx. 40:2, 17
bEx. 40:34
cNum. 17:7
dEx. 13:21, 22

15 Now on ^athe day that the tabernacle was erected ^bthe cloud covered the tabernacle, the ^ctent of the testimony, and ^din the evening it was like the appearance of fire over the tabernacle, until morning.

16 aEx. 40:34; Neh. 9:12

16 So it was continuously; ^athe cloud would cover it *by day,* and the appearance of fire by night.

17 aEx. 40:36-38; Num. 10:11, 12

17 ^aAnd whenever the cloud was lifted from over the tent, afterward the sons of Israel would then set out; and in the place where the cloud settled down, there the sons of Israel would camp.

18 a1 Cor. 10:1

18 At the command of the LORD the sons of Israel would set out, and at the command of the LORD they would camp; ^aas long as the cloud settled over the tabernacle, they remained camped.

19 Even when the cloud lingered over the tabernacle for many days, the sons of Israel would keep the LORD's charge and not set out.

20 If sometimes the cloud remained a few days over the tabernacle, ^aaccording to the command of the LORD they remained camped. Then according to the command of the LORD they set out.

20 aPs. 48:14; Prov. 3:5, 6

21 If sometimes the cloud remained from evening until morning, when the cloud was lifted in the morning, they would move out; or *if it remained* in the daytime and at night, whenever the cloud was lifted, they would set out.

22 Whether it was two days or a month or a year that the cloud lingered over the tabernacle, staying above it, the sons of Israel remained camped and did not set out; but ^awhen it was lifted, they did set out.

22 aEx. 40:36, 37

23 ^aAt the command of the LORD they camped, and at the command of the LORD they set out; they kept the LORD's charge, according to the command of the LORD through Moses.

23 aPs. 73:24; 107:7; Is. 63:14

10 The LORD spoke further to Moses, saying,

2 "Make yourself two trumpets of silver, of hammered work you shall make them; and you shall use them for ^asummoning the congregation and for having the camps set out.

★ 2 aIs. 1:13

3 "And ^awhen both are blown, all the congregation shall gather themselves to you at the doorway of the tent of meeting.

3 aJer. 4:5; Joel 2:15

4 "Yet if *only* one is blown, then the ^aleaders, the heads of the divisions of Israel, shall assemble before you.

4 aEx. 18:21; Num. 1:16; 7:2

5 "But when you blow an alarm, the camps that are pitched ^aon the east side shall set out.

★ 5-6

5 aNum. 10:14

6 "And when you blow an alarm the second time, the camps that are pitched on ^athe south

6 aNum. 10:18

9:15 The *cloud* was the sign of the presence of the Lord, and its movement was the means by which He guided Israel (see notes on Exod. 13:21 and 40:34).

10:2 *two trumpets of silver.* According to representations on Jewish coins and on the Arch of

Titus in Rome, these were long, straight tubes, flared at the end. They were used either to summon the people to the tabernacle or to alert them that they were about to break camp.

10:5-6 See note on 2:17.

side shall set out; an alarm is to be blown for them to set out.

⁷ ^aJoel 2:1

7 "When convening the assembly, however, you shall blow without ^asounding an alarm.

⁸ ^aNum. 31:6; Josh. 6:4; 2 Chr. 13:12

8 "^aThe priestly sons of Aaron, moreover, shall blow the trumpets; and this shall be for you a perpetual statute throughout your generations.

⁹ ^aJudg. 2:18; 1 Sam. 10:18; Ps. 106:42 ^bGen. 8:1; Ps. 106:4

9 "And when you go to war in your land against the adversary who ^aattacks you, then you shall sound an alarm with the trumpets, that you may be ^bremembered before the LORD your God, and be saved from your enemies.

¹⁰ ^aPs. 81:3-5

10 "Also in the day of your gladness and in your appointed feasts, and on the first *days* of your months, ^ayou shall blow the trumpets over your burnt offerings, and over the sacrifices of your peace offerings; and they shall be as a reminder of you before your God. I am the LORD your God."

II ISRAEL MARCHING TO KADESH-BARNEA, 10:11–12:16

A The March Begun, 10:11–36

¹¹ ^aEx. 40:17

11 Now it came about in ^athe second year, in the second month, on the twentieth of the month, that the cloud was lifted from over the tabernacle of the testimony;

¹² ^aEx. 40:36 ^bGen. 21:21; Num. 12:16

12 and the sons of Israel set out on ^atheir journeys from the wilderness of Sinai. Then the cloud settled down in the ^bwilderness of Paran.

¹³ ^aDeut. 1:6

13 ^aSo they moved out for the first time according to the commandment of the LORD through Moses.

¹⁴ ^aNum. 2:3-9

14 And the standard of the camp of the sons of Judah, according to their armies, ^aset out first, with Nahshon the son of Amminadab, over its army,

15 and Nethanel the son of Zuar, over the tribal army of the sons of Issachar;

16 and Eliab the son of Helon over the tribal army of the sons of Zebulun.

¹⁷ ^aNum. 4:21-32

17 ^aThen the tabernacle was taken down; and the sons of Gershon and the sons of Merari, who were carrying the tabernacle, set out.

¹⁸ ^aNum. 2:10-16

18 Next ^athe standard of the camp of Reuben, according to their armies, set out with Elizur the son of Shedeur, over its army,

19 and Shelumiel the son of Zurishaddai over the tribal army of the sons of Simeon,

20 and Eliasaph the son of Deuel was over the tribal army of the sons of Gad.

²¹ ^aNum. 4:4-20 ^bNum. 10:17

21 ^aThen the Kohathites set out, carrying the holy *objects;* and ^bthe tabernacle was set up before their arrival.

²² ^aNum. 2:18-24

22 ^aNext the standard of the camp of the sons of Ephraim, according to their armies, was set out, with Elishama the son of Ammihud over its army,

23 and Gamaliel the son of Pedahzur over the tribal army of the sons of Manasseh;

24 and Abidan the son of Gideoni over the tribal army of the sons of Benjamin.

²⁵ ^aNum. 2:25-31 ^bJosh. 6:9, 13

25 ^aThen the standard of the camp of the sons of Dan, according to their armies, *which formed* the ^brear guard for all the camps, set out, with Ahiezer the son of Ammishaddai over its army,

26 and Pagiel the son of Ochran over the tribal army of the sons of Asher;

27 and Ahira the son of Enan over the tribal army of the sons of Naphtali.

28 This was the order of march of the sons of Israel by their armies as they set out.

★29-32

²⁹ ^aJudg. 4:11 ^bEx. 2:18; 3:1; 18:12 ^cGen. 12:7; Ex. 6:4-8 ^dPs. 95:1-7; 100:1-5 ^eDeut. 4:40; 30:5

29 Then Moses said to ^aHobab the son of ^bReuel the Midian-

10:29-32 Moses asked *Hobab,* his brother-in-law (see note on Exod. 2:18), to accompany them and give them the benefit of his knowledge of that area. This paragraph does not say that he agreed, though apparently he did, because the people of the Midianite family, the Kenites, eventually settled in Canaan (cf. Judg. 1:16; 4:11). Divine guidance does not exclude using human help.

ite, Moses' father-in-law, "We are setting out to the place of which the LORD said, 'cI will give it to you'; dcome with us and we will do you good, for the LORD ehas promised good concerning Israel."

30 aJudg. 1:16; Matt. 21:28, 29

30 But he said to him, "aI will not come, but rather will go to my *own* land and relatives."

31 aJob 29:15

31 Then he said, "Please do not leave us, inasmuch as you know where we should camp in the wilderness, and you awill be as eyes for us.

32 aPs. 22:27-31; 67:5-7 bLev. 19:34; Deut. 10:18

32 "So it will be, if you go with us, it will come about that awhatever good the LORD does for us, bwe will do for you."

33 aNum. 10:12 bDeut. 1:33 cIs. 11:10

33 aThus they set out from the mount of the LORD three days' journey, with bthe ark of the covenant of the LORD journeying in front of them for the three days, to seek out ca resting place for them.

34 aNum. 9:15-23

34 aAnd the cloud of the LORD was over them by day, when they set out from the camp.

35 aPs. 68:1, 2; Is. 17:12-14 bDeut. 7:10; 32:41

35 Then it came about when the ark set out that Moses said,
"aRise up, O LORD!
And let Thine enemies
   be scattered,
And let those bwho hate
   Thee flee before
   Thee."

36 aIs. 63:17 bDeut. 1:10

36 And when it came to rest, he said,
"aReturn Thou, O LORD
To the myriad bthousands of Israel."

B The Murmurings Begun,
11:1–12:16

1 The murmuring of the
people (the 70 elders
and the quails),
11:1–35

★ 1-3
1 aNum. 14:2; 16:11; 17:5 bNum. 11:18; 14:28

11 Now the people became like athose who complain

of adversity bin the hearing of the LORD; and when the LORD heard *it*, His anger was kindled, and the fire of the LORD burned among them and consumed *some* of the outskirts of the camp.

2 aNum. 12:11, 13; 21:7

2 aThe people therefore cried out to Moses, and Moses prayed to the LORD, and the fire died out.

3 aDeut. 9:22

3 So the name of that place was called aTaberah, because the fire of the LORD burned among them.

★ 4 aEx. 12:38; 1 Cor. 10:6 bPs. 78:20

4 And the arabble who were among them had greedy desires; and also the sons of Israel wept again and said, "bWho will give us meat to eat?

★ 5 aEx. 16:3

5 "aWe remember the fish which we used to eat free in Egypt, the cucumbers and the melons and the leeks and the onions and the garlic,

6 aNum. 21:5

6 but now aour appetite is gone. There is nothing at all to look at except this manna."

★ 7 aEx. 16:31 bGen. 2:12

7 aNow the manna was like coriander seed, and its appearance like that of bbdellium.

8 The people would go about and gather *it* and grind *it* between two millstones or beat *it* in the mortar, and boil *it* in the pot and make cakes with it; and its taste was as the taste of cakes baked with oil.

9 aEx. 16:13, 14

9 aAnd when the dew fell on the camp at night, the manna would fall with it.

10 Now Moses heard the people weeping throughout their families, each man at the doorway of his tent; and the anger of the LORD was kindled greatly, and Moses was displeased.

11 aEx. 5:22; Deut. 1:12

11 aSo Moses said to the LORD, "Why hast Thou been so hard on Thy servant? And why have I not found favor in Thy

---

11:1-3 It is not said whether the fire of God's judgment extended only to tents on the outskirts of the camp, or to people, or (most likely) to both. *Taberah* means "burning."
11:4 *the rabble.* See note on Exod. 12:38.
11:5 They craved tasty food instead of the plain

manna. *leeks* had an onionlike bulb and stem, both of which were used for food.
11:7 *manna.* See note on Exod. 16:15. *coriander seed* is round and gray. *bdellium* is pearl-like, grayish-white.

sight, that Thou hast laid the burden of all this people on me?

12 "Was it I who conceived all this people? Was it I who brought them forth, that Thou shouldest say to me, 'Carry them in your bosom as a ᵃnurse carries a nursing infant, to the land which ᵇThou didst swear to their fathers'?

13 "Where am I to get meat to give to ᵃall this people? For they weep before me, saying, 'Give us meat that we may eat!'

14 "ᵃI alone am not able to carry all this people, because it is too burdensome for me.

15 "ᵃSo if Thou art going to deal thus with me, please kill me at once, if I have found favor in Thy sight, and do not let me see my wretchedness."

16 The LORD therefore said to Moses, "Gather for Me ᵃseventy men from the elders of Israel, ᵇwhom you know to be the elders of the people and their officers and bring them to the tent of meeting, and let them take their stand there with you.

17 "ᵃThen I will come down and speak with you there, and I will take of ᵇthe Spirit who is upon you, and will put *Him* upon them; and they shall bear the burden of the people with you, so that you shall not bear *it* all alone.

18 "And say to the people, 'ᵃConsecrate yourselves for tomorrow, and you shall eat meat; for you have wept ᵇin the ears of the LORD, saying, "Oh that someone would give us meat to eat! For we were well-off in Egypt." Therefore the LORD will give you meat and you shall eat.

19 'You shall eat, not one day, nor two days, nor five days, nor ten days, nor twenty days,

20 but a whole month, until it comes out of your nostrils and becomes loathsome to you; because ᵃyou have rejected the LORD who

is among you and have wept before Him, saying, "Why did we ever leave Egypt?" ' "

21 But Moses said, "The people, among whom I am, are 600,000 on foot; yet Thou hast said, 'I will give them meat in order that they may eat for a whole month.'

22 "Should flocks and herds be slaughtered for them, to be sufficient for them? Or should all the fish of the sea be gathered together for them, to be sufficient for them?"

23 And the LORD said to Moses, "Is ᵃthe LORD's power limited? Now you shall see whether ᵇMy word will come true for you or not."

24 So Moses went out and ᵃtold the people the words of the LORD. Also, he gathered seventy men of the elders of the people, and stationed them around the tent.

25 ᵃThen the LORD came down in the cloud and spoke to him; and He took of the Spirit who was upon him and placed *Him* upon the seventy elders. And it came about that when the Spirit rested upon them, they prophesied. But they did not do *it* again.

26 But two men had remained in the camp; the name of one was Eldad and the name of the other Medad. And ᵃthe Spirit rested upon them (now they were among those who had been registered, but had not gone out to the tent), and they prophesied in the camp.

27 So a young man ran and told Moses and said, "Eldad and Medad are prophesying in the camp."

28 Then ᵃJoshua the son of Nun, the attendant of Moses from his youth, answered and said, "ᵇMoses, my lord, restrain them."

---

12 ᵃ2 Kin. 10:1, 5; Is. 49:23 ᵇGen. 24:7; Ex. 13:5, 11; 33:1

13 ᵃNum. 11:21, 22; John 6:5-9

14 ᵃEx. 18:18; Deut. 1:12

15 ᵃEx. 32:32

★**16-17**

16 ᵃEx. 24:1, 9 ᵇEx. 18:25

17 ᵃNum. 11:25 ᵇ1 Sam. 10:6; Joel 2:28

★**18-20**

18 ᵃEx. 19:10, 22 ᵇNum. 11:1

20 ᵃJosh. 24:27; 1 Sam. 10:19

23 ᵃIs. 50:2; 59:1 ᵇEzek. 12:25; 24:14

24 ᵃNum. 11:16

25 ᵃNum. 11:17; 12:5

26 ᵃNum. 24:2; 1 Sam. 10:6; 2 Chr. 15:1; Neh. 9:30

28 ᵃEx. 33:11; Josh. 1:1 ᵇMark 9:38-40

11:16-17 God helped His overwrought prophet by giving him the assistance of 70 elders.
11:18-20 God answered the complaint of the people by promising they would soon be surfeited with *meat.*

★**29** *a*1 Cor. 14:5

29 But Moses said to him, "Are you jealous for my sake? *a*Would that all the LORD's people were prophets, that the LORD would put His Spirit upon them!"

30 Then Moses returned to the camp, *both* he and the elders of Israel.

★**31** *a*Ex. 16:13; Ps. 78:26-28; 105:40

31 *a*Now there went forth a wind from the LORD, and it brought quail from the sea, and let *them* fall beside the camp, about a day's journey on this side and a day's journey on the other side, all around the camp, and about two cubits *deep* on the surface of the ground.

★**32** *a*Ezek. 45:11

32 And the people spent all day and all night and all the next day, and gathered the quail (he who gathered least gathered ten *a*homers) and they spread *them* out for themselves all around the camp.

33 *a*Ps. 78:29-31; 106:15

33 *a*While the meat was still between their teeth, before it was chewed, the anger of the LORD was kindled against the people, and the LORD struck the people with a very severe plague.

★**34** *a*Deut. 9:22

34 So the name of that place was called *a*Kibroth-hattaavah, because there they buried the people who had been greedy.

35 *a*Num. 33:17

35 From Kibroth-hattaavah *a*the people set out for Hazeroth, and they remained at Hazeroth.

2 The murmuring of Miriam and Aaron (the leprosy of Miriam), 12:1-16

★**1** *a*Ex. 2:21

12 Then Miriam and Aaron spoke against Moses because of the Cushite woman whom he had married (for he had married a *a*Cushite woman);

2 *a*and they said, "Has the LORD indeed spoken only through Moses? Has He not spoken through us as well?" And the LORD heard it.

2 *a*Num. 16:3

3 (Now the man Moses was *a*very humble, more than any man who was on the face of the earth.)

3 *a*Matt. 11:29

4 And suddenly the LORD said to Moses and Aaron and to Miriam, "You three come out to the tent of meeting." So the three of them came out.

5 *a*Then the LORD came down in a pillar of cloud and stood at the doorway of the tent, and He called Aaron and Miriam. When they had both come forward,

5 *a*Ex. 19:9; 34:5

6 He said,
"Hear now My words:
If there is a prophet among you,
I, the LORD, shall make Myself known to him in a *a*vision.
I shall speak with him in a *b*dream.

★ **6-8**

6 *a*Gen. 46:2; 1 Sam. 3:15 *b*Gen. 31:11; 1 Kin. 3:5, 15

7 "Not so, with *a*My servant Moses,
*b*He is faithful in all My household;

7 *a*Josh. 1:1 *b*Heb. 3:2, 5

8 *a*With him I speak mouth to mouth,
Even openly, and not in dark sayings,
And he beholds *b*the form of the LORD.
Why then were you not afraid
To speak against My servant, against Moses?"

8 *a*Deut. 34:10; Hos. 12:13 *b*Ex. 20:4; 24:10, 11; Deut. 5:8; Ps. 17:15

9 So the anger of the LORD burned against them and *a*He departed.

9 *a*Gen. 17:22; 18:33

11:29 Moses' magnanimous reply to Joshua's suggestion that he silence the two prophets, Eldad and Medad, showed that he was not motivated by any desire for self-exaltation.

11:31 *two cubits deep* (better, high). The quail flew about 3 feet off the ground so that the people could knock them down and kill them easily.

11:32 *ten homers.* Over 100 bushels.

11:34 *Kibroth-hattaavah.* Literally, "graves of craving."

12:1 *spoke.* The verb is feminine singular, indicating that Miriam led in this criticism. The pretext used was Moses' marriage to a foreign woman (this could refer to Zipporah, Exod. 2:21, though likely it refers to a second marriage after her death), but the real cause was jealousy (v. 2).

12:6-8 The meaning is this: God spoke to prophets through *visions* and *dreams*; but He spoke to Moses directly, *openly* and not in riddles.

10 ªDeut.
24:9 ᵇEx.
4:6; 2 Kin.
5:27
10 But when the cloud had withdrawn from over the tent, behold, ªMiriam *was* leprous, as ᵇ*white as* snow. As Aaron turned toward Miriam, behold, she *was* leprous.

11 ª2 Sam.
19:19; 24:10
11 Then Aaron said to Moses, "Oh, my lord, I beg you, ªdo not account *this* sin to us, in which we have acted foolishly and in which we have sinned.

12 "Oh, do not let her be like one dead, whose flesh is half eaten away when he comes from his mother's womb!"

13 ªPs. 30:2;
41:4; Is.
30:26; Jer.
17:14
13 And Moses cried out to the LORD, saying, "O God, ªheal her, I pray!"

★14 ªDeut.
25:9; Job
17:6; 30:10;
Is. 50:6
ᵇNum. 5:1-4
14 But the LORD said to Moses, "If her father had but ªspit in her face, would she not bear her shame for seven days? Let her be shut up for seven days ᵇoutside the camp, and afterward she may be received again."

15 ªDeut.
24:9
15 So ªMiriam was shut up outside the camp for seven days, and the people did not move on until Miriam was received again.

16 Afterward, however, the people moved out from Hazeroth and camped in the wilderness of Paran.

III ISRAEL AT KADESH-BARNEA, 13:1–20:13

A The Defiance of God, 13:1–14:45

1 The reconnaissance and report of the spies, 13:1–33

1 ªDeut.
1:22, 23
13 Then ªthe LORD spoke to Moses saying,

★ 2 ªDeut.
1:22; 9:23
2 "ªSend out for yourself men so that they may spy out the land of Canaan, which I am going to give to the sons of Israel; you shall send a man from each of their fathers' tribes, every one a leader among them."

3 So Moses sent them from the wilderness of Paran at the command of the LORD, all of them men who were heads of the sons of Israel.

4 These then *were* their names: from the tribe of Reuben, Shammua the son of Zaccur;

5 from the tribe of Simeon, Shaphat the son of Hori;

6 from the tribe of Judah, ªCaleb the son of Jephunneh;
6 ªNum.
14:6, 30;
Josh. 14:6

7 from the tribe of Issachar, Igal the son of Joseph;

8 from the tribe of Ephraim, ªHoshea the son of Nun;
8 ªNum.
13:16; Deut.
32:44

9 from the tribe of Benjamin, Palti the son of Raphu;

10 from the tribe of Zebulun, Gaddiel the son of Sodi;

11 from the tribe of Joseph, from the tribe of Manasseh, Gaddi the son of Susi;

12 from the tribe of Dan, Ammiel the son of Gemalli;

13 from the tribe of Asher, Sethur the son of Michael;

14 from the tribe of Naphtali, Nahbi the son of Vophsi;

15 from the tribe of Gad, Geuel the son of Machi.

16 These are the names of the men whom Moses sent to spy out the land; but Moses called ªHoshea the son of Nun, Joshua.
★16 ªNum.
13:8; Deut.
32:44

17 When Moses sent them to spy out the land of Canaan, he said to them, "Go up there into ªthe Negev; then go up into the hill country.
17 ªGen.
12:9; 13:1, 3

18 "And see what the land is like, and whether the people who live in it are strong *or* weak, whether they are few or many.

19 "And how is the land in which they live, is it good or bad? And how are the cities in which

---

12:14 *If her father had but spit in her face.* If a father had to rebuke a daughter in this manner, a period of shame would follow (cf. Deut. 25:9; Isa. 50:6); how much more should Miriam be shamed seven days for flouting God's authority. The public nature of her sin called for public punishment (cf. 1 Tim. 5:20).

13:2 Cf. Deut. 1:22. Apparently the command of the Lord was given after the people requested spies be sent.

13:16 *Hoshea* means "salvation." To this is prefixed an abbreviation of the covenant name of God (Yahweh). Thus, Joshua means "God is salvation."

they live, are *they* like *open* camps or with fortifications?

20 "And ªhow is the land, is it fat or lean? Are there trees in it or not? Make an ᵇeffort then to get some of the fruit of the land." Now the time was the time of the first ripe grapes.

21 So they went up and spied out the land from ªthe wilderness of Zin as far as Rehob, ᵇat Lebo-hamath.

22 When they had gone up into ªthe Negev, they came to He-bron where ᵇAhiman, Sheshai and Talmai, the descendants of ᶜAnak were. (Now Hebron was built seven years before ᵈZoan in Egypt.)

23 Then they came to the val-ley of ªEshcol and from there cut down a branch with a single clus-ter of grapes; and they carried it on a pole between two *men*, with some of the pomegranates and the figs.

24 That place was called the valley of Eshcol, because of the cluster which the sons of Israel cut down from there.

25 When they returned from spying out the land, at the end of forty days,

26 they proceeded to come to Moses and Aaron and to all the congregation of the sons of Israel in the wilderness of Paran, at ªKa-desh; and they brought back word to them and to all the con-gregation and showed them the fruit of the land.

27 Thus they told him, and said, "We went in to the land where you sent us; and ªit cer-tainly does flow with milk and honey, and ᵇthis is its fruit.

28 "Nevertheless, ªthe people who live in the land are strong, and the cities are fortified *and* very large; and moreover, we saw ᵇthe descendants of Anak there.

29 "Amalek is living in the land of ªthe Negev and the Hit-tites and the Jebusites and ᵇthe Amorites are living in the hill country, and ᶜthe Canaanites are living by the sea and by the side of the Jordan."

30 Then Caleb quieted the people before Moses, and said, "We should by all means go up and take possession of it, for we shall surely overcome it."

31 But the men who had gone up with him said, "ªWe are not able to go up against the people, for they are too strong for us."

32 So they gave out to the sons of Israel ªa bad report of the land which they had spied out, saying, "The land through which we have gone, in spying it out, is ᵇa land that devours its inhabi-tants; and ᶜall the people whom we saw in it are men of *great* size.

33 "There also we saw the ªNephilim (the sons of Anak are part of the Nephilim); and ᵇwe became like grasshoppers in our own sight, and so we were in their sight."

2 The reaction and judgment of the people, 14:1-45

14 Then all the congregation lifted up their voices and cried, and the people wept that night.

2 And all the sons of Israel ªgrumbled against Moses and Aaron; and the whole

Marginal references

20 ªDeut. 1:24, 25
ᵇDeut. 31:6, 23

★21 ªNum. 20:1; 27:14; 33:36 ᵇJosh. 13:5

22 ªNum. 13:17 ᵇJosh. 15:14 ᶜNum. 13:28, 33 ᵈPs. 78:12, 43

23 ªGen. 14:13; Num. 13:24; 32:9; Deut. 1:24

★24

26 ªNum. 20:1, 14; 32:8

★27-29

27 ªEx. 3:8, 17; 13:5 ᵇDeut. 1:25

28 ªDeut. 1:28; 9:1, 2 ᵇNum. 13:33

29 ªNum. 13:17; 14:25, 45 ᵇJosh. 10:6 ᶜNum. 14:43, 45

31 ªDeut. 1:28; 9:1-3

★32 ªNum. 14:36, 37; Ps. 106:24 ᵇEzek. 36:13, 14 ᶜAmos 2:9

★33 ªGen. 6:4 ᵇDeut. 1:28; 9:2; Josh. 11:21

2 ªNum. 11:1 ᵇNum. 11:5; 16:13; 20:3, 4; 21:5

13:21 *the wilderness of Zin.* The northern half of the Negev. *Rehob.* A town in Lebanon. The spies went from south to north.

13:24 *the valley of Eshcol.* Lit., the wadi (a dried river bed) Eshcol (meaning "cluster"). Situated N. of Hebron, this wadi is still noted for its grapes.

13:27-29 The report of the spies was factual: the land was fruitful, the cities were fortified, and the population mixed. All had the same facts; but Joshua and Caleb also had faith (cf. Heb. 3:19).

13:32 *a land that devours its inhabitants.* Var-ious groups fought to possess it because it was such a good land.

13:33 *Nephilim* (the sons of Anak are part of the Nephilim). Anak was a tribe that lived near Hebron in the S. of Palestine. Some remained even after Joshua's conquest of the land (Josh. 11:21-22). They were apparently large of stat-ure (cf. Deut. 2:10). The only other occurrence of Nephilim in the O.T. refers to an antedilu-vian race (Gen. 6:4).

congregation said to them, "ᵇWould that we had died in the land of Egypt! Or would that we had died in this wilderness!

3 ᵃEx. 5:21; 16:3 ᵇNum. 14:31; Deut. 1:39

3 "And why is the LORD bringing us into this land, ᵃto fall by the sword? ᵇOur wives and our little ones will become plunder; would it not be better for us to return to Egypt?"

4 ᵃNeh. 9:17

4 So they said to one another, "ᵃLet us appoint a leader and return to Egypt."

5 ᵃNum. 16:4

5 ᵃThen Moses and Aaron fell on their faces in the presence of all the assembly of the congregation of the sons of Israel.

★ **6**

6 And Joshua the son of Nun and Caleb the son of Jephunneh, of those who had spied out the land, tore their clothes;

7 ᵃNum. 13:27; Deut. 1:25

7 and they spoke to all the congregation of the sons of Israel, saying, "ᵃThe land which we passed through to spy out is an exceedingly good land.

8 ᵃDeut. 10:15 ᵇEx. 3:8; Num. 13:27

8 "ᵃIf the LORD is pleased with us, then He will bring us into this land, and give it to us—ᵇa land which flows with milk and honey.

9 ᵃDeut. 1:26; 9:23, 24 ᵇDeut. 1:21, 29

9 "Only ᵃdo not rebel against the LORD; and do not ᵇfear the people of the land, for they shall be our prey. Their protection has been removed from them, and the LORD is with us; do not fear them."

10 ᵃEx. 17:4 ᵇEx. 16:10; Lev. 9:23

10 ᵃBut all the congregation said to stone them with stones. Then ᵇthe glory of the LORD appeared in the tent of meeting to all the sons of Israel.

★ **11** ᵃEx. 32:9-13 ᵇPs. 106:24

11 ᵃAnd the LORD said to Moses, "How long will this people spurn Me? And how long will ᵇthey not believe in Me, despite all the signs which I have performed in their midst?

★ **12** ᵃLev. 26:25; Deut. 28:21 ᵇEx. 32:10

12 "I will smite them with ᵃpestilence and dispossess them,

and I ᵇwill make you into a nation greater and mightier than they."

13 ᵃBut Moses said to the LORD, "Then the Egyptians will hear of it, for by Thy strength Thou didst bring up this people from their midst,

13 ᵃEx. 32:11-14; Ps. 106:23

14 and they will tell *it* to the inhabitants of this land. They have heard that Thou, O LORD, art in the midst of this people, for ᵃThou, O LORD, art seen eye to eye, while Thy cloud stands over them; and Thou dost go before them in a pillar of cloud by day and in a pillar of fire by night.

14 ᵃEx. 13:21; Deut. 5:4

15 "Now if Thou dost slay this people as one man, ᵃthen the nations who have heard of Thy fame will say,

15 ᵃEx. 32:12

16 'Because the LORD ᵃcould not bring this people into the land which He promised them by oath, therefore He slaughtered them in the wilderness.'

16 ᵃJosh. 7:7

17 "But now, I pray, let the power of the Lord be great, just as Thou hast declared,

18 'ᵃThe LORD is slow to anger and abundant in lovingkindness, forgiving iniquity and transgression; but ᵇHe will by no means clear *the guilty,* ᶜvisiting the iniquity of the fathers on the children to the third and the fourth *generations.*'

★ **18** ᵃEx. 20:6; 34:6, 7; Deut. 5:10; 7:9; Ps. 103:8; 145:8; Jon. 4:2 ᵇEx. 20:5; Deut. 5:9; 7:10 ᶜEx. 34:7

19 "ᵃPardon, I pray, the iniquity of this people according to the greatness of Thy lovingkindness, just as Thou also hast forgiven this people, from Egypt even until now."

19 ᵃEx. 32:32; 34:9

20 So the LORD said, "ᵃI have pardoned *them* according to your word;

20 ᵃMic. 7:18-20

21 but indeed, ᵃas I live, ᵇall the earth will be filled with the glory of the LORD.

21 ᵃNum. 14:28; Deut. 32:40; Is. 49:18 ᵇIs. 6:3; Hab. 2:14

22 "Surely ᵃall the men who have seen My glory and My signs, which I performed in Egypt and

★ **22** ᵃ1 Cor. 10:5 ᵇEx. 5:21; 14:11; 15:24; 16:2; 17:2, 3; 32:1; Num. 11:1, 4; 12:1; 14:2

14:6 *tore their clothes.* As a sign of mourning (cf. Lev. 10:6).

14:11 The purpose of *signs* performed in Egypt was to encourage the people's faith in God (see Exod. 4:5).

14:12 For the second time God offered to make of Moses a new nation in place of this one (see

Exod. 32:10).

14:18 *lovingkindness.* Heb., *hesed,* referring to God's steadfast, loyal love. See note on Hos. 2:19.

14:22 *these ten times.* (1) At the Red Sea (Exod. 14:11-12), (2) at Marah (Exod. 15:23-24), (3) in the wilderness of Sin (Exod. 16:2), (4) and (5)

in the wilderness, yet *b*have put Me to the test these ten times and have not listened to My voice,

23 *a*shall by no means see the land which I swore to their fathers, nor shall any of those who spurned Me see it.

24 "But My servant Caleb, *a*because he has had a different spirit and has followed Me fully, *b*I will bring into the land which he entered, and his descendants shall take possession of it.

25 "*a*Now the Amalekites and the Canaanites live in the valleys; turn tomorrow and set out to the wilderness by the way of the Red Sea."

26 And the LORD spoke to Moses and Aaron, saying,

27 "How long *shall I bear* with this evil congregation who are *a*grumbling against Me? I have heard the complaints of the sons of Israel, which they are making against Me.

28 "Say to them, '*a*As I live,' says the LORD, 'just as *b*you have spoken in My hearing, so I will surely do to you;

29 *a*your corpses shall fall in this wilderness, even all *b*your numbered men, according to your complete number from twenty years old and upward, who have grumbled against Me.

30 'Surely you shall not come into the land in which I swore to settle you, *a*except Caleb the son of Jephunneh and Joshua the son of Nun.

31 '*a*Your children, however, whom you said would become a prey—I will bring them in, and they shall know the land which you have rejected.

32 '*a*But as for you, your corpses shall fall in this wilderness.

33 'And your sons shall be shepherds for *a*forty years in the wilderness, and they shall suffer *for* your unfaithfulness, until your corpses lie in the wilderness.

34 'According to the *a*number of days which you spied out the land, forty days, for every day you shall bear your guilt a year, *even* forty years, and you shall know My opposition.

35 '*a*I, the LORD, have spoken, surely this I will do to all this evil congregation who are gathered together against Me. In this wilderness they shall be destroyed, and there they shall die.' "

36 *a*As for the men whom Moses sent to spy out the land and who returned and made all the congregation grumble against him by bringing out a bad report concerning the land,

37 even *a*those men who brought out the very bad report of the land died by a *b*plague before the LORD.

38 But Joshua the son of Nun and Caleb the son of Jephunneh remained alive out of those men who went to spy out the land.

39 And when Moses spoke *a*these words to all the sons of Israel, *b*the people mourned greatly.

40 In the morning, however, they rose up early and went up to the ridge of the hill country, saying, "*a*Here we are; we have indeed sinned, but we will go up to the place which the LORD has promised."

41 But Moses said, "*a*Why then are you transgressing the commandment of the LORD, when it will not succeed?

42 "*a*Do not go up, lest you be struck down before your enemies, for the LORD is not among you.

Marginal references (left column):

23 *a*Num. 26:65; 32:11; Heb. 3:18

★24 *a*Num. 14:6-9 *b*Num. 26:65; 32:12; Deut. 1:36; Josh. 14:6-15

★25 *a*Num. 13:29

27 *a*Num. 11:1

28 *a*Num. 14:21 *b*Num. 14:2; Deut. 2:14, 15; Heb. 3:17

29 *a*Heb. 3:17 *b*Num. 1:45, 46

30 *a*Num. 14:24

31 *a*Num. 14:3

32 *a*Num. 26:64, 65; 32:13; 1 Cor. 10:5

Marginal references (right column):

33 *a*Deut. 2:7; 8:2, 4; 29:5

34 *a*Num. 13:25

35 *a*Num. 23:19

36 *a*Num. 13:4-16, 32

37 *a*1 Cor. 10:10; Heb. 3:17, 18 *b*Num. 16:49

39 *a*Num. 14:28-35 *b*Ex. 33:4

40 *a*Deut. 1:41-44

41 *a*2 Chr. 24:20

42 *a*Deut. 1:42

---

in connection with manna (Exod. 16:20 and 16:27), (6) at Rephidim (Exod. 17:1-3), (7) at Horeb (Exod. 32:7), (8) at Taberah (Num. 11:1), (9) the complaint of the mixed multitude (Num. 11:4), and (10) at Kadesh-barnea (Num. 14).
14:24 The fulfillment of this promise is recorded in Josh. 14:6-15.

14:25 Though the Israelites were at the edge of the promised land, they were commanded to turn back into the wilderness where all who were 20 years of age and older would die (except Joshua and Caleb, cf. vv. 29-30) and where they would wander for 40 more years (cf. v. 33).

43 "For the Amalekites and the Canaanites will be there in front of you, and you will fall by the sword, inasmuch as you have turned back from following the LORD. And the LORD will not be with you."

44 *a*Num. 31:6

44 But they went up heedlessly to the ridge of the hill country; neither *a*the ark of the covenant of the LORD nor Moses left the camp.

45 *a*Num. 21:3

45 Then the Amalekites and the Canaanites who lived in that hill country came down, and struck them and beat them down as far as *a*Hormah.

B   The Discipline from God,
15:1–20:13
1 Miscellaneous laws concerning offerings, Sabbath-breaking, and garment fringes,
15:1–41

★ 2 *a*Lev. 23:10

15 Now the LORD spoke to Moses, saying,

2 "*a*Speak to the sons of Israel, and say to them, 'When you enter the land where you are to live, which I am giving you,

3 *a*Lev. 1:2, 3 *b*Lev. 22:21 *c*Lev. 23:1-44 *d*Gen. 8:21; 2 Cor. 2:15, 16; Phil. 4:18

3 then make *a*an offering by fire to the LORD, a burnt offering or a sacrifice to *b*fulfill a special vow, or as a freewill offering or in your *c*appointed times, to make a *d*soothing aroma to the LORD, from the herd or from the flock.

★ 4 *a*Num. 28:1-29:40

4 '*a*And the one who presents his offering shall present to the LORD a grain offering of one-tenth *of an ephah* of fine flour mixed with one-fourth of a hin of oil,

5 *a*Lev. 1:10; 3:6; Num. 15:11

5 and you shall prepare wine for the libation, one-fourth of a hin, with the burnt offering or for the sacrifice, for *a*each lamb.

6 'Or for a ram you shall prepare as a grain offering two-tenths *of an ephah* of fine flour mixed with one-third of a hin of oil;

7 and for the libation you shall offer one-third of a hin of wine as a soothing aroma to the LORD.

8 *a*Lev. 1:3; 3:1

8 'And when you prepare *a*a bull as a burnt offering or a sacrifice, to fulfill a special vow, or for peace offerings to the LORD,

9 then you shall offer with the bull a grain offering of three-tenths *of an ephah* of fine flour mixed with one-half a hin of oil;

10 and you shall offer as the libation one-half a hin of wine as an offering by fire, as a soothing aroma to the LORD.

11 'Thus it shall be done for each ox, or for each ram, or for each of the male lambs, or of the goats.

12 'According to the number that you prepare, so you shall do for everyone according to their number.

13 'All who are native shall do these things in this manner, in presenting an offering by fire, as a soothing aroma to the LORD.

★ 14

14 'And if an alien sojourns with you, or one who may be among you throughout your generations, and he *wishes to* make an offering by fire, as a soothing aroma to the LORD, just as you do, so he shall do.

15 *a*Num. 9:14; 15:29

15 'As for the assembly, there shall be *a*one statute for you and for the alien who sojourns *with you,* a perpetual statute throughout your generations; as you are, so shall the alien be before the LORD.

16 *a*Lev. 24:22

16 'There is to be *a*one law and one ordinance for you and for the alien who sojourns with you.' "

15:2 In spite of their disobedience, God would fulfill His promise to Abraham to give Israel the *land* of Canaan (cf. Gen. 15:18–21).

15:4 *one-tenth of an ephah.* About 2 quarts. *one-fourth of a hin.* About 2 pints. Note that the amounts of oil, flour, and wine increase with the size of the animal offered (vv. 6–7 and 9–10).

15:14 The *alien* was welcome to live among the Israelites and to worship according to God's law.

17 Then the LORD spoke to Moses, saying,

18 "Speak to the sons of Israel, and say to them, 'When you enter the land where I bring you,

★19-21

19 aJosh. 5:11, 12

19 then it shall be, that when you eat of the ᵃfood of the land, you shall lift up an offering to the LORD.

20 aEx. 34:26; Lev. 23:14 bDeut. 14:22, 23; 16:13

20 'ᵃOf the first of your dough you shall lift up a cake as an offering; as ᵇthe offering of the threshing floor, so you shall lift it up.

21 'From the first of your dough you shall give to the LORD an offering throughout your generations.

★22-29

22 aLev. 4:2

22 'But when you ᵃunwittingly fail and do not observe all these commandments, which the LORD has spoken to Moses,

23 *even* all that the LORD has commanded you through Moses, from the day when the LORD gave commandment and onward throughout your generations,

24 aLev. 4:2, 22, 27; 5:15, 18 bNum. 15:8-10

24 then it shall be, if it is done ᵃunintentionally, without the knowledge of the congregation, that all the congregation shall offer one bull for a burnt offering, as a soothing aroma to the LORD, ᵇwith its grain offering, and its libation, according to the ordinance, and one male goat for a sin offering.

25 aLev. 4:20; Heb. 2:17

25 'Then ᵃthe priest shall make atonement for all the congregation of the sons of Israel, and they shall be forgiven; for it was an error, and they have brought their offering, an offering by fire to the LORD, and their sin offering before the LORD, for their error.

26 aNum. 15:24

26 'So all the congregation of the sons of Israel will be forgiven, with the alien who sojourns among them, for *it happened* to all the people through ᵃerror.

27 aLev. 4:27-31; Luke 12:48

27 'Also if one person sins ᵃunintentionally, then he shall offer a one year old female goat for a sin offering.

28 aLev. 4:35

28 'And ᵃthe priest shall make atonement before the LORD for the person who goes astray when he sins unintentionally, making atonement for him that he may be forgiven.

29 'You shall have one law for him who does *anything* unintentionally, for him who is native among the sons of Israel and for the alien who sojourns among them.

★30-31

30 aNum. 14:40-44; Deut. 1:43; 17:12, 13

30 'But the person who does *anything* ᵃdefiantly, whether he is native or an alien, that one is blaspheming the LORD; and that person shall be cut off from among his people.

31 a2 Sam. 12:9; Prov. 13:13 bEzek. 18:20

31 'Because he has ᵃdespised the word of the LORD and has broken His commandment, that person shall be completely cut off; ᵇhis guilt *shall be* on him.' "

★32-36

32 aEx. 31:14, 15; 35:2, 3

32 Now while the sons of Israel were in the wilderness, they found a man ᵃgathering wood on the sabbath day.

33 And those who found him gathering wood brought him to Moses and Aaron, and to all the congregation;

34 aNum. 9:8

34 and they put him in custody ᵃbecause it had not been declared what should be done to him.

35 aLev. 20:2, 27; 24:14-23; Deut. 21:21

35 Then the LORD said to Moses, "The man shall surely be put to death; ᵃall the congregation shall stone him with stones outside the camp."

36 So all the congregation brought him outside the camp, and stoned him to death with

---

15:19-21 The *offering* (lit., heave offering) symbolically set aside the animal (see note on Lev. 7:32) or grain (as here) as a contribution to the Lord. Apparently it was for the priest to eat.

15:22-29 These verses describe the offerings to be brought when a man sinned unwittingly or unintentionally.

15:30-31 No propitiatory offering, only judg-ment, awaited the one who sinned *defiantly* (lit., with a high hand; i.e, with a raised, clenched fist in defiance of God and His commands). See note on Exod. 14:8 (where the same word is used).

15:32-36 These verses furnish an example of a sin committed with a high hand and the punishment that resulted (cf. Exod. 35:2).

stones, just as the LORD had commanded Moses.

★37-41
37 The LORD also spoke to Moses, saying,

38 aDeut. 22:12; Matt. 23:5
38 "Speak to the sons of Israel, and tell them that they shall make for themselves ªtassels on the corners of their garments throughout their generations, and that they shall put on the tassel of each corner a cord of blue.

39 aDeut. 4:23; 6:12; 8:11, 14, 19
39 "And it shall be a tassel for you to look at and ªremember all the commandments of the LORD, so as to do them and not follow after your own heart and your own eyes, after which you played the harlot,

40 aLev. 11:44, 45
40 in order that you may remember to do all My commandments, and ªbe holy to your God.

41 "I am the LORD your God who brought you out from the land of Egypt to be your God; I am the LORD your God."

2 The rebellion of Korah, 16:1-50

★ 1-3
1 aEx. 6:21; Jude 11 bNum. 26:9; Deut. 11:6
16 Now ªKorah the son of Izhar, the son of Kohath, the son of Levi, with ᵇDathan and Abiram, the sons of Eliab, and On the son of Peleth, sons of Reuben, took action,

2 aNum. 1:16; 26:9
2 and they rose up before Moses, together with some of the sons of Israel, two hundred and fifty leaders of the congregation, ªchosen in the assembly, men of renown.

3 aNum. 12:2; Ps. 106:16 bNum. 16:7 cNum. 5:3
3 And they assembled together ªagainst Moses and Aaron, and said to them, "ᵇYou have gone far enough, for all the congregation are holy, every one of them, and ᶜthe LORD is in their midst; so why do you exalt yourselves above the assembly of the LORD?"

4 aNum. 14:5
4 When Moses heard this, ªhe fell on his face;

5 aLev. 10:3; Ps. 65:4 bNum. 17:5, 8
5 and he spoke to Korah and all his company, saying, "Tomorrow morning the LORD will show who is His, and ªwho is holy, and will bring him near to Himself; even ᵇthe one whom He will choose, He will bring near to Himself.

6 "Do this: take censers for yourselves, Korah and all your company,

7 aNum. 16:3
7 and put fire in them, and lay incense upon them in the presence of the LORD tomorrow; and the man whom the LORD chooses shall be the one who is holy. ªYou have gone far enough, you sons of Levi!"

8 Then Moses said to Korah, "Hear now, you sons of Levi,

★ 9-10
9 aIs. 7:13 bNum. 3:6, 9; Deut. 10:8
9 ªis it not enough for you that the God of Israel has separated you from the rest of the congregation of Israel, ᵇto bring you near to Himself, to do the service of the tabernacle of the LORD, and to stand before the congregation to minister to them;

10 aNum. 3:10; 18:1-7
10 and that He has brought you near, Korah, and all your brothers, sons of Levi, with you? And are you ªseeking for the priesthood also?

11 aEx. 16:7 b1 Cor. 10:10
11 "Therefore you and all your company are gathered together ªagainst the LORD; but as for Aaron, who is he that ᵇyou grumble against him?"

★12-14
12 Then Moses sent a summons to Dathan and Abiram, the

15:37-41 Like "tying a string around the finger," the tassels and cord of blue on the edges of their garments were to remind Israel to obey God's commands.

16:1-3 Korah, a great-grandson of Levi and younger contemporary of Moses, was joined in this attempted revolt against the authority of Moses and Aaron by Dathan and Abiram (who were also Levites), by On (not a Levite), and by 250 representatives of the tribes of Israel. They charged that Moses and Aaron took too much authority to themselves in view of the fact that all the congregation are holy. Though it was true that all the congregation was holy (cf. Exod. 19:6), they failed to recognize that Moses and Aaron were God-appointed leaders (see note on Jude 11).

16:9-10 The important service of the Kohathites is described in 4:1-20. But they coveted more, namely, the priestly functions assigned to Aaron.

16:12-14 Dathan and Abiram, when summoned by Moses, charged him with ambitions of wanting to lord it over the people and of

sons of Eliab; but they said, "We will not come up.

13 "Is it not enough that you have brought us up out of a ªland flowing with milk and honey ᵇto have us die in the wilderness, but you would also lord it over us?

14 "Indeed, you have not brought us ªinto a land flowing with milk and honey, nor have you given us an inheritance of ᵇfields and vineyards. Would you ᶜput out the eyes of these men? We will not come up!"

15 Then Moses became very angry and said to the Lᴏʀᴅ, "ªDo not regard their offering! ᵇI have not taken a single donkey from them, nor have I done harm to any of them."

16 And Moses said to Korah, "You and all your company be present before the Lᴏʀᴅ tomorrow, both you and they along with Aaron.

17 "And each of you take his firepan and put incense on it, and each of you bring his censer before the Lᴏʀᴅ, two hundred and fifty firepans; also you and Aaron *shall* each *bring* his firepan."

18 So they each took his *own* censer and put fire on it, and laid incense on it; and they stood at the doorway of the tent of meeting, with Moses and Aaron.

19 Thus Korah assembled all the congregation against them at the doorway of the tent of meeting. And ªthe glory of the Lᴏʀᴅ appeared to all the congregation.

20 Then the Lᴏʀᴅ spoke to Moses and Aaron, saying,

21 "ªSeparate yourselves from among this congregation, ᵇthat I may consume them instantly."

22 But they fell on their faces, and said, "O God, ªThou God of the spirits of all flesh, ᵇwhen one man sins, wilt Thou be angry with the entire congregation?"

23 Then the Lᴏʀᴅ spoke to Moses, saying,

24 "Speak to the congregation, saying, 'ªGet back from around the dwellings of Korah, Dathan and Abiram.' "

25 Then Moses arose and went to Dathan and Abiram, with the elders of Israel following him,

26 and he spoke to the congregation, saying, "ªDepart now from the tents of these wicked men, and touch nothing that belongs to them, ᵇlest you be swept away in all their sin."

27 So they got back from around the dwellings of Korah, Dathan and Abiram; and Dathan and Abiram came out *and* stood at the doorway of their tents, along with their wives and ªtheir sons and their little ones.

28 And Moses said, "By this you shall know that ªthe Lᴏʀᴅ has sent me to do all these deeds; for this is not my doing.

29 "If these men die the death of all men, or if they suffer the ªfate of all men, *then* the Lᴏʀᴅ has not sent me.

30 "But ªif the Lᴏʀᴅ brings about an entirely new thing and the ground opens its mouth and swallows them up with all that is theirs, and they ᵇdescend alive into Sheol, then you will understand that these men have spurned the Lᴏʀᴅ."

31 Then it came about as he finished speaking all these words, that the ground that was under them split open;

32 and ªthe earth opened its mouth and swallowed them up, and their households, and ᵇall the men who belonged to Korah, with *their* possessions.

33 So they and all that belonged to them went down alive to Sheol; and the earth closed over them, and they perished from the midst of the assembly.

Marginal references (left column):

13 ªEx. 16:3;
Num. 11:4-6
ᵇNum.
14:2, 3

14 ªNum.
13:27; 14:8
ᵇEx. 22:5;
23:10, 11;
Num. 20:5
ᶜJudg.
16:21;
1 Sam. 11:2

15 ªGen.
4:4, 5
ᵇ1 Sam. 12:3

19 ªNum.
14:10; 16:42;
20:6

★20-22

21 ªNum.
16:45 ᵇEx.
32:10, 12

22 ªNum.
27:16 ᵇGen.
18:23-32;
Lev. 4:3

Marginal references (right column):

24 ªNum.
16:45

26 ªIs. 52:11
ᵇGen. 19:15,
17

27 ªNum.
26:11

28 ªEx.
3:12-15;
4:12, 15

29 ªEccl.
3:19

★30 ªJob
31:2, 3 ᵇPs.
55:15

★32 ªNum.
26:10; Deut.
11:6; Ps.
106:17
ᵇNum. 26:11

---

throwing dust in their eyes (this is the meaning of *put out the eyes,* v. 14). In fact, however, this charge was a cover-up for their own selfish ambitions.
16:20-22 Only Moses' and Aaron's intercession saved the entire nation from destruction.

16:30 *Sheol.* I.e., the grave (see note on Gen. 37:35).
16:32 The sons of Korah, who likely did not take part in their father's crime, did not die with him (26:11).

34 And all Israel who *were* around them fled at their outcry, for they said, "The earth may swallow us up!"

35 [a]Fire also came forth from the LORD and consumed the [b]two hundred and fifty men who were offering the incense.

36 Then the LORD spoke to Moses, saying,

37 "Say to Eleazar, the son of Aaron the priest, that he shall take up the censers out of the midst of the blaze, for they are holy; and you scatter the burning coals abroad.

38 "As for the censers of these men who have sinned at the cost of their lives, let them be made into hammered sheets for a plating of the altar, since they did present them before the LORD and they are holy; and [a]they shall be for a sign to the sons of Israel."

39 So Eleazar the priest took the bronze censers which the men who were burned had offered; and they hammered them out as a plating for the altar,

40 as a reminder to the sons of Israel that [a]no layman who is not of the descendants of Aaron should come near [b]to burn incense before the LORD; that he might not become like Korah and his company—just as the LORD had spoken to him through Moses.

41 But on the next day all the congregation of the sons of Israel [a]grumbled against Moses and Aaron, saying, "You are the ones who have caused the death of the LORD's people."

42 It came about, however, when the congregation had assembled against Moses and Aaron, that they turned toward the tent of meeting, and behold, the cloud covered it and [a]the glory of the LORD appeared.

43 Then Moses and Aaron came to the front of the tent of meeting,

44 and the LORD spoke to Moses, saying,

45 "[a]Get away from among this congregation, that I may consume them instantly." Then they fell on their faces.

46 And Moses said to Aaron, "Take your censer and put in it fire from the altar, and lay incense *on it;* then bring it quickly to the congregation and [a]make atonement for them, for [b]wrath has gone forth from the LORD, the plague has begun!"

47 Then Aaron took *it* as Moses had spoken, and ran into the midst of the assembly, for behold, the plague had begun among the people. [a]So he put *on* the incense and made atonement for the people.

48 And he took his stand between the dead and the living, so that the plague was checked.

49 [a]But those who died by the plague were 14,700, besides those who [b]died on account of Korah.

50 Then Aaron returned to Moses at the doorway of the tent of meeting, for the plague had been checked.

3 Validation of the Aaronic priesthood: Aaron's rod that budded, 17:1-13

17 Then the LORD spoke to Moses, saying,

2 "Speak to the sons of Israel, and get from them a rod for each father's household: twelve rods, from all their leaders according to their fathers' households. You shall write each name on his rod,

3 and write Aaron's name on the rod of Levi; for there is one

---

Marginal references:

35 [a]Num. 11:1-3; 26:10 [b]Num. 16:2

★36-40

38 [a]Ezek. 14:8; 2 Pet. 2:6

40 [a]Num. 1:51 [b]Ex. 30:7-10

★41-50

41 [a]Num. 16:3

42 [a]Num. 16:19

45 [a]Num. 16:21, 24

46 [a]Num. 25:13; Is. 6:6; 7 [b]Num. 18:5; Deut. 9:22

47 [a]Num. 25:6-8, 13

49 [a]Num. 25:9 [b]Num. 16:32, 35

16:36-40 The rebels' censers, because they had been used illegally, were beaten into plates to cover the altar and thus to be a constant warning to others who might be tempted to follow Korah's example.

16:41-50 The people blamed Moses and Aaron for the deaths of the rebels. Once again God prepared to destroy the nation. Aaron quickly took his censer (which carried the legitimate fire and incense) and made atonement for the people. Nevertheless, 14,700 people died.

rod for the head *of each* of their fathers' households.

4 "You shall then deposit them in the tent of meeting in front of ªthe testimony, where I meet with you.

5 "And it will come about that the rod of ªthe man whom I choose will sprout. Thus I shall lessen from upon Myself the grumblings of the sons of Israel, who are grumbling against you."

6 Moses therefore spoke to the sons of Israel, and all their leaders gave him a rod apiece, for each leader according to their fathers' households, twelve rods, with the rod of Aaron among their rods.

7 So Moses deposited the rods before the LORD in ªthe tent of the testimony.

8 Now it came about on the next day that Moses went into the tent of the testimony; and behold, ªthe rod of Aaron for the house of Levi had sprouted and put forth buds and produced blossoms, and it bore ripe almonds.

9 Moses then brought out all the rods from the presence of the LORD to all the sons of Israel; and they looked, and each man took his rod.

10 But the LORD said to Moses, "Put back the rod of Aaron ªbefore the testimony to be kept as a sign against the ᵇrebels, that you may put an end to their grumblings against Me, so that they should not die."

11 Thus Moses did; just as the LORD had commanded him, so he did.

12 Then the sons of Israel spoke to Moses, saying, "ªBehold, we perish, we are dying, we are all dying!

13 "ªEveryone who comes near, who comes near to the tab-

ernacle of the LORD, must die. Are we to perish completely?"

4 *The duties and support of the Levites,* 18:1–32

18 So the LORD said to Aaron, "You and your sons and your father's household with you shall ªbear the guilt in connection with the sanctuary; and you and your sons with you shall bear the guilt in connection with your priesthood.

2 "But bring with you also your brothers, the tribe of Levi, the tribe of your father, that they may be ªjoined with you and serve you, while you and your sons with you are before the tent of the testimony.

3 "And they shall thus attend to your obligation and the obligation of all the tent, but ªthey shall not come near to the furnishings of the sanctuary and ᵇthe altar, lest both they and you die.

4 "And they shall be joined with you and attend to the obligations of the tent of meeting, for all the service of the tent; but an outsider may not come near you.

5 "So you shall attend to the ªobligations of the sanctuary and the obligations of the altar, ᵇthat there may no longer be wrath on the sons of Israel.

6 "And behold, I Myself ªhave taken your fellow Levites from among the sons of Israel; they are ᵇa gift to you, dedicated to the LORD, to perform the service for the tent of meeting.

7 "But you and your sons with you shall ªattend to your priesthood for everything concerning the altar and inside the veil, and you are to perform service. I am giving you the priesthood as ᵇa bestowed service, but

Marginal references:

4 ªEx. 25:16, 21, 22; Num. 17:7

5 ªNum. 16:5

7 ªNum. 1:50, 53; 9:15

★ **8** ªEzek. 17:24; Heb. 9:4

10 ªNum. 17:4 ᵇDeut. 9:7, 24

★ **12-13**

12 ªIs. 6:5

13 ªNum. 1:51

★ **1** ªEx. 28:38; Lev. 10:17; 22:16

★ **2-7**

2 ªNum. 3:5-10

3 ªNum. 4:15-20 ᵇNum. 1:51; 18:7

5 ªEx. 27:21; Lev. 24:3 ᵇNum. 16:46

6 ªNum. 3:12, 45 ᵇNum. 3:9

7 ªEx. 29:9 ᵇNum. 18:20; Deut. 18:2; Matt. 10:8; 1 Pet. 5:2, 3 ᶜNum. 1:51

17:8 *on the next day.* The brief time that elapsed gave added evidence of the miraculous nature of this blossoming.

17:12–13 The people were still pitying themselves rather than praising God for His power and deliverance.

18:1 Aaron and his sons, who were responsible

for priestly ministries, were also responsible for the consequences of any defilement that might come to them or the sanctuary (cf. Exod. 28:38; Lev. 22:16).

18:2–7 Other Levites were given to Aaron and his sons (v. 6), to serve them while they officiated in the tabernacle (v. 7).

^cthe outsider who comes near shall be put to death."

★ 8-20

8 ^aLev.
6:16, 18;
7:28-34

8 Then the Lord spoke to Aaron, "Now behold, I Myself have given you charge of My ^aofferings, even all the holy gifts of the sons of Israel, I have given them to you as a portion, and to your sons as a perpetual allotment.

9 ^aLev. 2:1-
16 ^bLev.
6:30

9 "This shall be yours from the most holy *gifts, reserved* from the fire; every offering of theirs, even ^aevery grain offering and every ^bsin offering and every guilt offering, which they shall render to Me, shall be most holy for you and for your sons.

10 "As the most holy *gifts* you shall eat it; every male shall eat it. It shall be holy to you.

11 ^aNum.
18:1; Deut.
18:3 ^bLev.
22:1-16

11 "This also is yours, ^athe offering of their gift, even all the wave offerings of the sons of Israel; I have ^bgiven them to you and to your sons and daughters with you, as a perpetual allotment. Everyone of your household who is clean may eat it.

12 ^aDeut.
18:4; 32:14;
Ps. 81:16;
147:14

12 "^aAll the best of the fresh oil and all the best of the fresh wine and of the grain, the first fruits of those which they give to the Lord, I give them to you.

13 ^aEx.
22:29; 23:19;
34:26

13 "^aThe first ripe fruits of all that is in their land, which they bring to the Lord, shall be yours; everyone of your household who is clean may eat it.

14 ^aLev.
27:1-33

14 "^aEvery devoted thing in Israel shall be yours.

15 ^aEx.
13:13, 15;
Num. 3:46

15 "^aEvery first issue of the womb of all flesh, whether man or animal, which they offer to the Lord, shall be yours; nevertheless the first-born of man you shall surely redeem, and the first-born of unclean animals you shall redeem.

16 "And as to their redemption price, from a month old you shall redeem them, by your valuation, five shekels in silver, according to the shekel of the sanctuary, which is twenty gerahs.

17 ^aDeut.
15:19 ^bLev.
3:2

17 "But ^athe first-born of an ox or the first-born of a sheep or the first-born of a goat, you shall not redeem; they are holy. ^bYou shall sprinkle their blood on the altar and shall offer up their fat in smoke *as* an offering by fire, for a soothing aroma to the Lord.

18 ^aLev.
7:31

18 "And their meat shall be yours; it shall be yours like the ^abreast of a wave offering and like the right thigh.

19 ^aNum.
18:11
^b2 Chr. 13:5

19 "^aAll the offerings of the holy *gifts,* which the sons of Israel offer to the Lord, I have given to you and your sons and your daughters with you, as a perpetual allotment. It is ^ban everlasting covenant of salt before the Lord to you and your descendants with you."

20 ^aDeut.
10:9; 12:12;
14:27, 29
^bDeut. 18:2;
Josh. 13:33;
Ezek. 44:28

20 Then the Lord said to Aaron, "^aYou shall have no inheritance in their land, nor own any portion among them; ^bI am your portion and your inheritance among the sons of Israel.

21 ^aLev.
27:30-33;
Deut. 14:22-
29

21 "And to the sons of Levi, behold, I have given all the ^atithe in Israel for an inheritance, in return for their service which they perform, the service of the tent of meeting.

22 ^aNum.
1:51

22 "And ^athe sons of Israel shall not come near the tent of meeting again, lest they bear sin and die.

23 ^aNum.
18:1 ^bNum.
18:20

23 "Only the Levites shall perform the service of the tent of meeting, and they shall ^abear their iniquity; it shall be a perpetual statute throughout your generations, and among the sons of

---

18:8-20 These verses give instructions for the maintenance of the priests by the various offerings brought by the people. Included were *offerings* (lit., heave offerings, v. 8; cf. note on 15:19); whatever was not consumed by the altar fire (v. 9; see notes on Lev. 6:19, 24); every *wave* offering (vv. 11-13; see note on Lev. 7:30); *devoted* things (v. 14; see note on Lev. 27:28); and the revenue from the redemption of the firstborn of man and beast (vv. 15-18; see note on Exod. 22:29). These arrangements formed a *covenant of salt* (v. 19; an indissoluble arrangement, see note on Lev. 2:13).

Israel [b]they shall have no inheritance.

24 [a]Deut. 10:9

24 "For the tithe of the sons of Israel, which they offer as an offering to the LORD, I have given to the Levites for an inheritance; therefore I have said concerning them, '[a]They shall have no inheritance among the sons of Israel.'"

25 Then the LORD spoke to Moses, saying,

26 [a]Num. 18:21 [b]Neh. 10:38

26 "Moreover, you shall speak to the Levites and say to them, 'When you take from the sons of Israel [a]the tithe which I have given you from them for your inheritance, then you shall present an offering from it to the LORD, a [b]tithe of the tithe.

27 'And your offering shall be reckoned to you as the grain from the threshing floor or the full produce from the wine vat.

28 'So you shall also present an offering to the LORD from your tithes, which you receive from the sons of Israel; and from it you shall give the LORD's offering to Aaron the priest.

29 'Out of all your gifts you shall present every offering due to the LORD, from all the best of them, the sacred part from them.'

30 "And you shall say to them, 'When you have offered from it the best of it, then the rest shall be reckoned to the Levites as the product of the threshing floor, and as the product of the wine vat.

31 'And you may eat it anywhere, you and your households, for it is your compensation in return for your service in the tent of meeting.

32 [a]Lev. 22:15, 16

32 'And you shall bear no sin by reason of it, when you have offered the best of it. But you shall not [a]profane the sacred gifts of the sons of Israel, lest you die.'"

5 The red heifer sacrifice, 19:1–22

19 Then the LORD spoke to Moses and Aaron, saying,

★ 2-10

2 "This is the statute of the law which the LORD has commanded, saying, 'Speak to the sons of Israel that they bring you an [a]unblemished red heifer in which is no defect, and [b]on which a yoke has never been placed.

2 [a]Lev. 22:20-25 [b]Deut. 21:3

3 'And you shall give it to [a]Eleazar the priest, and it shall [b]be brought outside the camp and be slaughtered in his presence.

3 [a]Num. 3:4 [b]Lev. 4:11, 12, 21; Num. 19:9

4 'Next Eleazar the priest shall take some of its blood with his finger, and [a]sprinkle some of its blood toward the front of the tent of meeting seven times.

4 [a]Lev. 4:6, 17; 16:14

5 'Then the heifer shall be burned in his sight; [a]its hide and its flesh and its blood, with its refuse, shall be burned.

5 [a]Ex. 29:14; Lev. 4:11, 12

6 'And the priest shall take [a]cedar wood and hyssop and scarlet material, and cast it into the midst of the burning heifer.

6 [a]Lev. 14:4

7 'The priest [a]shall then wash his clothes and bathe his body in water, and afterward come into the camp, but the priest shall be unclean until evening.

7 [a]Lev. 16:26, 28; 22:6

8 'The one who burns it shall also wash his clothes in water and bathe his body in water, and shall be unclean until evening.

9 'Now a man who is clean shall gather up the ashes of the heifer and deposit them outside the camp in a clean place, and the congregation of the sons of Israel shall keep it as [a]water to remove impurity; it is purification from sin.

9 [a]Num. 8:7; 31:23

10 'And the one who gathers the ashes of the heifer [a]shall wash his clothes and be unclean until evening; and it shall be a perpetual statute to the sons of Israel

10 [a]Num. 19:7

19:2-10 The ritual of the red heifer provided cleansing for those who were defiled because of contact with a corpse. Preparations for the ritual required that the ashes of an unblemished, unyoked red heifer be mixed with water (called water to remove impurity). This served as a purification from sin (lit., a sin offering, as also in v. 17).

and to the alien who sojourns among them.

11 '*a*The one who touches the corpse of any person shall be unclean for seven days.

12 'That one shall *a*purify himself from uncleanness with the water on the third day and on the seventh day, *and then* he shall be clean; but if he does not purify himself on the third day and on the seventh day, he shall not be clean.

13 '*a*Anyone who touches a corpse, the body of a man who has died, and does not purify himself, *b*defiles the tabernacle of the LORD; and that person shall be cut off from Israel. Because the water for impurity was not *c*sprinkled on him, he shall be unclean; his uncleanness is still on him.

14 'This is the law when a man dies in a tent: everyone who comes into the tent and everyone who is in the tent shall be unclean for seven days.

15 'And every open vessel, which has no covering tied down on it, shall be unclean.

16 '*a*Also, anyone who in the open field touches one who has been slain with a sword or who has died *naturally,* or a human bone or a grave, shall be unclean for seven days.

17 'Then for the unclean *person* they shall take some of the ashes of the burnt *a*purification from sin and flowing water shall be added to them in a vessel.

18 'And a clean person shall take hyssop and dip *it* in the water, and sprinkle *it* on the tent and on all the furnishings and on the persons who were there, and on the one who touched the bone or

the one slain or the one dying *naturally* or the grave.

19 'Then the clean *person* *a*shall sprinkle on the unclean on the third day and on the seventh day; and on the seventh day he shall purify him from uncleanness, and he shall wash his clothes and bathe *himself* in water and shall be clean by evening.

20 'But the man who is unclean and does not purify himself from uncleanness, that person shall be cut off from the midst of the assembly, because he has *a*defiled the sanctuary of the LORD; the water for impurity has not been sprinkled on him, he is unclean.

21 'So it shall be a perpetual statute for them. And he *a*who sprinkles the water for impurity shall wash his clothes, and he who touches the water for impurity shall be unclean until evening.

22 '*a*Furthermore, anything that the unclean *person* touches shall be unclean; and the person who touches *it* shall be unclean until evening.' "

6 The sin of Moses, 20:1–13

20 Then the sons of Israel, the whole congregation, came to the *a*wilderness of Zin in the first month; and the people stayed at Kadesh. Now Miriam died there and was buried there.

2 *a*And there was no water for the congregation; *b*and they assembled themselves against Moses and Aaron.

3 *a*The people thus contended with Moses and spoke, saying, "*b*If only we had perished *c*when our brothers perished before the LORD!

Marginal references (left column):

11 *a*Lev. 21:1, 11; Num. 5:2; 6:6; Acts 21:26, 27

★**12** *a*Num. 19:19; 31:19

★**13** *a*Lev. 7:21; 22:3-7 *b*Lev. 15:31; 20:3; Num. 19:20 *c*Num. 19:19

★**16-19**

16 *a*Num. 31:19

17 *a*Num. 19:9

Marginal references (right column):

19 *a*Ezek. 36:25; Heb. 10:22

20 *a*Num. 19:13

21 *a*Num. 19:7

22 *a*Lev. 5:2, 3; 7:21; 22:5, 6

★ 1 *a*Num. 13:21; 27:14; 33:36

2 *a*Ex. 17:1 *b*Num. 16:19, 42

3 *a*Ex. 17:2 *b*Num. 14:2, 3 *c*Num. 16:31-35

19:12 *purify.* Lit., "de-sin" or "un-sin" as also in 8:21.

19:13 A defilement that was not cleansed would pollute the tabernacle as well. *sprinkled on him.* Lit., thrown or dashed on him.

19:16–19 People could not help becoming defiled occasionally; thus, the water was always available and any undefiled person (not just a

priest) could dash it on the one defiled. This ritual pictured the cleansing power of the blood of Christ (cf. Heb. 9:13-14; 1 John 1:7-9).

20:1 *Then.* Forty years after the Exodus from Egypt. *wilderness of Zin.* See note on 13:21. *Miriam.* The elder sister of Moses and Aaron (see also notes on Exod. 15:20 and Num. 12:1).

4 aEx. 17:3

4 "aWhy then have you brought the LORD's assembly into this wilderness, for us and our beasts to die here?

5 aNum. 16:14

5 "And why have you made us come up from Egypt, to bring us in to this wretched place? aIt is not a place of grain or figs or vines or pomegranates, nor is there water to drink."

6 aNum. 14:5

6 Then Moses and Aaron came in from the presence of the assembly to the doorway of the tent of meeting, and afell on their faces. Then the glory of the LORD appeared to them;

7 and the LORD spoke to Moses, saying,

★ 8 aEx. 4:17, 20; 17:5, 6

8 "Take athe rod; and you and your brother Aaron assemble the congregation and speak to the rock before their eyes, that it may yield its water. You shall thus bring forth water for them out of the rock and let the congregation and their beasts drink."

9 aNum. 17:10

9 So Moses took the rod afrom before the LORD, just as He had commanded him;

10 aPs. 106:33

10 and Moses and Aaron gathered the assembly before the rock. And he said to them, "aListen now, you rebels; shall we bring forth water for you out of this rock?"

11 aPs. 78:16; Is. 48:21; 1 Cor. 10:4

11 Then Moses lifted up his hand and struck the rock twice with his rod; and awater came forth abundantly, and the congregation and their beasts drank.

★12 aNum. 20:24; 27:14; Deut. 1:37; 3:26, 27

12 But the LORD said to Moses and Aaron, "aBecause you have not believed Me, to treat Me as holy in the sight of the sons of Israel, therefore you shall not bring this assembly into the land which I have given them."

★13 aEx. 17:7; Ps. 95:8

13 Those *were* the waters of aMeribah, because the sons of Israel contended with the LORD, and He proved Himself holy among them.

IV ISRAEL MARCHING TO MOAB, 20:14–21:35

A The Defiance of Edom, 20:14–22

★14 aGen. 36:31-39; Deut. 2:4 bJosh. 2:9, 10; 9:9, 10, 24

14 From Kadesh Moses then sent messengers to athe king of Edom: "Thus your brother Israel has said, 'You bknow all the hardship that has befallen us;

15 that our fathers went down to Egypt, and we stayed in Egypt a long time, and the Egyptians treated us and our fathers badly.

16 aEx. 2:23; 3:7 bEx. 14:19

16 'But awhen we cried out to the LORD, He heard our voice and sent ban angel and brought us out from Egypt; now behold, we are at Kadesh, a town on the edge of your territory.

★17 aNum. 21:22

17 'Please alet us pass through your land. We shall not pass through field or through vineyard; we shall not even drink water from a well. We shall go along the king's highway, not turning to the right or left, until we pass through your territory.' "

18 aNum. 24:18

18 aEdom, however, said to him, "You shall not pass through us, lest I come out with the sword against you."

19 aEx. 12:38 bDeut. 2:6, 28

19 Again, the sons of Israel said to him, "We shall go up by the highway, and if I and amy livestock do drink any of your water, bthen I will pay its price. Let me only pass through on my feet, nothing *else*."

20:8 *the rod.* The same rod with which Moses had performed previous miracles (cf. Exod. 7:20; 14:16). God instructed Moses and Aaron (the verb is plural) to *speak* to the rock, not strike it. In anger and self-glorification, Moses struck it (v. 11; cf. Psalm 106:32–33).
20:12 Because of their sin, Moses and Aaron were not permitted to enter the promised land. Here is a warning to us that forgiveness of sin does not always carry with it alleviation of the consequences of that sin.

20:13 *Meribah.* A play (in the Hebrew) on the verb "to strive."
20:14 *Edom.* See the Introduction to the Book of Obadiah and notes on Gen. 25:22. The Israelites wanted to go east from Kadesh, through Edom, which occupied the territory S. of the Dead Sea (cf. v. 17). Their request was refused with a show of force (v. 20).
20:17 *the king's highway.* A public caravan route.

20 aJudg.
11:17

20 But he said, "aYou shall not pass through." And Edom came out against him with a heavy force, and with a strong hand.

21 aJudg.
11:17 bDeut.
2:8

21 aThus Edom refused to allow Israel to pass through his territory; bso Israel turned away from him.

★22 aNum.
20:1, 14

22 Now when they set out from aKadesh, the sons of Israel, the whole congregation, came to Mount Hor.

B The Death of Aaron, 20:23-29

23 aNum.
33:37

23 Then the Lord spoke to Moses and Aaron at aMount Hor by the border of the land of Edom, saying,

24 aGen.
25:8 bNum.
20:5, 10

24 "Aaron shall be agathered to his people; for he shall not enter the land which I have given to the sons of Israel, because byou rebelled against My command at the waters of Meribah.

25 aNum.
3:4

25 "Take Aaron and his son aEleazar, and bring them up to Mount Hor;

26 aNum.
20:24

26 and strip Aaron of his garments and put them on his son Eleazar. So Aaron will be agathered *to his people*, and will die there."

27 So Moses did just as the Lord had commanded, and they went up to Mount Hor in the sight of all the congregation.

★28-29

28 aEx.
29:29 bNum.
33:38; Deut.
10:6; 32:50

28 And after Moses had stripped Aaron of his garments and aput them on his son Eleazar, bAaron died there on the mountain top. Then Moses and Eleazar came down from the mountain.

29 aGen.
1:5; 50:3, 10;
Deut. 34:8

29 And when all the congregation saw that Aaron had died,

all the house of Israel wept for Aaron thirty adays.

C The Defeat of Arad, 21:1-3

1 aNum.
33:40; Josh.
12:14; Judg.
1:16

21 When the Canaanite, the king of aArad, who lived in the Negev, heard that Israel was coming by the way of Atharim, then he fought against Israel, and took some of them captive.

2 aGen.
28:20; Judg.
11:30

2 So aIsrael made a vow to the Lord, and said, "If Thou wilt indeed deliver this people into my hand, then I will utterly destroy their cities."

★ 3 aNum.
14:45

3 And the Lord heard the voice of Israel, and delivered up the Canaanites; then they utterly destroyed them and their cities. Thus the name of the place was called aHormah.

D The Discipline of Israel: the Bronze Serpent, 21:4-9

★ 4 aDeut.
2:8

4 Then they set out from Mount Hor by the way of the Red Sea, to ago around the land of Edom; and the people became impatient because of the journey.

5 aNum.
14:2, 3
bNum. 11:6

5 And the people spoke against God and Moses, "aWhy have you brought us up out of Egypt to die in the wilderness? For there is no food and no water, and bwe loathe this miserable food."

★ 6 aDeut.
8:15 bJer.
8:17 c1 Cor.
10:9
7 aNum.
11:2; Ps.
78:34; Is.
26:16; Hos.
5:15 bEx.
8:8; 1 Sam.
12:19; Acts
8:24

6 aAnd the Lord sent fiery serpents among the people and bthey bit the people, so that cmany people of Israel died.

7 aSo the people came to Moses and said, "We have sinned, because we have spoken against the Lord and you; binter-

---

20:22 The location of *Mount Hor* is uncertain, though it apparently was on the border of Edom near Kadesh. Here the Israelites began their detour around Edom.

20:28-29 The death of Aaron was in the 40th year after the Exodus. His death at the age of 123 (see 33:38-39) stands in sharp contrast to the eternal priesthood of Christ (cf. Heb.

7:23-24).

21:3 *Hormah* means "destruction." The area was about 25 miles S. of Hebron.

21:4 *the Red Sea.* I.e., the NE. prong of the Red Sea, the Gulf of Aqaba.

21:6 *fiery serpents.* Venomous snakes with a burning, lethal bite.

cede with the Lord, that He may remove the serpents from us." And Moses interceded for the people.

★ 8-9   8 Then the Lord said to Moses, "Make a ªfiery *serpent,* and set it on a standard; and it shall come about, that everyone who is bitten, when he looks at it, he shall live."

9 ª2 Kin. 18:4; John 3:14, 15   9 And Moses made a ªbronze serpent and set it on the standard; and it came about, that if a serpent bit any man, when he looked to the bronze serpent, he lived.

E The Defeat of Sihon and Og, 21:10-35

10 ªNum. 33:43, 44   10 ªNow the sons of Israel moved out and camped in Oboth.

11 And they journeyed from Oboth, and camped at Iyeabarim, in the wilderness which is opposite Moab, to the east.

12 ªNum. 33:45   12 ªFrom there they set out and camped in Wadi Zered.

13 ªNum. 22:36; Judg. 11:18   13 From there they journeyed and camped on the other side of the Arnon, which is in the wilderness that comes out of the border of the Amorites, ªfor the Arnon is the border of Moab, between Moab and the Amorites.

★14   14 Therefore it is said in the Book of the Wars of the Lord,
"Waheb in Suphah,
And the wadis of the Arnon,

15 ªNum. 21:28; Deut. 2:9, 18, 29   15 And the slope of the wadis
That extends to the site of ªAr,
And leans to the border of Moab."

16 ªAnd from there *they continued* to Beer, that is the well where the Lord said to Moses, "Assemble the people, that I may give them water."

16 ªNum. 33:46-49

17 ªThen Israel sang this song:
"Spring up, O well! Sing to it!

17 ªEx. 15:1; Ps. 105:2

18 "The well, which the leaders sank,
Which the nobles of the people dug,
With the scepter *and* with their staffs."
And from the wilderness *they continued* to Mattanah,

19 and from Mattanah to Nahaliel, and from Nahaliel to Bamoth,

20 and from Bamoth to the valley that is in the land of Moab, at the top of Pisgah which overlooks the wasteland.

21 ªThen Israel sent messengers to Sihon, king of the Amorites, saying,

★21 ªDeut. 2:26-37; Judg. 11:19

22 "ªLet me pass through your land. We will not turn off into field or vineyard; we will not drink water from wells. We will go by the king's highway until we have passed through your border."

22 ªNum. 20:16, 17

23 ªBut Sihon would not permit Israel to pass through his border. So Sihon gathered all his people and went out against Israel in the wilderness, and came to ᵇJahaz and fought against Israel.

★23 ªNum. 20:21 ᵇDeut. 2:32

24 Then ªIsrael struck him with the edge of the sword, and took possession of his land from the Arnon to the Jabbok, as far as the sons of Ammon; for the ᵇborder of the sons of Ammon *was* Jazer.

★24 ªAmos 2:9 ᵇDeut. 2:37

21:8-9 Only those who believed God and looked on the bronze serpent lived. The N.T. uses this incident as an illustration of Christ's vicarious death on the cross and of the necessity of personal faith for salvation (John 3:14-15).

21:14 *the Book of the Wars of the Lord.* Apparently a collection of war songs.

21:21 *the Amorites.* See notes on Gen. 14:5 and Amos 2:9. They inhabited the area N. of the Arnon river (cf. v. 13), which flowed into the Dead Sea just N. of its midpoint.

21:23 *Jahaz.* Just N. of the Arnon.

21:24 *the Jabbok.* A tributary of the Jordan, flowing into it about 24 miles N. of the Dead Sea.

★25-26
25 aAmos
2:10

25 And Israel took all these cities and aIsrael lived in all the cities of the Amorites, in Heshbon, and in all her villages.

26 For Heshbon was the city of Sihon, king of the Amorites, who had fought against the former king of Moab and had taken all his land out of his hand, as far as the Arnon.

27 Therefore those who use proverbs say,

"Come to Heshbon! Let it be built!
So let the city of Sihon be established.

28 aJer.
48:45 bNum.
21:15 cNum.
22:41; Is.
15:2; 16:12

28 "aFor a fire went forth from Heshbon,
A flame from the town of Sihon;
It devoured bAr of Moab,
The cdominant heights of the Arnon.

29 aJer.
48:46 bJudg.
11:24; 1 Kin.
11:33; 2 Kin.
23:13 cIs.
15:5 dIs.
16:2

29 "aWoe to you, O Moab!
You are ruined, O people of bChemosh!
cHe has given his sons as fugitives,
dAnd his daughters into captivity,
To an Amorite king, Sihon.

30 aNum.
32:3, 34; Jer.
48:18, 22

30 "But we have cast them down,
Heshbon is ruined as far as aDibon,
Then we have laid waste even to Nophah,
Which reaches to Medeba."

31 Thus Israel lived in the land of the Amorites.

32 aNum.
32:1, 3, 35;
Jer. 48:32

32 And Moses sent to spy out aJazer, and they captured its villages and dispossessed the Amorites who were there.

★33 aDeut.
3:1-7 bJosh.
13:12

33 aThen they turned and went up by the way of Bashan, and Og the king of Bashan went out with all his people, for battle at bEdrei.

34 But the LORD said to Moses, "aDo not fear him, for I have given him into your hand, and all his people and his land; and you shall do to him as you did to Sihon, king of the Amorites, who lived at Heshbon." 34 aDeut.
3:2

35 So athey killed him and his sons and all his people, until there was no remnant left him; and they possessed his land. 35 aDeut.
3:3, 4

V ISRAEL ON THE PLAINS OF MOAB, 22:1-36:13

A Balak Propositions Balaam to Curse Israel, 22:1-41

22 aThen the sons of Israel journeyed, and camped in the plains of Moab beyond the Jordan opposite Jericho. ★ 1 aNum.
33:48, 49

2 Now aBalak the son of Zippor saw all that Israel had done to the Amorites. 2 aJudg.
11:25

3 aSo Moab was in great fear because of the people, for they were numerous; and Moab was in dread of the sons of Israel. 3 aEx.
15:15

4 And Moab said to the elders of aMidian, "Now this horde will lick up all that is around us, as the ox licks up the grass of the field." And Balak the son of Zippor was king of Moab at that time. ★ 4 aNum.
25:15-18;
31:1-3

5 So he sent messengers to aBalaam the son of Beor, at bPethor, which is near the River, in the land of the sons of his people, to call him, saying, "Behold, a people came out of Egypt; behold, they cover the surface of the land, and they are living opposite me. ★ 5 aJosh.
24:9; 2 Pet.
2:15f.; Jude
11 bDeut.
23:4

21:25-26 These two verses give the historical facts on which the poem in verses 27-30 is based. The essence of the poem is, "You Amorites have beaten the Moabites, but we Israelites have beaten you."

21:33 *Bashan* occupied the area E. of the Sea of Galilee and the Jordan River. Israel controlled the land from the Arnon to Mt. Hermon (cf.

Deut. 3:8).

22:1 *Moab.* See notes on Gen. 19:31 and Amos 2:1.

22:4 Because of his fear of the Israelites, Balak sought an alliance with the Midianites to the east (see note on Exod. 2:15).

22:5 *Pethor.* Located on the W. bank of the Euphrates in northern Mesopotamia (Deut. 23:4).

★ 6-7

6 aNum. 22:17; 23:7, 8 bNum. 22:12; 24:9

6 "aNow, therefore, please come, bcurse this people for me since they are too mighty for me; perhaps I may be able to defeat them and drive them out of the land. For I know that he whom you bless is blessed, and he whom you curse is cursed."

7 aNum. 23:23; 24:1; Josh. 13:22

7 So the elders of Moab and the elders of Midian departed with the *fees for* adivination in their hand; and they came to Balaam and repeated Balak's words to him.

8 And he said to them, "Spend the night here, and I will bring word back to you as the LORD may speak to me." And the leaders of Moab stayed with Balaam.

★ 9-20

9 aGen. 20:3

9 Then aGod came to Balaam and said, "Who are these men with you?"

10 And Balaam said to God, "Balak the son of Zippor, king of Moab, has sent *word* to me,

11 'Behold, there is a people who came out of Egypt and they cover the surface of the land; now come, curse them for me; perhaps I may be able to fight against them, and drive them out.' "

12 aNum. 23:8; 24:9 bGen. 12:2; 22:17

12 And God said to Balaam, "Do not go with them; ayou shall not curse the people; for they bare blessed."

13 So Balaam arose in the morning and said to Balak's leaders, "Go back to your land, for the LORD has refused to let me go with you."

14 And the leaders of Moab arose and went to Balak, and said, "Balaam refused to come with us."

15 Then Balak again sent leaders, more numerous and more distinguished than the former.

16 And they came to Balaam and said to him, "Thus says Balak the son of Zippor, 'Let nothing, I beg you, hinder you from coming to me;

17 aNum. 22:6

17 for I will indeed honor you richly, and I will do whatever you say to me. aPlease come then, curse this people for me.' "

18 aNum. 22:38; 24:13; 1 Kin. 22:14; 2 Chr. 18:13

18 And Balaam answered and said to the servants of Balak, "aThough Balak were to give me his house full of silver and gold, I could not do anything, either small or great, contrary to the command of the LORD my God.

19 "And now please, you also stay here tonight, and I will find out what else the LORD will speak to me."

20 aNum. 22:35; 23:5, 12, 16, 26; 24:13

20 And God came to Balaam at night and said to him, "If the men have come to call you, rise up *and* go with them; but aonly the word which I speak to you shall you do."

21 a2 Pet. 2:15

21 aSo Balaam arose in the morning, and saddled his donkey, and went with the leaders of Moab.

★ 22-35

22 aEx. 23:20

22 But God was angry because he was going, aand the angel of the LORD took his stand in the way as an adversary against him. Now he was riding on his donkey and his two servants were with him.

23 When the donkey saw the angel of the LORD standing in the way with his drawn sword in his hand, the donkey turned off from the way and went into the field; but Balaam struck the donkey to turn her back into the way.

24 Then the angel of the LORD stood in a narrow path of the

22:6–7 Apparently Balaam enjoyed considerable reputation as a successful prophet. *fees for divination.* I.e., payment for his services.

22:9–20 Balaam knew the true God, though he also used omens (v. 7; 24:1) and soothsaying (Josh. 13:22). *what else* (v. 19). These words belie the grandiose affirmation of verse 18, for though the Lord had told him not to go (v. 12), Balaam was hoping He would change His mind and permit him to go. God did grant permission (v. 20), but also expressed His displeasure with Balaam for his love of money (v. 22; cf. 2 Pet. 2:15).

22:22–35 The experience with his donkey and the angel of the Lord (see note on Gen. 16:10) was designed to reinforce God's displeasure with Balaam's motive for going. Balaam offered to return home (v. 34), but God told him to go on.

vineyards, *with* a wall on this side and a wall on that side.

25 When the donkey saw the angel of the Lord, she pressed herself to the wall and pressed Balaam's foot against the wall, so he struck her again.

26 And the angel of the Lord went further, and stood in a narrow place where there was no way to turn to the right hand or the left.

27 When the donkey saw the angel of the Lord, she lay down under Balaam; so *a*Balaam was angry and struck the donkey with his stick.

28 And *a*the Lord opened the mouth of the donkey, and she said to Balaam, "What have I done to you, that you have struck me these three times?"

29 Then Balaam said to the donkey, "Because you have made a mockery of me! If there had been a sword in my hand, *a*I would have killed you by now."

30 And the donkey said to Balaam, "Am I not your donkey on which you have ridden all your life to this day? Have I ever been accustomed to do so to you?" And he said, "No."

31 Then the Lord opened the eyes of Balaam, and he saw *a*the angel of the Lord standing in the way with his drawn sword in his hand; and he bowed all the way to the ground.

32 And the angel of the Lord said to him, "Why have you struck your donkey these three times? Behold, I have come out as an adversary, because your way was *a*contrary to me.

33 "But the donkey saw me and turned aside from me these three times. If she had not turned aside from me, I would surely have killed you just now, and let her live."

34 And Balaam said to the angel of the Lord, "*a*I have sinned, for I did not know that you were

standing in the way against me. Now then, if it is displeasing to you, I will turn back."

35 But the angel of the Lord said to Balaam, "Go with the men, but *a*you shall speak only the word which I shall tell you." So Balaam went along with the leaders of Balak.

36 When Balak heard that Balaam was coming, he went out to meet him at the city of Moab, which is on the Arnon border, at the extreme end of the border.

37 Then Balak said to Balaam, "Did I not urgently send to you to call you? Why did you not come to me? Am I really unable to honor you?"

38 So Balaam said to Balak, "Behold, I have come now to you! *a*Am I able to speak anything at all? The word that God puts in my mouth, that I shall speak."

39 And Balaam went with Balak, and they came to Kiriath-huzoth.

40 And Balak sacrificed oxen and sheep, and sent *some* to Balaam and the leaders who were with him.

41 Then it came about in the morning that Balak took Balaam, and brought him up to *a*the high places of Baal; and he saw from there a *b*portion of the people.

B Balaam Blesses Israel,
23:1–24:25

23 Then Balaam said to Balak, "Build seven altars for me here, and prepare seven bulls and seven rams for me here."

2 And Balak did just as Balaam had spoken, and Balak and Balaam offered up a bull and a ram on each altar.

3 Then Balaam said to Balak, "Stand beside your burnt offering, and I will go; perhaps the Lord will come to me, and what-

Margin references
27 *a*James 1:19
28 *a*2 Pet. 2:16
29 *a*Prov. 12:10; Matt. 15:19
31 *a*Josh. 5:13-15
32 *a*2 Pet. 2:15
34 *a*Num. 14:40
35 *a*Num. 22:20
★37-38
38 *a*Num. 22:18
41 *a*Num. 21:28 *b*Num. 23:13

22:37-38 Balak assumed that Balaam's presence meant he would curse Israel, and Balaam's reply is deftly ambiguous. Perhaps he yet hoped God would allow him to curse Israel and so obtain the promised rewards.

ever He shows me I will tell you."
So he went to a bare hill.

4 Now God met Balaam, and
he said to Him, "I have set up the
seven altars, and I have offered up
a bull and a ram on each altar."

5 Then the LORD [a]put a word
in Balaam's mouth and said, "Return to Balak, and you shall speak
thus."

6 So he returned to him, and
behold, he was standing beside
his burnt offering, he and all the
leaders of Moab.

★ 7-10

7 And he took up his discourse and said,

> "From [a]Aram Balak has
>> brought me,
> Moab's king from the
>> mountains of the East,
> '[b]Come curse Jacob for
>> me,
> And come, denounce Israel!'

8 "[a]How shall I curse,
> whom God has not
> cursed?
> And how can I denounce, whom the
> LORD has not denounced?

9 "As I see him from the
> top of the rocks,
> And I look at him from
> the hills;
> [a]Behold, a people who
> dwells apart,
> And shall not be reckoned among the nations.

10 "[a]Who can count the
> dust of Jacob,
> Or number the fourth
> part of Israel?
> [b]Let me die the death of
> the upright,
> [c]And let my end be like
> his!"

11 Then Balak said to Balaam, "What have you done to
me? [a]I took you to curse my enemies, but behold, you have actually blessed them!"

12 And he answered and said,
"Must I not be careful to speak
[a]what the LORD puts in my
mouth?"

13 Then Balak said to him,
"Please come with me to another
place from where you may see
them, although you will only see
the extreme end of them, and will
not see all of them; and curse
them for me from there."

14 So he took him to the field ★14
of Zophim, to the top of Pisgah,
and built seven altars and offered
a bull and a ram on each altar.

15 And he said to Balak,
"Stand here beside your burnt offering, while I myself meet the
LORD yonder."

16 Then the LORD met Balaam
and [a]put a word in his mouth and
said, "Return to Balak, and thus
you shall speak."

17 And he came to him, and
behold, he was standing beside
his burnt offering, and the leaders
of Moab with him. And Balak
said to him, "What has the LORD
spoken?"

18 Then he took up his discourse and said,

> "Arise, O Balak, and
>> hear;
> Give ear to me, O son of
>> Zippor!

19 "[a]God is not a man, that
> He should lie,
> Nor a son of man, that
> He should repent;
> [b]Has He said, and will
> He not do it?
> Or has He spoken, and
> will He not make it
> good?

Cross references (margin):

5 [a]Num. 22:20; Deut. 18:18; Jer. 1:9

★ 7-10

7 [a]Num. 22:5; Deut. 23:4 [b]Num. 22:6

8 [a]Num. 22:12

9 [a]Deut. 32:8; 33:28

10 [a]Gen. 13:16; 28:14 [b]Is. 57:1 [c]Ps. 37:37

11 [a]Neh. 13:2

12 [a]Num. 22:20

★14

16 [a]Num. 22:20

19 [a]1 Sam. 15:29 [b]Is. 40:8; 55:11

23:7-10 Balaam's first oration (in the form of a
poem) stated that Israel could not be cursed,
that she was a nation separate from all other
nations, that she was a large nation so that
even the *fourth part* (v. 10) of what he could
see could not be numbered, and that he
wished he might die sharing Israel's blessings.
23:14 *Pisgah* is sometimes identified with Mt.

Nebo (Deut. 34:1). Here it may refer to the
range of mountains that extend toward the
NE. corner of the Dead Sea, of which Nebo is
the highest peak. From this vantage point, Balaam saw another part of the camp of Israel.
Once again he predicted blessing, not cursing,
for Israel (vv. 18-24).

20 aGen.
12:2; 22:17;
Num. 22:12
bIs. 43:13

20 "Behold, I have received a command to bless;
aWhen He has blessed, then bI cannot revoke it.

★21 aNum.
14:18, 19,
34; Ps. 32:2,
5 bDeut.
9:24; 32:5;
Jer. 50:20
cEx. 3:12;
Deut. 31:23
dDeut. 33:5;
Ps. 89:15-18

21 "aHe has not observed misfortune in Jacob;
bNor has He seen trouble in Israel;
cThe LORD his God is with him,
dAnd the shout of a king is among them.

22 aNum.
24:8 bDeut.
33:17

22 "aGod brings them out of Egypt,
He is for them like the bhorns of the wild ox.

23 aNum.
22:7; 24:1;
Josh. 13:22

23 "aFor there is no omen against Jacob,
Nor is there any divination against Israel;
At the proper time it shall be said to Jacob
And to Israel, what God has done.

24 aGen.
49:9; Nah.
2:11, 12

24 "aBehold, a people rises like a lioness,
And as a lion it lifts itself;
It shall not lie down until it devours the prey,
And drinks the blood of the slain."

25 Then Balak said to Balaam, "Do not curse them at all nor bless them at all!"

26 aNum.
22:18

26 But Balaam answered and said to Balak, "Did I not tell you, 'aWhatever the LORD speaks, that I must do'?"

27 Then Balak said to Balaam, "Please come, I will take you to another place; perhaps it will be agreeable with God that you curse them for me from there."

★28

28 So Balak took Balaam to the top of Peor which overlooks the wasteland.

29 And Balaam said to Balak, "Build seven altars for me here and prepare seven bulls and seven rams for me here."

30 And Balak did just as Balaam had said, and offered up a bull and a ram on each altar.

24 When Balaam saw that it pleased the LORD to bless Israel, he did not go as at other times to seek aomens but he set his face toward the bwilderness.

1 aNum.
22:7; 23:23
bNum. 23:28

2 And Balaam lifted up his eyes and saw Israel camping tribe by tribe; and athe Spirit of God came upon him.

2 aNum.
11:26;
1 Sam.
19:20; Rev.
1:10

3 And he took up his discourse and said,
"aThe oracle of Balaam the son of Beor,
And the oracle of the man whose eye is opened;

3 aNum.
24:15, 16

4 The oracle of him who ahears the words of God,
Who sees the bvision of the Almighty,
Falling down, yet having his eyes uncovered,

★ 4 aNum.
22:20 bGen.
15:1; Num.
12:6

5 How fair are your tents, O Jacob,
Your dwellings, O Israel!

6 "Like valleys that stretch out,
Like gardens beside the river,
Like aaloes planted by the LORD,
Like bcedars beside the waters.

★ 6 aPs.
45:8 bPs.
1:3

7 "Water shall flow from his buckets,
And his seed shall be by many waters,
And his king shall be higher than aAgag,
bAnd his kingdom shall be exalted.

★ 7 aNum.
24:20;
1 Sam. 15:8
bPs. 145:11-
13

23:21 the shout of a king. A shout of triumph.
23:28 Peor. In the northern part of the range (see note on 23:14), from which Balaam could see the camp of Israel (24:2). It also overlooked the wasteland.
24:4 Almighty. Heb., shaddai (see note on Gen. 17:1). This time Balaam received a vision from God as he lay prostrate with his eyes uncov-

ered; i.e., with uncluttered spiritual vision.
24:6 aloes. A very valuable 100 to 120-foot-high tree whose resinous wood was used in perfume (Psalm 45:8). Balaam was predicting prosperity for Israel.
24:7 Agag was the king whom Samuel killed (1 Sam. 15:32-33). Balaam here predicts Israel's dominance.

8 aNum.
23:22 bNum.
23:24; Ps.
2:9 cPs. 45:5
8 "aGod brings him out of
    Egypt,
He is for him like the
    horns of the wild ox.
bHe shall devour the na-
    tions *who are* his ad-
    versaries,
And shall crush their
    bones in pieces,
And shatter *them* with
    his carrows.

9 aGen.
49:9; Num.
23:24 bGen.
12:3; 27:29
9 "aHe couches, he lies
    down as a lion,
And as a lion, who dares
    rouse him?
bBlessed is everyone
    who blesses you,
And cursed is everyone
    who curses you."

10 Then Balak's anger
burned against Balaam, and he
struck his hands together; and Balak said to Balaam, "I called you
to curse my enemies, but behold,
you have persisted in blessing
them these three times!
11 "Therefore, flee to your
place now. I said I would honor
you greatly, but behold, the LORD
has held you back from honor."

12 aNum.
22:18
12 And Balaam said to Balak,
"aDid I not tell your messengers
whom you had sent to me, saying,
13 aNum.
16:28 bNum.
22:20
13 'Though Balak were to give
me his house full of silver and
gold, I could not do anything contrary to the command of the LORD,
either good or bad, aof my own
accord. bWhat the LORD speaks,
that I will speak'?
14 aNum.
31:8, 16;
Josh. 13:22
14 "And now behold, aI am
going to my people; come, *and* I
will advise you what this people
will do to your people in the days
to come."

★15-25
15 And he took up his discourse and said,
15 aNum.
24:3, 4
        "aThe oracle of Balaam
            the son of Beor,
        And the oracle of the
            man whose eye is
            opened,

16   The oracle of him who
            hears the words of
            God,
        And knows the knowl-
            edge of the Most
            High,
        Who sees the vision of
            the Almighty,
        Falling down, yet having
            his eyes uncovered.
17   "I see him, but not now;
        I behold him, but not
            near;
        A star shall come forth
            from Jacob,
        aAnd a scepter shall rise
            from Israel,
        bAnd shall crush
            through the forehead
            of Moab,
        And tear down all the
            sons of Sheth.
18   "aAnd Edom shall be a
            possession,
        bSeir, its enemies, also
            shall be a possession,
        While Israel performs
            valiantly.
19   "One from Jacob shall
            have dominion,
        And shall destroy the
            remnant from the
            city."

20 And he looked at Amalek
and took up his discourse and
said,
        "Amalek was the first of
            the nations,
        aBut his end *shall be* de-
            struction."
21 And he looked at the aKe-
nite, and took up his discourse
and said,
        "Your dwelling place is
            enduring,
        And your nest is set in
            the cliff.
22   "Nevertheless Kain shall
            be consumed;
        How long shall aAsshur
            keep you captive?"

17 aGen.
49:10 bNum.
21:29; Is.
15:1-16:14

18 aGen.
27:29; Amos
9:11, 12
bGen. 32:3

20 aNum.
24:24

21 aGen.
15:19

22 aGen.
10:21, 22

24:15-25 Before Balaam left for home, he predicted (1) the coming of the Messiah-Ruler of
Israel (v. 17; *the sons of Sheth* is a general
reference to tumult); (2) victory over Moab,
Edom, the Amalekites, and the Kenites (vv.
17-21); (3) the Assyrian (= *Asshur*) captivity
of Israel (v. 22); (4) the affliction of Assyria and
Eber (the Hebrews) by people from the Mediterranean area (*Kittim*, v. 24).

23 And he took up his discourse and said,

"Alas, who can live except God has ordained it?

24 aGen. 10:4; Ezek. 27:6 bGen. 10:21 cNum. 24:20

24 "But ships *shall come* from the coast of aKittim,
And they shall afflict Asshur and shall afflict bEber;
cSo they also *shall come* to destruction."

25 aNum. 24:14

25 Then Balaam arose and departed and returned to ahis place, and Balak also went his way.

C Israel Worships Baal of Peor, 25:1-18

★ **1** aNum. 33:49; Josh. 2:1 bNum. 31:16; 1 Cor. 10:8; Rev. 2:14
★ **2** aEx. 34:15; Deut. 32:38

25 While Israel remained at aShittim, the people began bto play the harlot with the daughters of Moab.
2 For athey invited the people to the sacrifices of their gods, and the people ate and bowed down to their gods.

★ **3** aPs. 106:28, 29; Hos. 9:10

3 So aIsrael joined themselves to Baal of Peor, and the LORD was angry against Israel.

★ **4** aDeut. 13:17

4 And the LORD said to Moses, "Take all the leaders of the people and execute them in broad daylight before the LORD, aso that the fierce anger of the LORD may turn away from Israel."

5 aEx. 32:27

5 So Moses said to the judges of Israel, "Each of you aslay his men who have joined themselves to Baal of Peor."

6 aNum. 22:4 bJoel 2:17

6 Then behold, one of the sons of Israel came and brought to his relatives a aMidianite woman, in the sight of Moses and in the sight of all the congregation of the sons of Israel, bwhile they

were weeping at the doorway of the tent of meeting.

7 aWhen Phinehas the son of Eleazar, the son of Aaron the priest, saw it, he arose from the midst of the congregation, and took a spear in his hand;

7 aPs. 106:30

8 and he went after the man of Israel into the tent, and pierced both of them through, the man of Israel and the woman, through the body. aSo the plague on the sons of Israel was checked.

8 aNum. 16:46-48

9 aAnd those who died by the plague were 24,000.

★ **9** aNum. 14:37; 16:48-50; 31:16

10 Then the LORD spoke to Moses, saying,

11 "aPhinehas the son of Eleazar, the son of Aaron the priest, has turned away My wrath from the sons of Israel, in that he was jealous with My jealousy among them, so that I did not destroy the sons of Israel bin My jealousy.

11 aPs. 106:30 bEx. 20:5

12 "Therefore say, 'aBehold, I give him My bcovenant of peace;

12 aPs. 106:30, 31 bIs. 54:10; Ezek. 34:25; 37:26

13 and it shall be for him and his descendants after him, a covenant of a aperpetual priesthood, because he was jealous for his God, and bmade atonement for the sons of Israel.'"

★ **13** aEx. 29:9 bNum. 16:46

14 Now the name of the slain man of Israel who was slain with the Midianite woman, was Zimri the son of Salu, a leader of a father's household among the Simeonites.

15 And the name of the Midianite woman who was slain was aCozbi the daughter of bZur, who was head of the people of a father's household in Midian.

★ **15** aNum. 25:18 bNum. 31:8

16 Then the LORD spoke to Moses, saying,

17 "aBe hostile to the Midianites and strike them;

17 aNum. 25:1; 22:4; 31:1-3

18 for they have been hostile to you with their tricks, with

25:1 *Shittim* was the last stop before Israel crossed the Jordan (Josh. 2:1).

25:2 *they* is feminine, referring to the women of Moab. Apparently Balaam advised this (cf. 31:16) in order to compromise Israel, whom he could not curse (cf. Rev. 2:14).

25:3 *Baal of Peor.* The local, heathen god Baal that was worshiped at Peor. Prostitution (cf. v. 1) was part of that worship.

25:4 The Israelite *leaders* of the Baal worship were to be publicly executed.

25:9 See note on 1 Cor. 10:8.

25:13 Because of his hatred of sin (vv. 7-8), Phinehas' family was promised the high priesthood in Israel.

25:15 *Cozbi* means "deceiver." She was the daughter of a chieftain.

which they have deceived you in the affair of Peor, and in the affair of Cozbi, the daughter of the leader of Midian, their sister who was slain on the day of the plague because of Peor."

D The New Generation Numbered, 26:1-65

1 aNum. 25:9

26 Then it came about after the a plague, that the LORD spoke to Moses and to Eleazar the son of Aaron the priest, saying,

2 aEx. 30:11-16; 38:25, 26; Num. 1:2

2 "a Take a census of all the congregation of the sons of Israel from twenty years old and upward, by their fathers' households, whoever is able to go out to war in Israel."

3 aNum. 22:1; 33:48; 35:1

3 So Moses and Eleazar the priest spoke with them a in the plains of Moab by the Jordan at Jericho, saying,

4 "*Take a census of the people* from twenty years old and upward, as the LORD has commanded Moses."

Now the sons of Israel who came out of the land of Egypt *were:*

★ 5-51

5 Reuben, Israel's first-born, the sons of Reuben: *of* Hanoch, the family of the Hanochites; of Pallu, the family of the Palluites;

6 of Hezron, the family of the Hezronites; of Carmi, the family of the Carmites.

7 aNum. 1:21

7 These are the families of the Reubenites, and those who were numbered of them were a 43,730.

8 And the son of Pallu: Eliab.

9 aNum. 1:16; 16:2

9 And the sons of Eliab: Nemuel and Dathan and Abiram. These are the Dathan and Abiram

who were a called by the congregation, who contended against Moses and against Aaron in the company of Korah, when they contended against the LORD,

10 aNum. 16:32 bNum. 16:35, 38

10 and a the earth opened its mouth and swallowed them up along with Korah, when that company died, b when the fire devoured 250 men, so that they became a warning.

11 aNum. 16:27, 33; Deut. 24:16

11 a The sons of Korah, however, did not die.

12 The sons of Simeon according to their families: of Nemuel, the family of the Nemuelites; of Jamin, the family of the Jaminites; of Jachin, the family of the Jachinites;

13 of Zerah, the family of the Zerahites; of Shaul, the family of the Shaulites.

14 aNum. 1:23

14 These are the families of the Simeonites, a 22,200.

15 The sons of Gad according to their families: of Zephon, the family of the Zephonites; of Haggi, the family of the Haggites; of Shuni, the family of the Shunites;

16 of Ozni, the family of the Oznites; of Eri, the family of the Erites;

17 of Arod, the family of the Arodites; of Areli, the family of the Arelites.

18 aNum. 1:25

18 These are the families of the sons of Gad according to those who were numbered of them, a 40,500.

19 aGen. 38:2; 46:12

19 The a sons of Judah *were* Er and Onan, but Er and Onan died in the land of Canaan.

20 aGen. 49:8; 1 Chr. 2:3; Rev. 7:5

20 And the a sons of Judah according to their families were: of Shelah, the family of the Shelanites; of Perez, the family of the Perezites; of Zerah, the family of the Zerahites.

26:5-51. In comparing this census with the one taken 38 years earlier, we note the following: Reuben had decreased by 2,770 (v. 7; cf. 1:21), Simeon had lost 37,100 (v. 14; cf. 1:23), Gad had decreased by 5,150 (v. 18; cf. 1:25), Judah had gained 1,900 (v. 22; cf. 1:27), Issachar had gained 9,900 (v. 25; cf. 1:29), Zebulun had gained 3,100 (v. 27; cf. 1:31), Manasseh had gained 20,500 (v. 34; cf. 1:35), Ephraim had lost

8,000 (v. 37; cf. 1:33), Benjamin had increased by 10,200 (v. 41; cf. 1:37), Dan had gained 1,700 (v. 43; cf. 1:39), Asher had gained 11,900 (v. 47; cf. 1:41), and Naphtali had decreased by 8,000 (v. 50; cf. 1:43). The total number of adult males had decreased by 1,820 (v. 51; cf. 1:46), and during the years of wandering 1,200,000 people had died.

21 And the sons of Perez were: of Hezron, the family of the Hezronites; of Hamul, the family of the Hamulites.

22 aNum. 1:27
22 These are the families of Judah according to those who were numbered of them, ª76,500.

23 aGen. 46:13; 1 Chr. 7:1
23 The ªsons of Issachar according to their families: of Tola, the family of the Tolaites; of Puvah, the family of the Punites;

24 of Jashub, the family of the Jashubites; of Shimron, the family of the Shimronites.

25 aNum. 1:29
25 These are the families of Issachar according to those who were numbered of them, ª64,300.

26 aGen. 46:14
26 The ªsons of Zebulun according to their families: of Sered, the family of the Seredites; of Elon, the family of the Elonites; of Jahleel, the family of the Jahleelites.

27 aNum. 1:31
27 These are the families of the Zebulunites according to those who were numbered of them, ª60,500.

28 aGen. 46:20; Deut. 33:16f.
28 The ªsons of Joseph according to their families: Manasseh and Ephraim.

29 aJosh. 17:1; 1 Chr. 7:14f.
29 The sons of Manasseh: of Machir, the family of the Machirites; and ªMachir became the father of Gilead: of Gilead, the family of the Gileadites.

30 aJudg. 6:11, 24, 34
30 These are the sons of Gilead: of Iezer, the family of the ªIezerites; of Helek, the family of the Helekites;

31 and of Asriel, the family of the Asrielites; and of Shechem, the family of the Shechemites;

32 and of Shemida, the family of the Shemidaites; and of Hepher, the family of the Hepherites.

33 aNum. 27:1
33 Now Zelophehad the son of Hepher had no sons, but only daughters; and ªthe names of the daughters of Zelophehad were Mahlah, Noah, Hoglah, Milcah and Tirzah.

34 aNum. 1:35
34 These are the families of Manasseh; and those who were numbered of them were ª52,700.

35 These are the sons of Ephraim according to their families: of Shuthelah, the family of the Shuthelahites; of Becher, the family of the Becherites; of Tahan, the family of the Tahanites.

36 And these are the sons of Shuthelah: of Eran, the family of the Eranites.

37 aNum. 1:33
37 These are the families of the sons of Ephraim according to those who were numbered of them, ª32,500. These are the sons of Joseph according to their families.

38 The sons of Benjamin according to their families: of Bela, the family of the Belaites; of Ashbel, the family of the Ashbelites; of Ahiram, the family of the Ahiramites;

39 of Shephupham, the family of the Shuphamites; of Hupham, the family of the Huphamites.

40 And the sons of Bela were Ard and Naaman: of Ard, the family of the Ardites; of Naaman, the family of the Naamites.

41 aNum. 1:37
41 These are the sons of Benjamin according to their families; and those who were numbered of them were ª45,600.

42 These are the sons of Dan according to their families: of Shuham, the family of the Shuhamites. These are the families of Dan according to their families.

43 aNum. 1:39
43 All the families of the Shuhamites, according to those who were numbered of them, were ª64,400.

44 aGen. 46:17; 1 Chr. 7:30
44 The ªsons of Asher according to their families: of Imnah, the family of the Imnites; of Ishvi, the family of the Ishvites; of Beriah, the family of the Beriites.

45 Of the sons of Beriah: of Heber, the family of the Heberites; of Malchiel, the family of the Malchielites.

46 And the name of the daughter of Asher was Serah.

47 aNum. 1:41
47 These are the families of the sons of Asher according to those who were numbered of them, ª53,400.

48 aGen. 46:24; 1 Chr. 7:13
48 The ªsons of Naphtali according to their families: of Jahzeel, the family of the Jahzeelites; of Guni, the family of the Gunites;

49 ^a1 Chr. 7:13

49 of Jezer, the family of the Jezerites; of ^aShillem, the family of the Shillemites.

50 ^aNum. 1:43

50 These are the families of Naphtali according to their families; and those who were numbered of them were ^a45,400.

51 ^aEx. 12:37; 38:26; Num. 1:46; 11:21

51 These are those who were numbered of the sons of Israel, ^a601,730.

52 Then the LORD spoke to Moses, saying,

★53-54

53 "Among these the land shall be divided for an inheritance according to the number of names.

54 ^aNum. 33:54

54 "^aTo the larger *group* you shall increase their inheritance, and to the smaller *group* you shall diminish their inheritance; each shall be given their inheritance according to those who were numbered of them.

55 ^aNum. 33:54; 34:13

55 "But the land shall be ^adivided by lot. They shall receive their inheritance according to the names of the tribes of their fathers.

56 "According to the selection by lot, their inheritance shall be divided between the larger and the smaller *groups.*"

57 ^aGen. 46:11; Ex. 6:16; 1 Chr. 6:1, 16

57 And ^athese are those who were numbered of the Levites according to their families: of Gershon, the family of the Gershonites; of Kohath, the family of the Kohathites; of Merari, the family of the Merarites.

58 ^aEx. 6:20

58 These are the families of Levi: the family of the Libnites, the family of the Hebronites, the family of the Mahlites, the family of the Mushites, the family of the Korahites. ^aAnd Kohath became the father of Amram.

59 ^aEx. 2:1, 2; 6:20

59 And the name of Amram's wife ^awas Jochebed, the daughter of Levi, who was born to Levi in Egypt; and she bore to Amram: Aaron and Moses and their sister Miriam.

60 ^aNum. 3:2

60 ^aAnd to Aaron were born Nadab and Abihu, Eleazar and Ithamar.

61 ^aLev. 10:1, 2; Num. 3:4

61 ^aBut Nadab and Abihu died when they offered strange fire before the LORD.

62 ^aNum. 3:39 ^bNum. 1:47 ^cNum. 18:23, 24

62 And those who were numbered of them were ^a23,000, every male from a month old and upward, for ^bthey were not numbered among the sons of Israel ^csince no inheritance was given to them among the sons of Israel.

63 These are those who were numbered by Moses and Eleazar the priest, who numbered the sons of Israel in the plains of Moab by the Jordan at Jericho.

64 ^aNum. 14:29-35; Deut. 2:14-16; Heb. 3:17

64 ^aBut among these there was not a man of those who were numbered by Moses and Aaron the priest, who numbered the sons of Israel in the wilderness of Sinai.

65 ^aNum. 14:26-35; Ps. 90:3-10; 1 Cor. 10:5 ^bDeut. 1:36; Josh. 14:6-10

65 For the LORD had said of them, "^aThey shall surely die in the wilderness." And not a man was left of them, ^bexcept Caleb the son of Jephunneh, and Joshua the son of Nun.

E   The People Instructed,
27:1–30:16
1   The laws of inheritance,
27:1–11

1 ^aNum. 26:33; 36:1 ^bNum. 26:33

27 Then ^athe daughters of Zelophehad, the son of Hepher, the son of Gilead, the son of Machir, the son of Manasseh, of the families of Manasseh the son of Joseph, came near; and these are ^bthe names of his daughters: Mahlah, Noah and Hoglah and Milcah and Tirzah.

2 And they stood before Moses and before Eleazar the priest and before the leaders and all the congregation, at the doorway of the tent of meeting, saying,

★ 3 ^aNum. 26:64, 65 ^bNum. 26:33

3 "Our father ^adied in the wilderness, yet he was not among

26:53-54 This census furnished the basis for dividing the land, each tribe receiving more or less land, depending on its size. The actual location was decided by lot.
27:3 The question brought to Moses was this:

What would happen to the property of a man who died *in his own sin* (i.e., he shared the general sin of those who balked at Kadesh) without sons?

the company of those who gathered themselves together against the LORD in the company of Korah; but he died in his own sin, and ᵇhe had no sons.

4 "Why should the name of our father be withdrawn from among his family because he had no son? Give us a possession among our father's brothers."

5 ᵃNum. 9:8; 27:21

5 ᵃAnd Moses brought their case before the LORD.

6 Then the LORD spoke to Moses, saying,

★ 7-11

7 ᵃNum. 36:2; Josh. 17:4

7 "ᵃThe daughters of Zelophehad are right in *their* statements. You shall surely give them a hereditary possession among their father's brothers, and you shall transfer the inheritance of their father to them.

8 "Further, you shall speak to the sons of Israel, saying, 'If a man dies and has no son, then you shall transfer his inheritance to his daughter.

9 'And if he has no daughter, then you shall give his inheritance to his brothers.

10 'And if he has no brothers, then you shall give his inheritance to his father's brothers.

11 ᵃNum. 35:29

11 'And if his father has no brothers, then you shall give his inheritance to his nearest relative in his own family, and he shall possess it; and it shall be a ᵃstatutory ordinance to the sons of Israel, just as the LORD commanded Moses.' "

2 The appointment of Joshua, 27:12-23

★12 ᵃDeut. 3:23-27; 32:48-52 ᵇNum. 33:47, 48

12 ᵃThen the LORD said to Moses, "Go up to this ᵇmountain of Abarim, and see the land which I have given to the sons of Israel.

13 ᵃNum. 31:2 ᵇNum. 20:24, 28; Deut. 10:6

13 "And when you have seen it, you too ᵃshall be gathered to your people, ᵇas Aaron your brother was;

14 for in the wilderness of Zin, during the strife of the congregation, ᵃyou rebelled against My command to treat Me as holy before their eyes at the water." (These are the waters of Meribah of Kadesh in the wilderness of Zin.)

★**14** ᵃNum. 20:12; Deut. 32:51; Ps. 106:32

15 Then Moses spoke to the LORD, saying,

16 "ᵃMay the LORD, the God of the spirits of all flesh, appoint a man over the congregation,

16 ᵃNum. 16:22

17 who ᵃwill go out and come in before them, and who will lead them out and bring them in, that the congregation of the LORD may not be ᵇlike sheep which have no shepherd."

17 ᵃDeut. 31:2; 2 Chr. 1:10 ᵇ1 Kin. 22:17; Ezek. 34:5; Matt. 9:36; Mark 6:34

18 So the LORD said to Moses, "Take Joshua the son of Nun, a man ᵃin whom is the Spirit, and ᵇlay your hand on him;

18 ᵃNum. 11:25-29; Deut. 34:9 ᵇNum. 27:23

19 and have him stand before Eleazar the priest and before all the congregation; and ᵃcommission him in their sight.

19 ᵃDeut. 3:28; 31:3, 7, 8, 23

20 "And you shall put some of your authority on him, in order that all the congregation of the sons of Israel may obey *him.*

21 "Moreover, he shall stand before Eleazar the priest, who shall inquire for him ᵃby the judgment of the Urim before the LORD. At his command they shall go out and at his command they shall come in, *both* he and the sons of Israel with him, even all the congregation."

★**21** ᵃEx. 28:30; 1 Sam. 28:6

22 And Moses did just as the LORD commanded him; and he took Joshua and set him before Eleazar the priest, and before all the congregation.

23 Then he laid his hands on him and ᵃcommissioned him, just as the LORD had spoken through Moses.

23 ᵃDeut. 31:23

27:7-11 Moses announced a new law of inheritance whereby a daughter could inherit.

27:12 *Abarim.* The range of mountains overlooking (from the east) the Jordan valley and the Dead Sea (see note on 23:14).

27:14 See notes on 20:8 and 20:13.

27:21 God's will for Joshua was discovered through the use of the *Urim,* rather than directly, as in the case of Moses (see note on Exod. 28:30).

3 The order of offerings and festivals, 28:1-29:40

★ 1-2

28 Then the LORD spoke to Moses, saying,

2 aLev. 3:11

2 "Command the sons of Israel and say to them, 'You shall be careful to present My offering, My ᵃfood for My offerings by fire, of a soothing aroma to Me, at their appointed time.'

★ 3-8

3 aEx. 29:38-42

3 "ᵃAnd you shall say to them, 'This is the offering by fire which you shall offer to the LORD; two male lambs one year old without defect as a continual burnt offering every day.

4 'You shall offer the one lamb in the morning, and the other lamb you shall offer at twilight;

5 aEx. 16:36; Num. 15:4 bLev. 2:1

5 also ᵃa tenth of an ephah of fine flour for a ᵇgrain offering, mixed with a fourth of a hin of beaten oil.

6 'It is a continual burnt offering which was ordained in Mount Sinai as a soothing aroma, an offering by fire to the LORD.

7 aEx. 29:42

7 'Then the libation with it shall be a fourth of a hin for each lamb, ᵃin the holy place you shall pour out a libation of strong drink to the LORD.

8 'And the other lamb you shall offer at twilight; as the grain offering of the morning and as its libation, you shall offer it, an offering by fire, a soothing aroma to the LORD.

★ 9-10

9 'Then on the sabbath day two male lambs one year old without defect, and two-tenths of an ephah of fine flour mixed with oil as a grain offering, and its libation:

10 aNum. 28:3

10 'This is the burnt offering of every sabbath in addition to the ᵃcontinual burnt offering and its libation.

11 'Then ᵃat the beginning of each of your months you shall present a burnt offering to the LORD; two bulls and one ram, seven male lambs one year old without defect,

12 ᵃand three-tenths of an ephah of fine flour for a grain offering, mixed with oil, for each bull; and two-tenths of fine flour for a grain offering, mixed with oil, for the one ram;

13 and a tenth of an ephah of fine flour mixed with oil for a grain offering for each lamb, for a burnt offering of a soothing aroma, an offering by fire to the LORD.

14 'And their libations shall be half a hin of wine for a bull and a third of a hin for the ram and a fourth of a hin for a lamb; this is the burnt offering of each month throughout the months of the year.

15 'And one male goat for a sin offering to the LORD; it shall be offered with its libation in addition to the ᵃcontinual burnt offering.

16 'ᵃThen on the fourteenth day of the first month shall be the LORD's Passover.

17 'And ᵃon the fifteenth day of this month shall be a ᵇfeast, unleavened bread shall be eaten for seven days.

18 'On the ᵃfirst day shall be a holy convocation; you shall do no laborious work.

19 'And you shall present an offering by fire, a burnt offering to the LORD: two bulls and one ram and seven male lambs one year old, ᵃhaving them without defect.

20 'And for their grain offering, you shall offer fine flour

★11-15

11 aNum. 10:10; Ezek. 46:6, 7

12 aNum. 15:4-12

15 aNum. 28:3

16 aEx. 12:1-20; Lev. 23:5-8; Deut. 16:1-8

★17-25

17 aLev. 23:6 bEx. 23:15; 34:18; Deut. 16:3-8

18 aLev. 23:7

19 aDeut. 15:21

28:1-2 The regulations concerning sacrifices and festivals are stated again in chapters 28 and 29, just before Israel entered the land of Canaan.

28:3-8 These verses describe the daily offerings (see notes on Exod. 29:38 and Lev. 6:19). at twilight (v. 4). Lit., between the evenings (see note on Exod. 12:6).

28:9-10 On the Sabbath, special offerings were made in addition to the daily ones.

28:11-15 At the beginning of each month, a substantial burnt offering plus grain, drink, and sin offerings were made. The trumpets were also blown (see 10:10).

28:17-25 For the Feast of Unleavened Bread, see note on Exod. 12:15. Substantial offerings were brought each day for seven days (vv. 19-24).

mixed with oil: three-tenths *of an ephah* for a bull and two-tenths for the ram.

21 'A tenth *of an ephah* you shall offer for each of the seven lambs,

22 and one male goat for a [a]sin offering, to make atonement for you.

23 'You shall present these besides [a]the burnt offering of the morning, which is for a continual burnt offering.

24 'After this manner you shall present daily, for seven days, [a]the food of the offering by fire, of a soothing aroma to the LORD; it shall be presented with its libation in addition to the [b]continual burnt offering.

25 'And on the seventh day you shall have a holy convocation; [a]you shall do no laborious work.

26 'Also on [a]the day of the first fruits, when you present a new grain offering to the LORD in your *Feast of* Weeks, you shall have a holy convocation; [b]you shall do no laborious work.

27 'And you shall offer a burnt offering for a soothing aroma to the LORD, two young bulls, one ram, seven male lambs one year old,

28 and their grain offering, fine flour mixed with oil, three-tenths *of an ephah* for each bull, two-tenths for the one ram,

29 a tenth for each of the seven lambs,

30 one male goat to make atonement for you.

31 '[a]Besides the continual burnt offering and its grain offering, you shall present *them* with their libations. They shall be without defect.

29 '[a]Now in the seventh month, on the first day of the month, you shall also have a

holy convocation; [b]you shall do no laborious work. It will be to you a day for blowing trumpets.

2 'And you shall offer a burnt offering as a soothing aroma to the LORD: one bull, one ram, *and* seven male lambs one year old without defect;

3 also their grain offering, fine flour mixed with oil, three-tenths *of an ephah* for the bull, two-tenths for the ram,

4 and one-tenth for each of the seven lambs.

5 'And *offer* one male goat for a sin offering, to make atonement for you,

6 [a]besides the burnt offering of the new moon, and its grain offering, and the [b]continual burnt offering and its grain offering, and their libations, according to their ordinance, for a soothing aroma, an offering by fire to the LORD.

7 'Then on [a]the tenth day of this seventh month you shall have a holy convocation, and you shall humble yourselves; you shall not do any work.

8 'And you shall present a burnt offering to the LORD *as a* soothing aroma: one bull, one ram, seven male lambs one year old, [a]having them without defect;

9 and their grain offering, fine flour mixed with oil, three-tenths *of an ephah* for the bull, two-tenths for the one ram,

10 a tenth for each of the seven lambs;

11 one male goat for a sin offering, besides [a]the sin offering of atonement and [b]the continual burnt offering and its grain offering, and their libations.

12 'Then on [a]the fifteenth day of the seventh month you shall have a holy convocation; you [b]shall do no laborious work, and you shall observe a feast to the LORD for seven days.

Cross references (margin)

- **22** [a]Lev. 16:18; Rom. 8:3; Gal. 4:4f.
- **23** [a]Num. 28:3
- **24** [a]Lev. 3:11 [b]Num. 28:3
- **25** [a]Num. 28:18
- **★26** [a]Ex. 23:16; 34:22; Lev. 23:15-21; Deut. 16:9-12 [b]Num. 28:18
- **31** [a]Num. 28:3
- **★ 1-6**
- **1** [a]Ex. 23:16; 34:22; Lev. 23:23-25 [b]Num. 28:26
- **6** [a]Num. 28:27 [b]Num. 28:3
- **★ 7-11**
- **7** [a]Lev. 16:29-34; 23:26-32
- **8** [a]Lev. 22:20; Deut. 15:21; 17:1
- **11** [a]Lev. 16:3, 5 [b]Num. 28:3
- **★12-38**
- **12** [a]Lev. 23:33-35; Deut. 16:13-15 [b]Num. 29:1

28:26 *on the day of the first fruits.* I.e., 50 days after the Feast of Unleavened Bread, or on the day of Pentecost (see note on Lev. 23:15).

29:1-6 For the Feast of Trumpets, see note on Lev. 23:24.

29:7-11 For the Day of Atonement, see notes on Lev. 16.

29:12-38 For the Feast of Tabernacles, or Booths, see note on Lev. 23:34. Except for Passover and the Day of Atonement, these festivals were happy occasions for the people.

13 'And you shall present a burnt offering, an offering by fire as a soothing aroma to the Lord: thirteen bulls, two rams, fourteen male lambs one year old, which are without defect,

14 and their grain offering, fine flour mixed with oil, three-tenths *of an ephah* for each of the thirteen bulls, two-tenths for each of the two rams,

15 and a tenth for each of the fourteen lambs;

16 *a*Num. 28:3
16 and one male goat for a sin offering, *a*besides the continual burnt offering, its grain offering and its libation.

17 *a*Lev. 23:36
17 Then on *a*the second day: twelve bulls, two rams, fourteen male lambs one year old without defect;

18 *a*Lev. 2:1-16
18 and their grain offering and their libations for the bulls, for the rams and for the lambs, by their number *a*according to the ordinance;

19 *a*Num. 28:8
19 and one male goat for a sin offering, *a*besides the continual burnt offering and its grain offering, and their libations.

20 Then on the third day: eleven bulls, two rams, fourteen male lambs one year old without defect;

21 and their grain offering and their libations for the bulls, for the rams and for the lambs, their number according to the ordinance;

22 and one male goat for a sin offering, besides the continual burnt offering and its grain offering and its libation.

23 Then on the fourth day: ten bulls, two rams, fourteen male lambs one year old without defect;

24 their grain offering and their libations for the bulls, for the rams and for the lambs, by their number according to the ordinance;

25 and one male goat for a sin offering, besides the continual burnt offering, its grain offering and its libation.

26 *a*Heb. 7:26
26 'Then on the fifth day: nine bulls, two rams, fourteen male lambs one year old *a*without defect;

27 and their grain offering and their libations for the bulls, for the rams and for the lambs, by their number according to the ordinance;

28 and one male goat for a sin offering, besides the continual burnt offering and its grain offering and its libation.

29 'Then on the sixth day: eight bulls, two rams, fourteen male lambs one year old without defect;

30 and their grain offering and their libations for the bulls, for the rams and for the lambs, by their number according to the ordinance;

31 and one male goat for a sin offering, besides the continual burnt offering, its grain offering and its libations.

32 'Then on the seventh day: seven bulls, two rams, fourteen male lambs one year old without defect;

33 and their grain offering and their libations for the bulls, for the rams and for the lambs, by their number according to the ordinance;

34 and one male goat for a sin offering, besides the continual burnt offering, its grain offering and its libation.

35 *a*Lev. 23:36
35 '*a*On the eighth day you shall have a solemn assembly; you shall do no laborious work.

36 'But you shall present a burnt offering, an offering by fire, as a soothing aroma to the Lord: one bull, one ram, seven male lambs one year old without defect;

37 their grain offering and their libations for the bull, for the ram and for the lambs, by their number according to the ordinance;

38 and one male goat for a sin offering, besides the continual burnt offering and its grain offering and its libation.

★39 *a*Lev.
23:2

39 'You shall present these to the LORD at your *a*appointed times, besides your votive offerings and your freewill offerings, for your burnt offerings and for your grain offerings and for your libations and for your peace offerings.' "

40 And Moses spoke to the sons of Israel in accordance with all that the LORD had commanded Moses.

4 The law for vows, 30:1–16

1 *a*Num.
1:4, 16; 7:2

30 Then Moses spoke to *a*the heads of the tribes of the sons of Israel, saying, "This is the word which the LORD has commanded.

★ 2 *a*Deut.
23:21-23;
Matt. 5:33

2 "*a*If a man makes a vow to the LORD, or takes an oath to bind himself with a binding obligation, he shall not violate his word; he shall do according to all that proceeds out of his mouth.

★ 3-16

3 "Also if a woman makes a vow to the LORD, and binds herself by an obligation in her father's house in her youth,

4 and her father hears her vow and her obligation by which she has bound herself, and her father says nothing to her, then all her vows shall stand, and every obligation by which she has bound herself shall stand.

5 "But if her father should forbid her on the day he hears *of it,* none of her vows or her obligations by which she has bound herself shall stand; and the LORD will forgive her because her father had forbidden her.

6 "However, if she should marry while under her vows or the rash statement of her lips by which she has bound herself,

7 and her husband hears of it and says nothing to her on the day he hears *it,* then her vows

shall stand and her obligations by which she has bound herself shall stand.

8 "But if on the day her husband hears *of it,* he forbids her, then he shall annul her vow which she is under and the rash statement of her lips by which she has bound herself; and the LORD will forgive her.

9 "But the vow of a widow or of a divorced woman, everything by which she has bound herself, shall stand against her.

10 "However, if she vowed in her husband's house, or bound herself by an obligation with an oath,

11 and her husband heard *it,* but said nothing to her *and* did not forbid her, then all her vows shall stand, and every obligation by which she bound herself shall stand.

12 "But if her husband indeed annuls them on the day he hears *them,* then whatever proceeds out of her lips concerning her vows or concerning the obligation of herself, shall not stand; her husband has annulled them, and the LORD will forgive her.

13 "Every vow and every binding oath to humble herself, her husband may confirm it or her husband may annul it.

14 "But if her husband indeed says nothing to her from day to day, then he confirms all her vows or all her obligations which are on her; he has confirmed them, because he said nothing to her on the day he heard them.

15 "But if he indeed annuls   **★15**
them after he has heard them, then he shall bear her guilt."

16 These are the statutes which the LORD commanded Moses, *as* between a man and his wife, *and as* between a father and his daughter, *while she is* in her youth in her father's house.

29:39 Private offerings (*votive* and *freewill*) were made in addition to the ones prescribed for the festivals.
30:2 A man was unconditionally bound by any vow he made.
30:3–16 A vow made by a woman could be in-

validated by her father (in the case of an unmarried daughter) or by her husband (in the case of a wife). A widow or divorced woman was responsible for her own vows (v. 9).
30:15 If a husband invalidated his wife's vow some time later, he was held responsible.

F The People Defeat the Midianites, 31:1-54

31 Then the LORD spoke to Moses, saying,

★ **2** aNum. 25:1, 16, 17 bNum. 20:24, 26; 27:13

2 "aTake full vengeance for the sons of Israel on the Midianites; afterward you will be bgathered to your people."

3 aLev. 26:25

3 And Moses spoke to the people, saying, "Arm men from among you for the war, that they may go against Midian, to execute athe LORD's vengeance on Midian.

4 "A thousand from each tribe of all the tribes of Israel you shall send to the war."

5 So there were furnished from the thousands of Israel, a thousand from each tribe, twelve thousand armed for war.

6 aNum. 14:44 bNum. 10:8, 9

6 And Moses sent them, a thousand from each tribe, to the war, and Phinehas the son of Eleazar the priest, to the war with them, aand the holy vessels and bthe trumpets for the alarm in his hand.

7 aDeut. 20:13; Judg. 21:11; 1 Kin. 11:15, 16

7 So they made war against Midian, just as the LORD had commanded Moses, and athey killed every male.

8 aJosh. 13:21 bNum. 25:15 cNum. 31:16; Josh. 13:22

8 And they killed the kings of Midian along with the *rest of* their slain: aEvi and Rekem and bZur and Hur and Reba, the five kings of Midian; they also killed cBalaam the son of Beor with the sword.

9 And the sons of Israel captured the women of Midian and their little ones; and all their cattle and all their flocks and all their goods, they plundered.

10 Then they burned all their cities where they lived and all their camps with fire.

11 aDeut. 20:14

11 And athey took all the spoil and all the prey, both of man and of beast.

12 And they brought the captives and the prey and the spoil to Moses, and to Eleazar the priest and to the congregation of the sons of Israel, to the camp at the plains of Moab, which are by the Jordan opposite Jericho.

13 And Moses and Eleazar the priest and all the leaders of the congregation went out to meet them outside the camp.

14 And Moses was angry with the officers of the army, the captains of thousands and the captains of hundreds, who had come from service in the war.

15 And Moses said to them, "Have you spared aall the women?

15 aDeut. 20:14

16 "aBehold, these caused the sons of Israel, through the counsel of bBalaam, to trespass against the LORD in the matter of Peor, so the plague was among the congregation of the LORD.

16 aNum. 25:1-9 bNum. 31:8

17 "aNow therefore, kill every male among the little ones, and kill every woman who has known man intimately.

★**17-18**

17 aDeut. 7:2; 20:16-18

18 "But all the girls who have not known man intimately, spare for yourselves.

19 "aAnd you, camp outside the camp seven days; whoever has killed any person, and whoever has touched any slain, purify yourselves, you and your captives, on the third day and on the seventh day.

★**19-24**

19 aNum. 19:11-22

20 "And you shall purify for yourselves every garment and every article of leather and all the work of goats' *hair*, and all articles of wood."

21 Then Eleazar the priest said to the men of war who had gone to battle, "This is the statute of the law which the LORD has commanded Moses:

22 only the gold and the

31:2 The time had come to carry out the command of 25:16-18. The *Midianites* were responsible for corrupting Israel through adultery and idolatry, and therefore had to be destroyed.

31:17-18 All male Midianite children were to be killed, lest they endanger the inheritance of

Israel's sons by being allowed to grow up among the Israelites. Only virgin girls who could be assimilated into Israel were spared.

31:19-24 Every soldier and every thing had to be purified, the former with the water mixed with the ashes of the red heifer (see note on 19:2) and the latter by fire and water.

silver, the bronze, the iron, the tin and the lead,

²³ ^aNum. 19:9, 17

23 everything that can stand the fire, you shall pass through the fire, and it shall be clean, but it shall be purified with ^awater for impurity. But whatever cannot stand the fire you shall pass through the water.

24 "And you shall wash your clothes on the seventh day and be clean, and afterward you may enter the camp."

★25-27

25 Then the Lord spoke to Moses, saying,

26 "You and Eleazar the priest and the heads of the fathers' *households* of the congregation, take a count of the booty that was captured, both of man and of animal;

²⁷ ^aJosh. 22:8

27 and ^adivide the booty between the warriors who went out to battle and all the congregation.

★28-29

²⁸ ^aNum. 18:21-30

28 "^aAnd levy a tax for the Lord from the men of war who went out to battle, one in five hundred of the persons and of the cattle and of the donkeys and of the sheep;

29 take it from their half and give it to Eleazar the priest, as an offering to the Lord.

★30-31

³⁰ ^aNum. 3:7, 8, 25, 26, 31, 36, 37; 18:3, 4

30 "And from the sons of Israel's half, you shall take one drawn out of every fifty of the persons, of the cattle, of the donkeys and of the sheep, from all the animals, and give them to the Levites who ^akeep charge of the tabernacle of the Lord."

31 And Moses and Eleazar the priest did just as the Lord had commanded Moses.

32 Now the booty that remained from the spoil which the men of war had plundered was 675,000 sheep,

33 and 72,000 cattle,

34 and 61,000 donkeys,

35 and of human beings, of the women who had not known man intimately, all the persons were 32,000.

36 And the half, the portion of those who went out to war, was *as follows:* the number of sheep was 337,500,

37 and the Lord's levy of the sheep was 675,

38 and the cattle were 36,000, from which the Lord's levy was 72.

39 And the donkeys were 30,500, from which the Lord's levy was 61.

40 And the human beings were 16,000, from whom the Lord's levy was 32 persons.

⁴¹ ^aNum. 5:9, 10; 18:19

41 And Moses gave the levy *which was* the Lord's offering to Eleazar the priest, just ^aas the Lord had commanded Moses.

42 As for the sons of Israel's half, which Moses separated from the men who had gone to war—

43 now the congregation's half was 337,500 sheep,

44 and 36,000 cattle,

45 and 30,500 donkeys,

46 and the human beings were 16,000—

47 and from the sons of Israel's half, Moses took one drawn out of every fifty, both of man and of animals, and gave them to the Levites, who kept charge of the tabernacle of the Lord, just as the Lord had commanded Moses.

48 Then the officers who were over the thousands of the army, the captains of thousands and the captains of hundreds, approached Moses;

49 and they said to Moses, "Your servants have taken a census of men of war who are in our charge, and no man of us is missing.

⁵⁰ ^aEx. 30:12-16

50 "So we have brought as an offering to the Lord what each man found, articles of gold, armlets and bracelets, signet rings,

---

31:25-27 The spoil was divided equally between those who fought and those who stayed at home (cf. 1 Sam. 30:24-25).

31:28-29 The soldiers were to dedicate one out of every 500 captured persons and animals to the Lord.

31:30-31 Those who stayed home gave one out of every 50 captive persons and animals to the Levites.

earrings and necklaces, ᵃto make atonement for ourselves before the Lᴏʀᴅ."

51 And Moses and Eleazar the priest took the gold from them, all kinds of wrought articles.

★52   **52** And all the gold of the offering which they offered up to the Lᴏʀᴅ, from the captains of thousands and the captains of hundreds, was 16,750 shekels.

53 ᵃNum.
31:32; Deut.
20:14   **53** ᵃThe men of war had taken booty, every man for himself.

54 ᵃEx.
30:16   **54** So Moses and Eleazar the priest took the gold from the captains of thousands and of hundreds, and brought it to the tent of meeting as ᵃa memorial for the sons of Israel before the Lᴏʀᴅ.

G   Transjordan Settled by Two and a Half Tribes, 32:1-42

★ 1 ᵃEx.
12:38 ᵇNum.
21:32   **32** Now the sons of Reuben and the sons of Gad had an ᵃexceedingly large number of livestock. So when they saw the land of ᵇJazer and the land of Gilead, that it was indeed a place suitable for livestock,

2 the sons of Gad and the sons of Reuben came and spoke to Moses and to Eleazar the priest and to the leaders of the congregation, saying,

3 ᵃNum.
32:34-38   **3** "ᵃAtaroth, Dibon, Jazer, Nimrah, Heshbon, Elealeh, Sebam, Nebo and Beon,

4 ᵃNum.
21:34   **4** the land ᵃwhich the Lᴏʀᴅ conquered before the congregation of Israel, is a land for livestock; and your servants have livestock."

5 And they said, "If we have found favor in your sight, let this land be given to your servants as a possession; do not take us across the Jordan."

★ 6-15   **6** But Moses said to the sons of Gad and to the sons of Reuben, "Shall your brothers go to war while you yourselves sit here?

7 ᵃNum.
13:27-14:4   **7** "ᵃNow why are you discouraging the sons of Israel from crossing over into the land which the Lᴏʀᴅ has given them?

8 ᵃNum.
13:3, 26;
Deut. 1:19-
25   **8** "This is what your fathers did when I sent them from ᵃKadesh-barnea to see the land.

9 ᵃNum.
13:24; Deut.
1:24   **9** "For when they went up to ᵃthe valley of Eshcol and saw the land, they discouraged the sons of Israel so that they did not go into the land which the Lᴏʀᴅ had given them.

10 ᵃNum.
14:11f.; Deut.
1:34   **10** "So ᵃthe Lᴏʀᴅ's anger burned in that day, and He swore, saying,

11 ᵃNum.
14:28-30   **11** 'ᵃNone of the men who came up from Egypt, from twenty years old and upward, shall see the land which I swore to Abraham, to Isaac and to Jacob; for they did not follow Me fully,

12 ᵃDeut.
1:36; Josh.
14:8f.   **12** except Caleb the son of Jephunneh the Kenizzite and Joshua the son of Nun, ᵃfor they have followed the Lᴏʀᴅ fully.'

13 ᵃNum.
14:33-35   **13** "ᵃSo the Lᴏʀᴅ's anger burned against Israel, and He made them wander in the wilderness forty years, until the entire generation of those who had done evil in the sight of the Lᴏʀᴅ was destroyed.

14 ᵃDeut.
1:34f.   **14** "Now behold, you have risen up in your fathers' place, a brood of sinful men, to add still more to the burning ᵃanger of the Lᴏʀᴅ against Israel.

15 ᵃDeut.
30:17, 18;
2 Chr. 7:19,
20   **15** "For if you ᵃturn away from following Him, He will once more abandon them in the wilderness; and you will destroy all these people."

16 Then they came near to him and said, "We will build here sheepfolds for our livestock and cities for our little ones;

31:52 The gold booty was approximately 6,700 oz., an enormous amount.
32:1 The tribes of *Reuben* and *Gad* requested permission of Moses to settle in *Jazer* and *Gilead* (E. of the Jordan River), a good area for raising cattle.

32:6-15 Moses feared that the proposal of the sons of Gad and the sons of Reuben (vv. 2-5) would not proceed to conquer the land W. of the Jordan. It would be the defection at Kadesh (14:1-10) all over again.

17 ^abut we ourselves will be armed ready *to go* before the sons of Israel, until we have brought them to their place, while our little ones live in the fortified cities because of the inhabitants of the land.

18 "^aWe will not return to our homes until every one of the sons of Israel has possessed his inheritance.

19 "For we will not have an inheritance with them on the other side of the Jordan and beyond, because our inheritance has fallen to us ^aon this side of the Jordan toward the east."

20 ^aSo Moses said to them, "If you will do this, if you will arm yourselves before the LORD for the war,

21 and all of you armed men cross over the Jordan before the LORD until He has driven His enemies out from before Him,

22 ^aand the land is subdued before the LORD, then afterward you shall return and be free of obligation toward the LORD and toward Israel, and this land shall be yours for a possession before the LORD.

23 "But if you will not do so, behold, you have sinned against the LORD, and be sure ^ayour sin will find you out.

24 "Build yourselves cities for your little ones, and sheepfolds for your sheep; and ^ado what you have promised."

25 And the sons of Gad and the sons of Reuben spoke to Moses, saying, "Your servants will do just as my lord commands.

26 "^aOur little ones, our wives, our livestock and all our cattle shall remain there in the cities of Gilead;

27 while your servants, everyone who is armed for war, will ^across over in the presence of the LORD to battle, just as my lord says."

28 So Moses gave command concerning them to Eleazar the priest, and to Joshua the son of Nun, and to the heads of the fathers' *households* of the tribes of the sons of Israel.

29 And Moses said to them, "If the sons of Gad and the sons of Reuben, everyone who is armed for battle, will cross with you over the Jordan in the presence of the LORD, and the land will be subdued before you, then you shall give them the land of Gilead for a possession;

30 but if they will not cross over with you armed, they shall have possessions among you in the land of Canaan."

31 And the sons of Gad and the sons of Reuben answered, saying, "As the LORD has said to your servants, so we will do.

32 "We ourselves will cross over armed in the presence of the LORD into the land of Canaan, and the possession of our inheritance *shall remain* with us across the Jordan."

33 ^aSo Moses gave to them, to the sons of Gad and to the sons of Reuben and to the half-tribe of Joseph's son Manasseh, the kingdom of Sihon, king of the Amorites and the kingdom of Og, the king of Bashan, the land with its cities with *their* territories, the cities of the surrounding land.

34 And the sons of Gad built Dibon and Ataroth and ^aAroer,

35 and Atroth-shophan and Jazer and Jogbehah,

36 and ^aBeth-nimrah and Beth-haran as fortified cities, and sheepfolds for sheep.

37 And the sons of Reuben built Heshbon and Elealeh and Kiriathaim,

38 and ^aNebo and Baal-meon—*their* names being changed—and Sibmah, and they gave *other* names to the cities which they built.

32:23 *be sure your sin will find you out.* I.e., "if you fail to keep your agreement to assist in the conquest of the land W. of the Jordan before settling yourselves E. of the Jordan."

17 ^aJosh. 4:12, 13
18 ^aJosh. 22:1-4
19 ^aJosh. 12:1; 13:8
20 ^aDeut. 3:18
22 ^aDeut. 3:20
★23 ^aGen. 4:7; 44:16; Is. 59:12
24 ^aNum. 30:2
26 ^aJosh. 1:14
27 ^aJosh. 4:12
33 ^aDeut. 3:8-17; Josh. 12:1-6
34 ^aDeut. 2:36
36 ^aNum. 32:3
38 ^aIs. 46:1

★39 ªGen.
50:23

39 And the sons of ªMachir the son of Manasseh went to Gilead and took it, and dispossessed the Amorites who were in it.

40 ªDeut.
3:12, 13, 15;
Josh. 17:1

40 So Moses gave ªGilead to Machir the son of Manasseh, and he lived in it.

41 ªDeut.
3:14; Judg.
10:4

41 And Jair the son of Manasseh went and took its towns, and called them ªHavvoth-jair.

42 ª2 Sam.
18:18; Ps.
49:11

42 And Nobah went and took Kenath and its villages, and called it Nobah after ªhis own name.

H   The Journey from Egypt to Moab Reviewed, 33:1–49

★ 1ff.

1 ªPs.
77:20;
105:26; Mic.
6:4

33 These are the journeys of the sons of Israel, by which they came out from the land of Egypt by their armies, under ªthe leadership of Moses and Aaron.

★ 2

2 And Moses recorded their starting places according to their journeys by the command of the LORD, and these are their journeys according to their starting places.

3 ªEx.
12:37 ᵇEx.
14:8

3 ªAnd they journeyed from Rameses in the first month, on the fifteenth day of the first month; on the next day after the Passover the sons of Israel ᵇstarted out boldly in the sight of all the Egyptians,

4 ªEx.
12:12

4 while the Egyptians were burying all their first-born whom the LORD had struck down among them. The LORD had also executed judgments ªon their gods.

5 ªEx.
12:37

5 Then ªthe sons of Israel journeyed from Rameses, and camped in Succoth.

6 ªEx.
13:20

6 ªAnd they journeyed from Succoth, and camped in Etham, which is on the edge of the wilderness.

7 ªEx.
14:1, 2

7 ªAnd they journeyed from Etham, and turned back to Pihahiroth, which faces Baal-zephon; and they camped before Migdol.

8 ªAnd they journeyed from before Hahiroth, and passed through the midst of the sea into the wilderness; and ᵇthey went three days' journey in the wilderness of Etham, and camped at Marah.

8 ªEx.
14:22 ᵇEx.
15:22, 23

9 ªAnd they journeyed from Marah, and came to Elim; and in Elim there were twelve springs of water and seventy palm trees; and they camped there.

9 ªEx.
15:27

10 And they journeyed from Elim, and camped by the Red Sea.

11 And they journeyed from the Red Sea, and camped in ªthe wilderness of Sin.

11 ªEx. 16:1

12 And they journeyed from the wilderness of Sin, and camped at Dophkah.

13 And they journeyed from Dophkah, and camped at Alush.

14 And they journeyed from Alush, and camped ªat Rephidim; now it was there that the people had no water to drink.

14 ªEx. 17:1

15 And they journeyed from Rephidim, and camped in ªthe wilderness of Sinai.

15 ªEx. 19:1

16 And they journeyed from the wilderness of Sinai, and camped at ªKibroth-hattaavah.

16 ªNum.
11:34

17 And they journeyed from Kibroth-hattaavah, and camped at ªHazeroth.

17 ªNum.
11:35

18 And they journeyed from Hazeroth, and camped at Rithmah.

19 And they journeyed from Rithmah, and camped at Rimmon-perez.

20 And they journeyed from Rimmon-perez, and camped at ªLibnah.

20 ªDeut.
1:1

21 And they journeyed from Libnah, and camped at Rissah.

22 And they journeyed from Rissah, and camped in Kehelathah.

23 And they journeyed from Kehelathah, and camped at Mount Shepher.

32:39 *Manasseh.* This tribe was also given permission to settle E. of the Jordan because she had conquered some of that territory. She had a share on the W. side as well (cf. Josh. 22:7).
33:1ff. This chapter records the itinerary of the Israelites from Egypt to the Jordan. Listed are 41 stages in their journey of 40 years.
33:2 *their starting places.* Lit., the plucking up, or breaking camp.

24 And they journeyed from Mount Shepher, and camped at Haradah.

25 And they journeyed from Haradah, and camped at Makheloth.

26 And they journeyed from Makheloth, and camped at Tahath.

27 And they journeyed from Tahath, and camped at Terah.

28 And they journeyed from Terah, and camped at Mithkah.

29 And they journeyed from Mithkah, and camped at Hashmonah.

30 And they journeyed from Hashmonah, and camped at ^aMoseroth.

31 And they journeyed from Moseroth, and camped at Benejaakan.

32 And they journeyed from ^aBene-jaakan, and camped at Hor-haggidgad.

33 And they journeyed from Hor-haggidgad, and camped at ^aJotbathah.

34 And they journeyed from Jotbathah, and camped at Abronah.

35 And they journeyed from Abronah, and camped at ^aEzion-geber.

36 And they journeyed from Ezion-geber, and camped in the wilderness of ^aZin, that is, Kadesh.

37 And they journeyed from Kadesh, and camped at ^aMount Hor, ^bat the edge of the land of Edom.

38 ^aThen Aaron the priest went up to Mount Hor at the command of the LORD, and died there, in the fortieth year after the sons of Israel had come from the land of Egypt on the first *day* in the fifth month.

39 And Aaron was one hundred twenty-three years old when he died on Mount Hor.

40 Now the Canaanite, the king of ^aArad who lived in the Negev in the land of Canaan,

heard of the coming of the sons of Israel.

41 Then they journeyed from Mount Hor, and camped at Zalmonah.

42 And they journeyed from Zalmonah, and camped at Punon.

43 And they journeyed from Punon, and camped at ^aOboth.

44 And they journeyed from Oboth, and camped at Iye-abarim, at the border of Moab.

45 And they journeyed from Iyim, and camped at Dibon-gad.

46 And they journeyed from Dibon-gad, and camped at Almon-diblathaim.

47 And they journeyed from Almon-diblathaim, and camped in the mountains of ^aAbarim, before Nebo.

48 And they journeyed from the mountains of Abarim, and ^acamped in the plains of Moab by the Jordan *opposite* Jericho.

49 And they camped by the Jordan, from Beth-jeshimoth as far as ^aAbel-shittim in the plains of Moab.

I Instructions for Possessing the Land, 33:50–56

50 Then the LORD spoke to Moses in the plains of Moab by the Jordan *opposite* Jericho, saying,

51 "Speak to the sons of Israel and say to them, '^aWhen you cross over the Jordan into the land of Canaan,

52 then you shall drive out all the inhabitants of the land from before you, and ^adestroy all their figured stones, and destroy all their molten images and demolish all their high places;

53 ^aand you shall take possession of the land and live in it, for I have given the land to you to possess it.

54 '^aAnd you shall inherit the land by lot according to your families; to the larger you shall give more inheritance, and to the

---

30 ^aDeut. 10:6

32 ^aGen. 36:27; Deut. 10:6; 1 Chr. 1:42

33 ^aDeut. 10:7

35 ^aDeut. 2:8

36 ^aNum. 20:1

37 ^aNum. 20:22 ^bNum. 20:16

★**38** ^aNum. 20:28; Deut. 10:6

40 ^aNum. 21:1

43 ^aNum. 21:10, 11

47 ^aNum. 27:12

48 ^aNum. 22:1

49 ^aNum. 25:1

51 ^aJosh. 3:17

52 ^aEx. 23:24; Lev. 26:1; Deut. 7:5; 12:3, 30; Ps. 106:34-36

53 ^aDeut. 11:31; 17:14; Josh. 21:43

★**54** ^aNum. 26:53-56

33:38 See note on 20:22.   **33:54** See note on 26:53.

smaller you shall give less inheritance. Wherever the lot falls to anyone, that shall be his. You shall inherit according to the tribes of your fathers.

★55 *a*Josh. 23:13

55 'But if you do not drive out the inhabitants of the land from before you, then it shall come about that those whom you let remain of them *will become* *a*as pricks in your eyes and as thorns in your sides, and they shall trouble you in the land in which you live.

56 'And it shall come about that as I plan to do to them, so I will do to you.'"

J The Division of the Land of Canaan, 34:1-36:13

1 The boundaries, 34:1-12

2 *a*Gen. 17:8; Ps. 78:54, 55; 105:11

34 Then the LORD spoke to Moses, saying,

2 "Command the sons of Israel and say to them, 'When you enter *a*the land of Canaan, this is the land that shall fall to you as an inheritance, *even the* land of Canaan according to its borders.

★ 3-5

3 *a*Josh. 15:1-3 *b*Josh. 15:5

3 '*a*Your southern sector shall extend from the wilderness of Zin along the side of Edom, and your southern border shall extend from the end of the Salt Sea *b*eastward.

4 *a*Num. 32:8

4 'Then your border shall turn *direction* from the south to the ascent of Akrabbim, and continue to Zin, and its termination shall be to the south of *a*Kadesh-barnea; and it shall reach Hazaraddar, and continue to Azmon.

5 *a*Josh. 15:4

5 'And the border shall turn *direction* from Azmon to the brook of Egypt, and its termination shall be at *a*the sea.

★ 6

6 'As for the western border, you shall have the Great Sea, that is, *its* coastline; this shall be your west border.

★ 7-9

7 *a*Ezek. 47:15-17

7 '*a*And this shall be your north border: you shall draw your *border* line from the Great Sea to Mount Hor.

8 *a*Josh. 13:5

8 'You shall draw a line from Mount Hor to *a*the Lebo-hamath, and the termination of the border shall be at Zedad;

9 and the border shall proceed to Ziphron, and its termination shall be at Hazar-enan. This shall be your north border.

10 'For your eastern border you shall also draw a line from Hazar-enan to Shepham,

★11 *a*2 Kin. 23:33 *b*Deut. 3:17; Josh. 13:27

11 and the border shall go down from Shepham to *a*Riblah on the east side of Ain; and the border shall go down and reach to the slope on the east side of the Sea of *b*Chinnereth.

12 'And the border shall go down to the Jordan and its termination shall be at the Salt Sea. This shall be your land according to its borders all around.'"

2 The allotment, 34:13-29

13 *a*Gen. 15:18; Num. 26:52-56; Deut. 11:24; Josh. 14:1-5

13 So Moses commanded the sons of Israel, saying, "*a*This is the land that you are to apportion by lot among you as a possession, which the LORD has commanded to give to the nine and a half tribes.

14 *a*Num. 32:33

14 "*a*For the tribe of the sons of Reuben have received *theirs* according to their fathers' households, and the tribe of the sons of Gad according to their fathers'

33:55 Israel did fail to completely exterminate the Canaanites, whose pernicious influence plagued Israel and eventually resulted in the Assyrian and Babylonian captivities.

34:3-5 The southern boundary of Canaan ran from the *Salt Sea* (Dead Sea) SW. along the border of *Edom*, across the wilderness of *Zin* (see note on 13:21) to *Kadesh-barnea*, then NW. to the *brook of Egypt* (the Wadi el Arish).

34:6 The Mediterranean Sea formed the western

border.

34:7-9 The northern border included Mt. *Hor* (possibly Mt. Hermon, but not the Hor of 20:22, where Aaron died), *Lebo-hamath* (a town in what is today southern Syria), *Zedad* (possibly a town about 65 miles NE. of Damascus), *Ziphron* and *Hazar-enan* (possibly towns about 75 miles NE. of Damascus).

34:11 *the Sea of Chinnereth.* The Sea of Galilee. From there the eastern boundary followed the Jordan to the Dead Sea.

households, and the half-tribe of Manasseh have received their possession.

★15   15 "The two and a half tribes have received their possession across the Jordan opposite Jericho, eastward toward the sunrising."

★16-29   16 Then the LORD spoke to Moses, saying,

17 ªJosh. 14:1, 2   17 "ªThese are the names of the men who shall apportion the land to you for inheritance: Eleazar the priest and Joshua the son of Nun.

18 "And you shall take one leader of every tribe to apportion the land for inheritance.

19 ªGen. 29:35; Deut. 33:7; Ps. 60:7 ᵇNum. 13:6, 30; 26:65; Deut. 1:36   19 "And these are the names of the men: of the tribe of ªJudah, ᵇCaleb the son of Jephunneh.

20 ªGen. 29:33; 49:5; Ezek. 48:24   20 "And of the tribe of the sons of ªSimeon, Samuel the son of Ammihud.

21 ªGen. 49:27; Deut. 33:12; Ps. 68:27   21 "Of the tribe of ªBenjamin, Elidad the son of Chislon.

22 "And of the tribe of the sons of Dan a leader, Bukki the son of Jogli.

23 "Of the sons of Joseph: of the tribe of the sons of Manasseh a leader, Hanniel the son of E-phod.

24 "And of the tribe of the sons of Ephraim a leader, Kemuel the son of Shiphtan.

25 "And of the tribe of the sons of Zebulun a leader, Eliza-phan the son of Parnach.

26 "And of the tribe of the sons of Issachar a leader, Paltiel the son of Azzan.

27 "And of the tribe of the sons of Asher a leader, Ahihud the son of Shelomi.

28 "And of the tribe of the sons of Naphtali a leader, Pedahel the son of Ammihud."

29 These are those whom the LORD commanded to apportion the inheritance to the sons of Israel in the land of Canaan.

3   The cities of the Levites, 35:1-8

1 ªLev. 25:32-34   35 ªNow the LORD spoke to Moses in the plains of Moab by the Jordan opposite Jericho, saying,

★2   2 "Command the sons of Israel that they give to the Levites from the inheritance of their possession, cities to live in; and you shall give to the Levites pasture lands around the cities.

3 "And the cities shall be theirs to live in; and their pasture lands shall be for their cattle and for their herds and for all their beasts.

★4-5   4 "And the pasture lands of the cities which you shall give to the Levites shall extend from the wall of the city outward a thousand cubits around.

5 "You shall also measure outside the city on the east side two thousand cubits, and on the south side two thousand cubits, and on the west side two thousand cubits, and on the north side two thousand cubits, with the city in the center. This shall become theirs as pasture lands for the cities.

6 ªJosh. 20:7-9   6 "And the cities which you shall give to the Levites shall be the ªsix cities of refuge, which you shall give for the manslayer to flee to; and in addition to them you shall give forty-two cities.

7 ªJosh. 21:41   7 "All the cities which you shall give to the Levites shall be ªforty-eight cities, together with their pasture lands.

8 ªLev. 25:32-34; Num. 26:54; 33:54; Josh. 21:1-42   8 "ªAs for the cities which you shall give from the possession of the sons of Israel, you shall

---

34:15 across the Jordan opposite Jericho, eastward. The entire area of the Jordan is here associated with the most commanding fortress in the valley, Jericho.

34:16-29 The allotment of the land was to be supervised by Eleazar, Joshua, and one leader from each of the tribes.

35:2 Since all the Levites were not occupied at the tabernacle, they were given 48 cities in which to live and pasture lands around them.

35:4-5 The pasture lands included two areas around each city: one was 1,000 cubits (500 yards) from the wall of the city outward on each side, and the second was 2,000 additional cubits (1,000 yards) beyond the first one.

take more from the larger and you shall take less from the smaller; each shall give some of his cities to the Levites in proportion to his possession which he inherits."

4 The cities of refuge, 35:9-34

9 Then the LORD spoke to Moses, saying,

10 a Josh. 20:1-9

10 "a Speak to the sons of Israel and say to them, 'When you cross the Jordan into the land of Canaan,

★11-12

11 a Deut. 19:1-13
b Josh. 20:2f.
c Ex. 21:13;
Lev. 4:2f.,
22f.; Num. 35:22-25

11 a then you shall select for yourselves cities to be your b cities of refuge, that the manslayer who has killed any person c unintentionally may flee there.

12 a Deut. 19:4-6; Josh. 20:2, 3

12 'And a the cities shall be to you as a refuge from the avenger, so that the manslayer may not die until he stands before the congregation for trial.

13 'And the cities which you are to give shall be your six cities of refuge.

14 a Deut. 4:41

14 'You a shall give three cities across the Jordan and three cities in the land of Canaan; they are to be cities of refuge.

15 a Num. 35:11

15 'These six cities shall be for refuge for the sons of Israel, and for the alien and for the sojourner among them; that anyone who kills a person a unintentionally may flee there.

★16-24

16 a Ex. 21:12, 14;
Lev. 24:17

16 'a But if he struck him down with an iron object, so that he died, he is a murderer; the murderer shall surely be put to death.

17 a Num. 35:31

17 'And if he struck him down with a stone in the hand, by which he may die, and as a result he died, he is a murderer; the

murderer a shall surely be put to death.

18 'Or if he struck him with a wooden object in the hand, by which he may die, and as a result he died, he is a murderer; the murderer shall surely be put to death.

19 'The blood avenger himself shall put the murderer to death; he shall put him to death when he meets him.

20 a Gen. 4:8, 2 Sam. 3:27; 20:10
b Ex. 21:14;
Deut. 19:11

20 'And a if he pushed him of hatred, or threw something at him b lying in wait and as a result he died,

21 or if he struck him down with his hand in enmity, and as a result he died, the one who struck him shall surely be put to death, he is a murderer; the blood avenger shall put the murderer to death when he meets him.

22 a Num. 35:11

22 'a But if he pushed him suddenly without enmity, or threw something at him without lying in wait,

23 or with any deadly object of stone, and without seeing it dropped on him so that he died, while he was not his enemy nor seeking his injury,

24 a Josh. 20:6

24 then a the congregation shall judge between the slayer and the blood avenger according to these ordinances.

★25-34

25 'And the congregation shall deliver the manslayer from the hand of the blood avenger, and the congregation shall restore him to his city of refuge to which he fled; and he shall live in it until the death of the high priest who was anointed with the holy oil.

26 'But if the manslayer shall at any time go beyond the border

---

35:11-12 The Lord provided six *cities of refuge,* in which those guilty of accidental homicide might seek refuge from the *avenger* (the nearest relative of the murdered person) until they could be tried.

35:16-24 These verses differentiate deliberate and accidental homicide (murder and manslaughter).

35:25-34 These verses list criteria for judging various types of cases. If a verdict was man-

slaughter, the slayer could live as long as he stayed within a city of refuge until the death of the high priest; after that, he could safely return home (v. 28). More than one witness to a murder was required (v. 30). No ransom was permitted so that the life of a murderer could be spared (v. 31) or so that the one guilty of manslaughter could return home (v. 32), because killing polluted the land (v. 33).

of his city of refuge to which he may flee,

27 and the blood avenger finds him outside the border of his city of refuge, and the blood avenger kills the manslayer, he shall not be guilty of blood

28 because he should have remained in his city of refuge until the death of the high priest. But after the death of the high priest the manslayer shall return to the land of his possession.

29 'And these things shall be for a ªstatutory ordinance to you throughout your generations in all your dwellings.

30 'ªIf anyone kills a person, the murderer shall be put to death at the evidence of witnesses, but ᵇno person shall be put to death on the testimony of one witness.

31 'Moreover, you shall not take ransom for the life of a murderer who is guilty of death, but he shall surely be put to death.

32 'And you shall not take ransom for him who has fled to his city of refuge, that he may return to live in the land before the death of the priest.

33 'ªSo you shall not pollute the land in which you are; for blood pollutes the land and no expiation can be made for the land for the blood that is shed on it, except ᵇby the blood of him who shed it.

34 'And you shall not ªdefile the land in which you live, in the midst of which ᵇI dwell; for I the LORD am dwelling in the midst of the sons of Israel.' "

5 *The inheritance of women,*
36:1-13

36 ªAnd the heads of the fathers' *households* of the family of the sons of Gilead, the son of Machir, the son of Manas-

seh, of the families of the sons of Joseph, came near and spoke before Moses and before the leaders, the heads of the fathers' *households* of the sons of Israel,

2 and they said, "The LORD commanded my lord to give the land by lot to the sons of Israel as an inheritance, and my lord ªwas commanded by the LORD to give the inheritance of Zelophehad our brother to his daughters.

3 "But if they marry one of the sons of the *other* tribes of the sons of Israel, their inheritance will be withdrawn from the inheritance of our fathers and will be added to the inheritance of the tribe to which they belong; thus it will be withdrawn from our allotted inheritance.

4 "And when the ªjubilee of the sons of Israel comes, then their inheritance will be added to the inheritance of the tribe to which they belong; so their inheritance will be withdrawn from the inheritance of the tribe of our fathers."

5 Then Moses commanded the sons of Israel according to the word of the LORD, saying, "The tribe of the sons of Joseph are right in *their* statements.

6 "ªThis is what the LORD has commanded concerning the daughters of Zelophehad, saying, 'Let them marry whom they wish; only they must marry within the family of the tribe of their father.'

7 "Thus ªno inheritance of the sons of Israel shall be transferred from tribe to tribe, for the sons of Israel shall each hold to the inheritance of the tribe of his fathers.

8 "ªAnd every daughter who comes into possession of an inheritance of any tribe of the sons of Israel, shall be wife to one of the family of the tribe of her fa-

---

Marginal references (left column):

29 ªNum. 27:11

30 ªNum. 35:16 ᵇDeut. 17:6; 19:15; Matt. 18:16; John 7:51; 8:17, 18

33 ªDeut. 21:7, 8; Ps. 106:38 ᵇGen. 9:6

34 ªLev. 18:24, 25 ᵇNum. 5:3

★ 1-9

1 ªNum. 27:1

Marginal references (right column):

2 ªNum. 27:5-7

4 ªLev. 25:10

6 ªNum. 27:7

7 ª1 Kin. 21:3

8 ª1 Chr. 23:22

36:1-9 An additional question arose concerning the right of daughters to inherit their fathers' land if they had no brothers (cf. 27:1-11). If such an heiress married someone from another tribe, her land would have become the property of that other tribe, and permanently so after the year of jubilee (cf. Lev. 25:10). To prevent this from happening, Moses commanded that an heiress should marry within her father's tribe (v. 8).

ther, so that the sons of Israel each may possess the inheritance of his fathers.

9 "Thus no inheritance shall be transferred from one tribe to another tribe, for the tribes of the sons of Israel shall each hold to his own inheritance."

10 Just as the LORD had commanded Moses, so the daughters of Zelophehad did:

11 ^aMahlah, Tirzah, Hoglah, Milcah and Noah, the daughters of Zelophehad married their uncles' sons.

12 They married *those* from the families of the sons of Manasseh the son of Joseph, and their inheritance remained with the tribe of the family of their father.

13 ^aThese are the commandments and the ordinances which the LORD commanded to the sons of Israel through Moses in the plains of Moab by the Jordan *opposite* Jericho.

11 ªNum. 26:33

13 ªLev. 26:46; 27:34; Num. 22:1

INTRODUCTION TO
THE BOOK OF DEUTERONOMY

AUTHOR: Moses   DATE: 1410 B.C.

Title   *The English title, Deuteronomy (from the Greek Septuagint) means "second law-giving" and comes from the mistranslation of 17:18, which actually says "a copy of this law." The Jewish title (which means "words") comes from the first verse and is typical of the beginning of ancient suzerainty treaties (see note on Exod. 19:3). Much of the material in the book follows the treaty pattern, elaborating the responsibilities of Israel as God's covenant people. Included are repetitions of many of the laws contained in Exodus, Leviticus, and Numbers.*

Historical Setting   *The book contains the addresses that Moses gave during the final months of his life, when the Israelites were encamped in the plains of Moab prior to their entrance into the promised land. The people were facing war, temptations, and a new, settled way of life—all under the unproved leadership of Joshua. Moses' congregation here had not personally experienced the deliverance at the Red Sea or the giving of the Law at Sinai; they needed to be reminded of God's power and God's laws.*

Authorship of Chapter 34   *The account of Moses' death in chapter 34 could not have been written by Moses, but this obvious truth in no way negates the Mosaic authorship of the rest of the book. It was quite customary to append an obituary to the final work of a great man, and it is unthinkable that someone (most likely Joshua) would not have made such an addition to the last writing of Moses.*

Contents   *The book may be viewed as a constitution for the theocracy of Israel once she was established in the land. Its structure parallels that of a typical suzerainty treaty of that period: (1) preamble, 1:1-5; (2) historical prologue, 1:6-4:49; (3) main provisions, 5:1-26:19; (4) curses and blessings, 27:1-30:20; and (5) arrangements for continuation of the covenant, 31:1-33:29.*

Jesus Christ quoted from this book to refute the devil (Matt. 4:1-11) and to summarize the Law (Matt. 22:37). Of the 27 books of the N.T., 17 quote from Deuteronomy.

Some especially important passages include: 5:6-21 (the Ten Commandments); 6:4-9 (the Shema, "Hear, O Israel"); 13:1-5 (on false prophets); 18:9-15 (on false diviners); 29:1-30:20 (the Palestinian covenant).

OUTLINE OF DEUTERONOMY

THE BOOK OF DEUTERONOMY

I INTRODUCTION, 1:1-5

★ 1 *a*Deut.
4:46 *b*Deut.
2:8

1 These are the words which Moses spoke to all Israel *a*across the Jordan in the wilderness, in the *b*Arabah opposite Suph, between Paran and Tophel and Laban and Hazeroth and Dizahab.

★ 2 *a*Ex.
3:1; 17:6
*b*Gen. 32:3
*c*Num.
13:26; 32:8;
Deut. 9:23

2 It is eleven days' *journey* from *a*Horeb by the way of Mount *b*Seir to *c*Kadesh-barnea.

3 *a*Num.
33:38 *b*Deut.
4:1, 2

3 And it came about in the *a*fortieth year, on the first day of the eleventh month, that Moses spoke to the children of Israel, *b*according to all that the LORD had commanded him *to give* to them,

4 *a*Num.
21:21-26;
Deut. 2:26-
35; Josh.
13:10; Neh.
9:22 *b*Num.
21:33-35;
Josh. 13:12
*c*Josh. 12:4

4 after he had *a*defeated Sihon the king of the Amorites, who lived in Heshbon, and *b*Og the king of Bashan, who lived in *c*Ashtaroth and Edrei.

5 Across the Jordan in the land of Moab, Moses undertook to expound this law, saying,

II RECAPITULATION OF ISRAEL'S WANDERINGS: HISTORICAL, 1:6-4:43

A Israel at Sinai, 1:6-18

6 *a*Num.
10:11-13

6 "The LORD our God *a*spoke to us at Horeb, saying, 'You have stayed long enough at this mountain.

7 'Turn and set your journey, and go to *a*the hill country of the Amorites, and to all their neighbors in the Arabah, in the hill country and in the lowland and in *b*the Negev and by the seacoast, the land of the Canaanites, and Lebanon, as far as the great river, the river Euphrates.

★ 7 *a*Gen.
15:18; Deut.
11:24; Josh.
10:40 *b*Gen.
12:9

8 'See, I have placed the land before you; go in and possess the land which the LORD *a*swore to give to your fathers, to Abraham, to Isaac, and to Jacob, to them and their descendants after them.'

★ 8 *a*Gen.
12:7; 26:3;
28:13; Ex.
33:1; Num.
14:23; 32:11;
Heb. 6:13,
14

9 "And I spoke to you at that time, saying, '*a*I am not able to bear *the burden* of you alone.

★ 9-18
9 *a*Ex.
12:7; 26:3;
Num. 11:14

10 'The LORD your God has *a*multiplied you, and behold, you are this day as the stars of heaven for multitude.

10 *a*Gen.
15:5; 22:17;
Ex. 32:13;
Deut. 7:7;
10:22; 26:5;
28:62

11 'May the LORD, the God of your fathers, increase you a thousand-fold more than you are, and bless you, *a*just as He has promised you!

11 *a*Deut.
1:8, 10

12 'How can I alone bear the load and burden of you and your strife?

13 '*a*Choose wise and discerning and experienced men from your tribes, and I will appoint them as your heads.'

13 *a*Ex.
18:21

1:1 *across the Jordan.* I.e., Transjordan. See note on Num. 34:15.

1:2 *Horeb* is another name for Mt. Sinai (Exod. 3:1, 12; cf. Exod. 19:1). *Kadesh-barnea,* the place where Israel refused to believe God and enter Canaan from the SW., was located about 50 miles SW. of Beersheba. Now, 38 years later, Israel was poised on the eastern frontier of

Canaan.

1:7 *the lowland.* Situated between the coastal plain and the central highlands. It is known as the Shephelah. *the Negev.* About 4,500 sq. mi. of desert in the southern part of Canaan.

1:8 See note on Gen. 15:18.

1:9-18 See note on Exod. 18:13-27.

14 "And you answered me and said, 'The thing which you have said to do is good.'

15 "So I took the heads of your tribes, wise and experienced men, and appointed them heads over you, leaders of thousands, and of hundreds, of fifties and of tens, and officers for your tribes.

16 "Then I charged your judges at that time, saying, 'Hear *the cases* between your fellow countrymen, and ᵃjudge righteously between a man and his fellow countryman, or the alien who is with him.

17 "ᵃYou shall not show partiality in judgment; you shall hear the small and the great alike. You shall ᵇnot fear man, for the judgment is God's. And ᶜthe case that is too hard for you, you shall bring to me, and I will hear it.'

18 "ᵃAnd I commanded you at that time all the things that you should do.

B Israel at Kadesh-barnea, 1:19–46

19 "Then we set out from ᵃHoreb, and went through all that ᵇgreat and terrible wilderness which you saw, on the way to the ᶜhill country of the Amorites, just as the LORD our God had commanded us; and we came to ᵈKadesh-barnea.

20 "And I said to you, 'You have come to the hill country of the Amorites which the LORD our God is about to give us.

21 'See, the LORD your God has placed the land before you; go up, take possession, as the LORD, the God of your fathers, has spoken to you. ᵃDo not fear or be dismayed.'

22 "ᵃThen all of you approached me and said, 'Let us send men before us, that they may search out the land for us, and bring back to us word of the way by which we should go up, and the cities which we shall enter.'

23 "And the thing pleased me and I took twelve of your men, one man for each tribe.

24 "And ᵃthey turned and went up into the hill country, and came to the valley of Eshcol, and spied it out.

25 "Then they took *some* of the fruit of the land in their hands and brought it down to us; and they brought us back a report and said, 'It is a good land which the LORD our God is about to give us.'

26 "ᵃYet you were not willing to go up, but ᵇrebelled against the command of the LORD your God;

27 and ᵃyou grumbled in your tents and said, 'Because the LORD hates us, He has brought us out of the land of Egypt to deliver us into the hand of the Amorites to destroy us.

28 'Where can we go up? Our brethren have made our hearts melt, saying, "The people are bigger and taller than we; the cities are large and fortified to heaven. And besides, we saw ᵃthe sons of the Anakim there." '

29 "Then I said to you, 'Do not be shocked, nor fear them.

30 'The LORD your God who goes before you will ᵃHimself fight on your behalf, just as He did for you in Egypt before your eyes,

31 and in the wilderness where you saw how ᵃthe LORD your God carried you, just as a man carries his son, in all the way which you have walked, until you came to this place.'

32 "But ᵃfor all this, you did not trust the LORD your God,

33 ᵃwho goes before you on *your* way, ᵇto seek out a place for you to encamp, in fire by night and cloud by day, to show you the way in which you should go.

Cross references (margin)

16 ᵃDeut. 16:18; John 7:24

17 ᵃDeut. 10:17; 16:19; 24:17; 2 Chr. 19:5, 6; Prov. 24:23-26; Acts 10:34; James 2:1, 9 ᵇProv. 29:25 ᶜEx. 18:22, 26

18 ᵃEx. 18:20

★19-46

19 ᵃDeut. 1:2 ᵇDeut. 2:7; 8:15; 32:10; Jer. 2:6 ᶜDeut. 1:7 ᵈDeut. 1:2

21 ᵃJosh. 1:6, 9

22 ᵃNum. 13:1-3

24 ᵃNum. 13:21-25

26 ᵃNum. 14:1-4 ᵇDeut. 9:23

27 ᵃDeut. 9:28; Ps. 106:25

28 ᵃNum. 13:28, 33; Deut. 9:2

30 ᵃEx. 14:14; Deut. 3:22; 20:4; Neh. 4:20

31 ᵃDeut. 32:10-12; Is. 46:3, 4; 63:9; Hos. 11:3; Acts 13:18

32 ᵃNum. 14:11; Ps. 106:24; Heb. 3:19; 4:2; Jude 5

33 ᵃEx. 13:21; Num. 9:15-23; Neh. 9:12; Ps. 78:14 ᵇNum. 10:33

1:19-46 See notes on Num. 13 and 14. Moses repeatedly emphasized that it was a *good land* that God was about to *give* them (v. 25; 3:25; 4:21, 22; 6:18; 8:7, 10; 9:6; 11:17). *sons of the Anakim* (1:28). See note on Num. 13:33.

34 aNum.
14:28-30;
Heb. 3:18
34 "Then the LORD heard the sound of your words, and He was angry and ^atook an oath, saying,

35 aPs.
95:11;
106:26;
Ezek. 20:15;
1 Cor. 10:5;
Heb. 3:14-19
35 '^aNot one of these men, this evil generation, shall see the good land which I swore to give your fathers,

36 aNum.
14:24; Josh.
14:9
36 except Caleb the son of Jephunneh; he shall see it, and ^ato him and to his sons I will give the land on which he has set foot, because he has followed the LORD fully.'

★37 aNum.
20:12; Deut.
3:26; 4:21
bNum.
27:13, 18
37 "^aThe LORD was angry with me also on your account, saying, '^bNot even you shall enter there.

38 aNum.
14:30 bNum.
34:17; Deut.
3:28; 31:7;
Josh. 11:23
38 'Joshua the son of Nun, who stands before you, ^ahe shall enter there; encourage him, for ^bhe shall cause Israel to inherit it.

39 aNum.
14:3, 31 bIs.
7:15, 16
39 'Moreover, ^ayour little ones who you said would become a prey, and your sons, who this day have ^bno knowledge of good or evil, shall enter there, and I will give it to them, and they shall possess it.

40 aNum.
14:25
40 'But as for you, ^aturn around and set out for the wilderness by the way to the Red Sea.'

41 aNum.
14:40
41 "^aThen you answered and said to me, 'We have sinned against the LORD; we will indeed go up and fight, just as the LORD our God commanded us.' And every man of you girded on his weapons of war, and regarded it as easy to go up into the hill country.

42 aNum.
14:41-43
42 "^aAnd the LORD said to me, 'Say to them, "Do not go up, nor fight, for I am not among you; lest you be defeated before your enemies." '

43 aNum.
14:40
43 "So I spoke to you, but you would not listen. Instead ^ayou rebelled against the command of the LORD, and acted presumptuously and went up into the hill country.

44 aNum.
14:45 bPs.
118:12
44 "^aAnd the Amorites who lived in that hill country came out against you, and chased you ^bas bees do, and crushed you from Seir to Hormah.

45 aJob
27:8, 9; Ps.
66:18; John
9:31
45 "Then you returned and wept before the LORD; but the ^aLORD did not listen to your voice, nor give ear to you.

46 aNum.
20:1, 22;
Deut. 2:7, 14;
Judg. 11:17
46 "So you remained in ^aKadesh many days, the days that you spent *there*.

C　Israel's Journey from Kadesh to Moab, 2:1–3:29

1　The journey to Transjordan, 2:1-23

1 aNum.
21:4 bDeut.
1:2
2 "^aThen we turned and set out for the wilderness by the way to the Red Sea, as the LORD spoke to me, and circled ^bMount Seir for many days.

2 "And the LORD spoke to me, saying,

3 'You have circled this mountain long enough. Now turn north,

4 aNum.
20:14-21
bGen. 36:8
cEx. 15:15,
16
4 ^aand command the people, saying, "You will pass through the ^bterritory of your brothers the sons of Esau who live in Seir; and ^cthey will be afraid of you. So be very careful;

★ 5 aGen.
36:8; Josh.
24:4
5 do not provoke them, for I will not give you any of their land, even *as little as* a footstep ^abecause I have given Mount Seir to Esau as a possession.

6 "You shall buy food from them with money so that you may eat, and you shall also purchase water from them with money so that you may drink.

7 aDeut.
1:19 bNum.
14:33, 34;
32:13; Deut.
2:14
7 "For the LORD your God has blessed you in all that you have done; He has known your wanderings through this ^agreat wilderness. These ^bforty years the LORD your God has been with you; you have not lacked a thing." '

1:37 Though the announcement of Moses' exclusion from the land occurred 38 years after that of the Israelites at Kadesh, the reasons for them were the same—unbelief (cf. v. 32 with Num. 20:12).

2:5 The descendants of *Esau* were given the land of *Seir* (the entire area of Edom, the mountainous region S. of the Dead Sea; see Gen. 36:6-8).

★ 8 aDeut.
1:1 bNum.
33:35; 1 Kin.
9:26

8 "So we passed beyond our brothers the sons of Esau, who live in Seir, away from the aArabah road, away from Elath and bfrom Ezion-geber. And we turned and passed through by the way of the wilderness of Moab.

★ 9 aNum.
21:15, 28;
Deut. 2:18,
29 bGen.
19:36, 37

9 "Then the LORD said to me, 'Do not harass Moab, nor provoke them to war, for I will not give you any of their land as a possession, because I have given aAr to bthe sons of Lot as a possession.

10 aGen.
14:5

10 (The aEmim lived there formerly, a people as great, numerous, and tall as the Anakim.

11 aGen.
14:5; Deut.
2:20

11 Like the Anakim, they are also regarded as aRephaim, but the Moabites call them Emim.

12 aGen.
36:20; Deut.
2:22 bNum.
21:25, 35

12 aThe Horites formerly lived in Seir, but the sons of Esau dispossessed them and destroyed them from before them, and settled in their place, bjust as Israel did to the land of their possession which the LORD gave to them.)

13 'Now arise and cross over the brook Zered yourselves.' So we crossed over the brook Zered.

14 aDeut.
2:7 bNum.
14:29-35;
26:64, 65;
Ps. 106:26;
1 Cor. 10:5
cDeut. 1:34,
35

14 "Now the time that it took for us to come from Kadeshbarnea, until we crossed over the brook Zered, was athirty-eight years; until ball the generation of the men of war perished from within the camp, as cthe LORD had sworn to them.

15 aJude 5

15 "aMoreover the hand of the LORD was against them, to destroy them from within the camp, until they all perished.

16 aDeut.
2:14

16 "So it came about when aall the men of war had finally perished from among the people,

17 that the LORD spoke to me, saying,

18 aDeut.
2:9

18 'You shall cross over aAr, the border of Moab, today.

19 'And when you come opposite the asons of Ammon, do not harass them nor provoke them, for I will not give you any of the land of the sons of Ammon as a possession, because I have given it to bthe sons of Lot as a possession.'

★19 aGen.
19:38 bDeut.
2:9

20 (It is also regarded as the land of the aRephaim, for Rephaim formerly lived in it, but the Ammonites call them Zamzummin,

★20 aDeut.
2:11

21 a people as great, numerous, and tall as the Anakim, but the LORD destroyed them before them. And they dispossessed them and settled in their place,

22 just as He did for the sons of Esau, who alive in Seir, when He destroyed bthe Horites from before them; and they dispossessed them, and settled in their place even to this day.

22 aGen.
36:8; Deut.
2:5 bDeut.
2:12

23 And the aAvvim, who lived in villages as far as Gaza, the bCaphtorim who came from cCaphtor, destroyed them and lived in their place.)

23 aJosh.
13:3 bGen.
10:14; 1 Chr.
1:12 cJer.
47:4; Amos
9:7

2 The conquest of Transjordan, 2:24–3:11

24 'Arise, set out, and pass through the avalley of Arnon. Look! I have given Sihon the Amorite, king of Heshbon, and his land into your hand; begin to take possession and contend with him in battle.

★24-37

24 aNum.
21:13, 14;
Judg. 11:18

25 'This day I will begin to put athe dread and fear of you upon the peoples everywhere under the heavens, who, when they hear the report of you, bshall tremble and be in anguish because of you.'

25 aEx.
23:27; Deut.
11:25; Josh.
2:9 bEx.
15:14-16

26 "aSo I sent messengers from the wilderness of Kedemoth

26 aNum.
21:21-32;
Deut. 1:4;
Judg. 11:19-
21

2:8 The Edomites refused Israel passage across their territory (see note on Num. 20:14).

2:9 Concerning the Moabites, see notes on Gen. 19:31-38 and Amos 2:1.

2:19 Concerning the Ammonites, see notes on Gen. 19:31-38 and Amos 1:13.

2:20 the land of the Rephaim. Refers to a race of people who inhabited Palestine on both sides of the Jordan (see note on Gen. 14:5).

2:24-37 Compare Num. 21:21-32. The Amorites were an alien race (not related to the Israelites) who had spread across the E. side of the Jordan. As a result of sinking into idolatry, they had to be destroyed (see note on Gen. 15:13-16).

to Sihon king of Heshbon with words of peace, saying,

27 'Let me pass through your land, I will travel only on the highway; I will not turn aside to the right or to the left.

28 'You will sell me food for money so that I may eat, and give me water for money so that I may drink, ^aonly let me pass through on foot,

29 just as the sons of Esau who live in Seir and the Moabites who live in ^aAr did for me, until I cross over the Jordan into the land which the Lord our God is giving to us.'

30 "But ^aSihon king of Heshbon was not willing for us to pass through his land; for the ^bLord your God hardened his spirit and made his heart obstinate, in order to deliver him into your hand, as *he is* today.

31 "And the Lord said to me, 'See, I have begun to deliver Sihon and his land over to you. Begin to occupy, that you may possess his land.'

32 "Then Sihon with all his people came out to meet us in battle at Jahaz.

33 "And ^athe Lord our God delivered him over to us; and we ^bdefeated him with his sons and all his people.

34 "So we captured all his cities at that time, and ^autterly destroyed the men, women and children of every city. We left no survivor.

35 "We took ^aonly the animals as our booty and the spoil of the cities which we had captured.

36 "From ^aAroer which is on the edge of the valley of Arnon and *from* the city which is in the valley, even to Gilead, there was no city that was too high for us; the Lord our God delivered all over to us.

37 "^aOnly you did not go near to the land of the sons of Ammon, all along the river ^bJabbok and the cities of the hill country, and wherever the Lord our God had commanded us.

3 "^aThen we turned and went up the road to Bashan, and Og, king of Bashan, with all his people came out to meet us in battle at Edrei.

2 "But the Lord said to me, 'Do not fear him, for I have delivered him and all his people and his land into your hand; and you shall do to him just as you did to Sihon king of the Amorites, who lived at Heshbon.'

3 "So the Lord our God delivered Og also, king of Bashan, with all his people into our hand, and we smote them until no survivor was left.

4 "And we captured all his cities at that time; there was not a city which we did not take from them: sixty cities, all the region of ^aArgob, the kingdom of Og in Bashan.

5 "All these were cities fortified with high walls, gates and bars, besides a great many unwalled towns.

6 "And we utterly destroyed them, as we did to ^aSihon king of Heshbon, ^butterly destroying the men, women and children of every city.

7 "^aBut all the animals and the spoil of the cities we took as our booty.

8 "^aThus we took the land at that time from the hand of the two kings of the Amorites who were beyond the Jordan, from the valley of Arnon to Mount Hermon

9 (Sidonians ^acall Hermon ^bSirion, and the Amorites call it ^cSenir):

10 all the cities of the tableland and all Gilead and ^aall Bashan, as far as Salecah and Edrei, cities of the kingdom of Og in Bashan.

Cross references (margin):

28 ^aNum. 20:19

29 ^aDeut. 2:9

30 ^aNum. 21:23 ^bEx. 4:21; Josh. 11:20

33 ^aEx. 23:31; Deut. 7:2 ^bDeut. 29:7

34 ^aDeut. 3:6; 7:2

35 ^aDeut. 3:7

36 ^aDeut. 3:12; 4:48; Josh. 12:2; 13:9

37 ^aDeut. 2:19 ^bGen. 32:22; Num. 21:24; Deut. 3:16

★ 1 ^aNum. 21:33-35

★ 3

4 ^aDeut. 3:13, 14; 1 Kin. 4:13

6 ^aDeut. 1:4 ^bDeut. 2:34

7 ^aDeut. 2:35

8 ^aNum. 32:33; Josh. 12:1-7; 13:8-12

9 ^aDeut. 4:48; Josh. 11:17; Ps. 42:6; 133:3 ^bPs. 29:6 ^c1 Chr. 5:23

10 ^aJosh. 13:11

3:1 *Bashan.* See note on Num. 21:33.
3:3 The people rightly attributed this victory to the Lord, as they also did the one over Sihon (2:33).

★11 aGen.
14:5; Deut.
2:11, 20
b2 Sam.
11:1; 12:26;
Jer. 49:2

11 (For only Og king of Bashan was left of the remnant of the aRephaim. Behold, his bedstead was an iron bedstead; it is in bRabbah of the sons of Ammon. Its length was nine cubits and its width four cubits by ordinary cubit.)

3 The allotment of Transjordan, 3:12-29

★12-17
12 aDeut.
2:36 bNum.
32:32-38;
Josh. 13:8-
13

12 "So we took possession of this land at that time. From aAroer, which is by the valley of Arnon, and half the hill country of bGilead and its cities, I gave to the Reubenites and to the Gadites.

13 "And the rest of Gilead, and all Bashan, the kingdom of Og, I gave to the half-tribe of Manasseh, all the region of Argob (concerning all Bashan, it is called the land of Rephaim.

14 aNum.
32:41; 1 Chr.
2:22

14 aJair the son of Manasseh took all the region of Argob as far as the border of the Geshurites and the Maacathites, and called it, that is, Bashan, after his own name, Havvoth-jair, as it is to this day.)

15 aNum.
32:39, 40

15 "aAnd to Machir I gave Gilead.

16 aNum.
21:24; Deut.
2:37

16 "And to the Reubenites and to the Gadites, I gave from Gilead even as far as the valley of Arnon, the middle of the valley as a border and as far as the river aJabbok, the border of the sons of Ammon;

17 aNum.
34:11; Josh.
13:27 bJosh.
12:3 cGen.
14:3; Josh.
3:16

17 the Arabah also, with the Jordan as a border, from aChinnereth beven as far as the sea of the Arabah, cthe Salt Sea, at the foot of the slopes of Pisgah on the east.

★18-20
18 aJosh.
1:13 bNum.
32:20; Josh.
4:12, 13

18 "Then I commanded you at that time, saying, 'aThe LORD your God has given you this land to possess it; ball you valiant men shall cross over armed before your brothers, the sons of Israel.

19 aJosh.
1:14 bEx.
12:38

19 'aBut your wives and your little ones and your livestock (I know that you have bmuch livestock), shall remain in your cities which I have given you,

20 aJosh.
1:15 bJosh.
22:4

20 auntil the LORD gives rest to your fellow countrymen as to you, and they also possess the land which the LORD your God will give them beyond the Jordan. bThen you may return every man to his possession, which I have given you.'

21 "And I commanded Joshua at that time, saying, 'Your eyes have seen all that the LORD your God has done to these two kings; so the LORD shall do to all the kingdoms into which you are about to cross.

22 aEx.
14:14; Deut.
1:30; 20:4;
Neh. 4:20

22 'Do not fear them, for the LORD your God ais the one fighting for you.'

23 "I also pleaded with the LORD at that time, saying,

24 aDeut.
11:2 bEx.
8:10; 15:11;
2 Sam. 7:22;
Ps. 71:19;
86:8

24 'O Lord GOD, Thou hast begun to show Thy servant aThy greatness and Thy strong hand; for what bgod is there in heaven or on earth who can do such works and mighty acts as Thine?

25 aDeut.
4:22

25 'Let me, I pray, cross over and see the afair land that is beyond the Jordan, that good hill country and Lebanon.'

★26 aDeut.
1:37

26 "But athe LORD was angry with me on your account, and would not listen to me; and the LORD said to me, 'Enough! Speak to Me no more of this matter.

27 aNum.
23:14; 27:12
bDeut. 1:37

27 'Go up to the top of aPisgah and lift up your eyes to the west and north and south and east, and see it with your eyes, bfor you shall not cross over this Jordan.

3:11 Og. The last of the Rephaim or giant race that inhabited Palestine (see note on 2:20). His iron bedstead has been understood as an iron-trimmed stone coffin or an iron-decorated couch to be placed in his tomb or as a monument made of basalt (an iron-bearing rock). In any case, it was 13½ feet × 6 feet, indicating how huge Og was.
3:12-17 See notes on Num. 32. Chinnereth. The

Sea of Galilee. the Salt Sea. The Dead Sea.
3:18-20 The condition placed on Reuben, Gad, and Manasseh was that the men must join those of the other tribes in conquering the land W. of the Jordan before they could settle in the land Moses gave them E. of the Jordan.
3:26 the LORD was angry with me. For Moses' disobedience and disbelief at Meribah (see note on Num. 20:13).

28 aNum.
27:18; Deut.
31:3, 7, 8, 23
bDeut. 1:38

29 aNum.
25:1-3; Deut.
4:46; 34:6

1 aDeut.
1:3 bLev.
18:5; Deut.
5:33; 8:1;
16:20; 30:16,
19; Ezek.
20:11; Rom.
10:5

★ 2 aDeut.
12:32; Prov.
30:6; Rev.
22:18 bDeut.
4:5, 14, 40

★ 3-4

3 aNum.
25:1-9

5 aLev.
26:46; 27:34

6 aDeut.
30:19, 20;
32:46, 47;
Job 28:28;
Ps. 19:7;
111:10; Prov.
1:7; 2 Tim.
3:15

28 'aBut charge Joshua and encourage him and strengthen him; bfor he shall go across at the head of this people, and he shall give them as an inheritance the land which you will see.'

29 "So we remained in the valley opposite aBeth-peor.

D Israel on the Plains of Moab, 4:1-43

1 A call to obedience, 4:1-40

4 "And now, O Israel, listen to the statutes and the judgments which aI am teaching you to perform, in order that byou may live and go in and take possession of the land which the LORD, the God of your fathers, is giving you.

2 "aYou shall not add to the word which bI am commanding you, nor take away from it, that you may keep the commandments of the LORD your God which I command you.

3 "aYour eyes have seen what the LORD has done in the case of Baal-peor, for all the men who followed Baal-peor, the LORD your God has destroyed them from among you.

4 "But you who held fast to the LORD your God are alive today, every one of you.

5 "See, I have taught you statutes and judgments ajust as the LORD my God commanded me, that you should do thus in the land where you are entering to possess it.

6 "So keep and do them, afor that is your wisdom and your understanding in the sight of the peoples who will hear all these statutes and say, 'Surely this great

nation is a wise and understanding people.'

7 "For awhat great nation is there that has a god bso near to it as is the LORD our God cwhenever we call on Him?

8 "Or what great nation is there that has astatutes and judgments as righteous as this whole law which I am setting before you today?

9 "Only agive heed to yourself and keep your soul diligently, lest you forget the things which your eyes have seen, and lest they depart from your heart ball the days of your life; but cmake them known to your sons and your grandsons.

10 "Remember the day you stood before the LORD your God at Horeb, when the LORD said to me, 'Assemble the people to Me, that I may let them hear My words aso they may learn to fear Me all the days they live on the earth, and that they may bteach their children.'

11 "And you came near and stood at the foot of the mountain, aand the mountain burned with fire to the very heart of the heavens: darkness, cloud and thick gloom.

12 "Then the LORD spoke to you from the midst of the fire; you heard the sound of words, but you saw no form—only a voice.

13 "So He declared to you His covenant which He commanded you to perform, that is, athe ten commandments; and bHe wrote them on two tablets of stone.

14 "And the LORD commanded me at that time to teach you statutes and judgments, that you might perform them in the land

7 aDeut.
4:32-34;
2 Sam. 7:23
bPs. 34:17,
18; 145:18;
148:14; Is.
55:6 cPs.
34:18; 85:9

★ 8 aPs.
89:14; 97:2;
119:144,
160, 172

9 aDeut.
4:23; 6:12;
8:11, 14, 19;
Prov. 4:23;
23:19 bDeut.
6:2; 12:1;
16:3 cGen.
18:19; Deut.
4:10; 6:7, 20-
25; 11:19;
32:46; Ps.
78:5, 6; Prov.
22:6; Eph.
6:4

★10 aDeut.
14:23; 17:19;
31:12, 13
bDeut. 4:9

11 aEx.
19:18; Heb.
12:18, 19

13 aEx.
34:28; Deut.
10:4 bEx.
31:18; 34:1,
28

4:2 This same warning against adding to or abridging God's Law is repeated in 12:32 and Rev. 22:18-19.

4:3-4 The story is in Num. 25:1-9 (see note there). A total of 24,000 died in the plague.

4:8 The Mosaic Law was given to the nation Israel not to be a burden but to distinguish her people from all others by making her wise, great, and pleasing to a holy God. As a rule of life for God's people, the Mosaic code has

been replaced for the Christian by the law of Christ (see note on 2 Cor. 3:11), though some of the specific commands of the old code are reincorporated as requirements of the new code (cf. Rom. 13:9). As part of the inspired Scripture, the old as well as the new code is profitable to people of all times (cf. 1 Tim. 1:8-10; 2 Tim. 3:16).

4:10 Horeb. Mt. Sinai; the story is found in Exod. 19.

where you are going over to possess it.

15 "So [a]watch yourselves carefully, since you did not see any [b]form on the day the LORD spoke to you at Horeb from the midst of the fire,

16 lest you [a]act corruptly and [b]make a graven image for yourselves in the form of any figure, the likeness of male or female,

17 the likeness of any animal that is on the earth, the likeness of [a]any winged bird that flies in the sky,

18 the likeness of anything that creeps on the ground, the likeness of any fish that is in the water below the earth.

19 "And *beware*, lest you lift up your eyes to heaven and see the sun and the moon and the stars, [a]all the host of heaven, [b]and be drawn away and worship them and serve them, those which the LORD your God has allotted to all the peoples under the whole heaven.

20 "But the LORD has taken you and brought you out of [a]the iron furnace, from Egypt, to [b]be a people for His own possession, as today.

21 "[a]Now the LORD was angry with me on your account, and swore that I should not cross the Jordan, and that I should not enter the good land which the LORD your God is giving you as an inheritance.

22 "For [a]I shall die in this land, I shall not cross the Jordan, but you shall cross and take possession of this [b]good land.

23 "So watch yourselves, [a]lest you forget the covenant of the LORD your God, which He made with you, and [b]make for yourselves a graven image in the form of anything *against* which the LORD your God has commanded you.

24 "For the LORD your God is a [a]consuming fire, a [b]jealous God.

25 "When you become the father of children and children's children and have remained long in the land, and [a]act corruptly, and [b]make an idol in the form of anything, and [c]do that which is evil in the sight of the LORD your God *so as* to provoke Him to anger,

26 I [a]call heaven and earth to witness against you today, that you shall [b]surely perish quickly from the land where you are going over the Jordan to possess it. You shall not live long on it, but shall be utterly destroyed.

27 "And the LORD will [a]scatter you among the peoples, and you shall be left few in number among the nations, where the LORD shall drive you.

28 "And [a]there you will serve gods, the work of man's hands, [b]wood and stone, [c]which neither see nor hear nor eat nor smell.

29 "[a]But from there you will seek the LORD your God, and you will find *Him* if you search for Him [b]with all your heart and all your soul.

30 "When you [a]are in distress and all these things have come upon you, [b]in the latter days, [c]you will return to the LORD your God and listen to His voice.

31 "For the LORD your God is a [a]compassionate God; [b]He will not fail you nor [c]destroy you nor [d]forget the covenant with your fathers which He swore to them.

32 "Indeed, [a]ask now concerning the former days which were

15 [a]Josh. 23:11 [b]Is. 40:18

[*]16 [a]Deut. 4:25; 9:12; 31:29 [b]Ex. 20:4; Lev. 26:1; Deut. 5:8, 9; 27:15; Rom. 1:23

17 [a]Rom. 1:23

[*]19 [a]Gen. 2:1; Deut. 17:3; 2 Kin. 17:16; 21:3 [b]Deut. 13:5, 10; Job 31:26-28

20 [a]1 Kin. 8:51; Jer. 11:4 [b]Ex. 19:5; Deut. 7:6; 14:2; 26:18; Titus 2:14; 1 Pet. 2:9

21 [a]Num. 20:12; Deut. 1:37

22 [a]Num. 27:13, 14 [b]Deut. 3:25

23 [a]Deut. 4:9 [b]Deut. 4:16

[*]24 [a]Ex. 24:17; Deut. 9:3; Is. 30:27; 33:14; Heb. 12:29 [b]Deut. 5:9; 6:15

25 [a]Deut. 4:16 [b]Deut. 4:23 [c]2 Kin. 17:17

26 [a]Deut. 30:19; 31:28; 32:1; Is. 1:2; Mic. 6:2 [b]Deut. 7:4; 8:19, 20
[*]27-31
27 [a]Lev. 26:33; Deut. 28:64; 29:28; Neh. 1:8
28 [a]Deut. 28:36, 64; Jer. 16:13 [b]Deut. 29:17 [c]Ps. 115:4-8; 135:15-18; Is. 44:12-20
29 [a]Deut. 30:1-3, 10; 2 Chr. 15:4; Is. 55:6; Jer. 29:13 [b]Deut. 6:5; 10:12
30 [a]Ps. 18:6; 59:16; 107:6, 13 [b]Deut. 31:29; Jer. 23:20; Hos. 3:5; Heb. 1:2 [c]Jer. 4:1, 2
31 [a]Ex. 34:6; 2 Chr. 30:9; Neh. 9:31; Ps. 103:8; 111:4; 116:5; Jon. 4:2 [b]Deut. 31:6, 8; Josh. 1:5; 1 Chr. 28:20; Heb. 13:5 [c]Jer. 30:11 [d]Lev. 26:45
32 [a]Deut. 32:7; Job 8:8 [b]Gen. 1:27; Is. 45:12 [c]Deut. 28:64; Matt. 24:31 [d]Deut. 4:7; 2 Sam. 7:23

4:16 *a graven image.* See note on Exod. 20:4-6.
4:19 Astral worship was common in the Near East at that time. The last part of this verse means that the stars were created for the benefit of all, not as powers controlling men's destinies.
4:24 *fire.* A symbol of God's holiness. *a jealous God.* Here the term has the connotation of a God who maintains His rights.
4:27-31 Here is Moses' first prophecy of Israel's removal from the land if she proved disobedient. Yet, if she would turn to God, He would be merciful and restore her. Israel experienced such removals in the Assyrian and Babylonian captivities as well as in her dispersion after her rejection of Christ. *latter days.* Times subsequent to the prophet's message and culminating in the final restoration of Israel at the second coming of Jesus Christ.

before you, since the [b]day that God created man on the earth, and *inquire* [c]from one end of the heavens to the other. [d]Has *anything* been done like this great thing, or has *anything* been heard like it?

33 aEx. 20:22; Deut. 5:24, 26

33 "[a]Has *any* people heard the voice of God speaking from the midst of the fire, as you have heard *it*, and survived?

34 aEx. 14:30; Deut. 33:29 bDeut. 7:19 cDeut. 5:15; 6:21; Ps. 136:12

34 "[a]Or has a god tried to go to take for himself a nation from within *another* nation [b]by trials, by signs and wonders and by war and [c]by a mighty hand and by an outstretched arm and by great terrors, as the Lord your God did for you in Egypt before your eyes?

★35 aEx. 8:10; 9:14; Deut. 4:39; 32:12, 39; 1 Sam. 2:2; Is. 43:10-12; 44:6-8; 45:5-7; Mark 12:32

35 "To you it was shown that you might know that the Lord, He is God; [a]there is no other besides Him.

36 aEx. 19:9, 19; 20:18, 22; Deut. 4:33; Neh. 9:13; Heb. 12:25 bDeut. 8:5

36 "[a]Out of the heavens He let you hear His voice [b]to discipline you; and on earth He let you see His great fire, and you heard His words from the midst of the fire.

37 aDeut. 7:7, 8; 10:15; 33:3 bEx. 33:14; Is. 63:9

37 "[a]Because He loved your fathers, therefore He chose their descendants after them. And He [b]personally brought you from Egypt by His great power,

38 aNum. 32:4; 34:14, 15

38 driving out from before you nations greater and mightier than you, to bring you in *and* [a]to give you their land for an inheritance, as it is today.

39 aDeut. 4:35; Josh. 2:11

39 "Know therefore today, and take it to your heart, that [a]the Lord, He is God in heaven above and on the earth below; there is no other.

40 aLev. 22:31; Deut. 4:2; Ps. 105:45 bDeut. 4:1; 5:16, 29, 33; 6:3, 18; 12:25, 28; 22:7 cEx. 23:26; Deut. 32:47

40 "[a]So you shall keep His statutes and His commandments which I am giving you today, that [b]it may go well with you and with your children after you, and [c]that you may live long on the land which the Lord your God is giving you for all time."

2 The cities of refuge, 4:41-43

★41-43
41 aNum. 35:6; Deut. 19:2-13; Josh. 20:7-9

41 [a]Then Moses set apart three cities across the Jordan to the east,

42 that a manslayer might flee there, who unintentionally slew his neighbor without having enmity toward him in time past; and by fleeing to one of these cities he might live:

43 aJosh. 20:8

43 [a]Bezer in the wilderness on the plateau for the Reubenites, and Ramoth in Gilead for the Gadites, and Golan in Bashan for the Manassites.

III REHEARSAL OF ISRAEL'S LAW: LEGAL, 4:44-26:19

A Commands Concerning God, 4:44-12:32

1 The Ten Commandments, 4:44-5:33

44 Now this is the law which Moses set before the sons of Israel;

45 these are the testimonies and the statutes and the ordinances which Moses spoke to the sons of Israel, when they came out from Egypt,

46 aDeut. 3:29 bNum. 21:21-25

46 across the Jordan, in the valley [a]opposite Beth-peor, in the land of [b]Sihon king of the Amorites who lived at Heshbon, whom Moses and the sons of Israel defeated when they came out from Egypt.

47 aDeut. 1:4; 3:3, 4

47 And they took possession of his land and the land of [a]Og king of Bashan, the two kings of the Amorites, *who were* across the Jordan to the east,

★48 aDeut. 2:36; 3:12 bDeut. 3:9; Ps. 133:3

48 from [a]Aroer, which is on the edge of the valley of Arnon, even as far as [b]Mount Sion (that is, Hermon),

49 with all the Arabah across the Jordan to the east, even as far as the sea of the Arabah, at the foot of the slopes of Pisgah.

4:35 A clear declaration of absolute monotheism (as also v. 39).

4:41-43 Moses *set apart* three cities of refuge in Transjordan (see note on Num. 35:11). Three

cities on the W. side of the Jordan were also designated as cities of refuge (cf. 19:1-13).

4:48 *Sion.* Better, Sirion, a Canaanite name for Mt. Hermon, in the N. (cf. 3:9).

5 Then Moses summoned all Israel, and said to them, "Hear, O Israel, the statutes and the ordinances which I am speaking today in your hearing, that you may learn them and observe them carefully.

2 aEx. 19:5; Mal. 4:4

2 "The LORD our God made aa covenant with us at Horeb.

★ 3 aJer. 31:32; Heb. 8:9

3 "aThe LORD did not make this covenant with our fathers, but with us, *with* all those of us alive here today.

4 aNum. 14:14; Deut. 34:10 bDeut. 4:33

4 "The LORD spoke to you aface to face at the mountain bfrom the midst of the fire,

5 aGal. 3:19 bEx. 19:16, 21-24; 20:18; Heb. 12:18-21

5 *while* aI was standing between the LORD and you at that time, to declare to you the word of the LORD; bfor you were afraid because of the fire and did not go up the mountain. He said,

★ 6-21

6 aEx. 20:2-17; Lev. 26:1; Deut. 6:4; Ps. 81:10

6 'aI am the LORD your God, who brought you out of the land of Egypt, out of the house of slavery.

7 aEx. 20:3

7 'aYou shall have no other gods before Me.

8 aEx. 20:4-6; Lev. 26:1; Deut. 4:15-18; 27:15; Ps. 97:7

8 'aYou shall not make for yourself an idol, *or* any likeness *of* what is in heaven above or on the earth beneath or in the water under the earth.

9 aEx. 34:7; Num. 14:18; Deut. 7:10

9 'You shall not worship them or serve them; for I, the LORD your God, am a jealous God, avisiting the iniquity of the fathers on the children, and on the third and the fourth *generations* of those who hate Me,

10 aNum. 14:18; Deut. 7:9; Jer. 32:18

10 but ashowing lovingkindness to thousands, to those who love Me and keep My commandments.

11 aEx. 20:7; Lev. 19:12; Deut. 6:13; 10:20; Matt. 5:33

11 'aYou shall not take the name of the LORD your God in vain, for the LORD will not leave him unpunished who takes His name in vain.

12 'aObserve the sabbath day to keep it holy, as the LORD your God commanded you.

13 'Six days you shall labor and do all your work,

14 but athe seventh day is a sabbath of the LORD your God; *in it* you shall not do any work, you or your son or your daughter or your male servant or your female servant or your ox or your donkey or any of your cattle or your sojourner who stays with you, so that your male servant and your female servant may rest as well as you.

15 'aAnd you shall remember that you were a slave in the land of Egypt, and the LORD your God brought you out of there by a mighty hand and by an outstretched arm; therefore the LORD your God commanded you to observe the sabbath day.

16 'aHonor your father and your mother, as the LORD your God has commanded you, bthat your days may be prolonged, and that it may go well with you on the land which the LORD your God gives you.

17 'aYou shall not murder.

18 'aYou shall not commit adultery.

19 'aYou shall not steal.

20 'aYou shall not bear false witness against your neighbor.

21 'aYou shall not covet your neighbor's wife, and you shall not desire your neighbor's house, his field or his male servant or his female servant, his ox or his donkey or anything that belongs to your neighbor.'

22 "These words the LORD spoke to all your assembly at the mountain from the midst of the fire, *of* the cloud and *of* the thick gloom, with a great voice, and He added no more. And aHe wrote

12 aEx. 16:23-30; 20:8-11; 31:13f.; Mark 2:27f.

14 aGen. 2:2; Heb. 4:4

15 aEx. 20:11

16 aEx. 20:12; Lev. 19:3; Deut. 27:16; Matt. 15:4; 19:19; Mark 7:10; 10:19; Luke 18:20; Eph. 6:2, 3; Col. 3:20 bDeut. 4:40

17 aGen. 9:6; Ex. 20:13; Lev. 24:17; Matt. 5:21f., 19:18; Mark 10:19; Rom. 13:9; James 2:11

18 aEx. 20:14; Lev. 20:10; Matt. 5:27f.; 19:18; Mark 10:19; Luke 18:20; Rom. 13:9; James 2:11

19 aEx. 20:15; Lev. 19:11

20 aEx. 20:16, 23:1; Matt. 19:18

21 aEx. 20:17; Rom. 7:7; 13:9

★22-31

22 aEx. 24:12; 31:18; Deut. 4:13

5:3 The verse may mean (1) the covenant was not given only to those who were at Sinai but also to the generation Moses was now addressing, or (2) the Sinaitic covenant was not given to the patriarchs (they had the Abrahamic covenant, cf. 4:31), but to those who came out of Egypt (5:6).

5:6-21 The Ten Commandments are reiterated.

For an exposition of them, see the notes on Exod. 20. To the tenth commandment Moses added a prohibition against coveting another's *field* (v. 21), since the people were about to become landowners.

5:22-31 The scene at Sinai that Moses recalled was of the overpowering awesomeness of the holiness of God.

them on two tablets of stone and gave them to me.

23 "And it came about, when you heard the voice from the midst of the darkness, while the mountain was burning with fire, that you came near to me, all the heads of your tribes and your elders.

24 "And you said, 'Behold, the LORD our God has shown us His glory and His greatness, and we have heard His voice from the midst of the fire; we have seen today that God speaks with man, yet he lives.

25 aEx. 20:18, 19; Deut. 18:16

25 'aNow then why should we die? For this great fire will consume us; if we hear the voice of the LORD our God any longer, then we shall die.

26 aDeut. 4:33

26 'For awho is there of all flesh, who has heard the voice of the living God speaking from the midst of the fire, as we *have*, and lived?

27 'Go near and hear all that the LORD our God says; then speak to us all that the LORD our God will speak to you, and we will hear and do *it*.'

28 aDeut. 18:17

28 "And the LORD heard the voice of your words when you spoke to me, aand the LORD said to me, 'I have heard the voice of the words of this people which they have spoken to you. They have done well in all that they have spoken.

29 aPs. 81:13; Is. 48:18 bDeut. 11:1 cDeut. 5:16, 33

29 'aOh that they had such a heart in them, that they would fear Me, and bkeep all My commandments always, that cit may be well with them and with their sons forever!

30 'Go, say to them, "Return to your tents."

31 'aBut as for you, stand here by Me, that I may speak to you all the commandments and the statutes and the judgments which you shall teach them, that they may observe *them* in the land which I give them to possess.'

31 aEx. 24:12

32 "So you shall observe to do just as the LORD your God has commanded you; ayou shall not turn aside to the right or to the left.

32 aDeut. 17:20; 28:14; Josh. 1:7; 23:6; Prov. 4:27

33 "aYou shall walk in all the way which the LORD your God has commanded you, bthat you may live, and that it may be well with you, and that you may prolong *your* days in the land which you shall possess.

33 aDeut. 10:12; Jer. 7:23; Luke 1:6 bDeut. 4:1, 40; 12:25, 28; 22:7; Eph. 6:3

2   The command to love the LORD, 6:1-25

6 "Now this is the commandment, the statutes and the judgments which the LORD your God has commanded me to teach you, that you might do *them* in the land where you are going over to possess it,

2 so that you and your son and your grandson might afear the LORD your God, to keep all His statutes and His commandments, which I command you, ball the days of your life, and that your days may be prolonged.

2 aEx. 20:20; Deut. 10:12; Ps. 111:10; 128:1; Eccl. 12:13 bDeut. 4:9

3 "O Israel, you should listen and be careful to do *it*, that ait may be well with you and that you may multiply greatly, just as the LORD, the God of your fathers, has promised you, *in* ba land flowing with milk and honey.

★ **3** aDeut. 5:33 bEx. 3:8, 17
★ **4** aMatt. 22:37; Mark 12:29, 30; Luke 10:27 bDeut. 4:35, 39; John 10:30; 1 Cor. 8:4; Eph. 4:6
★ **5** aMatt. 22:37; Mark 12:30; Luke 10:27 bDeut. 4:29; 10:12

4 "aHear, O Israel! The LORD is our God, the bLORD is one!

5 "And ayou shall love the LORD your God bwith all your

6:3 A *land flowing with milk and honey* was a desert-dweller's dream, for it implied a land well watered (this phrase is repeated in 11:9; 26:9, 15; 27:3; 31:20). See note on Exod. 3:8.

6:4 Here begins the celebrated *Shema* (from the first word, *"Hear"*), which became Judaism's basic confession of faith. According to rabbinic tradition, the Shema originally consisted only of verse 4, but was later expanded to include verses 5-9, 11:13-21, and Num. 15:37-41. According to rabbinic law, it was to be recited morning and night (cf. v. 7). Verse 4

is subject to various translations, though the statement is likely stressing the uniqueness of Yahweh and should be translated, "The LORD is our God, the LORD alone." A secondary emphasis, His indivisibility, is apparent in most English translations. The Lord's uniqueness precludes the worship of any other, and demands a total love commitment (v. 5).

6:5 Jesus Christ called this the first and great commandment and added to it the phrase "with all your mind" (Mark 12:30).

heart and with all your soul and with all your might.

6 "And ªthese words, which I am commanding you today, shall be on your heart;

7 and ªyou shall teach them diligently to your sons and shall talk of them when you sit in your house and when you walk by the way and when you lie down and when you rise up.

8 "ªAnd you shall bind them as a sign on your hand and they shall be as frontals on your forehead.

9 "ªAnd you shall write them on the doorposts of your house and on your gates.

10 "Then it shall come about when the LORD your God brings you into the land which He swore to your fathers, Abraham, Isaac and Jacob, to give you, ªgreat and splendid cities which you did not build,

11 and houses full of all good things which you did not fill, and hewn cisterns which you did not dig, vineyards and olive trees which you did not plant, and ªyou shall eat and be satisfied,

12 then watch yourself, lest ªyou forget the LORD who brought you from the land of Egypt, out of the house of slavery.

13 "ªYou shall fear *only* the LORD your God; and you shall worship Him, and ᵇswear by His name.

14 "ªYou shall not follow other gods, any of the gods of the peoples who surround you,

15 for the LORD your God in the midst of you is a ªjealous God; otherwise the anger of the LORD your God will be kindled against you, and He will wipe you off the face of the earth.

16 "ªYou shall not put the LORD your God to the test, ᵇas you tested *Him* at Massah.

17 "ªYou should diligently keep the commandments of the LORD your God, and His testimonies and His statutes which He has commanded you.

18 "And you shall do what is right and good in the sight of the LORD, that ªit may be well with you and that you may go in and possess the good land which the LORD swore to *give* your fathers,

19 by driving out all your enemies from before you, as the LORD has spoken.

20 "ªWhen your son asks you in time to come, saying, 'What *do* the testimonies and the statutes and the judgments *mean* which the LORD commanded you?'

21 then you shall say to your son, 'We were slaves to Pharaoh in Egypt; and the LORD brought us from Egypt with a mighty hand.

22 'Moreover, the LORD showed great and distressing signs and wonders before our eyes against Egypt, Pharaoh and all his household;

23 and He brought us out from there in order to bring us in, to give us the land which He had sworn to our fathers.'

24 "So the LORD commanded us to observe all these statutes, ªto fear the LORD our God for our good always and ᵇfor our survival, as *it is* today.

25 "And ªit will be righteousness for us if we are careful to observe all this commandment before the LORD our God, just as He commanded us.

6 ªDeut. 11:18
7 ªDeut. 4:9; 11:19; Eph. 6:4
★ **8** ªEx. 12:14; 13:9, 16; Deut. 11:18; Prov. 3:3; 6:21; 7:3
★ **9** ªDeut. 11:20
10 ªDeut. 9:1; 19:1; Josh. 24:13; Ps. 105:44
11 ªDeut. 8:10; 11:15; 14:29
12 ªDeut. 4:9
13 ªDeut. 13:4; Matt. 4:10; Luke 4:8 ᵇDeut. 5:11; 10:20; Ps. 63:11; Matt. 5:33
★**14** ªJer. 25:6
15 ªDeut. 4:24; 5:9

★**16** ªMatt. 4:7; Luke 4:12 ᵇEx. 17:7
17 ªDeut. 11:22; Ps. 119:4
18 ªDeut. 4:40
20 ªEx. 13:8, 14
24 ªDeut. 10:12; Jer. 32:39 ᵇPs. 41:2; Luke 10:28
★**25** ªDeut. 24:13; Rom. 10:3

6:8 See note on Exod. 13:9. The Jews practiced this commandment later by wearing phylacteries.

6:9 Later the Jews placed a copy of the Shema in a small metal box or skin bag and placed it on the door. It is called a "mezuzah" (= doorpost).

6:14 The people were warned against entanglement with the gods of Canaan.

6:16 See note on Exod. 17:2.

6:25 *it will be righteousness for us.* I.e., obedience to the Law could not guarantee eternal life, but such obedience constituted the right to the blessings of the covenant, particularly title to the land.

3 The command to destroy the Canaanites, 7:1-26

7 [a]"When the LORD your God shall bring you into the land where you are entering to possess it, and shall clear away many nations before you, the Hittites and the Girgashites and the Amorites and the Canaanites and the Perizzites and the Hivites and the Jebusites, [b]seven nations greater and stronger than you,

2 and when the LORD your God shall deliver them before you, and you shall defeat them, [a]then you shall utterly destroy them. [b]You shall make no covenant with them [c]and show no favor to them.

3 "Furthermore, [a]you shall not intermarry with them; you shall not give your daughters to their sons, nor shall you take their daughters for your sons.

4 "For they will turn your sons away from following Me to serve other gods; then the anger of the LORD will be kindled against you, and [a]He will quickly destroy you.

5 "But thus you shall do to them: [a]you shall tear down their altars, and smash their *sacred* pillars, and hew down their Asherim, and burn their graven images with fire.

6 "For you are [a]a holy people to the LORD your God; the LORD your God has chosen you to be [b]a people for His own possession out of all the peoples who are on the face of the earth.

7 "[a]The LORD did not set His love on you nor choose you because you were more in number than any of the peoples, for you were the fewest of all peoples,

8 but because the LORD loved you and kept the [a]oath which He swore to your forefathers, [b]the LORD brought you out by a mighty hand, and redeemed you from the house of slavery, from the hand of Pharaoh king of Egypt.

9 "Know therefore that the LORD your God, [a]He is God, [b]the faithful God, [c]who keeps His covenant and His lovingkindness to a thousandth generation with those who [d]love Him and keep His commandments;

10 but [a]repays those who hate Him to their faces, to destroy them; He will not delay with him who hates Him, He will repay him to his face.

11 "Therefore, you shall keep the commandment and the statutes and the judgments which I am commanding you today, to do them.

12 "[a]Then it shall come about, because you listen to these judgments and keep and do them, that the LORD your God will keep with you His covenant and His lovingkindness which He swore to your forefathers.

13 "And He will [a]love you and bless you and [b]multiply you; He will also bless the fruit of your womb and the fruit of your ground, your grain and your new wine and your oil, the increase of your herd and the young of your flock, in the land which He swore to your forefathers to give you.

14 "You shall be blessed above all peoples; there shall be no male or female [a]barren among you or among your cattle.

Cross references

1 [a]Deut. 20:16-18 [b]Acts 13:19

★ 2 [a]Num. 31:17; Josh. 11:11 [b]Ex. 23:32 [c]Deut. 7:16; 13:8

★ 3-4
3 [a]Ex. 34:15, 16; Josh. 23:12; Ezra 9:2

4 [a]Deut. 4:26

★ 5 [a]Ex. 23:24; 34:13; Deut. 12:3

★ 6-11
6 [a]Ex. 19:6; Deut. 14:2, 21; Ps. 50:5; Jer. 2:3 [b]Ex. 19:5; Deut. 4:20; 14:2; 26:18; Ps. 135:4; Titus 2:14; 1 Pet. 2:9
7 [a]Deut. 4:37

8 [a]Ex. 32:13 [b]Ex. 13:3

9 [a]Deut. 4:35, 39 [b]Is. 49:7; 1 Cor. 1:9; 1 Thess. 5:24; 2 Tim. 2:13 [c]Ex. 20:6; Dan. 9:4 [d]Deut. 5:10

10 [a]Is. 59:18; Nah. 1:2

★12-13
12 [a]Lev. 26:3-13; Deut. 28:1-14

13 [a]Ps. 146:8; Prov. 15:9; John 14:21 [b]Lev. 26:9; Deut. 13:17; 30:5

14 [a]Ex. 23:26

7:2 *utterly destroy.* From the Hebrew root word for "devote," meaning here "to devote to destruction, to exterminate."

7:3-4 Marriage to a heathen would almost inevitably result in worshiping the heathen's gods (cf. Mal. 2:11).

7:5 *pillars . . . Asherim.* Pillars were associated with Baal worship and Asherim were images of Asherah, the mother of 70 gods, including Baal.

7:6-11 God's sovereign choice of Israel was not based on the size of the nation (Abraham received the promise while still childless, and Jacob's immediate family consisted of only 70 individuals) but stemmed from His love and from faithfulness to His covenant purpose for them. *lovingkindness* (v. 9). See note on Hos. 2:19.

7:12-13 Enjoyment of the blessings of God's unconditional relationship to His people was conditioned on their obedience.

15 "And [a]the Lord will remove from you all sickness; and He will not put on you any of the harmful diseases of Egypt which you have known, but He will lay them on all who hate you.

16 "And you shall consume all the peoples whom the Lord your God will deliver to you; [a]your eye shall not pity them, neither shall you serve their gods, for that *would be* [b]a snare to you.

17 "If you should say in your heart, 'These nations are greater than I; how can I [a]dispossess them?'

18 you shall not be afraid of them; you shall well [a]remember what the Lord your God did to Pharaoh and to all Egypt:

19 [a]the great trials which your eyes saw and the signs and the wonders and the mighty hand and the outstretched arm by which the Lord your God brought you out. So shall the Lord your God do to all the peoples of whom you are afraid.

20 "Moreover, the Lord your God will send [a]the hornet against them, until those who are left and hide themselves from you perish.

21 "You shall not dread them, for [a]the Lord your God is in your midst, [b]a great and awesome God.

22 "And the Lord your God will clear away these nations before you little by little; you will not be able to put an end to them quickly, lest the wild beasts grow too numerous for you.

23 "But the Lord your God shall deliver them before you, and will throw them into great confusion until they are destroyed.

24 "And He will deliver their kings into your hand so that you shall make their name perish from under heaven; [b]no man will be able to stand before you until you have destroyed them.

25 "The graven images of their gods you are to [a]burn with fire; you shall [b]not covet the silver or the gold that is on them, nor take it for yourselves, lest you be [c]snared by it, for it is an [d]abomination to the Lord your God.

26 "And you shall not bring an abomination into your house, and like it come under the [a]ban; you shall utterly detest it and you shall utterly abhor it, for it is something banned.

4 The command to remember God's past dealings, 8:1-10:11

8 "All the commandments that I am commanding you today you shall be careful to do, that you [a]may live and multiply, and go in and possess the land which the Lord swore *to give* to your forefathers.

2 "And you shall remember all the way which the Lord your God has [b]led you in the wilderness these forty years, that He might humble you, [c]testing you, to know what was in your heart, whether you would keep His commandments or not.

3 "And He humbled you and let you be hungry, and fed you with manna which you did not know, nor did your fathers know, that He might make you understand that [a]man does not live by bread alone, but man lives by everything that proceeds out of the mouth of the Lord.

4 "Your clothing did not wear out on you, nor did your foot swell these forty years.

5 "Thus you are to know in your heart that the Lord your

Margin references
★15 [a]Ex. 15:26
16 [a]Deut. 7:2 [b]Ex. 23:33; Judg. 8:27; Ps. 106:36
17 [a]Num. 33:53
18 [a]Ps. 105:5
19 [a]Deut. 4:34
★20 [a]Ex. 23:28; Josh. 24:12
21 [a]Ex. 29:45; Josh. 3:10 [b]Deut. 10:17; Neh. 1:5; 9:32
★22 [a]Ex. 23:29, 30
23 [a]Ex. 23:27; Josh. 10:10
24 [a]Josh. 6:2; 10:23-25 [b]Deut. 11:25; Josh. 1:5; 10:8; 23:9
25 [a]Ex. 32:20; Deut. 12:3; 1 Chr. 14:12 [b]Ex. 20:17 [c]Deut. 7:16; Judg. 8:27 [d]Deut. 17:1
★26 [a]Lev. 27:28f.
1 [a]Deut. 4:1
2 [a]Deut. 8:16 [b]Ps. 136:16; Amos 2:10 [c]Ex. 15:25; 20:20; 2 Chr. 32:31
★ 3 [a]Matt. 4:4; Luke 4:4
★ 4 [a]Deut. 29:5; Neh. 9:21
5 [a]Deut. 4:36; 2 Sam. 7:14; Prov. 3:12; Heb. 12:6; Rev. 3:19

7:15 *the harmful diseases of Egypt.* These included ophthalmia, dysentery, smallpox, and elephantiasis.

7:20 *the hornet.* See note on Exod. 23:28.

7:22 The conquest of Canaan would be progressive so that there would not be an excessive accumulation of corpses and desolate land to attract dangerous animals.

7:26 Achan disobeyed this admonition (Josh. 7:1).

8:3 *manna.* See notes on Exod. 16:15 and Num. 11:7. Manna was given to Israel as the source of all sustenance. Jesus quoted the latter part of this verse when tempted by the devil (Matt. 4:4).

8:4 Even their clothing was adequately supplied (perhaps partly through bartering with other people and partly miraculously, cf. 29:5).

God was disciplining you just as a man disciplines his son.

6 "Therefore, you shall keep the commandments of the LORD your God, to walk in His ways and to fear Him.

7 aDeut. 11:9-12; Jer. 2:7

7 "For athe LORD your God is bringing you into a good land, a land of brooks of water, of fountains and springs, flowing forth in valleys and hills;

8 a land of wheat and barley, of vines and fig trees and pomegranates, a land of olive oil and honey;

★ 9

9 a land where you shall eat food without scarcity, in which you shall not lack anything; a land whose stones are iron, and out of whose hills you can dig copper.

10 aDeut. 6:11

10 "When ayou have eaten and are satisfied, you shall bless the LORD your God for the good land which He has given you.

11 aDeut. 4:9

11 "Beware lest you aforget the LORD your God by not keeping His commandments and His ordinances and His statutes which I am commanding you today;

12 aProv. 30:9; Hos. 13:6

12 lest, awhen you have eaten and are satisfied, and have built good houses and lived in them,

13 and when your herds and your flocks multiply, and your silver and gold multiply, and all that you have multiplies,

14 aDeut. 8:11; Ps. 106:21

14 then your heart becomes proud, and you aforget the LORD your God who brought you out from the land of Egypt, out of the house of slavery.

15 aDeut. 1:19; Jer. 2:6 bNum. 21:6 cEx. 17:6; Num. 20:11; Deut. 32:13; Ps. 78:15; 114:8

15 "He led you through athe great and terrible wilderness, with its bfiery serpents and scorpions and thirsty ground where there was no water; He cbrought water for you out of the rock of flint.

16 aEx. 16:15 bDeut. 8:2

16 "In the wilderness He fed you manna awhich your fathers did not know, that He might humble you and that He might btest you, to do good for you in the end.

17 "Otherwise, ayou may say in your heart, 'My power and the strength of my hand made me this wealth.'

17 aDeut. 9:4

18 "But you shall remember the LORD your God, for ait is He who is giving you power to make wealth, that He may confirm His covenant which He swore to your fathers, as it is this day.

★18 aProv. 10:22; Hos. 2:8

19 "And it shall come about if you ever forget the LORD your God, and go after other gods and serve them and worship them, aI testify against you today that you shall surely perish.

19 aDeut. 4:26; 30:18

20 "Like the nations that the LORD makes to perish before you, so ayou shall perish; because you would not listen to the voice of the LORD your God.

20 aEzek. 5:5-17

9 "Hear, O Israel! You are crossing over the Jordan today to go in to dispossess anations greater and mightier than you, great cities bfortified to heaven,

1 aDeut. 4:38; 7:1; 11:23 bDeut. 1:28

2 a people great and tall, the sons of the Anakim, whom you know and of whom you have heard it said, 'aWho can stand before the sons of Anak?'

★ 2 aNum. 13:22, 28, 33; Josh. 11:21, 22

3 "Know therefore today that ait is the LORD your God who is crossing over before you as ba consuming fire. He will destroy them and He will subdue them before you, so that cyou may drive them out and destroy them quickly, just as the LORD has spoken to you.

3 aDeut. 31:3; Josh. 3:11 bDeut. 4:24; Heb. 12:29 cEx. 23:31; Deut. 7:24

4 "aDo not say in your heart when the LORD your God has driven them out before you, 'Because of my righteousness the LORD has brought me in to possess this land,' but it is bbecause of the wickedness of these nations that the LORD is dispossessing them before you.

4 aDeut. 8:17; 9:7, 24; 31:27 bLev. 18:3, 24-30; Deut. 12:31; 18:9-14

5 "It is anot for your righteousness or for the uprightness of your heart that you are going to possess their land, but it is because of the wickedness of these

★ 5 aTitus 3:5 bGen. 12:7; 13:15; 15:7; 17:8; 26:4; 28:13

8:9 Both iron and copper are found in Palestine.
8:18 This is an important lesson to remember: all we have is of God's grace (cf. 1 Cor. 4:7).

9:2 See note on Num. 13:33 regarding the Anakim.
9:5 confirm the oath. I.e., of Gen. 13:15.

nations *that* the Lord your God is driving them out before you, in order to confirm [b]the oath which the Lord swore to your fathers, to Abraham, Isaac and Jacob.

★ 6 [a]Deut. 9:13; 10:16; 31:27

6 "Know, then, *it is* not because of your righteousness *that* the Lord your God is giving you this good land to possess, for you are [a]a stubborn people.

7 [a]Ex. 14:10f.; Num. 14:22

7 "Remember, do not forget how you provoked the Lord your God to wrath in the wilderness; [a]from the day that you left the land of Egypt until you arrived at this place, you have been rebellious against the Lord.

★ 8-21

8 [a]Ex. 32:7-10; Ps. 106:19

8 "Even [a]at Horeb you provoked the Lord to wrath, and the Lord was so angry with you that He would have destroyed you.

9 [a]Ex. 24:18; 34:28; Deut. 8:3; 9:18

9 "When I went up to the mountain to receive the tablets of stone, the tablets of the covenant which the Lord had made with you, then I remained on the mountain forty days and nights; [a]I neither ate bread nor drank water.

10 [a]Deut. 4:13

10 "And the Lord gave me the two tablets of stone [a]written by the finger of God; and on them *were* all the words which the Lord had spoken with you at the mountain from the midst of the fire on the day of the assembly.

11 [a]Deut. 9:9

11 "And it came about [a]at the end of forty days and nights that the Lord gave me the two tablets of stone, the tablets of the covenant.

12 [a]Ex. 32:7, 8 [b]Judg. 2:17

12 "[a]Then the Lord said to me, 'Arise, go down from here quickly, for your people whom you brought out of Egypt have acted corruptly. They have [b]quickly turned aside from the way which I commanded them; they have made a molten image for themselves.'

13 [a]Ex. 32:9 [b]Deut. 10:16; 31:27; 2 Kin. 17:14

13 "The [a]Lord spoke further to me, saying, 'I have seen this peo-

ple, and indeed, it is a [b]stubborn people.

14 [a]Ex. 32:10 [b]Ps. 9:5; 109:13

14 '[a]Let Me alone, that I may destroy them and [b]blot out their name from under heaven; and I will make of you a nation mightier and greater than they.'

15 [a]Ex. 32:15-19

15 "[a]So I turned and came down from the mountain while the mountain was burning with fire, and the two tablets of the covenant were in my two hands.

16 "And I saw that you had indeed sinned against the Lord your God. You had made for yourselves a molten calf; you had turned aside quickly from the way which the Lord had commanded you.

17 "And I took hold of the two tablets and threw them from my hands, and smashed them before your eyes.

18 [a]Ex. 34:28 [b]Deut. 10:10 [c]Deut. 9:9 [d]Ex. 34:9

18 "[a]And I fell down before the Lord, [b]as at the first, forty days and nights; [c]I neither ate bread nor drank water, [d]because of all your sin which you had committed in doing what was evil in the sight of the Lord to provoke Him to anger.

19 [a]Ex. 32:10f.; Heb. 12:21 [b]Ex. 34:10; Deut. 10:10

19 "For [a]I was afraid of the anger and hot displeasure with which the Lord was wrathful against you in order to destroy you, [b]but the Lord listened to me that time also.

20 "And the Lord was angry enough with Aaron to destroy him; so I also prayed for Aaron at the same time.

21 [a]Ex. 32:20

21 "[a]And I took your sinful thing, the calf which you had made, and burned it with fire and crushed it, grinding it very small until it was as fine as dust; and I threw its dust into the brook that came down from the mountain.

★22 [a]Num. 11:3 [b]Ex. 17:7 [c]Num. 11:34

22 "Again at [a]Taberah and at [b]Massah and at [c]Kibroth-hatta-avah you provoked the Lord to wrath.

9:6 *stubborn.* The figure is that of a stubborn ox who refuses to submit to the yoke.

9:8-21 Moses reminded the people of the sin of making the golden calf (cf. Exod. 32). God's anger with Aaron (Deut. 9:20) is not men-

tioned in Exodus.

9:22 The incident at *Taberah* is recorded in Num. 11:1-3; at *Massah,* in Exod. 17:1-7; and at *Kibroth-hattaavah,* in Num. 11:31-34.

★23 *a*Deut.
1:2 *b*Deut.
1:21 *c*Deut.
1:26; Ps.
106:24

23 "And when the LORD sent you from *a*Kadesh-barnea, saying, '*b*Go up and possess the land which I have given you,' then you rebelled against the command of the LORD your God; *c*you neither believed Him nor listened to His voice.

24 *a*Deut.
9:7; 31:27

24 "*a*You have been rebellious against the LORD from the day I knew you.

25 *a*Deut.
9:18

25 "*a*So I fell down before the LORD the forty days and nights, which I did because the LORD had said He would destroy you.

26 *a*Ex.
32:11-13;
1 Sam. 7:9;
Jer. 15:1

26 "*a*And I prayed to the LORD, and said, 'O Lord GOD, do not destroy Thy people, even Thine inheritance, whom Thou hast redeemed through Thy greatness, whom Thou hast brought out of Egypt with a mighty hand.

27 'Remember Thy servants, Abraham, Isaac, and Jacob; do not look at the stubbornness of this people or at their wickedness or their sin.

28 *a*Ex.
32:12; Num.
14:16

28 'Otherwise the land from which Thou didst bring us may say, '*a*Because the LORD was not able to bring them into the land which He had promised them and because He hated them He has brought them out to slay them in the wilderness.'

29 *a*Deut.
4:20; 1 Kin.
8:51; Neh.
1:10; Ps.
106:40
*b*Deut. 4:34

29 'Yet they are Thy people, even *a*Thine inheritance, whom Thou hast brought out by Thy *b*great power and Thine outstretched arm.'

1 *a*Ex. 34:1
*b*Ex. 25:10

10 "At that time the LORD said to me, '*a*Cut out for yourself two tablets of stone like the former ones, and come up to Me on the mountain, and *b*make an ark of wood for yourself.

2 *a*Deut.
4:13 *b*Ex.
25:16

2 'And *a*I will write on the tablets the words that were on the former tablets which you shattered, and *b*you shall put them in the ark.'

★ 3 *a*Ex.
25:5; 37:1-9
*b*Ex. 34:4

3 "So *a*I made an ark of acacia wood and *b*cut out two tablets of stone like the former ones, and

went up on the mountain with the two tablets in my hand.

4 *a*Ex.
34:28; Deut.
4:13 *b*Ex.
20:1 *c*Deut.
9:10; 18:16

4 "And He wrote on the tablets, like the former writing, *a*the Ten Commandments *b*which the LORD had spoken to you on the mountain from the midst of the fire *c*on the day of the assembly; and the LORD gave them to me.

5 *a*Ex.
34:29 *b*Ex.
40:20, *c*1 Kin.
8:9

5 "Then I turned and *a*came down from the mountain, and *b*put the tablets in the ark which I had made; *c*and there they are, as the LORD commanded me."

6 *a*Num.
33:30, 31
*b*Num.
20:25-28;
33:38

6 (Now the sons of Israel set out from Beeroth *a*Bene-jaakan to Moserah. *b*There Aaron died and there he was buried and Eleazar his son ministered as priest in his place.

7 *a*Num.
33:33, 34

7 *a*From there they set out to Gudgodah; and from Gudgodah to Jotbathah, a land of brooks of water.

8 *a*Num.
3:6; 18:1-7;
Deut. 31:9
*b*Deut.
17:12; 18:5;
21:5

8 *a*At that time the LORD set apart the tribe of Levi to carry the ark of the covenant of the LORD, to stand before the LORD *b*to serve Him and to bless in His name until this day.

9 *a*Num.
18:20, 24;
Deut. 18:1, 2;
Ezek. 44:28

9 *a*Therefore, Levi does not have a portion or inheritance with his brothers; the LORD is his inheritance, just as the LORD your God spoke to him.)

10 *a*Ex.
34:28; Deut.
9:18

10 "*a*I, moreover, stayed on the mountain forty days and forty nights like the first time, and the LORD listened to me that time also; the LORD was not willing to destroy you.

11 "Then the LORD said to me, 'Arise, proceed on your journey ahead of the people, that they may go in and possess the land which I swore to their fathers to give them.'

5   The call to commitment,
   10:12–11:32

12 *a*Mic. 6:8
*b*Deut. 6:5;
Matt. 22:37;
1 Tim. 1:5
*c*Deut. 4:29

12 "*a*And now, Israel, what does the LORD your God require from you, but to fear the LORD your God, to walk in all His ways

---

9:23 Unbelief was their cardinal sin (cf. Heb. 3-4).

10:3 *acacia wood.* See note on Exod. 25:1-7. *ark.* See note on Exod. 25:10-16.

and ᵇlove Him, and to serve the LORD your God with ᶜall your heart and with all your soul,

13 *and* to keep the LORD's commandments and His statutes which I am commanding you today for your good?

14 "Behold, ᵃto the LORD your God belong heaven and the highest heavens, ᵇthe earth and all that is in it.

15 "ᵃYet on your fathers did the LORD set His affection to love them, and He chose their descendants after them, *even* you above all peoples, as *it is* this day.

16 "ᵃCircumcise then your heart, and ᵇstiffen your neck no more.

17 "ᵃFor the LORD your God is the God of gods and the ᵇLord of lords, the great, the mighty, and the awesome God ᶜwho does not show partiality, nor ᵈtake a bribe.

18 "He executes justice for ᵃthe orphan and the widow, and shows His love for the alien by giving him food and clothing.

19 "ᵃSo show your love for the alien, for you were aliens in the land of Egypt.

20 "You shall fear the LORD your God; you shall serve Him and ᵃcling to Him, and ᵇyou shall swear by His name.

21 "He is ᵃyour praise and He is your God, who has done these great and awesome things for you which your eyes have seen.

22 "ᵃYour fathers went down to Egypt seventy persons *in all*, ᵇand now the LORD your God has made you as numerous as the stars of heaven.

11 "You shall therefore ᵃlove the LORD your God, and always ᵇkeep His charge, His statutes, His ordinances, and His commandments.

2 "And know this day ᵃthat I am not *speaking* with your sons who have not known and who have not seen the discipline of the LORD your God—His greatness, His mighty hand, and His outstretched arm,

3 and ᵃHis signs and His works which He did in the midst of Egypt to Pharaoh the king of Egypt and to all his land;

4 and what He did to Egypt's army, to its horses and its chariots, ᵃwhen He made the water of the Red Sea to engulf them while they were pursuing you, and the LORD completely destroyed them;

5 and what He did to you in the wilderness until you came to this place;

6 and ᵃwhat He did to Dathan and Abiram, the sons of Eliab, the son of Reuben, when the earth opened its mouth and swallowed them, their households, their tents, and ᵇevery living thing that followed them, among all Israel—

7 but your own eyes have seen all the great work of the LORD which He did.

8 "You shall therefore keep every commandment which I am commanding you today, ᵃso that you may be strong and go in and possess the land into which you are about to cross to possess it;

9 ᵃso that you may prolong *your* days on the land which the LORD swore to your fathers to give to them and to their descendants, ᵇa land flowing with milk and honey.

10 "For the land, into which you are entering to possess it, is not like the land of Egypt from which you came, where you used to sow your seed and water it

---

Marginal references (left column):

14 ᵃ1 Kin. 8:27; Neh. 9:6; Ps. 68:33; 115:16 ᵇPs. 24:1

15 ᵃDeut. 4:37

★16 ᵃLev. 26:41; Jer. 4:4 ᵇDeut. 9:6

★17 ᵃJosh. 22:22; Ps. 136:2; Dan. 2:47; 1 Tim. 6:15; Rev. 19:16 ᵇRev. 17:14 ᶜDeut. 1:17; Acts 10:34; Rom. 2:11; Gal. 2:6; Eph. 6:9 ᵈDeut. 16:19

18 ᵃEx. 22:22-24; Ps. 68:5; 146:9

19 ᵃLev. 19:34; Ezek. 47:22, 23

20 ᵃDeut. 11:22; 13:4 ᵇDeut. 5:11; 6:13; Ps. 63:11

21 ᵃPs. 109:1; 148:14; Jer. 17:14

★22 ᵃGen. 46:27 ᵇGen. 15:5; 22:17; Deut. 1:10

1 ᵃDeut. 6:5; 10:12 ᵇLev. 18:30; 22:9

Marginal references (right column):

★ 2 ᵃDeut. 4:34

3 ᵃEx. 7:8-21

★ 4 ᵃEx. 14:28; Deut. 1:40; 2:1

★ 6 ᵃNum. 16:1-35; Ps. 106:16-18 ᵇNum. 26:10, 11

8 ᵃDeut. 31:6, 7, 23; Josh. 1:6, 7

9 ᵃDeut. 4:40; 5:16, 33; 6:2; Prov. 10:27 ᵇEx. 3:8

★10-11

10:16 Circumcision (see note on Gen. 17:9-14) is here used figuratively, meaning "separate yourselves from sin" (see note on Jer. 4:4).

10:17 The LORD (Yahweh; see notes on Exod. 3:14, 15) was no mere local deity, but the God of the universe (v. 14). He is also a righteous Judge (v. 18) and Lord of the events of history (cf. v. 21).

10:22 See note on Gen. 46:27.

11:2 *His outstretched arm.* A vivid figure of protection. Moses was particularly reminding those who were under 20 years old at the time of the Exodus of the great miracles they witnessed in connection with their flight from Egypt (cf. v. 7).

11:4 *the Red Sea.* See note on Exod. 13:18.

11:6 See note on Num. 16:12.

11:10-11 *water it with your foot.* Agriculture in

with your foot like a vegetable garden.

11 "But ªthe land into which you are about to cross to possess it, a land of hills and valleys, drinks water from the rain of heaven,

12 a land for which the LORD your God cares; ªthe eyes of the LORD your God are always on it, from the beginning even to the end of the year.

13 "And it shall come about, ªif you listen obediently to my commandments which I am commanding you today, ᵇto love the LORD your God and to serve Him ᶜwith all your heart and all your soul,

14 that 'ªHe will give the rain for your land in its season, the ᵇearly and late rain, that you may gather in your grain and your new wine and your oil.

15 'And ªHe will give grass in your fields for your cattle, and ᵇyou shall eat and be satisfied.'

16 "ªBeware, lest your hearts be deceived and you turn away and serve other gods and worship them.

17 "Or ªthe anger of the LORD will be kindled against you, and He will ᵇshut up the heavens ᶜso that there will be no rain and the ground will not yield its fruit; and ᵈyou will perish quickly from the good land which the LORD is giving you.

18 "ªYou shall therefore impress these words of mine on your heart and on your soul; and you shall bind them as a sign on your hand, and they shall be as frontals on your forehead.

19 "ªAnd you shall teach them to your sons, talking of them when you sit in your house and when you walk along the road and when you lie down and when you rise up.

20 "ªAnd you shall write them on the doorposts of your house and on your gates,

21 so that ªyour days and the days of your sons may be multiplied on the land which the LORD swore to your fathers to give them, as ᵇlong as the heavens remain above the earth.

22 "For if you are ªcareful to keep all this commandment which I am commanding you, to do it, ᵇto love the LORD your God, to walk in all His ways and ᶜhold fast to Him;

23 then the LORD will ªdrive out all these nations from before you, and you will ᵇdispossess nations greater and mightier than you.

24 "ªEvery place on which the sole of your foot shall tread shall be yours; ᵇyour border shall be from the wilderness to Lebanon, *and* from the river, the river Euphrates, as far as the western sea.

25 "ªThere shall no man be able to stand before you; the LORD your God shall lay the dread of you and the fear of you on all the land on which you set foot, as He has spoken to you.

26 "ªSee, I am setting before you today a blessing and a curse:

27 the ªblessing, if you listen to the commandments of the LORD your God, which I am commanding you today;

28 and the ªcurse, if you do not listen to the commandments of the LORD your God, but turn aside from the way which I am commanding you today, by following other gods which you have not known.

29 "And it shall come about, when the LORD your God brings

Cross references (margin)

11 ªDeut. 8:7
12 ª1 Kin. 9:3
13 ªLev. 26:3; Deut. 7:12 ᵇDeut. 11:1 ᶜDeut. 4:29
★14 ªLev. 26:4; Deut. 28:12 ᵇJoel 2:23; James 5:7
15 ªPs. 104:14 ᵇDeut. 6:11
16 ªJob 31:27
17 ªDeut. 6:15; 9:19 ᵇ1 Kin. 8:35; 2 Chr. 6:26; 7:13 ᶜDeut. 28:24 ᵈDeut. 4:26
★18-20
18 ªEx. 13:9, 16; Deut. 6:8
19 ªDeut. 4:9, 10; 6:7; Prov. 22:6
20 ªDeut. 6:9
21 ªProv. 3:2; 4:10; 9:11 ᵇPs. 72:5
22 ªDeut. 6:17 ᵇDeut. 11:1 ᶜDeut. 10:20
23 ªDeut. 4:38 ᵇDeut. 9:1
★24 ªJosh. 1:3; 14:9 ᵇGen. 15:18; Ex. 23:31; Deut. 1:7, 8
25 ªEx. 23:27; Deut. 7:24
26 ªDeut. 30:1, 19
27 ªDeut. 28:1-14
28 ªDeut. 28:15-68
★29 ªDeut. 27:12; Josh. 8:33

Egypt was dependent on irrigation; the reference may be to waterwheels turned by the feet or to turning the water into small channels with the foot. By contrast, Palestine is watered by rain.

11:14 *the early* rain fell in autumn (Sept.-Oct.), and the *late rain,* in the spring (Mar.-Apr.).

11:18-20 *bind them . . . write them.* See notes on 6:8 and 6:9.

11:24 *the western sea.* I.e., the Mediterranean.

See note on Gen. 15:18.

11:29 The choice between blessing and cursing (vv. 26-28) was dramatized by relating it to the cleavage between two mountains in the central part of Palestine which rise about 3,000 feet on either side of Shechem: Mt. *Gerizim* (which stood for blessing) and Mt. *Ebal* (which stood for cursing). This is elaborated on in Deut. 27.

you into the land where you are entering to possess it, ªthat you shall place the blessing on Mount Gerizim and the curse on Mount Ebal.

30 "Are they not across the Jordan, west of the way toward the sunset, in the land of the Canaanites who live in the Arabah, opposite ªGilgal, beside ᵇthe oaks of Moreh?

31 "For you are about to cross the Jordan to go in to possess the land which the LORD your God is giving you, and ªyou shall possess it and live in it,

32 and you shall be careful to do all the statutes and the judgments which I am setting before you today.

6 The command concerning the central sanctuary, 12:1–32

12 "These are the statutes and the judgments which you shall carefully observe in the land which the LORD, the God of your fathers, has given you to possess ªas long as you live on the earth.

2 "You shall utterly destroy all the places where the nations whom you shall dispossess serve their gods, on the ªhigh mountains and on the hills and under every green tree.

3 "And ªyou shall tear down their altars and smash their *sacred* pillars and burn their Asherim with fire, and you shall cut down the engraved images of their gods, and you shall ᵇobliterate their name from that place.

4 "You shall not act like this toward the LORD your God.

5 "ªBut you shall seek *the* LORD at the place which the LORD your God shall choose from all your tribes, to establish His name

there for His dwelling, and there you shall come.

6 "And there you shall bring your burnt offerings, your sacrifices, ªyour tithes, the contribution of your hand, your votive offerings, your freewill offerings, and the first-born of your herd and of your flock.

7 "There also you and your households shall eat before the LORD your God, and ªrejoice in all your undertakings in which the LORD your God has blessed you.

8 "You shall not do at all what we are doing here today, every man *doing* whatever is right in his own eyes;

9 for you have not as yet come to ªthe resting place and the ᵇinheritance which the LORD your God is giving you.

10 "When you cross the Jordan and live in the land which the LORD your God is giving you to inherit, and ªHe gives you rest from all your enemies around *you* so that you live in security,

11 ªthen it shall come about that the place in which the LORD your God shall choose for His name to dwell, there you shall bring all that I command you: your burnt offerings and your sacrifices, your tithes and the contribution of your hand, and all your choice votive offerings which you will vow to the LORD.

12 "And you shall ªrejoice before the LORD your God, you and your sons and daughters, your male and female servants, and the ᵇLevite who is within your gates, since ᶜhe has no portion or inheritance with you.

13 "ªBe careful that you do not offer your burnt offerings in every *cultic* place you see,

14 but in the place which the LORD chooses in one of your tribes, there you shall offer your

---

Marginal references (left column):

30 ªJosh. 4:19 ᵇGen. 12:6

31 ªDeut. 17:14; Josh. 21:43

1 ªDeut. 4:9, 10; 1 Kin. 8:40

2 ª2 Kin. 16:4; 17:10, 11

★ **3** ªNum. 33:52; Deut. 7:5; Judg. 2:2 ᵇEx. 23:13; Ps. 16:4; Zech. 13:2

★ **5** ªEx. 20:24; Deut. 12:11; 13; 2 Chr. 7:12; Ps. 78:68

Marginal references (right column):

★ **6** ªDeut. 14:22

7 ªLev. 23:40; Deut. 12:12, 18; 14:26; 28:47; Eccl. 3:12; 13; 5:18-20

9 ªDeut. 3:20, 25:19; Ps. 95:11 ᵇDeut. 4:21

10 ªJosh. 11:23

11 ªDeut. 12:5; 15:20; 16:2; 17:8; 18:6

12 ªDeut. 12:7 ᵇDeut. 12:18, 19; 26:11-13 ᶜDeut. 10:9; 14:29

13 ªDeut. 12:5, 11

12:3 All vestiges of idolatry must be destroyed throughout the land. On *pillars* and *Asherim,* see note on 7:5.

12:5 In contrast to heathen worship at various sites throughout the land, the worship of the LORD (Yahweh) was to be centered in the place of His designation. Gilgal, Bethel, and Shiloh

were temporary centers before the Temple was built in Jerusalem. Today worship is centered in the Word (Christ) who became flesh.

12:6 *burnt offerings.* See note on Lev. 1:3. *tithes.* See note on Lev. 27:30. *contribution.* See note on Lev. 7:32. *votive offerings.* See note on Lev. 7:12–17.

burnt offerings, and there you shall do all that I command you.

15 "ªHowever, you may slaughter and eat meat within any of your gates, whatever you desire, according to the blessing of the LORD your God which He has given you; the unclean and the clean may eat of it, as of ᵇthe gazelle and the deer.

16 "ªOnly you shall not eat the blood; ᵇyou are to pour it out on the ground like water.

17 "ªYou are not allowed to eat within your gates the tithe of your grain, or new wine, or oil, or the first-born of your herd or flock, or any of your votive offerings which you vow, or your freewill offerings, or the contribution of your hand.

18 "But ªyou shall eat them before the LORD your God in ᵇthe place which the LORD your God will choose, you and your son and daughter, and your male and female servants, and the ᶜLevite who is within your gates; and you shall ᵈrejoice before the LORD your God in all your undertakings.

19 "ªBe careful that you do not forsake the Levite as long as you live in your land.

20 "When the LORD your God extends your border ªas He has promised you, and you say, 'I will eat meat,' because you desire to eat meat, *then* you may eat meat, whatever you desire.

21 "If the place which the LORD your God chooses to put His name is too far from you, then you may slaughter of your herd and flock which the LORD has given you, as I have commanded you; and you may eat within your gates whatever you desire.

22 "Just as a gazelle or a deer is eaten, so you shall eat it; the un-

clean and the clean alike may eat of it.

23 "Only be sure ªnot to eat the blood, for the blood is the life, and you shall not eat the life with the flesh.

24 "You shall not eat it; you shall pour it out on the ground like water.

25 "You shall not eat it, in order that ªit may be well with you and your sons after you, for ᵇyou will be doing what is right in the sight of the LORD.

26 "ªOnly your holy things which you may have and your votive offerings, you shall take and go to the place which the LORD chooses.

27 "And ªyou shall offer your burnt offerings, the flesh and the blood, on the altar of the LORD your God; and the blood of your sacrifices shall be poured out on the altar of the LORD your God, and ᵇyou shall eat the flesh.

28 "Be careful to listen to all these words which I command you, in order that ªit may be well with you and your sons after you forever, for you will be doing what is good and right in the sight of the LORD your God.

29 "When ªthe LORD your God cuts off before you the nations which you are going in to dispossess, and you dispossess them and dwell in their land,

30 beware that you are not ensnared to follow them, after they are destroyed before you, and that you do not inquire after their gods, saying, 'How do these nations serve their gods, that I also may do likewise?'

31 "ªYou shall not behave thus toward the LORD your God, for every abominable act which the LORD hates they have done for their gods; for ᵇthey even burn

---

Cross-references (margin):

★15 ªDeut. 12:20-23 ᵇDeut. 12:22; 14:5; 15:22

★16 ªGen. 9:4; Lev. 7:26; 17:10-12; 1 Sam. 14:33f.; Acts 15:20, 29 ᵇDeut. 15:23

★17-18

17 ªDeut. 12:26

18 ªDeut. 14:23 ᵇDeut. 12:5 ᶜDeut. 12:12 ᵈDeut. 12:7; Eccl. 3:12f.; 5:18-20

19 ªDeut. 14:27

20 ªGen. 15:18; Deut. 11:24; 19:8

23 ªGen. 9:4; Lev. 17:10-14; Deut. 12:16

25 ªDeut. 4:40; Is. 3:10 ᵇEx. 15:26; 1.Kin. 11:38

26 ªNum. 5:9f.; 18:19; Deut. 12:17

27 ªLev. 1:9, 13 ᵇLev. 3:1-17

28 ªDeut. 4:40; Eccl. 8:12

29 ªJosh. 23:4

★30

31 ªDeut. 9:5 ᵇLev. 18:21; Deut. 18:10; Ps. 106:37; Jer. 32:35

12:15 Family feasts could, of course, be held at home. Meat was not prominent in the diet of most Israelites.

12:16 Two reasons for this restriction are given in the note on Lev. 17:11.

12:17-18 The *tithe* had to be taken to the central sanctuary. This referred to what was known as

the second tithe (see note on Mal. 3:8 and further elaboration of this command in 14:22-29).

12:30 The Israelites were not even to inquire about the worship of the Canaanites, lest they be tempted to incorporate aspects of it into their worship of God (cf. a similar admonition in Rom. 16:19).

their sons and daughters in the fire to their gods.

32 aDeut. 4:2; Josh. 1:7 bProv. 30:6; Rev. 22:18

32 "aWhatever I command you, you shall be careful to do; byou shall not add to nor take away from it.

B Commands Concerning False Prophets, 13:1-18

1 aMatt. 24:24; Mark 13:22; 2 Thess. 2:9

13 "aIf a prophet or a dreamer of dreams arises among you and gives you a sign or a wonder,

★ 2 aDeut. 13:6, 13

2 and the sign or the wonder comes true, concerning which he spoke to you, saying, 'aLet us go after other gods (whom you have not known) and let us serve them,'

3 aEx. 20:20; Deut. 8:2, 16; 1 Cor. 11:19 bDeut. 6:5

3 you shall not listen to the words of that prophet or that dreamer of dreams; for the Lord your God is atesting you to find out if byou love the Lord your God with all your heart and with all your soul.

4 a2 Kin. 23:3; 2 Chr. 34:31; 2 John 6 bDeut. 10:20

4 "aYou shall follow the Lord your God and fear Him; and you shall keep His commandments, listen to His voice, serve Him, and bcling to Him.

5 aDeut. 13:9, 15; 17:5; 1 Kin. 18:40 bDeut. 4:19; 13:10 c1 Cor. 5:13

5 "But that prophet or that dreamer of dreams shall be aput to death, because he has counseled rebellion against the Lord your God who brought you from the land of Egypt and redeemed you from the house of slavery, bto seduce you from the way in which the Lord your God commanded you to walk. cSo you shall purge the evil from among you.

6 aDeut. 17:2-7; 29:18 bDeut. 13:2

6 "aIf your brother, your mother's son, or your son or daughter, or the wife you cherish, or your friend who is as your own soul, entice you secretly, saying, 'bLet us go and serve other gods' (whom neither you nor your fathers have known),

7 of the gods of the peoples who are around you, near you or far from you, from one end of the earth to the other end),

8 aProv. 1:10 bDeut. 7:2

8 ayou shall not yield to him or listen to him; band your eye shall not pity him, nor shall you spare or conceal him.

★ 9 aDeut. 13:5 bLev. 24:14; Deut. 17:7

9 "aBut you shall surely kill him; byour hand shall be first against him to put him to death, and afterwards the hand of all the people.

10 aDeut. 13:5

10 "So you shall stone him to death because he has sought ato seduce you from the Lord your God who brought you out from the land of Egypt, out of the house of slavery.

11 aDeut. 19:20

11 "Then aall Israel will hear and be afraid, and will never again do such a wicked thing among you.

12 "If you hear in one of your cities, which the Lord your God is giving you to live in, anyone saying that

★13-18

13 aDeut. 13:2

13 some worthless men have gone out from among you and have seduced the inhabitants of their city, saying, 'aLet us go and serve other gods' (whom you have not known),

14 then you shall investigate and search out and inquire thoroughly. And if it is true and the matter established that this abomination has been done among you,

15 aDeut. 13:5

15 ayou shall surely strike the inhabitants of that city with the edge of the sword, utterly destroying it and all that is in it and

---

13:2 *the sign or the wonder.* I.e., a prediction concerning the future. Note that a false prophet's prediction might very well come to pass. The determination of whether he was a true or false prophet was not made on this basis, but on whether or not he led the people away from God. The success of false prophets was permitted in order to test God's people (v. 3).

13:9 A person who enticed another to idolatry was subject to capital punishment.

13:13-18 If a city was enticed to idolatry by *worthless men*, then it was to be completely destroyed. God places first priority on undivided loyalty to Himself.

its cattle with the edge of the sword.

16 "ªThen you shall gather all its booty into the middle of its open square and burn the city and all its booty with fire as a whole burnt offering to the LORD your God; and it shall be ᵇruin forever. It shall never be rebuilt.

17 "And nothing from that which is put under the ban shall cling to your hand, in order that the LORD may turn from ªHis burning anger and ᵇshow mercy to you, and have compassion on you and ᶜmake you increase, just ᵈas He has sworn to your fathers,

18 if you will listen to the voice of the LORD your God, keeping all His commandments which I am commanding you today, and doing what is right in the sight of the LORD your God.

C　Commands Concerning Food, 14:1-21

14 "You are ªthe sons of the LORD your God; ᵇyou shall not cut yourselves nor shave your forehead for the sake of the dead.

2 "For you are ªa holy people to the LORD your God; and the LORD has chosen you to be a ᵇpeople for His own possession out of all the peoples who are on the face of the earth.

3 "ªYou shall not eat any detestable thing.

4 "ªThese are the animals which you may eat: the ox, the sheep, the goat,

5 the deer, the gazelle, the roebuck, the wild goat, the ibex, the antelope and the mountain sheep.

6 "And any animal that divides the hoof and has the hoof split in two *and* chews the cud,

among the animals, that you may eat.

7 "Nevertheless, you are not to eat of these among those which chew the cud, or among those that divide the hoof in two: the camel and the rabbit and the rock-badger, for though they chew the cud, they do not divide the hoof; they are unclean for you.

8 "And the pig, because it divides the hoof but *does* not *chew* the cud, it is unclean for you. You shall not eat any of their flesh nor touch their carcasses.

9 "These you may eat of all that are in water: anything that has fins and scales you may eat,

10 but anything that does not have fins and scales you shall not eat; it is unclean for you.

11 "You may eat any clean bird.

12 "But ªthese are the ones which you shall not eat: the eagle and the vulture and the buzzard,

13 and the red kite, the falcon, and the kite in their kinds,

14 and every raven in its kind,

15 and the ostrich, the owl, the sea gull, and the hawk in their kinds,

16 the little owl, the great owl, the white owl,

17 the pelican, the carrion vulture, the cormorant,

18 the stork, and the heron in their kinds, and the hoopoe and the bat.

19 "And all the teeming life with wings are unclean to you; they shall not be eaten.

20 "You may eat any clean bird.

21 "ªYou shall not eat anything which dies *of itself.* You may give it to the alien who is in your town, so that he may eat it, or you may sell it to a foreigner, for you are ᵇa holy people to the

Cross references (margin)

16 ªDeut. 7:25, 26; ᵇJosh. 8:28; Is. 17:1; 25:2; Jer. 49:2

17 ªEx. 32:12; Num. 25:4 ᵇDeut. 30:3 ᶜDeut. 7:13 ᵈGen. 22:17; 26:4, 24; 28:14

★ **1** ªRom. 8:16; 9:8, 26; Gal. 3:26; 1 John 3:1 ᵇLev. 19:28; 21:5; Jer. 16:6; 41:5

2 ªLev. 20:26; Deut. 7:6; Rom. 12:1 ᵇEx. 19:5; Deut. 4:20; 26:18; Titus 2:14; 1 Pet. 2:9

★ **3** ªEzek. 4:14

4 ªLev. 11:2-45; Acts 10:14

★ **5**

★**12-18**

12 ªLev. 11:13

21 ªLev. 17:15; 22:8; Ezek. 4:14; 44:31 ᵇDeut. 14:2 ᶜEx. 23:19; 34:26

14:1 These signs of mourning for the dead, which were practiced by the Canaanites as an acknowledgment of the divinity of the dead person, were strictly forbidden to God's people (cf. Lev. 19:27-28; Jer. 16:6).

14:3 *detestable.* I.e., unclean. On distinctions be-

tween clean and unclean animals, see the notes on Lev. 11.

14:5 *ibex.* Or, antelope. *antelope.* Or, wild ox.

14:12-18 These birds are identified in the note on Lev. 11:13.

LORD your God. cYou shall not boil a kid in its mother's milk.

D   Commands Concerning Tithes, 14:22-29

★22-27

22 aLev. 27:30; Deut. 12:6, 17; Neh. 10:37

22 "You ashall surely tithe all the produce from what you sow, which comes out of the field every year.

23 aDeut. 12:5 bDeut. 4:10; Ps. 2:11; 111:10; 147:11; Is. 8:13; Jer. 32:38-40

23 "And you shall eat in the presence of the LORD your God, aat the place where He chooses to establish His name, the tithe of your grain, your new wine, your oil, and the first-born of your herd and your flock, in order that you may blearn to fear the LORD your God always.

24 aDeut. 12:5, 21

24 "And if the distance is so great for you that you are not able to bring the tithe, since the place where the LORD your God chooses ato set His name is too far away from you when the LORD your God blesses you,

25 then you shall exchange it for money, and bind the money in your hand and go to the place which the LORD your God chooses.

26 aDeut. 12:7

26 "And you may spend the money for whatever your heart desires, for oxen, or sheep, or wine, or strong drink, or whatever your heart desires; and athere you shall eat in the presence of the LORD your God and rejoice, you and your household.

27 aDeut. 12:12 bNum. 18:20; Deut. 10:9; 18:12

27 "Also you shall not neglect athe Levite who is in your town, bfor he has no portion or inheritance among you.

★28-29

28 aDeut. 26:12

28 "aAt the end of every third year you shall bring out all the tithe of your produce in that year, and shall deposit it in your town.

29 "And the Levite, abecause he has no portion or inheritance among you, and bthe alien, the orphan and the widow who are in your town, shall come and ceat and be satisfied, in order that dthe LORD your God may bless you in all the work of your hand which you do.

29 aDeut. 10:9 bDeut. 16:11, 14; 24:19-21; 26:12; Ps. 94:6; Is. 1:17 cDeut. 6:11 dDeut. 15:10; Mal. 3:10

E   Commands Concerning the Sabbatical Year, 15:1-23

15 "aAt the end of every seven years you shall grant a remission of debts.

★1-6

1 aDeut. 31:10

2 "And this is the manner of remission: every creditor shall release what he has loaned to his neighbor; he shall not exact it of his neighbor and his brother, because the LORD's remission has been proclaimed.

3 "aFrom a foreigner you may exact it, but your hand shall release whatever of yours is with your brother.

3 aDeut. 23:20

4 "However, there shall be no poor among you, since athe LORD will surely bless you in the land which the LORD your God is giving you as an inheritance to possess,

4 aDeut. 28:8

5 if only you listen obediently to the voice of the LORD your God, to observe carefully all this commandment which I am commanding you today.

6 "aFor the LORD your God shall bless you as He has promised you, and you will lend to many nations, but you will not borrow; and you will rule over many nations, but they will not rule over you.

6 aDeut. 28:12, 13

7 "If there is aa poor man with you, one of your brothers, in any of your towns in your land which the LORD your God is giving

7 aLev. 25:35; Deut. 15:11 b1 John 3:17

14:22-27 This command was considered by Jewish interpreters to be for a second tithe (see Lev. 27:30 and Num. 18:21 for the first; also the note on Mal. 3:8), which was brought to the central sanctuary either in kind or in money. Apparently the offerer could use a part of this tithe for a feast at the sanctuary (vv. 26-27).

14:28-29 Every third year, the second tithe was not brought to the sanctuary but kept at home and used to feed the Levites and the poor.

15:1-6 Every seventh year, there was to be an unconditional remission of the debts of fellow Israelites. Foreigners still had to pay, for unlike sojourners, who were permanent members of the community, foreigners were temporary, commercial visitors. These regulations helped keep poverty out of the nation.

you, [b]you shall not harden your heart, nor close your hand from your poor brother;

8 but [a]you shall freely open your hand to him, and shall generously lend him sufficient for his need *in* whatever he lacks.

9 "Beware, lest there is a base thought in your heart, saying, '[a]The seventh year, the year of remission, is near,' and [b]your eye is hostile toward your poor brother, and you give him nothing; then he [c]may cry to the LORD against you, and it will be a sin in you.

10 "You shall generously give to him, and your heart shall not be grieved when you give to him, because [a]for this thing the LORD your God will bless you in all your work and in all your undertakings.

11 "[a]For the poor will never cease *to be* in the land; therefore I command you, saying, 'You shall freely open your hand to your brother, to your needy and poor in your land.'

12 "[a]If your kinsman, a Hebrew man or woman, is sold to you, then he shall serve you six years, but in the seventh year you shall set him free.

13 "And when you set him free, you shall not send him away empty-handed.

14 "You shall furnish him liberally from your flock and from your threshing floor and from your wine vat; you shall give to him as the LORD your God has blessed you.

15 "And you shall remember that you were a slave in the land of Egypt, and the LORD your God redeemed you; therefore I command you this today.

16 "And it shall come about [a]if he says to you, 'I will not go out

from you,' because he loves you and your household, since he fares well with you;

17 then you shall take an awl and pierce it through his ear into the door, and he shall be your servant forever. And also you shall do likewise to your maidservant.

18 "It shall not seem hard to you when you set him free, for he has given you six years *with* double the service of a hired man; so the LORD your God will bless you in whatever you do.

19 "[a]You shall consecrate to the LORD your God all the first-born males that are born of your herd and of your flock; you shall not work with the first-born of your herd, nor shear the first-born of your flock.

20 "[a]You and your household shall eat it every year before the LORD your God in the place which the LORD chooses.

21 "[a]But if it has any defect, *such as* lameness or blindness, *or* any serious defect, you shall not sacrifice it to the LORD your God.

22 "You shall eat it within your gates; [a]the unclean and the clean alike *may eat it*, as [a]a gazelle or a deer.

23 "Only [a]you shall not eat its blood; you are to pour it out on the ground like water.

F Commands Concerning Festivals, 16:1-17

16 "Observe [a]the month of Abib and [b]celebrate the Passover to the LORD your God, for in the month of Abib the LORD your God brought you out of Egypt by night.

2 "And you shall sacrifice the Passover to the LORD your God

---

8 [a]Matt. 5:42; Luke 6:34; Gal. 2:10

★ **9** [a]Deut. 15:1 [b]Matt. 20:15 [c]Ex. 22:23; Deut. 24:15; Job 34:28; Ps. 12:5; James 5:4

10 [a]Deut. 14:29; Ps. 41:1; Prov. 22:9

11 [a]Matt. 26:11; Mark 14:7; John 12:8

★**12-18**

12 [a]Ex. 21:2-6; Lev. 25:39-43; Jer. 34:14

16 [a]Ex. 21:5, 6

★**19-22**

19 [a]Ex. 13:2, 12

20 [a]Lev. 7:15-18; Deut. 12:5; 14:23

21 [a]Lev. 22:19-25; Deut. 17:1

22 [a]Deut. 12:15, 16, 22

23 [a]Gen. 9:4; Lev. 7:26; 17:10; 19:26; Deut. 12:16, 23

★ **1-17**

1 [a]Ex. 12:2 [b]Num. 28:16

15:9 It was a *sin* to refuse to help the poor just because the seventh year was at hand when the debt would be canceled.

15:12-18 See note on Exod. 21:1-6.

15:19-22 Firstborn of the animals belonged to the Lord; however, to be accepted they had to be without blemish (cf. Exod. 22:29; Num. 18:17-18; Mal. 1:8).

16:1-17 These verses give instructions concerning the three annual pilgrimages that men were to make to the central sanctuary (see note on Exod. 23:14-17): Passover and Unleavened Bread (Deut. 16:1-8, see notes on Exod. 12); Weeks or Pentecost (Deut. 16:9-12, see note on Lev. 23:15-23); and Tabernacles (Deut. 16:13-15, see note on Lev. 23:34-43).

from the flock and the herd, in the place where the LORD chooses to establish His name.

3 "ªYou shall not eat leavened bread with it; seven days you shall eat with it unleavened bread, the bread of affliction (for you came out of the land of Egypt in haste), in order that you may remember ᵇall the days of your life the day when you came out of the land of Egypt.

4 "For seven days no leaven shall be seen with you in all your territory, and ªnone of the flesh which you sacrifice on the evening of the first day shall remain overnight until morning.

5 "You are not allowed to sacrifice the Passover in any of your towns which the LORD your God is giving you;

6 but ªat the place where the LORD your God chooses to establish His name, you shall sacrifice the Passover in the evening at sunset, at the time that you came out of Egypt.

7 "And you shall ªcook and eat *it* in the place which the LORD your God chooses. And in the morning you are to return to your tents.

8 "Six days you shall eat unleavened bread, and ªon the seventh day there shall be ᵇa solemn assembly to the LORD your God; you shall do no work *on it.*

9 "ªYou shall count seven weeks for yourself; you shall begin to count seven weeks from the time you begin to put the sickle to the standing grain.

10 "Then you shall celebrate the Feast of Weeks to the LORD your God with a tribute of a freewill offering of your hand, which you shall give just as the LORD your God blesses you;

11 and you shall ªrejoice before the LORD your God, you and your son and your daughter and your male and female servants and ᵇthe Levite who is in your

town, and ᶜthe stranger and the orphan and the widow who are in your midst, in the place where the LORD your God chooses to establish His name.

12 "And ªyou shall remember that you were a slave in Egypt, and you shall be careful to observe these statutes.

13 "ªYou shall celebrate the Feast of Booths seven days after you have gathered in from your threshing floor and your wine vat;

14 and you shall ªrejoice in your feast, you and your son and your daughter and your male and female servants and the Levite and the stranger and the orphan and the widow who are in your towns.

15 "Seven days you shall celebrate a feast to the LORD your God in the place which the LORD chooses, because the LORD your God will bless you in all your produce and in all the work of your hands, so that you shall be altogether joyful.

16 "ªThree times in a year all your males shall appear before the LORD your God in the place which He chooses, at the Feast of Unleavened Bread and at the Feast of Weeks and at the Feast of Booths, and ᵇthey shall not appear before the LORD empty-handed.

17 "Every man shall give as he is able, according to the blessing of the LORD your God which He has given you.

G   Commands Concerning Leaders, 16:18–18:22

1   *Judges,* 16:18–17:13

18 "You shall appoint for yourself judges and officers in all your towns which the LORD your God is giving you, according to your tribes, and they shall judge the people with righteous judgment.

---

3 ªEx. 12:8, 15, 19, 39; 13:3; 34:18 ᵇDeut. 4:9

4 ªEx. 12:8, 10; 34:25

6 ªDeut. 12:5

7 ªEx. 12:8; 2 Chr. 35:13

8 ªNum. 28:25 ᵇEx. 12:16; 13:6; Lev. 23:8, 36

9 ªEx. 23:16; 34:22; Lev. 23:15; Num. 28:26

11 ªDeut. 12:7 ᵇDeut. 12:12 ᶜDeut. 14:29

12 ªDeut. 15:15

13 ªLev. 23:34-43

14 ªDeut. 16:11

16 ªEx. 23:14-17; 34:23, 24 ᵇEx. 34:20

*18

16:18 *officers.* Baliffs who assisted in executing   the sentences of the *judges.*

19 aEx. 23:2; Lev. 19:15; Deut. 1:17; 10:17 bProv. 24:23 cEx. 23:8; Prov. 17:23; Eccl. 7:7

19 "aYou shall not distort justice; byou shall not be partial, and cyou shall not take a bribe, for a bribe blinds the eyes of the wise and perverts the words of the righteous.

20 aDeut. 4:1

20 "Justice, *and only* justice, you shall pursue, that ayou may live and possess the land which the LORD your God is giving you.

★21 aDeut. 7:5; 2 Kin. 17:16; 21:3; 2 Chr. 33:3

★**21** "aYou shall not plant for yourself an Asherah of any kind of tree beside the altar of the LORD your God, which you shall make for yourself.

22 aLev. 26:1

22 "aNeither shall you set up for yourself a *sacred* pillar which the LORD your God hates.

1 aDeut. 15:21

17 "aYou shall not sacrifice to the LORD your God an ox or a sheep which has a blemish or any defect, for that is a detestable thing to the LORD your God.

2 aDeut. 13:6-11

2 "aIf there is found in your midst, in any of your towns, which the LORD your God is giving you, a man or a woman who does what is evil in the sight of the LORD your God, by transgressing His covenant,

★ 3 aEx. 22:20 bJob 31:26-28 cJer. 7:22

3 and has gone and aserved other gods and worshiped them, bor the sun or the moon or any of the heavenly host, cwhich I have not commanded,

4 and if it is told you and you have heard of it, then you shall inquire thoroughly. And behold, if it is true and the thing certain that this detestable thing has been done in Israel,

5 aLev. 24:14; Josh. 7:25

5 then you shall bring out that man or that woman who has done this evil deed, to your gates, *that is*, the man or the woman, and ayou shall stone them to death.

6 "aOn the evidence of two witnesses or three witnesses, he who is to die shall be put to death; he shall not be put to death on the evidence of one witness.

7 "aThe hand of the witnesses shall be first against him to put him to death, and afterward the hand of all the people. bSo you shall purge the evil from your midst.

8 "aIf any case is too difficult for you to decide, between one kind of homicide or another, between one kind of lawsuit or another, and between one kind of assault or another, being cases of dispute in your courts, then you shall arise and go up to bthe place which the LORD your God chooses.

9 "So you shall come to athe Levitical priest or the judge who is *in office* in those days, and you shall inquire *of them*, and they will declare to you the verdict in the case.

10 "And you shall do according to the terms of the verdict which they declare to you from that place which the LORD chooses; and you shall be careful to observe according to all that they teach you.

11 "aAccording to the terms of the law which they teach you, and according to the verdict which they tell you, you shall do; you shall not turn aside from the word which they declare to you, to the right or the left.

12 "And the man who acts apresumptuously by not listening to the priest who stands there to serve the LORD your God, nor to the judge, that man shall die; thus you shall purge the evil from Israel.

★ 6-7

6 aNum. 35:30; Deut. 19:15; Matt. 18:16; John 8:17; 2 Cor. 13:1; 1 Tim. 5:19; Heb. 10:28

7 aLev. 24:14; Deut. 13:9 b1 Cor. 5:13

★ 8-13

8 a2 Chr. 19:10; Hag. 2:11 bDeut. 12:5; Ps. 122:5

9 aDeut. 19:17

11 aDeut. 25:1

12 aNum. 15:30; Deut. 1:43; 17:13; 18:20; Hos. 4:4

16:21 *Asherah.* See note on 7:5.

17:3 On the worship of the stars, see note on 4:19.

17:6-7 A minimum of two witnesses was required, and they had to be sure enough of their own testimony to be willing to cast the first stones. In a stoning, the victim was stripped naked and his hands bound; then he was paraded out of town, where he was placed on a scaffold about nine feet high. The first

witness pushed him off the scaffold; the second dropped a large stone on his head or chest. Then bystanders pelted the dying man with stones. No mourning was permitted for the dead man.

17:8-13 Any case (v. 8) that proved too difficult for the local court to decide was taken to the priests and judges at the central sanctuary. Their decisions were binding.

13 aDeut. 17:12

13 "Then all the people will hear and be afraid, and will not act apresumptuously again.

2 Kings, 17:14-20

★**14** aDeut. 11:31; Josh. 21:43
b1 Sam. 8:5, 19, 20; 10:19

14 "When you enter the land which the LORD your God gives you, and you apossess it and live in it, and you say, 'bI will set a king over me like all the nations who are around me,'

★**15-20**

15 aJer. 30:21

15 you shall surely set a king over you whom the LORD your God chooses, one afrom among your countrymen you shall set as king over yourselves; you may not put a foreigner over yourselves who is not your countryman.

16 a1 Kin. 4:26; 10:26-29; Ps. 20:7
bIs. 31:1; Ezek. 17:15
cEx. 13:17, 18; Hos. 11:5

16 "aMoreover, he shall not multiply horses for himself, nor shall he bcause the people to return to Egypt to multiply horses, since cthe LORD has said to you, 'You shall never again return that way.'

17 a2 Sam. 5:13; 12:11; 1 Kin. 11:3, 4

17 "aNeither shall he multiply wives for himself, lest his heart turn away; nor shall he greatly increase silver and gold for himself.

18 aDeut. 31:24-26

18 "Now it shall come about when he sits on the throne of his kingdom, he shall write for himself a copy of this law on a scroll ain the presence of the Levitical priests.

19 aDeut. 4:9, 10; Josh. 1:8

19 "And it shall be with him, and he shall read it aall the days of his life, that he may learn to fear the LORD his God, by carefully observing all the words of this law and these statutes,

20 aDeut. 5:32; 1 Kin. 15:5

20 that his heart may not be lifted up above his countrymen aand that he may not turn aside from the commandment, to the right or the left; in order that he

and his sons may continue long in his kingdom in the midst of Israel.

3 Levites, 18:1-8

★**1** aDeut. 10:9; 1 Cor. 9:13

18 "aThe Levitical priests, the whole tribe of Levi, shall have no portion or inheritance with Israel; they shall eat the LORD's offerings by fire and His portion.

2 aNum. 18:20

2 "aAnd they shall have no inheritance among their countrymen; the LORD is their inheritance, as He promised them.

3 aLev. 7:32-34; Num. 18:11, 12

3 "aNow this shall be the priests' due from the people, from those who offer a sacrifice, either an ox or a sheep, of which they shall give to the priest the shoulder and the two cheeks and the stomach.

4 aNum. 18:12

4 "You shall give him the afirst fruits of your grain, your new wine, and your oil, and the first shearing of your sheep.

5 aEx. 29:9
bDeut. 10:8

5 "aFor the LORD your God has chosen him and his sons from all your tribes, to bstand and serve in the name of the LORD forever.

★ **6-8**

6 aNum. 35:2, 3

6 "Now if a Levite comes from any of your towns throughout Israel where he aresides, and comes whenever he desires to the place which the LORD chooses,

7 then he shall serve in the name of the LORD his God, like all his fellow Levites who stand there before the LORD.

8 aLev. 27:30-33; Num. 18:21-24; 2 Chr. 31:4; Neh. 12:44

8 "aThey shall eat equal portions, except *what they receive* from the sale of their fathers' *estates.*

4 False Diviners, 18:9-14

9 aDeut. 9:5

9 "When you enter the land which the LORD your God gives you, you shall not learn to aimi-

---

17:14 The Israelites did this very thing (1 Sam. 8:5).

17:15-20 In the future, the king was (1) to be chosen by God, (2) to be an Israelite, (3) not to imitate royal courts of other nations in his desire for horses, wives, and money (cf. 1 Kings 10:28–11:4), (4) to have a copy of the Law (the original was deposited in the central sanctuary, cf. Deut. 31:9) and obey it.

18:1 *The Levitical priests* were the special class of qualified ministering priests chosen from among the *whole tribe of Levi.* Their portion of the offerings is assigned in verses 3–5.

18:6-8 If a *Levite* decided to serve at the central sanctuary, he had a right to his share of work and remuneration. He could also keep anything received from the sale of property at home (see also Lev. 25:33).

tate the detestable things of those nations.

★10-11

10 aDeut.
12:31 bEx.
22:18; Lev.
19:26, 31;
20:6; Jer.
27:9, 10;
Mal. 3:5

10 "There shall not be found among you anyone awho makes his son or his daughter pass through the fire, one who uses divination, one bwho practices witchcraft, or one who interprets omens, or a sorcerer,

11 aLev.
19:31

11 or one who casts a spell, aor a medium, or a spiritist, or one who calls up the dead.

12 aLev.
18:24

12 "For whoever does these things is detestable to the LORD; and abecause of these detestable things the LORD your God will drive them out before you.

13 aGen.
6:9; 17:1;
Matt. 5:48

13 "aYou shall be blameless before the LORD your God.

14 a2 Kin.
21:6

14 "For those nations, which you shall dispossess, listen to those who apractice witchcraft and to diviners, but as for you, the LORD your God has not allowed you to do so.

5 Messiah, 18:15-19

★15 aMatt.
21:11; Luke
2:25-34;
7:16; 24:19;
John 1:21,
25; 4:19;
Acts 3:22;
7:37

15 "aThe LORD your God will raise up for you a prophet like me from among you, from your countrymen, you shall listen to him.

16 aEx.
20:18, 19;
Deut. 5:23-
27

16 "This is aaccording to all that you asked of the LORD your God in Horeb on the day of the assembly, saying, 'Let me not hear again the voice of the LORD my God, let me not see this great fire anymore, lest I die.'

17 aDeut.
5:28

17 "aAnd the LORD said to me, 'They have spoken well.

18 aIs.
51:16; John
17:8 bJohn
4:25; 8:28;
12:49, 50

18 'I will raise up a prophet from among their countrymen like you, and aI will put My words

in his mouth, and bhe shall speak to them all that I command him.

19 aActs
3:23; Heb.
12:25

19 'aAnd it shall come about that whoever will not listen to My words which he shall speak in My name, I Myself will require it of him.

6 Prophets, 18:20-22

★20 aDeut.
13:5; 17:12
bDeut. 13:1,
2; Jer. 14:14;
Zech. 13:3

20 'But the prophet who shall speak a word apresumptuously in My name which I have not commanded him to speak, or bwhich he shall speak in the name of other gods, that prophet shall die.'

21 "And you may say in your heart, 'How shall we know the word which the LORD has not spoken?'

22 aJer. 28:9
bDeut. 18:20

22 "aWhen a prophet speaks in the name of the LORD, if the thing does not come about or come true, that is the thing which the LORD has not spoken. The prophet has spoken it bpresumptuously; you shall not be afraid of him.

H Commands Concerning Human Relationships, 19:1-26:19

1 The cities of refuge, 19:1-13

1 aDeut.
6:10, 11

19 "aWhen the LORD your God cuts off the nations, whose land the LORD your God gives you, and you dispossess them and settle in their cities and in their houses,

★ 2 aDeut.
4:41; Josh.
20:2

2 ayou shall set aside three cities for yourself in the midst of your land, which the LORD your God gives you to possess.

★ 3

3 "You shall prepare the roads for yourself, and divide into

18:10-11 pass through the fire. The worship of Molech sometimes involved human sacrifice in the fire. divination. A general term covering the types of magic that follow. one who practices witchcraft. The idea is that of practicing hidden arts. one who interprets omens. Balaam did this (cf. Num. 24:1). sorcerer. A practitioner of spells and occult magic. a spiritist. One who pretends to know about the unseen world.

18:15 a prophet. This role was ultimately fulfilled by Jesus of Nazareth (see note on Acts 3:22). like me. Moses was a type of Christ in

his service (Heb. 3:2) and in his office as a prophet (cf. Deut. 34:10 with Luke 24:19).

18:20 False prophets had to die (13:1-11). They would be exposed by the failure of their prophecies to come to pass (18:22). However, a prophet's prediction coming to pass did not prove he was of God (see note on 13:2).

19:2 Having already set aside three cities of refuge on the E. side of the Jordan, Moses did the same for the W. side (see notes on 4:41 and Num. 35:11).

19:3 roads. Those leading to the cities of refuge.

three parts the territory of your land, which the LORD your God will give you as a possession, so that any manslayer may flee there.

4 "ᵃNow this is the case of the manslayer who may flee there and live: when he kills his friend unintentionally, not hating him previously—

5 as when a man goes into the forest with his friend to cut wood, and his hand swings the axe to cut down the tree, and the iron head slips off the handle and strikes his friend so that he dies— he may flee to one of these cities and live;

6 lest the avenger of blood pursue the manslayer in the heat of his anger, and overtake him, because the way is long, and take his life, though he was not deserving of death, since he had not hated him previously.

7 "Therefore, I command you, saying, 'You shall set aside three cities for yourself.'

8 "And if the LORD your God ᵃenlarges your territory, just as He has sworn to your fathers, and gives you all the land which He promised to give your fathers—

9 if you carefully observe all this commandment, which I command you today, ᵃto love the LORD your God, and to walk in His ways always—ᵇthen you shall add three more cities for yourself, besides these three.

10 "So innocent blood will not be shed in the midst of your land which the LORD your God gives you as an inheritance, and ᵃbloodguiltiness be on you.

11 "But ᵃif there is a man who hates his neighbor and lies in wait for him and rises up against him

and strikes him so that he dies, and he flees to one of these cities,

12 then the elders of his city shall send and take him from there and deliver him into the hand of the avenger of blood, that he may die.

13 "ᵃYou shall not pity him, but ᵇyou shall purge the blood of the innocent from Israel, that it may go well with you.

2   The boundary mark, 19:14

14 "ᵃYou shall not move your neighbor's boundary mark, which the ancestors have set, in your inheritance which you shall inherit in the land that the LORD your God gives you to possess.

3   Witnesses, 19:15-21

15 "ᵃA single witness shall not rise up against a man on account of any iniquity or any sin which he has committed; on the evidence of two or three witnesses a matter shall be confirmed.

16 "ᵃIf a malicious witness rises up against a man to accuse him of wrongdoing,

17 then both the men who have the dispute shall stand ᵃbefore the LORD, before the priests and the judges who will be in office in those days.

18 "And the judges ᵃshall investigate thoroughly; and if the witness is a false witness and he has accused his brother falsely,

19 then ᵃyou shall do to him just as he had intended to do to his brother. Thus you shall purge the evil from among you.

20 "And ᵃthe rest will hear and be afraid, and will never again do such an evil thing among you.

Cross references (margin)

4 ᵃNum. 35:9-34

★ 6

8 ᵃGen. 15:18

★ 9 ᵃDeut. 6:5 ᵇJosh. 20:7

10 ᵃNum. 35:33; Deut. 21:1-9

11 ᵃEx. 21:12; Num. 35:16; 1 John 3:15

13 ᵃDeut. 7:2 ᵇ1 Kin. 2:31

★14 ᵃDeut. 27:17; Job 24:2; Prov. 22:28; Hos. 5:10

★15-21

15 ᵃNum. 35:30; Deut. 17:6; Matt. 18:16; John 8:17; 2 Cor. 13:1; 1 Tim. 5:19; Heb. 10:28

16 ᵃEx. 23:1; Ps. 27:12

17 ᵃDeut. 17:9

18 ᵃDeut. 25:1

19 ᵃProv. 19:5

20 ᵃDeut. 17:13; 21:21

19:6 the avenger of blood. The nearest relative of the deceased.

19:9 three more cities. In addition to the six already designated. These were never added, because Israel did not occupy all the territory promised to Abraham (cf. Gen. 15:18). David subdued and took tribute from that larger area, and Solomon inherited it (cf. 1 Kings

4:21), but it remained foreign and was soon lost.

19:14 To do this was equivalent to stealing (cf. 27:17; Job. 24:2; Prov. 22:28).

19:15-21 The requirements concerning evidence, already given for capital cases (cf. 17:6), were extended to all criminal cases. On the lex talionis (v. 21), see note on Lev. 24:20.

21 "Thus [a]you shall not show pity: [b]life for life, [c]eye for eye, tooth for tooth, hand for hand, foot for foot.

4 Warfare, 20:1-20

20 "When you go out to battle against your enemies and see [a]horses and chariots and people more numerous than you, [b]do not be afraid of them; for the LORD your God, who brought you up from the land of Egypt, is with you.

2 "Now it shall come about that when you are approaching the battle, the priest shall come near and speak to the people.

3 "And he shall say to them, 'Hear, O Israel, you are approaching the battle against your enemies today. Do not be fainthearted. [a]Do not be afraid, or panic, or tremble before them,

4 for the LORD your God [a]is the one who goes with you, to fight for you against your enemies, to save you.'

5 "The officers also shall speak to the people, saying, 'Who is the man that has built a new house and has not [a]dedicated it? Let him depart and return to his house, lest he die in the battle and another man dedicate it.

6 'And who is the man that has planted a vineyard and has not begun to use its fruit? Let him depart and return to his house, lest he die in the battle and another man begin to use its fruit.

7 '[a]And who is the man that is engaged to a woman and has not married her? Let him depart and return to his house, lest he die in the battle and another man marry her.'

8 "Then the officers shall speak further to the people, and they shall say, '[a]Who is the man that is afraid and fainthearted? Let him depart and return to his house, so that he might not make his brothers' hearts melt like his heart.'

9 "And it shall come about that when the officers have finished speaking to the people, they shall appoint commanders of armies at the head of the people.

10 "When you approach a city to fight against it, you shall offer it terms of peace.

11 "And it shall come about, if it agrees to make peace with you and opens to you, then it shall be that all the people who are found in it shall become your [a]forced labor and shall serve you.

12 "However, if it does not make peace with you, but makes war against you, then you shall besiege it.

13 "When the LORD your God gives it into your hand, [a]you shall strike all the men in it with the edge of the sword.

14 "Only the women and the children and [a]the animals and all that is in the city, all its spoil, you shall take as booty for yourself; and you shall use the spoil of your enemies which the LORD your God has given you.

15 "Thus you shall do to all the cities that are very far from you, which are not of the cities of these nations nearby.

16 "[a]Only in the cities of these peoples that the LORD your God is giving you as an inheritance, you shall not leave alive anything that breathes.

17 "But you shall utterly destroy them, the Hittite and the Amorite, the Canaanite and the Perizzite, the Hivite and the Jebusite, as the LORD your God has commanded you,

18 in order that they may not teach you to do [a]according to all their detestable things which they

21 [a]Deut. 19:13 [b]Ex. 21:23; Lev. 24:20 [c]Matt. 5:38

★ **1** [a]Deut. 3:22; 7:18; 31:6, 8; Ps. 20:7; Is. 31:1 [b]2 Chr. 32:7, 8; Ps. 23:4; Is. 41:10

3 [a]Deut. 20:1; Josh. 23:10

4 [a]Deut. 1:30; 3:22; Josh. 23:10

★ **5-9**

5 [a]Neh. 12:27

7 [a]Deut. 24:5

8 [a]Judg. 7:3

★**10-15**

11 [a]1 Kin. 9:21

13 [a]Num. 31:7

14 [a]Josh. 8:2

★**16-18**

16 [a]Ex. 23:31-33; Num. 21:2, 3; Deut. 7:1-5; Josh. 11:14

18 [a]Ex. 34:12-16; Deut. 7:4; 9:5; 12:30, 31 [b]Ex. 23:33; 2 Kin. 21:3-15; Ps. 106:34-41

20:1 Moses often used the deliverance from Egypt to encourage noble purposes in the lives of the Israelites (see also 4:20; 5:15; 6:12; 8:14; 10:19; 11:2-3; 24:18, 22; 26:5, 8).

20:5-9 These exemptions helped insure that victory would be ascribed to the Lord (cf. v. 4)

and showed that military matters were not paramount. On verse 8, see Judg. 7:2-3.

20:10-15 This procedure applied only to cities outside of Canaan.

20:16-18 Canaanite cities had to be utterly destroyed (see note on 7:2).

have done for their gods, so that you would [b]sin against the Lord your God.

19 "When you besiege a city a long time, to make war against it in order to capture it, you shall not destroy its trees by swinging an axe against them; for you may eat from them, and you shall not cut them down. For is the tree of the field a man, that it should be besieged by you?

[*20] **20** "Only the trees which you know are not fruit trees you shall destroy and cut down, that you may construct siegeworks against the city that is making war with you until it falls.

5 Manslaughter, 21:1-9

[* 1-9]
21 "If a slain person is found lying in the open country in the land which the Lord your God gives you to possess, *and* it is not known who has struck him,

2 then your elders and your judges shall go out and measure *the distance* to the cities which are around the slain one.

3 "And it shall be that the city which is nearest to the slain man, that is, the elders of that city, shall take a heifer of the herd, which has not been worked and which has not pulled in a yoke;

4 and the elders of that city shall bring the heifer down to a valley with running water, which has not been plowed or sown, and shall break the heifer's neck there in the valley.

[5 aDeut. 17:9-11; 19:17; 1 Chr. 23:13] **5** "Then [a]the priests, the sons of Levi, shall come near, for the Lord your God has chosen them to serve Him and to bless in the name of the Lord; and every dispute and every assault shall be settled by them.

[6 aMatt. 27:24] **6** "And all the elders of that city which is nearest to the slain

man shall [a]wash their hands over the heifer whose neck was broken in the valley;

7 and they shall answer and say, 'Our hands have not shed this blood, nor did our eyes see *it.*

8 'Forgive Thy people Israel whom Thou hast redeemed, O Lord, and do not place the guilt of [a]innocent blood in the midst of Thy people Israel.' And the bloodguiltiness shall be forgiven them. [★ 8 aNum. 35:33, 34; Jon. 1:14]

9 "[a]So you shall remove the guilt of innocent blood from your midst, when you do what is right in the eyes of the Lord. [9 aDeut. 19:13]

6 Marriage and family life, 21:10-22:30

10 "When you go out to battle against your enemies, and [a]the Lord your God delivers them into your hands, and you take them away captive, [10 aJosh. 21:44]

11 and see among the captives a beautiful woman, and have a desire for her and would take her as a wife for yourself,

12 then you shall bring her home to your house, and she shall [a]shave her head and trim her nails. [12 aLev. 14:8, 9; Num. 6:9]

13 "She shall also remove the clothes of her captivity and shall remain in your house, and [a]mourn her father and mother a full month; and after that you may go in to her and be her husband and she shall be your wife. [13 aPs. 45:10]

14 "And it shall be, if you are not pleased with her, then you shall let her go wherever she wishes; but you shall certainly not sell her for money, you shall not mistreat her, because you have [a]humbled her. [★14 aGen. 34:2]

15 "If a man has two wives, the one loved and [a]the other unloved, and *both* the loved and the [★15 aGen. 29:33]

20:20 Fruit-bearing trees were to be spared in a siege.

21:1-9 In the event of undetected homicide in the open countryside, the elders of the nearest city had to make atonement according to this prescribed ritual, under the jurisdiction of the priests.

21:8 *forgiven.* Apparently the city incurred guilt by not making nearby roads safe for travel.

21:14 *let her go.* This assumes granting a divorce according to 24:1-4.

21:15 *unloved.* Relatively speaking, in comparison to the other wife.

unloved have borne him sons, if the first-born son belongs to the unloved,

16 then it shall be in the day he wills what he has to his sons, he cannot make the son of the loved the first-born before the son of the unloved, who is the first-born.

17 "But he shall acknowledge the first-born, the son of the unloved, by giving him a double portion of all that he has, for he is the ᵃbeginning of his strength; ᵇto him belongs the right of the first-born.

18 "If any man has a stubborn and rebellious son who will ᵃnot obey his father or his mother, and when they chastise him, he will not even listen to them,

19 then his father and mother shall seize him, and bring him out to the elders of his city at the gateway of his home town.

20 "And they shall say to the elders of his city, 'This son of ours is stubborn and rebellious, he will not obey us, he is a glutton and a drunkard.'

21 "ᵃThen all the men of his city shall stone him to death; so ᵇyou shall remove the evil from your midst, and ᶜall Israel shall hear of it and fear.

22 "And if a man has committed a sin ᵃworthy of death, and he is put to death, and you hang him on a tree,

23 ᵃhis corpse shall not hang all night on the tree, but you shall surely bury him on the same day (for ᵇhe who is hanged is accursed of God), so that you ᶜdo not defile your land which the LORD your God gives you as an inheritance.

22 "ᵃYou shall not see your countryman's ox or his sheep straying away, and pay no attention to them; you shall certainly bring them back to your countryman.

2 "And if your countryman is not near you, or if you do not know him, then you shall bring it home to your house, and it shall remain with you until your countryman looks for it; then you shall restore it to him.

3 "And thus you shall do with his donkey, and you shall do the same with his garment, and you shall do likewise with anything lost by your countryman, which he has lost and you have found. You are not allowed to neglect *them*.

4 "You shall not see your countryman's donkey or his ox fallen down on the way, and pay no attention to them; you shall certainly help him to raise *them* up.

5 "A woman shall not wear man's clothing, nor shall a man put on a woman's clothing; for whoever does these things is an abomination to the LORD your God.

6 "If you happen to come upon a bird's nest along the way, in any tree or on the ground, with young ones or eggs, and the mother sitting on the young or on the eggs, ᵃyou shall not take the mother with the young;

7 you shall certainly let the mother go, but the young you may take for yourself, ᵃin order that it may be well with you, and that you may prolong your days.

8 "When you build a new house, you shall make a parapet

★17 ᵃGen. 49:3 ᵇGen. 25:31

★18-21

18 ᵃEx. 20:12; Lev. 19:3; Prov. 1:8; Eph. 6:1-3

21 ᵃLev. 20:2, 27; 24:14-23; Num. 15:25, 36 ᵇDeut. 19:19 ᶜDeut. 13:11

★22-23

22 ᵃDeut. 22:26; Matt. 26:66; Mark 14:64; Acts 23:29

23 ᵃJosh. 8:29; 10:26, 27; John 19:31 ᵇGal. 3:13 ᶜLev. 18:25; Num. 35:34

1 ᵃEx. 23:4, 5; Prov. 27:10; Zech. 7:9

★5

6 ᵃLev. 22:28

7 ᵃDeut. 4:40

★8

21:17 The firstborn received a double share of the father's estate (cf. Gen. 48:22; 1 Chron. 5:1).

21:18-21 An example of rebellion was given in 13:6-11. Anarchy in the home breeds anarchy in society; that is why this was such a serious matter. However, the elders were the final authority, not the father. According to Jewish tradition, this punishment was never carried out, though it was a strong deterrent to juvenile delinquency!

21:22-23 Hanging was not the usual means of death but a sequel to death, in order to expose the corpse to ultimate disgrace (see note on Gal. 3:13).

22:5 In that society male and female dress were similar, making distinctive styles for the sexes especially important.

22:8 *parapet.* A wall to keep anyone on the flat roof from falling off.

for your roof, that you may not bring bloodguilt on your house if anyone falls from it.

9 "ᵃYou shall not sow your vineyard with two kinds of seed, lest all the produce of the seed which you have sown, and the increase of the vineyard become defiled.

10 "ᵃYou shall not plow with an ox and a donkey together.

11 "ᵃYou shall not wear a material mixed of wool and linen together.

12 "ᵃYou shall make yourself tassels on the four corners of your garment with which you cover yourself.

13 "ᵃIf any man takes a wife and goes in to her and *then* turns against her,

14 and charges her with shameful deeds and publicly defames her, and says, 'I took this woman, *but* when I came near her, I did not find her a virgin,'

15 then the girl's father and her mother shall take and bring out the *evidence* of the girl's virginity to the elders of the city at the gate.

16 "And the girl's father shall say to the elders, 'I gave my daughter to this man for a wife, but he turned against her;

17 and behold, he has charged her with shameful deeds, saying, "I did not find your daughter a virgin." But this is the *evidence* of my daughter's virginity.' And they shall spread the garment before the elders of the city.

18 "So ᵃthe elders of that city shall take the man and chastise him,

19 and they shall fine him a hundred *shekels* of silver and give it to the girl's father, because he

publicly defamed a virgin of Israel. And she shall remain his wife; he cannot divorce her all his days.

20 "But if this ᵃcharge is true, that the girl was not found a virgin,

21 then they shall bring out the girl to the doorway of her father's house, and the men of her city shall stone her to death because she has ᵃcommitted an act of folly in Israel, by playing the harlot in her father's house; thus ᵇyou shall purge the evil from among you.

22 "ᵃIf a man is found lying with a married woman, then both of them shall die, the man who lay with the woman, and the woman; thus you shall purge the evil from Israel.

23 "ᵃIf there is a girl who is a virgin engaged to a man, and *another* man finds her in the city and lies with her,

24 then you shall bring them both out to the gate of that city and you shall stone them to death; the girl, because she did not cry out in the city, and the man, because he has violated his neighbor's wife. Thus you shall purge the evil from among you.

25 "But if in the field the man finds the girl who is engaged, and the man forces her and lies with her, then only the man who lies with her shall die.

26 "But you shall do nothing to the girl; there is no sin in the girl worthy of death, for just as a man rises against his neighbor and murders him, so is this case.

27 "When he found her in the field, the engaged girl cried out, but there was no one to save her.

28 "ᵃIf a man finds a girl who is a virgin, who is not engaged,

---

9 ᵃLev. 19:19

★10 ᵃ2 Cor. 6:14-16

★11 ᵃLev. 19:19

★12 ᵃNum. 15:37-41; Matt. 23:5

13 ᵃGen. 29:21; Deut. 24:1; Judg. 15:1

★18 ᵃEx. 18:21; Deut. 1:9-18

★19

20 ᵃDeut. 17:4

21 ᵃGen. 34:7; Lev. 19:29; 21:9; Deut. 23:17, 18; Judg. 20:5-10; 2 Sam. 13:12, 13 ᵇDeut. 13:5; 17:7; 19:19

22 ᵃLev. 20:10; Ezek. 16:38; Matt. 5:27, 28; John 8:5; 1 Cor. 6:9; Heb. 13:4

★23 ᵃLev. 19:20-22; Matt. 1:18, 19

★25-27

★28-29
28 ᵃEx. 22:16

22:10 The step and pull of the two beasts is unequal.
22:11 It is said that idolatrous priests wore garments of this mixture, thinking it to be magical.
22:12 See note on Num. 15:37.
22:18 *chastise him* by whipping him with 40 stripes (cf. 25:3).

22:19 The fine was equivalent to about 50 oz. of silver.
22:23 Betrothal was considered equally as binding as marriage.
22:25-27 Rape of a betrothed girl demanded the death of the man involved.
22:28-29 Rape of a virgin obliged the man to marry her.

and seizes her and lies with her and they are discovered,

29 then the man who lay with her shall give to the girl's father fifty *shekels* of silver, and she shall become his wife because he has violated her; he cannot divorce her all his days.

30 "[a]A man shall not take his father's wife so that he shall not uncover his father's skirt.

7 *The congregation, 23:1-18*

23 "[a]No one who is emasculated, or has his male organ cut off, shall enter the assembly of the LORD.

2 "No one of illegitimate birth shall enter the assembly of the LORD; none of his *descendants,* even to the tenth generation, shall enter the assembly of the LORD.

3 "[a]No Ammonite or Moabite shall enter the assembly of the LORD; none of their *descendants,* even to the tenth generation, shall ever enter the assembly of the LORD,

4 [a]because they did not meet you with food and water on the way when you came out of Egypt, and because they hired against you [b]Balaam the son of Beor from Pethor of Mesopotamia, to curse you.

5 "Nevertheless, the LORD your God was not willing to listen to Balaam, but the LORD your God [a]turned the curse into a blessing for you because the LORD your God [b]loves you.

6 "[a]You shall never seek their peace or their prosperity all your days.

7 "You shall not detest an Edomite, for [a]he is your brother; you shall not detest an Egyptian, [b]because you were an alien in his land.

8 "The sons of the third generation who are born to them may enter the assembly of the LORD.

9 "When you go out as an army against your enemies, then you shall keep yourself from every evil thing.

10 "[a]If there is among you any man who is unclean because of a nocturnal emission, then he must go outside the camp; he may not reenter the camp.

11 "But it shall be when evening approaches, he shall bathe himself with water, and at sundown he may reenter the camp.

12 "You shall also have a place outside the camp and go out there,

13 and you shall have a spade among your tools, and it shall be when you sit down outside, you shall dig with it and shall turn to cover up your excrement.

14 "Since [a]the LORD your God walks in the midst of your camp to deliver you and to defeat your enemies before you, therefore your camp must be [b]holy; and He must not see anything indecent among you lest He turn away from you.

15 "[a]You shall not hand over to his master a slave who has escaped from his master to you.

16 "He shall live with you in your midst, in the place which he shall choose in one of your towns where it pleases him; [a]you shall not mistreat him.

17 "[a]None of the daughters of

Cross-references (margin)

★**30** [a]Lev. 18:8; 20:11; Deut. 27:20; 1 Cor. 5:1

★ **1** [a]Lev. 21:20; 22:24

★ **3-6**

3 [a]Neh. 13:1, 2

4 [a]Neh. 13:2 [b]Num. 22:5; 23:7; Josh. 24:9; 2 Pet. 2:15; Jude 11

5 [a]Prov. 26:2 [b]Deut. 4:37

6 [a]Ezra 9:12

★ **7** [a]Gen. 25:24-26; Obad. 10, 12 [b]Ex. 22:21; 23:9; Lev. 19:34; Deut. 10:19

10 [a]Lev. 15:16

★**13**

14 [a]Lev. 26:12 [b]Ex. 3:5

★**15-16**

15 [a]1 Sam. 30:15

16 [a]Ex. 22:21; Prov. 22:22

★**17** [a]Lev. 19:29; Deut. 22:21 [b]Gen. 19:5; 2 Kin. 23:7

22:30 Marrying one's stepmother was prohibited (see notes on Lev. 18:6 and 18:8).

23:1 This restriction concerning emasculated persons and eunuchs was perhaps partially designed to prevent the copying of certain heathen practices.

23:3-6 The masculine forms indicate that a male *Ammonite or Moabite* is meant. Female proselytes, like Ruth of Moab, could marry male Israelites.

23:7 The Edomites descended from Esau, the *brother* of Jacob (see notes on Gen. 25:22 and Introduction to Obadiah).

23:13 This important sanitary rule related to the army on maneuvers.

23:15-16 This regulation refers to a non-Israelite slave fleeing from a cruel Canaanite master.

23:17 Both female and male cult prostitutes were common in Canaanite religion.

Israel shall be a cult prostitute, [b]nor shall any of the sons of Israel be a cult prostitute.

★18 [a]Lev. 18:22; 20:13

18 "You shall not bring the hire of a harlot or the wages of a [a]dog into the house of the LORD your God for any votive offering, for both of these are an abomination to the LORD your God.

8 Protection for the weak, 23:19–25:19

19 [a]Ex. 22:25; Lev. 25:35-37; Neh. 5:2-7; Ps. 15:5

19 "[a]You shall not charge interest to your countrymen: interest on money, food, or anything that may be loaned at interest.

20 [a]Deut. 28:12 [b]Deut. 15:10

20 "[a]You may charge interest to a foreigner, but to your countryman you shall not charge interest, so that [b]the LORD your God may bless you in all that you undertake in the land which you are about to enter to possess.

21 [a]Num. 30:1, 2; Job 22:27; Ps. 61:8; Eccl. 5:4, 5; Matt. 5:33

21 "[a]When you make a vow to the LORD your God, you shall not delay to pay it, for it would be sin in you, and the LORD your God will surely require it of you.

22 "However, if you refrain from vowing, it would not be sin in you.

23 "You shall be careful to perform what goes out from your lips, just as you have voluntarily vowed to the LORD your God, what you have promised.

★24-25

24 "When you enter your neighbor's vineyard, then you may eat grapes until you are fully satisfied, but you shall not put any in your basket.

25 [a]Matt. 12:1; Mark 2:23; Luke 6:1

25 "[a]When you enter your neighbor's standing grain, then you may pluck the heads with your hand, but you shall not wield a sickle in your neighbor's standing grain.

24 "When a man takes a wife and marries her, and it happens that she finds no favor in his eyes because he has found some [a]indecency in her, and [b]he writes her a certificate of divorce and puts it in her hand and sends her out from his house,

★ 1-4

1 [a]Num. 5:12, 28; Deut. 22:13-21 [b]Matt. 5:31; 19:7-9; Mark 10:4, 5

2 and she leaves his house and goes and becomes another man's wife,

3 and if the latter husband turns against her and writes her a certificate of divorce and puts it in her hand and sends her out of his house, or if the latter husband dies who took her to be his wife,

4 then her [a]former husband who sent her away is not allowed to take her again to be his wife, since she has been defiled; for that is an abomination before the LORD, and you shall not bring sin on the land which the LORD your God gives you as an inheritance.

4 [a]Jer. 3:1

5 "[a]When a man takes a new wife, he shall not go out with the army, nor be charged with any duty; he shall be free at home one year and shall [b]give happiness to his wife whom he has taken.

5 [a]Deut. 20:7 [b]Prov. 5:18

6 "No one shall take a hand-mill or an upper millstone in pledge, for he would be taking a life in pledge.

★ 6

7 "[a]If a man is caught kidnapping any of his countrymen of the sons of Israel, and he deals with him violently, or sells him, then that thief shall die; so you shall purge the evil from among you.

7 [a]Ex. 21:16

23:18 *dog.* A Hebrew epithet for a male prostitute or sodomite.

23:24-25 This liberty, which allowed a man to take from his neighbor's vineyard or field what he needed to eat, was kept from becoming license by prohibiting him from carrying anything away. See note on Matt. 12:2.

24:1-4 The meaning of this central O.T. passage on divorce is this: if the events of verses 1-3 take place (i.e., a woman is divorced from her first husband and marries a second one who also divorces her or dies), then the restriction of verse 4 applies (i.e., her first husband cannot remarry her). The passage cannot be construed as commanding divorce, only as regulating an existing practice. See notes on Matt. 19:3-11. *indecency.* Apparently this meant some repulsive or indecent exposure, rather than adultery (for which there was a test, Num. 5:11-31).

24:6 If either stone were removed, then grain necessary for daily food could not be ground (see note on Matt. 18:6).

★ 8 aLev.
13:1-14, 57

8 "aBe careful against an infection of leprosy, that you diligently observe and do according to all that the Levitical priests shall teach you; as I have commanded them, so you shall be careful to do.

9 aNum.
12:10

9 "Remember what the Lord your God did ato Miriam on the way as you came out of Egypt.

★10-13

10 aEx.
22:26, 27

10 "aWhen you make your neighbor a loan of any sort, you shall not enter his house to take his pledge.

11 "You shall remain outside, and the man to whom you make the loan shall bring the pledge out to you.

12 "And if he is a poor man, you shall not sleep with his pledge.

13 aEx.
22:26 bDeut.
6:25; Ps.
106:31; Dan.
4:27

13 "aWhen the sun goes down you shall surely return the pledge to him, that he may sleep in his cloak and bless you; and bit will be righteousness for you before the Lord your God.

14 aLev.
19:13; 25:35-
43; Deut.
15:7-18;
Prov. 14:31;
Amos 4:1;
1 Tim. 5:18

14 "aYou shall not oppress a hired servant *who is* poor and needy, whether *he is* one of your countrymen or one of your aliens who is in your land in your towns.

15 aLev.
19:13; Jer.
22:13; James
5:4 bEx.
22:23; Deut.
15:9; Job
35:9; James
5:4

15 "aYou shall give him his wages on his day before the sun sets, for he is poor and sets his heart on it; so that bhe may not cry against you to the Lord and it become sin in you.

16 a2 Kin.
14:6; 2 Chr.
25:4; Jer.
31:29, 30;
Ezek. 18:20

16 "aFathers shall not be put to death for *their* sons, nor shall sons be put to death for *their* fathers; everyone shall be put to death for his own sin.

17 aEx. 23:9;
Lev. 19:33;
Deut. 1:17;
10:17; 16:19;
27:19 bEx.
22:22

17 "aYou shall not pervert the justice due an alien *or* an orphan, nor btake a widow's garment in pledge.

18 "But you shall remember that you were a slave in Egypt, and that the Lord your God redeemed you from there; therefore I am commanding you to do this thing.

19 "aWhen you reap your harvest in your field and have forgotten a sheaf in the field, you shall not go back to get it; it shall be bfor the alien, for the orphan, and for the widow, in order that the Lord your God cmay bless you in all the work of your hands.

★19 aLev.
19:9, 10;
23:22 bDeut.
14:29 cProv.
19:17

20 "aWhen you beat your olive tree, you shall not go over the boughs again; it shall be bfor the alien, for the orphan, and for the widow.

20 aLev.
19:10 bDeut.
24:19

21 "When you gather the grapes of your vineyard, you shall not go over it again; it shall be for the alien, for the orphan, and for the widow.

22 "And you shall remember that you were a slave in the land of Egypt; therefore I am commanding you to do this thing.

25 "aIf there is a dispute between men and they go to court, and the judges decide their case, band they justify the righteous and condemn the wicked,

1 aDeut.
17:8-13;
19:17 bDeut.
1:16, 17

2 then it shall be if the wicked man adeserves to be beaten, the judge shall then make him lie down and be beaten in his presence with the number of stripes according to his guilt.

2 aProv.
19:29; Luke
12:48

3 "aHe may beat him forty times *but* no more, lest he beat him with many more stripes than these, and your brother be bdegraded in your eyes.

★ 3 a2 Cor.
11:24 bJob
18:3

4 "aYou shall not muzzle the ox while he is threshing.

★ 4 aProv.
12:10; 1 Cor.
9:9; 1 Tim.
5:18

5 "When brothers live together and one of them dies and

★ 5-10
5 aMatt.
22:24; Mark
12:19; Luke
20:28

24:8 *leprosy.* See note on Lev. 13:2.
24:10-13 Though a fellow Israelite could not be charged interest on a loan, a pledge could be taken, but no pledge that would jeopardize his livelihood or his life (e.g., a millstone, v. 6; or his mantle used as a cover when asleep, v. 13, cf. Amos 2:8; or his daily wage, Deut. 24:14–15).
24:19 Ruth benefited from this law (cf. Ruth 2:3).

25:3 *forty times.* See note on 2 Cor. 11:24.
25:4 Paul used this verse to show that the human laborer is also worthy of his hire (1 Cor. 9:9–10; 1 Tim. 5:18).
25:5-10 These verses announce the law of levirate (from the Latin meaning "husband's brother") marriage, designed to prevent extinction of the family name. See note on Matt. 22:24.

has no son, the wife of the deceased shall not be *married* outside *the family* to a strange man. [a]Her husband's brother shall go in to her and take her to himself as wife and perform the duty of a husband's brother to her.

6 [a]Ruth 4:5, 10

6 "And it shall be that the first-born whom she bears shall assume the name of his dead brother, that [a]his name may not be blotted out from Israel.

7 [a]Ruth 4:5, 6

7 "[a]But if the man does not desire to take his brother's wife, then his brother's wife shall go up to the gate to the elders and say, 'My husband's brother refuses to establish a name for his brother in Israel; he is not willing to perform the duty of a husband's brother to me.'

8 "Then the elders of his city shall summon him and speak to him. And if he persists and says, 'I do not desire to take her,'

★ 9 [a]Ruth 4:7, 8 [b]Num. 12:14

9 [a]then his brother's wife shall come to him in the sight of the elders, and pull his sandal off his foot and [b]spit in his face; and she shall declare, 'Thus it is done to the man who does not build up his brother's house.'

10 "And in Israel his name shall be called, 'The house of him whose sandal is removed.'

11 "If *two* men, a man and his countryman, are struggling together, and the wife of one comes near to deliver her husband from the hand of the one who is striking him, and puts out her hand and seizes his genitals,

12 [a]Deut. 7:2; 19:13

12 then you shall cut off her hand; [a]you shall not show pity.

13 [a]Lev. 19:35-37; Prov. 11:1; 20:23; Ezek. 45:10; Mic. 6:11

13 "[a]You shall not have in your bag differing weights, a large and a small.

14 "You shall not have in your house differing measures, a large and a small.

15 [a]Ex. 20:12

15 "You shall have a full and just weight; you shall have a full and just measure, [a]that your days may be prolonged in the land which the LORD your God gives you.

16 [a]Prov. 11:1

16 "For [a]everyone who does these things, everyone who acts unjustly is an abomination to the LORD your God.

★17 [a]Ex. 17:8-16

17 "[a]Remember what Amalek did to you along the way when you came out from Egypt,

18 [a]Ps. 36:1; Rom. 3:18

18 how he met you along the way and attacked among you all the stragglers at your rear when you were faint and weary; and he [a]did not fear God.

19 [a]Deut. 12:9

19 "Therefore it shall come about when the LORD your God has given you [a]rest from all your surrounding enemies, in the land which the LORD your God gives you as an inheritance to possess, you shall blot out the memory of Amalek from under heaven; you must not forget.

9 First fruits, 26:1-19

★ 1-11

26 "Then it shall be, when you enter the land which the LORD your God gives you as an inheritance, and you possess it and live in it,

2 [a]Ex. 22:29; 23:16, 19; Num. 18:13; Prov. 3:9 [b]Deut. 12:5

2 that you shall take some of [a]the first of all the produce of the ground which you shall bring in from your land that the LORD your God gives you, and you shall put *it* in a basket and [b]go to the place where the LORD your God chooses to establish His name.

3 "And you shall go to the priest who is in office at that time, and say to him, 'I declare this day to the LORD my God that I have

---

25:9 *pull his sandal off his foot.* This act signified the transfer of his rights (cf. Ruth 4:7-8). *spit in his face.* A sign of contempt.
25:17 *Amalek.* See note on Exod. 17:8. The Amalekites were perhaps the most savage and inhumane of the Canaanites.
26:1-11 These verses describe another dimension to the meaning of the Feast of First Fruits

(see note on Lev. 23:10-14). It was not only a pledge of the full harvest to come, but also a reminder of the rise of the nation from its meager beginnings (cf. Deut. 26:5). *a wandering Aramean.* A reference to Jacob, who resided for a long time in Aram (Mesopotamia, cf. Gen. 28:5) and whose family ties were for the most part with Paddan-aram.

entered the land which the LORD swore to our fathers to give us.'

4 "Then the priest shall take the basket from your hand and set it down before the altar of the LORD your God.

5 *a*Gen. 43:1-14
*b*Gen. 46:27
*c*Deut. 1:10; 10:22

5 "And you shall answer and say before the LORD your God, '*a*My father was a wandering Aramean, and he went down to Egypt and sojourned there, *b*few in number; but there he became a *c*great, mighty and populous nation.

6 *a*Ex. 1:8-11

6 'And the *a*Egyptians treated us harshly and afflicted us, and imposed hard labor on us.

7 *a*Ex. 2:23-25; 3:9

7 'Then *a*we cried to the LORD, the God of our fathers, and the LORD heard our voice and saw our affliction and our toil and our oppression;

8 *a*Deut. 4:34; 34:11, 12

8 *a*and the LORD brought us out of Egypt with a mighty hand and an outstretched arm and with great terror and with signs and wonders;

9 *a*Ex. 3:8, 17

9 and He has brought us to this place, and has given us this land, *a*a land flowing with milk and honey.

10 *a*Deut. 8:18; Prov. 10:22

10 'And now behold, I have brought the first of the produce of the ground *a*which Thou, O LORD hast given me.' And you shall set it down before the LORD your God, and worship before the LORD your God;

11 *a*Deut. 12:12 *b*Deut. 12:7; 16:11; Eccl. 3:12, 13; 5:18-20

11 and you and *a*the Levite and the alien who is among you shall *b*rejoice in all the good which the LORD your God has given you and your household.

★12 *a*Lev. 27:30; Num. 18:24; Deut. 14:28, 29; Heb. 7:5, 9, 10

12 "*a*When you have finished paying all the tithe of your increase in the third year, the year of tithing, then you shall give it to the Levite, to the stranger, to the orphan and to the widow, that they may eat in your towns, and be satisfied.

★13-14
13 *a*Ps. 119:141, 153, 176

13 "And you shall say before the LORD your God, 'I have removed the sacred *portion* from

my house, and also have given it to the Levite and the alien, the orphan and the widow, according to all Thy commandments which Thou hast commanded me; *a*I have not transgressed or forgotten any of Thy commandments.

14 'I have not eaten of it while mourning, nor have I removed any of it while I was unclean, nor offered any of it to the dead. I have listened to the voice of the LORD my God; I have done according to all that Thou hast commanded me.

15 *a*Ps. 80:14; Is. 63:15; Zech. 2:13 *b*Deut. 26:9

15 '*a*Look down from Thy holy habitation, from heaven, and bless Thy people Israel, and the ground which Thou hast given us, *b*a land flowing with milk and honey, as Thou didst swear to our fathers.'

16 *a*Deut. 4:29

16 "This day the LORD your God commands you to do these statutes and ordinances. You shall therefore be careful to do them *a*with all your heart and with all your soul.

17 *a*Ps. 48:14

17 "*a*You have today declared the LORD to be your God, and that you would walk in His ways and keep His statutes, His commandments and His ordinances, and listen to His voice.

18 *a*Ex. 6:7; 19:5; Deut. 4:20; 7:6; 14:2; 28:9; 29:13; Titus 2:14; 1 Pet. 2:9

18 "And the LORD has today declared you to be *a*His people, a treasured possession, as He has promised you, and that you should keep all His commandments;

19 *a*Deut. 4:7, 8; 28:1, 13 *b*Ex. 19:6; Deut. 7:6; Is. 62:12; Jer. 2:3; 1 Pet. 2:9

19 and that He shall *a*set you high above all nations which He has made, for praise, fame, and honor; and that you shall be *b*a consecrated people to the LORD your God, as He has spoken."

IV RATIFICATION OF ISRAEL'S COVENANT, 27:1-30:20
A Prerequisite Ceremonies, 27:1-26

27 Then Moses and the elders of Israel charged the

26:12 *the third year.* See note on 14:28.
26:13-14 The worshiper had to attest that he had given the tithe to the poor and had not

used it for any purpose that God did not approve.

people, saying, "Keep all the commandments which I command you today.

★ 2 ªJosh. 8:30-32

2 "ªSo it shall be on the day when you shall cross the Jordan to the land which the Lord your God gives you, that you shall set up for yourself large stones, and coat them with lime

3 ªDeut. 26:9

3 and write on them all the words of this law, when you cross over, in order that you may enter the land which the Lord your God gives you, ªa land flowing with milk and honey, as the Lord, the God of your fathers, promised you.

★ 4 ªDeut. 11:29; Josh. 8:30

4 "So it shall be when you cross the Jordan, you shall set up ªon Mount Ebal, these stones, as I am commanding you today, and you shall coat them with lime.

5 ªEx. 20:25; Josh. 8:31

5 "Moreover, you shall build there an altar to the Lord your God, an altar of stones; you ªshall not wield an iron tool on them.

★ 6

6 "You shall build the altar of the Lord your God of uncut stones; and you shall offer on it burnt offerings to the Lord your God;

7 ªDeut. 26:11

7 and you shall sacrifice peace offerings and eat there, and you shall ªrejoice before the Lord your God.

★ 8

8 "And you shall write on the stones all the words of this law very distinctly."

9 Then Moses and the Levitical priests spoke to all Israel, saying, "Be silent and listen, O Israel! This day you have become a people for the Lord your God.

10 "You shall therefore obey the Lord your God, and do His commandments and His statutes which I command you today."

★11-26

11 Moses also charged the people on that day, saying,

12 "When you cross the Jordan, these shall stand on ªMount Gerizim to bless the people: ᵇSimeon, Levi, Judah, Issachar, Joseph, and Benjamin.

12 ªDeut. 11:29 ᵇJosh. 8:33-35

13 "And for the curse, these shall stand on Mount Ebal: Reuben, Gad, Asher, Zebulun, Dan, and Naphtali.

14 "The Levites shall then answer and say to all the men of Israel with a loud voice,

15 'Cursed is the man who makes ªan idol or a molten image, an abomination to the Lord, the work of the hands of the craftsman, and sets it up in secret.' And ᵇall the people shall answer and say, 'Amen.'

15 ªEx. 20:4, 23; 34:17; Lev. 19:4; 26:1; Deut. 4:16, 23; 5:8; Is. 44:9 ᵇ1 Cor. 14:16

16 'ªCursed is he who dishonors his father or mother.' And all the people shall say, 'Amen.'

16 ªEx. 20:12; 21:17; Lev. 19:3; 20:9; Deut. 5:16; Ezek. 22:7

17 'ªCursed is he who moves his neighbor's boundary mark.' And all the people shall say, 'Amen.'

17 ªDeut. 19:14; Prov. 22:28

18 'ªCursed is he who misleads a blind person on the road.' And all the people shall say, 'Amen.'

18 ªLev. 19:14

19 'ªCursed is he who distorts the justice due an alien, orphan, and widow.' And all the people shall say, 'Amen.'

19 ªEx. 22:21; 23:9; Lev. 19:33; Deut. 10:18; 24:17

20 'ªCursed is he who lies with his father's wife, because he has uncovered his father's skirt.' And all the people shall say, 'Amen.'

20 ªLev. 18:8; 20:11; Deut. 22:30; 1 Cor. 5:1

21 'ªCursed is he who lies with any animal.' And all the people shall say, 'Amen.'

21 ªEx. 22:19; Lev. 18:23; 20:15

22 'ªCursed is he who lies with his sister, the daughter of his father or of his mother.' And all the people shall say, 'Amen.'

22 ªLev. 18:9; 20:17

23 'ªCursed is he who lies with his mother-in-law.' And all the people shall say, 'Amen.'

23 ªLev. 20:14

27:2 lime. Produced by roasting gypsum, which was available in the Jordan and Dead Sea valleys.
27:4 Mount Ebal. See note on 11:29.
27:6 uncut stones. In accordance with Exod. 20:25.
27:8 all the words of this law. Probably a reference to the curses and blessings of this and the following chapter.
27:11-26 This passage describes a ceremony of ratification of the covenant. Six tribes stood on Gerizim and six on Ebal, and the Levites in the valley between. The Levites spoke the 12 curses and, after each, all the people responded with Amen (lit., firm or assured; thus, "be it assured").

24 aEx.
21:12; Lev.
24:17; Num.
35:30, 31

25 aEx. 23:7;
Deut. 10:17;
Ps. 15:5;
Ezek. 22:12

26 aPs.
119:21; Jer.
11:3; Gal.
3:10

24 'aCursed is he who strikes his neighbor in secret.' And all the people shall say, 'Amen.'

25 'aCursed is he who accepts a bribe to strike down an innocent person.' And all the people shall say, 'Amen.'

26 'aCursed is he who does not confirm the words of this law by doing them.' And all the people shall say, 'Amen.'

B Promise of Blessings, 28:1-14

1 aEx.
15:26, 23:22-
27; Lev.
26:3-13;
Deut. 7:12-
26; 11:13
bDeut.
28:13; 26:19;
1 Chr. 14:2

2 aZech.
1:6

3 aGen.
39:5

6 aPs.
121:8

8 aDeut.
15:10

9 aEx. 19:5

28 "aNow it shall be, if you will diligently obey the LORD your God, being careful to do all His commandments which I command you today, the LORD your God bwill set you high above all the nations of the earth.

2 "And all these blessings shall come upon you and aovertake you, if you will obey the LORD your God.

3 "Blessed shall you be in the city, and blessed shall you be ain the country.

4 "Blessed shall be the offspring of your body and the produce of your ground and the offspring of your beasts, the increase of your herd and the young of your flock.

5 "Blessed shall be your basket and your kneading bowl.

6 "Blessed shall you be awhen you come in, and blessed shall you be when you go out.

7 "The LORD will cause your enemies who rise up against you to be defeated before you; they shall come out against you one way and shall flee before you seven ways.

8 "The LORD will command the blessing upon you in your barns and in aall that you put your hand to, and He will bless you in the land which the LORD your God gives you.

9 "aThe LORD will establish you as a holy people to Himself, as He swore to you, if you will keep the commandments of the LORD your God, and walk in His ways.

10 "So all the peoples of the earth shall see that ayou are called by the name of the LORD; and they shall be afraid of you.

11 "aAnd the LORD will make you abound in prosperity, in the offspring of your body and in the offspring of your beast and in the produce of your ground, in the land which the LORD swore to your fathers to give you.

12 "The LORD will open for you His good storehouse, the heavens, to give rain to your land in its season and to bless all the work of your hand; and ayou shall lend to many nations, but you shall not borrow.

13 "aAnd the LORD shall make you the head and not the tail, and you only shall be above, and you shall not be underneath, if you will listen to the commandments of the LORD your God, which I charge you today, to observe them carefully,

14 and ado not turn aside from any of the words which I command you today, to the right or to the left, to go after other gods to serve them.

C Promise of Curses, 28:15-68

15 "aBut it shall come about, if you will not obey the LORD your God, to observe to do all His commandments and His statutes with which I charge you today, that all these curses shall come upon you and overtake you.

16 "aCursed shall you be in the city, and cursed shall you be in the country.

17 "aCursed shall be your basket and your kneading bowl.

18 "aCursed shall be the offspring of your body and the produce of your ground, the increase of your herd and the young of your flock.

10 a2 Chr.
7:14

11 aDeut.
28:4; Prov.
10:22

12 aDeut.
23:20

★13 aDeut.
28:1, 44

14 aDeut.
5:32; Josh.
1:7

15 aLev.
26:14-43;
Josh. 23:15;
Dan. 9:11

16 aDeut.
28:3

17 aDeut.
28:5

18 aDeut.
28:4

28:13 the head and not the tail. An expression to indicate that, if obedient, Israel would be an independent power.

19 *Deut. 28:6*

19 "ᵃCursed *shall* you *be* when you come in, and cursed *shall* you *be* when you go out.

20 *Deut. 28:8; Mal. 2:2* ᵇPs. 80:16; Is. 51:20; 66:15 ᶜDeut. 4:26

20 "ᵃThe LORD will send upon you curses, confusion, and ᵇrebuke, in all you undertake to do, until you are destroyed and until ᶜyou perish quickly, on account of the evil of your deeds, because you have forsaken Me.

★21 *Lev. 26:25; Num. 14:12; Jer. 24:10; Amos 4:10*

21 "ᵃThe LORD will make the pestilence cling to you until He has consumed you from the land, where you are entering to possess it.

★22 *Lev. 26:16* ᵇAmos 4:9 ᶜDeut. 4:26

22 "ᵃThe LORD will smite you with consumption and with fever and with inflammation and with fiery heat and with the sword and ᵇwith blight and with mildew, and they shall pursue you until ᶜyou perish.

★23

23 "And the heaven which is over your head shall be bronze, and the earth which is under you, iron.

★24 *Deut. 11:17; 28:12*

24 "ᵃThe LORD will make the rain of your land powder and dust; from heaven it shall come down on you until you are destroyed.

25 *Deut. 28:7; Is. 30:17* ᵇ2 Chr. 29:8; Jer. 15:4; 24:9; Ezek. 23:46

25 "ᵃThe LORD will cause you to be defeated before your enemies; you shall go out one way against them, but you shall flee seven ways before them, and you shall ᵇbe *an example of* terror to all the kingdoms of the earth.

26 *Jer. 7:33; 16:4; 19:7; 34:20*

26 "ᵃAnd your carcasses shall be food to all birds of the sky and to the beasts of the earth, and there shall be no one to frighten *them* away.

★27 *Ex. 9:9; Deut. 7:15; 28:60, 61* ᵇ1 Sam. 5:6

27 "ᵃThe LORD will smite you with the boils of Egypt and with ᵇtumors and with the scab and with the itch, from which you cannot be healed.

28 "The LORD will smite you with madness and with blindness and with bewilderment of heart;

29 *Ex. 10:21*

29 and you shall ᵃgrope at noon, as the blind man gropes in darkness, and you shall not prosper in your ways; but you shall only be oppressed and robbed continually, with none to save you.

30 *Job 31:10; Jer. 8:10* ᵇAmos 5:11

30 "ᵃYou shall betroth a wife, but another man shall violate her; ᵇyou shall build a house, but you shall not live in it; you shall plant a vineyard, but you shall not use its fruit.

31 "Your ox shall be slaughtered before your eyes, but you shall not eat of it; your donkey shall be torn away from you, and shall not be restored to you; your sheep shall be given to your enemies, and you shall have none to save you.

32 *Deut. 28:41*

32 "ᵃYour sons and your daughters shall be given to another people, while your eyes shall look on and yearn for them continually; but there shall be nothing you can do.

33 *Jer. 5:15, 17*

33 "ᵃA people whom you do not know shall eat up the produce of your ground and all your labors, and you shall never be anything but oppressed and crushed continually.

34 "And you shall be driven mad by the sight of what you see.

35 *Deut. 28:27*

35 "ᵃThe LORD will strike you on the knees and legs with sore boils, from which you cannot be healed, from the sole of your foot to the crown of your head.

★36 *2 Kin. 17:4, 6; 24:12, 14; 25:7, 11; 2 Chr. 36:1-21; Jer. 39:1-9* ᵇDeut. 4:28; Jer. 16:13

36 "ᵃThe LORD will bring you and your king, whom you shall set over you, to a nation which neither you nor your fathers have known, and there you shall serve other gods, ᵇwood and stone.

37 *1 Kin. 9:7, 8; Jer. 19:8; 24:9; 25:9; 29:18*

37 "And ᵃyou shall become a horror, a proverb, and a taunt among all the people where the LORD will drive you.

28:21 *pestilence.* I.e., an epidemic.
28:22 *consumption.* A disease that would cause them to waste away.
28:23 These figures are used to characterize a long drought.
28:24 *powder and dust.* The "rain" would be one of sand and dust from the desert.
28:27 *the scab.* Scurvy. *the itch.* Probably scabies.
28:36 A prediction of the Assyrian and Babylonian captivities, which would be more than 700 years in the future. *king.* See 17:14.

38 "*a*You shall bring out much seed to the field but you shall gather in little, for *b*the locust shall consume it.

39 "*a*You shall plant and cultivate vineyards, but you shall neither drink of the wine nor gather *the grapes,* for the worm shall devour them.

40 "*a*You shall have olive trees throughout your territory but you shall not anoint yourself with the oil, for your olives shall drop off.

41 "*a*You shall have sons and daughters but they shall not be yours, for they shall go into captivity.

42 "*a*The cricket shall possess all your trees and the produce of your ground.

43 "*a*The alien who is among you shall rise above you higher and higher, but you shall go down lower and lower.

44 "*a*He shall lend to you, but you shall not lend to him; *b*he shall be the head, and you shall be the tail.

45 "So all these curses shall come on you and pursue you and overtake you *a*until you are destroyed, because you would not obey the Lord your God by keeping His commandments and His statutes which He commanded you.

46 "And they shall become *a*a sign and a wonder on you and your descendants forever.

47 "*a*Because you did not serve the Lord your God with joy and a glad heart, for the abundance of all things;

48 therefore you shall serve your enemies whom the Lord shall send against you, *a*in hunger, in thirst, in nakedness, and in the lack of all things; and He *b*will put an iron yoke on your neck until He has destroyed you.

49 "*a*The Lord will bring a nation against you from afar, from the end of the earth, *b*as the eagle swoops down, a nation whose language you shall not understand,

50 a nation of fierce countenance who shall *a*have no respect for the old, nor show favor to the young.

51 "Moreover, it shall eat the offspring of your herd and the produce of your ground until you are destroyed, who also leaves you no grain, new wine, or oil, nor the increase of your herd or the young of your flock until they have caused you to perish.

52 "*a*And it shall besiege you in all your towns until your high and fortified walls in which you trusted come down throughout your land, and it shall besiege you in all your towns throughout your land which the Lord your God has given you.

53 "*a*Then you shall eat the offspring of your own body, the flesh of your sons and of your daughters whom the Lord your God has given you, during the siege and the distress by which your enemy shall oppress you.

54 "The man who is refined and very delicate among you shall be hostile toward his brother and toward the wife he cherishes and toward the rest of his children who remain,

55 so that he will not give *even* one of them any of the flesh of his children which he shall eat, since he has nothing *else* left, during the siege and the distress by which your enemy shall oppress you in all your towns.

56 "*a*The refined and delicate woman among you, who would not venture to set the sole of her foot on the ground for delicateness and refinement, shall be hostile toward the husband she cherishes and toward her son and daughter,

57 and toward her afterbirth which issues from between her

28:49 *a nation.* Evidently Babylon, which is likened to an *eagle.* There follows, in verses 52–57, a description of the Babylonian siege of Jerusalem (cf. Lam. 4). This prophecy may also have had other fulfillments in other sieges of Jerusalem, especially that by the Romans in A.D. 70.

---

38 *a*Is. 5:10; Mic. 6:15; Hag. 1:6 *b*Ex. 10:4; Joel 1:4

39 *a*Is. 5:10; 17:10, 11

40 *a*Jer. 11:16; Mic. 6:15

41 *a*Deut. 28:32

42 *a*Deut. 28:38

43 *a*Deut. 28:13

44 *a*Deut. 28:12 *b*Deut. 28:13

45 *a*Deut. 4:25, 26

46 *a*Num. 26:10; Is. 8:18; Ezek. 5:15; 14:8

47 *a*Deut. 12:7; Neh. 9:35-37

48 *a*Lam. 4:4-6 *b*Jer. 28:13, 14

★**49** *a*Is. 5:26-30; 7:18-20; Jer. 5:15; 6:22, 23 *b*Jer. 48:40; 49:22; Lam. 4:19; Hos. 8:1

50 *a*Is. 47:6

52 *a*Jer. 10:17, 18; Zeph. 1:15, 16

53 *a*Lev. 26:29; 2 Kin. 6:28, 29; Jer. 19:9; Lam. 2:20; 4:10

56 *a*Lam. 4:10

57 *a*2 Kin. 6:28, 29; Lam. 4:10

legs and toward her children whom she bears; for ªshe shall eat them secretly for lack of anything *else*, during the siege and the distress by which your enemy shall oppress you in your towns.

58 aPs. 99:3;
Mal. 1:14
bIs. 42:8

58 "If you are not careful to observe all the words of this law which are written in this book, to ªfear this honored and awesome ᵇname, the Lᴏʀᴅ your God,

59 then the Lᴏʀᴅ will bring extraordinary plagues on you and your descendants, even severe and lasting plagues, and miserable and chronic sicknesses.

60 aDeut.
28:27

60 "ªAnd He will bring back on you all the diseases of Egypt of which you were afraid, and they shall cling to you.

61 aDeut.
4:25, 26

61 "Also every sickness and every plague which, not written in the book of this law, the Lᴏʀᴅ will bring on you ªuntil you are destroyed.

62 aDeut.
1:10; Neh.
9:23

62 "Then you shall be left few in number, ªwhereas you were as the stars of heaven for multitude, because you did not obey the Lᴏʀᴅ your God.

63 a Jer.
32:41 bProv.
1:26 c Jer.
12:14; 45:4

63 "And it shall come about that as the Lᴏʀᴅ ªdelighted over you to prosper you, and multiply you, so the Lᴏʀᴅ will ᵇdelight over you to make you perish and destroy you; and you shall be ᶜtorn from the land where you are entering to possess it.

★64-68

64 aLev.
26:33; Deut.
4:27; Neh.
1:8 bDeut.
4:28; 29:26;
32:17

64 "Moreover, the Lᴏʀᴅ will ªscatter you among all peoples, from one end of the earth to the other end of the earth; and there you shall ᵇserve other gods, wood and stone, which you or your fathers have not known.

65 aLam. 1:3
bLev. 26:36

65 "And ªamong those nations you shall find no rest, and there shall be no resting place for the sole of your foot; but there ᵇthe Lᴏʀᴅ will give you a trembling

heart, failing of eyes, and despair of soul.

66 "So your life shall hang in doubt before you; and you shall be in dread night and day, and shall have no assurance of your life.

67 "ªIn the morning you shall say, 'Would that it were evening!' And at evening you shall say, 'Would that it were morning!' because of the dread of your heart which you dread, and for the sight of your eyes which you shall see.

67 aJob 7:4

68 "And the Lᴏʀᴅ will bring you back to Egypt in ships, by the way about which I spoke to you, 'You will never see it again!' And there you shall offer yourselves for sale to your enemies as male and female slaves, but there will be no buyer."

D Provisions of the Palestinian Covenant, 29:1–30:20

29 ªThese are the words of the covenant which the Lᴏʀᴅ commanded Moses to make with the sons of Israel in the land of Moab, besides the ᵇcovenant which He had made with them at Horeb.

★ 1 aLev.
26:46; 27:34
bDeut. 5:2, 3

2 And Moses summoned all Israel and said to them, "You have seen all that the Lᴏʀᴅ did before your eyes in the land of Egypt to Pharaoh and all his servants and all his land;

3 ªthe great trials which your eyes have seen, those great signs and wonders.

3 aDeut.
4:34; 7:19

4 "Yet to this day ªthe Lᴏʀᴅ has not given you a heart to know, nor eyes to see, nor ears to hear.

★ 4 aIs. 6:9,
10; Ezek.
12:2; Matt.
13:14; Acts
28:26, 27;
Rom. 11:8

5 "And I have led you forty years in the wilderness; ªyour

★ 5 aDeut.
8:4

28:64-68 A prophecy of the dispersion of the Jewish people among *all peoples* after the destruction of Jerusalem by the Romans in A.D. 70. At that time, too, many were consigned to slavery and transported in *ships* to Egypt (v. 68).

29:1 *the covenant.* Moses now details the agree-

ment under which the people would enter the land of Palestine. This Palestinian covenant was in addition to the Mosaic covenant given at Sinai (*Horeb*).

29:4 The people were blind to the meaning of all that God had done for them (cf. Psalm 106:7).

29:5 See note on 8:4.

clothes have not worn out on you, and your sandal has not worn out on your foot.

6 *a*Deut. 8:3

6 "*a*You have not eaten bread, nor have you drunk wine or strong drink, in order that you might know that I am the LORD your God.

★ 7-8
7 *a*Num. 21:21-24, 33, 35; Deut. 2:26-3:17

7 "*a*When you reached this place, Sihon the king of Heshbon and Og the king of Bashan came out to meet us for battle, but we defeated them;

8 *a*Num. 32:32, 33; Deut. 3:12, 13

8 and we took their land and *a*gave it as an inheritance to the Reubenites, the Gadites, and the half-tribe of the Manassites.

9 *a*Deut. 4:6; 1 Kin. 2:3 *b*Josh. 1:7

9 "*a*So keep the words of this covenant to do them, *b*that you may prosper in all that you do.

10 "You stand today, all of you, before the LORD your God: your chiefs, your tribes, your elders and your officers, *even* all the men of Israel,

11 *a*Josh. 9:21, 23, 27

11 your little ones, your wives, and the alien who is within your camps, from *a*the one who chops your wood to the one who draws your water,

12 that you may enter into the covenant with the LORD your God, and into His oath which the LORD your God is making with you today,

13 *a*Gen. 17:7; Ex. 6:7

13 in order that He may establish you today as His people and that *a*He may be your God, just as He spoke to you and as He swore to your fathers, to Abraham, Isaac, and Jacob.

14 *a*Jer. 31:31; Heb. 8:7, 8

14 "Now not with you alone am I *a*making this covenant and this oath,

15 *a*Acts 2:39

15 *a*but both with those who stand here with us today in the presence of the LORD our God and with those who are not with us here today

★16

16 (for you know how we lived in the land of Egypt, and how we came through the midst

of the nations through which you passed.

17 *a*Ex. 20:23; Deut. 4:28; 28:36

17 "Moreover, you have seen their abominations and their idols of *a*wood, stone, silver, and gold, which *they had* with them);

★18 *a*Deut. 13:6 *b*Deut. 32:32; Heb. 12:15

18 *a*lest there shall be among you a man or woman, or family or tribe, whose heart turns away today from the LORD our God, to go and serve the gods of those nations; lest there shall be among you *b*a root bearing poisonous fruit and wormwood.

19 "And it shall be when he hears the words of this curse, that he will boast, saying, 'I have peace though I walk in the stubbornness of my heart in order to destroy the watered *land* with the dry.'

20 *a*Ps. 79:5; Ezek. 23:25 *b*Ps. 74:1; 80:4 *c*Ex. 32:33; Deut. 9:14; 2 Kin. 14:27

20 "The LORD shall never be willing to forgive him, but rather the anger of the LORD and *a*His jealousy will *b*burn against that man, and every curse which is written in this book will rest on him, and the LORD will *c*blot out his name from under heaven.

21 *a*Deut. 30:10

21 "Then the LORD will single him out for adversity from all the tribes of Israel, according to all the curses of the covenant *a*which are written in this book of the law.

22 *a*Jer. 19:8; 49:17; 50:13

22 "Now the generation to come, your sons who rise up after you and *a*the foreigner who comes from a distant land, when they see the plagues of the land and the diseases with which the LORD has afflicted it, will say,

★23 *a*Gen. 19:24; Is. 34:9; Jer. 17:6; Zeph. 2:9 *b*Is. 1:7; 64:11 *c*Jude 7

23 'All its land is *a*brimstone and salt, *b*a burning waste, unsown and unproductive, and no grass grows in it, like the overthrow of *c*Sodom and Gomorrah, Admah and Zeboiim, which the LORD overthrew in His anger and in His wrath.'

24 *a*1 Kin. 9:8; Jer. 22:8

24 "And all the nations shall say, '*a*Why has the LORD done

29:7-8 See notes on Num. 21:21-33 and Num. 32.
29:16 *the nations.* Edom, Ammon, and Moab.
29:18 *wormwood.* A bitter plant. A similar

warning is found in Heb. 12:15.
29:23 *brimstone.* Sulphur or the stifling sulfurous gases that come from volcanic eruption. *Admah . . . Zeboiim.* See note on Gen. 14:2.

thus to this land? Why this great outburst of anger?'

25 a2 Kin.
17:9-23;
2 Chr. 36:13-
21

25 "Then *men* shall say, '*a*Because they forsook the covenant of the LORD, the God of their fathers, which He made with them when He brought them out of the land of Egypt.

26 'And they went and served other gods and worshiped them, gods whom they have not known and whom He had not allotted to them.

27 aDan.
9:11

27 'Therefore, the anger of the LORD burned against that land, *a*to bring upon it every curse which is written in this book;

28 a2 Chr.
7:20; Ps.
52:5; Prov.
2:22; Ezek.
19:12, 13

28 and *a*the LORD uprooted them from their land in anger and in fury and in great wrath, and cast them into another land, as *it is* this day.'

★29 aActs
1:7 bJohn
5:39; Acts
17:11; 2 Tim.
3:16

29 "*a*The secret things belong to the LORD our God, but *b*the things revealed belong to us and to our sons forever, that we may observe all the words of this law.

★ 1-10

1 aDeut.
11:26; 30:15,
19 bLev.
26:40-45;
Deut. 28:64;
29:28; 1 Kin.
8:47

30 "So it shall be when all of these things have come upon you, *a*the blessing and the curse which I have set before you, and you call *them* to mind *b*in all nations where the LORD your God has banished you,

2 aDeut.
4:29, 30;
Neh. 1:9
bDeut. 4:29

2 and you *a*return to the LORD your God and obey Him *b*with all your heart and soul according to all that I command you today, you and your sons,

3 aGen.
28:15; 48:21;
Ps. 126:1, 4;
Jer. 29:14
bPs. 147:2;
Jer. 32:37;
Ezek. 34:13
cDeut. 4:27

3 then the LORD your God will *a*restore you from captivity, and have compassion on you, and *b*will gather you again from all the peoples where the LORD your God has *c*scattered you.

4 aNeh.
1:9; Is. 43:6;
48:20; 62:11

4 "If your outcasts are at the ends of the earth, *a*from there the

LORD your God will gather you, and from there He will bring you back.

5 aJer.
29:14; 30:3
bDeut. 7:13;
13:17

5 "And *a*the LORD your God will bring you into the land which your fathers possessed, and you shall possess it; and He will prosper you and *b*multiply you more than your fathers.

6 aDeut.
10:16 bDeut.
6:5

6 "Moreover *a*the LORD your God will circumcise your heart and the heart of your descendants, *b*to love the LORD your God with all your heart and with all your soul, in order that you may live.

7 aDeut.
7:15

7 "*a*And the LORD your God will inflict all these curses on your enemies and on those who hate you, who persecuted you.

8 "And you shall again obey the LORD, and observe all His commandments which I command you today.

9 aJer.
31:27, 28
bJer. 32:41

9 "*a*Then the LORD your God will prosper you abundantly in all the work of your hand, in the offspring of your body and in the offspring of your cattle and in the produce of your ground, for *b*the LORD will again rejoice over you for good, just as He rejoiced over your fathers;

10 aDeut.
29:21 bDeut.
4:29

10 if you obey the LORD your God to keep His commandments and His statutes which *a*are written in this book of the law, if you turn to the LORD your God *b*with all your heart and soul.

★11-14

11 "For this commandment which I command you today is not too difficult for you, nor is it out of reach.

12 aRom.
10:6-8

12 "It is not in heaven, that you should say, '*a*Who will go up to heaven for us to get it for us and make us hear it, that we may observe it?'

29:29 This important verse sets the limits and purpose of God's revelation: some things He chooses to keep to Himself, but what He has revealed (through the Law, in this instance) is the business of His children to obey.

30:1-10 A prediction of the regathering of Israel from all the nations to which she was scattered. This regathering will occur at the second coming of Christ (v. 3; cf. Mark 13:26-27) and will include: (1) restoration to the land of Palestine (v. 5), (2) a work of grace in the peo-

ple's hearts (v. 6, see notes on 10:16 and Jer. 31:31-34), (3) judgment of Israel's enemies (v. 7; cf. Joel 3:1-2), and (4) prosperity in the land (v. 9, cf. Amos 9:11-15).

30:11-14 Some things are known only to God (29:29), but the commands of His voice (30:8) written down for all to read (30:10), were His clear revelation to Israel, to be accepted in the heart. See Paul's use of this passage in Rom. 10:6-10.

13 "Nor is it beyond the sea, that you should say, 'Who will cross the sea for us to get it for us and make us hear it, that we may observe it?'

14 "But the word is very near you, in your mouth and in your heart, that you may observe it.

15 aDeut. 11:26
15 "See, [a]I have set before you today life and prosperity, and death and adversity;

16 aDeut. 6:5 bDeut. 4:1; 30:19
16 in that I command you to-day [a]to love the LORD your God, to walk in His ways and to keep His commandments and His statutes and His judgments, that you [b]may live and multiply, and that the LORD your God may bless you in the land where you are entering to possess it.

17 "But if your heart turns away and you will not obey, but are drawn away and worship other gods and serve them,

18 aDeut. 4:26; 8:19
18 I declare to you today that [a]you shall surely perish. You shall not prolong *your* days in the land where you are crossing the Jordan to enter and possess it.

19 aDeut. 4:26 bDeut. 30:1
19 "[a]I call heaven and earth to witness against you today, that I have set before you life and death, [b]the blessing and the curse. So choose life in order that you may live, you and your descendants,

20 aDeut. 6:5 bDeut. 10:20 cDeut. 4:1; 32:47; Acts 17:25, 28 dGen. 12:7; 17:1-8
20 [a]by loving the LORD your God, by obeying His voice, and [b]by holding fast to Him; [c]for this is your life and the length of your days, that you may live in [d]the land which the LORD swore to your fathers, to Abraham, Isaac, and Jacob, to give them."

V CONCLUSION, 31:1–34:12

A Charges Related to Moses, 31:1–29

31 So Moses went and spoke these words to all Israel.

2 And he said to them, "I am [a]a hundred and twenty years old today; [b]I am no longer able to come and go, and the LORD has said to me, '[c]You shall not cross this Jordan.'

★ 2 aDeut. 34:7 bNum. 27:17; 1 Kin. 3:7 cDeut. 1:37; 3:27

3 "[a]It is the LORD your God who will cross ahead of you; He will destroy these nations before you, and you shall dispossess them. [b]Joshua is the one who will cross ahead of you, just as the LORD has spoken.

3 aDeut. 9:3 bNum. 27:18

4 "And the LORD will do to them just as He did to Sihon and Og, the kings of the Amorites, and to their land, when He destroyed them.

5 "And [a]the LORD will deliver them up before you, and you shall do to them according to all the commandments which I have commanded you.

5 aDeut. 7:2

6 "[a]Be strong and courageous, [b]do not be afraid or tremble at them, for [c]the LORD your God is the one who goes with you. [d]He will not fail you or forsake you."

6 aJosh. 10:25; 1 Chr. 22:13 bDeut. 1:29; 7:18; 20:1 cDeut. 20:4 dJosh. 1:5; Heb. 13:5

7 Then Moses called to Joshua and said to him in the sight of all Israel, "[a]Be strong and courageous, for you shall go with this people into the land which the LORD has sworn to their fathers to give them, and you shall give it to them as an inheritance.

★ 7-8

7 aDeut. 1:38; 3:28

8 "And [a]the LORD is the one who goes ahead of you; He will be with you. [b]He will not fail you or forsake you. Do not fear, or be dismayed."

8 aEx. 13:21; 33:14 bDeut. 31:6; Josh. 1:5; Heb. 13:5

9 So Moses wrote this law and gave it to the priests, the sons of Levi [a]who carried the ark of the covenant of the LORD, and to all the elders of Israel.

★ 9-13

9 aNum. 4:5, 6, 15; Deut. 10:8; 31:25, 26; Josh. 3:3

10 Then Moses commanded them, saying, "At the end of *every* seven years, at the time of [a]the year of remission of debts, at the [b]Feast of Booths,

10 aDeut. 15:1, 2 bLev. 23:34; Deut. 16:13

31:2 *I am no longer able to come and go.* Physically, Moses was capable (34:7), but he had been forbidden to go into the promised land with the people (Num. 20:12).

31:7-8 Long before, Joshua had been made leader of the army (Exod. 17:9), and more recently had been invested with some of Moses'

authority (Num. 27:18-23).

31:9-13 The deposit of a written copy with the *priests* (v. 9, symbolizing the transfer of responsibility for enforcement to the priests), and the regulation for reading the covenant periodically (v. 10) were typical conditions of imperial treaties of that time.

11 when all Israel comes ato appear before the Lord your God at bthe place which He will choose, cyou shall read this law in front of all Israel in their hearing.

12 "Assemble the people, the men and the women and children and the alien who is in your town, in order that they may hear and alearn and fear the Lord your God, and be careful to observe all the words of this law.

13 "And their children, who have not known, will hear and learn to fear the Lord your God, as long as you live on the land which you are about to cross the Jordan to possess."

14 Then the Lord said to Moses, "Behold, athe time for you to die is near; call Joshua, and present yourselves at the tent of meeting, that I may commission him." bSo Moses and Joshua went and presented themselves at the tent of meeting.

15 aAnd the Lord appeared in the tent in a pillar of cloud, and the pillar of cloud stood at the doorway of the tent.

16 And the Lord said to Moses, "Behold, ayou are about to lie down with your fathers; and bthis people will arise and play the harlot with the strange gods of the land, into the midst of which they are going, and cwill forsake Me and break My covenant which I have made with them.

17 "aThen My anger will be kindled against them in that day, and bI will forsake them and chide My face from them, and they shall be consumed, and many evils and troubles shall come upon them; so that they will say in that day, 'dIs it not because our God is not among us that these evils have come upon us?'

18 "But I will surely hide My face in that day because of all the

evil which they will do, for they will turn to other gods.

19 "Now therefore, awrite this song for yourselves, and teach it to the sons of Israel; put it on their lips, in order that this song may be a witness for Me against the sons of Israel.

20 "aFor when I bring them into the land flowing with milk and honey, which I swore to their fathers, and they have eaten and are satisfied and bbecome prosperous, then they will turn to other gods and serve them, and spurn Me and break My covenant.

21 "Then it shall come about, awhen many evils and troubles have come upon them, that this song will testify before them as a witness (for it shall not be forgotten from the lips of their descendants); for bI know their intent which they are developing today, before I have brought them into the land which I swore."

22 aSo Moses wrote this song the same day, and taught it to the sons of Israel.

23 aThen He commissioned Joshua the son of Nun, and said, "bBe strong and courageous, for you shall bring the sons of Israel into the land which I swore to them, and cI will be with you."

24 And it came about, when Moses finished writing the words of this law in a book until they were complete,

25 that Moses commanded the Levites awho carried the ark of the covenant of the Lord, saying,

26 "Take this book of the law and place it beside the ark of the covenant of the Lord your God, that it may remain there as a witness against you.

27 "For I know ayour rebellion and byour stubbornness; behold, while I am still alive with you today, you have been rebellious

---

31:14 At this point, God spoke to Moses face to face for the last time on earth.
31:19 Moses and Joshua (the verb is plural) are commissioned to write a *song*, a means of

helping the people remember more easily the requirements of the covenant.
31:23 Joshua was now directly commissioned by God.

against the LORD; how much more, then, after my death?

28 "Assemble to me all the elders of your tribes and your officers, that I may speak these words in their hearing and [a]call the heavens and the earth to witness against them.

29 "For I know that after my death you will [a]act corruptly and turn from the way which I have commanded you; and evil will befall you in the latter days, for you will do that which is evil in the sight of the LORD, provoking Him to anger with the work of your hands."

B Song of Moses, 31:30–32:47

30 Then Moses spoke in the hearing of all the assembly of Israel the words of this song, until they were complete:

32 "[a]Give ear, O heavens, and let me speak;
And let the earth hear the words of my mouth.

2 "[a]Let my teaching drop as the rain,
My speech distill as the dew,
[b]As the droplets on the fresh grass
And as the showers on the herb.

3 "[a]For I proclaim the name of the LORD;
[b]Ascribe greatness to our God!

4 "[a]The Rock! His work is perfect,
[b]For all His ways are just;
[c]A God of faithfulness and without injustice,
Righteous and upright is He.

5 "[a]They have acted corruptly toward Him,
They are not His children, because of their defect;
[b]But are a perverse and crooked generation.

6 "Do you thus [a]repay the LORD,
[b]O foolish and unwise people?
[c]Is not He your Father who has bought you?
[d]He has made you and established you.

7 "Remember the days of old,
Consider the years of all generations.
[a]Ask your father, and he will inform you,
Your elders, and they will tell you.

8 "[a]When the Most High gave the nations their inheritance,
When He separated the sons of man,
He set the boundaries of the peoples
[b]According to the number of the sons of Israel.

9 "[a]For the LORD's portion is His people;
Jacob is the allotment of His inheritance.

10 "[a]He found him in a desert land,
And in the howling waste of a wilderness;
He encircled him, He cared for him,
He guarded him as [b]the pupil of His eye.

11 "[a]Like an eagle that stirs up its nest,
That hovers over its young,
[b]He spread His wings and caught them,

Cross references (left margin):

28 [a]Deut. 4:26; 30:19; 32:1
29 [a]Judg. 2:19
1 [a]Deut. 4:26; Ps. 50:4; Is. 1:2; Jer. 6:19
2 [a]Is. 55:10, 11 [b]Ps. 72:6
3 [a]Ex. 33:19; 34:5, 6 [b]Deut. 3:24; 5:24
★ 4 [a]Deut. 32:15, 18, 30; 2 Sam. 22:31 [b]Gen. 18:25; Dan. 4:37 [c]Deut. 7:9

Cross references (right margin):

5 [a]Deut. 4:25; 31:29 [b]Matt. 17:17
6 [a]Ps. 116:12 [b]Deut. 32:28 [c]Deut. 1:31; Ps. 74:2; Is. 63:16 [d]Deut. 32:15
★ 7-14
7 [a]Ex. 12:26; Ps. 78:5-8
8 [a]Acts 17:26 [b]Num. 23:9; Deut. 33:28
9 [a]1 Sam. 10:1; 1 Kin. 8:51, 53; Jer. 10:16
10 [a]Deut. 1:19 [b]Ps. 17:8; Prov. 7:2; Zech. 2:8
11 [a]Ex. 19:4; Deut. 33:12 [b]Ps. 18:10-18

32:4 *Rock.* A symbol of God's power as a refuge for frail men (see also vv. 13, 15, 18, 30, 31, 37).

32:7-14 These verses furnish an historical background: the dividing of the nations (v. 8; cf. Gen. 10-11), the choosing of Jacob (v. 9), and the deliverance from Egypt (v. 12). *the pupil of His eye* (v. 10). See Zech. 2:8. The protection and training of Israel are described in the illustration of the *eagle* (v. 11). Verses 13-14 refer to experiences in Transjordan, where the people had enjoyed *honey* and olive *oil* (the olive tree yields abundantly when growing on limestone terraces, *flinty rock*), dairy products, meat (concerning *Bashan,* see note on Amos 4:1), the richest grain, and *wine.*

He carried them on His pinions.

12 ^aDeut. 4:35, 39 ^bDeut. 32:39; Is. 43:12

12 "^aThe LORD alone guided him,
^bAnd there was no foreign god with him.

13 ^aIs. 58:14 ^bDeut. 8:8; Ps. 81:16 ^cJob 29:6

13 "^aHe made him ride on the high places of the earth,
And he ate the produce of the field;
^bAnd He made him suck honey from the rock,
And ^coil from the flinty rock,

14 ^aPs. 81:16; 147:14 ^bGen. 49:11

14 Curds of cows, and milk of the flock,
With fat of lambs,
And rams, the breed of Bashan, and goats,
^aWith the finest of the wheat—
And of the ^bblood of grapes you drank wine.

★15-18

15 ^aDeut. 31:20 ^bJudg. 10:6 ^cDeut. 32:6 ^dDeut. 32:4; Ps. 89:26

15 "^aBut Jeshurun grew fat and kicked—
You are grown fat, thick, and sleek—
^bThen he forsook God ^cwho made him,
And scorned ^dthe Rock of his salvation.

16 ^aPs. 78:58 ^bPs. 106:29

16 "^aThey made Him jealous with strange *gods;*
^bWith abominations they provoked Him to anger.

17 ^aLev. 17:7; 1 Cor. 10:20 ^bDeut. 28:64 ^cJudg. 5:8

17 "^aThey sacrificed to demons *who were* not God,
^bTo gods whom they have not known,
^cNew *gods* who came lately,
Whom your fathers did not dread.

18 ^aDeut. 32:4 ^bPs. 106:21

18 "You neglected ^athe Rock who begot you,
^bAnd forgot the God who gave you birth.

19 ^aLev. 26:30; Ps. 106:40 ^bJer. 44:21-23

19 "^aAnd the LORD saw *this,* and spurned *them*

^bBecause of the provocation of His sons and daughters.

20 ^aDeut. 31:29 ^bDeut. 32:5 ^cDeut. 9:23

20 "Then He said, 'I will hide My face from them,
^aI will see what their end shall *be;*
^bFor they are a perverse generation,
^cSons in whom is no faithfulness.

21 ^aDeut. 32:16; 1 Cor. 10:22 ^bDeut. 32:17; 1 Kin. 16:13, 26 ^cRom. 10:19

21 '^aThey have made Me jealous with *what* is not God;
They have provoked Me to anger with their ^bidols.
^cSo I will make them jealous with *those who* are not a people;
I will provoke them to anger with a foolish nation,

★**22** ^aNum. 16:33-35; Ps. 18:7, 8; Lam. 4:11 ^bLev. 26:20

22 ^aFor a fire is kindled in My anger,
And burns to the lowest part of Sheol,
^bAnd consumes the earth with its yield,
And sets on fire the foundations of the mountains.

23 ^aDeut. 29:21 ^bPs. 18:14; 45:5

23 '^aI will heap misfortunes on them;
^bI will use My arrows on them.

24 ^aDeut. 28:22, 48 ^bPs. 91:6 ^cLev. 26:22 ^dAmos 5:18, 19

24 '^aThey shall *be* wasted by famine, and consumed by plague
^bAnd bitter destruction;
^cAnd the teeth of beasts I will send upon them,
^dWith the venom of crawling things of the dust.

25 ^aLam. 1:20; Ezek. 7:15 ^b2 Chr. 36:17; Lam. 2:21

25 '^aOutside the sword shall bereave,
And inside terror—
^bBoth young man and virgin,
The nursling with the man of gray hair.

26 ^aDeut. 4:27; 28:64 ^bDeut. 9:14

26 'I would have said, "^aI will cut them to pieces,

32:15-18 Details of Israel's rebellion. *Jeshurun* means "upright one" and is a term of endearment (see note on Isa. 44:2). On verse 17, see

Lev. 17:7 and Psalm 106:37.
32:22 *Sheol.* See note on Gen. 37:35.

ᵇI will remove the memory of them from men,"

27 Had I not feared the provocation by the enemy,
Lest their adversaries should misjudge,
Lest they should say, "ᵃOur hand is triumphant,
And the LORD has not done all this.' '

28 "ᵃFor they are a nation lacking in counsel,
And there is no understanding in them.

29 "ᵃWould that they were wise, that they understood this,
ᵇThat they would discern their future!

30 "ᵃHow could one chase a thousand,
And two put ten thousand to flight,
Unless their ᵇRock had sold them,
And the LORD had given them up?

31 "Indeed their rock is not like our Rock,
ᵃEven our enemies themselves judge this.

32 "For their vine is from the vine of Sodom,
And from the fields of Gomorrah;
Their grapes are grapes of ᵃpoison,
Their clusters, bitter.

33 "Their wine is the venom of serpents,
And the deadly poison of cobras.

34 'Is it not laid up in store with Me,
Sealed up in My treasuries?
35 'ᵃVengeance is Mine, and retribution,

ᵇIn due time their foot will slip;
ᶜFor the day of their calamity is near,
And the impending things are hastening upon them.'

36 "ᵃFor the LORD will vindicate His people,
ᵇAnd will have compassion on His servants;
When He sees that their strength is gone,
And there is none remaining, bond or free.

37 "And He will say, 'ᵃWhere are their gods,
The rock in which they sought refuge?

38 'ᵃWho ate the fat of their sacrifices,
And drank the wine of their libation?
ᵇLet them rise up and help you,
Let them be your hiding place!

39 'ᵃSee now that I, I am He,
ᵇAnd there is no god besides Me;
ᶜIt is I who put to death and give life.
ᵈI have wounded, and it is I who heal;
ᵉAnd there is no one who can deliver from My hand.

40 'Indeed, ᵃI lift up My hand to heaven,
And say, as I live forever,

41 ᵃIf I sharpen My flashing sword,
And My hand takes hold on justice,
ᵇI will render vengeance on My adversaries,
And I will repay those who hate Me.

42 'ᵃI will make My arrows drunk with blood,

32:27-31 *Our hand is triumphant.* God would limit the victories of Israel's enemies over her, lest they think they accomplished these in their own power and thus take glory from God. Moses longed for Israel to understand that God used her enemies for His purposes.

32:32 The heathen are characterized as coming from wicked stock.

32:39-43 God is absolutely sovereign (v. 39) and will ultimately judge Israel's enemies and restore His chosen people.

ᵇAnd My sword shall devour flesh,
With the blood of the slain and the captives,
From the long-haired leaders of the enemy.'

43 "ᵃRejoice, O nations, *with* His people;
ᵇFor He will avenge the blood of His servants,
ᶜAnd will render vengeance on His adversaries,
ᵈAnd will atone for His land *and* His people."

44 Then Moses came and spoke all the words of this song in the hearing of the people, he, with ᵃJoshua the son of Nun.

45 When Moses had finished speaking all these words to all Israel,

46 he said to them, "ᵃTake to your heart all the words with which I am warning you today, which you shall command ᵇyour sons to observe carefully, *even* all the words of this law.

47 "For it is not an idle word for you; indeed ᵃit is your life. And ᵇby this word you shall prolong your days in the land, which you are about to cross the Jordan to possess."

C   Testament of Moses,
32:48–33:29

48 And ᵃthe LORD spoke to Moses that very same day, saying,

49 "ᵃGo up to this mountain of the Abarim, Mount Nebo, which is in the land of Moab opposite Jericho, and look at the land of Canaan, which I am giving to the sons of Israel for a possession.

50 "Then die on the mountain where you ascend, and be ᵃgathered to your people, as Aaron your brother died on Mount Hor and was gathered to his people,

51 ᵃbecause you broke faith with Me in the midst of the sons of Israel at the waters of Meribah-kadesh, in the ᵇwilderness of Zin, because you did not treat Me as holy in the midst of the sons of Israel.

52 "ᵃFor you shall see the land at a distance, but ᵇyou shall not go there, into the land which I am giving the sons of Israel."

33
Now this is the blessing with which Moses ᵃthe man of God blessed the sons of Israel before his death.

2   And he said,
"ᵃThe LORD came from Sinai,
ᵇAnd dawned on them from Seir;
ᶜHe shone forth from Mount Paran,
And He came from ᵈthe midst of ten thousand holy ones;
ᵉAt His right hand there was flashing lightning for them.

3   "ᵃIndeed, He loves the people;
ᵇAll Thy holy ones are in Thy hand,
ᶜAnd they followed in Thy steps;
Everyone receives of Thy words.

4   "ᵃMoses charged us with a law,
ᵇA possession for the assembly of Jacob.

5   "ᵃAnd He was king in Jeshurun,
When the heads of the people were gathered,
The tribes of Israel together.

---

43 ᵃRom. 15:10 ᵇ2 Kin. 9:7; Rev. 6:10; 19:2 cls. 1:24, 25 ᵈPs. 65:3; 79:9; 85:1

★44 ᵃNum. 13:8, 16

46 ᵃEzek. 40:4; 44:5 ᵇDeut. 4:9

47 ᵃDeut. 8:3; 30:20 ᵇDeut. 4:40; 33:25

48 ᵃNum. 27:12

★49 ᵃNum. 27:12-14; Deut. 3:27

★50 ᵃGen. 25:8

★51 ᵃNum. 20:12 ᵇNum. 27:14

52 ᵃDeut. 34:1-3 ᵇDeut. 1:37; 3:27

★ 1-5

1 ᵃJosh. 14:6

2 ᵃEx. 19:18, 20; Ps. 68:8, 17 ᵇJudg. 5:4 ᶜNum. 10:12; Hab. 3:3 ᵈDan. 7:10; Acts 7:53 ᵉEx. 23:20-22

3 ᵃDeut. 4:37; Mal. 1:2 ᵇDeut. 7:6; 14:2 ᶜDeut. 6:1-9; Luke 10:39

4 ᵃDeut. 4:2; John 7:19 ᵇPs. 119:111

5 ᵃNum. 23:21

32:44 *Joshua.* Lit., Hoshea. See note on Num. 13:16.
32:49 *Abarim.* See note on Num. 27:12. *Nebo.* See note on Num. 23:14.
32:50 *Hor.* See note on Num. 20:22.
32:51 See note on Num. 20:13.
33:1-5 Moses, in introducing his *blessing* (cf. Jacob's in Gen. 49), recounts God's advancing with His people from *Sinai, Seir* (Edom), and *Paran* (NE. part of the Sinai Peninsula). He came *from the midst of . . . holy ones.* A reference to angels. However, the *holy ones* in verse 3 refer to Israel, God's separated people. *Jeshurun.* See note on 32:15.

★ 6 aGen.
49:3, 4

6 "aMay Reuben live and
not die,
Nor his men be few."

★ 7 aGen.
49:8-12

7 aAnd this regarding Judah;
so he said,
"Hear, O Lord, the voice
of Judah,
And bring him to his
people.
With his hands he con-
tended for them;
And mayest Thou be a
help against his adver-
saries."

★ 8 aEx.
28:30; Lev.
8:8 bPs.
106:16 cEx.
17:7; Num.
20:13, 24;
Deut. 6:16

8 And of Levi he said,
"Let Thy aThummim and
Thy Urim belong to
Thy bgodly man,
cWhom Thou didst
prove at Massah,
With whom Thou didst
contend at the waters
of Meribah;

9 aEx.
32:27-29
bMal. 2:5

9 aWho said of his father
and his mother,
'I did not consider them';
And he did not ac-
knowledge his broth-
ers,
Nor did he regard his
own sons,
For bthey observed Thy
word,
And kept Thy covenant.

10 aLev.
10:11; Deut.
31:9-13
bLev. 16:12,
13 cPs.
51:19

10 "aThey shall teach Thine
ordinances to Jacob,
And Thy law to Israel.
bThey shall put incense
before Thee,
And cwhole burnt offer-
ings on Thine altar.

11 "O Lord, bless his substance,

And accept the work of
his hands;
Shatter the loins of
those who rise up
against him,
And those who hate
him, so that they may
not rise again."

12 Of Benjamin he said,
"aMay the beloved of the
Lord dwell in security
by Him,
bWho shields him all the
day,
cAnd he dwells between
His shoulders."

★12 aDeut.
4:37f.; 12:10
bDeut. 32:11
cEx. 28:12

13 And of Joseph he said,
"aBlessed of the Lord be
his land,
With the choice things
of heaven, with the
dew,
And from the deep lying
beneath,

★13-17

13 aGen.
27:27, 28;
49:22-26

14 And with the choice
yield of the sun,
And with the choice
produce of the
months.

15 "And with the best things
of athe ancient moun-
tains,
And with the choice
things of the ever-
lasting hills,

15 aHab. 3:6

16 And with the choice
things of the earth
and its fulness,
And the favor aof Him
who dwelt in the
bush.
Let it come to the head
of Joseph,

16 aEx. 2:2-
6; 3:2, 4

33:6 The prayer for Reuben reflects the danger of the tribe's decline, exposed as it was to Moab on the E. side of the Jordan. The Septuagint makes the last half of the verse refer to Simeon, who is omitted from the list. This omission was probably because Simeon's portion of land in Canaan was within the border of Judah (Josh. 19:1-9).

33:7 Moses prayed that Judah would take her place of leadership in Israel (cf. Gen. 49:8-12).

33:8 Concerning the Urim and Thummim, see

note on Exod. 28:30. Levi was to be faithful, as Moses was at Massah and Meribah (see note on Exod. 17:2). The Levites' duties are listed in verses 10-11.

33:12 The site of the future Temple in Jerusalem would be situated in the territory of Benjamin. he dwells. I.e., the Lord shall dwell.

33:13-17 Joseph, represented by his two sons Ephraim and Manasseh (v. 17), would have the choicest part of the land.

And to the crown of the
head of the one dis-
tinguished among his
brothers.

17 aNum.
23:22
b1 Kin.
22:11; Ps.
44:5

17 "As the first-born of his
ox, majesty is his,
And his horns are the
horns of ªthe wild ox;
With them he shall
ᵇpush the peoples,
All at once, to the ends
of the earth.
And those are the ten
thousands of Ephra-
im,
And those are the thou-
sands of Manasseh."

★18-19

18 aGen.
49:13-15

18 ªAnd of Zebulun he said,
"Rejoice, Zebulun, in
your going forth,
And, Issachar, in your
tents.

19 aEx.
15:17; Ps.
2:6; Is. 2:3
bPs. 4:5;
51:19 cIs.
60:5

19 "ªThey shall call peoples
to the mountain;
There they shall offer
ᵇrighteous sacrifices;
For they shall draw out
ᶜthe abundance of the
seas,
And the hidden trea-
sures of the sand."

★20-21

20 aGen.
49:19 bGen.
49:9

20 ªAnd of Gad he said,
"Blessed is the one who
enlarges Gad;
He lies down ᵇas a lion,
And tears the arm, also
the crown of the head.

21 aNum.
32:1-5
bNum. 34:14
cJosh. 4:12
dJosh.
22:1-3
★22 aGen.
49:16 bEzek.
19:2, 3

21 "ªThen he provided the
first part for himself,
ᵇFor there the ruler's
portion was reserved;
ᶜAnd he came with the
leaders of the people;
ᵈHe executed the justice
of the Lᴏʀᴅ,

And His ordinances with
Israel."

22 ªAnd of Dan he said,
"Dan is ᵇa lion's whelp,
That leaps forth from
Bashan."

23 And of Naphtali he said,
"ªO Naphtali, satisfied
with favor,
And full of the blessing
of the Lᴏʀᴅ,
Take possession of the
sea and the south."

★23 aGen.
49:21

24 ªAnd of Asher he said,
"More blessed than sons
is Asher;
May he be favored by
his brothers,
ᵇAnd may he dip his
foot in oil.

★24-25

24 aGen.
49:20 bJob
29:6

25 "ªYour locks shall be iron
and bronze,
ᵇAnd according to your
days, so shall your lei-
surely walk be.

25 aPs.
147:13
bDeut. 4:40;
32:47

26 "ªThere is none like the
God of Jeshurun,
ᵇWho rides the heavens
to your help,
And through the skies
in His majesty.

★26-29

26 aEx.
15:11; Deut.
4:35; Ps.
86:8; Jer.
10:6 bDeut.
10:14; Ps.
68:33, 34;
104:3; Hab.
3:8

27 "ªThe eternal God is a
dwelling place,
ᵇAnd underneath are
the everlasting arms;
ᶜAnd He drove out the
enemy from before
you,
ᵈAnd said, 'Destroy!'

27 aPs. 90:1,
2 bGen.
49:24 cEx.
34:11; Josh.
24:18 dDeut.
7:2

28 "ªSo Israel dwells in security,
ᵇThe fountain of Jacob
secluded,
ᶜIn a land of grain and
new wine;

28 aDeut.
33:12; Jer.
23:6 bNum.
23:9; Deut.
32:8 cGen.
27:28, 37
dDeut. 33:13

33:18-19 *Zebulun* was assured success in commercial dealings, including sea trade, and *Issachar*, in his agricultural pursuits (*in your
tents*).
33:20-21 *Gad*, swift and strong *as a lion* (v. 20),
got a piece of land fit for a ruler, yet he helped
the other tribes in the conquest of Canaan (cf.
v. 21b).
33:22 *Dan*, like an aggressive *lion's whelp* (cub),
established a foothold in *Bashan* in the N.,

though his original allotment was in the S. (see
Judg. 18).
33:23 *Naphtali* occupied the fertile land W. and
S. of the Lake of Galilee.
33:24-25 The territory of *Asher* was famous for
its olives (*oil*). Asher would be given strength
to secure Israel's northern border (v. 25).
33:26-29 God is above, beneath, and before His
people, an eternal refuge.

*d*His heavens also drop down dew.

29 *a*Ps. 1:1;
32:1, 2
*b*Deut. 4:32;
2 Sam. 7:23
*c*Gen. 15:1;
Ps. 33:20;
115:9-11
*d*Ps. 68:34
*e*Ps. 66:3
f Num. 33:52

29 "*a*Blessed are you, O Israel;

*b*Who is like you, a people saved by the LORD,

*c*Who is the shield of your help,

*d*And the sword of your majesty!

*e*So your enemies shall cringe before you,

*f*And you shall tread upon their high places."

D Death of Moses, 34:1-12

★ 1 *a*Deut.
32:49 *b*Deut.
32:52

34 *a*Now Moses went up from the plains of Moab to Mount Nebo, to the top of Pisgah, which is opposite Jericho. And the LORD *b*showed him all the land, Gilead as far as Dan,

★ 2-3

2 *a*Deut.
11:24

2 and all Naphtali and the land of Ephraim and Manasseh, and all the land of Judah as far as the *a*western sea,

3 *a*Judg.
1:16; 3:13;
2 Chr. 28:15

3 and the Negev and the plain in the valley of Jericho, *a*the city of palm trees, as far as Zoar.

4 *a*Gen.
12:7; 26:3;
28:13

4 Then the LORD said to him, "This is the land which *a*I swore to Abraham, Isaac, and Jacob, saying, 'I will give it to your descendants'; I have let you see *it*

with your eyes, but you shall not go over there."

5 *a*Num.
12:7; Josh.
1:1, 2 *b*Deut.
32:50

5 So Moses *a*the servant of the LORD *b*died there in the land of Moab, according to the word of the LORD.

★ 6 *a*Deut.
3:29; 4:46
*b*Jude 9

6 And He buried him in the valley in the land of Moab, *a*opposite Beth-peor; but *b*no man knows his burial place to this day.

★ 7 *a*Deut.
31:2 *b*Gen.
27:1; 48:10

7 Although Moses was *a*one hundred and twenty years old when he died, *b*his eye was not dim, nor his vigor abated.

8 So the sons of Israel wept for Moses in the plains of Moab thirty days; then the days of weeping *and* mourning for Moses came to an end.

9 *a*Num.
27:18, 23; Is.
11:2

9 Now Joshua the son of Nun was *a*filled with the spirit of wisdom, for Moses had laid his hands on him; and the sons of Israel listened to him and did as the LORD had commanded Moses.

★10 *a*Deut.
18:15, 18
*b*Ex. 33:11;
Num. 12:8;
Deut. 5:4

10 Since then *a*no prophet has risen in Israel like Moses, whom *b*the LORD knew face to face,

11 for all the signs and wonders which the LORD sent him to perform in the land of Egypt against Pharaoh, all his servants, and all his land,

12 and for all the mighty power and for all the great terror which Moses performed in the sight of all Israel.

34:1 *Pisgah.* See note on Num. 23:14.
34:2-3 *the western sea.* The Mediterranean. Moses' panorama was toward the NE., then W. and S., and finally back to the plain between Jericho and Nebo. *Zoar.* Located at the S. end of the Dead Sea.
34:6 Though Moses' exact burial place is unknown, it was in the area where the people

were camped (*Beth-peor,* about 10 miles E. of the Jordan at its mouth, cf. 3:29; 4:46).
34:7 See note on 31:2.
34:10 With Moses, God spoke *face to face* (cf. Exod. 33:11; Num. 12:8). Joshua needed the priests' help in order to discover the will of God (cf. Num. 27:21).

INTRODUCTION TO
THE BOOK OF JOSHUA

AUTHOR: Joshua DATE: 1400–1370 B.C.

Authorship Basically the book was composed by Joshua himself. To be sure, a few sections—such as 15:13-17 (cf. Judg. 1:9-13) and Josh. 24:29-31—could not have been written by him. These were probably added by Eleazar the priest or by Phinehas, his son. But Joshua is specifically identified as the author of 24:1-26, and clearly the author was an eyewitness of many of the events recorded—see, for example, 5:1 (contains we in some mss.) and 5:6 (us). It is also evident that the book was written not long after the events happened (6:25).

Background The book describes the conquest and division of the land of Canaan and is set against the background of the corrupt and brutal features of Canaanite religion, depicted clearly in the Ras Shamra Tablets. Prostitution of both sexes, infant sacrifice, and religious syncretism were some of the evils for which God commanded the Israelites to exterminate the inhabitants of Canaan. Much of the later spiritual declension in Israel was due to the fact that the Canaanites were not completely destroyed. As a result, their religion was tolerated and frequently absorbed by the Israelites.

The events of Joshua begin where those of Deuteronomy conclude. For a discussion of the time of the conquest, see the Introduction to the Book of Exodus.

Joshua the Man Evidently born in Egypt, Joshua (whose name means "Yahweh is salvation"; see note on Num. 13:16) may have served in Pharaoh's army. In any case, he was well qualified to command the Israelite forces against the Amalekites at Rephidim (Exod. 17:8-16). He served as personal attendant to Moses during the year at Mt. Sinai (Exod. 24:13). As the representative of the tribe of Ephraim, he scouted the land of Canaan with the other 11 spies and, with Caleb, opposed the majority report not to try to conquer the land (Num. 14:6-9). Before Moses' death he was commissioned as successor (Num. 27:18-23), and led the people in their conquest of Canaan. His outstanding qualities were faith, courage, obedience, and devotion to the law of God.

Date Assuming the earlier date for the Exodus from Egypt (see Introduction to the Book of Exodus), the conquest of Canaan under Joshua took place around 1400 B.C. The later date for the Exodus places the conquest of Canaan around 1240, a date more difficult to harmonize with the slight mention in the book of Joshua (13:2-3) of the Philistines, who were strong in Palestine around 1200.

Important Emphases The book emphasizes (1) the faithfulness of God to give Israel the land of Canaan (cf. Gen. 13:15); (2) the importance of the written Law of God (Josh. 1:8; 8:32-35; 23:6-16; 24:26-27); and (3) the holiness of God in judging the sins of the Canaanites (cf. Deut. 7:1-6).

OUTLINE OF JOSHUA

THE BOOK OF JOSHUA

I ENTERING THE LAND OF CANAAN, 1:1-5:15
A The Commission of God to Joshua, 1:1-9

1 Now it came about after the death of Moses the servant of the LORD that the LORD spoke to Joshua the son of Nun, Moses' servant, saying,

2 "Moses ᵃMy servant is dead; now therefore arise, ᵇcross this Jordan, you and all this people, to the land which I am giving to them, to the sons of Israel.

3 "ᵃEvery place on which the sole of your foot treads, I have given it to you, just as I spoke to Moses.

4 "ᵃFrom the wilderness and this Lebanon, even as far as the great river, the river Euphrates, all the land of the Hittites, and as far as the Great Sea toward the setting of the sun, will be your territory.

5 "ᵃNo man will *be able to* stand before you all the days of your life. Just as I have been with Moses, I will be with you; ᵇI will not fail you or forsake you.

6 "ᵃBe strong and courageous, for you shall give this people possession of the land which I swore to their fathers to give them.

7 "Only be strong and very courageous; ᵃbe careful to do according to all the law which Moses My servant commanded you; do not turn from it to the right or to the left, so that you may have success wherever you go.

8 "ᵃThis book of the law shall not depart from your mouth, but you shall meditate on it day and night, so that you may be careful to do according to all that is written in it; ᵇfor then you will make your way prosperous, and then you will have success.

9 "Have I not commanded you? ᵃBe strong and courageous! ᵇDo not tremble or be dismayed, for the LORD your God is with you wherever you go."

B The Command of Joshua to the People, 1:10-18

10 Then Joshua commanded the officers of the people, saying,

11 "Pass through the midst of the camp and command the people, saying, 'Prepare provisions

---

Marginal references:

★ 2 ᵃNum. 12:7; Deut. 34:5 ᵇJosh. 1:11

3 ᵃDeut. 11:24

★ 4 ᵃGen. 15:18; Num. 34:3

5 ᵃDeut. 7:24 ᵇDeut. 31:6, 7; Heb. 13:5

6 ᵃDeut. 31:6, 7, 23

7 ᵃDeut. 5:32

★ 8 ᵃDeut. 31:24; Josh. 8:34 ᵇDeut. 29:9; Ps. 1:1-3

9 ᵃJosh. 1:7 ᵇDeut. 31:8

★11 ᵃJosh. 3:2

1:2 *Moses* was forbidden to enter Palestine because of his unbelief (see Num. 20:12). The *Jordan,* then at flood stage (Josh. 3:15), would be difficult to cross.

1:4 The southern boundary of the land was the *wilderness* of Arabia; the northern, *Lebanon;* the eastern, the *Euphrates* River; and the western, the Mediterranean. *the land of the Hittites* is usually understood to mean N. Syria, though this phrase is not found in this verse in the Septuagint (Greek translation of the Hebrew Scriptures), nor in Deut. 11:24. This was the land promised to Abraham (see note on Gen. 15:18-21).

1:8 The success of Joshua's mission would lie in his personal obedience to the *law* of God. *meditate.* To ponder, muse, involving half-aloud reading and rereading of the Word (Psalm 1:2). Notice that the Law was already *written* at this time and was held to be authoritative.

1:11 *within three days.* The mission of the spies (chap. 2) apparently took place before this command to prepare was given. What is described in 3:2 may be the same as in 1:11, or may have followed it.

for yourselves, for within [a]three days you are to cross this Jordan, to go in to possess the land which the Lord your God is giving you, to possess it.' "

★12-15

12 aNum. 32:20-22

12 [a]And to the Reubenites and to the Gadites and to the half-tribe of Manasseh, Joshua said,

13 aDeut. 3:18-20

13 "Remember the word which Moses the servant of the Lord commanded you, saying, '[a]The Lord your God gives you rest, and will give you this land.'

14 "Your wives, your little ones, and your cattle shall remain in the land which Moses gave you beyond the Jordan, but you shall cross before your brothers in battle array, all your valiant warriors, and shall help them,

15 aJosh. 22:4 bJosh. 1:1

15 until the Lord gives your brothers rest, as He gives you, and they also possess the land which the Lord your God is giving them. [a]Then you shall return to your own land, and possess that which Moses [b]the servant of the Lord gave you beyond the Jordan toward the sunrise."

16 And they answered Joshua, saying, "All that you have commanded us we will do, and wherever you send us we will go.

17 aJosh. 1:5, 9

17 "Just as we obeyed Moses in all things, so we will obey you; only [a]may the Lord your God be with you, as He was with Moses.

18 "Anyone who rebels against your command and does not obey your words in all that you command him, shall be put to death; only be strong and courageous."

C   The Canvassing of Jericho: Rahab and the Spies, 2:1-24

2 Then Joshua the son of Nun sent two men as spies secretly from [a]Shittim, saying, "Go, view the land, especially Jericho." So they went and came into the house of [b]a harlot whose name was Rahab, and lodged there.

★ 1 aNum. 25:1; Josh. 3:1 bHeb. 11:31; James 2:25

2 And it was told the king of Jericho, saying, "Behold, men from the sons of Israel have come here tonight to search out the land."

★ 2

3 And the king of Jericho sent *word* to Rahab, saying, "Bring out the men who have come to you, who have entered your house, for they have come to search out all the land."

4 But the [a]woman had taken the two men and hidden them, and she said, "Yes, the men came to me, but I did not know where they were from.

★4-5

4 a2 Sam. 17:19

5 "And it came about when *it was time* to shut the gate, at dark, that the men went out; I do not know where the men went. Pursue them quickly, for you will overtake them."

6 But [a]she had brought them up to the roof and hidden them in the stalks of flax which she had laid in order on the roof.

★ 6 aJames 2:25

7 So the men pursued them on the road to the Jordan to the fords; and as soon as those who were pursuing them had gone out, they shut the gate.

★ 7

1:12-15 See notes on Num. 32.

2:1 *secretly.* Joshua, having learned an important lesson from his experience at Kadesh-barnea (Num. 13-14), concealed the spy mission even from the Israelites, so that if an unfavorable report were returned, the people would not be disheartened. *Shittim.* See note on Num. 25:1.

2:2 *the king of Jericho.* The local chief of the city-state of Jericho, not a ruler of an extensive area.

2:4-5 Rahab's actions, though not in conformity with the scriptural prohibition against lying, were evidence that she believed the God of

Israel was the true God (vv. 10-13). The Bible commends her faith, not her lying (Heb. 11:31; James 2:25). God's grace is remarkably demonstrated in giving her faith, sparing her, and including her in the Messianic line (Matt. 1:5).

2:6 *stalks of flax.* Three- or four-foot stems, previously soaked in water, laid out on the flat roof to dry.

2:7 *the fords* were to the E. of the city. Rahab's house was apparently on the western wall (toward the mountains, v. 16). She sent the soldiers in the opposite direction from the spies.

8 Now before they lay down, she came up to them on the roof,

★ **9** aNum. 20:24; Josh. 9:24 bEx. 23:27; Deut. 2:25; Josh. 9:9, 10

9 and said to the men, "aI know that the LORD has given you the land, and that the bterror of you has fallen on us, and that all the inhabitants of the land have melted away before you.

★**10** aEx. 14:21; Num. 23:22; 24:8 bNum. 21:21-35

10 "aFor we have heard how the LORD dried up the water of the Red Sea before you when you came out of Egypt, and bwhat you did to the two kings of the Amorites who were beyond the Jordan, to Sihon and Og, whom you utterly destroyed.

11 aJosh. 5:1; 7:5; Ps. 22:14; Is. 13:7; 19:1 bDeut. 4:39

11 "And when we heard it, aour hearts melted and no courage remained in any man any longer because of you; for the bLORD your God, He is God in heaven above and on earth beneath.

★**12** aJosh. 2:18, 19

12 "Now therefore, please swear to me by the LORD, since I have dealt kindly with you, that you also will deal kindly with my father's household, and give me a apledge of truth,

13 and spare my father and my mother and my brothers and my sisters, with all who belong to them, and deliver our lives from death."

★**14** aGen. 24:49

14 So the men said to her, "Our life for yours if you do not tell this business of ours; and it shall come about when the LORD gives us the land that we will adeal kindly and faithfully with you."

★**15**

15 Then she let them down by a rope through the window, for her house was on the city wall, so that she was living on the wall.

16 aJames 2:25

16 And she said to them, "aGo to the hill country, lest the pursuers happen upon you, and hide yourselves there for three days, until the pursuers return. Then afterward you may go on your way."

17 And the men said to her, "aWe shall be free from this oath to you which you have made us swear,

17 aGen. 24:8

18 unless, when we come into the land, you tie this cord of scarlet thread in the window through which you let us down, and agather to yourself into the house your father and your mother and your brothers and all your father's household.

★**18** aJosh. 2:12

19 "And it shall come about that anyone who goes out of the doors of your house into the street, his blood shall be on his own head, and we shall be free; but anyone who is with you in the house, ahis blood shall be on our head, if a hand is laid on him.

19 aMatt. 27:25

20 "But if you tell this business of ours, then we shall be free from the oath which you have made us swear."

21 And she said, "According to your words, so be it." So she sent them away, and they departed; and she tied the scarlet cord in the window.

22 And they departed and came to the hill country, and remained there for three days until the pursuers returned. Now the pursuers had sought them all along the road, but had not found them.

23 Then the two men returned and came down from the hill country and crossed over and came to Joshua the son of Nun, and they related to him all that had happened to them.

24 And they said to Joshua, "Surely the LORD has given all the land into our hands, and aall the inhabitants of the land, moreover, have melted away before us."

24 aJosh. 2:9

2:9 See the promise of Deut. 2:25.
2:10 See notes on Exod. 14:19–22, Num. 21:21, and Deut. 3:11.
2:12 dealt kindly. Heb., hesed. Steadfast loyalty, here between human beings, though usually between God and Israel (see note on Hos. 2:19).

2:14 The meaning is this: May we die instead of you if we fail to keep our bargain.
2:15 a rope. A different word than used in verse 18.
2:18 The scarlet thread would enable the invading Israelites to identify the house they were to spare.

D The Crossing of the Jordan River, 3:1-17

1 *a*Josh. 2:1

3 Then Joshua rose early in the morning; and he and all the sons of Israel set out from *a*Shittim and came to the Jordan, and they lodged there before they crossed.

2 *a*Josh. 1:11

2 And it came about *a*at the end of three days that the officers went through the midst of the camp;

★ **3** *a*Deut. 31:9

3 and they commanded the people, saying, "When you see the *a*ark of the covenant of the Lord your God with the Levitical priests carrying it, then you shall set out from your place and go after it.

★ **4**

4 "However, there shall be between you and it a distance of about 2,000 cubits by measure. Do not come near it, that you may know the way by which you shall go, for you have not passed this way before."

5 *a*Ex. 19:10, 11; Josh. 7:13

5 Then Joshua said to the people, "*a*Consecrate yourselves, for tomorrow the Lord will do wonders among you."

6 And Joshua spoke to the priests, saying, "Take up the ark of the covenant and cross over ahead of the people." So they took up the ark of the covenant and went ahead of the people.

7 *a*Josh. 4:14

7 Now the Lord said to Joshua, "This day I will begin to *a*exalt you in the sight of all Israel, that they may know that just as I have been with Moses, I will be with you.

8 "You shall, moreover, command the priests who are carrying the ark of the covenant, saying,

'When you come to the edge of the waters of the Jordan, you shall stand *still* in the Jordan.' "

9 Then Joshua said to the sons of Israel, "Come here, and hear the words of the Lord your God."

10 And Joshua said, "By this you shall know that *a*the living God is among you, and that He will assuredly *b*dispossess from before you the Canaanite, the Hittite, the Hivite, the Perizzite, the Girgashite, the Amorite, and the Jebusite.

11 "Behold, the ark of the covenant of *a*the Lord of all the earth is crossing over ahead of you into the Jordan.

12 "Now then, *a*take for yourselves twelve men from the tribes of Israel, one man for each tribe.

13 "And it shall come about when the soles of the feet of the priests who carry the ark of the Lord, the Lord of all the earth, shall rest in the waters of the Jordan, the waters of the Jordan shall be cut off, *and* the waters which are flowing down from above shall *a*stand in one heap."

14 So it came about when the people set out from their tents to cross the Jordan with the priests carrying *a*the ark of the covenant before the people,

15 and when those who carried the ark came into the Jordan, and the feet of the priests carrying the ark were dipped in the edge of the water (for the *a*Jordan overflows all its banks all the days of harvest),

16 *a*that the waters which were flowing down from above stood *and* rose up in *b*one heap, a

★**10** *a*Deut. 5:26; 1 Thess. 1:9 *b*Ex. 33:2; Deut. 7:1

11 *a*Job 41:11; Ps. 24:1; Zech. 6:5

12 *a*Josh. 4:2

13 *a*Ex. 15:8

14 *a*Ps. 132:8; Acts 7:44f.

15 *a*1 Chr. 12:15; Jer. 12:5; 49:19

★**16** *a*Ps. 66:6; 74:15; 114:3, 5 *b*Josh. 3:13 *c*Deut. 1:1

3:3 Normally the Kohathites carried the Ark, but on this extraordinary occasion the Levites who were priests carried it (as also in 6:6; 1 Kings 8:3-6).

3:4 The people were to be spread around at a distance of 3,000 feet from the Ark so that all could see it and be guided by it.

3:10 The destruction of the Canaanites was (1) to punish them for their gross wickedness (see notes on Deut. 7:2, 5) and (2) to prevent Israel from being infected by their evil religions.

3:16 The waters of the Jordan were dammed up at the city of Adam, 15 miles up river from where the Israelites crossed. In addition, the streams that flowed into the Jordan S. of Adam were also stopped. While it is true that a landslide could have stopped the Jordan, this would not have blocked these other streams, certainly not immediately, nor have allowed the river to begin to flow again immediately (4:18), nor permitted the people to walk on dry ground (3:17).

great distance away at Adam, the city that is beside Zarethan; and those which were flowing down toward the sea of the ᶜArabah, the Salt Sea, were completely cut off. So the people crossed opposite Jericho.

17 And the priests who carried the ark of the covenant of the LORD stood firm ᵃon dry ground in the middle of the Jordan while all Israel crossed on dry ground, until all the nation had finished crossing the Jordan.

E The Commemoration of the Crossing, 4:1-24

4 Now it came about when all the nation had finished crossing the ᵃJordan, that the LORD spoke to Joshua, saying,

2 "ᵃTake for yourselves twelve men from the people, one man from each tribe,

3 and command them, saying, 'Take up for yourselves twelve stones from here out of the middle of the Jordan, from the place where the priests' feet are standing firm, and carry them over with you, and lay them down in ᵃthe lodging place where you will lodge tonight.'"

4 So Joshua called the twelve men whom he had appointed from the sons of Israel, one man from each tribe;

5 and Joshua said to them, "Cross again to the ark of the LORD your God into the middle of the Jordan, and each of you take up a stone on his shoulder, according to the number of the tribes of the sons of Israel.

6 "Let this be a sign among you, so that ᵃwhen your children ask later, saying, 'What do these stones mean to you?'

7 then you shall say to them, 'Because the ᵃwaters of the Jordan

were cut off before the ark of the covenant of the LORD; when it crossed the Jordan, the waters of the Jordan were cut off.' So these stones shall become a ᵇmemorial to the sons of Israel forever."

8 And thus the sons of Israel did, as Joshua commanded, and took up twelve stones from the middle of the Jordan, just as the LORD spoke to Joshua, according to the number of the tribes of the sons of Israel; and they carried them over with them to ᵃthe lodging place, and put them down there.

9 Then Joshua set up twelve ᵃstones in the middle of the Jordan at the place where the feet of the priests who carried the ark of the covenant were standing, and they are there to this day.

10 For the priests who carried the ark were standing in the middle of the Jordan until everything was completed that the LORD had commanded Joshua to speak to the people, according to all that Moses had commanded Joshua. And the people hurried and crossed;

11 and it came about when all the people had finished crossing, that the ark of the LORD and the priests crossed before the people.

12 ᵃAnd the sons of Reuben and the sons of Gad and the half-tribe of Manasseh crossed over in battle array before the sons of Israel, just as Moses had spoken to them;

13 about 40,000, equipped for war, crossed for battle before the LORD to the desert plains of Jericho.

14 ᵃOn that day the LORD exalted Joshua in the sight of all Israel; so that they revered him, just as they had revered Moses all the days of his life.

15 Now the LORD said to Joshua,

---

17 ᵃEx. 14:21, 22, 29

★ 1-8
1 ᵃDeut. 27:2; Josh. 3:17
2 ᵃJosh. 3:12
3 ᵃJosh. 4:20

6 ᵃEx. 12:26; 13:14; Josh. 4:21

7 ᵃJosh. 3:13 ᵇEx. 12:14; Num. 16:40

8 ᵃJosh. 4:20

★ 9 ᵃGen. 28:18; Josh. 24:26f.; 1 Sam. 7:12

★12-13
12 ᵃNum. 32:17

14 ᵃJosh. 3:7

4:1-8 The 12 men, previously chosen (3:12), returned to where the priests were standing, to retrieve 12 stones with which to erect a memorial at Gilgal (4:20).
4:9 A second memorial of 12 stones was placed in the Jordan itself.

4:12-13 This was less than half the total number of fighting men in these tribes, the others remaining on the E. side of the Jordan to protect their lands and families. These 40,000 men led the crossing.

16 "Command the priests who carry ᵃthe ark of the testimony that they come up from the Jordan."

17 So Joshua commanded the priests, saying, "Come up from the Jordan."

18 And it came about when the priests who carried the ark of the covenant of the LORD had come up from the middle of the Jordan, and the soles of the priests' feet were lifted up to the dry ground, that the waters of the Jordan returned to their place, and went over all its banks as before.

19 Now the people came up from the Jordan on the ᵃtenth of the first month and camped at Gilgal on the eastern edge of Jericho.

20 ᵃAnd those twelve stones which they had taken from the Jordan, Joshua set up ᵇat Gilgal.

21 And he said to the sons of Israel, "When your children ask their fathers in time to come, saying, 'What are these stones?'

22 then you shall inform your children, saying, 'Israel crossed this Jordan on ᵃdry ground.'

23 "For the LORD your God dried up the waters of the Jordan before you until you had crossed, just as the LORD your God had done to the Red Sea, ᵃwhich He dried up before us until we had crossed;

24 that ᵃall the peoples of the earth may know that the ᵇhand of the LORD is mighty, so that you may ᶜfear the LORD your God forever."

F The Circumcision of the People, 5:1-12

5 Now it came about when all the kings of the Amorites who *were* beyond the Jordan to the west, and all the kings of the ᵃCanaanites who *were* by the sea, ᵇheard how the LORD had dried up the waters of the Jordan before the sons of Israel until they had crossed, that their hearts melted, and there was no spirit in them any longer, because of the sons of Israel.

2 At that time the LORD said to Joshua, "Make for yourself ᵃflint knives and circumcise again the sons of Israel the second time."

3 So Joshua made himself flint knives and circumcised the sons of Israel at Gibeath-haaraloth.

4 And this is the reason why Joshua circumcised them: ᵃall the people who came out of Egypt who were males, all the men of war, died in the wilderness along the way, after they came out of Egypt.

5 For all the people who came out were circumcised, but all the people who were born in the wilderness along the way as they came out of Egypt had not been circumcised.

6 For the sons of Israel walked ᵃforty years in the wilderness, until all the nation, *that is,* the men of war who came out of Egypt, perished because they did not listen to the voice of the LORD, ᵇto whom the LORD had sworn

---

16 ᵃEx. 25:16

★**19** ᵃDeut. 1:3

20 ᵃJosh. 4:8 ᵇJosh. 4:3, 8

22 ᵃJosh. 3:17

23 ᵃEx. 14:21

24 ᵃ1 Kin. 8:42; 2 Kin. 19:19; Ps. 106:8 ᵇEx. 15:16; 1 Chr. 29:12; Ps. 89:13 ᶜEx. 14:31; Ps. 76:71; Jer. 10:7

★**1** ᵃNum. 13:29 ᵇJosh. 2:10, 11

★**2** ᵃEx. 4:25

4 ᵃDeut. 2:14

6 ᵃDeut. 2:7, 14 ᵇNum. 14:29-35; 26:63-65

4:19 *Gilgal* was about 1¼ miles from *Jericho.* The Israelites arrived just in time to select the Passover lamb (see notes on Exod. 12), 40 years after the former generation had left Egypt.

5:1 The people of Canaan had counted on the Jordan acting as a barrier against invasion of their land by the Israelites.

5:2 *circumcise.* The sign of faith in the covenant

made with Abraham (see note on Gen. 17:9-14). During the wilderness experience, the rite had not been performed, the nation being under judgment. Now, before taking possession of the land, it was necessary to circumcise all males under 38 (i.e., who were under 20 at Kadesh, 18 years previous to this time).

that He would not let them see the land which the LORD had sworn to their fathers to give us, a land flowing with milk and honey.

7 And their children whom He raised up in their place, Joshua circumcised; for they were uncircumcised, because they had not circumcised them along the way.

8 Now it came about when they had finished circumcising all the nation, that they remained in their places in the camp until they were healed.

★ **9** *a*Zeph. 2:8

9 Then the LORD said to Joshua, "Today I have rolled away *a*the reproach of Egypt from you." So the name of that place is called Gilgal to this day.

10 *a*Ex. 12:18 *b*Josh. 4:19

10 While the sons of Israel camped at Gilgal, *a*they observed the Passover on the evening of the *b*fourteenth day of the month on the desert plains of Jericho.

★**11**

11 And on the day after the Passover, on that very day, they ate some of the produce of the land, unleavened cakes and parched grain.

★**12** *a*Ex. 16:35

12 And *a*the manna ceased on the day after they had eaten some of the produce of the land, so that the sons of Israel no longer had manna, but they ate some of the yield of the land of Canaan during that year.

G The Captain of the LORD's Army, 5:13–15

★**13** *a*Gen. 18:1, 2; 32:24, 30; Num. 22:31

13 Now it came about when Joshua was by Jericho, that he lifted up his eyes and looked, and behold, *a*a man was standing opposite him with his sword drawn in his hand, and Joshua went to him and said to him, "Are you for us or for our adversaries?"

★**14** *a*Gen. 17:3

14 And he said, "No, rather I indeed come now *as* captain of the host of the LORD." And Joshua *a*fell on his face to the earth, and bowed down, and said to him, "What has my lord to say to his servant?"

★**15** *a*Ex. 3:5

15 And the captain of the LORD's host said to Joshua, "*a*Remove your sandals from your feet, for the place where you are standing is holy." And Joshua did so.

II CONQUERING THE LAND OF CANAAN, 6:1–12:24
A Conquest of Central Canaan, 6:1–8:35
1 Victory at Jericho, 6:1–27

6 Now Jericho was tightly shut because of the sons of Israel; no one went out and no one came in.

★ **2-5**

2 *a*Deut. 7:24

2 And the LORD said to Joshua, "See, I have given Jericho into your hand, with *a*its king *and* the valiant warriors.

3 "And you shall march around the city, all the men of war circling the city once. You shall do so for six days.

4 *a*Lev. 25:9

4 "Also seven priests shall carry seven *a*trumpets of rams' horns before the ark; then on the seventh day you shall march around the city seven times, and

---

5:9 *the reproach of Egypt.* The taunts leveled by the Egyptians at the Israelites for their failure to gain their promised land. This reproach had now been *rolled away* (*Gilgal* means "the rolling").

5:11 *the produce.* I.e., crops of the harvest being gathered at that very time.

5:12 The *manna* had sustained them for 40 years (see note on Exod. 16:15).

5:13 With retreat back across the Jordan now impossible, Joshua was preoccupied with the coming battle, and so did not recognize his visitor.

5:14 Joshua worshiped the *captain of the host of* the LORD as God (6:2), acknowledging that this was His war and that the Israelites were but a part of the Lord's hosts (which also included angels and the forces of nature).

5:15 Cf. Exod. 3:5.

6:2-5 These verses record the important information the captain of the Lord's hosts communicated to Joshua about taking Jericho. The divine plan to march around Jericho for 7 days would test Israel's faith and would accentuate the fear already present in the people of Jericho (2:9). The city covered only about 8.5 acres, making it easy to march around seven times.

the priests shall blow the trumpets.

5 "And it shall be that when they make a long blast with the ram's horn, and when you hear the sound of the trumpet, all the people shall shout with a great shout; and the wall of the city will fall down flat, and the people will go up every man straight ahead."

6 So Joshua the son of Nun called the priests and said to them, "Take up the ark of the covenant, and let seven priests carry seven trumpets of rams' horns before the ark of the LORD."

7 Then he said to the people, "Go forward, and march around the city, and let the armed men go on before the ark of the LORD."

8 And it was so, that when Joshua had spoken to the people, the seven priests carrying the seven trumpets of rams' horns before the LORD went forward and blew the trumpets; and the ark of the covenant of the LORD followed them.

9 And the armed men went before the priests who blew the trumpets, and ªthe rear guard came after the ark, while they continued to blow the trumpets.

10 But Joshua commanded the people, saying, "You shall not shout nor let your voice be heard, nor let a word proceed out of your mouth, until the day I tell you, 'Shout!' Then you shall shout!"

11 So he had the ark of the LORD taken around the city, circling it once; then they came into the camp and spent the night in the camp.

12 Now Joshua rose early in the morning, and the priests took up the ark of the LORD.

13 And ªthe seven priests carrying the seven trumpets of rams'

horns before the ark of the LORD went on continually, and blew the trumpets; and the armed men went before them, and ᵇthe rear guard came after the ark of the LORD, while they continued to blow the trumpets.

14 Thus the second day they marched around the city once and returned to the camp; they did so for six days.

15 Then it came about on the seventh day that they rose early at the dawning of the day and marched around the city in the same manner seven times; only on that day they marched around the city seven times.

16 And it came about at the seventh time, when the priests blew the trumpets, Joshua said to the people, "ªShout! For the LORD has given you the city.

17 "And the city shall be ªunder the ban, it and all that is in it belongs to the LORD; only Rahab the harlot and all who are with her in the house shall live, because she hid the messengers whom we sent.

18 "But as for you, only keep yourselves from the things under the ban, lest you covet them and ªtake some of the things under the ban, so you would make the camp of Israel accursed and bring trouble on it.

19 "ªBut all the silver and gold and articles of bronze and iron are holy to the LORD; they shall go into the treasury of the LORD."

20 So the people shouted, and priests blew the trumpets; and it came about, when the people heard the sound of the trumpet, that the people shouted with a great shout and the ªwall fell down flat, so that the people went up into the city, every man

9 ªJosh. 6:13; Is. 52:12

13 ªJosh. 6:4 ᵇJosh. 6:9

16 ª2 Chr. 13:14f.

★17 ªLev. 27:28; Deut. 20:17

18 ªJosh. 7:1

19 ªNum. 31:11, 12, 21-23

★20 ªHeb. 11:30

6:17 *under the ban.* The same Hebrew word (*herem*) is translated "utterly destroyed" in verse 21. It means "to ban, destroy, devote," in the sense of belonging to a god or, as here, to the true God. Jericho was completely devoted to God as the first fruits of Canaan, and no booty was to be taken by the people (vv. 18-19). See note on Lev. 27:28-29.
6:20 *the wall fell down flat.* It may originally

have been as high as 30 feet. The part of the wall on which Rahab's house was built did not collapse. Some interpreters claim that an earthquake caused the destruction. If so, it was a remarkable miracle of timing and localization since the camp at Gilgal (a little more than a mile away) and Rahab's house remained intact.

straight ahead, and they took the city.

21 a Deut. 20:16

21 ^aAnd they utterly destroyed everything in the city, both man and woman, young and old, and ox and sheep and donkey, with the edge of the sword.

22 a Josh. 2:12-19

22 And Joshua said to the two men who had spied out the land, "^aGo into the harlot's house and bring the woman and all she has out of there, as you have sworn to her."

23 a Heb. 11:31

23 So the young men who were spies went in and ^abrought out Rahab and her father and her mother and her brothers and all she had; they also brought out all her relatives, and placed them outside the camp of Israel.

24 a Deut. 20:16-18

24 ^aAnd they burned the city with fire, and all that was in it. Only the silver and gold and articles of bronze and iron, they put into the treasury of the house of the LORD.

25 a Heb. 11:31 b Josh. 2:6

25 However, ^aRahab the harlot and her father's household and all she had, Joshua spared; and she has lived in the midst of Israel to this day, for ^bshe hid the messengers whom Joshua sent to spy out Jericho.

★26 a 1 Kin. 16:34

26 Then Joshua made them take an oath at that time, saying, "^aCursed before the LORD is the man who rises up and builds this city Jericho; with *the loss of* his first-born he shall lay its foundation, and with *the loss of* his youngest son he shall set up its gates."

27 a Gen. 39:2; Judg. 1:19 b Josh. 9:1, 3

27 So ^athe LORD was with Joshua, and his ^bfame was in all the land.

2   Defeat at Ai: Achan's sin, 7:1-26

★ 1 a Josh. 6:17-19

7 ^aBut the sons of Israel acted unfaithfully in regard to the things under the ban, for Achan, the son of Carmi, the son of Zabdi, the son of Zerah, from the

tribe of Judah, took some of the things under the ban, therefore the anger of the LORD burned against the sons of Israel.

★ 2 a Josh. 18:12; 1 Sam. 13:5; 14:23

2 Now Joshua sent men from Jericho to Ai, which is near ^aBeth-aven, east of Bethel, and said to them, "Go up and spy out the land." So the men went up and spied out Ai.

★ 3

3 And they returned to Joshua and said to him, "Do not let all the people go up; *only* about two or three thousand men need go up to Ai; do not make all the people toil up there, for they are few."

4 a Lev. 26:17; Deut. 28:25

4 So about three thousand men from the people went up there, but ^athey fled from the men of Ai.

5 a Lev. 26:36; Josh. 2:11; Ezek. 21:7; Nah. 2:10

5 And the men of Ai struck down about thirty-six of their men, and pursued them from the gate as far as Shebarim, and struck them down on the descent, so the ^ahearts of the people melted and became as water.

6 a Job 2:12 b Job 42:6; Lam. 2:10; Rev. 18:19

6 Then Joshua ^atore his clothes and fell to the earth on his face before the ark of the LORD until the evening, *both* he and the elders of Israel; and ^bthey put dust on their heads.

7 And Joshua said, "Alas, O Lord GOD, why didst Thou ever bring this people over the Jordan, *only* to deliver us into the hand of the Amorites, to destroy us? If only we had been willing to dwell beyond the Jordan!

8 "O Lord, what can I say since Israel has turned *their* back before their enemies?

9 a Ex. 32:12; Deut. 9:28

9 "^aFor the Canaanites and all the inhabitants of the land will hear of it, and they will surround us and cut off our name from the earth. And what wilt Thou do for Thy great name?"

10 So the LORD said to Joshua, "Rise up! Why is it that you have fallen on your face?

6:26 The curse relates to rebuilding Jericho as a fortified city, not to inhabiting it, and was fulfilled on Hiel around 870 B.C. (1 Kings 16:34).
7:1 *acted unfaithfully.* Lit., broke faith. Achan's

action was a breach of covenant law (v. 11).
7:2 *Ai* was located in the central hill country of Palestine, E. of Bethel.
7:3 *few.* See 8:25.

11 aJosh. 6:18, 19

12 aNum. 14:39, 45; Judg. 2:14

13 aJosh. 3:5 bJosh. 6:18

14 aProv. 16:33

15 a1 Sam. 14:38f. bGen. 34:7; Judg. 20:6

11 "Israel has sinned, and athey have also transgressed My covenant which I commanded them. And they have even taken some of the things under the ban and have both stolen and deceived. Moreover, they have also put *them* among their own things.

12 "Therefore the asons of Israel cannot stand before their enemies; they turn *their* backs before their enemies, for they have become accursed. I will not be with you anymore unless you destroy the things under the ban from your midst.

13 "Rise up! aConsecrate the people and say, 'Consecrate yourselves for tomorrow, for thus the LORD, the God of Israel, has said, "bThere are things under the ban in your midst, O Israel. You cannot stand before your enemies until you have removed the things under the ban from your midst."

14 'In the morning then you shall come near by your tribes. And it shall be that the tribe which athe LORD takes *by lot* shall come near by families, and the family which the LORD takes shall come near by households, and the household which the LORD takes shall come near man by man.

15 'And ait shall be that the one who is taken with the things under the ban shall be burned with fire, he and all that belongs to him, because he has transgressed the covenant of the LORD, and because he bhas committed a disgraceful thing in Israel.'"

16 So Joshua arose early in the morning and brought Israel near by tribes, and the tribe of Judah was taken.

17 And he brought the family of Judah near, and he took the family of the Zerahites; and he brought the family of the Zera-

hites near man by man, and Zabdi was taken.

18 And he brought his household near man by man; and aAchan, son of Carmi, son of Zabdi, son of Zerah, from the tribe of Judah, was taken.

19 Then Joshua said to Achan, "My son, I implore you, agive glory to the LORD, the God of Israel, and give praise to Him; and tell me now what you have done. Do not hide it from me."

20 So Achan answered Joshua and said, "Truly, I have sinned against the LORD, the God of Israel, and this is what I did:

21 when I saw among the spoil a beautiful mantle from Shinar and two hundred shekels of silver and a bar of gold fifty shekels in weight, then I acoveted them and took them; and behold, they are concealed in the earth inside my tent with the silver underneath it."

22 So Joshua sent messengers, and they ran to the tent; and behold, it was concealed in his tent with the silver underneath it.

23 And they took them from inside the tent and brought them to Joshua and to all the sons of Israel, and they poured them out before the LORD.

24 Then Joshua and all Israel with him, took Achan the son of Zerah, the silver, the mantle, the bar of gold, his sons, his daughters, his oxen, his donkeys, his sheep, his tent and all that belonged to him; and they brought them up to athe valley of Achor.

25 And Joshua said, "Why have you atroubled us? The LORD will trouble you this day." And all Israel stoned them with stones; and they burned them with fire after they had stoned them with stones.

26 And they raised over him a great heap of stones that stands to

18 aNum. 32:23; Acts 5:1-10

19 a1 Sam. 6:5; 2 Chr. 30:22; Jer. 13:16; John 9:24

21 aEph. 5:5; 1 Tim. 6:10

24 aJosh. 15:7

25 aJosh. 6:18

26 aIs. 65:10; Hos. 2:15

7:11 The sin of Achan was imputed to the nation.

7:21 *a beautiful mantle from Shinar.* A long robe woven of gold and silk threads. *shekels.* Each weighed about one-half ounce. A *bar of gold.* Such a bar, probably similar to Achan's

and measuring $10 \times 1 \times \frac{1}{2}$ inches, has been unearthed.

7:24 Achan's family must have been accomplices (cf. Deut. 24:16).

7:26 *Achor* means "trouble." The valley is about 1 mile S. of Jericho.

this day, and the LORD turned from the fierceness of His anger. Therefore the name of that place has been called ªthe valley of A-chor to this day.

3 Victory at Ai, 8:1-29

1 ªJosh. 1:9; 10:8
b Josh. 6:2

8 Now the LORD said to Joshua, "ªDo not fear or be dismayed. Take all the people of war with you and arise, go up to Ai; see, ᵇI have given into your hand the king of Ai, his people, his city, and his land.

★ 2 ªDeut. 20:14; Josh. 8:27

2 "And you shall do to Ai and its king just as you did to Jericho and its king; you shall ªtake only its spoil and its cattle as plunder for yourselves. Set an ambush for the city behind it."

★ 3

3 So Joshua rose with all the people of war to go up to Ai; and Joshua chose 30,000 men, valiant warriors, and sent them out at night.

★ 4 ªJudg. 20:29

4 And he commanded them, saying, "See, you are ªgoing to ambush the city from behind it. Do not go very far from the city, but all of you be ready.

5 ªJudg. 20:32

5 "Then I and all the people who are with me will approach the city. And it will come about when they come out to meet us as at the first, that ªwe will flee before them.

6 "And they will come out after us until we have drawn them away from the city, for they will say, 'They are fleeing before us as at the first.' So we will flee before them.

7 "And you shall rise from your ambush and take possession of the city, for the LORD your God will deliver it into your hand.

8 ªDeut. 20:16-18; Josh. 8:2

8 "Then it will be when you have seized the city, that you shall set the city on fire. You shall do it ªaccording to the word of the

LORD. See, I have commanded you."

9 So Joshua sent them away, and they went to the place of ambush and remained between Bethel and Ai, on the west side of Ai; but Joshua spent that night among the people.

10 ªGen. 22:3

10 Now Joshua ªrose early in the morning and mustered the people, and he went up with the elders of Israel before the people to Ai.

11 Then all the people of war who were with him went up and drew near and arrived in front of the city, and camped on the north side of Ai. Now there was a valley between him and Ai.

★12 ªGen. 12:8; 28:19; Judg. 1:22

12 And he took about 5,000 men and set them in ambush between ªBethel and Ai, on the west side of the city.

13 So they stationed the people, all the army that was on the north side of the city, and its rear guard on the west side of the city, and Joshua spent that night in the midst of the valley.

14 And it came about when the king of Ai saw it, that the men of the city hurried and rose up early and went out to meet Israel in battle, he and all his people at the appointed place before the desert plain. But he did not know that there was an ambush against him behind the city.

15 ªJosh. 15:61; 16:1; 18:12

15 And Joshua and all Israel pretended to be beaten before them, and fled ªby the way of the wilderness.

16 ªJudg. 20:31

16 And all the people who were in the city were called together to pursue them, and they pursued Joshua, and ªwere drawn away from the city.

17 So not a man was left in Ai or Bethel who had not gone out after Israel, and they left the city unguarded and pursued Israel.

8:2 This time the Israelites could keep the spoil. Achan should have been more patient!

8:3 30,000. A seemingly large number for an ambush. It has been suggested that "thousand" should read "chief." If so, Joshua sent 30 chiefs on a commando-type ambush.

8:4 behind it. I.e., on the W. side (v. 9).

8:12 This second force of 5,000 was sent to prevent attack by the men of Bethel. Joshua's main army on the north (v. 11) was to decoy the men of Ai out of their city.

★18-19

18 *a*Ex.
14:16; 17:9-
13; Josh.
8:26

18 Then the LORD said to Joshua, "*a*Stretch out the javelin that is in your hand toward Ai, for I will give it into your hand." So Joshua stretched out the javelin that was in his hand toward the city.

19 And the *men in* ambush rose quickly from their place, and when he had stretched out his hand, they ran and entered the city and captured it; and they quickly set the city on fire.

20 When the men of Ai turned back and looked, behold, the smoke of the city ascended to the sky, and they had no place to flee this way or that, for the people who had been fleeing to the wilderness turned against the pursuers.

21 When Joshua and all Israel saw that the *men in* ambush had captured the city and that the smoke of the city ascended, they turned back and slew the men of Ai.

22 *a*Josh.
8:8

22 And the others came out from the city to encounter them, so that they were *trapped* in the midst of Israel, some on this side and some on that side; and they slew them until *a*no one was left of those who survived or escaped.

23 But they took alive the king of Ai and brought him to Joshua.

24 Now it came about when Israel had finished killing all the inhabitants of Ai in the field in the wilderness where they pursued them, and all of them were fallen by the edge of the sword until they were destroyed, then all Israel returned to Ai and struck it with the edge of the sword.

25 *a*Deut.
20:16-18

25 *a*And all who fell that day, both men and women, were 12,000—all the people of Ai.

26 *a*Ex.
17:11, 12

26 For Joshua *a*did not withdraw his hand with which he stretched out the javelin until he had utterly destroyed all the inhabitants of Ai.

27 *a*Israel took only the cattle and the spoil of that city as plunder for themselves, according to the word of the LORD which He had commanded Joshua.

27 *a*Josh.
8:2

28 So Joshua burned Ai and made it *a*a heap forever, a desolation until this day.

28 *a*Deut.
13:16

29 *a*And he hanged the king of Ai on a tree until evening; and at sunset Joshua gave command and they took his body down from the tree, and threw it at the entrance of the city gate, and raised over it a great heap of stones *that stands* to this day.

★29 *a*Deut.
21:22, 23

4   Worship at Ebal, 8:30-35

30 Then Joshua built an altar to the LORD, the God of Israel, in *a*Mount Ebal,

★30 *a*Deut.
27:2-8

31 just as Moses the servant of the LORD had commanded the sons of Israel, as it is written in the book of the law of Moses, *a*an altar of uncut stones, on which no man had wielded an iron *tool;* and they offered burnt offerings on it to the LORD, and sacrificed peace offerings.

★31 *a*Ex.
20:25

32 And he *a*wrote there on the stones a copy of the law of Moses, which he had written, in the presence of the sons of Israel.

★32 *a*Deut.
27:2, 3, 8

33 *a*And all Israel with their elders and officers and their judges were standing on both sides of the ark before the Levitical priests who carried the ark of the covenant of the LORD, the stranger as well as the native. Half of them *stood* in front of *b*Mount Gerizim and half of them in front of Mount Ebal, just as Moses the servant of the LORD had given command at first to bless the people of Israel.

33 *a*Deut.
27:11-14
*b*Deut. 11:29

34 Then afterward he read all the words of the law, the blessing and the curse, according to all

34 *a*Josh.
1:8

8:18-19 Joshua's *javelin* signaled the ambushing party by reflecting the sun from its flat blade.
8:29 *hanged.* See note on Deut. 21:22-23.
8:30 *Ebal.* See note on Deut. 11:29.

8:31 *an altar.* See note on Exod. 20:24-26.
8:32 *the stones.* Not of the altar, but of a large pillar.

that is written in ªthe book of the law.

35 There was not a word of all that Moses had commanded which Joshua did not read before all the assembly of Israel ªwith the women and the little ones and the strangers who were living among them.

B Conquest of Southern Canaan, 9:1-10:43

1 Deception of the Gibeonites, 9:1-27

9 Now it came about when ªall the kings who were beyond the Jordan, in the hill country and in the lowland and on all the ᵇcoast of the Great Sea toward Lebanon, ᶜthe Hittite and the Amorite, the Canaanite, the Perizzite, the Hivite and the Jebusite, heard of it,

2 that they gathered themselves together with ªone accord to fight with Joshua and with Israel.

3 When the inhabitants of ªGibeon heard what Joshua had done to Jericho and to Ai,

4 they also acted craftily and set out as envoys, and took worn-out sacks on their donkeys, and wineskins, worn-out and torn and mended,

5 and worn-out and patched sandals on their feet, and worn-out clothes on themselves; and all the bread of their provision was dry and had become crumbled.

6 And they went to Joshua ᵃto the camp at Gilgal, and said to him and to the men of Israel, "We have come from a far country; now therefore, make a covenant with us."

7 And the men of Israel said to the ªHivites, "Perhaps you are living within our land; ᵇhow then shall we make a covenant with you?"

8 But they said to Joshua, "ªWe are your servants." Then Joshua said to them, "Who are you, and where do you come from?"

9 And they said to him, "Your servants have come from ªa very far country because of the fame of the Lᴏʀᴅ your God; for ᵇwe have heard the report of Him and all that He did in Egypt,

10 and all that He did to the two kings of the Amorites who were beyond the Jordan, to Sihon king of Heshbon and to Og king of Bashan who was at Ashtaroth.

11 "So our elders and all the inhabitants of our country spoke to us, saying, 'Take provisions in your hand for the journey, and go to meet them and say to them, "ªWe are your servants; now then, make a covenant with us." '

12 "This our bread was warm when we took it for our provisions out of our houses on the day that we left to come to you; but now behold, it is dry and has become crumbled.

13 "And these wineskins which we filled were new, and behold, they are torn; and these our clothes and our sandals are worn out because of the very long journey."

14 So the men of Israel took some of their provisions, and ªdid not ask for the counsel of the Lᴏʀᴅ.

15 ªAnd Joshua made peace with them and made a covenant with them, to let them live; and

Margin references

35 ªEx. 12:38; Deut. 31:12; Zech. 8:23

1 ªNum. 13:29; Josh. 3:10 ᵇNum. 34:6 ᶜEx. 3:17; 23:23

2 ªPs. 83:3, 5

★ **3ff.**

3 ªJosh. 9:17, 22; 10:2; 21:17

6 ªJosh. 5:10

★ **7** ªJosh. 9:1; 11:19 ᵇEx. 23:32; Deut. 7:2

8 ªDeut. 20:11; 2 Kin. 10:5

9 ªJosh. 9:16, 17 ᵇJosh. 2:9; 9:24

★**10**

11 ªJosh. 9:8

★**14** ªNum. 27:21

15 ªEx. 23:32

9:3ff. Though Israel could make peace with more distant cities, she was obliged to destroy the cities of the Canaanites (Deut. 7:1-2; 20:11-15). Since Gibeon was located just 6½ miles SW. of Ai, its envoys had to pretend they came from a great distance if they were to have any hope of escaping the invading Israelites.

9:7 Hivites were apparently the same as the Ho-

rites (cf. Gen. 36:2, 20) who are identified as Hurrians, settlers in Palestine before the time of Joshua.

9:10 The Gibeonites were clever not to mention Israel's recent victories—news they would not have known had they come a long distance.

9:14 Israel's sin was in not asking the Lord's counsel in the matter.

the leaders of the congregation swore *an oath* to them.

16 And it came about at the end of three days after they had made a covenant with them, that they heard that they were neighbors and that they were living within their land.

17 Then the sons of Israel set out and came to their cities on the third day. Now their cities *were* [a]Gibeon and Chephirah and Beeroth and Kiriath-jearim.

18 And the sons of Israel did not strike them because the leaders of the congregation had sworn to them by the LORD the God of Israel. And the whole congregation grumbled against the leaders.

19 But all the leaders said to the whole congregation, "We have sworn to them by the LORD, the God of Israel, and now we cannot touch them.

20 "This we will do to them, even let them live, lest wrath be upon us for the oath which we swore to them."

21 And the leaders said to them, "Let them live." So they became [a]hewers of wood and drawers of water for the whole congregation, just as the leaders had spoken to them.

22 Then Joshua called for them and spoke to them, saying, "Why have you deceived us, saying, 'We are very far from you,' [a]when you are living within our land?

23 "Now therefore, you are [a]cursed, and you shall never cease being slaves, both hewers of wood and drawers of water for the house of my God."

24 So they answered Joshua and said, "[a]Because it was certainly told your servants that the LORD your God had commanded His servant Moses to give you all the land, and to destroy all the inhabitants of the land before you; therefore we feared greatly for

our lives because of you, and have done this thing.

25 "And now behold, [a]we are in your hands; do as it seems good and right in your sight to do to us."

26 Thus he did to them, and delivered them from the hands of the sons of Israel, and they did not kill them.

27 But Joshua made them that day hewers of wood and drawers of water for the congregation and for the altar of the LORD, to this day, [a]in the place which He would choose.

2 Destruction of the Amorite coalition, 10:1–43

10 Now it came about when Adoni-zedek king of Jerusalem heard that Joshua had captured Ai, and had utterly destroyed it (just [a]as he had done to Jericho and its king, so he had done to Ai and its king), and that the inhabitants of Gibeon had [b]made peace with Israel and were within their land,

2 that he [a]feared greatly, because Gibeon *was* a great city, like one of the royal cities, and because it was greater than Ai, and all its men *were* mighty.

3 Therefore Adoni-zedek of Jerusalem sent *word* [a]to Hoham king of Hebron and to Piram king of Jarmuth and to Japhia king of Lachish and to Debir king of Eglon, saying,

4 "Come up to me and help me, and let us attack Gibeon, for it has [a]made peace with Joshua and with the sons of Israel."

5 So the five kings of [a]the Amorites, the king of Jerusalem, the king of Hebron, the king of Jarmuth, the king of Lachish, *and* the king of Eglon, gathered together and went up, they with all their armies, and camped by Gibeon and fought against it.

---

17 [a]Josh. 18:25

*20-21

21 [a]Deut. 29:11

22 [a]Josh. 9:16

23 [a]Gen. 9:25

24 [a]Josh. 9:9

25 [a]Gen. 16:6

27 [a]Deut. 12:5

*1-6

1 [a]Josh. 8:21f. [b]Josh. 9:15

2 [a]Ex. 15:14-16

3 [a]Josh. 10:23

4 [a]Josh. 9:15

5 [a]Num. 13:29

9:20-21 The Gibeonites were allowed to live because of *the oath* (cf. Num. 30:2), but had to become wood choppers and water carriers for the tabernacle (see note on Ezra 2:43).

10:1-6 News of the treaty between the Gibeonites and Israelites prompted five of the kings of the Amorites to unite and attack the Gibeonites, who then called for help from Joshua.

6 Then the men of Gibeon sent *word* to Joshua to the camp at Gilgal, saying, "Do not abandon your servants; come up to us quickly and save us and help us, for all the kings of the Amorites that live in the hill country have assembled against us."

7 aJosh. 8:1

7 So Joshua went up from Gilgal, he and ªall the people of war with him and all the valiant warriors.

8 aJosh. 1:5, 9

8 And the LORD said to Joshua, "ªDo not fear them, for I have given them into your hands; not one of them shall stand before you."

★ 9-11

9 So Joshua came upon them suddenly by marching all night from Gilgal.

10 aDeut. 7:23

10 ªAnd the LORD confounded them before Israel, and He slew them with a great slaughter at Gibeon, and pursued them by the way of the ascent of Beth-horon, and struck them as far as Azekah and Makkedah.

11 aPs. 18:12f.; Is. 28:2

11 And it came about as they fled from before Israel, *while* they were at the descent of Beth-horon, that ªthe LORD threw large stones from heaven on them as far as Azekah, and they died; *there were* more who died from the hailstones than those whom the sons of Israel killed with the sword.

★12-14

12 aHab. 3:11

12 Then Joshua spoke to the LORD in the day when the LORD delivered up the Amorites before the sons of Israel, and he said in the sight of Israel,

"O ªsun, stand still at Gibeon,
And O moon in the valley of Aijalon."

13

13 aHab. 3:11 b2 Sam. 1:18 cIs. 38:8

13 ªSo the sun stood still, and the moon stopped, Until the nation avenged themselves of their enemies.

Is it not written in ᵇthe book of Jashar? And ᶜthe sun stopped in the middle of the sky, and did not hasten to go *down* for about a whole day.

14 aEx. 14:14; Deut. 1:30; Josh. 10:42

14 And there was no day like that before it or after it, when the LORD listened to the voice of a man; for ªthe LORD fought for Israel.

15 Then Joshua and all Israel with him returned to the camp to Gilgal.

16 aJosh. 10:5

16 Now these ªfive kings had fled and hidden themselves in the cave at Makkedah.

17 And it was told Joshua, saying, "The five kings have been found hidden in the cave at Makkedah."

18 And Joshua said, "Roll large stones against the mouth of the cave, and assign men by it to guard them,

19 but do not stay *there* yourselves; pursue your enemies and attack them in the rear. Do not allow them to enter their cities,

---

10:9-11 After marching 25 miles uphill during the night, Joshua routed the coalition of kings, and the Lord sent *hailstones* to kill even more. Miraculously, none of the hailstones harmed the Israelites.

10:12-14 Views concerning this phenomenon fall into two categories. The first assumes a slowing or suspending of the normal rotation of the earth so that there were extra hours that day (either 12 or 24). God did this so that Joshua's forces could complete their victory before the enemy had a night for rest and regrouping. The Hebrew for "stood still" (v. 13) is a verb of motion, indicating a slowing or stopping of the rotation of the earth on its axis (which would not affect the earth's movement around the sun). Verse 14 indicates this was a unique day in the history of the world. The second category includes views that assume no irregularity in the rotation of the earth. One such view argues for the prolonging of daylight by some sort of unusual refraction of the sun's rays. Thus, there were more daylight hours but not more hours in the day. Another view supposes a prolonging of semi-darkness to give Joshua's men relief from the blazing summer sun, accomplished by God's sending an unusual summer hailstorm. This view takes *stood still* in verse 13 to mean "be still" or "cease," indicating that the sun was clouded by the storm and no extra hours were added to the day. Verses 12-15 are quoted from the *book of Jashar,* a collection of songs praising the heroes of Israel (also in 2 Sam. 1:18).

for the LORD your God has delivered them into your hand."

20 *a*Deut. 20:16

20 And it came about when Joshua and the sons of Israel had finished slaying them with a very great slaughter, *a*until they were destroyed, and the survivors *who* remained of them had entered the fortified cities,

21 that all the people returned to the camp to Joshua at Makkedah in peace. No one uttered a word against any of the sons of Israel.

22 Then Joshua said, "Open the mouth of the cave and bring these five kings out to me from the cave."

23 *a*Deut. 7:24

23 And they did so, and *a*brought these five kings out to him from the cave: the king of Jerusalem, the king of Hebron, the king of Jarmuth, the king of Lachish, *and* the king of Eglon.

★24 *a*Mal. 4:3

24 And it came about when they brought these kings out to Joshua, that Joshua called for all the men of Israel, and said to the chiefs of the men of war who had gone with him, "Come near, *a*put your feet on the necks of these kings." So they came near and put their feet on their necks.

25 *a*Josh. 10:8

25 Joshua then said to them, "*a*Do not fear or be dismayed! Be strong and courageous, for thus the LORD will do to all your enemies with whom you fight."

26 *a*Josh. 8:29

26 So afterward Joshua struck them and put them to death, and he *a*hanged them on five trees; and they hung on the trees until evening.

27 *a*Deut. 21:22, 23

27 And it came about at sunset that Joshua commanded, and *a*they took them down from the trees and threw them into the cave where they had hidden themselves, and put large stones over the mouth of the cave, to this very day.

★28-40

28 *a*Deut. 20:16 *b*Josh. 6:21

28 Now Joshua captured Makkedah on that day, and struck it and its king with the

edge of the sword; *a*he utterly destroyed it and every person who was in it. He left no survivor. Thus he did to the king of Makkedah *b*just as he had done to the king of Jericho.

29 *a*Josh. 15:42; 21:13

29 Then Joshua and all Israel with him passed on from Makkedah to *a*Libnah, and fought against Libnah.

30 And the LORD gave it also with its king into the hands of Israel, and he struck it and every person who *was* in it with the edge of the sword. He left no survivor in it. Thus he did to its king just as he had done to the king of Jericho.

31 And Joshua and all Israel with him passed on from Libnah to Lachish, and they camped by it and fought against it.

32 And the LORD gave Lachish into the hands of Israel; and he captured it on the second day, and struck it and every person who *was* in it with the edge of the sword, according to all that he had done to Libnah.

33 *a*Josh. 16:3, 10; Judg. 1:29; 1 Kin. 9:16f.

33 Then Horam king of *a*Gezer came up to help Lachish, and Joshua defeated him and his people until he had left him no survivor.

34 And Joshua and all Israel with him passed on from Lachish to Eglon, and they camped by it and fought against it.

35 And they captured it on that day and struck it with the edge of the sword; and he utterly destroyed that day every person who *was* in it, according to all that he had done to Lachish.

36 *a*Num. 13:22; Judg. 1:10, 20; 2 Sam. 5:1, 3, 5, 13; 2 Chr. 11:10

36 Then Joshua and all Israel with him went up from Eglon to *a*Hebron, and they fought against it.

37 And they captured it and struck it and its king and all its cities and all the persons who *were* in it with the edge of the sword. He left no survivor, according to all that he had done to

---

10:24 *put your feet on the necks.* A symbol of complete subjugation.
10:28-40 Joshua now used lightning-like raids

against key cities in the southern part of Canaan, W. of the Dead Sea. *Makkedah* was about 20 miles SW. of Jerusalem (v. 28).

Eglon. And he utterly destroyed it and every person who *was* in it.

38 Then Joshua and all Israel with him returned to ᵃDebir, and they fought against it.

39 And he captured it and its king and all its cities, and they struck them with the edge of the sword, and utterly destroyed every person *who was* in it. He left no survivor. Just as he had done to Hebron, so he did to Debir and its king, as he had also done to Libnah and its king.

40 Thus Joshua struck all the land, ᵃthe hill country and the Negev and the lowland and the slopes and ᵇall their kings. He left no survivor, but ᶜhe utterly destroyed all who breathed, just as the Lord, the God of Israel, had commanded.

41 And Joshua struck them from Kadesh-barnea even as far as Gaza, and all the country of ᵃGoshen even as far as Gibeon.

42 And Joshua captured all these kings and their lands at one time, because ᵃthe Lord, the God of Israel, fought for Israel.

43 So Joshua and all Israel with him returned to the camp at Gilgal.

C Conquest of Northern Canaan, 11:1-15

11 Then it came about, when Jabin king of ᵃHazor heard *of it,* that he sent to Jobab king of Madon and to the king of Shimron and to the king of Achshaph,

2 and to the kings who were of the north in the hill country, and in the ᵃArabah—south of Chinneroth and in the lowland and on the heights of Dor on the west—

3 to the Canaanite on the east and on the west, and the Amorite and the Hittite and the Perizzite and the Jebusite in the hill country, and ᵃthe Hivite at the foot of ᵇHermon in the land of ᶜMizpeh.

4 And they came out, they and all their armies with them, ᵃas many people as the sand that is on the seashore, with very many horses and chariots.

5 So all of these kings having agreed to meet, came and encamped together at the waters of Merom, to fight against Israel.

6 Then the Lord said to Joshua, "ᵃDo not be afraid because of them, for tomorrow at this time I will deliver all of them slain before Israel; you shall ᵇhamstring their horses and burn their chariots with fire."

7 So Joshua and all the people of war with him came upon them suddenly by the waters of Merom, and attacked them.

8 And the Lord delivered them into the hand of Israel, so that they defeated them, and pursued them as far as Great Sidon and ᵃMisrephoth-maim and the valley of ᵇMizpeh to the east; and they struck them until no survivor was left to them.

9 And Joshua did to them as the Lord had told him; he ᵃhamstrung their horses, and burned their chariots with fire.

10 Then Joshua turned back at that time, and captured ᵃHazor and struck its king with the sword; for Hazor formerly was the head of all these kingdoms.

Marginal references

38 ᵃJosh. 15:15; Judg. 1:11; 1 Chr. 6:58

40 ᵃDeut. 1:7 ᵇDeut. 7:24 ᶜDeut. 20:16

★41 ᵃJosh. 11:16; 15:51

42 ᵃJosh. 10:14

★ 1 ᵃJosh. 11:10

★ 2 ᵃJosh. 12:3; 13:27

3 ᵃDeut. 7:1; Judg. 3:3, 5; 1 Kin. 9:20 ᵇJosh. 11:17; 13:5, 11 ᶜJosh. 15:38; 18:26

4 ᵃJudg. 7:12

★5

★ 6 ᵃJosh. 10:8 ᵇ2 Sam. 8:4

8 ᵃJosh. 13:6 ᵇJosh. 11:3

9 ᵃJosh. 11:6

10 ᵃJosh. 11:1

10:41 This thrust was even further south and west.

11:1 News of Joshua's victories in the south prompted the kings of the city-states in the areas of Galilee and westward to form a coalition. This alliance was led by the king of *Hazor,* a city 5 miles SW. of the now-drained Lake Huleh, 10 miles N. of the Sea of Galilee.

11:2 *Chinneroth* is the Sea of Galilee. *Dor* was on the Mediterranean coast between Caesarea and Mt. Carmel.

11:5 *the waters of Merom.* Evidently not Lake Huleh, but an area of copious springs between Huleh and the Sea of Galilee, about 10 miles W. Here the armies of the northern coalition massed.

11:6 *hamstring.* Joshua was commanded to cripple the enemies' horses and burn their chariots, rather than capture them. In this way the Israelites would not put their trust in horses and chariots.

11 aDeut. 20:16

11 aAnd they struck every person who was in it with the edge of the sword, utterly destroying *them;* there was no one left who breathed. And he burned Hazor with fire.

12 aNum. 33:50-52; Deut. 7:2; 20:16f.

12 And Joshua captured all the cities of these kings, and all their kings, and he struck them with the edge of the sword, *and* utterly destroyed them; just aas Moses the servant of the LORD had commanded.

13 However, Israel did not burn any cities that stood on their mounds, except Hazor alone, *which* Joshua burned.

14 aNum. 31:11, 12

14 aAnd all the spoil of these cities and the cattle, the sons of Israel took as their plunder; but they struck every man with the edge of the sword, until they had destroyed them. They left no one who breathed.

15 Just as the LORD had commanded Moses his servant, so Moses commanded Joshua, and so Joshua did; he left nothing undone of all that the LORD had commanded Moses.

D Summary of the Conquest,
11:16-12:24

16 aJosh. 10:40, 41 bJosh. 11:2

16 Thus Joshua took all that land: athe hill country and all the Negev, all that land of Goshen, the lowland, bthe Arabah, the hill country of Israel and its lowland

★17 aJosh. 12:7 bDeut. 7:24

17 from aMount Halak, that rises toward Seir, even as far as Baal-gad in the valley of Lebanon at the foot of Mount Hermon. And he captured ball their kings and struck them down and put them to death.

18 Joshua waged war a long time with all these kings.

19 aJosh. 9:3, 7

19 There was not a city which made peace with the sons of Israel

except athe Hivites living in Gibeon; they took them all in battle.

20 aEx. 14:17 bDeut. 7:16

20 aFor it was of the LORD to harden their hearts, to meet Israel in battle in order that he might butterly destroy them, that they might receive no mercy, but that he might destroy them, just as the LORD had commanded Moses.

★21 aNum. 13:33; Deut. 9:2

21 Then Joshua came at that time and cut off athe Anakim from the hill country, from Hebron, from Debir, from Anab and from all the hill country of Judah and from all the hill country of Israel. Joshua utterly destroyed them with their cities.

22 a1 Sam. 17:4; 1 Kin. 2:39; 1 Chr. 8:13 bJosh. 15:46f.; 1 Sam. 5:1; Is. 20:1

22 There were no Anakim left in the land of the sons of Israel; only in Gaza, in aGath, and in bAshdod some remained.

23 aDeut. 1:38 bDeut. 12:9, 10; 25:19; Heb. 4:8

23 So Joshua took the whole land, according to all that the LORD had spoken to Moses, and aJoshua gave it for an inheritance to Israel according to their divisions by their tribes. bThus the land had rest from war.

★ 1-6

1 aNum. 32:33; Deut. 3:8-17

12 Now these are the akings of the land whom the sons of Israel defeated, and whose land they possessed beyond the Jordan toward the sunrise, from the valley of the Arnon as far as Mount Hermon, and all the Arabah to the east:

2 aDeut. 2:36

2 Sihon king of the Amorites, who lived in Heshbon, *and* ruled afrom Aroer, which is on the edge of the valley of the Arnon, both the middle of the valley and half of Gilead, even as far as the brook Jabbok, the border of the sons of Ammon;

3 aJosh. 11:2 bJosh. 13:20

3 and the aArabah as far as the Sea of Chinneroth toward the east, and as far as the sea of the Arabah, *even* the Salt Sea, eastward toward bBeth-jeshimoth, and on the south, at the foot of the slopes of Pisgah;

11:17 *Halak* was about 23 miles SE. of Beersheba in the south. *Hermon* is about 40 miles NE. of the Sea of Galilee in the north. Joshua had subdued the whole land.

11:21 *Anakim.* Giants living in the south who

had terrified the spies more than 40 years before (see note on Num. 13:33).

12:1-6 Summary of the victories under Moses on the E. side of the Jordan (see notes on Num. 21 and Deut. 2:24-3:17).

4 aDeut.
3:11 bDeut.
1:4

4 and the territory of Og king of Bashan, one of athe remnant of Rephaim, who lived at bAshtaroth and at Edrei,

5 aDeut.
3:10; Josh.
13:11; 1 Chr.
5:11 bDeut.
3:14; 1 Sam.
27:8

5 and ruled over Mount Hermon and aSalecah and all Bashan, as far as bthe border of the Geshurites and the Maacathites, and half of Gilead, *as far as* the border of Sihon king of Heshbon.

6 aNum.
32:33; Deut.
3:12

6 Moses the servant of the LORD and the sons of Israel defeated them; and aMoses the servant of the LORD gave it to the Reubenites and the Gadites, and the half-tribe of Manasseh as a possession.

7 aJosh.
11:17

7 Now these are the kings of the land whom Joshua and the sons of Israel defeated beyond the Jordan toward the west, from Baal-gad in the valley of Lebanon even as far as aMount Halak, which rises toward Seir; and Joshua gave it to the tribes of Israel as a possession according to their divisions,

8 aJosh.
11:16

8 in athe hill country, in the lowland, in the Arabah, on the slopes, and in the wilderness, and in the Negev; the Hittite, the Amorite and the Canaanite, the Perizzite, the Hivite and the Jebusite:

★ **9-16**

9 aJosh.
6:2 bJosh.
8:29

9 the aking of Jericho, one; the bking of Ai, which is beside Bethel, one;

10 aJosh.
10:23

10 the aking of Jerusalem, one; the king of Hebron, one;

11 the king of Jarmuth, one; the king of Lachish, one;

12 the king of Eglon, one; the king of Gezer, one;

13 the king of Debir, one; the king of Geder, one;

14 aNum.
21:1

14 the king of Hormah, one; the king of aArad, one;

15 the king of Libnah, one; the king of Adullam, one;

16 the king of Makkedah, one; the king of Bethel, one;

17 the king of Tappuah, one; the aking of Hepher, one;

★ **17-24**

17 a1 Kin.
4:10

18 the king of aAphek, one; the king of Lasharon, one;

18 aJosh.
13:4; 2 Kin.
13:17

19 the king of Madon, one; the king of Hazor, one;

20 the king of Shimron-meron, one; the king of Achshaph, one;

21 the king of Taanach, one; the king of Megiddo, one;

22 the king of aKedesh, one; the king of Jokneam in Carmel, one;

22 aJosh.
19:37; 20:7;
21:32

23 the king of Dor in the heights of Dor, one; the king of aGoiim in Gilgal, one;

23 aGen. 4:1

24 the king of Tirzah, one: ain all, thirty-one kings.

24 aDeut.
7:24

III DIVIDING THE LAND OF CANAAN, 13:1–24:33
A Instructions to Joshua, 13:1–7

13 Now aJoshua was old *and* advanced in years when the LORD said to him, "You are old *and* advanced in years, and very much of the land remains to be possessed.

★ **1** aJosh.
14:10

2 "This is the land that remains: all the regions *of* the Philistines and all *those of* the aGeshurites;

★ **2** aJosh.
13:11;
1 Sam. 27:8

3 from the Shihor which is east of Egypt, even as far as the border of Ekron to the north (it is counted as Canaanite); the afive lords of the Philistines: the Gazite, the Ashdodite, the Ashkelonite, the Gittite, the Ekronite; and the Avvite

★ **3** a1 Sam.
6:4, 16

4 to the south, all the land of the Canaanite, and Mearah that belongs to the Sidonians, as far as

4 aJosh.
12:18; 19:30,
1 Sam. 4:1;
1 Kin. 20:26,
30 bEzek.
16:3; Amos
2:10

12:9-16 Kings in southern Canaan.
12:17-24 Kings in northern Canaan. All these victories were accomplished through the power of the living God as His people trusted in Him.
13:1 Joshua was 90 or 100 years old at this time (cf. 23:1; 24:29). *to be possessed.* The area yet to be subdued by the tribes is described in

verses 2–6, moving from S. to N.
13:2 Mention of the *Philistines* (see note on Gen. 21:32) may be an editorial note explaining that what was later their territory belonged to the Canaanites in Joshua's day.
13:3 *Shihor* may refer to the easternmost branch of the Nile or to the River of Egypt (Wadi-el-Arish).

^aAphek, to the border of the ^bAmorite;

5 and the land of the ^aGebalite, and all of Lebanon, toward the east, ^bfrom Baal-gad below Mount Hermon as far as Lebo-hamath.

6 "All the inhabitants of the hill country from Lebanon as far as ^aMisrephoth-maim, all the Sidonians, I will drive them out from before the sons of Israel; ^bonly allot it to Israel for an inheritance as I have commanded you.

7 "Now therefore, apportion this land for an inheritance to the nine tribes, and the half-tribe of Manasseh."

B Division of Transjordan, 13:8-33

8 With the other half-tribe, the Reubenites and the Gadites received their inheritance which Moses gave them ^abeyond the Jordan to the east, just as Moses the servant of the LORD gave to them;

9 from Aroer, which is on the edge of the valley of the Arnon, with the city which is in the middle of the valley, and all the plain of Medeba, as far as Dibon;

10 and all the cities of Sihon king of the Amorites, who reigned in Heshbon, as far as the border of the sons of Ammon;

11 and ^aGilead, and the territory of the Geshurites and Maacathites, and all Mount Hermon, and all Bashan as far as Salecah;

12 all the kingdom of ^aOg in Bashan, who reigned in Ashtaroth and in Edrei (he alone was left of the remnant of the Rephaim); for Moses ^bstruck them and dispossessed them.

13 But the sons of Israel did not dispossess the Geshurites or the Maacathites; for Geshur and Maacath live among Israel until this day.

14 ^aOnly to the tribe of Levi he did not give an inheritance; the offerings by fire to the LORD, the God of Israel, are their inheritance, as He spoke to him.

15 So Moses gave an inheritance to the tribe of the sons of Reuben according to their families.

16 And their territory was ^afrom Aroer, which is on the edge of the valley of the Arnon, with the city which is in the middle of the valley and all the plain by Medeba;

17 Heshbon, and all its cities which are on the plain: Dibon and Bamoth-baal and Beth-baal-meon,

18 and ^aJahaz and Kedemoth and Mephaath,

19 and ^aKiriathaim and Sibmah and Zereth-shahar on the hill of the valley,

20 and Beth-peor and the slopes of Pisgah and Beth-jeshimoth,

21 even all the cities of the plain and all the kingdom of Sihon king of the Amorites who reigned in Heshbon, whom Moses struck with the chiefs of Midian, ^aEvi and Rekem and Zur and Hur and Reba, the princes of Sihon, who lived in the land.

22 The sons of Israel also killed ^aBalaam the son of Beor, the diviner, with the sword among *the rest of* their slain.

23 And the border of the sons of Reuben was the Jordan. This was the inheritance of the sons of Reuben according to their families, the cities and their villages.

24 Moses also gave an inheritance to the tribe of Gad, to the sons of Gad, according to their families.

25 And their territory was ^aJazer, and all the cities of Gilead, and half the land of the sons of

Cross references (margin)

5 ^a1 Kin. 5:18 ^bJosh. 12:7

6 ^aJosh. 11:8 ^bNum. 33:54

★ 8 ^aJosh. 12:1-6

11 ^aGen. 37:25; Num. 32:29; Josh. 13:25; 17:5f.

12 ^aDeut. 3:11 ^bNum. 21:24

14 ^aDeut. 18:1, 2

★15-23

16 ^aJosh. 13:9

18 ^aNum. 21:23; Judg. 11:20; Is. 15:4; Jer. 48:34

19 ^aNum. 32:37; Jer. 48:1, 23; Ezek. 25:9

21 ^aNum. 31:8

22 ^aNum. 31:8

★24-28

25 ^aNum. 21:32; Josh. 21:39; 2 Sam. 24:5; 1 Chr. 6:81, 26:31; Is. 16:8f.; Jer. 48:32

13:8 *which Moses gave them.* See notes on Num. 32:1 and 32:39.

13:15-23 The territory given to Reuben, previously occupied by Moab, was just to the E. of the Dead Sea.

13:24-28 The area given to the tribe of Gad, N. of the Dead Sea, was originally a part of Gilead.

Ammon, as far as Aroer which is before Rabbah;

26 and from Heshbon as far as Ramath-mizpeh and Betonim, and from Mahanaim as far as the border of Debir;

27 ^aNum. 34:11; Deut. 3:17   27 and in the valley, Beth-haram and Beth-nimrah and Succoth and Zaphon, the rest of the kingdom of Sihon king of Heshbon, with the Jordan as a border, as far as the *lower* end of the Sea of ^aChinnereth beyond the Jordan to the east.

*28-33   28 This is the inheritance of the sons of Gad according to their families, the cities and their villages.

29 Moses also gave *an inheritance* to the half-tribe of Manasseh; and it was for the half-tribe of the sons of Manasseh according to their families.

30 ^aNum. 32:41   30 And their territory was from Mahanaim, all Bashan, all the kingdom of Og king of Bashan, and all ^athe towns of Jair, which are in Bashan, sixty cities;

31 ^aJosh. 9:10; 12:4; 13:12; Judg. 10:6; 1 Sam. 7:3f.; 12:10; 1 Chr. 6:71   31 also half of Gilead, with ^aAshtaroth and Edrei, the cities of the kingdom of Og in Bashan, *were* for the sons of Machir the son of Manasseh, for half of the sons of Machir according to their families.

32 These are *the territories* which Moses apportioned for an inheritance in the plains of Moab, beyond the Jordan at Jericho to the east.

33 ^aDeut. 18:1f.; Josh. 13:14   33 But ^ato the tribe of Levi, Moses did not give an inheritance; the LORD, the God of Israel, is their inheritance, as He had promised to them.

C Division of Canaan, 14:1–19:51

1 Introduction, 14:1–5

14 Now these are *the territories* which the sons of Israel inherited in the land of Canaan, which ^aEleazar the priest, and Joshua the son of Nun, and the heads of the households of the tribes of the sons of Israel apportioned to them for an inheritance,

*1 ^aNum. 34:16-29

2 by the ^alot of their inheritance, as the LORD commanded through Moses, for the nine tribes and the half-tribe.

2 ^aNum. 26:55; 33:54; 34:13

3 For ^aMoses had given the inheritance of the two tribes and the half-tribe beyond the Jordan; but ^bhe did not give an inheritance to the Levites among them.

3 ^aNum. 32:33 ^bJosh. 13:14

4 For the sons of Joseph were two tribes, ^aManasseh and Ephraim, and they did not give a portion to the Levites in the land, except cities to live in, with their pasture lands for their livestock and for their property.

*4 ^aGen. 41:51f.; 46:20; 48:1, 5; Num. 26:28, 2 Chr. 30:1

5 Thus the sons of Israel did just ^aas the LORD had commanded Moses, and they divided the land.

5 ^aNum. 35:1f.; Josh. 21:2

2 Inheritance of Judah, 14:6–15:63

6 Then the sons of Judah drew near to Joshua in Gilgal, and ^aCaleb the son of Jephunneh the Kenizzite said to him, "You know the word which the LORD spoke to Moses the man of God concerning you and me in Kadesh-barnea.

*6-15

6 ^aNum. 13:6, 30; 14:6, 24, 30

13:28-33 Half of the tribe of Manasseh settled E. of the Jordan; the other half chose to settle W. of the Jordan.

14:1 See note on Num. 34:16–29.

14:4 The double-portion right of the firstborn was given to Joseph's two sons (see note on Gen. 48:5). The Levites were given certain *cities* and *pasture lands* (see notes on Num.

35:2 and 35:4–5).

14:6-15 Caleb, who with Joshua had brought the minority report at Kadesh-barnea, asked for and received the city of Hebron as his special inheritance (cf. 15:13). Still vigorous at 85, he helped drive out the *Anakim* (14:12), and later willingly gave up Hebron to the Levites and lived in the suburbs (21:12).

7 "I was forty years old when *Moses the servant of the Lord sent me from Kadesh-barnea to spy out the land, and I brought word back to him as *it was* in my heart.

8 "Nevertheless my brethren who went up with me made the heart of the people melt with fear; but *I followed the Lord my God fully.

9 "So Moses swore on that day, saying, 'Surely *the land on which your foot has trodden shall be an inheritance to you and to your children forever, because you have followed the Lord my God fully.'

10 "And now behold, the Lord has let me live, just as He spoke, these forty-five years, from the time that the Lord spoke this word to Moses, when Israel walked in the wilderness; and now behold, I am eighty-five years old today.

11 "*I am still as strong today as I was in the day Moses sent me; as my strength was then, so my strength is now, for war and for *going out and coming in.

12 "Now then, give me this hill country about which the Lord spoke on that day, for you heard on that day that *Anakim *were* there, with great fortified cities; perhaps the Lord will be with me, and I shall drive them out as the Lord has spoken."

13 So Joshua *blessed him, and *gave Hebron to Caleb the son of Jephunneh for an inheritance.

14 Therefore, Hebron became the inheritance of Caleb the son of Jephunneh the Kenizzite until this day, because he followed the Lord God of Israel fully.

15 Now the name of Hebron was formerly Kiriath-arba; *for Arba* was the greatest man among the Anakim. *Then the land had rest from war.

15 Now *the lot for the tribe of the sons of Judah according to their families reached the *border of Edom, southward to the *wilderness of Zin at the extreme south.

2 And their south border was from the lower end of the Salt Sea, from the bay that turns to the south.

3 Then it proceeded southward to the ascent of Akrabbim and continued to Zin, then went up by the south of Kadesh-barnea and continued to Hezron, and went up to Addar and turned about to Karka.

4 And it *continued to Azmon and proceeded to the *brook of Egypt; and the border ended at the sea. This shall be your south border.

5 And the *east border *was* the Salt Sea, as far as the mouth of the Jordan. And the *border of the north side was from the bay of the sea at the mouth of the Jordan.

6 Then the border went up to Beth-hoglah, and continued on the north of Beth-arabah, and the border went up to the stone of Bohan the son of Reuben.

7 And the border went up to Debir from *the valley of Achor, and turned northward toward Gilgal which is opposite the ascent of Adummim, which is on the south of the valley; and the border continued to the waters of En-shemesh, and it ended at En-rogel.

8 Then the border went up the valley of Ben-hinnom to the slope of the *Jebusite on the south (that is, Jerusalem); and the border went up to the top of the mountain which is before the valley of Hinnom to the west, which is at the end of the valley of Rephaim toward the north.

9 And from the top of the mountain the border curved to the spring of the waters of Neph-

Marginal references

7 *Num. 13:1-31
8 *Num. 14:24; Deut. 1:36
9 *Deut. 1:36
11 *Deut. 34:7 *Deut. 31:2
12 *Num. 13:33
13 *Josh. 22:6 *Judg. 1:20; 1 Chr. 6:55f.
15 *Josh. 11:23

★ 1-12
1 *Num. 34:3, 4 *Num. 20:16 *Deut. 32:51
4 *Num. 34:5 *Gen. 15:18; 1 Kin. 8:65
5 *Num. 34:3, 10-12 *Josh. 18:15-19
7 *Josh. 7:24
8 *Josh. 15:63
9 *1 Chr. 13:6 *Judg. 18:12

15:1-12 Judah's southern border extended from the S. end of the *Salt Sea* (Dead Sea) westward to the *brook of Egypt.* Her northern border extended from the N. tip of the Dead Sea to the Mediterranean (these representing the E. and W. limits).

toah and proceeded to the cities of Mount Ephron, then the border curved to ^aBaalah (that is, ^bKiriath-jearim).

10 And the border turned about from Baalah westward to Mount Seir, and continued to the slope of Mount Jearim on the north (that is, Chesalon), and went down to Beth-shemesh and continued through ^aTimnah.

11 And the border proceeded to the side of Ekron northward. Then the border curved to Shikkeron and continued to Mount Baalah and proceeded to Jabneel, and the border ended at the sea.

12 And the west border *was* ^aat the Great Sea, even *its* coastline. This is the border around the sons of Judah according to their families.

13 Now ^ahe gave to Caleb the son of Jephunneh a portion ^bamong the sons of Judah, according to the command of the Lord to Joshua, *namely,* Kiriath-arba, *Arba being* the father of Anak (that is, Hebron).

14 And ^aCaleb drove out from there the three ^bsons of Anak: Sheshai and Ahiman and Talmai, the children of Anak.

15 Then ^ahe went up from there against the inhabitants of Debir; now the name of Debir formerly was Kiriath-sepher.

16 And Caleb said, "The one who attacks Kiriath-sepher and captures it, I will give him Achsah my daughter as a wife."

17 And ^aOthniel the son of Kenaz, the brother of Caleb, captured it; so he gave him Achsah his daughter as a wife.

18 ^aAnd it came about that when she came *to him,* she persuaded him to ask her father for a field. So she alighted from the donkey, and Caleb said to her, "What do you want?"

19 Then she said, "Give me a blessing; since you have given me the land of the Negev, give me also springs of water." So he gave her the upper springs and the lower springs.

20 This is the inheritance of the tribe of the sons of Judah according to their families.

21 Now the cities at the extremity of the tribe of the sons of Judah toward the border of Edom in the south were Kabzeel and ^aEder and Jagur,

22 and Kinah and Dimonah and Adadah,

23 and Kedesh and Hazor and Ithnan,

24 Ziph and Telem and Bealoth,

25 and Hazor-hadattah and Kerioth-hezron (that is, Hazor),

26 Amam and Shema and Moladah,

27 and Hazar-gaddah and Heshmon and Beth-pelet,

28 and Hazar-shual and ^aBeersheba and Biziothiah,

29 Baalah and Iim and Ezem,

30 and Eltolad and Chesil and Hormah,

31 and ^aZiklag and Madmannah and Sansannah,

32 and Lebaoth and Shilhim and Ain and Rimmon; in all, twenty-nine cities with their villages.

33 In the lowland: ^aEshtaol and Zorah and Ashnah,

34 and Zanoah and Engannim, Tappuah and Enam,

35 Jarmuth and ^aAdullam, Socoh and Azekah,

36 and Shaaraim and Adithaim and Gederah and Gederothaim; fourteen cities with their villages.

37 Zenan and Hadashah and Migdal-gad,

38 and Dilean and Mizpeh and Joktheel,

Margin references:

10 ^aGen. 38:13; Judg. 14:1

12 ^aNum. 34:6

*13-19

13 ^aJosh. 14:13-15 ^bNum. 13:6

14 ^aJosh. 11:21, 22 ^bNum. 13:33; Deut. 9:2

15 ^aJosh. 10:38

17 ^aJudg. 1:13; 3:9

18 ^aJudg. 1:14

*20-62

21 ^aGen. 35:21

28 ^aGen. 21:31

31 ^a1 Sam. 27:6; 30:1

*32

33 ^aJudg. 13:25; 16:31

35 ^a1 Sam. 22:1

15:13-19 *Othniel* made a second assault on Debir after Joshua's lightning attack (10:38-39). He later became a judge of Israel (Judg. 3:9-11).

15:20-62 The cities of Judah are listed by four geographical areas: (1) the south (vv. 20-32); (2) the Shephelah (foothills, vv. 33-47); (3) the hill country (vv. 48-60); and (4) the wilderness of Judea that slopes down to the Dead Sea (vv. 61-62).

15:32 *twenty-nine cities.* Since 38 locations are listed, perhaps nine of these were too small to be called "cities," or they may have been in part of Simeon's territory (19:9).

39 aJosh.
10:3; 2 Kin.
14:19

39 aLachish and Bozkath and Eglon,

40 and Cabbon and Lahmas and Chitlish,

41 and Gederoth, Beth-dagon and Naamah and Makkedah; sixteen cities with their villages.

42 Libnah and Ether and A-shan,

43 and Iphtah and Ashnah and Nezib,

44 and Keilah and Achzib and Mareshah; nine cities with their villages.

45 Ekron, with its towns and its villages;

46 from Ekron even to the sea, all that were by the side of Ashdod, with their villages.

47 aJosh.
15:4

47 Ashdod, its towns and its villages; Gaza, its towns and its villages; as far as athe brook of Egypt and the Great Sea, even *its* coastline.

48 And in the hill country: Shamir and Jattir and Socoh,

49 and Dannah and Kiriath-sannah (that is, Debir),

50 and Anab and Eshtemoh and Anim,

51 and Goshen and Holon and Giloh; eleven cities with their villages.

52 Arab and Dumah and E-shan,

53 and Janum and Beth-tappuah and Aphekah,

54 and Humtah and Kiriath-arba (that is, Hebron), and Zior; nine cities with their villages.

55 Maon, Carmel and Ziph and Juttah,

56 and Jezreel and Jokdeam and Zanoah,

57 Kain, Gibeah and Timnah; ten cities with their villages.

58 Halhul, Beth-zur and Ge-dor,

59 and Maarath and Beth-anoth and Eltekon; six cities with their villages.

60 Kiriath-baal (that is, Kiri-ath-jearim), and Rabbah; two cities with their villages.

61 In the wilderness: Beth-arabah, Middin and Secacah,

62 and Nibshan and the City of Salt and Engedi; six cities with their villages.

63 Now as for the aJebusites, the inhabitants of Jerusalem, the sons of Judah could not drive them out; so the Jebusites live with the sons of Judah at Jerusalem until this day.

★**63** aJudg.
1:21; 2 Sam.
5:6; 1 Chr.
11:4

3 Inheritance of Ephraim,
16:1–10

16 Then the lot for the sons of Joseph went from the Jordan at Jericho to the waters of Jericho on the east into athe wilderness, going up from Jericho through the hill country to Bethel.

1 aJosh.
8:15; 18:12

2 And it went from Bethel to Luz, and acontinued to the border of the Archites at Ataroth.

2 aJosh.
18:13

3 And it went down westward to the territory of the Japhletites, as far as the territory of lower aBeth-horon even to bGezer, and it ended at the sea.

3 aJosh.
18:13; 1 Kin.
9:17 bJosh.
10:33

4 And the asons of Joseph, Manasseh and Ephraim, received their inheritance.

4 aJosh.
17:14

5 Now *this* was the territory of the sons of Ephraim according to their families: the border of their inheritance eastward was aAtaroth-addar, as far as upper Beth-horon.

★ **5-10**

5 aJosh.
18:13

6 Then the border went westward at aMichmethath on the north, and the border turned about eastward to Taanath-shiloh, and continued *beyond* it to the east of Janoah.

6 aJosh.
17:7

7 And it went down from Ja-noah to Ataroth and to aNaarah, then reached Jericho and came out at the Jordan.

7 a1 Chr.
7:28

8 From aTappuah the border continued westward to the brook

8 aJosh.
17:8

15:63 The men of Judah did capture the lower city (Judg. 1:8, 21), but only later did King David capture the upper city and eliminate the Jebusites (2 Sam. 5:6-7).

16:5-10 Ephraim was allotted the southern part of the central hill country, from the Jordan to the Mediterranean.

of Kanah, and it ended at the sea. This is the inheritance of the tribe of the sons of Ephraim according to their families,

9 *together* with the cities which were set apart for the sons of Ephraim in the midst of the inheritance of the sons of Manasseh, all the cities with their villages.

10 ᵃBut they did not drive out the Canaanites who lived in Gezer, so ᵇthe Canaanites live in the midst of Ephraim to this day, and they became forced laborers.

4 Inheritance of half-tribe of Manasseh, 17:1-18

17 Now *this* was the lot for the tribe of ᵃManasseh, for he was the first-born of Joseph. To Machir the first-born of Manasseh, the father of Gilead, was allotted Gilead and Bashan, because he was a man of war.

2 So *the lot* was *made* for the rest of the sons of Manasseh according to their families: for the sons of Abiezer and for the sons of Helek and for the sons of Asriel and for the sons of Shechem and for the sons of Hepher and for the sons of Shemida; these *were* the male *descendants* of Manasseh the son of Joseph according to their families.

3 However, ᵃZelophehad, the son of Hepher, the son of Gilead, the son of Machir, the son of Manasseh, had no sons, only daughters; and these are the names of his daughters: Mahlah and Noah, Hoglah, Milcah and Tirzah.

4 And they came near before Eleazar the priest and before Joshua the son of Nun and before the leaders, saying, "The LORD commanded Moses to give us an inheritance among our brothers." So ᵃaccording to the command of the LORD he gave them an inheritance among their father's brothers.

5 Thus there fell ten portions to Manasseh, besides the land of Gilead and Bashan, which is beyond the Jordan,

6 because the daughters of Manasseh received an inheritance among his sons. And the ᵃland of Gilead belonged to the rest of the sons of Manasseh.

7 And the border of Manasseh ran from Asher to Michmethath which was east of Shechem; then the border went southward to the inhabitants of En-tappuah.

8 The land of Tappuah belonged to Manasseh, but ᵃTappuah on the border of Manasseh *belonged* to the sons of Ephraim.

9 And the ᵃborder went down to the brook of Kanah, southward of the brook (these cities *belonged* to Ephraim among the cities of Manasseh), and the border of Manasseh *was* on the north side of the brook, and it ended at the sea.

10 The south side *belonged* to Ephraim and the north side to Manasseh, and the sea was their border; and they reached to Asher on the north and to Issachar on the east.

11 And in Issachar and in Asher, ᵃManasseh had Bethshean and its towns and Ibleam and its towns, and the inhabitants of Dor and its towns, and the inhabitants of En-dor and its towns, and the inhabitants of Taanach and its towns, and the inhabitants of Megiddo and its towns, the third is ᵇNapheth.

12 ᵃBut the sons of Manasseh could not take possession of these

---

Marginal references:

10 ᵃJudg. 1:29; 1 Kin. 9:16 ᵇJosh. 17:12, 13

1 ᵃGen. 41:51; 46:20; 48:17f.

★ 3-4

3 ᵃNum. 26:33; 27:1-7

4 ᵃNum. 27:5-7

★ 5

6 ᵃJosh. 13:30, 31

★ 7-11

8 ᵃJosh. 16:8

9 ᵃJosh. 16:8f.

11 ᵃ1 Chr. 7:29 ᵇJosh. 11:2; 12:23

★12-18
12 ᵃJudg. 1:27

17:3-4 Moses had said that a daughter could inherit from her father (see notes on Num. 27:3 and 27:7-11).

17:5 See note on 13:24-28.

17:7-11 Manasseh controlled the northern part of the central hill country up to the valley of Jezreel. *the third is Napheth* (v. 11). The word *Napheth* (countries) does not occur elsewhere. It may refer to three districts, towns, or mountains, or it may be explaining that Dor (third on the list) is Naphath-dor.

17:12-18 The children of Joseph did not eliminate the Canaanites in their territory but put them under tribute; then they complained about not having enough land. Joshua suggested that they clear trees and settle in the forested hill country. *chariots of iron*. I.e., chariots armed with projecting iron blades.

cities, because the Canaanites persisted in living in that land.

13 aJosh. 16:10

13 And it came about when the sons of Israel became strong, athey put the Canaanites to forced labor, but they did not drive them out completely.

14 aNum. 13:7

14 Then the asons of Joseph spoke to Joshua, saying, "Why have you given me only one lot and one portion for an inheritance, since I am a numerous people whom the LORD has thus far blessed?"

15 And Joshua said to them, "If you are a numerous people, go up to the forest and clear a place for yourself there in the land of the Perizzites and of the Rephaim, since the hill country of Ephraim is too narrow for you."

16 aJosh. 17:18; Judg. 1:19, 4:3, 13

16 And the sons of Joseph said, "The hill country is not enough for us, and all the Canaanites who live in the valley land have achariots of iron, both those who are in Beth-shean and its towns, and those who are in the valley of Jezreel."

17 And Joshua spoke to the house of Joseph, to Ephraim and Manasseh, saying, "You are a numerous people and have great power; you shall not have one lot *only,*

18 aJosh. 17:16

18 but the hill country shall be yours. For though it is a forest, you shall clear it, and to its farthest borders it shall be yours; for you shall drive out the Canaanites, even though they have achariots of iron *and* though they are strong."

5 Survey of remaining land, 18:1-10

★ 1 aJudg. 21:19, Jer. 7:12, 26:6, 9

18 Then the whole congregation of the sons of Israel assembled themselves at aShiloh, and set up the tent of meeting there; and the land was subdued before them.

2 And there remained among the sons of Israel seven tribes who had not divided their inheritance.

★ 2-9

3 aJudg. 18:9

3 So Joshua said to the sons of Israel, "aHow long will you put off entering to take possession of the land which the LORD, the God of your fathers, has given you?

4 "Provide for yourselves three men from each tribe that I may send them, and that they may arise and walk through the land and write a description of it according to their inheritance; then they shall return to me.

5 aJosh. 15:1

5 "And they shall divide it into seven portions; aJudah shall stay in its territory on the south, and the house of Joseph shall stay in their territory on the north.

6 aJosh. 14:2

6 "And you shall describe the land in seven divisions, and bring *the description* here to me. aAnd I will cast lots for you here before the LORD our God.

7 aNum. 18:7, 20; Josh. 13:33

7 "For athe Levites have no portion among you, because the priesthood of the LORD is their inheritance. Gad and Reuben and the half-tribe of Manasseh also have received their inheritance eastward beyond the Jordan, which Moses the servant of the LORD gave them."

8 aJosh. 18:1

8 Then the men arose and went, and Joshua commanded those who went to describe the land, saying, "Go and walk through the land and describe it, and return to me; then I will cast lots for you here before the LORD in aShiloh."

9 So the men went and passed through the land, and described it by cities in seven divisions in a book; and they came to Joshua to the camp at Shiloh.

10 aNum. 34:16-29; Josh. 19:51

10 And aJoshua cast lots for them in Shiloh before the LORD, and there Joshua divided the land to the sons of Israel according to their divisions.

18:1 From Gilgal the congregation moved to Shiloh, 10 miles N. of Bethel, pitching the tabernacle there, where it remained during the period of the judges (see 22:9, 12; 1 Sam. 1:3).

18:2-9 Joshua appointed a commission of 21 men to survey the land not already allotted to Judah, Manasseh, and Ephraim.

6 Inheritance of Benjamin,
18:11-28

*11-28

11 Now the lot of the tribe of the sons of Benjamin came up according to their families, and the territory of their lot lay between the sons of Judah and the sons of Joseph.

12 aJosh.
16:1

12 And ᵃtheir border on the north side was from the Jordan, then the border went up to the side of Jericho on the north, and went up through the hill country westward; and it ended at the wilderness of Beth-aven.

13 aGen.
28:19; Judg.
1:23 bJosh.
16:3

13 And from there the border continued to ᵃLuz, to the side of Luz (that is, Bethel) southward; and the border went down to Ataroth-addar, near the hill which lies on the south of ᵇlower Beth-horon.

14 And the border extended from there, and turned round on the west side southward, from the hill which lies before Beth-horon southward; and it ended at Kiriath-baal (that is, Kiriath-jearim), a city of the sons of Judah. This was the west side.

15 aJosh.
15:5-9

15 Then the ᵃsouth side was from the edge of Kiriath-jearim, and the border went westward and went to the fountain of the waters of Nephtoah.

16 a2 Kin.
23:10

16 And the border went down to the edge of the hill which is in the ᵃvalley of Ben-hinnom, which is in the valley of Rephaim northward; and it went down to the valley of Hinnom, to the slope of the Jebusite southward, and went down to En-rogel.

17 aJosh.
15:6

17 And it extended northward and went to En-shemesh and went to Geliloth, which is opposite the ascent of Adummim, and it went down to the ᵃstone of Bohan the son of Reuben.

18 And it continued to the side in front of the Arabah northward, and went down to the Arabah.

19 And the border continued to the side of Beth-hoglah northward; and the border ended at the north bay of the Salt Sea, at the south end of the Jordan. This was the south border.

20 Moreover, the Jordan was its border on the east side. This was the inheritance of the sons of Benjamin, according to their families and according to its borders all around.

21 Now the cities of the tribe of the sons of Benjamin according to their families were Jericho and Beth-hoglah and Emek-keziz,

22 and Beth-arabah and Zemaraim and Bethel,

23 and Avvim and Parah and Ophrah,

24 and Chephar-ammoni and Ophni and ᵃGeba; twelve cities with their villages.

24 aEzra
2:26; Is.
10:29

25 Gibeon and Ramah and Beeroth,

26 and Mizpeh and Chephirah and Mozah,

27 and Rekem and Irpeel and Taralah,

28 and ᵃZelah, Haeleph and the Jebusite (that is, Jerusalem), Gibeah, Kiriath; fourteen cities with their villages. This is the inheritance of the ᵇsons of Benjamin according to their families.

28 a2 Sam.
21:14 bNum.
26:38

7 Inheritance of Simeon, 19:1-9

19 Then the second lot fell to Simeon, to the tribe of the sons of Simeon according to their families, and their inheritance was in the midst of the inheritance of the sons of Judah.

* 1-9

2 So they had as their inheritance Beersheba and Sheba and Moladah,

3 and Hazar-shual and Balah and Ezem,

4 and Eltolad and Bethul and Hormah,

18:11-28 Benjamin drew an allotment of land between the territories of Judah and Ephraim, including Jerusalem (in fulfillment of Deut. 33:12).

19:1-9 Simeon was given land in the southern section of Judah's territory in fulfillment of Jacob's prophecy (see note on Gen. 49:5).

5 and Ziklag and Beth-marcaboth and Hazar-susah,

6 and Beth-lebaoth and Sharuhen, thirteen cities with their villages;

7 Ain, Rimmon and Ether and Ashan, four cities with their villages;

8 and all the villages which *were* around these cities as far as Baalath-beer, Ramah of the Negev. This *was* the inheritance of the tribe of the sons of Simeon according to their families.

9 The inheritance of the sons of Simeon *was taken* from the portion of the sons of Judah, for the share of the sons of Judah was too large for them; so the sons of Simeon received *an* inheritance in the midst of Judah's inheritance.

8 Inheritance of Zebulun, 19:10-16

★10-16   **10** Now the third lot came up for the sons of Zebulun according to their families. And the territory of their inheritance was as far as Sarid.

11 Then their border went up to the west and to Maralah, it then touched Dabbesheth, and reached to the brook that is before Jokneam.

12 Then it turned from Sarid to the east toward the sunrise as far as the border of Chisloth-tabor, and it proceeded to Daberath and up to Japhia.

13 And from there it continued eastward toward the sunrise to Gath-hepher, to Eth-kazin, and it proceeded to Rimmon which stretches to Neah.

14 And the border circled around it on the north to Hannathon, and it ended at the valley of Iphtahel.

15 *Included* also *were* Kattah and Nahalal and Shimron and Id-

alah and Bethlehem; twelve cities with their villages.

16 This *was* the inheritance of the sons of Zebulun according to their families, these cities with their villages.

9 Inheritance of Issachar, 19:17-23

17 The fourth lot fell to Issachar, to the sons of Issachar according to their families.   ★17-23

18 And their territory was to Jezreel and *included* Chesulloth and ᵃShunem,   18 ᵃ1 Sam. 28:4; 2 Kin. 4:8

19 and Hapharaim and Shion and Anaharath,

20 and Rabbith and Kishion and Ebez,

21 and Remeth and Engannim and En-haddah and Beth-pazzez.

22 And the border reached to ᵃTabor and Shahazumah and Beth-shemesh, and their border ended at the Jordan; sixteen cities with their villages.   22 ᵃJudg. 4:6; Ps. 89:12

23 This *was* the inheritance of the tribe of the sons of Issachar according to their families, the cities with their villages.

10 Inheritance of Asher, 19:24-31

24 Now the fifth lot fell to the tribe of the sons of Asher according to their families.   ★24-31

25 And their territory was Helkath and Hali and Beten and Achshaph,

26 and Allammelech and Amad and Mishal; and it reached to Carmel on the west and to Shihor-libnath.

27 And it turned toward the east to Beth-dagon, and reached to Zebulun, and to the valley of Iphtahel northward to Beth-emek and Neiel; then it proceeded on north to ᵃCabul,   27 ᵃ1 Kin. 9:13

19:10-16 *Zebulun* was allotted a landlocked area in lower Galilee which included Nazareth and which was traversed by trade routes.

19:17-23 The territory of *Issachar* was N. of that given to Manasseh and reached from Mt. Ta-

bor on the W. to the southern tip of the Sea of Galilee.

19:24-31 *Asher* settled along the Mediterranean coast from Mt. Carmel N. to Tyre where the Phoenicians were.

28 aGen.
10:19; Judg.
1:31; Acts
27:3

28 and Ebron and Rehob and Hammon and Kanah, as far as Great aSidon.

29 aJudg.
1:31

29 And the border turned to Ramah, and to the fortified city of Tyre; then the border turned to Hosah, and it ended at the sea by the region of aAchzib.

30 Included also were Ummah, and Aphek and Rehob; twenty-two cities with their villages.

31 This was the inheritance of the tribe of the sons of Asher according to their families, these cities with their villages.

11 Inheritance of Naphtali,
19:32-39

★32-39

32 The sixth lot fell to the sons of Naphtali; to the sons of Naphtali according to their families.

33 And their border was from Heleph, from the oak in Zaanannim and Adami-nekeb and Jabneel, as far as Lakkum; and it ended at the Jordan.

34 Then the border turned westward to Aznoth-tabor, and proceeded from there to Hukkok; and it reached to Zebulun on the south and touched Asher on the west, and to Judah at the Jordan toward the east.

35 aGen.
10:18; 1 Kin.
8:65 bDeut.
3:17

35 And the fortified cities were Ziddim, Zer and aHammath, Rakkath and bChinnereth,

36 and Adamah and Ramah and Hazor,

37 and Kedesh and Edrei and En-hazor,

38 and Yiron and Migdal-el, Horem and Beth-anath and Beth-shemesh; nineteen cities with their villages.

39 This was the inheritance of the tribe of the sons of Naphtali according to their families, the cities with their villages.

12 Inheritance of Dan,
19:40-48

★40-48

40 The seventh lot fell to the tribe of the sons of Dan according to their families.

41 And the territory of their inheritance was Zorah and Eshtaol and Ir-shemesh,

42 and Shaalabbin and Aijalon and Ithlah,

43 and Elon and Timnah and Ekron,

44 and Eltekeh and Gibbethon and Baalath,

45 and Jehud and Bene-berak and Gath-rimmon,

46 and Me-jarkon and Rakkon, with the territory over against Joppa.

47 aJudg.
18:1 bJudg.
18:29

47 And the territory of the asons of Dan proceeded beyond them; for the sons of Dan went up and fought with Leshem and captured it. Then they struck it with the edge of the sword and possessed it and settled in it; and they called bLeshem Dan after the name of Dan their father.

48 This was the inheritance of the tribe of the sons of Dan according to their families, these cities with their villages.

13 Special inheritances,
19:49-51

★49-50

49 When they finished apportioning the land for inheritance by its borders, the sons of Israel gave an inheritance in their midst to Joshua the son of Nun.

50 aNum.
13:8; Josh.
24:30

50 In accordance with the command of the LORD they gave him the city for which he asked, aTimnath-serah in the hill country of Ephraim. So he built the city and settled in it.

51 aJosh.
18:10

51 aThese are the inheritances which Eleazar the priest and Joshua the son of Nun and the heads of the households of

---

19:32-39 To the E. of Asher was the territory of Naphtali.

19:40-48 Dan was allotted a small section between the territory of Benjamin and the Mediterranean (cf. Judg. 1:34; 18:1-31).

19:49-50 After all the land had been allocated, the people gave Joshua Timnath-serah, in the hill country of Ephraim, about 12 miles NE. of Lydda (Lod).

the tribes of the sons of Israel distributed by lot in Shiloh before the LORD, at the doorway of the tent of meeting. So they finished dividing the land.

D Cities of Refuge, 20:1-9

★ 1-9

20 Then the LORD spoke to Joshua, saying,

2 a Num. 35:6-34; Deut. 4:41-43; 19:2ff.

2 "Speak to the sons of Israel, saying, 'Designate ^athe cities of refuge, of which I spoke to you through Moses,

3 that the manslayer who kills any person unintentionally, without premeditation, may flee there, and they shall become your refuge from the avenger of blood.

4 a Ruth 4:1; Job 5:4; Jer. 38:7

4 'And he shall flee to one of these cities, and shall stand at the entrance of the ^agate of the city and state his case in the hearing of the elders of that city; and they shall take him into the city to them and give him a place, so that he may dwell among them.

5 a Num. 35:12

5 'Now ^aif the avenger of blood pursues him, then they shall not deliver the manslayer into his hand, because he struck his neighbor without premeditation and did not hate him beforehand.

6 a Num. 35:12

6 'And he shall dwell in that city ^auntil he stands before the congregation for judgment, until the death of the one who is high priest in those days. Then the manslayer shall return to his own city and to his own house, to the city from which he fled.' "

7 a Josh. 21:32; 1 Chr. 6:76 **b**Josh. 21:11; Luke 1:39

7 So they set apart ^aKedesh in Galilee in the hill country of Naphtali and Shechem in the hill country of Ephraim, and Kiriath-

arba (that is, Hebron) in ^bthe hill country of Judah.

8 And beyond the Jordan east of Jericho, they designated Bezer in the wilderness on the plain from the tribe of Reuben, and Ramoth in Gilead from the tribe of Gad, and Golan in Bashan from the tribe of Manasseh.

9 a Num. 35:13ff.

9 ^aThese were the appointed cities for all the sons of Israel and for the stranger who sojourns among them, that whoever kills any person unintentionally may flee there, and not die by the hand of the avenger of blood until he stands before the congregation.

E Cities of the Levites, 21:1-45

1 a Num. 35:1-8

21 Then the heads of households of ^athe Levites approached Eleazar the priest and Joshua the son of Nun and the heads of households of the tribes of the sons of Israel.

★ 2 a Num. 35:2

2 And they spoke to them at Shiloh in the land of Canaan, saying, "^aThe LORD commanded through Moses to give us cities to live in, with their pasture lands for our cattle."

3 So the sons of Israel gave the Levites from their inheritance these cities with their pasture lands, according to the command of the LORD.

4 Then the lot came out for the families of the Kohathites. And the sons of Aaron the priest, who were of the Levites, received thirteen cities by lot from the tribe of Judah and from the tribe of the Simeonites and from the tribe of Benjamin.

20:1-9 Six *cities of refuge* are designated (as Moses had instructed; see note on Num. 35:11), three on each side of the Jordan, for protection of the unwitting slayer. This protection was provided only in cases of unpremeditated murder. The procedure indicated in verse 6 required that a person fleeing to one of these cities later had to stand trial in the community nearest the scene of the crime. If found innocent of premeditated murder, he

was returned to the city of refuge. After the death of the high priest, he was free to return with impunity to his home city. See Num. 35:25-34 for criteria for judging.

21:2 See notes on Num. 35:2 and 35:4-5. The Levites were given 48 cities with their *pasture lands*. This distribution provided a spiritual influence over all the people, since no one lived more than 10 miles from a city in which Levites lived.

5 And the rest of the sons of Kohath received ten cities by lot from the families of the tribe of Ephraim and from the tribe of Dan and from the half-tribe of Manasseh.

6 And the sons of Gershon received thirteen cities by lot from the families of the tribe of Issachar and from the tribe of Asher and from the tribe of Naphtali and from the half-tribe of Manasseh in Bashan.

7 The sons of Merari according to their families received twelve cities from the tribe of Reuben and from the tribe of Gad and from the tribe of Zebulun.

8 Now the *a*sons of Israel gave by lot to the Levites these cities with their pasture lands, as the Lord had commanded through Moses.

9 And they gave these cities which are *here* mentioned by name from the tribe of the sons of Judah and from the tribe of the sons of Simeon;

10 and they were for the sons of Aaron, one of the families of the Kohathites, of the sons of Levi, for the lot was theirs first.

11 Thus *a*they gave them Kiriath-arba, *Arba being* the *b*father of Anak (that is, Hebron), in the hill country of Judah, with its surrounding pasture lands.

12 But the fields of the city and its villages, they gave to Caleb the son of Jephunneh as his possession.

13 So *a*to the sons of Aaron the priest they gave *b*Hebron, the city of refuge for the manslayer, with its pasture lands, and *c*Libnah with its pasture lands,

14 and *a*Jattir with its pasture lands and *b*Eshtemoa with its pasture lands,

15 and Holon with its pasture lands and *a*Debir with its pasture lands,

16 and Ain with its pasture lands and *a*Juttah with its pasture lands *and* *b*Beth-shemesh with its pasture lands; nine cities from these two tribes.

17 And from the tribe of Benjamin, *a*Gibeon with its pasture lands, *b*Geba with its pasture lands,

18 Anathoth with its pasture lands and Almon with its pasture lands; four cities.

19 All the cities of the sons of Aaron, the priests, were thirteen cities with their pasture lands.

20 Then the cities from the tribe of Ephraim were allotted to the *a*families of the sons of Kohath, the Levites, *even to* the rest of the sons of Kohath.

21 And they gave them *a*Shechem, the city of refuge for the manslayer, with its pasture lands, in the hill country of Ephraim, and Gezer with its pasture lands,

22 and Kibzaim with its pasture lands and Beth-horon with its pasture lands; four cities.

23 And from the tribe of Dan, Elteke with its pasture lands, Gibbethon with its pasture lands,

24 Aijalon with its pasture lands, Gath-rimmon with its pasture lands; four cities.

25 And from the half-tribe of Manasseh, *they allotted* Taanach with its pasture lands and Gathrimmon with its pasture lands; two cities.

26 All the cities with their pasture lands for the families of the rest of the sons of Kohath were ten.

27 And *a*to the sons of Gershon, one of the families of the Levites, from the half-tribe of Manasseh, *they gave* Golan in Bashan, the city of refuge for the manslayer, with its pasture lands, and Be-eshterah with its pasture lands; two cities.

28 And from the tribe of Issachar, *they gave* Kishion with its pasture lands, Daberath with its pasture lands,

29 Jarmuth with its pasture lands, En-gannim with its pasture lands; four cities.

30 And from the tribe of Asher, *they gave* Mishal with its pasture lands, Abdon with its pasture lands,

31 Helkath with its pasture lands and Rehob with its pasture lands; four cities.

8 *a*Gen. 49:5ff.

11 *a*1 Chr. 6:55 *b*Josh. 14:15; 15:13

13 *a*1 Chr. 6:57 *b*Josh. 15:54 *c*Josh. 15:42

14 *a*Josh. 15:48 *b*Josh. 15:50

15 *a*Josh. 15:49

16 *a*Josh. 15:55 *b*Josh. 15:10

17 *a*Josh. 18:25 *b*Josh. 18:24

20 *a*1 Chr. 6:66

21 *a*Josh. 20:7

27 *a*1 Chr. 6:71

32 And from the tribe of Naphtali, *they gave* [a]Kedesh in Galilee, the city of refuge for the manslayer, with its pasture lands and Hammoth-dor with its pasture lands and Kartan with its pasture lands; three cities.

33 All the cities of the Gershonites according to their families were thirteen cities with their pasture lands.

34 And to the families of [a]the sons of Merari, the rest of the Levites, *they gave* from the tribe of Zebulun, Jokneam with its pasture lands and Kartah with its pasture lands.

35 Dimnah with its pasture lands, Nahalal with its pasture lands; four cities.

36 And from the tribe of Reuben, *they gave* [a]Bezer with its pasture lands and Jahaz with its pasture lands,

37 Kedemoth with its pasture lands and Mephaath with its pasture lands; four cities.

38 And from the tribe of Gad, *they gave* [a]Ramoth in Gilead, the city of refuge for the manslayer, with its pasture lands and [b]Mahanaim with its pasture lands,

39 Heshbon with its pasture lands, Jazer with its pasture lands; four cities in all.

40 All *these were* the cities of the sons of Merari according to their families, the rest of the families of the Levites; and their lot was twelve cities.

41 [a]All the cities of the Levites in the midst of the possession of the sons of Israel were forty-eight cities with their pasture lands.

42 These cities each had its surrounding pasture lands; thus *it was* with all these cities.

43 [a]So the LORD gave Israel all the land which He had sworn to give to their fathers, and [b]they possessed it and lived in it.

44 And the LORD [a]gave them rest on every side, according to all that He had sworn to their fathers, and [b]no one of all their enemies stood before them; [c]the LORD gave all their enemies into their hand.

45 [a]Not one of the good promises which the LORD had made to the house of Israel failed; all came to pass.

F Joshua's Farewell Messages, 22:1–24:28

1 To the two-and-a-half tribes, 22:1–34

22 [a]Then Joshua summoned the Reubenites and the Gadites and the half-tribe of Manasseh,

2 and said to them, "You have kept all that Moses the servant of the LORD commanded you, [a]and have listened to my voice in all that I commanded you.

3 "You have not forsaken your brothers these many days to this day, but have kept the charge of the commandment of the LORD your God.

4 "And now [a]the LORD your God has given rest to your brothers, as He spoke to them; therefore turn now and go to your tents, to the land of your possession, which Moses the servant of the LORD gave you beyond the Jordan.

5 "Only be very careful to observe the commandment and the law which Moses the servant of the LORD commanded you, to [a]love the LORD your God and walk

Margin references

32 [a]Josh. 20:7

34 [a]1 Chr. 6:77

36 [a]Deut. 4:43; Josh. 20:8

38 [a]Deut. 4:43; 1 Kin. 4:13 [b]Gen. 32:2; 2 Sam. 2:8

41 [a]Num. 35:7

★43-45

43 [a]Deut. 34:4 [b]Num. 33:53; Deut. 11:31; 17:14

44 [a]Josh. 1:13; 23:1 [b]Deut. 7:24 [c]Ex. 23:31

45 [a]Josh. 23:14; 1 Kin. 8:56

1 [a]Num. 32:20-22

★ 2 [a]Josh. 1:12-18

4 [a]Num. 32:18; Deut. 3:20

★ 5 [a]Deut. 5:10 [b]Deut. 4:29

21:43-45 God had kept His promise to give Israel the land of Canaan (Gen. 17:8). It is true that the Israelites had not yet fully conquered it, but God had told them they would do so gradually (see note on Deut. 7:22).

22:2 *all that Moses . . . commanded.* See notes on Num. 32. Read also of their obedience in Josh. 1:16-18 and 4:12-14.

22:5 Having discharged their military commitments, the 2½ tribes are reminded by Joshua of their continuing spiritual responsibilities. It is unnecessary to suppose that these tribes were not in God's will in settling E. of the Jordan. God had given them that land (24:8), and it was part of Palestine, the mountains of Gilead, E. of the Jordan (and not the Jordan itself), being the eastern boundary of Palestine.

in all His ways and keep His commandments and hold fast to Him and serve Him [b]with all your heart and with all your soul."

6 aGen.
47:7; Josh.
14:13;
2 Sam. 6:18;
Luke 24:50

6 So Joshua [a]blessed them and sent them away, and they went to their tents.

7 aNum.
32:33 bJosh.
17:1-13

7 Now [a]to the one half-tribe of Manasseh Moses had given *a possession* in Bashan, but [b]to the other half Joshua gave *a possession* among their brothers westward beyond the Jordan. So when Joshua sent them away to their tents, he blessed them,

8 aNum.
31:27;
1 Sam. 30:16

8 and said to them, "Return to your tents with great riches and with very much livestock, with silver, gold, bronze, iron, and with very many clothes; [a]divide the spoil of your enemies with your brothers."

9 aNum.
32:1, 26, 29

9 And the sons of Reuben and the sons of Gad and the half-tribe of Manasseh returned *home* and departed from the sons of Israel at Shiloh which is in the land of Canaan, to go to the [a]land of Gilead, to the land of *their* possession which they had possessed, according to the command of the LORD through Moses.

★10-11

10 And when they came to the region of the Jordan which is in the land of Canaan, the sons of Reuben and the sons of Gad and the half-tribe of Manasseh built an altar there by the Jordan, a large altar in appearance.

11 aDeut.
12:5; Josh.
22:19

11 And the sons of Israel heard *it* said, "Behold, the sons of Reuben and the sons of Gad and the half-tribe of Manasseh have [a]built an altar at the frontier of the land of Canaan, in the region of the Jordan, on the side *belonging to* the sons of Israel."

★12-20
12 aJosh.
18:1

12 And when the sons of Israel heard *of it,* the whole congregation of the sons of Israel gathered themselves at [a]Shiloh, to go up against them in war.

13 aNum.
25:7, 11;
31:6

13 Then the sons of Israel sent to the sons of Reuben and to the sons of Gad and to the half-tribe of Manasseh, into the land of Gilead, [a]Phinehas the son of Eleazar the priest,

14 aNum.
1:4

14 and with him ten chiefs, one chief for each father's household from each of the tribes of Israel; and [a]each one of them *was* the head of his father's household among the thousands of Israel.

15 And they came to the sons of Reuben and to the sons of Gad and to the half-tribe of Manasseh, to the land of Gilead, and they spoke with them saying,

16 aJosh.
22:11

16 "Thus says the whole congregation of the LORD, 'What is this unfaithful act which you have committed against the God of Israel, turning away from following the LORD this day, by [a]building yourselves an altar, to rebel against the LORD this day?

17 aNum.
25:1-9

17 'Is not [a]the iniquity of Peor enough for us, from which we have not cleansed ourselves to this day, although a plague came on the congregation of the LORD,

18 aNum.
16:22

18 that you must turn away this day from following the LORD? And it will come about if you rebel against the LORD today, that [a]He will be angry with the whole congregation of Israel tomorrow.

19 aJosh.
22:11

19 'If, however, the land of your possession is unclean, then cross into the land of the possession of the LORD, where the LORD's tabernacle stands, and take possession among us. Only do not rebel against the LORD, or rebel against us by [a]building an altar for yourselves, besides the altar of the LORD our God.

22:10-11 The 2½ tribes unwisely, but innocently, built an altar on the W. side of the Jordan before crossing over, to serve as a witness that they too shared in the inheritance of the Lord. It was a needless act, for God had ordained that all the males should appear at the sanctuary three times each year (see note on Exod. 23:14) in order to preserve the unity of the tribes.

22:12-20 The other tribes, ready to go to war over the matter of the altar, wisely sent a delegation headed by *Phinehas* (v. 13) to investigate first. *unfaithful act* (v. 16). The same word was used of Achan's sin (v. 20; 7:1). Regarding *the iniquity of Peor* (v. 17), which was idolatry and disobedience, see notes on Num. 25.

20 aJosh.
7:1-26

20 'Did not aAchan the son of Zerah act unfaithfully in the things under the ban, and wrath fall on all the congregation of Israel? And that man did not perish alone in his iniquity.' "

21 Then the sons of Reuben and the sons of Gad and the half-tribe of Manasseh answered, and spoke to the heads of the families of Israel.

★**22** aDeut.
10:17
b1 Kin. 8:39;
Job 10:7; Ps.
44:21

22 "The aMighty One, God, the LORD, the Mighty One, God, the LORD! bHe knows, and may Israel itself know. If it was in rebellion, or if in an unfaithful act against the LORD do not Thou save us this day!

23 aDeut.
12:11

23 "If we have built us an altar to turn away from following the LORD, or if to aoffer a burnt offering or grain offering on it, or if to offer sacrifices of peace offerings on it, may the LORD Himself require it.

24 "But truly we have done this out of concern, for a reason, saying, 'In time to come your sons may say to our sons, "What have you to do with the LORD, the God of Israel?

25 "For the LORD has made the Jordan a border between us and you, you sons of Reuben and sons of Gad; you have no portion in the LORD." So your sons may make our sons stop fearing the LORD.'

26 "Therefore we said, 'Let us build an altar, not for burnt offering or for sacrifice;

27 aGen.
31:48; Josh.
24:27 bDeut.
12:6, 11, 26f.

27 rather it shall be aa witness between us and you and between our generations after us, that we are to bperform the service of the LORD before Him with our burnt offerings, and with our sacrifices and with our peace offerings, that your sons may not say to our sons in time to come, "You have no portion in the LORD." '

28 "Therefore we said, 'It shall also come about if they say this to us or to our generations in time to come, then we shall say, "See the copy of the altar of the LORD which our fathers made, not for burnt offering or for sacrifice; rather it is a witness between us and you." '

29 aDeut.
12:13f.

29 "Far be it from us that we should rebel against the LORD and turn away from following the LORD this day, by abuilding an altar for burnt offering, for grain offering or for sacrifice, besides the altar of the LORD our God which is before His tabernacle."

30 So when Phinehas the priest and the leaders of the congregation, even the heads of the families of Israel who were with him, heard the words which the sons of Reuben and the sons of Gad and the sons of Manasseh spoke, it pleased them.

31 aEx. 25:8;
Lev. 26:11f.;
2 Chr. 15:2

31 And Phinehas the son of Eleazar the priest said to the sons of Reuben and to the sons of Gad and to the sons of Manasseh, "Today we know that the aLORD is in our midst, because you have not committed this unfaithful act against the LORD; now you have delivered the sons of Israel from the hand of the LORD."

32 Then Phinehas the son of Eleazar the priest and the leaders returned from the sons of Reuben and from the sons of Gad, from the land of Gilead, to the land of Canaan, to the sons of Israel, and brought back word to them.

33 a1 Chr.
29:20; Dan.
2:19; Luke
2:28

33 And the word pleased the sons of Israel, and the sons of Israel ablessed God; and they did not speak of going up against them in war, to destroy the land in which the sons of Reuben and the sons of Gad were living.

34 aGen.
31:47-49

34 And the sons of Reuben and the sons of Gad acalled the altar Witness; "For," they said, "it is a witness between us that the LORD is God."

2   To the rulers, 23:1-16

1 aJosh.
21:44

23 Now it came about after many days, when the LORD

22:22 The 2½ tribes swore their innocence by combining three names of God (El, Elohim, Yahweh) and repeating the combination twice. The matter had a happy ending (vv. 33-34).

had given ᵃrest to Israel from all their enemies on every side, and Joshua was old, advanced in years,

2 that ᵃJoshua called for all Israel, for their elders and their heads and their judges and their officers, and said to them, "I am old, advanced in years.

3 "And you have seen all that the LORD your God has done to all these nations because of you, for ᵃthe LORD your God is He who has been fighting for you.

4 "See, ᵃI have apportioned to you these nations which remain as an inheritance for your tribes, with all the nations which I have cut off, from the Jordan even to the Great Sea toward the setting of the sun.

5 "And the LORD your God, He shall thrust them out from before you and ᵃdrive them from before you; and ᵇyou shall possess their land, just as the LORD your God promised you.

6 "ᵃBe very firm, then, to keep and do all that is written in the book of the law of Moses, so that you may not turn aside from it to the right hand or to the left,

7 in order that you may not associate with these nations, these which remain among you, or ᵃmention the name of their gods, or ᵇmake *anyone* swear *by them*, or ᶜserve them, or bow down to them.

8 "But you are to cling to the LORD your God, as you have done to this day.

9 "ᵃFor the LORD has driven out great and strong nations from before you; and as for you, ᵇno man has stood before you to this day.

10 "ᵃOne of your men puts to flight a thousand, for the LORD your God is ᵇHe who fights for you, just as He promised you.

11 "So take diligent heed to yourselves to love the LORD your God.

12 "For if you ever go back and ᵃcling to the rest of these nations, these which remain among you, and ᵇintermarry with them, so that you associate with them and they with you,

13 know with certainty that the LORD your God will not continue to drive these nations out from before you; but they shall be a ᵃsnare and a trap to you, and a whip on your sides and thorns in your eyes, until you perish from off this good land which the LORD your God has given you.

14 "Now behold, today ᵃI am going the way of all the earth, and you know in all your hearts and in all your souls that ᵇnot one word of all the good words which the LORD your God spoke concerning you has failed; all have been fulfilled for you, not one of them has failed.

15 "And it shall come about that just as all the good words which the LORD your God spoke to you have come upon you, so ᵃthe LORD will bring upon you all the threats, until He has destroyed you from off this good land which the LORD your God has given you.

16 "ᵃWhen you transgress the covenant of the LORD your God, which He commanded you, and go and serve other gods, and bow down to them, then the anger of the LORD will burn against you, and you shall perish quickly from off the good land which He has given you."

3 To the people, 24:1-28

24 Then ᵃJoshua gathered all the tribes of Israel to Shechem, and called for the elders of Israel and for their heads and

---

Margin references (left column):

2 ᵃJosh. 24:1

3 ᵃDeut. 1:30

4 ᵃEx. 23:30

5 ᵃEx. 23:20 ᵇNum. 33:53

6 ᵃDeut. 5:32; Josh. 1:7

★ 7 ᵃEx. 23:13; Ps. 16:4 ᵇDeut. 6:13; 10:20 ᶜEx. 20:5

9 ᵃEx. 23:23, 30 ᵇDeut. 7:24

10 ᵃLev. 26:8; Deut. 28:7; 32:20 ᵇDeut. 3:22; Josh. 23:3

Margin references (right column):

12 ᵃEx. 34:15, 16; Ps. 106:34, 35 ᵇDeut. 7:3, 4; Ezra 9:2; Neh. 13:25

13 ᵃEx. 23:33; 34:12; Deut. 7:16

14 ᵃ1 Kin. 2:2 ᵇJosh. 21:45

15 ᵃLev. 26:14-33; Deut. 28:15

16 ᵃDeut. 4:25, 26

★ 1 ᵃJosh. 23:2

23:7 *in order that you may not associate with these nations.* I.e., do not mix with them.

24:1 Joshua called on the people to reaffirm their commitment to God and His covenant. The chapter takes the customary form of a suzerainty treaty (between a king and his vassals; see notes on Exod. 19:3 and Deut. 31:9–14).

The form includes a preamble (vv. 1–2), historical prologue (vv. 2–13), stipulations of the covenant (vv. 14–24), and the writing and depositing of the agreement (vv. 25–28). The reaffirmation was made at *Shechem* (v. 1), where Abraham built his first altar to the Lord in Canaan (see note on Gen. 12:6).

their judges and their officers; and they presented themselves before God.

2 And Joshua said to all the people, "Thus says the Lord, the God of Israel, 'From ancient times your fathers lived beyond the River, namely, ªTerah, the father of Abraham and the father of Nahor, and they served other gods.

3 Then ªI took your father Abraham from beyond the River, and led him through all the land of Canaan, and ᵇmultiplied his descendants and gave him ᶜIsaac.

4 'And to Isaac I gave ªJacob and Esau, and ᵇto Esau I gave Mount Seir, to possess it; but ᶜJacob and his sons went down to Egypt.

5 Then ªI sent Moses and Aaron, and I plagued Egypt by what I did in its midst; and afterward I brought you out.

6 'And I brought your fathers out of Egypt, and ªyou came to the sea; and Egypt pursued your fathers with chariots and horsemen to the Red Sea.

7 'But when they cried out to the Lord, He put darkness between you and the Egyptians, and brought the sea upon them and covered them; and your own eyes saw what I did in Egypt. And ªyou lived in the wilderness for a long time.

8 Then ªI brought you into the land of the Amorites who lived beyond the Jordan, and they fought with you; and I gave them into your hand, and you took possession of their land when I destroyed them before you.

9 Then ªBalak the son of Zippor, king of Moab, arose and fought against Israel, and he sent and summoned Balaam the son of Beor to curse you.

10 'But I ªwas not willing to listen to Balaam. So he had to bless you, and I delivered you from his hand.

11 'And ªyou crossed the Jordan and came to Jericho; and the citizens of Jericho fought against you, and ᵇthe Amorite and the Perizzite and the Canaanite and the Hittite and the Girgashite, the Hivite and the Jebusite. Thus ᶜI gave them into your hand.

12 Then I ªsent the hornet before you and it drove out the two kings of the Amorites from before you, but ᵇnot by your sword or your bow.

13 'And ªI gave you a land on which you had not labored, and cities which you had not built, and you have lived in them; you are eating of vineyards and olive groves which you did not plant.'

14 "Now, therefore, ªfear the Lord and serve Him in sincerity and truth; and put away the gods which your fathers served beyond the River and in Egypt, and serve the Lord.

15 "And if it is disagreeable in your sight to serve the Lord, choose for yourselves today whom you will serve: whether the gods which your fathers served which were beyond the River, or ªthe gods of the Amorites in whose land you are living; but as for me and my house, we will serve the Lord."

16 And the people answered and said, "Far be it from us that we should forsake the Lord to serve other gods;

17 for the Lord our God is He who brought us and our fathers up out of the land of Egypt, from the house of bondage, and who did these great signs in our sight and preserved us through all the way in which we went and among all the peoples through whose midst we passed.

18 "And the Lord drove out from before us all the peoples, even the Amorites who lived in the land. We also will serve the Lord, for He is our God."

---

2 ªGen. 11:27-32

★ **3** ªGen. 12:1; 24:7 ᵇGen. 15:5 ᶜGen. 21:3

4 ªGen. 25:25, 26 ᵇGen. 36:8; Deut. 2:5 ᶜGen. 46:6, 7

5 ªEx. 4:14-17

6 ªEx. 14:2-31

7 ªDeut. 1:46; 2:14

8 ªNum. 21:21-32

★ **9-10**

9 ªNum. 22:2-6

10 ªDeut. 23:5

11 ªJosh. 3:14-17 ᵇEx. 23:23, 28; Deut. 7:1 ᶜEx. 23:31

★ **12** ªEx. 23:28; Deut. 7:20 ᵇPs. 44:3

13 ªDeut. 6:10, 11

14 ªDeut. 10:12; 18:13; 1 Sam. 12:24

15 ªJudg. 6:10

24:3 *from beyond the River.* I.e., from the area N. and E. of the Euphrates.

24:9-10 See the notes on Num. 22–24.
24:12 *the hornet.* See note on Exod. 23:28.

19 Then Joshua said to the people, "You will not be able to serve the LORD, ªfor He is a holy God. He is ᵇa jealous God; ᶜHe will not forgive your transgression or your sins.

20 "ªIf you forsake the LORD and serve foreign gods, then He will turn and do you harm and consume you after He has done good to you."

21 And the people said to Joshua, "No, but we will serve the LORD."

22 And Joshua said to the people, "You are witnesses against yourselves that ªyou have chosen for yourselves the LORD, to serve Him." And they said, "We are witnesses."

23 "Now therefore, put away the foreign gods which are in your midst, and ªincline your hearts to the LORD, the God of Israel."

24 ªAnd the people said to Joshua, "We will serve the LORD our God and we will obey His voice."

25 ªSo Joshua made a covenant with the people that day, and made for them a statute and an ordinance in Shechem.

26 And Joshua ªwrote these words in the book of the law of God; and he took a large stone and set it up there under the oak that was by the sanctuary of the LORD.

27 And Joshua said to all the people, "Behold, ªthis stone shall be for a witness against us, for it has heard all the words of the LORD which He spoke to us; thus it shall be for a witness against you, lest you deny your God."

28 Then Joshua dismissed the people, each to his inheritance.

G The Death of Joshua, 24:29–33

29 And it came about after these things that Joshua the son of Nun, the servant of the LORD, died, being one hundred and ten years old.

30 And they buried him in the territory of his inheritance in ªTimnath-serah, which is in the hill country of Ephraim, on the north of Mount Gaash.

31 And ªIsrael served the LORD all the days of Joshua and all the days of the elders who survived Joshua, and had known all the deeds of the LORD which He had done for Israel.

32 Now ªthey buried the bones of Joseph, which the sons of Israel brought up from Egypt, at Shechem, in the piece of ground ᵇwhich Jacob had bought from the sons of Hamor the father of Shechem for one hundred pieces of money; and they became the inheritance of Joseph's sons.

33 And Eleazar the son of Aaron died; and they buried him at Gibeah of ªPhinehas his son, which was given him in the hill country of Ephraim.

Marginal references:

19 ªLev. 19:2; 20:7, 26 ᵇEx. 20:5; 34:14 ᶜEx. 23:21
20 ªDeut. 4:25, 26
22 ªPs. 119:173
23 ª1 Kin. 8:57, 58; Ps. 119:36; 141:4
24 ªEx. 19:8; 24:3, 7; Deut. 5:27
25 ªEx. 24:8
★26 ªDeut. 31:24
27 ªJosh. 22:27, 34
30 ªJosh. 19:50
31 ªJudg. 2:6f.
★32 ªGen. 50:24, 25; Ex. 13:19 ᵇGen. 33:19; John 4:5; Acts 7:15f.
33 ªJosh. 22:13

24:26 *by the sanctuary of the LORD.* Perhaps a reference to an old altar still standing, perhaps to an altar Joshua built on nearby Mt. Ebal (8:30), or perhaps the translation should be "beneath the oak tree which was sacred to the Lord" (cf. Gen. 12:6). The important fact is that the covenant, written on the stone, could be read by all (Josh. 24:27).

24:32 The burial of the body of *Joseph* is a reminder of Joseph's faith in God's promise to give Israel the land of Canaan, and of God's faithfulness in fulfilling His promise.

INTRODUCTION TO
THE BOOK OF JUDGES

AUTHOR: Anonymous   DATE: 1050-1000 B.C.

Historical Background *The events of this book cover the turbulent period in Israel's history from about 1380 to 1050 B.C., from the conquest of Palestine to the beginnings of the monarchy. Though the land had been generally conquered and occupied under Joshua, many important Canaanite strongholds had been bypassed, leaving their subjugation to individual Israelite tribes. The Book of Judges describes this warfare, as the Hebrews tried to complete their occupation of the land.*

The judges were military and civil leaders ruling during this time when the nation was a loose confederacy. Some of the judges ruled concurrently since each one did not necessarily rule over the entire land.

Authorship and Date *Though the author of the book is unknown, the Talmud suggests Samuel, and it is possible that he may have written portions. Judges was written after the death of Samson and after the coronation of King Saul, but before the conquest of Jerusalem by David about 990 B.C. (see 1:21; 17:6; 18:1; 19:1; 21:25).*

Purpose *Historically, the book serves to link the conquest of Palestine and the monarchy. Theologically, it provides many examples of the principle that obedience to the law brings peace, while disobedience means oppression and death. Spiritually, the faithfulness of God in forgiving His penitent people is seen even in this period when "every man did what was right in his own eyes" (17:6; 21:25).*

A Suggested Chronology of Oppressing Nations and Delivering Judges

Oppressor	Dates	Judge	Dates	Scripture
Mesopotamia	1361-1353	Othniel	1353-1313	3:7-11
Moab	1313-1295	Ehud	1295-1215	3:12-30
Philistia	?	Shamgar	?	3:31
Canaan	1215-1195	Deborah and Barak	1195-1155	4:1-5:31
Midian	1155-1148	Gideon	1148-1108	6:1-8:28
		Abimelech	1108-1105	9:1-57
Ammon	1105	Jephthah	1105-1099	10:6-12:7
Philistia	1099-1059	Samson	1085-1065	13:1-16:31

OUTLINE OF JUDGES

I. **Background of the Period of the Judges, 1:1-3:6**
A. The Political Background, 1:1-36
B. The Spiritual Background, 2:1-3:6
II. **History of the Period of the Judges, 3:7-16:31**
A. Mesopotamian Oppression and Othniel's Deliverance, 3:7-11
B. Moabite Oppression and Ehud's Deliverance, 3:12-30
C. Shamgar's Victory over the Philistines, 3:31
D. Canaanite Oppression and Deliverance by Deborah and Barak, 4:1-5:31
  1. The story, 4:1-24
  2. The song, 5:1-31
E. Midianite Oppression and Gideon's Deliverance, 6:1-8:35
  1. Gideon's call, 6:1-40
  2. Gideon's conquests, 7:1-8:35

F. Abimelech's Tyranny, 9:1-57
G. Tola's Judgeship, 10:1-2
H. Jair's Judgeship, 10:3-5
I. Ammonite Oppression and Jephthah's Deliverance, 10:6-12:7
J. Ibzan's Judgeship, 12:8-10
K. Elon's Judgeship, 12:11-12
L. Abdon's Judgeship, 12:13-15
M. Philistine Oppression and Samson's Career, 13:1-16:31
  1. Annunciation and birth of Samson, 13:1-25
  2. Marriage of Samson, 14:1-20
  3. Exploits of Samson, 15:1-20
  4. Fall of Samson, 16:1-31
III. **Apostasy of the Period of the Judges, 17:1-21:25**
A. Micah and the Migration of the Danites, 17:1-18:31

THE BOOK OF JUDGES

I BACKGROUND OF THE PERIOD OF THE JUDGES, 1:1-3:6

A The Political Background, 1:1-36

★ 1 aNum. 27:21 bJudg. 1:27; 2:21-23; 3:1-6

1 Now it came about after the death of Joshua that the sons of Israel ainquired of the LORD, saying, "Who shall go up first for us bagainst the Canaanites, to fight against them?"

2 aGen. 49:8

2 And the LORD said, "aJudah shall go up; behold, I have given the land into his hand."

★ 3

3 Then Judah said to Simeon his brother, "Come up with me into the territory allotted me, that we may fight against the Canaanites; and I in turn will go with you into the territory allotted you."

★ 4 aPs. 44:2; 78:55

4 And Judah went up, and athe LORD gave the Canaanites and the Perizzites into their hands; and they defeated ten thousand men at Bezek.

5 And they found Adoni-bezek in Bezek and fought against him and they defeated the Canaanites and the Perizzites.

★ 6-7

6 But Adoni-bezek fled; and they pursued him and caught him and cut off his thumbs and big toes.

7 aLev. 24:19

7 And Adoni-bezek said, "Seventy kings with their thumbs and their big toes cut off used to gather up scraps under my table; aas I have done, so God has repaid

me." So they brought him to Jerusalem and he died there.

★ 8 aJosh. 15:63; Judg. 1:21

8 Then the sons of Judah fought against aJerusalem and captured it and struck it with the edge of the sword and set the city on fire.

★ 9

9 And afterward the sons of Judah went down to fight against the Canaanites living in the hill country and in the Negev and in the lowland.

10 aJosh. 15:13-19

10 aSo Judah went against the Canaanites who lived in Hebron (now the name of Hebron formerly was Kiriath-arba); and they struck Sheshai and Ahiman and Talmai.

11 aJosh. 15:15

11 Then afrom there he went against the inhabitants of Debir (now the name of Debir formerly was Kiriath-sepher).

★12-13

12 And Caleb said, "The one who attacks Kiriath-sepher and captures it, I will even give him my daughter Achsah for a wife."

13 aJudg. 3:9

13 And aOthniel the son of Kenaz, Caleb's younger brother, captured it; so he gave him his daughter Achsah for a wife.

14 aJosh. 15:18

14 Then ait came about when she came to him, that she persuaded him to ask her father for a field. Then she alighted from her donkey, and Caleb said to her, "What do you want?"

1:1 With the death of Joshua, another era closed, as previously with the death of Moses (Josh. 1:1). *Canaanites.* Includes all the ethnic groups of Canaan.
1:3 *Judah said to Simeon.* The tribes are referred to under the names of their ancestors. Judah had been given a large territory (see note on Josh. 15:1-12), and Simeon was virtually incorporated into Judah (see note on Josh. 19:1-9).
1:4 The *Perizzites* may have been a people of a race different from the Canaanites.
1:6-7 Cutting off *thumbs* and *big toes* served two purposes: degradation, and inability to

use weapons.
1:8 Jerusalem was only temporarily and partially captured (cf. v. 21 and note on Josh. 15:63).
1:9 *the hill country.* The Judean mountain range, including Jerusalem (2,500 ft. high) and Hebron (3,040 ft. high). *the Negev.* The semi-desert area that begins just S. of Hebron. *the lowland.* The Shephelah, the foothills between the coast and the Judean mountains, the scene of many battles between the Israelites and the Philistines.
1:12-13 See note on Josh. 15:13.

15 And she said to him, "Give me a blessing, since you have given me the land of the Negev, give me also springs of water." So Caleb gave her the upper springs and the lower springs.

★16 aNum. 10:29-32; Judg. 4:11 bDeut. 34:3; Judg. 3:13 cNum. 21:1

16 And the descendants of athe Kenite, Moses' father-in-law, went up from the bcity of palms with the sons of Judah, to the wilderness of Judah which is in the south of cArad; and they went and lived with the people.

17 aNum. 21:3

17 Then Judah went with Simeon his brother, and they struck the Canaanites living in Zephath, and utterly destroyed it. So the name of the city was called aHormah.

★18 aJosh. 11:22

18 And Judah took aGaza with its territory and Ashkelon with its territory and Ekron with its territory.

19 aJosh. 17:16; Judg. 4:3, 13

19 Now the LORD was with Judah, and they took possession of the hill country; but they could not drive out the inhabitants of the valley because they had airon chariots.

★20 aJosh. 14:9 bJosh. 15:14; Judg. 1:10

20 Then they gave Hebron to Caleb, aas Moses had promised; and he drove out from there bthe three sons of Anak.

21 aJosh. 15:63; Judg. 1:8 b1 Chr. 11:4

21 aBut the sons of Benjamin did not drive out the bJebusites who lived in Jerusalem; so the Jebusites have lived with the sons of Benjamin in Jerusalem to this day.

★22

22 Likewise the house of Joseph went up against Bethel, and the LORD was with them.

23 aGen. 28:19

23 And the house of Joseph spied out Bethel (anow the name of the city was formerly Luz).

24 aJosh. 2:12

24 And the spies saw a man coming out of the city, and they said to him, "Please show us the entrance to the city and awe will treat you kindly."

25 aJosh. 6:25

25 So he showed them the entrance to the city, and they struck the city with the edge of the sword, abut they let the man and all his family go free.

★26

26 And the man went into the land of the Hittites and built a city and named it Luz which is its name to this day.

★27 aJosh. 17:12 bJudg. 1:1

27 aBut Manasseh did not take possession of Beth-shean and its villages, or Taanach and its villages, or the inhabitants of Dor and its villages, or the inhabitants of Ibleam and its villages, or the inhabitants of Megiddo and its villages; so bthe Canaanites persisted in living in that land.

28 And it came about when Israel became strong, that they put the Canaanites to forced labor, but they did not drive them out completely.

29 aJosh. 16:10

29 aNeither did Ephraim drive out the Canaanites who were living in Gezer; so the Canaanites lived in Gezer among them.

30 Zebulun did not drive out the inhabitants of Kitron, or the inhabitants of Nahalol; so the Canaanites lived among them and became subject to forced labor.

★31

31 Asher did not drive out the inhabitants of Acco, or the inhabitants of Sidon, or of Ahlab, or of Achzib, or of Helbah, or of Aphik, or of Rehob.

32 So the Asherites lived among the Canaanites, the inhabitants of the land; for they did not drive them out.

33 Naphtali did not drive out the inhabitants of Beth-shemesh, or the inhabitants of Beth-anath, but lived among the Canaanites, the inhabitants of the land; and

---

1:16 the Kenite. Jethro (see note on Num. 10:29–32). city of palms. Jericho (see note on Josh. 6:26).

1:18 Gaza . . . Ashkelon . . . Ekron. The principal coastal cities of the Philistines.

1:20 Regarding Anak see notes on Num. 13:33.

1:22 the house of Joseph. I.e., the tribes of Ephraim and Manasseh. The action now centers in central Palestine. On Bethel see note on Gen. 28:19.

1:26 the land of the Hittites. N. Syria (cf. Josh. 1:4).

1:27 These cities formed an E. to W. line of Canaanite fortifications along the plain of Esdraelon.

1:31 Acco. The N.T. city of Ptolemais (Acts 21:7), or present-day Acre.

the inhabitants of Beth-shemesh and Beth-anath became forced labor for them.

★34 **34** Then the Amorites forced the sons of Dan into the hill country, for they did not allow them to come down to the valley;

35 yet the Amorites persisted in living in Mount Heres, in Aijalon and in Shaalbim; but when the power of the house of Joseph grew strong, they became forced labor.

36 aJosh. 15:3 **36** And the border of the Amorites ran from the aascent of Akrabbim, from Sela and upward.

B The Spiritual Background, 2:1-3:6

★ 1 aJudg. 6:11; 13:2-21 bJudg. 2:5 cEx. 20:2 dGen. 17:7, 8; Lev. 26:42, 44; Deut. 7:9

2 Now athe angel of the Lord came up from Gilgal to bBochim. And he said, "cI brought you up out of Egypt and led you into the land which I have sworn to your fathers; and I said, 'dI will never break My covenant with you,

★ 2 aEx. 23:32; Deut. 7:2-5 bEx. 34:12, 13

2 and as for you, ayou shall make no covenant with the inhabitants of this land; byou shall tear down their altars.' But you have not obeyed Me; what is this you have done?

3 aJosh. 23:13 bNum. 33:55

3 "Therefore I also said, 'aI will not drive them out before you; but they shall become bas thorns in your sides, and their gods shall be a snare to you.' "

4 And it came about when the angel of the Lord spoke these words to all the sons of Israel, that the people lifted up their voices and wept.

5 So they named that place Bochim; and there they sacrificed to the Lord.

6 aWhen Joshua had dismissed the people, the sons of Israel went each to his inheritance to possess the land.

6 aJosh. 24:28-31

7 And the people served the Lord all the days of Joshua, and all the days of the elders who survived Joshua, who had seen all the great work of the Lord which He had done for Israel.

8 Then Joshua the son of Nun, the servant of the Lord, died at the age of one hundred and ten.

9 And they buried him in the territory of ahis inheritance in Timnath-heres, in the hill country of Ephraim, north of Mount Gaash.

9 aJosh. 19:49f.

10 And all that generation also were gathered to their fathers; and there arose another generation after them who adid not know the Lord, nor yet the work which He had done for Israel.

10 aEx. 5:2; 1 Sam. 2:12

11 Then the sons of Israel did aevil in the sight of the Lord, and served the bBaals,

11 aJudg. 3:7, 12; 4:1; 6:1 bJudg. 6:25; 8:33; 10:6

12 and athey forsook the Lord, the God of their fathers, who had brought them out of the land of Egypt, and followed other gods from among the gods of the peoples who were around them, and bowed themselves down to them; thus they provoked the Lord to anger.

12 aDeut. 31:16

13 So they forsook the Lord and aserved Baal and the Ashtaroth.

★13 aJudg. 10:6

14 aAnd the anger of the Lord burned against Israel, and He gave them into the hands of plunderers who plundered them; and bHe sold them into the hands of their enemies around them, so that they could no longer stand before their enemies.

14 aDeut. 31:17; Ps. 106:40-42 bDeut. 28:25; 32:30

1:34 Dan was eventually forced to search for new territory to the north (18:1-31).

2:1 angel of the Lord. The Lord Himself. See note on Gen. 16:10. Bochim (lit., the weepers, cf. v. 4) was near Gilgal (see note on Josh. 4:19).

2:2 Israel failed to fulfill part of her covenant responsibility (Deut. 7:1-6).

2:13 Baal. The rain and fertility god of the Ca-

naanites. The plural, Baals (v. 11), may include all the false deities of the land, for there were many local Baals. Ashtaroth. Plural of Ashtareth, the female consort of Baal. See note on Hos. 2:13. The worship of these false gods and goddesses included animal sacrifices, male and female prostitution, and sometimes human sacrifices.

15 *a*Lev.
26:14-39;
Deut. 28:15-
68

15 Wherever they went, the hand of the Lᴏʀᴅ was against them for evil, as the Lᴏʀᴅ had spoken and *a*as the Lᴏʀᴅ had sworn to them, so that they were severely distressed.

★**16** *a*Ps.
106:43-45

16 *a*Then the Lᴏʀᴅ raised up judges who delivered them from the hands of those who plundered them.

17 *a*Judg.
2:7

17 And yet they did not listen to their judges, for they played the harlot after other gods and bowed themselves down to them. They turned aside quickly from the way *a*in which their fathers had walked in obeying the commandments of the Lᴏʀᴅ; they did not do as *their fathers.*

★**18-19**

18 *a*Josh.
1:5 *b*Deut.
32:36; Ps.
106:44

18 And when the Lᴏʀᴅ raised up judges for them, *a*the Lᴏʀᴅ was with the judge and delivered them from the hand of their enemies all the days of the judge; for the Lᴏʀᴅ was *b*moved to pity by their groaning because of those who oppressed and afflicted them.

19 But it came about when the judge died, that they would turn back and act more corruptly than their fathers, in following other gods to serve them and bow down to them; they did not abandon their practices or their stubborn ways.

20 *a*Judg.
2:14

20 *a*So the anger of the Lᴏʀᴅ burned against Israel, and He said, "Because this nation has transgressed My covenant which I commanded their fathers, and has not listened to My voice,

21 *a*Josh.
23:4, 5, 13

21 *a*I also will no longer drive out before them any of the nations which Joshua left when he died,

22 *a*Deut.
8:2; 13:3

22 in order to *a*test Israel by them, whether they will keep the

way of the Lᴏʀᴅ to walk in it as their fathers did, or not."

23 So the Lᴏʀᴅ allowed those nations to remain, not driving them out quickly; and He did not give them into the hand of Joshua.

3 *a*Now these are the nations which the Lᴏʀᴅ left, to test Israel by them (*that is,* all who had not experienced any of the wars of Canaan;

★ **1-5**

1 *a*Judg.
1:1; 2:21, 22

2 only in order that the generations of the sons of Israel might be taught war, those who had not experienced it formerly).

3 *These nations are:* the five lords of the Philistines and all the Canaanites and the Sidonians and *a*the Hivites who lived in Mount Lebanon, from Mount Baal-hermon as far as Lebo-hamath.

★ **3** *a*Josh.
9:7; 11:19

4 And they were for *a*testing Israel, to find out if they would obey the commandments of the Lᴏʀᴅ, which He had commanded their fathers through Moses.

4 *a*Deut.
8:2

5 And *a*the sons of Israel lived among the Canaanites, the Hittites, the Amorites, the Perizzites, the Hivites, and the Jebusites;

5 *a*Ps.
106:35

6 and *a*they took their daughters for themselves as wives, and gave their own daughters to their sons, and served their gods.

6 *a*Ex.
34:15, 16;
Deut. 7:3, 4;
Josh. 23:12

II HISTORY OF THE PERIOD OF THE JUDGES, 3:7-16:31

A Mesopotamian Oppression and Othniel's Deliverance, 3:7-11

7 And the sons of Israel did *a*what was evil in the sight of the Lᴏʀᴅ, and *b*forgot the Lᴏʀᴅ their

★ **7** *a*Judg.
2:11 *b*Deut.
4:9 *c*Judg.
2:13

2:16 The *judges* God graciously gave Israel are also called deliverers or saviors (3:9, 15). They served as spiritual, military, and governmental leaders for the people, but were often ignored or rejected (2:17).

2:18-19 A description of the recurring cycle of Israel's history during this period.

3:1-5 In His providence, God used the failure of the Israelites to drive out the Canaanites by

using these pagans to teach the art of warfare to the Israelites who had not been involved in the initial wars under Joshua.

3:3 These were the *lords* of Ashdod, Ashkelon, Ekron, Gath, and Gaza. *Baal-hermon.* Mt. Hermon. *Lebo-hamath* was about 14 miles NE. of Baalbek in Syria.

3:7 *Asheroth.* Some kind of wooden representation of the female deity. See note on Jer. 17:2.

God, and cserved the Baals and the Asheroth.

★ 8   **8** Then the anger of the LORD was kindled against Israel, so that He sold them into the hands of Cushan-rishathaim king of Mesopotamia; and the sons of Israel served Cushan-rishathaim eight years.

★ 9 aJudg.
1:13   **9** And when the sons of Israel cried to the LORD, the LORD raised up a deliverer for the sons of Israel to deliver them, aOthniel the son of Kenaz, Caleb's younger brother.

★10 aNum.
11:25-29;
24:2   **10** And athe Spirit of the LORD came upon him, and he judged Israel. When he went out to war, the LORD gave Cushan-rishathaim king of Mesopotamia into his hand, so that he prevailed over Cushan-rishathaim.

11 Then the land had rest forty years. And Othniel the son of Kenaz died.

B Moabite Oppression and Ehud's Deliverance, 3:12-30

12 aJudg.
2:11 bJudg.
2:14   **12** Now the sons of Israel again adid evil in the sight of the LORD. So bthe LORD strengthened Eglon the king of Moab against Israel, because they had done evil in the sight of the LORD.

★13 aDeut.
34:3; Judg.
1:16   **13** And he gathered to himself the sons of Ammon and Amalek; and he went and defeated Israel, and they possessed athe city of the palm trees.

14 And the sons of Israel served Eglon the king of Moab eighteen years.

15 aPs.
78:34   **15** But when the sons of Israel acried to the LORD, the LORD

raised up a deliverer for them, Ehud the son of Gera, the Benjamite, a left-handed man. And the sons of Israel sent tribute by him to Eglon the king of Moab.

16 And Ehud made himself a sword which had two edges, a cubit in length; and he bound it on his right thigh under his cloak.   ★16

17 And he presented the tribute to Eglon king of Moab. Now Eglon was a very fat man.

18 And it came about when he had finished presenting the tribute, that he sent away the people who had carried the tribute.

19 But he himself turned back from the idols which were at Gilgal, and said, "I have a secret message for you, O king." And he said, "Keep silence." And all who attended him left him.

20 And Ehud came to him while he was sitting alone in his cool roof chamber. And Ehud said, "I have a message from God for you." And he arose from his seat.

21 And Ehud stretched out his left hand, took the sword from his right thigh and thrust it into his belly.

22 The handle also went in after the blade, and the fat closed over the blade, for he did not draw the sword out of his belly; and the refuse came out.   ★22

23 Then Ehud went out into the vestibule and shut the doors of the roof chamber behind him, and locked them.

24 When he had gone out, his servants came and looked, and behold, the doors of the roof chamber were locked; and they   24 a1 Sam.
24:3

3:8 *Cushan-rishathaim* means "doubly-wicked Cushan."

3:9 *Othniel* was already a proven conqueror (see note on Josh. 15:13–19).

3:10 The *Spirit of the LORD* came upon many in O.T. times as here with Othniel (see Judg. 6:34; 11:29; 13:25; 1 Sam. 10:9-10; 16:13; 1 Chron. 12:18). He was also in some people (Num. 27:18; Dan. 4:8; 6:3; 1 Pet. 1:11) and filled some for special service (Exod. 31:3; 35:31). These relationships are characterized

by the Lord, as the Spirit, being "with" them, in contrast to His permanent indwelling of all believers from the day of Pentecost on (John 14:17).

3:13 *Ammon* was E. and N. of Moab. Regarding *Amalek* see notes on Exod. 17:8 and Esther 3:1. *the city of the palm trees.* Jericho (cf. 1:16).

3:16 *a cubit.* Not the usual Hebrew word for cubit. This dagger was about a foot long.

3:22 *refuse.* Excrement came out when the dagger plunged through Eglon's fat body.

said, "ᵃHe is only relieving himself in the cool room."

25 And they waited until they became anxious; but behold, they did not open the doors of the roof chamber. Therefore they took the key and opened them, and behold, their master had fallen to the floor dead.

26 Now Ehud escaped while they were delaying, and he passed by the idols and escaped to Seirah.

27 And it came about when he had arrived, that ᵃhe blew the trumpet in the hill country of Ephraim; and the sons of Israel went down with him from the hill country, and he *was* in front of them.

28 And he said to them, "Pursue *them*, for the LORD has given your enemies the Moabites into your hands." So they went down after him and seized ᵃthe fords of the Jordan opposite Moab, and did not allow anyone to cross.

29 And they struck down at that time about ten thousand Moabites, all robust and valiant men; and no one escaped.

30 So Moab was subdued that day under the hand of Israel. And the land was undisturbed for eighty years.

C Shamgar's Victory over the Philistines, 3:31

31 And after him came ᵃShamgar the son of Anath, who struck down six hundred Philistines with an oxgoad; and he also saved Israel.

D Canaanite Oppression and Deliverance by Deborah and Barak, 4:1–5:31

1 The story, 4:1–24

4 Then ᵃthe sons of Israel again did evil in the sight of the LORD, after Ehud died.

2 And the LORD sold them into the hand of ᵃJabin king of Canaan, who reigned in Hazor; and the commander of his army was Sisera, who lived in ᵇHarosheth-hagoyim.

3 And the sons of Israel cried to the LORD; for he had nine hundred ᵃiron chariots, and he oppressed the sons of Israel severely for twenty years.

4 Now Deborah, a prophetess, the wife of Lappidoth, was judging Israel at that time.

5 And she used to sit under the ᵃpalm tree of Deborah between Ramah and Bethel in the hill country of Ephraim; and the sons of Israel came up to her for judgment.

6 Now she sent and summoned ᵃBarak the son of Abinoam from Kedesh-naphtali, and said to him, "Behold, the LORD, the God of Israel, has commanded, 'Go and march to Mount Tabor, and take with you ten thousand men from the sons of Naphtali and from the sons of Zebulun.

7 'And I will draw out to you Sisera, the commander of Jabin's army, with his chariots and his many *troops* to the river Kishon; and ᵃI will give him into your hand.'"

8 Then Barak said to her, "If you will go with me, then I will go; but if you will not go with me, I will not go."

9 And she said, "I will surely go with you; nevertheless, the honor shall not be yours on the journey that you are about to take, ᵃfor the LORD will sell Sisera into the hands of a woman." Then Deborah arose and went with Barak to Kedesh.

10 And Barak called ᵃZebulun and Naphtali together to Kedesh, and ten thousand men went

---

27 ᵃJudg. 6:34, 1 Sam. 13:3

28 ᵃJudg. 7:24; 12:5

★**31** ᵃJudg. 5:6

1 ᵃJudg. 2:19

★ **2** ᵃJosh. 11:1, 10 ᵇJudg. 4:13, 16

3 ᵃJudg. 1:19

5 ᵃGen. 35:8

6 ᵃHeb. 11:32

★ **7** ᵃPs. 83:9

9 ᵃJudg. 4:21

10 ᵃJudg. 5:18 ᵇJudg. 4:14, 5:15

3:31 An *oxgoad* might have been as long as eight feet with a spoke on one end and a chisel-shaped blade on the other. Normally used for cleaning a plow, it substituted nicely for a spear.

4:2 This *Jabin* ruled about a century later than the one mentioned in Josh. 11. *Hazor,* the most important stronghold in northern Canaan, was 4 miles SW. of Lake Huleh on a principal trade route.

4:7 *the river Kishon.* A stream which flows through the valley of Jezreel.

up *b*with him; Deborah also went up with him.

★11 *a*Judg.
1:16 *b*Josh.
19:33

11 Now Heber *a*the Kenite had separated himself from the Kenites, from the sons of Hobab the father-in-law of Moses, and had pitched his tent as far away as the oak in *b*Zaanannim, which is near Kedesh.

12 Then they told Sisera that Barak the son of Abinoam had gone up to Mount Tabor.

13 *a*Judg.
4:3 *b*Judg.
4:2

13 And Sisera called together all his chariots, *a*nine hundred iron chariots, and all the people who *were* with him, from *b*Harosheth-hagoyim to the river Kishon.

14 *a*Deut.
9:3; 2 Sam.
5:24; Ps.
68:7

14 And Deborah said to Barak, "Arise! For this is the day in which the LORD has given Sisera into your hands; behold, *a*the LORD has gone out before you." So Barak went down from Mount Tabor with ten thousand men following him.

★15 *a*Deut.
7:23; Josh.
10:10

15 *a*And the LORD routed Sisera and all *his* chariots and all *his* army, with the edge of the sword before Barak; and Sisera alighted from *his* chariot and fled away on foot.

16 *a*Ex.
14:28; Ps.
83:9

16 But Barak pursued the chariots and the army as far as Harosheth-hagoyim, and all the army of Sisera fell by the edge of the sword; *a*not even one was left.

17 Now Sisera fled away on foot to the tent of Jael the wife of Heber the Kenite, for *there was* peace between Jabin the king of Hazor and the house of Heber the Kenite.

18 And Jael went out to meet Sisera, and said to him, "Turn aside, my master, turn aside to me! Do not be afraid." And he turned aside to her into the tent, and she covered him with a rug.

19 *a*Judg.
5:24-27

19 *a*And he said to her, "Please give me a little water to drink, for I am thirsty." So she opened a bottle of milk and gave him a drink; then she covered him.

20 And he said to her, "Stand in the doorway of the tent, and it shall be if anyone comes and inquires of you, and says, 'Is there anyone here?' that you shall say, 'No.'"

★21 *a*Judg.
5:26

21 But Jael, Heber's wife, *a*took a tent peg and seized a hammer in her hand, and went secretly to him and drove the peg into his temple, and it went through into the ground; for he was sound asleep and exhausted. So he died.

22 And behold, as Barak pursued Sisera, Jael came out to meet him and said to him, "Come, and I will show you the man whom you are seeking." And he entered with her, and behold Sisera was lying dead with the tent peg in his temple.

23 *a*Neh.
9:24; Ps.
18:47

23 So *a*God subdued on that day Jabin the king of Canaan before the sons of Israel.

24 And the hand of the sons of Israel pressed heavier and heavier upon Jabin the king of Canaan, until they had destroyed Jabin the king of Canaan.

2 The song, 5:1-31

★ 1 *a*Ex.
15:1

5 *a*Then Deborah and Barak the son of Abinoam sang on that day, saying,

2 *a*Judg.
5:9 *b*Ps.
110:3

2　"*a*That the leaders led in Israel,
　　That *b*the people volunteered,
　　Bless the LORD!

3 *a*Ps. 27:6

3　"Hear, O kings; give ear, O rulers!
　　*a*I—to the LORD, I will sing,
　　I will sing praise to the LORD, the God of Israel.

4:11 A parenthetical note introducing the family of Jael (v. 17; see note on 1:16).

4:15 According to 5:21 the Lord sent rain which flooded the stream and valley, neutralizing the chariots. A similar thing happened when Napoleon defeated the Turks in the same place in A.D. 1799.

4:21 Cf. 5:26 for more details. The mallet and tent peg were easily accessible, since pitching a tent was the woman's job.

5:1 This chapter contains the poetic version of the prose account of chapter 4.

4 aDeut.
33:2; Ps.
68:7 bPs.
68:8, 9

4 "aLORD, when Thou didst
go out from Seir,
When Thou didst march
from the field of
Edom,
bThe earth quaked, the
heavens also dripped,
Even the clouds dripped
water.

5 aEx.
19:18 bPs.
68:8

5 "aThe mountains quaked
at the presence of the
LORD,
bThis Sinai, at the pres-
ence of the LORD, the
God of Israel.

★ **6** aJudg.
3:31 bJudg.
4:17

6 "In the days of aShamgar
the son of Anath,
In the days of bJael, the
highways were de-
serted,
And travelers went by
roundabout ways.

7 "The peasantry ceased,
they ceased in Israel,
Until I, Deborah, arose,
Until I arose, a mother
in Israel.

★ **8** aDeut.
32:17

8 "aNew gods were chosen;
Then war was in the
gates.
Not a shield or a spear
was seen
Among forty thousand
in Israel.

9 aJudg.
5:2

9 "My heart goes out to
athe commanders of
Israel,
The volunteers among
the people;
Bless the LORD!

10 aJudg.
10:4; 12:14

10 "aYou who ride on white
donkeys,
You who sit on rich car-
pets,
And you who travel on
the road—sing!

11 aGen.
24:11; 29:2,
3 b1 Sam.
12:7; Mic.
6:5 cJudg.
5:8

11 "At the sound of those
who divide flocks
among athe watering
places,
There they shall recount
bthe righteous deeds
of the LORD,

The righteous deeds for
His peasantry in Is-
rael.
Then the people of the
LORD went down cto
the gates.

12 aPs. 57:8
bPs. 68:18;
Eph. 4:8

12 "aAwake, awake, Deborah;
Awake, awake, sing a
song!
Arise, Barak, and btake
away your captives, O
son of Abinoam.

13 "Then survivors came
down to the nobles;
The people of the LORD
came down to me as
warriors.

14 aJudg.
12:15

14 "From Ephraim those
whose root is ain
Amalek came down,
Following you, Benja-
min, with your peo-
ples;
From Machir command-
ers came down,
And from Zebulun
those who wield the
staff of office.

★**15-17**

15 aJudg.
4:10

15 "And the princes of Issa-
char were with Deb-
orah;
As was Issachar, so was
Barak;
Into the valley they
rushed aat his heels;
Among the divisions of
Reuben
There were great re-
solves of heart.

16 aNum.
32:1, 2, 24,
36

16 "Why did you sit among
athe sheepfolds,
To hear the piping for
the flocks?
Among the divisions of
Reuben
There were great search-
ings of heart.

17 aJosh.
22:9

17 "aGilead remained across
the Jordan;
And why did Dan stay
in ships?

5:6 Shamgar. See 3:31. Since the Canaanites
controlled the highways, the Israelites had to
use other routes.

5:8 Israel turned to idolatry and was unarmed.
5:15-17 Reuben, Gilead, Dan, and Asher refused to join in the battle against Sisera.

Asher sat at the sea-
shore,
And remained by its
landings.

18 *a*Judg.
4:6, 10

18 "*a*Zebulun *was* a people
who despised their
lives *even* to death,
And Naphtali also, on
the high places of the
field.

19 *a*Josh.
11:1-5; Judg.
4:13 *b*Judg.
1:27 *c*Judg.
5:30

19 "*a*The kings came *and*
fought;
Then fought the kings
of Canaan
*b*At Taanach near the
waters of Megiddo;
*c*They took no plunder
in silver.

★20 *a*Josh.
10:12-14

20 "*a*The stars fought from
heaven,
From their courses they
fought against Sisera.

21 *a*Ex. 15:2;
Ps. 44:5

21 "The torrent of Kishon
swept them away,
The ancient torrent, the
torrent Kishon.
*a*O my soul, march on
with strength.

★22 *a*Job
39:19-25

22 "*a*Then the horses' hoofs
beat
From the dashing, the
dashing of his valiant
steeds.

★23 *a*Judg.
5:13

23 'Curse Meroz,' said the
angel of the LORD,
'Utterly curse its inhabitants;
*a*Because they did not
come to the help of
the LORD,
To the help of the LORD
against the warriors.'

24 *a*Judg.
4:19-21

24 "*a*Most blessed of women
is Jael,
The wife of Heber the
Kenite;
Most blessed is she of
women in the tent.

25 "He asked for water *and*
she gave him milk;

In a magnificent bowl
she brought him
curds.

26 "She reached out her
hand for the tent peg,
And her right hand for
the workmen's ham-
mer.
Then she struck Sisera,
she smashed his head;
And she shattered and
pierced his temple.

27 "Between her feet he
bowed, he fell, he lay;
Between her feet he
bowed, he fell;
Where he bowed, there
he fell dead.

28 "Out of the window she   ★28-30
looked and lamented,
The mother of Sisera
through the lattice,
'Why does his chariot
delay in coming?
Why do the hoofbeats
of his chariots tarry?'

29 "Her wise princesses
would answer her,
Indeed she repeats her
words to herself,

30 '*a*Are they not finding,   30 *a*Ex. 15:9
are they not dividing
the spoil?
A maiden, two maidens
for every warrior;
To Sisera a spoil of dyed
work,
A spoil of dyed work
embroidered,
Dyed work of double
embroidery on the
neck of the spoiler?'

31 "*a*Thus let all Thine en-   31 *a*Ps. 68:2;
emies perish, O LORD;   92:9 *b*Ps.
*b*But let those who love   19:4-6;
Him be like the rising   89:36, 37
of the sun in its
might."

And the land was undisturbed for
forty years.

5:20 A reference to the cloudburst God sent.

5:22 Apparently the hooves of the horses
stamped the ground in their effort to escape
the flood of water.

5:23 The town of *Meroz* did not help the Israelites and was cursed for it.

5:28-30 The scene shifts to Sisera's home. His
mother's concern is abated by the assurance
that the delay in Sisera's return was caused by
the dividing of the spoils.

E Midianite Oppression and
Gideon's Deliverance,
6:1–8:35

1 *Gideon's call*, 6:1–40

★ 1 aJudg. 2:11 bNum. 22:4; 25:15-18; 31:1-3

6 Then the sons of Israel ªdid what was evil in the sight of the Lord; and the Lord gave them into the hands of ᵇMidian seven years.

2 a1 Sam. 13:6; Heb. 11:38

2 And the power of Midian prevailed against Israel. Because of Midian the sons of Israel made for themselves ªthe dens which were in the mountains and the caves and the strongholds.

★ 3

3 For it was when Israel had sown, that the Midianites would come up with the Amalekites and the sons of the east and go against them.

4 aLev. 26:16 bDeut. 28:31

4 So they would camp against them and ªdestroy the produce of the earth as far as Gaza, and ᵇleave no sustenance in Israel as well as no sheep, ox, or donkey.

★ 5 aJudg. 7:12; 8:10

5 For they would come up with their livestock and their tents, they would come in ªlike locusts for number, both they and their camels were innumerable; and they came into the land to devastate it.

6 aDeut. 28:43

6 So Israel was brought ªvery low because of Midian, and the sons of Israel cried to the Lord.

7 Now it came about when the sons of Israel cried to the Lord on account of Midian,

8 aJudg. 2:1, 2

8 that the Lord sent a prophet to the sons of Israel, and ªhe said to them, "Thus says the Lord, the God of Israel, 'It was I who brought you up from Egypt, and brought you out from the house of slavery.

9 'And I delivered you from the hands of the Egyptians and from the hands of all your oppressors, and dispossessed them before you and gave you their land,

10 a2 Kin. 17:35; Jer. 10:2

10 and I said to you, "I am the Lord your God; you ªshall not fear the gods of the Amorites in whose land you live. But you have not obeyed Me." ' "

★11 aJudg. 2:1; 6:14; 13:3 bJosh. 17:2; Judg. 6:15 cHeb. 11:32

11 Then ªthe angel of the Lord came and sat under the oak that was in Ophrah, which belonged to Joash the ᵇAbiezrite as his son ᶜGideon was beating out wheat in the wine press in order to save *it* from the Midianites.

12 And the angel of the Lord appeared to him and said to him, "The Lord is with you, O valiant warrior."

13 aJudg. 6:1; Ps. 44:9

13 Then Gideon said to him, "O my lord, if the Lord is with us, why then has all this happened to us? And where are all His miracles which our fathers told us about, saying, 'Did not the Lord bring us up from Egypt?' But ªnow the Lord has abandoned us and given us into the hand of Midian."

14 aHeb. 11:32-34

14 And the Lord looked at him and said, "ªGo in this your strength and deliver Israel from the hand of Midian. Have I not sent you?"

15 aEx. 3:11 bJudg. 6:11

15 ªAnd he said to Him, "O Lord, how shall I deliver Israel? Behold, my family is the least in ᵇManasseh, and I am the youngest in my father's house."

16 aEx. 3:12; Josh. 1:5

16 ªBut the Lord said to him, "Surely I will be with you, and you shall defeat Midian as one man."

17 aJudg. 6:37; Is. 38:7, 8

17 So Gideon said to Him, "If now I have found favor in Thy sight, then show me ªa sign that it is Thou who speakest with me.

18 "Please do not depart from here, until I come *back* to Thee, and bring out my offering and lay

---

6:1 *Midian*. See notes on Exod. 2:15 and Num. 31:2.

6:3 *Amalekites*. See 3:13. The *sons of the east* included other nomads from the Syrian desert region.

6:5 The use of camels made long distance raids possible.

6:11 *the angel of the Lord*. Another theophany. See 2:1 and the note on Gen. 16:10. Abiezer was a son of Manasseh (Josh. 17:2). Gideon's *beating out wheat in the wine press* was an act of desperation, lest the Midianites discover and seize even the small amount that could be threshed that way.

it before Thee." And He said, "I will remain until you return."

19 Then Gideon went in and [a]prepared a kid and unleavened bread from an ephah of flour; he put the meat in a basket and the broth in a pot, and brought *them* out to him under the oak, and presented *them*.

20 And the angel of God said to him, "Take the meat and the unleavened bread and lay them on this rock, and pour out the broth." And he did so.

21 Then the angel of the LORD put out the end of the staff that was in his hand and touched the meat and the unleavened bread; and [a]fire sprang up from the rock and consumed the meat and the unleavened bread. Then the angel of the LORD vanished from his sight.

22 [a]When Gideon saw that he was the angel of the LORD, he said, "Alas, O Lord GOD! For now I have seen the angel of the LORD face to face."

23 And the LORD said to him, "Peace to you, do not fear; you shall not die."

24 Then Gideon built an altar there to the LORD and named it The LORD is Peace. To this day it is still [a]in Ophrah of the Abiezrites.

25 Now the same night it came about that the LORD said to him, "Take your father's bull and a second bull seven years old, and pull down the altar of Baal which belongs to your father, and cut down the [a]Asherah that is beside it;

26 and build an altar to the LORD your God on the top of this stronghold in an orderly manner, and take a second bull and offer a burnt offering with the wood of the Asherah which you shall cut down."

27 Then Gideon took ten men of his servants and did as the LORD had spoken to him; and it came about, because he was too afraid of his father's household and the men of the city to do it by day, that he did it by night.

28 When the men of the city arose early in the morning, behold, the altar of Baal was torn down, and the Asherah which was beside it was cut down, and the second bull was offered on the altar which had been built.

29 And they said to one another, "Who did this thing?" And when they searched about and inquired, they said, "Gideon the son of Joash did this thing."

30 Then the men of the city said to Joash, "Bring out your son, that he may die, for he has torn down the altar of Baal, and indeed, he has cut down the Asherah which was beside it."

31 But Joash said to all who stood against him, "Will you contend for Baal, or will you deliver him? Whoever will plead for him shall be put to death by morning. If he is a god, let him contend for himself, because someone has torn down his altar."

32 Therefore on that day he named him [a]Jerubbaal, that is to say, "Let Baal contend against him," because he had torn down his altar.

33 Then all the Midianites and the Amalekites and the sons of the east assembled themselves; and they crossed over and camped in [a]the valley of Jezreel.

34 So [a]the Spirit of the LORD came upon Gideon; and he [b]blew a trumpet, and the Abiezrites were called together to follow him.

Cross references (margin):

19 [a]Gen. 18:6-8
★21 [a]Lev. 9:24
22 [a]Gen. 32:30; Ex. 33:20; Judg. 13:21, 22
24 [a]Judg. 8:32
25 [a]Ex. 34:13
★26
★30
★31
★32 [a]Judg. 7:1
★33 [a]Josh. 17:16
★34 [a]Judg. 3:10 [b]Judg. 3:27

6:21 *fire.* The sign of divine acceptance of Gideon's offering (Lev. 9:24).
6:26 *the wood of the Asherah.* See note on 3:7.
6:30 So deep was their commitment to idolatry that these men were eager to kill the one who destroyed *the altar of Baal.*
6:31 Joash's logic is irrefutable: a god who can't save himself is not worth worshiping.
6:32 *Jerubbaal* means "let Baal contend."
6:33 *Jezreel* is the eastern part of the plain of Megiddo, an historic battleground in the heart of Palestine.
6:34 Here it is said that the Spirit literally clothed Gideon. See note on 3:10.

35 ^aJudg. 4:6, 10; 5:18 ^bJudg. 7:3

35 And he sent messengers throughout Manasseh, and they also were called together to follow him; and he sent messengers to Asher, ^aZebulun, and Naphtali, and ^bthey came up to meet them.

36 ^aJudg. 6:14, 16, 17

36 Then Gideon said to God, "^aIf Thou wilt deliver Israel through me, as Thou hast spoken,

37 behold, I will put a fleece of wool on the threshing floor. If there is dew on the fleece only, and it is dry on all the ground, then I will know that Thou wilt deliver Israel through me, as Thou hast spoken."

38 And it was so. When he arose early the next morning and squeezed the fleece, he drained the dew from the fleece, a bowl full of water.

★**39** ^aGen. 18:32

39 Then Gideon said to God, "^aDo not let Thine anger burn against me that I may speak once more; please let me make a test once more with the fleece, let it now be dry only on the fleece, and let there be dew on all the ground."

40 And God did so that night; for it was dry only on the fleece, and dew was on all the ground.

2 Gideon's conquests, 7:1-8:35

1 ^aJudg. 6:32 ^bGen. 12:6; Deut. 11:30

7 Then ^aJerubbaal (that is, Gideon) and all the people who were with him, rose early and camped beside the spring of Harod; and the camp of Midian was on the north side of them by the hill of ^bMoreh in the valley.

2 ^aDeut. 8:17, 18

2 And the LORD said to Gideon, "The people who are with you are too many for Me to give Midian into their hands, ^alest Israel become boastful, saying, 'My own power has delivered me.'

★ **3** ^aDeut. 20:8

3 "Now therefore come, proclaim in the hearing of the people,

saying, '^aWhoever is afraid and trembling, let him return and depart from Mount Gilead.'" So 22,000 people returned, but 10,000 remained.

4 ^aThen the LORD said to Gideon, "The people are still too many; bring them down to the water and I will test them for you there. Therefore it shall be that he of whom I say to you, 'This one shall go with you,' he shall go with you; but everyone of whom I say to you, 'This one shall not go with you,' he shall not go."

4 ^a1 Sam. 14:6

5 So he brought the people down to the water. And the LORD said to Gideon, "You shall separate everyone who laps the water with his tongue, as a dog laps, as well as everyone who kneels to drink."

★ **5**

6 Now the number of those who lapped, putting their hand to their mouth, was 300 men; but all the rest of the people kneeled to drink water.

7 And the LORD said to Gideon, "I will deliver you ^awith the 300 men who lapped and will give the Midianites into your hands; so let all the *other* people go, each man to his home."

7 ^a1 Sam. 14:6

8 So the 300 men took the people's provisions and their trumpets into their hands. And Gideon sent all the *other* men of Israel, each to his tent, but retained the 300 men; and the camp of Midian was below him in the valley.

9 Now the same night it came about that the LORD said to him, "^aArise, go down against the camp, ^afor I have given it into your hands.

9 ^aJosh. 2:24; 10:8; 11:6

10 "But if you are afraid to go down, go with Purah your servant down to the camp,

11 and you will hear what they say; and ^aafterward your

11 ^aJudg. 7:15; 1 Sam. 14:9, 10

6:39 Gideon evidently realized that the previous sign may not have been a sign at all (v. 38), since the ground would naturally have dried before the fleece. *fleece.* Shorn wool.
7:3 The well-known *Mount Gilead* is E. of the Jordan. This may be another one, otherwise unmentioned; or perhaps "from" should be

translated "toward."
7:5 *as a dog laps.* Evidently the 300 used their hands to bring the water to their mouths while standing upright, just as a dog uses his tongue to bring the water to his mouth. This proved them to be watchful and alert in contrast to those who knelt.

hands will be strengthened that you may go down against the camp." So he went with Purah his servant down to the outposts of the army that was in the camp.

12 Now the Midianites and the Amalekites and all the sons of the east were lying in the valley ^aas numerous as locusts; and their camels were without number, ^bas numerous as the sand on the seashore.

13 When Gideon came, behold, a man was relating a dream to his friend. And he said, "Behold, I had a dream; a loaf of barley bread was tumbling into the camp of Midian, and it came to the tent and struck it so that it fell, and turned it upside down so that the tent lay flat."

14 And his friend answered and said, "This is nothing less than the sword of Gideon the son of Joash, a man of Israel; God has given Midian and all the camp ^ainto his hand."

15 And it came about when Gideon heard the account of the dream and its interpretation, that he bowed in worship. He returned to the camp of Israel and said, "Arise, for the LORD has given the camp of Midian into your hands."

16 And he divided the 300 men into three companies, and he put trumpets and empty pitchers into the hands of all of them, with torches inside the pitchers.

17 And he said to them, "Look at me, and do likewise. And behold, when I come to the outskirts of the camp, do as I do.

18 "When I and all who are with me blow the trumpet, then you also blow the trumpets all around the camp, and say, 'For the LORD and for Gideon.'"

19 So Gideon and the hundred men who were with him came to the outskirts of the camp at the beginning of the middle watch, when they had just posted the watch; and they blew the trumpets and smashed the pitchers that were in their hands.

20 When the three companies blew the trumpets and broke the pitchers, they held the torches in their left hands and the trumpets in their right hands for blowing, and cried, "A sword for the LORD and for Gideon!"

21 And each stood in his place around the camp; and ^aall the army ran, crying out as they fled.

22 And when they blew 300 trumpets, the ^aLORD set the sword of one against another even throughout the whole army; and the army fled as far as Beth-shittah toward Zererah, as far as the edge of ^bAbel-meholah, by Tabbath.

23 And the men of Israel were summoned from ^aNaphtali and Asher and all Manasseh, and they pursued Midian.

24 And Gideon sent messengers throughout all the hill country of Ephraim, saying, "Come down against Midian and ^atake the waters before them, as far as Beth-barah and the Jordan." So all the men of Ephraim were summoned, and they took the waters as far as Beth-barah and the Jordan.

25 And they captured the two leaders of Midian, ^aOreb and Zeeb, and they killed Oreb at the rock of Oreb, and they killed Zeeb at the wine press of Zeeb, while they pursued Midian; and they brought the heads of Oreb and Zeeb to Gideon ^bfrom across the Jordan.

8 Then the men of Ephraim said to him, "^aWhat is this thing you have done to us, not calling us when you went to fight

12 ^aJudg. 6:5; 8:10 ^bJosh. 11:4

14 ^aJosh. 2:9

★16

★19

21 ^a2 Kin. 7:7

22 ^a1 Sam. 14:20 ^b1 Kin. 4:12; 19:16

23 ^aJudg. 6:35

24 ^aJudg. 3:28

25 ^aPs. 83:11; Is. 10:26 ^bJudg. 8:4

★ 1-3

1 ^aJudg. 12:1

7:16 *trumpets.* Rams' horns. *pitchers.* Earthenware vessels in which the provisions mentioned in verse 8 were possibly carried.
7:19 *the beginning of the middle watch.* About 10 P.M. The smashing of the *pitchers* not only made noise but allowed the lights to be seen

suddenly.
8:1-3 The Ephraimites complained that they had not been in on the initial rout of the Midianites. Gideon's soft answer, reminding them that they had captured two Midianite chiefs (7:24-25), calmed them.

against Midian?" And they contended with him vigorously.

2 But he said to them, "What have I done now in comparison with you? Is not the gleaning *of the grapes* of Ephraim better than the vintage of Abiezer?

3 "God has given the leaders of Midian, Oreb and Zeeb into your hands; and what was I able to do in comparison with you?" Then their anger toward him subsided when he said that.

4 Then Gideon and the 300 men who were with him came *a*to the Jordan *and* crossed over, weary yet pursuing.

5 And he said to the men of *a*Succoth, "Please give loaves of bread to the people who are following me, for they are weary, and I am pursuing Zebah and Zalmunna, the kings of Midian."

6 And the leaders of Succoth said, "*a*Are the hands of Zebah and Zalmunna already in your hands, that we should give bread to your army?"

7 And Gideon said, "All right, *a*when the Lord has given Zebah and Zalmunna into my hand, then I will thrash your bodies with the thorns of the wilderness and with briers."

8 And he went up from there to *a*Penuel, and spoke similarly to them; and the men of Penuel answered him just as the men of Succoth had answered.

9 So he spoke also to the men of Penuel, saying, "When I return safely, *a*I will tear down this tower."

10 Now Zebah and Zalmunna were in Karkor, and their armies with them, about 15,000 men, all who were left of the entire army of the sons of the east; *a*for the fallen were 120,000 swordsmen.

11 And Gideon went up by the way of those who lived in tents on the east of Nobah and Jogbehah, and attacked the camp, when the camp was unsuspecting.

12 When Zebah and Zalmunna fled, he pursued them and captured the two kings of Midian, Zebah and Zalmunna, and routed the whole army.

13 Then Gideon the son of Joash returned from the battle by the ascent of Heres.

14 And he captured a youth from Succoth and questioned him. Then *the youth* wrote down for him the princes of Succoth and its elders, seventy-seven men.

15 And he came to the men of Succoth and said, "Behold Zebah and Zalmunna, concerning whom you taunted me, saying, '*a*Are the hands of Zebah and Zalmunna already in your hand, that we should give bread to your men who are weary?'"

16 And he took the elders of the city, and thorns of the wilderness and briers, and he disciplined the men of Succoth with them.

17 *a*And he tore down the tower of Penuel and killed the men of the city.

18 Then he said to Zebah and Zalmunna, "What kind of men *were* they whom you killed at Tabor?" And they said, "They were like you, each one resembling the son of a king."

19 And he said, "They *were* my brothers, the sons of my mother. *As* the Lord lives, if only you had let them live, I would not kill you."

20 So he said to Jether his first-born, "Rise, kill them." But the youth did not draw his sword, for he was afraid, because he was still a youth.

Marginal references:
4 *a*Judg. 7:25
★ 5-6
5 *a*Gen. 33:17
6 *a*Judg. 8:15
7 *a*Judg. 7:15
★ 8 *a*Gen. 32:31
9 *a*Judg. 8:17
10 *a*Judg. 6:5; 7:12; Is. 9:4
15 *a*Judg. 8:6
★16
17 *a*Judg. 8:9
★20

8:5-6 *Succoth* was E. of the Jordan and N. of the Jabbok River. The residents did not wish to take a chance helping Gideon until they were certain that he had captured the Midianite chiefs.

8:8 *Penuel* was 4 miles E. of Succoth. These people also tried to remain neutral. See note on Gen. 32:30.

8:16 Gideon had the leaders of Succoth dragged over thorns, which probably resulted in their deaths.

8:20 For Jether to have performed the execution would have been an honor for the boy and greater humiliation for those to be slain.

★21 aPs.
83:11 bJudg.
8:26

21 Then Zebah and Zalmunna said, "Rise up yourself, and fall on us; for as the man, so is his strength." aSo Gideon arose and killed Zebah and Zalmunna, and btook the crescent ornaments which were on their camels' necks.

22 Then the men of Israel said to Gideon, "Rule over us, both you and your son, also your son's son, for you have delivered us from the hand of Midian."

23 a1 Sam.
8:7; 10:19;
12:12; Ps.
10:16

23 But Gideon said to them, "I will not rule over you, nor shall my son rule over you; athe LORD shall rule over you."

★24 aGen.
25:13-16

24 Yet Gideon said to them, "I would request of you, that each of you give me an earring from his spoil." (For they had gold earrings, because they were aIshmaelites.)

25 And they said, "We will surely give them." So they spread out a garment, and every one of them threw an earring there from his spoil.

★26

26 And the weight of the gold earrings that he requested was 1,700 shekels of gold, besides the crescent ornaments and the pendants and the purple robes which were on the kings of Midian, and besides the neck bands that were on their camels' necks.

★27 aEx.
28:6-35;
Judg. 17:5;
18:14-20

27 And Gideon made it into aan ephod, and placed it in his city, Ophrah, and all Israel played the harlot with it there, so that it became a snare to Gideon and his household.

28 So Midian was subdued before the sons of Israel, and they did not lift up their heads anymore. And the land was undisturbed for forty years in the days of Gideon.

29 Then aJerubbaal the son of Joash went and lived in his own house.

29 aJudg.
7:1

30 Now Gideon had aseventy sons who were his direct descendants, for he had many wives.

30 aJudg.
9:2, 5

31 And his concubine who was in Shechem also bore him a son, and he named him Abimelech.

32 And Gideon the son of Joash died at a ripe old age and was buried in the tomb of his father Joash, in Ophrah of the Abiezrites.

33 Then it came about, as soon as Gideon was dead, athat the sons of Israel again played the harlot with the Baals, and made bBaal-berith their god.

33 aJudg.
2:11, 12
bJudg. 9:4,
27, 46

34 Thus the sons of Israel adid not remember the LORD their God, who had delivered them from the hands of all their enemies on every side;

34 aDeut.
4:9; Judg.
3:7

35 anor did they show kindness to the household of Jerubbaal (that is, Gideon), in accord with all the good that he had done to Israel.

35 aJudg.
9:16-18

F   Abimelech's Tyranny, 9:1-57

9 And aAbimelech the son of Jerubbaal went to Shechem to his mother's relatives, and spoke to them and to the whole clan of the household of his mother's father, saying,

★ 1-6

1 aJudg.
8:31, 35

2 "Speak, now, in the hearing of all the leaders of Shechem, 'Which is better for you, that aseventy men, all the sons of Jerubbaal, rule over you, or that one man rule over you?' Also, remember that I am byour bone and your flesh."

2 aJudg.
8:30; 9:5, 18
bGen. 29:14

8:21 The ornaments were worn as amulets (cf. Isa. 3:18).

8:24 because they were Ishmaelites. A term for nomadic traders, which the Midianites were (see note on Gen. 37:25).

8:26 This was at least 350 ounces of gold, more if the reference is to the "heavy" shekel.

8:27 The form of the ephod is not known, but clearly it became an object of idolatrous worship.

9:1-6 Though Gideon declined to start a dynasty, Abimelech (his son by a concubine from Shechem) had other ideas. He appealed to his family ties in Shechem, received silver from the idol temple treasury, killed all but one of Gideon's other sons, and was made king. on one stone (v. 5) implies that the execution was public.

3 aGen.
29:15

3 And his mother's relatives spoke all these words on his behalf in the hearing of all the leaders of Shechem; and they were inclined to follow Abimelech, for they said, "He is ªour relative."

4 aJudg.
8:33

4 And they gave him seventy *pieces* of silver from the house of ªBaal-berith with which Abimelech hired worthless and reckless fellows, and they followed him.

5 aJudg.
8:30; 9:2, 18;
2 Kin. 11:1, 2

5 Then he went to his father's house at Ophrah, and ªkilled his brothers the sons of Jerubbaal, ᵇseventy men, on one stone. But Jotham the youngest son of Jerubbaal was left, for he hid himself.

6 And all the men of Shechem and all Beth-millo assembled together, and they went and made Abimelech king, by the oak of the pillar which was in Shechem.

★ 7 aDeut.
11:29, 30

7 Now when they told Jotham, he went and stood on the top of ªMount Gerizim, and lifted his voice and called out. Thus he said to them, "Listen to me, O men of Shechem, that God may listen to you.

8 "Once the trees went forth to anoint a king over them, and they said to the olive tree, 'Reign over us!'

9 "But the olive tree said to them, 'Shall I leave my fatness with which God and men are honored, and go to wave over the trees?'

10 "Then the trees said to the fig tree, 'You come, reign over us!'

11 "But the fig tree said to them, 'Shall I leave my sweetness and my good fruit, and go to wave over the trees?'

12 "Then the trees said to the vine, 'You come, reign over us!'

13 "But the vine said to them, 'Shall I leave my new wine, which cheers God and men, and go to wave over the trees?'

14 "Finally all the trees said to the bramble, 'You come, reign over us!'

★15

15 "And the bramble said to the trees, 'If in truth you are anointing me as king over you, come and take refuge in my shade; but if not, may fire come out from the bramble and consume the cedars of Lebanon.'

16 aJudg.
8:35

16 "Now therefore, if you have dealt in truth and integrity in making Abimelech king, and if you have dealt well with ªJerubbaal and his house, and have dealt with him as he deserved—

17 for my father fought for you and risked his life and delivered you from the hand of Midian;

18 aJudg.
8:30; 9:2, 5
bJudg. 8:31

18 but you have risen against my father's house today and have killed ªhis sons, seventy men, on one stone, and have made Abimelech, ᵇthe son of his maidservant, king over the men of Shechem, because he is your relative—

19 if then you have dealt in truth and integrity with Jerubbaal and his house this day, rejoice in Abimelech, and let him also rejoice in you.

20 "But if not, let fire come out from Abimelech and consume the men of Shechem and Beth-millo; and let fire come out from the men of Shechem and from Bethmillo, and consume Abimelech."

★21

21 Then Jotham escaped and fled, and went to Beer and remained there because of Abimelech his brother.

22 Now Abimelech ruled over Israel three years.

★23 a1 Sam.
16:14; Is.
19:2, 14 bIs.
33:1

23 ªThen God sent an evil spirit between Abimelech and the men of Shechem; and the men of Shechem ᵇdealt treacherously with Abimelech,

---

9:7 By his standing on a lower slope of Mt. Gerizim overlooking Shechem, Jotham's parable could be heard by the people of Shechem.

9:15 The point of Jotham's warning is simply that Abimelech, like a bramble, could offer no real security to the people of Shechem; in-stead, he would be both the cause and the means of their destruction (see vv. 42–49, 57).

9:21 *Beer* means "well."

9:23 *an evil spirit.* A demon, as also in 1 Sam. 16:14 and 2 Cor. 12:7.

24 *ain order that the violence done to the seventy sons of Jerubbaal might come, and *btheir blood might be laid on Abimelech their brother, who killed them, and on the men of Shechem, who strengthened his hands to kill his brothers.

25 And the men of Shechem set men in ambush against him on the tops of the mountains, and they robbed all who might pass by them along the road; and it was told to Abimelech.

26 Now Gaal the son of Ebed came with his relatives, and crossed over into Shechem; and the men of Shechem put their trust in him.

27 And they went out into the field and gathered *the grapes of* their vineyards and trod *them,* and held a festival; and they went into the house of *atheir god, and ate and drank and cursed Abimelech.

28 Then Gaal the son of Ebed said, "Who is Abimelech, and who is Shechem, that we should serve him? Is he not the son of Jerubbaal, and *is* Zebul *not* his lieutenant? Serve the men of *aHamor the father of Shechem; but why should we serve him?

29 "*aWould, therefore, that this people were under my authority! Then I would remove Abimelech." And he said to Abimelech, "Increase your army, and come out."

30 And when Zebul the ruler of the city heard the words of Gaal the son of Ebed, his anger burned.

31 And he sent messengers to Abimelech deceitfully, saying, "Behold, Gaal the son of Ebed and his relatives have come to Shechem; and behold, they are stirring up the city against you.

32 "Now therefore, arise by night, you and the people who are with you, and lie in wait in the field.

33 "And it shall come about in the morning, as soon as the sun is up, that you shall rise early and rush upon the city; and behold, when he and the people who are with him come out against you, you shall *ado to them whatever you can."

34 So Abimelech and all the people who *were* with him arose by night and lay in wait against Shechem in four companies.

35 Now Gaal the son of Ebed went out and stood in the entrance of the city gate; and Abimelech and the people who *were* with him arose from the ambush.

36 And when Gaal saw the people, he said to Zebul, "Look, people are coming down from the tops of the mountains." But Zebul said to him, "You are seeing the shadow of the mountains as *if they were* men."

37 And Gaal spoke again and said, "Behold, people are coming down from *athe highest part of the land, and one company comes by the way of the diviners' oak."

38 Then Zebul said to him, "Where is your boasting now with which you said, 'Who is Abimelech that we should serve him?' Is this not the people whom you despised? Go out now and fight with them!"

39 So Gaal went out before the leaders of Shechem and fought with Abimelech.

40 And Abimelech chased him, and he fled before him; and many fell wounded up to the entrance of the gate.

41 Then Abimelech remained at Arumah, but Zebul drove out Gaal and his relatives so that they could not remain in Shechem.

42 Now it came about the next day, that the people went out to the field, and it was told to Abimelech.

43 So he took his people and divided them into three

---

24 *aDeut. 27:25; Judg. 9:56, 57 *bNum. 35:33

★**27** *aJudg. 8:33; 9:46

★**28-29**

28 *aGen. 34:2

29 *a2 Sam. 15:4

33 *a1 Sam. 10:7

37 *aEzek. 38:12

9:27 This was at the end of summer.
9:28-29 Gaal appealed to the people to restore the ancient Shechemite aristocracy (regarding Hamor, see note on Gen. 34:25-29), hinting that he himself would be a good man to lead them!

companies, and lay in wait in the field; when he looked and saw the people coming out from the city, he arose against them and slew them.

44 Then Abimelech and the company who was with him dashed forward and stood in the entrance of the city gate; the other two companies then dashed against all who *were* in the field and slew them.

★45 *a* 2 Kin. 3:25

45 And Abimelech fought against the city all that day, and he captured the city and killed the people who *were* in it; then he *a* razed the city and sowed it with salt.

★46 *a* Judg. 8:33

46 When all the leaders of the tower of Shechem heard of *it,* they entered the inner chamber of the temple of *a* El-berith.

47 And it was told Abimelech that all the leaders of the tower of Shechem were gathered together.

48 *a* Ps. 68:14

48 So Abimelech went up to Mount *a* Zalmon, he and all the people who *were* with him; and Abimelech took an axe in his hand and cut down a branch from the trees, and lifted it and laid *it* on his shoulder. Then he said to the people who *were* with him, "What you have seen me do, hurry *and* do likewise."

49 And all the people also cut down each one his branch and followed Abimelech, and put *them* on the inner chamber and set the inner chamber on fire over those *inside,* so that all the men of the tower of Shechem also died, about a thousand men and women.

50 Then Abimelech went to Thebez, and he camped against Thebez and captured it.

51 But there was a strong tower in the center of the city, and all the men and women with all the leaders of the city fled there and shut themselves in; and they went up on the roof of the tower.

52 So Abimelech came to the tower and fought against it, and approached the entrance of the tower to burn it with fire.

53 But *a* certain woman threw an upper millstone on Abimelech's head, crushing his skull.

★53 *a* 2 Sam. 11:21

54 Then *a* he called quickly to the young man, his armor bearer, and said to him, "Draw your sword and kill me, lest it be said of me, 'A woman slew him.' " So the young man pierced him through, and he died.

★54 *a* 1 Sam. 31:4

55 And when the men of Israel saw that Abimelech was dead, each departed to his home.

56 Thus *a* God repaid the wickedness of Abimelech, which he had done to his father, in killing his seventy brothers.

56 *a* Gen. 9:5, 6; Ps 94:23

57 Also God returned all the wickedness of the men of Shechem on their heads, and the curse of Jotham the son of Jerubbaal came upon them.

★57

G　Tola's Judgeship, 10:1-2

10 Now after Abimelech died, Tola the son of Puah, the son of Dodo, a man of Issachar, *a* arose to save Israel; and he lived in Shamir in the hill country of Ephraim.

1 *a* Judg. 2:16

2 And he judged Israel twenty-three years. Then he died and was buried in Shamir.

H　Jair's Judgeship, 10:3-5

3 And after him, Jair the Gileadite arose, and judged Israel twenty-two years.

9:45 *sowed it with salt.* A symbolic ritual, with obvious direct effects, that condemned the land to desolation. Later, Shechem was rebuilt by Jeroboam (1 Kings 12:25).

9:46 *the tower.* Apparently a stronghold outside the city. The nearby temple of Baal, to which the men of the tower fled, was burned down by Abimelech and his men (v. 49).

9:53 On the size of a *millstone* see the note on Matt. 18:6.

9:54 Abimelech wanted to avoid the disgrace of dying at the hands of a woman.

9:57 *the curse of Jotham.* See verse 20.

★ **4** *a*Num.
32:41

4 And he had thirty sons who rode on thirty donkeys, and they had thirty cities in the land of Gilead *a*that are called Havvoth-jair to this day.

5 And Jair died and was buried in Kamon.

I Ammonite Oppression and Jephthah's Deliverance, 10:6-12:7

6 *a*Judg.
2:13 *b*Judg.
11:24 *c*Deut.
31:16, 17;
32:15

6 Then the sons of Israel again did evil in the sight of the LORD, *a*served the Baals and the Ashtaroth, the gods of Aram, the gods of Sidon, the gods of Moab, *b*the gods of the sons of Ammon, and the gods of the Philistines; thus *c*they forsook the LORD and did not serve Him.

★ **7** *a*1 Sam.
12:9

7 And the anger of the LORD burned against Israel, and He *a*sold them into the hands of the Philistines, and into the hands of the sons of Ammon.

8 And they afflicted and crushed the sons of Israel that year; for eighteen years they *afflicted* all the sons of Israel who were beyond the Jordan in Gilead in the land of the Amorites.

9 And the sons of Ammon crossed the Jordan to fight also against Judah, Benjamin, and the house of Ephraim, so that Israel was greatly distressed.

10 *a*1 Sam.
12:10

10 Then the *a*sons of Israel cried out to the LORD, saying, "We have sinned against Thee, for indeed, we have forsaken our God and served the Baals."

11 *a*Judg.
2:12 *b*Num.
21:21-25
*c*Judg. 3:13

11 And the LORD said to the sons of Israel, "*Did I* not *deliver* you *a*from the Egyptians, *b*the Amorites, *c*the sons of Ammon, and the Philistines?

12 *a*Ps.
106:42

12 "Also when the Sidonians, the Amalekites and the Maonites *a*oppressed you, you cried out to

Me, and I delivered you from their hands.

13 "Yet *a*you have forsaken Me and served other gods; therefore I will deliver you no more.

13 *a*Jer. 2:13

14 "*a*Go and cry out to the gods which you have chosen; let them deliver you in the time of your distress."

14 *a*Deut.
32:37

15 And the sons of Israel said to the LORD, "We have sinned, *a*do to us whatever seems good to Thee; only please deliver us this day."

★**15-16**

15 *a*1 Sam.
3:18

16 *a*So they put away the foreign gods from among them, and served the LORD; and *b*He could bear the misery of Israel no longer.

16 *a*Josh.
24:23 *b*Deut.
32:36

17 Then the sons of Ammon were summoned, and they camped in Gilead. And the sons of Israel gathered together, and camped in *a*Mizpah.

★**17** *a*Judg.
11:29

18 And the people, the leaders of Gilead, said to one another, "Who is the man who will begin to fight against the sons of Ammon? He shall become head over all the inhabitants of Gilead."

11 Now *a*Jephthah the Gileadite was a valiant warrior, but he was the son of a harlot. And Gilead was the father of Jephthah.

1 *a*Heb.
11:32

2 And Gilead's wife bore him sons; and when his wife's sons grew up, they drove Jephthah out and said to him, "You shall not have an inheritance in our father's house, for you are the son of another woman."

3 So Jephthah fled from his brothers and lived in the land of *a*Tob; and worthless fellows gathered themselves about Jephthah, and they went out with him.

★ **3** *a*2 Sam.
10:6, 8

4 And it came about after a while that *a*the sons of Ammon fought against Israel.

4 *a*Judg.
10:9, 17

5 And it happened when the sons of Ammon fought against

10:4 This family had considerable affluence.
10:7 Regarding *Ammon* see notes on 3:13; Gen. 19:31-38; and Amos 1:13.
10:15-16 The confession was accompanied by a renunciation of the false gods.

10:17 *Mizpah* means "watchtower" and could indicate one of several places.
11:3 Jephthah became a kind of bandit chief in the outlying area of *Tob*, N. of Ammon.

Israel that the elders of Gilead went to get Jephthah from the land of Tob;

6 and they said to Jephthah, "Come and be our chief that we may fight against the sons of Ammon."

7 *a*Gen. 26:27

7 Then Jephthah said to the elders of Gilead, "*a*Did you not hate me and drive me from my father's house? So why have you come to me now when you are in trouble?"

8 *a*Judg. 10:18

8 And the elders of Gilead said to Jephthah, "For this reason we have now returned to you, that you may go with us and fight with the sons of Ammon and *a*become head over all the inhabitants of Gilead."

9 So Jephthah said to the elders of Gilead, "If you take me back to fight against the sons of Ammon and the LORD gives them up to me, will I become your head?"

10 *a*Gen. 31:50; Jer. 29:23; 42:5; Mic. 1:2

10 And the elders of Gilead said to Jephthah, "*a*The LORD is witness between us; surely we will do as you have said."

★11 *a*Judg. 10:17; 11:29; 20:1; 1 Sam. 10:17

11 Then Jephthah went with the elders of Gilead, and the people made him head and chief over them; and Jephthah spoke all his words before the LORD at *a*Mizpah.

12 Now Jephthah sent messengers to the king of the sons of Ammon, saying, "What is between you and me, that you have come to me to fight against my land?"

13 *a*Num. 21:24 *b*Gen. 32:22

13 And the king of the sons of Ammon said to the messengers of Jephthah, "Because Israel *a*took away my land when they came up from Egypt, from the Arnon as far as the *b*Jabbok and the Jordan; therefore, return them peaceably now."

★14-23

14 But Jephthah sent messengers again to the king of the sons of Ammon,

15 and they said to him, "Thus says Jephthah, 'Israel did not take away the land of Moab, nor the land of the sons of Ammon.

16 *a*Num. 14:25; Deut. 1:40 *b*Num. 20:1, 4-21

16 'For when they came up from Egypt, and Israel *a*went through the wilderness to the Red Sea and *b*came to Kadesh,

17 *a*Num. 20:14-21 *b*Josh. 24:9

17 then Israel *a*sent messengers to the king of Edom, saying, "Please let us pass through your land," but the king of Edom would not listen. *b*And they also sent to the king of Moab, but he would not consent. So Israel remained at Kadesh.

18 *a*Num. 21:4; Deut. 2:8 *b*Deut. 2:9, 18, 19

18 'Then they went through the wilderness and *a*around the land of Edom and the land of Moab, and came to the east side of the land of Moab, and they camped beyond the Arnon; but they *b*did not enter the territory of Moab, for the Arnon *was* the border of Moab.

19 *a*Num. 21:21-32; Deut. 2:26-36

19 'And Israel sent *a*messengers to Sihon king of the Amorites, the king of Heshbon, and Israel said to him, "Please let us pass through your land to our place."

20 'But Sihon did not trust Israel to pass through his territory; so Sihon gathered all his people and camped in Jahaz, and fought with Israel.

21 *a*Num. 21:24; Deut. 2:32-34

21 'And the LORD, the God of Israel, gave Sihon and all his people into the hand of Israel, and they *a*defeated them; so Israel possessed all the land of the Amorites, the inhabitants of that country.

22 *a*Deut. 2:36, 37

22 '*a*So they possessed all the territory of the Amorites, from the Arnon as far as the Jabbok, and from the wilderness as far as the Jordan.

23 'Since now the LORD, the God of Israel, drove out the Amorites from before His people Israel, are you then to possess it?

11:11 *spoke all his words before the LORD.* To solemnize the agreement between Jephthah and the elders of Gilead that they would make him their ruler.

11:14-23 Jephthah states the correct facts concerning the Ammonites' claim to the disputed land (v. 13). When Israel first captured it, it belonged to the Amorites, not the Ammonites.

24 'Do you not possess what ᵃChemosh your god gives you to possess? So whatever the LORD our God has driven out before us, we will possess it.

25 'And now are you any better than ᵃBalak the son of Zippor, king of Moab? Did he ever strive with Israel, or did he ever fight against them?

26 'ᵃWhile Israel lived in Heshbon and its villages, and in Aroer and its villages, and in all the cities that are on the banks of the Arnon, three hundred years, why did you not recover them within that time?

27 'I therefore have not sinned against you, but you are doing me wrong by making war against me; ᵃmay the LORD, the Judge, judge today between the sons of Israel and the sons of Ammon.' "

28 But the king of the sons of Ammon disregarded the message which Jephthah sent him.

29 Now ᵃthe Spirit of the LORD came upon Jephthah, so that he passed through Gilead and Manasseh; then he passed through Mizpah of Gilead, and from Mizpah of Gilead he went on to the sons of Ammon.

30 And Jephthah made a vow to the LORD and said, "If Thou wilt indeed give the sons of Ammon into my hand,

31 then it shall be that whatever comes out of the doors of my house to meet me when I return in peace from the sons of Ammon, it shall be the LORD's, and I will offer it up as a burnt offering."

32 So Jephthah crossed over to the sons of Ammon to fight against them; and the LORD gave them into his hand.

33 And he struck them with a very great slaughter from Aroer to the entrance of ᵃMinnith, twenty cities, and as far as Abel-keramin. So the sons of Ammon were subdued before the sons of Israel.

34 When Jephthah came to his house at ᵃMizpah, behold, his daughter was coming out to meet him ᵇwith tambourines and with dancing. Now she was his one and only child; besides her he had neither son nor daughter.

35 And it came about when he saw her, that he tore his clothes and said, "Alas, my daughter! You have brought me very low, and you are among those who trouble me; for I have given my word to the LORD, and ᵃI cannot take it back."

36 So she said to him, "My father, you have given your word to the LORD; ᵃdo to me as you have said, since the LORD has avenged you of your enemies, the sons of Ammon."

37 And she said to her father, "Let this thing be done for me; let me alone two months, that I may go to the mountains and weep because of ᵃmy virginity, I and my companions."

38 Then he said, "Go." So he sent her away for two months; and she left with her companions, and wept on the mountains because of her virginity.

39 And it came about at the end of two months that she returned to her father, who did to her according to the vow which he had made; and she had no

---

★24 ᵃNum. 21:29; 1 Kin. 11:7

★25 ᵃNum. 22:2; Josh. 24:9; Mic. 6:5

26 ᵃNum. 21:25, 26; Deut. 2:36

27 ᵃGen. 16:5; 18:25; 31:53; 1 Sam. 24:12, 15

29 ᵃJudg. 3:10

★31

33 ᵃEzek. 27:17

34 ᵃJudg. 10:17; 11:11 ᵇEx. 15:20; 1 Sam. 18:6; Jer. 31:4

★35 ᵃNum. 30:2; Eccl. 5:4, 5

36 ᵃNum. 30:2

37 ᵃGen. 30:23; Luke 1:25

★38

★39

11:24 *Chemosh* was the god of Moab, and Milcom (or Molech) of Ammon, though Molech may be a title for Chemosh, who was worshiped by both peoples (since they had much in common).

11:25 Moab made no attempt to regain the territory Israel captured from Sihon until some 300 years later.

11:31 The latter part of the verse may be translated: ". . . shall surely be the Lord's (if a human being comes first), or I will offer it up for a burnt offering (if an animal appears first)."

See note on verse 39.

11:35 The joy of victory was suddenly turned to sorrow when Jephthah saw his daughter and remembered his vow (v. 31).

11:38 *wept . . . because of her virginity.* She would never bear children.

11:39 Some understand that Jephthah's daughter was only dedicated to the service of God in a life of celibacy and not actually slain. Others hold that she was killed according to Canaanite practices which Jephthah had embraced.

relations with a man. Thus it became a custom in Israel,

40 that the daughters of Israel went yearly to commemorate the daughter of Jephthah the Gileadite four days in the year.

★ 1-3
1 ªJudg.
8:1

12 Then the men of Ephraim were summoned, and they crossed to Zaphon and ªsaid to Jephthah, "Why did you cross over to fight against the sons of Ammon without calling us to go with you? We will burn your house down on you."

2 And Jephthah said to them, "I and my people were at great strife with the sons of Ammon; when I called you, you did not deliver me from their hand.

3 ª1 Sam.
19:5; 28:21;
Job 13:14

3 "And when I saw that you would not deliver me, I ªtook my life in my hands and crossed over against the sons of Ammon, and the LORD gave them into my hand. Why then have you come up to me this day, to fight against me?"

★ 4

4 Then Jephthah gathered all the men of Gilead and fought Ephraim; and the men of Gilead defeated Ephraim, because they said, "You are fugitives of Ephraim, O Gileadites, in the midst of Ephraim and in the midst of Manasseh."

★ 5-6
5 ªJudg.
3:28

5 And the Gileadites ªcaptured the fords of the Jordan opposite Ephraim. And it happened when any of the fugitives of Ephraim said, "Let me cross over," the men of Gilead would say to him, "Are you an Ephraimite?" If he said, "No,"

6 then they would say to him, "Say now, 'Shibboleth.' " But he said, "Sibboleth," for he could not pronounce it correctly. Then they seized him and slew

him at the fords of the Jordan. Thus there fell at that time 42,000 of Ephraim.

7 And Jephthah judged Israel six years. Then Jephthah the Gileadite died and was buried in *one of* the cities of Gilead.

J Ibzan's Judgeship, 12:8–10

8 Now Ibzan of Bethlehem judged Israel after him.

9 And he had thirty sons, and thirty daughters *whom* he gave in marriage outside *the family,* and he brought in thirty daughters from outside for his sons. And he judged Israel seven years.

10 Then Ibzan died and was buried in Bethlehem.

K Elon's Judgeship, 12:11–12

11 Now Elon the Zebulunite judged Israel after him; and he judged Israel ten years.

12 Then Elon the Zebulunite died and was buried at Aijalon in the land of Zebulun.

L Abdon's Judgeship, 12:13–15

13 Now Abdon the son of Hillel the Pirathonite judged Israel after him.

14 And he had forty sons and thirty grandsons who rode on seventy donkeys; and he judged Israel eight years.   ★14

15 Then Abdon the son of Hillel the Pirathonite died and was buried at Pirathon in the land of Ephraim, in the hill country of the Amalekites.

12:1–3 The Ephraimites complained again (cf. 8:1) that they had not been called on to help fight against the Ammonites, which charge Jephthah denied.

12:4 The taunt of the last part of this verse implies that the tribes on the E. of Jordan had deserted from Ephraim and Manasseh on the

W. side.

12:5–6 Blocking the fords of the Jordan, the Gileadites applied a linguistic test to screen out the Ephraimites, who pronounced *Shibboleth* as *Sibboleth.*

12:14 *seventy donkeys.* A sign of rank and affluence (cf. 10:4).

M   Philistine Oppression and Samson's Career,
13:1–16:31
1   Annunciation and birth of Samson, 13:1-25

1 *a*Judg. 2:11

13 Now the sons of Israel *a*again did evil in the sight of the LORD, so that the LORD gave them into the hands of the Philistines forty years.

2 *a*Josh. 19:41

2 And there was a certain man of *a*Zorah, of the family of the Danites, whose name was Manoah; and his wife was barren and had borne no *children.*

★ 3 *a*Judg. 6:11, 14; 13:6, 8, 10, 11; Luke 1:11-13

3 *a*Then the angel of the LORD appeared to the woman, and said to her, "Behold now, you are barren and have borne no *children,* but you shall conceive and give birth to a son.

4 *a*Num. 6:2, 3; Luke 1:15

4 "Now therefore, be careful *a*not to drink wine or strong drink, nor eat any unclean thing.

★ 5 *a*Luke 1:15 *b*Num. 6:2-5

5 "*a*For behold, you shall conceive and give birth to a son, and no razor shall come upon his head, for the boy shall be a *b*Nazirite to God from the womb; and he shall begin to deliver Israel from the hands of the Philistines."

6 *a*Judg. 6:11; 13:8, 10, 11

6 Then the woman came and told her husband, saying, "*a*A man of God came to me and his appearance was like the appearance of the angel of God, very awesome. And I did not ask him where he *came* from, nor did he tell me his name.

7 "But he said to me, 'Behold, you shall conceive and give birth to a son, and now you shall not drink wine or strong drink nor eat any unclean thing, for the boy shall be a Nazirite to God from the womb to the day of his death.'"

8 *a*Judg. 13:3, 7

8 Then Manoah entreated the LORD and said, "O Lord, please let *a*the man of God whom Thou hast sent come to us again

that he may teach us what to do for the boy who is to be born."

9 And God listened to the voice of Manoah; and *a*the angel of God came again to the woman as she was sitting in the field, but Manoah her husband was not with her.

9 *a*Judg. 13:8

10 So the woman ran quickly and told her husband, "Behold, *a*the man who came the *other* day has appeared to me."

10 *a*Judg. 13:9

11 Then Manoah arose and followed his wife, and when he came to the man he said to him, "Are you *a*the man who spoke to the woman?" And he said, "I am."

11 *a*Judg. 13:8

12 And Manoah said, "Now when your words come *to pass,* what shall be the boy's mode of life and his vocation?"

13 So *a*the angel of the LORD said to Manoah, "*b*Let the woman pay attention to all that I said.

13 *a*Judg. 13:11 *b*Judg. 13:4

14 "She should not eat anything that comes from the *a*vine nor drink wine or strong drink, nor eat any unclean thing; let her observe all that I commanded."

14 *a*Num. 6:4

15 Then Manoah said to *a*the angel of the LORD, "Please let us detain you so that we may prepare a kid for you."

15 *a*Judg. 13:3

16 And the angel of the LORD said to Manoah, "Though you detain me, *a*I will not eat your food, but if you prepare a burnt offering, *then* offer it to the LORD." For Manoah did not know that he was the angel of the LORD.

16 *a*Judg. 6:20

17 And Manoah said to the angel of the LORD, "*a*What is your name, so that when your words come *to pass,* we may honor you?"

17 *a*Gen. 32:29

18 But the angel of the LORD said to him, "Why do you ask my name, seeing it is *a*wonderful?"

★18 *a*Is. 9:6

19 So *a*Manoah took the kid with the grain offering and offered it on the rock to the LORD,

★19 *a*Judg. 6:20, 21

13:3 *the angel of the LORD.* See note on Gen. 16:10.

13:5 On the *Nazirite* vow see the note on Num. 6:1. In this instance it was a lifelong vow.

13:18 *it is wonderful.* The Hebrew is from a root meaning "surpassing," "ineffable."

13:19 *grain offering.* See note on Lev. 2:1.

and He performed wonders while Manoah and his wife looked on.

20 For it came about when the flame went up from the altar toward heaven, that the angel of the LORD ascended in the flame of the altar. When Manoah and his wife saw *this*, they ªfell on their faces to the ground.

21 Now the angel of the LORD appeared no more to Manoah or his wife. ªThen Manoah knew that he was the angel of the LORD.

22 So Manoah said to his wife, "ªWe shall surely die, for we have seen God."

23 But his wife said to him, "If the LORD had desired to kill us, He would not have accepted a burnt offering and a grain offering from our hands, nor would He have ªshown us all these things, nor would He have let us hear *things* like this at this time."

24 Then the woman gave birth to a son and named him Samson; and the ªchild grew up and the LORD blessed him.

25 And ªthe Spirit of the LORD began to stir him in ᵇMahaneh-dan, between Zorah and Eshtaol.

2 *Marriage of Samson*, 14:1-20

14 Then Samson went down to Timnah and saw a woman in Timnah, *one* of the daughters of the Philistines.

2 So he came back and told his father and mother, "I saw a woman in Timnah, *one* of the daughters of the Philistines; now therefore, get her for me as a wife."

3 Then his father and his mother said to him, "Is there no woman among the daughters of your ªrelatives, or among all our people, that you go to ᵇtake a wife from the uncircumcised Philistines?" But Samson said to his fa-

ther, "Get her for me, for she looks good to me."

4 However, his father and mother did not know that ªit was of the LORD, for He was seeking an occasion against the Philistines. Now at that time the Philistines were ruling over Israel.

5 Then Samson went down to Timnah with his father and mother, and came as far as the vineyards of Timnah; and behold, a young lion *came* roaring toward him.

6 And ªthe Spirit of the LORD came upon him mightily, so that ᵇhe tore him as one tears a kid though he had nothing in his hand; but he did not tell his father or mother what he had done.

7 So he went down and talked to the woman; and she looked good to Samson.

8 When he returned later to take her, he turned aside to look at the carcass of the lion; and behold, a swarm of bees and honey were in the body of the lion.

9 So he scraped the honey into his hands and went on, eating as he went. When he came to his father and mother, he gave *some* to them and they ate *it;* but he did not tell them that he had scraped the honey out of the body of the lion.

10 Then his father went down to the woman; and Samson made a feast there, for the young men customarily did this.

11 And it came about when they saw him that they brought thirty companions to be with him.

12 Then Samson said to them, "Let me now ªpropound a riddle to you; if you will indeed tell it to me within the seven days of the feast, and find it out, then I will give you thirty linen wraps and thirty ᵇchanges of clothes.

13 "But if you are unable to tell me, then you shall give me

Marginal references:

20 ªLev. 9:24; 1 Chr. 21:16; Ezek. 1:28; Matt. 17:6

21 ªJudg. 13:16

22 ªGen. 32:30; Deut. 5:26; Judg. 6:22

23 ªPs. 25:14

24 ª1 Sam. 3:19; Luke 1:80

25 ªJudg. 3:10 ᵇJudg. 18:11, 12

★**1**

3 ªGen. 24:3, 4 ᵇEx. 34:16; Deut. 7:3

★**4** ªJosh. 11:20

6 ªJudg. 3:10 ᵇ1 Sam. 17:34-36

★**8-9**

★**12** ªEzek. 17:2 ᵇGen. 45:22; 2 Kin. 5:22

14:1 *Timnath*, though occupied by the Philistines, was only about 4 miles SW. of Zorah, Samson's home.

14:4 The undesirable marriage to a Philistine was ultimately used by God for His purposes.

14:8-9 In the summer heat the carcass dried

quickly, leaving a suitable cavity for the bees. To touch the carcass was a violation of the law of the Nazirites (Num. 6:6).

14:12 *linen wraps*. Large rectangular sheets worn next to the skin or slept in at night.

thirty linen wraps and thirty changes of clothes." And they said to him, "Propound your riddle, that we may hear it."

14 So he said to them,

"Out of the eater came
something to eat,
And out of the strong
came something
sweet."

But they could not tell the riddle in three days.

15 Then it came about on the fourth day that they said to Samson's wife, "ªEntice your husband, that he may tell us the riddle, ᵇlest we burn you and your father's house with fire. Have you invited us to impoverish us? Is this not *so?*"

16 And Samson's wife wept before him and said, "ªYou only hate me, and you do not love me; you have propounded a riddle to the sons of my people, and have not told *it* to me." And he said to her, "Behold, I have not told *it* to my father or mother; so should I tell you?"

17 However she wept before him seven days while their feast lasted. And it came about on the seventh day that he told her because she pressed him so hard. She then told the riddle to the sons of her people.

18 So the men of the city said to him on the seventh day before the sun went down,

"What is sweeter than
honey?
And what is stronger
than a lion?"

And he said to them,

"If you had not plowed
with my heifer,
You would not have
found out my riddle."

19 Then ªthe Spirit of the LORD came upon him mightily, and he went down to Ashkelon and killed thirty of them and took

their spoil, and gave the changes *of clothes* to those who told the riddle. And his anger burned, and he went up to his father's house.

20 But Samson's wife was ªgiven to his companion who had been his friend.

3 Exploits of Samson, 15:1-20

15 But after a while, in the time of wheat harvest, it came about that Samson visited his wife ªwith a young goat, and said, "I will go in to my wife in *her* room." But her father did not let him enter.

2 And her father said, "I really thought that you hated her intensely; so I ªgave her to your companion. Is not her younger sister more beautiful than she? Please let her be yours instead."

3 Samson then said to them, "This time I shall be blameless in regard to the Philistines when I do them harm."

4 And Samson went and caught three hundred foxes, and took torches, and turned *the foxes* tail to tail, and put one torch in the middle between two tails.

5 When he had set fire to the torches, he released the foxes into the standing grain of the Philistines, thus burning up both the shocks and the standing grain, along with the vineyards *and* groves.

6 Then the Philistines said, "Who did this?" And they said, "Samson, the son-in-law of the Timnite, because he took his wife and gave her to his companion." So the Philistines came up and ªburned her and her father with fire.

7 And Samson said to them, "Since you act like this, I will surely take revenge on you, but after that I will quit."

Marginal references:

15 ªJudg. 16:5 ᵇJudg. 15:6

16 ªJudg. 16:15

★18

★19 ªJudg. 3:10; 13:25

★20 ªJudg. 15:2

★ 1 ªGen. 38:17

2 ªJudg. 14:20

6 ªJudg. 14:15

14:18 *my heifer.* A scornful reference to Samson's wife.

14:19 *Ashkelon,* a Philistine city, was on the Mediterranean coast about 23 miles away.

14:20 The best man, rather than Samson, consummated the marriage.

15:1 *the time of the wheat harvest.* I.e., May.

*8   8 And he struck them ruth-
lessly with a great slaughter; and
he went down and lived in the
cleft of the rock of Etam.

9 Then the Philistines went
up and camped in Judah, and
spread out in Lehi.

10 And the men of Judah
said, "Why have you come up
against us?" And they said, "We
have come up to bind Samson in
order to do to him as he did to
us."

11 aLev.
26:25; Deut.
28:43f.;
Judg. 13:1;
14:4; Ps.
106:40-42
11 Then 3,000 men of Judah
went down to the cleft of the rock
of Etam and said to Samson, "Do
you not know a that the Philistines
are rulers over us? What then is
this that you have done to us?"
And he said to them, "As they did
to me, so I have done to them."

*12   12 And they said to him, "We
have come down to bind you so
that we may give you into the
hands of the Philistines." And
Samson said to them, "Swear to
me that you will not kill me."

13 So they said to him, "No,
but we will bind you fast and give
you into their hands; yet surely
we will not kill you." Then they
bound him with two new ropes
and brought him up from the
rock.

14 aJudg.
14:19;
1 Sam. 11:6
14 When he came to Lehi, the
Philistines shouted as they met
him. And a the Spirit of the Lord
came upon him mightily so that
the ropes that were on his arms
were as flax that is burned with
fire, and his bonds dropped from
his hands.

15 aLev.
26:8; Josh.
23:10
15 And he found a fresh jawbone of a donkey, so he reached
out and took it and killed a a thousand men with it.

16 Then Samson said,
    "With the jawbone of a
        donkey,

Heaps upon heaps,
With the jawbone of a
    donkey
I have killed a thousand
    men."

17 And it came about when   *17
he had finished speaking, that he
threw the jawbone from his hand;
and he named that place Ramath-
lehi.

18 Then he became very   18 aJudg.
16:28
thirsty, and he a called to the Lord
and said, "Thou hast given this
great deliverance by the hand of
Thy servant, and now shall I die
of thirst and fall into the hands of
the uncircumcised?"

19 But God split the hollow   *19 als.
40:29
place that is in Lehi so that water
came out of it. When he drank,
a his strength returned and he revived. Therefore, he named it En-
hakkore, which is in Lehi to this
day.

20 So   a he judged Israel   20 aJudg.
16:31;
twenty years in b the days of the   Heb. 11:32
Philistines.   bJudg. 13:1

4 Fall of Samson, 16:1–31

16 Now Samson went to a Ga-   * 1 aJosh.
za and saw a harlot there,   15:47
and went in to her.

2 When it was told to the   2 a1 Sam.
23:26; Ps.
Gazites, saying, "Samson has   118:10-12
come here," they a surrounded the
place and lay in wait for him all
night at the gate of the city. And
they kept silent all night, saying,
"Let us wait until the morning
light, then we will kill him."

3 Now Samson lay until   * 3
midnight, and at midnight he
arose and took hold of the doors
of the city gate and the two posts
and pulled them up along with
the bars; then he put them on his
shoulders and carried them up to
the top of the mountain which is
opposite Hebron.

15:8 *ruthlessly.* Lit., leg on thigh, a wrestling figure indicating a slaughter using brute force.
15:12 *kill me.* Lit., fall upon me yourselves.
Samson asked that the Israelites not attack
him, so that he would not be obliged to retali-
ate and shed Jewish blood.
15:17 *Ramath-lehi* means "the height (hill) of
the jawbone."

15:19 *En-hakkore* means "the spring of the
caller."
16:1 Gaza was the southernmost of the five principal Philistine cities.
16:3 What incredible strength and endurance
Samson had! He carried the doors, doorposts,
and bar that secured the doors for a distance
of 38 miles (mostly uphill) to Hebron.

4 After this it came about that he loved a woman in the valley of Sorek, whose name was Delilah.

★ 5 *a*Josh.
13:3 *b*Judg.
14:15

5 And the *a*lords of the Philistines came up to her, and said to her, "*b*Entice him, and see where his great strength *lies* and how we may overpower him that we may bind him to afflict him. Then we will each give you eleven hundred *pieces* of silver."

6 So Delilah said to Samson, "Please tell me where your great strength is and how you may be bound to afflict you."

★ 7

7 And Samson said to her, "If they bind me with seven fresh cords that have not been dried, then I shall become weak and be like any *other* man."

8 Then the lords of the Philistines brought up to her seven fresh cords that had not been dried, and she bound him with them.

★ 9

9 Now she had *men* lying in wait in an inner room. And she said to him, "The Philistines are upon you, Samson!" But he snapped the cords as a string of tow snaps when it touches fire. So his strength was not discovered.

10 Then Delilah said to Samson, "Behold, you have deceived me and told me lies; now please tell me, how you may be bound."

11 And he said to her, "If they bind me tightly with new ropes which have not been used, then I shall become weak and be like any *other* man."

12 So Delilah took new ropes and bound him with them and said to him, "The Philistines are upon you, Samson!" For the *men* were lying in wait in the inner room. But he snapped the ropes from his arms like a thread.

★13-14

13 Then Delilah said to Samson, "Up to now you have deceived me and told me lies; tell me how you may be bound." And he said to her, "If you weave the seven locks of my hair with the web [and fasten it with a pin, then I shall become weak and be like any other man."

14 So while he slept, Delilah took the seven locks of his hair and wove them into the web]. And she fastened *it* with the pin, and said to him, "The Philistines are upon you, Samson!" But he awoke from his sleep and pulled out the pin of the loom and the web.

15 Then she said to him, "*a*How can you say, 'I love you,' when your heart is not with me? You have deceived me these three times and have not told me where your great strength is."

15 *a*Judg.
14:16

16 And it came about when she pressed him daily with her words and urged him, that his soul was annoyed to death.

17 So he told her all *that was* in his heart and said to her, "A razor has never come on my head, for I have been a *a*Nazirite to God from my mother's womb. If I am shaved, then my strength will leave me and I shall become weak and be like any *other* man."

17 *a*Num.
6:2, 5;
Judg. 13:5

18 When Delilah saw that he had told her all *that was* in his heart, she sent and called the lords of the Philistines, saying, "Come up once more, for he has told me all *that is* in his heart." Then the lords of the Philistines came up to her, and brought the money in their hands.

19 And she made him sleep on her knees, and called for a man and had him shave off the seven locks of his hair. Then she began to afflict him, and his strength left him.

20 And she said, "The Philistines are upon you, Samson!"

20 *a*Num.
14:42, 43;
Josh. 7:12;
1 Sam. 16:14

16:5 *eleven hundred pieces of silver.* I.e., 1100 shekels or about 34 pounds of silver. Delilah was promised this amount from each of the five lords of the Philistines.

16:7 *fresh cords.* Fresh bowstrings made of twisted gut.

16:9 *tow.* Raw flax fibers used for wicks.

16:13-14 Since Samson was lying with his head in her lap, Delilah could easily begin to weave his hair into the material.

And he awoke from his sleep and said, "I will go out as at other times and shake myself free." But he did not know that ªthe LORD had departed from him.

★21 21 Then the Philistines seized him and gouged out his eyes; and they brought him down to Gaza and bound him with bronze chains, and he was a grinder in the prison.

22 However, the hair of his head began to grow again after it was shaved off.

★23 ª1 Sam.
5:2 23 Now the lords of the Philistines assembled to offer a great sacrifice to ªDagon their god, and to rejoice, for they said,

> "Our god has given Samson our enemy into our hands."

24 ª1 Sam.
31:9; 1 Chr.
10:9; Ps.
97:7 24 When the people saw him, ªthey praised their god, for they said,

> "Our god has given our enemy into our hands,
> Even the destroyer of our country,
> Who has slain many of us."

25 It so happened when they were in high spirits, that they said, "Call for Samson, that he may amuse us." So they called for Samson from the prison, and he entertained them. And they made him stand between the pillars.

★26 26 Then Samson said to the boy who was holding his hand, "Let me feel the pillars on which the house rests, that I may lean against them."

27 Now the house was full of men and women, and all the lords of the Philistines were there. And about 3,000 men and women

were on the roof looking on while Samson was amusing *them*.

28 ªThen Samson called to the LORD and said, "O Lord GOD, please remember me and please strengthen me just this time, O God, that I may at once ªbe avenged of the Philistines for my two eyes." | 28 ªJudg.
15:18 ªJer.
15:15

29 And Samson grasped the two middle pillars on which the house rested, and braced himself against them, the one with his right hand and the other with his left.

30 And Samson said, "Let me die with the Philistines!" And he bent with all his might so that the house fell on the lords and all the people who were in it. So the dead whom he killed at his death were more than those whom he killed in his life. | **★30-31**

31 Then his brothers and all his father's household came down, took him, brought him up, and buried him between Zorah and Eshtaol in the tomb of Manoah his father. ªThus he had judged Israel twenty years. | 31 ªJudg.
15:20

III APOSTASY OF THE PERIOD OF THE JUDGES, 17:1–21:25

A Micah and the Migration of the Danites, 17:1–18:31

1 Micah and his private priest, 17:1–13

17 Now there was a man of the hill country of Ephraim whose name was Micah. | **★ 1**

2 And he said to his mother, "The eleven hundred *pieces* of silver which were taken from you, about which you uttered a curse | **★ 2-3**

16:21 Samson was reduced to humiliating slave labor, doing a woman's work.

16:23 *Dagon.* A vegetation god of the Philistines.

16:26 The flat roof, supported by wooden pillars set on stone bases, was made of logs laid from wall to wall.

16:30-31 Samson, a study in contrasts, exemplifies those who, though greatly endowed by God, fail to use His gifts to His greatest glory.

17:1 The remaining chapters of the book are ap-

pendices, not in chronological order, that give insights into Israelite life during the period of the judges.

17:2-3 Micah, fearing the curse his mother had placed on the thief who stole her 1100 shekels of silver (see note on 16:5), confessed to the crime. Then, hoping to neutralize the curse, his mother dedicated the money to the Lord and ordered that a *graven image* (wood overlaid with silver) and a *molten image* (of solid silver) be made.

in my hearing, behold, the silver is with me; I took it." And his mother said, "Blessed be my son by the Lord."

3 He then returned the eleven hundred *pieces* of silver to his mother, and his mother said, "I wholly dedicate the silver from my hand to the Lord for my son [a]to make a graven image and a molten image; now therefore, I will return them to you."

4 So when he returned the silver to his mother, his mother took two hundred *pieces* of silver and gave them to the silversmith who made them into a graven image and a molten image, and they were in the house of Micah.

5 And the man Micah had a [a]shrine and he made an [b]ephod and [c]household idols and consecrated one of his sons, [d]that he might become his priest.

6 In those days [a]there was no king in Israel; [b]every man did what was right in his own eyes.

7 Now there was a young man from [a]Bethlehem in Judah, of the family of Judah, who was a Levite; and he was staying there.

8 Then the man departed from the city, from Bethlehem in Judah, to stay wherever he might find a *place*; and as he made his journey, he came to the [a]hill country of Ephraim to the house of Micah.

9 And Micah said to him, "Where do you come from?" And he said to him, "I am a Levite from Bethlehem in Judah, and I am going to stay wherever I may find a *place*."

10 Micah then said to him, "Dwell with me and be [a]a father and a priest to me, and I will give you ten *pieces* of silver a year, a suit of clothes, and your maintenance." So the Levite went *in*.

11 And the Levite agreed to live with the man; and the young man became to him like one of his sons.

12 So Micah consecrated the Levite, and the young man [a]became his priest and lived in the house of Micah.

13 Then Micah said, "Now I know that the Lord will prosper me, seeing I have a Levite as priest."

2 Danite migration, 18:1-31

18 [a]In those days there was no king of Israel; and [b]in those days the tribe of the Danites was seeking an inheritance for themselves to live in, for until that day an inheritance had not been allotted to them as a possession among the tribes of Israel.

2 So the sons of Dan sent from their family five men out of their whole number, valiant men from [a]Zorah and Eshtaol, to spy out the land and to search it; and they said to them, "Go, search the land." And they came to [b]the hill country of Ephraim, to the house of Micah, and lodged there.

3 When they were near the house of Micah, they recognized the voice of the young man, the Levite; and they turned aside there, and said to him, "Who brought you here? And what are you doing in this *place*? And what do you have here?"

4 And he said to them, "Thus and so has Micah done to me, and he has hired me, and [a]I have become his priest."

5 And they said to him, "Inquire of God, please, that we may know whether our way on which we are going will be prosperous."

6 And the priest said to them, "Go in peace; your way in which you are going has the Lord's approval."

Margin references

3 [a]Ex. 20:4, 23; 34:17

★ 5 [a]Judg. 18:24 [b]Judg. 8:27; 18:14 [c]Gen. 31:19 [d]Num. 3:10

6 [a]Judg. 18:1; 19:1 [b]Deut. 12:8; Judg. 21:25

7 [a]Judg. 19:1; Ruth 1:1, 2; Mic. 5:2; Matt. 2:1

8 [a]Josh. 24:33

10 [a]Judg. 18:19

★12-13

12 [a]Num. 16:10; 18:1-7

★ 1 [a]Judg. 17:6; 19:1 [b]Josh. 19:40-48

2 [a]Judg. 13:25 [b]Judg. 17:1

4 [a]Judg. 17:12

17:5 *ephod.* See note on Hos. 3:4. *household idols.* See note on Gen. 31:19.
17:12-13 Micah now had all the external features of syncretistic religion, along with self-

sufficient superstitious belief.
18:1 The Amorites had forced the *Danites* into the mountain areas of their allotted territory (1:34).

★ 7 ᵃJosh.
19:47; Judg.
18:29

7 Then the five men departed and came to ᵃLaish and saw the people who were in it living in security, after the manner of the Sidonians, quiet and secure; for there was no ruler humiliating *them* for anything in the land, and they were far from the Sidonians and had no dealings with anyone.

8 When they came back to their brothers at Zorah and Eshtaol, their brothers said to them, "What *do* you *report?*"

9 And they said, "Arise, and let us go up against them; for we have seen the land, and behold, it is very good. And will you sit still? Do not delay to go, to enter, to possess the land.

10 ᵃDeut.
8:9

10 "When you enter, you shall come to a secure people with a spacious land; for God has given it into your hand, ᵃa place where there is no lack of anything that is on the earth."

11 Then from the family of the Danites, from Zorah and from Eshtaol, six hundred men armed with weapons of war set out.

12 ᵃJudg.
13:25

12 And they went up and camped at Kiriath-jearim in Judah. Therefore they called that place ᵃMahaneh-dan to this day; behold, it is west of Kiriath-jearim.

13 And they passed from there to the hill country of Ephraim and came to the house of Micah.

14 ᵃJudg.
17:5

14 Then the five men who went to spy out the country of Laish answered and said to their kinsmen, "Do you know that there are in these houses ᵃan ephod and household idols and a graven image and a molten image? Now therefore, consider what you should do."

15 And they turned aside there and came to the house of the young man, the Levite, to the house of Micah, and asked him of his welfare.

16 And the six hundred men armed with their weapons of war, who were of the sons of Dan, stood by the entrance of the gate.

17 ᵃGen.
31:19, 30; Is.
41:29; Mic.
5:13

17 Now the five men who went to spy out the land went up *and* entered there, *and* took ᵃthe graven image and the ephod and household idols and the molten image, while the priest stood by the entrance of the gate with the six hundred men armed with weapons of war.

18 And when these went into Micah's house and took the graven image, the ephod and household idols and the molten image, the priest said to them, "What are you doing?"

19 ᵃJob
21:5; 29:9;
40:4
ᵇJudg. 17:10

19 And they said to him, "Be silent, ᵃput your hand over your mouth and come with us, and be to us ᵇa father and a priest. Is it better for you to be a priest to the house of one man, or to be priest to a tribe and a family in Israel?"

20 And the priest's heart was glad, and he took the ephod and household idols and the graven image, and went among the people.

21 Then they turned and departed, and put the little ones and the livestock and the valuables in front of them.

★22-26

22 When they had gone some distance from the house of Micah, the men who *were* in the houses near Micah's house assembled and overtook the sons of Dan.

23 And they cried to the sons of Dan, who turned around and said to Micah, "What is *the matter* with you, that you have assembled together?"

24 And he said, "You have taken away my gods which I made, and the priest, and have

---

18:7 *Laish*. The Leshem of Josh. 19:47, a town N. of Israel which later became known as Dan. It had no internal government and was isolated from other tribes.
18:22-26 Micah and some friends chased the Danites in order to try and recover his objects of worship and his priest. But when the Danites threatened their lives, they returned home. Note Micah's bankrupt spiritual condition, as he complained that in taking away the gods he had made, the Danites had taken away everything (v. 24).

gone away, and what do I have besides? So how can you say to me, 'What is *the matter* with you?' "

25 And the sons of Dan said to him, "Do not let your voice be heard among us, lest fierce men fall upon you and you lose your life, with the lives of your household."

26 So the sons of Dan went on their way; and when Micah saw that they were too strong for him, he turned and went back to his house.

27 *a*Josh. 19:47; Judg. 18:7

27 Then they took what Micah had made and the priest who had belonged to him, and came to *a*Laish, to a people quiet and secure, and struck them with the edge of the sword; and they burned the city with fire.

28 *a*2 Sam. 10:6

28 And there was no one to deliver *them*, because it was far from Sidon and they had no dealings with anyone, and it was in the valley which is near *a*Bethrehob. And they rebuilt the city and lived in it.

29 *a*Josh. 19:47

29 And *a*they called the name of the city Dan, after the name of Dan their father who was born in Israel; however, the name of the city formerly was Laish.

★30 *a*Judg. 17:3, 5 *b*Ex. 2:22; 18:3 *c*Judg. 17:3, 5

30 And the sons of Dan set up for themselves *a*the graven image; and Jonathan, the son of *b*Gershom, the son of Manasseh, *c*he and his sons were priests to the tribe of the Danites until the day of the captivity of the land.

31 *a*Josh. 18:1

31 So they set up for themselves Micah's graven image which he had made, all the time that the *a*house of God was at Shiloh.

B The Benjamite War,
19:1–21:25
1 The reason for the war,
19:1–20:14

1 *a*Judg. 18:1

19 Now it came about in those days, when *a*there was no king in Israel, that there was a certain Levite staying in the remote part of the hill country of Ephraim, who took a concubine for himself from Bethlehem in Judah.

2 But his concubine played the harlot against him, and she went away from him to her father's house in Bethlehem in Judah, and was there for a period of four months.

3 *a*Gen. 34:3; 50:21

3 Then her husband arose and went after her to *a*speak tenderly to her in order to bring her back, taking with him his servant and a pair of donkeys. So she brought him into her father's house, and when the girl's father saw him, he was glad to meet him.

4 And his father-in-law, the girl's father, detained him; and he remained with him three days. So they ate and drank and lodged there.

5 *a*Gen. 18:5; Judg. 19:8

5 Now it came about on the fourth day that they got up early in the morning, and he prepared to go; and the girl's father said to his son-in-law, "*a*Sustain yourself with a piece of bread, and afterward you may go."

6 *a*Judg. 16:25; 19:9, 22; Ruth 3:7; 1 Kin. 21:7; Esth. 1:10

6 So both of them sat down and ate and drank together; and the girl's father said to the man, "Please be willing to spend the night, and *a*let your heart be merry."

18:30 *son of Manasseh.* Better, son of Moses. The Danite priests traced their lineage to Moses. *until the day of the captivity of the land.* Either a reference to the deportation by Tiglath-pileser III of Assyria in 733–732 (2 Kings 15:29) or to the time of the exile of the Ark from Shiloh in the eleventh century B.C. (1 Sam. 4:11). Verse 31 seems to favor the latter view.

7 Then the man arose to go, but his father-in-law urged him so that he spent the night there again.

8 And on the fifth day he arose to go early in the morning, and the girl's father said, "Please sustain yourself, and wait until afternoon"; so both of them ate.

9 When the man arose to go along with his concubine and servant, his father-in-law, the girl's father, said to him, "Behold now, the day has drawn to a close; please spend the night. Lo, the day is coming to an end; spend the night here that your heart may be merry. Then tomorrow you may arise early for your journey so that you may go home."

★10 *a*1 Chr. 11:4, 5

10 But the man was not willing to spend the night, so he arose and departed and came to *a place* opposite ªJebus (that is, Jerusalem). And there were with him a pair of saddled donkeys; his concubine also was with him.

11 *a*Judg. 19:19

11 When they *were* near Jebus, the day was almost gone; and ªthe servant said to his master, "Please come, and let us turn aside into this city of the Jebusites and spend the night in it."

12 However, his master said to him, "We will not turn aside into the city of foreigners who are not of the sons of Israel; but we will go on as far as Gibeah."

13 And he said to his servant, "Come and let us approach one of these places; and we will spend the night in Gibeah or Ramah."

14 So they passed along and went their way, and the sun set on them near Gibeah which belongs to Benjamin.

★15-21

15 And they turned aside there in order to enter *and* lodge in Gibeah. When they entered, they sat down in the open square

of the city, for no one took them into *his* house to spend the night.

16 Then behold, an old man was coming out of the field from his work at evening. Now the man was from ªthe hill country of Ephraim, and he was staying in Gibeah, but the men of the place ᵇwere Benjamites.

16 ªJudg. 19:1 ᵇJudg. 19:14

17 And he lifted up his eyes and saw the traveler in the open square of the city; and the old man said, "Where are you going, and where do you come from?"

18 And he said to him, "We are passing from Bethlehem in Judah to the remote part of the hill country of Ephraim, *for* I am from there, and I went to Bethlehem in Judah. But I am *now* going to my house, and no man will take me into his house.

19 "Yet there is both straw and fodder for our donkeys, and also bread and wine for me, your maidservant, and ªthe young man who is with your servants; there is no lack of anything."

19 ªJudg. 19:11

20 And the old man said, "ªPeace to you. Only let me *take care of* all your needs; however, do not spend the night in the open square."

20 ªGen. 43:23; Judg. 6:23

21 ªSo he took him into his house and gave the donkeys fodder, and they washed their feet and ate and drank.

21 ªGen. 24:32, 33

22 While they were making merry, behold, ªthe men of the city, certain ᵇworthless fellows, surrounded the house, pounding the door; and they spoke to the owner of the house, the old man, saying, "Bring out the man who came into your house that we may have relations with him."

★22 ªGen. 19:4, 5; Ezek. 16:46-48 ᵇDeut. 13:13; 1 Sam. 2:12; 1 Kin. 21:10; 2 Cor. 6:15

23 Then the man, the owner of the house, went out to them and said to them, "No, my fellows, please do not act so wick-

★23-24
23 ªGen. 34:7; Deut. 22:21; Judg. 20:6; 2 Sam. 13:12

19:10 Jerusalem is called *Jebus* here and in 1 Chron. 11:4-5, since it was occupied by the Jebusites (cf. Judg. 1:21).

19:15-21 Though they waited in the *open square of the city*, none of the people of Gibeah offered them hospitality, as they should have done. Finally, an Ephraimite sojourning

in Gibeah took them in.

19:22 *worthless fellows*. Lit., sons of Belial; better, worthless men. An O.T. phrase used of those involved in idolatry (Deut. 13:13), drunkenness (1 Sam. 1:16), rebellion (1 Sam. 2:12), and sodomy (as in this case).

19:23-24 See the note on Gen. 19:8.

edly; since this man has come into my house, ᵃdo not commit this act of folly.

24 ᵃGen. 19:8

24 "ᵃHere is my virgin daughter and his concubine. Please let me bring them out that you may ravish them and do to them whatever you wish. But do not commit such an act of folly against this man."

25 But the men would not listen to him, so the man seized his concubine and brought her out to them. And they raped her and abused her all night until morning, then let her go at the approach of dawn.

26 As the day began to dawn, the woman came and fell down at the doorway of the man's house where her master was, until full daylight.

27 When her master arose in the morning and opened the doors of the house and went out to go on his way, then behold, his concubine was lying at the doorway of the house, with her hands on the threshold.

★28 ᵃJudg. 20:5

28 And he said to her, "Get up and let us go," ᵃbut there was no answer. Then he placed her on the donkey; and the man arose and went to his home.

★29 ᵃ1 Sam. 11:7

29 When he entered his house, he took a knife and laid hold of his concubine and ᵃcut her in twelve pieces, limb by limb, and sent her throughout the territory of Israel.

30 ᵃJudg. 20:7; Prov. 13:10

30 And it came about that all who saw it said, "Nothing like this has ever happened or been seen from the day when the sons of Israel came up from the land of Egypt to this day. Consider it, ᵃtake counsel and speak up!"

★ 1 ᵃ1 Sam. 7:5

20 Then all the sons of Israel from Dan to Beersheba, including the land of Gilead, came out, and the congregation assembled as one man to the LORD at ᵃMizpah.

2 And the chiefs of all the people, even of all the tribes of Israel, took their stand in the assembly of the people of God, 400,000 foot soldiers ᵃwho drew the sword.

2 ᵃJudg. 8:10

3 (Now the sons of Benjamin heard that the sons of Israel had gone up to Mizpah.) And the sons of Israel said, "Tell us, how did this wickedness take place?"

4 So the Levite, the husband of the woman who was murdered, answered and said, "I came with my concubine to spend the night at Gibeah which belongs to Benjamin.

5 "But the ᵃmen of Gibeah rose up against me and surrounded the house at night because of me. They intended to kill me; instead, they ᵇravished my concubine so that she died.

5 ᵃJudg. 19:22 ᵇJudg. 19:25f.

6 "And I ᵃtook hold of my concubine and cut her in pieces and sent her throughout the land of Israel's inheritance; for ᵇthey have committed a lewd and disgraceful act in Israel.

6 ᵃJudg. 19:29 ᵇGen. 34:7; Josh. 7:15

7 "Behold, all you sons of Israel, ᵃgive your advice and counsel here."

7 ᵃJudg. 19:30

8 Then all the people arose as one man, saying, "Not one of us will go to his tent, nor will any of us return to his house.

9 "But now this is the thing which we will do to Gibeah; we will go up against it by lot.

10 "And we will take 10 men out of 100 throughout the tribes of Israel, and 100 out of 1,000, and 1,000 out of 10,000 to supply food for the people, that when they come to Gibeah of Benjamin, they may punish them for all the disgraceful acts that they have committed in Israel."

19:28 there was no answer. Because she was dead.
19:29 The dismemberment and distribution of the body served as a call to action (cf. 1 Sam. 11:7).

20:1 as one man. With one exception (see 21:8-9). Mizpah. Not the one E. of the Jordan (cf. 10:17), but the one about 8 miles N. of Jerusalem and about 3 miles from Gibeah.

11 Thus all the men of Israel were gathered against the city, united as one man.

12 Then the tribes of Israel sent men through the entire tribe of Benjamin, saying, "What is this wickedness that has taken place among you?

13 "Now then, deliver up the men, the [a]worthless fellows in Gibeah, that we may put them to death and [b]remove *this* wickedness from Israel." But the sons of Benjamin would not listen to the voice of their brothers, the sons of Israel.

14 And the sons of Benjamin gathered from the cities to Gibeah, to go out to battle against the sons of Israel.

2 The execution of the war, 20:15-48

15 And from the cities on that day the [a]sons of Benjamin were numbered, 26,000 men who draw the sword, besides the inhabitants of Gibeah who were numbered, 700 choice men.

16 Out of all these people 700 [a]choice men were left-handed; each one could sling a stone at a hair and not miss.

17 Then the men of Israel besides Benjamin were numbered, 400,000 men who draw the sword; all these were men of war.

18 Now the sons of Israel arose, went up to Bethel, and [a]inquired of God, and said, "Who shall go up first for us to battle against the sons of Benjamin?" Then the Lord said, "Judah *shall go up* first."

19 So the sons of Israel arose in the morning and camped against Gibeah.

20 And the men of Israel went out to battle against Benjamin, and the men of Israel arrayed for battle against them at Gibeah.

21 Then the sons of Benjamin came out of Gibeah and [a]felled to the ground on that day 22,000 men of Israel.

22 But the people, the men of Israel, encouraged themselves and arrayed for battle again in the place where they had arrayed themselves the first day.

23 [a]And the sons of Israel went up and wept before the Lord until evening, and [b]inquired of the Lord, saying, "Shall we again draw near for battle against the sons of my brother Benjamin?" And the Lord said, "Go up against him."

24 Then the sons of Israel came against the sons of Benjamin the second day.

25 And Benjamin went out against them from Gibeah the second day and felled to the ground again 18,000 men of the sons of Israel; all these drew the sword.

26 Then [a]all the sons of Israel and all the people went up and came to Bethel and wept; thus they remained there before the Lord and fasted that day until evening. And they offered burnt offerings and peace offerings before the Lord.

27 And the sons of Israel [a]inquired of the Lord (for the ark of the covenant of God *was* there in those days,

28 and Phinehas the son of Eleazar, Aaron's son, stood before it to *minister* in those days), saying, "Shall I yet again go out to battle against the sons of my brother Benjamin, or shall I cease?" And the Lord said, "Go up, [a]for tomorrow I will deliver them into your hand."

29 [a]So Israel set men in ambush around Gibeah.

30 And the sons of Israel went up against the sons of Benjamin on the third day and ar-

Reference notes (margin)

13 [a]2 Cor. 6:15 [b]Deut. 13:5; 17:12; 1 Cor. 5:13

15 [a]Num. 1:36, 37; 2:23; 26:41

16 [a]Judg. 3:15; 1 Chr. 12:2

18 [a]Num. 27:21; Judg. 20:23, 27

21 [a]Judg. 20:25

23 [a]Josh. 7:6, 7 [b]Judg. 20:18

26 [a]Judg. 20:23; 21:2

★27-28

27 [a]Judg. 20:18

28 [a]Judg. 7:9

29 [a]Josh. 8:4

20:27-28 The presence of the *ark* at Bethel (before its more permanent location at Shiloh) and the mention of *Phinehas* (see Josh. 22:13) indicate that these events happened early in the period of the judges.

rayed themselves against Gibeah, as at other times.

31 [a]And the sons of Benjamin went out against the people and were drawn away from the city, and they began to strike and kill some of the people, as at other times, on the highways, one of which goes up to Bethel and the other to Gibeah, *and* in the field, about thirty men of Israel.

32 And the sons of Benjamin said, "They are struck down before us, as at the first." But the sons of Israel said, "Let us flee that we may draw them away from the city to the highways."

33 Then all the men of Israel arose from their place and arrayed themselves at Baal-tamar; [a]and the men of Israel in ambush broke out of their place, even out of Maareh-geba.

34 When ten thousand choice men from all Israel came against Gibeah, the battle became fierce; [a]but Benjamin did not know that disaster was close to them.

35 And the LORD struck Benjamin before Israel, so that the sons of Israel destroyed 25,100 men of Benjamin that day, all who draw the sword.

36 So the sons of Benjamin saw that they were defeated. [a]When the men of Israel gave ground to Benjamin because they relied on the men in ambush whom they had set against Gibeah,

37 [a]the men in ambush hurried and rushed against Gibeah; the men in ambush also deployed and struck all the city with the edge of the sword.

38 Now the appointed sign between the men of Israel and the men in ambush was [a]that they should make a great cloud of smoke rise from the city.

39 Then the men of Israel turned in the battle, and Benjamin began to strike and kill about thirty men of Israel, [a]for they said, "Surely they are defeated before us, as in the first battle."

40 But when the cloud began to rise from the city in a column of smoke, Benjamin looked [a]behind them; and behold, the whole city was going up *in smoke* to heaven.

41 Then the men of Israel turned, and the men of Benjamin were terrified; for they saw that [a]disaster was close to them.

42 Therefore, they turned their backs before the men of Israel [a]toward the direction of the wilderness, but the battle overtook them while those who came out of the cities destroyed them in the midst of them.

43 [a]They surrounded Benjamin, pursued them without rest *and* trod them down opposite Gibeah toward the east.

44 Thus 18,000 men of Benjamin fell; all these were valiant warriors.

45 The rest turned and fled toward the wilderness to the rock of [a]Rimmon, but they caught 5,000 of them on the highways and overtook them at Gidom and killed 2,000 of them.

46 So all of Benjamin who fell that day were 25,000 men who draw the sword; all these were valiant warriors.

47 But 600 men turned and fled toward the wilderness to the rock of Rimmon, and they remained at the rock of Rimmon four months.

48 The men of Israel then turned back against the sons of Benjamin and struck them with the edge of the sword, both the entire city with the cattle and all that they found; they also set on fire all the cities which they found.

---

31 [a]Josh. 8:16
33 [a]Josh. 8:19
34 [a]Josh. 8:14; Job 21:13
36 [a]Josh. 8:15
*37-42
37 [a]Josh. 8:19
38 [a]Josh. 8:20
39 [a]Judg. 20:32
40 [a]Josh. 8:20
41 [a]Prov. 5:22; 11:5, 6; 29:6
42 [a]Josh. 8:15, 24
43 [a]Hos. 9:9; 10:9
45 [a]Judg. 21:13

20:37-42 As Joshua had done at Ai (Josh. 8:4-29), the Israelites here set an ambush. Gibeah was taken when its army, pursuing the main body of the Israelites as they feigned retreat, left the city undefended. Upon seeing the city ablaze, the main Israelite army knew that the ambush had been a success.

3 *The results of the war,*
21:1-25

★ 1-7

1 *a* Judg.
21:7, 18

21 Now the men of Israel *a* had sworn in Mizpah, saying, "None of us shall give his daughter to Benjamin in marriage."

2 *a* Judg.
20:26

2 *a* So the people came to Bethel and sat there before God until evening, and lifted up their voices and wept bitterly.

3 And they said, "Why, O Lord, God of Israel, has this come about in Israel, so that one tribe should be *missing* today in Israel?"

4 *a* Deut.
12:5; 2 Sam.
24:25

4 And it came about the next day that the people arose early and built *a* an altar there, and offered burnt offerings and peace offerings.

5 *a* Judg.
5:23

5 Then the sons of Israel said, "Who is there among all the tribes of Israel who did not come up in the assembly to the Lord?" For they had taken a great oath concerning him *a* who did not come up to the Lord at Mizpah, saying, "He shall surely be put to death."

6 And the sons of Israel were sorry for their brother Benjamin and said, "One tribe is cut off from Israel today.

7 *a* Judg.
21:1

7 "What shall we do for wives for those who are left, since we have *a* sworn by the Lord not to give them any of our daughters in marriage?"

★ 8

8 And they said, "What one is there of the tribes of Israel who did not come up to the Lord at Mizpah?" And behold, no one had come to the camp from Jabesh-gilead to the assembly.

9 For when the people were numbered, behold, not one of the inhabitants of Jabesh-gilead was there.

10 *a* Num.
31:17; Judg.
5:23; 1 Sam.
11:7

10 And the congregation sent 12,000 of the valiant warriors there, and commanded them, saying, "Go and *a* strike the inhabitants of Jabesh-gilead with the edge of the sword, with the women and the little ones.

11 *a* Num.
31:17

11 "And this is the thing that you shall do: you *a* shall utterly destroy every man and every woman who has lain with a man."

12 And they found among the inhabitants of Jabesh-gilead 400 young virgins who had not known a man by lying with him; and they brought them to the camp at Shiloh, which is in the land of Canaan.

13 *a* Judg.
20:47
b Deut. 20:10

13 Then the whole congregation sent *word* and spoke to the sons of Benjamin who were *a* at the rock of Rimmon, and *b* proclaimed peace to them.

14 And Benjamin returned at that time, and they gave them the women whom they had kept alive from the women of Jabesh-gilead; yet they were not enough for them.

15 And the people were sorry for Benjamin because the Lord had made a breach in the tribes of Israel.

16 Then the elders of the congregation said, "What shall we do for wives for those who are left, since the women are destroyed out of Benjamin?"

17 And they said, "*There must be* an inheritance for the survivors of Benjamin, that a tribe may not be blotted out from Israel.

18 *a* Judg
21:1

18 "But we cannot give them wives of our daughters." For the sons of Israel *a* had sworn, saying, "Cursed is he who gives a wife to Benjamin."

19 *a* Josh.
18:1; Judg.
18:31;
1 Sam. 1:3

19 So they said, "Behold, there is a feast of the Lord from

21:1-7 Since almost all the men of Benjamin had been killed (cf. 20:47), and since the other tribes had sworn not to let any of their girls marry a Benjamite, this tribe faced the challenge of preserving themselves from total extinction.

21:8 *Jabesh-gilead.* Since this town, on the E. side of the Jordan, had sent no troops (cf. 20:1), all its inhabitants were destroyed except 400 virgins, who were given to the Benjamite men who remained (v. 12).

year to year in ªShiloh, which is
on the north side of Bethel, on the
east side of the highway that goes
up from Bethel to Shechem, and
on the south side of Lebonah."

20 And they commanded the
sons of Benjamin, saying, "Go
and lie in wait in the vineyards,
21 and watch; and behold, if
the daughters of Shiloh come out
to ªtake part in the dances, then
you shall come out of the vineyards and each of you shall catch
his wife from the daughters of
Shiloh, and go to the land of Benjamin.

22 "And it shall come about,
when their fathers or their brothers come to complain to us, that
we shall say to them, 'Give them

to us voluntarily, because we did
not take for each man of Benjamin a wife in battle, ªnor did you
give *them* to them, *else* you
would now be guilty.' "

23 And the sons of Benjamin
did so, and took wives according
to their number from those who
danced, whom they carried away.
And they went and returned to
their inheritance, and ªrebuilt the
cities and lived in them.

24 And the sons of Israel departed from there at that time, every man to his tribe and family,
and each one of them went out
from there to his inheritance.

25 ªIn those days there was
no king in Israel; everyone did
what was right in his own eyes.

*21-22

21 ªEx.
15:20; Judg.
11:34

22 ªJudg.
21:1, 18

23 ªJudg.
20:48

*25 ªJudg.
17:6; 18:1;
19:1

21:21-22 The 200 male Benjamites still left
without wives were told to "take" wives from
among the maidens of Shiloh who danced at
the annual festival. This action allowed the

men of Shiloh to keep their oath not to "give"
(voluntarily) their girls to the Benjamites.
21:25 The verse appropriately summarizes the
events of this book!

INTRODUCTION TO
THE BOOK OF RUTH

Author: Uncertain　　　　　Date: c. 1000 b.c.

Authorship　*The author is unknown to us, though Samuel is suggested by some.*

Date　*Though the events of the book occurred during the period of the judges (the latter part of the twelfth century b.c.), the book itself was not written until later. (Notice that the author felt compelled to explain customs no longer practiced, 4:6-8.) The last verses of the book trace Ruth's descendants only to King David, strongly suggesting that the book was written during his reign. If it had been written later, we would expect the genealogy to be extended beyond David to include Solomon.*

Background　*The book provides a glimpse into the lives of ordinary, though godly, people during the turbulent period of the judges (see Introduction to the Book of Judges). It shows an oasis of faithfulness in an age marked by idolatry and unfaithfulness.*

Themes　*(1) Ruth herself shows that Gentiles could believe in the true God. (2) The book gives a partial lineage of David, and thus of Christ, and shows that Gentile blood was in the line of the One who became the Savior for all mankind. (3) Boaz, as the kinsman-redeemer (see note on 3:9), serves as a beautiful type of Christ, in that (a) he was a blood relative (Rom. 1:3; Heb. 2:14); (b) he had the price with which to purchase the forfeited inheritance (1 Pet. 1:18-19); (c) he was willing to redeem (Heb. 10:7). (4) The book is a moving example of the sovereignty of God in caring for His people (Ruth 2:12).*

OUTLINE OF RUTH

I. Ruth's Resolve, 1:1-22
A. Her Background, 1:1-5
B. Her Choice, 1:6-18
C. Her Arrival in Bethlehem, 1:19-22
II. Ruth's Rights, 2:1-23
A. Her Right to Glean, 2:1-3
B. The Results of her Gleaning, 2:4-17
1. Boaz meets Ruth, 2:4-7
2. Boaz protects Ruth, 2:8-13
3. Boaz provides for Ruth, 2:14-17

C. The Report of her Gleaning, 2:18-23
III. Ruth's Request, 3:1-18
A. Suggested by Naomi, 3:1-5
B. Executed by Ruth, 3:6-9
C. Agreed to by Boaz, 3:10-18
IV. Ruth's Reward, 4:1-22
A. A Husband, 4:1-12
B. A Son, 4:13-17
C. A Lineage, 4:18-22

THE BOOK OF RUTH

I　RUTH'S RESOLVE, 1:1-22

★ 1-2　**A　Her Background, 1:1-5**

1 aJudg.
2:16-18
bGen. 12:10;
26:1; 2 Kin.
8:1　cJudg.
17:8; Mic.
5:2

1 Now it came about in the days ᵃwhen the judges governed, that there was ᵇa famine in the land. And a certain man ᶜof

Bethlehem in Judah went to sojourn in the land of Moab with his wife and his two sons.

2　And the name of the man *was* Elimelech, and the name of his wife, Naomi; and the names of

2 aJudg.
3:30

1:1-2 The beautiful romance of Ruth is set against the dark background of the apostasy and foreign oppression of the period of the judges. Because of a local *famine*, *Elimelech* (= my God is King) took his wife *Naomi* (= pleasant, lovely) and his two sons, appropri-

ately named *Mahlon* ("puny") and *Chilion* ("pining"), to *sojourn*, i.e., to visit temporarily, in nearby *Moab* (see note on Amos 2:1). *Ephrathites*. A designation for inhabitants of Bethlehem (1 Sam. 17:12).

his two sons *were* Mahlon and Chilion, Ephrathites of Bethlehem in Judah. Now they ᵃentered the land of Moab and remained there.

3 Then Elimelech, Naomi's husband, died; and she was left with her two sons.

★ **4**   **4** And they took for themselves Moabite women *as* wives; the name of the one was Orpah and the name of the other Ruth. And they lived there about ten years.

5 Then both Mahlon and Chilion also died; and the woman was bereft of her two children and her husband.

B Her Choice, 1:6–18

6 ᵃEx. 4:31;
Jer. 29:10;
Zeph. 2:7
ᵇPs. 132:15;
Matt. 6:11

6 Then she arose with her daughters-in-law that she might return from the land of Moab, for she had heard in the land of Moab that the Lᴏʀᴅ had ᵃvisited His people in ᵇgiving them food.

7 So she departed from the place where she was, and her two daughters-in-law with her; and they went on the way to return to the land of Judah.

★ **8** ᵃ2 Tim.
1:16

8 And Naomi said to her two daughters-in-law, "Go, return each of you to her mother's house. ᵃMay the Lᴏʀᴅ deal kindly with you as you have dealt with the dead and with me.

★ **9**   **9** "May the Lᴏʀᴅ grant that you may find rest, each in the house of her husband." Then she

kissed them, and they lifted up their voices and wept.

10 And they said to her, "*No*, but we will surely return with you to your people."

11 But Naomi said, "Return, my daughters. Why should you go with me? Have I yet sons in my womb, that ᵃthey may be your husbands?

★11-12

11 ᵃGen.
38:11; Deut.
25:5

12 "Return, my daughters! Go, for I am too old to have a husband. If I said I have hope, if I should even have a husband tonight and also bear sons,

13 would you therefore wait until they were grown? Would you therefore refrain from marrying? No, my daughters; for it is harder for me than for you, for ᵃthe hand of the Lᴏʀᴅ has gone forth against me."

★13 ᵃJudg.
2:15; Job
19:21; Ps.
32:4

14 And they lifted up their voices and wept again; and Orpah kissed her mother-in-law, but Ruth clung to her.

15 Then she said, "Behold, your sister-in-law has gone back to her people and her ᵃgods; return after your sister-in-law."

★15 ᵃJosh.
24:15; Judg.
11:24

16 But Ruth said, "Do not urge me to leave you *or* turn back from following you; for where you go, I will go, and where you lodge, I will lodge. Your people *shall be* my people, and your God, my God.

★16-17

17 "Where you die, I will die, and there I will be buried. Thus may ᵃthe Lᴏʀᴅ do to me, and

17 ᵃ1 Sam.
3:17; 2 Kin.
6:31

1:4 *took . . . wives.* While such mixed marriages were not specifically forbidden in the Mosaic Law, condemnation is implied in the restrictions placed on the offspring (Deut. 23:3).
1:8 *the Lᴏʀᴅ deal kindly with you.* The Hebrew word *hesed* ("deal kindly," as also in 2:20 and 3:10) expresses Naomi's prayer that the Lᴏʀᴅ (lit., Yahweh, the covenant name of God with Israel; see note on Gen. 2:4) would show His faithful, covenant-keeping love to these two Moabite widows (see note on Hos. 2:19).
1:9 *find rest.* I.e., by finding a second husband.
1:11-12 Naomi's reference to the hopelessness of her having additional sons apparently relates to the custom of levirate marriage, by which the brother of the husband who died childless would marry the widow, so the de-

ceased would have an heir (see note on Deut. 25:5–10).
1:13 *the hand of the Lᴏʀᴅ.* A common expression for God's activity.
1:15 *her gods.* Chemosh was the national god of Moab (Num. 21:29 and 1 Kings 11:7; see note on 2 Kings 3:26–27).
1:16-17 Ruth's statement of commitment is perhaps the most beautiful in all literature, well deserving of the place it receives in many Christian wedding ceremonies. Ruth's leaving meant final severance from her nation and her religion. *Thus may the Lᴏʀᴅ do to me.* A formula invoking divine punishment, the addition of *and worse* indicating the worst possible consequences if Ruth were not true to her vow.

worse, if *anything but* death parts you and me."

18 aActs 21:14   **18** When ashe saw that she was determined to go with her, she said no more to her.

C   Her Arrival in Bethlehem, 1:19-22

★**19** aMatt. 21:10   **19** So they both went until they came to Bethlehem. And it came about when they had come to Bethlehem, that aall the city was stirred because of them, and the women said, "Is this Naomi?"

★**20** aEx. 6:3; Job 6:4   **20** And she said to them, "Do not call me Naomi; call me Mara, for athe Almighty has dealt very bitterly with me.

21 aJob 1:21   **21** "I went out full, but athe LORD has brought me back empty. Why do you call me Naomi, since the LORD has witnessed against me and the Almighty has afflicted me?"

★**22** aEx. 9:31; Lev. 23:10, 11   **22** So Naomi returned, and with her Ruth the Moabitess, her daughter-in-law, who returned from the land of Moab. And they came to Bethlehem at athe beginning of barley harvest.

II   RUTH'S RIGHTS, 2:1-23
A   Her Right to Glean, 2:1-3

★**1** aRuth 1:2   **2** Now Naomi had a kinsman of her husband, a man of great wealth, of the family of aE-limelech, whose name was Boaz.

★**2** aLev. 19:9, 10; 23:22; Deut. 24:19; Ruth 2:7   **2** And Ruth the Moabitess said to Naomi, "Please let me go to the field and aglean among the ears of grain after one in whose sight I may find favor." And she said to her, "Go, my daughter."

3 So she departed and went ★**3** and gleaned in the field after the reapers; and she happened to come to the portion of the field belonging to Boaz, who was of the family of Elimelech.

B   The Results of her Gleaning, 2:4-17
1   *Boaz meets Ruth,* 2:4-7

4 Now behold, Boaz came **4** aJudg. 6:12; Ps. 129:8; Luke 1:28; 2 Thess. 3:16 from Bethlehem and said to the reapers, "aMay the LORD be with you." And they said to him, "May the LORD bless you."

5 Then Boaz said to his servant who was in charge of the reapers, "Whose young woman is this?"

6 And the servant in charge of the reapers answered and said, "She is the young Moabite woman who returned with Naomi from the land of Moab.

7 "And she said, 'Please let ★**7** me glean and gather after the reapers among the sheaves.' Thus she came and has remained from the morning until now; she has been sitting in the house for a little while."

2   *Boaz protects Ruth,* 2:8-13

8 Then Boaz said to Ruth, "Listen carefully, my daughter. Do not go to glean in another field; furthermore, do not go on from this one, but stay here with my maids.

9 "Let your eyes be on the ★**9** field which they reap, and go after them. Indeed, I have commanded the servants not to touch you. When you are thirsty, go to the

---

1:19 *all the city.* Mostly the women because the men were out harvesting (v. 22).
1:20 *Naomi* means "pleasant," while *Mara* means "bitter."
1:22 *the beginning of barley harvest.* Toward the end of April.
2:1 The lineage of Boaz, Elimelech's relative, is traced to Perez, a son of Judah, in 4:18–22. Boaz was a *man of great wealth,* a phrase meaning that he possessed the finest of qualities.

2:2 *glean.* I.e., pick up the *grain,* in this case barley (v. 17), which the reapers left on purpose for the poor, as provided in the law (Lev. 19:9; 23:22).
2:3 In the providence of God, Ruth came to the field of her relative, Boaz.
2:7 *sheaves* = bundles of grain. The *house* was probably a temporary shelter for the workers.
2:9 Boaz promised to protect and provide for Ruth.

water jars and drink from what the servants draw."

10 *a*1 Sam. 25:23   **10** Then she *a*fell on her face, bowing to the ground and said to him, "Why have I found favor in your sight that you should take notice of me, since I am a foreigner?"

11 And Boaz answered and said to her, "All that you have done for your mother-in-law after the death of your husband has been fully reported to me, and how you left your father and your mother and the land of your birth, and came to a people that you did not previously know.

★12 *a*1 Sam. 24:19 *b*Ruth 1:16; Ps. 17:8, 36:7; 57:1; 61:4; 63:7; 91:4   **12** "*a*May the LORD reward your work, and your wages be full from the LORD, the God of Israel, *b*under whose wings you have come to seek refuge."

13 Then she said, "I have found favor in your sight, my lord, for you have comforted me and indeed have spoken kindly to your maidservant, though I am not like one of your maidservants."

3   Boaz provides for Ruth, 2:14-17

★14 *a*Ruth 2:18   **14** And at mealtime Boaz said to her, "Come here, that you may eat of the bread and dip your piece of bread in the vinegar." So she sat beside the reapers; and he served her roasted grain, and she ate and was satisfied *a*and had some left.

★15-16   **15** When she rose to glean, Boaz commanded his servants, saying, "Let her glean even among the sheaves, and do not insult her.

16 "And also you shall purposely pull out for her *some grain*

from the bundles and leave *it* that she may glean, and do not rebuke her."

17 So she gleaned in the field **★17** until evening. Then she beat out what she had gleaned, and it was about an ephah of barley.

C   The Report of her Gleaning, 2:18-23

18 And she took *it* up and **18 *a*Ruth 2:14** went into the city, and her mother-in-law saw what she had gleaned. She also took *it* out and *a*gave Naomi what she had left after she was satisfied.

19 Her mother-in-law then **★19 *a*Ps. 41:1** said to her, "Where did you glean today and where did you work? May he who *a*took notice of you be blessed." So she told her mother-in-law with whom she had worked and said, "The name of the man with whom I worked today is Boaz."

20 And Naomi said to her **★20 *a*2 Sam. 2:5** daughter-in-law, "*a*May he be blessed of the LORD who has not withdrawn his kindness to the living and to the dead." Again Naomi said to her, "The man is our relative, he is one of our closest relatives."

21 Then Ruth the Moabitess said, "Furthermore, he said to me, 'You should stay close to my servants until they have finished all my harvest.'"

22 And Naomi said to Ruth her daughter-in-law, "It is good, my daughter, that you go out with his maids, lest *others* fall upon you in another field."

23 So she stayed close by the **23 *a*Deut. 16:9** maids of Boaz in order to glean until *a*the end of the barley

---

2:12 *under whose wings.* As a mother bird protects her young by spreading her wings over them, so the Lord protects His people. This figure is also used in Psalms 17:8; 36:7; 57:1; 61:4; 63:7; 91:1, 4; Matt. 23:37.

2:14 The meal consisted of *vinegar* (a sour wine) and *roasted grain.*

2:15-16 Boaz's kindness exceeded Ruth's legal rights by not only allowing her to glean where the reapers were still working (*among the*

sheaves), but also by commanding that loose grain be intentionally left for her.

2:17 After Ruth *beat out* (threshed) her barley, she had an *ephah,* about half a bushel, enough to feed herself and Naomi for about five days.

2:19 Naomi recognized that the unusually large amount of grain was due to a special favor.

2:20 *relatives.* Here Naomi used the word *goel,* "kinsman-redeemer" (see note on 3:9).

harvest and the wheat harvest. And she lived with her mother-in-law.

III RUTH'S REQUEST, 3:1-18
A Suggested by Naomi, 3:1-5

★ 1 **3** Then Naomi her mother-in-law said to her, "My daughter, shall I not seek security for you, that it may be well with you?

★ 2-3 **2** "And now is not Boaz [a]our kinsman, with whose maids you were? Behold, he winnows barley at the threshing floor tonight.

3 "Wash yourself therefore, and anoint yourself and put on your *best* clothes, and go down to the threshing floor; *but* do not make yourself known to the man until he has finished eating and drinking.

★ 4 **4** "And it shall be when he lies down, that you shall notice the place where he lies, and you shall go and uncover his feet and lie down; then he will tell you what you shall do."

5 And she said to her, "[a]All that you say I will do."

B Executed by Ruth, 3:6-9

6 So she went down to the threshing floor and did according to all that her mother-in-law had commanded her.

7 When Boaz had eaten and drunk and [a]his heart was merry, he went to lie down at the end of the heap of grain; and she came secretly, and uncovered his feet and lay down.

8 And it happened in the middle of the night that the man was startled and bent forward; and behold, a woman was lying at his feet.

9 And he said, "Who are you?" And she answered, "I am Ruth your maid. So spread your covering over your maid, for you are a close relative."

C Agreed to by Boaz, 3:10-18

10 Then he said, "[a]May you be blessed of the LORD, my daughter. You have shown your last kindness to be better than the first by not going after young men, whether poor or rich.

11 "And now, my daughter, do not fear. I will do for you whatever you ask, for all my people in the city know that you are [a]a woman of excellence.

12 "And now it is true I am a close relative; however, there is a relative closer than I.

13 "Remain this night, and when morning comes, [a]if he will redeem you, good; let him redeem you. But if he does not wish to

Margin references
★ 1

★ 2-3
2 [a]Deut. 25:5-10

5 [a]Eph. 6:1; Col. 3:20

★ 7 [a]Judg. 19:6, 9; 2 Sam. 13:28; 1 Kin. 21:7; Esth. 1:10

★ 9

★ 10 [a]Ruth 2:20

11 [a]Prov. 12:4; 31:10

★ 12

★ 13 [a]Deut. 25:5; Matt. 22:24 [b]Judg. 8:19; Jer. 4:2; 12:16

3:1 *security.* I.e., marriage.

3:2-3 The grain had to be threshed and then guarded, both activities being accompanied by festivity. *best clothes.* Likely, a large outer garment to provide warmth during the night.

3:4 *uncover his feet.* I.e., remove Boaz's outer garment so that he would eventually wake up and notice her.

3:7 Boaz slept by the grain in order to protect it.

3:9 *spread your covering over your maid.* As a pledge that he would marry her. This expression is used of God's relation to Israel in Ezek. 16:8. The reason for Ruth's request is that Boaz was a *close relative* (Heb., *goel,* redeemer, see note on Isa. 59:17-21). The responsibilities of the kinsman-redeemer included (1) redeeming family property that had changed ownership, and (2) marrying a childless widow to raise up children in her dead husband's name. According to the law of levirate marriage (see note on 1:11-12), when

there was no brother to raise up children in the name of the deceased, the responsibility was extended to the next of kin. Ruth's action was in accord with this law, which required the initiative of the widow in seeking the marriage (Deut. 25:5, 7-10). Ruth was indicating that night her desire to have Boaz, who had given every evidence of willingness to perform the duties of kinsman-redeemer.

3:10 Ruth's *kindness* (Heb., *hesed* as in 1:8 and 2:20) at *first* was her consideration for her mother-in-law. Her kindness at the *last* was wishing to marry Boaz (who evidently belonged to her father-in-law's generation), rather than one of the *young men.*

3:12 The desired arrangement was complicated by the fact that Boaz was not Elimelech's nearest relative.

3:13 *redeem* . . . I.e., fulfill the role of kinsman-redeemer and marry Ruth.

redeem you, then I will redeem you, [b]as the LORD lives. Lie down until morning."

★14 *a*Rom. 14:16; 2 Cor. 8:21

14 So she lay at his feet until morning and rose before one could recognize another; and he said, "[a]Let it not be known that the woman came to the threshing floor."

★15

15 Again he said, "Give me the cloak that is on you and hold it." So she held it, and he measured six *measures* of barley and laid *it* on her. Then she went into the city.

16 And when she came to her mother-in-law, she said, "How did it go, my daughter?" And she told her all that the man had done for her.

17 And she said, "These six *measures* of barley he gave to me, for he said, 'Do not go to your mother-in-law empty-handed.'"

★18

18 Then she said, "Wait, my daughter, until you know how the matter turns out; for the man will not rest until he has settled it today."

IV RUTH'S REWARD, 4:1-22
A   A Husband, 4:1-12

★ 1 *a*Ruth 3:12

4 Now Boaz went up to the gate and sat down there, and behold, [a]the close relative of whom Boaz spoke was passing by, so he said, "Turn aside, friend, sit down here." And he turned aside and sat down.

★ 2 *a*1 Kin. 21:8; Prov. 31:23

2 And he took ten men of the [a]elders of the city and said, "Sit down here." So they sat down.

3 *a*Lev. 25:25

3 Then he said to the closest relative, "Naomi, who has come back from the land of Moab, has to sell the piece of land [a]which belonged to our brother Elimelech.

4 "So I thought to inform you, saying, '[a]Buy *it* before those who are sitting *here,* and before the elders of my people. If you will redeem *it,* redeem *it;* but if not, tell me that I may know; for [b]there is no one but you to redeem *it,* and I am after you.'" And he said, "I will redeem *it.*"

★ 4-6

4 *a*Jer. 32:7f. *b*Lev. 25:25

5 Then Boaz said, "On the day you buy the field from the hand of Naomi, you must also acquire Ruth the Moabitess, the widow of the deceased, in order [a]to raise up the name of the deceased on his inheritance."

5 *a*Gen. 38:8; Deut. 25:5f.; Matt. 22:24

6 And [a]the closest relative said, "I cannot redeem it for myself, lest I jeopardize my own inheritance. Redeem *it* for yourself; you *may have* my right of redemption, for I cannot redeem *it.*"

6 *a*Lev. 25:25

7 Now this was [a]*the custom* in former times in Israel concerning the redemption and the exchange *of land* to confirm any matter: a man removed his sandal and gave it to another; and this was the *manner of* attestation in Israel.

★ 7 *a*Deut. 25:8-10

8 So the closest relative said to Boaz, "Buy *it* for yourself." And he removed his sandal.

9 Then Boaz said to the elders and all the people, "You are witnesses today that I have bought from the hand of Naomi all that belonged to Elimelech and all that belonged to Chilion and Mahlon.

10 "Moreover, I have acquired Ruth the Moabitess, the widow of

10 *a*Deut. 25:6

3:14 Boaz wished to protect Ruth from gossip.

3:15 A gift to Naomi of goodwill and assurance, probably carried on Ruth's head.

3:18 *the man.* I.e., Boaz wouldn't rest until the matter was settled.

4:1 The city *gate* functioned as a forum for public business, especially the kind described in this chapter.

4:2 *ten men* are called on to witness this transaction.

4:4-6 The nearer kinsman agreed to pay the price of purchasing the land of Elimelech, until he found out that it involved the responsibility of marrying and supporting the widow Ruth. This would *jeopardize* his own inheritance, being a double financial burden by (1) buying the field for Ruth's heir, rather than for his own, and (2) providing for Ruth and her family.

4:7 Handing over the sandal symbolized handing over the right of redemption to Boaz, like signing "on the dotted line."

Mahlon, to be my wife in order to raise up the name of the deceased on his inheritance, so ᵃthat the name of the deceased may not be cut off from his brothers or from the court of his *birth* place; you are witnesses today."

★11 ᵃGen. 29:25-30   **11** And all the people who were in the court, and the elders, said, "*We are* witnesses. May the Lᴏʀᴅ make the woman who is coming into your home ᵃlike Rachel and Leah, both of whom built the house of Israel; and may you achieve wealth in Ephrathah and become famous in Bethlehem.

★12 ᵃGen. 38:29; 46:12; Ruth 4:18   **12** "Moreover, may your house be like the house of ᵃPerez whom Tamar bore to Judah, through the offspring which the Lᴏʀᴅ shall give you by this young woman."

B A Son, 4:13-17

★13 ᵃGen. 29:31; 33:5   **13** So Boaz took Ruth, and she became his wife, and he went in to her. And ᵃthe Lᴏʀᴅ enabled her to conceive, and she gave birth to a son.

★14 ᵃLuke 1:58   **14** Then the ᵃwomen said to Naomi, "Blessed is the Lᴏʀᴅ who has not left you without a redeemer today, and may his name become famous in Israel.

15 "May he also be to you a restorer of life and a sustainer of your old age; for your daughter-in-law, who loves you ᵃand is better to you than seven sons, has given birth to him."   **★15** ᵃRuth 1:16, 17; 2:11, 12

16 Then Naomi took the child and laid him in her lap, and became his nurse.

17 And the neighbor women gave him a name, saying, "A son has been born to Naomi!" So they named him Obed. He is the father of Jesse, the father of David.

C A Lineage, 4:18-22

18 Now these are the generations of Perez: ᵃto Perez was born Hezron,   **★18-22**   **18** ᵃMatt. 1:3-6

19 and to Hezron was born Ram, and to Ram, Amminadab,

20 and to Amminadab was born Nahshon, and to Nahshon, Salmon,

21 and to Salmon was born Boaz, and to Boaz, Obed,

22 and to Obed was born Jesse, and to Jesse, David.

4:11 *like Rachel and Leah.* The witnesses hoped that Boaz would be rewarded with a large family, as was Jacob.

4:12 *house of Perez.* From whom Boaz descended, 4:18-22.

4:13 *the Lᴏʀᴅ enabled her to conceive.* That children are a gift from God needs to be reemphasized in modern times.

4:14 This *redeemer* (better, "kinsman, heir") is Naomi's grandson, Obed (meaning "servant"), the grandfather of David (v. 17).

4:15 Since having seven sons would indicate the blessing of God (1 Sam. 2:5; Job 1:2), to describe Ruth the Moabitess as *better . . . than seven sons* was high praise indeed!

4:18-22 This genealogy traces the line of Judah from Perez, son of Tamar, through Boaz to David.

INTRODUCTION TO
THE FIRST BOOK OF SAMUEL

AUTHORS: Samuel and others   DATE: 930 B.C. and later

Authors *Though the two books of Samuel are named for the key figure of the early chapters, Samuel could not have written more than part of 1 Samuel since his death is recorded in chapter 25. That he did in fact write a book is attested to in 1 Samuel 10:25. First Chronicles 29:29 indicates that Nathan and Gad also wrote about the events recorded in Samuel.*

Historical Background *Samuel emerged as the last judge in the 350-year span of the judges. The book covers a period of about 115 years, from the childhood of Samuel to the beginning of the reign of King David. Appearing on the scene during one of the darkest periods of Israel's history, Samuel called the people to a revival of the true worship of Yahweh (the LORD; Acts 3:24). He was also a king-maker, anointing both Saul (10:1) and David (16:13). Thus 1 Samuel forms the link between the judges and the monarchy.*

Contents *First Samuel focuses on three principal characters: Samuel, Saul, and David (2 Samuel centers exclusively on David). The principal lesson of the book has to do with the effects of sin and holiness in relation to the people and their leaders. Well-known stories in the book include that of David and Goliath (chap. 17), David and Jonathan (chap. 18), and Saul and the witch of Endor (chap. 28).*

OUTLINE OF 1 SAMUEL

I. **Samuel, the Last Judge, 1:1-8:22**
A. His Early Life and Call, 1:1-3:21
  1. His mother, 1:1-2:10
    a. Her sorrow, 1:1-8
    b. Her supplication, 1:9-18
    c. Her son, 1:19-23
    d. Her sacrifice, 1:24-28
    e. Her song, 2:1-10
  2. His ministry, 2:11-3:21
    a. The situation at Shiloh, 2:11-36
    b. The summons to Samuel, 3:1-21
B. His War with the Philistines, 4:1-7:2
  1. The capture of the ark by the Philistines, 4:1-22
    a. The defeat of Israel, 4:1-11
    b. The death of Eli, 4:12-18
    c. The departure of the glory: Ichabod, 4:19-22
  2. The curse of the ark on the Philistines, 5:1-12
  3. The return of the ark by the Philistines, 6:1-7:2
C. His Revival Ministry to Israel, 7:3-17
D. His Warning to Israel Concerning their Demand for a King, 8:1-22
II. **Saul, the First King, 9:1-31:13**
A. The Rise of Saul, 9:1-11:15
  1. The choosing of Saul, 9:1-27
  2. The coronation of Saul, 10:1-27
  3. The conquest of the Ammonites, 11:1-15
B. The Reminder by Samuel, 12:1-25

C. The Rejection of Saul, 13:1-15:35
  1. His sinful offering, 13:1-23
  2. His rash vows, 14:1-52
  3. His partial obedience, 15:1-35
D. The Replacement of Saul by David, 16:1-23
  1. David chosen and anointed, 16:1-13
  2. David employed at Saul's court, 16:14-23
E. The Rise of David over Saul, 17:1-18:30
  1. David's defeat of Goliath, 17:1-58
  2. David's friendship with Jonathan, 18:1-4
  3. David's relations with Saul, 18:5-16
  4. David's marriage, 18:17-30
F. The Rejection of David by Saul, 19:1-26:25
  1. David protected by Jonathan, 19:1-10
  2. David protected by Michal, 19:11-17
  3. David protected by Samuel, 19:18-24
  4. David protected by Jonathan, 20:1-42
  5. David protected by Ahimelech, 21:1-9
  6. David protected by Achish, 21:10-15
  7. David and his band of men, 22:1-26:25
    a. In the cave of Adullam and in Mizpah, 22:1-5
    b. Saul slays the priests, 22:6-23
    c. At Keilah, 23:1-12
    d. In the wilderness of Ziph, 23:13-29
    e. At Engedi, David spares Saul, 24:1-22
    f. David and Abigail, 25:1-44
    g. In the wilderness of Ziph, David spares Saul again, 26:1-25

THE FIRST BOOK OF SAMUEL

I SAMUEL, THE LAST JUDGE,
1:1-8:22

A His Early Life and Call,
1:1-3:21

1 His mother, 1:1-2:10

a Her sorrow, 1:1-8

★ **1** *a*1 Sam.
1:19 *b*Josh.
17:17, 18;
24:33
*c*1 Chr. 6:22-
28, 33-38

1 Now there was a certain man from *a*Ramathaim-zophim from the *b*hill country of Ephraim, and his name was *c*Elkanah the son of Jeroham, the son of Elihu, the son of Tohu, the son of Zuph, an Ephraimite.

★ **2** *a*Deut.
21:15-17
*b*Luke 2:36

2 And he had *a*two wives: the name of one was *b*Hannah and the name of the other Peninnah; and Peninnah had children, but Hannah had no children.

★ **3** *a*Ex.
34:23;
1 Sam. 1:21;
Luke 2:41
*b*Ex. 23:14;
Deut. 12:5-7;
16:16 *c*Josh.
18:1

3 Now this man would go up from his city *a*yearly *b*to worship and to sacrifice to the LORD of hosts in *c*Shiloh. And the two sons of Eli, Hophni and Phinehas were priests to the LORD there.

4 *a*Deut.
12:17, 18

4 And when the day came that Elkanah sacrificed, he *a*would give portions to Peninnah his wife and to all her sons and her daughters;

5 *a*Gen.
16:1; 30:1

5 but to Hannah he would give a double portion, for he loved Hannah, *a*but the LORD had closed her womb.

6 *a*Job
24:21

6 Her rival, however, *a*would provoke her bitterly to irritate her, because the LORD had closed her womb.

7 And it happened year after year, as often as she went up to the house of the LORD, she would provoke her, so she wept and would not eat.

★ **8** *a*Ruth
4:15

8 Then Elkanah her husband said to her, "Hannah, why do you weep and why do you not eat and why is your heart sad? *a*Am I not better to you than ten sons?"

b Her supplication, 1:9-18

9 *a*1 Sam.
3:3

9 Then Hannah rose after eating and drinking in Shiloh. Now Eli the priest was sitting on the seat by the doorpost of *a*the temple of the LORD.

10 And she, greatly distressed, prayed to the LORD and wept bitterly.

★**11** *a*Num.
30:6-11
*b*Gen. 29:32
*c*Num. 6:5;
Judg. 13:5

11 And she *a*made a vow and said, "O LORD of hosts, if Thou wilt indeed *b*look on the affliction of Thy maidservant and remember me, and not forget Thy maidservant, but wilt give Thy maidservant a son, then I will give him to the LORD all the days of his life,

---

1:1 *Ramathaim-zophim.* Lit., the heights of the Zuphite. A longer name for Ramah (1:19), a city in the hill country of Ephraim, 5 miles N. of Jerusalem.

1:2 Though at variance with God's ideal for marriage (Gen. 2:24), polygamy was allowed in the case of a childless first marriage (cf. Deut. 21:15-17) and of a levirate marriage (Deut. 25:5-10), but the practice often caused great misery (cf. 1 Sam. 1:6-7).

1:3 *LORD of hosts.* A military figure, referring to God as the One who commands the angelic armies of heaven (1 Kings 22:19; Luke 2:13;

Rev. 19:14) and the armies of Israel (1 Sam. 17:45). The term emphasizes the sovereignty and omnipotence of God. *Shiloh.* The location of the tabernacle (Josh. 18:1) and the religious center of the nation until the loss of the Ark (1 Sam. 4). It was 20 miles N. of Jerusalem.

1:8 Elkanah considered his love and care for her a greater blessing than a large family!

1:11 Hannah vowed that if she were given a son, he would be dedicated to lifelong levitical service (cf. Num. 4:2-3) and become a lifelong Nazirite (see note on Num. 6:1-8).

and *c*a razor shall never come on his head."

12 Now it came about, as she continued praying before the LORD, that Eli was watching her mouth.

13 As for Hannah, *a*she was speaking in her heart, only her lips were moving, but her voice was not heard. So Eli thought she was drunk.

14 Then Eli said to her, "*a*How long will you make yourself drunk? Put away your wine from you."

15 But Hannah answered and said, "No, my lord, I am a woman oppressed in spirit; I have drunk neither wine nor strong drink, but I *a*have poured out my soul before the LORD.

16 "Do not consider your maidservant as a worthless woman; for I have spoken until now out of my great concern and provocation."

17 Then Eli answered and said, "*a*Go in peace; and may the God of Israel *b*grant your petition that you have asked of Him."

18 And she said, "*a*Let your maidservant find favor in your sight." So the woman went her way and ate, and *b*her face was no longer sad.

c Her son, 1:19-23

19 Then they arose early in the morning and worshiped before the LORD, and returned again to their house in *a*Ramah. And Elkanah had relations with Hannah his wife, and *b*the LORD remembered her.

20 And it came about in due time, after Hannah had conceived, that she gave birth to a son; and she named him Samuel, *saying,* "*a*Because I have asked him of the LORD."

21 Then the man Elkanah *a*went up with all his household to offer to the LORD the yearly sacrifice and *pay* his vow.

22 But Hannah did not go up, for she said to her husband, "*I will not go up* until the child is weaned; then I will *a*bring him, that he may appear before the LORD and *b*stay there forever."

23 And *a*Elkanah her husband said to her, "Do what seems best to you. Remain until you have weaned him; only *b*may the LORD confirm His word." So the woman remained and nursed her son until she weaned him.

d Her sacrifice, 1:24-28

24 Now when she had weaned him, *a*she took him up with her, with a three-year-old bull and one ephah of flour and a jug of wine, and brought him to *b*the house of the LORD in Shiloh, although the child was young.

25 Then *a*they slaughtered the bull, and *b*brought the boy to Eli.

26 And she said, "Oh, my lord! *a*As your soul lives, my lord, I am the woman who stood here beside you, praying to the LORD.

27 "*a*For this boy I prayed, and the LORD has given me my petition which I asked of Him.

28 "*a*So I have also dedicated him to the LORD; as long as he lives he is dedicated to the LORD." And *b*he worshiped the LORD there.

Cross references (margin):

13 *a*Gen. 24:42-45

14 *a*Acts 2:4, 13

★15 *a*Job 30:16; Ps. 42:4; 62:8; Lam. 2:19

17 *a*Judg. 18:6; 1 Sam. 25:35; 2 Kin. 5:19; Mark 5:34; Luke 7:50 *b*Ps. 20:3-5

18 *a*Gen. 33:15; Ruth 2:13 *b*Rom. 15:13

19 *a*1 Sam. 1:1; 2:11 *b*Gen. 21:1; 30:22

★20 *a*Gen. 41:51, 52; Ex. 2:10, 22; Matt. 1:21

21 *a*Deut. 12:11; 1 Sam. 1:3

★22 *a*Luke 2:22 *b*1 Sam. 1:11, 28

23 *a*Num. 30:7, 10, 11 *b*1 Sam. 1:17

★24 *a*Num. 15:9, 10; Deut. 12:5, 6 *b*Josh. 18:1; 1 Sam. 4:3, 4

25 *a*Lev. 1:5 *b*Luke 2:22

26 *a*2 Kin. 2:2, 4, 6, 4:30

27 *a*1 Sam. 1:11-13; Ps. 6:9; 66:19, 20

★28 *a*1 Sam. 1:11, 22 *b*Gen. 24:26, 52

1:15 The outpouring of one's soul before God is an excellent description of fervent prayer (cf. Phil. 4:6-7; 1 Pet. 5:7).

1:20 Samuel means "name of God," and serves as a continual reminder of God's mercy toward those who call upon His name.

1:22 *weaned.* Lit., dealt fully with. The word may include the idea of spiritual training as well. Hebrew children were normally weaned at two to three years (cf. 2 Maccabees 7:27).

1:24 *a three-year-old bull.* Better, three bulls. *ephah.* A dry measure estimated to be about two-thirds of a bushel.

1:28 *dedicated.* Lit., made him over to. The idea is that of a complete and irrevocable giving up of the child to the Lord. Hannah was careful to pay the vow even at great cost (cf. Eccl. 5:4-5).

e *Her song, 2:1-10*

★1-10
★ 1 aI Sam.
2:1-10; Luke
1:46-55
bDeut.
33:17; Job
16:15; Ps.
75:10; 89:17,
24; 92:10;
112:9 cPs.
9:14; 13:5;
35:9; Is.
12:2, 3

2 Then Hannah aprayed and said,

"My heart exults in the LORD;
bMy horn is exalted in the LORD,
My mouth speaks boldly against my enemies,
Because cI rejoice in Thy salvation.

2 aEx.
15:11; Lev.
19:2; Ps.
86:8 b2 Sam.
22:32 cDeut.
32:30, 31

2 "aThere is no one holy like the LORD,
Indeed, bthere is no one besides Thee,
cNor is there any rock like our God.

3 aProv.
8:13 b1 Sam.
16:7; 1 Kin.
8:39 cProv.
16:2; 24:12

3 "Boast no more so very proudly,
aDo not let arrogance come out of your mouth;
bFor the LORD is a God of knowledge,
cAnd with Him actions are weighed.

4 aPs.
37:15; 46:9
bPs. 18:39;
Heb. 11:32-
34

4 "aThe bows of the mighty are shattered,
bBut the feeble gird on strength.

★ 5 aRuth
4:15; Ps.
113:9
bJer. 15:9

5 "Those who were full hire themselves out for bread,
But those who were hungry cease *to* hunger.
aEven the barren gives birth to seven,
But bshe who has many children languishes.

★ 6 aDeut.
32:39; 2 Kin.
5:7; Rev.
1:18 bIs.
26:19

6 "aThe LORD kills and makes alive;
bHe brings down to Sheol and raises up.

7 "aThe LORD makes poor and rich;
bHe brings low, He also exalts.

7 aDeut.
8:17, 18
bJob 5:11;
Ps. 75:7;
James 4:10

8 "aHe raises the poor from the dust,
bHe lifts the needy from the ash heap
cTo make them sit with nobles,
And inherit a seat of honor;
dFor the pillars of the earth are the LORD's,
And He set the world on them.

★ 8 aJob
42:10-12; Ps.
75:7; 113:7
b2 Sam. 7:8;
Dan. 2:48;
James 2:5
cJob 36:7;
Ps. 113:8
dJob 38:4-6;
Ps. 75:3;
104:5

9 "aHe keeps the feet of His godly ones,
bBut the wicked ones are silenced in darkness;
cFor not by might shall a man prevail.

9 aPs.
91:11, 12;
121:3; Prov.
3:26; 1 Pet.
1:5 bMatt.
8:12 cPs.
33:16, 17

10 "aThose who contend with the LORD will be shattered;
bAgainst them He will thunder in the heavens,
cThe LORD will judge the ends of the earth;
dAnd He will give strength to His king,
eAnd will exalt the horn of His anointed."

10 aEx. 15:6;
Ps. 2:9
b1 Sam.
7:10; 2 Sam.
22:14; Ps.
18:13, 14
cPs. 96:13;
98:9; Matt.
25:31, 32
dPs. 21:1, 7
ePs. 89:24

2 *His ministry, 2:11-3:21*
a *The situation at Shiloh,*
2:11-36

11 Then Elkanah went to his home at aRamah. bBut the boy ministered to the LORD before Eli the priest.

11 aI Sam.
1:1, 19
b1 Sam.
1:28; 2:18;
3:1

12 Now the sons of Eli were aworthless men; they did not know the LORD

12 aJer. 2:8;
9:3, 6; 2 Cor.
6:15
★13-17
13 aLev.
7:29-34

13 aand the custom of the

2:1-10 Hannah's praise is in response to God's answer to her prayer, and was probably delivered before the congregation of worshipers. The theme of Hannah's praise is her confidence in God's sovereignty. Hannah praises God for His holiness (v. 2), knowledge (v. 3), power (vv. 4-8), and judgment (vv. 9-10).

2:1 *horn.* An image of invincible strength (cf. Dan. 7:21).

2:5 God often reverses human circumstances, humbling the proud and exalting the humble (Prov. 16:18; 18:12).

2:6 *Sheol.* The place of the dead awaiting the resurrection and the great white throne judgment; equivalent to Hades in the N.T. (see note on Gen. 37:35).

2:8 *pillars of the earth.* I.e., world leaders (cf. Dan. 4:25, 32).

2:13-17 The sons of Eli were guilty of taking more of the sacrifice than their allotted portion (Lev. 7:34), of taking the meat before the fat had been burned as a sacrifice to God (Lev. 3:3, 5), and of generally despising the offerings of the Lord (2:17).

priests with the people. When any man was offering a sacrifice, the priest's servant would come while the meat was boiling, with a three-pronged fork in his hand.

14 Then he would thrust it into the pan, or kettle, or caldron, or pot; all that the fork brought up the priest would take for himself. Thus they did in Shiloh to all the Israelites who came there.

15 aLev. 3:3-5, 16

15 Also, before athey burned the fat, the priest's servant would come and say to the man who was sacrificing, "Give the priest meat for roasting, as he will not take boiled meat from you, only raw."

16 And if the man said to him, "They must surely burn the fat first, and then take as much as you desire," then he would say, "No, but you shall give it to me now; and if not, I will take it by force."

17 aMal. 2:7-9

17 Thus the sin of the young men was very great before the LORD, for the men adespised the offering of the LORD.

★18 a1 Sam. 2:11; 3:1 b1 Sam. 2:28; 22:18; 2 Sam. 6:14; 1 Chr. 15:27

18 Now aSamuel was ministering before the LORD, as a boy bwearing a linen ephod.

19 aEx. 28:31 b1 Sam. 1:3, 21

19 And his mother would make him a little arobe and bring it to him from year to year when she would come up with her husband to offer bthe yearly sacrifice.

20 aLuke 2:34 b1 Sam. 1:11, 27, 28

20 Then Eli would abless Elkanah and his wife and say, "May the LORD give you children from this woman in place of the one she bdedicated to the LORD." And they went to their own home.

★21 aGen. 21:1 bJudg. 13:24; 1 Sam. 2:26; 3:19-21; Luke 1:80; 2:40

21 And athe LORD visited Hannah; and she conceived and gave birth to three sons and two daughters. And bthe boy Samuel grew before the LORD.

22 a1 Sam. 2:13-17 bEx. 38:8

22 Now Eli was very old; and he heard aall that his sons were

doing to all Israel, and how they lay with bthe women who served at the doorway of the tent of meeting.

23 And he said to them, "Why do you do such things, the evil things that I hear from all these people?

24 "No, my sons; for the report is not good awhich I hear the LORD's people circulating.

★24 a1 Kin. 15:26

25 "If one man sins against another, aGod will mediate for him; but bif a man sins against the LORD, who can intercede for him?" But they would not listen to the voice of their father, for the cLORD desired to put them to death.

★25 aDeut. 1:17 bNum. 15:30; 1 Sam. 3:14; Heb. 10:26, 27 cJosh. 11:20

26 Now the boy aSamuel was growing in stature and in favor both with the LORD and with men.

26 a1 Sam. 2:21; Luke 2:52

27 Then aa man of God came to Eli and said to him, "Thus says the LORD, 'bDid I not indeed reveal Myself to the house of your father when they were in Egypt in bondage to Pharaoh's house?

★27 aDeut. 33:1; Judg. 13:6 bEx. 4:14-16; 12:1, 43

28 'And adid I not choose them from all the tribes of Israel to be My priests, to go up to My altar, to burn incense, to carry an ephod before Me; and did I not bgive to the house of your father all the fire offerings of the sons of Israel?

28 aEx. 28:1-4; 30:7, 8; Lev. 8:7, 8 bLev. 7:35, 36

29 'Why do you akick at My sacrifice and at My offering bwhich I have commanded in My cdwelling above Me, by making yourselves fat with the choicest of every offering of My people Israel?'

29 a1 Sam. 2:13-17 bDeut. 12:5-9 cPs. 26:8 dMatt. 10:37

30 "Therefore the LORD God of Israel declares, 'aI did indeed say that your house and the house of your father should walk before Me forever'; but now the LORD declares, 'Far be it from Me—for bthose who honor Me I will

30 aEx. 29:9; Num. 25:13 bPs. 50:23 cMal. 2:9

2:18 linen ephod. A close-fitting, sleeveless, apron-like garment, extending to the hips and worn almost exclusively by the priest; used when officiating before the altar (2:28; see note on Exod. 28:6–14).

2:21 Hannah provides an example for fervent prayer (1:10–11, 15), obedience (1:28), worship (2:1–10), and devotion to family (1:24; 2:18–19) which resulted in God's blessing.

2:24 the LORD's people circulating. Lit., causing the people of the LORD to transgress.

2:25 for the LORD. The preposition may denote result, i.e., "therefore the Lord. . . ." Note the severe consequences of this sinning against God.

2:27 a man of God. I.e., a spokesman for the Lord (see note on 1 Chron. 23:14).

honor, and those ^cwho despise Me will be lightly esteemed.

★31-35

31 a1 Sam. 4:11-18; 22:17-20

31 'Behold, ^athe days are coming when I will break your strength and the strength of your father's house so that there will not be an old man in your house.

32 a1 Kin. 2:26, 27
bZech. 8:4

32 'And you will see ^athe distress of My dwelling, in *spite of* all that I do good for Israel; and an ^bold man will not be in your house forever.

33 'Yet I will not cut off every man of yours from My altar that your eyes may fail *from weeping* and your soul grieve, and all the increase of your house will die in the prime of life.

34 a1 Sam. 10:7-9; 1 Kin. 13:3 b1 Sam. 4:11, 17

34 'And this will be ^athe sign to you which shall come concerning your two sons, Hophni and Phinehas: ^bon the same day both of them shall die.

35 a1 Sam. 3:1; 7:9; 9:12, 13 b1 Sam. 8:3-5; 25:28; 2 Sam. 7:11, 27; 1 Kin. 11:38 c1 Sam. 10:9, 10; 12:3; 16:13

35 'But ^aI will raise up for Myself a faithful priest who will do according to what is in My heart and in My soul; and ^bI will build him an enduring house, and he will walk before ^cMy anointed always.

36 'And it shall come about that everyone who is left in your house shall come and bow down to him for a piece of silver or a loaf of bread, and say, "Please assign me to one of the priest's offices so that I may eat a piece of bread." ' "

b The summons to Samuel, 3:1-21

★ 1 a1 Sam. 2:11, 18 bPs. 74:9; Ezek. 7:26; Amos 8:11, 12

3 Now ^athe boy Samuel was ministering to the LORD before Eli. And ^bword from the LORD was rare in those days, visions were infrequent.

2 aGen. 27:1; 48:10; 1 Sam. 4:15

2 And it happened at that time as Eli was lying down in his place (now ^ahis eyesight had begun to grow dim *and* he could not see well),

★ 3 aEx. 25:31-37; Lev. 24:2, 3

3 and ^athe lamp of God had not yet gone out, and Samuel was lying down in the temple of the LORD where the ark of God *was*,

4 aIs. 6:8

4 that the LORD called Samuel; and he said, "^aHere I am."

5 Then he ran to Eli and said, "Here I am, for you called me." But he said, "I did not call, lie down again." So he went and lay down.

6 And the LORD called yet again, "Samuel!" So Samuel arose and went to Eli, and said, "Here I am, for you called me." But he answered, "I did not call, my son, lie down again."

7 aActs 19:2; 1 Cor. 13:11

7 ^aNow Samuel did not yet know the LORD, nor had the word of the LORD yet been revealed to him.

8 So the LORD called Samuel again for the third time. And he arose and went to Eli, and said, "Here I am, for you called me." Then Eli discerned that the LORD was calling the boy.

9 And Eli said to Samuel, "Go lie down, and it shall be if He calls you, that you shall say, 'Speak, LORD, for Thy servant is listening.' " So Samuel went and lay down in his place.

★10

10 Then the LORD came and stood and called as at other times, "Samuel! Samuel!" And Samuel said, "Speak, for Thy servant is listening."

★11-14 11 a2 Kin. 21:12; Jer. 19:3

11 And the LORD said to Samuel, "Behold, ^aI am about to do a thing in Israel at which both ears

---

2:31-35 The prophet predicts the destruction of the priestly family of Eli, partially fulfilled in the massacre of the priests of Nob (1 Sam. 22:11-19) and in the transfer of the priesthood to the family of Zadok in the time of Solomon (1 Kings 2:26-27, 35). The death of Eli's two sons on the same day would be a sign to validate the prophecy.
3:1 Apostasy and prophetic inactivity characterized the days of Eli.
3:3 The lamp burned from evening to morning

outside the veil (Lev. 24:3; Exod. 27:20-21). In the early morning hours, while Samuel lay near the Ark, the Lord commissioned him for his prophetic ministry.
3:10 *listening.* The word means "to hear with a view to obeying." Samuel was listening to God's Word and was determined to obey it.
3:11-14 Samuel's first test as a prophet was to bring an ear-tingling message of doom to Eli. He passed the test (3:18).

of everyone who hears it will tingle.

12 "In that day [a]I will carry out against Eli all that I have spoken concerning his house, from beginning to end.

13 "For [a]I have told him that I am about to judge his house forever for [b]the iniquity which he knew, because [c]his sons brought a curse on themselves and [d]he did not rebuke them.

14 "And therefore I have sworn to the house of Eli that [a]the iniquity of Eli's house shall not be atoned for by sacrifice or offering forever."

15 So Samuel lay down until morning. Then he [a]opened the doors of the house of the LORD. But Samuel was afraid to tell [b]the vision to Eli.

16 Then Eli called Samuel and said, "Samuel, my son." And he said, "Here I am."

17 And he said, "What is the word that He spoke to you? Please do not hide it from me. [a]May God do so to you, and more also, if you hide anything from me of all the words that He spoke to you."

18 So Samuel told him everything and hid nothing from him. And he said, "[a]It is the LORD; let Him do what seems good to Him."

19 Thus [a]Samuel grew and [b]the LORD was with him and [c]let none of his words fail.

20 And all Israel [a]from Dan even to Beersheba knew that Samuel was confirmed as a prophet of the LORD.

21 And [a]the LORD appeared again at Shiloh, [b]because the LORD

revealed Himself to Samuel at Shiloh by the word of the LORD.

B His War with the Philistines, 4:1–7:2

1 The capture of the ark by the Philistines, 4:1–22

a The defeat of Israel, 4:1–11

4 Thus the word of Samuel came to all Israel. Now Israel went out to meet the Philistines in battle and camped beside [a]Ebenezer while the Philistines camped in [b]Aphek.

2 And the Philistines drew up in battle array to meet Israel. When the battle spread, Israel was defeated before the Philistines who killed about four thousand men on the battlefield.

3 When the people came into the camp, the elders of Israel said, "[a]Why has the LORD defeated us today before the Philistines? [b]Let us take to ourselves from Shiloh the ark of the covenant of the LORD, that it may come among us and deliver us from the power of our enemies."

4 So the people sent to Shiloh, and from there they carried the ark of the covenant of the LORD of hosts [a]who sits *above* the cherubim; and the two sons of Eli, Hophni and Phinehas, *were* there with the ark of the covenant of God.

5 And it happened as the ark of the covenant of the LORD came into the camp, that [a]all Israel shouted with a great shout, so that the earth resounded.

Cross references (left column):

12 [a]1 Sam. 2:27-36

★13 [a]1 Sam. 2:29-31 [b]1 Sam. 2:22 [c]1 Sam. 2:12, 17, 22 [d]Deut. 17:12; 21:18

14 [a]Lev. 15:31; Is. 22:14

15 [a]1 Chr. 15:23 [b]1 Sam. 3:10

17 [a]2 Sam. 3:35

18 [a]Ex. 34:5-7; Lev. 10:3; Job 2:10; Is. 39:8

19 [a]1 Sam. 2:21 [b]Gen. 21:22; 28:15; 39:2 [c]1 Sam. 9:6

★20 [a]Judg. 20:1

21 [a]Gen. 12:7 [b]1 Sam. 3:10

Cross references (right column):

★ 1 [a]1 Sam. 7:12 [b]Josh. 12:18; 1 Sam. 29:1

★ 3 [a]Josh. 7:7, 8 [b]Num. 10:35; Josh. 6:6

4 [a]Ex. 25:22; 2 Sam. 6:2; Ps. 80:1

5 [a]Josh. 6:5, 20

3:13 The epitome of a tragic family situation: rebellious children and failure in the area of parental discipline.

3:20 The expression "from Dan to Beersheba" (about 150 miles) denotes the whole territory of Israel from its northernmost to its southernmost extremity (cf. Judg. 20:1).

4:1 *Philistines.* The Philistine or "Sea People" migrated from Crete (Caphtor, Amos 9:7) and other Aegean islands to the eastern Mediterranean coast and settled on the southern coastal plain of Palestine, a region which became

known as Philistia. The Philistines were a powerful military people and were the greatest threat to the Israelites during the days of Samuel, Saul, and David. *Ebenezer* means "stone of help" (cf. 7:12). *Aphek.* A strategic border city at the northern edge of the Philistine territory, 11 miles NE. of Joppa.

4:3 The Ark symbolized the presence and power of God, but the Israelites used it superstitiously by placing their faith in it rather than in God himself.

6 And when the Philistines heard the noise of the shout, they said, "What *does* the noise of this great shout in the camp of the Hebrews *mean?*" Then they understood that the ark of the LORD had come into the camp.

★ 7-8
7 ^aEx. 15:14

7 And the Philistines were afraid, for they said, "God has come into the camp." And they said, "^aWoe to us! For nothing like this has happened before.

8 "Woe to us! Who shall deliver us from the hand of these mighty gods? These are the gods who smote the Egyptians with all *kinds of* plagues in the wilderness.

9 ^a1 Cor. 16:13 ^bJudg. 13:1; 1 Sam. 14:21

9 "^aTake courage and be men, O Philistines, lest you become slaves to the Hebrews, ^bas they have been slaves to you; therefore, be men and fight."

10 ^aDeut. 28:15, 25; 1 Sam. 4:2 ^b2 Sam. 18:17; 19:8; 2 Kin. 14:12; 2 Chr. 25:22

10 So the Philistines fought and ^aIsrael was defeated, and ^bevery man fled to his tent, and the slaughter was very great; for there fell of Israel thirty thousand foot soldiers.

11 ^a1 Sam. 2:34; Ps. 78:56-64

11 And the ark of God was taken; and ^athe two sons of Eli, Hophni and Phinehas, died.

b The death of Eli, 4:12-18

★12 ^aJosh. 7:6; 2 Sam. 1:2; 15:32; Neh. 9:1; Job 2:12

12 Now a man of Benjamin ran from the battle line and came to Shiloh the same day with ^ahis clothes torn and dust on his head.

13 ^a1 Sam. 1:9; 4:18

13 When he came, behold, ^aEli was sitting on *his* seat by the road eagerly watching, because his heart was trembling for the ark of God. So the man came to tell *it* in the city, and all the city cried out.

14 When Eli heard the noise of the outcry, he said, "What *does* the noise of this commotion *mean?*" Then the man came hurriedly and told Eli.

15 ^a1 Sam. 3:2; 1 Kin. 14:4

15 Now Eli was ninety-eight years old, and ^ahis eyes were set so that he could not see.

16 ^a2 Sam. 1:4

16 And the man said to Eli, "I am the one who came from the battle line. Indeed, I escaped from the battle line today." And he said, "^aHow did things go, my son?"

17 Then the one who brought the news answered and said, "Israel has fled before the Philistines and there has also been a great slaughter among the people, and your two sons also, Hophni and Phinehas, are dead, and the ark of God has been taken."

★18 ^a1 Sam. 4:13

18 And it came about when he mentioned the ark of God that ^aEli fell off the seat backward beside the gate, and his neck was broken and he died, for he was old and heavy. Thus he judged Israel forty years.

c The departure of the glory: Ichabod, 4:19-22

19 Now his daughter-in-law, Phinehas' wife, was pregnant and about to give birth; and when she heard the news that the ark of God was taken and that her father-in-law and her husband had died, she kneeled down and gave birth, for her pains came upon her.

20 ^aGen. 35:16-19

20 And about the time of her death the women who stood by her said to her, "^aDo not be afraid, for you have given birth to a son." But she did not answer or pay attention.

★21 ^aPs. 26:8; Jer. 2:11 ^b1 Sam. 4:11

21 And she called the boy Ichabod, saying, "^aThe glory has departed from Israel," because ^bthe ark of God was taken and because of her father-in-law and her husband.

4:7-8 The Philistines looked upon the Ark as an idol, an Israelite god.

4:12 Torn clothing and dust on the head were the signs of mourning for the dead or for national calamity.

4:18 Only here is it indicated that Eli served as a judge as well as a priest.

4:21 *Ichabod* means "no glory." The loss of the Ark meant the absence of glory in Israel.

22 And she said, "The glory has departed from Israel, for the ark of God was taken."

2　The curse of the ark on the Philistines, 5:1-12

5 Now the Philistines took the ark of God and [a]brought it from Ebenezer to [b]Ashdod.

2 Then the Philistines took the ark of God and brought it to [a]the house of Dagon, and set it by Dagon.

3 When the Ashdodites arose early the next morning, behold, [a]Dagon had fallen on his face to the ground before the ark of the LORD. So they took Dagon and [b]set him in his place again.

4 But when they arose early the next morning, behold, [a]Dagon had fallen on his face to the ground before the ark of the LORD. And the head of Dagon and both the palms of his hands *were* cut off on the threshold; only the trunk of Dagon was left to him.

5 Therefore neither the priests of Dagon nor all who enter Dagon's house [a]tread on the threshold of Dagon in Ashdod to this day.

6 Now [a]the hand of the LORD was heavy on the Ashdodites, and [b]He ravaged them and smote them with [c]tumors, both Ashdod and its territories.

7 When the men of Ashdod saw that it was so, they said, "The ark of the God of Israel must not remain with us, for His hand is severe on us and on Dagon our god."

8 So they sent and [a]gathered all the lords of the Philistines to

them and said, "What shall we do with the ark of the God of Israel?" And they said, "Let the ark of the God of Israel be brought around to Gath." And they brought the ark of the God of Israel *around*.

9 And it came about that after they had brought it around, [a]the hand of the LORD was against the city with very great confusion; and He smote the men of the city, both young and old, so that [b]tumors broke out on them.

10 So they sent the ark of God to Ekron. And it happened as the ark of God came to Ekron that the Ekronites cried out, saying, "They have brought the ark of the God of Israel around to us, to kill us and our people."

11 They [a]sent therefore and gathered all the lords of the Philistines and said, "Send away the ark of the God of Israel, and let it return to its own place, that it may not kill us and our people." For there was a deadly confusion throughout the city; [b]the hand of God was very heavy there.

12 And the men who did not die were smitten with tumors and [a]the cry of the city went up to heaven.

3　The return of the ark by the Philistines, 6:1-7:2

6 Now the ark of the LORD had been in the country of the Philistines seven months.

2 And [a]the Philistines called for the priests and the diviners, saying, "What shall we do with the ark of the LORD? Tell us how we shall send it to its place."

3 And they said, "If you send away the ark of the God of

---

1 [a]1 Sam. 4:1; 7:12 [b]Josh. 13:3

★ **2** [a]Judg. 16:23-30; 1 Chr. 10:8-10

3 [a]Is. 19:1; 46:1, 2 [b]Is. 46:7

★ **4** [a]Ezek. 6:4, 6; Mic. 1:7

5 [a]Zeph. 1:9

★ **6** [a]Ex. 9:3; 1 Sam. 5:7, 11; Ps. 32:4; 145:20; 147:6; Acts 13:11 [b]1 Sam. 6:5 [c]Deut. 28:27; Ps. 78:66

★ **8** [a]1 Sam. 5:11; 29:6-11

★ **9** [a]Deut. 2:15; 1 Sam. 5:11; 7:13; 12:15 [b]1 Sam. 5:6

★**10**

11 [a]1 Sam. 5:8 [b]1 Sam. 5:6, 9

★**12** [a]Ex. 12:30; Is. 15:3

2 [a]Gen. 41:8; Ex. 7:11; Is. 2:6

3 [a]Ex. 23:15; Deut. 16:16 [b]Lev. 5:15, 16

5:1 *Ashdod,* located on the Mediterranean coast 33 miles W. of Jerusalem, was one of the five *major Philistine cities* (cf. *6:17*).

5:2 *Dagon* was a Philistine vegetation god. In ancient literature Baal is sometimes referred to as the "son of Dagon."

5:4 The idol fell before the Ark twice. The second time it was destroyed, as divine judgment on the Philistine deity.

5:6 *tumors.* Or boils. Perhaps the sores were the symptoms of bubonic plague, for mice rav-

aged the land (*6:5*).

5:8 *Gath.* Another of the five Philistine cities (*6:17*), was 12 miles E. of Ashdod.

5:9 *tumors.* See note on *5:6*.

5:10 *Ekron.* Another of the five Philistine cities (*6:17*), six miles N. of Gath.

5:12 *tumors.* See note on *5:6*. One lesson from the experience of the Philistines with the Ark seems clear: no matter how sacred, that which is acquired by improper means can never bring blessing to the possessor.

Israel, [a]do not send it empty; but you shall surely [b]return to Him a guilt offering. Then you shall be healed and it shall be known to you why His hand is not removed from you."

★ **4-5**

4 ¹ª1 Sam. 5:6, 9, 12; 6:17 ᵇJosh. 13:3; Judg. 3:3; 1 Sam. 6:17, 18

4 Then they said, "What shall be the guilt offering which we shall return to Him?" And they said, "Five golden [a]tumors and five golden mice [b]according to the number of the lords of the Philistines, for one plague was on all of you and on your lords.

5 ªJosh. 7:19; 1 Chr. 16:28, 29; Is. 42:12; Jer. 13:16; John 9:24; Rev. 14:7 ᵇ1 Sam. 5:6, 11 ᶜ1 Sam. 5:3, 4, 7

5 "So you shall make likenesses of your tumors and likenesses of your mice that ravage the land, and [a]you shall give glory to the God of Israel; perhaps [b]He will ease His hand from you, [c]your gods, and your land.

6 ªEx. 7:13; 8:15, 32; 9:34; 14:17 ᵇEx. 12:31

6 "Why then do you harden your hearts [a]as the Egyptians and Pharaoh hardened their hearts? When He had severely dealt with them, [b]did they not allow the people to go, and they departed?

★ **7** ª2 Sam. 6:3 ᵇNum. 19:2; Deut. 21:3, 4

7 "Now therefore take and [a]prepare a new cart and two milch cows on which there [b]has never been a yoke; and hitch the cows to the cart and take their calves home, away from them.

8 ª1 Sam. 6:4, 5 ᵇ1 Sam. 6:3

8 "And take the ark of the LORD and place it on the cart; and put [a]the articles of gold which you return to Him as [b]a guilt offering in a box by its side. Then send it away that it may go.

★ **9** ªJosh. 15:10; 21:16 ᵇ1 Sam. 6:3

9 "And watch, if it goes up by the way of its own territory to [a]Beth-shemesh, then He has done us this great evil. But if not, then [b]we shall know that it was not His hand that struck us; it happened to us by chance."

10 Then the men did so, and took two milch cows and hitched them to the cart, and shut up their calves at home.

11 And they put the ark of the LORD on the cart, and the box with the golden mice and the likenesses of their tumors.

12 And the cows took the straight way in the direction of [a]Beth-shemesh; they went along [b]the highway, lowing as they went, and did not turn aside to the right or to the left. And the lords of the Philistines followed them to the border of Beth-shemesh.

★**12** ª1 Sam. 6:9 ᵇNum. 20:19

13 Now *the people of* Beth-shemesh were reaping their wheat harvest in the valley, and they raised their eyes and saw the ark and were glad to see *it*.

14 And the cart came into the field of Joshua the Beth-shemite and stood there where there *was* a large stone; and they split the wood of the cart and [a]offered the cows as a burnt offering to the LORD.

14 ª2 Sam. 24:22; 1 Kin. 19:21

15 And [a]the Levites took down the ark of the LORD and the box that was with it, in which were the articles of gold, and put them on the large stone; and the men of Beth-shemesh offered burnt offerings and sacrificed sacrifices that day to the LORD.

15 ªJosh. 3:3

16 And when the [a]five lords of the Philistines saw it, they returned to Ekron that day.

16 ªJosh. 13:3; Judg. 3:3

17 And [a]these are the golden tumors which the Philistines returned for a guilt offering to the LORD: one for Ashdod, one for Gaza, one for Ashkelon, one for Gath, one for Ekron;

★**17** ª1 Sam. 6:4

18 and the golden mice, according to the number of all the cities of the Philistines belonging to the five lords, [a]both of fortified

18 ªDeut. 3:5 ᵇ1 Sam. 6:14, 15

6:4-5 The Philistine priests and diviners suggested that an offering of golden images of the mice and sores would appease the God of Israel and bring an end to the severe judgment.
6:7 *milch cows.* Milk cows still nursing their young.
6:9 The cows going away from their calves *would be a clear indication* that they were being led by a supernatural power, and would signify to the Philistines that the plague had

indeed been the judgment of God.
6:12 *Beth-shemesh* was a levitical city (Josh. 21:16) of the Israelites in the Sorek Valley, 8 miles E. of Ekron, 15 miles W. of Jerusalem.
6:17 *Ashkelon* is located on the Mediterranean coast, 9½ miles S. of Ashdod. *Gaza* is also on the coast, 12 miles S. of Ashkelon. There is no indication that the Ark was in Ashkelon or Gaza, but they came under the plague which fell on all the Philistines (6:4).

cities and of country villages. ᵇThe large stone on which they set the ark of the Lᴏʀᴅ *is a witness* to this day in the field of Joshua the Beth-shemite.

19 And ᵃHe struck down some of the men of Beth-shemesh because they had looked into the ark of the Lᴏʀᴅ. He struck down of all the people, 50,070 men, and the people mourned because the Lᴏʀᴅ had struck the people with a great slaughter.

20 And the men of Beth-shemesh said, "ᵃWho is able to stand before the Lᴏʀᴅ, this holy God? And to whom shall He go up from us?"

21 So they sent messengers to the inhabitants of ᵃKiriath-jearim, saying, "The Philistines have brought back the ark of the Lᴏʀᴅ; come down and take it up to you."

7 And the men of Kiriath-jearim came and took the ark of the Lᴏʀᴅ and ᵃbrought it into the house of Abinadab on the hill, and consecrated Eleazar his son to keep the ark of the Lᴏʀᴅ.

2 And it came about from the day that the ark remained at Kiriath-jearim that the time was long, for it was twenty years; and all the house of Israel lamented after the Lᴏʀᴅ.

C His Revival Ministry to Israel, 7:3-17

3 Then Samuel spoke to all the house of Israel, saying, "ᵃIf you return to the Lᴏʀᴅ with all your heart, ᵇremove the foreign gods and the ᶜAshtaroth from among you and ᵈdirect your hearts to the Lᴏʀᴅ and ᵉserve Him alone; and He will deliver you from the hand of the Philistines."

4 So the sons of Israel removed the Baals and the Ashtaroth and served the Lᴏʀᴅ alone.

5 Then Samuel said, "Gather all Israel to ᵃMizpah, and ᵇI will pray to the Lᴏʀᴅ for you."

6 And they gathered to Mizpah, and drew water and ᵃpoured it out before the Lᴏʀᴅ, and ᵇfasted on that day, and said there, "ᶜWe have sinned against the Lᴏʀᴅ." And Samuel judged the sons of Israel at Mizpah.

7 Now when the Philistines heard that the sons of Israel had gathered to Mizpah, the lords of the Philistines went up against Israel. And when the sons of Israel heard it, ᵃthey were afraid of the Philistines.

8 Then the sons of Israel said to Samuel, "ᵃDo not cease to cry to the Lᴏʀᴅ our God for us, that He may save us from the hand of the Philistines."

9 And Samuel took ᵃa suckling lamb and offered it for a whole burnt offering to the Lᴏʀᴅ; and Samuel cried to the Lᴏʀᴅ for Israel and ᵇthe Lᴏʀᴅ answered him.

10 Now Samuel was offering up the burnt offering, and the Philistines drew near to battle against Israel. But ᵃthe Lᴏʀᴅ thundered with a great thunder on that day against the Philistines

---

Marginal references

★19 ᵃEx. 19:21; Num. 4:5, 15, 20; 2 Sam. 6:7

20 ᵃLev. 11:44, 45; 2 Sam. 6:9; Mal. 3:2; Rev. 6:17

★21 ᵃJosh. 9:17; 15:9, 60; 1 Chr. 13:5, 6

1 ᵃ2 Sam. 6:3, 4

★3 ᵃ1 Kin. 8:48; Is. 55:7; Hos. 6:1; Joel 2:12-14 ᵇGen. 35:2; Josh. 24:14, 23; Judg. 10:16 ᶜJudg. 2:13; 1 Sam. 31:10 ᵈDeut. 13:4; 2 Chr. 19:3 ᵉDeut. 6:13; 10:20; 13:4; Josh. 24:14; Matt. 4:10; Luke 4:8

★4

★5 ᵃJudg. 10:17; 20:1 ᵇ1 Sam. 8:6; 12:17-19

★6 ᵃ1 Sam. 1:15; Ps. 62:8; Lam. 2:19 ᵇLev. 16:29; Neh. 9:1 ᶜJudg. 10:10; 1 Kin. 8:47; Ps. 106:6

7 ᵃ1 Sam. 13:6; 17:11

8 ᵃ1 Sam. 12:19-24; Is. 37:4

9 ᵃLev. 22:27 ᵇPs. 99:6; Jer. 15:1

10 ᵃ1 Sam. 2:10; 2 Sam. 22:14, 15; Ps. 29:3, 4 ᵇJosh. 10:10; Ps. 18:14

6:19 The men of Beth-shemesh were guilty of the presumptuous sin of gazing into the Ark, apparently a violation of Num. 4:20 (cf. Num. 4:5-6, 15-20). The number 50,070 is doubted by conservative scholars and is probably a *copyist's error. The number in the LXX* (Greek O.T.) and the writings of Josephus (*Antiq.* 6.1.4) is 70.

6:21 *Kiriath-jearim* is located 10 miles W. of Jerusalem. The Ark was not returned to Shiloh, for archaeological data indicates that the city was destroyed about 1050 B.C. (cf. Jer. 26:9), perhaps after the battle at Aphek (1 Sam. 4).

7:3 *Ashtaroth.* The plural form of Ashtareth, a Canaanite fertility goddess and the female counterpart of Baal (see note on Hos. 2:13). Canaanite cultic religion had filtered into Israelite worship. Samuel promised deliverance for repentance.

7:4 *Baals.* The plural of Baal, the supreme fertility deity of the Canaanites, whose domain was the sky, from which he fertilized the land.

7:5 *Mizpah*, located at Tell en-Nasbeh, about 7 miles N. of Jerusalem. Samuel was a praying prophet (cf. 8:6; 12:19, 23; Jer. 15:1).

7:6 The outpouring of water was a sign of repentance.

and [b]confused them, so that they were routed before Israel.

11 And the men of Israel went out of Mizpah and pursued the Philistines, and struck them down as far as below Beth-car.

★12 [a]Gen. 35:14; Josh. 4:9; 24:26

12 Then Samuel [a]took a stone and set it between Mizpah and Shen, and named it Ebenezer, saying, "Thus far the Lord has helped us."

13 [a]Judg. 13:1-15
[b]1 Sam. 13:5

13 [a]So the Philistines were subdued and [b]they did not come anymore within the border of Israel. And the hand of the Lord was against the Philistines all the days of Samuel.

★14 [a]Num. 13:29; Josh. 10:5-10

14 And the cities which the Philistines had taken from Israel were restored to Israel, from Ekron even to Gath; and Israel delivered their territory from the hand of the Philistines. So there was peace between Israel and [a]the Amorites.

15 [a]1 Sam. 7:6

15 Now Samuel [a]judged Israel all the days of his life.

★16-17
16 [a]Gen. 28:19; 35:6
[b]Josh. 5:9, 10
[c]1 Sam. 7:5

16 And he used to go annually on circuit to [a]Bethel and [b]Gilgal and [c]Mizpah, and he judged Israel in all these places.

17 [a]1 Sam. 1:1, 19; 2:11
[b]Judg. 21:4

17 Then his return was to [a]Ramah, for his house was there, and there he judged Israel; and he [b]built there an altar to the Lord.

D His Warning to Israel Concerning their Demand for a King, 8:1-22

1 [a]Deut. 16:18, 19

8 And it came about when Samuel was old that [a]he appointed his sons judges over Israel.

★ 2 [a]Gen. 22:19; 1 Kin. 19:3; Amos 5:5

2 Now the name of his first-born was Joel, and the name of his second, Abijah; they were judging in [a]Beersheba.

★ 3 [a]Ex. 23:6, 8; Deut. 16:19

3 His sons, however, did not walk in his ways, but turned aside after dishonest gain and [a]took bribes and perverted justice.

4 [a]1 Sam. 7:17

4 Then all the elders of Israel gathered together and came to Samuel at [a]Ramah;

★ 5 [a]Deut. 17:14, 15

5 and they said to him, "Behold, you have grown old, and your sons do not walk in your ways. Now [a]appoint a king for us to judge us like all the nations."

6 [a]1 Sam. 12:17
[b]1 Sam. 15:11

6 But the thing was [a]displeasing in the sight of Samuel when they said, "Give us a king to judge us." And [b]Samuel prayed to the Lord.

7 [a]Ex. 16:8; 1 Sam. 10:19

7 And the Lord said to Samuel, "Listen to the voice of the people in regard to all that they say to you, for [a]they have not rejected you, but they have rejected Me from being king over them.

8 "Like all the deeds which they have done since the day that I brought them up from Egypt even to this day—in that they have forsaken Me and served other gods—so they are doing to you also.

9 [a]Ezek. 3:18 [b]1 Sam. 8:11-18; 10:25

9 "Now then, listen to their voice; [a]however, you shall solemnly warn them and tell them of [b]the procedure of the king who will reign over them."

★10-18

10 [a]1 Sam. 8:4

10 So Samuel spoke all the words of the Lord to [a]the people who had asked of him a king.

7:12 *Ebenezer.* Lit., stone of help (cf. 4:1).

7:14 The third major battle with the Philistines resulted in a victory for Israel and the recovery of Israelite territory as far W. as Ekron and Gath. *Amorites.* A general name for the original inhabitants of Canaan (see note on Gen. 14:5-7).

7:16-17 Samuel was a circuit-rider judge. He had civil (7:16), religious (7:6, 17), and military responsibilities (12:11).

8:2 *Beersheba.* A city located at the southern extremity of Israel (cf. 3:20), 48 miles S. of Jerusalem.

8:3 Samuel's sons used their office and authority for personal gain. This corruption is a reflec-

tion on Samuel who was perhaps too involved in his ministry to watch over the spiritual welfare of his family. As a result, God was dishonored.

8:5 Three reasons are given for the elders' request: (1) the corruption of Samuel's sons, (2) the desire to conform to the pattern of others, (3) the need for a military commander (8:20). God had made provision in the law for the appointment of a king (Deut. 17:14-15), but the error of the elders was in their attitude and in their failure to recognize God as their true King (8:7; 12:12).

8:10-18 The Lord revealed to Samuel the problems that having a king would bring: the

11 And he said, "*a*This will be the procedure of the king who will reign over you: *b*he will take your sons and place *them* for himself in his chariots and among his horsemen and *c*they will run before his chariots.

12 "And *a*he will appoint for himself commanders of thousands and of fifties, and *some* to do his plowing and to reap his harvest and to make his weapons of war and equipment for his chariots.

13 "He will also take your daughters for perfumers and cooks and bakers.

14 "And *a*he will take the best of your fields and your vineyards and your olive groves, and give *them* to his servants.

15 "And he will take a tenth of your seed and of your vineyards, and give to his officers and to his servants.

16 "He will also take your male servants and your female servants and your best young men and your donkeys, and use *them* for his work.

17 "He will take a tenth of your flocks, and you yourselves will become his servants.

18 "Then *a*you will cry out in that day because of your king whom you have chosen for yourselves, but *b*the LORD will not answer you in that day."

19 Nevertheless, the people *a*refused to listen to the voice of Samuel, and they said, "No, but there shall be a king over us,

20 *a*that we also may be like all the nations, that our king may judge us and go out before us and fight our battles."

21 Now after Samuel had heard all the words of the people, *a*he repeated them in the LORD's hearing.

22 And the LORD said to Samuel, "*a*Listen to their voice, and appoint them a king." So Samuel said to the men of Israel, "Go every man to his city."

II SAUL, THE FIRST KING, 9:1–31:13
A The Rise of Saul, 9:1–11:15
1 The choosing of Saul, 9:1–27

9 Now there was a man of Benjamin whose name was *a*Kish the son of Abiel, the son of Zeror, the son of Becorath, the son of Aphiah, the son of a Benjamite, a mighty man of valor.

2 And he had a son whose name was *a*Saul, a *a*choice and handsome *man,* and there was not a more handsome person than he among the sons of Israel; *b*from his shoulders and up he was taller than any of the people.

3 Now the donkeys of Kish, Saul's father, were lost. So Kish said to his son Saul, "Take now with you one of the servants, and arise, go search for the donkeys."

4 And he passed through *a*the hill country of Ephraim and passed through the land of *b*Shalishah, but they did not find *them.* Then they passed through the land of *c*Shaalim, but *they were*

Cross references (margin)

11 *a*Deut. 17:14-20; 1 Sam. 10:25 *b*1 Sam. 14:52 *c*2 Sam. 15:1

12 *a*Num. 31:14; 1 Sam. 22:7

14 *a*1 Kin. 21:7; Ezek. 46:18

18 *a*Is. 8:21 *b*Prov. 1:25-28; Is. 1:15; Mic. 3:4

19 *a*Is. 66:4; Jer. 44:16

★**20** *a*1 Sam. 8:5

21 *a*Judg. 11:11

★**22** *a*1 Sam. 8:7

1 *a*1 Sam. 14:51; 1 Chr. 8:33; 9:36-39

2 *a*1 Sam. 10:24 *b*1 Sam. 10:23

★**4** *a*Josh. 24:33 *b*2 Kin. 4:42 *c*Josh. 19:42

---

drafting of young men and women (vv. 11–13), the taxation of crops and flocks (vv. 14–15, 17a), the appropriation of servants and animals (v. 16), and the loss of personal liberty (v. 17b).

8:20 Conformity to the ways of unbelievers is displeasing to the Lord and indicates spiritual decline (cf. 3 John 11).

8:22 Was it God's will for Israel to have a king? Prophecies dating back to Moses indicate that it was (Gen. 49:10; Num. 24:17; Deut. 17:14-20). It was not God's preceptive will for Israel to acquire a king in the manner in which they were doing it (i.e., at the wrong time and from improper motives), but God allowed it

because this was within His permissive will. God in His sovereignty allows even the evil deeds of men to accomplish His purposes (cf. Gen. 50:20; Acts 2:23). With respect to sin and evil, God wills to permit it, but not to effect it, for He cannot commit evil (see note on Isa. 45:7).

9:4 The search would have taken Saul north from his home at Gibeah (10:26) through *Shalishah* and *Shaalim* (unidentified) where he then circled back through Benjamin to Ramah, the home of Samuel (7:17; 9:18). Having been privately anointed by Samuel, he returned home by way of Gibeath-haelohim ("hill of God," 10:5, 10).

not *there.* Then he passed through the land of the Benjamites, but they did not find *them.*

★ **5** *a*1 Sam. 1:1 *b*1 Sam. 10:2

5 When they came to the land of *a*Zuph, Saul said to his servant who was with him, "Come, and let us return, *b*lest my father cease *to be concerned* about the donkeys and become anxious for us."

6 *a*Deut. 33:1; 1 Kin. 13:1; 2 Kin. 5:8 *b*1 Sam. 3:19 *c*Gen. 24:42

6 And he said to him, "Behold now, there is *a*a man of God in this city, and the man is held in honor; *b*all that he says surely comes true. Now let us go there, *c*perhaps he can tell us about our journey on which we have set out."

7 *a*1 Kin. 14:3; 2 Kin. 5:15; 8:8, 9; Ezek. 13:19

7 Then Saul said to his servant, "But behold, if we go, what shall we bring the man? For the bread is gone from our sack and there is *a*no present to bring to the man of God. What do we have?"

8 *a*1 Sam. 9:6

8 And the servant answered Saul again and said, "Behold, I have in my hand a fourth of a shekel of silver; I will give *it* to the man of God and he will *a*tell us our way."

★ **9** *a*2 Sam. 24:11; 2 Kin. 17:13; 1 Chr. 9:22; 26:28; 29:29; Is. 30:10; Amos 7:12

9 (Formerly in Israel, when a man went to inquire of God, he used to say, "Come, and let us go to the seer"; for *he who is called* a prophet now was formerly called *a*a seer.)

10 Then Saul said to his servant, "Well said; come, let us go." So they went to the city where the man of God was.

11 *a*Gen. 24:11, 15; 29:8, 9; Ex. 2:16

11 As they went up the slope to the city, *a*they found young women going out to draw water, and said to them, "Is the seer here?"

★ **12** *a*Gen. 31:54; Num. 28:11-15; 1 Kin. 3:2 *b*1 Sam. 7:17; 10:5

12 And they answered them and said, "He is; see, *he is* ahead of you. Hurry now, for he has come into the city today, for *a*the people have a sacrifice on *b*the high place today.

13 *a*Luke 9:16; John 6:11

13 "As soon as you enter the city you will find him before he goes up to the high place to eat, for the people will not eat until he comes, because *a*he must bless the sacrifice; afterward those who are invited will eat. Now therefore, go up for you will find him at once."

14 So they went up to the city. As they came into the city, behold, Samuel was coming out toward them to go up to the high place.

15 *a*1 Sam. 15:1; Acts 13:21

15 Now a day before Saul's coming, *a*the LORD had revealed *this* to Samuel saying,

★ **16** *a*1 Sam. 10:1 *b*Ex. 3:7, 9

16 "About this time tomorrow I will send you a man from the land of Benjamin, and *a*you shall anoint him to be prince over My people Israel; and he shall deliver My people from the hand of the Philistines. For *b*I have regarded My people, because their cry has come to Me."

17 *a*1 Sam. 16:12

17 When Samuel saw Saul, the LORD said to him, "*a*Behold, the man of whom I spoke to you! This one shall rule over My people."

★ **18**

18 Then Saul approached Samuel in the gate, and said, "Please tell me where the seer's house is."

19 And Samuel answered Saul and said, "I am the seer. Go up before me to the high place, for you shall eat with me today; and in the morning I will let you go, and will tell you all that is on your mind.

9:5 *Zuph.* A region of the hill country of Ephraim (cf. 1:1).

9:9 This explanatory information clarifies for later readers that a "seer" (from "to see") became known in later times as a "prophet." There may once have been a distinction, but not at the time of this writing (cf. v. 11).

9:12 *high place.* An elevated place of worship and sacrifice located on a hill or an artificial platform. The idea was essentially Canaanite

(cf. Deut. 12:2-5), but Israel used such facilities before the construction of the Temple (see note on 1 Kings 3:2).

9:16 Anointing involved a consecration or setting apart for service. It was a religious act which established a special relationship between God and the king who served as His representative and ruler over the people.

9:18 The providence of God in bringing Saul to Samuel is very clear. God was in control.

20 "And [a]as for your donkeys which were lost three days ago, do not set your mind on them, for they have been found. And [b]for whom is all that is desirable in Israel? Is it not for you and for all your father's household?"

21 And Saul answered and said, "[a]Am I not a Benjamite, of [b]the smallest of the tribes of Israel, and my family the least of all the families of the tribe of Benjamin? Why then do you speak to me in this way?"

22 Then Samuel took Saul and his servant and brought them into the hall, and gave them a place at the head of those who were invited, who were about thirty men.

23 And Samuel said to the cook, "Bring the portion that I gave you, concerning which I said to you, 'Set it aside.'"

24 Then the cook [a]took up the leg with what was on it and set it before Saul. And Samuel said, "Here is what has been reserved! Set it before you and eat, because it has been kept for you until the appointed time, since I said I have invited the people." So Saul ate with Samuel that day.

25 When they came down from the high place into the city, Samuel spoke with Saul [a]on the roof.

26 And they arose early; and it came about at daybreak that Samuel called to Saul on the roof, saying, "Get up, that I may send you away." So Saul arose, and both he and Samuel went out into the street.

27 As they were going down to the edge of the city, Samuel said to Saul, "Say to the servant that he might go ahead of us and pass on, but you remain standing now, that I may proclaim the word of God to you."

2   The coronation of Saul,
10:1-27

10 Then [a]Samuel took the flask of oil, poured it on his head, [b]kissed him and said, "Has not [c]the LORD anointed you a ruler over [d]His inheritance?

2 "When you go from me today, then you will find two men close to [a]Rachel's tomb in the territory of Benjamin at Zelzah; and they will say to you, '[b]The donkeys which you went to look for have been found. Now behold, your father has ceased to be concerned about the donkeys and is anxious for you, saying, "What shall I do about my son?"'

3 "Then you will go on further from there, and you will come as far as the [a]oak of Tabor, and there three men going up [b]to God at Bethel will meet you, one carrying three kids, another carrying three loaves of bread, and another carrying a jug of wine;

4 and they will greet you and give you two loaves of bread, which you will accept from their hand.

5 "Afterward you will come to [a]the hill of God where the Philistine garrison is; and it shall be as soon as you have come there to the city, that you will meet [b]a group of prophets coming down from the high place with harp, tambourine, flute, and a lyre before them, and [c]they will be prophesying.

6 "Then [a]the Spirit of the LORD will come upon you mightily, and [b]you shall prophesy with them and be changed into another man.

★20 [a]1 Sam. 9:3 [b]1 Sam. 8:5; 12:13

21 [a]1 Sam. 15:17 [b]Judg. 20:46-48

★24 [a]Ex. 29:22, 27; Lev. 7:32, 33; Num. 18:18

25 [a]Deut. 22:8; Luke 5:19; Acts 10:9

1 [a]Ex. 30:23-33; 1 Sam. 16:13; 2 Kin. 9:3, 6 [b]Ps. 2:12 [c]1 Sam. 16:13; 26:9; 2 Sam. 1:14 [d]Deut. 32:9; Ps. 78:71

★ 2-5

2 [a]Gen. 35:16-20; 48:7 [b]1 Sam. 9:3-5

3 [a]Gen. 35:8 [b]Gen. 28:19; 35:1, 3, 7

5 [a]1 Sam. 13:2, 3 [b]1 Sam. 19:20; 2 Kin. 2:3, 5, 15 [c]2 Kin. 3:15; 1 Chr. 25:1-6; 1 Cor. 14:1

★ 6 [a]Num. 11:25, 29; Judg. 14:6 [b]1 Sam. 10:10; 19:23, 24

9:20 The contrast is between the lost donkeys and all that is precious or desirable.

9:24 Giving Saul the shoulder of the sacrifice (cf. Lev. 7:32-33) was intended to honor him above all the other guests.

10:2-5 Saul was promised three signs, which would serve to authenticate Samuel's authority to anoint him king and to confirm God's will in the matter.

10:6 The Spirit coming upon Saul designated him as the true successor to the judges (see note on Judg. 3:10).

★ 7-8

7 aEccl.
9:10 bJosh.
1:5; Judg.
6:12; Heb.
13:5

8 a1 Sam.
11:14; 13:8
b1 Sam.
11:15
c1 Sam. 13:8

★ 9 a1 Sam.
10:6

10 a1 Sam.
10:5, 6;
19:20

★11-12

11 a1 Sam.
19:24; Amos
7:14, 15;
Matt. 13:54-
57; John
7:15

12 a1 Sam.
19:23, 24

14 a1 Sam.
14:50
b1 Sam.
9:3-6

16 a1 Sam.
9:20

7 "And it shall be when these signs come to you, ado for yourself what the occasion requires; for bGod is with you.

8 "And ayou shall go down before me to Gilgal; and behold, I will come down to you to offer burnt offerings and bsacrifice peace offerings. cYou shall wait seven days until I come to you and show you what you should do."

9 Then it happened when he turned his back to leave Samuel, God achanged his heart; and all those signs came about on that day.

10 aWhen they came to the hill there, behold, a group of prophets met him; and the Spirit of God came upon him mightily, so that he prophesied among them.

11 And it came about, when all who knew him previously saw that he prophesied now with the prophets, that the people said to one another, "What has happened to the son of Kish? aIs Saul also among the prophets?"

12 And a man there answered and said, "Now, who is their father?" Therefore it became a proverb: "aIs Saul also among the prophets?"

13 When he had finished prophesying, he came to the high place.

14 Now aSaul's uncle said to him and his servant, "Where did you go?" And he said, "bTo look for the donkeys. When we saw that they could not be found, we went to Samuel."

15 And Saul's uncle said, "Please tell me what Samuel said to you."

16 So Saul said to his uncle, "aHe told us plainly that the donkeys had been found." But he did not tell him about the matter of the kingdom which Samuel had mentioned.

17 Thereafter Samuel called the apeople together to the Lord at Mizpah;

18 and he said to the sons of Israel, "aThus says the Lord, the God of Israel, 'I brought Israel up from Egypt, and I delivered you from the hand of the Egyptians, and from the power of all the kingdoms that were oppressing you.'

19 "But you atoday rejected your God, who delivers you from all your calamities and your distresses; yet you have said, 'No, but set a king over us!' Now therefore, bpresent yourselves before the Lord by your tribes and by your clans."

20 Thus Samuel brought all the tribes of Israel near, and the tribe of Benjamin was taken by lot.

21 Then he brought the tribe of Benjamin near by its families, and the Matrite family was taken. And Saul the son of Kish was taken; but when they looked for him, he could not be found.

22 Therefore athey inquired further of the Lord, "Has the man come here yet?" So the Lord said, "Behold, he is hiding himself by the baggage."

23 So they ran and took him from there, and when he stood among the people, ahe was taller than any of the people from his shoulders upward.

24 And Samuel said to all the people, "Do you see him awhom the Lord has chosen? Surely there is no one like him among all the people." So all the people shouted and said, "bLong live the king!"

★17 aJudg.
20:1; 1 Sam.
7:5

18 aJudg.
6:8, 9

19 a1 Sam.
8:6, 7; 12:12
bJosh. 7:14-
18; 24:1;
Prov. 16:33

★20-21

22 a1 Sam.
23:2, 4

23 a1 Sam.
9:2

24 aDeut.
17:15;
2 Sam. 21:6
b1 Kin. 1:25,
34, 39

10:7-8 Saul was instructed to do nothing independently of Samuel, but he disobeyed (13:8-10).

10:9 *God changed his heart.* God gave Saul the qualities necessary to be king and deliverer of Israel.

10:11-12 Some who had known Saul previously were surprised to see someone of a higher class acting like one of the ecstatic prophets, who were of dubious parentage.

10:17 *Mizpah.* See 7:5.

10:20-21 *was taken by lot.* Lot casting was a means of determining God's will through yes and no questions (Josh. 7:15-18), a practice used prior to the permanent indwelling ministry of the Holy Spirit (Acts 1:26).

25 Then Samuel told the people [a]the ordinances of the kingdom, and wrote *them* in the book and [b]placed *it* before the LORD. And Samuel sent all the people away, each one to his house.

26 And Saul also went [a]to his house at Gibeah; and the valiant *men* whose hearts God had touched went with him.

27 But certain [a]worthless men said, "How can this one deliver us?" And they despised him and [b]did not bring him any present. But he kept silent.

3 The conquest of the Ammonites, 11:1-15

11 Now [a]Nahash the Ammonite came up and besieged [b]Jabesh-gilead; and all the men of Jabesh said to Nahash, "Make [c]a covenant with us and we will serve you."

2 But Nahash the Ammonite said to them, "I will make *it* with you on this condition, [a]that I will gouge out the right eye of every one of you, thus I will make it [b]a reproach on all Israel."

3 And [a]the elders of Jabesh said to him, "Let us alone for seven days, that we may send messengers throughout the territory of Israel. Then, if there is no one to deliver us, we will come out to you."

4 Then the messengers came [a]to Gibeah of Saul and spoke these words in the hearing of the people, and all the people [b]lifted up their voices and wept.

5 Now behold, Saul was coming from the field [a]behind the oxen; and he said, "What is *the*

matter with the people that they weep?" So they related to him the words of the men of Jabesh.

6 Then [a]the Spirit of God came upon Saul mightily when he heard these words, and he became very angry.

7 And he took a yoke of oxen and [a]cut them in pieces, and sent *them* throughout the territory of Israel by the hand of messengers, saying, "[b]Whoever does not come out after Saul and after Samuel, so shall it be done to his oxen." Then the dread of the LORD fell on the people, and they came out [c]as one man.

8 And he numbered them in [a]Bezek; and the [b]sons of Israel were 300,000, and the men of Judah 30,000.

9 And they said to the messengers who had come, "Thus you shall say to the men of Jabesh-gilead, 'Tomorrow, by the time the sun is hot, you shall have deliverance.'" So the messengers went and told the men of Jabesh; and they were glad.

10 Then the men of Jabesh said, "[a]Tomorrow we will come out to you, and you may do to us whatever seems good to you."

11 And it happened the next morning that Saul put the people [a]in three companies; and they came into the midst of the camp at the morning watch, and struck down the Ammonites until the heat of the day. And it came about that those who survived were scattered, so that no two of them were left together.

12 Then the people said to Samuel, "[a]Who is he that said, 'Shall Saul reign over us?' [b]Bring

---

10:26 *Gibeah,* located just 3 miles N. of Jerusalem on the main road to Shechem, was Saul's home and the first capital of the monarchy.

10:27 Saul had his supporters (10:26) and his political enemies as well, but he held his peace in order not to provoke the situation.

11:1 Chapter 11 shows how the initial opposition against Saul was overcome, and how the king proved himself. Both Jabesh-gilead and the territory of the Ammonites were located E. of the Jordan.

11:2 The loss of the right eye would disable a

warrior, for the left eye was generally concealed behind his shield.

11:3 Nahash agreed to the proposal, for he was apparently not prepared to take the city by force and did not expect any help to come to the inhabitants of Jabesh.

11:8 *Bezek* was 17 miles N. of Shechem.

11:11 *morning watch.* The last of three night watches (Lam. 2:19; Judg. 7:19; Exod. 14:24-27), in the early morning hours. Saul employed a surprise tactic.

Marginal references:

25 [a]Deut. 17:14-20; 1 Sam. 8:11-18 [b]Deut. 31:26

★**26** [a]1 Sam. 11:4; 15:34

★**27** [a]Deut. 13:13; 1 Sam. 25:17 [b]1 Kin. 10:25; 2 Chr. 17:5

★ **1** [a]1 Sam. 12:12 [b]Judg. 21:8; 1 Sam. 31:11 [c]Gen. 26:28; 1 Kin. 20:34; Job 41:4; Ezek. 17:13

★ **2** [a]Num. 16:14 [b]1 Sam. 17:26; Ps. 44:13

★ **3** [a]1 Sam. 8:4

4 [a]1 Sam. 10:26; 15:34 [b]Gen. 27:38; Judg. 2:4; 20:23, 26; 21:2; 1 Sam. 30:4

5 [a]1 Kin. 19:19

6 [a]Judg. 3:10; 6:34; 11:29; 13:25; 14:6; 1 Sam. 10:10; 16:13

7 [a]Judg. 19:29 [b]Judg. 21:5, 8 [c]Judg. 20:1

★ **8** [a]Judg. 1:5 [b]Judg. 20:2

10 [a]1 Sam. 11:3

★**11** [a]Judg. 7:16, 20

12 [a]1 Sam. 10:27 [b]Luke 19:27

the men, that we may put them to death."

13 But Saul said, "[a]Not a man shall be put to death this day, for today [b]the LORD has accomplished deliverance in Israel."

14 Then Samuel said to the people, "Come and let us go to [a]Gilgal and [b]renew the kingdom there."

15 So all the people went to Gilgal, and there they made Saul king [a]before the LORD in Gilgal. There they also [b]offered sacrifices of peace offerings before the LORD; and there Saul and all the men of Israel rejoiced greatly.

B The Reminder by Samuel, 12:1-25

12 Then Samuel said to all Israel, "Behold, [a]I have listened to your voice in all that you said to me, and I [b]have appointed a king over you.

2 "And now, [a]here is the king walking before you, but [b]I am old and gray, and behold [c]my sons are with you. And [d]I have walked before you from my youth even to this day.

3 "Here I am; bear witness against me before the LORD and [a]His anointed. [b]Whose ox have I taken, or whose donkey have I taken, or whom have I defrauded? Whom have I oppressed, or [c]from whose hand have I taken a bribe to blind my eyes with it? I will restore it to you."

4 And they said, "You have not defrauded us, or oppressed us, or taken anything from any man's hand."

5 And he said to them, "The LORD is witness against you, and His anointed is witness this day that [a]you have found nothing [b]in my hand." And they said, "[a]He is witness."

6 Then Samuel said to the people, "It is the LORD who [a]appointed Moses and Aaron and who brought your fathers up from the land of Egypt.

7 "So now, take your stand, [a]that I may plead with you before the LORD concerning all the righteous acts of the LORD which He did for you and your fathers.

8 "[a]When Jacob went into Egypt and [b]your fathers cried out to the LORD, then [c]the LORD sent Moses and Aaron [d]who brought your fathers out of Egypt and settled them in this place.

9 "But [a]they forgot the LORD their God, so [b]He sold them into the hand of Sisera, captain of the army of Hazor, and [c]into the hand of the Philistines and [d]into the hand of the king of Moab, and they fought against them.

10 "And [a]they cried out to the LORD and said, 'We have sinned because we have forsaken the LORD and have served [b]the Baals and the Ashtaroth; but [c]now deliver us from the hands of our enemies, and we will serve Thee.'

11 "Then the LORD sent [a]Jerubbaal and [b]Bedan and [c]Jephthah and [d]Samuel, and delivered you from the hands of your enemies all around, so that you lived in security.

12 "When you saw [a]that Nahash the king of the sons of Ammon came against you, you said to me, '[b]No, but a king shall reign

Center cross-references

13 [a]1 Sam. 10:27; 2 Sam. 19:22 [b]Ex. 14:13; 30; 1 Sam. 19:5

★**14-15**

14 [a]1 Sam. 7:16; 10:8 [b]1 Sam. 10:25

15 [a]1 Sam. 10:17 [b]1 Sam. 10:8

★ **1** [a]1 Sam. 8:7, 9, 22 [b]1 Sam. 10:24; 11:14, 15

2 [a]1 Sam. 8:20 [b]1 Sam. 8:1, 5 [c]1 Sam. 8:3 [d]1 Sam. 3:10, 19, 20

★ **3** [a]1 Sam. 10:1; 24:6; 2 Sam. 1:14 [b]Ex. 20:17; Num. 16:15; Acts 20:33 [c]Ex. 23:8; Deut. 16:19

5 [a]Acts 23:9, 24:20 [b]Ex. 22:4

★ **6-12**

6 [a]Ex. 6:26; Mic. 6:4

7 [a]Ezek. 20:35; Mic. 6:1-5

8 [a]Gen. 46:5, 6 [b]Ex. 2:23-25 [c]Ex. 3:10; 4:14-16 [d]1 Sam. 10:18

9 [a]Deut. 32:18; Judg. 3:7 [b]Judg. 4:2 [c]Judg. 3:31; 10:7; 13:1 [d]Judg. 3:12-30

★**10** [a]Judg. 10:10 [b]Judg. 2:13; 3:7 [c]Judg. 10:15, 16

★**11** [a]Judg. 6:31, 32; 7:1 [b]Judg. 4:6; 11:1 [c]Judg. 11:29 [d]1 Sam. 3:20

12 [a]1 Sam. 11:1, 2 [b]1 Sam. 8:6, 19 [c]Judg. 8:23; 1 Sam. 8:7

11:14-15 The ceremonies at Gilgal involved a confirmation of the kingdom in the hands of Saul, and an affirmation of commitment to the king.

12:1 In Samuel's farewell address he defended his judicial administration and relinquished leadership of the tribes to Saul. Samuel did, however, continue his priestly and prophetic functions.

12:3 Samuel reminded the people of his own honesty and integrity (in contrast to his sons' failures, cf. 8:3, 5).

12:6-12 Samuel proceeded to rehearse the history of God's righteous acts toward Israel.

12:10 *Baals and the Ashtaroth.* See note on 7:4.

12:11 *Bedan.* Possibly an unknown judge (but what purpose would this serve in the argument?) but probably a copyist's error and intended to be a reference to Barak (so LXX and Syriac; cf. Heb. 11:32).

over us,' calthough the LORD your God *was* your king.

★13-18
13 a1 Sam.
10:24
b1 Sam. 8:5;
12:17, 19;
Hos. 13:11

13 "Now therefore, ahere is the king whom you have chosen, bwhom you have asked for, and behold, the LORD has set a king over you.

14 aJosh.
24:14

14 "aIf you will fear the LORD and serve Him, and listen to His voice and not rebel against the command of the LORD, then both you and also the king who reigns over you will follow the LORD your God.

15 aLev.
26:14, 15;
Josh. 24:20;
Is. 1:20
b1 Sam. 5:9
c1 Sam. 12:9

15 "And aif you will not listen to the voice of the LORD, but rebel against the command of the LORD, then bthe hand of the LORD will be against you, cas it was against your fathers.

16 aEx.
14:13, 31

16 "Even now, atake your stand and see this great thing which the LORD will do before your eyes.

★17-18

17 aProv.
26:1 b1 Sam.
7:9, 10;
James 5:16ff.
c1 Sam. 8:7

17 "aIs it not the wheat harvest today? bI will call to the LORD, that He may send thunder and rain. Then you will know and see that cyour wickedness is great which you have done in the sight of the LORD by asking for yourselves a king."

18 aEx.
14:31

18 So Samuel called to the LORD, and the LORD sent thunder and rain that day; and aall the people greatly feared the LORD and Samuel.

19 aEx. 9:28;
1 Sam.
12:23; Jer.
15:1; 1 John
5:16 b1 Sam.
12:17, 20

19 Then all the people said to Samuel, "aPray for your servants to the LORD your God, so that we may not die, for we have added to all our sins bthis evil by asking for ourselves a king."

20 aDeut.
11:16

20 And Samuel said to the people, "Do not fear. You have committed all this evil, yet ado

not turn aside from following the LORD, but serve the LORD with all your heart.

21 aDeut.
11:16; Is.
41:29; Hab.
2:18

21 "And you must not turn aside, for *then you would go* after afutile things which can not profit or deliver, because they are futile.

★22 aDeut.
31:6; 1 Kin.
6:13 bEx.
32:12; Num.
14:13; Josh.
7:9; Ps.
106:8; Jer.
14:21 cDeut.
7:6-11; 1 Pet.
2:9

22 "For athe LORD will not abandon His people bon account of His great name, because the LORD chas been pleased to make you a people for Himself.

★23 aRom.
1:9; 1 Cor.
9:16; Col.
1:9; 1 Thess.
3:10; 2 Tim.
1:3 b1 Kin.
8:36; Ps.
34:11; Prov.
4:11

23 "Moreover, as for me, afar be it from me that I should sin against the LORD by ceasing to pray for you; but bI will instruct you in the good and right way.

24 aEccl.
12:13 bDeut.
10:21; Is.
5:12

24 "aOnly fear the LORD and serve Him in truth with all your heart; for consider bwhat great things He has done for you.

25 aIs. 1:20;
3:11 bJosh.
24:20
c1 Sam.
31:1-5; Hos.
10:3

25 "aBut if you still do wickedly, bboth you and your king cshall be swept away."

C The Rejection of Saul, 13:1–15:35

1 *His sinful offering*, 13:1-23

13 Saul was *forty* years old when he began to reign, and he reigned *thirty*-two years over Israel. ★ 1

2 a1 Sam.
13:5; 14:31
b1 Sam.
10:26

2 Now Saul chose for himself 3,000 men of Israel, of which 2,000 were with Saul in aMichmash and in the hill country of Bethel, while 1,000 were with Jonathan at bGibeah of Benjamin. But he sent away the rest of the people, each to his tent.

★ 3 a1 Sam.
10:5 b1 Sam.
13:16; 14:5
cJudg. 3:27;
6:34

3 And Jonathan smote athe garrison of the Philistines that was in bGeba, and the Philistines heard of *it*. Then Saul cblew the

---

12:13-18 Samuel warned Israel that the king would procure the anticipated deliverance only if they would fear the Lord and give up their rebellion against God.

12:17-18 Since rain during the wheat harvest (May-June) was uncommon, this thunderstorm was considered a sign from God.

12:22 God's name signifies His reputation and character.

12:23 Samuel regarded failure to pray as a sin against the Lord.

13:1 The original numbers in this verse have ap-

parently been lost in transmission. One way to understand the verse is this: "Saul was _____ years old when he began to reign, and he reigned _____ and two years over Israel." Another suggestion renders it: "Saul was one and _____ years old when he began to reign, and when he had reigned two years over Israel then Saul chose for himself 3,000 men of Israel . . ."

13:3 *Let the Hebrews hear.* I.e., of Jonathan's victory.

trumpet throughout the land, saying, "Let the Hebrews hear."

★ 4 ᵃGen. 34:30; Ex. 5:21; 2 Sam. 10:6

4 And all Israel heard the news that Saul had smitten the garrison of the Philistines, and also that Israel ᵃhad become odious to the Philistines. The people were then summoned to Saul at Gilgal.

★ 5 ᵃJosh. 11:4 ᵇJosh. 18:12; 1 Sam. 14:23

5 Now the Philistines assembled to fight with Israel, 30,000 chariots and 6,000 horsemen, and ᵃpeople like the sand which is on the seashore in abundance; and they came up and camped in Michmash, east of ᵇBeth-aven.

6 ᵃJudg. 6:2

6 When the men of Israel saw that they were in a strait (for the people were hard-pressed), then ᵃthe people hid themselves in caves, in thickets, in cliffs, in cellars, and in pits.

7 ᵃNum. 32:33

7 Also *some of* the Hebrews crossed the Jordan into the land of ᵃGad and Gilead. But as for Saul, he *was* still in Gilgal, and all the people followed him trembling.

★ 8-9

8 ᵃ1 Sam. 10:8

8 Now ᵃhe waited seven days, according to the appointed time set by Samuel, but Samuel did not come to Gilgal; and the people were scattering from him.

9 ᵃDeut. 12:5-14; 2 Sam. 24:25; 1 Kin. 3:4

9 So Saul said, "Bring to me the burnt offering and the peace offerings." And ᵃhe offered the burnt offering.

10 ᵃ1 Sam. 15:13

10 And it came about as soon as he finished offering the burnt offering, that behold, Samuel came; and ᵃSaul went out to meet him *and* to greet him.

★11-12

11 ᵃ1 Sam. 13:2, 5, 16, 23

11 But Samuel said, "What have you done?" And Saul said, "Because I saw that the people were scattering from me, and that

you did not come within the appointed days, and that ᵃthe Philistines were assembling at Michmash,

12 therefore I said, 'Now the Philistines will come down against me at Gilgal, and I have not asked the favor of the LORD.' So I forced myself and offered the burnt offering."

13 And Samuel said to Saul, "ᵃYou have acted foolishly; ᵇyou have not kept the commandment of the LORD your God, which He commanded you, for now the LORD would have established your kingdom over Israel ᶜforever.

★13-14

13 ᵃ2 Chr. 16:9 ᵇ1 Sam. 15:11, 22, 28 ᶜ1 Sam. 1:22

14 "But ᵃnow your kingdom shall not endure. ᵇThe LORD has sought out for Himself a man after His own heart, and the LORD has appointed him as ruler over His people, because you have not kept what the LORD commanded you."

14 ᵃ1 Sam. 15:28 ᵇActs 7:46; 13:22

15 Then Samuel arose and went up from Gilgal to ᵃGibeah of Benjamin. And Saul numbered the people who were present with him, ᵇabout six hundred men.

★15 ᵃ1 Sam. 13:2 ᵇ1 Sam. 13:2, 6, 7; 14:2

16 Now Saul and his son Jonathan and the people who were present with them were staying in ᵃGeba of Benjamin while the Philistines camped at Michmash.

16 ᵃ1 Sam. 13:2, 3

17 And ᵃthe raiders came from the camp of the Philistines in three companies: one company turned toward ᵇOphrah, to the land of Shual,

★17 ᵃ1 Sam. 14:15 ᵇJosh. 18:23

18 and another company turned toward ᵃBeth-horon, and another company turned toward the border which overlooks the

18 ᵃJosh. 16:3; 18:13, 14 ᵇNeh. 11:34

13:4 *the garrison.* This word may be translated "prefect," the assassination of whom was the signal for revolt.

13:5 Some translations read "3,000 chariots" instead of 30,000. The hill country where the battle was fought would not accommodate the larger number.

13:8-9 Saul was disobedient to God's spokesman. Rather than waiting on Samuel (10:8), he offered a burnt offering to unite the people and prepare for war. He resorted to situation ethics rather than biblical ethics, and then of-

fered excuses for his conduct (but no valid reasons, 13:10-12).

13:11-12 Saul tried to justify himself instead of confessing his sin.

13:13-14 Disobedience may eliminate opportunities for service by disqualifying one from a position of leadership.

13:15 *arose and went up.* From Gilgal in the valley to Gibeah in the mountains.

13:17 *raiders* = destroyers. Philistine reinforcements carrying out punitive expeditions against Israel to the N., W., and E. (vv. 17-18).

valley of [b]Zeboim toward the wilderness.

★19 a Judg.
5:8; 2 Kin.
24:14; Jer.
24:1; 29:2
b Judg. 5:8

19 Now [a]no blacksmith could be found in all the land of Israel, for the Philistines said, "Lest the Hebrews make [b]swords or spears."

★20

20 So all Israel went down to the Philistines, each to sharpen his plowshare, his mattock, his axe, and his hoe.

★21

21 And the charge was two-thirds of a shekel for the plowshares, the mattocks, the forks, and the axes, and to fix the hoes.

22 a Judg.
5:8

22 So it came about on the day of battle that [a]neither sword nor spear was found in the hands of any of the people who *were* with Saul and Jonathan, but they were found with Saul and his son Jonathan.

23 a 1 Sam.
14:1; 2 Sam.
23:14
b 1 Sam.
14:4, 5; Is.
10:28

23 And [a]the garrison of the Philistines went out to [b]the pass of Michmash.

2 *His rash vows,* 14:1-52

2 a 1 Sam.
13:15, 16
b Is. 10:28
c 1 Sam.
13:15

14 Now the day came that Jonathan, the son of Saul, said to the young man who was carrying his armor, "Come and let us cross over to the Philistines' garrison that is on yonder side." But he did not tell his father.

2 And Saul was staying in the outskirts of [a]Gibeah under the pomegranate tree which is in [b]Migron. And the people who *were* with him *were* [c]about six hundred men,

★ 3 a 1 Sam.
22:9-12, 20
b 1 Sam. 4:21
c 1 Sam. 1:3
d 1 Sam. 2:28

3 and Ahijah, the [a]son of Ahitub, [b]Ichabod's brother, the son of Phinehas, the son of Eli, the priest of the LORD at [c]Shiloh, [d]was wearing an ephod. And the people did not know that Jonathan had gone.

4 And [a]between the passes by which Jonathan sought to cross over to the Philistines' garrison, there was a sharp crag on the one side, and a sharp crag on the other side, and the name of the one was Bozez, and the name of the other Seneh.

4 a 1 Sam.
13:23

5 The one crag rose on the north opposite Michmash, and the other on the south opposite Geba.

6 Then Jonathan said to the young man who was carrying his armor, "Come and let us cross over to the garrison of [a]these uncircumcised; perhaps the LORD will work for us, for [b]the LORD is not restrained to save by many or by few."

6 a 1 Sam.
17:26, 36;
Jer. 9:25, 26
b Judg. 7:4,
7; 1 Sam.
17:46, 47;
Ps. 115:3;
135:6; Zech.
4:6; Matt.
19:26

7 And his armor bearer said to him, "Do all that is in your heart; turn yourself, *and* here I am with you according to your desire."

8 Then Jonathan said, "[a]Behold, we will cross over to the men and reveal ourselves to them.

8 a Judg.
7:9-14

9 "If they say to us, 'Wait until we come to you'; then we will stand in our place and not go up to them.

10 "But if they say, 'Come up to us,' then we will go up, for the LORD has given them into our hands; and [a]this shall be the sign to us."

10 a Gen.
24:14; Judg.
6:36

11 And when both of them revealed themselves to the garrison of the Philistines, the Philistines said, "Behold, [a]Hebrews are coming out of the holes where they have hidden themselves."

11 a 1 Sam.
13:6; 14:22

12 So the men of the garrison hailed Jonathan and his armor bearer and said, "Come up to us and [a]we will tell you something." And Jonathan said to his armor

12 a 1 Sam.
17:43, 44
b 2 Sam. 5:24

13:19 *blacksmith.* The Philistines had a monopoly on iron and metal-working craftsmen until the time of David (1 Chron. 22:3), accounting in large measure for their superior military power.

13:20 *mattock* = pickax.

13:21 A better translation would be: "And the charge was a pim (2/3 shekel) for the goads and mattocks, for the forks and axes, and to fix the goad points." For sharpening potential

weapons to be used against them, the Philistines naturally charged a high price.

14:3 *ephod.* The ephod was used to consult God in a time of crisis. This was probably done by means of the Urim and Thummim attached to the breastplate of the ephod (see notes on Exod. 28:6-30). By yes and no questions the wrong choice between two alternatives could be eliminated.

bearer, "Come up after me, for [b]the Lord has given them into the hands of Israel."

13 Then Jonathan climbed up on his hands and feet, with his armor bearer behind him; and they fell before Jonathan, and his armor bearer put some to death after him.

★14 **14** And that first slaughter which Jonathan and his armor bearer made was about twenty men within about half a furrow in an acre of land.

15 [a]1 Sam. 13:17, 18
[b]1 Sam. 7:10
[c]Gen. 35:5;
2 Kin. 7:6

15 And there was a trembling in the camp, in the field, and among all the people. Even the garrison and [a]the raiders trembled, and [b]the earth quaked so [c]that it became a great trembling.

★16 **16** Now Saul's watchmen in Gibeah of Benjamin looked, and behold, the multitude melted away; and they went here and there.

17 And Saul said to the people who *were* with him, "Number now and see who has gone from us." And when they had numbered, behold, Jonathan and his armor bearer were not *there.*

★18 [a]1 Sam. 23:9; 30:7

18 Then Saul said to Ahijah, "[a]Bring the ark of God here." For the ark of God was at that time with the sons of Israel.

★19 [a]Num. 27:21

19 And it happened [a]while Saul talked to the priest, that the commotion in the camp of the Philistines continued and increased; so Saul said to the priest, "Withdraw your hand."

20 [a]Judg. 7:22; 2 Chr. 20:23

20 Then Saul and all the people who *were* with him rallied and came to the battle; and behold, [a]every man's sword was against his fellow, *and there was* very great confusion.

★21-22

21 [a]1 Sam. 29:4

21 Now the Hebrews *who* were with the Philistines previously, who went up with them all around in the camp, even [a]they also *turned* to be with the Israelites who *were* with Saul and Jonathan.

22 [a]1 Sam. 13:6

22 When all the [a]men of Israel who had hidden themselves in the hill country of Ephraim heard that the Philistines had fled, even they also pursued them closely in the battle.

23 [a]Ex. 14:30;
1 Sam. 10:19; 14:23;
1 Chr. 11:14;
2 Chr. 32:22;
Ps. 44:7
[b]1 Sam. 13:5

23 So [a]the Lord delivered Israel that day, and the battle spread beyond [b]Beth-aven.

★24-30

★24 [a]Josh. 6:26

24 Now the men of Israel were hard-pressed on that day, for Saul had [a]put the people under oath, saying, "Cursed be the man who eats food before evening, and until I have avenged myself on my enemies." So none of the people tasted food.

25 And all *the people of* the land entered the forest, and there was honey on the ground.

26 [a]Matt. 3:4

26 When the people entered the forest, behold, [a]*there was* a flow of honey; but no man put his hand to his mouth, for the people feared the oath.

27 [a]1 Sam. 14:43
[b]1 Sam. 30:12

27 But Jonathan had not heard when his father put the people under oath; therefore, [a]he put out the end of the staff that *was* in his hand and dipped it in the honeycomb, and put his hand to his mouth, and [b]his eyes brightened.

28 Then one of the people answered and said, "Your father strictly put the people under oath, saying, 'Cursed be the man who eats food today.'" And the people were weary.

14:14 The site of the skirmish is identified by its relatively small land area.

14:16 Saul's spies observed how the Philistine camp was in confusion due to the attack by Jonathan.

14:18 *ark.* The Ark at this time was at Kiriathjearim from which it was not removed for 20 years (7:2). It may, however, have been brought to Gibeah temporarily. The LXX reads "ephod," an object which could have been used for decision-making (cf. 14:3).

14:19 *Withdraw your hand.* I.e., "Don't consult God now; there is no time!"

14:21-22 With the report of victory the Israelite deserters (or mercenaries) returned, and those who had avoided the initial confrontation joined in the battle.

14:24-30 So desirous was Saul of avenging himself against his enemies that he neglected the needs of his own men and swore a foolish oath which almost cost the life of his son.

14:24 *hard-pressed.* I.e., fatigued.

29 ^aJosh. 7:25; 1 Kin. 18:18

29 Then Jonathan said, "^aMy father has troubled the land. See now, how my eyes have brightened because I tasted a little of this honey.

30 "How much more, if only the people had eaten freely today of the spoil of their enemies which they found! For now the slaughter among the Philistines has not been great."

31 ^a1 Sam. 14:5 ^bJosh. 10:12

31 And they struck among the Philistines that day from ^aMichmash to ^bAijalon. And the people were very weary.

★32 ^a1 Sam. 15:19 ^bGen. 9:4; Lev. 3:17; 17:10-14; 19:26; Deut. 12:16, 23; Acts 15:20

32 And ^athe people rushed greedily upon the spoil, and took sheep and oxen and calves, and slew *them* on the ground; and the people ate *them* ^bwith the blood.

33 ^aLev. 7:26, 27; 19:26; Deut. 12:16, 23-25; 15:23

33 Then they told Saul, saying, "Behold, the people are ^asinning against the LORD by eating with the blood." And he said, "You have acted treacherously; roll a great stone to me today."

★34

34 And Saul said, "Disperse yourselves among the people and say to them, 'Each one of you bring me his ox or his sheep, and slaughter *it* here and eat; and do not sin against the LORD by eating with the blood.' " So all the people that night brought each one his ox with him, and slaughtered *it* there.

35 ^a1 Sam. 7:12, 17; 2 Sam. 24:25; James 4:8

35 And ^aSaul built an altar to the LORD; it was the first altar that he built to the LORD.

36 ^a1 Sam. 14:3, 18, 19

36 Then Saul said, "Let us go down after the Philistines by night and take spoil among them until the morning light, and let us not leave a man of them." And they said, "Do whatever seems good to you." So ^athe priest said, "Let us draw near to God here."

37 ^a1 Sam. 10:22 ^b1 Sam. 28:6

37 And Saul ^ainquired of God, "Shall I go down after the Philistines? Wilt Thou give them into the hand of Israel?" But ^bHe did not answer him on that day.

38 And Saul said, "^aDraw near here, all you chiefs of the people, and investigate and see how this sin has happened today.

38 ^aJosh. 7:11, 12; 1 Sam. 10:19, 20

39 "For ^aas the LORD lives, who delivers Israel, though it is in Jonathan my son, he shall surely die." But not one of all the people answered him.

★39 ^a1 Sam. 14:24, 44; 2 Sam. 12:5

40 Then he said to all Israel, "You shall be on one side and I and Jonathan my son will be on the other side." And the people said to Saul, "Do what seems good to you."

41 Therefore, Saul said to the LORD, the God of Israel, "^aGive a perfect *lot*." And Jonathan and Saul were taken, but the people escaped.

★41-42

41 ^aActs 1:24

42 And Saul said, "Cast *lots* between me and Jonathan my son." And Jonathan was taken.

43 Then Saul said to Jonathan, "^aTell me what you have done." So Jonathan told him and said, "^bI indeed tasted a little honey with the end of the staff that was in my hand. Here I am, I must die!"

43 ^aJosh. 7:19 ^b1 Sam. 14:27

44 And Saul said, "^aMay God do this *to me* and more also, for ^byou shall surely die, Jonathan."

44 ^aRuth 1:17; 1 Sam. 25:22 ^b1 Sam. 14:39

45 But the people said to Saul, "Must Jonathan die, who has brought about this great deliverance in Israel? Far from it! As the LORD lives, ^athere shall not one hair of his head fall to the ground, for ^bhe has worked with God this day." So the people rescued Jonathan and he did not die.

45 ^a2 Sam. 14:11; 1 Kin. 1:52; Luke 21:18; Acts 27:34 ^b2 Cor. 6:1

46 Then Saul went up from pursuing the Philistines, and the Philistines went to their own place.

14:32 Physically weakened, they disobeyed the prohibition against eating meat with blood (Lev. 17:10-14).

14:34 Saul had the animals slain on an altar so the blood could be drained.

14:39 Another foolish oath by Saul! Beware of making foolish promises that are impossible or extremely costly to keep.

14:41-42 By casting lots it was determined that Jonathan was the one in violation of Saul's foolish oath.

14:47 Saul expanded his kingdom to the south (Edom), east (Ammon and Moab), north (Zobah), and west (Philistia). *inflicted punishment.* Lit., smote; i.e., defeated.

47 Now when Saul had taken the kingdom over Israel, he fought against all his enemies on every side, against Moab, *a*the sons of Ammon, Edom, *b*the kings of Zobah, and *c*the Philistines; and wherever he turned, he inflicted punishment.

48 And he acted valiantly and *a*defeated the Amalekites, and delivered Israel from the hands of those who plundered them.

49 Now *a*the sons of Saul were Jonathan and Ishvi and Malchi-shua; and the names of his two daughters *were these:* the name of the first-born *b*Merab and the name of the younger *c*Michal.

50 And the name of Saul's wife was Ahinoam the daughter of Ahimaaz. And *a*the name of the captain of his army was Abner the son of Ner, Saul's uncle.

51 *a*And Kish *was* the father of Saul, and Ner the father of Abner *was* the son of Abiel.

52 Now the war against the Philistines was severe all the days of Saul; and when Saul saw any mighty man or any valiant man, he *a*attached him to his staff.

3　His partial obedience,
15:1-35

15 Then Samuel said to Saul, "*a*The LORD sent me to anoint you as king over His people, over Israel; now therefore, listen to the words of the LORD.

2 "Thus says the LORD of hosts, 'I will punish Amalek *a*for what he did to Israel, how he set himself against him on the way while he was coming up from Egypt.

3 'Now go and strike Amalek and *a*utterly destroy all that he has, and do not spare him; but *b*put to death both man and woman, child and infant, ox and sheep, camel and donkey.' "

4 Then Saul summoned the people and numbered them in *a*Telaim, 200,000 foot soldiers and 10,000 men of Judah.

5 And Saul came to the city of Amalek, and set an ambush in the valley.

6 And Saul said to *a*the Kenites, "Go, depart, go down from among the Amalekites, lest I destroy you with them; for *b*you showed kindness to all the sons of Israel when they came up from Egypt." So the Kenites departed from among the Amalekites.

7 So *a*Saul defeated the Amalekites, from *b*Havilah as you go to *c*Shur, which is east of Egypt.

8 And he captured *a*Agag the king of the Amalekites alive, and *b*utterly destroyed all the people with the edge of the sword.

9 But Saul and the people *a*spared Agag and the best of the sheep, the oxen, the fatlings, the lambs, and all that was good, and were not willing to destroy them utterly; but everything despised and worthless, that they utterly destroyed.

10 Then the word of the LORD came to Samuel, saying,

11 "*a*I regret that I have made

14:48 *Amalekites.* Nomadic descendants of Esau (Gen. 36:12) who fought against Israel at Rephidim (Exod. 17:8-13) and were placed under divine judgment (Deut. 25:19).

15:1 *listen.* I.e., with a view to obeying.

15:3 *utterly destroy.* Lit., put under a ban. A ban involved devoting cities, persons, animals, and possessions to the Lord for destruction in accordance with Deut. 7:2-6; 12:2-3; 20:16-18 (see note on Josh. 6:17). While this practice was severe, it was a just punishment.

15:4 *Telaim.* Possibly the Telem of Josh. 15:24, a city located in the Negev a few miles N. of Beersheba.

15:6 *Kenites.* Nomadic Midianites who were well disposed toward Israel from ancient times (Exod. 2:16-18; 18:9-12; Num. 10:29-32; Judg. 1:16).

15:7 The campaign proceeded from *Havilah* (in NW. Arabia) E. toward *Shur,* which is near the eastern border of Egypt.

15:8-9 By sparing Agag and the best of the spoil, Saul violated the ban and disobeyed God's word through Samuel.

15:11 *I regret.* Not an indication of changeableness in God's nature (15:29; cf. James 1:17), but an expression of sorrow (cf. Gen. 6:6) at the sinful rebellion of Saul.

Saul king, for [b]he has turned back from following Me, and has not carried out My commands." And Samuel was distressed and [c]cried out to the LORD all night.

12 And Samuel rose early in the morning to meet Saul; and it was told Samuel, saying, "Saul came to [a]Carmel, and behold, he set up a monument for himself, then turned and proceeded on down to [b]Gilgal."

13 And Samuel came to Saul, and Saul said to him, "[a]Blessed are you of the LORD! I have carried out the command of the LORD."

14 But Samuel said, "[a]What then is this bleating of the sheep in my ears, and the lowing of the oxen which I hear?"

15 And Saul said, "They have brought them from the Amalekites, for [a]the people spared the best of the sheep and oxen, to sacrifice to the LORD your God; but the rest we have utterly destroyed."

16 Then Samuel said to Saul, "Wait, and let me tell you what the LORD said to me last night." And he said to him, "Speak!"

17 And Samuel said, "Is it not true, [a]though you were little in your own eyes, you were *made* the head of the tribes of Israel? And the LORD anointed you king over Israel,

18 and the LORD sent you on a mission, and said, '[a]Go and utterly destroy the sinners, the Amalekites, and fight against them until they are exterminated.'

19 "Why then did you not obey the voice of the LORD, [a]but rushed upon the spoil and did what was evil in the sight of the LORD?"

20 Then Saul said to Samuel, "[a]I did obey the voice of the LORD, and went on the mission on which the LORD sent me, and have brought back Agag the king of Amalek, and have utterly destroyed the Amalekites.

21 "But [a]the people took *some* of the spoil, sheep and oxen, the choicest of the things devoted to destruction, to sacrifice to the LORD your God at Gilgal."

22 And Samuel said,
"[a]Has the LORD as much
delight in burnt offerings and sacrifices
As in obeying the voice of the LORD?
Behold, [b]to obey is better than sacrifice,
And to heed than the fat of rams.

23 "For rebellion is as the sin of [a]divination,
And insubordination is as [b]iniquity and idolatry.
Because you have rejected the word of the LORD,
[c]He has also rejected you from *being* king."

24 Then Saul said to Samuel, "[a]I have sinned; [b]I have indeed transgressed the command of the LORD and your words, because I feared the people and listened to their voice.

25 "Now therefore, [a]please pardon my sin and return with me, that I may worship the LORD."

26 But Samuel said to Saul, "I will not return with you; for [a]you have rejected the word of the LORD, and the LORD has rejected you from being king over Israel."

27 And as Samuel turned to go, [a]Saul seized the edge of his robe, and it tore.

28 So Samuel said to him, "[a]The LORD has torn the kingdom of Israel from you today, and has given it to your neighbor who is better than you.

★12 [a]Josh. 15:55; 1 Sam. 25:2 [b]1 Sam. 13:12, 15

★13-15
13 [a]Gen. 14:19; Judg. 17:2; Ruth 3:10; 2 Sam. 2:5
14 [a]Ex. 32:21-24

15 [a]Gen. 3:12, 13; Ex. 32:22, 23; 1 Sam. 15:9, 21

17 [a]1 Sam. 9:21; 10:22

18 [a]1 Sam. 15:3

★19 [a]1 Sam. 14:32

20 [a]1 Sam. 15:13

21 [a]Ex. 32:22, 23; 1 Sam. 15:15

22 [a]Ps. 40:6-8; 51:16, 17; Is. 1:11-15; Mic. 6:6-8; Heb. 10:6-9 [b]Jer. 7:22, 23; Hos. 6:6; Matt. 12:7; Mark 12:33

★23 [a]Deut. 18:10 [b]Gen. 31:19, 34 [c]1 Sam. 13:14

24 [a]Num. 22:34; 2 Sam. 12:13; Ps. 51:4 [b]Prov. 29:25; Is. 51:12, 13

25 [a]Ex. 10:17

★26 [a]1 Sam. 13:14; 16:1

27 [a]1 Kin. 11:30, 31

28 [a]1 Sam. 28:17, 18; 1 Kin. 11:31

15:12 *Carmel* was located 7½ miles S. of Hebron.
15:13-15 Saul excused himself and blamed the people (cf. 15:20-21).
15:19 *rushed upon.* I.e., swooped down on like a bird of prey.

15:23 *divination.* See note on Deut. 18:10-11. *insubordination.* Arrogance or presumption.
15:26 Though Saul was qualified in many ways to be a great leader, his self-willed spirit prevented fulfillment of that potential.

★29 ªI Chr.
29:11 ᵇNum.
23:19; Ezek.
24:14; Titus
1:2
29 "And also the ªGlory of Israel ᵇwill not lie or change His mind; for He is not a man that He should change His mind."

★30 ªJohn
5:44; 12:43
ᵇIs. 29:13
30 Then he said, "I have sinned; ª but please honor me now before the elders of my people and before Israel, and go back with me, ᵇthat I may worship the Lᴏʀᴅ your God."

31 So Samuel went back following Saul, and Saul worshiped the Lᴏʀᴅ.

★32
32 Then Samuel said, "Bring me Agag, the king of the Amalekites." And Agag came to him cheerfully. And Agag said, "Surely the bitterness of death is past."

33 ªGen.
9:6; Judg.
1:7; Matt. 7:2
33 But Samuel said, "ªAs your sword has made women childless, so shall your mother be childless among women." And Samuel hewed Agag to pieces before the Lᴏʀᴅ at Gilgal.

34 ªI Sam.
7:17. ᵇI Sam.
11:4
34 Then Samuel went to ªRamah, but Saul went up to his house at ᵇGibeah of Saul.

35 ªI Sam.
19:24
ᵇI Sam. 16:1
35 And ªSamuel did not see Saul again until the day of his death; for Samuel ᵇgrieved over Saul. And the Lᴏʀᴅ regretted that He had made Saul king over Israel.

★ 1 ªI Sam.
15:35
ᵇI Sam.
13:13, 14;
15:23
ᶜI Sam.
9:16; 10:1;
2 Kin. 9:1
ᵈRuth 4:17-
22 ᵉPs.
78:70, 71;
Acts 13:22

D The Replacement of Saul by David, 16:1-23

1 David chosen and anointed, 16:1-13

16 Now the Lᴏʀᴅ said to Samuel, "ªHow long will you grieve over Saul, since ᵇI have rejected him from being king over Israel? ᶜFill your horn with oil, and go; I will send you to ᵈJesse the Bethlehemite, for I have ᵉselected a king for Myself among his sons."

★ 2 ªI Sam.
20:29
2 But Samuel said, "How can I go? When Saul hears of it, he will kill me." And the Lᴏʀᴅ said, "ªTake a heifer with you, and say, 'I have come to sacrifice to the Lᴏʀᴅ.'

3 ªEx. 4:15;
Acts 9:6
ᵇDeut.
17:14, 15;
1 Sam. 9:16
3 "And you shall invite Jesse to the sacrifice, and ªI will show you what you shall do; and ᵇyou shall anoint for Me the one whom I designate to you."

★ 4 ªGen.
48:7; Luke
2:4 ᵇI Kin.
2:13; 2 Kin.
9:22; 1 Chr.
12:17, 18
4 So Samuel did what the Lᴏʀᴅ said, and came to ªBethlehem. And the elders of the city came trembling to meet him and said, "ᵇDo you come in peace?"

★ 5 ªGen.
35:2; Ex.
19:10
5 And he said, "In peace; I have come to sacrifice to the Lᴏʀᴅ. ªConsecrate yourselves and come with me to the sacrifice." He also consecrated Jesse and his sons, and invited them to the sacrifice.

6 ªI Sam.
17:13
6 Then it came about when they entered, that he looked at ªEliab and thought, "Surely the Lᴏʀᴅ's anointed is before Him."

★ 7 ªI Sam.
2:3; 1 Kin.
8:39; 1 Chr.
28:9; Luke
16:15
7 But the Lᴏʀᴅ said to Samuel, "Do not look at his appearance or at the height of his stature, because I have rejected him; for God sees not as man sees, for man looks at the outward appearance, ªbut the Lᴏʀᴅ looks at the heart."

8 ªI Sam.
17:13
8 Then Jesse called ªAbinadab, and made him pass before Samuel. And he said, "Neither has the Lᴏʀᴅ chosen this one."

15:29 *the Glory of Israel.* A unique designation for God, emphasizing His eternal nature. The title is particularly appropriate in this context, which stresses His immutability.

15:30 Saul was concerned that it not appear he had lost Samuel's support.

15:32 *cheerfully.* The Hebrew is unclear. It may mean "trembling" or "in fetters." *Surely the bitterness of death is past* might better be translated, "Now comes bitter death."

16:1 The rest of 1 Samuel (chaps. 16-31) portrays the relationship of Saul and David, and David's preparation for kingship.

16:2 Samuel's fear of Saul was probably justified

(18:11). The Lord did not suggest deception, but simply told Samuel to take care of the anointing while he was in Bethlehem on official business.

16:4 *Bethlehem* is located about five miles S. of Jerusalem. The visit of Samuel was unexpected, and the town elders may have thought he had come to pronounce and execute judgment (7:15-16; 15:33).

16:5 *Consecrate.* I.e., set yourselves apart by means of ceremonial washings and purifications.

16:7 Note the contrast between the divine and human perspectives.

9 *a*1 Sam.
17:13

9 Next Jesse made *a*Shammah pass by. And he said, "Neither has the LORD chosen this one."

10 Thus Jesse made seven of his sons pass before Samuel. But Samuel said to Jesse, "The LORD has not chosen these."

11 *a*1 Sam.
17:12;
2 Sam. 13:3

11 And Samuel said to Jesse, "Are these all the children?" And he said, "*a*There remains yet the youngest, and behold, he is tending the sheep." Then Samuel said to Jesse, "Send and bring him; for we will not sit down until he comes here."

★12 *a*Gen.
39:6; Ex. 2:2;
Acts 7:20
*b*1 Sam. 9:17

12 So he sent and brought him in. Now he was ruddy, with *a*beautiful eyes and a handsome appearance. And the LORD said, "*b*Arise, anoint him; for this is he."

★13 *a*1 Sam.
10:1 *b*Num.
27:18;
1 Sam. 10:6,
9, 10

13 Then Samuel took the horn of oil and *a*anointed him in the midst of his brothers; and *b*the Spirit of the LORD came mightily upon David from that day forward. And Samuel arose and went to Ramah.

2 David employed at Saul's court, 16:14-23

★14 *a*Judg.
16:20;
1 Sam. 11:6;
18:12; 28:15
*b*Judg. 9:23;
1 Sam.
16:15, 16;
18:10; 19:9;
1 Kin. 22:19-
22

14 *a*Now the Spirit of the LORD departed from Saul, and *b*an evil spirit from the LORD terrorized him.

15 Saul's servants then said to him, "Behold now, an evil spirit from God is terrorizing you.

16 *a*1 Sam.
18:10; 19:9;
2 Kin. 3:15

16 "Let our lord now command your servants who are before you. Let them seek a man who is a skillful player on the harp; and it shall come about when the evil spirit from God is on you, that

*a*he shall play *the harp* with his hand, and you will be well."

17 So Saul said to his servants, "Provide for me now a man who can play well, and bring *him* to me."

18 *a*1 Sam.
17:32-36
*b*1 Sam. 3:19

18 Then one of the young men answered and said, "Behold, I have seen a son of Jesse the Bethlehemite who is a skillful musician, *a*a mighty man of valor, a warrior, one prudent in speech, and a handsome man; and *b*the LORD is with him."

19 So Saul sent messengers to Jesse, and said, "Send me your son David who is with the flock."

20 *a*1 Sam.
10:4, 27;
Prov. 18:16

20 And Jesse *a*took a donkey *loaded with* bread and a jug of wine and a young goat, and sent *them* to Saul by David his son.

21 *a*Gen.
41:46; Prov.
22:29

21 Then David came to Saul and *a*attended him, and Saul loved him greatly; and he became his armor bearer.

22 And Saul sent to Jesse, saying, "Let David now stand before me; for he has found favor in my sight."

★23 *a*1 Sam.
16:14-16

23 So it came about whenever *a*the *evil* spirit from God came to Saul, David would take the harp and play *it* with his hand; and Saul would be refreshed and be well, and the evil spirit would depart from him.

E The Rise of David over Saul, 17:1-18:30

1 David's defeat of Goliath, 17:1-58

★ 1-3

1 *a*1 Sam.
13:5 *b*Josh.
15:35; 2 Chr.
28:18 *c*Josh.
10:10
*d*1 Chr.
11:13

17 Now *a*the Philistines gathered their armies for battle; and they were gathered at

---

16:12 *ruddy.* I.e., reddish. A reference to the color of his hair and complexion, regarded as beautiful in areas where hair and complexion are usually dark.

16:13 This private anointing was the first of three anointings for David. His second came as king of Judah (2 Sam. 2:4) and his third as king over all Israel (2 Sam. 5:3).

16:14 *departed.* The presence of the Holy Spirit in the O.T. was selective and temporary, while today it is universal and permanent among be-

lievers (see note on Judg. 3:10). The *evil spirit* was used by God as the instrument of judgment on Saul, resulting in a mental disturbance bordering on madness.

16:23 Whatever Saul's malady (cf. 16:14), it was temporarily relieved by music.

17:1-3 The armies were camped on either side of the Elah Valley, 15 miles W. of Bethlehem. The Philistines were apparently on the hill to the S. of the valley, and the Israelites were on the hill to the N.

Socoh which belongs to Judah, and they camped between ^bSocoh and ^cAzekah, in ^dEphes-dammim.

2 And Saul and the men of Israel were gathered, and camped in ^athe valley of Elah, and drew up in battle array to encounter the Philistines.

3 And the Philistines stood on the mountain on one side while Israel stood on the mountain on the other side, with the valley between them.

4 Then a champion came out from the armies of the Philistines named ^aGoliath, from ^bGath, whose height was six cubits and a span.

5 And *he had* a bronze helmet on his head, and he was clothed with scale-armor which weighed five thousand shekels of bronze.

6 *He* also *had* bronze greaves on his legs and a ^abronze javelin *slung* between his shoulders.

7 And ^athe shaft of his spear was like a weaver's beam, and the head of his spear *weighed* six hundred shekels of iron; ^bhis shield-carrier also walked before him.

8 And he stood and shouted to the ranks of Israel, and said to them, "Why do you come out to draw up in battle array? Am I not the Philistine and you ^aservants of Saul? Choose a man for yourselves and let him come down to me.

9 "^aIf he is able to fight with me and kill me, then we will become your servants; but if I prevail against him and kill him, then you shall become our servants and serve us."

10 Again the Philistine said, "^aI defy the ranks of Israel this day; give me a man that we may fight together."

11 When Saul and all Israel heard these words of the Philistine, they were dismayed and greatly afraid.

12 Now David was ^athe son of the ^bEphrathite of Bethlehem in Judah, whose name was Jesse, and ^che had eight sons. And Jesse was old in the days of Saul, advanced *in years* among men.

13 And the three older sons of Jesse had gone after Saul to the battle. And ^athe names of his three sons who went to the battle were Eliab the first-born, and the second to him Abinadab, and the third Shammah.

14 And ^aDavid was the youngest. Now the three oldest followed Saul,

15 ^abut David went back and forth from Saul ^bto tend his father's flock at Bethlehem.

16 And the Philistine came forward morning and evening for forty days, and took his stand.

17 Then Jesse said to David his son, "^aTake now for your brothers an ephah of this roasted grain and these ten loaves, and run to the camp to your brothers.

18 "^aBring also these ten cuts of cheese to the commander of *their* thousand, ^band look into the welfare of your brothers, and bring back news of them.

19 "For Saul and they and all the men of Israel are in the valley of Elah, fighting with the Philistines."

20 So David arose early in the morning and left the flock with a keeper and took *the supplies* and went as Jesse had commanded him. And he came to the ^acircle of

2 ^a1 Sam. 21:9

4 ^a2 Sam. 21:19 ^bJosh. 11:22

5

6 ^a1 Sam. 17:45

7 ^a2 Sam. 21:19; 1 Chr. 11:23 ^b1 Sam. 17:41

8-10

8 ^a1 Sam. 8:17

9 ^a2 Sam. 2:12-16

10 ^a1 Sam. 17:26, 36, 45; 2 Sam. 21:21

12 ^aRuth 4:22; 1 Sam. 16:18 ^bGen. 35:19 ^c1 Sam. 16:10, 11; 1 Chr. 2:13-15

13 ^a1 Sam. 16:6, 8, 9

14 ^a1 Sam. 16:11

15 ^a1 Sam. 16:21-23 ^b1 Sam. 16:11, 19

17 ^a1 Sam. 25:18

18 ^a1 Sam. 16:20 ^bGen. 37:13, 14

20 ^a1 Sam. 26:5, 7

17:4 A cubit was 18 inches and a span, 9 inches. Goliath was 9 feet 9 inches tall!

17:5 Goliath's coat of armor weighed about 125 pounds.

17:6 *bronze greaves.* Bronze shin guards.

17:7 *a weaver's beam* was stout and heavy (about 17 pounds). The spearhead weighed about 16 pounds. An attendant, carrying a large protective shield, went ahead of Goliath.

17:8-10. Goliath suggested a contest between individual warriors on behalf of the armies. In ancient times battles were sometimes decided by such a contest.

17:17 *ephah.* A dry measure equivalent to 5.8 gallons.

17:20 *circle of the camp.* A circle of wagons which formed a kind of fortification around the camp.

the camp while the army was going out in battle array shouting the war cry.

21 And Israel and the Philistines drew up in battle array, army against army.

22 Then David left his [a]baggage in the care of the baggage keeper, and ran to the battle line and entered in order to greet his brothers.

23 As he was talking with them, behold, the champion, the Philistine from Gath named Goliath, was coming up from the army of the Philistines, and he spoke [a]these same words; and David heard *them*.

24 When all the men of Israel saw the man, they fled from him and were greatly afraid.

★25 And the men of Israel said, "Have you seen this man who is coming up? Surely he is coming up to defy Israel. And it will be that the king will enrich the man who kills him with great riches and [a]will give him his daughter and make his father's house free in Israel."

26 Then David spoke to the men who were standing by him, saying, "What will be done for the man who kills this Philistine, and takes away [a]the reproach from Israel? For who is this [b]uncircumcised Philistine, that he should [c]taunt the armies of [d]the living God?"

27 And the people answered him in accord with this word, saying, "[a]Thus it will be done for the man who kills him."

28 Now Eliab his oldest brother heard when he spoke to the men; and [a]Eliab's anger burned against David and he said, "Why have you come down? And with whom have you left those few sheep in the wilderness? I know your insolence and the wickedness of your heart; for you have come down in order to see the battle."

29 But David said, "What have I done now? Was it not just a question?"

30 Then he turned away from him to another and [a]said the same thing; and the people answered the same thing as before.

31 When the words which David spoke were heard, they told *them* to Saul, and he sent for him.

32 And David said to Saul, "[a]Let no man's heart fail on account of him; [b]your servant will go and fight with this Philistine."

33 Then Saul said to David, "[a]You are not able to go against this Philistine to fight with him; for you are *but* a youth while he has been a warrior from his youth."

34 But David said to Saul, "Your servant was tending his father's sheep. When a lion or a bear came and took a lamb from the flock,

35 I went out after him and attacked him, and [a]rescued *it* from his mouth; and when he rose up against me, I seized *him* by his beard and struck him and killed him.

36 "Your servant has killed both the lion and the bear; and this uncircumcised Philistine will be like one of them, since he has taunted the armies of the living God."

37 And David said, "[a]The LORD who delivered me from the paw of the lion and from the paw of the bear, He will deliver me from the hand of this Philistine." And Saul said to David, "[b]Go, and may the LORD be with you."

38 Then Saul clothed David with his garments and put a bronze helmet on his head, and he clothed him with armor.

39 And David girded his sword over his armor and tried to walk, for he had not tested *them*. So David said to Saul, "I cannot go with these, for I have not

---

22 [a]Judg. 18:21; Is. 10:28

23 [a]1 Sam. 17:8-10

★25 [a]Josh. 15:16

26 [a]1 Sam. 11:2 [b]1 Sam. 14:6; 17:36; Jer. 9:25, 26 [c]1 Sam. 17:10 [d]Deut. 5:26; 2 Kin. 19:4; Jer. 10:10

27 [a]1 Sam. 17:25

28 [a]Gen. 37:4, 8-36; Prov. 18:19; Matt. 10:36

30 [a]1 Sam. 17:26, 27

32 [a]Deut. 20:1-4 [b]1 Sam. 16:18

33 [a]Num. 13:31

35 [a]Amos 3:12

37 [a]2 Cor. 1:10; 2 Tim. 4:17, 18 [b]1 Sam. 20:13; 1 Chr. 22:11, 16

17:25 *free.* I.e., from taxes and forced labor.

tested *them*." And David took them off.

40 And he took his stick in his hand and chose for himself five smooth stones from the brook, and put them in the shepherd's bag which he had, even in *his* pouch, and [a]his sling was in his hand; and he approached the Philistine.

41 Then the Philistine came on and approached David, with the shield-bearer in front of him.

42 When the Philistine looked and saw David, [a]he disdained him; for he was *but* a youth, and [b]ruddy, with a handsome appearance.

43 And the Philistine said to David, "[a]Am I a dog, that you come to me with sticks?" And [b]the Philistine cursed David by his gods.

44 The Philistine also said to David, "Come to me, and I will give your flesh [a]to the birds of the sky and the beasts of the field."

45 Then David said to the Philistine, "You come to me with a sword, a spear, and a javelin, [a]but I come to you in the name of the LORD of hosts, the God of the armies of Israel, whom you have taunted.

46 "This day the LORD will deliver you up into my hands, and I will strike you down and remove your head from you. And I will give the [a]dead bodies of the army of the Philistines this day to the birds of the sky and the wild beasts of the earth, [b]that all the earth may know that there is a God in Israel,

47 and that all this assembly may know that [a]the LORD does not deliver by sword or by spear; [b]for the battle is the LORD's and He will give you into our hands."

48 Then it happened when the Philistine rose and came and drew near to meet David, that [a]David ran quickly toward the battle line to meet the Philistine.

49 And David put his hand into his bag and took from it a stone and slung *it*, and struck the Philistine on his forehead. And the stone sank into his forehead, so that he fell on his face to the ground.

50 Thus David prevailed over the Philistine with a sling and a stone, and he struck the Philistine and killed him; but there was no sword in David's hand.

51 Then David ran and stood over the Philistine and [a]took his sword and drew it out of its sheath and killed him, and cut off his head with it. [b]When the Philistines saw that their champion was dead, they fled.

52 And the men of Israel and Judah arose and shouted and pursued the Philistines as far as the valley, and to the gates of [a]Ekron. And the slain Philistines lay along the way to [b]Shaaraim, even to Gath and Ekron.

53 And the sons of Israel returned from chasing the Philistines and plundered their camps.

54 Then David took the Philistine's head and brought it to Jerusalem, but he put his weapons in his tent.

55 Now when Saul saw David going out against the Philistine, he said to Abner the commander of the army, "Abner, whose son is [a]this young man?" And Abner said, "By your life, O king, I do not know."

56 And the king said, "You inquire whose son the youth is."

Marginal references (left column):

40 [a]Judg. 20:16

★42 [a]Ps. 123:4; Prov. 16:18 [b]1 Sam. 16:12

43 [a]1 Sam. 24:14; 2 Sam. 3:8; 2 Kin. 8:13 [b]1 Kin. 20:10

44 [a]1 Sam. 17:46

45 [a]2 Sam. 22:35; 2 Chr. 32:8; Ps. 124:8; Heb. 11:32-34

★46-47

46 [a]Deut. 28:26 [b]Josh. 4:24; 1 Kin. 8:43; 18:36; 2 Kin. 19:19; Is. 37:20

47 [a]1 Sam. 14:6; 2 Chr. 14:11; 20:15; Ps. 44:6; Hos. 1:7; Zech. 4:6 [b]2 Chr. 20:15

Marginal references (right column):

48 [a]Ps. 27:3

★50

51 [a]1 Sam. 21:9; 2 Sam. 23:21 [b]Heb. 11:34

52 [a]Josh. 15:11 [b]Josh. 15:36

★54

★55 [a]1 Sam. 16:12, 21, 22

17:42 *ruddy*. See note on 16:12.
17:46-47 David intended that his victory teach that the LORD (Yahweh) is the true God and that He delivers His people.
17:50 A *sling* could be used with deadly accuracy (see Judg. 20:16).
17:54 *Jerusalem*. This must be a reference to the Israelite portion of Jerusalem (Josh. 15:63; Judg. 1:8) outside the Jebusite fortress which

was not taken until David had become king (2 Sam. 5:6-9). *tent*. Perhaps a reference to David's home in Bethlehem. The sword was later deposited in a sanctuary at Nob (cf. 21:9).
17:55 Saul knew David well from contact with him in his court (16:18-23), but evidently had forgotten the name of David's father and needed to know it to reward David's family for the victory (17:25).

57 So when David returned from killing the Philistine, Abner took him and [a]brought him before Saul with the Philistine's head in his hand.

58 And Saul said to him, "Whose son are you, young man?" And David answered, "[a]I am the son of your servant Jesse the Bethlehemite."

2　David's friendship with Jonathan, 18:1-4

18 Now it came about when he had finished speaking to Saul, that [a]the soul of Jonathan was knit to the soul of David, and [b]Jonathan loved him as himself.

2 And Saul took him that day and [a]did not let him return to his father's house.

3 Then [a]Jonathan made a covenant with David because he loved him as himself.

4 And [a]Jonathan stripped himself of the robe that was on him and gave it to David, with his armor, including his sword and his bow and his belt.

3　David's relations with Saul, 18:5-16

5 So David went out wherever Saul sent him, *and* prospered; and Saul set him over the men of war. And it was pleasing in the sight of all the people and also in the sight of Saul's servants.

6 And it happened as they were coming, when David returned from killing the Philistine, that [a]the women came out of all the cities of Israel, singing and dancing, to meet King Saul, with tambourines, with joy and with musical instruments.

7 And the women [a]sang as they played, and said,

"[b]Saul has slain his thousands,

[c]And David his ten thousands."

8 Then Saul became very angry, for this saying displeased him; and he said, "They have ascribed to David ten thousands, but to me they have ascribed thousands. Now [a]what more can he have but the kingdom?"

9 And Saul looked at David with suspicion from that day on.

10 Now it came about on the next day that [a]an evil spirit from God came mightily upon Saul, and [b]he raved in the midst of the house, while David was playing *the harp* with his hand, [c]as usual; and [d]a spear *was* in Saul's hand.

11 And [a]Saul hurled the spear for he thought, "I will pin David to the wall." But David escaped from his presence twice.

12 Now [a]Saul was afraid of David, [b]for the LORD was with him but [c]had departed from Saul.

13 Therefore Saul removed him from his presence, and appointed him as his commander of a thousand; and [a]he went out and came in before the people.

14 And David was prospering in all his ways for [a]the LORD *was* with him.

15 When Saul saw that he was prospering greatly, he dreaded him.

16 But [a]all Israel and Judah loved David, and he went out and came in before them.

4　David's marriage, 18:17-30

17 Then Saul said to David, "[a]Here is my older daughter Merab; I will give her to you as a wife, only be a valiant man for me and fight [b]the LORD's battles." For Saul thought, "My hand shall not

---

18:1 Chapters 18–20 describe David's service in Saul's court. The story is told in terms of the relationship between David and Jonathan.
18:3 The covenant was unilateral, Jonathan committing himself to the Lord's anointed.
18:8 *angry.* Saul's jealousy of David was a significant factor in destroying his relationship

with David and in bringing about his own decline.
18:17 *as a wife.* Saul had promised his daughter to the slayer of Goliath (17:25), but now the reward is conditioned on further conquests. Saul was hoping that David would fall at the hand of the Philistines.

57 [a]1 Sam. 17:54
58 [a]1 Sam. 17:12
★ 1 [a]Gen. 44:30 [b]Deut. 13:6; 1 Sam. 20:17; 2 Sam. 1:26
2 [a]1 Sam. 17:15
★ 3 [a]1 Sam. 20:8-17
4 [a]Gen. 41:42; 1 Sam. 17:38; Esth. 6:8
6 [a]Ex. 15:20, 21; Judg. 11:34; Ps. 68:25; 149:3
7 [a]Ex. 15:21; 1 Sam. 21:11; 29:5 [b]1 Sam. 21:11 [c]2 Sam. 18:3
★ 8 [a]1 Sam. 15:28
10 [a]1 Sam. 16:14 [b]1 Sam. 19:23, 24 [c]1 Sam. 16:23 [d]1 Sam. 19:9
11 [a]1 Sam. 19:10; 20:33
12 [a]1 Sam. 18:15, 29 [b]1 Sam. 16:13, 18 [c]1 Sam. 16:14; 28:15
13 [a]Num. 27:17; 1 Sam. 18:16; 2 Sam. 5:2
14 [a]Gen. 39:2, 3, 23; Josh. 6:27; 1 Sam. 16:18
16 [a]1 Sam. 18:5
★17 [a]1 Sam. 17:25 [b]Num. 21:14; 1 Sam. 17:36, 47; 25:28 [c]1 Sam. 18:21, 25

be against him, but ^clet the hand of the Philistines be against him."

18 But David said to Saul, "^aWho am I, and what is my life or my father's family in Israel, that I should be the king's son-in-law?"

19 So it came about at the time when Merab, Saul's daughter, should have been given to David, that she was given to ^aAdriel ^bthe Meholathite for a wife.

20 Now ^aMichal, Saul's daughter, loved David. When they told Saul, the thing was agreeable to him.

21 And Saul thought, "I will give her to him that she may become a snare to him, and ^athat the hand of the Philistines may be against him." Therefore Saul said to David, "^bFor a second time you may be my son-in-law today."

22 Then Saul commanded his servants, "Speak to David secretly, saying, 'Behold, the king delights in you, and all his servants love you; now therefore, become the king's son-in-law.' "

23 So Saul's servants spoke these words to David. But David said, "Is it trivial in your sight to become the king's son-in-law, ^asince I am a poor man and lightly esteemed?"

24 And the servants of Saul reported to him according to these words *which* David spoke.

25 Saul then said, "Thus you shall say to David, 'The king does not desire any ^adowry except a hundred foreskins of the Philistines, ^bto take vengeance on the king's enemies.' " Now ^cSaul planned to make David fall by the hand of the Philistines.

26 When his servants told David these words, it pleased David to become the king's son-in-law. ^aBefore the days had expired

27 David rose up and went, ^ahe and his men, and struck down two hundred men among the Philistines. Then ^bDavid brought their foreskins, and they gave them in full number to the king, that he might become the king's son-in-law. So Saul gave him Michal his daughter for a wife.

28 When Saul saw and knew that the LORD was with David, and *that* Michal, Saul's daughter, loved him,

29 then Saul was even more afraid of David. Thus Saul was David's enemy continually.

30 Then the commanders of the Philistines ^awent out *to battle*, and it happened as often as they went out, that David ^bbehaved himself more wisely than all the servants of Saul. So his name was highly esteemed.

F The Rejection of David by Saul, 19:1–26:25

1 David protected by Jonathan, 19:1–10

19 Now Saul told Jonathan his son and all his servants ^ato put David to death. But ^bJonathan, Saul's son, greatly delighted in David.

2 So Jonathan told David saying, "Saul my father is seeking to put you to death. Now therefore, please be on guard in the morning, and stay in a secret place and hide yourself.

3 "And I will go out and stand beside my father in the field where you are, and I will speak with my father about you; ^aif I find out anything, then I shall tell you."

4 Then Jonathan ^aspoke well of David to Saul his father, and said to him, "^bDo not let the king sin against his servant David,

★18 ^a1 Sam. 9:21; 18:23; 2 Sam. 7:18

19 ^a2 Sam. 21:8 ^bJudg. 7:22; 1 Kin. 19:16

20 ^a1 Sam. 18:28

★21 ^a1 Sam. 18:17 ^b1 Sam. 18:26

23 ^aGen. 29:20; 34:12

★25 ^aGen. 34:12; Ex. 22:17 ^b1 Sam. 14:24 ^c1 Sam. 18:17

★26 ^a1 Sam. 18:21

27 ^a1 Sam. 18:17 ^b2 Sam. 3:14

30 ^a2 Sam. 11:1 ^b1 Sam. 18:5

1 ^a1 Sam. 18:8, 9 ^b1 Sam. 18:1-3

3 ^a1 Sam. 20:9, 13

4 ^a1 Sam. 20:32; Prov. 31:8, 9 ^bGen. 42:22; Prov. 17:13; Jer. 18:20

18:18 Saul furthered his dishonesty by actually giving to another the daughter he had promised David.

18:21 *For a second time.* Better, in a second way; i.e., by an alternative other than the traditional dowry (cf. 18:25).

18:25 *hundred foreskins.* Tangible proof that 100 Philistines had been slain.

18:26 *days.* The period before the appointed time for the delivery of the dowry and marriage.

since he has not sinned against you, and since his deeds *have been* very beneficial to you.

5 "For ªhe took his life in his hand and struck the Philistine, and ᵇthe LORD brought about a great deliverance for all Israel; you saw *it* and rejoiced. ᶜWhy then will you sin against innocent blood, by putting David to death without a cause?"

6 And Saul listened to the voice of Jonathan, and Saul vowed, "As the LORD lives, he shall not be put to death."

7 Then Jonathan called David, and Jonathan told him all these words. And Jonathan brought David to Saul, and he was in his presence as ªformerly.

8 When there was war again, David went out and fought with the Philistines, and defeated them with great slaughter, so that they fled before him.

9 Now there was ªan evil spirit from the LORD on Saul as he was sitting in his house ᵇwith his spear in his hand, ᶜand David was playing *the harp* with *his* hand.

10 ªAnd Saul tried to pin David to the wall with the spear, but he slipped away out of Saul's presence, so that he struck the spear into the wall. And David fled and escaped that night.

2 David protected by Michal,
19:11-17

11 Then ªSaul sent messengers to David's house to watch him, in order to put him to death in the morning. But Michal, David's wife, told him, saying, "If you do not save your life tonight, tomorrow you will be put to death."

12 ªSo Michal let David down through a window, and he went out and fled and escaped.

13 And Michal took ªthe household idol and laid *it* on the bed, and put a quilt of goats' *hair* at its head, and covered *it* with clothes.

14 When Saul sent messengers to take David, she said, "ªHe is sick."

15 Then Saul sent messengers to see David, saying, "Bring him up to me on his bed, that I may put him to death."

16 When the messengers entered, behold, the household idol *was* on the bed with the quilt of goats' *hair* at its head.

17 So Saul said to Michal, "Why have you deceived me like this and let my enemy go, so that he has escaped?" And Michal said to Saul, "He said to me, 'Let me go! ªWhy should I put you to death?' "

3 David protected by Samuel,
19:18-24

18 Now David fled and escaped and came ªto Samuel at Ramah, and told him all that Saul had done to him. And he and Samuel went and stayed in ᵇNaioth.

19 And it was told Saul, saying, "Behold, David is at Naioth in Ramah."

20 Then ªSaul sent messengers to take David, but when they saw ᵇthe company of the prophets prophesying, with Samuel standing *and* presiding over them, the Spirit of God came upon the messengers of Saul; and ᶜthey also prophesied.

21 And when it was told Saul, he sent other messengers, and they also prophesied. So Saul sent messengers again the third time, and they also prophesied.

22 Then he himself went to Ramah, and came as far as the

Marginal references (left column):

5 ªJudg. 9:17; 1 Sam. 17:49, 50; 28:21; Ps. 119:109
ᵇ1 Sam. 11:13; 1 Chr. 11:14 ᶜDeut. 19:10-13; 1 Sam. 20:32; Ps. 94:21; Matt. 27:4

7 ª1 Sam. 16:21; 18:2, 10, 13

9 ª1 Sam. 16:14; 18:10, 11 ᵇ1 Sam. 18:10 ᶜ1 Sam. 16:16

10 ª1 Sam. 18:11; 20:33; Prov. 1:16

11 ªJudg. 16:2; Ps. 59:title

12 ªJosh. 2:15; Acts 9:25; 2 Cor. 11:33

Marginal references (right column):

★13 ªGen. 31:19; Judg. 18:14, 17

★14 ªJosh. 2:5

17 ª2 Sam. 2:22

★18 ª1 Sam. 7:17 ᵇ1 Sam. 19:22, 23

★20-21
20 ª1 Sam. 19:11, 14; John 7:32 ᵇ1 Sam. 10:5, 6, 10 ᶜNum. 11:25; Joel 2:28

19:13 *household idol.* Heb., *teraphim,* an idol kept in a household shrine (see note on Gen. 31:19).
19:14 Lies and idolatry marred the character of Michal (cf. 19:17).
19:18 *Naioth,* a community in Ramah where the school of the prophets was located (19:19-20).
19:20-21 The evil intent of Saul's messengers was thwarted by the Spirit of God. They all joined the school of the prophets and prophesied in spite of themselves.

large well that is in Secu; and he asked and said, "Where are Samuel and David?" And *someone* said, "Behold, they are at Naioth in Ramah."

23 And he proceeded there to Naioth in Ramah; and ªthe Spirit of God came upon him also, so that he went along prophesying continually until he came to Naioth in Ramah.

24 And he also stripped off his clothes, and he too prophesied before Samuel and lay down ªnaked all that day and all that night. Therefore they say, "ᵇIs Saul also among the prophets?"

4 David protected by Jonathan, 20:1-42

20 Then David fled from Naioth in Ramah, and came and ªsaid to Jonathan, "What have I done? What is my iniquity? And what is my sin before your father, that he is seeking my life?"

2 And he said to him, "Far from it, you shall not die. Behold, my father does nothing either great or small without disclosing it to me. So why should my father hide this thing from me? It is not so!"

3 Yet David ªvowed again, saying, "Your father knows well that I have found favor in your sight, and he has said, 'Do not let Jonathan know this, lest he be grieved.' But truly ᵇas the LORD lives and as your soul lives, there is hardly a step between me and death."

4 Then Jonathan said to David, "Whatever you say, I will do for you."

5 So David said to Jonathan, "Behold, tomorrow is ªthe new moon, and I ought ᵇto sit down to eat with the king. But let me go,

ᶜthat I may hide myself in the field until the third evening.

6 "If your father misses me at all, then say, 'David earnestly asked *leave* of me to run to ªBethlehem his city, because it is ᵇthe yearly sacrifice there for the whole family.'

7 "If he says, 'It is good,' your servant *shall be* safe; but if he is very angry, ªknow that he has decided on evil.

8 "Therefore deal kindly with your servant, for ªyou have brought your servant into a covenant of the LORD with you. But ᵇif there is iniquity in me, put me to death yourself; for why then should you bring me to your father?"

9 And Jonathan said, "Far be it from you! For if I should indeed learn that evil has been decided by my father to come upon you, then would I not tell you about it?"

10 Then David said to Jonathan, "Who will tell me if your father answers you harshly?"

11 And Jonathan said to David, "Come, and let us go out into the field." So both of them went out to the field.

12 Then Jonathan said to David, "The LORD, the God of Israel, *be witness!* When I have sounded out my father about this time tomorrow, *or* the third day, behold, if there is good *feeling* toward David, shall I not then send to you and make it known to you?

13 "If it please my father to do you harm, ªmay the LORD do so to Jonathan and more also, if I do not make it known to you and send you away, that you may go in safety. And ᵇmay the LORD be with you as He has been with my father.

14 "And if I am still alive, will you not show me the lovingkind-

---

Cross references (left margin):

23 ª1 Sam. 10:10

24 ª2 Sam. 6:20; Is. 20:2; Mic. 1:8 ᵇ1 Sam. 10:10-12

1 ª1 Sam. 24:9

3 ªDeut. 6:13 ᵇ1 Sam. 25:26; 2 Kin. 2:6

★ 5 ªNum. 10:10; 28:11-15; Amos 8:5 ᵇ1 Sam. 20:24, 27 ᶜ1 Sam. 19:2

Cross references (right margin):

6 ª1 Sam. 17:58 ᵇDeut. 12:5; 1 Sam. 9:12

7 ª1 Sam. 25:17

8 ª1 Sam. 18:3; 23:18 ᵇ2 Sam. 14:32

13 ªRuth 1:17; 1 Sam. 3:17 ᵇJosh. 1:5; 1 Sam. 17:37; 18:12; 1 Chr. 22:11, 16

★14-15

20:5 *new moon.* I.e., the new moon sacrificial meal (see note on Amos 8:5), which was both a religious and civil festival.

20:14-15 *lovingkindness.* Heb., *hesed* (see note on Hos. 2:19). Love and loyalty, the two essen-

tial aspects of a covenant relationship, are bound together in this word. Jonathan recognized that David would one day be king and requested protection for himself and his family when David would take the throne.

ness of the LORD, that I may not die?

15 "And [a]you shall not cut off your lovingkindness from my house forever, not even when the LORD cuts off every one of the enemies of David from the face of the earth."

16 So Jonathan made a *covenant* with the house of David, *saying*, "[a]May the LORD require *it* at the hands of David's enemies."

17 And Jonathan made David vow again because of his love for him, because [a]he loved him as he loved his own life.

18 Then Jonathan said to him, "[a]Tomorrow is the new moon, and you will be missed because your seat will be empty.

19 "When you have stayed for three days, you shall go down quickly and come to the place where you hid yourself on that eventful day, and you shall remain by the stone Ezel.

20 "And I will shoot three arrows to the side, as though I shot at a target.

21 "And behold, I will send the lad, *saying*, 'Go, find the arrows.' If I specifically say to the lad, 'Behold, the arrows are on this side of you, get them,' then come; for there is safety for you and no harm, as the LORD lives.

22 "But if I say to the youth, '[a]Behold, the arrows are beyond you,' go, for the LORD has sent you away.

23 "[a]As for the agreement of which you and I have spoken, behold, [b]the LORD is between you and me forever."

24 So David hid in the field; and when the new moon came, the king sat down to eat food.

25 And the king sat on his seat as usual, the seat by the wall; then Jonathan rose up and Abner sat down by Saul's side, but [a]David's place was empty.

26 Nevertheless Saul did not speak anything that day, for he thought, "It is an accident, [a]he is not clean, surely *he is* not clean."

27 And it came about the next day, the second *day* of the new moon, that David's place was empty; so Saul said to Jonathan his son, "Why has the son of Jesse not come to the meal, either yesterday or today?"

28 Jonathan then answered Saul, "[a]David earnestly asked leave of me *to go* to Bethlehem,

29 for he said, 'Please let me go, since our family has a sacrifice in the city, and my brother has commanded me to attend. And now, if I have found favor in your sight, please let me get away that I may see my brothers.' For this reason he has not come to the king's table."

30 Then Saul's anger burned against Jonathan and he said to him, "You son of a perverse, rebellious woman! Do I not know that you are choosing the son of Jesse to your own shame and to the shame of your mother's nakedness?

31 "For as long as the son of Jesse lives on the earth, neither you nor your kingdom will be established. Therefore now, send and bring him to me, for [a]he must surely die."

32 But Jonathan answered Saul his father and said to him, "[a]Why should he be put to death? What has he done?"

33 Then [a]Saul hurled his spear at him to strike him down; [b]so Jonathan knew that his father had decided to put David to death.

34 Then Jonathan arose from the table in fierce anger, and did not eat food on the second day of

---

15 [a]2 Sam. 9:1, 3
★16 [a]Deut. 23:21; 1 Sam. 25:22
17 [a]1 Sam. 18:1
18 [a]1 Sam. 20:5, 25
★19
22 [a]1 Sam. 20:37
23 [a]1 Sam. 20:14, 15 [b]Gen. 31:49, 53; 1 Sam. 20:42
25 [a]1 Sam. 20:18
★26 [a]Lev. 7:20, 21; 15:5; 1 Sam. 16:5
28 [a]1 Sam. 20:6
★30
31 [a]2 Sam. 12:5
32 [a]Gen. 31:36; 1 Sam. 19:5; Prov. 31:9; Matt. 27:23
33 [a]1 Sam. 18:11; 19:10 [b]1 Sam. 20:7

20:16 *require it.* I.e., bring it to pass (even in the face of opposition).
20:19 *on that eventful day.* Either a reference to 19:2 or to some unrecorded occasion when Saul schemed to kill David.
20:26 *not clean.* Ritually defiled and thus unable to partake of the festival meal (Lev. 15:16).
20:30 *shame.* Saul vented his anger with the most offensive language. *to the shame of your mother's nakedness.* An expression meaning, "Your mother will be ashamed that she brought you into the world."

the new moon, for he was grieved over David because his father had dishonored him.

35 Now it came about in the morning that Jonathan went out into the field for the appointment with David, and a little lad *was* with him.

36 And he said to his lad, "ᵃRun, find now the arrows which I am about to shoot." As the lad was running, he shot an arrow past him.

37 When the lad reached the place of the arrow which Jonathan had shot, Jonathan called after the lad, and said, "ᵃIs not the arrow beyond you?"

38 And Jonathan called after the lad, "Hurry, be quick, do not stay!" And Jonathan's lad picked up the arrow and came to his master.

39 But the lad was not aware of anything; only Jonathan and David knew about the matter.

40 Then Jonathan gave his weapons to his lad and said to him, "Go, bring *them* to the city."

41 When the lad was gone, David rose from the south side and fell on his face to the ground, and ᵃbowed three times. And they kissed each other and wept together, but ᵇDavid more.

42 And Jonathan said to David, "ᵃGo in safety, inasmuch as we have sworn to each other in the name of the LORD, saying, 'ᵇThe LORD will be between me and you, and between my descendants and your descendants forever.'" Then he rose and departed, while Jonathan went into the city.

5 David protected by Ahimelech, 21:1-9

21 Then David came to ᵃNob to Ahimelech the priest; and Ahimelech ᵇcame trembling to meet David, and said to him, "Why are you alone and no one with you?"

2 And David said to Ahimelech the priest, "The king has commissioned me with a matter, and has said to me, 'ᵃLet no one know anything about the matter on which I am sending you and with which I have commissioned you; and I have directed the young men to a certain place.'

3 "Now therefore, what do you have on hand? Give me five loaves of bread, or whatever can be found."

4 And the priest answered David and said, "There is no ordinary bread on hand, but there is ᵃconsecrated bread; if only the young men have ᵇkept themselves from women."

5 And David answered the priest and said to him, "ᵃSurely women have been kept from us as previously when I set out and the ᵇvessels of the young men were holy, though it was an ordinary journey; how much more then today will their vessels *be* holy?"

6 So ᵃthe priest gave him consecrated *bread*; for there was no bread there but the ᵇbread of the Presence which was removed from before the LORD, in order to put hot bread *in its place* when it was taken away.

Margin references

36 ᵃ1 Sam. 20:20, 21
37 ᵃ1 Sam. 20:22
★41 ᵃGen. 42:6 ᵇ1 Sam. 18:3
★42 ᵃ1 Sam. 20:22 ᵇ1 Sam. 20:15, 16, 23

★ 1 ᵃ1 Sam. 22:19; Neh. 11:32; Is. 10:32 ᵇ1 Sam. 16:4
★ 2 ᵃPs. 141:3
★ 4 ᵃEx. 25:30; Lev. 24:5-9; Matt. 12:4 ᵇEx. 19:15
★ 5 ᵃEx. 19:14, 15 ᵇ1 Thess. 4:4
★ 6 ᵃMatt. 12:3, 4; Luke 6:3, 4 ᵇLev. 24:5-9

20:41 *but David more.* I.e., David broke down with grief.
20:42 From this point on until Saul's death, David was an outcast from the royal court.
21:1 *Nob.* A small town inhabited by priests, just N. of Jerusalem (probably on Mt. Scopus). Here *Ahimelech* (= Ahijah of 14:3) innocently gave David the sacred bread and the sword of Goliath.
21:2 David's lying and deception eventuated in the tragic deaths of the priests (22:9-18).
21:4 *consecrated bread.* The bread of the Presence (see notes on Exod. 25:23-30 and Matt.

12:4).
21:5 Though the journey had no religious purpose, David assured the priest that the men were ceremonially clean, certainly on this special mission. *vessels.* Perhaps a euphemism for their bodies (as in 1 Thess. 4:4).
21:6 The priest recognized that his moral obligation to preserve David's life by providing bread superceded the ceremonial regulation concerning who could eat the showbread (Lev. 24:5-9). Christ referred to this example when teaching the true meaning of the Sabbath law.

★ 7 *a*1 Sam.
14:47; 22:9;
Ps. 52: title
*b*1 Chr.
27:29, 31

7 Now one of the servants of Saul was there that day, detained before the LORD; and his name was *a*Doeg the Edomite, the *b*chief of Saul's shepherds.

8 And David said to Ahimelech, "Now is there not a spear or a sword on hand? For I brought neither my sword nor my weapons with me, because the king's matter was urgent."

★ 9 *a*1 Sam.
17:51, 54
*b*1 Sam. 17:2

9 Then the priest said, "*a*The sword of Goliath the Philistine, whom you killed *b*in the valley of Elah, behold, it is wrapped in a cloth behind the ephod; if you would take it for yourself, take *it*. For there is no other except it here." And David said, "There is none like it; give it to me."

6 David protected by Achish, 21:10-15

★10 *a*Ps.
34:title

10 Then David arose and fled that day from Saul, and went to *a*Achish king of Gath.

★11 *a*Ps.
56:title
*b*1 Sam.
18:7; 29:5

11 But the *a*servants of Achish said to him, "Is this not David the king of the land? *b*Did they not sing of this one as they danced, saying,

'Saul has slain his thousands,
And David his ten thousands'?"

12 *a*Luke
2:19

12 And David *a*took these words to heart, and greatly feared Achish king of Gath.

★13 *a*Ps.
34:title

13 So he *a*disguised his sanity before them, and acted insanely in their hands, and scribbled on the doors of the gate, and let his saliva run down into his beard.

14 Then Achish said to his servants, "Behold, you see the man behaving as a madman. Why do you bring him to me?

15 "Do I lack madmen, that you have brought this one to act the madman in my presence? Shall this one come into my house?"

7 David and his band of men, 22:1-26:25
a In the cave of Adullam and in Mizpah, 22:1-5

22 So David departed from there and *a*escaped to *b*the cave of Adullam; and when his brothers and all his father's household heard *of it*, they went down there to him.

★ 1 *a*Ps.
57:title
*b*Josh.
12:15; 15:35;
2 Sam.
23:13; Ps.
142:title

2 And everyone who was in distress, and everyone who was in debt, and everyone who was discontented, gathered to him; and he became captain over them. Now there were *a*about four hundred men with him.

2 *a*1 Sam.
23:13; 25:13

3 And David went from there to Mizpah of Moab; and he said to the king of Moab, "Please let my father and my mother come *and stay* with you until I know what God will do for me."

★ 3

4 Then he left them with the king of Moab; and they stayed with him all the time that David was in the stronghold.

5 And *a*the prophet Gad said to David, "Do not stay in the stronghold; depart, and go into the land of Judah." So David departed and went into the forest of Hereth.

★ 5 *a*2 Sam.
24:11; 1 Chr.
21:9; 29:29;
2 Chr. 29:25

b Saul slays the priests, 22:6-23

6 Then Saul heard that David and the men who were with

6 *a*Judg.
4:5; 1 Sam.
14:2

21:7 *Doeg* was detained at the sanctuary at Nob because of a vow, a need for cleansing, or because he was suspected of leprosy (Lev. 13:4).
21:9 *ephod.* Cf. 2:18.
21:10 David fled for refuge to Philistine territory, wearing Goliath's sword!
21:11 The anointing of David would not have been known to the Philistines, but his well-known exploits commended him as king.
21:13 *scribbled.* David feigned insanity to persuade Achish to let him leave.

22:1 *cave of Adullam.* A cave near a strategic city at the western edge of the hill country, not far from the Philistine border (10 miles SE. of Gath).
22:3 David took his family to Moab, across the Dead Sea, so that they might be out of reach of Saul. Ruth 1:4 and 4:21-22 record David's family ties with Moab.
22:5 *the forest of Hereth*, to which David returned after his trip to Moab, was only a few miles E. of Adullam.

him had been discovered. Now ᵃSaul was sitting in Gibeah, under the tamarisk tree on the height with his spear in his hand, and all his servants were standing around him.

7 And Saul said to his servants who stood around him, "Hear now, O Benjamites! Will the son of Jesse also give to all of you fields and vineyards? ᵃWill he make you all commanders of thousands and commanders of hundreds?

8 "For all of you have conspired against me so that there is no one who discloses to me ᵃwhen my son makes a *covenant* with the son of Jesse, and there is none of you ᵇwho is sorry for me or discloses to me that my son has stirred up my servant against me to lie in ambush, as *it is* this day."

9 Then ᵃDoeg the Edomite, who was standing by the servants of Saul, answered and said, "ᵇI saw the son of Jesse coming to Nob, to ᶜAhimelech the son of Ahitub.

10 "And ᵃhe inquired of the LORD for him, ᵇgave him provisions, and ᶜgave him the sword of Goliath the Philistine."

11 Then the king sent someone to summon Ahimelech the priest, the son of Ahitub, and all his father's household, the priests who were in Nob; and all of them came to the king.

12 And Saul said, "Listen now, son of Ahitub." And he answered, "Here I am, my lord."

13 Saul then said to him, "Why have you and the son of Jesse conspired against me, in that you have given him bread and a sword and have inquired of God for him, that he should rise up

against me ᵃby lying in ambush as *it is* this day?"

14 ᵃThen Ahimelech answered the king and said, "And who among all your servants is as faithful as David, even the king's son-in-law, who is captain over your guard, and is honored in your house?

15 "Did I *just* begin ᵃto inquire of God for him today? Far be it from me! ᵇDo not let the king impute anything to his servant or to any of the household of my father, for your servant knows nothing at all of this whole affair."

16 But the king said, "You shall surely die, Ahimelech, you and all your father's household!"

17 And ᵃthe king said to the guards who were attending him, "Turn around and put the priests of the LORD to death, because their hand also is with David and because they knew that he was fleeing and did not reveal it to me." But the ᵇservants of the king were not willing to put forth their hands to attack the priests of the LORD.

18 Then the king said to Doeg, "You turn around and attack the priests." And Doeg the Edomite turned around and attacked the priests, and ᵃhe killed that day eighty-five men ᵇwho wore the linen ephod.

19 And ᵃhe struck Nob the city of the priests with the edge of the sword, both men and women, children and infants; also oxen, donkeys, and sheep, he struck with the edge of the sword.

20 But ᵃone son of Ahimelech the son of Ahitub, named Abiathar, ᵇescaped and fled after David.

22:7 Appealing to tribal jealousies, Saul reminded his fellow Benjamites that only he, not David, would favor them.
22:8 *lie in ambush.* Saul claimed that David was a revolutionary, not merely a fugitive.
22:14 *who is captain over your guard.* Lit., who turns aside to your bodyguard; i.e., who has access to your bodyguard. The idea is that,

since David had free access to those who protected Saul's life, how could he be considered an enemy?
22:20 *Abiathar,* who in Mark 2:26 is related to the incident of giving bread to David (21:6), evidently served as coadjutor with his father Ahimelech.

21 And Abiathar told David that Saul had killed the priests of the LORD.

★**22** *a*1 Sam. 21:7
22 Then David said to Abiathar, "I knew on that day, when *a*Doeg the Edomite was there, that he would surely tell Saul. I have brought about *the death* of every person in your father's household.

23 *a*1 Kin. 2:26
23 "Stay with me, do not be afraid, for *a*he who seeks my life seeks your life; for you are safe with me."

c At Keilah, 23:1-12

★ **1** *a*Josh. 15:44; Neh. 3:17, 18
23 Then they told David, saying, "Behold, the Philistines are fighting against *a*Keilah, and are plundering the threshing floors."

2 *a*1 Sam. 23:4, 6, 9-12; 2 Sam. 5:19, 23
2 So David *a*inquired of the LORD, saying, "Shall I go and attack these Philistines?" And the LORD said to David, "Go and attack the Philistines, and deliver Keilah."

3 But David's men said to him, "Behold, we are afraid here in Judah. How much more then if we go to Keilah against the ranks of the Philistines?"

4 *a*Josh. 8:7; Judg. 7:7
4 Then David inquired of the LORD once more. And the LORD answered him and said, "Arise, go down to Keilah, for *a*I will give the Philistines into your hand."

5 So David and his men went to Keilah and fought with the Philistines; and he led away their livestock and struck them with a great slaughter. Thus David delivered the inhabitants of Keilah.

★ **6** *a*1 Sam. 22:20
6 Now it came about, when Abiathar the son of Ahimelech *a*fled to David at Keilah, *that* he came down *with* an ephod in his hand.

7 When it was told Saul that David had come to Keilah, Saul said, "God has delivered him into my hand, for he shut himself in by entering a city with double gates and bars."

8 So Saul summoned all the people for war, to go down to Keilah to besiege David and his men.

9 *a*1 Sam. 22:20
*b*1 Sam. 23:6; 30:7
9 Now David knew that Saul was plotting evil against him; so he said to *a*Abiathar the priest, "*b*Bring the ephod here."

10 Then David said, "O LORD God of Israel, Thy servant has heard for certain that Saul is seeking to come to Keilah to destroy the city on my account.

11 "Will the men of Keilah surrender me into his hand? Will Saul come down just as Thy servant has heard? O LORD God of Israel, I pray, tell Thy servant." And the LORD said, "He will come down."

12 *a*Judg. 15:10-13; 1 Sam. 23:20
12 Then David said, "Will the men of Keilah surrender me and my men into the hand of Saul?" And the LORD said, "*a*They will surrender you."

d In the wilderness of Ziph, 23:13-29

13 *a*1 Sam. 22:2; 25:13
*b*2 Sam. 15:20
13 Then David and his men, *a*about six hundred, arose and departed from Keilah, and they went *b*wherever they could go. When it was told Saul that David had escaped from Keilah, he gave up the pursuit.

★**14** *a*Josh. 15:55; 2 Chr. 11:8 *b*Ps. 32:7
14 And David stayed in the wilderness in the strongholds, and remained in the hill country in the wilderness of *a*Ziph. And Saul

---

22:22 David's deception (21:2) brought devastating consequences, for which he assumed full responsibility.
23:1 *Keilah,* a city of Judah about 3 miles S. of Adullam, bordered on the territory of the Philistines, who would raid the threshing floors after the Israelites had done the hard work of harvesting and processing the grain.

23:6 On the *ephod* see 2:18.
23:14 The *wilderness* of Judah is a desolate, barren area between the hill country and the Dead Sea. David and his men used the many ravines and caves in this area as refuge from Saul. *wilderness of Ziph.* A barren plateau 4 miles SE. of Hebron.

sought him every day, but [b]God did not deliver him into his hand.

★15 **15** Now David became aware that Saul had come out to seek his life while David was in the wilderness of Ziph at Horesh.

★16 [a]1 Sam. 30:6; Neh. 2:18
16 And Jonathan, Saul's son, arose and went to David at Horesh, and [a]encouraged him in God.

17 [a]Ps. 27:1, 3; 118:6; Is. 54:17; Heb. 13:6 [b]1 Sam. 20:31; 24:20
17 Thus he said to him, "[a]Do not be afraid, because the hand of Saul my father shall not find you, and you will be king over Israel and I will be next to you; and [b]Saul my father knows that also."

18 [a]1 Sam. 18:3; 20:12-17, 42; 2 Sam. 9:1; 21:7
18 So [a]the two of them made a covenant before the LORD; and David stayed at Horesh while Jonathan went to his house.

★19 [a]1 Sam. 26:1; Ps. 54:title [b]1 Sam. 26:3
19 Then [a]Ziphites came up to Saul at Gibeah, saying, "Is David not hiding with us in the strongholds at Horesh, on [b]the hill of Hachilah, which is on the south of Jeshimon?

20 [a]1 Sam. 23:12
20 "Now then, O king, come down according to all the desire of your soul to do so; and [a]our part *shall be* to surrender him into the king's hand."

21 [a]1 Sam. 22:8
21 And Saul said, "May you be blessed of the LORD; [a]for you have had compassion on me.

22 "Go now, make more sure, and investigate and see his place where his haunt is, *and* who has seen him there; for I am told that he is very cunning.

23 "So look, and learn about all the hiding places where he hides himself, and return to me with certainty, and I will go with you; and it shall come about if he is in the land that I will search him out among all the thousands of Judah."

★24 [a]Josh. 15:55; 1 Sam. 25:2
24 Then they arose and went to Ziph before Saul. Now David and his men were in the wilder-

ness of [a]Maon, in the Arabah to the south of Jeshimon.

25 When Saul and his men went to seek *him*, they told David, and he came down to the rock and stayed in the wilderness of Maon. And when Saul heard *it*, he pursued David in the wilderness of Maon.

26 [a]Ps. 17:9
26 And Saul went on one side of the mountain, and David and his men on the other side of the mountain; and David was hurrying to get away from Saul, for Saul and his men [a]were surrounding David and his men to seize them.

27 But a messenger came to Saul, saying, "Hurry and come, for the Philistines have made a raid on the land."

28 So Saul returned from pursuing David, and went to meet the Philistines; therefore they called that place the Rock of Escape.

★29 [a]Josh. 15:62; 2 Chr. 20:2
29 And David went up from there and stayed in the strongholds of [a]Engedi.

e At Engedi, David spares Saul, 24:1-22

24 [1] [a]1 Sam. 23:28, 29 [b]1 Sam. 23:19
Now it came about [a]when Saul returned from pursuing the Philistines, [b]he was told, saying, "Behold, David is in the wilderness of Engedi."

2 [a]1 Sam. 26:2
2 Then [a]Saul took three thousand chosen men from all Israel, and went to seek David and his men in front of the Rocks of the Wild Goats.

3 [a]Judg. 3:24 [b]Ps. 57:title; 142:title
3 And he came to the sheepfolds on the way, where there *was* a cave; and Saul [a]went in to relieve himself. Now [b]David and his men were sitting in the inner recesses of the cave.

23:15 *at Horesh.* Somewhere in the area of Ziph.
23:16 Though Saul could not find David, Jonathan located him for this their last meeting.
23:19 *Jeshimon* means "desert" or "waste" and refers to the wilderness SE. of Hebron (23:24; 26:1, 3).
23:24 *wilderness of Maon.* The wilderness near

the city of Maon, 5 miles S. of Ziph. *Arabah* means "wasteland," the Rift Valley N. and S. of the Dead Sea, but here defined as an area in the wilderness of Judah.
23:29 *Engedi.* I.e., the spring of the kid, an oasis E. of Hebron above the shores of the Dead Sea; known for its lush vineyards (Song 1:14).

★ 4 *a*1 Sam.
23:17; 25:28-
30 *b*1 Sam.
26:8, 11

4 And the men of David said to him, "Behold, *a this is* the day of which the LORD said to you, 'Behold; *b*I am about to give your enemy into your hand, and you shall do to him as it seems good to you.' " Then David arose and cut off the edge of Saul's robe secretly.

★ 5 *a*2 Sam.
24:10

5 And it came about afterward that *a*David's conscience bothered him because he had cut off the edge of Saul's *robe.*

6 *a*1 Sam.
26:11

6 So he said to his men, "*a*Far be it from me because of the LORD that I should do this thing to my lord, the LORD's anointed, to stretch out my hand against him, since he is the LORD's anointed."

7 And David persuaded his men with *these* words and did not allow them to rise up against Saul. And Saul arose, left the cave, and went on *his* way.

★ 8 *a*1 Sam.
25:23, 24;
1 Kin. 1:31

8 Now afterward David arose and went out of the cave and called after Saul, saying, "My lord the king!" And when Saul looked behind him, *a*David bowed with his face to the ground and prostrated himself.

9 And David said to Saul, "Why do you listen to the words of men, saying, 'Behold, David seeks to harm you'?

10 *a*Ps. 7:3,
4 *b*1 Sam.
24:4

10 "*a*Behold, this day your eyes have seen that the LORD had given you today into my hand in the cave, and *b*some said to kill you, but *my eye* had pity on you; and I said, 'I will not stretch out my hand against my lord, for he is the LORD's anointed.'

11 *a*2 Kin.
5:13 *b*1 Sam.
23:14, 23;
26:20

11 "Now, *a*my father, see! Indeed, see the edge of your robe in my hand! For in that I cut off the edge of your robe and did not kill you, know and perceive that there

is no evil or rebellion in my hands, and I have not sinned against you, though you *b*are lying in wait for my life to take it.

12 "*a*May the LORD judge between you and me, and may the LORD avenge me on you; but my hand shall not be against you.

13 "As the proverb of the ancients says, '*a*Out of the wicked comes forth wickedness'; but my hand shall not be against you.

14 "After whom has the king of Israel come out? Whom are you pursuing? *a*A dead dog, *b*a single flea?

15 "*a*The LORD therefore be judge and decide between you and me; and may He see and *b*plead my cause, and deliver me from your hand."

16 Now it came about when David had finished speaking these words to Saul, that Saul said, "*a*Is this your voice, my son David?" Then Saul lifted up his voice and wept.

17 *a*And he said to David, "You are more righteous than I; for *b*you have dealt well with me, while I have dealt wickedly with you.

18 "And you have declared today that you have done good to me, that *a*the LORD delivered me into your hand and *yet* you did not kill me.

19 "For if a man *a*finds his enemy, will he let him go away safely? May the LORD therefore reward you with good in return for what you have done to me this day.

20 "And now, behold, *a*I know that you shall surely be king, and that *b*the kingdom of Israel shall be established in your hand.

21 "So now *a*swear to me by the LORD that you will not cut off

12 *a*Gen.
16:5; 31:53;
Judg. 11:27;
1 Sam.
26:10, 23

13 *a*Matt.
7:16-20

★14 *a*2 Sam.
9:8 *b*1 Sam.
26:20

15 *a*1 Sam.
24:12 *b*Ps.
35:1; 43:1;
119:154;
Mic. 7:9

16 *a*1 Sam.
26:17

★17 *a*1 Sam.
26:21 *b*Matt.
5:44

18 *a*1 Sam.
26:23

19 *a*1 Sam.
23:17

20 *a*1 Sam.
23:17
*b*1 Sam.
13:14
21 *a*Gen.
21:23;
1 Sam.
20:14-17;
2 Sam.
21:6-8

24:4 Apparently Saul laid his robe to the side when he entered the cave, and David was able to cut off a piece unobserved.
24:5 David's conscience was troubled, for touching Saul's clothing was tantamount to touching his person, and David knew it was wrong to lift up a hand against the Lord's anointed king (24:6, 10).

24:8 David honored Saul as king of Israel, though Saul was his enemy (cf. 1 Pet. 2:13, 17).
24:14 David described himself as perfectly harmless to King Saul.
24:17 Saul apparently felt genuinely sorry for the way he treated David, but his remorse was temporary (26:1-2).

my descendants after me, and that you will not destroy my name from my father's household."

^{22 a1 Sam.
23:29}

22 And David swore to Saul. And Saul went to his home, but David and his men went up to ^athe stronghold.

f David and Abigail, 25:1–44

^{★ 1 a1 Sam.
28:3 bNum.
20:29; Deut.
34:8 c2 Kin.
21:18; 2 Chr.
33:20 dGen.
21:21; Num.
10:12; 13:3}

25 ^aThen Samuel died; and all Israel gathered together and ^bmourned for him, and ^cburied him at his house in Ramah. And David arose and went down to the ^dwilderness of Paran.

^{★ 2 a1 Sam.
23:24 bJosh.
15:55 cGen.
38:13;
2 Sam. 13:23}

2 Now *there was* a man in ^aMaon whose business was in ^bCarmel; and the man was very rich, and he had three thousand sheep and a thousand goats. And it came about while ^che was shearing his sheep in Carmel

^{★ 3 aProv.
31:10 bJosh.
15:13;
1 Sam. 30:14}

3 (now the man's name was Nabal, and his ^awife's name was Abigail. And the woman was intelligent and beautiful in appearance, but the man was harsh and evil in *his* dealings, and he was ^ba Calebite),

4 that David heard in the wilderness that Nabal was shearing his sheep.

5 So David sent ten young men, and David said to the young men, "Go up to Carmel, visit Nabal and greet him in my name;

^{6 a1 Chr.
12:18; Ps.
122:7; Luke
10:5}

6 and thus you shall say, 'Have a long life, ^apeace be to you, and peace be to your house, and peace be to all that you have.

^{7 a2 Sam.
13:23, 24
b1 Sam.
25:15; 21}

7 'And now I have heard ^athat you have shearers; now your shepherds have been with us and we have not insulted them, ^bnor

have they missed anything all the days they were in Carmel.

8 'Ask your young men and they will tell you. Therefore let *my* young men find favor in your eyes, for we have come on ^aa festive day. Please give whatever you find at hand to your servants and to your son David.' "

^{★ 8 aNeh.
8:10-12;
Esth. 9:19,
22}

9 When David's young men came, they spoke to Nabal according to all these words in David's name; then they waited.

10 But Nabal answered David's servants, and said, "^aWho is David? And who is the son of Jesse? There are many servants today who are each breaking away from his master.

^{10 aJudg.
9:28}

11 "Shall I then ^atake my bread and my water and my meat that I have slaughtered for my shearers, and give it to men whose origin I do not know?"

^{★11 aJudg.
8:6, 15}

12 So David's young men retraced their way and went back; and they came and told him according to all these words.

13 And David said to his men, "Each *of you* gird on his sword." So each man girded on his sword. And David also girded on his sword, and about ^afour hundred men went up behind David while two hundred ^bstayed with the baggage.

^{13 a1 Sam.
23:13
b1 Sam.
30:24}

14 But one of the young men told Abigail, Nabal's wife, saying, "Behold, David sent messengers from the wilderness to ^agreet our master, and he scorned them.

^{★14 a1 Sam.
13:10; 15:13}

15 "Yet the men were very good to us, and we were not ^ainsulted, nor did we miss anything as long as we went about with them, while we were in the fields.

^{15 a1 Sam.
25:7, 21}

16 "^aThey were a wall to us both by night and by day, all the

^{16 aEx.
14:22; Job
1:10}

25:1 *wilderness of Paran.* A desert area in the Sinai Peninsula, far to the SW. of Palestine. The LXX reads "wilderness of Maon" (cf. v. 2).
25:2 Nabal's place of business was in Carmel (not the Mt. Carmel near Galilee, but a place 7 miles S. of Hebron), while his home was actually in Maon, a mile farther S.
25:3 *Nabal* means "fool," and his manner of conducting himself indicates that the name was appropriate.

25:8 *festive.* Lit., good. I.e., a day of prosperity and celebration at shearing time (cf. v. 36). David and his men had been protecting the flocks and possessions of Nabal (25:15-16, 21) in return for provisions, and payday had finally arrived.
25:11 Nabal not only refused to pay, but pretended not to know of David or of their agreement.
25:14 *scorned.* Lit., yelled or screamed at.

time we were with them tending the sheep.

17 "Now therefore, know and consider what you should do, for evil is plotted against our master and against all his household; and he is such a worthless man that no one can speak to him."

18 a2 Sam. 16:1; 1 Chr. 12:40

18 Then Abigail hurried and atook two hundred *loaves* of bread and two jugs of wine and five sheep already prepared and five measures of roasted grain and a hundred clusters of raisins and two hundred cakes of figs, and loaded *them* on donkeys.

19 aGen. 32:16, 20

19 And she said to her young men, "aGo on before me; behold, I am coming after you." But she did not tell her husband Nabal.

20 And it came about as she was riding on her donkey and coming down by the hidden part of the mountain, that behold, David and his men were coming down toward her; so she met them.

21 aPs. 109:5; Prov. 17:13

21 Now David had said, "Surely in vain I have guarded all that this *man* has in the wilderness, so that nothing was missed of all that belonged to him; and he has areturned me evil for good.

22 a1 Sam. 3:17; 20:13 b1 Kin. 14:10

22 "aMay God do so to the enemies of David, and more also, bif by morning I leave *as much as* one male of any who belong to him."

23 a1 Sam. 20:41

23 When Abigail saw David, she hurried and dismounted from her donkey, and fell on her face before David, aand bowed herself to the ground.

24 And she fell at his feet and said, "On me alone, my lord, be the blame. And please let your maidservant speak to you, and listen to the words of your maidservant.

25 "Please do not let my lord pay attention to this worthless man, Nabal, for as his name is, so is he. Nabal is his name and folly

is with him; but I your maidservant did not see the young men of my lord whom you sent.

26 aHeb. 10:30 b2 Sam. 18:32

26 "Now therefore, my lord, as the LORD lives, and as your soul lives, since the LORD has restrained you from shedding blood, and afrom avenging yourself by your own hand, now then blet your enemies, and those who seek evil against my lord, be as Nabal.

27 aGen. 33:11; 1 Sam. 30:26

27 "And now let athis gift which your maidservant has brought to my lord be given to the young men who accompany my lord.

28 a1 Sam. 25:24 b1 Sam. 22:14; 2 Sam. 7:11, 16 c1 Sam. 18:17 d1 Sam. 24:11; Ps. 7:3

28 "Please forgive athe transgression of your maidservant; for bthe LORD will certainly make for my lord an enduring house, because my lord is cfighting the battles of the LORD, and devil shall not be found in you all your days.

★29 aJer. 10:18

29 "And should anyone rise up to pursue you and to seek your life, then the life of my lord shall be bound in the bundle of the living with the LORD your God; but the lives of your enemies aHe will sling out as from the hollow of a sling.

30 a1 Sam. 13:14

30 "And it shall come about when the LORD shall do for my lord according to all the good that He has spoken concerning you, and ashall appoint you ruler over Israel,

★31 aGen. 40:14; 1 Sam. 25:30

31 that this will not cause grief or a troubled heart to my lord, both by having shed blood without cause and by my lord having avenged himself. aWhen the LORD shall deal well with my lord, then remember your maidservant."

32 aEx. 18:10; 1 Kin. 1:48; Ps. 41:13; 72:18; 106:48; Luke 1:68

32 Then David said to Abigail, "aBlessed be the LORD God of Israel, who sent you this day to meet me,

33 a1 Sam. 25:26

33 and blessed be your discernment, and blessed be you, awho have kept me this day from

---

25:29 The figure is taken from the custom of binding valuables in a bundle to protect them from injury. God cares for His own as a man does his treasure.

25:31 Abigail argued that the needless shedding of blood at this time would not be in David's best interests.

bloodshed, and from avenging myself by my own hand.

34 "Nevertheless, as the Lord God of Israel lives, ᵃwho has restrained me from harming you, unless you had come quickly to meet me, surely there would not have been left to Nabal until the morning light *as much as* one male."

35 So David received from her hand what she had brought him, and he said to her, "ᵃGo up to your house in peace. See, I have listened to you and ᵇgranted your request."

36 Then Abigail came to Nabal, and behold, he was holding ᵃa feast in his house, like the feast of a king. And Nabal's heart was merry within him, ᵇfor he was very drunk; so ᶜshe did not tell him anything at all until the morning light.

37 But it came about in the morning, when the wine had gone out of Nabal, that his wife told him these things, and his heart died within him so that he became *as* a stone.

38 And about ten days later, it happened that ᵃthe Lord struck Nabal, and he died.

39 When David heard that Nabal was dead, he said, "Blessed be the Lord, who has ᵃpleaded the cause of my reproach from the hand of Nabal, and ᵇhas kept back His servant from evil. The Lord has also returned the evildoing of Nabal on his own head." Then David sent ᶜa proposal to Abigail, to take her as his wife.

40 When the servants of David came to Abigail at Carmel, they spoke to her, saying, "David has sent us to you, to take you as his wife."

41 And she arose ᵃand bowed with her face to the ground and said, "Behold, your maidservant is a maid ᵇto wash the feet of my lord's servants."

42 Then ᵃAbigail quickly arose, and rode on a donkey, with her five maidens who attended her; and she followed the messengers of David, and became his wife.

43 David had also taken Ahinoam of ᵃJezreel, and ᵇthey both became his wives.

44 Now Saul had given ᵃMichal his daughter, David's wife, to Palti the son of Laish, who was from ᵇGallim.

g *In the wilderness of Ziph, David spares Saul again, 26:1-25*

26 Then the Ziphites came to Saul at Gibeah, saying, "ᵃIs not David hiding on the hill of Hachilah, *which is* before Jeshimon?"

2 So Saul arose ᵃand went down to the wilderness of Ziph, having with him ᵃthree thousand chosen men of Israel, to search for David in the wilderness of Ziph.

3 And Saul camped in the hill of Hachilah, which is before Jeshimon, ᵃbeside the road, and David was staying in the wilderness. When ᵇhe saw that Saul came after him into the wilderness,

4 David sent out spies, and he knew that Saul was definitely coming.

5 David then arose and came to the place where Saul had camped. And David saw the place where Saul lay, and ᵃAbner the son of Ner, the commander of his army; and Saul was lying in the circle of the camp, and the people were camped around him.

6 Then David answered and said to Ahimelech ᵃthe Hittite and to ᵇAbishai the son of Zeruiah, Joab's brother, saying, "Who ᶜwill go down with me to Saul in the camp?" And Abishai said, "I will go down with you."

34 ᵃ1 Sam. 25:26

35 ᵃ1 Sam. 20:42; 2 Kin. 5:19 ᵇGen. 19:21

36 ᵃ2 Sam. 13:28 ᵇProv. 20:1; Is. 5:11; Hos. 4:11 ᶜ1 Sam. 25:19

★**37**

38 ᵃ1 Sam. 26:10; 2 Sam. 6:7; Ps. 104:29

39 ᵃ1 Sam. 24:15; Prov. 22:23 ᵇ1 Sam. 25:26, 34 ᶜSong 8:8

41 ᵃ1 Sam. 25:23 ᵇMark 1:7

42 ᵃGen. 24:61-67

★**43** ᵃJosh. 15:56 ᵇ1 Sam. 27:3; 30:5

44 ᵃ1 Sam. 18:27; 2 Sam. 3:14 ᵇIs. 10:30

★ **1** ᵃ1 Sam. 23:19; Ps. 54:title

★ **2** ᵃ1 Sam. 13:2; 24:2

3 ᵃ1 Sam. 24:3 ᵇ1 Sam. 23:15

5 ᵃ1 Sam. 14:50, 51; 17:55

6 ᵃGen. 23:3; 26:34; Josh. 3:10; 1 Kin. 10:29; 2 Kin. 7:6 ᵇ1 Chr. 2:16 ᶜJudg. 7:10, 11

25:37 Nabal apparently suffered a stroke and was paralyzed.
25:43 For note on polygamy, see 1:2.
26:1 The incidents related in chapters 24 and 26

are similar, but the differences are sufficient to establish that the events are in fact separate. *Jeshimon*. See note on 23:19.
26:2 *wilderness of Ziph*. See note on 23:14.

7 So David and Abishai came to the people by night, and behold, Saul lay sleeping inside the circle of the camp, with his spear stuck in the ground at his head; and Abner and the people were lying around him.

8 Then Abishai said to David, "Today God has delivered your enemy into your hand; now therefore, please let me strike him with the spear to the ground with one stroke, and I will not strike him the second time."

9 But David said to Abishai, "Do not destroy him, for ªwho can stretch out his hand against the LORD's anointed and be without guilt?"

10 David also said, "As the LORD lives, ªsurely the LORD will strike him, or ᵇhis day will come that he dies, or ᶜhe will go down into battle and perish.

11 "ªThe LORD forbid that I should stretch out my hand against the LORD's anointed; but now please take the spear that is at his head and the jug of water, and let us go."

12 So David took the spear and the jug of water from *beside* Saul's head, and they went away, but no one saw or knew *it,* nor did any awake, for they were all asleep, because ªa sound sleep from the LORD had fallen on them.

13 Then David crossed over to the other side, and stood on top of the mountain at a distance *with* a large area between them.

14 And David called to the people and to Abner the son of Ner, saying, "Will you not answer, Abner?" Then Abner answered and said, "Who are you who calls to the king?"

15 So David said to Abner, "Are you not a man? And who is like you in Israel? Why then have you not guarded your lord the king? For one of the people came to destroy the king your lord.

16 "This thing that you have done is not good. As the LORD lives, *all* of you ªmust surely die, because you did not guard your lord, the LORD's anointed. And now, see where the king's spear is, and the jug of water that was at his head."

17 Then Saul recognized David's voice and said, "ªIs this your voice, my son David?" And David said, "It is my voice, my lord the king."

18 He also said, "ªWhy then is my lord pursuing his servant? For what have I done? Or what evil is in my hand?

19 "Now therefore, please let my lord the king listen to the words of his servant. If ªthe LORD has stirred you up against me, ᵇlet Him accept an offering; but ᶜif it is men, cursed are they before the LORD, for ᵈthey have driven me out today that I should have no attachment with the inheritance of the LORD, saying, 'Go, serve other gods.'

20 "Now then, do not let my blood fall to the ground away from the presence of the LORD; for the king of Israel has come out to search for ªa single flea, just as one hunts a partridge in the mountains."

21 Then Saul said, "ªI have sinned. Return, my son David, for I will not harm you again because my life was precious in your sight this day. Behold, I have played the fool and have committed a serious error."

22 And David answered and said, "Behold the spear of the

Cross-references (margin):

★ **9-10**

9 ªl Sam. 24:6, 7; 2 Sam. 1:14, 16

10 ªDeut. 32:35; 1 Sam. 25:26, 38; Rom. 12:19; Heb. 10:30 ᵇGen. 47:29; Deut. 31:14; Ps. 37:13 ᶜl Sam. 31:6

11 ªl Sam. 24:6, 12; Rom. 12:17, 19; 1 Pet. 3:9

12 ªGen. 2:21; 15:12; Is. 29:10

16 ªl Sam. 20:31

17 ªl Sam. 24:16

18 ªl Sam. 24:9, 11-14

★ **19** ª2 Sam. 16:11 ᵇGen. 8:21 ᶜl Sam. 24:9 ᵈJosh. 22:25-27

★ **20** ªl Sam. 24:14

21 ªEx. 9:27; 1 Sam. 15:24, 30; 24:17

26:9-10 David recognized God's sovereignty over the life of Saul and believed that God would remove him from office in His own perfect time.

26:19 *let Him accept an offering.* David would be willing to offer an atoning sacrifice to God if there were any offense on his own part. But if other *men* (i.e., evil men) were the cause of

Saul's hostility toward him, they should be judged. *Go, serve other gods.* David felt that his exile from the land, the inheritance from God, was equivalent to forcing him to abandon the worship of the Lord, for there were no sanctuaries of the Lord outside Israelite territory.

26:20 See 24:14.

king! Now let one of the young men come over and take it.

²³ ^a1 Sam. 24:19; Ps. 7:8; 18:20; 62:12 ^b1 Sam. 24:12

23 "And ^athe LORD will repay each man *for* his righteousness and his faithfulness; for the LORD delivered you into *my* hand today, but ^bI refused to stretch out my hand against the LORD's anointed.

²⁴ ^a1 Sam. 18:30 ^bPs. 54:7

24 "Now behold, as your life was ^ahighly valued in my sight this day, so may my life be highly valued in the sight of the LORD, and may He ^bdeliver me from all distress."

²⁵ ^a1 Sam. 24:19 ^b1 Sam. 24:22

25 Then Saul said to David, "^aBlessed are you, my son David; you will both accomplish much and surely prevail." So ^bDavid went on his way, and Saul returned to his place.

G The Refuge of David in Philistine Territory, 27:1–31:13

1 David becomes a Philistine vassal, 27:1–28:2

★ 1 ^a1 Sam. 26:19

27 Then David said to himself, "Now I will perish one day by the hand of Saul. ^aThere is nothing better for me than to escape into the land of the Philistines. Saul then will despair of searching for me anymore in all the territory of Israel, and I will escape from his hand."

★ 2 ^a1 Sam. 25:13 ^b1 Sam. 21:10; 1 Kin. 2:39

2 So David arose and crossed over, he and ^athe six hundred men who were with him, to ^bAchish the son of Maoch, king of Gath.

3 ^a1 Sam. 30:3; 2 Sam. 2:3 ^b1 Sam. 25:42, 43

3 And David lived with Achish at Gath, he and his men, ^aeach with his household, *even* David with ^bhis two wives, Ahinoam the Jezreelitess, and

Abigail the Carmelitess, Nabal's widow.

4 Now it was told Saul that David had fled to Gath, so he no longer searched for him.

5 Then David said to Achish, "If now I have found favor in your sight, let them give me a place in one of the cities in the country, that I may live there; for why should your servant live in the royal city with you?"

6 So Achish gave him Ziklag that day; therefore ^aZiklag has belonged to the kings of Judah to this day.

★ 6 ^aJosh. 15:31; 19:5; Neh. 11:28

7 And the number of days that David lived in the country of the Philistines was ^aa year and four months.

7 ^a1 Sam. 29:3

8 Now David and his men went up and raided ^athe Geshurites and the Girzites and ^bthe Amalekites; for they were the inhabitants of the land from ancient times, as you come to ^cShur even as far as the land of Egypt.

★ 8-10

8 ^aJosh. 13:2, 13 ^bEx. 17:8; 1 Sam. 15:7, 8 ^cEx. 15:22

9 And David attacked the land and did not leave a man or a woman alive, and he ^atook away the sheep, the cattle, the donkeys, the camels, and the clothing. Then he returned and came to Achish.

9 ^a1 Sam. 15:3; Job 1:3

10 Now Achish said, "Where have you ^amade a raid today?" And David said, "Against the Negev of Judah and against the Negev of ^bthe Jerahmeelites and against the Negev of ^cthe Kenites."

★10 ^a1 Sam. 23:27 ^b1 Sam. 30:29, 1 Chr. 2:9, 25 ^cJudg. 1:16; 4:11

11 And David did not leave a man or a woman alive, to bring to Gath, saying, "Lest they should tell about us, saying, 'So has David done and so *has been* his practice all the time he has lived

---

27:1 David, placing no confidence in Saul's blessing (26:25), sought refuge from Saul outside Israelite territory.

27:2 David returned to Achish, king of Gath (cf. 21:10-15), who welcomed him, no doubt having heard of the split between David and Saul and desirous of strengthening his army with David's 600 fighting men. *Gath.* See 5:8.

27:6 *Ziklag.* A city located about 12 miles N. of Beersheba. The move was probably motivated

by David's desire to be free from Philistine surveillance and to avoid pagan influence.

27:8-10 David used Ziklag as a base for his raids on the northern Sinai desert tribes which were enemies of Judah, while he pretended to serve the interests of Achish.

27:10 *Negev.* The geographical region S. of the hill country of Judah, the center of which is Beersheba.

in the country of the Philistines.' "

12 So Achish believed David, saying, "He has surely made himself odious among his people Israel; therefore he will become my servant forever."

28 Now it came about in those days that ᵃthe Philistines gathered their armed camps for war, to fight against Israel. And Achish said to David, "Know assuredly that you will go out with me in the camp, you and your men."

2 And David said to Achish, "Very well, you shall know what your servant can do." So Achish said to David, "Very well, I will make you my bodyguard ᵃfor life."

2 Saul consults the medium at Endor, 28:3–25

3 Now ᵃSamuel was dead, and all Israel had lamented him and buried him ᵇin Ramah his own city. And Saul had removed from the land those who ᶜwere mediums and spiritists.

4 So the Philistines gathered together and came and camped ᵃin Shunem; and Saul gathered all Israel together and they camped in ᵇGilboa.

5 When Saul saw the camp of the Philistines, he was afraid and his heart trembled greatly.

6 ᵃWhen Saul inquired of the LORD, ᵇthe LORD did not answer him, either by ᶜdreams or by ᵈUrim or by prophets.

7 Then Saul said to his servants, "Seek for me a woman who is a medium, that I may go to her and inquire of her." And his servants said to him, "Behold, ᵃthere is a woman who is a medium at ᵇEn-dor."

8 Then Saul ᵃdisguised himself by putting on other clothes, and went, he and two men with him, and they came to the woman by night; and he said, "ᵇConjure up for me, please, and ᶜbring up for me whom I shall name to you."

9 But the woman said to him, "Behold, you know ᵃwhat Saul has done, how he has cut off those who are mediums and spiritists from the land. Why are you then laying a snare for my life to bring about my death?"

10 And Saul vowed to her by the LORD, saying, "As the LORD lives, there shall no punishment come upon you for this thing."

11 Then the woman said, "Whom shall I bring up for you?" And he said, "Bring up Samuel for me."

12 When the woman saw Samuel, she cried out with a loud voice; and the woman spoke to Saul, saying, "Why have you deceived me? For you are Saul."

13 And the king said to her, "Do not be afraid; but what do you see?" And the woman said to Saul, "I see a divine being coming up out of the earth."

Marginal references (left column):

1 ᵃ1 Sam. 29:1

★ 2 ᵃ1 Sam. 1:22, 28

★ 3 ᵃ1 Sam. 25:1 ᵇ1 Sam. 7:17 ᶜLev. 19:31; 20:27; Deut. 18:10; 1 Sam. 15:23

★ 4-5
4 ᵃJosh. 19:18; 1 Sam. 28:4; 1 Kin. 1:3; 2 Kin. 4:8
ᵇ1 Sam. 31:1 ★ 6 ᵃ1 Chr. 10:13, 14 ᵇ1 Sam. 14:37; Prov. 1:24-31 ᶜNum. 12:6; Joel 2:28 ᵈEx. 28:30; Num. 27:21

Marginal references (right column):

★ 7 ᵃActs 16:16 ᵇJosh. 17:11; Ps. 83:10

8 ᵃ2 Chr. 18:29; 35:22 ᵇ1 Chr. 10:13; Is. 8:19 ᶜDeut. 18:10, 11

9 ᵃ1 Sam. 28:3

★12

★13

28:2 David's response to Achish's summons to join in war against the Israelites was ambiguous. He dared not refuse; yet to accede would have pitted him against his own people. This aspect of the story resumes in 29:1.

28:3 In obedience to the law, Saul had removed those who practiced spiritism (see notes on Exod. 22:18 and Deut. 18:10-11).

28:4-5 Saul was in panic because the Philistines were poised at *Shunem* (seven miles E. of Megiddo), ready to battle the Israelites in the plain of Jezreel, where their sophisticated weapons could be used more advantageously to crush the Israelites.

28:6 *Urim.* See notes on 14:3 and Exod. 28:30. Saul may have set up under Zadok a rival priesthood to Abiathar's and so could get no guidance from God.

28:7 *a woman who is a medium.* One who practices necromancy, consulting the dead to determine the future, strictly forbidden by the law (Lev. 19:31). At *En-dor,* between Mt. Tabor and the Hill of Moreh, lived a medium who had escaped Saul's purge.

28:12 The medium shrieked with fear when Samuel actually appeared, rather than some spirit that would impersonate him. On this occasion God miraculously permitted the actual spirit of Samuel to speak and announce Saul's imminent death (v. 19).

28:13 *a divine being.* A superhuman figure or spirit of the dead (Samuel).

14 a1 Sam.
15:27
b1 Sam. 24:8

14 And he said to her, "What is his form?" And she said, "An old man is coming up, and ᵃhe is wrapped with a robe." And Saul knew that it was Samuel, and ᵇhe bowed with his face to the ground and did homage.

15 a1 Sam.
16:14; 18:12
b1 Sam. 28:6

15 Then Samuel said to Saul, "Why have you disturbed me by bringing me up?" And Saul answered, "I am greatly distressed; for the Philistines are waging war against me, and ᵃGod has departed from me and ᵇanswers me no more, either through prophets or by dreams; therefore I have called you, that you may make known to me what I should do."

16 And Samuel said, "Why then do you ask me, since the LORD has departed from you and has become your adversary?

17 a1 Sam.
15:28

17 "And the LORD has done according ᵃas He spoke through me; for the LORD has torn the kingdom out of your hand and given it to your neighbor, to David.

★18 a1 Sam.
15:20, 26;
1 Kin. 20:42

18 "As ᵃyou did not obey the LORD and did not execute His fierce wrath on Amalek, so the LORD has done this thing to you this day.

★19 a1 Sam.
31:2; Job
3:17-19

19 "Moreover the LORD will also give over Israel along with you into the hands of the Philistines, therefore tomorrow ᵃyou and your sons will be with me. Indeed the LORD will give over the army of Israel into the hands of the Philistines!"

20 Then Saul immediately fell full length upon the ground and was very afraid because of the words of Samuel; also there was no strength in him, for he had eaten no food all day and all night.

21 aJudg.
12:3; 1 Sam.
19:5; Job
13:14

21 And the woman came to Saul and saw that he was terrified, and said to him, "Behold, your maidservant has obeyed you, and ᵃI have taken my life in my hand,

and have listened to your words which you spoke to me.

22 "So now also, please listen to the voice of your maidservant, and let me set a piece of bread before you that *you may* eat and have strength when you go on *your* way."

23 a1 Kin.
21:4 b2 Kin.
5:13 cEsth.
1:6; Ezek.
23:41

23 But he refused and said, "ᵃI will not eat." ᵇHowever, his servants together with the woman urged him, and he listened to them. So he arose from the ground and sat on ᶜthe bed.

24 aGen.
18:7; Luke
15:23, 27, 30
bGen. 18:6

24 And the woman had a ᵃfattened calf in the house, and she quickly slaughtered it; and she ᵇtook flour, kneaded it, and baked unleavened bread from it.

25 And she brought *it* before Saul and his servants, and they ate. Then they arose and went away that night.

3 David dismissed by the Philistines, 29:1-11

1 a1 Sam.
28:1 bJosh.
12:18; 19:30;
1 Sam. 4:1;
1 Kin. 20:30
c1 Kin. 21:1;
2 Kin. 9:30

29 Now ᵃthe Philistines gathered together all their armies to ᵇAphek, while the Israelites were camping by the spring which is in ᶜJezreel.

★ 2 a1 Sam.
28:1, 2

2 And the lords of the Philistines were proceeding on by hundreds and by thousands, and ᵃDavid and his men were proceeding on in the rear with Achish.

3 a1 Sam.
27:7 b1 Sam.
27:1-6;
1 Chr. 12:19,
20; Dan. 6:5

3 Then the commanders of the Philistines said, "What *are* these Hebrews *doing here?*" And Achish said to the commanders of the Philistines, "Is this not David, the servant of Saul the king of Israel, ᵃwho has been with me these days, or *rather* these years, and ᵇI have found no fault in him from the day he deserted *to me* to this day?"

4 a1 Sam.
27:6 b1 Sam.
14:21

4 But the commanders of the Philistines were angry with him, and the commanders of the Philistines said to him, "Make the man go back, that he may return

---

28:18 On *Amalek* see notes on Exod. 17:8 and 1 Sam. 30:1.
28:19 *with me.* I.e., in death.

29:2 *the lords of the Philistines.* Civil rulers of the Philistine cities (of whom Achish was one).

a to his place where you have assigned him, and do not let him go down to battle with us, b lest in the battle he become an adversary to us. For with what could this *man* make himself acceptable to his lord? *Would it* not *be* with the heads of these men?

5 a1 Sam. 18:7; 21:11

5 "Is this not David, a of whom they sing in the dances, saying,

'Saul has slain his thousands,
And David his ten thousands'?"

6 a2 Sam. 3:25; 2 Kin. 19:27; Is. 37:28 b1 Sam. 27:8-12; 29:3

6 Then Achish called David and said to him, "*As* the LORD lives, you *have been* upright, and a your going out and your coming in with me in the army are pleasing in my sight; b for I have not found evil in you from the day of your coming to me to this day. Nevertheless, you are not pleasing in the sight of the lords.

7 "Now therefore return, and go in peace, that you may not displease the lords of the Philistines."

8 a1 Sam. 27:10-12

8 And David said to Achish, "a But what have I done? And what have you found in your servant from the day when I came before you to this day, that I may not go and fight against the enemies of my lord the king?"

9 a2 Sam. 14:17, 20; 19:27 b1 Sam. 29:4

9 But Achish answered and said to David, "I know that you are pleasing in my sight, a like an angel of God; nevertheless b the commanders of the Philistines have said, 'He must not go up with us to the battle.'

10 a1 Chr. 12:19, 22

10 "Now then arise early in the morning a with the servants of your lord who have come with you, and as soon as you have arisen early in the morning and have light, depart."

★11

11 So David arose early, he and his men, to depart in the morning, to return to the land of the Philistines. And the Philistines went up to Jezreel.

4 *David destroys the Amalekites,* 30:1–31

★ 1 a1 Sam. 29:4, 11 b1 Sam. 15:7; 27:8-10 c1 Sam. 27:6, 8

30 Then it happened when David and his men came to a Ziklag on the third day, that b the Amalekites had made a raid on the Negev and on c Ziklag, and had overthrown Ziklag and burned it with fire;

★ 2 a1 Sam. 27:11

2 and they took captive the women *and all* who were in it, both small and great, a without killing anyone, and carried *them* off and went their way.

3 And when David and his men came to the city, behold, it was burned with fire, and their wives and their sons and their daughters had been taken captive.

4 a Num. 14:1

4 Then David and the people who were with him a lifted their voices and wept until there was no strength in them to weep.

5 a1 Sam. 25:42, 43; 2 Sam. 2:2

5 Now a David's two wives had been taken captive, Ahinoam the Jezreelitess and Abigail the widow of Nabal the Carmelite.

6 a Ex. 17:4; John 8:59 b1 Sam. 23:16; Ps. 18:2; 27:14; 31:24; 71:4, 5; Rom. 4:20

6 Moreover David was greatly distressed because a the people spoke of stoning him, for all the people were embittered, each one because of his sons and his daughters. But b David strengthened himself in the LORD his God.

★ 7 a1 Sam. 23:6, 9 b1 Sam. 22:20-23

7 Then a David said to b Abiathar the priest, the son of Ahimelech, "Please bring me the ephod." So Abiathar brought the ephod to David.

8 a1 Sam. 23:2, 4; Ps. 50:15; 91:15 b Ex. 15:9 c1 Sam. 30:18

8 And a David inquired of the LORD, saying, "b Shall I pursue this band? Shall I overtake them?" And He said to him, "Pursue, for

---

29:9 *like an angel of God.* A common expression of courtesy.

29:11 The Lord used the suspicion of the Philistines to deliver David from the distressing predicament of fighting Israel or being killed by Achish for disloyalty.

30:1 The Amalekites, whom Saul failed to destroy completely (15:2-3, 10-19), continued to be a curse to the Israelites.

30:2 They intended to make their captives slaves.

30:7 *ephod.* See 14:3.

you shall surely overtake them, ^cand you shall surely rescue *all.*"

★ **9** ^a1 Sam. 27:2

9 So David went, ^ahe and the six hundred men who were with him, and came to the brook Besor, *where* those left behind remained.

10 ^a1 Sam. 30:9, 21

10 But David pursued, he and four hundred men, for ^atwo hundred who were too exhausted to cross the brook Besor, remained *behind.*

11 Now they found an Egyptian in the field and brought him to David, and gave him bread and he ate, and they provided him water to drink.

12 ^aJudg. 15:19

12 And they gave him a piece of fig cake and two clusters of raisins, and he ate; ^athen his spirit revived. For he had not eaten bread or drunk water for three days and three nights.

13 And David said to him, "To whom do you belong? And where are you from?" And he said, "I am a young man of Egypt, a servant of an Amalekite; and my master left me behind when I fell sick three days ago.

14 ^a1 Sam. 30:1, 16; 2 Sam. 8:18; 1 Kin. 1:38, 44; Ezek. 25:16; Zeph. 2:5 ^bJosh. 14:13; 15:13; 21:12 ^c1 Sam. 30:1

14 "We made a raid on ^athe Negev of the Cherethites, and on that which belongs to Judah, and on ^bthe Negev of Caleb, and ^cwe burned Ziklag with fire."

15 Then David said to him, "Will you bring me down to this band?" And he said, "Swear to me by God that you will not kill me or deliver me into the hands of my master, and I will bring you down to this band."

16 ^aLuke 12:19; 17:27f. ^b1 Sam. 30:14

16 And when he had brought him down, behold, they were spread over all the land, ^aeating and drinking and dancing because of ^ball the great spoil that they had taken from the land of the Philistines and from the land of Judah.

17 ^a1 Sam. 11:11 ^bJudg. 7:12; 1 Sam. 15:3

17 And David slaughtered them ^afrom the twilight until the evening of the next day; and not a man of them escaped, except four hundred young men who rode on ^bcamels and fled.

18 ^aGen. 14:16

18 So David ^arecovered all that the Amalekites had taken, and rescued his two wives.

19 ^a1 Sam. 30:8

19 But nothing of theirs was missing, whether small or great, sons or daughters, spoil or anything that they had taken for themselves; ^aDavid brought *it* all back.

★**20** ^a1 Sam. 30:26-31

20 So David had captured all the sheep and the cattle *which the people* drove ahead of the *other* livestock, and they said, "^aThis is David's spoil."

21 ^a1 Sam. 30:10

21 When ^aDavid came to the two hundred men who were too exhausted to follow David, who had also been left at the brook Besor, and they went out to meet David and to meet the people who were with him, then David approached the people and greeted them.

22 Then all the wicked and worthless men among those who went with David answered and said, "Because they did not go with us, we will not give them any of the spoil that we have recovered, except to every man his wife and his children, that they may lead *them* away and depart."

23 Then David said, "You must not do so, my brothers, with what the LORD has given us, who has kept us and delivered into our hand the band that came against us.

24 ^aNum. 31:27; Josh. 22:8

24 "And who will listen to you in this matter? For ^aas his share is who goes down to the battle, so shall his share be who stays by the baggage; they shall share alike."

25 And so it has been from that day forward, that he made it a statute and an ordinance for Israel to this day.

30:9 The brook Besor is the major wadi (a usually dry river bed) which drains the Negev and empties into the Mediterranean just S. of Gaza.

30:20 David used his *spoil* as presents for his friends in Judah (vv. 26–31).

26 Now when David came to Ziklag, he sent *some* of the spoil to the elders of Judah, to his friends, saying, "Behold, ᵃa gift for you from the spoil of ᵇthe enemies of the Lᴏʀᴅ:

27 to those who were in ᵃBethel, and to those who were in ᵇRamoth of the Negev, and to those who were in ᶜJattir,

28 and to those who were in ᵃAroer, and to those who were in Siphmoth, and to those who were in ᵇEshtemoa,

29 and to those who were in Racal, and to those who were in the cities of ᵃthe Jerahmeelites, and to those who were in the cities of ᵇthe Kenites,

30 and to those who were in ᵃHormah, and to those who were in ᵇBor-ashan, and to those who were in Athach,

31 and to those who were in ᵃHebron, and to all the places where David himself and his men were accustomed to ᵇgo."

5 The Philistines and the death of Saul, 31:1-13

31 ᵃNow the Philistines were fighting against Israel, and the men of Israel fled from before the Philistines and fell slain ᵇon Mount Gilboa.

2 And the Philistines overtook Saul and his sons; and the Philistines killed ᵃJonathan and Abinadab and Malchi-shua the sons of Saul.

3 And ᵃthe battle went heavily against Saul, and the archers

hit him; and he was badly wounded by the archers.

4 ᵃThen Saul said to his armor bearer, "Draw your sword and pierce me through with it, lest ᵇthese uncircumcised come and pierce me through and make sport of me." But his armor bearer would not, for he was greatly afraid. ᶜSo Saul took his sword and fell on it.

5 And when his armor bearer saw that Saul was dead, he also fell on his sword and died with him.

6 Thus Saul died with his three sons, his armor bearer, and all his men on that day together.

7 And when the men of Israel who were on the other side of the valley, with those who were beyond the Jordan, saw that the men of Israel had fled and that Saul and his sons were dead, they abandoned the cities and fled; then the Philistines came and lived in them.

8 And it came about on the next day when the Philistines came to strip the slain, that they found Saul and his three sons fallen on Mount Gilboa.

9 And they cut off his head, and stripped off his weapons, and sent *them* throughout the land of the Philistines, ᵃto carry the good news ᵇto the house of their idols and to the people.

10 And they put his weapons in the temple of ᵃAshtaroth, and ᵇthey fastened his body to the wall of ᶜBeth-shan.

11 Now when ᵃthe

30:26-31 David reestablished contact with the citizens of Judah who were later to name him king (2 Sam. 2:1-4). All the cities mentioned were in the territory of Judah and Simeon.

30:27 *Bethel.* Not the Bethel in the territory of Benjamin, but probably the Bethul of Josh. 19:4.

31:1 Mount Gilboa is 1,696 feet high, located in the Valley of Jezreel.

31:2 This "Waterloo" of Saul and his sons fulfilled Samuel's prophecy (28:19).

31:4 *uncircumcised . . .make sport of me.* Remembering how the Philistines abused and tormented Samson, Saul wished to prevent such from happening to him, especially since

he was the Lord's anointed.

31:7 *valley.* Of Jezreel.

31:10 The house of *Ashtaroth* was the temple of Ashtarte, the Canaanite fertility goddess and counterpart of Baal, and was located in the strategic city of *Beth-shan* (at the junction of the Jezreel and Jordan valleys). The bodies of the fallen warriors were hung on the wall along the open square of the city (cf. 2 Sam. 21:12).

31:11-13 The bodies were recovered and buried by the men of Jabesh-gilead, who had not forgotten how Saul had once rescued them (11:1-11).

inhabitants of Jabesh-gilead heard what the Philistines had done to Saul,

★12 *a*2 Sam. 2:4-7 *b*2 Chr. 16:14

12 *a*all the valiant men rose and walked all night, and took the body of Saul and the bodies of his sons from the wall of Beth-shan, and they came to Jabesh, and *b*burned them there.

13 And they took their bones and *a*buried them under *b*the tamarisk tree at Jabesh, and *c*fasted seven days.

★13 *a*2 Sam. 21:12-14 *b*1 Sam. 22:6 *c*2 Sam. 1:12

31:12 Cremation was not the general Hebrew practice except in the case of criminals (Josh. 7:25). The bodies may have been burned because they had been badly mutilated; even so, the bones were preserved and buried.

31:13 The week of fasting was a sign of public mourning for the king of Israel. Saul's great failure as king was his disobedience, which eventually disqualified him from holding the office. Had Saul been obedient to God, perhaps his life would have ended in great glory rather than in dark, tragic defeat (cf. John 14:15).

INTRODUCTION TO
THE SECOND BOOK OF SAMUEL

AUTHORS: Samuel and others   DATE: 930 B.C. and later

Relation to 1 Samuel *In the Hebrew Bible, 1 and 2 Samuel form a single book. On matters of authorship, date, and background see the Introduction to 1 Samuel.*

Contents *First Samuel closes with the death of Israel's first king, Saul. Second Samuel records the history of King David's reign, including his making Jerusalem the political and religious center of the nation, the establishing of the Davidic dynasty, David's great military victories, his shameful sin with Bathsheba, and his mistake in numbering the people. Second Samuel 7:4-14 records the important (and still partly unfulfilled) covenant God made with David and his posterity.*

OUTLINE OF 2 SAMUEL

THE SECOND BOOK OF SAMUEL

I DAVID'S CORONATION OVER THE KINGDOM, 1:1–5:6

A The Time of the Coronation (after Saul's Death), 1:1–27

1 The report of Saul's death, 1:1–10

★ 1 a1 Sam. 31:6 b1 Sam. 30:1, 17, 26

1 Now it came about after ᵃthe death of Saul, when David had returned from ᵇthe slaughter of the Amalekites, that David remained two days in Ziklag.

★ 2 a2 Sam. 4:10 b1 Sam. 4:12 c1 Sam. 25:23

2 And it happened on the third day, that behold, ᵃa man came out of the camp from Saul, ᵇwith his clothes torn and dust on his head. And it came about when he came to David that ᶜhe fell to the ground and prostrated himself.

3 Then David said to him, "From where do you come?" And he said to him, "I have escaped from the camp of Israel."

4 a1 Sam. 4:16

4 And David said to him, "ᵃHow did things go? Please tell me." And he said, "The people have fled from the battle, and also many of the people have fallen and are dead; and Saul and Jonathan his son are dead also."

5 So David said to the young man who told him, "How do you know that Saul and his son Jonathan are dead?"

★ 6-10

6 a1 Sam. 28:4; 31:1-6; 1 Chr. 10:4-10 b1 Sam. 31:2-4

6 And the young man who told him said, "By chance I happened to be on ᵃMount Gilboa, and behold, ᵇSaul was leaning on his spear. And behold, the chariots and the horsemen pursued him closely.

7 "And when he looked behind him, he saw me and called to me. And I said, 'Here I am.'

8 "And he said to me, 'Who are you?' And I answered him, 'ᵃI am an Amalekite.'

8 a1 Sam. 15:3; 30:1, 13, 17

9 "Then he said to me, 'Please stand beside me and kill me; for agony has seized me because my life still lingers in me.'

10 "So I stood beside him ᵃand killed him, because I knew that he could not live after he had fallen. And ᵇI took the crown which was on his head and the bracelet which was on his arm, and I have brought them here to my lord."

10 a Judg. 9:54 b2 Kin. 11:12

2 The reaction to Saul's death, 1:11–16

11 Then ᵃDavid took hold of his clothes and tore them, and so also did all the men who were with him.

★11 a Gen. 37:29, 34; Josh. 7:6; 2 Chr. 34:27; Ezra 9:3

12 And they mourned and wept and ᵃfasted until evening for Saul and his son Jonathan and for the people of the LORD and the house of Israel, because they had fallen by the sword.

12 a2 Sam. 3:35

13 And David said to the young man who told him, "Where are you from?" And he answered, "ᵃI am the son of an alien, an Amalekite."

13 a2 Sam. 1:8

14 Then David said to him, "How is it you were not afraid ᵃto stretch out your hand to destroy the LORD's anointed?"

14 a1 Sam. 24:6; 26:9, 11, 16

15 And David called one of the young men and said, "Go, cut him down." ᵃSo he struck him and he died.

★15-16

15 a2 Sam. 4:10, 12

16 a1 Sam. 26:9; 2 Sam. 3:28, 29; 1 Kin. 2:32 b2 Sam. 1:10; Luke 19:22

16 And David said to him, "ᵃYour blood is on your head, for ᵇyour mouth has testified against

---

1:1 *Ziklag* was located in the Negev about 12 miles N. of Beersheba.

1:2 *dust on his head.* A sign of mourning, because of the death of Saul.

1:6-10 The Amalekite's story is at variance with the record of 1 Sam. 31:3–6 and is clearly a fabrication. He apparently sought recognition or reward for claiming to have killed Saul

(who in reality committed suicide). As a mercenary or looter, he came across Saul's body and took the king's crown and bracelet to substantiate his fabrication.

1:11 *tore.* A sign of mourning.

1:15-16 David apparently believed the account and had the Amalekite executed on the basis of his own testimony of having slain the king.

you, saying, 'I have killed the LORD's anointed.' "

3 The remorse over Saul's death, 1:17-27

17 `a`2 Chr. 35:25

17 Then David `a`chanted with this lament over Saul and Jonathan his son,

★**18** `a`Josh. 10:13

18 and he told *them* to teach the sons of Judah *the song of* the bow; behold, it is written in `a`the book of Jashar.

★**19** `a`2 Sam. 1:25, 27

19 "Your beauty, O Israel, is slain on your high places!
`a`How have the mighty fallen!

20 `a`1 Sam. 31:8-13; Mic. 1:10 `b`Ex. 15:20, 21; 1 Sam. 18:6 `c`1 Sam. 14:6

20 "`a`Tell *it* not in Gath,
Proclaim it not in the streets of Ashkelon;
Lest `b`the daughters of the Philistines rejoice,
Lest the daughters of `c`the uncircumcised exult.

★**21** `a`1 Sam. 31:1 `b`Ezek. 31:15 `c`Is. 21:5

21 "`a`O mountains of Gilboa,
`b`Let not dew or rain be on you, nor fields of offerings;
For there the shield of the mighty was defiled,
The shield of Saul, not `c`anointed with oil.

22 `a`Deut. 32:42; Is. 34:6 `b`1 Sam. 18:4

22 "`a`From the blood of the slain, from the fat of the mighty,
`b`The bow of Jonathan did not turn back,
And the sword of Saul did not return empty.

23 `a`Jer. 4:13 `b`Judg. 14:18

23 "Saul and Jonathan, beloved and pleasant in their life,
And in their death they were not parted;
`a`They were swifter than eagles,

`b`They were stronger than lions.

24 "O daughters of Israel, weep over Saul,
Who clothed you luxuriously in scarlet,
Who put ornaments of gold on your apparel.

25 "`a`How have the mighty fallen in the midst of the battle!
Jonathan is slain on your high places.

25 `a`2 Sam. 1:19, 27

26 "I am distressed for you, my brother Jonathan;
You have been very pleasant to me.
`a`Your love to me was more wonderful
Than the love of women.

26 `a`1 Sam. 18:1-4

27 "`a`How have the mighty fallen,
And `b`the weapons of war perished!"

★**27** `a`2 Sam. 1:19, 25 `b`Is. 13:5

B The Extent of the Kingdom (over Judah), 2:1-7

2 Then it came about afterwards that `a`David inquired of the LORD, saying, "Shall I go up to one of the cities of Judah?" And the LORD said to him, "Go up." So David said, "Where shall I go up?" And He said, "`b`To Hebron."

★**1** `a`1 Sam. 23:2, 4, 9-12 `b`Josh. 14:13; 1 Sam. 30:31

2 So David went up there, and `a`his two wives also, Ahinoam the Jezreelitess and Abigail the widow of Nabal the Carmelite.

2 `a`1 Sam. 25:42, 43

3 And `a`David brought up his men who *were* with him, each with his household; and they lived in the cities of Hebron.

3 `a`1 Sam. 30:9; 1 Chr. 12:1

4 Then the men of Judah came and there `a`anointed David king over the house of Judah.

★**4** `a`1 Sam. 16:13; 2 Sam. 5:3, 5 `b`1 Sam. 31:11-13

1:18 *book of Jashar.* A history of Israel's wars in which some important events and great men were commemorated poetically (cf. Josh. 10:13).

1:19 *high places.* I.e., Mt. Gilboa, where Saul died.

1:21 *not anointed with oil.* Saul's shield was not cleansed and polished with oil, but was discarded.

1:27 *weapons of war.* A figurative reference to the fallen warriors, Saul and Jonathan.

2:1 Chapters 2-4 record the conflict between two rivals: David, who took the throne of Judah, and Ish-bosheth, Saul's surviving son, who occupied the throne in Israel.

2:4 This was David's second anointing (cf. 1 Sam. 16:13).

And they told David, saying, "It was [b]the men of Jabesh-gilead who buried Saul."

5 [a]1 Sam. 23:21; Ps. 115:15

5 And David sent messengers to the men of Jabesh-gilead, and said to them, "[a]May you be blessed of the LORD because you have shown this kindness to Saul your lord, and have buried him.

6 [a]Ex. 34:6; 2 Tim. 1:16

6 "And now [a]may the LORD show lovingkindness and truth to you; and I also will show this goodness to you, because you have done this thing.

★ 7

7 "Now therefore, let your hands be strong, and be valiant; for Saul your lord is dead, and also the house of Judah has anointed me king over them."

C The Effort to Include the Other Tribes, 2:8–4:12

1 The rival, Ish-bosheth, 2:8–11

★ 8-9

8 [a]1 Sam. 14:50 [b]Gen. 32:2; 2 Sam. 17:24

8 But [a]Abner the son of Ner, commander of Saul's army, had taken Ish-bosheth the son of Saul, and brought him over to [b]Mahanaim.

9 [a]Josh. 22:9 [b]Judg. 1:32 [c]1 Sam. 29:1

9 And he made him king over [a]Gilead, over the [b]Ashurites, over [c]Jezreel, over Ephraim, and over Benjamin, even over all Israel.

★10-11

10 Ish-bosheth, Saul's son, was forty years old when he became king over Israel, and he was king for two years. The house of Judah, however, followed David.

11 [a]2 Sam. 5:5

11 And [a]the time that David was king in Hebron over the house of Judah was seven years and six months.

2 The civil war, 2:12–4:12

a Abner vs. Joab, 2:12–32

12 [a]Josh. 10:12; 18:25

12 Now Abner the son of Ner, went out from Mahanaim to [a]Gibeon with the servants of Ish-bosheth the son of Saul.

13 [a]2 Sam. 8:16; 1 Chr. 2:16; 11:6

13 And [a]Joab the son of Zeruiah and the servants of David went out and met them by the pool of Gibeon; and they sat down, one on the one side of the pool and the other on the other side of the pool.

★14 [a]2 Sam. 2:16, 17

14 Then Abner said to Joab, "Now let the young men arise and [a]hold a contest before us." And Joab said, "Let them arise."

15 So they arose and went over by count, twelve for Benjamin and Ish-bosheth the son of Saul, and twelve of the servants of David.

16 And each one of them ★16 seized his opponent by the head, and thrust his sword in his opponent's side; so they fell down together. Therefore that place was called Helkath-hazzurim, which is in Gibeon.

17 [a]2 Sam. 3:1

17 And that day the battle was very severe, and [a]Abner and the men of Israel were beaten before the servants of David.

★18 [a]1 Chr. 2:16 [b]1 Chr. 12:8; Hab. 3:19

18 Now [a]the three sons of Zeruiah were there, Joab and Abishai and Asahel; and Asahel was [b]as swift-footed as one of the gazelles which is in the field.

19 And Asahel pursued Abner and did not turn to the right or to the left from following Abner.

2:7 This tacit invitation to the people of Jabesh-gilead to join his kingdom was also a shrewd ploy by David, since the people lived to the N. of Ish-bosheth's capital, Mahanaim (v. 8; cf. Gen. 32:1-2).

2:8-9 Ish-bosheth ("man of shame") was crowned king over the northern tribes and Transjordan (see note on 1 Chron. 8:34).

2:10-11 The difference in lengths of reigns (Ish-bosheth, 2 years; David, 7½ years) may be because Ish-bosheth did not take the throne immediately, but required five years to recover the northern territory from the Philistines.

2:14 hold a contest. I.e., between champions in behalf of the opposing armies.

2:16 Helkath-hazzurim = Field of Sword-edges. The death of all 24 contestants made the representative battle inconclusive and a general battle was necessary (v. 17).

2:18 Zeruiah. David's sister (1 Chron. 2:16).

20 Then Abner looked behind him and said, "Is that you, Asahel?" And he answered, "It is I."

21 So Abner said to him, "Turn to your right or to your left, and take hold of one of the young men for yourself, and take for yourself his spoil." But Asahel was not willing to turn aside from following him.

22 And Abner repeated again to Asahel, "Turn aside from following me. Why should I strike you to the ground? ^aHow then could I lift up my face to your brother Joab?"

23 However, he refused to turn aside; therefore Abner struck him in the belly with the butt end of the spear, so that the spear came out at his back. And he fell there and died on the spot. And it came about that all who came to the place where ^aAsahel had fallen and died, stood still.

24 But Joab and Abishai pursued Abner, and when the sun was going down, they came to the hill of Ammah, which is in front of Giah by the way of the wilderness of Gibeon.

25 And the sons of Benjamin gathered together behind Abner and became one band, and they stood on the top of a certain hill.

26 Then Abner called to Joab and said, "Shall the sword devour forever? Do you not know that it will be bitter in the end? How long will you refrain from telling the people to turn back from following their brothers?"

27 And Joab said, "As God lives, if you had not spoken, surely then the people would have gone away in the morning, each from following his brother."

28 So Joab blew the trumpet; and all the people halted and pursued Israel no longer, ^anor did they continue to fight anymore.

29 Abner and his men then went through the Arabah all that night; so they crossed the Jordan, walked all morning, and came to ^aMahanaim.

30 Then Joab returned from following Abner; when he had gathered all the people together, nineteen of David's servants besides Asahel were missing.

31 But the servants of David had struck down many of Benjamin and Abner's men, so that three hundred and sixty men died.

32 And they took up Asahel and buried him ^ain his father's tomb which was in Bethlehem. Then Joab and his men went all night until the day dawned at Hebron.

b *Abner deserts Ish-bosheth,*
   3:1-21

3 Now ^athere was a long war between the house of Saul and the house of David; and David grew steadily stronger, but the house of Saul grew weaker continually.

2 ^aSons were born to David at Hebron: his first-born was Amnon, by ^bAhinoam the Jezreelitess;

3 and his second, Chileab, by Abigail the widow of Nabal the Carmelite; and the third, Absalom the son of ^aMaacah, the daughter of Talmai, king of ^bGeshur;

4 and the fourth, ^aAdonijah the son of Haggith; and the fifth, Shephatiah the son of Abital;

5 and the sixth, Ithream, by David's wife Eglah. These were born to David at Hebron.

6 And it came about while there was war between the house of Saul and the house of David that ^aAbner was making himself strong in the house of Saul.

22 ^a2 Sam. 3:27

★23 ^a2 Sam. 20:12

★27

28 ^a2 Sam. 3:1

★29 ^a2 Sam. 2:8

32 ^aGen. 47:29, 30; Judg. 8:32

1 ^a1 Kin. 14:30; Ps. 46:9

2 ^a1 Chr. 3:1-3 ^b1 Sam. 25:42, 43

3 ^a1 Sam. 27:8; 1 Chr. 3:2 ^b2 Sam. 14:32; 15:8

4 ^a1 Kin. 1:5

6 ^a2 Sam. 2:8, 9

2:23 The butt end of the spear was pointed so that it might be stuck in the ground (1 Sam. 26:7). *stood still* to mourn his death.
2:27 Had Abner not issued a challenge (2:14),

the conflict would have been avoided altogether.
2:29 *Arabah.* The wasteland of the Rift Valley N. and S. of the Dead Sea.

★ **7** *a*2 Sam.
21:8-11

7 Now Saul had a concubine whose name was *a*Rizpah, the daughter of Aiah; and Ish-bosheth said to Abner, "Why have you gone in to my father's concubine?"

★ **8** *a*1 Sam.
24:14;
2 Sam. 9:8

8 Then Abner was very angry over the words of Ish-bosheth and said, "*a*Am I a dog's head that belongs to Judah? Today I show kindness to the house of Saul your father, to his brothers and to his friends, and have not delivered you into the hands of David; and yet today you charge me with a guilt concerning the woman.

9 *a*1 Kin.
19:2 *b*1 Sam.
15:28

9 "*a*May God do so to Abner, and more also, if *b*as the Lord has sworn to David, I do not accomplish this for him,

10 *a*1 Sam.
15:28
*b*1 Sam. 3:20

10 *a*to transfer the kingdom from the house of Saul, and to establish the throne of David over Israel and over Judah, *b*from Dan even to Beersheba."

11 And he could no longer answer Abner a word, because he was afraid of him.

12 Then Abner sent messengers to David in his place, saying, "Whose is the land? Make your covenant with me, and behold, my hand shall be with you to bring all Israel over to you."

★**13** *a*Gen.
43:3 *b*1 Sam.
18:20; 19:11

13 And he said, "Good! I will make a covenant with you, but I demand one thing of you, namely, *a*you shall not see my face unless you *b*first bring Michal, Saul's daughter, when you come to see me."

14 *a*1 Sam.
18:25, 27

14 So David sent messengers to Ish-bosheth, Saul's son, saying, "Give me my wife Michal, to whom I was betrothed *a*for a hundred foreskins of the Philistines."

15 And Ish-bosheth sent and took her from *her* husband, from Paltiel the son of Laish.

16 *a*2 Sam.
16:5; 19:16

16 But her husband went with her, weeping as he went, and followed her as far as *a*Bahurim. Then Abner said to him, "Go, return." So he returned.

17 *a*1 Sam.
8:4

17 Now Abner had consultation with *a*the elders of Israel, saying, "In times past you were seeking for David to be king over you.

18 *a*1 Sam.
9:16; 15:28

18 "Now then, do *it*! For the Lord has spoken of David, saying, '*a*By the hand of My servant David I will save My people Israel from the hand of the Philistines and from the hand of all their enemies.'"

19 *a*1 Sam.
10:20, 21;
1 Chr. 12:29

19 And Abner also spoke in the hearing of Benjamin; and in addition Abner went to speak in the hearing of David in Hebron all that seemed good to Israel and to *a*the whole house of Benjamin.

20 Then Abner and twenty men with him came to David at Hebron. And David made a feast for Abner and the men who were with him.

21 *a*2 Sam.
3:10, 12
*b*1 Kin.
11:37

21 And Abner said to David, "Let me arise and go, and *a*gather all Israel to my lord the king that they may make a covenant with you, and that *b*you may be king over all that your soul desires." So David sent Abner away, and he went in peace.

c Joab murders Abner, 3:22-39

22 *a*1 Sam.
27:8

22 And behold, *a*the servants of David and Joab came from a raid and brought much spoil with them; but Abner was not with David in Hebron, for he had sent him away, and he had gone in peace.

23 When Joab and all the army that was with him arrived, they told Joab, saying, "Abner the son of Ner came to the king, and he has sent him away, and he has gone in peace."

24 Then Joab came to the king and said, "What have you

3:7 *concubine.* A slave woman who was the legal chattel of her master, and often served to raise him an heir. By the time of the kings, the possession of concubines appears to have been a royal prerogative. Having intercourse with a king's concubine was a treasonous act, for it was in essence making a claim to the throne (cf. 16:20-21).

3:8 *Am I a dog's head that belongs to Judah?* I.e., am I a contemptible traitor?

3:13 David wanted his wife back in order to strengthen his claim to Saul's throne.

done? Behold, Abner came to you; why then have you sent him away and he is already gone?

25 aDeut.
28:6; 1 Sam.
29:6; Is.
37:28

25 "You know Abner the son of Ner, that he came to deceive you and to learn of ayour going out and coming in, and to find out all that you are doing."

26 When Joab came out from David, he sent messengers after Abner, and they brought him back from the well of Sirah; but David did not know it.

★**27** a2 Sam.
2:23; 20:9,
10; 1 Kin. 2:5

27 So when Abner returned to Hebron, Joab took him aside into the middle of the gate to speak with him privately, and there ahe struck him in the belly so that he died on account of the blood of Asahel his brother.

28 And afterward when David heard it, he said, "I and my kingdom are innocent before the LORD forever of the blood of Abner the son of Ner.

★**29** aDeut.
21:6-9; 1 Kin.
2:31-33
bLev. 13:46

29 "aMay it fall on the head of Joab and on all his father's house; and may there not fail from the house of Joab bone who has a discharge, or who is a leper, or who takes hold of a distaff, or who falls by the sword, or who lacks bread."

30 a2 Sam.
2:23

30 So Joab and Abishai his brother killed Abner abecause he had put their brother Asahel to death in the battle at Gibeon.

31 aGen.
37:34; Judg.
11:35

31 Then David said to Joab and to all the people who were with him, "aTear your clothes and gird on sackcloth and lament before Abner." And King David walked behind the bier.

32 aJob
31:28, 29;
Prov. 24:17

32 Thus they buried Abner in Hebron; and the king lifted up his voice and wept at athe grave of Abner, and all the people wept.

★**33-34**

33 a2 Sam.
1:17; 2 Chr.
35:25

33 And athe king chanted a *lament* for Abner and said,
　　"Should Abner die as a
　　　　fool dies?

34 "Your hands were not
　　　bound, nor your feet
　　　put in fetters;
　　As one falls before the
　　　wicked, you have
　　　fallen."
And all the people wept again over him.

35 Then all the people came ato persuade David to eat bread while it was still day; but David vowed, saying, "bMay God do so to me, and more also, if I taste bread or anything else cbefore the sun goes down."

35 a2 Sam.
12:17
b1 Sam. 3:17
c2 Sam. 1:12

36 Now all the people took note of it, and it pleased them, just as everything the king did pleased all the people.

37 So all the people and all Israel understood that day that it had not been *the will* of the king to put Abner the son of Ner to death.

38 Then the king said to his servants, "Do you not know that a prince and a great man has fallen this day in Israel?

39 "And I am aweak today, though anointed king; and these men bthe sons of Zeruiah are too difficult for me. cMay the LORD repay the evildoer according to his evil."

39 a1 Chr.
29:1; 2 Chr.
13:7 b2 Sam.
19:5-7
c1 Kin. 2:32-
34

d　*The murder of Ish-bosheth,*
　　　　4:1-12

4 Now when Ish-bosheth, Saul's son, heard that aAbner had died in Hebron, bhe lost courage, and all Israel was disturbed.

1 a2 Sam.
3:27 bEzra
4:4

2 And Saul's son *had* two men who were commanders of bands: the name of the one was Baanah and the name of the other Rechab, sons of Rimmon the Beerothite, of the sons of Benjamin (for aBeeroth is also considered bpart of Benjamin,

2 aJosh.
9:17 bJosh.
18:25

3:27 The murder was Joab's vengeance for Abner's slaying Asahel during battle (2:23).
3:29 The strong curse uttered by David indicates that he did not consider Joab's actions in the least justified. Hebron, where Joab slew Abner, was a city of refuge (Josh. 21:13), and in such a city not even a blood avenger could

slay a murderer without a trial (Num. 35:22-25). *who takes hold of a distaff.* I.e., one fit for women's work; effeminate.
3:33-34 The meaning is this: only because of treachery could such an ignoble death, befitting a fool, be the fate of so great a warrior.

3 aNeh.
11:33

3 and the Beerothites fled to aGittaim, and have been aliens there until this day).

★ 4 a2 Sam.
9:3, 6
b1 Sam.
31:1-4
c1 Chr. 8:34;
9:40

4 Now aJonathan, Saul's son, had a son crippled in his feet. He was five years old when the breport of Saul and Jonathan came from Jezreel, and his nurse took him up and fled. And it happened that in her hurry to flee, he fell and became lame. And his name was cMephibosheth.

5 a2 Sam.
2:8

5 So the sons of Rimmon the Beerothite, Rechab and Baanah, departed and came to the house of aIsh-bosheth in the heat of the day while he was taking his midday rest.

6 a2 Sam.
2:23

6 And they came to the middle of the house as if to get wheat, and athey struck him in the belly; and Rechab and Baanah his brother escaped.

7 a2 Sam.
2:29

7 Now when they came into the house, as he was lying on his bed in his bedroom, they struck him and killed him and beheaded him. And they took his head and atraveled by way of the Arabah all night.

8 a1 Sam.
24:4; 25:29

8 Then they brought the head of Ish-bosheth to David at Hebron, and said to the king, "Behold, the head of Ish-bosheth, athe son of Saul, your enemy, who sought your life; thus the LORD has given my lord the king vengeance this day on Saul and his descendants."

9 aGen.
48:16; 1 Kin.
1:29; Ps.
31:7

9 And David answered Rechab and Baanah his brother, sons of Rimmon the Beerothite, and said to them, "As the LORD lives, awho has redeemed my life from all distress,

10 a2 Sam.
1:2, 4, 15

10 awhen one told me, saying, 'Behold, Saul is dead,' and thought he was bringing good news, I seized him and killed him in Ziklag, which was the reward I gave him for his news.

11 "How much more, when wicked men have killed a righteous man in his own house on his bed, shall I not now arequire his blood from your hand, and destroy you from the earth?"

★11 aGen.
9:5; Ps. 9:12

12 Then aDavid commanded the young men, and they killed them and cut off their hands and feet, and hung them up beside the pool in Hebron. But they took the head of Ish-bosheth band buried it in the grave of Abner in Hebron.

12 a2 Sam.
1:15 b2 Sam.
3:32

D David Enthroned over All the Tribes, 5:1-6

5 aThen all the tribes of Israel came to David at Hebron and said, "Behold, we are byour bone and your flesh.

★ 1 a1 Chr.
11:1-3
b2 Sam.
19:13

2 "Previously, when Saul was king over us, ayou were the one who led Israel out and in. And the LORD said to you, 'bYou will shepherd My people Israel, and you will be ca ruler over Israel.'"

2 a1 Sam.
18:5, 13, 16
bGen. 49:24;
2 Sam. 7:7
c1 Sam.
25:30

3 So all the elders of Israel came to the king at Hebron, and King David amade a covenant with them before the LORD at Hebron; then bthey anointed David king over Israel.

★ 3 a2 Sam.
3:21 b1 Sam.
16:13;
2 Sam. 2:4

4 David was athirty years old when he became king, and bhe reigned forty years.

4 aGen.
41:46; Num.
4:3; Luke
3:23 b1 Kin.
2:11; 1 Chr.
26:31

5 At Hebron ahe reigned over Judah seven years and six months, and in Jerusalem he reigned thirty-three years over all Israel and Judah.

5 a2 Sam.
2:11; 1 Chr.
3:4; 29:27

6 aNow the king and his men went to bJerusalem against

★ 6 a1 Chr.
11:4-9
bJosh.
15:63; 18:28;
Judg. 1:21

4:4 *Jezreel.* The plain where the Philistines engaged Israel in battle (1 Sam. 29:1, 11). Regarding the name *Mephibosheth* see note on 1 Chron. 8:34. His story is resumed in 2 Sam. 9.

4:11 Ish-bosheth was called *righteous* in that he was not guilty of any wicked deed or crime. He had merely assumed the throne upon Saul's death, at the encouragement of Abner.

5:1 Chapters 5–10 recount the reign of David over all Israel at Jerusalem. During these years he enjoyed great prosperity and blessing from God.

5:3 This was David's third anointing, and resulted in the unification of the twelve tribes under one king (cf. 1 Sam. 16:13; 2 Sam. 2:4).

5:6 The Jebusites boasted that the blind and the lame could easily defend Jerusalem, but the city was taken by entering through the water tunnel.

the Jebusites, the inhabitants of the land, and they said to David, "You shall not come in here, but the blind and lame shall turn you away"; thinking, "David cannot enter here."

II DAVID'S CONSOLIDATION OF THE KINGDOM, 5:7–6:23
A The Government Established in Jerusalem, 5:7–25

★ **7** ᵃ2 Sam. 6:12, 16; 1 Kin. 2:10; 9:24

7 Nevertheless, David captured the stronghold of Zion, that is ᵃthe city of David.

8 And David said on that day, "Whoever would strike the Jebusites, let him reach the lame and the blind, who are hated by David's soul, through the water tunnel." Therefore they say, "The blind or the lame shall not come into the house."

★ **9** ᵃ2 Sam. 5:7 ᵇ1 Kin. 9:15, 24

9 So David lived in the stronghold, and called it ᵃthe city of David. And David built all around from the ᵇMillo and inward.

10 ᵃ2 Sam. 3:1

10 And ᵃDavid became greater and greater, for the LORD God of hosts was with him.

11 ᵃ1 Kin. 5:1, 10, 18; 1 Chr. 14:1 ᵇPs. 30:title

11 ᵃThen Hiram king of Tyre sent messengers to David with cedar trees and carpenters and stonemasons; and ᵇthey built a house for David.

12 And David realized that the LORD had established him as king over Israel, and that He had exalted his kingdom for the sake of His people Israel.

★**13** ᵃDeut. 17:17; 1 Chr. 3:9

13 Meanwhile ᵃDavid took more concubines and wives from Jerusalem, after he came from Hebron; and more sons and daughters were born to David.

14 ᵃ1 Chr. 3:5-8

14 Now ᵃthese are the names of those who were born to him in Jerusalem: Shammua, Shobab, Nathan, Solomon,

15 Ibhar, Elishua, Nepheg, Japhia,

16 Elishama, Eliada and Eliphelet.

★**17** ᵃ1 Sam. 29:1 ᵇ2 Sam. 23:14; 1 Chr. 11:16

17 When the Philistines heard that they had anointed David king over Israel, ᵃall the Philistines went up to seek out David; and when David heard of it, he went down to the ᵇstronghold.

★**18** ᵃGen. 14:5; Josh. 15:8; 17:15; 18:16

18 Now the Philistines came and spread themselves out in ᵃthe valley of Rephaim.

19 ᵃ1 Sam. 23:2 ᵇ2 Sam. 2:1

19 Then ᵃDavid inquired of the LORD, saying, "Shall I go up against the Philistines? Wilt Thou give them into my hand?" And ᵇthe LORD said to David, "Go up, for I will certainly give the Philistines into your hand."

★**20** ᵃ1 Chr. 14:11; Is. 28:21

20 So David came to ᵃBaal-perazim, and defeated them there; and he said, "The LORD has broken through my enemies before me like the breakthrough of waters." Therefore he named that place Baal-perazim.

21 ᵃ1 Chr. 14:12

21 And they abandoned their idols there, so ᵃDavid and his men carried them away.

22 ᵃ2 Sam. 5:18

22 Now ᵃthe Philistines came up once again and spread themselves out in the valley of Rephaim.

★**23-24**

23 ᵃ2 Sam. 5:19

23 And when ᵃDavid inquired of the LORD, He said, "You shall not go directly up; circle around behind them and come at them in front of the balsam trees.

5:7 David established his capital in neutral territory between Israel and Judah. Jerusalem was an excellent fortress city, for it was naturally defensible on the S., E., and W. (due to valleys) and had a good water supply, the Gihon spring.

5:9 Millo. From the Hebrew "to fill"; hence a "mound" or "terrace." It served as part of Jerusalem's northern defenses (1 Kings 9:24).

5:13 The multiplication of David's wives was a direct violation of Deut. 17:17. In antiquity, international alliances were often sealed by the marriage of a king's daughter to the other participant in the treaty. This practice accounts for some of David's and Solomon's many wives (cf. 1 Kings 11:1-3).

5:17 stronghold. The cave of Adullam (23:13-14), or possibly Jerusalem (5:7).

5:18 the valley of Rephaim. The most direct approach to Jerusalem from Philistia.

5:20 Baal-perazim. Lit., the Lord of breaking forth. The image is of flooding waters breaking through a dam, as David's troops broke through the Philistine assault.

5:23-24 balsam trees. Baka-shrubs, from which sap or resin came.

24 a2 Kin.
7:6 bJudg.
4:14

24 "And it shall be, when ᵃyou hear the sound of marching in the tops of the balsam trees, then you shall act promptly, for then ᵇthe LORD will have gone out before you to strike the army of the Philistines."

★25 aIs.
28:21 bJosh.
12:12; 21:21

25 Then David did so, just as the LORD had commanded him, and struck down the Philistines from ᵃGeba as far as ᵇGezer.

B The ark Brought to Jerusalem, 6:1-23

1 a1 Chr.
13:5-14

6 ᵃNow David again gathered all the chosen men of Israel, thirty thousand.

★ 2 aJosh.
15:9, 10;
1 Sam. 7:1
bLev. 24:16
cEx. 25:22

2 And David arose and went with all the people who were with him to ᵃBaale-judah, to bring up from there the ark of God which is called by the ᵇName, the very name of the LORD of hosts who ᶜis enthroned *above* the cherubim.

★ 3 aNum.
7:4-9; 1 Sam.
6:7

3 And they placed the ark of God on ᵃa new cart that they might bring it from the house of Abinadab which was on the hill; and Uzzah and Ahio, the sons of Abinadab, were leading the new cart.

4 a1 Sam.
7:1; 1 Chr.
13:7

4 So ᵃthey brought it with the ark of God from the house of Abinadab, which was on the hill; and Ahio was walking ahead of the ark.

5 a1 Sam.
18:6, 7
b1 Chr. 13:8

5 Meanwhile, David and all the house of Israel ᵃwere celebrating before the LORD ᵇwith all kinds of *instruments made* of fir wood, and with lyres, harps, tambourines, castanets and cymbals.

6 But when they came to the ᵃthreshing floor of Nacon, Uzzah ᵇreached out toward the ark of God and took hold of it, for the oxen nearly upset *it.*

★ 6-7

6 a1 Chr.
13:9 bNum.
4:15, 19, 20

7 And the anger of the LORD burned against Uzzah, and ᵃGod struck him down there for his irreverence; and he died there by the ark of God.

7 a1 Sam.
6:19

8 And David became angry because of the LORD's outburst against Uzzah, and that place is called Perez-uzzah to this day.

★ 8

9 So ᵃDavid was afraid of the LORD that day; and he said, "How can the ark of the LORD come to me?"

9 aPs.
119:120;
Luke 5:8

10 And David was unwilling to move the ark of the LORD into the city of David with him; but David took it aside to the house of ᵃObed-edom the Gittite.

10 a1 Chr.
26:4-8

11 Thus the ark of the LORD remained in the house of Obed-edom the Gittite three months, and the LORD ᵃblessed Obed-edom and all his household.

11 aGen.
30:27; 39:5

12 Now it was told King David, saying, "The LORD has blessed the house of Obed-edom and all that belongs to him, on account of the ark of God." ᵃAnd David went and brought up the ark of God from the house of Obed-edom into ᵇthe city of David with gladness.

12 a1 Chr.
15:25-16:3
b1 Kin. 8:1

13 And so it was, that when the ᵃbearers of the ark of the LORD had gone six paces, he sacrificed an ᵇox and a fatling.

★13 aNum.
4:15; Josh.
3:3; 1 Chr.
15:2, 15
b1 Kin. 8:5

14 And ᵃDavid was dancing before the LORD with all *his* might, and David was ᵇwearing a linen ephod.

★14 aEx.
15:20, 21;
Judg. 11:34
bEx. 19:6;
1 Sam. 2:18,
28

5:25 After mopping up the nearby Philistine opposition, David was free to take further steps to build his kingdom into an empire.

6:2 *Baale-judah.* Also known as Kiriath-jearim (1 Sam. 7:1).

6:3 The Ark was to be carried by the sons of Kohath (Exod. 25:14-15; Num. 3:30-31; 4:15; 7:9), not by a cart or vehicle. David adopted a Philistine expediency (cf. 1 Sam. 6:7-8). See 1 Chron. 13 and 15 for a parallel account.

6:6-7 The sin of Uzzah in touching the Ark (cf. Num. 4:15) arose from the fact that it was not being carried by the Levites as God had directed. The violation of God's holiness, represented by the Ark, cost him his life.

6:8 David's anger was not directed against the Lord, but arose because of the calamity which occurred through his own carelessness.

6:13 In David's second attempt to bring the Ark to Jerusalem, it was transferred in the prescribed manner (cf. 6:3).

6:14 *linen ephod.* A sleeveless priestly garment extending to the hips and used when officiating before the altar (see note on 1 Sam. 2:18).

15 So David and all the house of Israel were bringing up the ark of the LORD with shouting and the sound of the trumpet.

16 Then it happened *as* the ark of the LORD came into the city of David that [a]Michal the daughter of Saul looked out of the window and saw King David leaping and dancing before the LORD; and she despised him in her heart.

17 So they brought in the ark of the LORD and set it [a]in its place inside the tent which David had pitched for it; and [b]David offered burnt offerings and peace offerings before the LORD.

18 And when David had finished offering the burnt offering and the peace offering, [a]he blessed the people in the name of the LORD of hosts.

19 Further, he distributed to all the people, to all the multitude of Israel, both to men and women, a cake of bread and one of dates and one of raisins to each one. Then all the people departed each to his house.

20 But when David returned to bless his household, Michal the daughter of Saul came out to meet David and said, "How the king of Israel distinguished himself today! [a]He uncovered himself today in the eyes of his servants' maids as one of the [b]foolish ones shamelessly uncovers himself!"

21 So David said to Michal, "[a]It *was* before the LORD, who chose me above your father and above all his house, to appoint me ruler over the people of the LORD, over Israel; therefore I will celebrate before the LORD.

22 "And I will be more lightly esteemed than this and will be humble in my own eyes, but with the maids of whom you have spoken, with them I will be distinguished."

23 And Michal the daughter of Saul had no child to the day of her death.

III DAVID'S COVENANT CONCERNING THE KINGDOM, 7:1-29
A David's Proposal, 7:1-3

7 [a]Now it came about when the king lived in his house, and the LORD had given him rest on every side from all his enemies,

2 that the king said to [a]Nathan the prophet, "See now, I dwell in [b]a house of cedar, but the ark of God [c]dwells within tent curtains."

3 And Nathan said to the king, "[a]Go, do all that is in your mind, for the LORD is with you."

B God's Disposal, 7:4-29
1 God's promise, 7:4-17

4 But it came about in the same night that the word of the LORD came to Nathan, saying,

5 "Go and say to My servant David, 'Thus says the LORD, "[a]Are you the one who should build Me a house to dwell in?

6 "For [a]I have not dwelt in a house since the day I brought up the sons of Israel from Egypt, even to this day; but I have been moving about [b]in a tent, even in a tabernacle.

7 "[a]Wherever I have gone with all the sons of Israel, did I speak a word with one of the tribes of Israel, [b]which I commanded to shepherd My people Israel, saying, 'Why have you not built Me a house of cedar?' " '

Marginal references:
*16 [a]2 Sam. 3:14
*17 [a]1 Chr. 15:1; 2 Chr. 1:4 [b]1 Kin. 8:62-65
18 [a]1 Kin. 8:14, 15
*20 [a]2 Sam. 6:14, 16; Eccl. 7:17 [b]Judg. 9:4
21 [a]1 Sam. 13:14; 15:28
*22
*23
1 [a]1 Chr. 17:1-27
* 2 [a]2 Sam. 7:17; 12:1; 1 Kin. 1:22; 1 Chr. 29:29; 2 Chr. 9:29 [b]2 Sam. 5:11 [c]Ex. 26:1
3 [a]1 Kin. 8:17, 18; 1 Chr. 22:7
5 [a]1 Kin. 5:3, 4; 8:19
6 [a]Josh. 18:1; 1 Kin. 8:16 [b]Ex. 40:18, 34
7 [a]Lev. 26:11, 12 [b]2 Sam. 5:2

6:16 *dancing.* Lit., whirling around.
6:17 David was entitled to do these things because he was king (cf. 1 Kings 8:62-65).
6:20 Michal sarcastically rebuked David for celebrating with the people in a manner which she considered unbefitting a king. *uncovered.* David had appeared clothed only in an ephod (v. 14), rather than in his royal robes.
6:22 David was quite willing to be lowly esteemed and humbled, realizing the Lord exalts such ones (1 Sam. 2:7-8; cf. Matt. 23:12).
6:23 The Lord condemned Michal to the disgrace of childlessness.
7:2 David's zeal for the Lord is evidenced by his desire to build a temple to house the Ark.

8 *a*1 Sam.
16:11, 12;
Ps. 78:70, 71
*b*2 Sam. 6:21

9 *a*1 Sam.
5:10 *b*Ps.
18:37-42

10 *a*Ex.
15:17; Is.
5:2, 7 *b*Ps.
89:22, 23; Is.
60:18

★**11** *a*Judg.
2:14-16;
1 Sam. 12:9-
11 *b*2 Sam.
7:1 *c*1 Sam.
25:28;
2 Sam. 7:27

★**12-16**

12 *a*1 Kin.
2:1 *b*Deut.
31:16; Acts
13:36 *c*1 Kin.
8:20; Ps.
132:11

13 *a*1 Kin.
6:12; 8:19
*b*Is. 9:7; 49:8

14 *a*Ps.
89:26, 27;
2 Cor. 6:18;
Heb. 1:5
*b*1 Kin.
11:34; Ps.
89:30-33

8 "Now therefore, thus you shall say to My servant David, 'Thus says the LORD of hosts, "*a*I took you from the pasture, from following the sheep, *b*that you should be ruler over My people Israel.

9 "And *a*I have been with you wherever you have gone and *b*have cut off all your enemies from before you; and I will make you a great name, like the names of the great men who are on the earth.

10 "I will also appoint a place for My people Israel and *a*will plant them, that they may live in their own place and not be disturbed again; *b*nor will the wicked afflict them any more as formerly,

11 even *a*from the day that I commanded judges to be over My people Israel; and *b*I will give you rest from all your enemies. The LORD also declares to you that *c*the LORD will make a house for you.

12 "*a*When your days are complete and you *b*lie down with your fathers, *c*I will raise up your descendant after you, who will come forth from you, and I will establish his kingdom.

13 "*a*He shall build a house for My name, and *b*I will establish the throne of his kingdom forever.

14 "*a*I will be a father to him and he will be a son to Me; *b*when he commits iniquity, I will correct him with the rod of men and the strokes of the sons of men,

15 but My lovingkindness shall not depart from him, *a*as I took *it* away from Saul, whom I removed from before you.

16 "And *a*your house and your kingdom shall endure before Me forever; your throne shall be established forever." ' "

17 In accordance with all these words and all this vision, so Nathan spoke to David.

2 David's praise, 7:18-29

18 Then David the king went in and sat before the LORD, and he said, "*a*Who am I, O Lord GOD, and what is my house, that Thou hast brought me this far?

19 "And yet this was insignificant in Thine eyes, O Lord GOD, *a*for Thou hast spoken also of the house of Thy servant concerning the distant future. And *b*this is the custom of man, O Lord GOD.

20 "And again what more can David say to Thee? For *a*Thou knowest Thy servant, O Lord GOD!

21 "*a*For the sake of Thy word, and according to Thine own heart, Thou hast done all this greatness to let Thy servant know.

22 "For this reason *a*Thou art great, O Lord GOD; for *b*there is none like Thee, and there is no God besides Thee, *c*according to

15 *a*1 Sam.
15:23; 16:14

16 *a*2 Sam.
7:13; Ps.
89:36, 37

★**18-29**

★**18** *a*Ex.
3:11; 1 Sam.
18:18

19 *a*2 Sam.
7:11-16;
1 Chr. 17:17
*b*Is. 55:8, 9

20 *a*1 Sam.
16:7; John
21:17

21 *a*1 Chr.
17:19; Eph.
4:32

22 *a*Deut.
3:24; Ps.
48:1; 86:10
*b*Ex. 15:11;
1 Sam. 2:2
*c*Ex. 10:2;
Ps. 44:1

7:11 David was denied his request to build a house for the Lord, but God promised instead that He would build a house for David (i.e., a dynasty).

7:12-16 This great covenant which God graciously made with David included the following provisions: (1) David would have a son who would succeed him and establish his kingdom (v. 12); (2) that son (Solomon), rather than David, would build the Temple (v. 13a); (3) the throne of Solomon's kingdom would be established forever (v. 13b); (4) though David's sins justified chastening, God's *lovingkindness* (Heb., *hesed*, steadfast love; see note on Hos. 2:19) would be forever (vv. 14-15); (5) David's house, kingdom, and throne would be established forever (v. 16). The covenant did not guarantee uninterrupted rule by David's fam-

ily (and, in fact, the Babylonian Exile interrupted it), but did promise that the right to rule would always remain with David's dynasty. Jesus Christ is the ultimate fulfillment of these promises (Luke 1:31-33) and, although at this present time He is not ruling from the throne of David (Heb. 12:2), at His second coming He will assume this throne (see notes on Matt. 1:11; 19:28; Acts 15:15).

7:18-29 David's prayer exemplifies the proper response of a believer to God's revealed will. Rather than mourn the loss of the privilege of building the Temple, David rejoiced in the promise of future blessing and acknowledged God's sovereignty.

7:18 *sat.* I.e., sat back on his heels in a position of prayer.

all that we have heard with our ears.

23 "And *a*what one nation on the earth is like Thy people Israel, whom God went to redeem for Himself as a people and to make a name for Himself, and *b*to do a great thing for Thee and awesome things for Thy land, before *c*Thy people whom *d*Thou hast redeemed for Thyself from Egypt, *from* nations and their gods?

24 "For *a*Thou hast established for Thyself Thy people Israel as Thine own people forever, and *b*Thou, O Lord, hast become their God.

25 "Now therefore, O Lord God, the word that Thou hast spoken concerning Thy servant and his house, confirm *it* forever, and do as Thou hast spoken,

26 *a*that Thy name may be magnified forever, by saying, 'The Lord of hosts is God over Israel'; and may the house of Thy servant David be established before Thee.

27 "For Thou, O Lord of hosts, the God of Israel, hast made a revelation to Thy servant, saying, '*a*I will build you a house'; therefore Thy servant has found courage to pray this prayer to Thee.

28 "And now, O Lord God, Thou art God, and *a*Thy words are truth, and Thou hast promised this good thing to Thy servant.

29 "Now therefore, may it please Thee to bless the house of Thy servant, that it may continue forever before Thee. For Thou, O Lord God, hast spoken; and *a*with Thy blessing may the house of Thy servant be blessed forever."

Side references left column:
23 *a*Deut. 4:32-38 *b*Deut. 10:21 *c*Deut. 15:15 *d*Deut. 9:26

24 *a*Deut. 32:6 *b*Gen. 17:7, 8; Ex. 6:7

26 *a*Ps. 72:18, 19; Matt. 6:9

27 *a*2 Sam. 7:13

28 *a*Ex. 34:6; John 17:17

29 *a*Num. 6:24-26

IV DAVID'S CONQUESTS FOR THE KINGDOM, 8:1-10:19

A He Defeats Philistia, Moab, Zobah, Syria, Edom, 8:1-18

8 *a*Now after this it came about that David defeated the Philistines and subdued them; and David took control of the chief city from the hand of the Philistines.

2 And *a*he defeated *b*Moab, and measured them with the line, making them lie down on the ground; and he measured two lines to put to death and one full line to keep alive. And *c*the Moabites became servants to David, *d*bringing tribute.

3 Then David defeated *a*Hadadezer, the son of Rehob king of Zobah, as *b*he went to restore his rule at the River.

4 And David captured from him 1,700 horsemen and 20,000 foot soldiers; and David *a*hamstrung the chariot horses, but reserved *enough* of them for 100 chariots.

5 And when *a*the Arameans of Damascus came to help Hadadezer, king of Zobah, David killed 22,000 Arameans.

6 Then David put garrisons among the Arameans of Damascus, and *a*the Arameans became servants to David, bringing tribute. And *b*the Lord helped David wherever he went.

7 And David took the shields of gold which were carried by the servants of Hadadezer, and brought them to Jerusalem.

8 And from Betah and from *a*Berothai, cities of Hadadezer,

Side references right column:
★ 1 *a*1 Chr. 18

★ 2 *a*Num. 24:17 *b*1 Sam. 22:3, 4 *c*2 Sam. 8:6; 1 Kin. 4:21 *d*2 Kin. 3:4; 17:3

★ 3 *a*1 Sam. 14:47; 2 Sam. 10:16, 19 *b*2 Sam. 10:15-19

★ 4 *a*Josh. 11:6, 9

★ 5 *a*1 Kin. 11:23-25

6 *a*2 Sam. 8:2 *b*2 Sam. 3:18

★ 8 *a*Ezek. 47:16

8:1 This chapter records the expansion of David's kingdom under the blessing of God. *control of the chief city.* Heb., *Metheg-ammah;* probably a reference to Gath (1 Chron. 18:1), a key Philistine city which David captured and controlled.

8:2 The verse may be understood to mean that David spared the young Moabites (whose heights were equal to that of one measuring *line*) and executed the adults (whose heights were equal to two lines). Or it may mean that one out of three rows of soldiers was spared.

8:3 *Zobah.* An Aramean kingdom N. of Damascus.

8:4 *1,700 horsemen.* Apparently a copyist's error in place of 1,000 chariots and 7,000 horsemen (cf. LXX and 1 Chron. 18:4). *hamstrung.* I.e., disabled them for military activity by cutting the back sinews of the hind legs.

8:5 *Arameans.* Syrians. As a political entity, Syria began in the Hellenistic period (332 B.C.–63 B.C.). In the O.T. the region was called Aram, and the people Arameans.

8:8 *Betah* = Tibhath of 1 Chron. 18:8.

King David took a very large amount of bronze.

★ 9 *a*1 Kin.
8:65; 2 Chr.
8:4

9 Now when Toi king of *a*Hamath heard that David had defeated all the army of Hadadezer,

10 Toi sent Joram his son to King David to greet him and bless him, because he had fought against Hadadezer and defeated him; for Hadadezer had been at war with Toi. And *Joram* brought with him articles of silver, of gold and of bronze.

11 *a*1 Kin.
7:51

11 King David also *a*dedicated these to the LORD, with the silver and gold that he had dedicated from all the nations which he had subdued:

12 *a*2 Sam.
8:2 *b*2 Sam.
10:14
*c*2 Sam.
5:17-25
*d*1 Sam.
27:8; 30:17-
20

12 from Aram and *a*Moab and *b*the sons of Ammon and *c*the Philistines and *d*Amalek, and from the spoil of Hadadezer, son of Rehob, king of Zobah.

★13 *a*2 Sam.
7:9 *b*2 Kin.
14:7

13 So *a*David made a name for himself when he returned from killing 18,000 Arameans in *b*the Valley of Salt.

14 *a*Gen.
27:37-40;
Num. 24:17,
18 *b*2 Sam.
8:6

14 And he put garrisons in Edom. In all Edom he put garrisons, and *a*all the Edomites became servants to David. And *b*the LORD helped David wherever he went.

15 So David reigned over all Israel; and David administered justice and righteousness for all his people.

16 *a*1 Chr.
11:6 *b*1 Kin.
4:3 *c*2 Kin.
18:18, 37

16 And *a*Joab the son of Zeruiah *was* over the army, and *b*Jehoshaphat the son of Ahilud was *c*recorder.

17 *a*1 Chr.
6:4-8 *b*1 Chr.
16:39, 40
*c*2 Kin. 18:18
18 *a*1 Kin.
4:4 *b*1 Sam.
30:14;
2 Sam.
15:18; 20:7,
23; 1 Kin.
1:38, 44
*c*1 Chr.
18:17

17 And *a*Zadok the son of Ahitub and Ahimelech the son of Abiathar *were* *b*priests, and Seraiah *was* *c*secretary.

18 And *a*Benaiah the son of Jehoiada was over the *b*Cherethites and the Pelethites; and David's sons were *c*chief ministers.

B He Shows Kindness to Mephibosheth, 9:1-13

9 Then David said, "Is there yet anyone left of the house of Saul, *a*that I may show him kindness for Jonathan's sake?"

★ 1 *a*1 Sam.
20:14-17, 42

2 Now there was a servant of the house of Saul whose name was Ziba, and they called him to David; and the king said to him, "Are you *a*Ziba?" And he said, "I am your servant."

2 *a*2 Sam.
16:1-4;
19:17, 29

3 And the king said, "Is there not yet anyone of the house of Saul to whom I may show the *a*kindness of God?" And Ziba said to the king, "*b*There is still a son of Jonathan who is crippled in both feet."

3 *a*1 Sam.
20:14
*b*2 Sam. 4:4

4 So the king said to him, "Where is he?" And Ziba said to the king, "Behold, he is *a*in the house of Machir the son of Ammiel in Lo-debar."

4 *a*2 Sam.
17:27-29

5 Then King David sent and brought him from the house of Machir the son of Ammiel, from Lo-debar.

6 And *a*Mephibosheth, the son of Jonathan the son of Saul, came to David and *b*fell on his face and prostrated himself. And David said, "Mephibosheth." And he said, "Here is your servant!"

6 *a*2 Sam.
16:4; 19:24-
30 *b*1 Sam.
25:23

7 And David said to him, "Do not fear, for *a*I will surely show kindness to you for the sake of your father Jonathan, and *b*will restore to you all the land of your grandfather Saul; and *c*you shall eat at my table regularly."

7 *a*2 Sam.
9:1, 3
*b*2 Sam. 12:8
*c*2 Sam.
19:28; 1 Kin.
2:7; 2 Kin.
25:29

8 Again he prostrated himself and said, "What is your servant, that you should regard *a*a dead dog like me?"

★ 8 *a*2 Sam.
16:9; 24:14

9 Then the king called Saul's servant Ziba, and said to him, "*a*All that belonged to Saul

9 *a*2 Sam.
16:4; 19:29

8:9 *Hamath* was another Aramean state located about 100 miles N. of Damascus.

8:13 *Arameans.* Probably a copyist's error and a reference to Edom rather than Aram (cf. 1 Chron. 18:12; Psalm 60, title).

9:1 *kindness.* Loyal love (Heb. *hesed,* here and v. 3; see note on Hos. 2:19). David displayed

covenant loyalty (1 Sam. 20:42) toward Mephibosheth, the crippled son of Jonathan, by restoring his property and providing for his physical needs, thereby giving a beautiful illustration of grace.

9:8 *a dead dog.* I.e., someone contemptible and useless.

★10 a2 Sam.
9:7, 11, 13
b2 Sam.
19:28; 1 Kin.
2:7

and to all his house I have given to your master's grandson.

10 "And you and your sons and your servants shall cultivate the land for him, and you shall bring in the produce so that your master's grandson may have food; nevertheless aMephibosheth your master's grandson bshall eat at my table regularly." Now Ziba had fifteen sons and twenty servants.

11 a2 Sam.
16:1-4;
19:24-30

11 Then Ziba said to the king, "According ato all that my lord the king commands his servant so your servant will do." So Mephibosheth ate at David's table as one of the king's sons.

12 And Mephibosheth had a young son whose name was Mica. And all who lived in the house of Ziba were servants to Mephibosheth.

13 a2 Sam.
9:7, 11
b2 Sam. 9:3

13 So Mephibosheth lived in Jerusalem, for ahe ate at the king's table regularly. Now bhe was lame in both feet.

C He Defeats Ammon, 10:1-19

★ 1. a1 Chr.
19:1-19
b1 Sam. 11:1

10 aNow it happened afterwards that bthe king of the Ammonites died, and Hanun his son became king in his place.

★ 2 a1 Sam.
11:1

2 Then David said, "I will show kindness to Hanun the son of aNahash, just as his father showed kindness to me." So David sent some of his servants to console him concerning his father. But when David's servants came to the land of the Ammonites,

3 aGen.
42:9, 16

3 the princes of the Ammonites said to Hanun their lord, "Do you think that David is honoring your father because he has sent consolers to you? aHas David not

sent his servants to you in order to search the city, to spy it out and overthrow it?"

4 So Hanun took David's servants and ashaved off half of their beards, and bcut off their garments in the middle as far as their hips, and sent them away.

★ 4 aIs.
15:2; Jer.
41:5; bIs.
20:4

5 When they told it to David, he sent to meet them, for the men were greatly humiliated. And the king said, "Stay at Jericho until your beards grow, and then return."

6 Now when the sons of Ammon saw that athey had become odious to David, the sons of Ammon sent and bhired the Arameans of cBeth-rehob and the dArameans of Zobah, 20,000 foot soldiers, and the king of eMaacah with 1,000 men, and the men of Tob with 12,000 men.

★ 6 aGen.
34:30;
1 Sam. 27:12
b2 Sam. 8:3,
5; 2 Kin. 7:6
cJudg. 18:28
d2 Sam. 8:3
eDeut. 3:14

7 When David heard of it, he sent Joab and all the army, the mighty men.

8 And the sons of Ammon came out and drew up in battle array aat the entrance of the city, while the Arameans of Zobah and of Rehob and the men of bTob and Maacah were by themselves in the field.

8 a1 Chr.
19:9 bJudg.
11:3, 5

9 Now when Joab saw that the battle was set against him in front and in the rear, he selected from all the choice men of Israel, and arrayed them against the Arameans.

10 But the remainder of the people he placed in the hand of Abishai his brother, and he arrayed them against the sons of Ammon.

11 And he said, "If the Arameans are too strong for me, then you shall help me, but if the sons of Ammon are too strong for you, then I will come to help you.

9:10 This meant that while David would provide the necessities of life for Mephibosheth, Mephibosheth had to care for the maintenance of his family and servants (v. 12).

10:1 Chapter 10 records the details of David's conflict with the Ammonites and Arameans, incidentally mentioned in 8:12. It also fur-

nishes the backdrop against which the drama of David's great sin will be enacted (chap. 11).

10:2 as his father showed kindness. Perhaps when David was a refugee.

10:4 Shaving off a person's beard is still regarded by the Arabs as a great indignity.

10:6 Arameans. Syrians (see note on 8:5).

12 aDeut.
31:6; Josh.
1:6; 1 Cor.
16:13
b1 Sam. 3:18

12 "aBe strong, and let us show ourselves courageous for the sake of our people and for the cities of our God; and bmay the LORD do what is good in His sight."

13 a1 Kin.
20:13-21

13 So Joab and the people who were with him drew near to the battle against the Arameans, and athey fled before him.

14 a2 Sam.
11:1

14 When the sons of Ammon saw that the Arameans fled, they also fled before Abishai and entered the city. aThen Joab returned from fighting against the sons of Ammon and came to Jerusalem.

*15-18

15 When the Arameans saw that they had been defeated by Israel, they gathered themselves together.

16 a2 Sam.
8:3-8 b1 Chr.
19:16

16 aAnd Hadadezer sent and brought out the Arameans who were beyond the River, and they came to Helam; and bShobach the commander of the army of Hadadezer led them.

17 Now when it was told David, he gathered all Israel together and crossed the Jordan, and came to Helam. And the Arameans arrayed themselves to meet David and fought against him.

*18 a1 Chr.
19:18

18 But the Arameans fled before Israel, and David killed a700 charioteers of the Arameans and 40,000 horsemen and struck down Shobach the commander of their army, and he died there.

19 a2 Sam.
8:6

19 When all the kings, servants of Hadadezer, saw that they were defeated by Israel, athey made peace with Israel and served them. So the Arameans feared to help the sons of Ammon anymore.

V DAVID'S CRIMES WITHIN THE KINGDOM, 11:1-27

A Adultery, 11:1-13

11 aThen it happened bin the spring, at the time when kings go out to battle, that David sent Joab and his servants with him and all Israel, and they destroyed the sons of Ammon and cbesieged Rabbah. But David stayed at Jerusalem.

★ 1 a1 Chr.
20:1 b2 Sam.
10:14; 1 Kin.
20:22, 26
c2 Sam.
12:26-29;
Jer. 49:2, 3;
Amos 1:14

2 Now when evening came David arose from his bed and walked around on athe roof of the king's house, and from the roof he saw a woman bathing; and the woman was very beautiful in appearance.

★ 2 aDeut.
22:8; 1 Sam.
9:25; Matt.
24:17; Acts
10:9

3 So David sent and inquired about the woman. And one said, "Is this not aBathsheba, the daughter of Eliam, the wife of bUriah the Hittite?"

★ 3 a1 Chr.
3:5 b2 Sam.
23:39

4 And David sent messengers and took her, and when she came to him, ahe lay with her; band when she had purified herself from her uncleanness, she returned to her house.

★ 4 aPs.
51:title;
James 1:14,
15 bLev.
12:2-5;
15:18-28;
18:19

5 And the woman conceived; and she sent and told David, and said, "aI am pregnant."

5 aLev.
20:10; Deut.
22:22

6 Then David sent to Joab, saying, "Send me Uriah the Hittite." So Joab sent Uriah to David.

7 When Uriah came to him, aDavid asked concerning the wel-

7 aGen.
37:14;
1 Sam. 17:22

10:15-18 In the second campaign, Hadadezer enlisted the support of the Arameans beyond the Euphrates. The armies were engaged at Helam, in Transjordan, where David brought Israel another victory.

10:18 *700.* Probably a copyist's error, in place of 7,000 (cf. 1 Chron. 19:18).

11:1 Chapters 11-20 record David's troubles in the areas of morals, politics, and family relationships, and illustrates repeatedly the inevitable and devastating consequences of sin.

11:2 Oriental homes had an enclosed courtyard that was considered part of the house. Bathsheba, bathing herself by lamplight, was not immodest for she was in her house. However, the interior of the courtyard could be seen from the roof of David's house, situated as it was on the higher elevation of Mt. Zion.

11:3 There were three steps to David's sin: (1) he saw (v. 2); (2) he inquired (v. 3); (3) he yielded to temptation (v. 4). David was carried away by his lust, which gave birth to sin, which resulted in judgment (death; cf. James 1:14-15). *Uriah the Hittite.* Though a Hittite, Uriah must have worshiped Yahweh (the LORD), since his name means "Yahweh is my light."

11:4 Purification after intercourse was required by Mosaic Law (Lev. 15:18).

fare of Joab and the people and the state of the war.

8 Then David said to Uriah, "Go down to your house, and *a*wash your feet." And Uriah went out of the king's house, and a present from the king was sent out after him.

9 But Uriah slept *a*at the door of the king's house with all the servants of his lord, and did not go down to his house.

10 Now when they told David, saying, "Uriah did not go down to his house," David said to Uriah, "Have you not come from a journey? Why did you not go down to your house?"

11 And Uriah said to David, "*a*The ark and Israel and Judah are staying in temporary shelters, and my lord Joab and *b*the servants of my lord are camping in the open field. Shall I then go to my house to eat and to drink and to lie with my wife? By your life and the life of your soul, I will not do this thing."

12 Then David said to Uriah, "*a*Stay here today also, and tomorrow I will let you go." So Uriah remained in Jerusalem that day and the next.

13 Now David called him, and he ate and drank before him, and he *a*made him drunk; and in the evening he went out to lie on his bed *b*with his lord's servants, but he did not go down to his house.

B　Murder, 11:14-27

14 Now it came about in the morning that David *a*wrote a letter to Joab, and sent *it* by the hand of Uriah.

15 And *a*he had written in the letter, saying, "Place Uriah in the front line of the fiercest battle and withdraw from him, *b*so that he may be struck down and die."

16 So it was as Joab kept watch on the city, that he put Uriah at the place where he knew there *were* valiant men.

17 And the men of the city went out and fought against Joab, and some of the people among David's servants fell; and *a*Uriah the Hittite also died.

18 Then Joab sent and reported to David all the events of the war.

19 And he charged the messenger, saying, "When you have finished telling all the events of the war to the king,

20 and if it happens that the king's wrath rises and he says to you, 'Why did you go so near to the city to fight? Did you not know that they would shoot from the wall?

21 'Who *a*struck down Abimelech the son of Jerubbesheth? Did not a woman throw an upper millstone on him from the wall so that he died at Thebez? Why did you go so near the wall?'—then you shall say, 'Your servant Uriah the Hittite is dead also.' "

22 So the messenger departed and came and reported to David all that Joab had sent him *to tell.*

23 And the messenger said to David, "The men prevailed against us and came out against us in the field, but we pressed them as far as the entrance of the gate.

24 "Moreover, the archers shot at your servants from the wall; so some of the king's servants are dead, and your servant Uriah the Hittite is also dead."

25 Then David said to the messenger, "Thus you shall say to Joab, 'Do not let this thing displease you, for the sword devours one as well as another; make your battle against the city stronger

---

★ 8 *a*Gen. 43:24; Luke 7:44

9 *a*1 Kin. 14:27, 28

★11 *a*2 Sam. 7:2, 6　*b*2 Sam. 20:6

12 *a*Job 20:12-14

13 *a*Prov. 20:1; 23:29-35　*b*2 Sam. 11:9

★14 *a*1 Kin. 21:8-10

15 *a*Eccl. 8:11; Jer. 17:9　*b*2 Sam. 12:9

17 *a*2 Sam. 11:21

★21 *a*Judg. 9:50-54

11:8 *wash your feet.* A contemporary idiom meaning "spend some time at home."
11:11 Uriah exemplified the epitome of dedication to his men and to his mission (see also v. 13).
11:14 David now resorted to Uriah's murder and coldly sent the letter of instructions by the victim himself.
11:21 *Jerubbesheth* is a variation of Jerubbaal of Judg. 9:57 (= Gideon, Judg. 7:1).

and overthrow it;' and *so* encourage him."

26 *a*Gen. 50:10; Deut. 34:8; 1 Sam. 31:13

26 Now when the wife of Uriah heard that Uriah her husband was dead, *a*she mourned for her husband.

★**27** *a*2 Sam. 12:9 *b*Ps. 51:4, 5

27 When the *time of* mourning was over, David sent and brought her to his house and *a*she became his wife; then she bore him a son. But *b*the thing that David had done was evil in the sight of the Lord.

VI DAVID'S CONFLICTS IN THE KINGDOM, 12:1–20:26
A The Death of his Baby and the Restoration to Power, 12:1–31

★ **1** *a*2 Sam. 7:2, 4, 17 *b*Ps. 51:title

12 Then the Lord sent *a*Nathan to David. And *b*he came to him, and said,

"There were two men in one city, the one rich and the other poor.

2 "The rich man had a great many flocks and herds.

3 *a*2 Sam. 11:3

3 "But the poor man had nothing except *a*one little ewe lamb
Which he bought and nourished;
And it grew up together with him and his children.
It would eat of his bread and drink of his cup and lie in his bosom,
And was like a daughter to him.

4 "Now a traveler came to the rich man,
And he was unwilling to take from his own flock or his own herd,
To prepare for the wayfarer who had come to him;

Rather he took the poor man's ewe lamb and prepared it for the man who had come to him."

5 Then David's anger burned greatly against the man, and he said to Nathan, "As the Lord lives, surely the man who has done this *a*deserves to die.

★ **5** *a*1 Sam. 26:16

6 "And he must make restitution for the lamb *a*fourfold, because he did this thing and had no compassion."

★ **6** *a*Ex. 22:1; Luke 19:8

7 Nathan then said to David, "*a*You are the man! Thus says the Lord God of Israel, '*b*It is I who anointed you king over Israel and it is I who delivered you from the hand of Saul.

7 *a*1 Kin. 20:42 *b*1 Sam. 16:13

8 'I also gave you *a*your master's house and your master's wives into your care, and I gave you the house of Israel and Judah; and if *that had been* too little, I would have added to you many more things like these!

8 *a*2 Sam. 9:7

9 'Why *a*have you despised the word of the Lord by doing evil in His sight? *b*You have struck down Uriah the Hittite with the sword, *c*have taken his wife to be your wife, and have killed him with the sword of the sons of Ammon.

9 *a*1 Sam. 15:23, 26 *b*2 Sam. 11:14–17 *c*2 Sam. 11:27

10 'Now therefore, *a*the sword shall never depart from your house, because you have despised Me and have taken the wife of Uriah the Hittite to be your wife.'

★**10-11**

10 *a*2 Sam. 13:28; 18:14; 1 Kin. 2:25

11 "Thus says the Lord, 'Behold, I will raise up evil against you from your own household; *a*I will even take your wives before your eyes, and give *them* to your companion, and he shall lie with your wives in broad daylight.

11 *a*Deut. 28:30; 2 Sam. 16:21, 22

12 'Indeed *a*you did it secretly, but *b*I will do this thing before all Israel, and under the sun.' "

12 *a*2 Sam. 11:4–15 *b*2 Sam. 16:22

11:27 While sin may be concealed from the public, the omniscient God sees it.

12:1 Nathan the prophet used a parable to lead David to condemn his own actions and bring about repentance.

12:5 David himself deserved death for adultery (Lev. 20:10) and murder (Lev. 24:17).

12:6 David demanded restitution according to the Mosaic Law (Exod 22:1).

12:10-11 These predictions of judgment were fulfilled in the violent deaths of Amnon (13:28–29) and Absalom (18:15), and in Absalom's public appropriation of David's royal concubines (16:22).

13 Then David said to Nathan, "ªI have sinned against the LORD." And Nathan said to David, "The LORD also has ᵇtaken away your sin; you shall not die.

14 "However, because by this deed you have ªgiven occasion to the enemies of the LORD to blaspheme, the child also that is born to you shall surely die."

15 So Nathan went to his house.

Then the LORD struck the child that Uriah's widow bore to David, so that he was *very* sick.

16 David therefore inquired of God for the child; and David ªfasted and went and ᵇlay all night on the ground.

17 And ªthe elders of his household stood beside him in order to raise him up from the ground, but he was unwilling and would not eat food with them.

18 Then it happened on the seventh day that the child died. And the servants of David were afraid to tell him that the child was dead, for they said, "Behold, while the child was *still* alive, we spoke to him and he did not listen to our voice. How then can we tell him that the child is dead, since he might do *himself* harm!"

19 But when David saw that his servants were whispering together, David perceived that the child was dead; so David said to his servants, "Is the child dead?" And they said, "He is dead."

20 So David arose from the ground, ªwashed, anointed *himself*, and changed his clothes; and he came into the house of the LORD and ᵇworshiped. Then he came to his own house, and when he requested, they set food before him and he ate.

21 Then his servants said to him, "What is this thing that you have done? While the child was alive, you fasted and wept; but when the child died, you arose and ate food."

22 And he said, "While the child was *still* alive, ªI fasted and wept; for I said, ᵇWho knows, the LORD may be gracious to me, that the child may live.'

23 "But now he has died; why should I fast? Can I bring him back again? ªI shall go to him, but ᵇhe will not return to me."

24 Then David comforted his wife Bathsheba, and went in to her and lay with her; and she gave birth to a son, and ªhe named him Solomon. Now the LORD loved him

25 and sent *word* through Nathan the prophet, and he named him Jedidiah for the LORD's sake.

26 ªNow Joab fought against ᵇRabbah of the sons of Ammon, and captured the royal city.

27 And Joab sent messengers to David and said, "I have fought against Rabbah, I have even captured the city of waters.

28 "Now therefore, gather the rest of the people together and camp against the city and capture it, lest I capture the city myself and it be named after me."

29 So David gathered all the people and went to Rabbah, fought against it, and captured it.

30 Then ªhe took the crown of their king from his head; and its weight *was* a talent of gold, and *in it was* a precious stone; and it was *placed* on David's head.

Cross references (margin):

★**13** ª1 Sam. 15:24, 30; 2 Sam. 24:10; Luke 18:13 ᵇLev. 20:10; 24:17; Prov. 28:13; Mic. 7:18

★**14** ªIs. 52:5; Rom. 2:24

16 ªNeh. 1:4 ᵇ2 Sam. 13:31

17 ªGen. 24:2

20 ªRuth 3:3; Matt. 6:17 ᵇPs. 95:6-8; 103:1, 8-17; Prov. 3:7

22 ªIs. 38:1-3 ᵇJon. 3:9

★**23** ªGen. 37:35 ᵇJob 7:8-10

24 ª1 Chr. 22:9; Matt. 1:6

★**25**

26 ª1 Chr. 20:1-3 ᵇDeut. 3:11

★**27**

★**30** ª1 Chr. 20:2

12:13 David's confession (given fuller expression in Psalm 51) was immediate, as was God's gracious forgiveness.

12:14 For the sake of God's holy reputation among the nations, the sin of adultery had to be judged.

12:23 While the verse may lend support to the view that infants who die are taken to heaven, the emphasis here is not on existence after death, but on the inevitability of death. The child could not return to life, but David would someday join his son in death.

12:25 *Jedidiah* means "beloved of the Lord." The name marked Solomon as successor to the throne.

12:27 *the city of waters.* That part of Rabbah which linked it to its water supply.

12:30 *a talent of gold.* About 75 lbs.

And he brought out the spoil of the city in great amounts.

★31 *a* 1 Chr. 20:3; Heb. 11:37

31 He also brought out the people who were in it, and *a*set *them* under saws, sharp iron instruments, and iron axes, and made them pass through the brickkiln. And thus he did to all the cities of the sons of Ammon. Then David and all the people returned *to* Jerusalem.

B The Incest of Amnon, 13:1-39

★ 1-29

1 *a* 2 Sam. 3:2, 3; 1 Chr. 3:2 *b* 1 Chr. 3:9 *c* 2 Sam. 3:2

13 Now it was after this that *a*Absalom the son of David had a beautiful sister whose name was *b*Tamar, and *c*Amnon the son of David loved her.

★ 2

2 And Amnon was so frustrated because of his sister Tamar that he made himself ill, for she was a virgin, and it seemed hard to Amnon to do anything to her.

3 *a* 1 Sam. 16:9

3 But Amnon had a friend whose name was Jonadab, the son of *a*Shimeah, David's brother; and Jonadab was a very shrewd man.

4 And he said to him, "O son of the king, why are you so depressed morning after morning? Will you not tell me?" Then Amnon said to him, "I am in love with Tamar, the sister of my brother Absalom."

5 Jonadab then said to him, "Lie down on your bed and pretend to be ill; when your father comes to see you, say to him, 'Please let my sister Tamar come and give me *some* food to eat, and let her prepare the food in my sight, that I may see *it* and eat from her hand.'"

6 *a* Gen. 18:6

6 So Amnon lay down and pretended to be ill; when the king came to see him, Amnon said to the king, "Please let my sister Tamar come and *a*make me a couple of cakes in my sight, that I may eat from her hand."

7 Then David sent to the house for Tamar, saying, "Go now to your brother Amnon's house, and prepare food for him."

8 So Tamar went to her brother Amnon's house, and he was lying down. And she took dough, kneaded *it*, made cakes in his sight, and baked the cakes.

9 *a* Gen. 45:1

9 And she took the pan and dished *them* out before him, but he refused to eat. And Amnon said, "*a*Have everyone go out from me." So everyone went out from him.

10 Then Amnon said to Tamar, "Bring the food into the bedroom, that I may eat from your hand." So Tamar took the cakes which she had made and brought them into the bedroom to her brother Amnon.

11 *a* Gen. 39:12

11 When she brought *them* to him to eat, he *a*took hold of her and said to her, "Come, lie with me, my sister."

12 *a* Lev. 20:17 *b* Judg. 19:23; 20:6

12 But she answered him, "No, my brother, do not violate me, for *a*such a thing is not done in Israel; do not do this *b*disgraceful thing!

13 *a* Gen. 20:12

13 "As for me, where could I get rid of my reproach? And as for you, you will be like one of the fools in Israel. Now therefore, please speak to the king, for *a*he will not withhold me from you."

14 *a* Lev. 18:9; Deut. 22:25, 27:22; 2 Sam. 12:11

14 However, he would not listen to her; since he was stronger than she, he *a*violated her and lay with her.

★15

15 Then Amnon hated her with a very great hatred; for the

12:31 There are two views as to the meaning of this verse: (1) David imposed hard labor on the captives. However, this would require a change of "pass through" to "toil at." (2) David had them killed in accordance with cruel Ammonite ways (cf. 1 Sam. 11:2; Amos 1:13).

13:1-29 The tragedy of the rape of Tamar and murder of Amnon is clearly a fulfillment of God's promised judgment on David for his sin

with Bathsheba (12:11). Amnon and Tamar were David's children by Ahinoam (3:2) and Maacah (3:3) respectively.

13:2 *frustrated.* I.e., sexually frustrated. A marriage relationship with one's half-sister was forbidden by the Mosaic Law (Lev. 18:11).

13:15 Amnon's "love" was really lust, which when gratified turned to hatred.

hatred with which he hated her was greater than the love with which he had loved her. And Amnon said to her, "Get up, go away!"

16 But she said to him, "No, because this wrong in sending me away is greater than the other that you have done to me!" Yet he would not listen to her.

17 Then he called his young man who attended him and said, "Now throw this woman out of my *presence*, and lock the door behind her."

18 Now she had on ᵃa long-sleeved garment; for in this manner the virgin daughters of the king dressed themselves in robes. Then his attendant took her out and locked the door behind her.

19 And ᵃTamar put ashes on her head, and ᵇtore her long-sleeved garment which *was* on her; and ᶜshe put her hand on her head and went away, crying aloud as she went.

20 Then Absalom her brother said to her, "Has Amnon your brother been with you? But now keep silent, my sister, he is your brother; do not take this matter to heart." So Tamar remained and was desolate in her brother Absalom's house.

21 Now when King David heard of all these matters, he was very angry.

22 But Absalom did not speak to Amnon ᵃeither good or bad; for ᵇAbsalom hated Amnon because he had violated his sister Tamar.

23 Now it came about after two full years that Absalom ᵃhad sheepshearers in Baal-hazor, which is near Ephraim, and Absalom invited all the king's sons.

24 And Absalom came to the king and said, "Behold now, your servant has sheepshearers; please

let the king and his servants go with your servant."

25 But the king said to Absalom, "No, my son, we should not all go, lest we be burdensome to you." Although he urged him, he would not go, but blessed him.

26 Then ᵃAbsalom said, "If not, please let my brother Amnon go with us." And the king said to him, "Why should he go with you?"

27 But when Absalom urged him, he let Amnon and all the king's sons go with him.

28 And Absalom commanded his servants, saying, "See now, ᵃwhen Amnon's heart is merry with wine, and when I say to you, 'Strike Amnon,' then put him to death. Do not fear; have not I myself commanded you? Be courageous and be valiant."

29 And the servants of Absalom did to Amnon just as Absalom had commanded. Then all the king's sons arose and each mounted ᵃhis mule and fled.

30 Now it was while they were on the way that the report came to David, saying, "Absalom has struck down all the king's sons, and not one of them is left."

31 Then the king arose, ᵃtore his clothes and ᵇlay on the ground; and all his servants were standing by with clothes torn.

32 And ᵃJonadab, the son of Shimeah, David's brother, responded, "Do not let my lord suppose they have put to death all the young men, the king's sons, for Amnon alone is dead; because by the intent of Absalom this has been determined since the day that he violated his sister Tamar.

33 "Now therefore, do not let my lord the king ᵃtake the report to heart, namely, 'all the king's

Cross references (margin):
18 ᵃGen. 37:3, 23
★19 ᵃ1 Sam. 4:12; Esth. 4:1 ᵇGen. 37:29; 2 Sam. 1:11 ᶜJer. 2:37
★20
★21
22 ᵃGen. 31:24 ᵇLev. 19:17; 1 John 2:9, 11; 3:10, 12, 15
23 ᵃ1 Sam. 25:7
26 ᵃ2 Sam. 3:27; 11:13-15
28 ᵃJudg. 19:6, 9, 22; 1 Sam. 25:36-38
29 ᵃ2 Sam. 18:9; 1 Kin. 1:33, 38
★30-33
31 ᵃ2 Sam. 1:11 ᵇ2 Sam. 12:16
32 ᵃ2 Sam. 13:3-5
33 ᵃ2 Sam. 19:19

13:19 Tamar's actions were those of a widow mourning for her husband.

13:20 Absalom quieted the matter, determining to take revenge when Amnon least expected (v. 22).

13:21 David was angry but did not execute Amnon as he should have (Lev. 20:17). This may

be due to the fact that Amnon was David's firstborn (1 Chron. 3:1) and would be expected to inherit the throne.

13:30-33 The report received by David was exaggerated, but Jonadab perceived the truth and reassured the king.

sons are dead,' for only Amnon is dead."

34 Now [a]Absalom had fled. And [b]the young man who was the watchman raised his eyes and looked, and behold, many people were coming from the road behind him by the side of the mountain.

35 And Jonadab said to the king, "Behold, the king's sons have come; according to your servant's word, so it happened."

36 And it came about as soon as he had finished speaking, that behold, the king's sons came and lifted their voices and wept; and also the king and all his servants wept very bitterly.

37 Now [a]Absalom fled and went to [b]Talmai the son of Ammihud, the king of [c]Geshur. And *David* mourned for his son every day.

38 [a]So Absalom had fled and gone to Geshur, and was there three years.

39 And *the heart of* King David longed to go out to Absalom; for [a]he was comforted concerning Amnon, since he was dead.

C The Rebellion of Absalom, 14:1–18:33

1 *Absalom returns,* 14:1–33

14 Now Joab the son of Zeruiah perceived that [a]the king's heart *was* inclined toward Absalom.

2 So Joab sent to [a]Tekoa and brought a wise woman from there and said to her, "Please pretend to be a mourner, and put on mourning garments now, and do not [b]anoint yourself with oil, but like a woman who has been mourning for the dead many days;

3 then go to the king and speak to him in this manner." So Joab put [a]the words in her mouth.

4 Now when the woman of Tekoa spoke to the king, she fell on her face to the ground and [a]prostrated herself and said, "[b]Help, O king."

5 And the king said to her, "What is your trouble?" And she answered, "Truly I am a widow, for my husband is dead.

6 "And your maidservant had two sons, but the two of them struggled together in the field, and there was no one to separate them, so one struck the other and killed him.

7 "Now behold, [a]the whole family has risen against your maidservant, and they say, 'Hand over the one who struck his brother, that we may put him to death for the life of his brother whom he killed, [b]and destroy the heir also.' Thus they will extinguish my coal which is left, so as to leave my husband neither name nor remnant on the face of the earth."

8 Then the king said to the woman, "Go to your house, and I will give orders concerning you."

9 And the woman of Tekoa said to the king, "O my lord, the king, [a]the iniquity is on me and my father's house, but [b]the king and his throne are guiltless."

10 So the king said, "Whoever speaks to you, bring him to me, and he will not touch you anymore."

11 Then she said, "Please let the king remember the LORD your

Cross references

34 [a]2 Sam. 13:37, 38 [b]2 Sam. 18:24

37 [a]2 Sam. 13:34 [b]2 Sam. 3:3 [c]2 Sam. 14:23, 32

38 [a]2 Sam. 13:34

★**39** [a]2 Sam. 12:19-23

★ **1-20**
1 [a]2 Sam. 13:39

★ **2** [a]2 Sam. 23:26; 2 Chr. 11:6; Amos 1:1 [b]2 Sam. 12:20

3 [a]2 Sam. 14:19

4 [a]1 Sam. 25:23 [b]2 Kin. 6:26-28

★ **7** [a]Num. 35:19; Deut. 19:12, 13 [b]Matt. 21:38

★ **8-9**

9 [a]Gen. 43:9; 1 Sam. 25:24 [b]1 Kin. 2:33

★**10**

★**11** [a]Num. 35:19, 21; Deut. 19:4-10 [b]1 Sam. 14:45; 1 Kin. 1:52; Matt. 10:30

13:39 David gradually accepted the fact of Amnon's death, and became anxious to see Absalom again.

14:1-20 Joab used a subtle method to enable David to be reunited with Absalom after a three-year separation.

14:2 On *Tekoa* see Introduction to the Book of Amos.

14:7 The extinction of a family line on account of the absence of an heir was regarded as a terrible misfortune. The surviving son is compared to the last *coal* left among the embers.

14:8-9 David was apparently putting the woman off, seeking to avoid becoming blameworthy himself by defending a guilty son. The persistent woman expressed her willingness to bear any guilt in place of the king.

14:10 David authorized the woman to bring her persecutors before him for judgment.

14:11 *the avenger of blood.* See note on Num. 35:11-12.

God, ᵃso that the avenger of blood may not continue to destroy, lest they destroy my son." And he said, "ᵇAs the Lᴏʀᴅ lives, not one hair of your son shall fall to the ground."

12 Then the woman said, "Please let your maidservant speak a word to my lord the king." And he said, "Speak."

13 And the woman said, "ᵃWhy then have you planned such a thing against the people of God? For in speaking this word the king is as one who is guilty, in that the king does not bring back ᵇhis banished one.

14 "For ᵃwe shall surely die and are ᵇlike water spilled on the ground which cannot be gathered up again. Yet God does not take away life, but plans ways so that ᶜthe banished one may not be cast out from him.

15 "Now the reason I have come to speak this word to my lord the king is because the people have made me afraid; so your maidservant said, 'Let me now speak to the king, perhaps the king will perform the request of his maidservant.

16 'For the king will hear and deliver his maidservant from the hand of the man who would destroy both me and my son from ᵃthe inheritance of God.'

17 "Then your maidservant said, 'Please let the word of my lord the king be comforting, for as ᵃthe angel of God, so is my lord the king to discern good and evil. And may the Lᴏʀᴅ your God be with you.'"

18 Then the king answered and said to the woman, "Please do not hide anything from me that I am about to ask you." And the woman said, "Let my lord the king please speak."

19 So the king said, "Is the hand of Joab with you in all this?" And the woman answered and said, "As your soul lives, my lord the king, no one can turn to the right or to the left from anything that my lord the king has spoken. Indeed, it was ᵃyour servant Joab who commanded me, and it was he who put all these words in the mouth of your maidservant;

20 in order to change the appearance of things your servant Joab has done this thing. But my lord is wise, ᵃlike the wisdom of the angel of God, to know all that is in the earth."

21 Then the king said to Joab, "Behold now, ᵃI will surely do this thing; go therefore, bring back the young man Absalom."

22 And Joab fell on his face to the ground, prostrated himself and blessed the king; then Joab said, "Today your servant knows that I have found favor in your sight, O my lord, the king, in that the king has performed the request of his servant."

23 So Joab arose and went to ᵃGeshur, and brought Absalom to Jerusalem.

24 However the king said, "Let him turn to ᵃhis own house, and let him not see my face." So Absalom turned to his own house and did not see the king's face.

25 Now in all Israel was no one as handsome as Absalom, so highly praised; ᵃfrom the sole of his foot to the crown of his head there was no defect in him.

26 And when he ᵃcut the hair of his head (and it was at the end of every year that he cut it, for it was heavy on him so he cut it), he weighed the hair of his head at 200 shekels by the king's weight.

27 And ᵃto Absalom there were born three sons, and one daughter whose name was

---

Margin references:

★**13** ᵃ2 Sam. 12:7; 1 Kin. 20:40-42
ᵇ2 Sam. 13:37, 38

14 ᵃJob 30:23; 34:15; Heb. 9:27
ᵇPs. 58:7
ᶜNum. 35:15, 25, 28

16 ᵃDeut. 32:9; 1 Sam. 26:19

17 ᵃ1 Sam. 29:9; 2 Sam. 14:20; 19:27

19 ᵃ2 Sam. 14:3

20 ᵃ2 Sam. 14:17; 19:27

21 ᵃ2 Sam. 14:11

23 ᵃDeut. 3:14; 2 Sam. 13:37, 38

★**24** ᵃ2 Sam. 13:20

25 ᵃDeut. 28:35; Job 2:7; Is. 1:6

★**26** ᵃEzek. 44:20

★**27** ᵃ2 Sam. 18:18
ᵇ2 Sam. 13:1

14:13 The woman applied the principle of David's judgment to his own situation with Absalom.
14:24 David's unwillingness to forgive completely and to restore Absalom to the court generated bitterness in the heart of Absalom.
14:26 The weight of Absalom's hair clippings was 3½ to 4 lbs.
14:27 Absalom's sons predeceased him (18:18). Concerning *Tamar* see note on 1 Kings 15:1-2.

*b*Tamar; she was a woman of beautiful appearance.

28 Now Absalom lived two full years in Jerusalem, *a*and did not see the king's face.

29 Then Absalom sent for Joab, to send him to the king, but he would not come to him. So he sent again a second time, but he would not come.

30 Therefore he said to his servants, "See, *a*Joab's field is next to mine, and he has barley there; go and set it on fire." So Absalom's servants set the field on fire.

31 Then Joab arose, came to Absalom at his house and said to him, "Why have your servants set my field on fire?"

32 And Absalom answered Joab, "Behold, I sent for you, saying, 'Come here, that I may send you to the king, to say, "Why have I come from Geshur? It would be better for me still to be there." ' Now therefore, let me see the king's face; *a*and if there is iniquity in me, let him put me to death."

33 So when Joab came to the king and told him, he called for Absalom. Thus he came to the king and prostrated himself on his face to the ground before the king, and *a*the king kissed Absalom.

2 *Absalom revolts,* 15:1-12

15 Now it came about after this that *a*Absalom provided for himself a chariot and horses, and fifty men as runners before him.

2 And Absalom used to rise early and *a*stand beside the way to the gate; and it happened that when any man had a suit to come to the king for judgment, Absalom would call to him and say, "From what city are you?" And he would say, "Your servant is from one of the tribes of Israel."

3 Then Absalom would say to him, "See, *a*your claims are good and right, but no man listens to you on the part of the king."

4 Moreover, Absalom would say, "*a*Oh that one would appoint me judge in the land, then every man who has any suit or cause could come to me, and I would give him justice."

5 And it happened that when a man came near to prostrate himself before him, he would put out his hand and take hold of him and *a*kiss him.

6 And in this manner Absalom dealt with all Israel who came to the king for judgment; *a*so Absalom stole away the hearts of the men of Israel.

7 Now it came about at the end of forty years that Absalom said to the king, "Please let me go and pay my vow which I have vowed to the LORD, in *a*Hebron.

8 "For your servant *a*vowed a vow while I was living at Geshur in Aram, saying, '*b*If the LORD shall indeed bring me back to Jerusalem, then I will serve the LORD.' "

9 And the king said to him, "Go in peace." So he arose and went to Hebron.

10 But Absalom sent spies throughout all the tribes of Israel, saying, "As soon as you hear the sound of the trumpet, then you shall say, '*a*Absalom is king in Hebron.' "

11 Then two hundred men went with Absalom from Jerusalem, *a*who were invited and *b*went innocently, and they did not know anything.

Margin references:

28 *a*2 Sam. 14:24
30 *a*Judg. 15:3-5
32 *a*1 Sam. 20:8; Prov. 28:13
★33 *a*Gen. 33:4; Luke 15:20
★ 1-23
1 *a*1 Kin. 1:5
2 *a*Ruth 4:1; 2 Sam. 19:8
3 *a*Prov. 12:2
4 *a*Judg. 9:29
5 *a*2 Sam. 14:33; 20:9
6 *a*Rom. 16:18
★ 7 *a*2 Sam. 3:2, 3
8 *a*2 Sam. 13:37, 38 *b*Gen. 28:20, 21
10 *a*1 Kin. 1:34; 2 Kin. 9:13
11 *a*1 Sam. 9:13 *b*1 Sam. 22:15

14:33 After two years Absalom was restored to favor with David and again enjoyed full court privileges.

15:1-23 During the three years of separation from David, Absalom had grown bitter. This eventually erupted in rebellion, which forced David to flee Jerusalem when Absalom usurped the throne.

15:7 *forty years.* Probably a copyist's error and should read "four years" with the LXX, Syriac, and writings of Josephus (*Antiq.* 7.9.1). The period probably began with Absalom's return from Geshur.

12 ᵃ2 Sam.
15:31 ᵇJosh.
15:51 ᶜPs.
3:1

12 And Absalom sent for ᵃAhithophel the Gilonite, David's counselor, from his city ᵇGiloh, while he was offering the sacrifices. And the conspiracy was strong, for ᶜthe people increased continually with Absalom.

3 Absalom routs David,
15:13–16:14

13 ᵃJudg.
9:3; 2 Sam.
15:6

13 Then a messenger came to David, saying, "ᵃThe hearts of the men of Israel are with Absalom."

★**14** ᵃ2 Sam.
12:11; Ps.
3:title

14 And David said to all his servants who were with him at Jerusalem, "ᵃArise and let us flee, for *otherwise* none of us shall escape from Absalom. Go in haste, lest he overtake us quickly and bring down calamity on us and strike the city with the edge of the sword."

15 Then the king's servants said to the king, "Behold, your servants *are ready to do* whatever my lord the king chooses."

16 ᵃ2 Sam.
16:21, 22

16 So the king went out and all his household with him. But ᵃthe king left ten concubines to keep the house.

17 And the king went out and all the people with him, and they stopped at the last house.

18 ᵃ2 Sam.
8:18 ᵇ1 Sam.
23:13; 25:13;
30:1, 9

18 Now all his servants passed on beside him, ᵃall the Cherethites, all the Pelethites, and all the Gittites, ᵇsix hundred men who had come with him from Gath, passed on before the king.

★**19** ᵃ2 Sam.
18:2

19 Then the king said to ᵃIttai the Gittite, "Why will you also go with us? Return and remain with the king, for you are a foreigner and also an exile; *return* to your own place.

20 ᵃ1 Sam.
23:13
ᵇ2 Sam. 2:6

20 "You came *only* yesterday, and shall I today make you wander with us, while ᵃI go where I will? Return and take back your brothers; ᵇmercy and truth be with you."

21 But Ittai answered the king and said, "As the LORD lives, and as my lord the king lives, surely ᵃwherever my lord the king may be, whether for death or for life, there also your servant will be."

22 Therefore David said to Ittai, "Go and pass over." So Ittai the Gittite passed over with all his men and all the little ones who *were* with him.

23 While all the country was weeping with a loud voice, all the people passed over. The king also passed over ᵃthe brook Kidron, and all the people passed over toward ᵇthe way of the wilderness.

24 Now behold, ᵃZadok also *came,* and all the Levites with him ᵇcarrying the ark of the covenant of God. And they set down the ark of God, and ᶜAbiathar came up until all the people had finished passing from the city.

25 And the king said to Zadok, "Return the ark of God to the city. If I find favor in the sight of the LORD, then ᵃHe will bring me back again, and show me both it and ᵇHis habitation.

26 "But if He should say thus, 'ᵃI have no delight in you,' behold, here I am, ᵇlet Him do to me as seems good to Him."

27 The king said also to Zadok the priest, "Are you *not* ᵃa seer? Return to the city in peace and your ᵇtwo sons with you, your son Ahimaaz and Jonathan the son of Abiathar.

28 "See, I am going to wait ᵃat the fords of the wilderness until word comes from you to inform me."

29 Therefore Zadok and Abiathar returned the ark of God to Jerusalem and remained there.

21 ᵃRuth
1:16, 17;
Prov. 17:17

★**23** ᵃ1 Kin.
15:13; 2 Chr.
29:16
ᵇ2 Sam.
15:28; 16:2

24 ᵃ2 Sam.
8:17; 20:25
ᵇNum. 4:15;
1 Sam. 4:4, 5
ᶜ1 Sam.
22:20

25 ᵃPs. 43:3
ᵇEx. 15:13;
Jer. 25:30

26 ᵃ2 Sam.
11:27; 1 Chr.
21:7 ᵇ1 Sam.
3:18

27 ᵃ1 Sam.
9:6-9
ᵇ2 Sam.
17:17

★**28** ᵃJosh.
5:10; 2 Sam.
17:16

15:14 David fled for his life and for fear of an attack on Jerusalem if he remained at the city. Perhaps he was seeking to avert civil war and bloodshed. But he obviously expected to return to Jerusalem, for he left ten concubines to keep house (v. 16 and 16:21–22).
15:19 Although David did not recognize Absalom as king, he encouraged Ittai to remain with whomever God should appoint king (cf. 15:25–26).
15:23 *the way of the wilderness.* In Judea, between Jerusalem and the Jordan River.
15:28 *the fords of the wilderness.* Where they could retreat across the Jordan, if necessary.

30 And David went up the ascent of the *Mount of Olives,* and wept as he went, and [a]his head was covered and he walked [b]barefoot. Then all the people who were with him each covered his head and went up weeping as they went.

31 Now someone told David, saying, "[a]Ahithophel is among the conspirators with Absalom." And David said, "O LORD, I pray, [b]make the counsel of Ahithophel foolishness."

32 It happened as David was coming to the summit, where God was worshiped, that behold, Hushai the [a]Archite met him with his coat torn, and dust on his head.

33 And David said to him, "If you pass over with me, then you will be [a]a burden to me.

34 "But if you return to the city, and [a]say to Absalom, 'I will be your servant, O king; as I have been your father's servant in time past, so I will now be your servant,' then you can thwart the counsel of Ahithophel for me.

35 "And are not Zadok and Abiathar the priests with you there? So it shall be that [a]whatever you hear from the king's house, you shall report to Zadok and Abiathar the priests.

36 "Behold [a]their two sons are with them there, Ahimaaz, Zadok's son and Jonathan, Abiathar's son; and [b]by them you shall send me everything that you hear."

37 So Hushai, [a]David's friend, came into the city, and [b]Absalom came into Jerusalem.

16 Now when David had passed [a]a little beyond the summit, behold, [b]Ziba the servant of Mephibosheth met him [c]with a couple of saddled donkeys, and on them *were* two hundred loaves of bread, a hundred clusters of raisins, a hundred summer fruits, and a jug of wine.

2 And the king said to Ziba, "Why do you have these?" And Ziba said, "[a]The donkeys are for the king's household to ride, and the bread and summer fruit for the young men to eat, and the wine, [b]for whoever is faint in the wilderness to drink."

3 Then the king said, "And where is [a]your master's son?" And [b]Ziba said to the king, "Behold, he is staying in Jerusalem, for he said, 'Today the house of Israel will restore the kingdom of my father to me.' "

4 So the king said to Ziba, "Behold, all that belongs to Mephibosheth is yours." And Ziba said, "I prostrate myself; let me find favor in your sight, O my lord, the king!"

5 When King David came to [a]Bahurim, behold, there came out from there a man of the family of the house of Saul [b]whose name was Shimei, the son of Gera; he came out [c]cursing continually as he came.

6 And he threw stones at David and at all the servants of King David; and all the people and all the mighty men were at his right hand and at his left.

7 And thus Shimei said when he cursed, "Get out, get out, [a]you man of bloodshed, and worthless fellow!

8 "[a]The LORD has returned upon you all [b]the bloodshed of the house of Saul, in whose place you have reigned; and the LORD has given the kingdom into the hand of your son Absalom. And behold, you are *taken* in your own evil, for you are a man of bloodshed!"

9 Then [a]Abishai the son of Zeruiah said to the king, "Why should [b]this dead dog [c]curse my

---

30 [a]Esth. 6:12; Ezek. 24:17, 23 [b]Is. 20:2-4

★**31-32**

31 [a]2 Sam. 15:12 [b]2 Sam. 16:23; 17:14, 23

32 [a]Josh. 16:2

33 [a]2 Sam. 19:35

34 [a]2 Sam. 16:19

35 [a]2 Sam. 17:15, 16

36 [a]2 Sam. 15:27 [b]2 Sam. 17:17

37 [a]2 Sam. 16:16; 1 Chr. 27:33 [b]2 Sam. 16:15

★**1-4**

1 [a]2 Sam. 15:32 [b]2 Sam. 9:2-13 [c]1 Sam. 25:18

2 [a]Judg. 10:4 [b]2 Sam. 17:29

3 [a]2 Sam. 9:9, 10 [b]2 Sam. 19:26, 27

★**5** [a]2 Sam. 3:16; 17:18 [b]2 Sam. 19:16-23; 1 Kin. 2:8, 9, 44 [c]Ex. 22:28; 1 Sam. 17:43

7 [a]2 Sam. 12:9

8 [a]2 Sam. 21:1-9 [b]2 Sam. 1:16; 3:28, 29; 4:11, 12

★**9** [a]1 Sam. 26:8; 2 Sam. 19:21; Luke 9:54 [b]2 Sam. 9:8 [c]Ex. 22:28

15:31-32 Ahithophel's defection was counterbalanced by the loyalty of Hushai, who remained in Jerusalem to function as an informant for David.

16:1-4 Ziba's accusation of Mephibosheth's disloyalty was, according to 19:24-28, false. He was evidently trying to commend himself in the eyes of David.

16:5 *Bahurim.* A village E. of the Mount of Olives.

16:9 *Abishai* was Joab's brother (2:18). *dead dog.* I.e., contemptible person.

lord the king? Let me go over now, and cut off his head."

★10 *a*2 Sam. 3:39; 19:22 *b*John 18:11 *c*Rom. 9:20

10 But the king said, "*a*What have I to do with you, O sons of Zeruiah? *b*If he curses, and if the LORD has told him, 'Curse David,' *c*then who shall say, 'Why have you done so?' "

11 *a*2 Sam. 12:11 *b*Gen. 45:5; 1 Sam. 26:19

11 Then David said to Abishai and to all his servants, "Behold, *a*my son who came out from me seeks my life; how much more now this Benjamite? Let him alone and let him curse, *b*for the LORD has told him.

12 *a*Deut. 23:5; Rom. 8:28

12 "Perhaps the LORD will look on my affliction and *a*return good to me instead of his cursing this day."

13 So David and his men went on the way; and Shimei went along on the hillside parallel with him and as he went he cursed, and cast stones and threw dust at him.

14 And the king and all the people who were with him arrived weary and he refreshed himself there.

4 Absalom rules in Jerusalem, 16:15-17:23

15 *a*2 Sam. 15:12, 37

15 *a*Then Absalom and all the people, the men of Israel, entered Jerusalem, and Ahithophel with him.

16 *a*2 Sam. 15:37 *b*2 Sam. 15:34 *c*1 Sam. 10:24; 2 Kin. 11:12

16 Now it came about when *a*Hushai the Archite, David's friend, came to Absalom, that *b*Hushai said to Absalom, "*c*Long live the king! Long live the king!"

17 *a*2 Sam. 19:25

17 And Absalom said to Hushai, "Is this your loyalty to your friend? *a*Why did you not go with your friend?"

★18-19

18 Then Hushai said to Absalom, "No! For whom the LORD,

this people, and all the men of Israel have chosen, his will I be, and with him I will remain.

19 *a*2 Sam. 15:34

19 "And besides, *a*whom should I serve? Should I not serve in the presence of his son? As I have served in your father's presence, so I will be in your presence."

20 Then Absalom said to Ahithophel, "Give your advice. What shall we do?"

★21-22

21 *a*2 Sam. 15:16; 20:3

21 And Ahithophel said to Absalom, "*a*Go in to your father's concubines, whom he has left to keep the house; then all Israel will hear that you have made yourself odious to your father. The hands of all who are with you will also be strengthened."

22 *a*2 Sam. 15:16; 20:3 *b*2 Sam. 12:11, 12

22 So they pitched a tent for Absalom on the roof, *a*and Absalom went in to his father's concubines *b*in the sight of all Israel.

★23 *a*2 Sam. 17:14, 23 *b*2 Sam. 15:12

23 And *a*the advice of Ahithophel, which he gave in those days, *was* as if one inquired of the word of God; *b*so was all the advice of Ahithophel *regarded* by both David and Absalom.

★ 1-14

17 Furthermore, Ahithophel said to Absalom, "Please let me choose 12,000 men that I may arise and pursue David tonight.

2 *a*2 Sam. 16:14 *b*1 Kin. 22:31

2 "And *a*I will come upon him while he is weary and exhausted and will terrify him so that all the people who are with him will flee. Then *b*I will strike down the king alone,

★ 3 *a*Jer. 6:14

3 and I will bring back all the people to you. The return of everyone depends on the man you seek; *then* all the people shall be at *a*peace."

4 So the plan pleased Absalom and all the elders of Israel.

16:10 David regarded Shimei's cursing as ordained of God, who would ultimately requite him (v. 12).

16:18-19 Hushai, David's spy, cleverly ingratiated himself with Absalom by suggesting he (Absalom), as David's son, had a legitimate, if premature, claim to the throne.

16:21-22 In ancient times the appropriation of the royal harem demonstrated possession of the throne (cf. 3:7). The deed would also re-

move any possibility of reconciliation between Absalom and David.

16:23 The counsel of Ahithophel was received by both David and Absalom as equivalent to a word from the Lord.

17:1-4 God used Hushai, David's loyal friend, to thwart the counsel of Ahithophel and lead Absalom to his death.

17:3 The idea is, the return of the whole nation depends on seeking out and destroying David.

5 Then Absalom said, "Now call ^aHushai the Archite also, and let us hear what he has to say."

6 When Hushai had come to Absalom, Absalom said to him, "Ahithophel has spoken thus. Shall we carry out his plan? If not, you speak."

7 So Hushai said to Absalom, "^aThis time the advice that Ahithophel has given is not good."

8 Moreover, Hushai said, "You know your father and his men, that they are mighty men and they are fierce, ^alike a bear robbed of her cubs in the field. And your father is an expert in warfare, and will not spend the night with the people.

9 "Behold, he has now hidden himself in one of the caves or in another place; and it will be when he falls on them at the first attack, that whoever hears it will say, 'There has been a slaughter among the people who follow Absalom.'

10 "And even the one who is valiant, whose heart is like the heart of a lion, ^awill completely lose heart; for all Israel knows that your father is a mighty man and those who are with him are valiant men.

11 "But I counsel that all Israel be surely gathered to you, ^afrom Dan even to Beersheba, ^bas the sand that is by the sea in abundance, and that you personally go into battle.

12 "So we shall come to him in one of the places where he can be found, and we will fall on him ^aas the dew falls on the ground; and of him and of all the men who are with him, not even one will be left.

13 "And if he withdraws into a city, then all Israel shall bring ropes to that city, and we will ^adrag it into the valley until not even a small stone is found there."

14 Then Absalom and all the men of Israel said, "The counsel of Hushai the Archite is better than the counsel of Ahithophel." For ^athe LORD had ordained to thwart the good counsel of Ahithophel, in order that the LORD might bring calamity on Absalom.

15 Then ^aHushai said to Zadok and to Abiathar the priests, "This is what Ahithophel counseled Absalom and the elders of Israel, and this is what I have counseled.

16 "Now therefore, send quickly and tell David, saying, '^aDo not spend the night at the fords of the wilderness, but by all means cross over, lest the king and all the people who are with him be destroyed.'"

17 ^aNow Jonathan and Ahimaaz were staying at ^bEn-rogel, and a maidservant would go and tell them, and they would go and tell King David, for they could not be seen entering the city.

18 But a lad did see them, and told Absalom; so the two of them departed quickly and came to the house of a man ^ain Bahurim, who had a well in his courtyard, and they went down into it.

19 And ^athe woman took a covering and spread it over the well's mouth and scattered grain on it, so that nothing was known.

20 Then Absalom's servants came to the woman at the house and said, "Where are Ahimaaz and Jonathan?" And ^athe woman said to them, "They have crossed the brook of water." And when they searched and could not find them, they returned to Jerusalem.

21 And it came about after they had departed that they came up out of the well and went and told King David; and they said to

---

Marginal references (left column):

5 ^a2 Sam. 15:32-34

★ 7-14

7 ^a2 Sam. 16:21

8 ^aHos. 13:8

10 ^aJosh. 2:9-11

11 ^a1 Sam. 3:20 ^bGen. 22:17; 1 Sam. 13:5

12 ^aPs. 110:3; Mic. 5:7

13 ^aMic. 1:6

Marginal references (right column):

★14 ^a2 Sam. 15:31, 34; Ps. 9:15, 16

★15-22

15 ^a2 Sam. 15:35, 36

16 ^a2 Sam. 15:28

★17 ^a2 Sam. 15:27, 36 ^bJosh. 15:7; 18:16

★18 ^a2 Sam. 3:16; 16:5

19 ^aJosh. 2:4-6

20 ^aLev. 19:11; Josh. 2:3-5; 1 Sam. 19:12-17

21 ^a2 Sam. 17:15, 16

17:7-14 Hushai's counsel was designed to buy time for David and to flatter Absalom into taking personal command of the campaign.
17:14 God was controlling the decision of these men.

17:15-22 David is informed of Absalom's decision through his intelligence channels.
17:17 En-rogel is located just a short distance SE. of Jerusalem.
17:18 well. Probably a dry cistern.

David, "aArise and cross over the water quickly for thus Ahithophel has counseled against you."

22 Then David and all the people who *were* with him arose and crossed the Jordan; and by dawn not even one remained who had not crossed the Jordan.

★23 a2 Sam.
15:12
b2 Kin. 20:1
cMatt. 27:5

23 Now when Ahithophel saw that his counsel was not followed, he saddled *his* donkey and arose and went to his home, to ªhis city, and bset his house in order, and cstrangled himself; thus he died and was buried in the grave of his father.

5 Absalom is defeated and dies, 17:24–18:33

★24 aGen.
32:2, 10;
2 Sam. 2:8

24 Then David came to ªMahanaim. And Absalom crossed the Jordan, he and all the men of Israel with him.

25 a2 Sam.
19:13; 20:9-
12; 1 Kin.
2:5, 32
b1 Chr. 2:16

25 And Absalom set ªAmasa over the army in place of Joab. Now Amasa was the son of a man whose name was Ithra the Israelite, who went in to Abigail the daughter of bNahash, sister of Zeruiah, Joab's mother.

26 And Israel and Absalom camped in the land of Gilead.

27 a1 Sam.
11:1; 2 Sam.
10:1, 2
b2 Sam.
12:26, 29
c2 Sam. 9:4
d2 Sam.
19:31-39;
1 Kin. 2:7

27 Now when David had come to Mahanaim, Shobi ªthe son of Nahash from bRabbah of the sons of Ammon, cMachir the son of Ammiel from Lo-debar, and dBarzillai the Gileadite from Rogelim,

28 aProv.
11:25; Matt.
5:7

28 brought ªbeds, basins, pottery, wheat, barley, flour, parched *grain,* beans, lentils, parched *seeds,*

29 a2 Sam.
16:2, 14;
Prov. 21:26;
Eccl. 11:1;
Rom. 12:13

29 honey, curds, sheep, and cheese of the herd, for David and for the people who *were* with him, ªto eat; for they said, "The people are hungry and weary and thirsty in the wilderness."

18 Then David numbered the people who were with him and ªset over them commanders of thousands and commanders of hundreds.

★ 1 aEx.
18:25; Num.
31:14;
1 Sam. 22:7

2 And David sent the people out, ªone third under the command of Joab, one third under the command of Abishai the son of Zeruiah, Joab's brother, and one third under the command of bIttai the Gittite. And the king said to the people, "I myself will surely go out with you also."

2 aJudg.
7:16; 1 Sam.
11:11
b2 Sam.
15:19-22

3 But the people said, "ªYou should not go out; for if we indeed flee, they will not care about us; even if half of us die, they will not care about us. But you are worth ten thousand of us; therefore now it is better that you *be* ready to help us from the city."

3 a2 Sam.
21:17

4 Then the king said to them, "Whatever seems best to you I will do." So ªthe king stood beside the gate, and all the people went out by hundreds and thousands.

4 a2 Sam.
18:24

5 And the king charged Joab and Abishai and Ittai, saying, "*Deal* gently for my sake with the young man Absalom." And ªall the people heard when the king charged all the commanders concerning Absalom.

5 a2 Sam.
18:12

6 Then the people went out into the field against Israel, and the battle took place in ªthe forest of Ephraim.

★ 6 aJosh.
17:15, 18;
2 Sam. 17:26

7 And the people of Israel were defeated there before the servants of David, and the slaughter there that day was great, 20,000 men.

8 For the battle there was spread over the whole countryside, and the forest devoured more people that day than the sword devoured.

★ 8

17:23 Ahithophel, perceptive to the end, realized that his cause was lost. Other suicides recorded in the Bible are those of Abimelech (Judg. 9:54), Samson (Judg. 16:30), Saul (1 Sam. 31:4), Zimri (1 Kings 16:18), and Judas (Matt. 27:5).

17:24 David's forces were mobilized in the north (on *Mahanaim* see 2:7).

18:1 *numbered.* I.e., counted and mustered.

18:6 The battle took place in the treacherous forest of Ephraim, N. of the Jabbok River in Transjordan.

18:8 Because of the rugged nature of the terrain, the pursuit through the forest caused more deaths than the battle.

★ 9 *a*2 Sam.
14:26

9 Now Absalom happened to meet the servants of David. For Absalom was riding on *his* mule, and the mule went under the thick branches of a great oak. And *a*his head caught fast in the oak, so he was left hanging between heaven and earth, while the mule that was under him kept going.

10 When a certain man saw *it*, he told Joab and said, "Behold, I saw Absalom hanging in an oak."

11 Then Joab said to the man who had told him, "Now behold, you saw *him!* Why then did you not strike him there to the ground? And I would have given you ten *pieces* of silver and a belt."

12 *a*2 Sam.
18:5

12 And the man said to Joab, "Even if I should receive a thousand *pieces* of silver in my hand, I would not put out my hand against the king's son; for *a*in our hearing the king charged you and Abishai and Ittai, saying, 'Protect for me the young man Absalom!'

★13 *a*2 Sam.
14:19, 20

13 "Otherwise, if I had dealt treacherously against his life (and *a*there is nothing hidden from the king), then you yourself would have stood aloof."

★14-15

14 *a*2 Sam.
14:30

14 Then Joab said, "I will not waste time here with you." *a*So he took three spears in his hand and thrust them through the heart of Absalom while he was yet alive in the midst of the oak.

15 And ten young men who carried Joab's armor gathered around and struck Absalom and killed him.

16 *a*2 Sam.
2:28; 20:22

16 Then *a*Joab blew the trumpet, and the people returned from pursuing Israel, for Joab restrained the people.

17 *a*Deut.
21:20, 21;
Josh. 7:26;
8:29 *b*2 Sam.
19:8; 20:1,
22

17 And they took Absalom and cast him into a deep pit in the forest and *a*erected over him a very great heap of stones. And *b*all Israel fled, each to his tent.

18 *a*1 Sam.
15:12 *b*Gen.
14:17
*c*2 Sam.
14:27

18 Now Absalom in his lifetime had taken and *a*set up for himself a pillar which is in *b*the King's Valley, for he said, "*c*I have no son to preserve my name." So he named the pillar after his own name, and it is called Absalom's monument to this day.

19 *a*2 Sam.
15:36
*b*2 Sam.
18:31

19 Then *a*Ahimaaz the son of Zadok said, "Please let me run and bring the king news *b*that the Lᴏʀᴅ has freed him from the hand of his enemies."

20 But Joab said to him, "You are not the man to carry news this day, but you shall carry news another day; however, you shall carry no news today because the king's son is dead."

★21

21 Then Joab said to the Cushite, "Go, tell the king what you have seen." So the Cushite bowed to Joab and ran.

22 *a*2 Sam.
18:29

22 Now Ahimaaz the son of Zadok said once more to Joab, "But whatever happens, please let me also run after the Cushite." And Joab said, "Why would you run, my son, since *a*you will have no reward for going?"

23 "But whatever happens," *he said*, "I will run." So he said to him, "Run." Then Ahimaaz ran by way of the plain and passed up the Cushite.

24 *a*2 Sam.
19:8 *b*2 Sam.
13:34; 2 Kin.
9:17

24 Now *a*David was sitting between the two gates; and *b*the watchman went up to the roof of the gate by the wall, and raised his eyes and looked, and behold, a man running by himself.

25 And the watchman called and told the king. And the king said, "If he is by himself there is good news in his mouth." And he came nearer and nearer.

26 Then the watchman saw another man running; and the watchman called to the gatekeeper and said, "Behold, *another*

18:9 The tradition that Absalom was caught by his hair comes from Josephus (*Antiq.* 7.10.2), but it seems reasonable in light of 14:26.

18:13 *against his life.* Perhaps better, against my life.

18:14-15 The slaying of Absalom was contrary to the king's explicit orders (v. 5).

18:21 Joab wanted the Cushite slave to report the incident, in case David reacted with violence.

man running by himself." And the king said, "This one also is bringing good news."

27   And the watchman said, "I think the running of the first one ^ais like the running of Ahimaaz the son of Zadok." And the king said, "^bThis is a good man and comes with good news."

28   And Ahimaaz called and said to the king, "All is well." And ^ahe prostrated himself before the king with his face to the ground. And he said, "^bBlessed is the LORD your God, who has delivered up the men who lifted their hands against my lord the king."

29   And the king said, "^aIs it well with the young man Absalom?" And Ahimaaz answered, "When Joab sent the king's servant, and your servant, I saw a great tumult, but ^bI did not know what it was."

30   Then the king said, "Turn aside and stand here." So he turned aside and stood still.

31   And behold, the Cushite arrived, and the Cushite said, "Let my lord the king receive good news, for ^athe LORD has freed you this day from the hand of all those who rose up against you."

32   Then the king said to the Cushite, "^aIs it well with the young man Absalom?" And the Cushite answered, "^bLet the enemies of my lord the king, and all who rise up against you for evil, be as that young man!"

33   And the king was deeply moved and went up to the chamber over the gate and wept. And thus he said as he walked, "^aO my son Absalom, my son, my son Absalom! ^bWould I had died instead of you, O Absalom, my son, my son!"

D   Disorder in the Kingdom, 19:1–39

19   Then it was told Joab, "Behold, ^athe king is weeping and mourns for Absalom."

2   And the victory that day was turned to mourning for all the people, for the people heard it said that day, "The king is grieved for his son."

3   So the people went by stealth into the city that day, as people who are humiliated steal away when they flee in battle.

4   And the king ^acovered his face and cried out with a loud voice, "^bO my son Absalom, O Absalom, my son, my son!"

5   Then Joab came into the house to the king and said, "Today you have covered with shame the faces of all your servants, who today have saved your life and the lives of your sons and daughters, the lives of your wives, and the lives of your concubines,

6   by loving those who hate you, and by hating those who love you. For you have shown today that princes and servants are nothing to you; for I know this day that if Absalom were alive and all of us were dead today, then you would be pleased.

7   "Now therefore arise, go out and speak kindly to your servants, for I swear by the LORD, if you do not go out, surely ^anot a man will pass the night with you, and this will be worse for you than all the evil that has come upon you from your youth until now."

8   So the king arose and sat in the gate. When they told all the people, saying, "Behold, the king is ^asitting in the gate," then all the people came before the king.

Cross-references (margin)

27 ^a2 Kin. 9:20 ^b1 Kin. 1:42

28 ^a1 Sam. 25:23; 2 Sam. 14:4 ^b1 Sam. 17:46

★29 ^a2 Sam. 20:9; 2 Kin. 4:26 ^b2 Sam. 18:22

31 ^aJudg. 5:31; 2 Sam. 18:19

★32 ^a2 Sam. 18:29 ^b1 Sam. 25:26

★33 ^a2 Sam. 19:4 ^bEx. 32:32; Rom. 9:3

1 ^a2 Sam. 18:5, 14

4 ^a2 Sam. 15:30 ^b2 Sam. 18:33

★ 7 ^aProv. 14:28

★ 8 ^a2 Sam. 15:2; 18:24 ^b2 Sam. 18:17

18:29 Ahimaaz was lying, for Joab had told him explicitly that the king's son was dead (v. 20).
18:32 The Cushite, unlike Ahimaaz, answered plainly but courteously that Absalom was dead.
18:33 The tragedy of Absalom was the consequence of David's sin with Bathsheba (cf. 12:11–12). Sin may be forgiven, but one still reaps its inevitable consequences.
19:7 Joab warned that David's unrestrained grief could lead to political disaster.
19:8 in the gate. Where the king granted audiences to his subjects. Now Israel. Better, But Israel. The people who had followed Absalom returned home.

Now [b]Israel had fled, each to his tent.

9 And all the people were quarreling throughout all the tribes of Israel, saying, "[a]The king delivered us from the hand of our enemies and [b]saved us from the hand of the Philistines, but now [c]he has fled out of the land from Absalom.

10 "However, Absalom, whom we anointed over us, has died in battle. Now then, why are you silent about bringing the king back?"

11 Then King David sent to [a]Zadok and Abiathar the priests, saying, "Speak to the elders of Judah, saying, 'Why are you the last to bring the king back to his house, since the word of all Israel has come to the king, *even* to his house?

12 'You are my brothers; [a]you are my bone and my flesh. Why then should you be the last to bring back the king?'

13 "And say to [a]Amasa, 'Are you not my bone and my flesh? [b]May God do so to me, and more also, if you will not be [c]commander of the army before me continually [d]in place of Joab.' "

14 Thus he turned the hearts of all the men of Judah [a]as one man, so that they sent *word* to the king, *saying*, "Return, you and all your servants."

15 The king then returned and came as far as the Jordan. And Judah came to [a]Gilgal in order to go to meet the king, to bring the king across the Jordan.

16 Then [a]Shimei the son of Gera, the Benjamite who was from Bahurim, hurried and came down with the men of Judah to meet King David.

17 And there were a thousand men of Benjamin with him, with [a]Ziba the servant of the house of Saul, and his fifteen sons and his twenty servants with him; and they rushed to the Jordan before the king.

18 Then they kept crossing the ford to bring over the king's household, and to do what was good in his sight. And Shimei the son of Gera fell down before the king as he was about to cross the Jordan.

19 So he said to the king, "[a]Let not my lord consider me guilty, nor remember what your servant did wrong on the day when my lord the king came out from Jerusalem, so that the king should take *it* to heart.

20 "For your servant knows that I have sinned; therefore behold, I have come today, [a]the first of all the house of Joseph to go down to meet my lord the king."

21 But Abishai the son of Zeruiah answered and said, "[a]Should not Shimei be put to death for this, [b]because he cursed the LORD's anointed?"

22 David then said, "[a]What have I to do with you, O sons of Zeruiah, that you should this day be an adversary to me? [b]Should any man be put to death in Israel today? For do I not know that I am king over Israel today?"

23 And the king said to Shimei, "[a]You shall not die." Thus the king swore to him.

24 Then [a]Mephibosheth the son of Saul came down to meet the king; and [b]he had neither cared for his feet, nor trimmed his mustache, nor [c]washed his clothes, from the day the king de-

---

Marginal references (left column):

9 [a]2 Sam. 8:1-14
[b]2 Sam. 5:20; 8:1
[c]2 Sam. 15:14

★**11** [a]2 Sam. 15:29

12 [a]2 Sam. 5:1

★**13** [a]2 Sam. 17:25
[b]1 Kin. 19:2
[c]2 Sam. 8:16
[d]2 Sam. 3:27-39; 19:5-7

14 [a]Judg. 20:1

★**15-40**

15 [a]Josh. 5:9; 1 Sam. 11:14, 15

16 [a]2 Sam. 16:5-13; 1 Kin. 2:8

Marginal references (right column):

17 [a]2 Sam. 16:1-4; 19:26, 27

★**18-19**

19 [a]1 Sam. 22:15; 2 Sam. 16:6-8

★**20** [a]2 Sam. 16:5

21 [a]2 Sam. 16:7, 8 [b]Ex. 22:28

22 [a]2 Sam. 3:39; 16:9, 10 [b]1 Sam. 11:13

23 [a]1 Kin. 2:8

★**24** [a]2 Sam. 9:6-10 [b]2 Sam. 12:20 [c]Ex. 19:10

19:11 The elders of Judah were reticent to invite David to return, perhaps because of the part they had played in Absalom's insurrection (cf. 15:10-11).

19:13 David replaced his commander Joab with Amasa, the commander of Absalom's army (17:25), to secure the allegiance of the rebel army and to discipline Joab for slaying Absalom.

19:15-40 Returning to Jerusalem from exile, Da-

vid was met at the Jordan by his supporters.

19:18-19 Shimei had cursed David as he fled from Jerusalem (16:5-8).

19:20 *house of Joseph.* A reference to the tribe of Ephraim (the offspring of Joseph's son), a large tribe and representative of the ten northern tribes.

19:24 Mephibosheth exhibited signs of extreme and extended mourning.

parted until the day he came *home* in peace.

25 *a*2 Sam. 16:17

25 And it was when he came from Jerusalem to meet the king, that the king said to him, "*a*Why did you not go with me, Mephibosheth?"

26 *a*2 Sam. 9:3

26 So he answered, "O my lord, the king, my servant deceived me; for your servant said, 'I will saddle a donkey for myself that I may ride on it and go with the king,' *a*because your servant is lame.

27 *a*2 Sam. 16:3, 4 *b*2 Sam. 14:17, 20

27 "Moreover, *a*he has slandered your servant to my lord the king; but my lord the king is *b*like the angel of God, therefore do what is good in your sight.

28 *a*2 Sam. 21:6-9 *b*2 Sam. 9:7, 10, 13

28 "For *a*all my father's household was nothing but dead men before my lord the king; *b*yet you set your servant among those who ate at your own table. What right do I have yet that I should complain anymore to the king?"

★**29**

29 So the king said to him, "Why do you still speak of your affairs? I have decided, 'You and Ziba shall divide the land.' "

30 And Mephibosheth said to the king, "Let him even take it all, since my lord the king has come safely to his own house.

31 *a*2 Sam. 17:27-29; 1 Kin. 2:7

31 Now *a*Barzillai the Gileadite had come down from Rogelim; and he went on to the Jordan with the king to escort him over the Jordan.

32 *a*2 Sam. 17:27-29

32 Now Barzillai was very old, being eighty years old; and he had *a*sustained the king while he stayed at Mahanaim, for he was a very great man.

33 And the king said to Barzillai, "You cross over with me and I will sustain you in Jerusalem with me."

34 *a*Gen. 47:8

34 But Barzillai said to the king, "*a*How long have I yet to live, that I should go up with the king to Jerusalem?

35 "I am now *a*eighty years old. Can I distinguish between good and bad? Or can your servant taste what I eat or what I drink? Or can I hear anymore *b*the voice of singing men and women? *c*Why then should your servant be an added burden to my lord the king?

35 *a*Ps. 90:10 *b*Eccl. 2:8; Is. 5:11, 12 *c*2 Sam. 15:33

36 "Your servant would merely cross over the Jordan with the king. Why should the king compensate me *with* this reward?

37 "Please let your servant return, that I may die in my own city near the grave of my father and my mother. However, here is your servant *a*Chimham, let him cross over with my lord the king, and do for him what is good in your sight."

★**37** *a*2 Sam. 19:40; 1 Kin. 2:7; Jer. 41:17

38 And the king answered, "Chimham shall cross over with me, and I will do for him what is good in your sight; and whatever you require of me, I will do for you."

39 All the people crossed over the Jordan and the king crossed too. The king then *a*kissed Barzillai and blessed him, and he returned to his place.

39 *a*Gen. 31:55; Ruth 1:14; 2 Sam. 14:33

E   Revolution in the Kingdom, 19:40–20:26

40 Now the king went on to Gilgal, and Chimham went on with him; and all the people of Judah and also *a*half the people of Israel accompanied the king.

40 *a*2 Sam. 19:9, 10

41 And behold, all the men of Israel came to the king and said to the king, "*a*Why had our brothers *b*the men of Judah stolen you away, and brought the king and his household and all David's men with him over the Jordan?"

41 *a*Judg. 8:1; 12:1 *b*2 Sam. 19:11, 12

42 Then all the men of Judah answered the men of Israel, "Because *a*the king is a close relative

42 *a*2 Sam. 19:12

19:29 David rebuffed Mephibosheth and decided to divide his property. David either (1) made a bad judgment, (2) was trying to keep from alienating Ziba, or (3) did not believe

Mephibosheth to be totally innocent. **19:37** *Chimham* was apparently Barzilai's son (cf. 1 Kings 2:7).

to us. Why then are you angry about this matter? Have we eaten at all at the king's *expense*, or has anything been taken for us?"

43 But the men of Israel answered the men of Judah and said, "ᵃWe have ten parts in the king, therefore we also have more *claim* on David than you. Why then did you treat us with contempt? Was it not our advice first to bring back our king?" Yet the words of the men of Judah were harsher than the words of the men of Israel.

20 Now ᵃa worthless fellow happened to be there whose name was Sheba, the son of ᵇBichri, a Benjamite; and he blew the trumpet and said,
"ᶜWe have no portion in David,
Nor do we have inheritance in ᵈthe son of Jesse;
ᵉEvery man to his tents, O Israel!"

2 So all the men of Israel withdrew from following David, *and* followed Sheba the son of Bichri; but the men of Judah remained steadfast to their king, from the Jordan even to Jerusalem.

3 Then David came to his house at Jerusalem, and ᵃthe king took the ten women, the concubines whom he had left to keep the house, and placed them under guard and provided them with sustenance, but did not go in to them. So they were shut up until the day of their death, living as widows.

4 Then the king said to ᵃAmasa, "Call out the men of Judah for me within three days, and be present here yourself."

5 So Amasa went to call out *the men of* Judah, but he ᵃdelayed longer than the set time which he had appointed him.

6 And David said to ᵃAbishai, "Now Sheba the son of Bichri will do us more harm than Absalom; ᵇtake your lord's servants and pursue him, lest he find for himself fortified cities and escape from our sight."

7 So Joab's men went out after him, ᵃalong with the Cherethites and the Pelethites and all the mighty men; and they went out from Jerusalem to pursue Sheba the son of Bichri.

8 When they were at the large stone which is in ᵃGibeon, Amasa came to meet them. Now Joab was dressed in his military attire, and over it was a belt with a sword in its sheath fastened at his waist; and as he went forward, it fell out.

9 And Joab said to Amasa, "Is it well with you, my brother?" And ᵃJoab took Amasa by the beard with his right hand to kiss him.

10 But Amasa was not on guard against the sword which was in Joab's hand so ᵃhe struck him in the belly with it and poured out his inward parts on the ground, and did not *strike* him again; and he died. Then Joab and Abishai his brother pursued Sheba the son of Bichri.

11 Now there stood by him one of Joab's young men, and said, "Whoever favors Joab and whoever is for David, ᵃlet him follow Joab."

12 But Amasa lay wallowing in *his* blood in the middle of the highway. And when the man saw

---

19:43 The dispute between Israel and Judah gave rise to Sheba's rebellion.
20:1 *Every man to his tents.* I.e., Let's go home, and from there we will resist the king.
20:4–10 Amasa's slowness to carry out orders (vv. 4–5) could have resulted in another disaster, and it provided Joab with the opportunity to kill him and regain his lost position.
20:8 Joab apparently contrived to let his sword fall out of its sheath so that as he picked it up,

seemingly innocently, he could stab the unsuspecting Amasa.
20:9 Taking hold of someone's beard and kissing his cheek was a customary Oriental greeting.
20:11–22 Command of David's army transferred again to Joab (v. 13; cf. v. 23), who pursued Sheba to Abel Beth-maacah, about 25 miles N. of the Sea of Galilee in the Hula Valley. There Sheba was slain.

★**43** ᵃ2 Sam. 5:1; 1 Kin. 11:30, 31

★ **1** ᵃ2 Sam. 16:7 ᵇGen. 46:21
ᶜ2 Sam. 19:43; 1 Kin. 12:16
ᵈ1 Sam. 22:7-9
ᵉ1 Sam. 13:2; 2 Sam. 18:17; 2 Chr. 10:16

3 ᵃ2 Sam. 15:16; 16:21, 22

★ **4-10**
4 ᵃ2 Sam. 17:25; 19:13

5 ᵃ1 Sam. 13:8

6 ᵃ2 Sam. 21:17 ᵇ2 Sam. 11:11; 1 Kin. 1:33

7 ᵃ2 Sam. 8:18; 1 Kin. 1:38

★ **8** ᵃ2 Sam. 2:13; 3:30

★ **9** ᵃMatt. 26:49

10 ᵃ2 Sam. 2:23; 3:27; 1 Kin. 2:5

★**11-22**
11 ᵃ2 Sam. 20:13

that all the people stood still, he removed Amasa from the highway into the field and threw a garment over him when he saw that everyone who came by him stood still.

13 As soon as he was removed from the highway, all the men passed on after Joab to pursue Sheba the son of Bichri.

14 Now he went through all the tribes of Israel to Abel even to Beth-maacah and all the Berites; and they were gathered together and also went after him.

★15 a1 Kin. 15:20; 2 Kin. 15:29 b2 Kin. 19:32; Ezek. 4:2

15 And they came and besieged him in aAbel Beth-maacah, and bthey cast up a mound against the city, and it stood by the rampart; and all the people who were with Joab were wreaking destruction in order to topple the wall.

16 a2 Sam. 14:2

16 Then aa wise woman called from the city, "Hear, hear! Please tell Joab, 'Come here that I may speak with you.' "

17 So he approached her, and the woman said, "Are you Joab?" And he answered, "I am." Then she said to him, "Listen to the words of your maidservant." And he answered, "I am listening."

★18

18 Then she spoke, saying, "Formerly they used to say, 'They will surely ask advice at Abel,' and thus they ended the dispute.

★19 aDeut. 20:10 b1 Sam. 26:19; 2 Sam. 14:16; 21:3

19 "I am of those who are peaceable and faithful in Israel. aYou are seeking to destroy a city even a mother in Israel. Why would you swallow up bthe inheritance of the LORD?"

20 And Joab answered and said, "Far be it, far be it from me

that I should swallow up or destroy!

21 aJosh. 24:33 b2 Sam. 20:2

21 "Such is not the case. But a man from athe hill country of E-phraim, bSheba the son of Bichri by name, has lifted up his hand against King David. Only hand him over, and I will depart from the city." And the woman said to Joab, "Behold, his head will be thrown to you over the wall."

22 a2 Sam. 20:16; Eccl. 9:13-16 b2 Sam. 20:1

22 Then the woman awisely came to all the people. And they cut off the head of Sheba the son of Bichri and threw it to Joab. So bhe blew the trumpet, and they were dispersed from the city, each to his tent. Joab also returned to the king at Jerusalem.

23 a2 Sam. 8:16-18; 1 Kin. 4:3-6

23 aNow Joab was over the whole army of Israel, and Benaiah the son of Jehoiada was over the Cherethites and the Pelethites;

★24 a1 Kin. 4:3

24 and Adoram was over the forced labor, and aJehoshaphat the son of Ahilud was the recorder;

25 a1 Kin. 4:4

25 and Sheva was scribe, and Zadok and aAbiathar were priests;

26 and Ira the Jairite was also a priest to David.

VII DAVID'S CONCLUSION IN THE KINGDOM, 21:1-24:25

A The Famine, 21:1-14

★21:1-24:5 **★ 1-2**

1 aGen. 12:10; 26:1; 42:5 bNum. 27:21

21 Now there was aa famine in the days of David for three years, year after year; and bDavid sought the presence of the LORD. And the LORD said, "It is for Saul and his bloody house, because he put the Gibeonites to death."

20:15 The purpose of the mound, was to help them reach the top part of the wall, break through, and gain entrance to the city.

20:18 The proverb indicates that the people of Abel were well-known for their wisdom.

20:19 a mother in Israel. I.e., a mother city or capital; the prominent city of its region. The woman questioned Joab's failure to submit to the citizens' terms of peace in accordance with Deut. 20:10.

20:24 Adoram. Adoniram of 1 Kings 4:6. Samuel had predicted that tribute (including forced la-

bor) would be one of the evils of having a king (1 Sam. 8:11-16).

21:1-24:25 This section is a nonchronological appendix to the book and records many events that occurred earlier in David's reign.

21:1-2 David recognized this famine as divine chastening (cf. Deut. 28:47-48) and asked God the reason. The sin was that Saul, zealous to exterminate the heathen from Israel, had slain some of the Gibeonites with whom Israel had made a treaty (cf. Josh. 9:3-27).

2 *a*Josh.
9:3, 15-20

2 So the king called the Gibeonites and spoke to them (now the Gibeonites were not of the sons of Israel but of the remnant of the Amorites, and *a*the sons of Israel made a covenant with them, but Saul had sought to kill them in his zeal for the sons of Israel and Judah).

★ 3 *a*1 Sam.
26:19;
2 Sam. 20:19

3 Thus David said to the Gibeonites, "What should I do for you? And how can I make atonement that you may bless *a*the inheritance of the LORD?"

4 *a*Num.
35:31, 32

4 Then the Gibeonites said to him, "*a*We have no *concern* of silver or gold with Saul or his house, nor is it for us to put any man to death in Israel." And he said, "I will do for you whatever you say."

5 *a*2 Sam.
21:1

5 So they said to the king, "*a*The man who consumed us, and who planned to exterminate us from remaining within any border of Israel,

★ 6 *a*Num.
25:4 *b*1 Sam.
10:24

6 let seven men from his sons be given to us, and we will hang them *a*before the LORD in Gibeah of Saul, *b*the chosen of the LORD." And the king said, "I will give *them.*"

7 *a*2 Sam.
4:4; 9:10
*b*1 Sam.
18:3; 20:12-
17; 23:18;
2 Sam. 9:1-7

7 But the king spared *a*Mephibosheth, the son of Jonathan the son of Saul, *b*because of the oath of the LORD which was between them, between David and Saul's son Jonathan.

8 *a*2 Sam.
3:7 *b*1 Sam.
18:19 *c*1 Kin.
19:16

8 So the king took the two sons of *a*Rizpah the daughter of Aiah, Armoni and Mephibosheth whom she had born to Saul, and the five sons of *b*Merab the daughter of Saul, whom she had born to Adriel the son of Barzillai the *c*Meholathite.

★ 9 *a*Ex.
9:31, 32

9 Then he gave them into the hands of the Gibeonites, and they hanged them in the mountain before the LORD, so that the seven of them fell together; and they were put to death in the first days of harvest at *a*the beginning of barley harvest.

10 *a*And Rizpah the daughter of Aiah took sackcloth and spread it for herself on the rock, from the beginning of harvest until it rained on them from the sky; and *b*she allowed neither the birds of the sky to rest on them by day nor the beasts of the field by night.

★10 *a*Deut.
21:23
*b*1 Sam.
17:44, 46

11 When it was told David what Rizpah the daughter of Aiah, the concubine of Saul, had done,

12 then David went and took *a*the bones of Saul and the bones of Jonathan his son from the men of Jabesh-gilead, who had stolen them from the open square of *b*Beth-shan, *c*where the Philistines had hanged them on the day *d*the Philistines struck down Saul in Gilboa.

12 *a*1 Sam.
31:11-13
*b*Josh. 17:11
*c*1 Sam.
31:10
*d*1 Sam.
31:3, 4

13 And he brought up the bones of Saul and the bones of Jonathan his son from there, and they gathered the bones of those who had been hanged.

14 And they buried the bones of Saul and Jonathan his son in the country of Benjamin in *a*Zela, in the grave of Kish his father; thus they did all that the king commanded, and after that *b*God was moved by entreaty for the land.

★14 *a*Josh.
18:28 *b*Josh.
7:26; 2 Sam.
24:25

B   The Exploits, 21:15-22

15 Now when *a*the Philistines were at war again with Israel, David went down and his servants

★15-22

15 *a*2 Sam.
5:17-25

21:3 David asked the Gibeonites what they would accept as settlement for the injustice.
21:6 The Gibeonites demanded justice in keeping with the principle of Num. 35:31; a life demands a life. In light of Deut. 24:16 it is probable that the seven sons were directly implicated in the attack upon the Gibeonites. *hang.* The word indicates some form of execution involving the exposure of the dead bodies, a dishonoring and severe penalty.
21:9 *hanged.* See note on 21:6
21:10 From the barley harvest of April to the early rains of October, *Rizpah* protected the exposed bodies from scavengers.
21:14 In due time the famine ended and God restored the land to prosperity.
21:15-22 The rest of the chapter records David's exploits against the Philistines.

with him; and as they fought against the Philistines, David became weary.

★16 *a*Num. 13:22, 28; Josh. 15:14; 2 Sam. 21:18-22

16 Then Ishbi-benob, who was *a*among the descendants of the giant, the weight of whose spear was three hundred *shekels* of bronze in weight, was girded with a new *sword*, and he intended to kill David.

★17 *a*2 Sam. 20:6-10 *b*2 Sam. 18:3 *c*2 Sam. 22:29; 1 Kin. 11:36

17 But *a*Abishai the son of Zeruiah helped him, and struck the Philistine and killed him. Then the men of David swore to him, saying, "*b*You shall not go out again with us to battle, that you may not extinguish *c*the lamp of Israel."

18 *a*1 Chr. 20:4-8 *b*1 Chr. 11:29; 27:11

18 *a*Now it came about after this that there was war again with the Philistines at Gob; then *b*Sibbecai the Hushathite struck down Saph, who was among the descendants of the giant.

★19 *a*1 Sam. 17:7

19 And there was war with the Philistines again at Gob, and Elhanan the son of Jaare-oregim the Bethlehemite killed Goliath the Gittite, *a*the shaft of whose spear was like a weaver's beam.

20 *a*2 Sam. 21:16, 18

20 And there was war at Gath again, where there was a man of *great* stature who had six fingers on each hand and six toes on each foot, twenty-four in number; and he also had been born *a*to the giant.

21 And when he defied Israel, Jonathan the son of Shimei, David's brother, struck him down.

22 *a*1 Chr. 20:8

22 *a*These four were born to the giant in Gath, and they fell by the hand of David and by the hand of his servants.

C   The Song of David, 22:1-51

22 *a*And David spoke *b*the words of this song to the LORD in the day that the LORD delivered him from the hand of all his enemies and from the hand of Saul.

★1 *a*Ps. 18:2-50 *b*Ex. 15:1; Deut. 31:30

2 And he said,
"*a*The LORD is my rock and my fortress and my deliverer;

2 *a*1 Sam. 23:25; 24:2; Ps. 31:3; 71:3

3 *a*My God, my rock, in whom I take refuge;
My *b*shield and *c*the horn of my salvation, my stronghold and *d*my refuge;
My savior, Thou dost save me from violence.

★3 *a*Deut. 32:4, 37; 1 Sam. 2:2 *b*Gen. 15:1; Deut. 33:29 *c*Luke 1:69 *d*Ps. 9:9

4 "I call upon the LORD, *a*who is worthy to be praised;
And I am saved from my enemies.

4 *a*Ps. 48:1; 96:4

5 "For *a*the waves of death encompassed me;
*b*The torrents of destruction overwhelmed me;

★ 5-6

5 *a*Ps. 93:4; Jon. 2:3 *b*Ps. 69:14, 15

6 *a*The cords of Sheol surrounded me;
The snares of death confronted me.

6 *a*Ps. 116:3

7 "*a*In my distress I called upon the LORD,
Yes, I cried to my God;
And from His temple He heard my voice,
And my cry for help came into His ears.

★ 7-19

7 *a*Ps. 116:4; 120:1

8 "Then *a*the earth shook and quaked,

8 *a*Judg. 5:4; Ps. 97:4 *b*Job 26:11

21:16 The spear of Ishbi-benob weighed about 8 lbs.

21:17 I.e., David, whose life and actions brought well-being to the people.

21:19 The Hebrew text attributes the slaying of Goliath to Elhanan, in contradiction to 1 Sam. 17:50. There is evidence of a copyist's error (cf. 1 Chron. 20:5), and it is probable that Elhanan killed "the brother of" Goliath. Others suggest that Elhanan and David are different names for the same person, just as Solomon had another name (cf. 12:24). Or it is possible that there were two Goliaths.

22:1 This hymn of praise is almost identical to Psalm 18 and is David's response to God's goodness in delivering him from his enemies and from the vicious King Saul.

22:3 *the horn of my salvation.* The figure denoting power is borrowed from animals whose horns are for protection and defense (see note on Luke 1:69).

22:5-6 David reflected on the circumstances in which he almost lost his life.

22:7-19 David reported God's deliverance. God is described as He appeared to Moses at Sinai, with earthquakes, thunder, darkness, and lightning.

*b*The foundations of heaven were trembling
And were shaken, because He was angry.

9 "Smoke went up out of His nostrils,
*a*And fire from His mouth devoured;
*b*Coals were kindled by it.

10 "He bowed the heavens also, and came down
With *a*thick darkness under His feet.

11 "*a*And He rode on a cherub and flew;
And He appeared on *b*the wings of the wind.

12 "*a*And He made darkness canopies around Him,
A mass of waters, thick clouds of the sky.

13 "From the brightness before Him
*a*Coals of fire were kindled.

14 "*a*The LORD thundered from heaven,
And the Most High uttered His voice.

15 "*a*And He sent out arrows, and scattered them,
Lightning, and routed them.

16 "Then the channels of the sea appeared,
The foundations of the world were laid bare,
By the rebuke of the LORD,
*a*At the blast of the breath of His nostrils.

17 "*a*He sent from on high, He took me;
*b*He drew me out of many waters.

18 "He delivered me from my strong enemy,
From those who hated me, for they were too strong for me.

19 "They confronted me in the day of my calamity,
*a*But the LORD was my support.

20 "*a*He also brought me forth into a broad place;
He rescued me, *b*because He delighted in me.

21 "*a*The LORD has rewarded me according to my righteousness;
*b*According to the cleanness of my hands He has recompensed me.

22 "*a*For I have kept the ways of the LORD,
And have not acted wickedly against my God.

23 "*a*For all His ordinances *were* before me;
And *as for* His statutes, I did not depart from them.

24 "*a*I was also blameless toward Him,
And I kept myself from my iniquity.

25 "*a*Therefore the LORD has recompensed me according to my righteousness,
According to my cleanness before His eyes.

26 "*a*With the kind Thou dost show Thyself kind,
With the blameless Thou dost show Thyself blameless;

27 *a*With the pure Thou dost show Thyself pure,
*b*And with the perverted Thou dost show Thyself astute.

28 "*a*And Thou dost save an afflicted people;
*b*But Thine eyes are on the haughty *whom* Thou dost abase.

---

9 *a*Ps. 97:3; Heb. 12:29 *b*2 Sam. 22:13
10 *a*Ex. 19:16; 1 Kin. 8:12; Ps. 97:2; Nah. 1:3
11 *a*2 Sam. 6:2 *b*Ps. 104:3
12 *a*Job 36:29
13 *a*2 Sam. 22:9
14 *a*Job 37:2-5; Ps. 29:3
15 *a*Deut. 32:23; Josh. 10:10; 1 Sam. 7:10
16 *a*Ex. 15:8; Nah. 1:4
17 *a*Ps. 144:7 *b*Ex. 2:10

19 *a*Ps. 23:4
★20-28
20 *a*Ps. 31:8; 118:5 *b*2 Sam. 15:26
21 *a*1 Sam. 26:23; 1 Kin. 8:32 *b*Ps. 24:4
22 *a*Gen. 18:19; Ps. 128:1; Prov. 8:32
23 *a*Deut. 6:6-9; Ps. 119:30, 102
24 *a*Gen. 6:9; 7:1; Eph. 1:4; Col. 1:21, 22
★25-26
25 *a*2 Sam. 22:21
26 *a*Matt. 5:7
★27 *a*Matt. 5:8; 1 John 3:3 *b*Lev. 26:23, 24; Rom. 1:28
28 *a*Ex. 3:7, 8; Ps. 72:12, 13 *b*Is. 2:11, 12, 17; 5:15

22:20-28 David presented the reasons for God's condescension and deliverance.
22:25-26 God promised blessing for obedience and judgment for disobedience (Deut. 28:30), and David rejoiced because God blessed him for his obedience.
22:27 Those who insist on devious ways are given up to their perversity (cf. Rom. 1:28).

★29-46

29 *a*2 Sam. 21:17; 1 Kin. 11:36; Ps. 27:1

29 "*a*For Thou art my lamp, O Lord;
And the Lord illumines my darkness.

30 *a*2 Sam. 5:6-8

30 "*a*For by Thee I can run upon a troop;
By my God I can leap over a wall.

31 *a*Deut. 32:4; Matt. 5:48 *b*Ps. 12:6; 119:140; Prov. 30:5 *c*2 Sam. 22:3; Ps. 84:9

31 "*a*As for God, His way is blameless;
*b*The word of the Lord is tested;
*c*He is a shield to all who take refuge in Him.

32 *a*1 Sam. 2:2 *b*2 Sam. 22:2

32 "*a*For who is God, besides the Lord?
*b*And who is a rock, besides our God?

33 *a*2 Sam. 22:2; Ps. 31:3, 4

33 "*a*God is my strong fortress;
And He sets the blameless in His way.

34 *a*2 Sam. 2:18; Hab. 3:19 *b*Deut. 32:13

34 "*a*He makes my feet like hinds' *feet*,
*b*And sets me on my high places.

35 *a*Ps. 144:1 *b*Job 20:24

35 "*a*He trains my hands for battle,
*b*So that my arms can bend a bow of bronze.

36 *a*Eph. 6:16, 17

36 "Thou hast also given me *a*the shield of Thy salvation,
And Thy help makes me great.

37 *a*2 Sam. 22:20; Prov. 4:12

37 "*a*Thou dost enlarge my steps under me,
And my feet have not slipped.

38 *a*Ex. 15:9

38 "I pursued my enemies and *a*destroyed them,
And I did not turn back until they were consumed.

★39 *a*Mal. 4:3

39 "And I have devoured them and shattered them, so that they did not rise;
And *a*they fell under my feet.

40 "For Thou hast girded me with strength for battle;
Thou hast subdued under me *a*those who rose up against me.

40 *a*Ps. 44:5

41 "Thou hast also *a*made my enemies turn *their* backs to me,
And I destroyed those who hated me.

★41 *a*Ex. 23:27; Josh. 10:24

42 "*a*They looked, but there was none to save;
*b*Even to the Lord, but He did not answer them.

42 *a*Is. 17:7, 8 *b*Is. 28:6; Is. 1:15

43 "*a*Then I pulverized them as the dust of the earth,
*b*I crushed *and* stamped them as the mire of the streets.

43 *a*2 Kin. 13:7 *b*Is. 10:6; Mic. 7:10

44 "*a*Thou hast also delivered me from the contentions of my people;
*b*Thou hast kept me as head of the nations;
*c*A people whom I have not known serve me.

44 *a*2 Sam. 3:1; 19:9, 14 *b*2 Sam. 8:1-14 *c*Is. 55:5

45 "*a*Foreigners pretend obedience to me;
As soon as they hear, they obey me.

45 *a*Ps. 66:3; 81:15

46 "Foreigners lose heart,
*a*And come trembling out of their fortresses.

★46 *a*1 Sam. 14:11; Mic. 7:17

47 "The Lord lives, and blessed be my rock;
And exalted be *a*God, the rock of my salvation,

★47-50

47 *a*2 Sam. 22:3; Ps. 89:26

48 *a*The God who executes vengeance for me,
*b*And brings down peoples under me,

48 *a*1 Sam. 24:12; 25:39; 2 Sam. 4:8; Ps. 94:1 *b*Ps. 144:2

49 Who also brings me out from my enemies;
Thou dost even lift me above *a*those who rise up against me;

49 *a*Ps. 44:5 *b*Ps. 140:1, 4, 11

22:29-46 David described what he could do by the Lord's enablement—the O.T. equivalent of Phil. 4:13.
22:39 *shattered*. Lit., beat to pieces.
22:41 *turn their backs to*. I.e., flee from.

22:46 *lose heart.* I.e., despair.
22:47-50 David closed this psalm of thanksgiving with renewed praise for God's glorious deeds.

^bThou dost rescue me from the violent man.

50 ^aRom. 15:9

50 "^aTherefore I will give thanks to Thee, O Lord, among the nations,
And I will sing praises to Thy name.

51 ^aPs. 144:10 ^bPs. 89:24 ^c2 Sam. 7:12-16

51 "^aHe is a tower of deliverance to His king,
And ^bshows lovingkindness to His anointed,
^cTo David and his descendants forever."

D The Last Words of David, 23:1-7

★ 1-7
1 ^a2 Sam. 7:8, 9; Ps. 78:70, 71 ^b1 Sam. 16:12, 13; Ps. 89:20

23 Now these are the last words of David.
David the son of Jesse declares,
^aAnd the man who was raised on high declares,
^bThe anointed of the God of Jacob,
And the sweet psalmist of Israel,

★ 2 ^aMatt. 22:43; 2 Pet. 1:21

2 "^aThe Spirit of the Lord spoke by me,
And His word was on my tongue.

3 ^a2 Sam. 22:2, 3, 32 ^bPs. 72:1-3; Is. 11:1-5 ^c2 Chr. 19:7, 9

3 "The God of Israel said,
^aThe Rock of Israel spoke to me,
'^bHe who rules over men righteously,
^cWho rules in the fear of God,

4 ^aJudg. 5:31; Ps. 72:6

4 ^aIs as the light of the morning when the sun rises,
A morning without clouds,
When the tender grass springs out of the earth,

Through sunshine after rain.'

5 "Truly is not my house so with God?
For ^aHe has made an everlasting covenant with me,
Ordered in all things, and secured;
For all my salvation and all my desire,
Will He not indeed make it grow?

★ 5 ^a2 Sam. 7:12-16; Ps. 89:29; Is. 55:3

6 "^aBut the worthless, every one of them will be thrust away like thorns,
Because they cannot be taken in hand;

★ 6-7
6 ^aMatt. 13:41

7 But the man who touches them
Must be armed with iron and the shaft of a spear,
And ^athey will be completely burned with fire in their place."

7 ^aMatt. 3:10; 13:30; Heb. 6:8

E The Deeds of David's Mighty Men, 23:8-39

8 ^aThese are the names of the mighty men whom David had: Josheb-basshebeth a Tahchemonite, chief of the captains, he was called Adino the Eznite, because of eight hundred slain by him at one time;

★ 8 ^a1 Chr. 11:11-47

9 and after him was Eleazar the son of ^aDodo the ^bAhohite, one of the three mighty men with David when they defied the Philistines who were gathered there to battle and the men of Israel had withdrawn.

9 ^a1 Chr. 27:4 ^b1 Chr. 8:4

10 ^aHe arose and struck the Philistines until his hand was

10 ^a1 Chr. 11:13 ^b1 Sam. 11:13; 19:5

23:1-7 *last words.* Probably David's last formal utterance, expressing praise to God, the righteous Ruler and Covenant-Keeper.
23:2 David affirmed the divine inspiration of his writings.
23:5 *grow.* I.e., prosper. David expressed faith that God would consummate the covenant established in 7:12-16.

23:6-7 David anticipated judgment on the ungodly who persecute Abraham's seed (cf. Gen. 12:3).
23:8 Here (through v. 39) David presents the names and achievements of 37 of his bravest warriors. According to 1 Chron. 11:10, these men helped David become king. *at one time.* I.e., during one battle.

weary and clung to the sword, and ᵇthe Lᴏʀᴅ brought about a great victory that day; and the people returned after him only to strip *the slain.*

11 Now after him was Shammah the son of Agee a ᵃHararite. And the Philistines were gathered into a troop, where there was a plot of ground full of lentils, and the people fled from the Philistines.

12 But he took his stand in the midst of the plot, defended it and struck the Philistines; and ᵃthe Lᴏʀᴅ brought about a great victory.

13 Then three of the thirty chief men went down and came to David in the harvest time to the ᵃcave of Adullam, while the troop of the Philistines was camping in ᵇthe valley of Rephaim.

14 And David was then ᵃin the stronghold, while the garrison of the Philistines was then in Bethlehem.

15 ᵃAnd David had a craving and said, "Oh that someone would give me water to drink from the well of Bethlehem which is by the gate!"

16 ᵃSo the three mighty men broke through the camp of the Philistines, and drew water from the well of Bethlehem which was by the gate, and took *it* and brought *it* to David. Nevertheless he would not drink it, but ᵇpoured it out to the Lᴏʀᴅ;

17 and he said, "Be it far from me, O Lᴏʀᴅ, that I should do this. ᵃ*Shall I drink* the blood of the men who went in *jeopardy* of their lives?" Therefore he would not drink it. These things the three mighty men did.

18 And ᵃAbishai, the brother of Joab, the son of Zeruiah, was ᵇchief of the thirty. And he swung his spear against three hundred and killed *them,* and had a name as well as the three.

19 He was most honored of the thirty, therefore he became their commander; however, he did not attain to the three.

20 Then ᵃBenaiah the son of Jehoiada, the son of a valiant man of ᵇKabzeel, who had done mighty deeds, killed the two *sons* of Ariel of Moab. He also went down and killed a lion in the middle of a pit on a snowy day.

21 And he killed an Egyptian, an impressive man. Now the Egyptian *had* a spear in his hand, but he went down to him with a club and snatched the spear from the Egyptian's hand, and killed him with his own spear.

22 These *things* ᵃBenaiah the son of Jehoiada did, and had a name as well as the three mighty men.

23 He was honored among the thirty, but he did not attain to the three. And David appointed him over his guard.

24 ᵃAsahel the brother of Joab was among the thirty; Elhanan the son of Dodo of Bethlehem,

25 ᵃShammah the ᵇHarodite, Elika the Harodite,

26 Helez the Paltite, Ira the son of Ikkesh the ᵃTekoite,

27 Abiezer the ᵃAnathothite, Mebunnai the Hushathite,

28 Zalmon the Ahohite, Maharai the ᵃNetophathite,

29 ᵃHeleb the son of Baanah the Netophathite, Ittai the son of Ribai of ᵇGibeah of the sons of Benjamin,

30 Benaiah a ᵃPirathonite, Hiddai of the brooks of ᵇGaash,

31 Abi-albon the Arbathite, Azmaveth the ᵃBarhumite,

32 Eliahba the ᵃShaalbonite, the sons of Jashen, Jonathan,

33 ᵃShammah the Hararite, Ahiam the son of Sharar the Ararite,

34 Eliphelet the son of Ahasbai, the son of ᵃthe Maacathite,

Side references (left column):
11 ᵃ2 Sam. 23:33
12 ᵃ2 Sam. 23:10
13 ᵃ1 Sam. 22:1 ᵇ2 Sam. 5:18
14 ᵃ1 Sam. 22:4, 5
15 ᵃ1 Chr. 11:17
16 ᵃ1 Chr. 11:18 ᵇGen. 35:14
17 ᵃLev. 17:10
18 ᵃ2 Sam. 10:10, 14; 18:2 ᵇ1 Chr. 11:20, 21

Side references (right column):
★20 ᵃ2 Sam. 8:18; 20:23 ᵇJosh. 15:21
22 ᵃ2 Sam. 23:20
★24 ᵃ2 Sam. 2:18; 1 Chr. 27:7
25 ᵃ1 Chr. 11:27 ᵇJudg. 7:1
26 ᵃ2 Sam. 14:2
27 ᵃJosh. 21:18
28 ᵃ2 Kin. 25:23
29 ᵃ1 Chr. 11:30 ᵇJosh. 18:28
30 ᵃJudg. 12:13, 15 ᵇJosh. 24:30
31 ᵃ2 Sam. 3:16
32 ᵃJosh. 19:42
33 ᵃ2 Sam. 23:11
34 ᵃ2 Sam. 10:6, 8; 20:14 ᵇ2 Sam. 11:3 ᶜ2 Sam. 15:12

23:20 *two sons of Ariel of Moab.* Lit., the two of Ariel of Moab; i.e., two Moabite champions.
23:24 The "thirty" composed the elite core of David's mighty men, to which replacements were added as men were killed. The active number was kept at thirty warriors; hence the list contains more than thirty names.

ᵇEliam the son of ᶜAhithophel the Gilonite,

35 ᵃ1 Chr.
11:37 ᵇJosh.
15:55
35　ᵃHezro the ᵇCarmelite, Paarai the Arbite,

36 ᵃ2 Sam.
8:3
36　Igal the son of Nathan of ᵃZobah, Bani the Gadite,

37 ᵃ2 Sam.
4:2
37　Zelek the Ammonite, Naharai the ᵃBeerothite, armor bearers of Joab the son of Zeruiah,

38 ᵃ1 Chr.
2:53
38　Ira the ᵃIthrite, Gareb the Ithrite,

★39 ᵃ2 Sam.
11:3, 6
39　ᵃUriah the Hittite; thirty-seven in all.

F　The Census and Plague, 24:1-25

★ 1 ᵃ1 Chr.
21:1 ᵇ2 Sam.
21:1, 2
ᶜ1 Chr.
27:23, 24
24 ᵃNow ᵇagain the anger of the LORD burned against Israel, and it incited David against them to say, "ᶜGo, number Israel and Judah."

2 ᵃJudg.
20:1; 2 Sam.
3:10
2　And the king said to Joab the commander of the army who was with him, "Go about now through all the tribes of Israel, ᵃfrom Dan to Beersheba, and register the people, that I may know the number of the people."

3 ᵃDeut.
1:11
3　But Joab said to the king, "ᵃNow may the LORD your God add to the people a hundred times as many as they are, while the eyes of my lord the king *still* see; but why does my lord the king delight in this thing?"

4　Nevertheless, the king's word prevailed against Joab and against the commanders of the army. So Joab and the commanders of the army went out from the presence of the king, to register the people of Israel.

5 ᵃDeut.
2:36; Josh.
13:9, 16
ᵇNum.
21:32; 32:35
5　And they crossed the Jordan and camped in ᵃAroer, on the right side of the city that is in the middle of the valley of Gad, and toward ᵇJazer.

6　Then they came to Gilead and to the land of Tahtim-hodshi, and they came to Dan-jaan and around to ᵃSidon,

6 ᵃJosh.
19:28; Judg.
1:31

7　and came to the ᵃfortress of Tyre and to all the cities of the ᵇHivites and of the Canaanites, and they went out to the south of Judah, *to* ᶜBeersheba.

7 ᵃJosh.
19:29 ᵇJosh.
11:3; Judg.
3:3 ᶜGen.
21:22-33

8　So when they had gone about through the whole land, they came to Jerusalem at the end of nine months and twenty days.

9　And Joab gave ᵃthe number of the registration of the people to the king; and there were in Israel ᵇeight hundred thousand valiant men who drew the sword, and the men of Judah were five hundred thousand men.

★ 9 ᵃNum.
1:44-46
ᵇ1 Chr. 21:5

10　Now ᵃDavid's heart troubled him after he had numbered the people. So David said to the LORD, "ᵇI have sinned greatly in what I have done. But now, O LORD, please take away the iniquity of Thy servant, for ᶜI have acted very foolishly."

★10 ᵃ1 Sam.
24:5 ᵇ2 Sam.
12:13
ᶜ1 Sam.
13:13; 2 Chr.
16:9

11　When David arose in the morning, the word of the LORD came to ᵃthe prophet Gad, David's ᵇseer, saying,

11 ᵃ1 Sam.
22:5; 1 Chr.
29:29
ᵇ1 Sam. 9:9

12　"Go and speak to David, 'Thus the LORD says, "I am offering you three things; choose for yourself one of them, which I may do to you." ' "

13　So Gad came to David and told him, and said to him, "Shall ᵃseven years of famine come to you in your land? Or will you flee

★13 ᵃ1 Chr.
21:12; Ezek.
14:21

23:39 The 37 include "the three" (vv. 8-12), Abishai, Benaiah (vv. 18-23), the thirty-one warriors (vv. 24-39), and David's commander, Joab (v. 37).

24:1 David's numbering of the people, usually done for purposes of taxation or military draft, is included to describe the events which led David to buy the ground upon which the Temple would be built. David's sin was in putting his faith in numbers rather than in God. Even Joab recognized this as a foolish move (v. 3). *incited.* It was Satan who actually prompted David to number the people (see note on 1 Chron. 21:1-4).

24:9 *eight hundred thousand.* See note on 1 Chron. 21:5.

24:10 Almost 10 months passed before David realized his sin.

24:13 *seven years of famine.* According to 1 Chron. 21:12 and the LXX, this should read "three years."

three months before your foes while they pursue you? Or shall there be three days' pestilence in your land? Now consider and see what answer I shall return to Him who sent me."

★14 *a*Ps. 51:1; 130:4, 7

14 Then David said to Gad, "I am in great distress. Let us now fall into the hand of the Lord *a*for His mercies are great, but do not let me fall into the hand of man."

15 *a*1 Chr. 21:14; 27:24 *b*2 Sam. 24:2

15 So *a*the Lord sent a pestilence upon Israel from the morning until the appointed time; and seventy thousand men of the people *b*from Dan to Beersheba died.

★16 *a*Ex. 12:23; 2 Kin. 19:35; Acts 12:23 *b*Ex. 32:14; 1 Sam. 15:11

16 *a*When the angel stretched out his hand toward Jerusalem to destroy it, *b*the Lord relented from the calamity, and said to the angel who destroyed the people, "It is enough! Now relax your hand!" And the angel of the Lord was by the threshing floor of A-raunah the Jebusite.

17 *a*2 Sam. 24:10 *b*2 Sam. 7:8; Ps. 74:1

17 Then David spoke to the Lord when he saw the angel who was striking down the people, and said, "Behold, *a*it is I who have sinned, and it is I who have done wrong; but *b*these sheep, what have they done? Please let Thy hand be against me and against my father's house."

18 *a*1 Chr. 21:18

18 So Gad came to David that day and said to him, "*a*Go up, erect an altar to the Lord on the threshing floor of Araunah the Jebusite."

19 And David went up according to the word of Gad, just as the Lord had commanded.

20 And Araunah looked down and saw the king and his servants crossing over toward him; and Araunah went out and bowed his face to the ground before the king.

21 *a*Num. 16:44-50

21 Then Araunah said, "Why has my lord the king come to his servant?" And David said, "To buy the threshing floor from you, in order to build an altar to the Lord, *a*that the plague may be held back from the people."

22 *a*1 Sam. 6:14; 1 Kin. 19:21

22 And Araunah said to David, "Let my lord the king take and offer up what is good in his sight. Look, *a*the oxen for the burnt offering, the threshing sledges and the yokes of the oxen for the wood.

23 *a*Ezek. 20:40, 41

23 "Everything, O king, Araunah gives to the king." And Araunah said to the king, "May the Lord your God *a*accept you."

★24 *a*Mal. 1:13, 14 *b*1 Chr. 21:24, 25

24 However, the king said to Araunah, "No, but I will surely buy it from you for a price, for *a*I will not offer burnt offerings to the Lord my God which cost me nothing." So *b*David bought the threshing floor and the oxen for fifty shekels of silver.

★25 *a*2 Sam. 21:14

25 And David built there an altar to the Lord, and offered burnt offerings and peace offerings. *a*Thus the Lord was moved by entreaty for the land, and the plague was held back from Israel.

24:14 David knew God to be more merciful than men and he wisely took the third option.
24:16 *relented.* Lit., repented. Not an indication of changeableness in God's character (cf. 1 Sam. 15:29; James 1:17), but an expression of sorrow concerning evil.
24:24 Here is an important principle of sacrificial giving.
24:25 The threshing floor was on Mount Moriah, a hill in the region of Moriah, where Abraham offered Isaac (see note on Gen. 22:2) and where Solomon later built the Temple (2 Chron. 3:1).

INTRODUCTION TO
THE FIRST BOOK OF THE KINGS

AUTHOR: Jeremiah   DATE: c. 550 B.C.

Title   *Originally one book, 1 and 2 Kings are appropriately titled from their subject matter, which traces the history of the kings of Israel and Judah from Solomon to the Babylonian captivity. First Kings concludes abruptly with the beginning of the reign of Ahaziah in 853.*

Author   *Jewish tradition attributes the book to the prophet Jeremiah. Clearly the author used historical sources in compiling the book (11:41; 14:19, 29), and the last chapter of 2 Kings must have been written by someone living in Babylon rather than Egypt, where Jeremiah died.*

Purpose   *The purpose of the book was not only to record the history of these kings, but to show that the success of any king (and of the nation as a whole) depended on the measure of his allegiance to God's law. Failure resulted in decline and captivity.*

Contents   *Important passages in 1 Kings include the description of Solomon's great wisdom (chaps. 3-4), the dedication of Solomon's Temple (chap. 8), the visit of the Queen of Sheba (chap. 10), and the ministry of Elijah (particularly his confrontation with the priests of Baal on Mt. Carmel, chap. 18).*

OUTLINE OF 1 KINGS

THE FIRST BOOK OF THE KINGS

I THE UNITED KINGDOM, 1:1-11:43

A The Accession of Solomon (2 Chron. 1:1-17), 1:1-3:1

1 The struggle for the succession, 1:1-53

★ 1 **1** Now King David was old, advanced in age; and they covered him with clothes, but he could not keep warm.

2 So his servants said to him, "Let them seek a young virgin for my lord the king, and let her attend the king and become his nurse; and let her lie in your bosom, that my lord the king may keep warm."

3 So they searched for a beautiful girl throughout all the territory of Israel, and found Abishag the ᵃShunammite, and brought her to the king.

4 And the girl was very beautiful; and she became the king's nurse and served him, but the king did not cohabit with her.

5 Now ᵃAdonijah the son of Haggith exalted himself, saying, "I will be king." So ᵇhe prepared for himself chariots and horsemen with fifty men to run before him.

6 And his father had never crossed him at any time by asking, "Why have you done so?" And he was also a very handsome man; and ᵃhe was born after Absalom.

7 And he had conferred with ᵃJoab the son of Zeruiah and with ᵇAbiathar the priest; and following ᶜAdonijah they helped him.

8 But ᵃZadok the priest, ᵇBenaiah the son of Jehoiada, ᶜNathan the prophet, ᵈShimei, Rei, and ᵉthe mighty men who belonged to David, were not with Adonijah.

9 And Adonijah sacrificed sheep and oxen and fatlings by the stone of Zoheleth, which is beside ᵃEn-rogel; and he invited all his brothers, the king's sons, and all the men of Judah, the king's servants.

10 But he did not invite Nathan the prophet, Benaiah, the mighty men, and ᵃSolomon his brother.

11 Then Nathan spoke to ᵃBathsheba the mother of Solomon, saying, "Have you not heard that Adonijah the son of Haggith has become king, and David our lord does not know *it?*

12 "So now come, please let me ᵃgive you counsel and save

Marginal references

3 ᵃJosh. 19:18; 1 Sam. 28:4

★ 5 ᵃ2 Sam. 3:4 ᵇ2 Sam. 15:1

★ 6 ᵃ2 Sam. 3:3, 4

7 ᵃ1 Chr. 11:6 ᵇ1 Sam. 22:20, 23; 2 Sam. 20:25 ᶜ1 Kin. 2:22

8 ᵃ2 Sam. 20:25; 1 Chr. 16:39 ᵇ2 Sam. 8:18 ᶜ2 Sam. 12:1 ᵈ1 Kin. 4:18 ᵉ2 Sam. 23:8-39

★ 9-10

9 ᵃJosh. 15:7; 18:16; 2 Sam. 17:17

10 ᵃ2 Sam. 12:24

11 ᵃ2 Sam. 12:24

12 ᵃProv. 15:22

1:1 *David was old.* About 70 (2 Sam. 5:4). *clothes.* Better, bed clothes.
1:5 *Adonijah* apparently was David's oldest living son (cf. 2 Sam. 3:2-4; 13:28; 18:14).
1:6 *had never crossed him.* I.e., David had not disciplined him; Adonijah was a spoiled child.

1:9-10 As a prelude to taking over the throne, Adonijah held a feast but failed to invite *Nathan* and *Solomon.* He apparently was planning to kill them, for had they eaten together, he would have been obliged to protect them.

your life and the life of your son Solomon.

13 "Go at once to King David and say to him, 'Have you not, my lord, O king, sworn to your maidservant, saying, "[a]Surely Solomon your son shall be king after me, and he shall sit on my throne"? Why then has Adonijah become king?'

14 "Behold, while you are still there speaking with the king, I will come in after you and confirm your words."

15 So Bathsheba went in to the king in the bedroom. Now [a]the king was very old, and Abishag the Shunammite was ministering to the king.

16 Then Bathsheba bowed and prostrated herself before the king. And the king said, "What do you wish?"

17 And she said to him, "My lord, you swore to your maidservant by the LORD your God, saying, '[a]Surely your son Solomon shall be king after me and he shall sit on my throne.'

18 "And now, behold, Adonijah is king; and now, my lord the king, you do not know it.

19 "And [a]he has sacrificed oxen and fatlings and sheep in abundance, and has invited all the sons of the king and Abiathar the priest and Joab the commander of the army; but he has not invited Solomon your servant.

20 "And as for you now, my lord the king, the eyes of all Israel are on you, to tell them who shall sit on the throne of my lord the king after him.

21 "Otherwise it will come about, [a]as soon as my lord the king sleeps with his fathers, that I and my son Solomon will be considered offenders."

22 And behold, while she was still speaking with the king, Nathan the prophet came in.

23 And they told the king, saying, "Here is Nathan the prophet." And when he came in before the king, he prostrated himself before the king with his face to the ground.

24 Then Nathan said, "My lord the king, have you said, 'Adonijah shall be king after me, and he shall sit on my throne'?

25 "[a]For he has gone down today and has sacrificed oxen and fatlings and sheep in abundance, and has invited all the king's sons and the commanders of the army and Abiathar the priest, and behold, they are eating and drinking before him; and they say, '[b]Long live King Adonijah!'

26 "[a]But me, even me your servant, and Zadok the priest and Benaiah the son of Jehoiada and your servant Solomon, he has not invited.

27 "Has this thing been done by my lord the king, and you have not shown to your servants who should sit on the throne of my lord the king after him?"

28 Then King David answered and said, "Call Bathsheba to me." And she came into the king's presence and stood before the king.

29 And the king vowed and said, "[a]As the LORD lives, who has redeemed my life from all distress,

30 surely as [a]I vowed to you by the LORD the God of Israel, saying, 'Your son Solomon shall be king after me, and he shall sit on my throne in my place'; I will indeed do so this day."

31 Then Bathsheba bowed with her face to the ground, and prostrated herself before the king and said, "[a]May my lord King David live forever."

32 Then King David said, "Call to me [a]Zadok the priest, Nathan the prophet, and Benaiah the son of Jehoiada." And they came into the king's presence.

33 And the king said to them, "Take with you [a]the servants of

Cross-references (margin)

13 [a]1 Kin. 1:30; 1 Chr. 22:9-13
15 [a]1 Kin. 1:1
17 [a]1 Kin. 1:13
19 [a]1 Kin. 1:9
21 [a]Deut. 31:16; 2 Sam. 7:12; 1 Kin. 2:10
25 [a]1 Kin. 1:9 [b]1 Sam. 10:24
26 [a]1 Kin. 1:8, 10
29 [a]2 Sam. 4:9
30 [a]1 Kin. 1:13, 17
31 [a]Dan. 2:4; 3:9
32 [a]1 Kin. 1:8
★33-34
33 [a]2 Sam. 20:6, 7 [b]2 Chr. 32:30; 33:14

1:33-34 *my own mule.* A sign that Solomon was David's choice to succeed him. *Gihon* was in the upper part of the Kidron Valley. David was bypassing preliminary steps to Solomon's accession and arranging for his actual coronation. This would put Adonijah, who had only

your lord, and have my son Solomon ride on my own mule, and bring him down to ᵇGihon.

34 "And let Zadok the priest and Nathan the prophet ᵃanoint him there as king over Israel, and ᵇblow the trumpet and say, 'ᶜLong live King Solomon!'

35 "Then you shall come up after him, and he shall come and sit on my throne and be king in my place; for I have appointed him to be ruler over Israel and Judah."

36 And Benaiah the son of Jehoiada answered the king and said, "Amen! Thus may the Lᴏʀᴅ, the God of my lord the king, say.

37 "ᵃAs the Lᴏʀᴅ has been with my lord the king, so may He be with Solomon, and ᵇmake his throne greater than the throne of my lord King David!"

38 So ᵃZadok the priest, Nathan the prophet, Benaiah the son of Jehoiada, ᵇthe Cherethites, and the Pelethites went down and had Solomon ride on King David's mule, and brought him to ᶜGihon.

39 Zadok the priest then ᵃtook the horn of oil from the tent and ᵇanointed Solomon. Then they ᶜblew the trumpet, and all the people said, "ᵈLong live King Solomon!"

40 And all the people went up after him, and the people were playing on flutes and rejoicing with great joy, so that the earth shook at their noise.

41 Now Adonijah and all the guests who were with him heard it, as they finished eating. When Joab heard the sound of the trumpet, he said, "Why is the city making such an uproar?"

42 While he was still speaking, behold, ᵃJonathan the son of Abiathar the priest came. Then Adonijah said, "Come in, for ᵇyou are a valiant man and bring good news."

43 But Jonathan answered and said to Adonijah, "No! Our lord King David has made Solomon king.

44 "The king has also sent with him Zadok the priest, Nathan the prophet, Benaiah the son of Jehoiada, the Cherethites, and the Pelethites; and they have made him ride on the king's mule.

45 "And Zadok the priest and Nathan the prophet have anointed him king in Gihon, and they have come up from there rejoicing, ᵃso that the city is in an uproar. This is the noise which you have heard.

46 "Besides, ᵃSolomon has even taken his seat on the throne of the kingdom.

47 "And moreover, the king's servants came to bless our lord King David, saying, 'May ᵃyour God make the name of Solomon better than your name and his throne greater than your throne!' And ᵇthe king bowed himself on the bed.

48 "The king has also said thus, 'Blessed be the Lᴏʀᴅ, the God of Israel, who ᵃhas granted one to sit on my throne today while my own eyes see it.' "

49 Then all the guests of Adonijah were terrified; and they arose and each went on his way.

50 And Adonijah was afraid of Solomon, and he arose, went and ᵃtook hold of the horns of the altar.

51 Now it was told Solomon, saying, "Behold, Adonijah is afraid of King Solomon, for behold, he has taken hold of the horns of the altar, saying, 'Let King Solomon swear to me today that he will not put his servant to death with the sword.' "

52 And Solomon said, "If he will be a worthy man, ᵃnot one of his hairs will fall to the ground;

---

34 ᵃ1 Sam. 10:1; 16:3, 12; 2 Sam. 5:3; 1 Kin. 19:16; 2 Kin. 9:3 ᵇ2 Sam. 15:10 ᶜ1 Kin. 1:25

37 ᵃJosh. 1:5, 17; 1 Sam. 20:13 ᵇ1 Kin. 1:47

38 ᵃ1 Kin. 1:8 ᵇ2 Sam. 8:18 ᶜ1 Kin. 1:33

39 ᵃEx. 30:23-32; Ps. 89:20 ᵇ1 Chr. 29:22 ᶜ1 Kin. 1:34 ᵈ1 Sam. 10:24

42 ᵃ2 Sam. 15:27, 36; 17:17 ᵇ2 Sam. 18:27

45 ᵃ1 Kin. 1:40

46 ᵃ1 Chr. 29:23

47 ᵃ1 Kin. 1:37 ᵇGen. 47:31

48 ᵃ2 Sam. 7:12; 1 Kin. 3:6

★49

★50 ᵃEx. 27:2; 30:10; 1 Kin. 2:28

52 ᵃ1 Sam. 14:45; 2 Sam. 14:11; Acts 27:34

---

taken preliminary steps, in the position of having to overthrow Solomon if he wished to be king.
1:49 Those who associated with Adonijah would

be considered co-conspirators.
1:50 *took hold of the horns of the altar.* A claim to protection (which was not automatically guaranteed, Exod. 21:14; 1 Kings 2:28-34).

but if wickedness is found in him, he will die."

53 So King Solomon sent, and they brought him down from the altar. And he came and prostrated himself before King Solomon, and Solomon said to him, "Go to your house."

2 *The final charge of David to Solomon*, 2:1-12

1 aGen. 47:29; Deut. 31:14

2 2 As David's atime to die drew near, he charged Solomon his son, saying,

2 "aI am going the way of all the earth. bBe strong, therefore, and show yourself a man.

2 aJosh. 23:14 bDeut. 31:7, 23; Josh. 1:6, 7

3 aDeut. 17:18-20 b1 Chr. 22:12, 13

3 "And keep the charge of the LORD your God, to walk in His ways, to keep His statutes, His commandments, His ordinances, and His testimonies, aaccording to what is written in the law of Moses, that byou may succeed in all that you do and wherever you turn,

4 aso that athe LORD may carry out His promise which He spoke concerning me, saying, b'If your sons are careful of their way, cto walk before Me in truth with all their heart and with all their soul, dyou shall not lack a man on the throne of Israel.'

4 a2 Sam. 7:25 bPs. 132:12 c2 Kin. 20:3 d2 Sam. 7:12, 13; 1 Kin. 8:25; 9:5

★ 5-6

5 a2 Sam. 2:13, 18 b2 Sam. 3:27; 1 Kin. 2:32 c2 Sam. 20:10

5 "Now you also know what Joab the ason of Zeruiah did to me, what he did to the two commanders of the armies of Israel, to bAbner the son of Ner, and to cAmasa the son of Jether, whom he killed; he also shed the blood of war in peace. And he put the blood of war on his belt about his waist, and on his sandals on his feet.

6 a1 Kin. 2:9

6 "aSo act according to your wisdom, and do not let his gray hair go down to Sheol in peace.

7 "But ashow kindness to the sons of Barzillai the Gileadite, and blet them be among those who eat at your table; cfor they assisted me when I fled from Absalom your brother.

★ 7 a2 Sam. 19:31-38 b2 Sam. 9:7, 10 c2 Sam. 17:27-29

8 "And behold, athere is with you Shimei the son of Gera the Benjamite, of Bahurim; now it was he who cursed me with a violent curse on the day I went to Mahanaim. But when bhe came down to me at the Jordan, I swore to him by the LORD, saying, 'I will not put you to death with the sword.'

★ 8 a2 Sam. 16:5-8 b2 Sam. 19:18-23

9 "Now therefore, do not let him go unpunished, afor you are a wise man; and you will know what you ought to do to him, and you will bring his gray hair down to Sheol with blood."

9 a1 Kin. 2:6

10 Then aDavid slept with his fathers and was buried in bthe city of David.

10 aActs 2:29; 13:36 b2 Sam. 5:7; 1 Kin. 3:1

11 And athe days that David reigned over Israel *were* forty years: bseven years he reigned in Hebron, and thirty-three years he reigned in Jerusalem.

11 a2 Sam. 5:4, 5; 1 Chr. 3:4; 29:26, 27 b2 Sam. 5:5

12 And aSolomon sat on the throne of David his father, and his kingdom was firmly established.

12 a1 Chr. 29:23; 2 Chr. 1:1

3 *The purge initiated by Solomon*, 2:13-46

13 Now Adonijah the son of Haggith came to Bathsheba the mother of Solomon. And she said, "aDo you come peacefully?" And he said, "Peacefully."

★13-25

13 a1 Sam. 16:4

14 Then he said, "I have something *to say* to you." And she said, "Speak."

15 So he said, "You know that athe kingdom was mine and bthat all Israel expected me to be king; chowever, the kingdom has

15 a2 Sam. 3:3, 4; 1 Kin. 2:22 b1 Kin. 1:5-25 c1 Kin. 1:38-50 d1 Chr. 22:9, 10; 28:5-7

2:5-6 Joab was guilty of murdering two generals in times of peace (2 Sam. 3:27; 20:10). *Sheol.* See note on Gen. 37:35.
2:7 Without their kindness David might have starved to death (2 Sam. 17:27-29).
2:8 On the curse of Shimei, see 2 Sam. 16:5-13 and 19:16-23. Cursing a ruler was a capital

crime (Exod. 22:28).
2:13-25 Solomon saw through Adonijah's request to marry Abishag (part of David's harem and thus an inheritor, 1:3-4) as a scheme to gain the throne, and so ordered him put to death.

turned about and become my brother's, *d*for it was his from the LORD.

16 "And now I am making one request of you; do not refuse me." And she said to him, "Speak."

17 17 Then he said, "Please speak to Solomon the king, for he will not refuse you, that he may give me *a*Abishag the Shunammite as a wife."

18 And Bathsheba said, "Very well; I will speak to the king for you."

19 19 So Bathsheba went to King Solomon to speak to him for Adonijah. And the king arose to meet her, bowed before her, and sat on his throne; then he *a*had a throne set for the king's mother, and *b*she sat on his right.

20 20 Then she said, "I am making one small request of you; *a*do not refuse me." And the king said to her, "Ask, my mother, for I will not refuse you."

21 21 So she said, "*a*Let Abishag the Shunammite be given to Adonijah your brother as a wife."

22 22 And King Solomon answered and said to his mother, "And why are you asking Abishag the Shunammite for Adonijah? *a*Ask for him also the kingdom—*b*for he is my older brother—even for him, for *c*Abiathar the priest, and for Joab the son of Zeruiah!"

23 23 Then King Solomon swore by the LORD, saying, "May God do so to me and more also, if Adonijah has *a*not spoken this word against his own life.

24 24 "Now therefore, as the LORD lives, who has established me and set me on the throne of David my father, and *a*who has made me a house as He promised, surely Adonijah will be put to death today."

25 So King Solomon *a*sent Benaiah the son of Jehoiada; and he fell upon him so that he died.

26 Then to Abiathar the priest the king said, "*a*Go to Anathoth to your own field, *b*for you deserve to die; but I will not put you to death at this time, because *c*you carried the ark of the Lord GOD before my father David, and because *d*you were afflicted in everything with which my father was afflicted."

27 So Solomon dismissed Abiathar from being priest to the LORD, in order to fulfill *a*the word of the LORD, which He had spoken concerning the house of Eli in Shiloh.

28 Now the news came to Joab, *a*for Joab had followed Adonijah, *b*although he had not followed Absalom. And Joab fled to the tent of the LORD and *c*took hold of the horns of the altar.

29 And it was told King Solomon that Joab had fled to the tent of the LORD, and behold, he is beside the altar. Then Solomon *a*sent Benaiah the son of Jehoiada, saying, "*b*Go, fall upon him."

30 So Benaiah came to the tent of the LORD, and said to him, "Thus the king has said, 'Come out.'" But he said, "No, for I will die here." And Benaiah brought the king word again, saying, "Thus spoke Joab, and thus he answered me."

31 And the king said to him, "*a*Do as he has spoken and fall upon him and bury him, *b*that you may remove from me and from my father's house the blood which Joab shed without cause.

32 "And *a*the LORD will return his blood on his own head, *b*because he fell upon two men more righteous and better than he and killed them with the sword, while my father David did not know *it*:

Marginal references (left column):

17 *a*1 Kin. 1:3, 4

19 *a*1 Kin. 15:13 *b*Ps. 45:9

20 *a*1 Kin. 2:16

21 *a*1 Kin. 1:3, 4

22 *a*2 Sam. 12:8 *b*1 Kin. 1:6; 2:15; 1 Chr. 3:2, 5 *c*1 Kin. 1:7

23 *a*Ruth 1:17

24 *a*2 Sam. 7:11, 13; 1 Chr. 22:10

Marginal references (right column):

25 *a*2 Sam. 8:18

★26-27

26 *a*Josh. 21:18; Jer. 1:1 *b*1 Sam. 26:16 *c*1 Sam. 23:6; 2 Sam. 15:24-29 *d*1 Sam. 22:20-23; 23:8, 9

27 *a*1 Sam. 2:27-36

★28-35

28 *a*1 Kin. 1:7 *b*2 Sam. 17:25; 18:2 *c*1 Kin. 1:50

29 *a*1 Kin. 2:25 *b*Ex. 21:14

31 *a*Ex. 21:14 *b*Num. 35:33; Deut. 19:13; 21:8, 9

32 *a*Gen. 9:6; Judg. 9:24, 57; Ps. 7:16 *b*2 Chr. 21:13, 14 *c*2 Sam. 3:27 *d*2 Sam. 20:9, 10

2:26-27 Abiathar, a priest of the line of Eli, was banished to his home town *Anathoth* (Josh. 21:18; Jer. 1:1) for his part in Adonijah's attempt to gain the throne. He was spared execution because he remained faithful to David during Absalom's rebellion (2 Sam. 15:24ff.). The doom foretold on the house of Eli was thus fulfilled (1 Sam. 2:30-35). 2:28-35 See notes on 1:50 and 2:5-6.

ᶜAbner the son of Ner, commander of the army of Israel, and ᵈAmasa the son of Jether, commander of the army of Judah.

33 33 "ᵃSo shall their blood return
3:29 on the head of Joab and on the head of his descendants forever; but to David and his descendants and his house and his throne, may there be peace from the LORD forever."

34 ᵃ1 Kin.
2:25 ᵇJosh.
15:61; Matt.
3:1 **34** Then ᵃBenaiah the son of Jehoiada went up and fell upon him and put him to death, and he was buried at his own house ᵇin the wilderness.

35 ᵃ1 Kin.
4:4 ᵇ1 Chr.
6:53; 24:3;
29:22 ᶜ1 Kin.
2:27 **35** And ᵃthe king appointed Benaiah the son of Jehoiada over the army in his place, and the king appointed ᵇZadok the priest ᶜin the place of Abiathar.

36 ᵃ2 Sam.
16:5; 1 Kin.
2:8 **36** Now the king sent and called for ᵃShimei and said to him, "Build for yourself a house in Jerusalem and live there, and do not go out from there to any place.

★**37** ᵃ2 Sam.
15:23; 2 Kin.
23:6; John
18:1 ᵇJosh.
2:19; 2 Sam.
1:16; Ezek.
18:13 **37** "For it will happen on the day you go out and ᵃcross over the brook Kidron, you will know for certain that you shall surely die; ᵇyour blood shall be on your own head."

38 Shimei then said to the king, "The word is good. As my lord the king has said, so your servant will do." So Shimei lived in Jerusalem many days.

39 ᵃ1 Sam.
27:2 **39** But it came about at the end of three years, that two of the servants of Shimei ran away ᵃto Achish son of Maacah, king of Gath. And they told Shimei, saying, "Behold, your servants are in Gath."

★**40** **40** Then Shimei arose and saddled his donkey, and went to Gath to Achish to look for his servants. And Shimei went and brought his servants from Gath.

41 And it was told Solomon

that Shimei had gone from Jerusalem to Gath, and had returned.

42 So the king sent and called for Shimei and said to him, "Did I not make you swear by the LORD and solemnly warn you, saying, 'You will know for certain that on the day you depart and go anywhere, you shall surely die'? And you said to me, 'The word which I have heard is good.'

43 "Why then have you not kept the oath of the LORD, and the command which I have laid on you?"

44 The king also said to Shimei, "ᵃYou know all the evil which you acknowledge in your heart, which you did to my father David; therefore ᵇthe LORD shall return your evil on your own head.

44 ᵃ2 Sam.
16:5-13
ᵇ1 Sam.
25:39; 2 Kin.
11:1, 12-16;
Ps. 7:16

45 "But King Solomon shall be blessed, and ᵃthe throne of David shall be established before the LORD forever."

45 ᵃ2 Sam.
7:13; Prov.
25:5

46 ᵃSo the king commanded Benaiah the son of Jehoiada, and he went out and fell upon him so that he died. ᵇThus the kingdom was established in the hands of Solomon.

46 ᵃ1 Kin.
2:25, 34
ᵇ1 Kin. 2:12;
2 Chr. 1:1

4   The marriage of Solomon, 3:1

3 Then ᵃSolomon formed a marriage alliance with Pharaoh king of Egypt, and took Pharaoh's daughter ᵇand brought her to the city of David, ᶜuntil he had finished building his own house and the house of the LORD and ᵈthe wall around Jerusalem.

1 ᵃ1 Kin.
7:8; 9:16, 24;
2 Chr. 8:11
ᵇ1 Kin. 9:24
ᶜ1 Kin. 7:1;
9:10 ᵈ1 Kin.
9:15

B   The Wisdom of Solomon, 3:2–4:34

1   Solomon's request for wisdom, 3:2-15

2 ᵃThe people were still sacrificing on the high places, be-

★ **2** ᵃLev.
17:3-5; Deut.
12:2, 13, 14;
1 Kin. 22:43

2:37 This restriction kept Shimei from returning to his home across the Kidron in the territory of Benjamin, and kept him under the king's surveillance.
2:40 Gath was about 30 miles SW. of Jerusalem, but not across the Kidron. Though Shimei

may have gone in good faith, he violated the command not to leave Jerusalem.
3:2 The use of *high places* to worship the Lord before the Temple was built in Jerusalem was not now an abomination as it later became.

cause there was no house built for the name of the LORD until those days.

3 Now *a*Solomon loved the LORD, *b*walking in the statutes of his father David, except he sacrificed and burned incense on the high places.

4 *a*And the king went to *b*Gibeon to sacrifice there, *c*for that was the great high place; Solomon offered a thousand burnt offerings on that altar.

5 *a*In Gibeon the LORD appeared to Solomon *b*in a dream at night; and God said, "*c*Ask what *you wish* me to give you."

6 Then Solomon said, "*a*Thou hast shown great lovingkindness to Thy servant David my father, *b*according as he walked before Thee in truth and righteousness and uprightness of heart toward Thee; and *c*Thou hast reserved for him this great lovingkindness, that Thou hast given him a son to sit on his throne, as *it is* this day.

7 "And now, O LORD my God, *a*Thou hast made Thy servant king in place of my father David, yet *b*I am but a little child; *c*I do not know how to go out or come in.

8 "And *a*Thy servant is in the midst of Thy people which Thou hast chosen, *b*a great people who cannot be numbered or counted for multitude.

9 "So *a*give Thy servant an understanding heart to judge Thy people *b*to discern between good and evil. For who is able to judge this great people of Thine?"

10 And it was pleasing in the sight of the Lord that Solomon had asked this thing.

11 And God said to him, "Because you have asked this thing and have *a*not asked for yourself long life, nor have asked riches for yourself, nor have you asked for the life of your enemies, but have asked for yourself discernment to understand justice,

12 behold, *a*I have done according to your words. Behold, *b*I have given you a wise and discerning heart, so that there has been no one like you before you, nor shall one like you arise after you.

13 "*a*And I have also given you what you have not asked, both *b*riches and honor, so that there will not be any among the kings like you all your days.

14 "And *a*if you walk in My ways, keeping My statutes and commandments, as your father David walked, then I will *b*prolong your days."

15 Then *a*Solomon awoke, and behold, it was a dream. And he came to Jerusalem and stood before the ark of the covenant of the Lord, and offered burnt offerings and made peace offerings, and *b*made a feast for all his servants.

2 Solomon's display of wisdom, 3:16-28

16 Then two women who were harlots came to the king and stood before him.

17 And the one woman said, "Oh, my lord, this woman and I live in the same house; and I gave birth to a child while she *was* in the house.

18 "And it happened on the third day after I gave birth, that this woman also gave birth to a child, and we were together. There was no stranger with us in the house, only the two of us in the house.

19 "And this woman's son died in the night, because she lay on it.

20 "So she arose in the middle of the night and took my son from beside me while your maidservant slept, and laid him in her bosom, and laid her dead son in my bosom.

21 "And when I rose in the morning to nurse my son, behold,

3 *a*Deut. 6:5; 10:12, 13; 11:13; 30:16; Ps. 31:23; 145:20; 1 Cor. 8:3
*b*1 Kin. 2:3; 9:4; 11:4, 6, 38
★ **4** *a*2 Chr. 1:3 *b*Josh. 18:21-25
*c*1 Chr. 16:39; 21:29
5 *a*1 Kin. 9:2; 11:9
*b*Num. 12:6; Matt. 1:20; 2:13 *c*John 15:7
6 *a*2 Sam. 7:8-17; 2 Chr. 1:8
*b*1 Kin. 9:4
*c*1 Kin. 1:48

★ **7** *a*1 Chr. 22:9-13
*b*1 Chr. 29:1; Jer. 1:6, 7
*c*Num. 27:17

8 *a*Ex. 19:6; Deut. 7:6
*b*Gen. 15:5; 22:17

9 *a*2 Chr. 1:10; Ps. 72:1, 2; Prov. 2:3-9; James 1:5 *b*2 Sam. 14:17; Heb. 5:14

11 *a*James 4:3

12 *a*1 John 5:14, 15
*b*1 Kin. 4:29-31; 5:12; 10:23, 24; Eccl. 1:16

13 *a*1 Kin. 4:21-24; 10:23, 27; Matt. 6:33; Eph. 3:20
*b*Prov. 3:16

14 *a*1 Kin. 3:6 *b*Ps. 91:16; Prov. 3:2

15 *a*Gen. 41:7 *b*1 Kin. 8:65

3:4 *Gibeon* was about 6 miles NW. of Jerusalem.
3:7 *I am but a little child.* Not in age (he was about 20, cf. 1 Chron. 29:1) but in experience.

he was dead; but when I looked at him carefully in the morning, behold, he was not my son, whom I had borne."

22 Then the other woman said, "No! For the living one is my son, and the dead one is your son." But the first woman said, "No! For the dead one is your son, and the living one is my son." Thus they spoke before the king.

23 Then the king said, "The one says, 'This is my son who is living, and your son is the dead one'; and the other says, 'No! For your son is the dead one, and my son is the living one.'"

24 And the king said, "Get me a sword." So they brought a sword before the king.

25 And the king said, "Divide the living child in two, and give half to the one and half to the other."

26 Then the woman whose child was the living one spoke to the king, for ªshe was deeply stirred over her son and said, "Oh, my lord, give her the living child, and by no means kill him." But the other said, "He shall be neither mine nor yours; divide him!"

27 Then the king answered and said, "Give the first woman the living child, and by no means kill him. She is his mother."

28 When all Israel heard of the judgment which the king had handed down, they feared the king; for ªthey saw that the wisdom of God was in him to administer justice.

3 Solomon's administration, 4:1-28

4 Now King Solomon was king over all Israel.

2 And these were his officials: Azariah the son of Zadok was ªthe priest;

3 Elihoreph and Ahijah, the sons of Shisha were secretaries; ªJehoshaphat the son of Ahilud was the recorder;

4 and ªBenaiah the son of Jehoiada was over the army; and Zadok and ᵇAbiathar were priests;

5 and Azariah the son of Nathan was over ªthe deputies; and Zabud the son of Nathan, a priest, was the king's friend;

6 and Ahishar was over the household; and Adoniram the son of Abda was over the men subject to forced labor.

7 And Solomon had twelve deputies over all Israel, who provided for the king and his household; each man had to provide for a month in the year.

8 And these are their names: Ben-hur, in the ªhill country of Ephraim;

9 Ben-deker in Makaz and ªShaalbim and ᵇBeth-shemesh and Elonbeth-hanan;

10 Ben-hesed, in Arubboth (ªSocoh was his and all the land of ᵇHepher);

11 Ben-abinadab, in all the ªheight of Dor (Taphath the daughter of Solomon was his wife);

12 Baana the son of Ahilud, in ªTaanach and Megiddo, and all ᵇBeth-shean which is beside ᶜZarethan below Jezreel, from Bethshean to ᵈAbel-meholah as far as the other side of ᵉJokmeam;

13 Ben-geber, in ªRamothgilead (ᵇthe towns of Jair, the son of Manasseh, which are in Gilead were his; ᶜthe region of Argob, which is in Bashan, sixty great cities with walls and bronze bars were his);

14 Ahinadab the son of Iddo, in ªMahanaim;

15 ªAhimaaz, in Naphtali (he also married Basemath the daughter of Solomon);

Margin references:
26 ªGen. 43:30; Is. 49:15; Jer. 31:20; Hos. 11:8

28 ª1 Kin. 3:9, 11, 12; Dan. 1:17; Col. 2:2, 3

★ 2 ª1 Chr. 6:10

3 ª2 Sam. 8:16

★ 4 ª1 Kin. 2:35 ᵇ1 Kin. 2:27

5 ª1 Kin. 4:7

★ 7

8 ªJosh. 24:33

9 ªJudg. 1:35 ᵇJosh. 21:16

10 ªJosh. 15:35 ᵇJosh. 12:17

11 ªJosh. 11:1, 2

12 ªJudg. 5:19 ᵇJosh. 17:11 ᶜJosh. 3:16 ᵈ1 Kin. 19:16 ᵉ1 Chr. 6:68

13 ª1 Kin. 22:3-15 ᵇNum. 32:41 ᶜDeut. 3:4

14 ªJosh. 13:26

15 ª2 Sam. 15:27

4:2 Azariah was actually the grandson of Zadok (1 Chron. 6:8-9), a not uncommon meaning for the word son. Zadok was probably elderly at this time and gave many of his duties to his grandson.

4:4 Abiathar, though banished (2:26-27), still retained the title of priest.

4:7 Each officer, in rotation, was responsible to see that the king's household was supplied for one month.

16 a2 Sam. 15:32

16 Baana the son of aHushai, in Asher and Bealoth;

17 Jehoshaphat the son of Paruah, in Issachar;

18 a1 Kin. 1:8

18 aShimei the son of Ela, in Benjamin;

19 aDeut. 3:8-10

19 Geber the son of Uri, in the land of Gilead, athe country of Sihon king of the Amorites and of Og king of Bashan; and *he was* the only deputy who *was* in the land.

20 aGen. 22:17; 32:12; 1 Kin. 3:8

20 aJudah and Israel *were* as numerous as the sand that is on the seashore in abundance; *they* were eating and drinking and rejoicing.

★21 a2 Chr. 9:26 bGen. 15:18; Josh. 1:4 c2 Sam. 8:2, 6

21 aNow Solomon ruled over all the kingdoms bfrom the River *to* the land of the Philistines and to the border of Egypt; cthey brought tribute and served Solomon all the days of his life.

★22

22 And Solomon's provision for one day was thirty kors of fine flour and sixty kors of meal,

23 ten fat oxen, twenty pasture-fed oxen, a hundred sheep besides deer, gazelles, roebucks, and fattened fowl.

★24 aJudg. 1:18 bPs. 72:11

24 For he had dominion over everything west of the River, from Tiphsah even to aGaza, bover all the kings west of the River; and che had peace on all sides around about him.

★25 aJer. 23:6; Mic. 4:4; Zech. 3:10 b1 Sam. 3:20

25 aSo Judah and Israel lived in safety, every man under his vine and his fig tree, bfrom Dan even to Beersheba, all the days of Solomon.

★26 a1 Kin. 10:26; 2 Chr. 1:14

26 aAnd Solomon had 40,000 stalls of horses for his chariots, and 12,000 horsemen.

★27

27 And those deputies provided for King Solomon and all who came to King Solomon's ta-

ble, each in his month; they left nothing lacking.

28 aEsth. 8:10, 14; Mic. 1:13

28 They also brought barley and straw for the horses and aswift steeds to the place where it should be, each according to his charge.

4 Solomon's fame, 4:29-34

29 a1 Kin. 3:12 b1 Kin. 4:20

29 Now aGod gave Solomon wisdom and very great discernment and breadth of mind, blike the sand that is on the seashore.

30 aGen. 29:1; Judg. 6:33 bIs. 19:11; Acts 7:22

30 And Solomon's wisdom surpassed the wisdom of all athe sons of the east and ball the wisdom of Egypt.

★31 a1 Kin. 3:12 b1 Chr. 15:19; Ps. 89 title c1 Chr. 2:6

31 For ahe was wiser than all men, than bEthan the Ezrahite, Heman, cCalcol and Darda, the sons of Mahol; and his fame was *known* in all the surrounding nations.

★32 aProv. 1:1; 10:1; 25:1; Eccl. 12:9; Song 1:1

32 aHe also spoke 3,000 proverbs, and his songs were 1,005.

33 And he spoke of trees, from the cedar that is in Lebanon even to the hyssop that grows on the wall; he spoke also of animals and birds and creeping things and fish.

34 a1 Kin. 10:1; 2 Chr. 9:23

34 And men acame from all peoples to hear the wisdom of Solomon, from all the kings of the earth who had heard of his wisdom.

C The Temple of Solomon (2 Chron. 2:1–7:22), 5:1–8:66

1 Preparations for the Temple, 5:1–18

★ 1 a2 Chr. 2:3 b2 Sam. 5:11; 1 Chr. 14:1

5 Now Hiram king of Tyre sent his servants to Solomon, when he heard that they had

---

4:21 *the River.* The Euphrates. Solomon reigned over almost all the territory promised to Abraham (see note on Gen. 15:18-21 and observe that the river of Egypt there and *the border of Egypt* here are not the same; cf. 8:65 where the wadi el-Arish is indicated).
4:22 One *kor* = 6.25 bushels or 58 gallons.
4:24 *Tiphsah* was a large town on the W. side of the Euphrates.
4:25 *under his vine and his fig tree.* A proverbial expression for idyllic conditions (Mic. 4:4).

4:26 No one seemed to be concerned that Solomon was disobeying God (Deut. 17:16).
4:27 *all who came to King Solomon's table.* Perhaps 4,000-5,000 people who were cared for at court.
4:31 Who these wise men were is unknown.
4:32 Many of Solomon's *proverbs* are recorded in the book of Proverbs. Some of his *songs* may be reflected in the Song of Solomon.
5:1 Hiram had sent David laborers and wood for his public works (2 Sam. 5:11).

anointed him king in place of his father, for [b]Hiram had always been a friend of David.

2   Then [a]Solomon sent *word* to Hiram, saying,

3   "You know that [a]David my father was unable to build a house for the name of the LORD his God because of the wars which surrounded him, until the LORD put them under the soles of his feet.

4   "But now [a]the LORD my God has given me rest on every side; there is neither adversary nor misfortune.

5   "And behold, [a]I intend to build a house for the name of the LORD my God, as the LORD spoke to David my father, saying, 'Your son, whom I will set on your throne in your place, he will build the house for My name.'

6   "Now therefore, command that they cut for me [a]cedars from Lebanon, and my servants will be with your servants; and I will give you wages for your servants according to all that you say, for you know that there is no one among us who knows how to cut timber like the Sidonians."

7   And it came about when Hiram heard the words of Solomon, that he rejoiced greatly and said, "Blessed be the LORD today, who has given to David a wise son over this great people."

8   So Hiram sent *word* to Solomon, saying, "I have heard *the message* which you have sent me; I will do what you desire concerning the cedar and cypress timber.

9   "My servants will bring *them* down from Lebanon to the sea; and I will make them into rafts *to go* by sea [a]to the place where you direct me, and I will have them broken up there, and you shall carry *them* away. Then [b]you shall accomplish my desire by giving food to my household."

10   So Hiram gave Solomon as much as he desired of the cedar and cypress timber.

11   [a]Solomon then gave Hiram 20,000 kors of wheat as food for his household, and twenty kors of beaten oil; thus Solomon would give Hiram year by year.

12   And [a]the LORD gave wisdom to Solomon, just as He promised him; and there was peace between Hiram and Solomon, and the two of them made a covenant.

13   Now [a]King Solomon levied forced laborers from all Israel; and the forced laborers numbered 30,000 men.

14   And he sent them to Lebanon, 10,000 a month in relays; they were in Lebanon a month *and* two months at home. And [a]Adoniram *was* over the forced laborers.

15   Now [a]Solomon had 70,000 transporters, and 80,000 hewers *of stone* in the mountains,

16   [a]besides Solomon's 3,300 chief deputies who *were* over the project *and* who ruled over the people who were doing the work.

17   Then [a]the king commanded, and they quarried great stones, costly stones, to lay the foundation of the house with cut stones.

18   So Solomon's builders and Hiram's builders and [a]the Gebalites cut them, and prepared the timbers and the stones to build the house.

2   Description and construction of the Temple, 6:1–38

6 [a]Now it came about in the four hundred and eightieth year after the sons of Israel came out of the land of Egypt, in the fourth year of Solomon's reign over Israel, in the month of Ziv which is the second month, that

---

Side references (left column):

2   [a]2 Chr. 2:3

3   [a]2 Sam. 7:5; 1 Chr. 28:2, 3

4   [a]1 Kin. 4:24; 1 Chr. 22:9

5   [a]2 Sam. 7:12, 13; 1 Chr. 17:12; 22:10; 28:6; 2 Chr. 2:4

6   [a]2 Chr. 2:8

★ 9   [a]2 Chr. 2:16 [b]Ezra 3:7; Ezek. 27:17

Side references (right column):

★11   [a]2 Chr. 2:10

12   [a]1 Kin. 3:12

13   [a]1 Kin. 4:6; 9:15

14   [a]1 Kin. 4:6; 12:18

15   [a]1 Kin. 9:20-22; 2 Chr. 2:17, 18

16   [a]1 Kin. 9:23

17   [a]1 Kin. 6:7; 1 Chr. 22:2

18   [a]Josh. 13:5; Ezek. 27:9

★ 1   [a]2 Chr. 3:1, 2

5:9 The lumber was floated on *rafts* from Lebanon to Palestine.
5:11 On *kors* see note on 4:22.
6:1 The date is 967 B.C. and *Ziv* is the second

month (April-May). On the relation of this date to the Exodus see the Introduction to Exodus.

he began to build the house of the LORD.

★ 2   **2**   As for the house which King Solomon built for the LORD, its length *was* sixty cubits and its width twenty *cubits* and its height thirty cubits.

3   And the porch in front of the nave of the house *was* twenty cubits in length, corresponding to the width of the house, *and* its depth along the front of the house *was* ten cubits.

4 ªEzek. 40:16; 41:16   **4**   Also for the house ªhe made windows with *artistic* frames.

★ 5-6   **5**   And ªagainst the wall of the house he built stories encom-
5 ªEzek. 41:6 ᵇ1 Kin. 6:16, 19, 20 ᶜEzek. 41:5   passing the walls of the house around both the nave and the ᵇin- ner sanctuary; thus he made ᶜside chambers all around.

6   The lowest story *was* five cubits wide, and the middle *was* six cubits wide, and the third *was* seven cubits wide; for on the out- side he made offsets *in the wall* of the house all around in order that *the beams* should not be inserted in the walls of the house.

★ 7 ªEx. 20:25; Deut. 27:5, 6   **7**   And ªthe house, while it was being built, was built of stone prepared at the quarry, and there was neither hammer nor axe nor any iron tool heard in the house while it was being built.

8   The doorway for the low- est side chamber *was* on the right side of the house; and they would go up by winding stairs to the middle *story*, and from the mid- dle to the third.

9 ª1 Kin. 6:14, 38   **9**   So ªhe built the house and finished it; and he covered the house with beams and planks of cedar.

10   He also built the stories against the whole house, each five cubits high; and they were fas- tened to the house with timbers of cedar.

11   Now the word of the LORD came to Solomon saying,

12   "*Concerning* this house which you are building, ªif you will walk in My statutes and ex- ecute My ordinances and keep all My commandments by walking in them, then I will carry out My word with you which I spoke to David your father.

12 ª2 Sam. 7:5-16; 1 Kin. 9:4

13   "And ªI will dwell among the sons of Israel, and ᵇwill not forsake My people Israel."

13 ªEx. 25:8; 29:45; Lev. 26:11 ᵇDeut. 31:6; Josh. 1:5; Heb. 13:5

14   ªSo Solomon built the house and finished it.

★14 ª1 Kin. 6:9, 38

15   Then he ªbuilt the walls of the house on the inside with boards of cedar; from the floor of the house to the ceiling he over- laid *the walls* on the inside with wood, and he overlaid the floor of the house with boards of cypress.

15 ª1 Kin. 7:7

16   ªAnd he built twenty cu- bits on the rear part of the house with boards of cedar from the floor to the ceiling; he built *them* for it on the inside as an inner sanctuary, *even* as ᵇthe most holy place.

★16-17

16 ª2 Chr. 3:8 ᵇEx. 26:33, 34; Lev. 16:2; 1 Kin. 8:6; Heb. 9:3

17   And the house, that is, the nave in front of *the inner sanctu- ary*, was forty cubits *long*.

18   And there was cedar on the house within, carved *in the shape* of ªgourds and open flow- ers; all was cedar, there was no stone seen.

★18 ª1 Kin. 7:24

19   Then he prepared an inner sanctuary within the house in or- der to place there the ark of the covenant of the LORD.

20   And the inner sanctuary *was* twenty cubits in length, twenty cubits in width, and twenty cubits in height, and he

---

6:2 Normally the cubit was 18 inches; however, 2 Chron. 3:3 may indicate that a longer cubit (20.9 inches) was used in this construction. In either case the structure was not a large one, probably measuring 90 to 105 feet long, 30 to 35 feet wide, and 45 to 52½ feet high.
6:5-6 A triple-decker arrangement of rooms buttressed the walls, with access by a winding staircase (v. 8).

6:7 The stones were prepared at a quarry which Solomon had on the outskirts of Jerusalem.
6:14 This Temple stood until destroyed by the Babylonians in 586.
6:16-17 The Holy of Holies occupied one-third of the interior space of the Temple, and the Holy Place, two-thirds.
6:18 *gourds* = knobs.

overlaid it with pure gold. He also overlaid the altar with cedar.

21 So Solomon overlaid the inside of the house with pure gold. And he drew chains of gold across the front of the inner sanctuary; and he overlaid it with gold.

22 And he overlaid the whole house with gold, until all the house was finished. Also *the whole altar which was by the inner sanctuary he overlaid with gold.

23 *Also in the inner sanctuary he made two cherubim of olive wood, each ten cubits high.

24 And five cubits *was* the one wing of the cherub and five cubits the other wing of the cherub; from the end of one wing to the end of the other wing *were* ten cubits.

25 And the other cherub *was* ten cubits; both the cherubim were of the same measure and the same form.

26 The height of the one cherub *was* ten cubits, and so *was* the other cherub.

27 And he placed the cherubim in the midst of the inner house, and *the wings of the cherubim were spread out, so that the wing of the one was touching the one wall, and the wing of the other cherub was touching the other wall. So their wings were touching each other in the center of the house.

28 He also overlaid the cherubim with gold.

29 Then he carved all the walls of the house round about with carved engravings of cherubim, palm trees, and open flowers, inner and outer *sanctuaries*.

30 And he overlaid the floor of the house with gold, inner and outer *sanctuaries*.

31 And for the entrance of the inner sanctuary he made doors of olive wood, the lintel *and* five-sided doorposts.

32 So *he made* two doors of olive wood, and he carved on them carvings of cherubim, palm trees, and open flowers, and overlaid them with gold; and he spread the gold on the cherubim and on the palm trees.

33 So also he made for the entrance of the nave four-sided doorposts of olive wood

34 and *two doors of cypress wood; the two leaves of the one door turned on pivots, and the two leaves of the other door turned on pivots.

35 And he carved *on it* cherubim, palm trees, and open flowers; and he overlaid *them* with gold evenly applied on the engraved work.

36 And *he built the inner court with three rows of cut stone and a row of cedar beams.

37 *In the fourth year the foundation of the house of the LORD was laid, in the month of Ziv.

38 And in the eleventh year, in the month of Bul, which is the eighth month, the house was finished throughout all its parts and according to all its plans. So he was seven years in building it.

3 Construction of other buildings, 7:1–12

7 Now *Solomon was building his own house thirteen years, and he finished all his house.

2 And *he built the house of the forest of Lebanon; its length was 100 cubits and its width 50

Marginal references

22 *Ex. 30:1, 3, 6
23 *Ex. 37:7-9; 2 Chr. 3:10-12
27 *Ex. 25:20; 37:9; 1 Kin. 8:7
★31-35
34 *Ezek. 41:23-25
36 *1 Kin. 7:12; Jer. 36:10
37 *1 Kin. 6:1
★38
★ 1-12
1 *1 Kin. 3:1; 9:10; 2 Chr. 8:1
2 *1 Kin. 10:17, 21; 2 Chr. 9:16

6:31-35 Olivewood doors separated the Holy of Holies from the Holy Place (apparently there was also a curtain, 2 Chron. 3:14), and the doors to the Temple proper matched them.

6:38 Seven years later, in *Bul* (Oct.-Nov.), the Temple was completed.

7:1-12 *his house.* I.e., the total complex of buildings described in these verses, which included

the house of the forest of Lebanon (apparently an armory, 10:16-17) connected by a colonnade (v. 6) to a throne room containing a gold and ivory throne approached by six steps (10:18-19). Solomon's own house and one for the daughter of Pharaoh (v. 8; cf. 3:1) completed the complex.

cubits and its height 30 cubits, on four rows of cedar pillars with cedar beams on the pillars.

3 And it was paneled with cedar above the side chambers which were on the 45 pillars, 15 in each row.

4 And *there were artistic window* frames in three rows, and window was opposite window in three ranks.

5 And all the doorways and doorposts had squared *artistic* frames, and window was opposite window in three ranks.

6 Then he made ªthe hall of pillars; its length was 50 cubits and its width 30 cubits, and a porch *was* in front of them and pillars and a ᵇthreshold in front of them.

7 And he made the hall of the ªthrone where he was to judge, the hall of judgment, and ᵇit was paneled with cedar from floor to floor.

8 And his house where he was to live, the other court inward from the hall, was of the same workmanship. ªHe also made a house like this hall for Pharaoh's daughter, ᵇwhom Solomon had married.

9 All these were of costly stones, of stone cut according to measure, sawed with saws, inside and outside; even from the foundation to the coping, and so on the outside to the great court.

10 And the foundation was of costly stones, *even* large stones, stones of ten cubits and stones of eight cubits.

11 And above were costly stones, stone cut according to measure, and cedar.

12 So ªthe great court all around had three rows of cut stone and a row of cedar beams even as the inner court of the house of the LORD, and ᵇthe porch of the house.

4 *Furnishing the Temple,* 7:13-51

13 Now ªKing Solomon sent and brought Hiram from Tyre.

14 ªHe was a widow's son from the tribe of Naphtali, and his father was a man of Tyre, a worker in bronze; and ᵇhe was filled with wisdom and understanding and skill for doing any work in bronze. So he came to King Solomon and ᶜperformed all his work.

15 And he fashioned ªthe two pillars of bronze; ᵇeighteen cubits was the height of one pillar, and a line of twelve cubits measured the circumference of both.

16 He also made two capitals of molten bronze to set on the tops of the pillars; the height of the one capital was five cubits and the height of the other capital was five cubits.

17 *There were* nets of network and twisted threads of chainwork for the capitals which were on the top of the pillars; seven for the one capital and seven for the other capital.

18 So he made the pillars, and two rows around on the one network to cover the capitals which were on the top of the pomegranates; and so he did for the other capital.

19 And the capitals which *were* on the top of the pillars in the porch were of lily design, four cubits.

20 And *there were* capitals also on the two pillars, close to the rounded projection which was beside the network; and ªthe pomegranates *numbered* two hundred in rows around both capitals.

21 ªThus he set up the pillars at the ᵇporch of the nave; and he set up the right pillar and named

---

6 ª1 Kin. 7:12 ᵇEzek. 41:25, 26

7 ªPs. 122:5; Prov. 20:8 ᵇ1 Kin. 6:15, 16

8 ª1 Kin. 9:24; 2 Chr. 8:11 ᵇ1 Kin. 3:1

12 ª1 Kin. 6:36 ᵇ1 Kin. 7:6

★**13-14**
13 ª2 Chr. 2:13, 14; 4:11

14 ª2 Chr. 2:14 ᵇEx. 28:3; 31:3-5; 35:31; 36:1 ᶜ2 Chr. 4:11-16

15 ª2 Kin. 25:17; 2 Chr. 3:15; 4:12; Jer. 52:21 ᵇ1 Kin. 7:41

20 ª1 Kin. 7:42; 2 Chr. 3:16; 4:13; Jer. 52:23

★**21** ª2 Chr. 3:17 ᵇ1 Kin. 6:3

7:13-14 *Hiram.* Not King Hiram (5:1), but a half-Jewish artisan. *from the tribe of Naphtali.* In 2 Chron. 2:14 it is said that Hiram's mother was of the tribe of Dan. Probably she was born in Dan but her deceased first husband

was of Naphtali. Or perhaps she was a native of Dan but a resident of Naphtali, or vice versa.
7:21 *Jachin* means "he establishes," and *Boaz* means "in him is strength."

it Jachin, and he set up the left pillar and named it Boaz.

22 And on the top of the pillars was lily design. So the work of the pillars was finished.

★23-26

23 *a*Now he made the sea of *b*cast *metal* ten cubits from brim to brim, circular in form, and its height was five cubits, and thirty cubits in circumference.

23 *a*2 Chr. 4:2 *b*2 Kin. 16:17; 25:13

24 And under its brim *a*gourds went around encircling it ten to a cubit, *b*completely surrounding the sea; the gourds were in two rows, cast with the rest.

24 *a*1 Kin. 6:18 *b*2 Chr. 4:3

25 *a*It stood on twelve oxen, three facing north, three facing west, three facing south, and three facing east; and the sea *was* set on top of them, and all their rear parts *turned* inward.

25 *a*2 Chr. 4:4, 5; Jer. 52:20

26 And it was a handbreadth thick, and its brim was made like the brim of a cup, *as* a lily blossom; it could hold two thousand baths.

★27 *a*1 Kin. 7:38; 2 Kin. 25:13; 2 Chr. 4:14

27 Then *a*he made the ten stands of bronze; the length of each stand was four cubits and its width four cubits and its height three cubits.

28 And this was the design of the stands: they had borders, even borders between the frames,

29 and on the borders which were between the frames *were* lions, oxen and cherubim; and on the frames there *was* a pedestal above, and beneath the lions and oxen *were* wreaths of hanging work.

30 Now each stand had four bronze wheels with bronze axles, and its four feet had supports; beneath the basin *were* cast supports with wreaths at each side.

31 And its opening inside the crown at the top *was* a cubit, and its opening *was* round like the design of a pedestal, a cubit and a half; and also on its opening *there*

were engravings, and their borders were square, not round.

32 And the four wheels *were* underneath the borders, and the axles of the wheels *were* on the stand. And the height of a wheel *was* a cubit and a half.

33 And the workmanship of the wheels *was* like the workmanship of a chariot wheel. Their axles, their rims, their spokes, and their hubs *were* all cast.

34 Now *there were* four supports at the four corners of each stand; its supports *were* part of the stand itself.

35 And on the top of the stand *there was* a circular form half a cubit high, and on the top of the stand its stays and its borders *were* part of it.

36 And he engraved on the plates of its stays and on its borders, cherubim, lions and palm trees, according to the clear space on each, with wreaths *all* around.

37 *a*He made the ten stands like this: all of them had one casting, one measure and one form.

37 *a*2 Chr. 4:14

38 *a*And he made ten basins of bronze, one basin held forty baths; each basin *was* four cubits, *and* on each of the ten stands *was* one basin.

38 *a*Ex. 30:18; 2 Chr. 4:6

39 Then he set the stands, five on the right side of the house and five on the left side of the house; and he set the sea of cast metal on the right side of the house eastward toward the south.

40 Now Hiram made the basins and the shovels and the bowls. So Hiram finished doing all the work which he performed for King Solomon *in* the house of the LORD:

41 the two pillars and the two bowls of the capitals which *were* on the top of the *a*two pillars, and the two networks to cover the two

41 *a*1 Kin. 7:17, 18

7:23-26 This gigantic laver for the priests' washing was ten cubits (14½ ft.) across when measured from outside rim to outside rim, but the inside measurement was two handbreadths (6 in.) less (v. 26). This inside measurement was apparently used when calculating the circumference as 30 cubits (52½ ft.). It contained 2,000 *baths* (a bath was about 5.8 gallons).

7:27 *stands*. Bases for the movable lavers described in verses 38-39, each containing about 200 gallons of water.

bowls of the capitals which *were* on the top of the pillars;

42 ᵃ1 Kin. 7:20   **42** and the ᵃfour hundred pomegranates for the two networks, two rows of pomegranates for each network to cover the two bowls of the capitals which *were* on the tops of the pillars;

43 and the ten stands with the ten basins on the stands;

44 ᵃ1 Kin. 7:23, 25   **44** and ᵃthe one sea and the twelve oxen under the sea;

45 ᵃEx. 27:3; 2 Chr. 4:16   **45** and ᵃthe pails and the shovels and the bowls; even all these utensils which Hiram made for King Solomon *in* the house of the LORD *were* of polished bronze.

★46 ᵃ2 Chr. 4:17 ᵇGen. 33:17; Josh. 13:27 ᶜJosh. 3:16   **46** ᵃIn the plain of the Jordan the king cast them, in the clay ground between ᵇSuccoth and ᶜZarethan.

47 ᵃ1 Chr. 22:3, 14   **47** And Solomon left all the utensils *unweighed*, because *they were* too many; ᵃthe weight of the bronze could not be ascertained.

★48-50

48 ᵃEx. 30:1-3; 37:10-29; 2 Chr. 4:8 ᵇEx. 25:30   **48** And Solomon made all the furniture which *was in* the house of the LORD: ᵃthe golden altar and the golden table on which *was* the ᵇbread of the Presence;

49 ᵃEx. 25:31-38   **49** and the lampstands, five on the right side and five on the left, in front of the inner sanctuary, of pure gold; and ᵃthe flowers and the lamps and the tongs, of gold;

50 ᵃEx. 27:3; 2 Kin. 25:15   **50** and the cups and the snuffers and the bowls and the spoons and the ᵃfirepans, of pure gold; and the hinges both for the doors of the inner house, the most holy place, *and* for the doors of the house, *that is,* of the nave, of gold.

51 ᵃ2 Chr. 5:1 ᵇ2 Sam. 8:11; 1 Chr. 18:11; 2 Chr. 5:1   **51** ᵃThus all the work that King Solomon performed *in* the house of the LORD was finished. And ᵇSolomon brought in the things dedicated by his father David, the silver and the gold and

the utensils, *and* he put them in the treasuries of the house of the LORD.

5   Dedication of the Temple, 8:1-66

8 ᵃ Then Solomon assembled the elders of Israel and all ᵇthe heads of the tribes, the leaders of the fathers' *households* of the sons of Israel, to King Solomon in Jerusalem, ᶜto bring up the ark of the covenant of the LORD from ᵈthe city of David, which is Zion.

1 ᵃ2 Chr. 5:2-10 ᵇNum. 1:4; 7:2 ᶜ2 Sam. 6:12-17; 1 Chr. 15:25-29 ᵈ2 Sam. 5:7

2 And all the men of Israel assembled themselves to King Solomon at ᵃthe feast, in the month Ethanim, which is the seventh month.

★ 2 ᵃLev. 23:34; 1 Kin. 8:65; 2 Chr. 7:8-10

3 Then all the elders of Israel came, and ᵃthe priests took up the ark.

3 ᵃNum. 7:9; Deut. 31:9; Josh. 3:3, 6

4 And they brought up the ark of the LORD and ᵃthe tent of meeting and all the holy utensils, which were in the tent; and the priests and the Levites brought them up.

4 ᵃ1 Kin. 3:4; 2 Chr. 1:3

5 And King Solomon and all the congregation of Israel, who were assembled to him, ᵃwere with him before the ark, sacrificing so many sheep and oxen they could not be counted or numbered.

5 ᵃ2 Sam. 6:13; 2 Chr. 1:6

6 Then ᵃthe priests brought the ark of the covenant of the LORD ᵇto its place, into the inner sanctuary of the house, to the most holy place, ᶜunder the wings of the cherubim.

6 ᵃ1 Kin. 8:3 ᵇ1 Kin. 6:19 ᶜ1 Kin. 6:27

7 For the cherubim spread their wings over the place of the ark, and the cherubim made a covering over the ark and its poles from above.

★7-8

8 But ᵃthe poles were so long that the ends of the poles could be seen from the holy place

8 ᵃEx. 25:13-15; 37:4, 5

7:46 Excavations have shown that this area (*Succoth* was E. of the Jordan and just N. of the Jabbok River) was a center of metallurgy.

7:48-50 On the articles in the tabernacle similar to these, see notes on Exod. 25.

8:2 *the month Ethanim.* Tishri or Sept.-Oct. (see note on Exod. 12:2), 11 months after the com-

pletion of the Temple (6:38).

8:7-8 The Ark was placed lengthwise beneath the wings of the cherubim, and the staves extended beyond the area obscured by the veil but not so that they could be seen from the outside porch.

before the inner sanctuary, but they could not be seen outside; they are there to this day.

★ 9 ^aEx. 25:16, 21; Deut. 10:2-5; Heb. 9:4 ^bEx. 24:7, 8; 40:20; Deut. 4:13

9 ^aThere was nothing in the ark except the two tablets of stone which Moses put there at Horeb, where ^bthe LORD made a covenant with the sons of Israel, when they came out of the land of Egypt.

10 ^aEx. 40:34, 35; 2 Chr. 7:1, 2

10 And it came about when the priests came from the holy place, that ^athe cloud filled the house of the LORD,

11 so that the priests could not stand to minister because of the cloud, for the glory of the LORD filled the house of the LORD.

★12 ^a2 Chr. 6:1 ^bLev. 16:2; Ps. 18:11; 97:2

12 ^aThen Solomon said,
"The LORD has said that
^bHe would dwell in
the thick cloud.

13 ^a2 Sam. 7:13 ^bEx. 15:17; Ps. 132:14

13 "^aI have surely built Thee
a lofty house,
^bA place for Thy dwell-
ing forever."

14 ^a2 Sam. 6:18; 1 Kin. 8:55

14 Then the king faced about and ^ablessed all the assembly of Israel, while all the assembly of Israel was standing.

15 ^a1 Chr. 29:10, 20; Neh. 9:5; Luke 1:68 ^b2 Sam. 7:12, 13; 1 Chr. 22:10

15 And he said, "^aBlessed be the LORD, the God of Israel, ^bwho spoke with His mouth to my father David and has fulfilled *it* with His hand, saying,

16 ^a2 Sam. 7:4, 5; 1 Chr. 17:3-10; 2 Chr. 6:5 ^bDeut. 12:5, 11 ^c1 Sam. 16:1; 2 Sam. 7:8

16 '^aSince the day that I brought My people Israel from Egypt, I did not choose a city out of all the tribes of Israel *in which* to build a house that ^bMy name might be there, but ^cI chose David to be over My people Israel.'

17 ^a2 Sam. 7:2, 3; 1 Chr. 17:1, 2

17 "^aNow it was in the heart of my father David to build a house for the name of the LORD, the God of Israel.

18 'But the LORD said to my father David, 'Because it was in your heart to build a house for My name, you did well that it was in your heart.

19 ^a2 Sam. 7:5, 12, 13; 1 Kin. 5:3, 5; 1 Chr. 17:11, 12; 22:8-10

19 'Nevertheless you shall not build the house, but your son who shall be born to you, he shall build the house for My name.'

20 ^a1 Chr. 28:5, 6

20 "Now the LORD has fulfilled His word which He spoke; for ^aI have risen in place of my father David and sit on the throne of Israel, as the LORD promised, and have built the house for the name of the LORD, the God of Israel.

21 ^aDeut. 31:26; 1 Kin. 8:9

21 "And there I have set a place for the ark, ^ain which is the covenant of the LORD, which He made with our fathers when He brought them from the land of Egypt."

22 ^a1 Kin. 8:54; 2 Chr. 6:12 ^bEx. 9:33; Ezra 9:5

22 Then ^aSolomon stood before the altar of the LORD in the presence of all the assembly of Israel and ^bspread out his hands toward heaven.

★23-53

23 ^a1 Sam. 2:2; 2 Sam. 7:22 ^bDeut. 7:9; Neh. 1:5; 9:32; Dan. 9:4

23 And he said, "O LORD, the God of Israel, ^athere is no God like Thee in heaven above or on earth beneath, ^bwho art keeping covenant and showing lovingkindness to Thy servants who walk before Thee with all their heart,

24 who hast kept with Thy servant, my father David, that which Thou hast promised him; indeed, Thou hast spoken with

---

8:9 See Heb. 9:4, which refers to the contents of the Ark when it stood in the tabernacle and contained the law, Aaron's rod, and manna. Apparently the latter two items had been lost by this time. (Some think they were never placed *in* the Ark but alongside it; cf. Exod. 16:33-34; Num. 17:10.)

8:12 Solomon recognized the cloud as the symbol of God's presence and favor (Exod. 19:9; Lev. 16:2).

8:23-53 Solomon's great prayer (much longer than his previous sermon!) began with thanksgiving for the uniqueness (v. 23a) and faithfulness (vv. 23b-24, on *lovingkindness* see note on Hos. 2:19) of God's promise. He then asked

God for His continued presence and protection (vv. 25-30); for a continuous demonstration of His holiness (vv. 31-32); for forgiveness, restoration, and succor in times of distress upon confession of sin (vv. 33-40); for answered prayer for the *foreigner* (vv. 41-43; Heb., *nokri*, does not mean the settled alien, but the non-Israelite who came to worship); for victory in battle (vv. 44-45); and for return from captivity (vv. 46-53). Three different words for sin are used in verse 47: *sinned* (missed the mark); *committed iniquity* (deliberately disobeyed); and *acted wickedly* (failed to conform to a true standard).

Thy mouth and hast fulfilled it with Thy hand as it is this day.

25 "Now therefore, O LORD, the God of Israel, keep with Thy servant David my father that which Thou hast promised him, saying, 'ᵃYou shall not lack a man to sit on the throne of Israel, if only your sons take heed to their way to walk before Me as you have walked.'

26 "Now therefore, O God of Israel, let Thy word, I pray Thee, be confirmed ᵃwhich Thou hast spoken to Thy servant, my father David.

27 "But will God indeed dwell on the earth? Behold, ᵃheaven and the highest heaven cannot contain Thee, how much less this house which I have built!

28 "Yet have regard to the ᵃprayer of Thy servant and to his supplication, O LORD my God, to listen to the cry and to the prayer which Thy servant prays before Thee today;

29 ᵃthat Thine eyes may be open toward this house night and day, toward ᵇthe place of which Thou hast said, 'My name shall be there,' to listen to the prayer which Thy servant shall pray toward this place.

30 "And ᵃlisten to the supplication of Thy servant and of Thy people Israel, ᵇwhen they pray toward this place; hear Thou in heaven Thy dwelling place; hear and ᶜforgive.

31 "ᵃIf a man sins against his neighbor and is made to take an oath, and he comes and takes an oath before Thine altar in this house,

32 then hear Thou in heaven and act and judge Thy servants, ᵃcondemning the wicked by bringing his way on his own head and justifying the righteous by giving him according to his righteousness.

33 "ᵃWhen Thy people Israel are defeated before an enemy, because they have sinned against Thee, ᵇif they turn to Thee again and confess Thy name and pray and make supplication to Thee in this house,

34 then hear Thou in heaven, and forgive the sin of Thy people Israel, and bring them back to the land which Thou didst give to their fathers.

35 "ᵃWhen the heavens are shut up and there is no rain, because they have sinned against Thee, and they pray toward this place and confess Thy name and turn from their sin when Thou dost afflict them,

36 then hear Thou in heaven and forgive the sin of Thy servants and of Thy people Israel, ᵃindeed, teach them the good way in which they should walk. And ᵇsend rain on Thy land, which Thou hast given Thy people for an inheritance.

37 "ᵃIf there is famine in the land, if there is pestilence, if there is blight or mildew, locust or grasshopper, if their enemy besieges them in the land of their cities, whatever plague, whatever sickness there is,

38 whatever prayer or supplication is made by any man or by all Thy people Israel, each knowing the affliction of his own heart, and spreading his hands toward this house;

39 then hear Thou in heaven Thy dwelling place, and forgive and act and render to each according to all his ways, ᵃwhose heart Thou knowest, for ᵇThou alone dost know the hearts of all the sons of men,

40 that they may fear Thee all the days that they live in the land which Thou hast given to our fathers.

41 "Also concerning the foreigner who is not of Thy people Israel, when he comes from a far country for Thy name's sake

42 (for they will hear of Thy great name ᵃand Thy mighty hand, and of Thine outstretched arm); when he comes and prays toward this house,

43 hear Thou in heaven Thy dwelling place, and do according to all for which the foreigner calls

---

25 ᵃ1 Kin. 2:4

26 ᵃ2 Sam. 7:25

27 ᵃ2 Chr. 2:6; Ps. 139:7-16; Is. 66:1; Jer. 23:24; Acts 7:49

28 ᵃPhil. 4:6

29 ᵃ2 Chr. 7:15; Neh. 1:6 ᵇDeut. 12:11

30 ᵃNeh. 1:6 ᵇDan. 6:10 ᶜEx. 34:6, 7; Ps. 85:2; Dan. 9:9; 1 John 1:9

31 ᵃEx. 22:8-11

32 ᵃDeut. 25:1

33 ᵃLev. 26:17, 25; Deut. 28:25, 48 ᵇLev. 26:40-42

35 ᵃLev. 26:19; Deut. 11:16, 17; 2 Sam. 24:10-13

36 ᵃ1 Sam. 12:23; Ps. 5:8; 25:4, 5; 27:11; 86:11; 119:133; Jer. 6:16 ᵇ1 Kin. 18:1, 41-45; Jer. 14:22

37 ᵃLev. 26:16, 25, 26; Deut. 28:21-23, 38-42

39 ᵃ1 Sam. 2:3; 16:7 ᵇ1 Chr. 28:9; Ps. 11:4; Jer. 17:10; John 2:24, 25; Acts 1:24

42 ᵃEx. 13:3; Deut. 3:24

43 ᵃJosh. 4:23, 24; 1 Sam. 17:46; Ps. 67:2

to Thee, in order [a]that all the peoples of the earth may know Thy name, to fear Thee, as *do* Thy people Israel, and that they may know that this house which I have built is called by Thy name.

44 "When Thy people go out to battle against their enemy, by whatever way Thou shalt send them, and [a]they pray to the LORD toward the city which Thou hast chosen and the house which I have built for Thy name,

45 then hear in heaven their prayer and their supplication, and maintain their cause.

46 "When they sin against Thee (for [a]there is no man who does not sin) and Thou art angry with them and dost deliver them to an enemy, so that they take them away captive [b]to the land of the enemy, far off or near;

47 [a]if they take thought in the land where they have been taken captive, and repent and make supplication to Thee in the land of those who have taken them captive, saying, '[b]We have sinned and have committed iniquity, we have acted wickedly';

48 [a]if they return to Thee with all their heart and with all their soul in the land of their enemies who have taken them captive, and [b]pray to Thee toward their land which Thou hast given to their fathers, the city which Thou hast chosen, and the house which I have built for Thy name;

49 then hear their prayer and their supplication in heaven Thy dwelling place, and maintain their cause,

50 and forgive Thy people who have sinned against Thee and all their transgressions which they have transgressed against Thee, and [a]make them *objects of compassion* before those who have taken them captive, that they may have compassion on them

51 ([a]for they are Thy people and Thine inheritance which Thou hast brought forth from Egypt, [b]from the midst of the iron furnace),

52 [a]that Thine eyes may be open to the supplication of Thy servant and to the supplication of Thy people Israel, to listen to them whenever they call to Thee.

53 "For Thou hast separated them from all the peoples of the earth as Thine inheritance, [a]as Thou didst speak through Moses Thy servant, when Thou didst bring our fathers forth from Egypt, O Lord GOD."

54 [a]And it came about that when Solomon had finished praying this entire prayer and supplication to the LORD, [b]he arose from before the altar of the LORD, from kneeling on his knees with his hands spread toward heaven.

55 And he stood and [a]blessed all the assembly of Israel with a loud voice, saying,

56 "Blessed be the LORD, who has given rest to His people Israel, [a]according to all that He promised; [b]not one word has failed of all His good promise, which He promised through Moses His servant.

57 "May the LORD our God be with us, as He was with our fathers; [a]may He not leave us or forsake us,

58 that [a]He may incline our hearts to Himself, to walk in all His ways and to keep His commandments and His statutes and His ordinances, which He commanded our fathers.

59 "And may these words of mine, with which I have made supplication before the LORD, be near to the LORD our God day and night, that He may maintain the cause of His servant and the cause of His people Israel, as each day requires,

60 so [a]that all the peoples of the earth may know that [b]the LORD is God; there is no one else.

61 "[a]Let your heart therefore be wholly devoted to the LORD our God, to walk in His statutes and to keep His commandments, as at this day."

62 [a]Now the king and all Israel with him [b]offered sacrifice before the LORD.

---

44 [a]2 Chr. 14:11

46 [a]Ps. 130:3, 4; 143:2; Prov. 20:9; Eccl. 7:20; Rom. 3:23; 1 John 1:8-10 [b]Lev. 26:34-39; 2 Kin. 17:6, 18; 25:21

47 [a]Lev. 26:40-42; Neh. 9:2 [b]Ezra 9:6, 7; Neh. 1:6; Ps. 106:6; Dan. 9:5

48 [a]Deut. 4:29; 1 Sam. 7:3, 4; Neh. 1:9 [b]Dan. 6:10; Jon. 2:4

50 [a]2 Chr. 30:9; Ps. 106:46; Acts 7:10

51 [a]Ex. 32:11, 12; Deut. 9:26-29 [b]Deut. 4:20; Jer. 11:4

52 [a]1 Kin. 8:29

53 [a]Ex. 19:5, 6; Deut. 9:26-29

54 [a]2 Chr. 7:1 [b]2 Chr. 6:13

55 [a]Num. 6:23-26; 2 Sam. 6:18; 1 Kin. 8:14

56 [a]Deut. 12:10 [b]Josh. 21:45; 23:14, 15

57 [a]Deut. 31:6, 17; Josh. 1:5; 1 Sam. 12:22; Rom. 8:31; Heb. 13:5

58 [a]Ps. 119:36; Jer. 31:33

60 [a]Josh. 4:24; 1 Sam. 17:46; 1 Kin. 8:43; 2 Kin. 19:19 [b]Deut. 4:35; 1 Kin. 18:39; Jer. 10:10-12

61 [a]Deut. 18:13; 1 Kin. 11:4; 2 Kin. 20:3

62 [a]2 Chr. 7:4-10 [b]2 Sam. 6:17-19; Ezra 6:16, 17

★63 ᵃEzra
6:15-18;
Neh. 12:27

64 ᵃ2 Chr.
4:1

★65 ᵃLev.
23:34-42;
1 Kin. 8:2
ᵇNum. 34:8;
Josh. 13:5;
Judg. 3:3;
2 Kin. 14:25
ᶜGen. 15:18;
Ex. 23:31;
Num. 34:5;
Josh. 13:3

1 ᵃ2 Chr.
7:11 ᵇ1 Kin.
7:1, 2
ᶜ2 Chr. 8:6

2 ᵃ1 Kin.
3:5; 11:9;
2 Chr. 1:7

63 And Solomon offered for the sacrifice of peace offerings, which he offered to the LORD, 22,000 oxen and 120,000 sheep. ᵃSo the king and all the sons of Israel dedicated the house of the LORD.

64 On the same day the king consecrated the middle of the court that *was* before the house of the LORD, because there he offered the burnt offering and the grain offering and the fat of the peace offerings; for ᵃthe bronze altar that *was* before the LORD *was* too small to hold the burnt offering and the grain offering and the fat of the peace offerings.

65 So ᵃSolomon observed the feast at that time, and all Israel with him, a great assembly ᵇfrom the entrance of Hamath ᶜto the brook of Egypt, before the LORD our God, for seven days and seven *more* days, *even* fourteen days.

66 On the eighth day he sent the people away and they blessed the king. Then they went to their tents joyful and glad of heart for all the goodness that the LORD had shown to David His servant and to Israel His people.

D The Fame of Solomon
(2 Chron. 8:1-9:28),
9:1-10:29

1 *His covenant from God,*
9:1-9

9 ᵃNow it came about when Solomon had finished building the house of the LORD, and ᵇthe king's house, and ᶜall that Solomon desired to do,

2 that ᵃthe LORD appeared to Solomon a second time, as He had appeared to him at Gibeon.

3 ᵃ2 Kin.
20:5; Ps.
10:17; 34:17
ᵇ1 Kin. 8:29
ᶜDeut.
11:12; 2 Chr.
6:40

4 ᵃ1 Kin.
3:6, 14; 11:4,
6, 8; 2 Kin.
20:3; Ps.
128:1

5 ᵃ2 Sam.
7:12, 16;
1 Kin. 2:4;
6:12; 1 Chr.
22:10

★6-7

6 ᵃ2 Sam.
7:14-16;
1 Chr. 28:9;
Ps. 89:30ff.

7 ᵃLev.
18:24-29;
Deut. 4:26;
2 Kin. 17:23
ᵇJer. 7:4-14
ᶜDeut.
28:37; Ps.
44:14; Jer.
24:9

★ 8 ᵃ2 Kin.
25:9; 2 Chr.
36:19 ᵇDeut.
29:24-26;
2 Chr. 7:21;
Jer.
22:8, 9, 28

9 ᵃDeut.
29:25-28;
Jer. 2:10-13

3 And the LORD said to him, "ᵃI have heard your prayer and your supplication, which you have made before Me; I have consecrated this house which you have built ᵇby putting My name there forever, and ᶜMy eyes and My heart will be there perpetually.

4 "And as for you, ᵃif you will walk before Me as your father David walked, in integrity of heart and uprightness, doing according to all that I have commanded you *and* will keep My statutes and My ordinances,

5 then ᵃI will establish the throne of your kingdom over Israel forever, just as I promised to your father David, saying, 'You shall not lack a man on the throne of Israel.'

6 "ᵃBut if you or your sons shall indeed turn away from following Me, and shall not keep My commandments and My statutes which I have set before you and shall go and serve other gods and worship them,

7 ᵃthen I will cut off Israel from the land which I have given them, and ᵇthe house which I have consecrated for My name, I will cast out of My sight. So ᶜIsrael will become a proverb and a byword among all peoples.

8 "And this house will become ᵃa heap of ruins; everyone who passes by will be astonished and hiss and say, 'ᵇWhy has the LORD done thus to this land and to this house?'

9 "And they will say, 'ᵃBecause they forsook the LORD their God, who brought their fathers out of the land of Egypt, and adopted other gods and worshiped them and served them,

---

8:63 The large number of sacrifices was certainly appropriate for this magnificent occasion, and was easily financed out of Solomon's great wealth.

8:65 *from the entrance of Hamath.* The northern boundary of Israel, 14 miles NE. of Baalbek. *the brook of Egypt.* The wadi el-Arish (see note on 4:21). The dedication of the Temple lasted *seven days* and the Feast of Tabernacles another *seven days* (see 2 Chron.

7:9-10).

9:6-7 As far as the Temple and people are concerned, it is clearly stated that it will be destroyed and they will go into captivity if they are unfaithful; but the Davidic dynasty will not be set aside (Psalm 89:30-37).

9:8 *a heap of ruins.* The text is uncertain, though the meaning is that the revered Temple will be destroyed (cf. 2 Chron. 7:21).

therefore the LORD has brought all this adversity on them.' "

2 His gift to Hiram, 9:10-14

★10-14

10 ²Chr. 8:1 ᵇ1 Kin. 6:37, 38; 7:1; 9:1

10 ªAnd it came about ᵇat the end of twenty years in which Solomon had built the two houses, the house of the LORD and the king's house
11 (Hiram king of Tyre had supplied Solomon with cedar and cypress timber and gold according to all his desire), then King Solomon gave Hiram twenty cities in the land of Galilee.
12 So Hiram came out from Tyre to see the cities which Solomon had given him, and they did not please him.

13 ªJosh. 19:27

13 And he said, "What are these cities which you have given me, my brother?" So they were called the land of ªCabul to this day.

14 ª1 Kin. 9:11

14 ªAnd Hiram sent to the king 120 talents of gold.

3 His subjects, 9:15-25

★15 ª1 Kin. 5:13 ᵇ2 Sam. 5:9; 1 Kin. 9:24 ᶜJosh. 11:1; 19:36 ᵈJosh. 17:11 ᵉJudg. 1:29

15 Now this is the account of the forced labor which King Solomon ªlevied to build the house of the LORD, his own house, the ᵇMillo, the wall of Jerusalem, ᶜHazor, ᵈMegiddo, and ᵉGezer.

16 ªJosh. 16:10 ᵇ1 Kin. 3:1; 7:8

16 For Pharaoh king of Egypt had gone up and captured Gezer, and burned it with fire, and killed the ªCanaanites who lived in the city, and had ᵇgiven it as a dowry to his daughter, Solomon's wife.

17 ªJosh. 10:10; 16:3; 21:22; 2 Chr. 8:5

17 So Solomon rebuilt Gezer and the lower ªBeth-horon

18 ★18 ªJosh. 19:44

18 and ªBaalath and Tamar in the wilderness, in the land of Judah,

19 and all the storage cities which Solomon had, even ªthe cities for his chariots and the cities for ᵇhis horsemen, and ᶜall that it pleased Solomon to build in Jerusalem, in Lebanon, and in all the land under his rule.

19 ª1 Kin. 10:26; 2 Chr. 1:14 ᵇ1 Kin. 4:26 ᶜ1 Kin. 9:1

20 As for all the people who were left of the Amorites, the Hittites, the Perizzites, the Hivites and the Jebusites, who were not of the sons of Israel,

21 ªtheir descendants who were left after them in the land ᵇwhom the sons of Israel were unable to destroy utterly, ᶜfrom them Solomon levied ᵈforced laborers, even to this day.

21 ªJudg. 1:21-29; 3:1 ᵇJosh. 15:63; 17:12, 13 ᶜJudg. 1:28, 35 ᵈGen. 9:25, 26; Ezra 2:55, 58

22 But Solomon ªdid not make slaves of the sons of Israel; for they were men of war, his servants, his princes, his captains, his chariot commanders, and his horsemen.

22 ªLev. 25:39

23 These were the ªchief officers who were over Solomon's work, five hundred and fifty, ᵇwho ruled over the people doing the work.

23 ª2 Chr. 8:10 ᵇ1 Kin. 5:16

24 As soon as ªPharaoh's daughter came up from the city of David to her house which Solomon had built for her, ᵇthen he built the Millo.

★24 ª1 Kin. 3:1; 7:8 ᵇ2 Sam. 5:9; 1 Kin. 9:15; 11:27; 2 Chr. 32:5

25 Now ªthree times in a year Solomon offered burnt offerings and peace offerings on the altar which he built to the LORD, burning incense with them on the altar which was before the LORD. So he finished the house.

★25 ªEx. 23:14-17; Deut. 16:16

4 His navy, 9:26-28

26 King Solomon also built ªfleet of ships in ᵇEzion-geber,

★26 ª1 Kin. 22:48 ᵇNum. 33:35; Deut. 2:8; 1 Kin. 22:48

9:10-14 Solomon's treasury being depleted, he gave Hiram 20 cities in northern Galilee, which area Hiram called Cabul (understood by some to mean "worthless" or "good for nothing"). Evidently Solomon later regained possession of the region (2 Chron. 8:2). Hiram sent Solomon about 144,000 ounces of gold.
9:15 Megiddo. An important fortification controlling a pass between the plains of Esdraelon and Sharon and the site of the future battle of Armageddon (see note on Rev. 16:16).

9:18 Tamar. On the road from Hebron to Elath. Some identify it as Tadmor (2 Chron. 8:4), the city later known as Palmyra.
9:24 Millo. A fortress incorporated into the wall of Jerusalem.
9:25 three times in a year. I.e., the feasts of Unleavened Bread, Pentecost, and Tabernacles.
9:26 Ezion-geber is between modern Elath and Aqaba on the N. end of the E. arm of the Red Sea.

which is near Eloth on the shore of the Red Sea, in the land of Edom.

27ª1 Kin. 5:6, 9; 10:11

27 ªAnd Hiram sent his servants with the fleet, sailors who knew the sea, along with the servants of Solomon.

★28 ª1 Chr. 29:4; 2 Chr. 8:18

28 And they went to ªOphir, and took four hundred and twenty talents of gold from there, and brought it to King Solomon.

5 His visit from the queen of Sheba, 10:1-13

★ 1 ª2 Chr. 9:1; Matt. 12:42; Luke 11:31 ᵇGen. 10:7, 28; Ps. 72:10, 15 ᶜJudg. 14:12-14; Ps. 49:4

10 Now when the ªqueen of ᵇSheba heard about the fame of Solomon concerning the name of the LORD, she came ᶜto test him with difficult questions.

2 ª1 Kin. 10:10

2 So she came to Jerusalem with a very large retinue, with camels ªcarrying spices and very much gold and precious stones. When she came to Solomon, she spoke with him about all that was in her heart.

3 And Solomon answered all her questions; nothing was hidden from the king which he did not explain to her.

4 When the queen of Sheba perceived all the wisdom of Solomon, the house that he had built,

★ 5

5 the food of his table, the seating of his servants, the attendance of his waiters and their attire, his cupbearers, and his stairway by which he went up to the house of the LORD, there was no more spirit in her.

6 Then she said to the king, "It was a true report which I heard in my own land about your words and your wisdom.

7 "Nevertheless I did not believe the reports, until I came and my eyes had seen it. And behold,

the half was not told me. You exceed in wisdom and prosperity the report which I heard.

8 "How ªblessed are your men, how blessed are these your servants who stand before you continually and hear your wisdom.

8 ªProv. 8:34

9 "ªBlessed be the LORD your God who delighted in you to set you on the throne of Israel; ᵇbecause the LORD loved Israel forever, therefore He made you king, ᶜto do justice and righteousness."

9 ª1 Kin. 5:7 ᵇ1 Chr. 17:22; 2 Chr. 2:11 ᶜ2 Sam. 8:15; 23:3; Ps. 72:2

10 And ªshe gave the king a hundred and twenty talents of gold, and a very great amount of spices and precious stones. Never again did such abundance of spices come in as that which the queen of Sheba gave King Solomon.

★10-11

10 ª1 Kin. 10:2

11 ªAnd also the ships of Hiram, which brought gold from Ophir, brought in from Ophir a very great number of almug trees and precious stones.

11 ª1 Kin. 9:27, 28; Job 22:24

12 And ªthe king made of the almug trees supports for the house of the LORD and for the king's house, also lyres and harps for the singers; such almug trees have not come in again, nor have they been seen to this day.

12 ª2 Chr. 9:11

13 And King Solomon gave to the queen of Sheba all her desire which she requested, besides what he gave her according to his royal bounty. Then she turned and went to her own land together with her servants.

6 His wealth, 10:14-29

14 ªNow the weight of gold which came in to Solomon in one year was 666 talents of gold,

★14 ª2 Chr. 9:13-28

9:28 *Ophir* has been variously identified as S. Arabia, E. Africa, or India. The gold amounted to about 504,000 ounces.

10:1 *the queen of Sheba.* Ruler of the Sabeans in the southern part of Arabia. She travelled 1,200 miles on camelback to visit King Solomon, probably because his presence on the Gulf of Aqaba threatened the caravan routes which made S. Arabia rich.

10:5 *his stairway.* A reference either to the burnt

offering or to the stairway leading to the Temple. *there was no more spirit in her* because she discovered she could not get the best of Solomon (cf. Josh. 5:1).

10:10-11 *a hundred and twenty talents.* About 144,000 ounces. *almug* (or algum). Probably the red sandalwood tree, which grows up to 20 feet in height and is still used in making musical instruments.

10:14 *666 talents.* Nearly 800,000 ounces.

15 *a*2 Chr. 9:14

15 besides *that* from the traders and the wares of the merchants and all the kings of the *a*Arabs and the governors of the country.

★**16** *a*1 Kin. 14:26-28; 2 Chr. 12:9, 10

16 And *a*King Solomon made 200 large shields of beaten gold, using 600 *shekels of* gold on each large shield.

★**17** *a*1 Kin. 14:26
*b*1 Kin. 7:2

17 And *he made* *a*300 shields of beaten gold, using three minas of gold on each shield, and *b*the king put them in the house of the forest of Lebanon.

18 *a*1 Kin. 10:22; 2 Chr. 9:17; Ps. 45:8

18 Moreover, the king made a great throne of *a*ivory and overlaid it with refined gold.

19 There *were* six steps to the throne and a round top to the throne at its rear, and arms on each side of the seat, and two lions standing beside the arms.

20 And twelve lions were standing there on the six steps on the one side and on the other; nothing like *it* was made for any other kingdom.

★**21**

21 And all King Solomon's drinking vessels *were* of gold, and all the vessels of the house of the forest of Lebanon *were* of pure gold. None was of silver; it was not considered valuable in the days of Solomon.

★**22** *a*1 Kin. 9:26-28; 22:48; 2 Chr. 20:36

22 For *a*the king had at sea the ships of Tarshish with the ships of Hiram; once every three years the ships of Tarshish came bringing gold and silver, ivory and apes and peacocks.

23 *a*1 Kin. 3:12, 13; 4:30

23 *a*So King Solomon became greater than all the kings of the earth in riches and in wisdom.

24 *a*1 Kin. 3:9, 12, 28

24 And all the earth was seeking the presence of Solomon, *a*to hear his wisdom which God had put in his heart.

25 *a*Ps. 68:29

25 And *a*they brought every man his gift, articles of silver and gold, garments, weapons, spices,

horses, and mules, so much year by year.

26 *a*1 Kin. 4:26; 2 Chr. 1:14-17; 9:25
*b*1 Kin. 9:19

26 *a*Now Solomon gathered chariots and horsemen; and he had 1,400 chariots and 12,000 horsemen, and he stationed them in the *b*chariot cities and with the king in Jerusalem.

27 *a*Deut. 17:17; 2 Chr. 1:15

27 *a*And the king made silver *as common* as stones in Jerusalem, and he made cedars as plentiful as sycamore trees that are in the lowland.

28 *a*Deut. 17:16; 2 Chr. 1:16; 9:28

28 *a*Also Solomon's import of horses was from Egypt and Kue, and the king's merchants procured *them* from Kue for a price.

★**29** *a*2 Kin. 7:6, 7

29 And a chariot was imported from Egypt for 600 *shekels* of silver, and a horse for 150; and by the same means they exported them *a*to all the kings of the Hittites and to the kings of the Arameans.

E The Downfall of Solomon, 11:1-43

1 The reasons, 11:1-8

★ **1-4**

1 *a*Deut. 17:17; Neh. 13:23-27

11 Now *a*King Solomon loved many foreign women along with the daughter of Pharaoh: Moabite, Ammonite, Edomite, Sidonian, and Hittite women,

2 *a*Ex. 23:31-33; 34:12-16; Deut. 7:3

2 from the nations concerning which the LORD had said to the sons of Israel, "*a*You shall not associate with them, neither shall they associate with you, for they will surely turn your heart away after their gods." Solomon held fast to these in love.

3 *a*2 Sam. 5:13-16

3 *a*And he had seven hundred wives, princesses, and three hundred concubines, and his wives turned his heart away.

4 *a*1 Kin. 9:4

4 For it came about when Solomon was old, his wives turned his heart away after other gods; and *a*his heart was not

---

10:16 *large shields.* Each of these shields contained about 15 lbs. of gold.
10:17 *shields.* A smaller shield, which weighed about 5 lbs.
10:21 *the house of the forest of Lebanon.* See note on 7:1.
10:22 *ships of Tarshish.* Especially large and sea-

worthy ships. See note on Isa. 2:16.
10:29 An imported *chariot* cost 15 lbs. of silver; a *horse*, 3¾ lbs.
11:1-4 Solomon was obliged to allow his foreign wives to worship their own gods, a contagion which ultimately affected the king himself.

wholly devoted to the LORD his God, as the heart of David his father *had been.*

★ 5-7

5 a Judg. 2:13; 10:6; 1 Sam. 7:3, 4 **b**1 Kin. 11:7

5 For Solomon went after **a**Ashtoreth the goddess of the Sidonians and after **b**Milcom the detestable idol of the Ammonites.

6 And Solomon did what was evil in the sight of the LORD, and did not follow the LORD fully, as David his father *had done.*

7 a Num. 21:29; Judg. 11:24; 2 Kin. 23:13 **b**Lev. 20:2-5; 2 Kin. 23:10; Acts 7:43

7 Then Solomon built a high place for **a**Chemosh the detestable idol of Moab, on the mountain which is east of Jerusalem, and for **b**Molech the detestable idol of the sons of Ammon.

8 Thus also he did for all his foreign wives, who burned incense and sacrificed to their gods.

2 The warning, 11:9-13

9 a Ps. 90:7 **b**1 Kin. 11:2, 4 **c**1 Kin. 3:5; 9:2

9 Now **a**the LORD was angry with Solomon **b**because his heart was turned away from the LORD, the God of Israel, **c**who had appeared to him twice,

10 a1 Kin. 6:12; 9:6, 7

10 and **a**had commanded him concerning this thing, that he should not go after other gods; but he did not observe what the LORD had commanded.

11 a1 Sam. 2:30; 1 Kin. 11:29-31; 12:15, 16, 20; 2 Kin. 17:15, 21

11 So the LORD said to Solomon, "Because you have done this, and you have not kept My covenant and My statutes, which I have commanded you, **a**I will surely tear the kingdom from you, and will give it to your servant.

12 "Nevertheless I will not do it in your days for the sake of your father David, *but* I will tear it out of the hand of your son.

★13 a2 Sam. 7:15; 1 Chr. 17:13; Ps. 89:33 **b**1 Kin. 11:32, 36; 12:20 **c**1 Kin. 8:29

13 "However, **a**I will not tear away all the kingdom, but **b**I will give one tribe to your son for the sake of My servant David and

cfor the sake of Jerusalem which I have chosen."

3 The adversaries, 11:14-28

14 Then the LORD raised up an adversary to Solomon, Hadad the Edomite; he was of the royal line in Edom.

★15 a2 Sam. 8:14; 1 Chr. 18:12, 13 **b**Deut. 20:13

15 For it came about, **a**when David was in Edom, and Joab the commander of the army had gone up to bury the slain, and had **b**struck down every male in Edom

16 (for Joab and all Israel stayed there six months, until he had cut off every male in Edom),

17 that Hadad fled to Egypt, he and certain Edomites of his father's servants with him, while Hadad *was* a young boy.

18 a Num. 10:12; Deut. 1:1

18 And they arose from Midian and came to **a**Paran; and they took men with them from Paran and came to Egypt, to Pharaoh king of Egypt, who gave him a house and assigned him food and gave him land.

19 Now Hadad found great favor before Pharaoh, so that he gave him in marriage the sister of his own wife, the sister of Tahpenes the queen.

20 And the sister of Tahpenes bore his son Genubath, whom Tahpenes weaned in Pharaoh's house; and Genubath was in Pharaoh's house among the sons of Pharaoh.

21 a1 Kin. 2:10

21 But **a**when Hadad heard in Egypt that David slept with his fathers, and that Joab the commander of the army was dead, Hadad said to Pharaoh, "Send me away, that I may go to my own country."

22 Then Pharaoh said to him, "But what have you lacked with me, that behold, you are seeking to go to your own country?" And

---

11:5-7 Concerning *Ashtoreth* see notes on Judg. 2:13 and Hos. 2:13. Concerning *Milcom* and *Chemosh* see note on Judg. 11:24. On *Molech* see note on Lev. 18:21. *the mountain which is east of Jerusalem.* The Mount of Olives.

11:13 *one tribe.* I.e., Judah, to which Benjamin was indissolubly connected, since Jerusalem

straddled the territory of both tribes (cf. 11:32 and 12:21). Simeon, the tribe S. of Judah, had apparently migrated N. and was counted with the 10 northern tribes (cf. 1 Chron. 12:23-25; 2 Chron. 15:9; 34:6).

11:15 See 2 Sam. 8:14.

he answered, "Nothing; nevertheless you must surely let me go."

23 ªGod also raised up *another* adversary to him, Rezon the son of Eliada, who had fled from his lord ᵇHadadezer king of Zobah.

24 And he gathered men to himself and became leader of a marauding band, ªafter David slew them of *Zobah;* and they went to Damascus and stayed there, and reigned in Damascus.

25 So he was an adversary to Israel all the days of Solomon, along with the evil that Hadad *did;* and he abhorred Israel and reigned over Aram.

26 Then ªJeroboam the son of Nebat, an Ephraimite of Zeredah, Solomon's servant, whose mother's name was Zeruah, a widow, ᵇalso rebelled against the king.

27 Now this was the reason why he rebelled against the king: ªSolomon built the Millo, *and* closed up the breach of the city of his father David.

28 Now the man Jeroboam was a valiant warrior, and when ªSolomon saw that the young man was industrious, he appointed him over all the forced labor of the house of Joseph.

4 The prophecy of Ahijah, 11:29-40

29 And it came about at that time, when Jeroboam went out of Jerusalem, that ªthe prophet Ahijah the Shilonite found him on the road. Now Ahijah had clothed himself with a new cloak; and both of them were alone in the field.

30 Then ªAhijah took hold of the new cloak which was on him, and tore it into twelve pieces.

31 And he said to Jeroboam, "Take for yourself ten pieces; for thus says the Lᴏʀᴅ, the God of Is-

rael, ʰBehold, ªI will tear the kingdom out of the hand of Solomon and give you ten tribes

32 (ªbut he will have one tribe, for the sake of My servant David and for the sake of Jerusalem, ᵇthe city which I have chosen from all the tribes of Israel),

33 because they have forsaken Me, and ªhave worshiped Ashtoreth the goddess of the Sidonians, ᵇChemosh the god of Moab, and Milcom the god of the sons of Ammon; and they have not walked in My ways, doing what is right in My sight and *observing* My statutes and My ordinances, as his father David *did.*

34 'Nevertheless I will not take the whole kingdom out of his hand, but I will make him ruler all the days of his life, for the sake of My servant David whom I chose, who observed My commandments and My statutes;

35 but ªI will take the kingdom from his son's hand and give it to you, *even* ten tribes.

36 'But ªto his son I will give one tribe, ᵇthat My servant David may have a lamp always before Me in Jerusalem, ᶜthe city where I have chosen for Myself to put My name.

37 'And I will take you, and you shall reign over whatever you desire, and you shall be king over Israel.

38 'Then it will be, that if you listen to all that I command you and walk in My ways, and do what is right in My sight by observing My statutes and My commandments, as My servant David did, then ªI will be with you and ᵇbuild you an enduring house as I built for David, and I will give Israel to you.

39 'Thus I will afflict the descendants of David for this, but not always.' "

11:25 While the S. part of Solomon's kingdom was taken by Hadad, Rezon whittled away at it in the N.

11:27-28 On the building of *Millo* see note on 9:24. *the forced labor.* Labor which the Israel-

ites performed part of each year.

11:36 *a lamp.* I.e., posterity. David's line would not be eradicated, though his descendants would be afflicted (v. 39).

Margin references:

23 ª1 Kin. 11:14
ᵇ2 Sam. 8:3; 10:16

24 ª2 Sam. 10:8, 18

★25

26 ª1 Kin. 11:11, 28; 12:2, 20; 2 Chr. 13:6
ᵇ2 Sam. 20:21

★27-28

27 ª1 Kin. 9:15, 24

28 ªProv. 22:29

29 ª1 Kin. 12:15; 14:2; 2 Chr. 9:29

30 ª1 Sam. 15:27, 28

31 ª1 Kin. 11:11, 12

32 ª1 Kin. 11:13; 12:21
ᵇ1 Kin. 11:13; 14:21

33 ª1 Sam. 7:3; 1 Kin. 11:5-8
ᵇNum. 21:29; Jer. 48:7, 13

35 ª1 Kin. 11:12; 12:16, 17

★36 ª1 Kin. 11:13
ᵇ1 Kin. 15:4; 2 Kin. 8:19; Ps. 132:17
ᶜ1 Kin. 11:13

38 ªDeut. 31:8; Josh. 1:5 ᵇ2 Sam. 7:11, 27

40 Solomon sought therefore to put Jeroboam to death; but Jeroboam arose and fled to Egypt to ªShishak king of Egypt, and he was in Egypt until the death of Solomon.

★40 ª1 Kin. 14:25; 2 Chr. 12:2-9

5 The death of Solomon, 11:41-43

41 ªNow the rest of the acts of Solomon and whatever he did, and his wisdom, are they not written in the book of the acts of Solomon?

41 ª2 Chr. 9:29

42 Thus ªthe time that Solomon reigned in Jerusalem over all Israel was forty years.

42 ª2 Chr. 9:30

43 And Solomon ªslept with his fathers and was buried in the city of his father David, and his son ᵇRehoboam reigned in his place.

43 ª1 Kin. 2:10; 2 Chr. 9:31 ᵇ1 Kin. 14:21; Matt. 1:7

II THE DIVIDED KINGDOM, 12:1-22:53
A The Rupture in the Kingdom, 12:1-24
1 The request of the northern tribes, 12:1-4

12 ªThen Rehoboam went to Shechem, for all Israel had come to ᵇShechem to make him king.

★ 1 ª2 Chr. 10:1 ᵇJudg. 9:6

2 Now it came about ªwhen Jeroboam the son of Nebat heard of it, that he was living in Egypt (for he was yet in Egypt, where he had fled from the presence of King Solomon).

★ 2 ª1 Kin. 11:26, 40

3 Then they sent and called him, and Jeroboam and all the assembly of Israel came and spoke to Rehoboam, saying,

4 "ªYour father made our yoke hard; therefore lighten the hard service of your father and his heavy yoke which he put on us, and we will serve you."

4 ª1 Sam. 8:11-18; 1 Kin. 4:7, 21-25; 9:15

2 The reply of Rehoboam, 12:5-15

5 Then he said to them, "ªDepart for three days, then return to me." So the people departed.

5 ª1 Kin. 12:12

6 And King Rehoboam ªconsulted with the elders who had served his father Solomon while he was still alive, saying, "How do you counsel *me* to answer this people?"

6 ª1 Kin. 4:1-6; Job 12:12; 32:7

7 Then they spoke to him, saying, "ªIf you will be a servant to this people today, will serve them, grant them their petition, and speak good words to them, then they will be your servants forever."

7 ª2 Chr. 10:7; Prov. 15:1

8 But he forsook the counsel of the elders which they had given him, and consulted with the young men who grew up with him and served him.

9 So he said to them, "What counsel do you give that we may answer this people who have spoken to me, saying, 'Lighten the yoke which your father put on us'?"

10 And the young men who grew up with him spoke to him, saying, "Thus you shall say to this people who spoke to you, saying, 'Your father made our yoke heavy, now you make it lighter for us!' But you shall speak to them, 'My little finger is thicker than my father's loins!

★10

11 'Whereas my father loaded you with a heavy yoke, I will add to your yoke; my father disciplined you with whips, but I will discipline you with scorpions.' "

★11

12 Then Jeroboam and all the people came to Rehoboam on the third day as the king had directed, saying, "ªReturn to me on the third day."

12 ª1 Kin. 12:5

11:40 *Shishak.* Sheshonk I, who reigned 945-924 and gave political asylum to Jeroboam. Later (925) he invaded Palestine, exacting heavy tribute from Judah (14:25-26).

12:1 *Shechem.* First mentioned in Gen. 12:6, it was in the territory of Ephraim, near present-day Nablus (see also Judg. 9:1).

12:2 *Jeroboam.* See 11:26-40. He became the

spokesman to present the grievances of the people to the king.

12:10 *young men.* About 40 years old (cf. 14:21). *My little finger . . .* A proverbial expression meaning, "My power will be greater than my father's."

12:11 *scorpions.* Whips with barbed points or bits of metal attached.

13 And the king answered the people harshly, for he forsook the advice of the elders which they had given him,

14 ªEx. 1:13, 14; 5:5-9, 16-18

14 and he spoke to them according to the advice of the young men, saying, "ªMy father made your yoke heavy, but I will add to your yoke; my father disciplined you with whips, but I will discipline you with scorpions."

★15 ªDeut. 2:30; Judg. 14:4; 1 Kin. 12:24; 2 Chr. 10:15 ᵇ1 Kin. 11:11, 31

15 So the king did not listen to the people; ªfor it was a turn *of events* from the LORD, ᵇthat He might establish His word, which the LORD spoke through Ahijah the Shilonite to Jeroboam the son of Nebat.

3 The revolt of the northern tribes, 12:16-24

16 ª2 Sam. 20:1

16 When all Israel *saw* that the king did not listen to them, the people answered the king, saying,

"What portion do we
have in David?
We have no inheritance
in the son of Jesse;
ªTo your tents, O Israel!
Now look after your
own house, David!"

So Israel departed to their tents.

17 ª1 Kin. 11:13, 36

17 But ªas for the sons of Israel who lived in the cities of Judah, Rehoboam reigned over them.

★18 ª2 Sam. 20:24; 1 Kin. 4:6; 5:14

18 Then King Rehoboam sent ªAdoram, who was over the forced labor, and all Israel stoned him to death. And King Rehoboam made haste to mount his chariot to flee to Jerusalem.

19 ª2 Kin. 17:21

19 ªSo Israel has been in rebellion against the house of David to this day.

★20 ª1 Kin. 11:13, 32, 36

20 And it came about when all Israel heard that Jeroboam had returned, that they sent and called him to the assembly and made him king over all Israel. ªNone but the tribe of Judah followed the house of David.

21 ª2 Chr. 11:1

21 ªNow when Rehoboam had come to Jerusalem, he assembled all the house of Judah and the tribe of Benjamin, 180,000 chosen men who were warriors, to fight against the house of Israel to restore the kingdom to Rehoboam the son of Solomon.

22 ª2 Chr. 11:2; 12:5-7

22 But the word of God came to ªShemaiah the man of God, saying,

23 ª1 Kin. 12:17

23 "Speak to Rehoboam the son of Solomon, king of Judah, and to all the house of Judah and Benjamin and to the ªrest of the people, saying,

24 ª1 Kin. 12:15

24 'Thus says the LORD, "You must not go up and fight against your relatives the sons of Israel; return every man to his house, ªfor this thing has come from Me." ' " So they listened to the word of the LORD, and returned and went *their way* according to the word of the LORD.

B The Reign of Jeroboam in Israel (931-910), 12:25-14:20

1 Establishing religious centers and worship, 12:25-33

★25 ªGen. 12:6; Judg. 9:45-49 ᵇGen. 32:30, 31; Judg. 8:8, 17

25 Then ªJeroboam built Shechem in the hill country of Ephraim, and lived there. And he went out from there and built ᵇPenuel.

26 And Jeroboam said in his heart, "Now the kingdom will return to the house of David.

27 ªDeut. 12:5-7, 14

27 "ªIf this people go up to offer sacrifices in the house of the LORD at Jerusalem, then the heart of this people will return to their lord, *even* to Rehoboam king of Judah; and they will kill me and return to Rehoboam king of Judah."

12:15 The Lord was using these events to accomplish His will (cf. 11:11, 30).

12:18 Rehoboam, not realizing that the break was final, sent the worst possible representative, *Adoram* (the Adoniram of 4:6; 5:14), who had been in charge of the forced labor.

12:20 *None but the tribe of Judah.* See note on 11:13.

12:25 *Penuel.* Located E. of the Jordan, it served to keep those tribes who lived in that area from being invaded by Rehoboam or Shishak (14:25).

★28 a2 Kin.
10:29; 17:16;
Hos. 8:4-7
bHos. 10:5
cEx. 32:4, 8

28 So the king consulted, and amade two golden bcalves, and he said to them, "It is too much for you to go up to Jerusalem; cbehold your gods, O Israel, that brought you up from the land of Egypt."

★29 aHos.
10:5 bGen.
28:19 cJudg.
18:26-31
30 a1 Kin.
13:34; 2 Kin.
17:21
★31 a1 Kin.
13:32
b1 Kin.
13:33; 2 Kin.
17:32; 2 Chr.
11:15; 13:9

29 And he set aone in bBethel, and the other he put in cDan.

30 Now athis thing became a sin, for the people went to worship before the one as far as Dan.

31 And ahe made houses on high places, and bmade priests from among all the people who were not of the sons of Levi.

★32 aLev.
23:33, 34;
Num. 29:12;
1 Kin. 8:2, 5
bAmos 7:10-
13

32 And Jeroboam instituted a feast in the eighth month on the fifteenth day of the month, alike the feast which is in Judah, and he went up to the altar; thus he did in Bethel, sacrificing to the calves which he had made. And he stationed in Bethel bthe priests of the high places which he had made.

33 aNum.
15:39
b1 Kin. 13:1

33 Then he went up to the altar which he had made in Bethel on the fifteenth day in the eighth month, even in the month which he had adevised in his own heart; and he instituted a feast for the sons of Israel, and went up to the altar bto burn incense.

2 Encountering the man of God, 13:1-32

1 a1 Kin.
12:22; 2 Kin.
23:17
b1 Kin.
12:33

13 Now behold, there came aa man of God from Judah to Bethel by the word of the Lord, while Jeroboam was standing by the altar bto burn incense.

★ 2 a1 Kin.
13:32
b2 Kin.
23:15, 16

2 And ahe cried against the altar by the word of the Lord, and said, "O altar, altar, thus says the Lord, 'Behold, a son shall be born to the house of David, bJosiah by name; and on you he shall sacrifice the priests of the high places

who burn incense on you, and human bones shall be burned on you.' "

3 Then he gave a sign the same day, saying, "aThis is the sign which the Lord has spoken, 'Behold, the altar shall be split apart and the ashes which are on it shall be poured out.' "

3 aEx. 4:1-
5; Judg.
6:17; Is.
38:7; John
2:18; 1 Cor.
1:22

4 Now it came about when the king heard the saying of the man of God, which he cried against the altar in Bethel, that Jeroboam stretched out his hand from the altar, saying, "Seize him." But his hand which he stretched out against him dried up, so that he could not draw it back to himself.

★ 4

5 The altar also was split apart and the ashes were poured out from the altar, according to the sign which the man of God had given by the word of the Lord.

6 And the king answered and said to the man of God, "Please aentreat the Lord your God, and pray for me, that my hand may be restored to me." So bthe man of God entreated the Lord, and the king's hand was restored to him, and it became as it was before.

6 aEx. 8:8,
28; 9:28;
10:17; Acts
8:24; James
5:16 bLuke
6:27, 28

7 Then the king said to the man of God, "Come home with me and refresh yourself, and aI will give you a reward."

7 a1 Sam.
9:7, 8; 2 Kin.
5:15

8 But the man of God said to the king, "aIf you were to give me half your house I would not go with you, nor would I eat bread or drink water in this place.

8 aNum.
22:18; 24:13;
1 Kin. 13:16,
17

9 "For so it was commanded me by the word of the Lord, saying, 'You shall eat no bread, nor drink water, nor return by the way which you came.' "

12:28 two golden calves. Perhaps the people at first did not actually worship the calves, but thought of God as invisibly riding on them.

12:29 Jeroboam cleverly placed one golden calf in Bethel, which was on the road to Jerusalem and 11 miles N., and the other calf in the northernmost part of his kingdom, Dan.

12:31 Jeroboam also infiltrated the priesthood

with non-Levites.

12:32 the feast. Probably Tabernacles, observed one month late (Lev. 23:34).

13:2 This remarkable prediction, specifically naming Josiah, was fulfilled about 300 years later (2 Kings 23:15-20).

13:4 dried up. Stiffened, paralyzed.

10 So he went another way, and did not return by the way which he came to Bethel.

11 Now [a]an old prophet was living in Bethel; and his sons came and told him all the deeds which the man of God had done that day in Bethel; the words which he had spoken to the king, these also they related to their father.

12 And their father said to them, "Which way did he go?" Now his sons had seen the way which the man of God who came from Judah had gone.

13 Then he said to his sons, "Saddle the donkey for me." So they saddled the donkey for him and he rode away on it.

14 So he went after the man of God and found him sitting under an oak; and he said to him, "Are you the man of God who came from Judah?" And he said, "I am."

15 Then he said to him, "Come home with me and eat bread."

16 And he said, "[a]I cannot return with you, nor go with you, nor will I eat bread or drink water with you in this place.

17 "For a command *came* to me [a]by the word of the LORD, 'You shall eat no bread, nor drink water there; do not return by going the way which you came.'"

18 And he said to him, "[a]I also am a prophet like you, and [b]an angel spoke to me by the word of the LORD, saying, 'Bring him back with you to your house, that he may eat bread and drink water.'" *But* [c]he lied to him.

19 So he went back with him, and ate bread in his house and drank water.

20 Now it came about, as they were sitting down at the table, that the word of the LORD came to the prophet who had brought him back;

21 and he cried to the man of God who came from Judah, saying, "Thus says the LORD, 'Because you have disobeyed the command of the LORD, and have not observed the commandment which the LORD your God commanded you,

22 but have returned and eaten bread and drunk water in the place of which He said to you, "Eat no bread and drink no water"; your body shall not come to the grave of your fathers.'"

23 And it came about after he had eaten bread and after he had drunk, that he saddled the donkey for him, for the prophet whom he had brought back.

24 Now when he had gone, [a]a lion met him on the way and killed him, and his body was thrown on the road, with the donkey standing beside it; the lion also was standing beside the body.

25 And behold, men passed by and saw the body thrown on the road, and the lion standing beside the body; so they came and told *it* in the city where [a]the old prophet lived.

26 Now when the prophet who brought him back from the way heard *it*, he said, "It is the man of God, who disobeyed the command of the LORD; therefore the LORD has given him to the lion, which has torn him and killed him, according to the word of the LORD which He spoke to him."

27 Then he spoke to his sons, saying, "Saddle the donkey for me." And they saddled *it.*

28 And he went and found his body thrown on the road with the donkey and the lion standing beside the body; the lion had not eaten the body nor torn the donkey.

29 So the prophet took up the body of the man of God and laid

---

11 [a]1 Kin. 13:25; 2 Kin. 23:18

16 [a]1 Kin. 13:8, 9

17 [a]1 Kin. 20:35

★**18-22**

18 [a]Matt. 7:15; 1 John 4:1 [b]Gal. 1:8 [c]Prov. 12:19, 22; 19:5; Jer. 29:31, 32; Ezek. 13:8, 9; 1 Tim. 4:1, 2

24 [a]1 Kin. 20:36

25 [a]1 Kin. 13:11

13:18-22 Like Balaam, this prophet had true prophetic gifts but was guilty of worldly self-promotion. So he lied in order to get the prophet from Judah to stay with him, then announced his doom, thus currying favor with Jeroboam.

it on the donkey, and brought it back and he came to the city of the old prophet to mourn and to bury him.

30 And he laid his body in his own grave, and they mourned over him, *saying*, "ᵃAlas, my brother!"

31 And it came about after he had buried him, that he spoke to his sons, saying, "When I die, bury me in the grave in which the man of God is buried; ᵃlay my bones beside his bones.

32 "ᵃFor the thing shall surely come to pass which he cried by the word of the Lord against the altar in Bethel and ᵇagainst all the houses of the high places which are in the cities of ᶜSamaria."

3 Elevating non-Levites to the priesthood, 13:33-34

33 After this event Jeroboam did not return from his evil way, but ᵃagain he made priests of the high places from among all the people; ᵇany who would, he ordained, to be priests of the high places.

34 ᵃAnd this event became sin to the house of Jeroboam, ᵇeven to blot *it* out and destroy *it* from off the face of the earth.

4 Experiencing his son's sickness and Ahijah's prophecy, 14:1-18

14 At that time Abijah the son of Jeroboam became sick.

2 And Jeroboam said to his wife, "Arise now, and ᵃdisguise yourself so that they may not know that you are the wife of Jeroboam, and go to ᵇShiloh; behold, Ahijah the prophet is there, who ᶜspoke concerning me *that I would be* king over this people.

3 "ᵃAnd take ten loaves with you, *some* cakes and a jar of honey, and go to him. He will tell you what will happen to the boy."

4 And Jeroboam's wife did so, and arose and went to ᵃShiloh, and came to the house of ᵇAhijah. Now Ahijah could not see, ᶜfor his eyes were dim because of his age.

5 Now the Lord had said to Ahijah, "Behold, the wife of Jeroboam is coming to inquire of you concerning her son, for he is sick. You shall say thus and thus to her, for it will be when she arrives that ᵃshe will pretend to be another woman."

6 And it came about when Ahijah heard the sound of her feet coming in the doorway, that he said, "Come in, wife of Jeroboam, why do you pretend to be another woman? For I am sent to you *with* a harsh *message*.

7 "Go, say to Jeroboam, 'Thus says the Lord God of Israel, "ᵃBecause I exalted you from among the people and made you leader over My people Israel,

8 and ᵃtore the kingdom away from the house of David and gave it to you—ᵇyet you have not been like My servant David, who kept My commandments and who followed Me with all his heart, ᶜto do only that which was right in My sight;

9 you also have done more evil than all who were before you, and ᵃhave gone and made for yourself other gods and ᵇmolten images to provoke Me to anger, and have ᶜcast Me behind your back—

10 therefore behold, I am bringing calamity on the house of Jeroboam, and ᵃwill cut off from Jeroboam every male person, ᵇboth bond and free in Israel, and I ᶜwill make a clean sweep of the house of Jeroboam, as one sweeps away dung until it is all gone.

11 "ᵃAnyone belonging to Jeroboam who dies in the city the dogs will eat. And he who dies in the field the birds of the heavens

---

Cross references (margin):

30 ᵃJer. 22:18

31 ᵃRuth 1:17; 2 Kin. 23:17, 18

32 ᵃ1 Kin. 13:2 ᵇLev. 26:30; 1 Kin. 12:31 ᶜ1 Kin. 16:24; John 4:5; Acts 8:14

33 ᵃ1 Kin. 12:31, 32 ᵇJudg. 17:5

34 ᵃ1 Kin. 12:30; 2 Kin. 17:21 ᵇ1 Kin. 14:10; 15:29, 30

2 ᵃ1 Sam. 28:8; 2 Sam. 14:2; 2 Chr. 18:29 ᵇJosh. 18:1 ᶜ1 Kin. 11:29-31

3 ᵃ1 Sam. 9:7, 8; 1 Kin. 13:7; 2 Kin. 4:42

4 ᵃ1 Kin. 14:2 ᵇ1 Kin. 11:29 ᶜ1 Sam. 3:2; 4:15

5 ᵃ2 Sam. 14:2

7 ᵃ2 Sam. 12:7; 1 Kin. 11:28-31; 16:2

8 ᵃ1 Kin. 11:31 ᵇ1 Kin. 11:33, 38 ᶜ1 Kin. 15:5

9 ᵃ1 Kin. 12:28; 2 Chr. 11:15 ᵇEx. 34:17 ᶜNeh. 9:26; Ps. 50:17; Ezek. 23:35

10 ᵃ1 Kin. 21:21; 2 Kin. 9:8 ᵇDeut. 32:36; 2 Kin. 14:26 ᶜ1 Kin. 15:29

★**11-13**

11 ᵃ1 Kin. 16:4; 21:24

14:11-13 Only the sick son Abijah, of all the male descendants of Jeroboam, would be buried; the others would suffer the indignity of having their bodies devoured by scavengers.

will eat; for the Lord has spoken it." '

12 *a*1 Kin. 14:17

12 "Now you arise, go to your house. *a*When your feet enter the city the child will die.

13 *a*2 Chr. 19:3

13 "And all Israel shall mourn for him and bury him, for he alone of Jeroboam's *family* shall come to the grave, because in him *a*something good was found toward the Lord God of Israel in the house of Jeroboam.

★**14** *a*1 Kin. 15:27-29

14 "Moreover, *a*the Lord will raise up for Himself a king over Israel who shall cut off the house of Jeroboam this day and from now on.

★**15** *a*Deut. 29:28; 2 Kin. 17:6; Ps. 52:5 *b*Josh. 23:15, 16 *c*2 Kin. 15:29 *d*Ex. 34:13, 14; Deut. 12:3, 4

15 "For the Lord will strike Israel, as a reed is shaken in the water; and *a*He will uproot Israel from *b*this good land which He gave to their fathers, and *c*will scatter them beyond the *Euphrates* River, *d*because they have made their Asherim, provoking the Lord to anger.

16 *a*1 Kin. 12:30; 13:34; 15:30, 34; 16:2

16 "And He will give up Israel *a*on account of the sins of Jeroboam, which he committed and with which he made Israel to sin."

★**17** *a*1 Kin. 15:21, 33; 16:6-9, 15, 23; Song 6:4 *b*1 Kin. 14:12

17 Then Jeroboam's wife arose and departed and came to *a*Tirzah. *b*As she was entering the threshold of the house, the child died.

18 *a*1 Kin. 14:13

18 *a*And all Israel buried him and mourned for him, according to the word of the Lord which He spoke through His servant Ahijah the prophet.

5   *Expiring,* 14:19-20

19 *a*1 Kin. 14:30; 2 Chr. 13:2-20

19 Now the rest of the acts of Jeroboam, *a*how he made war and how he reigned, behold, they are written in the Book of the Chronicles of the Kings of Israel.

20 And the time that Jeroboam reigned *was* twenty-two years; and he slept with his fathers, and Nadab his son reigned in his place.

C   The Reign of Rehoboam in Judah (931-913; 2 Chron. 10:1-12:16), 14:21-31

1   *Apostasy in Judah,* 14:21-24

21 *a*Now Rehoboam the son of Solomon reigned in Judah. Rehoboam was forty-one years old when he became king, and he reigned seventeen years in Jerusalem, *b*the city which the Lord had chosen from all the tribes of Israel to put His name there. And his mother's name was Naamah the Ammonitess.

21 *a*2 Chr. 12:13 *b*1 Kin. 11:32, 36

22 *a*And Judah did evil in the sight of the Lord, and they *b*provoked Him to jealousy more than all that their fathers had done, with the sins which they committed.

22 *a*2 Chr. 12:1, 14 *b*Deut. 32:21; Ps. 78:58; 1 Cor. 10:22

23 For they also built for themselves *a*high places and *sacred* *b*pillars and *c*Asherim on every high hill and *d*beneath every luxuriant tree.

23 *a*Deut. 12:2; Ezek. 16:24 *b*Deut. 16:22 *c*1 Kin. 14:15 *d*2 Kin. 17:10; Is. 57:5; Jer. 2:20

24 And there were also *a*male cult prostitutes in the land. They did according to all the abominations of the nations which the Lord dispossessed before the sons of Israel.

24 *a*Gen. 19:5; Deut. 23:17; 1 Kin. 15:12; 22:46; 2 Kin. 23:7

2   *Attack by Shishak of Egypt,* 14:25-28

25 *a*Now it came about in the fifth year of King Rehoboam, that Shishak the king of Egypt came up against Jerusalem.

★**25-26**

25 *a*1 Kin. 11:40; 2 Chr. 12:2, 9

26 And he took away the treasures of the house of the Lord and the treasures of the king's house, and *a*he took everything, *b*even taking all the shields of gold which Solomon had made.

26 *a*1 Kin. 15:18; 2 Chr. 12:9 *b*1 Kin. 10:17; 2 Chr. 9:15, 16

27 So King Rehoboam made shields of bronze in their place, and *a*committed them to the care of the commanders of the guard who guarded the doorway of the king's house.

27 *a*1 Sam. 8:11; 22:17

14:14 *and from now on.* I.e., the judgment is at hand.
14:15 *Asherim.* See note on Deut. 7:5.
14:17 *Tirzah,* the residence of the king, super-

seded Shechem as capital of the Northern Kingdom (15:21).
14:25-26 *Shishak.* See note on 11:40. *shields.* See notes on 10:16,17.

28 Then it happened as often as the king entered the house of the LORD, that the guards would carry them and would bring them back into the guards' room.

3 Death of Rehoboam, 14:29-31

29 [a]2 Chr. 12:15, 16

29 [a]Now the rest of the acts of Rehoboam and all that he did, are they not written in the Book of the Chronicles of the Kings of Judah?

30 [a]1 Kin. 12:21; 15:6

30 [a]And there was war between Rehoboam and Jeroboam continually.

31 [a]1 Kin. 14:21

31 And Rehoboam slept with his fathers, and was buried with his fathers in the city of David; and [a]his mother's name was Naamah the Ammonitess. And Abijam his son became king in his place.

D The Reign of Abijam (Abijah) in Judah (913–911; 2 Chron. 13:1-22), 15:1-8

★ 1-2
1 [a]2 Chr. 13:1

15 [a]Now in the eighteenth year of King Jeroboam, the son of Nebat, Abijam became king over Judah.

2 [a]2 Chr. 13:2 [b]2 Chr. 11:21

2 He reigned three years in Jerusalem; and his mother's name was [a]Maacah the daughter of [b]Abishalom.

3 [a]1 Kin. 11:4; Ps. 119:80

3 And he walked in all the sins of his father which he had committed before him; and [a]his heart was not wholly devoted to the LORD his God, like the heart of his father David.

★ 4 [a]2 Sam. 21:17; 1 Kin. 11:36; 2 Chr. 21:7

4 But for David's sake the LORD his God gave him a [a]lamp in Jerusalem, to raise up his son after him and to establish Jerusalem;

5 [a]because David did what was right in the sight of the LORD, and had not turned aside from anything that He commanded him all the days of his life, [b]except in the case of Uriah the Hittite.

6 [a]And there was war between Rehoboam and Jeroboam all the days of his life.

7 Now [a]the rest of the acts of Abijam and all that he did, are they not written in the Book of the Chronicles of the Kings of Judah? [b]And there was war between Abijam and Jeroboam.

8 [a]And Abijam slept with his fathers and they buried him in the city of David; and Asa his son became king in his place.

E The Reign of Asa in Judah (911–870; 2 Chron. 14:1-16:14), 15:9-24

1 His reforms, 15:9-15

9 So in the twentieth year of Jeroboam the king of Israel, Asa began to reign as king of Judah.

10 And he reigned forty-one years in Jerusalem; and [a]his mother's name was Maacah the daughter of Abishalom.

11 And [a]Asa did what was right in the sight of the LORD, like David his father.

12 [a]He also put away the male cult prostitutes from the land, and [b]removed all the idols which his fathers had made.

13 [a]And he also removed Maacah his mother from being queen mother, because she had made a horrid image as an Asherah; and Asa cut down her horrid image and [b]burned it at the brook Kidron.

5 [a]1 Kin. 9:4; 14:8; Luke 1:6 [b]2 Sam. 11:3f., 15-17; 12:9, 10

6 [a]1 Kin. 14:30; 2 Chr. 12:15-13:20

7 [a]2 Chr. 13:2, 21, 22 [b]2 Chr. 13:3-20

8 [a]2 Chr. 14:1

10 [a]1 Kin. 15:2

11 [a]2 Chr. 14:2

12 [a]Deut. 23:17; 1 Kin. 14:24; 22:46 [b]1 Kin. 11:7, 8; 14:23; 2 Chr. 14:2-5 ★13 [a]2 Chr. 15:16-18 [b]Ex. 32:20

15:1-2 Abijam. The Abijah of 2 Chron. 13:1, who reigned 913–911 and was the son of Maacah (= Micaiah of 2 Chron. 13:2), who was the granddaughter of Abishalom (= Absalom whose daughter Tamar married Uriel).
15:4 a lamp. See note on 11:36.
15:13 The reforms of Asa included deposing the

Queen Mother, Maacah (the word mother here indicates his grandmother, not an uncommon usage). The Hebrew word for queen is not the one usually used, and may indicate special authority; it is also used of the Queen of Sheba.

14 ᵃBut the high places were not taken away; nevertheless ᵇthe heart of Asa was wholly devoted to the LORD all his days. **15** And ᵃhe brought into the house of the LORD the dedicated things of his father and his own dedicated things: silver and gold and utensils.

2 His war with Baasha, 15:16-24

16 ᵃNow there was war between Asa and Baasha king of Israel all their days. **17** ᵃAnd Baasha king of Israel went up against Judah and ᵇfortified Ramah ᶜin order to prevent *anyone* from going out or coming in to Asa king of Judah. **18** Then ᵃAsa took all the silver and the gold which were left in the treasuries of the house of the LORD and the treasuries of the king's house, and delivered them into the hand of his servants. And ᵇKing Asa sent them to Benhadad the son of Tabrimmon, the son of Hezion, king of Aram, who lived in ᶜDamascus, saying, **19** "*Let there be* a ᵃtreaty between you and me, *as* between my father and your father. Behold, I have sent you a present of silver and gold; go, break your treaty with Baasha king of Israel so that he will withdraw from me." **20** So Ben-hadad listened to King Asa and sent the commanders of his armies against the cities of Israel, and conquered ᵃIjon, ᵇDan, ᶜAbel-beth-maacah and all ᵈChinneroth, besides all the land of Naphtali. **21** And it came about when Baasha heard *of it* that ᵃhe ceased fortifying Ramah, and remained in ᵇTirzah. **22** Then King Asa made a proclamation to all Judah—none was exempt—and they carried away the stones of Ramah and its timber with which Baasha had built. And King Asa built with them ᵃGeba of Benjamin and Mizpah.

23 ᵃNow the rest of all the acts of Asa and all his might and all that he did and the cities which he built, are they not written in the Book of the Chronicles of the Kings of Judah? But in the time of his old age he was diseased in his feet. **24** And Asa slept with his fathers and was buried with his fathers in the city of David his father; and ᵃJehoshaphat his son reigned in his place.

F The Reign of Nadab in Israel (910-909), 15:25-31

25 Now ᵃNadab the son of Jeroboam became king over Israel in the second year of Asa king of Judah, and he reigned over Israel two years. **26** And he did evil in the sight of the LORD, and ᵃwalked in the way of his father and ᵇin his sin which he made Israel sin. **27** Then ᵃBaasha the son of Ahijah of the house of Issachar conspired against him, and Baasha struck him down at ᵇGibbethon, which belonged to the Philistines, while Nadab and all Israel were laying siege to Gibbethon. **28** So Baasha killed him in the third year of Asa king of Judah, and reigned in his place. **29** And it came about, as soon as he was king, he struck down all the household of Jeroboam. He did not leave to Jeroboam any persons alive, until he had destroyed them, ᵃaccording to the word of the LORD, which He spoke by His servant Ahijah the Shilonite, **30** *and* because of the sins of Jeroboam which he sinned, and

---

15:17 *Ramah.* About 4 miles N. of Jerusalem. This was a defiant action by Baasha.
15:18-20 To take the pressure off Baasha's encroachment on Judah (by building Ramah), Asa entered into a foreign alliance with Aram (Syria), who, in turn, attacked towns in the Galilee area, causing Israel to stop fortifying Ramah.
15:21 *Tirzah.* See note on 14:17.
15:29 The prophecy of 14:10-13 is now fulfilled.

^awhich he made Israel sin, because of his provocation with which he provoked the Lord God of Israel to anger.

31 ^aNow the rest of the acts of Nadab and all that he did, are they not written in the Book of the Chronicles of the Kings of Israel?

G The Reign of Baasha in Israel (909–886), 15:32–16:7

32 ^aAnd there was war between Asa and Baasha king of Israel all their days.

33 In the third year of Asa king of Judah, Baasha the son of Ahijah became king over all Israel at Tirzah, and reigned twenty-four years.

34 And he did evil in the sight of the Lord, and ^awalked in the way of Jeroboam and in his sin which he made Israel sin.

16 Now the word of the Lord came to ^aJehu the son of ^bHanani against Baasha, saying,

2 "Inasmuch as I ^aexalted you from the dust and made you leader over My people Israel, and ^byou have walked in the way of Jeroboam and have made My people Israel sin, provoking Me to anger with their sins,

3 behold, ^aI will consume ^bBaasha and his house, and ^cI will make your house like the house of Jeroboam the son of Nebat.

4 "^aAnyone of Baasha who dies in the city the dogs shall eat, and anyone of his who dies in the field the birds of the heavens will eat."

5 ^aNow the rest of the acts of Baasha and what he did and his might, are they not written in the Book of the Chronicles of the Kings of Israel?

6 And Baasha slept with his fathers and was buried in ^aTirzah,

and Elah his son became king in his place.

7 Moreover, the word of the Lord through ^athe prophet Jehu the son of Hanani also came against Baasha and his household, both because of all the evil which he did in the sight of the Lord, provoking Him to anger with ^bthe work of his hands, in being like the house of Jeroboam, and because ^che struck it.

H The Reign of Elah in Israel (886–885), 16:8–14

8 In the twenty-sixth year of Asa king of Judah, Elah the son of Baasha became king over Israel at Tirzah, *and reigned* two years.

9 And his servant ^aZimri, commander of half his chariots, conspired against him. Now he *was* at Tirzah drinking himself drunk in the house of Arza, ^bwho *was* over the household at Tirzah.

10 Then Zimri went in and struck him and put him to death, in the twenty-seventh year of Asa king of Judah, and became king in his place.

11 And it came about, when he became king, as soon as he sat on his throne, that ^ahe killed all the household of Baasha; he did not leave a single male, neither of his relatives nor of his friends.

12 Thus Zimri destroyed all the household of Baasha, ^aaccording to the word of the Lord, which He spoke against Baasha through ^bJehu the prophet,

13 for all the sins of Baasha and the sins of Elah his son, which they sinned and which they made Israel sin, ^aprovoking the Lord God of Israel to anger with their idols.

14 ^aNow the rest of the acts of Elah and all that he did, are they not written in the Book of the Chronicles of the Kings of Israel?

Marginal references (left column):
31 ^a1 Kin. 14:19
32 ^a1 Kin. 15:16
34 ^a1 Kin. 15:26
★ 1-5
1 ^a1 Kin. 16:7; 2 Chr. 19:2; 20:34 ^b2 Chr. 16:7-10
2 ^a1 Sam. 2:8; 1 Kin. 14:7 ^b1 Kin. 15:34
3 ^a1 Kin. 14:10; 21:21 ^b1 Kin. 16:11 ^c1 Kin. 15:29
4 ^a1 Kin. 14:11; 21:24
5 ^a1 Kin. 14:19; 15:31
6 ^a1 Kin. 14:17; 15:21

Marginal references (right column):
7 ^a1 Kin. 16:1 ^bPs. 115:4; Is. 2:8 ^c1 Kin. 14:14; 15:27, 29
9 ^a2 Kin. 9:30-33 ^bGen. 24:2; 39:4; 1 Kin. 18:3
11 ^a1 Kin. 15:29; 16:3
★12 ^a1 Kin. 16:3 ^b2 Chr. 19:2; 20:34
13 ^aDeut. 32:21; 1 Kin. 15:30
14 ^a1 Kin. 16:5

16:1-5 Since Baasha chose to live in sin like Jeroboam, he would suffer the same ignominious fate of Jeroboam's family (cf. vv. 11–12 and 14:10–13).

16:12 Two dynasties (Jeroboam's and Baasha's) had risen and fallen in Israel in 46 years. The third, Zimri's, lasted only 7 days (v. 15)!

I The Reign of Zimri in Israel (885), 16:15-20

15 In the twenty-seventh year of Asa king of Judah, Zimri reigned seven days at Tirzah. Now the people were camped against ᵃGibbethon, which belonged to the Philistines.

16 And the people who were camped heard it said, "Zimri has conspired and has also struck down the king." Therefore all Israel made Omri, the commander of the army, king over Israel that day in the camp.

17 Then Omri and all Israel with him went up from Gibbethon, and they besieged Tirzah.

18 And it came about, when Zimri saw that the city was taken, that he went into the citadel of the king's house and burned the king's house over him with fire, and ᵃdied,

19 because of his sins which he sinned, doing evil in the sight of the Lord, ᵃwalking in the way of Jeroboam, and in his sin which he did, making Israel sin.

20 ᵃNow the rest of the acts of Zimri and his conspiracy which he carried out, are they not written in the Book of the Chronicles of the Kings of Israel?

J The Reign of Omri in Israel (885-874), 16:21-28

21 Then the people of Israel were divided into two parts: half of the people followed Tibni the son of Ginath, to make him king; the *other* half followed Omri.

22 But the people who followed Omri prevailed over the people who followed Tibni the son of Ginath. And Tibni died and Omri became king.

23 In the thirty-first year of Asa king of Judah, Omri became king over Israel, and reigned twelve years; he reigned six years at ᵃTirzah.

24 And he bought the hill Samaria from Shemer for two talents of silver; and he built on the hill, and named the city which he built ᵃSamaria, after the name of Shemer, the owner of the hill.

25 And ᵃOmri did evil in the sight of the Lord, and ᵇacted more wickedly than all who *were* before him.

26 For he ᵃwalked in all the way of Jeroboam the son of Nebat and in his sins which he made Israel sin, provoking the Lord God of Israel with their idols.

27 Now the rest of the acts of Omri which he did and his might which he showed, are they not written in the Book of the Chronicles of the Kings of Israel?

28 So Omri slept with his fathers, and was buried in Samaria; and Ahab his son became king in his place.

K The Reign of Ahab in Israel (874-853), 16:29-22:40

1 The beginning of Ahab's reign, 16:29-34

29 Now Ahab the son of Omri became king over Israel in the thirty-eighth year of Asa king of Judah, and Ahab the son of Omri reigned over Israel in Samaria twenty-two years.

30 And Ahab the son of Omri did evil in the sight of the Lord ᵃmore than all who were before him.

31 And it came about, as though it had been a trivial thing for him to walk in the sins of Jeroboam the son of Nebat, that

---

Margin references:

15 ᵃ1 Kin. 15:27
18 ᵃ1 Sam. 31:4, 5; 2 Sam. 17:23
19 ᵃ1 Kin. 12:28; 14:16; 15:26
20 ᵃ1 Kin. 16:5, 14, 27
23 ᵃ1 Kin. 15:21
★24-25
24 ᵃ1 Kin. 16:28, 29, 32
25 ᵃMic. 6:16 ᵇ1 Kin. 14:9; 16:30-33
26 ᵃ1 Kin. 16:19
★29-31
30 ᵃ1 Kin. 14:9; 16:25
31 ᵃDeut. 7:1-5 ᵇJudg. 18:7; 1 Kin. 11:1-5; 2 Kin. 10:18; 17:16

16:24-25 Omri is remembered for two things: he built Samaria, making it the capital and giving its name to the entire Northern Kingdom; and he became the most wicked king up to that time, though his son Ahab outdid him (v. 33). Samaria, located about 7 miles NW. of Shechem, became the center of idolatrous worship (16:32; Hos. 8:5-6; Amos 3:12-15; 6:1-6; Mic. 1:5-7). It fell to the Assyrians in 722 (2 Kings 17:5).

16:29-31 Ahab is remembered for two things: his wickedness and his marriage to Jezebel, who advanced Baal worship into Israel.

[a]he married Jezebel the daughter of Ethbaal king of the [b]Sidonians, and went to serve Baal and worshiped him. **32** So he erected an altar for Baal in [a]the house of Baal, which he built in Samaria.

33 And Ahab also made [a]the Asherah. Thus [b]Ahab did more to provoke the LORD God of Israel than all the kings of Israel who were before him.

34 [a]In his days Hiel the Bethelite built Jericho; he laid its foundations with the *loss of* Abiram his first-born, and set up its gates with the *loss of* his youngest son Segub, according to the word of the LORD, which He spoke by Joshua the son of Nun.

2 Elijah's prediction of drought, 17:1

17 Now Elijah the Tishbite, who was of [a]the settlers of Gilead, said to Ahab, "[b]As the LORD, the God of Israel lives, before whom I stand, surely [c]there shall be neither dew nor rain these years, except by my word."

3 God's provision for Elijah, 17:2-24

2 And the word of the LORD came to him, saying,

3 "Go away from here and turn eastward, and hide yourself by the brook Cherith, which is east of the Jordan.

4 "And it shall be that you shall drink of the brook, and [a]I have commanded the ravens to provide for you there."

5 So he went and did according to the word of the LORD, for he went and lived by the brook Cherith, which is east of the Jordan.

6 And the ravens brought him bread and meat in the morning and bread and meat in the evening, and he would drink from the brook.

7 And it happened after a while, that the brook dried up, because there was no rain in the land.

8 Then the word of the LORD came to him, saying,

9 "Arise, go to [a]Zarephath, which belongs to Sidon, and stay there; behold, [b]I have commanded a widow there to provide for you."

10 So he arose and went to Zarephath, and when he came to the gate of the city, behold, a widow was there gathering sticks; and [a]he called to her and said, "Please get me a little water in a jar, that I may drink."

11 And as she was going to get *it*, he called to her and said, "Please bring me a piece of bread in your hand."

12 But she said, "[a]As the LORD your God lives, [b]I have no bread, only a handful of flour in the bowl and a little oil in the jar; and behold, I am gathering a few sticks that I may go in and prepare for me and my son, that we may eat it and [c]die."

13 Then Elijah said to her, "Do not fear; go, do as you have said, but make me a little bread cake from it first, and bring *it* out to me, and afterward you may make *one* for yourself and for your son.

14 "For thus says the LORD God of Israel, 'The bowl of flour shall

---

Cross references (left margin):

32 [a]2 Kin. 10:21, 26, 27

★**33** [a]2 Kin. 13:6 [b]1 Kin. 14:9; 16:29, 30; 21:25

★**34** [a]Josh. 6:26

★ **1** [a]Judg. 12:4 [b]1 Kin. 18:10; 22:14; 2 Kin. 3:14; 5:20 [c]1 Kin. 18:1; Luke 4:25; James 5:17

★ **3**

4 [a]1 Kin. 17:9

Cross references (right margin):

★ **9** [a]Obad. 20; Luke 4:26 [b]1 Kin. 17:4

10 [a]Gen. 24:17; John 4:7

★**12** [a]1 Kin. 17:1 [b]2 Kin. 4:2-7 [c]Gen. 21:15, 16

16:33 *the Asherah.* The chief goddess of Tyre, and mother of Baal (see notes on Deut. 7:5; Jer. 17:2).

16:34 *Hiel* tried to defy God's curse on anyone who fortified Jericho (the setting up of *gates* showed that this was his intention) with the result that his two sons died (either by being sacrificed in the process of building, or by direct divine judgment on them).

17:1 *Elijah* means "Yahweh is God," a significant name in a time when Baal worship threatened to extinguish the worship of Yahweh in Israel.

17:3 *Cherith.* A stream in Gilead, E. of the Jordan.

17:9 *Zarephath.* A town on the Mediterranean coast between Tyre and Sidon.

17:12 The famine had extended this far north and the widow was preparing her last meal. The oath shows that she worshiped the God of Israel. God sent Elijah to a Gentile widow to rebuke the apostasy of Israel (Luke 4:24-26).

not be exhausted, nor shall the jar of oil be empty, until the day that the LORD sends rain on the face of the earth.' "

15 So she went and did according to the word of Elijah, and she and he and her household ate for *many* days.

16 The bowl of flour was not exhausted nor did the jar of oil become empty, according to the word of the LORD which He spoke through Elijah.

★17 **17** Now it came about after these things, that the son of the woman, the mistress of the house, became sick; and his sickness was so severe, that there was no breath left in him.

★18 *a*2 Sam. 16:10; 2 Kin. 3:13; Luke 4:34; John 2:4 *b*1 Kin. 12:22
18 So she said to Elijah, "*a*What do I have to do with you, O *b*man of God? You have come to me to bring my iniquity to remembrance, and to put my son to death!"

★19 **19** And he said to her, "Give me your son." Then he took him from her bosom and carried him up to the upper room where he was living, and laid him on his own bed.

20 And he called to the LORD and said, "O LORD my God, hast Thou also brought calamity to the widow with whom I am staying, by causing her son to die?"

21 *a*2 Kin. 4:34, 35; Acts 20:10
21 *a*Then he stretched himself upon the child three times, and called to the LORD, and said, "O LORD my God, I pray Thee, let this child's life return to him."

22 *a*Luke 7:14; Heb. 11:35
22 And the LORD heard the voice of Elijah, *a*and the life of the child returned to him and he revived.

23 And Elijah took the child, and brought him down from the upper room into the house and gave him to his mother; and Elijah said, "See, your son is alive."

24 Then the woman said to Elijah, "*a*Now I know that you are a man of God, and that the word of the LORD in your mouth is truth."

24 *a*John 2:11; 3:2; 16:30

4 Elijah's challenge to the priests of Baal, 18:1-46

18 Now it came about *a*after many days, that the word of the LORD came to Elijah in the third year, saying, "Go, show yourself to Ahab, and *b*I will send rain on the face of the earth."

★ 1 *a*1 Kin. 17:1; Luke 4:25; James 5:17 *b*Deut. 28:12

2 So Elijah went to show himself to Ahab. Now the famine *was* severe in Samaria.

3 And Ahab called Obadiah *a*who *was* over the household. (Now Obadiah *b*feared the LORD greatly;

3 *a*1 Kin. 16:9 *b*Neh. 7:2; Job 28:28

4 for it came about, *a*when Jezebel destroyed the prophets of the LORD, that Obadiah took a hundred prophets and hid them by fifties in a cave, and *b*provided them with bread and water.)

4 *a*1 Kin. 18:13 *b*Matt. 10:40-42

5 Then Ahab said to Obadiah, "Go through the land to all the springs of water and to all the valleys; perhaps we will find grass and keep the horses and mules alive, and not have to kill some of the cattle."

★ 5

6 So they divided the land between them to survey it; Ahab went one way by himself and Obadiah went another way by himself.

7 Now as Obadiah was on the way, behold, Elijah met him, *a*and he recognized him and fell on his face and said, "Is this you, Elijah my master?"

★ 7-16

7 *a*2 Kin. 1:6-8

17:17 *there was no breath left in him.* He was actually dead (vv. 18, 20).

17:18 The mother thought her son had died because of some sin she had committed.

17:19 *upper room.* Likely a room on the roof with an outside stair.

18:1 Three years at Zarephath + the time at Cherith = the 3½ years of Luke 4:25 and James 5:17.

18:5 We know from secular records that Ahab must have had several thousand *horses.*

18:7-16 Obadiah feared for his life if he told Ahab that he had found Elijah, particularly if Elijah should then disappear. But Elijah assured him that he would confront Ahab that very day.

8 And he said to him, "It is I. Go, say to your master, 'Behold, Elijah *is here.*' "

9 And he said, "What sin have I committed, that you are giving your servant into the hand of Ahab, to put me to death?

10 *a*1 Kin. 17:1

10 "*a*As the LORD your God lives, there is no nation or kingdom where my master has not sent to search for you; and when they said, 'He is not *here,*' he made the kingdom or nation swear that they could not find you.

11 "And now you are saying, 'Go, say to your master, "Behold, Elijah *is here.*" '

12 *a*2 Kin. 2:16; Ezek. 3:12, 14; Acts 8:39

12 "And it will come about when I leave you *a*that the Spirit of the LORD will carry you where I do not know; so when I come and tell Ahab and he cannot find you, he will kill me, although *I* your servant have feared the LORD from my youth.

13 *a*1 Kin. 18:4

13 "*a*Has it not been told to my master what I did when Jezebel killed the prophets of the LORD, that I hid a hundred prophets of the LORD by fifties in a cave, and provided them with bread and water?

14 "And now you are saying, 'Go, say to your master, "Behold, Elijah *is here*" '; he will then kill me."

15 *a*1 Kin. 17:1

15 And Elijah said, "*a*As the LORD of hosts lives, before whom I stand, I will surely show myself to him today."

16 So Obadiah went to meet Ahab, and told him; and Ahab went to meet Elijah.

17 *a*Josh. 7:25; 1 Kin. 21:20

17 And it came about, when Ahab saw Elijah that *a*Ahab said to him, "Is this you, you troubler of Israel?"

★18 *a*1 Kin. 9:9; 2 Chr. 15:2 *b*1 Kin. 16:31; 21:25, 26

18 And he said, "I have not troubled Israel, but you and your father's house *have,* because *a*you have forsaken the commandments of the LORD, and *b*you have followed the Baals.

★19 *a*Josh. 19:26; 2 Kin. 2:25 *b*1 Kin. 18:22 *c*1 Kin. 16:33

19 "Now then send *and* gather to me all Israel at *a*Mount Carmel, *b*together with 450 prophets of Baal and 400 prophets of *c*the A- sherah, who eat at Jezebel's ta- ble."

20 So Ahab sent *a message* among all the sons of Israel, and brought the prophets together at Mount Carmel.

★21 *a*2 Kin. 17:41; Matt. 6:24 *b*Josh. 24:15

21 And Elijah came near to all the people and said, "*a*How long *will* you hesitate between two opinions? *b*If the LORD is God, fol- low Him; but if Baal, follow him." But the people did not answer him a word.

22 *a*1 Kin. 19:10, 14 *b*1 Kin. 18:19

22 Then Elijah said to the people, "I *a*alone am left a prophet of the LORD, but Baal's prophets are *b*450 men.

23 "Now let them give us two oxen; and let them choose one ox for themselves and cut it up, and place it on the wood, but put no fire *under it*; and I will prepare the other ox, and lay it on the wood, and I will not put a fire *un- der it.*

24 *a*1 Kin. 18:38

24 "Then you call on the name of your god, and I will call on the name of the LORD, and *a*the God who answers by fire, He is God." And all the people answered and said, "That is a good idea."

25 So Elijah said to the prophets of Baal, "Choose one ox for yourselves and prepare it first for you are many, and call on the name of your god, but put no fire *under it.*"

26 *a*Ps. 115:4, 5; Jer. 10:5

26 Then they took the ox which was given them and they prepared it and called on the name of Baal from morning until noon saying, "O Baal, answer us." But there was *a*no voice and no one answered. And they leaped about the altar which they made.

18:18 *Baals.* See note on Judg. 2:13.

18:19 *Carmel.* A mountain range, rising to 1,800 feet, which juts into the Mediterranean near modern Haifa. *of the Asherah.* See note on 16:33.

18:21 *How long will you hesitate between two opinions?* Lit., how long are you hopping be- tween two forks? Israel's sin was not that of totally rejecting Yahweh, but of seeking to combine His worship with Baal worship.

27 And it came about at noon, that Elijah mocked them and said, "Call out with a loud voice, for he is a god; either he is occupied or gone aside, or is on a journey, or perhaps he is asleep and needs to be awakened."

28 So they cried with a loud voice and [a]cut themselves according to their custom with swords and lances until the blood gushed out on them.

29 And it came about when midday was past, that they raved [a]until the time of the offering of the *evening* sacrifice; but there was no voice, no one answered, and no one paid attention.

30 Then Elijah said to all the people, "Come near to me." So all the people came near to him. And [a]he repaired the altar of the LORD which had been torn down.

31 And Elijah took twelve stones according to the number of the tribes of the sons of Jacob, to whom the word of the LORD had come, saying, "[a]Israel shall be your name."

32 So with the stones he built an altar in [a]the name of the LORD, and he made a trench around the altar, large enough to hold two measures of seed.

33 [a]Then he arranged the wood and cut the ox in pieces and laid *it* on the wood. And he said, "Fill four pitchers with water and pour *it* on the burnt offering and on the wood."

34 And he said, "Do it a second time," and they did it a second time. And he said, "Do it a third time," and they did it a third time.

35 And the water flowed around the altar, and he also filled the trench with water.

36 Then it came about [a]at the time of the offering of the *evening*

sacrifice, that Elijah the prophet came near and said, "[b]O LORD, the God of Abraham, Isaac and Israel, today let it be known that [c]Thou art God in Israel, and that I am Thy servant, and [d]that I have done all these things at Thy word.

37 "Answer me, O LORD, answer me, that this people may know that Thou, O LORD, art God, and *that* Thou hast turned their heart back again."

38 Then the [a]fire of the LORD fell, and consumed the burnt offering and the wood and the stones and the dust, and licked up the water that was in the trench.

39 And when all the people saw it, they fell on their faces; and they said, "[a]The LORD, He is God; the LORD, He is God."

40 Then Elijah said to them, "Seize the prophets of Baal; do not let one of them escape." So they seized them; and Elijah brought them down to [a]the brook Kishon, [b]and slew them there.

41 Now Elijah said to Ahab, "Go up, eat and drink; for there is the sound of the roar of a *heavy* shower."

42 So Ahab went up to eat and drink. But Elijah went up to the top of [a]Carmel; and he [b]crouched down on the earth, and put his face between his knees.

43 And he said to his servant, "Go up now, look toward the sea." So he went up and looked and said, "There is nothing." And he said, "Go back" seven times.

44 And it came about at the seventh *time*, that he said, "Behold, [a]a cloud as small as a man's hand is coming up from the sea." And he said, "Go up, say to Ahab, 'Prepare *your chariot* and go down, so that the *heavy* shower does not stop you.'"

Marginal references:

28 [a]Lev. 19:28; Deut. 14:1

★29 [a]Ex. 29:39, 41

30 [a]1 Kin. 19:10, 14; 2 Chr. 33:16

31 [a]Gen. 32:28; 35:10; 2 Kin. 17:34

★32 [a]Col. 3:17

★33 [a]Gen. 22:9; Lev. 1:7, 8

36 [a]1 Kin. 18:29 [b]Gen. 28:13; Ex. 3:6; 4:5; Matt. 22:32 [c]1 Kin. 8:43 [d]Num. 16:28-32

38 [a]Gen. 15:17; Lev. 9:24; 10:1, 2; Judg. 6:21; 2 Kin. 1:12; 1 Chr. 21:26; 2 Chr. 7:1; Job 1:16

39 [a]1 Kin. 18:21, 24

40 [a]Judg. 4:7; 5:21 [b]Deut. 13:5; 18:20; 2 Kin. 10:24, 25

42 [a]1 Kin. 18:19, 20 [b]James 5:18

44 [a]Luke 12:54

18:29 The prophets of Baal put on their frenzied show from noon until 3 P.M.

18:32 *two measures of seed*. About 5 gallons. Because this seems too small a trench, some suggest that the trench on each of the four sides of the altar was this size, while others

think the trench was large enough for sowing (as in a furrow) five gallons of seed.

18:33 There is a perennial spring near this traditional site, from which the *water* may have been brought.

★45-46
45 *a*Josh.
17:16; Judg.
6:33

46 *a*2 Kin.
3:15; Is.
8:11; Ezek.
3:14 *b*2 Kin.
4:29; Jer.
1:17; 1 Pet.
1:13

45 So it came about in a little while, that the sky grew black with clouds and wind, and there was a heavy shower. And Ahab rode and went to *a*Jezreel.

46 Then *a*the hand of the LORD was on Elijah, and *b*he girded up his loins and outran Ahab to Jezreel.

5 Elijah's flight to Horeb, 19:1-18

1 *a*1 Kin.
18:40

★ 2 *a*Ruth
1:17; 1 Kin.
20:10; 2 Kin.
6:31

3 *a*Gen.
21:31

★ 4 *a*Num.
11:15; Jer.
20:14-18;
Jon. 4:3, 8

5 *a*Gen.
28:12

19 Now Ahab told Jezebel all that Elijah had done, and *a*how he had killed all the prophets with the sword.

2 Then Jezebel sent a messenger to Elijah, saying, "*a*So may the gods do to me and even more, if I do not make your life as the life of one of them by tomorrow about this time."

3 And he was afraid and arose and ran for his life and came to *a*Beersheba, which belongs to Judah, and left his servant there.

4 But he himself went a day's journey into the wilderness, and came and sat down under a juniper tree; and *a*he requested for himself that he might die, and said, "It is enough; now, O LORD, take my life, for I am not better than my fathers."

5 And he lay down and slept under a juniper tree; and behold, there was *a*an angel touching him, and he said to him, "Arise, eat."

6 Then he looked and behold, there was at his head a bread cake *baked on* hot stones, and a jar of water. So he ate and drank and lay down again.

7 And the angel of the LORD came again a second time and touched him and said, "Arise, eat, because the journey is too great for you."

8 So he arose and ate and drank, and went in the strength of that food *a*forty days and forty nights to *b*Horeb, the mountain of God.

9 Then he came there to a cave, and lodged there; and behold, *a*the word of the LORD *came* to him, and He said to him, "What are you doing here, Elijah?"

10 And he said, "*a*I have been very zealous for the LORD, the God of hosts; for the sons of Israel have forsaken Thy covenant, *b*torn down Thine altars and killed Thy prophets with the sword. And *c*I alone am left; and they seek my life, to take it away."

11 So He said, "*a*Go forth, and stand on the mountain before the LORD." And behold, the LORD was passing by! And *b*a great and strong wind was rending the mountains and breaking in pieces the rocks before the LORD; *but* the LORD *was* not in the wind. And after the wind an earthquake, *but* the LORD *was* not in the earthquake.

12 And after the earthquake a fire, *but* the LORD *was* not in the fire; and after the fire *a*a sound of a gentle blowing.

13 And it came about when Elijah heard *it*, that *a*he wrapped his face in his mantle, and went out and stood in the entrance of the cave. And behold, *b*a voice *came* to him and said, "What are you doing here, Elijah?"

14 Then he said, "*a*I have been very zealous for the LORD, the God of hosts; for the sons of Israel have forsaken Thy covenant, torn down Thine altars and killed Thy prophets with the sword. And I alone am left; and

★ 8 *a*Ex.
24:18; 34:28;
Deut. 9:9-11,
18; Matt. 4:2
*b*Ex. 3:1;
4:27

9 *a*Ex.
33:21, 22

10 *a*Ex. 20:5;
34:14 *b*Rom.
11:3, 4
*c*1 Kin. 18:22

11 *a*Ex.
19:20; 24:12,
18 *b*Ezek.
1:4

★12 *a*Job
4:16; Zech.
4:6

13 *a*Ex. 3:6
*b*1 Kin. 19:9

14 *a*1 Kin.
19:10

18:45-46 *Jezreel.* A winter residence of Ahab, about 17 miles from Carmel. Elijah was granted supernatural power to run this distance.

19:2 *as the life of one of them.* I.e., as one of the prophets of Baal whom Elijah killed.

19:4 *juniper tree.* A desert shrub that sometimes

grows 10 feet high.

19:8 The journey to *Horeb* (Sinai, see note on Exod. 3:1) took *forty days* because Elijah was alternately wandering and hiding due to his despondent condition.

19:12 *a sound of a gentle blowing.* Lit., the sound of gentle stillness.

they seek my life, to take it away."

★15-17
15 a2 Kin. 8:8-15

15 And the LORD said to him, "Go, return on your way to the wilderness of Damascus, and when you have arrived, ^ayou shall anoint Hazael king over Aram;

16 a2 Kin. 9:1-10 b1 Kin. 19:19-21; 2 Kin. 2:9, 15

16 and ^aJehu the son of Nimshi you shall anoint king over Israel; and ^bElisha the son of Shaphat of Abel-meholah you shall anoint as prophet in your place.

17 a2 Kin. 8:12; 13:3, 22 b2 Kin. 9:14-10:25

17 "And it shall come about, the ^aone who escapes from the sword of Hazael, Jehu ^bshall put to death, and the one who escapes from the sword of Jehu, Elisha shall put to death.

★18 aRom. 11:4 bHos. 13:2

18 "^aYet I will leave 7,000 in Israel, all the knees that have not bowed to Baal and every mouth that has not ^bkissed him."

6 Elijah's appointment of Elisha, 19:19-21

★19 a1 Sam. 28:14; 2 Kin. 2:8, 13, 14

19 So he departed from there and found Elisha the son of Shaphat, while he was plowing with twelve pairs of oxen before him, and he with the twelfth. And Elijah passed over to him and threw ^ahis mantle on him.

20 aMatt. 8:21, 22; Luke 9:61, 62; Acts 20:37

20 And he left the oxen and ran after Elijah and said, "Please ^alet me kiss my father and my mother, then I will follow you." And he said to him, "Go back again, for what have I done to you?"

21 a2 Sam. 24:22

21 So he returned from following him, and took the pair of oxen and sacrificed them and ^aboiled their flesh with the implements of the oxen, and gave it to the people and they ate. Then he arose and followed Elijah and ministered to him.

7 Ahab's Syrian victories, 20:1-43

20 Now ^aBen-hadad king of Aram gathered all his army, ^band there were thirty-two kings with him, and horses and chariots. And he went up and ^cbesieged Samaria, and fought against it.

★ 1 a1 Kin. 15:18, 20; 2 Kin. 6:24 b1 Kin. 22:31 c1 Kin. 16:24; 2 Kin. 6:24

2 Then he sent messengers to the city to Ahab king of Israel, and said to him, "Thus says Ben-hadad,

★ 2-9

3 'Your silver and your gold are mine; your most beautiful wives and children are also mine.' "

4 And the king of Israel answered and said, "It is according to your word, my lord, O king; I am yours, and all that I have."

5 Then the messengers returned and said, "Thus says Ben-hadad, 'Surely, I sent to you saying, "You shall give me your silver and your gold and your wives and your children,"

6 but about this time tomorrow I will send my servants to you, and they will search your house and the houses of your servants; and it shall come about, whatever is desirable in your eyes, they will take in their hand and carry away.' "

7 Then the king of Israel called all the elders of the land and said, "Please observe and ^asee how this man is looking for trouble; for he sent to me for my wives and my children and my

7 a2 Kin. 5:7

19:15-17 Elijah was instructed to *anoint* (i.e., commission for the purpose of destroying Baal worship in Israel) *Hazael* as king of Syria (Aram; 2 Kings 8:7-15; 10:32-33; 13:3, 22-25), *Jehu* as king of Israel (2 Kings 9:1-3; 10:1-36), and *Elisha* as his own successor.
19:18 *kissed him.* Part of the worship (Hos. 13:2).
19:19 *Elisha* means "God is salvation." His ministry spanned the reigns of Jehoram, Jehu, Jehoahaz, and Jehoash of the Northern Kingdom. He headed schools of prophets (2 Kings 4:38-44; 6:1-7) and performed more recorded miracles than anyone other than Jesus Christ. When called by Elijah he was plowing, and responded by immediately sacrificing a pair of oxen (v. 21).
20:1 *Ben-hadad.* A dynasty of kings of Syria, though this particular king was likely the same mentioned in 15:18, who now renewed his war against Israel.
20:2-9 The conditions of peace Ben-hadad offered were rejected by Ahab and the elders of Israel.

silver and my gold, and I did not refuse him."

8 And all the elders and all the people said to him, "Do not listen or consent."

9 So he said to the messengers of Ben-hadad, "Tell my lord the king, 'All that you sent for to your servant at the first I will do, but this thing I cannot do.' " And the messengers departed and brought him word again.

10 And Ben-hadad sent to him and said, "May ªthe gods do so to me and more also, if the dust of Samaria shall suffice for handfuls for all the people who follow me."

11 Then the king of Israel answered and said, "Tell *him,* 'ªLet not him who girds on *his armor* boast like him who takes *it off.*' "

12 And it came about when Ben-hadad heard this message, as ªhe was drinking with the kings in the temporary shelters, that he said to his servants, "Station yourselves." So they stationed *themselves* against the city.

13 Now behold, a prophet approached Ahab king of Israel and said, "Thus says the Lᴏʀᴅ, 'Have you seen all this great multitude? Behold, ªI will deliver them into your hand today, and ᵇyou shall know that I am the Lᴏʀᴅ.' "

14 And Ahab said, "By whom?" So he said, "Thus says the Lᴏʀᴅ, 'By the young men of the rulers of the provinces.' " Then he said, "Who shall begin the battle?" And he answered, "You."

15 Then he mustered the young men of the rulers of the provinces, and there were 232; and after them he mustered all the people, *even* all the sons of Israel, 7,000.

16 And they went out at noon, while ªBen-hadad was drinking himself drunk in the temporary shelters with the thirty-two kings who helped him.

17 And the young men of the rulers of the provinces went out first; and Ben-hadad sent out and they told him, saying, "Men have come out from Samaria."

18 ªThen he said, "If they have come out for peace, take them alive; or if they have come out for war, take them alive."

19 So these went out from the city, the young men of the rulers of the provinces, and the army which followed them.

20 And they killed each his man; and the Arameans fled, and Israel pursued them, and Ben-hadad king of Aram escaped on a horse with horsemen.

21 And the king of Israel went out and struck the horses and chariots, and killed the Arameans with a great slaughter.

22 Then ªthe prophet came near to the king of Israel, and said to him, "Go, strengthen yourself and observe and see what you have to do; for ᵇat the turn of the year the king of Aram will come up against you."

23 Now the servants of the king of Aram said to him, "ªTheir gods are gods of the mountains, therefore they were stronger than we; but rather let us fight against them in the plain, *and* surely we shall be stronger than they.

24 "And do this thing: remove the kings, each from his place, and put captains in their place,

25 and muster an army like the army that you have lost, horse for horse, and chariot for chariot. Then we will fight against them in the plain, and surely we shall be stronger than they." And he listened to their voice and did so.

26 So it came about ªat the turn of the year, that Ben-hadad

★10 ª1 Kin. 19:2; 2 Kin. 6:31

★11 ªProv. 27:1

12 ª1 Kin. 16:9; Prov. 31:4, 5

13 ª1 Kin. 20:28 ᵇ1 Kin. 18:36

★16 ª1 Kin. 16:9; 20:12; Prov. 20:1

18 ª2 Kin. 14:8-12

★22 ª1 Kin. 20:13 ᵇ2 Sam. 11:1; 1 Kin. 20:26

23 ª1 Kin. 14:23; Jer. 16:19-21; Rom. 1:21-23

★26 ª1 Kin. 20:22 ᵇ2 Kin. 13:17

20:10 *if the dust of Samaria . . .* I.e., if each soldier took only a handful of earth, Samaria would be levelled.
20:11 This proverbial saying means, "Let not the one who begins a fight boast of victory prematurely."

20:16 Attacking at noon, when the Syrians (Arameans) and their allies were drinking and resting, Ahab's forces routed the enemy.
20:22 *at the turn of the year.* I.e., in the spring.
20:26 *Aphek.* The location is uncertain, though probably E. of Galilee.

mustered the Arameans and went up to [b]Aphek to fight against Israel.

27 And the sons of Israel were mustered and were provisioned and went to meet them; and the sons of Israel camped before them like two little flocks of goats, [a]but the Arameans filled the country.

28 Then [a]a man of God came near and spoke to the king of Israel and said, "Thus says the LORD, 'Because the Arameans have said, "[b]The LORD is a god of the mountains, but He is not a god of the valleys"; therefore [c]I will give all this great multitude into your hand, and you shall know that I am the LORD.' "

29 So they camped one over against the other seven days. And it came about that on the seventh day, the battle was joined, and the sons of Israel killed of the Arameans 100,000 foot soldiers in one day.

30 But the rest fled to [a]Aphek into the city, and the wall fell on 27,000 men who were left. And Ben-hadad fled and came into the city [b]into an inner chamber.

31 And [a]his servants said to him, "Behold now, we have heard that the kings of the house of Israel are merciful kings, please let us [b]put sackcloth on our loins and ropes on our heads, and go out to the king of Israel; perhaps he will save your life."

32 So [a]they girded sackcloth on their loins and put ropes on their heads, and came to the king of Israel and said, "[b]Your servant Ben-hadad says, 'Please let me live.' " And he said, "Is he still alive? He is my brother."

33 Now the men took this as an omen, and quickly catching his word said, "Your brother Ben-

hadad." Then he said, "Go, bring him." Then Ben-hadad came out to him, and he took him up into the chariot.

34 And Ben-hadad said to him, "[a]The cities which my father took from your father I will restore, and you shall make streets for yourself in Damascus, as my father made in Samaria." Ahab said, "And I will let you go with this covenant." So he made a covenant with him and let him go.

35 Now a certain man of [a]the sons of the prophets said to another [b]by the word of the LORD, "Please strike me." But the man refused to strike him.

36 Then he said to him, "Because you have not listened to the voice of the LORD, behold, as soon as you have departed from me, [a]a lion will kill you." And as soon as he had departed from him a lion found him, and killed him.

37 Then he found another man and said, "Please strike me." And the man struck him, wounding him.

38 So the prophet departed and waited for the king by the way, and [a]disguised himself with a bandage over his eyes.

39 And as the king passed by, he cried to the king and said, "Your servant went out into the midst of the battle; and behold, a man turned aside and brought a man to me and said, 'Guard this man; if for any reason he is missing, [a]then your life shall be for his life, or else you shall pay a talent of silver.'

40 "And while your servant was busy here and there, he was gone." And the king of Israel said to him, "So shall your judgment be; you yourself have decided it."

Marginal references (left column):

27 [a]Judg. 6:3-5; 1 Sam. 13:5-8
★28 [a]1 Kin. 17:18 [b]1 Kin. 20:23 [c]1 Kin. 20:13
30 [a]1 Kin. 20:26 [b]1 Kin. 22:25; 2 Chr. 18:24
★31 [a]1 Kin. 20:23-26 [b]Gen. 37:34; 2 Sam. 3:31
★32 [a]1 Kin. 20:31 [b]1 Kin. 20:3-6

Marginal references (right column):

★34 [a]1 Kin. 15:20
★35-37
35 [a]2 Kin. 2:3-7 [b]1 Kin. 13:17, 18
36 [a]1 Kin. 13:24
38 [a]1 Kin. 14:2
★39-43
39 [a]2 Kin. 10:24

20:28 God would teach the Arameans that, as an omnipresent Being, He is not confined either to the hills or to the valleys (v. 23).

20:31 The sackcloth and ropes were signs of submission. The conqueror could use the rope to hang his victim if he chose not to show mercy.

20:32 my brother. I.e., my fellow-king (cf. 9:13).

20:34 you shall make streets for yourself in Da-

mascus. Sections of Damascus would be set aside for commercial purposes.

20:35-37 The prophet needed to be wounded so as to appear that he had been in battle.

20:39-43 The meaning is this: just as a soldier must not allow a prisoner of war to escape, so Ahab should not have allowed Ben-hadad to live.

41 Then he hastily took the bandage away from his eyes, and the king of Israel recognized him that he was of the prophets.

42 ᵃ1 Kin. 20:39

42 And he said to him, "Thus says the LORD, 'Because you have let go out of *your* hand the man whom I had devoted to destruction, therefore ᵃyour life shall go for his life, and your people for his people.' "

43 ᵃ1 Kin. 21:4

43 So ᵃthe king of Israel went to his house sullen and vexed, and came to Samaria.

8 Ahab's desire to have Naboth's vineyard, 21:1-29

1 ᵃJudg. 6:33; 1 Kin. 18:45, 46

21 Now it came about after these things, that Naboth the Jezreelite had a vineyard which *was* in ᵃJezreel beside the palace of Ahab king of Samaria.

2 ᵃ1 Sam. 8:14

2 And Ahab spoke to Naboth, saying, "ᵃGive me your vineyard, that I may have it for a vegetable garden because it is close beside my house, and I will give you a better vineyard than it in its place; if you like, I will give you the price of it in money."

★ 3 ᵃLev. 25:23; Num. 36:7; Ezek. 46:18

3 But Naboth said to Ahab, "The LORD forbid me ᵃthat I should give you the inheritance of my fathers."

4 ᵃ1 Kin. 20:43

4 ᵃSo Ahab came into his house sullen and vexed because of the word which Naboth the Jezreelite had spoken to him; for he said, "I will not give you the inheritance of my fathers." And he lay down on his bed and turned away his face and ate no food.

5 But Jezebel his wife came to him and said to him, "How is it that your spirit is so sullen that you are not eating food?"

6 So he said to her, "Because I spoke to Naboth the Jezreelite, and said to him, 'Give me your vineyard for money; or else, if it pleases you, I will give you a vineyard in its place.' But he said, 'I will not give you my vineyard.' "

7 And Jezebel his wife said to him, "ᵃDo you now reign over Israel? Arise, eat bread, and let your heart be joyful; I will give you the vineyard of Naboth the Jezreelite."

7 ᵃ1 Sam. 8:14

8 ᵃSo she wrote letters in Ahab's name and sealed them with his seal, and sent letters to ᵇthe elders and to the nobles who were living with Naboth in his city.

8 ᵃEsth. 3:12; 8:8, 10 ᵇ1 Kin. 20:7

9 Now she wrote in the letters, saying, "Proclaim a fast, and seat Naboth at the head of the people;

10 and seat two ᵃworthless men before him, and let them testify against him, saying, 'ᵇYou cursed God and the king.' Then take him out and ᶜstone him to death."

★10 ᵃ1 Sam. 2:12; 2 Sam. 20:1 ᵇEx. 22:28; Lev. 24:15, 16; Acts 6:11 ᶜLev. 24:14

11 So the men of his city, the elders and the nobles who lived in his city, did as Jezebel had sent *word* to them, just as it was written in the letters which she had sent them.

12 They ᵃproclaimed a fast and seated Naboth at the head of the people.

12 ᵃIs. 58:4

13 Then the two worthless men came in and sat before him; and the worthless men testified against him, even against Naboth, before the people, saying, "Naboth cursed God and the king." ᵃSo they took him outside the city and stoned him to death with stones.

13 ᵃ2 Kin. 9:26; 2 Chr. 24:21; Acts 7:58, 59; Heb. 11:37

14 Then they sent *word* to Jezebel, saying, "Naboth has been stoned, and is dead."

15 And it came about when Jezebel heard that Naboth had been stoned and was dead, that Jezebel said to Ahab, "Arise, take possession of the vineyard of Naboth, the Jezreelite, which he refused to give you for money; for Naboth is not alive, but dead."

21:3 Naboth refused to sell his property for religious reasons (Lev. 25:23-28; Num. 36:7-8).
21:10 *worthless men.* See note on Judg. 19:22.

Jezebel saw to it that the procedure used to kill Naboth was technically according to the law (Deut. 17:5-6).

16 And it came about when Ahab heard that Naboth was dead, that Ahab arose to go down to the vineyard of Naboth the Jezreelite, to take possession of it.

17 Then the word of the Lord came to Elijah the Tishbite, saying,

18 "Arise, go down to meet Ahab king of Israel, ᵃwho is in Samaria; behold, he is in the vineyard of Naboth where he has gone down to take possession of it.

19 "And you shall speak to him, saying, 'Thus says the Lord, "ᵃHave you murdered, and also taken possession?"' And you shall speak to him, saying, 'Thus says the Lord, "ᵇIn the place where the dogs licked up the blood of Naboth the dogs shall lick up your blood, even yours."'"

20 And Ahab said to Elijah, "ᵃHave you found me, O my enemy?" And he answered, "I have found you, ᵇbecause you have sold yourself to do evil in the sight of the Lord.

21 "Behold, I will bring evil upon you, and ᵃwill utterly sweep you away, and will cut off from Ahab every male, both bond and free in Israel;

22 and ᵃI will make your house ᵇlike the house of Jeroboam the son of Nebat, and like the house of Baasha the son of Ahijah, because of the provocation with which you have provoked Me to anger, and because you ᶜhave made Israel sin.

23 "And of Jezebel also has the Lord spoken, saying, 'ᵃThe dogs shall eat Jezebel in the district of Jezreel.'

24 "ᵃThe one belonging to Ahab, who dies in the city, the dogs shall eat, and the one who dies in the field the birds of heaven shall eat."

25 ᵃSurely there was no one like Ahab who sold himself to do evil in the sight of the Lord, because Jezebel his wife incited him.

26 And ᵃhe acted very abominably in following idols, ᵇaccording to all that the Amorites had done, whom the Lord cast out before the sons of Israel.

27 And it came about when Ahab heard these words, that ᵃhe tore his clothes and put on sackcloth and fasted, and he lay in sackcloth and went about despondently.

28 Then the word of the Lord came to Elijah the Tishbite, saying,

29 "Do you see how Ahab has humbled himself before Me? Because he has humbled himself before Me, I will not bring the evil in his days, but I will bring the evil upon his house ᵃin his son's days."

9 Ahab's final battle, 22:1-40

22 And three years passed without war between Aram and Israel.

2 ᵃAnd it came about in the third year, that ᵇJehoshaphat the king of Judah came down to the king of Israel.

3 Now the king of Israel said to his servants, "Do you know that ᵃRamoth-gilead belongs to us, and we are still doing nothing to take it out of the hand of the king of Aram?"

Marginal references:

18 ᵃ1 Kin. 16:29
★19 ᵃ2 Sam. 12:9 ᵇ1 Kin. 22:38; 2 Kin. 9:26
20 ᵃ1 Kin. 18:17 ᵇ1 Kin. 21:25; 2 Kin. 17:17; Rom. 7:14
21 ᵃ1 Kin. 14:10; 2 Kin. 9:8
★22 ᵃ1 Kin. 15:29 ᵇ1 Kin. 16:3, 11 ᶜ1 Kin. 12:30; 13:34; 14:16
★23 ᵃ2 Kin. 9:10, 30-37
24 ᵃ1 Kin. 14:11; 16:4
25 ᵃ1 Kin. 16:30-33; 21:20
26 ᵃ1 Kin. 15:12; 2 Kin. 17:12 ᵇGen. 15:16; Lev. 18:25-30; 2 Kin. 21:11
★27 ᵃGen. 37:34; 2 Sam. 3:31; 2 Kin. 6:30
★29 ᵃ2 Kin. 9:25-37
2 ᵃ2 Chr. 18:2 ᵇ1 Kin. 15:24
★ 3-4
3 ᵃDeut. 4:43; Josh. 21:38; 1 Kin. 4:13

21:19 *In the place.* I.e., outside the city. Naboth was executed outside Jezreel (v. 13) and Ahab's blood was licked up outside Samaria (22:38, the "pool" being outside the city).

21:22 On the punishment of *Jeroboam* see 14:11, and on *Baasha*, 16:4.

21:23 Packs of dogs running wild acted as scavengers. On the fulfillment see 2 Kings 9:35-37.

21:27 Ahab's repentance was not accompanied by acts (such as restoring Naboth's vineyard to his family or tearing down the altars to Baal) that would prove it was genuine.

21:29 The whole penalty was not inflicted on Ahab (v. 19); some was reserved for Jehoram (2 Kings 9:24-25).

22:3-4 *Ramoth-gilead.* Apparently it had not been restored to Israel after the treaty of 20:34. Jehoshaphat agreed to join Ahab in this campaign.

4 ^a2 Kin.
3:7

4 And he said to Jehoshaphat, "Will you go with me to battle at Ramoth-gilead?" And Jehoshaphat said to the king of Israel, "^aI am as you are, my people as your people, my horses as your horses."

5 Moreover, Jehoshaphat said to the king of Israel, "Please inquire first for the word of the LORD."

★ **6** ^a1 Kin.
18:19

6 Then ^athe king of Israel gathered the prophets together, about four hundred men, and said to them, "Shall I go against Ramoth-gilead to battle or shall I refrain?" And they said, "Go up, for the Lord will give it into the hand of the king."

7 ^a2 Kin.
3:11

7 But ^aJehoshaphat said, "Is there not yet a prophet of the LORD here, that we may inquire of him?"

8 And the king of Israel said to Jehoshaphat, "There is yet one man by whom we may inquire of the LORD, but I hate him, because he does not prophesy good concerning me, but evil. He is Micaiah son of Imlah." But Jehoshaphat said, "Let not the king say so."

9 Then the king of Israel called an officer and said, "Bring quickly Micaiah son of Imlah."

10 ^a1 Kin.
22:6

10 Now the king of Israel and Jehoshaphat king of Judah were sitting each on his throne, arrayed in their robes, at the threshing floor at the entrance of the gate of Samaria; and ^aall the prophets were prophesying before them.

11 ^aZech.
1:18-21
^bDeut. 33:17

11 Then Zedekiah the son of Chenaanah made ^ahorns of iron for himself and said, "Thus says the LORD, '^bWith these you shall gore the Arameans until they are consumed.' "

12 And all the prophets were prophesying thus, saying, "Go up to Ramoth-gilead and prosper, for the LORD will give it into the hand of the king."

13 Then the messenger who went to summon Micaiah spoke to him saying, "Behold now, the words of the prophets are uniformly favorable to the king. Please let your word be like the word of one of them, and speak favorably."

14 But Micaiah said, "^aAs the LORD lives, what ^bthe LORD says to me, that I will speak."

14 ^a1 Kin.
18:10, 15
^bNum.
22:18; 24:13

15 When he came to the king, the king said to him, "Micaiah, shall we go to Ramoth-gilead to battle, or shall we refrain?" And he answered him, "^aGo up and succeed, and the LORD will give it into the hand of the king."

★**15** ^a1 Kin.
22:12

16 Then the king said to him, "How many times must I adjure you to speak to me nothing but the truth in the name of the LORD?"

17 So he said,
"I saw all Israel
  Scattered on the mountains,
  ^aLike sheep which have no shepherd.
And the LORD said,
  'These have no master.
Let each of them return to his house in peace.' "

★**17** ^aNum.
27:17; 1 Kin.
22:34-36;
2 Chr. 18:16;
Matt. 9:36;
Mark 6:34

18 Then the king of Israel said to Jehoshaphat, "^aDid I not tell you that he would not prophesy good concerning me, but evil?"

18 ^a1 Kin.
22:8

19 And Micaiah said, "Therefore, hear the word of the LORD. ^aI saw the LORD sitting on His throne, and ^ball the host of heaven standing by Him on His right and on His left.

19 ^aIs. 6:1;
Ezek. 1:26-
28; Dan. 7:9,
10 ^bJob 1:6;
2:1; Ps.
103:20, 21;
Dan. 7:10;
Matt. 18:10;
Heb. 1:7, 14

20 "And the LORD said, 'Who will entice Ahab to go up and fall at Ramoth-gilead?' And one said this while another said that.

22:6 the prophets. Not Jezebel's 400 prophets of Baal, but prophets of the Lord. Yet because they were on Ahab's payroll, they said what they knew the king wanted to hear.
22:15 Apparently Micaiah's tone of voice and gestures showed that he spoke sarcastically (cf. v. 16).
22:17 The truth was that Ahab would be killed and his army scattered.

★21-23

21 "Then a spirit came forward and stood before the LORD and said, 'I will entice him.'

22 *a*Judg.
9:23; 1 Sam.
16:14; 18:10;
19:9; Ezek.
14:9;
2 Thess. 2:11

22 "And the LORD said to him, 'How?' And he said, 'I will go out and *a*be a deceiving spirit in the mouth of all his prophets.' Then He said, 'You are to entice *him* and also prevail. Go and do so.'

23 *a*Ezek.
14:9

23 "Now therefore, behold, *a*the LORD has put a deceiving spirit in the mouth of all these your prophets; and the LORD has proclaimed disaster against you."

★24-25

24 *a*1 Kin.
22:11; Matt.
5:39; Acts
23:2, 3
*b*2 Chr.
18:23

24 Then *a*Zedekiah the son of Chenaanah came near and struck Micaiah on the cheek and said, "*b*How did the Spirit of the LORD pass from me to speak to you?"

25 *a*1 Kin.
20:30

25 And Micaiah said, "Behold, you shall see on that day when you *a*enter an inner room to hide yourself."

26 Then the king of Israel said, "Take Micaiah and return him to Amon the governor of the city and to Joash the king's son;

27 *a*2 Chr.
16:10; 18:25-
27

27 and say, 'Thus says the king, "*a*Put this man in prison, and feed him sparingly with bread and water until I return safely." ' "

28 *a*Deut.
18:22 *b*Mic.
1:2

28 And Micaiah said, "*a*If you indeed return safely the LORD has not spoken by me." And he said, "*b*Listen, all you people."

29 *a*1 Kin.
22:3, 4

29 So *a*the king of Israel and Jehoshaphat king of Judah went up against Ramoth-gilead.

★30 *a*2 Chr.
35:22

30 And the king of Israel said to Jehoshaphat, "*a*I will disguise myself and go into the battle, but you put on your robes." So the king of Israel disguised himself and went into the battle.

31 *a*1 Kin.
20:1, 16, 24;
2 Chr. 18:30

31 Now *a*the king of Aram had commanded the thirty-two captains of his chariots, saying, "Do not fight with small or great, but with the king of Israel alone."

32 So it came about, when the captains of the chariots saw Jehoshaphat, that they said, "Surely it is the king of Israel," and they turned aside to fight against him, and Jehoshaphat cried out.

33 Then it happened, when the captains of the chariots saw that it was not the king of Israel, that they turned back from pursuing him.

34 Now a certain man drew his bow at random and struck the king of Israel in a joint of the armor. So he said to the driver of his chariot, "Turn around, and take me out of the fight; *a*for I am severely wounded."

★34 *a*2 Chr.
35:23

35 And the battle raged that day, and the king was propped up in his chariot in front of the Arameans, and died at evening, and the blood from the wound ran into the bottom of the chariot.

36 *a*Then a cry passed throughout the army close to sunset, saying, "Every man to his city and every man to his country."

36 *a*2 Kin.
14:12

37 So the king died and was brought to Samaria, and they buried the king in Samaria.

38 And they washed the chariot by the pool of Samaria, and the dogs licked up his blood (now the harlots bathed themselves *there*), *a*according to the word of the LORD which He spoke.

★38 *a*1 Kin.
21:19

39 Now the rest of the acts of Ahab and all that he did and *a*the ivory house which he built and all the cities which he built, are they not written in the Book of the Chronicles of the Kings of Israel?

★39 *a*Amos
3:15

40 So Ahab slept with his fathers, and Ahaziah his son became king in his place.

22:21-23 The Lord permitted *a deceiving spirit* to control the prophets and give Ahab the wrong advice. Nonetheless, Ahab made a responsible choice, having been warned of the truth by Micaiah.
22:24-25 To Zedekiah's challenge of Micaiah's authority, the true prophet predicted that when Israel was defeated Zedekiah would re-

alize the truth.
22:30 By this cowardly suggestion Ahab showed that he secretly feared Micaiah's prophecy might be true.
22:34 *at random*. Without taking specific aim.
22:38 See note on 21:19.
22:39 *the ivory house*. Excavations of Ahab's palace have uncovered many ivory items.

L   The Reign of Jehoshaphat in Judah (873–848; 2 Chron. 17:1–20:37), 22:41–50

★41-50
41 *²Chr. 20:31*   **41** ᵃNow Jehoshaphat the son of Asa became king over Judah in the fourth year of Ahab king of Israel.

42 Jehoshaphat was thirty-five years old when he became king, and he reigned twenty-five years in Jerusalem. And his mother's name was Azubah the daughter of Shilhi.

43 *²Chr. 17:3 ᵇ1 Kin. 15:14; 2 Kin. 12:3*   **43** ᵃAnd he walked in all the way of Asa his father; he did not turn aside from it, doing right in the sight of the Lᴏʀᴅ. ᵇHowever, the high places were not taken away; the people still sacrificed and burnt incense on the high places.

44 *ᵃ1 Kin. 22:2; 2 Kin. 8:16, 18; 2 Chr. 19:2*   **44** ᵃJehoshaphat also made peace with the king of Israel.

45 *ᵃ2 Chr. 20:34*   **45** Now the rest of the acts of Jehoshaphat, and his might which he showed and how he warred, are they not written ᵃin the Book of the Chronicles of the Kings of Judah?

46 *ᵃGen. 19:5; Deut. 23:17; 1 Kin. 14:24; 15:12; Jude 7*   **46** And the remnant of ᵃthe sodomites who remained in the days of his father Asa, he expelled from the land.

47 *ᵃ2 Sam. 8:14; 2 Kin. 3:9*   **47** Now ᵃthere was no king in Edom; a deputy was king.

48 Jehoshaphat made ᵃships of Tarshish to go to ᵇOphir for gold, but ᶜthey did not go for the ships were broken at ᵈEzion-geber.

★48 *ᵃ1 Kin. 10:22; 2 Chr. 20:36 ᵇ1 Kin. 9:28 ᶜ2 Chr. 20:37 ᵈ1 Kin. 9:26*

49 Then Ahaziah the son of Ahab said to Jehoshaphat, "Let my servants go with your servants in the ships." But Jehoshaphat was not willing.

50 *ᵃ2 Chr. 21:1*   **50** ᵃAnd Jehoshaphat slept with his fathers and was buried with his fathers in the city of his father David, and Jehoram his son became king in his place.

M   The Reign of Ahaziah in Israel (841), 22:51–53

★51-53
51 *ᵃ1 Kin. 22:40*   **51** Ahaziah the son of Ahab ᵃbecame king over Israel in Samaria in the seventeenth year of Jehoshaphat king of Judah, and he reigned two years over Israel.

52 *ᵃ1 Kin. 15:26; 21:25*   **52** And he did evil in the sight of the Lᴏʀᴅ and ᵃwalked in the way of his father and in the way of his mother and in the way of Jeroboam the son of Nebat, who caused Israel to sin.

53 *ᵃJudg. 2:11; 1 Kin. 16:30-32*   **53** ᵃSo he served Baal and worshiped him and provoked the Lᴏʀᴅ God of Israel to anger according to all that his father had done.

22:41-50 A much more detailed account of good King Jehoshaphat's reign in Judah (873–848) is given in 2 Chron. 17–20. His son Jehoram married Athaliah, the daughter of Ahab and Jezebel (2 Kings 8:16–18), opening the door to Baal worship in Judah.
22:48 *ships of Tarshish.* Especially large ships (see note on 10:22). On *Ophir* see note on 9:28. *were broken.* I.e., somehow destroyed (see 2 Chron. 20:35–37). *Ezion-geber.* See note on 9:26.
22:51-53 Cf. 2 Chron. 20:35–21:1. *Ahaziah* is described in the worst possible way.

INTRODUCTION TO
THE SECOND BOOK OF THE KINGS

AUTHOR: Jeremiah   DATE: c. 550 B.C.

Title, Author and Date *Since 1 and 2 Kings were originally one book, see the Introduction to 1 Kings for a discussion of these matters.*

Contents *Continuing where 1 Kings concluded (with Ahaziah), 2 Kings traces the decline and captivity of both Israel and Judah. Israel endured a succession of evil kings reigning during a 130-year period until the Assyrian captivity. Briefly told is the history of Judah, culminating in the Babylonian captivity. The book also records the miracle-filled ministry of Elisha. Well-known passages include the raising of the Shunammite's son (chap. 4), the healing of Naaman, the Syrian leper (chap. 5), the death of Jezebel (chap. 9), the revivals under Hezekiah (chap. 18) and under Josiah (chap. 23).*

During this period Amos and Hosea prophesied in Israel, and Obadiah, Joel, Isaiah, Micah, Nahum, Habakkuk, Zephaniah, and Jeremiah in Judah.

OUTLINE OF 2 KINGS

THE SECOND BOOK OF THE KINGS

I THE DIVIDED KINGDOM, 1:1–17:41

A The Reign of Ahaziah in Israel (853–852), 1:1–18

1 Now *a*Moab rebelled against Israel after the death of Ahab.

2 And Ahaziah fell through the lattice in his upper chamber which *was* in Samaria, and became ill. So he sent messengers and said to them, "Go, *a*inquire of Baal-zebub, the god of Ekron, *b*whether I shall recover from this sickness."

3 But the angel of the LORD said to *a*Elijah the Tishbite, "Arise, go up to meet the messengers of the king of Samaria and say to them, 'Is it because there is no God in Israel *that* you are going to inquire of *b*Baal-zebub, the god of Ekron?'

4 "Now therefore thus says the LORD, '*a*You shall not come down from the bed where you have gone up, but you shall surely die.'" Then Elijah departed.

5 When the messengers returned to him he said to them, "Why have you returned?"

6 And they said to him, "A man came up to meet us and said to us, 'Go, return to the king who sent you and say to him, "Thus says the LORD, 'Is it because there is no God in Israel *that* you are sending *a*to inquire of Baal-zebub, the god of Ekron? Therefore you shall not come down from the bed where you have gone up, but shall surely die.'"'"

7 And he said to them, "What kind of man was he who came up to meet you and spoke these words to you?"

8 And they answered him, "*a*He *was* a hairy man with a leather girdle bound about his loins." And he said, "It is Elijah the Tishbite."

9 Then the king *a*sent to him a captain of fifty with his fifty. And he went up to him, and behold, he was sitting on the top of the hill. And he said to him, "O man of God, the king says, 'Come down.'"

10 And Elijah answered and said to the captain of fifty, "If I am a man of God, *a*let fire come down from heaven and consume you and your fifty." *b*Then fire came down from heaven and consumed him and his fifty.

11 So he again sent to him another captain of fifty with his fifty. And he answered and said

Cross references

1 *a*2 Sam. 8:2; 2 Kin. 3:5

★ 2 *a*2 Kin. 1:3, 6, 16; Matt. 10:25; Mark 3:22 *b*2 Kin. 8:7-10

★ 3 *a*1 Kin. 17:1; 21:17 *b*2 Kin. 1:2

4 *a*2 Kin. 1:6, 16

6 *a*2 Kin. 1:2

★ 8 *a*Zech. 13:4; Matt. 3:4; Mark 1:6

9 *a*2 Kin. 6:13, 14

10 *a*1 Kin. 18:36-38; Luke 9:54 *b*Job 1:16

1:2 *lattice.* The crossed bars which covered a window to keep out the sun while allowing ventilation. *Baal-zebub* means "Lord of the flies," though here it probably represents a spelling change from Baal-zebul, which means "Baal the prince." *Ekron* was about 15 miles S.

of Joppa.

1:3 *the angel of the LORD.* See note on Gen. 16:10.

1:8 *a hairy man.* I.e., wearing a garment of sheep or goat skin with the hair left on.

to him, "O man of God, thus says the king, 'Come down quickly.' "

12 And Elijah answered and said to them, "If I am a man of God, let fire come down from heaven and consume you and your fifty." Then the fire of God came down from heaven and consumed him and his fifty.

13 So he ªagain sent the captain of a third fifty with his fifty. When the third captain of fifty went up, he came and bowed down on his knees before Elijah, and begged him and said to him, "O man of God, please let my life and the lives of these fifty servants of yours be precious in your sight.

14 "Behold fire came down from heaven, and consumed the first two captains of fifty with their fifties; but now let my life be precious in your sight."

15 And ªthe angel of the Lord said to Elijah, "Go down with him; ᵇdo not be afraid of him." So he arose and went down with him to the king.

16 Then he said to him, "Thus says the Lord, 'Because you have sent messengers ªto inquire of Baal-zebub, the god of Ekron—is it because there is no God in Israel to inquire of His word?—therefore you shall not come down from the bed where you have gone up, but shall surely die.' "

17 So Ahaziah died according to the word of the Lord which Elijah had spoken. And because he had no son, Jehoram became king in his place ªin the second year of Jehoram the son of Jehoshaphat, king of Judah.

18 Now the rest of the acts of Ahaziah which he did, are they not written in the Book of the Chronicles of the Kings of Israel?

B The Reign of Jehoram (Joram) in Israel (852–841), 2:1–8:15

1 *The translation of Elijah,* 2:1–11

2 And it came about when the Lord was about to ªtake up Elijah by a whirlwind to heaven, that Elijah went with ᵇElisha from ᶜGilgal.

2 And Elijah said to Elisha, "ªStay here please, for the Lord has sent me as far as ᵇBethel." But Elisha said, "ᶜAs the Lord lives and as you yourself live, I will not leave you." So they went down to Bethel.

3 Then ªthe sons of the prophets who *were at* Bethel came out to Elisha and said to him, "Do you know that the Lord will take away your master from over you today?" And he said, "Yes, I know; be still."

4 And Elijah said to him, "Elisha, please ªstay here, for the Lord has sent me to ᵇJericho." But he said, "ᶜAs the Lord lives, and as you yourself live, I will not leave you." So they came to Jericho.

5 And ªthe sons of the prophets who *were* at Jericho approached Elisha and said to him, "ᵇDo you know that the Lord will take away your master from over you today?" And he answered, "Yes, I know; be still."

6 Then Elijah said to him, "Please ªstay here, for the Lord has sent me to ᵇthe Jordan." And he said, "As the Lord lives, and as you yourself live, I will not leave you." So the two of them went on.

7 Now ªfifty men of the sons of the prophets went and stood opposite *them* at a distance, while

---

Margin references:

13 ªIs. 1:5; Jer. 5:3

15 ª2 Kin. 1:3 ᵇIs. 51:12; Jer. 1:17; Ezek. 2:6

16 ª2 Kin. 1:3

17 ª2 Kin. 3:1; 8:16

★ 1 ªGen. 5:24; Heb. 11:5 ᵇ1 Kin. 19:16-21 ᶜJosh. 4:19

2 ªRuth 1:15 ᵇ1 Kin. 12:28, 29 ᶜ1 Sam. 1:26; 2 Kin. 2:4, 6

3 ª2 Kin. 4:1, 38; 5:22

4 ª2 Kin. 2:2 ᵇJosh. 6:26 ᶜ2 Kin. 2:2

★ 5 ª2 Kin. 2:3 ᵇ2 Kin. 2:3

6 ª2 Kin. 2:2 ᵇJosh. 3:8, 15-17

7 ª2 Kin. 2:15, 16

2:1 Apparently not the *Gilgal* in the Jordan Valley (Josh. 4:19), but one in the hill country of Ephraim, about 8 miles NW. of Bethel.

2:5 *the sons of the prophets.* Apprentices to the prophets.

the two of them stood by the Jordan.

8 And Elijah ^atook his mantle and folded it together and ^bstruck the waters, and they were divided here and there, so that the two of them crossed over on dry ground.

9 Now it came about when they had crossed over, that Elijah said to Elisha, "Ask what I shall do for you before I am taken from you." And Elisha said, "Please, let a ^adouble portion of your spirit be upon me."

10 And he said, "You have asked a hard thing. *Nevertheless,* if you ^asee me when I am taken from you, it shall be so for you; but if not, it shall not be *so.*"

11 Then it came about as they were going along and talking, that behold, *there appeared* ^aa chariot of fire and horses of fire which separated the two of them. And Elijah went up by a whirlwind to heaven.

2 The beginning of Elisha's ministry, 2:12-25

12 And Elisha saw *it* and cried out, "^aMy father, my father, the chariots of Israel and its horsemen!" And he saw him no more. Then ^bhe took hold of his own clothes and tore them in two pieces.

13 He also took up the mantle of Elijah that fell from him, and returned and stood by the bank of the Jordan.

14 And he took the mantle of Elijah that fell from him, and struck the waters and said, "Where is the Lord, the God of Elijah?" And when he also had ^astruck the waters, they were divided here and there; and Elisha crossed over.

15 Now when ^athe sons of the prophets who *were* at Jericho opposite *him* saw him, they said, "The spirit of Elijah rests on Elisha." And they came to meet him and bowed themselves to the ground before him.

16 And they said to him, "Behold now, there are with your servants fifty strong men, please let them go and search for your master; perhaps ^athe Spirit of the Lord has taken him up and cast him on some mountain or into some valley." And he said, "You shall not send."

17 But when ^athey urged him until he was ashamed, he said, "Send." They sent therefore fifty men; and they searched three days, but did not find him.

18 And they returned to him while he was staying at Jericho; and he said to them, "Did I not say to you, 'Do not go'?"

19 Then the men of the city said to Elisha, "Behold now, the situation of this city is pleasant, as my lord sees; but the water is bad, and the land is unfruitful."

20 And he said, "Bring me a new jar, and put salt in it." So they brought *it* to him.

21 And he went out to the spring of water, and ^athrew salt in it and said, "Thus says the Lord, 'I have purified these waters; there shall not be from there death or unfruitfulness any longer.' "

22 So the waters have been purified to this day, according to

Marginal references

8 ^a1 Kin. 19:13, 19
^bEx. 14:21, 22; 2 Kin. 2:14

★**9** ^aNum. 11:17-25; Deut. 21:17

★**10** ^aActs 1:10

★**11** ^a2 Kin. 6:17

★**12** ^a2 Kin. 13:14 ^bGen. 37:34; Job 1:20

14 ^a2 Kin. 2:8

15 ^a2 Kin. 2:7

★**16-18**

16 ^a1 Kin. 18:12; Acts 8:39

17 ^a2 Kin. 8:11

21 ^aEx. 15:25, 26; 2 Kin. 4:41; 6:6

2:9 *let a double portion of your spirit be upon me.* Not a request that Elisha have or do twice as much as Elijah, but a plea that he might be the recognized heir of Elijah in the prophetic office (the firstborn received a double portion of his father's inheritance, Deut. 21:17).

2:10 What Elisha requested was not Elijah's to bestow.

2:11 Elijah, like Enoch (see note on Gen. 5:22-24), was taken to heaven without dying. This will also be the experience of believers living at the time of Christ's return (1 Cor. 15:51; 1 Thess. 4:17).

2:12 *the chariots of Israel and its horsemen!* I.e., Elijah was the strongest instrument of God's power for Israel (just as the chariot was the mightiest military weapon of the nation).

2:16-18 The sons of the prophets did not believe what Elisha apparently had told them had happened to Elijah and insisted on sending out a search party.

the word of Elisha which he spoke.

★23 *a*2 Chr. 36:16; Ps. 31:17, 18

23 Then he went up from there to Bethel; and as he was going up by the way, young lads came out from the city and *a*mocked him and said to him, "Go up, you baldhead; go up, you baldhead!"

24 *a*Neh. 13:25-27

24 When he looked behind him and saw them, he *a*cursed them in the name of the Lord. Then two female bears came out of the woods and tore up forty-two lads of their number.

25 *a*1 Kin. 18:19, 20; 2 Kin. 4:25

25 And he went from there to *a*Mount Carmel, and from there he returned to Samaria.

3 Jehoram's expedition against Moab, 3:1-27

★ 1 *a*2 Kin. 1:17

3 Now Jehoram the son of Ahab became king over Israel at Samaria *a*in the eighteenth year of Jehoshaphat king of Judah, and reigned twelve years.

★ 2 *a*Ex. 23:24; 2 Kin. 10:18, 26-28 *b*1 Kin. 16:31, 32

2 And he did evil in the sight of the Lord, though not like his father and his mother; for *a*he put away the *sacred* pillar of Baal *b*which his father had made.

★ 3 *a*1 Kin. 12:28-32 *b*1 Kin. 14:9, 16

3 Nevertheless, *a*he clung to the sins of Jeroboam the son of Nebat, *b*which he made Israel sin; he did not depart from them.

★ 4-5

4 *a*2 Sam. 8:2; Is. 16:1, 2

4 Now Mesha king of Moab was a sheep breeder, and *a*used to pay the king of Israel 100,000 lambs and the wool of 100,000 rams.

5 *a*2 Kin. 1:1

5 But it came about, *a*when Ahab died, the king of Moab rebelled against the king of Israel.

6 And King Jehoram went out of Samaria at that time and mustered all Israel.

7 Then he went and sent *word* to Jehoshaphat the king of Judah, saying, "The king of Moab has rebelled against me. Will you go with me to fight against Moab?" And he said, "I will go up; *a*I am as you are, my people as your people, my horses as your horses."

7 *a*1 Kin. 22:4

8 And he said, "Which way shall we go up?" And he answered, "The way of the wilderness of Edom."

9 So *a*the king of Israel went with *b*the king of Judah and *c*the king of Edom; and they made a circuit of seven days' journey, and there was no water for the army or for the cattle that followed them.

9 *a*2 Kin. 3:1 *b*2 Kin. 3:7 *c*1 Kin. 22:47

10 Then the king of Israel said, "Alas! For the Lord has called these three kings to give them into the hand of Moab."

★10

11 But Jehoshaphat said, "*a*Is there not a prophet of the Lord here, that we may inquire of the Lord by him?" And one of the king of Israel's servants answered and said, "*b*Elisha the son of Shaphat is here, *c*who used to pour water on the hands of Elijah."

11 *a*1 Kin. 22:7 *b*2 Kin. 2:25 *c*1 Kin. 19:21; John 13:4, 5, 13, 14

12 And Jehoshaphat said, "The word of the Lord is with him." So the king of Israel and Jehoshaphat and the king of Edom went down to him.

13 Now Elisha said to the king of Israel, "What do I have to do with you? *a*Go to the prophets of your father and to the prophets of your mother." And the king of Israel said to him, "No, for the Lord has called these three kings *together* to give them into the hand of Moab."

13 *a*1 Kin. 18:19; 22:6-11, 22-25

2:23 *young lads.* Young men, not irresponsible youngsters. They were challenging Elisha's prophetic office. *Go up.* I.e., ascend, as you claimed Elijah did. *baldhead.* Whether Elisha was bald at this time or not is beside the point (he did live 50 more years, 13:14); the young men were in effect cursing Elisha (cf. Isa. 3:17, 24).
3:1 The double dating of the accession of *Jehoram* (cf. 1:17) indicates a coregency with Je-

hoshaphat in Judah.
3:2 *his mother.* Jezebel, who lived throughout his entire reign (9:30).
3:3 *the sins of Jeroboam.* See 1 Kings 12:26-33.
3:4-5 An inscription on the Moabite Stone, discovered in 1868, describes this revolt on the part of Mesha in refusing to continue to pay tribute.
3:10 Impious Jehoram blamed God for his predicament.

14 a1 Kin.
17:1; 2 Kin.
5:16
14 And Elisha said, "aAs the LORD of hosts lives, before whom I stand, were it not that I regard the presence of Jehoshaphat the king of Judah, I would not look at you nor see you.

*15 a1 Sam.
16:23; 1 Chr.
25:1 b1 Kin.
18:46; Ezek.
1:3
15 "But now abring me a minstrel." And it came about, when the minstrel played, that bthe hand of the LORD came upon him.

16 And he said, "Thus says the LORD, 'Make this valley full of trenches.'

17 aPs.
107:35
17 "For thus says the LORD, 'You shall not see wind nor shall you see rain; yet that valley ashall be filled with water, so that you shall drink, both you and your cattle and your beasts.

18 aJer.
32:17, 27;
Mark 10:27;
Luke 1:37
18 'And this is but a aslight thing in the sight of the LORD; He shall also give the Moabites into your hand.

19 a2 Kin.
3:25
19 'aThen you shall strike every fortified city and every choice city, and fell every good tree and stop all springs of water, and mar every good piece of land with stones.'"

20 aEx.
29:39, 40
20 And it happened in the morning aabout the time of offering the sacrifice, that behold, water came by the way of Edom, and the country was filled with water.

21 Now all the Moabites heard that the kings had come up to fight against them. And all who were able to put on armor and older were summoned, and stood on the border.

*22
22 And they rose early in the morning, and the sun shone on the water, and the Moabites saw the water opposite *them* as red as blood.

23 Then they said, "This is blood; the kings have surely fought together, and they have slain one another. Now therefore, Moab, to the spoil!"

24 But when they came to the camp of Israel, the Israelites arose and struck the Moabites, so that they fled before them; and they went forward into the land, slaughtering the Moabites.

*25 a2 Kin.
3:19 bIs.
16:7; Jer.
48:31, 36
25 aThus they destroyed the cities; and each one threw a stone on every piece of good land and filled it. So they stopped all the springs of water and felled all the good trees, until in bKir-hareseth *only* they left its stones; however, the slingers went about *it* and struck it.

*26-27
26 When the king of Moab saw that the battle was too fierce for him, he took with him 700 men who drew swords, to break through to the king of Edom; but they could not.

27 aAmos
2:1; Mic. 6:7
27 Then he took his oldest son who was to reign in his place, and aoffered him as a burnt offering on the wall. And there came great wrath against Israel, and they departed from him and returned to their own land.

4 Elisha's ministry, 4:1–8:15
a Elisha aids a widow, 4:1-7

* 1 a2 Kin.
2:3 bLev.
25:39-41, 48;
1 Sam. 22:2;
Neh. 5:2-5
4 Now a certain woman of the wives of athe sons of the prophets cried out to Elisha, "Your servant my husband is dead, and you know that your servant feared the LORD; and bthe creditor has come to take my two children to be his slaves."

2 a1 Kin.
17:12
2 And Elisha said to her, "What shall I do for you? Tell me, what do you have in the house?" And she said, "Your maidservant has nothing in the house except aa jar of oil."

3:15 *minstrel.* A player of a stringed instrument, called in order to calm Elisha's perturbed spirit (vv. 13–14) that he might hear God speaking to him.

3:22 *red as blood.* Caused either by the soil or the early morning sun or both.

3:25 *felled all the good trees.* A veritable scorched earth policy, not normally permitted (Deut. 20:19). *Kir-hareseth.* The chief city in the southern part of Moab.

3:26-27 Hoping for a turn in his fortunes, the king of Moab made the supreme sacrifice in offering his son to Chemosh, the god of Moab (Deut. 12:31). The Israelites were so frightened at what an aroused Moabite army might do that they retreated.

4:1 *sons of the prophets.* Obviously not unmarried monks. The sons would have had to work off their father's debt (Lev. 25:39ff.).

3 Then he said, "Go, borrow vessels at large for yourself from all your neighbors, *even* empty vessels; do not get a few.

4 "And you shall go in and shut the door behind you and your sons, and pour out into all these vessels; and you shall set aside what is full."

5 So she went from him and shut the door behind her and her sons; they were bringing *the vessels* to her and she poured.

★ **6** ^aMatt. 14:20

6 And it came about when ^athe vessels were full, that she said to her son, "Bring me another vessel." And he said to her, "There is not one vessel more." And the oil stopped.

7 ^a1 Kin. 12:22

7 Then she came and told ^athe man of God. And he said, "Go, sell the oil and pay your debt, and you *and* your sons can live on the rest."

b Elisha and the Shunammite woman, 4:8–37

★ **8** ^aJosh. 19:18

8 Now there came a day when Elisha passed over to ^aShunem, where there was a prominent woman, and she persuaded him to eat food. And so it was, as often as he passed by, he turned in there to eat food.

9 ^a2 Kin. 4:7

9 And she said to her husband, "Behold now, I perceive that this is a holy ^aman of God passing by us continually.

★**10** ^aMatt. 10:41, 42; 25:40; Rom. 12:13

10 "Please, let us ^amake a little walled upper chamber and let us set a bed for him there, and a table and a chair and a lampstand; and it shall be, when he comes to us, *that* he can turn in there."

11 One day he came there and turned in to the upper chamber and rested.

12 ^a2 Kin. 4:29-31; 5:20-27; 8:4, 5

12 Then he said to ^aGehazi his servant, "Call this Shunammite." And when he had called her, she stood before him.

13 And he said to him, "Say now to her, 'Behold, you have been careful for us with all this care; what can I do for you? Would you be spoken for to the king or to the captain of the army?'" And she answered, "I live among my own people."

14 So he said, "What then is to be done for her?" And Gehazi answered, "Truly she has no son and her husband is old."

15 And he said, "Call her." When he had called her, she stood in the doorway.

16 ^aGen. 18:14 ^b2 Kin. 4:28

16 Then he said, "^aAt this season next year you shall embrace a son." And she said, "No, my lord, O man of God, ^bdo not lie to your maidservant."

17 And the woman conceived and bore a son at that season the next year, as Elisha had said to her.

18 When the child was grown, the day came that he went out to his father to the reapers.

★**19**

19 And he said to his father, "My head, my head." And he said to his servant, "Carry him to his mother."

20 When he had taken him and brought him to his mother, he sat on her lap until noon, and *then* died.

21 ^a2 Kin. 4:32 ^b2 Kin. 4:7

21 And she went up and ^alaid him on the bed of ^bthe man of God, and shut *the door* behind him, and went out.

22 Then she called to her husband and said, "Please send me one of the servants and one of the donkeys, that I may run to the man of God and return."

23 ^aNum. 10:10; 28:11; 1 Chr. 23:31

23 And he said, "Why will you go to him today? It is neither ^anew moon nor sabbath." And she said, "*It will be* well."

24 Then she saddled a donkey and said to her servant, "Drive and go forward; do not

---

4:6 God's supply was as large as the woman's faith and obedience.
4:8 *Shunem.* Seven miles E. of Megiddo, overlooking the valley of Jezreel.

4:10 *a little walled upper chamber.* A weatherproof room on the flat roof of the house.
4:19 *My head, my head.* Perhaps he suffered a sunstroke.

slow down the pace for me unless I tell you."

★25 *a*2 Kin. 2:25

25 So she went and came to the man of God to *a*Mount Carmel. And it came about when the man of God saw her at a distance, that he said to Gehazi his servant, "Behold, yonder is the Shunammite.

26 "Please run now to meet her and say to her, 'Is it well with you? Is it well with your husband? Is it well with the child?' " And she answered, "It is well."

★27 *a*2 Kin. 4:25

27 When she came to the man of God *a*to the hill, she caught hold of his feet. And Gehazi came near to push her away; but the man of God said, "Let her alone, for her soul is troubled within her; and the LORD has hidden it from me and has not told me."

28 *a*2 Kin. 4:16

28 Then she said, "Did I ask for a son from my lord? Did I not say, '*a*Do not deceive me'?"

29 *a*1 Kin. 18:46; 2 Kin. 9:1 *b*Ex. 4:17; 2 Kin. 2:14 *c*Luke 10:4 *d*Ex. 7:19, 20; 14:16

29 Then he said to Gehazi, "*a*Gird up your loins and *b*take my staff in your hand, and go your way; if you meet any man, do not *c*salute him, and if anyone salutes you, do not answer him; and *d*lay my staff on the lad's face."

30 *a*2 Kin. 2:2, 4

30 And the mother of the lad said, "*a*As the LORD lives and as you yourself live, I will not leave you." And he arose and followed her.

★31 *a*John 11:11

31 Then Gehazi passed on before them and laid the staff on the lad's face, but there was neither sound nor response. So he returned to meet him and told him, "The lad *a*has not awakened."

32 When Elisha came into the house, behold the lad was dead and laid on his bed.

33 *a*2 Kin. 4:4; Matt. 6:6; Luke 8:51

33 So he entered and *a*shut the door behind them both, and prayed to the LORD.

34 And *a*he went up and lay on the child, and put his mouth on his mouth and his eyes on his eyes and his hands on his hands, and he stretched himself on him; and the flesh of the child became warm.

34 *a*1 Kin. 17:21-23

35 Then he returned and walked in the house once back and forth, and went up and *a*stretched himself on him; and the lad sneezed seven times and the lad opened his eyes.

★35 *a*1 Kin. 17:21

36 And he called Gehazi and said, "Call this Shunammite." So he called her. And when she came in to him, he said, "Take up your son."

37 Then she went in and fell at his feet and bowed herself to the ground, and *a*she took up her son and went out.

37 *a*Heb. 11:35

c Elisha at Gilgal, 4:38–44

38 When Elisha returned to *a*Gilgal, *there was* *b*a famine in the land. As *c*the sons of the prophets *d*were sitting before him, he said to his servant, "*e*Put on the large pot and boil stew for the sons of the prophets."

38 *a*2 Kin. 2:1 *b*2 Kin. 8:1 *c*2 Kin. 2:3 *d*Luke 10:39; Acts 22:3 *e*Ezek. 11:3, 7, 11; 24:3

39 Then one went out into the field to gather herbs, and found a wild vine and gathered from it his lap full of wild gourds, and came and sliced them into the pot of stew, for they did not know *what they were.*

★39

40 So they poured *it* out for the men to eat. And it came about as they were eating of the stew, that they cried out and said, "O man of God, there is *a*death in the pot." And they were unable to eat.

40 *a*Ex. 10:17

41 But he said, "Now bring meal." *a*And he threw it into the pot, and he said, "Pour *it* out for the people that they may eat." Then there was no harm in the pot.

41 *a*Ex. 15:25; 2 Kin. 2:21

4:25 The distance was about 25 miles.
4:27 Elisha did not yet know that her son had died.
4:31 Elisha's instruction to Gehazi was designed to teach the people that the power to work miracles was not magically inherent in Elisha's staff.

4:35 *he returned.* Elisha got off the bed and *walked* around the chamber in excitement and anticipation. This was not cardiopulmonary resuscitation, but a spectacular miracle of restoring life to one who had been dead for some hours.
4:39 *wild gourds.* Wild cucumbers.

42 aMatt.
14:16-21;
15:32-38

42 Now a man came from Baal-shalishah, and brought the man of God bread of the first fruits, twenty loaves of barley and fresh ears of grain in his sack. And he said, "aGive *them* to the people that they may eat."

43 aLuke
9:13; John
6:9

43 And his attendant said, "What, ashall I set this before a hundred men?" But he said, "Give *them* to the people that they may eat, for thus says the LORD, 'They shall eat and have *some* left over.'"

44 aMatt.
14:20; 15:37;
John 6:13

44 So he set *it* before them, and they ate and ahad *some* left over, according to the word of the LORD.

*d Elisha and Naaman the leper,
5:1-27*

1 aLuke
4:27

5 Now aNaaman, captain of the army of the king of Aram, was a great man with his master, and highly respected, because by him the LORD had given victory to Aram. The man was also a valiant warrior, *but he was* a leper.

2 a2 Kin.
6:23; 13:20

2 Now the Arameans had gone out ain bands, and had taken captive a little girl from the land of Israel; and she waited on Naaman's wife.

3 And she said to her mistress, "I wish that my master were with the prophet who is in Samaria! Then he would cure him of his leprosy."

4 And Naaman went in and told his master, saying, "Thus and thus spoke the girl who is from the land of Israel."

★ **5** a1 Sam.
9:7; 2 Kin.
4:42 bJudg.
14:12; 2 Kin.
5:22, 23

5 Then the king of Aram said, "Go now, and I will send a letter to the king of Israel." And he departed and atook with him ten talents of silver and six thousand *shekels* of gold and ten bchanges of clothes.

6 And he brought the letter to the king of Israel, saying, "And now as this letter comes to you,

behold, I have sent Naaman my servant to you, that you may cure him of his leprosy."

7 And it came about when the king of Israel read the letter, that ahe tore his clothes and said, "bAm I God, to kill and to make alive, that this man is sending *word* to me to cure a man of his leprosy? But cconsider now, and see how he is seeking a quarrel against me."

7 aGen.
37:29 bGen.
30:2; 1 Sam.
2:6 c1 Kin.
20:7; Luke
11:54

8 And it happened when Elisha athe man of God heard that the king of Israel had torn his clothes, that he sent *word* to the king, saying, "Why have you torn your clothes? Now let him come to me, and he shall know that there is a prophet in Israel."

8 a1 Kin.
12:22

9 So Naaman came with his horses and his chariots, and stood at the doorway of the house of Elisha.

10 And Elisha sent a messenger to him, saying, "aGo and wash in the Jordan seven times, and your flesh shall be restored to you and *you shall* be clean."

10 aJohn 9:7

11 But Naaman was furious and went away and said, "Behold, I thought, 'He will surely come out to me, and stand and call on the name of the LORD his God, and wave his hand over the place, and cure the leper.'

12 "Are not Abanah and Pharpar, the rivers of Damascus, better than all the waters of Israel? Could I not wash in them and be clean?" So he turned and awent away in a rage.

★ **12** aProv.
14:17; 16:32;
19:11

13 aThen his servants came near and spoke to him and said, "bMy father, had the prophet told you *to do some* great thing, would you not have done *it*? How much more *then*, when he says to you, 'Wash, and be clean'?"

13 a1 Sam.
28:23
b2 Kin. 2:12;
6:21; 8:9

14 So he went down and dipped *himself* seven times in the Jordan, according to the word of the man of God; and ahis flesh

14 a2 Kin.
5:10; Job
33:25 bLuke
4:27; 5:13

5:5 *ten talents of silver.* 30,000 shekels, about 15,000 ounces. *six thousand shekels.* About 3,000 ounces, a handsome gift.
5:12 The *Abanah* is the present-day Barada,

which flows through the center of Damascus, and the *Pharpar* is the Awaj, which flows further S. Both are clear streams, in contrast to the turbid Jordan.

was restored like the flesh of a little child, and *b*he was clean.

15 When he returned to the man of God with all his company, and came and stood before him, he said, "Behold now, *a*I know that there is no God in all the earth, but in Israel; so please *b*take a present from your servant now."

16 But he said, "*a*As the LORD lives, before whom I stand, *b*I will take nothing." And he urged him to take *it,* but he refused.

17 And Naaman said, "If not, please let your servant at least be given two mules' load of *a*earth; for your servant will no more offer burnt offering nor will he sacrifice to other gods, but to the LORD.

18 "In this matter may the LORD pardon your servant: when my master goes into the house of Rimmon to worship there, and *a*he leans on my hand and I bow myself in the house of Rimmon, when I bow myself in the house of Rimmon, the LORD pardon your servant in this matter."

19 And he said to him, "*a*Go in peace." So he departed from him some distance.

20 But *a*Gehazi, the servant of Elisha the man of God, thought, "Behold, my master has spared this Naaman the Aramean, by not receiving from his hands what he brought. *b*As the LORD lives, I will run after him and take something from him."

21 So Gehazi pursued Naaman. When Naaman saw one running after him, he came down from the chariot to meet him and said, "Is all well?"

22 And he said, "*a*All is well. My master has sent me, saying, 'Behold, just now two young men of the sons of the prophets have come to me from *b*the hill country of Ephraim. Please give them a talent of silver and *c*two changes of clothes.' "

23 And Naaman said, "*a*Be pleased to take two talents." And he urged him, and bound two talents of silver in two bags with two changes of clothes, and gave them to two of his servants; and they carried *them* before him.

24 When he came to the hill, he took them from their hand and *a*deposited them in the house, and he sent the men away, and they departed.

25 But he went in and stood before his master. And Elisha said to him, "Where have you been, Gehazi?" And he said, "*a*Your servant went nowhere."

26 Then he said to him, "Did not my heart go *with you,* when the man turned from his chariot to meet you? *a*Is it a time to receive money and to receive clothes and olive groves and vineyards and sheep and oxen and male and female servants?

27 "Therefore, the leprosy of Naaman shall cleave to you and to your descendants forever." So he went out from his presence *a*a leper *as white* as snow.

e Elisha recovers the axe head,
6:1-7

6 Now *a*the sons of the prophets said to Elisha, "Behold now, the place before you where we are living is too limited for us.

2 "Please let us go to the Jordan, and each of us take from there a beam, and let us make a place there for ourselves where we may live." So he said, "Go."

3 Then one said, "Please be willing to go with your servants." And he answered, "I shall go."

Marginal references (left column):

15 *a*Josh. 2:11; 1 Sam. 17:46, 47; 2 Kin. 5:8
*b*1 Sam. 25:27

16 *a*2 Kin. 3:14 *b*Gen. 14:22, 23; 2 Kin. 5:20, 26

★17-18

17 *a*Ex. 20:24

18 *a*2 Kin. 7:2, 17

19 *a*Ex. 4:18; 1 Sam. 1:17; Mark 5:34

20 *a*2 Kin. 4:12, 31, 36 *b*Ex. 20:7; 2 Kin. 6:31

★22 *a*2 Kin. 4:26 *b*Josh. 24:33 *c*2 Kin. 5:5

Marginal references (right column):

23 *a*2 Kin. 6:3

24 *a*Josh. 7:1, 11, 12, 21; 1 Kin. 21:16

25 *a*2 Kin. 5:22

26 *a*2 Kin. 5:16

27 *a*Ex. 4:6; Num. 12:10

★ 1 *a*2 Kin. 2:3

5:17-18 Naaman wanted to take soil from the Holy Land back home to use in worshiping Yahweh. Nevertheless, he was required to go into the *house of Rimmon,* the god of Damascus, with the king. Elisha assured him that God would understand (v. 19).
5:22 *a talent of silver.* About 1,500 ounces. Ge-

hazi's greed blinded him to the seriousness of his sin in letting Naaman think he paid for his healing, which God had freely given him.
6:1 *too limited.* The number of the sons of the prophets had increased, making their quarters too small.

★ 5

6 *a*Ex.
15:25; 2 Kin.
2:21; 4:41

4 So he went with them; and when they came to the Jordan, they cut down trees.

5 But as one was felling a beam, the axe head fell into the water; and he cried out and said, "Alas, my master! For it was borrowed."

6 Then the man of God said, "Where did it fall?" And when he showed him the place, *a*he cut off a stick, and threw *it* in there, and made the iron float.

7 And he said, "Take it up for yourself." So he put out his hand and took it.

f Elisha thwarts Syria, 6:8–8:6

★ 8-14

9 *a*2 Kin.
4:1, 7; 6:12

13 *a*Gen.
37:17

8 Now the king of Aram was warring against Israel; and he counseled with his servants saying, "In such and such a place shall be my camp."

9 And *a*the man of God sent word to the king of Israel saying, "Beware that you do not pass this place, for the Arameans are coming down there."

10 And the king of Israel sent to the place about which the man of God had told him; thus he warned him, so that he guarded himself there, more than once or twice.

11 Now the heart of the king of Aram was enraged over this thing; and he called his servants and said to them, "Will you tell me which of us is for the king of Israel?"

12 And one of his servants said, "No, my lord, O king; but Elisha, the prophet who is in Israel, tells the king of Israel the words that you speak in your bedroom."

13 So he said, "Go and see where he is, that I may send and take him." And it was told him,

saying, "Behold, he is in *a*Dothan."

14 And he sent horses and chariots and a great army there, and they came by night and surrounded the city.

15 Now when the attendant of the man of God had risen early and gone out, behold, an army with horses and chariots was circling the city. And his servant said to him, "Alas, my master! What shall we do?"

16 So he answered, "*a*Do not fear, for *b*those who are with us are more than those who are with them."

17 Then Elisha prayed and said, "*a*O Lord, I pray, open his eyes that he may see." And the Lord opened the servant's eyes, and he saw; and behold, the mountain was full of *b*horses and chariots of fire all around Elisha.

18 And when they came down to him, Elisha prayed to the Lord and said, "Strike this people with blindness, I pray." So He *a*struck them with blindness according to the word of Elisha.

19 Then Elisha said to them, "This is not the way, nor is this the city; follow me and I will bring you to the man whom you seek." And he brought them to Samaria.

20 And it came about when they had come into Samaria, that Elisha said, "O *a*Lord, open the eyes of these *men,* that they may see." So the Lord opened their eyes, and they saw; and behold, they were in the midst of Samaria.

21 Then the king of Israel when he saw them, said to Elisha, "*a*My father, shall I kill them? Shall I kill them?"

22 And he answered, "You shall not kill *them.* Would you

16 *a*Ex.
14:13
*b*2 Chr. 32:7,
8; Rom. 8:31

17 *a*2 Kin.
6:20 *b*2 Kin.
2:11; Ps.
68:17; Zech.
6:1-7

★18 *a*Gen.
19:11

20 *a*2 Kin.
6:17

★21-23
21 *a*2 Kin.
2:12; 5:13;
8:9

22 *a*Deut.
20:11-16;
2 Chr. 28:8-
15 *b*Rom.
12:20

6:5 *it was borrowed.* This suggests they were too poor to own axes.

6:8-14 His predatory raids being thwarted by Elisha's advice to the king of Israel, the king of Syria planned to capture Elisha.

6:18 *blindness.* See the note on Gen. 19:11,

where the only other occurrence of the Hebrew word is found.

6:21-23 The purpose of blinding and then restoring sight to the Aramean soldiers was to cause their king to acknowledge the mighty power of God.

ªkill those you have taken captive with your sword and with your bow? ᵇSet bread and water before them, that they may eat and drink and go to their master."

23 So he prepared a great feast for them; and when they had eaten and drunk he sent them away, and they went to their master. And ªthe marauding bands of Arameans did not come again into the land of Israel.

24 Now it came about after this, that ªBen-hadad king of Aram gathered all his army and went up and besieged Samaria.

25 And there was a great ªfamine in Samaria; and behold, they besieged it, until a donkey's head was sold for eighty *shekels* of silver, and a fourth of a *kab* of dove's dung for five *shekels* of silver.

26 And as the king of Israel was passing by on the wall a woman cried out to him, saying, "Help, my lord, O king!"

27 And he said, "If the Lᴏʀᴅ does not help you, from where shall I help you? From the threshing floor, or from the wine press?"

28 And the king said to her, "ªWhat is the matter with you?" And she answered, "This woman said to me, 'Give your son that we may eat him today, and we will eat my son tomorrow.'

29 "ªSo we boiled my son and ate him; and I said to her on the next day, 'Give your son, that we may eat him'; but she has hidden her son."

30 And it came about when the king heard the words of the woman, that ªhe tore his clothes—now he was passing by on the wall—and the people looked, and behold, he had sackcloth beneath on his body.

31 Then he said, "May ªGod do so to me and more also, if the head of Elisha the son of Shaphat remains on him today."

32 Now Elisha was sitting in his house, and ªthe elders were sitting with him. And *the king* sent a man from his presence; but before the messenger came to him, he said to the elders, "Do you ᵇsee how this son of a murderer has sent to take away my head? Look, when the messenger comes, shut the door and hold the door shut against him. Is not the sound of his master's feet coming behind him?"

33 And while he was still talking with them, behold, the messenger came down to him, and he said, "ªBehold, this evil is from the Lᴏʀᴅ; why should I wait for the Lᴏʀᴅ any longer?"

7 Then Elisha said, "Listen to the word of the Lᴏʀᴅ; thus says the Lᴏʀᴅ, 'ªTomorrow about this time a measure of fine flour shall be *sold* for a shekel, and two measures of barley for a shekel, in the gate of Samaria.' "

2 And ªthe royal officer on whose hand the king was leaning answered the man of God and said, "Behold, ᵇif the Lᴏʀᴅ should make windows in heaven, could this thing be?" Then he said, "Behold you shall see it with your own eyes, but you shall not eat of it."

3 Now there were four ªleprous men at the entrance of the gate; and they said to one another, "Why do we sit here until we die?

4 "If we say, 'We will enter the city,' then the famine is in the city and we shall die there; and if we sit here, we die also. Now

Cross references (margin)

23 ª2 Kin. 5:2; 24:2
24 ª1 Kin. 20:1
★25 ªLev. 26:26
28 ªJudg. 18:23
29 ªLev. 26:27-29; Deut. 28:52, 53, 57; Lam. 4:10
30 ª1 Kin. 21:27
31 ªRuth 1:17; 1 Kin. 19:2
★32 ªEzek. 8:1; 14:1; 20:1
ᵇ1 Kin. 18:4, 13, 14; 21:10, 13
★33 ªIs. 8:21
★ 1 ª2 Kin. 7:18
2 ª2 Kin. 5:18; 7:17, 19 ᵇGen. 7:11; Mal. 3:10
★ 3-4
3 ªLev. 13:45, 46; Num. 5:2-4; 12:10-14
4 ª2 Kin. 6:24

6:25 *a donkey's head.* So severe was the famine that the head of this unclean animal sold for 40 ounces of silver. One-fourth of a *kab* (a measure of uncertain quantity) may have been 1 or 2 pints.

6:32 *son of a murderer.* An idiom for murderer or possibly a reference to Ahab's murder of Naboth (1 Kings 21).

6:33 Apparently Elisha had told the king to wait

for the Lord's deliverance, but the king, feeling that the situation was beyond hope, saw no other option but to surrender to Aram.

7:1 *a measure.* One-third of an ephah, 5–7 quarts. Suddenly food would be plentiful and inexpensive, courtesy of the fleeing Aramean army leaving their supplies behind (cf. 6:25).

7:3-4 Lepers were required to live outside cities (see note on Lev. 13:46).

therefore come, and let us go over to ᵃthe camp of the Arameans. If they spare us, we shall live; and if they kill us, we shall but die."

5 And they arose at twilight to go to the camp of the Arameans; when they came to the outskirts of the camp of the Arameans, behold, there was no one there.

★ **6** ᵃ2 Sam. 5:24 ᵇ1 Kin. 10:29 ᶜ2 Chr. 12:2, 3; Is. 31:1; 36:9

6 For ᵃthe Lord had caused the army of the Arameans to hear a sound of chariots and a sound of horses, *even* the sound of a great army, so that they said to one another, "Behold, the king of Israel has hired against us ᵇthe kings of the Hittites and ᶜthe kings of the Egyptians, to come upon us."

7 ᵃPs. 48:4-6; Prov. 28:1

7 Therefore they ᵃarose and fled in the twilight, and left their tents and their horses and their donkeys, even the camp just as it was, and fled for their life.

8 ᵃJosh. 7:21

8 When these lepers came to the outskirts of the camp, they entered one tent and ate and drank, and ᵃcarried from there silver and gold and clothes, and went and hid *them*; and they returned and entered another tent and carried from there *also*, and went and hid *them*.

9 Then they said to one another, "We are not doing right. This day is a day of good news, but we are keeping silent; if we wait until morning light, punishment will overtake us. Now therefore come, let us go and tell the king's household."

10 So they came and called to the gatekeepers of the city, and they told them, saying, "We came to the camp of the Arameans, and behold, there was no one there, nor the voice of man, only the horses tied and the donkeys tied, and the tents just as they were."

11 And the gatekeepers called, and told *it* within the king's household.

12 Then the king arose in the night and said to his servants, "I will now tell you what the Arameans have done to us. They know that ᵃwe are hungry; therefore they have gone from the camp ᵇto hide themselves in the field, saying, 'When they come out of the city, we shall capture them alive and get into the city.' "

13 And one of his servants answered and said, "Please, let some *men* take five of the horses which remain, which are left in the city. Behold, they *will be in any case* like all the multitude of Israel who are left in it; behold, they *will be in any case* like all the multitude of Israel who have already perished, so let us send and see."

14 They took therefore two chariots with horses, and the king sent after the army of the Arameans, saying, "Go and see."

15 And they went after them to the Jordan, and behold, all the way was full of clothes and equipment, which the Arameans had thrown away in their haste. Then the messengers returned and told the king.

16 So the people went out and plundered the camp of the Arameans. Then a measure of fine flour *was sold* for a shekel and two measures of barley for a shekel, ᵃaccording to the word of the Lᴏʀᴅ.

17 Now the king appointed ᵃthe royal officer on whose hand he leaned to have charge of the gate; but the people trampled on him at the gate, and he died just as the man of God had said, ᵇwho spoke when the king came down to him.

18 And it came about just as the man of God had spoken to the king, saying, "ᵃTwo measures of barley for a shekel and a measure of fine flour for a shekel, shall be

★**12-13**

12 ᵃ2 Kin. 6:25-29 ᵇJosh. 8:4-12

16 ᵃ2 Kin. 7:1

★**17** ᵃ2 Kin. 7:2 ᵇ2 Kin. 6:32

18 ᵃ2 Kin. 7:1

7:6 God produced a sound which frightened the Arameans away (cf. 19:7; 2 Sam. 5:24).
7:12-13 The king suspected an Aramean plot, but was advised to send in a few men who, if

not killed by the Arameans, would soon die of starvation anyway.
7:17 Death was the judgment for scoffing at Elisha's prophecy (v. 2).

sold tomorrow about this time at the gate of Samaria."

19 Then the royal officer answered the man of God and said, "Now behold, ^aif the Lord should make windows in heaven, could such a thing be?" And he said, "Behold, you shall see it with your own eyes, but you shall not eat of it."

20 And so it happened to him, for the people trampled on him at the gate, and he died.

8 Now ^aElisha spoke to the woman whose son he had restored to life, saying, "Arise and go with your household, and sojourn wherever you can sojourn; for the ^bLord has called for a famine, and ^cit shall even come on the land for seven years."

2 So the woman arose and did according to the word of the man of God, and she went with her household and sojourned in the land of the Philistines seven years.

3 And it came about at the end of seven years, that the woman returned from the land of the Philistines; and she went out to appeal to the king for her house and for her field.

4 Now the king was talking with ^aGehazi, the servant of the man of God, saying, "Please relate to me all the great things that Elisha has done."

5 And it came about, as he was relating to the king ^ahow he had restored to life the one who was dead, that behold, the woman whose son he had restored to life, appealed to the king for her house and for her field. And Gehazi said, "My lord, O king, this is the woman and this is her son, whom Elisha restored to life."

6 When the king asked the woman, she related *it* to him. So

the king appointed for her a certain officer, saying, "Restore all that was hers and all the produce of the field from the day that she left the land even until now."

g Elisha in Damascus, 8:7-15

7 Then Elisha came to ^aDamascus. Now ^bBen-hadad king of Aram was sick, and it was told him, saying, "^cThe man of God has come here."

8 And the king said to ^aHazael, "^bTake a gift in your hand and go to meet the man of God, and ^cinquire of the Lord by him, saying, 'Will I recover from this sickness?'"

9 So Hazael went to meet him and took a gift in his hand, even every kind of good thing of Damascus, forty camels' loads; and he came and stood before him and said, "^aYour son Ben-hadad king of Aram has sent me to you, saying, 'Will I recover from this sickness?'"

10 Then Elisha said to him, "^aGo, say to him, 'You shall surely recover,' but the ^bLord has shown me that he will certainly die."

11 And he fixed his gaze steadily *on him* ^auntil he was ashamed, and ^bthe man of God wept.

12 And Hazael said, "Why does my lord weep?" Then he answered, "Because ^aI know the evil that you will do to the sons of Israel: their strongholds you will set on fire, and their young men you will kill with the sword, and their little ones you ^bwill dash in pieces, and their women with child you will rip up."

13 Then Hazael said, "But what is your servant, ^a*who is but*

Cross references (left margin)
19 ^a2 Kin. 7:2

★ **1** ^a2 Kin. 4:18, 31-35; ^bPs. 105:16; Hag. 1:11 ^cGen. 41:27, 54

4 ^a2 Kin. 4:12; 5:20-27

5 ^a2 Kin. 4:35

Cross references (right margin)
7 ^a1 Kin. 11:24 ^b2 Kin. 6:24 ^c2 Kin. 5:20

8 ^a1 Kin. 19:15, 17 ^b1 Kin. 14:3 ^c2 Kin. 1:2

★ **9** ^a2 Kin. 5:13

10 ^a2 Kin. 8:14 ^b2 Kin. 8:15

★**11** ^a2 Kin. 2:17 ^bLuke 19:41

★**12** ^a2 Kin. 10:32, 33; 12:17; 13:3, 7 ^b2 Kin. 15:16; Nah. 3:10

★**13** ^a1 Sam. 17:43; 2 Sam. 9:8 ^b1 Kin. 19:15

8:1 Here continues the story of the Shunammite woman in 4:8-37, though the seven-year famine must have ended before Gehazi became a leper (5:27). Apparently Gehazi's form of leprosy did not require isolation (2 Kings 8:4-5).
8:9 *forty camels' loads.* A very large gift, with which the king apparently hoped to buy healing from Elisha.

8:11 *And he (Elisha) fixed his gaze steadily on him (Hazael) was ashamed.*
8:12 Hazael became guilty of these crimes (10:32; 13:3-7, 22; cf. Amos 1:3-5).
8:13 *But what is your servant, who is but a dog.* This was a common cliché of humility. *you will be king over Aram.* Cf. 1 Kings 19:15. Hazael reigned c. 843-796.

a dog, that he should do this great thing?" And Elisha answered, "ᵇThe Lord has shown me that you will be king over Aram."

14   So he departed from Elisha and returned to his master, who said to him, "What did Elisha say to you?" And he answered, "He told me that ᵃyou would surely recover."

15   And it came about on the morrow, that he took the cover and dipped it in water and spread it on his face, ᵃso that he died. And Hazael became king in his place.

C   The Reign of Jehoram (Joram) in Judah (848–841; 2 Chron. 21:1–20), 8:16–24

16   Now in the fifth year of ᵃJoram the son of Ahab king of Israel, Jehoshaphat being then the king of Judah, Jehoram the son of Jehoshaphat king of Judah became king.

17   He was ᵃthirty-two years old when he became king, and he reigned eight years in Jerusalem.

18   And he walked in the way of the kings of Israel, just as the house of Ahab had done, for ᵃthe daughter of Ahab became his wife; and he did evil in the sight of the Lord.

19   However, the Lord was not willing to destroy Judah, for the sake of David His servant, ᵃsince He had promised him to give a lamp to him through his sons always.

20   In his days ᵃEdom revolted from under the hand of Judah, and made a king over themselves.

21   Then Joram crossed over to Zair, and all his chariots with him. And it came about that he arose by night and struck the Edomites who had surrounded him and the captains of the chariots; ᵃbut *his* army fled to their tents.

22   ᵃSo Edom revolted against Judah to this day. Then ᵇLibnah revolted at the same time.

23   And the rest of the acts of Joram and all that he did, are they not written in the Book of the Chronicles of the Kings of Judah?

24   So Joram slept with his fathers, and ᵃwas buried with his fathers in the city of David; and ᵇAhaziah his son became king in his place.

D   The Reign of Ahaziah in Judah (841; 2 Chron. 22:1–9), 8:25–29

25   ᵃIn the twelfth year of Joram the son of Ahab king of Israel, Ahaziah the son of Jehoram king of Judah began to reign.

26   ᵃAhaziah *was* twenty-two years old when he became king, and he reigned one year in Jerusalem. And his mother's name *was* Athaliah the granddaughter of Omri king of Israel.

27   And ᵃhe walked in the way of the house of Ahab, and did evil in the sight of the Lord, like the house of Ahab *had done,* because he was a son-in-law of the house of Ahab.

28   Then he went with Joram the son of Ahab to war against ᵃHazael king of Aram at ᵇRamoth-gilead, and the Arameans wounded Joram.

29   So ᵃKing Joram returned to be healed in Jezreel of the wounds which the Arameans had inflicted on him at ᵇRamah, when he fought against Hazael king of Aram. Then ᶜAhaziah the son of Jehoram king of Judah went down to see Joram the son of Ahab in Jezreel because he was sick.

Marginal references:

14 ª2 Kin. 8:10
★15 ª2 Kin. 8:10
★16 ª2 Kin. 1:17; 3:1
17 ª2 Chr. 21:5-10
18 ª2 Kin. 8:27
★19 ª2 Sam. 7:12-15; 1 Kin. 11:36
20 ª1 Kin. 22:47; 2 Kin. 3:9, 26, 27; 8:22
21 ª2 Sam. 18:17; 19:8
22 ªGen. 27:40 ᵇJosh. 21:13; 2 Kin. 19:8
24 ª2 Chr. 21:20 ᵇ2 Chr. 21:1, 7
25 ª2 Chr. 22:1-6
26 ª2 Chr. 22:2
27 ª2 Chr. 22:3
★28 ª2 Kin. 8:15 ᵇ1 Kin. 22:3, 29
29 ª2 Kin. 9:15 ᵇ2 Kin. 8:28; 2 Chr. 22:5, 6 ᶜ2 Kin. 9:16

8:15 *the cover.* The thick bed quilt, made even heavier when soaked with water, suffocated the king.
8:16 Jehoram began a coregency with his father.
8:19 *a lamp.* See note on 1 Kings 11:36.

8:28 *Ramoth-gilead.* An important town E. of the Jordan, near the Aramean border and which changed hands between Israel and Aram a number of times.

E The Reign of Jehu in Israel (841-814), 9:1-10:36

1 Jehu anointed by Elisha, 9:1-10

1 *a*2 Kin. 2:3 *b*2 Kin. 4:29 *c*1 Sam. 10:1; 16:1; 1 Kin. 1:39 *d*2 Kin. 8:28, 29

9 Now Elisha the prophet called one of *a*the sons of the prophets, and said to him, "*b*Gird up your loins, and *c*take this flask of oil in your hand, and go to *d*Ramoth-gilead.

2 *a*1 Kin. 19:16, 17; 2 Kin. 9:14, 20 *b*2 Kin. 9:5, 11

2 "When you arrive there, search out *a*Jehu the son of Jehoshaphat the son of Nimshi, and go in and *b*bid him arise from among his brothers, and bring him to an inner room.

★ **3** *a*2 Chr. 22:7

3 "Then take the flask of oil and pour it on his head and say, 'Thus says the LORD, "*a*I have anointed you king over Israel." ' Then open the door and flee and do not wait."

4 *a*2 Kin. 9:1

4 So *a*the young man, the servant of the prophet, went to Ramoth-gilead.

5 When he came, behold, the captains of the army were sitting, and he said, "I have a word for you, O captain." And Jehu said, "For which one of us?" And he said, "For you, O captain."

6 *a*1 Sam. 2:7, 8; 1 Kin. 19:16; 2 Kin. 9:3; 2 Chr. 22:7

6 And he arose and went into the house, and he poured the oil on his head and said to him, "Thus says the LORD, the God of Israel, '*a*I have anointed you king over the people of the LORD, *even* over Israel.

7 *a*Deut. 32:35, 43 *b*1 Kin. 18:4; 21:15, 21, 25 *c*2 Kin. 9:32-37

7 'And you shall strike the house of Ahab your master, *a*that I may avenge *b*the blood of My servants the prophets, and the blood of all the servants of the LORD, *c*at the hand of Jezebel.

8 *a*1 Kin. 21:21; 2 Kin. 10:17 *b*1 Sam. 25:22 *c*Deut. 32:36; 2 Kin. 14:26

8 'For the whole house of Ahab shall perish, and *a*I will cut off from Ahab *b*every male person *c*both bond and free in Israel.

9 *a*1 Kin. 14:10, 11; 15:29 *b*1 Kin. 16:3-5, 11, 12

9 'And *a*I will make the house of Ahab like the house of Jeroboam the son of Nebat, and *b*like the house of Baasha the son of Ahijah.

★**10** *a*1 Kin. 21:23; 2 Kin. 9:35, 36

10 'And *a*the dogs shall eat Jezebel in the territory of Jezreel, and none shall bury *her.*' " Then he opened the door and fled.

2 Jehu defeats Jehoram of Israel, 9:11-10:17

★**11** *a*2 Kin. 9:17, 19, 22 *b*Jer. 29:26; Hos. 9:7; Mark 3:21

11 Now Jehu came out to the servants of his master, and one said to him, "*a*Is all well? Why did this *b*mad fellow come to you?" And he said to them, "You know very well the man and his talk."

12 And they said, "It is a lie, tell us now." And he said, "Thus and thus he said to me, 'Thus says the LORD, "I have anointed you king over Israel." ' "

★**13** *a*Matt. 21:7, 8; Mark 11:7, 8 *b*2 Sam. 15:10; 1 Kin. 1:34, 39

13 Then *a*they hurried and each man took his garment and placed it under him on the bare steps, and *b*blew the trumpet, saying, "Jehu is king!"

14 *a*1 Kin. 22:3; 2 Kin. 8:28

14 So Jehu the son of Jehoshaphat the son of Nimshi conspired against Joram. *a*Now Joram with all Israel was defending Ramoth-gilead against Hazael king of Aram,

15 *a*2 Kin. 8:29

15 but *a*King Joram had returned to Jezreel to be healed of the wounds which the Arameans had inflicted on him when he fought with Hazael king of Aram. So Jehu said, "If this is your mind, *then* let no one escape *or* leave the city to go tell *it* in Jezreel."

16 *a*2 Kin. 8:29

16 Then Jehu rode in a chariot and went to Jezreel, for Joram was lying there. *a*And Ahaziah king of Judah had come down to see Joram.

17 Now the watchman was standing on the tower in Jezreel and he saw the company of Jehu as he came, and said, "I see a company." And Joram said, "Take a horseman and send him

---

9:3 See 1 Kings 19:16. Jehu is portrayed in the Black Obelisk of Shalmaneser III (dated 841) as bringing tribute to that Assyrian monarch.
9:10 See verses 35-37 and 1 Kings 21:23.
9:11 *this mad fellow.* The servants' impression of the prophet. *You know very well the man.*

Jehu thought his fellow officers had sent the prophet to anoint him so that he would lead a revolt against Joram.
9:13 *under him.* A token of their homage to Jehu.

to meet them and let him say, 'Is it peace?' "

★18 a 2 Kin. 9:19, 22

18 So a horseman went to meet him and said, "Thus says the king, 'Is it peace?' " And Jehu said, "aWhat have you to do with peace? Turn behind me." And the watchman reported, "The messenger came to them, but he did not return."

19 Then he sent out a second horseman, who came to them and said, "Thus says the king, 'Is it peace?' " And Jehu answered, "What have you to do with peace? Turn behind me."

20 a 2 Sam. 18:27 b 1 Kin. 19:17

20 And the watchman reported, "He came even to them, and he did not return; and athe driving is like the driving of bJehu the son of Nimshi, for he drives furiously."

21 a 2 Chr. 22:7 b 1 Kin. 21:1-7, 15-19; 2 Kin. 9:26

21 Then Joram said, "Get ready." And they made his chariot ready. aAnd Joram king of Israel and Ahaziah king of Judah went out, each in his chariot, and they went out to meet Jehu and found him in the bproperty of Naboth the Jezreelite.

22 a 1 Kin. 16:30-33; 18:19; 2 Chr. 21:13

22 And it came about, when Joram saw Jehu, that he said, "Is it peace, Jehu?" And he answered, "What peace, aso long as the harlotries of your mother Jezebel and her witchcrafts are so many?"

23 a 2 Kin. 11:14

23 So Joram reined about and fled and said to Ahaziah, "aThere is treachery, O Ahaziah!"

★24 a 1 Kin. 22:34

24 And aJehu drew his bow with his full strength and shot Joram between his arms; and the arrow went through his heart, and he sank in his chariot.

★25 a 1 Kin. 21:1 b 1 Kin. 21:19, 24-29 c ls. 13:1

25 Then Jehu said to Bidkar his officer, "Take him up and acast him into the property of the field of Naboth the Jezreelite, for I

remember when you and I were riding together after Ahab his father, that the bLord laid this coracle against him:

26 a 1 Kin. 21:13, 19 b 2 Kin. 9:21, 25

26 'Surely aI have seen yesterday the blood of Naboth and the blood of his sons,' says the Lord, 'and bI will repay you in this property,' says the Lord. Now then, take and cast him into the property, according to the word of the Lord."

27 a 2 Chr. 22:7, 9 b Josh. 17:11; Judg. 1:27

27 aWhen Ahaziah the king of Judah saw this, he fled by the way of the garden house. And Jehu pursued him and said, "Shoot him too, in the chariot." So they shot him at the ascent of Gur, which is at bIbleam. But he fled to Megiddo and died there.

28 a 2 Kin. 23:30

28 aThen his servants carried him in a chariot to Jerusalem, and buried him in his grave with his fathers in the city of David.

29 a 2 Kin. 8:25

29 Now in athe eleventh year of Joram, the son of Ahab, Ahaziah became king over Judah.

★30 a Jer. 4:30; Ezek. 23:40

30 When Jehu came to Jezreel, Jezebel heard of it, and ashe painted her eyes and adorned her head, and looked out the window.

★31 a 1 Kin. 16:9-20; 2 Kin. 9:18-22

31 And as Jehu entered the gate, she said, "aIs it well, Zimri, your master's murderer?"

32 Then he lifted up his face to the window and said, "Who is on my side? Who?" And two or three officials looked down at him.

33 And he said, "Throw her down." So they threw her down, and some of her blood was sprinkled on the wall and on the horses, and he trampled her under foot.

★34-37

34 a 1 Kin. 21:25 b 1 Kin. 16:31

34 When he came in, he ate and drank; and he said, "See now to athis cursed woman and bury her, for bshe is a king's daughter."

9:18 *Turn behind me.* I.e., fall in at the rear. Jehu was taking no chances that word of the purpose of his coming might get back to Joram.

9:24 *between his arms.* I.e., between his shoulders.

9:25 See note on 1 Kings 21:19.

9:30 Jezebel wanted to die like a Phoenician queen, all made up.

9:31 With bitter sarcasm Jezebel called Jehu *Zimri*, who wiped out the house of Baasha and who himself was killed a week later (1 Kings 16:11, 18).

9:34-37 As a king's daughter (1 Kings 16:31), Jezebel deserved to be buried, but during the delay caused by Jehu's feasting, scavenger dogs had eaten her body in fulfillment of 1 Kings 21:23.

35 And they went to bury her, but they found no more of her than the skull and the feet and the palms of her hands.

36 Therefore they returned and told him. And he said, "This is the word of the LORD, which He spoke by His servant Elijah the Tishbite, saying, 'ªIn the property of Jezreel the dogs shall eat the flesh of Jezebel;

37 and ªthe corpse of Jezebel shall be as dung on the face of the field in the property of Jezreel, so they cannot say, "This is Jezebel." ' "

10 Now Ahab had seventy sons in ªSamaria. And Jehu wrote letters and sent *them* to Samaria, to the rulers of Jezreel, the elders, and to the guardians of *the children of* Ahab, saying,

2 "And now, ªwhen this letter comes to you, since your master's sons are with you, as well as the chariots and horses and a fortified city and the weapons,

3 select the best and fittest of your master's sons, and set *him* on his father's throne, and fight for your master's house."

4 But they feared greatly and said, "Behold, ªthe two kings did not stand before him; how then can we stand?"

5 And the one who *was* over the household, and he who *was* over the city, the elders, and the guardians of *the children,* sent word to Jehu, saying, "ªWe are your servants, all that you say to us we will do, we will not make any man king; do what is good in your sight."

6 Then he wrote a letter to them a second time saying, "If you are on my side, and you will listen to my voice, take the heads of the men, your master's sons, and come to me at Jezreel tomor-row about this time." Now the king's sons, seventy persons, *were* with the great men of the city, *who* were rearing them.

7 And it came about when the letter came to them, that they took the king's sons, and ªslaughtered *them,* seventy persons, and put their heads in baskets, and sent *them* to him at Jezreel.

8 When the messenger came and told him, saying, "They have brought the heads of the king's sons," he said, "Put them in two heaps at the entrance of the gate until morning."

9 Now it came about in the morning, that he went out and stood, and said to all the people, "You are innocent; behold, ªI conspired against my master and killed him, but ᵇwho killed all these?

10 "Know then that ªthere shall fall to the earth nothing of the word of the LORD, which the LORD spoke concerning the house of Ahab, for the LORD has done ᵇwhat He spoke through His servant Elijah."

11 So Jehu killed all who remained of the house of Ahab in ªJezreel, and all his great men and his acquaintances and his priests, until he left him without a survivor.

12 Then he arose and departed, and went to Samaria. On the way while he was at Beth-eked of the shepherds,

13 ªJehu met the relatives of Ahaziah king of Judah and said, "Who are you?" And they answered, "We are the relatives of Ahaziah; and we have come down to greet the sons of the king and the sons of the queen mother."

14 And he said, "Take them alive." So they took them alive, and killed them at the pit of

---

Marginal references:

36 ªl Kin. 21:23

37 ªJer. 8:1-3

★ 1-11
1 ªl Kin. 16:24-29

2 ª2 Kin. 5:6

4 ª2 Kin. 9:24, 27

5 ªJosh. 9:8, 11; 1 Kin. 20:4, 32; 2 Kin. 18:14

7 ªJudg. 9:5; 2 Kin. 11:1

9 ª2 Kin. 9:14-24
ᵇ2 Kin. 10:6

10 ª2 Kin. 9:7-10
ᵇl Kin. 21:19-29

11 ªHos. 1:4

★12

13 ª2 Kin. 8:24, 29; 2 Chr. 21:17; 22:8

10:1-11 To secure his dynasty Jehu challenged the nobles and foster fathers of Ahab's 70 sons to put one on the throne. They wisely refused and accepted Jehu's terms of surrender, which involved sending him the heads of Ahab's sons. Jehu assured the people that they and he were innocent (v. 9); the slaying of Ahab's sons was a fulfillment of Elijah's prophecy (1 Kings 19:17).
10:12 *Beth-eked.* About 16 miles NE. of Samaria.

Beth-eked, forty-two men; and he left none of them.

15 Now when he had departed from there, he met aJehonadab the son of bRechab *coming* to meet him; and he greeted him and said to him, "Is your heart right, as my heart is with your heart?" And Jehonadab answered, "It is." *Jehu said*, "If it is, cgive *me* your hand." And he gave him his hand, and he took him up to him into the chariot.

16 And he said, "Come with me and asee my zeal for the LORD." So he made him ride in his chariot.

17 And when he came to Samaria, ahe killed all who remained to Ahab in Samaria, until he had destroyed him, baccording to the word of the LORD, which He spoke to Elijah.

3 Jehu destroys Baal
worshipers,
10:18-36

18 Then Jehu gathered all the people and said to them, "aAhab served Baal a little; Jehu will serve him much.

19 "And now, asummon all the prophets of Baal, all his worshipers and all his priests; let no one be missing, for I have a great sacrifice for Baal; whoever is missing shall not live." But Jehu did it in cunning, in order that he might destroy the worshipers of Baal.

20 And Jehu said, "aSanctify a solemn assembly for Baal." And bthey proclaimed *it.*

21 Then Jehu sent throughout Israel and all the worshipers of Baal came, so that there was not a man left who did not come. And when they went into athe house of Baal, the house of Baal was filled from one end to the other.

22 And he said to the one who *was* in charge of the ward-

robe, "Bring out garments for all the worshipers of Baal." So he brought out garments for them.

23 And Jehu went into the house of Baal with Jehonadab the son of Rechab; and he said to the worshipers of Baal, "Search and see that there may be here with you none of the servants of the LORD, but only the worshipers of Baal."

24 Then they went in to offer sacrifices and burnt offerings. Now Jehu had stationed for himself eighty men outside, and he had said, "aThe one who permits any of the men whom I bring into your hands to escape, shall give up his life in exchange."

25 Then it came about, as soon as he had finished offering the burnt offering, that Jehu said to the aguard and to the royal officers, "bGo in, kill them; let none come out." And they killed them with the edge of the sword; and the guard and the royal officers threw *them* out, and went to the inner room of the house of Baal.

26 And they brought out the sacred apillars of the house of Baal, and burned them.

27 They also broke down the sacred pillar of Baal and broke down the house of Baal, and amade it a latrine to this day.

28 Thus Jehu eradicated Baal out of Israel.

29 However, aas for the sins of Jeroboam the son of Nebat, which he made Israel sin, from these Jehu did not depart, *even* the bgolden calves that *were* at Bethel and that *were* at Dan.

30 And the LORD said to Jehu, "Because you have done well in executing what is right in My eyes, *and* have done to the house of Ahab according to all that *was* in My heart, ayour sons of the fourth generation shall sit on the throne of Israel."

10:15 *Jehonadab* (the longer form of Jonadab). The founder of a strict sect of nomadic Israelites who protested the corrupting influences of the Canaanites (cf. Jer. 35:1-11). He accompanied Jehu to Samaria and participated in the destruction of the worshipers of Baal.

10:29 Though Jehu destroyed Baal worship, he did not eradicate the idolatry of Jeroboam (see notes on 1 Kings 12:28 and 12:29) nor walk in the law of God (v. 31).

31 aProv.
4:23 b2 Kin.
10:29

31 But Jehu ªwas not careful to walk in the law of the LORD, the God of Israel, with all his heart; ᵇhe did not depart from the sins of Jeroboam, which he made Israel sin.

32 a2 Kin.
13:25; 14:25
b1 Kin.
19:17; 2 Kin.
8:12; 13:22

32 In those days the ªLORD began to cut off *portions* from Israel; and ᵇHazael defeated them throughout the territory of Israel:

★33 aDeut.
2:36 bAmos
1:3-5

33 from the Jordan eastward, all the land of Gilead, the Gadites and the Reubenites and the Manassites, from ªAroer, which is by the valley of the Arnon, even ᵇGilead and Bashan.

34 Now the rest of the acts of Jehu and all that he did and all his might, are they not written in the Book of the Chronicles of the Kings of Israel?

35 And Jehu slept with his fathers, and they buried him in Samaria. And Jehoahaz his son became king in his place.

36 Now the time which Jehu reigned over Israel in Samaria *was* twenty-eight years.

F The Reign of Athaliah in Judah (841-835; 2 Chron. 22:10-23:15), 11:1-16

★ 1 a2 Chr.
22:10-12

11 ªWhen Athaliah the mother of Ahaziah saw that her son was dead, she rose and destroyed all the royal offspring.

★ 2 a2 Kin.
11:21; 12:1

2 But Jehosheba, the daughter of King Joram, sister of Ahaziah, ªtook Joash the son of Ahaziah and stole him from among the king's sons who were being put to death, and placed him and his nurse in the bedroom. So they hid him from Athaliah, and he was not put to death.

3 So he was hidden with her in the house of the LORD six years, while Athaliah was reigning over the land.

4 ªNow in the seventh year Jehoiada sent and brought the captains of hundreds of ᵇthe Carites and of the guard, and brought them to him in the house of the LORD. Then he made a covenant with them and put them under oath in the house of the LORD, and showed them the king's son.

5 And he commanded them, saying, "This is the thing that you shall do: ªone third of you, who come in on the sabbath and keep watch over the king's house

6 (one third also *shall be* at the gate Sur, and one third at the gate behind the guards), shall keep watch over the house for defense.

7 "And two parts of you, *even* all who go out on the sabbath, shall also keep watch over the house of the LORD for the king.

8 "Then you shall surround the king, each with his weapons in his hand; and whoever comes within the ranks shall be put to death. And ªbe with the king when he goes out and when he comes in."

9 So the captains of hundreds ªdid according to all that Jehoiada the priest commanded. And each one of them took his men who were to come in on the sabbath, with those who were to go out on the sabbath, and came to Jehoiada the priest.

10 And ªthe priest gave to the captains of hundreds the spears and shields that had been King David's, which *were* in the house of the LORD.

11 And the guards stood each with his weapons in his hand, from the right side of the house to the left side of the house, by the altar and by the house, around the king.

★ 4 a2 Chr.
23:1-21
b2 Sam.
20:23; 2 Kin.
11:19

5 a1 Chr.
9:25

8 aNum.
27:16, 17

9 a2 Chr.
23:8

10 a2 Sam.
8:7; 1 Chr.
18:7

10:33 The weakness of Israel made it possible for Hazael to take Israel's territory E. of the Jordan.

11:1 The story of Ahaziah is resumed from 9:27. Athaliah was the daughter of Ahab and Jezebel and the wife of Jehoram.

11:2 Athaliah's attempt to exterminate all rivals to the throne was thwarted by the hiding of *Joash* (= Jehoash of v. 21) in the *bedroom* (a room where mattresses and couches were stored).

11:4 *Jehoiada*. The high priest (v. 9).

★12 a2 Sam.
1:10 bEx.
25:16; 31:18
c1 Sam.
10:24

12 Then he brought the king's son out and aput the crown on him, and gave him bthe testimony; and they made him king and anointed him, and they clapped their hands and said, "cLong live the king!"

13 a2 Chr.
23:12

13 aWhen Athaliah heard the noise of the guard and of the people, she came to the people in the house of the LORD.

14 a2 Kin.
23:3; 2 Chr.
34:31
b1 Kin. 1:39,
40 cGen.
37:29; 44:13
d2 Kin. 9:23

14 And she looked and behold, the king was standing aby the pillar, according to the custom, with the captains and the trumpeters beside the king; and ball the people of the land rejoiced and blew trumpets. Then Athaliah ctore her clothes and cried, "dTreason! Treason!"

15 And Jehoiada the priest commanded the captains of hundreds who were appointed over the army, and said to them, "Bring her out between the ranks, and whoever follows her put to death with the sword." For the priest said, "Let her not be put to death in the house of the LORD."

16 aGen.
9:6; Lev.
24:17

16 So they seized her, and when she arrived at the horses' entrance of the king's house, she was aput to death there.

G The Reign of Jehoash (Joash) in Judah (835-796; 2 Chron. 23:16-24:27), 11:17-12:21

17 aJosh.
24:25; 2 Chr.
15:12-14;
34:31
b1 Sam.
10:25;
2 Sam. 5:3

17 Then aJehoiada made a covenant between the LORD and the king and the people, that they should be the LORD's people, also bbetween the king and the people.

18 a2 Kin.
10:26, 27
bDeut. 12:2,
3 c1 Kin.
18:40

18 And all the people of the land went to athe house of Baal, and tore it down; bhis altars and his images they broke in pieces

thoroughly, and ckilled Mattan the priest of Baal before the altars. And the priest appointed officers over the house of the LORD.

19 And he took the captains of hundreds and the aCarites and the guards and all the people of the land; and they brought the king down from the house of the LORD, and came by the way of bthe gate of the guards to the king's house. And he sat on the throne of the kings.

20 So aall the people of the land rejoiced and the city was quiet. For they had put Athaliah to death with the sword at the king's house.

21 aJehoash was seven years old when he became king.

12 In the seventh year of Jehu, aJehoash became king, and he reigned forty years in Jerusalem; and his mother's name was Zibiah of Beersheba.

2 And Jehoash did right in the sight of the LORD all his days in which Jehoiada the priest instructed him.

3 Only athe high places were not taken away; the people still sacrificed and burned incense on the high places.

4 Then Jehoash said to the priests, "All the money of the sacred things awhich is brought into the house of the LORD, in current money, both bthe money of each man's assessment and all the money which any man's heart prompts him to bring into the house of the LORD,

5 let the priests take it for themselves, each from his acquaintance; and they shall repair the damages of the house wherever any damage may be found.

6 But it came about that in the twenty-third year of King Jehoash athe priests had not repaired the damages of the house.

19 a2 Kin.
11:4 b2 Kin.
11:6

20 aProv.
11:10

21 a2 Chr.
24:1-14

1 a2 Chr.
24:1

★ 2

3 a2 Kin.
14:4; 15:35

★ 4 a2 Kin.
22:4 bEx.
30:13-16;
35:5, 22, 29;
1 Chr. 29:3-9

★ 6 a2 Chr.
24:5

11:12 *the testimony.* Probably a copy of the Mosaic Law to remind the king of his obligations.
12:2 Jehoash served the Lord as long as *Jehoiada* lived to instruct him (2 Chron. 24:2).
12:4 The law concerning this money is described

in a note on Lev. 27:2. Freewill offerings were also brought.
12:6 We are not told how long before the twenty-third year the collection had begun.

★ 7

7 Then King Jehoash called for Jehoiada the priest, and for the *other* priests and said to them, "Why do you not repair the damages of the house? Now therefore take no *more* money from your acquaintances, but pay it for the damages of the house."

8 So the priests agreed that they should take no *more* money from the people, nor repair the damages of the house.

9 ᵃMark 12:41; Luke 21:1

9 But ᵃJehoiada the priest took a chest and bored a hole in its lid, and put it beside the altar, on the right side as one comes into the house of the LORD; and the priests who guarded the threshold put in it all the money which was brought into the house of the LORD.

★10 ᵃ2 Sam. 8:17; 2 Kin. 19:2; 22:3, 4, 12

10 And when they saw that there was much money in the chest, ᵃthe king's scribe and the high priest came up and tied *it* in bags and counted the money which was found in the house of the LORD.

11 And they gave the money which was weighed out into the hands of those who did the work, who had the oversight of the house of the LORD; and they paid it out to the carpenters and the builders, who worked on the house of the LORD;

12 ᵃ2 Kin. 22:5, 6

12 and ᵃto the masons and the stonecutters, and for buying timber and hewn stone to repair the damages to the house of the LORD, and for all that was laid out for the house to repair it.

★13 ᵃ2 Chr. 24:14
ᵇ1 Kin. 7:48, 50

13 But ᵃthere were not made for the house of the LORD ᵇsilver cups, snuffers, bowls, trumpets, any vessels of gold, or vessels of silver from the money which was

brought into the house of the LORD;

14 for they gave that to those who did the work, and with it they repaired the house of the LORD.

15 Moreover, ᵃthey did not require an accounting from the men into whose hand they gave the money to pay to those who did the work, for they dealt faithfully.

15 ᵃ2 Kin. 22:7; 1 Cor. 4:2; 2 Cor. 8:20

16 The ᵃmoney from the guilt offerings and ᵇthe money from the sin offerings, was not brought into the house of the LORD; ᶜit was for the priests.

★16 ᵃLev. 5:15-18
ᵇLev. 4:24, 29 ᶜLev. 7:7; Num. 18:19

17 Then ᵃHazael king of Aram went up and fought against Gath and captured it, and ᵇHazael set his face to go up to Jerusalem.

17 ᵃ1 Kin. 19:17; 2 Kin. 8:12; 10:32, 33 ᵇ2 Chr. 24:23, 24

18 And ᵃJehoash king of Judah took all the sacred things that Jehoshaphat and Jehoram and Ahaziah, his fathers, kings of Judah, had dedicated, and ᵇhis own sacred things and all the gold that was found among the treasuries of the house of the LORD and of the king's house, and sent *them* to Hazael king of Aram. Then he went away from Jerusalem.

18 ᵃ1 Kin. 14:26; 15:18; 2 Kin. 16:8; 18:15, 16 ᵇ2 Kin. 12:4

19 Now the rest of the acts of Joash and all that he did, are they not written in the Book of the Chronicles of the Kings of Judah?

20 ᵃAnd his servants arose and made a conspiracy, and ᵇstruck down Joash at ᶜthe house of Millo *as he was* going down to Silla.

★20 ᵃ2 Chr. 24:25-27
ᵇ2 Kin. 14:5 ᶜJudg. 9:6; 2 Sam. 5:9; 1 Kin. 11:27

21 For Jozacar the son of Shimeath, and Jehozabad the son of ᵃShomer, his servants, struck *him*, and he died; and they buried him with his fathers in the city of David, and ᵇAmaziah his son became king in his place.

21 ᵃ2 Chr. 24:26
ᵇ2 Kin. 14:1

12:7 *from your acquaintances.* Assessors who fixed the value of the offerings. Because the project had been delayed, the king took it out of the hands of the priests, ordering instead that the money be placed in a chest (v. 9) and paid directly to those who repaired the Temple (v. 11).

12:10 *money.* Precious metals, for coinage had not yet been invented.

12:13 After the Temple was repaired, the surplus money was used for these furnishings (2 Chron. 24:14).

12:16 *money from the guilt offerings.* See note on Lev. 5:15-16.

12:20 The details as to why Joash's servants conspired against him are recorded in 2 Chron. 24:17-26. *the house of Millo.* See note on 1 Kings 9:24.

H The Reign of Jehoahaz in Israel (814–798), 13:1–9

13 In the twenty-third year of Joash the son of Ahaziah, king of Judah, Jehoahaz the son of Jehu became king over Israel at Samaria, *and he reigned* seventeen years.

★ **2** *a*1 Kin. 12:26-33

2 And he did evil in the sight of the LORD, and followed the sins of Jeroboam the son of Nebat, *a*with which he made Israel sin; he did not turn from them.

3 *a*Judg. 2:14 *b*2 Kin. 12:17 *c*2 Kin. 13:24, 25

3 *a*So the anger of the LORD was kindled against Israel, and He gave them continually into the hand of *b*Hazael king of Aram, and into the hand of *c*Ben-hadad the son of Hazael.

4 *a*Num. 21:7-9 *b*Ex. 3:7, 9; 2 Kin. 14:26

4 Then *a*Jehoahaz entreated the favor of the LORD, and the LORD listened to him; for *b*He saw the oppression of Israel, how the king of Aram oppressed them.

★ **5** *a*2 Kin. 13:25; 14:25, 27; Neh. 9:27

5 And the LORD gave Israel a *a*deliverer, so that they escaped from under the hand of the Arameans; and the sons of Israel lived in their tents as formerly.

6 *a*2 Kin. 13:2 *b*1 Kin. 16:33

6 Nevertheless they did not turn away from the sins of the house of Jeroboam, *a*with which he made Israel sin, but walked in them; and *b*the Asherah also remained standing in Samaria.

7 *a*Amos 1:3

7 For he left to Jehoahaz of the army not more than fifty horsemen and ten chariots and 10,000 footmen, for the king of Aram had destroyed them and *a*made them like the dust at threshing.

8 Now the rest of the acts of Jehoahaz, and all that he did and his might, are they not written in the Book of the Chronicles of the Kings of Israel?

9 And Jehoahaz slept with his fathers, and they buried him in Samaria; and Joash his son became king in his place.

I The Reign of Jehoash (Joash) in Israel (798–782), 13:10–25

★**10-13**

10 In the thirty-seventh year of Joash king of Judah, Jehoash the son of Jehoahaz, became king over Israel in Samaria, *and reigned* sixteen years.

11 And he did evil in the sight of the LORD; he did not turn away from all the sins of Jeroboam the son of Nebat, with which he made Israel sin, but he walked in them.

12 *a*2 Kin. 13:14-19; 14:8-15

12 *a*Now the rest of the acts of Joash and all that he did and his might with which he fought against Amaziah king of Judah, are they not written in the Book of the Chronicles of the Kings of Israel?

13 So Joash slept with his fathers, and Jeroboam sat on his throne; and Joash was buried in Samaria with the kings of Israel.

★**14** *a*2 Kin. 2:12

14 When Elisha became sick with the illness of which he was to die, Joash the king of Israel came down to him and wept over him and said, "*a*My father, my father, the chariots of Israel and its horsemen!"

15 And Elisha said to him, "Take a bow and arrows." So he took a bow and arrows.

16 Then he said to the king of Israel, "Put your hand on the bow." And he put his hand *on it,* then Elisha laid his hands on the king's hands.

★**17** *a*1 Kin. 20:26

17 And he said, "Open the window toward the east," and he opened *it.* Then Elisha said, "Shoot!" And he shot. And he said, "The LORD's arrow of victory, even the arrow of victory over

---

13:2 On the sins of Jeroboam see notes on 1 Kings 12:28, 29, 31.
13:5 *a deliverer.* Perhaps an unnamed general.
13:10-13 There were two kings named Joash (or Jehoash). This one was king of Israel (northern tribes); the other was king of Judah, in the south (11:2; 12:1).
13:14 *the chariots of Israel.* See note on 2:12.
13:17 *Aphek.* A town in Bashan, E. of the Sea of Galilee.

Aram; for you shall defeat the Arameans at [a]Aphek until you have destroyed *them*."

18 Then he said, "Take the arrows," and he took them. And he said to the king of Israel, "Strike the ground," and he struck *it* three times and stopped.

★19 [a]2 Kin. 5:20 [b]2 Kin. 13:25

19 So [a]the man of God was angry with him and said, "You should have struck five or six times, then you would have struck Aram until you would have destroyed *it*. But now you shall strike Aram [b]only three times."

20 [a]2 Kin. 3:7; 24:2

20 And Elisha died, and they buried him. Now [a]the bands of the Moabites would invade the land in the spring of the year.

★21 [a]Matt. 27:52

21 And as they were burying a man, behold, they saw a marauding band; and they cast the man into the grave of Elisha. And when the man touched the bones of Elisha he [a]revived and stood up on his feet.

22 [a]2 Kin. 8:12, 13

22 Now [a]Hazael king of Aram had oppressed Israel all the days of Jehoahaz.

23 [a]2 Kin. 14:27 [b]1 Kin. 8:28 [c]Gen. 13:16, 17; 17:2-5

23 But the [a]LORD was gracious to them and [b]had compassion on them and turned to them because of [c]His covenant with Abraham, Isaac, and Jacob, and would not destroy them or cast them from His presence until now.

24 When Hazael king of Aram died, Ben-hadad his son became king in his place.

25 [a]2 Kin. 10:32, 33; 14:25 [b]2 Kin. 13:18, 19

25 Then [a]Jehoash the son of Jehoahaz took again from the hand of Ben-hadad the son of Hazael the cities which he had taken in war from the hand of Jehoahaz his father. [b]Three times Joash defeated him and recovered the cities of Israel.

J The Reign of Amaziah in Judah (796-767; 2 Chron. 25:1-28), 14:1-22

14 [a]In the second year of Joash son of Joahaz king of Israel, [b]Amaziah the son of Joash king of Judah became king.

1 [a]2 Chr. 25:1 [b]2 Kin. 13:10

2 He was twenty-five years old when he became king, and he reigned twenty-nine years in Jerusalem. And his mother's name was Jehoaddin of Jerusalem.

3 And he did right in the sight of the LORD, yet not like David his father; he did according to all that Joash his father had done.

★ 3

4 Only [a]the high places were not taken away; [b]the people still sacrificed and burned incense on the high places.

4 [a]2 Kin. 12:3 [b]2 Kin. 16:4

5 Now it came about, as soon as the kingdom was firmly in his hand, that he [a]killed his servants who had slain the king his father.

★ 5 [a]2 Kin. 12:20

6 But the sons of the slayers he did not put to death, according to what is written in the book of the law of Moses, as the LORD commanded, saying, "[a]The fathers shall not be put to death for the sons, nor the sons be put to death for the fathers; but [b]each shall be put to death for his own sin."

★ 6 [a]Deut. 24:16 [b]Jer. 31:30; Ezek. 18:4, 20

7 He killed *of* Edom in [a]the Valley of Salt 10,000 and took [b]Sela by war, and named it [c]Joktheel to this day.

★ 7 [a]2 Sam. 8:13; 1 Chr. 18:12; 2 Chr. 25:11 [b]Is. 16:1 [c]Josh. 15:38

8 [a]Then Amaziah sent messengers to Jehoash, the son of Jehoahaz son of Jehu, king of Israel, saying, "[b]Come, let us face each other."

★ 8 [a]2 Chr. 25:17-24 [b]2 Sam. 2:14-17

13:19 *three times.* Had he struck the ground more times (v. 18), Joash's conquest of Aram would have been more complete (see v. 25).

13:21 *he revived.* Lit., he lived. This miracle confirmed Elisha's promise to Joash of victory over Aram.

14:3 *not like David.* See 2 Chron. 25:14-16.

14:5 *his servants.* See 12:20.

14:6 This was in accord with the law of Deut. 24:16. This reference also shows that Deuteronomy was not written as late as some critics of the Bible hold.

14:7 *Valley of Salt.* The area S. of the Dead Sea. *Sela.* Petra.

14:8 *face each other.* I.e., Amaziah challenged Jehoash to battle.

★ 9-10

9 aJudg.
9:8-15

9 And Jehoash king of Israel sent to Amaziah king of Judah, saying, "aThe thorn bush which was in Lebanon sent to the cedar which was in Lebanon, saying, 'Give your daughter to my son in marriage.' But there passed by a wild beast that was in Lebanon, and trampled the thorn bush.

10 a2 Kin.
14:7 bDeut.
8:14; 2 Chr.
26:16

10 "aYou have indeed defeated Edom, and byour heart has become proud. Enjoy your glory and stay at home; for why should you provoke trouble so that you, even you, should fall, and Judah with you?"

11 aJosh.
19:38

11 But Amaziah would not listen. So Jehoash king of Israel went up; and he and Amaziah king of Judah faced each other at aBeth-shemesh, which belongs to Judah.

12 a2 Sam.
18:17

12 And Judah was defeated by Israel, and athey fled each to his tent.

13 aNeh.
8:16; 12:39
b2 Chr.
25:23

13 Then Jehoash king of Israel captured Amaziah king of Judah, the son of Jehoash the son of Ahaziah, at Beth-shemesh, and came to Jerusalem and tore down the wall of Jerusalem from athe Gate of Ephraim to bthe Corner Gate, 400 cubits.

14 a1 Kin.
14:26; 2 Kin.
12:18

14 And ahe took all the gold and silver and all the utensils which were found in the house of the LORD, and in the treasuries of the king's house, the hostages also, and returned to Samaria.

15 a2 Kin.
13:12, 13

15 aNow the rest of the acts of Jehoash which he did, and his might and how he fought with Amaziah king of Judah, are they not written in the Book of the Chronicles of the Kings of Israel?

16 So Jehoash slept with his fathers and was buried in Samaria with the kings of Israel; and Jeroboam his son became king in his place.

17 a2 Chr.
25:25-28

17 aAnd Amaziah the son of Joash king of Judah lived fifteen years after the death of Jehoash son of Jehoahaz king of Israel.

18 Now the rest of the acts of Amaziah, are they not written in the Book of the Chronicles of the Kings of Judah?

★19 aJosh.
10:31; 2 Kin.
18:14, 17

19 And they conspired against him in Jerusalem, and he fled to aLachish; but they sent after him to Lachish and killed him there.

20 Then they brought him on horses and he was buried at Jerusalem with his fathers in the city of David.

★21

21 And all the people of Judah took Azariah, who was sixteen years old, and made him king in the place of his father Amaziah.

22 a1 Kin.
9:26; 2 Kin.
16:6; 2 Chr.
8:17

22 aHe built Elath and restored it to Judah, after the king slept with his fathers.

K   The Reign of Jeroboam II in Israel (794–753), 14:23–29

23 In the fifteenth year of Amaziah the son of Joash king of Judah, Jeroboam the son of Joash king of Israel became king in Samaria, *and reigned* forty-one years.

24 And he did evil in the sight of the LORD; he did not depart from all the sins of Jeroboam the son of Nebat, which he made Israel sin.

★25 a2 Kin.
10:32; 13:25
b1 Kin. 8:65
cDeut. 3:17
dJon. 1:1;
Matt. 12:39,
40 eJosh.
19:13

25 aHe restored the border of Israel from bthe entrance of Hamath as far as cthe Sea of the Arabah, according to dthe word of the LORD, the God of Israel, which

---

14:9-10 Jehoash tried to cut Amaziah down to size with this parable: a thistle tried to make himself equal with a cedar tree until a wild beast accidently stepped on him and stopped his ambitious plans. Likewise Amaziah should stay home and be content with his little trophies.

14:19 *Lachish.* 25 miles SW. of Jerusalem.
14:21 *Azariah.* The Uzziah of 2 Chron. 26:1 and Isa. 1:1.
14:25 *the entrance of Hamath.* See note on 1 Kings 8:65. *Sea of the Arabah.* The Dead Sea.

He spoke through His servant ᵈJonah the son of Amittai, the prophet, who was of ᵉGath-hepher.

26 For the ᵃLORD saw the affliction of Israel, *which was* very bitter; for ᵇthere was neither bond nor free, nor was there any helper for Israel.

27 And the ᵃLORD did not say that He would blot out the name of Israel from under heaven, but He saved them by the hand of Jeroboam the son of Joash.

28 Now the rest of the acts of Jeroboam and all that he did and his might, how he fought and how he recovered for Israel, ᵃDamascus and ᵇHamath, *which had belonged* to Judah, are they not written in the Book of the Chronicles of the Kings of Israel?

29 And Jeroboam slept with his fathers, even with the kings of Israel, and Zechariah his son became king in his place.

L The Reign of Azariah (Uzziah) in Judah (790–739; 2 Chron. 26:1–23), 15:1–7

15 ᵃIn the twenty-seventh year of Jeroboam king of Israel, Azariah son of Amaziah king of Judah became king.

2 He was ᵃsixteen years old when he became king, and he reigned fifty-two years in Jerusalem; and his mother's name was Jecoliah of Jerusalem.

3 And he did right in the sight of the LORD, according to all that his father Amaziah had done.

4 Only ᵃthe high places were not taken away; the people still sacrificed and burned incense on the high places.

5 ᵃAnd the LORD struck the king, so that he was a leper to the day of his death. And he ᵇlived in a separate house, while Jotham the king's son was over the

household, judging the people of the land.

6 Now the rest of the acts of Azariah and all that he did, are they not written in the Book of the Chronicles of the Kings of Judah?

7 And Azariah slept with his fathers, and they buried him with his fathers in the city of David, and Jotham his son became king in his place.

M The Reign of Zechariah in Israel (753), 15:8–12

8 ᵃIn the thirty-eighth year of Azariah king of Judah, Zechariah the son of Jeroboam became king over Israel in Samaria *for* six months.

9 And he did evil in the sight of the LORD, as his fathers had done; he did not depart from the sins of Jeroboam the son of Nebat, which he made Israel sin.

10 Then Shallum the son of Jabesh conspired against him and ᵃstruck him before the people and killed him, and reigned in his place.

11 Now the rest of the acts of Zechariah, behold they are written in the Book of the Chronicles of the Kings of Israel.

12 This is ᵃthe word of the LORD which He spoke to Jehu, saying, "Your sons to the fourth generation shall sit on the throne of Israel." And so it was.

N The Reign of Shallum in Israel (752), 15:13–15

13 Shallum son of Jabesh became king in the ᵃthirty-ninth year of Uzziah king of Judah, and he reigned one month in ᵇSamaria.

14 Then Menahem son of Gadi went up from ᵃTirzah and came to Samaria, and struck Shallum son of Jabesh in Samaria, and

---

Marginal references:

26 ᵃ2 Kin. 13:4 ᵇDeut. 32:36
27 ᵃ2 Kin. 13:23
28 ᵃ1 Kin. 11:24 ᵇ2 Chr. 8:3
1 ᵃ2 Kin. 14:17
2 ᵃ2 Chr. 26:3, 4
4 ᵃ2 Kin. 12:3
★ 5 ᵃ2 Chr. 26:21-23 ᵇLev. 13:46; Num. 12:14
8 ᵃ2 Kin. 15:1
10 ᵃAmos 7:9
★12 ᵃ2 Kin. 10:30
13 ᵃ2 Kin. 15:1, 8 ᵇ1 Kin. 16:24
14 ᵃ1 Kin. 14:17

15:5 Uzziah was made a *leper* because he usurped functions that belonged to the priests (2 Chron. 26:17-21).

15:12 *the fourth generation.* As predicted in 10:30.

killed him and became king in his place.

15 Now the rest of the acts of Shallum and his conspiracy which he made, behold they are written in the Book of the Chronicles of the Kings of Israel.

O The Reign of Menahem in Israel (752–742), 15:16–22

★16 ª2 Kin. 8:12; Hos. 13:16   **16** Then Menahem struck Tiphsah and all who were in it and its borders from Tirzah, because they did not open to him, therefore he struck it; and he ripped up ªall its women who were with child.

17 ª2 Kin. 15:1, 8, 13   **17** In the ªthirty-ninth year of Azariah king of Judah, Menahem son of Gadi became king over Israel and reigned ten years in Samaria.

18 And he did evil in the sight of the LORD; he did not depart all his days from the sins of Jeroboam the son of Nebat, which he made Israel sin.

★19–20

19 ª1 Chr. 5:25, 26 ᵇ2 Kin. 14:5   **19** ªPul, king of Assyria, came against the land, and Menahem gave Pul a thousand talents of silver so that his hand might be with him to ᵇstrengthen the kingdom under his rule.

20 Then Menahem exacted the money from Israel, even from all the mighty men of wealth, from each man fifty shekels of silver to pay the king of Assyria. So the king of Assyria returned and did not remain there in the land.

21 Now the rest of the acts of Menahem and all that he did, are they not written in the Book of the Chronicles of the Kings of Israel?

22 And Menahem slept with his fathers, and Pekahiah his son became king in his place.

P The Reign of Pekahiah in Israel (742–740), 15:23–26

23 ª2 Kin. 15:1, 8, 13, 17   **23** In ªthe fiftieth year of Azariah king of Judah, Pekahiah son of Menahem became king over Israel in Samaria, and reigned two years.

24 And he did evil in the sight of the LORD; he did not depart from the sins of Jeroboam son of Nebat, which he made Israel sin.

25 ª1 Kin. 16:18   **25** Then Pekah son of Remaliah, his officer, conspired against him and struck him in Samaria, in ªthe castle of the king's house with Argob and Arieh; and with him were fifty men of the Gileadites, and he killed him and became king in his place.

26 Now the rest of the acts of Pekahiah and all that he did, behold they are written in the Book of the Chronicles of the Kings of Israel.

Q The Reign of Pekah in Israel (752–732), 15:27–31

★27–31

27 ª2 Kin. 15:23 ᵇ2 Chr. 28:6; Is. 7:1   **27** In ªthe fifty-second year of Azariah king of Judah, ᵇPekah son of Remaliah became king over Israel in Samaria, and reigned twenty years.

28 And he did evil in the sight of the LORD; he did not depart from the sins of Jeroboam son of Nebat, which he made Israel sin.

15:16 *Tiphsah.* A town near Tirzah in Samaria. Not the Tiphsah of 1 Kings 4:24, which was on the Euphrates River.

15:19–20 *Pul.* Tiglath-pileser III (1 Chron. 5:26), a general who took the reins of the Assyrian government and made its army into an efficient military machine. *a thousand talents* = 3,000,000 shekels. Therefore about 60,000 men contributed to this levy.

15:27–31 A year after *Pekah* began to reign, Uzziah, king of Judah, died as a leper, and Isaiah saw the great vision recorded in Isa. 6. Because Judah refused to join an anti-Assyrian alliance

with Israel, she was successfully invaded by Israel (2 Chron. 28:5–15). A second invasion a few months later was not successful because *Tiglath-pileser* (III) of Assyria attacked northern Israel about 733 (v. 29; Isa. 7), thus marking the beginning of the end for the Northern Kingdom. *Hoshea*, a puppet king and the last king of Israel, attempted an alliance with Egypt and was imprisoned by the Assyrians who besieged Samaria, the capital, conquering it in 722 and ending the history of the Northern Kingdom of Israel.

29 In the days of Pekah king of Israel, [a]Tiglath-pileser king of Assyria came and captured Ijon and Abel-beth-maacah and Janoah and Kedesh and Hazor and Gilead and Galilee, all the land of Naphtali; and [b]he carried them captive to Assyria.

30 And Hoshea the son of Elah made a conspiracy against Pekah the son of Remaliah, and struck him and put him to death and became king in his place, in the twentieth year of Jotham the son of Uzziah.

31 Now the rest of the acts of Pekah and all that he did, behold, they are written in the Book of the Chronicles of the Kings of Israel.

R The Reign of Jotham in Judah (750-731; 2 Chron. 27:1-9), 15:32-38

32 In the second year of Pekah the son of Remaliah king of Israel, Jotham the son of Uzziah king of Judah became king.

33 [a]He was twenty-five years old when he became king, and he reigned sixteen years in Jerusalem; and his mother's name was Jerusha the daughter of Zadok.

34 And [a]he did what was right in the sight of the LORD; he did according to all that his father Uzziah had done.

35 Only [a]the high places were not taken away; the people still sacrificed and burned incense on the high places. [b]He built the upper gate of the house of the LORD.

36 Now the rest of the acts of Jotham and all that he did, are they not written in the Book of the Chronicles of the Kings of Judah?

37 In those days [a]the LORD began to send Rezin king of Aram and Pekah the son of Remaliah against Judah.

38 And Jotham slept with his fathers, and he was buried with his fathers in the city of David his father; and Ahaz his son became king in his place.

S The Reign of Ahaz in Judah (731-715; 2 Chron. 28:1-27), 16:1-20

16 In the seventeenth year of Pekah the son of Remaliah, [a]Ahaz the son of Jotham, king of Judah, became king.

2 [a]Ahaz *was* twenty years old when he became king, and he reigned sixteen years in Jerusalem; and he did not do what was right in the sight of the LORD his God, as his father David *had* done.

3 But he walked in the way of the kings of Israel, [a]and even made his son pass through the fire, [b]according to the abominations of the nations whom the LORD had driven out from before the sons of Israel.

4 And he [a]sacrificed and burned incense on the high places and on the hills and under every green tree.

5 Then [a]Rezin king of Aram and Pekah son of Remaliah, king of Israel, came up to Jerusalem to wage war; and they besieged Ahaz, [b]but could not overcome him.

6 At that time Rezin king of Aram recovered [a]Elath for Aram, and cleared the Judeans out of Elath entirely; and the Arameans came to Elath, and have lived there to this day.

7 [a]So Ahaz sent messengers to [b]Tiglath-pileser king of Assyria, saying, "I am your servant and your son; come up and deliver me from the hand of the king of Aram, and from the hand of the king of Israel, who are rising up against me."

Cross references (margin)

29 [a]2 Kin. 15:19
[b]2 Kin. 17:6
33 [a]2 Chr. 27:1
34 [a]2 Kin. 15:3, 4; 2 Chr. 26:4, 5
★35 [a]2 Kin. 12:3 [b]2 Chr. 23:20; 27:3
37 [a]2 Kin. 16:5; Is. 7:1
1 [a]2 Chr. 28:1
2 [a]2 Chr. 28:1-4
★ 3 [a]Lev. 18:21; 2 Kin. 17:17; 21:6 [b]Deut. 12:31; 2 Kin. 21:2, 11
4 [a]Deut. 12:2; 2 Kin. 14:4
★ 5-9
5 [a]2 Kin. 15:37; Is. 7:1 [b]2 Chr. 28:5, 6
6 [a]2 Kin. 14:22; 2 Chr. 26:2
7 [a]2 Chr. 28:16 [b]2 Kin. 15:29

15:35 *the upper gate.* On the N. side of the Temple.
16:3 *pass through the fire.* Ahaz actually sacrificed his son to Molech (see notes on Lev. 18:21 and Isa. 30:33).
16:5-9 See notes on Isa. 7.

8 a2 Kin.
12:17, 18;
18:15

8 And [a]Ahaz took the silver and gold that was found in the house of the LORD and in the treasuries of the king's house, and sent a present to the king of Assyria.

9 a2 Chr.
28:21 bAmos
1:3-5 cIs.
22:6; Amos
9:7

9 [a]So the king of Assyria listened to him; and the king of Assyria went up against Damascus and [b]captured it, and carried the people of it away into exile to [c]Kir, and put Rezin to death.

★10-11

10 Now King Ahaz went to Damascus to meet [a]Tiglath-pileser king of Assyria, and saw the altar which was at Damascus; and King Ahaz sent to [b]Urijah the priest the pattern of the altar and its model, according to all its workmanship.

10 a2 Kin.
15:29 bIs.
8:2

11 So Urijah the priest built an altar; according to all that King Ahaz had sent from Damascus, thus Urijah the priest made it, before the coming of King Ahaz from Damascus.

12 a2 Chr.
26:16, 19

12 And when the king came from Damascus, the king saw the altar; then [a]the king approached the altar and went up to it,

13 and burned his burnt offering and his meal offering, and poured his libation and sprinkled the blood of his peace offerings on the altar.

14 aEx. 27:1,
2; 40:6, 29;
2 Chr. 4:1
b2 Kin.
16:11

14 And [a]the bronze altar, which was before the LORD, he brought from the front of the house, from between [b]his altar and the house of the LORD, and he put it on the north side of his altar.

★15 aEx.
29:39-41
b2 Kin.
16:14

15 Then King Ahaz commanded Urijah the priest, saying, "Upon the great altar burn [a]the morning burnt offering and the evening meal offering and the king's burnt offering and his meal offering, with the burnt offering

of all the people of the land and their meal offering and their libations; and sprinkle on it all the blood of the burnt offering and all the blood of the sacrifice. But [b]the bronze altar shall be for me to inquire by."

16 So Urijah the priest did according to all that King Ahaz commanded.

17 Then King Ahaz [a]cut off the borders of the stands, and removed the laver from them; he also [b]took down the sea from the bronze oxen which were under it, and put it on a pavement of stone.

★17-18

17 a1 Kin.
7:27, 28, 38
b1 Kin. 7:23,
25

18 And the covered way for the sabbath which they had built in the house, and the outer entry of the king, he removed from the house of the LORD because of the king of Assyria.

19 Now the rest of the acts of Ahaz which he did, are they not written [a]in the Book of the Chronicles of the Kings of Judah?

19 a2 Chr.
28:26

20 So [a]Ahaz slept with his fathers, and [b]was buried with his fathers in the city of David; and his son Hezekiah reigned in his place.

20 aIs. 14:28
b2 Chr.
28:27

T The Reign of Hoshea in Israel (732-722), 17:1-41

1 The defeat of Israel, 17:1-6

17 In the twelfth year of Ahaz king of Judah, [a]Hoshea the son of Elah became king over Israel in Samaria, and reigned nine years.

1 a2 Kin.
15:30

2 And he did evil in the sight of the LORD, only not as the kings of Israel who were before him.

3 [a]Shalmaneser king of Assyria came up [b]against him, and Hoshea became his servant and paid him tribute.

★ 3 aHos.
10:14
b2 Kin. 18:9-
12

16:10-11 Ahaz was likely in Damascus to pay tribute to Tiglath-pileser when he saw the heathen altar and commissioned his high priest to duplicate it for use in the worship in Jerusalem.

16:15 for me to inquire by. The king would receive oracles there.

16:17-18 The king broke up the furniture

(1 Kings 7:23-39) to use the metal for paying tribute. the covered way for the sabbath. Perhaps some kind of covered walkway used by the king when attending the Temple on the Sabbath.

17:3 Shalmaneser. Shalmaneser V, son of and successor to Tiglath-pileser III, reigned 727-722.

★ 4 4 But the king of Assyria found conspiracy in Hoshea, who had sent messengers to So king of Egypt and had offered no tribute to the king of Assyria, as *he had done* year by year; so the king of Assyria shut him up and bound him in prison.

5 *a*Hos. 13:16 5 Then the king of Assyria invaded the whole land and went up to *a*Samaria and besieged it three years.

★ 6 *a*Hos. 13:16 *b*Deut. 28:64; 29:27, 28 *c*2 Kin. 18:11; 1 Chr. 5:26 *d*Is. 37:12 *e*Is. 13:17; 21:2 6 In the ninth year of Hoshea, *a*the king of Assyria captured Samaria and *b*carried Israel away into exile to Assyria, and *c*settled them in Halah and Habor, *on* the river of *d*Gozan, and *e*in the cities of the Medes.

2 The sins of Israel, 17:7-23

7 *a*Josh. 23:16 *b*Ex. 14:15-30 *c*Judg. 6:10 7 Now *a*this came about, because the sons of Israel had sinned against the LORD their God, *b*who had brought them up from the land of Egypt from under the hand of Pharaoh, king of Egypt, *c*and they had feared other gods

8 *a*Lev. 18:3; Deut. 18:9 *b*2 Kin. 16:3; 17:19 8 and *a*walked in the customs of the nations whom the LORD had driven out before the sons of Israel, and *in the customs* *b*of the kings of Israel which they had introduced.

9 *a*2 Kin. 18:8 9 And the sons of Israel did things secretly which were not right, against the LORD their God. Moreover, they built for themselves high places in all their towns, from *a*watchtower to fortified city.

★10 *a*Ex. 34:12-14 *b*1 Kin. 14:23; Mic. 5:14 10 And *a*they set for themselves *sacred* pillars and *b*Asherim on every high hill and under every green tree,

11 and there they burned incense on all the high places as the nations did which the LORD had carried away to exile before them; and they did evil things provoking the LORD.

12 *a*Ex. 20:4 12 And they served idols, *a*concerning which the LORD had said to them, "You shall not do this thing."

13 *a*Neh. 9:29, 30 *b*2 Kin. 17:23 *c*1 Sam. 9:9 *d*Jer. 7:3-7; 18:11; Ezek. 18:31 13 Yet the *a*LORD warned Israel and Judah, *b*through all His prophets *and* *c*every seer, saying, "*d*Turn from your evil ways and keep My commandments, My statutes according to all the law which I commanded your fathers, and which I sent to you through My servants the prophets."

14 *a*Ex. 32:9; 33:3; Acts 7:51 14 However, they did not listen, but *a*stiffened their neck like their fathers, who did not believe in the LORD their God.

15 *a*Jer. 8:9 *b*Ex. 24:6-8; Deut. 29:25 *c*Deut. 32:21 *d*Jer. 2:5; Rom. 1:21-23 *e*Deut. 12:30, 31 15 And *a*they rejected His statutes and *b*His covenant which He made with their fathers, and His warnings with which He warned them. And *c*they followed vanity and *d*became vain, and *went* after the nations which surrounded them, concerning which the *e*LORD had commanded them not to do like them.

16 *a*1 Kin. 12:28 *b*1 Kin. 14:15, 23 *c*Deut. 4:19; 2 Kin. 21:3 *d*1 Kin. 16:31 16 And they forsook all the commandments of the LORD their God and made for themselves molten images, *even* *a*two calves, and *b*made an Asherah and *c*worshiped all the host of heaven and *d*served Baal.

17 *a*2 Kin. 16:3 *b*Lev. 19:26; Deut. 18:10-12 *c*1 Kin. 21:20 17 Then *a*they made their sons and their daughters pass through the fire, and *b*practiced divination and enchantments, and *c*sold themselves to do evil in the sight of the LORD, provoking Him.

18 *a*2 Kin. 17:6 *b*1 Kin. 11:13, 32, 36 18 So the LORD was very angry with Israel, and *a*removed them from His sight; *b*none was left except the tribe of Judah.

17:4 *to So king of Egypt.* Probably should be translated, "to So, to the king of Egypt," So being a political center. On this conspiracy see note on 15:27.

17:6 *the king of Assyria.* I.e., Shalmaneser, though Sargon II (722-705, Isa. 20:1) takes credit in his annals for the actual conquest of Samaria. Perhaps they were both involved, Shalmaneser as the king and Sargon as the general (see 18:10, "they"). *Halah.* An unidentified city or district in Mesopotamia. *Habor.* The modern Khabur River, one of the tributaries of the upper Euphrates, the area of Gozan (= Guzani in Assyrian records).

17:10 See note on Judg. 3:7. In this section (through v. 23) the author lists the sins which led to the Assyrian captivity.

19 Also ^aJudah did not keep the commandments of the LORD their God, but ^bwalked in the customs which Israel had introduced.

20 And the LORD rejected all the descendants of Israel and afflicted them and ^agave them into the hand of plunderers, until He had cast them out of His sight.

21 When ^aHe had torn Israel from the house of David, ^bthey made Jeroboam the son of Nebat king. Then ^cJeroboam drove Israel away from following the LORD, and made them commit a great sin.

22 And the sons of Israel walked in all the sins of Jeroboam which he did; they did not depart from them,

23 ^auntil the LORD removed Israel from His sight, ^bas He spoke through all His servants the prophets. ^cSo Israel was carried away into exile from their own land to Assyria until this day.

3 The resettlement of Israel, 17:24–41

24 ^aAnd the king of Assyria brought *men* from Babylon and from Cuthah and from ^bAvva and from ^cHamath and Sephar-vaim, and settled *them* in the cities of Samaria in place of the sons of Israel. So they possessed Samaria and lived in its cities.

25 And it came about at the beginning of their living there, that they ^adid not fear the LORD; therefore the LORD sent lions among them which killed some of them.

26 So they spoke to the king of Assyria, saying, "The nations whom you have carried away into exile in the cities of Samaria do not know the custom of the god of the land; so he has sent lions among them, and behold, they kill them because they do not know the custom of the god of the land."

27 Then the king of Assyria commanded, saying, "Take there one of the priests whom you carried away into exile, and let him go and live there; and let him teach them the custom of the god of the land."

28 So one of the priests whom they had carried away into exile from Samaria came and lived at Bethel, and taught them how they should fear the LORD.

29 But every nation still made gods of its own and put them ^ain the houses of the high places which the people of Samaria had made, every nation in their cities in which they lived.

30 And ^athe men of Babylon made Succoth-benoth, the men of Cuth made Nergal, the men of Hamath made Ashima,

31 and the Avvites made Nibhaz and Tartak; and ^athe Sepharvites burned their children in the fire to ^bAdrammelech and Anammelech the gods of ^cSepharvaim.

32 ^aThey also feared the LORD and ^bappointed from among themselves priests of the high places, who acted for them in the houses of the high places.

17:24 After the fall of Samaria, it was repopulated with people from *Cuthah* (in Babylon), *Avva* (on the Orontes River), *Hamath* (between Aleppo and Damascus), and *Sepharvaim* (possibly on the border between Damascus and Hamath). These people, by intermarriage with those left in Israel, began the new mongrel race known as the Samaritans (see note on Luke 10:33).

17:26–33 Because of the havoc wrought by the *lions*, the Samaritans asked for a priest to be sent to teach them about Yahweh. The result was a mixture of paganism and Yahweh worship, the people retaining their native gods (vv. 30–31) along with a defective fear of the Lord (vv. 33–34). *Succoth-benoth.* Perhaps the pagan god Marduk or his consort. *Nergal.* A pagan god, lord of the underworld. *Ashima.* The identification is uncertain, possibly the goddess Asherah. *Nibhaz.* Unknown pagan god. *Tartak.* Unknown pagan god. *Adrammelech.* Probably means "Adad is king," Adad being a Babylonian god. *Anammelech* means "Anu is king," Anu also being a Babylonian deity.

Marginal references:

19 ^a1 Kin. 14:22, 23 ^b2 Kin. 16:3

20 ^a2 Kin. 15:29

21 ^a1 Kin. 11:11, 31 ^b1 Kin. 12:20 ^c1 Kin. 12:28-33

23 ^a2 Kin. 17:6 ^b2 Kin. 17:13 ^c2 Kin. 17:6

★24 ^aEzra 4:2, 10 ^b2 Kin. 18:34 ^c1 Kin. 8:65

25 ^a2 Kin. 17:32-41

★26-33

29 ^a1 Kin. 12:31; 13:32

30 ^a2 Kin. 17:24

31 ^a2 Kin. 17:17 ^b2 Kin. 19:37 ^c2 Kin. 17:24

32 ^aZeph. 1:5 ^b1 Kin. 12:31

33 They feared the LORD and served their own gods according to the custom of the nations from among whom they had been carried away into exile.

34 To this day they do according to the earlier customs: they do not fear the LORD, nor do they follow their statutes or their ordinances or the law, or the commandments which the LORD commanded the sons of Jacob, ^awhom He named Israel;

35 with whom the LORD made a covenant and commanded them, saying, "^aYou shall not fear other gods, nor ^bbow down yourselves to them nor ^cserve them nor sacrifice to them.

36 "But the LORD, ^awho brought you up from the land of Egypt with great power and with ^ban outstretched arm, ^cHim you shall fear, and to Him you shall bow yourselves down, and to Him you shall sacrifice.

37 "And the statutes and the ordinances and the law and the commandment, which He wrote for you, ^ayou shall observe to do forever; and you shall not fear other gods.

38 "And the covenant that I have made with you, ^ayou shall not forget, nor shall you fear other gods.

39 "But the LORD your God you shall fear; and He will deliver you from the hand of all your enemies."

40 However, they did not listen, but they did according to their earlier custom.

41 ^aSo while these nations feared the LORD, they also served their idols; their children likewise and their grandchildren, as their fathers did, so they do to this day.

Marginal references (left column):
34 ^aGen. 32:28; 35:10
★35-39
35 ^aJudg. 6:10 ^bEx. 20:5 ^cDeut. 5:9
36 ^aEx. 14:15-30 ^bEx. 6:6; 9:15 ^cLev. 19:32; Deut. 6:13
37 ^aDeut. 5:32
38 ^aDeut. 4:23; 6:12
41 ^aZeph. 1:5; Matt. 6:24

II THE SURVIVING KINGDOM OF JUDAH, 18:1-25:30

A The Reign of Hezekiah (715-686; 2 Chron. 29:1-32:33), 18:1-20:21

1 His reforms, 18:1-12

18 Now it came about ^ain the third year of Hoshea, the son of Elah king of Israel, that ^bHezekiah the son of Ahaz king of Judah became king.

2 He was ^atwenty-five years old when he became king, and he reigned twenty-nine years in Jerusalem; and his mother's name was Abi the daughter of Zechariah.

3 ^aAnd he did right in the sight of the LORD, according to all that his father David had done.

4 ^aHe removed the high places and broke down the *sacred* pillars and cut down the Asherah. He also broke in pieces ^bthe bronze serpent that Moses had made, for until those days the sons of Israel burned incense to it; and it was called Nehushtan.

5 ^aHe trusted in the LORD, the God of Israel; ^bso that after him there was none like him among all the kings of Judah, nor *among those* who were before him.

6 For he ^aclung to the LORD; he did not depart from following Him, but kept His commandments, which the LORD had commanded Moses.

7 ^aAnd the LORD was with him; wherever he went he prospered. And ^bhe rebelled against the king of Assyria and did not serve him.

8 ^aHe defeated the Philistines as far as Gaza and its

Marginal references (right column):
★ 1 ^a2 Kin. 16:2; 17:1 ^b2 Chr. 28:27
2 ^a2 Chr. 29:1, 2
3 ^a2 Kin. 20:3; 2 Chr. 31:20
★ 4 ^a2 Kin. 18:22; 2 Chr. 31:1 ^bNum. 21:8, 9
5 ^a2 Kin. 19:10 ^b2 Kin. 23:25
6 ^aDeut. 10:20; Josh. 23:8
7 ^aGen. 39:2, 3; 1 Sam. 18:14 ^b2 Kin. 16:7
8 ^a2 Chr. 28:18; Is. 14:29 ^b2 Kin. 17:9

17:35-39 This passage consists of quotations from Exod. 20:5, 7, 20; 6:6; 20:23; Deut. 4:34; 5:15; 13:5; 28:14.

18:1 *Hezekiah*, one of Judah's best kings, pursued an anti-Assyrian policy which brought a campaign against Judah by Sennacherib, resulting first in Hezekiah's paying tribute, and then in the miraculous defeat of the Assyrian army (chaps. 18-20; 2 Chron. 29-32; Isa. 36-39).

18:4 *the bronze serpent.* What seven hundred years before was a means of healing (Num. 21:8-9) had become an idol that was worshiped. *Nehushtan* means "a mere piece of bronze"—a contemptuous unmasking of what the relic really was. To destroy it was the only wise course of action (see note on Rom. 13:14).

territory, from [b]watchtower to fortified city.

9 Now it came about in the fourth year of King Hezekiah, which was the seventh year of Hoshea son of Elah king of Israel, that [a]Shalmaneser king of Assyria came up against Samaria and besieged it.

10 And at the end of three years they captured it; in the sixth year of Hezekiah, which was [a]the ninth year of Hoshea king of Israel, Samaria was captured.

11 Then the king of Assyria carried Israel away into exile to Assyria, and put them in [a]Halah and on the Habor, the river of Gozan, and in the cities of the Medes,

12 because they [a]did not obey the voice of the Lord their God, but transgressed His covenant, even all that Moses the servant of the Lord commanded; they would neither listen, nor do it.

2 His deliverance from Sennacherib's two invasions, 18:13–19:37

13 [a]Now in the fourteenth year of King Hezekiah, Sennacherib king of Assyria came up against all the fortified cities of Judah and seized them.

14 Then Hezekiah king of Judah sent to the king of Assyria at Lachish, saying, "[a]I have done wrong. Withdraw from me; whatever you impose on me I will bear." So the king of Assyria required of Hezekiah king of Judah three hundred talents of silver and thirty talents of gold.

15 And [a]Hezekiah gave him all the silver which was found in the house of the Lord, and in the treasuries of the king's house.

16 At that time Hezekiah cut off *the gold from* the doors of the temple of the Lord, and *from* the doorposts which Hezekiah king of Judah had overlaid, and gave it to the king of Assyria.

17 Then the king of Assyria sent [a]Tartan and Rab-saris and Rabshakeh from Lachish to King Hezekiah with a large army to Jerusalem. So they went up and came to Jerusalem. And when they went up, they came and stood by the [b]conduit of the upper pool, which is on the highway of the fuller's field.

18 When they called to the king, [a]Eliakim the son of Hilkiah, who was over the household, and [b]Shebnah the scribe and Joah the son of Asaph the recorder, came out to them.

19 Then Rabshakeh said to them, "Say now to Hezekiah, 'Thus says the great king, the king of Assyria, "[a]What is this confidence that you have?

20 "You say (but *they are* only empty words), '*I have* counsel and strength for the war.' Now on whom do you rely, [a]that you have rebelled against me?

21 "Now behold, you [a]rely on the staff of this crushed reed, *even* on Egypt; on which if a man leans, it will go into his hand and pierce it. So is Pharaoh king of Egypt to all who rely on him.

22 "But if you say to me, 'We trust in the Lord our God,' is it not He whose high places and [a]whose altars Hezekiah has taken away, and has said to Judah and to Jerusalem, 'You shall worship before this altar in Jerusalem'?

23 "Now therefore, come, make a bargain with my master the king of Assyria, and I will give you two thousand horses, if you

9 [a]2 Kin. 17:3-7 ★

10 [a]2 Kin. 17:6

11 [a]1 Chr. 5:26

12 [a]1 Kin. 9:6; Dan. 9:6, 10

13 [a]2 Chr. 32:1; Is. 36:1-39:8

14 [a]2 Kin. 18:7 ★

15 [a]1 Kin. 15:18, 19; 2 Kin. 12:18; 16:8

17 [a]Is. 20:1 [b]2 Kin. 20:20; Is. 7:3 ★

18 [a]2 Kin. 19:2; Is. 22:20 [b]Is. 22:15

19 [a]2 Chr. 32:10

20 [a]2 Kin. 18:7

21 [a]Is. 30:2, 3, 7; Ezek. 29:6, 7

22 [a]2 Kin. 18:4; 2 Chr. 31:1

23 ★

18:9 The contrast is startling: under Hezekiah, Judah was being led back to God at the same time that Israel, under Hoshea, was being taken into captivity.

18:14 The tribute amounted to about 360,000 ounces of silver and 36,000 ounces of gold.

18:17 *Tartan.* General of the army (see note on

Isa. 20:1). The meeting place, the same one where Isaiah confronted wicked Ahaz 33 years earlier (Isa. 7:3), had sufficient water for *fullers* (launderers).

18:23 Rabshakeh (not a proper name, but a word meaning commander) insinuates that Hezekiah doesn't even have 2,000 horsemen.

are able on your part to set riders on them.

24 "How then can you repulse one official of the least of my master's servants, and rely on Egypt for chariots and for horsemen?

★25   **25** "Have I now come up without the LORD's approval against this place to destroy it? The LORD said to me, 'Go up against this land and destroy it.' " ' "

★26 *a*Ezra 4:7; Dan. 2:4   **26** Then Eliakim the son of Hilkiah, and Shebnah and Joah, said to Rabshakeh, "Speak now to your servants in Aramaic, for we understand *it*; and do not speak with us in *a*Judean, in the hearing of the people who are on the wall."

27 But Rabshakeh said to them, "Has my master sent me only to your master and to you to speak these words, *and* not to the men who sit on the wall, *doomed* to eat their own dung and drink their own urine with you?"

28 Then Rabshakeh stood and cried with a loud voice in Judean, saying, "Hear the word of the great king, the king of Assyria.

29 *a*2 Chr. 32:15   **29** "Thus says the king, '*a*Do not let Hezekiah deceive you, for he will not be able to deliver you from my hand;

30 nor let Hezekiah make you trust in the LORD, saying, "The LORD will surely deliver us, and this city shall not be given into the hand of the king of Assyria."

★31-32

31 *a*1 Kin. 4:20, 25   **31** 'Do not listen to Hezekiah, for thus says the king of Assyria, "Make your peace with me and come out to me, and eat *a*each of his vine and each of his fig tree and drink each of the waters of his own cistern,

32 *a*Deut. 8:7-9; 11:12   **32** until I come and take you away *a*to a land like your own

land, a land of grain and new wine, a land of bread and vineyards, a land of olive trees and honey, that you may live and not die." But do not listen to Hezekiah, when he misleads you, saying, "The LORD will deliver us."

33 '*a*Has any one of the gods of the nations delivered his land from the hand of the king of Assyria?   33 *a*2 Kin. 19:12; Is. 10:10, 11

34 '*a*Where are the gods of Hamath and *b*Arpad? Where are the gods of Sepharvaim, Hena and *c*Ivvah? Have they delivered Samaria from my hand?   34 *a*2 Kin. 19:13 *b*Is. 10:9 *c*2 Kin. 17:24

35 'Who among all the gods of the lands have delivered their land from my hand, *a*that the LORD should deliver Jerusalem from my hand?' "   35 *a*Ps. 2:1-3; 59:7

36 But the people were silent and answered him not a word, for the king's commandment was, "Do not answer him."

37 Then *a*Eliakim the son of Hilkiah, who was over the household, and Shebna the scribe and Joah the son of Asaph, the recorder, came to Hezekiah *b*with their clothes torn and told him the words of Rabshakeh.   37 *a*2 Kin. 18:26 *b*2 Kin. 6:30

19 *a*And when King Hezekiah heard *it*, he *b*tore his clothes, *c*covered himself with sackcloth and entered the house of the LORD.   1 *a*2 Chr. 32:20-22; Is. 37:1 *b*2 Kin. 18:37 *c*1 Kin. 21:27

2 Then he sent Eliakim who was over the household with Shebna the scribe and the elders of the priests, *a*covered with sackcloth, to *b*Isaiah the prophet the son of Amoz.   2 *a*2 Sam. 3:31 *b*Is. 1:1; 2:1

3 And they said to him, "Thus says Hezekiah, 'This day is a day of distress, rebuke, and rejection; for children have come to

---

18:25 The commander further claimed that he had come against Judah by command of the Lord.

18:26 The Hebrew officials asked the Assyrians to speak in *Aramaic,* the commercial and diplomatic language of the day, so that bystanders would not understand what was being

said. Evidently the Rabshakeh (commander) himself was speaking in Hebrew or through an interpreter.

18:31-32 Addressing the populace directly, the Rabshakeh insisted that they would stay alive only by surrendering and going into what he pictured as a rather pleasant exile.

birth, and there is no strength to *deliver.*

4 a Josh.
14:12;
2 Sam. 16:12
b 2 Kin.
18:35 c Is.
1:9

4 '[a]Perhaps the LORD your God will hear all the words of Rabshakeh, whom his master the king of Assyria has sent [b]to reproach the living God, and will rebuke the words which the LORD your God has heard. Therefore, offer a prayer for [c]the remnant that is left.'"

5 So the servants of King Hezekiah came to Isaiah.

6 a 2 Kin.
18:17
b 2 Kin.
18:22-25;
30:35

6 And Isaiah said to them, "Thus you shall say to your master, 'Thus says the LORD, "Do not be afraid because of the words that you have heard, with which the [a]servants of the king of Assyria [b]have blasphemed Me.

7 a 2 Kin.
7:6 b 2 Kin.
19:37

7 "Behold, I will put a spirit in him so that [a]he shall hear a rumor and return to his own land. And [b]I will make him fall by the sword in his own land." ' "

★ 8 a Josh.
10:29
b 2 Kin.
18:14

8 Then Rabshakeh returned and found the king of Assyria fighting against [a]Libnah, for he had heard that the king had left [b]Lachish.

★ 9

9 When he heard *them* say concerning Tirhakah king of Cush, "Behold, he has come out to fight against you," he sent messengers again to Hezekiah saying,

10 a 2 Kin.
18:5 b 2 Kin.
18:30

10 "Thus you shall say to Hezekiah king of Judah, 'Do not [a]let your God in whom you trust deceive you saying, "[b]Jerusalem shall not be given into the hand of the king of Assyria."

11 'Behold, you have heard what the kings of Assyria have done to all the lands, destroying

them completely. So will you be spared?

12 '[a]Did the gods of those nations which my fathers destroyed deliver them, *even* [b]Gozan and [c]Haran and Rezeph and [d]the sons of Eden who *were* in Telassar?

13 '[a]Where is the king of Hamath, the king of Arpad, the king of the city of Sepharvaim, and *of* Hena and Ivvah?' "

14 Then [a]Hezekiah took the letter from the hand of the messengers and read it, and he went up to the house of the LORD and spread it out before the LORD.

15 And Hezekiah prayed before the LORD and said, "O LORD, the God of Israel, [a]who art enthroned *above* the cherubim, [b]Thou art the God, Thou alone, of all the kingdoms of the earth. Thou hast made heaven and earth.

16 "[a]Incline Thine ear, O LORD, and hear; [b]open Thine eyes, O LORD, and see; and listen to the words of Sennacherib, which he has sent [c]to reproach the living God.

17 "Truly, O LORD, the kings of Assyria have devastated the nations and their lands

18 and have cast their gods into the fire, [a]for they were not gods but the work of men's hands, wood and stone. So they have destroyed them.

19 "And now, O LORD our God, I pray, deliver us from his hand [a]that all the kingdoms of the earth may know that Thou alone, O [b]LORD, art God."

20 Then Isaiah the son of Amoz sent to Hezekiah saying,

★ 12-13

12 a 2 Kin.
18:33
b 2 Kin. 17:6
c Gen. 11:31
d Is. 37:12

13 a 2 Kin.
18:34

★ 14-19

14 a Is. 37:14

15 a Ex.
25:22; Is.
37:14
b 2 Kin. 5:15

16 a Ps. 31:2;
Is. 37:17
b 1 Kin. 8:29;
2 Chr. 6:40
c 2 Kin. 19:4

18 a Is. 44:9-
20; Acts
17:29

19 a 1 Kin.
8:42, 43
b 2 Kin.
19:15

★ 20-34
20 a 2 Kin.
20:5

19:8 *Libnah.* See note on Isa. 37:8.
19:9 *Tirhakah.* If this is related to a single campaign of Sennacherib against Judah in 701, then Tirhakah was then a general, though he is designated by the title of king which he later assumed. If there were two separate campaigns (a 13- or 14-year break coming between 18:16 and 18:17), then he was king at this time. In any case, this threat from Egypt made it urgent for Sennacherib to press Judah to surrender.
19:12-13 Recounts of previous conquests of Sennacherib.

19:14-19 In this childlike prayer, Hezekiah acknowledged God's sovereignty (v. 15), mentioned Sennacherib's defiance of God and the impotence of his gods (vv. 16-18), and beseeched God for deliverance (v. 19).
19:20-34 In His answer, God assured Hezekiah (1) that Sennacherib was but an instrument in God's hand (vv. 20-28; on v. 25 see note on Isa. 10:5); (2) that a remnant would survive (vv. 29-31, though they might lose two years' harvest); (3) that Jerusalem would not fall to the Assyrians (vv. 32-34).

"Thus says the LORD, the God of Israel, 'Because you have prayed to Me about Sennacherib king of Assyria, [a]I have heard you.'

21 "This is the word that the LORD has spoken against him:

'She has despised you
    and mocked you,
[a]The virgin daughter of
    Zion;
She [b]has shaken her
    head behind you,
The daughter of Jerusa-
    lem!

22 'Whom have you [a]re-
    proached and [b]blas-
    phemed?
And against whom have
    you raised your voice,
And haughtily lifted up
    your eyes?
Against the [c]Holy One
    of Israel!

23 '[a]Through your messen-
    gers you have re-
    proached the Lord,
And you have said,
    "With my many
    chariots
I came up to the heights
    of the mountains,
To the remotest parts of
    Lebanon;
And I cut down its tall
    cedars and its choice
    cypresses.
And I entered its far-
    thest lodging place, its
    [b]thickest forest.

24 "I dug wells and drank
    foreign waters,
And with the sole of my
    feet I [a]dried up
All the rivers of Egypt."

25 '[a]Have you not heard?
Long ago I did it;
From ancient times I
    planned it.
[b]Now I have brought it
    to pass,
That you should turn
    fortified cities into
    ruinous heaps.

26 "Therefore their inhabi-
    tants were short of
    strength,

They were dismayed
    and put to shame;
They were [a]as the vege-
    tation of the field and
    as the green herb,
As grass on the house-
    tops is scorched be-
    fore it is grown up.

27 "But [a]I know your sitting
    down,
And your going out and
    your coming in,
And your raging against
    Me.

28 'Because of your raging
    against Me,
And because your arro-
    gance has come up to
    My ears,
Therefore I [a]will put My
    hook in your nose,
And My bridle in your
    lips,
And [b]I will turn you
    back by the way
    which you came.

29 'Then this shall be [a]the sign for you: you shall eat this year what grows of itself, in the second year what springs from the same, and in the third year sow, reap, plant vineyards, and eat their fruit.

30 '[a]And the surviving rem-nant of the house of Judah shall again take root downward and bear fruit upward.

31 'For out of Jerusalem shall go forth a remnant, and [a]out of Mount Zion survivors. [b]The zeal of the LORD shall perform this.

32 'Therefore thus says the LORD concerning the king of As-syria, "[a]He shall not come to this city or shoot an arrow there; nei-ther shall he come before it with a shield, nor throw up a mound against it.

33 "[a]By the way that he came, by the same he shall return, and he shall not come to this city," ' declares the LORD.

34 '[a]For I will defend this city to save it for My own sake and [b]for My servant David's sake.' "

21 [a]Jer.
14:17; Lam.
2:13 [b]Ps.
109:25; Matt.
27:39

22 [a]2 Kin.
19:4 [b]2 Kin.
19:6 [c]Is.
5:24; 30:11-
15

23 [a]2 Kin.
18:17
[b]2 Chr.
26:10; Is.
10:18

24 [a]Is. 19:6

25 [a]Is. 45:7
[b]Is. 10:5

26 [a]Ps.
129:6

27 [a]Ps.
139:1

28 [a]Ezek.
19:9; 29:4
[b]2 Kin.
19:33, 36

29 [a]Ex. 3:12;
2 Kin. 20:8, 9

30 [a]2 Kin.
19:4; 2 Chr.
32:22, 23

31 [a]Is. 10:20
[b]Is. 9:7

32 [a]Is. 8:7-
10

33 [a]2 Kin.
19:28

34 [a]2 Kin.
20:6; Is. 31:5
[b]1 Kin.
11:12, 13

★35 a2 Sam.
24:16; 2 Chr.
32:21

35 a Then it happened that night that the angel of the LORD went out, and struck 185,000 in the camp of the Assyrians; and when men rose early in the morning, behold, all of them were dead.

36 a2 Kin.
19:7, 28, 33
b Jon. 1:2

36 So a Sennacherib king of Assyria departed and returned home, and lived at b Nineveh.

37 a2 Kin.
19:17, 31
b Gen. 8:4;
Jer. 51:27
c Ezra 4:2

37 And it came about as he was worshiping in the house of Nisroch his god, that a Adrammelech and Sharezer killed him with the sword; and they escaped into b the land of Ararat. And c Esarhaddon his son became king in his place.

3 His illness and recovery, 20:1-11

★ 1 a2 Chr.
32:24; Is.
38:1-22
b2 Sam.
17:23

20 a In those days Hezekiah became mortally ill. And Isaiah the prophet the son of Amoz came to him and said to him, "Thus says the LORD, 'b Set your house in order, for you shall die and not live.'"

2 Then he turned his face to the wall, and prayed to the LORD, saying,

3 a Neh.
5:19; 13:14,
22, 31
b2 Kin. 18:3-
6 c2 Sam.
12:21, 22

3 "a Remember now, O LORD, I beseech Thee, b how I have walked before Thee in truth and with a whole heart, and have done what is good in Thy sight." And c Hezekiah wept bitterly.

4 And it came about before Isaiah had gone out of the middle court, that the word of the LORD came to him, saying,

5 a1 Sam.
9:16; 10:1
b2 Kin.
19:20 c Ps.
39:12

5 "Return and say to a Hezekiah the leader of My people, 'Thus says the LORD, the God of your father David, "b I have heard your prayer, c I have seen your tears; behold, I will heal you. On the third day you shall go up to the house of the LORD.

6 a2 Kin.
19:34

6 "And I will add fifteen years to your life, and I will deliver you and this city from the hand of the king of Assyria; and a I will defend this city for My own sake and for My servant David's sake."'"

7 Then Isaiah said, "Take a cake of figs." And they took and laid it on the boil, and he recovered.

8 Now Hezekiah said to Isaiah, "What will be the sign that the LORD will heal me, and that I shall go up to the house of the LORD the third day?"

9 a Is. 38:7

9 And Isaiah said, "a This shall be the sign to you from the LORD, that the LORD will do the thing that He has spoken: shall the shadow go forward ten steps or go back ten steps?"

10 So Hezekiah answered, "It is easy for the shadow to decline ten steps; no, but let the shadow turn backward ten steps."

★11 a Josh.
10:12-14; Is.
38:8

11 And Isaiah the prophet cried to the LORD, and a He brought the shadow on the stairway back ten steps by which it had gone down on the stairway of Ahaz.

4 His foolishness before the Babylonians, 20:12-21

★12 a2 Chr.
32:31; Is.
39:1-8

12 a At that time Berodachbaladan a son of Baladan, king of Babylon, sent letters and a present to Hezekiah, for he heard that Hezekiah had been sick.

13 a2 Chr.
32:27

13 And Hezekiah listened to them, and showed them a all his treasure house, the silver and the gold and the spices and the precious oil and the house of his armor and all that was found in his treasuries. There was nothing in his house, nor in all his dominion, that Hezekiah did not show them.

14 Then Isaiah the prophet came to King Hezekiah and said

19:35 See note on Isa. 37:36.
20:1 In those days. I.e., when Sennacherib first began to attack Judah (cf. v. 6).
20:11 See note on Isa. 38:8. Second Chronicles 32:31 indicates this was a geographically localized miracle, nonetheless spectacular, but not involving the reversal of the earth's rotation

which would have affected the entire world.
20:12 Berodach-baladan. A misspelling for Merodach-baladan (Isa. 39:1), twice king of Babylon (722-710 and 703-702), who apparently sent this delegation to enlist Hezekiah's aid against Assyria.

to him, "What did these men say, and from where have they come to you?" And Hezekiah said, "They have come from a far country, from Babylon."

15 And he said, "What have they seen in your house?" So Hezekiah answered, "They have seen all that is in my house; there is nothing among my treasuries that I have not shown them."

16 Then Isaiah said to Hezekiah, "Hear the word of the LORD.

★17-18
17 a2 Kin. 24:13; 25:13-15; 2 Chr. 36:10; Jer. 52:17-19

17 'Behold, the days are coming when all that is in your house, and all that your fathers have laid up in store to this day shall be carried to Babylon; nothing shall be left,' says the LORD.

18 a2 Kin. 24:12; 2 Chr. 33:11 bDan. 1:3-7

18 'And some aof your sons who shall issue from you, whom you shall beget, shall be taken away; and they shall become boffcials in the palace of the king of Babylon.' "

★19 a1 Sam. 3:18

19 Then Hezekiah said to Isaiah, "The word of the LORD which you have spoken is agood." For he thought, "Is it not so, if there shall be peace and truth in my days?"

★20 a2 Chr. 32:32 bNeh. 3:16

20 aNow the rest of the acts of Hezekiah and all his might, and how he bmade the pool and the conduit, and brought water into the city, are they not written in the Book of the Chronicles of the Kings of Judah?

21 a2 Chr. 32:33

21 aSo Hezekiah slept with his fathers, and Manasseh his son became king in his place.

B The Reign of Manasseh (695–642; 2 Chron. 33:1-20), 21:1-18

★ 1 a2 Chr. 33:1-9

21 aManasseh was twelve years old when he became king, and he reigned fifty-five

years in Jerusalem; and his mother's name was Hephzibah.

2 aJer. 15:4 b2 Kin. 16:3

2 And ahe did evil in the sight of the LORD, baccording to the abominations of the nations whom the LORD dispossessed before the sons of Israel.

3 a2 Kin. 18:4 b1 Kin. 16:31-33 cDeut. 17:2-5; 2 Kin. 17:16; 23:5

3 For ahe rebuilt the high places which Hezekiah his father had destroyed; and bhe erected altars for Baal and made an Asherah, as Ahab king of Israel had done, and cworshiped all the host of heaven and served them.

4 a2 Kin. 16:10-16 b2 Sam. 7:13; 1 Kin. 8:29

4 And ahe built altars in the house of the LORD, of which the LORD had said, "bIn Jerusalem I will put My name."

5 a2 Kin. 23:4, 5 b1 Kin. 7:12; 2 Kin. 23:12

5 For he built altars for aall the host of heaven in bthe two courts of the house of the LORD.

★ 6 aLev. 18:21; 2 Kin. 16:3; 17:17 bLev. 19:26, 31; Deut. 18:10-14

6 And ahe made his son pass through the fire, bpracticed witchcraft and used divination, and dealt with mediums and spiritists. He did much evil in the sight of the LORD provoking *Him to anger*.

★ 7 aDeut. 16:21; 2 Kin. 23:6 b1 Kin. 8:29; 9:3; 2 Chr. 7:12, 16

7 Then ahe set the carved image of Asherah that he had made, in the house of which the LORD said to David and to his son Solomon, "bIn this house and in Jerusalem, which I have chosen from all the tribes of Israel, I will put My name forever.

8 a2 Sam. 7:10; 2 Kin. 18:11, 12

8 "And I awill not make the feet of Israel wander anymore from the land which I gave their fathers, if only they will observe to do according to all that I have commanded them, and according to all the law that My servant Moses commanded them."

9 aProv. 29:12

9 But they did not listen, and Manasseh aseduced them to do evil more than the nations whom the LORD destroyed before the sons of Israel.

10 Now the LORD spoke through His servants the prophets, saying,

---

20:17-18 See note on Isa. 39:6.
20:19 Rather than confessing his sin, Hezekiah was satisfied simply to enjoy peace for the rest of his own life.
20:20 See note on 2 Chron. 32:30.
21:1 Though he had the advantage of a godly

father with whom he reigned as coregent for 10 years, *Manasseh* was Judah's worst and longest reigning king (cf. 24:3).
21:6 See note on 16:3.
21:7 *Asherah.* See note on Jer. 17:2. She was the mother of 70 gods, including Baal.

★11 *a*2 Kin.
21:2; 24:3, 4
*b*Gen. 15:16;
1 Kin. 21:26
*c*2 Kin. 21:16
*d*2 Kin. 21:21

11 "*a*Because Manasseh king of Judah has done these abominations, *b*having done wickedly more than all the Amorites did who *were* before him, and *c*has also made Judah sin *d*with his idols;

★12 *a*1 Sam.
3:11; Jer.
19:3

12 therefore thus says the LORD, the God of Israel, 'Behold, I am bringing *such* calamity on Jerusalem and Judah, that whoever hears of it, *a*both his ears shall tingle.

★13 *a*Is.
34:11; Amos
7:7, 8

13 '*a*And I will stretch over Jerusalem the line of Samaria and the plummet of the house of Ahab, and I will wipe Jerusalem as one wipes a dish, wiping it and turning it upside down.
14 'And I will abandon the remnant of My inheritance and deliver them into the hand of their enemies, and they shall become as plunder and spoil to all their enemies;
15 because they have done evil in My sight, and have been provoking Me to anger, since the day their fathers came from Egypt, even to this day.' "

★16 *a*2 Kin.
24:4 *b*2 Kin.
21:11

16 *a*Moreover, Manasseh shed very much innocent blood until he had filled Jerusalem from one end to another; besides his sin *b*with which he made Judah sin, in doing evil in the sight of the LORD.

17 *a*2 Chr.
33:11-19

17 *a*Now the rest of the acts of Manasseh and all that he did and his sin which he committed, are they not written in the Book of the Chronicles of the Kings of Judah?

18 *a*2 Chr.
33:20
*b*2 Kin.
21:26

18 *a*And Manasseh slept with his fathers and was buried in the garden of his own house, *b*in the garden of Uzza, and Amon his son became king in his place.

C The Reign of Amon (642–640; 2 Chron. 33:21–25), 21:19–26

19 *a*2 Chr.
33:21-23

19 *a*Amon was twenty-two years old when he became king, and he reigned two years in Jerusalem; and his mother's name *was* Meshullemeth the daughter of Haruz of Jotbah.

20 *a*2 Kin.
21:2-6, 11,
16

20 And he did evil in the sight of the LORD, *a*as Manasseh his father had done.
21 For he walked in all the way that his father had walked, and served the idols that his father had served and worshiped them.

22 *a*2 Kin.
22:17; 1 Chr.
28:9

22 So *a*he forsook the LORD, the God of his fathers, and did not walk in the way of the LORD.

23 *a*2 Kin.
12:20; 14:19

23 And *a*the servants of Amon conspired against him and killed the king in his own house.

24 *a*2 Kin.
14:5

24 Then *a*the people of the land killed all those who had conspired against King Amon, and the people of the land made Josiah his son king in his place.
25 Now the rest of the acts of Amon which he did, are they not written in the Book of the Chronicles of the Kings of Judah?

26 *a*2 Kin.
21:18

26 And he was buried in his grave *a*in the garden of Uzza, and Josiah his son became king in his place.

D The Reign of Josiah (640–609; 2 Chron. 34:1–35:27), 22:1–23:30

1 He repairs the Temple, 22:1–7

1 *a*2 Chr.
34:1 *b*Josh.
15:39

22 *a*Josiah was eight years old when he became king, and

21:11 *the Amorites.* The epitome of evil. See note on Gen. 15:13–16.
21:12 The harsh news of the captivity would make ears *tingle.*
21:13 Jerusalem would be judged according to the same righteous standard as were Samaria and Ahab, and as a result would be destroyed.
21:16 According to tradition, Manasseh killed Isaiah (see Introduction to Isaiah).

he reigned thirty-one years in Jerusalem; and his mother's name *was* Jedidah the daughter of Adaiah of *b*Bozkath.

2 And he did right in the sight of the LORD and walked in all the way of his father David, nor did he *a*turn aside to the right or to the left.

3 Now *a*it came about in the eighteenth year of King Josiah that the king sent Shaphan, the son of Azaliah the son of Meshullam the scribe, to the house of the LORD saying,

4 "*a*Go up to Hilkiah the high priest that he may count the money brought in to the house of the LORD which the doorkeepers have gathered from the people.

5 "*a*And let them deliver it into the hand of the workmen who have the oversight of the house of the LORD, and let them give it to the workmen who are in the house of the LORD to repair the damages of the house,

6 to the carpenters and the builders and the masons and for buying timber and hewn stone to repair the house.

7 "Only *a*no accounting shall be made with them for the money delivered into their hands, for they deal faithfully."

2   He recovers the law, 22:8-20

8 Then Hilkiah the high priest said to Shaphan the scribe, "*a*I have found the book of the law in the house of the LORD." And Hilkiah gave the book to Shaphan who read it.

9 And Shaphan the scribe came to the king and brought back word to the king and said, "Your servants have emptied out the money that was found in the house, and have delivered it into the hand of the workmen who have the oversight of the house of the LORD."

10 Moreover, Shaphan the scribe told the king saying, "Hilkiah the priest has given me a book." And Shaphan read it in the presence of the king.

11 And it came about when the king heard the words of the book of the law, that *a*he tore his clothes.

12 Then the king commanded Hilkiah the priest, *a*Ahikam the son of Shaphan, *b*Achbor the son of Micaiah, Shaphan the scribe, and Asaiah the king's servant saying,

13 "Go, inquire of the LORD for me and the people and all Judah concerning the words of this book that has been found, for *a*great is the wrath of the LORD that burns against us, because our fathers have not listened to the words of this book, to do according to all that is written concerning us."

14 So Hilkiah the priest, Ahikam, Achbor, Shaphan, and Asaiah went to Huldah the prophetess, the wife of Shallum the son of *a*Tikvah, the son of Harhas, keeper of the wardrobe (now she lived in Jerusalem in the *b*Second Quarter); and they spoke to her.

15 And she said to them, "Thus says the LORD God of Israel, 'Tell the man who sent you to me,

16 thus says the LORD, "Behold, I *a*bring evil on this place and on its inhabitants, *even* all the words of the book which the king of Judah has read.

17 "*a*Because they have forsaken Me and have burned incense to other gods that they

Marginal references

2 *a*Deut. 5:32; Josh. 1:7

3 *a*2 Chr. 34:8

★4-7

4 *a*2 Kin. 12:4, 9, 10

5 *a*2 Kin. 12:11-14

7 *a*2 Kin. 12:15; 1 Cor. 4:2

★ 8 *a*Deut. 31:24-26; 2 Chr. 34:14, 15

11 *a*Gen. 37:34; Josh. 7:6

12 *a*2 Kin. 25:22; Jer. 26:24 *b*2 Chr. 34:20

13 *a*Deut. 29:23-28; 31:17, 18

★14 *a*2 Chr. 34:22 *b*Zeph. 1:10

16 *a*Deut. 29:27; Dan. 9:11-14

17 *a*Deut. 29:25, 26; 2 Kin. 21:22

Footnotes

22:4-7 Jehoash used a similar procedure (see notes on 12:7-15). The money came from the southern tribes and from the remnants of Israel (2 Chron. 34:8-9).

22:8 *the book of the law.* Possibly the entire Pentateuch or perhaps the book of Deuteronomy or Scripture portions such as Lev. 26 and Deut. 28, which speak of judgment. Manasseh

had doubtless destroyed all the copies that had not been hidden.

22:14 Only rarely did God speak to the nation through a woman (cf. Miriam, Exod. 15 and Deborah, Judg. 5). *keeper of the wardrobe.* Either the royal wardrobe or that of the priests. *the Second Quarter.* A suburb of the city of Jerusalem.

might provoke Me to anger with all the work of their hands, therefore My wrath burns against this place, and it shall not be quenched." '

18 18 "But to ^athe king of Judah who sent you to inquire of the LORD thus shall you say to him, 'Thus says the LORD God of Israel, "*Regarding* the words which you have heard,

18 *a*2 Chr. 34:26

19 *a*because your heart was tender and *b*you humbled yourself before the LORD when you heard what I spoke against this place and against its inhabitants that they should become *c*a desolation and a *d*curse, and you have *e*torn your clothes and wept before Me, I truly have heard you," declares the LORD.

19 *a*1 Sam. 24:5; Ps. 51:17 *b*Ex. 10:3; 1 Kin. 21:29 *c*Lev. 26:31 *d*Jer. 26:6 *e*2 Kin. 22:11

20 "Therefore, behold, I will gather you to your fathers, and *a*you shall be gathered to your grave in peace, neither shall your eyes see all the evil which I will bring on this place." ' " So they brought back word to the king.

★20 *a*2 Kin. 23:30

3 He renews the covenant,
23:1-3

23 ^aThen the king sent, and they gathered to him all the elders of Judah and of Jerusalem.

1 *a*2 Chr. 34:29-32

2 And the king went up to the house of the LORD and all the men of Judah and all the inhabitants of Jerusalem with him, and the priests and the prophets and all the people, both small and great; and *a*he read in their hearing all the words of the book of the covenant, *b*which was found in the house of the LORD.

2 *a*Deut. 31:10-13 *b*2 Kin. 22:8

3 And *a*the king stood by the pillar and made a covenant before the LORD, *b*to walk after the LORD, and to keep His commandments and His testimonies and His statutes with all *his* heart and all *his* soul, to carry out the words of this

3 *a*2 Kin. 11:14, 17 *b*Deut. 13:4

covenant that were written in this book. And all the people entered into the covenant.

4 He reforms the nation,
23:4-30

4 Then the king commanded Hilkiah the high priest and *a*the priests of the second order and the doorkeepers, *b*to bring out of the temple of the LORD all the vessels that were made for Baal, for Asherah, and for all the host of heaven; and *c*he burned them outside Jerusalem in the fields of the Kidron, and carried their ashes to Bethel.

★ 4 *a*2 Kin. 25:18; Jer. 52:24 *b*2 Kin. 21:37; 2 Chr. 33:3 *c*2 Kin. 23:15

5 And he did away with the idolatrous priests whom the kings of Judah had appointed to burn incense in the high places in the cities of Judah and in the surrounding area of Jerusalem, also those who burned incense to Baal, to the sun and to the moon and to the constellations and to all the *a*host of heaven.

★ 5 *a*2 Kin. 21:3

6 And he brought out the Asherah from the house of the LORD outside Jerusalem to the brook Kidron, and burned it at the brook Kidron, and *a*ground *it* to dust, and *b*threw its dust on the graves of the common people.

6 *a*2 Kin. 23:15 *b*2 Chr. 34:4

7 He also broke down the houses of the *a*male cult prostitutes which *were* in the house of the LORD, where *b*the women were weaving hangings for the Asherah.

7 *a*1 Kin. 14:24; 15:12 *b*Ex. 35:25, 26; Ezek. 16:16

8 Then he brought all the priests from the cities of Judah, and defiled the high places where the priests had burned incense, from *a*Geba to Beersheba; and he broke down the high places of the gates which *were* at the entrance of the gate of Joshua the governor of the city, which *were* on one's left at the city gate.

8 *a*Josh. 21:17; 1 Kin. 15:22

9 Nevertheless *a*the priests of the high places did not go up to the altar of the LORD in Jerusalem,

★ 9 *a*Ezek. 44:10-14

22:20 *in peace.* I.e., in fellowship with God; not in peaceful circumstances, for Josiah was killed in battle (2 Chron. 35:23).
23:4 *Asherah.* See note on 21:7; also vv. 6, 7.

23:5 The Hebrew word for *priests* refers to priests of a heathen religion.
23:9 Apparently these false priests were given sustenance, though not allowed to sacrifice.

but they ate unleavened bread among their brothers.

10 ᵃHe also defiled Topheth, which is in the valley of the son of Hinnom, ᵇthat no man might make his son or his daughter pass through the fire for ᶜMolech.

11 And he did away with the horses which the kings of Judah had given to the ᵃsun, at the entrance of the house of the LORD, by the chamber of Nathan-melech the official, which *was* in the precincts; and he burned the chariots of the sun with fire.

12 And ᵃthe altars which *were* on the roof, the upper chamber of Ahaz, which the kings of Judah had made, and ᵇthe altars which Manasseh had made in the two courts of the house of the LORD, the king broke down; and he smashed them there, and ᶜthrew their dust into the brook Kidron.

13 And the high places which *were* before Jerusalem, which *were* on the right of ᵃthe mount of destruction which Solomon the king of Israel had built for ᵇAsh-toreth the abomination of the Sidonians, and for ᶜChemosh the abomination of Moab, and for Milcom the abomination of the sons of Ammon, the king defiled.

14 And ᵃhe broke in pieces the *sacred* pillars and cut down the Asherim and ᵇfilled their places with human bones.

15 Furthermore, ᵃthe altar that *was* at Bethel *and* the ᵇhigh place which Jeroboam the son of Nebat, who made Israel sin, had made, even that altar and the high place he broke down. Then he ᶜdemolished its stones, ground them to dust, and burned the A-sherah.

16 Now when Josiah turned, he saw the graves that *were* there on the mountain, and he sent and took the bones from the graves and burned *them* on the altar and defiled it ᵃaccording to the word of the LORD which the man of God proclaimed, who proclaimed these things.

17 Then he said, "What is this monument that I see?" And the men of the city told him, "ᵃIt is the grave of the man of God who came from Judah and proclaimed these things which you have done against the altar of Bethel."

18 And he said, "Let him alone; let no one disturb his bones." So they left his bones undisturbed ᵃwith the bones of the prophet who came from Samaria.

19 And Josiah also removed all the houses of the high places which *were* ᵃin the cities of Samaria, which the kings of Israel had made provoking the LORD; and he did to them just as he had done in Bethel.

20 And all the priests of the high places who *were* there ᵃhe slaughtered on the altars and burned human bones on them; then he returned to Jerusalem.

21 Then the king commanded all the people saying, "ᵃCelebrate the Passover to the LORD your God ᵇas it is written in this book of the covenant."

22 ᵃSurely such a Passover had not been celebrated from the days of the judges who judged Israel, nor in all the days of the kings of Israel and of the kings of Judah.

Cross references (margin):

★10 ᵃIs. 30:33; Jer. 7:31, 32; 19:4-6 ᵇLev. 18:21 ᶜ1 Kin. 11:7

★11 ᵃDeut. 4:19; Job 31:26; Ezek. 8:16

12 ᵃJer. 19:13; Zeph. 1:5 ᵇ2 Kin. 21:5; 2 Chr. 33:5 ᶜ2 Kin. 23:4, 6

★13 ᵃ1 Kin. 11:7 ᵇ1 Kin. 11:5 ᶜNum. 21:29

14 ᵃDeut. 7:5, 25 ᵇ2 Kin. 23:16

15 ᵃ1 Kin. 13:1 ᵇ1 Kin. 12:28-33 ᶜ2 Kin. 23:6

★16 ᵃ1 Kin. 13:2

17 ᵃ1 Kin. 13:1, 30, 31

★18 ᵃ1 Kin. 13:11, 31

19 ᵃ2 Chr. 34:6, 7

20 ᵃ2 Kin. 10:25; 11:18

21 ᵃ2 Chr. 35:1-17 ᵇNum. 9:2-4; Deut. 16:2-8

★22 ᵃ2 Chr. 35:18, 19

23:10 *Topheth.* A place in the valley of Hinnom (Gehenna), just S. of Jerusalem, where child sacrifices were made to Molech (see notes on 16:3 and Jer. 7:31).

23:11 Sun worship was stopped.

23:13 *the mount of destruction.* The Mount of Olives, where heathen temples then stood (see note on 1 Kings 11:5-7). The presence of the bones of the dead made these places unclean, thus assuring that they would not be used for Hebrew religious purposes.

23:16 Josiah ransacked the sepulchres of idolatrous priests and burned the bones on the heathen altars before demolishing them (1 Kings 13:2).

23:18 See 1 Kings 13:31-32.

23:22 *such a Passover.* None had been observed in strict conformity to the law since the days of the judges, though the Passover was observed by Hezekiah, 2 Chron. 30. Further details of this Passover are recorded in 2 Chron. 35.

23 But in the eighteenth year of King Josiah, this Passover was observed to the LORD in Jerusalem.

24 Moreover, Josiah removed [a]the mediums and the spiritists and the [b]teraphim and [c]the idols and all the abominations that were seen in the land of Judah and in Jerusalem, [d]that he might confirm the words of the law which were written [e]in the book that Hilkiah the priest found in the house of the LORD.

25 And before him there was no king [a]like him who turned to the LORD with all his heart and with all his soul and with all his might, according to all the law of Moses; nor did any like him arise after him.

26 However, the LORD did not turn from the fierceness of His great wrath with which His anger burned against Judah, [a]because of all the provocations with which Manasseh had provoked Him.

27 And the LORD said, "I will remove Judah also from My sight, [a]as I have removed Israel. And [b]I will cast off Jerusalem, this city which I have chosen, and the temple of which I said, 'My name shall be there.'"

28 Now the rest of the acts of Josiah and all that he did, are they not written in the Book of the Chronicles of the Kings of Judah?

29 [a]In his days [b]Pharaoh Neco king of Egypt went up to the king of Assyria to the river Euphrates. And King Josiah went to meet him, and when *Pharaoh Neco* saw him he killed him at [c]Megiddo.

30 And [a]his servants drove his body in a chariot from Megiddo, and brought him to Jerusalem and buried him in his own tomb. [b]Then the people of the land took Jehoahaz the son of Josiah and anointed him and made him king in place of his father.

E The Reign of Jehoahaz (609; 2 Chron. 36:1-4), 23:31-33

31 [a]Jehoahaz was twenty-three years old when he became king, and he reigned three months in Jerusalem; and his mother's name was [b]Hamutal the daughter of Jeremiah of Libnah.

32 And he did evil in the sight of the LORD, [a]according to all that his fathers had done.

33 And [a]Pharaoh Neco imprisoned him at [b]Riblah in the land of [c]Hamath, that he might not reign in Jerusalem; and he imposed on the land a fine of one hundred talents of silver and a talent of gold.

F The Reign of Jehoiakim (Eliakim; 609-597; 2 Chron. 36:5-8), 23:34-24:7

34 And Pharaoh Neco made [a]Eliakim the son of Josiah king in the place of Josiah his father, and [b]changed his name to Jehoiakim. But he took Jehoahaz away and [c]brought *him* to Egypt, and he died there.

35 So Jehoiakim [a]gave the silver and gold to Pharaoh, but he taxed the land in order to give the money at the command of Pharaoh. He exacted the silver and gold from the people of the land, each according to his valuation, to give it to Pharaoh Neco.

36 [a]Jehoiakim was twenty-five years old when he became

Margin references:

24 [a]Lev. 19:31; 2 Kin. 21:6 [b]Gen. 31:19 mg. [c]2 Kin. 21:11, 21 [d]Deut. 18:10-22 [e]2 Kin. 22:8

25 [a]2 Kin. 18:5

26 [a]2 Kin. 21:11-13; Jer. 15:4

27 [a]2 Kin. 18:11 [b]2 Kin. 21:13, 14

★29 [a]2 Chr. 35:20-24 [b]Jer. 46:2 [c]Judg. 5:19

30 [a]2 Kin. 9:28 [b]2 Chr. 36:1-4

★31 [a]1 Chr. 3:15; Jer. 22:11 [b]2 Kin. 24:18

32 [a]2 Kin. 21:2-7

★33 [a]2 Kin. 23:29 [b]2 Kin. 25:6 [c]1 Kin. 8:65

34 [a]1 Chr. 3:15 [b]2 Kin. 24:17; 2 Chr. 36:4 [c]Jer. 22:11, 12; Ezek. 19:3, 4

★35 [a]2 Kin. 23:33

36 [a]2 Chr. 36:5; Jer. 22:18, 19; 26:1

23:29 *Pharaoh Neco king of Egypt (609-594) went up to the king of Assyria* to help him against Nabopolassar, king of Babylon. Additional details are found in 2 Chron. 35:20-24.

23:31 *Jehoahaz* = Shallum (see note on Jer. 22:10).

23:33 *Riblah.* About 65 miles N. of Damascus. See also 25:6-7, 18-21. The tribute was about 120,000 ounces of silver and 1,200 ounces of gold.

23:35 *Jehoiakim* became a vassal to Egypt for four years, exacting the tribute from all the people (though he built a luxurious palace for himself, Jer. 22:13-14). See notes on Jer. 25:1 and Dan. 1:1.

king, and he reigned eleven years in Jerusalem; and his mother's name *was* Zebidah the daughter of Pedaiah of Rumah.

37 a 2 Kin. 23:32

37 And he did evil in the sight of the LORD, ^aaccording to all that his fathers had done.

★ 1 a 2 Chr. 36:6; Jer. 25:1; Dan. 1:1, 2

24 ^aIn his days Nebuchadnezzar king of Babylon came up, and Jehoiakim became his servant *for* three years; then he turned and rebelled against him.

2 a Jer. 35:11f.
b 2 Kin. 6:23
c 2 Kin. 13:20
d 2 Kin. 23:27

2 And the LORD sent against him ^abands of Chaldeans, ^bbands of Arameans, ^cbands of Moabites, and bands of Ammonites. So He sent them against Judah to destroy it, ^daccording to the word of the LORD, which He had spoken through His servants the prophets.

3 a 2 Kin. 18:25
b 2 Kin. 23:26

3 ^aSurely at the command of the LORD it came upon Judah, to remove *them* from His sight ^bbecause of the sins of Manasseh, according to all that he had done,

4 a 2 Kin. 21:16

4 and ^aalso for the innocent blood which he shed, for he filled Jerusalem with innocent blood; and the LORD would not forgive.

5 Now the rest of the acts of Jehoiakim and all that he did, are they not written in the Book of the Chronicles of the Kings of Judah?

6 a Jer. 22:18, 19

6 So ^aJehoiakim slept with his fathers, and Jehoiachin his son became king in his place.

7 a Jer. 37:5-7 b Jer. 46:2 c Gen. 15:18

7 And ^athe king of Egypt did not come out of his land again, ^bfor the king of Babylon had taken all that belonged to the king of Egypt from ^cthe brook of Egypt to the river Euphrates.

G The Reign of Jehoiachin (597; 2 Chron. 36:9–10), 24:8–16

8 a 1 Chr. 3:16 b 2 Chr. 36:9

8 ^aJehoiachin was ^beighteen years old when he became king,

and he reigned three months in Jerusalem; and his mother's name *was* Nehushta the daughter of Elnathan of Jerusalem.

9 a 2 Kin. 21:2-7

9 And he did evil in the sight of the LORD, ^aaccording to all that his father had done.

★10

10 At that time the servants of Nebuchadnezzar king of Babylon went up to Jerusalem, and the city came under siege.

11 And Nebuchadnezzar the king of Babylon came to the city, while his servants were besieging it.

12 a Jer. 22:24-30; 24:1; 29:1, 2
b 2 Chr. 36:10

12 And ^aJehoiachin the king of Judah went out to the king of Babylon, he and his mother and his servants and his captains and his officials. So ^bthe king of Babylon took him captive in the eighth year of his reign.

★13 a 2 Kin. 20:17; Is. 39:6 b 2 Kin. 25:13-15
c 1 Kin. 7:48-50

13 And ^ahe carried out from there all the treasures of the house of the LORD, and the treasures of the king's house, and ^bcut in pieces all the vessels of gold ^cwhich Solomon king of Israel had made in the temple of the LORD, just as the LORD had said.

14 a Jer. 24:1
b 2 Kin. 24:16; Jer. 52:28 c Jer. 24:1; 29:2
d 2 Kin. 25:12

14 Then ^ahe led away into exile all Jerusalem and all the captains and all the mighty men of valor, ^bten thousand captives, and ^call the craftsmen and the smiths. None remained ^dexcept the poorest people of the land.

15 a 2 Chr. 36:10; Jer. 22:24-28; Ezek. 17:12

15 So ^ahe led Jehoiachin away into exile to Babylon; also the king's mother and the king's wives and his officials and the leading men of the land, he led away into exile from Jerusalem to Babylon.

16 a 2 Kin. 24:14

16 And all the men of valor, ^aseven thousand, and the craftsmen and the smiths, one thousand, all strong and fit for war, and these the king of Babylon brought into exile to Babylon.

24:1 After the battle of Carchemish in 605 (which ended the rule of Egypt), Nebuchadnezzar entered Jerusalem, made Jehoiakim a vassal, and took Daniel and others to Babylon.

24:10 The second invasion of Jerusalem by Nebuchadnezzar, in 597. See Introduction to Jeremiah for the chronology.
24:13 See note on Dan. 1:2.

H   The Reign of Zedekiah (Mattaniah; 597–586; 2 Chron. 36:11–21), 24:17–25:21

1   Rebellion against Babylon and destruction of the Temple, 24:17–25:10

17 [a]Then the king of Babylon made his uncle Mattaniah, king in his place, and changed his name to Zedekiah.

18 [a]Zedekiah was twenty-one years old when he became king, and he reigned eleven years in Jerusalem; and his mother's name *was* [b]Hamutal the daughter of Jeremiah of Libnah.

19 And he did evil in the sight of the Lord, [a]according to all that Jehoiakim had done.

20 For [a]through the anger of the Lord *this* came about in Jerusalem and Judah until He cast them out from His presence. And [b]Zedekiah rebelled against the king of Babylon.

25 [a]Now it came about in the ninth year of his reign, on the tenth day of the tenth month, that [b]Nebuchadnezzar king of Babylon came, he and all his army, against Jerusalem, camped against it, and [c]built a siege wall all around it.

2 So the city was under siege until the eleventh year of King Zedekiah.

3 On the ninth day of the *fourth* month [a]the famine was so severe in the city that there was no food for the people of the land.

4 [a]Then the city was broken into, and all the men of war fled by night by way of the gate between the two walls beside [b]the king's garden, though the Chaldeans were all around the city. And they went by way of the Arabah.

5 But the army of the Chaldeans pursued the king and overtook him in the plains of Jericho

and all his army was scattered from him.

6 Then [a]they captured the king and [b]brought him to the king of Babylon at [c]Riblah, and he passed sentence on him.

7 And [a]they slaughtered the sons of Zedekiah before his eyes, then [b]put out the eyes of Zedekiah and bound him with bronze fetters and brought him to Babylon.

8 [a]Now on the seventh day of the [b]fifth month, which was the nineteenth year of King Nebuchadnezzar, king of Babylon, Nebuzaradan the captain of the guard, a servant of the king of Babylon, came to Jerusalem.

9 And [a]he burned the house of the Lord, [b]the king's house, and all the houses of Jerusalem; even every great house he burned with fire.

10 So all the army of the Chaldeans who *were with* the captain of the guard [a]broke down the walls around Jerusalem.

2   Third deportation to Babylon, 25:11–21

11 Then [a]the rest of the people who were left in the city and the deserters who had deserted to the king of Babylon and the rest of the multitude, Nebuzaradan the captain of the guard carried away into exile.

12 But the captain of the guard left some of [a]the poorest of the land to be vinedressers and plowmen.

13 [a]Now the bronze pillars which were in the house of the Lord, and the stands and [b]the bronze sea which were in the house of the Lord, the Chaldeans broke in pieces and carried the bronze to Babylon.

14 [a]And they took away the pots, the shovels, the snuffers, the

---

Cross-references (margin):

17 [a]2 Chr. 36:10-13; Jer. 37:1

18 [a]Jer. 27:1; 28:1; 52:1 [b]2 Kin. 23:31

19 [a]2 Kin. 23:37

20 [a]Deut. 4:24; 29:27; 2 Kin. 23:26 [b]2 Chr. 36:13; Ezek. 17:15

★ 1 [a]2 Chr. 36:17-20; Jer. 39:1-7 [b]Jer. 21:2; 34:1, 2; Ezek. 24:2 [c]Ezek. 21:22

3 [a]2 Kin. 6:24, 25; Lam. 4:9, 10

★ 4 [a]Ezek. 33:21 [b]Neh. 3:15

★ 6 [a]Jer. 34:21, 22 [b]Jer. 32:4 [c]2 Kin. 23:33

★ 7 [a]Jer. 39:6, 7 [b]Ezek. 12:13

8 [a]Jer. 52:12 [b]Jer. 39:8-12

9 [a]1 Kin. 9:8; 2 Chr. 36:19; Ps. 74:3-7 [b]Amos 2:5

10 [a]2 Kin. 14:13; Neh. 1:3

11 [a]2 Chr. 36:20

12 [a]2 Kin. 24:14; Jer. 40:7

13 [a]1 Kin. 7:15-22; 2 Kin. 20:17; 2 Chr. 3:15-17; 36:18 [b]1 Kin. 7:23-26; 2 Chr. 4:2-4

14 [a]Ex. 27:3; 1 Kin. 7:47-50; 2 Chr. 4:16

25:1 The final siege of Jerusalem began in January 588 and lasted a year and a half.

25:4 *of the Arabah.* The Jordan Valley. King Zedekiah was captured at Jericho (v. 5).

24:6 *Riblah.* See note on 23:33.

25:7 Jeremiah had warned Zedekiah that he would see Nebuchadnezzar (Jer. 32:4; 34:3), but Ezekiel predicted that he would not see Babylon (Ezek. 12:13). How accurately both these prophecies were fulfilled!

spoons, and all the bronze vessels which were used in *temple* service.

15 The captain of the guard also took away the firepans and the basins, what was fine gold and what was fine silver.

★16 *a*1 Kin. 7:47

16 The two pillars, the one sea, and the stands which Solomon had made for the house of the LORD—*a*the bronze of all these vessels was beyond weight.

17 *a*1 Kin. 7:15-22

17 *a*The height of the one pillar was eighteen cubits, and a bronze capital was on it; the height of the capital was three cubits, with a network and pomegranates on the capital all around, all of bronze. And the second pillar was like these with network.

★18-21

18 *a*1 Chr. 6:14; Ezra 7:1 *b*Jer. 21:1; 29:25, 29

18 Then the captain of the guard took *a*Seraiah the chief priest and *b*Zephaniah the second priest, with the three officers of the temple.

19 *a*Esth. 1:14

19 And from the city he took one official who was overseer of the men of war, and *a*five of the king's advisers who were found in the city; and the scribe of the captain of the army, who mustered the people of the land; and sixty men of the people of the land who were found in the city.

20 *a*2 Kin. 23:33

20 And Nebuzaradan the captain of the guard took them and brought them to the king of Babylon at *a*Riblah.

21 *a*Deut. 28:64; 2 Kin. 23:27

21 Then the king of Babylon struck them down and put them to death at Riblah in the land of Hamath. *a*So Judah was led away into exile from its land.

I   Gedaliah, the Puppet Governor (586), 25:22-26

★22 *a*Jer. 39:14; 40:7-9

22 Now *as for* the people who were left in the land of Judah,

whom Nebuchadnezzar king of Babylon had left, he appointed *a*Gedaliah the son of Ahikam, the son of Shaphan over them.

23 *a*When all the captains of the forces, they and *their* men, heard that the king of Babylon had appointed Gedaliah *governor,* they came to Gedaliah to *b*Mizpah, namely, Ishmael the son of Nethaniah, and Johanan the son of Kareah, and Seraiah the son of Tanhumeth the Netophathite, and Jaazaniah the son of the Maacathite, they and their men.

23 *a*Jer. 40:7-9 *b*Josh. 18:26

24 And Gedaliah swore to them and their men and said to them, "Do not be afraid of the servants of the Chaldeans; live in the land and serve the king of Babylon, and it will be well with you."

25 *a*But it came about in the seventh month, that Ishmael the son of Nethaniah, the son of Elishama, of the royal family, came with ten men and struck Gedaliah down so that he died along with the Jews and the Chaldeans who were with him at Mizpah.

25 *a*Jer. 41:1, 2

26 *a*Then all the people, both small and great, and the captains of the forces arose and went to Egypt; for they were afraid of the Chaldeans.

26 *a*Jer. 43:4-7

J   The Release of Jehoiachin in Babylon, 25:27-30

27 *a*Now it came about in the thirty-seventh year of *b*the exile of Jehoiachin king of Judah, in the twelfth month, on the twenty-seventh *day* of the month, that Evil-merodach king of Babylon, in the year that he became king, *c*released Jehoiachin king of Judah from prison;

★27-30

27 *a*Jer. 52:31-34 *b*2 Kin. 24:12, 15 *c*Gen. 40:13, 20

25:16 *which Solomon had made.* The account is in 1 Kings 7:15-50.
25:18-21 These men had probably been ringleaders in the revolt against Nebuchadnezzar or had been leaders in defending the city.
25:22 *Gedaliah.* A friend of Jeremiah (Jer. 39:14), he was a worthy governor, but was assassinated because he placed trust in unworthy

men (v. 23; cf. Jer. 40:14).
25:27-30 Babylonian tablets confirm that Jehoiachin, his sons, and others received rations from Nebuchadnezzar's stores. After the death of Nebuchadnezzar, Evil-merodach, attempting to gain favor with the captive Jews, released Jehoiachin from prison and treated him well.

598

28 aDan.
2:37; 5:18,
19

28 and he aspoke kindly to him and set his throne above the throne of the kings who *were* with him in Babylon.

29 a2 Sam.
9:7

29 And Jehoiachin changed his prison clothes, and ahad his

meals in the king's presence regularly all the days of his life;

30 and for his aallowance, a regular allowance was given him by the king, a portion for each day, all the days of his life.

30 aNeh.
11:23; 12:47

INTRODUCTION TO
THE FIRST BOOK OF THE CHRONICLES

AUTHOR: Ezra   DATE: 450–425 B.C.

Title *Originally one book with 2 Chronicles (until 180 B.C.), the book's Hebrew title means "the words (affairs) of the days," i.e., the annals of Israel from Adam to the Babylonian captivity and Cyrus' decree allowing the exiled Jews to return. In a sense it is a "miniature Old Testament," tracing in capsule form the flow of O.T. history.*

Authorship *Though not specified by name in the book, Ezra has traditionally been assumed to be the author. Unquestionably, he used sources in compiling the book, including prophetic records by Samuel (1 Chron. 29:29), Isaiah (2 Chron. 32:32), and others (2 Chron. 9:29; 12:15; 20:34; 33:19); but particularly a source called "the Book of the Kings of Judah and Israel" (2 Chron. 16:11; 25:26). However, this is not the canonical 1 and 2 Kings, but likely some earlier court record.*

Purpose *Ezra, who led a group of exiles back to Palestine in 458, was concerned about building a true spiritual foundation for the people. To further that purpose he evidently compiled the Chronicles in order to emphasize the importance of racial and religious purity, the proper place of the law, the Temple, and the priesthood. Thus he omits detailed activities of the kings and prophets, stressing instead the rich heritage of the people and the blessing of their covenant relationship to God.*

Contents *1 Chronicles is heavily weighted with genealogies, and focuses on the reign of King David. Important sections include the statement of the great covenant with David (17:11-14) and David's magnificent prayer of praise in 29:10-19.*

OUTLINE OF 1 CHRONICLES

THE FIRST BOOK OF THE CHRONICLES

I GENEALOGIES FROM ADAM TO DAVID, 1:1-9:44

A Adam to Abraham, 1:1-27

★ 1 ᵃGen. 4:25-5:32

1 ᵃAdam, Seth, Enosh,
2 Kenan, Mahalalel, Jared,

★ 3   3 Enoch, Methuselah, Lamech,
4 Noah, Shem, Ham and Japheth.

★ 5-23   5 ᵃThe sons of Japheth were

5 ᵃGen. 10:2-4
Gomer, Magog, Madai, Javan, Tubal, Meshech, and Tiras.
6 And the sons of Gomer were Ashkenaz, Diphath, and Togarmah.
7 And the sons of Javan were Elishah, Tarshish, Kittim, and Rodanim.
8 The sons of Ham were Cush, Mizraim, Put, and Canaan.
9 And the sons of Cush were Seba, Havilah, Sabta, Raama, and Sabteca; and the sons of Raamah were Sheba and Dedan.

★10   10 And Cush became the father of Nimrod; he began to be a mighty one in the earth.

11 ᵃGen. 10:13-18
11 ᵃAnd Mizraim became the father of the people of Lud, Anam, Lehab, Naphtuh,

★12   12 Pathrus, Casluh, from which the Philistines came, and Caphtor.
13 And Canaan became the father of Sidon, his first-born, Heth,
14 and the Jebusites, the Amorites, the Girgashites,

15 the Hivites, the Arkites, the Sinites,
16 the Arvadites, the Zemarites, and the Hamathites.

17 ᵃGen. 10:22-29
17 ᵃThe sons of Shem were Elam, Asshur, Arpachshad, Lud, Aram, Uz, Hul, Gether, and Meshech.
18 And Arpachshad became the father of Shelah and Shelah became the father of Eber.

★19   19 And two sons were born to Eber, the name of the one was Peleg, for in his days the earth was divided, and his brother's name was Joktan.
20 And Joktan became the father of Almodad, Sheleph, Hazarmaveth, Jerah,
21 Hadoram, Uzal, Diklah,
22 Ebal, Abimael, Sheba,
23 Ophir, Havilah, and Jobab; all these were the sons of Joktan.

24 ᵃGen. 11:10-26, Luke 3:34-36
24 ᵃShem, Arpachshad, Shelah,
25 Eber, Peleg, Reu,
26 Serug, Nahor, Terah,
27 Abram, that is Abraham.   ★27

B Abraham to Jacob, 1:28-54

28 The sons of Abraham were Isaac and Ishmael.

★29-33   29 ᵃThese are their genealogies: the first-born of Ishmael

29 ᵃGen. 25:13-16
was Nebaioth, then Kedar, Adbeel, Mibsam,
30 Mishma, Dumah, Massa, Hadad, Tema,

1:1 This most extensive (through 9:44) collection of genealogical tables in the O.T. serves to show the ancestry of the tribes of Israel, to focus on the importance of the Davidic line from which Messiah came, to emphasize the tribe of Levi from which the priests came, and to remind Israel of the importance of racial and religious purity.

1:3 *Enoch.* Who did not die (see note on Gen. 5:22-24). Notice that the ungodly line of Cain is omitted.

1:5-23 A reproduction of the records of Gen. 10, with minor differences of spelling. Regarding

verse 5 see notes on Ezek. 38:2 and 38:5-6.

1:10 *Nimrod* was *mighty* as an extraordinary hunter and city builder (Gen. 10:8-12).

1:12 *Philistines.* See note on Gen. 21:32.

1:19 *Peleg* means "division," and refers to the scattering of Gen. 11:9, which occurred during his times.

1:27 On the meaning of *Abram* and *Abraham* see note on Gen. 11:27.

1:29-33 The sons of *Ishmael* and *Keturah* began many of the tribes that later formed into the Arabs.

31 Jetur, Naphish and Kedemah; these *were* the sons of Ishmael.

32 ᵃAnd the sons of Keturah, Abraham's concubine, *whom* she bore, *were* Zimran, Jokshan, Medan, Midian, Ishbak, and Shuah. And the sons of Jokshan *were* Sheba and Dedan.

33 And the sons of Midian *were* Ephah, Epher, Hanoch, Abida, and Eldaah. All these were the sons of Keturah.

34 And ᵃAbraham became the father of Isaac. The sons of Isaac *were* ᵇEsau and Israel.

35 ᵃThe sons of Esau *were* Eliphaz, Reuel, Jeush, Jalam, and Korah.

36 The sons of Eliphaz *were* Teman, Omar, Zephi, Gatam, Kenaz, Timna, and Amalek.

37 The sons of Reuel *were* Nahath, Zerah, Shammah, and Mizzah.

38 ᵃAnd the sons of Seir *were* Lotan, Shobal, Zibeon, Anah, Dishon, Ezer, and Dishan.

39 And the sons of Lotan *were* Hori and Homam; and Lotan's sister *was* Timna.

40 The sons of Shobal *were* Alian, Manahath, Ebal, Shephi, and Onam. And the sons of Zibeon *were* Aiah and Anah.

41 The son of Anah *was* Dishon. And the sons of Dishon *were* Hamran, Eshban, Ithran, and Cheran.

42 The sons of Ezer *were* Bilhan, Zaavan and Jaakan. The sons of Dishan *were* Uz and Aran.

43 ᵃNow these are the kings who reigned in the land of Edom before any king of the sons of Israel reigned. Bela *was* the son of Beor, and the name of his city was Dinhabah.

44 When Bela died, Jobab the son of Zerah of ᵃBozrah became king in his place.

45 When Jobab died, Husham of the land of ᵃthe Temanites became king in his place.

46 When Husham died, Hadad the son of Bedad, who defeated Midian in the field of Moab, became king in his place; and the name of his city *was* Avith.

47 When Hadad died, Samlah of Masrekah became king in his place.

48 When Samlah died, Shaul of Rehoboth by the River became king in his place.

49 When Shaul died, Baalhanan the son of Achbor became king in his place.

50 When Baal-hanan died, Hadad became king in his place; and the name of his city was Pai, and his wife's name was Mehetabel, the daughter of Matred, the daughter of Mezahab.

51 Then Hadad died. Now the chiefs of Edom were: chief Timna, chief Aliah, chief Jetheth,

52 chief Oholibamah, chief Elah, chief Pinon,

53 chief Kenaz, chief Teman, chief Mibzar,

54 chief Magdiel, chief Iram. These *were* the chiefs of Edom.

C Jacob to David, 2:1-55

2 ᵃThese are the sons of Israel: Reuben, Simeon, Levi, Judah, Issachar, Zebulun,

2 Dan, Joseph, Benjamin, Naphtali, Gad, and Asher.

3 ᵃThe sons of Judah *were* Er, Onan, and Shelah; *these* three were born to him by Bath-shua the Canaanitess. And Er, Judah's first-born, was wicked in the sight of the LORD, so He put him to death.

Marginal references
32 ᵃGen. 25:1-4
★34 ᵃ1 Chr. 1:28 ᵇGen. 25:25, 26; 32:28
★35 ᵃGen. 36:4-10
38 ᵃGen. 36:20-28
43 ᵃGen. 36:31-43
44 ᵃIs. 34:6
45 ᵃJob 2:11
★51
1 ᵃGen. 35:22-26; 46:8-25
★ 3 ᵃGen. 38:2-10

1:34 Notice that Jacob is called *Israel* here (see note on Gen. 32:25-28).
1:35 Brief mention (through v. 54) is made of the descendants of Esau, though the writer's primary interest focuses on the descendants of Jacob (Israel). *Esau* is Edom (see note on Gen. 25:22).
1:51 *chiefs.* Tribal heads or leaders.
2:3 *Bath-shua.* Better, a daughter of Shua, as in Gen. 38:2.

4 ^aGen. 38:13-30

★ 7 ^aJosh. 7:1

★15

★18

4 And ^aTamar his daughter-in-law bore him Perez and Zerah. Judah had five sons in all.

5 The sons of Perez *were* Hezron and Hamul.

6 And the sons of Zerah *were* Zimri, Ethan, Heman, Calcol, and Dara; five of them in all.

7 And the son of Carmi *was* ^aAchar, the troubler of Israel, who violated the ban.

8 And the son of Ethan *was* Azariah.

9 Now the sons of Hezron, who were born to him *were* Jerahmeel, Ram, and Chelubai.

10 And Ram became the father of Amminadab, and Amminadab became the father of Nahshon, leader of the sons of Judah;

11 Nahshon became the father of Salma, Salma became the father of Boaz,

12 Boaz became the father of Obed, and Obed became the father of Jesse;

13 and Jesse became the father of Eliab his first-born, then Abinadab the second, Shimea the third,

14 Nethanel the fourth, Raddai the fifth,

15 Ozem the sixth, David the seventh;

16 and their sisters *were* Zeruiah and Abigail. And the three sons of Zeruiah *were* Abshai, Joab, and Asahel.

17 And Abigail bore Amasa, and the father of Amasa was Jether the Ishmaelite.

18 Now Caleb the son of Hezron had sons by Azubah *his* wife, and by Jerioth; and these were her sons: Jesher, Shobab, and Ardon.

19 When Azubah died, Caleb married Ephrath, who bore him Hur.

20 And Hur became the father of Uri, and Uri became the father of Bezalel.

21 Afterward Hezron went in to the daughter of Machir the father of Gilead, whom he married when he was sixty years old; and she bore him Segub.

22 And Segub became the father of Jair, who had twenty-three cities in the land of Gilead.

23 But Geshur and Aram took the towns of Jair from them, with Kenath and its villages, *even* sixty cities. All these were the sons of Machir, the father of Gilead.

24 And after the death of Hezron in Caleb-ephrathah, Abijah, Hezron's wife, bore him Ashhur the father of Tekoa.

25 Now the sons of Jerahmeel the first-born of Hezron *were* Ram the first-born, then Bunah, Oren, Ozem, *and* Ahijah.

26 And Jerahmeel had another wife, whose name was Atarah; she was the mother of Onam.

27 And the sons of Ram, the first-born of Jerahmeel, were Maaz, Jamin, and Eker.

28 And the sons of Onam were Shammai and Jada. And the sons of Shammai *were* Nadab and Abishur.

29 And the name of Abishur's wife *was* Abihail, and she bore him Ahban and Molid.

30 And the sons of Nadab *were* Seled and Appaim, and Seled died without sons.

31 And the son of Appaim *was* Ishi. And the son of Ishi *was* Sheshan. And the son of Sheshan *was* Ahlai.

32 And the sons of Jada the brother of Shammai *were* Jether and Jonathan, and Jether died without sons.

33 And the sons of Jonathan *were* Peleth and Zaza. These were the sons of Jerahmeel.

34 Now Sheshan had no sons, only daughters. And Sheshan had an Egyptian servant whose name was Jarha.

2:7 *Achar* = Achan. See note on Josh. 7:1.
2:15 *David the seventh.* According to 1 Sam. 16:10-11, Jesse had eight sons. One probably died in childhood and therefore is not mentioned in this genealogy.
2:18 *Caleb.* Not the same as the faithful spy who lived 100 years later and is mentioned in 4:15.

35 And Sheshan gave his daughter to Jarha his servant in marriage, and she bore him Attai. **36** And Attai became the father of Nathan, and Nathan became the father of Zabad, **37** and Zabad became the father of Ephlal, and Ephlal became the father of Obed, **38** and Obed became the father of Jehu, and Jehu became the father of Azariah, **39** and Azariah became the father of Helez, and Helez became the father of Eleasah, **40** and Eleasah became the father of Sismai, and Sismai became the father of Shallum, **41** and Shallum became the father of Jekamiah, and Jekamiah became the father of Elishama.

42 Now the sons of Caleb, the brother of Jerahmeel, *were* Mesha his first-born, who was the father of Ziph; and his son was Mareshah, the father of Hebron. **43** And the sons of Hebron *were* Korah and Tappuah and Rekem and Shema. **44** And Shema became the father of Raham, the father of Jorkeam; and Rekem became the father of Shammai. **45** And the son of Shammai was Maon, and Maon *was* the father of Bethzur.

46 And Ephah, Caleb's concubine, bore Haran, Moza, and Gazez; and Haran became the father of Gazez. **47** And the sons of Jahdai *were* Regem, Jotham, Geshan, Pelet, Ephah, and Shaaph. **48** Maacah, Caleb's concubine, bore Sheber and Tirhanah. **49** She also bore Shaaph the father of Madmannah, Sheva the father of Machbena and the father of Gibea; and the daughter of Caleb *was* Achsah.

50 These were the sons of Caleb.

The sons of Hur, the first-born of Ephrathah, *were* Shobal the father of Kiriath-jearim, **51** Salma the father of Bethlehem *and* Hareph the father of Beth-gader. **52** And Shobal the father of Kiriath-jearim had sons: Haroeh, half of the Manahathites, **53** and the families of Kiriath-jearim: the Ithrites, the Puthites, the Shumathites, and the Mishraites; from these came the Zorathites and the Eshtaolites. **54** The sons of Salma *were* Bethlehem and the Netophathites, Atroth-beth-joab and half of the Manahathites, the Zorites. **55** And the families of scribes who lived at Jabez *were* the Tirathites, the Shimeathites, *and* the Sucathites. Those are the Kenites who came from Hammath, the father of the house of Rechab. ★**55**

D David to the Captivity, 3:1-24

3 ᵃ Now these were the sons of David who were born to him in Hebron: the first-born *was* Amnon, by Ahinoam the Jezreelitess; the second *was* Daniel, by Abigail the Carmelitess; **2** the third *was* Absalom the son of Maacah, the daughter of Talmai king of Geshur; the fourth *was* Adonijah the son of Haggith; **3** the fifth *was* Shephatiah, by Abital; the sixth *was* Ithream, by his wife Eglah. **4** Six were born to him in Hebron, and ᵃthere he reigned seven years and six months. And in Jerusalem he reigned thirty-three years. **5** ᵃAnd these were born to him in Jerusalem: Shimea, Shobab, Nathan, and ᵇSolomon, four,

★ **1** a 2 Sam. 3:2-5

4 a 2 Sam. 2:11; 5:4, 5; 1 Kin. 2:11; 1 Chr. 29:27
5 a 2 Sam. 5:14-16; 1 Chr. 14:4-7
b 2 Sam. 12:24, 25
c 2 Sam. 11:3

2:55 *Kenites.* See notes on Num. 10:29–32 and Judg. 1:16.
3:1 This chapter traces the line of David to about 500 B.C. Though Jer. 22:30 predicted that no solely human descendant would sit on the throne of David, leaders like Zerubbabel came from the family of David, as did ultimately the God-man, Jesus Christ. *Daniel.* The Chileab of 2 Sam. 3:3.

by ^cBath-shua the daughter of Ammiel;

6 and Ibhar, Elishama, Eliphelet,

7 Nogah, Nepheg, and Japhia,

8 Elishama, Eliada, and Eliphelet, nine.

★ **9** ^a2 Sam. 13:1   **9** All *these were* the sons of David, besides the sons of the concubines; and ^aTamar *was* their sister.

10 Now Solomon's son *was* Rehoboam, Abijah *was* his son, Asa his son, Jehoshaphat his son,

11 Joram his son, Ahaziah his son, Joash his son,

12 Amaziah his son, Azariah his son, Jotham his son,

13 Ahaz his son, Hezekiah his son, Manasseh his son,

14 Amon his son, Josiah his son.

15 And the sons of Josiah *were* Johanan the first-born, and the second *was* Jehoiakim, the third Zedekiah, the fourth Shallum.

16 And the sons of Jehoiakim *were* Jeconiah his son, Zedekiah his son.

17 And the sons of Jeconiah, the prisoner, *were* Shealtiel his son,

18 and Malchiram, Pedaiah, Shenazzar, Jekamiah, Hoshama, and Nedabiah.

★19   **19** And the sons of Pedaiah *were* Zerubbabel and Shimei. And the sons of Zerubbabel *were* Meshullam and Hananiah, and Shelomith *was* their sister;

20 and Hashubah, Ohel, Berechiah, Hasadiah, and Jushabhesed, five.

21 And the sons of Hananiah *were* Pelatiah and Jeshaiah, the sons of Rephaiah, the sons of Arnan, the sons of Obadiah, the sons of Shecaniah.

22 And the son of Shecaniah *was* Shemaiah, and the sons of

Shemaiah *were* Hattush, Igal, Bariah, Neariah, and Shaphat, six.

23 And the sons of Neariah *were* Elioenai, Hizkiah, and Azrikam, three.

24 And the sons of Elioenai *were* Hodaviah, Eliashib, Pelaiah, Akkub, Johanan, Delaiah, and Anani, seven.

E   Genealogies of the Twelve Tribes, 4:1—8:40

1   *Judah,* 4:1-23

4 ^aThe sons of Judah *were* Perez, Hezron, Carmi, Hur, and Shobal.   ★ **1** ^a1 Chr. 2:3

2 And Reaiah the son of Shobal became the father of Jahath, and Jahath became the father of Ahumai and Lahad. These *were* the families of the Zorathites.

3 And these *were* the sons of Etam: Jezreel, Ishma, and Idbash; and the name of their sister *was* Hazzelelponi.

4 And Penuel *was* the father of Gedor, and Ezer the father of Hushah. These *were* the sons of Hur, the first-born of Ephrathah, the father of Bethlehem.

5 And Ashhur, the father of Tekoa, had two wives, Helah and Naarah.

6 And Naarah bore him Ahuzzam, Hepher, Temeni, and Haahashtari. These were the sons of Naarah.

7 And the sons of Helah *were* Zereth, Izhar and Ethnan.

8 And Koz became the father of Anub and Zobebah, and the families of Aharhel the son of Harum.

9 And Jabez was more honorable than his brothers, and his mother named him Jabez saying, "Because I bore *him* with pain."   ★9-10

3:9 For the story of *Tamar* see 2 Sam. 13.

3:19 On *Zerubbabel's* father, see note on Ezra 5:2.

4:1 *sons of Judah.* Only *Perez* was actually a son; the others were leaders of various clans, but

not brothers.

4:9-10 *Jabez.* Through the prayer of faith, he overcame the sorrow indicated by the meaning of his name.

10 Now Jabez called on the God of Israel, saying, "Oh that Thou wouldst bless me indeed, and enlarge my border, and that Thy hand might be with me, and that Thou wouldst keep *me* from harm, that *it* may not pain me!" And God granted him what he requested.

11 And Chelub the brother of Shuhah became the father of Mehir, who was the father of Eshton.

12 And Eshton became the father of Beth-rapha and Paseah, and Tehinnah the father of Irnahash. These are the men of Recah.

13 Now the sons of Kenaz *were* Othniel and Seraiah. And the son of Othniel *was* Hathath.

14 And Meonothai became the father of Ophrah, and Seraiah became the father of Joab the father of Ge-harashim, for they were craftsmen.

15 And the sons of Caleb the son of Jephunneh *were* Iru, Elah and Naam; and the son of Elah *was* Kenaz.

16 And the sons of Jehallelel *were* Ziph and Ziphah, Tiria and Asarel.

17 And the sons of Ezrah *were* Jether, Mered, Epher, and Jalon. (And these are the sons of Bithia the daughter of Pharaoh, whom Mered took) and she conceived and *bore* Miriam, Shammai, and Ishbah the father of Eshtemoa.

18 And his Jewish wife bore Jered the father of Gedor, and Heber the father of Soco, and Jekuthiel the father of Zanoah.

19 And the sons of the wife of Hodiah, the sister of Naham, *were* the fathers of Keilah the Garmite and Eshtemoa the Maacathite.

20 And the sons of Shimon *were* Amnon and Rinnah, Benhanan and Tilon. And the sons of Ishi *were* Zoheth and Ben-zoheth.

★21   **21** The sons of Shelah the son of Judah *were* Er the father of Lecah and Laadah the father of Mareshah, and the families of the house of the linen workers at Beth-ashbea;

22 and Jokim, the men of Cozeba, Joash, Saraph, who ruled in Moab, and Jashubi-lehem. And the records are ancient.

23 These were the potters and the inhabitants of Netaim and Gederah; they lived there with the king for his work.

2 *Simeon,* 4:24–43

24 The sons of Simeon *were* ★24 Nemuel and Jamin, Jarib, Zerah, Shaul;

25 Shallum his son, Mibsam his son, Mishma his son.

26 And the sons of Mishma *were* Hammuel his son, Zaccur his son, Shimei his son.

27 Now Shimei had sixteen sons and six daughters; but his brothers did not have many sons, nor did all their family multiply like the sons of Judah.

28 And they lived at Beersheba, Moladah, and Hazar-shual,

29 at Bilhah, Ezem, Tolad,

30 Bethuel, Hormah, Ziklag,

31 Beth-marcaboth, Hazar-susim, Beth-biri, and Shaaraim. These *were* their cities until the reign of David.

32 And their villages *were* Etam, Ain, Rimmon, Tochen, and Ashan, five cities;

33 and all their villages that *were* around the same cities as far as Baal. These *were* their settlements, and they have their genealogy.

34 And Meshobab and Jamlech and Joshah the son of Amaziah,

35 and Joel and Jehu the son of Joshibiah, the son of Seraiah, the son of Asiel,

36 and Elioenai, Jaakobah, Jeshohaiah, Asaiah, Adiel, Jesimiel, Benaiah,

37 Ziza the son of Shiphi, the son of Allon, the son of Jedaiah,

---

4:21 *Shelah.* The third son of Judah (2:3).
4:24 *Simeon.* See notes on Josh. 19:1–9 and

1 Kings 11:13.

the son of Shimri, the son of Shemaiah;

38 these mentioned by name *were* leaders in their families; and their fathers' houses increased greatly.

39 And they went to the entrance of Gedor, even to the east side of the valley, to seek pasture for their flocks.

40 ^aJudg. 18:7-10

40 And they found rich and good pasture, and ^athe land was broad and quiet and peaceful; for those who lived there formerly *were* Hamites.

★**41** ^a1 Chr. 4:33-38

41 And ^athese, recorded by name, came in the days of Hezekiah king of Judah, and attacked their tents, and the Meunites who were found there, and destroyed them utterly to this day, and lived in their place; because there was pasture for their flocks.

42 ^aGen. 36:8, 9

42 And from them, from the sons of Simeon, five hundred men went to ^aMount Seir, with Pelatiah, Neariah, Rephaiah, and Uzziel, the sons of Ishi, as their leaders.

43 ^a1 Sam. 15:7, 8; 30:17

43 And ^athey destroyed the remnant of the Amalekites who escaped, and have lived there to this day.

3 Reuben, 5:1-10

★ **1** ^aGen. 29:32; 1 Chr. 2:1 ^bGen. 35:22; 49:4 ^cGen. 48:15-22

5 Now the sons of Reuben the first-born of Israel (for ^ahe was the first-born, but because ^bhe defiled his father's bed, ^chis birthright was given to the sons of Joseph the son of Israel; so that he is not enrolled in the genealogy according to the birthright.

2 ^aGen. 49:8-10; Ps. 60:7; 108:8 ^bMic. 5:2; Matt. 2:6

2 ^aThough Judah prevailed over his brothers, and ^bfrom him *came* the leader, yet the birthright belonged to Joseph),

3 ^aGen. 46:9; Ex. 6:14; Num. 26:5-9

3 ^athe sons of Reuben the first-born of Israel *were* Hanoch and Pallu, Hezron and Carmi.

4 The sons of Joel *were* Shemaiah his son, Gog his son, ^aShimei his son,

4 ^a1 Chr. 5:8

5 Micah his son, Reaiah his son, Baal his son,

6 Beerah his son, whom Tilgath-pilneser king of Assyria carried away into exile; he was leader of the Reubenites.

★ **6**

7 And his kinsmen by their families, ^ain the genealogy of their generations, *were* Jeiel the chief, then Zechariah

7 ^a1 Chr. 5:17

8 and Bela the son of Azaz, the son of Shema, the son of Joel, who lived in ^aAroer, even to Nebo and Baal-meon.

8 ^aNum. 32:34; Josh. 12:2

9 And to the east he settled as far as the entrance of the wilderness from the river Euphrates, ^abecause their cattle had increased in the land of Gilead.

9 ^aJosh. 22:8, 9

10 And in the days of Saul ^athey made war with the Hagrites, who fell by their hand, so that they occupied their tents throughout all the land east of Gilead.

★**10** ^a1 Chr. 5:18-21

4 Gad, 5:11-22

11 Now the sons of Gad lived opposite them in the land of ^aBashan as far as ^bSalecah.

★**11** ^aJosh. 13:11 ^bDeut. 3:10

12 Joel *was* the chief, and Shapham the second, then Janai and Shaphat in Bashan.

13 And their kinsmen of their fathers' households *were* Michael, Meshullam, Sheba, Jorai, Jacan, Zia, and Eber, seven.

14 These *were* the sons of Abihail, the son of Huri, the son of Jaroah, the son of Gilead, the son of Michael, the son of Jeshishai, the son of Jahdo, the son of Buz;

15 Ahi the son of Abdiel, the son of Guni, *was* head of their fathers' households.

16 And they lived in Gilead, in Bashan and in its towns, and in

16 ^a1 Chr. 27:29; Song 2:1; Is. 35:2; 65:10

4:41 *the Meunites.* An Edomite tribe.
5:1 *Reuben.* See note on Gen. 49:3-4.
5:6 *Tilgath-pilneser.* Tiglath-pileser, king of Assyria, who attacked northern Israel in 733. See note on 2 Kings 15:27-31.

5:10 *Hagrites.* Not necessarily descendants of Hagar, Ishmael's mother, but simply a tribe or tribes living in the Aramean and N. Arabian desert.
5:11 *Gad.* See note on Num. 32:1.

all the pasture lands of ªSharon, as far as their borders.

17 All of these were enrolled in the genealogies in the days of ªJotham king of Judah and in the days of ᵇJeroboam king of Israel.

18 The sons of Reuben and the Gadites and the half-tribe of Manasseh, *consisting* of valiant men, men who bore shield and sword and shot with bow, and *were* skillful in battle, *were* 44,760, who ªwent to war.

19 And they made war against ªthe Hagrites, ᵇJetur, Naphish, and Nodab.

20 And they were helped against them, and the Hagrites and all who *were* with them were given into their hand; for ªthey cried out to God in the battle, and He was entreated for them, because ᵇthey trusted in Him.

21 And they took away their cattle: their 50,000 camels, 250,000 sheep, 2,000 donkeys, and 100,000 men.

22 For many fell slain, because ªthe war *was* of God. And ᵇthey settled in their place until the ᶜexile.

5 Manasseh, 5:23-26

23 Now the sons of the half-tribe of Manasseh lived in the land; from Bashan to Baalhermon and ªSenir and Mount Hermon they were numerous.

24 And these were the heads of their fathers' households, even Epher, Ishi, Eliel, Azriel, Jeremiah, Hodaviah, and Jahdiel, mighty men of valor, famous men, heads of their fathers' households.

25 But they ªacted treacherously against the God of their fathers, and ᵇplayed the harlot ᶜafter the gods of the peoples of the land, whom God had destroyed before them.

26 So the God of Israel stirred up the spirit of ªPul, king of Assyria, even the spirit of Tilgathpilneser king of Assyria, and he ᵇcarried them away into exile, namely the Reubenites, the Gadites, and the half-tribe of Manasseh, and brought them to Halah, Habor, Hara, and to the river of Gozan, to this day.

6 Levi, 6:1-81

6 ªThe sons of Levi *were* Gershon, Kohath and Merari.

2 And the sons of Kohath *were* Amram, Izhar, Hebron, and Uzziel.

3 And the children of Amram *were* Aaron, Moses, and Miriam. And the sons of Aaron *were* Nadab, Abihu, Eleazar, and Ithamar.

4 Eleazar became the father of Phinehas, *and* Phinehas became the father of Abishua,

5 and Abishua became the father of Bukki, and Bukki became the father of Uzzi,

6 and Uzzi became the father of Zerahiah, and Zerahiah became the father of Meraioth,

7 Meraioth became the father of Amariah, and Amariah became the father of Ahitub,

8 and ªAhitub became the father of Zadok, and Zadok ᵇbecame the father of Ahimaaz,

9 and Ahimaaz became the father of Azariah, and Azariah became the father of Johanan,

10 and Johanan became the father of Azariah (ªit was he who served as the priest in the house

---

★17 ª2 Kin. 15:5, 32 ᵇ2 Kin. 14:16, 28

18 ªNum. 1:3

19 ª1 Chr. 5:10 ᵇGen. 25:15; 1 Chr. 1:31

20 ª2 Chr. 14:11-13 ᵇPs. 9:10; 20:7, 8; 22:4, 5

★22 ªJosh. 23:10; 2 Chr. 32:8; Rom. 8:31 ᵇ1 Chr. 4:41 ᶜ2 Kin. 15:29; 17:6

23 ªDeut. 3:9

25 ªDeut. 32:15-18 ᵇEx. 34:15 ᶜ2 Kin. 17:7

★26 ª2 Kin. 15:19, 29; 2 Chr. 28:20 ᵇ2 Kin. 17:6

★ 1 ªGen. 46:11; Ex. 6:16-25

★ 8 ª2 Sam. 8:17 ᵇ2 Sam. 15:27

★10 ª2 Chr. 26:17 ᵇ1 Kin. 6:1; 2 Chr. 3:1

5:17 *Jotham* reigned 750-731 and *Jeroboam II*, 794-753.
5:22 *until the exile.* The Assyrian captivity that began in 722.
5:26 *Pul.* The name of Tiglath-pileser before his accession (see note on 2 Kings 15:19-20).
6:1 *Levi.* See note on Gen. 49:5-7. Ezra was of this tribe (Ezra 7:1-5). The high priestly line is listed, though incompletely, in verses 3-15,

49-53; the three clans of Levi in verses 16-30; the singers in verses 31-48; and the lands assigned to the Levites in verses 54-81. Chapters 23-26 contain additional information about the Levites.
6:8 *Zadok.* High priest under David and Solomon.
6:10 See the account in 2 Chron. 26:17ff.

*b*which Solomon built in Jerusalem),

11 *a*Ezra 7:3

11 and *a*Azariah became the father of Amariah, and Amariah became the father of Ahitub,

12 and Ahitub became the father of Zadok, and Zadok became the father of Shallum,

★13 **13** and Shallum became the father of Hilkiah, and Hilkiah became the father of Azariah,

14 *a*Neh. 11:11

14 and Azariah became the father of *a*Seraiah, and Seraiah became the father of Jehozadak;

★15 **15** and Jehozadak went *along* when the LORD carried Judah and Jerusalem away into exile by Nebuchadnezzar.

16 *a*Gen. 46:11; Ex. 6:16

16 *a*The sons of Levi *were* Gershom, Kohath, and Merari.

17 And these are the names of the sons of Gershom: Libni and Shimei.

18 And the sons of Kohath *were* Amram, Izhar, Hebron, and Uzziel.

19 *a*Num. 3:33; 1 Chr. 23:21

19 The sons of *a*Merari *were* Mahli and Mushi. And these are the families of the Levites according to their fathers' *households.*

20 Of Gershom: Libni his son, Jahath his son, Zimmah his son,

21 Joah his son, Iddo his son, Zerah his son, Jeatherai his son.

22 The sons of Kohath *were* Amminadab his son, Korah his son, Assir his son,

23 Elkanah his son, Ebiasaph his son, and Assir his son,

24 Tahath his son, Uriel his son, Uzziah his son, and Shaul his son.

25 And the sons of Elkanah *were* Amasai and Ahimoth.

26 *As for* Elkanah, the sons of Elkanah *were* Zophai his son and Nahath his son,

27 Eliab his son, Jeroham his son, Elkanah his son.

28 And the sons of Samuel *were* *a*Joel, the first-born and Abijah, the second.

29 The sons of Merari *were* Mahli, Libni his son, Shimei his son, Uzzah his son,

30 Shimea his son, Haggiah his son, Asaiah his son.

31 *a*Now these are those whom David appointed over the service of song in the house of the LORD, *b*after the ark rested *there.*

32 And they ministered with song before the tabernacle of the tent of meeting, until Solomon had built the house of the LORD in Jerusalem; and they served in their office according to their order.

33 And these are those who served with their sons. From the sons of the Kohathites *were* Heman the singer, the son of Joel, the son of Samuel,

34 the son of Elkanah, the son of Jeroham, the son of Eliel, the son of Toah,

35 the son of Zuph, the son of Elkanah, the son of Mahath, the son of Amasai,

36 the son of Elkanah, the son of Joel, the son of Azariah, the son of Zephaniah,

37 the son of Tahath, the son of Assir, the son of Ebiasaph, the son of Korah,

38 the son of Izhar, the son of Kohath, the son of Levi, the son of Israel.

39 And *Heman's* brother Asaph stood at his right hand, even Asaph the son of Berechiah, the son of Shimea,

40 the son of Michael, the son of Baaseiah, the son of Malchijah,

41 the son of Ethni, the son of Zerah, the son of Adaiah,

42 the son of Ethan, the son of Zimmah, the son of Shimei,

28 *a*1 Sam. 8:2; 1 Chr. 6:33

31 *a*1 Chr. 15:16-22, 27; 16:4-6 *b*2 Sam. 6:17; 1 Kin. 8:4; 1 Chr. 15:25-16:1

★33

6:13 *Hilkiah.* The high priest who discovered the book of the law which resulted in Josiah's reformation (see note on 2 Kings 22:8).

6:15 *Jehozadak* = Jozadak (Ezra 3:2; Neh. 12:26). Joshua, the high priest who returned from exile with Zerubbabel, was his son.

6:33 *Kohathites.* Some were responsible for moving the vessels of the tabernacle (Num. 4:1-20), some were designated by David to bring the Ark to Jerusalem (15:4-5), and some (as here) were assigned to a ministry of praise.

43 the son of Jahath, the son of Gershom, the son of Levi.

44 And on the left hand *were* their kinsmen the sons of Merari: Ethan the son of Kishi, the son of Abdi, the son of Malluch,

45 the son of Hashabiah, the son of Amaziah, the son of Hilkiah,

46 the son of Amzi, the son of Bani, the son of Shemer,

47 the son of Mahli, the son of Mushi, the son of Merari, the son of Levi.

48 And their kinsmen the Levites were appointed for all the service of the tabernacle of the house of God.

49 aEx. 27:1-8 bEx. 30:1-7 cEx. 30:10-16 **49** But Aaron and his sons aoffered on the altar of burnt offering and bon the altar of incense, for all the work of the most holy place, and cto make atonement for Israel, according to all that Moses the servant of God had commanded.

50 a1 Chr. 6:4-8; Ezra 7:5 **50** aAnd these are the sons of Aaron: Eleazar his son, Phinehas his son, Abishua his son,

51 Bukki his son, Uzzi his son, Zerahiah his son,

52 Meraioth his son, Amariah his son, Ahitub his son,

53 Zadok his son, Ahimaaz his son.

54 aJosh. 21:4, 10 **54** Now these are their settlements according to their camps within their borders. To the sons of Aaron of the families of the Kohathites (for theirs was the afirst lot),

55 aJosh. 14:13; 21:11f. **55** to them they gave aHebron in the land of Judah, and its pasture lands around it;

★**56** aJosh. 15:13 **56** abut the fields of the city and its villages, they gave to Caleb the son of Jephunneh.

★**57** aJosh. 21:13, 19 **57** And ato the sons of Aaron they gave the *following* cities of refuge: Hebron, Libnah also with its pasture lands, Jattir, Eshtemoa with its pasture lands,

58 Hilen with its pasture lands, Debir with its pasture lands,

59 Ashan with its pasture lands, and Beth-shemesh with its pasture lands;

60 and from the tribe of Benjamin: Geba with its pasture lands, Allemeth with its pasture lands, and Anathoth with its pasture lands. All their cities throughout their families were thirteen cities.

61 aJosh. 21:5; 1 Chr. 6:66-70 **61** aThen to the rest of the sons of Kohath *were given* by lot, from the family of the tribe, from the half-tribe, the half of Manasseh, ten cities.

62 And to the sons of Gershom, according to their families, *were given* from the tribe of Issachar and from the tribe of Asher, the tribe of Naphtali, and the tribe of Manasseh, thirteen cities in Bashan.

63 aJosh. 21:7, 34-40 **63** aTo the sons of Merari *were given* by lot, according to their families, from the tribe of Reuben, the tribe of Gad, and the tribe of Zebulun, twelve cities.

64 aNum. 35:1-8; Josh. 21:3, 41, 42 **64** aSo the sons of Israel gave to the Levites the cities with their pasture lands.

65 a1 Chr. 6:57-60 **65** And they gave by lot from the tribe of the sons of Judah, the tribe of the sons of Simeon, and the tribe of the sons of Benjamin, athese cities which are mentioned by name.

66 aJosh. 21:20-26 **66** aNow some of the families of the sons of Kohath had cities of their territory from the tribe of Ephraim.

67 And they gave to them the *following* cities of refuge: Shechem in the hill country of Ephraim with its pasture lands, Gezer also with its pasture lands,

68 Jokmeam with its pasture lands, Beth-horon with its pasture lands,

69 Aijalon with its pasture lands, and Gath-rimmon with its pasture lands;

70 and from the half-tribe of Manasseh: Aner with its pasture lands and Bileam with its pasture

---

6:56 See note on Josh. 14:6-15.
6:57 *cities of refuge.* See notes on Num. 35:11-12; Josh. 20:1-9.

lands, for the rest of the family of the sons of Kohath.

71 To the sons of Gershom were given, from the family of the half-tribe of Manasseh: Golan in Bashan with its pasture lands and Ashtaroth with its pasture lands;

72 and from the tribe of Issachar: Kedesh with its pasture lands, Daberath with its pasture lands,

73 and Ramoth with its pasture lands, Anem with its pasture lands;

74 and from the tribe of Asher: Mashal with its pasture lands, Abdon with its pasture lands,

75 Hukok with its pasture lands, and Rehob with its pasture lands;

76 and from the tribe of Naphtali: Kedesh in Galilee with its pasture lands, Hammon with its pasture lands, and Kiriathaim with its pasture lands.

77 To the rest of the Levites, the sons of Merari, were given, from the tribe of Zebulun: Rimmono with its pasture lands, Tabor with its pasture lands;

78 and beyond the Jordan at Jericho, on the east side of the Jordan, were given them, from the tribe of Reuben: Bezer in the wilderness with its pasture lands, Jahzah with its pasture lands,

79 Kedemoth with its pasture lands, and Mephaath with its pasture lands;

80 and from the tribe of Gad: Ramoth in Gilead with its pasture lands, Mahanaim with its pasture lands,

81 Heshbon with its pasture lands, and Jazer with its pasture lands.

7 Issachar, 7:1-5

★ 1-5 **7** Now the sons of Issachar were four: Tola, Puah, Jashub, and Shimron.

2 And the sons of Tola were Uzzi, Rephaiah, Jeriel, Jahmai, Ibsam, and Samuel, heads of their fathers' households. The sons of Tola were mighty men of valor in their generations; [a]their number in the days of David was 22,600.

3 And the son of Uzzi was Izrahiah. And the sons of Izrahiah were Michael, Obadiah, Joel, Isshiah; all five of them were [a]chief men.

4 And with them by their generations according to their fathers' households were 36,000 troops of the army for war, for they had many wives and sons.

5 And their relatives among all the families of Issachar were mighty men of valor, enrolled by genealogy, in all 87,000.

8 Benjamin, 7:6-12

6 [a]The sons of Benjamin were three: Bela and Becher and Jediael.

7 And the sons of Bela were five: Ezbon, Uzzi, Uzziel, Jerimoth, and Iri. They were heads of fathers' households, mighty men of valor, and were 22,034 enrolled by genealogy.

8 And the sons of Becher were Zemirah, Joash, Eliezer, Elioenai, Omri, Jeremoth, Abijah, Anathoth, and Alemeth. All these were the sons of Becher.

9 And they were enrolled by genealogy, according to their generations, heads of their fathers' households, 20,200 mighty men of valor.

10 And the son of Jediael was Bilhan. And the sons of Bilhan were Jeush, Benjamin, Ehud, Chenaanah, Zethan, Tarshish, and Ahishahar.

11 All these were sons of Jediael, according to the heads of their fathers' households, 17,200 mighty men of valor, who were ready to go out with the army to war.

Marginal references:
2 [a]2 Sam. 24:1-9
3 [a]1 Chr. 5:24
★6-12
6 [a]1 Chr. 8:1-40

7:1-5 sons of Issachar. See Gen. 46:13; Num. 26:23-25.
7:6-12 sons of Benjamin. See Gen. 46:21; Num. 26:38-41 and supplementary information in 8:1ff.

12 And Shuppim and Huppim *were* the sons of Ir; Hushim *was* the son of Aher.

9 Naphtali, 7:13

*13 13 The sons of Naphtali *were* Jahziel, Guni, Jezer, and Shallum, the sons of Bilhah.

10 Manasseh, 7:14-19

*14-19 14 The sons of Manasseh *were* Asriel, whom his Aramean concubine bore; she bore Machir the father of Gilead.

15 And Machir took a wife for Huppim and Shuppim, whose sister's name was Maacah. And the name of the second was Zelophehad, and Zelophehad had daughters.

16 And Maacah the wife of Machir bore a son, and she named him Peresh; and the name of his brother *was* Sheresh, and his sons *were* Ulam and Rakem.

17 And the son of Ulam *was* Bedan. These *were* the sons of Gilead the son of Machir, the son of Manasseh.

18 And his sister Hammolecheth bore Ishhod and Abiezer and Mahlah.

19 And the sons of Shemida were Ahian and Shechem and Likhi and Aniam.

11 Ephraim, 7:20-29

*20-29 20 And ᵃthe sons of Ephraim *were* Shuthelah and Bered his son, Tahath his son, Eleadah his son, Tahath his son,
20 ᵃNum. 26:35, 36

21 Zabad his son, Shuthelah his son, and Ezer and Elead whom the men of Gath who were born in the land killed, because they came down to take their livestock.

22 And their father Ephraim ᵃmourned many days, and his relatives ᵇcame to comfort him.
22 ᵃGen. 37:34 ᵇJob 2:11; John 11:19

23 Then he went in to his wife, and she conceived and bore a son, and he named him Beriah, because misfortune had come upon his house.

24 And his daughter was Sheerah, ᵃwho built lower and upper Beth-horon, also Uzzen-sheerah.
24 ᵃJosh. 16:3, 5; 2 Chr. 8:5

25 And Rephah was his son along with Resheph, Telah his son, Tahan his son,

26 Ladan his son, Ammihud his son, Elishama his son,

27 Non his son, and ᵃJoshua his son.
27 ᵃEx. 17:9-14; 24:13

28 And ᵃtheir possessions and settlements *were* Bethel with its towns, and to the east Naaran, and to the west Gezer with its towns, and Shechem with its towns as far as Ayyah with its towns,
28 ᵃJosh. 16:2

29 and along the borders of the sons of Manasseh, Beth-shean with its towns, Taanach with its towns, Megiddo with its towns, Dor with its towns. In these lived the ᵃsons of Joseph the son of Israel.
29 ᵃJudg. 1:22-29

12 Asher, 7:30-40

30 ᵃThe sons of Asher *were* Imnah, Ishvah, Ishvi and Beriah, and Serah their sister.
*30-40
30 ᵃGen. 46:17; Num. 26:44-46

31 And the sons of Beriah *were* Heber and Malchiel, who was the father of Birzaith.

32 And Heber became the father of Japhlet, Shomer and Hotham, and Shua their sister.

33 And the sons of Japhlet *were* Pasach, Bimhal, and Ashvath. These were the sons of Japhlet.

34 And the sons of Shemer *were* Ahi and Rohgah, Jehubbah and Aram.

35 And the sons of his brother Helem *were* Zophah, Imna, Shelesh, and Amal.

36 The sons of Zophah *were* Suah, Harnepher, Shual, Beri, and Imrah,

37 Bezer, Hod, Shamma, Shilshah, Ithran, and Beera.

7:13 *sons of Naphtali.* See Gen. 46:24; Num. 26:48-50.
7:14-19 *sons of Manasseh.* See Num. 26:29-34.

7:20-29 *sons of Ephraim.* See Num. 26:35-37.
7:30-40 *sons of Asher.* See Gen. 46:17; Num. 26:44-47.

38 And the sons of Jether *were* Jephunneh, Pispa, and Ara.

39 And the sons of Ulla *were* Arah, Hanniel, and Rizia.

40 All these *were* the sons of Asher, heads of the fathers' houses, choice and mighty men of valor, heads of the princes. And the number of them enrolled by genealogy for service in war was 26,000 men.

13 Benjamin, 8:1-40

8 And ᵃBenjamin became the father of Bela his first-born, Ashbel the second, ᵇAharah the third,

2 Nohah the fourth, and Rapha the fifth.

3 And Bela had sons: Addar, Gera, Abihud,

4 Abishua, Naaman, Ahoah,

5 Gera, Shephuphan, and Huram.

6 And these are the sons of Ehud: these are the heads of fathers' *households* of the inhabitants of Geba, and they carried them into exile to Manahath,

7 namely, Naaman, Ahijah, and Gera—he carried them into exile; and he became the father of Uzza and Ahihud.

8 And Shaharaim became the father of children in the country of Moab, after he had sent away Hushim and Baara his wives.

9 And by Hodesh his wife he became the father of Jobab, Zibia, Mesha, Malcam,

10 Jeuz, Sachia, Mirmah. These were his sons, heads of fathers' *households*.

11 And by Hushim he became the father of Abitub and Elpaal.

12 And the sons of Elpaal *were* Eber, Misham, and Shemed, who built Ono and Lod, with its towns;

13 and Beriah and Shema,

[margin note: ★ 1 ᵃGen. 46:21; 1 Chr. 7:6-12 ᵇ1 Chr. 7:12]

who were heads of fathers' *households* of the inhabitants of Aijalon, who put to flight the inhabitants of Gath;

14 and Ahio, Shashak, and Jeremoth.

15 And Zebadiah, Arad, Eder,

16 Michael, Ishpah, and Joha *were* the sons of Beriah.

17 And Zebadiah, Meshullam, Hizki, Heber,

18 Ishmerai, Izliah, and Jobab *were* the sons of Elpaal.

19 And Jakim, Zichri, Zabdi,

20 Elienai, Zillethai, Eliel,

21 Adaiah, Beraiah, and Shimrath *were* the sons of Shimei.

22 And Ishpan, Eber, Eliel,

23 Abdon, Zichri, Hanan,

24 Hananiah, Elam, Anthothijah,

25 Iphdeiah, and Penuel *were* the sons of Shashak.

26 And Shamsherai, Shehariah, Athaliah,

27 Jaareshiah, Elijah, and Zichri *were* the sons of Jeroham.

28 These were heads of the fathers' *households* according to their generations, chief men, who lived in Jerusalem.

29 ᵃNow in Gibeon, *Jeiel,* the father of Gibeon lived, and his wife's name was Maacah;

30 and his first-born son *was* Abdon, then Zur, Kish, Baal, Nadab,

31 Gedor, Ahio, and Zecher.

32 And Mikloth became the father of Shimeah. And they also lived with their relatives in Jerusalem opposite their *other* relatives.

33 ᵃAnd Ner became the father of Kish, and Kish became the father of Saul, and Saul became the father of Jonathan, Malchishua, Abinadab, and Eshbaal.

34 And the son of Jonathan *was* Merib-baal, and Merib-baal became the father of Micah.

[margin note: ★29-40   29 ᵃ1 Chr. 9:35-38]

[margin note: 33 ᵃ1 Chr. 9:39-44]

[margin note: ★34]

8:1 This chapter supplements the information given in 7:6-12 about the important tribe of Benjamin, which gave Israel her first king (Saul) and which showed loyalty to the Da-vidic dynasty.

8:29-40 The house of Saul (virtually the same as 9:35-44).

8:34 *Merib-baal* = Mephibosheth (2 Sam. 4:4).

35 And the sons of Micah *were* Pithon, Melech, Tarea, and Ahaz.

36 And Ahaz became the father of Jehoaddah, and Jehoaddah became the father of Alemeth, Azmaveth, and Zimri; and Zimri became the father of Moza.

37 And Moza became the father of Binea; Raphah *was* his son, Eleasah his son, Azel his son.

38 And Azel had six sons, and these *were* their names: Azrikam, Bocheru, Ishmael, Sheariah, Obadiah and Hanan. All these *were* the sons of Azel.

39 And the sons of Eshek his brother *were* Ulam his first-born, Jeush the second, and Eliphelet the third.

40 And the sons of Ulam were mighty men of valor, archers, and had many sons and grandsons, 150 *of them*. All these *were* of the sons of Benjamin.

F Jerusalem's Inhabitants, 9:1-34

9 So all Israel was enrolled by genealogies; and behold, they are written in the Book of the Kings of Israel. And ªJudah was carried away into exile to Babylon for their unfaithfulness.

2 ªNow the first who lived in their possessions in their cities *were* Israel, the priests, the Levites and ᵇthe temple servants.

3 And some of the sons of Judah, of the sons of Benjamin, and of the sons of Ephraim and Manasseh lived in ªJerusalem:

4 Uthai the son of Ammihud, the son of Omri, the son of Imri, the son of Bani, from the sons of Perez the ªson of Judah.

5 And from the Shilonites *were* Asaiah the first-born and his sons.

6 And from the sons of Zerah *were* Jeuel and their relatives, 690 *of them*.

7 And from the sons of Benjamin *were* Sallu the son of Meshullam, the son of Hodaviah, the son of Hassenuah,

8 and Ibneiah the son of Jeroham, and Elah the son of Uzzi, the son of Michri, and Meshullam the son of Shephatiah, the son of Reuel, the son of Ibnijah;

9 and their relatives according to their generations, ª956. All these *were* heads of fathers' *households* according to their fathers' houses.

10 ªAnd from the priests *were* Jedaiah, Jehoiarib, Jachin,

11 and Azariah the son of Hilkiah, the son of Meshullam, the son of Zadok, the son of Meraioth, the son of Ahitub, ªthe chief officer of the house of God;

12 and Adaiah the son of Jeroham, the son of Pashhur, the son of Malchijah, and Maasai the son of Adiel, the son of Jahzerah, the son of Meshullam, the son of Meshillemith, the son of Immer;

13 and their relatives, heads of their fathers' households, 1,760 very able men for the work of the service of the house of God.

14 ªAnd of the Levites *were* Shemaiah the son of Hasshub, the son of Azrikam, the son of Hashabiah, of the sons of Merari;

15 and Bakbakkar, Heresh and Galal and Mattaniah the son of Mica, the son of Zichri, the son of Asaph,

16 and Obadiah the son of Shemaiah, the son of Galal, the son of Jeduthun, and Berechiah the son of Asa, the son of Elkanah, who lived in the villages of the Netophathites.

17 Now the gatekeepers *were* Shallum and Akkub and Talmon

★ 1 ª1 Chr. 5:25, 26

★ 2 ªEzra 2:70; Neh. 7:73; 11:3-22 ᵇEzra 2:43, 58; 8:20

3 ªNeh. 11:1

4 ªGen. 46:12; Num. 26:20

9 ªNeh. 11:8

10 ªNeh. 11:10-14

11 ªJer. 20:1

14 ªNeh. 11:15-19

When the boy was named, Baal may have had no reference to the idol Baal, but rather to God (since the basic meaning is "master"). However, *bosheth* (Heb., meaning "shame") was substituted as a euphemism for the word Baal.

9:1 *in the Book of the Kings of Israel.* Not our 1 and 2 Kings, but court records and registers now lost.

9:2 *the first who lived.* This list records those who first returned to Palestine after the Babylonian captivity (cf. Neh. 11:3). On the *temple servants* see note on Ezra 2:43.

and Ahiman and their relatives (Shallum the chief

★18 *a*Ezek. 44:1; 46:1, 2

18 *being stationed* until now at *a*the king's gate to the east). These *were* the gatekeepers for the camp of the sons of Levi.

19 And Shallum the son of Kore, the son of Ebiasaph, the son of Korah, and his relatives, of his father's house, the Korahites, *were* over the work of the service, keepers of the thresholds of the tent; and their fathers had been over the camp of the LORD, keepers of the entrance.

20 *a*Num. 25:7-13

20 And *a*Phinehas the son of Eleazar was ruler over them previously, *and* the LORD was with him.

21 *a*1 Chr. 26:2, 14

21 *a*Zechariah the son of Meshelemiah was gatekeeper of the entrance of the tent of meeting.

★22 *a*1 Chr. 26:1 *b*2 Chr. 31:15, 18

22 All these who were chosen to be gatekeepers in the thresholds were 212. These were enrolled by genealogy in their villages, *a*whom David and Samuel the seer appointed *b*in their office of trust.

23 So they and their sons had charge of the gates of the house of the LORD, *even* the house of the tent, as guards.

24 The gatekeepers were on the four sides, to the east, west, north, and south.

25 *a*2 Kin. 11:5, 7; 2 Chr. 23:8

25 And their relatives in their villages *a were* to come in every seven days from time to time *to be* with them;

26 for the four chief gatekeepers who *were* Levites, were in an office of trust, and were over the chambers and over the treasuries in the house of God.

27 *a*1 Chr. 23:30-32

27 And they spent the night around the house of God, *a*because the watch was committed to them; and they *were* in charge of opening *it* morning by morning.

28 Now some of them had charge of the utensils of service,

for they counted them when they brought them in and when they took them out.

29 Some of them also were appointed over the furniture and over all the utensils of the sanctuary and *a*over the fine flour and the wine and the oil and the frankincense and the spices.

29 *a*1 Chr. 23:29

30 And some of *a*the sons of the priests prepared the mixing of the spices.

30 *a*Ex. 30:23-25

31 And Mattithiah, one of the Levites, who was the first-born of Shallum the Korahite, had *a*the responsibility over the things which were baked in pans.

31 *a*1 Chr. 9:22

32 And some of their relatives of the sons of the Kohathites *a were* over the showbread to prepare it every sabbath.

32 *a*Lev. 24:5-8

33 Now these are *a*the singers, heads of fathers' *households* of the Levites, *who lived* in the chambers *of the temple* free *from other service;* for they were engaged *b*in their work day and night.

★33 *a*1 Chr. 6:31-47; 25:1 *b*Ps. 134:1

34 These were heads of fathers' *households* of the Levites according to their generations, chief men, who lived in Jerusalem.

G The Family of Saul, 9:35–44

35 *a*And in Gibeon Jeiel the father of Gibeon lived, and his wife's name was Maacah,

35 *a*1 Chr. 8:29-32

36 and his first-born son *was* Abdon, then Zur, Kish, Baal, Ner, Nadab,

37 Gedor, Ahio, Zechariah, and Mikloth.

38 And Mikloth became the father of Shimeam. And they also lived with their relatives in Jerusalem opposite their *other* relatives.

39 *a*And Ner became the father of Kish, and Kish became the

39 *a*1 Chr. 8:33-38

9:18 *gatekeepers for the camp of the sons of Levi.* Guards around the doors of the tabernacle and the Temple.

9:22 *Samuel* arranged a rotation system for the gatekeepers. As a child he had performed this

duty himself (1 Sam. 3:15).

9:33 *the singers.* Listed in verses 14-15 (cf. Neh. 11:17), they figure prominently in chapters 15-16.

father of Saul, and Saul became the father of Jonathan, Malchi-shua, Abinadab, and Eshbaal.

40 And the son of Jonathan *was* Merib-baal; and Merib-baal became the father of Micah.

41 And the sons of Micah *were* Pithon, Melech, Tahrea, *and Ahaz.*

42 And Ahaz became the father of Jarah, and Jarah became the father of Alemeth, Azmaveth, and Zimri; and Zimri became the father of Moza,

43 and Moza became the father of Binea and Rephaiah his son, Eleasah his son, Azel his son.

44 And Azel had six sons whose names are these: Azrikam, Bocheru and Ishmael and Sheari-ah and Obadiah and Hanan. These were the sons of Azel.

II DAVID'S ANOINTING, 10:1-12:40

A The Death of Saul, 10:1-14

10 ªNow the Philistines fought against Israel; and the men of Israel fled before the Philistines, and fell slain on Mount Gilboa.

2 And the Philistines closely pursued Saul and his sons, and the Philistines struck down Jonathan, ªAbinadab and Malchi-shua, the sons of Saul.

3 And the battle became heavy against Saul, and the archers overtook him; and he was wounded by the archers.

4 Then Saul said to his armor bearer, "Draw your sword and thrust me through with it, lest these uncircumcised come and abuse me." But his armor bearer would not, for he was greatly afraid. ªTherefore Saul took his sword and fell on it.

5 And when his armor bearer saw that Saul was dead, he likewise fell on his sword and died.

6 ªThus Saul died with his three sons, and all *those* of his house died together.

7 When all the men of Israel who were in the valley saw that they had fled, and that Saul and his sons were dead, they forsook their cities and fled; and the Philistines came and lived in them.

8 And it came about the next day, when the Philistines came to strip the slain, that they found Saul and his sons fallen on Mount Gilboa.

9 ªSo they stripped him and took his head and his armor and sent *messengers* around the land of the Philistines, to carry the good news to their idols and to the people.

10 And they put his armor in the house of their gods and fastened his head in the house of Dagon.

11 When all Jabesh-gilead heard all that the Philistines had done to Saul,

12 ªall the valiant men arose and took away the body of Saul and the bodies of his sons, and brought them to Jabesh and buried their bones under the oak in Jabesh, and fasted seven days.

13 ªSo Saul died for his trespass which he committed against the LORD, because of the word of the LORD which he did not keep; and also ᵇbecause he asked counsel of a medium, making inquiry *of it,*

14 and did not inquire of the LORD. Therefore He killed him, and ªturned the kingdom to David the son of Jesse.

Margin references:

41 ª1 Chr. 8:35-37

★ 1-14
1 ª1 Sam. 31:1-13
2 ª1 Sam. 31:4
4 ª1 Sam. 31:4

★ 6 ª1 Sam. 31:6
9 ª1 Sam. 31:9
★10
12 ª1 Sam. 31:12f.
★13 ª1 Sam. 13:13, 14; 15:23 ᵇLev. 19:31; 20:6; 1 Sam. 28:7
14 ª1 Sam. 15:28; 1 Chr. 12:23

10:1-14 This chapter on the death of Saul is parallel to 1 Sam. 31 (see notes there).
10:6 *all those of his house.* I.e., all the men who fought with him. Some of his sons and troops did survive (2 Sam. 2:8; 21:8).

10:10 *Dagon.* See note on 1 Sam. 5:2.
10:13 Saul's death was due to disobedience in not following Samuel's commands (1 Sam. 13:8-9; 15:3, 9) and in seeking counsel of a spirit (1 Sam. 28).

B The Accession of David,
11:1–3

★ 1-3
1 *a*2 Sam.
5:1, 3, 6-10

11 *a*Then all Israel gathered to David at Hebron and said, "Behold, we are your bone and your flesh.

2 *a*2 Sam.
5:2; 7:7

2 "In times past, even when Saul was king, you *were* the one who led out and brought in Israel; and the Lord your God said to you, '*a*You shall shepherd My people Israel, and you shall be prince over My people Israel.' "

3 *a*2 Sam.
2:4; 5:3, 5
*b*1 Sam.
16:1, 3, 12,
13

3 So all the elders of Israel came to the king at Hebron, and David made a covenant with them in Hebron before the Lord; and *a*they anointed David king over Israel, *b*according to the word of the Lord through Samuel.

C The Capture of Jerusalem,
11:4–9

★ 4 *a*Josh.
15:8, 63;
Judg. 1:21

4 Then David and all Israel went to Jerusalem (*a*that is, Jebus); and the Jebusites, the inhabitants of the land, *were* there.

★ 5

5 And the inhabitants of Jebus said to David, "You shall not enter here." Nevertheless David captured the stronghold of Zion (that is, the city of David).

6 *a*2 Sam.
8:16

6 Now David had said, "Whoever strikes down a Jebusite first shall be chief and commander." *a*And Joab the son of Zeruiah went up first, so he became chief.

7 Then David dwelt in the stronghold; therefore it was called the city of David.

8 And he built the city all around, from the Millo even to the surrounding area; and Joab repaired the rest of the city.

9 And *a*David became greater and greater, for the Lord of hosts *was* with him.

9 *a*2 Sam.
3:1

D The Heroes of David,
11:10–12:40

10 *a*2 Sam.
23:8-39
*b*1 Chr. 11:3

10 *a*Now these are the heads of the mighty men whom David had, who gave him strong support in his kingdom, together with all Israel, to make him king, *b*according to the word of the Lord concerning Israel.

11 *a*2 Sam.
23:8 *b*1 Chr.
12:18

11 And these *constitute* the list of the mighty men whom David had: *a*Jashobeam, the son of a Hachmonite, *b*the chief of the thirty; he lifted up his spear against three hundred whom he killed at one time.

12 *a*1 Chr.
27:4

12 And after him was Eleazar the son of *a*Dodo, the Ahohite, who *was* one of the three mighty men.

13 *a*2 Sam.
23:11, 12

13 He was with David at Pasdammim *a*when the Philistines were gathered together there to battle, and there was a plot of ground full of barley; and the people fled before the Philistines.

14 And they took their stand in the midst of the plot, and defended it, and struck down the Philistines; and the Lord saved them by a great victory.

★15 *a*1 Chr.
14:9

15 Now three of the thirty chief men went down to the rock to David, into the cave of Adullam, while *a*the army of the Philistines was camping in the valley of Rephaim.

16 *a*1 Sam.
10:5

16 And David was then in the stronghold, while *a*the garrison of the Philistines *was* then in Bethlehem.

11:1-3 For 7½ years David had been king of Judah (2 Sam. 2:4), while Saul's son, Ish-bosheth, was king over Israel and Transjordan (2 Sam. 2:8-9). Here he is listed as king over the reunited nation. *David made a covenant with them.* I.e., an agreement as to his own prerogatives and the people's rights, somewhat like a constitutional monarchy. *Samuel* had anointed David 20 years before (see note on 1 Sam. 16:13).
11:4 *Jebus.* See note on Judg. 19:10.
11:5 See notes on Josh. 15:63 and 2 Sam. 5:6 and 5:7.
11:15 *the cave of Adullam.* See note on 1 Sam. 22:1. *Rephaim.* A valley in the vicinity of Jerusalem toward Bethlehem.

17 And David had a craving and said, "Oh that someone would give me water to drink from the well of Bethlehem, which is by the gate!"

18 So the three broke through the camp of the Philistines, and drew water from the well of Bethlehem which *was* by the gate, and took *it* and brought *it* to David; nevertheless David would not drink it, but poured it out to the Lord;

19 and he said, "Be it far from me before my God that I should do this. Shall I drink the blood of these men *who went* at the risk of their lives? For at the risk of their lives they brought it." Therefore he would not drink it. These things the three mighty men did.

20 As for Abshai the brother of Joab, he was chief of the thirty, and he swung his spear against three hundred and killed them; and he had a name as well as the thirty.

21 Of the three in the second *rank* he was the most honored, and became their commander; however, he did not attain to the *first* three.

22 ᵃBenaiah the son of Jehoiada, the son of a valiant man of Kabzeel, mighty in deeds, struck down the two *sons of* Ariel of Moab. He also went down and killed a lion inside a pit on a snowy day.

23 And he killed an Egyptian, a man of *great* stature five cubits tall. Now in the Egyptian's hand *was* ᵃa spear like a weaver's beam, but he went down to him with a club and snatched the spear from the Egyptian's hand, and killed him with his own spear.

24 These *things* Benaiah the son of Jehoiada did, and had a name as well as the three mighty men.

25 Behold, he was honored among the thirty, but he did not attain to the three; and David appointed him over his guard.

26 Now the mighty men of the armies *were* Asahel the brother of Joab, Elhanan the son of Dodo of Bethlehem,

27 Shammoth the Harorite, Helez the Pelonite,

28 Ira the son of Ikkesh the Tekoite, Abiezer the Anathothite,

29 Sibbecai the Hushathite, Ilai the Ahohite,

30 Maharai the Netophathite, Heled the son of Baanah the Netophathite,

31 Ithai the son of Ribai of Gibeah of the sons of Benjamin, Benaiah the Pirathonite,

32 Hurai of the brooks of Gaash, Abiel the Arbathite,

33 Azmaveth the Baharumite, Eliahba the Shaalbonite,

34 the sons of Hashem the Gizonite, Jonathan the son of Shagee the Hararite,

35 Ahiam the son of Sacar the Hararite, Eliphal the son of Ur,

36 Hepher the Mecherathite, Ahijah the Pelonite,

37 Hezro the Carmelite, Naarai the son of Ezbai,

38 Joel the brother of Nathan, Mibhar the son of Hagri,

39 Zelek the Ammonite, Naharai the Berothite, the armor bearer of Joab the son of Zeruiah,

40 Ira the Ithrite, Gareb the Ithrite,

41 Uriah the Hittite, Zabad ⋆41 the son of Ahlai,

42 Adina the son of Shiza the Reubenite, a chief of the Reubenites, and thirty with him,

43 Hanan the son of Maacah and Joshaphat the Mithnite,

44 Uzzia the Ashterathite, Shama and Jeiel the sons of Hotham the Aroerite,

45 Jediael the son of Shimri and Joha his brother, the Tizite,

46 Eliel the Mahavite and Jeribai and Joshaviah, the sons of Elnaam, and Ithmah the Moabite,

47 Eliel and Obed and Jaasiel the Mezobaite.

---

22 ᵃ2 Sam. 8:18

⋆23 ᵃ1 Sam. 17:7

11:23 The Egyptian was about 7½ feet tall; his spear weighed about 17 lbs.

11:41 The story of what happened to *Uriah* is found in 2 Sam. 11.

1 *a*1 Sam.
27:2-6

12 *a*Now these are the ones who came to David at Ziklag, while he was still restricted because of Saul the son of Kish; and they were among the mighty men who helped *him* in war.

2 *a*Judg.
3:15; 20:16
*b*1 Chr.
12:29

2 They were equipped with bows, *a*using both the right hand and the left *to sling* stones and *to shoot* arrows from the bow; *b*they were Saul's kinsmen from Benjamin.

3 The chief was Ahiezer, then Joash, the sons of Shemaah the Gibeathite; and Jeziel and Pelet, the sons of Azmaveth, and Beracah and Jehu the Anathothite,

4 and Ishmaiah the Gibeonite, a mighty man among the thirty, and over the thirty. Then Jeremiah, Jahaziel, Johanan, Jozabad the Gederathite,

5 Eluzai, Jerimoth, Bealiah, Shemariah, Shephatiah the Haruphite,

6 Elkanah, Isshiah, Azarel, Joezer, Jashobeam, the Korahites,

7 and Joelah and Zebadiah, the sons of Jeroham of Gedor.

★ **8** *a*2 Sam.
2:18

8 And from the Gadites there came over to David in the stronghold in the wilderness, mighty men of valor, men trained for war, who could handle shield and spear, and whose faces were like the faces of lions, and *a*they were as swift as the gazelles on the mountains.

9 Ezer *was* the first, Obadiah the second, Eliab the third,

★**10**

10 Mishmannah the fourth, Jeremiah the fifth,

11 Attai the sixth, Eliel the seventh,

12 Johanan the eighth, Elzabad the ninth,

13 Jeremiah the tenth, Machbannai the eleventh.

14 *a*Deut.
32:30

14 These of the sons of Gad were captains of the army; *a*he who was least was equal to a hundred and the greatest to a thousand.

15 *a*These are the ones who crossed the Jordan in the first month when it was overflowing all its banks and they put to flight all those in the valleys, both to the east and to the west.

★**15** *a*Josh.
3:15; 4:18

16 Then some of the sons of Benjamin and Judah came to the stronghold to David.

17 And David went out to meet them, and answered and said to them, "If you come peacefully to me to help me, my heart shall be united with you; but if to betray me to my adversaries, since there is no wrong in my hands, may the God of our fathers look on *it* and decide."

18 Then *a*the Spirit came upon *b*Amasai, who was the chief of the thirty, *and he said,*

> "*We* are yours, O David,
>   And with you, O son of Jesse!
> *c*Peace, peace to you,
>   And peace to him who helps you;
> Indeed, your God helps you!"

★**18** *a*Judg.
3:10; 6:34
*b*1 Chr. 2:17
*c*1 Sam.
25:5, 6

Then David received them and made them captains of the band.

19 *a*From Manasseh also some defected to David, when he was about to go to battle with the Philistines against Saul. But they did not help them, for the lords of the Philistines after consultation sent him away, saying, "At *the cost of* our heads he may defect to his master Saul."

19 *a*1 Sam.
29:2-9

20 As he went to Ziklag, there defected to him from Manasseh: Adnah, Jozabad, Jediael, Michael, Jozabad, Elihu, and Zillethai, captains of thousands who belonged to Manasseh.

21 And they helped David against *a*the band of raiders, for

21 *a*1 Sam.
30:1

12:8 *in the stronghold.* The cave of Adullam (11:15).
12:10 In the Hebrew, *Jeremiah* is here spelled differently from the way it is in verse 13.
12:15 *the first month.* March-April, when the

Jordan was flooding, making their action even more brave.
12:18 On the Spirit's work in the O.T., see note on Judg. 3:10.

they were all mighty men of valor, and were captains in the army.

22 aGen. 32:2; Josh. 5:13-15

22 For day by day *men* came to David to help him, until there was a great army ªlike the army of God.

★23 a2 Sam. 2:3, 4 b1 Chr. 10:14 c1 Chr. 11:10

23 Now these are the numbers of the divisions equipped for war, ªwho came to David at Hebron, bto turn the kingdom of Saul to him, caccording to the word of the LORD.

24 The sons of Judah who bore shield and spear *were* 6,800, equipped for war.

25 Of the sons of Simeon, mighty men of valor for war, 7,100.

26 Of the sons of Levi 4,600.

27 Now Jehoiada was the leader of *the house of* Aaron, and with him were 3,700,

28 a2 Sam. 8:17; 1 Chr. 6:8, 53

28 also ªZadok, a young man mighty of valor, and of his father's house twenty-two captains.

29 a1 Chr. 12:2 b2 Sam. 2:8, 9

29 And of the sons of Benjamin, ªSaul's kinsmen, 3,000; for until now bthe greatest part of them had kept their allegiance to the house of Saul.

30 And of the sons of Ephraim 20,800, mighty men of valor, famous men in their fathers' households.

31 And of the half-tribe of Manasseh 18,000, who were designated by name to come and make David king.

32 aEsth. 1:13

32 And of the sons of Issachar, ªmen who understood the times, with knowledge of what Israel should do, their chiefs were two hundred; and all their kinsmen were at their command.

33 aPs. 12:2

33 Of Zebulun, there were 50,000 who went out in the army, who could draw up in battle formation with all kinds of weapons of war and helped *David* with ªan undivided heart.

34 And of Naphtali *there were* 1,000 captains, and with them 37,000 with shield and spear.

35 And of the Danites who could draw up in battle formation, *there were* 28,600.

36 And of Asher *there were* 40,000 who went out in the army to draw up in battle formation.

37 And from the other side of the Jordan, of the Reubenites and the Gadites and of the half-tribe of Manasseh, *there were* 120,000 with all *kinds* of weapons of war for the battle.

38 a2 Sam. 5:1-3; 1 Chr. 12:33

38 All these, being men of war, who could draw up in battle formation, came to Hebron with ªa perfect heart, to make David king over all Israel; and all the rest also of Israel were of one mind to make David king.

39 And they were there with David three days, eating and drinking; for their kinsmen had prepared for them.

40 a1 Sam. 25:18

40 Moreover those who were near to them, *even* as far as Issachar and Zebulun and Naphtali, ªbrought food on donkeys, camels, mules, and on oxen, great quantities of flour cakes, fig cakes and bunches of raisins, wine, oil, oxen and sheep. There was joy indeed in Israel.

III DAVID'S REIGN, 13:1–29:21

A David and the Ark, 13:1–17:27

1 David brings the Ark to Chidon: Uzza's death, 13:1–14

13 Then David consulted with the captains of the thousands and the hundreds, even with every leader.

2 And David said to all the assembly of Israel, "If it seems good to you, and if it is from the LORD our God, let us send everywhere to our kinsmen who remain in all the land of Israel, also to the priests and Levites who are with them in their cities with

---

12:23 The total number of warriors was about 350,000 (the number that came from Issachar is not specified, v. 32).

pasture lands, that they may meet with us;

3 a1 Sam. 7:1, 2

3 and let us bring back the ark of our God to us, afor we did not seek it in the days of Saul."

4 Then all the assembly said that they would do so, for the thing was right in the eyes of all the people.

★ **5** a2 Sam. 6:1; 1 Kin. 8:65; 1 Chr. 15:3 b1 Sam. 6:21; 7:1

5 aSo David assembled all Israel together, from the Shihor of Egypt even to the entrance of Hamath, bto bring the ark of God from Kiriath-jearim.

6 a2 Sam. 6:2-11 bJosh. 15:9 cEx. 25:22; 2 Kin. 19:15

6 aAnd David and all Israel went up to bBaalah, *that is,* to Kiriath-jearim, which belongs to Judah, to bring up from there the ark of God, the LORD cwho is enthroned *above* the cherubim, where His name is called.

★ **7** a1 Sam. 7:1

7 And they carried the ark of God on a new cart from athe house of Abinadab, and Uzza and Ahio drove the cart.

8 a1 Chr. 15:16

8 And David and all Israel were celebrating before God with all *their* might, aeven with songs and with lyres, harps, tambourines, cymbals, and with trumpets.

9 a2 Sam. 6:6

9 When they came to athe threshing floor of Chidon, Uzza put out his hand to hold the ark, because the oxen nearly upset *it.*

10 a1 Chr. 15:13, 15 bLev. 10:2

10 And the anger of the LORD burned against Uzza, so He struck him down abecause he put out his hand to the ark; band he died there before God.

11 Then David became angry because of the LORD's outburst against Uzza; and he called that place Perez-uzza to this day.

12 And David was afraid of God that day, saying, "How can I bring the ark of God *home* to me?"

13 a2 Chr. 15:25

13 So David did not take the ark with him to the city of David, but took it aside ato the house of Obed-edom the Gittite.

14 Thus the ark of God remained with the family of Obed-edom in his house three months; and athe LORD blessed the family of Obed-edom with all that he had.

14 a1 Chr. 26:4, 5

2 David's fame and victory over the Philistines, 14:1-17

14 aNow Hiram king of Tyre sent messengers to David with cedar trees, masons, and carpenters, to build a house for him.

★ **1** a2 Sam. 5:11

2 And David realized that the LORD had established him as king over Israel, *and* that his kingdom was highly exalted, for the sake of His people Israel.

3 Then David took more wives at Jerusalem, and David became the father of more sons and daughters.

★ **3**

4 aAnd these are the names of the children born *to him* in Jerusalem: Shammua, Shobab, Nathan, Solomon,

4 a1 Chr. 3:5-8

5 Ibhar, Elishua, Elpelet,

6 Nogah, Nepheg, Japhia,

7 Elishama, Beeliada and Eliphelet.

8 When the Philistines heard that David had been anointed king over all Israel, all the Philistines went up in search of David; and David heard of it and went out against them.

9 Now the Philistines had come and amade a raid in the valley of Rephaim.

9 a1 Chr. 11:15; 14:13

10 And David inquired of God, saying, "Shall I go up against the Philistines? And wilt Thou give them into my hand?" Then the LORD said to him, "Go up, for I will give them into your hand."

11 So they came up to Baal-perazim, and David defeated them there; and David said, "God has broken through my enemies

★ **11**

13:5 *Shihor of Egypt.* The southern boundary of Israel. *Hamath.* See note on 1 Kings 8:65.
13:7 The Ark was to be carried by hand not by any vehicle, and was not to be touched by those carrying it (Num. 4:15). God had once allowed the Philistines to transport the Ark on

a cart (1 Sam. 6:7), but His exception did not set aside His revealed will.
14:1 Cf. the note on 1 Kings 5:1.
14:3 On David's taking many wives, see note on 2 Sam. 5:13.
14:11 *Baal-perazim.* See note on 2 Sam. 5:20.

by my hand, like the breakthrough of waters." Therefore they named that place Baal-perazim.

★12 **12** And they abandoned their gods there; so David gave the order and they were burned with fire.

13 a1 Chr. 14:9 **13** And the Philistines made a yet another raid in the valley.

★14 **14** And David inquired again of God, and God said to him, "You shall not go up after them; circle around behind them, and come at them in front of the balsam trees.

15 "And it shall be when you hear the sound of marching in the tops of the balsam trees, then you shall go out to battle, for God will have gone out before you to strike the army of the Philistines."

16 And David did just as God had commanded him, and they struck down the army of the Philistines from Gibeon even as far as Gezer.

17 aEx. 15:14-16; Deut. 2:25 **17** Then the fame of David went out into all the lands; and a the LORD brought the fear of him on all the nations.

3 David brings the Ark to Jerusalem, 15:1-29

1 a1 Chr. 15:3; 16:1; 17:1-5 **15** Now *David* built houses for himself in the city of David; and he prepared a place for the ark of God, and a pitched a tent for it.

★ 2 aNum. 4:15; Deut. 10:8 **2** Then David said, "a No one is to carry the ark of God but the Levites; for the LORD chose them to carry the ark of God, and to minister to Him forever."

3 a1 Kin. 8:1; 1 Chr. 13:5 bEx. 40:20f.; 2 Sam. 6:12, 17; 1 Chr. 15:1, 12 **3** And a David assembled all Israel at Jerusalem, to bring up the ark of the LORD b to its place, which he had prepared for it.

4 And David gathered together the sons of Aaron, and a the Levites:

4 a1 Chr. 6:16-30; 12:26

5 of the sons of Kohath, Uriel the chief, and 120 of his relatives;

6 of the sons of Merari, Asaiah the chief, and 220 of his relatives;

7 of the sons of Gershom, Joel the chief, and 130 of his relatives;

8 of the sons of Elizaphan, Shemaiah the chief, and 200 of his relatives;

9 of the sons of Hebron, Eliel the chief, and 80 of his relatives;

10 of the sons of Uzziel, Amminadab the chief, and 112 of his relatives.

11 Then David called for a Zadok and b Abiathar the priests, and for the Levites, for Uriel, Asaiah, Joel, Shemaiah, Eliel, and Amminadab,

11 a1 Chr. 12:28 b1 Sam. 22:20-23; 1 Kin. 2:26, 35

12 and said to them, "You are the heads of the fathers' *households* of the Levites; a consecrate yourselves both you and your relatives, that you may bring up the ark of the LORD God of Israel, b to *the place* that I have prepared for it.

★12 aEx. 19:14, 15; 2 Chr. 35:6 b1 Chr. 15:1, 3

13 "a Because you did not *carry* it at the first, the LORD our God made an outburst on us, for we did not seek Him according to the ordinance."

13 a2 Sam. 6:3; 1 Chr. 13:7

14 a So the priests and the Levites consecrated themselves to bring up the ark of the LORD God of Israel.

14 a1 Chr. 15:12

15 And the sons of a the Levites carried the ark of God on their shoulders, with the poles thereon as Moses had commanded according to the word of the LORD.

15 aEx. 25:14; Num. 4:5f.

14:12 *burned.* According to the law (Deut. 7:5, 25).

14:14 *balsam trees.* Lit., Baka trees, from which sap or resin came.

15:2 David learned from the mistake he had made in his first attempt to bring the Ark to Jerusalem (see note on 13:7).

15:12 *consecrate yourselves.* By washing (Exod. 19:10, 14), avoiding defilement (Lev. 11:44), and refraining from intercourse (Exod. 19:15).

16 *a*1 Chr. 13:8; 25:1

16 Then David spoke to the chiefs of the Levites *a*to appoint their relatives the singers, with instruments of music, harps, lyres, loud-sounding cymbals, to raise sounds of joy.

17 *a*1 Chr. 25:1

17 So *a*the Levites appointed Heman the son of Joel, and from his relatives, Asaph the son of Berechiah; and from the sons of Merari their relatives, Ethan the son of Kushaiah,

18 and with them their relatives of the second rank, Zechariah, Ben, Jaaziel, Shemiramoth, Jehiel, Unni, Eliab, Benaiah, Maaseiah, Mattithiah, Eliphelehu, Mikneiah, Obed-edom, and Jeiel, the gatekeepers.

19 So the singers, Heman, Asaph, and Ethan *were appointed* to sound aloud cymbals of bronze;

20 *a*Ps. 46:title

20 and Zechariah, Aziel, Shemiramoth, Jehiel, Unni, Eliab, Maaseiah, and Benaiah, with harps *tuned* to *a*alamoth;

21 *a*Ps. 6:title

21 and Mattithiah, Eliphelehu, Mikneiah, Obed-edom, Jeiel, and Azaziah, to lead with lyres tuned to *a*the sheminith.

22 And Chenaniah, chief of the Levites, was *in charge of* the singing; he gave instruction in singing because he was skillful.

23 And Berechiah and Elkanah were gatekeepers for the ark.

24 *a*1 Chr. 15:28; 16:6

24 And Shebaniah, Joshaphat, Nethanel, Amasai, Zechariah, Benaiah, and Eliezer, the priests, *a*blew the trumpets before the ark of God. Obed-edom and Jehiah also *were* gatekeepers for the ark.

25 *a*2 Sam. 6:12, 15
*b*1 Chr. 13:13

25 *a*So *it was* David, with the elders of Israel and the captains over thousands, who went to bring up the ark of the covenant of the Lord from *b*the house of Obed-edom with joy.

26 *a*Num. 23:1-4, 29

26 And it came about because God was helping the Levites who were carrying the ark of the covenant of the Lord, that they sacrificed *a*seven bulls and seven rams.

27 Now David was clothed with a robe of fine linen with all the Levites who were carrying the ark, and the singers and Chenaniah the leader of the singing *with* the singers. *a*David also wore an ephod of linen.

★27 *a*2 Sam. 6:14

28 Thus all Israel brought up the ark of the covenant of the Lord with shouting, and with sound of the horn, with trumpets, with loud-sounding cymbals, with harps and lyres.

29 And it happened when the ark of the covenant of the Lord came to the city of David, that *a*Michal the daughter of Saul looked out of the window, and saw King David leaping and making merry; and she despised him in her heart.

★29 *a*2 Sam. 3:13f.; 6:16

4 David's celebration and arrangements for the Ark, 16:1-43

16 And they brought in the ark of God and *a*placed it inside the tent which David had pitched for it, and they offered burnt offerings and peace offerings before God.

1 *a*1 Chr. 15:1

2 When David had finished offering the burnt offering and the peace offerings, he blessed the people in the name of the Lord.

3 And he distributed to everyone of Israel, both man and woman, to everyone a loaf of bread and a portion *of meat* and a raisin cake.

4 And he appointed some of the Levites *as* ministers before the ark of the Lord, even to celebrate and to thank and praise the Lord God of Israel:

5 Asaph the chief, and second to him Zechariah, *then* Jeiel, Shemiramoth, Jehiel, Mattithiah, Eliab, Benaiah, Obed-edom, and Jeiel, with musical instruments, harps, lyres; also Asaph *played* loud-sounding cymbals,

★ 5

15:27 *an ephod of linen.* See note on 2 Sam. 6:14.

15:29 See notes on 2 Sam. 6:20 through 6:23.
16:5 *Asaph.* See note on Ezra 2:41.

★ 6

6 and Benaiah and Jahaziel the priests *blew* trumpets continually before the ark of the covenant of God.

★ 7 a2
Sam. 22:1;
23:1

7 Then on that day David ªfirst assigned Asaph and his relatives to give thanks to the LORD.

8 a1 Chr.
16:8-36; Ps.
105:1-15
b1 Kin. 8:43;
2 Kin. 19:19

8 ªOh give thanks to the LORD, call upon His name;
ᵇMake known His deeds among the peoples.

9 Sing to Him, sing praises to Him;
Speak of all His wonders.

10 Glory in His holy name;
Let the heart of those who seek the LORD be glad.

11 aPs. 24:6

11 ªSeek the LORD and His strength;
Seek His face continually.

12 aPs.
103:2 bPs.
78:43-68

12 ªRemember His wonderful deeds which He has done,
ᵇHis marvels and the judgments from His mouth,

13 O seed of Israel His servant,
Sons of Jacob, His chosen ones!

14 aPs.
48:10

14 He is the LORD our God;
ªHis judgments are in all the earth.

15 Remember His covenant forever,
The word which He commanded to a thousand generations,

★16-18

16 aGen.
12:7; 17:2;
22:16-18;
26:3

17 aGen.
35:11, 12

16 ª*The covenant* which He made with Abraham,
And His oath to Isaac.

17 ªHe also confirmed it to Jacob for a statute,
To Israel as an everlasting covenant,

18 aGen.
13:15

18 Saying, "ªTo you I will give the land of Canaan,

As the portion of your inheritance."

19 aGen.
34:30; Deut.
7:7

19 ªWhen they were only a few in number,
Very few, and strangers in it,

20 And they wandered about from nation to nation,
And from *one* kingdom to another people,

21 aGen.
12:17; 20:3;
Ex. 7:15-18

21 He permitted no man to oppress them,
And ªHe reproved kings for their sakes, *saying,*

22 aGen.
20:7

22 "Do not touch My anointed ones,
And ªdo My prophets no harm."

23 aPs.
96:1-13

23 ªSing to the LORD, all the earth;
Proclaim good tidings of His salvation from day to day.

24 Tell of His glory among the nations,
His wonderful deeds among all the peoples.

25 aPs.
144:3-6 bPs.
89:7

25 For ªgreat is the LORD, and greatly to be praised;
He also is ᵇto be feared above all gods.

26 aLev.
19:4 bPs.
102:25

26 For all the gods of the peoples are ªidols,
ᵇBut the LORD made the heavens.

27 Splendor and majesty are before Him,
Strength and joy are in His place.

28 Ascribe to the LORD, O families of the peoples,
Ascribe to the LORD glory and strength.

29 aPs. 29:2

29 Ascribe to the LORD the glory due His name;
Bring an offering, and come before Him;
ªWorship the LORD in holy array.

16:6 *continually.* Does not mean constantly, but a certain fixed and regularly recurring service.
16:7 This psalm (through v. 36) consists, with slight variations, of Psalms 105:1-15; 96; and 106:1, 47-48, perhaps indicating that David was their author (though they are listed anonymously in the Psalter).
16:16-18 On the Abrahamic covenant see notes on Gen. 12:2, 3; 15:18-21; 17:7-8; 26:24-25.

30 Tremble before Him, all the earth;
Indeed, the world is firmly established, it will not be moved.

31 ^aLet the heavens be glad, and let the earth rejoice;
And let them say among the nations, "^bThe Lord reigns."

32 ^aLet the sea roar, and all it contains;
Let the field exult, and all that is in it.

33 Then the trees of the forest will sing for joy before the Lord;
For He is coming to judge the earth.

34 ^aO give thanks to the Lord, for He is good;
For His lovingkindness is everlasting.

35 ^aThen say, "Save us, O God of our salvation,
And gather us and deliver us from the nations,
To give thanks to Thy holy name,
And glory in Thy praise."

36 ^aBlessed be the Lord, the God of Israel,
From everlasting even to everlasting.
Then all the people ^bsaid, "Amen," and praised the Lord.

37 So he left Asaph and his relatives there ^abefore the ark of the covenant of the Lord, to minister before the ark continually, ^bas every day's work required;

38 and ^aObed-edom with his 68 relatives; Obed-edom, also the son of Jeduthun, and ^bHosah as gatekeepers.

39 And he left ^aZadok the priest and his relatives the priests ^bbefore the tabernacle of the Lord in the high place which was at Gibeon,

40 to offer burnt offerings to the Lord on the altar of burnt offering continually morning and evening, ^aeven according to all that is written in the law of the Lord, which He commanded Israel.

41 And with them were ^aHeman and Jeduthun, and ^bthe rest who were chosen, who were designated by name, to ^cgive thanks to the Lord, because His lovingkindness is everlasting.

42 And with them were Heman and Jeduthun with trumpets and cymbals for those who should sound aloud, and with instruments for ^athe songs of God, and the sons of Jeduthun for the gate.

43 ^aThen all the people departed each to his house, and David returned to bless his household.

5 David's desire to build a temple: the Davidic covenant, 17:1-27

17 ^aAnd it came about, when David dwelt in his house, that David said to Nathan the prophet, "Behold, I am dwelling in a house of cedar, but the ark of the covenant of the Lord is under curtains."

2 Then Nathan said to David, "Do all that is in your heart, for God is with you."

3 And it came about the same night, that the word of God came to Nathan, saying,

4 "Go and tell David My servant, 'Thus says the Lord, ^a"You shall not build a house for Me to dwell in;

5 for I have not dwelt in a house since the day that I brought up Israel to this day, ^abut I have

---

Marginal references:
31 ^aIs. 44:23; 49:13 ^bPs. 93:1; 96:10
32 ^aPs. 98:7
34 ^a2 Chr. 5:13; 7:3; Ezra 3:11; Ps. 106:1; 136:1; Jer. 33:11
35 ^aPs. 106:47, 48
★36 ^a1 Kin. 8:15, 56; Ps. 72:18 ^bDeut. 27:15; Neh. 8:6
★37 ^a1 Chr. 16:4, 5 ^b2 Chr. 8:14; Ezra 3:4
38 ^a1 Chr. 13:14 ^b1 Chr. 26:10
39 ^a1 Chr. 15:11 ^b1 Kin. 3:4
40 ^aEx. 29:38-42; Num. 28:3, 4
★41 ^a1 Chr. 6:33 ^b1 Chr. 25:1-6 ^c2 Chr. 5:13
42 ^a1 Chr. 25:7; 2 Chr. 7:6; 29:27
43 ^a2 Sam. 6:19
★ 1 ^a2 Sam. 7:1-29
4 ^a1 Chr. 28:2, 3
5 ^aEx. 40:2, 3; 2 Sam. 7:6

16:36 Amen means "firmness" (and thus "true") and is derived from the Hebrew verb that means "to believe" (see note on Gen. 15:6).
16:37 before the ark. Which was now in Jerusalem, though the tabernacle itself was still in Gibeon (v. 39). They were not united until Solomon's Temple was built (1 Kings 8:4).
16:41 lovingkindness. See note on Hos. 2:19.
17:1 under curtains. I.e., in a tent.

gone from tent to tent and from *one* dwelling place *to another.*

6 *a*2 Sam.
7:7

6 "In all places where I have walked with all Israel, have I spoken a word *a*with any of the judges of Israel, whom I commanded to shepherd My people, saying, 'Why have you not built for Me a house of cedar?' " '

7 "Now, therefore, thus shall you say to My servant David, 'Thus says the Lord of hosts, "I took you from the pasture, from following the sheep, that you should be leader over My people Israel.

8 "And I have been with you wherever you have gone, and have cut off all your enemies from before you; and I will make you a name like the name of the great ones who are in the earth.

9 "And I will appoint a place for My people Israel, and will plant them, that they may dwell in their own place and be moved no more; neither shall the wicked waste them anymore as formerly,

10 even from the day that I commanded judges *to be* over My people Israel. And I will subdue all your enemies. Moreover, I tell you that the Lord will build a house for you.

★11-14

11 "And it shall come about when your days are fulfilled that you must go *to be* with your fathers, that I will set up *one of* your descendants after you, who shall be of your sons; and I will establish his kingdom.

12 "He shall build for Me a house, and I will establish his throne forever.

13 *a*2 Cor.
6:18; Heb.
1:5 *b*1 Chr.
10:14

13 "*a*I will be his father, and he shall be My son; and I will not take My lovingkindness away from him, *b*as I took it from him who was before you.

14 "But I will settle him in My house and in My kingdom forever, and his throne shall be established forever." ' "

15 According to all these words and according to all this vision, so Nathan spoke to David.

★16 *a*2 Sam.
7:18

16 Then David the king went in and sat before the Lord and said, "*a*Who am I, O Lord God, and what is my house that Thou hast brought me this far?

17 "And this was a small thing in Thine eyes, O God; but Thou hast spoken of Thy servant's house for a great while to come, and hast regarded me according to the standard of a man of high degree, O Lord God.

18 "What more can David still *say* to Thee concerning the honor *bestowed* on Thy servant? For Thou knowest Thy servant.

19 *a*2 Sam.
7:21; Is.
37:35

19 "O Lord, *a*for Thy servant's sake, and according to Thine own heart, Thou hast wrought all this greatness, to make known all these great things.

20 "O Lord, there is none like Thee, neither is there any God besides Thee, according to all that we have heard with our ears.

21 "And what one nation in the earth is like Thy people Israel, whom God went to redeem for Himself *as* a people, to make Thee a name by great and terrible things, in driving out nations from before Thy people, whom Thou didst redeem out of Egypt?

22 *a*Ex.
19:5, 6

22 "*a*For Thy people Israel Thou didst make Thine own people forever, and Thou, O Lord, didst become their God.

23 "And now, O Lord, let the word that Thou hast spoken concerning Thy servant and concerning his house, be established forever, and do as Thou hast spoken.

24 "And let Thy name be established and magnified forever, saying, 'The Lord of hosts is the God of Israel, *even* a God to Israel; and the house of David Thy servant is established before Thee.'

17:11-14 For an explanation of this great covenant with David, see the note on 2 Sam. 7:12-16.

17:16 *before the Lord.* In the tent he had erected for the Ark.

25 "For Thou, O my God, hast revealed to Thy servant that Thou wilt build for him a house; therefore Thy servant hath found *courage* to pray before Thee.

26 "And now, O LORD, Thou art God, and hast promised this good thing to Thy servant.

27 "And now it hath pleased Thee to bless the house of Thy servant, that it may continue forever before Thee; for Thou, O LORD, hast blessed, and it is blessed forever."

B David's Wars, 18:1-20:8

1 *a*2 Sam. 8:1-18

18 Now after this *a*it came about that David defeated the Philistines and subdued them and took Gath and its towns from the hand of the Philistines.

2 And he defeated Moab, and the Moabites became servants to David, bringing tribute.

★ 3

3 David also defeated Hadadezer king of Zobah *as far as* Hamath, as he went to establish his rule to the Euphrates River.

★ 4

4 And David took from him 1,000 chariots and 7,000 horsemen and 20,000 foot soldiers, and David hamstrung all the chariot horses, but reserved *enough* of them for 100 chariots.

5 *a*1 Chr. 19:6

5 When the Arameans of Damascus came to help Hadadezer king *a*of Zobah, David killed 22,000 men of the Arameans.

6 Then David put *garrisons* among the Arameans of Damascus; and the Arameans became servants to David, bringing tribute. And the LORD helped David wherever he went.

7 And David took the shields of gold which were carried by the servants of Hadadezer, and brought them to Jerusalem.

8 Also from Tibhath and from Cun, cities of Hadadezer, David took a very large amount of bronze, with which *a*Solomon made the bronze sea and the pillars and the bronze utensils.

★ 8 *a*1 Kin. 7:40-47; 2 Chr. 4:11-18

9 Now when Tou king of Hamath heard that David had defeated all the army of Hadadezer king of Zobah,

10 he sent Hadoram his son to King David, to greet him and to bless him, because he had fought against Hadadezer and had defeated him; for Hadadezer had been at war with Tou. And *Hadoram brought* all kinds of articles of gold and silver and bronze.

11 King David also dedicated these to the LORD with the silver and the gold which he had carried away from all the nations: from Edom, Moab, the sons of Ammon, the Philistines, and from Amalek.

12 Moreover Abishai the son of Zeruiah defeated 18,000 Edomites in the Valley of Salt.

★12

13 Then he put garrisons in Edom, and all the Edomites became servants to David. And the LORD helped David wherever he went.

14 So David reigned over all Israel; and he administered justice and righteousness for all his people.

15 And *a*Joab the son of Zeruiah *was* over the army, and Jehoshaphat the son of Ahilud *was* recorder;

★15 *a*1 Chr. 11:6

16 and Zadok the son of Ahitub and Abimelech the son of Abiathar *were* priests, and Shavsha *was* secretary;

★16

17 and Benaiah the son of Jehoiada *was* over the Cherethites

---

18:3 *Zobah.* A territory NE. of Damascus.
18:4 *hamstrung.* So that the horses were disabled. See note on 2 Sam. 8:4.
18:8 *Solomon made . . .* See note on 1 Kings 7:23-26.
18:12 *Abishai.* A cousin of David and brother of Joab, who, according to the title of Psalm 60, was also involved in this victory. The *Valley of*

Salt. In the vicinity (probably S.) of the Dead Sea.
18:15 *recorder.* A kind of public relations officer, who arranged royal ceremonies, appointments, and travels.
18:16 *Abimelech.* Should read Ahimelech (2 Sam. 8:17).

and the Pelethites, and the sons of David *were* chiefs at the king's side.

1 *a*2 Sam. 10:1-19

19 *a*Now it came about after this, that Nahash the king of the sons of Ammon died, and his son became king in his place.

★ **2**   **2** Then David said, "I will show kindness to Hanun the son of Nahash, because his father showed kindness to me." So David sent messengers to console him concerning his father. And David's servants came into the land of the sons of Ammon to Hanun, to console him.

3 But the princes of the sons of Ammon said to Hanun, "Do you think that David is honoring your father, in that he has sent comforters to you? Have not his servants come to you to search and to overthrow and to spy out the land?"

★ **4**   **4** So Hanun took David's servants and shaved them, and cut off their garments in the middle as far as their hips, and sent them away.

5 Then *certain persons* went and told David about the men. And he sent to meet them, for the men were greatly humiliated. And the king said, "Stay at Jericho until your beards grow, and *then* return."

★ **6** *a*1 Chr. 18:5, 9

6 When the sons of Ammon saw that they had made themselves odious to David, Hanun and the sons of Ammon sent 1,000 talents of silver to hire for themselves chariots and horsemen from Mesopotamia, from Aram-maacah, and *a*from Zobah.

★ **7** *a*Num. 21:30; Josh. 13:9, 16

7 So they hired for themselves 32,000 chariots, and the king of Maacah and his people, who came and camped before *a*Medeba. And the sons of Am-

mon gathered together from their cities and came to battle.

8 When David heard *of it,* he sent Joab and all the army, the mighty men.

9 And the sons of Ammon came out and drew up in battle array at the entrance of the city, and the kings who had come were by themselves in the field.

10 Now when Joab saw that the battle was set against him in front and in the rear, he selected from all the choice men of Israel and they arrayed themselves against the Arameans.

11 But the remainder of the people he placed in the hand of Abshai his brother; and they arrayed themselves against the sons of Ammon.

12 And he said, "If the Arameans are too strong for me, then you shall help me; but if the sons of Ammon are too strong for you, then I will help you.

13 "Be strong, and let us show ourselves courageous for the sake of our people and for the cities of our God; and may the LORD do what is good in His sight."

14 So Joab and the people who were with him drew near to the battle against the Arameans, and they fled before him.

15 When the sons of Ammon saw that the Arameans fled, they also fled before Abshai his brother, and entered the city. Then Joab came to Jerusalem.

16 When the Arameans saw that they had been defeated by Israel, they sent messengers, and brought out the Arameans who were beyond the River, with Shophach the commander of the army of Hadadezer leading them.

17 When it was told David, he gathered all Israel together and crossed the Jordan, and came

---

19:2 *the sons of Ammon.* See notes on Gen. 19:31-38 and Amos 1:13.
19:4 *shaved them.* Specifically, shaved off half their beards (see note on 2 Sam. 10:4).
19:6 *1,000 talents of silver.* Approximately 1.2 million ounces. *Mesopotamia.* The territory

between the Tigris and Euphrates rivers. *Aram-maachah.* Between Damascus and Galilee.
19:7 *Medeba.* A city about 20 miles SW of Amman (the present capital of Jordan).

upon them and drew up in formation against them. And when David drew up in battle array against the Arameans, they fought against him.

18 And the Arameans fled before Israel, and David killed of the Arameans 7,000 charioteers and 40,000 foot soldiers, and put to death Shophach the commander of the army.

19 So when the servants of Hadadezer saw that they were defeated by Israel, they made peace with David and served him. Thus the Arameans were not willing to help the sons of Ammon anymore.

20 ªThen it happened in the spring, at the time when kings go out to battle, that Joab led out the army and ravaged the land of the sons of Ammon, and came and besieged Rabbah. But David stayed at Jerusalem. And ᵇJoab struck Rabbah and overthrew it.

2 ªAnd David took the crown of their king from his head, and he found it to weigh a talent of gold, and there was a precious stone in it; and it was placed on David's head. And he brought out the spoil of the city, a very great amount.

3 And he brought out the people who were in it, ªand cut them with saws and with sharp instruments and with axes. And thus David did to all the cities of the sons of Ammon. Then David and all the people returned to Jerusalem.

4 ªNow it came about after this, that war broke out at Gezer with the Philistines; then Sibbecai the Hushathite killed Sippai, one of the descendants of the giants, and they were subdued.

5 And there was war with the Philistines again, and Elhanan the son of ªJair killed Lahmi the brother of Goliath the Gittite, the ᵇshaft of whose spear was like a weaver's beam.

6 And again there was war at Gath, where there was a man of great stature who had twenty-four fingers and toes, six fingers on each hand and six toes on each foot; and he also was descended from the giants.

7 And when he taunted Israel, Jonathan the son of Shimea, David's brother, killed him.

8 These were descended from the giants in Gath, and they fell by the hand of David and by the hand of his servants.

C David's Sinful Census, 21:1-30

21 ªThen Satan stood up against Israel and moved David to number Israel.

2 So David said to Joab and to the princes of the people, "ªGo, number Israel from Beersheba even to Dan, and bring me word that I may know their number."

3 And Joab said, "ªMay the LORD add to His people a hundred times as many as they are! But, my lord the king, are they not all my lord's servants? Why does my lord seek this thing? Why should he be a cause of guilt to Israel?"

4 Nevertheless, the king's word prevailed against Joab. Therefore, Joab departed and went throughout all Israel, and came to Jerusalem.

Margin references:

★ 1 ª2 Sam. 11:1 ᵇ2 Sam. 12:26
★ 2 ª2 Sam. 12:30, 31
★ 3 ª2 Sam. 12:31
★ 4 ª2 Sam. 21:18-22
★ 5 ª2 Sam. 21:19 ᵇ1 Sam. 17:7; 1 Chr. 11:23
★ 1-4
1 ª2 Sam. 24:1-25
2 ª1 Chr. 27:23, 24
3 ªDeut. 1:11

20:1 *David stayed at Jerusalem.* The scandal of David's adultery with Bathsheba and his murder of her husband, Uriah (2 Sam. 11), occurred during this time. *Rabbah.* The chief city of the Ammonites, now called Amman, the capital of Jordan.
20:2 *a talent of gold.* About 1,200 ounces.
20:3 See note on 2 Sam. 12:31.
20:4 *the descendants of the giants.* Heb., *Rephaim.* See notes on Deut. 2:20 and 3:11.

20:5 *the brother of Goliath.* See note on 2 Sam. 21:19. *a weaver's beam* weighed about 17 lbs.
21:1-4 Actually God permitted Satan to prompt David to take a census of the people, and David insisted on doing it, contrary to Joab's advice (see note on 2 Sam. 24:1). Though not inherently wrong, the action demonstrated David's reliance on numbers of warriors rather than on God. The census took about ten months to complete (2 Sam. 24:5-8).

★ 5 a2 Sam.
24:9

5 And Joab gave the number of the census of all the people to David. And ªall Israel were 1,100,000 men who drew the sword; and Judah was 470,000 men who drew the sword.

6 a1 Chr.
27:24

6 ªBut he did not number Levi and Benjamin among them, for the king's command was abhorrent to Joab.

7 And God was displeased with this thing, so He struck Israel.

8 a2 Sam.
12:13

8 And David said to God, "I have sinned greatly, in that I have done this thing. ªBut now, please take away the iniquity of Thy servant, for I have done very foolishly."

9 a2 Sam.
24:11; 1 Chr.
29:29
b1 Sam. 9:9

9 And the Lord spoke to ªGad, David's bseer, saying,

10 "Go and speak to David, saying, 'Thus says the Lord, "I offer you three things; choose for yourself one of them, that I may do it to you." ' "

11 So Gad came to David and said to him, "Thus says the Lord, 'Take for yourself

12 a2 Sam.
24:13

12 ªeither three years of famine, or three months to be swept away before your foes, while the sword of your enemies overtakes you, or else three days of the sword of the Lord, even pestilence in the land, and the angel of the Lord destroying throughout all the territory of Israel.' Now, therefore, consider what answer I shall return to Him who sent me."

13 aPs. 51:1;
130:4, 7

13 And David said to Gad, "I am in great distress; please let me fall into the hand of the Lord, ªfor His mercies are very great. But do not let me fall into the hand of man."

★14 a1 Chr.
27:24

14 ªSo the Lord sent a pestilence on Israel; 70,000 men of Israel fell.

★15 aEx.
32:14;
1 Sam.
15:11; Jon.
3:10

15 And God sent an angel to Jerusalem to destroy it; but as he was about to destroy it, the Lord saw and ªwas sorry over the calamity, and said to the destroying angel, "It is enough; now relax your hand." And the angel of the Lord was standing by the threshing floor of Ornan the Jebusite.

16 a1 Kin.
21:27

16 Then David lifted up his eyes and saw the angel of the Lord standing between earth and heaven, with his drawn sword in his hand stretched out over Jerusalem. Then David and the elders, ªcovered with sackcloth, fell on their faces.

17 a2 Sam.
7:8; Ps. 74:1

17 And David said to God, "Is it not I who commanded to count the people? Indeed, I am the one who has sinned and done very wickedly, ªbut these sheep, what have they done? O Lord my God, please let Thy hand be against me and my father's household, but not against Thy people that they should be plagued."

18 a2 Chr.
3:1

18 ªThen the angel of the Lord commanded Gad to say to David, that David should go up and build an altar to the Lord on the threshing floor of Ornan the Jebusite.

19 So David went up at the word of Gad, which he spoke in the name of the Lord.

20 Now Ornan turned back and saw the angel, and his four sons who were with him hid themselves. And Ornan was threshing wheat.

21 And as David came to Ornan, Ornan looked and saw David, and went out from the threshing floor, and prostrated himself before David with his face to the ground.

22 Then David said to Ornan, "Give me the site of this threshing floor, that I may build on it an altar to the Lord; for the full price you shall give it to me, that the plague may be restrained from the people."

21:5 The 800,000 from Israel in 2 Sam. 24:9 may not have included the 300,000 listed in 1 Chron. 27, which would make the total (as here) 1,100,000. The 470,000 in Judah may not have included the 30,000 of 2 Sam. 6:1, which would bring the total (as here) to 500,000. Or perhaps the Chronicles figure represents a round number.
21:14 The consequences of sin often affect others.
21:15 Ornan = Araunah of 2 Sam. 24:16.

23 And Ornan said to David, "Take *it* for yourself; and let my lord the king do what is good in his sight. See, I will give the oxen for burnt offerings and the threshing sledges for wood and the wheat for the grain offering; I will give *it* all."

24 But King David said to Ornan, "No, but I will surely buy *it* for the full price; for I will not take what is yours for the LORD, or offer a burnt offering which costs me nothing."

★**25** ᵃ2 Sam. 24:24
25 So ᵃDavid gave Ornan 600 shekels of gold by weight for the site.

26 ᵃLev. 9:24; Judg. 6:21
26 Then David built an altar to the LORD there, and offered burnt offerings and peace offerings. And he called to the LORD and ᵃHe answered him with fire from heaven on the altar of burnt offering.

27 And the LORD commanded the angel, and he put his sword back in its sheath.

28 At that time, when David saw that the LORD had answered him on the threshing floor of Ornan the Jebusite, he offered sacrifice there.

29 ᵃ1 Kin. 3:4; 1 Chr. 16:39
29 ᵃFor the tabernacle of the LORD, which Moses had made in the wilderness, and the altar of burnt offering *were* in the high place at Gibeon at that time.

30 But David could not go before it to inquire of God, for he was terrified by the sword of the angel of the LORD.

D David's Preparations for the Temple, 22:1–23:1

1 ᵃ1 Chr. 21:18-28; 2 Chr. 3:1
★ **2** ᵃ1 Kin. 9:20, 21; 2 Chr. 2:17
ᵇ1 Kin. 5:17, 18

22 Then David said, "ᵃThis is the house of the LORD God, and this is the altar of burnt offering for Israel."

2 So David gave orders to gather ᵃthe foreigners who were in the land of Israel, and ᵇhe set stonecutters to hew out stones to build the house of God.

3 ᵃ1 Chr. 29:2, 7 ᵇ1 Chr. 22:14
3 And David ᵃprepared large quantities of iron to make the nails for the doors of the gates and for the clamps, and more ᵇbronze than could be weighed;

4 ᵃ1 Kin. 5:6-10
4 and timbers of cedar logs beyond number, for ᵃthe Sidonians and Tyrians brought large quantities of cedar timber to David.

★ **5** ᵃ1 Kin. 3:7; 1 Chr. 29:1
5 And David said, "My son ᵃSolomon is young and inexperienced, and the house that is to be built for the LORD shall be exceedingly magnificent, famous and glorious throughout all lands. Therefore I will make preparation for it." So David made ample preparations before his death.

6 ᵃ1 Kin. 2:1
6 Then ᵃhe called for his son Solomon, and charged him to build a house for the LORD God of Israel.

7 ᵃ2 Sam. 7:2, 3; 1 Chr. 17:1
7 And David said to Solomon, "ᵃMy son, I had intended to build a house to the name of the LORD my God.

8 ᵃ1 Chr. 28:3
8 "But the word of the LORD came to me, saying, 'ᵃYou have shed much blood, and have waged great wars; you shall not build a house to My name, because you have shed *so* much blood on the earth before Me.

9 ᵃ1 Kin. 4:20, 25 ᵇ2 Sam. 12:24, 25
9 'Behold, a son shall be born to you, who shall be a man of rest; and ᵃI will give him rest from all his enemies on every side; for ᵇhis name shall be Solomon, and I will give peace and quiet to Israel in his days.

10 ᵃ2 Sam. 7:13, 14; 1 Chr. 17:12
10 'ᵃHe shall build a house for My name, and he shall be My son, and I will be his father; and I will establish the throne of his kingdom over Israel forever.'

11 ᵃ1 Chr. 22:16
11 "Now, my son, ᵃthe LORD be with you that you may be successful, and build the house of

---

21:25 The amount was about 300 ounces of gold and paid for the whole property on which the Temple would be built. 2 Sam. 24:24 records only the purchase of the threshingfloor and oxen.
22:2 *foreigners.* Resident alien Canaanites.
22:5 *young and inexperienced.* See note on 1 Kings 3:7.

the Lord your God just as He has spoken concerning you.

12 aKin. 3-9-12; 2 Chr. 1:10 b1 Kin. 2:3

12 "aOnly the Lord give you discretion and understanding, and give you charge over Israel, so that you may bkeep the law of the Lord your God.

13 a1 Chr. 28:7 bJosh. 1:6-9

13 "aThen you shall prosper, if you are careful to observe the statutes and the ordinances which the Lord commanded Moses concerning Israel. bBe strong and courageous, do not fear nor be dismayed.

★**14** a1 Chr. 29:4 b1 Chr. 22:3

14 "Now behold, with great pains I have prepared for the house of the Lord a100,000 talents of gold and 1,000,000 talents of silver, and bbronze and iron beyond weight, for they are in great quantity; also timber and stone I have prepared, and you may add to them.

15 "Moreover, there are many workmen with you, stonecutters and masons of stone and carpenters, and all men who are skillful in every kind of work.

16 a1 Chr. 22:11

16 "Of the gold, the silver and the bronze and the iron, there is no limit. Arise and work, and may athe Lord be with you."

17 a1 Chr. 28:1-6

17 aDavid also commanded all the leaders of Israel to help his son Solomon, saying,

18 a1 Chr. 22:9; 23:25

18 "Is not the Lord your God with you? And ahas He not given you rest on every side? For He has given the inhabitants of the land into my hand, and the land is subdued before the Lord and before His people.

19 a1 Chr. 28:9 b1 Kin. 8:6, 21; 2 Chr. 5:7 c1 Chr. 22:7

19 "Now aset your heart and your soul to seek the Lord your God; arise, therefore, and build the sanctuary of the Lord God, bso that you may bring the ark of the covenant of the Lord, and the holy vessels of God into the house that is to be built cfor the name of the Lord."

23 aNow when David reached old age, bhe made his son Solomon king over Israel.

★**1** a1 Chr. 29:28 b1 Kin. 1:1-40; 2:12; 1 Chr. 28:5; 29:22

E   David's Organization of the Levites, 23:2-26:32

1   Numbering of and duties of the Levites, 23:2-32

2 And he gathered together all the leaders of Israel with the priests and the Levites.

3 And athe Levites were numbered from thirty years old and upward, and btheir number by census of men was 38,000.

★**3** aNum. 4:3-49 bNum. 4:48; 1 Chr. 23:24

4 Of these, 24,000 were ato oversee the work of the house of the Lord; and 6,000 were bofficers and judges,

4 aEzra 3:8, 9 b1 Chr. 26:29

5 and 4,000 were gatekeepers, and a4,000 were praising the Lord with the instruments which David made for giving praise.

★**5** a1 Chr. 15:16

6 And David divided them into divisions aaccording to the sons of Levi: Gershon, Kohath, and Merari.

6 a1 Chr. 6:1

7 Of the Gershonites were Ladan and Shimei.

8 The sons of Ladan were Jehiel the first and Zetham and Joel, three.

9 The sons of Shimei were Shelomoth and Haziel and Haran, three. These were the heads of the fathers' households of Ladan.

10 And the sons of Shimei were Jahath, Zina, Jeush, and Beriah. These four were the sons of Shimei.

11 And Jahath was the first, and Zizah the second; but Jeush and Beriah did not have many sons, so they became a father's household, one class.

12 The sons of Kohath were four: Amram, Izhar, Hebron and Uzziel.

22:14 *100,000 talents of gold.* About 120 million ounces! *1,000,000 talents of silver.* About 1.2 billion ounces! The total value today would amount to 16-17 billion dollars.
23:1 The events surrounding the disputed suc-cession are not included here. See note on 1 Kings 1:33-34.
23:3 *thirty years.* See note on Num. 4:2.
23:5 *the instruments which David made.* He was long remembered for these (Amos 6:5).

13 aEx. 6:20
bEx. 28:1
cEx. 30:6-10

13 [a]The sons of Amram were Aaron and Moses. And [b]Aaron was set apart to sanctify him as most holy, he and his sons forever, [c]to burn incense before the LORD, to minister to Him and to bless in His name forever.

★14 aDeut.
33:1; Ps.
90:title

14 But as for [a]Moses the man of God, his sons were named among the tribe of Levi.

15 The sons of Moses were Gershom and Eliezer.

16 The son of Gershom was Shebuel the chief.

17 And the son of Eliezer was Rehabiah the chief; and Eliezer had no other sons, but the sons of Rehabiah were very many.

18 The son of Izhar was Shelomith the chief.

19 The sons of Hebron were Jeriah the first, Amariah the second, Jahaziel the third and Jekameam the fourth.

20 The sons of Uzziel were Micah the first and Isshiah the second.

21 The sons of Merari were Mahli and Mushi. The sons of Mahli were Eleazar and Kish.

22 And Eleazar died and had no sons, but daughters only, so their brothers, the sons of Kish, took them as wives.

23 The sons of Mushi were three: Mahli, Eder, and Jeremoth.

★24 aNum.
10:17, 21
b1 Chr. 23:3

24 [a]These were the sons of Levi according to their fathers' households, even the heads of the fathers' households of those of them who were counted, in the number of names by their census, doing the work for the service of the house of the LORD, [b]from twenty years old and upward.

25 a1 Chr.
22:18

25 For David said, "The LORD God of Israel [a]has given rest to His people, and He dwells in Jerusalem forever.

26 aNum.
4:5, 15; 7:9;
Deut. 10:8

26 "And also, [a]the Levites will no longer need to carry the tabernacle and all its utensils for its service."

27 For by the last words of David the sons of Levi were numbered, from twenty years old and upward.

28 For their office is to assist the sons of Aaron with the service of the house of the LORD, in the courts and in the chambers and in the purifying of all holy things, even the work of the service of the house of God,

29 [a]and with the showbread, and [b]the fine flour for a grain offering, and unleavened wafers, or [c]what is baked in the pan, or [d]what is well-mixed, and [e]all measures of volume and size.

29 aLev.
24:5-9 bLev.
6:20 c1 Chr.
9:31 dLev.
6:21 eLev.
19:35, 36

30 And they are to stand every morning to thank and to praise the LORD, and likewise at evening,

31 and to offer all burnt offerings to the LORD, [a]on the sabbaths, the new moons and [b]the fixed festivals in the number set by the ordinance concerning them, continually before the LORD.

31 aIs. 1:13,
14 bLev.
23:2-4

32 Thus [a]they are to keep charge of the tent of meeting, and charge of the holy place, and [b]charge of the sons of Aaron their relatives, for the service of the house of the LORD.

32 aNum.
1:53; 1 Chr.
9:27 bNum.
3:6-9, 38

2 Dividing the Levites into 24 groups, 24:1-31

24 Now the divisions of the descendants of Aaron were these: [a]the sons of Aaron were Nadab, Abihu, Eleazar, and Ithamar.

1 aEx. 6:23

2 [a]But Nadab and Abihu died before their father and had no sons. So Eleazar and Ithamar served as priests.

★ 2 aLev.
10:2

3 And David, with [a]Zadok of the sons of Eleazar and Ahime-

★ 3 a1 Chr.
3:31; 6:8

23:14 man of God. I.e., one charged with a mission by God. Cf. Deut. 33:1; Josh. 14:6; Psalm 90 (title); 1 Tim. 6:11.

23:24 Foreseeing the need for added manpower when the Temple would be built, David lowered the age of service to 20.

24:2 Nadab and Abihu died. See note on Lev. 10:1.

24:3 Ahimelech. The son of Abiathar (v. 6) and the grandson of another Ahimelech (1 Sam. 22:20).

lech of the sons of Ithamar, divided them according to their offices for their ministry.

★ 4   **4** Since more chief men were found from the descendants of Eleazar than the descendants of Ithamar, they divided them thus: *there were* sixteen heads of fathers' households of the descendants of Eleazar, and eight of the descendants of Ithamar according to their fathers' households.

5 *a*1 Chr.
24:31   **5** *a*Thus they were divided by lot, the one as the other; for they were officers of the sanctuary and officers of God, both from the descendants of Eleazar and the descendants of Ithamar.

6 *a*1 Chr.
18:16   **6** And Shemaiah, the son of Nethanel the scribe, from the Levites, recorded them in the presence of the king, the princes, Zadok the priest, *a*Ahimelech the son of Abiathar, and the heads of the fathers' *households* of the priests and of the Levites; one father's household taken for Eleazar and one taken for Ithamar.

7 Now the first lot came out for Jehoiarib, the second for Jedaiah,

8 the third for Harim, the fourth for Seorim,

9 the fifth for Malchijah, the sixth for Mijamin,

10 *a*Neh.
12:4; Luke
1:5   **10** the seventh for Hakkoz, the eighth for *a*Abijah,

11 the ninth for Jeshua, the tenth for Shecaniah,

12 the eleventh for Eliashib, the twelfth for Jakim,

13 the thirteenth for Huppah, the fourteenth for Jeshebeab,

14 the fifteenth for Bilgah, the sixteenth for Immer,

15 the seventeenth for Hezir, the eighteenth for Happizzez,

16 the nineteenth for Pethahiah, the twentieth for Jehezkel,

17 the twenty-first for Jachin, the twenty-second for Gamul,

18 the twenty-third for Delaiah, the twenty-fourth for Maaziah.

19 *a*1 Chr.
9:25   **19** *a*These were their offices for their ministry, when *they* came in to the house of the LORD according to the ordinance *given* to them through Aaron their father, just as the LORD God of Israel had commanded him.

20 Now for the rest of the sons of Levi: of the sons of Amram, Shubael; of the sons of Shubael, Jehdeiah.

21 Of Rehabiah: of the sons of Rehabiah, Isshiah the first.

22 Of the Izharites, Shelomoth; of the sons of Shelomoth, Jahath.

23 *a*1 Chr.
23:19   **23** And the sons *a*of *Hebron:* Jeriah *the first,* Amariah the second, Jahaziel the third, Jekameam the fourth.

24 *Of* the sons of Uzziel, Micah; of the sons of Micah, Shamir.

25 The brother of Micah, Isshiah; of the sons of Isshiah, Zechariah.

26 The sons of Merari, Mahli and Mushi; the sons of Jaaziah, Beno.

27 The sons of Merari: by Jaaziah *were* Beno, Shoham, Zaccur, and Ibri.

28 By Mahli: Eleazar, who had no sons.

29 By Kish: the sons of Kish, Jerahmeel.

30 And the sons of Mushi: Mahli, Eder, and Jerimoth. These *were* the sons of the Levites according to their fathers' households.

31 *a*1 Chr.
24:5, 6
*b*1 Chr. 24:6   **31** *a*These also cast lots just as their relatives the sons of Aaron in the presence of David the king, *b*Zadok, Ahimelech, and the heads of the fathers' *households* of the priests and of the Levites— the head of fathers' *households* as

---

24:4 Dividing the priests into 24 groups meant that each group would serve for two weeks out of the year. The way the Jewish year was divided meant that their service would gradually move around the calendar. This arrangement was reinstituted after the exile and continued into N.T. times (see note on Luke 1:5).

well as those of his younger brother.

3 Assigning the musicians, 25:1-31

★ 1 *a*1 Chr. 6:33, 39
*b*2 Kin. 3:15
*c*1 Chr. 15:16

25 Moreover, David and the commanders of the army set apart for the service *some* of the sons of *a*Asaph and of Heman and of Jeduthun, who *were* to *b*prophesy with lyres, *c*harps, and cymbals; and the number of those who performed their service was:

2 Of the sons of Asaph: Zaccur, Joseph, Nethaniah, and Asharelah; the sons of Asaph *were* under the direction of Asaph, who prophesied under the direction of the king.

3 *a*1 Chr. 16:41, 42

3 *a*Of Jeduthun, the sons of Jeduthun: Gedaliah, Zeri, Jeshaiah, Shimei, Hashabiah, and Mattithiah, six, under the direction of their father Jeduthun with the harp, who prophesied in giving thanks and praising the LORD.

★ 4

4 Of Heman, the sons of Heman: Bukkiah, Mattaniah, Uzziel, Shebuel and Jerimoth, Hananiah, Hanani, Eliathah, Giddalti and Romamti-ezer, Joshbekashah, Mallothi, Hothir, Mahazioth.

★ 5 *a*2 Sam. 24:11; 1 Chr. 21:9

5 All these *were* the sons of Heman *a*the king's seer to exalt him according to the words of God, for God gave fourteen sons and three daughters to Heman.

6 *a*1 Chr. 15:16
*b*1 Chr. 15:19

6 All these were under the direction of their father to sing in the house of the LORD, *a*with cymbals, harps and lyres, for the service of the house of God. *b*Asaph, Jeduthun and Heman *were* under the direction of the king.

7 *a*1 Chr. 23:5

7 And their number who were trained in singing to the

LORD, with their relatives, all who were skillful, *was* *a*288.

★ 8 *a*1 Chr. 26:13

8 And *a*they cast lots for their duties, all alike, the small as well as the great, the teacher *as well as* the pupil.

9 Now the first lot came out for Asaph to Joseph, the second for Gedaliah, he with his relatives and sons *were* twelve;

10 the third to Zaccur, his sons and his relatives, twelve;

11 the fourth to Izri, his sons and his relatives, twelve;

12 the fifth to Nethaniah, his sons and his relatives, twelve;

13 the sixth to Bukkiah, his sons and his relatives, twelve;

14 the seventh to Jesharelah, his sons and his relatives, twelve;

15 the eighth to Jeshaiah, his sons and his relatives, twelve;

16 the ninth to Mattaniah, his sons and his relatives, twelve;

17 the tenth to Shimei, his sons and his relatives, twelve;

18 the eleventh to Azarel, his sons and his relatives, twelve;

19 the twelfth to Hashabiah, his sons and his relatives, twelve;

20 for the thirteenth, Shubael, his sons and his relatives, twelve;

21 for the fourteenth, Mattithiah, his sons and his relatives, twelve;

22 for the fifteenth to Jeremoth, his sons and his relatives, twelve;

23 for the sixteenth to Hananiah, his sons and his relatives, twelve;

24 for the seventeenth to Joshbekashah, his sons and his relatives, twelve;

25 for the eighteenth to Ha-

25:1 On these who were appointed chief musicians see 16:5. *who were to prophesy.* Notice that prophecy sometimes was given as poetry and with music (cf. 1 Sam. 10:5).

25:4 Some think that the last nine words are not to be taken as proper names; rather, they relate to Heman's prayer, which goes something like this: "Be gracious, O Lord, be gracious to me. Thou art my God whom I magnify and exalt for helping. Though sitting forlorn, I

have proclaimed highest visions."

25:5 *to exalt him.* This may refer to blowing an actual horn or to the fact that Heman's sons helped him.

25:8 The teachers (skilled ones) were the 288 of verse 7, and the scholars or pupils were the 4,000 of 23:5. They cast lots to determine the order of the 24 groups to match the 24 courses of priests.

nani, his sons and his relatives, twelve;

26 for the nineteenth to Mallothi, his sons and his relatives, twelve;

27 for the twentieth to Eliathah, his sons and his relatives, twelve;

28 for the twenty-first to Hothir, his sons and his relatives, twelve;

29 for the twenty-second to Giddalti, his sons and his relatives, twelve;

30 for the twenty-third to Mahazioth, his sons and his relatives, twelve;

31 for the twenty-fourth to Romamti-ezer, his sons and his relatives, twelve.

4 Appointing guards, 26:1–19

★1 **26** For the divisions of the gatekeepers *there were* of the Korahites, Meshelemiah the son of Kore, of the sons of Asaph.

2 And Meshelemiah had sons: Zechariah the first-born, Jediael the second, Zebadiah the third, Jathniel the fourth,

3 Elam the fifth, Johanan the sixth, Eliehoenai the seventh.

4 And ªObed-edom had sons: Shemaiah the first-born, Jehozabad the second, Joah the third, Sacar the fourth, Nethanel the fifth,

5 Ammiel the sixth, Issachar the seventh, *and* Peullethai the eighth; God had indeed blessed him.

6 Also to his son Shemaiah sons were born who ruled over the house of their father, for they were mighty men of valor.

7 The sons of Shemaiah *were* Othni, Rephael, Obed, and

Elzabad, whose brothers, Elihu and Semachiah, were valiant men.

8 All these *were* of the sons of Obed-edom; they and their sons and their relatives *were* able men with strength for the service, 62 from Obed-edom.

9 And Meshelemiah had sons and relatives, 18 valiant men.

10 Also ªHosah, *one* of the sons of Merari had sons: Shimri the first (although he was not the first-born, his father made him first),

11 Hilkiah the second, Tebaliah the third, Zechariah the fourth; all the sons and relatives of Hosah *were* 13.

12 To these divisions of the gatekeepers, the chief men, *were* given duties like their relatives to minister in the house of the LORD.

13 ªAnd they cast lots, the small and the great alike, according to their fathers' households, for every gate.

14 And the lot to the east fell to Shelemiah. Then they cast lots *for* his son Zechariah, a counselor with insight, and his lot came out to the north.

15 For Obed-edom *it fell* to the south, and to his sons went the storehouse.

16 For Shuppim and Hosah *it was* to the west, by the gate of Shallecheth, on the ascending highway. Guard corresponded to guard.

17 On the east there were six Levites, on the north four daily, on the south four daily, and at the storehouse two by two.

18 At the ªParbar on the west *there were* four at the highway and two at the Parbar.

19 These were the divisions of the gatekeepers of the sons of Korah and of the sons of Merari.

Marginal references:

4 ª2 Sam. 6:11; 1 Chr. 13:14

10 ª1 Chr. 16:38

13 ª1 Chr. 24:5, 31; 25:8

★14

★18 ª2 Kin. 23:11

26:1 Four thousand (23:5) *gatekeepers* were involved in guarding the Temple day and night to prevent unauthorized persons from entering and profaning it. Various numbers of leaders of these gatekeepers are mentioned in vv.

8, 9, 11 and 9:22.

26:14 They cast lots to determine which gates would be guarded by whom.

26:18 *Parbar.* Probably some kind of cloistered area on the W. side of the temple area.

5 Assigning the treasures, 26:20-28

20 And the Levites, their relatives, had ª charge of the treasures of the house of God, and of the treasures of the dedicated gifts. **21** The sons of Ladan, the sons of the Gershonites belonging to Ladan, namely, the Jehielites, were the heads of the fathers' households, belonging to Ladan the Gershonite. **22** The sons of Jehieli, Zetham and Joel his brother, had charge of the treasures of the house of the LORD. **23** As for the Amramites, the Izharites, the Hebronites, and the Uzzielites, **24** Shebuel the son of Gershom, the son of Moses, was officer over the treasures. **25** And his relatives by Eliezer were Rehabiah his son, Jeshaiah his son, Joram his son, Zichri his son, and Shelomoth his son. **26** This Shelomoth and his relatives had charge of all the treasures of the dedicated gifts, ª which King David and the heads of the fathers' households, the commanders of thousands and hundreds, and commanders of the army, had dedicated. **27** They dedicated part of the spoil won in battles to repair the house of the LORD. **28** And all that Samuel the seer had dedicated and Saul the son of Kish, Abner the son of Ner and Joab the son of Zeruiah, everyone who had dedicated anything, all of this was in the care of Shelomoth and his relatives.

6 Delegating magistrates, 26:29-32

29 As for the Izharites, Chenaniah and his sons ª were assigned to outside duties for Israel, as ᵇ officers and judges. **30** As for the Hebronites, ª Hashabiah and his relatives, 1,700 capable men, had charge of the affairs of Israel west of the Jordan, for all the work of the LORD and the service of the king. **31** As for the Hebronites, ª Jerijah the chief (these Hebronites were investigated according to their genealogies and fathers' households, in the fortieth year of David's reign, and men of outstanding capability were found among them at ᵇ Jazer of Gilead) **32** and his relatives, capable men, were 2,700 in number, heads of fathers' households. And King David made them overseers of the Reubenites, the Gadites and the half-tribe of the Manassites ª concerning all the affairs of God and of the king.

F David's Civil Leaders, 27:1-34

27 Now this is the enumeration of the sons of Israel, the heads of fathers' households, the commanders of thousands and of hundreds, and their officers who served the king in all the affairs of the divisions which came in and went out month by month throughout all the months of the year, each division numbering 24,000.

26:20 treasures of the house of God. Ordinary revenues that came to the Temple from prescribed contributions and special gifts (Lev. 27; Num. 18:16; 1 Chron. 29:7-8). treasures of the dedicated gifts. See verses 26-28; 18:11 and 2 Chron. 5:1.

26:29 officers and judges. Scribes or secretaries and magistrates who adjudicated cases on the basis of the law, and who were likely involved in the collection of taxes and tithes. Altogether there were 6,000 (23:4).

27:1-15 David had an army of 288,000 men, consisting of twelve divisions of 24,000 men, each of which served in turn for one month out of the year. Eight of the twelve generals belonged to the tribe of Judah.

★20 ª1 Chr. 26:22, 24, 26; 28:12; Ezra 2:69

26 ª2 Sam. 8:11

★29 ªNeh. 11:16 ᵇ1 Chr. 23:4

30 ª1 Chr. 27:17

31 ª1 Chr. 23:19 ᵇ1 Chr. 6:81

32 ª2 Chr. 19:11

★ 1-15

2 ^a2 Sam. 23:8-30; 1 Chr. 11:11-31

2 Jashobeam the son of Zabdiel ^ahad charge of the first division for the first month; and in his division *were* 24,000.

3 *He was* from the sons of Perez, *and was* chief of all the commanders of the army for the first month.

4 Dodai the Ahohite and his division had charge of the division for the second month, Mikloth *being* the chief officer; and in his division *were* 24,000.

5 The third commander of the army for the third month *was* Benaiah, the son of Jehoiada the priest, *as* chief; and in his division *were* 24,000.

6 This Benaiah *was* the mighty man of the thirty, and had charge of thirty; and over his division was Ammizabad his son.

7 The fourth for the fourth month *was* Asahel the brother of Joab, and Zebadiah his son after him; and in his division *were* 24,000.

8 The fifth for the fifth month *was* the commander Shamhuth the Izrahite; and in his division *were* 24,000.

9 The sixth for the sixth month *was* Ira the son of Ikkesh the Tekoite; and in his division *were* 24,000.

10 The seventh for the seventh month *was* Helez the Pelonite of the sons of Ephraim; and in his division *were* 24,000.

11 The eighth for the eighth month *was* Sibbecai the Hushathite of the Zerahites; and in his division *were* 24,000.

12 The ninth for the ninth month *was* Abiezer the Anathothite of the Benjamites; and in his division *were* 24,000.

13 The tenth for the tenth month *was* Maharai the Netophathite of the Zerahites; and in his division *were* 24,000.

14 The eleventh for the eleventh month *was* Benaiah the Pirathonite of the sons of Ephraim; and in his division *were* 24,000.

15 The twelfth for the twelfth month *was* Heldai the Netophathite of Othniel; and in his division *were* 24,000.

16 Now in charge of the tribes of Israel: chief officer for the Reubenites was Eliezer the son of Zichri; for the Simeonites, Shephatiah the son of Maacah;

17 for Levi, Hashabiah the son of Kemuel; for Aaron, Zadok;

18 for Judah, Elihu, *one* of David's brothers; for Issachar, Omri the son of Michael;

19 for Zebulun, Ishmaiah the son of Obadiah; for Naphtali, Jeremoth the son of Azriel;

20 for the sons of Ephraim, Hoshea the son of Azaziah; for the half-tribe of Manasseh, Joel the son of Pedaiah;

21 for the half-tribe of Manasseh in Gilead, Iddo the son of Zechariah; for Benjamin, Jaasiel the son of Abner;

22 for Dan, Azarel the son of Jeroham. ^aThese *were* the princes of the tribes of Israel.

22 ^a1 Chr. 28:1

23 But David did not count those twenty years of age and under, ^abecause the LORD had said He would multiply Israel ^bas the stars of heaven.

✶23 ^a1 Chr. 21:2-5 ^bGen. 15:5; 22:17; 26:4

24 Joab the son of Zeruiah had begun to count *them*, but did not finish; and because of ^athis, wrath came upon Israel, and the number was not included in the account of the chronicles of King David.

✶24 ^a2 Sam. 24:12-15; 1 Chr. 21:1-7

25 Now Azmaveth the son of Adiel had charge of the king's storehouses. And Jonathan the son of Uzziah had charge of the storehouses in the country, in the cities, in the villages, and in the towers.

✶25-31

27:23 David only took a census of the fighting men (cf. Num. 1:3), but even this showed lack of faith in God's power to protect his kingdom. To have numbered all the people would have displayed doubt in God's promise (Gen.

22:17).
27:24 See note on 21:1.
27:25-31 These acted as overseers of David's estates and properties.

26 And Ezri the son of Chelub had charge of the agricultural workers who tilled the soil.

27 And Shimei the Ramathite had charge of the vineyards; and Zabdi the Shiphmite had charge of the produce of the vineyards *stored* in the wine cellars.

28 And Baal-hanan the Gederite had charge of the olive and *a*sycamore trees in the Shephelah; and Joash had charge of the stores of oil.

29 And Shitrai the Sharonite had charge of the cattle which were grazing in *a*Sharon; and Shaphat the son of Adlai had charge of the cattle in the valleys.

30 And Obil the Ishmaelite had charge of the camels; and Jehdeiah the Meronothite had charge of the donkeys.

31 And Jaziz the *a*Hagrite had charge of the flocks. All these were overseers of the property which belonged to King David.

32 Also Jonathan, David's uncle, *was* a counselor, a man of understanding, and a scribe; and Jehiel the son of Hachmoni tutored the king's sons.

33 And *a*Ahithophel was counselor to the king; and *b*Hushai the Archite was the king's friend.

34 And Jehoiada the son of *a*Benaiah, and *b*Abiathar succeeded Ahithophel; and Joab was the *c*commander of the king's army.

G David's Last Instructions to the People and to Solomon, 28:1-21

28 Now *a*David assembled at Jerusalem all the officials of Israel, the princes of the tribes, and the commanders of the divisions that served the king, and the commanders of thousands, and the commanders of hun-

dreds, and the overseers of all the property and livestock belonging to the king and his sons, with the officials and *b*the mighty men, even all the valiant men.

2 Then King David rose to his feet and said, "Listen to me, my brethren and my people; I *a*had intended to build a permanent home for the ark of the covenant of the Lord and for *b*the footstool of our God. So I had made preparations to build *it*.

3 "But God said to me, '*a*You shall not build a house for My name because you are a man of war and have shed blood.'

4 "Yet, the Lord, the God of Israel, *a*chose me from all the house of my father to be king over Israel *b*forever. For *c*He has chosen Judah to be a leader; and *d*in the house of Judah, my father's house, and among the sons of my father He took pleasure in me to make *me* king over all Israel.

5 "And *a*of all my sons (for the Lord has given me many sons), *b*He has chosen my son Solomon to sit on the throne of the kingdom of the Lord over Israel.

6 "And He said to me, 'Your son *a*Solomon is the one who shall build My house and My courts; for I have chosen him to be a son to Me, and I will be a father to him.

7 'And I will establish his kingdom forever, *a*if he resolutely performs My commandments and My ordinances, as is done now.'

8 "So now, in the sight of all Israel, the assembly of the Lord, and in the hearing of our God, observe and seek after all the commandments of the Lord your God in order that you may possess the good land and bequeath *it* to your sons after you forever.

9 "As for you, my son Solomon, know the God of your father, and *a*serve Him with a whole

28 *a*1 Kin. 10:27; 2 Chr. 1:15

29 *a*1 Chr. 5:16

31 *a*1 Chr. 5:10

★32-34

33 *a*2 Sam. 15:12 *b*2 Sam. 15:32, 37

34 *a*1 Chr. 27:5 *b*1 Kin. 1:7 *c*1 Chr. 11:6

1 *a*1 Chr. 23:2; 27:1-31 *b*1 Chr. 11:10-47

★2 *a*1 Chr. 17:1, 2 *b*Ps. 132:7; Is. 66:1

3 *a*1 Chr. 22:8

4 *a*1 Sam. 16:6-13 *b*1 Chr. 17:23, 27 *c*Gen. 49:8-10; 1 Chr. 5:2 *d*1 Sam. 16:1

★5 *a*1 Chr. 3:1-9; 14:3-7 *b*1 Chr. 22:9, 10

6 *a*2 Sam. 7:13, 14

7 *a*1 Chr. 22:13

9 *a*1 Kin. 8:61; 1 Chr. 29:17-19 *b*1 Sam. 16:7 *c*2 Chr. 15:2; Jer. 29:13

27:32-34 These were the king's close counselors.
28:2 *the footstool of our God.* The mercy seat of the Ark.

28:5 *the kingdom of the Lord.* The king was only God's deputy in His kingdom.

heart and a willing mind; [b]for the LORD searches all hearts, and understands every intent of the thoughts. [c]If you seek Him, He will let you find Him; but if you forsake Him, He will reject you forever.

10 [a]1 Chr. 22:13

10 "Consider now, for the LORD has chosen you to build a house for the sanctuary; [a]be courageous and act."

11 [a]Ex. 25:40; 1 Chr. 28:12, 19
[b]1 Kin. 6:3
[c]Ex. 25:17-22

11 Then David gave to his son Solomon [a]the plan of [b]the porch of the temple, its buildings, its storehouses, its upper rooms, its inner rooms, and [c]the room for the mercy seat;

12 [a]1 Chr. 26:20, 28

12 and the plan of all that he had in mind, for the courts of the house of the LORD, and for all the surrounding rooms, for [a]the storehouses of the house of God, and for the storehouses of the dedicated things;

13 [a]1 Chr. 24:1 [b]1 Chr. 23:6

13 also for [a]the divisions of the priests and [b]the Levites and for all the work of the service of the house of the LORD and for all the utensils of service in the house of the LORD;

14 for the golden *utensils*, the weight of gold for all utensils for every kind of service; for the silver utensils, the weight *of silver* for all utensils for every kind of service;

15 [a]Ex. 25:31-39

15 and the weight *of gold* for the [a]golden lampstands and their golden lamps, with the weight of each lampstand and its lamps; and *the weight of silver* for the silver lampstands, with the weight of each lampstand and its lamps according to the use of each lampstand;

16 and the gold by weight for the tables of showbread, for each table; and silver for the silver tables;

17 and the forks, the basins, and the pitchers of pure gold; and for the golden bowls with the weight for each bowl; and for the silver bowls with the weight for each bowl;

18 [a]Ex. 30:1-10 [b]Ex. 25:18-22

18 and for [a]the altar of incense refined gold by weight; and gold for the model of the chariot, even [b]the cherubim, that spread out *their wings*, and covered the ark of the covenant of the LORD.

*19 [a]1 Chr. 28:11, 12

19 "All *this*," said David, "the LORD made me understand in writing by His hand upon me, [a]all the details of this pattern."

20 [a]1 Chr. 22:13 [b]Josh. 1:5; Heb. 13:5

20 Then David said to his son Solomon, "[a]Be strong and courageous, and act; do not fear nor be dismayed, for the LORD God, my God, is with you. [b]He will not fail you nor forsake you until all the work for the service of the house of the LORD is finished.

21 [a]1 Chr. 28:13 [b]Ex. 35:25-35; 36:1, 2

21 "Now behold, [a]there are the divisions of the priests and the Levites for all the service of the house of God, and [b]every willing man of any skill will be with you in all the work for all kinds of service. The officials also and all the people will be entirely at your command."

H David's Offerings and Worship, 29:1-21

*1 [a]1 Chr. 22:5 [b]1 Chr. 29:19

29 Then King David said to the entire assembly, "My son Solomon, whom alone God has chosen, [a]is still young and inexperienced and the work is great; for [b]the temple is not for man, but for the LORD God.

2 [a]1 Chr. 22:3-5

2 "Now [a]with all my ability I have provided for the house of my God the gold for the *things of* gold, and the silver for the *things of* silver, and the bronze for the *things of* bronze, the iron for the *things of* iron, and wood for the *things of* wood, onyx stones and inlaid *stones*, stones of antimony, and stones of various colors, and all kinds of precious stones, and alabaster in abundance.

28:19 Apparently David, in a vision, had seen the entire edifice and had sketched it for Solomon.

29:1 *young and inexperienced*. See note on 1 Kings 3:7.

3 "And moreover, in my delight in the house of my God, the treasure I have of gold and silver, I give to the house of my God, over and above all that I have already provided for the holy temple,

4 namely, [a]3,000 talents of gold, of [b]the gold of Ophir, and 7,000 talents of refined silver, to overlay the walls of the buildings;

5 of gold for the things of gold, and of silver for the things of silver, that is, for all the work done by the craftsmen. Who then is willing to consecrate himself this day to the LORD?"

6 Then [a]the rulers of the fathers' households, and the princes of the tribes of Israel, and the commanders of thousands and of hundreds, with [b]the overseers over the king's work, offered willingly;

7 and for the service for the house of God they gave 5,000 talents and 10,000 [a]darics of gold, and 10,000 talents of silver, and 18,000 talents of brass, and 100,000 talents of iron.

8 And whoever possessed precious stones gave them to the treasury of the house of the LORD, in care of [a]Jehiel the Gershonite.

9 Then the people rejoiced because they had offered so willingly, for they had made their offering to the LORD [a]with a whole heart, and King David also rejoiced greatly.

10 So David blessed the LORD in the sight of all the assembly; and David said, "Blessed art Thou, O LORD God of Israel our father, forever and ever.

11 "[a]Thine, O LORD, is the greatness and the power and the glory and the victory and the majesty, indeed everything that is in the heavens and the earth; Thine is the dominion, O LORD, and

Thou dost exalt Thyself as head over all.

12 "[a]Both riches and honor come from Thee, and Thou dost rule over all, and [b]in Thy hand is power and might; and it lies in Thy hand to make great, and to strengthen everyone.

13 "Now therefore, our God, we thank Thee, and praise Thy glorious name.

14 "But who am I and who are my people that we should be able to offer as generously as this? For all things come from Thee, and from Thy hand we have given Thee.

15 "For [a]we are sojourners before Thee, and tenants, as all our fathers were; [b]our days on the earth are like a shadow, and there is no hope.

16 "O LORD our God, all this abundance that we have provided to build Thee a house for Thy holy name, it is from Thy hand, and all is Thine.

17 "Since I know, O my God, that [a]Thou triest the heart and [b]delightest in uprightness, I, in the integrity of my heart, have willingly offered all these things; so now with joy I have seen Thy people, who are present here, make their offerings willingly to Thee.

18 "O LORD, the God of Abraham, Isaac, and Israel, our fathers, preserve this forever in the intentions of the heart of Thy people, and direct their heart to Thee;

19 "and [a]give to my son Solomon a perfect heart to keep Thy commandments, Thy testimonies, and Thy statutes, and to do them all, and [b]to build the temple, for which I have made provision."

20 Then David said to all the assembly, "Now bless the LORD your God." And [a]all the assembly blessed the LORD, the God of their

---

★ 4 [a]1 Chr. 22:14 [b]1 Kin. 9:28

6 [a]1 Chr. 27:1; 28:1 [b]1 Chr. 27:25-31

★ 7 [a]Ezra 2:69; Neh. 7:70

8 [a]1 Chr. 23:8

★ 9 [a]1 Kin. 8:61; 2 Cor. 9:7

11 [a]Matt. 6:13; Rev. 5:13

12 [a]2 Chr. 1:12 [b]2 Chr. 20:6

15 [a]Lev. 25:23 [b]Job 14:2, 10-12

17 [a]1 Chr. 28:9 [b]Ps. 15:2

19 [a]1 Chr. 28:9; Ps. 72:1 [b]1 Chr. 29:1, 2

20 [a]Josh. 22:33 [b]Ex. 4:31

29:4 The gold was about 3.6 million ounces and the silver about 8.4 million ounces. On Ophir see note on 1 Kings 9:28. to overlay. See 2 Chron. 3:4-8.
29:7 5,000 talents. About 6 million ounces. 10,000 darics. About 45,500 ounces (see note

on Ezra 2:69). The silver amounted to about 12 million ounces. The brass equalled approximately 1.35 million lbs., and the iron, 7.5 million lbs. (3,750 tons).
29:9 they had offered so willingly. An attitude in giving which pleases God (2 Cor. 9:7).

fathers, and [b]bowed low and did homage to the Lord and to the king.

21 And on the next day [a]they made sacrifices to the Lord and offered burnt offerings to the Lord, 1,000 bulls, 1,000 rams *and* 1,000 lambs, with their libations and sacrifices in abundance for all Israel.

21 [a]1 Kin. 8:62, 63

IV THE ACCESSION OF SOLOMON AND DEATH OF DAVID, 29:22-30

★22 [a]1 Chr. 23:1 [b]1 Kin. 1:33-39

22 So they ate and drank that day before the Lord with great gladness.

And they made Solomon the son of David king [a]a second time, and they [b]anointed *him* as ruler for the Lord and Zadok as priest.

23 [a]1 Kin. 2:12

23 Then [a]Solomon sat on the throne of the Lord as king instead of David his father; and he prospered, and all Israel obeyed him.

24 And all the officials, the mighty men, and also all the sons of King David pledged allegiance to King Solomon.

25 And [a]the Lord highly exalted Solomon in the sight of all Israel, and [b]bestowed on him royal majesty which had not been on any king before him in Israel.

25 [a]2 Chr. 1:1 [b]1 Kin. 3:13; 2 Chr. 1:12

26 Now [a]David the son of Jesse reigned over all Israel.

26 [a]1 Chr. 18:14

27 [a]And the period which he reigned over Israel *was* forty years; he reigned in Hebron seven years and in Jerusalem thirty-three *years.*

27 [a]2 Sam. 5:4, 5; 1 Kin. 2:11; 1 Chr. 3:4

28 Then he died in [a]a ripe old age, [b]full of days, riches and honor; and his son Solomon reigned in his place.

28 [a]Gen. 15:15; Acts 13:36 [b]1 Chr. 23:1

29 Now the acts of King David, from first to last, are written in the chronicles of [a]Samuel the seer, in the chronicles of [b]Nathan the prophet, and in the chronicles of [c]Gad the seer,

★29 [a]1 Sam. 9:9 [b]2 Sam. 7:2-4; 12:1-7 [c]1 Sam. 22:5

30 with all his reign, his power, and the circumstances which came on him, on Israel, and on all the kingdoms of the lands.

29:22 *a second time.* The same as 23:1, the first time being related in 1 Kings 1:33. *Zadok* was confirmed as high priest, Abiathar having disqualified himself by being involved in plots (see note on 1 Kings 2:26-27).

29:29 These refer to source materials used in compiling Chronicles.

INTRODUCTION TO
THE SECOND BOOK OF THE CHRONICLES

AUTHOR: Ezra   DATE: 450–425 B.C.

Title, Authorship, Purpose   *Since 1 and 2 Chronicles were originally one book, see the Introduction to 1 Chronicles for a discussion of these matters.*

Contents   *Beginning where 1 Chronicles concludes, 2 Chronicles records the history of the reign of King Solomon (971–931) and of all the kings of Judah from Rehoboam (931) through Zedekiah (586). Thus the book covers the same period as 1 and 2 Kings, though 2 Chronicles focuses only on the kings of Judah and excludes those of Israel. Disobedience to the Mosaic Law was the reason for the Babylonian captivity. The book concludes with a brief reference to the decree of Cyrus in 539 which permitted the Jews to return to Judea and build their Temple.*

Significant passages include Solomon's prayer for wisdom (1:7–12), the dedication of Solomon's magnificent Temple (chaps. 5–7), the visit of the Queen of Sheba (9:1–12), and the prediction of the length of the captivity (36:20–21). Favorite verses are found in 7:14 and 16:9.

OUTLINE OF 2 CHRONICLES

I. **The Reign of Solomon, 1:1–9:31**
  A. Solomon's Inauguration, 1:1–17
    1. His worship and prayer for wisdom,
      1:1–13
    2. His wealth, 1:14–17
  B. Solomon's Temple, 2:1–7:22
    1. Preparations for the Temple, 2:1–18
    2. Construction of the Temple, 3:1–4:22
    3. Dedication of the Temple, 5:1–7:22
      a. Installing the Ark, 5:1–14
      b. Speaking to the people, 6:1–11
      c. Praying to God, 6:12–42
      d. God's glory, 7:1–3
      e. The sacrifices and feast, 7:4–11
      f. God speaks to Solomon, 7:12–22
  C. Solomon's Fame, 8:1–9:28
    1. His cities, 8:1–6
    2. His subjects, 8:7–11
    3. His offerings, 8:12–13
    4. His organization of the Levites, 8:14–16
    5. His navy, 8:17–18
    6. His visit from the queen of Sheba,
      9:1–12
    7. His wealth, 9:13–28
  D. Solomon's Death, 9:29–31
II. **The Kings of Judah, 10:1–36:21**
  A. Rehoboam (931–913; 1 Kings 14:21–31),
    10:1–12:16
    1. Rehoboam causes division, 10:1–19
    2. Rehoboam follows the Lord, 11:1–23
    3. Rehoboam forsakes the Lord, 12:1–16
  B. Abijah (Abijam, 913–911; 1 Kings 15:1–8),
    13:1–22
  C. Asa (911–870; 1 Kings 15:9–24), 14:1–16:14
    1. Early reforms, 14:1–8
    2. War with Ethiopians, 14:9–15
    3. Reliance on the Lord, 15:1–19
    4. War with Baasha of Israel, 16:1–10

    5. Death, 16:11–14
  D. Jehoshaphat (873–848; 1 Kings 22:41–50),
    17:1–20:37
    1. His revival, 17:1–19
    2. His alliance with Ahab, 18:1–19:3
    3. His reforms, 19:4–11
    4. His victory over Moab and Ammon,
      20:1–30
    5. His last days, 20:31–37
  E. Jehoram (Joram, 848–841; 2 Kings 8:16–24),
    21:1–20
  F. Ahaziah (841; 2 Kings 8:25–29), 22:1–9
  G. Athaliah (841–835; 2 Kings 11:1–16),
    22:10–23:15
  H. Joash (Jehoash, 835–796; 2 Kings 13:10–25),
    23:16–24:27
    1. Following the Lord, 23:16–24:16
    2. Forsaking the Lord, 24:17–27
  I. Amaziah (796–767; 2 Kings 14:1–22),
    25:1–28
    1. Following the Lord, 25:1–13
    2. Forsaking the Lord, 25:14–28
  J. Uzziah (Azariah, 790–739; 2 Kings 15:1–7),
    26:1–23
    1. Following the Lord, 26:1–15
    2. Forsaking the Lord, 26:16–23
  K. Jotham (750–731; 2 Kings 15:32–38), 27:1–9
  L. Ahaz (731–715; 2 Kings 16:1–20), 28:1–27
  M. Hezekiah (715–686; 2 Kings 18:1–20:21),
    29:1–32:33
    1. His revival, 29:1–31:21
    2. His victory over the Assyrians, 32:1–23
    3. His last days, 32:24–33
  N. Manasseh (695–642; 2 Kings 21:1–18),
    33:1–20
  O. Amon (642–640; 2 Kings 21:19–26),
    33:21–25

P. Josiah (640–609; 2 Kings 22:1–23:30), 34:1–35:27
  1. His reforms, 34:1–13
  2. His discovery of the law, 34:14–33
  3. His observance of the Passover, 35:1–19
  4. His death, 35:20–27
Q. Joahaz (609; 2 Kings 23:31–33), 36:1–4

R. Jehoiakim (Eliakim, 609–597; 2 Kings 23:34–24:7), 36:5–8
S. Jehoiachin (597; 2 Kings 24:8–16), 36:9–10
T. Zedekiah (597–586, 2 Kings 24:17–25:21), 36:11–21
III. The Decree of Cyrus, 36:22–23

THE SECOND BOOK OF THE CHRONICLES

I THE REIGN OF SOLOMON, 1:1–9:31
A Solomon's Inauguration, 1:1–17

1 His worship and prayer for wisdom, 1:1–13

1 Now ªSolomon the son of David established himself securely over his kingdom, and the LORD his God *was* with him and ᵇexalted him greatly.

2 And Solomon spoke to all Israel, ªto the commanders of thousands and of hundreds and to the judges and to every leader in all Israel, the heads of the fathers' *households.*

3 Then Solomon, and all the assembly with him, went to ªthe high place which was at Gibeon; ᵇfor God's tent of meeting was there, which Moses the servant of the LORD had made in the wilderness.

4 However, David had brought up ªthe ark of God from Kiriath-jearim to ᵇthe place he had prepared for it; for he had pitched a tent for it in Jerusalem.

5 Now ªthe bronze altar, which Bezalel the son of Uri, the son of Hur, had made, was there before the tabernacle of the LORD, and Solomon and the assembly sought it out.

6 And Solomon went up there before the LORD to the bronze altar which *was* at the tent of meeting, and ªoffered a thousand burnt offerings on it.

7 ªIn that night God appeared to Solomon and said to him, "Ask what I shall give you."

8 And Solomon said to God, "Thou hast dealt with my father David with great lovingkindness, and ªhast made me king in his place.

9 "Now, O LORD God, ªThy promise to my father David is fulfilled; for Thou hast made me king over ᵇa people as numerous as the dust of the earth.

10 "ªGive me now wisdom and knowledge, ᵇthat I may go out and come in before this people; for who can rule this great people of Thine?"

11 ªAnd God said to Solomon, "Because you had this in mind, and did not ask for riches, wealth, or honor, or the life of those who hate you, nor have you even asked for long life, but you have asked for yourself wisdom and knowledge, that you may rule My people, over whom I have made you king,

12 wisdom and knowledge have been granted to you. And ªI will give you riches and wealth and honor, such as none of the kings who were before you has possessed, nor those who will come after you."

★ **1** ª1 Kin. 2:12, 46 ᵇ1 Chr. 29:25
2 ª1 Chr. 28:1
★ **3** ª1 Kin. 3:4 ᵇEx. 36:8
★ **4** ª1 Chr. 15:25-28 ᵇ2 Chr. 6:2
★ **5** ªEx. 31:9; 38:1-7
6 ª1 Kin. 3:4
7 ª1 Kin. 3:5-14
8 ª1 Chr. 28:5
9 ª2 Sam. 7:12-16 ᵇGen. 13:16; 22:17; 28:14
★ **10** ª1 Kin. 3:9 ᵇNum. 27:17; 2 Sam. 5:2
11 ª1 Kin. 3:11
12 ª1 Chr. 29:25; 2 Chr. 9:22

1:1 *established himself.* Solomon firmly grasped the reigns of power. The details of how he did this are in 1 Kings 1–2 (note 2:46).
1:3 The tabernacle was at Gibeon (6 miles NW. of Jerusalem; 1 Chron. 16:39), though the Ark was at Jerusalem (v. 4).
1:4 See notes on 1 Chron. 15.
1:5 *the bronze altar.* See note on Exod. 27:1–8.
1:10 Solomon's *wisdom* (the ability to apply knowledge correctly) was unique (1 Kings 3:12).

13 [a]2 Chr. 1:3

13 [a]So Solomon went from the high place which was at Gibeon, from the tent of meeting, to Jerusalem, and he reigned over Israel.

2 His wealth, 1:14-17

14 [a]1 Kin. 10:26-29
[b]1 Kin. 4:26
[c]1 Kin. 9:19

14 [a]And Solomon amassed chariots and horsemen. [b]He had 1,400 chariots, and 12,000 horsemen, and he stationed them in [c]the chariot cities and with the king at Jerusalem.

15 [a]1 Kin. 10:27 [b]Deut. 17:17

15 And [a]the king made [b]silver and gold as plentiful in Jerusalem as stones, and he made cedars as plentiful as sycamores in the lowland.

★**16** [a]Deut. 17:16

16 And Solomon's [a]horses were imported from Egypt and from Kue; the king's traders procured them from Kue for a price.

★**17**

17 And they imported chariots from Egypt for 600 shekels of silver apiece, and horses for 150 apiece, and by the same means they exported them to all the kings of the Hittites and the kings of Aram.

B Solomon's Temple, 2:1-7:22

1 Preparations for the Temple, 2:1-18

1 [a]1 Kin. 5:5

2 [a]Now Solomon decided to build a house for the name of the Lord, and a royal palace for himself.

★**2** [a]1 Kin. 5:15, 16; 2 Chr. 2:18

2 So [a]Solomon assigned 70,000 men to carry loads, and 80,000 men to quarry stone in the mountains, and 3,600 to supervise them.

★**3** [a]1 Kin. 5:2-11 [b]1 Chr. 14:1

3 [a]Then Solomon sent word to Huram the king of Tyre, saying, "[b]As you dealt with David my father, and sent him cedars to build him a house to dwell in, so do for me.

4 "Behold, I am about to build a house for the name of the Lord my God, dedicating it to Him, [a]to burn fragrant incense before Him, and to set out [b]the showbread continually, and to offer [c]burnt offerings morning and evening, [d]on sabbaths and on new moons and on the appointed feasts of the Lord our God, this being required forever in Israel.

4 [a]Ex. 30:7
[b]Ex. 25:30
[c]Ex. 29:38-42 [d]Num. 28:9, 10

5 "And the house which I am about to build will be great; for [a]greater is our God than all the gods.

5 [a]Ex. 15:11; 1 Chr. 16:25

6 "But [a]who is able to build a house for Him, for the heavens and the highest heavens cannot contain Him? So who am I, that I should build a house for Him, except to burn incense before Him?

★**6** [a]1 Kin. 8:27; 2 Chr. 6:18

7 "And now [a]send me a skilled man to work in gold, silver, brass and iron, and in purple, crimson and violet fabrics, and who knows how to make engravings, to work with the skilled men [b]whom I have in Judah and Jerusalem, whom David my father provided.

7 [a]Ex. 31:3-5; 2 Chr. 2:13, 14 [b]1 Chr. 22:15

8 "[a]Send me also cedar, cypress and algum timber from Lebanon, for I know that your servants know how to cut timber of Lebanon; and indeed, [b]my servants will work with your servants,

★**8** [a]1 Kin. 5:6 [b]2 Chr. 9:10, 11

9 to prepare timber in abundance for me, for the house which I am about to build will be great and wonderful.

10 "Now behold, [a]I will give to your servants, the woodsmen who cut the timber, 20,000 kors of crushed wheat, and 20,000 kors of barley, and 20,000 baths of wine, and 20,000 baths of oil."

★**10** [a]1 Kin. 5:11

1:16 Buying so many horses was prohibited by the law (Deut. 17:16). and from Kue. Cilicia, in SE. Asia Minor.
1:17 See note on 1 Kings 10:29.
2:2 These were resident aliens (see note on 1 Chron. 22:2).
2:3 Huram. A variant form of Hiram. See note on 1 Kings 5:1.

2:6 With great humility Solomon realized that the omnipresent God could not be confined to a Temple, but rather that the Temple served as a place in which His people could worship Him.
2:8 algum. See note on 1 Kings 10:10-11.
2:10 A bath was about 5.8 gallons.

11 Then Huram, king of Tyre, answered in a letter sent to Solomon: "[a]Because the LORD loves His people, He has made you king over them."

12 Then Huram continued, "Blessed be [a]the LORD, the God of Israel, who has made heaven and earth, who has given King David a wise son, endowed with discretion and understanding, [b]who will build a house for the LORD and a royal palace for himself.

13 "And now I am sending a skilled man, endowed with understanding, Huram-abi;

14 [a]the son of a Danite woman and a Tyrian father, who knows how to work in gold, silver, bronze, iron, stone and wood, *and* in purple, violet, linen and crimson fabrics, and *who knows how* to make all kinds of engravings and to execute any design which may be assigned to him, *to work* with your skilled men, and with those of my lord David your father.

15 "Now then, let my lord send to his servants wheat and barley, oil and wine, of [a]which he has spoken.

16 "And [a]we will cut whatever timber you need from Lebanon, and bring it to you on rafts by sea to Joppa, so that you may carry it up to Jerusalem."

17 And Solomon numbered all the aliens who *were* in the land of Israel, [a]following the census which his father David had taken; and 153,600 were found.

18 [a]And he appointed 70,000 of them to carry loads, and 80,000 to quarry *stones* in the mountains, and 3,600 supervisors to make the people work.

2 Construction of the Temple, 3:1–4:22

3 [a]Then Solomon began to build the house of the LORD in Jerusalem on Mount Moriah, where *the* LORD had appeared to his father David, at the place that David had prepared, [b]on the threshing floor of Ornan the Jebusite.

2 And he began to build on the second *day* in the second month of the fourth year of his reign.

3 Now these are the foundations which [a]Solomon laid for building the house of God. The length in cubits, according to the old standard *was* sixty cubits, and the width twenty cubits.

4 And the porch which was in front of the house [a]was as long as the width of the house, twenty cubits, and the height 120; and inside he overlaid it with pure gold.

5 And he overlaid [a]the main room with cypress wood and overlaid it with fine gold, and ornamented it with palm trees and chains.

6 Further, he adorned the house with precious stones; and the gold was gold from Parvaim.

7 [a]He also overlaid the house with gold—the beams, the thresholds, and its walls, and its doors; and he [b]carved cherubim on the walls.

8 Now he made [a]the room of the holy of holies: its length, across the width of the house, *was* twenty cubits, and its width *was* twenty cubits; and he overlaid it with fine gold, *amounting* to 600 talents.

Marginal references:

11 [a]1 Kin. 10:9; 2 Chr. 9:8

12 [a]Ps. 33:6; 102:25 [b]2 Chr. 2:1

★**13**

★**14** [a]1 Kin. 7:14

15 [a]2 Chr. 2:10

16 [a]1 Kin. 5:8, 9

17 [a]1 Chr. 22:2

18 [a]2 Chr. 2:2

★ **1** [a]1 Kin. 6:1 [b]1 Chr. 21:18

★ **2**

★ **3** [a]1 Kin. 6:2

★ **4** [a]1 Kin. 6:3

★ **5** [a]1 Kin. 6:17

★ **6**

7 [a]1 Kin. 6:20-22 [b]1 Kin. 6:29-35

★ **8** [a]Ex. 26:33; 1 Kin. 6:16

2:13 *Huram-abi* (= Hiram, my father). A master craftsman named Hiram, who was entitled to the designation "father" because of his skill.

2:14 See note on 1 Kings 7:13-14.

3:1 *Moriah.* See note on Gen. 22:2.

3:2 *second month of* . . . April-May, 967.

3:3 *cubits.* See note on 1 Kings 6:2.

3:4 *the height.* The tower was about 209 feet high, though some think 120 is a copyist's error and should read "20 cubits."

3:5 *the main room.* The Holy Place (in contrast to the Holy of Holies of v. 8).

3:6 *Parvaim.* Unidentified, perhaps Arabia.

3:8 *600 talents.* About 720,000 ounces.

★ 9 a1 Chr.
28:11

9 And the weight of the nails was fifty shekels of gold. He also overlaid ᵃthe upper rooms with gold.

10 aEx.
25:18-20;
1 Kin. 6:23-
28

10 ᵃThen he made two sculptured cherubim in the room of the holy of holies and overlaid them with gold.

11 And the wingspan of the cherubim *was* twenty cubits; the wing of one, of five cubits, touched the wall of the house, and *its* other wing, of five cubits, touched the wing of the other cherub.

12 And the wing of the other cherub, of five cubits, touched the wall of the house; and *its* other wing of five cubits, was attached to the wing of the first cherub.

13 The wings of these cherubim extended twenty cubits, and they stood on their feet facing the *main* room.

14 aEx.
26:31

14 ᵃAnd he made the veil of violet, purple, crimson and fine linen, and he worked cherubim on it.

15 a1 Kin.
7:15-20

15 ᵃHe also made two pillars for the front of the house, thirty-five cubits high, and the capital on the top of each *was* five cubits.

16 And he made chains in the inner sanctuary, and placed *them* on the tops of the pillars; and he made one hundred pomegranates and placed *them* on the chains.

★17 a1 Kin.
7:21

17 ᵃAnd he erected the pillars in front of the temple, one on the right and the other on the left, and named the one on the right Jachin and the one on the left Boaz.

★ 1 aEx.
27:1, 2;
2 Kin. 16:14

4 Then ᵃhe made a bronze altar, twenty cubits in length and twenty cubits in width and ten cubits in height.

★ 2 a1 Kin.
7:23-26

2 ᵃAlso he made the cast *metal* sea, ten cubits from brim to brim, circular in form, and its height *was* five cubits and its circumference thirty cubits.

3 Now figures like oxen *were* under it *and* all around it, ten cubits, entirely encircling the sea. The oxen *were* in two rows, cast in one piece.

4 It stood on twelve oxen, three facing the north, three facing west, three facing south, and three facing east; and the sea *was* set on top of them, and all their hindquarters turned inwards.

5 And it was a handbreadth thick, and its brim was made like the brim of a cup, *like* a lily blossom; it ᵃcould hold 3,000 baths.

★ 5 a1 Kin.
7:26

6 ᵃHe also made ten basins in which to wash, and he set five on the right side and five on the left, to rinse things for the burnt offering; but the sea *was* for the priests to wash in.

6 aEx.
30:17-21;
1 Kin. 7:38,
40

7 Then ᵃhe made the ten golden lampstands in the way prescribed for them, and he set them in the temple, five on the right side and five on the left.

★ 7-8

7 aEx.
25:31-40;
1 Kin. 7:49

8 He also made ᵃten tables and placed them in the temple, five on the right side and five on the left. And he made one hundred golden bowls.

8 a1 Kin.
7:48

9 Then he made ᵃthe court of the priests and ᵇthe great court and doors for the court, and overlaid their doors with bronze.

9 a1 Kin.
6:36 b2 Kin.
21:5

10 And ᵃhe set the sea on the right side *of the house* toward the southeast.

10 a1 Kin.
7:39

11 ᵃHuram also made the pails, the shovels, and the bowls. So Huram finished doing the work which he performed for King Solomon in the house of God:

11 a1 Kin.
7:40-51

12 the two pillars, the bowls and the two capitals on top of the pillars, and the two networks to cover the two bowls of the capi-

---

3:9 *fifty shekels.* About 25 ounces.
3:17 *Jachin . . . Boaz.* See note on 1 Kings 7:21.
4:1 The *altar* of burnt offering is described in Exod. 27:1.
4:2 the *cast metal sea.* A laver. See note on 1 Kings 7:23-26.
4:5 *3,000 baths.* About 17,400 gallons. 1 Kings 7:26 states that this laver held only 2,000

baths. The difference may be that, while the laver itself only held 2,000, an additional 1,000 baths were needed to supply the system which included the smaller lavers (vv. 6, 14).
4:7-8 The Temple contained ten lampstands and ten tables (for the showbread) instead of one each as in the tabernacle.

tals which were on top of the pillars,

13 *a*1 Kin.
7:20

13 and *a*the four hundred pomegranates for the two networks, two rows of pomegranates for each network to cover the two bowls of the capitals which were on the pillars.

14 *a*1 Kin.
7:27-43

14 *a*He also made the stands and he made the basins on the stands,

15 *and* the one sea with the twelve oxen under it.

16 *a*1 Kin.
7:14; 2 Chr.
2:13

16 And the pails, the shovels, the forks, and all its utensils, *a*Huram-abi made of polished bronze for King Solomon for the house of the LORD.

★**17**

17 On the plain of the Jordan the king cast them, in the clay ground between Succoth and Zeredah.

18 *a*1 Kin.
7:47

18 *a*Thus Solomon made all these utensils in great quantities, for the weight of the bronze could not be found out.

★**19** *a*2 Chr.
4:8

19 Solomon also made all the things that *were* in the house of God: even the golden altar, *a*the tables with the bread of the Presence on them,

20 *a*Ex.
25:31-37;
2 Chr. 5:7

20 the lampstands with their lamps of pure gold, *a*to burn in front of the inner sanctuary in the way prescribed;

21 the flowers, the lamps, and the tongs of gold, of purest gold;

22 and the snuffers, the bowls, the spoons, and the firepans of pure gold; and the entrance of the house, its inner doors for the holy of holies, and the doors of the house, *that is,* of the nave, of gold.

3 Dedication of the Temple, 5:1-7:22

a Installing the Ark, 5:1-14

★ **1** *a*1 Kin.
7:51 *b*2 Sam.
8:11; 1 Chr.
18:11

5 *a*Thus all the work that Solomon performed for the house

of the LORD was finished. And Solomon brought in the *b*things that David his father had dedicated, even the silver and the gold and all the utensils, *and* put them in the treasuries of the house of God.

★ **2** *a*1 Kin.
8:1-9
*b*2 Sam.
6:12-15;
1 Chr. 15:25-
28; 2 Chr.
1:4

2 *a*Then Solomon assembled to Jerusalem the elders of Israel and all the heads of the tribes, the leaders of the fathers' *households* of the sons of Israel, *b*to bring up the ark of the covenant of the LORD out of the city of David, which is Zion.

★ **3** *a*1 Kin.
8:2 *b*2 Kin.
7:8-10

3 And *a*all the men of Israel assembled themselves to the king at *b*the feast, that is *in* the seventh month.

4 *a*Josh.
3:6; 2 Chr.
5:7

4 Then all the elders of Israel came, and *a*the Levites took up the ark.

5 And they brought up the ark and the tent of meeting and all the holy utensils which *were* in the tent; the Levitical priests brought them up.

6 And King Solomon and all the congregation of Israel who were assembled with him before the ark were sacrificing so many sheep and oxen, that they could not be counted or numbered.

7 Then the priests brought the ark of the covenant of the LORD to its place, into the inner sanctuary of the house, to the holy of holies, under the wings of the cherubim.

★ **8-9**

8 For the cherubim spread their wings over the place of the ark, so that the cherubim made a covering over the ark and its poles.

9 *a*1 Kin.
8:8, 9

9 And the poles were so long that *a*the ends of the poles of the ark could be seen in front of the inner sanctuary, but they could not be seen outside; and they are there to this day.

4:17 *Zeredah* = Zarethan (see note on 1 Kings 7:46).
4:19 *bread of the Presence.* See note on Exod. 25:23-30.
5:1 *the things that David . . . had dedicated.* See 1 Chron. 29:2-5.
5:2 *Zion.* A name for Jerusalem or, as here, the

portion of it located in the SE. part (2 Sam. 5:6-7). Moriah, where the Temple was, is N. of this area.
5:3 *the feast* of Tabernacles (see note on Lev. 23:34-43) *in the seventh month* (Sept.-Oct.). See note on 1 Kings 8:2.
5:8-9 See note on 1 Kings 8:7-8.

★10 *a*Deut.
10:2-5; Heb.
9:4

10 *a*There was nothing in the ark except the two tablets which Moses put *there* at Horeb, where the LORD made a covenant with the sons of Israel, when they came out of Egypt.

★11 *a*1 Chr.
24:1-5

11 And when the priests came forth from the holy place (for all the priests who were present had sanctified themselves, without regard *a*to divisions),

12 *a*1 Chr.
25:1-4
*b*1 Chr. 13:8;
15:16, 24
*c*2 Chr. 7:6

12 and all the Levitical singers, *a*Asaph, Heman, Jeduthun, and their sons and kinsmen, clothed in fine linen, *b*with cymbals, harps, and lyres, standing east of the altar, and with them one hundred and twenty priests *c*blowing trumpets

13 *a*1 Chr.
16:42
*b*1 Chr.
16:34; 2 Chr.
7:3; Ezra
3:11; Ps.
100:5; Jer.
33:11

13 in unison when the trumpeters and the singers were to make themselves heard with one voice to praise and to glorify the LORD, and when they lifted up their voice *a*accompanied by trumpets and cymbals and instruments of music, and when they praised the LORD *saying, "*b*He* indeed is good for His lovingkindness is everlasting," then the house, the house of the LORD, was filled with a cloud,

14 *a*Ex.
40:35; 1 Kin.
8:11

14 so that the priests could not stand to minister because of the cloud, for *a*the glory of the LORD filled the house of God.

b *Speaking to the people,*
      6:1-11

1 *a*1 Kin.
8:12-50

6 *a*Then Solomon said,
    "The LORD has said that He would dwell in the thick cloud.

2 "I have built Thee a lofty house,
    And a place for Thy dwelling forever."

3 Then the king faced about and blessed all the assembly of Israel, while all the assembly of Israel was standing.

4 And he said, "Blessed be the LORD, the God of Israel, who spoke with His mouth to my father David and has fulfilled *it* with His hands, saying,

5 'Since the day that I brought My people from the land of Egypt, I did not choose a city out of all the tribes of Israel *in which* to build a house that My name might be there, nor did I choose any man for a leader over My people Israel;

6 but *a*I have chosen Jerusalem that My name might be there, and I *b*have chosen David to be over My people Israel.'

★6 *a*2 Chr.
12:13
*b*1 Chr. 28:4

7 "*a*Now it was in the heart of my father David to build a house for the name of the LORD, the God of Israel.

7 *a*1 Kin.
5:3; 1 Chr.
28:2

8 "But the LORD said to my father David, 'Because it was in your heart to build a house for My name, you did well that it was in your heart.

9 'Nevertheless you shall not build the house, but your son who shall be born to you, he shall build the house for My name.'

10 "Now the LORD has fulfilled His word which He spoke; for I have risen in the place of my father David and sit on the throne of Israel, as the LORD promised, and have built the house for the name of the LORD, the God of Israel.

11 "And there I have set the ark, *a*in which is the covenant of the LORD, which He made with the sons of Israel."

11 *a*2 Chr.
5:7, 10

c *Praying to God,* 6:12-42

12 Then he stood before the altar of the LORD in the presence of all the assembly of Israel and spread out his hands.

13 *a*Now Solomon had made a bronze platform, five cubits long, five cubits wide, and three cubits high, and had set it in the midst of the court; and he stood

13 *a*Neh. 8:4
*b*1 Kin. 8:54

5:10 See note on 1 Kings 8:9.
5:11 *without regard to divisions.* I.e., priests from all 24 courses helped on this occasion

(see note on 1 Chron. 24:4).
6:6 See note on 2 Sam. 7:12-16.

on it, [b]knelt on his knees in the presence of all the assembly of Israel, and spread out his hands toward heaven.

★14 [a]Ex. 15:11; Deut. 3:24 [b]Deut. 7:9

14 And he said, "O Lord, the God of Israel, [a]there is no god like Thee in heaven or on earth, [b]keeping covenant and showing lovingkindness to Thy servants who walk before Thee with all their heart;

15 [a]1 Chr. 22:9, 10

15 [a]who has kept with Thy servant David, my father, that which Thou hast promised him; indeed, Thou hast spoken with Thy mouth, and hast fulfilled it with Thy hand, as it is this day.

16 [a]1 Kin. 2:4; 2 Chr. 7:18

16 "Now therefore, O Lord, the God of Israel, keep with Thy servant David, my father, that which Thou hast promised him, saying, '[a]You shall not lack a man to sit on the throne of Israel, if only your sons take heed to their way, to walk in My law as you have walked before Me.'

17 "Now therefore, O Lord, the God of Israel, let Thy word be confirmed which Thou hast spoken to Thy servant David.

18 [a]Ps. 113:5, 6 [b]2 Chr. 2:6; Is. 66:1; Acts 7:49

18 "But [a]will God indeed dwell with mankind on the earth? Behold, [b]heaven and the highest heaven cannot contain Thee; how much less this house which I have built.

19 "Yet have regard to the prayer of Thy servant and to his supplication, O Lord my God, to listen to the cry and to the prayer which Thy servant prays before Thee;

★20 [a]Ps. 33:18; 34:15 [b]Deut. 12:11

20 that Thine [a]eyes may be open toward this house day and night, toward [b]the place of which Thou hast said that Thou wouldst put Thy name there, to listen to the prayer which Thy servant shall pray toward this place.

21 [a]Is. 43:25; 44:22; Mic. 7:18

21 "And listen to the supplications of Thy servant and of Thy people Israel, when they pray toward this place; hear Thou from

Thy dwelling place, from heaven; [a]hear Thou and forgive.

22 "If a man sins against his neighbor, and is made to take an oath, and he comes and takes an oath before Thine altar in this house,

23 [a]Is. 3:11; Rom. 2:8, 9

23 then hear Thou from heaven and act and judge Thy servants, [a]punishing the wicked by bringing his way on his own head and justifying the righteous by giving him according to his righteousness.

24 [a]Ps. 51:4

24 "And if Thy people Israel are defeated before an enemy, because [a]they have sinned against Thee, and they return to Thee and confess Thy name, and pray and make supplication before Thee in this house,

25 then hear Thou from heaven and forgive the sin of Thy people Israel, and bring them back to the land which Thou hast given to them and to their fathers.

26 [a]1 Kin. 17:1

26 "When the [a]heavens are shut up and there is no rain because they have sinned against Thee, and they pray toward this place and confess Thy name, and turn from their sin when Thou dost afflict them;

27 [a]Ps. 94:12

27 then hear Thou in heaven and forgive the sin of Thy servants and Thy people Israel, indeed, [a]teach them the good way in which they should walk. And send rain on Thy land, which Thou hast given to Thy people for an inheritance.

28 [a]2 Chr. 20:9

28 "If there is [a]famine in the land, if there is pestilence, if there is blight or mildew, if there is locust or grasshopper, if their enemies besiege them in the land of their cities, whatever plague or whatever sickness there is,

29 whatever prayer or supplication is made by any man or by all Thy people Israel, each knowing his own affliction and his own pain, and spreading his hands toward this house,

---

6:14 On the movement of thought in Solomon's great prayer, see note on 1 Kings 8:23-53.
6:20 *toward this place.* Jews, understanding this literally, prayed in the direction of Jerusalem (cf. v. 38 and note on Dan. 6:10).

30 *a*1 Sam. 16:7; 1 Chr. 28:9

30 then hear Thou from heaven Thy dwelling place, and forgive, and render to each according to all his ways, whose heart Thou knowest *a*for Thou alone dost know the hearts of the sons of men,

31 that they may fear Thee, to walk in Thy ways as long as they live in the land which Thou hast given to our fathers.

32 *a*Is. 56:3-8

32 "Also concerning *a*the foreigner who is not from Thy people Israel, when he comes from a far country for Thy great name's sake and Thy mighty hand and Thine outstretched arm, when they come and pray toward this house;

33 *a*2 Chr. 7:14

33 then hear Thou from heaven, from Thy dwelling place, and do according to all for which the foreigner calls to Thee, in order that all the peoples of the earth may know Thy name, and fear Thee, as *do* Thy people Israel, and that they may know that this house which I have built is *a*called by Thy name.

34 "When Thy people go out to battle against their enemies, by whatever way Thou shalt send them, and they pray to Thee toward this city which Thou hast chosen, and the house which I have built for Thy name,

35 then hear Thou from heaven their prayer and their supplication, and maintain their cause.

★36 *a*Job 15:14-16; James 3:2; 1 John 1:8-10

36 "When they sin against Thee (*a*for there is no man who does not sin) and Thou art angry with them and dost deliver them to an enemy, so that they take them away captive to a land far off or near,

37 if they take thought in the land where they are taken captive, and repent and make supplication to Thee in the land of their captivity, saying, 'We have sinned, we have committed iniquity, and have acted wickedly';

38 *a*Jer. 29:12, 13

38 *a*if they return to Thee with all their heart and with all their soul in the land of their captivity, where they have been taken captive, and pray toward their land which Thou hast given to their fathers, and the city which Thou hast chosen, and toward the house which I have built for Thy name,

39 then hear from heaven, from Thy dwelling place, their prayer and supplications, and maintain their cause, and forgive Thy people who have sinned against Thee.

40 *a*2 Chr. 7:15; Neh. 1:6, 11 *b*Ps. 17:1

40 "Now, O my God, I pray Thee, *a*let Thine eyes be open, and *b*Thine ears attentive to the prayer *offered* in this place.

41 *a*Ps. 132:8, 9

41 "*a*Now therefore arise, O LORD God, to Thy resting place, Thou and the ark of Thy might; let Thy priests, O LORD God, be clothed with salvation, and let Thy godly ones rejoice in what is good.

★42 *a*Ps. 89:24, 28; 132:10-12; Is. 55:3

42 "O LORD God, do not turn away the face of Thine anointed; *a*remember *Thy* lovingkindness to Thy servant David."

d   God's glory, 7:1-3

★ 1 *a*1 Kin. 8:54 *b*Lev. 9:23f.; 1 Kin. 18:24, 38

7 *a*Now when Solomon had finished praying, *b*fire came down from heaven and consumed the burnt offering and the sacrifices; and the glory of the LORD filled the house.

2 *a*2 Chr. 5:14

2 And *a*the priests could not enter into the house of the LORD, because the glory of the LORD filled the LORD's house.

3 *a*2 Chr. 5:13; 20:21

3 And all the sons of Israel, seeing the fire come down and the glory of the LORD upon the house, bowed down on the pavement with their faces to the ground,

---

6:36 Notice this clear O.T. statement of the universal sinfulness of man.
6:42 *Thy lovingkindness.* Heb., *hesed* (see note on Hos. 2:19). I.e., the promises made to

David.
7:1 *fire came down.* As also happened at the inauguration of the tabernacle (Lev. 9:24).

and they worshiped and gave praise to the LORD, *saying*, "ªTruly He is good, truly His lovingkindness is everlasting."

e   The sacrifices and feast,
7:4-11

4 ª1 Kin.
8:62, 63

4 ªThen the king and all the people offered sacrifice before the LORD.

★ **5**

5 And King Solomon offered a sacrifice of 22,000 oxen, and 120,000 sheep. Thus the king and all the people dedicated the house of God.

6 ª1 Chr.
15:16-21
*b*2 Chr. 5:12

6 And the priests stood at their posts and ªthe Levites, with the instruments of music to the LORD, which King David had made for giving praise to the LORD—"for His lovingkindness is everlasting"—whenever he gave praise by their means, while *b*the priests on the other side blew trumpets; and all Israel was standing.

7 ª1 Kin.
8:64-66

7 ªThen Solomon consecrated the middle of the court that *was* before the house of the LORD, for there he offered the burnt offerings and the fat of the peace offerings, because the bronze altar which Solomon had made was not able to contain the burnt offering, the grain offering, and the fat.

★ **8** ª1 Kin.
8:65 *b*Gen.
15:18

8 So ªSolomon observed the feast at that time for seven days, and all Israel with him, a very great assembly, *who came* from the entrance of Hamath to the *b*brook of Egypt.

9 ªLev.
23:36

9 And on the eighth day they held ªa solemn assembly, for the dedication of the altar they observed seven days, and the feast seven days.

10 Then on the twenty-third day of the seventh month he sent the people to their tents, rejoicing and happy of heart because of the goodness that the LORD had shown to David and to Solomon and to His people Israel.

11 ªThus Solomon finished the house of the LORD and the king's palace, and successfully completed all that he had planned on doing in the house of the LORD and in his palace.

11 ª1 Kin.
9:1-9

f   God speaks to Solomon,
7:12-22

12 Then the LORD appeared to Solomon at night and said to him, "I have heard your prayer, and ªhave chosen this place for Myself as a house of sacrifice.

12 ªDeut.
12:5, 11

13 "ªIf I shut up the heavens so that there is no rain, or if I command the locust to devour the land, or if I send pestilence among My people,

13 ª2 Chr.
6:26-28

14 ªand My people who are called by My name humble themselves and pray, and seek My face and turn from their wicked ways, then I will hear from heaven, will forgive their sin, and will heal their land.

★ **14** ª2 Chr.
6:37-39;
James 4:10

15 "ªNow My eyes shall be open and My ears attentive to the prayer *offered* in this place.

15 ª2 Chr.
6:20, 40

16 "For ªnow I have chosen and consecrated this house that My name may be there forever, and My eyes and My heart will be there perpetually.

16 ª2 Chr.
7:12

17 "And as for you, if you walk before Me as your father David walked even to do according to all that I have commanded you and will keep My statutes and My ordinances,

18 then I will establish your royal throne as I covenanted with your father David, saying, 'ªYou shall not lack a man *to be* ruler in Israel.'

★ **18** ª1 Kin.
2:4; 2 Chr.
6:16

19 "ªBut if you turn away and forsake My statutes and My

19 ªLev.
26:14, 33;
Deut. 28:15

7:5 According to 1 Kings 8:63 these were peace offerings which provided food for the people during the two weeks of celebration (2 Chron. 7:9-10).

7:8 See note on 1 Kings 8:65.

7:14 This well-known verse states God's requirements for blessing: humility, prayer, devotion, and repentance.

7:18 See note on 1 Kings 9:6-7.

commandments which I have set before you and shall go and serve other gods and worship them,

20 *aDeut. 29:28; 1 Kin. 14:15* *bDeut. 28:37* **20** ªthen I will uproot you from My land which I have given you, and this house which I have consecrated for My name I will cast out of My sight, and I will make it ᵇa proverb and a byword among all peoples.

21 *aDeut. 29:24-27* **21** "As for this house, which was exalted, everyone who passes by it will be astonished and say, 'ªWhy has the LORD done thus to this land and to this house?'

22 *aJudg. 2:13* **22** "And they will say, 'Because ªthey forsook the LORD, the God of their fathers, who brought them from the land of Egypt, and they adopted other gods and worshiped them and served them, therefore He has brought all this adversity on them.' "

C Solomon's Fame, 8:1–9:28

1 His cities, 8:1-6

1 *a1 Kin. 9:10-28* **8** ª Now it came about at the end of the twenty years in which Solomon had built the house of the LORD and his own house

★ 2 **2** that he built the cities which Huram had given to him, and settled the sons of Israel there.

★ 3 **3** Then Solomon went to Hamath-zobah and captured it.

★ 4 **4** And he built Tadmor in the wilderness and all the storage cities which he had built in Hamath.

★ 5 *a1 Chr. 7:24* *b2 Chr. 14:7* **5** He also built upper ªBeth-horon and lower Beth-horon, ᵇfortified cities *with* walls, gates, and bars;

6 and Baalath and all the storage cities that Solomon had, and all the cities for his chariots and cities for his horsemen, and

all that it pleased Solomon to build in Jerusalem, in Lebanon, and in all the land under his rule.

2 His subjects, 8:7-11

7 ªAll of the people who were left of the Hittites, the Amorites, the Perizzites, the Hivites, and the Jebusites, who were not of Israel, *7 aGen.*

8 namely, from their descendants who were left after them in the land whom the sons of Israel had not destroyed, ªthem Solomon raised as forced laborers to this day. *8 a1 Kin. 4:6; 9:21*

9 But Solomon did not make slaves for his work from the sons of Israel; they were men of war, his chief captains, and commanders of his chariots and his horsemen.

10 And these were the chief officers of King Solomon, two hundred and fifty who ruled over the people. *★10*

11 ªThen Solomon brought Pharaoh's daughter up from the city of David to the house which he had built for her; for he said, "My wife shall not dwell in the house of David king of Israel, because the places are holy where the ark of the LORD has entered." *★11 a1 Kin. 3:1; 7:8*

3 His offerings, 8:12-13

12 Then Solomon offered burnt offerings to the LORD on ªthe altar of the LORD which he had built before the porch; *12 a2 Chr. 4:1*

13 and ªdid *so* according to the daily rule, offering *them* up ᵇaccording to the commandment of Moses, for ᶜthe sabbaths, ᵈthe new moons, and the ᵉthree annual feasts—the Feast of Unleavened Bread, the Feast of Weeks, and the Feast of Booths. *13 aEx. 29:38-42* *bNum. 28:3* *cNum. 28:9, 10* *dNum. 28:11* *eEx. 23:14-17; 34:22, 23; Deut. 16:16*

8:2 *the cities.* See note on 1 Kings 9:10–14.
8:3 *Hamath-zobah.* See note on 1 Chron. 18:3.
8:4 *Tadmor.* About 135 miles NE. of Damascus.
8:5 The twin cities of *Beth-horon* controlled a pass NW. of Jerusalem that led to Joppa.
8:10 *two hundred and fifty.* One would not ex-

pect the number to remain constant throughout Solomon's reign; hence the different number in 1 Kings 9:23.
8:11 *the house which he had built for her.* See 1 Kings 3:1 and note on 7:1–12.

4 His organization of the Levites, 8:14-16

14 a1 Chr.
24:1 b1 Chr.
25:1 c1 Chr.
26:1 dNeh.
12:24, 36

14 Now according to the ordinance of his father David, he appointed ^athe divisions of the priests for their service, and ^bthe Levites for their duties of praise and ministering before the priests according to the daily rule, and ^cthe gatekeepers by their divisions at every gate; for ^dDavid the man of God had so commanded.

15 And they did not depart from the commandment of the king to the priests and Levites in any manner or concerning the storehouses.

16 Thus all the work of Solomon was carried out from the day of the foundation of the house of the LORD, and until it was finished. So the house of the LORD was completed.

5 His navy, 8:17-18

★17 a1 Kin.
9:26 b2 Kin.
14:22

17 Then Solomon went to ^aEzion-geber and to ^bEloth on the seashore in the land of Edom.

★18 a2 Chr.
9:10, 13

18 And Huram by his servants sent him ships and servants who knew the sea; and they went with Solomon's servants to Ophir, and ^atook from there four hundred and fifty talents of gold, and brought them to King Solomon.

6 His visit from the queen of Sheba, 9:1-12

★ 1 a1 Kin.
10:1-13;
Matt. 12:42;
Luke 11:31

9 ^aNow when the queen of Sheba heard of the fame of Solomon, she came to Jerusalem to test Solomon with difficult questions. She had a very large retinue, with camels carrying spices, and a large amount of gold and precious stones; and when she came to Solomon, she spoke with him about all that was on her heart.

2 And Solomon answered all her questions; nothing was hidden from Solomon which he did not explain to her.

3 And when the queen of Sheba had seen the wisdom of Solomon, the house which he had built,

4 the food at his table, the seating of his servants, the attendance of his ministers and their attire, his cupbearers and their attire, and his stairway by which he went up to the house of the LORD, she was breathless.

5 Then she said to the king, "It was a true report which I heard in my own land about your words and your wisdom.

6 "Nevertheless I did not believe their reports until I came and my eyes had seen it. And behold, the half of the greatness of your wisdom was not told me. You surpass the report that I heard.

7 "How blessed are your men, how blessed are these your servants who stand before you continually and hear your wisdom.

8 a1 Chr.
28:5; 29:23
bDeut. 7:8;
2 Chr. 2:11

8 "Blessed be the LORD your God who delighted in you, ^asetting you on His throne as king for the LORD your God; ^bbecause your God loved Israel establishing them forever, therefore He made you king over them, to do justice and righteousness."

9 Then she gave the king one hundred and twenty talents of gold, and a very great *amount of* spices and precious stones; there had never been spice like that which the queen of Sheba gave to King Solomon.

★10 a1 Kin.
10:11; 2 Chr.
8:18

10 And the servants of Huram and the servants of Solomon ^awho brought gold from Ophir,

★ 4

★ 9

8:17 See note on 1 Kings 9:26.
8:18 *Ophir.* See note on 1 Kings 9:28. The difference between 450 talents here and 420 in 1 Kings is likely a copyist's error.
9:1 *the queen of Sheba.* See note on 1 Kings 10:1. *with difficult questions.* I.e., riddles

(Judg. 14:12).
9:4 *his stairway.* See note on 1 Kings 10:5.
9:9 The gift amounted to about 144,000 ounces of gold.
9:10 *algum trees.* See note on 1 Kings 10:10.

also brought algum trees and precious stones.

11 And from the algum the king made steps for the house of the Lord and for the king's palace, and lyres and harps for the singers; and none like that was seen before in the land of Judah.

12 And King Solomon gave to the queen of Sheba all her desire which she requested besides *a return for* what she had brought to the king. Then she turned and went to her own land with her servants.

7 His wealth, 9:13–28

★13 *a*1 Kin. 10:14-28

13 *a*Now the weight of gold which came to Solomon in one year was 666 talents of gold,

14 *a*Ps. 68:29; 72:10

14 besides that which the traders and merchants brought; and all *a*the kings of Arabia and the governors of the country brought gold and silver to Solomon.

★15-16

15 And King Solomon made 200 large shields of beaten gold, using 600 *shekels of* beaten gold on each large shield.

16 And *he made* 300 shields of beaten gold, using three hundred shekels of gold on each shield, and the king put them in the house of the forest of Lebanon.

17 Moreover, the king made a great throne of ivory and overlaid it with pure gold.

18 And *there were* six steps to the throne and a footstool in gold attached to the throne, and arms on each side of the seat, and two lions standing beside the arms.

19 And twelve lions were standing there on the six steps on the one side and on the other; nothing like *it* was made for any *other* kingdom.

20 And all King Solomon's drinking vessels *were* of gold, and all the vessels of the house of the forest of Lebanon *were* of pure gold; silver was not considered valuable in the days of Solomon.

21 *a*For the king had ships which went to Tarshish with the servants of Huram; once every three years the ships of Tarshish came bringing gold and silver, ivory and apes and peacocks.

21 *a*2 Chr. 20:36, 37

22 *a*So King Solomon became greater than all the kings of the earth in riches and wisdom.

22 *a*1 Kin. 3:13; 2 Chr. 1:12

23 And all the kings of the earth were seeking the presence of Solomon, to hear his wisdom which God had put in his heart.

24 And *a*they brought every man his gift, articles of silver and gold, garments, weapons, spices, horses, and mules, so much year by year.

24 *a*Ps. 72:10

25 Now Solomon had *a*4,000 stalls for horses and chariots and 12,000 horsemen, and he stationed them in the chariot cities and with the king in Jerusalem.

25 *a*Deut. 17:16; 1 Kin. 4:26; 10:26; 2 Chr. 1:14

26 *a*And he was the ruler over all the kings from the Euphrates River even to the land of the Philistines, and as far as the border of Egypt.

★26 *a*Gen. 15:18; 1 Kin. 4:21, 24

27 *a*And the king made silver *as common* as stones in Jerusalem, and he made cedars as plentiful as sycamore trees that are in the lowland.

27 *a*2 Chr. 1:15-17

28 *a*And they were bringing horses for Solomon from Egypt and from all countries.

28 *a*2 Chr. 1:16

D Solomon's Death, 9:29–31

29 *a*Now the rest of the acts of Solomon, from first to last, *b*are they not written in the records of Nathan the prophet, and in the prophecy of Ahijah the Shilonite, and in the visions of Iddo the seer concerning Jeroboam the son of Nebat?

★29 *a*1 Kin. 11:41-43 *b*1 Chr. 29:29

9:13 *666 talents.* About 799,200 ounces.
9:15-16 See notes on 1 Kings 10:16, 17. *the house of the forest of Lebanon.* See note on 1 Kings 7:1.
9:26 On the extent of Solomon's kingdom see note on 1 Kings 4:21.
9:29 These were some of the sources used in compiling Chronicles (see Introduction to 1 Chronicles).

30 *a*1 Kin. 11:42, 43   **30** And *a*Solomon reigned forty years in Jerusalem over all Israel.

31 *a*1 Kin. 2:10   **31** And Solomon slept with his fathers and was buried in *a*the city of his father David; and his son Rehoboam reigned in his place.

II THE KINGS OF JUDAH, 10:1–36:21

A Rehoboam (931–913; 1 Kings 14:21–31), 10:1–12:16

1 Rehoboam causes division, 10:1–19

★ **1** *a*1 Kin. 12:1-20

10 *a*Then Rehoboam went to Shechem, for all Israel had come to Shechem to make him king.

2 *a*1 Kin. 11:40   **2** And it came about when Jeroboam the son of Nebat heard *of it* (for *a*he was in Egypt where he had fled from the presence of King Solomon), that Jeroboam returned from Egypt.

3 So they sent and summoned him. When Jeroboam and all Israel came, they spoke to Rehoboam, saying,

4 *a*1 Kin. 5:13-16   **4** "Your father made our *a*yoke hard; now therefore lighten the hard service of your father and his heavy yoke which he put on us, and we will serve you."

5 And he said to them, "Return to me again in three days." So the people departed.

6 *a*Job 8:8, 9; 32:7   **6** Then King Rehoboam *a*consulted with the elders who had served his father Solomon while he was still alive, saying, "How do you counsel *me* to answer this people?"

7 *a*Prov. 15:1   **7** And they spoke to him, saying, "If you will be kind to this people and please them and *a*speak good words to them, then they will be your servants forever."

8 *a*2 Sam. 17:14; Prov. 13:20   **8** But he *a*forsook the counsel of the elders which they had given him, and consulted with the young men who grew up with him and served him.

9 So he said to them, "What counsel do you give that we may answer this people, who have spoken to me, saying, 'Lighten the yoke which your father put on us'?"

10 And the young men who grew up with him spoke to him, saying, "Thus you shall say to the people who spoke to you, saying, 'Your father made our yoke heavy, but you make it lighter for us.' Thus you shall say to them, 'My little finger is thicker than my father's loins!

11 'Whereas my father loaded you with a heavy yoke, I will add to your yoke; my father disciplined you with whips, but I *will discipline you* with scorpions.' "

12 So Jeroboam and all the people came to Rehoboam on the third day as the king had directed, saying, "Return to me on the third day."

13 And the king answered them harshly, and King Rehoboam forsook the counsel of the elders.

14 And he spoke to them according to the advice of the young men, saying, "My father made your yoke heavy, but I will add to it; my father disciplined you with whips, but I *will discipline you* with scorpions."

15 *a*2 Chr. 25:16-20 *b*1 Kin. 11:29-39   **15** So the king did not listen to the people, *a*for it was a turn *of events* from God *b*that the LORD might establish His word, which He spoke through Ahijah the Shilonite to Jeroboam the son of Nebat.

16 *a*2 Sam. 20:1 *b*2 Chr. 10:19   **16** And when all Israel *saw* that the king did not listen to them the people answered the king, saying,
"*a*What portion do we
    have in David?
We have no inheritance
    in the son of Jesse.

10:1 This chapter describes the division of the kingdom of Judah from the majority of Israel. Because the northern division (Israel) was apostate from the beginning, the chronicler does not mention Jeroboam's being made king (1 Kings 12:20). See notes on 1 Kings 12.

Every man to your tents,
O Israel;
Now look after your
own house, David."
ᵇSo all Israel departed to their
tents.

17 But as for the sons of Israel
who lived in the cities of Judah,
Rehoboam reigned over them.

★18 ᵃ1 Kin.
4:6; 5:14

18 Then King Rehoboam sent
Hadoram, who was ᵃover the
forced labor, and the sons of Israel stoned him to death. And
King Rehoboam made haste to
mount his chariot to flee to Jerusalem.

19 ᵃ1 Kin.
12:19

19 So ᵃIsrael has been in rebellion against the house of David
to this day.

2 Rehoboam follows the Lord, 11:1-23

1 ᵃ1 Kin.
12:21-24

11 ᵃNow when Rehoboam had
come to Jerusalem, he as-
sembled the house of Judah and
Benjamin, 180,000 chosen men
who were warriors, to fight
against Israel to restore the kingdom to Rehoboam.

2 ᵃ2 Chr.
12:5-7, 15

2 But the word of the LORD
came to ᵃShemaiah the man of
God, saying,

3 "Speak to Rehoboam the
son of Solomon, king of Judah,
and to all Israel in Judah and Benjamin, saying,

4 ᵃ2 Chr.
28:8-11
ᵇ2 Chr.
10:15

4 'Thus says the LORD, "You
shall not go up or fight against
ᵃyour relatives; return every man
to his house, ᵇfor this thing is
from Me." ' " So they listened to
the words of the LORD and returned from going against Jeroboam.

★ 5-12

5 ᵃ2 Chr.
8:2-6; 11:23

5 Rehoboam lived in Jerusalem and ᵃbuilt cities for defense
in Judah.

6 Thus he built Bethlehem,
Etam, Tekoa,

7 Beth-zur, Soco, Adullam,

8 Gath, Mareshah, Ziph,

9 Adoraim, Lachish, Azekah,

10 Zorah, Aijalon, and Hebron, which are fortified cities in
Judah and in Benjamin.

11 He also strengthened the
fortresses and put officers in them
and stores of food, oil and wine.

12 And *he put* shields and
spears in every city and
strengthened them greatly. So he
held Judah and Benjamin.

13 Moreover, the priests and
the Levites who were in all Israel
stood with him from all their districts.

★13-14

14 For ᵃthe Levites left their
pasture lands and their property
and came to Judah and Jerusalem,
for ᵇJeroboam and his sons had
excluded them from serving as
priests to the LORD.

14 ᵃNum.
35:2-5
ᵇ1 Kin.
12:28-33;
2 Chr. 13:9

15 And ᵃhe set up priests of
his own for the high places, for
the satyrs, and for the calves
which he had made.

★15 ᵃ1 Kin.
12:31; 13:33

16 And ᵃthose from all the
tribes of Israel who set their
hearts on seeking the LORD God of
Israel, followed them to Jerusalem
to sacrifice to the LORD God of
their fathers.

16 ᵃ2 Chr.
15:9

17 ᵃAnd they strengthened
the kingdom of Judah and supported Rehoboam the son of
Solomon for three years, for they
walked in the way of David and
Solomon for three years.

17 ᵃ2 Chr.
12:1

18 Then Rehoboam took as a
wife Mahalath the daughter of
Jerimoth the son of David *and of*
Abihail the daughter of ᵃEliab the
son of Jesse,

18 ᵃ1 Sam.
16:6

19 and she bore him sons:
Jeush, Shemariah, and Zaham.

20 And after her he took
ᵃMaacah the daughter of Absalom, and she bore him Abijah,
Attai, Ziza, and Shelomith.

★20 ᵃ1 Kin.
15:2; 2 Chr.
13:2

10:18 *Hadoram* = Adoram of 1 Kings 12:18.

11:5-12 Not in 1 Kings, this paragraph describes Rehoboam's fortification of cities in the south-ern and western part of his land because of danger from Egypt (12:2-4).

11:13-14 Immigration of faithful priests and Le-vites from Israel to Judah occurred immedi-ately after Jeroboam's accession (see note on 1 Kings 12:31) and later (notice "and his sons," v. 14).

11:15 *for the satyrs.* Goat-like idols (see note on Lev. 17:1-7). *calves.* See note on 1 Kings 12:28.

11:20 *Maacah.* The granddaughter of Absalom (see note on 1 Kings 15:1-2).

★21 *a*Deut. 17:17

21 And Rehoboam loved Maacah the daughter of Absalom more than all his *other* wives and concubines. For *a*he had taken eighteen wives and sixty concubines and fathered twenty-eight sons and sixty daughters.

22 *a*Deut. 21:15-17

22 And *a*Rehoboam appointed Abijah the son of Maacah as head and leader among his brothers, for he *intended* to make him king.

★23

23 And he acted wisely and distributed some of his sons through all the territories of Judah and Benjamin to all the fortified cities, and he gave them food in abundance. And he sought many wives *for them.*

3 Rehoboam forsakes the Lord, 12:1-16

★ 1 *a*2 Chr. 11:17; 12:13 *b*2 Chr. 26:13-16

12 It took place *a*when the kingdom of Rehoboam was established and strong that *b*he and all Israel with him forsook the law of the LORD.

★ 2 *a*1 Kin. 14:25 *b*1 Kin. 11:40

2 *a*And it came about in King Rehoboam's fifth year, because they had been unfaithful to the LORD, that *b*Shishak king of Egypt came up against Jerusalem

★ 3 *a*2 Chr. 16:8; Nah. 3:9

3 with 1,200 chariots and 60,000 horsemen. And the people who came with him from Egypt were without number: *a*the Lubim, the Sukkiim, and the Ethiopians.

4 *a*2 Chr. 11:5-12

4 And he captured *a*the fortified cities of Judah and came as far as Jerusalem.

5 *a*2 Chr. 11:2 *b*Deut. 28:15; 2 Chr. 15:2

5 Then *a*Shemaiah the prophet came to Rehoboam and the princes of Judah who had gathered at Jerusalem because of Shishak, and he said to them, "Thus says the LORD, '*b*You have

forsaken Me, so I also have forsaken you to Shishak.' "

6 So the princes of Israel and the king humbled themselves and said, "The *a*LORD is righteous."

★ 6-7

6 *a*Ex. 9:27; Dan. 9:14

7 And when the LORD saw that they humbled themselves, the word of the LORD came to Shemaiah, saying, "*a*They have humbled themselves so I will not destroy them, but I will grant them some *measure* of deliverance, and *b*My wrath shall not be poured out on Jerusalem by means of Shishak.

7 *a*1 Kin. 21:29 *b*2 Chr. 34:25-27; Ps. 78:38

8 "But they will become his slaves so *a*that they may learn *the difference between* My service and the service of the kingdoms of the countries."

8 *a*Deut. 28:47, 48

9 *a*So Shishak king of Egypt came up against Jerusalem, and took the treasures of the house of the LORD and the treasures of the king's palace. He took everything; *b*he even took the golden shields which Solomon had made.

★ 9 *a*1 Kin. 14:26-28 *b*1 Kin. 10:16, 17; 2 Chr. 9:15, 16

10 Then King Rehoboam made shields of bronze in their place, and committed them to the care of the commanders of the guard who guarded the door of the king's house.

11 And it happened as often as the king entered the house of the LORD, the guards came and carried them and *then* brought them back into the guards' room.

12 And *a*when he humbled himself, the anger of the LORD turned away from him, so as not to destroy *him* completely; and also conditions *b*were good in Judah.

12 *a*2 Chr. 12:6, 7 *b*2 Chr. 19:3

13 *a*So King Rehoboam strengthened himself in Jerusalem, and reigned. Now Rehoboam was forty-one years old when he

13 *a*1 Kin. 14:21

11:21 Like his father Solomon, Rehoboam violated the law in taking so many wives (cf. 1 Kings 11:1; Deut. 17:17).

11:23 The meaning is this: Rehoboam made his sons deputies throughout the kingdom and sought wives for them.

12:1 *forsook the law.* By practicing Canaanite idolatry (1 Kings 14:22-23).

12:2 *Shishak.* See note on 1 Kings 11:40. This attack took place in 925, and an account of it is

engraved on the wall of the temple at Karnak.

12:3 *Lubim.* Lybians of N. Africa. *Sukkiim.* Unidentified, though perhaps also of Lybian origin. Israel, as well as Judah, was overrun in this invasion.

12:6-7 Here is an illustration of a fulfillment of the promise of 7:14.

12:9 *the golden shields.* See notes on 1 Kings 10:16, 17.

began to reign, and he reigned seventeen years in Jerusalem, the city which the LORD had chosen from all the tribes of Israel, to put His name there. And his mother's name was Naamah the Ammonitess.

14 a2 Chr. 19:3

14 And he did evil ªbecause he did not set his heart to seek the LORD.

**★15 a1 Kin. 14:29
b2 Chr. 12:5
c2 Chr. 9:29**

15 ªNow the acts of Rehoboam, from first to last, are they not written in the records of ᵇShemaiah the prophet and of ᶜIddo the seer, according to genealogical enrollment? And *there were* wars between Rehoboam and Jeroboam continually.

16 a2 Chr. 11:20

16 And Rehoboam slept with his fathers, and was buried in the city of David; and his son ªAbijah became king in his place.

B Abijah (Abijam, 913–911; 1 Kings 15:1–8), 13:1–22

**★ 1-2
1 a1 Kin. 15:1, 2
2 a1 Kin. 15:7**

13 ªIn the eighteenth year of King Jeroboam, Abijah became king over Judah.

2 He reigned three years in Jerusalem; and his mother's name was Micaiah the daughter of Uriel of Gibeah. ªAnd there was war between Abijah and Jeroboam.

3 And Abijah began the battle with an army of valiant warriors, 400,000 chosen men, while Jeroboam drew up in battle formation against him with 800,000 chosen men *who were* valiant warriors.

★ 4 aJosh. 18:22

4 Then Abijah stood on Mount ªZemaraim, which is in the hill country of Ephraim, and said, "Listen to me, Jeroboam and all Israel:

**★ 5 a2 Sam. 7:12-16
bLev. 2:13;
Num. 18:19**

5 "Do you not know that ªthe LORD God of Israel gave the rule over Israel forever to David and his sons by ᵇa covenant of salt?

6 a1 Kin. 11:26

6 "Yet ªJeroboam the son of Nebat, the servant of Solomon the son of David, rose up and rebelled against his master,

★ 7 a2 Chr. 12:13

7 and worthless men gathered about him, scoundrels, who proved too strong for Rehoboam, the son of Solomon, when ªhe was young and timid and could not hold his own against them.

8 a1 Kin. 12:28; 2 Chr. 11:15

8 "So now you intend to resist the kingdom of the LORD through the sons of David, being a great multitude and *having* with you ªthe golden calves which Jeroboam made for gods for you.

**9 a2 Chr. 11:14, 15
bEx. 29:29-33 cJer. 2:11; 5:7**

9 "ªHave you not driven out the priests of the LORD, the sons of Aaron and the Levites, and made for yourselves priests like the peoples of *other* lands? Whoever comes ᵇto consecrate himself with a young bull and seven rams, even he may become a priest of *what are* ᶜno gods.

10 "But as for us, the LORD is our God, and we have not forsaken Him; and the sons of Aaron are ministering to the LORD as priests, and the Levites attend to their work.

11 aEx. 29:38; 2 Chr. 2:4 bEx. 25:30-39; Lev. 24:5-9

11 "And every morning and evening ªthey burn to the LORD burnt offerings and fragrant incense, and ᵇthe showbread is *set* on the clean table, and the golden lampstand with its lamps is *ready* to light every evening; for we keep the charge of the LORD our God, but you have forsaken Him.

12 aNum. 10:8, 9

12 "Now behold, God is with us at *our* head and ªHis priests with the signal trumpets to sound the alarm against you. O sons of Israel, do not fight against the LORD God of your fathers, for you will not succeed."

13 aJosh. 8:4-9

13 But Jeroboam ªhad set an ambush to come from the rear, so that *Israel* was in front of Judah,

---

12:15 *Shemaiah's* records provided some of the source material for the book (11:2; 12:5).
13:1-2 *Abijah* = Abijam of 1 Kings 15:1–8 (see notes there).
13:4 *Zemaraim.* A mountain in the hill country of Ephraim near the border of Benjamin.
13:5 The permanency of the Davidic covenant

(see note on 2 Sam. 7:12–16) is emphasized by referring to it as *a covenant of salt* (see notes on Lev. 2:13 and Num. 18:8–20).
13:7 *worthless men.* See note on Judg. 19:22. *young and timid.* Rehoboam was actually 41, but was very immature.

and the ambush was behind them.

14 a2 Chr. 14:11

14 When Judah turned around, behold, they were attacked both front and rear; so ^athey cried to the LORD, and the priests blew the trumpets.

★15-20

15 a2 Chr. 14:12

15 Then the men of Judah raised a war cry, and when the men of Judah raised the war cry, then it was that God ^arouted Jeroboam and all Israel before Abijah and Judah.

16 a2 Chr. 16:8

16 And when the sons of Israel fled before Judah, ^aGod gave them into their hand.

17 And Abijah and his people defeated them with a great slaughter, so that 500,000 chosen men of Israel fell slain.

18 a2 Chr. 14:11

18 Thus the sons of Israel were subdued at that time, and the sons of Judah conquered ^abecause they trusted in the LORD, the God of their fathers.

19 And Abijah pursued Jeroboam, and captured from him *several* cities, Bethel with its villages, Jeshanah with its villages, and Ephron with its villages.

20 a1 Sam. 25:38 b1 Kin. 14:20

20 And Jeroboam did not again recover strength in the days of Abijah; and the ^aLORD struck him and ^bhe died.

21 But Abijah became powerful, and took fourteen wives to himself; and became the father of twenty-two sons and sixteen daughters.

22 a2 Chr. 24:27 b2 Chr. 9:29

22 Now the rest of the acts of Abijah, and his ways and his words are written in ^athe treatise of ^bthe prophet Iddo.

C Asa (911–870; 1 Kings 15:9–24), 14:1–16:14

1 Early reforms, 14:1–8

1 a1 Kin. 15:8

14 ^aSo Abijah slept with his fathers, and they buried

him in the city of David, and his son Asa became king in his place. The land was undisturbed for ten years during his days.

2 And Asa did good and right in the sight of the LORD his God,

★ 3 aDeut. 7:5 b1 Kin. 15:12-14 cEx. 34:13

3 for he removed ^athe foreign altars and ^bhigh places, tore down the *sacred* pillars, cut down the ^cAsherim,

4 and commanded Judah to seek the LORD God of their fathers and to observe the law and the commandment.

5 a2 Chr. 34:4, 7

5 He also removed the high places and the ^aincense altars from all the cities of Judah. And the kingdom was undisturbed under him.

6 a2 Chr. 11:5 b2 Chr. 15:15

6 And ^ahe built fortified cities in Judah, since the land was undisturbed, and there was no one at war with him during those years, ^bbecause the LORD had given him rest.

7 a2 Chr. 8:5

7 For he said to Judah, "^aLet us build these cities and surround *them* with walls and towers, gates and bars. The land is still ours, because we have sought the LORD our God; we have sought Him, and He has given us rest on every side." So they built and prospered.

★ 8 a2 Chr. 13:3

8 Now Asa had an army of ^a300,000 from Judah, bearing large shields and spears, and 280,000 from Benjamin, bearing shields and wielding bows; all of them were valiant warriors.

2 War with Ethiopians, 14:9–15

★ 9 a2 Chr. 12:2, 3; 16:8 b2 Chr. 11:8

9 Now Zerah the Ethiopian ^acame out against them with an army of a million men and 300 chariots, and he came to ^bMareshah.

★10

10 So Asa went out to meet him, and they drew up in battle

13:15–20 God apparently intervened in some supernatural way to give Judah victory. The death of half a million soldiers severely crippled the Northern Kingdom (vv. 17, 20).
14:3 *sacred pillars . . . Asherim.* See note on Deut. 7:5.
14:8 *shields.* Ones that covered the whole body.

14:9 *the Ethiopian.* Lit., the Cushite. Not from what is modern Ethiopia but the Sudan, immediately S. of Egypt.
14:10 *at Mareshah.* A city halfway between Gaza and Jerusalem which Rehoboam had fortified (11:9).

formation in the valley of Zepha-thah at Mareshah.

11 Then Asa [a]called to the LORD his God, and said, "LORD, there is no one besides Thee to help *in the battle* between the powerful and those who have no strength; so help us, O LORD our God, [b]for we trust in Thee, and in Thy name have come against this multitude. O LORD, Thou art our God; let not man prevail against Thee."

12 So [a]the LORD routed the Ethiopians before Asa and before Judah, and the Ethiopians fled.

13 And Asa and the people who *were* with him pursued them as far as [a]Gerar; and so many Ethiopians fell that they could not recover, for they were shattered before the LORD, and before His army. And they carried away very much plunder.

14 And they destroyed all the cities around Gerar, [a]for the dread of the LORD had fallen on them; and they despoiled all the cities, for there was much plunder in them.

15 They also struck down those who owned livestock, and they carried away large numbers of sheep and camels. Then they returned to Jerusalem.

3 *Reliance on the Lord,* 15:1-19

15 Now [a]the Spirit of God came on Azariah the son of Oded,

2 and he went out to meet Asa and said to him, "Listen to me, Asa, and all Judah and Benja-min: [a]the LORD is with you when you are with Him. And [b]if you seek Him, He will let you find Him; but if you forsake Him, He will forsake you.

3 "And [a]for many days Israel was without the true God and without [b]a teaching priest and without law.

4 "But [a]in their distress they turned to the LORD God of Israel, and they sought Him, and He let them find Him.

5 "[a]And in those times there was no peace to him who went out or to him who came in, for many disturbances afflicted all the inhabitants of the lands.

6 "And [a]nation was crushed by nation, and city by city, for God troubled them with every kind of distress.

7 "But you, [a]be strong and do not lose courage, for there is [b]re-ward for your work."

8 Now when Asa heard these words and the prophecy which Azariah the son of Oded the prophet spoke, he took cour-age and removed the abominable idols from all the land of Judah and Benjamin and from [a]the cities which he had captured in the hill country of Ephraim. [b]He then re-stored the altar of the LORD which was in front of the porch of the LORD.

9 And he gathered all Judah and Benjamin and those from E-phraim, Manasseh, and Simeon [a]who resided with them, for many defected to him from Israel when they saw that the LORD his God was with him.

10 So they assembled at Jeru-salem in the third month of the fifteenth year of Asa's reign.

11 And [a]they sacrificed to the LORD that day 700 oxen and 7,000 sheep from the spoil they had brought.

12 And [a]they entered into the covenant to seek the LORD God of their fathers with all their heart and soul;

---

11 [a]2 Chr. 13:14
[b]2 Chr. 13:18

12 [a]2 Chr. 13:15

★13 [a]Gen. 10:19

14 [a]2 Chr. 17:10

1 [a]2 Chr. 20:14; 24:20

2 [a]2 Chr. 20:17
[b]2 Chr. 15:4, 15

★ 3-6
3 [a]1 Kin. 12:28-33
[b]Lev. 10:8-11; 2 Chr. 17:9
4 [a]Deut. 4:29

5 [a]Judg. 5:6

6 [a]Matt. 24:7

7 [a]Josh. 1:7, 9 [b]Ps. 58:11

8 [a]2 Chr. 13:19
[b]2 Chr. 4:1; 8:12

★ 9 [a]2 Chr. 11:16

★10

11 [a]2 Chr. 14:13-15

12 [a]2 Chr. 23:16

14:13 *Gerar.* About 10 miles S. of Gaza (Gen. 20:1).
15:3-6 *These verses* evidently refer to the period of the judges.
15:9 On the tribe of *Simeon* being associated

with the North, see note on 1 Kings 11:13. Many from the northern tribes defected to the South because of the apostasy in the North. **15:10** *in the third month.* May-June.

13 aEx. 22:20; Deut. 13:6-9

13 and whoever would not seek the LORD God of Israel ᵃshould be put to death, whether small or great, man or woman.

14 Moreover, they made an oath to the LORD with a loud voice, with shouting, with trumpets, and with horns.

15 a2 Chr. 14:7

15 And all Judah rejoiced concerning the oath, for they had sworn with their whole heart and had sought Him earnestly, and He let them find Him. So ᵃthe LORD gave them rest on every side.

★16 a1 Kin. 15:13-15 bEx. 34:13 c2 Chr. 14:2-5

16 ᵃAnd he also removed Maacah, the mother of King Asa, from the *position of* queen mother, because she had made a horrid image as ᵇan Asherah, and ᶜAsa cut down her horrid image, crushed *it* and burned *it* at the brook Kidron.

17 But the high places were not removed from Israel; nevertheless Asa's heart was blameless all his days.

18 And he brought into the house of God the dedicated things of his father and his own dedicated things: silver and gold and utensils.

★19

19 And there was no more war until the thirty-fifth year of Asa's reign.

4 War with Baasha of Israel, 16:1-10

★ 1-6

1 a1 Kin. 15:17-22

16 In the thirty-sixth year of Asa's reign ᵃBaasha king of Israel came up against Judah and fortified Ramah in order to prevent *anyone* from going out or coming in to Asa king of Judah.

2 Then Asa brought out silver and gold from the treasuries of the house of the LORD and the king's house, and sent them to Ben-hadad king of Aram, who lived in Damascus, saying,

3 "*Let there be* a treaty between you and me, *as* between my father and your father. Behold, I have sent you silver and gold; go, break your treaty with Baasha king of Israel so that he will withdraw from me."

4 aEx. 1:11

4 So Ben-hadad listened to King Asa and sent the commanders of his armies against the cities of Israel, and they conquered Ijon, Dan, Abel-maim, and all ᵃthe store cities of Naphtali.

5 And it came about when Baasha heard *of it* that he ceased fortifying Ramah and stopped his work.

6 Then King Asa brought all Judah, and they carried away the stones of Ramah and its timber with which Baasha had been building, and with them he fortified Geba and Mizpah.

7 a1 Kin. 16:1; 2 Chr. 19:2 b2 Chr. 14:11; 32:7, 8

7 At that time ᵃHanani the seer came to Asa king of Judah and said to him, "ᵇBecause you have relied on the king of Aram and have not relied on the LORD your God, therefore the army of the king of Aram has escaped out of your hand.

★ 8 a2 Chr. 14:9 b2 Chr. 12:3 c2 Chr. 13:16, 18

8 "Were not ᵃthe Ethiopians and the Lubim ᵇan immense army with very many chariots and horsemen? Yet, ᶜbecause you relied on the LORD, He delivered them into your hand.

★ 9 aProv. 15:3; Jer. 16:17; Zech. 4:10 b2 Chr. 15:17

9 "For ᵃthe eyes of the LORD move to and fro throughout the earth that He may strongly support those ᵇwhose heart is completely His. You have acted foolishly in this. Indeed, from now on you will surely have wars."

★10

10 Then Asa was angry with the seer and put him in prison, for he was enraged at him for this. And Asa oppressed some of the people at the same time.

15:16 See note on 1 Kings 15:13.
15:19 Apparently a reference to the 35th year after the division of the kingdom, not the 35th year of Asa's reign. The same is true of the 36th year referred to in 16:1.
16:1-6 See notes on 1 Kings 15:17, 18-20.
16:8 *Ethiopians and the Lubim.* See notes on

14:9 and 12:3.
16:9 *completely His.* Lit., whole; i.e., wholeheartedly devoted to Him.
16:10 Asa's kingly pride had been offended by this forthright reminder that he had failed to trust God.

5 *Death,* 16:11-14

11 *a* 1 Kin. 15:23, 24

11 *a* And now, the acts of Asa from first to last, behold, they are written in the Book of the Kings of Judah and Israel.

★**12** *a* Jer. 17:5

12 And in the thirty-ninth year of his reign Asa became diseased in his feet. His disease was severe, yet even in his disease he *a* did not seek the LORD, but the physicians.

13 So Asa slept with his fathers, having died in the forty-first year of his reign.

★**14** *a* Gen. 50:2; John 19:39, 40
b 2 Chr. 21:19

14 And they buried him in his own tomb which he had cut out for himself in the city of David, and they laid him in the resting place which he had filled *a* with spices of various kinds blended by the perfumers' art; and *b* they made a very great fire for him.

D Jehoshaphat (873-848; 1 Kings 22:41-50), 17:1-20:37

1 *His revival,* 17:1-19

1 *a* 1 Kin. 15:24

17 *a* Jehoshaphat his son then became king in his place, and made his position over Israel firm.

2 *a* 2 Chr. 11:5 *b* 2 Chr. 15:8

2 He placed troops in all *a* the fortified cities of Judah, and set garrisons in the land of Judah, and in the cities of Ephraim *b* which Asa his father had captured.

★ **3**

3 And the LORD was with Jehoshaphat because he followed the example of his father David's earlier days and did not seek the Baals,

4 *a* 1 Kin. 12:28

4 but sought the God of his father, followed His commandments, *a* and did not act as Israel did.

5 *a* 2 Chr. 18:1

5 So the LORD established the kingdom in his control, and all Judah brought tribute to Jehoshaphat, and *a* he had great riches and honor.

6 *a* 2 Chr. 15:17

6 And he took great pride in the ways of the LORD and again *a* removed the high places and the Asherim from Judah.

7 *a* 2 Chr. 15:3; 35:3

7 Then in the third year of his reign he sent his officials, Benhail, Obadiah, Zechariah, Nethanel, and Micaiah, *a* to teach in the cities of Judah;

8 *a* 2 Chr. 19:8

8 and with them *a* the Levites, Shemaiah, Nethaniah, Zebadiah, Asahel, Shemiramoth, Jehonathan, Adonijah, Tobijah, and Tobadonijah, the Levites; and with them Elishama and Jehoram, the priests.

9 *a* Deut. 6:4-9

9 And they taught in Judah, having *a* the book of the law of the LORD with them; and they went throughout all the cities of Judah and taught among the people.

10 *a* 2 Chr. 14:14

10 Now *a* the dread of the LORD was on all the kingdoms of the lands which *were* around Judah, so that they did not make war against Jehoshaphat.

11 *a* 2 Chr. 9:14; 26:8

11 And some of the Philistines *a* brought gifts and silver as tribute to Jehoshaphat; the Arabians also brought him flocks, 7,700 rams and 7,700 male goats.

12 So Jehoshaphat grew greater and greater, and he built fortresses and store cities in Judah.

13 And he had large supplies in the cities of Judah, and warriors, valiant men, in Jerusalem.

★**14-19**

14 And this was their muster according to their fathers' households: of Judah, commanders of thousands, Adnah *was* the commander, and with him 300,000 valiant warriors;

15 and next to him *was* Johanan the commander, and with him 280,000;

16 *a* Judg. 5:2, 9; 1 Chr. 29:9

16 and next to him Amasiah the son of Zichri, *a* who volun-

16:12 *the physicians.* These doubtless used more magic than medicine. Again Asa failed to seek the Lord regarding his problem.

16:14 *a very great fire.* Not cremation but burning of spices near the body.

17:3 *the Baals.* The various local adaptations of Baal (see note on Judg. 2:13).

17:14-19 This large number (1,160,000) is doubtless the number of males available for military duty, rather than actual enlisted men.

teered for the LORD, and with him 200,000 valiant warriors;

17 and of Benjamin, Eliada a valiant warrior, and with him 200,000 armed with bow and shield;

18 and next to him Jehozabad, and with him 180,000 equipped for war.

19 *a*2 Chr. 17:2

19 These are they who served the king, apart from *a*those whom the king put in the fortified cities through all Judah.

2 His alliance with Ahab, 18:1–19:3

★ 1-3

1 *a*2 Chr. 17:5

18 Now *a*Jehoshaphat had great riches and honor; and he allied himself by marriage with Ahab.

2 *a*1 Kin. 22:2-35

2 *a*And some years later he went down to *visit* Ahab at Samaria. And Ahab slaughtered many sheep and oxen for him and the people who were with him, and induced him to go up against Ramoth-gilead.

3 And Ahab king of Israel said to Jehoshaphat king of Judah, "Will you go with me *against* Ramoth-gilead?" And he said to him, "I am as you are, and my people as your people, and *we will be* with you in the battle."

★ 4-27

4 Moreover, Jehoshaphat said to the king of Israel, "Please inquire first for the word of the LORD."

5 Then the king of Israel assembled the prophets, four hundred men, and said to them, "Shall we go against Ramoth-gilead to battle, or shall I refrain?" And they said, "Go up, for God will give *it* into the hand of the king."

6 But Jehoshaphat said, "Is there not yet a prophet of the LORD here that we may inquire of him?"

7 And the king of Israel said to Jehoshaphat, "There is yet one man by whom we may inquire of the LORD, but I hate him, for he never prophesies good concerning me but always evil. He is Micaiah, son of Imla." But Jehoshaphat said, "Let not the king say so."

8 Then the king of Israel called an officer and said, "Bring quickly Micaiah, Imla's son."

9 *a*Ruth 4:1

9 Now the king of Israel and Jehoshaphat the king of Judah were sitting each on his throne, arrayed in *their* robes, and *they* were sitting *a*at the threshing floor at the entrance of the gate of Samaria; and all the prophets were prophesying before them.

10 And Zedekiah the son of Chenaanah made horns of iron for himself and said, "Thus says the LORD, 'With these you shall gore the Arameans, until they are consumed.'"

11 And all the prophets were prophesying thus, saying, "Go up to Ramoth-gilead and succeed, for the LORD will give *it* into the hand of the king."

12 Then the messenger who went to summon Micaiah spoke to him saying, "Behold, the words of the prophets are uniformly favorable to the king. So please let your word be like one of them and speak favorably."

13 *a*Num. 22:18-20, 35

13 But Micaiah said, "As the LORD lives, *a*what my God says, that I will speak."

14 And when he came to the king, the king said to him, "Micaiah, shall we go to Ramoth-gilead to battle, or shall I refrain?" He said, "Go up and succeed, for they will be given into your hand."

15 Then the king said to him, "How many times must I adjure you to speak to me nothing but the truth in the name of the LORD?"

16 *a*Num. 27:17; 1 Kin. 22:17; Ezek. 34:5; 35:4-8; Matt. 9:36; Mark 6:34

16 So he said,
"I saw all Israel

18:1-3 Good King Jehoshaphat made three disastrous alliances with apostate Israel: the marriage of his son Jehoram to a daughter of Ahab (21:6), a commercial alliance (20:35-37), and this military alliance (see note on 1 Kings 22:3-4).

18:4-27 Concerning Micaiah's true prophecy see the notes on 1 Kings 22:6 through 22:24-25.

Scattered on the mountains,
aLike sheep which have no shepherd;
And the LORD said,
'These have no master.
Let each of them return to his house in peace.'"

17 Then the king of Israel said to Jehoshaphat, "Did I not tell you that he would not prophesy good concerning me, but evil?"

18 And Micaiah said, "Therefore, hear the word of the LORD. aI saw the LORD sitting on His throne, and all the host of heaven standing on His right and on His left.

19 "And the LORD said, 'Who will entice Ahab king of Israel to go up and fall at Ramoth-gilead?' And one said this while another said that.

20 "Then a aspirit came forward and stood before the LORD and said, 'I will entice him.' And the LORD said to him, 'How?'

21 "And he said, 'I will go and be aa deceiving spirit in the mouth of all his prophets.' Then He said, 'You are to entice *him* and prevail also. Go and do so.'

22 "Now therefore, athe LORD has put a deceiving spirit in the mouth of these your prophets; for the LORD has proclaimed disaster against you."

23 Then Zedekiah the son of Chenaanah came near and astruck Micaiah on the cheek and said, "How did the Spirit of the LORD pass from me to speak to you?"

24 And Micaiah said, "Behold, you shall see on that day, when you enter an inner room to hide yourself."

25 Then the king of Israel said, "aTake Micaiah and return him to Amon bthe governor of the city, and to Joash the king's son;

26 and say, 'Thus says the king, "aPut this *man* in prison, and feed him sparingly with bread and water until I return safely." ' "

27 And Micaiah said, "If you indeed return safely, the LORD has not spoken by me." And he said, "aListen, all you people."

28 So the king of Israel and Jehoshaphat king of Judah went up against Ramoth-gilead.

29 And the king of Israel said to Jehoshaphat, "I will disguise myself and go into battle, but you put on your robes." So the king of Israel disguised himself, and they went into battle.

30 Now the king of Aram had commanded the captains of his chariots, saying, "Do not fight with small or great, but with the king of Israel alone."

31 So it came about when the captains of the chariots saw Jehoshaphat, that they said, "It is the king of Israel," and they turned aside to fight against him. But Jehoshaphat acried out, and the LORD helped him, and God diverted them from him.

32 Then it happened when the captains of the chariots saw that it was not the king of Israel, that they turned back from pursuing him.

33 And a certain man drew his bow at random and struck the king of Israel in a joint of the armor. So he said to the driver of the chariot, "Turn around, and take me out of the fight; for I am severely wounded."

34 And the battle raged that day, and the king of Israel propped himself up in his chariot in front of the Arameans until evening; and at sunset he died.

19 Then Jehoshaphat the king of Judah returned in safety to his house in Jerusalem.

2 And aJehu the son of Hanani the seer went out to meet him and said to King Jehosha-

---

Marginal references:

18 aIs. 6:1-5; Dan. 7:9, 10
20 aJob 1:6; 2 Thess. 2:9
21 aJohn 8:44
22 aIs. 19:14; Ezek. 14:9
23 aJer. 20:2; Mark 14:65; Acts 23:2
25 a2 Chr. 18:8 b2 Chr. 34:8
26 a2 Chr. 16:10
27 aMic. 1:2
★28-34
31 a2 Chr. 13:14, 15
★ 2 a1 Kin. 16:1; 2 Chr. 20:34 b2 Chr. 18:1, 3 c2 Chr. 24:18

18:28-34 On the death of Ahab see the notes on 1 Kings 22:30, 34.
19:2 *Jehu* had prophesied against Baasha 25 years before (1 Kings 16:1). The *wrath* predicted came in the form of invasion and commercial reversals (20:1, 37).

phat, "*b*Should you help the wicked and love those who hate the Lord and *c*so *bring* wrath on yourself from the Lord?

3 asidebar 2 Chr.
12:12
b2 Chr. 17:6
c2 Chr.
12:14

3 "But *a*there is *some* good in you, for *b*you have removed the Asheroth from the land and you *c*have set your heart to seek God."

3 His reforms, 19:4-11

4 a2 Chr.
15:8-13

4 So Jehoshaphat lived in Jerusalem and went out again among the people from Beersheba to the hill country of Ephraim and *a*brought them back to the Lord, the God of their fathers.

5 aDeut.
16:18-20

5 And he appointed *a*judges in the land in all the fortified cities of Judah, city by city.

6 aLev.
19:15; Deut.
1:17

6 And he said to the judges, "Consider what you are doing, for *a*you do not judge for man but for the Lord who is with you when you render judgment.

7 aGen.
18:25; Deut.
32:4 bDeut.
10:17, 18

7 "Now then let the fear of the Lord be upon you; be very careful what you do, for the Lord our God will *a*have no part in unrighteousness, *b*or partiality, or the taking of a bribe."

★ **8** a2 Chr.
17:8, 9

8 And in Jerusalem also Jehoshaphat appointed some *a*of the Levites and priests, and some of the heads of the fathers' *households* of Israel, for the judgment of the Lord and to judge disputes among the inhabitants of Jerusalem.

9 Then he charged them saying, "Thus you shall do in the fear of the Lord, faithfully and wholeheartedly.

★**10** aDeut.
17:8 b2 Chr.
19:2

10 "*a*And whenever any dispute comes to you from your brethren who live in their cities, between blood and blood, between law and commandment,

statutes and ordinances, you shall warn them that they may not be guilty before the Lord, and *b*wrath may *not* come on you and your brethren. Thus you shall do and you will not be guilty.

★**11** a2 Chr.
19:8 b1 Chr.
28:20

11 "And behold, Amariah the chief priest will be over you in *a*all that pertains to the Lord; and Zebadiah the son of Ishmael, the ruler of the house of Judah, in all that pertains to the king. Also the Levites shall be officers before you. *b*Act resolutely, and the Lord be with the upright."

4 His victory over Moab and Ammon, 20:1-30

★ **1** a1 Chr.
4:41; 2 Chr.
26:7

20 Now it came about after this that the sons of Moab and the sons of Ammon, together with some of the *a*Meunites, came to make war against Jehoshaphat.

★ **2** aGen.
14:7

2 Then some came and reported to Jehoshaphat, saying, "A great multitude is coming against you from beyond the sea, out of Aram and behold, they are in *a*Hazazon-tamar (that is Engedi)."

3 a2 Chr.
19:3 b1 Sam.
7:6; Ezra
8:21

3 And Jehoshaphat was afraid and *a*turned his attention to seek the Lord; and *b*proclaimed a fast throughout all Judah.

4 aJoel
1:14

4 So Judah gathered together to *a*seek help from the Lord; they even came from all the cities of Judah to seek the Lord.

★ **5**

5 Then Jehoshaphat stood in the assembly of Judah and Jerusalem, in the house of the Lord before the new court,

6 aDeut.
4:39 b1 Chr.
29:11

6 and he said, "O Lord, the God of our fathers, *a*art Thou not God in the heavens? And *b*art Thou not ruler over all the kingdoms of the nations? Power and might are in Thy hand so that no one can stand against Thee.

19:8 *for the judgment of the Lord.* Matters covered in the law. *disputes.* Civil cases.
19:10 *between blood and blood.* Homicide cases.
19:11 *Amariah* acted as presiding judge in matters pertaining to the law, while *Zebadiah* acted in civil cases.
20:1 *Moab.* See note on Amos 2:1. *Ammon.* See

note on Amos 1:13. *the Meunites.* Their capital was Maan, 12 miles SE. of Petra.
20:2 *Aram.* The text should read "Edom." The invaders marched around the S. end of the Dead Sea.
20:5 *the new court.* Probably the same as the great court of 4:9.

7 "Didst Thou not, O our God, drive out the inhabitants of this land before Thy people Israel, and ªgive it to the descendants of ᵇAbraham Thy friend forever?

8 "And they lived in it, and have built Thee a sanctuary there for Thy name, saying,

9 'ªShould evil come upon us, the sword, *or* judgment, or pestilence, or famine, we will stand before this house and before Thee (for ᵇThy name is in this house) and cry to Thee in our distress, and Thou wilt hear and deliver *us*.'

10 "And now behold, ªthe sons of Ammon and Moab and Mount Seir, ᵇwhom Thou didst not let Israel invade when they came out of the land of Egypt (they turned aside from them and did not destroy them),

11 behold *how* they are rewarding us, by ªcoming to drive us out from Thy possession which Thou hast given us as an inheritance.

12 "O our God, ªwilt Thou not judge them? For we are powerless before this great multitude who are coming against us; nor do we know what to do, but ᵇour eyes are on Thee."

13 And all Judah was standing before the Lᴏʀᴅ, with their infants, their wives, and their children.

14 Then in the midst of the assembly ªthe Spirit of the Lᴏʀᴅ came upon Jahaziel the son of Zechariah, the son of Benaiah, the son of Jeiel, the son of Mattaniah, the Levite of the sons of Asaph;

15 and he said, "Listen, all Judah and the inhabitants of Jerusalem and King Jehoshaphat: thus says the Lᴏʀᴅ to you, 'ªDo not fear or be dismayed because of this great multitude, for ᵇthe battle is not yours but God's.

16 Tomorrow go down against them. Behold, they will come up by the ascent of Ziz, and you will find them at the end of the valley in front of the wilderness of Jeruel.

17 'You *need* not fight in this *battle;* station yourselves, ªstand and see the salvation of the Lᴏʀᴅ on your behalf, O Judah and Jerusalem.' Do not fear or be dismayed; tomorrow go out to face them, ᵇfor the Lᴏʀᴅ is with you."

18 And Jehoshaphat ªbowed his head with *his* face to the ground, and all Judah and the inhabitants of Jerusalem fell down before the Lᴏʀᴅ, worshiping the Lᴏʀᴅ.

19 And the Levites, from the sons of the Kohathites and of the sons of the Korahites, stood up to praise the Lᴏʀᴅ God of Israel, with a very loud voice.

20 And they rose early in the morning and went out to the wilderness of Tekoa; and when they went out, Jehoshaphat stood and said, "Listen to me, O Judah and inhabitants of Jerusalem, ªput your trust in the Lᴏʀᴅ your God, and you will be established. Put your trust in His prophets and succeed."

21 And when he had consulted with the people, he appointed those who sang to the Lᴏʀᴅ and those who ªpraised *Him* in holy attire, as they went out before the army and said, "ᵇGive thanks to the Lᴏʀᴅ, for His lovingkindness is everlasting."

22 And when they began singing and praising, the Lᴏʀᴅ ªset ambushes against the sons of ᵇAmmon, Moab, and Mount Seir, who had come against Judah; so they were routed.

23 For the sons of Ammon and Moab rose up against the inhabitants of Mount Seir destroying *them* completely, and when they had finished with the inhabitants of Seir, ªthey helped to destroy one another.

24 When Judah came to the lookout of the wilderness, they

Cross references (margin):

★ **7** ªIs. 41:8 ᵇJames 2:23

9 ª2 Chr. 6:28-30 ᵇ2 Chr. 6:20

10 ª2 Chr. 20:1, 22 ᵇNum. 20:17-21

11 ªPs. 83:12

12 ªJudg. 11:27 ᵇPs. 25:15; 121:1, 2

14 ª2 Chr. 15:1; 24:20

15 ªEx. 14:13; Deut. 20:1-4; 2 Chr. 32:7, 8 ᵇ1 Sam. 17:47

17 ªEx. 14:13 ᵇ2 Chr. 15:2

18 ªEx. 4:31

★ **20** ªIs. 7:9

21 ª1 Chr. 16:29; Ps. 29:2 ᵇ1 Chr. 16:34

★ **22** ª2 Chr. 13:13 ᵇ2 Chr. 20:10

23 ªJudg. 7:22; 1 Sam. 14:20

20:7 *this land.* This promise was part of the Abrahamic covenant (see note on Gen. 15:18–21).

20:20 *the wilderness of Tekoa.* S. of Bethlehem.
20:22 Either angelic creatures or inhabitants of the area ambushed the invaders.

looked toward the multitude; and behold, they *were* corpses lying on the ground, and no one had escaped.

25 And when Jehoshaphat and his people came to take their spoil, they found much among them, *including* goods, garments, and valuable things which they took for themselves, more than they could carry. And they were three days taking the spoil because there was so much.

★26 26 Then on the fourth day they assembled in the valley of Beracah, for there they blessed the LORD. Therefore they have named that place "The Valley of Beracah" until today.

27 *a*Neh. 12:43 27 And every man of Judah and Jerusalem returned with Jehoshaphat at their head, returning to Jerusalem with joy, *a*for the LORD had made them to rejoice over their enemies.

28 And they came to Jerusalem with harps, lyres, and trumpets to the house of the LORD.

29 *a*2 Chr. 14:14; 17:10 29 And *a*the dread of God was on all the kingdoms of the lands when they heard that the LORD had fought against the enemies of Israel.

30 *a*2 Chr. 14:6, 7; 15:15 30 So the kingdom of Jehoshaphat was at peace, *a*for his God gave him rest on all sides.

5 *His last days,* 20:31–37

31 *a*1 Kin. 22:41-43 31 *a*Now Jehoshaphat reigned over Judah. He *was* thirty-five years old when he became king, and he reigned in Jerusalem twenty-five years. And his mother's name *was* Azubah the daughter of Shilhi.

32 And he walked in the way of his father Asa and did not depart from it, doing right in the sight of the LORD.

★33 *a*2 Chr. 17:6 *b*2 Chr. 19:3 33 *a*The high places, however, were not removed; *b*the people had not yet directed their hearts to the God of their fathers.

34 Now the rest of the acts of Jehoshaphat, first to last, behold, they are written in the annals of *a*Jehu the son of Hanani, which is recorded in the Book of the Kings of Israel.

34 *a*2 Chr. 19:2

35 *a*And after this Jehoshaphat king of Judah allied himself with Ahaziah king of Israel. He acted wickedly in so doing.

35 *a*1 Kin. 22:48, 49

36 So he allied himself with him to make ships to go *a*to Tarshish, and they made the ships in Ezion-geber.

★36 *a*2 Chr. 9:21

37 Then Eliezer the son of Dodavahu of Mareshah prophesied against Jehoshaphat saying, "Because you have allied yourself with Ahaziah, the LORD has destroyed your works." So the ships were broken and could not go to Tarshish.

E   Jehoram (Joram, 848-841; 2 Kings 8:16-24), 21:1-20

21 *a*Then Jehoshaphat slept with his fathers and was buried with his fathers in the city of David, and Jehoram his son became king in his place.

★ 1 *a*1 Kin. 22:50

2 And he had brothers, the sons of Jehoshaphat: Azariah, Jehiel, Zechariah, Azaryahu, Michael, and Shephatiah. All these *were* the sons of Jehoshaphat king *a*of Israel.

2 *a*2 Chr. 12:6; 23:2

3 And their father gave them many gifts of silver, gold and precious things, *a*with fortified cities in Judah, but he gave the kingdom to Jehoram because he was the first-born.

3 *a*2 Chr. 11:5

4 Now when Jehoram had taken over the kingdom of his father and made himself secure, he *a*killed all his brothers with the sword, and some of the rulers of Israel also.

4 *a*Gen. 4:8; Judg. 9:5

5 *a*Jehoram *was* thirty-two years old when he became king,

5 *a*2 Kin. 8:17-22

20:26 *the valley of Beracah.* About 6 miles SW. of Bethlehem. The word means "blessing."
20:33 Apparently the people resisted Jehoshaphat's decree of 17:6.

20:36 See note on 1 Kings 22:48.
21:1 Jehoram began his solo reign in 848, though he had been coregent since 853.

and he reigned eight years in Jerusalem.

★ 6 *a*1 Kin. 12:28-30 *b*2 Chr. 18:1

6 *a*And he walked in the way of the kings of Israel, just as the house of Ahab did (*b*for Ahab's daughter was his wife), and he did evil in the sight of the LORD.

★ 7 *a*2 Sam. 7:12-17; 1 Kin. 11:13, 36

7 Yet the LORD was not willing to destroy the house of David because of the covenant which he had made with David, *a*and since He had promised to give a lamp to him and his sons forever.

8 *a*2 Chr. 20:22, 23; 21:10

8 In his days *a*Edom revolted against the rule of Judah, and set up a king over themselves.

9 Then Jehoram crossed over with his commanders and all his chariots with him. And it came about that he arose by night and struck down the Edomites who were surrounding him and the commanders of the chariots.

★10

10 So Edom revolted against Judah to this day. Then Libnah revolted at the same time against his rule, because he had forsaken the LORD God of his fathers.

★11 *a*1 Kin. 11:7 *b*Lev. 20:5

11 Moreover, *a*he made high places in the mountains of Judah, and caused the inhabitants of Jerusalem *b*to play the harlot and led Judah astray.

★12 *a*2 Chr. 17:3, 4 *b*2 Chr. 14:2-5

12 Then a letter came to him from Elijah the prophet saying, "Thus says the LORD God of your father David, 'Because *a*you have not walked in the ways of Jehoshaphat your father *b*and the ways of Asa king of Judah,

13 *a*2 Chr. 21:6 *b*1 Kin. 16:31-33 *c*2 Chr. 21:4

13 but *a*have walked in the way of the kings of Israel, and have caused Judah and the inhabitants of Israel to play the harlot *b*as the house of Ahab played the harlot, and you *c*have also

killed your brothers, your own family, who were better than you,

14 behold, the LORD is going to strike your people, your sons, your wives, and all your possessions with a great calamity;

15 *a*2 Chr. 21:18, 19

15 and *a*you will suffer severe sickness, a disease of your bowels, until your bowels come out because of the sickness, day by day.' "

★16 *a*2 Chr. 33:11 *b*2 Chr. 17:11; 22:1

16 Then *a*the LORD stirred up against Jehoram the spirit of the Philistines and *b*the Arabs who bordered the Ethiopians;

17 *a*2 Chr. 25:23

17 and they came against Judah and invaded it, and carried away all the possessions found in the king's house together with his sons and his wives, so that no son was left to him except *a*Jehoahaz, the youngest of his sons.

18 *a*2 Chr. 21:15

18 So after all this the LORD smote him *a*in his bowels with an incurable sickness.

★19-20

19 *a*2 Chr. 16:14

19 Now it came about in the course of time, at the end of two years, that his bowels came out because of his sickness and he died in great pain. And his people made no fire for him like *a*the fire for his fathers.

20 *a*Jer. 22:18, 28 *b*2 Chr. 24:25; 28:27

20 He was thirty-two years old when he became king, and he reigned in Jerusalem eight years; and he departed *a*with no one's regret, and they buried him in the city of David, *b*but not in the tombs of the kings.

F Ahaziah (841; 2 Kings 8:25-29), 22:1-9

★ 1 *a*2 Kin. 8:24-29 *b*2 Chr. 21:16

22 *a*Then the inhabitants of Jerusalem made Ahaziah,

21:6 Jehoram not only married a daughter of wicked Ahab but also became wedded to her godless practices (see note on Mal. 2:11).
21:7 Here the promises made to David (2 Sam. 7:12; 1 Chron. 17:11) are designated a *covenant. a lamp.* See note on 1 Kings 11:36.
21:10 *Libnah,* about 25 miles SW. of Jerusalem, joined the Edomites in the revolt.
21:11 *to play the harlot.* Not physical but spiritual unfaithfulness (James 4:4).
21:12 Elijah had been translated into heaven by

the time this *letter* was delivered to Jehoram.
21:16 *the Ethiopians.* Lit., the Cushites. See note on 14:9.
21:19-20 *no fire.* This customary honor was not given him (see note on 16:14). He was not even buried where kings normally were.
22:1 *Ahaziah* (= Jehoahaz, 21:17), a nephew of King Ahaziah of the Northern Kingdom and grandson of Ahab, followed Ahab's wicked ways.

his youngest son, king in his place, for the band of men who came with *b*the Arabs to the camp had slain all the older *sons.* So A-haziah the son of Jehoram king of Judah began to reign.

2 Ahaziah *was* twenty-two years old when he became king, and he reigned one year in Jerusalem. And his mother's name was Athaliah, the granddaughter of Omri.

3 He also walked in the ways of the house of Ahab, for his mother was his counselor to do wickedly.

4 And he did evil in the sight of the Lord like the house of Ahab, for they were his counselors after the death of his father, to *a*his destruction.

5 He also walked according to their counsel, and went with Jehoram the son of Ahab king of Israel to wage war against Hazael king of Aram at Ramoth-gilead. But the *a*Arameans wounded Joram.

6 So he returned to be healed in Jezreel of the wounds which they had inflicted on him at Ramah, when he fought against Hazael king of Aram. And Ahaziah, the son of Jehoram king of Judah, went down to see Jehoram the son of Ahab in Jezreel, because he was sick.

7 Now *a*the destruction of Ahaziah was from God, in that he went to Joram. For when he came, *b*he went out with Jehoram against Jehu the son of Nimshi, *c*whom the Lord had anointed to cut off the house of Ahab.

8 *a*And it came about when Jehu was executing judgment on the house of Ahab, he found the princes of Judah and the sons of Ahaziah's brothers, ministering to Ahaziah, and slew them.

9 *a*He also sought Ahaziah, and they caught him while he was hiding in Samaria; they brought him to Jehu, put him to death, *b*and buried him. For they said, "He is the son of Jehoshaphat, *c*who sought the Lord with all his heart." So there was no one of the house of Ahaziah to retain the power of the kingdom.

G   Athaliah (841-835; 2 Kings 11:1-16), 22:10-23:15

10 *a*Now when Athaliah the mother of Ahaziah saw that her son was dead, she rose and destroyed all the royal offspring of the house of Judah.

11 But Jehoshabeath the king's daughter took Joash the son of Ahaziah, and stole him from among the king's sons who were being put to death, and placed him and his nurse in the bedroom. So Jehoshabeath, the daughter of King Jehoram, the wife of Jehoiada the priest (for she was the sister of Ahaziah), hid him from Athaliah so that she would not put him to death.

12 And he was hidden with them in the house of God six years while Athaliah reigned over the land.

23 *a*Now in the seventh year Jehoiada strengthened himself, and took captains of hundreds: Azariah the son of Jeroham, Ishmael the son of Johanan, Azariah the son of Obed, Maaseiah the son of Adaiah, and Elishaphat the son of Zichri, *and* they *entered* into a covenant with him.

2 And they went throughout Judah and gathered the Levites from all the cities of Judah, and the heads of the fathers' *households* of *a*Israel, and they came to Jerusalem.

3 Then all the assembly made a covenant with the king in

Marginal references

4 *a*Prov. 13:20

★ 5 *a*2 Kin. 8:28

★ 7 *a*2 Chr. 10:15
*b*2 Kin. 9:21
*c*2 Kin. 9:6, 7

8 *a*2 Kin. 10:11-14

9 *a*2 Kin. 9:27 *b*2 Kin. 9:28 *c*2 Chr. 17:4

★10 *a*2 Kin. 11:1-3

★ 1 *a*2 Kin. 11:4-20

2 *a*2 Chr. 11:13-17; 21:2

3 *a*2 Sam. 7:12; 2 Chr. 21:7

Footnotes

22:5 *Ramoth-gilead.* See note on 2 Kings 8:28. *Ramah* (2 Chron. 22:6) refers to the same place.
22:7 Read 2 Kings 9 for additional details.
22:10 Athaliah's attempt to kill all her grandchildren so that she could rule was eventually thwarted by the hiding of Joash, who took the throne six years later (see note on 2 Kings 11:2).
23:1 *Jehoiada.* The high priest.

the house of God. And Jehoiada said to them, "Behold, the king's son shall reign, ᵃas the Lord has spoken concerning the sons of David.

4 ᵃ1 Chr. 9:25

4 "This is the thing which you shall do: one third of you, of the priests and Levites ᵃwho come in on the sabbath, *shall be* gate-keepers,

5 and one third *shall be* at the king's house, and a third at the Gate of the Foundation; and all the people *shall be* in the courts of the house of the Lord.

6 ᵃ1 Chr. 23:28-32

6 "But let no one enter the house of the Lord except the priests and ᵃthe ministering Levites; they may enter, for they are holy. And let all the people keep the charge of the Lord.

7 "And the Levites will surround the king, each man with his weapons in his hand; and whoever enters the house, let him be killed. Thus be with the king when he comes in and when he goes out."

8 ᵃ1 Chr. 24:1

8 So the Levites and all Judah did according to all that Jehoiada the priest commanded. And each one of them took his men who were to come in on the sabbath, with those who were to go out on the sabbath, for Jehoiada the priest did not dismiss any of ᵃthe divisions.

9 Then Jehoiada the priest gave to the captains of hundreds the spears and the large and small shields which had been King David's, which *were* in the house of God.

10 And he stationed all the people, each man with his weapon in his hand, from the right side of the house to the left side of the house, by the altar and by the house, around the king.

★11 ᵃEx. 25:16, 21
ᵇ1 Sam. 10:24

11 Then they brought out the king's son and put the crown on him, and *gave him* ᵃthe testimony, and made him king. And

Jehoiada and his sons anointed him and said, "ᵇLong live the king!"

12 When Athaliah heard the noise of the people running and praising the king, she came into the house of the Lord to the people.

13 And she looked, and behold, the king was standing by his pillar at the entrance, and the captains and the trumpeters *were* beside the king. And all the people of the land rejoiced and blew trumpets, the singers with *their* musical instruments leading the praise. Then Athaliah tore her clothes and said, "Treason! Treason!"

14 And Jehoiada the priest brought out the captains of hundreds who were appointed over the army, and said to them, "Bring her out between the ranks; and whoever follows her, put to death with the sword." For the priest said, "Let her not be put to death in the house of the Lord."

★14

15 So they seized her, and when she arrived at the entrance of ᵃthe Horse Gate of the king's house, they ᵇput her to death there.

15 ᵃNeh. 3:28; Jer. 31:40
ᵇ2 Chr. 22:10

H Joash (Jehoash, 835-796; 2 Kings 13:10-25), 23:16-24:27

1 *Following the Lord,* 23:16-24:16

16 Then ᵃJehoiada made a covenant between himself and all the people and the king, that they should be the Lord's people.

16 ᵃ2 Kin. 11:17

17 And all the people went to the house of Baal, and tore it down, and they broke in pieces his altars and his images, and ᵃkilled Mattan the priest of Baal before the altars.

17 ᵃDeut. 13:6-9; 1 Kin. 18:40

18 Moreover, Jehoiada placed the offices of the house of the Lord under the authority of ᵃthe

★18 ᵃ2 Chr. 5:5 ᵇ1 Chr. 23:6, 25-31
ᶜ1 Chr. 25:1

23:11 *the testimony.* Probably a copy of the Law.
23:14 *Bring her out between the ranks.* I.e., March Athaliah out of the Temple between

the ranks of soldiers and kill any who might try to rescue her.
23:18 First Chronicles 24-25 describes this orderly arrangement.

Levitical priests, [b]whom David had assigned over the house of the LORD, to offer the burnt offerings of the LORD, as it is written in the law of Moses—[c]with rejoicing and singing according to the order of David.

19 And he stationed [a]the gatekeepers of the house of the LORD, so that no one should enter who was in any way unclean.

20 And [a]he took the captains of hundreds, the nobles, the rulers of the people, and all the people of the land, and brought the king down from the house of the LORD, and came through the upper gate to the king's house. And they placed the king upon the royal throne.

21 So [a]all of the people of the land rejoiced and the city was quiet. For they had put Athaliah to death with the sword.

24 [a]Joash was seven years old when he became king, and he reigned forty years in Jerusalem; his mother's name was Zibiah from Beersheba.

2 And [a]Joash did what was right in the sight of the LORD all the days of Jehoiada the priest.

3 And Jehoiada took two wives for him, and he became the father of sons and daughters.

4 Now it came about after this that Joash decided [a]to restore the house of the LORD.

5 And he gathered the priests and Levites, and said to them, "Go out to the cities of Judah, and collect money from all [a]Israel to repair the house of your God annually, and you shall do the matter quickly." But the Levites did not act quickly.

6 So the king summoned Jehoiada the chief priest and said to him, "Why have you not required the Levites to bring in from Judah and from Jerusalem [a]the levy fixed by Moses the servant of the LORD on the congregation of Israel [b]for the tent of the testimony?"

7 For [a]the sons of the wicked Athaliah had broken into the house of God and even used the holy things of the house of the LORD for the Baals.

8 So the king commanded, and [a]they made a chest and set it outside by the gate of the house of the LORD.

9 And [a]they made a proclamation in Judah and Jerusalem to bring to the LORD [b]the levy fixed by Moses the servant of God on Israel in the wilderness.

10 And all the officers and all the people rejoiced and brought in their levies and dropped them into the chest until they had finished.

11 And it came about whenever the chest was brought in to the king's officer by the Levites, and when [a]they saw that there was much money, then the king's scribe and the chief priest's officer would come, empty the chest, take it, and return it to its place. Thus they did daily and collected much money.

12 And the king and Jehoiada gave it to those who did the work of the service of the house of the LORD; and they hired masons and carpenters to restore the house of the LORD, and also workers in iron and bronze to repair the house of the LORD.

13 So the workmen labored, and the repair work progressed in their hands, and they restored the house of God according to its specifications, and strengthened it.

14 And when they had finished, they brought the rest of the money before the king and Jehoiada; and it was made into utensils for the house of the LORD, utensils for the service and the burnt offering, and pans and utensils of gold and silver. And they offered burnt offerings in the house of the LORD continually all the days of Jehoiada.

Margin references:

19 [a]1 Chr. 9:22
20 [a]2 Kin. 11:19
21 [a]2 Kin. 11:20
1 [a]2 Kin. 11:21; 12:1-15
2 [a]2 Chr. 26:4, 5
★ 4-14
4 [a]2 Chr. 24:7
5 [a]2 Chr. 21:2
6 [a]Ex. 30:12-16 [b]Num. 1:50
7 [a]2 Chr. 21:17
8 [a]2 Kin. 12:9
9 [a]2 Chr. 36:22 [b]2 Chr. 24:6
11 [a]2 Kin. 12:10

24:4-14 On Joash's (= Jehoash) zeal to repair the Temple see notes on 2 Kings 12:2-13.

15 Now when Jehoiada reached a ripe old age he died; he was one hundred and thirty years old at his death.

16 And they buried him [a]in the city of David among the kings, because he had done well in [b]Israel and to God and His house.

2 Forsaking the Lord, 24:17-27

17 But after the death of Jehoiada the officials of Judah came and bowed down to the king, and the king listened to them.

18 And they abandoned [a]the house of the LORD, the God of their fathers, and [b]served the Asherim and the idols; so [c]wrath came upon Judah and Jerusalem for this their guilt.

19 Yet [a]He sent prophets to them to bring them back to the LORD; though they testified against them, they would not listen.

20 [a]Then the Spirit of God came on Zechariah the son of Jehoiada the priest; and he stood above the people and said to them, "Thus God has said, '[b]Why do you transgress the commandments of the LORD and do not prosper? [c]Because you have forsaken the LORD, He has also forsaken you.'"

21 So [a]they conspired against him and at the command of the king they stoned him to death in the court of the house of the LORD.

22 Thus Joash the king did not remember the kindness which his father Jehoiada had shown him, but he murdered his son. And as he died he said, "May [a]the LORD see and avenge!"

23 Now it came about at the turn of the year that [a]the army of the Arameans came up against

him; and they came to Judah and Jerusalem, destroyed all the officials of the people from among the people, and sent all their spoil to the king of Damascus.

24 Indeed the army of the Arameans came with a small number of men; yet [a]the LORD delivered a very great army into their hands, [b]because they had forsaken the LORD, the God of their fathers. Thus they executed judgment on Joash.

25 [a]And when they had departed from him (for they left him very sick), his own servants conspired against him because of the blood of the son of Jehoiada the priest, and murdered him on his bed. So he died, and they buried him in the city of David, but they did not bury him in the tombs of the kings.

26 Now these are those who conspired against him: Zabad the son of Shimeath the Ammonitess, and Jehozabad the son of Shimrith the Moabitess.

27 As to his sons and the many oracles against him and [a]the rebuilding of the house of God, behold, they are written in the [b]treatise of the Book of the Kings. Then Amaziah his son became king in his place.

I Amaziah (796-767; 2 Kings 14:1-22), 25:1-28

1 Following the Lord, 25:1-13

25 [a]Amaziah was twenty-five years old when he became king, and he reigned twenty-nine years in Jerusalem. And his mother's name was Jehoaddan of Jerusalem.

2 And he did right in the sight of the LORD, [a]yet not with a whole heart.

3 Now [a]it came about as soon as the kingdom was firmly

Margin references:

16 [a]2 Chr. 21:20 [b]2 Chr. 21:2

18 [a]2 Chr. 24:4 [b]Ex. 34:12-14 [c]Josh. 22:20

19 [a]Jer. 7:25

★20 [a]2 Chr. 20:14 [b]Num. 14:41 [c]2 Chr. 15:2

21 [a]Neh. 9:26; Matt. 23:34, 35

22 [a]Gen. 9:5

23 [a]2 Kin. 12:17

24 [a]2 Chr. 16:7, 8 [b]2 Chr. 24:20

25 [a]2 Kin. 12:20, 21

★27 [a]2 Chr. 24:12 [b]2 Chr. 13:22

1 [a]2 Kin. 14:1-6

2 [a]2 Chr. 25:14

3 [a]2 Kin. 14:5

24:20 On the Spirit's work in the O.T. see note on Judg. 3:10. *Zechariah the son of Jehoiada.* Not the prophet Zechariah, but likely the grandson of Jehoiada (see note on Matt.

23:35).
24:27 *oracles.* Threatening prophecies against him (cf. v. 19).

in his grasp, that he killed his servants who had slain his father the king.

★ 4 ªDeut. 24:16

4 However, he did not put their children to death, but *did* as it is written in the law in the book of Moses, which the LORD commanded, saying, "ªFathers shall not be put to death for sons, nor sons be put to death for fathers, but each shall be put to death for his own sin."

5 ªNum. 1:3 ᵇ2 Chr. 26:13

5 Moreover, Amaziah assembled Judah and appointed them according to *their* fathers' households under commanders of thousands and commanders of hundreds throughout Judah and Benjamin; and he took a census of those ªfrom twenty years old and upward, and found them to be ᵇ300,000 choice men, *able* to go to war *and* handle spear and shield.

★ 6-10

6 He hired also 100,000 valiant warriors out of Israel for one hundred talents of silver.

7 ª2 Kin. 4:9

7 But ªa man of God came to him saying, "O king, do not let the army of Israel go with you, for the LORD is not with Israel *nor with* any of the sons of Ephraim.

8 ª2 Chr. 14:11; 20:6

8 "But if you do go, do *it*, be strong for the battle; *yet* God will bring you down before the enemy, ªfor God has power to help and to bring down."

9 ªDeut. 8:18; Prov. 10:22

9 And Amaziah said to the man of God, "But what *shall we* do for the hundred talents which I have given to the troops of Israel?" And the man of God answered, "ªThe LORD has much more to give you than this."

10 Then Amaziah dismissed them, the troops which came to him from Ephraim, to go home; so their anger burned against Judah and they returned home in fierce anger.

★11 ª2 Kin. 14:7

11 Now Amaziah strengthened himself, and led his people

forth, and went to ªthe Valley of Salt, and struck down 10,000 of the sons of Seir.

12 The sons of Judah also captured 10,000 alive and brought them to the top of the cliff, and threw them down from the top of the cliff so that they were all dashed to pieces.

13 But the troops whom Amaziah sent back from going with him to battle, raided the cities of Judah, from Samaria to Beth-horon, and struck down 3,000 of them, and plundered much spoil.

2 Forsaking the Lord, 25:14-28

14 Now it came about after Amaziah came from slaughtering the Edomites that ªhe brought the gods of the sons of Seir, set them up as his gods, bowed down before them, and burned incense to them.

★14 ª2 Chr. 28:23

15 Then the anger of the LORD burned against Amaziah, and He sent him a prophet who said to him, "Why have you sought the gods of the people ªwho have not delivered their own people from your hand?"

15 ª2 Chr. 25:11, 12

16 And it came about as he was talking with him that the king said to him, "Have we appointed you a royal counselor? Stop! Why should you be struck down?" Then the prophet stopped and said, "I know that God has planned to destroy you, because you have done this, and have not listened to my counsel."

17 ªThen Amaziah king of Judah took counsel and sent to Joash the son of Jehoahaz the son of Jehu, the king of Israel, saying, "Come, let us face each other."

17 ª2 Kin. 14:8-14

18 And Joash the king of Israel sent to Amaziah king of

★18 ªJudg. 9:8-15

25:4 See note on 2 Kings 14:6.
25:6–10 A man of God warned Amaziah to send home the 100,000 mercenaries he hired out of the northern tribes for the 100 talents (120,000 ounces) of silver lest he lose God's help and blessing.

25:11 *the Valley of Salt*. The S. end of the Dead Sea. He also captured the capital of Edom, Petra (2 Kings 14:7).
25:14 *Seir*. Edom.
25:18 For the meaning of Joash's (= Jehoash) parable, see note on 2 Kings 14:9–10.

Judah, saying, "ᵃThe thorn bush which was in Lebanon sent to the cedar which was in Lebanon, saying, 'Give your daughter to my son in marriage.' But there passed by a wild beast that was in Lebanon, and trampled the thorn bush.

19 ᵃ2 Chr. 26:16; 32:25

19 "You said, 'Behold, you have defeated Edom.' And ᵃyour heart has become proud in boasting. Now stay at home; for why should you provoke trouble that you, even you, should fall and Judah with you?"

20 But Amaziah would not listen, for it was from God, that He might deliver them into the hand of Joash because they had sought the gods of Edom.

★**21**

21 So Joash king of Israel went up, and he and Amaziah king of Judah faced each other at Beth-shemesh, which belonged to Judah.

22 And Judah was defeated by Israel, and they fled each to his tent.

★**23** ᵃ2 Chr. 21:17; 22:1

23 Then Joash king of Israel captured Amaziah king of Judah, the son of Joash the son of ᵃJehoahaz, at Beth-shemesh, and brought him to Jerusalem, and tore down the wall of Jerusalem from the Gate of Ephraim to the Corner Gate, 400 cubits.

★**24** ᵃ1 Chr. 26:15

24 And he took all the gold and silver, and all the utensils which were found in the house of God with ᵃObed-edom, and the treasures of the king's house, the hostages also, and returned to Samaria.

25 ᵃ2 Kin. 14:17-22

25 ᵃAnd Amaziah, the son of Joash king of Judah, lived fifteen years after the death of Joash, son of Jehoahaz, king of Israel.

26 Now the rest of the acts of Amaziah, from first to last, be-

hold, are they not written in the Book of the Kings of Judah and Israel?

27 And from the time that ★**27** Amaziah turned away from following the LORD they conspired against him in Jerusalem, and he fled to Lachish; but they sent after him to Lachish and killed him there.

28 Then they brought him on horses and buried him with his fathers in the city of Judah.

J Uzziah (Azariah, 790-739; 2 Kings 15:1-7), 26:1-23

1 Following the Lord, 26:1-15

26 And all the people of Judah took Uzziah, who was sixteen years old, and made him king in the place of his father Amaziah.　　★**1**

2 He built Eloth and restored ★**2** it to Judah after the king slept with his fathers.

3 Uzziah was ᵃsixteen years old when he became king, and he reigned fifty-two years in Jerusalem; and his mother's name was Jechiliah of Jerusalem.　　**3** ᵃ2 Kin. 15:2, 3

4 And he did right in the sight of the LORD according to all that his father Amaziah had done.

5 And ᵃhe continued to seek God in the days of Zechariah, ᵇwho had understanding through the vision of God; and ᶜas long as he sought the LORD, God prospered him.　　★ **5** ᵃ2 Chr. 24:2 ᵇDan. 1:17 ᶜ2 Chr. 15:2

6 Now he went out and ᵃwarred against the Philistines, and broke down the wall of Gath and the wall of Jabneh and the wall of Ashdod; and he built cities in the area of Ashdod and among the Philistines.　　**6** ᵃIs. 14:29

25:21 faced each other. I.e., engaged in battle.
25:23 Amaziah was defeated in his own territory, Beth-shemesh being about 15 miles W. of Jerusalem.
25:24 with (the family of) Obed-edom who served as doorkeepers (1 Chron. 26:4-8).
25:27 Lachish. 25 miles SW. of Jerusalem.

26:1 Uzziah. Called Azariah in 2 Kings 14:21.
26:2 Eloth. Elath, a valuable port on the Gulf of Aqaba.
26:5 Zechariah. Not the postexilic prophet Zechariah, but another, unknown to us, by the same name.

7 And ªGod helped him against the Philistines, and against the Arabians who lived in Gur-baal, and the Meunites.

8 The Ammonites also gave ªtribute to Uzziah, and his fame extended to the border of Egypt, for he became very strong.

9 Moreover, Uzziah built towers in Jerusalem at ªthe Corner Gate and at the ᵇValley Gate and at the corner buttress and fortified them.

10 And he built towers in the wilderness and ªhewed many cisterns, for he had much livestock, both in the lowland and in the plain. *He also had* plowmen and vinedressers in the hill country and the fertile fields, for he loved the soil.

11 Moreover, Uzziah had an army ready for battle, which entered combat by divisions, according to the number of their muster, prepared by Jeiel the scribe and Maaseiah the official, under the direction of Hananiah, one of the king's officers.

12 The total number of the heads of the *households,* of valiant warriors, was 2,600.

13 And under their direction was an elite army of ª307,500, who could wage war with great power, to help the king against the enemy.

14 Moreover, Uzziah prepared for all the army shields, spears, helmets, body armor, bows and sling stones.

15 And in Jerusalem he made engines *of war* invented by skillful men to be on the towers and on the corners, for the purpose of shooting arrows and great stones. Hence his fame spread afar, for he was marvelously helped until he *was* strong.

2 *Forsaking the Lord,* 26:16–23

16 But ªwhen he became strong, his heart was so proud that he acted corruptly, and he was unfaithful to the LORD his God, for ᵇhe entered the temple of the LORD to burn incense on the altar of incense.

17 Then ªAzariah the priest entered after him and with him eighty priests of the LORD, valiant men.

18 And ªthey opposed Uzziah the king and said to him, "ᵇIt is not for you, Uzziah, to burn incense to the LORD, ᶜbut for the priests, the sons of Aaron who are consecrated to burn incense. Get out of the sanctuary, for you have been unfaithful, and will have no honor from the LORD God."

19 But Uzziah, with a censer in his hand for burning incense, was enraged; and while he was enraged with the priests, ªthe leprosy broke out on his forehead before the priests in the house of the LORD, beside the altar of incense.

20 And Azariah the chief priest and all the priests looked at him, and behold, he *was* leprous on his forehead; and they hurried him out of there, and he himself also hastened to get out because the LORD had smitten him.

21 ªAnd King Uzziah was a leper to the day of his death; and he lived in ᵇa separate house, being a leper, for he was cut off from the house of the LORD. And Jotham his son *was* over the king's house judging the people of the land.

22 Now the rest of the acts of Uzziah, first to last, the prophet

---

Cross references (margin):

★ 7 ª2 Chr. 21:16
8 ª2 Chr. 17:11
9 ª2 Chr. 25:23 ᵇNeh. 2:13, 15; 3:13
★10 ªGen. 26:18-21
13 ª2 Chr. 25:5
★15
★16-20
16 ªDeut. 32:15; 2 Chr. 25:19 ᵇ1 Kin. 13:1-4
17 ª1 Chr. 6:10
18 ª2 Chr. 19:2 ᵇNum. 3:10; 16:39, 40 ᶜEx. 30:7, 8
19 ª2 Kin. 5:25-27
21 ª2 Kin. 15:5-7 ᵇLev. 13:46
22 ªIs. 1:1

26:7 The *Arabians* lived on Judah's SE. border (see note on 20:1).
26:10 *in the wilderness.* S. Judah. *in the lowland.* The Shephelah, the foothills. *in the plain.* The tableland E. of the Jordan.

26:15 *engines.* Catapults.
26:16-20 God judged Uzziah by making him a leper because he usurped prerogatives that had been assigned to the priests (see note on Exod. 30:1-10).

ªIsaiah, the son of Amoz, has written.

23 So Uzziah slept with his fathers, and they buried him with his fathers ªin the field of the grave which belonged to the kings, for they said, "He is a leper." And Jotham his son became king in his place.

K Jotham (750–731; 2 Kings 15:32–38), 27:1–9

27 ªJotham was twenty-five years old when he became king, and he reigned sixteen years in Jerusalem. And his mother's name was Jerushah the daughter of Zadok.

2 And he did right in the sight of the Lord, according to all that his father Uzziah had done; ªhowever he did not enter the temple of the Lord. But the people continued acting corruptly.

3 He built the upper gate of the house of the Lord, and he built extensively the wall of ªOphel.

4 Moreover, he built ªcities in the hill country of Judah, and he built fortresses and towers on the wooded *hills*.

5 He fought also with the king of the Ammonites and prevailed over them so that the Ammonites gave him during that year one hundred talents of silver, ten thousand kors of wheat and ten thousand of barley. The Ammonites also paid him this *amount* in the second and in the third year.

6 ªSo Jotham became mighty because he ordered his ways before the Lord his God.

7 ªNow the rest of the acts of Jotham, even all his wars and his acts, behold, they are written in the Book of the Kings of Israel and Judah.

8 He was ªtwenty-five years old when he became king, and he reigned sixteen years in Jerusalem.

9 And Jotham slept with his fathers, and they buried him in the city of David; and Ahaz his son became king in his place.

L Ahaz (731–715; 2 Kings 16:1–20), 28:1–27

28 ªAhaz *was* twenty years old when he became king, and he reigned sixteen years in Jerusalem; and ᵇhe did not do right in the sight of the Lord as David his father *had done*.

2 ªBut he walked in the ways of the kings of Israel; he also ᵇmade molten images for the Baals.

3 Moreover, ªhe burned incense in the valley of Ben-hinnom, and ᵇburned his sons in fire, ᶜaccording to the abominations of the nations whom the Lord had driven out before the sons of Israel.

4 And he sacrificed and ªburned incense on the high places, on the hills, and under every green tree.

5 Wherefore, ªthe Lord his God delivered him into the hand of the king of Aram; and they defeated him and carried away from him a great number of captives, and brought *them* to Damascus. And he was also delivered into the hand of the king of Israel, who inflicted him with heavy casualties.

6 For ªPekah the son of Remaliah slew in Judah 120,000 in one day, all valiant men, because they had forsaken the Lord God of their fathers.

7 And Zichri, a mighty man of Ephraim, slew Maaseiah the

Cross-references (margin):

23 ª2 Chr. 21:20; 28:27; Is. 6:1

1 ª2 Kin. 15:33-35

2 ª2 Chr. 26:16

★ 3 ª2 Chr. 33:14; Neh. 3:26

4 ª2 Chr. 11:5

★ 5

6 ª2 Chr. 26:5

7 ª2 Kin. 15:36

8 ª2 Chr. 27:1

1 ª2 Kin. 16:2-4
ᵇ2 Chr. 27:2

2 ª2 Chr. 22:3 ᵇEx. 34:17

★ 3 ªJosh. 15:8 ᵇLev. 18:21; 2 Chr. 33:6 ᶜ2 Chr. 33:2

4 ª2 Chr. 28:25

5 ª2 Kin. 16:5; 2 Chr. 24:24; Is. 7:1

★ 6-8

6 ª2 Kin. 16:5

27:3 *upper gate.* On the N. side of the Temple. *the wall of Ophel.* S. of the Temple and part of the old city of David.

27:5 The silver was equivalent to 120,000 ounces. Ten thousand *kors* is equivalent to 62,500 bushels or 2.2 million liters. The Lord did what was promised in 25:9!

28:3 *burned his sons.* A generalized expression for his offspring; in particular, 2 Kings 16:3 states it was his son.

28:6–8 See notes on Isa. 7.

king's son, and Azrikam the ruler of the house and Elkanah the second to the king.

8 And [a]the sons of Israel carried away captive of [b]their brethren 200,000 women, sons, and daughters; and took also a great deal of spoil from them, and they brought the spoil to Samaria.

★ 9-15

9 But a prophet of the LORD was there, whose name was Oded; and [a]he went out to meet the army which came to Samaria and said to them, "Behold, because the LORD, the God of your fathers, [b]was angry with Judah, He has delivered them into your hand, and you have slain them in a rage [c]which has even reached heaven.

10 "And now you are proposing to [a]subjugate for yourselves the people of Judah and Jerusalem for male and female slaves. Surely, do you not have transgressions of your own against the LORD your God?

11 "Now therefore, listen to me and return the captives [a]whom you captured from your brothers, [b]for the burning anger of the LORD is against you."

12 Then some of the heads of the sons of Ephraim—Azariah the son of Johanan, Berechiah the son of Meshillemoth, Jehizkiah the son of Shallum, and Amasa the son of Hadlai—arose against those who were coming from the battle,

13 and said to them, "You must not bring the captives in here, for you are proposing to bring upon us guilt against the LORD adding to our sins and our guilt; for our guilt is great so that His burning anger is against Israel."

14 So the armed men left the captives and the spoil before the officers and all the assembly.

15 Then [a]the men who were designated by name arose, took the captives, and they clothed all their naked ones from the spoil; and they gave them clothes and sandals, fed them and [b]gave them drink, anointed them with oil, led all their feeble ones on donkeys, and brought them to Jericho, [c]the city of palm trees, to their brothers; then they returned to Samaria.

16 [a]At that time King Ahaz sent to the kings of Assyria for help.

17 [a]For again the Edomites had come and attacked Judah, and carried away captives.

18 [a]The Philistines also had invaded the cities of the lowland and of the Negev of Judah, and had taken Beth-shemesh, Aijalon, Gederoth, and Soco with its villages, Timnah with its villages, and Gimzo with its villages, and they settled there.

19 For the LORD humbled Judah because of Ahaz king of [a]Israel, for he had brought about a lack of restraint in Judah and was very unfaithful to the LORD.

20 So [a]Tilgath-pilneser king of Assyria came against him and afflicted him instead of strengthening him.

21 [a]And Ahaz took a portion out of the house of the LORD and out of the palace of the king and of the princes, and gave it to the king of Assyria; but it did not help him.

22 Now in the time of his distress this same King Ahaz [a]became yet more unfaithful to the LORD.

23 [a]For he sacrificed to the gods of Damascus which had defeated him, and said, "[b]Because the gods of the kings of Aram helped them, I will sacrifice to them that they may help me." But

---

8 [a]Deut. 28:25, 41; [b]2 Chr. 11:4
9 [a]2 Chr. 25:15 [b]Is. 47:6 [c]Ezra 9:6; Rev. 18:5
10 [a]Lev. 25:39
11 [a]2 Chr. 28:8 [b]James 2:13

15 [a]2 Chr. 28:12 [b]2 Kin. 6:22; Prov. 25:21, 22 [c]Deut. 34:3
★16-21
16 [a]2 Kin. 16:7
17 [a]Obad. 10, 14
18 [a]Ezek. 16:57
19 [a]2 Chr. 21:2
20 [a]1 Chr. 5:26
21 [a]2 Kin. 16:8, 9
22 [a]Is. 1:5; Jer. 5:3; Rev. 16:11
23 [a]2 Chr. 25:14 [b]Jer. 44:17, 18

28:9-15 This paragraph, not found in 2 Kings, relates how an otherwise unknown prophet, *Oded*, led a protest against the Northern Kingdom's retaining the prisoners of war from the Southern Kingdom because they were brothers. The result was that the prisoners were clothed, cared for, and returned to Jericho.
28:16-21 See note on 2 Kings 15:27-31. *afflicted him* (v. 20). By the tribute demanded.

they became the downfall of him and all Israel.

★24 *a*2 Kin. 16:17 *b*2 Chr. 29:7 *c*2 Chr. 30:14; 33:3-5

24 Moreover, when Ahaz gathered together the utensils of the house of God, he *a*cut the utensils of the house of God in pieces; and he *b*closed the doors of the house of the LORD, and *c*made altars for himself in every corner of Jerusalem.

25 And in every city of Judah he made high places to burn incense to other gods, and provoked the LORD, the God of his fathers, to anger.

26 *a*2 Kin. 16:19, 20

26 *a*Now the rest of his acts and all his ways, from first to last, behold, they are written in the Book of the Kings of Judah and Israel.

27 *a*2 Kin. 16:20; 2 Chr. 24:25; Is. 14:28 *b*2 Chr. 21:2

27 *a*So Ahaz slept with his fathers, and they buried him in the city, in Jerusalem, for they did not bring him into the tombs of the kings of *b*Israel; and Hezekiah his son reigned in his place.

M Hezekiah (715-686; 2 Kings 18:1-20:21), 29:1-32:33

1 His revival, 29:1-31:21

1 *a*2 Kin. 18:1-3

29 *a*Hezekiah became king *when he was* twenty-five years old; and he reigned twenty-nine years in Jerusalem. And his mother's name *was* Abijah, the daughter of Zechariah.

2 *a*2 Chr. 28:1; 34:2

2 And *a*he did right in the sight of the LORD, according to all that his father David had done.

★ 3 *a*2 Chr. 28:24; 29:7

3 In the first year of his reign, in the first month, he *a*opened the doors of the house of the LORD and repaired them.

★ 4

4 And he brought in the priests and the Levites, and gathered them into the square on the east.

★ 5 *a*2 Chr. 29:15, 34; 35:6

5 Then he said to them, "Listen to me, O Levites. *a*Conse-

crate yourselves now, and consecrate the house of the LORD, the God of your fathers, and carry the uncleanness out from the holy place.

6 *a*Ezek. 8:16

6 "For our fathers have been unfaithful and have done evil in the sight of the LORD our God, and have forsaken Him and *a*turned their faces away from the dwelling place of the LORD, and have turned *their* backs.

7 *a*2 Chr. 28:24

7 "They have also *a*shut the doors of the porch and put out the lamps, and have not burned incense or offered burnt offerings in the holy place to the God of Israel.

8 *a*2 Chr. 24:20 *b*Jer. 25:9, 18

8 "Therefore *a*the wrath of the LORD was against Judah and Jerusalem, and He has made them an object of terror, of horror, and of *b*hissing, as you see with your own eyes.

9 *a*2 Chr. 28:5-8, 17

9 "For behold, *a*our fathers have fallen by the sword, and our sons and our daughters and our wives are in captivity for this.

10 *a*2 Chr. 23:16

10 "Now it is in my heart *a*to make a covenant with the LORD God of Israel, that His burning anger may turn away from us.

11 *a*Num. 3:6; 8:6

11 "My sons, do not be negligent now, for *a*the LORD has chosen you to stand before Him, to minister to Him, and to be His ministers and burn incense."

12 *a*2 Chr. 31:13 *b*Num. 3:19, 20

12 Then the Levites arose: *a*Mahath, the son of Amasai and Joel the son of Azariah, from the sons of *b*the Kohathites; and from the sons of Merari, Kish the son of Abdi and Azariah the son of Jehallelel; and from the Gershonites, Joah the son of Zimmah and Eden the son of Joah;

13 and from the sons of Elizaphan, Shimri and Jeiel; and from the sons of Asaph, Zechariah and Mattaniah;

14 and from the sons of Heman, Jehiel and Shimei; and from

28:24 For details of Ahaz's attempt to displace the worship of Yahweh, see the notes on 2 Kings 16:10-11, 15, 17-18.

29:3 *opened the doors.* Wicked Ahaz had closed them (28:24).

29:4 *the square on the east.* An open area in front of the east gate of the Temple.

29:5 *Consecrate yourselves now.* See note on 1 Chron. 15:12.

the sons of Jeduthun, Shemaiah and Uzziel.

★15 *a*2 Chr. 29:5 *b*1 Chr. 23:28 *c*2 Chr. 30:12

15 And they assembled their brothers, *a*consecrated themselves, and went in *b*to cleanse the house of the LORD, according to the commandment of the king *c*by the words of the LORD.

★16 *a*2 Chr. 15:16

16 So the priests went in to the inner part of the house of the LORD to cleanse *it,* and every unclean thing which they found in the temple of the LORD they brought out to the court of the house of the LORD. Then the Levites received *it* to carry out to *a*the Kidron valley.

17 *a*2 Chr. 29:3

17 Now they began the consecration *a*on the first *day* of the first month, and on the eighth day of the month they entered the porch of the LORD. Then they consecrated the house of the LORD in eight days, and finished on the sixteenth day of the first month.

18 Then they went in to King Hezekiah and said, "We have cleansed the whole house of the LORD, the altar of burnt offering with all of its utensils, and the table of showbread with all of its utensils.

19 *a*2 Chr. 28:24

19 "Moreover, *a*all the utensils which King Ahaz had discarded during his reign in his unfaithfulness, we have prepared and consecrated; and behold, they are before the altar of the LORD."

20 Then King Hezekiah arose early and assembled the princes of the city and went up to the house of the LORD.

★21 *a*Lev. 4:3-14

21 And they brought seven bulls, seven rams, seven lambs, and seven male goats *a*for a sin offering for the kingdom, the sanctuary, and Judah. And he ordered the priests, the sons of Aaron, to offer *them* on the altar of the LORD.

22 *a*Lev. 4:18

22 So they slaughtered the bulls, and the priests took the blood and sprinkled it on the altar. They also slaughtered the rams and sprinkled the blood on the altar; they slaughtered the lambs also and *a*sprinkled the blood on the altar.

23 Then they brought the male goats of the sin offering before the king and the assembly, and *a*they laid their hands on them.

23 *a*Lev. 4:15

24 And the priests slaughtered them and purged the altar with their blood *a*to atone for all Israel, for the king ordered the burnt offering and the sin offering for all Israel.

★24 *a*Lev. 4:26

25 *a*He then stationed the Levites in the house of the LORD with cymbals, with harps, and with lyres, *b*according to the command of David and of *c*Gad the king's seer, and of *d*Nathan the prophet; for the command was from the LORD through His prophets.

25 *a*1 Chr. 25:6 *b*2 Chr. 8:14 *c*2 Sam. 24:11 *d*2 Sam. 7:2

26 And the Levites stood with *a*the *musical* instruments of David, and *b*the priests with the trumpets.

26 *a*1 Chr. 23:5 *b*2 Chr. 5:12

27 Then Hezekiah gave the order to offer the burnt offering on the altar. When the burnt offering began, *a*the song to the LORD also began with the trumpets, *accompanied* by the instruments of David, king of Israel.

27 *a*2 Chr. 23:18

28 While the whole assembly worshiped, the singers also sang and the trumpets sounded; all this *continued* until the burnt offering was finished.

29 Now at the completion of the burnt offerings, *a*the king and all who were present with him bowed down and worshiped.

29 *a*2 Chr. 20:18

30 Moreover, King Hezekiah and the officials ordered the Levites to sing praises to the LORD with the words of David and Asaph the seer. *a*So they sang praises with joy, and bowed down and worshiped.

30 *a*Ps. 100:1; 106:12

29:15 *by the words of the LORD* as previously recorded in the Law (Deut. 12:2-4).
29:16 *every unclean thing.* Accumulated dirt as well as implements of Ahaz's idolatrous worship (2 Kings 16:15).
29:21 *sin offering.* See note on Lev. 4:2.
29:24 *burnt offering.* See note on Lev. 1:3-4.

31 *a*2 Chr.
13:9 *b*Ex.
35:5, 22

31 Then Hezekiah answered and said, "*a*Now *that* you have consecrated yourselves to the LORD, come near and bring sacrifices and thank offerings to the house of the LORD." And the assembly brought sacrifices and thank offerings, and *b*all those who were willing *brought* burnt offerings.

32 And the number of the burnt offerings which the assembly brought was 70 bulls, 100 rams, and 200 lambs; all these were for a burnt offering to the LORD.

33 And the consecrated things were 600 bulls and 3,000 sheep.

★34 *a*2 Chr.
35:11
*b*2 Chr. 30:3

34 But the priests were too few, so that they were unable to skin all the burnt offerings; *a*therefore their brothers the Levites helped them until the work was completed, and until the *other* priests had consecrated themselves. For *b*the Levites were more conscientious to consecrate themselves than the priests.

★35 *a*2 Chr.
29:32
*b*Lev. 3:16
*c*Num. 15:5-
10

35 And there *were* also *a*many burnt offerings with *b*the fat of the peace offerings and with *c*the libations for the burnt offerings. Thus the service of the house of the LORD was established *again.*

36 Then Hezekiah and all the people rejoiced over what God had prepared for the people, because the thing came about suddenly.

★ 1

30 Now Hezekiah sent to all Israel and Judah and wrote letters also to Ephraim and Manasseh, that they should come to the house of the LORD at Jerusalem to celebrate the Passover to the LORD God of Israel.

2 For the king and his princes and all the assembly in Jerusalem had decided *a*to celebrate the Passover in the second month,

3 since they could not celebrate it *a*at that time, because the priests had not consecrated themselves in sufficient numbers, nor had the people been gathered to Jerusalem.

4 Thus the thing was right in the sight of the king and all the assembly.

5 So they established a decree to circulate a proclamation throughout all Israel *a*from Beersheba even to Dan, that they should come to celebrate the Passover to the LORD God of Israel at Jerusalem. For they had not celebrated *it* in great numbers as it was prescribed.

6 And *a*the couriers went throughout all Israel and Judah with the letters from the hand of the king and his princes, even according to the command of the king, saying, "O sons of Israel, return to the LORD God of Abraham, Isaac, and Israel, that He may return to those of you who escaped *and* are left from *b*the hand of the kings of Assyria.

7 "*a*And do not be like your fathers and your brothers, who were unfaithful to the LORD God of their fathers, so that *b*He made them a horror, as you see.

8 "Now do not *a*stiffen your neck like your fathers, but yield to the LORD and enter His sanctuary which He has consecrated forever, and serve the LORD your God, *b*that His burning anger may turn away from you.

9 "For *a*if you return to the LORD, your brothers and your sons *will find* compassion before

★ 2 *a*Num.
9:10, 11;
2 Chr. 30:13,
15

3 *a*2 Chr.
29:17, 34

5 *a*Judg.
20:1

6 *a*Esth.
8:14; Job
9:25; Jer.
51:31
*b*2 Chr.
28:20

7 *a*Ezek.
20:13
*b*2 Chr. 29:8

8 *a*Ex. 32:9
*b*2 Chr.
29:10

9 *a*Deut.
30:2 *b*Ex.
34:6, 7; Mic.
7:18

29:34 *the Levites were more conscientious.* Since they apparently had not followed Uriah and the other priests who cooperated with Ahaz (2 Kings 16:10).
29:35 *peace offerings.* See note on Lev. 3:1. *burnt offerings.* See note on Lev. 23:13.
30:1 Those in the Northern Kingdom (*Ephraim and Manasseh*) who had not been taken into

captivity by the Assyrians (2 Kings 17:6) were invited to join Judah in celebrating the Passover. Verses 10-11 record their response.
30:2 If circumstances required it (v. 3; 29:17), the celebration of Passover could be postponed from the first month to the second (Num. 9:10-11).

those who led them captive, and will return to this land. [b]For the LORD your God is gracious and compassionate, and will not turn His face away from you if you return to Him."

10 So the couriers passed from city to city through the country of Ephraim and Manasseh, and as far as Zebulun, but [a]they laughed them to scorn, and mocked them.

11 Nevertheless [a]some men of Asher, Manasseh, and Zebulun humbled themselves and came to Jerusalem.

12 The [a]hand of God was also on Judah to give them one heart to do what the king and the princes commanded by the word of the LORD.

13 Now many people were gathered at Jerusalem to celebrate the Feast of Unleavened Bread [a]in the second month, a very large assembly.

14 And they arose and removed the altars which *were* in Jerusalem; they also [a]removed all the incense altars and [b]cast *them* into the brook Kidron.

15 Then [a]they slaughtered the Passover *lambs* on the fourteenth of the second month. And [b]the priests and Levites were ashamed of themselves and consecrated themselves, and brought burnt offerings to the house of the LORD.

16 And [a]they stood at their stations after their custom, according to the law of Moses the man of God; the priests sprinkled the blood *which they received* from the hand of the Levites.

17 For *there were* many in the assembly who had not consecrated themselves; therefore, [a]the Levites *were* over the slaughter of the Passover *lambs* for everyone who *was* unclean, in order to consecrate *them* to the LORD.

18 For a multitude of the people, [a]*even* many from Ephraim and Manasseh, Issachar and Zebulun, had not purified themselves, [b]yet they ate the Passover [c]otherwise than prescribed. For Hezekiah prayed for them, saying, "May the good LORD pardon

19 [a]everyone who prepares his heart to seek God, the LORD God of his fathers, though not according to the purification *rules* of the sanctuary."

20 So the LORD heard Hezekiah and [a]healed the people.

21 And the sons of Israel present in Jerusalem [a]celebrated the Feast of Unleavened Bread *for* seven days with great joy, and the Levites and the priests praised the LORD day after day with loud instruments to the LORD.

22 Then Hezekiah [a]spoke encouragingly to all the Levites who showed good insight *in the things* of the LORD. So they ate for the appointed seven days, sacrificing peace offerings and [b]giving thanks to the LORD God of their fathers.

23 Then the whole assembly [a]decided to celebrate *the feast* another seven days, so they celebrated the seven days with joy.

24 For [a]Hezekiah king of Judah had contributed to the assembly 1,000 bulls and 7,000 sheep, and the princes had contributed to the assembly 1,000 bulls and 10,000 sheep; and [b]a large number of priests consecrated themselves.

25 And all the assembly of Judah rejoiced, with the priests and the Levites, and [a]all the assembly that came from Israel, both the sojourners who came from the land of Israel and those living in Judah.

---

10 [a]2 Chr. 36:16

11 [a]2 Chr. 30:18, 21, 25

12 [a]2 Cor. 3:5; Phil. 2:13; Heb. 13:20, 21

★**13** [a]2 Chr. 30:2

★**14** [a]2 Chr. 28:24 [b]2 Chr. 29:16

15 [a]2 Chr. 30:2, 3 [b]2 Chr. 29:34

★**16** [a]2 Chr. 35:10, 15

17 [a]2 Chr. 29:34

18 [a]2 Chr. 30:11, 25 [b]Num. 9:10 [c]Ex. 12:43-49

19 [a]2 Chr. 19:3

20 [a]James 5:16

21 [a]Ex. 12:15; 13:6

22 [a]2 Chr. 32:6 [b]Ezra 10:11

★**23** [a]1 Kin. 8:65

24 [a]2 Chr. 35:7, 8 [b]2 Chr. 29:34; 30:3

25 [a]2 Chr. 30:11, 18

30:13 the Feast of Unleavened Bread. See note on Exod. 12:15–20.

30:14 Just as the priests had previously cleansed the Temple, the people now stripped the city of all the paraphernalia of Ahaz's idolatry (28:25).

30:16 On the ritual of the Passover see notes on Exod. 12.

30:23 The Feast of Unleavened Bread was observed an extra seven days, marking the rededication of the Temple (see note on 1 Kings 8:65).

26 a2 Chr. 7:8-10

26 So there was great joy in Jerusalem, because there was nothing like this in Jerusalem asince the days of Solomon the son of David, king of Israel.

27 a2 Chr. 23:18 bNum. 6:23 cDeut. 26:15; Ps. 68:5

27 Then aThe Levitical priests arose and bblessed the people; and their voice was heard and their prayer came to cHis holy dwelling place, to heaven.

★ **1** a2 Kin. 18:4

31 Now when all this was finished, all Israel who were present went out to the cities of Judah, abroke the pillars in pieces, cut down the Asherim, and pulled down the high places and the altars throughout all Judah and Benjamin, as well as in Ephraim and Manasseh, until they had destroyed them all. Then all the sons of Israel returned to their cities, each to his possession.

★ **2** a1 Chr. 24:1 b1 Chr. 23:28-31

2 And Hezekiah appointed aThe divisions of the priests and the Levites by their divisions, each according to his service, both the priests and the Levites, bfor burnt offerings and for peace offerings, to minister and to give thanks and to praise in the gates of the camp of the LORD.

3 a2 Chr. 35:7 bNum. 28:1-29:40

3 He also appointed aThe king's portion of his goods for the burnt offerings, namely, for the morning and evening burnt offerings, and the burnt offerings for the sabbaths and for the new moons and for the fixed festivals, bas it is written in the law of the LORD.

★ **4** aNum. 18:8 bMal. 2:7

4 Also he commanded the people who lived in Jerusalem to give aThe portion due to the priests and the Levites, that they might devote themselves to bthe law of the LORD.

5 aNeh. 13:12

5 And as soon as the order spread, the sons of Israel provided in abundance the first fruits of grain, new wine, oil, honey, and of all the produce of the field; and they brought in abundantly aThe tithe of all.

6 And the sons of Israel and Judah who lived in the cities of Judah, also brought in the tithe of oxen and sheep, and aThe tithe of sacred gifts which were consecrated to the LORD their God, and placed them in heaps.

6 aLev. 27:30; Deut. 14:28

7 In the third month they began to make the heaps, and finished them by the seventh month.

★ **7-19**

8 And when Hezekiah and the rulers came and saw the heaps, they blessed the LORD and aHis people Israel.

8 aDeut. 33:29; Ps. 33:12; 144:15

9 Then Hezekiah questioned the priests and the Levites concerning the heaps.

10 And Azariah the chief priest aof the house of Zadok said to him, "bSince the contributions began to be brought into the house of the LORD, we have had enough to eat with plenty left over, for the LORD has blessed His people, and this great quantity is left over."

10 a1 Chr. 6:8, 9 bMal. 3:10

11 Then Hezekiah commanded them to prepare aRooms in the house of the LORD, and they prepared them.

11 a1 Kin. 6:5, 8

12 And they faithfully brought in the contributions and the tithes and the consecrated things; and Conaniah the Levite was the officer in charge aof them and his brother Shimei was second.

12 a2 Chr. 35:9

13 And Jehiel, Azaziah, Nahath, Asahel, Jerimoth, Jozabad, Eliel, Ismachiah, Mahath, and Benaiah were overseers under the authority of Conaniah and Shimei his brother by the appointment of King Hezekiah, and aAzariah was the chief officer of the house of God.

13 a2 Chr. 31:10

14 And Kore the son of Imnah the Levite, the keeper of the eastern gate, was over the freewill

---

31:1 pillars . . . Asherim. See note on Deut. 7:5.
31:2 divisions of the priests. See note on 1 Chron. 24:4.
31:4 the portion. For supporting the priesthood. See note on Num. 18:8-20.
31:7-19 From the third month (May-June) to the seventh month (Sept.-Oct.) the people brought their tithes in such abundance that Hezekiah ordered storehouses prepared (so that the food would not have to be left outside in heaps) and lists made of those entitled to receive the supplies.

offerings of God, to apportion the contributions for the LORD and the most holy things.

15 And under his authority were ᵃEden, Miniamin, Jeshua, Shemaiah, Amariah, and Shecaniah in ᵇthe cities of the priests, to distribute faithfully *their portions* to their brothers by divisions, whether great or small,

16 without regard to their genealogical enrollment, to the males from ᵃthirty years old and upward—everyone who entered the house of the LORD ᵇfor his daily obligations—for their work in their duties according to their divisions;

17 as well as the priests who were enrolled genealogically according to their fathers' households, and the Levites ᵃfrom twenty years old and upwards, by their duties *and* their divisions.

18 And the genealogical enrollment *included* all their little children, their wives, their sons, and their daughters, for the whole assembly, for they consecrated themselves faithfully in holiness.

19 Also for the sons of Aaron the priests *who were* in ᵃthe pasture lands of their cities, or in each and every city, ᵇthere were men who were designated by name to distribute portions to every male among the priests and to everyone genealogically enrolled among the Levites.

20 And thus Hezekiah did throughout all Judah; and ᵃhe did what *was* good, right, and true before the LORD his God.

21 And every work which he began in the service of the house of God in law and in commandment, seeking his God, he did with all his heart and ᵃprospered.

2 His victory over the Assyrians, 32:1-23

32 After these acts of faithfulness ᵃSennacherib king

of Assyria came and invaded Judah and besieged the fortified cities, and thought to break into them for himself.

2 Now when Hezekiah saw that Sennacherib had come, and that he intended to make war on Jerusalem,

3 he decided with his officers and his warriors to cut off the *supply of* water from the springs which *were* outside the city, and they helped him.

4 So many people assembled ᵃand stopped up all the springs and ᵇthe stream which flowed through the region, saying, "Why should the kings of Assyria come and find abundant water?"

5 And he took courage and ᵃrebuilt all the wall that had been broken down, and erected towers on it, and *built* ᵇanother outside wall, and strengthened the ᶜMillo in the city of David, and made weapons and shields in great number.

6 And he appointed military officers over the people, and gathered them to him in the square at the city gate, and ᵃspoke encouragingly to them, saying,

7 "ᵃBe strong and courageous, do not fear or be dismayed because of the king of Assyria, nor because of all the multitude which is with him; ᵇfor the one with us is greater than the one with him.

8 "With him is *only* ᵃan arm of flesh, but ᵇwith us is the LORD our God to help us and to fight our battles." And the people relied on the words of Hezekiah king of Judah.

9 After this ᵃSennacherib king of Assyria sent his servants to Jerusalem while he *was* besieging Lachish with all his forces with him, against Hezekiah king of Judah and against all Judah who *were* at Jerusalem, saying,

10 "Thus says Sennacherib king of Assyria, 'On what are you

15 ᵃ2 Chr. 29:12 ᵇJosh. 21:9-19

16 ᵃ1 Chr. 23:3 ᵇEzra 3:4

17 ᵃ1 Chr. 23:24

19 ᵃLev. 25:34; Num. 35:2-5 ᵇ2 Chr. 31:12-15

20 ᵃ2 Kin. 20:3; 22:2

21 ᵃDeut. 29:9; Prov. 3:9, 10

1 ᵃ2 Kin. 18:13-19, 37; Is. 36:1-37:38

4 ᵃ2 Kin. 20:20 ᵇ2 Chr. 32:30

★ **5** ᵃ2 Chr. 25:23 ᵇ2 Kin. 25:4 ᶜ1 Kin. 9:24

6 ᵃ2 Chr. 30:22

7 ᵃ1 Chr. 22:13 ᵇ2 Kin. 6:16

8 ᵃJer. 17:5 ᵇ2 Chr. 20:17

★ **9-19**
9 ᵃ2 Kin. 18:17

32:5 *Millo.* See note on 1 Kings 9:24. This passage does not mention the tribute Hezekiah paid to Sennacherib (see note on 2 Kings 18:14).

32:9-19 See notes on 2 Kings 18:17-32 and 19:8-13.

trusting that you are remaining in Jerusalem under siege?

11 'Is not Hezekiah misleading you to give yourselves over to die by hunger and by thirst, saying, "The LORD our God will deliver us from the hand of the king of Assyria"?

12 'ᵃHas not the same Hezekiah taken away His high places and His altars, and said to Judah and Jerusalem, "You shall worship before one altar, and on it you shall burn incense"?

13 'Do you not know what I and my fathers have done to all the peoples of the lands? ᵃWere the gods of the nations of the lands able at all to deliver their land from my hand?

14 'ᵃWho *was there* among all the gods of those nations which my fathers utterly destroyed who could deliver his people out of my hand, that your God should be able to deliver you from my hand?

15 'Now therefore, do not let Hezekiah deceive you or mislead you like this, and do not believe him, for ᵃno god of any nation or kingdom was able to deliver his people from my hand or from the hand of my fathers. How much less shall your God deliver you from my hand?' "

16 And his servants spoke further against the LORD God and against His servant Hezekiah.

17 He also wrote letters to insult the LORD God of Israel, and to speak against Him, saying, "ᵃAs the gods of the nations of the lands have not delivered their people from my hand, so the God of Hezekiah shall not deliver His people from my hand."

18 And ᵃthey called this out with a loud voice in the language of Judah to the people of Jerusalem who were on the wall, to frighten and terrify them, so that they might take the city.

19 And they spoke of the God of Jerusalem as of ᵃthe gods of the peoples of the earth, the work of men's hands.

20 But King Hezekiah and Isaiah the prophet, the son of Amoz, prayed about this and cried out to heaven.

21 And the LORD sent an angel who destroyed every mighty warrior, commander and officer in the camp of the king of Assyria. So he returned in shame to his own land. And when he had entered the temple of his god, some of his own children killed him there with the sword.

22 So the LORD ᵃsaved Hezekiah and the inhabitants of Jerusalem from the hand of Sennacherib the king of Assyria, and from the hand of all *others,* and guided them on every side.

23 And ᵃmany were bringing gifts to the LORD at Jerusalem and choice presents to Hezekiah king of Judah, so that ᵇhe was exalted in the sight of all nations thereafter.

3 His last days, 32:24–33

24 ᵃIn those days Hezekiah became mortally ill; and he prayed to the LORD, and the LORD spoke to him and gave him a sign.

25 But Hezekiah gave no return for the benefit he received, ᵃbecause his heart was proud; ᵇtherefore wrath came on him and on Judah and Jerusalem.

26 However, ᵃHezekiah humbled the pride of his heart, both he and the inhabitants of Jerusalem, so that the wrath of the LORD did not come on them in the days of Hezekiah.

Cross references (margin):

12 ᵃ2 Chr. 31:1
13 ᵃ2 Kin. 18:33-35
14 ᵃIs. 10:9-11
15 ᵃEx. 5:2; Is. 36:18-20; Dan. 3:15
17 ᵃ2 Chr. 32:14
18 ᵃ2 Kin. 18:28
19 ᵃPs. 115:4-8
★21
22 ᵃIs. 31:5
23 ᵃ2 Sam. 8:10 ᵇ2 Chr. 1:1
★24 ᵃ2 Kin. 20:1-11; Is. 38:1-8
25 ᵃ2 Chr. 26:16; 32:31 ᵇ2 Chr. 24:18
26 ᵃJer. 26:18, 19

32:21 For this supernatural deliverance see note on Isa. 37:36. Sennacherib's own sons killed him (Isa. 37:38).

32:24 On Hezekiah's sickness and the sign God gave him, see the note on 2 Kings 20:11.

27 Now Hezekiah had immense riches and honor; and he made for himself treasuries for silver, gold, precious stones, spices, shields and all kinds of valuable articles,

28 storehouses also for the produce of grain, wine and oil, pens for all kinds of cattle and sheepfolds for the flocks.

29 ^a1 Chr. 29:12

29 And he made cities for himself, and acquired flocks and herds in abundance; for ^aGod had given him very great wealth.

★30 ^a2 Kin. 20:20
^b1 Kin. 1:33

30 It was Hezekiah who ^astopped the upper outlet of the waters of ^bGihon and directed them to the west side of the city of David. And Hezekiah prospered in all that he did.

★31 ^a2 Kin. 20:12; Is. 39:1 ^b2 Chr. 32:24; Is. 38:7, 8 ^cDeut. 8:16

31 And even *in the matter of* ^athe envoys of the rulers of Babylon, who sent to him to inquire of ^bthe wonder that had happened in the land, God left him *alone only* ^cto test him, that He might know all that was in his heart.

32 Now the rest of the acts of Hezekiah and his deeds of devotion, behold, they are written in the vision of Isaiah the prophet, the son of Amoz, in the Book of the Kings of Judah and Israel.

33 ^aPs. 112:6; Prov. 10:7

33 So Hezekiah slept with his fathers, and they buried him in the upper section of the tombs of the sons of David; and all Judah and the inhabitants of Jerusalem ^ahonored him at his death. And his son Manasseh became king in his place.

N   Manasseh (695–642; 2 Kings 21:1–18), 33:1–20

★ 1-2
1 ^a2 Kin. 21:1-9

33 ^aManasseh was twelve years old when he became king, and he reigned fifty-five years in Jerusalem.

2 ^a2 Chr. 28:3; Jer. 15:4

2 And ^ahe did evil in the sight of the LORD according to the abominations of the nations whom the LORD dispossessed before the sons of Israel.

★ 3 ^a2 Chr. 31:1 ^bDeut. 16:21; 2 Kin. 23:5, 6

3 For ^ahe rebuilt the high places which Hezekiah his father had broken down; ^bhe also erected altars for the Baals and made Asherim, and worshiped all the host of heaven and served them.

4 ^a2 Chr. 28:24 ^b2 Sam. 7:13; 2 Chr. 7:16

4 And ^ahe built altars in the house of the LORD of which the LORD had said, "My name shall be ^bin Jerusalem forever."

5 ^a2 Chr. 4:9

5 For he built altars for all the host of heaven in ^athe two courts of the house of the LORD.

★ 6 ^a2 Chr. 28:3 ^bLev. 19:31; 20:27

6 And ^ahe made his sons pass through the fire in the valley of Ben-hinnom; and he practiced witchcraft, used divination, practiced sorcery, and ^bdealt with mediums and spiritists. He did much evil in the sight of the LORD, provoking Him *to anger.*

7 ^a2 Chr. 33:15 ^b1 Kin. 9:3-5; 2 Chr. 7:16; 33:4

7 Then he put ^athe carved image of the idol which he had made in the house of God, of which God had said to David and to Solomon his son, "^bIn this house and in Jerusalem, which I have chosen from all the tribes of Israel, I will put My name forever;

8 ^a2 Sam. 7:10

8 and I will not again remove the foot of Israel from the land ^awhich I have appointed for your fathers, if only they will observe to do all that I have commanded them according to all the law, the statutes, and the ordinances *given* through Moses."

9 Thus Manasseh misled Judah and the inhabitants of Jerusalem to do more evil than the

---

32:30 An inscription found in 1880 near the mouth of the Siloam tunnel describes this remarkable engineering feat by which water was brought from the Spring of Gihon to a place inside the city. Diggers worked from both ends, meeting almost exactly in the middle of this 1,200 cubit-long tunnel (since it measures 1,777 feet, we know that the cubit was about

18 inches).
32:31 See notes on 2 Kings 20:12, 17–18, 19.
33:1-2 *Manasseh.* See note on 2 Kings 21:1.
33:3 On astral worship see note on Deut. 4:19.
33:6 *Ben-hinnom.* See notes on 2 Kings 23:10 and Jer. 7:31. On these various facets of *witchcraft* see note on Deut. 18:10–11.

nations whom the LORD destroyed before the sons of Israel.

10 aNeh. 9:29; Jer. 25:4

10 And the LORD spoke to Manasseh and his people, but athey paid no attention.

★**11** aDeut. 28:36 b2 Chr. 36:6

11 aTherefore the LORD brought the commanders of the army of the king of Assyria against them, and they captured Manasseh with hooks, bbound him with bronze *chains*, and took him to Babylon.

12 aPs. 118:5; 120:1; 130:1, 2 b2 Chr. 32:26

12 And when ahe was in distress, he entreated the LORD his God and bhumbled himself greatly before the God of his fathers.

13 a2 Chr. 20; Ezra 8:23 bDan. 4:32

13 When he prayed to Him, aHe was moved by his entreaty and heard his supplication, and brought him again to Jerusalem to his kingdom. Then Manasseh bknew that the LORD *was* God.

14 a1 Kin. 1:33 bNeh. 3:3 c2 Chr. 27:3

14 Now after this he built the outer wall of the city of David on the west side of aGihon, in the valley, even to the entrance of the bFish Gate; and he encircled the cOphel *with it* and made it very high. Then he put army commanders in all the fortified cities of Judah.

15 a2 Chr. 33:3-7

15 He also aremoved the foreign gods and the idol from the house of the LORD, as well as all the altars which he had built on the mountain of the house of the LORD and in Jerusalem, and he threw *them* outside the city.

16 aLev. 7:11-18

16 And he set up the altar of the LORD and sacrificed apeace offerings and thank offerings on it; and he ordered Judah to serve the LORD God of Israel.

★**17** a2 Chr. 32:12

17 Nevertheless athe people still sacrificed in the high places, *although* only to the LORD their God.

18 Now the rest of the acts of Manasseh even ahis prayer to his God, and the words of bthe seers who spoke to him in the name of the LORD God of Israel, behold, they are among the records of the kings of cIsrael.

18 a2 Chr. 33:12, 13 b2 Chr. 33:10 c2 Chr. 21:2

19 His prayer also and a*how* God was entreated by him, and all his sin, his unfaithfulness, and bthe sites on which he built high places and erected the Asherim and the carved images, before he humbled himself, behold, they are written in the records of the Hozai.

19 a2 Chr. 33:13 b2 Chr. 33:3

20 So Manasseh slept with his fathers, and they buried him in his own house. And Amon his son became king in his place.

O   Amon (642-640; 2 Kings 21:19-26), 33:21-25

21 aAmon *was* twenty-two years old when he became king, and he reigned two years in Jerusalem.

21 a2 Kin. 21:19-24

22 And he did evil in the sight of the LORD as Manasseh his father ahad done, and Amon sacrificed to all bthe carved images which his father Manasseh had made, and he served them.

22 a2 Chr. 33:2-7 b2 Chr. 34:3, 4

23 Moreover, he did not humble himself before the LORD aas his father Manasseh had done, but Amon multiplied guilt.

23 a2 Chr. 33:12, 19

24 Finally ahis servants conspired against him and put him to death in his own house.

24 a2 Chr. 25:27

25 But the people of the land killed all the conspirators against King Amon, and the people of the land made Josiah his son king in his place.

33:11 This probably occurred during the reign of Ashurbanipal (648). *hooks.* Placed through the nostrils of important prisoners (2 Kings 19:28).

33:17 Even though the *high places* were used to worship Yahweh, such localized worship was contrary to the law concerning worship in a central sanctuary (see note on Deut. 12:5).

P Josiah (640-609; 2 Kings 22:1-23:30), 34:1-35:27

1 His reforms, 34:1-13

1 a2 Kin. 22:1, 2; Jer. 1:2; 3:6

34 ^aJosiah *was* eight years old when he became king, and he reigned thirty-one years in Jerusalem.

2 a2 Chr. 29:2

2 And ^ahe did right in the sight of the Lord, and walked in the ways of his father David and did not turn aside to the right or to the left.

3 a2 Chr. 15:2; Prov. 8:17 b1 Kin. 13:2; 2 Chr. 33:22

3 For in the eighth year of his reign while he was still a youth, he began to ^aseek the God of his father David; and in the twelfth year he began ^bto purge Judah and Jerusalem of the high places, the Asherim, the carved images, and the molten images.

4 a2 Kin. 23:4, 5, 11 bEx. 32:20

4 And they tore down the altars of the Baals in his presence, and ^athe incense altars that were high above them he chopped down; also the Asherim, the carved images, and the molten images he broke in pieces and ^bground to powder and scattered *it* on the graves of those who had sacrificed to them.

★ 5 a1 Kin. 13:2; 2 Kin. 23:20

5 Then ^ahe burned the bones of the priests on their altars, and purged Judah and Jerusalem.

6 a2 Kin. 23:15, 19

6 And ^ain the cities of Manasseh, Ephraim, Simeon, even as far as Naphtali, in their surrounding ruins,

7 a2 Chr. 31:1

7 he also tore down the altars and ^abeat the Asherim and the carved images into powder, and chopped down all the incense altars throughout the land of Israel. Then he returned to Jerusalem.

★ 8-13

8 a2 Kin. 22:3-20 b2 Chr. 18:25

8 ^aNow in the eighteenth year of his reign, when he had purged the land and the house, he sent Shaphan the son of Azaliah, and Maaseiah ^ban official of the city, and Joah the son of Joahaz the recorder, to repair the house of the Lord his God.

9 And they came to ^aHilkiah the high priest and delivered the money that was brought into the house of God, which the Levites, the doorkeepers, had collected from ^bManasseh and Ephraim, and from all the remnant of Israel, and from all Judah and Benjamin and the inhabitants of Jerusalem.

9 a2 Chr. 35:8 b2 Chr. 30:10, 18

10 Then they gave *it* into the hands of the workmen who had the oversight of the house of the Lord, and the workmen who were working in the house of the Lord used it to restore and repair the house.

11 They in turn gave *it* to the carpenters and to the builders to buy quarried stone and timber for couplings and to make beams for the houses ^awhich the kings of Judah had let go to ruin.

11 a2 Chr. 33:4-7

12 And ^athe men did the work faithfully with foremen over them to supervise: Jahath and Obadiah, the Levites of the sons of Merari, Zechariah and Meshullam of the sons of the Kohathites, and ^bthe Levites, all who were skillful with musical instruments.

12 a2 Kin. 12:15 b1 Chr. 25:1

13 *They were* also over ^athe burden bearers, and supervised all the workmen from job to job; and *some* of the Levites *were* scribes and officials and gatekeepers.

13 aNeh. 4:10

2 His discovery of the law, 34:14-33

14 When they were bringing out the money which had been brought into the house of the Lord, ^aHilkiah the priest found the book of the law of the Lord *given* by Moses.

★14 a2 Chr. 34:9

15 And Hilkiah responded and said to Shaphan the scribe, "I have found the book of the law in the house of the Lord." And Hilkiah gave the book to Shaphan.

16 Then Shaphan brought the book to the king and reported

34:5 See notes on 2 Kings 23:14, 16.
34:8-13 See note on 2 Kings 22:4-7.

34:14 *book of the law.* See note on 2 Kings 22:8.

further word to the king, saying, "Everything that was entrusted to your servants they are doing.

17 "They have also emptied out the money which was found in the house of the Lord, and have delivered it into the hands of the supervisors and the workmen."

18 Moreover, Shaphan the scribe told the king saying, "Hilkiah the priest gave me a book." And Shaphan read from it in the presence of the king.

19 And it came about when the king heard *the words of the law that *bhe tore his clothes.

20 Then the king commanded Hilkiah, Ahikam the son of Shaphan, Abdon the son of Micah, Shaphan the scribe, and Asaiah the king's servant, saying,

21 "Go, inquire of the Lord for me and for those who are left in Israel and in Judah, concerning the words of the book which has been found; for *great is the wrath of the Lord which is poured out on us because our fathers have not observed the word of the Lord, to do according to all that is written in this book."

22 So Hilkiah and *those* whom the king had told went to Huldah the prophetess, the wife of Shallum the son of Tokhath, the son of Hasrah, the keeper of the wardrobe (now she lived in Jerusalem in the Second Quarter); and they spoke to her regarding this.

23 And she said to them, "Thus says the Lord, the God of Israel, 'Tell the man who sent you to Me,

24 thus says the Lord, "Behold, *I am bringing evil on this place and on its inhabitants, *even* all *bthe curses written in the book which they have read in the presence of the king of Judah.

25 "*aBecause they have forsaken Me and have burned incense to other gods, that they

might provoke Me to anger with all the works of their hands, therefore My wrath will be poured out on this place, and it shall not be quenched." '

26 "But to the king of Judah who sent you to inquire of the Lord, thus you will say to him, 'Thus says the Lord God of Israel *regarding* the words which you have heard,

27 "*aBecause your heart was tender and you humbled yourself before God, when you heard His words against this place and against its inhabitants, and *because* you humbled yourself before Me, tore your clothes, and wept before Me, I truly have heard you," declares the Lord.

28 "Behold, I will gather you to your fathers and you shall be gathered to your grave in peace, so your eyes shall not see all the evil which I will bring on this place and on its inhabitants."' " And they brought back word to the king.

29 *aThen the king sent and gathered all the elders of Judah and Jerusalem.

30 And the king went up to the house of the Lord and *all the men of Judah, the inhabitants of Jerusalem, the priests, the Levites, and all the people, from the greatest to the least; and he read in their hearing all the words of the book of the covenant which was found in the house of the Lord.

31 Then the king *astood in his place and *bmade a covenant before the Lord to walk after the Lord, and to keep His commandments and His testimonies and His statutes with all his heart and with all his soul, to perform the words of the covenant written in this book.

32 Moreover, he made all who were present in Jerusalem and Benjamin to stand *with him.* So the inhabitants of Jerusalem did according to the covenant of God, the God of their fathers.

Cross references (margin):

19 aDeut. 28:3-68
bJosh. 7:6

21 a2 Chr. 29:8

★22

24 a2 Chr. 36:14-20
bDeut. 28:15-68

25 a2 Chr. 33:3

27 a2 Kin. 22:19; 2 Chr. 12:7; 32:26

★28

29 a2 Kin. 23:1-3

30 aNeh. 8:1-3

31 a2 Kin. 11:14; 23:3; 2 Chr. 30:16
b2 Chr. 23:16; 29:10

34:22 *Huldah the prophetess.* See note on 2 Kings 22:14.

34:28 *in peace.* See note on 2 Kings 22:20.

★33 ᵃ2 Chr.
34:3-7

33 And Josiah ᵃremoved all the abominations from all the lands belonging to the sons of Israel, and made all who were present in Israel to serve the Lᴏʀᴅ their God. Throughout his lifetime they did not turn from following the Lᴏʀᴅ God of their fathers.

3 His observance of the Passover, 35:1-19

1 ᵃ2 Kin.
23:21 ᵇEx.
12:6; Num.
9:3

35 Then Josiah ᵃcelebrated the Passover to the Lᴏʀᴅ in Jerusalem, and ᵇthey slaughtered the Passover *animals* on the fourteenth *day* of the first month.

2 ᵃ2 Chr.
29:11

2 And he set the priests in their offices and ᵃencouraged them in the service of the house of the Lᴏʀᴅ.

★ 3 ᵃ2 Chr.
17:8, 9; Neh.
8:7 ᵇ1 Chr.
23:26

3 He also said to ᵃthe Levites who taught all Israel *and* who were holy to the Lᴏʀᴅ, "Put the holy ark in the house which Solomon the son of David king of Israel built; ᵇit will be a burden on *your* shoulders no longer. Now serve the Lᴏʀᴅ your God and His people Israel.

★ 4 ᵃ1 Chr.
9:10-13
ᵇ2 Chr. 8:14

4 "And ᵃprepare *yourselves* by your fathers' households in your divisions, according to the writing of David king of Israel and ᵇaccording to the writing of his son Solomon.

5 ᵃEzra
6:18

5 "Moreover, ᵃstand in the holy place according to the sections of the fathers' households of your brethren the lay people, and according to the Levites, by division of a father's household.

6 ᵃ2 Chr.
35:1 ᵇ2 Chr.
29:5

6 "Now ᵃslaughter the Passover *animals*, ᵇsanctify yourselves, and prepare for your brethren to do according to the word of the Lᴏʀᴅ by Moses."

7 And Josiah contributed to the lay people, to all who were present, flocks of lambs and kids, all for the Passover offerings, numbering 30,000 plus 3,000

bulls; these were from the king's possessions.

8 ᵃ2 Chr.
31:13

8 His officers also contributed a freewill offering to the people, the priests, and the Levites. Hilkiah and Zechariah and Jehiel, ᵃthe officials of the house of God, gave to the priests for the Passover offerings 2,600 *from the flocks* and 300 bulls.

9 ᵃ2 Chr.
31:12

9 ᵃConaniah also, and Shemaiah and Nethanel, his brothers, and Hashabiah and Jeiel and Jozabad, the officers of the Levites, contributed to the Levites for the Passover offerings 5,000 *from the flocks* and 500 bulls.

10 ᵃ2 Chr.
35:5

10 So the service was prepared, and ᵃthe priests stood at their stations and the Levites by their divisions according to the king's command.

11 ᵃ2 Chr.
35:1, 6
ᵇ2 Chr.
29:22
ᶜ2 Chr.
29:34

11 And ᵃthey slaughtered the Passover *animals*, and while ᵇthe priests sprinkled the blood received from their hand, ᶜthe Levites skinned them.

★12

12 Then they removed the burnt offerings that *they* might give them to the sections of the fathers' households of the lay people to present to the Lᴏʀᴅ, as it is written in the book of Moses. They did this also with the bulls.

13 ᵃEx. 12:8,
9 ᵇLev. 6:28

13 So ᵃthey roasted the Passover *animals* on the fire according to the ordinance, and they boiled ᵇthe holy things in pots, in kettles, in pans, and carried *them* speedily to all the lay people.

14 And afterwards they prepared for themselves and for the priests, because the priests, the sons of Aaron, *were* offering the burnt offerings and the fat until night; therefore the Levites prepared for themselves and for the priests, the sons of Aaron.

15 ᵃ1 Chr.
25:1 ᵇ1 Chr.
26:12-19

15 The singers, the sons of Asaph, *were* also at their stations ᵃaccording to the command of David, Asaph, Heman, and Jeduthun the king's seer; and ᵇthe

---

34:33 For details of Josiah's removal of the idolatrous *abominations* see 2 Kings 23:4-14.
35:3 The Ark apparently had been removed (probably during the reign of Manasseh) to

keep it from being profaned (33:7).
35:4 *in your divisions.* See note on 1 Chron. 24:4.
35:12 See note on Lev. 3:3.

gatekeepers at each gate did not have to depart from their service, because the Levites their brethren prepared for them.

16 So all the service of the LORD was prepared on that day to celebrate the Passover, and to offer burnt offerings on the altar of the LORD according to the command of King Josiah.

17 Thus [a]the sons of Israel who were present celebrated the Passover at that time, and the Feast of Unleavened Bread seven days.

18 And [a]there had not been celebrated a Passover like it in Israel since the days of Samuel the prophet; nor had any of the kings of Israel celebrated such a Passover as Josiah did with the priests, the Levites, all Judah and Israel who were present, and the inhabitants of Jerusalem.

19 In the eighteenth year of Josiah's reign this Passover was celebrated.

4 His death, 35:20-27

20 [a]After all this, when Josiah had set the temple in order, Neco king of Egypt came up to make war at [b]Carchemish on the Euphrates, and Josiah went out to engage him.

21 But Neco sent messengers to him, saying, "[a]What have we to do with each other, O King of Judah? I am not coming against you today but against the house with which I am at war, and God has ordered me to hurry. Stop for your own sake from interfering with God who is with me, that He may not destroy you."

22 However, Josiah would not turn away from him, but [a]disguised himself in order to make war with him; nor did he listen to the words of Neco [b]from the

mouth of God, but came to make war on the plain of [c]Megiddo.

23 And the archers shot King Josiah, and the king said to his servants, "Take me away, for I am badly wounded."

24 So his servants took him out of the chariot and carried him in the second chariot which he had, and brought him to Jerusalem where he died and was buried in the tombs of his fathers. [a]And all Judah and Jerusalem mourned for Josiah.

25 Then [a]Jeremiah chanted a lament for Josiah. And all the male and female singers speak about Josiah in their lamentations to this day. And they made them an ordinance in Israel; behold, they are also written in the Lamentations.

26 Now the rest of the acts of Josiah and his deeds of devotion as written in the law of the LORD,

27 and his acts, first to last, behold, they are written in the Book of the Kings of Israel and Judah.

Q Joahaz (609; 2 Kings 23:31-33), 36:1-4

36 [a]Then the people of the land took [b]Joahaz the son of Josiah, and made him king in place of his father in Jerusalem.

2 Joahaz was twenty-three years old when he became king, and he reigned three months in Jerusalem.

3 Then the king of Egypt deposed him at Jerusalem, and imposed on the land a fine of one hundred talents of silver and one talent of gold.

4 And the king of Egypt made Eliakim his brother king over Judah and Jerusalem, and changed his name to Jehoiakim. But [a]Neco took Joahaz his brother and brought him to Egypt.

Side references:

17 [a]Ex. 12:1-20; 2 Chr. 30:21

★18 [a]2 Kin. 23:21; 2 Chr. 30:5

★20 [a]2 Kin. 23:29, 30 [b]Is. 10:9; Jer. 46:2

★21-22

21 [a]2 Chr. 25:19

22 [a]2 Chr. 18:29 [b]2 Chr. 35:21 [c]Judg. 5:19

24 [a]Zech. 12:11

25 [a]Jer. 22:10; Lam. 4:20

1 [a]2 Kin. 23:30-34 [b]Jer. 22:11

★ 3

★ 4 [a]Jer. 22:10-12

35:18 See note on 2 Kings 23:22.
35:20 *Neco.* See note on 2 Kings 23:29.
35:21-22 Neco only wished to move his army through Palestine, without engaging in battle; however, Josiah refused to believe this even though the message was *from the mouth of*

God. Megiddo. See note on 1 Kings 9:15.
36:3 The silver amounted to 120,000 ounces, and the gold, 1,200 ounces.
36:4 On the chronology of these rulers see the Introduction to Jeremiah. On Jehoiakim see notes on 2 Kings 23:35 and 24:1.

R Jehoiakim (Eliakim, 609-597; 2 Kings 23:34-24:7), 36:5-8

5 a 2 Kin. 23:36, 37; Jer. 22:13- 19; 26:1; 35:1

5 aJehoiakim was twenty-five years old when he became king, and he reigned eleven years in Jerusalem; and he did evil in the sight of the Lord his God.

★ 6-7
6 a 2 Kin. 24:1; Jer. 25:1-9
b 2 Chr. 33:11

6 Nebuchadnezzar king of Babylon came up aagainst him and bbound him with bronze *chains* to take him to Babylon.

7 a 2 Kin. 24:13

7 aNebuchadnezzar also brought *some* of the articles of the house of the Lord to Babylon and put them in his temple at Babylon.

8 a 2 Kin. 24:5

8 aNow the rest of the acts of Jehoiakim and the abominations which he did, and what was found against him, behold, they are written in the Book of the Kings of Israel and Judah. And Jehoiachin his son became king in his place.

S Jehoiachin (597; 2 Kings 24:8-16), 36:9-10

9 a 2 Kin. 24:8-17

9 aJehoiachin was eight years old when he became king, and he reigned three months and ten days in Jerusalem, and he did evil in the sight of the Lord.

10 a 2 Sam. 11:1; Jer. 22:25; 24:1; 29:1; Ezek. 17:12 b Jer. 37:1

10 And aat the turn of the year King Nebuchadnezzar sent and brought him to Babylon with the valuable articles of the house of the Lord, and he made his kinsman bZedekiah king over Judah and Jerusalem.

T Zedekiah (597-586; 2 Kings 24:17-25:21), 36:11-21

11 a 2 Kin. 24:18-20; Jer. 27:1; 28:1; 52:1

11 aZedekiah was twenty-one years old when he became king, and he reigned eleven years in Jerusalem.

12 And he did evil in the sight of the Lord his God; ahe did not humble himself bbefore Jeremiah the prophet who spoke for the Lord.

12 a 2 Chr. 33:23 b Jer. 21:3-7

13 And ahe also rebelled against King Nebuchadnezzar who had made him swear *allegiance* by God. But bhe stiffened his neck and hardened his heart against turning to the Lord God of Israel.

★13 a Jer. 52:3; Ezek. 17:15 b 2 Chr. 30:8

14 Furthermore, all the officials of the priests and the people were very unfaithful *following* all the abominations of the nations; and they defiled the house of the Lord which He had sanctified in Jerusalem.

★14-21

15 And the Lord, the God of their fathers, asent *word* to them again and again by His messengers, because He had compassion on His people and on His dwelling place;

15 a Jer. 7:13; 25:3

16 but they *continually* amocked the messengers of God, bdespised His words and scoffed at His prophets, cuntil the wrath of the Lord arose against His people, until there was no remedy.

16 a 2 Chr. 30:10; Jer. 5:12, 13 b Prov. 1:24-32 c Ezra 5:12

17 aTherefore He brought up against them the king of the Chaldeans who slew their young men with the sword in the house of their sanctuary, and had no compassion on young man or virgin, old man or infirm; He gave *them* all into his hand.

17 a 2 Kin. 25:1-7; Jer. 21:1-10

18 And aall the articles of the house of God, great and small, and the treasures of the house of the Lord, and the treasures of the king and of his officers, he brought *them* all to Babylon.

18 a 2 Chr. 36:7, 10

19 Then athey burned the house of God, and broke down the wall of Jerusalem and burned all its fortified buildings with fire, and destroyed all its valuable articles.

19 a 1 Kin. 9:8; 2 Kin. 25:9; Jer. 52:13

36:6-7 This refers to Nebuchadnezzar's first invasion of Jerusalem, in 605.
36:13 On Zedekiah's fate see note on 2 Kings 25:7.
36:14-21 Two reasons are given here for the Babylonian captivity: continued idolatry, and failure to give the land 70 sabbatical years of rest (see note on Lev. 25:2-7). For the completion of the 70 years of captivity see note on Ezra 3:8.

20 ^a2 Kin.
25:11 ^bJer.
27:7

20 And those who had escaped from the sword he ^acarried away to Babylon; and ^bthey were servants to him and to his sons until the rule of the kingdom of Persia,

21 ^aJer.
29:10 ^bLev.
26:34 ^cLev.
25:4 ^dJer.
25:11
★**22** ^aEzra
1:1-3 ^bJer.
25:12; 29:10
^cIs. 44:28

21 ^ato fulfill the word of the LORD by the mouth of Jeremiah, until ^bthe land had enjoyed its sabbaths. ^cAll the days of its desolation it kept sabbath ^duntil seventy years were complete.

III THE DECREE OF CYRUS, 36:22-23

22 ^aNow in the first year of Cyrus king of Persia—in order to fulfill the word of the LORD ^bby the mouth of Jeremiah—the LORD ^cstirred up the spirit of Cyrus king of Persia, so that he sent a proclamation throughout his kingdom, and also *put it* in writing, saying,

23 "Thus says Cyrus king of Persia, 'The LORD, the God of heaven, has given me all the kingdoms of the earth, and He has appointed me to build Him a house in Jerusalem, which is in Judah. Whoever there is among you of all His people, may the LORD his God be with him, and let him go up!' "

36:22 *in the first year.* I.e., the first year that Cyrus was ruler of the conquered Babylonian Empire (538, though he had been king of Persia since 559). Verses 22-23 (identical to Ezra 1:1-2) lead the reader directly to the continuing historical account in the book of Ezra.

INTRODUCTION TO
THE BOOK OF EZRA

AUTHOR: Ezra   DATE: 456–444 B.C.

Title and Authorship *The book, named after its principal character, originally formed one work with the books of Nehemiah and Chronicles. Although Ezra is not mentioned in the book as its author, he most likely did write the book using various documents (e.g., 4:7-16), genealogies (e.g., 2:1-70), and personal memoirs (e.g., 7:27-9:15) and his sources. In the Vulgate (Latin Bible), Ezra and Nehemiah are titled 1 and 2 Esdras, while the apocryphal book called 1 Esdras in the English text is 3 Esdras in the Vulgate.*

Date *Although some date the book around 330 B.C., its linguistic similarities with the fifth century Aramaic papyri from the Jewish community at Elephantine, Egypt, argue for an earlier date during the lifetime of Ezra (who lived to the time of Nehemiah, Neh. 8:1-9; 12:36). Ezra probably finished the book between 456 (when the events of 10:17-44 took place) and 444, when Nehemiah arrived in Jerusalem.*

Historical Background *The book records the fulfillment of God's promise to restore Israel to her land after the 70 years of captivity in Babylon (Jer. 25:11). This was accomplished through the help of three Persian kings (Cyrus, Darius, and Artaxerxes) as well as Jewish leaders such as Zerubbabel, Joshua, Haggai, Zechariah, and Ezra. Cyrus overthrew Babylon in October 539, and in accord with his policy of encouraging subject people to return to their homelands, he issued a decree in 538 allowing the Jews to do the same (see Introduction to Zechariah). About 50,000 did return under the leadership of Zerubbabel, and the foundation of the Temple was laid, though it was not completed until 515 in the reign of Darius. Ezra 1-6 describe these events. Chapters 7-10 describe Ezra's return to Jerusalem under the favor of Artaxerxes to help bring spiritual revival to the people.*
The Persian kings involved in this period (in relation to Ezra and other portions of the O.T.) are as follows:

King (dates)		Corresponding Chapters in Ezra	Relation to Other Books of O.T.
Cyrus	538–530		
Cambyses	530–522	Chapters 1-6 (though there is	Haggai (520)
Smerdis	522	no mention of Cambyses or	Zechariah (520-515)
Darius I	521–486	Smerdis).	
Xerxes I (Ahasuerus)	486–465	4:6	Esther (474)
Artaxerxes I	464–423	4:7-23 and chaps. 7-10	Malachi (450-400)
Darius II	423–404		Nehemiah (445-425)

OUTLINE OF EZRA

I. The Return under Zerubbabel, 1:1-6:22
  A. The Decree of Cyrus, 1:1-11
  B. The Census of the People, 2:1-70
    1. Leaders, 2:1-2
    2. Families, 2:3-20
    3. Cities, 2:21-35
    4. Priests, 2:36-39
    5. Levites, 2:40-42
    6. Nethinim, 2:43-54
    7. Solomon's servants, 2:55-58
    8. Uncertain genealogies, 2:59-63
    9. Totals, 2:64-70
  C. The Construction of the Temple Begun, 3:1-13
    1. Sacrifices begun, 3:1-6

    2. Foundation begun, 3:7-13
  D. The Opposition, 4:1-24
    1. The compromise, 4:1-3
    2. The campaign, 4:4-5
    3. The climax, 4:6-24
  E. The Construction Renewed, 5:1-6:12
    1. The preaching of the prophets, 5:1-2
    2. The protest of Tattenai, 5:3-17
    3. The decree of Darius, 6:1-12
  F. The Temple Completed, 6:13-22
    1. The completion, 6:13-15
    2. The dedication, 6:16-18
    3. The Passover, 6:19-22
II. The Return under Ezra, 7:1-10:44
  A. The Return to Jerusalem, 7:1-8:36

THE BOOK OF EZRA

I THE RETURN UNDER ZERUBBABEL, 1:1-6:22

A The Decree of Cyrus, 1:1-11

★ 1 a2 Chr. 36:22; Jer. 25:12; 29:10
b Ezra 5:13

1 [a]Now in the first year of Cyrus king of Persia, in order to fulfill the word of the LORD by the mouth of Jeremiah, the LORD stirred up the spirit of Cyrus king of Persia, so that he [b]sent a proclamation throughout all his kingdom, and also *put it* in writing, saying,

★ 2 a Is. 44:28; 45:1, 12, 13

2 "Thus says Cyrus king of Persia, 'The LORD, the God of heaven, has given me all the kingdoms of the earth, and [a]He has appointed me to build Him a house in Jerusalem, which is in Judah.

3 a1 Kin. 8:23; 18:39; Is. 37:16; Dan. 6:26

3 'Whoever there is among you of all His people, may his God be with him! Let him go up to Jerusalem which is in Judah, and rebuild the house of the LORD, the God of Israel; [a]He is the God who is in Jerusalem.

★ 4

4 'And every survivor, at whatever place he may live, let the men of that place support him with silver and gold, with goods and cattle, together with a freewill offering for the house of God which is in Jerusalem.' "

★ 5 a Ezra 1:1, 2

5 Then the heads of fathers' *households* of Judah and Benjamin and the priests and the Levites arose, [a]even everyone whose spirit God had stirred to go up and rebuild the house of the LORD which is in Jerusalem.

6 a Neh. 6:9; Is. 35:3

6 And all those about them [a]encouraged them with articles of silver, with gold, with goods, with cattle, and with valuables, aside from all that was given as a freewill offering.

★ 7 a Ezra 5:14; 6:5
b 2 Kin. 24:13; 2 Chr. 36:7

7 [a]Also King Cyrus brought out the articles of the house of the LORD, [b]which Nebuchadnezzar had carried away from Jerusalem and put in the house of his gods;

★ 8 a Ezra 5:14

8 and Cyrus, king of Persia, had them brought out by the hand of Mithredath the treasurer, and he counted them out to [a]Sheshbazzar, the prince of Judah.

★ 9-11

9 a Ezra 8:27

9 Now this *was* their number: 30 [a]gold dishes, 1,000 silver dishes, 29 duplicates;

10 30 gold bowls, 410 silver bowls of a second *kind, and* 1,000 other articles.

11 All the articles of gold and silver *numbered* 5,400. Sheshbazzar brought them all up with the exiles who went up from Babylon to Jerusalem.

1:1 The action of *Cyrus,* predicted about 200 years before (see notes on Isa. 44:21-28; 45:1, 5 and Introduction to Zechariah), fulfilled the prophecy of *Jeremiah* (25:12).
1:2 This acknowledgment (cf. vv. 3, 4) of Yahweh provides no clear proof that Cyrus was a believer (see note on Isa. 45:5), but is evidence of his policy to conciliate captive peoples and their religions, as described in the Cyrus Cylinder. This decree was discovered by Darius I some 20 years later (6:2).
1:4 *let the men.* I.e., Gentile neighbors were to *help* by their donations (v. 6).
1:5 Although 49,897 chose to go (2:64-65), many

remained in Babylon.
1:7 Some of these *articles* had been looted and taken to Babylon in 605 (Dan. 1:2), others in 597 (2 Kings 24:13), and the rest in 586 (2 Kings 25:14-15; Jer. 27:16-22). The Temple furniture had been destroyed in 586 (2 Kings 25:13; Jer. 3:16).
1:8 *Sheshbazzar.* Zerubbabel's Babylonian name (cf. 5:16 with Zech. 4:9). He was the godly grandson of wicked King Jeconiah (1 Chron. 3:17-19; cf. Hag. 2:23).
1:9-11 The vessels totalled 5,400, of which the 2,499 listed in vv. 9-10 were evidently the largest or most important.

B The Census of the People, 2:1-70

1 Leaders, 2:1-2

1 *a* 2 Kin. 24:14-16; 25:11; 2 Chr. 36:20; Neh. 7:6-73

2 *a*Now these are the people of the province who came up out of the captivity of the exiles whom Nebuchadnezzar the king of Babylon had carried away to Babylon, and returned to Jerusalem and Judah, each to his city.

★ 2

2 These came with Zerubbabel, Jeshua, Nehemiah, Seraiah, Reelaiah, Mordecai, Bilshan, Mispar, Bigvai, Rehum, and Baanah.
The number of the men of the people of Israel:

2 Families, 2:3-20

★ 3-19

3   the sons of Parosh, 2,172;
4   the sons of Shephatiah, 372;

5 *a*Neh. 7:10
6 *a*Neh. 7:11

5   the sons of *a*Arah, 775;
6   the sons of *a*Pahath-moab of the sons of Jeshua *and* Joab, 2,812;
7   the sons of Elam, 1,254;
8   the sons of Zattu, 945;
9   the sons of Zaccai, 760;
10   the sons of Bani, 642;
11   the sons of Bebai, 623;
12   the sons of Azgad, 1,222;

13 *a*Ezra 8:13

13   the sons of *a*Adonikam, 666;
14   the sons of Bigvai, 2,056;
15   the sons of Adin, 454;
16   the sons of Ater of Hezekiah, 98;
17   the sons of Bezai, 323;
18   the sons of Jorah, 112;
19   the sons of Hashum, 223;
20   the sons of Gibbar, 95;

3 Cities, 2:21-35

21   the men of *a*Bethlehem, 123;

21 *a*Gen. 35:19; Matt. 2:6

22   the men of Netophah, 56;
23   the men of Anathoth, 128;
24   the sons of Azmaveth, 42;
25   the sons of Kiriath-arim, Chephirah, and Beeroth, 743;
26   the sons of *a*Ramah and Geba, 621;

26 *a*Josh. 18:25

27   the men of Michmas, 122;
28   the men of Bethel and Ai, 223;
29   the sons of Nebo, 52;
30   the sons of Magbish, 156;
31   the sons of the other Elam, 1,254;
32   the sons of Harim, 320;
33   the sons of Lod, Hadid, and Ono, 725;
34   the men of *a*Jericho, 345;
35   the sons of Senaah, 3,630.

34 *a*1 Kin. 16:34; 2 Chr. 28:15

4 Priests, 2:36-39

36   *a*The priests: the sons of Jedaiah of the house of Jeshua, 973;

36 *a*1 Chr. 24:7-18

37   the sons of *a*Immer, 1,052;

37 *a*1 Chr. 24:14

38   *a*the sons of Pashhur, 1,247;

38 *a*1 Chr. 9:12

39   the sons of *a*Harim, 1,017.

39 *a*1 Chr. 24:8

5 Levites, 2:40-42

40   The Levites: the sons of Jeshua and Kadmiel, of the sons of Hodaviah, 74.

★40

41   The singers: the sons of Asaph, 128.

★41

42   The sons of the gatekeepers: the sons of Shallum, the sons of Ater, the sons of Talmon, the

★42

2:2 *Jeshua.* The high priest (3:2). *Nehemiah.* Not the famous governor who went 80 years later. *Mordecai.* Not the one in the book of Esther and who remained in Persia.
2:3-19 These are apparently names of families, some members of which returned with Zerubbabel in 536 and others later with Ezra (cf. Ezra 8, 10; Neh. 10).
2:40 Only 74 Levites had chosen to return, in contrast with 4,289 priests (vv. 36-39). Ezra found the same reluctance on the part of the

Levites in his day (8:15), probably due to their inferior status in comparison to ministering priests.
2:41 *of Asaph.* An outstanding musician in the time of King David, who was appointed minister of music in the Temple (1 Chron. 15:19; 16:5) and whose descendants were also official musicians. Psalms 50, 73-83 are attributed to Asaph.
2:42 *gatekeepers.* Kept unauthorized people from entering forbidden areas in the Temple.

sons of Akkub, the sons of Hatita, the sons of Shobai, in all 139.

6 Nethinim, 2:43-54

★43 [a]1 Chr. 9:2

43 The [a]temple servants: the sons of Ziha, the sons of Hasupha, the sons of Tabbaoth,

44 the sons of Keros, the sons of Siaha, the sons of Padon,

45 the sons of Lebanah, the sons of Hagabah, the sons of Akkub,

46 the sons of Hagab, the sons of Shalmai, the sons of Hanan,

47 the sons of Giddel, the sons of Gahar, the sons of Reaiah,

48 the sons of Rezin, the sons of Nekoda, the sons of Gazzam,

49 the sons of Uzza, the sons of Paseah, the sons of Besai,

50 the sons of Asnah, the sons of Meunim, the sons of Nephisim,

51 the sons of Bakbuk, the sons of Hakupha, the sons of Harhur,

52 the sons of Bazluth, the sons of Mehida, the sons of Harsha,

53 the sons of Barkos, the sons of Sisera, the sons of Temah,

54 the sons of Neziah, the sons of Hatipha.

7 Solomon's servants, 2:55-58

55 [a]1 Kin. 9:21

55 The sons of [a]Solomon's servants: the sons of Sotai, the sons of Hassophereth, the sons of Peruda,

56 the sons of Jaalah, the sons of Darkon, the sons of Giddel,

57 the sons of Shephatiah, the sons of Hattil, the sons of Pochereth-hazzebaim, the sons of Ami.

★58 [a]1 Chr. 9:2 [b]1 Kin. 9:21

58 All the [a]temple servants, and the sons of [b]Solomon's servants, were 392.

8 Uncertain genealogies, 2:59-63

59 Now these are those who came up from Tel-melah, Tel-harsha, Cherub, Addan, and Immer, but they were not able to give evidence of their fathers' households, and their descendants, whether they were of Israel:

60 the sons of Delaiah, the sons of Tobiah, the sons of Nekoda, 652.

61 [a]2 Sam. 17:27; 1 Kin. 2:7

61 And of the sons of the priests: the sons of Habaiah, the sons of Hakkoz, the sons of [a]Barzillai, who took a wife from the daughters of Barzillai the Gileadite, and he was called by their name.

62 [a]Num. 16:39, 40

62 These searched among their ancestral registration, but they could not be located; [a]therefore they were considered unclean and excluded from the priesthood.

★63 [a]Lev. 2:3, 10 [b]Ex. 28:30; Num. 27:21

63 And the governor said to them [a]that they should not eat from the most holy things until a priest stood up with [b]Urim and Thummim.

9 Totals, 2:64-70

64 The whole assembly numbered 42,360,

65 [a]2 Chr. 35:25

65 besides their male and female servants, who numbered 7,337; and they had 200 [a]singing men and women.

66 Their horses were 736; their mules, 245;

67 their camels, 435; their donkeys, 6,720.

68 And some of the heads of fathers' households, when they arrived at the house of the Lord which is in Jerusalem, offered willingly for the house of God to restore it on its foundation.

2:43 *The temple servants.* Descendants of the Gibeonites (Josh. 9).
2:58 *Solomon's servants.* His prisoners of war.

2:63 *Urim and Thummim.* See note on Exod. 28:30.

★69 aEzra
8:25-34

69 According to their ability they gave ato the treasury for the work 61,000 gold drachmas, and 5,000 silver minas, and 100 priestly garments.

70 a1 Chr.
9:2; Neh.
11:3

70 aNow the priests and the Levites, some of the people, the singers, the gatekeepers, and the temple servants lived in their cities, and all Israel in their cities.

C The Construction of the Temple Begun, 3:1-13

1 Sacrifices begun, 3:1-6

★ 1 aNeh.
7:73; 8:1

3 Now when the seventh month came, and athe sons of Israel *were* in the cities, the people gathered together as one man to Jerusalem.

★ 2 aNeh.
12:1, 8
bEzra 2:2;
Hag. 1:1; 2:2
c1 Chr. 3:17
dEx. 27:1
eDeut.
12:5, 6

2 Then aJeshua the son of Jozadak and his brothers the priests, and bZerubbabel the son cof Shealtiel, and his brothers arose and dbuilt the altar of the God of Israel, to offer burnt offerings on it, eas it is written in the law of Moses, the man of God.

3 aEzra 4:4
bNum. 28:2

3 So they set up the altar on its foundation, for athey were terrified because of the peoples of the lands; and they boffered burnt offerings on it to the LORD, burnt offerings morning and evening.

★ 4 aNeh.
8:14; Zech.
14:16 bEx.
23:16 cNum.
29:12

4 And they celebrated the aFeast of Booths, bas it is written, and *offered* the fixed number of burnt offerings daily, caccording to the ordinance, as each day required;

★ 5 aEx.
29:38; Num.
28:3 bNum.
28:11 cNum.
29:39

5 and afterward *there was* a acontinual burnt offering, also bfor the new moons and cfor all the fixed festivals of the LORD that were consecrated, and from everyone who offered a freewill offering to the LORD.

6 From the first day of the seventh month they began to offer burnt offerings to the LORD, but the foundation of the temple of the LORD had not been laid.

2 Foundation begun, 3:7-13

★ 7 a2 Chr.
2:10; Acts
12:20
b2 Chr. 2:16
cActs 9:36
dEzra 1:2;
6:3

7 Then they gave money to the masons and carpenters, and afood, drink, and oil to the Sidonians and to the Tyrians, bto bring cedar wood from Lebanon to the sea at cJoppa, according to the permission they had from dCyrus king of Persia.

★ 8 aEzra
3:2; 4:3
b1 Chr. 23:4,
24

8 Now in the second year of their coming to the house of God at Jerusalem in the second month, aZerubbabel the son of Shealtiel and Jeshua the son of Jozadak and the rest of their brothers the priests and the Levites, and all who came from the captivity to Jerusalem, began *the work* and bappointed the Levites from twenty years and older to oversee the work of the house of the LORD.

9 aEzra
2:40

9 Then aJeshua *with* his sons and brothers stood united *with* Kadmiel and his sons, the sons of Judah *and* the sons of Henadad *with* their sons and brothers the Levites, to oversee the workmen in the temple of God.

10 aZech.
4:6-10
b1 Chr. 6:31;
25:1

10 Now when the builders had alaid the foundation of the temple of the LORD, the priests stood in their apparel with

---

2:69 *drachmas*. Lit., darics, a thick gold Persian coin weighing 130 grams, or 4.55 ounces. Thus the gifts amounted to 277,550 ounces of gold. *minas*. A mina was equivalent to 1.25 pounds, making a total of 6,250 pounds of silver.
3:1 The journey of 530 direct miles from Babylon to Palestine (about 900 traveling miles) would have taken at least 4 months (cf. 7:8-9).
3:2 The *altar* was erected on the first day of the seventh month (v. 6), which was the beginning of the Feast of Trumpets (Num. 29:1-6), an interesting foreshadowing of Israel's final regathering (see note on Lev. 23:24). *burnt offerings*. See note on Lev. 1:2. These were of-

fered morning and evening (v. 3; see note on Exod. 29:38-41).
3:4 *the Feast of Booths*. Lasting from the 15th to the 22nd of the seventh month (Sept.-Oct.; see note on Lev. 23:34-43).
3:5 *new moons*. See note on Amos 8:5, as well as Num. 28:11-15.
3:7 This pattern followed that of the building of Solomon's Temple (1 Kings 5:7-12). The details of Cyrus' decree are recorded in 6:3-5.
3:8 *twenty years*. See note on Num. 4:2, and 1 Chron. 23:24. The foundation was laid in the spring of 535, bringing to a close the 70 years of captivity, which had begun in 605.

trumpets, and the Levites, the sons of Asaph, with cymbals, to praise the LORD [b]according to the directions of King David of Israel.

11 [a]2 Chr. 7:3; Neh. 12:24, 40 **[b]**1 Chr. 16:34; 2 Chr. 5:13; Ps. 100:5; 106:1; 107:1; 118:1; 131:1; Jer. 33:11

11 And [a]they sang, praising and giving thanks to the LORD, saying, "[b]For He is good, for His lovingkindness is upon Israel forever." And all the people shouted with a great shout when they praised the LORD because the foundation of the house of the LORD was laid.

★12 [a]Hag. 2:3

12 Yet many of the priests and Levites and heads of fathers' households, [a]the old men who had seen the first temple, wept with a loud voice when the foundation of this house was laid before their eyes, while many shouted aloud for joy;

13 so that the people could not distinguish the sound of the shout of joy from the sound of the weeping of the people, for the people shouted with a loud shout, and the sound was heard far away.

D The Opposition, 4:1–24
1 The compromise, 4:1–3

★ 1-2

1 [a]Ezra 4:7-10 **[b]**Ezra 1:11

4 Now when [a]the enemies of Judah and Benjamin heard that [b]the people of the exile were building a temple to the LORD God of Israel,

2 [a]2 Kin. 17:32 **[b]**2 Kin. 19:37

2 they approached Zerubbabel and the heads of fathers' households, and said to them, "Let us build with you, for we, like you, seek your God; [a]and we

have been sacrificing to Him since the days of [b]Esarhaddon king of Assyria, who brought us up here."

3 [a]Neh. 2:20 **[b]**Ezra 1:1, 2

3 But Zerubbabel and Jeshua and the rest of the heads of fathers' households of Israel said to them, "[a]You have nothing in common with us in building a house to our God; but we ourselves will together build to the LORD God of Israel, [b]as King Cyrus, the king of Persia has commanded us."

2 The campaign, 4:4–5

4 [a]Ezra 3:3

4 Then [a]the people of the land discouraged the people of Judah, and frightened them from building,

★ 5

5 and hired counselors against them to frustrate their counsel all the days of Cyrus king of Persia, even until the reign of Darius king of Persia.

3 The climax, 4:6–24

★ 6 [a]Esth. 1:1; Dan. 9:1

6 Now in the reign of [a]Ahasuerus, in the beginning of his reign, they wrote an accusation against the inhabitants of Judah and Jerusalem.

★ 7 [a]2 Kin. 18:26; Dan. 2:4

7 And in the days of Artaxerxes, Bishlam, Mithredath, Tabeel, and the rest of his colleagues, wrote to Artaxerxes king of Persia; and the text of the letter was written in Aramaic and translated [a]from Aramaic.

8 Rehum the commander and Shimshai the scribe wrote a

3:12 Many older men who remembered the grandeur of Solomon's Temple (destroyed about 50 years before) wept because this Temple was smaller and less magnificent. The same reaction occurred 15 years later when construction was renewed (see note on Hag. 2:3).

4:1-2 the enemies. Descendants from the intermarriages of Israelites and foreigners who were transplanted to Samaria by Esarhaddon, king of Assyria, in 669 in fulfillment of the prophecy of Isa. 7:8, uttered in 734 (2 Kings 17:24). This procedure by the Assyrians effectively stifled nationalistic spirit and created a

syncretistic religion. Zerubbabel and Joshua refused the offer of help.

4:5 hired counselors. Probably public relations experts at the court in Shushan. Since Daniel was dead, the Jews had no one at court to counter the enemies' propaganda.

4:6 Ahasuerus. Xerxes I. See "Historical Background" in the Introduction to Ezra. Nowhere else mentioned, this event took place in 486.

4:7 Artaxerxes (464-423). Tabeel. Perhaps the same person as Tobiah in Neh. 2:19. Aramaic. The commercial language of the time. Ezra 4:8-6:18 was originally written in Aramaic. See note on Dan. 2:4.

letter against Jerusalem to King Artaxerxes, as follows—

★ **9** ᵃ2 Kin. 17:24 ᵇEzra 5:6; 6:6

9 then *wrote* Rehum the commander and Shimshai the scribe and ᵃthe rest of their colleagues, the judges and ᵇthe lesser governors, the officials, the secretaries, the men of Erech, the Babylonians, the men of Susa, that is, the Elamites,

★**10** ᵃEzra 4:11, 17; 7:12

10 and the rest of the nations which the great and honorable Osnappar deported and settled in the city of Samaria, and in the rest of the region beyond the River. ᵃAnd now

11 this is the copy of the letter which they sent to him: "To King Artaxerxes: Your servants, the men in the region beyond the River, and now

12 ᵃ2 Chr. 36:13 ᵇEzra 5:3, 9

12 let it be known to the king, that the Jews who came up from you have come to us at Jerusalem; they are rebuilding ᵃthe rebellious and evil city, and ᵇare finishing the walls and repairing the foundations.

★**13-16**

13 ᵃEzra 4:20; 7:24

13 "Now let it be known to the king, that if that city is rebuilt and the walls are finished, ᵃthey will not pay tribute, custom, or toll, and it will damage the revenue of the kings.

14 "Now because we are in the service of the palace, and it is not fitting for us to see the king's dishonor, therefore we have sent and informed the king,

15 so that a search may be made in the record books of your fathers. And you will discover in the record books, and learn that that city is a rebellious city and ᵃdamaging to kings and provinces, and that they have incited revolt within it in past days; therefore that city was laid waste.

16 "We inform the king that, if that city is rebuilt and the walls finished, as a result you will have no possession in *the province* beyond the River."

17 *Then* the king sent an answer to Rehum the commander, to Shimshai the scribe, and to the rest of their colleagues who live in Samaria and in the rest of *the provinces* beyond the River: "Peace. And now

18 the document which you sent to us has been ᵃtranslated and read before me.

18 ᵃNeh. 8:8

19 "And a decree has been issued by me, and a search has been made and it has been discovered that that city has risen up against the kings in past days, that rebellion and revolt have been perpetrated in it,

20 ᵃthat mighty kings have ruled over Jerusalem, governing all *the provinces* ᵇbeyond the River, and that ᶜtribute, custom, and toll were paid to them.

20 ᵃ1 Kin. 4:21; 1 Chr. 18:3 ᵇGen. 15:18; Josh. 1:4 ᶜEzra 4:13; 7:24

21 "So, now issue a decree to make these men stop *work*, that the city may not be rebuilt until a decree is issued by me.

★**21**

22 "And beware of being negligent in carrying out this *matter*; why should damage increase to the detriment of the kings?"

23 Then as soon as the copy of King Artaxerxes' document was read before Rehum and Shimshai the scribe and their colleagues, they went in haste to Jerusalem to the Jews and stopped them by force of arms.

24 Then work on the house of God in Jerusalem ceased, and it was stopped until the second year of the reign of Darius king of Persia.

★**24**

4:9 This imposing list added authority to their letter.

4:10 *Osnappar.* Ashurbanipal, king of Assyria (668–626), who completed the transplanting of the people begun by Esarhaddon (vv. 1–2). *the River.* The Euphrates. *And now.* Equivalent to "etc." (See also in vv. 11, 17; 7:12).

4:13-16 Notice the three-pronged appeal: if the Jews were not stopped, the king would suffer

financially (v. 13), his honor would be damaged (v. 14), and he would lose that part of his kingdom (vv. 15–16).

4:21 The king did in fact revoke this decision later (Neh. 2).

4:24 The work on the Temple was halted until 520. This verse connects chronologically with v. 5 (vv. 6–23 are a parenthesis tracing the history of opposition).

E　The Construction Renewed,
5:1–6:12

1　The preaching of the prophets, 5:1-2

1 aHag. 1:1
bZech. 1:1

5 When the prophets, aHaggai the prophet and bZechariah the son of Iddo, prophesied to the Jews who were in Judah and Jerusalem, in the name of the God of Israel, who was over them,

★ 2 aEzra
3:2; Hag.
1:12; Zech.
4:6-9 bEzra
6:14; Hag.
2:4; Zech.
3:1

2　then aZerubbabel the son of Shealtiel and Jeshua the son of Jozadak arose and began to rebuild the house of God which is in Jerusalem; and bthe prophets of God were with them supporting them.

2　The protest of Tattenai, 5:3-17

★ 3 aEzra
6:6, 13 bEz-
ra 1:3; 5:9

3　At that time aTattenai, the governor of the province beyond the River, and Shethar-bozenai and their colleagues came to them and spoke to them thus, "bWho issued you a decree to rebuild this temple and to finish this structure?"

4 aEzra
5:10

4　aThen we told them accordingly what the names of the men were who were reconstructing this building.

5 aEzra 7:6,
28

5　But athe eye of their God was on the elders of the Jews, and they did not stop them until a report should come to Darius, and then a written reply be returned concerning it.

★ 6 aEzra
5:3 bEzra
4:9

6　This is the copy of the letter which aTattenai, the governor of the province beyond the River, and Shethar-bozenai and his colleagues bthe officials, who were beyond the River, sent to Darius the king.

7　They sent a report to him in which it was written thus: "To Darius the king, all peace.

★ 8

8　"Let it be known to the king, that we have gone to the province of Judah, to the house of the great God, which is being built with huge stones, and beams are being laid in the walls; and this work is going on with great care and is succeeding in their hands.

9　"Then we asked those elders and said to them thus, 'Who issued you a decree to rebuild this temple and to finish this structure?'

10　"We also asked them their names so as to inform you, and that we might write down the names of the men who were at their head.

★11-15

11　"And thus they answered us, saying, 'We are the servants of the God of heaven and earth and are rebuilding the temple that was built many years ago, awhich a great king of Israel built and finished.

11 a1 Kin.
6:1, 38

12　'But abecause our fathers had provoked the God of heaven to wrath, bHe gave them into the hand of Nebuchadnezzar king of Babylon, the Chaldean, who destroyed this temple and deported the people to Babylon.

12 a2 Chr.
36:16, 17
b2 Kin. 25:8-
11; Jer.
52:12-15

13　'However, ain the first year of Cyrus king of Babylon, King Cyrus bissued a decree to rebuild this house of God.

13 aEzra 1:1
bEzra 1:1-4

14　'And also athe gold and silver utensils of the house of God which Nebuchadnezzar had taken from the temple in Jerusalem, and brought them to the temple of Babylon, these King Cyrus took from the temple of Babylon, and they were given to one bwhose

14 aEzra 1:7;
6:5; Dan. 5:2
bEzra 1:8;
5:16

5:2 Zerubbabel. Designated as the son of both Shealtiel and Shealtiel's brother Pedaiah (1 Chron. 3:17-19), suggesting a case of levirate marriage (see note on Deut. 25:5-10).

5:3 Tattenai. The Persian governor for the territory W. of the Euphrates. Shethar-bozenai. Apparently his executive aide.

5:6 the officials (lit., Apharsachites). Possibly settlers or officials who were especially devoted to the king (cf. 4:9).

5:8 huge stones. Lit., stones of rolling; i.e., stones so large they had to be moved on rollers.

5:11-15 Quoting the Jews' answer to Tattenai, the letter relates the history of the Temple from the time of its completion under Solomon (v. 11), through its destruction in 586 (v. 12), and to the decree to rebuild it in 538 (vv. 13-15).

name was Sheshbazzar, whom he had appointed governor.

15 'And he said to him, "Take these utensils, go *and* deposit them in the temple in Jerusalem, and let the house of God be rebuilt in its place."

^{16 aEzra 3:8,}
^{10 bEzra}
^{6:15}

16 'Then that Sheshbazzar came *and* ᵃlaid the foundations of the house of God in Jerusalem; and from then until now it has been under construction, and it is ᵇnot *yet* completed.'

^{17 aEzra}
^{6:1, 2}

17 "And now, if it pleases the king ᵃlet a search be conducted in the king's treasure house, which is there in Babylon, if it be that a decree was issued by King Cyrus to rebuild this house of God at Jerusalem; and let the king send to us his decision concerning this *matter.*"

3 The decree of Darius, 6:1-12

^{1 aEzra}
^{5:17}

6 Then King Darius issued a decree, and ᵃsearch was made in the archives, where the treasures were stored in Babylon.

^{★ 2 a2 Kin.}
^{17:6}

2 And in Ecbatana in the fortress, which is ᵃin the province of Media, a scroll was found and there was written in it as follows: "Memorandum—

^{★ 3-5}

^{3 aEzra 1:1;}
^{5:13}

3 "ᵃIn the first year of King Cyrus, Cyrus the king issued a decree: '*Concerning* the house of God at Jerusalem, let the temple, the place where sacrifices are offered, be rebuilt and let its foundations be retained, its height being 60 cubits and its width 60 cubits;

^{4 a1 Kin.}
^{6:36}

4 ᵃwith three layers of huge stones, and one layer of timbers. And let the cost be paid from the royal treasury.

^{5 aEzra 1:7;}
^{5:14}

5 'And also let ᵃthe gold and silver utensils of the temple of God, which Nebuchadnezzar took from the temple in Jerusalem and brought to Babylon, be returned and brought to their places in the temple in Jerusalem; and you shall put *them* in the house of God.'

6 "Now therefore, ᵃTattenai, governor of *the province* beyond the River, Shethar-bozenai, and your colleagues, the officials of *the provinces* beyond the River, keep away from there.

^{6 aEzra 5:3;}
^{6:13}

7 "Leave this work on the house of God alone; let the governor of the Jews and the elders of the Jews rebuild this house of God on its site.

8 "Moreover, ᵃI issue a decree concerning what you are to do for these elders of Judah in the rebuilding of this house of God: the full cost is to be paid to these people from the royal treasury out of the taxes of *the provinces* beyond the River, and that without delay.

^{★ 8-9}

^{8 aEzra 6:4;}
^{7:14-22}

9 "And whatever is needed, both young bulls, rams, and lambs for a burnt offering to the God of heaven, and wheat, salt, wine, and anointing oil, as the priests in Jerusalem request, *it* is to be given to them daily without fail,

10 that they may offer acceptable sacrifices to the God of heaven and ᵃpray for the life of the king and his sons.

^{10 aEzra}
^{7:23; Jer.}
^{29:7; 1 Tim.}
^{2:1, 2}

11 "And I issued a decree that ᵃany man who violates this edict, a timber shall be drawn from his house and he shall be impaled on it and ᵇhis house shall be made a refuse heap on account of this.

^{11 aEzra}
^{7:26 bDan.}
^{2:5; 3:29}

12 "And may the God who ᵃhas caused His name to dwell there overthrow any king or people who attempts to change *it*, so as to destroy this house of God in Jerusalem. I, Darius, have issued *this* decree, let *it* be carried out with all diligence!"

^{12 aDeut.}
^{12:5, 11;}
^{1 Kin. 9:3}

6:2 The efficient Persian government kept its records on scrolls of papyrus or leather at *Ecbatana,* modern Hamadan on the road from Baghdad to Teheran. It was a city at 6,000 feet elevation, with a climate conducive to the preservation of scrolls.

6:3-5 These added details, appropriate to the official memorandum, were not included in the public proclamation of 1:2-4.

6:8-9 Darius not only confirmed Cyrus' previous decree, but added one of his own, which provided for some of the *taxes* to be given to the Jews—a provision which must have shocked Tattenai, since it cut into his share.

F The Temple Completed, 6:13–22

1 The completion, 6:13–15

13 ᵃEzra 6:6

13 Then ᵃTattenai, the governor of *the province* beyond the River, Shethar-bozenai, and their colleagues carried out *the decree* with all diligence, just as King Darius had sent.

14 ᵃEzra 5:1, 2 ᵇEzra 1:1; 5:13 ᶜEzra 4:24; 6:12 ᵈEzra 7:1

14 And ᵃthe elders of the Jews were successful in building through the prophesying of Haggai the prophet and Zechariah the son of Iddo. And they finished building according to the command of the God of Israel and the decree ᵇof Cyrus, ᶜDarius, and ᵈArtaxerxes king of Persia.

★15 ᵃEsth. 3:7

15 And this temple was completed on the third day of the ᵃmonth Adar; it was the sixth year of the reign of King Darius.

2 The dedication, 6:16–18

16 ᵃ1 Kin. 8:63; 2 Chr. 7:5

16 And the sons of Israel, the priests, the Levites, and the rest of the exiles, ᵃcelebrated the dedication of this house of God with joy.

★17 ᵃEzra 8:35

17 And they offered for the dedication of this temple of God 100 bulls, 200 rams, 400 lambs, and as a sin offering for all Israel ᵃ12 male goats, corresponding to the number of the tribes of Israel.

18 ᵃ1 Chr. 24:1; 2 Chr. 35:5 ᵇ1 Chr. 23:6 ᶜNum. 3:6; 8:9

18 Then they appointed the priests to ᵃtheir divisions and the Levites in ᵇtheir orders for the service of God in Jerusalem, ᶜas it is written in the book of Moses.

3 The Passover, 6:19–22

★19 ᵃEzra 1:11 ᵇEx. 12:6

19 And ᵃthe exiles observed the Passover on ᵇthe fourteenth of the first month.

20 ᵃ2 Chr. 29:34; 30:15 ᵇ2 Chr. 35:11

20 ᵃFor the priests and the Levites had purified themselves together; all of them were pure. Then ᵇthey slaughtered the Passover *lamb* for all the exiles, both for their brothers the priests and for themselves.

★21 ᵃNeh. 9:2; 10:28 ᵇEzra 9:11

21 And the sons of Israel who returned from exile and ᵃall those who had separated themselves from ᵇthe impurity of the nations of the land to *join* them, to seek the LORD God of Israel, ate *the Passover.*

★22 ᵃEx. 12:15 ᵇEzra 7:27; Prov. 21:1 ᶜEzra 1:1; 6:1

22 And ᵃthey observed the Feast of Unleavened Bread seven days with joy, for the LORD had caused them to rejoice, and ᵇhad turned the heart of ᶜthe king of Assyria toward them to encourage them in the work of the house of God, the God of Israel.

II THE RETURN UNDER EZRA, 7:1–10:44

A The Return to Jerusalem, 7:1–8:36

1 The leader, Ezra, 7:1–10

★ 1 ᵃ1 Chr. 6:4-14 ᵇEzra 7:12, 21; Neh. 2:1

7 ᵃNow after these things, in the reign of ᵇArtaxerxes king of Persia, *there went up* Ezra son of Seraiah, son of Azariah, son of Hilkiah,

2 son of Shallum, son of Zadok, son of Ahitub,

3 son of Amariah, son of Azariah, son of Meraioth,

4 son of Zerahiah, son of Uzzi, son of Bukki,

★ 5

5 son of Abishua, son of Phinehas, son of Eleazar, son of Aaron the chief priest.

★ 6 ᵃEzra 7:11, 12, 21 ᵇEzra 7:9, 28; 8:22

6 This Ezra went up from Babylon, and he was a ᵃscribe skilled in the law of Moses, which

---

6:15 The Temple was completed on March 12, 515 B.C.

6:17 The offerings were on a much less lavish scale than those at the dedication of the Temple of Solomon, which involved more than 200 times as many oxen and sheep (1 Kings 8:63). The people were much poorer and fewer in number at this time.

6:19 *Passover.* See note on Exod. 12:11.

6:21 Two groups are indicated here: the returnees, and the residents of the land who had re-

mained separate from heathen practices.

6:22 *Unleavened Bread.* See note on Exod. 12:15-20.

7:1 *after these things.* I.e., 58 years after the events of chapter 6. *Seraiah.* High priest at the time of deportation in 586 (2 Kings 25:18).

7:5 Ezra's abbreviated genealogy is traced back to *Aaron.*

7:6 *scribe.* His duties are indicated in v. 10. Also see note on Matt. 2:4.

the LORD God of Israel had given; and the king granted him all he requested *b*because the hand of the LORD his God *was* upon him.

★ 7 *a*Ezra 8:1-20

7 And *a*some of the sons of Israel and some of the priests, the Levites, the singers, the gatekeepers, and the temple servants went up to Jerusalem in the seventh year of King Artaxerxes.

★ 8-9

8 And he came to Jerusalem in the fifth month, which was in the seventh year of the king.

9 *a*Ezra 7:6; Neh. 2:8

9 For on the first of the first month he began to go up from Babylon; and on the first of the fifth month he came to Jerusalem, *a*because the good hand of his God *was* upon him.

10 *a*Deut. 33:10; Ezra 7:25; Neh. 8:1

10 For Ezra had set his heart to study the law of the LORD, and to practice *it,* and *a*to teach *His* statutes and ordinances in Israel.

2 The letter of Artaxerxes, 7:11-28

★11

11 Now this is the copy of the decree which King Artaxerxes gave to Ezra the priest, the scribe, learned in the words of the commandments of the LORD and His statutes to Israel:

12 *a*Ezek. 26:7; Dan. 2:37

12 "Artaxerxes, *a*king of kings, to Ezra the priest, the scribe of the law of the God of heaven, perfect *peace.* And now

13 *a*Ezra 6:1

13 *a*I have issued a decree that any of the people of Israel and their priests and the Levites in my kingdom who are willing to go to Jerusalem, may go with you.

★14 *a*Ezra 7:15, 28; 8:25

14 "Forasmuch as you are sent by the king and his *a*seven counselors to inquire concerning Judah and Jerusalem according to the law of your God which is in your hand,

15 *a*2 Chr. 6:2; Ezra 6:12; Ps. 135:21

15 and to bring the silver and

gold, which the king and his counselors have freely offered to the God of Israel, *a*whose dwelling is in Jerusalem,

16 *a*Ezra 8:25 *b*Ezra 1:4, 6 *c*1 Chr. 29:6

16 with *a*all the silver and gold which you shall find in the whole province of Babylon, along *b*with the freewill offering of the people and of the priests, who *c*offered willingly for the house of their God which is in Jerusalem;

17 *a*Num. 15:4-13 *b*Deut. 12:5-11

17 with this money, therefore, you shall diligently buy bulls, rams, and lambs, *a*with their grain offerings and their libations and *b*offer them on the altar of the house of your God which is in Jerusalem.

18 "And whatever seems good to you and to your brothers to do with the rest of the silver and gold, you may do according to the will of your God.

19 "Also the utensils which are given to you for the service of the house of your God, deliver in full before the God of Jerusalem.

20 *a*Ezra 6:4

20 "And the rest of the needs for the house of your God, for which you may have occasion to provide, *a*provide *for it* from the royal treasury.

21 *a*Ezra 7:6

21 "And I, even I King Artaxerxes, issue a decree to all the treasurers who are *in the provinces* beyond the River, that whatever Ezra the priest, *a*the scribe of the law of the God of heaven, may require of you, it shall be done diligently,

★22

22 *even* up to 100 talents of silver, 100 kors of wheat, 100 baths of wine, 100 baths of oil, and salt as needed.

23 *a*Ezra 6:10

23 "Whatever is commanded by the God of heaven, let it be done with zeal for the house of the God of heaven, *a*lest there be wrath against the kingdom of the king and his sons.

7:7 *temple servants.* See note on 2:43.
7:8-9 The journey lasted from March 27 to July 24, 457.
7:11 Artaxerxes' letter (through v. 26) extended generous support to the Jews, a small price to pay for peace in that part of his empire (v. 23).

7:14 *his seven counselors.* See Esther 1:14.
7:22 *100 talents of silver.* One talent was about 75 pounds. *100 kors of wheat.* From 400-600 bushels. One *bath* was equivalent to 5½ gallons.

★24 aEzra
4:13, 20
bEzra 7:7

24 "We also inform you that ait is not allowed to impose tax, tribute or toll bon any of the priests, Levites, singers, doorkeepers, Nethinim, or servants of this house of God.

25 aEx.
18:21; Deut.
16:18 bEzra
7:10; Mal.
2:7; Col. 1:28

25 "And you, Ezra, according to the wisdom of your God which is in your hand, aappoint magistrates and judges that they may judge all the people who are in the province beyond the River, even all those who know the laws of your God; and you may bteach anyone who is ignorant of them.

26 aEzra
6:11, 12

26 "And awhoever will not observe the law of your God and the law of the king, let judgment be executed upon him strictly, whether for death or for banishment or for confiscation of goods or for imprisonment."

27 aEzra
6:22

27 Blessed be the LORD, the God of our fathers, awho has put such a thing as this in the king's heart, to adorn the house of the LORD which is in Jerusalem,

28 aEzra 9:9
bEzra 5:5

28 and ahas extended lovingkindness to me before the king and his counselors and before all the king's mighty princes. Thus I was strengthened according to bthe hand of the LORD my God upon me, and I gathered leading men from Israel to go up with me.

3 The journey, 8:1-36

8 Now these are the heads of their fathers' households and the genealogical enrollment of those who went up with me from Babylon in the reign of King Artaxerxes:

2 a1 Chr.
3:22

2 of the sons of Phinehas, Gershom; of the sons of Ithamar, Daniel; of the sons of David, aHattush;

★ 3 aEzra
2:3

3 of the sons of Shecaniah who was of the sons of aParosh, Zechariah and with him 150

males who were in the genealogical list;

4 of the sons of Pahathmoab, Eliehoenai the son of Zerahiah and 200 males with him;

5 of the sons of Shecaniah, the son of Jahaziel and 300 males with him;

6 and of the sons of aAdin, Ebed the son of Jonathan and 50 males with him;

6 aEzra
2:15; Neh.
7:20; 10:16

7 and of the sons of Elam, Jeshaiah the son of Athaliah and 70 males with him;

8 and of the sons of Shephatiah, Zebadiah the son of Michael and 80 males with him;

9 of the sons of Joab, Obadiah the son of Jehiel and 218 males with him;

10 and of the sons of Shelomith, the son of Josiphiah and 160 males with him;

11 and of the sons of Bebai, Zechariah the son of Bebai and 28 males with him;

12 and of the sons of Azgad, Johanan the son of Hakkatan and 110 males with him;

13 and of the sons of Adonikam, the last ones, these being their names, Eliphelet, Jeuel, and Shemaiah and 60 males with them;

14 and of the sons of Bigvai, Uthai and Zabbud and 70 males with them.

15 Now I assembled them at athe river that runs to Ahava, where we camped for three days; and when I observed the people and the priests, I bdid not find any Levites there.

★15 aEzra
8:21, 31
bEzra 7:7;
8:2

16 So I sent for Eliezer, Ariel, Shemaiah, Elnathan, Jarib, Elnathan, Nathan, Zechariah, and Meshullam, leading men, and for Joiarib and Elnathan, teachers.

17 And I sent them to Iddo the leading man at the place Casiphia; and I told them what to

★17 aEzra
2:43

7:24 All those who ministered in the Temple were now exempted from taxation.

8:3 These are names of families, not individuals. See note on 2:3. The total (vv. 3-14) is 1,496.

8:15 Ahava. The location is uncertain. I did not find any Levites. See note on 2:40 for a possi-

ble reason.

8:17 Casiphia. Unidentifiable, though a colony of Levites and Nethinim (Temple servants) must have been there. Forty Levites and 200 servants responded to Ezra's call to enlist (vv. 18-20).

say to Iddo *and* his brothers, ᵃthe temple servants at the place Casiphia, *that is,* to bring ministers to us for the house of our God.

18   **18** And ᵃaccording to the good hand of our God upon us they brought us a ᵇman of insight of the sons of Mahli, the son of Levi, the son of Israel, namely Sherebiah, and his sons and brothers, 18 men;

19   and Hashabiah and Jeshaiah of the sons of Merari, with his brothers and their sons, 20 men;

20   **20** and 220 of ᵃthe temple servants, whom David and the princes had given for the service of the Levites, all of them designated by name.

21   **21** Then I proclaimed ᵃa fast there at ᵇthe river of Ahava, that we might ᶜhumble ourselves before our God to seek from Him a safe journey for us, our little ones, and all our possessions.

22   **22** For I was ashamed to request from the king troops and horsemen to protect us from the enemy on the way, because we had said to the king, "ᵃThe hand of our God is favorably disposed to all those who seek Him, but ᵇHis power and His anger are against all those who ᶜforsake Him."

23   **23** So we fasted and sought our God concerning this *matter,* and He ᵃlistened to our entreaty.

24   **24** Then I set apart twelve of the leading priests, ᵃSherebiah, Hashabiah, and with them ten of their brothers;

25   **25** and I ᵃweighed out to them ᵇthe silver, the gold, and the utensils, the offering for the house of our God which the king and ᶜhis counselors and his princes, and all Israel present *there,* had offered.

26   **26** ᵃThus I weighed into their hands 650 talents of silver, and silver utensils *worth* 100 talents, *and* gold talents,

27   **27** and 20 gold bowls, *worth* 1,000 darics; and two utensils of fine shiny bronze, precious as gold.

28   **28** Then I said to them, "ᵃYou are holy to the Lᴏʀᴅ, and the ᵇutensils are holy; and the silver and the gold are a freewill offering to the Lᴏʀᴅ God of your fathers.

29   **29** "Watch and keep *them* ᵃuntil you weigh *them* before the leading priests, the Levites, and the heads of the fathers' *households* of Israel at Jerusalem, *in* the chambers of the house of the Lᴏʀᴅ."

30   **30** So the priests and the Levites ᵃaccepted the weighed out silver and gold and the utensils, to bring *them* to Jerusalem to the house of our God.

31   **31** Then we journeyed from ᵃthe river Ahava on ᵇthe twelfth of the first month to go to Jerusalem; and ᶜthe hand of our God was over us, and He delivered us from the hand of the enemy and the ambushes by the way.

32   **32** ᵃThus we came to Jerusalem and remained there three days.

33   **33** And on the fourth day the silver and the gold and the utensils ᵃwere weighed out in the house of our God into the hand of ᵇMeremoth the son of Uriah the priest, and with him *was* Eleazar the son of Phinehas; and with them *were* the Levites, Jozabad the son of Jeshua and Noadiah the son of Binnui.

34   **34** Everything *was* numbered and weighed, and all the weight was recorded at that time.

35   **35** ᵃThe exiles who had come from the captivity offered burnt offerings to the God of Israel: ᵇ12

---

18 ᵃEzra 7:6, 28 ᵇ2 Chr. 30:22
20 ᵃEzra 2:43; 7:7
21 ᵃ1 Sam. 7:6; 2 Chr. 20:3 ᵇEzra 8:15, 31 ᶜLev. 16:29; 23:29; Is. 58:3, 5
★22 ᵃEzra 7:6, 9, 28 ᵇJosh. 22:16 ᶜ2 Chr. 15:2
23 ᵃ1 Chr. 5:20; 2 Chr. 33:13
24 ᵃEzra 8:18, 19
25 ᵃEzra 8:33 ᵇEzra 7:15, 16 ᶜEzra 7:14
★26 ᵃEzra 1:9-11
★27
28 ᵃLev. 21:6-8 ᵇLev. 22:2, 3
★29 ᵃEzra 8:33, 34
30 ᵃEzra 1:9
31 ᵃEzra 8:15, 21 ᵇEzra 7:9 ᶜEzra 8:22
32 ᵃNeh. 2:11
★33-34
33 ᵃEzra 8:30 ᵇNeh. 3:4, 21
35 ᵃEzra 2:1 ᵇEzra 6:17

8:22 Ezra showed complete trust in the Lord by not asking for military escort (though this would not necessarily have been wrong; cf. Neh. 2:9).

8:26 One talent was about 75 pounds.

8:27 *darics.* See note on 2:69.

8:29 Ezra expected the 24 men (v. 24) among whom the treasure was divided to give an accounting when they reached Jerusalem. The equivalent value of the gold and silver today would be around $20 million.

8:33-34 Notice how carefully the accounting was done (cf. 2 Cor. 8:21).

bulls for all Israel, 96 rams, 77 lambs, 12 male goats for a sin offering, all as a burnt offering to the LORD.

36 *aEzra 7:21-24 *bEzra 4:7; 5:6* **36** Then *a*they delivered the king's edicts to *b*the king's satraps, and to the governors *in the provinces* beyond the River, and they supported the people and the house of God.

B The Revival in Jerusalem, 9:1-10:44
1 The condition of the people, 9:1-4

★ 1-4

1 *aEzra 6:21; Neh. 9:2 bLev. 18:24-30*

9 Now when these things had been completed, the princes approached me, saying, "The people of Israel and the priests and the Levites have not *a*separated themselves from the peoples of the lands, *b*according to their abominations, *those* of the Canaanites, the Hittites, the Perizzites, the Jebusites, the Ammonites, the Moabites, the Egyptians, and the Amorites.

2 *aDeut. 7:3; Ezra 10:2, 18 bEx. 22:31; Deut. 14:2; 2 Cor. 6:14 cNeh. 13:3* **2** "For *a*they have taken some of their daughters *as wives* for themselves and for their sons, so that *b*the holy race has *c*intermingled with the peoples of the lands; indeed, the hands of the princes and the rulers have been foremost in this unfaithfulness."

3 *a2 Kin. 18:37 bNeh. 1:4* **3** And when I heard about this matter, I *a*tore my garment and my robe, and pulled some of the hair from my head and my beard, and *b*sat down appalled.

4 *aEzra 10:3; Is. 66:2 bEx. 29:39* **4** Then *a*everyone who trembled at the words of the God of Israel on account of the unfaithfulness of the exiles gathered to

me, and I sat appalled until *b*the evening offering.

2 The confession of Ezra, 9:5-15

★ 5-15

5 *aEx. 9:29* **5** But at the evening offering I arose from my humiliation, even with my garment and my robe torn, and I fell on my knees and *a*stretched out my hands to the LORD my God;

6 *a2 Chr. 28:9; Ezra 9:13, 15; Rev. 18:5* **6** and I said, "O my God, I am ashamed and embarrassed to lift up my face to Thee, my God, for our iniquities have risen above our heads, and our *a*guilt has grown even to the heavens.

7 *a2 Chr. 29:6; Ps. 106:6 bDan. 9:7* **7** "*a*Since the days of our fathers to this day we *have been* in great guilt, and on account of our iniquities we, our kings *and* our priests have been given into the hand of the kings of the lands, to the sword, to captivity, and to plunder and to *b*open shame, as *it is* this day.

8 *aEzra 9:13-15 bIs. 22:23 cPs. 13:3* **8** "But now for a brief moment grace has been *shown* from the LORD our God, *a*to leave us an escaped remnant and to give us a *b*peg in His holy place, that our God may *c*enlighten our eyes and grant us a little reviving in our bondage.

9 *aNeh. 9:36 bEzra 7:28* **9** "*a*For we are slaves; yet in our bondage, our God has not forsaken us, but *b*has extended lovingkindness to us in the sight of the kings of Persia, to give us reviving to raise up the house of our God, to restore its ruins, and to give us a wall in Judah and Jerusalem.

9:1-4 Ezra had been in Jerusalem about 4½ months (8:31; 10:9) when the officials brought the problem of mixed marriages to his attention (see note on Deut. 7:3-4). The sin had plagued Israel before (Judg. 3:5-6) and would again later, in the time of Nehemiah and Malachi (Neh. 13:23-28; Mal. 2:11). Ezra inflicted signs of mourning and indignation on himself (cf. Lev. 10:6; Isa. 50:6; Neh. 13:25), fully realizing the gravity of the situation.
9:5-15 Similar to the prayers in Dan. 9 and Neh.

9, this is also one of the great prayers of confession in the Bible. Only in verse 6 does Ezra use singular pronouns ("I," "my"); in the remainder of the prayer, though he is personally guiltless, Ezra associates himself with the guilt of his people. He acknowledges past sins (v. 7), present deliverance (vv. 8-9; the Temple was the *peg* that supported the whole nation), present sins (vv. 10-12), deserved punishment (vv. 13-14), and the righteousness of God (v. 15).

10 "And now, our God, what shall we say after this? For we have forsaken Thy commandments,

11 aEzra 6:21

11 which Thou hast commanded by Thy servants the prophets, saying, 'The land which you are entering to possess is an unclean land with the uncleanness of the peoples of the lands, with their abominations which have filled it from end to end and awith their impurity.

12 aEx. 34:15, 16; Deut. 7:3; Ezra 9:2 bDeut. 23:6 cProv. 13:22

12 'So now do not agive your daughters to their sons nor take their daughters to your sons, and bnever seek their peace or their prosperity, that you may be strong and eat the good *things* of the land and cleave *it* as an inheritance to your sons forever.'

13 aEzra 9:6, 7 bEzra 9:8

13 "And after all that has come upon us for our evil deeds and aour great guilt, since Thou our God hast requited *us* less than our iniquities *deserve,* and hast given us ban escaped remnant as this,

14 aEzra 9:2 bDeut. 9:8, 14

14 ashall we again break Thy commandments and intermarry with the peoples who commit these abominations? bWouldst Thou not be angry with us to the point of destruction, until there is no remnant nor any who escape?

15 aNeh. 9:33; Dan. 9:7 bEzra 9:6 cJob 9:2; Ps. 130:3

15 "O Lord God of Israel, aThou art righteous, for we have been left an escaped remnant, as *it is* this day; behold, we are before Thee in bour guilt, for cno one can stand before Thee because of this."

3   *The covenant of the people,* 10:1-8

1 aDan. 9:4, 20 b2 Chr. 20:9

10 Now awhile Ezra was praying and making confession, weeping and prostrating himself bbefore the house of God,

a very large assembly, men, women, and children, gathered to him from Israel; for the people wept bitterly.

2 And Shecaniah the son of Jehiel, one of the sons of Elam, answered and said to Ezra, "aWe have been unfaithful to our God, and have married foreign women from the peoples of the land; yet now there is hope for Israel in spite of this.

★ 2 aEzra 9:2; Neh. 13:27

3 "So now alet us make a covenant with our God to put away all the wives and btheir children, according to the counsel of my lord and of cthose who tremble at the commandment of our God; and let it be done daccording to the law.

★ 3 a2 Chr. 34:31 bEzra 10:44 cEzra 9:4 dDeut. 7:2, 3

4 "Arise! For *this* matter is your responsibility, but we will be with you; abe courageous and act."

4 a1 Chr. 28:10

5 Then Ezra rose and amade the leading priests, the Levites, and all Israel, take oath that they would do according to this proposal; so they took the oath.

5 aNeh. 5:12; 13:25

6 Then Ezra arose from before the house of God and went into the chamber of Jehohanan the son of Eliashib. Although he went there, bhe did not eat bread, nor drink water, for he was mourning over the unfaithfulness of the exiles.

★ 6 aEzra 10:1 bDeut. 9:18

7 And they made a proclamation throughout Judah and Jerusalem to all the exiles, that they should assemble at Jerusalem,

8 and that whoever would not come within three days, according to the counsel of the leaders and the elders, all his possessions should be forfeited and he himself excluded from the assembly of the exiles.

★ 8

10:2 *Shecaniah.* Spokesman for the offenders, he does not appear in the list of those who had married foreign wives. He may have based his *hope* on the promise of Deut. 30:8-10.
10:3 *covenant.* The most binding form of self-committal they could make.
10:6 According to Josephus, Joiakim was high

priest at this time, but it is entirely possible that his son, *Eliashib,* and great-grandson, *Jehohanan* (Neh. 12:10), had private rooms in the Temple precincts.
10:8 Notice the haste with which the matter was expedited. *forfeited.* I.e., devoted to the Temple (Lev. 27:28).

4 The cleansing of the people,
10:9–44

★ **9** *a*1 Sam.
12:18; Ezra
9:4; 10:3

9 So all the men of Judah and Benjamin assembled at Jerusalem within the three days. It was the ninth month on the twentieth of the month, and all the people sat in the open square *before* the house of God, *a*trembling because of this matter and the heavy rain.

10 Then Ezra the priest stood up and said to them, "You have been unfaithful and have married foreign wives adding to the guilt of Israel.

11 *a*Lev.
26:40; Prov.
28:13 *b*Rom.
12:2 *c*Ezra
10:3

11 "Now, therefore, *a*make confession to the LORD God of your fathers, and *b*do His will; and *c*separate yourselves from the peoples of the land and from the foreign wives."

12 Then all the assembly answered and said with a loud voice, "That's right! As you have said, so it is our duty to *do*.

★**13-14**

13 "But there are many people, it is the rainy season, and we are not able to stand in the open. Nor can the task be done in one or two days, for we have transgressed greatly in this matter.

14 *a*2 Kin.
23:26; 2 Chr.
28:11-13;
29:10; 30:8

14 "Let our leaders represent the whole assembly and let all those in our cities who have married foreign wives come at appointed times, together with the elders and judges of each city, until the *a*fierce anger of our God on account of this matter is turned away from us."

★**15**

15 Only Jonathan the son of Asahel and Jahzeiah the son of Tikvah opposed this, with Meshullam and Shabbethai the Levite supporting them.

★**16-17**

16 But the exiles did so. And Ezra the priest selected men *who* were heads of fathers' *households* for each of their father's *households*, all of them by name. So they convened on the first day of the tenth month to investigate the matter.

17 And they finished *investigating* all the men who had married foreign wives by the first of the first month.

★**18-44**

18 *a*Ezra 5:2;
Hag. 1:1, 12;
2:4; Zech.
3:1; 6:11

18 And among the sons of the priests who had married foreign wives were found of the sons of *a*Jeshua the son of Jozadak, and his brothers: Maaseiah, Eliezer, Jarib, and Gedaliah.

★**19** *a*Lev.
5:15; 6:6

19 And they pledged to put away their wives, and being guilty, *a they offered* a ram of the flock for their offense.

20 And of the sons of Immer *there were* Hanani and Zebadiah;

21 and of the sons of Harim: Maaseiah, Elijah, Shemaiah, Jehiel, and Uzziah;

22 and of the sons of Pashhur: Elioenai, Maaseiah, Ishmael, Nethanel, Jozabad, and Elasah.

23 And of Levites *there were* Jozabad, Shimei, Kelaiah (that is, Kelita), Pethahiah, Judah, and Eliezer.

24 And of the singers *there was* Eliashib; and of the gatekeepers: Shallum, Telem, and Uri.

25 *a*Ezra 2:3;
8:3; Neh. 7:8

25 And of Israel, of the sons of *a*Parosh *there were* Ramiah, Izziah, Malchijah, Mijamin, Eleazar, Malchijah, and Benaiah;

26 and of the sons of Elam: Mattaniah, Zechariah, Jehiel, Abdi, Jeremoth, and Elijah;

27 *a*Ezra 2:8;
Neh. 7:13

27 and of the sons of *a*Zattu: Elioenai, Eliashib, Mattaniah, Jeremoth, Zabad, and Aziza;

28 and of the sons of Bebai: Jehohanan, Hananiah, Zabbai, *and* Athlai;

10:9 Gathering together on Dec. 8, 457, the people trembled because of fear of God's punishment and because of the chilling *rain* characteristic of that time of the year.

10:13-14 Because of the rain and the time needed to straighten out the many cases, the procedure of verse 14 was agreed upon.

10:15 Only four men opposed the plan.

10:16-17 Three months were required to complete the investigations.

10:18-44 The names of 113 individuals are listed in these verses (17 priests, 10 Levites, and 86 others).

10:19 *a ram.* According to the requirement in Lev. 6:4, 6.

*29   **29** and of the sons of Bani: Meshullam, Malluch, and Adaiah, Jashub, Sheal, *and* Jeremoth;

30 and of the sons of Pahath-moab: Adna, Chelal, Benaiah, Maaseiah, Mattaniah, Bezalel, Binnui, and Manasseh;

31 aNeh. 3:11   **31** and *of* the sons of Harim: Eliezer, Isshijah, aMalchijah, Shemaiah, Shimeon,

32 Benjamin, Malluch, *and* Shemariah;

33 of the sons of Hashum: Mattenai, Mattattah, Zabad, Eliphelet, Jeremai, Manasseh, *and* Shimei;

34 of the sons of Bani: Maadai, Amram, Uel,

35 Benaiah, Bedeiah, Cheluhi,

36 Vaniah, Meremoth, Eliashib,

37 Mattaniah, Mattenai, Jaasu,

38 Bani, Binnui, Shimei,

39 Shelemiah, Nathan, Adaiah,

40 Machnadebai, Shashai, Sharai,

41 Azarel, Shelemiah, Shemariah,

42 Shallum, Amariah, *and* Joseph.

43 Of the sons of aNebo *there were* Jeiel, Mattithiah, Zabad, Zebina, Jaddai, Joel, *and* Benaiah.   **43** aNum. 32:38; Ezra 2:29

44 All these had married aforeign wives, and some of them had wives *by whom* they had children.   ***44** a1 Kin. 11:1-3; Ezra 10:3

10:29 *Meshullam* gave up his foreign wife, though he had opposed the agreement (v. 15).
10:44 The presence of children in some families made the separations more complicated. For the moment the nation was purified, though the sin returned 12 years later (Neh. 10:30), and again 30 years later (Neh. 13:23).

INTRODUCTION TO
THE BOOK OF NEHEMIAH

AUTHOR: Nehemiah   DATE: 445–425 B.C.

The Man Nehemiah *As cupbearer to King Artaxerxes I, Nehemiah's position was a responsible one (certifying that none of the wine the king drank was poisoned) and an influential one (since such a trusted servant often became a close advisor). Having heard that the walls of Jerusalem had not been rebuilt, and having received permission from the king to go to Jerusalem to correct the situation, he demonstrated unmatched skills in leadership and organization. In 52 days the rebuilding job was completed. As governor of Judah Nehemiah exhibited humility, integrity, patriotism, energy, piety, and unselfishness. After 12 years in this capacity he returned briefly to Artaxerxes' court (1:1; 13:6) and then returned to Judah, where he called the people to repentance.*

Much of the material in the book comes from what must have been Nehemiah's personal diary, so frank and vivid is the reporting. For the connection between this book and Ezra, see the Introduction to Ezra.

Historical Background *Refer to the Introduction to Ezra. The Elephantine Papyri, discovered in 1903, confirm the historicity of the book of Nehemiah, mentioning Sanballat (2:19) and Johohanan (6:18; 12:23). These sources also tell us that Nehemiah ceased to be governor of Judah before 408 B.C.*

Contents *The book completes the history of the restoration of the returned remnant from exile in Babylon, a restoration begun under Ezra's leadership. It also marks the beginning of Daniel's "seventy weeks" (see note on Dan. 9:25), and provides historical background for the book of Malachi.*

OUTLINE OF NEHEMIAH

THE BOOK OF NEHEMIAH

I REBUILDING THE WALLS (UNDER NEHEMIAH), 1:1-7:73

A The Return to Jerusalem, 1:1-2:20

1 The condition of Jerusalem, 1:1-7

1 The words of [a]Nehemiah the son of Hacaliah.

Now it happened in [b]the month Chislev, [c]in the twentieth year, while I was in [d]Susa the capitol, 2 that [a]Hanani, one of my brothers, and some men from Judah came; and I asked them concerning the Jews who had escaped *and* had survived the captivity, and about Jerusalem.

3 And they said to me, "The remnant there in the [a]province who survived the captivity are in great distress and [b]reproach, and [c]the wall of Jerusalem is broken down and [d]its gates are burned with fire."

4 Now it came about when I heard these words, [a]I sat down and wept and mourned for days; and I was fasting and praying before [b]the God of heaven.

5 And I said, "I beseech Thee, O LORD God of heaven, [a]the great and awesome God, [b]who preserves the covenant and lovingkindness for those who love Him and keep His commandments,

6 [a]let Thine ear now be attentive and Thine eyes open to hear the prayer of Thy servant which I am praying before Thee now, day and night, on behalf of the sons of Israel Thy servants, [b]confessing the sins of the sons of Israel which we have sinned against Thee; [c]I and my father's house have sinned.

7 "[a]We have acted very corruptly against Thee and have not kept the commandments, nor the statutes, nor the ordinances [b]which Thou didst command Thy servant Moses.

2 The petition of Nehemiah, 1:8-11

8 "Remember the word which Thou didst command Thy servant Moses, saying, '[a]If you are unfaithful I will scatter you among the peoples;

9 [a]but if you return to Me and keep My commandments and do them, though those of you who have been scattered were in the most remote part of the heavens, I [b]will gather them from there and will bring them [c]to the place where I have chosen to cause My name to dwell.'

10 "And [a]they are Thy servants and Thy people whom Thou didst redeem by Thy great power and by Thy strong hand.

11 "O Lord, I beseech Thee, [a]may Thine ear be attentive to the prayer of Thy servant and the prayer of Thy servants who delight to revere Thy name, and make Thy servant successful today, and grant him compassion before this man."

Now I was the [b]cupbearer to the king.

★ 1 [a]Neh. 10:1 [b]Zech. 7:1 [c]Neh. 2:1 [d]Esth. 1:2; Dan. 8:2

★ 2 [a]Neh. 7:2.

3 [a]Neh. 7:6 [b]Neh. 2:17 [c]Neh. 2:17 [d]Neh. 2:3

★ 4-11

4 [a]Ezra 9:3; 10:1 [b]Neh. 2:4

5 [a]Neh. 4:14; 9:32; Dan. 9:4 [b]Ex. 20:6; Ps. 89:2, 3

6 [a]Dan. 9:17 [b]Ezra 10:1; Dan. 9:20 [c]2 Chr. 29:6

7 [a]Dan. 9:5 [b]Deut. 28:14

8 [a]Lev. 26:33

9 [a]Deut. 30:2, 3 [b]Deut. 30:4 [c]Deut. 12:5

10 [a]Ex. 32:11; Deut. 9:29

11 [a]Neh. 1:6 [b]Gen. 40:21; Neh. 2:1

1:1 *The words.* I.e., Nehemiah's own memoirs. *Nehemiah* means "Yahweh consoles." Though nothing is known about Nehemiah's father, the words *son of Hacaliah* distinguish him from other Nehemiahs (3:16; Ezra 2:2). *Chislev.* Nov.-Dec. (see note on Exod. 12:2). *the twentieth year.* Of Artaxerxes, 445 B.C. *Susa.* See notes on Dan. 8:2 and Esther 1:2.
1:2 *Hanani.* Evidently a blood brother (7:2), he brought Nehemiah the report of conditions in Jerusalem due to the opposition recorded in Ezra 4:23-24.

1:4-11 Nehemiah's prayer involved (1) pleading the *lovingkindness* of God (Heb., *hesed;* see note on Hos. 2:19); (2) confessing sin (notice that Nehemiah, like Ezra, 9:5-15, and Daniel, 9:3-19, identifies himself with his people); (3) acknowledging the rightness of God's judgment (on Neh. 1:8-9 cf. Lev. 26:33-45 and Deut. 30:1-5); and (4) asking for success in the next step (which would require the king, *this man* of Neh. 1:11, to reverse the decision he had made as recorded in Ezra 4:21).

3 The commission of Artaxerxes, 2:1-10

★ 1 *a*Neh. 1:1 *b*Ezra 7:1 *c*Neh. 1:11

2 And it came about in the month Nisan, *a*in the twentieth year of King *b*Artaxerxes, that wine *was* before him, and *c*I took up the wine and gave it to the king. Now I had not been sad in his presence.

★ 2 *a*Prov. 15:13

2 So the king said to me, "Why is your face sad though you are not sick? *a*This is nothing but sadness of heart." Then I was very much afraid.

3 *a*Dan. 2:4 *b*2 Kin. 25:8-10; 2 Chr. 36:19; Neh. 1:3; Jer. 52:12-14

3 And I said to the king, "*a*Let the king live forever. Why should my face not be sad *b*when the city, the place of my fathers' tombs, lies desolate and its gates have been consumed by fire?"

★ 4 *a*Neh. 1:4

4 Then the king said to me, "What would you request?" *a*So I prayed to the God of heaven.

5 And I said to the king, "If it please the king, and if your servant has found favor before you, send me to Judah, to the city of my fathers' tombs, that I may rebuild it."

★ 6 *a*Neh. 13:6

6 Then the king said to me, the queen sitting beside him, "How long will your journey be, and when will you return?" So it pleased the king to send me, and *a*I gave him a definite time.

★ 7-9

7 *a*Ezra 7:21; 8:36

7 And I said to the king, "If it please the king, let letters be given me *a*for the governors *of the provinces* beyond the River,

that they may allow me to pass through until I come to Judah,

8 and a letter to Asaph the keeper of the king's *a*forest, that he may give me timber to make beams for the gates of *b*the fortress which is by the temple, for the wall of the city, and for the house to which I will go." And the king granted *them* to me because *c*the good hand of my God *was* on me.

8 *a*Eccl. 2:5, 6 *b*Neh. 7:2 *c*Ezra 7:6; Neh. 2:18

9 Then I came to *a*the governors *of the provinces* beyond the River and gave them the king's letters. Now *b*the king had sent with me officers of the army and horsemen.

9 *a*Neh. 2:7 *b*Ezra 8:22

10 And when *a*Sanballat the Horonite and Tobiah the Ammonite official heard *about it,* it was very displeasing to them that someone had come to seek the welfare of the sons of Israel.

★10 *a*Neh. 2:19; 4:1

4 The inspection of the walls, 2:11-20

11 So I *a*came to Jerusalem and was there three days.

11 *a*Ezra 8:32

12 And I arose in the night, I and a few men with me. I did not tell anyone what my God was putting into my mind to do for Jerusalem and there was no animal with me except the animal on which I was riding.

13 So I went out at night by *a*the Valley Gate in the direction of the Dragon's Well and *on* to

★13-15

13 *a*Neh. 3:13 *b*Neh. 1:3 *c*Neh. 2:3, 17

2:1 *Nisan.* Mar.-Apr. (of 444 B.C.), four months after Nehemiah began praying, but still in the twentieth year of Artaxerxes' reign (1:1), since his official year began and ended in Tishri (Sept.-Oct.; see note on Exod. 12:2).

2:2 A sad countenance was not tolerated in the royal presence, so Nehemiah had good reason to be afraid (cf. Esther 4:2).

2:4 Though Nehemiah's prayer was (of necessity) brief and silent, it had been preceded by a long period of petition to the Lord (1:4-11).

2:6 *I gave him a definite time.* Nehemiah probably agreed to return after a relatively short time, which was later extended, for he stayed 12 years (5:14).

2:7-9 These *letters,* granting concessions to Nehemiah, form the decree of Dan. 9:25. *the fortress* protected the Temple. *the house.* I.e., the

governor's home. Nehemiah was also given an armed escort (Neh. 2:9; cf. note on Ezra 8:22).

2:10 *Sanballat.* Also mentioned in the Elephantine Papyri as governor of Samaria, he assessed Nehemiah's arrival as a threat to Samaria's control of Judea. *Tobiah.* Probably an ex-slave, now governor of Ammon.

2:13-15 Nehemiah's nocturnal reconnaissance began at the SW. *Valley Gate,* proceeded eastward to the *King's Pool* (probably the Pool of Siloam), then up the *ravine* (the Kidron Valley), since his donkey or mule could not make it over the rubble of the eastern wall. It is unclear from verse 15 whether he then turned westward, then S., making the complete circuit back to his original starting point; or whether he retraced his steps S., then W., back to the *Valley Gate.*

the Refuse Gate, inspecting the walls of Jerusalem ᵇwhich were broken down and its ᶜgates which were consumed by fire.

14 aNeh. 3:15 b2 Kin. 20:20

14 Then I passed on to ᵃthe Fountain Gate and ᵇthe King's Pool, but there was no place for my mount to pass.

15 aJohn 18:1

15 So I went up at night by the ᵃravine and inspected the wall. Then I entered the Valley Gate again and returned.

16 And the officials did not know where I had gone or what I had done; nor had I as yet told the Jews, the priests, the nobles, the officials, or the rest who did the work.

17 aNeh. 1:3

17 Then I said to them, "You see the bad situation we are in, that ᵃJerusalem is desolate and its gates burned by fire. Come, let us rebuild the wall of Jerusalem that we may no longer be a reproach."

18 a2 Sam. 2:7

18 And I told them how the hand of my God had been favorable to me, and also about the king's words which he had spoken to me. Then they said, "Let us arise and build." ᵃSo they put their hands to the good *work.*

★19 aNeh. 6:6 bNeh. 4:1 cNeh. 6:6

19 But when Sanballat the Horonite, and Tobiah the Ammonite official, and ᵃGeshem the Arab heard *it,* ᵇthey mocked us and despised us and said, "What is this thing you are doing? ᶜAre you rebelling against the king?"

20 aEzra 4:3 bNeh. 2:4; Acts 8:21

20 So I answered them and said to them, "ᵃThe God of heaven will give us success; therefore we His servants will arise and build, ᵇbut you have no portion, right, or memorial in Jerusalem."

B The Rebuilding of the Walls, 3:1–7:4

1 *The work assigned,* 3:1–32

3 Then ᵃEliashib the high priest arose with his brothers the priests and built ᵇthe Sheep Gate; they consecrated it and ᶜhung its doors. They consecrated the wall to ᵈthe Tower of the Hundred *and* ᵉthe Tower of Hananel.

★ 1 aNeh. 3:20; 13:28 bNeh. 3:32; 12:39 cNeh. 6:1; 7:1 dNeh. 12:39 eJer. 31:38

2 And next to him ᵃthe men of Jericho built, and next to them Zaccur the son of Imri built.

2 aNeh. 7:36

3 Now the sons of Hassenaah built ᵃthe Fish Gate; they laid its beams and hung its doors with its bolts and bars.

★ 3 aNeh. 12:39

4 And next to them Meremoth the son of Uriah the son of Hakkoz made repairs. And next to him Meshullam the son of Berechiah the son of Meshezabel made repairs. And next to him Zadok the son of Baana also made repairs.

★ 4

5 Moreover, next to him the Tekoites made repairs, but their nobles did not support the work of their masters.

★ 5

6 And Joiada the son of Paseah and Meshullam the son of Besodeiah repaired ᵃthe Old Gate; they laid its beams and hung its doors, with its bolts and its bars.

★ 6 aNeh. 12:39

7 Next to them Melatiah the Gibeonite and Jadon the Meronothite, the men of Gibeon and of Mizpah, also made repairs for the official seat of the ᵃgovernor *of the province* beyond the River.

7 aNeh. 2:7

8 Next to him Uzziel the son of Harhaiah of the ᵃgoldsmiths

★ 8 aNeh. 3:31, 32 bNeh. 12:38

2:19 *Geshem.* A powerful chieftain of Dedan in NW. Arabia. Nehemiah was surrounded by enemies who tried to intimidate him by insinuating that he wanted to rebel against the king of Persia.

3:1 *Eliashib* (see note on Ezra 10:6) energetically helped Nehemiah in constructing the walls, but later caused him trouble by allowing alliances with the Samaritans (13:4). *Sheep Gate.* At the NE. corner of the city. *Tower of the Hundred.* A short distance to the W., while the *Tower of Hananeel* was further W. All classes of people participated in the building: priests (v. 1), goldsmiths and perfumers (v. 8),

rulers and women (v. 12), Levites (v. 17), and merchants (v. 32).

3:3 *Fish Gate.* Located in the northern section of the wall, just W. of the Tower of Hananeel.

3:4 Some men, such as *Meremoth,* accepted a second allotment of work (cf. vv. 21, 5, 27).

3:5 The *nobles* of Tekoa (the birthplace of Amos, 10 miles S. of Jerusalem) refused to work, perhaps fearing reprisals from Sanballat. *masters.* Referring to their overlords or perhaps "lord," referring to Nehemiah.

3:6 *Old Gate.* Situated at the NW. corner of the city.

3:8 *Broad Wall.* The western wall.

made repairs. And next to him Hananiah, one of the perfumers, made repairs, and they restored Jerusalem as far as [b]the Broad Wall.

9 And next to them Rephaiah the son of Hur, [a]the official of half the district of Jerusalem, made repairs.

10 Next to them Jedaiah the son of Harumaph made repairs opposite his house. And next to him Hattush the son of Hashabneiah made repairs.

11 Malchijah the son of Harim and Hasshub the son of Pahath-moab repaired another section and [a]the Tower of Furnaces.

12 And next to him Shallum the son of Hallohesh, [a]the official of half the district of Jerusalem, made repairs, he and his daughters.

13 Hanun and the inhabitants of Zanoah repaired [a]the Valley Gate. They built it and hung its doors with its bolts and its bars, and a thousand cubits of the wall to the Refuse Gate.

14 And Malchijah the son of Rechab, the official of the district of [a]Beth-haccherem repaired the [b]Refuse Gate. He built it and hung its doors with its bolts and its bars.

15 Shallum the son of Colhozeh, the official of the district of Mizpah, [a]repaired the Fountain Gate. He built it, covered it, and hung its doors with its bolts and its bars, and the wall of the Pool of Shelah at [b]the king's garden as far as [c]the steps that descend from the city of David.

16 After him Nehemiah the son of Azbuk, [a]official of half the district of Beth-zur, made repairs as far as a point opposite the tombs of David, and as far as [b]the artificial pool and the house of the mighty men.

17 After him the Levites carried out repairs under Rehum the son of Bani. Next to him Hashabiah, the official of half the district of Keilah, carried out repairs for his district.

18 After him their brothers carried out repairs under Bavvai the son of Henadad, official of the other half of the district of Keilah.

19 And next to him Ezer the son of Jeshua, [a]the official of Mizpah, repaired another section, in front of the ascent of the armory [b]at the Angle.

20 After him Baruch the son of Zabbai zealously repaired another section, from the Angle to the doorway of the house of [a]Eliashib the high priest.

21 After him Meremoth the son of Uriah the son of Hakkoz repaired another section, from the doorway of Eliashib's house even as far as the end of his house.

22 And after him the priests, [a]the men of the valley, carried out repairs.

23 After them Benjamin and Hasshub carried out repairs in front of their house. After them Azariah the son of Maaseiah, son of Ananiah carried out repairs beside his house.

24 After him Binnui the son of Henadad repaired another section, from the house of Azariah as far as [a]the Angle and as far as the corner.

25 Palal the son of Uzai made repairs in front of the Angle and the tower projecting from the upper house of the king, which is by [a]the court of the guard. After him Pedaiah the son of Parosh made repairs.

26 And [a]the temple servants living in [b]Ophel made repairs as far as the front of [c]the Water Gate toward the east and the projecting tower.

Cross references (margin)

- 9 [a]Neh. 3:12, 17
- ★11 [a]Neh. 12:38
- 12 [a]Neh. 3:9
- ★13 [a]Neh. 2:13
- 14 [a]Jer. 6:1 [b]Neh. 2:13
- ★15 [a]Neh. 2:17 [b]2 Kin. 25:4 [c]Neh. 12:37
- 16 [a]Neh. 3:9, 12, 17 [b]2 Kin. 20:20; Is. 7:3
- 19 [a]Neh. 3:15 [b]2 Chr. 26:9
- 20 [a]Neh. 3:1
- 22 [a]Neh. 12:28
- 24 [a]Neh. 3:19
- 25 [a]Jer. 32:2
- ★26 [a]Neh. 7:46 [b]Neh. 11:21 [c]Neh. 8:1

3:11 Malchijah. A restored wrongdoer (cf. Ezra 10:31), he helped build the Tower of Furnaces (SW. corner, just N. of the Valley Gate, v. 13).

3:13 Through the Refuse Gate, at the S. tip of the city near the Pool of Siloam, refuse was carted to the Valley of Hinnom to be burned.

3:15 Fountain Gate. Just N. of the S. tip of the city, near the Pool of Siloam.

3:26 Water Gate. On the E.; nearby was a tower adjacent to the wall guarding the eastern side of Ophel (i.e., Mt. Zion, immediately S. of the Temple).

27 ᵃNeh. 3:5

27 After him ᵃthe Tekoites repaired another section in front of the great projecting tower and as far as the wall of Ophel.

★28-31

28 ᵃ2 Kin. 11:16; 2 Chr. 23:15; Jer. 31:40

28 Above ᵃthe Horse Gate the priests carried out repairs, each in front of his house.

29 After them Zadok the son of Immer carried out repairs in front of his house. And after him Shemaiah the son of Shecaniah, the keeper of the East Gate, carried out repairs.

30 After him Hananiah the son of Shelemiah, and Hanun the sixth son of Zalaph, repaired another section. After him Meshullam the son of Berechiah carried out repairs in front of his own quarters.

31 ᵃNeh. 3:8, 32

31 After him Malchijah one of ᵃthe goldsmiths, carried out repairs as far as the house of the temple servants and of the merchants, in front of the Inspection Gate and as far as the upper room of the corner.

32 ᵃNeh. 3:1; 12:39

32 And between the upper room of the corner and ᵃthe Sheep Gate the goldsmiths and the merchants carried out repairs.

2 The work attacked, 4:1-6:14
a By mockery, 4:1-6

1 ᵃNeh. 2:10

4 Now it came about that when ᵃSanballat heard that we were rebuilding the wall, he became furious and very angry and mocked the Jews.

★ 2 ᵃEzra 4:9, 10
ᵇNeh. 4:10

2 And he spoke in the presence of his brothers and ᵃthe wealthy men of Samaria and said, "What are these feeble Jews doing? Are they going to restore it for themselves? Can they offer sacrifices? Can they finish in a day? Can they revive the stones

from the ᵇdusty rubble even the burned ones?"

3 ᵃLam. 5:18

3 Now Tobiah the Ammonite was near him and he said, "Even what they are building—ᵃif a fox should jump on it, he would break their stone wall down!"

★ 4-5

4 ᵃPs. 123:3, 4
ᵇPs. 79:12

4 ᵃHear, O our God, how we are despised! ᵇReturn their reproach on their own heads and give them up for plunder in a land of captivity.

5 ᵃPs. 69:27, 28; Jer. 18:23

5 Do not ᵃforgive their iniquity and let not their sin be blotted out before Thee, for they have demoralized the builders.

★ 6-9

6 So we built the wall and the whole wall was joined together to half its height, for the people had a mind to work.

b By conspiracy, 4:7-23

7 Now it came about when Sanballat, Tobiah, the Arabs, the Ammonites, and the Ashdodites heard that the repair of the walls of Jerusalem went on, and that the breaches began to be closed, they were very angry.

8 ᵃPs. 83:3

8 And all of them ᵃconspired together to come and fight against Jerusalem and to cause a disturbance in it.

9 ᵃNeh. 4:11

9 But we prayed to our God, and because of them we ᵃset up a guard against them day and night.

★10-12

10 Thus in Judah it was said,
"The strength of the burden bearers is failing,
Yet there is much rubbish;
And we ourselves are unable
To rebuild the wall."

11 And our enemies said, "They will not know or see until

3:28-31 Horse Gate. Near the Temple on the E. Further N. was the East Gate, and still further N. the Inspection Gate (near the present Golden Gate). Jesus may have entered Jerusalem in His triumphal entry through the Inspection Gate or the East Gate (Matt. 21:10).
4:2 burned. Fire would weaken and crack the limestone.
4:4-5 The fact that God was being challenged explains the harsh tone of Nehemiah's prayer.

4:6-9 With the walls half built (v. 6), mere jeering was insufficient and an open attack was now planned (v. 8), necessitating both prayer and constant vigil (v. 9).
4:10-12 The persistent rumor of imminent attack discouraged the workers. in Judah. I.e., among the Jews. Neighboring Jews repeatedly urged those who were building to leave their work and return home to protect their families (v. 12).

we come among them, kill them, and put a stop to the work."

12 And it came about when the Jews who lived near them came and told us ten times, "They will come up against us from every place where you may turn,"

13 *a*Neh. 4:17, 18

13 then I stationed *men* in the lowest parts of the space behind the wall, the exposed places, and I *a*stationed the people in families with their swords, spears, and bows.

14 *a*Num. 14:9; Deut. 1:29, 30 *b*2 Sam. 10:12

14 When I saw *their fear,* I rose and spoke to the nobles, the officials, and the rest of the people: "*a*Do not be afraid of them; remember the Lord who is great and awesome, and *b*fight for your brothers, your sons, your daughters, your wives, and your houses."

15 *a*2 Sam. 17:14

15 And it happened when our enemies heard that it was known to us, and that *a*God had frustrated their plan, then all of us returned to the wall, each one to his work.

★**16-23**

16 And it came about from that day on, that half of my servants carried on the work while half of them held the spears, the shields, the bows, and the breastplates; and the captains *were* behind the whole house of Judah.

17 Those who were rebuilding the wall and those who carried burdens took *their* load with one hand doing the work and the other holding a weapon.

18 As for the builders, each *wore* his sword girded at his side as he built, while the trumpeter *stood* near me.

19 And I said to the nobles, the officials, and the rest of the people, "The work is great and extensive, and we are separated on the wall far from one another.

20 *a*Ex. 14:14; Deut. 1:30

20 "At whatever place you hear the sound of the trumpet, rally to us there. *a*Our God will fight for us."

21 So we carried on the work with half of them holding spears from dawn until the stars appeared.

22 At that time I also said to the people, "Let each man with his servant spend the night within Jerusalem so that they may be a guard for us by night and a laborer by day."

23 So neither I, my brothers, my servants, nor the men of the guard who followed me, none of us removed our clothes, each *took* his weapon *even to* the water.

c By extortion, 5:1–19

★ **1-5**

1 *a*Lev. 25:35 *b*Deut. 15:7

5 Now *a*there was a great outcry of the people and of their wives against their *b*Jewish brothers.

2 *a*Hag. 1:6

2 For there were those who said, "We, our sons and our daughters, are many; therefore let us *a*get grain that we may eat and live."

3 And there were others who said, "We are mortgaging our fields, our vineyards, and our houses that we might get grain because of the famine."

4 *a*Ezra 4:13; 7:24

4 Also there were those who said, "We have borrowed money *a*for the king's tax *on* our fields and our vineyards.

5 *a*Gen. 37:27 *b*Lev. 25:39

5 "And now *a*our flesh is like the flesh of our brothers, our chil-

---

4:16-23 Measures Nehemiah took included seeing that half of his own bodyguard was always armed, alerting each ruler to be ready to lead his group in case of attack (v. 16), arming the laborers (v. 17), seeing that each builder had a sword at his side (v. 18), having a trumpeter always ready to sound the alarm (v. 18), and urging all who could possibly do so to remain in Jerusalem at night (v. 22).

5:1-5 It *is* uncertain whether the events of this chapter happened during the time the walls were being built (when normal means of gaining income would have been interrupted) or later (which v. 7, the calling of a great assembly, and v. 14 may indicate—although v. 16 seems to indicate otherwise). The landless were short of food (v. 2); the landowners were forced to mortgage their land because of a famine (v. 3); and borrowing was necessary to pay a property tax imposed by the Persians. On usury and slavery see notes on Exod. 21:1-6; 22:25-27; Lev. 25:35-46; Deut. 24:10-13.

dren like their children. Yet behold, [b]we are forcing our sons and our daughters to be slaves, and some of our daughters are forced into bondage *already*, and we are helpless because our fields and vineyards belong to others."

6   **6** Then I was very [a]angry when I had heard their outcry and these words.

7   **7** And I consulted with myself, and contended with the nobles and the rulers and said to them, "[a]You are exacting usury, each from his brother!" Therefore, I held a great assembly against them.

8   **8** And I said to them, "We according to our ability [a]have redeemed our Jewish brothers who were sold to the nations; now would you even sell your brothers that they may be sold to us?" Then they were silent and could not find a word *to say*.

9   **9** Again I said, "The thing which you are doing is not good; should you not walk in the fear of our God because of [a]the reproach of the nations, our enemies?

10-11   **10** "And likewise I, my brothers and my servants, are lending them money and grain. Please, let us leave off this usury.

11 "Please, give back to them this very day their fields, their vineyards, their olive groves, and their houses, also the hundredth *part* of the money and of the grain, the new wine, and the oil that you are exacting from them."

12   **12** Then they said, "We [a]will give *it* back and [b]will require nothing from them; we will do exactly as you say." So I called the priests and [c]took an oath from them that they would do according to this promise.

13 I [a]also shook out the front of my garment and said, "Thus may God shake out every man from his house and from his possessions who does not fulfill this promise; even thus may he be shaken out and emptied." And [b]all the assembly said, "Amen!" And they praised the LORD. Then the people did according to this promise.

14 Moreover, from the day that I was appointed to be their governor in the land of Judah, from [a]the twentieth year to the [b]thirty-second year of King Artaxerxes, *for* twelve years, neither I nor my kinsmen have eaten the governor's food *allowance*.

15 But the former governors who were before me laid burdens on the people and took from them bread and wine *besides* forty shekels of silver; even their servants domineered the people. But I did not do so [a]because of the fear of God.

16 And I also applied myself to the work on this wall; we did not buy any land, and all my servants were gathered there for the work.

17 Moreover, [a]*there were* at my table one hundred and fifty Jews and officials, besides those who came to us from the nations that were around us.

18 Now [a]that which was prepared for each day was one ox *and* six choice sheep, also birds were prepared for me; and once in ten days all sorts of wine *were* furnished in abundance. Yet for all this [b]I did not demand the governor's food *allowance*, because the servitude was heavy on this people.

Margin references:

6 [a]Ex. 11:8

7 [a]Ex. 22:25; Lev. 25:36; Deut. 23:19, 20

★ 8 [a]Lev. 25:48

9 [a]Neh. 4:4

★10-11

12 [a]2 Chr. 28:15 [b]Neh. 10:31 [c]Ezra 10:5

★13 [a]Acts 18:6 [b]Neh. 8:6

★14 [a]Neh. 1:1 [b]Neh. 13:6

★15 [a]Neh. 5:9; Job 31:23

17 [a]1 Kin. 18:19

★18 [a]1 Kin. 4:22, 23 [b]2 Thess. 3:8

5:8 Nehemiah himself had bought back Jews sold into slavery to heathens.

5:10-11 Nehemiah urged the return of property held in pledge and the forgiveness of interest payments, so that those in debt could begin to pay off the principal. *the hundredth part of the money.* Interest at the rate of 1% per month or 12% per year.

5:13 *I also shook out the front of my garment.* A gesture symbolizing complete rejection of any

who might violate this agreement.

5:14 During the entire 12 years of his first term as governor, Nehemiah did not take any salary or allowance from the people as former Persian governors had done.

5:15 *shekels.* One shekel is approximately one-half ounce.

5:18 Nehemiah set an unselfish example for all the people.

19 ᵃNeh.
13:14, 22, 31

19 ᵃRemember me, O my God, for good, *according to* all that I have done for this people.

d   By compromise, 6:1-4

★ 1 ᵃNeh.
3:1, 3

6 Now it came about when it was reported to Sanballat, Tobiah, to Geshem the Arab, and to the rest of our enemies that I had rebuilt the wall, and *that* no breach remained in it, ᵃalthough at that time I had not set up the doors in the gates,

★ 2 ᵃ1 Chr.
8:12

2 that Sanballat and Geshem sent a message to me, saying, "Come, let us meet together at Chephirim in the plain of ᵃOno." But they were planning to harm me.

3 So I sent messengers to them, saying, "I am doing a great work and I cannot come down. Why should the work stop while I leave it and come down to you?"

4 And they sent *messages* to me four times in this manner, and I answered them in the same way.

e   By slander, 6:5-9

★ 5-6

5 Then Sanballat sent his servant to me in the same manner a fifth time with an open letter in his hand.

6 ᵃNeh.
2:19

6 In it was written, "It is reported among the nations, and Gashmu says, that ᵃyou and the Jews are planning to rebel; therefore you are rebuilding the wall. And you are to be their king, according to these reports.

★ 7

7 "And you have also appointed prophets to proclaim in Jerusalem concerning you, 'A king is in Judah!' And now it will be reported to the king according to these reports. So come now, let us take counsel together."

8 Then I sent a *message* to him saying, "Such things as you are saying have not been done, but you are ᵃinventing them in your own mind."

8 ᵃJob
13:4; Ps.
52:2

9 For all of them were *trying* to frighten us, thinking, "They will become discouraged with the work and it will not be done." But now, ᵃO God, strengthen my hands.

9 ᵃPs.
138:3

f   By treachery, 6:10-14

10 And when I entered the house of Shemaiah the son of Delaiah, son of Mehetabel, ᵃwho was confined at home, he said, "Let us meet together in the house of God, within the temple, and let us close the doors of the temple, for they are coming to kill you, and they are coming to kill you at night."

★10-14

10 ᵃJer. 36:5

11 But I said, "ᵃShould a man like me flee? And could one such as I go into the temple to save his life? I will not go in."

11 ᵃProv.
28:1

12 Then I perceived that surely God had not sent him, but he uttered *his* prophecy against me because Tobiah and Sanballat had hired him.

13 He was hired for this reason, ᵃthat I might become frightened and act accordingly and sin, so that they might have an evil report in order that they could reproach me.

13 ᵃNeh. 6:6

14 ᵃRemember, O my God, Tobiah and Sanballat according to these works of theirs, and also Noadiah ᵇthe prophetess and the

14 ᵃNeh.
13:29 ᵇEzek.
13:17

6:1 On these men, see notes on 2:10 and 2:19.
6:2 Since progress on the wall had lessened the danger of attack, Nehemiah's enemies tried to lure him to the *plain of Ono,* 19 miles N. of Jerusalem, where they could more easily assassinate him or attack Jerusalem in his absence.
6:5-6 Having failed to draw Nehemiah outside Jerusalem, *Sanballat* sent an *open letter,* which was either posted or read publicly, accusing Nehemiah of wanting to be king.
6:7 Perhaps Malachi was prophesying at this time, and Sanballat deliberately twisted his message about Messiah the King and applied it to Nehemiah.
6:10-14 *Shemaiah* claimed to have a special revelation about a plot against Nehemiah's life and suggested that the Holy Place in the Temple would be the only safe place for Nehemiah. But the suggestion unmasked Shemaiah's treachery, since only the priests could enter the Holy Place (Num. 18:7). If Nehemiah had done so, his testimony would have been ruined.

rest of the prophets who were *trying* to frighten me.

3 The work accomplished, 6:15–7:4

★15 ᵃNeh. 4:1, 2

15 So ᵃthe wall was completed on the twenty-fifth of *the month* Elul, in fifty-two days.

16 ᵃNeh. 2:10; 4:1, 7 ᵇEx. 14:25

16 And it came about ᵃwhen all our enemies heard *of it,* and all the nations surrounding us saw *it,* they lost their confidence; for ᵇthey recognized that this work had been accomplished with the help of our God.

17 Also in those days many letters went from the nobles of Judah to Tobiah, and Tobiah's *letters* came to them.

★18

18 For many in Judah were bound by oath to him because he was the son-in-law of Shecaniah the son of Arah, and his son Jehohanan had married the daughter of Meshullam the son of Berechiah.

19 Moreover, they were speaking about his good deeds in my presence and reported my words to him. Then Tobiah sent letters to frighten me.

★ 1 ᵃNeh. 6:1, 15

7 Now it came about when ᵃthe wall was rebuilt and I had set up the doors, and the gatekeepers and the singers and the Levites were appointed,

★ 2 ᵃNeh. 1:2 ᵇNeh. 10:23 ᶜNeh. 2:8 ᵈNeh. 13:13

2 that I put ᵃHanani my brother, and ᵇHananiah the commander of ᶜthe fortress, in charge of Jerusalem, for he was ᵈa faithful man and feared God more than many.

3 Then I said to them, "Do not let the gates of Jerusalem be opened until the sun is hot, and while they are standing *guard,* let them shut and bolt the doors. Also appoint guards from the inhabitants of Jerusalem, each at his post, and each in front of his own house."

4 Now the city was large and spacious, but the people in it were few and the houses were not built.

C The Register of the People, 7:5–73

★ 5-73

5 ᵃThen my God put it into my heart to assemble the nobles, the officials, and the people to be enrolled by genealogies. Then I found the book of the genealogy of those who came up first in which I found the following record:

5 ᵃProv. 2:6; 3:6

6 ᵃThese are the people of the province who came up from the captivity of the exiles whom Nebuchadnezzar the king of Babylon had carried away, and who returned to Jerusalem and Judah, each to his city,

6 ᵃEzra 2:1-70

7 who came with Zerubbabel, Jeshua, Nehemiah, Azariah, Raamiah, Nahamani, Mordecai, Bilshan, Mispereth, Bigvai, Nehum, Baanah.

The number of men of the people of Israel:

8 the sons of Parosh, 2,172;

9 the sons of Shephatiah, 372;

10 the sons of Arah, 652;

11 the sons of Pahath-moab of the sons of Jeshua and Joab, 2,818;

12 the sons of Elam, 1,254;

13 the sons of Zattu, 845;

14 the sons of Zaccai, 760;

15 the sons of Binnui, 648;

16 the sons of Bebai, 628;

6:15 To finish in 52 days was a tremendous accomplishment, and one that was recognized as due to the power of God (v. 16). *Elul* was Aug.-Sept.

6:18 Both through his wife and his daughter-in-law, Tobiah had links with influential families in Jerusalem (cf. Ezra 2:5 for *Arah* and Neh. 3:4, 30 for *Meshullam*). Nehemiah had to face a fifth column within his own ranks!

7:1 *doors.* In the gates (cf. 6:1). *gatekeepers and the singers and the Levites.* Appointed to guard the gates (v. 3).

7:2 *the fortress.* See note on 2:7-9.

7:5-73 This record, probably stored in the Temple archives, is virtually the same as in Ezra 2 and was likely the basis for Nehemiah's populating Jerusalem with those of pure ancestry (11:1).

17 the sons of Azgad, 2,322;
18 the sons of Adonikam, 667;
19 the sons of Bigvai, 2,067;
20 the sons of Adin, 655;
21 the sons of Ater, of Hezekiah, 98;
22 the sons of Hashum, 328;
23 the sons of Bezai, 324;
24 the sons of Hariph, 112;
25 the sons of Gibeon, 95;
26 the men of Bethlehem and Netophah, 188;
27 the men of Anathoth, 128;
28 the men of Beth-azmaveth, 42;
29 the men of Kiriath-jearim, Chephirah, and Beeroth, 743;
30 the men of Ramah and Geba, 621;
31 the men of Michmas, 122;
32 the men of Bethel and Ai, 123;
33 the men of the other Nebo, 52;
34 the sons of the other Elam, 1,254;
35 the sons of Harim, 320;
36 the men of Jericho, 345;
37 the sons of Lod, Hadid, and Ono, 721;
38 the sons of Senaah, 3,930.
39 The priests: the sons of Jedaiah of the house of Jeshua, 973;
40 the sons of Immer, 1,052;
41 the sons of Pashhur, 1,247;
42 the sons of Harim, 1,017.
43 The Levites: the sons of Jeshua, of Kadmiel, of the sons of Hodevah, 74.
44 The singers: the sons of Asaph, 148.
45 The gatekeepers: the sons of Shallum, the sons of Ater, the sons of Talmon, the sons of Akkub, the sons of Hatita, the sons of Shobai, 138.
46 The temple servants: the sons of Ziha, the sons of Hasupha, the sons of Tabbaoth,
47 the sons of Keros, the sons of Sia, the sons of Padon,
48 the sons of Lebana, the sons of Hagaba, the sons of Shalmai,
49 the sons of Hanan, the sons of Giddel, the sons of Gahar,

50 the sons of Reaiah, the sons of Rezin, the sons of Nekoda,
51 the sons of Gazzam, the sons of Uzza, the sons of Paseah,
52 the sons of Besai, the sons of Meunim, the sons of Nephushesim,
53 the sons of Bakbuk, the sons of Hakupha, the sons of Harhur,
54 the sons of Bazlith, the sons of Mehida, the sons of Harsha,
55 the sons of Barkos, the sons of Sisera, the sons of Temah,
56 the sons of Neziah, the sons of Hatipha.
57 The sons of Solomon's servants: the sons of Sotai, the sons of Sophereth, the sons of Perida,
58 the sons of Jaala, the sons of Darkon, the sons of Giddel,
59 the sons of Shephatiah, the sons of Hattil, the sons of Pochereth-hazzebaim, the sons of Amon.
60 All the temple servants and the sons of Solomon's servants were 392.
61 And these were they who came up from Tel-melah, Tel-harsha, Cherub, Addon, and Immer; but they could not show their fathers' houses or their descendants, whether they were of Israel:
62 the sons of Delaiah, the sons of Tobiah, the sons of Nekoda, 642.
63 And of the priests: the sons of Hobaiah, the sons of Hakkoz, the sons of Barzillai, who took a wife of the daughters of Barzillai, the Gileadite, and was named after them.
64 These searched among their ancestral registration, but it could not be located; therefore they were considered unclean and excluded from the priesthood.
65 And [a]the governor said to them that they should not eat from the most holy things until a priest arose with [b]Urim and Thummim.

65 [a]Neh. 8:9; 10:1
[b]Ex. 28:30; Deut. 33:8

66 The whole assembly together *was* 42,360,

67 besides their male and their female servants, of whom there were 7,337; and they had 245 male and female singers.

68 *a*Ezra 2:66

68 *a*Their horses were 736; their mules, 245;

69 *their* camels, 435; *their* donkeys, 6,720.

70 *a*Neh. 7:65; 8:9

70 And some from among the heads of fathers' *households* gave to the work. The *a*governor gave to the treasury 1,000 gold drachmas, 50 basins, 530 priests' garments.

71 And some of the heads of fathers' *households* gave into the treasury of the work 20,000 gold drachmas, and 2,200 silver minas.

72 And that which the rest of the people gave was 20,000 gold drachmas and 2,000 silver minas, and 67 priests' garments.

73 *a*1 Chr. 9:2 *b*Ezra 3:1

73 Now *a*the priests, the Levites, the gatekeepers, the singers, some of the people, the temple servants, and all Israel, lived in their cities.

*b*And when the seventh month came, the sons of Israel *were* in their cities.

II RENEWING THE COVENANT (UNDER EZRA), 8:1-10:39

A The Reading of the Law, 8:1-8

1 *a*Neh. 3:26 *b*Ezra 7:6 *c*2 Chr. 34:15

8 And all the people gathered as one man at the square which was in front of *a*the Water Gate, and they asked *b*Ezra the scribe to bring *c*the book of the law of Moses which the LORD had given to Israel.

★ 2 *a*Deut. 31:9-11; Neh. 8:9 *b*Lev. 23:24

2 Then *a*Ezra the priest brought the law before the assembly of men, women, and all

who *could* listen with understanding, on *b*the first day of the seventh month.

3 *a*Neh. 8:1

3 And he read from it before the square which was in front of *a*the Water Gate from early morning until midday, in the presence of men and women, those who could understand; and all the people were attentive to the book of the law.

★ 4

4 And Ezra the scribe stood at a wooden podium which they had made for the purpose. And beside him stood Mattithiah, Shema, Anaiah, Uriah, Hilkiah, and Maaseiah on his right hand; and Pedaiah, Mishael, Malchijah, Hashum, Hashbaddanah, Zechariah, *and* Meshullam on his left hand.

5 *a*Neh. 8:3 *b*Judg. 3:20; 1 Kin. 8:12-14

5 And Ezra opened *a*the book in the sight of all the people for he was standing above all the people; and when he opened it, all the people *b*stood up.

6 *a*Neh. 5:13 *b*Ex. 4:31

6 Then Ezra blessed the LORD the great God. And all the people answered, "*a*Amen, Amen!" while lifting up their hands; then *b*they bowed low and worshiped the LORD with *their* faces to the ground.

★ 7-8

7 Also Jeshua, Bani, Sherebiah, Jamin, Akkub, Shabbethai, Hodiah, Maaseiah, Kelita, Azariah, Jozabad, Hanan, Pelaiah, and the Levites, explained the law to the people while the people *remained* in their place.

8 And they read from the book, from the law of God, translating to give the sense so that they understood the reading.

B The Response of the People, 8:9-18

★ 9 *a*Neh. 7:65, 70 *b*Neh. 12:26 *c*Neh. 8:2 *d*Deut. 12:7, 12

9 Then Nehemiah, who was the *a*governor, and Ezra *b*the

8:2 *the first day of the seventh month.* The time of the Feast of Trumpets (see note on Lev. 23:24).

8:4 This is the first mention of a *podium* in the Bible; it was strong enough to support Ezra and 13 others.

8:7-8 The reading of the Law was interspersed with explanation; indeed, the Law was also

translated from Hebrew into Aramaic, the only language some of the people may have understood (cf. 13:24).

8:9 Conviction of sin caused the people to *weep*, appropriate to the Day of Atonement (on the tenth day of the month) but not to the Feast of Trumpets and the celebration of the completion of the wall.

priest *and* scribe, and the Levites who taught the people said to all the people, "ᶜThis day is holy to the Lᴏʀᴅ your God; ᵈdo not mourn or weep." For all the people were weeping when they heard the words of the law.

10 aDeut. 26:11-13

10 Then he said to them, "Go, eat of the fat, drink of the sweet, and ᵃsend portions to him who has nothing prepared; for this day is holy to our Lord. Do not be grieved, for the joy of the Lᴏʀᴅ is your strength."

11 So the Levites calmed all the people, saying, "Be still, for the day is holy; do not be grieved."

12 aNeh. 8:10 bNeh. 8:7, 8

12 And all the people went away to eat, to drink, ᵃto send portions and to celebrate a great festival, ᵇbecause they understood the words which had been made known to them.

★13-18

13 Then on the second day the heads of fathers' *households* of all the people, the priests, and the Levites were gathered to Ezra the scribe that they might gain insight into the words of the law.

14 aLev. 23:34, 40, 42

14 And they found written in the law how the Lᴏʀᴅ had commanded through Moses that the sons of Israel ᵃshould live in booths during the feast of the seventh month.

15 aLev. 23:34 bDeut. 16:16 cLev. 23:40

15 ᵃSo they proclaimed and circulated a proclamation in all their cities and ᵇin Jerusalem, saying, "ᶜGo out to the hills, and bring olive branches, and wild olive branches, myrtle branches, palm branches, and branches of *other* leafy trees, to make booths, as it is written."

16 aJer. 32:29 bNeh. 8:1 c2 Kin. 14:13; Neh. 12:39

16 So the people went out and brought *them* and made booths for themselves, each ᵃon his roof, and in their courts, and in the courts of the house of God,

and in the square at ᵇthe Water Gate, and in the square at ᶜthe Gate of Ephraim.

17 And the entire assembly of those who had returned from the captivity made booths and lived in them. The sons of Israel ᵃhad indeed not done so from the days of Joshua the son of Nun to that day. And ᵇthere was great rejoicing.

17 a2 Chr. 7:8; 8:13 b2 Chr. 30:21

18 And ᵃhe read from the book of the law of God daily, from the first day to the last day. And they ᵇcelebrated the feast seven days, and on ᶜthe eighth day *there was* a solemn assembly according to the ordinance.

18 aDeut. 31:11 bLev. 23:36 cNum. 29:35

C The Repentance of the People, 9:1-38

9 Now on the twenty-fourth day of ᵃthis month the sons of Israel assembled ᵇwith fasting, in sackcloth, and with ᶜdirt upon them.

★ 1 aNeh. 8:2 bEzra 8:23 c1 Sam. 4:12

2 And the ᵃdescendants of Israel separated themselves from all foreigners, and stood and ᵇconfessed their sins and the iniquities of their fathers.

2 aEzra 10:11; Neh. 13:3 bProv. 28:13; Jer. 3:13

3 While ᵃthey stood in their place, they read from the book of the law of the Lᴏʀᴅ their God for a fourth of the day; and for *another* fourth they confessed and worshiped the Lᴏʀᴅ their God.

★ 3 aNeh. 8:4

4 ᵃNow on the Levites' platform stood Jeshua, Bani, Kadmiel, Shebaniah, Bunni, Sherebiah, Bani, *and* Chenani, and they cried with a loud voice to the Lᴏʀᴅ their God.

4 aNeh. 8:7

5 Then the Levites, Jeshua, Kadmiel, Bani, Hashabneiah, Sherebiah, Hodiah, Shebaniah, *and* Pethahiah, said, "Arise, bless the Lᴏʀᴅ your God forever and ever!

★ 5-38

8:13-18 Further study of the Law revealed that during the Feast of Tabernacles (see note on Lev. 23:34) everybody was to dwell in booths; so preparations for that time of celebration were ordered. The feast had been observed since the days of Joshua (1 Kings 8:65; 2 Chron. 7:9; Ezra 3:4), but not by *the entire*

assembly (Neh. 8:17).
9:1 Two days after the conclusion of the Feast of Tabernacles, the people began to acknowledge their sins before God. *sackcloth.* See note on Gen. 37:34.
9:3 *a fourth of the day.* Three daylight hours.
9:5-38 Ezra's prayer began with an acknowledg-

O may Thy glorious name
be blessed
And exalted above all
blessing and praise!

6 a Deut.
6:4; 2 Kin.
19:15 **b**Gen.
1:1 **c**Col.
1:16f.

6 "aThou alone art the LORD.
bThou hast made the heavens,
The heaven of heavens
with all their host,
The earth and all that is on
it,
The seas and all that is in
them.
cThou dost give life to all
of them
And the heavenly host
bows down before
Thee.

7 a Gen.
12:1 **b**Gen.
11:31 **c**Gen.
17:5

7 "Thou art the LORD God,
aWho chose Abram
And brought him out from
bUr of the Chaldees,
And cgave him the name
Abraham.

8 a Gen.
15:6, 18-21
bJosh.
21:43-45

8 "And Thou didst find ahis
heart faithful before
Thee,
And didst make a covenant with him
To give him the land of the
Canaanite,
Of the Hittite and the Amorite,
Of the Perizzite, the Jebusite, and the Girgashite—
To give it to his descendants.
And Thou bhast fulfilled
Thy promise,
For Thou art righteous.

9 a Ex. 3:7
bEx. 14:10-
14, 31

9 "aThou didst see the affliction of our fathers in
Egypt,
And didst bhear their cry
by the Red Sea.

10 a Ex. 5:2;
7:8-12:32
bEx. 9:16

10 "Then Thou didst perform
asigns and wonders
against Pharaoh,

Against all his servants
and all the people of
his land;
For Thou didst know that
athey acted arrogantly
toward them,
And bdidst make a name
for Thyself as it is this
day.

11 a Ex.
14:21 **b**Ex.
15:1, 5, 10

11 "And aThou didst divide
the sea before them,
So they passed through the
midst of the sea on
dry ground;
And btheir pursuers Thou
didst hurl into the
depths,
Like a stone into raging
waters.

12 a Ex.
13:21, 22

12 "And with a pillar of cloud
aThou didst lead them
by day,
And with a pillar of fire by
night
To light for them the way
In which they were to go.

13 a Ex.
19:11, 18-20
bEx. 20:1
cPs. 19:7-9

13 "Then aThou didst come
down on Mount Sinai,
And didst bspeak with
them from heaven;
Thou didst give to them
cjust ordinances and
true laws,
Good statutes and commandments.

14 a Ex.
16:23; 20:8

14 "So Thou didst make
known to them aThy
holy sabbath,
And didst lay down for
them commandments,
statutes, and law,
Through Thy servant
Moses.

15 a Ex. 16:4,
14, 15 **b**Ex.
17:6; Num.
20:7-13
cDeut. 1:8,
21

15 "Thou didst aprovide bread
from heaven for them
for their hunger,
Thou didst bbring forth
water from a rock for
them for their thirst,

---

ment of God's majesty (v. 6) and continued
with a recital of the major points of Israel's
history: the Abrahamic covenant (vv. 7-8, see
notes on Gen. 12:2; 15:17), the events of the
Exodus from Egypt and the years of wandering in the desert (vv. 9-23), and the conquest
of Canaan and subsequent backsliding (vv.
24-31). It concluded with a confession of sin
(vv. 32-37) and a commitment to keep God's
laws (v. 38).

And Thou didst ^ctell them
to enter in order to
possess
The land which Thou didst
swear to give them.

16 aNeh.
9:10 bDeut.
1:26-33;
31:27; Neh.
9:29

16 "But they, our fathers,
^aacted arrogantly;
They ^bbecame stubborn
and would not listen
to Thy command-
ments.

17 aPs.
78:11, 42-55
bNum. 14:4
cEx. 34:6, 7;
Num. 14:18

17 "And they refused to listen,
And ^adid not remember
Thy wondrous deeds
which Thou hadst
performed among
them;
So they became stubborn
and ^bappointed a
leader to return to
their slavery in Egypt.
But Thou art a God ^cof
forgiveness,
Gracious and compassion-
ate,
Slow to anger, and
abounding in loving-
kindness;
And Thou didst not for-
sake them.

18 aEx.
32:4-8, 31

18 "Even when they ^amade for
themselves
A calf of molten metal
And said, 'This is your
God
Who brought you up from
Egypt,'
And committed great blas-
phemies,

19 aDeut.
8:2-4; Neh.
9:27, 31
bNeh. 9:12

19 ^aThou, in Thy great compassion,
Didst not forsake them in
the wilderness;
^bThe pillar of cloud did not
leave them by day,
To guide them on their
way,
Nor the pillar of fire by
night, to light for
them the way in
which they were to
go.

20 aNum.
11:17; Neh.
9:30; Is.
63:11-14

20 "And ^aThou didst give Thy
good Spirit to instruct
them,

Thy manna Thou didst not
withhold from their
mouth,
And Thou didst give them
water for their thirst.

21 "Indeed, ^aforty years Thou
didst provide for them
in the wilderness *and*
they were not in want;
Their clothes did not wear
out, nor did their feet
swell.

21 aDeut.
2:7

22 "Thou didst also give them
kingdoms and peo-
ples,
And Thou didst allot *them*
to them as a bound-
ary.
^aAnd they took possession
of the land of Sihon
the king of Heshbon,
And the land of Og the
king of Bashan.

22 aNum.
21:21-35

23 "And Thou didst make
their sons numerous
as ^athe stars of
heaven,
And Thou didst bring
them into the land
Which Thou hadst told
their fathers to enter
and possess.

23 aGen.
15:5; 22:17

24 "^aSo their sons entered and
possessed the land.
And ^bThou didst subdue
before them the in-
habitants of the land,
the Canaanites,
And Thou didst give them
into their hand, with
their kings, and the
peoples of the land,
To do with them as they
desired.

24 aJosh.
11:23; 21:43
bJosh. 18:1

25 "And ^athey captured fortified cities and a ^bfer-
tile land.
They took possession of
^chouses full of every
good thing,
Hewn cisterns, vineyards,
olive groves,
Fruit trees in abundance.
So they ate, were filled,
and ^dgrew fat,
And ^ereveled in Thy great
goodness.

25 aDeut.
3:5 bNum.
13:27 cDeut.
6:11 dDeut.
32:15 e1 Kin.
8:66

26 *a*Judg.
2:11 *b*1 Kin.
14:9 *c*2 Chr.
36:16 *d*Neh.
9:30 *e*Neh.
9:18

26 "*a*But they became disobedient and rebelled against Thee,
And *b*cast Thy law behind their backs
And *c*killed Thy prophets who had *d*admonished them
So that they might return to Thee,
And *e*they committed great blasphemies.

27 *a*Judg.
2:14 *b*Deut.
4:29 *c*Judg.
2:16

27 "Therefore Thou didst *a*deliver them into the hand of their oppressors who oppressed them,
But when they cried to Thee *b*in the time of their distress,
Thou didst hear from heaven, and according to Thy great compassion
Thou didst *c*give them deliverers who delivered them from the hand of their oppressors.

28 *a*Judg.
3:11 *b*Ps.
106:43

28 "But *a*as soon as they had rest, they did evil again before Thee;
Therefore Thou didst abandon them to the hand of their enemies, so that they ruled over them.
When they cried again to Thee, Thou didst hear from heaven,
And *b*many times Thou didst rescue them according to Thy compassion,

29 *a*Neh.
9:26, 30
*b*Neh. 9:10,
16 *c*Lev.
18:5 *d*Zech.
7:11

29 And *a*admonished them in order to turn them back to Thy law.
Yet *b*they acted arrogantly and did not listen to Thy commandments but sinned against Thine ordinances,
By *c*which if a man observes them he shall live.
And they *d*turned a stubborn shoulder and stiffened their neck, and would not listen.

30 *a*Ps.
95:10; Acts
13:18
*b*2 Kin.
17:13-18;
2 Chr. 36:15,
16; Neh.
9:26, 29
*c*Neh. 9:20

30 "*a*However, Thou didst bear with them for many years,
And *b*admonished them by *c*Thy Spirit through Thy prophets,
Yet they would not give ear.
Therefore Thou didst give them into the hand of the peoples of the lands.

31 *a*Jer. 4:27
*b*Neh. 9:17

31 "Nevertheless, in Thy great compassion Thou *a*didst not make an end of them or forsake them,
For Thou art *b*a gracious and compassionate God.

32 *a*Neh. 1:5
*b*2 Kin.
15:19, 29;
2 Kin. 17:3-6;
Ezra 4:2, 10

32 "Now therefore, our God, *a*the great, the mighty, and the awesome God, who dost keep covenant and lovingkindness,
Do not let all the hardship seem insignificant before Thee,
Which has come upon us, our kings, our princes, our priests, our prophets, our fathers, and on all Thy people,
*b*From the days of the kings of Assyria to this day.

33 *a*Gen.
18:25; Jer.
12:1

33 "However, *a*Thou art just in all that has come upon us;
For Thou hast dealt faithfully, but we have acted wickedly.

34 "For our kings, our leaders, our priests, and our fathers have not kept Thy law
Or paid attention to Thy commandments and Thine admonitions with which Thou hast admonished them.

35 *a*Deut.
28:47 *b*Neh.
9:25

35 "But *a*they, in their own kingdom,
*b*With Thy great goodness which Thou didst give them,

With the broad and rich
land which Thou didst
set before them,
Did not serve Thee or turn
from their evil deeds.

36 aDeut.
28:48

36 "Behold, awe are slaves today,
And as to the land which
Thou didst give to our
fathers to eat of its
fruit and its bounty,
Behold, we are slaves on it.

37 aDeut.
28:33

37 "And aits abundant produce
is for the kings
Whom Thou hast set over
us because of our sins;
They also rule over our
bodies
And over our cattle as they
please,
So we are in great distress.

38 aNeh.
10:29 bNeh.
10:1

38 "Now because of all this
aWe are making an agree-
ment in writing;
And on the bsealed docu-
ment *are the names of*
our leaders, our Le-
vites *and* our priests."

D   The Ratification of the Covenant, 10:1–27

1 aNeh.
9:38

10 Now on the asealed document *were the names of:*
Nehemiah the governor, the son
of Hacaliah, and Zedekiah,
2 Seraiah, Azariah, Jeremiah,
3 Pashhur, Amariah, Mal-
chijah,
4 Hattush, Shebaniah, Malluch,
5 Harim, Meremoth, Oba-
diah,
6 Daniel, Ginnethon, Baruch,
7 Meshullam, Abijah, Mijamin,
8 Maaziah, Bilgai, Shemaiah.
These *were* the priests.
9 And the Levites: Jeshua the
son of Azaniah, Binnui of the
sons of Henadad, Kadmiel;

10 also their brothers Shebaniah, Hodiah, Kelita, Pelaiah, Hanan,
11 Mica, Rehob, Hashabiah,
12 Zaccur, Sherebiah, Shebaniah,
13 Hodiah, Bani, Beninu.
14 The leaders of the people:
Parosh, Pahath-moab, Elam, Zattu, Bani,
15 Bunni, Azgad, Bebai,
16 Adonijah, Bigvai, Adin,
17 Ater, Hezekiah, Azzur,
18 Hodiah, Hashum, Bezai,
19 Hariph, Anathoth, Nebai,
20 Magpiash,   Meshullam,
Hezir,
21 Meshezabel, Zadok, Jaddua,
22 Pelatiah, Hanan, Anaiah,
23 Hoshea, Hananiah, Hasshub,
24 Hallohesh, Pilha, Shobek,
25 Rehum, Hashabnah, Maaseiah,
26 Ahiah, Hanan, Anan,
27 Malluch, Harim, Baanah.

E   The Responsibilities of the Covenant, 10:28–39

28 Now athe rest of the people, the priests, the Levites, the
gatekeepers, the singers, the temple servants, and ball those who
had separated themselves from
the peoples of the lands to the law
of God, their wives, their sons and
their daughters, all those who had
knowledge and understanding,

★28 aEzra
2:36-58
bNeh. 9:2

29 are joining with their kinsmen, their nobles, and are ataking
on themselves a curse and an oath
to walk in God's law, which was
given through Moses, God's servant, and to keep and to observe
all the commandments of GOD
our Lord, and His ordinances and
His statutes;

★29 aNeh.
5:12

30 and athat we will not give
our daughters to the peoples of
the land or take their daughters
for our sons.

★30-39
30 aEx.
34:16; Deut.
7:3

10:28 *the temple servants.* See note on Ezra 2:43.
10:29 *curse.* The penalty for violating the oath
they took in binding themselves to keep God's

laws.
10:30-39 The people agreed (1) not to marry
heathens (see note on Deut. 7:3-4), (2) to keep

31 aNeh.
13:15-22
bEx. 23:10,
11; Lev.
25:1-7
cDeut.
15:1, 2

31 As afor the peoples of the land who bring wares or any grain on the sabbath day to sell, we will not buy from them on the sabbath or a holy day; and we will forego *the crops* the bseventh year and the cexaction of every debt.

★32 aEx.
30:11-16;
Matt. 17:24

32 We also placed ourselves under obligation to contribute yearly aone third of a shekel for the service of the house of our God:

33 aLev.
24:5, 6;
2 Chr. 2:4

33 for the ashowbread, for the continual grain offering, for the continual burnt offering, the sabbaths, the new moon, for the appointed times, for the holy things and for the sin offerings to make atonement for Israel, and all the work of the house of our God.

★34 aNeh.
11:1 bNeh.
13:31

34 Likewise awe cast lots bfor the supply of wood *among* the priests, the Levites, and the people in order that they might bring it to the house of our God, according to our fathers' households, at fixed times annually, to burn on the altar of the LORD our God as it is written in the law;

35 aEx.
23:19; 34:26;
Deut. 26:2

35 and in order that they might bring the first fruits of our ground and athe first fruits of all the fruit of every tree to the house of the LORD annually,

36 aEx. 13:2

36 and abring to the house of our God the first-born of our sons and of our cattle, and the first-born of our herds and our flocks as it is written in the law, for the priests who are ministering in the house of our God.

37 aLev.
23:17 bNeh.
13:5, 9 cLev.
27:30; Num.
18:21

37 aWe will also bring the first of our dough, our contribu-tions, the fruit of every tree, the new wine and the oil bto the priests at the chambers of the house of our God; and the ctithe of our ground to the Levites, for the Levites are they who receive the tithes in all the rural towns.

38 And athe priest, the son of Aaron, shall be with the Levites when the Levites receive tithes, and the Levites shall bring up the tenth of the tithes to the house of our God, to the chambers of bthe storehouse.

★38-39

38 aNum.
18:26 bNeh.
13:12, 13

39 For the sons of Israel and the sons of Levi shall bring the acontribution of the grain, the new wine and the oil, to the chambers; there are the utensils of the sanctuary, the priests who are ministering, the gatekeepers, and the singers. Thus bwe will not neglect the house of our God.

39 aDeut.
12:6 bNeh.
13:10, 11

III   REFORMING THE NATION, 11:1-13:31

A   Repopulating the Cities, 11:1-12:26

1   *Jerusalem*, 11:1-24

11 Now athe leaders of the people lived in Jerusalem, but the rest of the people bcast lots to bring one out of ten to live in Jerusalem, cthe holy city, while nine-tenths *remained* in the *other* cities.

★ 1-2

1 aNeh. 7:4
bNeh. 10:34
cNeh. 11:18;
Is. 48:2

2 And the people blessed all the men who avolunteered to live in Jerusalem.

2 aJudg.
5:9
★ 3-24
3 a1 Chr.
9:2-34 bNeh.
7:73; 11:20
cEzra 2:43
dNeh. 7:57

3 aNow these are the heads of the provinces who lived in

---

the Sabbath and holy days free of commercial activity (see notes on Exod. 20:8-11 and Amos 8:5), (3) to observe the sabbatical year (see note on Exod. 23:10-11), and (4) to support the Temple.

10:32 The one-third shekel tax was a revival of an earlier command (though requiring a lesser amount than previously; see note on Exod. 30:11-16). The reduced rate may indicate something of the poverty of the people at this time.

10:34 *supply of wood.* Necessary to keep the fire going on the altar (Lev. 6:12).

10:38-39 On the tithe see notes on Lev. 27:30-33 and Mal. 3:8. The Levites had to tithe the tithes given to them in order to support the serving priests, porters, and singers.

11:1-2 Now that Jerusalem (here first referred to as *the holy city*) was secured with walls, it needed to be repopulated, so *lots* were cast to bring one-tenth of the country's population into the city. Others apparently moved voluntarily (v. 2).

11:3-24 These verses (cf. 1 Chron. 9:2-17) apparently list those already resident in Jerusalem, including laymen (vv. 3-9), priests (vv. 10-14), Levites (vv. 15-18), gatekeepers (v. 19), Temple servants (v. 21; on *Ophel* see note on 3:26), and certain other individuals (vv. 22-24; on *the sons of Asaph* see note on Ezra 2:41).

Jerusalem, but in the cities of Judah *each lived on his own property in their cities—the Israelites, the priests, the Levites, the ᶜtemple servants and the ᵈdescendants of Solomon's servants.

4 And some of the sons of Judah and some of the sons of Benjamin lived in Jerusalem. From the sons of Judah: Athaiah the son of Uzziah, the son of Zechariah, the son of Amariah, the son of Shephatiah, the son of Mahalalel, of the sons of Perez;

5 and Maaseiah the son of Baruch, the son of Col-hozeh, the son of Hazaiah, the son of Adaiah, the son of Joiarib, the son of Zechariah, the son of the Shilonite.

6 All the sons of Perez who lived in Jerusalem were 468 able men.

7 Now these are the sons of Benjamin: Sallu the son of Meshullam, the son of Joed, the son of Pedaiah, the son of Kolaiah, the son of Maaseiah, the son of Ithiel, the son of Jeshaiah;

8 and after him Gabbai *and* Sallai, 928.

9 And Joel the son of Zichri was their overseer, and Judah the son of Hassenuah was second in command of the city.

10 From the priests: Jedaiah the son of Joiarib, Jachin,

11 Seraiah the son of Hilkiah, the son of Meshullam, the son of Zadok, the son of Meraioth, the son of Ahitub, the leader of the house of God,

12 and their kinsmen who performed the work of the temple, 822; and Adaiah the son of Jeroham, the son of Pelaliah, the son of Amzi, the son of Zechariah, the son of Pashhur, the son of Malchijah,

13 and his kinsmen, heads of fathers' *households,* 242; and Amashsai the son of Azarel, the son of Ahzai, the son of Meshillemoth, the son of Immer,

14 and their brothers, valiant warriors, 128. And their overseer was Zabdiel, the son of Haggedolim.

15 Now from the Levites: Shemaiah the son of Hasshub, the son of Azrikam, the son of Hashabiah, the son of Bunni;

16 and Shabbethai and Jozabad, from the leaders of the Levites, who were in charge of ᵃthe outside work of the house of God;

17 and Mattaniah the son of Mica, the son of Zabdi, the son of Asaph, who was the leader in beginning the thanksgiving in prayer, and Bakbukiah, the second among his brethren; and Abda the son of Shammua, the son of Galal, the son of Jeduthun.

18 All the Levites in ᵃthe holy city *were* 284.

19 Also the gatekeepers, Akkub, Talmon, and their brethren, who kept watch at the gates, *were* 172.

20 And the rest of Israel, of the priests, *and* of the Levites, *were* in all the cities of Judah, each ᵃon his own inheritance.

21 But ᵃthe temple servants were living in Ophel, and Ziha and Gishpa were in charge of the temple servants.

22 Now ᵃthe overseer of the Levites in Jerusalem was Uzzi the son of Bani, the son of Hashabiah, the son of Mattaniah, the son of Mica, from the sons of Asaph, who were the singers for the service of the house of God.

23 ᵃFor *there was* a commandment from the king concerning them and a firm regulation for the song leaders ᵇday by day.

24 And Pethahiah the son of Meshezabel, of the sons ᵃof Zerah the son of Judah, was the ᵇking's representative in all matters concerning the people.

2 Other cities, 11:25-36

25 Now as for the villages with their fields, some of the sons

16 ᵃ1 Chr. 26:29

18 ᵃNeh. 11:1

20 ᵃNeh. 11:3

21 ᵃNeh. 3:26

22 ᵃNeh. 11:9, 14

23 ᵃEzra 6:8; 7:20 ᵇNeh. 12:47

24 ᵃGen. 38:30 ᵇ1 Chr. 18:17

★25-26
25 ᵃJosh. 14:15 ᵇJosh. 13:9, 17

11:25-26 These verses list towns in the former territories of Judah (vv. 25-30) and Benjamin (vv. 31-36), where other Jews lived.

of Judah lived in [a]Kiriath-arba and its towns, in [b]Dibon and its towns, and in Jekabzeel and its villages,

26 and in Jeshua, in Moladah and Beth-pelet,

27 and in Hazar-shual, in Beersheba and its towns,

28 and in Ziklag, in Meconah and in its towns,

29 and in En-rimmon, in Zorah and in Jarmuth,

30 Zanoah, Adullam, and their villages, Lachish and its fields, Azekah and its towns. So they encamped from Beersheba as far as the valley of Hinnom.

31 The sons of Benjamin also *lived* from Geba *onward,* at Michmash and Aija, at Bethel and its towns,

32 at Anathoth, Nob, Ananiah,

33 Hazor, Ramah, Gittaim,

34 Hadid, Zeboim, Neballat,

35 Lod and Ono, the valley of craftsmen.

36 And from the Levites, *some* divisions in Judah belonged to Benjamin.

3 Priests and Levites, 12:1-26

★ 1-9
1 [a]Ezra 2:1;
7:7

12 Now these are [a]the priests and the Levites who came up with Zerubbabel the son of Shealtiel, and Jeshua: Seraiah, Jeremiah, Ezra,

2 Amariah, Malluch, Hattush,

3 Shecaniah, Rehum, Meremoth,

4 Iddo, Ginnethoi, Abijah,

5 Mijamin, Maadiah, Bilgah,

6 Shemaiah and Joiarib, Jedaiah,

7 Sallu, Amok, Hilkiah, and Jedaiah. These were the heads of the priests and their kinsmen in the days of Jeshua.

8 And the Levites *were* Jeshua, Binnui, Kadmiel, Sherebiah, Judah, *and* Mattaniah *who was* in charge of the songs of thanksgiving, he and his brothers.

9 Also Bakbukiah and Unni, their brothers, stood opposite them [a]in *their* service divisions.

9 [a]Neh. 12:24

10 And Jeshua became the father of Joiakim, and Joiakim became the father of Eliashib, and Eliashib became the father of Joiada,

★10-11

11 and Joiada became the father of Jonathan, and Jonathan became the father of Jaddua.

12 Now in the days of Joiakim the priests, the heads of fathers' *households* were: of Seraiah, Meraiah; of Jeremiah, Hananiah;

★12

13 of Ezra, Meshullam; of Amariah, Jehohanan;

14 of Malluchi, Jonathan; of Shebaniah, Joseph;

15 of Harim, Adna; of Meraioth, Helkai;

16 of Iddo, Zechariah; of Ginnethon, Meshullam;

★16

17 of Abijah, Zichri; of Miniamin, of Moadiah, Piltai;

18 of Bilgah, Shammua; of Shemaiah, Jehonathan;

19 of Joiarib, Mattenai; of Jedaiah, Uzzi;

20 of Sallai, Kallai; of Amok, Eber;

21 of Hilkiah, Hashabiah; of Jedaiah, Nethanel.

22 As for the Levites, the heads of fathers' *households* were registered in the days of Eliashib, Joiada, and Johanan, and Jaddua; so *were* the priests in the reign of Darius the Persian.

★22

12:1-9 The priests and Levites who returned with Zerubbabel and Joshua (Ezra 2:2, 36-40) are listed in this section. *stood opposite them in their service divisions* (v. 9). Refers either to antiphonal singing or alternate shifts of service.

12:10-11 A listing of the line of high priests from Joshua to Jaddua (see note on v. 22).

12:12 *Joiakim.* Joshua's successor as high priest (v. 10).

12:16 *Zechariah.* The famous prophet (Ezra 5:1).

12:22 *Eliashib.* A contemporary of Nehemiah and the grandson of Joshua, the high priest in Zerubbabel's day. *Johanan.* The same as Jonathan of v. 11. *Jaddua.* Many identify him as the man who, according to Josephus, was high

23 The sons of Levi, the heads of fathers' *households,* were registered in the Book of the Chronicles up to the days of Johanan the son of Eliashib.

24 And the heads of the Levites *were* Hashabiah, Sherebiah, and Jeshua the son of Kadmiel, with their brothers opposite them, ªto praise *and* give thanks, as prescribed by David the man of God, ᵇdivision corresponding to division.

25 Mattaniah, and Bakbukiah, Obadiah, Meshullam, Talmon, *and* Akkub were gatekeepers keeping watch at ªthe storehouses of the gates.

26 These *served* in the days of Joiakim the son of Jeshua, the son of Jozadak, and in the days of ªNehemiah the governor and of Ezra the priest *and* scribe.

B Rededicating the Wall, 12:27–47

27 Now at the dedication of the wall of Jerusalem they sought out the Levites from all their places, to bring them to Jerusalem so that they might celebrate the dedication with gladness, with hymns of thanksgiving and with songs ªto the accompaniment of cymbals, harps, and lyres.

28 So the sons of the singers were assembled from the district around Jerusalem, and from ªthe villages of the Netophathites,

29 from Beth-gilgal, and from *their* fields in Geba and Azmaveth, for the singers had built themselves villages around Jerusalem.

30 And the priests and the Levites ªpurified themselves; they also purified the people, the gates, and the wall.

31 Then I had the leaders of Judah come up on top of the wall, and I appointed two great choirs, ªthe first proceeding to the right on top of the wall toward ᵇthe Refuse Gate.

32 Hoshaiah and half of the leaders of Judah followed them,

33 with Azariah, Ezra, Meshullam,

34 Judah, Benjamin, Shemaiah, Jeremiah,

35 and some of the sons of the priests with trumpets; *and* Zechariah the son of Jonathan, the son of Shemaiah, the son of Mattaniah, the son of Micaiah, the son of Zaccur, the son of Asaph,

36 and his kinsmen, Shemaiah, Azarel, Milalai, Gilalai, Maai, Nethanel, Judah *and* Hanani, ªwith the musical instruments of David the man of God. And Ezra the scribe went before them.

37 And at ªthe Fountain Gate they went directly up ᵇthe steps of the city of David by the stairway of the wall above the house

---

Cross references (margin)

24 ªNeh. 11:17 ᵇNeh. 12:9
25 ª1 Chr. 26:15
26 ªNeh. 8:9
27 ª1 Chr. 15:16, 28
★28-29
28 ª1 Chr. 9:16
★30 ªNeh. 13:22, 30
★31-37
31 ªNeh. 12:38 ᵇNeh. 2:13
36 ªNeh. 12:24
37 ªNeh. 2:14 ᵇNeh. 3:15 ᶜNeh. 3:26

---

priest when Alexander the Great invaded Persia (333 B.C.). If so, the *Darius* of this verse was Darius III (335–331 B.C.), and a copyist, not Nehemiah, added this part of the genealogy. It is quite possible, however, that there were two high priests with the same name and that Nehemiah knew this Jaddua as a young man, if not as high priest (though this is possible as well, since, according to the Elephantine Papyri, Johanan was high priest in 408, and Nehemiah may have lived until about 400 and seen Jaddua become high priest sometime between 408 and 400). If this is an earlier Jaddua, then

the *Darius* mentioned was Darius II (423–404 B.C.).

12:28-29 The places named were all near Jerusalem.

12:30 The purification of the wall would have been done by sprinkling sacrificial blood on it.

12:31-37 Nehemiah organized two groups to encircle the city. The first, led by Ezra, proceeded from the SW. corner of the city wall E., then N., led by singers (v. 31), followed by princes (vv. 32-33), then priests with trumpets (vv. 35, 41) and Levites with stringed instruments (v. 36).

of David to ᶜthe Water Gate on the east.

★38-43
38 ªNeh. 12:31 ᵇNeh. 3:11 ᶜNeh. 3:8

38 ªThe second choir proceeded to the left, while I followed them with half of the people on the wall, ᵇabove the Tower of Furnaces, to ᶜthe Broad Wall,

39 ªNeh. 8:16 ᵇNeh. 3:6 ᶜNeh. 3:3 ᵈNeh. 3:1 ᵉNeh. 3:25

39 and above ªthe Gate of Ephraim, by ᵇthe Old Gate, by the ᶜFish Gate, ᵈthe Tower of Hananel, and the Tower of the Hundred, as far as the Sheep Gate, and they stopped at ᵉthe Gate of the Guard.

40 Then the two choirs took their stand in the house of God. So did I and half of the officials with me;

41 and the priests, Eliakim, Maaseiah, Miniamin, Micaiah, Elioenai, Zechariah, and Hananiah, with the trumpets;

42 and Maaseiah, Shemaiah, Eleazar, Uzzi, Jehohanan, Malchijah, Elam, and Ezer. And the singers sang, with Jezrahiah *their* leader,

43 ªPs. 9:2; 92:4

43 and on that day they offered great sacrifices and rejoiced because ªGod had given them great joy, even the women and children rejoiced, so that the joy of Jerusalem was heard from afar.

44 ªNeh. 13:4, 5, 12, 13

44 On that day ªmen were also appointed over the chambers for the stores, the contributions, the first fruits, and the tithes, to gather into them from the fields of the cities the portions required by the law for the priests and Levites; for Judah rejoiced over the priests and Levites who served.

45 ª1 Chr. 25:1

45 For they performed the worship of their God and the service of purification, together with the singers and the gatekeepers

ªin accordance with the command of David *and* of his son Solomon.

46 For in the days of David and ªAsaph, in ancient times, *there were* ᵇleaders of the singers, songs of praise and hymns of thanksgiving to God.

★46 ª2 Chr. 29:30 ᵇ1 Chr. 9:33

47 And so all Israel in the days of Zerubbabel and Nehemiah gave the portions due the singers and the gatekeepers ªas each day required, and ᵇset apart the consecrated *portion* for the Levites, and the Levites set apart the consecrated *portion* for the sons of Aaron.

★47 ªNeh. 11:23 ᵇNum. 18:21

C   Reviving the People, 13:1-31
1   *Reforms in relation to non-Jews, 13:1-3*

13 On that day ªthey read aloud from the book of Moses in the hearing of the people; and there was found written in it that ᵇno Ammonite or Moabite should ever enter the assembly of God,

★ 1-3
1 ªNeh. 9:3 ᵇDeut. 23:3-5; Neh. 13:23

2 because they did not meet the sons of Israel with bread and water, but ªhired Balaam against them to curse them. However, ᵇour God turned the curse into a blessing.

2 ªNum. 22:3-11 ᵇDeut. 23:5

3 So it came about, that when they heard the law, ªthey excluded ᵇall foreigners from Israel.

3 ªNeh. 9:2; 10:28 ᵇEx. 12:38

2   *Reforms in relation to the priesthood, 13:4-14*

4 Now prior to this, Eliashib the priest, ªwho was appointed over the chambers of the house of

★ 4-6
4 ªNeh. 12:44 ᵇ2:10; 6:1, 17, 18

12:38-43 The other group proceeded N., then E. to the Temple area, meeting the first group in the Temple courts (v. 40), where they offered sacrifices and praised God (vv. 41-43). For the location of the various gates *see* notes on chapter 3.

12:46 *See* note on Ezra 2:41.

12:47 *See* note on 10:38-39.

13:1-3 *See* note on Deut. 23:3-6 for this restriction on the *Ammonite* and *Moabite. all foreigners.* Included heathen who attached themselves to the Jews by marriage, commerce, or religious observances (*see* note on Exod. 12:38).

13:4-6 *Tobiah.* An Ammonite (2:19) to whom Eliashib had turned over a *large room* in the court of the Temple during Nehemiah's absence from Jerusalem. *king of Babylon.* Artaxerxes, who was probably in Babylon at that time, since it was an administrative center of the Persian Empire.

our God, being related to [b]Tobiah,

5 aNum. 18:21

5 had prepared a large room for him, where formerly they put the grain offerings, the frankincense, the utensils, and the tithes of grain, wine and oil [a]prescribed for the Levites, the singers and the gatekeepers, and the contributions for the priests.

6 aNeh. 5:14 bEzra 6:22

6 But during all this *time* I was not in Jerusalem, for in [a]the thirty-second year of [b]Artaxerxes king of Babylon I had gone to the king. After some time, however, I asked leave from the king,

★ 7-9

7 aNeh. 13:5

7 and I came to Jerusalem and learned about the evil that Eliashib had done for Tobiah, [a]by preparing a room for him in the courts of the house of God.

8 aJohn 2:13-16

8 And it was very displeasing to me, so I [a]threw all of Tobiah's household goods out of the room.

9 a2 Chr. 29:5, 15, 16

9 Then I gave an order and [a]they cleansed the rooms; and I returned there the utensils of the house of God with the grain offerings and the frankincense.

★10 aDeut. 12:19; Neh. 10:37 bNeh. 12:28, 29

10 I also discovered that [a]the portions of the Levites had not been given *them*, so that the Levites and the singers who performed the service had gone away, [b]each to his own field.

11 aNeh. 13:17, 25 bNeh. 10:39

11 So I [a]reprimanded the officials and said, "[b]Why is the house of God forsaken?" Then I gathered them together and restored them to their posts.

12 aNeh. 10:37; 12:44; Mal. 3:10

12 All Judah then brought [a]the tithe of the grain, wine, and oil into the storehouses.

13 aNeh. 7:2

13 And in charge of the storehouses I appointed Shelemiah the priest, Zadok the scribe, and Pedaiah of the Levites, and in addition to them was Hanan the son

of Zaccur, the son of Mattaniah; for [a]they were considered reliable, and it was their task to distribute to their kinsmen.

14 [a]Remember me for this, O my God, and do not blot out my loyal deeds which I have performed for the house of my God and its services.

14 aNeh. 5:19; 13:22, 31

3   Reforms in relation to the Sabbath, 13:15-22

★15-22

15 In those days I saw in Judah some who were treading wine presses [a]on the sabbath, and bringing in sacks of grain and loading *them* on donkeys, as well as wine, grapes, figs, and all kinds of loads, [b]and they brought *them* into Jerusalem on the sabbath day. So [c]I admonished *them* on the day they sold food.

15 aEx. 20:8; 34:21; Deut. 5:12-14; Jer. 17:22 bNeh. 10:31; Jer. 17:21 cNeh. 9:29; 13:21

16 Also men of Tyre were living there who imported fish and all kinds of merchandise, and sold *them* to the sons of Judah on the sabbath, even in Jerusalem.

17 Then [a]I reprimanded the nobles of Judah and said to them, "What is this evil thing you are doing, by profaning the sabbath day?

17 aNeh. 13:11, 25

18 "[a]Did not your fathers do the same so that our God brought on us, and on this city, all this trouble? Yet you are adding to the wrath on Israel by profaning the sabbath."

18 aEzra 9:13; Jer. 17:21

19 [a]And it came about that just as it grew dark at the gates of Jerusalem before the sabbath, I commanded that the doors should be shut and that they should not open them until after the sabbath. Then I stationed some of my servants at the gates *that* no load should enter on the sabbath day.

19 aLev. 23:32

20 Once or twice the traders

13:7-9 When Nehemiah returned and discovered, to his horror, what Eliashib had done, he threw Tobiah's belongings out and ceremonially cleansed the room.

13:10 Nehemiah discovered that, in spite of the oath the people had taken, the Levites (and presumably also the priests) had not been receiving their tithes and, as a result, had to

work in the fields. To rectify this, he appointed four reliable treasurers over the *storehouses* (v. 13).

13:15-22 Also in violation of the covenant (10:30-31), some Jews were preparing and transporting wares on the Sabbath (v. 15) and Phoenician traders were actually selling on the Sabbath (v. 16).

and merchants of every kind of merchandise spent the night outside Jerusalem.

21 Then [a]I warned them and said to them, "Why do you spend the night in front of the wall? If you do so again, I will use force against you." From that time on they did not come on the sabbath.

22 And I commanded the Levites that [a]they should purify themselves and come as gatekeepers to sanctify the sabbath day. *For* this also [b]remember me, O my God, and have compassion on me according to the greatness of Thy lovingkindness.

4 Reforms in relation to marriage, 13:23–31

23 In those days I also saw that the Jews had [a]married women from [b]Ashdod, [c]Ammon, *and* Moab.

24 As for their children, half spoke in the language of Ashdod, and none of them was able to speak the language of Judah, but the language of his own people.

25 So [a]I contended with them and cursed them and [b]struck some of them and pulled out their hair, and [c]made them swear by God, "You shall not give your daughters to their sons, nor take of their daughters for your sons or for yourselves.

26 "[a]Did not Solomon king of Israel sin regarding these things? [b]Yet among the many nations there was no king like him, and [c]he was loved by his God, and God made him king over all Israel; nevertheless the foreign women caused even him to sin.

27 "Do we then hear about you that you have committed all this great evil [a]by acting unfaithfully against our God by marrying foreign women?"

28 Even one of the sons of Joiada, the son of Eliashib the high priest, was a son-in-law of [a]Sanballat the Horonite, so I drove him away from me.

29 [a]Remember them, O my God, because they have defiled the priesthood and the [b]covenant of the priesthood and the Levites.

30 [a]Thus I purified them from everything foreign and appointed duties for the priests and the Levites, each in his task,

31 and *I arranged* [a]for the supply of wood at appointed times and for the first fruits. [b]Remember me, O my God, for good.

13:23-25 The sin of mixed marriages had erupted again (see notes on Ezra 9:1–4 and 10:44), and the children of these marriages could not speak Hebrew. Nehemiah dealt firmly with the offenders (on pulling out the hair, see note on Isa. 50:4–9).

13:26 Foreign wives had proved to be Solomon's downfall (1 Kings 11:1–8).

13:28 One of the younger sons of Joiada (Johanan was the oldest son, 12:11, 22) married a daughter of *Sanballat* (see note on 2:10). He deserved to be expelled, because the priestly line was not to be contaminated by intermarriage (Lev. 21:6–8, 14–15).

Marginal references:

21 [a]Neh. 13:15

22 [a]1 Chr. 15:12; Neh. 12:30 [b]Neh. 13:14, 31

★23-25

23 [a]Ex. 34:11-16; Deut. 7:1-5; Ezra 9:2; Neh. 10:30 [b]Neh. 4:7 [c]Ezra 9:1; Neh. 13:1

25 [a]Neh. 13:11, 17 [b]Deut. 25:2 [c]Neh. 10:29, 30

★26 [a]1 Kin. 11:1 [b]1 Kin. 3:13; 2 Chr. 1:12 [c]2 Sam. 12:24, 25

27 [a]Ezra 10:2; Neh. 13:23

★28 [a]Neh. 2:10, 19; 4:1

29 [a]Neh. 6:14 [b]Num. 25:13

30 [a]Neh. 10:30

31 [a]Neh. 10:34 [b]Neh. 13:14, 22

INTRODUCTION TO
THE BOOK OF ESTHER

AUTHOR: Uncertain   DATE: c. 465 B.C.

Authorship   *Though his name is unknown to us, the author was evidently a Jew (Jewish nationalism permeates the book) who was personally acquainted with details of the reign of Ahasuerus and the palace in Shushan. He must have written the book shortly after the close of Ahasuerus' reign, since that administration is spoken of in the past tense (10:2-3).*

Historical Setting   *The events of this book cover a 10-year portion (483-473) of the reign of Xerxes I (486-465). Ahasuerus is the Hebrew form of his name, equivalent to the Persian Khshayarsha and the Greek Xerxes. The events occurred between those recorded in the sixth and seventh chapters of Ezra (see the Introduction to Ezra for further background).*

Theme   *Though the name of God is nowhere mentioned in the book, His sovereignty and providence are evident throughout. Vashti's dismissal, Esther's regal position, Xerxes' indebtedness to Mordecai discovered during a sleepless night, and the miraculous deliverance of the Jews all demonstrate God's control and care for His people (Psalm 121:4). The book also explains the origin of the Feast of Purim (2 Maccab. 15:36) on the 13th and 14th days of Adar (Feb.-Mar.), when Jews celebrate the deliverance from Haman.*

Historical Accuracy   *Objections raised about the historicity of Esther include the following: (1) Secular history fails to mention Vashti or Esther as queens during the reign of Xerxes. However, Herodotus, who often omits mention of important people (like Belshazzar, Dan. 5), does report that Xerxes sought consolation in his harem after his defeat at Salamis, which was in the year Esther was made queen (Esther 2:16; Herodotus 7.7). (2) It is alleged (from Esther 2:5-6) that Xerxes was a near successor to Nebuchadnezzar, since this passage appears to say that Mordecai was deported by Nebuchadnezzar in 597 and yet was still living during the reign of Xerxes. However, the antecedent of who in verse 6 is not Mordecai but Kish, his great-grandfather. (3) Objection is raised concerning the account of the slaying of 75,000 enemies of the Jews in one day, and without apparent interference from the Persians (Esther 9:16-17). Though unusual, this was by no means impossible, in light of known Persian callousness toward human life and of the pre-planned arming of the Jews (8:13).*

Contents   *Undoubtedly 4:14 is the best known verse in the book, emphasizing the theme of God's control of all events.*

OUTLINE OF ESTHER

I. The Danger to God's People, 1:1-3:15
  A. The Divorce of Vashti, 1:1-22
  B. The Discovery of Esther, 2:1-20
  C. The Devotion of Mordecai, 2:21-23
  D. The Decree of Haman, 3:1-15
II. The Decision of God's Servant, 4:1-5:14
  A. Mordecai's Appeal to Esther, 4:1-14
  B. Esther's Answer to Mordecai, 4:15-17
  C. Esther's Audience with Ahasuerus, 5:1-8
  D. Haman's Arrogance over Mordecai, 5:9-14

III. The Deliverance of God's People, 6:1-10:3
  A. The Defeat of Haman, 6:1-7:10
    1. Haman humbled, 6:1-14
    2. Haman hanged, 7:1-10
  B. The Decree of Ahasuerus and Mordecai, 8:1-17
  C. The Defeat of Israel's Enemies, 9:1-19
  D. The Days of Purim, 9:20-32
  E. The Description of Mordecai's Fame, 10:1-3

THE BOOK OF ESTHER

I THE DANGER TO GOD'S PEOPLE,
1:1–3:15
A The Divorce of Vashti,
1:1–22

★ 1 *a*Ezra 4:6; Dan. 9:1 *b*Esth. 8:9 *c*Esth. 9:30

1 Now it took place in the days of *a*Ahasuerus, the Ahasuerus who reigned *b*from India to Ethiopia over *c*127 provinces,

★ 2 *a*1 Kin. 1:46 *b*Neh. 1:1; Dan. 8:2

2 in those days as King Ahasuerus *a*sat on his royal throne which *was* in *b*Susa the capital,

★ 3-12

3 *a*Esth. 2:18

3 in the third year of his reign, *a*he gave a banquet for all his princes and attendants, the army *officers* of Persia and Media, the nobles, and the princes of his provinces being in his presence.

4 And he displayed the riches of his royal glory and the splendor of his great majesty for many days, 180 days.

5 *a*Esth. 7:7, 8

5 And when these days were completed, the king gave a banquet lasting seven days for all the people who were present in Susa the capital, from the greatest to the least, in the court of *a*the garden of the king's palace.

6 *a*Ezek. 23:41; Amos 6:4

6 *There were hangings of* fine white and violet linen held by cords of fine purple linen on silver rings and marble columns, *and* *a*couches of gold and silver on a mosaic pavement of porphyry, marble, mother-of-pearl, and precious stones.

7 *a*Esth. 2:18

7 Drinks were served in golden vessels of various kinds, and the royal wine was plentiful *a*according to the king's bounty.

8 And the drinking was *done* according to the law, there was no compulsion, for so the king had given orders to each official of his household that he should do according to the desires of each person.

9 Queen Vashti also gave a banquet for the women in the palace which belonged to King Ahasuerus.

10 *a*Judg. 16:25

10 On the seventh day, when the heart of the king was *a*merry with wine, he commanded Mehuman, Biztha, Harbona, Bigtha, Abagtha, Zethar, and Carkas, the seven eunuchs who served in the presence of King Ahasuerus,

11 *a*Esth. 2:17; 6:8

11 to bring Queen Vashti before the king with *her* royal *a*crown in order to display her beauty to the people and the princes, for she was beautiful.

12 But Queen Vashti refused to come at the king's command delivered by the eunuchs. Then the king became very angry and his wrath burned within him.

★13 *a*Jer. 10:7; Dan. 2:2 *b*1 Chr. 12:32

13 Then the king said to *a*the wise men *b*who understood the times—for it was the custom of the king so *to speak* before all who knew law and justice,

14 *a*2 Kin. 25:19; Matt. 18:10

14 and were close to him: Carshena, Shethar, Admatha, Tarshish, Meres, Marsena, and Memucan, the seven princes of Persia and Media *a*who had access to the king's presence and sat in the first place in the kingdom—

15 "According to law, what is to be done with Queen Vashti, because she did not obey the command of King Ahasuerus *delivered* by the eunuchs?"

1:1 *India.* The area drained by the Indus River, in present-day Pakistan. *Ethiopia.* Or Cush, presently N. Sudan.

1:2 *Susa.* One of the main capitals of the empire, 150 miles N. of the Persian Gulf (cf. Neh. 1:1).

1:3-12 For 6 months (in the year 482 B.C.) the king exhibited the grandeur of his court, during which time he probably planned with the military and civil leaders his proposed invasion of Greece (which occurred in 480 B.C.). At the conclusion, a 7-day drinking feast was held (vv. 3, 5; though no one was compelled to drink, v. 8), the queen holding a separate feast for the women guests (v. 9). On the last day of the feast, the drunken king summoned his queen, presumably to make a lewd display of her before his guests, but she refused to obey.

1:13 *wise men who understood the times.* I.e., astrologers. They also knew the Law of Moses (cf. Ezra 7:14).

★16-19

16 And in the presence of the king and the princes, Memucan said, "Queen Vashti has wronged not only the king but *also* all the princes, and all the peoples who are in all the provinces of King Ahasuerus.

17 "For the queen's conduct will become known to all the women causing them to look with contempt on their husbands by saying, 'King Ahasuerus commanded Queen Vashti to be brought in to his presence, but she did not come.'

18 "And this day the ladies of Persia and Media who have heard of the queen's conduct will speak in *the same way* to all the king's princes, and there will be plenty of contempt and anger.

19 *a*Esth.
8:8; Dan. 6:8

19 "If it pleases the king, let a royal edict be issued by him and let it be written in the laws of Persia and Media so *a*that it cannot be repealed, that Vashti should come no more into the presence of King Ahasuerus, and let the king give her royal position to another who is more worthy than she.

20 *a*Eph.
5:22; Col.
3:18

20 "And when the king's edict which he shall make is heard throughout all his kingdom, great as it is, then *a*all women will give honor to their husbands, great and small."

21 And *this* word pleased the king and the princes, and the king did as Memucan proposed.

★22 *a*Esth.
3:12; 8:9
*b*Eph. 5:22-24

22 So he sent letters to all the king's provinces, *a*to each province according to its script and to every people according to their language, that every man should *b*be the master in his own house and the one who speaks in the language of his own people.

B   The Discovery of Esther, 2:1-20

2 After these things *a*when the anger of King Ahasuerus had subsided, he remembered Vashti and what she had done and *b*what had been decreed against her.

★ 1 *a*Esth.
7:10 *b*Esth.
1:19, 20

2 Then the king's attendants, who served him, said, "*a*Let beautiful young virgins be sought for the king.

2 *a*1 Kin.
1:2

3 "And let the king appoint overseers in *a*all the provinces of his kingdom that they may gather every beautiful young virgin to Susa the capital, to the harem, into the custody of *b*Hegai, the king's eunuch, who was in charge of the women; and *c*let their cosmetics be given *them*.

3 *a*Esth.
1:1, 2 *b*Esth.
2:8, 15
*c*Esth. 2:9,
12

4 "Then let the young lady who pleases the king be queen in place of Vashti." And the matter pleased the king, and he did accordingly.

5 *Now* there was a Jew in Susa the capital whose name was *a*Mordecai, the son of Jair, the son of Shimei, the son of Kish, a Benjamite,

5 *a*Esth. 3:2

6 *a*who had been taken into exile from Jerusalem with the captives who had been exiled with Jeconiah king of Judah, whom Nebuchadnezzar the king of Babylon had exiled.

★ 6 *a*2 Kin.
24:14, 15;
2 Chr. 36:10

7 And he was bringing up Hadassah, that is *a*Esther, his uncle's daughter, for she had neither father nor mother. Now the young lady was beautiful of form and face, and when her father and her mother died, Mordecai took her as his own daughter.

★ 7 *a*Esth.
2:15

8 So it came about when the command and decree of the king were heard and *a*many young la-

★ 8-11
8 *a*Esth. 2:3
*b*Esth. 2:3,
15

1:16-19 The counsellors turned the matter into a national crisis threatening male supremacy!
1:22 The king solemnly decreed (how could it ever have been enforced!) that every man was to rule his own household and that his native language was to be spoken in that home.
2:1 *After these things.* After Ahasuerus' defeat at Plataea in 479, he probably began to long for his queen again.

2:6 See Introduction, "Historical Accuracy."
2:7 *Hadassah,* meaning "myrtle," was her Hebrew name; her Persian name (Esther) meant "star."
2:8-11 Esther was taken into the king's *harem* and instructed by Mordecai (her cousin who reared her) not to reveal her nationality. Perhaps he feared for her life (v. 11), or for his own position (v. 19).

dies were gathered to Susa the capital into the custody of [b]Hegai, that Esther was taken to the king's palace into the custody of Hegai, who was in charge of the women.

9 Now the young lady pleased him and found favor with him. So he quickly provided her with her [a]cosmetics and food, gave her seven choice maids from the king's palace, and transferred her and her maids to the best place in the harem.

10 [a]Esther did not make known her people or her kindred, for Mordecai had instructed her that she should not make *them* known.

11 And every day Mordecai walked back and forth in front of the court of the harem to learn how Esther was and how she fared.

12 Now when the turn of each young lady came to go in to King Ahasuerus, after the end of her twelve months under the regulations for the women—for the days of their beautification were completed as follows: six months with oil of myrrh and six months with spices and the cosmetics for women—

13 the young lady would go in to the king in this way: anything that she desired was given her to take with her from the harem to the king's palace.

14 In the evening she would go in and in the morning she would return to the second harem, to the custody of Shaashgaz, the king's eunuch who was in charge of the concubines. She would not again go in to the king unless the king delighted in her and she was summoned by name.

15 Now when the turn of Esther, [a]the daughter of Abihail the uncle of Mordecai who had taken her as his daughter, came to go in to the king, she did not request anything except what [b]Hegai, the king's eunuch who was in charge of the women, advised. And Esther found favor in the eyes of all who saw her.

16 So Esther was taken to King Ahasuerus to his royal palace in the tenth month which is the month Tebeth, in the seventh year of his reign.

17 And the king loved Esther more than all the women, and she found favor and kindness with him more than all the virgins, so that [a]he set the royal crown on her head and made her queen instead of Vashti.

18 Then [a]the king gave a great banquet, Esther's banquet, for all his princes and his servants; he also made a holiday for the provinces and gave gifts [b]according to the king's bounty.

19 And [a]when the virgins were gathered together the second time, then Mordecai [b]was sitting at the king's gate.

20 [a]Esther had not yet made known her kindred or her people, even as Mordecai had commanded her, for Esther did what Mordecai told her as she had done [b]when under his care.

C The Devotion of Mordecai, 2:21–23

21 In those days, while Mordecai was sitting at the king's gate, [a]Bigthan and Teresh, two of the king's officials from those who guarded the door, became

---

9 [a]Esth. 2:3, 12

10 [a]Esth. 2:20

★**15-17**

15 [a]Esth. 2:7; 9:29 [b]Esth. 2:3, 8

17 [a]Esth. 1:11

★**18** [a]Esth. 1:3 [b]Esth. 1:7

★**19** [a]Esth. 2:3, 4 [b]Esth. 2:21; 3:2

20 [a]Esth. 2:10 [b]Esth. 2:7

★**21-23**

21 [a]Esth. 6:2

2:15-17 Each concubine waited to be summoned by the king. Esther's turn came in the month of Tebeth (the Babylonian name for Dec.-Jan.), 479 B.C. She was crowned queen four years after Vashti's divorce and after Ahasuerus had suffered crushing defeat at the hands of the Greeks (See Introduction, "Historical Accuracy.")

2:18 *made a holiday.* This could mean a release from taxes, a holiday, or a release of prisoners.
2:19 *the second time.* Another occasion when Ahasuerus added to his harem, after Esther had been made queen.
2:21-23 Mordecai foiled an assassination plot against the king, and the report of this service was duly recorded in the king's diary (6:1-2).

angry and sought to lay hands on King Ahasuerus.

22 aEsth. 6:1, 2

22 But the plot became known to Mordecai, and ahe told Queen Esther, and Esther informed the king in Mordecai's name.

23 aEsth. 10:2

23 Now when the plot was investigated and found *to be so,* they were both hanged on a gallows; and it *was* written in athe Book of the Chronicles in the king's presence.

D The Decree of Haman, 3:1-15

★ **1** aEsth. 5:11 bEsth. 3:10; 8:3 cEsth. 5:11

3 After these events King Ahasuerus apromoted Haman, the son of Hammedatha bthe Agagite, and cadvanced him and established his authority over all the princes who *were* with him.

★ **2** aEsth. 2:19; 5:9

2 And all the king's servants who were at the king's gate bowed down and paid homage to Haman; for so the king had commanded concerning him. But aMordecai neither bowed down nor paid homage.

3 aEsth. 2:19 bEsth. 3:2

3 Then the king's servants who were at athe king's gate said to Mordecai, "bWhy are you transgressing the king's command?"

4 Now it was when they had spoken daily to him and he would not listen to them, that they told

Haman to see whether Mordecai's reason would stand; for he had told them that he was a Jew.

5 aEsth. 5:9

5 When Haman saw that aMordecai neither bowed down nor paid homage to him, Haman was filled with rage.

★ **6** aPs. 83:4

6 But he disdained to lay hands on Mordecai alone, for they had told him *who* the people of Mordecai *were;* therefore Haman asought to destroy all the Jews, the people of Mordecai, who *were* throughout the whole kingdom of Ahasuerus.

★ **7** aEsth. 9:24-26 bEzra 6:15

7 In the first month, which is the month Nisan, in the twelfth year of King Ahasuerus, Pur, that is the lot, was acast before Haman from day to day and from month *to month,* until the twelfth month, that is bthe month Adar.

8 aEzra 4:12-15; Acts 16:20, 21

8 Then Haman said to King Ahasuerus, "There is a certain people scattered and dispersed among the peoples in all the provinces of your kingdom; atheir laws are different from *those* of all *other* people, and they do not observe the king's laws, so it is not in the king's interest to let them remain.

★ **9**

9 "If it is pleasing to the king, let it be decreed that they be destroyed, and I will pay ten thousand talents of silver into the hands of those who carry on the king's business, to put into the king's treasuries."

★**10-11** **10** aGen. 41:42; Esth. 8:2 bEsth. 3:1 cEsth. 7:6

10 Then athe king took his

3:1 *the Agagite.* Possibly related to the Amalekites (1 Sam. 15:8, 33). If so, Haman was a descendant of Esau, an enemy of the descendants of Isaac (see note on Exod. 17:8).

3:2 Apparently Mordecai did not bow to Haman because Haman claimed some sort of divine honors, as did the Persian kings. As a faithful Jew, Mordecai could not give such honor (Deut. 6:13-14).

3:6 Haman realized that to kill only Mordecai would not solve his problem.

3:7 *first month . . . twelfth year.* Mar.-Apr., 474, more than 4 years after Esther had become queen. *Pur.* An Assyrian word meaning "lot." The plural, Purim, gives its name to the feast commemorating the Jews' deliverance from Haman (see Introduction, under "Theme"). Haman, being very superstitious, cast the lot in order to determine the most propitious time

for carrying out his plot against the Jews. The lot fell on the *twelfth month* (Feb.-Mar.) which not only gave Haman time to prepare but also, in the overruling providence of God, gave the Jews time to thwart his plan.

3:9 In reality Haman offered a bribe to the king, the amount of which he expected to cover by confiscating the property of the Jews. *ten thousand talents of silver.* A talent weighed from 58-80 pounds (see note on Matt. 18:24). Using an average figure of 75 pounds, this would amount to 12 million ounces of silver.

3:10-11 The king, not even interested enough to inquire who the people were, gave Haman his *ring* (on which was the official seal, the equivalent of the king's signature) and permission to do whatever he wished with the people and their money.

signet ring from his hand and gave it to Haman, the son of Hammedatha [b]the Agagite, [c]the enemy of the Jews.

11 And the king said to Haman, "The silver is yours, and the people *also,* to do with them as you please."

12 [a]Then the king's scribes were summoned on the thirteenth day of the first month, and it was written just as Haman commanded to [b]the king's satraps, to the governors who were over each province, and to the princes of each people, each province according to its script, each people according to its language, being written [c]in the name of King Ahasuerus and sealed with the king's signet ring.

13 And letters were sent by [a]couriers to all the king's provinces [b]to destroy, to kill, and to annihilate all the Jews, both young and old, women and children, [c]in one day, the thirteenth *day* of the twelfth month, which is the month Adar, and to [d]seize their possessions as plunder.

14 [a]A copy of the edict to be issued as law in every province was published to all the peoples so that they should be ready for this day.

15 The couriers went out impelled by the king's command while the decree was issued in Susa the capital; and while the king and Haman sat down to drink, [a]the city of Susa was in confusion.

II THE DECISION OF GOD'S SERVANT, 4:1–5:14
A Mordecai's Appeal to Esther, 4:1–14

4 When Mordecai learned [a]all that had been done, he tore his clothes, put on sackcloth and ashes, and went out into the midst of the city and wailed loudly and bitterly.

2 And he went as far as the king's gate, for no one was to enter the king's gate clothed in sackcloth.

3 And in each and every province where the command and decree of the king came, there was great mourning among the Jews, with [a]fasting, weeping, and wailing; and many lay on sackcloth and ashes.

4 Then Esther's maidens and her eunuchs came and told her, and the queen writhed in great anguish. And she sent garments to clothe Mordecai that he might remove his sackcloth from him, but he did not accept *them.*

5 Then Esther summoned Hathach from the king's eunuchs, whom the king had appointed to attend her, and ordered him *to go* to Mordecai to learn what this *was* and why it *was.*

6 So Hathach went out to Mordecai to the city square in front of the king's gate.

7 And Mordecai told him all that had happened to him, and [a]the exact amount of money that Haman had promised to pay to the king's treasuries for the destruction of the Jews.

8 He also gave him [a]a copy of the text of the edict which had been issued in Susa for their destruction, that he might show Esther and inform her, and to order her to go in to the king to implore his favor and to plead with him for her people.

9 And Hathach came back and related Mordecai's words to Esther.

10 Then Esther spoke to Hathach and ordered him *to reply* to Mordecai:

★12-13
12 [a]Esth. 8:9
[b]Ezra 8:36
[c]1 Kin. 21:8;
Esth. 8:8, 10

13 [a]2 Chr. 30:6; Esth. 8:10, 14
[b]Esth. 7:4
[c]Esth. 8:12
[d]Esth. 8:11; 9:10

14 [a]Esth. 8:13, 14

15 [a]Esth. 8:15

★ 1 [a]2 Sam. 1:11; Esth. 3:8-10; Jon. 3:5,6

★ 2

3 [a]Esth. 4:16

7 [a]Esth. 3:9

★ 8 [a]Esth. 3:14

3:12-13 The edict was drawn up and letters were sent immediately by a postal system employing riders stationed at various intervals who passed messages along to each other, thus allowing the letters to reach the remotest part of the empire in time to prepare for the execution of the Jews.

4:1 *sackcloth.* See note on Gen. 37:34.
4:2 See note on Neh. 2:2.
4:8 *for her people.* Hathach now knew that Esther was a Jewess.

11 aEsth.
5:1; 6:4
bDan. 2:9
cEsth. 5:2;
8:4

11 "All the king's servants and the people of the king's provinces know that for any man or woman who acomes to the king to the inner court who is not summoned, bhe has but one law, that he be put to death, unless the king holds out cto him the golden scepter so that he may live. And I have not been summoned to come to the king for these thirty days."

12 And they related Esther's words to Mordecai.

★13   13 Then Mordecai told *them* to reply to Esther, "Do not imagine that you in the king's palace can escape any more than all the Jews.

★14 aLev.
26:42; 2 Kin.
13:5

14 "For if you remain silent at this time, relief and adeliverance will arise for the Jews from another place and you and your father's house will perish. And who knows whether you have not attained royalty for such a time as this?"

B   Esther's Answer to Mordecai, 4:15-17

15 Then Esther told *them* to reply to Mordecai,

★16 aJoel
1:14; 2:12
bEsth. 5:1

16 "Go, assemble all the Jews who are found in Susa, and fast for me; ado not eat or drink for bthree days, night or day. I and my maidens also will fast in the same way. And thus I will go in to the king, which is not according to the law; and if I perish, I perish."

17 So Mordecai went away and did just as Esther had commanded him.

C   Esther's Audience with Ahasuerus, 5:1-8

5 Now it came about aon the third day that Esther put on her royal robes and stood bin the inner court of the king's palace in front of the king's rooms, and the king was sitting on his royal throne in the throne room, opposite the entrance to the palace.

★ 1 aEsth.
4:16 bEsth.
4:11; 6:4

2 And it happened when the king saw Esther the queen standing in the court, ashe obtained favor in his sight; and bthe king extended to Esther the golden scepter which was in his hand. So Esther came near and touched the top of the scepter.

2 aEsth. 2:9
bEsth. 4:11;
8:4

3 Then the king said to her, "What is *troubling* you, Queen Esther? And what is your request? aEven to half of the kingdom it will be given to you."

3 aEsth.
7:2; Mark
6:23

4 And Esther said, "If it please the king, may the king and Haman come this day to the banquet that I have prepared for him."

5 Then the king said, "aBring Haman quickly that we may do as Esther desires." So the king and Haman came to the banquet which Esther had prepared.

★ 5-8

5 aEsth.
6:14

6 And, as they drank their wine at the banquet, athe king said to Esther, "bWhat is your petition, for it shall be granted to you. And what is your request? Even to half of the kingdom it shall be done."

6 aEsth. 7:2
bEsth. 5:3

7 So Esther answered and said, "My petition and my request is:

8 aif I have found favor in the sight of the king, and if it

8 aEsth.
7:3; 8:5
bEsth. 6:14

4:13 Mordecai put pressure on Esther, reminding her that she risked death whether she approached the king or not.

4:14 Mordecai was convinced that God would somehow save the Jewish nation, whether through Esther or otherwise.

4:16 Prayer was no doubt the purpose for this *fast,* indicating Esther's sense of dependence on God.

5:1 *on the third day.* A part of a day was counted as a whole day, explaining how the

fast could extend for three days, night and day (4:16), and yet terminate on the third day (see note on Matt. 12:40).

5:5-8 It was providential that Esther apparently lost the courage to expose Haman before the king at her first banquet, and so held a second one the next day. During the intervening night, the events of chapter 6 took place, making it much easier for Esther to expose Haman at the second banquet.

please the king to grant my petition and do what I request, may the king and Haman come to [b]the banquet which I shall prepare for them, and tomorrow I will do as the king says."

D   Haman's Arrogance over Mordecai, 5:9-14

9 Then Haman went out that day glad and pleased of heart; but when Haman saw Mordecai [a]in the king's gate, and [b]that he did not stand up or tremble before him, Haman was filled with anger against Mordecai.

10 Haman controlled himself, however, went to his house, and sent for his friends and his wife [a]Zeresh.

11 Then Haman recounted to them the glory of his riches, and the [a]number of his sons, and every *instance* where the king had magnified him, and how he had [b]promoted him above the princes and servants of the king.

12 Haman also said, "Even Esther the queen let no one but me come with the king to the banquet which she had prepared; and [a]tomorrow also I am invited by her with the king.

13 "Yet all of this does not satisfy me every time I see Mordecai the Jew sitting at [a]the king's gate."

14 Then Zeresh his wife and all his friends said to him, "[a]Have a gallows fifty cubits high made and in the morning ask the king to have Mordecai hanged on it, then go joyfully with the king to the banquet." And the advice pleased Haman, so he had the gallows made.

III THE DELIVERANCE OF GOD'S PEOPLE, 6:1-10:3

A   The Defeat of Haman, 6:1-7:10

1 *Haman humbled,* 6:1-14

6 During that night the king [a]could not sleep so he gave an order to bring [b]the book of records, the chronicles, and they were read before the king.

2 And it was found written what [a]Mordecai had reported concerning Bigthana and Teresh, two of the king's eunuchs who were doorkeepers, that they had sought to lay hands on King Ahasuerus.

3 And the king said, "What honor or dignity has been bestowed on Mordecai for this?" Then the king's servants who attended him said, "Nothing has been done for him."

4 So the king said, "Who is in the court?" Now Haman had just [a]entered the outer court of the king's palace in order to speak to the king about [b]hanging Mordecai on the gallows which he had prepared for him.

5 And the king's servants said to him, "Behold, Haman is standing in the court." And the king said, "Let him come in."

6 So Haman came in and the king said to him, "What is to be done for the man [a]whom the king desires to honor?" And Haman said to himself, "Whom would the king desire to honor more than me?"

7 Then Haman said to the king, "For the man whom the king desires to honor,

8 let them bring a royal robe which the king has worn, and [a]the horse on which the king has

Marginal references

9 [a]Esth. 2:19 [b]Esth. 3:5

10 [a]Esth. 6:13

★11 [a]Esth. 9:7-10 [b]Esth. 3:1

12 [a]Esth. 5:8

13 [a]Esth. 5:9

★14 [a]Esth. 6:4; 7:9, 10

★ 1 [a]Dan. 6:18 [b]Esth. 2:23; 10:2

2 [a]Esth. 2:21, 22

★ 4-5

4 [a]Esth. 4:11 [b]Esth. 5:14

6 [a]Esth. 6:7, 9, 11

★ 8 [a]1 Kin. 1:33 [b]Esth. 1:11; 2:17

5:11 *his sons.* Haman had 10 sons (9:10).
5:14 *fifty cubits high.* 75 feet high, an excessive height, almost the height of the city walls.
6:1 *could not sleep.* Lit., sleep fled from him. Once again God overruled. *the chronicles.* Cf. 2:21.

6:4-5 By divine arrangement, Haman was at court early to seek permission to have Mordecai executed on the gallows he had had built during the night.
6:8 Assyrian reliefs depict the practice of setting crown-like headdresses on horses.

ridden, and on whose head [b]a royal crown has been placed;

9 [a]Gen. 41:43

9 and let the robe and the horse be handed over to one of the king's most noble princes and let them array the man whom the king desires to honor and lead him on horseback through the city square, [a]and proclaim before him, 'Thus it shall be done to the man whom the king desires to honor.' "

10 Then the king said to Haman, "Take quickly the robes and the horse as you have said, and do so for Mordecai the Jew, who is sitting at the king's gate; do not fall short in anything of all that you have said."

11 So Haman took the robe and the horse, and arrayed Mordecai, and led him *on horseback* through the city square, and proclaimed before him, "Thus it shall be done to the man whom the king desires to honor."

12 [a]2 Sam. 15:30

12 Then Mordecai returned to the king's gate. But Haman hurried home, mourning, [a]with *his* head covered.

★**13** [a]Esth. 5:10

13 And Haman recounted [a]to Zeresh his wife and all his friends everything that had happened to him. Then his wise men and Zeresh his wife said to him, "If Mordecai, before whom you have begun to fall, is of Jewish origin, you will not overcome him, but will surely fall before him."

★**14** [a]Esth. 5:8

14 While they were still talking with him, the king's eunuchs arrived and hastily [a]brought Haman to the banquet which Esther had prepared.

2 Haman hanged, 7:1-10

7 Now the king and Haman came to drink *wine* with Esther the queen.

2 [a]Esth. 5:6; 9:12 [b]Esth. 5:3

2 And the king said to Esther on the second day also as they drank their wine at the banquet, "[a]What is your petition, Queen Esther? It shall be granted you. And what is your request? [b]Even to half of the kingdom it shall be done."

3 [a]Esth. 5:8; 8:5

3 Then Queen Esther answered and said, "[a]If I have found favor in your sight, O king, and if it please the king, let my life be given me as my petition, and my people as my request;

★**4** [a]Esth. 3:9 [b]Esth. 3:13

4 for [a]we have been sold, I and my people, to be destroyed, [b]to be killed and to be annihilated. Now if we had only been sold as slaves, men and women, I would have remained silent, for the trouble would not be commensurate with the annoyance to the king."

5 Then King Ahasuerus asked Queen Esther, "Who is he, and where is he, who would presume to do thus?"

6 [a]Esth. 3:10

6 And Esther said, "[a]A foe and an enemy, is this wicked Haman!" Then Haman became terrified before the king and queen.

7 [a]Esth. 1:12 [b]Esth. 1:5

7 And the king arose [a]in his anger from drinking wine *and went* into [b]the palace garden; but Haman stayed to beg for his life from Queen Esther, for he saw that harm had been determined against him by the king.

★**8** [a]Esth. 1:6

8 Now when the king returned from the palace garden into the place where they were drinking wine, Haman was falling on [a]the couch where Esther was. Then the king said, "Will he even assault the queen with me in the house?" As the word went out of the king's mouth, they covered Haman's face.

★**9** [a]Esth. 5:14 [b]Esth. 2:22

9 Then Harbonah, one of the eunuchs who *were* before the king said, "Behold indeed, [a]the

---

6:13 Haman's wife and his wise men apparently just now suspected that Mordecai was a Jew, and predicted doom for Haman if this were so.
6:14 Guests were customarily sent for and escorted to oriental banquets.
7:4 *sold.* Referring to Haman's bribe (3:9; 4:7).
7:8 When the king returned, he found Haman

pleading for his life before Esther, who was reclining on the *couch* at the banquet table. The king placed the worst possible construction on the situation. *the word.* I.e., to execute Haman.
7:9 *Harbonah.* See 1:10.

gallows standing at Haman's house fifty cubits high, which Haman made for Mordecai ^bwho spoke good on behalf of the king!" And the king said, "Hang him on it."

10 ^aSo they hanged Haman on the gallows which he had prepared for Mordecai, ^band the king's anger subsided.

B   The Decree of Ahasuerus and Mordecai, 8:1–17

8 On that day King Ahasuerus gave the house of Haman, ^athe enemy of the Jews, to Queen Esther; and Mordecai came before the king, for Esther had disclosed ^bwhat he was to her.

2 ^aAnd the king took off his signet ring which he had taken away from Haman, and gave it to Mordecai. And Esther set Mordecai over the house of Haman.

3 Then Esther spoke again to the king, fell at his feet, wept, and implored him to avert the evil *scheme* of Haman the Agagite and his plot which he had devised against the Jews.

4 ^aAnd the king extended the golden scepter to Esther. So Esther arose and stood before the king.

5 Then she said, "^aIf it pleases the king and if I have found favor before him and the matter *seems* proper to the king and I am pleasing in his sight, let it be written to revoke the ^bletters devised by Haman, the son of Hammedatha the Agagite, which he wrote to destroy the Jews who are in all the king's provinces.

6 "For ^ahow can I endure to see the calamity which shall befall my people, and how can I endure to see the destruction of my kindred?"

7 So King Ahasuerus said to Queen Esther and to Mordecai the Jew, "Behold, ^aI have given the house of Haman to Esther, and him they have hanged on the gallows because he had stretched out his hands against the Jews.

8 "Now you write to the Jews as you see fit, in the king's name, and ^aseal *it* with the king's signet ring; for a decree which is written in the name of the king and sealed with the king's signet ring ^bmay not be revoked."

9 ^aSo the king's scribes were called at that time in the third month (that is, the month Sivan), on the twenty-third day; and it was written according to all that Mordecai commanded to the Jews, the satraps, the governors, and the princes of the provinces which *extended* ^bfrom India to Ethiopia, 127 provinces, to ^cevery province according to its script, and to every people according to their language, as well as to the Jews according to their script and their language.

10 And he wrote in the name of King Ahasuerus, and sealed it with the king's signet ring, and sent letters by couriers on ^ahorses, riding on steeds sired by the royal stud.

11 In them the king granted the Jews who were in each and every city *the right* ^ato assemble and to defend their lives, ^bto destroy, to kill, and to annihilate the entire army of any people or province which might attack them, including children and women, and ^cto plunder their spoil,

12 on ^aone day in all the provinces of King Ahasuerus, the thirteenth *day* of the twelfth month (that is, the month Adar).

13 ^aA copy of the edict to be issued as law in each and every

---

Cross references (margin):

10 ^aPs. 7:16; 94:23 ^bEsth. 7:7, 8

★ 1 ^aEsth. 7:6 ^bEsth. 2:7, 15

2 ^aEsth. 3:10

4 ^aEsth. 4:11; 5:2

5 ^aEsth. 5:8; 7:3 ^bEsth. 3:13

6 ^aEsth. 7:4; 9:1

7 ^aEsth. 8:1

★ 8-14

8 ^aEsth. 3:12; 8:10 ^bEsth. 1:19

9 ^aEsth. 3:12 ^bEsth. 1:1 ^cEsth. 1:22; 3:12

10 ^a1 Kin. 4:28

11 ^aEsth. 9:2 ^bEsth. 3:13 ^cEsth. 9:10

12 ^aEsth. 3:13; 9:1

13 ^aEsth. 3:14

8:1 *what he was to her.* I.e., her cousin and guardian.
8:8–14 Though the king could not revoke the previous decree Haman had devised (cf. Dan. 6:8, 12, 15), there was no reason why a counterdecree could not be issued. Mordecai proceeded to issue such a decree with the king's

approval, thereby permitting the Jews to defend themselves, kill their attackers, and take spoils on the day Haman's decree was to become effective. The counterdecree was issued in June and disseminated posthaste, allowing the Jews about 8 months to prepare to defend themselves.

province, was published to all the peoples, so that the Jews should be ready for this day to avenge themselves on their enemies.

14 The couriers, hastened and impelled by the king's command, went out, riding on the royal steeds; and the decree was given out in Susa the capital.

15 aEsth.
5:11 bGen.
41:42 cEsth.
3:15

15 Then Mordecai went out from the presence of the king ªin royal robes of blue and white, with a large crown of gold and ba garment of fine linen and purple; and cthe city of Susa shouted and rejoiced.

16 aPs.
97:11; 112:4

16 For the Jews there was ªlight and gladness and joy and honor.

★17 aEsth.
9:19 bEsth.
9:27

17 And in each and every province, and in each and every city, wherever the king's commandment and his decree arrived, there was gladness and joy for the Jews, a feast and a ªholiday. And bmany among the peoples of the land became Jews, for the dread of the Jews had fallen on them.

C The Defeat of Israel's Enemies, 9:1-19

★1 aEsth.
8:12 bEsth.
9:17 cEsth.
3:13

9 Now ªin the twelfth month (that is, the month Adar), on bthe thirteenth day cwhen the king's command and edict were about to be executed, on the day when the enemies of the Jews hoped to gain the mastery over them, it was turned to the contrary so that the Jews themselves gained the mastery over those who hated them.

2 aEsth.
8:11; 9:15-18
bEsth. 8:17

2 ªThe Jews assembled in their cities throughout all the provinces of King Ahasuerus to lay hands on those who sought

their harm; and no one could stand before them, bfor the dread of them had fallen on all the peoples.

3 Even all the princes of the provinces, ªthe satraps, the governors, and those who were doing the king's business assisted the Jews, because the dread of Mordecai had fallen on them.

★3 aEzra
8:36

4 Indeed, Mordecai was great in the king's house, and his fame spread throughout all the provinces; for the man Mordecai ªbecame greater and greater.

4 a2 Sam.
3:1; 1 Chr.
11:9

5 Thus ªthe Jews struck all their enemies with the sword, killing and destroying; and they did what they pleased to those who hated them.

5 aEsth.
3:13

6 And in Susa the capital the Jews killed and destroyed five hundred men,

7 and Parshandatha, Dalphon, Aspatha,

8 Poratha, Adalia, Aridatha,

9 Parmashta, Arisai, Aridai, and Vaizatha,

10 ªthe ten sons of Haman the son of Hammedatha, the Jews' enemy; but bthey did not lay their hands on the plunder.

★10 aEsth.
5:11 bEsth.
8:11

11 On that day the number of those who were killed in Susa the capital was reported to the king.

12 And the king said to Queen Esther, "The Jews have killed and destroyed five hundred men and the ten sons of Haman in Susa the capital. What then have they done in the rest of the king's provinces! ªNow what is your petition? It shall even be granted you. And what is your further request? It shall also be done."

12 aEsth.
5:6; 7:2

13 Then said Esther, "If it

★13 aEsth.
8:11; 9:15

8:17 *became Jews.* I.e., embraced the religion of Judaism as proselytes.

9:1 *it was turned to the contrary.* Another indication of the sovereign providence of God.

9:3 The rulers, torn between two contradictory decrees, wisely decided, in view of his popularity, to obey the one issued by Mordecai!

9:10 Though the Jews had a right to the spoil, they did not take it (8:11; 9:15-16).

9:13 Why Esther asked permission to continue the massacre in Susa for a second day is not stated. Perhaps she was simply being vindictive, or perhaps she had learned of further attacks being planned against the Jews.

pleases the king, [a]let tomorrow also be granted to the Jews who are in Susa to do according to the edict of today; and let Haman's ten sons be hanged on the gallows."

14 So the king commanded that it should be done so; and an edict was issued in Susa, and Haman's ten sons were hanged.

15 And the Jews who were in Susa assembled also on the fourteenth day of the month Adar and killed [a]three hundred men in Susa, but [b]they did not lay their hands on the plunder.

16 Now [a]the rest of the Jews who were in the king's provinces [b]assembled, to defend their lives and rid themselves of their enemies, and kill 75,000 of those who hated them; but they did not lay their hands on the plunder.

17 This was done on [a]the thirteenth day of the month Adar, and [b]on the fourteenth day they rested and made it a day of feasting and rejoicing.

18 But the Jews who were in Susa [a]assembled on the thirteenth and [b]the fourteenth of the same month, and they rested on the fifteenth day and made it a day of feasting and rejoicing.

19 Therefore the Jews of the rural areas, who live in [a]the rural towns, make the fourteenth day of the month Adar a [b]holiday for rejoicing and feasting and [c]sending portions of food to one another.

D The Days of Purim, 9:20-32

20 Then Mordecai recorded these events, and he sent letters to all the Jews who were in all the provinces of King Ahasuerus, both near and far,

21 obliging them to celebrate the fourteenth day of the month Adar, and the fifteenth day of the same month, annually,

22 because on those days the Jews rid themselves of their enemies, and it was a month which was [a]turned for them from sorrow into gladness and from mourning into a holiday; that they should make them days of feasting and rejoicing and [b]sending portions of food to one another and gifts to the poor.

23 Thus the Jews undertook what they had started to do, and what Mordecai had written to them.

24 For Haman the son of Hammedatha, the Agagite, the adversary of all the Jews, had schemed against the Jews to destroy them, and [a]had cast Pur, that is the lot, to disturb them and destroy them.

25 But [a]when it came to the king's attention, he commanded by letter [b]that his wicked scheme which he had devised against the Jews, [c]should return on his own head, and that he and his sons should be hanged on the gallows.

26 Therefore they called these days Purim after the name of Pur. And [a]because of the instructions in this letter, both what they had seen in this regard and what had happened to them,

27 the Jews established and made a custom for themselves, and for their descendants, and for [a]all those who allied themselves with them, so that they should not fail [b]to celebrate these two days according to their regulation, and according to their appointed time annually.

28 So these days were to be remembered and celebrated throughout every generation, every family, every province, and every city; and these days of Purim were not to fail from among the Jews, or their memory fade from their descendants.

Marginal references:

15 [a]Esth. 9:12 [b]Esth. 9:10
16 [a]Esth. 9:2 [b]Lev. 26:7, 8; Esth. 8:11
★17-22
17 [a]Esth. 9:1 [b]Esth. 9:21
18 [a]Esth. 8:11; 9:2 [b]Esth. 9:21
19 [a]Deut. 3:5; Zech. 2:4 [b]Esth. 9:22 [c]Neh. 8:10
22 [a]Ps. 30:11 [b]Neh. 8:12
24 [a]Esth. 3:7
25 [a]Esth. 7:4-10 [b]Esth. 3:6-15 [c]Ps. 7:16
26 [a]Esth. 9:20
27 [a]Esth. 8:17 [b]Esth. 9:20, 21

9:17-22 Jews in the provinces celebrated their victory on the 14th day of Adar, while Jews in Susa waited until the 15th (because of the events of v. 15). Eventually Mordecai ordered that both days should be observed annually as the Feast of Purim (see note on 3:7).

29 Then Queen Esther, [a]daughter of Abihail, with Mordecai the Jew, wrote with full authority to confirm [b]this second letter about Purim.

30 And he sent letters to all the Jews, [a]to the 127 provinces of the kingdom of Ahasuerus, namely, words of peace and truth,

31 to establish these days of Purim at their appointed times, just as Mordecai the Jew and Queen Esther had established for them, and just as they had established for themselves and for their descendants with instructions [a]for their times of fasting and their lamentations.

32 And the command of Esther established these customs for [a]Purim, and it was written in the book.

E The Description of Mordecai's Fame, 10:1-3

10 Now King Ahasuerus laid a tribute on the land and on the [a]coastlands of the sea.

2 And all the accomplishments of his authority and strength, and the full account of the greatness of Mordecai, [a]to which the king advanced him, are they not written in [b]the Book of the Chronicles of the Kings of Media and Persia?

3 For Mordecai the Jew was [a]second *only* to King Ahasuerus and great among the Jews, and in favor with the multitude of his kinsmen, [b]one who sought the good of his people and one who spoke for the welfare of his whole nation.

9:29-31 Later, a second letter was written by Esther and Mordecai together, in which they enjoined fasting (which they had personally been observing) on all Jews in connection with Purim.

10:3 Mordecai held the office of first minister no longer than 8 years, for secular history records that another man was in that office in 465.

Marginal references:

★29-31
29 [a]Esth. 2:15 [b]Esth. 9:20, 21
30 [a]Esth. 1:1
31 [a]Esth. 4:3
32 [a]Esth. 9:26

1 [a]Is. 11:11; 24:15
2 [a]Esth. 8:15; 9:4 [b]Esth. 2:23
★ 3 [a]Gen. 41:43, 44 [b]Neh. 2:10

INTRODUCTION TO
THE BOOK OF JOB

AUTHOR: Uncertain   DATE: Uncertain

Author   *Though we know the title of the book comes from its principal character, and that Job was an historical person (Ezek. 14:14, 20; James 5:11), we do not know for certain who actually wrote the book. Suggestions include Job himself, Elihu, Moses, and Solomon.*

Date   *The date of the events in the book and the date of the writing of the book are two different matters. The events may have taken place in a patriarchal society in the second millennium B.C., around the time of Abraham. Several facts support this dating: (1) Job lived more than 140 years (42:16), a not uncommon lifespan during the patriarchal period; (2) the economy of Job's day, in which wealth was measured in terms of livestock (1:3), was the type that existed in this period; (3) like Abraham, Isaac, and Jacob, Job was the priest of his family (1:5); (4) the absence of any reference to the nation Israel or the Mosaic Law suggests a pre-Mosaic date (before 1500 B.C.).*

Three principal views exist concerning the date of writing: (1) in the patriarchal age, shortly after the events happened; (2) in the time of Solomon (950 B.C.); (3) at the time of the Exile or after, though the mention of Job by Ezekiel (Ezek. 14:14) negates such a late date. The detailed report of the speeches of Job and his friends seems to argue for the book's being written shortly after the events occurred. On the other hand, the book shares characteristics of other wisdom literature (e.g., Psalms 88, 89) written during the Solomonic age, and should be regarded as a dramatic poem describing real events, rather than a verbatim report.

Theme   *The book wrestles with the age-old question: Why do righteous men suffer, if God is a God of love and mercy? It clearly teaches the sovereignty of God and the need for man to acknowledge such. Job's three friends gave essentially the same answer: all suffering is due to sin. Elihu, however, declared that suffering is often the means of purifying the righteous. God's purpose, therefore, was to strip away all of Job's self-righteousness and to bring him to the place of complete trust in Him.*

Contents   *The book gives important insights into the work of Satan (1:6-2:10). The best-known verses in the book are 19:25-26.*

OUTLINE OF JOB

I. **The Disasters of Job, 1:1-2:13**
  A. Job's Circumstances, 1:1-5
  B. Job's Calamities, 1:6-2:10
    1. Satan's proposal, 1:6-11
    2. God's permission, 1:12-22
    3. Satan's persistence, 2:1-6
    4. Job's patience, 2:7-10
  C. Job's Comforters, 2:11-13
II. **The Dialogues with Job, 3:1-42:6**
  A. Job's Lament, 3:1-26
  B. Eliphaz' First Speech, 4:1-5:27
  C. Job's Reply to Eliphaz, 6:1-7:21
  D. Bildad's First Speech, 8:1-22
  E. Job's Reply to Bildad, 9:1-10:22
  F. Zophar's First Speech, 11:1-20
  G. Job's Reply to Zophar, 12:1-14:22
  H. Eliphaz' Second Speech, 15:1-35
  I. Job's Second Reply to Eliphaz, 16:1-17:16
  J. Bildad's Second Speech, 18:1-21
  K. Job's Second Reply to Bildad, 19:1-29
  L. Zophar's Second Speech, 20:1-29
  M. Job's Second Reply to Zophar, 21:1-34
  N. Eliphaz' Third Speech, 22:1-30

  O. Job's Third Reply to Eliphaz, 23:1-24:25
  P. Bildad's Third Speech, 25:1-6
  Q. Job's Third Reply to Bildad, 26:1-14
  R. Job's Last Reply to his Friends, 27:1-31:40
    1. A protestation of innocence, 27:1-23
    2. A pronouncement concerning wisdom, 28:1-28
    3. A panorama of his life, 29:1-31:40
  S. Elihu's Speeches, 32:1-37:24
    1. His first speech, 32:1-33:33
    2. His second speech, 34:1-37
    3. His third speech, 35:1-16
    4. His fourth speech, 36:1-37:24
  T. God's Speeches, 38:1-42:6
    1. God's first speech: His knowledge, 38:1-40:2
    2. Job's wise silence, 40:3-5
    3. God's second speech: His power, 40:6-41:34
    4. Job's repentance, 42:1-6
III. **The Deliverance of Job, 42:7-17**
  A. In Relation to his Friends, 42:7-9
  B. In Relation to his Family, 42:10-17

THE BOOK OF JOB

I THE DISASTERS OF JOB, 1:1–2:13

A Job's Circumstances, 1:1–5

★ **1** aJer. 25:20; Lam. 4:21 bEzek. 14:14, 20; James 5:11 cGen. 6:9; 17:1; Deut. 18:13 dGen. 22:12; 42:18; Ex. 18:21; Prov. 8:13 eJob 28:28
2 aJob 42:13
★ **3** aJob 42:12 bJob 29:25

1 There was a man in the aland of Uz, whose name was bJob, and that man was cblameless, upright, dfearing God, and eturning away from evil.

2 aAnd seven sons and three daughters were born to him.

3 aHis possessions also were 7,000 sheep, 3,000 camels, 500 yoke of oxen, 500 female donkeys, and very many servants; and that man was bthe greatest of all the men of the east.

4 And his sons used to go and hold a feast in the house of each one on his day, and they would send and invite their three sisters to eat and drink with them.

★ **5** aGen. 8:20; Job 42:8 bJob 8:4 c1 Kin. 21:10, 13

5 And it came about, when the days of feasting had completed their cycle, that Job would send and consecrate them, rising up early in the morning and offering aburnt offerings *according to* the number of them all; for Job said, "bPerhaps my sons have sinned and ccursed God in their hearts." Thus Job did continually.

B Job's Calamities, 1:6–2:10

1 Satan's proposal, 1:6–11

6 aNow there was a day when the bsons of God came to present themselves before the LORD, and Satan also came among them.

★ **6** aJob 2:1 bJob 38:7

7 And the LORD said to Satan, "From where do you come?" Then Satan answered the LORD and said, "aFrom roaming about on the earth and walking around on it."

★ **7** a1 Pet. 5:8

8 And the LORD said to Satan, "Have you considered aMy servant Job? For there is no one like him on the earth, ba blameless and upright man, fearing God and turning away from evil."

8 aNum. 12:7; Josh. 1:2, 7; Job 42:7, 8 bJob 1:1

9 Then aSatan answered the LORD, "Does Job fear God for nothing?

9 aRev. 12:9f.

10 "aHast Thou not made a hedge about him and his house and all that he has, on every side? bThou hast blessed the work of his hands, and his cpossessions have increased in the land.

10 aJob 29:2-6; Ps. 34:7 bJob 31:25 cJob 1:3; 31:25

11 "aBut put forth Thy hand now and btouch all that he has; he will surely curse Thee to Thy face."

11 aJob 2:5 bJob 19:21

1:1 *the land of Uz.* Job lived in the area to the SE. of the Dead Sea. In Lam. 4:21 Uz is referred to as the same territory as Edom. This area was also identified with Uz by Ptolemy, a Greek general under Alexander the Great, in the third century B.C. *Job.* The meaning of Job's name is somewhat uncertain. It may mean "the one who turns back to God" or "the assailed or persecuted one." *blameless.* Job was not perfect in the sense of being sinless. The Bible teaches (and experience supports the fact) that every person falls short of God's standard of perfection (Rom. 3:23). The writer is asserting here that Job could not be justly charged with any moral failure by his fellow men. From the human point of view he was without blame.

1:3 *the greatest of all the men of the east.* Job's greatness consisted in his moral and spiritual qualities (v. 1) as well as his wealth (v. 3).

1:5 Job functioned as priest for his family.

1:6 *the sons of God.* I.e., angels. The phrase is used of angels elsewhere in Scripture (38:7;

see note on Gen. 6:2). This interpretation harmonizes with the fact that Satan, himself an angelic being, joined them on this occasion. **1:7** *Satan.* It is clear from this passage that Satan is a person, not just an evil influence. (1) He conversed with the Lord, which requires intellect. (2) He was antagonistic toward Job (vv. 9–11), showing that he has emotions. (3) He purposed to destroy Job and disgrace God (1:11; 2:4-5, 7), thus demonstrating Satan has a will. Satan's activities, however, are limited by the sovereign control of God (1:12; 2:6). Consistently throughout Scripture Satan is presented as both a real person and a spirit being. His name means "adversary," characterizing his basic nature, which is to oppose God's Person, His plan, and His people. *on the earth.* Satan had access to the earth and freedom to roam around on it. He still has this freedom and will continue to exercise it until he is bound for a thousand years during the Millennium (Rev. 20:2) and then cast into the lake of fire forever (Matt. 25:41).

2 God's permission, 1:12-22

12 Then the LORD said to Satan, "Behold, all that he has is in your power, only do not put forth your hand on him." So Satan departed from the presence of the LORD.

13 Now it happened on the day when his sons and his daughters were eating and drinking wine in their oldest brother's house,

14 that a messenger came to Job and said, "The oxen were plowing and the donkeys feeding beside them,

15 and the [a]Sabeans attacked and took them. They also slew the servants with the edge of the sword, and I alone have escaped to tell you."

16 While he was still speaking, another also came and said, "[a]The fire of God fell from heaven and burned up the sheep and the servants and consumed them, and I alone have escaped to tell you."

17 While he was still speaking, another also came and said, "The [a]Chaldeans formed three bands and made a raid on the camels and took them and slew the servants with the edge of the sword; and I alone have escaped to tell you."

18 While he was still speaking, another also came and said, "Your sons and your daughters were eating and drinking wine in their oldest brother's house,

19 and behold, a great wind came from across the wilderness and struck the four corners of the house, and it fell on the young people and they died; and I alone have escaped to tell you."

20 Then Job arose and [a]tore his robe and shaved his head, and he fell to the ground and worshiped.

21 And he said,
"[a]Naked I came from my
   mother's womb,
And naked I shall return
   there.
The [b]LORD gave and the
   LORD has taken away.
Blessed be the name of
   the LORD."

22 [a]Through all this Job did not sin nor did he blame God.

3 Satan's persistence, 2:1-6

2 [a]Again there was a day when the sons of God came to present themselves before the LORD, and Satan also came among them to present himself before the LORD.

2 And the LORD said to Satan, "Where have you come from?" Then Satan answered the LORD and said, "From roaming about on the earth, and walking around on it."

3 And the LORD said to Satan, "Have you considered My servant Job? For there is no one like him on the earth, a blameless and upright man fearing God and turning away from evil. And he still [a]holds fast his integrity, although you incited Me against him, to ruin him without cause."

4 And Satan answered the LORD and said, "Skin for skin!

---

marginal references:

★15 [a]Gen. 10:7; Job 6:19

★16 [a]Gen. 19:24; Lev. 10:2; Num. 11:1-3

★17 [a]Gen. 11:28, 31

★20 [a]Gen. 37:29, 34; Josh. 7:6

★21-22

21 [a]Eccl. 5:15 [b]1 Sam. 2:7, 8; Job 2:10

22 [a]Job 2:10

1 [a]Job 1:6-8

3 [a]Job 27:5, 6

★4

1:15 *the Sabeans.* Nomadic bedouins living in the area of Uz and to the S.

1:16 *The fire of God.* Perhaps lightning.

1:17 *The Chaldeans.* Another regional group of nomadic marauders, not to be confused with the later Chaldeans, who lived in (and for a time ruled) the Babylonian Empire (7th and 6th centuries B.C.).

1:20 *tore his robe and shaved his head.* Expressions of grief common at this time (2:12; Gen. 37:34). *worshiped.* Grief and worship can often accompany one another.

1:21-22 Satan's first attack was against Job's possessions. It was designed to expose Job's true motives for serving God, which Satan contended were selfish. This test took place only after God gave Satan permission to try Job. Job recognized God's hand in his affairs and evidenced a proper attitude toward his possessions. They were a gracious gift from God, not things he had earned and therefore had a right to keep.

2:4 *Skin for skin.* Satan charged Job with callousness; i.e., being willing to give up the skin of his animals, servants, and children in order to save his own skin.

Yes, all that a man has he will give for his life.

5 "[a]However, put forth Thy hand, now, and [b]touch his bone and his flesh; he will curse Thee to Thy face."

★ 6 6 So the LORD said to Satan, "Behold, he is in your power, only spare his life."

4 Job's patience, 2:7-10

★ 7 7 Then Satan went out from the presence of the LORD, and smote Job with [a]sore boils from the sole of his foot to the crown of his head.

★ 8 8 And he took a potsherd to scrape himself while [a]he was sitting among the ashes.

★ 9 9 Then his wife said to him, "Do you still hold fast your integrity? Curse God and die!"

10 But he said to her, "You speak as one of the foolish women speaks. [a]Shall we indeed accept good from God and not accept adversity?" [b]In all this Job did not sin with his lips.

C Job's Comforters, 2:11-13

★11 11 Now when Job's three friends heard of all this adversity that had come upon him, they came each one from his own place, Eliphaz the [a]Temanite, Bildad the [b]Shuhite, and Zophar the Naamathite; and they made an appointment together to come to [c]sympathize with him and comfort him.

12 And when they lifted up their eyes at a distance, and did not recognize him, they raised their voices and wept. And each of them [a]tore his robe, and they [b]threw dust over their heads toward the sky.

13 [a]Then they sat down on the ground with him for seven days and seven nights with no one speaking a word to him, for they saw that *his* pain was very great.

II THE DIALOGUES WITH JOB,
3:1–42:6

A Job's Lament, 3:1–26

3 Afterward Job opened his mouth and cursed the day of his *birth*. **★ 1**

2 And Job said,

3 "[a]Let the day perish on which I was to be born,
And the night *which* said,
'A boy is conceived.'

Marginal references:
5 [a]Job 1:11 [b]Job 19:20
7 [a]Deut. 28:35; Job 7:5; 13:28; 30:17, 18, 30
8 [a]Job 42:6; Jer. 6:26; Ezek. 27:30; Jon. 3:6
10 [a]Job 1:21 [b]Job 1:22; Ps. 39:1; James 1:12
11 [a]Gen. 36:11; Job 6:19; Jer. 49:7 [b]Gen. 25:2 [c]Job 42:11; Rom. 12:15
12 [a]Job 1:20 [b]Josh. 7:6; Neh. 9:1; Lam. 2:10; Ezek. 27:30
13 [a]Gen. 50:10; Ezek. 3:15
3 [a]Jer. 20:14-18

2:6 *spare his life.* Satan was only permitted to go so far (cf. 1 Cor. 10:13).

2:7 *sore boils.* Satan's second test was against Job's person (cf. note on 1:22). Job's condition was characterized by several symptoms. The skin covering his entire body was affected (v. 7), he itched intensely (v. 8), and he was in acute pain (v. 13). His flesh attracted worms and became crusty and hard (7:5). It oozed serum and turned darker in color (7:5; 30:30). Job also experienced fever and aching bones (30:17, 30). He may have had elephantiasis or a leukemia of the skin. The good will of God included physical suffering for Job at this time, as it does for many today.

2:8 *potsherd.* A piece of broken pottery. Job was not only ill, but his sickness made him unclean and therefore a social outcast.

2:9 Job's wife concluded that he was suffering because God was unfair—a popular explanation for suffering but totally contrary to the character of God. Job called her view foolishness (v. 10). Many people arrive at her conclusion when they consider only empirical evidence (that which we gain by observation). Unless we also consider revelational evidence (that which comes from God), we are likely to reason as Job's wife did.

2:11 *the Temanite.* Eliphaz was a resident of the city of Teman in Uz (Edom). This town became famous for its wise men (Jer. 49:7). *the Shuhite.* Bildad lived in the area nearby, inhabited by the descendants of Shuah, one of Abraham's sons by Keturah (Gen. 25:1-2). *the Naamathite.* Zophar also lived nearby, in the area of Naamath. All three men were probably outstanding in their areas and time, since they were friends of "the greatest of all the men of the east" (1:3).

3:1 Whereas the introductory two chapters were written in prose, here begins a long section of poetry (3:1-42:6), though the conclusion (42:7-17) is prose. This chapter introduces the debate which follows. In it Job says some things that move his friends to break their long silence and suggest to him why he may be suffering. Job speaks out of great physical and mental anguish. His own basic presuppo-

4 "May that day be darkness;
Let not God above care for
it,
Nor light shine on it.

5 "Let ᵃdarkness and black
gloom claim it;
Let a cloud settle on it;
Let the blackness of the
day terrify it.

6 "As for that night, let darkness seize it;
Let it not rejoice among
the days of the year;
Let it not come into the
number of the
months.

7 "Behold, let that night be
barren;
Let no joyful shout enter
it.

8 "Let those curse it who
curse the day,
Who are prepared to
ᵃrouse Leviathan.

9 "Let the stars of its twilight
be darkened;
Let it wait for light but
have none,
Neither let it see the
breaking dawn;

10 Because it did not shut the
opening of my moth-
er's womb,
Or hide trouble from my
eyes.

11 "ᵃWhy did I not die at
birth,
Come forth from the
womb and expire?

12 "Why did the knees receive
me,
And why the breasts, that I
should suck?

13 "For now I ᵃwould have lain
down and been quiet;
I would have slept then, I
would have been at
rest,

14 With ᵃkings and with
ᵇcounselors of the
earth,
Who rebuilt ᶜruins for
themselves;

15 Or with ᵃprinces ᵇwho had
gold,
Who were filling their
houses with silver.

16 "Or like a miscarriage
which is discarded, I
would not be,
As infants that never saw
light.

17 "There the wicked cease
from raging,
And there the weary are at
ᵃrest.

18 "The prisoners are at ease
together;
They do not hear the voice
of the taskmaster.

19 "The small and the great
are there,
And the slave is free from
his master.

20 "Why is ᵃlight given to him
who suffers,
And life to the bitter of
soul;

21 Who ᵃlong for death, but
there is none,
And dig for it more than
for ᵇhidden treasures;

22 Who rejoice greatly,
They exult when they find
the grave?

23 "Why is light given to a
man ᵃwhose way is
hidden,
And whom ᵇGod has
hedged in?

24 "For ᵃmy groaning comes at
the sight of my food,
And ᵇmy cries pour out
like water.

Cross-references (margin)

5 ᵃJer. 13:16
★ 8 ᵃJob 41:1, 25
11 ᵃJob 10:18, 19
★12
13 ᵃJob 3:13-19; 7:8-10, 21; 10:21, 22; 14:10-15, 20-22; 16:22; 17:13-16; 19:25-27; 21:13, 23-26; 24:19, 20; 26:5, 6; 34:22
14 ᵃJob 12:18 ᵇJob 12:17 ᶜJob 15:28; Is. 58:12
15 ᵃJob 12:21 ᵇJob 27:16, 17
★16
17 ᵃJob 17:16
20 ᵃJer. 20:18
21 ᵃRev. 9:6 ᵇProv. 2:4
23 ᵃJob 19:6, 8, 12 ᵇJob 19:8; Ps. 88:8; Lam. 3:7
24 ᵃJob 6:7; 33:20 ᵇJob 30:16; Ps. 42:4

---

sition, that God always blesses the righteous and afflicts the wicked, has proven faulty. If he judges by his experience, he must conclude that his theology is wrong, for he cannot put what he believes to be true of God together with what is happening to him. Though at times Job reacts with hostility, he always turns back to God. Much of what he says later is exaggerated, untrue, and virtually blasphe-mous, but he never renounces God.

3:8 Let those curse it . . . I.e., the sorcerers who were thought to be able to make a day un-lucky. to rouse Leviathan. A mythological sea monster capable of devouring on a large scale.

3:12 Why did the knees receive me. Probably a reference to the father's knees, on which a newborn child was laid (Gen. 50:23).

3:16 Job wishes he had been stillborn.

25 ^aJob
9:28; 30:15

25 "For ^awhat I fear comes
upon me,
And what I dread befalls
me.

26 ^aJob
7:13, 14

26 "I ^aam not at ease, nor am I
quiet,
And I am not at rest, but
turmoil comes."

B Eliphaz' First Speech,
4:1–5:27

★ 1

2 ^aJob
32:18-20

4 Then Eliphaz the Temanite
answered,
2 "If one ventures a word
with you, will you be-
come impatient?
But ^awho can refrain from
speaking?

3 ^aJob 4:3,
4; 29:15, 16,
21, 25

3 "Behold ^ayou have admonished many,
And you have strength-
ened weak hands.

4 "Your words have helped
the tottering to stand,
And you have strength-
ened feeble knees.

★ 5 ^aJob
6:14 ^bJob
19:21

5 "But now it has come to
you, and you ^aare impatient;
It ^btouches you, and you
are dismayed.

6 ^aJob 1:1
^bProv. 3:26

6 "Is not your ^afear of God
^byour confidence,
And the integrity of your
ways your hope?

7 ^aJob
8:20; 36:6, 7;
Ps. 37:25

7 "Remember now, ^awho
ever perished being
innocent?
Or where were the upright
destroyed?

8 ^aJob
15:31, 35;
Prov. 22:8;
Hos. 10:13;
Gal. 6:7
9 ^aJob
15:30; Is.
11:4; 30:33;
2 Thess. 2:8
^bJob 40:11-
13

8 "According to what I have
seen, ^athose who plow
iniquity
And those who sow trou-
ble harvest it.

9 "By ^athe breath of God they
perish,

And ^bby the blast of His
anger they come to an
end.

★10-11
10 ^aJob
5:15; Ps.
58:6

10 "The ^aroaring of the lion
and the voice of the
fierce lion,
And the teeth of the young
lions are broken.

11 ^aJob
29:17; Ps.
34:10 ^bJob
5:4; 20:10;
27:14

11 "The ^alion perishes for lack
of prey,
And the ^bwhelps of the
lioness are scattered.

★12-21
12 ^aJob
4:12-17;
33:15-18
^bJob 26:14

12 "Now a word ^awas brought
to me stealthily,
And my ear received a
^bwhisper of it.

13 ^aJob
33:15

13 "Amid   disquieting
^athoughts from the vi-
sions of the night,
When deep sleep falls on
men,

14 Dread came upon me, and
trembling,
And made all my bones
shake.

15 "Then a spirit passed by my
face;
The hair of my flesh bris-
tled up.

16 "It stood still, but I could
not discern its appear-
ance;
A form was before my
eyes;
There was silence, then I
heard a voice:

17 ^aJob 9:2;
25:4 ^bJob
31:15; 32:22;
35:10; 36:3

17 'Can ^amankind be just before God?
Can a man be pure before
his ^bMaker?

18 ^aJob
15:15

18 '^aHe puts no trust even in
His servants;
And against His angels He
charges error.

19 ^aJob
10:9; 33:6
^bGen. 2:7;
3:19; Job
22:16

19 'How much more those
who dwell in ^ahouses
of clay,

4:1 Eliphaz. The most sympathetic of Job's three
friends, who speaks first and appeals to experience for authority. He was likely the eldest
(15:10).
4:5 It. I.e., the calamity that had befallen Job.
4:10-11 The meaning is this: although wicked
men may be strong, they cannot ultimately
prosper.

4:12-21 Eliphaz tried to bolster his argument by
relating it to a vision he had had (vv. 15-16).
He asks, "If angels cannot be considered trustworthy, how can man be?" (vv. 18-19). before
the moth. I.e., sooner than the moth. their
tent-cord. Death is likened to the collapse of a
tent when the tent-cord is pulled up.

Whose *b*foundation is in
the dust,
Who are crushed before
the moth!

20 '*a*Between morning and
evening they are bro-
ken in pieces;
Unobserved, they *b*perish
forever.

21 'Is not their *a*tent-cord
plucked up within
them?
They die, yet *b*without
wisdom.'

5 "Call now, is there anyone
who will answer you?
And to which of the *a*holy
ones will you turn?

2 "For *a*vexation slays the
foolish man,
And anger kills the simple.

3 "I have seen the *a*foolish
taking root,
And I *b*cursed his abode
immediately.

4 "His *a*sons are far from
safety,
They are even oppressed
in the gate,
Neither is there a deliverer.

5 "His harvest the hungry devour,
And take it to a *place of*
thorns;
And the *a*schemer is eager
for their wealth.

6 "For *a*affliction does not
come from the dust,
Neither does trouble
sprout from the
ground,

7 For *a*man is born for trouble,
As sparks fly upward.

8 "But as for me, I would
*a*seek God,
And I would place my
cause before God;

9 Who *a*does great and unsearchable things,
Wonders without number.

10 "He *a*gives rain on the
earth,
And sends water on the
fields,

11 So that *a*He sets on high
those who are lowly,
And those who mourn are
lifted to safety.

12 "He *a*frustrates the plotting
of the shrewd,
So that their hands cannot
attain success.

13 "He *a*captures the wise by
their own shrewdness
And the advice of the cunning is quickly
thwarted.

14 "By day they *a*meet with
darkness,
And grope at noon as in
the night.

15 "But He saves from *a*the
sword of their mouth,
And *b*the poor from the
hand of the mighty.

16 "So the helpless has hope,
And *a*unrighteousness
must shut its mouth.

17 "Behold, how *a*happy is the
man whom God re-
proves,
So do not despise the *b*discipline of the Al-
mighty.

18 "For *a*He inflicts pain, and
gives relief;
He wounds, and His hands
also heal.

19 "From six troubles *a*He will
deliver you,
Even in seven *b*evil will not
touch you.

20 "In *a*famine He will redeem
you from death,
And *b*in war from the
power of the sword.

Marginal references (left column):

20 *a*Job 14:2
*b*Job 14:20;
20:7

21 *a*Job 8:22
*b*Job 18:21;
36:12

★ 1 *a*Job
15:15

2 *a*Prov.
12:16; 27:3

★ 3-7

3 *a*Jer. 12:2
*b*Job 24:18;
31:30

4 *a*Job 4:11

5 *a*Job
18:8-10;
22:10

6 *a*Job
15:35

7 *a*Job 14:1

★ 8-27

8 *a*Job
13:2, 3; Ps.
50:15

Marginal references (right column):

9 *a*Job
9:10; 37:14,
16; 42:3

10 *a*Job
36:27-29;
37:6-11;
38:26

11 *a*Job
22:29; 36:7

12 *a*Ps.
33:10

13 *a*Job
37:24; 1 Cor.
3:19

14 *a*Job
12:25; 15:30;
18:18; 20:26;
24:13

15 *a*Job
4:10, 11; Ps.
35:10 *b*Job
29:17; 34:28;
36:6, 15;
38:15

16 *a*Ps.
107:42

17 *a*Ps.
94:12 *b*Job
36:15, 16;
Prov. 3:11;
Heb. 12:5-
11; James
1:12

18 *a*Deut.
32:39;
1 Sam. 2:6;
Is. 30:26;
Hos. 6:1

19 *a*Ps.
34:19 *b*Ps.
91:10

20 *a*Ps.
33:19; 37:19
*b*Ps. 144:10

5:1 Eliphaz warns Job against appealing his case
to angels (*holy ones*).
5:3-7 Eliphaz cites from personal experience
(the basis of all his pronouncements) the case
of a foolish man who began to prosper and

was then cursed. Trouble, he concludes,
comes from a man himself.
5:8-27 Eliphaz urges Job to submit to God, who
would bless him if he would repent. *From six
troubles* (v. 19). I.e., in all possible trouble.

21 aJob
5:15; Ps.
31:20 bPs.
91:5, 6

21 "You will be ahidden from
    the scourge of the
    tongue,
    bNeither will you be afraid
    of violence when it
    comes.

22 aJob 8:21
bPs. 91:13;
Ezek. 34:25;
Hos. 2:18

22 "You will alaugh at violence
    and famine,
    bNeither will you be afraid
    of wild beasts.

23 aIs. 11:6-
9; 65:25

23 "For you will be in league
    with the stones of the
    field;
    And athe beasts of the
    field will be at peace
    with you.

24 aJob 8:6

24 "And you will know that
    your atent is secure,
    For you will visit your
    abode and fear no
    loss.

25 aPs.
112:2 bIs.
44:3, 4;
48:19

25 "You will know also that
    your   adescendants
    will be many,
    And byour offspring as the
    grass of the earth.

26 aJob
42:17

26 "You will acome to the
    grave in full vigor,
    Like the stacking of grain
    in its season.

27 "Behold this, we have in-
    vestigated it, thus it is;
    Hear it, and know for
    yourself."

C   Job's Reply to Eliphaz,
6:1-7:21

★ 1-4
2 aJob 31:6

6 Then Job answered,
2 "aOh that my vexation
    were   actually
    weighed,
    And laid in the balances
    together with my in-
    iquity!

3 aJob 23:2

3 "For then it would be
    aheavier than the sand
    of the seas,
    Therefore my words have
    been rash.

4 "For the aarrows of the Al-
    mighty are within me;
    Their bpoison my spirit
    drinks;
    The cterrors of God are ar-
    rayed against me.

4 aJob
16:13; Ps.
38:2 bJob
20:16; 21:20
cJob 30:15

5 "Does the awild donkey
    bray over his grass,
    Or does the ox low over
    his fodder?

★ 5 aJob
39:5-8

6 "Can something tasteless be
    eaten without salt,
    Or is there any taste in the
    white of an egg?

★ 6-7

7 "My soul arefuses to touch
    them;
    They are like loathsome
    food to me.

7 aJob
3:24; 33:20

8 "Oh that my request might
    come to pass,
    And that God would grant
    my longing!

9 "Would that God were
    awilling to crush me;
    That He would loose His
    hand and cut me off!

9 aNum.
11:15; 1 Kin.
19:4; Job
7:16; 9:21;
10:1

10 "But it is still my consola-
    tion,
    And I rejoice in unsparing
    pain,
    That I ahave not denied
    the words of the Holy
    One.

10 aJob
22:22; 23:11,
12

11 "What is my strength, that I
    should wait?
    And what is my end, that I
    should aendure?

11 aJob 21:4

12 "Is my strength the strength
    of stones,
    Or is my flesh bronze?

13 "Is it that my ahelp is not
    within me,
    And that bdeliverance is
    driven from me?

13 aJob 26:2
bJob 26:3

14 "For the adespairing man
    there should be kind-
    ness from his friend;
    Lest he bforsake the fear of
    the Almighty.

★14-30

14 aJob 4:5
bJob 1:5;
15:4

6:1-4 Job pleads that the impatience with which
he has been charged be weighed against the
calamity he has experienced.
6:5 Just as animals do not complain without adequate cause, so Job has not.

6:6-7 Job has lost his taste for life.
6:14-30 Job expresses how deeply he has been
hurt by his friends' unkindness, though he is
unmoved by their arguments.

15 *a*Jer. 15:18

15 "My brothers have acted
    *a*deceitfully like a
    wadi,
    Like the torrents of wadis
    which vanish,

16 Which are turbid because
    of ice,
    And into which the snow
    melts.

17 *a*Job 24:19

17 "When *a*they become wa-
    terless, they are silent,
    When it is hot, they vanish
    from their place.

18 "The paths of their course
    wind along,
    They go up into nothing
    and perish.

19 *a*Gen. 25:15; Is. 21:14; Jer. 25:23 *b*Job 1:15

19 "The caravans of *a*Tema
    looked,
    The travelers of *b*Sheba
    hoped for them.

20 *a*Jer. 14:3

20 "They *a*were disappointed
    for they had trusted,
    They came there and were
    confounded.

21 *a*Ps. 38:11

21 "Indeed, you have now be-
    come such,
    *a*You see a terror and are
    afraid.

22 "Have I said, 'Give me
    something,'
    Or, 'Offer a bribe for me
    from your wealth,'

23 Or, 'Deliver me from the
    hand of the adver-
    sary,'
    Or, 'Redeem me from the
    hand of the tyrants'?

24 *a*Ps. 39:1

24 "Teach me, and *a*I will be
    silent;
    And show me how I have
    erred.

25 "How painful are honest
    words!
    But what does your argu-
    ment prove?

26 *a*Job 8:2; 15:2; 16:3

26 "Do you intend to reprove
    my words,
    When the *a*words of one in
    despair belong to the
    wind?

27 "You would even *a*cast *lots*
    for *b*the orphans,
    And *c*barter over your
    friend.

27 *a*Joel 3:3; Nah. 3:10 *b*Job 22:9; 24:3, 9 *c*2 Pet. 2:3

28 "And now please look at
    me,
    And *see* if I *a*lie to your
    face.

28 *a*Job 27:4; 33:3; 36:4

29 "Desist now, let there be no
    injustice;
    Even desist, *a*my right-
    eousness is yet in it.

★29 *a*Job 13:18; 19:6; 23:10; 27:5, 6; 34:5; 42:1-6

30 "Is there injustice on my
    tongue?
    Cannot *a*my palate discern
    calamities?

30 *a*Job 12:11

7 "Is not man *a*forced to labor
    on earth,
    And *are not* his days like
    the days of *b*a hired
    man?

★ 1-6

1 *a*Job 5:7; 10:17; 14:1, 14 *b*Job 14:6

2 "As a slave who pants for
    the shade,
    And as a hired man who
    eagerly waits for his
    wages,

3 So am I allotted months of
    vanity,
    And *a*nights of trouble are
    appointed me.

3 *a*Job 16:7

4 "When I *a*lie down I say,
    'When shall I arise?'
    But the night continues,
    And I am continually toss-
    ing until dawn.

4 *a*Deut. 28:67; Job 7:13, 14

5 "My *a*flesh is clothed with
    worms and a crust of
    dirt;
    My skin hardens and runs.

5 *a*Job 2:7; 17:14

6 "My days are *a*swifter than
    a weaver's shuttle,
    And come to an end *b*with-
    out hope.

6 *a*Job 9:25 *b*Job 13:15; 14:19; 17:15, 16; 19:10

7 "Remember that my life *a*is
    but breath,
    My eye will *b*not again see
    good.

7 *a*Job 7:16; Ps. 78:39; James 4:14 *b*Job 9:25

8 "The *a*eye of him who sees
    me will behold me no
    more;
    Thine eyes *will be* on me,
    but *b*I will not be.

8 *a*Job 8:18; 20:9 *b*Job 7:21

6:29 *Desist.* I.e., change your course; seek some
other explanation of my troubles rather than
the unfair presupposition that I am guilty.

7:1–6 Job likens his existence to the weary grind
of a hired laborer.

★ 9-10
9 aJob
30:15 bJob
3:13-19
c2 Sam.
12:23; Job
11:8; 14:13;
17:13, 16
10 aJob
8:18; 20:9;
27:21, 23

9 "When a acloud vanishes, it
  is gone,
So bhe who goes down to
  cSheol does not come
  up.

10 "He will not return again to
  his house,
Nor will ahis place know
  him anymore.

11 aJob
10:1; 21:4;
23:2; Ps.
40:9

11 "Therefore, aI will not restrain my mouth;
I will speak in the anguish
  of my spirit,
I will complain in the bitterness of my soul.

★12 aEzek.
32:2, 3

12 "Am I the sea, or athe sea
  monster,
That Thou dost set a guard
  over me?

13 aJob 7:4;
Ps. 6:6

13 "If I say, 'aMy bed will comfort me,
My couch will ease my
  complaint,'

14 Then Thou dost frighten
  me with dreams
And terrify me by visions;

15 So that my soul would
  choose suffocation,
Death rather than my
  pains.

16 aJob 6:9;
9:21; 10:1
bJob 7:7

16 "I awaste away; I will not
  live forever.
Leave me alone, bfor my
  days are but a breath.

17 aJob
22:2; Ps. 8:4;
144:3; Heb.
2:6

17 "aWhat is man that Thou
  dost magnify him,
And that Thou art con-
  cerned about him,

18 aJob 14:3

18 That aThou dost examine
  him every morning,
And try him every mo-
  ment?

★19 aJob
9:18, 10:20;
14:6

19 "aWilt Thou never turn Thy
  gaze away from me,
Nor let me alone until I
  swallow my spittle?

20 aJob
35:3, 6 bPs.
36:6

20 "aHave I sinned? What have
  I done to Thee,

O bwatcher of men?
Why hast Thou set me as
  Thy target,
So that I am a burden to
  myself?

21 "Why then adost Thou not
  pardon my transgres-
  sion
And take away my iniq-
  uity?
For now I will blie down in
  the dust;
And Thou wilt seek me,
  cbut I will not be."

21 aJob
9:28; 10:14
bJob 10:9
cJob 7:8

D Bildad's First Speech, 8:1-22

8 Then Bildad the Shuhite answered,

★ 1-7

2 "How long will you say
  these things,
And the awords of your
  mouth be a mighty
  wind?

2 aJob 6:26

3 "Does aGod pervert justice
Or does the Almighty per-
  vert what is right?

3 aGen.
18:25; Deut.
32:4; 2 Chr.
19:7; Job
34:10, 12;
36:23; 37:23;
Rom. 3:5

4 "aIf your sons sinned
  against Him,
Then He delivered them
  into the power of their
  transgression.

4 aJob 1:5,
18, 19

5 "If you would aseek God
And implore the compas-
  sion of the Almighty,

5 aJob
5:17-27

6 If you are pure and up-
  right,
Surely now aHe would
  rouse Himself for you
And restore your righteous
  bestate.

6 aJob
22:27; 34:28;
Ps. 7:6 bJob
5:24

7 "Though your beginning
  was insignificant,
Yet your aend will increase
  greatly.

7 aJob
42:12

8 "Please ainquire of past
  generations,

★ 8-10
8 aDeut.
4:32; 32:7;
Job 15:18;
20:4

7:9-10 The meaning is that, after death, there is
no return to the familiar scenes of earth.
7:12 Job complains about the restraint being
placed on him as if he were upsetting the stability of the universe.
7:19 until I swallow my spittle. An expression
meaning, "for a single moment."
8:1-7 Bildad. Less sensitive than Eliphaz, he im-

plies that Job's children were killed because of
their sins (v. 4). His diagnosis of Job's problem
is basically the same as Eliphaz's; i.e., Job was
suffering because of his sin (vv. 5-7). Shuhite.
A descendant of Shuah, son of Abraham and
Keturah (Gen. 25:2); an Arab.
8:8-10 For authority, Bildad appeals to the
teachings of his predecessors.

And consider the things searched out by their fathers.

9 a Job 14:2

9 "For we are *only* of yesterday and know nothing,
Because a our days on earth are as a shadow.

10 "Will they not teach you *and* tell you,
And bring forth words from their minds?

11 "Can the papyrus grow up without marsh?
Can the rushes grow without water?

12 "While it is still green *and* not cut down,
Yet it withers before any *other* plant.

13 a Ps. 9:17
b Job 11:20; 13:16; 15:34; 20:5; 27:8

13 "So are the paths of a all who forget God,
And the b hope of the godless will perish.

14 a Is. 59:5, 6

14 Whose confidence is fragile,
And whose trust a spider's web.

15 a Job 8:22; 27:18; Ps. 49:11

15 "He trusts in his a house, but it does not stand;
He holds fast to it, but it does not endure.

16 a Ps. 37:35; Jer. 11:16 b Ps. 80:11

16 "He a thrives before the sun,
And his b shoots spread out over his garden.

17 "His roots wrap around a rock pile,
He grasps a house of stones.

18 a Job 7:10 b Job 7:8

18 "If he is removed from a his place,
Then it will deny him, *saying,* 'b I never saw you.'

★19 a Job 20:5

19 "Behold, a this is the joy of His way;
And out of the dust others will spring.

20 "Lo, a God will not reject a man of integrity,
Nor b will He support the evildoers.

20 a Job 4:7 b Job 21:30

21 "He will yet fill a your mouth with laughter,
And your lips with shouting.

21 a Job 5:22; Ps. 126:1, 2

22 "Those who hate you will be a clothed with shame;
And the b tent of the wicked will be no more."

22 a Ps. 132:18 b Job 8:15; 15:34; 18:14; 21:28

E   Job's Reply to Bildad,
9:1–10:22

9 Then Job answered,

★ 1

2 "In truth I know that this is so,
But how can a a man be in the right before God?

★ 2 a Job 4:17; 25:4

3 "If one wished to a dispute with Him,
He could not answer Him once in a thousand *times.*

3 a Job 10:2; 13:19; 23:6; 40:2

4 "a Wise in heart and b mighty in strength,
Who has c defied Him without harm?

4 a Job 11:6; 12:13; 28:23; 38:36; 37 b Job 9:19; 23:6 c 2 Chr. 13:12; Prov. 29:1

5 "a It is God who removes the mountains, they know not *how,*
When He overturns them in His anger;

5 a Job 9:5-10; 26:6-14; 41:11

6 Who a shakes the earth out of its place,
And its b pillars tremble;

6 a Is. 2:19, 21; 13:13; Hag. 2:6 b Ps. 75:3

7 Who commands the a sun not to shine,
And sets a seal upon the stars;

7 a Is. 13:10; Ezek. 32:7, 8

8 Who alone a stretches out the heavens,
And b tramples down the waves of the sea;

8 a Gen. 1:1; Job 37:18; Ps. 104:2; Is. 40:22 b Job 38:16; Ps. 77:19

8:19 *joy of His way.* Better, his (i.e., a wicked man's) way. Probably an ironical statement meaning that the wicked can only look forward to the "joy" of calamity.

9:1 In his reply to Bildad (to 10:22), Job points out that tradition is not our best source of knowledge; God has revealed much about Himself even in nature (9:4–12). While we

should listen to the wisdom of our elders, we must remember that they are finite mortals who have grasped only a part of reality.

9:2 This question puzzles most people and is one of the great questions of life. The answer is that we are made just before God only by the substitutionary death of His Son for our sins (Rom. 3:21–28).

★ 9 ªJob 38:31, 32; Amos 5:8 ᵇJob 37:9

10 ªJob 5:9

11 ªJob 23:8, 9; 35:14

12 ªJob 10:7; 11:10 ᵇIs. 45:9

★13 ªJob 26:12; Ps. 89:10; Is. 30:7; 51:9

14 ªJob 9:3, 32

15 ªJob 9:20, 21; 10:15 ᵇJob 8:5

16

17 ªJob 16:12, 14; 30:22

18 ªJob 7:19; 10:20 ᵇJob 13:26; 27:2

19 ªJob 9:4

9 Who makes the ªBear, Orion, and the Pleiades,
And the ᵇchambers of the south;

10 Who ªdoes great things, unfathomable,
And wondrous works without number.

11 "Were He to pass by me, ªI would not see Him;
Were He to move past *me,*
I would not perceive Him.

12 "Were He to snatch away, who could ªrestrain Him?
Who could say to Him, 'ᵇWhat art Thou doing?'

13 "God will not turn back His anger;
Beneath Him crouch the helpers of ªRahab.

14 "How then can ªI answer Him,
And choose my words before Him?

15 "For ªthough I were right, I could not answer;
I would have to ᵇimplore the mercy of my judge.

16 "If I called and He answered me,
I could not believe that He was listening to my voice.

17 "For He ªbruises me with a tempest,
And multiplies my wounds without cause.

18 "He will ªnot allow me to get my breath,
But saturates me with ᵇbitterness.

19 "If *it is a matter* of power, ªbehold, *He is* the strong one!

And if *it is a matter* of justice, who can summon Him?

20 "ªThough I am righteous, my mouth will ᵇcondemn me;
Though I am guiltless, He will declare me guilty.

21 "I am ªguiltless;
I do not take notice of myself;
I ᵇdespise my life.

22 "It is *all* one; therefore I say, 'He ªdestroys the guiltless and the wicked.'

23 "If the scourge kills suddenly,
He ªmocks the despair of the innocent.

24 "The earth ªis given into the hand of the wicked;
He ᵇcovers the faces of its judges.
If *it is* not *He,* then who is it?

25 "Now ªmy days are swifter than a runner;
They flee away, ᵇthey see no good.

26 "They slip by like ªreed boats,
Like an ᵇeagle that swoops on its prey.

27 "Though I say, 'I will forget ªmy complaint,
I will leave off my *sad* countenance and be cheerful,'

28 I am ªafraid of all my pains,
I know that ᵇThou wilt not acquit me.

29 "I am accounted ªwicked,
Why then should I toil in vain?

30 "If I should ªwash myself with snow
And cleanse ᵇmy hands with lye,

20 ªJob 9:15 ᵇJob 9:29; 15:6

21 ªJob 1:1; 12:4; 13:18 ᵇJob 7:16

22 ªJob 10:7, 8

23 ªJob 24:12

★24 ªJob 10:3; 12:6; 16:11 ᵇJob 12:17

25 ªJob 7:6 ᵇJob 7:7

26 ªIs. 18:2 ᵇJob 39:29; Hab. 1:8

27 ªJob 7:11

28 ªJob 3:25 ᵇJob 7:21; 10:14

29 ªJob 10:2; Ps. 37:33

30 ªJer. 2:22 ᵇJob 31:7

9:9 *the Bear, Orion and the Pleiades.* Constellations.
9:13 *Rahab.* A mythological monster who was subdued by Marduk, and thus a figurative expression for pride.
9:24 Job goes on to deny flatly his friends' whole interpretation of life, since the wicked do not always suffer but frequently prosper.

31 Yet Thou wouldst plunge
me into the pit,
And my own clothes
would abhor me.

32-33

32 "For ᵃHe is not a man as I
am that ᵇI may answer
Him,
That we may go to court
together.

33 "There is no ᵃumpire between us,
Who may lay his hand
upon us both.

34 "Let Him ᵃremove His rod
from me,
And let not dread of Him
terrify me.

35 "Then I ᵃwould speak and
not fear Him;
But I am not like that in
myself.

10 "ᵃI loathe my own life;
I will give full vent to ᵇmy
complaint;
I will speak in the bitterness of my soul.

2 "I will say to God, 'ᵃDo not
condemn me;
Let me know why Thou
dost contend with me.

3 'Is it right for Thee indeed
to ᵃoppress,
To reject ᵇthe labor of Thy
hands,
And to look favorably on
ᶜthe schemes of the
wicked?

4 'Hast Thou eyes of flesh?
Or dost Thou ᵃsee as a
man sees?

5 'Are Thy days as the days
of a mortal,
Or ᵃThy years as man's
years,

6 That ᵃThou shouldst seek
for my guilt,
And search after my sin?

7 'According to Thy knowledge ᵃI am indeed not
guilty;

Yet there is ᵇno deliver-
ance from Thy hand.

8 'ᵃThy hands fashioned and
made me altogether,
ᵇAnd wouldst Thou de-
stroy me?

9 'Remember now, that Thou
hast made me as
ᵃclay;
And wouldst Thou ᵇturn
me into dust again?

10 'Didst Thou not pour me
out like milk,
And curdle me like cheese;

11 Clothe me with skin and
flesh,
And knit me together with
bones and sinews?

12 'Thou hast ᵃgranted me life
and lovingkindness;
And Thy care has pre-
served my spirit.

13 'Yet ᵃthese things Thou
hast concealed in Thy
heart;
I know that this is within
Thee:

14 If I sin, then Thou wouldst
ᵃtake note of me,
And ᵇwouldst not acquit
me of my guilt.

15 'If ᵃI am wicked, woe to me!
And ᵇif I am righteous, I
dare not lift up my
head.
I am sated with disgrace
and conscious of my
misery.

16 'And should my head be
lifted up, ᵃThou
wouldst hunt me like
a lion;
And again Thou wouldst
show Thy ᵇpower
against me.

17 'Thou dost renew ᵃThy witnesses against me,
And increase Thine anger
toward me,
ᵇHardship after hardship is
with me.

Cross-references (left column)

32 ᵃEccl.
6:10 ᵇJob
9:3; Rom.
9:20

33 ᵃ1 Sam.
2:25; Job
9:19; Is. 1:18

34 ᵃJob
13:21

35 ᵃJob
13:22

1-7
1 ᵃJob 7:16
ᵇJob 7:11

2 ᵃJob 9:29

3 ᵃJob
9:22-24;
16:11; 19:6;
27:2 ᵇJob
10:8; 14:15;
Ps. 138:8; Is.
64:8 ᶜJob
21:16; 22:18

4 ᵃ1 Sam.
16:7; Job
28:24; 34:21

5 ᵃJob
36:26

6 ᵃJob
14:16

7 ᵃJob
9:21; 13:18
ᵇJob 9:12;
23:13; 27:22

Cross-references (right column)

8 ᵃJob
10:3; Ps.
119:73 ᵇJob
9:22

9 ᵃJob
4:19; 33:6
ᵇJob 7:21

10

12 ᵃJob 33:4

13 ᵃJob
23:13

14 ᵃJob 7:20
ᵇJob 7:21;
9:28

15 ᵃJob
10:7; Is. 3:11
ᵇJob 6:29

16 ᵃIs.
38:13; Lam.
3:10; Hos.
13:7 ᵇJob
5:9

17 ᵃRuth
1:21; Job
16:8 ᵇJob
7:1

9:32-33 Job's words about God's transcendence
(being aloof and detached from His creation)
reflect a feeling of helplessness. This led him
to cry out for an *umpire* or arbitrator, someone who understands both God and man and
can bring them together in harmony. God has
provided one in His Son, the God-Man, Jesus

Christ (1 Tim. 2:5).
10:1-7 Job thinks of every possible reason why
God might be afflicting him and concludes
that God must know that he is a man of integrity (v. 7).
10:10 A reference to God's care of the embryo.

★18 ªJob
3:11-13

18 'ªWhy then hast Thou brought me out of the womb?
Would that I had died and no eye had seen me!

19 'I should have been as though I had not been,
Carried from womb to tomb.'

★20-22

20 ªJob 14:1
bJob 7:16,
19

20 "Would He not let ªmy few days alone?
bWithdraw from me that I may have a little cheer

21 ª2 Sam.
12:23; Job
3:13-19;
16:22 bPs.
88:12 cJob
10:22; 34:22;
38:17; Ps.
23:4

21 Before I go—ªand I shall not return—
bTo the land of darkness and cdeep shadow;

22 The land of utter gloom as darkness *itself,*
Of deep shadow without order,
And which shines as the darkness."

F Zophar's First Speech, 11:1-20

★ 1-3

2 ªJob 8:2;
15:2; 18:2

11 Then Zophar the Naamathite answered,

2 "Shall a multitude of words go unanswered,
And a ªtalkative man be acquitted?

3 ªJob
17:2; 21:3

3 "Shall your boasts silence men?
And shall you ªscoff and none rebuke?

4 ªJob 6:10
bJob 10:7

4 "For ªyou have said, 'My teaching is pure,
And bI am innocent in your eyes.'

5 "But would that God might speak,

And open His lips against you,

6 And show you the secrets of wisdom!
For sound wisdom ªhas two sides.
Know then that God forgets a part of byour iniquity.

★ 6 ªJob
9:4 bJob
15:5; 22:5

7 "ªCan you discover the depths of God?
Can you discover the limits of the Almighty?

7 ªJob
33:12, 13;
36:26; 37:5,
23; Rom.
11:33

8 "*They are* ªhigh as the heavens, what can you do?
Deeper than bSheol, what can you know?

8 ªJob
22:12; 35:5
bJob 26:6;
38:17

9 "Its measure is longer than the earth,
And broader than the sea.

10 "If He passes by or shuts up,
Or calls an assembly, ªwho can restrain Him?

10 ªJob 9:12

11 "For ªHe knows false men,
And He bsees iniquity without investigating.

11 ªJob
34:21-23
bJob 24:23;
28:24; 31:4

12 "And ªan idiot will become intelligent
When the foal of a bwild donkey is born a man.

12 ªPs. 39:5,
11; 62:9;
144:4; Eccl.
1:2; 11:10
bJob 39:5

13 "ªIf you would bdirect your heart right,
And cspread out your hand to Him;

★13-20

13 ªJob
5:17-27;
11:13-20
b1 Sam. 7:3;
Ps. 78:8
cJob 22:27;
Ps. 88:9;
143:6

14 If iniquity is in your hand, ªput it far away,
And do not let wickedness dwell in your tents.

14 ªJob
22:23

15 "Then, indeed, you could ªlift up your face without *moral* defect,

15 ªJob
22:26 bPs.
27:3; 46:2

10:18 Again Job wishes he had not been born (cf. 3:11).

10:20-22 Job begs that God would leave him alone just for a little while before he dies.

11:1-3 *Zophar.* More blunt and harsh than the other two friends, he also concludes that Job is suffering because of his sins. In fact, he says that God has given Job only a fraction of what he deserves (v. 6). To his simple way of thinking, all Job needed to do was repent and everything would change (vv. 13-15). Zophar's authority was not religious experience or tradition, but intuition or common sense. His ul-timate authority, therefore, was really himself; what appeared right to him was considered to be indeed right. This kind of person sees all issues as either black or white. Zophar was not interested in probing the mysteries of God's working. He not only called Job a sinner, but rebuked and insulted him for attempting to understand God's ways (v. 12).

11:6 *has two sides.* Divine wisdom has two sides to it: one which man sees, and another known only to God.

11:13-20 Zophar also calls on Job to repent and assures him of rich rewards if he will do so.

And you would be steadfast and [b]not fear.

16 "For you would [a]forget your trouble,
As [b]waters that have passed by, you would remember it.

17 "And your life would be [a]brighter than noonday;
Darkness would be like the morning.

18 "Then you would trust, because there is hope;
And you would look around and rest securely.

19 "You would [a]lie down and none would disturb you,
And many would [b]entreat your favor.

20 "But the [a]eyes of the wicked will fail,
And there will [b]be no escape for them;
And their [c]hope is [d]to breathe their last."

G Job's Reply to Zophar, 12:1–14:22

★ 1
12 Then Job responded,
2 "Truly then [a]you are the people,
And with you wisdom will die!

3 "But [a]I have intelligence as well as you;
I am not inferior to you.
And who does not know such things as these?

4 "I am a [a]joke to my friends.
The one who called on God, and He answered him;
The just and [b]blameless man is a joke.

★ 5
5 "He who is at ease holds calamity in contempt,

As prepared for those whose feet slip.

6 "The [a]tents of the destroyers prosper,
And those who provoke God [b]are secure,
Whom God brings [c]into their power.

7 "But now ask the beasts, and let them teach you;
And the birds of the heavens, and let them tell you.

8 "Or speak to the earth, and let it teach you;
And let the fish of the sea declare to you.

9 "Who among all these does not know
That [a]the hand of the LORD has done this,

10 [a]In whose hand is the life of every living thing,
And [b]the breath of all mankind?

11 "Does not [a]the ear test words,
As the palate tastes its food?

12 "Wisdom is with [a]aged men,
With long life is understanding.

13 "With Him are [a]wisdom and [b]might;
To Him belong counsel and [c]understanding.

14 "Behold, He [a]tears down, and it cannot be rebuilt;
He [b]imprisons a man, and there can be no release.

15 "Behold, He [a]restrains the waters, and they dry up;

16 [a]Is. 65:16
[b]Job 22:11

17 [a]Job 22:26

19 [a]Lev. 26:6; Is. 17:2; Mic. 4:4; Zeph. 3:13 [b]Is. 45:14

20 [a]Deut. 28:65; Job 17:5 [b]Job 27:22; 34:22 [c]Job 8:13 [d]Job 6:9

2 [a]Job 17:10

3 [a]Job 13:2

4 [a]Job 17:6; 30:1, 9, 10; 34:7 [b]Job 6:29

★ 6 [a]Job 9:24; 21:7-9 [b]Job 24:23 [c]Job 22:18

9 [a]Is. 41:20

10 [a]Acts 17:28 [b]Job 27:3; 33:4

11 [a]Job 34:3

★12 [a]Job 15:10; 32:7

13 [a]Job 9:4 [b]Job 9:4 [c]Job 11:6; 26:12; 32:8; 36:5; 38:36

14 [a]Job 19:10; Is. 25:2 [b]Job 37:7

15 [a]Deut. 11:17; 1 Kin. 8:35; 17:1 [b]Gen. 7:11-24

12:1 Job now replies to his friends (through 14:22). He severely criticizes them (12:1-13:12), declares his own righteousness (13:13-19), and then appeals to God (13:20-14:22).
12:5 The meaning of this difficult verse seems to be this: it is easy for you, living in your comfortable world, to mock me.
12:6 The last phrase could read, "who bring their god in their hand." I.e, the god of robbers is the weapon in their hand.
12:12 These phrases should probably be understood as questions: "Is wisdom with aged men or understanding with long life?"

And He [b]sends them out,
and they inundate the
earth.

16 "With Him are strength and
sound wisdom,
The [a]misled and the mis-
leader belong to Him.

17 "He makes [a]counselors
walk barefoot,
And makes fools of
[b]judges.

18 "He [a]loosens the bond of
kings,
And binds their loins with
a girdle.

19 "He makes priests walk
barefoot,
And overthrows [a]the se-
cure ones.

20 "He deprives the trusted
ones of speech,
And [a]takes away the discernment of the el-
ders.

21 "He [a]pours contempt on
nobles,
And [b]loosens the belt of
the strong.

22 "He [a]reveals mysteries from
the darkness,
And brings the deep dark-
ness into light.

23 "He [a]makes the nations
great, then destroys
them;
He enlarges the nations,
then leads them away.

24 "He [a]deprives of intelligence the chiefs of the
earth's people,
And makes them wander
in a pathless waste.

25 "They [a]grope in darkness
with no light,
And He makes them [b]stag-
ger like a drunken
man.

13 "[a]Behold, my eye has seen
all this,
My ear has heard and un-
derstood it.

2 "[a]What you know I also
know.
I am not inferior to you.

3 "But [a]I would speak to the
Almighty,
And I desire to [b]argue with
God.

4 "But you [a]smear with lies;
You are all [b]worthless
physicians.

5 "O that you would [a]be
completely silent,
And that it would become
your wisdom!

6 "Please hear my argument,
And listen to the conten-
tions of my lips.

7 "Will you [a]speak what is
unjust for God,
And speak what is deceit-
ful for Him?

8 "Will you [a]show partiality
for Him?
Will you contend for God?

9 "Will it be well when He
examines you?
Or [a]will you deceive Him
as one deceives a
man?

10 "He will surely reprove you,
If you secretly [a]show partiality.

11 "Will not [a]His majesty terrify you,
And the dread of Him fall
on you?

12 "Your memorable sayings
are proverbs of ashes,
Your defenses are defenses
of clay.

13 "[a]Be silent before me so
that I may speak;
Then let come on me what
may.

14 "Why should I take my
flesh in my teeth,
And [a]put my life in my
hands?

15 "[a]Though He slay me,
I will hope in Him.

Cross references (left margin):

16 [a]Job 13:7, 9
★17 [a]Job 3:14 [b]Job 9:24
18 [a]Ps. 116:16
19 [a]Job 24:22; 34:24-28; 35:9
20 [a]Job 17:4; 32:9
21 [a]Job 34:19; Ps. 107:40 [b]Job 12:18
22 [a]Dan. 2:22; 1 Cor. 4:5
23 [a]Is. 9:3; 26:15
24 [a]Job 12:20
25 [a]Job 5:14 [b]Is. 24:20
1 [a]Job 12:9

Cross references (right margin):

2 [a]Job 12:3
3 [a]Job 13:22; 23:4 [b]Job 13:15
★ 4-12
4 [a]Ps. 119:69 [b]Jer. 23:32
5 [a]Job 13:13; 21:5; Prov. 17:28
7 [a]Job 27:4
8 [a]Lev. 19:15; Prov. 24:23
9 [a]Job 12:16
10 [a]Job 13:8; 32:21; 34:19
11 [a]Job 31:23
13 [a]Job 13:5
14 [a]Ps. 119:109
★15 [a]Job 7:6 [b]Job 27:5

12:17 *barefoot.* I.e., sometimes rulers are driven
to their wits' end.
13:4–12 Job severely castigates the motives of
his friends. Prov. 17:28 expresses the same sarcasm as here in verse 5. Job also reminds them
(v. 9) that they too face a heart-searching God.
13:15 The text is uncertain and may be translated, "He will slay me; I wait for Him (to

Nevertheless I *b*will argue
my ways before Him.

16 "This also will be my *a*salvation,

For *b*a godless man may
not come before His
presence.

17 "Listen carefully to my
speech,

And let my declaration *fill*
your ears.

18 "Behold now, I have *a*prepared my case;

I know that *b*I will be vindicated.

19 "*a*Who will contend with
me?

For then I would be silent
and *a*die.

20 "Only two things do not do
to me,

Then I will not hide from
Thy face:

21 *a*Remove Thy hand from
me,

And let not the dread of
Thee terrify me.

22 "Then call, and *a*I will answer;

Or let me speak, then re-
ply to me.

23 "*a*How many are my iniquities and sins?

Make known to me my re-
bellion and my sin.

24 "Why dost Thou *a*hide Thy
face,

And consider me *b*Thine
enemy?

25 "Wilt Thou cause a *a*driven
leaf to tremble?

Or wilt Thou pursue the
dry *b*chaff?

26 "For Thou dost write *a*bitter
things against me,

And dost *b*make me to inherit the iniquities of
my youth.

27 "Thou *a*dost put my feet in
the stocks,

And dost watch all my
paths;

Thou dost set a limit for
the soles of my feet,

28 While I am decaying like a
*a*rotten thing,

Like a garment that is
moth-eaten.

14 "*a*Man, who is born of
woman,

Is short-lived and *b*full of
turmoil.

2 "*a*Like a flower he comes
forth and withers.

He also flees like *b*a
shadow and does not
remain.

3 "Thou also dost *a*open
Thine eyes on him,

And *b*bring him into judgment with Thyself.

4 "*a*Who can make the clean
out of the unclean?

No one!

5 "Since his days are determined,

The *a*number of his
months is with Thee,

And his limits Thou hast
set so that he cannot
pass.

6 "*a*Turn Thy gaze from him
that he may rest,

Until he fulfills his day like
a hired man.

7 "For there is hope for a tree,
When it is cut down, that
it will sprout again,
And its shoots will not fail.

8 "Though its roots grow old
in the ground,
And its stump dies in the
dry soil,

9 At the scent of water it will
flourish
And put forth sprigs like a
plant.

10 "But *a*man dies and lies
prostrate.
Man *b*expires, and where is
he?

Margin references (left column):
16 *a*Job 23:7; Is. 12:1, 2 *b*Job 34:21-23
18 *a*Job 23:4 *b*Job 9:21; 10:7; 12:4
19 *a*Job 7:21; 10:8; Is. 50:8
21 *a*Job 9:34; Ps. 39:10
22 *a*Job 9:16; 14:15
★23-26
23 *a*Job 7:21
24 *a*Ps. 13:1; 44:24; 88:14; Is. 8:17 *b*Job 19:11; 33:10; Lam. 2:5
25 *a*Lev. 26:36 *b*Job 21:18
26 *a*Job 9:18 *b*Ps. 25:7
27 *a*Job 33:11

Margin references (right column):
28 *a*Job 2:7
1 *a*Job 5:7 *b*Eccl. 2:23
2 *a*Ps. 90:5, 6; 103:15; Is. 40:6, 7; James 1:10; 1 Pet. 1:24 *b*Job 8:9
3 *a*Ps. 8:4; 144:3 *b*Ps. 143:2
4 *a*Job 15:14; 25:4; Ps. 51:5
5 *a*Job 21:21
6 *a*Job 7:19; Ps. 39:13
★ 7-12
10 *a*Job 3:13; 14:10-15 *b*Job 13:9

---

strike)"; i.e., "I have no hope." Or it may
mean, "Though He slay me, I will not delay."
In any case, the general sense is clear: the fear
of death would not deter Job from saying "Not
guilty" to God.

13:23-26 Job wants to know why he is being afflicted.
14:7-12 In his despair Job claims that the fate of
a tree is better than the fate of a man, since a
tree can sprout again.

11 aIs. 19:5

11 "As ᵃwater evaporates from the sea,
And a river becomes parched and dried up,

12 aJob 3:13

12 So ᵃman lies down and does not rise.
Until the heavens be no more,
He will not awake nor be aroused out of his sleep.

★13-14

13 aIs. 26:20

13 "Oh that Thou wouldst hide me in Sheol,
That Thou wouldst conceal me ᵃuntil Thy wrath returns to Thee,
That Thou wouldst set a limit for me and remember me!

14 "If a man dies, will he live again?
All the days of my struggle I will wait,
Until my change comes.

15 aJob 10:3

15 "Thou wilt call, and I will answer Thee;
Thou wilt long for ᵃthe work of Thy hands.

16 aJob
31:4; 34:21;
Ps. 139:1-3;
Prov. 5:21
bJob 10:6

16 "For now Thou dost ᵃnumber my steps,
Thou dost not ᵇobserve my sin.

17 aDeut.
32:32-34

17 "My transgression is ᵃsealed up in a bag,
And Thou dost wrap up my iniquity.

18 "But the falling mountain crumbles away,
And the rock moves from its place;

19 aJob 7:6

19 Water wears away stones,
Its torrents wash away the dust of the earth;
So Thou dost ᵃdestroy man's hope.

20 aJob
4:20; 20:7

20 "Thou dost forever overpower him and he ᵃdeparts;
Thou dost change his appearance and send him away.

21 aEccl. 9:5

21 "His sons achieve honor, but ᵃhe does not know it;
Or they become insignificant, but he does not perceive it.

★22

22 "But his body pains him,
And he mourns only for himself."

H   Eliphaz' Second Speech, 15:1-35

★ 1-16

15 Then Eliphaz the Temanite responded,

2 aJob 6:26

2 "Should a wise man answer with windy knowledge,
ᵃAnd fill himself with the east wind?

3 "Should he argue with useless talk,
Or with words which are not profitable?

4 "Indeed, you do away with reverence,
And hinder meditation before God.

5 aJob 22:5
bJob 5:12,
13

5 "For ᵃyour guilt teaches your mouth,
And you choose the language of ᵇthe crafty.

6 aJob 18:7

6 "Your ᵃown mouth condemns you, and not I;
And your own lips testify against you.

7 aJob
38:4, 21;
Prov. 8:25

7 "Were you the first man to be born,
Or ᵃwere you brought forth before the hills?

14:13-14 Sheol. See note on Gen. 37:35. Job longs for death as a relief from his present sufferings. If he could hope that beyond Sheol there were some sort of resurrection, then he could endure his present problems.

14:22 Here ends the first round of debate between Job and his three friends. They have all concluded that Job is suffering because of his sins. Job has rejected their assumption, seeing death as his only way out. But the ire of his friends has been aroused and they are eager to say more.

15:1-16 Eliphaz, now directly censorious, accuses Job of being a windbag (vv. 1-6), of ignoring the wisdom of age (vv. 7-13), and of ignoring the sinfulness of man (vv. 14-16). the consolations of God (v. 11). Eliphaz's description of his own ministry of comfort to Job!

8 *a*Job
29:4; Rom.
11:34; 1 Cor.
2:11

9 *a*Job
12:3; 13:2

10 *a*Job
12:12;
32:6, 7

11 *a*Job
5:17-19;
36:15, 16
*b*Job 6:10;
23:12

12 *a*Job
11:13; 36:13

14 *a*Job
14:4; Prov.
20:9; Eccl.
7:20 *b*Job
25:4

15 *a*Job 5:1
*b*Job 25:5

16 *a*Ps. 14:1
*b*Job 34:7;
Prov. 19:28

★17-35

18 *a*Job 8:8;
20:4

20 *a*Job
15:24 *b*Job
24:1; 27:13

8 "Do you hear the *a*secret
counsel of God,
And limit wisdom to your-
self?
9 "*a*What do you know that
we do not know?
What do you understand
that we do not?
10 "Both the *a*gray-haired and
the aged are among
us,
Older than your father.
11 "Are *a*the consolations of
God too small for you,
Even the *b*word *spoken*
gently with you?
12 "Why does your *a*heart carry you away?
And why do your eyes
flash,
13 That you should turn your
spirit against God,
And allow *such* words to
go out of your mouth?
14 "What is man, that *a*he
should be pure,
Or *b*he who is born of a
woman, that he
should be righteous?
15 "Behold, He puts no trust in
His *a*holy ones,
And the *b*heavens are not
pure in His sight;
16 How much less one who is
*a*detestable and cor-
rupt,
Man, who *b*drinks iniquity
like water!

17 "I will tell you, listen to me;
And what I have seen I will
also declare;
18 What wise men have told,
And have not concealed
from *a*their fathers,
19 To whom alone the land
was given,
And no alien passed
among them.
20 "The wicked man writhes
*a*in pain all *his* days,

And numbered are the
years *b*stored up for
the ruthless.
21 "Sounds of *a*terror are in his
ears,
*b*While at peace the de-
stroyer comes upon
him.
22 "He does not believe that
he will *a*return from
darkness,
And he is destined for *b*the
sword.
23 "He wanders about for
food, saying, 'Where
is it?'
He knows that a day of
*a*darkness is at hand.
24 "Distress and anguish terrify him,
They overpower him like a
king ready for the at-
tack,
25 Because he has stretched
out his hand against
God,
And conducts himself *a*arrogantly against the
Almighty.
26 "He rushes headlong at
Him
With his massive shield.
27 "For he has *a*covered his
face with his fat,
And made his thighs
heavy with flesh.
28 "And he has *a*lived in desolate cities,
In houses no one would inhabit,
Which are destined to be-
come ruins.
29 "He *a*will not become rich,
nor will his wealth en-
dure;
And his grain will not
bend down to the
ground.
30 "He will *a*not escape from
darkness;
The *b*flame will wither his
shoots,

21 *a*Job
15:24; 18:11;
20:25; 24:17;
27:20 *b*Job
20:21;
1 Thess. 5:3

22 *a*Job
15:30 *b*Job
19:29; 27:14;
33:18; 36:12

23 *a*Job
15:22, 30

25 *a*Job 36:9

27 *a*Ps. 73:7;
119:70

28 *a*Job
3:14; Is.
5:8, 9

29 *a*Job
27:16, 17

30 *a*Job
5:14; 15:22
*b*Job 15:34;
20:26; 22:20;
31:12 *c*Job
4:9

15:17-35 Eliphaz now debates Job's statement
(12:6) that wicked men prosper. Rather, he
says, they experience pain (v. 20), threat of calamity (v. 21), anguish (vv. 22-24), and premature death (v. 32). He numbers Job among this
group.

And by ^cthe breath of His
mouth he will go
away.

31 ^aJob
35:13; Is.
59:4

31 "Let him not ^atrust in emptiness, deceiving him-
self;
For emptiness will be his
reward.

32 ^aJob
22:16; Eccl.
7:17 ^bJob
18:16

32 "It will be accomplished
^abefore his time,
And his palm ^bbranch will
not be green.

33 ^aJob 14:2

33 "He will drop off his unripe
grape like the vine,
And will ^acast off his
flower like the olive
tree.

34 ^aJob 8:13
^bJob 8:22

34 "For the company of ^athe
godless is barren,
And fire consumes ^bthe
tents of the corrupt.

35 ^aPs. 7:14;
Is. 59:4

35 "They ^aconceive mischief
and bring forth iniq-
uity,
And their mind prepares
deception."

**I Job's Second Reply to
Eliphaz, 16:1–17:16**

★ **1-5**
2 ^aJob
13:4; 21:34

16 Then Job answered,
2 "I have heard many
such things;
^aSorry comforters are you
all.

3 ^aJob 6:26

3 "Is there *no* limit to ^awindy
words?
Or what plagues you that
you answer?

4 ^aPs. 22:7;
109:25;
Zeph. 2:15;
Matt. 27:39

4 "I too could speak like you,
If I were in your place.
I could compose words
against you,
And ^ashake my head at
you.

5 "I could strengthen you
with my mouth,
And the solace of my lips
could lessen *your
pain.*

★ **6-17**
6 ^aJob
9:27, 28

6 "If I speak, ^amy pain is not
lessened,

And if I hold back, what
has left me?

7 ^aJob 7:3
^bJob 16:20;
19:13-15

7 "But now He has ^aexhaust-
ed me;
Thou hast laid ^bwaste all
my company.

8 ^aJob
10:17 ^bJob
19:20; Ps.
109:24

8 "And Thou hast shriveled
me up,
^aIt has become a witness;
And my ^bleanness rises up
against me,
It testifies to my face.

9 ^aJob
19:11; Hos.
6:1 ^bPs.
35:16; Lam.
2:16; Acts
7:54 ^cJob
13:24; 33:10

9 "His anger has ^atorn me
and hunted me down,
He has ^bgnashed at me
with His teeth;
My ^cadversary glares at
me.

10 ^aPs.
22:13 ^bIs.
50:6; Lam.
3:30; Acts
23:2 ^cJob
30:12; Ps.
35:15

10 "They have ^agaped at me
with their mouth,
They have ^bslapped me on
the cheek with con-
tempt;
They have ^cmassed themselves against me.

11 "God hands me over to ruf-
fians,
And tosses me into the
hands of the wicked.

12 ^aJob 9:17
^bJob 7:20;
Lam. 3:12

12 "I was at ease, but ^aHe shattered me;
And He has grasped me by
the neck and shaken
me to pieces;
He has also set me up as
His ^btarget.

13 ^aJob 6:4;
19:12; 25:3
^bJob 20:25

13 "His ^aarrows surround me.
Without mercy He splits
my kidneys open;
He pours out ^bmy gall on
the ground.

14 ^aJob 9:17
^bJoel 2:7

14 "He ^abreaks through me
with breach after
breach;
He ^bruns at me like a warrior.

15 ^aGen.
37:34; Ps.
69:11 ^bPs.
7:5

15 "I have sewed ^asackcloth
over my skin,
And ^bthrust my horn in
the dust.

16 ^aJob
16:20 ^bJob
24:17

16 "My face is flushed from
^aweeping,
^bAnd deep darkness is on
my eyelids,

16:1-5 Job spurns the "comfort" of his friends.
16:6-17 Once again Job describes his desperate
situation.

17 Although there is no ^aviolence in my hands,
And ^bmy prayer is pure.

18 "O earth, do not cover my blood,
And let there be no *resting* place for my cry.

19 "Even now, behold, ^amy witness is in heaven,
And my advocate is ^bon high.

20 "My friends are my scoffers;
^aMy eye weeps to God.

21 "O that a man might plead with God
As a man with his neighbor!

22 "For when a few years are past,
I shall go the way ^aof no return.

17 "My spirit is broken, my days are extinguished,
The ^agrave is *ready* for me.

2 "^aSurely mockers are with me,
And my eye gazes on their provocation.

3 "Lay down, now, a pledge ^afor me with Thyself;
Who is there that will be my guarantor?

4 "For Thou hast ^akept their heart from understanding;
Therefore Thou wilt not exalt *them*.

5 "He who ^ainforms against friends for a share *of the spoil*,
The ^beyes of his children also shall languish.

6 "But He has made me a ^abyword of the people,
And I am one at whom men ^bspit.

7 "My eye has also grown ^adim because of grief,
And all my ^bmembers are as a shadow.

8 "The upright shall be appalled at this,
And the ^ainnocent shall stir up himself against the godless.

9 "Nevertheless ^athe righteous shall hold to his way,
And ^bhe who has clean hands shall grow stronger and stronger.

10 "But come again all of you now,
For I ^ado not find a wise man among you.

11 "My ^adays are past, my plans are torn apart,
Even the wishes of my heart.

12 "They make night into day, *saying,*
'The light is near,' in the presence of darkness.

13 "If I look for ^aSheol as my home,
I make my bed in the darkness;

14 If I call to the ^apit, 'You are my father';
To the ^bworm, 'my mother and my sister';

15 Where now is ^amy hope?
And who regards my hope?

16 "Will it go down with me to Sheol?
Shall we together ^ago down into the dust?"

J　Bildad's Second Speech, 18:1–21

18 Then Bildad the Shuhite responded,

2 "How long will you hunt for words?
Show understanding and then we can talk.

16:18 Job's innocence cries for vindication (cf. Gen. 4:10).
16:21 Job longs for a divine helper (cf. 1 John 2:1-2).
17:3-5 Job asks God to be the *pledge* with Himself of Job's innocence.
17:6 *at whom men spit.* An abhorring.
17:13-14 Again Job expresses his longing for death.

Marginal references:

17 ^aIs. 59:6; Jon. 3:8 ^bJob 27:4
★18
19 ^aGen. 31:50; Job 19:25-27; Rom. 1:9; Phil. 1:8; 1 Thess. 2:5 ^bJob 31:2
20 ^aJob 17:7
★21
22 ^aJob 3:13
1 ^aPs. 88:3, 4
2 ^aJob 12:4; 17:6
★ 3-5
3 ^aPs. 119:122; Is. 38:14
4 ^aJob 12:20
5 ^aLev. 19:13, 16 ^bJob 11:20
★ 6 ^aJob 17:2 ^bJob 30:10
7 ^aJob 16:16 ^bJob 16:8
8 ^aJob 22:19
9 ^aProv. 4:18 ^bJob 22:30; 31:7
10 ^aJob 12:2
11 ^aJob 7:6
★13-14
13 ^aJob 3:13
14 ^aJob 7:5; 13:28; 30:30 ^bJob 21:26; 25:6
15 ^aJob 7:6
16 ^aJob 3:17; 21:33

3 aPs. 73:22

3 "Why are we aregarded as beasts,
As stupid in your eyes?
4 "O you who tear yourself in your anger—
For your sake is the earth to be abandoned,
Or the rock to be moved from its place?

★ 5-21
5 aJob 21:17; Prov. 13:9; 20:20; 24:20
6 aJob 12:25

5 "Indeed, the alight of the wicked goes out,
And the flame of his fire gives no light.
6 "The light in his tent is adarkened,
And his lamp goes out above him.

7 aJob 15:6

7 "His vigorous stride is shortened,
And his aown scheme brings him down.

8 aJob 22:10; Ps. 9:15; 35:8; Is. 24:17, 18

8 "For he is athrown into the net by his own feet,
And he steps on the webbing.
9 "A snare seizes him by the heel,
And a trap snaps shut on him.
10 "A noose for him is hidden in the ground,
And a trap for him on the path.

11 aJob 15:21 bJob 18:18; 20:8

11 "All around aterrors frighten him,
And bharry him at every step.

12 aIs. 8:21

12 "His strength is afamished,
And calamity is ready at his side.

13 aZech. 14:12

13 "His skin is devoured by disease,
The first-born of death adevours his limbs.

14 aJob 8:22; 18:6 bJob 15:21

14 "He is atorn from the security of his tent,
And they march him before the king of bterrors.

15 aPs. 11:6

15 "There dwells in his tent nothing of his;
aBrimstone is scattered on his habitation.

16 "His aroots are dried below,
And his bbranch is cut off above.
17 "aMemory of him perishes from the earth,
And he has no name abroad.
18 "He is driven from light ainto darkness,
And bchased from the inhabited world.
19 "He has no aoffspring or posterity among his people,
Nor any survivor where he sojourned.
20 "Those in the west are appalled at ahis fate,
And those in the east are seized with horror.
21 "Surely such are the adwellings of the wicked,
And this is the place of him who does not know God."

16 aIs. 5:24; Hos. 9:16; Amos 2:9; Mal. 4:1 bJob 15:30, 32
17 aJob 24:20; Ps. 34:16; Prov. 10:7
18 aJob 5:14; Is. 8:22; 15:30 bJob 20:8; 27:21-23
19 aJob 27:14, 15; Is. 14:22
20 aPs. 37:13; Jer. 50:27; Obad. 12
21 aJob 21:28

K Job's Second Reply to Bildad, 19:1-29

19 Then Job responded,
2 "How long will you torment me,
And crush me with words?
3 "These ten times you have insulted me,
You are not ashamed to wrong me.
4 "Even if I have truly erred,
My error lodges with me.
5 "If indeed you avaunt yourselves against me,
And prove my disgrace to me,
6 Know then that aGod has wronged me,
And has closed bHis net around me.

7 "Behold, aI cry, 'Violence!' but I get no answer;
I shout for help, but there is no justice.

★ 3
5 aPs. 35:26; 38:16; 55:12, 13
6 aJob 16:11; 27:2 bJob 18:8-10; Ps. 66:11; Lam. 1:13
7 aJob 9:24; 30:20, 24; Hab. 1:2

18:5-21 Bildad paints the fate of "wicked" Job as being consumed by the first-born of death (v. 13; i.e., deadly disease), as going into oblivion (vv. 16-19), and as being cursed by God (Brimstone, v. 15, was a symbol of this; cf. Gen. 19:24; Deut. 29:23).
19:3 These ten times. I.e., often (Gen. 31:7).

8 "He has ᵃwalled up my way
so that I cannot pass;
And He has put ᵇdarkness
on my paths.

9 "He has ᵃstripped my honor
from me,
And removed the ᵇcrown
from my head.

10 "He ᵃbreaks me down on
every side, and I am
gone;
And He has uprooted my
ᵇhope ᶜlike a tree.

11 "He has also ᵃkindled His
anger against me,
And ᵇconsidered me as His
enemy.

12 "His ᵃtroops come together,
And ᵇbuild up their way
against me,
And camp around my tent.

13 "He has ᵃremoved my
brothers far from me,
And my ᵇacquaintances
are completely es-
tranged from me.

14 "My relatives have failed,
And my ᵃintimate friends
have forgotten me.

15 "Those who live in my
house and my maids
consider me a stran-
ger.
I am a foreigner in their
sight.

16 "I call to my servant, but he
does not answer,
I have to implore him with
my mouth.

17 "My breath is offensive to
my wife,
And I am loathsome to my
own brothers.

18 "Even young children despise me;
I rise up and they speak
against me.

19 "All my ᵃassociates abhor
me,
And those I love have
turned against me.

20 "My ᵃbone clings to my
skin and my flesh,
And I have escaped *only*
by the skin of my
teeth.

21 "Pity me, pity me, O you
my friends,
For the ᵃhand of God has
struck me.

22 "Why do you ᵃpersecute me
as God *does*,
And are not satisfied with
my flesh?

23 "Oh that my words were
written!
Oh that they were ᵃin-
scribed in a book!

24 "That with an iron stylus
and lead
They were engraved in the
rock forever!

25 "And as for me, I know that
ᵃmy Redeemer lives,
And at the last He will
take His stand on the
earth.

26 "Even after my skin is destroyed,
Yet from my flesh I shall
ᵃsee God;

27 Whom I myself shall behold,
And whom my eyes shall
see and not another.
My heart ᵃfaints within
me.

Cross references (margin):

8 ᵃJob 3:23; Lam. 3:7, 9 ᵇJob 30:26

9 ᵃJob 12:17, 19; Ps. 89:44 ᵇJob 16:15; Ps. 89:39; Lam. 5:16

10 ᵃJob 12:14 ᵇJob 7:6 ᶜJob 24:20

11 ᵃJob 16:9 ᵇJob 13:24; 33:10

12 ᵃJob 16:13 ᵇJob 30:12

★13-22

13 ᵃJob 16:7; Ps. 69:8 ᵇJob 16:20; Ps. 88:8, 18

14 ᵃJob 19:19

19 ᵃPs. 38:11; 55:12, 13

20 ᵃJob 16:8; 33:21; Ps. 102:5; Lam. 4:8

21 ᵃJob 1:11; Ps. 38:2

22 ᵃJob 13:24, 25; 16:11; 19:6; Ps. 69:26

★23-24

23 ᵃIs. 30:8; Jer. 36:2

★25-27

25 ᵃJob 16:19; Ps. 78:35; Prov. 23:11; Is. 43:14; Jer. 50:34

26 ᵃPs. 17:15; Matt. 5:8; 1 Cor. 13:12; 1 John 3:2

27 ᵃPs. 73:26

19:13-22 Job, isolated from those dearest to him, longs for affection.

19:23-24 Job, despairing of justice in his life-time, wishes that his case could be *inscribed* (engraved) *in a book.* Then, realizing that ordinary writing is perishable, he desires that it be cut on a leaden tablet or on a rock.

19:25-27 *Redeemer.* Heb., *goel.* See notes on Ruth 3:9 and Isa. 59:17-21. Job believed in a living God who would vindicate his case even after his death. *at the last.* In the future. *on the earth.* Lit., upon dust, referring to the dust of the earth or to the dust of Job's grave. *from my flesh.* Although the Hebrew preposition,

min, sometimes means "without" (in which case Job expected vindication in a disembodied state), when it is used with the verb "to see" it may indicate the vantage point from which a person sees (in which case Job expected to be in a body when he was received in the resurrection). The last phrase of verse 27 is an exclamation something like, "I'm overwhelmed at the thought." This great expression of hope marks the turning point in Job's attitude. He has seen his sufferings in the perspective of certain future vindication of his case.

28 "If you say, 'How shall we ^apersecute him?'
And 'What pretext for a case against him can we find?'

29 *Then* be afraid of ^athe sword for yourselves,
For wrath *brings* the punishment of the sword,
So that you may know ^bthere is judgment."

L Zophar's Second Speech, 20:1-29

20 Then Zophar the Naamathite answered,

2 "Therefore my disquieting thoughts make me respond,
Even because of my inward agitation.

3 "I listened to ^athe reproof which insults me,
And the spirit of my understanding makes me answer.

4 "Do you know this from ^aof old,
From the establishment of man on earth,

5 That the ^atriumphing of the wicked is short,
And ^bthe joy of the godless momentary?

6 "Though his loftiness ^areaches the heavens,
And his head touches the clouds,

7 He ^aperishes forever like his refuse;
Those who have seen him ^bwill say, 'Where is he?'

8 "He flies away like a ^adream, and they cannot find him;
Even like a vision of the night he is ^bchased away.

9 "The ^aeye which saw him sees him no more,
And ^bhis place no longer beholds him.

10 "His ^asons favor the poor,
And his hands ^bgive back his wealth.

11 "His ^abones are full of his youthful vigor,
But it lies down with him in the dust.

12 "Though ^aevil is sweet in his mouth,
And he hides it under his tongue,

13 *Though* he desires it and will not let it go,
But holds it ^ain his mouth,

14 *Yet* his food in his stomach is changed
To the venom of cobras within him.

15 "He swallows riches,
But will ^avomit them up;
God will expel them from his belly.

16 "He sucks ^athe poison of cobras;
The viper's tongue slays him.

17 "He does not look at ^athe streams,
The rivers flowing with honey and curds.

18 "He ^areturns what he has attained
And cannot swallow *it;*
As to the riches of his trading,
He cannot even enjoy *them.*

19 "For he has ^aoppressed *and* forsaken the poor;
He has seized a house which he has not built.

20 "Because he knew no quiet within him
He does ^anot retain anything he desires.

20:1-2 Zophar, seething with anger because of Job's warnings (19:28-29), tells Job that a wicked man's prosperity is brief (v. 5). He attempts to make suffering Job appear to be sinning Job.

20:19 Apparently Job's friends could not produce any proof of Job's guilt, so the best Zophar can do is accuse him of land-grabbing and oppressing the poor. There is no evidence that Job did these things.

21 aJob
15:29

21 "Nothing remains for him
     to devour,
   Therefore ahis prosperity
     does not endure.

22 aJob 5:5

22 "In the fulness of his plenty
     he will be cramped;
   The ahand of everyone
     who suffers will come
     against him.

23 aJob
20:13, 14
bNum.
11:18-20, 33;
Ps. 78:30, 31

23 "When he afills his belly,
   God will send His fierce
     anger on him
   And will brain it on him
     while he is eating.

24 aIs.
24:18; Amos
5:19

24 "He may aflee from the iron
     weapon,
   But the bronze bow will
     pierce him.

25 aJob
16:13 bJob
18:11, 14

25 "It is drawn forth and
     comes out of his back,
   Even the glittering point
     from ahis gall.
   bTerrors come upon him,

26 aJob
18:18 bJob
15:30; Ps.
21:9

26 Complete adarkness is
     held in reserve for his
     treasures,
   And unfanned bfire will
     devour him;
   It will consume the survi-
     vor in his tent.

27 aDeut.
31:28; Is.
26:21

27 "The aheavens will reveal
     his iniquity,
   And the earth will rise up
     against him.

28 aDeut.
28:31 bJob
20:15; 21:30

28 "The aincrease of his house
     will depart;
   His possessions will flow
     away bin the day of
     His anger.

29 aJob
27:13;
31:2, 3

29 "This is the wicked man's
     aportion from God,
   Even the heritage decreed
     to him by God."

M Job's Second Reply to Zophar, 21:1-34

★ 1-6

21 Then Job answered,
  2 "Listen carefully to
       my speech,
     And let this be your way
       of consolation.

3 aJob
11:3; 17:2

3 "Bear with me that I may
     speak;
   Then after I have spoken,
     you may amock.

4 aJob 7:11
bJob 6:11

4 "As for me, is amy com-
     plaint to man?
   And bwhy should I not be
     impatient?

5 aJudg.
18:19; Job
13:5; 29:9;
40:4

5 "Look at me, and be aston-
     ished,
   And aput your hand over
     your mouth.

6 aPs. 55:5

6 "Even when I remember, I
     am disturbed,
   And ahorror takes hold of
     my flesh.

★ 7-16
7 aJob
9:24; Ps.
73:3; Jer.
12:1; Hab.
1:13 bJob
12:19

7 "Why ado the wicked still
     live,
   Continue on, also become
     very bpowerful?

8 aPs.
17:14

8 "Their adescendants are es-
     tablished with them
     in their sight,
   And their offspring before
     their eyes,

9 aJob 12:6

9 Their houses aare safe
     from fear,
   Neither is the rod of God
     on them.

10 "His ox mates without fail;
    His cow calves and does
      not abort.

11 "They send forth their little
      ones like the flock,
    And their children skip
      about.

12 "They sing to the timbrel
      and harp
    And rejoice at the sound of
      the flute.

13 aJob
21:23; 36:11

13 "They aspend their days in
      prosperity,
    And suddenly they go
      down to Sheol.

14 aJob
22:17

14 "And they say to God, 'aDe-
      part from us!
    We do not even desire the
      knowledge of Thy
      ways.

15 aJob
22:17; 34:9

15 'Who is the Almighty, that
      we should serve Him,
    And awhat would we gain
      if we entreat Him?'

21:1-6 Job, now taking the initiative, demands
the attention of his accusers.
21:7-16 Contrary to Zophar's thesis, the wicked
often prosper. Verse 13 means that, prosper-

ous to the end, the wicked sometimes die
without a struggle. In verse 16 Job acknowledges that even the prosperity of the wicked
comes from the Lord who governs all men.

16 *a*Job
22:18

16 "Behold, their prosperity is not in their hand;
The *a*counsel of the wicked is far from me.

★17 *a*Job
18:5, 6 *b*Job
31:2, 3

17 "How often is *a*the lamp of the wicked put out,
Or *does* their *b*calamity fall on them?
Does God apportion destruction in His anger?

18 *a*Job
13:25; Ps.
83:13 *b*Ps.
1:4; 35:5; Is.
17:13; Hos.
13:3

18 "Are they as *a*straw before the wind,
And like *b*chaff which the storm carries away?

★19 *a*Ex.
20:5; Jer.
31:29; Ezek.
18:2

19 "*You say,* '*a*God stores away a man's iniquity for his sons.'
Let God repay him so that he may know *it.*

20 *a*Num.
14:28-32;
Jer. 31:30;
Ezek. 18:4
*b*Ps. 60:3; Is.
51:17; Jer.
25:15; Rev.
14:10

20 "Let his *a*own eyes see his decay,
And let him *b*drink of the wrath of the Almighty.

21 "For what does he care for his household after him,
When the number of his months is cut off?

22 *a*Job
35:11; 36:22;
Is. 40:14;
Rom. 11:34
*b*Job 4:18;
15:15; Ps.
82:1

22 "Can anyone *a*teach God knowledge,
In that He *b*judges those on high?

23 *a*Job
20:11; 21:13

23 "One *a*dies in his full strength,
Being wholly at ease and satisfied;

★24 *a*Prov.
3:8

24 His sides are filled out with fat,
And the *a*marrow of his bones is moist,

25 While another dies with a bitter soul,
Never even tasting *anything* good.

26 *a*Job
3:13; 20:11;
Eccl. 9:2
*b*Job 24:20;
Is. 14:11

26 "Together they *a*lie down in the dust,
And *b*worms cover them.

27 "Behold, I know your thoughts,
And the plans by which you would wrong me.

28 *a*Job 1:3;
31:37 *b*Job
8:22; 18:21

28 "For you say, 'Where is the house of *a*the nobleman,
And where is the *b*tent, the dwelling places of the wicked?'

29 "Have you not asked wayfaring men,
And do you not recognize their witness?

30 *a*Job
20:29; Prov.
16:4; 2 Pet.
2:9 *b*Job
21:17, 20;
40:11

30 "For the *a*wicked is reserved for the day of calamity;
They will be led forth at *b*the day of fury.

31 "Who will confront him with his actions,
And who will repay him for what he has done?

★32-33

32 "While he is carried to the grave,
Men will keep watch over *his* tomb.

33 *a*Job
3:22; 17:16
*b*Job 3:19;
24:24

33 "The *a*clods of the valley will gently cover him;
Moreover, *b*all men will follow after him,
While countless ones *go* before him.

34 *a*Job 16:2

34 "How then will you vainly *a*comfort me,
For your answers remain *full* of falsehood?"

N Eliphaz' Third Speech, 22:1-30

★ 1

22 Then Eliphaz the Temanite responded,

2 *a*Job
35:7; Luke
17:10

2 "Can a vigorous *a*man be of use to God,
Or a wise man be useful to himself?

21:17 The verse is a skeptical question. How often, Job asks, does this really happen?

21:19 *iniquity.* I.e., the punishment of a man's iniquity is often borne by his children.

21:24 *sides.* The word, occurring only here, may refer to milk pails or, figuratively, to the fatness of the body.

21:32-33 Even the repulsiveness of death is softened for the prosperous wicked man.

22:1 In the third round of the debate (through 26:14) we find Eliphaz and Bildad trying harder than ever to prove that Job is a great sinner (22:5).

3 "Is there any pleasure to the Almighty if you are righteous,
Or profit if you make your ways perfect?

4 *a*Job 14:3; 19:29

4 "Is it because of your reverence that He reproves you,
That He *a*enters into judgment against you?

5 *a*Job 11:6; 15:5

5 "Is not *a*your wickedness great,
And your iniquities without end?

★ **6-9**
6 *a*Ex. 22:26; Deut. 24:6, 17; Job 24:3, 9; Ezek. 18:16
*b*Job 31:19, 20

6 "For you have *a*taken pledges of your brothers without cause,
And *b*stripped men naked.

7 *a*Job 31:16, 17
*b*Job 31:31

7 "To the weary you have *a*given no water to drink,
And from the hungry you have *b*withheld bread.

8 *a*Job 9:24
*b*Job 12:19
*c*Is. 3:3; 9:15

8 "But the earth *a*belongs to the *b*mighty man,
And *c*the honorable man dwells in it.

9 *a*Job 24:3, 21; 29:13; 31:16, 18 *b*Job 6:27

9 "You have sent *a*widows away empty,
And the strength of the *b*orphans has been crushed.

10 *a*Job 18:8
*b*Job 15:21

10 "Therefore *a*snares surround you,
And sudden *b*dread terrifies you,

11 *a*Job 5:14
*b*Job 38:34; Ps. 69:2; 124:5; Lam. 3:54

11 Or *a*darkness, so that you cannot see,
And an *b*abundance of water covers you.

★ **12-14**
12 *a*Job 11:7-9

12 "Is not God *a*in the height of heaven?
Look also at the distant stars, how high they are!

13 *a*Ps. 10:11; 59:7; 64:5; 94:7; Is. 29:15; Ezek. 8:12

13 "And you say, '*a*What does God know?
Can He judge through the thick darkness?

14 '*a*Clouds are a hiding place for Him, so that He cannot see;
And He walks on the vault of heaven.'

14 *a*Job 26:9

15 "Will you keep to the ancient path
Which *a*wicked men have trod,

15 *a*Job 34:36

16 Who were snatched away *a*before their time,
Whose *b*foundations were washed away by a river?

16 *a*Job 15:32; 21:13, 18 *b*Job 14:19; Ps. 90:5; Is. 28:2; Matt. 7:26, 27

17 "They *a*said to God, 'Depart from us!'
And 'What can the Almighty do to them?'

17 *a*Job 21:14, 15

18 "Yet He *a*filled their houses with good *things*;
But *b*the counsel of the wicked is far from me.

18 *a*Job 12:6
*b*Job 21:16

19 "The *a*righteous see and are glad,
And the innocent mock them,

19 *a*Ps. 52:6; 58:10; 107:42

20 *Saying*, 'Truly our adversaries are cut off,
And their abundance *a*the fire has consumed.'

20 *a*Job 15:30

21 "*a*Yield now and be at peace with Him;
Thereby good will come to you.

★**21-30**

21 *a*Ps. 34:10

22 "Please receive *a*instruction from His mouth,
And establish His words in your heart.

22 *a*Job 6:10; 23:12; Prov. 2:6

23 "If you *a*return to the Almighty, you will be restored;
If you *b*remove unrighteousness far from your tent,

23 *a*Job 8:5; 11:13; Is. 19:22; 31:6; Zech. 1:3
*b*Job 11:14

24 And *a*place *your* gold in the dust,
And the gold of Ophir among the stones of the brooks,

24 *a*Job 31:24, 25

22:6-9 Eliphaz accuses Job of gaining his now lost wealth by robbing the poor (cf. 20:19). **naked.** Without the outer garment which could be taken as a pledge, but not kept overnight (see notes on Exod. 22:25-27 and Amos 2:8).

22:12-14 Eliphaz presumes to accuse Job of secretly thinking that God is so exalted and removed that wicked man has nothing to fear from Him.
22:21-30 Again Job is urged to repent. *Ophir* (v. 24). See note on 1 Kings 9:28.

25 Then the Almighty will be
    your gold
    And choice silver to you.

26 *a*Job
27:10; Ps.
37:4; Is.
58:14

26 "For then you will *a*delight
    in the Almighty,
    And lift up your face to
    God.

27 *a*Job
11:13; 33:26;
Is. 58:9 *b*Job
34:28

27 "You will *a*pray to Him, and
    *b*He will hear you;
    And you will pay your
    vows.

28 *a*Job
11:17; Ps.
112:4

28 "You will also decree a
    thing, and it will be
    established for you;
    And *a*light will shine on
    your ways.

29 *a*Job
5:11; 36:7;
Matt. 23:12;
James 4:6;
1 Pet. 5:5

29 "When you are cast down,
    you will speak with
    confidence
    And the *a*humble person
    He will save.

30 *a*Job
42:7, 8; Ps.
18:20;
24:3, 4

30 "He will deliver one who is
    not innocent,
    And he will be *a*delivered
    through the cleanness
    of your hands."

O Job's Third Reply to Eliphaz, 23:1–24:25

★ 1-7

2 *a*Job 7:11
*b*Job 6:2, 3;
Ps. 32:4

23 Then Job replied,
    2 "Even today my
    *a*complaint is rebel-
    lion;
    His hand is *b*heavy despite
    my groaning.

3 "Oh that I knew where I
    might find Him,
    That I might come to His
    seat!

4 *a*Job
13:18

4 "I would *a*present *my* case
    before Him
    And fill my mouth with ar-
    guments.

5 "I would learn the words
    which He would an-
    swer,
    And perceive what He
    would say to me.

6 "Would He contend with
    me by *a*the greatness
    of *His* power?
    No, surely He would pay
    attention to me.

6 *a*Job 9:4

7 "There the upright would
    *a*reason with Him;
    And I would be *b*delivered
    forever from my
    Judge.

7 *a*Job 13:3
*b*Job 13:16;
23:10

8 "Behold, I go forward but
    He is not *there,*
    And backward, but I *a*can-
    not perceive Him;

8 *a*Job
9:11; 35:14

9 When He acts on the left, I
    cannot behold *Him;*
    He turns on the right, I
    cannot see Him.

10 "But He knows the way I
    take;
    When He has *a*tried me, I
    shall come forth as
    gold.

★10 *a*Job
7:18; Ps. 7:9;
11:5; 66:10;
Zech. 13:9;
1 Pet. 1:7

11 "My foot has *a*held fast to
    His path;
    I have kept His way and
    not turned aside.

★11-12

11 *a*Job
31:7; Ps.
17:5; 44:18

12 "I have not departed from
    the command of His
    lips;
    I have treasured the
    *a*words of His mouth
    more than my neces-
    sary food.

12 *a*Job
6:10; 22:22

13 "But He is unique and who
    can turn Him?
    And *what* His soul desires,
    that He does.

14 "For He performs what is
    appointed for me,
    And many such *decrees*
    are with Him.

★14-16

15 "Therefore, I would be dis-
    mayed at His pres-
    ence;
    When I consider, I am ter-
    rified of Him.

16 "*It is* God *who* has made my
    *a*heart faint,

16 *a*Deut.
20:3; Job
27:2; Jer.
51:46

23:1-7 Job declares his longing for God and asserts once again his innocence.
23:10 *the way I take.* Lit., the way that is in me;
i.e., my conduct. The last part of the verse
does not refer to the refining effect of suffering, but to his innocence. When the "Assayer"
tries him, He will find not secret dross cleverly

concealed from men (as his friends charged),
but gold.
23:11-12 Job claims to have kept God's law
(contrary to Eliphaz's charge, 22:22).
23:14-16 Job acknowledges that his sufferings
are in the will of God, though the thought
troubles him.

And the Almighty *who* has dismissed me,

17 *a*Job 10:18, 19 *b*Job 19:8

17 But I *a*am not silenced by the darkness,
Nor *b*deep gloom *which* covers me.

★ 1 *a*Acts 1:7 *b*Is. 2:12; Jer. 46:10; Obad. 15; Zeph. 1:7

24 "*a*Why are times not stored up by the Almighty,
And why do those who know Him not see *b*His days?

★ 2-24

2 *a*Deut. 19:14; 27:17; Prov. 23:10

2 "Some *a*remove the landmarks;
They seize and devour flocks.

3 *a*Job 6:27 *b*Deut. 24:17; Job 22:9

3 "They drive away the donkeys of the *a*orphans;
They take the *b*widow's ox for a pledge.

4 *a*Job 24:14; 29:16; 30:25; 31:19 *b*Job 29:12; Ps. 41:1; Prov. 14:31; 28:28; Amos 8:4

4 "They push *a*the needy aside from the road;
The *b*poor of the land are made to hide themselves altogether.

5 *a*Job 39:5-8 *b*Ps. 104:23

5 "Behold, as *a*wild donkeys in the wilderness
They *b*go forth seeking food in their activity,
As bread for *their* children in the desert.

6 "They harvest their fodder in the field,
And they glean the vineyard of the wicked.

7 *a*Ex. 22:26; Job 22:6

7 "*a*They spend the night naked, without clothing,
And have no covering against the cold.

8 "They are wet with the mountain rains,
And they hug the rock for want of a shelter.

9 *a*Job 6:27

9 "Others snatch the *a*orphan from the breast,
And against the poor they take a pledge.

10 "They cause *the poor* to go about naked without clothing,
And they take away the sheaves from the hungry,

11 "Within the walls they produce oil;
They tread wine presses but thirst.

12 *a*Job 9:23, 24

12 "From the city men groan,
And the souls of the wounded cry out;
Yet God *a*does not pay attention to folly.

13 "Others have been with those who rebel against the light;
They do not want to know its ways,
Nor abide in its paths.

14 *a*Mic. 2:1 *b*Ps. 10:8

14 "The murderer *a*arises at dawn;
He *b*kills the poor and the needy,
And at night he is as a thief.

15 *a*Prov. 7:9

15 "And the eye of the *a*adulterer waits for the twilight,
Saying, 'No eye will see me.'
And he disguises his face.

16 *a*Ex. 22:2; Matt. 6:19 *b*John 3:20

16 "In the dark they *a*dig into houses,
They *b*shut themselves up by day;
They do not know the light.

17 *a*Job 15:21

17 "For the morning is the same to him as thick darkness,
For he is familiar with the *a*terrors of thick darkness.

18 *a*Job 22:11, 16; 27:20 *b*Job 5:3 *c*Job 24:6, 11

18 "They are *a*insignificant on the surface of the water;
Their portion is *b*cursed on the earth.
They do not turn toward the *c*vineyards.

19 *a*Job 6:16, 17 *b*Job 21:13

19 "Drought and heat *a*consume the snow waters,
So does *b*Sheol *those who* have sinned.

24:1 Job complains that God does not have fixed times for the punishment of evildoers (cf. v. 12).

24:2-24 Job describes the rampant evil in the world which God apparently tolerates.

20 ^aIs. 49:15
^bJob 21:26
^cJob 18:17;
Ps. 34:16;
Prov. 10:7
^dJob 19:10;
Dan. 4:14

20 "A ^amother will forget him;
The ^bworm feeds sweetly
till he is remembered
^cno more.
And wickedness will be
broken ^dlike a tree.

21 ^aJob 22:9

21 "He wrongs the barren
woman,
And does no good for ^athe
widow.

22 ^aJob 9:4
^bJob 18:20

22 "But He drags off the valiant by ^aHis power;
He rises, but ^bno one has
assurance of life.

23 ^aJob 12:6
^bJob 10:4;
11:11

23 "He provides them ^awith
security, and they are
supported;
And His ^beyes are on their
ways.

24 ^aPs.
37:10 ^bJob
14:21

24 "They are exalted a ^alittle
while, then they are
gone;
Moreover, they are
^bbrought low and like
everything gathered
up;
Even like the heads of
grain they are cut off.

★25 ^aJob
6:28; 27:4

25 "Now if it is not so, ^awho
can prove me a liar,
And make my speech
worthless?"

P   Bildad's Third Speech, 25:1-6

★ 1-6

2 ^aJob 9:4;
36:5, 22;
37:23; 42:2
^bJob 16:19;
31:2

25 Then Bildad the Shuhite
answered,
2 "^aDominion and awe belong to Him
Who establishes peace in
^bHis heights.

3 ^aJob
16:13

3 "Is there any number to
^aHis troops?
And upon whom does His
light not rise?

4 ^aJob
4:17; 9:2
^bJob 14:4

4 "How then can a man be
^ajust with God?

Or how can he be ^bclean
who is born of
woman?

5 ^aJob
31:26 ^bJob
15:15

5 "If even ^athe moon has no
brightness
And the ^bstars are not pure
in His sight,

6 ^aJob 7:17
^bJob 17:14

6 How much less ^aman, *that*
^bmaggot,
And the son of man, *that*
worm!"

Q   Job's Third Reply to Bildad, 26:1-14

★ 1-4

2 ^aJob
6:11, 12
^bPs. 71:9

26 Then Job responded,
2 "What a help you
are to ^athe weak!
How you have saved the
arm   ^bwithout
strength!

3 "What counsel you have
given to *one* without
wisdom!
What helpful insight you
have abundantly pro-
vided!

4 "To whom have you uttered
words?
And whose spirit was ex-
pressed through you?

5 ^aJob
3:13; Ps.
88:10

5 "The ^adeparted spirits
tremble
Under the waters and their
inhabitants.

★ 6 ^aJob
9:5-10; 26:6-
14; 38:17;
41:11 ^bJob
28:22; 31:12

6 "Naked is ^aSheol before
Him
And ^bAbaddon has no
covering.

★ 7 ^aJob
9:8

7 "He ^astretches out the north
over empty space,
And hangs the earth on
nothing.

★ 8 ^aJob
37:11; Prov.
30:4

8 "He ^awraps up the waters in
His clouds;
And the cloud does not
burst under them.

24:25 Job challenges his friends to disagree with
him.
25:1-6 Bildad does not attempt to prove Job
wrong but simply declares that Job is presumptuous in thinking he can argue with God.
On verse 4 see note on 9:2.
26:1-4 Job sarcastically accuses Bildad of not
having an original thought in his head!

26:6 *Abaddon.* The place of destruction, a synonym for Sheol.
26:7 A remarkable description of what we now
know to be a scientifically accurate description
of the earth.
26:8 Here may be a reference to the same state
described in Gen. 1:7.

★ **9** *a* Job 22:14; Ps. 97:2; 105:39

9 "He ^aobscures the face of the full moon,
And spreads His cloud over it.

10 *a* Job 38:1–11; Prov. 8:29 *b* Job 38:19, 20, 24

10 "He has inscribed a ^acircle on the surface of the waters,
At the ^bboundary of light and darkness.

11 "The pillars of heaven tremble,
And are amazed at His rebuke.

★**12** *a* Is. 51:15; Jer. 31:35 *b* Job 12:13 *c* Job 9:13

12 "He ^aquieted the sea with His power,
And by His ^bunderstanding He shattered ^cRahab.

★**13** *a* Job 9:8 *b* Is. 27:1

13 "By His breath the ^aheavens are cleared;
His hand has pierced ^bthe fleeing serpent.

★**14** *a* Job 4:12 *b* Job 36:29; 37:4, 5

14 "Behold, these are the fringes of His ways;
And how faint ^aa word we hear of Him!
But His mighty ^bthunder, who can understand?"

R Job's Last Reply to his Friends, 27:1–31:40

1 A protestation of innocence, 27:1–23

1 *a* Job 13:12; 29:1

27 Then Job continued his ^adiscourse and said,

2 *a* Job 16:11; 34:5 *b* Job 9:18

2 "As God lives, ^awho has taken away my right,
And the Almighty, ^bwho has embittered my soul,

3 For as long as life is in me,
And the ^abreath of God is in my nostrils,

★ **3** *a* Job 32:8; 33:4

4 My lips certainly will not speak unjustly,
Nor will ^amy tongue mutter deceit.

4 *a* Job 6:28; 33:3

5 "Far be it from me that I should declare you right;
Till I die ^aI will not put away my integrity from me.

5 *a* Job 6:29

6 "I ^ahold fast my righteousness and will not let it go.
My heart does not reproach any of my days.

6 *a* Job 2:3; 13:18

7 "May my enemy be as the wicked,
And my opponent as the unjust.

8 "For what is ^athe hope of the godless when he is cut off,
When God requires ^bhis life?

★ **8-23**

8 *a* Job 8:13; 11:20 *b* Job 12:10

9 "Will God ^ahear his cry,
When ^bdistress comes upon him?

9 *a* Job 35:12, 13; Ps. 18:41; Prov. 1:28; Is. 1:15; Jer. 14:12; Mic. 3:4 *b* Prov. 1:27

10 "Will he take ^adelight in the Almighty,
Will he call on God at all times?

10 *a* Job 22:26, 27; Ps. 37:4; Is. 58:14

11 "I will instruct you in the power of God;
What is with the Almighty I will not conceal.

12 "Behold, all of you have seen *it*;

26:9 *full moon* (or throne). The meaning is that God veils the heavens with clouds.
26:12 *Rahab.* A figurative expression for pride. See note on 9:13.
26:13 *By His breath.* I.e., the wind blows away the storm clouds so the *heavens are cleared.*
26:14 Job's magnificent conclusion is this: how much knowledge of God there is beyond what we can see and hear.
27:3 Job declares he will maintain his innocence until death.
27:8-23 Some think this is Zophar's third speech (though he is not introduced by name), and others that Job is sarcastically arguing Zophar's case for him (cf. chap. 20). This may in

fact be Job's less pressured acknowledgment that the wicked do not always or ultimately prosper, though they may for a time. They will be condemned (v. 8), they have no present help from God (vv. 9–10), they cannot be assured of passing on their prosperity to their children (vv. 14–18). The *widows* of verse 15 are the widows of the sons killed by the plague, and they enjoy no lasting prosperity (vv. 18–23). *as a hut which the watchman has made* (v. 18). A flimsy shelter of boughs, made by a watchman in the vineyard. Destruction comes on the wicked man suddenly (v. 19). *clap their hands* (v. 23). A sign of indignation (Num. 24:10).

Why then do you act foolishly?

13 aJob 20:29 bJob 15:20

13 "This is athe portion of a wicked man from God,
And the inheritance which btyrants receive from the Almighty.

14 aJob 15:22; 18:19 bJob 20:10

14 "Though his sons are many, they are destined afor the sword;
And his bdescendants will not be satisfied with bread.

15 aPs. 78:64

15 "His survivors will be buried because of the plague,
And their awidows will not be able to weep.

16 "Though he piles up silver like dust,
And prepares garments as plentiful as the clay;

17 aJob 20:18-21

17 He may prepare it, abut the just will wear it,
And the innocent will divide the silver.

18 aJob 8:15; 18:14

18 "He has built his ahouse like the spider's web,
Or as a hut which the watchman has made.

19 aJob 7:8; 21; 20:7

19 "He lies down rich, but never again;
He opens his eyes, and ait is no more.

20 aJob 15:21 bJob 20:8; 34:20

20 "aTerrors overtake him like a flood;
A tempest steals him away bin the night.

21 aJob 21:18 bJob 7:10

21 "The east awind carries him away, and he is gone,
For it whirls him baway from his place.

22 aJer. 13:14; Ezek. 5:11; 24:14 bJob 11:20

22 "For it will hurl at him awithout sparing;
He will surely try to bflee from its power.

23 aJob 18:18; 20:8

23 "Men will clap their hands at him,
And will ahiss him from his place.

2 A pronouncement concerning wisdom, 28:1-28

28 "Surely there is a mine for silver,
And a place where they refine gold.
2 "Iron is taken from the dust,
And from rock copper is smelted.

3 aEccl. 1:13

3 "Man puts an end to darkness,
And ato the farthest limit he searches out
The rock in gloom and deep shadow.

★ 4

4 "He sinks a shaft far from habitation,
Forgotten by the foot;
They hang and swing to and fro far from men.
5 "The earth, from it comes food,
And underneath it is turned up as fire.

★ 6-11

6 "Its rocks are the source of sapphires,
And its dust contains gold.
7 "The path no bird of prey knows,
Nor has the falcon's eye caught sight of it.
8 "The proud beasts have not trodden it,
Nor has the fierce lion passed over it.
9 "He puts his hand on the flint;
He overturns the mountains at the base.
10 "He hews out channels through the rocks;
And his eye sees anything precious.
11 "He dams up the streams from flowing;
And what is hidden he brings out to the light.

12 aJob 28:23, 28; Eccl. 7:24

12 "But awhere can wisdom be found?

28:4 The verse apparently describes descent into a mine shaft by means of a swinging basket.
28:6-11 Man with his ingenuity has unearthed the treasures of the earth, but he cannot find wisdom (vv. 12-14).

And where is the place of
understanding?

13 a Matt.
13:44-46

13 "ªMan does not know its
value,
Nor is it found in the land
of the living.

14 "The deep says, 'It is not in
me';
And the sea says, 'It is not
with me.'

15 a Prov.
3:13, 14;
8:10, 11;
16:16

15 "ªPure gold cannot be given
in exchange for it,
Nor can silver be weighed
as its price.

★**16**

16 "It cannot be valued in the
gold of Ophir,
In precious onyx, or sap-
phire.

17 a Prov.
8:10; 16:16

17 "ªGold or glass cannot
equal it,
Nor can it be exchanged
for articles of fine
gold.

18 a Prov.
8:11

18 "Coral and crystal are not to
be mentioned;
And the acquisition of
ªwisdom is above *that
of* pearls.

19 a Prov.
8:19

19 "The topaz of Ethiopia cannot equal it,
Nor can it be valued in
ªpure gold.

20 a Job
28:23, 28

20 "ªWhere then does wisdom
come from?
And where is the place of
understanding?

21 "Thus it is hidden from the
eyes of all living,
And concealed from the
birds of the sky.

22 a Job
26:6; Prov.
8:32-36

22 "ªAbaddon and Death say,
'With our ears we have
heard a report of it.'

23 a Job 9:4;
Prov. 8:22-36

23 "ªGod understands its way;
And He knows its place.

24 a Ps. 11:4;
33:13, 14;
66:7; Prov.
15:3

24 "For He ªlooks to the ends
of the earth,
And sees everything under
the heavens.

25 "When He imparted
ªweight to the wind,
And ᵇmeted out the waters
by measure,

★**25** a Ps.
135:7 ᵇ Job
12:15; 38:8-
11

26 When He set a ªlimit for
the rain,
And a course for the
ᵇthunderbolt,

26 a Job
37:6, 11, 12;
38:26-28
ᵇ Job 37:3;
38:25

27 Then He saw it and declared it;
He established it and also
searched it out.

28 "And to man He said, 'Behold, the ªfear of the
Lord, that is wisdom;
And to depart from evil is
understanding.'"

★**28** a Ps.
111:10; Prov.
1:7; 9:10;
Eccl. 12:13

3 A panorama of his life,
     29:1-31:40

29 And Job again took up his
ªdiscourse and said,

1 a Num.
23:7; 24:3;
Job 13:12;
27:1

2 "Oh that I were as in
months gone by,
As in the days when God
ªwatched over me;

2 a Jer.
31:28

3 When ªHis lamp shone
over my head,
And ᵇby His light I walked
through darkness;

3 a Job 18:6
ᵇ Job 11:17

4 As I was in the prime of
my days,
When the ªfriendship of
God *was* over my tent;

★ **4** a Job
15:8; Ps.
25:14; Prov.
3:32

5 When the Almighty was
yet with me,
And my children were
around me;

6 When my steps were
bathed in ªbutter,
And the ᵇrock poured out
for me streams of oil!

★ **6** a Deut.
32:14; Job
20:17 ᵇ Deut.
32:13; Ps.
81:16

7 "When I went out to ªthe
gate of the city,
When I took my seat in
the square;

7 a Job
31:21

8 The young men saw me
and hid themselves,

28:16 *Ophir.* See note on 1 Kings 9:28.
28:25 God controls all the elements of nature, of which the *wind* and *waters* are examples.
28:28 True wisdom is fearing (showing holy respect and reverence for) God and shunning evil.
29:4 *the prime of my days.* Before his tribula-

tion, Job had reached the autumn of his life.
the friendship of God. Lit., the counsel of God (guided his home). Job, recalling the happiness of those days, recognizes that it centered in his fellowship with God.
29:6 Hyperbolic expressions of the abundance which Job enjoyed.

And the old men arose *and* stood.

9 "The princes ^astopped talking,
　And ^bput *their* hands on their mouths;

10 The voice of the nobles was ^ahushed,
　And their ^btongue stuck to their palate.

11 "For when ^athe ear heard, it called me blessed;
　And when the eye saw, it gave witness of me,

12 Because I delivered ^athe poor who cried for help,
　And the ^borphan who had no helper.

13 "The blessing of the one ^aready to perish came upon me,
　And I made the ^bwidow's heart sing for joy.

14 "I ^aput on righteousness, and it clothed me;
　My justice was like a robe and a turban.

15 "I was ^aeyes to the blind,
　And feet to the lame.

16 "I was a father to ^athe needy,
　And I investigated the case which I did not know.

17 "And I ^abroke the jaws of the wicked,
　And snatched the prey from his teeth.

18 "Then I thought, 'I shall die in my nest,
　And I shall multiply *my* days as the sand.

19 'My ^aroot is spread out to the waters,
　And ^bdew lies all night on my branch.

20 'My glory is *ever* new with me,
　And my ^abow is renewed in my hand.'

21 "To me ^athey listened and waited,

And kept silent for my counsel.

22 "After my words they did not ^aspeak again,
　And ^bmy speech dropped on them.

23 "And they waited for me as for the rain,
　And opened their mouth as for the spring rain.

24 "I smiled on them when they did not believe,
　And the light of my face they did not cast down.

25 "I chose a way for them and sat as ^achief,
　And dwelt as a king among the troops,
　As one who ^bcomforted the mourners.

30 "But now those younger than I ^amock me,
　Whose fathers I disdained to put with the dogs of my flock.

2 "Indeed, what *good was* the strength of their hands to me?
　Vigor had perished from them.

3 "From want and famine they are gaunt
　Who gnaw the dry ground by night in waste and desolation,

4 Who pluck mallow by the bushes,
　And whose food is the root of the broom shrub.

5 "They are driven from the community;
　They shout against them as *against* a thief,

6 So that they dwell in dreadful valleys,
　In holes of the earth and of the rocks.

7 "Among the bushes they cry out;
　Under the nettles they are gathered together.

Marginal references:

9 ^aJob 29:21 ^bJob 21:5
10 ^aJob 29:22 ^bPs. 137:6
★12 ^aJob 24:4, 9; 34:28; Ps. 72:12; Prov. 21:13 ^bJob 31:17, 21
13 ^aJob 31:19 ^bJob 22:9
14 ^aJob 27:5, 6; Ps. 132:9; Is. 59:17; 61:10; Eph. 6:14
15 ^aNum. 10:31
16 ^aJob 24:4; Prov. 29:7
17 ^aPs. 3:7
19 ^aJer. 17:8 ^bHos. 14:5
20 ^aGen. 49:24; Ps. 18:34
21 ^aJob 4:3; 29:9
22 ^aJob 29:10 ^bDeut. 32:2
★24
25 ^aJob 1:3; 31:37 ^bJob 4:4; 16:5
★ 1-15
1 ^aJob 12:4

29:12 Job denies the charge that he oppressed the poor (20:19; 22:6-9).
29:24 The meaning is this: people looked to Job with such great deference that they could not believe he would smile on them.
30:1-15 The lowest people whom he had befriended (29:11-17), now insult him.

8 "Fools, even those without a
name,
They were scourged from
the land.

9 aJob 12:4
bJob 17:6;
Ps. 69:11;
Lam. 3:14,
63

9 "And now I have become
their ataunt,
I have even become a bby-
word to them.

10 aNum.
12:14; Deut.
25:9; Job
17:6; Is.
50:6; Matt.
26:67

10 "They abhor me *and* stand
aloof from me,
And they do not refrain
from aspitting at my
face.

11 aRuth
1:21; Ps.
88:7 bPs.
32:9

11 "Because He has loosed His
bowstring and aaf-
flicted me,
They have cast off bthe
bridle before me.

12 aPs.
140:4, 5
bJob 19:12

12 "On the right hand their
brood arises;
They athrust aside my feet
band build up against
me their ways of de-
struction.

13 aIs. 3:12

13 "They abreak up my path,
They profit from my de-
struction,
No one restrains them.

14 "As *through* a wide breach
they come,
Amid the tempest they roll
on.

15 aJob
3:25; 31:23;
Ps. 55:3-5
bJob 7:9;
Hos. 13:3

15 "aTerrors are turned against
me,
They pursue my honor as
the wind,
And my prosperity has
passed away blike a
cloud.

16 a1 Sam.
1:15; Job
3:24; Ps.
22:14; 42:4;
Is. 53:12

16 "And now amy soul is
poured out within me;
Days of affliction have
seized me.

17 aJob
30:30

17 "At night it pierces amy
bones within me,
And my gnawing *pains*
take no rest.

★18 aJob
2:7

18 "By a great force my garment is adistorted;
It binds me about as the
collar of my coat.

19 aPs. 69:2,
14

19 "He has cast me into the
amire,
And I have become like
dust and ashes.

20 aJob 19:7

20 "I acry out to Thee for help,
but Thou dost not an-
swer me;
I stand up, and Thou dost
turn Thy attention
against me.

21 aJob
10:3; 16:9,
14; 19:6, 22

21 "Thou hast become cruel to
me;
With the might of Thy
hand Thou dost aper-
secute me.

22 aJob
9:17; 27:21

22 "Thou dost alift me up to
the wind *and* cause
me to ride;
And Thou dost dissolve
me in a storm.

23 aJob
9:22; 10:8
bJob 3:19;
Eccl. 12:5

23 "For I know that Thou awilt
bring me to death
And to the bhouse of
meeting for all living.

24 aJob 19:7

24 "Yet does not one in a heap
of ruins stretch out *his*
hand,
Or in his disaster therefore
acry out for help?

25 aPs.
35:13, 14;
Rom. 12:15
bJob 24:4

25 "Have I not awept for the
one whose life is
hard?
Was not my soul grieved
for bthe needy?

26 aJob
3:25, 26; Jer.
8:15 bJob
19:8

26 "When I aexpected good,
then evil came;
When I waited for light,
bthen darkness came.

★27 aLam.
2:11

27 "I am seething awithin, and
cannot relax;
Days of affliction confront
me.

28 aJob
30:31; Ps.
38:6; 42:9;
43:2 bJob
19:7

28 "I go about amourning
without comfort;
I stand up in the assembly
and bcry out for help.

★29 aPs.
44:19; Mic.
1:8

29 "I have become a brother to
ajackals,
And a companion of os-
triches.

★30 aJob
2:7 bPs.
102:3

30 "My askin turns black on
me,

30:18 Some understand this verse to mean that
Job's clothes hung loosely over his emaciated
body; others, that because of Job's writhing in
pain, his clothes became twisted about him.
Clearly, his physical torment was great.
30:27 *I am seething within.* Not a reference to
his disease, but to the turmoil of his inner
feelings.
30:29 Job's wails were akin to those of the *jackals* and *ostriches.*
30:30 *on me.* Lit., from upon me; i.e., his skin
was peeling.

And my [b]bones burn with fever.

31 "Therefore my [a]harp is turned to mourning,
And my flute to the sound of those who weep.

31 "I have made a covenant with my [a]eyes;
How then could I gaze at a virgin?

2 "And what is [a]the portion of God from above
Or the heritage of the Almighty from on high?

3 "Is it not [a]calamity to the unjust,
And disaster to [b]those who work iniquity?

4 "Does He not [a]see my ways,
And [b]number all my steps?

5 "If I have [a]walked with falsehood,
And my foot has hastened after deceit,

6 Let Him [a]weigh me with accurate scales,
And let God know [b]my integrity.

7 "If my step has [a]turned from the way,
Or my heart followed my eyes,
Or if any [b]spot has stuck to my hands,

8 Let me [a]sow and another eat,
And let my [b]crops be uprooted.

9 "If my heart has been [a]enticed by a woman,
Or I have lurked at my neighbor's doorway,

10 May my wife [a]grind for another,
And let [b]others kneel down over her.

11 "For that would be a [a]lustful crime;

Moreover, it would be [b]an iniquity *punishable by* judges.

12 "For it would be [a]fire that consumes to [b]Abaddon,
And would [c]uproot all my increase.

13 "If I have [a]despised the claim of my male or female slaves
When they filed a complaint against me,

14 What then could I do when God arises,
And when He calls me to account, what will I answer Him?

15 "Did not [a]He who made me in the womb make him,
And the same one fashion us in the womb?

16 "If I have kept [a]the poor from *their* desire,
Or have caused the eyes of [b]the widow to fail,

17 Or have [a]eaten my morsel alone,
And [b]the orphan has not shared it

18 (But from my youth he grew up with me as with a father,
And from infancy I guided her),

19 If I have seen anyone perish [a]for lack of clothing,
Or that [b]the needy had no covering,

20 If his loins have not thanked me,
And if he has not been warmed with the fleece of my sheep,

21 If I have lifted up my hand against [a]the orphan,

31:1 Job once again declares his innocence: in his personal life (vv. 1–12), toward his neighbors (vv. 13–23), and toward God (vv. 24–34). In verses 1–12 he disclaims lust (v. 1), deceit (v. 5), and covetousness (v. 7).
31:10 *May my wife grind for another.* The low-est slave did the grinding (Exod. 11:5).
31:21 *Because I saw I had support in the gate.* Though Job knew he could use his influence to pervert justice (the gate of the city was the place where disputes were adjudicated), he never did so.

Because I saw I had sup-
port ᵇin the gate,

22 Let my shoulder fall from
the socket,
And my ᵃarm be broken
off at the elbow.

23 "For ᵃcalamity from God is
a terror to me,
And because of ᵇHis maj-
esty I can do nothing.

24 "If I have put my confidence in ᵃgold,
And called fine gold my
trust,

25 If I have ᵃgloated because
my wealth was great,
And because my hand had
secured so much;

26 If I have ᵃlooked at the sun
when it shone,
Or the moon going in
splendor,

27 And my heart became secretly enticed,
And my hand threw a kiss
from my mouth,

28 That too would have been
ᵃan iniquity calling for
judgment,
For I would have ᵇdenied
God above.

29 "Have I ᵃrejoiced at the extinction of my enemy,
Or exulted when evil be-
fell him?

30 "No, ᵃI have not allowed my
mouth to sin
By asking for his life in ᵇa
curse.

31 "Have the men of my tent
not said,
'Who can find one who has
not been ᵃsatisfied
with his meat'?

32 "The alien has not lodged
outside,
For I have opened my
doors to the traveler.

33 "Have I ᵃcovered my transgressions like Adam,
By hiding my iniquity in
my bosom,

34 Because I ᵃfeared the great
multitude,
And the contempt of fam-
ilies terrified me,
And kept silent and did
not go out of doors?

35 "Oh that I had one to hear
me!
Behold, here is my signa-
ture;
ᵃLet the Almighty answer
me!
And the indictment which
my ᵇadversary has
written,

36 Surely I would carry it on
my shoulder;
I would bind it to myself
like a crown.

37 "I would declare to Him
ᵃthe number of my
steps;
Like ᵇa prince I would approach Him.

38 "If my ᵃland cries out
against me,
And its furrows weep to-
gether;

39 If I have ᵃeaten its fruit
without money,
Or have ᵇcaused its owners
to lose their lives,

40 Let ᵃbriars grow instead of
wheat,
And stinkweed instead of
barley."
The words of Job are ended.

Cross references (margin):

22 ᵃJob 38:15

23 ᵃJob 31:3 ᵇJob 13:11

24 ᵃJob 22:24; Mark 10:23-25

25 ᵃJob 1:3, 10; Ps. 62:10

★26-27
26 ᵃDeut. 4:19; 17:3; Ezek. 8:16

28 ᵃDeut. 17:2-7; Job 31:11 ᵇJosh. 24:27; Is. 59:13

29 ᵃProv. 17:5; 24:17; Obad. 12

30 ᵃPs. 7:4 ᵇJob 5:3

★31 ᵃJob 22:7

★33 ᵃGen. 3:10; Prov. 28:13

34 ᵃEx. 23:2

35 ᵃJob 19:7; 30:20, 24, 28; 35:14 ᵇJob 27:7

37 ᵃJob 31:4 ᵇJob 1:3; 29:25

38 ᵃJob 24:2

39 ᵃJob 24:6, 10-12; James 5:4 ᵇ1 Kin. 21:19

40 ᵃJob 32:13; Is. 5:6

31:26-27 Job disclaimed ever having become entangled in the pagan worship of heavenly bodies. Verse 27 refers to throwing a kiss of adoration.
31:31 The last part of the verse should read,
"Who hath not been satisfied with his flesh?"
I.e., the flesh of animals which Job provided
for food.

31:33 in my bosom. Lit., in my hiding place. The
verb form of the Hebrew word is found in
Gen. 3:8, 10, in relation to Adam's hiding from
God. Job had no secret sin to hide. Some understand Adam as referring not to the individual but to mankind in general.

S Elihu's Speeches, 32:1–37:24

1 His first speech, 32:1–33:33

1 aJob 10:7; 13:18; 27:5, 6; 31:6

32 Then these three men ceased answering Job, because he was ªrighteous in his own eyes.

★ **2** aGen. 22:21 bJob 27:5, 6 cJob 30:21

2 But the anger of Elihu the son of Barachel the ªBuzite, of the family of Ram burned; against Job his anger burned, bbecause he justified himself cbefore God.

3 And his anger burned against his three friends because they had found no answer, and yet had condemned Job.

4 Now Elihu had waited to speak to Job because they were years older than he.

5 And when Elihu saw that there was no answer in the mouth of the three men his anger burned.

6 aJob 15:10

6 So Elihu the son of Barachel the Buzite spoke out and said,

"I am young in years and you are ªold;
Therefore I was shy and afraid to tell you what I think.

7 aJob 8:8, 9

7 "I thought ªage should speak,
And increased years should teach wisdom.

★ **8-9**

8 aJob 33:4 bJob 38:36

8 "But it is a spirit in man,
And the ªbreath of the Almighty gives them bunderstanding.

9 aJob 32:7

9 "The abundant *in years* may not be wise,
Nor may ªelders understand justice.

10 "So I say, 'Listen to me,
I too will tell what I think.'

11 "Behold, I waited for your words,
I listened to your reasonings,

While you pondered what to say.

12 "I even paid close attention to you,
Indeed, there was no one who refuted Job,
Not one of you who answered his words.

13 aJer. 9:23

13 "Do not say,
'ªWe have found wisdom;
God will rout him, not man.'

14 "For he has not arranged *his* words against me;
Nor will I reply to him with your arguments.

15 "They are dismayed, they answer no more;
Words have failed them.

16 "And shall I wait, because they do not speak,
Because they stop *and* answer no more?

17 "I too will answer my share,
I also will tell my opinion.

18 "For I am full of words;
The spirit within me constrains me.

19 "Behold, my belly is like unvented wine,
Like new wineskins it is about to burst.

20 "Let me speak that I may get relief;
Let me open my lips and answer.

21 aLev. 19:15; Job 13:8, 10; 34:19

21 "Let me now ªbe partial to no one;
Nor flatter *any* man.

22 "For I do not know how to flatter,
Else my Maker would soon take me away.

33 "However now, Job, please ªhear my speech,
And listen to all my words.

1 aJob 13:6

2 "Behold now, I open my mouth,

32:2 *Elihu,* a descendant of Buz, the nephew of Abraham (Gen. 22:21), can restrain himself no longer from speaking, apparently having witnessed the entire confrontation between Job and his three friends. He had refrained from speaking because he was younger (v. 6). Since the older men had failed to convince Job (v.

12), he felt compelled to speak (v. 18).
32:8-9 Wisdom always comes from God, but not always from older men. Job's friends, Elihu declares, are obviously not wise, in spite of their age, since they failed to convince Job that his suffering was due to sin.

My tongue in my mouth
speaks.

3 "My words are *from* the uprightness of my heart;
And my lips speak
^aknowledge sincerely.

4 "The ^aSpirit of God has
made me,
And the ^bbreath of the Almighty gives me life.

5 "^aRefute me if you can;
Array yourselves before
me, take your stand.

6 "Behold, I belong to God
like you;
I too have been formed out
of the ^aclay.

7 "Behold, ^ano fear of me
should terrify you,
Nor should my pressure
weigh heavily on you.

8 "Surely you have spoken in
my hearing,
And I have heard the
sound of *your* words:

9 'I am ^apure, ^bwithout transgression;
I am innocent and there ^cis
no guilt in me.

10 'Behold, He invents pre-
texts against me;
He ^acounts me as His enemy.

11 'He ^aputs my feet in the
stocks;
He watches all my paths.'

12 "Behold, let me tell you,
^ayou are not right in
this,
For God is greater than
man.

13 "Why do you ^acomplain
against Him,
That He does not give an
account of all His do-
ings?

14 "Indeed ^aGod speaks once,
Or twice, *yet* no one no-
tices it.

15 "In a ^adream, a vision of the
night,
When sound sleep falls on
men,
While they slumber in
their beds,

16 Then ^aHe opens the ears
of men,
And seals their instruction,

17 That He may turn man
aside *from his* con-
duct,
And keep man from pride;

18 He ^akeeps back his soul
from the pit,
And his life from passing
over ^binto Sheol.

19 "Man is also chastened with
^apain on his bed,
And with unceasing com-
plaint in his bones;

20 So that his life ^aloathes
bread,
And his soul favorite food.

21 "His ^aflesh wastes away
from sight,
And his ^bbones which
were not seen stick
out.

22 "Then ^ahis soul draws near
to the pit,
And his life to those who
bring death.

23 "If there is an angel *as* ^ame-
diator for him,
One out of a thousand,
To remind a man what is
right for him,

24 Then let him be gracious
to him, and say,
'Deliver him from ^agoing
down to the pit,
I have found a ^bransom';

25 Let his flesh become fresh-
er than in youth,
Let him return to the days
of his youthful vigor;

26 Then he will ^apray to God,
and He will accept
him,

Cross references (left margin):

3 ^aJob
6:28; 27:4;
36:4

4 ^aGen.
2:7; Job
10:3; 32:8
^bJob 27:3

5 ^aJob
33:32

★ 6-7

6 ^aJob 4:19

7 ^aJob
13:21

★ 8-13

9 ^aJob
9:21; 10:7;
13:18; 16:17
^bJob 7:21;
13:23; 14:17
^cJob 10:14

10 ^aJob
13:24

11 ^aJob
13:27

12 ^aEccl.
7:20

13 ^aJob
40:2; Is. 45:9

★14-24
14 ^aJob
33:29; 40:5;
Ps. 62:11

Cross references (right margin):

15 ^aJob
4:12-17;
33:15-18

16 ^aJob
36:10, 15

18 ^aJob
33:22, 24,
28, 30 ^bJob
15:22

19 ^aJob
30:17

20 ^aJob
3:24; 6:7; Ps.
107:18

21 ^aJob 16:8
^bJob 19:20;
Ps. 22:17;
102:5

22 ^aJob
33:18, 28

23 ^aGen.
40:8

24 ^aJob
33:18, 28; Is.
38:17 ^bJob
36:18; Ps.
49:7

★25-28

26 ^aJob
22:27; 34:28;
Ps. 50:14, 15
^bJob 22:26

33:6-7 Elihu declares that since he is a man like
Job, his presence will not overpower Job with
terror (cf. 9:34; 13:21).
33:8-13 Elihu represents Job's position accurately and rebukes him for charging God with
hostility toward him.

33:14-24 God speaks to men through dreams
and visions (vv. 15-16), through pain (vv.
19-22), and through angels (v. 23).
33:25-28 The man who responds submissively
to God's dealings with him will regain health
and joy.

That [b]he may see His face
with joy,
And He may restore His
righteousness to man.

27 "He will sing to men and
say,
'I [a]have sinned and perverted what is right,
And it is not [b]proper for
me.

28 'He has redeemed my soul
from going to the pit,
And my life shall [a]see the
light.'

29 "Behold, God does [a]all
these oftentimes with
men,

30 To [a]bring back his soul
from the pit,
That he may be enlight-
ened with the light of
life.

31 "Pay attention, O Job, listen
to me;
Keep silent and let me
speak.

32 "Then if you have anything
to say, answer me;
Speak, for I desire to justify you.

33 "If not, [a]listen to me;
Keep silent, and I will
teach you wisdom."

2   His second speech, 34:1-37

34 Then Elihu continued and
said,

2 "Hear my words, you wise
men,
And listen to me, you who
know.

3 "For [a]the ear tests words,
As the palate tastes food.

4 "Let us choose for ourselves
what is right;
Let us know among our-
selves what is good.

5 "For Job has said, '[a]I am
righteous,
But [b]God has taken away
my right;

6 Should I lie concerning my
right?
My [a]wound is incurable,
though I am without
transgression.'

7 "What man is like Job,
Who [a]drinks up derision
like water,

8 Who goes [a]in company
with the workers of
iniquity,
And walks with wicked
men?

9 "For he has said, '[a]It profits
a man nothing
When he is pleased with
God.'

10 "Therefore, listen to me,
you men of under-
standing.
Far be it from God to [a]do
wickedness,
And from the Almighty to
do wrong.

11 "For He pays a man according to [a]his work,
And makes him find it ac-
cording to his way.

12 "Surely, [a]God will not act
wickedly,
And the Almighty will not
pervert justice.

13 "Who [a]gave Him authority
over the earth?
And who [b]has laid on Him
the whole world?

14 "If He should determine to
do so,
If He should [a]gather to
Himself His spirit and
His breath,

15 All [a]flesh would perish together,
And man would [b]return to
dust.

16 "But if you have understanding, hear this;
Listen to the sound of my
words.

Margin references

27 [a]2 Sam. 12:13; Luke 15:21 [b]Rom. 6:21
28 [a]Job 22:28
29 [a]Eph. 1:11; Phil. 2:13
30 [a]Job 33:18; Zech. 9:11
33 [a]Ps. 34:11
3 [a]Job 12:11
★ 5-9
5 [a]Job 13:18; 33:9 [b]Job 27:2
6 [a]Job 6:4
7 [a]Job 15:16
8 [a]Job 22:15
9 [a]Job 21:15; 35:3; Ps. 50:18
★10-28
10 [a]Gen. 18:25; Deut. 32:4; Job 8:3; 34:12; Rom. 9:14
11 [a]Job 34:25; Ps. 62:12; Prov. 24:12; Jer. 32:19; Ezek. 33:20; Matt. 16:27; Rom. 2:6; 2 Cor. 5:10; Rev. 22:12
12 [a]Job 34:10
13 [a]Job 38:4 [b]Job 38:5
14 [a]Job 12:10; Ps. 104:29; Eccl. 12:7
15 [a]Gen. 7:21; Job 9:22 [b]Gen. 3:19; Job 10:9

34:5-9 Again Elihu accurately represents Job's
contention that God has wronged an innocent
man (vv. 5-6) and that it is useless for a man
to be a friend of God, because the wicked
prosper and the righteous suffer (v. 9).
34:10-28 The theme of these verses is that God,
the Ruler of the universe, cannot be unjust.

17 *a*2 Sam.
23:3; Job
34:30 *b*Job
40:8

17 "Shall *a*one who hates justice rule?
And *b*will you condemn a
righteous mighty one,

18 Who says to a king,
'Worthless one,'
To nobles, 'Wicked ones';

19 *a*Lev.
19:15; Deut.
10:17; 2 Chr.
19:7; Acts
10:34; Rom.
2:11; Gal.
2:6; Eph. 6:9;
Col. 3:25;
1 Pet. 1:17
*b*Job 10:3

19 Who shows no *a*partiality
to princes,
Nor regards the rich above
the poor,
For they all are the *b*work
of His hands?

20 *a*Ex.
12:29; Job
34:25; 36:20
*b*Job 12:19

20 "In a moment they die, and
*a*at midnight
People are shaken and
pass away,
And *b*the mighty are taken
away without a hand.

21 *a*Job
24:23; 31:4;
Prov. 5:21;
15:3; Jer.
16:17

21 "For *a*His eyes are upon the
ways of a man,
And He sees all his steps.

22 *a*Ps.
139:11, 12;
Amos 9:2, 3

22 "There is *a*no darkness or
deep shadow
Where the workers of in-
iquity may hide them-
selves.

23 *a*Job
11:11

23 "For He does not *a*need to
consider a man fur-
ther,
That he should go before
God in judgment.

24 *a*Job
12:19

24 "He breaks in pieces
*a*mighty men without
inquiry,
And sets others in their
place.

25 *a*Job
34:11 *b*Job
34:20

25 "Therefore He *a*knows their
works,
And *b*He overthrows *them*
in the night,
And they are crushed.

26 *a*Ps. 9:5;
11:5

26 "He *a*strikes them like the
wicked
In a public place,

27 *a*1 Sam.
15:11 *b*Job
21:14

27 Because they *a*turned aside
from following Him,
And *b*had no regard for
any of His ways;

28 *a*Job
35:9; James
5:4 *b*Ex.
22:23; Job
22:27

28 So that they caused *a*the
cry of the poor to
come to Him,

And that He might *b*hear
the cry of the af-
flicted—

29 When He keeps quiet,
who then can con-
demn?
And when He hides His
face, who then can
behold Him,
That is, in regard to both
nation and man?—

30 *a*Job
5:15; 20:5;
34:17; Prov.
29:2-12

30 So that *a*godless men
should not rule,
Nor be snares of the peo-
ple.

31 "For has anyone said to
God,
'I have borne *chastisement*;
I will not offend *anymore*;

32 *a*Job
33:27

32 Teach Thou me what I do
not see;
If I have *a*done iniquity,
I will do it no more'?

33 *a*Job
41:11

33 "Shall He *a*recompense on
your terms, because
you have rejected *it*?
For you must choose, and
not I;
Therefore declare what
you know.

34 "Men of understanding will
say to me,
And a wise man who hears
me,

35 *a*Job
35:16; 38:2

35 'Job *a*speaks without
knowledge,
And his words are without
wisdom.

★36-37

36 *a*Job
22:15

36 'Job ought to be tried to the
limit,
Because he answers *a*like
wicked men.

37 *a*Job 23:2
*b*Job 27:23

37 'For he adds *a*rebellion to
his sin;
He *b*claps his hands among
us,
And multiplies his words
against God.' "

34:36-37 Elihu hopes that Job's trials will continue either until he recants or, if he does not

recant, until he dies.

3 *His third speech,* 35:1-16

★ 1-4

35 Then Elihu continued and said,

2 a Job 27:2

2 "Do you think this is according to ª justice?
Do you say, 'My righteousness is more than God's'?

3 a Job 34:9
b Job 9:30, 31

3 "For you say, 'ª What advantage will it be to You?
b What profit shall I have, more than if I had sinned?'

4 "I will answer you,
And your friends with you.

★ 5-8

5 a Gen. 15:5; Ps. 8:3
b Job 22:12

5 "ª Look at the heavens and see;
And behold b the clouds—they are higher than you.

6 a Job 7:20; Prov. 8:36; Jer. 7:19

6 "If you have sinned, ª what do you accomplish against Him?
And if your transgressions are many, what do you do to Him?

7 a Job 22:2, 3; Prov. 9:12; Luke 17:10; Rom. 11:35

7 "If you are righteous, ª what do you give to Him?
Or what does He receive from your hand?

8 "Your wickedness is for a man like yourself,
And your righteousness is for a son of man.

★ 9-16

9 a Ex. 2:23
b Job 12:19

9 "Because of the ª multitude of oppressions they cry out;
They cry for help because of the arm b of the mighty.

10 a Job 21:14; 27:10; 36:13; Is. 51:13 b Job 8:21; Ps. 42:8; 77:6; 149:5; Acts 16:25

10 "But ª no one says, 'Where is God my Maker,
Who b gives songs in the night,

11 a Job 36:22; Ps. 94:12; Jer. 32:33

11 Who ª teaches us more than the beasts of the earth,
And makes us wiser than the birds of the heavens?'

12 a Prov. 1:28

12 "There ª they cry out, but He does not answer
Because of the pride of evil men.

13 a Job 27:9; Prov. 15:29; Is. 1:15; Jer. 11:11; Mic. 3:4

13 "Surely ª God will not listen to an empty *cry*,
Nor will the Almighty regard it.

14 a Job 9:11; 23:8, 9 b Job 31:35

14 "How much less when ª you say you do not behold Him,
The b case is before Him, and you must wait for Him!

15 "And now, because He has not visited *in* His anger,
Nor has He acknowledged transgression well,

16 a Job 34:35; 38:2

16 So Job opens his mouth emptily;
He multiplies words ª without knowledge."

4 *His fourth speech,* 36:1-37:24

★ 1-23

36 Then Elihu continued and said,

2 "Wait for me a little, and I will show you
That there is yet more to be said in God's behalf.

3 a Job 8:3; 37:23

3 "I will fetch my knowledge from afar,
And I will ascribe ª righteousness to my Maker.

4 a Job 33:3 b Job 37:16

4 "For truly ª my words are not false;
One who is b perfect in knowledge is with you.

35:1-4 Elihu states Job's complaint that godliness avails a man nothing.
35:5-8 Elihu declares that God is too lofty to be affected either by godliness or ungodliness, which only affect other people (v. 8).
35:9-16 Elihu states his belief that unanswered prayer—even that of a righteous man—is due to lack of faith (v. 10) and to the emptiness of the prayer (v. 13; cf. James 4:3).

36:1-23 Elihu extols the greatness and providence of God, urging Job to recognize God's purpose in his sufferings and to join with others in exalting Him. Verse 18b means, "Don't let the greatness of your afflictions (*ransom*) keep you from accepting them. Submit to whatever God requires." In verse 21 Elihu accuses Job of rebelling, rather than submitting to his affliction in meekness.

5 aPs.
22:24; 69:33;
102:17 bJob
12:13

6 aJob
8:22; 34:26
bJob 5:15

7 aPs.
33:18; 34:15
bJob 5:11;
Ps. 113:8

8 aJob
36:15, 21

9 aJob
15:25

10 aJob
33:16; 36:15
b2 Kin.
17:13; Job
36:21; Jon.
3:8

11 a1 Tim.
4:8 bPs.
16:11

12 aJob
15:22 bJob
4:21

14 aDeut.
23:17

15 aJob
36:8, 21
bJob 36:10

5 "Behold, God is mighty but
    does not adespise *any*;
    He is bmighty in strength
    of understanding.
6 "He does not akeep the
    wicked alive,
    But gives justice to bthe af-
    flicted.
7 "He does not awithdraw His
    eyes from the right-
    eous;
    But bwith kings on the
    throne
    He has seated them for-
    ever, and they are ex-
    alted.
8 "And if they are bound in
    fetters,
    And are caught in the
    cords of aaffliction,
9 Then he declares to them
    their work
    And their transgressions,
    that they have amag-
    nified themselves.
10 "And aHe opens their ear to
    instruction,
    And bcommands that they
    return from evil.
11 "If they hear and serve
    Him,
    They shall aend their days
    in prosperity,
    And their years in bplea-
    sures.
12 "But if they do not hear,
    they shall perish aby
    the sword,
    And they shall bdie with-
    out knowledge.
13 "But the godless in heart lay
    up anger;
    They do not cry for help
    when He binds them.
14 "They die in youth,
    And their life *perishes*
    among the acult pros-
    titutes.
15 "He delivers the afflicted in
    their aaffliction,
    And bopens their ear in
    time of oppression.

16 "Then indeed, He aenticed
    you from the mouth
    of distress,
    Instead of it, a broad place
    with no constraint;
    And that which was set on
    your table was full of
    fatness.
17 "But you were full of ajudg-
    ment on the wicked;
    Judgment and justice take
    hold *of you.*
18 "*Beware* lest awrath entice
    you to scoffing;
    And do not let the great-
    ness of the bransom
    turn you aside.
19 "Will your riches keep *you*
    from distress,
    Or all the forces of *your*
    strength?
20 "Do not long for athe night,
    When people vanish in
    their place.
21 "Be careful, do anot turn to
    evil;
    For you have preferred this
    to baffliction.
22 "Behold, God is exalted in
    His power;
    Who is a ateacher like
    Him?
23 "Who has appointed Him
    His way,
    And who has said, 'aThou
    hast done wrong'?
24 "Remember that you
    should aexalt His
    work,
    Of which men have bsung.
25 "All men have seen it;
    Man beholds from afar.
26 "Behold, God is aexalted,
    and bwe do not know
    Him;
    The cnumber of His years
    is unsearchable.
27 "For aHe draws up the
    drops of water,
    They distill rain from the
    mist,

16 aHos.
2:14

17 aJob
22:5, 10, 11

18 aJon. 4:4,
9 bJob 33:24

20 aJob
34:20, 25

21 aJob
36:10; Ps.
31:6; 66:18
bJob 36:8,
15; Heb.
11:25

22 aJob
35:11

23 aDeut.
32:4; Job 8:3

24 aPs. 92:5;
Rev. 15:3
bEx. 15:1;
Judg. 5:1;
1 Chr. 16:9;
Ps. 59:16;
138:5
★36:26-
37:13

26 aJob
11:7-9; 37:23
b1 Cor.
13:12 cJob
10:5; Ps.
90:2; 102:24,
27; Heb.
1:12

27 aJob
5:10; 36:26-
29; 37:6, 11;
38:28; Ps.
147:8

36:26-37:13 These phenomena of nature witness to the greatness of God: (1) the rain cycle
of evaporation and precipitation (36:27-28); (2)
thunderstorms (36:29-37:4); (3) snow and ice
(37:5-10); and (4) the clouds (37:11-13).

28 Which the clouds pour
down,
They drip upon man
abundantly.

29 "Can anyone understand
the ªspreading of the
clouds,
The ᵇthundering of His pavilion?

★30 30 "Behold, He spreads His
lightning about Him,
And He covers the depths
of the sea.

31 "For by these He ªjudges
peoples;
He ᵇgives food in abun-
dance.

32 "He covers *His* hands with
the lightning,
And ªcommands it to
strike the mark.

33 "Its ªnoise declares His
presence;
The cattle also, concerning
what is coming up.

37 "At this also my heart
trembles,
And leaps from its place.

2 "Listen closely to the ªthunder of His voice,
And the rumbling that
goes out from His
mouth.

3 "Under the whole heaven
He lets it loose,
And His lightning to the
ªends of the earth.

4 "After it, a voice roars;
He thunders with His ma-
jestic voice;
And He does not restrain
the lightnings when
His voice is heard.

5 "God ªthunders with His
voice wondrously,
Doing ᵇgreat things which
we cannot compre-
hend.

6 "For to ªthe snow He says,
'Fall on the earth,'
And to the ᵇdownpour and
the rain, 'Be strong.'

7 "He ªseals the hand of ev-
ery man,
That ᵇall men may know
His work.

8 "Then the beast goes into
its ªlair,
And remains in its den.

9 "Out of the ªsouth comes
the storm,
And out of the north the
cold.

10 "From the breath of God
ªice is made,
And the expanse of the
waters is frozen.

11 "Also with moisture He
ªloads the thick cloud;
He ᵇdisperses ᶜthe cloud of
His lightning.

12 "And it changes direction,
turning around by His
guidance,
That it may do whatever
He ªcommands it
On the ᵇface of the inhabited earth.

13 "Whether for ªcorrection,
or for ᵇHis world,
Or for ᶜlovingkindness, He
causes it to happen.

14 "Listen to this, O Job,
Stand and consider the
wonders of God.

15 "Do you know how God establishes them,
And makes the lightning
of His cloud to shine?

16 "Do you know about the
layers of the thick
clouds,
The ªwonders of one ᵇper-
fect in knowledge,

17 You whose garments are
hot,
When the land is still because of the south
wind?

18 "Can you, with Him,
ªspread out the skies,
Strong as a molten mirror?

36:30 *And He covers the depths of the sea.* The
sea may refer to the masses of thunderclouds
in the heavens which enshroud God, or it may
refer to the sea on earth which is drawn up

into the clouds by evaporation.
37:14-24 Elihu appeals to Job to consider reverently the wonders of God's creation and to
turn from his rebellious ways.

Marginal references (left column):

29 ªJob 37:11, 16
ᵇJob 26:14

★30

31 ªJob 37:13 ᵇPs. 104:27; 136:25; Acts 14:17

32 ªJob 37:11, 12, 15

33 ªJob 37:2

2 ªJob 36:33; 37:4, 5; Ps. 29:3-9

3 ªJob 28:24; 37:11, 12; 38:13

5 ªJob 26:14 ᵇJob 5:9; 37:14, 16, 23

6 ªJob 38:22 ᵇJob 36:27

Marginal references (right column):

7 ªJob 12:14 ᵇPs. 111:2

8 ªJob 38:40; Ps. 104:21, 22

9 ªJob 9:9

10 ªJob 38:29; Ps. 147:17

11 ªJob 36:27 ᵇJob 36:29 ᶜJob 37:15

12 ªJob 36:32; Ps. 148:8 ᵇIs. 14:21; 27:6

13 ªEx. 9:18, 23; 1 Sam. 12:18, 19 ᵇJob 38:26, 27 ᶜ1 Kin. 18:41-46

★14-24

16 ªJob 37:5, 14, 23 ᵇJob 36:4

18 ªJob 9:8; Ps. 104:2; Is. 44:24; 45:12; Jer. 10:12; Zech. 12:1

19 *a*Job
9:14; Rom.
8:26

19 "Teach us what we shall say
to Him;
We *a*cannot arrange *our
case* because of dark-
ness.

20 "Shall it be told Him that I
would speak?
Or should a man say that
he would be swal-
lowed up?

21 "And now men do not see
the light which is
bright in the skies;
But the wind has passed
and cleared them.

22 "Out of the north comes
golden *splendor;*
Around God is awesome
majesty.

23 *a*Job
11:7, 8; Rom.
11:33; 1 Tim.
6:16 *b*Job
9:4; 36:5 *c*Is.
63:9; Lam.
3:33; Ezek.
18:23, 32;
33:11 *d*Job
8:3

23 "The Almighty—*a*we cannot find Him;
He is *b*exalted in power;
And *c*He will not do violence *d*to justice and
abundant righteous-
ness.

24 *a*Matt.
10:28 *b*Job
5:13; Matt.
11:25; 1 Cor.
1:26

24 "Therefore men *a*fear Him;
He does not *b*regard any
who are wise of
heart."

T   God's Speeches, 38:1–42:6
*1   God's first speech: His
knowledge,* 38:1–40:2

★ 1 *a*Job
40:6

38 Then the LORD *a*answered
Job out of the whirlwind
and said,

★ 2 *a*Job
35:16; 42:3

2 "Who is this that *a*darkens
counsel
By words without knowl-
edge?

★ 3 *a*Job
40:7 *b*Job
42:4

3 "Now *a*gird up your loins
like a man,
And *b*I will ask you, and
you instruct Me!

4 *a*Job
15:7; Ps.
104:5; Prov.
8:29; 30:4

4 "Where were you *a*when I
laid the foundation of
the earth!

Tell *Me,* if you have understanding,

5 Who set its *a*measure-
ments, since you
know?
Or who stretched the line
on it?

5 *a*Prov.
8:29; Is.
40:12

6 "On what *a*were its bases
sunk?
Or who laid its corner-
stone,

6 *a*Job 26:7

7 When the morning stars
sang together,
And all the *a*sons of God
shouted for joy?

★ 7 *a*Job
1:6

8 "Or *who* *a*enclosed the sea
with doors,
When, bursting forth, it
went out from the
womb;

8 *a*Gen.
1:9; Ps.
104:6-9;
Prov. 8:29;
Jer. 5:22

9 When I made a cloud its
garment,
And thick darkness its
swaddling band,

10 And I *a*placed boundaries
on it,
And I set a bolt and doors,

10 *a*Gen.
1:9; Ps. 33:7;
104:9; Prov.
8:29; Jer.
5:22

11 And I said, 'Thus far you
shall come, but no
farther;
And here shall your proud
waves stop'?

12 "Have you ever in your life
commanded the
morning,
And caused the dawn to
know its place;

13 That it might take hold of
*a*the ends of the earth,
And *b*the wicked be
shaken out of it?

★13 *a*Job
28:24; 37:3
*b*Job 34:25,
26; 36:6

14 "It is changed like clay *under* the seal;
And they stand forth like a
garment.

★14

15 "And *a*from the wicked
their light is withheld,

15 *a*Job 5:14
*b*Num.
15:30; Ps
10:15; 37:17

38:1 Finally God breaks His silence and speaks
to Job directly.
38:2 How absurd to think that a creature should
become the critic of the Creator.
38:3 *like a man.* Heb., *geber,* denoting man in
his strength as a combatant. God accepts Job's
challenge (9:34; 10:2ff.; 13:3; 23:3ff.; 31:35ff.).
38:7 Stars and angels (*sons of God,* see note on

1:6) joined in praise when the earth was created.
38:13 Personified dawn is represented as taking
the cover of darkness off the earth and shaking the wicked out of it like dust.
38:14 When dawn comes, the dark earth stands
out in clear relief as shapeless clay does when
stamped with a seal.

And the ^buplifted arm is broken.

16 aGen. 7:11; 8:2; Prov. 8:24, 28

16 "Have you entered into ^athe springs of the sea?
Or have you walked in the recesses of the deep?

17 aJob 10:21; 26:6; 34:22

17 "Have the gates of death been revealed to you?
Or have you seen the gates of ^adeep darkness?

18 aJob 28:24

18 "Have you understood the expanse of ^athe earth?
Tell *Me*, if you know all this.

19 "Where is the way to the dwelling of light?
And darkness, where is its place,

20 aJob 26:10

20 That you may take it to ^aits territory,
And that you may discern the paths to its home?

★21 aJob 15:7

21 "You know, for ^ayou were born then,
And the number of your days is great!

★22-30

22 aJob 37:6 bEx. 9:18; Josh. 10:11; Is. 30:30; Ezek. 13:11, 13; Rev. 16:21

22 "Have you entered the storehouses ^aof the snow,
Or have you seen the storehouses of the ^bhail,

23 Which I have reserved for the time of distress,
For the day of war and battle?

24 aJob 26:10

24 "Where is the way that ^athe light is divided,
Or the east wind scattered on the earth?

25 "Who has cleft a channel for the flood,
Or a way for the thunderbolt;

26 aJob 36:27

26 To bring ^arain on a land without people,
On a desert without a man in it,

27 aPs. 104:13, 14; 107:35

27 To ^asatisfy the waste and desolate land,
And to make the seeds of grass to sprout?

28 aJob 36:27, 28; Ps. 147:8; Jer. 14:22

28 "Has ^athe rain a father?
Or who has begotten the drops of dew?

29 aJob 37:10; Ps. 147:17

29 "From whose womb has come the ^aice?
And the frost of heaven, who has given it birth?

30 "Water becomes hard like stone,
And the surface of the deep is imprisoned.

★31 aJob 9:9; Amos 5:8

31 "Can you bind the chains of the ^aPleiades,
Or loose the cords of Orion?

★32

32 "Can you lead forth a constellation in its season,
And guide the Bear with her satellites?

33 aPs. 148:6; Jer. 31:35, 36

33 "Do you know the ^aordinances of the heavens,
Or fix their rule over the earth?

34 aJob 22:11; 36:27, 28; 38:37

34 "Can you lift up your voice to the clouds,
So that an ^aabundance of water may cover you?

35 aJob 36:32; 37:3

35 "Can you ^asend forth lightnings that they may go
And say to you, 'Here we are'?

36 aJob 9:4; Ps. 51:6; Eccl. 2:26 bJob 32:8

36 "Who has ^aput wisdom in the innermost being,
Or has given ^bunderstanding to the mind?

37 aJob 38:34

37 "Who can count the clouds by wisdom,
Or ^atip the water jars of the heavens,

38 When the dust hardens into a mass,
And the clods stick together?

38:21 God speaks here with great irony.
38:22–30 Job cannot understand even such common things as snow, hail, wind, rain, lightning, frost, and ice.
38:31 *chains.* The idea is: Does Job determine the movements of the constellations in the heavens?
38:32 *the Bear.* A large bright star or constellation (see 9:9).

★39 ªPs.
104:21

39 "Can you hunt the ªprey
for the lion,
Or satisfy the appetite of
the young lions,

40 ªJob 37:8

40 When they ªcrouch in
their dens,
And lie in wait in *their*
lair?

41 ªPs.
147:9; Matt.
6:26; Luke
12:24

41 "Who prepares for ªthe ra-
ven its nourishment,
When its young cry to
God,
And wander about without
food?

1 ªDeut.
14:5; 1 Sam.
24:2; Ps.
104:18 ªPs.
29:9

39 "Do you know the time
the ªmountain goats
give birth?
Do you observe the calving
of the ªdeer?

2 "Can you count the months
they fulfill,
Or do you know the time
they give birth?

3 "They kneel down, they
bring forth their
young,
They get rid of their labor
pains.

4 "Their offspring become
strong, they grow up
in the open field;
They leave and do not re-
turn to them.

★ 5 ªJob
6:5; 11:12;
24:5; Ps.
104:11

5 "Who sent out the ªwild
donkey free?
And who loosed the bonds
of the swift donkey,

6 ªJob
24:5; Jer.
2:24; Hos.
8:9

6 To whom I gave ªthe wilderness for a home,
And the salt land for his
dwelling place?

7 "He scorns the tumult of
the city,
The shoutings of the driver
he does not hear.

8 "He explores the mountains
for his pasture,
And he searches after ev-
ery green thing.

9 "Will the ªwild ox consent
to serve you?
Or will he spend the night
at your manger?

9 ªNum.
23:22; Deut.
33:17; Ps.
22:21; 29:6;
92:10; Is.
34:7

10 "Can you bind the wild ox
in a furrow with
ropes?
Or will he harrow the valleys after you?

11 "Will you trust him because
his strength is great
And leave your labor to
him?

12 "Will you have faith in him
that he will return
your grain,
And gather *it from* your
threshing floor?

13 "The ostriches' wings flap
joyously
With the pinion and plum-
age of love,

★13-17

14 For she abandons her eggs
to the earth,
And warms them in the
dust,

15 And she forgets that a foot
may crush them,
Or that a wild beast may
trample them.

16 "She treats her young ªcru-
elly, as if *they* were
not hers;
Though her labor be in
vain, *she* is uncon-
cerned;

16 ªLam. 4:3

17 Because God has made her
forget wisdom,
And has not given her a
share of understand-
ing.

38:39 God now confronts Job (through 39:30)
with mysteries of the animal kingdom in order
to make him more aware of his ignorance and
thus of his inability to be a competent judge of
the works of God. The lion, raven, wild goat,
deer, wild donkey, wild ox, ostrich, horse,
hawk, and eagle are all paraded before Job's
mind.
39:5 *wild donkey.* Unlike the domestic donkey,
it is fleet of foot and graceful.

39:13-17 It appears to man that the ostrich is
unconcerned about her young, leaving some
of her eggs uncovered (though only by day
when the heat of the sand helps incubate
them) and unhatched (thereby serving as food
for her young). Her seeming lack of wisdom is
not apart from God's plan, just as behind the
trials of the godly, which seem so unreasonable to Job, lies the wise purpose of God.

18 "When she lifts herself on
　　high,
　　She laughs at the horse
　　and his rider.

19 "Do you give the horse *his*
　　might?
　　Do you clothe his neck
　　with a mane?

20 aJoel 2:5
bJer. 8:16

20 "Do you make him ªleap
　　like the locust?
　　His majestic ᵇsnorting is
　　terrible.

21 aJer. 8:6

21 "He paws in the valley,
　　and rejoices in *his*
　　strength;
　　He ªgoes out to meet the
　　weapons.

22 "He laughs at fear and is
　　not dismayed;
　　And he does not turn back
　　from the sword.

23 "The quiver rattles against
　　him,
　　The flashing spear and
　　javelin.

24 "With shaking and rage he
　　races over the ground;
　　And he does not stand still
　　at the voice of the
　　trumpet.

25 "As often as the trumpet
　　sounds he says, 'Aha!'
　　And he scents the battle
　　from afar,
　　And thunder of the cap-
　　tains, and the war cry.

★26

26 "Is it by your understand-
　　ing that the hawk
　　soars,
　　Stretching his wings
　　toward the south?

27 aJer.
49:16;
Obad. 4

27 "Is it at your command that
　　the eagle mounts up,
　　And makes ªhis nest on
　　high?

28 "On the cliff he dwells and
　　lodges,
　　Upon the rocky crag, an
　　inaccessible place.

29 "From there he ªspies out
　　food;
　　His eyes see *it* from afar.

29 aJob 9:26

30 "His young ones also suck
　　up blood;
　　And ªwhere the slain are,
　　there is he."

30 aMatt.
24:28; Luke
17:37

40

Then the Lᴏʀᴅ said to Job,
　2 "Will the faultfinder
　　ªcontend with the Al-
　　mighty?
　Let him who ᵇreproves
　　God answer it."

★ 2 aJob
9:3; 10:2;
33:13; Is.
45:9 bJob
13:3; 23:4;
31:35

2 Job's wise silence, 40:3–5

　3 Then Job answered the
Lᴏʀᴅ and said,
　4 "Behold, I am insignificant;
　　what can I reply to
　　Thee?
　I ªlay my hand on my
　　mouth.

4 aJob
21:5; 29:9

　5 "Once I have spoken, and ªI
　　will not answer;
　Even twice, and I will add
　　no more."

5 aJob 9:3;
15

3 God's second speech: His power, 40:6–41:34

　6 Then the ªLᴏʀᴅ answered
Job out of the storm, and said,
　7 "Now ªgird up your loins
　　like a man;
　I will ᵇask you, and you in-
　　struct Me.

★ 6-14
6 aJob 38:1

7 aJob 38:3
bJob 38:3;
42:4

　8 "Will you really ªannul My
　　judgment?
　Will you ᵇcondemn Me
　　ᶜthat you may be jus-
　　tified?

8 aRom.
3:4 bJob
10:3; 7;
16:11; 19:6;
27:2 cJob
13:18; 27:6

　9 "Or do you have an arm
　　like God,
　And can you ªthunder
　　with a voice like His?

9 aJob
37:5; Ps.
29:3

10 "ªAdorn yourself with emi-
　　nence and dignity;
　And clothe yourself with
　　honor and majesty.

10 aPs. 93:1;
104:1

11 "Pour out ªthe overflowings
　　of your anger;

11 aIs.
42:25; Nah.
1:6, 8 bIs.
2:12; Dan.
4:37

39:26 *toward the south.* Refers to the migratory
instinct of the bird.
40:2 Though God challenges Job to answer, Job
wisely declines.
40:6–14 When Job criticized God's ways, he was
in effect trying to usurp God's position as governor of the world. In this paragraph full of
irony, God asks if Job can really perform those
things which only God can do.

And look on everyone who is [b]proud, and make him low.

12 "Look on everyone who is proud, *and* [a]humble him;
And [b]tread down the wicked where they stand.

13 "[a]Hide them in the dust together;
Bind them in the hidden *place*.

14 "Then I will also confess to you,
That your own right hand can save you.

15 "Behold now, Behemoth, which [a]I made as well as you;
He eats grass like an ox.

16 "Behold now, his strength in his loins,
And his power in the muscles of his belly.

17 "He bends his tail like a cedar;
The sinews of his thighs are knit together.

18 "His bones are tubes of bronze;
His limbs are like bars of iron.

19 "He is the [a]first of the ways of God;
Let his [b]maker bring near his sword.

20 "Surely the mountains [a]bring him food,
And all the beasts of the field [b]play there.

21 "Under the lotus plants he lies down,
In the covert of the reeds and the marsh.

22 "The lotus plants cover him with shade;
The willows of the brook surround him.

23 "If a river rages, he is not alarmed;
He is confident, though the [a]Jordan rushes to his mouth.

24 "Can anyone capture him when he is on watch,
With barbs can anyone pierce *his* nose?

41 "Can you draw out [a]Leviathan with a fishhook?
Or press down his tongue with a cord?

2 "Can you [a]put a rope in his nose?
Or pierce his jaw with a hook?

3 "Will he make many supplications to you?
Or will he speak to you soft words?

4 "Will he make a covenant with you?
Will you take him for a servant forever?

5 "Will you play with him as with a bird?
Or will you bind him for your maidens?

6 "Will the traders bargain over him?
Will they divide him among the merchants?

7 "Can you fill his skin with harpoons,
Or his head with fishing spears?

8 "Lay your hand on him;
Remember the battle; you will not do it again!

9 "Behold, your expectation is false;
Will you be laid low even at the sight of him?

10 "No one is so fierce that he dares to [a]arouse him;
Who then is he that can stand before Me?

11 "Who has [a]given to Me that I should repay *him*?
Whatever is [b]under the whole heaven is Mine.

Cross references (left margin):

12 [a]1 Sam. 2:7; Is. 2:12; 13:11; Dan. 4:37 [b]Is. 63:3
13 [a]Is. 2:10-12
★15 [a]Job 40:19
19 [a]Job 41:33 [b]Job 40:15
20 [a]Ps. 104:14 [b]Ps. 104:26

Cross references (right margin):

23 [a]Gen. 13:10
★ 1 [a]Job 3:8; Ps. 74:14; 104:26; Is. 27:1
2 [a]2 Kin. 19:28; Is. 37:29
10 [a]Job 3:8
11 [a]Rom. 11:35 [b]Ex. 19:5; Deut. 10:14; Job 9:5-10; 26:6-14; 28:24; Ps. 24:1; 50:12; 1 Cor. 10:26

40:15 Job is invited to consider the *Behemoth*, usually considered to be the hippopotamus. The Lord's point is this: Since I made both the Behemoth and you, Job, and you cannot control even this fellow creature, how dare you think of usurping My place!

41:1 Using a second illustration, *Leviathan*, usually identified as the crocodile (though sometimes used symbolically, as in Isa. 27:1), God makes the same point as in 40:15.

12 "I will not keep silence concerning his limbs,
Or his mighty strength, or his orderly frame.

13 "Who can strip off his outer armor?
Who can come within his double mail?

14 "Who can open the doors of his face?
Around his teeth there is terror.

15 "*His* strong scales are *his* pride,
Shut up *as with* a tight seal.

16 "One is so near to another,
That no air can come between them.

17 "They are joined one to another;
They clasp each other and cannot be separated.

18 ªJob 3:9   **18** "His sneezes flash forth light,
And his eyes are like the ªeyelids of the morning.

19 "Out of his mouth go burning torches;
Sparks of fire leap forth.

20 "Out of his nostrils smoke goes forth,
As *from* a boiling pot and *burning* rushes.

21 "His breath kindles coals,
And a flame goes forth from his mouth.

★22   **22** "In his neck lodges strength,
And dismay leaps before him.

23 "The folds of his flesh are joined together,
Firm on him and immovable.

24 "His heart is as hard as a stone;
Even as hard as a lower millstone.

25 "When he raises himself up, the mighty fear;
Because of the crashing they are bewildered.

26 "The sword that reaches him cannot avail;
Nor the spear, the dart, or the javelin.

27 "He regards iron as straw,
Bronze as rotten wood.

28 "The arrow cannot make him flee;
Slingstones are turned into stubble for him.

29 "Clubs are regarded as stubble;
He laughs at the rattling of the javelin.

30 "His underparts are *like* sharp potsherds;   ★30
He spreads out *like* a threshing sledge on the mire.

31 "He makes the depths boil like a pot;   ★31
He makes the sea like a jar of ointment.

32 "Behind him he makes a wake to shine;
One would think the deep to be gray-haired.

33 "ªNothing on earth is like him,   33 ªJob 40:19
One made without fear.

34 "He looks on everything that is high;   34 ªJob 28:8
He is king over all the ªsons of pride."

4   *Job's repentance*, 42:1–6

42 Then Job answered the Lord, and said,   ★ 1-6

41:22 *dismay leaps before him*. Better, fear dances before him. A graphic description of the terror which the presence of Leviathan brings to other creatures, including man.

41:30 The crocodile's scales leave an impression on the mud as if a threshing board had passed over it.

41:31 When he swims he makes a commotion like boiling water or like the foaming from mixtures in a medicine bowl.

42:1–6 Job repents of his pride and rebellion and finds contentment in the knowledge that he has God's fellowship. This is the great lesson of the book: If we know God, we do not need to know why He allows us to experience what we do. He is not only in control of the universe and all its facets but also of our lives; and He loves us. Though His ways are sometimes beyond our comprehension, we should not criticize Him for His dealings with us or with others. God is always in control of all things, even when He appears not to be.

2 aGen.
18:14; Matt.
19:26

2 "I know that aThou canst
do all things,
And that no purpose of
Thine can be
thwarted.

3 aJob 38:2
bPs. 40:5;
131:1; 139:6

3 'Who is this that ahides
counsel without
knowledge?'
"Therefore I have declared
that which I did not
understand,
Things btoo wonderful for
me, which I did not
know."

4 aJob
38:3; 40:7

4 'Hear, now, and I will
speak;
I will aask Thee, and do
Thou instruct me.'

★ 5 aJob
26:14; Rom.
10:17 bls.
6:5; Eph.
1:17, 18

5 "I have aheard of Thee by
the hearing of the ear;
But now my beye sees
Thee;

6 Therefore I retract,
And I repent in dust and
ashes."

III THE DELIVERANCE OF JOB,
42:7–17
A In Relation to his Friends,
42:7–9

★ 7-8
7 aJob
40:3-5;
42:1-6

7 And it came about after
the LORD had spoken these words
to Job, that the LORD said to Eliphaz the Temanite, "My wrath is
kindled against you and against
your two friends, because you
have not spoken of Me what is
right aas My servant Job has.

8 aNum.
23:1 bJob
1:5 cGen.
20:17; James
5:16; 1 John
5:16 dJob
22:30

8 "Now therefore, take for
yourselves aseven bulls and seven
rams, and go to My servant Job,
and offer up a bburnt offering for
yourselves, and My servant Job
will cpray for you. dFor I will accept him so that I may not do
with you according to your folly,
because you have not spoken of
Me what is right, as My servant
Job has."

9 So Eliphaz the Temanite
and Bildad the Shuhite and Zophar the Naamathite went and
did as the LORD told them; and the
LORD accepted Job.

B In Relation to his Family,
42:10–17

10 aDeut.
30:3; Job
1:2, 3; Ps.
14:7; 85:1-3;
126:1-6

10 And the LORD arestored
the fortunes of Job when he
prayed for his friends, and the
LORD increased all that Job had
twofold.

★11 aJob
19:13 bJob
2:11

11 Then all his abrothers, and
all his sisters, and all who had
known him before, came to him,
and they ate bread with him in
his house; and they bconsoled
him and comforted him for all the
evil that the LORD had brought on
him. And each one gave him one
piece of money, and each a ring of
gold.

★12-13

12 aJob
1:10; 8:7;
James 5:11
bJob 1:3

12 aAnd the LORD blessed the
latter days of Job more than his
beginning, band he had 14,000
sheep, and 6,000 camels, and
1,000 yoke of oxen, and 1,000 female donkeys.

13 aJob 1:2

13 And ahe had seven sons
and three daughters.

14 And he named the first Je-
mimah, and the second Keziah,
and the third Keren-happuch.

★15

15 And in all the land no
women were found so fair as Job's
daughters; and their father gave
them inheritance among their
brothers.

★16

16 And after this Job lived
140 years, and saw his sons, and
his grandsons, four generations.

17 aGen.
15:15; 25:8;
Job 5:26

17 aAnd Job died, an old man
and full of days.

42:5 No form of God appeared in the whirlwind,
but what God revealed about Himself enabled
Job to see Him.
42:7-8 Four times in these verses God refers to
Job as My servant, a vindication of God's confidence in Job when originally challenged by
Satan (1:8).
42:11 Such presents were customarily given
when visiting an important person, especially
after a calamity (cf. 2 Chron. 32:23).
42:12-13 Job was given twice as many animals

as he had originally owned (1:2-3) but only
the same number of children, since the ten
who died (1:19) he fully expected to see in the
resurrection (cf. 19:26).
42:15 Giving his daughters a share in the inheritance was an unusual favor, granted later under the law only if there were no sons (Num.
27:8).
42:16 Since Job lived to such a great age, he obviously fully recovered his health.

INTRODUCTION TO
THE BOOK OF PSALMS

AUTHORS: Various   DATES: Various

Title   *The variety of songs, laments, and praises in this book caused it to be left unnamed in the O.T. The Jews referred to it as "The Book of Praises," while the Septuagint entitled it "The Book of Psalms" (from a Greek word indicating songs sung to the accompaniment of stringed instruments). The book was the hymnal of the Jewish people.*

Authorship and Date   *The titles to the various psalms relate 73 of them to David, two to Solomon, twelve to the sons of Korah (see notes on Num. 16; also see Num. 26:9-11), twelve to Asaph (see note on Ezra 2:41), one to Heman (1 Kings 4:31), one to Ethan (1 Chron. 15:19), and one to Moses. The majority of the psalms were written during the times of David and Solomon (10th century B.C.).*

Nature of Hebrew Poetry   *Unlike much Western poetry, Hebrew poetry is not based on rhyme or meter, but on rhythm and parallelism. The rhythm is not achieved by balanced numbers of accented and unaccented syllables, but by tonal stress or accent on important words.*

In parallelism, the poet states an idea in the first line, then reinforces it by various means in the succeeding line or lines. The most common type is synonymous parallelism, in which the second line essentially repeats the idea of the first (Psalm 3:1). In antithetic parallelism, the second line contains an idea opposite to that in the first (Psalm 1:6). In synthetic parallelism, the second or succeeding lines add to or develop the idea of the first (Psalm 1:1-2). In emblematic parallelism, the second line elevates the thought of the first, often by using a simile (Psalm 42:1). Parallelism is not restricted to two lines, but may extend to strophes (smaller units of a few lines) and stanzas (longer units). The alphabetical acrostic is also used (Psalm 119; Introduction to Lamentations).

Classification of the Psalms   *The most generally agreed upon categories of the psalms are: (1) the lament or petition psalms, either individual (Ps. 3) or communal (Ps. 44); (2) thanksgiving or praise psalms, either individual (Ps. 30) or communal (Ps. 65); (3) psalms of trust in God (Ps. 4); (4) hymns which include psalms on the enthronement of Yahweh (see note on Gen. 2:4; Ps. 47), psalms concerning Jerusalem (Ps. 48), and royal psalms (some of which are Messianic; Pss. 2, 110); and (5) didactic and wisdom psalms (Pss. 1, 37, 119). Psalms may also be classified according to themes; e.g., creation (Pss. 8, 19), the Exodus (Ps. 78), imprecation (Ps. 7), penitence (Ps. 6), psalms of pilgrims (Ps. 120). Psalms which include important prophecies concerning Messiah include 2, 8, 16, 22, 40, 45, 72, 110, 118.*

Titles and Technical Terms   *All but 34 of the psalms have titles or superscriptions which normally comprise the first verse of the Hebrew text. They are editorial titles, added after the psalms were written, but are historically accurate.*

The two most frequently used technical terms are: (1) Selah (occurring 71 times in the Psalms and three times in Hab. 3), which is probably a musical notation signaling an interlude or change of musical accompaniment; and (2) For the choir director, which is attached to 55 psalms (and Hab. 3:19), suggesting that a collection of psalms existed for the choir director, possibly for use on special occasions. Other titles and terms are discussed at particular psalms.

Imprecatory Psalms   *These psalms (7, 35, 55, 58, 59, 69, 79, 109, 137, 139), which invoke judgment or curses on one's enemies perplex many. Consider, however, that the purposes of these imprecations are (1) to demonstrate God's just and righteous judgment toward the wicked (58:11); (2) to show the authority of God over the wicked (59:13); (3) to lead the wicked to seek the Lord (83:16); (4) to cause the righteous to praise God (7:17). Therefore, out of zeal for God and abhorrence of sin, the psalmist calls on God to punish the wicked and to vindicate His righteousness.*

Contents   *The psalms are divided into five books, each ending with a doxology (1-41; 42-72; 73-89; 90-106; 107-150). A summary of the contents appears as the beginning note on each psalm.*

THE BOOK OF PSALMS

The following expressions occur often in the Psalms:

Selah   May mean *Pause, Crescendo* or *Musical Interlude*
Maskil   Possibly, *Contemplative,* or *Didactic,* or *Skillful Psalm*
Mikhtam   Possibly, *Epigrammatic Poem,* or *Atonement Psalm*
Sheol   The nether world

BOOK 1

PSALM 1

★ 1-3

1 a Prov. 4:14 b Ps. 5:9, 10; 10:2-11; 36:1-4 c Ps. 17:4; 119:104 d Ps. 26:4, 5; Jer. 15:17

HOW blessed is the man who
     a does not walk in the
     b counsel of the
     wicked,
Nor stand in the c path of
     sinners,
Nor d sit in the seat of
     scoffers!

2 a Ps. 119:14, 16, 35 b Josh. 1:8 c Ps. 25:5 d Ps. 63:5, 6

2 But his a delight is b in the
     law of the LORD,
And in His law he medi-
     tates c day and d night.

3 a Ps. 92:12-14; Jer. 17:8; Ezek. 19:10 b Gen. 39:2, 3, 23; Ps. 128:2

3 And he will be like a a tree
     firmly planted by
     streams of water,
Which yields its fruit in its
     season,
And its leaf does not
     wither;
And in whatever he does,
     b he prospers.

★4-6

4 a Job 21:18; Ps. 35:5; Is. 17:13

4 The wicked are not so,
But they are like a chaff
     which the wind drives
     away.

5 a Ps. 5:5 b Ps. 9:7, 8, 16 c Ps. 89:5, 7

5 Therefore a the wicked will
     not stand in the
     b judgment,
Nor sinners in c the assem-
     bly of the righteous.

6 a Ps. 37:18; Nah. 1:7; John 10:14; 2 Tim. 2:19 b Ps. 9:5, 6; 11:6

6 For the LORD a knows the
     way of the righteous,
But the way of b the wicked
     will perish.

PSALM 2

1 a Ps. 46:6; 83:2-5; Acts 4:25, 26 b Ps. 21:11

WHY are a the nations in an
     uproar,
And the peoples b devising
     a vain thing?

2 a Ps. 48:4-6 b Ps. 74:18, 23 c John 1:41

2 The a kings of the earth
     take their stand,
And the rulers take coun-
     sel together
b Against the LORD and
     against His c Anoint-
     ed:

3 a Jer. 5:5

3 "Let us a tear their fetters
     apart,
And cast away their cords
     from us!"

★ 4 a Ps. 37:13 b Ps. 59:8

4 He who sits in the heavens
     a laughs,
The Lord b scoffs at them.

Psalm 1 This anonymous wisdom psalm stands as a faithful doorkeeper to the entire Psalter. It reminds those who enter of the righteous behavior and fruitful life that are characteristic of the one who delights in God's law (vv. 1-3), in contrast with the life and destiny of the ungodly, who will perish (vv. 4-6). For similar N.T. contrasts, see Matt. 7:13-14 and 1 John 5:12.
1:1-3 Negatively, the righteous man does not believe like, behave like, or belong to the realm of wicked men (v. 1). Positively, the Word of God is his hallmark of faith and practice (v. 2). Therefore, he is spiritually healthy and fruitful (v. 3). *How blessed* (v. 1). The Heb. word is in the plural and means, "Oh, how very happy!"
1:4-6 In contrast, the wicked are spiritually dead and guilty before God. As the wind blows away the fragments of straw when the grain is

winnowed, so the wicked will not stand acquitted, either in this world or in the world to come.
Psalm 2 In this royal psalm (so designated because the theme is the supreme King, as in also Psalms 18, 20, 21, 45, 72, 89, 101, 110, 132, 144), David (cf. Acts 4:25) unveils the resolve of world rulers to rebel against the Lord and His anointed King (vv. 1-3), reveals the Lord's purpose to set His King on Mt. Zion (vv. 4-6), reports the resolve of the King (Jesus Christ, v. 7) to recite the decree spoken to Him by the Lord on the day of His coronation giving Him authority to rule the earth in righteousness (vv. 7-9), and exhorts the world rulers to submit to the Son to avoid His wrath (vv. 10-12).
2:4 *The Lord.* Heb., *Adonai,* meaning "sovereign." Little wonder that opposition is to Him, laughably pathetic. See note on Gen. 15:2.

5 aPs. 21:8,
9; 76:7 bPs.
78:49, 50

5 Then He will speak to
them in His aanger
And bterrify them in His
fury:

★ 6 aPs.
45:6 bPs.
48:1, 2

6 "But as for Me, I have installed aMy King
Upon Zion, bMy holy
mountain."

★ 7 aActs
13:33; Heb.
1:5; 5:5

7 "I will surely tell of the de-
cree of the LORD:
He said to Me, 'Thou art
aMy Son,
Today I have begotten
Thee.

8 aPs. 21:1,
2 bPs. 22:27
cPs. 67:7

8 'Ask of Me, and aI will
surely give bthe na-
tions as Thine inheri-
tance,
And the very cends of the
earth as Thy posses-
sion.

★ 9 aPs.
89:23; 110:5,
6; Rev. 2:26,
27; 12:5;
19:15 bPs.
28:5; 52:5;
72:4

9 'Thou shalt abreak them
with a rod of iron,
Thou shalt bshatter them
like earthenware.' "

10 aProv.
8:15; 27:11

10 Now therefore, O kings,
ashow discernment;
Take warning, O judges of
the earth.

11 aPs. 5:7
bPs.
119:119, 120

11 Worship the LORD with
areverence,
And rejoice with btrem-
bling.

12 aPs. 2:7
bRev. 6:16,
17 cPs. 5:11;
34:22

12 Do homage to athe Son,
lest He become angry,
and you perish in the
way,
For bHis wrath may soon
be kindled.
How blessed are all who
ctake refuge in Him!

PSALM 3

A Psalm of David, when he
fled from Absalom his son.

O LORD, how amy adversaries
have increased!
Many are rising up against
me.

1 a2 Sam.
15:12; Ps.
69:4

2 Many are saying of my
soul,
"There is no adeliverance
for him in God."
[Selah.

★ 2 aPs.
22:7, 8;
71:11

3 But Thou, O LORD, art aa
shield about me,
My bglory, and the One
who clifts my head.

3 aPs. 5:12;
28:7 bPs.
62:7 cPs.
9:13; 27:6

4 I was crying to the LORD
with my voice,
And He aanswered me
from bHis holy
mountain. [Selah.

4 aPs. 4:3;
34:4 bPs.
2:6; 15:1;
43:3

5 I alay down and slept;
I awoke, for the LORD sustains me.

5 aLev.
26:6; Ps. 4:8;
Prov. 3:24

6 I will anot be afraid of ten
thousands of people
Who have bset themselves
against me round
about.

6 aPs. 23:4;
27:3 bPs.
118:10-13

7 aArise, O LORD; bsave me,
O my God!
For Thou hast csmitten all
my enemies on the
cheek;
Thou hast dshattered the
teeth of the wicked.

7 aPs. 7:6
bPs. 6:4;
22:21 cJob
16:10 dPs.
57:4; 58:6

8 aSalvation belongs to the
LORD;
Thy bblessing be upon
Thy people! [Selah.

8 aPs. 28:8;
35:3; Is.
43:11 bPs.
29:11

2:6 installed. Into office as king. Zion. Jerusalem,
where Messiah will reign during the Millennium (Isa. 2:3).
2:7 Today I have begotten Thee. The day of
coronation. The N.T. relates this to Christ's
resurrection (Acts 13:33-34; Rom. 1:4; Heb.
1:5; 5:5).
2:9 Messiah will break and shatter when He

comes again (Rev. 2:27).
Psalm 3 In this individual lament psalm,
David is encouraged by God's protection in the
face of Absalom's rebellion (vv. 1-3), praises
God for delivering him (vv. 4-6), and seeks further victory from God (vv. 7-8).
3:2 Selah. See Introduction, "Titles and Technical Terms."

PSALM 4

For the choir director; on stringed instruments. A Psalm of David.

[a]1 [a]Ps.
3:4; 17:6
[b]Ps. 18:6
[c]Ps. 18:18,
19 [d]Ps.
25:16 [e]Ps.
17:6; 39:12

[a]**A**NSWER me when [b]I call, O God of my righteousness!

Thou hast [c]relieved me in my distress;

Be [d]gracious to me and [e]hear my prayer.

[a]2 [a]Ps. 3:3
[b]Ps. 69:7-
10, 19, 20
[c]Ps. 12:2;
31:6 [d]Ps.
31:18

2 O sons of men, how long will [a]my honor become [b]a reproach?

How long will you love [c]what is worthless and aim at [d]deception?   [Selah.

3 [a]Ps.
135:4 [b]Ps.
31:23, 50:5;
79:2 [c]Ps.
6:8, 9; 17:6

3 But know that the LORD has [a]set apart the [b]godly man for Himself;

The LORD [c]hears when I call to Him.

4 [a]Ps. 99:1
[b]Ps. 119:11;
Eph. 4:26
[c]Ps. 77:6

4 [a]Tremble, [b]and do not sin; [c]Meditate in your heart upon your bed, and be still.   [Selah.

5 [a]Deut.
33:19; Ps.
51:19 [b]Ps.
37:3, 5; 62:8

5 Offer the [a]sacrifices of righteousness,

And [b]trust in the LORD.

★ 6 [a]Job
7:7; 9:25
[b]Num. 6:26;
Ps. 80:3, 7,
19

6 Many are saying, "[a]Who will show us *any* good?"

[b]Lift up the light of Thy countenance upon us, O LORD!

7 [a]Ps.
97:11, 12; Is.
9:3; Acts
14:17

7 Thou hast put [a]gladness in my heart,

More than when their grain and new wine abound.

8 [a]Job
11:19; Ps.
3:5 [b]Lev.
25:18; Deut.
12:10; Ps.
16:9

8 In peace I will both [a]lie down and sleep,

For Thou alone, O LORD, dost make me to [b]dwell in safety.

PSALM 5

For the choir director; for flute accompaniment. A Psalm of David.

[a]**G**IVE ear to my words, O LORD, Consider my [b]groaning.

★ 1 [a]Ps.
54:2 [b]Ps.
104:34

2 Heed [a]the sound of my cry for help, [b]my King and my God,

For to Thee do I pray.

2 [a]Ps.
140:6 [b]Ps.
84:3

3 In the morning, O LORD, Thou wilt hear my voice;

In the [a]morning I will order *my prayer* to Thee and *eagerly* [b]watch.

3 [a]Ps.
88:13 [b]Ps.
130:5

4 For Thou art not a God [a]who takes pleasure in wickedness;

[b]No evil dwells with Thee.

4 [a]Ps. 11:5;
34:16 [b]Ps.
92:15

5 The [a]boastful shall not [b]stand before Thine eyes;

Thou [c]dost hate all who do iniquity.

5 [a]Ps. 73:3;
75:4 [b]Ps.
1:5 [c]Ps.
11:5; 45:7

6 Thou [a]dost destroy those who speak falsehood;

The LORD abhors [b]the man of bloodshed and deceit.

6 [a]Ps. 52:4,
5 [b]Ps. 55:23

7 But as for me, [a]by Thine abundant lovingkindness I will enter Thy house,

★ 7 [a]Ps.
69:13 [b]Ps.
115:11, 13

Psalm 4 In this song of trust, David seeks God's help (v. 1), warns his enemies and exhorts them to trust God (vv. 2-5), and, in spite of opposition, expresses his trust in the Lord, who gives him joy, peace, and security (vv. 6-8).
4:1 *relieved me.* Lit., made room for me in tight places.
4:2 The background of this psalm is likely the same as of Psalm 3; i.e., Absalom's revolt. David appeals to the rebels to have second thoughts about supporting Absalom.

4:6 *Lift up the light of Thy countenance upon us.* Show favor toward us.
Psalm 5 In this individual lament psalm, David entreats God to answer his morning prayer (vv. 1-3), describes God's hatred of sin (vv. 4-6), asks God to guide him in righteousness (vv. 7-10), and rejoices in God's protection and blessing (vv. 11-12).
5:1 *groaning.* See note on Josh. 1:8.
5:7 *lovingkindness.* Heb., *hesed,* meaning "steadfast love." See note on Hos. 2:19.

At Thy holy temple I will
^bbow in ^creverence
for Thee.

8 ^aPs. 31:3
^bPs. 31:1
^cPs. 27:11

8   O Lord, ^alead me ^bin Thy
     righteousness ^cbe-
     cause of my foes;
     Make Thy way straight be-
     fore me.

★ **9** ^aPs.
52:3 ^bPs.
7:14 ^cRom.
3:13

9   There is ^anothing reliable
     in what they say;
     Their ^binward part is de-
     struction *itself*;
     Their ^cthroat is an open
     grave;
     They flatter with their
     tongue.

10 ^aPs. 9:16
^bPs. 36:12
^cPs. 107:10,
11

10   Hold them guilty, O God;
     ^aBy their own devices let
     them fall!
     In the multitude of their
     transgressions ^bthrust
     them out,
     For they are ^crebellious
     against Thee.

11 ^aPs. 2:12
^bPs. 33:1;
64:10 ^cPs.
12:7 ^dPs.
69:36

11   But let all who ^atake ref-
     uge in Thee ^bbe glad,
     Let them ever sing for joy;
     And mayest Thou ^cshelter
     them,
     That those who ^dlove Thy
     name may exult in
     Thee.

12 ^aPs.
29:11 ^bPs.
32:7, 10

12   For it is Thou who dost
     ^abless the righteous
     man, O Lord,
     Thou dost ^bsurround him
     with favor as with a
     shield.

PSALM 6

For the choir director; with
   stringed instruments,
upon an eight-stringed lyre.
   A Psalm of David.

O LORD, ^ado not rebuke me in
      Thine anger,
   Nor chasten me in Thy
      wrath.

1 ^aPs. 38:1;
118:18

2   Be gracious to me, O Lord,
        for I *am* ^apining away;
     ^bHeal me, O Lord, for ^cmy
        bones are dismayed.

★ **2-3**
2 ^aPs.
102:4, 11
^bPs. 41:4;
147:3; Hos.
6:1 ^cPs.
22:14; 31:10

3   And my ^asoul is greatly
        dismayed;
     But Thou, O Lord—^bhow
        long?

3 ^aPs. 88:3;
John 12:27
^bPs. 90:13

4   Return, O Lord, ^arescue
        my soul;
     Save me because of Thy
        lovingkindness.

★ **4-5**
4 ^aPs.
17:13

5   For ^athere is no mention of
        Thee in death;
     In Sheol who will give
        Thee thanks?

5 ^aPs. 30:9;
88:10-12;
115:17; Eccl.
9:10; Is.
38:18

6   I am ^aweary with my sigh-
        ing;
     Every night I make my bed
        swim,
     I dissolve my couch with
        ^bmy tears.

6 ^aPs. 69:3
^bPs. 42:3

7   My ^aeye has wasted away
        with grief;
     It has become old because
        of all my adversaries.

7 ^aJob
17:7; Ps.
31:9; 38:10

8   ^aDepart from me, all you
        who do iniquity,

★ **8** ^aPs.
119:115;
Matt. 7:23;
Luke 13:27
^bPs. 3:4;
28:6

5:9 *an open grave.* I.e., corrupt and dangerous.
   Psalm 6 In this individual lament psalm,
David expresses his distress that God uses his
adversaries to chasten him (vv. 1-3), petitions
God for deliverance (vv. 4-5), laments his sufferings (vv. 6-7), and warns his enemies to depart,
confident that the Lord will answer his prayer
(vv. 8-10). This is the first of the penitential
psalms (also Psalms 32, 38, 51, 102, 130, 143). In
these, the distress afflicting the psalmist is his
sin, and so the lament is a confession of sin.
   6:2-3 In his dismay, David asks God *how long*
this chastening will last. David's extremity (vv.

6-7) is God's opportunity (vv. 9-10).
   6:4-5 David offers two reasons why God should
deliver him: (1) God's *lovingkindness* (loyal
love, see note on Hos. 2:19), and (2) David's
inability to praise God in *Sheol* (the grave; see
note on Gen. 37:35). David is not here discussing the question of whether there is consciousness after death; he is simply stating
that only the living can publicly give thanks to
God here on earth.
   6:8 David speaks as a king purging his kingdom
of evildoers. Christ quoted the verse in a similar way (Matt. 7:23).

For the LORD [b]has heard the voice of my weeping.

9 aPs.
116:1 bPs.
66:19, 20

9 The LORD [a]has heard my supplication,
The LORD [b]receives my prayer.

★10 aPs.
71:13, 24
bPs. 73:19

10 All my enemies shall [a]be ashamed and greatly dismayed;
They shall turn back, they shall [b]suddenly be ashamed.

PSALM 7

A Shiggaion of David, which he sang to the Lord concerning Cush, a Benjamite.

1 aPs. 31:1;
71:1 bPs.
31:15

O LORD my God, [a]in Thee I have taken refuge;
Save me from all those who pursue me, and [b]deliver me,

★ 2 aPs.
57:4; Is.
38:13

2 Lest he tear my soul [a]like a lion,
Dragging me away, while there is none to deliver.

3 a1 Sam.
24:11

3 O LORD my God, if I have done this,
If there is [a]injustice in my hands,

4 aPs.
109:4, 5
b1 Sam.
24:7; 26:9

4 If I have [a]rewarded evil to my friend,
Or have [b]plundered him who without cause was my adversary,

5 Let the enemy pursue my soul and overtake it;
And let him trample my life down to the ground,

And lay my glory in the dust.   [Selah.

6 aPs. 3:7
bPs. 94:2
cPs. 138:7
dPs. 35:23;
44:23

6 [a]Arise, O LORD, in Thine anger;
[b]Lift up Thyself against [c]the rage of my adversaries,
And [d]arouse Thyself for me; Thou hast appointed judgment.

7 aPs.
22:27

7 And let the assembly of the [a]peoples encompass Thee;
And over them return Thou on high.

8 aPs.
96:13; 98:9
bPs. 18:20;
26:1; 35:24;
43:1

8 The LORD [a]judges the peoples;
[b]Vindicate me, O LORD, according to my righteousness and my integrity that is in me.

★ 9 aPs.
34:21; 94:23
bPs. 37:23;
40:2 cPs.
11:4, 5; Jer.
11:20; Rev.
2:23

9 O let [a]the evil of the wicked come to an end, but [b]establish the righteous;
For the righteous God [c]tries the hearts and minds.

10 aPs. 18:2,
30 bPs.
97:10, 11;
125:4

10 My [a]shield is with God,
Who [b]saves the upright in heart.

11 aPs. 50:6
bPs. 90:9

11 God is a [a]righteous judge,
And a God who has [b]indignation every day.

★12-14
12 aPs. 58:5
bDeut. 32:41
cPs. 64:7

12 If a man [a]does not repent,
He will [b]sharpen His sword;
He has [c]bent His bow and made it ready.

13 aPs.
18:14; 45:5

13 He has also prepared for Himself deadly weapons;
He makes His [a]arrows fiery shafts.

6:10 *dismayed.* A description of David in verses 2–3, but here it describes his enemies.

Psalm 7 In this individual lament psalm, David confidently seeks God for deliverance (vv. 1–2), affirms his innocence (vv. 3–5), appeals to God to vindicate him from slander (vv. 6–10) and bring judgment on his wicked enemies (vv. 11–16), and resolves to praise God for His righteousness (v. 17). This is the first of the imprecatory psalms, which contain an invocation of judgment, calamity, or curse against one's enemies who are viewed as the enemies of God (see Introduction). *Shiggaion.* An obscure term,

perhaps indicating an ecstatic song. *Cush.* Not mentioned elsewhere; probably he was one of Saul's henchmen sent to kill David.

7:2 This particular enemy was violent *like a lion.*

7:9 *tries.* I.e., tests. *the hearts and minds.* Lit., kidneys; together referring to man's entire immaterial being.

7:12-14 God is the subject of the actions of verse 13, but verse 14 again describes the actions of the wicked man, where the fertility of evil is compared to the process of childbearing.

14 [a]Job 15:35; Is. 59:4; James 1:15

14 Behold, he travails with wickedness,
And he [a]conceives mischief, and brings forth falsehood.

15 [a]Job 4:8; Ps. 57:6

15 He has dug a pit and hollowed it out,
And has [a]fallen into the hole which he made.

16 [a]Esth. 9:25; Ps. 140:9 [b]Ps. 140:11

16 His [a]mischief will return upon his own head,
And his [b]violence will descend upon his own pate.

17 [a]Ps. 71:15, 16 [b]Ps. 9:2; 66:1, 2, 4

17 I will give thanks to the LORD [a]according to His righteousness,
And will [b]sing praise to the name of the LORD Most High.

PSALM 8

For the choir director; on the Gittith.
A Psalm of David.

1 [a]Ps. 57:5, 11; 113:4; 148:13

O LORD, our Lord,
How majestic is Thy name in all the earth,
Who hast [a]displayed Thy splendor above the heavens!

★ 2-3

2 [a]Matt. 21:16; 1 Cor. 1:27 [b]Ps. 29:1; 118:14 [c]Ps. 44:16

2 [a]From the mouth of infants and nursing babes Thou hast established [b]strength,
Because of Thine adversaries,
To make [c]the enemy and the revengeful cease.

3 When I [a]consider [b]Thy heavens, the work of Thy fingers,
The [c]moon and the stars, which Thou hast ordained;

3 [a]Ps. 111:2 [b]Ps. 89:11; 144:5 [c]Ps. 136:9

4 [a]What is man, that Thou dost take thought of him?
And the son of man, that Thou dost care for him?

4 [a]Job 7:17; Ps. 144:3; Heb. 2:6-8

5 Yet Thou hast made him a [a]little lower than God,
And [b]dost crown him with [c]glory and majesty!

★ **5** [a]Gen. 1:26; Ps. 82:6 [b]Ps. 103:4 [c]Ps. 21:5

6 Thou dost make him to [a]rule over the works of Thy hands;
Thou hast [b]put all things under his feet,

6 [a]Gen. 1:26, 28 [b]1 Cor. 15:27; Eph. 1:22; Heb. 2:8

7 All sheep and oxen,
And also the beasts of the field,

8 The birds of the heavens, and the fish of the sea,
Whatever passes through the paths of the seas.

9 [a]O LORD, our Lord,
How majestic is Thy name in all the earth!

9 [a]Ps. 8:1

PSALM 9

For the choir director; on Muth-labben.
A Psalm of David.

1 [a]Ps. 86:12 [b]Ps. 26:7

I WILL give thanks to the LORD with all [a]my heart;

Psalm 8 In this hymn of praise, David marvels at the majesty of the Lord, who uses the weak (*infants,* v. 2) to overthrow the mighty (vv. 1-2), ponders the thought that God has entrusted His creation to the dominion of man (vv. 3-8), and concludes with a note of praise (v. 9). The meaning of *Gittith* is uncertain. It is derived from "Gath" and may indicate a tune or instrument connected with that place.
8:2-3 From nursing babies to heavenly bodies, God is Lord of all!
8:5 *God.* Heb., *Elohim,* usually translated, as here, "God." The psalmist views man, created in God's image, as a little lower than God. In Heb. 2:6-8, the passage is applied to Christ as Son of Man.
Psalm 9 Here David praises the Lord, the righteous Judge, for destroying the wicked (vv. 1-10), exhorts the people to praise Him (vv. 11-12), and calls upon God to destroy the wicked so the righteous may be delivered (vv. 13-20). Together with Psalm 10, this forms a partially alphabetic acrostic in the Hebrew text, every alternate verse (for the most part) beginning with the next successive letter of the Hebrew alphabet. *Muth-labben.* Means "death for (or of) the son," but what it refers to is uncertain.

I will [b]tell of all Thy wonders.

2 aPs. 5:11;
104:34 bPs.
66:2, 4 cPs.
83:18; 92:1

2 I will be glad and [a]exult in Thee;
I will [b]sing praise to Thy name, O [c]Most High.

3 aPs. 27:2

3 When my enemies turn back,
They stumble and [a]perish before Thee.

4 aPs.
140:12 bPs.
50:6

4 For Thou hast [a]maintained my just cause;
Thou dost sit on the throne [b]judging righteously.

★ **5-6**

5 aPs.
119:21 bPs.
69:28; Prov.
10:7

5 Thou hast [a]rebuked the nations; Thou hast destroyed the wicked;
Thou hast [b]blotted out their name forever and ever.

6 aPs.
34:16

6 The enemy has come to an end in perpetual ruins,
And Thou hast uprooted the cities;
The very [a]memory of them has perished.

7 aPs.
10:16 bPs.
89:14

7 But the [a]LORD abides forever;
He has established His [b]throne for judgment,

8 aPs.
96:13; 98:9

8 And He will [a]judge the world in righteousness;
He will execute judgment for the peoples with equity.

9 aPs. 32:7;
59:9, 16, 17

9 The LORD also will be a [a]stronghold for the oppressed,
A stronghold in times of trouble,

10 aPs.
91:14 bPs.
37:28; 94:14

10 And those who [a]know Thy name will put their trust in Thee;

For Thou, O LORD, hast not [b]forsaken those who seek Thee.

11 aPs. 76:2
bPs. 105:1;
107:22

11 Sing praises to the LORD, who [a]dwells in Zion;
[b]Declare among the peoples His deeds.

★**12** aGen.
9:5; Ps.
72:14 bPs.
9:18

12 For [a]He who requires blood remembers them;
He does not forget [b]the cry of the afflicted.

13 aPs.
38:19 bPs.
30:3; 86:13

13 Be gracious to me, O LORD;
Behold my affliction from those [a]who hate me,
Thou who [b]dost lift me up from the gates of death;

14 aPs.
106:2 bPs.
13:5; 20:5;
35:9; 51:12

14 That I may tell of [a]all Thy praises,
That in the gates of the daughter of Zion
I may [b]rejoice in Thy salvation.

15 aPs. 7:15,
16 bPs. 57:6

15 The nations have sunk down [a]in the pit which they have made;
In the [b]net which they hid, their own foot has been caught.

★**16** aEx. 7:5
bPs. 9:4

16 The LORD has [a]made Himself known;
He has [b]executed judgment.
In the work of his own hands the wicked is snared.
[Higgaion Selah.

★**17** aPs.
49:14 bJob
8:13; Ps.
50:22

17 The wicked will [a]return to Sheol,
Even all the nations who [b]forget God.

18 aPs. 9:12;
12:5 bPs.
62:5; 71:5;
Prov. 23:18

18 For the [a]needy will not always be forgotten,
Nor the [b]hope of the afflicted perish forever.

9:5-6 These verses teach that the wicked are to be punished forever.

9:12 *requires blood.* I.e., avenges blood by requiring capital punishment (cf. Gen. 9:5-6).

9:16 *Higgaion.* May mean "meditation," or may indicate the use of quieter instruments.

9:17 *Sheol.* See note on Gen. 37:35.

Psalm 10 In this individual lament psalm, the psalmist elaborates on the ungodliness and unrighteousness of the wicked who oppress the afflicted (vv. 1-11), petitions the Lord to deliver the afflicted and to destroy the wicked (vv. 12-15), and expresses confidence that the Lord has answered his prayer (vv. 16-18). Although this psalm lacks a superscription, David is likely the author, in view of the close relationship between this psalm and Psalm 9.

19 aNum.
10:35 bPs.
9:5

19 aArise, O Lord, do not let
man prevail;
Let the nations be bjudged
before Thee.

20 aPs. 14:5
bPs. 62:9

20 Put them ain fear, O Lord;
Let the nations know that
they are bbut men.
[Selah.

PSALM 10*

1 aPs. 22:1
bPs. 13:1;
55:1

Why adost Thou stand afar
off, O Lord?
Why bdost Thou hide
Thyself in times of
trouble?

2 aPs. 73:6,
8 bPs. 7:16;
9:16

2 In apride the wicked hotly
pursue the afflicted;
Let them be bcaught in the
plots which they have
devised.

3 aPs. 49:6;
94:3, 4 bPs.
112:10 cPs.
10:13

3 For the wicked aboasts of
his bheart's desire,
And the greedy man
curses and cspurns the
Lord.

4 aPs.
10:13; 36:2
bPs. 14:1;
36:1

4 The wicked, in the haughtiness of his counte-
nance, adoes not seek
Him.
All his thoughts are,
"bThere is no God."

5 aPs. 52:7
bPs. 28:5

5 His ways aprosper at all
times;
Thy judgments are on
high, bout of his sight;
As for all his adversaries,
he snorts at them.

6 aPs.
49:11; Eccl.
8:11 bRev.
18:7

6 He says to himself, "aI
shall not be moved;
Throughout all genera-
tions bI shall not be in
adversity."

7 aRom.
3:14 bPs.
73:8 cJob
20:12; Ps.
140:3

7 His amouth is full of curses
and deceit and bop-
pression;
cUnder his tongue is mis-
chief and wickedness.

8 aPs. 11:2
bPs. 94:6
cPs. 72:12

8 He sits in the alurking
places of the villages;
In the hiding places he
bkills the innocent;

His eyes stealthily watch
for the cunfortunate.

9 aPs.
17:12 bPs.
59:3; Mic.
7:2 cPs. 10:2
dPs. 140:5

9 He lurks in a hiding place
as aa lion in his lair;
He blurks to catch cthe afflicted;
He catches the afflicted
when he draws him
into his dnet.

10 He crouches, he bows
down,
And the unfortunate fall
by his mighty ones.

11 aPs. 10:4

11 He asays to himself, "God
has forgotten;
He has hidden His face; He
will never see it."

12 aPs. 17:7;
Mic. 5:9 bPs.
9:12

12 Arise, O Lord; O God, alift
up Thy hand.
bDo not forget the af-
flicted.

13 aPs. 10:3

13 Why has the wicked
aspurned God?
He has said to himself,
"Thou wilt not re-
quire it."

14 aPs. 10:7
bPs. 22:11
cPs. 68:5

14 Thou hast seen it, for
Thou hast beheld
amischief and vex-
ation to take it into
Thy hand.
The bunfortunate commits
himself to Thee;
Thou hast been the chelp-
er of the orphan.

★15 aPs.
37:17 bPs.
140:11

15 aBreak the arm of the
wicked and the
evildoer,
bSeek out his wickedness
until Thou dost find
none.

16 aPs.
29:10 bDeut.
8:20

16 The Lord is aKing forever
and ever;
bNations have perished
from His land.

17 aPs. 9:18
b1 Chr.
29:18 cPs.
34:15

17 O Lord, Thou hast heard
the adesire of the
humble;
Thou wilt bstrengthen
their heart, cThou wilt
incline Thine ear

18 aPs.
146:9 bPs.
9:9; 74:21
cIs. 29:20

18 To vindicate the aorphan
and the boppressed,

---

*See note, p. 805.

10:15 arm. A symbol of power.

That man who is of the
earth may cause ᶜter-
ror no more.

PSALM 11

For the choir director. *A Psalm*
of David.

★ **1-3**
1 ᵃPs. 2:12
ᵇPs. 121:1

IN the LORD I ᵃtake refuge;
How can you say to my
soul, "Flee *as* a bird to
your ᵇmountain;

2 ᵃPs. 7:12;
37:14 ᵇPs.
64:3 ᶜPs.
64:4

2 For, behold, the wicked
ᵃbend the bow,
They ᵇmake ready their
arrow upon the string,
To ᶜshoot in darkness at
the upright in heart.

3 ᵃPs. 82:5;
87:1;
119:152

3 If the ᵃfoundations are destroyed,
What can the righteous
do?"

★ **4-7**
4 ᵃPs. 18:6;
Mic. 1:2;
Hab. 2:20
ᵇPs. 103:19;
Is. 66:1;
Matt. 5:34;
Rev. 4:2 ᶜPs.
33:18; 34:15,
16

4 The LORD is in His ᵃholy
temple; the LORD's
ᵇthrone is in heaven;
His ᶜeyes behold, His eyelids test the sons of
men.

5 ᵃGen.
22:1; Ps.
34:19; James
1:12 ᵇPs.
5:5

5 The LORD ᵃtests the righteous and ᵇthe wicked,
And the one who loves
violence His soul
hates.

★ **6** ᵃPs.
18:13, 14
ᵇGen. 19:24;
Ezek. 38:22
ᶜJer. 4:11,
12 ᵈPs. 75:8

6 Upon the wicked He will
ᵃrain snares;
ᵇFire and brimstone and
ᶜburning wind will be
the portion of ᵈtheir
cup.

7 ᵃPs. 7:9,
11 ᵇPs.
33:5; 45:7
ᶜPs. 16:11;
17:15

7 For the LORD is ᵃrighteous;
ᵇHe loves righteous-
ness;

The upright will ᶜbehold
His face.

PSALM 12

For the choir director; upon an
eight-stringed lyre.
A Psalm of David.

★ **1** ᵃIs.
57:1; Mic.
7:2

HELP, LORD, for ᵃthe godly
man ceases to be,
For the faithful disappear
from among the sons
of men.

2 ᵃPs. 10:7;
41:6 ᵇPs.
28:3; 55:21;
Jer. 9:8;
Rom. 16:18

2 They ᵃspeak falsehood to
one another;
With ᵇflattering lips and
with a double heart
they speak.

★ **2-4**

3 ᵃDan.
7:8; Rev.
13:5

3 May the LORD cut off all
flattering lips,
The tongue that ᵃspeaks
great things;

4 ᵃPs.
73:8, 9

4 Who ᵃhave said, "With
our tongue we will
prevail;
Our lips are our own; who
is lord over us?"

★ **5** ᵃPs.
9:9; 10:18
ᵇIs. 33:10
ᶜPs. 34:6;
35:10

5 "Because of the ᵃdevasta-
tion of the afflicted,
because of the groan-
ing of the needy,
Now ᵇI will arise," says the
LORD; "I will ᶜset him
in the safety for which
he longs."

★ **6** ᵃ2 Sam.
22:31; Ps.
18:30; 19:8,
10; 119:140
ᵇProv. 30:5

6 The ᵃwords of the LORD
are pure words;
As silver ᵇtried in a furnace on the earth, re-
fined seven times.

7 ᵃPs.
37:28; 97:10

7 Thou, O LORD, wilt keep
them;

Psalm 11 In this song of trust, David, faced
with the temptation to flee (vv. 1–3), expresses
his faith in the Lord, who will destroy the wicked
and deliver the righteous (vv. 4–7). The setting
may be Saul's attempt to kill David (1 Sam. 18:11
and 19:10).
11:1–3 *How can you say.* Evidently the advice of
well-meaning friends to yield to expediency
and flee. *foundations.* Of society.
11:4–7 David prefers the way of faith. God's
eyelids narrow as He scrutinizes men.
11:6 *snares.* Possibly burning coals, or perhaps
traps.
Psalm 12 In this lament psalm, David con-

trasts the trouble caused by the wicked words of
evil men (vv. 1–5) with his trust in the true
words of the Lord (vv. 6–8).
12:1 The aggressiveness of wickedness makes it
seem to David that the righteous have disappeared from the earth.
12:2–4 The words of evil men manipulate rather
than communicate, and are described as empty talk (*falsehood*), smooth talk (*flattering*),
double talk, and big talk (v. 4).
12:5 The Lord promises deliverance for the *afflicted* and *needy*.
12:6 God's words are as pure and valuable as
fully refined *silver*.

Thou wilt ^apreserve him from this generation forever.

★ **8** *a*Ps. 55:10, 11 *b*Is. 32:5

8 The ^awicked strut about on every side,
When ^bvileness is exalted among the sons of men.

PSALM 13

For the choir director. A Psalm of David.

★ **1-2**

1 *a*Ps. 44:24 *b*Job 13:24; Ps. 89:46

H OW long, O LORD? Wilt Thou ^aforget me forever?
How long ^bwilt Thou hide Thy face from me?

2 *a*Ps. 42:4 *b*Ps. 42:9

2 How long shall I ^atake counsel in my soul,
Having ^bsorrow in my heart all the day?
How long will my enemy be exalted over me?

3 *a*Ps. 5:1 *b*1 Sam. 14:29; Ezra 9:8; Job 33:30; Ps. 18:28 *c*Jer. 51:39

3 ^aConsider *and* answer me, O LORD, my God;
^bEnlighten my eyes, lest I ^csleep the *sleep of* death,

4 *a*Ps. 12:4 *b*Ps. 25:2; 38:16

4 Lest my enemy ^asay, "I have overcome him,"
Lest ^bmy adversaries rejoice when I am shaken.

★ **5-6**

5 *a*Ps. 52:8 *b*Ps. 9:14

5 But I have ^atrusted in Thy lovingkindness;
My heart shall ^brejoice in Thy salvation.

6 *a*Ps. 96:1, 2 *b*Ps. 116:7; 119:17; 142:7

6 I will ^asing to the LORD,
Because He has ^bdealt bountifully with me.

PSALM 14

For the choir director. *A Psalm* of David.

T HE fool has ^asaid in his heart, "There is no God."
They are corrupt, they have committed abominable deeds;
There is ^bno one who does good.

★ **1** *a*Ps. 10:4; 53:1 *b*Ps. 14:1-3; 130:3; Rom. 3:10-12

2 The LORD has ^alooked down from heaven upon the sons of men,
To see if there are any who ^bunderstand,
Who ^cseek after God.

★ **2-3**

2 *a*Ps. 33:13, 14; 102:19 *b*Ps. 92:6 *c*1 Chr. 22:19

3 They have all ^aturned aside; together they have become corrupt;
There is ^bno one who does good, not even one.

3 *a*Ps. 58:3 *b*Ps. 143:2

4 Do all the workers of wickedness ^anot know,
Who ^beat up my people *as* they eat bread,
And ^cdo not call upon the Lord?

4 *a*Ps. 82:5 *b*Ps. 27:2; Jer. 10:25; Mic. 3:3 *c*Ps. 79:6; Is. 64:7

5 There they are in great dread,
For God is with the ^arighteous generation.

5 *a*Ps. 73:15; 112:2

6 You would put to shame the counsel of the afflicted,
But the LORD is his ^arefuge.

6 *a*Ps. 9:9; 40:17; 46:1; 142:5

7 Oh, that ^athe salvation of Israel would come out of Zion!

★ **7** *a*Ps. 53:6 *b*Ps. 85:1, 2

12:8 *strut.* Arrogantly.

Psalm 13 Here David laments his oppression by the enemy (vv. 1-2), petitions God to deliver him (vv. 3-4), and confidently resolves to praise God for that deliverance (vv. 5-6).

13:1-2 The fourfold repetition of *How long* indicates the extremity of David's misery.

13:5-6 David trusts in God's loyal love (*lovingkindness,* see note on Hos. 2:19), His *salvation,* and His bountiful care.

Psalm 14 David laments the moral foolishness and corruption of the whole human race (vv. 1-6), and longs for the establishment of the

righteous kingdom of the Lord on earth (v. 7). This psalm, with only slight changes in verses 5-6, is identical to Psalm 53.

14:1 *The fool* (one who is morally perverse, not mentally deficient) is described as to his belief ("no God") and behavior ("no good"). His is a practical rather than a theoretical atheism.

14:2-3 Paul cites these verses in Rom. 3:10-12 in support of the universal and perennial sinfulness of mankind.

14:7 David longs for the establishing of the Messianic kingdom on earth (cf. Isa. 59:20-21; Rom. 11:26-27).

When the LORD [b]restores
His captive people,
Jacob will rejoice, Israel
will be glad.

PSALM 15

A Psalm of David.

1 [a]Ps. 27:5,
6; 61:4 [b]Ps.
24:3

O LORD, who may abide [a]in
Thy tent?
Who may dwell on Thy
[b]holy hill?

2 [a]Ps. 24:4;
Is. 33:15
[b]Zech. 8:16;
Eph. 4:25

2 He who [a]walks with integrity, and works right-
eousness,
And [b]speaks truth in his
heart.

3 [a]Ps.
50:20 [b]Ps.
28:3 [c]Ps.
23:1

3 He [a]does not slander with
his tongue,
Nor [b]does evil to his
neighbor,
Nor [c]takes up a reproach
against his friend;

4 [a]Acts
28:10 [b]Judg.
11:35

4 In whose eyes a reprobate
is despised,
But who [a]honors those
who fear the LORD;
He [b]swears to his own
hurt, and does not
change;

★ **5** [a]Ex.
22:25; Lev.
25:36; Deut.
23:20; Ezek.
18:8 [b]Ex.
23:8; Deut.
16:19 [c]2 Pet.
1:10

5 He [a]does not put out his
money at interest,
Nor [b]does he take a bribe
against the innocent.
[c]He who does these things
will never be shaken.

PSALM 16

A Mikhtam of David.

1 [a]Ps. 17:8
[b]Ps. 7:1

P RESERVE me, O God, for [b]I
take refuge in Thee.

2 [a]Ps.
73:25

2 I said to the LORD, "Thou
art my Lord;
I [a]have no good besides
Thee."

★ **3** [a]Ps.
101:6 [b]Ps.
119:63

3 As for the [a]saints who are
in the earth,
They are the majestic ones
[b]in whom is all my
delight.

4 [a]Ps.
32:10 [b]Ps.
106:37, 38
[c]Ex. 23:13;
Josh. 23:7

4 The [a]sorrows of those who
have bartered for an-
other god will be mul-
tiplied;
I shall not pour out their
libations of [b]blood,
Nor shall I [c]take their
names upon my lips.

★ **5-6**
5 [a]Ps.
73:26;
119:57;
142:5; Lam.
3:24 [b]Ps.
23:5 [c]Ps.
125:3 mg.

5 The LORD is the [a]portion of
my inheritance and
my [b]cup;
Thou dost support my [c]lot.

6 [a]Ps.
78:55 [b]Jer.
3:19

6 The [a]lines have fallen to
me in pleasant places;
Indeed, my heritage is
[b]beautiful to me.

★ **7** [a]Ps.
73:24 [b]Ps.
77:6

7 I will bless the LORD who
has [a]counseled me;
Indeed, my [b]mind instructs
me in the night.

Psalm 15 Here David describes the character of the person who qualifies to be a guest of
God. The synonymous, parallel questions of
verse 1 are answered in the following verses by
an elevenfold description of the righteous man
who is upright in deed, word, attitude, and finances. These qualities, not natural to men, are
imparted by God.
15:5 *at interest.* See notes on Lev. 25:35–46 and
Deut. 24:10–13.
Psalm 16 In this song of trust, David declares that as he has trusted the Lord to be his
portion in life (vv. 1–8), so will he trust Him to
preserve him in death (vv. 9–11). The meaning of
Mikhtam (also used in the headings of Psalms

56–60) is uncertain. It is apparently derived from
a verb meaning "to cover," and may indicate
psalms dealing with protection (covering) from
one's enemies or psalms recited silently (with
lips covering the mouth).
16:3 David delights not only in God but also in
the people of God.
16:5-6 David describes the beauty of his spiritual inheritance in terms similar to the divine
allotment of the promised land to Israel. *lines.*
Measuring cords by which the various allot-
ments were measured.
16:7 Sleepless nights provide opportunity for instruction (facing hard facts).

★ 8-10

8 *a*Ps.
16:8-11; Acts
2:25-28 *b*Ps.
27:8; 123:1;
2 *c*Ps. 73:23;
110:5; 121:5
*d*Ps. 112:6

9 *a*Ps. 4:7;
13:5 *b*Ps.
30:12; 57:8;
108:1 *c*Ps.
4:8

10 *a*Ps.
49:15; 86:13
*b*Acts 13:35

11 *a*Ps.
139:24; Matt.
7:14 *b*Ps.
21:6; 43:4
*c*Job 36:11;
Ps. 36:7, 8;
46:4

8 *a*I have *b*set the LORD continually before me;
Because He is *c*at my right hand, *d*I will not be shaken.

9 Therefore *a*my heart is glad, and *b*my glory rejoices;
My flesh also will *c*dwell securely.

10 For Thou *a*wilt not abandon my soul to Sheol;
Neither wilt Thou *b*allow Thy Holy One to undergo decay.

11 Thou wilt make known to me *a*the path of life;
In *b*Thy presence is fulness of joy;
In Thy right hand there are *c*pleasures forever.

PSALM 17

A Prayer of David.

1 *a*Ps. 9:4
*b*Ps. 61:1;
142:6 *c*Ps.
88:2 *d*Is.
29:13

2 *a*Ps.
103:6 *b*Ps.
98:9; 99:4

★ 3 *a*Ps.
26:1, 2 *b*Job
23:10; Ps.
66:10; Zech.
13:9; 1 Pet.
1:7 *c*Jer.
50:20 *d*Ps.
39:1

HEAR a *a*just cause, O LORD,
*b*give heed to my cry;
*c*Give ear to my prayer, which is not from *d*deceitful lips.

2 Let *a*my judgment come forth from Thy presence;
Let Thine eyes look with *b*equity.

3 Thou hast *a*tried my heart;
Thou hast visited *me* by night;
Thou hast *b*tested me and *c*dost find nothing;

I have *d*purposed that my mouth will not transgress.

4 As for the deeds of men, *a*by the word of Thy lips
I have kept from the *b*paths of the violent.

5 My *a*steps have held fast to Thy paths.
My *b*feet have not slipped.

6 I have *a*called upon Thee, for Thou wilt answer me, O God;
*b*Incline Thine ear to me, hear my speech.

7 *a*Wondrously show Thy lovingkindness,
O *b*Savior of those who take refuge at Thy right hand
From those who rise up *against them.*

8 Keep me as the *a*apple of the eye;
Hide me *b*in the shadow of Thy wings,

9 From the *a*wicked who despoil me,
My *b*deadly enemies, who surround me.

10 They have *a*closed their unfeeling *heart*;
With their mouth they *b*speak proudly.

11 They have now *a*surrounded us in our steps;
They set their eyes *b*to cast *us* down to the ground.

★ 4 *a*Ps.
119:9, 101
*b*Ps. 10:5-11

5 *a*Job
23:11; Ps.
44:18;
119:133 *b*Ps.
18:36; 37:31

6 *a*Ps. 86:7;
116:2 *b*Ps.
88:2

7 *a*Ps.
31:21 *b*Ps.
20:6

★ 8 *a*Deut.
32:10; Zech.
2:8 *b*Ruth
2:12; Ps.
36:7; 57:1;
61:4; 63:7;
91:1, 4
9 *a*Ps.
31:20 *b*Ps.
27:12

★10-12
10 *a*Job
15:27; Ps.
73:7 *b*1 Sam.
2:3; Ps.
31:18; 73:8
11 *a*Ps.
88:17 *b*Ps.
37:14

16:8–10 These verses are cited by Peter in Acts 2:25–28, 31, and verse 10 is cited by Paul in Acts 13:35 as referring to the resurrection of Christ. *at my right hand* (v. 8). The position of a protector or defender. The language here (termed typico-prophetically Messianic) refers initially to the psalmist's own experience, but the ultimate fulfillment is only in Jesus Christ (also Psalm 22:11–18). Thus David's hyperbolic language about his own deliverance from death, or more probably about his own future resurrection, finds its complete fulfillment in Christ's deliverance out of death by resurrection, for only Christ has not seen corruption. *Sheol* (v. 10). Here, the grave (see note on Gen. 37:35).

Psalm 17   In this lament David presents his credentials of uprightness (vv. 1–5) and petitions the Lord for protection from wicked men (vv. 6–14) in view of his hope for the future (v. 15). Although a large number of the psalms are prayers, only five are so designated (17, 86, 90, 102, 142).

17:3 David does not here claim sinlessness, but the justice of his case against the wicked.

17:4 Perhaps David had in mind the incident of 1 Sam. 25:32ff.

17:8 *as the apple of the eye.* I.e., the pupil of the eye, an emblem of that which is tenderest and dearest. *wings.* An oft-used figure for protection.

17:10–12 The imagery of the predator describes the heartlessness of David's wicked enemies (cf. 22:12–18).

12 aPs. 7:2
bPs. 10:9

12 He is ^alike a lion that is eager to tear, And as a young lion ^blurking in hiding places.

★13-15

13 aPs. 3:7
bPs. 55:23
cPs. 22:20
dPs. 7:12

13 ^aArise, O Lord, confront him, ^bbring him low; ^cDeliver my soul from the wicked with ^dThy sword,

14 aPs. 17:7
bPs. 73:3-7;
Luke 16:25
cPs. 49:6

14 From men with ^aThy hand, O Lord, From men of the world, ^bwhose portion is in *this* life; And whose belly Thou ^cdost fill with Thy treasure; They are satisfied with children, And leave their abundance to their babes.

15 aPs. 11:7;
16:11;
140:13;
1 John 3:2
bPs. 4:6, 7
cNum. 12:8

15 As for me, I shall ^abehold Thy face in righteousness; ^bI will be satisfied with Thy ^clikeness when I awake.

PSALM 18

For the choir director. *A Psalm* of David the servant of the Lord, who spoke to the Lord the words of this song in the day that the Lord delivered him from the hand of all his enemies and from the hand of Saul. And he said,

1 aPs.
59:17

★ 2 aDeut.
32:18;
1 Sam. 2:2;
Ps. 18:31,
46; 28:1;
31:3; 42:9;
71:3; 78:15
bPs. 144:2
cPs. 19:14
dPs. 28:7;
33:20; 59:11;
84:9, 11;
Prov. 30:5
ePs. 75:10
fPs. 59:9

"I LOVE Thee, O Lord, ^amy strength."

2 The Lord is ^amy rock and ^bmy fortress and my ^cdeliverer, My God, my rock, in whom I take refuge;

My ^dshield and the ^ehorn of my salvation, my ^fstronghold.

3 aPs. 48:1;
96:4; 145:3
bPs. 34:6

3 I call upon the Lord, who is ^aworthy to be praised, And I am ^bsaved from my enemies.

4 aPs.
116:3 bPs.
69:2;
124:3, 4

4 The ^acords of death encompassed me, And the ^btorrents of ungodliness terrified me.

5 aPs.
116:3

5 The ^acords of Sheol surrounded me; The snares of death confronted me.

6 aPs.
50:15; 120:1
bPs. 3:4
cPs. 34:15

6 In my ^adistress I called upon the Lord, And cried to my God for help; He heard my voice ^bout of His temple, And my ^ccry for help before Him came into His ears.

★7-15

7 aJudg.
5:4; Ps. 68:7,
8; Is. 13:13;
Hag. 2:6
bPs.
114:4, 6

7 Then the ^aearth shook and quaked; And the ^bfoundations of the mountains were trembling And were shaken, because He was angry.

8 aPs. 50:3

8 Smoke went up out of His nostrils, And ^afire from His mouth devoured; Coals were kindled by it.

9 aPs.
144:5 bPs.
97:2

9 He ^abowed the heavens also, and came down With thick ^bdarkness under His feet.

10 aPs. 80:1;
99:1 bPs.
104:3

10 And He rode upon a ^acherub and flew; And He sped upon the ^bwings of the wind.

17:13-15 The *treasure* which God allows the wicked to have is transitory; by contrast (v. 15), resurrection (*awake*) in the presence of God is eternal.

Psalm 18 In this victory song, David relates what the Lord is to him (vv. 1-3), rehearses God's deliverance (vv. 4-19), relates the basis for that deliverance (vv. 20-30), further rehearses the victory (vv. 31-48), and resolves anew to continue praising God (vv. 49-50). Fourth longest in

the Psalter, this psalm, also found in 2 Sam. 22, was written after the death of Saul and the securing of David's kingdom. Thus it commemorates David's overall deliverance from his enemies rather than a specific victory. *the servant of the Lord* (in superscription). See note on Psalm 36.

18:2 Notice the many emblems of protection. *horn.* See note on 2 Sam. 22:3.

18:7-15 See note on 2 Sam. 22:7-19.

11   He made ᵃdarkness His hiding place, ᵇHis canopy around Him, Darkness of waters, thick clouds of the skies.

12   From the ᵃbrightness before Him passed His thick clouds, Hailstones and ᵇcoals of fire.

13   The LORD also ᵃthundered in the heavens, And the Most High uttered His voice, Hailstones and coals of fire.

14   And He ᵃsent out His arrows, and scattered them, And lightning flashes in abundance, and routed them.

15   Then the ᵃchannels of water appeared, And the foundations of the world were laid bare At Thy ᵇrebuke, O LORD, At the blast of the ᶜbreath of Thy nostrils.

16   He ᵃsent from on high, He took me; He drew me out of ᵇmany waters.

17   He ᵃdelivered me from my strong enemy, And from those who hated me, for they were ᵇtoo mighty for me.

18   They confronted me in ᵃthe day of my calamity, But ᵇthe LORD was my stay.

19   He brought me forth also into a ᵃbroad place; He rescued me, because ᵇHe delighted in me.

20   The LORD has ᵃrewarded me according to my righteousness; According to the ᵇcleanness of my hands He has recompensed me.

21   For I have ᵃkept the ways of the LORD, And have ᵇnot wickedly departed from my God.

22   For all ᵃHis ordinances were before me, And I did not put away His ᵇstatutes from me.

23   I was also ᵃblameless with Him, And I ᵇkept myself from my iniquity.

24   Therefore the LORD has ᵃrecompensed me according to my righteousness, According to the cleanness of my hands in His eyes.

25   With ᵃthe kind Thou dost show Thyself kind; With the blameless ᵇThou dost show Thyself blameless;

26   With the pure Thou dost show Thyself ᵃpure; And with the crooked ᵇThou dost show Thyself astute.

27   For Thou dost ᵃsave an afflicted people; But ᵇhaughty eyes Thou dost abase.

28   For Thou dost ᵃlight my lamp; The LORD my God ᵇillumines my darkness.

29   For by Thee I can ᵃrun upon a troop; And by my God I can ᵇleap over a wall.

30   As for God, His way is ᵃblameless; The ᵇword of the LORD is tried; He is a ᶜshield to all who take refuge in Him.

31   For ᵃwho is God, but the LORD? And who is a ᵇrock, except our God,

---

Cross references (left column):

11 ᵃDeut. 4:11 ᵇPs. 97:2

12 ᵃPs. 104:2 ᵇPs. 97:3; 140:10; Hab. 3:4

13 ᵃPs. 29:3; 104:7

14 ᵃPs. 144:6; Hab. 3:11

15 ᵃPs. 106:9 ᵇPs. 76:6 ᶜPs. 18:8

16 ᵃPs. 144:7 ᵇPs. 32:6

17 ᵃPs. 59:1 ᵇPs. 35:10; 142:6

18 ᵃPs. 59:16 ᵇPs. 16:8

19 ᵃPs. 4:1; 31:8; 118:5 ᵇPs. 37:23; 41:11

20 ᵃ1 Sam. 24:19; Job 33:26; Ps. 7:8 ᵇJob 22:30; Ps. 24:4

Cross references (right column):

21 ᵃPs. 37:34; 119:33; Prov. 8:32 ᵇ2 Chr. 34:33; Ps. 119:102

22 ᵃPs. 119:30 ᵇPs. 119:83

23 ᵃPs. 18:32 ᵇPs. 19:12, 13; 25:11; 66:18

24 ᵃ1 Sam. 26:23; Ps. 18:20

25 ᵃ1 Kin. 8:32; Ps. 62:12; Matt. 5:7 ᵇPs. 18:30

★26 ᵃJob 25:5; Hab. 1:13 ᵇLev. 26:23, 24, 27, 28; Prov. 3:34

27 ᵃPs. 72:12 ᵇPs. 101:5; Prov. 6:17

28 ᵃ1 Kin. 15:4; Job 18:6; Ps. 132:17 ᵇPs. 27:1

29 ᵃPs. 118:10-12 ᵇPs. 18:33; 40:2

30 ᵃDeut. 32:4; Ps. 19:7; 145:17; Rev. 15:3 ᵇPs. 12:6 ᶜPs. 17:7; 91:4

31 ᵃDeut. 32:39; 1 Sam. 2:2; Ps. 86:8-10; Is. 45:5 ᵇDeut. 32:31; Ps. 18:2; 62:2

18:26 With the *crooked* (perverse) God shows Himself *astute* (lit., twisted); i.e., He is at cross-purposes with those who are at cross-purposes with Him.

32 The God who [a]girds me
with strength,
And makes my way
[b]blameless?

33 He [a]makes my feet like
hinds' *feet*,
And [b]sets me upon my
high places.

34 He [a]trains my hands for
battle,
So that my arms can [b]bend
a bow of bronze.

35 Thou hast also given me
[a]the shield of Thy sal-
vation,
And Thy [b]right hand up-
holds me;
And [c]Thy gentleness
makes me great.

36 Thou dost [a]enlarge my
steps under me,
And my [b]feet have not
slipped.

37 I [a]pursued my enemies
and overtook them,
And I did not turn back
[b]until they were con-
sumed.

38 I shattered them, so that
they were [a]not able to
rise;
They fell [b]under my feet.

39 For Thou hast [a]girded me
with strength for bat-
tle;
Thou hast [b]subdued under
me those who rose up
against me.

40 Thou hast also made my
enemies [a]turn their
backs to me,
And I [b]destroyed those
who hated me.

41 They cried for help, but
there was [a]none to
save,

Even to the LORD, but [b]He
did not answer them.

42 Then I beat them fine as
the [a]dust before the
wind;
I emptied them out as the
mire of the streets.

43 Thou hast delivered me
from the [a]contentions
of the people;
Thou hast placed me as
[b]head of the nations;
A [c]people whom I have
not known serve me.

44 As soon as they hear, they
obey me;
Foreigners [a]submit to me.

45 Foreigners [a]fade away,
And [b]come trembling out
of their fortresses.

46 The LORD [a]lives, and
blessed be [b]my rock;
And exalted be [c]the God
of my salvation,

47 The God who [a]executes
vengeance for me,
And [b]subdues peoples under me.

48 He [a]delivers me from my
enemies;
Surely Thou [b]dost lift me
above those who rise
up against me;
Thou dost rescue me from
the [c]violent man.

49 Therefore I will [a]give
thanks to Thee among
the nations, O LORD,
And I will [b]sing praises to
Thy name.

50 He gives great [a]deliverance
to His king,
And shows lovingkindness
to [b]His anointed,
To David and [c]his de-
scendants forever.

18:43 Not only had David quelled civil war (2 Sam. 3:1), but God had made him the head of many nations (2 Sam. 8).
18:49-50 Paul saw Messianic implications in this statement (Rom. 15:9), supported by the term *anointed* (Heb., *messiah*) used of the royal line which culminated in Christ.

Marginal references:

32 [a]Ps. 18:39; Is. 45:5 [b]Ps. 18:23

33 [a]Hab. 3:19 [b]Deut. 32:13

34 [a]Ps. 144:1 [b]Job 29:20

35 [a]Ps. 33:20 [b]Ps. 63:8; 119:117 [c]Ps. 138:6

36 [a]Ps. 18:33 [b]Ps. 66:9; Prov. 4:12

37 [a]Ps. 44:5 [b]Ps. 37:20

38 [a]Ps. 36:12 [b]Ps. 47:3

39 [a]Ps. 18:32 [b]Ps. 18:47

40 [a]Ps. 21:12 [b]Ps. 94:23

41 [a]Ps. 50:22 [b]Job 27:9; Prov. 1:28

42 [a]Ps. 83:13

★43 [a]2 Sam. 3:1; 19:9; Ps. 35:1 [b]2 Sam. 8:1-18; Ps. 89:27 [c]Is. 55:5

44 [a]Ps. 66:3

45 [a]Ps. 37:2 [b]Mic. 7:17

46 [a]Job 19:25 [b]Ps. 18:2 [c]Ps. 51:14

47 [a]Ps. 94:1 [b]Ps. 18:43; 47:3; 144:2

48 [a]Ps. 3:7 [b]Ps. 27:6; 59:1 [c]Ps. 11:5

★49-50

49 [a]Rom. 15:9 [b]Ps. 108:1

50 [a]Ps. 21:1; 144:10 [b]Ps. 28:8 [c]Ps. 89:4

PSALM 19

For the choir director. A
Psalm of David.

★ 1-2
1 aPs. 8:1;
50:6; Rom.
1:19, 20
bGen. 1:6, 7

Tᴴᴱ aheavens are telling of the
     glory of God;
     And their bexpanse is de-
     claring the work of
     His hands.

2 aPs.
74:16 bPs.
139:12

2 Day to aday pours forth
     speech,
     And bnight to night reveals
     knowledge.

★ 3

3 There is no speech, nor are
     there words;
     Their voice is not heard.

4 aRom.
10:18 bPs.
104:2

4 Their aline has gone out
     through all the earth,
     And their utterances to the
     end of the world.
     In them He has bplaced a
     tent for the sun,

5 Which is as a bridegroom
     coming out of his
     chamber;
     It rejoices as a strong man
     to run his course.

★ 6 aPs.
113:3; Eccl.
1:5

6 Its arising is from one end
     of the heavens,
     And its circuit to the other
     end of them;
     And there is nothing hid-
     den from its heat.

★ 7-9

7 aPs.
111:7 bPs.
119:160 cPs.
23:3 dPs.
93:5 ePs.
119:98-100

7 aThe law of the Lᴏʀᴅ is
     bperfect, crestoring
     the soul;
     The testimony of the Lᴏʀᴅ
     is dsure, making ewise
     the simple.

8 aPs.
119:128 bPs.
119:14 cPs.
12:6 dPs.
36:9

8 The precepts of the Lᴏʀᴅ
     are aright, brejoicing
     the heart;
     The commandment of the
     Lᴏʀᴅ is cpure, den-
     lightening the eyes.

9 aPs.
119:142 bPs.
119:138

9 The fear of the Lᴏʀᴅ is
     clean, enduring for-
     ever;
     The judgments of the Lᴏʀᴅ
     are atrue; they are
     brighteous altogether.

10 aPs.
119:72, 127
bPs. 119:103

10 They are more desirable
     than agold, yes, than
     much fine gold;
     bSweeter also than honey
     and the drippings of
     the honeycomb.

11 aPs. 17:4
bPs. 24:5, 6;
Prov. 29:18

11 Moreover, by them aThy
     servant is warned;
     In keeping them there is
     great breward.

★12 aPs.
40:12; 139:6
bPs. 51:1, 2
cPs. 90:8;
139:23, 24

12 Who can adiscern his er-
     rors? bAcquit me of
     chidden faults.

★13 aNum.
15:30 bPs.
119:133 cPs.
18:32 dPs.
25:11

13 Also keep back Thy ser-
     vant afrom presump-
     tuous sins;
     Let them not brule over
     me;
     Then I shall be cblameless,
     And I shall be acquitted of
     dgreat transgression.

14 aPs.
104:34 bPs.
18:2 cPs.
31:5; Is. 47:4

14 Let the words of my mouth
     and athe meditation of
     my heart
     Be acceptable in Thy sight,
     O Lᴏʀᴅ, bmy rock and my
     cRedeemer.

Psalm 19 In this hymn of praise, David reflects on the glory of God in natural revelation
(vv. 1-6) and the glory of the law as God's special
revelation (vv. 7-9), which alone meets man's
spiritual needs (vv. 10-14).
19:1-2 Day and night the created universe
broadcasts its silent but eloquent symphony to
the glory of the Creator.
19:3 The communication is nonverbal.
19:6 Even a blind man can feel the heat of the
sun.

19:7-9 A sixfold description of God's special
revelation. law. I.e., His revealed will. testimony. His truth. precepts. I.e., particular in-
junctions. commandment. Authoritative
words. fear. I.e., reverential trust which God's
words foster in His people. judgments. I.e., decisions relating to human situations.
19:12 errors and hidden faults refer to sins of
ignorance (see note on Lev. 4:2).
19:13 presumptuous sins are deliberate violations (see note on Num. 15:30-31).

PSALM 20

For the choir director. A Psalm of David.

★ 1-6
1 *a*Ps. 50:15 *b*Ps. 91:14 *c*Ps. 46:7, 11

M AY the LORD answer you *a*in the day of trouble! May the *b*name of the *c*God of Jacob set you *securely* on high!

2 *a*Ps. 3:4 *b*Ps. 110:2

2 May He send you help *a*from the sanctuary, And *b*support you from Zion!

3 *a*Acts 10:4 *b*Ps. 51:19

3 May He *a*remember all your meal offerings, And *b*find your burnt offering acceptable! [Selah.

4 *a*Ps. 21:2 *b*Ps. 145:19

4 May He grant you your *a*heart's desire, And *b*fulfill all your counsel!

5 *a*Ps. 9:14 *b*Ps. 60:4 *c*1 Sam. 1:17

5 We will *a*sing for joy over your victory, And in the name of our God we will *b*set up our banners. May the LORD *c*fulfill all your petitions.

6 *a*Ps. 41:11 *b*Is. 58:9 *c*Ps. 28:8

6 Now *a*I know that the LORD saves His anointed; He will *b*answer him from His holy heaven, With the *c*saving strength of His right hand.

7 *a*Ps. 33:17 *b*2 Chr. 32:8

7 Some *boast* in chariots, and some in *a*horses; But *b*we will boast in the name of the LORD, our God.

8 *a*Is. 2:11, 17 *b*Ps. 37:24; Mic. 7:8

8 They have *a*bowed down and fallen;

But we have *b*risen and stood upright.

9 *a*Ps. 3:7 *b*Ps. 17:6

9 *a*Save, O LORD; May the *b*King answer us in the day we call.

PSALM 21

For the choir director. A Psalm of David.

1 *a*Ps. 59:16, 17

O LORD, in Thy strength the king will *a*be glad, And in Thy salvation how greatly he will rejoice!

2 *a*Ps. 20:4; 37:4

2 Thou hast *a*given him his heart's desire, And Thou hast not withheld the request of his lips. [Selah.

★ 3 *a*Ps. 59:10 *b*2 Sam. 12:30

3 For Thou *a*dost meet him with the blessings of good things; Thou dost set a *b*crown of fine gold on his head.

4 *a*Ps. 61:6; 133:3 *b*Ps. 91:16

4 He asked life of Thee, Thou *a*didst give it to him, *b*Length of days forever and ever.

5 *a*Ps. 9:14; 20:5 *b*Ps. 8:5; 96:6

5 His *a*glory is great through Thy salvation, *b*Splendor and majesty Thou dost place upon him.

6 *a*1 Chr. 17:27 *b*Ps. 43:4

6 For Thou dost make him most *a*blessed forever; Thou dost make him joyful *b*with gladness in Thy presence.

★ 7 *a*Ps. 125:1 *b*Ps. 112:6

7 For the king *a*trusts in the LORD, And through the lovingkindness of the Most High *b*he will not be shaken.

Psalm 20 In this royal psalm, David relays the people's prayer for his victory in battle (vv. 1–5), rehearses his own trust in God for victory (vv. 6–8), and reiterates the people's prayer to the Lord, their King (v. 9).
20:1-6 Throughout these verses *you* refers to the *anointed* king (v. 6).
Psalm 21 In this royal thanksgiving psalm, David acknowledges that God has established his kingdom (vv. 1–7), rehearses the people's anticipation of his further success as their king (vv.

8–12), and records their praise to the Lord (v. 13). The psalm is partly Messianic (e.g., vv. 4–6, 10–12), the language of these verses being hyperbolic in relation to David, but literally true of Christ.
21:3 *dost meet.* God confronts David with blessing (cf. 18:35).
21:7 *lovingkindness.* Heb., *hesed;* see note on Hos. 2:19. *the Most High.* Heb., *Elyon;* see note on Gen. 14:18.

8 Your hand will ^afind out
all your enemies;
Your right hand will find
out those who hate
you.

9 You will make them ^aas a
fiery oven in the time
of your anger;
The LORD will ^bswallow
them up in His wrath,
And ^cfire will devour
them.

10 Their offspring Thou wilt
destroy from the
earth,
And their ^adescendants
from among the sons
of men.

11 Though they ^aintended
evil against Thee,
And ^bdevised a plot,
They will not succeed.

12 For Thou wilt ^amake them
turn their back;
Thou wilt aim ^bwith Thy
bowstrings at their
faces.

13 Be Thou exalted, O LORD,
in Thy strength;
We will ^asing and praise
Thy power.

PSALM 22

For the choir director; upon
Aijeleth Hashshahar. A Psalm
of David.

^aM<small>Y</small> God, my God, why hast
Thou forsaken me?
^bFar from my deliverance
are the words of my
^cgroaning.

2 O my God, I ^acry by day,
but Thou dost not an-
swer;
And by night, but I have
no rest.

3 Yet ^aThou art holy,
O Thou who art enthroned
upon ^bthe praises of
Israel.

4 In Thee our fathers ^atrust-
ed;
They trusted, and Thou
didst ^bdeliver them.

5 To Thee they cried out,
and were delivered;
^aIn Thee they trusted, and
were not disap-
pointed.

6 But I am a ^aworm, and not
a man,
A ^breproach of men, and
^cdespised by the peo-
ple.

7 All who see me ^asneer at
me;
They separate with the lip,
they ^bwag the head,
saying,

8 "Commit *yourself* to the
LORD; ^alet Him deliver
him;
Let Him rescue him, be-
cause He delights in
him."

9 Yet Thou art He who
^adidst bring me forth
from the womb;
Thou didst make me trust
when upon my moth-
er's breasts.

10 Upon Thee I was cast
^afrom birth;

21:8 *will find out.* In the sense of "overthrow."
21:10-12 *Thou* and *Thee* in these verses probably refer to the king, with ultimate reference
to Christ.
Psalm 22 In this lament psalm, David expresses his trust in God (vv. 3–5, 9–10) in spite of
his apparent rejection by God (vv. 1–2) and by
men (vv. 6–8), petitions God's help and deliverance (vv. 11, 19–21) in the face of attacks by his
enemies (vv. 11–18), confidently resolves to
praise God (vv. 22, 25), invites others to join in
that praise (vv. 23, 26) because God has heard his
prayer (v. 24), and predicts the future worldwide

worship of the Lord (vv. 27–31). *upon Aijeleth
Hashshahar* (in superscription). Lit., upon the
hind of the dawn. Probably the name of a tune.
The psalm is typico-prophetically Messianic (see
note on Psalm 16:8) and is one of the most
quoted psalms in the N.T.
22:1 Jesus quoted this first phrase on the cross
(see note on Matt. 27:46).
22:3 *the praises of Israel.* A figure of speech for
the sanctuary, where Israel praised the Lord.
22:7 *separate with the lip.* A mocking gesture,
similar to "stick out the tongue."

Thou hast been my God from my mother's womb.

11 [a]Be not far from me, for trouble is near;
For there is [b]none to help.

12 Many [a]bulls have surrounded me;
Strong *bulls* of [b]Bashan have encircled me.

13 They [a]open wide their mouth at me,
As a ravening and a roaring [b]lion.

14 I am [a]poured out like water,
And all my [b]bones are out of joint;
My [c]heart is like wax;
It is melted within me.

15 My [a]strength is dried up like a potsherd,
And [b]my tongue cleaves to my jaws;
And Thou dost [c]lay me in the dust of death.

16 For [a]dogs have surrounded me;
A band of evildoers has encompassed me;
They [b]pierced my hands and my feet.

17 I can count all my bones.
[a]They look, they stare at me;

18 They [a]divide my garments among them,
And for my clothing they cast lots.

19 But Thou, O Lord, [a]be not far off;
O Thou my help, [b]hasten to my assistance.

20 Deliver my soul from [a]the sword,
My [b]only *life* from the power of the dog.

21 Save me from the [a]lion's mouth;
And from the horns of the [b]wild oxen Thou dost [c]answer me.

22 I will [a]tell of Thy name to my brethren;
In the midst of the assembly I will praise Thee.

23 [a]You who fear the Lord, praise Him;
All you descendants of Jacob, [b]glorify Him,
And [c]stand in awe of Him, all you descendants of Israel.

24 For He has [a]not despised nor abhorred the affliction of the afflicted;
Neither has He [b]hidden His face from him;
But [c]when he cried to Him for help, He heard.

25 From Thee *comes* [a]my praise in the great assembly;
I shall [b]pay my vows before those who fear Him.

26 The afflicted shall eat and [a]be satisfied;
Those who seek Him will [b]praise the Lord.
Let your [c]heart live forever!

27 All the [a]ends of the earth will remember and turn to the Lord,

---

★11-18
11 [a]Ps. 71:12
[b]2 Kin. 14:26; Ps. 72:12; Is. 63:5
★12 [a]Ps. 22:21; 68:30
[b]Deut. 32:14; Amos 4:1
13 [a]Job 16:10; Ps. 35:21; Lam. 2:16; 3:46
[b]Ps. 10:9; 17:12
14 [a]Job 30:16 [b]Ps. 31:10; Dan. 5:6 [c]Josh. 7:5; Job 23:16; Ps. 73:26; Nah. 2:10
★15 [a]Ps. 38:10 [b]John 19:28 [c]Ps. 104:29

★16 [a]Ps. 59:6, 7
[b]Matt. 27:35; John 20:25

★17 [a]Luke 23:27, 35

★18 [a]Matt. 27:35; Mark 15:24; Luke 23:34; John 19:24

19 [a]Ps. 22:11 [b]Ps. 70:5

20 [a]Ps. 37:14 [b]Ps. 35:17

★21 [a]Ps. 22:13 [b]Ps. 22:12 [c]Ps. 34:4; 118:5; 120:1

★22-26
22 [a]Ps. 40:10; Heb. 2:12
23 [a]Ps. 135:19, 20 [b]Ps. 86:12 [c]Ps. 33:8
24 [a]Ps. 69:33 [b]Ps. 27:9; 69:17; 102:2 [c]Ps. 31:22; Heb. 5:7
25 [a]Ps. 35:18; 40:9, 10 [b]Ps. 61:8; Eccl. 5:4
26 [a]Ps. 107:9 [b]Ps. 40:16 [c]Ps. 69:32

★27-31
27 [a]Ps. 2:8; 82:8 [b]Ps. 86:9

22:11–18 David describes his struggle with death in language which is also appropriate to the suffering Messiah. Verses 14-16 prophetically describe crucifixion, a means of execution not known until Roman times: the pain, the extreme thirst, asphyxiation, and agony to the hands and feet.
22:12 *bulls of Bashan.* See note on Amos 4:1.
22:15 *potsherd.* A broken piece of an earthenware vessel.
22:16 *dogs,* who haunted streets as scavengers, well describe the savage enemies.

22:17 The victim was a living skeleton.
22:18 See note on Matt. 27:35. All these details of Jesus' crucifixion were carried out by people who had no knowledge of these predictions.
22:21 The deliverance of the Messiah was accomplished by His resurrection from the dead.
22:22-26 Gratitude was expressed publicly with a sacrifice (v. 25) and a feast (v. 26; cf. Lev. 7:16). Verse 22 is also (see note on 22:1) used of Christ (Heb. 2:12).
22:27-31 A description of millennial blessings. On the feast of verse 29, see note on Isa. 25:6.

And all the [b]families of the nations will worship before Thee.

28 aPs. 47:7; Obad. 21; Zech. 14:9; Matt. 6:13 bPs. 47:8

28 For the [a]kingdom is the LORD's,
And He [b]rules over the nations.

29 aPs. 17:10; 45:12; Hab. 1:16 bPs. 28:1; Is. 26:19 cPs. 89:48

29 All the [a]prosperous of the earth will eat and worship,
All those who [b]go down to the dust will bow before Him,
Even he who [c]cannot keep his soul alive.

30 aPs. 102:28 bPs. 102:18

30 [a]Posterity will serve Him;
It will be told of the Lord to [b]the *coming* generation.

31 aPs. 40:9; 71:18 bPs. 78:6

31 They will come and [a]will declare His righteousness
To a people [b]who will be born, that He has performed *it*.

PSALM 23

★ **1** aPs. 78:52; 80:1; Is. 40:11; Jer. 31:10; Ezek. 34:11-13; John 10:11; 1 Pet. 2:25 bPs. 34:9, 10; Phil. 4:19
★ **2** aPs. 65:11-13; Ezek. 34:14 bRev. 7:17 cPs. 36:8; 46:4

A Psalm of David.

THE LORD is my [a]shepherd,
I shall [b]not want.
2 He makes me lie down in [a]green pastures;
He [b]leads me beside [c]quiet waters.

3 He [a]restores my soul;
He [b]guides me in the [c]paths of righteousness
For His name's sake.

★ **3** aPs. 19:7 bPs. 5:8; 31:3 cPs. 85:13; Prov. 4:11; 8:20

4 Even though I [a]walk through the valley of the shadow of death,
I [b]fear no evil; for [c]Thou art with me;
Thy [d]rod and Thy staff, they comfort me.

★ **4** aJob 10:21, 22; Ps. 107:14 bPs. 3:6; 27:1 cPs. 16:8; Is. 43:2 dMic. 7:14

5 Thou dost [a]prepare a table before me in the presence of my enemies;
Thou hast [b]anointed my head with oil;
My [c]cup overflows.

★ **5** aPs. 78:19 bPs. 92:10; Luke 7:46 cPs. 16:5

6 Surely [a]goodness and lovingkindness will follow me all the days of my life,
And I will [b]dwell in the house of the LORD forever.

★ **6** aPs. 25:7, 10 bPs. 27:4-6

PSALM 24

A Psalm of David.

THE [a]earth is the LORD's, and all it contains,
The [b]world, and those who dwell in it.
2 For He has [a]founded it upon the seas,
And established it upon the rivers.

★ **1** a1 Cor. 10:26 bPs. 89:11

2 aPs. 104:3, 5; 136:6

Psalm 23 In his most beautiful song of trust, David pictures the Lord as the great Shepherd who provides for and protects His sheep (vv. 1-4) and as the gracious Host who protects and provides abundantly for His guests (vv. 5-6).
23:1 The figure of a *shepherd* depicts the Lord as guide, protector, and constant companion (cf. Gen. 48:15; Isa. 49:10; Jer. 31:9-10; Ezek. 34; Psalm 80:1; 95:7).
23:2 *quiet waters.* Inlets or ponds where rest and refreshment could be found.
23:3 *restores.* Through the provision of food and water (v. 2). God's leading is always in *paths* which are right in His eyes and which will honor His name (i.e., His holy person).
23:4 The shepherd protects his sheep with his *rod* or club (used to fight off wild beasts), and He guides straying sheep with his *staff* or crook.

23:5 As a gracious Host, God provides all that we need. *anointed.* A courtesy shown guests at a banquet.
23:6 David sees himself not merely as a guest-for-a-day, but as a recipient of God's covenant *lovingkindness* (see note on Hos. 2:19) *forever. the house of the Lord* is the place where God is.
Psalm 24 Beginning with a hymn of praise to God the Owner and Creator of the whole earth (vv. 1-2), David then instructs prospective worshipers (vv. 3-6) and concludes with an anthem to the King of glory (vv. 7-10). David may have composed this psalm when he brought the Ark to Jerusalem (2 Sam. 6; or on one of the anniversaries of that occasion).
24:1 God owns everything because He made everything.

3 aPs. 15:1
bPs. 2:6
cPs. 65:4

3 Who may ªascend into the
ᵇhill of the LORD?
And who may stand in His
holy ᶜplace?

★ **4** aJob
17:9; Ps.
22:30; 26:6
bPs. 51:10;
73:1; Matt.
5:8 cEzek.
18:15 dPs.
15:4

4 He who has ªclean hands
and a ᵇpure heart,
Who has not ᶜlifted up his
soul to falsehood,
And has not ᵈsworn de-
ceitfully.

5 aPs.
115:13 bPs.
36:10

5 He shall receive a ªblessing
from the LORD
And ᵇrighteousness from
the God of his salva-
tion.

★ **6** aPs.
27:4, 8

6 This is the generation of
those who ªseek Him,
Who seek Thy face—*even*
Jacob.   [Selah.

★ **7-10**

7 aPs.
118:20; Is.
26:2 bPs.
29:2, 9; 97:6;
Acts 7:2;
1 Cor. 2:8

7 ªLift up your heads, O
gates,
And be lifted up, O an-
cient doors,
That the King of ᵇglory
may come in!

8 aDeut.
4:34; Ps.
96:7 bEx.
15:3, 6; Ps.
76:3-6

8 Who is the King of glory?
The LORD ªstrong and
mighty,
The LORD ᵇmighty in bat-
tle.

9 aPs. 26:8;
57:11

9 Lift up your heads, O
gates,
And lift *them* up, O an-
cient doors,
That the King of ªglory
may come in!

10 aGen.
32:2; Josh.
5:14; 2 Sam.
5:10; Neh.
9:6

10 Who is this King of glory?
The LORD of ªhosts,
He is the King of glory.
[Selah.

PSALM 25

A Psalm of David.

1 aPs. 86:4;
143:8
2 aPs. 31:1
bPs. 25:20;
31:1 cPs.
13:4; 41:11

T O Thee, O LORD, I ªlift up my
soul.

2 O my God, in Thee ªI
trust,

Do not let me ᵇbe
ashamed;
Do not let my ᶜenemies
exult over me.

3 aPs. 37:9;
40:1; Is.
49:23 bPs.
119:158; Is.
21:2; Hab.
1:13

3 Indeed, ªnone of those
who wait for Thee
will be ashamed;
Those who ᵇdeal treacher-
ously without cause
will be ashamed.

4 aEx.
33:13; Ps.
27:11; 86:11

4 ªMake me know Thy
ways, O LORD;
Teach me Thy paths.

5 aPs.
25:10; 43:3
bPs. 79:9
cPs. 40:1

5 Lead me in ªThy truth and
teach me,
For Thou art the ᵇGod of
my salvation;
For Thee I ᶜwait all the
day.

6 aPs. 98:3
bPs. 103:17

6 ªRemember, O LORD, Thy
compassion and Thy
lovingkindnesses,
For they have been ᵇfrom
of old.

7 aJob
13:26; 20:11
bPs. 51:1
cPs. 31:19

7 Do not remember the ªsins
of my youth or my
transgressions;
ᵇAccording to Thy loving-
kindness remember
Thou me,
For Thy ᶜgoodness' sake,
O LORD.

8 aPs. 86:5
bPs. 92:15
cPs. 32:8

8 ªGood and ᵇupright is the
LORD;
Therefore He ᶜinstructs
sinners in the way.

9 aPs. 23:3
bPs. 27:11

9 He ªleads the humble in
justice,
And He ᵇteaches the hum-
ble His way.

10 aPs.
40:11 bPs.
103:18

10 All the paths of the LORD
are ªlovingkindness
and truth
To ᵇthose who keep His
covenant and His tes-
timonies.

11 aPs. 31:3;
79:9 bEx.
34:9

11 For ªThy name's sake, O
LORD,
ᵇPardon my iniquity, for it
is great.

24:4 Necessary qualities for holiness in worship.
24:6 *Jacob.* Better, like Jacob; referring to Gen.
32:30.
24:7-10 These verses speak prophetically of the
ascension of Christ after His victory over sin
and death and of His coming reign as King
over all the earth.

Psalm 25 In this psalm, David petitions the
Lord for protection, guidance, and pardon (vv.
1-7), describes some of the attributes of God (vv.
8-14), and prays for deliverance (vv. 15-22).
With minor exceptions, each verse of this alphabetic acrostic psalm begins with successive letters of the Hebrew alphabet.

12 Who is the man who
　　ᵃfears the LORD?
　He will ᵇinstruct him in
　　the way he should
　　choose.

13 His soul will ᵃabide in
　　prosperity,
　And his descendants will
　　ᵇinherit the land.

14 The ᵃsecret of the LORD is
　　for those who fear
　　Him,
　And He will ᵇmake them
　　know His covenant.

15 My ᵃeyes are continually
　　toward the LORD,
　For He will ᵇpluck my feet
　　out of the net.

16 ᵃTurn to me and be gra-
　　cious to me,
　For I am ᵇlonely and af-
　　flicted.

17 The ᵃtroubles of my heart
　　are enlarged;
　Bring me ᵇout of my dis-
　　tresses.

18 ᵃLook upon my affliction
　　and my trouble,
　And ᵇforgive all my sins.

19 Look upon my enemies,
　　for they ᵃare many;
　And they ᵇhate me with
　　violent hatred.

20 ᵃGuard my soul and de-
　　liver me;
　Do not let me ᵇbe
　　ashamed, for I take
　　refuge in Thee.

21 Let ᵃintegrity and upright-
　　ness preserve me,
　For ᵇI wait for Thee.

22 ᵃRedeem Israel, O God,
　　Out of all his troubles.

Left margin references

12 ᵃPs. 31:19 ᵇPs. 25:8; 37:23
13 ᵃProv. 1:33; Jer. 23:6 ᵇPs. 37:11; 69:36; Matt. 5:5
14 ᵃProv. 3:32; John 7:17 ᵇGen. 17:1, 2
15 ᵃPs. 123:2; 141:8 ᵇPs. 31:4; 124:7
16 ᵃPs. 69:16 ᵇPs. 143:4
17 ᵃPs. 40:12 ᵇPs. 107:6
18 ᵃ2 Sam. 16:12; Ps. 31:7 ᵇPs. 103:3
19 ᵃPs. 3:1 ᵇPs. 9:13
20 ᵃPs. 86:2 ᵇPs. 25:2
21 ᵃPs. 41:12 ᵇPs. 25:3
★22 ᵃPs. 130:8

PSALM 26

A Psalm of David.

VINDICATE me, O LORD, for I
　　have ᵇwalked in my
　　integrity;
　And I have ᶜtrusted in the
　　LORD ᵈwithout waver-
　　ing.

2 ᵃExamine me, O LORD, and
　　try me;
　ᵇTest my mind and my
　　heart.

3 For Thy ᵃlovingkindness is
　　before my eyes,
　And I have ᵇwalked in Thy
　　truth.

4 I do not ᵃsit with deceitful
　　men,
　Nor will I go with ᵇpre-
　　tenders.

5 I ᵃhate the assembly of
　　evildoers,
　And I will not sit with the
　　wicked.

6 I shall ᵃwash my hands in
　　innocence,
　And I will go about ᵇThine
　　altar, O LORD,

7 That I may proclaim with
　　the voice of ᵃthanks-
　　giving,
　And declare all Thy won-
　　ders.

8 O LORD, I ᵃlove the habita-
　　tion of Thy house,
　And the place where Thy
　　ᵇglory dwells.

9 ᵃDo not take my soul away
　　along with sinners,

Right margin references

★1 ᵃPs. 7:8 ᵇ2 Kin. 20:3; Prov. 20:7 ᶜPs. 13:5; 28:7 ᵈHeb. 10:23
★2 ᵃPs. 17:3; 139:23 ᵇPs. 7:9
3 ᵃPs. 48:9 ᵇ2 Kin. 20:3; Ps. 86:11
4 ᵃPs. 1:1 ᵇPs. 28:3
5 ᵃPs. 31:6; 139:21
6 ᵃPs. 73:13 ᵇPs. 43:3, 4
7 ᵃPs. 9:1
8 ᵃPs. 27:4 ᵇPs. 24:7
★9-10
9 ᵃPs. 28:3 ᵇPs. 139:19

25:22 What David has prayed for himself, he also prays for the nation.
　Psalm 26 David first seeks divine vindication of his integrity (vv. 1-8), then petitions God to deliver him from the fate of the wicked (vv. 9-11), and finally resolves to praise the Lord for answering (v. 12).
26:1 *integrity.* I.e., sincerity of purpose and sin-
gle-hearted devotion, not sinlessness.
26:2 David invites God to *examine* his claim of innocency of the charges of wickedness brought against him by others (see note on 17:3).
26:9-10 *Do not take.* David prays for a holy separation from sinners so that in the day of judgment he will not be taken with them.

10 aPs. 37:7
bPs. 15:5

Nor my life with ᵇmen of
   bloodshed,

10 In whose hands is a
   ᵃwicked scheme,
And whose right hand is
   full of ᵇbribes.

11 aPs. 26:1
bPs. 44:26;
69:18

11 But as for me, I shall ᵃwalk
   in my integrity;
ᵇRedeem me, and be gra-
   cious to me.

12 aPs. 40:2
bPs. 27:11
cPs. 22:22

12 ᵃMy foot stands on a ᵇlevel
   place;
In the ᶜcongregations I
   shall bless the LORD.

PSALM 27

A Psalm of David.

★ 1 aPs.
18:28; Is.
60:20; Mic.
7:8 bEx.
15:2; Ps.
62:7; 118:14;
Is. 33:2; Jon.
2:9 cPs. 28:8
dPs. 118:6
2 aPs. 14:4
bPs. 9:3

THE LORD is my ᵃlight and my
   ᵇsalvation;
Whom shall I fear?
The LORD is the ᶜdefense of
   my life;
ᵈWhom shall I dread?

2 When evildoers came
   upon me to ᵃdevour
   my flesh,
My adversaries and my en-
   emies, they ᵇstumbled
   and fell.

3 aPs. 3:6
bJob 4:6

3 Though a ᵃhost encamp
   against me,
My heart will not fear;
Though war arise against
   me,
In *spite of* this I shall be
   ᵇconfident.

4 aPs. 26:8
bPs. 23:6
cPs. 90:17
dPs. 18:6

4 ᵃOne thing I have asked
   from the LORD, that I
   shall seek:
That I may ᵇdwell in the
   house of the LORD all
   the days of my life,
To behold ᶜthe beauty of
   the LORD,

And to ᵈmeditate in His
   temple.

5 For in the ᵃday of trouble
He will ᵇconceal me in
   His tabernacle;
In the secret place of His
   tent He will ᶜhide me;
He will ᵈlift me up on a
   rock.

★ 5 aPs.
50:15 bPs.
31:20 cPs.
17:8 dPs.
40:2

6 And now ᵃmy head will be
   lifted up above my
   enemies around me;
And I will offer in His tent
   ᵇsacrifices with shouts
   of joy;
I will ᶜsing, yes, I will sing
   praises to the LORD.

★ 6 aPs. 3:3
bPs. 107:22
cPs. 13:6

7 ᵃHear, O LORD, when I cry
   with my voice,
And be gracious to me and
   ᵇanswer me.

7 aPs. 4:3;
61:1 bPs.
13:3

8 *When Thou didst say,*
   "ᵃSeek My face," my
   heart said to Thee,
"Thy face, O LORD, ᵇI shall
   seek."

8 aPs.
105:4; Amos
5:6 bPs.
34:4

9 ᵃDo not hide Thy face
   from me,
Do not turn Thy servant
   away in ᵇanger;
Thou hast been ᶜmy help;
ᵈDo not abandon me nor
   ᵉforsake me,
O God of my salvation!

9 aPs.
69:17 bPs.
6:1 cPs.
40:17 dPs.
94:14 ePs.
37:28

10 For my father and ᵃmy
   mother have forsaken
   me,
But ᵇthe LORD will take me
   up.

★10 aIs.
49:15 bIs.
40:11

11 ᵃTeach me Thy way, O
   LORD,
And lead me in a ᵇlevel
   path,
Because of my foes.

11 aPs. 25:4;
86:11 bPs.
5:8; 26:12

12 Do not deliver me over to
   the ᵃdesire of my ad-
   versaries;

12 aPs. 41:2
bDeut.
19:18; Ps.
35:11; Matt.
26:60 cActs
9:1

Psalm 27 In this great anthem of praise, David expresses his confidence in the Lord (vv. 1-6), prays for continued victory (vv. 7-12), and rejoices in his waiting on the Lord (vv. 13-14).
27:1 *light* dispels the anxieties and dangers of darkness; *salvation* guarantees the defeat of all adversaries; *defense* (stronghold) assures victory against all assaults.
27:5 *tabernacle.* Tent, a place of shelter.
27:6 *lifted up.* In victory.

27:10 The verse is probably conditional: "If my father . . ."
Psalm 28 In this lament psalm, David petitions the Lord to deliver him from the just judgment due his enemies (vv. 1-4), confidently predicts their punishment (v. 5), publicly praises God for the assurance of an answer to his prayer (vv. 6-8), and petitions the Lord to save Israel (v. 9).

For [b]false witnesses have
risen against me,
And such as [c]breathe out
violence.

13 *I would have despaired* unless I had believed
that I would see the
[a]goodness of the LORD
In the [b]land of the living.

14 [a]Wait for the LORD;
Be [b]strong, and let your
heart take courage;
Yes, wait for the LORD.

PSALM 28*

A Psalm of David.

1 TO Thee, O LORD, I call;
My [a]rock, do not be deaf
to me,
Lest, if Thou [b]be silent to
me,
I become like those who
[c]go down to the pit.

2 Hear the [a]voice of my supplications when I cry
to Thee for help,
When I [b]lift up my hands
[c]toward Thy holy
[d]sanctuary.

3 [a]Do not drag me away
with the wicked
And with those who work
iniquity;
Who [b]speak peace with
their neighbors,
While evil is in their
hearts.

4 Requite them [a]according
to their work and ac-
cording to the evil of
their practices;
Requite them according to
the deeds of their
hands;
Repay them their recom-
pense.

5 Because they [a]do not regard the works of the
LORD
Nor the deeds of His
hands,
He will tear them down
and not build them
up.

6 Blessed be the LORD,
Because He [a]has heard the
voice of my supplica-
tion.

7 The LORD is my [a]strength
and my [b]shield;
My heart [c]trusts in Him,
and I am helped;
Therefore [d]my heart ex-
ults,
And with [e]my song I shall
thank Him.

8 The LORD is their [a]strength,
And He is a [b]saving de-
fense to His anointed.

9 [a]Save Thy people, and
bless [b]Thine inheri-
tance;
Be their [c]shepherd also,
and [d]carry them for-
ever.

PSALM 29

A Psalm of David.

1 [a]ASCRIBE to the LORD, O sons
of the mighty,
Ascribe to the LORD glory
and strength.

2 Ascribe to the LORD the
glory due to His
name;
Worship the LORD [a]in holy
array.

Marginal references

13 [a]Ps. 31:19 [b]Job 28:13; Ps. 52:5; 116:9; 142:5; Is. 38:11; Jer. 11:19; Ezek. 26:20

14 [a]Ps. 25:3; 37:34; 40:1; 62:5; 130:5; Prov. 20:22; Is. 25:9 [b]Ps. 31:24

★ 1 [a]Ps. 18:2 [b]Ps. 35:22; 39:12; 83:1 [c]Ps. 88:4; 143:7; Prov. 1:12

★ 2 [a]Ps. 140:6 [b]Ps. 134:2; 141:2; Lam. 2:19; 1 Tim. 2:8 [c]Ps. 5:7; 138:2 [d]1 Kin. 6:5

3 [a]Ps. 26:9 [b]Ps. 12:2; 55:21; 62:4; Jer. 9:8

4 [a]Ps. 62:12; 2 Tim. 4:14; Rev. 18:6; 22:12

5 [a]Is. 5:12

6 [a]Ps. 28:2

7 [a]Ps. 18:2; 59:17 [b]Ps. 3:3 [c]Ps. 13:5; 112:7 [d]Ps. 16:9 [e]Ps. 40:3; 69:30

★ 8-9
8 [a]Ps. 20:6; 89:17 [b]Ps. 27:1; 140:7
9 [a]Ps. 106:47 [b]Deut. 9:29; 32:9; 1 Kin. 8:51; Ps. 33:12; 106:40 [c]Ps. 80:1 [d]Deut. 1:31; Is. 40:11; 46:3; 63:9

★ 1 [a]1 Chr. 16:28, 29; Ps. 96:7-9

★ 2 [a]2 Chr. 20:21; Ps. 110:3

---

*See note, p. 821.
28:1 *deaf.* In the sense of not answering.
28:2 *sanctuary.* Refers to the Holy of Holies.
28:8-9 The Lord provides the *strength* of a fortress and the care of a *shepherd.*
Psalm 29 This hymn of David ascribes glory
to the omnipotent Lord (vv. 1-2) who controls
and reveals Himself in nature (vv. 3-9) and in
blessing His people with strength and peace (vv.
10-11). The name of the Lord (Yahweh, LORD)

occurs 18 times in this brief psalm (see note on
Gen. 2:4).
29:1 *sons of the mighty.* Probably refers to angels (though some understand the reference to
be to the people of God).
29:2 *in holy array.* Or, in the beauty of holiness.
While the phrase may be translated either
way, it likely refers to God's holiness not
man's, and means, "Worship the Lord for the
splendor of His holiness."

★ 3-9
3 [a]Ps. 104:7 [b]Job 37:4, 5; Ps. 18:13 [c]Ps. 18:16; 107:23

3 The [a]voice of the LORD is upon the waters;
The God of glory [b]thunders,
The LORD is over [c]many waters.

4 [a]Ps. 68:33

4 The voice of the LORD is [a]powerful,
The voice of the LORD is majestic.

5 [a]Judg. 9:15; 1 Kin. 5:6; Ps. 104:16; Is. 2:13; 14:8

5 The voice of the LORD breaks the cedars;
Yes, the LORD breaks in pieces [a]the cedars of Lebanon.

6 [a]Ps. 114:4, 6 [b]Deut. 3:9

6 And He makes Lebanon [a]skip like a calf,
And [b]Sirion like a young wild ox.
7 The voice of the LORD hews out flames of fire.

8 [a]Num. 13:26

8 The voice of the LORD shakes the wilderness;
The LORD shakes the wilderness of [a]Kadesh.

9 [a]Job 39:1 [b]Ps. 26:8

9 The voice of the LORD makes [a]the deer to calve,
And strips the forests bare,
And [b]in His temple everything says, "Glory!"

★10 [a]Gen. 6:17 [b]Ps. 10:16

10 The LORD sat *as King* at the [a]flood;
Yes, the LORD sits as [b]King forever.

11 [a]Ps. 28:8; 68:35; Is. 40:29 [b]Ps. 37:11; 72:3

11 The LORD will give [a]strength to His people;
The LORD will bless His people with [b]peace.

PSALM 30

A Psalm; a Song at the Dedication of the House.
A Psalm of David.

1 [a]Ps. 118:28; 145:1 [b]Ps. 3:3 [c]Ps. 25:2; 35:19, 24

I WILL [a]extol Thee, O LORD, for Thou hast [b]lifted me up,
And hast not let my [c]enemies rejoice over me.

2 [a]Ps. 88:13 [b]Ps. 6:2; 103:3; Is. 53:5

2 O LORD my God,
I [a]cried to Thee for help, and Thou didst [b]heal me.

★ 3 [a]Ps. 86:13 [b]Ps. 28:1

3 O LORD, Thou hast [a]brought up my soul from Sheol;
Thou hast kept me alive, that I should not [b]go down to the pit.

4 [a]Ps. 149:1 [b]Ps. 50:5 [c]Ps. 97:12 [d]Ex. 3:15; Ps. 135:13; Hos. 12:5

4 [a]Sing praise to the LORD, you [b]His godly ones,
And [c]give thanks to His holy [d]name.

5 [a]Ps. 103:9; Is. 26:20; 54:7, 8 [b]Ps. 118:1 [c]Ps. 126:5; 2 Cor. 4:17

5 For [a]His anger is but for a moment,
His [b]favor is for a lifetime;
Weeping may [c]last for the night,
But a shout of joy *comes* in the morning.

★ 6-7
6 [a]Ps. 10:6; 62:2, 6

6 Now as for me, I said in my prosperity,
"I will [a]never be moved."

7 [a]Deut. 31:17; Ps. 104:29; 143:7

7 O LORD, by Thy favor Thou hast made my mountain to stand strong;
Thou didst [a]hide Thy face, I was dismayed.

29:3-9 David describes a mighty thunderstorm which rises from the W. over the Mediterranean (vv. 3-4), breaks in full fury over the mountains of *Lebanon* and *Sirion* (Mt. Hermon) and down the length of Canaan (vv. 5-7), and finally passes out of sight and sound into the desert of *Kadesh* (vv. 8-9). *flames of fire* (v. 7). Lightning.

29:10 The Hebrew word used here for *flood* is found elsewhere only in Gen. 6-11; thus David is apparently referring here to the Flood of Noah.

Psalm 30 In this individual thanksgiving psalm, David acknowledges God's deliverance, calling on the congregation to join in praise (vv. 1-5); he remembers his past sin (vv. 6-10), and renews his praise to God (vv. 11-12).

30:3 *Thou hast brought up my soul from Sheol.* I.e., God delivered him from the brink of death.

30:6-7 David reflects on his past distress caused by his self-sufficiency and by God's chastening. Some hold that this refers to the plague God sent on Israel because of David's census (2 Sam. 24; 1 Chron. 21). If so, 70,000 died because of his sin.

8 To Thee, O Lord, I called,
And to the Lord I made
supplication:

9 "What profit is there in my
blood, if I [a]go down to
the pit?
Will the [b]dust praise Thee?
Will it declare Thy
faithfulness?

10 "[a]Hear, O Lord, and be gracious to me;
O Lord, be Thou my
[b]helper."

11 Thou hast turned for me
[a]my mourning into
dancing;
Thou hast [b]loosed my
sackcloth and girded
me with [c]gladness;

12 That *my* [a]soul may sing
praise to Thee, and
not be silent.
O Lord my God, I will
[b]give thanks to Thee
forever.

PSALM 31

For the choir director. A
Psalm of David.

[a]IN Thee, O Lord, I have taken
refuge;
Let me never [b]be ashamed;
[c]In Thy righteousness deliver me.

2 [a]Incline Thine ear to me,
rescue me quickly;
Be Thou to me a [b]rock of
strength,
A stronghold to save me.

3 For Thou art my rock and
[a]my fortress;
For [b]Thy name's sake
Thou wilt lead me and
guide me.

4 Thou wilt [a]pull me out of
the net which they
have secretly laid for
me;
For Thou art my [b]strength.

5 [a]Into Thy hand I commit
my spirit;
Thou hast [b]ransomed me,
O Lord, [c]God of truth.

6 I hate those who [a]regard
vain idols;
But I [b]trust in the Lord.

7 I will [a]rejoice and be glad
in Thy lovingkind-
ness,
Because Thou hast [b]seen
my affliction;
Thou hast known the trou-
bles of my soul,

8 And Thou hast not [a]given
me over into the hand
of the enemy;
Thou hast set my feet in a
large place.

9 Be gracious to me, O Lord,
for [a]I am in distress;
My [b]eye is wasted away
from grief, [c]my soul
and my body *also*.

10 For my life is spent with
[a]sorrow,
And my years with sigh-
ing;
My [b]strength has failed
because of my iniq-
uity,
And [c]my body has wasted
away.

11 Because of all my adversaries, I have become
a [a]reproach,
Especially to my [b]neigh-
bors,
And an object of dread to
my acquaintances;
Those who see me in the
street flee from me.

Marginal references (left column):
- ★ 9 [a]Ps. 28:1 [b]Ps. 6:5
- 10 [a]Ps. 4:1; 27:7 [b]Ps. 27:9; 54:4
- 11 [a]Eccl. 3:4; Jer. 31:4, 13 [b]Is. 20:2 [c]Ps. 4:7
- 12 [a]Ps. 16:9; 57:8; 108:1 [b]Ps. 44:8
- 1 [a]Ps. 31:1-3; 71:1-3 [b]Ps. 25:2 [c]Ps. 143:1
- 2 [a]Ps. 17:6; 71:2; 86:1; 102:2 [b]Ps. 18:2; 71:3
- 3 [a]Ps. 18:2 [b]Ps. 23:3; 25:11

Marginal references (right column):
- 4 [a]Ps. 25:15 [b]Ps. 46:1
- ★ 5 [a]Luke 23:46; Acts 7:59 [b]Ps. 55:18; 71:23 [c]Deut. 32:4; Ps. 71:22
- 6 [a]Jon. 2:8 [b]Ps. 52:8
- 7 [a]Ps. 90:14 [b]Ps. 10:14
- 8 [a]Deut. 32:30; Ps. 37:33
- 9 [a]Ps. 66:14; 69:17 [b]Ps. 6:7 [c]Ps. 63:1
- 10 [a]Ps. 13:2 [b]Ps. 39:11 [c]Ps. 32:3; 38:3; 102:3
- 11 [a]Ps. 69:19 [b]Job 19:13; Ps. 38:11; 88:8, 18

30:9 The idea of this verse is that if David dies,
he cannot offer praise to God (see note on
6:4-5).

Psalm 31 In this lament psalm, David first
addresses his prayer to God (vv. 1-8), laments
his physical distress and danger (vv. 9-13), petitions the Lord to deliver him and silence his enemies (vv. 14-18), praises the Lord for delivering
His own (vv. 19-22), and exhorts the godly to
love the Lord and be strong (vv. 23-24).

31:5 Committing one's life to God is the epitome
of faith. Jesus made the supreme commitment
on the cross (Luke 23:46; cf. Acts 7:59).

12 aPs. 88:5

12 I am ^aforgotten as a dead man, out of mind,
I am like a broken vessel.

13 aPs.
50:20; Jer.
20:10 bLam.
2:22 cPs.
62:4; Matt.
27:1 dPs.
41:7

13 For I have heard the ^aslander of many,
^bTerror is on every side;
While they ^ctook counsel together against me,
They ^dschemed to take away my life.

14 aPs.
140:6

14 But as for me, I trust in Thee, O LORD,
I say, "^aThou art my God."

15 aJob
14:5; 24:1
bPs. 143:9

15 My ^atimes are in Thy hand;
^bDeliver me from the hand of my enemies, and from those who persecute me.

16 aNum.
6:25; Ps. 4:6;
80:3 bPs.
6:4

16 Make Thy ^aface to shine upon Thy servant;
^bSave me in Thy lovingkindness.

17 aPs. 25:2,
20 bPs. 25:3
c1 Sam. 2:9;
Ps. 94:17;
115:17

17 Let me not be ^aput to shame, O LORD, for I call upon Thee;
Let the ^bwicked be put to shame, let them ^cbe silent in Sheol.

18 aPs.
109:2; 120:2
b1 Sam. 2:3;
Ps. 94:4;
Jude 15

18 Let the ^alying lips be dumb,
Which ^bspeak arrogantly against the righteous
With pride and contempt.

19 aPs. 65:4;
145:7; Is.
64:4; Rom.
2:4; 11:22
bPs. 5:11
cPs. 23:5

19 How great is Thy ^agoodness,
Which Thou hast stored up for those who fear Thee,
Which Thou hast wrought for those who ^btake refuge in Thee,
^cBefore the sons of men!

20 aPs. 27:5
bPs. 37:12
cJob 5:21;
Ps. 31:13

20 Thou dost hide them in the ^asecret place of Thy presence from the ^bconspiracies of man;

Thou dost keep them secretly in a shelter from the ^cstrife of tongues.

21 ^aBlessed be the LORD,
For He has made ^bmarvelous His lovingkindness to me in a besieged ^ccity.

21 aPs. 28:6
bPs. 17:7
c1 Sam.
23:7; Ps.
87:5

22 As for me, ^aI said in my alarm,
"I am ^bcut off from before Thine eyes";
Nevertheless Thou didst ^chear the voice of my supplications
When I cried to Thee.

22 aPs.
116:11 bPs.
88:5; Is.
38:11, 12;
Lam. 3:54
cPs. 18:6;
66:19;
145:19

23 O love the LORD, all you ^aHis godly ones!
The LORD ^bpreserves the faithful,
And fully ^crecompenses the proud doer.

23 aPs. 30:4;
37:28; 50:5
bPs. 145:20;
Rev. 2:10
cDeut.
32:41; Ps.
94:2

24 ^aBe strong, and let your heart take courage,
All you who hope in the LORD.

24 aPs.
27:14

PSALM 32

A Psalm of David. A Maskil.

HOW blessed is he whose transgression is forgiven,
Whose sin is covered!

1 aPs. 85:2;
103:3; Rom.
4:7, 8

2 How blessed is the man to whom the LORD ^adoes not impute iniquity,
And in whose spirit there is ^bno deceit!

2 a2 Cor.
5:19 bJohn
1:47

3 When ^aI kept silent *about my sin,* ^bmy body wasted away
Through my ^cgroaning all day long.

★ 3-4

3 aPs. 39:2,
3 bPs. 31:10
cPs. 38:8

Psalm 32 This psalm of forgiveness is probably the sequel to Psalm 51, in which David confesses his sin with Bathsheba. Here he describes the blessing of forgiveness which followed chastening and confession (vv. 1-5), then encourages others to seek the Lord's deliverance rather than stubbornly refusing to follow Him (vv. 6-10), and finally exhorts them to rejoice in the Lord (v. 11). *Maskil.* Probably means a contemplative or didactic poem.
32:3-4 While David *kept silent* (did not immediately confess his sin), God chastened him physically and emotionally.

4 a1 Sam.
5:6; Job
23:2; 33:7;
Ps. 38:2;
39:10 bPs.
22:15

4 For day and night aThy hand was heavy upon me;

My bvitality was drained away as with the fever heat of summer. [Selah.

★ 5 aLev.
26:40 bJob
31:33 cPs.
38:18; Prov.
28:13;
1 John 1:9
dPs. 103:12

5 I aacknowledged my sin to Thee,

And my iniquity I bdid not hide;

I said, "cI will confess my transgressions to the LORD";

And Thou ddidst forgive the guilt of my sin. [Selah.

6 aPs.
69:13; Is.
55:6 bPs.
46:1-3; 69:1;
124:5; 144:7;
Is. 43:2

6 Therefore, let everyone who is godly pray to Thee ain a time when Thou mayest be found;

Surely bin a flood of great waters they shall not reach him.

7 aPs. 9:9;
31:20; 91:1;
119:114 bPs.
121:7 cEx.
15:1; Judg.
5:1; Ps. 40:3

7 Thou art amy hiding place; Thou bdost preserve me from trouble;

Thou dost surround me with csongs of deliverance. [Selah.

★ 8-10

8 aPs. 25:8
bPs. 33:18

8 I will ainstruct you and teach you in the way which you should go;

I will counsel you bwith My eye upon you.

9 aProv.
26:3

9 Do not be aas the horse or as the mule which have no understanding,

Whose trappings include bit and bridle to hold them in check,

Otherwise they will not come near to you.

10 aPs. 16:4;
Prov. 13:21;
Rom. 2:9
bPs. 5:11,
12; Prov.
16:20

10 Many are the asorrows of the wicked;

But bhe who trusts in the LORD, lovingkindness shall surround him.

11 Be aglad in the LORD and rejoice you righteous ones,

And shout for joy all you who are bupright in heart.

11 aPs.
64:10; 68:3;
97:12 bPs.
7:10; 64:10

PSALM 33

SING for joy in the LORD, O you righteous ones;

Praise is bbecoming to the upright.

1 aPs.
32:11; Phil.
3:1; 4:4 bPs.
92:1; 147:1

2 Give thanks to the LORD with the alyre;

Sing praises to Him with a bharp of ten strings.

2 aPs.
71:22; 147:7
bPs. 144:9

3 Sing to Him a anew song; Play skillfully with ba shout of joy.

3 aPs. 40:3;
96:1; 98:1;
144:9; Is.
42:10; Rev.
5:9 bPs.
98:4

4 For the word of the LORD ais upright;

And all His work is done bin faithfulness.

★ 4-5

4 aPs. 19:8
bPs. 119:90

5 He aloves righteousness and justice;

The bearth is full of the lovingkindness of the LORD.

5 aPs. 11:7;
37:28 bPs.
119:64

6 By the aword of the LORD the heavens were made,

And bby the breath of His mouth call their host.

6 aGen.
1:6; Ps.
148:5; Heb.
11:3 bPs.
104:30
cGen. 2:1

7 He gathers the awaters of the sea together as a heap;

He lays up the deeps in storehouses.

★ 7 aEx.
15:8; Josh.
3:16; Ps.
78:13

8 Let aall the earth fear the LORD;

Let all the inhabitants of the world bstand in awe of Him.

8 aPs. 67:7
bPs. 96:9

32:5 When he confessed, God forgave (1 John 1:9).

32:8-10 The speaker is David, who now instructs others on the basis of his own experience.

Psalm 33 In this anonymous hymn of praise, the psalmist calls on the righteous to praise the Lord (vv. 1-3) because of His dependability as Ruler (vv. 4-12) and Judge (vv. 13-19). Verses 20-22 are a final chorus of praise.

33:4-5 These verses summarize the heart of the psalm: God is dependable in all His words and works, which are characterized by righteousness, justice, and grace.

33:7 *the deeps.* The vast masses of turbulent water, which God controls.

9 aGen. 1:3; Ps. 148:5

9 For aHe spoke, and it was done;
He commanded, and it stood fast.

10 aPs. 2:1-3; Is. 8:10; 19:3

10 The LORD anullifies the counsel of the nations;
He frustrates the plans of the peoples.

11 aJob 23:12; Prov. 19:21 bPs. 40:5; 92:5; 139:17; Is. 55:8

11 The acounsel of the LORD stands forever,
The bplans of His heart from generation to generation.

12 aPs. 144:15 bEx. 19:5; Deut. 7:6; Ps. 28:9

12 Blessed is the anation whose God is the LORD,
The people whom He has bchosen for His own inheritance.

13 aJob 28:24; Ps. 14:2 bPs. 11:4

13 The LORD alooks from heaven;
He bsees all the sons of men;

14 a1 Kin. 8:39, 43; Ps. 102:19

14 From aHis dwelling place He looks out
On all the inhabitants of the earth,

15 aJob 10:8; Ps. 119:73 b2 Chr. 16:9; Job 34:21; Jer. 32:19 **16** aPs. 44:6; 60:11

15 He who afashions the hearts of them all,
He who bunderstands all their works.

16 aThe king is not saved by a mighty army;
A warrior is not delivered by great strength.

17 aPs. 20:7; 147:10; Prov. 21:31

17 A ahorse is a false hope for victory;
Nor does it deliver anyone by its great strength.

18 aJob 36:7; Ps. 32:8; 34:15; 1 Pet. 3:12 bPs. 32:10; 147:11

18 Behold, athe eye of the LORD is on those who fear Him,
On those who bhope for His lovingkindness,

19 aPs. 56:13; Acts 12:11 bJob 5:20; Ps. 37:19 **20** aPs. 62:1; 130:6; Is. 8:17 bPs. 115:9

19 To adeliver their soul from death,
And to keep them alive bin famine.

20 Our soul awaits for the LORD;

He is our bhelp and our shield.

21 aPs. 13:5; 28:7; Zech. 10:7; John 16:22

21 For our aheart rejoices in Him,
Because we trust in His holy name.

22 Let Thy lovingkindness, O LORD, be upon us,
According as we have hoped in Thee.

PSALM 34

A Psalm of David when he feigned madness before Abimelech, who drove him away and he departed.

1 aEph. 5:20; 1 Thess. 5:18 bPs. 71:6

I WILL abless the LORD at all times;
His bpraise shall continually be in my mouth.

2 aPs. 44:8; Jer. 9:24; 1 Cor. 1:31 bPs. 69:32

2 My soul shall amake its boast in the LORD;
The bhumble shall hear it and rejoice.

3 aPs. 35:27; 69:30; Luke 1:46 bPs. 18:46

3 O amagnify the LORD with me,
And let us bexalt His name together.

4 a2 Chr. 15:2; Ps. 9:10; Matt. 7:7 bPs. 34:6, 17, 19

4 I asought the LORD, and He answered me,
And bdelivered me from all my fears.

5 aPs. 36:9; Is. 60:5 bPs. 25:3

5 They alooked to Him and were radiant,
And their faces shall bnever be ashamed.

6 aPs. 34:4

6 This poor man cried and athe LORD heard him,
And saved him out of all his troubles.

7 aPs. 91:11; Dan. 6:22

7 The aangel of the LORD encamps around those who fear Him,
And rescues them.

8 aPs. 119:103; Heb. 6:5; 1 Pet. 2:3 bPs. 2:12

8 O ataste and see that the LORD is good;

Psalm 34 In this psalm of thanksgiving (an acrostic like Psalm 25), David calls on the congregation to praise the Lord for delivering him and for His goodness to His people (vv. 1-10), and then instructs the people concerning the righteous path to a long life (vv. 11-22). David *feigned madness* (in superscription) before Achish (1 Sam. 21:10-15), who is referred to here under the dynastic title *Abimelech* (see note on Gen. 26:1).

How ^bblessed is the man who takes refuge in Him!

9 O fear the Lord, you ^aHis saints;
For to those who fear Him, there is ^bno want.

10 The young lions do lack and suffer hunger;
But they who seek the Lord shall ^anot be in want of any good thing.

11 ^aCome, you children, listen to me;
^bI will teach you ^cthe fear of the Lord.

12 ^aWho is the man who desires life,
And loves *length of* days that he may ^bsee good?

13 Keep ^ayour tongue from evil,
And your lips from speaking ^bdeceit.

14 ^aDepart from evil, and do good;
Seek peace, and ^bpursue it.

15 The ^aeyes of the Lord are toward the righteous,
And His ears are *open* to their cry.

16 The ^aface of the Lord is against evildoers,
To ^bcut off the memory of them from the earth.

17 *The righteous* ^acry and the Lord hears,
And delivers them out of all their troubles.

18 The Lord ^ais near to the ^bbrokenhearted,
And saves those who are ^ccrushed in spirit.

19 ^aMany are the ^bafflictions of the righteous;
But the Lord ^cdelivers him out of them all.

20 He keeps all his bones;
^aNot one of them is broken.

21 ^aEvil shall slay the wicked;
And those who hate the righteous will be condemned.

22 The Lord ^aredeems the soul of His servants;
And none of those who ^btake refuge in Him will be condemned.

PSALM 35

A Psalm of David.

CONTEND, O Lord, with those who ^acontend with me;
Fight against those who ^bfight against me.

2 Take hold of ^abuckler and shield,
And rise up for ^bmy help.

3 Draw also the spear and the battle-axe to meet those who pursue me;
Say to my soul, "I am ^ayour salvation."

4 Let those be ^aashamed and dishonored who seek my life;
Let those be ^bturned back and humiliated who devise evil against me.

5 Let them be ^alike chaff before the wind,
With the angel of the Lord driving *them* on.

Marginal references:

9 ^aPs. 31:23 ^bPs. 23:1
★**10** ^aPs. 84:11
11 ^aPs. 66:16 ^bPs. 32:8 ^cPs. 111:10
★**12-14**
12 ^aPs. 34:12-16; 1 Pet. 3:10-12 ^bEccl. 3:13
13 ^aPs. 141:3; Prov. 13:3; James 1:26 ^b1 Pet. 2:22
14 ^aPs. 37:27; Is. 1:16, 17 ^bRom. 14:19; Heb. 12:14
15 ^aJob 36:7; Ps. 33:18
16 ^aLev. 17:10; Jer. 44:11; Amos 9:4 ^bJob 18:17; Ps. 9:6, 109:15; Prov. 10:7
17 ^aPs. 34:6; 145:19
18 ^aPs. 145:18 ^bPs. 147:3; Is. 61:1 ^cPs. 51:17; Is. 57:15

19 ^aProv. 24:16 ^bPs. 71:20; 2 Tim. 3:11f. ^cPs. 34:4, 6, 17
★**20** ^aJohn 19:33, 36
21 ^aPs. 94:23; 140:11; Prov. 24:16
22 ^a1 Kin. 1:29; Ps. 71:23 ^bPs. 37:40
1 ^aPs. 18:43; Is. 49:25 ^bPs. 56:2
2 ^aPs. 91:4 ^bPs. 44:26
3 ^aPs. 62:2
4 ^aPs. 70:2 ^bPs. 40:14; 129:5
★ **5** ^aJob 21:18; Ps. 83:13; Is. 29:5

34:10 Though the king of the beasts may starve, the Lord provides for His own (cf. 23:1).

34:12-14 David practiced what he preached (1 Sam. 25:14-16), and so should the Christian (1 Peter 3:10-12).

34:20 *He keeps all his bones.* I.e., God preserves the righteous man though he may be severely afflicted. This scripture had a unique fulfillment in the Righteous One, Jesus Christ (John 19:36).

Psalm 35 In this imprecatory psalm (see Introduction), David petitions the Lord to deliver him and to bring destruction on his enemies (vv. 1-10), laments the unjust hatred of his enemies against him (vv. 11-16), and further petitions the Lord for deliverance and justice (vv. 17-28). It was likely written during the time David was being hunted by Saul and is in a sense an elaboration of 1 Sam. 24:15. The imprecation is not against Saul himself (for David had spared his life), but against those who fomented Saul's insane jealousy against David.

35:5 *the angel of the Lord.* See note on Gen. 16:10.

6 aPs.
73:18; Jer.
23:12

★ 7-8

7 aPs. 69:4;
109:3; 140:5
bPs. 9:15

8 aPs.
55:23; Is.
47:11;
1 Thess. 5:3
bPs. 9:15
cPs. 73:18

9 aIs. 61:10
bPs. 9:14;
13:5; Luke
1:47

10 aPs. 51:8
bEx. 15:11;
Ps. 86:8;
Mic. 7:18
cPs. 18:17
dPs. 37:14;
109:16

11 aPs.
27:12

12 aPs.
38:20; 109:5;
Jer. 18:20;
John 10:32

13 aJob
30:25 bPs.
69:11 cPs.
69:10 dMatt.
10:13; Luke
10:6

14 aPs. 38:6

15 aObad.
12 bJob
30:1, 8, 12
cPs. 7:2

6 Let their way be dark and
   aslippery,
   With the angel of the LORD
   pursuing them.

7 For awithout cause they
   bhid their net for me;
   Without cause they dug a
   pit for my soul.

8 Let adestruction come
   upon him unawares;
   And blet the net which he
   hid catch himself;
   Into that very cdestruction
   let him fall.

9 And my soul shall arejoice
   in the LORD;
   It shall bexult in His salvation.

10 All my abones will say,
   "LORD, bwho is like
   Thee,
   Who delivers the aff⎽ted
   from him cwho is too
   strong for him,
   And dthe afflicted and the
   needy from him who
   robs him?"

11 aMalicious witnesses rise
   up;
   They ask me of things that
   I do not know.

12 They arepay me evil for
   good,
   To the bereavement of my
   soul.

13 But as for me, awhen they
   were sick, my bcloth-
   ing was sackcloth;
   I chumbled my soul with
   fasting;
   And my dprayer kept returning to my bosom.

14 I went about as though it
   were my friend or
   brother;
   I abowed down mourning,
   as one who sorrows
   for a mother.

15 But aat my stumbling they
   rejoiced, and gathered
   themselves together;

The bsmiters whom I did
   not know gathered to-
   gether against me,
   They cslandered me without ceasing.

16 Like godless jesters at a
   feast,
   They agnashed at me with
   their teeth.

17 Lord, ahow long wilt Thou
   look on?
   Rescue my soul bfrom
   their ravages,
   My conly life from the
   lions.

18 I will agive Thee thanks in
   the great congrega-
   tion;
   I will bpraise Thee among
   a mighty throng.

19 aDo not let those who are
   wrongfully bmy en-
   emies rejoice over me;
   Neither let those cwho
   hate me without cause
   dwink maliciously.

20 For they do not speak
   peace,
   But they devise adeceitful
   words against those
   who are quiet in the
   land.

21 And they aopened their
   mouth wide against
   me;
   They said, "bAha, aha, our
   eyes have seen it!"

22 aThou hast seen it, O
   LORD, bdo not keep si-
   lent;
   O Lord, cdo not be far
   from me.

23 aStir up Thyself, and
   awake to my right,
   And to my cause, my God
   and my Lord.

24 aJudge me, O LORD my
   God, according to Thy
   righteousness;
   And bdo not let them rejoice over me.

16 aJob
16:9; Ps.
37:12; Lam.
2:16

17 aPs. 13:1;
Hab. 1:13
bPs. 35:7
cPs. 22:20,
21

18 aPs.
22:22 bPs.
22:25

★19, 21

19 aPs. 13:4;
30:1; 38:16
bPs. 38:19;
69:4 cJohn
15:25 dProv.
6:13; 10:10

20 aPs.
55:21; Jer.
9:8; Mic.
6:12

21 aJob
16:10; Ps.
22:13 bPs.
40:15; 70:3

22 aEx. 3:7;
Ps. 10:14
bPs. 28:1
cPs. 10:1;
22:11; 38:21;
71:12

★23 aPs.
7:6; 44:23;
59:4; 80:2

24 aPs. 9:4;
26:1; 43:1
bPs. 35:19

35:7-8 A classic example of poetic justice.
35:19, 21 Both *wink maliciously* and *opened their mouth wide against me* signify gestures of malice and contempt.

35:23 *my God* (Elohim) *and my Lord* (Adonai). An appeal to the power and sovereignty of God (see notes on Gen. 1:1 and 15:2).

25 aPs.
35:21 bPs.
56:1; 124:3;
Prov. 1:12;
Lam. 2:16

25 Do not let them say in
their heart, "aAha,
our desire!"
Do not let them say, "We
have bswallowed him
up!"

26 aPs.
40:14 bPs.
109:29 cJob
19:5; Ps.
38:16

26 Let athose be ashamed and
humiliated altogether
who rejoice at my dis-
tress;
Let those be bclothed with
shame and dishonor
who cmagnify them-
selves over me.

27 aPs.
32:11 bPs.
9:4 cPs.
40:16; 70:4
dPs. 147:11;
149:4

27 Let them ashout for joy
and rejoice, who favor
bmy vindication;
And clet them say continually, "The LORD be
magnified,
Who ddelights in the prosperity of His servant."

28 aPs.
51:14; 71:15,
24

28 And amy tongue shall declare Thy righteous-
ness
And Thy praise all day
long.

PSALM 36

For the choir director. A
Psalm of David
the servant of the LORD.

★ 1 aRom.
3:18

TRANSGRESSION speaks to
the ungodly within
his heart;
There is ano fear of God
before his eyes.

2 aDeut.
29:19; Ps.
10:11; 49:18

2 For it aflatters him in his
own eyes,
Concerning the discovery
of his iniquity and the
hatred of it.

3 aPs. 10:7;
12:2 bPs.
94:8; Jer.
4:22

3 The awords of his mouth
are wickedness and
deceit;

He has bceased to be wise
and to do good.

4 He aplans wickedness
upon his bed;
He sets himself on a bpath
that is not good;
He cdoes not despise evil.

4 aProv.
4:16; Mic.
2:1 bIs. 65:2
cPs. 52:3;
Rom. 12:9

5 Thy alovingkindness, O
LORD, extends to the
heavens,
Thy faithfulness reaches to
the skies.

★ 5 aPs.
57:10;
103:11;
108:4

6 Thy arighteousness is like
the mountains of God;
Thy bjudgments are like a
great deep.
O LORD, Thou cpreservest
man and beast.

6 aPs.
71:19 bJob
11:8; Ps.
77:19; Rom.
11:33 cNeh.
9:6; Ps.
104:14, 15;
145:16

7 How aprecious is Thy
lovingkindness, O
God!
And the children of men
btake refuge in the
shadow of Thy wings.

★ 7 aPs.
40:5; 139:17
bRuth 2:12;
Ps. 17:8;
57:1; 91:4

8 They adrink their fill of the
abundance of Thy
house;
And Thou dost give them
to drink of the briver
of Thy delights.

8 aPs. 63:5;
65:4; Is.
25:6; Jer.
31:12-14
bJob 20:17;
Ps. 46:4;
Rev. 22:1

9 For with Thee is the afoun-
tain of life;
In Thy light we see light.

9 aJer. 2:13

10 O continue Thy loving-
kindness to athose
who know Thee,
And Thy brighteousness to
the upright in heart.

10 aJer.
22:16 bPs.
24:5

11 Let not the foot of pride
come upon me,
And let not the hand of
the wicked drive me
away.

12 There the doers of iniquity
have fallen;

12 aPs.
140:10; Is.
26:14

Psalm 36 Against the backdrop of the evil
schemes of wicked men (vv. 1-4), David voices
praise in a description of the attributes of God
working in behalf of man's salvation (vv. 5-9),
and petitions God to continue His protective love
(vv. 10-11) with a confident expression concerning the defeat of the wicked (v. 12). servant of
the LORD (in superscription). A title God gave
David as His anointed king (2 Sam. 3:18; 7:5, 8).

36:1 Transgression, rather than God, is viewed
as speaking within the heart of a wicked man
who regards it as an oracle (a divine utterance), assuring him that he need have no fear
of God.
36:5 lovingkindness. Heb., hesed, loyal love or
covenant faithfulness (also vv. 7, 10).
36:7 in the shadow of Thy wings. See note on
Ruth 2:12.

They have been thrust down and [a]cannot rise.

PSALM 37

A Psalm of David.

★ 1 [a]Prov. 23:17; 24:19 [b]Ps. 73:3; Prov. 3:31

★ 1 **D**O not fret because of evildoers,
Be not [b]envious toward wrongdoers.

2 [a]Job 14:2; Ps. 90:6; 92:7; James 1:11 [b]Ps. 129:6

2 For they will [a]wither quickly like the grass,
And [b]fade like the green herb.

3 [a]Ps. 62:8 [b]Deut. 30:20 [c]Is. 40:11; Ezek. 34:13, 14

3 [a]Trust in the LORD, and do good;
[b]Dwell in the land and [c]cultivate faithfulness.

4 [a]Job 22:26; Ps. 94:19; Is. 58:14 [b]Ps. 21:2; 145:19; Matt. 7:7, 8

4 [a]Delight yourself in the LORD;
And He will [b]give you the desires of your heart.

★ 5 [a]Ps. 55:22; Prov. 16:3; 1 Pet. 5:7

5 [a]Commit your way to the LORD,
Trust also in Him, and He will do it.

6 [a]Ps. 97:11; Is. 58:8, 10; Mic. 7:9 [b]Job 11:17

6 And He will bring forth [a]your righteousness as the light,
And your judgment [b]as the noonday.

7 [a]Ps. 40:1; 62:5; Lam. 3:26 [b]Ps. 37:1, 8 [c]Jer. 12:1

7 Rest in the LORD and [a]wait patiently for Him;
[b]Do not fret because of him who [c]prospers in his way,
Because of the man who carries out wicked schemes.

8 [a]Eph. 4:31; Col. 3:8

8 Cease from anger, and [a]forsake wrath;
Do not fret, *it leads* only to evildoing.

9 [a]Ps. 37:2, 22 [b]Ps. 25:13; Prov. 2:21; Is. 57:13; 60:21; Matt. 5:5

9 For [a]evildoers will be cut off,

But those who wait for the LORD, they will [b]inherit the land.

10 Yet [a]a little while and the wicked man will be no more;
And you will look carefully for [b]his place, and he will not be *there.*

10 [a]Job 24:24 [b]Job 7:10; Ps. 37:35, 36

11 But [a]the humble will inherit the land,
And will delight themselves in [b]abundant prosperity.

11 [a]Matt. 5:5 [b]Ps. 72:7

12 The wicked [a]plots against the righteous,
And [b]gnashes at him with his teeth.

12 [a]Ps. 31:13, 20 [b]Ps. 35:16

13 The Lord [a]laughs at him;
For He sees [b]his day is coming.

13 [a]Ps. 2:4 [b]1 Sam. 26:10; Job 18:20

14 The wicked have drawn the sword and [a]bent their bow,
To cast down the [b]afflicted and the needy,
To [c]slay those who are upright in conduct.

14 [a]Ps. 11:2; Lam. 2:4 [b]Ps. 35:10; 86:1 [c]Ps. 11:2

15 Their sword will enter their own heart,
And their [a]bows will be broken.

15 [a]1 Sam. 2:4; Ps. 46:9

16 [a]Better is the little of the righteous
Than the abundance of many wicked.

16 [a]Prov. 15:16; 16:8

17 For the [a]arms of the wicked will be broken;
But the LORD [b]sustains the righteous.

17 [a]Job 38:15; Ps. 10:15; Ezek. 30:21 [b]Ps. 71:6; 145:14

18 The LORD [a]knows the days of the blameless;
And their [b]inheritance will be forever.

18 [a]Ps. 1:6; 31:7 [b]Ps. 37:27, 29

19 They will not be ashamed in the time of evil;

19 [a]Job 5:20; Ps. 33:19

Psalm 37 In this wisdom psalm, David uses a series of proverbial expressions to exhort the righteous to trust in the Lord, who will cause them to inherit the land (vv. 9, 22, 29), and not to fret about the wicked, who will be rooted out from the earth (vv. 22, 28, 34, 38). This psalm is an alphabetic acrostic, every second verse beginning with successive letters of the Hebrew alphabet.

37:1 *Do not fret.* Do not be incensed, angry, or indignant.

37:5 *Commit.* See note on Prov. 16:3.

And ᵃin the days of famine they will have abundance.

20 But the ᵃwicked will perish;
And the enemies of the LORD will be like the glory of the pastures,
They vanish—ᵇlike smoke they vanish away.

21 The wicked borrows and does not pay back,
But the righteous ᵃis gracious and gives.

22 For ᵃthose blessed by Him will ᵇinherit the land;
But those ᶜcursed by Him will be cut off.

23 ᵃThe steps of a man are established by the LORD;
And He ᵇdelights in his way.

24 When ᵃhe falls, he shall not be hurled headlong;
Because ᵇthe LORD is the One who holds his hand.

25 I have been young, and now I am old;
Yet ᵃI have not seen the righteous forsaken,
Or ᵇhis descendants begging bread.

26 All day long ᵃhe is gracious and lends;
And ᵇhis descendants are a blessing.

27 ᵃDepart from evil, and do good,
So you will abide ᵇforever.

28 For the LORD ᵃloves justice,
And ᵇdoes not forsake His godly ones;
They are ᶜpreserved forever;
But the ᵈdescendants of the wicked will be cut off.

29 The righteous will ᵃinherit the land,
And ᵇdwell in it forever.

30 The mouth of the righteous ᵃutters wisdom,
And his tongue ᵇspeaks justice.

31 The ᵃlaw of his God is in his heart;
His ᵇsteps do not slip.

32 The ᵃwicked spies upon the righteous,
And ᵇseeks to kill him.

33 The LORD will ᵃnot leave him in his hand,
Or ᵇlet him be condemned when he is judged.

34 ᵃWait for the LORD, and keep His way,
And He will exalt you to inherit the land;
When the ᵇwicked are cut off, you will see it.

35 I have ᵃseen a violent, wicked man
Spreading himself like a ᵇluxuriant tree in its native soil.

36 Then he passed away, and lo, he ᵃwas no more;
I sought for him, but he could not be found.

37 Mark the ᵃblameless man, and behold the ᵇupright;
For the man of peace will have a ᶜposterity.

38 But transgressors will be altogether ᵃdestroyed;
The posterity of the wicked will be ᵇcut off.

39 But the ᵃsalvation of the righteous is from the LORD;
He is their strength ᵇin time of trouble.

40 And ᵃthe LORD helps them, and delivers them;
He ᵇdelivers them from the wicked, and saves them,
Because they ᶜtake refuge in Him.

20 ᵃPs. 73:27 ᵇPs. 68:2; 102:3
21 ᵃPs. 112:5, 9
★**22** ᵃProv. 3:33 ᵇPs. 37:9 ᶜJob 5:3
23 ᵃ1 Sam. 2:9; Ps. 40:2; 66:9; 119:5 ᵇPs. 147:11
24 ᵃPs. 145:14; Prov. 24:16; Mic. 7:8 ᵇPs. 147:6
25 ᵃPs. 37:28; Is. 41:17; Heb. 13:5 ᵇPs. 109:10
26 ᵃDeut. 15:8; Ps. 37:21 ᵇPs. 147:13
27 ᵃPs. 34:14 ᵇPs. 37:18; 102:28
28 ᵃPs. 11:7; 33:5 ᵇPs. 37:25 ᶜPs. 31:23 ᵈPs. 21:10; 37:9; Prov. 2:22; Is. 14:20
29 ᵃPs. 37:9; Prov. 2:21 ᵇPs. 37:18
★**30** ᵃPs. 49:3; Prov. 10:13 ᵇPs. 101:1; 119:13
31 ᵃDeut. 6:6; Ps. 40:8; 119:11; Is. 51:7; Jer. 31:33 ᵇPs. 26:1; 37:23
32 ᵃPs. 10:8; 17:11 ᵇPs. 37:14
33 ᵃPs. 31:8; 2 Pet. 2:9 ᵇPs. 34:22; 109:31
34 ᵃPs. 27:14; 37:9 ᵇPs. 52:5, 6; 91:8
★**35** ᵃJob 5:3; Jer. 12:2 ᵇJob 8:16
36 ᵃJob 20:5; Ps. 37:10
37 ᵃPs. 37:18 ᵇPs. 7:10 ᶜIs. 57:1, 2
38 ᵃPs. 1:4-6; 37:20, 28 ᵇPs. 37:9; 73:17
39 ᵃPs. 3:8; 62:1 ᵇPs. 9:9; 37:19
40 ᵃPs. 54:4 ᵇPs. 22:4; Is. 31:5; Dan. 3:17; 6:23 ᶜ1 Chr. 5:20; Ps. 34:22

37:22 A summary of the entire psalm.
37:30 The *mouth* gives evidence of one's character (cf. 36:3).

37:35 The wicked appear to be indestructible, *like a luxuriant tree in its native soil.*

PSALM 38

A Psalm of David, for a memorial.

O LORD, [a]rebuke me not in Thy wrath;
And chasten me not in Thy burning anger.

2 For Thine [a]arrows have sunk deep into me,
And [b]Thy hand has pressed down on me.

3 There is [a]no soundness in my flesh [b]because of Thine indignation;
There is no health [c]in my bones because of my sin.

4 For my [a]iniquities are gone over my head;
As a heavy burden they weigh too much for me.

5 My wounds grow foul and fester.
Because of [a]my folly,

6 I am bent over and [a]greatly bowed down;
I [b]go mourning all day long.

7 For my loins are filled with [a]burning;
And there is [b]no soundness in my flesh.

8 I am [a]benumbed and badly crushed;
I [b]groan because of the agitation of my heart.

9 Lord, all [a]my desire is before Thee;
And my [b]sighing is not hidden from Thee.

10 My heart throbs, [a]my strength fails me;

And the [b]light of my eyes, even that has gone from me.

11 My [a]loved ones and my friends stand aloof from my plague;
And my kinsmen [b]stand afar off.

12 Those who [a]seek my life [b]lay snares for me;
And those who [c]seek to injure me have threatened destruction,
And they [d]devise treachery all day long.

13 But I, like a deaf man, do not hear;
And I am like a [a]dumb man who does not open his mouth.

14 Yes, I am like a man who does not hear,
And in whose mouth are no arguments.

15 For [a]I hope in Thee, O LORD;
Thou [b]wilt answer, O Lord my God.

16 For I said, "May they not rejoice over me,
Who, when my foot slips, [a]would magnify themselves against me."

17 For I am [a]ready to fall,
And [b]my sorrow is continually before me.

18 For I [a]confess my iniquity;
I am full of [b]anxiety because of my sin.

19 But my [a]enemies are vigorous and strong;
And many are those who [b]hate me wrongfully.

20 And those who [a]repay evil for good,

Cross-references

1 [a]Ps. 6:1
2 [a]Job 6:4 [b]Ps. 32:4
★3 [a]Is. 1:6 [b]Ps. 102:10 [c]Job 33:19; Ps. 6:2; 31:10
4 [a]Ezra 9:6; Ps. 40:12
5 [a]Ps. 69:5
6 [a]Ps. 35:14 [b]Job 30:28; Ps. 42:9; 43:2
7 [a]Ps. 102:3 [b]Ps. 38:3
8 [a]Lam. 1:13, 20f.; 2:11; 5:17 [b]Job 3:24; Ps. 22:1; 32:3
9 [a]Ps. 10:17 [b]Ps. 6:6; 102:5
10 [a]Ps. 31:10 [b]Ps. 6:7; 69:3; 88:9
★11 [a]Ps. 31:11; 88:18 [b]Luke 23:49
12 [a]Ps. 54:3 [b]Ps. 140:5 [c]Ps. 35:4 [d]Ps. 35:20
★13-14
13 [a]Ps. 39:2, 9
15 [a]Ps. 39:7 [b]Ps. 17:6
16 [a]Ps. 35:26
17 [a]Ps. 35:15 [b]Ps. 13:2
★18 [a]Ps. 32:5 [b]2 Cor. 7:9, 10
19 [a]Ps. 18:17 [b]Ps. 35:19
20 [a]Ps. 35:12 [b]Ps. 109:5; 1 John 3:12

Psalm 38 This psalm falls into three divisions, each beginning with an address to God. The first (vv. 1–8) describes the sufferings from sin; the second (vv. 9–14), the loneliness of sin; and the third (vv. 15–22), the confession of sin. Like other penitential psalms (see note on Psalm 6), this lament focuses on David's sin and God's chastening as the cause of the distress. *for a memorial* (in superscription). See note on Psalm 70. **38:3** David's *sin* is not identified, though it is

likely different from that mentioned in Psalm 51.
38:11 *plague.* The word is used of leprosy, indicating that David's friends avoided him as if he were a leper.
38:13-14 David does not defend himself against his enemies' accusations (v. 12).
38:18 David confesses that his sin is the cause of his anxiety.

21 aPs.
22:19; 35:22

22 aPs.
40:13, 17
bPs. 27:1

They boppose me, because
    I follow what is good.

21 Do not forsake me, O
    LORD;
O my God, ado not be far
    from me!

22 Make ahaste to help me,
    O Lord, bmy salvation!

PSALM 39

For the choir director, for
Jeduthun.
A Psalm of David.

★ 1 a1 Kin.
2:4; 2 Kin.
10:31; Ps.
119:9 bJob
2:10; Ps.
34:13; James
3:5-12 cPs.
141:3; James
3:2

2 aPs.
38:13

3 aPs. 32:4;
Jer. 20:9;
Luke 24:32

★ 4 aJob
6:11; Ps.
90:12;
119:84 bPs.
78:39;
103:14

★ 5 aPs.
89:47 bPs.
144:4 cJob
14:2; Ps.
62:9; Eccl.
6:12

I SAID, "I will aguard my ways,
    That I bmay not sin with
    my tongue;
I will guard cmy mouth as
    with a muzzle,
While the wicked are in
    my presence."

2 I was adumb and silent,
I refrained *even* from
    good;
And my sorrow grew
    worse.

3 My aheart was hot within
    me;
While I was musing the
    fire burned;
Then I spoke with my
    tongue:

4 "LORD, make me to know
    amy end,
And what is the extent of
    my days,
Let me know how btran-
    sient I am.

5 "Behold, Thou hast made
    amy days *as* hand-
    breadths,
And my blifetime as noth-
    ing in Thy sight,

Surely every man at his
    best is a mere cbreath.
        [Selah.

6 "Surely every man awalks
    about as a phantom;
Surely they make an bup-
    roar for nothing;
He camasses *riches*, and
    does not know who
    will gather them.

7 "And now, Lord, for what
    do I wait?
My ahope is in Thee.

8 "aDeliver me from all my
    transgressions;
Make me not the bre-
    proach of the foolish.

9 "I have become adumb, I do
    not open my mouth,
Because it is bThou who
    hast done *it*.

10 "aRemove Thy plague from
    me;
Because of bthe opposition
    of Thy hand, I am
    perishing.

11 "With areproofs Thou dost
    chasten a man for in-
    iquity;
Thou dost bconsume as a
    moth what is precious
    to him;
Surely cevery man is a
    mere breath. [Selah.

12 "aHear my prayer, O LORD,
    and give ear to my
    cry;
Do not be silent bat my
    tears;
For I am ca stranger with
    Thee,
A dsojourner like all my
    fathers.

★ 6 a1 Cor.
7:31; James
1:10, 11;
1 Pet. 1:24
bPs. 127:2;
Eccl. 5:17
cPs. 49:10;
Eccl. 2:26;
5:14; Luke
12:20

7 aPs.
38:15

8 aPs. 51:9,
14; 79:9
bPs. 44:13;
79:4; 119:22

9 aPs. 39:2
b2 Sam.
16:10; Job
2:10

10 aJob
9:34; 13:21
bPs. 32:4

11 aEzek.
5:15; 2 Pet.
2:16 bJob
13:28; Ps.
90:7; Is. 50:9
cPs. 39:5

★12 aPs.
102:1; 143:1
b2 Kin. 20:5;
Ps. 56:8
cLev. 25:23;
1 Chr. 29:15;
Ps. 119:19;
Heb. 11:13;
1 Pet. 2:11
dGen. 47:9

Psalm 39 David asks God to help him accept
the brevity of life (vv. 1-6) and to cease chastening him in view of its shortness (vv. 7-13). *Jedu-*
thun. One of the choir directors appointed by
David to lead public worship (1 Chron. 16:41;
25:1-3; cf. the headings of Psalms 62, 77).
39:1 David's feeling that God was to blame for
the brevity of life was strong enough to be
taken for disloyalty if it had been vented before the *wicked.*

39:4 He asks that he may realize how certain it
is that life will end.
39:5 Life is only a few *handbreadths* (four fingers).
39:6 *as a phantom.* I.e., as a shadow, unsubstan-
tial.
39:12 He prays that God will be kind to him in
the same way He taught Israel to be kind to
the *stranger* and *sojourner* (Deut. 10:18-19).

★13 aJob
7:19; 10:20,
21; 14:6; Ps.
102:24

13 "aTurn Thy gaze away from
me, that I may smile
again,
Before I depart and am no
more."

PSALM 40

For the choir director. A
Psalm of David.

1 aPs. 25:5;
27:14; 37:7
bPs. 34:15

I aWAITED patiently for the
LORD;
And He inclined to me,
and bheard my cry.

★ 2 aPs.
69:2, 14; Jer.
38:6 bPs.
27:5 cPs.
37:23

2 He brought me up out of
the apit of destruction,
out of the miry clay;
And bHe set my feet upon
a rock cmaking my
footsteps firm.

3 aPs. 32:7;
33:3 bPs.
52:6; 64:9

3 And He put a anew song in
my mouth, a song of
praise to our God;
Many will bsee and fear,
And will trust in the LORD.

4 aPs. 34:8;
84:12 bJob
37:24 cPs.
125:5

4 How ablessed is the man
who has made the
LORD his trust,
And bhas not turned to the
proud, nor to those
who clapse into false-
hood.

5 aJob 5:9;
Ps. 136:4
bPs. 139:17;
Is. 55:8 cPs.
71:15;
139:18

5 Many, O LORD my God,
are athe wonders
which Thou hast
done,
And Thy bthoughts toward
us;
There is none to compare
with Thee;
If I would declare and
speak of them,

They cwould be too nu-
merous to count.

6 aSacrifice and meal offering Thou hast not de-
sired;
My ears Thou hast
opened;
Burnt offering and sin offering Thou hast not
required.

★ 6 a1 Sam.
15:22; Ps.
51:16; Is.
1:11; Jer.
6:20; 7:22,
23; Amos
5:22; Mic.
6:6-8; Heb.
10:5-7

7 Then I said, "Behold, I
come;
In the scroll of the book it
is written of me;

★ 7

8 aI delight to do Thy will, O
my God;
bThy Law is within my
heart."

8 aJohn
4:34 bPs.
37:31; Jer.
31:33; 2 Cor.
3:3

9 I have aproclaimed glad
tidings of righteous-
ness in the great con-
gregation;
Behold, I will bnot restrain
my lips,
O LORD, cThou knowest.

9 aPs.
22:22, 25
bPs. 119:13
cJosh.
22:22; Ps.
139:4

10 I have anot hidden Thy
righteousness within
my heart;
I have bspoken of Thy
faithfulness and Thy
salvation;
I have not concealed Thy
lovingkindness and
Thy truth from the
great congregation.

10 aActs
20:20, 27
bPs. 89:1

11 Thou, O LORD, wilt not
withhold Thy com-
passion from me;
Thy alovingkindness and
Thy truth will con-
tinually preserve me.

11 aPs. 43:3;
57:3; 61:7;
Prov. 20:28

12 For evils beyond number
have asurrounded me;

12 aPs. 18:5;
116:3 bPs.
38:4; 65:3
cPs. 69:4
dPs. 73:26

39:13 *Turn Thy gaze away from me.* In the
sense of diverting chastening for sin so that
his days may be enjoyable.

Psalm 40 In this psalm of praise (vv. 1-10)
and petition for deliverance (vv. 11-17), David
praises God for past deliverance (vv. 1-4) and
offers himself in dedication (vv. 5-10). Then David brings a new problem before the Lord (vv.
11-12), asking again for deliverance (vv. 13-17).
The words of David's dedication (vv. 6-8) go beyond him to the Lord Jesus, who came to be the
obedient Sacrifice to end all sacrifices (see Heb.
10:5-7 which quotes these verses).

40:2 David compares his plight to that of a pris-

oner confined in a *pit* and a traveler flounder-
ing in a treacherous quagmire of *clay*.

40:6 *My ears Thou hast opened.* An expression
signifying obedience, based either on the custom of piercing the ear as a sign of voluntary
perpetual service (Exod. 21:6) or on the idea of
hearing what God says (Isa. 50:4-5). Instead of
external ceremony only, David realizes that
God wants his heart. In effect, he is saying,
"Here I am to do what is prescribed to me as
my duty in the law, but to do it from the
heart."

40:7 *the book.* The Mosaic Law.

My [b]iniquities have overtaken me, so that I am
not able to see;
They are [c]more numerous
than the hairs of my
head;
And my [d]heart has failed
me.

★13-17

13 aPs. 70:1
bPs. 22:19;
71:12

13 [a]Be pleased, O Lord, to deliver me;
Make [b]haste, O Lord, to
help me.

14 aPs. 35:4,
26; 70:2;
71:13 bPs.
63:9

14 Let those be [a]ashamed and
humiliated together
Who [b]seek my life to destroy it;
Let those be turned back
and dishonored
Who delight in my hurt.

15 aPs. 70:3
bPs. 35:21;
70:3

15 Let those [a]be appalled because of their shame
Who [b]say to me, "Aha,
aha!"

16 aPs. 70:4
bPs. 35:27

16 [a]Let all who seek Thee rejoice and be glad in
Thee;
Let those who love Thy
salvation [b]say con-
tinually,
"The Lord be magnified!"

17 aPs. 70:5;
86:1; 109:22
bPs. 40:5;
1 Pet. 5:7

17 Since [a]I am afflicted and
needy,
[b]Let the Lord be mindful
of me;
Thou art my help and my
deliverer;
Do not delay, O my God.

PSALM 41

For the choir director. A
Psalm of David.

1 aPs. 82:3,
4; Prov.
14:21 bPs.
27:5; 37:19

[H]OW blessed is he who [a]con-
siders the helpless;
The Lord will deliver him
[b]in a day of trouble.

2 aPs.
37:28 bPs.
37:22 cPs.
27:12

2 The Lord will [a]protect
him, and keep him
alive,

And he shall be called
[b]blessed upon the
earth;
And [c]do not give him over
to the desire of his en-
emies.

3 The Lord will sustain him
upon his sickbed;
In his illness, Thou dost restore him to health.

4 aPs. 6:2;
103:3; 147:3
bPs. 51:4

4 As for me, I said, "O Lord,
be gracious to me;
[a]Heal my soul, for [b]I have
sinned against Thee."

5 aPs.
38:12

5 My enemies [a]speak evil
against me,
"When will he die, and his
name perish?"

6 aPs. 12:2;
62:4; Prov.
26:24-26

6 And when he comes to see
me, he [a]speaks false-
hood;
His heart gathers wicked-
ness to itself;
When he goes outside, he
tells it.

7 aPs. 56:5

7 All who hate me whisper
together against me;
Against me they [a]devise
my hurt, *saying,*

8 aPs
71:10, 11

8 "A wicked thing is poured
out upon him,
That when he lies down,
he will [a]not rise up
again."

★ 9 a2 Sam.
15:12; Job
19:13, 19;
Ps. 55:12,
13, 20; Jer.
20:10; Mic.
7:5; Matt.
26:23; Luke
22:21; John
13:18

9 Even my [a]close friend, in
whom I trusted,
Who ate my bread,
Has lifted up his heel
against me.

10 aPs. 3:3

10 But Thou, O Lord, be gracious to me, and [a]raise
me up,
That I may repay them.

11 aPs.
37:23;
147:11 bPs.
25:2

11 By this I know that [a]Thou
art pleased with me,
Because [b]my enemy does
not shout in triumph
over me.

40:13-17 These verses are essentially identical to
Psalm 70.
Psalm 41 David's amplification of the beati-
tude later recorded in Matt. 5:7 includes instructing the congregation that the merciful will receive mercy (vv. 1-3), recalling his experience

with those who did not show him mercy (vv.
4-9) and praising God, who did (vv. 10-12).
41:9 David's betrayal by a false friend pictures
Judas' betrayal of Christ (John 13:18-19, where
this verse is quoted, omitting the phrase "in
whom I trusted").

12 aPs.
18:32; 37:17;
63:8 bJob
36:7; Ps.
21:6

12 As for me, aThou dost uphold me in my integrity,
And Thou dost set me bin Thy presence forever.

★13 aPs.
72:18, 19;
89:52;
106:48;
150:6

13 aBlessed be the LORD, the God of Israel,
From everlasting to everlasting.
Amen, and Amen.

BOOK 2

PSALM 42

For the choir director.
A Maskil of the sons of Korah.

★ 1 aPs.
119:131
2 aPs. 63:1;
84:2; 143:6
bJosh. 3:10;
Ps. 84:2; Dan.
10:10; Matt.
26:63; Rom.
9:26;
1 Thess. 1:9
cEx. 23:17;
Ps. 43:4;
84:7
3 aPs. 80:5;
102:9 bPs.
79:10; 115:2;
Joel 2:17;
Mic. 7:10

As the deer pants for the water brooks,
So my soul apants for Thee, O God.

2 My soul athirsts for God, for the bliving God;
When shall I come and cappear before God?

3 My atears have been my food day and night,
While they bsay to me all day long, "Where is your God?"

4 a1 Sam.
1:15; Job
30:16; Ps.
62:8; Lam.
2:19 bPs.
55:14; 122:1;
Is. 30:29
cPs. 100:4

4 These things I remember, and I apour out my soul within me.
For I bused to go along with the throng and lead them in procession to the house of God,
With the voice of cjoy and thanksgiving, a multitude keeping festival.

5 aPs.
42:11; 43:5
bPs. 38:6;
Matt. 26:38
cPs. 77:3
dPs. 71:14;
Lam. 3:24
ePs. 44:3

5 aWhy are you bin despair, O my soul?
And why have you become cdisturbed within me?
dHope in God, for I shall again praise Him
For the ehelp of His presence.

★ 6 aPs.
61:2 b2 Sam.
17:22 cDeut.
3:8

6 O my God, my soul is in despair within me;
Therefore I aremember Thee from bthe land of the Jordan,
And the peaks of cHermon, from Mount Mizar.

★ 7 aPs.
69:1, 2; 88:7;
Jon. 2:3

7 Deep calls to deep at the sound of Thy waterfalls;
All Thy abreakers and Thy waves have rolled over me.

8 aPs. 57:3;
133:3 bJob
35:10; Ps.
16:7; 63:6;
77:6; 149:5
cEccl. 5:18;
8:15

8 The LORD will acommand His lovingkindness in the daytime;
And His song will be with me bin the night,
A prayer to cthe God of my life.

9 aPs. 18:2
bPs. 38:6
cPs. 17:9

9 I will say to God amy rock, "Why hast Thou forgotten me?
Why do I go bmourning because of the coppression of the enemy?"

10 aPs. 42:3;
Joel 2:17

10 As a shattering of my bones, my adversaries revile me;
While they asay to me all day long, "Where is your God?"

11 aPs. 42:5;
43:5

11 aWhy are you in despair, O my soul?

41:13 This doxology marks the close of Book I of the Psalms (see Introduction, "Contents"; cf. Psalms 72:18-19; 89:52; 106:48; 150:1-6).
Psalms 42 and 43 These psalms comprise a single, sadly beautiful poem in which the writer, exiled in the far north of Palestine (42:6), yearns to return to the Temple in Jerusalem. He first expresses this yearning for God (42:1-5), then reveals the depths of his distress (42:6-11) and prays that he might return (43:1-5). *Maskil.* See introductory note on Psalm 32. Twelve psalms (42-49, 84-85, 87-88) are dedicated to the de-

scendants of *Korah* (see note on Num. 16:1-3), who were singers in the Temple choir (2 Chron. 20:19).
42:1 The figure is that of a *deer* longing for water in the midst of a prolonged drought.
42:6 *the peaks of Hermon.* The 20-mile long ridge of Hermon, 40 miles NE. of the Sea of Galilee. *Mount Mizar.* Apparently in the same vicinity, but is unidentified.
42:7 *Deep calls to deep.* The floods and cataracts of the headwaters of the Jordan illustrate the waves of sorrow that overwhelm the writer.

And why have you become disturbed within me?
Hope in God, for I shall yet praise Him,
The help of my countenance, and my God.

PSALM 43

1 a Ps.
26:1; 35:24
b 1 Sam.
24:15; Ps.
35:1 c Ps.
5:6; 38:12

a V INDICATE me, O God, and b plead my case against an ungodly nation;
O deliver me from c the deceitful and unjust man!

2 a Ps. 18:1;
28:7; 31:4
b Ps. 44:9;
88:14 c Ps.
42:9

2 For Thou art the a God of my strength; why hast Thou b rejected me?
Why do I go c mourning because of the oppression of the enemy?

★ **3-4**

3 a Ps. 36:9
b Ps. 2:6;
3:4; 42:4;
46:4 c Ps.
84:1

3 O send out Thy a light and Thy truth, let them lead me;
Let them bring me to Thy b holy hill,
And to Thy c dwelling places.

4 a Ps. 26:6
b Ps. 21:6
c Ps. 33:2;
49:4; 57:8;
71:22

4 Then I will go to a the altar of God,
To God my exceeding b joy;
And upon the c lyre I shall praise Thee, O God, my God.

5 a Ps. 42:5,
11

5 a Why are you in despair, O my soul?
And why are you disturbed within me?
Hope in God, for I shall again praise Him,
The help of my countenance, and my God.

PSALM 44

For the choir director.
A Maskil of the sons of Korah.

1 a Ex.
12:26, 27;
Deut. 6:20;
Judg. 6:13;
Ps. 78:3
b Ps. 78:12
c Deut. 32:7;
Ps. 77:5; Is.
51:9; 63:9

O GOD, we have heard with our ears,
Our a fathers have told us,
The b work that Thou didst in their days,
In the c days of old.

★ **2** a Josh.
3:10; Neh.
9:24; Ps.
78:55; 80:8
b Ex. 15:17;
2 Sam. 7:10;
Jer. 24:6;
Amos 9:15
c Ps. 135:10-
12 d Ps.
80:9-11;
Zech. 2:6

2 Thou with Thine own hand didst a drive out the nations;
Then Thou didst b plant them;
Thou didst c afflict the peoples,
Then Thou didst d spread them abroad.

3 a Deut.
8:17, 18;
Josh. 24:12
b Ps. 77:15
c Ps. 4:6;
89:15 d Deut.
4:37; 7:7, 8;
10:15; Ps.
106:4

3 For by their own sword they a did not possess the land;
And their own arm did not save them;
But Thy right hand, and Thine b arm, and the c light of Thy presence,
For Thou didst d favor them.

4 a Ps.
74:12 b Ps.
42:8

4 Thou art a my King, O God;
b Command victories for Jacob.

5 a Deut.
33:17; Ps.
60:12; Dan.
8:4 b Ps.
108:13;
Zech. 10:5

5 Through Thee we will a push back our adversaries;
Through Thy name we will b trample down those who rise up against us.

6 a 1 Sam.
17:47; Ps.
33:16; Hos.
1:7

6 For I will a not trust in my bow,
Nor will my sword save me.

Psalm 43 See introductory note on Psalm 42.
43:1 The psalmist's mood changes to one of confidence and trust.
43:3-4 The *holy hill* and *the altar* serve as means to the highest end—fellowship with God Himself.
Psalm 44 In this psalm of national lament,

God's past care for Israel stimulates the praise (vv. 1-3) and confidence (vv. 4-8) the people have as they bring before the Lord their present defeat (vv. 9-16) and their petition for deliverance (vv. 17-26). *Maskil*. See note on Psalm 32. *sons of Korah*. See note on Psalm 42.
44:2 A reference to the conquest of Canaan under Joshua. *them*. I.e., Israel.

7 aPs.
136:24 bPs.
53:5

8 aPs. 34:2
bPs. 30:12

9 aPs. 43:2;
60:1, 10;
74:1; 89:38;
108:11 bPs.
69:19 cPs.
60:10;
108:11

10 aLev.
26:17; Josh.
7:8, 12; Ps.
89:43 bPs.
89:41

★11 aPs.
44:22; Rom.
8:36 bLev.
26:33; Deut.
4:27; 28:64;
Ps. 106:27;
Ezek. 20:23

12 aDeut.
32:30; Judg.
2:14, 3:8; Is.
52:3, 4; Jer.
15:13

13 aDeut.
28:37; Ps.
79:4; 89:41
bPs. 80:6;
Ezek. 23:32

14 aJob
17:6; Ps.
69:11; Jer.
24:9 b2 Kin.
19:21; Ps.
109:25

15 a2 Chr.
32:21; Ps.
69:7

16 aPs.
74:10 bPs.
8:2

7 But Thou [a]hast saved us from our adversaries,
And Thou hast [b]put to shame those who hate us.

8 In God we have [a]boasted all day long,
And we will [b]give thanks to Thy name forever. [Selah.

9 Yet Thou [a]hast rejected us and brought us to [b]dishonor,
And [c]dost not go out with our armies.

10 Thou dost cause us to [a]turn back from the adversary;
And those who hate us [b]have taken spoil for themselves.

11 Thou dost give us as [a]sheep to be eaten,
And hast [b]scattered us among the nations.

12 Thou dost [a]sell Thy people cheaply,
And hast not profited by their sale.

13 Thou dost make us a [a]reproach to our neighbors,
A scoffing and a [b]derision to those around us.

14 Thou dost make us [a]a byword among the nations,
A [b]laughingstock among the peoples.

15 All day long my dishonor is before me,
And my [a]humiliation has overwhelmed me,

16 Because of the voice of him who [a]reproaches and reviles,

Because of the presence of the [b]enemy and the avenger.

17 All this has come upon us, but we have [a]not forgotten Thee,
And we have not [b]dealt falsely with Thy covenant.

18 Our heart has not [a]turned back,
And our steps [b]have not deviated from Thy way,

19 Yet Thou hast [a]crushed us in a place of [b]jackals,
And covered us with [c]the shadow of death.

20 If we had [a]forgotten the name of our God,
Or extended our hands to [b]a strange god;

21 Would not God [a]find this out?
For He knows the secrets of the heart.

22 But [a]for Thy sake we are killed all day long;
We are considered as [b]sheep to be slaughtered.

23 [a]Arouse Thyself, why [b]dost Thou sleep, O Lord?
Awake, [c]do not reject us forever.

24 Why dost Thou [a]hide Thy face,
And [b]forget our affliction and our oppression?

25 For our [a]soul has sunk down into the dust;
Our body cleaves to the earth.

26 [a]Rise up, be our help,
And [b]redeem us for the sake of Thy lovingkindness.

★17-22

17 aPs. 78:7;
119:61, 83,
109, 141,
153, 176
bPs. 78:57

18 aPs.
78:57 bJob
23:11; Ps.
119:51, 157

19 aPs. 51:8;
94:5 bJob
30:29; Is.
13:22; Jer.
9:11 cJob
3:5; Ps. 23:4

20 aPs.
78:11 bDeut.
6:14; Ps.
81:9

21 aPs.
139:1, 2; Jer.
17:10

★22 aRom.
8:36 bIs.
53:7; Jer.
12:3

23 aPs. 7:6
bPs. 78:65
cPs. 77:7

24 aJob
13:24; Ps.
88:14 bPs.
42:9; Lam.
5:20

25 aPs.
119:25

★26 aPs.
35:2 bPs.
6:4; 25:22

44:11 Not likely referring to the Exile, but to some time of national peril.

44:17-22 A defense of the faithfulness of the nation, similar to the plea of innocence in some individual lament psalms (see note on 17:3).

44:22 An expression of the price of loyalty to God in a world at war with Him (quoted by Paul in Rom. 8:36).

44:26 *lovingkindness.* The people approach God on the basis of His covenant love (see note on Hos. 2:19).

PSALM 45

For the choir director; according to the Shoshannim. A Maskil of the sons of Korah. A Song of Love.

★ 1 *a*Ezra 7:6

MY heart overflows with a good theme;
I address my verses to the King;
My tongue is the pen of *a* ready writer.

2 *a*Luke 4:22 *b*Ps. 21:6

2 Thou art fairer than the sons of men;
*a*Grace is poured upon Thy lips;
Therefore God has *b*blessed Thee forever.

3 *a*Heb. 4:12; Rev. 1:16 *b*Is. 9:6

3 Gird *a*Thy sword on *Thy* thigh, O *b*Mighty One,
In Thy splendor and Thy majesty!

4 *a*Zeph. 2:3 *b*Ps. 21:8

4 And in Thy majesty ride on victoriously,
For the cause of truth and *a*meekness *and* righteousness;
Let Thy *b*right hand teach Thee awesome things.

5 *a*Ps. 18:14; 120:4; Is. 5:28; 7:13 *b*Ps. 92:9 *c*2 Sam. 18:14

5 Thine *a*arrows are sharp;
The *b*peoples fall under Thee;
Thine arrows are *c*in the heart of the King's enemies.

★ 6-7

6 *a*Ps. 93:2; Heb. 1:8, 9 *b*Ps. 98:9

6 *a*Thy throne, O God, is forever and ever;
A scepter of *b*uprightness is the scepter of Thy kingdom.

7 *a*Ps. 11:7; 33:5 *b*Ps. 2:2

7 Thou hast *a*loved righteousness, and hated wickedness;

Therefore God, Thy God, has *b*anointed Thee
With the oil of joy above Thy fellows.

8 *a*Song 4:14; John 19:39 *b*Ps. 150:4

8 All Thy garments are fragrant with *a*myrrh and aloes *and* cassia;
Out of ivory palaces *b*stringed instruments have made Thee glad.

★ 9 *a*Song 6:8 *b*1 Kin. 2:19 *c*1 Kin. 9:28; Is. 13:12

9 Kings' daughters are among *a*Thy noble ladies;
At Thy *b*right hand stands the queen in *c*gold from Ophir.

10 *a*Deut. 21:13; Ruth 1:16, 17

10 Listen, O daughter, give attention and incline your ear;
*a*Forget your people and your father's house;

11 *a*Gen. 18:12; 1 Pet. 3:6 *b*Eph. 5:33

11 Then the King will desire your beauty;
Because He is your *a*Lord, *b*bow down to Him.

12 *a*Ps. 87:4 *b*Ps. 22:29; 68:29; 72:10, 11; Is. 49:23

12 And the daughter of *a*Tyre *will come* with a gift;
The *b*rich among the people will entreat your favor.

13 *a*Ex. 39:2, 3

13 The King's daughter is all glorious within;
Her clothing is *a*interwoven with gold.

14 *a*Song 1:4 *b*Judg. 5:30; Ezek. 16:10 *c*Ps. 45:9

14 She will be *a*led to the King *b*in embroidered work;
The *c*virgins, her companions who follow her,
Will be brought to Thee.

15 They will be led forth with gladness and rejoicing;
They will enter into the King's palace.

Psalm 45 In this royal wedding psalm, the psalmist praises the king (vv. 1–9), exhorts (vv. 10–12) and describes the bride (vv. 13–15), and pronounces a benediction (vv. 16–17). *Shoshannim* means lilies, perhaps indicating a wedding tune. *Maskil.* See note on Psalm 32.
45:1 *overflows.* I.e., in composing this love song for the king.
45:6–7 The king is addressed as God in verse 6 and is distinguished from God in verse 7. Verse 6 was likely a royal hyperbole (extravagant exaggeration) of the king referred to (perhaps Solomon), but ultimately refers to Jesus Christ (Heb. 1:8–9). Capitalizing of the pronouns indicates they refer to Christ; not capitalized they refer to the historic king, who was being married at that time.
45:9 *gold from Ophir.* See note on 1 Kings 9:28.

★16-17

16 In place of your fathers
will be your sons;
You shall make them
princes in all the
earth.

17 *a*Mal.
1:11 *b*Ps.
138:4

17 I will cause *a*Thy name to
be remembered in all
generations;
Therefore the peoples *b*will
give Thee thanks for-
ever and ever.

PSALM 46

For the choir director. *A Psalm
of the sons of Korah,* set to
Alamoth. A Song.

1 *a*Ps. 14:6;
62:7, 8
*b*Deut. 4:7;
Ps. 145:18
*c*Ps. 9:9

Gᴏᴅ is our *a*refuge and
strength,
A very *b*present help *c*in
trouble.

★ 2-3

2 *a*Ps. 23:4;
27:1 *b*Ps.
82:5 *c*Ps.
18:7

2 Therefore we will *a*not
fear, though *b*the
earth should change,
And though *c*the moun-
tains slip into the
heart of the sea;

3 *a*Ps. 93:3,
4; Jer. 5:22

3 Though its *a*waters roar
and foam,
Though the mountains
quake at its swelling
pride. [Selah.

★ 4 *a*Ps.
36:8; 65:9;
Is. 8:6; Rev.
22:1 *b*Ps.
48:1; 87:3;
101:8; Is.
60:14; Rev.
3:12 *c*Ps.
43:3
5 *a*Deut.
23:14; Is.
12:6; Ezek.
43:7, 9; Hos.
11:9; Joel
2:27; Zech.
2:5 *b*Ps.
37:40; Is.
41:14; Luke
1:54

4 There is a *a*river whose
streams make glad the
*b*city of God,
The holy *c*dwelling places
of the Most High.

5 God is *a*in the midst of her,
she will not be moved;
God will *b*help her when
morning dawns.

6 The nations *a*made an uproar, the kingdoms
tottered;
He *b*raised His voice, the
earth *c*melted.

6 *a*Ps. 2:1,
2 *b*Ps.
18:13; 68:33;
Jer. 25:30;
Joel 2:11;
Amos 1:2
*c*Amos 9:5;
Mic. 1:4;
Nah. 1:5

7 The Lᴏʀᴅ of hosts *a*is with
us;
The God of Jacob is *b*our
stronghold. [Selah.

★ 7 *a*Num.
14:9; 2 Chr.
13:12 *b*Ps.
9:9; 48:3

8 Come, *a*behold the works
of the Lᴏʀᴅ,
Who has wrought *b*desolations in the earth.

★ 8 *a*Ps.
66:5 *b*Is.
61:4; Jer.
51:43

9 He *a*makes wars to cease to
the end of the earth;
He *b*breaks the bow and
cuts the spear in two;
He *c*burns the chariots
with fire.

9 *a*Is. 2:4;
Mic. 4:3
*b*1 Sam. 2:4;
Ps. 76:3 *c*Is.
9:5; Ezek.
39:9

10 "Cease *striving* and *a*know
that I am God;
I will be *b*exalted among
the nations, I will be
exalted in the earth."

★10 *a*Ps.
100:3 *b*Is.
2:11, 17

11 The Lᴏʀᴅ of hosts is with
us;
The God of Jacob is our
stronghold. [Selah.

PSALM 47

For the choir director.
A Psalm of the sons of Korah.

Oᴀ*a*CLAP your hands, all peoples;
*b*Shout to God with the
voice of joy.

1 *a*Ps. 98:8
*b*Ps. 106:47

2 For the Lᴏʀᴅ Most High is
to be *a*feared,
A *b*great King over all the
earth.

2 *a*Deut.
7:21; Neh.
1:5; Ps. 66:3,
5; 68:35
*b*Mal. 1:14

45:16-17 The poet wishes for the king a numerous and distinguished posterity.
Psalm 46 This psalm of trust and thanksgiving focuses on the God of Israel, their refuge (vv.
1-3), the city of God, their security (vv. 4-7), and
the deliverance of God, their peace (vv. 8-11).
While the invasion of Israel by Sennacherib during the reign of Hezekiah (2 Kings 18:13-19:37)
may form the historical background for this
psalm, it seems to anticipate Psalm 47, which is a
song of God's kingship, and thus ultimately refers to the millennial reign of Christ. *Alamoth.*
Lit., maidens, probably referring to soprano
voices.
46:2-3 The idea is, "whatever happens."

46:4 *a river* for physical and spiritual blessing,
particularly in relation to the millennial *city of
God,* Jerusalem (Ezek. 47:1; Zech. 14:8).
46:7 *The Lᴏʀᴅ of hosts.* See note on 1 Sam. 1:3.
46:8 Ultimately, only King Messiah can do such
things, during His future millennial reign (see
notes on Isa. 2:2-4; 11:6-9).
46:10 *Cease striving.* I.e., cease from warlike activities and acknowledge God's supremacy.
Psalm 47 This psalm of God's kingship celebrates the reign of the Lord over all the earth. As
Psalms 96-98, it looks forward to God's rule
through Christ during the Millennium (see note
on Psalm 96).

★ 3 aPs. 18:47
3 He asubdues peoples under us,
And nations under our feet.

4 a1 Pet. 1:4 bAmos 6:8; 8:7; Nah. 2:2
4 He chooses our ainheritance for us,
The bglory of Jacob whom He loves.   [Selah.

★ 5 aPs. 68:18 bPs. 98:6
5 God has aascended with a shout,
The Lord, with the bsound of a trumpet.

6 aPs. 68:4 bPs. 89:18
6 aSing praises to God, sing praises;
Sing praises to bour King, sing praises.

7 aZech. 14:9 b1 Cor. 14:15
7 For God is the aKing of all the earth;
Sing praises bwith a skillful psalm.

8 a1 Chr. 16:31; Ps. 22:28 bPs. 97:2
8 God areigns over the nations,
God sits on bHis holy throne.

★ 9 aPs. 72:11; 102:22; Is. 49:7, 23 bRom. 4:11, 12 cPs. 89:18 dPs. 97:9
9 The aprinces of the people have assembled themselves as the bpeople of the God of Abraham;
For the cshields of the earth belong to God;
He is dhighly exalted.

PSALM 48

A Song; a Psalm of the sons of Korah.

1 a1 Chr. 16:25; Ps. 96:4; 145:3 bPs. 46:4 cPs. 2:6; 87:1; Is. 2:3; Mic. 4:1; Zech. 8:3
aGREAT is the Lord, and greatly to be praised,
In the bcity of our God, His choly mountain.

★ 2 aPs. 50:2 bLam. 2:15 cMatt. 5:35
2 aBeautiful in elevation, bthe joy of the whole earth,

Is Mount Zion in the far north,
The ccity of the great King.

3 aPs. 46:7
3 God, in her palaces, Has made Himself known as a astronghold.

4 a2 Sam. 10:6-19
4 For, lo, the akings assembled themselves,
They passed by together.

5 aEx. 15:15
5 They saw it, then they were amazed;
They were aterrified, they fled in alarm.

6 aIs. 13:8
6 Panic seized them there, Anguish, as of aa woman in childbirth.

★ 7 aJer. 18:17 b1 Kin. 22:48 c1 Kin. 10:22; Ezek. 27:25
7 With the aeast wind Thou bdost break the cships of Tarshish.

8 aPs. 87:5
8 As we have heard, so have we seen
In the city of the Lord of hosts, in the city of our God;
God will aestablish her forever.   [Selah.

9 aPs. 26:3; 40:10
9 We have thought on aThy lovingkindness, O God,
In the midst of Thy temple.

10 aDeut. 28:58; Josh. 7:9; Mal. 1:11 bPs. 65:1, 2; 100:1 cIs. 41:10
10 As is Thy aname, O God, So is Thy bpraise to the ends of the earth;
Thy cright hand is full of righteousness.

★11 aPs. 97:8
11 Let Mount aZion be glad, Let the adaughters of Judah rejoice,
Because of Thy judgments.

12 aNeh. 3:1, 11, 25-27
12 Walk about Zion, and go around her;
Count her atowers;

47:3 *nations.* See Rev. 19:15.
47:5 *has ascended.* I.e., to His earthly throne.
47:9 *the shields of the earth.* I.e., the symbols of authority are His too.
Psalm 48 In this song of Zion, the psalmist praises God and Zion (Jerusalem) His dwelling place (vv. 1-3), describes the defeat of the city's enemies (vv. 4-7), offers thanksgiving (vv. 9-10), and invites the people to praise and trust God (vv. 11-14).

48:2 *in the far north.* In heathen lore, the abode of the gods (see note on Isa. 14:13-14); thus, this is a claim that Jerusalem is the place where the true God reigns.
48:7 *the ships of Tarshish.* Though the greatest of ancient ships, they could not withstand God's mighty power (see note on Isa. 2:16).
48:11 *the daughters of Judah.* Its cities and villages.

13 *a*Ps.
122:7 *b*Ps.
78:5-7

13 Consider her *a*ramparts;
Go through her palaces;
That you may *b*tell *it* to the
next generation.

14 *a*Ps. 23:4;
Is. 58:11

14 For such is God,
Our God forever and ever;
He will *a*guide us until
death.

PSALM 49

For the choir director.
A Psalm of the sons of Korah.

1 *a*Ps. 78:1;
Is. 1:2; Mic.
1:2 *b*Ps.
33:8

*a*HEAR this, all peoples;
Give ear, all *b*inhabitants
of the world,

2 *a*Ps. 62:9

2 Both *a*low and high,
Rich and poor together.

3 *a*Ps.
37:30 *b*Ps.
119:130

3 My mouth will *a*speak wisdom;
And the meditation of my
heart *will be* *b*under-
standing.

★ **4** *a*Ps.
78:2 *b*2 Kin.
3:15 *c*Num.
12:8

4 I will incline my ear to *a*a
proverb;
*b*I will express my *c*riddle
on the harp.

5 *a*Ps. 23:4;
27:1

5 Why should I *a*fear in days
of adversity,
When the iniquity of my
foes surrounds me,

6 *a*Job
31:24; Ps.
52:7; Prov.
11:28; Mark
10:24

6 Even those who *a*trust in
their wealth,
And boast in the abun-
dance of their riches?

★ **7-9**

7 *a*Matt.
25:8, 9 *b*Job
36:18, 19

7 No man can by any means
*a*redeem *his* brother,
Or give to God a *b*ransom
for him—

8 *a*Matt.
16:26

8 For *a*the redemption of his
soul is costly,
And he should cease *trying*
forever—

9 That he should *a*live on
eternally;
That he should not *b*un-
dergo decay.

9 *a*Ps.
22:29 *b*Ps.
16:10; 89:48

10 For he sees *that even* *a*wise
men die;
The *b*stupid and the senseless alike perish,
And *c*leave their wealth to
others.

10 *a*Eccl.
2:16 *b*Ps.
92:6; 94:8
*c*Ps. 39:6;
Eccl. 2:18,
21; Luke
12:20

11 Their *a*inner thought is,
that their houses *b*are
forever,
And their dwelling places
to all generations;
They have *c*called their
lands after their own
names.

11 *a*Ps. 64:6
*b*Ps. 10:6
*c*Gen. 4:17;
Deut. 3:14

12 But *a*man in *his* pomp will
not endure;
He is like the beasts that
perish.

★ **12** *a*Ps.
49:20

13 This is the *a*way of those
who are foolish,
And of those after them
who *b*approve their
words.   [Selah.

13 *a*Jer.
17:11 *b*Ps.
49:18

14 As sheep they are appointed *a*for Sheol;
Death shall be their shepherd;
And the *b*upright shall rule
over them in the
morning;
And their form shall be for
Sheol *c*to consume,
So that they have no habitation.

★ **14** *a*Ps.
9:17 *b*Dan.
7:18; Mal.
4:3; 1 Cor.
6:2; Rev.
2:26 *c*Job
24:19

15 But God will *a*redeem my
soul from the power
of Sheol;
For *b*He will receive me.
     [Selah.

★ **15** *a*Ps.
16:10; 56:13;
Hos. 13:14
*b*Gen. 5:24;
Ps. 16:11;
73:24

Psalm 49 This wisdom psalm, written to instruct men rather than to praise God, calls on the
world to hear the truth (vv. 1–4) concerning the
temporary glory and false security of the wicked
rich (vv. 5–14), whose doom is certain, in contrast to the everlasting hope of the righteous (vv.
15–20).
49:4 *proverb . . . riddle.* See note on Ezek. 17:2.
49:7-9 The thought is this: man cannot purchase
from God additional days in order to extend
his life.

49:12 This does not deal with the question of
life after death, but with the fact that the
hopes of wicked men are restricted to this life.
49:14 *Death shall be their shepherd.* I.e., guide
them directly to Sheol (see note on Gen.
37:35). The righteous will ultimately triumph
over the wicked, either in this life or in the life
to come (*morning*).
49:15 God pays the ransom which man could
not pay (vv. 7–8).

16 ªPs. 37:7

16 Do not be afraid ªwhen a
man becomes rich,
When the glory of his
house is increased;

17 ªPs.
17:14; 1 Tim.
6:7

17 For when he dies he will
ªcarry nothing away;
His glory will not descend
after him.

18 ªDeut.
29:19; Ps.
10:3, 6; Luke
12:19

18 Though while he lives he
ªcongratulates him-
self—
And though *men* praise
you when you do well
for yourself—

19 ªGen.
15:15 ᵇJob
33:30; Ps.
56:13

19 He shall ªgo to the generation of his fathers;
They shall never see ᵇthe
light.

20 ªPs.
49:12 ᵇEccl.
3:19

20 ªMan in *his* pomp, yet
without understand-
ing,
Is ᵇlike the beasts that perish.

PSALM 50

A Psalm of Asaph.

1 ªJosh.
22:22 ᵇPs.
113:3

ª

THE Mighty One, God, the
LORD, has spoken,
And summoned the earth
ᵇfrom the rising of the
sun to its setting.

2 ªPs. 48:2;
Lam. 2:15
ᵇDeut. 33:2;
Ps. 80:1;
94:1
3 ªPs.
96:13 ᵇLev.
10:2; Num.
16:35; Ps.
97:3; Dan.
7:10 ᶜPs.
18:12, 13
4 ªDeut.
4:26; 31:28;
32:1; Is. 1:2
★ 5 ªPs.
30:4; 37:28;
52:9 ᵇEx.
24:7; 2 Chr.
6:11; Ps.
25:10 ᶜPs.
50:8

2 Out of Zion, ªthe perfection of beauty,
God ᵇhas shone forth.

3 May our God ªcome and
not keep silence;
ᵇFire devours before Him,
And it is very ᶜtempestu-
ous around Him.

4 He ªsummons the heavens
above,
And the earth, to judge His
people;

5 "Gather My ªgodly ones to
Me,

Those who have made a
ᵇcovenant with Me by
ᶜsacrifice."

6 ªPs. 89:5;
97:6 ᵇPs.
75:7; 96:13

6 And the ªheavens declare
His righteousness,
For ᵇGod Himself is judge.
[Selah.

7 ªPs. 49:1;
81:8 ᵇEx.
20:2; Ps.
48:14

7 "ªHear, O My people, and I
will speak;
O Israel, I will testify
against you;
I am God, ᵇyour God.

★ 8-13
8 ªPs. 40:6;
51:16; Is.
1:11; Hos.
6:6

8 "I do ªnot reprove you for
your sacrifices,
And your burnt offerings
are continually before
Me.

9 ªPs.
69:31

9 "I shall take no ªyoung bull
out of your house,
Nor male goats out of your
folds.

10 ªPs.
104:24

10 "For ªevery beast of the forest is Mine,
The cattle on a thousand
hills.

11 ªMatt.
6:26

11 "I know every ªbird of the
mountains,
And everything that
moves in the field is
Mine.

12 ªEx. 19:5;
Deut. 10:14;
Ps. 24:1;
1 Cor. 10:26

12 "If I were hungry, I would
not tell you;
For the ªworld is Mine,
and all it contains.

13 ªPs. 50:9
14 ªPs. 27:6;
69:30;
107:22;
116:17; Hos.
14:2; Rom.
12:1; Heb.
13:15 ᵇNum.
30:2; Deut.
23:21; Ps.
22:25; 56:12;
61:8; 65:1;
76:11
15 ªPs.
91:15; 107:6,
13; Zech.
13:9 ᵇPs.
81:7 ᶜPs.
22:23

13 "Shall I eat the flesh of
ªbulls,
Or drink the blood of male
goats?

14 "Offer to God ªa sacrifice of
thanksgiving,
And ᵇpay your vows to the
Most High;

15 And ªcall upon Me in the
day of trouble;
I shall ᵇrescue you, and
you will ᶜhonor Me."

Psalm 50 This warning from Asaph reports
an appearance of God for judgment (vv. 1-6) and
presents God's indictment of His people for insincere sacrifices (vv. 7-13), with instruction for
correction (vv. 14-15), and His indictment for
unethical practices (vv. 16-21), with instruction
for correction (vv. 22-23). *Asaph.* Also wrote
Psalms 73-83 (see note on Ezra 2:41).

50:5 *godly ones.* I.e., Israel, with whom God
made the Mosaic *covenant* (Exod. 24:7) and
whom He accuses (v. 7).

50:8-13 God does not reprove them for failing
to bring their offerings (v. 8), but for bringing
them with the motive of trying to make the
God who owns everything dependent on their
generosity.

★16-17

16 ᵃIs. 29:13

17 ᵃProv.
5:12; 12:1;
Rom. 2:21,
22 ᵇ1 Kin.
14:9; Neh.
9:26

18 ᵃRom.
1:32 ᵇ1 Tim.
5:22

19 ᵃPs. 10:7
ᵇPs. 36:3;
52:2

20 ᵃJob
19:18; Matt.
10:21

★21 ᵃEccl.
8:11; Is.
42:14; 57:11
ᵇPs. 90:8

22 ᵃJob
8:13; Ps.
9:17 ᵇPs.
7:2

23 ᵃPs.
50:14 ᵇPs.
85:13 ᶜPs.
91:16

16 But to the wicked God says,
"What right have you to tell of My statutes,
And to take ᵃMy covenant in your mouth?
17 "For you ᵃhate discipline,
And you ᵇcast My words behind you.
18 "When you see a thief, you ᵃare pleased with him,
And you ᵇassociate with adulterers.
19 "You ᵃlet your mouth loose in evil,
And your ᵇtongue frames deceit.
20 "You sit and ᵃspeak against your brother;
You slander your own mother's son.
21 "These things you have done, and ᵃI kept silence;
You thought that I was just like you;
I will ᵇreprove you, and state *the case* in order before your eyes.
22 "Now consider this, you who ᵃforget God,
Lest I ᵇtear *you* in pieces, and there be none to deliver.
23 "He who ᵃoffers a sacrifice of thanksgiving honors Me;
And to him who ᵇorders *his* way *aright*
I shall ᶜshow the salvation of God."

PSALM 51

For the choir director. A Psalm of David, when Nathan the prophet came to him, after he had gone in to Bathsheba.

★1 ᵃPs.
4:1; 109:26
ᵇPs. 69:16,
106:45 ᶜPs.
51:9; Is.
43:25; 44:22;
Acts 3:19;
Col. 2:14

2 ᵃPs. 51:7;
Is. 1:16; 4:4;
Jer. 4:14;
Acts 22:16;
Rev. 1:5
ᵇJer. 33:8;
Ezek. 36:33;
Heb. 9:14;
1 John 1:7, 9

3 ᵃIs. 59:12

★4 ᵃGen.
20:6; 39:9;
2 Sam.
12:13; Ps.
41:4 ᵇLuke
15:21 ᶜRom.
3:4

★5 ᵃJob
14:4; 15:14;
Ps. 58:3;
Eph. 2:3

6 ᵃJob
38:36; Ps.
15:2 ᵇProv.
2:6; Eccl.
2:26; James
1:5

ᵃBE gracious to me, O God, according to Thy lovingkindness;
According to the greatness of ᵇThy compassion ᶜblot out my transgressions.
2 ᵃWash me thoroughly from my iniquity,
And ᵇcleanse me from my sin.
3 For I ᵃknow my transgressions,
And my sin is ever before me.
4 ᵃAgainst Thee, Thee only, I have sinned,
And done what is ᵇevil in Thy sight,
So that ᶜThou art justified when Thou dost speak,
And blameless when Thou dost judge.
5 Behold, I was ᵃbrought forth in iniquity,
And in sin my mother conceived me.
6 Behold, Thou dost desire ᵃtruth in the innermost being,
And in the hidden part Thou wilt ᵇmake me know wisdom.

50:16-17 God now accuses them of giving lip service to His laws (v. 16) while violating them (v. 17). Details are listed in verses 18-20.
50:21 They assumed that God's *silence* indicated that He was as lawless as they were!
Psalm 51 In this penitential psalm (see note on Psalm 6), David pleads for forgiveness and cleansing (vv. 1-2), confesses his guilt (vv. 3-6), prays for pardon and restoration (vv. 7-12), resolves to praise God (vv. 13-17), and prays for the continued prosperity of Jerusalem (vv. 18-19). The psalm elaborates David's confession

of his sin with Bathsheba (2 Sam. 11-12, especially 12:13).
51:1 In his unworthiness David pleads God's *lovingkindness* (love based on the covenant; see note on Hos. 2:19) and *compassion*.
51:4 Though David's sin involved others, he recognized that it was primarily against God.
51:5 *brought forth* (in birth). It is not that the acts of giving birth or conceiving are in themselves sinful, but that from the moment of conception a person possesses a sinful nature.

★ **7** aEx.
12:22; Lev.
14:4; Num.
19:18; Heb.
9:19 bIs.
1:18
8 aIs.
35:10; Joel
1:16 bPs.
35:10

9 aJer.
16:17

10 aEzek.
18:31; Eph.
2:10 bPs.
24:4; Matt.
5:8; Acts
15:9 cPs.
78:37
★**11** a2 Kin.
13:23; 24:20;
Jer. 7:15 bIs.
63:10, 11

12 aPs. 13:5
bPs. 110:3

13 aActs
9:21, 22
bPs. 22:27

★**14** a2 Sam.
12:9; Ps.
26:9 bPs.
25:5 cPs.
35:28; 71:15

15 aEx. 4:15
bPs. 9:14

16 a1 Sam.
15:22; Ps.
40:6

7 Purify me ᵃwith hyssop,
and I shall be clean;
Wash me, and I shall be
ᵇwhiter than snow.

8 Make me to hear ᵃjoy and
gladness,
Let the ᵇbones which Thou
hast broken rejoice.

9 ᵃHide Thy face from my
sins,
And blot out all my iniquities.

10 ᵃCreate in me a ᵇclean
heart, O God,
And renew a ᶜsteadfast
spirit within me.

11 ᵃDo not cast me away from
Thy presence,
And do not take Thy ᵇHo-
ly Spirit from me.

12 Restore to me the ᵃjoy of
Thy salvation,
And sustain me with a
ᵇwilling spirit.

13 Then I will ᵃteach transgressors Thy ways,
And sinners will be ᵇcon-
verted to Thee.

14 Deliver me from ᵃbloodguiltiness, O God,
Thou ᵇGod of my sal-
vation;
Then my ᶜtongue will joy-
fully sing of Thy
righteousness.

15 O LORD, ᵃopen my lips,
That my mouth may ᵇde-
clare Thy praise.

16 For Thou ᵃdost not delight
in sacrifice, otherwise
I would give it;
Thou art not pleased with
burnt offering.

17 The sacrifices of God are a
ᵃbroken spirit;
A broken and a contrite
heart, O God, Thou
wilt not despise.

18 ᵃBy Thy favor do good to
Zion;
ᵇBuild the walls of Jerusalem.

19 Then Thou wilt delight in
ᵃrighteous sacrifices,
In ᵇburnt offering and
whole burnt offering;
Then young bulls will be
offered on Thine altar.

PSALM 52

For the choir director.　A Maskil
of David, when Doeg the
Edomite came and told Saul, and
said to him, "David has come to
the house of Ahimelech."

WHY do you ᵃboast in evil, O
mighty man?
The ᵇlovingkindness of
God *endures* all day
long.

2 Your tongue devises ᵃde-
struction,
Like a ᵇsharp razor, ᶜO
worker of deceit.

3 You ᵃlove evil more than
good,
ᵇFalsehood more than
speaking what is
right.　　　[Selah.

4 You love all words that devour,
O ᵃdeceitful tongue.

5 But God will break you
down forever;

17 aPs.
34:18

18 aPs.
69:35; Is.
51:3 bPs.
102:16;
147:2

19 aPs. 4:5
bPs. 66:13,
15

1 aPs. 94:4
bPs. 52:8

2 aPs. 5:9
bPs. 57:4;
59:7 cPs.
101:7

3 aPs. 36:4
bPs. 58:3;
Jer. 9:5

4 aPs.
120:3

★ **5** aIs.
22:18, 19
bProv. 2:22
cPs. 27:13

51:7 *hyssop.* See note on Exod. 12:22. It was
used in cleansing the house of a leper (Lev.
14:49) and in purification from defilement by
death (Num. 19:18-19).
51:11 In the O.T. economy, the *Holy Spirit* was
particularly related to service, rather than salvation (cf. note on Judg. 3:10; Rom. 8:9). Here
David is asking God not to take away his service as the anointed king of Israel (cf. Saul,
1 Sam. 16:13-14).
51:14 *bloodguiltiness.* Lit., bloods; i.e., the sen-

tence of death for the murder of Uriah.
Psalm 52 Contrasting the wicked and the
righteous, this didactic psalm may be outlined
this way: the description of the wicked (vv. 1-4),
the doom of the wicked (v. 5), the delight of the
righteous (vv. 6-9). *Maskil.* See note on Psalm
32. First Sam. 21:1-22:19 furnishes the historical
background.
52:5 Four striking figures describe the doom of
the wicked.

He will snatch you up, and
ªtear you away from
your tent,
And ᵇuproot you from the
ᶜland of the living.
[Selah.

★ 6-7

6 ªPs.
37:34; 40:3
ᵇJob 22:19

6 And the righteous will ªsee
and fear,
And will ᵇlaugh at him,
saying,

7 ªPs. 49:6
ᵇPs. 10:6

7 "Behold, the man who
would not make God
his refuge,
But ªtrusted in the abun-
dance of his riches,
And ᵇwas strong in his evil
desire."

8 ªPs.
92:12; 128:3;
Jer. 11:16
ᵇPs. 13:5

8 But as for me, I am like a
ªgreen olive tree in
the house of God;
I ᵇtrust in the lovingkindness of God forever
and ever.

9 ªPs.
30:12 ᵇPs.
54:6

9 I will ªgive Thee thanks
forever, because Thou
hast done it,
And I will wait on Thy
name, ᵇfor it is good,
in the presence of Thy
godly ones.

PSALM 53

For the choir director; according
to Mahalath.
A Maskil of David.

1 ªPs. 10:4;
14:1-7; 53:1-
6 ᵇRom.
3:10

ª
THE fool has said in his heart,
"There is no God,"
They are corrupt, and have
committed abomina-
ble injustice;
ᵇThere is no one who does
good.

2 ªRom.
3:11 ᵇ2 Chr.
15:2

2 God has looked down
from heaven upon the
sons of men,
To see if there is ªanyone
who understands,
Who ᵇseeks after God.

3 ªRom.
3:12

3 ªEvery one of them has
turned aside; together
they have become
corrupt;
There is no one who does
good, not even one.

4 ªJer. 4:22

4 Have the workers of wickedness ªno knowl-
edge,
Who eat up My people as
though they ate
bread,
And have not called upon
God?

★ 5 ªLev.
26:17, 36;
Prov. 28:1
ᵇPs. 141:7;
Jer. 8:1, 2;
Ezek. 6:5
ᶜPs. 44:7
ᵈ2 Kin.
17:20; Jer.
6:30; Lam.
5:22

5 There they were in great
fear ªwhere no fear
had been;
For God ᵇscattered the
bones of him who en-
camped against you;
You ᶜput them to shame,
because ᵈGod had re-
jected them.

6 ªPs. 14:7

6 Oh, that ªthe salvation of
Israel would come out
of Zion!
When God restores His
captive people,
Let Jacob rejoice, let Israel
be glad.

PSALM 54

For the choir director; on
stringed instruments.
A Maskil of David, when the
Ziphites came and said
to Saul, "Is not David hiding
himself among us?"

1 ªPs. 20:1
ᵇ2 Chr. 20:6

S
AVE me, O God, by ªThy
name,

52:6-7 The righteous fear (stand in awe of) God
and laugh (in derision) at the wicked.

Psalm 53 In this psalm (essentially identical
with Psalm 14; see notes there), David laments
the moral foolishness and corruption of the human race (vv. 1-5) and longs for the establishing
of the righteous kingdom of the Lord on earth (v.
6). Mahalath. A term meaning "sickness" (also
in Psalm 88), possibly the first word of a well-
known tune to which this psalm was sung. Maskil. See note on Psalm 32.

53:5 This verse suggests a miraculous deliverance as the background for adapting Psalm 14
for the occasion (perhaps that of 2 Kings
7:6-7).

Psalm 54 Reflecting on the treachery of the
Ziphites, who revealed to Saul that David was
hiding among them (1 Sam. 23), David petitions
God for deliverance from his enemies (vv. 1-3)
and praises Him for the answer (vv. 4-7). Maskil.
See note on Psalm 32.

And vindicate me by [b]Thy
power.

2 [a]Hear my prayer, O God;
[b]Give ear to the words of
my mouth.

3 For strangers have [a]risen
against me,
And [b]violent men have
[c]sought my life;
They have [d]not set God
before them. [Selah.

4 Behold, [a]God is my helper;
The Lord is the [b]sustainer
of my soul.

5 He will [a]recompense the
evil to my foes;
[b]Destroy them [c]in Thy
faithfulness.

6 [a]Willingly I will sacrifice
to Thee;
I will give [b]thanks to Thy
name, O LORD, for it is
good.

7 For He has [a]delivered me
from all trouble;
And my eye has [b]looked
with satisfaction upon
my enemies.

PSALM 55

For the choir director; on
stringed instruments.
A Maskil of David.

[a]GIVE ear to my prayer, O God;
And [b]do not hide Thyself
from my supplication.

2 Give [a]heed to me, and answer me;
I am restless in my [b]com-
plaint and [c]am surely
distracted,

3 Because of the voice of the
enemy,
Because of the [a]pressure of
the wicked;

For they [b]bring down trouble upon me,
And in anger they [c]bear a
grudge against me.

4 My [a]heart is in anguish
within me,
And the terrors of [b]death
have fallen upon me.

5 Fear and [a]trembling come
upon me;
And [b]horror has over-
whelmed me.

6 And I said, "Oh, that I had
wings like a dove!
I would fly away and [a]be at
rest.

7 "Behold, I would wander far
away,
I would [a]lodge in the
wilderness. [Selah.

8 "I would hasten to my place
of refuge
From the [a]stormy wind
and tempest."

9 Confuse, O Lord, [a]divide
their tongues,
For I have seen [b]violence
and strife in the city.

10 Day and night they go
around her upon her
walls;
And iniquity and mischief
are in her midst.

11 [a]Destruction is in her
midst;
[b]Oppression and deceit do
not depart from her
streets.

12 For it is [a]not an enemy
who reproaches me,
Then I could bear it;
Nor is it one who hates me
who [b]has exalted him-
self against me,
Then I could hide myself
from him.

Marginal references

2 [a]Ps. 17:6;
55:1 [b]Ps.
5:1

3 [a]Ps.
86:14 [b]Ps.
18:48; 86:14;
140:1, 4, 11
[c]1 Sam.
20:1; 25:29;
Ps. 40:14;
63:9; 70:2
[d]Ps. 36:1

4 [a]Ps.
30:10; 37:40;
118:7 [b]Ps.
37:17, 24;
41:12; 51:12;
145:14; Is.
41:10

5 [a]Ps.
94:23 [b]Ps.
143:12 [c]Ps.
89:49; 96:13;
Is. 42:3

6 [a]Num.
15:3; Ps.
116:17 [b]Ps.
50:14

7 [a]Ps. 34:6
[b]Ps. 59:10;
92:11; 112:8;
118:7

1 [a]Ps. 54:2;
61:1; 86:6
[b]Ps. 27:9

2 [a]Ps.
66:19; 86:6,
7 [b]1 Sam.
1:16; Job
9:27; Ps.
64:1; 77:3;
142:2 [c]Is.
38:14; 59:11;
Ezek. 7:16
3 [a]Ps. 17:9
[b]2 Sam.
16:7, 8 [c]Ps.
71:11; 143:3

4 [a]Ps. 38:8
[b]Ps. 18:4, 5;
116:3

5 [a]Ps.
119:120
[b]Job 21:6;
Is. 21:4;
Ezek. 7:18

6 [a]Job 3:13

7 [a]1 Sam.
23:14

8 [a]Is. 4:6;
25:4; 29:6

★ 9 [a]Gen.
11:9 [b]Ps.
11:5; Jer. 6:7

★10-11

11 [a]Ps. 5:9
[b]Ps. 10:7;
17:9

12 [a]Ps. 41:9
[b]Ps. 35:26

Psalm 55 Because of the treachery of an intimate friend (vv. 12-13), David prays in anguish
(with respect to himself, vv. 1-8), in anger (with
respect to his enemies, vv. 9-15), and in assurance (with respect to God, vv. 16-23).
55:9 The meaning is this: may such confusion
and division as occurred at Babel happen to
my enemies (see notes on Gen. 11:7 and 9).
55:10-11 As king, David was especially concerned that the city had become a parade
ground for rebels and terrorists.

★13 a2 Sam.
15:12 bJob
19:14; Ps.
41:9

13 But it is you, a man my equal,
My acompanion and my bfamiliar friend.

14 aPs. 42:4

14 We who had sweet fellowship together,
aWalked in the house of God in the throng.

★15 aPs.
64:7; Prov.
6:15; Is.
47:11;
1 Thess. 5:3
bNum.
16:30, 33

15 Let death come adeceitfully upon them;
Let them bgo down alive to Sheol,
For evil is in their dwelling, in their midst.

16 aPs.
57:2, 3

16 As for me, I shall acall upon God,
And the Lord will save me.

17 aPs.
141:2; Dan.
6:10; Acts
3:1; 10:3, 30
bPs. 5:3;
88:13; 92:2
cActs 10:9

17 aEvening and bmorning and at cnoon, I will complain and murmur,
And He will hear my voice.

18 aPs.
103:4 bPs.
56:2

18 He will aredeem my soul in peace from the battle *which is* against me,
For they are bmany *who strive* with me.

19 aPs.
78:59 bDeut.
33:27; Ps.
90:2; 93:2
cPs. 36:1

19 God will ahear and answer them—
Even the one bwho sits enthroned from of old—
[Selah.
With whom there is no change,
And who cdo not fear God.

20 aPs. 7:4;
120:7 bNum.
30:2; Ps.
89:34

20 He has put forth his hands against athose who were at peace with him;
He has bviolated his covenant.

21 aPs. 12:2;
28:3; Prov.
5:3, 4 bPs.
57:4; 59:7

21 His speech was asmoother than butter,
But his heart was war;
His words were asofter than oil,

Yet they were drawn bswords.

22 aPs. 37:5;
1 Pet. 5:7
bPs. 37:24
cPs. 15:5;
112:6

22 aCast your burden upon the Lord, and He will sustain you;
bHe will never allow the righteous to cbe shaken.

23 aPs.
73:18; Is.
38:17; Ezek.
28:8 bPs.
5:6 cJob
15:32; Prov.
10:27 dPs.
25:2; 56:3

23 But Thou, O God, wilt bring them down to the apit of destruction;
bMen of bloodshed and deceit will cnot live out half their days.
But I will dtrust in Thee.

PSALM 56

For the choir director; according to Jonath elem rehokim. A Mikhtam of David, when the Philistines seized him in Gath.

1 aPs. 57:3
bPs. 17:9

BE gracious, O God, for man has atrampled upon me;
Fighting all day long he boppresses me.

2 aPs.
35:25; 57:3;
124:3 bPs.
35:1

2 My foes have atrampled upon me all day long,
For they are many who bfight proudly against me.

3 aPs. 55:4,
5 bPs. 11:1

3 When I am aafraid,
I will bput my trust in Thee.

★ 4 aPs.
56:10, 11
bPs. 118:6;
Heb. 13:6

4 aIn God, whose word I praise,
In God I have put my trust; I shall not be afraid.
bWhat can *mere* man do to me?

5 a2 Pet.
3:16 bPs.
41:7

5 All day long they adistort my words;
All their bthoughts are against me for evil.

55:13 We cannot be sure who this traitor was, though verses 20–21 tell us how he acted.

55:15 *Let them go down alive to Sheol.* I.e., let God's judgment be immediate and startling (as was that upon Korah, Num. 16:30–32), not for personal vindication but because the treachery was against God's appointed leader.

Psalm 56 This lament contains a plea for help (vv. 1–6), a petition for vengeance (vv.

7–11), and a promise to pay vows (vv. 12–13). *according to Jonath elem rehokim.* Probably means, "to the tune of 'the silent dove in far-off lands.'" *Mikhtam.* See note on Psalm 16. The historical background is David's feigning insanity *in Gath* (1 Sam. 21:10–15).

56:4 The implied answer to the question is, "Nothing that God does not permit." See also verse 11.

6 aPs. 59:3;
140:2; Is.
54:15 bPs.
17:11 cPs.
71:10

6 They ªattack, they lurk,
They ᵇwatch my steps,
As they have ᶜwaited to
    take my life.

7 aPs.
36:12; Prov.
19:5; Ezek.
17:15; Rom.
2:3 bPs.
55:23

7 Because of wickedness,
    ªcast them forth,
In anger ᵇput down the
    peoples, O God!

★ **8** aPs.
139:3
b2 Kin. 20:5;
Ps. 39:12
cMal. 3:16

8 Thou ªhast taken account
    of my wanderings;
Put my ᵇtears in Thy bot-
    tle;
Are they not in ᶜThy
    book?

9 aPs. 9:3
bPs. 102:2
cPs. 41:11;
118:6; Rom.
8:31

9 Then my enemies will
    ªturn back ᵇin the day
    when I call;
This I know, that ᶜGod is
    for me.
10 In God, whose word I
    praise,
In the LORD, whose word I
    praise,
11 In God I have put my trust,
    I shall not be afraid.
What can man do to me?

★**12** aPs.
50:14

12 Thy ªvows are binding
    upon me, O God;
I will render thank offer-
    ings to Thee.

13 aPs.
33:19; 49:15;
86:13 bPs.
116:8 cPs.
116:9 dJob
33:30

13 For Thou hast ªdelivered
    my soul from death,
Indeed ᵇmy feet from
    stumbling,
So that I may ᶜwalk before
    God
In the ᵈlight of the living.

PSALM 57

For the choir director; set to Al-
tashheth. A Mikhtam of David,
when he fled from Saul, in the
cave.

1 aPs. 2:12;
34:22 bRuth
2:12; Ps.
17:8; 36:7;
63:7; 91:4
cIs. 26:20

Be gracious to me, O God, be
    gracious to me,
For my soul ªtakes refuge
    in Thee;

And in the ᵇshadow of
    Thy wings I will take
    refuge,
Until destruction ᶜpasses
    by.

2 I will cry to God Most
    High,
To God who ªaccomplishes
    all things for me.

2 aPs.
138:8

3 He will ªsend from heaven
    and save me;
He reproaches him who
    ᵇtramples upon me.
                    [Selah.
God will send forth His
    ᶜlovingkindness and
    His truth.

★ **3** aPs.
18:16; 144:5;
7 bPs. 56:2
cPs. 25:10;
40:11

4 My soul is among ªlions;
I must lie among those
    who breathe forth
    fire,
Even the sons of men,
    whose ᵇteeth are
    spears and arrows,
And their ᶜtongue a sharp
    sword.

★ **4** aPs.
35:17; 58:6
bProv. 30:14
cPs. 55:21;
59:7; 64:3;
Prov. 12:18

5 ªBe exalted above the
    heavens, O God;
Let Thy glory be above all
    the earth.

5 aPs.
57:11; 108:5

6 They have prepared a ªnet
    for my steps;
My soul is ᵇbowed down;
They ᶜdug a pit before me;
They themselves have
    ᵈfallen into the midst
    of it.   [Selah.

6 aPs. 10:9;
31:4; 35:7;
140:5 bPs.
145:14 cPs.
7:15 dProv.
26:27; 28:10;
Eccl. 10:8

7 ªMy ᵇheart is steadfast, O
    God, my heart is
    steadfast;
I will sing, yes, I will sing
    praises!

7 aPs.
57:7-11;
108:1-5 bPs.
112:7

8 Awake, ªmy glory;
Awake, ᵇharp and lyre,
I will awaken the dawn!

8 aPs. 16:9;
30:12 bPs.
150:3

9 ªI will give thanks to Thee,
    O Lord, among the
    peoples;

9 aPs.
108:3

56:8 I.e., God is attentive to every detail of his
life.
56:12 thank offerings. Could be either actual
sacrifices (see note on Lev. 7:12-17) or songs of
praise (Psalm 26:7) or, as here, both.
Psalm 57 Fleeing Saul, David voices prayer
(vv. 1-6) and praise (vv. 7-11) for deliverance.

Al-tashheth. Lit., do not destroy; possibly a tune
indication (also Psalms 58-59, 75). Mikhtam. See
note on Psalm 16.
57:3 lovingkindness. God's steadfast love (see
note on Hos. 2:19).
57:4 David had to hide from men whose hearts
were aflame with enmity.

I will sing praises to Thee among the nations.

10 aPs. 36:5; 103:11; 108:4

10 For Thy alovingkindness is great to the heavens, And Thy truth to the clouds.

11 aPs. 57:5; 108:5

11 aBe exalted above the heavens, O God; *Let* Thy glory *be* above all the earth.

PSALM 58

For the choir director; *set to* Al-tashheth. A Mikhtam of David.

★ **1** aPs. 82:2

DO you indeed speak right-eousness, O gods? Do you ajudge uprightly, O sons of men?

2 aMal. 3:15 bPs. 94:20; Is. 10:1

2 No, in heart you awork un-righteousness; On earth you bweigh out the violence of your hands.

★ **3-5**

3 aPs. 51:5; Is. 48:8 bPs. 53:3

3 The wicked are estranged afrom the womb; These who speak lies bgo astray from birth.

4 aDeut. 32:33; Ps. 140:3

4 They have venom like the avenom of a serpent; Like a deaf cobra that stops up its ear,

5 aJer. 8:17 bEccl. 10:11

5 So that it adoes not hear the voice of bcharm-ers, *Or* a skillful caster of spells.

6 aJob 4:10; Ps. 3:7

6 O God, ashatter their teeth in their mouth; Break out the fangs of the young lions, O LORD.

7 Let them aflow away like water that runs off; *When* he baims his arrows, let them be as head-less shafts.

7 aJosh. 2:11; 7:5; Ps. 112:10; Is. 13:7; Ezek. 21:7 bPs. 64:3

8 *Let them be* as a snail which melts away as it goes along, *Like* the amiscarriages of a woman which never see the sun.

8 aJob 3:16; Eccl. 6:3

9 Before your apots can feel *the fire of* thorns, He will bsweep them away with a whirlwind, the green and the burning alike.

★ **9** aPs. 118:12; Eccl. 7:6 bJob 27:21; Ps. 83:15; Prov. 10:25

10 The arighteous will rejoice when he bsees the vengeance; He will cwash his feet in the blood of the wicked.

10 aJob 22:19; Ps. 32:11; 64:10; 107:42 bDeut. 32:43; Ps. 91:8; Jer. 11:20; 20:12 cPs. 68:23

11 And men will say, "Surely there is a areward for the righteous; Surely there is a God who bjudges on earth!"

11 aPs. 18:20; 19:11; Is. 3:10; Luke 6:23, 35 bPs. 9:8; 67:4; 75:7; 94:2

PSALM 59

For the choir director; *set to* Al-tashheth. A Mikhtam of David, when Saul sent *men,* and they watched the house in order to kill him.

1 aPs. 143:9 bPs. 20:1; 69:29

a

DELIVER me from my en-emies, O my God; bSet me *securely* on high away from those who rise up against me.

Psalm 58 An imprecatory psalm (see Intro-duction). David indicts unrighteous judges (vv. 1–5) and calls for their swift destruction (vv. 6–9) so the righteous can rejoice in God's justice (vv. 10–11). *Al-tashheth.* See note on Psalm 57. *Mikhtam.* See note on Psalm 16.
58:1 *gods.* Or, *mighty ones.* Though the mean-ing of the Hebrew word is obscure, the refer-ence is clearly to unrighteous judges, who ei-ther are being referred to sarcastically as "gods" or who had taken that as an honorific title.
58:3–5 *from the womb.* See note on 51:5. Be-cause of inborn sinfulness, men lie, poison

others, and are deaf to all appeals (like a snake who will not obey a snake charmer).
58:9 A reference to two kinds of branches for firewood, and picturing God's judgment on the wicked.
Psalm 59 In this imprecatory psalm (see In-troduction), David appeals for God's help (vv. 1–5), describes his dangerous situation (vv. 6–10), asks for judgment on his enemies (vv. 11–15), and ascribes praise to God (vv. 16–17). *Al-tashheth.* See note on Psalm 57. *Mikhtam.* See note on Psalm 16. For the historical back-ground, see 1 Sam. 19:11–12.

2 aPs. 28:3;
36:12; 53:4;
92:7; 94:16
bPs. 26:9;
139:19; Prov.
29:10

3 aPs. 56:6
b1 Sam.
24:11; Ps.
7:3, 4; 69:4

2 Deliver me from ᵃthose
who do iniquity,
And save me from ᵇmen of
bloodshed.

3 For behold, they ᵃhave set
an ambush for my
life;
Fierce men ᵃlaunch an at-
tack against me,
ᵇNot for my transgression
nor for my sin, O
LORD,

4 aPs.
35:19 bPs.
7:6; 35:23

4 ᵃFor no guilt of *mine*, they
run and set them-
selves against me.
ᵇArouse Thyself to help
me, and see!

5 aPs. 69:6;
80:4; 84:8
bPs. 9:5; Is.
26:14 cIs.
2:9; Jer.
18:23

5 And Thou, ᵃO LORD God
of hosts, the God of
Israel,
Awake to ᵇpunish all the
nations;
ᶜDo not be gracious to any
who are treacherous
in iniquity.   [Selah.

6 aPs.
59:14 bPs.
22:16

6 They ᵃreturn at evening,
they howl like a ᵇdog,
And go around the city.

7 aPs. 94:4;
Prov. 15:2,
28 bPs.
57:4; Prov.
12:18 cJob
22:13; Ps.
10:11; 73:11;
94:7

7 Behold, they ᵃbelch forth
with their mouth;
ᵇSwords are in their lips,
For, *they say,* "ᶜWho
hears?"

8 aPs.
37:13; Prov.
1:26 bPs.
2:4

8 But Thou, O LORD, dost
ᵃlaugh at them;
Thou dost ᵇscoff at all the
nations.

9 aPs.
18:17 bPs.
9:9; 62:2

9 *Because of* his ᵃstrength I
will watch for Thee,
For God is my ᵇstronghold.

10 aPs. 21:3
bPs. 54:7

10 My God ᵃin His lovingkindness will meet
me;
God will let me ᵇlook tri-
umphantly upon my
foes.

★11 aDeut.
4:9; 6:12
bPs. 106:27;
144:6; Is.
33:3 cPs.
84:9

11 Do not slay them, ᵃlest my
people forget;
ᵇScatter them by Thy
power, and bring
them down,
O Lord, ᶜour shield.

12 aProv.
12:13
bZeph. 3:11
cPs. 10:7

12 *On account of* the ᵃsin of
their mouth *and* the
words of their lips,
Let them even be ᵇcaught
in their pride,
And on account of ᶜcurses
and lies which they
utter.

13 aPs.
104:35 bPs.
83:18

13 ᵃDestroy *them* in wrath,
destroy *them,* that
they may be no more;
That *men* may ᵇknow that
God rules in Jacob,
To the ends of the earth.
[Selah.

14 aPs. 59:6

14 And they ᵃreturn at evening, they howl like a
dog,
And go around the city.

15 aJob
15:23

15 They ᵃwander about for
food,
And growl if they are not
satisfied.

16 aPs.
21:13 bPs.
101:1 cPs.
5:3; 88:13
dPs. 59:9
e2 Sam.
22:3; Ps.
46:1

16 But as for me, I shall ᵃsing
of Thy strength;
Yes, I shall ᵇjoyfully sing
of Thy lovingkindness
in the ᶜmorning,
For Thou hast been my
ᵈstronghold,
And a ᵉrefuge in the day of
my distress.

17 aPs. 59:9
bPs. 59:10

17 ᵃO my strength, I will sing
praises to Thee;
For God is my ᵇstronghold,
the God who shows
me lovingkindness.

PSALM 60

For the choir director; according
to Shushan Eduth.   A
Mikhtam of David, to teach;
when he struggled with Aram-
naharaim and with Aram-
zobah, and Joab returned, and
smote twelve thousand of
Edom in the Valley of Salt.

O GOD, ᵃThou hast rejected
us. Thou hast ᵇbroken
us;

1 aPs. 44:9
b2 Sam. 5:20
cPs. 79:5
dPs. 80:3

59:11 David asks that the punishment of the
wicked would be such as to teach the people
the seriousness of sin, especially sins of speech
(v. 12).

Psalm 60 While David was fighting in the
north with *Aram-naharaim* (Mesopotamia) and

2 aPs. 18:7
b2 Chr. 7:14;
Is. 30:26

3 aPs.
66:12; 71:20
bPs. 75:8; Is.
51:17, 22;
Jer. 25:15

★ 4 aPs.
20:5; Is.
5:26; 11:12;
13:2

5 aPs.
60:5-12;
108:6-13
bDeut.
33:12; Ps.
127:2; Is.
5:1; Jer.
11:15 cPs.
17:7

★ 6-7

6 aPs.
89:35 bGen.
12:6; 33:18;
Josh. 17:7
cGen. 33:17;
Josh. 13:27

7 aJosh.
13:31 bDeut.
33:17 cGen.
49:10

★ 8 a2 Sam.
8:2 b2 Sam.
8:14 c2 Sam.
8:1

Thou hast been cangry; O,
drestore us.

2 Thou hast made the aland
quake, Thou hast split
it open;
bHeal its breaches, for it
totters.

3 Thou hast amade Thy people experience hard-
ship;
Thou hast given us wine to
bdrink that makes us
stagger.

4 Thou hast given a abanner
to those who fear
Thee,
That it may be displayed
because of the truth.
[Selah.

5 aThat Thy bbeloved may
be delivered,
cSave with Thy right hand,
and answer us!

6 God has spoken in His
aholiness:
"I will exult, I will portion
out bShechem and
measure out the val-
ley of cSuccoth.

7 "aGilead is Mine, and Manasseh is Mine;
bEphraim also is the hel-
met of My head;
Judah is My cscepter.

8 "aMoab is My washbowl;
Over bEdom I shall throw
My shoe;
Shout loud, O cPhilistia,
because of Me!"

9 Who will bring me into
the besieged city?

Who will lead me to
Edom?

10 Hast not Thou Thyself, O
God, arejected us?
And bwilt Thou not go
forth with our armies,
O God?

11 O give us help against the
adversary,
For adeliverance by man is
in vain.

12 Through God we shall ado
valiantly,
And it is He who will
btread down our ad-
versaries.

PSALM 61

For the choir director; on a
stringed instrument.
A Psalm of David.

a

HEAR my cry, O God;
bGive heed to my prayer.

2 From the aend of the earth
I call to Thee, when
my heart is bfaint;
Lead me to cthe rock that
is higher than I.

3 For Thou hast been a arefuge for me,
A btower of strength
against the enemy.

4 Let me adwell in Thy tent
forever;
Let me btake refuge in the
shelter of Thy wings.
[Selah.

5 For Thou hast heard my
avows, O God;

10 aPs. 60:1;
108:11
bJosh. 7:12;
Ps. 44:9

11 aPs.
146:3

12 aNum.
24:18; Ps.
118:16 bPs.
44:5; Is. 63:3

★ 2-4

1 aPs. 64:1
bPs. 86:6

2 aPs. 42:6
bPs. 77:3
cPs. 18:2;
94:22

3 aPs. 62:7
bPs. 59:9;
Prov. 18:10

4 aPs. 23:6;
27:4 bPs.
17:8; 91:4
5 aJob
22:27; Ps.
56:12 bDeut.
28:58; Neh.
1:11; Ps.
86:11;
102:15; Is.
59:19; Mal.
2:5; 4:2

Aram-zobah (between Damascus and the Upper
Euphrates), Edom, invading from the south, defeated Israel. Joab was dispatched and achieved
an important victory over the Edomites (2 Sam.
8; 1 Chron. 18). Shushan Eduth. Lit., the lily of
the testimony, apparently a tune. Mikhtam. See
note on Psalm 16. The psalm may be outlined as
follows: the predicament of the nation (vv. 1-5),
the promise of God (vv. 6-8), and the petition of
David (vv. 9-12).
60:4 Since God had given a banner to summon
them to fight victoriously, their defeat seemed
inexplicable.
60:6-7 God assures them that He who apportioned the land is still in control of it.
60:8 Other nations are put in their places: Moab,

to bathe the feet; Edom, the servant to whom
the sandals are thrown; Philistia, to provide
the topic for a victory song.
Psalm 61 Disheartened, David prays for
strength and security (vv. 1-2), based on the
comfort that comes from God's character (vv.
3-4) and on the confidence that comes from His
faithfulness to His promises (vv. 5-7), all of
which motivates the psalmist to praise and give
thanks to God (v. 8).
61:2-4 the rock that is higher than I. An asylum
which gives protection and security. God is
that asylum, pictured by four figures of
speech: refuge, tower of strength, tent, and
shelter.

Thou hast given *me* the inheritance of those who [b]fear Thy name.

6 Thou wilt [a]prolong the king's life;
His years will be as many generations.

7 He will abide [a]before God forever;
Appoint [b]lovingkindness and truth, that they may preserve him.

8 So I will [a]sing praise to Thy name forever,
That I may [b]pay my vows day by day.

PSALM 62

For the choir director; according to Jeduthun.
A Psalm of David.

[a]MY soul *waits* in silence for God only;
From Him [b]is my salvation.

2 He only is my [a]rock and my salvation,
My [b]stronghold; I shall not be greatly shaken.

3 How long will you assail a man,
That you may murder *him*, all of you,
Like a [a]leaning wall, like a tottering fence?

4 They have counseled only to thrust him down from his high position;
They [a]delight in falsehood;
They [b]bless with their mouth,
But inwardly they curse. [Selah.

5 My soul, [a]wait in silence for God only,

For my hope is from Him.

6 He only is [a]my rock and my salvation,
My stronghold; I shall not be shaken.

7 On God my [a]salvation and my glory *rest*;
The rock of my strength, my [b]refuge is in God.

8 [a]Trust in Him at all times, O people;
[b]Pour out your heart before Him;
God is a refuge for us. [Selah.

9 Men of [a]low degree are only [b]vanity, and men of rank are a [c]lie;
In the [d]balances they go up;
They are together lighter than breath.

10 [a]Do not trust in oppression,
And do not vainly hope in [b]robbery;
If riches increase, [c]do not set *your* heart *upon* them.

11 Once God has [a]spoken;
Twice I have heard this:
That [b]power belongs to God;

12 And lovingkindness [a]is Thine, O Lord,
For Thou [b]dost recompense a man according to his work.

PSALM 63

A Psalm of David, when he was in the wilderness of Judah.

O GOD, [a]Thou art my God; I shall seek Thee earnestly;

Marginal references

★ 7-8
6 [a]Ps. 21:4
7 [a]Ps. 41:12 [b]Ps. 40:11
8 [a]Judg. 5:3; Ps. 30:4; 33:2; 71:22 [b]Ps. 65:1; Is. 19:21
1 [a]Ps. 33:20 [b]Ps. 37:39
2 [a]Ps. 89:26 [b]Ps. 59:17; 62:6
3 [a]Is. 30:13
4 [a]Ps. 4:2 [b]Ps. 28:3; 55:21
5 [a]Ps. 62:1
6 [a]Ps. 62:2
7 [a]Ps. 85:9; Jer. 3:23 [b]Ps. 46:1
8 [a]Ps. 37:3, 5; 52:8; Is. 26:4 [b]1 Sam. 1:15; Ps. 42:4; Lam. 2:19
★ 9 [a]Ps. 49:2 [b]Job 7:16; Ps. 39:5; Is. 40:17 [c]Ps. 116:11 [d]Is. 40:15
10 [a]Is. 30:12 [b]Is. 61:8; Ezek. 22:29; Nah. 3:1 [c]Job 31:25; Ps. 49:6; 52:7; Mark 10:24; Luke 12:15; 1 Tim. 6:10
11 [a]Job 33:14; 40:5 [b]Ps. 59:17; Rev. 19:1
12 [a]Ps. 86:5; 103:8; 130:7 [b]Job 34:11; Ps. 28:4; Jer. 17:10; Matt. 16:27; Rom. 2:6; 1 Cor. 3:8; Rev. 2:23
1 [a]Ps. 118:28 [b]Ps. 42:2; 84:2; Matt. 5:6 [c]Ps. 143:6

61:7-8 David appeals to God's covenant with him (2 Sam. 7:16).

Psalm 62 David waits on God (vv. 1-7) and warns others to put their trust in Him, rather than in the folly of ill-gotten gain or human strength (vv. 8-12). *Jeduthun.* See note on Psalm 39.

62:9 Place the wicked on a balance scale and their side goes up, since they weigh as much as breath!

Psalm 63 *in the wilderness of Judah,* separated from the sanctuary in Jerusalem, David fellowships with God, who is the desire of his being (vv. 1-4), the delight of his soul (vv. 5-8), and the defense of his life (vv. 9-11).

My soul [b]thirsts for Thee,
my flesh yearns for
Thee,
In a [c]dry and weary land
where there is no wa-
ter.

2 Thus I have [a]beheld Thee
in the sanctuary,
To see Thy power and Thy
glory.

3 Because Thy [a]lovingkind-
ness is better than life,
My lips will praise Thee.

4 So I will bless Thee [a]as
long as I live;
I will [b]lift up my hands in
Thy name.

5 My soul is [a]satisfied as
with marrow and fat-
ness,
And my mouth offers
[b]praises with joyful
lips.

6 When I remember Thee
[a]on my bed,
I meditate on Thee in the
[b]night watches,

7 For [a]Thou hast been my
help,
And in the [b]shadow of
Thy wings I sing for
joy.

8 My soul [a]clings to Thee;
Thy [b]right hand upholds
me.

9 But those who [a]seek my
life, to destroy it,
Will go into the [b]depths of
the earth.

10 They will be [a]delivered
over to the power of
the sword;
They will be a [b]prey for
foxes.

11 But the [a]king will rejoice
in God;
Everyone who [b]swears by
Him will glory,

For the [c]mouths of those
who speak lies will be
stopped.

PSALM 64

For the choir director.   A
Psalm of David.

HEAR my voice, O God, in
[a]my complaint;
[b]Preserve my life from
dread of the enemy.

2 Hide me from the [a]secret
counsel of evildoers,
From the tumult of [b]those
who do iniquity,

3 Who [a]have sharpened
their tongue like a
sword.
They [b]aimed bitter speech
as their arrow,

4 To [a]shoot from conceal-
ment at the blameless;
Suddenly they shoot at
him, and [b]do not fear.

5 They hold fast to themselves an evil purpose;
They talk of [a]laying snares
secretly;
They say, "[b]Who can see
them?"

6 They devise injustices,
saying,
"We are ready with a well-
conceived plot";
For the [a]inward thought
and the heart of a
man are deep.

7 But [a]God will shoot at
them with an arrow;
Suddenly they will be
wounded.

8 So they will [a]make him
stumble;
[b]Their own tongue is
against them;
All who see them will
[c]shake the head.

Margin references:

★ 2 [a]Ps. 27:4

3 [a]Ps. 69:16

4 [a]Ps. 104:33; 146:2 [b]Ps. 28:2; 143:6

5 [a]Ps. 36:8 [b]Ps. 71:23

6 [a]Ps. 4:4 [b]Ps. 16:7; 42:8; 119:55

7 [a]Ps. 27:9 [b]Ps. 17:8

8 [a]Num. 32:12; Deut. 1:36; Hos. 6:3 [b]Ps. 18:35; 41:12

9 [a]Ps. 40:14 [b]Ps. 55:15

★10 [a]Jer. 18:21; Ezek. 35:5 [b]Lam. 5:18

★11 [a]Ps. 21:1 [b]Deut. 6:13; Is. 45:23; 65:16 [c]Job 5:16; Ps. 107:42; Rom. 3:19

★ 1 [a]Ps. 55:2 [b]Ps. 140:1

2 [a]Ps. 56:6 [b]Ps. 59:2

★ 3 [a]Ps. 140:3 [b]Ps. 58:7

4 [a]Ps. 10:8; 11:2 [b]Ps. 55:19

5 [a]Ps. 140:5 [b]Job 22:13; Ps. 10:11

6 [a]Ps. 49:11

7 [a]Ps. 7:12, 13

★ 8 [a]Ps. 9:3 [b]Prov. 12:13; 18:7 [c]Ps. 22:7; 44:14; Jer. 18:16; 48:27; Lam. 2:15

63:2 *the sanctuary.* Not the Temple, as yet not
built, but the temporary place of the Ark.
63:10 *foxes.* Or, jackals; i.e., scavengers.
63:11 *the king.* I.e., David himself.
    Psalm 64 This psalm relates the plot of Da-
vid's enemies (vv. 1–6) and their punishment by

God (vv. 7–10).
64:1 *complaint.* I.e., troubled thoughts.
64:3 Sins of the tongue are again condemned
(see note on 59:11).
64:8 Their own tongues will eventually trip
them up.

9 aPs. 40:3
bJer. 51:10

9 Then all men will afear,
And will bdeclare the work
of God,
And will consider what He
has done.

10 aJob
22:19; Ps.
32:11 bPs.
11:1; 25:20

10 The righteous man will be
aglad in the LORD, and
will btake refuge in
Him;
And all the upright in
heart will glory.

PSALM 65

For the choir director. A
Psalm of David. A Song.

★ **1** aPs.
116:18

THERE will be silence before
Thee, *and* praise in
Zion, O God;
And to Thee the avow will
be performed.

2 aPs. 86:9;
145:21; Is.
66:23

2 O Thou who dost hear
prayer,
To Thee aall men come.

3 aPs. 38:4;
40:12 bPs.
79:9

3 aIniquities prevail against
me;
As for our transgressions,
Thou dost bforgive
them.

4 aPs.
33:12; 84:4
bPs. 4:3
cPs. 36:8

4 How ablessed is the one
whom Thou dost
bchoose, and bring
near *to Thee*,
To dwell in Thy courts.
We will be csatisfied with
the goodness of Thy
house,
Thy holy temple.

5 aPs. 45:4;
66:3 bPs.
85:4 cPs.
22:27; 48:10
dPs. 107:23

5 By aawesome *deeds* Thou
dost answer us in
righteousness, O
bGod of our salvation,
Thou who art the trust of
all the cends of the
earth and of the far-
thest dsea;

6 Who dost aestablish the
mountains by His
strength,
Being bgirded with might;

6 aPs. 95:4
bPs. 93:1

7 Who dost astill the roaring
of the seas,
The roaring of their waves,
And the btumult of the
peoples.

7 aPs. 89:9;
93:3, 4;
107:29; Matt.
8:26 bPs.
2:1; 74:23;
Is. 17:12, 13

8 And they who dwell in the
aends *of the earth*
stand in awe of Thy
signs;
Thou dost make the dawn
and the sunset shout
for joy.

8 aPs. 2:8;
139:9; Is.
24:16

9 Thou dost visit the earth,
and acause it to over-
flow;
Thou dost greatly benrich
it;
The cstream of God is full
of water;
Thou dost prepare their
dgrain, for thus Thou
dost prepare the
earth.

★ **9** aLev.
26:4; Job
5:10; Ps.
68:9; 104:13;
147:8; Jer.
5:24 bPs.
104:24 cPs.
46:4 dPs.
104:14;
147:14

10 Thou dost water its fur-
rows abundantly;
Thou dost settle its ridges;
Thou dost soften it awith
showers;
Thou dost bless its growth.

10 aDeut.
32:2; Ps.
72:6; 147:8

11 Thou hast crowned the
year with Thy aboun-
ty,
And Thy paths bdrip *with*
fatness.

11 aPs.
104:28 bJob
36:28; Ps.
147:14

12 aThe pastures of the wilderness drip,
And the bhills gird them-
selves with rejoicing.

12 aJob
38:26, 27;
Joel 2:22
bPs. 98:8; Is.
55:12

13 The meadows are aclothed
with flocks,
And the valleys are bcov-
ered with grain;
They cshout for joy, yes,
they sing.

13 aPs.
144:13; Is.
30:23 bPs.
72:16 cPs.
98:8; Is.
44:23; 55:12

Psalm 65 In this thanksgiving hymn, David praises God for His favor (vv. 1–4), for His greatness (vv. 5–8), and for His harvest (vv. 9–13). Thus God is magnified as Redeemer, Creator, and Provider.
65:1 *Zion.* Jerusalem. *vow.* See Lev. 22:21 and note on Lev. 7:12–17.
65:9 The first part of this verse is a summary statement, illustrated in the many examples given (through v. 13). God's presence provides the harvest of field and flock.

PSALM 66

For the choir director. A Song. A Psalm.

1 **S**HOUT joyfully to God, all the earth;

2 Sing the *a*glory of His name;
Make His *b*praise glorious.

3 Say to God, "How *a*awesome are Thy works!
Because of the greatness of Thy power Thine enemies will *b*give feigned obedience to Thee.

4 "*a*All the earth will worship Thee,
And will *b*sing praises to Thee;
They will sing praises to Thy name." [Selah.

5 *a*Come and see the works of God,
Who is *b*awesome in *His* deeds toward the sons of men.

6 He *a*turned the sea into dry land;
They passed through *b*the river on foot;
There let us *c*rejoice in Him!

7 He *a*rules by His might forever;
His *b*eyes keep watch on the nations;
Let not the rebellious *c*exalt themselves. [Selah.

8 Bless our God, O peoples,
And *a*sound His praise abroad,

9 Who *a*keeps us in life,
And *b*does not allow our feet to slip.

10 For Thou hast *a*tried us, O God;
Thou hast *b*refined us as silver is refined.

11 Thou *a*didst bring us into the net;
Thou didst lay an oppressive burden upon our loins.

12 Thou didst make men *a*ride over our heads;
We went through *b*fire and through water;
Yet Thou *c*didst bring us out into *a place of* abundance.

13 I shall *a*come into Thy house with burnt offerings;
I shall *b*pay Thee my vows,

14 Which my lips uttered
And my mouth spoke when I was *a*in distress.

15 I shall *a*offer to Thee burnt offerings of fat beasts,
With the smoke of *b*rams;
I shall make an *offering of* bulls with male goats.
[Selah.

16 *a*Come *and* hear, all who fear God,
And I will *b*tell of what He has done for my soul.

17 I cried to Him with my mouth,
And He was *a*extolled with my tongue.

18 If I *a*regard wickedness in my heart,
The *b*Lord will not hear;

19 But certainly *a*God has heard;

Marginal references:

a
1 *a*Ps. 81:1; 95:1; 98:4; 100:1
2 *a*Ps. 79:9; Is. 42:8 *b*Is. 42:12
3 *a*Ps. 47:2; 65:5; 145:6 *b*Ps. 18:44; 81:15
4 *a*Ps. 22:27; 67:7; 86:9; 117:1; Zech. 14:16 *b*Ps. 67:4
5 *a*Ps. 46:8 *b*Ps. 106:22
★ 6 *a*Ex. 14:21; Ps. 106:9 *b*Josh. 3:16; Ps. 114:3 *c*Ps. 105:43
7 *a*Ps. 145:13 *b*Ps. 11:4 *c*Ps. 140:8
8 *a*Ps. 98:4

9 *a*Ps. 30:3 *b*Ps. 121:3
10 *a*Job 23:10; Ps. 7:9; 17:3; 26:2 *b*Is. 48:10; Zech. 13:9; Mal. 3:3; 1 Pet. 1:7
11 *a*Lam. 1:13; Ezek. 12:13
★12 *a*Is. 51:23 *b*Ps. 78:21; Is. 43:2 *c*Ps. 18:19
★13 *a*Ps. 96:8; Jer. 17:26 *b*Ps. 22:25; 116:14; Eccl. 5:4
14 *a*Ps. 18:6
15 *a*Ps. 51:19 *b*Num. 6:14
16 *a*Ps. 34:11 *b*Ps. 71:15, 24
17 *a*Ps. 30:1
★18-19
18 *a*Job 36:21; John 9:31 *b*Job 27:9; Ps. 18:41; Prov. 1:28; 28:9; Is. 1:15; James 4:3
19 *a*Ps. 18:6; 116:1, 2

Psalm 66 In celebration of some national deliverance, the psalmist calls on all the earth to praise God (vv. 1-12) and, as the representative of the nation, he offers sacrifice and praise (vv. 13-15) and exhorts the people to prayer and praise (vv. 16-20).
66:6 A reference to the deliverance from Egypt (Exod. 14-15), an event viewed with the greatest awe in the Psalms (18:15-19; 68:7-8; 74:13-15; 77:16-20; 78:13, 52, 53; 89:7-10; 106:7-12; 136:10-15).
66:12 *ride over our heads.* Depicts the triumph of their enemies.
66:13 *burnt offerings.* See note on Lev. 1:3.
66:18-19 Sin disqualifies the suppliant; a blameless heart gives assurance that God hears our prayers (1 John 3:21).

He has given heed to the voice of my prayer.

20 ^aPs.
68:35 ^bPs.
22:24

20 ^aBlessed be God,
Who ^bhas not turned away my prayer,
Nor His lovingkindness from me.

PSALM 67

For the choir director; with stringed instruments. A Psalm. A Song.

1 ^aNum.
6:25 ^bPs.
4:6; 31:16;
80:3, 7, 19;
119:135

GOD be gracious to us and ^abless us,
And ^bcause His face to shine upon us—
[Selah.

2 ^aPs. 98:2;
Acts 18:25;
Titus 2:11
^bIs. 52:10

2 That ^aThy way may be known on the earth,
^bThy salvation among all nations.

3 ^aPs. 66:4

3 Let the ^apeoples praise Thee, O God;
Let all the peoples praise Thee.

4 ^aPs.
100:1, 2
^bPs. 9:8;
96:10, 13;
98:9 ^cPs.
47:8

4 Let the ^anations be glad and sing for joy;
For Thou wilt ^bjudge the peoples with uprightness,
And ^cguide the nations on the earth. [Selah.

5 ^aPs. 67:3

5 Let the ^apeoples praise Thee, O God;
Let all the peoples praise Thee.

★ 6 ^aLev.
26:4; Ps.
85:12; Ezek.
34:27; Zech.
8:12 ^bPs.
29:11;
115:12

6 The ^aearth has yielded its produce;
God, our God, ^bblesses us.

7 ^aPs.
22:27; 33:8

7 God blesses us,
That ^aall the ends of the earth may fear Him.

PSALM 68

For the choir director. A Psalm of David. A Song.

1 ^aNum.
10:35; Ps.
12:5; 132:8

LET ^aGod arise, let His enemies be scattered;
And let those who hate Him flee before Him.

2 ^aPs.
37:20; Is.
9:18; Hos.
13:3 ^bPs.
22:14; 97:5;
Mic. 1:4 ^cPs.
9:3; 37:20;
80:16

2 As ^asmoke is driven away, so drive them away;
As ^bwax melts before the fire,
So let the ^cwicked perish before God.

3 ^aPs.
32:11; 64:10;
97:12

3 But let the ^arighteous be glad; let them exult before God;
Yes, let them rejoice with gladness.

★ 4 ^aPs.
66:2 ^bIs.
57:14; 62:10
^cDeut.
33:26; Ps.
18:10; 68:33;
Is. 40:3 ^dEx.
6:3; Ps.
83:18

4 Sing to God, ^asing praises to His name;
^bCast up a highway for Him who ^crides through the deserts,
Whose ^dname is the LORD, and exult before Him.

5 ^aPs.
10:14; 146:9
^bDeut. 10:18
^cDeut. 26:15

5 A ^afather of the fatherless and a ^bjudge for the widows,
Is God in His ^choly habitation.

★ 6 ^aPs.
107:4-7;
113:9 ^bPs.
69:33;
102:20;
107:10, 14;
146:7; Acts
12:7; 16:26
^cPs. 78:17;
107:34, 40

6 God ^amakes a home for the lonely;
He ^bleads out the prisoners into prosperity,
Only ^cthe rebellious dwell in a parched land.

7 ^aEx.
13:21; Ps.
78:14; Hab.
3:13 ^bJudg.
5:4; Ps.
78:52

7 O God, when Thou ^adidst go forth before Thy people,

Psalm 67 This psalm of thanksgiving invokes God's continued blessing on Israel so that the nations may experience His salvation, justice, and bounty, and so praise Him.
67:6 *The earth has yielded.* An abundant harvest gave assurance of future blessing.
Psalm 68 This victorious hymn, probably composed for David's procession with the Ark from the house of Obed-edom to Jerusalem (2 Sam. 6:12), calls for the wicked to flee before God (vv. 1-6), celebrates God's victorious march from Egypt to Jerusalem (vv. 7-18) and His

power exercised in the choice of Jerusalem (vv. 19-31), and calls on the nations to praise Him (vv. 32-35).
68:4 *the LORD.* (JAH, an abbreviation for Yahweh; see notes on Gen. 2:4; Exod. 3:15). Other Hebrew names for God used in this psalm are: Elohim (v. 1), El Shaddai (v. 14), Yahweh (v. 16), Yah Elohim (v. 18), Adonai (v. 19), and Yahweh Adonai (v. 20).
68:6 *into prosperity.* Or, into singing. *the rebellious.* Who died in the wilderness, rather than entering Canaan.

When Thou didst [b]march
through the wilder-
ness,   [Selah.

8   The [a]earth quaked;
The [b]heavens also dropped
rain at the presence of
God;
[c]Sinai itself *quaked* at the
presence of God, the
God of Israel.

9   Thou didst [a]shed abroad a
plentiful rain, O God;
Thou didst confirm Thine
inheritance, when it
was parched.

10   Thy creatures settled in it;
Thou didst [a]provide in
Thy goodness for the
poor, O God.

11   The Lord gives the command;
The [a]women who proclaim
the *good* tidings are a
great host:

12   "[a]Kings of armies flee, they
flee,
And she who remains at
home will [b]divide the
spoil!"

13   When you lie down
[a]among the sheep-
folds,
You are like the wings of a
dove covered with sil-
ver,
And its pinions with glis-
tening gold.

14   When the Almighty [a]scat-
tered the kings there,
It was snowing in [b]Zal-
mon.

15   A [a]mountain of God is the
mountain of Bashan;
A mountain *of many*
peaks is the mountain
of Bashan.

16   Why do you look with
envy, O mountains
with *many* peaks,

At the mountain which
God has [a]desired for
His abode?
Surely, [b]the LORD will
dwell *there* forever.

17   The [a]chariots of God are
myriads, [b]thousands
upon thousands;
The Lord is among them *as
at* Sinai, in holiness.

18   Thou hast [a]ascended on
high, Thou hast [b]led
captive *Thy* captives;
Thou hast received gifts
among men,
Even *among* the rebellious
also, that the LORD
God may dwell *there.*

19   Blessed be the Lord, who
daily [a]bears our bur-
den,
[b]The God *who* is our
salvation.   [Selah.

20   God is to us a [a]God of de-
liverances;
And [b]to GOD the Lord belong escapes from
death.

21   Surely God will [a]shatter
the head of His en-
emies,
The hairy crown of him
who goes on in his
guilty deeds.

22   The Lord said, "[a]I will
bring *them* back from
Bashan.
I will bring *them* back
from the depths of the
sea;

23   That [a]your foot may shatter *them* in blood,
The tongue of your [b]dogs
may have its portion
from *your* enemies."

24   They have seen [a]Thy procession, O God;

Cross references (left margin):

8 [a]Ex. 19:18; Judg. 5:4; 2 Sam. 22:8; Ps. 77:18; Jer. 10:10 [b]Judg. 5:4; Ps. 18:9; Is. 45:8 [c]Ex. 19:18; Judg. 5:5

★ **9** [a]Lev. 26:4; Deut. 11:11; Job 5:10; Ezek. 34:26

10 [a]Ps. 65:9; 74:19; 78:20; 107:9

★**11** [a]Ex. 15:20; 1 Sam. 18:6

12 [a]Josh. 10:16; Judg. 5:19; Ps. 135:11 [b]Judg. 5:30; 1 Sam. 30:24

13 [a]Gen. 49:14; Judg. 5:16

★**14** [a]Josh. 10:10 [b]Judg. 9:48

★**15** [a]Ps. 36:6

16 [a]Deut. 12:5; Ps. 87:1, 2; 132:13 [b]Ps. 132:14

Cross references (right margin):

17 [a]2 Kin. 6:17; Hab. 3:8 [b]Deut. 33:2; Dan. 7:10

★**18** [a]Ps. 7:7; 47:5; Eph. 4:8 [b]Judg. 5:12

19 [a]Ps. 55:22; Is. 46:4 [b]Ps. 65:5

20 [a]Ps. 106:43 [b]Deut. 32:39; Ps. 49:15; 56:13

21 [a]Ps. 110:6; Hab. 3:13

22 [a]Num. 21:33; Amos 9:1-3

23 [a]Ps. 58:10 [b]1 Kin. 21:19; Jer. 15:3

24 [a]Ps. 77:13 [b]Ps. 63:2

68:9 *a plentiful rain* of manna and quails (Psalm 78:24, 27; see notes on Exod. 16:13 and 15).
68:11 Israel's victories were commonly cele-brated by women singing and dancing (Exod. 15:20; 1 Sam. 18:6-7).
68:14 When God dispersed the kings of Canaan, it was like snowflakes driven by the wind (or

melting) against the dark wooded slopes of Zalmon (a hill near Shechem).
68:15 *the mountain of Bashan.* Probably a refer-ence to 9,100 foot Mt. Hermon.
68:18 This Messianic verse looks forward to the ascension of Christ (see note on Eph. 4:8).

The procession of my God,
my King, [b]into the
sanctuary.

25 [a]1 Chr.
13:8; 15:6;
Ps. 47:6
[b]Ex. 15:20;
Judg. 11:34

25 The [a]singers went on, the
musicians after *them*,
In the midst of the [b]maid-
ens beating tambou-
rines.

26 [a]Ps.
22:22, 23;
26:12 [b]Deut.
33:28; Is.
48:1

26 [a]Bless God in the congregations,
Even the LORD, *you who
are* of the [b]fountain of
Israel.

★27 [a]Judg.
5:14; 1 Sam.
9:21 [b]Judg.
5:18

27 There is [a]Benjamin, the
youngest,   ruling
them,
The princes of Judah *in*
their throng,
The princes of [b]Zebulun,
the princes of Naph-
tali.

28 [a]Ps.
29:11; 44:4
[b]Is. 26:12

28 Your God has [a]command-
ed your strength;
Show Thyself strong, O
God, [b]who hast acted
on our behalf.

29 [a]1 Kin.
10:10, 25;
2 Chr. 32:23;
Ps. 45:12;
72:10; Is.
18:7

29 Because of Thy temple at
Jerusalem
[a]Kings will bring gifts to
Thee.

★30 [a]Job
40:21; Ezek.
29:3 [b]Ps.
22:12 [c]Ps.
18:14; 89:10

30 Rebuke the [a]beasts in the
reeds,
The herd of [b]bulls with the
calves of the peoples,
Trampling under foot the
pieces of silver;
He has [c]scattered the peoples who delight in
war.

31 [a]Is.
19:19, 21
[b]Is. 45:14;
Zeph. 3:10

31 Envoys will come out of
[a]Egypt;
[b]Ethiopia will quickly
stretch out her hands
to God.

32 Sing to God, O [a]kingdoms
of the earth;
[b]Sing praises to the Lord,
[Selah.

32 [a]Ps.
102:22 [b]Ps.
67:4

33 To Him who [a]rides upon
the [b]highest heavens,
which are from an-
cient times;
Behold, [c]He speaks forth
with His voice, a
[d]mighty voice.

33 [a]Deut.
33:26; Ps.
18:10; 104:3
[b]Deut.
10:14; 1 Kin.
8:27 [c]Ps.
46:6 [d]Ps.
29:4

34 [a]Ascribe strength to God;
His majesty is over Israel,
And [b]His strength is in the
skies.

34 [a]Ps. 29:1
[b]Ps. 150:1

35 O God, *Thou art* [a]awe-
some from Thy sanc-
tuary.
The God of Israel Himself
[b]gives strength and
power to the people.
[c]Blessed be God!

35 [a]Deut.
7:21; 10:17;
Ps. 47:2;
66:5 [b]Ps.
29:11; Is.
40:29 [c]Ps.
66:20; 2 Cor.
1:3

PSALM 69

For the choir director; according
to Shoshannim. *A Psalm* of
David.

SAVE me, O God,
For the [a]waters have
threatened my life.

1 [a]Job
22:11; Ps.
32:6; 42:7;
69:14, 15;
Jon. 2:5

2 I have sunk in deep [a]mire,
and there is no foot-
hold;
I have come into deep wa-
ters, and a [b]flood
overflows me.

2 [a]Ps. 40:2
[b]Jon. 2:3

3 I am [a]weary with my crying; my throat is
parched;
My [b]eyes fail while I wait
for my God.

3 [a]Ps. 6:6
[b]Deut.
28:32; Ps.
38:10;
119:82, 123;
Is. 38:14

4 Those [a]who hate me without a cause are more
than the hairs of my
head;

★ 4 [a]Ps.
35:19; John
15:25 [b]Ps.
35:19; 38:19;
59:3 [c]Ps.
35:11; Jer.
15:10

68:27 All the tribes are included, the examples
mentioned being the southernmost and the
northernmost.
68:30 *the beasts in the reeds*. Symbolic of the
Egyptians.
Psalm 69 This lament may be outlined as
follows: David's despair in persecution (vv.
1-12), his desire for punishment (of his enemies)
(vv. 13-28), and his declaration of praise (vv.
29-36). *Shoshannim*. See note on Psalm 45.

Psalm 69 is one of the most quoted psalms in the
N.T.
69:4 Though David encountered unjustified persecution, the sinless Lord Jesus experienced it
in the most supreme way (John 15:25). For
other Messianic implications, cf. verse 8 with
John 7:3-5; verse 9 with John 2:17 and Rom.
15:3; verse 21 with Matt. 27:34; verse 25 with
Matt. 23:38.

Those who would destroy me [b]are powerful,
[c]What I did not steal, I then have to restore.

**5 aPs. 38:5
bPs. 44:21**

5 O God, it is Thou who dost know [a]my folly,
And [b]my wrongs are not hidden from Thee.

6 a2 Sam. 12:14

6 May those who wait for Thee not [a]be ashamed through me, O Lord GOD of hosts;
May those who seek Thee not be dishonored through me, O God of Israel,

7 aJer. 15:15 bPs. 44:15; Is. 50:6; Jer. 51:51

7 Because [a]for Thy sake I have borne reproach;
[b]Dishonor has covered my face.

8 aJob 19:13-15; Ps. 31:11; 38:11

8 I have become [a]estranged from my brothers,
And an alien to my mother's sons.

9 aPs. 119:139; John 2:17 bPs. 89:41, 50; Rom. 15:3

9 For [a]zeal for Thy house has consumed me,
And [b]the reproaches of those who reproach Thee have fallen on me.

10 aPs. 35:13

10 When I wept [a]in my soul with fasting,
It became my reproach.

11 a1 Kin. 20:31; Ps. 35:13 b1 Kin. 9:7; Job 17:6; Ps. 44:14; Jer. 24:9

11 When I made [a]sackcloth my clothing,
I became [b]a byword to them.

12 aGen. 19:1; Ruth 4:1 bJob 30:9

12 Those who [a]sit in the gate talk about me,
And I am the [b]song of the drunkards.

13 aPs. 32:6; Is. 49:8; 2 Cor. 6:2 bPs. 51:1

13 But as for me, my prayer is to Thee, O LORD, [a]at an acceptable time;
O God, in the [b]greatness of Thy lovingkindness,
Answer me with Thy saving truth.

★14-15

14 aPs. 69:2 bPs. 144:7 cPs. 69:2

14 Deliver me from the [a]mire, and do not let me sink;

May I be [b]delivered from my foes, and from the [c]deep waters.

15 aPs. 124:4, 5 bNum.

15 May the [a]flood of water not overflow me,
And may the deep not swallow me up,
And may the [b]pit not shut its mouth on me.

16 aPs. 63:3; 109:21 bPs. 51:1; 106:45 cPs. 25:16; 86:16

16 Answer me, O LORD, for [a]Thy lovingkindness is good;
[b]According to the greatness of Thy compassion, [c]turn to me,

17 aPs. 27:9; 102:2; 143:7 bPs. 31:9; 66:14

17 And [a]do not hide Thy face from Thy servant,
For I am [b]in distress; answer me quickly.

18 a2 Sam. 4:9; Ps. 26:11; 49:15 bPs. 119:134

18 Oh draw near to my soul and [a]redeem it;
[b]Ransom me because of my enemies!

19 aPs. 22:6; 31:11

19 Thou dost know my [a]reproach and my shame and my dishonor;
All my adversaries are before Thee.

20 aJer. 23:9 bPs. 142:4; Is. 63:5 cJob 16:2

20 Reproach has [a]broken my heart, and I am so sick.
And [b]I looked for sympathy, but there was none,
And for [c]comforters, but I found none.

21 aDeut. 29:18 bMatt. 27:34, 48; Mark 15:23, 36; Luke 23:36; John 19:28-30

21 They also gave me [a]gall for my food,
And for my thirst they [b]gave me vinegar to drink.

22 aRom. 11:9, 10 b1 Thess. 5:3

22 May [a]their table before them become a snare;
And [b]when they are in peace, may it become a trap.

23 aIs. 6:10 bDan. 5:6

23 May their [a]eyes grow dim so that they cannot see,
And make their [b]loins shake continually.

69:14-15 David faced imminent death like a drowning man.

24 ªPs. 79:6;
Jer. 10:25;
Ezek. 20:8;
Hos. 5:10

24 ªPour out Thine indignation on them,
And may Thy burning an-
ger overtake them.

★25 ªMatt.
23:38; Luke
13:35; Acts
1:20

25 May their ªcamp be desolate;
May none dwell in their
tents.

26 ª2 Chr.
28:9; Zech.
1:15 ᵇIs.
53:4 ᶜPs.
109:22

26 For they have ªpersecuted
him whom ᵇThou
Thyself hast smitten,
And they tell of the pain of
those whom ᶜThou
hast wounded.

27 ªNeh.
4:5; Ps.
109:14; Rom.
1:28 ᵇIs.
26:10 ᶜPs.
103:17

27 Do Thou add ªiniquity to
their iniquity,
And ᵇmay they not come
into ᶜThy righteous-
ness.

28 ªEx.
32:32, 33;
Rev. 3:5
ᵇPhil. 4:3;
Rev. 13:8;
17:8; 20:15
ᶜPs. 87:6;
Ezek. 13:9;
Luke 10:20;
Heb. 12:23

28 May they be ªblotted out
of the ᵇbook of life,
And may they not be ᶜre-
corded with the right-
eous.

29 ªPs. 70:5
ᵇPs. 20:1;
59:1

29 But I am ªafflicted and in
pain;
May Thy salvation, O
God, ᵇset me *securely*
on high.

30 ªPs. 28:7
ᵇPs. 34:3
ᶜPs. 50:14

30 I will ªpraise the name of
God with song,
And shall ᵇmagnify Him
with ᶜthanksgiving.

31 ªPs.
50:13, 14;
51:16

31 And it will ªplease the
LORD better than an ox
Or a young bull with
horns and hoofs.

32 ªPs. 34:2
ᵇPs. 22:26

32 The ªhumble have seen *it*
and are glad;
You who seek God, ᵇlet
your heart revive.

33 ªPs. 12:5
ᵇPs. 68:6

33 For ªthe LORD hears the
needy,
And ᵇdoes not despise His
who are prisoners.

★34-35
34 ªPs.
96:11; 98:7;
148:1-13; Is.
44:23; 49:13
ᵇIs. 55:12

34 Let ªheaven and earth
praise Him,
The seas and ᵇeverything
that moves in them.

35 For God will ªsave Zion
and ᵇbuild the cities
of Judah,
That they may dwell there
and ᶜpossess it.

35 ªPs. 46:5;
51:18 ᵇPs.
147:2; Is.
44:26
ᶜObad. 17

36 And the ªdescendants of
His servants will in-
herit it,
And those who love His
name ᵇwill dwell in it.

36 ªPs.
25:13;
102:28 ᵇPs.
37:29

PSALM 70

For the choir director.
A Psalm of David;
for a memorial.

ᵃO GOD, *hasten* to deliver me;
O LORD, hasten to my help!
2 ªLet those be ashamed and
humiliated
Who seek my life;
Let those be turned back
and dishonored
Who delight in my hurt.
3 ªLet those be turned back
because of their
shame
Who say, "Aha, aha!"

1 ªPs.
40:13-17;
70:1-5

2 ªPs. 35:4,
26

3 ªPs.
40:15

4 Let all who seek Thee re-
joice and be glad in
Thee;
And let those who love
Thy salvation say con-
tinually,
"Let God be magnified."

5 But ªI am afflicted and
needy;
ᵇHasten to me, O God!
Thou art my help and my
deliverer;
O LORD, do not delay.

5 ªPs.
40:17 ᵇPs.
141:1

PSALM 71

ᵃIN Thee, O LORD, I have taken
refuge;
Let me never be ashamed.

1 ªPs. 25:2,
3; 31:1-3;
71:1-3

69:25 Peter applied this verse to Judas (Acts
1:20).
69:34-35 These verses anticipate millennial conditions of a rebuilt and repopulated Judah,
when all the earth will praise God.
Psalm 70 An urgent prayer for help, this
psalm is basically identical to Psalm 40:13-17. *for
a memorial.* Or, to bring to remembrance. Per-

haps a reference to laying this petition before
God for His attention and action.
Psalm 71 The unnamed, aged writer of this
psalm cries for help (vv. 1-3), prays for deliverance because of a confidence based on God's
lifelong care for him (vv. 4-13), and resolves to
continue praising God (vv. 14-24).

2 aPs. 31:1
bPs. 17:6

2 ^aIn Thy righteousness deliver me, and rescue me;
^bIncline Thine ear to me, and save me.

3 aPs. 31:2,
3 bDeut.
33:27; Ps.
90:1; 91:9
cPs. 7:6;
42:8 dPs.
18:2

3 ^aBe Thou to me a rock of ^bhabitation, to which I may continually come;
Thou hast given ^ccommandment to save me,
For Thou art ^dmy rock and my fortress.

4 aPs.
140:1, 4

4 ^aRescue me, O my God, out of the hand of the wicked,
Out of the grasp of the wrongdoer and ruthless man,

5 aPs. 39:7;
Jer. 14:8;
17:7, 13, 17;
50:7 bPs.
22:9

5 For Thou art my ^ahope;
O Lord God, *Thou art* my ^bconfidence from my youth.

6 aPs.
22:10; Is.
46:3 bJob
10:18; Ps.
22:9 cPs.
34:1

6 By Thee I have been ^asustained from *my* birth;
Thou art He who ^btook me from my mother's womb;
My ^cpraise is continually of Thee.

★ 7 aIs.
8:18; 1 Cor.
4:9 bPs.
61:3

7 I have become a ^amarvel to many;
For Thou art ^bmy strong refuge.

8 aPs.
35:28; 63:5
bPs. 96:6;
104:1

8 My ^amouth is filled with Thy praise,
And with ^bThy glory all day long.

9 aPs.
71:18; 92:14;
Is. 46:4

9 Do not cast me off in the ^atime of old age;
Do not forsake me when my strength fails.

10 aPs. 56:6
bPs. 31:13;
83:3; Matt.
27:1

10 For my enemies have spoken against me;
And those who ^awatch for my life ^bhave consulted together,

11 aPs. 3:2
bPs. 7:2

11 Saying, "^aGod has forsaken him;
Pursue and seize him, for

there is ^bno one to deliver."

12 aPs. 10:1;
22:11; 35:22;
38:21 bPs.
38:22; 40:13;
70:1; 5

12 O God, ^ado not be far from me;
O my God, ^bhasten to my help!

13 aPs. 35:4,
26; 40:14
bPs. 109:29
cEsth. 9:2;
Ps. 71:24

13 Let those who are adversaries of my soul be ^aashamed *and* consumed;
Let them be ^bcovered with reproach and dishonor, who ^cseek to injure me.

14 aPs.
130:7 bPs.
71:8

14 But as for me, I will ^ahope continually,
And will ^bpraise Thee yet more and more.

★15 aPs.
35:28 bPs.
96:2 cPs.
40:5

15 My ^amouth shall tell of Thy righteousness,
And of ^bThy salvation all day long;
For I ^cdo not know the sum *of them.*

16 aPs.
106:2 bPs.
51:14

16 I will come ^awith the mighty deeds of the Lord God;
I will ^bmake mention of Thy righteousness, Thine alone.

★17-18
17 aDeut.
4:5; 6:7 bPs.
26:7; 40:5;
119:27

17 O God, Thou ^ahast taught me from my youth;
And I still ^bdeclare Thy wondrous deeds.

18 aPs. 71:9
bPs. 22:31;
78:4, 6

18 And even when *I am* ^aold and gray, O God, do not forsake me,
Until I ^bdeclare Thy strength to *this* generation,
Thy power to all who are to come.

19 aPs. 36:6;
57:10 bPs.
126:2; Luke
1:49 cDeut.
3:24; Ps.
35:10
★20 aPs.
60:3 bPs.
80:18; 85:6;
119:25;
138:7; Hos.
6:1, 2 cPs.
86:13

19 For Thy ^arighteousness, O God, *reaches* to the heavens,
Thou who hast ^bdone great things;
O God, ^cwho is like Thee?

20 Thou, who hast ^ashown me many troubles and distresses,

71:7 Though men point to him as someone to be avoided or mocked (apparently the meaning of *marvel*), God is still his refuge.
71:15 *sum of them.* God's inexhaustible mercies cannot be counted.

71:17-18 An important ministry of older believers is to declare God's wondrous deeds as a testimony to the younger generation.
71:20 *revive.* Not a reference to resurrection but to deliverance from his present distress.

Wilt [b]revive me again,
And wilt bring me up
again [c]from the
depths of the earth.

21 Mayest Thou increase my
[a]greatness,
And turn to [b]comfort me.

22 I will also praise Thee with
[a]a harp,
Even Thy truth, O my
God;
To Thee I will sing praises
with the [b]lyre,
O Thou [c]Holy One of Is-
rael.

23 My lips will [a]shout for joy
when I sing praises to
Thee;
And my [b]soul, which Thou
hast redeemed.

24 My [a]tongue also will utter
Thy righteousness all
day long;
For they are [b]ashamed, for
they are humiliated
who seek my hurt.

PSALM 72

A Psalm of Solomon.

GIVE the king [a]Thy judgments, O God,
And [b]Thy righteousness to
the king's son.

2 May he [a]judge Thy people
with righteousness,
And [b]Thine afflicted with
justice.

3 Let the mountains bring
[a]peace to the people,
And the hills in righteousness.

4 May he [a]vindicate the afflicted of the people,

Save the children of the
needy,
And crush the oppressor.

5 Let them fear Thee [a]while
the sun endures,
And as long as the moon,
throughout all genera-
tions.

6 May he come down [a]like
rain upon the mown
grass,
Like [b]showers that water
the earth.

7 In his days may the [a]right-
eous flourish,
And [b]abundance of peace
till the moon is no
more.

8 May he also rule [a]from sea
to sea,
And from the River to the
ends of the earth.

9 Let [a]the nomads of the
desert [b]bow before
him;
And his enemies [c]lick the
dust.

10 Let the kings of [a]Tarshish
and of the [b]islands
bring presents;
The kings of [c]Sheba and
[d]Seba [e]offer gifts.

11 And let all [a]kings bow
down before him,
All [b]nations serve him.

12 For he will [a]deliver the
needy when he cries
for help,
The afflicted also, and him
who has no helper.

13 He will have [a]compassion
on the poor and
needy,

Margin references

21 [a]Ps. 18:35 [b]Ps. 23:4; 86:17; Is. 12:1; 49:13

22 [a]Ps. 33:2; 81:2; 92:1-3; 144:9 [b]Ps. 33:2; 147:7 [c]2 Kin. 19:22; Ps. 78:41; 89:18; Is. 1:4

23 [a]Ps. 5:11; 32:11; 132:9, 16 [b]Ps. 34:22; 55:18; 103:4

24 [a]Ps. 35:28 [b]Ps. 71:13

1 [a]1 Kin. 3:9; 1 Chr. 22:13 [b]Ps. 24:5

★ 2-11

2 [a]Is. 9:7; 11:2-5; 32:1 [b]Ps. 82:3

3 [a]Is. 2:4; 9:5, 6; Mic. 4:3, 4; Zech. 9:10

4 [a]Is. 11:4

5 [a]Ps. 72:17; 89:36, 37

6 [a]Deut. 32:2; 2 Sam. 23:4; Hos. 6:3 [b]Ps. 65:10

7 [a]Ps. 92:12 [b]Is. 2:4

★ 8 [a]Ex. 23:31; Zech. 9:10

★ 9 [a]Ps. 74:14; Is. 23:13 [b]Ps. 22:29 [c]Is. 49:23; Mic. 7:17

10 [a]2 Chr. 9:21; Ps. 48:7 [b]Ps. 97:1; Is. 42:4, 10; Zeph. 2:11 [c]1 Kin. 10:1; Job 6:19; Is. 60:6 [d]Gen. 10:7; Is. 43:3 [e]Ps. 45:12; 68:29

11 [a]Ps. 138:4; Is. 49:23 [b]Ps. 86:9

12 [a]Job 29:12; Ps. 72:4

13 [a]Prov. 19:17; 28:8

Psalm 72 In this royal psalm, Solomon prays that the king's reign will be characterized by righteousness (vv. 1-4), peace (vv. 5-7), power (vv. 8-11), compassion (vv. 12-15), and prosperity (vv. 16-17). The concluding notes of praise (vv. 18-20) close Book II of the Psalms (see Introduction, "Contents"). Like other royal psalms (cf. Psalm 2), this one is also Messianic, referring to an O. T. king (either Solomon or his son), but having its ultimate fulfillment in the ideal King,

Jesus Christ, David's greatest Son (Luke 1:31-33). *of Solomon.* Cf. Psalm 127, the only other attributed to Solomon.

72:2-11 May be translated (also vv. 15-17) as prayers: "May he judge . . ." "Let the mountains . . ."

72:8 This will not be fulfilled until the millennial reign of Christ (see also vv. 11 and 17).

72:9 *lick the dust.* A symbol of utter defeat.

And the lives of the needy
he will save.

14 He will [a]rescue their life
from oppression and
violence;
And their blood will be
[b]precious in his sight;

15 So may he live; and may
the [a]gold of Sheba be
given to him;
And let them pray for him
continually;
Let them bless him all day
long.

16 May there be abundance
of grain in the earth
on top of the moun-
tains;
Its fruit will wave like the
cedars of [a]Lebanon;
And may those from the
city flourish like [b]veg-
etation of the earth.

17 May his [a]name endure forever;
May his name increase [b]as
long as the sun shines;
And let men [c]bless themselves by him;
[d]Let all nations call him
blessed.

18 [a]Blessed be the LORD God,
the God of Israel,
Who alone [b]works won-
ders.

19 And blessed be His [a]glori-
ous name forever;
And may the whole [b]earth
be filled with His
glory.
[c]Amen, and Amen.

20 The prayers of David the
son of Jesse are ended.

BOOK 3

PSALM 73

A Psalm of Asaph.

SURELY God is [a]good to Israel,
To those who are [b]pure in
heart!

2 But as for me, [a]my feet
came close to stum-
bling;
My steps had almost
slipped.

3 For I was [a]envious of the
arrogant,
As I saw the [b]prosperity of
the wicked.

4 For there are no pains in
their death;
And their body is fat.

5 They are [a]not in trouble as
other men;
Nor are they [b]plagued like
mankind.

6 Therefore pride is [a]their
necklace;
The [b]garment of violence
covers them.

7 Their eye bulges from [a]fat-
ness;
The imaginations of their
heart run riot.

8 They [a]mock, and wickedly
speak of oppression;
They [b]speak from on high.

9 They have [a]set their
mouth against the
heavens,
And their tongue parades
through the earth.

10 Therefore his people return to this place;
And waters of [a]abundance
are drunk by them.

Reference column (left)

14 [a]Ps. 69:18
[b]1 Sam. 26:21; Ps. 116:15

15 [a]Is. 60:6

16 [a]Ps. 104:16 [b]Job 5:25

17 [a]Ex. 3:15; Ps. 135:13 [b]Ps. 89:36 [c]Gen. 12:3; 22:18 [d]Luke 1:48

18 [a]1 Chr. 29:10; Ps. 41:13; 89:52; 106:48 [b]Ex. 15:11; Job 5:9; Ps. 77:14; 86:10; 136:4

19 [a]Neh. 9:5; Ps. 96:8 [b]Num. 14:21 [c]Ps. 41:13

★20

Reference column (right)

★ 1 [a]Ps. 86:5 [b]Ps. 24:4; 51:10; Matt. 5:8

2 [a]Ps. 94:18

3 [a]Ps. 37:1; Prov. 23:17 [b]Job 21:7; Ps. 37:7; Jer. 12:1

5 [a]Job 21:9; Ps. 73:12 [b]Ps. 73:14

6 [a]Gen. 41:42; Prov. 1:9 [b]Ps. 109:18

7 [a]Job 15:27; Ps. 17:10; Jer. 5:28

8 [a]Ps. 1:1 [b]Ps. 17:10; 2 Pet. 2:18; Jude 16

★ 9 [a]Rev. 13:6

★10 [a]Ps. 23:5

72:20 *The prayers of David.* David was the chief,
though not sole, author of the psalms in Book
II.
   Psalm 73 Asaph (see note on Psalm 50) finds
the answer to the perplexing prosperity of the
wicked (vv. 1-14) in the contrast between their
destiny and that of the righteous (vv. 15-28).

73:1 This is the conclusion that came out of the
trial of his nearly lost faith (v. 2).
   73:9 The wicked mock God and lord it over other men.
   73:10 Even God's people are tempted to corrupt
practices.

11 aJob 22:13

11 And they say, "aHow does God know?
And is there knowledge with the Most High?"

12 aPs. 49:6; 52:7 bJer. 49:31; Ezek. 23:42

12 Behold, athese are the wicked;
And always bat ease, they have increased in wealth.

★13-14
13 aJob 21:15; 34:9; 35:3 bPs. 26:6

13 Surely ain vain I have kept my heart pure,
And bwashed my hands in innocence;

14 aPs. 38:6 bJob 33:19; Ps. 118:18

14 For I have been stricken aall day long,
And bchastened every morning.

★15-17
15 aPs. 14:5

15 If I had said, "I will speak thus,"
Behold, I should have betrayed the ageneration of Thy children.

16 aEccl. 8:17

16 When I apondered to understand this,
It was troublesome in my sight

17 aPs. 27:4; 77:13 bPs. 37:38

17 Until I came into the asanctuary of God;
Then I perceived their bend.

18 aPs. 35:6 bPs. 35:8; 36:12

18 Surely Thou dost set them in aslippery places;
Thou dost cast them down to bdestruction.

19 aNum. 16:21; Is. 47:11 bJob 18:11

19 How they are adestroyed in a moment!
They are utterly swept away by bsudden terrors!

20 aJob 20:8 bPs. 78:65 c1 Sam. 2:30

20 Like a adream when one awakes,
O Lord, when baroused, Thou wilt cdespise their form.

21 aJudg. 10:16 bActs 2:37

21 When my aheart was embittered,
And I was bpierced within,

22 aPs. 49:10; 92:6 bJob 18:3; Ps. 49:20; Eccl. 3:18

22 Then I was asenseless and ignorant;
I was like a bbeast before Thee.

23 aPs. 16:8

23 Nevertheless aI am continually with Thee;
Thou hast taken hold of my right hand.

24 aPs. 32:8; 48:14; Is. 58:11 bGen. 5:24; Ps. 49:15

24 With Thy counsel Thou wilt aguide me,
And afterward breceive me to glory.

25 aPs. 16:2; Phil. 3:8

25 aWhom have I in heaven but Thee?
And besides Thee, I desire nothing on earth.

26 aPs. 38:10; 40:12; 84:2; 119:81 bPs. 16:5

26 My aflesh and my heart may fail,
But God is the strength of my heart and my bportion forever.

27 aPs. 119:155 bPs. 37:20 cEx. 34:15; Num. 15:39; Ps. 106:39; Hos. 4:12; 9:1

27 For, behold, athose who are far from Thee will bperish;
Thou hast destroyed all those who care unfaithful to Thee.

28 aPs. 65:4; Heb. 10:22; James 4:8 bPs. 14:6; 71:7 cPs. 40:5; 107:22; 118:17

28 But as for me, athe nearness of God is my good;
I have made the Lord GOD my brefuge,
That I may ctell of all Thy works.

PSALM 74

A Maskil of Asaph.

1 aPs. 44:9; 77:7 bDeut. 29:20; Ps. 18:8; 89:46 cPs. 79:13; 95:7; 100:3

O GOD, why hast Thou arejected us forever?
Why does Thine anger bsmoke against the csheep of Thy pasture?

73:13–14 The problem of the life-long prosperity of the wicked is aggravated by the apparent lack of reward for those who live righteously.

73:15–17 The conditions described in verses 3–14 are misleading apart from God's viewpoint and His final word, which assures the destruction of the wicked (vv. 18–20, 27).

Psalm 74 Against the background of the Babylonian captivity and the destruction of the Temple in 586, this psalm relates the nation's cry for help (vv. 1–2), the conditions of the havoc (vv. 3–11), and the confidence of their hope (vv. 12–23). Maskil. See note on Psalm 32. Asaph, a contemporary of David, lived long before this psalm was written; thus the reference here is either to one of his descendants or to a choir guild that bore his name.

2 aEx.
15:16; Deut.
32:6 bEx.
15:13; Ps.
77:15;
106:10; Is.
63:9 cDeut.
32:9; Is.
63:17; Jer.
10:16; 51:19
dPs. 9:11;
68:16

2 Remember Thy congregation, which Thou hast ªpurchased of old,
Which Thou hast bredeemed to be the ctribe of Thine inheritance;
And Mount dZion, where Thou hast dwelt.

★ 3 aIs.
61:4 bPs.
79:1

3 Turn Thy footsteps toward the ªperpetual ruins;
The enemy bhas damaged everything within the sanctuary.

★ 4 aLam.
2:7 bNum.
2:2 cPs. 74:9

4 Thine adversaries have ªroared in the midst of Thy meeting place;
They have set up their bown standards cfor signs.

5 aJer.
46:22

5 It seems as if one had lifted up
His ªaxe in a forest of trees.

6 a1 Kin.
6:18, 29, 32,
35

6 And now all its ªcarved work
They smash with hatchet and hammers.

★ 7 a2 Kin.
25:9 bPs.
89:39; Lam.
2:2

7 They have ªburned Thy sanctuary to the ground;
They have bdefiled the dwelling place of Thy name.

★ 8 aPs.
83:4

8 They ªsaid in their heart, "Let us completely subdue them."
They have burned all the meeting places of God in the land.

9 aPs.
78:43
b1 Sam. 3:1;
Lam. 2:9;
Ezek. 7:26;
Amos 8:11
cPs. 6:3;
79:5; 80:4
10 aPs.
44:16; 79:12;
89:51 bLev.
24:16

9 We do not see our ªsigns;
There is bno longer any prophet,
Nor is there any among us who knows chow long.

10 How long, O God, will the adversary ªrevile,
And the enemy bspurn Thy name forever?

11 Why ªdost Thou withdraw Thy hand, even Thy right hand?
From within Thy bosom, bdestroy them!

11 aLam. 2:3
bPs. 59:13

12 Yet God is ªmy king from of old,
Who works deeds of deliverance in the midst of the earth.

12 aPs. 44:4

13 Thou didst ªdivide the sea by Thy strength;
Thou bdidst break the heads of the csea monsters in the waters.

★13-14

13 aEx.
14:21; Ps.
78:13 bIs.
51:9 cPs.
148:7; Jer.
51:34

14 Thou didst crush the heads of ªLeviathan;
Thou didst give him as food for the creatures bof the wilderness.

14 aJob
41:1; Ps.
104:26; Is.
27:1 bPs.
72:9

15 Thou didst ªbreak open springs and torrents;
Thou didst bdry up everflowing streams.

15 aEx. 17:5,
6; Num.
20:11; Ps.
78:15;
105:41;
114:8; Is.
48:21 bEx.
14:21, 22;
Josh. 2:10;
3:13; Ps.
114:3

16 Thine is the day, Thine is the night;
Thou hast ªprepared the light and the sun.

16 aGen.
1:14-18; Ps.
104:19;
136:7, 8

17 Thou hast ªestablished all the boundaries of the earth;
Thou hast made bsummer and winter.

17 aDeut.
32:8; Acts
17:26 bGen.
8:22; Ps.
147:16-18

18 Remember this, O LORD, that the enemy has ªreviled;
And a bfoolish people has spurned Thy name.

18 aPs.
74:10 bDeut.
32:6; Ps.
14:1; 39:8;
53:1

19 Do not deliver the soul of Thy ªturtledove to the wild beast;
bDo not forget the life of Thine afflicted forever.

★19 aSong
2:14 bPs.
9:18

74:3 They ask God to hasten to inspect the seemingly irreparable ruins of the Temple and the city of Jerusalem.
74:4 *their own standards for signs.* The enemies' standards in the Temple area replaced those emblems God had placed in the Temple (like Aaron's rod).
74:7 See 2 Kings 25:9-10.
74:8 *meeting places.* Not a reference to synagogues, which developed later, but to the Temple viewed as the last of God's successive meeting places.
74:13-14 God's destruction of the *sea monsters* and *Leviathan* (see note on Job 3:8) is a poetic description of His victory over the Egyptians at the time of the Exodus.
74:19 *Thy turtledove.* Defenseless, like Israel at this time in her history.

20 aGen.
17:7; Ps.
106:45 bPs.
88:6; 143:3

20 Consider the acovenant;
For the bdark places of the
land are full of the
habitations of vio-
lence.

21 aPs.
103:6 bPs.
35:10; Is.
41:17

21 Let not the aoppressed return dishonored;
Let the bafflicted and
needy praise Thy
name.

22 aPs. 43:1;
Is. 3:13;
43:26; Ezek.
20:35 bPs.
14:1; 53:1;
74:18

22 Do arise, O God, and
aplead Thine own
cause;
Remember how the bfool-
ish man reproaches
Thee all day long.

23 aPs.
74:10 bPs.
65:7

23 Do not forget the voice of
Thine aadversaries,
The buproar of those who
rise against Thee
which ascends con-
tinually.

PSALM 75

For the choir director; set to
Al-tashheth.
A Psalm of Asaph, a Song.

1 aPs.
79:13 bPs.
145:18 cPs.
26:7; 44:1;
71:17

WE agive thanks to Thee, O
God, we give thanks,
For Thy name is bnear;
Men declare cThy won-
drous works.

2 aPs.
102:13 bPs.
9:8; 67:4; Is.
11:4

2 "When I select an aappointed time,
It is I who bjudge with equity.

3 aPs. 46:6;
Is. 24:19
b1 Sam. 2:8

3 "The aearth and all who
dwell in it melt;
It is I who have firmly set
its bpillars.   [Selah.

★ 4 aZech.
1:21

4 "I said to the boastful, 'Do
not boast,'

And to the wicked, 'aDo
not lift up the horn;

5 a1 Sam.
2:3; Ps. 94:4

5 Do not lift up your horn
on high,
aDo not speak with inso-
lent pride.' "

★ 6 aPs. 3:3

6 For not from the east, nor
from the west,
Nor from the adesert
comes exaltation;

7 aPs. 50:6
b1 Sam. 2:7;
Ps. 147:6;
Dan. 2:21

7 But aGod is the Judge;
He bputs down one, and
exalts another.

8 aJob
21:20; Ps.
11:6; 60:3;
Jer. 25:15
bProv. 23:30
cObad. 16

8 For a acup is in the hand of
the LORD, and the
wine foams;
It is bwell mixed, and He
pours out of this;
Surely all the wicked of
the earth must drain
and cdrink down its
dregs.

9 aPs.
22:22; 40:10

9 But as for me, I will ade-
clare it forever;
I will sing praises to the
God of Jacob.

10 aPs.
101:8; Jer.
48:25
b1 Sam. 2:1;
Ps. 89:17;
92:10;
148:14

10 And all the ahorns of the
wicked He will cut off,
But bthe horns of the
righteous will be lifted
up.

PSALM 76

For the choir director; on
stringed instruments.
A Psalm of Asaph, a Song.

1 aPs. 48:3
bPs. 99:3

GOD is aknown in Judah;
His name is bgreat in Is-
rael.

★ 2 aPs.
27:5; Lam.
2:6 bGen.
14:18 cPs.
9:11; 132:13;
135:21

2 And His atabernacle is in
bSalem;
His cdwelling place also is
in Zion.

74:20 the covenant. Originally made with Abraham (see notes on Gen. 15:18–21 and 17:7–8).
Psalm 75 In this communal thanksgiving
psalm, Asaph praises God who will judge the
earth (vv. 1–3), warns the wicked of this judgment (vv. 4–8), and vows to praise God (vv.
9–10). Al-tashheth. See note on Psalm 57.
75:4 Do not lift up the horn. I.e., do not proudly
vaunt your strength.
75:6 No mention is made of the north (the desert was to the south), since the Assyrians were
approaching from that direction (Isa. 36–37 is

likely the background of this psalm).
Psalm 76 This hymn of thanksgiving records the voice of the people (vv. 1–3), the victory
of God (vv. 4–10), and the vows of the people
(vv. 11–12). As with Psalm 75, the victory celebrated is likely the defeat of the Assyrians in 701
B.C. (2 Kings 18:13–19:37; Isa. 36–37); therefore
the Asaph mentioned is either a descendant of
the Asaph of David's time or a reference to a
choir guild bearing his name.
76:2 Salem. A shortened form of Jerusalem, also
called Zion.

3 aPs. 46:9

3 There He ªbroke the flam-
    ing arrows,
The shield, and the sword,
    and the weapons of
    war.   [Selah.

★ 4

4 Thou art resplendent,
More majestic than the
    mountains of prey.

★ 5-6

5 als.
10:12; 46:12

5 The ªstouthearted were
    plundered;
They sank into sleep;
And none of the warriors
    could use his hands.

6 aPs.
80:16 bEx.
15:1, 21; Ps.
78:53

6 At Thy ªrebuke, O God of
    Jacob,
Both brider and horse were
    cast into a dead sleep.

7 a1 Chr.
16:25; Ps.
89:7; 96:4
bEzra 9:15;
Ps. 130:3;
Nah. 1:6;
Mal. 3:2;
Rev. 6:17

7 Thou, even Thou, art ªto
    be feared;
And bwho may stand in
    Thy presence when
    once Thou art angry?

8 a1 Chr.
16:30; 2 Chr.
20:29, 30;
Ps. 33:8

8 Thou didst cause judg-
    ment to be heard
    from heaven;
The earth ªfeared, and was
    still,

9 aPs. 9:7,
8; 74:22;
82:8

9 When God ªarose to judg-
    ment,
To save all the humble of
    the earth.   [Selah.

10 aEx. 9:16;
Rom. 9:17

10 For the ªwrath of man
    shall praise Thee;
With a remnant of wrath
    Thou shalt gird Thy-
    self.

11 aEccl.
5:4-6 bPs.
50:14
c2 Chr.
32:23; Ps.
68:29

11 ªMake vows to the LORD
    your God and bfulfill
    them;
Let all who are around
    Him cbring gifts to
    Him who is to be
    feared.

12 aPs. 47:2

12 He will cut off the spirit of
    princes;
He is ªfeared by the kings
    of the earth.

PSALM 77

For the choir director; according
    to Jeduthun.
A Psalm of Asaph.

M Y voice rises to God, and I
    will ªcry aloud;
My voice rises to God, and
    He will hear me.

2 In the ªday of my trouble I
    sought the Lord;
bIn the night my chand
    was stretched out
    without dweariness;
My soul drefused to be
    comforted.

3 When I remember God,
    then I am ªdisturbed;
When I bsigh, then cmy
    spirit grows faint.
                    [Selah.

4 Thou hast held my eyelids
    open;
I am so troubled that I
    ªcannot speak.

5 I have considered the
    ªdays of old,
The years of long ago.

6 I will remember my ªsong
    in the night;
I bwill meditate with my
    heart;
And my spirit ponders.

7 Will the Lord ªreject for-
    ever?
And will He bnever be fa-
    vorable again?

8 Has His ªlovingkindness
    ceased forever?
Has His bpromise come to
    an end forever?

9 Has God ªforgotten to be
    gracious?
Or has He in anger with-
    drawn His
    bcompassion? [Selah.

10 Then I said, "ªIt is my
    grief,

1 aPs. 3:4;
142:1

2 aPs.
50:15; 86:7
bPs. 63:6; Is.
26:9 cJob
11:13; Ps.
88:9 dGen.
37:35

★ 3 aPs.
42:5, 11;
43:5 bPs.
55:2; 142:2
cPs. 61:2;
143:4

4 aPs. 39:9

5 aDeut.
32:7; Ps.
44:1; 143:5;
Is. 51:9

6 aPs. 42:8
bPs. 4:4

7 aPs. 44:9
bPs. 85:1, 5

8 aPs.
89:49
b2 Pet. 3:9

9 als. 49:15
bPs. 25:6;
40:11; 51:1

10 aPs.
31:22; 73:14
bPs. 44:2, 3

76:4 the mountains of prey. The invaders.
76:5-6 This description remarkably fits the
judgment God brought on the armies of Sennacherib (2 Kings 19:35; Isa. 37:36).
Psalm 77 In this lament, we see the psalm-

ist's call for help (vv. 1-10) and the comfort of
history (vv. 11-20). Jeduthun. See note on Psalm
39.
77:3 disturbed. Because of the questions of
verses 7-9.

That the ᵇright hand of the Most High has changed."

11 ᵃPs. 105:5; 143:5

11 I shall remember the ᵃdeeds of the LORD;
Surely I will ᵃremember Thy wonders of old.

12 ᵃPs. 145:5

12 I will ᵃmeditate on all Thy work,
And muse on Thy deeds.

13 ᵃPs. 63:2; 73:17 ᵇEx. 15:11; Ps. 71:19; 86:8

13 Thy way, O God, is ᵃholy;
ᵇWhat god is great like our God?

14 ᵃPs. 72:18 ᵇPs. 106:8

14 Thou art the ᵃGod who workest wonders;
Thou hast ᵇmade known Thy strength among the peoples.

15 ᵃEx. 6:6; Deut. 9:29; Ps. 74:2; 78:42 ᵇPs. 80:1

15 Thou hast by Thy power ᵃredeemed Thy people,
The sons of Jacob and ᵇJoseph.   [Selah.

★16-20

16 ᵃEx. 14:21; Ps. 114:3; Hab. 3:8, 10

16 The ᵃwaters saw Thee, O God;
The waters saw Thee, they were in anguish;
The deeps also trembled.

17 ᵃJudg. 5:4 ᵇPs. 68:33 ᶜPs. 18:14

17 The ᵃclouds poured out water;
The skies ᵇgave forth a sound;
Thy ᶜarrows flashed here and there.

18 ᵃPs. 18:13; 104:7 ᵇPs. 97:4 ᶜJudg. 5:4; Ps. 18:7

18 The ᵃsound of Thy thunder was in the whirlwind;
The ᵇlightnings lit up the world;
The ᶜearth trembled and shook.

19 ᵃIs. 51:10; Hab. 3:15
20 ᵃEx. 13:21; 14:19; Ps. 78:52; 80:1; Is. 63:11-13 ᵇEx. 6:26; Ps. 105:26

19 Thy ᵃway was in the sea,
And Thy paths in the mighty waters,
And Thy footprints may not be known.

20 Thou ᵃdidst lead Thy people like a flock,

By the hand of ᵇMoses and Aaron.

PSALM 78

A Maskil of Asaph.

LISTEN, O my people, to my instruction;
ᵇIncline your ears to the words of my mouth.

1 ᵃIs. 51:4 ᵇIs. 55:3

2 I will ᵃopen my mouth in a parable;
I will utter ᵇdark sayings of old,

★ 2 ᵃPs. 49:4; Matt. 13:35 ᵇProv. 1:6

3 Which we have heard and known,
And ᵃour fathers have told us.

3 ᵃPs. 44:1

4 We will ᵃnot conceal them from their children,
But ᵇtell to the generation to come the praises of the LORD,
And His strength and His ᶜwondrous works that He has done.

4 ᵃEx. 12:26; Deut. 6:7; 11:19; Job 15:18; Ps. 145:4; Is. 38:19; Joel 1:3 ᵇEx. 13:8, 14; Ps. 22:30 ᶜJob 37:16; Ps. 26:7; 71:17

5 For He established a ᵃtestimony in Jacob,
And appointed a ᵇlaw in Israel,
Which He ᶜcommanded our fathers,
That they should ᵈteach them to their children,

5 ᵃPs. 19:7; 81:5; Is. 8:20 ᵇPs. 147:19 ᶜDeut. 6:4-9 ᵈDeut. 4:9

6 ᵃThat the generation to come might know, *even* ᵇthe children *yet* to be born,
That they may arise and ᶜtell *them* to their children,

6 ᵃPs. 102:18 ᵇPs. 22:31 ᶜDeut. 11:19

7 That they should put their confidence in God,
And ᵃnot forget the works of God,

7 ᵃDeut. 4:9; 6:12; 8:14 ᵇDeut. 4:2; 5:1, 29; 27:1; Josh. 22:5

77:16-20 See note on 66:6.
Psalm 78 Asaph recites the early history of the nation in order to warn future generations against a repetition of unfaithfulness. He invites (vv. 1-11) the people to recall their provocation of God in the wilderness experience (vv. 12-39), their ingratitude during the Exodus (vv. 40-55),

and their unfaithfulness during the period of the judges (vv. 56-72). *Maskil.* See note on Psalm 32.
78:2 On the meaning of *parable* and *dark sayings* (riddles) see note on Ezek. 17:2. This verse is quoted in Matt. 13:35 to describe Jesus' way of teaching.

But [b]keep His commandments,

8   And [a]not be like their fathers,
A [b]stubborn and rebellious generation,
A generation that [c]did not prepare its heart,
And whose spirit was not [d]faithful to God.

9   The sons of Ephraim were [a]archers equipped with bows,
Yet [b]they turned back in the day of battle.

10   They [a]did not keep the covenant of God,
And refused to [b]walk in His law;

11   And they [a]forgot His deeds,
And His miracles that He had shown them.

12   [a]He wrought wonders before their fathers,
In the land of Egypt, in the [b]field of Zoan.

13   He [a]divided the sea, and caused them to pass through;
And He made the waters stand [b]up like a heap.

14   Then He led them with the cloud by [a]day,
And all the night with a [b]light of fire.

15   He [a]split the rocks in the wilderness,
And gave *them* abundant drink like the ocean depths.

16   He [a]brought forth streams also from the rock,
And caused waters to run down like rivers.

17   Yet they still continued to sin against Him,
To [a]rebel against the Most High in the desert.

18   And in their heart they [a]put God to the test
By asking [b]food according to their desire.

19   Then they spoke against God;
They said, "[a]Can God prepare a table in the wilderness?

20   "Behold, He [a]struck the rock, so that waters gushed out,
And streams were overflowing;
Can He give bread also?
Will He provide [b]meat for His people?"

21   Therefore the LORD heard and was [a]full of wrath,
And a fire was kindled against Jacob,
And anger also mounted against Israel;

22   Because they [a]did not believe in God,
And did not trust in His salvation.

23   Yet He commanded the clouds above,
And [a]opened the doors of heaven;

24   And He [a]rained down manna upon them to eat,
And gave them [b]food from heaven.

25   Man did eat the bread of angels;
He sent them food [a]in abundance.

26   He [a]caused the east wind to blow in the heavens;
And by His power He directed the south wind.

27   When He rained meat upon them like the dust,
Even [a]winged fowl like the sand of the seas,

28   Then He let *them* fall in the midst of their camp,

Cross references (left margin):

8 [a]2 Kin. 17:14; 2 Chr. 30:7; Ezek. 20:18 [b]Ex. 32:9; Deut. 9:7, 24; 31:27; Judg. 2:19; Is. 30:9 [c]Job 11:13; Ps. 78:37 [d]Ps. 51:10

★ **9** [a]1 Chr. 12:2 [b]Judg. 20:39; Ps. 78:57

10 [a]Judg. 2:20; 1 Kin. 11:11; 2 Kin. 17:15; 18:12 [b]Ps. 119:1; Jer. 32:23; 44:10, 23

11 [a]Ps. 106:13

★**12** [a]Ex. chs. 7-12; Ps. 106:22 [b]Num. 13:22; Ps. 78:43; Is. 19:11; 30:4; Ezek. 30:14

13 [a]Ex. 14:21; Ps. 74:13; 136:13 [b]Ex. 15:8; Ps. 33:7

14 [a]Ex. 13:21; Ps. 105:39 [b]Ex. 14:24

15 [a]Ex. 17:6; Num. 20:11; Ps. 105:41; 114:8; Is. 48:21; 1 Cor. 10:4

16 [a]Num. 20:8, 10, 11

17 [a]Deut. 9:22; Is. 63:10; Heb. 3:16

18 [a]Ex. 17:6; Deut. 6:16; Ps. 78:41, 56; 95:9; 106:14; 1 Cor. 10:9 [b]Num. 11:4

Cross references (right margin):

19 [a]Ex. 16:3; Num. 11:4; 20:3; 21:5; Ps. 23:5

20 [a]Num. 20:11; Ps. 78:15, 16 [b]Num. 11:18

21 [a]Num. 11:1

22 [a]Deut. 1:32; 9:23; Heb. 3:18

23 [a]Gen. 7:11; Mal. 3:10

24 [a]Ex. 16:4 [b]Ps. 105:40; John 6:31

★**25** [a]Ex. 16:3

26 [a]Num. 11:31

27 [a]Ex. 16:13; Ps. 105:40

78:9 *turned back.* Not a reference to a specific occasion of cowardice in battle but to the fact that, like cowards, they retreated from obedience to God's law (vv. 10-11).

78:12 *Zoan.* See note on Isa. 19:11-14.
78:25 *the bread of angels.* Food from heaven, good enough for angels.

Round about their dwellings.

29 So they ᵃate and were well filled;
And their desire He gave to them.

30 Before they had satisfied their desire,
ᵃWhile their food was in their mouths,

31 The ᵃanger of God rose against them,
And killed some of their ᵇstoutest ones,
And subdued the choice men of Israel.

32 In spite of all this they ᵃstill sinned,
And ᵇdid not believe in His wonderful works.

33 So He brought ᵃtheir days to an end in futility,
And their years in sudden terror.

34 When He killed them, then they ᵃsought Him,
And returned and searched ᵇdiligently for God;

35 And they remembered that God was their ᵃrock,
And the Most High God their ᵇRedeemer.

36 But they ᵃdeceived Him with their mouth,
And ᵇlied to Him with their tongue.

37 For their heart was not ᵃsteadfast toward Him,
Nor were they faithful in His covenant.

38 But He, being ᵃcompassionate, ᵇforgave *their* iniquity, and did not destroy *them*;
And often He ᶜrestrained His anger,
And did not arouse all His wrath.

39 Thus ᵃHe remembered that they were but ᵇflesh,
A ᶜwind that passes and does not return.

40 How often they ᵃrebelled against Him in the wilderness,
And ᵇgrieved Him in the ᶜdesert!

41 And again and again they ᵃtempted God,
And pained the ᵇHoly One of Israel.

42 They ᵃdid not remember ᵇHis power,
The day when He ᶜredeemed them from the adversary,

43 When He performed His ᵃsigns in Egypt,
And His ᵇmarvels in the field of Zoan,

44 And ᵃturned their rivers to blood,
And their streams, they could not drink.

45 He sent among them swarms of ᵃflies, which devoured them,
And ᵇfrogs which destroyed them.

46 He gave also their crops to the ᵃgrasshopper,
And the product of their labor to the ᵇlocust.

47 He destroyed their vines with ᵃhailstones,
And their sycamore trees with frost.

48 He gave over their ᵃcattle also to the hailstones,
And their herds to bolts of lightning.

49 He ᵃsent upon them His burning anger,
Fury, and indignation, and trouble,
A band of destroying angels.

50 He leveled a path for His anger;
He did not spare their soul from death,

29 ᵃNum. 11:19, 20

30 ᵃNum. 11:33

31 ᵃNum. 11:33, 34; Job 20:23 ᵇIs. 10:16

32 ᵃNum. chs. 14, 16, 17 ᵇNum. 14:11; Ps. 78:11

★**33** ᵃNum. 14:29, 35

34 ᵃNum. 21:7; Hos. 5:15 ᵇPs. 63:1

35 ᵃDeut. 32:4 ᵇEx. 15:13; Deut. 9:26; Ps. 74:2; Is. 41:14

36 ᵃEx. 24:7, 8; Ezek. 33:31 ᵇEx. 32:7, 8; Is. 57:11

37 ᵃPs. 51:10; 78:8; Acts 8:21

38 ᵃEx. 34:6 ᵇNum. 14:18-20 ᶜIs. 48:9

39 ᵃJob 10:9; Ps. 103:14 ᵇGen. 6:3 ᶜJob 7:7, 16; Ps. 103:14; James 4:14

40 ᵃPs. 95:8, 9; 106:43; 107:11; Heb. 3:16 ᵇPs. 95:10; Is. 63:10; Eph. 4:30 ᶜPs. 106:14

41 ᵃNum. 14:22 ᵇ2 Kin. 19:22; Ps. 89:18

42 ᵃJudg. 8:34 ᵇPs. 44:3 ᶜPs. 106:10

43 ᵃPs. 105:27 ᵇEx. 4:21; 7:3

44 ᵃEx. 7:20; Ps. 105:29

45 ᵃEx. 8:24; Ps. 105:31 ᵇEx. 8:6; Ps. 105:30

46 ᵃ1 Kin. 8:37; Ps. 105:34 ᵇEx. 10:14

47 ᵃEx. 9:23-25; Ps. 105:32

48 ᵃEx. 9:19

49 ᵃEx. 15:7

50 ᵃEx. 12:29, 30

78:33 *futility.* A reference to the 40 years of wandering in the wilderness.

But ^agave over their life to the plague,

51 And ^asmote all the firstborn in Egypt,
The ^bfirst *issue* of their virility in the tents of ^cHam.

52 But He ^aled forth His own people like sheep,
And guided them in the wilderness ^blike a flock;

53 And He led them ^asafely, so that they did not fear;
But ^bthe sea engulfed their enemies.

54 So ^aHe brought them to His holy land,
To this ^bhill country ^cwhich His right hand had gained.

55 He also ^adrove out the nations before them,
And He ^bapportioned them for an inheritance by measurement,
And made the tribes of Israel dwell in their tents.

56 Yet they ^atempted and ^brebelled against the Most High God,
And did not keep His testimonies,

57 But turned back and ^aacted treacherously like their fathers;
They ^bturned aside like a treacherous bow.

58 For they ^aprovoked Him with their ^bhigh places,
And ^caroused His jealousy with their ^dgraven images.

59 When God heard, He was filled with ^awrath,
And greatly ^babhorred Israel;

60 So that He ^aabandoned the ^bdwelling place at Shiloh,
The tent which He had pitched among men,

61 And gave up His ^astrength to captivity,
And His glory ^binto the hand of the adversary.

62 He also ^adelivered His people to the sword,
And was filled with wrath at His inheritance.

63 ^aFire devoured His young men;
And His ^bvirgins had no wedding songs.

64 His ^apriests fell by the sword;
And His ^bwidows could not weep.

65 Then the Lord ^aawoke as *if from* sleep,
Like a ^bwarrior overcome by wine.

66 And He ^adrove His adversaries backward;
He put on them an everlasting reproach.

67 He also ^arejected the tent of Joseph,
And did not choose the tribe of Ephraim,

68 But chose the tribe of Judah,
Mount ^aZion which He loved.

69 And He ^abuilt His sanctuary like the heights,
Like the earth which He has founded forever.

70 He also ^achose David His servant,
And took him from the sheepfolds;

71 From ^athe care of the ewes ^bwith suckling lambs He brought him,
To ^cshepherd Jacob His people,

---

51 ^aEx. 12:29; Ps. 105:36; 135:8; 136:10
^bGen. 49:3
^cPs. 105:23, 27; 106:22
52 ^aEx. 15:22 ^bPs. 77:20
53 ^aEx. 14:19, 20 ^bEx. 14:27, 28; Ps. 106:11
54 ^aEx. 15:17 ^bPs. 68:16; Is. 11:9 ^cPs. 44:3
55 ^aJosh. 11:16-23; Ps. 44:2 ^bJosh. 13:7; 23:4; Ps. 105:11; 135:12
56 ^aPs. 78:18 ^bJudg. 2:11-13; Ps. 78:40
57 ^aEzek. 20:27, 28 ^bHos. 7:16
58 ^aDeut. 4:25; Judg. 2:12; 1 Kin. 14:9; Is. 65:3 ^bLev. 26:30; 1 Kin. 3:2; 2 Kin. 16:4; Jer. 17:3 ^cDeut. 32:16, 21; 1 Kin. 14:22 ^dEx. 20:4; Lev. 26:1; Deut. 4:25
59 ^aDeut. 1:34; 9:19; Ps. 106:40 ^bLev. 26:30; Deut. 32:19; Amos 6:8
60 ^a1 Sam. 4:11; Ps. 78:67; Jer. 7:12, 14; 26:6 ^bJosh. 18:1
*61 ^aPs. 63:2; 132:8 ^b1 Sam. 4:17
62 ^aJudg. 20:21; 1 Sam. 4:10
63 ^aNum. 11:1; 21:28; Is. 26:11; Jer. 48:45 ^bJer. 7:34; 16:9; Lam. 2:21
64 ^a1 Sam. 4:17; 22:18 ^bJob 27:15; Ezek. 24:23
65 ^aPs. 44:23; 73:20 ^bIs. 42:13
66 ^a1 Sam. 5:6
67 ^aPs. 78:60
*68-72
68 ^aPs. 87:2; 132:13
69 ^a1 Kin. 6:1-38
70 ^a1 Sam. 16:11, 12
71 ^a2 Sam. 7:8; Is. 40:11 ^bGen. 33:13 ^c2 Sam. 5:2; 1 Chr. 11:2; Ps. 28:9 ^d1 Sam. 10:1

78:61 The delivering of God's *strength to captivity* refers to the capture of the Ark by the Philistines (1 Sam. 4:1-7:1).
78:68-72 The hope of the nation rested on God's new choices of *Judah* (replacing Ephraim), *Zion* (then in enemy hands), and *David* (a shepherd lad).

And Israel ^dHis inheritance.

^{72 a}1 Kin. 9:4

72 So he shepherded them according to the ^aintegrity of his heart,
And guided them with his skillful hands.

PSALM 79

A Psalm of Asaph.

★ 1-5
^{1 a}Lam.
1:10 ^bPs.
74:2 ^cPs.
74:3, 7
^d2 Kin. 25:9,
10; 2 Chr.
36:17-19;
Jer. 26:18;
52:12-14;
Mic. 3:12
^{2 a}Deut.
28:26; Jer.
7:33; 16:4;
19:7; 34:20

O GOD, the ^anations have invaded ^bThine inheritance;
They have defiled Thy ^choly temple;
They have ^dlaid Jerusalem in ruins.

2 They have given the ^adead bodies of Thy servants for food to the birds of the heavens,
The flesh of Thy godly ones to the beasts of the earth.

^{3 a}Jer.
14:16; 16:4

3 They have poured out their blood like water round about Jerusalem;
And there was ^ano one to bury them.

^{4 a}Ps.
44:13; 80:6;
Dan. 9:16

4 We have become a ^areproach to our neighbors,
A scoffing and derision to those around us.

^{5 a}Ps. 13:1;
74:1, 9, 10;
85:5; 89:46
^bDeut.
29:20; Ezek.
36:5; 38:19
^cPs. 89:46;
Zeph. 3:8
^{6 a}Ps.
69:24; Jer.
10:25; Ezek.
21:31; Zeph.
3:8
^b1 Thess.
4:5; 2 Thess.
1:8 ^cPs.
14:4; 53:4

5 ^aHow long, O LORD? Wilt Thou be angry forever?
Will Thy ^bjealousy ^cburn like fire?

6 ^aPour out Thy wrath upon the nations which ^bdo not know Thee,
And upon the kingdoms which ^cdo not call upon Thy name.

7 For they have ^adevoured Jacob,
And ^blaid waste his habitation.

^{7 a}Ps. 53:4
^b2 Chr.
36:19; Jer.
39:8

8 ^aDo not remember the iniquities of our forefathers against us;
Let Thy compassion come quickly to ^bmeet us;
For we are ^cbrought very low.

★ 8-10
^{8 a}Ps.
106:6; Is.
64:9 ^bPs.
21:3 ^cDeut.
28:43; Ps.
116:6; 142:6;
Is. 26:5

9 ^aHelp us, O God of our salvation, for the glory of ^bThy name;
And deliver us, and ^cforgive our sins, ^dfor Thy name's sake.

^{9 a}2 Chr.
14:11 ^bPs.
31:3 ^cPs.
25:11; 65:3
^dJer. 14:7

10 ^aWhy should the nations say, "Where is their God?"
Let there be known among the nations in our sight,
^bVengeance for the blood of Thy servants, which has been shed.

^{10 a}Ps.
42:10; 115:2
^bPs. 94:1, 2

11 Let ^athe groaning of the prisoner come before Thee;
According to the greatness of Thy power preserve those who are ^adoomed to die.

^{11 a}Ps.
102:20

12 And return to our neighbors ^asevenfold ^binto their bosom
The ^creproach with which they have reproached Thee, O Lord.

^{12 a}Gen.
4:15; Lev.
26:21, 28;
Ps. 12:6;
119:164;
Prov. 6:31;
24:16; Is.
30:26 ^bPs.
35:13; Is.
65:6, 7; Jer.
32:18; Luke
6:38 ^cPs.
74:10, 18, 22

13 So we Thy people and the ^asheep of Thy pasture
Will ^bgive thanks to Thee forever;
To all generations we will ^ctell of Thy praise.

^{13 a}Ps. 74:1;
95:7; 100:3
^bPs. 44:8
^cPs. 89:1; Is.
43:21

Psalm 79 In this imprecatory psalm (see Introduction), Asaph bemoans the desecration of Jerusalem (vv. 1-5) and beseeches God to destroy Israel's enemies (vv. 6-13). *Asaph.* See note on Psalm 74.
79:1-5 These verses depict the destruction of Jerusalem by the armies of Babylon in 586.
79:8-10 The psalmist appeals to God's mercy (vv. 8-9) and to His honor (v. 10).
Psalm 80 Written against the background of the Assyrian captivity of the northern tribes of Israel (see note on 2 Kings 17:6), this psalm reveals the shock that event had in Jerusalem (where the Asaph singers lived). Now exposed to Assyria on the north, the people of Judah cry to God as the Shepherd of His sheep (vv. 1-7) and to God as the Husbandman of His vineyard (vv. 8-19). *Shoshannim.* See note on Psalm 45. *Eduth.* A testimony.

PSALM 80*

For the choir director; *set to*
El Shoshannim;
Eduth.
A Psalm of Asaph.

1 aPs. 23:1
bPs. 77:15;
78:67; Amos
5:15 cEx.
25:22;
1 Sam. 4:4;
2 Sam. 6:2;
Ps. 99:1

Oh, give ear, [a]Shepherd of Israel,
Thou who dost lead [b]Jo-
seph like a flock;
Thou who [c]art enthroned
above the cherubim,
shine forth!

2 aNum.
2:18-24 bPs.
35:23

2 Before [a]Ephraim and Benjamin and Manasseh,
[b]stir up Thy power,
And come to save us!

★ 3 aPs.
60:1; 80:7,
19; 85:4;
126:1; Lam.
5:21 bNum.
6:25; Ps. 4:6;
31:16

3 O God, [a]restore us,
And [b]cause Thy face to
shine *upon us,* and we
will be saved.

4 aPs. 59:5;
84:8 bPs.
79:5; 85:5

4 O [a]Lord God *of* hosts,
[b]How long wilt Thou be
angry with the prayer
of Thy people?

5 aPs. 42:3;
102:9; Is.
30:20

5 Thou hast fed them with
the [a]bread of tears,
And Thou hast made them
to drink tears in large
measure.

6 aPs.
44:13; 79:4

6 Thou dost make us an object of contention [a]to
our neighbors;
And our enemies laugh
among themselves.

★ 8-9
8 aPs.
80:15; Is.
5:1, 2, 7; Jer.
2:21; 12:10;
Ezek. 17:6;
19:10 bJosh.
13:6; 2 Chr.
20:7; Ps.
44:2; Acts
7:45 cJer.
11:17; 32:41;
Ezek. 17:23;
Amos 9:15
9 aEx.
23:28; Josh.
24:12; Is. 5:2
bHos. 14:5

7 O God *of* hosts, restore us,
And cause Thy face to
shine *upon us,* and we
will be saved.

8 Thou didst remove a [a]vine
from Egypt;
Thou didst [b]drive out the
nations, and didst
[c]plant it.

9 Thou didst [a]clear *the
ground* before it,

And it [b]took deep root and
filled the land.

10 aGen.
49:22

10 The mountains were covered with its shadow;
And the cedars of God
with its [a]boughs.

★11 aPs.
72:8

11 It was sending out its
branches [a]to the sea,
And its shoots to the River.

12 aPs.
89:40; Is. 5:5

12 Why hast Thou [a]broken
down its hedges,
So that all who pass *that
way* pick its *fruit?*

13 aJer. 5:6

13 A boar from the forest
[a]eats it away,
And whatever moves in
the field feeds on it.

14 aPs.
90:13 bPs.
102:19; Is.
63:15

14 O God *of* hosts, [a]turn
again now, we be-
seech Thee;
[b]Look down from heaven
and see, and take care
of this vine,

15 aPs. 80:8

15 Even the [a]shoot which Thy
right hand has
planted,
And on the son whom
Thou hast strength-
ened for Thyself.

16 a2 Chr.
36:19; Ps.
74:8; Jer.
52:13 bPs.
39:11; 76:6

16 It is [a]burned with fire, it is
cut down;
They perish at the [b]rebuke
of Thy countenance.

★17 aPs.
89:21 bPs.
80:15

17 Let [a]Thy hand be upon the
man of Thy right
hand,
Upon the son of man
whom Thou [b]didst
make strong for Thy-
self.

18 aIs. 50:5
bPs. 71:20

18 Then we shall not [a]turn
back from Thee;
[b]Revive us, and we will call
upon Thy name.

19 aPs. 80:3

19 O Lord God of hosts, [a]re-
store us;
Cause Thy face to shine
upon us, and we will
be saved.

---

*See note, p. 874.
80:3 *restore us.* More than a cry for national restoration, this includes a desire for spiritual revival (v. 18), and implies a confession of sin.
80:8-9 Israel, the vine, transplanted from Egypt,
had spread throughout Canaan.
80:11 The *sea* is the Mediterranean; the *River,*
the Euphrates.

80:17 *the son of man.* Here, used of Israel (cf.
Exod. 4:22).
Psalm 81 This psalm, associated with the
Feast of Tabernacles (see note on Lev. 23:34-43)
opens with a summons to praise (vv. 1-5), continues with an exhortation to remember (vv.
6-10), and concludes with a call to repent (vv.
11-16). *Gittith.* See note on Psalm 8.

PSALM 81*

For the choir director; on the
Gittith.
A Psalm of Asaph.

1 *a*Ps.
51:14; 59:16;
95:1 *b*Ps.
46:1 *c*Ps.
66:1; 95:2;
98:4 *d*Ps.
84:8

2 *a*Ex.
15:20; Ps.
149:3 *b*Ps.
92:3; 98:5;
147:7 *c*Ps.
108:2; 144:9

★ **3** *a*Num.
10:10 *b*Lev.
23:24

★ **5** *a*Ex.
11:4 *b*Deut.
28:49; Ps.
114:1; Jer.
5:15

6 *a*Is. 9:4;
10:27

7 *a*Ex. 2:23;
14:10; Ps.
50:15 *b*Ex.
19:19; 20:18
*c*Ex. 17:6, 7;
Num. 20:13;
Ps. 95:8

8 *a*Ps. 50:7
*b*Ps. 95:7

9 *a*Ex. 20:3;
Deut. 5:7;
32:12; Ps.
44:20; Is.
43:12

SING for joy to God our
*b*strength;
Shout *c*joyfully to the
*d*God of Jacob.
2 Raise a song, strike *a*the
timbrel,
The sweet sounding *b*lyre
with the *c*harp.
3 Blow the trumpet at the
*a*new moon,
At the full moon, on our
*b*feast day.
4 For it is a statute for Israel,
An ordinance of the God
of Jacob.
5 He established it for a testimony in Joseph,
When he *a*went through-
out the land of Egypt.
I heard a *b*language that I
did not know:
6 "I *a*relieved his shoulder of
the burden,
His hands were freed from
the basket.
7 "You *a*called in trouble, and
I rescued you;
I *b*answered you in the
hiding place of thun-
der;
I proved you at the *c*waters
of Meribah.   [Selah.
8 "*a*Hear, O My people, and I
will admonish you;
O Israel, if you *b*would listen to Me!
9 "Let there be no *a*strange
god among you;

Nor shall you worship any
foreign god.
10 "*a*I, the LORD, am your God,
Who brought you up from
the land of Egypt;
*b*Open your mouth wide
and I will *c*fill it.
11 "But My people *a*did not
listen to My voice;
And Israel did not obey
Me.
12 "So I *a*gave them over to the
stubbornness of their
heart,
To walk in their own de-
vices.
13 "Oh that My people *a*would
listen to Me,
That Israel would *b*walk in
My ways!
14 "I would quickly *a*subdue
their enemies,
And *b*turn My hand
against their adversar-
ies.
15 "*a*Those who hate the LORD
would *b*pretend obe-
dience to Him;
And their time *of punishment* would be for-
ever.
16 "But I would feed you with
the *a*finest of the
wheat;
And with *b*honey from the
rock I would satisfy
you."

10 *a*Ex. 20:2;
Deut. 5:6
*b*Job 29:23
*c*Ps. 37:4;
78:25; 107:9

11 *a*Deut.
32:15; Ps.
106:25

12 *a*Job 8:4;
Acts 7:42;
Rom. 1:24,
26

13 *a*Deut.
5:29; Ps.
81:8; Is.
48:18 *b*Ps.
128:1; Is.
42:24; Jer.
7:23

14 *a*Ps.
18:47; 47:3
*b*Amos 1:8

15 *a*Rom.
1:30 *b*Ps.
18:44; 66:3

16 *a*Deut.
32:14; Ps.
147:14
*b*Deut. 32:13

PSALM 82

A Psalm of Asaph.

★ **1** *a*Is.
3:13 *b*2 Chr.
19:6; Ps.
58:11 *c*Ex.
21:6; 22:8,
28

GOD takes His *a*stand in His
own congregation;
He *b*judges in the midst of
the *c*rulers.

---

*See note, p. 875.
81:3 *the new moon.* The beginning of the seventh month, when the trumpet was blown (see
note on Lev. 23:24). *At the full moon.* On the
fifteenth day, when the Feast of Tabernacles
began.
81:5 The *language* they did not know in Egypt
was the call to liberation from Egypt of verse
6.

Psalm 82 Like Psalm 58 this also relates to
the unjust judges who stand before God's judgment seat (v. 1) accused of injustice (vv. 2–5), and
who hear the divine verdict of death (vv. 6–7).
The psalmist petitions God to extend His just
judgment throughout the earth (v. 8).
82:1 *rulers.* A reference to the human rulers and
judges of the people (also v. 6; see notes on
Psalm 58:1 and John 10:34).

2 aPs. 58:1
bDeut. 1:17;
Prov. 18:5

2 How long will you ajudge
   unjustly,
   And bshow partiality to the
   wicked?   [Selah.

3 aDeut.
24:17; Ps.
10:18; Is.
11:4; Jer.
22:16

3 aVindicate the weak and
   fatherless;
   Do justice to the afflicted
   and destitute.

4 aJob
29:12

4 aRescue the weak and
   needy;
   Deliver them out of the
   hand of the wicked.

5 aPs. 14:4;
Jer. 4:22;
Mic. 3:1
bProv. 2:13;
Is. 59:9; Jer.
23:12 cPs.
11:3

5 They ado not know nor do
   they understand;
   They bwalk about in darkness;
   All the cfoundations of the
   earth are shaken.

6 aPs. 82:1;
John 10:34
bPs. 89:26

6 I asaid, "You are gods,
   And all of you are bsons of
   the Most High.

7 aJob
21:32; Ps.
49:12; Ezek.
31:14 bPs.
83:11

7 "Nevertheless ayou will die
   like men,
   And fall like any bone of
   the princes."

8 aPs. 12:5
bPs. 58:11;
96:13 cPs.
2:8; Rev.
11:15

8 aArise, O God, bjudge the
   earth!
   For it is Thou who dost
   cpossess all the na-
   tions.

PSALM 83

A Song, a Psalm of Asaph.

1 aPs. 28:1;
35:22 bPs.
109:1

O GOD, ado not remain quiet;
   bDo not be silent and, O
   God, do not be still.

2 aPs. 2:1;
Is. 17:12
bPs. 81:15
cJudg. 8:28;
Zech. 1:21

2 For, behold, Thine en-
   emies amake an up-
   roar;
   And bthose who hate Thee
   have cexalted them-
   selves.

3 aPs. 64:2;
Is. 29:15
bPs. 27:5;
31:20

3 They amake shrewd plans
   against Thy people,
   And conspire together
   against bThy trea-
   sured ones.

4 They have said, "Come,
   and alet us wipe them
   out as a nation,
   That the bname of Israel
   be remembered no
   more."

4 aEsth.
3:6; Ps. 74:8;
Jer. 48:2
bPs. 41:5;
Jer. 11:19

5 For they have aconspired
   together with one
   mind;
   Against Thee do they
   make a covenant:

5 aPs. 2:2;
Dan. 6:7

6 The tents of aEdom and
   the bIshmaelites;
   cMoab, and the dHagrites;

7 aGebal, and bAmmon, and
   cAmalek;
   dPhilistia with the inhabitants of eTyre;

★ 6-7
6 a2 Chr.
20:10; Ps.
137:7 bGen.
25:12-16
c2 Chr.
20:10
d1 Chr. 5:10
7 aJosh.
13:5; Ezek.
27:9 b2 Chr.
20:10
c1 Sam. 15:2
d1 Sam. 4:1;
29:1 eEzek.
27:3; Amos
1:9

8 aAssyria also has joined
   with them;
   They have become a help
   to the bchildren of
   Lot.   [Selah.

8 a2 Kin.
15:19 bDeut.
2:9

9 Deal with them aas with
   Midian,
   As bwith Sisera and Jabin,
   at the torrent of Ki-
   shon,

9 aJudg.
7:1-24
bJudg. 4:7,
15, 21-24

10 Who were destroyed at
   En-dor,
   Who abecame as dung for
   the ground.

10 aZeph.
1:17

11 Make their nobles like aO-
   reb and Zeeb,
   And all their princes like
   bZebah and Zal-
   munna,

11 aJudg.
7:25 bJudg.
8:12, 21

12 Who said, "aLet us possess
   for ourselves
   The bpastures of God."

12 a2 Chr.
20:11 bPs.
132:13

13 O my God, make them
   like the awhirling
   dust;
   Like bchaff before the
   wind.

13 aIs. 17:13
bJob 21:18;
Ps. 35:5; Is.
40:24; Jer.
13:24

14 Like afire that burns the
   forest,
   And like a flame that bsets
   the mountains on fire,

14 aIs. 9:18
bEx. 19:18;
Deut. 32:22

Psalm 83 Ringed by enemies, the psalmist
pleads with God for help (vv. 1-4), pictures the
confederacy (vv. 5-8), and prays for vengeance
(vv. 9-18).
83:6-7 *Edom.* See Introduction to the Book of
Obadiah. *Ishmaelites.* See note on Gen. 16:11.

Moab. See note on Amos 2:1. *Hagrites.* See
note on 1 Chron. 5:10. *Gebal.* An area between the Dead Sea and Petra. *Ammon.* See
note on Amos 1:13. *Amalek.* See note on
Exod. 17:8. *Philistia.* See note on 1 Sam. 4:1.
Tyre. See note on Ezek. 26:2.

15 *a*Job 9:17; Ps. 58:9

15 So pursue them *a*with Thy tempest,
And terrify them with Thy storm.

16 *a*Job 10:15; Ps. 109:29; 132:18

16 *a*Fill their faces with dishonor,
That they may seek Thy name, O LORD.

17 *a*Ps. 35:4; 70:2

17 Let them be *a*ashamed and dismayed forever;
And let them be humiliated and perish,

★18 *a*Ps. 59:13 *b*Ps. 86:10; Is. 45:21 *c*Ps. 9:2; 18:13; 97:9

18 That they may *a*know that *b*Thou alone, whose name is the LORD,
Art the *c*Most High over all the earth.

PSALM 84

For the choir director; on the Gittith.
A Psalm of the sons of Korah.

1 *a*Ps. 43:3; 132:5

HOW lovely are Thy *a*dwelling places,
O LORD of hosts!

2 *a*Ps. 42:1, 2; 63:1 *b*Ps. 42:2

2 My *a*soul longed and even yearned for the courts of the LORD;
My heart and my flesh sing for joy to the *b*living God.

3 *a*Ps. 43:4 *b*Ps. 5:2

3 The bird also has found a house,
And the swallow a nest for herself, where she may lay her young,
Even Thine *a*altars, O LORD of hosts,
*b*My King and my God.

4 *a*Ps. 65:4 *b*Ps. 42:5, 11

4 How *a*blessed are those who dwell in Thy house!

They are *b*ever praising Thee.   [Selah.

5 *a*Ps. 81:1 *b*Ps. 86:11; 122:1; Jer. 31:6

5 How blessed is the man whose *a*strength is in Thee;
In whose heart are the *b*highways *to Zion!*

★ 6 *a*Ps. 107:35; Joel 2:23

6 Passing through the valley of Baca, they make it a spring,
The *a*early rain also covers it with blessings.

7 *a*Prov. 4:18; Is. 40:31; John 1:16; 2 Cor. 3:18 *b*Ex. 34:23; Deut. 16:16; Ps. 42:2

7 They *a*go from strength to strength;
Every one of them *b*appears before God in Zion.

8 *a*Ps. 59:5; 80:4; 84:1 *b*Ps. 81:1

8 O *a*LORD God of hosts, hear my prayer;
Give ear, O *b*God of Jacob! [Selah.

★ 9 *a*Gen. 15:1; Ps. 3:3; 28:7; 59:11; 115:9-11 *b*1 Sam. 16:6; 2 Sam. 19:21; Ps. 2:2; 132:17

9 Behold our *a*shield, O God,
And look upon the face of *b*Thine anointed.

★10 *a*Ps. 27:4

10 For *a*a day in Thy courts is better than a thousand *outside.*
I would rather stand at the threshold of the house of my God,
Than dwell in the tents of wickedness.

11 *a*Is. 60:19, 20; Mal. 4:2; Rev. 21:23 *b*Gen. 15:1 *c*Ps. 85:9 *d*Ps. 34:9, 10

11 For the LORD God is *a*a sun and *b*shield;
The LORD gives grace and *c*glory;
*d*No good thing does He withhold from those who walk uprightly.

12 *a*Ps. 2:12; 40:4

12 O LORD of hosts,
How *a*blessed is the man who trusts in Thee!

83:18 *the LORD.* Heb., *Yahweh,* see note on Gen. 2:4.
 Psalm 84 This song of a pilgrim expresses his passion for God's house (vv. 1-4), his pilgrimage to God's house (vv. 5-8), and his praise in God's house (vv. 9-12). *Gittith.* See note on Psalm 8. *the sons of Korah.* See note on Psalm 42.
84:6 *the valley of Baca.* Not a specific place, but a reference either to a place of weeping (Baca

being from a root meaning "to weep") or a valley of desolation (Baca being the singular of "balsam trees," which grow in arid ground). The meaning is: the pilgrim turns his troubles into blessings.
84:9 *shield.* Speaks of protection. *anointed.* Refers immediately to the Davidic king (though ultimately to Christ).
84:10 *stand at the threshold.* As a humble suppliant.

PSALM 85

For the choir director.
A Psalm of the sons of Korah.

O LORD, Thou didst show [a]favor to Thy land;
Thou didst [b]restore the captivity of Jacob.

2 Thou didst [a]forgive the iniquity of Thy people;
Thou didst [b]cover all their sin. [Selah.

3 Thou didst [a]withdraw all Thy fury;
Thou didst [b]turn away from Thy burning anger.

4 [a]Restore us, O God of our salvation,
And [b]cause Thine indignation toward us to cease.

5 Wilt [a]Thou be angry with us forever?
Wilt Thou prolong Thine anger to all generations?

6 Wilt Thou not Thyself [a]revive us again,
That Thy people may [b]rejoice in Thee?

7 Show us Thy lovingkindness, O LORD,
And [a]grant us Thy salvation.

8 I will hear what God the LORD will say;
For He will [a]speak peace to His people, to His godly ones;
But let them not [b]turn back to folly.

9 Surely [a]His salvation is near to those who fear Him,
That [b]glory may dwell in our land.

10 [a]Lovingkindness and truth have met together;
[b]Righteousness and peace have kissed each other.

11 Truth [a]springs from the earth;
And righteousness looks down from heaven.

12 Indeed, [a]the LORD will give what is good;
And our [b]land will yield its produce.

13 [a]Righteousness will go before Him,
And will make His footsteps into a way.

PSALM 86

A Prayer of David.

INCLINE Thine ear, O LORD, and answer me;
For I am [b]afflicted and needy.

2 [a]Do preserve my soul, for I am a [b]godly man;
O Thou my God, save Thy servant who [c]trusts in Thee.

3 Be [a]gracious to me, O Lord,
For [b]to Thee I cry all day long.

4 Make glad the soul of Thy servant,
For to Thee, O Lord, [a]I lift up my soul.

5 For Thou, Lord, art [a]good, and [b]ready to forgive,
And [c]abundant in lovingkindness to all who call upon Thee.

Marginal references (left column):
1 [a]Ps. 77:7; 106:4 [b]Ezra 1:11; Ps. 14:7; 126:1; Jer. 30:18; Ezek. 39:25; Hos. 6:11; Joel 3:1
2 [a]Num. 14:19; 1 Kin. 8:34; Ps. 78:38; 103:3; Jer. 31:34 [b]Ps. 32:1
3 [a]Ps. 78:38; 106:23 [b]Ex. 32:12; Deut. 13:17; Ps. 106:23; Jon. 3:9
4 [a]Ps. 80:3,7 [b]Dan. 9:16
5 [a]Ps. 74:1; 79:5; 80:4
6 [a]Ps. 71:20; 80:18 [b]Ps. 33:1; 90:14; 149:2
7 [a]Ps. 106:4
8 [a]Ps. 29:11; Hag. 2:9; Zech. 9:10 [b]Ps. 78:57; 2 Pet. 2:21
★ 9-11
9 [a]Ps. 34:18; Is. 46:13 [b]Ps. 84:11; Hag. 2:7; Zech. 2:5; John 1:14

Marginal references (right column):
10 [a]Ps. 25:10; 89:14; Prov. 3:3 [b]Ps. 72:3; Is. 32:17
11 [a]Is. 45:8
12 [a]Ps. 84:11; James 1:17 [b]Lev. 26:4; Ps. 67:6; Ezek. 34:27; Zech. 8:12
13 [a]Ps. 89:14
1 [a]Ps. 17:6; 31:2; 71:2 [b]Ps. 40:17; 70:5
★ 2-15
2 [a]Ps. 25:20 [b]Ps. 4:3; 50:5 [c]Ps. 25:2; 31:14; 56:4
3 [a]Ps. 4:1; 57:1 [b]Ps. 25:5; 88:9
4 [a]Ps. 25:1; 143:8
5 [a]Ps. 25:8 [b]Ps. 130:4 [c]Ex. 34:6; Neh. 9:17; Ps. 103:8; 145:8; Joel 2:13; Jon. 4:2

Psalm 85 Written during some setback in the fortunes of the nation, this psalm recalls the deeds of God in the past (vv. 1-3), reflects on the distress of the present (vv. 4-7), and reassures concerning deliverance in the future (vv. 8-13).
85:9-11 When the *glory* (presence) of God reigns in the land, the people will experience the characteristics of verses 10-11 (fully so in the Millennium).

Psalm 86 The only psalm of David in Book III (see Introduction, "Contents"), this prayer opens (vv. 1-7) and closes (vv. 14-17) with petitions surrounding a section of adoration and thanksgiving (vv. 8-13).
86:2-15 *godly.* I.e., a loyal member of the people who enjoy God's covenant relationship and enjoy His *lovingkindness* (vv. 5, 13, 15; Heb., *hesed*, see note on Hos. 2:19).

6 aPs. 55:1

6 aGive ear, O Lord, to my prayer;
And give heed to the voice of my supplications!

7 aPs. 50:15; 77:2 bPs. 17:6

7 In athe day of my trouble I shall call upon Thee,
For bThou wilt answer me.

8 aEx. 15:11; 2 Sam. 7:22; 1 Kin. 8:23; Ps. 89:6; Jer. 10:6 bDeut. 3:24

8 There is ano one like Thee among the gods, O Lord;
Nor are there any works blike Thine.

9 aPs. 22:27; 66:4; Is. 66:23; Rev. 15:4

9 aAll nations whom Thou hast made shall come and worship before Thee, O Lord;
And they shall glorify Thy name.

10 aPs. 77:13 bEx. 15:11; Ps. 72:18; 77:14; 136:4 cDeut. 6:4; 32:39; Ps. 83:18; Is. 37:16; 44:6, 8; Mark 12:29; 1 Cor. 8:4

10 For Thou art agreat and bdoest wondrous deeds;
Thou alone cart God.

★11 aPs. 25:5 bJer. 32:39

11 aTeach me Thy way, O Lord;
I will walk in Thy truth;
bUnite my heart to fear Thy name.

12 aPs. 111:1

12 I will agive thanks to Thee, O Lord my God, with all my heart,
And will glorify Thy name forever.

13 aPs. 30:3

13 For Thy lovingkindness toward me is great,
And Thou hast adelivered my soul from the depths of Sheol.

14 aPs. 54:3

14 O God, arrogant men have arisen up against me,
And a band of violent men have sought my life,
And they have not set Thee before them.

15 aPs. 86:5

15 But Thou, O Lord, art a God amerciful and gracious,
Slow to anger and abundant in lovingkindness and truth.

16 aPs. 25:16 bPs. 68:35 cPs. 116:16

16 aTurn to me, and be gracious to me;
Oh bgrant Thy strength to Thy servant,
And save the cson of Thy handmaid.

17 aJudg. 6:17; Ps. 119:122 bPs. 112:10 cPs. 118:13

17 aShow me a sign for good, That those who hate me may bsee it, and be ashamed,
Because Thou, O Lord, chast helped me and comforted me.

PSALM 87

A Psalm of the sons of Korah. A Song.

★ 1-3

1 aPs. 78:69; Is. 28:16

His afoundation is in the holy mountains.

2 aPs. 78:67, 68

2 The Lord aloves the gates of Zion
More than all the *other* dwelling places of Jacob.

3 aIs. 60:1 bPs. 46:4; 48:8

3 aGlorious things are spoken of you,
O bcity of God. [Selah.

★ 4 aJob 9:13; Ps. 89:10; Is. 19:23-25 bPs. 45:12 cPs. 68:31

4 "I shall mention aRahab and Babylon among those who know Me;
Behold, Philistia and bTyre with cEthiopia:
'This one was born there.'"

5 aPs. 48:8

5 But of Zion it shall be said, "This one and that one were born in her";
And the Most High Himself will aestablish her.

6 aPs. 69:28; Is. 4:3; Ezek. 13:9

6 The Lord shall count when He aregisters the peoples,
"This one was born there." [Selah.

7 aPs. 68:25; 149:3 b2 Sam. 6:14; Ps. 30:11 cPs. 36:9

7 Then those who asing as well as those who bplay the flutes *shall say,*

86:11 *Unite my heart to fear Thy name.* I.e., May I have undivided reverence for Thee.

Psalm 87 In this psalm of praise of Jerusalem, the psalmist describes the glories of Zion (vv. 1-3), the nations and Zion (vv. 4-6), and the joy in Zion (v. 7).

87:1-3 God founded *Zion* (Isa. 14:32), God loves it, and God has spoken gloriously of it (Isa. 2:2-4; 4:2-6; 28:16).

87:4 *Rahab.* Stands for Egypt (see note on Isa. 51:9). In the Millennium all will be citizens (*born there*) of the kingdom.

"All my csprings *of joy* are in you."

PSALM 88

A Song. A Psalm of the sons of Korah.
For the choir director; according to Mahalath Leannoth.
A Maskil of Heman the Ezrahite.

1 aPs. 24:5;
27:9 bPs.
22:2; 86:3;
Luke 18:7

O LORD, the aGod of my salvation,
I have bcried out by day and in the night before Thee.

2 aPs. 18:6
bPs. 31:2;
86:1

2 Let my prayer acome before Thee;
bIncline Thine ear to my cry!

★ 3 aPs.
107:26 bPs.
107:18;
116:3

3 For my asoul has had enough troubles,
And bmy life has drawn near to Sheol.

4 aPs. 28:1;
143:7 bJob
29:12; Ps.
22:11

4 I am reckoned among those who ago down to the pit;
I have become like a man bwithout strength,

5 aPs.
31:12 Ps.
31:22; Is.
53:8

5 Forsaken aamong the dead,
Like the slain who lie in the grave,
Whom Thou dost remember no more,
And they are bcut off from Thy hand.

6 aPs.
86:13; Lam.
3:55 bPs.
143:3 cPs.
69:15

6 Thou hast put me in athe lowest pit,
In bdark places, in the cdepths.

7 aPs. 32:4;
39:10 bPs.
42:7

7 Thy wrath ahas rested upon me,
And Thou hast afflicted me with ball Thy waves. [Selah.

8 Thou hast removed amy acquaintances far from me;
Thou hast made me an bobject of loathing to them;
I am cshut up and cannot go out.

8 aJob
19:13, 19;
Ps. 31:11;
142:4 bJob
30:10 cPs.
142:7; Jer.
32:2; 36:5

9 My aeye has wasted away because of affliction;
I have bcalled upon Thee every day, O LORD;
I have cspread out my hands to Thee.

9 aPs. 6:7;
31:9 bPs.
22:2; 86:3
cJob 11:13;
Ps. 143:6

10 Wilt Thou perform wonders for the dead?
Will athe departed spirits rise *and* praise Thee? [Selah.

★10-12
10 aPs. 6:5;
30:9

11 Will Thy lovingkindness be declared in the grave,
Thy faithfulness in Abaddon?

12 Will Thy wonders be made known in the adarkness?
And Thy righteousness in the land of forgetfulness?

12 aJob
10:21; Ps.
88:6

13 But I, O LORD, have cried out ato Thee for help,
And bin the morning my prayer comes before Thee.

13 aPs. 30:2
bPs. 5:3;
119:147

14 O LORD, why adost Thou reject my soul?
Why dost Thou bhide Thy face from me?

14 aPs. 43:2;
44:9 bJob
13:24; Ps.
13:1; 44:24

15 I was afflicted and aabout to die from my youth on;
I suffer bThy terrors; I am overcome.

15 aProv.
24:11 bJob
6:4; 31:23

16 Thy aburning anger has passed over me;

16 a2 Chr.
28:11; Is.
13:13; Lam.
1:12 bLam.
3:54; Ezek.
37:11

Psalm 88 In this saddest psalm of the Psalter, the writer describes the calamities facing him (vv. 1-9) in the crisis that threatens his life (vv. 10-13), and expresses consternation concerning what is happening in his life (vv. 14-18). *Mahalath.* See note on Psalm 53. *Leannoth.* Means "to humble or afflict." *Maskil.* See note on Psalm 32. *Heman the Ezrahite.* A leader of the Korahite choral guild (1 Chron. 6:33, 37).
88:3 *Sheol.* That the psalmist's life was about to

terminate in death is seen by the number of words or concepts used that relate to the netherworld: *the pit* (vv. 4, 6), *the dead* (vv. 5, 10), *the grave* (not the word sheol, v. 5), *dark places* (v. 6), *depths* (v. 6), *Abaddon* (v. 11), *the darkness* (v. 12), and *the land of forgetfulness* (v. 12).
88:10-12 The point is the same as in Psalm 6:4-5 (see note there).

Thy terrors have [b]de-
stroyed me.

17 [a]Ps.
118:10-12
[b]Ps. 124:4
[c]Ps. 17:11;
22:12, 16

17 They have [a]surrounded
me [b]like water all day
long;
They have [c]encompassed
me altogether.

18 [a]Job
19:13; Ps.
88:8; 31:11;
38:11

18 Thou hast removed [a]lover
and friend far from
me;
My acquaintances are *in*
darkness.

PSALM 89

A Maskil of Ethan the Ezrahite.

1 [a]Ps.
59:16; 101:1
[b]Ps. 40:10
[c]Ps. 36:5;
88:11; 89:5,
8, 24, 33, 49;
92:2; 119:90;
Is. 25:1;
Lam. 3:23

I WILL [a]sing of the lovingkindness of the LORD for-
ever;
To all generations I will
[b]make known Thy
[c]faithfulness with my
mouth.

2 [a]Ps.
103:17 [b]Ps.
36:5; 119:90

2 For I have said, "[a]Loving-
kindness will be built
up forever;
In the heavens Thou wilt
establish Thy [b]faith-
fulness."

3 [a]1 Kin.
8:16 [b]Ps.
132:11

3 "I have made a covenant
with [a]My chosen;
I have [b]sworn to David My
servant,

4 [a]2 Sam.
7:16 [b]2 Sam.
7:13; Is. 9:7;
Luke 1:33

4 I will establish your [a]seed
forever,
And build up your [b]throne
to all generations."
[Selah.

★ 5-7

5 [a]Ps. 19:1;
97:6 [b]Ps.
149:1. [c]Job
5:1

5 And the [a]heavens will
praise Thy wonders,
O LORD;
Thy faithfulness also [b]in
the assembly of the
[c]holy ones.

6 For [a]who in the skies is
comparable to the
LORD?
Who among the [b]sons of
the mighty is like the
LORD,

6 [a]Ps. 86:8;
113:5 [b]Ps.
29:1; 82:1

7 A God [a]greatly feared in
the council of the [b]ho-
ly ones,
And [c]awesome above all
those who are around
Him?

7 [a]Ps. 47:2;
68:35; 76:7,
11 [b]Ps. 89:5
[c]Ps. 96:4

8 O Lord GOD of hosts, [a]who
is like Thee, O mighty
LORD?
Thy faithfulness also surrounds Thee.

8 [a]Ps.
35:10, 71:19

9 Thou dost rule the swelling of the sea;
When its waves rise, Thou
[a]dost still them.

9 [a]Ps. 65:7;
107:29

10 Thou Thyself didst crush
[a]Rahab like one who
is slain;
Thou didst [b]scatter Thine
enemies with Thy
mighty arm.

10 [a]Ps. 87:4;
Is. 30:7; 51:9
[b]Ps. 18:14;
68:1; 144:6

11 The [a]heavens are Thine,
the earth also is
Thine;
The [b]world and all it contains, Thou hast
founded them.

11 [a]Gen.
1:1; 1 Chr.
29:11; Ps.
96:5 [b]Ps.
24:1

12 The [a]north and the south,
Thou hast created
them;
[b]Tabor and [c]Hermon
[d]shout for joy at Thy
name.

12 [a]Job 26:7
[b]Josh.
19:22; Judg.
4:6; Jer.
46:18 [c]Deut.
3:8; Josh.
11:17; 12:1;
Ps. 133:3;
Song 4:8
[d]Ps. 98:8

13 Thou hast a strong arm;
Thy hand is mighty, Thy
[a]right hand is exalted.

13 [a]Ps. 98:1;
118:16

14 [a]Righteousness and justice
are the foundation of
Thy throne;

14 [a]Ps. 97:2
[b]Ps. 85:13

Psalm 89 In this royal psalm, the writer
praises the Lord for His covenant with David (vv.
1-4) and for His character (vv. 5-18); he then
rehearses the Davidic covenant in poetic form
(vv. 19-37; see note on 2 Sam. 7:12-16), laments
the king's present humiliating defeat (vv. 38-45),
and petitions the Lord to remember His covenant (vv. 46-51). *Maskil.* See note on Psalm 32.
Ethan the Ezrahite. Probably identical with Jeduthun (see note on Psalm 39) though referring
here to a descendant of the Ethan of David's
time (1 Chron. 15:19), since the disaster of verses
38-45 did not occur during David's reign but later, during the decline of Judah. Or the term may
refer to a choir guild bearing Ethan's name.
89:5-7 *holy ones . . . sons of the mighty . . . holy
ones.* References to angels (see note on Psalm
29:1).

^bLovingkindness and truth go before Thee.

15   How blessed are the people who know the ^ajoyful sound!
O LORD, they walk in the ^blight of Thy countenance.

16   In ^aThy name they rejoice all the day,
And by Thy righteousness they are exalted.

17   For Thou art the glory of ^atheir strength,
And by Thy favor our ^bhorn is exalted.

18   For our ^ashield belongs to the LORD,
And our king to the ^bHoly One of Israel.

19   Once Thou didst speak in vision to Thy godly ones,
And didst say, "I have given help to one who is ^amighty;
I have exalted one ^bchosen from the people.

20   "I have ^afound David My servant;
With My holy ^boil I have anointed him,

21   With whom ^aMy hand will be established;
My arm also will ^bstrengthen him.

22   "The enemy will not deceive him,
Nor the ^ason of wickedness afflict him.

23   "But I shall ^acrush his adversaries before him,
And strike those who hate him.

24   "And My ^afaithfulness and My lovingkindness will be with him,
And in My name his ^bhorn will be exalted.

25   "I shall also set his hand ^aon the sea,

And his right hand on the rivers.

26   "He will cry to Me, 'Thou art ^amy Father,
My God, and the ^brock of my salvation.'

27   "I also shall make him My ^afirst-born,
The ^bhighest of the kings of the earth.

28   "My ^alovingkindness I will keep for him forever,
And My ^bcovenant shall be confirmed to him.

29   "So I will establish his ^adescendants forever,
And his ^bthrone ^cas the days of heaven.

30   "If his sons ^aforsake My law,
And do not walk in My judgments,

31   If they violate My statutes,
And do not keep My commandments,

32   Then I will visit their transgression with the ^arod,
And their iniquity with stripes.

33   "But I will not break off ^aMy lovingkindness from him,
Nor deal falsely in My faithfulness.

34   "My ^acovenant I will not violate,
Nor will I ^balter the utterance of My lips.

35   "Once I have ^asworn by My holiness;
I will not lie to David.

36   "His ^adescendants shall endure forever,
And his ^bthrone ^cas the sun before Me.

37   "It shall be established forever ^alike the moon,
And the ^bwitness in the sky is faithful." [Selah.

Cross references (left margin):

15 ^aLev. 23:24; Num. 10:10; Ps. 98:6 ^bPs. 4:6; 44:3; 67:1; 80:3; 90:8

16 ^aPs. 105:3

★17 ^aPs. 28:8 ^bPs. 75:10; 92:10; 148:14

18 ^aPs. 47:9 ^bPs. 71:22; 78:41

★19 ^a2 Sam. 17:10 ^b1 Kin. 11:34; Ps. 78:70

20 ^a1 Sam. 13:14; 16:1-12; Acts 13:22 ^b1 Sam. 16:13

21 ^aPs. 18:35; 80:17 ^bPs. 18:32

22 ^a2 Sam. 7:10; Ps. 125:3

23 ^a2 Sam. 7:9; Ps. 18:40

24 ^aPs. 89:1 ^bPs. 132:17

25 ^aPs. 72:8

Cross references (right margin):

26 ^a2 Sam. 7:14; 1 Chr. 22:10; Jer. 3:19 ^b2 Sam. 22:47; Ps. 95:1

27 ^aEx. 4:22; Ps. 2:7; Jer. 31:9; Col. 1:15, 18 ^bNum. 24:7; Ps. 72:11; Rev. 19:16

28 ^aPs. 89:33 ^bPs. 89:3, 34

29 ^aPs. 18:50; 89:4, 36 ^b1 Kin. 2:4; Ps. 89:4; 132:12; Is. 9:7; Jer. 33:17 ^cDeut. 11:21

★30-37

30 ^a2 Sam. 7:14; Ps. 119:53

32 ^aJob 9:34; 21:9

33 ^a2 Sam. 7:15

34 ^aDeut. 7:9; Jer. 33:20, 21 ^bNum. 23:19

35 ^aPs. 60:6; Amos 4:2

36 ^aPs. 89:29; Luke 1:33 ^bPs. 72:5 ^cPs. 72:17

37 ^aPs. 72:5 ^bJob 16:19

89:17 *our horn.* Our strength.
89:19 *Thy godly ones.* If singular (as in some versions), the reference is to David; if plural, to the prophets Samuel and Nathan.

89:30-37 Though punishment will follow disobedience, the Davidic covenant will remain inviolable.

38 But Thou hast ᵃcast off and ᵇrejected,
Thou hast been full of wrath against Thine ᶜanointed.

39 Thou hast ᵃspurned the covenant of Thy servant;
Thou hast ᵇprofaned ᶜhis crown in the dust.

40 Thou hast ᵃbroken down all his walls;
Thou hast ᵇbrought his strongholds to ruin.

41 ᵃAll who pass along the way plunder him;
He has become a ᵇreproach to his neighbors.

42 Thou hast ᵃexalted the right hand of his adversaries;
Thou hast ᵇmade all his enemies rejoice.

43 Thou dost also turn back the edge of his sword,
And hast ᵃnot made him stand in battle.

44 Thou hast made his ᵃsplendor to cease,
And cast his throne to the ground.

45 Thou hast ᵃshortened the days of his youth;
Thou hast ᵇcovered him with shame.   [Selah.

46 ᵃHow long, O Lᴏʀᴅ?
Wilt Thou hide Thyself forever?
Will Thy ᵇwrath burn like fire?

47 ᵃRemember what my span of life is;
For what ᵇvanity Thou hast created all the sons of men!

48 What man can live and not ᵃsee death?

Can he ᵇdeliver his soul from the power of Sheol?   [Selah.

49 Where are Thy former lovingkindnesses, O Lord,
Which Thou didst ᵃswear to David in Thy faithfulness?

50 Remember, O Lord, the ᵃreproach of Thy servants;
How I do bear in my bosom *the reproach of* all the many peoples,

51 With which ᵃThine enemies have reproached, O Lᴏʀᴅ,
With which they have reproached the footsteps of ᵇThine anointed.

52 ᵃBlessed be the Lᴏʀᴅ forever!
Amen and Amen.

BOOK 4

Psalm 90

A Prayer of Moses the man of God.

Lᴏʀᴅ, Thou hast been our ᵃdwelling place in all generations.

2 Before ᵃthe mountains were born,
Or Thou ᵇdidst give birth to the earth and the world,
Even ᶜfrom everlasting to everlasting, Thou art God.

3 Thou dost ᵃturn man back into dust,

Marginal references:

★38-45
38 ᵃPs. 44:9
ᵇDeut. 32:19; 1 Chr. 28:9 ᶜPs. 20:6; 89:20, 51
39 ᵃPs. 78:59; Lam. 2:7 ᵇPs. 74:7 ᶜLam. 5:16
40 ᵃPs. 80:12 ᵇLam. 2:2, 5
41 ᵃPs. 80:12 ᵇPs. 44:13; 69:9, 19; 79:4
42 ᵃPs. 13:2 ᵇPs. 80:6
43 ᵃPs. 44:10
44 ᵃEzek. 28:7
45 ᵃPs. 102:23 ᵇPs. 44:15; 71:13; 109:29
46 ᵃPs. 13:1; 44:24 ᵇPs. 79:5; 80:4
47 ᵃJob 7:7; 10:9; 14:1 ᵇPs. 39:5; 62:9; Eccl. 1:2; 2:11
48 ᵃPs. 22:29; 49:9 ᵇPs. 49:15

49 ᵃ2 Sam. 7:15; Jer. 30:9; Ezek. 34:23
50 ᵃPs. 69:9; 74:18, 22
51 ᵃPs. 74:10, 18, 22 ᵇPs. 89:38
★52 ᵃPs. 41:13; 72:19; 106:48
1 ᵃDeut. 33:27; Ps. 71:3; 91:1; Ezek. 11:16
2 ᵃJob 15:7; Prov. 8:25 ᵇGen. 1:1; Ps. 102:25; 104:5 ᶜPs. 93:2; 102:24, 27; Jer. 10:10
★ 3 ᵃGen. 3:19; Job 34:14, 15; Ps. 104:29

89:38-45 This lament protests God's apparent spurning of His covenant because of some humiliating defeat suffered by the Davidic king.
89:52 This doxology closes Book III (see Introduction, "Contents").
Psalm 90 In this oldest of all the psalms, Moses acknowledges the eternality of God (vv.

1-2), the frailty of man (vv. 3-6), the sinfulness of man (vv. 7-8), the shortness of life (vv. 9-12), and prays for God's grace on His people (vv. 13-17).
90:3 In contrast to God, who is eternal (vv. 1-2), man is frail and will return to *dust,* according to the curse of Gen. 3:19.

★ 4 a2 Pet.
3:8 bPs.
39:5 cEx.
14:24; Judg.
7:19

And dost say, "Return, O children of men."

4 For ^aa thousand years in Thy sight
Are like ^byesterday when it passes by,
Or as a ^cwatch in the night.

5 aJob
22:16; 27:20
bJob 14:12;
20:8; Ps.
76:5 cPs.
103:15; Is.
40:6

5 Thou ^ahast swept them away like a flood, they ^bfall asleep;
In the morning they are like ^cgrass which sprouts anew.

6 aJob 14:2
bPs. 92:7;
Matt. 6:30
cJames 1:11

6 In the morning it ^aflourishes, and sprouts anew;
Toward evening it ^bfades, and ^cwithers away.

7 aPs.
39:11

7 For we have been ^aconsumed by Thine anger,
And by Thy wrath we have been dismayed.

8 aPs.
50:21; Jer.
16:17 bPs.
19:12; Eccl.
12:14

8 Thou hast ^aplaced our iniquities before Thee,
Our ^bsecret sins in the light of Thy presence.

9 aPs.
78:33

9 For ^aall our days have declined in Thy fury;
We have finished our years like a sigh.

★10 a2 Kin.
19:35 bEccl.
12:2-7; Jer.
20:18 cJob
20:8; Ps.
78:39

10 As for the days of our life, they contain seventy years,
Or if due to strength, ^aeighty years,
Yet their pride is but ^blabor and sorrow;
For soon it is gone and we ^cfly away.

★11 aPs.
76:7 bNeh.
5:9

11 Who understands the ^apower of Thine anger,
And Thy fury, according to the ^bfear that is due Thee?

12 So ^ateach us to number our days,
That we may ^bpresent to Thee a heart of wisdom.

★12 aDeut.
32:29; Ps.
39:4 bProv.
2:1-6

13 Do ^areturn, O LORD; ^bhow long will it be?
And be ^csorry for Thy servants.

13 aPs. 6:4;
80:14 bPs.
6:3; 74:10
cEx. 32:12;
Deut. 32:36;
Ps. 106:45;
135:14;
Amos 7:3, 6;
Jon. 3:9

14 O ^asatisfy us in the morning with Thy lovingkindness,
That we may ^bsing for joy and be glad all our days.

★14-17

14 aPs. 36:8;
65:4; 103:5;
Jer. 31:14
bPs. 31:7;
85:6

15 ^aMake us glad according to the days Thou hast afflicted us,
And the ^byears we have seen evil.

15 aPs. 86:4
bDeut. 2:14-
16; Ps. 31:10

16 Let Thy ^awork appear to Thy servants,
And Thy ^bmajesty to their children.

16 aDeut.
32:4; Ps.
44:1; 77:12;
92:4; Hab.
3:2 b1 Kin.
8:11; Is. 6:3

17 And let the ^afavor of the Lord our God be upon us;
And do ^bconfirm for us the work of our hands;
Yes, confirm the work of our hands.

17 aPs. 27:4
bPs. 37:23;
Is. 26:12;
1 Cor. 3:7

PSALM 91

He who dwells in the ^ashelter of the Most High
Will abide in the ^bshadow of the Almighty.

2 I will say to the LORD, "My ^arefuge and my ^bfortress,
My God, in whom I ^ctrust!"

3 For it is He who delivers you from the ^asnare of the trapper,

★ 1-2
1 aPs. 27:5;
31:20; 32:7
bPs. 17:8;
121:5; Is.
25:4; 32:2
2 aPs. 14:6;
91:9; 94:22;
142:5 bPs.
18:2; 31:3;
Jer. 16:19
cPs. 25:2;
56:4
3 aPs.
124:7; Prov.
6:5 b1 Kin.
8:37; 2 Chr.
20:9; Ps.
91:6

90:4 The longest span of any human life (Methuselah lived 969 years) is but a day to God, who is no more bound by time than is a man who sleeps through the night watch.
90:10 Extension of life is a mixed blessing.
90:11 Who takes to heart the intensity of God's wrath against sin and therefore gives Him due reverence?
90:12 Help us allot our days wisely.
90:14-17 When God deals with us in lovingkindness, life will be joyous (v. 14), it will be

viewed from His perspective (v. 16), and His blessing will be on our work (vv. 16-17).
Psalm 91 This psalm of trust may be outlined as follows: the bases of security found in the character (vv. 1-2) and care (vv. 3-8) of God; and the blessings of security (His protection, vv. 9-13, and His love, vv. 14-16).
91:1-2 Notice the four names for God: Most High (see note on Gen. 14:18), Almighty (see note on Gen. 17:1), LORD (see note on Gen. 2:4), God (see note on Gen. 1:1).

And from the deadly ^bpestilence.

^{4 a}Is. 51:16
^bPs. 17:8;
36:7; 57:1;
63:7 ^cPs.
40:11 ^dPs.
35:2

4 He will ^acover you with His pinions,
And ^bunder His wings you may seek refuge;
His ^cfaithfulness is a ^dshield and bulwark.

★ 5-7
^{5 a}Job
5:19-23; Ps.
23:4; 27:1
^bSong 3:8
^cPs. 64:4
^{6 a}2 Kin.
19:35; Ps.
91:10 ^bJob
5:22

5 You ^awill not be afraid of the ^bterror by night,
Or of the ^carrow that flies by day;

6 Of the ^apestilence that stalks in darkness,
Or of the ^bdestruction that lays waste at noon.

^{7 a}Gen.
7:23; Josh.
14:10

7 A thousand may fall at your side,
And ten thousand at your right hand;
But ^ait shall not approach you.

^{8 a}Ps.
37:34; 58:10

8 You will only look on with your eyes,
And ^asee the recompense of the wicked.

^{9 a}Ps. 91:2
^bPs. 90:1

9 For you have made the Lord, ^amy refuge,
Even the Most High, ^byour dwelling place.

^{10 a}Prov.
12:21

10 ^aNo evil will befall you,
Nor will any plague come near your tent.

★^{11 a}Ps.
34:7; Matt.
4:6; Luke
4:10, 11;
Heb. 1:14

11 For He will give ^aHis angels charge concerning you,
To guard you in all your ways.

^{12 a}Matt.
4:6; Luke
4:11

12 They will ^abear you up in their hands,
Lest you strike your foot against a stone.

^{13 a}Judg.
14:6; Dan.
6:22; Luke
10:19

13 You will ^atread upon the lion and cobra,
The young lion and the serpent you will trample down.

14 "^aBecause he has loved Me, therefore I will deliver him;
I will ^bset him securely on high, because he has ^cknown My name.

^{14 a}Ps.
145:20 ^bPs.
59:1 ^cPs.
9:10

15 "He will ^acall upon Me, and I will answer him;
I will be with him in trouble;
I will rescue him, and ^bhonor him.

^{15 a}Job
12:4; Ps.
50:15
^b1 Sam.
2:30; John
12:26

16 "With a ^along life I will satisfy him,
And ^blet him behold My salvation."

^{16 a}Deut.
6:2; Ps. 21:4;
Prov. 3:1, 2
^bPs. 50:23

PSALM 92

A Psalm, a Song for the Sabbath day.

^IT is ^agood to give thanks to the Lord,
And to ^bsing praises to Thy name, O Most High;

^{1 a}Ps.
147:1 ^bPs.
135:3

2 To ^adeclare Thy lovingkindness in the morning,
And Thy ^bfaithfulness by night,

^{2 a}Ps.
59:16 ^bPs.
89:1

3 With the ^aten-stringed lute, and with the ^aharp;
With resounding music upon the ^alyre.

★ ^{3 a}1 Sam.
10:5; 1 Chr.
13:8; Neh.
12:27; Ps.
33:2

4 For Thou, O Lord, hast made me glad by what Thou ^ahast done,
I will ^bsing for joy at the ^cworks of Thy hands.

^{4 a}Ps. 40:5;
90:16 ^bPs.
106:47 ^cPs.
8:6; 111:7;
143:5

5 How ^agreat are Thy works, O Lord!
Thy ^bthoughts are very ^cdeep.

^{5 a}Ps. 40:5;
111:2; Rev.
15:3 ^bPs.
33:11; 40:5;
139:17 ^cPs.
36:6; Rom.
11:33

91:5-7 In God we are secure at all times (v. 5), in all dangers (v. 6), and in all circumstances (v. 7).
91:11 See note on Heb. 1:14.
Psalm 92 Used on the Sabbath, this psalm of praise thanks God (vv. 1-3) for His judgment on the wicked (vv. 4-9) and His blessings on the righteous (vv. 10-15).
92:3 The use of instruments shows that this psalm was part of corporate worship.

★ 6 aPs.
49:10; 73:22;
94:8

6 A asenseless man has no
knowledge;
Nor does a astupid man
understand this:

7 aJob
12:6; Ps.
90:5 bPs.
94:4 cPs.
37:38

7 That when the wicked
asprouted up like
grass,
And all bwho did iniquity
flourished,
It was only that they might
be cdestroyed forever-
more.

8 aPs.
83:18; 93:4;
113:5

8 But Thou, O Lord, art aon
high forever.

9 aPs.
37:20 bPs.
68:1; 89:10

9 For, behold, Thine en-
emies, O Lord,
For, behold, aThine en-
emies will perish;
All who do iniquity will be
bscattered.

★10 aPs.
75:10; 89:17;
112:9 bPs.
23:5; 45:7

10 But Thou hast exalted my
ahorn like that of the
wild ox;
I have been banointed with
fresh oil.

11 aPs. 54:7;
91:8

11 And my eye has alooked
exultantly upon my
foes,
My ears hear of the evil-
doers who rise up
against me.

★12-14

12 aNum.
24:6; Ps. 1:3;
52:8; 72:7;
Jer. 17:8;
Hos. 14:5, 6
bPs. 104:16;
Ezek. 31:3
13 aPs.
80:15; Is.
60:21 bPs.
100:4;
116:19
14 aProv.
11:30; Is.
37:31; John
15:2; James
3:18
15 aPs. 25:8;
Job 34:10
bDeut. 32:4;
Ps. 18:2;
94:22 cRom.
9:14

12 The arighteous man will
flourish like the palm
tree,
He will grow like a bcedar
in Lebanon.

13 aPlanted in the house of
the Lord,
They will flourish bin the
courts of our God.

14 They will still ayield fruit
in old age;
They shall be full of sap
and very green,

15 To declare that athe Lord
is upright;

He is my brock, and there
is cno unrighteous-
ness in Him.

PSALM 93

THE Lord reigns, He is bclothed
with majesty;
The Lord has cclothed and
girded Himself with
strength;
Indeed, the dworld is
firmly established, it
will not be moved.

2 Thy athrone is established
from of old;
Thou bart from ever-
lasting.

3 The afloods have lifted up,
O Lord,
The floods have lifted up
their voice;
The floods lift up their
pounding waves.

4 More than the sounds of
many waters,
Than the mighty breakers
of the sea,
The Lord aon high is
mighty.

5 Thy atestimonies are fully
confirmed;
bHoliness befits Thy
house,
O Lord, forevermore.

PSALM 94

O LORD, God of avengeance;
God of vengeance, bshine
forth!
2 aRise up, O bJudge of the
earth;
Render recompense cto the
proud.

1 aPs.
96:10; 97:1;
99:1 bPs.
104:1 cPs.
65:6, Is. 51:9
dPs. 96:10

2 aPs. 45:6;
Lam. 5:19
bPs. 90:2

★ 3 aPs.
96:11;
98:7, 8

4 aPs. 65:7;
89:6, 9; 92:8

5 aPs. 19:7
bPs. 29:2;
96:9; 1 Cor.
3:17

1 aDeut.
32:35; Is.
35:4, Nah.
1:2, Rom.
12:19 bPs.
50:2; 80:1

2 aPs. 7:6
bGen. 18:25
cPs. 31:23

92:6 The senseless man fails to understand
God's majestic ways.
92:10 God exalts the horn (strength) of the
righteous and consecrates him for service
(anointed).
92:12–14 The righteous flourish and are strong
(v. 12); they are secure (v. 13) and fruitful (v.
14).
Psalm 93 In this psalm to God as King, the
psalmist exults in the sovereignty of God, who is

enthroned above the floods and who dwells in
the temple of holiness. He anticipates the millennial reign of Messiah.
93:3 The floods typify rebellious uprisings
against God.
Psalm 94 This lament may be outlined as
follows: the charge against the wicked (vv. 1–7);
the call to the wicked (vv. 8–11); the confidence
of the psalmist in God's justice (vv. 12–23).

3 aJob 20:5

3 How long shall the wicked,
O Lord,
How long shall the
awicked exult?

★ **4-7**

4 aPs.
31:18; 75:5
bPs. 10:3;
52:1

4 They pour forth *words*,
they aspeak arro-
gantly;
All who do wickedness
bvaunt themselves.

5 aIs. 3:15
bPs. 79:1

5 They acrush Thy people, O
Lord,
And baffict Thy heritage.

6 aIs. 10:2

6 They aslay the widow and
the stranger,
And murder the orphans.

7 aJob
22:13; Ps.
10:11

7 And athey have said, "The
Lord does not see,
Nor does the God of Jacob
pay heed."

8 aPs. 92:6

8 Pay heed, you asenseless
among the people;
And when will you under-
stand, astupid ones?

9 aEx. 4:11;
Prov. 20:12

9 He who aplanted the ear,
does He not hear?
He who formed the eye,
does He not see?

10 aPs. 44:2
bJob 35:11;
Is. 28:26

10 He who achastens the nations, will He not re-
buke,
Even He who bteaches
man knowledge?

11 aJob
11:11; 1 Cor.
3:20

11 The Lord aknows the
thoughts of man,
That they are a *mere*
breath.

12 aDeut.
8:5; Job
5:17; Ps.
119:71; Prov.
3:11, 12;
Heb. 12:5, 6
bPs. 119:171

12 Blessed is the man whom
aThou dost chasten, O
Lord,
And bdost teach out of
Thy law;

13 aJob
34:29; Hab.
3:16 bPs.
49:5 cPs.
9:15; 55:23

13 That Thou mayest grant
him arelief from the
bdays of adversity,
Until ca pit is dug for the
wicked.

14 a1 Sam.
12:22; Lam.
3:31; Rom.
11:2 bPs.
37:28

14 For athe Lord will not
abandon His people,
Nor will He bforsake His
inheritance.

15 For ajudgment will again
be righteous;
And all the upright in
heart will follow it.

15 aPs. 97:2;
Is. 42:3; Mic.
7:9

16 Who will astand up for me
against evildoers?
Who will take his stand for
me bagainst those
who do wickedness?

16 aNum.
10:35; Is.
28:21; 33:10
bPs. 17:13;
59:2

17 If athe Lord had not been
my help,
My soul would soon have
dwelt in *the abode of*
silence.

★**17** aPs.
124:1, 2

18 If I should say, "aMy foot
has slipped,"
Thy lovingkindness, O
Lord, will hold me up.

18 aPs.
38:16; 73:2

19 When my anxious
thoughts multiply
within me,
Thy aconsolations delight
my soul.

19 aIs.
57:18; 66:13

20 Can a athrone of destruction be allied with
Thee,
One bwhich devises mis-
chief by decree?

★**20-23**

20 aAmos
6:3 bPs.
50:16; 58:2

21 They aband themselves together against the life
of the righteous,
And bcondemn the inno-
cent to death.

21 aPs. 56:6;
59:3 bEx.
23:7; Ps.
106:38; Prov.
17:15; Matt.
27:4

22 But the Lord has been my
astronghold,
And my God the brock of
my refuge.

22 aPs. 9:9;
59:9 bPs.
18:2; 71:7

23 And He has abrought back
their wickedness upon
them,
And will bdestroy them in
their evil;
The Lord our God will de-
stroy them.

23 aPs. 7:16;
140:9, 11
bGen. 19:15

PSALM 95

O COME, let us asing for joy to
the Lord;

1 aPs. 66:1;
81:1 bPs.
89:26

94:4-7 The wicked are arrogant (v. 4) and cruel
(vv. 5-6), foolishly thinking that God does not
know what they are doing (v. 7; cf. v. 11).
94:17 *My soul would soon have dwelt in the
abode of silence.* I.e., I would soon have died.
94:20-23 The question of verse 20 (Why does

God allow evil rulers to use laws to make
wrong appear right?) is answered by acknowledging the existence of evil (v. 21), God's care
for His own (v. 22), and ultimate retribution
(v. 23).
Psalm 95 This hymn begins with a call to

Let us shout joyfully to *b*the rock of our salvation.

2 Let us *a*come before His presence *b*with thanksgiving;
Let us shout joyfully to Him *c*with psalms.

3 For the LORD is a *a*great God,
And a great King *b*above all gods,

4 In whose hand are the *a*depths of the earth;
The peaks of the mountains are His also.

5 The sea is His, for it was He *a*who made it;
And His hands formed the dry land.

6 Come, let us *a*worship and bow down;
Let us *b*kneel before the LORD our *c*Maker.

7 For He is our God,
And *a*we are the people of His *b*pasture, and the sheep of His hand.
*c*Today, if you would hear His voice,

8 Do not harden your hearts, as at *a*Meribah,
As in the day of *b*Massah in the wilderness;

9 "When your fathers *a*tested Me,
They tried Me, though they had seen My work.

10 "For *a*forty years I loathed *that* generation,
And said they are a people who err in their heart,

And they do not know My ways.

11 "Therefore I *a*swore in My anger,
Truly they shall not enter into My *b*rest."

PSALM 96

*a*SING to the LORD a *b*new song;
Sing to the LORD, all the earth.

2 Sing to the LORD, bless His name;
*a*Proclaim good tidings of His salvation from day to day.

3 Tell of *a*His glory among the nations,
His wonderful deeds among all the peoples.

4 For *a*great is the LORD, and *b*greatly to be praised;
He is to be *c*feared *d*above all gods.

5 For *a*all the gods of the peoples are idols,
But *b*the LORD made the heavens.

6 *a*Splendor and majesty are before Him,
Strength and beauty are in His sanctuary.

7 Ascribe to the LORD, O *a*families of the peoples,
*b*Ascribe to the LORD glory and strength.

8 Ascribe to the LORD the *a*glory of His name;
Bring an *b*offering, and come into His courts.

Cross-references (margin)

2 *a*Mic. 6:6; *b*Ps. 100:4; 147:7; Jon. 2:9 *c*Ps. 81:2; Eph. 5:19; James 5:13

3 *a*Ps. 48:1; 135:5; 145:3 *b*Ps. 96:4; 97:9

4 *a*Ps. 135:6

5 *a*Gen. 1:9, 10; Ps. 146:6; Jon. 1:9

6 *a*Ps. 96:9; 99:5, 9 *b*2 Chr. 6:13; Dan. 6:10; Phil. 2:10 *c*Ps. 100:3; 149:2; Is. 17:7; Hos. 8:14

★ 7 *a*Ps. 79:13 *b*Ps. 74:1 *c*Heb. 3:7-11, 15; 4:7

★ 8 *a*Ex. 17:2-7; Num. 20:13 *b*Ex. 17:7; Deut. 6:16

9 *a*Num. 14:22; Ps. 78:18; 1 Cor. 10:9

10 *a*Acts 7:36; 13:18; Heb. 3:10, 17

★11 *a*Num. 14:23, 28-30; Deut. 1:35; Heb. 4:3, 5 *b*Deut. 12:9

1 *a*1 Chr. 16:23-33 *b*Ps. 40:3

2 *a*Ps. 71:15

3 *a*Ps. 145:12

4 *a*Ps. 48:1; 145:3 *b*Ps. 18:3 *c*Ps. 89:7 *d*Ps. 95:3

★ 5 *a*1 Chr. 16:26; Jer. 10:11 *b*Ps. 115:15; Is. 42:5

6 *a*Ps. 104:1

7 *a*Ps. 22:27 *b*1 Chr. 16:28, 29; Ps. 29:1, 2

8 *a*Ps. 79:9; 115:1 *b*Ps. 45:12; 72:10

---

the people to praise the Lord (vv. 1–2) because of His sovereignty above all supposed gods (vv. 3–5); continues with a call to worship God (v. 6) because He is their Creator and Shepherd (v. 7a); and concludes with a warning to the present generation to avoid the unbelief of their forefathers (vv. 7b–11).

95:7 *hear.* Includes the idea of obedience.
95:8 *at Meribah.* See note on Exod. 17:2.
95:11 *My rest.* I.e., the promised land of Canaan, which the wilderness generation did not enter. See note on Heb. 4:5–9 for the application of this warning to the Christian.
Psalm 96 This psalm, parallel to 1 Chron.

16:23–33, contains three stanzas: the first, a call to the whole earth to praise the Lord (vv. 1–3) because of His righteousness (vv. 4–6); second, a call to the nations to worship the Lord (vv. 7–9) because of His righteous reign on the earth (v. 10); third, a call to nature to rejoice before the Lord (vv. 11–12) because He is coming to judge the earth in righteousness (v. 13). The psalm is Messianic in the sense that the future rule of God spoken of will be fulfilled in the rule of Messiah, who is Son of David and Son of God.
96:5 *idols.* Lit., nothings, denoting the unreality of the supposed gods of the nations.

9 aWorship the Lord in holy attire;
bTremble before Him, all the earth.

10 Say among the nations,
"aThe Lord reigns;
Indeed, the aworld is firmly established, it will not be moved;
He will bjudge the peoples with equity."

11 Let the aheavens be glad, and let the bearth rejoice;
Let cthe sea roar, and all it contains;

12 Let the afield exult, and all that is in it.
Then all the btrees of the forest will sing for joy

13 Before the Lord, afor He is coming;
For He is coming to judge the earth.
bHe will judge the world in righteousness,
And the peoples in His faithfulness.

Psalm 97

a
THE Lord reigns; let the bearth rejoice;
Let the many cislands be glad.

2 aClouds and thick darkness surround Him;
bRighteousness and justice are the foundation of His throne.

3 aFire goes before Him,
And bburns up His adversaries round about.

4 His alightnings lit up the world;

The earth saw and btrembled.

5 The mountains amelted like wax at the presence of the Lord,
At the presence of the bLord of the whole earth.

6 The aheavens declare His righteousness,
And ball the peoples have seen His glory.

7 Let all those be ashamed who serve agraven images,
Who boast themselves of bidols;
cWorship Him, all you gods.

8 Zion heard this and awas glad,
And the daughters of Judah have rejoiced
Because of Thy judgments, O Lord.

9 For Thou art the Lord aMost High over all the earth;
Thou art exalted far babove all gods.

10 aHate evil, you who love the Lord,
Who bpreserves the souls of His godly ones;
He cdelivers them from the hand of the wicked.

11 aLight is sown like seed for the righteous,
And bgladness for the upright in heart.

12 Be aglad in the Lord, you righteous ones;
And bgive thanks to His holy name.

96:9 in holy attire. See note on 29:2.
96:13 to judge. In the sense of govern.
Psalm 97 This hymn of God's kingship opens with a call for all the earth to rejoice at the establishment of the kingdom of the Lord (v. 1), whose presence is described in theophany-like language (vv. 2-6); describes the effects of His kingdom in relation to the wicked (v. 7) and the righteous (vv. 8-9); and concludes with an exhor-

tation to hate evil and praise the Lord (vv. 10-12).
97:2-6 The eschatological kingdom will be characterized by morality and universality.
97:7 gods (also in v. 9). Either a reference to angels (cf. Heb. 1:6) or to heathen gods (Psalm 96:5) or to all supernatural creatures, whether angels or nonexistent gods.

PSALM 98

A Psalm.

1 a Ps. 33:3
b Ps. 40:5;
96:3 c Ex.
15:6 d Is.
52:10

O SING to the LORD a *new song,
For He has done *b*wonderful things,
His *c*right hand and His *d*holy arm have gained the victory for Him.

2 a Is. 52:10
b Is. 62:2;
Rom. 3:25

2 *a*The LORD has made known His salvation;
He has *b*revealed His righteousness in the sight of the nations.

★ **3** a Luke
1:54, 72
b Ps. 22:27

3 He has *a*remembered His lovingkindness and His faithfulness to the house of Israel;
*b*All the ends of the earth have seen the salvation of our God.

4 a Ps.
100:1 b Is.
44:23

4 *a*Shout joyfully to the LORD, all the earth;
*b*Break forth and sing for joy and sing praises.

5 a Ps. 92:3
b Is. 51:3

5 Sing praises to the LORD with the *a*lyre;
With the lyre and the *b*sound of melody.

6 a Num.
10:10; 2 Chr.
15:14 b Ps.
66:1 c Ps.
47:7

6 With *a*trumpets and the sound of the horn
*b*Shout joyfully before *c*the King, the LORD.

★ **7-8**

7 a Ps.
96:11 b Ps.
24:1

7 Let the *a*sea roar and all it contains,
The *b*world and those who dwell in it.

8 a Ps. 93:3;
Is. 55:12
b Ps. 65:12;
89:12

8 Let the *a*rivers clap their hands;
Let the *b*mountains sing together for joy

9 a Ps.
96:13 b Ps.
96:10

9 Before the LORD; for He is coming to *a*judge the earth;
He will judge the world with righteousness,
And *b*the peoples with equity.

PSALM 99

★ **1** a Ps.
97:1 b Ex.
25:22;
1 Sam. 4:4;
Ps. 80:1

a THE LORD reigns, let the peoples tremble;
He *b*is enthroned *above* the cherubim, let the earth shake!

2 a Ps. 48:1;
Is. 12:6 b Ps.
97:9; 113:4

2 The LORD is *a*great in Zion,
And He is *b*exalted above all the peoples.

★ **3** a Deut.
28:58; Ps.
76:1 b Lev.
19:2; Josh.
24:19;
1 Sam. 2:2;
Ps. 22:3; Is.
6:3

3 Let them praise Thy *a*great and awesome name;
*b*Holy is He.

4 a Ps. 11:7;
33:5 b Ps.
17:2; 98:9
c Ps. 103:6;
146:7; Jer.
23:5

4 And the strength of the King *a*loves justice;
Thou hast established *b*equity;
Thou hast *c*executed justice and righteousness in Jacob.

5 a Ps. 34:3;
107:32;
118:28 b Ps.
132:7 c Ps.
99:3

5 *a*Exalt the LORD our God,
And *b*worship at His footstool;
*c*Holy is He.

6 a Jer. 15:1
b Ex. 24:6-8;
29:26; 40:23-
27; Lev. 8:1-
30 c Jer. 15:1
d 1 Sam. 7:9;
12:18; Ps.
22:4, 5 e Ex.
15:25; 32:30-
34

6 *a*Moses and Aaron were among His *b*priests,
And *c*Samuel was among those who *d*called on His name;
They *e*called upon the LORD, and He answered them.

★ **7-9**

7 a Ex. 33:9;
Num. 12:5
b Ps. 105:28

7 He *a*spoke to them in the pillar of cloud;
They *b*kept His testimonies,

Psalm 98 This hymn praises God as Deliverer (vv. 1–3), as King (vv. 4–6), and as Ruler (vv. 7–9).
98:3 *lovingkindness.* His covenant faithfulness (see note on Hos. 2:19).
98:7-8 Nature will rejoice in its release when Christ rules in His millennial kingdom (see note on Rom. 8:20).
Psalm 99 This hymn of God's kingship contains three stanzas: the declaration of the majesty of God (vv. 1–3), the description of the rule of

God (vv. 4–5), and the dealings with Israel of the God who is holy (vv. 6–9). The psalm views God's reign over Israel in O.T. times, as well as the future millennial reign of Christ.
99:1 *cherubim.* See note on Ezek. 1:5.
99:3 *Holy.* Basically means separation from what is common or unclean. Referring here (and vv. 5 and 9) to God, it denotes Him as the pure and eternal One, distinct from all others.
99:7-9 Yet this holy God answers prayers and forgives sinners.

And the statute that He gave them.

8 O Lord our God, Thou didst *a*answer them; Thou wast a *b*forgiving God to them, And *yet* an *c*avenger of their *evil* deeds.

9 Exalt the Lord our God, And worship at His holy hill; For holy is the Lord our God.

PSALM 100

A Psalm for Thanksgiving.

*a*SHOUT joyfully to the Lord, all the earth.

2 *a*Serve the Lord with gladness; *b*Come before Him with joyful singing.

3 Know that *a*the Lord Himself is God; It is He who has *b*made us, and not we ourselves; *We are* *c*His people and the sheep of His pasture.

4 Enter His gates *a*with thanksgiving, *And* His courts with praise. Give thanks to Him; *b*bless His name.

5 For *a*the Lord is good; *b*His lovingkindness is everlasting, And His *c*faithfulness to all generations.

PSALM 101

A Psalm of David.

I WILL *a*sing of lovingkindness and justice, To Thee, O Lord, I will sing praises.

2 I will *a*give heed to the blameless way. When wilt Thou come to me? I will walk within my house in the *b*integrity of my heart.

3 I will set no *a*worthless thing before my eyes; I hate the work of those who *b*fall away; It shall not fasten its grip on me.

4 A *a*perverse heart shall depart from me; I will know no evil.

5 Whoever secretly *a*slanders his neighbor, him I will destroy; No one who has a *b*haughty look and an arrogant heart will I endure.

6 My eyes shall be upon the faithful of the land, that they may dwell with me; He who walks in a *a*blameless way is the one who will minister to me.

7 He who *a*practices deceit shall not dwell within my house;

Marginal references:

8 *a*Ps. 106:44 *b*Num. 14:20; Ps. 78:38 *c*Ex. 32:28; Num. 20:12; Ps. 95:11; 107:12

1 *a*Ps. 95:1; 98:4, 6

2 *a*Deut. 12:11, 12; 28:47 *b*Ps. 95:2

★ 3 *a*Deut. 4:35; 1 Kin. 18:39; Ps. 46:10 *b*Job 10:3, 8; Ps. 95:6; 119:73 *c*Ps. 74:1, 2; 95:7; Is. 40:11; Ezek. 34:30, 31

4 *a*Ps. 95:2; 116:17 *b*Ps. 96:2

★ 5 *a*1 Chr. 16:34; 2 Chr. 5:13; 7:3; Ezra 3:11; Ps. 25:8; 86:5; 106:1; 107:1; 118:1; Jer. 33:11; Nah. 1:7 *b*Ps. 136:1 *c*Ps. 119:90

1 *a*Ps. 51:14; 89:1; 145:7

2 *a*1 Sam. 18:5, 14 *b*1 Kin. 9:4

3 *a*Deut. 15:9 *b*Josh. 23:6; Ps. 40:4

4 *a*Prov. 11:20

5 *a*Ps. 50:20; Jer. 9:4 *b*Ps. 10:4; 18:27; Prov. 6:17

★ 6-7

6 *a*Ps. 119:1

7 *a*Ps. 43:1; 52:2 *b*Ps. 52:4, 5

Psalm 100 This brief but beloved psalm calls on all men to praise and worship the Lord. (Yahweh; see note on Gen. 2:4) because He is God (vv. 1-3) and because He is good (vv. 4-5).
100:3 That Yahweh is the true God is seen by His power to create and to relate to Israel as Shepherd.
100:5 The goodness of God is seen in His steadfast *lovingkindness* (see note on Hos. 2:19)

and *faithfulness.*
Psalm 101 A manifesto of ethical standards of King David for himself (vv. 1-4) and for his administration (vv. 5-8), only perfectly practiced by Messiah in His future kingdom.
101:6-7 David resolves to surround himself with counsellors who are faithful, righteous, honest, and truthful.

He who speaks falsehood
*b*shall not maintain
his position before
me.

★ 8 *a*Jer.
21:12 *b*Ps.
75:10 *c*Ps.
118:10-12
*d*Ps. 46:4;
48:2, 8

8   *a*Every morning I will *b*destroy all the wicked of
the land,
So as to *c*cut off from the
*d*city of the Lord all
those who do iniquity.

PSALM 102

A Prayer of the Afflicted, when
he is faint, and
pours out his complaint before
the Lord.

1 *a*Ps.
39:12; 61:1
*b*Ex. 2:23;
1 Sam. 9:16

2 *a*Ps.
69:17 *b*Ps.
31:2 *c*Ps.
69:17

*a*HEAR my prayer, O Lord!
And let my cry for help
*b*come to Thee.

2   *a*Do not hide Thy face
from me in the day of
my distress;
*b*Incline Thine ear to me;
In the day when I call *c*answer me quickly.

★ 3-9
3 *a*Ps.
37:20; James
4:14 *b*Job
30:30; Lam.
1:13
4 *a*Ps. 90:5,
6 *b*Ps. 37:2;
Is. 40:7
*c*1 Sam. 1:7;
2 Sam.
12:17; Ezra
10:6; Job
33:20

5 *a*Job
19:20; Lam.
4:8

6 *a*Is.
34:11; Zeph.
2:14

7 *a*Ps. 77:4

3   For my days *a*have been
consumed in smoke,
And my *b*bones have been
scorched like a hearth.

4   My heart *a*has been smitten like grass and has
*b*withered away,
Indeed, I *c*forget to eat my
bread.

5   Because of the loudness of
my groaning
My *a*bones cling to my
flesh.

6   I resemble a *a*pelican of the
wilderness;
I have become like an owl
of the waste places.

7   I *a*lie awake,
I have become like a lonely
bird on a housetop.

8   My enemies *a*have reproached me all day
long;
Those who *b*deride me
have used my *name* as
a *c*curse.

8 *a*Ps.
31:11 *b*Acts
26:11
*c*2 Sam.
16:5; Is.
65:15; Jer.
29:22

9   For I have eaten ashes like
bread,
And *a*mingled my drink
with weeping,

9 *a*Ps. 42:3;
80:5

10   *a*Because of Thine indignation and Thy wrath;
For Thou hast *b*lifted me
up and cast me away.

10 *a*Ps. 38:3
*b*Job 27:21;
30:22

11   My days are like a *a*lengthened shadow;
And I *b*wither away like
grass.

11 *a*Job
14:2; Ps.
109:23 *b*Ps.
102:4

12   But Thou, O Lord, dost
*a*abide forever;
And Thy *b*name to all generations.

★12-22
12 *a*Ps. 9:7;
10:16; Lam.
5:19 *b*Ex.
3:15; Ps.
135:13

13   Thou wilt *a*arise *and* have
*b*compassion on Zion;
For *c*it is time to be gracious to her,
For the *d*appointed time
has come.

13 *a*Ps. 12:5;
44:26 *b*Is.
60:10; Zech.
1:12 *c*Ps.
119:126 *d*Ps.
75:2; Dan.
8:19

14   Surely Thy servants find
pleasure in her stones,
And feel pity for her dust.

15   So the *a*nations will fear
the name of the Lord,
And *b*all the kings of the
earth Thy glory.

15 *a*1 Kin.
8:43; Ps.
67:7 *b*Ps.
138:4

16   For the Lord has *a*built up
Zion;
He has *b*appeared in His
glory.

16 *a*Ps.
147:2 *b*Is.
60:1, 2

17   He has *a*regarded the
prayer of the desti-
tute,
And has not despised their
prayer.

17 *a*Neh.
1:6; Ps.
22:24

101:8 Justice would be dispensed daily.
Psalm 102 The psalmist here prays to God
in his distress (vv. 1-11), and finds his confidence
in the sovereign purpose of God (vv. 12-22) and
in His unchangeableness (vv. 23-28).
102:3-9 In these verses the psalmist describes
his fever (v. 3), his frailty (v. 4), his pain (v. 5),

his loneliness (v. 6), his sleeplessness (v. 7),
and his rejection and sorrow (vv. 8-9).
102:12-22 Two features of the millennial kingdom stand out in this paragraph: Jerusalem
will be restored, and the entire world will worship the Lord.

18 This will be ^awritten for the ^bgeneration to come;
That ^ca people yet to be created may praise the LORD.

19 For He ^alooked down from His holy height;
^bFrom heaven the LORD gazed upon the earth,

20 To hear the ^agroaning of the prisoner;
To ^bset free those who were doomed to death;

21 That *men* may ^atell of the name of the LORD in Zion,
And His praise in Jerusalem;

22 When ^athe peoples are gathered together,
And the kingdoms, to serve the LORD.

23 He has weakened my strength in the way;
He has ^ashortened my days.

24 I say, "O my God, ^ado not take me away in the midst of my days,
Thy ^byears are throughout all generations.

25 "Of old Thou didst ^afound the earth;
And the ^bheavens are the work of Thy hands.

26 "Even they will ^aperish, but Thou dost endure;
And all of them will wear out like a garment;
Like clothing Thou wilt change them, and they will be changed.

27 "But Thou art ^athe same,
And Thy years will not come to an end.

28 "The ^achildren of Thy servants will continue,
And their ^bdescendants will be established before Thee."

PSALM 103

A Psalm of David.

^aBLESS the LORD, O my soul;
And all that is within me,
bless His ^bholy name.

2 Bless the LORD, O my soul,
And ^aforget none of His benefits;

3 Who ^apardons all your iniquities;
Who ^bheals all your diseases;

4 Who ^aredeems your life from the pit;
Who ^bcrowns you with lovingkindness and compassion;

5 Who ^asatisfies your years with good things,
So that your youth is ^brenewed like the eagle.

6 The LORD ^aperforms righteous deeds,
And judgments for all who are ^boppressed.

7 He ^amade known His ways to Moses,
His ^bacts to the sons of Israel.

8 The LORD is ^acompassionate and gracious,
^bSlow to anger and abounding in lovingkindness.

9 He ^awill not always strive *with us;*

---

18. ^aDeut. 31:19; Rom. 15:4; 1 Cor. 10:11 ^bPs. 22:30; 48:13 ^cPs. 22:31; 78:6f.

19. ^aDeut. 26:15; Ps. 14:2; 53:2 ^bPs. 33:13

20. ^aPs. 79:11 ^bPs. 146:7

21. ^aPs. 22:22

22. ^aPs. 22:27; 86:9; Is. 49:22, 23; 60:3; Zech. 8:20-23

★23-28
23. ^aPs. 39:5

24. ^aPs. 39:13; Is. 38:10 ^bJob 36:26; Ps. 90:2; 102:12; Hab. 1:12

25. ^aGen. 1:1; Neh. 9:6; Heb. 1:10-12 ^bPs. 96:5

26. ^aIs. 34:4; 51:6; Matt. 24:35; 2 Pet. 3:10; Rev. 20:11

27. ^aIs. 41:4; 43:10; Mal. 3:6; James 1:17

28. ^aPs. 69:36 ^bPs. 89:4

★1 ^aPs. 104:1, 35 ^bPs. 33:21; 105:3; 145:21; Ezek. 36:21; 39:7
2 ^aDeut. 6:12; 8:11
★3 ^aEx. 34:7; 86:5; 130:8; Is. 43:25 ^bEx. 15:26; Ps. 30:2; Jer. 30:17
4 ^aPs. 49:15 ^bPs. 5:12
5 ^aPs. 107:9; 145:16 ^bIs. 40:31
6 ^aPs. 99:4; 146:7 ^bPs. 12:5
7 ^aEx. 33:13; Ps. 99:7; 147:19 ^bPs. 78:11; 106:22
8 ^aEx. 34:6; Num. 14:18; Neh. 9:17; Ps. 86:15; Jon. 4:2; James 5:11 ^bPs. 145:8; Joel 2:13; Nah. 1:3
★9 ^aPs. 30:5; Is. 57:16 ^bJer. 3:5, 12; Mic. 7:18

102:23-28 The psalmist contrasts the brevity of his own life (vv. 23-24) with the unchangeableness of the eternal God (vv. 25-27, attributed to Jesus Christ in Heb. 1:10-12).
Psalm 103 This magnificent hymn praises God for His personal blessings (vv. 1-5), for His national blessings (vv. 6-7), for His forgiving love (vv. 8-14), for His eternal love (vv. 15-18),

and concludes with a universal call to praise (vv. 19-22).
103:1 *Bless the LORD.* Adore and thank Him for all benefits.
103:3 *diseases.* Spiritual afflictions, parallel with *iniquities.*
103:9 God does not continue to nurse His grievances.

Nor will He ᵇkeep *His anger* forever.

10 He has ᵃnot dealt with us
according to our sins,
Nor rewarded us according
to our iniquities.

11 For as high ᵃas the heavens
are above the earth,
So great is His lovingkindness toward those
who fear Him.

12 As far as the east is from
the west,
So far has He ᵃremoved
our transgressions
from us.

13 Just ᵃas a father has compassion on *his* chil-
dren,
So the Lᴏʀᴅ has compas-
sion on those who
fear Him.

14 For ᵃHe Himself knows
our frame;
He ᵇis mindful that we are
but ᶜdust.

15 As for man, his days are
ᵃlike grass;
As a ᵇflower of the field, so
he flourishes.

16 When the ᵃwind has
passed over it, it is no
more;
And its ᵇplace acknowl-
edges it no longer.

17 But the ᵃlovingkindness of
the Lᴏʀᴅ is from ever-
lasting to everlasting
on those who fear
Him,
And His righteousness ᵇto
children's children,

18 To ᵃthose who keep His
covenant,
And who remember His
precepts to do them.

19 The Lᴏʀᴅ has established
His ᵃthrone in the
heavens;
And His ᵇsovereignty rules
over all.

20 Bless the Lᴏʀᴅ, you ᵃHis
angels,
ᵇMighty in strength, who
ᶜperform His word,
ᵈObeying the voice of His
word!

21 Bless the Lᴏʀᴅ, all you ᵃHis
hosts,
You ᵇwho serve Him,
doing His will.

22 Bless the Lᴏʀᴅ, ᵃall you
works of His,
In all places of His dominion;
Bless the Lᴏʀᴅ, O my soul!

PSALM 104

Bᴸᴇss the Lᴏʀᴅ, O my soul!
O Lᴏʀᴅ my God, Thou art
very great;
Thou art ᵇclothed with
splendor and majesty,

2 Covering Thyself with
ᵃlight as with a cloak,
ᵇStretching out heaven
like a *tent* curtain.

3 He ᵃlays the beams of His
upper chambers in the
waters;
He makes the ᵇclouds His
chariot;
He walks upon the ᶜwings
of the wind;

4 He makes ᵃthe winds His
messengers,
Flaming ᵇfire His minis-
ters.

5 He ᵃestablished the earth
upon its foundations,

Marginal references:

10 ᵃEzra 9:13; Lam. 3:22

★11 ᵃPs. 36:5; 57:10

12 ᵃ2 Sam. 12:13; Is. 38:17; 43:25; Zech. 3:9; Heb. 9:26

13 ᵃMal. 3:17

14 ᵃIs. 29:16 ᵇPs. 78:39 ᶜGen. 3:19; Eccl. 12:7

15 ᵃPs. 90:5; Is. 40:6; 1 Pet. 1:24 ᵇJob 14:2; James 1:10, 11

16 ᵃIs. 40:7 ᵇJob 7:10; 8:18; 20:9

★17 ᵃPs. 25:6 ᵇEx. 20:6; Deut. 5:10; Ps. 105:8

18 ᵃDeut. 7:9; Ps. 25:10

19 ᵃPs. 11:4 ᵇPs. 47:2, 8; Dan. 4:17, 25

20 ᵃPs. 148:2 ᵇPs. 29:1; 78:25 ᶜMatt. 6:10 ᵈPs. 91:11; Heb. 1:14

★21 ᵃ1 Kin. 22:19; Neh. 9:6; Ps. 148:2; Luke 2:13 ᵇPs. 104:4

22 ᵃPs. 145:10

1 ᵃPs. 103:22 ᵇPs. 93:1

2 ᵃDan. 7:9 ᵇIs. 40:22

3 ᵃAmos 9:6 ᵇIs. 19:1 ᶜPs. 18:10

★4 ᵃPs. 148:8; Heb. 1:7 ᵇ2 Kin. 2:11; 6:17

5 ᵃJob 38:4; Ps. 24:2

103:11 *fear.* Reverential awe and trust (also vv. 13, 17).
103:17 *from everlasting to everlasting.* The basis of His children's security.
103:21 *hosts, You who serve Him.* Other angels.
Psalm 104 In this hymn of praise, a poetic parallel to Gen. 1, the psalmist portrays the Lᴏʀᴅ as the One who created the heavens (vv. 1-4) and the earth (vv. 5-9), who adapted the earth for the needs of all living creatures (vv. 10-23), who has dominion over all creation (vv. 24-32), and is worthy of praise (vv. 33-35).
104:4 See note on Heb. 1:7.

So that it will not totter
forever and ever.

★ 6 aGen.
1:2

6 Thou ªdidst cover it with
the deep as with a
garment;
The waters were standing
above the mountains.

7 aPs.
18:15; 106:9;
Is. 50:2 bPs.
29:3; 77:18

7 At Thy ªrebuke they fled;
At the bsound of Thy
thunder they hurried
away.

8 aPs. 33:7

8 The mountains rose; the
valleys sank down
To the ªplace which Thou
didst establish for
them.

9 aJob
38:10, 11;
Jer. 5:22

9 Thou didst set a ªbounda-
ry that they may not
pass over;
That they may not return
to cover the earth.

10 aPs.
107:35; Is.
41:18

10 He sends forth ªsprings in
the valleys;
They flow between the
mountains;

11 aPs.
104:13 bJob
39:5

11 They ªgive drink to every
beast of the field;
The bwild donkeys quench
their thirst.

12 aMatt.
8:20

12 Beside them the birds of
the heavens ªdwell;
They lift up their voices
among the branches.

13 aPs. 65:9;
147:8 bJer.
10:13

13 He ªwaters the mountains
from His upper cham-
bers;
bThe earth is satisfied with
the fruit of His works.

14 aJob
38:27; Ps.
147:8 bGen.
1:29 cJob
28:5

14 He causes the ªgrass to
grow for the cattle,
And bvegetation for the labor of man,
So that he may bring forth
food cfrom the earth,

15 aJudg.
9:13; Prov.
31:6; Eccl.
10:19 bPs.
23:5; 92:10;
141:5; Luke
7:46 cGen.
18:5; Judg.
19:5, 8

15 And ªwine which makes
man's heart glad,
bSo that he may make his
face glisten with oil,
And food which csustains
man's heart.

16 The trees of the LORD drink
their fill,

The cedars of Lebanon
which He planted,

17 aPs.
104:12 bLev.
11:19

17 Where the ªbirds build
their nests,
And the bstork, whose
home is the fir trees.

18 aJob 39:1
bProv. 30:26
cLev. 11:5

18 The high mountains are
for the ªwild goats;
The bcliffs are a refuge for
the crock badgers.

19 aGen.
1:14 bPs.
19:6

19 He made the moon ªfor
the seasons;
The bsun knows the place
of its setting.

20 aPs.
74:16; Is.
45:7 bPs.
50:10; Is.
56:9; Mic.
5:8

20 Thou ªdost appoint darkness and it becomes
night,
In which all the bbeasts of
the forest prowl
about.

21 aJob
38:39 bPs.
145:15; Joel
1:20

21 The ªyoung lions roar after
their prey,
And bseek their food from
God.

22 aJob 37:8

22 When the sun rises they
withdraw,
And lie down in their
ªdens.

23 aGen.
3:19

23 Man goes forth to ªhis
work
And to his labor until evening.

24 aPs. 40:5
bPs. 136:5;
Prov. 3:19;
Jer. 10:12;
51:15 cPs.
65:9

24 O LORD, how ªmany are
Thy works!
In bwisdom Thou hast
made them all;
The cearth is full of Thy
possessions.

25 aPs. 8:8;
69:34

25 There is the ªsea, great and
broad,
In which are swarms with-
out number,
Animals both small and
great.

★26 aPs.
107:23;
Ezek. 27:9
bJob 41:1;
Ps. 74:14; Is.
27:1

26 There the ªships move
along,
And bLeviathan, which
Thou hast formed to
sport in it.

27 aPs.
145:15 bJob
36:31; 38:41;
Ps. 136:25;
147:9

27 They all ªwait for Thee,
To bgive them their food in
due season.

104:6 Not a reference to the Flood of Noah's
time, but to the third day of God's creative
activity (Gen. 1:9–10).

104:26 Leviathan. Here a sea monster; for other
uses see notes on Job 3:8 and 41:1.

28 Thou dost give to them,
they gather *it* up;
Thou ^adost open Thy
hand, they are satis-
fied with good.

29 Thou ^adost hide Thy face,
they are dismayed;
Thou ^bdost take away their
spirit, they expire,
And ^creturn to their dust.

30 Thou dost send forth Thy
^aSpirit, they are cre-
ated;
And Thou dost renew the
face of the ground.

31 Let the ^aglory of the LORD
endure forever;
Let the LORD ^bbe glad in
His works;

32 He ^alooks at the earth, and
it ^btrembles;
He ^ctouches the mountains, and they smoke.

33 I will sing to the LORD ^aas
long as I live;
I will ^bsing praise to my
God while I have my
being.

34 Let my ^ameditation be
pleasing to Him;
As for me, I shall ^bbe glad
in the LORD.

35 Let sinners be ^aconsumed
from the earth,
And let the ^bwicked be no
more.
^cBless the LORD, O my
soul.
^dPraise the LORD!

PSALM 105

OH ^agive thanks to the LORD,
^bcall upon His name;
^cMake known His deeds
among the peoples.

2 Sing to Him, ^asing praises
to Him;
^bSpeak of all His wonders.

3 Glory in His holy name;
Let the ^aheart of those who
seek the LORD be glad.

4 Seek the LORD and ^aHis
strength;
^bSeek His face continually.

5 Remember His ^awonders
which He has done,
His marvels, and the
^bjudgments uttered by
His mouth,

6 O seed of ^aAbraham, His
servant,
O sons of ^bJacob, His
^cchosen ones!

7 He is the LORD our God;
His ^ajudgments are in all
the earth.

8 He has ^aremembered His
covenant forever,
The word which He com-
manded to a ^bthou-
sand generations,

9 *The* ^a*covenant* which He
made with Abraham,
And His ^boath to Isaac.

10 Then He ^aconfirmed it to
Jacob for a statute,
To Israel as an everlasting
covenant,

11 Saying, "^aTo you I will
give the land of Ca-
naan
As the ^bportion of your inheritance,"

12 When they were only a
^afew men in number,
Very few, and ^bstrangers
in it.

13 And they wandered about
from nation to nation,
From *one* kingdom to an-
other people.

14 He ^apermitted no man to
oppress them,
And He ^breproved kings
for their sakes:

15 "^aDo not touch My
anointed ones,

Marginal references

28 ^aPs. 145:16

★29-30
29 ^aDeut. 31:17; Ps. 30:7 ^bJob 34:14, 15; Ps. 146:4; Eccl. 12:7 ^cGen. 3:19; Job 10:9; Ps. 90:3

30 ^aJob 33:4; Ezek. 37:9

31 ^aPs. 86:12; 111:10 ^bGen. 1:31

32 ^aJudg. 5:5; Ps. 97:4, 5; 114:7 ^bHab. 3:10 ^cEx. 19:18; Ps. 144:5
33 ^aPs. 63:4 ^bPs. 146:2

34 ^aPs. 19:14 ^bPs. 9:2

35 ^aPs. 59:13 ^bPs. 37:10 ^cPs. 104:1 ^dPs. 105:45; 106:48

1 ^a1 Chr. 16:8-22, 34; Ps. 106:1; Is. 12:4 ^bPs. 99:6 ^cPs. 145:12
2 ^aPs. 96:1; 98:5 ^bPs. 77:12; 119:27; 145:5

3 ^aPs. 33:21

4 ^aPs. 63:2 ^bPs. 27:8

5 ^aPs. 40:5; 77:11 ^bPs. 119:13

6 ^aPs. 105:42 ^bPs. 135:4 ^c1 Chr. 16:13; Ps. 106:5; 135:4
7 ^aIs. 26:9

8 ^aPs. 105:42; 106:45; Luke 1:72 ^bDeut. 7:9

9 ^aGen. 12:7; 17:2, 8; 22:16-18; Gal. 3:17 ^bGen. 26:3

10 ^aGen. 28:13-15

11 ^aGen. 13:15; 15:18 ^bJosh. 23:4; Ps. 78:55

12 ^aGen. 34:30; Deut. 7:7 ^bGen. 23:4; Heb. 11:9

14 ^aGen. 20:7; 35:5 ^bGen. 12:17; 20:3, 7

★15 ^aGen. 26:11

104:29-30 The *spirit* of every living thing depends on God's Spirit.
Psalm 105 This psalm of Israel's history
opens with a call to praise and remember God's
wondrous works (vv. 1-7); then highlights the
Abrahamic covenant (vv. 8-15), the life of Joseph
and Israel's settlement in Egypt (vv. 16-24), the
life of Moses and the deliverance from Egypt (vv.
25-38), God's care for them in the wilderness
(vv. 39-41), and the entrance into Canaan (vv.
42-45). Some of this psalm is quoted in connection with David's procession when bringing the
Ark to Jerusalem (1 Chron. 16:8-22).
105:15 Abraham is called a prophet in Gen. 20:7.

And do My prophets no
harm."

16   16 And He ªcalled for a famine upon the land;
He ᵇbroke the whole staff
of bread.

16 ªGen.
41:54 ᵇLev.
26:26; Is.
3:1; Ezek.
4:16

17 He ªsent a man before
them,
Joseph, *who* was ᵇsold as a
slave.

17 ªGen.
45:5 ᵇGen.
37:28, 36;
Acts 7:9

18 They afflicted his ªfeet
with fetters,
He himself was laid in
irons;

18 ªGen.
39:20; 40:15

19 Until the time that his
ªword came to pass,
The word of the Lᴏʀᴅ
ᵇtested him.

19 ªGen.
40:20, 21
ᵇPs. 66:10

20 The ªking sent and re-
leased him,
The ruler of peoples, and
set him free.

20 ªGen.
41:14

21 He ªmade him lord of his
house,
And ruler over all his possessions,

21 ªGen.
41:40-44

22 To imprison his princes ªat
will,
That he might teach his elders wisdom.

22 ªGen.
41:44

23 ªIsrael also came into
Egypt;
Thus Jacob ᵇsojourned in
the land of Ham.

23 ªGen.
46:6; Acts
7:15 ᵇActs
13:17

24 And He ªcaused His people to be very fruitful,
And made them stronger
than their adversaries.

24 ªEx.
1:7, 9

25 He ªturned their heart to
hate His people,
To ᵇdeal craftily with His
servants.

25 ªEx. 1:8;
4:21 ᵇEx.
1:10; Acts
7:19

26 He ªsent Moses His servant,
And ᵇAaron whom He had
chosen.

26 ªEx. 3:10;
4:12 ᵇEx.
4:14; Num.
16:5; 17:5-8

27 They ªperformed His wondrous acts among
them,
And miracles in the land of
Ham.

27 ªPs.
78:43-51;
105:27-36

28 He ªsent darkness and
made *it* dark;

28 ªEx.
10:21, 22
ᵇPs. 99:7

And they did not ᵇrebel
against His words.

29 He ªturned their waters
into blood,
And caused their fish to
die.

29 ªEx. 7:20,
21

30 Their land swarmed with
ªfrogs
Even in the ᵇchambers of
their kings.

30 ªEx. 8:6
ᵇEx. 8:3

31 He spoke, and there came
a ªswarm of flies
And ᵇgnats in all their territory.

★31 ªEx.
8:21 ᵇEx.
8:16, 17

32 He gave them ªhail for
rain,
And flaming fire in their
land.

32 ªEx.
9:23-25

33 He ªstruck down their
vines also and their fig
trees,
And shattered the trees of
their territory.

33 ªPs.
78:47

34 He spoke, and ªlocusts
came,
And young locusts, even
without number,

34 ªEx.
10:12-15

35 And ate up all vegetation
in their land,
And ate up the fruit of
their ground.

36 He also ªstruck down all
the first-born in their
land,
The ᵇfirst fruits of all their
vigor.

36 ªEx.
12:29; 13:15;
Ps. 135:8;
136:10
ᵇGen. 49:3

37 Then He brought them
out with ªsilver and
gold;
And among His tribes
there was not one
who stumbled.

37 ªEx.
12:35, 36

38 Egypt was ªglad when they
departed;
For the ᵇdread of them had
fallen upon them.

38 ªEx.
12:33 ᵇEx.
15:16

39 He spread a ªcloud for a
covering,
And ᵇfire to illumine by
night.

39 ªEx.
13:21; Neh.
9:12; Ps.
78:14; Is. 4:5
ᵇEx. 40:38

40 They ªasked, and He
brought ᵇquail,
And satisfied them with
the ᶜbread of heaven.

40 ªEx.
16:12; Ps.
78:18 ᵇEx.
16:13; Num.
11:31; Ps.
78:27 ᶜEx.
16:15; Neh.
9:15; Ps.
78:24; John
6:31

105:31 See note on Exod. 8:16.

41 *a*Ex. 17:6;
Num. 20:11;
Ps. 78:15;
114:8; Is.
48:21; 1 Cor.
10:4
★42 *a*Gen.
15:13, 14;
Ps. 105:8

43 *a*Ex. 15:1;
Ps. 106:12

44 *a*Josh.
11:16-23,
13:7; Ps.
78:55 *b*Deut.
6:10, 11

45 *a*Deut.
4:1, 40

41 He opened the rock, and
        *a*water flowed out;
        It ran in the dry places *like*
        a river.
42 For He *a*remembered His
        holy word
        With Abraham His ser-
        vant;
43 And He brought forth His
        people with joy,
        His chosen ones with a
        joyful *a*shout.
44 He *a*gave them also the
        lands of the nations,
        That they *b*might take pos-
        session of *the fruit of*
        the peoples' labor,
45 So that they might *a*keep
        His statutes,
        And observe His laws,
        Praise the LORD!

PSALM 106

1 *a*Ps.
105:1; 107:1;
118:1; 136:1;
Jer. 33:11
*b*2 Chr. 5:13;
7:3; Ezra
3:11; Ps.
100:5
*c*1 Chr.
16:34, 41

2 *a*Ps.
145:4, 12;
150:2

3 *a*Ps. 15:2

4 *a*Ps. 44:3;
119:132

5 *a*Ps. 1:3
*b*Ps. 118:15
*c*Ps. 105:3

P RAISE the LORD!
        Oh *a*give thanks to the
        LORD, for He *b*is good;
        For *c*His lovingkindness is
        everlasting.
2 Who can speak of the
        *a*mighty deeds of the
        LORD,
        Or can show forth all His
        praise?
3 How blessed are those
        who keep justice,
        Who *a*practice righteous-
        ness at all times!

4 Remember me, O LORD, in
        Thy *a*favor toward
        Thy people;
        Visit me with Thy salva-
        tion,
5 That I may see the *a*pros-
        perity of Thy chosen
        ones,
        That I may *b*rejoice in the
        gladness of Thy na-
        tion,

        That I may *c*glory with
        Thine inheritance.

6 *a*1 Kin.
8:47; Ezra
9:7; Neh. 1:7;
Jer. 3:25;
Dan. 9:5
*b*2 Chr. 30:7;
Neh. 9:2; Ps.
78:8, 57;
Zech. 1:4

7 *a*Judg.
3:7; Ps.
78:11, 42
*b*Ex. 14:11,
12; Ps. 78:17

8 *a*Ezek.
20:9 *b*Ex.
9:16

9 *a*Ps.
18:15; 78:13;
Is. 50:2; Nah.
1:4 *b*Ex.
14:21; Is.
51:10 *c*Is.
63:11-13

10 *a*Ex.
14:30 *b*Ps.
78:42; 107:2

11 *a*Ex.
14:27, 28,
15:5; Ps.
78:53

12 *a*Ex.
14:31 *b*Ex.
15:1-21; Ps.
105:43

13 *a*Ex.
15:24, 16:2;
17:2 *b*Ps.
107:11

14 *a*Num.
11:4; Ps.
78:18; 1 Cor.
10:6 *b*Ex.
17:2; 1 Cor.
10:9

15 *a*Num.
11:31; Ps.
78:29 *b*Is.
10:16

6 *a*We have sinned *b*like our
        fathers,
        We have committed iniq-
        uity, we have behaved
        wickedly.
7 Our fathers in Egypt did
        not understand Thy
        wonders;
        They *a*did not remember
        Thine abundant
        kindnesses,
        But *b*rebelled by the sea, at
        the Red Sea.
8 Nevertheless He saved
        them *a*for the sake of
        His name,
        That He might *b*make His
        power known.
9 Thus He *a*rebuked the Red
        Sea and it *b*dried up;
        And He *c*led them through
        the deeps, as through
        the wilderness.
10 So He *a*saved them from
        the hand of the one
        who hated *them,*
        And *b*redeemed them from
        the hand of the ene-
        my.
11 And *a*the waters covered
        their adversaries;
        Not one of them was left.
12 Then they *a*believed His
        words;
        They *b*sang His praise.

13 They quickly *a*forgot His
        works;
        They *b*did not wait for His
        counsel,
14 But *a*craved intensely in
        the wilderness,
        And *b*tempted God in the
        desert.
15 So He *a*gave them their re-
        quest,
        But *b*sent a wasting disease
        among them.

105:42 See note on Gen. 15:18-21.
  Psalm 106 After an opening call to praise
(vv. 1-3) and a brief prayer (vv. 4-5), the psalmist laments and confesses Israel's sins: their unbelief and murmuring at the Red Sea (vv. 7-12),
their murmuring for flesh to eat (vv. 13-15), their
jealousy over the authority of Moses and Aaron

(vv. 16-18), their worship of the calf (vv. 19-23),
their unbelief of the report of the spies (vv.
24-27), their participation in Moabite worship
(vv. 28-31), the murmuring at Meribah (vv.
32-33), and their continued disobedience after
entering Canaan (vv. 34-46). He concludes with
a petition and praise (vv. 47-48).

16 aNum.
16:1-3

16 When they became aenvi-
ous of Moses in the
camp,
And of Aaron, the holy
one of the LORD,

★17 aNum.
16:32; Deut.
11:6

17 The aearth opened and
swallowed up Dathan,
And engulfed the com-
pany of Abiram.

18 aNum.
16:35

18 And a afire blazed up in
their company;
The flame consumed the
wicked.

★19 aEx.
32:4; Deut.
9:8; Acts
7:41

19 They amade a calf in Horeb,
And worshiped a molten
image.

20 aJer.
2:11; Rom.
1:23

20 Thus they aexchanged
their glory
For the image of an ox that
eats grass.

21 aPs.
78:11; 106:7,
13 bDeut.
10:21

21 They aforgot God their
Savior,
Who had done bgreat
things in Egypt,

22 aPs.
105:27

22 aWonders in the land of
Ham,
And awesome things by
the Red Sea.

23 aEx.
32:10; Ezek.
20:8; 13
bEx. 32:11-
14; Deut.
9:25-29

23 Therefore aHe said that He
would destroy them,
Had not bMoses His cho-
sen one stood in the
breach before Him,
To turn away His wrath
from destroying them.

24 aNum.
14:31 bDeut.
8:7; Jer.
3:19; Ezek.
20:6 cDeut.
1:32; 9:23;
Heb. 3:19

24 Then they adespised the
bpleasant land;
They cdid not believe in
His word,

25 aNum.
14:2; Deut.
1:27

25 But agrumbled in their
tents;
They did not listen to the
voice of the LORD.

26 aNum.
14:28-35; Ps.
95:11; Ezek.
20:15; Heb.
3:11

26 Therefore He aswore to
them,
That He would cast them
down in the wilder-
ness,

★27 aDeut.
4:27 bLev.
26:33; Ps.
44:11

27 And that He would acast
their seed among the
nations,

And bscatter them in the
lands.

28 They ajoined themselves
also to Baal-peor,
And ate bsacrifices offered
to the dead.

★28 aNum.
25:3; Deut.
4:3; Hos.
9:10 bNum.
25:2

29 Thus they aprovoked Him
to anger with their
deeds;
And the plague broke out
among them.

29 aNum.
25:4

30 Then Phinehas astood up
and interposed;
And so the bplague was
stayed.

30 aNum.
25:7 bNum.
25:8

31 And it was areckoned to
him for righteousness,
To all generations forever.

31 aGen.
15:6; Num.
25:11-13

32 They also aprovoked Him
to wrath at the waters
of Meribah,
So that it bwent hard with
Moses on their ac-
count;

32 aNum.
20:2-13; Ps.
81:7; 95:9
bNum. 20:12

33 Because they awere rebellious against His
Spirit,
He spoke rashly with his
lips.

33 aNum.
20:3, 10; Ps.
78:40;
107:11

34 They adid not destroy the
peoples,
As bthe LORD commanded
them,

34 aJudg.
1:21, 27-36
bDeut. 7:2,
16

35 But athey mingled with the
nations,
And learned their prac-
tices,

35 aJudg.
3:5, 6

36 And aserved their idols,
bWhich became a snare to
them.

36 aJudg.
2:12 bDeut.
7:16

37 They even asacrificed their
sons and their daugh-
ters to the bdemons,

37 aDeut.
12:31; 32:17;
2 Kin. 16:3;
17:17; Ezek.
16:20, 21;
1 Cor. 10:20
bLev. 17:7

38 And shed ainnocent blood,
The blood of their bsons
and their daughters,
Whom they sacrificed to
the idols of Canaan;
And the land was cpol-
luted with the blood.

38 aPs.
94:21 bDeut.
18:10 cNum.
35:33; Is.
24:5; Jer.
3:1, 2

106:17 See note on Num. 16:12.
106:19 See note on Exod. 32:4.
106:27 *cast their seed.* I.e., disperse their descendants.
106:28 *Baal-peor.* See note on Num. 25:3.

★39 *a*Lev.
18:24; Ezek.
20:18 *b*Lev.
17:7; Num.
15:39; Judg.
2:17; Hos.
4:12

39 Thus they became *a*unclean in their practices,
And *b*played the harlot in their deeds.

★40-46
40 *a*Judg.
2:14; Ps.
78:59 *b*Lev.
26:30; Deut.
32:19 *c*Deut.
9:29; 32:9
41 *a*Judg.
2:14; Neh.
9:27

40 Therefore the *a*anger of the Lord was kindled against His people,
And He *b*abhorred His *c*inheritance.

41 Then *a*He gave them into the hand of the nations;
And those who hated them ruled over them.

42 *a*Judg.
4:3; 10:12

42 Their enemies also *a*oppressed them,
And they were subdued under their power.

43 *a*Judg.
2:16-18 *b*Ps.
81:12 *c*Judg.
6:6

43 Many times He would *a*deliver them;
They, however, were rebellious in their *b*counsel,
And so *c*sank down in their iniquity.

44 *a*Judg.
3:9; 6:7;
10:10

44 Nevertheless He looked upon their distress,
When He *a*heard their cry;

45 *a*Lev.
26:42; Ps.
105:8 *b*Judg.
2:18 *c*Ps.
69:16

45 And He *a*remembered His covenant for their sake,
And *b*relented *c*according to the greatness of His lovingkindness.

46 *a*1 Kin.
8:50; 2 Chr.
30:9; Ezra
9:9; Neh.
1:11; Jer.
42:12

46 He also made them *a*objects of compassion
In the presence of all their captors.

47 *a*1 Chr.
16:35, 36
*b*Ps. 147:2
*c*Ps. 47:1

47 *a*Save us, O Lord our God,
And *b*gather us from among the nations,

To give thanks to Thy holy name,
And *c*glory in Thy praise.

48 *a*Ps.
41:13; 72:18;
89:52

48 *a*Blessed be the Lord, the God of Israel,
From everlasting even to everlasting.
And let all the people say, "Amen."
Praise the Lord!

BOOK 5

PSALM 107

★ 1 *a*1 Chr.
16:34; Ps.
106:1; 118:1;
136:1; Jer.
33:11
*b*2 Chr. 5:13;
7:3; Ezra
3:11; Ps.
100:5

OH *a*give thanks to the Lord, for *b*He is good;
For His lovingkindness is everlasting.

2 *a*Is. 35:9,
10; 62:12;
63:4 *b*Ps.
78:42;
106:10

2 Let *a*the redeemed of the Lord say so,
Whom He has *b*redeemed from the hand of the adversary,

3 *a*Deut.
30:3; Neh.
1:9; Ps.
106:47; Is.
11:12; 43:5;
56:8; Ezek.
11:17; 20:34

3 And *a*gathered from the lands,
From the east and from the west,
From the north and from the south.

4 *a*Num.
14:33; 32:13;
Deut. 2:7;
32:10; Josh.
5:6; 14:10
*b*Ps. 107:7,
36

4 They *a*wandered in the wilderness in a desert region;
They did not find a way to an inhabited *b*city.

5 *a*Ps. 77:3

5 *They were* hungry and thirsty;
Their *a*soul fainted within them.

6 *a*Ps.
50:15;
107:13, 19,
28

6 Then they *a*cried out to the Lord in their trouble;
He delivered them out of their distresses.

106:39 Spiritual infidelity was a continuing problem from the time of Moses to the Babylonian captivity.
106:40-46 This section seems to describe in particular the period of the judges, with its cycles of foreign oppression and divine deliverance.
Psalm 107 Within the framework of a hymn with its opening call to praise (vv. 1-3) and concluding description of God's providence (vv. 33-43), the psalmist presents four pictures of the nation's deliverance from captivity (vv. 4-32). They are: travellers in distress being guided to a

city (vv. 4-9), prisoners in a dungeon being released (vv. 10-16), sick men being restored to health (vv. 17-22), and sailors safely brought to their destination (vv. 23-32). Each of these four vignettes contains a problem (vv. 4-5, 10-12, 17-18, 23-27), a prayer (vv. 6a, 13a, 19a, 28a), God's provision (vv. 6b-7, 13b-14, 19b-20, 28b-30), and praise (vv. 8-9, 15-16, 21-22, 31-32).
107:1 Note the frequent mention of God's *lovingkindness* (steadfast, covenant love; see note on Hos. 2:19) in vv. 8, 15, 21, 31, 43.

7 aEzra
8:21; Ps. 5:8;
Jer. 31:9
bPs. 107:4,
36

7 He led them also by a
ªstraight way,
To go to ªan inhabited
city.

8 aPs.
107:15, 21,
31

8 ªLet them give thanks to
the LORD for His
lovingkindness,
And for His wonders to
the sons of men!

9 aPs.
22:26; 34:10;
63:5; 103:5
bPs. 146:7;
Matt. 5:6;
Luke 1:53

9 For He has ªsatisfied the
thirsty soul,
And the ªhungry soul He
has filled with what is
good.

10 aPs.
143:3; Is.
42:7; Mic.
7:8; Luke
1:79 bJob
36:8; Ps.
102:20

10 There were those who
ªdwelt in darkness
and in the shadow of
death,
ªPrisoners in misery and
chains,

11 aPs.
78:40; 106:7;
Lam. 3:42
bNum.
15:31; 2 Chr.
36:16; Prov.
1:25; Is. 5:24
cPs. 73:24

11 Because they had ªrebelled
against the words of
God,
And ªspurned the ªcounsel
of the Most High.

12 aPs.
22:11; 72:12

12 Therefore He humbled
their heart with labor;
They stumbled and there
was ªnone to help.

13 aPs.
107:6

13 Then they ªcried out to the
LORD in their trouble;
He saved them out of their
distresses.

14 aPs.
86:13;
107:10 bPs.
116:16; Jer.
2:20; 30:8;
Nah. 1:13;
Luke 13:16;
Acts 12:7

14 He ªbrought them out of
darkness and the
shadow of death,
And ªbroke their bands
apart.

15 aPs.
107:8, 21, 31

15 ªLet them give thanks to
the LORD for His
lovingkindness,
And for His wonders to
the sons of men!

16 aIs.
45:1, 2

16 For He has ªshattered gates
of bronze,
And cut bars of iron asunder.

17 aIs. 65:6,
7; Jer. 30:14,
15; Lam.
3:39; Ezek.
24:23

17 Fools, because of their rebellious way,
And ªbecause of their iniquities, were afflicted.

18 aJob
33:20; Ps.
102:4 bJob
33:22; Ps.
88:3 cJob
38:17; Ps.
9:13

18 Their ªsoul abhorred all
kinds of food;
And they ªdrew near to
the ªgates of death.

19 Then they cried out to the
LORD in their trouble;
He saved them out of their
distresses.

20 aPs.
147:15, 18;
Matt. 8:8
b2 Kin. 20:5;
Ps. 30:2;
103:3; 147:3
cJob 33:28,
30; Ps. 30:3;
49:15; 56:13;
103:4

20 He ªsent His word and
ªhealed them,
And ªdelivered them from
their destructions.

21 aPs.
107:8, 15, 31

21 ªLet them give thanks to
the LORD for His
lovingkindness,
And for His wonders to
the sons of men!

22 aLev.
7:12; Ps.
50:14;
116:17 bPs.
9:11; 73:28;
118:17

22 Let them also offer ªsacri-
fices of thanksgiving,
And ªtell of His works
with joyful singing.

★23 aIs.
42:10; Jon.
1:3

23 Those who ªgo down to
the sea in ships,
Who do business on great
waters;

24 They have seen the works
of the LORD,
And His wonders in the
deep.

25 aPs.
105:31, 34
bPs. 148:8;
Jon. 1:4 cPs.
93:3, 4

25 For He ªspoke and raised
up a ªstormy wind,
Which ªlifted up the waves
of the sea.

26 aPs.
22:14;
119:28

26 They rose up to the heavens, they went down
to the depths;
Their soul ªmelted away in
their misery.

★27 aJob
12:25; Is.
24:20

27 They reeled and ªstag-
gered like a drunken
man,
And were at their wits'
end.

28 Then they cried to the
LORD in their trouble,
And He brought them out
of their distresses.

29 aPs. 65:7;
89:9; Matt.
8:26; Luke
8:24

29 He ªcaused the storm to be
still,
So that the waves of the
sea were hushed.

30 Then they were glad because they were quiet;

107:23 *go down to the sea in ships.* I.e., "to sail
the sea," the ocean being "down" from the
mountains of Israel.

107:27 *at their wits' end.* Their navigational skill
and seamanship was of no value.

So He guided them to their desired haven.

31 aPs.
107:8, 15, 21
bPs. 78:4;
111:4

31 ^aLet them give thanks to the LORD for His lovingkindness,
And for His ^bwonders to the sons of men!

32 aPs. 34:3;
99:5; Is. 25:1
bPs. 22:22,
25 cPs.
35:18

32 Let them ^aextol Him also ^bin the congregation of the people,
And ^cpraise Him at the seat of the elders.

33 a1 Kin.
17:1, 7; Ps.
74:15; Is.
42:15; 50:2

33 He ^achanges rivers into a wilderness,
And springs of water into a thirsty ground;

34 aGen.
13:10; 14:3;
19:24, 25;
Deut. 29:23
bJob 39:6;
Jer. 17:6

34 A ^afruitful land into a ^bsalt waste,
Because of the wickedness of those who dwell in it.

35 aPs.
105:41;
114:8; Is.
35:6, 7;
41:18

35 He ^achanges a wilderness into a pool of water,
And a dry land into springs of water;

36 aPs.
107:4, 7

36 And there He makes the hungry to dwell,
So that they may establish ^aan inhabited city,

37 a2 Kin.
19:29; Is.
65:21; Amos
9:14

37 And sow fields, and ^aplant vineyards,
And gather a fruitful harvest.

38 aGen.
12:2; 17:20;
Ex. 1:7; Deut.
1:10 bDeut.
7:14

38 Also He blesses them and they ^amultiply greatly;
And He ^bdoes not let their cattle decrease.

39 a2 Kin.
10:32; Ezek.
5:11; 29:15
bPs. 38:6;
44:25; 57:6

39 When they are ^adiminished and ^bbowed down
Through oppression, misery, and sorrow,

40 aJob
12:21 bJob
12:24 cDeut.
32:10

40 He ^apours contempt upon princes,
And ^bmakes them wander ^cin a pathless waste.

41 a1 Sam.
2:8; Ps. 59:1;
113:7, 8
bJob 21:11;
Ps. 78:52;
113:9

41 But He ^asets the needy securely on high away from affliction,
And ^bmakes *his* families like a flock.

42 The ^aupright see it, and are glad;
But all ^bunrighteousness shuts its mouth.

42 aJob
22:19; Ps.
52:6 bJob
5:16; Ps.
63:11; Rom.
3:19

43 Who is ^awise? Let him give heed to these things;
And consider the ^blovingkindnesses of the LORD.

43 aPs. 64:9;
Jer. 9:12;
Hos. 14:9
bPs. 107:1

PSALM 108

A Song, a Psalm of David.

^aMY heart is steadfast, O God;
I will sing, I will sing praises, even with my soul.

1 aPs.
57:7-11;
108:1-5

2 Awake, harp and lyre;
I will awaken the dawn!

3 I will give thanks to Thee, O LORD, among the peoples;
And I will sing praises to Thee among the nations.

4 For Thy ^alovingkindness is great ^babove the heavens;
And Thy truth *reaches* to the skies.

4 aNum.
14:18; Deut.
100:5; Mic.
7:18-20 bPs.
113:4

5 ^aBe exalted, O God, above the heavens,
And Thy glory above all the earth.

5 aPs. 57:5

6 ^aThat Thy beloved may be delivered,
Save with Thy right hand, and answer me!

6 aPs.
60:5-12;
108:6-13

7 God has spoken in His holiness:
"I will exult, I will portion out Shechem,
And measure out the valley of Succoth.

* 7-8

8 "Gilead is Mine, Manasseh is Mine;
Ephraim also is the helmet of My head;
^aJudah is My scepter.

8 aGen.
49:10

Psalm 108 David vows to praise God (vv. 1-5, which are virtually identical with 57:7-11) and voices his petition to God for deliverance (vv. 6-13, which are virtually identical with 60:5-12).
108:7-8 See note on 60:6-7.

★ 9

9 "Moab is My washbowl;
Over Edom I shall throw
My shoe;
Over Philistia I will shout
aloud."

10 aPs. 60:9

10 aWho will bring me into
the besieged city?
Who will lead me to
Edom?

11 aPs. 44:9

11 Hast not Thou Thyself, O
God, arejected us?
And wilt Thou not go
forth with our armies,
O God?

12 aIs. 30:3

12 Oh give us help against the
adversary,
For adeliverance by man is
in vain.

13 aIs. 60:12; 63:1-4

13 Through God we shall do
valiantly;
And ait is He who will
tread down our adver-
saries.

PSALM 109

For the choir director. A
Psalm of David.

1 aDeut. 10:21 bPs. 28:1; 83:1

O aGOD of my praise,
bDo not be silent!

2 aPs. 10:7; 52:4 bPs. 120:2

2 For they have opened the
wicked and adeceitful
mouth against me;
They have spoken against
me with a blying
tongue.

3 aPs. 35:7; 69:4; John 15:25

3 They have also surrounded
me with words of ha-
tred,
And fought against me
awithout cause.

4 aPs. 38:20 bPs. 69:13; 141:5

4 In return afor my love they
act as my accusers;
But bI am in prayer.

5 aPs. 35:12; 38:20 bJohn 7:7; 10:32

5 Thus they have arepaid me
evil for good,
And bhatred for my love.

6 Appoint a wicked man
over him;
And let an aaccuser stand
at his right hand.

★ 6-20

6 aZech. 3:1

7 When he is judged, let him
acome forth guilty;
And let his bprayer be-
come sin.

7 aPs. 1:5 bProv. 28:9

8 Let ahis days be few;
Let banother take his of-
fice.

8 aPs. 55:23 bActs 1:20

9 Let his achildren be fatherless,
And his bwife a widow.

★ 9-10

9 aEx. 22:24 bJer. 18:21

10 Let his achildren wander
about and beg;
And let them bseek suste-
nance far from their
ruined homes.

10 aGen. 4:12; Job 30:5-8; Ps. 59:15 bPs. 37:25

11 Let athe creditor seize all
that he has;
And let bstrangers plunder
the product of his la-
bor.

11 aNeh. 5:7; Job 5:5; 20:15 bIs. 1:7; Lam. 5:2; Ezek. 7:21

12 Let there be none to aex-
tend lovingkindness
to him,
Nor bany to be gracious to
his fatherless children.

12 aEzra 7:28; 9:9 bJob 5:4; Is. 9:17

13 Let his aposterity be cut
off;
In a following generation
let their bname be
blotted out.

13 aJob 18:19; Ps. 21:10; 37:28 bPs. 9:5; Prov. 10:7

14 Let athe iniquity of his fathers be remembered
before the LORD,
And do not let the sin of
his mother be bblotted
out.

14 aEx. 20:5; Num. 14:18; Is. 65:6, 7; Jer. 32:18 bNeh. 4:5; Jer. 18:23

15 Let athem be before the
LORD continually,
That He may bcut off their
memory from the
earth;

15 aPs. 90:8; Jer. 16:17 bJob 18:17; Ps. 34:16

16 Because he did not re-
member to show
lovingkindness,

16 aPs. 37:14 bPs. 34:18 cPs. 37:32; 94:6

108:9 See note on 60:8.
Psalm 109 In this imprecatory psalm (see Introduction), David cries out for God's judgment
on his false accusers (vv. 1-5), especially His
judgment on one whom he strongly curses (vv.
6-20); then he petitions God for deliverance (vv.
21-25) and judgment (vv. 26-29), closing with a
vow of praise (vv. 30-31).
109:6-20 Some hold that these are the curses

spoken by David's enemies against him. It is
simpler, however, to view them as David's imprecation against one of his enemies mentioned in verses 12-14. What happened to Judas was a fullfillment of these curses (cf. Acts
1:16-20).
109:9-10 Fathers' sins do affect their children
(cf. Exod. 20:5; Luke 19:41-44).

But persecuted the ^aafflicted and needy man,
And the ^bdespondent in heart, to ^cput *them* to death.

17   ^aProv. 14:14; Ezek. 35:9; Matt. 7:2

17 He also loved cursing, so ^ait came to him;
And he did not delight in blessing, so it was far from him.

18   ^aPs. 73:6; 109:29; Ezek. 7:27 ^bNum. 5:22

18 But he ^aclothed himself with cursing as with his garment,
And it ^bentered into his body like water,
And like oil into his bones.

19   ^aPs. 73:6; 109:29; Ezek. 7:27 ^b2 Sam. 22:40; Ps. 30:11; Is. 11:5

19 Let it be to him as ^aa garment with which he covers himself,
And for a belt with which he constantly ^bgirds himself.

20   ^aPs. 54:5; 94:23; Is. 3:11; 2 Tim. 4:14 ^bPs. 41:5; 71:10

20 Let this be the ^areward of my accusers from the LORD,
And of those who ^bspeak evil against my soul.

21   ^aPs. 23:3; 25:11; 79:9; 106:8; Ezek. 36:22 ^bPs. 69:16

21 But Thou, O GOD, the Lord, deal *kindly* with me ^afor Thy name's sake;
Because ^bThy lovingkindness is good, deliver me;

22   ^aPs. 40:17; 86:1 ^bJob 24:12; Ps. 143:4; Prov. 18:14

22 For ^aI am afflicted and needy,
And my heart is ^bwounded within me.

23   ^aPs. 102:11 ^bEx. 10:19; Job 39:20

23 I am passing ^alike a shadow when it lengthens;
I am shaken off ^blike the locust.

24   ^aHeb. 12:12 ^bPs. 35:13

24 My ^aknees are weak from ^bfasting;
And my flesh has grown lean, without fatness.

25   ^aPs. 22:6 ^bPs. 22:7; Jer. 18:16; Lam. 2:15; Matt. 27:39; Mark 15:29

25 I also have become a ^areproach to them;
When they see me, they ^bwag their head.

26   ^aPs. 119:86

26 ^aHelp me, O LORD my God;
Save me according to Thy lovingkindness.

27   ^aJob 37:7

27 And let them ^aknow that this is Thy hand;
Thou, LORD, hast done it.

28   ^a2 Sam. 16:11, 12 ^bIs. 65:14

28 ^aLet them curse, but do Thou bless;
When they arise, they shall be ashamed,
But Thy ^bservant shall be glad.

29   ^aJob 8:22; Ps. 132:18 ^bJob 8:22; Ps. 35:26

29 Let ^amy accusers be clothed with dishonor,
And let them ^bcover themselves with their own shame as with a robe.

30   ^aPs. 22:22; 35:18; 111:1

30 With my mouth I will give thanks abundantly to the LORD;
And in the midst of many ^aI will praise Him.

31   ^aPs. 16:8; 73:23; 110:5; 121:5 ^bPs. 37:33

31 For He stands ^aat the right hand of the needy,
To save him from those who ^bjudge his soul.

PSALM 110

A Psalm of David.

★ 1-2
1   ^aMatt. 22:44; Mark 12:36; Luke 20:42, 43; Acts 2:34, 35; Heb. 1:13 ^bMatt. 26:64; Eph. 1:20; Col. 3:1; Heb. 1:3; 8:1; 10:12; 12:2 ^c1 Cor. 15:25; Eph. 1:22

^aTHE LORD says to my Lord:
"^bSit at My right hand,
Until I make ^cThine enemies a footstool for Thy feet."

2   ^aPs. 45:6; Jer. 48:17; Ezek. 19:14 ^bPs. 2:9; 72:8; Dan. 7:13, 14

2 The LORD will stretch forth Thy strong ^ascepter from Zion, *saying*,
"^bRule in the midst of Thine enemies."

★ 3   ^aJudg. 5:2; Neh. 11:2 ^b1 Chr. 16:29; Ps. 96:9 ^c2 Sam. 17:12; Mic. 5:7

3 Thy ^apeople will volunteer freely in the day of Thy power;
^bIn holy array, from the womb of the dawn,
Thy youth are to Thee *as* the ^cdew.

Psalm 110 This short psalm, one of the most quoted in the N.T., pictures Messiah as King (vv. 1–3), as Priest (v. 4), and as victorious Warrior (vv. 5–7). See notes on Matt. 22:43 and 44.
110:1-2 Verse 1 refers to the present position of Christ sharing the Father's kingly authority; verse 2, to His rule on earth during the millennial kingdom.
110:3 The meaning is this: during the Millennium God's people will voluntarily rally to the Messiah, who will lead them with constantly renewed vigor. *holy array.* See note on 29:2.

★ 4 aHeb.
7:21 bNum.
23:19 cZech.
6:13; Heb.
5:6, 10; 6:20;
7:17, 21

4 aThe Lord has sworn and
will bnot change His
mind,
"Thou art a cpriest forever
According to the order of
Melchizedek."

★ 5-6
5 aPs. 16:8;
109:31 bPs.
68:14; 76:12
cPs. 2:5, 12;
Rom. 2:5;
Rev. 6:17

6 aIs. 2:4;
Joel 3:12;
Mic. 4:3 bIs.
66:24 cPs.
68:21

5 The Lord is aat Thy right
hand;
He will bshatter kings in
the cday of His wrath.
6 He will ajudge among the
nations,
He will fill *them* with
bcorpses,
He will cshatter the chief
men over a broad
country.

★ 7 aJudg.
7:5, 6 bPs.
27:6

7 He will adrink from the
brook by the wayside;
Therefore He will blift up
His head.

PSALM 111

1 aPs.
35:18; 138:1
bPs. 89:7;
149:1

PRAISE the Lord!
I awill give thanks to the
Lord with all *my*
heart,
In the bcompany of the upright and in the as-
sembly.

2 aPs. 92:5
bPs. 143:5

2 aGreat are the works of the
Lord;
They are bstudied by all
who delight in them.

3 aPs. 96:6;
145:5 bPs.
112:3, 9;
119:142

3 aSplendid and majestic is
His work;
And bHis righteousness
endures forever.

4 aPs. 86:5,
15; 103:8;
145:8

4 He has made His wonders
to be remembered;
The Lord is agracious and
compassionate.

5 He has agiven food to
those who fear Him;
He will bremember His
covenant forever.
6 He has made known to His
people the power of
His works,
In giving them the heritage
of the nations.

5 aMatt.
6:31-33 bPs.
105:8

7 The works of His hands
are atruth and justice;
All His precepts bare sure.
8 They are aupheld forever
and ever;
They are performed in
btruth and upright-
ness.

7 aRev.
15:3 bPs.
19:7; 93:5

8 aPs.
119:160; Is.
40:8; Matt.
5:18 bPs.
19:9

9 He has sent aredemption
to His people;
He has ordained His cov-
enant forever;
bHoly and awesome is His
name.

9 aLuke
1:68 bPs.
99:3; Luke
1:49

10 The afear of the Lord is the
beginning of wisdom;
A bgood understanding
have all those who do
His commandments;
His cpraise endures for-
ever.

★10 aJob
28:28; Prov.
1:7; 9:10;
Eccl. 12:13
bPs. 119:98;
Prov. 3:4
cPs. 145:2

PSALM 112

PRAISE the Lord!
How ablessed is the man
who fears the Lord,
Who greatly bdelights in
His commandments.
2 His adescendants will be
mighty on earth;
The generation of the bupright will be blessed.

★ 1 aPs.
128:1 bPs.
1:2; 119:14,
16

2 aPs.
102:28;
127:4 bPs.
128:4

110:4 Like Melchizedek, Christ combines the offices of priest and king (see notes on Gen.
14:18 and Zech. 6:12-13).
110:5-6 This will be fulfilled in the campaign of
Armageddon, climaxing in the second coming
of Christ (cf. Rev. 19:15).
110:7 This pictures Messiah refreshed and victorious.
Psalm 111 In this hymn the psalmist exhorts
others and resolves himself to praise the Lord (v.
1) because of His mighty works, which manifest
His power, righteousness, truth, and justice (vv.
2-9) and which lead men to fear and praise Him

(v. 10). This acrostic consists of 22 lines beginning in succession with the 22 letters of the Hebrew alphabet.
111:10 *The fear of the Lord.* See note on Prov.
1:7.
Psalm 112 An acrostic like the preceding
psalm, this one contrasts the blessings of the
righteous (vv. 1-9) and the judgment on the
wicked (v. 10).
112:1 Here the fear of the Lord is related to
obeying God's commands, which brings freedom from all other fears (vv. 7-8).

3 [a]Prov.
3:16; 8:18;
Matt. 6:33

3 [a]Wealth and riches are in his house,
And his righteousness endures forever.

★**4-9**

4 [a]Job
11:17; Ps.
97:11 [b]Ps.
37:26

4 Light arises in the darkness [a]for the upright;
He is [b]gracious and compassionate and righteous.

5 [a]Ps.
37:21

5 It is well with the man who [a]is gracious and lends;
He will maintain his cause in judgment.

6 [a]Ps. 15:5;
55:22 [b]Prov.
10:7

6 For he will [a]never be shaken;
The [b]righteous will be remembered forever.

7 [a]Prov.
1:33 [b]Ps.
57:7; 108:1
[c]Ps. 56:4

7 He will not fear [a]evil tidings;
His [b]heart is steadfast, [c]trusting in the LORD.

8 [a]Heb.
13:9 [b]Ps.
27:1; 56:11;
Prov. 1:33;
3:24; Is. 12:2
[c]Ps. 54:7;
59:10

8 His [a]heart is upheld, he [b]will not fear,
Until he [c]looks with satisfaction on his adversaries.

★ **9** [a]2 Cor.
9:9 [b]Ps.
75:10; 89:17;
92:10;
148:14

9 He [a]has given freely to the poor;
His righteousness endures forever;
His [b]horn will be exalted in honor.

10 [a]Ps.
86:17 [b]Ps.
35:16; 37:12;
Matt. 8:12;
25:30; Luke
13:28 [c]Ps.
58:7 [d]Job
8:13; Prov.
10:28; 11:7

10 The [a]wicked will see it and be vexed;
He will [b]gnash his teeth and [c]melt away;
The [d]desire of the wicked will perish.

PSALM 113

1 [a]Ps.
135:1 [b]Ps.
34:22; 69:36;
79:10; 90:13

PRAISE the LORD!
[a]Praise, O [b]servants of the LORD.
Praise the name of the LORD.

2 [a]Blessed be the name of the LORD
From this time forth and forever.

2 [a]Ps.
145:21; Dan.
2:20

3 [a]From the rising of the sun to its setting
The [b]name of the LORD is to be praised.

3 [a]Ps. 50:1;
Is. 59:19;
Mal. 1:11
[b]Ps. 18:3;
48:1, 10

4 The LORD is [a]high above all nations;
His [b]glory is above the heavens.

4 [a]Ps. 97:9;
99:2 [b]Ps.
8:1; 57:11;
148:13

5 [a]Who is like the LORD our God,
Who [b]is enthroned on high,

5 [a]Ex.
15:11; Ps.
35:10; 89:6
[b]Ps. 103:19

6 Who [a]humbles Himself to behold
The things that are in heaven and in the earth?

6 [a]Ps. 11:4;
138:6; Is.
57:15

7 He [a]raises the poor from the dust,
And lifts the needy from the ash heap,

7 [a]1 Sam.
2:8; Ps.
107:41

8 To make them [a]sit with princes,
With the princes of His people.

8 [a]Job 36:7

9 He [a]makes the barren woman abide in the house
As a joyful mother of children.
Praise the LORD!

9 [a]1 Sam.
2:5; Ps. 68:6;
Is. 54:1

PSALM 114

1 [a]Ex.
12:51; 13:3
[b]Ps. 81:5

WHEN Israel went forth [a]from Egypt,
The house of Jacob from a people of [b]strange language,

2 Judah became [a]His sanctuary,
Israel, [b]His dominion.

2 [a]Ex.
15:17; 29:45,
46; Ps.
78:68, 69
[b]Ex. 19:6

112:4-9 The righteous man is a blessing to others (v. 4), generous (vv. 5, 9), and stable in adversity (vv. 6-8).
112:9 *horn.* A symbol of strength.
Psalm 113 Psalms 113-118, known as the Egyptian (because of Psalm 114) Hallel (meaning "praise"), are sung in connection with the Passover, the first two before the meal and the remaining four after (see note on Mark 14:26). This hymn calls for praise to the Lord (vv. 1-3),

because He is exalted on high (vv. 4-5), yet condescends to exalt the lowly (vv. 6-9).
Psalm 114 This brief hymn commemorating God's mighty deeds in the Exodus may be divided as follows: the rehearsal of the facts (vv. 1-4), the interrogation of the (personified) waters and hills (vv. 5-6), the exhortation to the earth to tremble before the Lord of such wonders (vv. 7-8).

3 aEx.
14:21; Ps.
77:16 bJosh.
3:13, 16

4 aEx.
19:18; Judg.
5:5; Ps. 18:7;
29:6; Hab.
3:6

5 aHab. 3:8

7 aPs. 96:9

8 aEx. 17:6;
Num. 20:11;
Ps. 78:15;
105:41 bPs.
107:35
cDeut. 8:15

1 aIs.
48:11; Ezek.
36:22 bPs.
29:2; 96:8

2 aPs.
79:10 bPs.
42:3, 10

3 aPs.
103:19 bPs.
135:6; Dan.
4:35

★ **4-8**

4 aPs.
115:4-8;
135:15-18;
Jer. 10:4
bDeut. 4:28;
2 Kin. 19:18;
Is. 37:19;
44:10, 20;
Jer. 10:3

5 aJer. 10:5

3 The ᵃsea looked and fled;
   The ᵇJordan turned back.
4 The mountains ᵃskipped
   like rams,
   The hills, like lambs.
5 What ᵃails you, O sea, that
   you flee?
   O Jordan, that you turn
   back?
6 O mountains, that you
   skip like rams?
   O hills, like lambs?

7 ᵃTremble, O earth, before
   the Lord,
   Before the God of Jacob,
8 Who ᵃturned the rock into
   a ᵇpool of water,
   The ᶜflint into a fountain
   of water.

PSALM 115

ᵃ
NOT to us, O Lord, not to us,
   But ᵇto Thy name give
   glory
   Because of Thy loving-
   kindness, because of
   Thy truth.
2 ᵃWhy should the nations
   say,
   "ᵇWhere, now, is their
   God?"
3 But our ᵃGod is in the
   heavens;
   He ᵇdoes whatever He
   pleases.
4 Their ᵃidols are silver and
   gold,
   The ᵇwork of man's hands.
5 They have mouths, but
   they ᵃcannot speak;
   They have eyes, but they
   cannot see;
6 They have ears, but they
   cannot hear;
   They have noses, but they
   cannot smell;

7 They have hands, but they
   cannot feel;
   They have feet, but they
   cannot walk;
   They cannot make a sound
   with their throat.
8 ᵃThose who make them
   will become like
   them,
   Everyone who trusts in
   them.

9 O ᵃIsrael, ᵇtrust in the
   Lord;
   He is their ᶜhelp and their
   shield.
10 O house of ᵃAaron, trust
   in the Lord;
   He is their help and their
   shield.
11 You who ᵃfear the Lord,
   trust in the Lord;
   He is their help and their
   shield.
12 The Lord ᵃhas been mindful of us; He will bless
   us;
   He will bless the house of
   Israel;
   He will bless the house of
   Aaron.
13 He will ᵃbless those who
   fear the Lord,
   ᵇThe small together with
   the great.
14 May the Lord ᵃgive you increase,
   You and your children.
15 May you be blessed of the
   Lord,
   ᵃMaker of heaven and
   earth.

16 The heavens are ᵃthe
   heavens of the Lord;
   But ᵇthe earth He has giv-
   en to the sons of men.
17 The ᵃdead do not praise
   the Lord,

8 aPs.
135:18; Is.
44:9-11

★ **9** aPs.
118:2;
135:19 bPs.
37:3; 62:8
cPs. 33:20

10 aPs.
118:2;
135:19

11 aPs.
22:23;
103:11;
135:20

12 aPs. 98:3

13 aPs.
103:11;
112:1; 128:1
bRev. 11:18;
19:5

14 aDeut.
1:11

15 aGen.
1:1; Neh. 9:6;
Ps. 96:5;
102:25;
121:2; 124:8;
134:3; 146:6;
Acts 14:15;
Rev. 14:7

16 aPs.
89:11 bPs.
8:6

★**17** aPs.
6:5; 88:10-
12; Is. 38:18
bPs. 31:17

Psalm 115 The psalm consists of: a contrast (between the sovereign God and impotent idols, vv. 1-8), a call (to trust God, vv. 9-11), a confidence (in God's blessings, vv. 12-16), and a chorus (of praise, vv. 17-18).
115:4-8 See Isa. 44:9-20 (and note there) for another biting satire on idolatry.
115:9 The *shield* as a symbol of divine protection is as ancient as Abraham (Gen. 15:1).

115:17 While it is true that O.T. believers were given very little revelation concerning life after death, passages like this should not be understood to teach cessation of existence nor an unconscious or inactive state after death. The point is that the dead have left the sphere of earthly activities, the highest of which is to praise the Lord (see notes on 6:4 and 30:9).

Nor *do* any who go down
into [b]silence;

18 But as for us, we will
[a]bless the LORD
From this time forth and
forever.
Praise the LORD!

18 [a]Ps.
113:2; Dan.
2:20

PSALM 116

1 [a]Ps. 18:1
[b]Ps. 6:8;
66:19; Is.
37:17; Dan.
9:18

[a]I LOVE the LORD, because He
[b]hears
My voice *and* my supplications.

2 [a]Ps. 17:6;
31:2; 40:1

2 Because He has [a]inclined
His ear to me,
Therefore I shall call *upon
Him* as long as I live.

★ 3 [a]Ps.
18:4, 5

3 The [a]cords of death encompassed me,
And the terrors of Sheol
came upon me;
I found distress and sor-
row.

4 [a]Ps. 18:6;
118:5 [b]Ps.
17:13; 22:20

4 Then [a]I called upon the
name of the LORD:
"O LORD, I beseech Thee,
[b]save my life!"

5 [a]Ps.
86:15; 103:8
[b]Ezra 9:15;
Neh. 9:8; Ps.
119:137;
145:17; Jer.
12:1; Dan.
9:14 [c]Ex.
34:6

5 [a]Gracious is the LORD, and
[b]righteous;
Yes, our God is [c]compas-
sionate.

6 The LORD preserves [a]the
simple;
I was [b]brought low, and
He saved me.

★ 6 [a]Ps.
19:7; Prov.
1:4 [b]Ps.
79:8; 142:6
7 [a]Jer.
6:16; Matt.
11:29 [b]Ps.
13:6; 142:7

7 Return to your [a]rest, O my
soul,
For the LORD has [b]dealt
bountifully with you.

8 For Thou hast [a]rescued my
soul from death,
My eyes from tears,
My feet from stumbling.

8 [a]Ps.
49:15; 56:13;
86:13

9 I shall walk before the
LORD
In the [a]land of the living.

9 [a]Ps.
27:13

10 I [a]believed when I said,
"I am [b]greatly afflicted."

10 [a]2 Cor.
4:13 [b]Ps.
88:7

11 I [a]said in my alarm,
"[b]All men are liars."

11 [a]Ps.
31:22 [b]Ps.
62:9; Rom.
3:4

12 What shall I [a]render to the
LORD
For all His [b]benefits
toward me?

12 [a]2 Chr.
32:25;
1 Thess. 3:9
[b]Ps. 103:2

13 I shall lift up the [a]cup of
salvation,
And [b]call upon the name
of the LORD.

★13 [a]Ps.
16:5 [b]Ps.
80:18; 105:1

14 I shall [a]pay my vows to the
LORD,
Oh *may it be* [b]in the pres-
ence of all His people.

14 [a]Ps.
50:14;
116:18 [b]Ps.
22:25

15 [a]Precious in the sight of
the LORD
Is the death of His godly
ones.

★15 [a]Ps.
72:14

16 O LORD, surely I am [a]Thy
servant,
I am Thy servant, the [b]son
of Thy handmaid,
Thou hast [c]loosed my
bonds.

16 [a]Ps.
86:16;
119:125;
143:12 [b]Ps.
86:16 [c]Ps.
107:14

17 To Thee I shall offer [a]a
sacrifice of thanksgiv-
ing,
And [b]call upon the name
of the LORD.

17 [a]Lev.
7:12; Ps.
50:14 [b]Ps.
116:13

18 I shall [a]pay my vows to the
LORD,
Oh *may it be* in the pres-
ence of all His people,

18 [a]Ps.
116:14

19 In the [a]courts of the LORD's
house,
In the midst of you, O [b]Je-
rusalem.
Praise the LORD!

19 [a]Ps.
92:13; 96:8;
135:2 [b]Ps.
102:21

PSALM 117

[a]PRAISE the LORD, all nations;
Laud Him, all peoples!

1 [a]Rom.
15:11

Psalm 116 In this song of personal thanksgiving, the psalmist reiterates his love for the
Lord (vv. 1-2), rehearses his past distress (vv.
3-4), reports and reflects on his deliverance (vv.
5-11), and resolves anew to praise the Lord for
deliverance (vv. 12-19).
116:3 So severe was the psalmist's trouble that it
was likely to result in his death.
116:6 *the simple.* Those whose lack of wisdom
and experience exposes them to danger.

116:13 *I shall lift up the cup of salvation.* Perhaps an allusion to the drink offering offered
in gratitude for salvation.
116:15 The death of His saints is of concern to
the Lord.
Psalm 117 This shortest and middle chapter
of the Bible is a hymn in its simplest form—a
call to praise (v. 1) and the cause for that praise
(v. 2).

★ 2 aPs.
103:11 bPs.
100:5; 146:6

2 For His *a*lovingkindness is
great toward us,
And the *b*truth of the LORD
is everlasting.
Praise the LORD!

PSALM 118

1 a1 Chr.
16:8, 34; Ps.
106:1; 107:1;
Jer. 33:11
b2 Chr. 5:13;
7:3; Ezra
3:11; Ps.
100:5; 136:1-
26

2 aPs.
115:9

3 aPs.
115:10

4 aPs.
115:11

GIVE thanks to the LORD, for
*b*He is good;
For His lovingkindness is
everlasting.
2 Oh let *a*Israel say,
"His lovingkindness is everlasting."
3 Oh let the *a*house of Aaron
say,
"His lovingkindness is everlasting."
4 Oh let those *a*who fear the
LORD say,
"His lovingkindness is everlasting."

★ 5 aPs.
18:6; 86:7;
120:1 bPs.
18:19

6 aJob
19:27; Ps.
56:9; Heb.
13:6 bPs.
23:4; 27:1
cPs. 56:4, 11

7 aPs. 54:4
bPs. 54:7;
59:10

8 a2 Chr.
32:7, 8; Ps.
40:4; 108:12;
Is. 31:1, 3;
57:13; Jer.
17:5

9 aPs.
146:3

10 aPs. 3:6;
88:17 bPs.
18:40

5 From *my* *a*distress I called
upon the LORD;
The LORD answered me
and *b*set *me* in a large
place.
6 The LORD is *a*for me; I will
*b*not fear;
*c*What can man do to me?
7 The LORD is for me *a*among
those who help me;
Therefore I shall *b*look
with satisfaction on
those who hate me.
8 It is *a*better to take refuge
in the LORD
Than to trust in man.
9 It is *a*better to take refuge
in the LORD
Than to trust in princes.

10 All nations *a*surrounded
me;
In the name of the LORD I
will surely *b*cut them
off.

11 They *a*surrounded me, yes,
they surrounded me;
In the name of the LORD I
will surely cut them
off.
12 They surrounded me *a*like
bees;
They were extinguished as
a *b*fire of thorns;
In the name of the LORD I
will surely cut them
off.
13 You *a*pushed me violently
so that I was falling,
But the LORD *b*helped me.
14 *a*The LORD is my strength
and song,
And He has become *b*my
salvation.
15 The sound of *a*joyful
shouting and salva-
tion is in the tents of
the righteous;
The *b*right hand of the
LORD does valiantly.
16 The *a*right hand of the
LORD is exalted;
The right hand of the LORD
does valiantly.
17 I *a*shall not die, but live,
And *b*tell of the works of
the LORD.
18 The LORD has *a*disciplined
me severely,
But He has *b*not given me
over to death.
19 *a*Open to me the gates of
righteousness;
I shall enter through them,
I shall give thanks to
the LORD.
20 This is the gate of the
LORD;
The *a*righteous will enter
through it.
21 I shall give thanks to Thee,
for Thou hast *a*an-
swered me;

11 aPs.
88:17

12 aDeut.
1:44 bPs.
58:9; Nah.
1:10

★13 aPs.
140:4 bPs.
86:17

14 aEx. 15:2;
Is. 12:2 bPs.
27:1

15 aPs. 68:3
bEx. 15:6;
Ps. 89:13;
Luke 1:51

16 aEx. 15:6;
Ps. 89:13

17 aPs. 6:5;
116:8, 9;
Hab. 1:12
bPs. 73:28;
107:22

18 aPs.
73:14; Jer.
31:18; 1 Cor.
11:32; 2 Cor.
6:9 bPs.
86:13

19 aIs. 26:2

20 aPs. 15:1,
2; 24:3-6;
140:13; Is.
35:8; Rev.
22:14

21 aPs.
116:1; 118:5
bPs. 118:14

117:2 *lovingkindness.* Steadfast, loyal love (see
note on Hos. 2:19).
Psalm 118 This psalm of jubilant thanksgiving was sung by worshipers in procession to the
Temple. It contains an acclamation of praise (vv.
1-4), an acknowledgment of past distress, petition, and deliverance by God (vv. 5-21), and an

anticipation of the future day when the Foundation Stone will bring salvation (vv. 22-29).
118:5 In place of *distress* (lit., a tight place), the
Lord provides a *large place.*
118:13 *You pushed me violently.* The reference
is to Israel's enemies, who are addressed as an
individual.

And Thou hast [b]become
my salvation.

22 The [a]stone which the
builders rejected
Has become the chief cor-
ner *stone.*

23 This is the Lord's doing;
It is marvelous in our eyes.

24 This is the day which the
Lord has made;
Let us [a]rejoice and be glad
in it.

25 O Lord, [a]do save, we beseech Thee;
O Lord, we beseech Thee,
do send [b]prosperity!

26 [a]Blessed is the one who
comes in the name of
the Lord;
We have [b]blessed you
from the house of the
Lord.

27 [a]The Lord is God, and He
has given us [b]light;
Bind the festival sacrifice
with cords to the
[c]horns of the altar.

28 [a]Thou art my God, and I
give thanks to Thee;
Thou art my God, [b]I extol
Thee.

29 [a]Give thanks to the Lord,
for He is good;
For His lovingkindness is
everlasting.

PSALM 119

א Aleph.

HOW blessed are those whose
way is [a]blameless,

Who [b]walk in the law of
the Lord.

2 How blessed are those
who [a]observe His tes-
timonies,
Who [b]seek Him [c]with all
their heart.

3 They also [a]do no unrighteousness;
They walk in His ways.

4 Thou hast [a]ordained Thy
precepts,
That we should keep *them*
diligently.

5 Oh that my [a]ways may be
established
To [b]keep Thy statutes!

6 Then I [a]shall not be
ashamed
When I look upon all Thy
commandments.

7 I shall [a]give thanks to Thee
with uprightness of
heart,
When I learn Thy right-
eous judgments.

8 I shall keep Thy statutes;
Do not [a]forsake me utterly!

ב Beth.

9 How can a young man
keep his way pure?
By [a]keeping *it* according to
Thy word.

10 With [a]all my heart I have
sought Thee;
Do not let me [b]wander
from Thy command-
ments.

11 Thy word I have [a]trea-
sured in my heart,
That I may not sin against
Thee.

Cross-references (margin)

★22-23
22 [a]Matt.
21:42; Mark
12:10, 11;
Luke 20:17;
Acts 4:11;
Eph. 2:20;
1 Pet. 2:7
24 [a]Ps. 31:7

★25-26
25 [a]Ps.
106:47 [b]Ps.
122:6, 7
26 [a]Matt.
21:9; 23:39;
Mark 11:9;
Luke 13:35;
19:38; John
12:13 [b]Ps.
129:8
27 [a]1 Kin.
18:39 [b]Esth.
8:16; Ps.
18:28; 27:1;
1 Pet. 2:9
[c]Ex. 27:2
28 [a]Ps. 63:1;
140:6 [b]Ex.
15:2; Is. 25:1
29 [a]Ps. 118:1

1 [a]Ps.
101:2, 6;
Prov. 11:20;
13:6 [b]Ps.
128:1; Ezek.
11:20; 18:17;
Mic. 4:2

2 [a]Ps.
25:10; 99:7;
119:22, 168
[b]Deut. 4:29;
Ps. 119:10
[c]Deut. 6:5;
10:12; 11:13;
13:3; 30:2
3 [a]1 John
3:9; 5:18
4 [a]Deut.
4:13; Neh.
9:13
5 [a]Ps. 40:2;
Prov. 4:26
[b]Deut. 12:1;
2 Chr. 7:17
6 [a]Job
22:26; Ps.
119:80
7 [a]Ps.
119:62
8 [a]Ps.
38:21; 71:9,
18
9 [a]1 Kin.
2:4; 8:25;
2 Chr. 6:16
10 [a]2 Chr.
15:15; Ps.
119:2, 145
[b]Ps. 119:21,
118
11 [a]Ps.
37:31; 40:8;
Luke 2:19;
51

118:22-23 Christ applied these words to His own rejection (Matt. 21:42-44; cf. Peter's use in Acts 4:11 and 1 Pet. 2:7).
118:25-26 These words were spoken in praise of Christ by the populace at His triumphal entry (see note on Matt. 21:9), but in view of His rejection by the Jewish leaders, Christ announced the future fulfillment of this praise at His second coming (see notes on Matt. 23:39 and Luke 13:35).
Psalm 119 This wisdom psalm concerning the law of the Lord is an alphabetic acrostic in which each stanza of eight verses is devoted to successive letters of the Hebrew alphabet, each

verse of a particular stanza beginning with the same letter. The psalm conveys the thought that the Word of God contains everything man needs to know. Except for verses 1-3, 115, it is addressed to the Lord. The psalmist uses ten different terms for the law or Word of God, every verse except verses 90, 122 and 132 mentioning at least one of these terms: *law* (i.e., instruction or revelation), *testimonies* (or precepts), *ways*, *precepts* (or orders), *statutes* (or decrees), *commandments*, *judgments* (or ordinances), *word*, *path*, *word* (the last "word" meaning promise or utterance as in v. 11).

12 aPs.
119:26, 64,
108, 124,
135, 171

12 Blessed art Thou, O Lord;
    aTeach me Thy statutes.

13 aPs. 40:9
bPs. 119:72

13 With my lips I have atold of
    All the bordinances of Thy mouth.

14 aPs.
119:111, 162

14 I have arejoiced in the way of Thy testimonies,
    As much as in all riches.

15 aPs. 1:2;
119:23, 48,
78, 97, 148
bPs. 25:4;
27:11; Is
58:2

15 I will ameditate on Thy precepts,
    And regard bThy ways.

16 aPs. 1:2;
119:24, 35,
47, 70, 77,
92, 143, 174
bPs. 119:93

16 I shall adelight in Thy statutes;
    I shall bnot forget Thy word.

ג Gimel.

17 aPs. 13:6;
116:7

17 aDeal bountifully with Thy servant,
    That I may live and keep Thy word.

18 Open my eyes, that I may behold
    Wonderful things from Thy law.

19 aGen.
47:9; Lev.
25:23; 1 Chr.
29:15; Ps.
39:12;
119:54; Heb.
11:13

19 I am a astranger in the earth;
    Do not hide Thy commandments from me.

20 aPs. 42:1,
2; 63:1; 84:2;
119:40, 131

20 My soul is crushed awith longing
    After Thine ordinances at all times.

21 aPs.
68:30 bDeut.
27:26; Ps.
37:22 cPs.
119:10; 118

21 Thou dost arebuke the arrogant, the bcursed,
    Who cwander from Thy commandments.

22 aPs. 39:8;
119:39 bPs.
119:2

22 aTake away reproach and contempt from me,
    For I bobserve Thy testimonies.

23 aPs.
119:161 bPs.
119:15

23 Even though aprinces sit and talk against me,
    Thy servant bmeditates on Thy statutes.

24 aPs.
119:16

24 Thy testimonies also are my adelight;
    They are my counselors.

ד Daleth.

25 aPs.
44:25 bPs.
119:37, 40,
88, 93, 107,
149, 154,
156, 159,
143:11 cPs.
119:65

25 My asoul cleaves to the dust;
    bRevive me caccording to Thy word.

26 aPs. 25:4;
27:11; 86:11;
119:12

26 I have told of my ways, and Thou hast answered me;
    aTeach me Thy statutes.

27 Make me understand the way of Thy precepts,
    So I will ameditate on Thy wonders.

27 aPs.
105:2; 145:5

28 My asoul weeps because of grief;
    bStrengthen me according to Thy word.

28 aPs.
22:14;
107:26 bPs.
20:2; 1 Pet.
5:10

29 Remove the false way from me,
    And graciously grant me Thy law.

30 I have chosen the faithful way;
    I have placed Thine ordinances before me.

31 I acleave to Thy testimonies;
    O Lord, do not put me to shame!

31 aDeut.
11:22

32 I shall run the way of Thy commandments,
    For Thou wilt aenlarge my heart.

32 a1 Kin.
4:29; Is.
60:5; 2 Cor.
6:11, 13

ה He.

33 aTeach me, O Lord, the way of Thy statutes,
    And I shall observe it to the end.

33 aPs.
119:5, 12

34 aGive me understanding, that I may bobserve Thy law,
    And keep it cwith all my heart.

34 aPs.
119:27, 73,
125, 144,
169 b1 Chr.
22:12; Ezek.
44:24 cPs.
119:2, 69

35 Make me walk in the apath of Thy commandments,
    For I bdelight in it.

35 aPs. 25:4;
Is. 40:14
bPs. 112:1;
119:16

36 aIncline my heart to Thy testimonies,
    And not to bdishonest gain.

36 a1 Kin.
8:58 bEzek.
33:31; Mark
7:21, 22;
Luke 12:15;
Heb. 13:5

37 Turn away my aeyes from looking at vanity,
    And brevive me in Thy ways.

37 aIs. 33:15
bPs. 71:20;
119:25

38 aEstablish Thy word to Thy servant,
    As that which produces reverence for Thee.

38 a2 Sam.
7:25

39 aTurn away my reproach which I dread,
    For Thine ordinances are good.

39 aPs.
119:22

40 Behold, I along for Thy precepts;
    Revive me through Thy righteousness.

40 aPs.
119:20

ו Vav.

41 *a*Ps.
119:77 *b*Ps.
119:58, 76,
116, 170

41 May Thy *a*lovingkindnesses also come to me, O
Lord,
Thy salvation *b*according
to Thy word;

42 *a*Prov.
27:11 *b*Ps.
102:8;
119:39

42 So I shall have an *a*answer
for him who *b*re-
proaches me,
For I trust in Thy word.

43 *a*Ps.
119:49, 74,
81, 114, 147

43 And do not take the word
of truth utterly out of
my mouth,
For I *a*wait for Thine ordinances.

44 *a*Ps.
119:33

44 So I will *a*keep Thy law
continually,
Forever and ever.

45 *a*Prov.
4:12 *b*Ps.
119:94, 155

45 And I will *a*walk at liberty,
For I *b*seek Thy precepts.

46 *a*Matt.
10:18; Acts
26:1, 2

46 I will also speak of Thy
testimonies *a*before
kings,
And shall not be ashamed.

47 *a*Ps.
119:16 *b*Ps.
119:97, 127,
159

47 And I shall *a*delight in Thy
commandments,
Which I *b*love.

48 *a*Ps.
119:97, 127,
159 *b*Ps.
119:15

48 And I shall lift up my
hands to Thy com-
mandments,
Which I *a*love;
And I will *b*meditate on
Thy statutes.

ז Zayin.

49 Remember the word to
Thy servant,
In which Thou hast made
me hope.

50 *a*Job
6:10; Rom.
15:4

50 This is my *a*comfort in my
affliction,
That Thy word has revived
me.

51 *a*Job
30:1; Jer.
20:7 *b*Job
23:11; Ps.
44:18;
119:157

51 The arrogant *a*utterly deride me,
Yet I do not *b*turn aside
from Thy law.

52 *a*Ps.
103:18

52 I have *a*remembered Thine
ordinances from of
old, O Lord,
And comfort myself.

53 Burning *a*indignation has
seized me because of
the wicked,
Who *b*forsake Thy law.

54 Thy statutes are my songs
In the house of my *a*pilgrimage.

55 O Lord, I *a*remember Thy
name *b*in the night,
And keep Thy law.

56 This has become mine,
That I *a*observe Thy precepts.

53 *a*Ex.
32:19; Ezra
9:3; Neh.
13:25; Ps.
119:158 *b*Ps.
89:30

54 *a*Gen.
47:9; Ps.
119:19

55 *a*Ps. 63:6
*b*Ps. 42:8;
92:2; 119:62;
Is. 26:9; Acts
16:25

56 *a*Ps.
119:22, 69,
100

ח Heth.

57 The Lord is my *a*portion;
I have promised to *b*keep
Thy words.

58 I *a*entreated Thy favor
*b*with all *my* heart;
*c*Be gracious to me *d*according to Thy word.

59 I *a*considered my ways,
And turned my feet to Thy
testimonies.

60 I hastened and did not delay
To keep Thy command-
ments.

★57-64
57 *a*Ps. 16:5;
Lam. 3:24
*b*Deut. 33:9

58 *a*1 Kin.
13:6 *b*Ps.
119:2 *c*Ps.
41:4; 56:1;
57:1 *d*Ps.
119:41

59 *a*Mark
14:72; Luke
15:17

61 The *a*cords of the wicked
have encircled me,
But I have *b*not forgotten
Thy law.

62 At *a*midnight I shall rise to
give thanks to Thee
Because of Thy *b*righteous
ordinances.

63 I am a *a*companion of all
those who fear Thee,
And of those who keep
Thy precepts.

64 *a*The earth is full of Thy
lovingkindness,   O
Lord;
*b*Teach me Thy statutes.

61 *a*Job
36:8; Ps.
140:5 *b*Ps.
119:83, 141,
153, 176

62 *a*Ps.
119:55 *b*Ps.
119:7

63 *a*Ps.
101:6

64 *a*Ps. 33:5
*b*Ps. 119:12

ט Teth.

65 Thou hast dealt well with
Thy servant,
O Lord, according to Thy
word.

★65-72

119:57-64 The thought is that we cannot have
God without knowing His Word.
119:65-72 The goodness of God sometimes includes discipline. *covered with fat* (v. 70). I.e.,
insensible and incapable of receiving spiritual
truth.

66 *a*Phil. 1:9

66 Teach me good *a*discernment and knowledge,
For I believe in Thy commandments.

67 *a*Ps. 119:71, 75; Jer. 31:18, 19; Heb. 12:5-11
68 *a*Ps. 86:5; 100:5; 106:1; 107:1; Matt. 19:17 *b*Deut. 8:16; 28:63; 30:5; 125:4 *c*Ps. 119:12
69 *a*Job 13:4; Ps. 109:2 *b*Ps. 119:56

67 *a*Before I was afflicted I went astray,
But now I keep Thy word.
68 Thou art *a*good and *b*doest good;
*c*Teach me Thy statutes.
69 The arrogant have *a*forged a lie against me;
With all *my* heart I will *b*observe Thy precepts.

70 *a*Deut. 32:15; Job 15:27; Ps. 17:10; Is. 6:10; Jer. 5:28; Acts 28:27 *b*Ps. 119:16
71 *a*Ps. 119:67, 75
72 *a*Ps. 19:10; 119:127; Prov. 8:10, 11, 19

70 Their heart is *a*covered with fat,
But I *b*delight in Thy law.
71 It is *a*good for me that I was afflicted,
That I may learn Thy statutes.
72 The *a*law of Thy mouth is better to me
Than thousands of gold and silver *pieces.*

' Yodh.

73 *a*Job 10:8; 31:15; Ps. 100:3; 138:8; 139:15, 16 *b*Ps. 119:34
74 *a*Ps. 34:2; 35:27; 107:42 *b*Ps. 119:43
75 *a*Ps. 119:138 *b*Heb. 12:10

73 *a*Thy hands made me and fashioned me;
*b*Give me understanding, that I may learn Thy commandments.
74 May those who fear Thee *a*see me and be glad,
Because I *b*wait for Thy word.
75 I know, O Lord, that Thy judgments are *a*righteous,
And that *b*in faithfulness Thou hast afflicted me.
76 O may Thy lovingkindness comfort me,
According to Thy word to Thy servant.

77 *a*Ps. 119:41 *b*Ps. 119:16

77 May *a*Thy compassion come to me that I may live,
For Thy law is my *b*delight.

78 *a*Jer. 50:32 *b*Ps. 119:86 *c*Ps. 119:15

78 May *a*the arrogant be ashamed, for they subvert me *b*with a lie;

But I shall *c*meditate on Thy precepts.
79 May those who fear Thee turn to me,
Even those who know Thy testimonies.
80 May my heart be *a*blameless in Thy statutes,
That I may not *b*be ashamed.

80 *a*Ps. 119:1 *b*Ps. 119:46

 כ Kaph.

81 My *a*soul languishes for Thy salvation;
I *b*wait for Thy word.
82 My *a*eyes fail *with longing* for Thy word,
While I say, "When wilt Thou comfort me?"
83 Though I have *a*become like a wineskin in the smoke,
I do *b*not forget Thy statutes.
84 How many are the *a*days of Thy servant?
When wilt Thou *b*execute judgment on those who persecute me?
85 The arrogant have *a*dug pits for me,
Men who are not in accord with Thy law.
86 All Thy commandments are *a*faithful;
They have *b*persecuted me with a lie; *c*help me!
87 They almost destroyed me on earth,
But as for me, I *a*did not forsake Thy precepts.
88 Revive me according to Thy lovingkindness,
So that I may keep the testimony of Thy mouth.

81 *a*Ps. 84:2 *b*Ps. 119:43
82 *a*Ps. 69:3; 119:123; Is. 38:14; Lam. 2:11
★83 *a*Job 30:30 *b*Ps. 119:61
84 *a*Ps. 39:4 *b*Rev. 6:10
85 *a*Ps. 7:15; 35:7; 57:6; Jer. 18:22
86 *a*Ps. 119:138 *b*Ps. 119:78, 161 *c*Ps. 109:26
87 *a*Is. 58:2

ל Lamedh.

89 *a*Forever, O Lord,
Thy word is settled in heaven.
90 Thy *a*faithfulness *continues* throughout all generations;

89 *a*Ps. 89:2; 119:160; Is. 40:8; Matt. 24:35; 1 Pet. 1:25
90 *a*Ps. 36:5; 89:1, 2 *b*Ps. 148:6 *c*Eccl. 1:4

119:83 *like a wineskin in the smoke.* I.e., black,   shriveled, of no further use.

Thou didst [b]establish the earth, and it [c]stands.

91 They stand this day according to Thine [a]ordinances,
For [b]all things are Thy servants.

92 If Thy law had not been my [a]delight,
Then I would have perished [b]in my affliction.

93 I will [a]never forget Thy precepts,
For by them Thou hast [b]revived me.

94 I am Thine, [a]save me;
For I have [b]sought Thy precepts.

95 The wicked [a]wait for me to destroy me;
I shall diligently consider Thy testimonies.

96 I have seen a limit to all perfection;
Thy commandment is exceedingly broad.

 מ Mem.

97 O how I [a]love Thy law!
It is my [b]meditation all the day.

98 Thy [a]commandments make me wiser than my enemies,
For they are ever mine.

99 I have more insight than all my teachers,
For Thy testimonies are my [a]meditation.

100 I understand [a]more than the aged,
Because I have [b]observed Thy precepts.

101 I have [a]restrained my feet from every evil way,
That I may keep Thy word.

102 I have not [a]turned aside from Thine ordinances,
For Thou Thyself hast taught me.

103 How [a]sweet are Thy words to my taste!
Yes, sweeter than honey to my mouth!

104 From Thy precepts I [a]get understanding;
Therefore I [b]hate every false way.

נ Nun.

105 Thy word is a [a]lamp to my feet,
And a light to my path.

106 I have [a]sworn, and I will confirm it,
That I will keep Thy righteous ordinances.

107 I am exceedingly [a]afflicted;
[b]Revive me, O LORD, according to Thy word.

108 O accept the [a]freewill offerings of my mouth, O LORD,
And [b]teach me Thine ordinances.

109 My [a]life is continually in my hand,
Yet I do not [b]forget Thy law.

110 The wicked have [a]laid a snare for me,
Yet I have not [b]gone astray from Thy precepts.

111 I have [a]inherited Thy testimonies forever,
For they are the [b]joy of my heart.

112 I have [a]inclined my heart to perform Thy statutes
Forever, *even* [b]to the end.

ס Samekh.

113 I hate those who are [a]double-minded,
But I love Thy [b]law.

114 Thou art my [a]hiding place and my [b]shield;
I [c]wait for Thy word.

115 [a]Depart from me, evildoers,
That I may [b]observe the commandments of my God.

119:96 The meaning is this: all earthly things are limited but His Word is infinite.

119:105-112 The psalmist vows to follow God's Word always.

Marginal references:

91 [a]Jer. 31:35; 33:25 [b]Ps. 104:2-4

92 [a]Ps. 119:16 [b]Ps. 119:50

93 [a]Ps. 119:16, 83 [b]Ps. 119:25

94 [a]Ps. 119:146 [b]Ps. 119:45

95 [a]Ps. 40:14; Is. 32:7

★96

97 [a]Ps. 119:47, 48, 127, 163, 165 [b]Ps. 1:2, 119:15

98 [a]Deut. 4:6; Ps. 119:130

99 [a]Ps. 119:15

100 [a]Job 32:7-9 [b]Ps. 119:22, 56

101 [a]Prov. 1:15

102 [a]Deut. 17:20; Josh. 23:6; 1 Kin. 15:5

103 [a]Ps. 19:10; Prov. 8:11; 24:13, 14

104 [a]Ps. 119:130 [b]Ps. 119:128

★105-112
105 [a]Prov. 6:23

106 [a]Neh. 10:29

107 [a]Ps. 119:25, 50 [b]Ps. 119:25

108 [a]Hos. 14:2; Heb. 13:15 [b]Ps. 119:12

109 [a]Judg. 12:3; Job 13:14 [b]Ps. 119:16

110 [a]Ps. 91:3; 140:5; 141:9 [b]Ps. 119:10

111 [a]Deut. 33:4 [b]Ps. 119:14, 162

112 [a]Ps. 119:36 [b]Ps. 119:33

113 [a]1 Kin. 18:21; James 1:8; 4:8 [b]Ps. 119:47

114 [a]Ps. 31:20; 32:7; 61:4; 91:1 [b]Ps. 84:9 [c]Ps. 119:74

115 [a]Ps. 6:8; 139:19; Matt. 7:23 [b]Ps. 119:22

116 ^aSustain me according to
Thy word, that I may
live;
And ^bdo not let me be
ashamed of my hope.

117 Uphold me that I may be
^asafe,
That I may ^bhave regard
for Thy statutes con-
tinually.

118 Thou hast rejected all
those ^awho wander
from Thy statutes,
For their deceitfulness is
useless.

119 Thou hast removed all the
wicked of the earth
like ^adross;
Therefore I ^blove Thy testimonies.

120 My flesh ^atrembles for fear
of Thee,
And I am ^bafraid of Thy
judgments.

y Ayin.

121 I have ^adone justice and
righteousness;
Do not leave me to my op-
pressors.

122 Be ^asurety for Thy servant
for good;
Do not let the arrogant
^boppress me.

123 My ^aeyes fail *with longing*
for Thy salvation,
And for Thy righteous
word.

124 Deal with Thy servant ^aac-
cording to Thy loving-
kindness,
And ^bteach me Thy statutes.

125 ^aI am Thy servant; ^bgive
me understanding,
That I may know Thy tes-
timonies.

126 It is time for the LORD to
^aact,
For they have broken Thy
law.

127 Therefore I ^alove Thy
commandments
Above gold, yes, above
fine gold.

128 Therefore I esteem right all
Thy ^aprecepts con-
cerning everything,
I ^bhate every false way.

ם Pe.

129 Thy testimonies are ^awon-
derful;
Therefore my soul ^bob-
serves them.

130 The ^aunfolding of Thy
words gives light;
It gives ^bunderstanding to
the simple.

131 I ^aopened my mouth wide
and ^bpanted,
For I ^clonged for Thy commandments.

132 ^aTurn to me and be gracious to me,
After Thy manner with
those who love Thy
name.

133 Establish my ^afootsteps in
Thy word,
And do not let any iniq-
uity ^bhave dominion
over me.

134 ^aRedeem me from the oppression of man,
That I may keep Thy pre-
cepts.

135 ^aMake Thy face shine
upon Thy servant,
And ^bteach me Thy statutes.

136 My eyes shed ^astreams of
water,
Because they ^bdo not keep
Thy law.

צ Tsadhe.

137 ^aRighteous art Thou, O
LORD,
And upright are Thy judg-
ments.

138 Thou hast commanded
Thy testimonies in
^arighteousness
And exceeding ^bfaithful-
ness.

139 My ^azeal has consumed
me,
Because my adversaries
have forgotten Thy
words.

140 Thy ^aword is very pure,
Therefore Thy servant
^bloves it.

141 I am small and ^adespised,
Yet I do not ^bforget Thy
precepts.

---

116 ^aPs.
37:17, 24;
54:4 ^bPs.
25:2, 20;
31:1, 17;
Rom. 5:5;
9:33; Phil.
1:20

117 ^aPs.
12:5; Prov.
29:25 ^bPs.
119:6, 15

118 ^aPs.
119:10, 21

119 ^aIs.
1:22, 25;
Ezek. 22:18,
19 ^bPs.
119:47

120 ^aJob
4:14; Hab.
3:16 ^bPs.
119:161

121 ^a2 Sam.
8:15; Job
29:14

122 ^aJob
17:3; Heb.
7:22 ^bPs.
119:134

123 ^aPs.
119:82

124 ^aPs.
51:1; 106:45;
109:26;
119:88, 149,
159 ^bPs.
119:12

125 ^aPs.
116:16 ^bPs.
119:27

126 ^aJer.
18:23; Ezek.
31:11

127 ^aPs.
19:10;
119:47

128 ^aPs.
19:8 ^bPs.
119:104

129 ^aPs.
119:18 ^bPs.
119:22

130 ^aProv.
6:23 ^bPs.
19:7

131 ^aJob
29:23; Ps.
81:10 ^bPs.
42:1 ^cPs.
119:20

132 ^aPs.
25:16; 106:4

133 ^aPs.
17:5 ^bPs.
19:13; Rom.
6:12

134 ^aPs.
119:84;
142:6; Luke
1:74

135 ^aNum.
6:25; Ps. 4:6;
31:16; 67:1;
80:3, 7, 19
^bPs. 119:12

136 ^aJer.
9:1; 18;
14:17; Lam.
3:48 ^bPs.
119:158

137 ^aEzra
9:15; Neh.
9:33; Ps.
116:5; 129:4;
145:17; Jer.
12:1; Lam.
1:18; Dan.
9:7, 14

138 ^aPs.
19:7-9
119:144, 172
^bPs. 119:86,
90

139 ^aPs.
69:9; John
2:17

140 ^aPs.
12:6; 19:8
^bPs. 119:47

141 ^aPs.
22:6 ^bPs.
119:61

142   142 Thy righteousness is an
*a*Ps.   everlasting righteous-
19:9;   ness,
119:151, 160   And *a*Thy law is truth.

143   143 Trouble and anguish have
*a*Ps.   come upon me;
119:24   Yet Thy commandments
     are my *a*delight.

144   144 Thy *a*testimonies are right-
*a*Ps.   eous forever;
19:9 *b*Ps.   *b*Give me understanding
119:27   that I may live.

ק Qoph.

145   **145** I cried *a*with all my heart;
*a*Ps.   answer me, O LORD!
119:10 *b*Ps.   I will *b*observe Thy stat-
119:22, 55   utes.

146   146 I cried to Thee; *a*save me,
*a*Ps. 3:7   And I shall keep Thy testi-
     monies.

147   147 I *a*rise before dawn and cry
*a*Ps. 5:3;   for help;
57:8; 108:2   I wait for Thy words.

148   148 My eyes anticipate the
*a*Ps.   *a*night watches,
63:6 *b*Ps.   That I may *b*meditate on
119:15   Thy word.

149   149 Hear my voice *a*according
*a*Ps.   to Thy lovingkind-
119:124 *b*Ps.   ness;
119:25   *b*Revive me, O LORD, ac-
     cording to Thine ordi-
     nances.

150 Those who follow after
     wickedness draw
     near;
     They are far from Thy law.

151   151 Thou art *a*near, O LORD,
*a*Ps.   And all Thy command-
34:18;   ments are *b*truth.
145:18; Is.
50:8 *b*Ps.
119:142

152   152 Of old I have *a*known from
*a*Ps.   Thy testimonies,
119:125 *b*Ps.   That Thou hast founded
119:89; Luke   them *b*forever.
21:33

ר Resh.

153   **153** *a*Look upon my *b*affliction
*a*Lam.   and rescue me,
5:1 *b*Ps.   For I do not *c*forget Thy
119:50 *c*Ps.   law.
119:16; Prov.
3:1; Hos. 4:6

154   154 *a*Plead my cause and *b*re-
*a*1 Sam.   deem me;
24:15; Ps.   Revive me according to
35:1; Mic.   Thy word.
7:9 *b*Ps.
119:134

155 Salvation is *a*far from the
     wicked,
     For they *b*do not seek Thy
     statutes.

155 *a*Job 5:4
*b*Ps. 119:45,
94

156 *a*Great are Thy mercies, O
     LORD;
     Revive me according to
     Thine ordinances.

156 *a*2 Sam.
24:14

157 Many are my *a*persecutors
     and my adversaries,
     Yet I do not *b*turn aside
     from Thy testimonies.

157 *a*Ps. 7:1;
119:86, 161
*b*Ps. 119:51

158 I behold the *a*treacherous
     and *b*loathe *them*,
     Because they do not keep
     Thy word.

158 *a*Is.
21:2; 24:16
*b*Ps. 139:21

159 Consider how I *a*love Thy
     precepts;
     *b*Revive me, O LORD, ac-
     cording to Thy loving-
     kindness.

159 *a*Ps.
119:47 *b*Ps.
119:25

160 The *a*sum of Thy word is
     *b*truth,
     And every one of Thy
     righteous ordinances
     *c*is everlasting.

160 *a*Ps.
139:17 *b*Ps.
119:142 *c*Ps.
119:89, 152

ש Shin.

161   **161** *a*Princes persecute me
     without cause,
     But my heart *b*stands in
     awe of Thy words.

161 *a*1 Sam.
24:11; 26:18;
Ps. 119:23
*b*Ps. 119:120

162 I *a*rejoice at Thy word,
     As one who *b*finds great
     spoil.

162 *a*Ps.
119:14, 111
*b*1 Sam.
30:16; Is. 9:3

163 I *a*hate and despise false-
     hood,
     But I *b*love Thy law.

163 *a*Ps.
31:6;
119:104,
128; Prov.
13:5 *b*Ps.
119:47

164 Seven times a day I praise
     Thee,
     Because of Thy *a*righteous
     ordinances.

★164 *a*Ps.
119:7, 160

165 Those who love Thy law
     have *a*great peace,
     And *b*nothing causes them
     to stumble.

165 *a*Ps.
37:11; Is. Prov.
3:2; Is. 26:3;
32:17 *b*Prov.
3:23; Is.
63:13;
1 John 2:10

166 I *a*hope for Thy salvation,
     O LORD,
     And do Thy command-
     ments.

166 *a*Gen.
49:18; Ps.
119:81, 174

167 My *a*soul keeps Thy testi-
     monies,
     And I *b*love them exceed-
     ingly.

167 *a*Ps.
119:129 *b*Ps.
119:47

119:164 *Seven times.* Even more repeatedly than   the three times of 55:17.

168 aPs.
119:22 bJob
24:23; Ps.
139:3; Prov.
5:21

168 I akeep Thy precepts and Thy testimonies,
For all my bways are before Thee.

ת Tav.

★169-176
169 aJob
16:18; Ps.
18:6; 102:1
bPs. 119:27,
144 cPs.
119:65, 154

169 Let my acry come before Thee, O LORD;
bGive me understanding caccording to Thy word.

170 aPs.
28:2; 130:2;
140:6; 143:1
bPs. 22:20;
31:2; 59:1

170 Let my asupplication come before Thee;
bDeliver me according to Thy word.

171 aPs.
51:15; 63:3
bPs. 94:12;
119:12; Is.
2:3; Mic. 4:2

171 Let my alips utter praise,
For Thou bdost teach me Thy statutes.

172 aPs.
51:14 bPs.
119:138

172 Let my atongue sing of Thy word,
For all Thy bcommandments are righteousness.

173 aPs.
37:24; 73:23
bJosh.
24:22; Luke
10:42

173 Let Thy ahand be ready to help me,
For I have bchosen Thy precepts.

174 aPs.
119:166 bPs.
119:16, 24

174 I along for Thy salvation, O LORD,
And Thy law is my bdelight.

175 aIs. 55:3

175 Let my asoul live that it may praise Thee,
And let Thine ordinances help me.

176 aIs.
53:6; Jer.
50:6; Matt.
18:12; Luke
15:4 bPs.
119:16

176 I have agone astray like a lost sheep; seek Thy servant,
For I do bnot forget Thy commandments.

PSALM 120

A Song of Ascents.

IN my trouble I cried to the LORD,
And He answered me.

2 Deliver my soul, O LORD, from alying lips,
From a bdeceitful tongue.

3 What shall be given to you, and what more shall be done to you,
You adeceitful tongue?

4 aSharp arrows of the warrior,
With the burning bcoals of the broom tree.

5 Woe is me, for I sojourn in aMeshech,
For I dwell among the btents of cKedar!

6 Too long has my soul had its dwelling
With those who ahate peace.

7 I aam for peace, but when I speak,
They are bfor war.

1 aPs. 18:6;
66:14; 102:2;
Jon. 2:2

★ 2 aPs.
109:2; Prov.
12:22 bPs.
52:4; Zeph.
3:13

3 aPs. 52:4;
Zeph. 3:13

★ 4 aPs.
45:5; Prov.
25:18; Is.
5:28 bPs.
140:10

★ 5 aGen.
10:2; 1 Chr.
1:5; Ezek.
27:13; 38:2,
3; 39:1
bSong 1:5
cGen. 25:13;
Is. 21:16;
60:7; Jer.
2:10; 49:28;
Ezek. 27:21
6 aPs.
35:20
7 aPs.
109:4 bPs.
55:21

PSALM 121

A Song of Ascents.

I WILL alift up my eyes to bthe mountains;
From whence shall my help come?

★ 1-2

1 aPs.
123:1; Is.
40:26 bPs.
87:1

119:169-176 The word affects the mind (v. 169), the mouth (vv. 171-72), the will (v. 173), the emotions (v. 174), and the conscience (v. 176).
Psalm 120 In this lament, the psalmist cries for deliverance (vv. 1-2), for retribution (vv. 3-4), and for peace (vv. 5-7). *A Song of Ascents.* Psalms 120-134 formed a hymn book used by pilgrims going up to Jerusalem for the annual feasts of Passover, Pentecost, and Tabernacles.
120:2 The *lying lips* and *deceitful tongue* are those of his enemies.
120:4 God's judgment will burn like *coals of the broom tree,* which burns hot and long.
120:5 By referring to *Meshech* (see note on

Ezek. 38:2) and *Kedar* (see note on Isa. 21:16), the psalmist conveys that he lived in hostile surroundings.
Psalm 121 This pilgrim hymn (see note on Psalm 120) affirms that all true help comes from the Lord, who is the Keeper of Israel.
121:1-2 Whatever the psalmist's reason for looking to the *mountains,* whether as a potential refuge or as a menace (being the haunt of robbers), he affirms that his trust is in the Creator not only of those mountains but of the universe. *From whence* begins a new sentence, which is a question answered in verse 2.

2 My ^ahelp *comes* from the LORD,
Who ^bmade heaven and earth.

3 He will not ^aallow your foot to slip;
He who ^bkeeps you will not slumber.

4 Behold, He who keeps Israel
Will neither slumber nor sleep.

5 The LORD is your ^akeeper;
The LORD is your ^bshade on your right hand.

6 The ^asun will not smite you by day,
Nor the moon by night.

7 The LORD will ^aprotect you from all evil;
He will keep your soul.

8 The LORD will ^aguard your going out and your coming in
^bFrom this time forth and forever.

PSALM 122

A Song of Ascents, of David.

I WAS glad when they said to me,
"Let us ^ago to the house of the LORD."

2 Our feet are standing
Within your ^agates, O Jerusalem,

3 Jerusalem, that is ^abuilt
As a city that is ^bcompact together;

4 To which the tribes ^ago up,
even the tribes of the LORD—
An ordinance for Israel—
To give thanks to the name of the LORD.

5 For there ^athrones were set for judgment,
The thrones of the house of David.

6 Pray for the ^apeace of Jerusalem:
"May they prosper who ^blove you.

7 "May peace be within your ^awalls,
And prosperity within your ^bpalaces."

8 For the sake of my ^abrothers and my friends,
I will now say, "^bMay peace be within you."

9 For the sake of the house of the LORD our God
I will ^aseek your good.

PSALM 123

A Song of Ascents.

To Thee I ^alift up my eyes,
O Thou who ^bart enthroned in the heavens!

2 Behold, as the eyes of ^aservants *look* to the hand of their master,
As the eyes of a maid to the hand of her mistress;
So our ^beyes *look* to the LORD our God,
Until He shall be gracious to us.

3 ^aBe gracious to us, O LORD, be gracious to us;
For we are greatly filled ^bwith contempt.

4 Our soul is greatly filled
With the ^ascoffing of ^bthose who are at ease,

Marginal references

2 ^aPs. 124:8 ^bPs. 115:15
3 ^a1 Sam. 2:9; Ps. 66:9 ^bPs. 41:2; 127:1; Is. 27:3
★ 5-6
5 ^aPs. 91:4 ^bPs. 16:8; 91:1; Is. 25:4
6 ^aPs. 91:5; Is. 49:10; Jon. 4:8; Rev. 7:16
7 ^aPs. 41:2; 91:10-12
★ 8 ^aDeut. 28:6 ^bPs. 113:2; 115:18

1 ^aPs. 42:4; Is. 2:3; Mic. 4:2; Zech. 8:21
2 ^aPs. 9:14; 87:2; 116:19; Jer. 7:2
★ 3 ^aPs. 48:13; 147:2 ^b2 Sam. 5:9; Neh. 4:6
4 ^aEx. 23:17; Deut. 16:16; Ps. 84:5

5 ^aDeut. 17:8; 2 Chr. 19:8; Ps. 89:29
6 ^aPs. 29:11; Jer. 29:7 ^bPs. 102:14
7 ^aPs. 51:18; Is. 62:6 ^bPs. 48:3, 13; Jer. 17:27
8 ^aPs. 133:1 ^b1 Sam. 25:6; John 20:19
9 ^aNeh. 2:10; Esth. 10:3

1 ^aPs. 121:1; 141:8 ^bPs. 2:4; 11:4
★ 2 ^aProv. 27:18; Mal. 1:6 ^bPs. 25:15
3 ^aPs. 4:1; 51:1 ^bNeh. 4:4; Ps. 119:22
4 ^aNeh. 2:19; Ps. 79:4 ^bJob 12:5; Is. 32:9, 11; Amos 6:1 ^cNeh. 4:4; Ps. 119:22

121:5-6 The Lord is the *shade* (protection) from all adversaries of the day and night.
121:8 *your going out and your coming in.* A figure of speech for "everything you do." God watches over the believer all the time, in every circumstance, and forever.
Psalm 122 Here the psalmist recounts his joyful pilgrimage to Jerusalem (vv. 1-2), which he praises as the spiritual and civic center of the nation (vv. 3-5), calling for prayer for its peace

and prosperity (vv. 6-9).
122:3 *that is compact together.* I.e., that unifies the people.
Psalm 123 The psalmist expresses his confidence in God (vv. 1-2) and prays for the people's deliverance from those who have contempt for them (vv. 3-4).
123:2 *look to the hand.* I.e., for supply of all needs.

And with the ^ccontempt of the proud.

PSALM 124

A Song of Ascents, of David.

1 ^aPs.
94:17 ^bPs.
129:1

"^a**H**AD it not been the LORD
who was on our side,"
Let Israel now say,

2 "Had it not been the LORD
who was on our side,
When men rose up against
us;

3 ^aNum.
16:30; Ps.
35:25; 56:1;
57:3; Prov.
1:12 ^bGen.
39:19; Ps.
138:7

3 Then they would have
^aswallowed us alive,
When their ^banger was
kindled against us;

4 ^aJob
22:11; Ps.
18:16; 32:6;
69:2; 144:7

4 Then the ^awaters would
have engulfed us,
The stream would have
swept over our soul;

5 ^aJob
38:11

5 Then the ^araging waters
would have swept
over our soul."

6 ^aPs. 27:2;
Prov. 30:14

6 Blessed be the LORD,
Who has not given us to
be ^atorn by their
teeth.

7 ^aPs.
141:10;
2 Cor. 11:33;
Heb. 11:34
^bProv. 6:5
^cPs. 91:3;
Hos. 9:8

7 Our soul has ^aescaped ^bas
a bird out of the
^csnare of the trapper;
The snare is broken and
we have escaped.

8 ^aPs.
121:2 ^bGen.
1:1; Ps.
134:3

8 Our ^ahelp is in the name
of the LORD,
Who ^bmade heaven and
earth.

PSALM 125

A Song of Ascents.

1 ^aPs. 46:5
^bPs. 61:7;
Eccl. 1:4

THOSE who trust in the LORD
Are as Mount Zion, which
^acannot be moved,
but ^babides forever.

2 As the mountains surround Jerusalem,
So ^athe LORD surrounds
His people
^bFrom this time forth and
forever.

2 ^aZech.
2:5 ^bPs.
121:8

3 For the ^ascepter of wickedness shall not rest
upon the land of the
righteous;
That the righteous ^bmay
not put forth their
hands to do wrong.

★ **3** ^aPs.
89:22; Prov.
22:8; Is. 14:5
^b1 Sam.
24:10; Ps.
55:20; Acts
12:1

4 ^aDo good, O LORD, to
those who are good,
And to those who are ^bup-
right in their hearts.

4 ^aPs.
119:68 ^bPs.
7:10; 11:2;
32:11; 36:10;
94:15

5 But as for those who ^aturn
aside to their
^bcrooked ways,
The LORD will lead them
away with the ^cdoers
of iniquity.
^dPeace be upon Israel.

5 ^aJob
23:11; Ps.
40:4; 101:3
^bProv. 2:15;
Is. 59:8 ^cPs.
92:7; 94:4
^dPs. 128:6;
Gal. 6:16

PSALM 126

A Song of Ascents.

WHEN the LORD ^abrought
back the captive ones
of Zion,
We were ^blike those who
dream.

1 ^aPs. 85:1;
Jer. 29:14;
Hos. 6:11
^bActs 12:9

2 Then our ^amouth was
filled with laughter,
And our ^btongue with joyful shouting;
Then they said among the
nations,
"The LORD has ^cdone great
things for them."

2 ^aJob 8:21
^bPs. 51:14;
Is. 35:6
^c1 Sam.
12:24; Ps.
71:19; Luke
1:49

3 The LORD has done great
things for us;
We are ^aglad.

3 ^aIs. 25:9;
Zeph. 3:14

Psalm 124 In this thanksgiving psalm, the psalmist reflects on Israel's past needs which the Lord met (vv. 1-5), reports God's deliverance (vv. 6-7), and reaffirms his trust in the Lord (v. 8). The threats from his enemies are as the danger of drowning (vv. 3-5) and as confinement in a bird trap (vv. 6-7).

Psalm 125 In this song of trust, the psalmist compares the stability of believers with Mt. Zion (v. 1) and the security of the Lord's people with

that of Jerusalem (v. 2), reminding them that for-
eign domination is temporary (v. 3). He then prays for God's blessing on the righteous (v. 4) and predicts judgment on the wicked (v. 5). **125:3** *rest.* I.e., rest permanently.

Psalm 126 Here the restored exiles rejoice in the Lord's deliverance (vv. 1-3), pray for the restoration of others (v. 4), and take confidence in the principle of sowing and reaping (vv. 5-6).

4 Restore our captivity, O
Lord,
As the ªstreams in the
South.

5 Those who sow in ªtears
shall reap with ᵇjoyful
shouting.

6 He who goes to and fro
weeping, carrying *his*
bag of seed,
Shall indeed come again
with a shout of joy,
bringing his sheaves
with him.

PSALM 127

A Song of Ascents, of Solomon.

UNLESS the Lord ªbuilds the
house,
They labor in vain who
build it;
Unless the Lord ᵇguards
the city,
The watchman keeps
awake in vain.

2 It is vain for you to rise up
early,
To retire late,
To ªeat the bread of painful labors;
For He gives to His ᵇbe-
loved ᶜeven in his
sleep.

3 Behold, ªchildren are a gift
of the Lord;
The ᵇfruit of the womb is a
reward.

4 Like arrows in the hand of
a ªwarrior,

So are the children of one's
youth.

5 How ªblessed is the man
whose quiver is full of
them;
ᵇThey shall not be
ashamed,
When they ᶜspeak with
their enemies ᵈin the
gate.

PSALM 128

A Song of Ascents.

HOW blessed is everyone who
fears the Lord,
Who ᵇwalks in His ways.

2 When you shall ªeat of the
ᵇfruit of your hands,
You will be happy and ᶜit
will be well with you.

3 Your wife shall be like a
ªfruitful vine,
Within your house,
Your children like ᵇolive
plants
Around your table.

4 Behold, for thus shall the
man be blessed
Who fears the Lord.

5 ªThe Lord bless you ᵇfrom
Zion,
And may you see the pros-
perity of Jerusalem all
the days of your life.

6 Indeed, may you see your
ªchildren's children.
ᵇPeace be upon Israel!

126:4 The psalmist prays for a flood of returning exiles, like the seasonal torrents that fill normally dry streams in the desert.
126:5-6 The efforts of the exiles to reestablish the nation amid difficulties will someday come to fruition like a harvest, a principle applicable to Christian work as well.
Psalm 127 In this didactic psalm, the psalmist stresses that life should be lived in dependence on the Lord (vv. 1-2) and children regarded as a heritage from the Lord (vv. 3-5). *Solomon.* See note on Psalm 72.
127:1 House-building and city-guarding cannot succeed apart from God's help.
127:5 *they.* I.e., fathers of large families, who had more prestige in community affairs, which were conducted at the city *gate* (see note on Ruth 4:1).
Psalm 128 This psalm teaches the interrelatedness of blessings on the home (vv. 1-4) with blessings on the community (vv. 5-6).
128:1 *blessed.* Happy. This stems from reverence and obedience.
128:3 *Within your house.* Contrast the promiscuous wife (Prov. 7:11).

PSALM 129

A Song of Ascents.

1 "**M**ANY times they have ^apersecuted me from my ^byouth up,"
^cLet Israel now say,

2 "Many times they have persecuted me from my youth up;
Yet they have ^anot prevailed against me.

3 "The plowers plowed upon my back;
They lengthened their furrows."

4 The LORD ^ais righteous;
He has cut in two the ^bcords of the wicked.

5 May all who ^ahate Zion,
Be ^bput to shame and turned backward,

6 Let them be like ^agrass upon the housetops,
Which withers before it grows up;

7 With which the reaper does not fill his hand,
Or the binder of sheaves his ^abosom;

8 Nor do those who pass by say,
"The ^ablessing of the LORD be upon you;
We bless you in the name of the LORD."

PSALM 130

A Song of Ascents.

1 **O**UT of the ^adepths I have cried to Thee, O LORD.

2 Lord, ^ahear my voice!
Let ^bThine ears be attentive
To the ^cvoice of my supplications.

3 If Thou, LORD, shouldst mark iniquities,
O Lord, who could ^astand?

4 But there is ^aforgiveness with Thee,
That Thou mayest be ^bfeared.

5 I wait for the LORD, my ^asoul does wait,
And ^bin His word do I hope.

6 My soul *waits* for the Lord
More than the watchmen ^afor the morning;
Indeed, more than the watchmen for the morning.

7 O Israel, ^ahope in the LORD;
For with the LORD there is ^blovingkindness,
And with Him is ^cabundant redemption.

8 And He will ^aredeem Israel
From all his iniquities.

PSALM 131

A Song of Ascents, of David.

1 **O** LORD, my heart is not ^aproud, nor my eyes ^bhaughty;
Nor do I involve myself in ^cgreat matters,
Or in things ^dtoo difficult for me.

Cross references (margin)

1 ^aEx. 1:11; Judg. 3:8; Ps. 88:15 ^bIs. 47:12; Jer. 2:2; 22:21; Ezek. 16:22; Hos. 2:15; 11:1 ^cPs. 124:1
2 ^aJer. 1:19; 15:20; 20:11; Matt. 16:18; 2 Cor. 4:8, 9
★ **3**
4 ^aPs. 119:137 ^bPs. 140:5
5 ^aMic. 4:11 ^bPs. 70:3; 71:13
★ **6** ^a2 Kin. 19:26; Ps. 37:2; Is. 37:27
7 ^aPs. 79:12
★ **8** ^aRuth 2:4; Ps. 118:26
1 ^aPs. 42:7; 69:2; Lam. 3:55

2 ^aPs. 64:1; 119:149 ^b2 Chr. 6:40; Neh. 1:6, 11 ^cPs. 28:2; 140:6
3 ^aPs. 76:7; 143:2; Nah. 1:6; Mal. 3:2; Rev. 6:17
★ **4** ^aEx. 34:7; Neh. 9:17; Ps. 86:5; Is. 55:7; Dan. 9:9 ^b1 Kin. 8:39, 40; Jer. 33:8, 9
5 ^aPs. 27:14; 33:20; 40:1; 62:1, 5; Is. 8:17; 26:8 ^bPs. 119:74, 81
6 ^aPs. 63:6; 119:147
7 ^aPs. 131:3 ^bPs. 86:5; 103:4 ^cPs. 111:9; Rom. 3:24; Eph. 1:7
8 ^aPs. 103:3, 4; Luke 1:68; Titus 2:14
★ **1** ^a2 Sam. 22:28; Ps. 101:5; Is. 2:12; Zeph. 3:11 ^bProv. 30:13; Is. 5:15 ^cJer. 45:5; Rom. 12:16 ^dJob 42:3; Ps. 139:6

Psalm 129 This psalm of thanksgiving speaks of Israel's harassment (vv. 1-4) and Israel's hope (vv. 5-8).
129:3 Israel is pictured as a scourged man with welts on his back like *furrows* in a ploughed field.
129:6 *grass upon the housetops.* Having no soil, it quickly withers.
129:8 Zion's enemies will not hear the customary greeting of friends.
Psalm 130 This lament includes an entreaty for God's deliverance (vv. 1-2), expectation of God's forgiveness (vv. 3-6), and an exhortation to Israel to trust the Lord (vv. 7-8). This pilgrim psalm (see note on Psalm 120) is also a penitential psalm (see note on Psalm 6).
130:4 Note that the outcome of forgiveness is fear (reverence). Cf. 1 Pet. 2:9, 17.
Psalm 131 Here David expresses his childlike trust in the Lord (vv. 1-2) and calls on Israel to hope in the Lord (v. 3).
131:1 David declares himself free from haughtiness (*great matters*) and excessive ambition (*things too difficult*).

2 Surely I have ^acomposed and quieted my soul;
Like a weaned ^bchild *rests* against his mother,
My soul is like a weaned child within me.

3 O Israel, ^ahope in the LORD
^bFrom this time forth and forever.

PSALM 132

A Song of Ascents.

Rᴇᴍᴇᴍʙᴇʀ, O LORD, on David's behalf,
All ^ahis affliction;

2 How he swore to the LORD,
And vowed to ^athe Mighty One of Jacob,

3 "Surely I will not enter ^amy house,
Nor lie on my bed;

4 I will not ^agive sleep to my eyes,
Or slumber to my eyelids;

5 Until I find a ^aplace for the LORD,
A dwelling place for ^bthe Mighty One of Jacob."

6 Behold, we heard of it in ^aEphrathah;
We found it in the ^bfield of Jaar.

7 Let us go into His ^adwelling place;
Let us ^bworship at His ^cfootstool.

8 ^aArise, O LORD, to Thy ^bresting place;
Thou and the ark of Thy ^cstrength.

9 Let Thy priests be ^aclothed with righteousness;
And let Thy ^bgodly ones sing for joy.

10 For the sake of David Thy servant,
Do not turn away the face of Thine ^aanointed.

11 The LORD has ^asworn to David,
A truth from which He will not turn back;
"^bOf the fruit of your body I will set upon your throne.

12 "If your sons will keep My covenant,
And My testimony which I will teach them,
Their sons also shall ^asit upon your throne forever."

13 For the LORD has ^achosen Zion;
He has ^bdesired it for His habitation.

14 "This is My ^aresting place forever;
Here I will ^bdwell, for I have desired it.

15 "I will abundantly ^abless her provision;
I will ^bsatisfy her needy with bread.

16 "Her ^apriests also I will clothe with salvation;
And her ^agodly ones will sing aloud for joy.

17 "There I will cause the ^ahorn of David to spring forth;
I have prepared a ^blamp for Mine anointed.

Cross-references

★ **2** ^aPs. 62:1 ^bMatt. 18:3; 1 Cor. 14:20

3 ^aPs. 130:7 ^bPs. 113:2

1 ^aGen. 49:24; 2 Sam. 16:12

★ **2-5** ^aGen. 49:24; Is. 49:26; 60:16

3 ^aJob 21:28

4 ^aProv. 6:4

5 ^a1 Kin. 8:17; 1 Chr. 22:7; 26:8; Acts 7:46 ^bPs. 132:2

★ **6** ^aGen. 35:19; 1 Sam. 17:12 ^b1 Sam. 7:1

7 ^aPs. 43:3 ^bPs. 5:7; 99:5 ^c1 Chr. 28:2

8 ^aNum. 10:35; 2 Chr. 6:41; Ps. 68:1 ^bPs. 132:14 ^cPs. 78:61

9 ^aJob 29:14 ^bPs. 30:4; 132:16; 149:5

★ **10** ^aPs. 2:2; 132:17

★ **11-18**

11 ^aPs. 89:3, 35 ^b2 Sam. 7:12-16; 1 Chr. 17:11-14; 2 Chr. 6:16; Ps. 89:4; Acts 2:30

12 ^aLuke 1:32; Acts 2:30

13 ^aPs. 48:1, 2; 78:68 ^bPs. 68:16

14 ^aPs. 132:8 ^bPs. 68:16; Matt. 23:21

15 ^aPs. 147:14 ^bPs. 107:9

16 ^a2 Chr. 6:41; Ps. 132:9

17 ^aEzek. 29:21; Luke 1:69 ^b1 Kin. 11:36; 15:4; 2 Kin. 8:19; 2 Chr. 21:7; Ps. 18:28

Notes

131:2 As a child who has successfully gone through the troublesome process of weaning and found contentment, so David had been delivered from all self-seeking and had found contentment in the Lord.

Psalm 132 This royal psalm consists of two parts: the request that the Lord remember David's zeal in bringing the Ark to Jerusalem and thus bless his dynasty (vv. 1-10); and the response of the Lord promising to fulfill the Davidic covenant (vv. 11-18).

132:2-5 See note on 2 Sam. 7:2.

132:6 *Ephrathah.* Probably not here a reference to Bethlehem (as in Gen. 35:19) but to Kiriath-jearim (cf. 1 Sam. 6:21-7:2; 1 Chron. 13:6).

132:10 *anointed.* Refers to each successive Davidic king.

132:11-18 The ultimate fulfillment of the Davidic covenant (v. 11, see note on 2 Sam. 7:12-16) will come in the millennial kingdom, in which Messiah, ruling from Zion (Jerusalem), will bring peace and prosperity to the world. *horn of David* (v. 17). Messiah (cf. Jer. 23:5; 33:15; Ezek. 29:21; Zech. 3:8; 6:12). *lamp.* David's posterity is assured (see note on 1 Kings 11:36).

18 *a*Job
8:22; Ps.
35:26;
109:29 *b*Ps.
21:3

18 "His enemies I will *a*clothe
with shame;
But upon himself his
*b*crown shall shine."

PSALM 133

A Song of Ascents, of David.

1 *a*Gen.
13:8; Heb.
13:1

B EHOLD, how good and how
pleasant it is
For *a*brothers to dwell together in unity!

★ **2** *a*Ex.
29:7; 30:25,
30; Lev. 8:12
*b*Ex. 28:33;
39:24

2 It is like the precious *a*oil
upon the head,
Coming down upon the
beard,
Even Aaron's beard,
Coming down upon the
*b*edge of his robes.

3 *a*Prov.
19:12; Hos.
14:5; Mic.
5:7 *b*Deut.
3:9; 4:48
*c*Ps. 48:2;
74:2; 78:68
*d*Lev. 25:21;
Deut. 28:8;
Ps. 42:8 *e*Ps.
21:4

3 It is like the *a*dew of *b*Hermon,
Coming down upon the
*c*mountains of Zion;
For there the LORD *d*commanded the bless-
ing—*e*life forever.

PSALM 134

A Song of Ascents.

★ **1** *a*Ps.
103:21 *b*Ps.
135:1, 2
*c*Deut. 10:8;
1 Chr. 23:30;
2 Chr. 29:11
*d*1 Chr. 9:33
2 *a*Ps. 28:2;
1 Tim. 2:8
*b*Ps. 63:2

B EHOLD, *a*bless the LORD, all
*b*servants of the LORD,
Who *c*serve *d*by night in
the house of the LORD!
2 *a*Lift up your hands to the
*b*sanctuary,
And bless the LORD.

3 *a*Ps.
128:5 *b*Ps.
124:8

3 May the LORD *a*bless you
from Zion,
He who *b*made heaven and
earth.

PSALM 135

a

P RAISE the LORD!
Praise the name of the
LORD;
Praise *Him*, O *b*servants of
the LORD,

2 You who stand in the
house of the LORD,
In the *a*courts of the house
of our God!

3 Praise the LORD, for *a*the
LORD is good;
*b*Sing praises to His name,
*c*for it is lovely.

4 For the LORD has *a*chosen
Jacob for Himself,
Israel for His *b*own posses-
sion.

5 For I know that *a*the LORD
is great,
And that our Lord is
*b*above all gods.

6 *a*Whatever the LORD
pleases, He does,
In heaven and in earth, in
the seas and in all
deeps.

7 He *a*causes the vapors to
ascend from the ends
of the earth;
Who *b*makes lightnings for
the rain;
Who *c*brings forth the
wind from His trea-
suries.

8 He *a*smote the first-born
of Egypt,
Both of man and beast.

9 He sent *a*signs and wonders into your midst,
O Egypt,

1 *a*Ps.
113:1 *b*Ps.
134:1

2 *a*Ps.
92:13;
116:19

3 *a*Ps.
100:5;
119:68 *b*Ps.
68:4 *c*Ps.
147:1

4 *a*Deut.
7:6; 10:15;
Ps. 105:6
*b*Ex. 19:5;
Mal. 3:17;
Titus 2:14;
1 Pet. 2:9

5 *a*Ps. 48:1;
95:3; 145:3
*b*Ps. 97:9

6 *a*Ps.
115:3

7 *a*Jer.
10:13; 51:16
*b*Job 28:25,
26; 38:25,
26; Zech.
10:1 *c*Jer.
10:13; 51:16

8 *a*Ex.
12:12; Ps.
78:51;
105:36

9 *a*Ex. 7:10;
Deut. 6:22;
Ps. 78:43
*b*Ps. 136:15

Psalm 133 Unity of the brethren is pictured
as being as precious as the oil of priestly consecration and as refreshing as the early mountain
dew.
133:2 *oil.* See note on Exod. 30:32.
Psalm 134 This benedictory conclusion to
the pilgrim psalms (see note on Psalm 120) calls
on the priests to bless the Lord and be blessed by

Him.
134:1 *bless.* See note on 103:1.
Psalm 135 This anthology of praise begins
with a call to praise the Lord because of His
goodness and choice of Israel (vv. 1-4), because
of His greatness as Lord of creation (vv. 5-7) and
Lord of history (vv. 8-18), and concludes with a
renewed call to praise (vv. 19-21).

Upon *b*Pharaoh and all his servants.

10 *a*Num. 21:24; Ps. 135:10-12; 136:17-21
*b*Ps. 44:2
11 *a*Num. 21:21-26; Deut. 29:7
*b*Num. 21:33-35
*c*Josh. 12:7-24
12 *a*Deut. 29:8; Ps. 78:55; 136:21, 22
13 *a*Ex. 3:15; Ps. 102:12

10 *a*He *b*smote many nations,
And slew mighty kings,

11 *a*Sihon, king of the Amorites,
And *b*Og, king of Bashan,
And *c*all the kingdoms of Canaan;

12 And He *a*gave their land as a heritage,
A heritage to Israel His people.

13 Thy *a*name, O LORD, is everlasting,
Thy remembrance, O LORD, throughout all generations.

14 *a*Deut. 32:36; Ps. 50:4 *b*Ps. 90:13; 106:46

14 For the LORD will *a*judge His people,
And *b*will have compassion on His servants.

★15 *a*Ps. 115:4-8; 135:15-18

15 The *a*idols of the nations are *but* silver and gold,
The work of man's hands.

16 They have mouths, but they do not speak;
They have eyes, but they do not see;

17 They have ears, but they do not hear;
Nor is there any breath at all in their mouths.

18 Those who make them will be like them,
Yes, everyone who trusts in them.

19 *a*Ps. 115:9

19 O house of *a*Israel, bless the LORD;
O house of Aaron, bless the LORD;

20 *a*Ps. 118:4

20 O house of Levi, bless the LORD;
You *a*who revere the LORD, bless the LORD.

21 *a*Ps. 128:5; 134:3 *b*Ps. 132:14

21 Blessed be the LORD *a*from Zion,
Who *b*dwells in Jerusalem.
Praise the LORD!

PSALM 136

*a*GIVE thanks to the LORD, for *b*He is good;
For *c*His lovingkindness is everlasting.

2 Give thanks to the *a*God of gods,
For His lovingkindness is everlasting.

3 Give thanks to the *a*Lord of lords,
For His lovingkindness is everlasting.

4 To Him who *a*alone does great wonders,
For His lovingkindness is everlasting;

5 To Him who *a*made the heavens *b*with skill,
For His lovingkindness is everlasting;

6 To Him who *a*spread out the earth above the waters,
For His lovingkindness is everlasting;

7 To Him who *a*made *the* great lights,
For His lovingkindness is everlasting:

8 The *a*sun to rule by day,
For His lovingkindness is everlasting,

9 The *a*moon and stars to rule by night,
For His lovingkindness is everlasting.

10 To Him who *a*smote the Egyptians in their first-born,
For His lovingkindness is everlasting,

11 And *a*brought Israel out from their midst,
For His lovingkindness is everlasting,

12 With a *a*strong hand and an *b*outstretched arm,

1 *a*1 Chr. 16:34; Ps. 106:1; 107:1; 118:1; Jer. 33:11
*b*2 Chr. 5:13; 7:3; Ezra 3:11; Ps. 100:5
*c*1 Chr. 16:41; 2 Chr. 20:21; Ps. 118:1-4
2 *a*Deut. 10:17
3 *a*Deut. 10:17
4 *a*Deut. 6:22; Job 9:10; Ps. 72:18
5 *a*Gen. 1:1 *b*Ps. 104:24; Prov. 3:19; Jer. 10:12; 51:15
6 *a*Gen. 1:2, 6, 9; Ps. 24:2; Is. 42:5; 44:24; Jer. 10:12
7 *a*Gen. 1:14-18; Ps. 74:16
8 *a*Gen. 1:16
9 *a*Gen. 1:16
10 *a*Ex. 12:29; Ps. 78:51; 135:8
11 *a*Ex. 12:51; 13:3; Ps. 105:43
12 *a*Ex. 6:1; 13:9; 1 Kin. 8:42; Neh. 1:10; Ps. 44:3; Jer. 32:21 *b*Ex. 6:6; Deut. 4:34; 5:15; 7:19; 9:29; 11:2; 2 Kin. 17:36; 2 Chr. 6:32; Jer. 32:17

135:15 See note on 115:4.
Psalm 136 Punctuated by the refrain exalting the Lord's steadfast love (Heb., *hesed,* see note on Hos. 2:19), this hymn opens with a call to praise (vv. 1-3) because of God's great deeds in nature (vv. 4-9), His gracious actions in the history of Israel (vv. 10-22), and His mercy toward all (vv. 23-25), and closes with another call to praise (v. 26). This psalm was probably used antiphonally in Temple worship. In Jewish liturgy it is called "the Great Hallel," recited at the Passover meal after the "Lesser Hallel" (see note on Psalm 113).

For His lovingkindness is everlasting;

13 To Him who ªdivided the Red Sea asunder,
For His lovingkindness is everlasting,

13 ªEx.
14:21; Ps.
66:6; 78:13

14 And ªmade Israel pass through the midst of it,
For His lovingkindness is everlasting;

14 ªEx.
14:22; Ps.
106:9

15 But ªHe overthrew Pharaoh and his army in the Red Sea,
For His lovingkindness is everlasting,

15 ªEx.
14:27; Ps.
78:53;
106:11

16 To Him who ªled His people through the wilderness,
For His lovingkindness is everlasting;

16 ªEx.
13:18; 15:22;
Deut. 8:15;
Ps. 78:52

17 To Him who ªsmote great kings,
For His lovingkindness is everlasting,

17 ªPs.
135:10-12;
136:17-22

18 And ªslew mighty kings,
For His lovingkindness is everlasting:

18 ªDeut.
29:7

19 ªSihon, king of the Amorites,
For His lovingkindness is everlasting,

19 ªNum.
21:21-24

20 And ªOg, king of Bashan,
For His lovingkindness is everlasting,

20 ªNum.
21:33-35

21 And ªgave their land as a heritage,
For His lovingkindness is everlasting,

21 ªJosh.
12:1

22 Even a heritage to Israel His ªservant,
For His lovingkindness is everlasting.

22 ªPs.
105:6; Is.
41:8; 44:1;
45:4

23 Who ªremembered us in our low estate,
For His lovingkindness is everlasting,

23 ªPs. 9:12;
103:14;
106:45

24 And has ªrescued us from our adversaries,
For His lovingkindness is everlasting;

24 ªJudg.
6:9; Neh.
9:28; Ps.
107:2

25 Who ªgives food to all flesh,
For His lovingkindness is everlasting.

25 ªPs.
104:27;
145:15

26 Give thanks to the ªGod of heaven,
For His lovingkindness is everlasting.

26 ªGen.
24:3, 7;
2 Chr. 36:23;
Ezra 1:2;
5:11; Neh.
1:4

PSALM 137

BY the ªrivers of Babylon,
There we sat down and ᵇwept,
When we remembered Zion.
2 Upon the ªwillows in the midst of it
We ᵇhung our harps.
3 For there our captors ªdemanded of us songs,
And ᵇour tormentors mirth, *saying*,
"Sing us one of the songs of Zion."

★ **1** ªEzek.
1:1, 3 ᵇNeh.
1:4

2 ªLev.
23:40; Is.
44:4 ᵇJob
30:31; Is.
24:8; Ezek.
26:13

3 ªPs. 80:6
ᵇIs. 49:17

4 How can we sing ªthe Lord's song
In a foreign land?
5 If I ªforget you, O Jerusalem,
May my right hand forget *her skill.*
6 May my ªtongue cleave to the roof of my mouth,
If I do not remember you,
If I do not ᵇexalt Jerusalem
Above my chief joy.

4 ª2 Chr.
29:27; Neh.
12:46

5 ªIs. 65:11

6 ªJob
29:10; Ps.
22:15; Ezek.
3:26 ᵇNeh.
2:3
★ **7** ªPs.
83:4-8; Is.
34:5, 6; Jer.
49:7-22;
Lam. 4:21;
Ezek. 25:12-
14; 35:2;
Amos 1:11;
Obad. 10-14
ᵇPs. 74:7;
Hab. 3:13
★ **8-9**

7 Remember, O Lord, against the sons of ªEdom
The day of Jerusalem,
Who said, "Raze it, raze it,
ᵇTo its very foundation."
8 O daughter of Babylon, you ªdevastated one,
How blessed will be the one who ᵇrepays you

8 ªIs. 13:1-
22; 47:1-15;
Jer. 25:12;
50:1-46;
51:1-64
ᵇJer. 50:15;
51:24, 35,
36, 49; Rev.
18:6

Psalm 137 In this Song of the Exiles, the psalmist mourns the plight of captive Jews (vv. 1-4), expresses his love for Jerusalem (vv. 5-6), and imprecates against Israel's enemies (vv. 7-9). **137:1** *the rivers of Babylon.* The Euphrates and its tributaries, the Chebar (Ezek. 1:1), and nu-

merous canals of the area.
137:7 For details of Edom's crimes against Jerusalem, see note on Obad. 11-14.
137:8-9 The stern law of retaliation demanded that Babylon be treated as she had treated Jerusalem.

With the recompense with which you have repaid us.

9 How blessed will be the one who seizes and [a]dashes your little ones
Against the rock.

9 [a]2 Kin.
8:12; Is.
13:16; Hos.
13:16; Nah.
3:10

PSALM 138

A Psalm of David.

[a]

I WILL give Thee thanks with all my heart;
I will sing praises to Thee before the [b]gods.

★ 1 [a]Ps.
111:1 [b]Ps.
95:3; 96:4;
97:7

2 I will bow down [a]toward Thy holy temple,
And [b]give thanks to Thy name for Thy lovingkindness and Thy truth;
For Thou hast [c]magnified Thy word according to all Thy name.

★ 2 [a]1 Kin.
8:29; Ps. 5:7;
28:2 [b]Ps.
140:13 [c]Is.
42:21

3 On the day I [a]called Thou didst answer me;
Thou didst make me bold with [b]strength in my soul.

3 [a]Ps.
118:5 [b]Ps.
28:7; 46:1

4 [a]All the kings of the earth will give thanks to Thee, O LORD,
When they have heard the words of Thy mouth.

★ 4 [a]Ps.
72:11;
102:15

5 And they will [a]sing of the ways of the LORD.
For [b]great is the glory of the LORD.

5 [a]Ps.
145:7 [b]Ps.
21:5

6 For [a]though the LORD is exalted,

6 [a]Ps.
113:4-7
[b]Prov. 3:34;
Is. 57:15;
Luke 1:48;
James 4:6;
1 Pet. 5:5
[c]Ps. 40:4;
101:5

Yet He [b]regards the lowly;
But the [c]haughty He knows from afar.

7 Though I [a]walk in the midst of trouble,
Thou wilt [b]revive me;
Thou wilt [c]stretch forth Thy hand against the wrath of my enemies,
And Thy right hand will [d]save me.

7 [a]Ps. 23:4;
143:11 [b]Ezra
9:8, 9; Ps.
71:20; Is.
57:15 [c]Ex.
7:5; 15:12;
Is. 5:25; Jer.
51:25; Ezek.
6:14; 25:13
[d]Ps. 20:6;
60:5

8 The LORD will [a]accomplish what concerns me;
Thy [b]lovingkindness, O LORD, is everlasting;
[c]Do not forsake the [d]works of Thy hands.

★ 8 [a]Ps.
57:2; Phil.
1:6 [b]Ps.
136:1 [c]Job
10:8; Ps.
27:9; 71:9,
119:8 [d]Job
10:3; 14:15;
Ps. 100:3

PSALM 139

For the choir director. A Psalm of David.

O LORD, Thou hast [a]searched me and known *me*.

★ 1 [a]Ps.
17:3; 44:21;
Jer. 12:3

2 Thou [a]dost know when I sit down and when I rise up;
Thou [b]dost understand my thought from afar.

2 [a]2 Kin.
19:27 [b]Ps.
94:11; Is.
66:18; Matt.
9:4

3 Thou [a]dost scrutinize my path and my lying down,
And art intimately acquainted with all my ways.

3 [a]Job
14:16; 31:4

4 Even before there is a word on my tongue,
Behold, O LORD, Thou [a]dost know it all.

4 [a]Heb.
4:13

5 Thou hast [a]enclosed me behind and before,

★ 5 [a]Ps.
34:7; 125:2
[b]Job 9:33

Psalm 138 In this thanksgiving psalm, the psalmist praises God for answered prayer (vv. 1-3), for His plan for the world (vv. 4-6), and for His purposes for himself (vv. 7-8).
138:1 *gods*. Likely a reference to pagan idols, whose supposed might the psalmist challenges.
138:2 *word*. God's answer to the psalmist's prayer surpassed all that he had previously known His name to signify.
138:4 See note on 72:8.
138:8 The psalmist expresses confidence in the will of God whose *lovingkindness* is forever.

Psalm 139 This psalm focuses on four great attributes of God: His knowledge of all things (vv. 1-6), His presence everywhere (vv. 7-12), His power in the formation of man (vv. 13-18), and His holiness, which destroys evil men and searches the believer's heart (vv. 19-24).
139:1 *searched* (also in v. 23). Used of the careful scrutiny involved in mining operations (cf. Job 28:3) and in exploring a country (cf. Judg. 18:2).
139:5 *enclosed*. This may mean there is no escape from God's omniscience, or it may signify His knowledge protecting us.

And [b]laid Thy hand upon me.

6 aRom. 11:33 bJob 42:3

6 Such [a]knowledge is [b]too wonderful for me;
It is too high, I cannot attain to it.

7 aJer. 23:24

7 [a]Where can I go from Thy Spirit?
Or where can I flee from Thy presence?

★ 8 aAmos 9:2-4 bJob 26:6; Prov. 15:11

8 [a]If I ascend to heaven, Thou art there;
If I make my bed in Sheol, behold, [b]Thou art there.

9 If I take the wings of the dawn,
If I dwell in the remotest part of the sea,

10 aPs. 23:2, 3

10 Even there Thy hand will [a]lead me,
And Thy right hand will lay hold of me.

11 aJob 22:13

11 If I say, "Surely the [a]darkness will overwhelm me,
And the light around me will be night,"

★12 aJob 34:22; Dan. 2:22 b1 John 1:5

12 Even the [a]darkness is not dark to Thee,
And the night is as bright as the day.
[b]Darkness and light are alike to Thee.

★13 aPs. 119:73; Is. 44:24 bJob 10:11

13 For Thou didst [a]form my inward parts;
Thou didst [b]weave me in my mother's womb.

14 aPs. 40:5

14 I will give thanks to Thee, for I am fearfully and wonderfully made;
[a]Wonderful are Thy works,
And my soul knows it very well.

15 My [a]frame was not hidden from Thee,
When I was made in secret,
And skillfully wrought in the [b]depths of the earth.

★15 aJob 10:8-10; Eccl. 11:5 bPs. 63:9

16 Thine [a]eyes have seen my unformed substance;
And in [b]Thy book they were all written,
The [c]days that were ordained for me,
When as yet there was not one of them.

★16 aJob 10:8-10; Eccl. 11:5 bPs. 56:8 cJob 14:5

17 How precious also are Thy [a]thoughts to me, O God!
How vast is the sum of them!

17 aPs. 40:5; 92:5

18 If I should count them, they would [a]outnumber the sand.
When [b]I awake, I am still with Thee.

18 aPs. 40:5 bPs. 3:5

19 O that Thou wouldst [a]slay the wicked, O God;
[b]Depart from me, therefore, [c]men of bloodshed.

★19 aIs. 11:4 bPs. 6:8; 119:115 cPs. 5:6; 26:9

20 For they [a]speak against Thee wickedly,
And Thine enemies [b]take Thy name in vain.

20 aJude 15 bEx. 20:7; Deut. 5:11

21 Do I not [a]hate those who hate Thee, O LORD?
And do I not [b]loathe those who rise up against Thee?

21 a2 Chr. 19:2; Ps. 26:5; 31:6 bPs. 119:158

22 I hate them with the utmost hatred;
They have become my enemies.

23 [a]Search me, O God, and know my heart;

23 aJob 31:6; Ps. 26:2 bPs. 7:9; Prov. 17:3; Jer. 11:20; 1 Thess. 2:4

139:8 *Sheol.* Even the abode of the dead is not apart from God's omnipresence (cf. Rev. 14:10; on Sheol see note on Gen. 37:35).
139:12 God's all-seeing eyes can penetrate even the darkness.
139:13 *didst form.* Meaning to acquire by creation (Gen. 14:19; Deut. 32:6).
139:15 *My frame.* I.e., my bones or skeleton. *in the depths of the earth.* An allusion to the

womb, as mysterious as the netherworld.
139:16 *unformed substance.* Reference to the embryo. The last part of the verse means that the days of David's life were written in God's book, affirming God's prior knowledge and plan of everything in David's life.
139:19 *men of bloodshed.* I.e., violent, murderous men.

^bTry me and know my anxious thoughts;

24 And see if there be any ^ahurtful way in me,
And ^blead me in the ^ceverlasting way.

PSALM 140

For the choir director. A Psalm of David.

RESCUE me, O LORD, from evil men;
Preserve me from ^bviolent men,

2 Who ^adevise evil things in *their* hearts;
They ^bcontinually stir up wars.

3 They ^asharpen their tongues as a serpent;
^bPoison of a viper is under their lips. [Selah.

4 ^aKeep me, O LORD, from the hands of the wicked;
^bPreserve me from violent men,
Who have purposed to ^ctrip up my feet.

5 The proud have ^ahidden a trap for me, and cords;
They have spread a ^bnet by the wayside;
They have set ^csnares for me. [Selah.

6 I ^asaid to the LORD, "Thou art my God;
^bGive ear, O LORD, to the ^cvoice of my supplications.

7 "O GOD the Lord, ^athe strength of my salvation,

Thou hast ^bcovered my head in the day of battle.

8 "Do not grant, O LORD, the ^adesires of the wicked;
Do not promote ^bhis *evil* device, *lest* they be exalted. [Selah.

9 "As for the head of those who surround me,
May the ^amischief of their lips cover them.

10 "May ^aburning coals fall upon them;
May they be ^bcast into the fire,
Into deep pits from which they ^ccannot rise.

11 "May a slanderer not be established in the earth;
^aMay evil hunt the violent man speedily."

12 I know that the LORD will ^amaintain the cause of the afflicted,
And ^bjustice for the poor.

13 Surely the ^arighteous will give thanks to Thy name;
The ^bupright will dwell in Thy presence.

PSALM 141

A Psalm of David.

O LORD, I call upon Thee; ^ahasten to me!
^bGive ear to my voice when I call to Thee!

2 May my prayer be counted as ^aincense before Thee;
The ^blifting up of my hands as the ^cevening offering.

139:24 *everlasting way.* Stands in contrast to the way of the wicked, who will perish.
Psalm 140 This imprecatory psalm contains the cry of the psalmist for relief (vv. 1-7) and retribution (vv. 8-11), and the confidence of the psalmist that God will answer (vv. 12-13).
140:3 *viper.* Egyptian cobra, one of the most poisonous snakes.
140:10 David asks that the fall of his enemies be complete and irreversible.
Psalm 141 In this lament, David asks the Lord to hear him (vv. 1-2), to keep him from all ill-considered speech and actions (vv. 3-7), and to deliver him from his enemies (vv. 8-10).

Margin references:

★24 ^aPs. 146:9; Prov. 15:9; 28:10; Jer. 25:5; 36:3 ^bPs. 5:8; 143:10 ^cPs. 16:11

1 ^aPs. 17:13; 59:2; 71:4 ^bPs. 18:48; 86:14; 140:11

2 ^aPs. 7:14; 36:4; 52:2; Prov. 6:14; Is. 59:4; Hos. 7:15 ^bPs. 56:6

★3 ^aPs. 57:4; 64:3 ^bPs. 58:4; Rom. 3:13; James 3:8

4 ^aPs. 71:4 ^bPs. 140:1 ^cPs. 36:11

5 ^aJob 18:9; Ps. 35:7; 141:9; 142:3 ^bPs. 31:4; 57:6; Lam. 1:13 ^cPs. 141:9; Is. 8:14; Amos 3:5

6 ^aPs. 16:2; 31:14 ^bPs. 143:1 ^cPs. 116:1; 130:2

7 ^aPs. 28:8; 118:14 ^bPs. 144:10

8 ^aPs. 112:10 ^bEsth. 9:25; Ps. 10:2, 3

9 ^aPs. 7:16; Prov. 18:7

★10 ^aPs. 11:6 ^bPs. 21:9; Matt. 3:10 ^cPs. 36:12

11 ^aPs. 34:21

12 ^a1 Kin. 8:45, 49; Ps. 9:4; 18:27; 82:3 ^bPs. 12:5; 35:10

13 ^aPs. 97:12 ^bPs. 11:7; 16:11; 17:15

1 ^aPs. 22:19; 38:22; 70:5 ^bPs. 5:1; 143:1

2 ^aEx. 30:8; Luke 1:10; Rev. 5:8; 8:3, 4 ^b1 Tim. 2:8 ^cEx. 29:39, 41; 1 Kin. 18:29, 36; Dan. 9:21

★ 3-4
3 aPs.
34:13; 39:1;
Prov. 13:3;
21:23 bMic.
7:5
4 aPs.
119:36 bIs.
32:6; Hos.
6:8; Mal.
3:15 cProv.
23:6

3 Set a aguard, O Lord, over my mouth;
Keep watch over the bdoor of my lips.

4 aDo not incline my heart to any evil thing,
To practice deeds of wickedness
With men who bdo iniquity;
And cdo not let me eat of their delicacies.

★ 5 aProv.
9:8; 19:25;
25:12; 27:6;
Eccl. 7:5;
Gal. 6:1 bPs.
23:5; 133:2
cPs. 35:14

5 Let the arighteous smite me in kindness and reprove me;
It is boil upon the head;
Do not let my head refuse it,
For still my prayer cis against their wicked deeds.

★ 6-7
6 a2 Chr.
25:12

6 Their judges are athrown down by the sides of the rock,
And they hear my words, for they are pleasant.

7 aPs.
129:3 bPs.
53:5 cNum.
16:32, 33;
Ps. 88:3-5

7 As when one aplows and breaks open the earth,
Our bbones have been scattered at the cmouth of Sheol.

8 aPs.
25:15; 123:2
bPs. 2:12;
11:1 cPs.
27:9

8 For my aeyes are toward Thee, O God, the Lord;
In Thee I btake refuge; cdo not leave me defenseless.

9 aPs.
38:12; 64:5;
91:3;
119:110 bPs.
140:5

9 Keep me from the ajaws of the trap which they have set for me,
And from the bsnares of those who do iniquity.

10 aPs. 7:15;
35:8; 57:6
bPs. 124:7

10 Let the wicked afall into their own nets,
While I pass by bsafely.

PSALM 142

Maskil of David, when he was in the cave. A Prayer.

1 aPs. 77:1
bPs. 30:8

I aCRY aloud with my voice to the Lord;
I bmake supplication with my voice to the Lord.

2 aPs.
102:title bPs.
77:2

2 I apour out my complaint before Him;
I declare my btrouble before Him.

3 aPs. 77:3;
143:4 bPs.
140:5

3 When amy spirit was overwhelmed within me,
Thou didst know my path.
In the way where I walk
They have bhidden a trap for me.

4 aPs.
31:11; 88:8,
18 bJob
11:20; Jer.
25:35 cJer.
30:17

4 Look to the right and see;
For there is ano one who regards me;
There is no bescape for me;
cNo one cares for my soul.

5 aPs. 91:2,
9 bPs. 16:5;
73:26 cPs.
27:13

5 I cried out to Thee, O Lord;
I said, "Thou art amy refuge,
My bportion in the cland of the living.

6 aPs. 17:1
bPs. 79:8;
116:6 cPs.
18:17

6 "aGive heed to my cry,
For I am bbrought very low;
Deliver me from my persecutors,
For they are too cstrong for me.

★ 7 aPs.
143:11;
146:7 bPs.
13:6

7 "aBring my soul out of prison,
So that I may give thanks to Thy name;
The righteous will surround me,

141:3-4 David prays for a godly separation from the words, thoughts, practices, and fellowship (*do not let me eat of their delicacies*) of the ungodly.
141:5 David welcomes reproof from the godly lest he be tempted to compromise with evil.
141:6-7 When the leaders (*judges*) of the ungodly are judged and their *bones* scattered, then the ungodly will listen to David.
Psalm 142 The psalm consists of David's cry

to the Lord (vv. 1-2), his complaint that his foes seek to kill him and that no one cares (vv. 3-4), and his confidence in the Lord for deliverance (vv. 5-7). *Maskil.* See note on Psalm 32. *cave.* Perhaps that of Adullam (1 Sam. 22) or Engedi (1 Sam. 24). This is the last of eight psalms from the period of David's flight from Saul (34, 52, 54, 56, 57, 59, 63). *A Prayer.* See note on Psalm 17. **142:7** *prison.* Not a jail, but the confinement and restriction involved in hiding from Saul.

For Thou wilt [b]deal bountifully with me."

PSALM 143

A Psalm of David.

1 [a]Ps.
140:6 [b]Ps.
89:1, 2 [c]Ps.
71:2

HEAR my prayer, O LORD,
  [a]Give ear to my supplications!
Answer me in Thy [b]faithfulness, in Thy [c]righteousness!

2 [a]Job
14:3; 22:4
[b]1 Kin. 8:46;
Job 4:17;
9:2; 25:4; Ps.
130:3; Eccl.
7:20; Rom.
3:10, 20;
Gal. 2:16

2 And [a]do not enter into judgment with Thy servant,
For in Thy sight [b]no man living is righteous.

3 [a]Ps.
44:25 [b]Ps.
88:6; Lam.
3:6

3 For the enemy has persecuted my soul;
He has crushed my life [a]to the ground;
He [b]has made me dwell in dark places, like those who have long been dead.

4 [a]Ps. 77:3;
142:3 [b]Lam.
3:11

4 Therefore [a]my spirit is overwhelmed within me;
My heart is [b]appalled within me.

5 [a]Ps. 77:5,
10, 11 [b]Ps.
77:12 [c]Ps.
105:2

5 I [a]remember the days of old;
I [b]meditate on all Thy doings;
I [c]muse on the work of Thy hands.

6 [a]Job
11:13; Ps.
88:9 [b]Ps.
42:2; 63:1

6 I [a]stretch out my hands to Thee;
My [b]soul *longs* for Thee, as a parched land. [Selah.

7 [a]Ps.
69:17 [b]Ps.
73:26; 84:2;
Jer. 6:18;
Lam. 1:22
[c]Ps. 27:9;
69:17; 102:2
[d]Ps. 28:1;
88:4

7 [a]Answer me quickly, O LORD, my [b]spirit fails;
[c]Do not hide Thy face from me,
Lest I become like [d]those who go down to the pit.

8 [a]Ps.
90:14 [b]Ps.
46:5 [c]Ps.
25:2 [d]Ps.
27:11; 32:8;
86:11 [e]Ps.
25:1; 86:4

8 Let me hear Thy [a]lovingkindness [b]in the morning;
For I trust [c]in Thee;
Teach me the [d]way in which I should walk;
For to Thee I [e]lift up my soul.

9 [a]Ps.
31:15; 59:1

9 [a]Deliver me, O LORD, from my enemies;
I take refuge in Thee.

10 [a]Ps. 25:4,
5; 119:12
[b]Neh. 9:20
[c]Ps. 23:3

10 [a]Teach me to do Thy will,
For Thou art my God;
Let [b]Thy good Spirit [c]lead me on level ground.

★11-12

11 [a]Ps.
25:11 [b]Ps.
119:25 [c]Ps.
31:1; 71:2

11 [a]For the sake of Thy name, O LORD, [b]revive me.
[c]In Thy righteousness bring my soul out of trouble.

12 [a]Ps. 54:5
[b]Ps. 52:5
[c]Ps. 116:16

12 And in Thy lovingkindness [a]cut off my enemies,
And [b]destroy all those who afflict my soul;
For [c]I am Thy servant.

PSALM 144

A *Psalm* of David.

1 [a]Ps. 18:2
[b]2 Sam.
22:35; Ps.
18:34

BLESSED be the LORD, [a]my rock,
Who [b]trains my hands for war,
And my fingers for battle;

2 [a]Ps. 18:2;
91:2 [b]Ps.
59:9 [c]Ps.
3:3; 28:7;
84:9 [d]Ps.
18:39

2 My lovingkindness and [a]my fortress,
My [b]stronghold and my deliverer;
My [c]shield and He in whom I take refuge;
Who [d]subdues my people under me.

3 [a]Job
7:17; Ps. 8:4;
Heb. 2:6

3 O LORD, [a]what is man, that Thou dost take knowledge of him?

Psalm 143 Here David appeals for mercy (vv. 1-2), laments his present distress (vv. 3-4), longs for blessings like those of the past (vv. 5-6), and prays for deliverance, guidance, and vindication (vv. 7-12). A penitential psalm (see note on Psalm 6).
143:11-12 David prays that the Lord would re-

vive him (i.e., preserve his life) on the basis of God's *name,* His *righteousness,* and His *lovingkindness* (see note on Hos. 2:19).
Psalm 144 This royal song may be outlined as follows: praise for past victories (vv. 1-4), petition for present deliverance (vv. 5-11), a picture of future blessings (vv. 12-15).

Or the son of man, that Thou dost think of him?

4 4 ᵃMan is like a mere breath;
His ᵇdays are like a passing shadow.

4 ᵃPs. 39:11 ᵇJob 8:9; 14:2; Ps. 102:11; 109:23

5 5 ᵃBow Thy heavens, O LORD, and ᵇcome down;
ᶜTouch the mountains, that they may smoke.

5 ᵃPs. 18:9 ᵇIs. 64:1 ᶜPs. 104:32

6 6 Flash forth ᵃlightning and scatter them;
Send out Thine ᵇarrows and confuse them.

6 ᵃPs. 18:14 ᵇPs. 7:13; 58:7; Hab. 3:11; Zech. 9:14

7 7 Stretch forth Thy hand ᵃfrom on high;
Rescue me and ᵇdeliver me out of great waters,
Out of the hand of ᶜaliens

7 ᵃPs. 18:16 ᵇPs. 69:1, 14 ᶜPs. 18:44; 54:3

8 8 Whose mouths ᵃspeak deceit,
And whose ᵇright hand is a right hand of falsehood.

★ 8 ᵃPs. 12:2; 41:6 ᵇGen. 14:22; Deut. 32:40; Ps. 106:26; Is. 44:20

9 9 I will sing a ᵃnew song to Thee, O God;
Upon a ᵇharp of ten strings I will sing praises to Thee,

9 ᵃPs. 33:3; 40:3 ᵇPs. 33:2

10 10 Who dost ᵃgive salvation to kings;
Who ᵇdost rescue David His servant from the evil sword.

10 ᵃPs. 18:50 ᵇ2 Sam. 18:7; Ps. 140:7

11 11 Rescue me, and deliver me out of the hand of ᵃaliens,
Whose mouth ᵇspeaks deceit,
And whose ᶜright hand is a right hand of falsehood.

11 ᵃPs. 18:44; 54:3 ᵇPs. 12:2; 41:6 ᶜGen. 14:22; Deut. 32:40; Ps. 106:26; Is. 44:20

12 12 Let our sons in their youth be as ᵃgrown-up plants,

★12-15 12 ᵃPs. 92:12-14; 128:3 ᵇSong 4:4; 7:4

And our daughters as ᵇcorner pillars fashioned as for a palace;

13 13 Let our ᵃgarners be full, furnishing every kind of produce,
And our flocks bring forth thousands and ten thousands in our fields;

13 ᵃProv. 3:9, 10

14 14 Let our ᵃcattle bear,
Without ᵇmishap and without ᶜloss,
Let there be no ᵈoutcry in our streets!

14 ᵃProv. 14:4 ᵇ2 Kin. 25:10, 11 ᶜAmos 5:3 ᵈIs. 24:11; Jer. 14:2

15 15 How blessed are the people who are so situated;
How ᵃblessed are the people whose God is the LORD!

15 ᵃPs. 33:12

PSALM 145

A Psalm of Praise, of David.

I WILL ᵃextol Thee, ᵇmy God, O King;
And I will ᶜbless Thy name forever and ever.

1 ᵃPs. 30:1; 66:17 ᵇPs. 5:2 ᶜPs. 34:1

2 2 Every day I will bless Thee,
And I will ᵃpraise Thy name forever and ever.

2 ᵃPs. 71:6

3 3 ᵃGreat is the LORD, and highly to be praised;
And His ᵇgreatness is unsearchable.

3 ᵃPs. 48:1; 86:10; 147:5 ᵇJob 5:9; 9:10; 11:7; Is. 40:28; Rom. 11:33

4 4 One ᵃgeneration shall praise Thy works to another,
And shall declare Thy mighty acts.

4 ᵃPs. 22:30, 31; Is. 38:19

5 5 On the ᵃglorious splendor of Thy majesty,
And ᵇon Thy wonderful works, I will meditate.

5 ᵃPs. 145:12 ᵇPs. 119:27

144:8 David's enemies affirmed fidelity by raising or offering their *right hand,* but practiced treachery.
144:12-15 This picture of peace and prosperity involved vigorous sons, dependable daughters, full barns, healthy animals, and God's presence.
Psalm 145 This hymn of praise begins with a vow to praise God (vv. 1-2) for His greatness, about which one generation tells the next (vv. 3-7); continues with praise for the Lord's attributes (vv. 8-10), His everlasting kingdom (vv. 11-13), His providential mercies (vv. 14-16), and His righteous ways (vv. 17-20); and closes with a renewed resolve to praise the Lord (v. 21). An alphabetic acrostic psalm, each verse beginning with a successive letter of the Hebrew alphabet, except for the letter *nun,* missing between verses 13 and 14 (though found in the LXX and in a text from Qumran).

6 aDeut.
10:21; Ps.
66:3; 106:22
bDeut. 32:3

6 And men shall speak of the power of Thine aawesome acts;
And I will btell of Thy greatness.

7 aPs.
31:19; Is.
63:7 bPs.
51:14

7 They shall eagerly utter the memory of Thine aabundant goodness,
And shall bshout joyfully of Thy righteousness.

8 aEx. 34:6;
Num. 14:18;
Ps. 86:5, 15;
103:8

8 The LORD is agracious and merciful;
Slow to anger and great in lovingkindness.

9 aPs.
100:5; 136:1;
Jer. 33:11;
Nah. 1:7;
Matt. 19:17;
Mark 10:18
bPs. 145:15

9 The LORD is agood to all,
And His bmercies are over all His works.

10 aPs. 19:1;
103:22 bPs.
68:26

10 aAll Thy works shall give thanks to Thee, O LORD,
And Thy bgodly ones shall bless Thee.

11 aJer.
14:21

11 They shall speak of the aglory of Thy kingdom,
And talk of Thy power;

12 aPs.
105:1 bPs.
145:5; Is.
2:10, 19, 21

12 To amake known to the sons of men Thy mighty acts,
And the bglory of the majesty of Thy kingdom.

13 aPs.
10:16; 29:10;
1 Tim. 1:17;
2 Pet. 1:11

13 Thy kingdom is an aeverlasting kingdom,
And Thy dominion *endures* throughout all generations.

14 aPs.
37:24 bPs.
146:8

14 The LORD asustains all who fall,
And braises up all who are bowed down.

15 aPs.
104:27;
136:25

15 The eyes of all look to Thee,
And Thou adost give them their food in due time.

16 aPs.
104:28

16 Thou adost open Thy hand,
And dost satisfy the desire of every living thing.

17 The LORD is arighteous in all His ways,
And kind in all His deeds.

17 aPs.
116:5

18 The LORD is anear to all who call upon Him,
To all who call upon Him bin truth.

18 aDeut.
4:7; Ps.
34:18;
119:151
bJohn 4:24

19 He will afulfill the desire of those who fear Him;
He will also bhear their cry and will save them.

19 aPs. 21:2;
37:4 bPs.
10:17; Prov.
15:29;
1 John 5:14

20 The LORD akeeps all who love Him;
But all the bwicked, He will destroy.

20 aPs.
31:23; 91:14;
97:10 bPs.
9:5; 37:38

21 My amouth will speak the praise of the LORD;
And ball flesh will cbless His holy name forever and ever.

21 aPs. 71:8
bPs. 65:2;
150:6 cPs.
145:1, 2

PSALM 146

P RAISE the LORD!
aPraise the LORD, O my soul!

1 aPs.
103:1

2 I will praise the LORD awhile I live;
I will bsing praises to my God while I have my being.

2 aPs. 63:4
bPs. 104:33

3 aDo not trust in princes,
In mortal bman, in whom there is cno salvation.

★ **3** aPs.
118:9 bPs.
118:8; Is.
2:22 cPs.
60:11;
108:12

4 His aspirit departs, he breturns to the earth;
In that very day his cthoughts perish.

4 aPs.
104:29
bEccl. 12:7
cPs. 33:10;
1 Cor. 2:6

5 How ablessed is he whose help is the God of Jacob,
Whose bhope is in the LORD his God;

5 aPs.
144:15; Jer.
17:7 bPs.
71:5

6 Who amade heaven and earth,
The bsea and all that is in them;
Who ckeeps faith forever;

6 aPs.
115:15; Rev.
14:7 bActs
14:15 cPs.
117:2

7 Who aexecutes justice for the oppressed;

7 aPs.
103:6 bPs.
107:9;
145:15 cPs.
68:6; Is. 61:1

Psalm 146 This first of five joyous hymns of praise that close the Psalter, each beginning and ending with Hallelujah, opens with a call to praise (vv. 1–5) and lists the causes for praise as the greatness of God (v. 6) and the graciousness of God (vv. 7–10).
146:3 *princes.* Influential people who are in reality *mortal.*

Who ^bgives food to the hungry.

The LORD ^csets the prisoners free.

8   *Matt. 9:30; John 9:7 *Ps. 145:14 *Ps. 11:7*

8 The LORD ^aopens *the eyes* of the blind;

The LORD ^braises up those who are bowed down;

The LORD ^cloves the righteous;

9   *Ex. 22:21; Lev. 19:34 *Deut. 10:18; Ps. 68:5 *Ps. 147:6*

9 The LORD ^aprotects the strangers;

He ^bsupports the fatherless and the widow;

But He thwarts ^cthe way of the wicked.

10   *Ex. 15:18; Ps. 10:16*

10 The LORD will ^areign forever,

Thy God, O Zion, to all generations.

Praise the LORD!

PSALM 147

1   *Ps. 92:1; 135:3 *Ps. 33:1*

P RAISE the LORD!

For ^ait is good to sing praises to our God;

For it is pleasant *and* praise is ^bbecoming.

★ 2-5
2   *Ps. 51:18; 102:16 *Deut. 30:3; Ps. 106:47; Is. 11:12; 56:8; Ezek. 39:28*

2 The LORD ^abuilds up Jerusalem;

He ^bgathers the outcasts of Israel.

3   *Ps. 34:18; 51:17; Is. 61:1 *Job 5:18; Is. 30:26; Ezek. 34:16*

3 He heals the ^abrokenhearted,

And ^bbinds up their wounds.

4   *Gen. 15:5 *Is. 40:26*

4 He ^acounts the number of the stars;

He ^bgives names to all of them.

5   *Ps. 48:1; 145:3 *Is. 40:28*

5 ^aGreat is our Lord, and abundant in strength;

His ^bunderstanding is infinite.

6 The LORD ^asupports the afflicted;

He brings down the wicked to the ground.

6   *Ps. 37:24; 146:8, 9*

7 ^aSing to the LORD with thanksgiving;

Sing praises to our God on the lyre,

7   *Ps. 33:2; 95:1, 2*

8 Who ^acovers the heavens with clouds,

Who ^bprovides rain for the earth,

Who ^cmakes grass to grow on the mountains.

8   *Job 26:8 *Job 5:10; 38:26, Ps. 104:13 *Job 38:27; Ps. 104:14*

9 He ^agives to the beast its food,

And to the ^byoung ravens which cry.

9   *Ps. 104:27, 28; 145:15 *Job 38:41; Matt. 6:26*

10 He does not delight in the strength of the ^ahorse;

He ^bdoes not take pleasure in the legs of a man.

★10-11
10   *Ps. 33:17 *1 Sam. 16:7*

11 The LORD ^afavors those who fear Him,

^bThose who wait for His lovingkindness.

11   *Ps. 149:4 *Ps. 33:18*

12 Praise the LORD, O Jerusalem!

Praise your God, O Zion!

13 For He has strengthened the ^abars of your gates;

He has ^bblessed your sons within you.

13   *Neh. 3:3; 7:3 *Ps. 37:26*

14 He ^amakes peace in your borders;

He ^bsatisfies you with ^cthe finest of the wheat.

14   *Ps. 29:11; Is. 54:13; 60:17, 18 *Ps. 132:15 *Deut. 32:14; Ps. 81:16*

15 He sends forth His ^acommand to the earth;

His ^bword runs very swiftly.

★15-20
15   *Job 37:12; Ps. 148:5 *Ps. 104:4*

16 He gives ^asnow like wool;

He scatters the ^bfrost like ashes.

16   *Job 37:6; Ps. 148:8 *Job 38:29*

Psalm 147 This hymn contains three stanzas, each beginning with a call to praise followed by the causes for praise. The first (vv. 1-6) calls for praise because of God's grace to Jerusalem (vv. 2-3) and greatness in creation (vv. 4-6); the second (vv. 7-11), because of His greatness in creation (vv. 8-9) and grace to those who trust Him (vv. 10-11); the third (vv. 12-20), because He preserves Jerusalem (vv. 13-14) and gives His Word to man (vv. 15-20).

147:2-5 The Lord's care for His people (vv. 2-3) is guaranteed by His omnipotence (vv. 4-5). **147:10-11** The Lord does not take delight in physical strength but in reverential trust (on *fear* see note on 103:11; on *lovingkindness*, Hos. 2:19). **147:15-20** His Word commands the forces of nature (vv. 15-18), but particularly communicated His laws to Israel, thus distinguishing her from all other nations (vv. 19-20).

17 He casts forth His [a]ice as fragments;
Who can stand before His [b]cold?

18 He [a]sends forth His word and melts them;
He [b]causes His wind to blow and the waters to flow.

19 He [a]declares His words to Jacob,
His [b]statutes and His ordinances to Israel.

20 He [a]has not dealt thus with any nation;
And as for His ordinances, they have [b]not known them.
Praise the LORD!

PSALM 148

PRAISE the LORD!
Praise the LORD [a]from the heavens;
Praise Him [b]in the heights!

2 Praise Him, [a]all His angels;
Praise Him, [b]all His hosts!

3 Praise Him, sun and moon;
Praise Him, all stars of light!

4 Praise Him, [a]highest heavens,
And the [b]waters that are above the heavens!

5 Let them praise the name of the LORD,
For [a]He commanded and they were created.

6 He has also [a]established them forever and ever;
He has made a [b]decree which will not pass away.

7 Praise the LORD from the earth,
[a]Sea monsters and all [b]deeps;

8 [a]Fire and hail, [b]snow and [c]clouds;
[d]Stormy wind, [e]fulfilling His word;

9 [a]Mountains and all hills;
Fruit [b]trees and all cedars;

10 [a]Beasts and all cattle;
[b]Creeping things and winged fowl;

11 [a]Kings of the earth and all peoples;
Princes and all judges of the earth;

12 Both young men and virgins;
Old men and children.

13 Let them praise the name of the LORD,
For His [a]name alone is exalted;
His [b]glory is above earth and heaven.

14 And He has [a]lifted up a horn for His people,
[b]Praise for all His godly ones;
Even for the sons of Israel, a people [c]near to Him.
Praise the LORD!

PSALM 149

PRAISE the LORD!
Sing to the LORD a [a]new song,
And His praise [b]in the congregation of the godly ones.

2 Let Israel be glad in [a]his Maker;
Let the sons of Zion rejoice in their [b]King.

3 Let them praise His name with [a]dancing;
Let them sing praises to Him with [b]timbrel and lyre.

Cross-references (left column)

17 [a]Job 37:10 [b]Job 37:9

18 [a]Ps. 33:9; 107:20; 147:15 [b]Ps. 107:25

19 [a]Deut. 33:3, 4 [b]Mal. 4:4

20 [a]Deut. 4:7, 8, 32-34; Rom. 3:1, 2 [b]Ps. 79:6; Jer. 10:25

1 [a]Ps. 69:34 [b]Job 16:19; Ps. 102:19; Matt. 21:9

★ 2 [a]Ps. 103:20 [b]Ps. 103:21

★ 4 [a]Deut. 10:14; 1 Kin. 8:27; Neh. 9:6; Ps. 68:33 [b]Gen. 1:7

5 [a]Gen. 1:1; Ps. 33:6, 9

6 [a]Ps. 89:37; Jer. 31:35, 36; 33:20, 25 [b]Job 38:33

7 [a]Gen. 1:21; Ps. 74:13 [b]Gen. 1:2; Deut. 33:13; Hab. 3:10

Cross-references (right column)

8 [a]Ps. 18:12 [b]Ps. 147:16 [c]Ps. 135:7 [d]Ps. 107:25 [e]Job 37:12; Ps. 103:20

9 [a]Is. 44:23; 49:13 [b]Is. 55:12

10 [a]Is. 43:20 [b]Hos. 2:18

11 [a]Ps. 102:15

13 [a]Is. 12:4 [b]Ps. 8:1; 113:4

★14 [a]1 Sam. 2:1; Ps. 75:10 [b]Deut. 10:21; Ps. 109:1; Jer. 17:14 [c]Lev. 10:3; Eph. 2:17

1 [a]Ps. 33:3 [b]Ps. 35:18; 89:5

2 [a]Ps. 95:6 [b]Judg. 8:23; Ps. 47:6; Zech. 9:9

★ 3 [a]2 Sam. 6:14; Ps. 150:4 [b]Ex. 15:20; Ps. 81:2

Psalm 148 The psalmist calls on the heavens (vv. 1-6) and the earth (vv. 7-14) to praise the Lord.
148:2 *hosts.* Apparently a reference to angels.
148:4 *highest heavens.* Plurality of heavens may be hinted at (cf. 2 Cor. 12:2).
148:14 *horn.* Strength.

Psalm 149 This hymn is a summons to praise (vv. 1-4) and a song of triumph (vv. 5-9).
149:3 *dancing.* In the O.T., whirling motion done by a single individual or by a large group, not by couples (cf. 2 Sam. 6:16). *timbrel.* Tambourine.

4 aJob
36:11; Ps.
16:11; 35:27;
147:11 bPs.
132:16; Is.
61:3

4 For the Lord ᵃtakes pleasure in His people;
He will ᵇbeautify the afflicted ones with salvation.

5 aPs.
132:16 bJob
35:10; Ps.
42:8

5 Let the ᵃgodly ones exult in glory;
Let them ᵇsing for joy on their beds.

★ 6-9

6 aPs.
66:17 bHeb.
4:12 cNeh.
4:17

6 Let the ᵃhigh praises of God be in their mouth,
And a ᵇtwo-edged ᶜsword in their hand,

7 aEzek.
25:17; Mic.
5:15

7 To ᵃexecute vengeance on the nations,
And punishment on the peoples;

8 aJob 36:8
bNah. 3:10

8 To bind their kings ᵃwith chains,
And their ᵇnobles with fetters of iron;

9 aDeut.
7:1, 2; Ezek.
28:26 bPs.
112:9;
148:14

9 To ᵃexecute on them the judgment written;
This is an ᵇhonor for all His godly ones.
Praise the Lord!

PSALM 150

PRAISE the Lord!
Praise God in His ᵃsanctuary;
Praise Him in His mighty ᵇexpanse.

1 aPs.
73:17;
102:19 bPs.
19:1

2 Praise Him for His ᵃmighty deeds;
Praise Him according to His excellent ᵇgreatness.

2 aPs.
145:12
bDeut. 3:24;
Ps. 145:3

3 Praise Him with ᵃtrumpet sound;
Praise Him with ᵇharp and lyre.

★ 3-5

3 aPs. 98:6
bPs. 33:2

4 Praise Him with ᵃtimbrel and dancing;
Praise Him with ᵇstringed instruments and ᶜpipe.

4 aPs.
45:8; Is.
38:20 cGen.
4:21; Job
21:12

5 Praise Him with loud ᵃcymbals;
Praise Him with resounding cymbals.

5 a2 Sam.
6:5; 1 Chr.
13:8; 15:16;
Ezra 3:10;
Neh. 12:27

6 Let ᵃeverything that has breath praise the Lord.
Praise the Lord!

6 aPs.
103:22;
145:21

149:6–9 These verses look forward to the subjugation of the nations at the establishment of Christ's millennial kingdom (see notes on Isa. 54:11–17 and Mic. 5:4–15).
Psalm 150 In this final doxology, the psalmist calls for praise in God's sanctuary (v. 1) because of His deeds and His greatness (v. 2), with all kinds of musical instruments (vv. 3–5), and by everything that has breath (v. 6).
150:3–5 Israel's music was apparently loud and rhythmic, produced primarily by percussion and stringed instruments. *trumpet.* Shofar, or ram's horn. The *harp* and *lyre* were larger and smaller portable harps, which varied in size and number of strings. *timbrel.* Tambourine. *stringed instruments.* A general term. *pipe.* Flutelike instrument. *cymbals.* Of brass or silver; apparently there were larger, louder ones and smaller, higher-pitched ones.

INTRODUCTION TO
THE BOOK OF PROVERBS

AUTHORS: Solomon and Others   DATE: 950–700 B.C.

Authorship   *According to 1 Kings 4:32, Solomon spoke 3,000 proverbs and 1,005 songs. He wrote most of the collection of proverbs in this book. The section from 1:1–9:18 is ascribed to him as are the sections from 10:1–22:16 and 25:1–29:27, although the proverbs in the latter section were selected from Solomon's collection by King Hezekiah's committee (25:1). We know nothing of Agur, author of chapter 30, or of Lemuel, author of chapter 31.*

Characteristics   *The Hebrew term for "proverb" means a comparison, and it came to be used for any sage or moralistic pronouncement (cf. Ezek. 18:2; Psalm 49:4). Many proverbs are condensed parables. The sayings in this book form a library of instruction on how to live a godly life here on earth and how to be assured of reward in the life to come. Thus these proverbs are not so much popular sayings as they are a distillation of wisdom from those who knew the law of God.*
   This type of literature goes back in written form to about 2700 B.C. in Egypt. The section 22:17–24:34 is similar to the proverbs of an Egyptian writer, Amenemop, who apparently antedated Solomon.

Contents   *Though the theme running throughout the book is wisdom for living, the specific teachings include instruction on folly, sin, goodness, wealth, poverty, the tongue, pride, humility, justice, vengeance, strife, gluttony, love, lust, laziness, friends, the family, life, and death. Almost every facet of human relationships is mentioned, and the teaching of the book is applicable to all men everywhere.*

OUTLINE OF PROVERBS

THE BOOK OF PROVERBS

I INTRODUCTION, 1:1-7

A The Author, 1:1

★ **1** *a*1 Kin. 4:32; Prov. 10:1; 25:1; Eccl. 12:9 *b*Eccl. 1:1

1 The *a*proverbs of Solomon *b*the son of David, king of Israel:

B The Purpose, 1:2-6

★ **2-4**

★ **2** *a*Prov. 15:33 *b*Prov. 4:1

2 To know *a*wisdom and instruction,
To discern the sayings of *b*understanding,

★ **3** *a*Prov. 2:1; 19:20 *b*Prov. 2:9

3 To *a*receive instruction in wise behavior,
*b*Righteousness, justice and equity;

★ **4** *a*Prov. 8:5, 12 *b*Prov. 2:10, 11; 3:21

4 To give *a*prudence to the naive,
To the youth *b*knowledge and discretion,

★ **5-6**

5 *a*Prov. 9:9 *b*Prov. 14:6; Eccl. 9:11

5 A wise man will hear and *a*increase in learning,
And a *b*man of understanding will acquire wise counsel,

6 *a*Num. 12:8; Ps. 49:4; 78:2; Dan. 8:23

6 To understand a proverb and a figure,
The words of the wise and their *a*riddles.

C The Theme, 1:7

★ **7** *a*Job 28:28; Ps. 111:10; Prov. 9:10; 15:33; Eccl. 12:13

7 *a*The fear of the LORD is the beginning of knowledge;
Fools despise wisdom and instruction.

II THE PRECEPTS OF WISDOM, 1:8–9:18

A Avoid Bad Company, 1:8-19

★ **1:8-9:18**

★ **8** *a*Prov. 4:1 *b*Prov. 6:20

8 *a*Hear, my son, your father's instruction,
And *b*do not forsake your mother's teaching;

9 *a*Prov. 4:9 *b*Gen. 41:42; Dan. 5:29

9 Indeed, they are a *a*graceful wreath to your head,
And *b*ornaments about your neck.

★**10-19** **10** *a*Prov. 16:29 *b*Gen. 39:7-10; Deut. 13:8; Ps. 50:18; Eph. 5:11

10 My son, if sinners *a*entice you,
*b*Do not consent.

11 *a*Prov. 12:6; Jer. 5:26 *b*Ps. 10:8; Prov. 1:18

11 If they say, "Come with us, Let us *a*lie in wait for blood,
Let us *b*ambush the innocent without cause;

12 *a*Ps. 124:3 *b*Ps. 28:1

12 Let us *a*swallow them alive like Sheol,

1:1 *proverbs of Solomon.* Proverbs are sayings taken from everyday life intended to serve as practical guidelines for successful living. The ascription to Solomon does not mean that he wrote the whole book (cf. 22:17; 24:23; 30:1; 31:1), but identifies him as the major contributor.

1:2-4 The purpose of Proverbs is that the reader might know wisdom and allow it to govern his or her life.

1:2 *wisdom.* I.e., the use of knowledge in a practical and successful way. *instruction.* Training by word (24:32) or rod (23:13).

1:3 *instruction in wise behavior.* Training in wise dealings which lead to success.

1:4 *prudence.* I.e., a safeguard against being misled. *naive.* I.e., persons undecided in their views and easily influenced.

1:5-6 Proverbs benefit not only the simple, but the wise. *wise counsel.* Lit., "steerings"; i.e., the discernment to steer a right course through life. *proverb.* A description by way of comparison.

1:7 The motto of the wisdom teachers and theme of the book is that the fear of the Lord is the starting point and essence of wisdom. *fear of the LORD.* I.e., a reverence for God expressed in submission to His will (cf. Job 28:28; Eccles. 12:13; Psalm 111:10; Prov. 9:10; 15:33). Wisdom is not acquired by a mechanical formula but through a right relationship with God. *Fools.* I.e., easily led, gullible, silly persons; those who are both mentally naive and morally irresponsible.

1:8-9:18 The first major section of the book records discourses on wisdom in which the student is encouraged to consider and compare the ways of the foolish and the ways of the wise.

1:8 *Hear, my son.* A wise teacher is addressing his pupil. *Hear.* I.e., with a view to obedience.

1:10-19 The way of sinners is attractive (vv. 10-14), but it leads to destruction (vv. 15-19). You may gain the world but lose your soul (Mark 8:36).

1:12 *Sheol.* The grave or place of the dead (cf. Psalm 55:15).

Even whole, as those who
 *b*go down to the pit;

13 We shall find all *kinds* of
 precious wealth,
 We shall fill our houses
 with spoil;

14 Throw in your lot with us,
 We shall all have one
 purse,"

15 a Ps. 1:1;
Prov. 4:14
bPs. 119:101

15 My son, *a*do not walk in
 the way with them.
 *b*Keep your feet from their
 path,

16 a Prov.
6:17, 18; Is.
59:7

16 For *a*their feet run to evil,
 And they hasten to shed
 blood.

★17

17 Indeed, it is useless to
 spread the net
 In the eyes of any bird;

18 a Prov.
11:19

18 But they *a*lie in wait for
 their own blood;
 They ambush their own
 lives.

19 a Prov.
15:27

19 So are the ways of everyone who *a*gains by
 violence;
 It takes away the life of its
 possessors.

B Heed Wisdom's Advice,
 1:20-33

★20-23

20 a Prov.
8:1-3; 9:3

20 *a*Wisdom shouts in the
 street,
 She lifts her voice in the
 square;

21 At the head of the noisy
 streets she cries out;
 At the entrance of the
 gates in the city, she
 utters her sayings:

22 a Prov.
1:4, 32; 8:5;
9:4; 22:3
bPs. 1:1
cProv. 1:29;
5:12

22 "How long, O *a*naive ones,
 will you love simplic-
 ity?
 And *b*scoffers delight
 themselves in scoffing,
 And fools *c*hate knowl-
 edge?

23 "Turn to my reproof,
 Behold, I will *a*pour out my
 spirit on you;
 I will make my words
 known to you.

23 a Is.
32:15; Joel
2:28; John
7:39

24 Because *a*I called, and you
 *b*refused;
 I *c*stretched out my hand,
 and no one paid at-
 tention;

24 a Is.
65:12; 66:4;
Jer. 7:13
bZech. 7:11
cIs. 65:2;
Rom. 10:21

25 And you *a*neglected all my
 counsel,
 And did not *b*want my reproof;

25 a Ps.
107:11; Luke
7:30 **b**Prov.
15:10

26 I will even *a*laugh at your
 *b*calamity;
 I will mock when your
 *c*dread comes,

26 a Ps. 2:4
bProv. 6:15
cProv. 10:24

27 When your dread comes
 like a storm,
 And your calamity comes
 on like a *a*whirlwind,
 When distress *and* anguish
 come on you.

27 a Prov.
10:25

28 "Then they will *a*call on me,
 but I will not answer;
 They will *b*seek me diligently, but they shall
 not find me,

28 a1 Sam.
8:18; Job
27:9; 35:12;
Ps. 18:41; Is.
1:15; Jer.
11:11; 14:12;
Ezek. 8:18;
Mic. 3:4;
Zech. 7:13;
James 4:3
bProv. 8:17

29 Because they *a*hated
 knowledge,
 And did not choose the
 fear of the LORD.

29 a Job
21:14; Prov.
1:22

30 "They *a*would not accept
 my counsel,
 They spurned all my re-
 proof.

30 a Ps.
81:11; Prov.
1:25

31 "So they shall *a*eat of the
 fruit of their own way,
 And be *b*satiated with their
 own devices.

31 a Job 4:8;
Prov. 5:22,
23; 22:8; Is.
3:11; Jer.
6:19 **b**Prov.
14:14

32 "For the *a*waywardness of
 the naive shall kill
 them,
 And the complacency of
 fools shall destroy
 them.

32 a Jer. 2:19

33 "But *a*he who listens to me
 shall live securely,
 And shall be at ease from
 the dread of evil."

33 a Ps.
25:12, 13;
Prov. 3:24-26

1:17 If a bird knows enough to avoid an obvious trap, then surely a person must have as much sense!

1:20-23 Wisdom is personified as a woman inviting all to come to her and learn, but the majority refuse to heed her appeal.

C Avoid the Adulteress, 2:1-22

★ 1-22

1 aProv. 4:10 bProv. 3:1

2 My son, if you will ^areceive my sayings, And ^btreasure my commandments within you,

2 aProv. 22:17

2 ^aMake your ear attentive to wisdom, Incline your heart to understanding;

3 For if you cry for discernment, Lift your voice for understanding;

4 aProv. 3:14 bJob 3:21; Matt. 13:44

4 If you seek her as ^asilver, And search for her as for ^bhidden treasures;

5 aProv. 1:7

5 Then you will discern the ^afear of the LORD, And discover the knowledge of God.

★ 6-7

6 a1 Kin. 3:12; Job 32:8; James 1:5

6 For ^athe LORD gives wisdom; From His mouth *come* knowledge and understanding.

7 aPs. 84:11; Prov. 30:5

7 He stores up sound wisdom for the upright; *He is* a ^ashield to those who walk in integrity,

8 a1 Sam. 2:9; Ps. 66:9

8 Guarding the paths of justice, And He ^apreserves the way of His godly ones.

9 aProv. 8:20 bProv. 4:18

9 Then you will discern ^arighteousness and justice And equity *and* every ^bgood course.

★10-22

10 aProv. 14:33 bProv. 22:18

10 For ^awisdom will enter your heart, And ^bknowledge will be pleasant to your soul;

11 Discretion will ^aguard you, Understanding will watch over you,

11 aProv. 4:6; 6:22

12 To ^adeliver you from the way of evil, From the man who speaks ^bperverse things;

12 aProv. 28:26 bProv. 6:12

13 From those who ^aleave the paths of uprightness, To walk in the ^bways of darkness;

13 aProv. 21:16 bPs. 82:5; Prov. 4:19; John 3:19, 20

14 Who ^adelight in doing evil, And rejoice in the perversity of evil;

14 aProv. 10:23; Jer. 11:15

15 Whose paths are ^acrooked, And who are devious in their ways;

15 aPs. 125:5; Prov. 21:8

16 To ^adeliver you from the strange woman, From the ^badulteress who flatters with her words;

★16-19

★16 aProv. 6:24; 7:5 bProv. 23:27

17 That leaves the ^acompanion of her youth, And forgets the ^bcovenant of her God;

17 aMal. 2:14, 15 bGen. 2:24

18 For ^aher house sinks down to death, And her tracks *lead* to the dead;

18 aProv. 7:27

19 None ^awho go to her return again, Nor do they reach the ^bpaths of life.

19 aEccl. 7:26 bPs. 16:11; Prov. 5:6

20 So you will ^awalk in the way of good men, And keep to the ^bpaths of the righteous.

20 aHeb. 6:12 bProv. 4:18

21 For ^athe upright will live in the land, And ^bthe blameless will remain in it;

21 aPs. 37:9, 29; Prov. 10:30 bProv. 28:10

22 But ^athe wicked will be cut off from the land, And ^bthe treacherous will be ^cuprooted from it.

22 aPs. 37:38; Prov. 10:30 bProv. 11:3 cDeut. 28:63; Ps. 52:5

2:1-22 The master teacher speaks again and describes the happy results of pursuing and acquiring wisdom.

2:6-7 Wisdom is God-given, not the result of mere human effort or ability (cf. 1 Kings 3:9ff.; James 1:5).

2:10-22 Wisdom is beneficial in that it delivers one from the ways of evil men (vv. 10-15), from the arms of the adulteress (vv. 16-19), and preserves one's life and character (vv. 20-22).

2:16-19 What kind of woman is the adulteress? She is a flatterer (v. 16); unfaithful to her husband (v. 17); may have a religious background but is backslidden (v. 17); and offers a taste of life but delivers death (vv. 18-19).

2:16 *adulteress.* Lit., foreign woman; i.e., a woman outside the circle of a man's proper relationships, hence a harlot or adulteress.

D   Trust and Honor God, 3:1-12

★ 1-12
1 *a*Ps.
119:61; Prov.
4:5 *b*Ex.
20:6; Deut.
30:16
2 *a*Ps.
91:16; Prov.
3:16; 4:10;
9:11; 10:27

3 *a*2 Sam.
15:20; Prov.
14:22 *b*Deut.
6:8; 11:18;
Prov. 1:9;
6:21 *c*Prov.
7:3; Jer.
17:1; 2 Cor.
3:3

4 *a*1 Sam.
2:26; Prov.
8:35; Luke
2:52 *b*Ps.
111:10

5 *a*Ps. 37:3,
5; Prov.
22:19 *b*Prov.
23:4; Jer.
9:23

★ 6 *a*1 Chr.
28:9; Prov.
16:3; Phil.
4:6; Matt.
1:5 *b*Is.
45:13; Jer.
10:23

7 *a*Rom.
12:16 *b*Job
1:1; 28:28;
Prov. 8:13;
16:6

8 *a*Prov.
4:22 *b*Job
21:24

9 *a*Is. 43:23
*b*Ex. 23:19;
Deut. 26:2;
Mal. 3:10

10 *a*Deut.
28:8 *b*Joel
2:24

11 *a*Job
5:17; Heb.
12:5, 6

3 My son, *a*do not forget my teaching,
But let your heart *b*keep my commandments;

2 For *a*length of days and years of life,
And peace they will add to you.

3 Do not let *a*kindness and truth leave you;
*b*Bind them around your neck,
*c*Write them on the tablet of your heart.

4 So you will *a*find favor and *b*good repute
In the sight of God and man.

5 *a*Trust in the LORD with all your heart,
And *b*do not lean on your own understanding.

6 In all your ways *a*acknowledge Him,
And He will *b*make your paths straight.

7 *a*Do not be wise in your own eyes;
*b*Fear the LORD and turn away from evil.

8 It will be *a*healing to your body,
And *b*refreshment to your bones.

9 *a*Honor the LORD from your wealth,
And from the *b*first of all your produce;

10 So your *a*barns will be filled with plenty,
And your *b*vats will overflow with new wine.

11 *a*My son, do not reject the discipline of the LORD,
Or loathe His reproof,

12 For *a*whom the LORD loves He reproves,
Even *b*as a father, the son in whom he delights.

12 *a*Rev.
3:19 *b*Deut.
8:5; Prov.
13:24

E   Consider the Value of Wisdom, 3:13-20

13 *a*How blessed is the man who finds wisdom,
And the man who gains understanding.

14 For its *a*profit is better than the profit of silver,
And its gain than fine gold.

15 She is *a*more precious than jewels;
And nothing you desire compares with her.

16 *a*Long life is in her right hand;
In her left hand are *b*riches and honor.

17 Her *a*ways are pleasant ways,
And all her paths are *b*peace.

18 She is a *a*tree of life to those who take hold of her,
And happy are all who hold her fast.

19 The LORD *a*by wisdom founded the earth;
By understanding He *b*established the heavens.

20 By His knowledge the *a*deeps were broken up,
And the *b*skies drip with dew.

13 *a*Prov.
8:32, 34

14 *a*Job
28:15-19;
Prov. 8:10;
19; 16:16

15 *a*Job
28:18; Prov.
8:11

16 *a*Prov.
3:2 *b*Prov.
8:18; 22:4

17 *a*Matt.
11:29 *b*Ps.
119:165;
Prov. 16:7

★18 *a*Gen.
2:9; Prov.
11:30; 13:12;
15:4; Rev.
2:7

★19-26
19 *a*Ps.
104:24; Prov.
8:27 *b*Prov.
8:27, 28

20 *a*Gen.
7:11 *b*Deut.
33:28; Job
36:28

F   Be Kind and Generous to Others, 3:21-35

21 My son, *a*let them not depart from your sight;

21 *a*Prov.
4:21

3:1-12 Wisdom not only delivers one from evil but promises certain rewards: longevity and peace (vv. 1-2), favor with God and man (vv. 3-4), guidance (vv. 5-6), health and refreshment (vv. 7-8), prosperity (vv. 9-10), and a proper response to discipline (vv. 11-12).
3:6 *acknowledge.* Lit., know; i.e., know God personally and be in fellowship with Him. *make . . . straight.* I.e., clear obstructions and enable

one to go forward.
3:18 *tree of life.* I.e., a source of life (cf. Gen. 2:9; Rev. 2:7). Wisdom is a source of life to those who attain to her.
3:19-26 Wisdom played a dynamic part in the creation of the universe. By it God changed chaos to order. So also wisdom can have a dynamic effect on human life.

Keep sound wisdom and
   discretion,

22 So they will be ᵃlife to
   your soul,
And ᵇadornment to your
   neck.

23 Then you will ᵃwalk in
   your way securely,
And your foot will not
   ᵇstumble.

24 When you ᵃlie down, you
   will not be afraid;
When you lie down, your
   sleep will be sweet.

25 ᵃDo not be afraid of sudden fear,
Nor of the ᵇonslaught of
   the wicked when it
   comes;

26 For the Lᴏʀᴅ will be your
   confidence,
And will ᵃkeep your foot
   from being caught.

27 ᵃDo not withhold good
   from those to whom it
   is due,
When it is in your power
   to do *it.*

28 ᵃDo not say to your neighbor, "Go, and come
   back,
And tomorrow I will give
   it,"
When you have it with
   you.

29 ᵃDo not devise harm
   against your neighbor,
While he lives in security
   beside you.

30 ᵃDo not contend with a
   man without cause,
If he has done you no
   harm.

31 ᵃDo not envy a man of violence,
And do not choose any of
   his ways.

32 For the ᵃcrooked *man* is an
   abomination to the
   Lᴏʀᴅ;

But He is ᵇintimate with
   the upright.

33 The ᵃcurse of the Lᴏʀᴅ is
   on the house of the
   wicked,
But He ᵇblesses the dwelling of the righteous.

34 Though ᵃHe scoffs at the
   scoffers,
Yet ᵇHe gives grace to the
   afflicted.

35 ᵃThe wise will inherit hon-
   or,
But fools display dishonor.

G Acquire Wisdom, 4:1-9

4 Hear, O sons, the ᵃinstruction
   of a father,
And ᵇgive attention that
   you may gain under-
   standing,

2 For I give you sound
   ᵃteaching;
ᵇDo not abandon my in-
   struction.

3 When I was a son to my
   father,
ᵃTender and ᵇthe only son
   in the sight of my
   mother,

4 Then he ᵃtaught me and
   said to me,
"Let your heart ᵇhold fast
   my words;
ᶜKeep my commandments
   and live;

5 ᵃAcquire wisdom! ᵇAcquire understanding!
Do not forget, nor turn
   away from the words
   of my mouth.

6 "Do not forsake her, and
   she will guard you;
ᵃLove her, and she will
   watch over you.

7 "ᵃThe beginning of wisdom
   is: ᵇAcquire wisdom;
And with all your acquir-
   ing, get understand-
   ing.

Margin references (left column):

22 ᵃDeut. 32:47; Prov. 4:22; 8:35; 16:22; 21:21 ᵇProv. 1:9

23 ᵃProv. 4:12; 10:9 ᵇPs. 91:12; Is. 5:27; 63:13

24 ᵃJob 11:19; Ps. 3:5; Prov. 1:33; 6:22

25 ᵃPs. 91:5; 1 Pet. 3:14 ᵇJob 5:21

26 ᵃ1 Sam. 2:9

27 ᵃRom. 13:7; Gal. 6:10

28 ᵃLev. 19:13; Deut. 24:15

29 ᵃProv. 6:14; 14:22

30 ᵃProv. 26:17; Rom. 12:18

31 ᵃPs. 37:1; Prov. 24:1

★**32** ᵃProv. 11:20 ᵇJob 29:4; Ps. 25:14

Margin references (right column):

33 ᵃLev. 26:14, 16; Deut. 11:28; Zech. 5:3, 4; Mal. 2:2 ᵇJob 8:6; Ps. 1:3

34 ᵃJames 4:6 ᵇ1 Pet. 5:5

★**35b** ᵃDan. 12:3

★ **1-27**

1 ᵃPs. 34:11; Prov. 1:8 ᵇProv. 1:2; 2:2

2 ᵃDeut. 32:2; Job 11:4 ᵇPs. 89:30; 119:87; Prov. 3:1

3 ᵃ1 Chr. 22:5; 29:1 ᵇZech. 12:10

4 ᵃEph. 6:4 ᵇPs. 119:168 ᶜProv. 7:2

5 ᵃProv. 4:7 ᵇProv. 16:16

6 ᵃ2 Thess. 2:10

★ **7** ᵃProv. 8:23 ᵇProv. 23:23

3:32 Perverse individuals are an abomination to
God, but He deals with the righteous as His
intimate friends.

3:35b Lit., "but fools raise up (elevate, exalt)
shame (dishonor)." While the wise inherit
honor, fools promote the shame that is consistent with their character.

4:1-27 Wisdom provides many benefits:
watchcare and honor (vv. 1-9); guidance in the
way of righteousness (vv. 10-19); and life,
health, and integrity (vv. 20-27).

4:7 The first step in acquiring wisdom is to
make up your mind that you want it and will
strive to obtain it.

8 *a*1 Sam. 2:30

8 "*a*Prize her, and she will exalt you;
She will honor you if you embrace her.

9 *a*Prov. 1:9

9 "She will place *a*on your head a garland of grace;
She will present you with a crown of beauty."

H Avoid Bad Company, 4:10-19

10 *a*Prov. 2:1 *b*Prov. 3:2

10 Hear, my son, and *a*accept my sayings,
And the *b*years of your life will be many.

11 *a*1 Sam. 12:23

11 I have *a*directed you in the way of wisdom;
I have led you in upright paths.

★**12** *a*Job 18:7; Ps. 18:36 *b*Ps. 91:11; Prov. 3:23

12 When you walk, your *a*steps will not be impeded;
And if you run, you *b*will not stumble.

13 *a*Prov. 3:18 *b*Prov. 3:22; John 6:63

13 *a*Take hold of instruction; do not let go.
Guard her, for she is your *b*life.

14 *a*Ps. 1:1; Prov. 1:15

14 *a*Do not enter the path of the wicked,
And do not proceed in the way of evil men.

15 Avoid it, do not pass by it;
Turn away from it and pass on.

★**16** *a*Ps. 36:4; Mic. 2:1

16 For they *a*cannot sleep unless they do evil;
And they are robbed of sleep unless they make *someone* stumble.

17 *a*Prov. 13:2

17 For they *a*eat the bread of wickedness,

And drink the wine of violence.

★**18-19**
★**18** *a*Is. 26:7; Matt. 5:14; Phil. 2:15 *b*2 Sam. 23:4 *c*Dan. 12:3 *d*Job 11:17

18 But the *a*path of the righteous is like the *b*light of dawn,
That *c*shines brighter and brighter until the *d*full day.

19 *a*Job 18:5, 6; Prov. 2:13; Is. 59:9, 10; Jer. 23:12; John 12:35 *b*John 11:10

19 The *a*way of the wicked is like darkness;
They do not know over what they *b*stumble.

I Watch Yourself, 4:20-27

20 *a*Prov. 5:1 *b*Prov. 2:2

20 My son, *a*give attention to my words;
*b*Incline your ear to my sayings.

21 *a*Prov. 3:21 *b*Prov. 7:1, 2

21 *a*Do not let them depart from your sight;
*b*Keep them in the midst of your heart.

22 *a*Prov. 3:22 *b*Prov. 3:8; 12:18

22 For they are *a*life to those who find them,
And *b*health to all their whole body.

★**23** *a*Matt. 12:34; 15:18, 19; Mark 7:21; Luke 6:45

23 Watch over your heart with all diligence,
For *a*from it *flow* the springs of life.

24 *a*Prov. 6:12; 10:32 *b*Prov. 19:1

24 Put away from you a *a*deceitful mouth,
And *b*put devious lips far from you.

25 Let your eyes look directly ahead,
And let your gaze be fixed straight in front of you.

★**26b** *a*Prov. 5:21; Heb. 12:13 *b*Ps. 119:5

26 *a*Watch the path of your feet,
And all your *b*ways will be established.

27 *a*Deut. 5:32; 28:14 *b*Prov. 1:15; Is. 1:16

27 *a*Do not turn to the right nor to the left;
*b*Turn your foot from evil.

4:12 Wisdom's way is straight and level in contrast to the crooked and cluttered way of folly.

4:16 The wicked are unable to sleep because the day has passed without an opportunity to obtain gain from an act of violence.

4:18-19 While the righteous walk in increasing light, the wicked walk in darkness.

4:18 *full day.* Lit., "standing firm of day"; i.e., the noon time, when the sun is directly overhead and appears stationary.

4:23 *heart.* I.e., mind or inner being. *springs of life.* Lit., outgoings of life; i.e., spiritual vitality.

4:26b Perhaps better, "and let all your ways be established."

J Forsake Lust, 5:1–23

★ 1-6

1 aProv. 4:20 bProv. 22:17

5 My son, ªgive attention to my wisdom,
ᵇIncline your ear to my understanding;

2 aProv. 3:21 bMal. 2:7

2 That you may ªobserve discretion,
And your ᵇlips may reserve knowledge.

3 aProv. 2:16; 5:20; 7:5; 22:14 bSong 4:11 cPs. 55:21

3 For the lips of an ªadulteress ᵇdrip honey,
And ᶜsmoother than oil is her speech;

★ 4 aEccl. 7:26 bPs. 57:4; Heb. 4:12

4 But in the end she is ªbitter as wormwood,
ᵇSharp as a two-edged sword.

★ 5 aProv. 7:27

5 Her feet ªgo down to death,
Her steps lay hold of Sheol.

6 aProv. 4:26; 5:21 b2 Pet. 2:14 cProv. 30:20

6 She does not ponder the ªpath of life;
Her ways are ᵇunstable, she ᶜdoes not know it.

★ 7-23

7 aProv. 7:24 bPs. 119:102

7 ªNow then, my sons, listen to me,
And ᵇdo not depart from the words of my mouth.

★ 8 aProv. 7:25 bProv. 9:14

8 ªKeep your way far from her,
And do not go near the ᵇdoor of her house,

9 Lest you give your vigor to others,
And your years to the cruel one;

10 Lest strangers be filled with your strength,
And your hard-earned goods go to the house of an alien;

11 And you groan at your latter end,
When your flesh and your body are consumed;

12 And you say, "How I have ªhated instruction!
And my heart ᵇspurned reproof!

12 aProv. 1:7, 22, 29 bProv. 1:25; 12:1

13 "And I have not listened to the voice of my ªteachers,
Nor inclined my ear to my instructors!

13 aProv. 1:8

14 "I was almost in utter ruin
In the midst of the assembly and congregation."

★14

15 Drink water from your own cistern,
And fresh water from your own well.

★15

16 Should your ªsprings be dispersed abroad,
Streams of water in the streets?

★16 aProv. 5:18; 9:17; Song 4:12, 15

17 Let them be yours alone,
And not for strangers with you.

18 Let your ªfountain be blessed,
And ᵇrejoice in the ᶜwife of your youth.

★18-19

18 aProv. 9:17; Song 4:12, 15 bEccl. 9:9 cMal. 2:14

19 As a loving ªhind and a graceful doe,
Let her breasts satisfy you at all times;
Be exhilarated always with her love.

★19-20

19 aSong 2:9, 17; 4:5; 7:3

5:1-6 Wisdom helps guard against the adulteress.

5:4 *wormwood.* A shrub with a bitter taste; thus, the height of bitterness. The adulteress may appear sweet, but in reality she is exceedingly bitter.

5:5 *Sheol.* The abode of the dead. Her steps lead to death, and those who associate with her meet a like fate.

5:7-23 This section warns of the consequences of marital infidelity and points to the delights of a faithful marriage in contrast to its pathetic alternative.

5:8 Avoid enticing opportunities!

5:14 *in utter ruin.* I.e., at the point of utter ruin. The adulterer nearly lost his life as punishment for his sin (cf. Deut. 22:22).

5:15 The figurative language here refers to marital intercourse. The main point is to find contentment with your lawful wife.

5:16 The idea is, should you beget children by an adulteress, a woman of the street? *springs.* A reference to one's children.

5:18-19 The wise teacher presents a healthy view of sex. His counsel is to enjoy the delight of God-given sex only in marriage.

5:19-20 *doe.* Gazelle.

20 aProv.
5:3 bProv.
2:16; 6:24;
7:5; 23:27

20 For why should you, my
son, be exhilarated
with an aadulteress,
And embrace the bosom of
a bforeigner?

★**21** aJob
14:16; 31:4;
34:21; Ps.
119:168;
Prov. 15:3;
Jer. 16:17;
32:19; Hos.
7:2; Heb.
4:13 bProv.
4:26

21 For the aways of a man are
before the eyes of the
LORD,
And He bwatches all his
paths.

22 aNum.
32:23; Ps.
7:15; 9:15;
40:12; Prov.
1:31, 32

22 His aown iniquities will
capture the wicked,
And he will be held with
the cords of his sin.

★**23** aJob
4:21; 36:12

23 He will adie for lack of instruction,
And in the greatness of his
folly he will go astray.

K Avoid Surety, 6:1-5

★ **1-5**

★ **1** aProv.
11:15; 17:18;
20:16; 22:26;
27:13

6 My son, if you have become
asurety for your
neighbor,
Have given a pledge for a
stranger,

2 *If* you have been snared
with the words of
your mouth,
Have been caught with the
words of your mouth,

★ **3**

3 Do this then, my son, and
deliver yourself;
Since you have come into
the hand of your
neighbor,
Go, humble yourself, and
importune your
neighbor.

4 aPs.
132:4

4 Do not give asleep to your
eyes,
Nor slumber to your eye-
lids;

5 aPs. 91:3;
124:7

5 Deliver yourself like a gazelle from *the hunt-
er's* hand,
And like a abird from the
hand of the fowler.

L Shun Laziness, 6:6-19

6 Go to the aant, O bslug-
gard,
Observe her ways and be
wise,

★ **6-11**
6 aProv.
30:24, 25
bProv. 6:9;
10:26; 13:4;
20:4; 26:16

7 Which, having ano chief,
Officer or ruler,

7 aProv.
30:27

8 Prepares her food ain the
summer,
And gathers her provision
in the harvest.

8 aProv.
10:5

9 How long will you lie
down, O sluggard?
When will you arise from
your sleep?

10 "aA little sleep, a little
slumber,
A little folding of the
hands to rest"—

10 aProv.
24:33

11 aAnd your poverty will
come in like a vaga-
bond,
And your need like an
armed man.

★**11** aProv.
24:34

12 A aworthless person, a
wicked man,
Is the one who walks with
a bfalse mouth,

★**12-15**
12 aProv.
16:27 bProv.
4:24; 10:32

13 Who awinks with his eyes,
who signals with his
feet,
Who points with his fin-
gers;

13 aJob
15:12; Ps.
35:19; Prov.
10:10

14 Who *with* aperversity in
his heart bdevises evil
continually,
Who cspreads strife.

14 aProv.
17:20 bProv.
3:29; Mic.
2:1 cProv.
6:19; 16:28

15 Therefore ahis calamity
will come suddenly;
bInstantly he will be broken, and there will be
cno healing.

15 aProv.
24:22 bIs.
30:13, 14;
Jer. 19:11
c2 Chr.
36:16

5:21 *paths.* Lit., wagon tracks; i.e., habits.
5:23 The wicked will die for his failure to heed
divine instruction.
6:1-5 The master teacher warns against becoming liable for the financial obligations of another. The one solution he offers is, *deliver
yourself* (vv. 3, 5).
6:1 *surety.* A cosigner, one responsible for a
debt should the borrower default. *stranger.* A
neutral term; the borrower.

6:3 *importune your neighbor.* Lit., pester; i.e.,
strongly urge your neighbor.
6:6-11 The wise teacher rebukes the slothful
person, who characteristically does not begin
things (6:9), does not complete things (12:27),
and makes excuses for his laziness (22:13).
6:11 Procrastination will bring unexpected disaster.
6:12-15 This section reveals the character of the
wicked man.

★16

16 There are six things which the LORD hates,
Yes, seven which are an abomination to Him:

17 aPs. 18:27; 101:5; Prov. 21:4; 30:13 bPs. 31:18; 120:2; Prov. 12:22; 17:7 cDeut. 19:10; Prov. 28:17; Is. 1:15; 59:7

17 aHaughty eyes, a blying tongue,
And hands that cshed innocent blood,

18 aGen. 6:5; Prov. 24:2 bProv. 1:16; Is. 59:7; Rom. 3:15

18 A heart that devises awicked plans,
bFeet that run rapidly to evil,

19 aPs. 27:12; Prov. 12:17; 19:5, 9; 21:28 bProv. 6:14

19 A afalse witness who utters lies,
And one who bspreads strife among brothers.

M   Avoid Adultery, 6:20-35

★20-35

20 aEph. 6:1

20 aMy son, observe the commandment of your father,
And do not forsake the teaching of your mother;

21 aProv. 3:3

21 aBind them continually on your heart;
Tie them around your neck.

22 aProv. 3:23

22 When you awalk about, they will guide you;
When you sleep, they will watch over you;
And when you awake, they will talk to you.

23 aPs. 19:8; 119:105

23 For athe commandment is a lamp, and the teaching is light;
And reproofs for discipline are the way of life,

24 aProv. 5:3; 7:5, 21

24 To akeep you from the evil woman,
From the smooth tongue of the adulteress.

★25 aMatt. 5:28 b2 Kin. 9:30; Jer. 4:30; Ezek. 23:40

25 aDo not desire her beauty in your heart,
Nor let her catch you with her beyelids.

26 For aon account of a harlot one is reduced to a loaf of bread,
And an adulteress bhunts for the precious life.

26 aProv. 5:9, 10; 29:3 bProv. 7:23; Ezek. 13:18

27 Can a man take fire in his bosom,
And his clothes not be burned?

★27-29

28 Or can a man walk on hot coals,
And his feet not be scorched?

29 So is the one who agoes in to his neighbor's wife;
Whoever touches her bwill not go unpunished.

29 aEzek. 18:6; 33:26 bProv. 16:5

30 Men do not despise a thief if he steals
To asatisfy himself when he is hungry;

30 aJob 38:39

31 But when he is found, he must arepay sevenfold;
He must give all the substance of his house.

31 aEx. 22:1-4

32 The one who commits adultery with a woman is alacking sense;
He who would bdestroy himself does it.

32 aProv. 7:7; 9:4, 16; 10:13, 21; 11:12; 12:11 bProv. 7:22, 23

33 Wounds and disgrace he will find,
And his reproach will not be blotted out.

34 For ajealousy enrages a man,
And he will not spare in the bday of vengeance.

34 aProv. 27:4; Song 8:6 bProv. 11:4

35 He will not accept any ransom,
Nor will he be content though you give many gifts.

★35

6:16 *six . . . seven.* The list, though specific, is not exhaustive (cf. 30:15, 18).

6:20-35 The theme of this section is the 7th commandment, "You shall not commit adultery" (Exod. 20:14).

6:25 *catch.* I.e., captivate.

6:27-29 It is impossible to engage in this sin without suffering the consequences.

6:35 With a thief, restitution is possible (vv. 30-31) but with an adulterer it is not (vv. 34-35).

N Avoid the Harlot, 7:1-27

★ 1-27
1 *a*Prov. 2:1; 6:20

7 My son, *a*keep my words,
And treasure my commandments within you.

★ 2 *a*Prov. 4:4 *b*Deut. 32:10; Ps. 17:8; Zech. 2:8

2 *a*Keep my commandments and live,
And my teaching *b*as the apple of your eye.

3 *a*Deut. 6:8; 11:18; Prov. 6:21 *b*Prov. 3:3

3 *a*Bind them on your fingers;
*b*Write them on the tablet of your heart.

★4-5

4 Say to wisdom, "You are my sister,"
And call understanding *your* intimate friend;

5 That they may keep you from an adulteress,
From the foreigner who flatters with her words.

6 *a*Judg. 5:28 *b*Song 2:9

6 For *a*at the window of my house
I looked out *b*through my lattice,

7 *a*Prov. 1:22 *b*Prov. 6:32; 9:4

7 And I saw among the *a*naive,
I discerned among the youths,
A young man *b*lacking sense;

8 *a*Prov. 7:12 *b*Prov. 7:27

8 Passing through the street near *a*her corner;
And he takes the way to *b*her house,

9 *a*Job 24:15

9 In the *a*twilight, in the evening,
In the middle of the night and *in* the darkness.

10 *a*Gen. 38:14, 15; 1 Tim. 2:9

10 And behold, a woman *comes* to meet him,
*a*Dressed as a harlot and cunning of heart.

11 *a*Prov. 9:13 *b*1 Tim. 5:13; Titus 2:5

11 She is *a*boisterous and rebellious;

Her *b*feet do not remain at home;

12 *a*Prov. 9:14 *b*Prov. 23:28

12 *She is* now in the streets, now *a*in the squares,
And *b*lurks by every corner.

13 So she seizes him and kisses him,
And with a *a*brazen face she says to him:

★13-21

13 *a*Prov. 21:29

14 "I was due to offer *a*peace offerings;
Today I have *b*paid my vows.

★14 *a*Lev. 7:11 *b*Lev. 7:16

15 "Therefore I have come out to meet you,
To seek your presence earnestly, and I have found you.

16 "I have spread my couch with *a*coverings,
With colored *b*linens of Egypt.

16 *a*Prov. 31:22 *b*Is. 19:9; Ezek. 27:7

17 "I have sprinkled my bed With *a*myrrh, aloes and *b*cinnamon.

17 *a*Ps. 45:8 *b*Ex. 30:23

18 "Come, let us drink our fill of love until morning;
Let us delight ourselves with caresses.

19 "For the man is not at home,
He has gone on a long journey;

20 He has taken a *a*bag of money with him,
At full moon he will come home."

20 *a*Gen. 42:35

21 With her many persuasions she entices him;
With her *a*flattering lips she seduces him.

21 *a*Prov. 5:3; 6:24

22 Suddenly he follows her,
As an ox goes to the slaughter,
Or as *one in* fetters to the discipline of a fool,

★22

7:1-27 In chapter 7 the warnings against adultery are dramatized. The wise teacher describes how a simpleton succumbs to the temptations of the adulteress (vv. 6-23).

7:2 *apple of your eye.* Lit., pupil of your eye; i.e., a precious thing to be guarded with the utmost care.

7:4-5 As an intimate companion, wisdom will protect the susceptible person from the enticements of the adulteress.

7:13-21 Note carefully the enticing tactics of the adulteress: kisses (v. 13), flattery (v. 15), sensuality (vv. 16-18), reassurance (vv. 19-20).

7:14 *peace offerings.* Lit., sacrifices of peace offerings. Having offered sacrifices, she had a good supply of meat on hand and urged her victim to share it with her, since it had to be eaten right away (see note on Lev. 7:12-17).

7:22 *Or as one in fetters to the discipline of a fool.* Heb., like (one in) fetters to the correction a fool (goes). The young man proceeds on to a drastic fate.

23 *Eccl.
9:12

23 Until an arrow pierces
through his liver;
As a *bird hastens to the
snare,
So he does not know that
it *will cost him* his
life.

24 *Prov.
5:7

24 Now therefore, *my* sons,
*listen to me,
And pay attention to the
words of my mouth.

25 *Prov.
5:8

25 Do not let your heart *turn
aside to her ways,
Do not stray into her
paths.

26 *Prov.
9:18

26 For many are the victims
she has cast down,
And *numerous are all her
slain.

27 *Prov.
2:18; 5:5;
9:18; 1 Cor.
6:9, 10; Rev.
22:15

27 Her *house is the way to
Sheol,
Descending to the cham-
bers of death.

O Wisdom and Folly
Contrasted,
8:1–9:18

1 The qualities of wisdom,
8:1-21

★ 1-36
1 *Prov.
1:20, 21; 8:1-
3; 9:3; 1 Cor.
1:24

2 *Prov.
9:3, 14

8 Does not *wisdom call,
And understanding lift up
her voice?

2 On top of *the heights beside the way,
Where the paths meet, she
takes her stand;

3 *Job 29:7

3 Beside the *gates, at the
opening to the city,
At the entrance of the
doors, she cries out:

4 "To you, O men, I call,
And my voice is to the
sons of men.

5 *Prov.
1:4 *Prov.
1:22, 32;
3:35

5 "O *naive ones, discern
prudence;
And, O *fools, discern wisdom.

6 *Prov.
22:20 *Prov.
23:16

6 "Listen, for I shall speak
*noble things;

And the opening of my
lips *will produce*
*right things.

7 *Ps.
37:30; John
8:14; Rom.
15:8

7 "For my *mouth will utter
truth;
And wickedness is an
abomination to my
lips.

8 *Deut.
32:5; Prov.
2:15; Phil.
2:15

8 "All the utterances of my
mouth are in right-
eousness;
There is nothing *crooked
or perverted in them.

9 *Prov.
14:6 *Prov.
3:13

9 "They are all *straightforward to him who un-
derstands,
And right to those who
*find knowledge.

10 *Prov.
3:14, 15;
8:19

10 "Take my *instruction, and
not silver,
And knowledge rather
than choicest gold.

★11 *Job
28:15, 18;
Ps. 19:10
*Prov. 3:15

11 "For wisdom is *better than
jewels;
And *all desirable things
can not compare with
her.

12 *Prov.
8:5 *Prov.
1:4

12 "I, wisdom, *dwell with
prudence,
And I find *knowledge *and
discretion.

13 *Prov.
3:7; 16:6
*1 Sam. 2:3;
Prov. 16:18;
Is. 13:11
*Prov. 15:9
*Prov. 6:12

13 "The *fear of the Lord is to
hate evil;
*Pride and arrogance and
*the evil way,
And the *perverted mouth,
I hate.

14 *Prov.
1:25; 19:20;
Is. 28:29;
Jer. 32:19
*Prov. 2:7;
3:21; 18:1
*Eccl. 7:19;
9:16

14 "*Counsel is mine and
*sound wisdom;
I am understanding, *pow-
er is mine.

15 *2 Chr.
1:10; Prov.
29:4; Dan.
2:21; Matt.
28:18; Rom.
13:1

15 "By me *kings reign,
And rulers decree justice.

16 *1 Sam.
2:30; Prov.
4:6; John
14:21 *Prov.
2:4, 5; John
7:37; James
1:5

16 "By me *princes rule, and
nobles,
All who judge rightly.

17 *1 Sam.
2:30; Prov.
4:6; John
14:21 *Prov.
2:4, 5; John
7:37; James
1:5

17 "I *love those who love me;
And *those who diligently
seek me will find me.

18 *Prov.
3:16 *Ps.
112:3; Matt.
6:33

18 "*Riches and honor are with
me,
Enduring *wealth and
righteousness.

8:1-36 In chapter eight wisdom is exalted. As in
1:20-33, wisdom is personified and appeals for
all to receive her instruction.
8:11 *jewels.* Lit., corals.

19 "My fruit is ᵃbetter than gold, even pure gold, And my yield than ᵇchoicest silver.

20 "I walk in the way of righteousness, In the midst of the paths of justice,

21 To endow those who love me with wealth, That I may ᵃfill their treasuries.

2   The origin of wisdom, 8:22–31

22 "The Lᴏʀᴅ possessed me ᵃat the beginning of His way, Before His works of old.

23 "From everlasting I was ᵃestablished, From the beginning, ᵇfrom the earliest times of the earth.

24 "When there were no ᵃdepths I was brought forth, When there were no springs abounding with water.

25 "ᵃBefore the mountains were settled, Before the hills I was brought forth;

26 While He had not yet made the earth and the fields, Nor the first dust of the world.

27 "When He ᵃestablished the heavens, I was there, When ᵇHe inscribed a circle on the face of the deep,

28 When He made firm the skies above, When the springs of the deep became fixed,

29 When ᵃHe set for the sea its boundary, So that the water should not transgress His command, When He marked out ᵇthe foundations of the earth;

30 Then ᵃI was beside Him, as a master workman; And I was daily His delight, Rejoicing always before Him,

31 Rejoicing in the world, His earth, And having ᵃmy delight in the sons of men.

3   The man of wisdom, 8:32–36

32 "Now therefore, O sons, ᵃlisten to me, For ᵇblessed are they who keep my ways.

33 "ᵃHeed instruction and be wise, And do not neglect it.

34 "ᵃBlessed is the man who listens to me, Watching daily at my gates, Waiting at my doorposts.

35 "For ᵃhe who finds me finds life, And ᵇobtains favor from the Lᴏʀᴅ.

36 "But he who sins against me ᵃinjures himself; All those who ᵇhate me ᶜlove death."

8:22–31 This section has often been interpreted Christologically, as presenting a picture of Christ rather than simply the eternal character of wisdom. While Christ is the revelation of God's wisdom (1 Cor. 1:24) and possesses all wisdom and knowledge (Col. 2:3), there is no clear indication that Christ is revealed here. The passage shows that wisdom is older than creation and is fundamental to it (v. 23), that it assisted in creation as a master workman (v. 30), and that it rejoiced in creation (vv. 30–31). **8:22** *The Lᴏʀᴅ possessed me.* I.e., wisdom is

God's; it came forth from Him. **8:23** *from the earliest times of the earth.* Lit., from the origins of the earth. **8:27** *inscribed a circle.* I.e., marked out the circle of the horizon. The sky appears as a vaulted canopy to the earthly viewer. *face of the deep.* I.e., the ocean. **8:31** *the world, His earth.* Better, the world of His earth; i.e., the inhabited earth. **8:32–36** The chapter concludes with wisdom's closing appeal. **8:32** *listen.* Hear with a view to obedience.

Margin references:

19 ᵃJob 28:15; Prov. 3:14 ᵇProv. 10:20
21 ᵃProv. 24:4
★22–31
★22 ᵃJob 28:26–28; Ps. 104:24; Prov. 3:19
★23 ᵃJohn 1:1–3 ᵇJohn 17:5
24 ᵃGen. 1:2; Ex. 15:5; Job 38:16; Prov. 3:20
25 ᵃJob 15:7; Ps. 90:2
★27 ᵃProv. 3:19 ᵇJob 26:10
29 ᵃJob 38:10; Ps. 104:9 ᵇJob 38:6; Ps. 104:5
30 ᵃJohn 1:2, 3
★31 ᵃPs. 16:3; John 13:1
★32–36
★32 ᵃProv. 5:7; 7:24 ᵇPs. 119:1, 2; 128:1; Prov. 29:18; Luke 11:28
33 ᵃProv. 4:1
34 ᵃProv. 3:13, 18
35 ᵃProv. 4:22; John 17:3 ᵇProv. 3:4; 12:2
36 ᵃProv. 1:31, 32; 15:32 ᵇProv. 5:12; 12:1 ᶜProv. 21:6

4 The woman of foolishness,
9:1-18

★ 1-18
★ 1 a1 Cor.
3:9, 10; Eph.
2:20-22;
1 Pet. 2:5

9 Wisdom has a built her house,
She has hewn out her seven pillars;

2 aMatt.
22:4 bSong
8:2 cLuke
14:16, 17

2 She has a prepared her food, she has b mixed her wine;
She has also c set her table;

3 aPs.
68:11; Matt.
22:3 bProv.
8:1, 2 cProv.
9:14

3 She has a sent out her maidens, she b calls
From the c tops of the heights of the city:

4 aProv.
8:5; 9:16
bProv. 6:32

4 "a Whoever is naive, let him turn in here!"
To him who b lacks understanding she says,

5 aSong
5:1; Is. 55:1;
John 6:27

5 "Come, a eat of my food,
And drink of the wine I have mixed.

6 aProv.
8:35; 9:11
bEzek.
11:20; 37:24

6 "Forsake *your* folly and a live,
And b proceed in the way of understanding."

★ 7-12

7 He who a corrects a scoffer gets dishonor for himself,
And he who reproves a wicked man *gets* insults for himself.

7 aProv.
23:9

8 aProv.
15:12; Matt.
7:6 bPs.
141:5; Prov.
10:8

8 a Do not reprove a scoffer, lest he hate you,
b Reprove a wise man, and he will love you.

9 aProv.
1:5

9 Give *instruction* to a wise man, and he will be still wiser,
Teach a righteous man, and he will a increase *his* learning.

★10 aJob
28:28; Ps.
111:10; Prov.
1:7

10 The a fear of the LORD is the beginning of wisdom,
And the knowledge of the Holy One is understanding.

11 For a by me your days will be multiplied,
And years of life will be added to you.

11 aProv.
3:16; 10:27

12 If you are wise, you are wise a for yourself,
And if you b scoff, you alone will bear it.

★12 aJob
22:2; Prov.
14:14 bProv.
19:29

13 The woman of folly is a boisterous,
She is naive, and b knows nothing.

13 aProv.
7:11 bProv.
5:6

14 And she sits at the doorway of her house,
On a seat by a the high places of the city,

14 aProv.
9:3

15 Calling to those who pass by,
Who are making their paths straight:

★15

16 "a Whoever is naive, let him turn in here,"
And to him who lacks understanding she says,

16 aProv.
9:4

17 "Stolen water is sweet;
And a bread *eaten* in secret is pleasant."

★17 aProv.
20:17

18 But he does not know that the dead are there,
That her guests are in the a depths of Sheol.

18 aProv.
7:27

III   THE PROVERBS OF SOLOMON,
10:1-24:34

A   Proverbs which Contrast Righteous and Wicked Lives, 10:1-15:33

10 The a proverbs of Solomon.
b A wise son makes a father glad,
But c a foolish son is a grief to his mother.

★10:1-22:16

★ 1 aProv.
1:1 bProv.
15:20; 29:3
cProv. 17:25;
29:15

9:1-18 The teachings of the first eight chapters are summarized, as both wisdom (vv. 1-6) and folly (vv. 13-18) invite men to a banquet to partake of their benefits.
9:1 *seven pillars.* I.e., an ideally constructed house.
9:7-12 This section points out the contrasting ways of the scoffer and the wise.
9:10 The motto of the wise teacher and the theme of the book (1:7) is reiterated.
9:12 An individual may choose wisdom and reap

its reward, or scoff and incur the penalty.
9:15 *Who are making their paths straight* = straight on their ways; i.e., who are living in an upright manner.
9:17 The foolish woman promotes the attractiveness of what is forbidden; "stolen water" and "bread eaten in secret" may be figures of illicit intercourse (cf. 5:15-20; 30:20).
10:1-22:16 The discourses concerning wisdom and folly (chaps. 1-9) constitute a preface to the central portion of the book, which con-

2 aPs. 49:7;
Prov. 11:4;
21:6; Ezek.
7:19; Luke
12:19, 20

3 aPs. 34:9,
10; 37:25;
Prov. 28:25;
Matt. 6:33
bPs. 112:10;
Prov. 28:9

4 aProv.
13:4; 21:5

★ 6 aProv.
28:20 bProv.
10:11; Obad.
10

7 aPs.
112:6 bPs.
9:5, 6;
109:13; Eccl.
8:10

8 aProv.
9:8; Matt.
7:24

9 aPs. 23:4;
Prov. 3:23;
28:18; Is.
33:15, 16
bProv.
26:26; Matt.
10:26; 1 Tim.
5:25

10 aPs.
35:19; Prov.
6:13 bProv.
10:8

★11 aPs.
37:30; Prov.
13:14; 18:4
bProv. 10:6

2 aIll-gotten gains do not profit,
But righteousness delivers from death.

3 The LORD awill not allow the righteous to hunger,
But He bwill thrust *aside* the craving of the wicked.

4 Poor is he who works with a negligent hand,
But the ahand of the diligent makes rich.

5 He who gathers in summer is a son who acts wisely,
But he who sleeps in harvest is a son who acts shamefully.

6 aBlessings are on the head of the righteous,
But bthe mouth of the wicked conceals violence.

7 The amemory of the righteous is blessed,
But bthe name of the wicked will rot.

8 The awise of heart will receive commands,
But a babbling fool will be thrown down.

9 He awho walks in integrity walks securely,
But bhe who perverts his ways will be found out.

10 He awho winks the eye causes trouble,
And ba babbling fool will be thrown down.

11 The amouth of the righteous is a fountain of life,

But bthe mouth of the wicked conceals violence.

12 Hatred stirs up strife,
But alove covers all transgressions.

13 On athe lips of the discerning, wisdom is found,
But ba rod is for the back of him who lacks understanding.

14 Wise men astore up knowledge,
But with bthe mouth of the foolish, ruin is at hand.

15 The arich man's wealth is his fortress,
The bruin of the poor is their poverty.

16 The awages of the righteous is life,
The income of the wicked, punishment.

17 He ais *on* the path of life who heeds instruction,
But he who forsakes reproof goes astray.

18 He awho conceals hatred *has* lying lips,
And he who spreads slander is a fool.

19 When there are amany words, transgression is unavoidable,
But bhe who restrains his lips is wise.

20 The tongue of the righteous is *as* achoice silver,
The heart of the wicked is *worth* little.

21 The alips of the righteous feed many,

12 aProv.
17:9; 1 Cor.
13:4-7;
James 5:20;
1 Pet. 4:8

13 aProv.
10:31 bProv.
19:29; 26:3

14 aProv.
9:9 bProv.
10:8, 10;
13:3; 18:7

★15 aJob
31:24; Ps.
52:7; Prov.
18:11 bProv.
19:7

★16 aProv.
11:18, 19

17 aProv.
6:23

18 aProv.
26:24

19 aJob
11:2; Prov.
18:21; Eccl.
5:3 bProv.
17:27; James
1:19; 3:2

20 aProv.
8:19

21 aProv.
10:11 bProv.
5:23; Hos.
4:6

---

tains 375 of Solomon's proverbs. These proverbs are general principles and guidelines which may have exceptions. Any exception is not a problem of inerrancy, but a matter of the nature of proverbs. They are true as general rules.

10:1 *A wise son.* One who fears and obeys God and makes a successful application of knowledge in everyday dealings. *a foolish son.* One who is insensible, and insensitive to moral truth, acting without regard to it and to his own destruction.

10:6b Violent plans and language envelop the mouths of the wicked.

10:11 *fountain of life.* I.e., source of spiritual vitality. Better, "violence covers the mouth of the wicked."

10:15 Wealth can sometimes protect from trouble, while poverty is a liability which exposes one to misfortune.

10:16 The income of the righteous establishes life, while what is acquired by the crimes of the wicked yields sin and ultimately death.

But fools ᵇdie for lack of understanding.

★22 ᵃGen. 24:35; 26:12; Deut. 8:18; Prov. 8:21

22 It is the ᵃblessing of the LORD that makes rich, And He adds no sorrow to it.

23 ᵃProv. 2:14; 15:21

23 Doing wickedness is like ᵃsport to a fool; And so is wisdom to a man of understanding.

24 ᵃJob 15:21; Prov. 1:27; Is. 66:4 ᵇPs. 145:19; Prov. 15:8; Matt. 5:6; 1 John 5:14, 15

24 What ᵃthe wicked fears will come upon him, And the ᵇdesire of the righteous will be granted.

25 ᵃJob 21:18; Ps. 58:9; Prov. 12:7 ᵇPs. 15:5; Prov. 12:3; Matt. 7:24, 25

25 When the ᵃwhirlwind passes, the wicked is no more, But the ᵇrighteous has an everlasting foundation.

26 ᵃProv. 26:6

26 Like vinegar to the teeth and smoke to the eyes, So is the ᵃlazy one to those who send him.

27 ᵃProv. 3:2; 9:11; 14:27 ᵇJob 15:32, 33; 22:16; Ps. 55:23

27 The ᵃfear of the LORD prolongs life, But the ᵇyears of the wicked will be shortened.

28 ᵃProv. 11:23 ᵇJob 8:13; 11:20; Prov. 11:7

28 The ᵃhope of the righteous is gladness, But the ᵇexpectation of the wicked perishes.

29 ᵃProv. 13:6 ᵇProv. 21:15

29 The ᵃway of the LORD is a stronghold to the upright, But ᵇruin to the workers of iniquity.

30 ᵃPs. 37:29; 125:1; Prov. 2:21 ᵇProv. 2:22

30 The ᵃrighteous will never be shaken, But ᵇthe wicked will not dwell in the land.

31 ᵃPs. 37:30; Prov. 10:13 ᵇProv. 17:20

31 The ᵃmouth of the righteous flows with wisdom, But the ᵇperverted tongue will be cut out.

32 ᵃEccl. 12:10 ᵇProv. 2:12; 6:12

32 The lips of the righteous bring forth ᵃwhat is acceptable, But the ᵇmouth of the wicked, what is perverted.

11 A ᵃfalse balance is an abomination to the LORD, But a ᵇjust weight is His delight.

1 ᵃLev. 19:35, 36; Deut. 25:13-16; Prov. 20:10, 23; Mic. 6:11 ᵇProv. 16:11

2 When ᵃpride comes, then comes dishonor, But with the humble is wisdom.

★ 2 ᵃProv. 16:18; 18:12; 29:23

3 The ᵃintegrity of the upright will guide them, But the ᵇfalseness of the treacherous will destroy them.

3 ᵃProv. 13:6 ᵇProv. 19:3; 22:12

4 ᵃRiches do not profit in the day of wrath, But ᵇrighteousness delivers from death.

4 ᵃProv. 10:2; Ezek. 7:19; Zeph. 1:18 ᵇGen. 7:1

5 The ᵃrighteousness of the blameless will smooth his way, But ᵇthe wicked will fall by his own wickedness.

5 ᵃProv. 3:6 ᵇProv. 5:22

6 The righteousness of the upright will deliver them, But the treacherous will ᵃbe caught by their own greed.

6 ᵃPs. 7:15, 16; 9:15; Eccl. 10:8

7 When a wicked man dies, his ᵃexpectation will perish, And the ᵇhope of strong men perishes.

7 ᵃProv. 10:28 ᵇJob 8:13, 14

8 The righteous is delivered from trouble, But the wicked takes his place.

9 With his ᵃmouth the godless man destroys his neighbor, But through knowledge the ᵇrighteous will be delivered.

9 ᵃProv. 16:29 ᵇProv. 11:6

10 When it ᵃgoes well with the righteous, the city rejoices, And when the wicked perish, there is glad shouting.

10 ᵃProv. 28:12

11 By the blessing of the upright a city is exalted, But by the mouth of the wicked it is torn down.

10:22 Real prosperity is a divine blessing, accompanied by neither anxiety nor trouble.

11:2 humble. Submissive to God and man (cf. Micah 6:8).

12 He who despises his neighbor lacks sense,
But a man of understanding keeps silent.

13 He ^awho goes about as a talebearer reveals secrets,
But he who is trustworthy ^bconceals a matter.

14 Where there is no ^aguidance, the people fall,
But in abundance of counselors there is victory.

15 He who is ^asurety for a stranger will surely suffer for it,
But he who hates going surety is safe.

16 A ^agracious woman attains honor,
And violent men attain riches.

17 The ^amerciful man does himself good,
But the cruel man does himself harm.

18 The wicked earns deceptive wages,
But he who ^asows righteousness *gets* a true reward.

19 He who is steadfast in ^arighteousness *will attain* to life,
And ^bhe who pursues evil *will bring about* his own death.

20 The perverse in heart are an abomination to the Lord,
But the ^ablameless in *their* walk are His ^bdelight.

21 Assuredly, the evil man will not go unpunished,
But the descendants of the righteous will be delivered.

22 As a ^aring of gold in a swine's snout,
So is a beautiful woman who lacks discretion.

23 The desire of the righteous is only good,
But the ^aexpectation of the wicked is wrath.

24 There is one who scatters, yet increases all the more,
And there is one who withholds what is justly due, but *it results* only in want.

25 The ^agenerous man will be prosperous,
And he who ^bwaters will himself be watered.

26 He who withholds grain, the ^apeople will curse him,
But ^bblessing will be on the head of him who ^csells *it*.

27 He who diligently seeks good seeks favor,
But ^ahe who searches after evil, it will come to him.

28 He who ^atrusts in his riches will fall,
But ^bthe righteous will flourish like the *green* leaf.

29 He who ^atroubles his own house will ^binherit wind,
And ^cthe foolish will be servant to the wisehearted.

30 The fruit of the righteous is ^aa tree of life,
And ^bhe who is wise wins souls.

31 If ^athe righteous will be rewarded in the earth,

Cross-references

13 ^aLev. 19:16; Prov. 20:19; 1 Tim. 5:13 ^bProv. 19:11

★14 ^aProv. 15:22; 20:18; 24:6

★15-16
15 ^aProv. 6:1; 27:13

16 ^aProv. 31:28, 30

17 ^aMatt. 5:7; 25:34-36

★18 ^aHos. 10:12; Gal. 6:8, 9; James 3:18

19 ^aProv. 10:16; 12:28; 19:23 ^bProv. 21:16; Rom. 6:23; James 1:15

20 ^aPs. 119:1; Prov. 13:6 ^b1 Chr. 29:17

★21

★22 ^aGen. 24:47

23 ^aProv. 10:28; Rom. 2:8, 9

25 ^aProv. 3:9, 10; 2 Cor. 9:6, 7 ^bMatt. 5:7

26 ^aProv. 24:24 ^bJob 29:13 ^cGen. 42:6

27 ^aEsth. 7:10; Ps. 7:15, 16; 57:6

28 ^aPs. 49:6; Mark 10:25; 1 Tim. 6:17 ^bPs. 1:3; 92:12; Jer. 17:8

29 ^aProv. 15:27 ^bEccl. 5:16 ^cProv. 14:19

★30 ^aProv. 3:18 ^bProv. 14:25; Dan. 12:3; 1 Cor. 9:19-22; James 5:20
31 ^a2 Sam. 22:21, 25; Prov. 13:21; 1 Pet. 4:18

11:14 *guidance.* Lit., "steering," wise direction on the course of life.
11:15-16 Cf. 6:1. A quiet woman can win honor, while brute force will gain material possessions only.
11:18 The labor of the wicked has no blessing and brings no permanent gain, in contrast to the righteous, who will earn an enduring reward.

11:21 *Assuredly.* Lit., hand to hand; an allusion to shaking hands to confirm a matter.
11:22 *discretion.* Lit., taste; i.e., moral perception.
11:30 *tree of life.* I.e., source of life. *wins souls.* Not winning to salvation in this context, but attracting others and imparting to them wisdom.

How much more the wicked and the sinner!

★ 1

12 Whoever loves discipline loves knowledge,
But he who hates reproof is stupid.

2 A [a]good man will obtain favor from the LORD,
But He will condemn a man who devises evil.

3 A man will [a]not be established by wickedness,
But the root of the [b]righteous will not be moved.

4 An [a]excellent wife is the crown of her husband,
But she who shames *him* is as [b]rottenness in his bones.

5 The thoughts of the righteous are just,
But the counsels of the wicked are deceitful.

6 The [a]words of the wicked lie in wait for blood,
But the [b]mouth of the upright will deliver them.

7 The [a]wicked are overthrown and are no more,
But the [b]house of the righteous will stand.

8 A man will be praised according to his insight,
But one of perverse mind will be despised.

★ 9

9 Better is he who is lightly esteemed and has a servant,
Than he who honors himself and lacks bread.

10 A [a]righteous man has regard for the life of his beast,
But the compassion of the wicked is cruel.

11 He [a]who tills his land will have plenty of bread,
But he who pursues vain *things* lacks sense.

12 The [a]wicked desires the booty of evil men,
But the root of the righteous [b]yields *fruit*.

13 An evil man is ensnared by the transgression of his lips,
But the [a]righteous will escape from trouble.

14 A man will be [a]satisfied with good by the fruit of his words,
And the [b]deeds of a man's hands will return to him.

15 The [a]way of a fool is right in his own eyes,
But a wise man is he who listens to counsel.

16 A [a]fool's vexation is known at once,
But a prudent man conceals dishonor.

17 He who speaks truth tells what is right,
But a false witness, deceit.

18 There is one who [a]speaks rashly like the thrusts of a sword,
But the [b]tongue of the wise brings healing.

19 Truthful lips will be established forever,
But a [a]lying tongue is only for a moment.

20 Deceit is in the heart of those who devise evil,
But counselors of peace have joy.

21 [a]No harm befalls the righteous,

Marginal references

2 [a]Prov. 3:4; 8:35

3 [a]Prov. 11:5 [b]Prov. 10:25

★ **4** [a]Prov. 31:11; 1 Cor. 11:7 [b]Prov. 14:30; Hab. 3:16

★ **6** [a]Prov. 1:11, 16 [b]Prov. 14:3

7 [a]Job 34:25; Prov. 10:25 [b]Matt. 7:24-27

10 [a]Deut. 25:4

11 [a]Prov. 28:19

★**12** [a]Prov. 21:10 [b]Prov. 11:30

13 [a]Prov. 11:8; 21:23; 2 Pet. 2:9

★**14** [a]Prov. 13:2; 15:23; 18:20 [b]Job 34:11; Prov. 1:31; 24:12; Is. 3:10, 11; Hos. 4:9

15 [a]Prov. 14:12; 16:2; 21:2

★**16** [a]Prov. 14:33; 27:3; 29:11

18 [a]Ps. 57:4 [b]Prov. 4:22; 15:4

19 [a]Ps. 52:4, 5; Prov. 19:9

21 [a]Ps. 91:10; 121:7; Prov. 1:33; 1 Pet. 3:13

12:1 *discipline.* Training by word or deed.

12:4 *excellent wife.* A wife of noble and upright character (cf. 31:10-31).

12:6 While the wicked condemn men with false testimony, the righteous will speak the truth and deliver the innocent.

12:9 *has a servant.* Better, is a servant to himself. I.e., "Better is a man of humble circumstances who works for himself, than one who plays the big man and has nothing to eat."

12:12 *booty.* Probably, stronghold. *yields fruit.* Better, endures. The wicked covets the stronghold of other evil men in order to strengthen his own position. The righteous, however, depends upon his integrity and he endures.

12:14 Words bear fruit as do deeds.

12:16 *vexation* = anger. A fool loses his temper when offended, but a prudent man ignores an insult.

But the wicked are filled with trouble.

22 ^aLying lips are an abomination to the LORD,
But those who deal faithfully are His delight.

22 aRev. 22:15

23 A ^aprudent man conceals knowledge,
But the heart of fools proclaims folly.

★23 aProv. 10:14; 11:13; 13:16; 15:2; 29:11

24 The hand of the diligent will rule,
But the slack *hand* will be ^aput to forced labor.

24 aGen. 49:15; Judg. 1:28; 1 Kin. 9:21

25 ^aAnxiety in the heart of a man weighs it down,
But a ^bgood word makes it glad.

25 aProv. 15:13 bIs. 50:4

26 The righteous is a guide to his neighbor,
But the way of the wicked leads them astray.

★26

27 A slothful man does not roast his prey,
But the ^aprecious possession of a man *is* diligence.

27 aProv. 10:4; 13:4

28 ^aIn the way of righteousness is life,
And in *its* pathway there is no death.

★28 aDeut. 30:15f.; 32:46f.; Jer. 21:8

13 A ^awise son *accepts his* father's discipline,
But a ^bscoffer does not listen to rebuke.

1 aProv. 10:1; 15:20 bProv. 9:7, 8; 15:12

2 From the fruit of a man's mouth he ^aenjoys good,
But the desire of the treacherous is ^bviolence.

★ 2 aProv. 12:14 bProv. 1:31; Hos. 10:13

3 The one who ^aguards his mouth preserves his life;
The one who ^bopens wide his lips comes to ruin.

3 aProv. 18:21; 21:23; James 3:2 bProv. 18:7; 20:19

4 The soul of the sluggard craves and *gets* nothing,
But the soul of the diligent is made fat.

★ 4

5 A righteous man ^ahates falsehood,
But a wicked man ^bacts disgustingly and shamefully.

★ 5 aCol. 3:9 bProv. 3:35

6 Righteousness ^aguards the one whose way is blameless,
But wickedness subverts the sinner.

6 aProv. 11:3

7 There is one who ^apretends to be rich, but has nothing;
Another pretends to be ^bpoor, but has great wealth.

7 aProv. 11:24; Luke 12:20, 21 bLuke 12:33; 2 Cor. 6:10; James 2:5

8 The ransom of a man's life is his riches,
But the poor hears no rebuke.

★ 8

9 The ^alight of the righteous rejoices,
But the ^blamp of the wicked goes out.

★ 9 aJob 29:3; Prov. 4:18 bJob 18:5; Prov. 24:20

10 Through presumption comes nothing but strife,
But with those who receive counsel is wisdom.

11 Wealth *obtained* by fraud dwindles,
But the one who gathers by labor increases *it.*

12 Hope deferred makes the heart sick,
But desire fulfilled is a tree of life.

★12

13 The one who ^adespises the word will be in debt to it,

★13 aNum. 15:31; 2 Chr. 36:16 bProv. 13:21

12:23 The prudent man is cautious and reserved, while the fool rushes in and proclaims his ignorance.
12:26 Better, "The righteous investigates his neighbor, but the way of the wicked leads them astray." The investigation is necessary, for the way of the godless leads into error.
12:28 The verse alludes to the immortality of the righteous.
13:2 One's words will bring a tangible return.
13:4 *is made fat.* I.e., is abundantly satisfied.
13:5 *acts disgustingly and shamefully.* Lit.,

causes to stink and makes ashamed. The righteous detest falsehood, but the wicked cause shame.
13:8 A rich man may have to buy off his life while a poor man can ignore a threat.
13:9 *light . . . lamp.* I.e., joy and prosperity (cf. Esther 8:16). *rejoices.* I.e., burns merrily.
13:12 *tree of life.* See note on 3:18.
13:13 *word.* I.e., Word of God. *will be in debt to it.* Lit., is pledged to it, is obligated to obey the law lest he forfeit his pledge.

But the one who fears the
commandment will be
[b]rewarded.

★14 [a]Prov.
10:11; 14:27
[b]Ps. 18:5

14 The teaching of the wise is
a [a]fountain of life,
To turn aside from the
[b]snares of death.

★15 [a]Ps.
111:10; Prov.
3:4

15 [a]Good understanding produces favor,
But the way of the treacherous is hard.

16 [a]Prov.
12:23

16 Every [a]prudent man acts
with knowledge,
But a fool displays folly.

17 [a]Prov.
25:13

17 A wicked messenger falls
into adversity,
But [a]a faithful envoy
brings healing.

18 [a]Prov.
15:5, 32

18 Poverty and shame *will
come* to him who [a]ne-
glects discipline,
But he who regards re-
proof will be honored.

★19

19 Desire realized is sweet to
the soul,
But it is an abomination to
fools to depart from
evil.

20 [a]Prov.
2:20; 15:31

20 [a]He who walks with wise
men will be wise,
But the companion of fools
will suffer harm.

★21 [a]Ps.
32:10; 54:5;
Is. 47:11
[b]Prov.
11:31; 13:13;
Is. 3:10

21 [a]Adversity pursues sinners,
But the [b]righteous will be
rewarded with pros-
perity.

★22 [a]Ezra
9:12; Ps.
37:25 [b]Job
27:16, 17;
Prov. 28:8;
Eccl. 2:26

22 A good man [a]leaves an inheritance to his chil-
dren's children,
And the [b]wealth of the
sinner is stored up for
the righteous.

23 [a]Prov.
12:11

23 [a]Abundant food *is in* the
fallow ground of the
poor,

But it is swept away by injustice.

24 He who [a]spares his rod
hates his son,
But he who loves him [b]dis-
ciplines him dili-
gently.

★24 [a]Prov.
19:18; 22:15;
23:13, 14;
29:15, 17
[b]Deut. 8:5;
Prov. 3:12;
Heb. 12:7

25 The [a]righteous has enough
to satisfy his appetite,
But the stomach of the
[b]wicked is in want.

25 [a]Ps.
34:10; 103:5;
132:15; Prov.
10:3 [b]Prov.
13:18; Luke
15:14

14 The [a]wise woman builds
her house,
But the foolish tears it
down with her own
hands.

1 [a]Ruth
4:11; Prov.
31:10-27

2 He who [a]walks in his up-
rightness fears the
Lord,
But he who is [b]crooked in
his ways despises
Him.

2 [a]Prov.
19:1; 28:6
[b]Prov. 2:15

3 In the mouth of the foolish
is a rod for *his* back,
But [a]the lips of the wise
will preserve them.

★ 3 [a]Prov.
12:6

4 Where no oxen are, the
manger is clean,
But much increase comes
by the strength of the
ox.

★ 4

5 A [a]faithful witness will not
lie,
But a [b]false witness
[c]speaks lies.

5 [a]Rev. 1:5;
3:14 [b]Ex.
23:1; Deut.
19:16; Prov.
6:19; 12:17
[c]Prov. 19:5

6 A scoffer seeks wisdom,
and *finds* none,
But knowledge is easy to
him who has under-
standing.

7 Leave the [a]presence of a
fool,
Or you will not discern
words of knowledge.

7 [a]Prov.
23:9

13:14 *teaching.* Instruction. *fountain of life.* See
note on 10:11.
13:15 *hard.* Better, not lasting.
13:19 Nothing is so sweet as gaining some desired thing, but fools won't leave their evil
ways to do that.
13:21 *will be rewarded with prosperity.* Better,
he will reward with prosperity. The prospect
of just recompense for good or evil is a general
rule, but there are exceptions, as in the case of
Job.

13:22 Good men leave their wealth to their
grandchildren, but sinners lose it to more
righteous persons.
13:24 The discipline referred to here is training
either by word (15:5; 24:32) or deed (23:13).
14:3 *rod for his back.* Lit., rod of pride; i.e., hurt-
ful pride.
14:4 There is no milk without some manure.
Some disturbance is the price of growth and
accomplishment.

8 The wisdom of the prudent is to understand his way,
But ªthe folly of fools is deceit.

9 Fools mock at sin,
But ªamong the upright there is good will.

10 The heart knows its own ªbitterness,
And a stranger does not share its joy.

11 The ªhouse of the wicked will be destroyed,
But the tent of the upright will flourish.

12 There ªis a way which seems right to a man,
But its ᵇend is the way of death.

13 Even in laughter the heart may be in pain,
And the ªend of joy may be grief.

14 The backslider in heart will have his ªfill of his own ways,
But a good man will ᵇbe satisfied with his.

15 The naive believes everything,
But the prudent man considers his steps.

16 A wise man is cautious and ªturns away from evil,
But a fool is arrogant and careless.

17 A quick-tempered man acts foolishly,
And a man of evil devices is hated.

18 The naive inherit folly,
But the prudent are crowned with knowledge.

19 The ªevil will bow down before the good,
And the wicked at the gates of the righteous.

20 The ªpoor is hated even by his neighbor,
But those who love the rich are many.

21 He who ªdespises his neighbor sins,
But ᵇhappy is he who is gracious to the poor.

22 Will they not go astray who ªdevise evil?
But kindness and truth will be to those who devise good.

23 In all labor there is profit,
But mere talk leads only to poverty.

24 The ªcrown of the wise is their riches,
But the folly of fools is foolishness.

25 A truthful witness saves lives,
But he who ªspeaks lies is treacherous.

26 In the ªfear of the LORD there is strong confidence,
And his children will have refuge.

27 The fear of the LORD is a fountain of life,
That one may avoid the snares of death.

28 In a multitude of people is a king's glory,
But in the dearth of people is a prince's ruin.

29 He who is ªslow to anger has great understanding,
But he who is quick-tempered exalts folly.

30 A ªtranquil heart is life to the body,
But passion is ᵇrottenness to the bones.

Cross-references

★8 ª1 Cor. 3:19
9 ªProv. 3:34; 11:20
10 ª1 Sam. 1:10; Job 21:25
11 ªJob 8:15
★12 ªProv. 12:15; 16:25 ᵇRom. 6:21
★13 ªEccl. 2:1, 2
14 ªProv. 1:31; 12:21 ᵇProv. 12:14; 18:20
★15
★16 ªJob 28:28; Ps. 34:14; Prov. 3:7; 22:3
19 ª1 Sam. 2:36; Prov. 11:29
20 ªProv. 19:7
21 ªProv. 11:12 ᵇPs. 41:1; Prov. 19:17; 28:8
22 ªPs. 36:4; Prov. 3:29; 12:2; Mic. 2:1
★24 ªProv. 10:22; 13:8; 21:20
★25 ªProv. 14:5
★26 ªProv. 18:10; 19:23; Is. 33:6
★27
★29 ªProv. 16:32; 19:11; Eccl. 7:9; James 1:19
30 ªProv. 15:13 ᵇProv. 12:4; Hab. 3:16

14:8 The prudent man carefully considers his conduct and habits, but the foolish sidestep the truth of their frivolous lifestyle.

14:12 A shortcut to success may be a false trail leading to destruction.

14:13 While laughter may relieve the tension of one suffering grief, it is only a temporary escape from the reality of a tragedy.

14:15 The prudent man looks before he leaps.

14:16 *is arrogant.* Shows anger.

14:24 Wisdom yields riches, but nothing good can be expected from a fool.

14:25 A witness may save life or deceitfully destroy the innocent.

14:26 *his children.* I.e., the children of the one who fears the Lord.

14:27 *fountain of life.* See note on 10:11.

14:29 *quick-tempered.* Lit., short of spirit; i.e., impatient.

31 ᵃProv.
17:5; Matt.
25:40;
1 John 3:17
ᵇJob 31:15;
Prov. 22:2

31 He ᵃwho oppresses the poor reproaches ᵇhis Maker,
But he who is gracious to the needy honors Him.

★32 ᵃProv.
6:15; 24:16
ᵇGen. 49:18;
Ps. 16:11;
17:15; 37:37;
73:24; 2 Cor.
1:9; 5:8;
2 Tim. 4:18
★33

32 The wicked is ᵃthrust down by his wrong-doing,
But the ᵇrighteous has a refuge when he dies.

33 Wisdom rests in the heart of one who has understanding,
But in the bosom of fools it is made known.

34 Righteousness exalts a nation,
But sin is a disgrace to *any* people.

35 ᵃMatt.
24:45, 47;
25:21, 23

35 The king's favor is toward a ᵃservant who acts wisely,
But his anger is toward him who acts shamefully.

1 ᵃJudg.
8:1-3; Prov.
15:18; 25:15
ᵇ1 Sam.
25:10-13

15 A ᵃgentle answer turns away wrath,
But a ᵇharsh word stirs up anger.

2 ᵃProv.
15:7 ᵇProv.
12:23; 13:16;
15:28

2 The ᵃtongue of the wise makes knowledge acceptable,
But the ᵇmouth of fools spouts folly.

3 ᵃ2 Chr.
16:9; Job
31:4; Jer.
16:17; Zech.
4:10; Heb.
4:13
★ 4

3 The ᵃeyes of the LORD are in every place,
Watching the evil and the good.

4 A soothing tongue is a tree of life,
But perversion in it crushes the spirit.

5 A fool rejects his father's discipline,
But he who regards reproof is prudent.

6 ᵃProv.
8:21

6 Much wealth is *in* the house of the ᵃrighteous,

But trouble is in the income of the wicked.

7 The lips of the wise spread knowledge,
But the hearts of fools are not so.

8 The ᵃsacrifice of the wicked is an abomination to the LORD,
But ᵇthe prayer of the upright is His delight.

8 ᵃProv.
21:27; Eccl.
5:1; Is. 1:11;
Jer. 6:20;
Mic. 6:7
ᵇProv. 15:29

9 The way of the wicked is an abomination to the LORD,
But He loves him who ᵃpursues righteousness.

9 ᵃ1 Tim.
6:11

10 Stern discipline is for him who forsakes the way;
He who hates reproof will die.

11 ᵃSheol and Abaddon *lie open* before the LORD,
How much more the ᵇhearts of men!

★11 ᵃJob
26:6; Ps.
139:8
ᵇ1 Sam.
16:7; 2 Chr.
6:30; Ps.
44:21; Acts
1:24

12 A ᵃscoffer does not love one who reproves him,
He will not go to the wise.

★12 ᵃProv.
13:1; Amos
5:10

13 A ᵃjoyful heart makes a cheerful face,
But when the heart is ᵇsad, the ᶜspirit is broken.

★13 ᵃProv.
17:22 ᵇProv.
12:25 ᶜProv.
17:22; 18:14

14 The ᵃmind of the intelligent seeks knowledge,
But the mouth of fools feeds on folly.

14 ᵃProv.
18:15

15 All the days of the afflicted are bad,
But a cheerful heart *has* a continual feast.

★15

16 ᵃBetter is a little with the fear of the LORD,
Than great treasure and turmoil with it.

16 ᵃPs.
37:16; Prov.
16:8; Eccl.
4:6; 1 Tim.
6:6

17 ᵃBetter is a dish of vegetables where love is,
Than a ᵇfattened ox and hatred with it.

17 ᵃProv.
17:1 ᵇMatt.
22:4; Luke
15:23

14:32 The righteous put their confidence in God, believing death to be a place of refuge and immortality.
14:33 While the wise man does not parade his knowledge, the fool boasts of the little he has.
15:4 *soothing*. Lit., healing. *tree of life*. See note on 3:18.
15:11 *Sheol and Abaddon*. The two synonyms

have reference to the place of the dead, the grave. The verse points to God's omniscience (cf. Psalm 139:7–12).
15:12 He shuns the wise because he hates their reproof.
15:13 Sad thoughts crush the spirit.
15:15 One's temperament has a considerable effect on one's circumstances.

18 aProv.
16:28; 26:21;
29:22 bProv.
14:29 cGen.
13:8; Prov.
16:14; Eccl.
10:4

18　A ahot-tempered man stirs up strife,
But the bslow to anger cpacifies contention.

19　The way of the sluggard is as a hedge of thorns,
But the path of the upright is a highway.

20 aProv.
10:1; 29:3
bProv. 30:17

20　A awise son makes a father glad,
But a foolish man bdespises his mother.

21 aProv.
14:8; Eph.
5:15

21　Folly is joy to him who lacks sense,
But a man of understanding awalks straight.

22　Without consultation, plans are frustrated,
But with many counselors they succeed.

23 aProv.
12:14 bProv.
25:11; Is.
50:4

23　A aman has joy in an apt answer,
And how delightful is a timely bword!

24 aProv.
4:18

24　The apath of life leads upward for the wise,
That he may keep away from Sheol below.

25 aProv.
12:7; 14:11
bDeut.
19:14; Prov.
23:10 cPs.
68:5; 146:9

25　The Lord will atear down the house of the proud,
But He will bestablish the boundary of the cwidow.

26　Evil plans are an abomination to the Lord,
But pleasant words are pure.

27 aProv.
1:19; 28:25;
1 Tim. 6:10
bEx. 23:8;
Deut. 16:19;
1 Sam. 12:3;
Is. 33:15

27　He who aprofits illicitly troubles his own house,
But he who bhates bribes will live.

28 a1 Pet.
3:15 bProv.
10:32; 15:2

28　The heart of the righteous aponders how to answer,
But the bmouth of the wicked pours out evil things.

29　The Lord is afar from the wicked,
But He bhears the prayer of the righteous.

29 aPs.
18:41; Prov.
1:28 bPs.
145:18, 19

30　Bright eyes gladden the heart;
Good news puts fat on the bones.

★30

31　He whose ear listens to the life-giving reproof
Will dwell among the wise.

32　He who aneglects discipline bdespises himself,
But he who clistens to reproof acquires understanding.

32 aProv.
1:7; 8:33
bProv. 8:36
cProv. 15:5

33　The fear of the Lord is the instruction for wisdom,
And before honor comes humility.

B　Proverbs which Encourage Godly Lives, 16:1-22:16

16　The aplans of the heart belong to man,
But the answer of the tongue is from the Lord.

★ 1-9

★ 1 aProv.
16:9; 19:21

2　All the ways of a man are clean in his own sight,
But the aLord weighs the motives.

★ 2 a1 Sam.
16:7; Dan.
5:27

3　aCommit your works to the Lord,
And your plans will be established.

★ 3 aPs.
37:5; 55:22;
Prov. 3:6;
1 Pet. 5:7

4　The Lord ahas made everything for its own purpose,
Even the bwicked for the day of evil.

4 aGen.
1:31; Eccl.
3:11 bRom.
9:22

5　Everyone who is proud in heart is an abomination to the Lord;
Assuredly, he will not be unpunished.

★ 5

15:30 Bright eyes. I.e., the brightness which shines in the eyes when good news comes. puts fat on the bones. I.e., invigorates the body.
16:1-9 The topic of these verses is God and His ultimate control over human activity.
16:1 Man may make plans, but the execution of them, which becomes explicit in speech, fulfills God's designs.
16:2 motives. Lit., spirits; i.e., moral character or disposition.
16:3 Commit. Lit., Roll. Roll your burdens on the Lord; while they may cause you anxiety, they are not too great for Him.
16:5 Cf. 11:21.

6 By alovingkindness and truth iniquity is atoned for,
And by the bfear of the LORD one keeps away from evil.

7 When a man's ways are pleasing to the LORD,
He amakes even his enemies to be at peace with him.

8 Better is a little with righteousness
Than great income with injustice.

9 The mind of aman plans his way,
But bthe LORD directs his steps.

10 A divine adecision is in the lips of the king;
His mouth should not err in judgment.

11 A ajust balance and scales belong to the LORD;
All the weights of the bag are His concern.

12 It is an abomination for kings to commit wickedness,
For a athrone is established on righteousness.

13 Righteous lips are the delight of kings,
And he who speaks right is loved.

14 The wrath of a king is as messengers of death,
But a wise man will appease it.

15 In the light of a king's face is life,
And his favor is like a cloud with the aspring rain.

16 How much abetter it is to get wisdom than gold!
And to get understanding is to be chosen above silver.

17 The ahighway of the upright is to depart from evil;
He who watches his way preserves his life.

18 aPride goes before destruction,
And a haughty spirit before stumbling.

19 It is better to be of a ahumble spirit with the lowly,
Than to bdivide the spoil with the proud.

20 He who gives attention to the word shall afind good,
And bblessed is he who trusts in the LORD.

21 The awise in heart will be called discerning,
And sweetness of speech bincreases persuasiveness.

22 Understanding is a fountain of life to him who has it,
But the discipline of fools is folly.

23 The aheart of the wise teaches his mouth,
And adds persuasiveness to his lips.

24 aPleasant words are a honeycomb,
Sweet to the soul and bhealing to the bones.

25 aThere is a way which seems right to a man,

Cross references (left margin):

★ **6** aDan. 4:27; Luke 11:41 bProv. 8:13; 14:16

7 aGen. 33:4; 2 Chr. 17:10

9 aProv. 16:1; 19:21 bPs. 37:23; Prov. 20:24; Jer. 10:23

★**10-15**
★**10** a1 Kin. 3:28

★**11** aProv. 11:1

12 aProv. 25:5

★**14**

★**15** aJob 29:23

Cross references (right margin):

16 aProv. 8:10, 19

17 aIs. 35:8

18 aProv. 11:2; 18:12; Jer. 49:16; Obad. 3, 4

★**19** aProv. 3:34; 29:23; Is. 57:15 bEx. 15:9; Judg. 5:30; Prov. 1:13, 14

20 aProv. 19:8 bPs. 2:12; 34:8; Jer. 17:7

21 aHos. 14:9 bProv. 16:23

★**22**

23 aPs. 37:30; Prov. 15:28; Matt. 12:34

24 aPs. 19:10; Prov. 15:26; 24:13, 14 bProv. 4:22; 17:22

25 aProv. 12:15; 14:12

16:6 *lovingkindness.* Loyal love. *truth.* Faithfulness. The atonement for man's sin is the result of God's loyal love and faithfulness. The fear of the Lord motivates a man to turn away from sin when he is tempted.

16:10–15 A king's responsibility.

16:10 *divine decision.* The reference is to the finality of the king's words. Because of this it is necessary that he be careful not to err in judgment.

16:11 God is concerned with and in opposition to unfair trade practices.

16:14 It is wise to pacify a king rather than defy him.

16:15 *spring rain.* I.e., the rain which falls in the spring and assures the ripening of the crops.

16:19 It is better to live humbly with the lowly than to be enriched through improper means with the proud.

16:22 *fountain of life.* I.e., a source of spiritual vitality.

But its end is the way of death.

26 A worker's appetite works for him,
For his hunger urges him on.

27 A [a]worthless man digs up evil,
While his words are as a [b]scorching fire.

28 A perverse man spreads strife,
And a slanderer separates intimate friends.

29 A man of violence [a]entices his neighbor,
And leads him in a way that is not good.

30 He who winks his eyes *does so* to devise perverse things;
He who compresses his lips brings evil to pass.

31 A [a]gray head is a crown of glory;
It [b]is found in the way of righteousness.

32 He who is slow to anger is better than the mighty,
And he who rules his spirit, than he who captures a city.

33 The [a]lot is cast into the lap,
But its every [b]decision is from the LORD.

17 [a]Better is a dry morsel and quietness with it
Than a house full of feasting with strife.

2 A servant who acts wisely will rule over a son who acts shamefully,

And will share in the inheritance among brothers.

3 The [a]refining pot is for silver and the furnace for gold,
But [b]the LORD tests hearts.

4 An [a]evildoer listens to wicked lips,
A liar pays attention to a destructive tongue.

5 He who mocks the [a]poor reproaches his Maker;
He who [b]rejoices at calamity will not go unpunished.

6 [a]Grandchildren are the crown of old men,
And the [b]glory of sons is their fathers.

7 [a]Excellent speech is not fitting for a fool;
Much less are [b]lying lips to a prince.

8 A [a]bribe is a charm in the sight of its owner;
Wherever he turns, he prospers.

9 He who [a]covers a transgression seeks love,
But he who repeats a matter [b]separates intimate friends.

10 A rebuke goes deeper into one who has understanding
Than a hundred blows into a fool.

11 A rebellious man seeks only evil,
So a cruel messenger will be sent against him.

Side notes (left column):

27 [a]Prov. 6:12, 14, 18 [b]James 3:6

★28

29 [a]Prov. 1:10; 12:26

★30

31 [a]Prov. 20:29 [b]Prov. 3:1, 2

★33 [a]Prov. 18:18 [b]Prov. 29:26

★ 1 [a]Prov. 15:17

Side notes (right column):

★ 3 [a]Prov. 27:21 [b]1 Chr. 29:17; Ps. 26:2; Prov. 15:11; Jer. 17:10; Mal. 3:3

4 [a]Prov. 14:15

5 [a]Prov. 14:31 [b]Job 31:29; Prov. 24:17; Obad. 12

6 [a]Gen. 48:11; Prov. 13:22 [b]Ex. 20:12; Mal. 1:6

7 [a]Prov. 24:7 [b]Ps. 31:18; Prov. 12:22

★ 8 [a]Prov. 21:14; Is. 1:23; Amos 5:12

★ 9 [a]Prov. 10:12; James 5:20; 1 Pet. 4:8 [b]Prov. 16:28

★10

★11

16:28 *slanderer.* Better, backbiter.

16:30 *compresses his lips.* I.e., conveys an expression of malice without words. Much evil and perversity can be disseminated without a word being spoken.

16:33 God is sovereign over human affairs. What appears to be chance is really part of God's sovereign design.

17:1 *feasting.* I.e., feasting provided by the family's portion of a peace offering (see note on Lev. 7:12–17).

17:3 God's tests of character are constructive in their intention; cf. 1 Pet. 1:7; James 1:2–4.

17:8 A bribe may cause one to prosper, but the use of such a practice is certainly to be condemned (17:23).

17:9 Overlooking an offense may preserve a friendship, but one who takes advantage of such graciousness will cause the friendship to be broken.

17:10 *goes deeper into.* Lit., descends into; i.e., makes an impression.

17:11 *cruel messenger.* I.e., one to execute judgment.

12 aProv.
29:9 b2 Sam.
17:8; Hos.
13:8

12 Let a ^aman meet a ^bbear robbed of her cubs, Rather than a fool in his folly.

13 aPs.
35:12; 109:5;
Jer. 18:20
b2 Sam.
12:10; 1 Kin.
21:22; Prov.
13:21

13 He who ^areturns evil for good, ^bEvil will not depart from his house.

14 aProv.
20:3; 25:8;
1 Thess. 4:11

14 The beginning of strife is *like* letting out water, So ^aabandon the quarrel before it breaks out.

15 aEx. 23:7;
Prov. 18:5;
24:24; Is.
5:23

15 He who ^ajustifies the wicked, and he who condemns the righteous, Both of them alike are an abomination to the LORD.

★16 aProv.
23:23

16 Why is there a price in the hand of a fool to ^abuy wisdom, When he has no sense?

★17 aRuth
1:16; Prov.
18:24

17 A ^afriend loves at all times, And a brother is born for adversity.

★18 aProv.
6:1; 11:15;
22:26

18 A man lacking in sense ^apledges, And becomes surety in the presence of his neighbor.

★19 aProv.
29:22 bProv.
16:18; 29:23

19 He who ^aloves transgression loves strife; He who ^braises his door seeks destruction.

20 aProv.
24:20
b James 3:8

20 He who has a crooked mind ^afinds no good, And he who is ^bperverted in his language falls into evil.

21 aProv.
10:1; 17:25;
19:13

21 He who ^abegets a fool *does* so to his sorrow, And the father of a fool has no joy.

22 A ^ajoyful heart is good medicine, But a broken spirit ^bdries up the bones.

★22 aProv.
15:13 bPs.
22:15

23 A wicked man receives a ^abribe from the bosom To ^bpervert the ways of justice.

23 aProv.
17:8 bEx.
23:8; Mic.
3:11; 7:3

24 Wisdom is in the presence of the one who has understanding, But the ^aeyes of a fool are on the ends of the earth.

★24 aEccl.
2:14

25 A ^afoolish son is a grief to his father, And ^bbitterness to her who bore him.

25 aProv.
19:13 bProv.
10:1

26 It is also not good to ^afine the righteous, *Nor* to strike the noble for *their* uprightness.

26 aProv.
17:15; 18:5

27 He who ^arestrains his words has knowledge, And he who has a ^bcool spirit is a man of understanding.

27 aProv.
10:19; James
1:19 bProv.
14:29

28 Even a fool, when he ^akeeps silent, is considered wise; When he closes his lips, he is *counted* prudent.

28 aJob 13:5

18 He who separates himself seeks *his own* desire, He ^aquarrels against all sound wisdom.

1 aProv.
3:21; 8:14

2 A fool does not delight in understanding, But only ^ain revealing his own mind.

★ 2 aProv.
12:23; 13:16;
Eccl. 10:3

3 When a wicked man comes, contempt also comes,

★3

17:16 This picture of a fool trying to buy wisdom is satirical, for wisdom cannot be purchased at any price. Nor is it received through some mechanical formula, but only by a proper heart attitude.

17:17 When you are in trouble, you see who your friends are and how helpful a brother can be.

17:18 *pledges.* Lit., strike hands; i.e., confirms a contract by handshake. *surety.* A cosigner, one responsible for a debt should the borrower default.

17:19 *raises his door.* A figure referring to opening one's mouth with boastful, arrogant talk.

17:22 *is good medicine.* Lit., causes good healing.

17:24 Wisdom is easily accessible to the discerning man, but the fool keeps looking to other interests and never finds wisdom.

18:2 The fool has no desire to learn, but desires only to air his personal opinions.

18:3 Contempt, dishonor, and reproach are the three companions of wickedness.

And with dishonor *comes* reproach.

4 The words of a man's mouth are ᵃdeep waters;
The fountain of wisdom is a bubbling brook.

5 To ᵃshow partiality to the wicked is not good,
Nor to ᵇthrust aside the righteous in judgment.

6 A fool's lips bring strife,
And his mouth calls for ᵃblows.

7 A ᵃfool's mouth is his ruin,
And his lips are the snare of his soul.

8 The words of a whisperer are like dainty morsels,
And they go down into the innermost parts of the body.

9 He also who is ᵃslack in his work
ᵇIs brother to him who destroys.

10 The ᵃname of the Lᴏʀᴅ is a ᵇstrong tower;
The righteous runs into it and ᶜis safe.

11 A ᵃrich man's wealth is his strong city,
And like a high wall in his own imagination.

12 ᵃBefore destruction the heart of man is haughty,
But ᵇhumility *goes* before honor.

13 He who ᵃgives an answer before he hears,

It is folly and shame to him.

14 The ᵃspirit of a man can endure his sickness,
But a ᵇbroken spirit who can bear?

15 The ᵃmind of the prudent acquires knowledge,
And the ᵇear of the wise seeks knowledge.

16 A man's ᵃgift makes room for him,
And brings him before great men.

17 The first to plead his case *seems* just,
Until another comes and examines him.

18 The ᵃlot puts an end to contentions,
And decides between the mighty.

19 A brother offended *is harder to be won* than a strong city,
And contentions are like the bars of a castle.

20 With the ᵃfruit of a man's mouth his stomach will be satisfied;
ᵇHe will be satisfied *with* the product of his lips.

21 ᵃDeath and life are in the power of the tongue,
And those who love it will eat its ᵇfruit.

22 He who finds a ᵃwife finds a good thing,
And ᵇobtains favor from the Lᴏʀᴅ.

23 The ᵃpoor man utters supplications,

Cross references (left margin):

★ 4 ᵃProv. 20:5

5 ᵃLev. 19:15; Deut. 1:17; 16:19; Ps. 82:2; Prov. 17:15; 24:23; 28:21 ᵇEx. 23:2, 6; Prov. 17:26; 31:5; Mic. 3:9
6 ᵃProv. 19:29
7 ᵃPs. 64:8; 140:9; Prov. 10:14; 12:13; 13:3; Eccl. 10:12

9 ᵃProv. 10:4 ᵇProv. 28:24

★10 ᵃEx. 3:15 ᵇ2 Sam. 22:2, 3, 33; Ps. 18:2; 61:3; 91:2; 144:2 ᶜProv. 29:25

11 ᵃProv. 10:15

12 ᵃProv. 11:2; 16:18; 29:23 ᵇProv. 15:33

13 ᵃProv. 20:25; John 7:51

Cross references (right margin):

14 ᵃProv. 17:22 ᵇProv. 15:13

15 ᵃProv. 15:14; Eph. 1:17 ᵇProv. 15:31

★16 ᵃGen. 32:20; 1 Sam. 25:27

★17

★18 ᵃProv. 16:33

★19

★20-21
20 ᵃProv. 12:14 ᵇProv. 14:14
21 ᵃProv. 12:13; 13:3; Matt. 12:37 ᵇProv. 13:2; Is. 3:10; Hos. 10:13
22 ᵃGen. 2:18; Prov. 12:4; 19:14; 31:10-31 ᵇProv. 8:35
★23 ᵃProv. 19:7 ᵇJames 2:3, 6
ᶜ1 Kin. 12:13; 2 Chr. 10:13

18:4 *deep waters.* I.e., obscure, hidden (cf. 20:5). *bubbling brook.* I.e., clear. While some men's words are obscure, others are sources of wisdom and convey the clear truth.
18:10 The "name of the Lᴏʀᴅ" is used here for the Lord Himself. He is the Protector of the righteous.
18:16 *gift.* Here a more neutral term than "bribe"; refers to an innocent courtesy. A legitimate favor can smooth the way for a person (cf. 1 Sam. 17:18).
18:17 *case.* I.e., lawsuit. It is always wise to hear

both sides of the story before making a judgment.
18:18 The decision by lot separates opponents and allows for harmony to be restored.
18:19 *bars of a castle.* I.e., a barrier to friendly relations.
18:20-21 A man's tongue can yield satisfaction, life, or death. Those who are prone to use the tongue must take the consequences of their words.
18:23 This proverb simply reports the ugly realities of the world.

But the ᵇrich man ᶜanswers roughly.

24 A man of *many* friends *comes* to ruin, But there is ᵃa friend who sticks closer than a brother.

19 ¹ ᵃBetter is a poor man who ᵇwalks in his integrity Than he who is perverse in speech and is a fool.

2 Also it is not good for a person to be without knowledge, And he who makes ᵃhaste with his feet errs.

3 The ᵃfoolishness of man subverts his way, And his heart ᵇrages against the Lord.

4 ᵃWealth adds many friends, But a poor man is separated from his friend.

5 A ᵃfalse witness will not go unpunished, And he who ᵇtells lies will not escape.

6 ᵃMany will entreat the favor of a generous man, And every man is a friend to him who ᵇgives gifts.

7 All the brothers of a poor man hate him; How much more do his ᵃfriends go far from him! He ᵇpursues *them with* words, *but* they are gone.

8 He who gets wisdom loves his own soul; He who keeps understanding will ᵃfind good.

9 A ᵃfalse witness will not go unpunished, And he who tells lies will perish.

10 Luxury is ᵃnot fitting for a fool; Much less for a ᵇslave to rule over princes.

11 A man's ᵃdiscretion makes him slow to anger, And it is his glory ᵇto overlook a transgression.

12 The ᵃking's wrath is like the roaring of a lion, But his favor is like ᵇdew on the grass.

13 A ᵃfoolish son is destruction to his father, And the ᵇcontentions of a wife are a constant dripping.

14 House and wealth are an ᵃinheritance from fathers, But a prudent wife is from the Lord.

15 ᵃLaziness casts into a deep sleep, And an idle man will suffer hunger.

16 He who ᵃkeeps the commandment keeps his soul, *But* he who is careless of his ways will die.

17 He who ᵃis gracious to a poor man lends to the Lord, And He will repay him for his ᵇgood deed.

18 ᵃDiscipline your son while there is hope, And do not desire his death.

19 A *man of* great anger shall bear the penalty,

Cross references (left):

★24 ᵃProv. 17:17; John 15:14, 15

1 ᵃProv. 28:6 ᵇPs. 26:11; Prov. 14:2; 20:7

★2 ᵃProv. 21:5; 28:20; 29:20

★3 ᵃProv. 11:3 ᵇIs. 8:21

4 ᵃProv. 14:20

5 ᵃEx. 23:1; Deut. 19:16-19; Prov. 19:9; 21:28 ᵇProv. 6:19

6 ᵃProv. 29:26 ᵇProv. 18:16; 21:14

7 ᵃPs. 38:11 ᵇProv. 18:23

8 ᵃProv. 16:20

Cross references (right):

9 ᵃProv. 19:5; Dan. 6:24

★10 ᵃProv. 17:7; 26:1; Eccl. 10:6, 7 ᵇProv. 30:22

11 ᵃProv. 14:29; 16:32 ᵇMatt. 5:44; Eph. 4:32; Col. 3:13

12 ᵃProv. 16:14 ᵇGen. 27:28; Deut. 33:28; Ps. 133:3; Hos. 14:5; Mic. 5:7

13 ᵃProv. 17:25 ᵇProv. 21:9, 19; 27:15

14 ᵃ2 Cor. 12:14

15 ᵃProv. 6:9, 10; 24:33

★16 ᵃProv. 13:13; 16:17; Luke 10:28; 11:28

★17 ᵃDeut. 15:7, 8; Prov. 14:31; 28:27; Eccl. 11:1, 2; Matt. 10:42; 25:40; 2 Cor. 9:6-8; Heb. 6:10 ᵇProv. 12:14; Luke 6:38

★18 ᵃProv. 13:24; 23:13; 29:15, 17

★19

18:24 Probably better, "A man of (too) many friends will be broken in pieces." Indiscriminately chosen friends may bring trouble, but a genuine friend sticks with you through thick and thin.

19:2 *makes haste with his feet.* I.e., proceeds without caution and direction.

19:3 The foolish man blames the Lord for failures he has brought upon himself.

19:10 Comfort tends to confirm a fool in his folly.

19:16 Premature death is the lot of those who disregard the law and are careless with respect to proper living.

19:17 The Lord will recompense a lender for his kindness to the poor.

19:18 *And do not desire his death.* Lit., And to the causing him to die, do not lift up your soul; i.e., do not neglect child discipline and thereby bring on your son's death.

19:19 It is futile to rescue a man given to anger, for his temper will repeatedly land him in fresh trouble.

For if you rescue *him,* you will only have to do it again.

20 ^aListen to counsel and accept discipline,
That you may be wise the rest of your days.

21 Many are the ^aplans in a man's heart,
But the ^bcounsel of the LORD, it will stand.

22 What is desirable in a man is his kindness,
And *it is* better to be a poor man than a liar.

23 The ^afear of the LORD *leads* to life,
So that one may sleep ^bsatisfied, ^cuntouched by evil.

24 The ^asluggard buries his hand ^bin the dish,
And will not even bring it back to his mouth.

25 ^aStrike a scoffer and the naive may become shrewd,
But ^breprove one who has understanding and he will gain knowledge.

26 He ^awho assaults *his* father and drives *his* mother away
Is a shameful and disgraceful son.

27 Cease listening, my son, to discipline,
And you will stray from the words of knowledge.

28 A rascally witness makes a mockery of justice,

And the mouth of the wicked ^aspreads iniquity.

29 Judgments are prepared for ^ascoffers,
And ^bblows for the back of fools.

20 ^aWine is a mocker, ^bstrong drink a brawler,
And whoever is intoxicated by it is not wise.

2 The terror of a king is like the growling of a lion;
He who provokes him to anger ^aforfeits his own life.

3 ^aKeeping away from strife is an honor for a man,
But any fool will quarrel.

4 The ^asluggard does not plow after the autumn,
So he begs during the harvest and has nothing.

5 A plan in the heart of a man is *like* deep water,
But a man of understanding draws it out.

6 Many a man ^aproclaims his own loyalty,
But who can find a ^btrustworthy man?

7 A righteous man who ^awalks in his integrity—
^bHow blessed are his sons after him.

8 ^aA king who sits on the throne of justice
Disperses all evil with his eyes.

Cross-references (side margins):

20 ^aProv. 4:1; 8:33; 12:15

21 ^aProv. 16:1, 9 ^bPs. 33:10, 11; Is. 14:26, 27

23 ^aProv. 14:27; 1 Tim. 4:8 ^bPs. 25:13 ^cPs. 91:10; Prov. 12:21

★24 ^aProv. 26:15 ^bMatt. 26:23; Mark 14:20

★25 ^aProv. 21:11 ^bProv. 9:8

26 ^aProv. 28:24

★27

★28 ^aJob 15:16; 20:12, 13; 34:7

29 ^aPs. 1:1; Prov. 9:12 ^bProv. 10:13; 18:6; 26:3

★ 1 ^aGen. 9:21; Prov. 23:29, 30; Is. 28:7; Hos. 4:11 ^bProv. 31:4; Is. 5:22; 56:12

2 ^aNum. 16:38; 1 Kin. 2:23; Prov. 8:36; Hab. 2:10

3 ^aGen. 13:7f.; Prov. 17:14

★ 4 ^aProv. 13:4; 21:25

★5

6 ^aProv. 25:14; Matt. 6:2; Luke 18:11 ^bPs. 12:1; Luke 18:8

★ 7 ^aProv. 19:1 ^bPs. 37:26; 112:2

8 ^aProv. 20:26; 25:5

19:24 Having dipped his hand in the *dish,* the sluggard does not have the strength to take the food to his mouth.

19:25 A simpleton needs an object lesson in order to learn. He must see that the mocker suffers. A wise man needs only a word of reproof to set him right.

19:27 The man who stops hearing and obeying will soon go astray.

19:28 *spreads.* Lit., swallows. To practice evil is the enjoyment of the wicked.

20:1 *brawler.* Lit., one making an uproar. Wine and strong drink are personified as a drunkard.

20:4 *after the autumn.* Lit., from winter; i.e., from the beginning of winter on. In Israel the farmer waited for the October-November rains to start his plowing and planting of winter crops. The sluggard procrastinates because of the weather and consequently does not bring in a harvest.

20:5 A man's real intention may be hidden, but a wise person is able to penetrate and discern his inner thoughts.

20:7 This proverb is based on the principle of Exod. 20:5–6.

★ **9** a1 Kin.
8:46; 2 Chr.
6:36; Job
14:4; Eccl.
7:20; Rom.
3:9; 1 John
1:8

10 aProv.
11:1; 20:23

★**11** aMatt.
7:16

12 aEx. 4:11;
Ps. 94:9

13 aProv.
6:9, 10;
19:15; 24:33

★**16**

★**17** aProv.
9:17

18 aProv.
11:14; 15:22
bProv. 24:6;
Luke 14:31

★**19** aProv.
11:13 bProv.
13:3

9 aWho can say, "I have cleansed my heart, I am pure from my sin"?

10 aDiffering weights and differing measures, Both of them are abominable to the LORD.

11 It is by his deeds that a lad adistinguishes himself If his conduct is pure and right.

12 The hearing aear and the seeing eye, The LORD has made both of them.

13 aDo not love sleep, lest you become poor; Open your eyes, *and* you will be satisfied with food.

14 "Bad, bad," says the buyer; But when he goes his way, then he boasts.

15 There is gold, and an abundance of jewels; But the lips of knowledge are a more precious thing.

16 Take his garment when he becomes surety for a stranger; And for foreigners, hold him in pledge.

17 aBread obtained by falsehood is sweet to a man, But afterward his mouth will be filled with gravel.

18 Prepare aplans by consultation, And bmake war by wise guidance.

19 He who agoes about as a slanderer reveals secrets,

Therefore do not associate with ba gossip.

20 He who acurses his father or his mother, His blamp will go out in time of darkness.

21 An inheritance gained hurriedly at the beginning, Will not be blessed in the end.

22 aDo not say, "I will repay evil"; bWait for the LORD, and He will save you.

23 aDiffering weights are an abomination to the LORD, And a bfalse scale is not good.

24 aMan's steps are *ordained* by the LORD, How then can man understand his way?

25 It is a snare for a man to say rashly, "It is holy!" And aafter the vows to make inquiry.

26 A awise king winnows the wicked, And drives the bthreshing wheel over them.

27 The aspirit of man is the lamp of the LORD, Searching all the innermost parts of his being.

28 Loyalty and atruth preserve the king, And he upholds his throne by righteousness.

29 The glory of young men is their strength, And the ahonor of old men is their gray hair.

★**20** aEx.
21:17; Lev.
20:9; Prov.
30:11; Matt.
15:4 bJob
18:5; Prov.
13:9; 24:20

22 aProv.
24:29; Matt.
5:39; Rom.
12:17, 19;
1 Thess.
5:15; 1 Pet.
3:9 bPs.
27:14

23 aProv.
20:10 bProv.
11:1

★**24** aProv.
16:9

★**25** aEccl.
5:4, 5

★**26** aProv.
20:8 bIs.
28:27

★**27** a1 Cor.
2:11

28 aProv.
29:14

★**29** aProv.
16:31

20:9 The implied answer is "nobody," thus teaching the impossibility of sinless perfection.

20:11 The activities of a child in his early years point to the direction his life is taking.

20:16 The one who is *surety* (the person responsible should the borrower default) for a *stranger* or a *foreigner* should be certain he receives some collateral (see notes on Exod. 22:25–27 and Amos 2:8).

20:17 *Bread obtained by falsehood.* Obtained by dishonest means.

20:19 *a gossip.* A foolish babbler.

20:20 *lamp.* I.e., the lamp of life. See Exod. 21:17.

20:24 God's sovereignty over man's ways is beyond our full comprehension.

20:25 It is perilous to dedicate something to the Lord and then reconsider the vow.

20:26 *winnows.* I.e., punishes. *the threshing-wheel.* The wheel of the cart used in threshing (cf. Isa. 28:27).

20:27 The conscience searches the inner part of man to convict of sin.

20:29 *honor.* Splendor.

30 ^aStripes that wound scour away evil,
And strokes *reach* the innermost parts.

21 The king's heart is *like* channels of water in the hand of the Lord;
He ^aturns it wherever He wishes.

2 ^aEvery man's way is right in his own eyes,
But the Lord ^bweighs the hearts.

3 To do ^arighteousness and justice
Is desired by the Lord rather than sacrifice.

4 Haughty eyes and a proud heart,
The ^alamp of the wicked, is sin.

5 The plans of the ^adiligent *lead* surely to advantage,
But everyone ^bwho is hasty *comes* surely to poverty.

6 The ^agetting of treasures by a lying tongue
Is a fleeting vapor, the pursuit of ^bdeath.

7 The violence of the wicked will drag them away,
Because they ^arefuse to act with justice.

8 The way of a guilty man is ^acrooked,
But as for the pure, his conduct is upright.

9 It is better to live in a corner of a roof,
Than in a house shared with a contentious woman.

10 The soul of the wicked desires evil;

His ^aneighbor finds no favor in his eyes.

11 When the ^ascoffer is punished, the naive becomes wise;
But when the wise is instructed, he receives knowledge.

12 The righteous one considers the house of the wicked,
Turning the ^awicked to ruin.

13 He who ^ashuts his ear to the cry of the poor
Will also cry himself and not be ^banswered.

14 A ^agift in secret subdues anger,
And a bribe in the bosom, strong wrath.

15 The execution of justice is joy for the righteous,
But is ^aterror to the workers of iniquity.

16 A man who wanders from the way of understanding
Will ^arest in the assembly of the dead.

17 He who ^aloves pleasure *will become* a poor man;
He who loves wine and oil will not become rich.

18 The wicked is a ^aransom for the righteous,
And the ^btreacherous is in the place of the upright.

19 ^aIt is better to live in a desert land,
Than with a contentious and vexing woman.

20 There is precious ^atreasure and oil in the dwelling of the wise,

---

Cross references (left margin):
★30 ^aPs. 89:32; Prov. 22:15; Is. 53:5; 1 Pet. 2:24
1 ^aEzra 6:22
2 ^aProv. 16:2 ^bProv. 16:2; 24:12; Luke 16:15
3 ^a1 Sam. 15:22; Prov. 15:8; Is. 1:11, 16, 17; Hos. 6:6; Mic. 6:7, 8
★ 4 ^aProv. 24:20; Luke 11:34
5 ^aProv. 10:4; 13:4 ^bProv. 28:22
6 ^aProv. 13:11; 20:21 ^bProv. 8:36
7 ^aAmos 5:7; Mic. 3:9
8 ^aProv. 2:15
10 ^aPs. 52:3; Prov. 2:14; 14:21

Cross references (right margin):
11 ^aProv. 19:25
★12 ^aProv. 14:11
13 ^aMatt. 18:30-34; 1 John 3:17 ^bJames 2:13
★14 ^aProv. 18:16; 19:6
★15 ^aProv. 10:29
★16 ^aPs. 49:14
17 ^aProv. 23:21
★18 ^aIs. 43:3 ^bProv. 11:8
19 ^aProv. 21:9
★20 ^aPs. 112:3; 22:4 ^bJob 20:15, 18

20:30 *Stripes that wound.* Lit., blows of a bruise; i.e., severe blows that bruise. Physical discipline may cure a man of evil and cleanse his inner person.

21:4 *lamp.* I.e., (1) the standards which govern the lives of the wicked, or (2) their arrogant life.

21:12 Better, The Righteous One considers the house of the wicked, subverting the wicked to ruin.

21:14 The proverb does not promote bribery, but simply states a fact of experience.

21:15 The execution of justice brings joy to the righteous and dismay to the wicked.

21:16 Those who neglect wisdom shall soon find their way to the grave.

21:18 The wicked rather than the righteous will ultimately suffer judgment.

21:20 The wise man plans and saves for the future, but the foolish person squanders what he has.

But a foolish man [b]swallows it up.

21 He who [a]pursues righteousness and loyalty
Finds life, righteousness and honor.

22 A [a]wise man scales the city of the mighty,
And brings down the stronghold in which they trust.

23 He who [a]guards his mouth and his tongue,
Guards his soul from troubles.

24 "Proud," "Haughty," "[a]Scoffer," are his names,
Who acts with [b]insolent pride.

25 The [a]desire of the sluggard puts him to death,
For his hands refuse to work;

26 All day long he is craving,
While the righteous [a]gives and does not hold back.

27 The [a]sacrifice of the wicked is an abomination,
How much more when he brings it with evil intent!

28 A [a]false witness will perish,
But the man who listens to the truth will speak forever.

29 A wicked man [a]shows a bold face,
But as for the [b]upright, he makes his way sure.

30 There is [a]no wisdom and no understanding

And no counsel against the Lord.

31 The [a]horse is prepared for the day of battle,
But [b]victory belongs to the Lord.

22

1 A [a]good name is to be more desired than great riches,
Favor is better than silver and gold.

2 The rich and the poor have a common bond,
The Lord is the [a]maker of them all.

3 The [a]prudent sees the evil and hides himself,
But the naive go on, and are punished for it.

4 The reward of humility and the fear of the Lord
Are riches, honor and life.

5 [a]Thorns and snares are in the way of the perverse;
He who guards himself will be far from them.

6 [a]Train up a child in the way he should go,
Even when he is old he will not depart from it.

7 The [a]rich rules over the poor,
And the borrower becomes the lender's slave.

8 He who [a]sows iniquity will reap vanity,
And the [b]rod of his fury will perish.

9 He who is [a]generous will be blessed,

Cross references (left column):

21 [a]Prov. 15:9; Matt. 5:6; 1 Cor. 15:58

★22 [a]2 Sam. 5:6-9; Prov. 24:5; Eccl. 7:19; 9:15, 16

23 [a]Prov. 12:13; 13:3; 18:21; James 3:2

24 [a]Ps. 1:1; Prov. 1:22; 3:34; 24:9; Is. 29:20 [b]Is. 16:6; Jer. 48:29

25 [a]Prov. 13:4

★26 [a]Ps. 37:26; 112:5, 9; Matt. 5:42; Eph. 4:28

27 [a]Prov. 15:8; Is. 66:3; Jer. 6:20; Amos 5:22

★28 [a]Prov. 19:5, 9

★29 [a]Eccl. 8:1 [b]Ps. 119:5; Prov. 11:5

30 [a]Jer. 9:23; Acts 5:38, 39; 1 Cor. 3:19, 20

Cross references (right column):

31 [a]Ps. 20:7; 33:17; Is. 31:1 [b]Ps. 3:8; Jer. 3:23; 1 Cor. 15:57

★ 1 [a]Prov. 10:7; Eccl. 7:1

★ 2 [a]Job 31:15; Prov. 14:31

★ 3 [a]Prov. 14:16; 27:12; Is. 26:20

5 [a]Prov. 15:19

★ 6 [a]Eph. 6:4

7 [a]Prov. 18:23; James 2:6

★ 8 [a]Job 4:8 [b]Ps. 125:3

★ 9 [a]Prov. 19:17; 2 Cor. 9:6 [b]Luke 14:13

21:22 Wisdom is superior to physical strength.

21:26 While the sluggard craves his sleep, the righteous gives himself unreservedly to his work.

21:28 While the false witness will perish, the one who listens attentively will report accurately, and his testimony will stand.

21:29 *shows a bold face.* I.e., shows his defiance by his countenance.

22:1 *A good name.* Good character and the reputation that should go with it.

22:2 The rich and poor alike have a common origin and responsibility to God.

22:3 The prudent keep clear of evil, but the sim-ple charge right in and pay the penalty for doing so.

22:6 *in the way he should go.* Lit., according to his way; i.e., the child's habits and interests. The instruction must take into account his in-dividuality and inclinations, and be in keeping with his degree of physical and mental devel-opment.

22:8 *rod of his fury.* I.e., the capacity for exercis-ing anger. The wicked will reap what they sow and eventually perish.

22:9 *generous.* Lit., has a good eye; i.e., looks with kindness and benevolence.

For he [b]gives some of his food to the poor.

10 [a]Drive out the scoffer, and contention will go out,
Even strife and dishonor will cease.

11 He who loves [a]purity of heart
And whose speech is [b]gracious, the king is his friend.

12 The eyes of the LORD preserve knowledge,
But He overthrows the words of the treacherous man.

13 The [a]sluggard says, "There is a lion outside;
I shall be slain in the streets!"

14 The mouth of [a]an adulteress is a deep pit;
He who is [b]cursed of the LORD will fall into it.

15 Foolishness is bound up in the heart of a child;
The [a]rod of discipline will remove it far from him.

16 He [a]who oppresses the poor to make much for himself
Or who gives to the rich, [b]*will* only *come to* poverty.

C Proverbs which Concern Various Practices, 22:17–23:35

17 [a]Incline your ear and hear the words of the wise,
And apply your mind to my knowledge;

18 For it will be [a]pleasant if you keep them within you,

That they may be ready on your lips.

19 So that your [a]trust may be in the LORD,
I have taught you today, even you.

20 Have I not written to you [a]excellent things
Of counsels and knowledge,

21 To make you [a]know the certainty of the words of truth
That you may [b]correctly answer to him who sent you?

22 [a]Do not rob the poor because he is poor,
Or [b]crush the afflicted at the gate;

23 For the LORD will [a]plead their case,
And take the life of those who rob them.

24 Do not associate with a man *given* to anger;
Or go with a [a]hot-tempered man,

25 Lest you [a]learn his ways,
And find a snare for yourself.

26 Do not be among those who [a]give pledges,
Among those who become sureties for debts.

27 If you have nothing with which to pay,
Why should he [a]take your bed from under you?

28 [a]Do not move the ancient boundary
Which your fathers have set.

Marginal references (left column):
10 [a]Gen. 21:9, 10; Prov. 18:6; 26:20
11 [a]Ps. 24:4; Matt. 5:8 [b]Prov. 14:35; 16:13
★12
13 [a]Prov. 26:13
14 [a]Prov. 2:16; 5:3; 7:5; 23:27 [b]Eccl. 7:26
15 [a]Prov. 13:24; 23:14
★16 [a]Eccl. 5:8; James 2:13 [b]Prov. 28:22
★22:17–24:34
★17 [a]Prov. 5:1
★18-21
18 [a]Prov. 2:10

Marginal references (right column):
19 [a]Prov. 3:5
20 [a]Prov. 8:6
21 [a]Luke 1:3, 4 [b]Prov. 25:13; 1 Pet. 3:15
★22:22-23:14
22 [a]Ex. 23:6; Job 31:16; Prov. 22:16 [b]Zech. 7:10; Mal. 3:5
23 [a]1 Sam. 25:39; Ps. 35:10; 140:12; Prov. 23:11; Jer. 51:36
24 [a]Prov. 29:22
25 [a]1 Cor. 15:33
★26 [a]Prov. 17:18
★27 [a]Ex. 22:26; Prov. 20:16
28 [a]Deut. 19:14; 27:17; Job 24:2; Prov. 23:10

22:12 The Lord is the ultimate guardian of truth.
22:16 The exploitation of the poor for personal gain, and bribery of the rich will both lead to *poverty.*
22:17–24:34 This section records the "words of the wise." The teaching style returns to the pattern of chapters 1–9. The proverbial discourses, however, are not as expansive.
22:17 The wise teacher invites the pupil to hear the words of the wise.
22:18–21 The advantages of hearing the instruction of the wise are set forth.
22:22–23:14 The wise teacher sets forth a series of precepts and warnings.
22:26 *give pledges.* Lit., strike hands. I.e., confirm an agreement. *sureties.* Those responsible for the debts of a borrower should he default.
22:27 *he.* I.e., the harsh creditor.

29 Do you see a man skilled in his work?
He will ᵃstand before kings;
He will not stand before obscure men.

23 When you sit down to dine with a ruler,
Consider carefully what is before you;
2 And put a knife to your throat,
If you are a ᵃman of great appetite.
3 Do not ᵃdesire his delicacies,
For it is deceptive food.

4 ᵃDo not weary yourself to gain wealth,
ᵇCease from your consideration of it.
5 When you set your eyes on it, it is gone.
For ᵃwealth certainly makes itself wings,
Like an eagle that flies toward the heavens.

6 ᵃDo not eat the bread of a ᵇselfish man,
Or desire his delicacies;
7 For as he thinks within himself, so he is.
He says to you, "Eat and drink!"
But ᵃhis heart is not with you.
8 You will ᵃvomit up the morsel you have eaten,
And waste your compliments.

9 ᵃDo not speak in the hearing of a fool,
For he will ᵇdespise the wisdom of your words.

10 Do not move the ancient boundary,
Or ᵃgo into the fields of the fatherless;
11 For their ᵃRedeemer is strong;
ᵇHe will plead their case against you.

12 Apply your heart to discipline,
And your ears to words of knowledge.

13 ᵃDo not hold back discipline from the child,
Although you beat him with the rod, he will not die.
14 You shall beat him with the rod,
And ᵃdeliver his soul from Sheol.

15 My son, if your heart is ᵃwise,
My own heart also will be glad;
16 And my inmost being will rejoice,
When your lips speak ᵃwhat is right.

17 ᵃDo not let your heart envy sinners,
But live in the ᵇfear of the LORD always.

Marginal references (left column):
29 ᵃGen. 41:46; 1 Kin. 10:8
★ 1-3
2 ᵃProv. 23:20
3 ᵃPs. 141:4; Prov. 23:6; Dan. 1:5, 8, 13, 15, 16
★ 4-5
★ 4 ᵃProv. 15:27; 28:20; Matt. 6:19; 1 Tim. 6:9; Heb. 13:5; ᵇProv. 3:5, 7
★ 5 ᵃProv. 27:24; 1 Tim. 6:17
★ 6-8
6 ᵃPs. 141:4 ᵇDeut. 15:9; Prov. 28:22
7 ᵃProv. 26:24, 25
8 ᵃProv. 25:16

Marginal references (right column):
9 ᵃMatt. 7:6 ᵇProv. 1:7
★10-11
★10 ᵃJer. 22:3; Zech. 7:10
★11 ᵃJob 19:25; Jer. 50:34 ᵇProv. 22:23
★13-14
13 ᵃProv. 13:24; 19:18
★14 ᵃ1 Cor. 5:5
15 ᵃProv. 23:24f.; 27:11; 29:3
★16 ᵃProv. 8:6
17 ᵃPs. 37:1; Prov. 24:1, 19 ᵇProv. 28:14

23:1-3 One must exercise caution in the presence of a ruler, for he may entertain with ulterior motives. *put a knife to your throat.* I.e., restrain your appetite at all cost. The good hospitality may have a sinister purpose behind it.
23:4-5 The warning is against coveting riches.
23:4 *consideration.* Lit., understanding; i.e., insight directed towards becoming rich.
23:5 Riches are fleeting and elusive. You bank on them and suddenly they are gone.
23:6-8 A wise teacher warns against receiving favors from an insincere host.
23:10-11 A wise teacher warns against exploiting the defenseless poor.
23:10 *the ancient boundary.* I.e., boundary marker (see note on Deut. 19:14).
23:11 *Redeemer.* Lit., near kinsman; i.e., one who will protect the interests of the family (see notes on Lev. 25:25-28 and Ruth 3:9). The term may refer to God (see notes on Gen. 48:15-16; Exod. 6:6; Job 19:25-27).
23:13-14 A wise teacher warns of neglecting child discipline.
23:14 Discipline may deliver a child from an untimely death.
23:16 *inmost being.* Lit., kidneys; i.e., seat of emotion.

★18 aPs.
19:11; 58:11;
Prov. 24:14
bPs. 9:18

19 aProv.
6:6 bProv.
4:23; 9:6

20 aProv.
20:1; 23:29,
30; Is. 5:22;
Matt. 24:49;
Luke 21:34;
Rom. 13:13;
Eph. 5:18
bDeut.
21:20; Prov.
28:7

21 aProv.
21:17 bProv.
6:10, 11.

22 aProv.
1:8; Eph. 6:1
bProv.
15:20; 30:17

23 aProv.
4:7; 18:15;
Matt. 13:44

24 aProv.
10:1; 15:20;
29:3

25 aProv.
27:11

26 aProv.
3:1; 4:4 bPs.
1:2; 119:24

★27 aProv.
22:14 bProv.
5:20

18 Surely there is a ^afuture,
And your ^bhope will not
be cut off.

19 Listen, my son, and ^abe
wise,
And ^bdirect your heart in
the way.

20 Do not be with ^aheavy
drinkers of wine,
Or with ^bgluttonous eaters
of meat;

21 For the ^aheavy drinker and
the glutton will come
to poverty,
And ^bdrowsiness will
clothe *a man* with
rags.

22 ^aListen to your father who
begot you,
And ^bdo not despise your
mother when she is
old.

23 ^aBuy truth, and do not sell
it,
Get wisdom and instruc-
tion and understand-
ing.

24 The father of the righteous
will greatly rejoice,
And ^ahe who begets a wise
son will be glad in
him.

25 Let your ^afather and your
mother be glad,
And let her rejoice who
gave birth to you.

26 ^aGive me your heart, my
son,
And let your eyes ^bdelight
in my ways.

27 For a harlot is a ^adeep pit,

And an ^badulterous
woman is a narrow
well.

28 Surely she ^alurks as a robber,
And increases the faithless
among men.

29 Who has ^awoe? Who has
sorrow?
Who has contentions?
Who has complain-
ing?
Who has wounds without
cause?
Who has redness of eyes?

30 Those who ^alinger long
over wine,
Those who go to taste
^bmixed wine.

31 Do not look on the wine
when it is red,
When it sparkles in the
cup,
When it ^agoes down
smoothly;

32 At the last it ^abites like a
serpent,
And stings like a ^bviper.

33 Your eyes will see strange
things,
And your mind will ^autter
perverse things.

34 And you will be like one
who lies down in the
middle of the sea,
Or like one who lies down
on the top of a mast.

35 "They ^astruck me, *but* I did
not become ill;
They beat me, *but* I did
not know *it*.
When shall I awake?
I will ^bseek another drink."

28 aProv.
6:26; 7:12;
Eccl. 7:26

★29-35

29 aIs. 5:11,
22

30 a1 Sam.
25:36; Prov.
20:1; Is.
5:11; 28:7;
Eph. 5:18
bPs. 75:8

★31 aSong
7:9

★32 aJob
20:16; Prov.
20:1; Eph.
5:18 bPs.
91:13; Is.
11:8

33 aProv.
2:12

★34

★35 aProv.
27:22; Jer.
5:3 bProv.
26:11; Is.
56:12

23:18 Don't be unduly burdened by the problems of the present, but allow a proper perspective on the future to help you maintain a
buoyant attitude in the present.
23:27 Whoever is enticed by the harlot or adulteress comes to inescapable doom.
23:29-35 In warning against drunkenness, a
wise teacher presents a case study of a drunkard.

23:31 The warning is to avoid wine's enticements of beauty and taste.
23:32 *viper.* Poisonous snake.
23:34 The picture is of a drunken sailor who
falls into the sea and drowns, or goes to sleep
in the crow's nest.
23:35 A drunk may be involved in a fight, but
be in such a stupor that he does not feel the
blows on his body.

D Proverbs which Concern Various People, 24:1-34

24 Do not be ^aenvious of evil men,
Nor desire to ^bbe with them;

2 For their minds devise ^aviolence,
And their lips ^btalk of trouble.

3 ^aBy wisdom a house is built,
And by understanding it is established;

4 And by knowledge the rooms are ^afilled
With all precious and pleasant riches.

5 A ^awise man is strong,
And a man of knowledge increases power.

6 For ^aby wise guidance you will wage war,
And ^bin abundance of counselors there is victory.

7 Wisdom is ^atoo high for a fool,
He does not open his mouth ^bin the gate.

8 He who ^aplans to do evil,
Men will call him a schemer.

9 The ^adevising of folly is sin,
And the scoffer is an abomination to men.

10 If you ^aare slack in the day of distress,
Your strength is limited.

11 ^aDeliver those who are being taken away to death,
And those who are staggering to slaughter,
Oh hold *them* back.

12 If you say, "See, we did not know this,"
Does He not ^aconsider *it*
^bwho weighs the hearts?
And ^cdoes He not know *it*
who ^dkeeps your soul?
And will He not ^erender to man according to his work?

13 My son, eat ^ahoney, for it is good,
Yes, the ^bhoney from the comb is sweet to your taste;

14 Know *that* ^awisdom is thus for your soul;
If you find *it*, then there will be a ^bfuture,
And your hope will not be cut off.

15 ^aDo not lie in wait, O wicked man, against the dwelling of the righteous;
Do not destroy his resting place;

16 For a ^arighteous man falls seven times, and rises again,
But the ^bwicked stumble in *time of* calamity.

17 ^aDo not rejoice when your enemy falls,
And do not let your heart be glad when he stumbles;

18 Lest the LORD see *it* and be displeased,
And He turn away His anger from him.

19 ^aDo not fret because of evildoers,
Or be ^benvious of the wicked;

Cross references

1 ^aPs. 37:1; Prov. 3:31; 23:17; 24:19 ^bPs. 1:1; Prov. 1:15
★ **2** ^aIs. 30:12; Jer. 22:17 ^bJob 15:35; Ps. 10:7; 38:12
3 ^aProv. 9:1; 14:1
4 ^aProv. 8:21
5 ^aProv. 21:22
6 ^aProv. 20:18 ^bProv. 11:14
★ **7** ^aPs. 10:5; Prov. 14:6; 17:16 ^bJob 5:4; Ps. 127:5
★ **8** ^aProv. 6:14; 14:22; Rom. 1:30
9 ^aMatt. 15:19; Acts 8:22
★ **10** ^aDeut. 20:8; Job 4:5; Jer. 51:46; Heb. 12:3
11 ^aPs. 82:4; Is. 58:6, 7
★ **12-13**
★ **12** ^aEccl. 5:8 ^b1 Sam. 16:7; Prov. 21:2 ^cPs. 94:9-11 ^dPs. 121:3-8 ^eJob 34:11; Prov. 12:14
13 ^aPs. 19:10; 119:103; Prov. 25:16; Song 5:1 ^bProv. 16:24; 27:7; Song 4:11
14 ^aProv. 2:10 ^bProv. 23:18
15 ^aPs. 10:9, 10
16 ^aJob 5:19; Ps. 37:24; Mic. 7:8 ^bProv. 6:15; 14:32; 24:22; Jer. 18:17
17 ^aJob 31:29; Ps. 35:15, 19; Prov. 17:5; Obad. 12
19 ^aPs. 37:1 ^bProv. 23:17; 24:1

24:2 *devise.* Ponder.
24:7 *the gate.* The meeting place of the wise men and elders of the city (see note on Ruth 4:1).
24:8 *schemer.* Lit., possessor of evil plans.
24:10 *slack* = faint. If you are fainthearted in time of distress, your strength will be limited.
24:12-13 A wise teacher instructs of the delight and beneficial effect of wisdom.
24:12 The excuse of ignorance is not acceptable.

*20 aJob
15:31 bProv.
23:18 cJob
18:5, 6;
21:17; Prov.
13:9; 20:20

20 For ᵃthere will be no ᵇfuture for the evil man;
The ᶜlamp of the wicked will be put out.

*21 aRom.
13:1-7; 1 Pet.
2:17

21 My son, ᵃfear the LORD and the king;
Do not associate with those who are given to change;

22 aProv.
24:16

22 For their ᵃcalamity will rise suddenly,
And who knows the ruin *that comes* from both of them?

23 aProv.
1:6; 22:17
bProv. 18:5;
28:21

23 These also are ᵃsayings of the wise.
To ᵇshow partiality in judgment is not good.

24 aProv.
17:15; Is.
5:23 bProv.
11:26

24 He ᵃwho says to the wicked, "You are righteous,"
ᵇPeoples will curse him, nations will abhor him;

25 aProv.
28:23

25 But ᵃto those who rebuke the *wicked* will be delight,
And a good blessing will come upon them.

*26

26 He kisses the lips
Who gives a right answer.

*27 aProv.
27:23-27

27 Prepare your work outside,
And ᵃmake it ready for yourself in the field;
Afterwards, then, build your house.

28 aProv.
25:18 bLev.
6:2, 3; 19:11;
Eph. 4:25

28 Do not be a ᵃwitness against your neighbor without cause,
And ᵇdo not deceive with your lips.

29 ᵃDo not say, "Thus I shall do to him as he has done to me;
I will render to the man according to his work."

29 aProv.
20:22; Matt.
5:39; Rom.
12:17

30 I passed by the field of the sluggard,
And by the vineyard of the man ᵃlacking sense;

*30-34
30 aProv.
6:32

31 And behold, it was completely ᵃovergrown with thistles,
Its surface was covered with ᵇnettles,
And its stone ᶜwall was broken down.

31 aGen.
3:18 bJob
30:7 cIs. 5:5

32 When I saw, I reflected upon it;
I looked, *and* received instruction.

33 "ᵃA little sleep, a little slumber,
A little folding of the hands to rest,"

33 aProv.
6:10

34 Then your poverty will come *as* a robber,
And your want like an armed man.

*34

IV THE PROVERBS OF SOLOMON COPIED BY HEZEKIAH'S MEN, 25:1—29:27

A Proverbs Concerning Relationships with Others, 25:1—26:28

1 With kings, 25:1-7

25 These also are ᵃproverbs of Solomon which the men of Hezekiah, king of Judah, transcribed.

*25:1-29:27
* 1 aProv.
1:1

2 It is the glory of God to ᵃconceal a matter,
But the glory of ᵇkings is to search out a matter.

2 aDeut.
29:29; Rom.
11:33 bEzra
6:1

24:20 *lamp.* I.e., joy and prosperity (cf. Esther 8:16).

24:21 *those who are given to change.* I.e., those in opposition to civil authority.

24:26 As a kiss on the lips seals a matter between a couple, so an honest answer confirms a fair judgment.

24:27 *build your house.* I.e., marry and rear a family. Certain preparations need to be made before one begins a family.

24:30-34 The wise teacher presents a lesson on laziness from the sluggard's neglected vineyard. He makes an observation (vv. 30-31), an interpretation (v. 32), and an application (vv. 33-34). A wise man can learn a lesson even from a sluggard!

24:34 *a robber* = a vagabond.

25:1-29:27 In this section are proverbs of Solomon, arranged by an editorial committee set up by King Hezekiah.

25:1 *transcribed.* I.e., extracted from Solomon's works and incorporated into Proverbs.

★ 3

3 As the heavens for height
and the earth for
depth,
So the heart of kings is unsearchable.

4 aProv.
26:23; Ezek.
22:18 bMal.
3:2, 3

4 Take away the ªdross from
the silver,
And there comes out a
vessel for the bsmith;

5 aProv.
20:8 bProv.
16:12

5 Take away the ªwicked
from before the king,
And his bthrone will be established in right-
eousness.

★ 6

6 Do not claim honor in the
presence of the king,
And do not stand in the
place of great men;

7 aLuke
14:7-11

7 For ªit is better that it be
said to you, "Come up
here,"
Than that you should be
put lower in the pres-
ence of the prince,
Whom your eyes have
seen.

2 With neighbors, 25:8-20

★ 8 aProv.
17:14; Matt.
5:25

8 Do not go out ªhastily to
argue your case;
Otherwise, what will you
do in the end,
When your neighbor puts
you to shame?

★ 9 aMatt.
18:15 bProv.
11:13

9 ªArgue your case with
your neighbor,
And bdo not reveal the secret of another,

10 Lest he who hears it reproach you,
And the evil report about
you not pass away.

11 Like apples of gold in settings of silver
Is a ªword spoken in right
circumstances.

★11 aProv.
15:23

12 Like an ªearring of gold
and an bornament of
cfine gold
Is a wise reprover to a dlis-
tening ear.

★12 aEx.
32:2; 35:22;
Ezek. 16:12
b2 Sam. 1:24
cJob 28:17
dProv.
15:31; 20:12

13 Like the cold of snow in
the time of harvest
Is a ªfaithful messenger to
those who send him,
For he refreshes the soul of
his masters.

★13 aProv.
13:17

14 Like ªclouds and bwind
without rain
Is a man who boasts of his
gifts falsely.

★14 aJude
12 bJer.
5:13; Mic.
2:11

15 By ªforbearance a ruler
may be persuaded,
And a soft tongue breaks
the bone.

★15 aGen.
32:4; 1 Sam.
25:24; Eccl.
10:4

16 Have you ªfound honey?
Eat only what you
need,
Lest you have it in excess
and vomit it.

16 aJudg.
14:8; 1 Sam.
14:25

17 Let your foot rarely be in
your   neighbor's
house,
Lest he become weary of
you and hate you.

18 Like a club and a ªsword
and a sharp barrow
Is a man who bears cfalse
witness against his
neighbor.

18 aPs. 57:4;
Prov. 12:18
bJer. 9:8
cEx. 20:16;
Prov. 24:28

19 Like a bad tooth and an
unsteady foot
Is confidence in a ªfaithless
man in time of trou-
ble.

★19 aJob
6:15; Is. 36:6

25:3 As man cannot estimate the height of the
heavens or the depth of the earth, so he cannot comprehend the inner thoughts of a ruler.
25:6 Do not claim honor. Lit., Do not honor
yourself. The circumstance is a feast. Do not
take a position at the table which may be reserved for a more distinguished guest (cf. Luke
14:7-11).
25:8 argue your case. Lit., contend; i.e., conduct
a lawsuit.
25:9 Before taking a case to court, gather evidence and keep it confidential.
25:11 settings. Lit., sculptures. spoken in right
circumstances. Lit., spoken in its time. The

simile is obscure, but the message is clear.
25:12 listening. Hearing with a view to obedience.
25:13 cold of snow. I.e., cold ice water from the
mountain snow, or a cool mountain breeze.
25:14 The gift of the braggart does not compare
with what he promised.
25:15 forbearance. Self-restraint and gentle
speech are effective against stubborn opposition.
25:19 an unsteady foot. Lit., a slipping foot. Mis-
placed confidence can lead to trouble and disaster.

★20   20   *Like* one who takes off a garment on a cold day, *or like* vinegar on soda,

Is he who sings songs to a troubled heart.

3 *With enemies,* 25:21-24

★21-22
21 *a*Ex. 23:4, 5; 2 Kin. 6:22; 2 Chr. 28:15; Matt. 5:44; Rom. 12:20

21 *a*If your enemy is hungry, give him food to eat; And if he is thirsty, give him water to drink;

22 *a*2 Sam. 16:12; Matt. 6:4, 6

22 For you will heap burning coals on his head, And *a*the LORD will reward you.

23 *a*Ps. 101:5

23 The north wind brings forth rain, And a *a*backbiting tongue, an angry countenance.

24 *a*Prov. 21:9

24 It is *a*better to live in a corner of the roof Than in a house shared with a contentious woman.

4 *With yourself,* 25:25-26:2

25 *a*Prov. 15:30

25 *Like* cold water to a weary soul, So is *a*good news from a distant land.

★26 *a*Ezek. 32:2; 34:18, 19

26 *Like* a *a*trampled spring and a polluted well Is a righteous man who gives way before the wicked.

★27 *a*Prov. 27:2; Luke 14:11

27 It is not good to eat much honey, Nor is it glory to *a*search out one's own glory.

28 *Like* a *a*city that is broken into *and* without walls Is a man *b*who has no control over his spirit.

26

Like snow in summer and like *a*rain in harvest, So honor is not *b*fitting for a fool.

2 *Like* a *a*sparrow in *its* flitting, like a swallow in *its* flying, So a *b*curse without cause does not alight.

5 *With fools,* 26:3-12

3 A *a*whip is for the horse, a bridle for the donkey, And a *b*rod for the back of fools.

4 *a*Do not answer a fool according to his folly, Lest you also be like him.

5 *a*Answer a fool as his folly *deserves,* Lest he be *b*wise in his own eyes.

6 He cuts off *his own* feet, *and* drinks violence Who sends a message by the hand of a fool.

7 *Like* the legs *which* hang down from the lame, So is a proverb in the mouth of fools.

8 Like one who binds a stone in a sling, So is he who gives honor to a fool.

9 *Like* a thorn *which* falls into the hand of a drunkard, So is a proverb in the mouth of fools.

★28 *a*Prov. 16:32 *b*2 Chr. 32:5; Neh. 1:3

★ 1-12

★ 1 *a*1 Sam. 12:17 *b*Prov. 17:7

★ 2 *a*Prov. 27:8; Is. 16:2 *b*Num. 23:8; Deut. 23:5; 2 Sam. 16:12

3 *a*Ps. 32:9 *b*Prov. 10:13; 19:29

★ 4-5
4 *a*Prov. 23:9; 29:9; Is. 36:21; Matt. 7:6
5 *a*Matt. 16:1-4; 21:24-27 *b*Prov. 3:7; 28:11; Rom. 12:16

★ 6

★ 8

25:20 *troubled heart.* Lit., evil heart; i.e., a sad heart.

25:21-22 Kindness shown to an enemy will bring shame to him and blessing to the benefactor.

25:26 A righteous man's defection affects those who have learned to rely upon him.

25:27 The proverb warns against becoming too engrossed in one's share of honor. Excess, even of a good thing, is bad.

25:28 A man without self-control is an easy victim when attacked by his desires and impulses.

26:1-12 The first part of the chapter concerns fools.

26:1 *honor.* I.e., a place of honor.

26:2 An unjustified curse will never be effective.

26:4-5 These verses are complementary rather than contradictory. While it is unwise to argue with a fool at his level and to recognize his foolish suppositions, there are occasions when it is best to refute him soundly, lest his foolish opinions seem to be confirmed.

26:6 *cuts off his own feet.* I.e., a foolish messenger will, as it were, disable the sender so that his purpose cannot be accomplished.

26:8 *binds a stone in a sling.* A senseless act, for the stone should be free to fly from the sling.

10 *Like* an archer who wounds everyone,
So is he who hires a fool or who hires those who pass by.

11 *a*2 Pet. 2:22 *b*Ex. 8:15

11 Like *a*a dog that returns to its vomit
Is a fool who *b*repeats his folly.

12 *a*Prov. 3:7; 26:5 *b*Prov. 29:20

12 Do you see a man *a*wise in his own eyes?
*b*There is more hope for a fool than for him.

6 With sluggards, 26:13-16

★**13-16**

13 *a*Prov. 22:13

13 The *a*sluggard says, "There is a lion in the road! A lion is in the open square!"

14 *a*Prov. 6:9

14 *As* the door turns on its hinges,
So *does* the *a*sluggard on his bed.

15 *a*Prov. 19:24

15 The *a*sluggard buries his hand in the dish;
He is weary of bringing it to his mouth again.

16 *a*Prov. 27:11

16 The sluggard is *a*wiser in his own eyes
Than seven men who can give a discreet answer.

7 With gossips, 26:17-28

★**17-28**

★**17** *a*Prov. 3:30

17 *Like* one who takes a dog by the ears
Is he who passes by *and* meddles with *a*strife not belonging to him.

18 *a*Is. 50:11

18 Like a madman who throws
*a*Firebrands, arrows and death,

★**19** *a*Prov. 24:28 *b*Eph. 5:4

19 So is the man who *a*deceives his neighbor,

And says, "*b*Was I not joking?"

20 *a*Prov. 16:28 *b*Prov. 22:10

20 For lack of wood the fire goes out,
And where there is no *a*whisperer, *b*contention quiets down.

★**21** *a*Prov. 15:18; 29:22

21 *Like* charcoal to hot embers and wood to fire,
So is a *a*contentious man to kindle strife.

22 *a*Prov. 18:8

22 The *a*words of a whisperer are like dainty morsels,
And they go down into the innermost parts of the body.

★**23** *a*Matt. 23:27; Luke 11:39 *b*Prov. 25:4

23 *Like* an earthen *a*vessel overlaid with silver *b*dross
Are burning lips and a wicked heart.

★**24** *a*Ps. 41:6; Prov. 10:18 *b*Prov. 12:20

24 He who *a*hates disguises *it* with his lips,
But he lays up *b*deceit in his heart.

25 *a*Ps. 28:3; Prov. 26:23; Jer. 9:8

25 When he *a*speaks graciously, do not believe him,
For there are seven abominations in his heart.

★**26** *a*Matt. 23:28 *b*Luke 8:17

26 *Though his* hatred *a*covers itself with guile,
His wickedness will be *b*revealed before the assembly.

★**27** *a*Esth. 7:10; Prov. 28:10

27 He who *a*digs a pit will fall into it,
And he who rolls a stone, it will come back on him.

★**28** *a*Prov. 29:5

28 A lying tongue hates those it crushes,
And a *a*flattering mouth works ruin.

26:13-16 This section concerns the lazy person.
26:17-28 This section is about the scoundrel or mischievous person.
26:17 *meddles.* Lit., angers himself.
26:19 The person who makes a joke of his thoughtlessness is a dangerous person to be around.
26:21 The quarreler feeds the fires of contention.
26:23 *burning lips.* I.e., lips anxious to express

good. A false front may hide an ugly inner reality.
26:24 *disguises.* Pretends. He fakes it and waits for an opportune time to express his hatred.
26:26 Though a man may conceal his hatred, it will one day be exposed at a judicial assembly.
26:27 Ultimate retribution for evil is certain.
26:28 Those whose mouths are characterized by lies and flattery hate the victims they bring to ruin.

B Proverbs Concerning Actions, 27:1-29:27

1 In relation to life, 27:1-27

27 1 [a]Do not boast about tomorrow,
For you [b]do not know what a day may bring forth.

2 Let [a]another praise you, and not your own mouth;
A stranger, and not your own lips.

3 A stone is heavy and the sand weighty,
But the provocation of a fool is heavier than both of them.

4 Wrath is fierce and anger is a flood,
But [a]who can stand before jealousy?

5 Better is [a]open rebuke
Than love that is concealed.

6 Faithful are the [a]wounds of a friend,
But deceitful are the [b]kisses of an enemy.

7 A sated man loathes honey,
But to a famished man any bitter thing is sweet.

8 Like a [a]bird that wanders from her nest,
So is a man who [b]wanders from his home.

9 [a]Oil and perfume make the heart glad,
So a man's counsel is sweet to his friend.

10 Do not forsake your own [a]friend or [b]your father's friend,

And do not go to your brother's house in the day of your calamity;
Better is a neighbor who is near than a brother far away.

11 [a]Be wise, my son, and make my heart glad,
That I may [b]reply to him who reproaches me.

12 A prudent man sees evil and hides himself,
The naive proceed and pay the penalty.

13 [a]Take his garment when he becomes surety for a stranger;
And for an adulterous woman hold him in pledge.

14 [a]He who blesses his friend with a loud voice early in the morning,
It will be reckoned a curse to him.

15 A [a]constant dripping on a day of steady rain
And a contentious woman are alike;

16 He who would restrain her restrains the wind,
And grasps oil with his right hand.

17 Iron sharpens iron,
So one man sharpens another.

18 He who tends the [a]fig tree will eat its fruit;
And he who [b]cares for his master will be honored.

19 As in water face *reflects* face,
So the heart of man *reflects* man.

Cross references

1 [a]James 4:13-16 [b]Luke 12:19, 20; James 4:14
2 [a]Prov. 25:27; 2 Cor. 10:12, 18; 12:11
★ 3
4 [a]Prov. 6:34; 1 John 3:12
★ 5 [a]Prov. 28:23; Gal. 2:14
★ 6 [a]Ps. 141:5; Prov. 20:30 [b]Matt. 26:49
★ 7
8 [a]Prov. 26:2; Is. 16:2 [b]Gen. 21:14
9 [a]Ps. 23:5; 141:5
★10 [a]Prov. 18:24 [b]1 Kin. 12:6-8; 2 Chr. 10:6-8
★11 [a]Prov. 10:1; 23:15; 29:3 [b]Ps. 119:42
★13 [a]Prov. 20:16
14 [a]Ps. 122
15 [a]Prov. 19:13
★16
★17
18 [a]2 Kin. 18:31; Song 8:12; Is. 36:16; 1 Cor. 3:8; 9:7; 2 Tim. 2:6 [b]Luke 12:42-44; 19:17
★19

27:3 The anger that a fool provokes is almost unbearable.

27:5 Love that is concealed does not show itself in administering a needed reproof.

27:6 A loyal friend may correct an individual and the wounds will heal, while a deceitful enemy says sweet things that offer no real help.

27:7 While luxurious possessions may not satisfy, to those without them even cheap things look good.

27:10 The verse does not belittle a distant brother, but commends the close friend.

27:11 A master teacher desires the pupil to be wise so that no one will be able to criticize him as a poor teacher.

27:13 *surety.* I.e., one responsible for a debt should the borrower default.

27:16 The thought of the proverb is that it is impossible to hide or restrain the contentious woman (v. 15).

27:17 Social contacts have a stimulating effect on the mind and personality.

27:19 As water reflects the face, the heart of man reflects and reveals his inner person.

★20 aJob
26:6; Prov.
15:11 bProv.
30:15, 16;
Hab. 2:5
cEccl. 1:8;
4:8

20 aSheol and Abaddon are bnever satisfied,
Nor are the ceyes of man ever satisfied.

★21 aProv.
17:3 bLuke
6:26

21 The acrucible is for silver and the furnace for gold,
And a man bis tested by the praise accorded him.

★22 aProv.
23:35; 26:11;
Jer. 5:3

22 Though you apound a fool in a mortar with a pestle along with crushed grain,
Yet his folly will not depart from him.

★23-27
23 aJer.
31:10; Ezek.
34:12; John
10:3

24 aJob
19:9; Ps.
89:39; Jer.
13:18; Lam.
5:16; Ezek.
21:26

25 aIs. 17:5;
Jer. 40:10,
12

23 aKnow well the condition of your flocks,
And pay attention to your herds;

24 For riches are not forever,
Nor does a acrown endure to all generations.

25 When the grass disappears, the new growth is seen,
And the herbs of the mountains are agathered in,

26 The lambs will be for your clothing,
And the goats will bring the price of a field,

27 And there will be goats' milk enough for your food,
For the food of your household,
And sustenance for your maidens.

2 In relation to law, 28:1-10

★ 1 aLev.
26:17, 36;
Ps. 53:5

28 The wicked aflee when no one is pursuing,
But the righteous are bold as a lion.

2 By the transgression of a land amany are its princes,
But bby a man of understanding and knowledge, so it endures.

★ 2 a1 Kin.
16:8-28;
2 Kin. 15:8-
15 bProv.
11:11

3 A apoor man who oppresses the lowly
Is like a driving rain which leaves no food.

★ 3 aMatt.
18:28

4 Those who forsake the law apraise the wicked,
But those who keep the law bstrive with them.

★ 4 aPs.
49:18; Rom.
1:32 b1 Kin.
18:18; Neh.
13:11, 15;
Matt. 3:7;
14:4; Eph.
5:11
5 aPs. 92:6;
Is. 6:9; 44:18
bPs.
119:100;
Prov. 2:9;
John 7:17;
1 Cor. 2:15;
1 John 2:20,
27
6 aProv.
19:1

5 Evil men ado not understand justice,
But those who seek the LORD bunderstand all things.

6 aBetter is the poor who walks in his integrity,
Than he who is crooked though he be rich.

7 He who keeps the law is a discerning son,
But he who is a companion of agluttons humiliates his father.

★ 7 aProv.
23:20

8 He who increases his wealth by ainterest and usury,
Gathers it bfor him who is gracious to the poor.

★ 8 aEx.
22:25; Lev.
25:36 bJob
27:17; Prov.
13:22; 14:31

9 He who turns away his ear from listening to the law,
Even his aprayer is an abomination.

★ 9 aPs.
66:18; 109:7;
Prov. 15:8;
21:27

10 He who leads the upright astray in an evil way
Will ahimself fall into his own pit,
But the bblameless will inherit good.

10 aPs. 7:15;
Prov. 26:27
bMatt. 6:33;
Heb. 6:12;
1 Pet. 3:9

27:20 Sheol and Abaddon. See note on 15:11.
27:21 A man's response to praise is a test of his character. Self-depreciation may reflect false pride.
27:22 crushed grain. Better, grit.
27:23-27 The last verses of the chapter contain a brief treatise on the blessings of pastoral life and the sufficiency of God's provision.
28:1 bold. Lit., confident.
28:2 transgression of a land. I.e., national sin. National sin brings upheaval, but a wise ruler can bring national stability.
28:3 Oppression of the poor by obscure men is an absurd calamity, like rain that washes away crops instead of watering them.
28:4 One's attitude towards the law reflects one's attitude toward the wicked.
28:7 gluttons. Better, frivolous men.
28:8 The extortioner will lose his gains to a more just man who is kind to the poor.
28:9 Such hypocrisy is unacceptable to God.

3 In relation to wealth,
28:11-28

★11 aProv.
3:7; 26:5, 12

11 The rich man is ^awise in his own eyes,
But the poor who has understanding sees through him.

★12 aProv.
11:10; 29:2
bProv.
28:28; Eccl.
10:5, 6

12 When the ^arighteous triumph, there is great glory,
But ^bwhen the wicked rise, men hide themselves.

★13 aJob
31:33; Ps.
32:3 bPs.
32:5; 1 John
1:9

13 He who ^aconceals his transgressions will not prosper,
But he who ^bconfesses and forsakes *them* will find compassion.

★14 aProv.
23:17 bPs.
95:8; Rom.
2:5

14 How blessed is the man who ^afears always,
But he who ^bhardens his heart will fall into calamity.

15 aProv.
19:12; 1 Pet.
5:8 bEx.
1:14; Prov.
29:2; Matt.
2:16

15 *Like* a ^aroaring lion and a rushing bear
Is a ^bwicked ruler over a poor people.

16 aEccl.
10:16; Is.
3:12

16 A ^aleader who is a great oppressor lacks understanding,
But he who hates unjust gain will prolong *his* days.

★17 aGen.
9:6; Ex.
21:14

17 A man who is ^aladen with the guilt of human blood
Will be a fugitive until death; let no one support him.

18 aProv.
10:27

18 He who walks blamelessly will be delivered,
But he who is ^acrooked will fall all at once.

19 aProv.
12:11 bProv.
20:13

19 ^aHe who tills his land will ^bhave plenty of food,

But he who follows empty *pursuits* will have poverty in plenty.

20 A ^afaithful man will abound with blessings,
But he who ^bmakes haste to be rich will not go unpunished.

★20 aProv.
10:6; Matt.
24:45; 25:21
bProv.
20:21; 28:22;
1 Tim. 6:9

21 To ^ashow partiality is not good,
^bBecause for a piece of bread a man will transgress.

★21 aProv.
24:23 bEzek.
13:19

22 A man with an ^aevil eye ^bhastens after wealth,
And does not know that want will come upon him.

★22 aProv.
23:6 bProv.
21:5

23 He who ^arebukes a man will afterward find *more* favor
Than he who ^bflatters with the tongue.

23 aProv.
27:5, 6
bProv. 29:5

24 He who ^arobs his father or his mother,
And says, "It is not a transgression,"
Is the ^bcompanion of a man who destroys.

24 aProv.
19:26 bProv.
18:9

25 An arrogant man ^astirs up strife,
But he who ^btrusts in the Lord ^cwill prosper.

25 aProv.
15:18 bProv.
29:25; 1 Tim.
6:6 cProv.
11:25

26 He who ^atrusts in his own heart is a fool,
But he who walks wisely will be delivered.

26 aProv.
3:5

27 He who ^agives to the poor will never want,
But he who shuts his eyes will have many curses.

27 aProv.
11:24; 19:17

28 When the wicked rise, men hide themselves;
But when they perish, the righteous increase.

28:11 *sees through him.* I.e., examines him and makes an accurate evaluation of his knowledge.
28:12 *triumph.* Lit., exult. *men hide themselves.* Lit., men will be searched for; i.e., will be hidden. The righteous will hide from their wicked rulers.
28:13 *conceals.* I.e., refuses to admit his guilt (cf. Psalm 32:5).

28:14 *fears always.* I.e., fears sin and its consequences.
28:17 A murderer can find no escape until he dies.
28:20 Hastily acquired wealth usually comes through dishonest dealings.
28:21 For the smallest bribe some men will depart from strict justice.
28:22 *evil eye.* Selfish motives.

4 In relation to stubbornness, 29:1-27

29 A man who hardens *his* neck after ᵃmuch reproof
Will ᵇsuddenly be broken beyond remedy.

2 When the ᵃrighteous increase, the people rejoice,
But when a wicked man rules, people groan.

3 A man who ᵃloves wisdom makes his father glad,
But he who ᵇkeeps company with harlots wastes *his* wealth.

4 The ᵃking gives stability to the land by justice,
But a man who takes bribes overthrows it.

5 A man who ᵃflatters his neighbor
Is spreading a net for his steps.

6 By transgression an evil man is ᵃensnared,
But the righteous ᵇsings and rejoices.

7 The ᵃrighteous is concerned for the rights of the poor,
The wicked does not understand *such* concern.

8 Scorners ᵃset a city aflame,
But ᵇwise men turn away anger.

9 When a wise man has a controversy with a foolish man,
The foolish man either rages or laughs, and there is no rest.

10 Men of ᵃbloodshed hate the blameless,
But the upright are concerned for his life.

11 A ᵃfool always loses his temper,
But a ᵇwise man holds it back.

12 If a ᵃruler pays attention to falsehood,
All his ministers *become* wicked.

13 The ᵃpoor man and the oppressor have this in common:
The LORD gives ᵇlight to the eyes of both.

14 If a ᵃking judges the poor with truth,
His ᵇthrone will be established forever.

15 The ᵃrod and reproof give wisdom,
But a child who gets his own way ᵇbrings shame to his mother.

16 When the wicked increase, transgression increases;
But the ᵃrighteous will see their fall.

17 ᵃCorrect your son, and he will give you comfort;
He will also ᵇdelight your soul.

18 Where there is ᵃno vision, the people ᵇare unrestrained,
But ᶜhappy is he who keeps the law.

19 A slave will not be instructed by words *alone*;
For though he understands, there will be no response.

Marginal references

1 ᵃ1 Sam. 2:25; 2 Chr. 36:16; Prov. 1:24-31 ᵇProv. 6:15

★ **2** ᵃEsth. 8:15; Prov. 11:10; 28:12

3 ᵃProv. 10:1; 15:20; 27:11; 28:7 ᵇProv. 5:10; 6:26; Luke 15:30

4 ᵃ2 Chr. 9:8; Prov. 8:15; 29:14

★ **5** ᵃPs. 5:9

★ **6** ᵃProv. 22:5; Eccl. 9:12 ᵇEx. 15:1

★ **7** ᵃJob 29:16; Ps. 41:1; Prov. 31:8, 9

★ **8** ᵃProv. 11:11 ᵇProv. 16:14

★ **9**

★**10** ᵃGen. 4:5-8; 1 John 3:12

11 ᵃProv. 12:16; 14:33 ᵇProv. 19:11

12 ᵃ1 Kin. 12:14

★**13** ᵃProv. 22:2 ᵇEzra 9:8; Ps. 13:3

14 ᵃPs. 72:4; Is. 11:4 ᵇProv. 16:12; 25:5

15 ᵃProv. 13:24; 22:15 ᵇProv. 10:1; 17:25

★**16** ᵃPs. 37:34, 36; 58:10; 91:8; 92:11; Prov. 21:12

17 ᵃProv. 13:24; 29:15 ᵇProv. 10:1

★**18** ᵃ1 Sam. 3:1; Ps. 74:9; Amos 8:11, 12 ᵇEx. 32:25 ᶜPs. 1:1, 2; 106:3; 119:2; Prov. 8:32; John 13:17

★**19**

29:2 *increase.* Lit., become great.
29:5 *his steps.* Probably his own steps.
29:6 The trap set for the ruin of another often ensnares the schemer.
29:7 Lit., But the wicked does not understand knowledge. The righteous recognize the claims of the poor, but the godless have no knowledge with which to comprehend such claims.
29:8 *set a city aflame.* Lit., blow a city; i.e., stir up the city to the point of disorder.
29:9 *rest.* I.e., calmness. A controversy with a

fool is rarely a calm matter.
29:10 Better, . . . and as for the upright, they seek his life.
29:13 God's blessing of life *(light to the eyes)* is common to both the oppressor and the poor.
29:16 The righteous will outlive the wicked and see their fall.
29:18 *vision.* I.e., prophetic revelation. Without prophetic revelation from God people are unrestrained and fall under judgment.
29:19 It will take more than words to correct a stubborn servant.

20 *a*James
1:19 *b*Prov.
26:12

20 Do you see a man who is
 *a*hasty in his words?
There is *b*more hope for a
 fool than for him.

★21

21 He who pampers his slave
 from childhood
Will in the end find him to
 be a son.

22 *a*Prov.
15:18; 26:21

22 An *a*angry man stirs up
 strife,
And a hot-tempered man
 abounds in transgres-
 sion.

23 *a*Prov.
11:2; 16:18;
Dan. 4:30,
31; Matt.
23:12; James
4:6 *b*Prov.
15:33; 18:12;
22:4; Is.
66:2; Luke
14:11; 18:14;
James 4:10

24 *a*Lev. 5:1

★25 *a*Gen.
12:12; 20:2;
Luke 12:4;
John 12:42,
43 *b*Ps.
91:1-16;
Prov. 18:10;
28:25

26 *a*Prov.
19:6 *b*Is.
49:4; 1 Cor.
4:4

27 *a*Ps. 6:8;
139:21, 22;
Prov. 12:8
*b*Ps. 69:4;
Prov. 29:10;
Matt. 10:22;
24:9; John
15:18; 17:14;
1 John 3:13

23 A man's *a*pride will bring
 him low,
But a *b*humble spirit will
 obtain honor.

24 He who is a partner with a
 thief hates his own
 life;
He *a*hears the oath but
 tells nothing.

25 The *a*fear of man brings a
 snare,
But he who *b*trusts in the
 LORD will be exalted.

26 *a*Many seek the ruler's favor,
But *b*justice for man *comes*
 from the LORD.

27 An *a*unjust man is abominable to the righteous,
And he who is *b*upright in
 the way is abominable
 to the wicked.

V THE WORDS OF AGUR, 30:1-33

A Personal Words, 30:1-14

★ 1

2 *a*Ps.
49:10; 73:22;
Prov. 12:1

30 The words of Agur the son
of Jakeh, the oracle.
The man declares to Ithiel, to

★ 2-4

Ithiel and Ucal:
 2 Surely I am more *a*stupid
  than any man,

And I do not have the un-
 derstanding of a man.

3 Neither have I learned wisdom,
Nor do I have the *a*knowledge of the Holy One.

3 *a*Prov.
9:10

4 Who has *a*ascended into
 heaven and de-
 scended?
Who has gathered the
 *b*wind in His fists?
Who has *c*wrapped the
 waters in His gar-
 ment?
Who has *d*established all
 the ends of the earth?
What is His *e*name or His
 son's name?
Surely you know!

★ 4 *a*Ps.
68:18; John
3:13; Eph.
4:8 *b*Ex.
15:10; Ps.
135:7 *c*Job
26:8; 38:8, 9
*d*Ps. 24:2; Is.
45:18 *e*Rev.
19:12

5 Every *a*word of God is
 tested;
He is a *b*shield to those
 who take refuge in
 Him.

5 *a*Ps. 12:6;
18:30 *b*Ps.
3:3; 84:11;
Prov. 2:7

6 *a*Do not add to His words
Lest He reprove you, and
 you be proved a liar.

★ 6 *a*Deut.
4:2; 12:32;
Rev. 22:18

7 Two things I asked of
 Thee,
Do not refuse me before I
 die:

★ 7-9

8 Keep deception and lies far
 from me,
Give me neither poverty
 nor riches;
Feed me with the *a*food
 that is my portion,

8 *a*Job
23:12; Matt.
6:11

9 Lest I be *a*full and deny
 *b*Thee and say, "Who
 is the LORD?"
Or lest I be *c*in want and
 steal,
And *d*profane the name of
 my God.

9 *a*Deut.
8:12; 31:20;
Neh. 9:25;
Hos. 13:6
*b*Josh.
24:27; Job
31:28 *c*Prov.
6:30 *d*Ex.
20:7

29:21 The warning is clear but the prediction is elusive. The thought perhaps is that a pampered slave will become as an heir of the house, conducting himself as though he were free.

29:25 *exalted.* Better, be set securely on high. Man's fear is overcome by confidence in God.

30:1 Chapter 30 was authored by Agur ("gatherer"), whom the early rabbis and church fathers identified as Solomon; however, there is no factual basis for this suggestion. It is a pro-

phetic declaration giving lessons on wisdom.

30:2-4 Agur reflects on man's inability to comprehend the infinite God.

30:4 Man is not able to penetrate the depths of God's nature and ways.

30:6 Supplementing God's Word with man's speculations is foolish business.

30:7-9 Agur prays for good character and for circumstances which will not endanger that character.

10 aEccl.
7:21

10 Do not slander a slave to
his master,
Lest he ^acurse you and you
be found guilty.

★11-14

11 aEx.
21:17; Prov.
20:20

11 There is a kind of *man*
who ^acurses his father,
And does not bless his
mother.

12 aProv.
16:2; Is.
65:5; Luke
18:11; Titus
1:15, 16

12 There is a kind who is
^apure in his own eyes,
Yet is not washed from his
filthiness.

13 aProv.
6:17; Is.
2:11; 5:15

13 There is a kind—oh how
^alofty are his eyes!
And his eyelids are raised
in arrogance.

14 aPs. 57:4
bJob 29:17
cPs. 14:4;
Amos 8:4

14 There is a kind of *man*
whose ^ateeth are *like*
swords,
And his ^bjaw teeth *like*
knives,
To ^cdevour the afflicted
from the earth,
And the needy from
among men.

B Numerical Proverbs, 30:15-33

★15

15 The leech has two daugh-
ters,
"Give," "Give."
There are three things that
will not be satisfied,
Four that will not say,
"Enough":

16 aProv.
27:20 bGen.
30:1

16 ^aSheol, and the ^bbarren
womb,
Earth that is never satisfied
with water,
And fire that never says,
"Enough."

★17 aGen.
9:22 bProv.
15:20 cDeut.
28:26

17 The eye that ^amocks a father,
And ^bscorns a mother,

The ^cravens of the valley
will pick it out,
And the young ^ceagles will
eat it.

18 There are three things
which are too won-
derful for me,
Four which I do not understand:

19 The way of an ^aeagle in
the sky,
The way of a serpent on a
rock,
The way of a ship in the
middle of the sea,
And the way of a man
with a maid.

19 aDeut.
28:49; Jer.
48:40; 49:22

20 This is the way of an
^aadulterous woman:
She eats and wipes her
mouth,
And says, "I have done no
wrong."

20 aProv.
5:6

21 Under three things the
earth quakes,
And under four, it cannot
bear up:

★21-23

22 Under a ^aslave when he
becomes king,
And a fool when he is satisfied with food,

22 aProv.
19:10; Eccl.
10:7

23 Under an unloved woman
when she gets a hus-
band,
And a maidservant when
she supplants her mis-
tress.

★23

24 Four things are small on
the earth,
But they are exceedingly
wise:

★24-28

25 The ^aants are not a strong
folk,
But they prepare their food
in the summer;

25 aProv.
6:6

30:11-14 A picture of four kinds of evil men: the disrespectful, the hypocrite, the proud, and the greedy.

30:15 "Give" and "Give" are the names of the two daughters.

30:17 The judgment is that the body will lie unburied for the birds to feed on (cf. Deut. 28:26).

30:21-23 Four unbearable things are cited.

30:23 *unloved.* Lit., hated; i.e., an unpleasant woman.

30:24-28 Four small creatures which manifest wisdom. Ants have foresight to make provision; badgers find protective shelter; locusts have an ordered *(in ranks)* community; and the lizard is bold and fearless.

26 aLev. 11:5; Ps. 104:18

26 The ^abadgers are not mighty folk,
Yet they make their houses in the rocks;

27 aJoel 2:7

27 The locusts have no king,
Yet all of them go out in ^aranks;

28 The lizard you may grasp with the hands,
Yet it is in kings' palaces.

★29-31

29 There are three things which are stately in *their* march,
Even four which are stately when they walk:

30 aJudg. 14:18; 2 Sam. 1:23 bMic. 5:8

30 The lion *which* is ^amighty among beasts
And does not ^bretreat before any,

★31

31 The strutting cock, the male goat also,
And a king *when his* army is with him.

32 aJob 21:5; 40:4; Mic. 7:16

32 If you have been foolish in exalting yourself
Or if you have plotted *evil*, ^aput *your* hand on your mouth.

★33 aProv. 10:12; 29:22

33 For the churning of milk produces butter,
And pressing the nose brings forth blood;
So the churning of ^aanger produces strife.

VI THE WORDS OF LEMUEL, 31:1-9

★ 1-9

31 The words of King Lemuel, the oracle which his mother taught him.

2 What, O my son?
And what, O ^ason of my womb?
And what, O son of my ^bvows?

★ 2 aIs. 49:15 b1 Sam. 1:11

3 ^aDo not give your strength to women,
Or your ways to that which ^bdestroys kings.

★ 3 aProv. 5:9 bDeut. 17:17; 1 Kin. 11:1; Neh. 13:26

4 It is not for ^akings, O Lemuel,
It is not for kings to ^bdrink wine,
Or for rulers to desire strong drink,

★ 4-7

4 aEccl. 10:17 bProv. 20:1; Is. 5:22; Hos. 4:11

5 Lest they drink and forget what is decreed,
And ^apervert the rights of all the afflicted.

5 aEx. 23:6; Deut. 16:19; Prov. 17:15

6 Give strong drink to him who is ^aperishing,
And wine to him ^bwhose life is bitter.

★ 6-7

6 aJob 29:13 bJob 3:20; Is. 38:15

7 Let him drink and forget his poverty,
And remember his trouble no more.

8 ^aOpen your mouth for the dumb,
For the rights of all the unfortunate.

★ 8 aJob 29:12-17; Ps. 82

9 Open your mouth, ^ajudge righteously,
And defend the ^brights of the afflicted and needy.

9 aLev. 19:15; Deut. 1:16 bIs. 1:17; Jer. 22:16

VII THE CAPABLE WIFE, 31:10-31

★10-31 ★10 aRuth 3:11; Prov. 12:4; 19:14 bJob 28:18; Prov. 8:11

10 An ^aexcellent wife, who can find?

30:29-31 Four creatures that manifest dignity when they march.
30:31 The exhortation is to desist from evil.
30:33 One tempted to anger must exercise self-restraint in light of the certain results.
31:1-9 This section, and perhaps the acrostic poem that follows (vv. 10-31), is attributed to King Lemuel, of whom nothing is known. Some have suggested that Lemuel ("belonging to God") was Bathsheba's name for Solomon, but this is just a guess.
31:2 *son of my vows.* Lemuel was granted to his mother in response to her vows (cf. 1 Sam. 1:11).
31:3 Lemuel's mother warns against immorality and neglect of the affairs of state.

31:4-7 The king's mother warns against intemperance (see note on Lev. 10:9).
31:6-7 The verses do not condone intoxication but indicate the medicinal use of alcohol in ancient times.
31:8 *the dumb.* I.e., those unable to plead their own case.
31:10-31 The description of the worthy woman is an acrostic poem exalting the honor and dignity of womanhood. It may be by Lemuel or be an anonymous appendix to the book.
31:10 *excellent.* The adjective is used in different contexts with reference to strength, ability, efficiency, wealth, and valor. She is in every way an excellent woman. *jewels* = corals.

For her worth is far *b*above jewels.

11 The heart of her husband trusts in her,
And he will have no lack of gain.

12 She does him good and not evil
All the days of her life.

13 She looks for wool and flax,
And works with her hands in delight.

14 *aEzek. 27:25*

14 She is like *a*merchant ships;
She brings her food from afar.

15 *aProv. 20:13; Rom. 12:11 bLuke 12:42*

15 She *a*rises also while it is still night,
And *b*gives food to her household,
And portions to her maidens.

16 She considers a field and buys it;
From her earnings she plants a vineyard.

★17 *a1 Kin. 18:46; 2 Kin. 4:29; Job 38:3*

17 She *a*girds herself with strength,
And makes her arms strong.

★18

18 She senses that her gain is good;
Her lamp does not go out at night.

19 She stretches out her hands to the distaff,
And her hands grasp the spindle.

20 *aDeut. 15:11; Job 31:16-20; Prov. 22:9; Rom. 12:13; Eph. 4:28*

20 She *a*extends her hand to the poor;
And she stretches out her hands to the needy.

★21 *a2 Sam. 1:24*

21 She is not afraid of the snow for her household,
For all her household are *a*clothed with scarlet.

22 *aProv. 7:16 bGen. 41:42; Rev. 19:8, 14 cJudg. 8:26; Luke 16:19*

22 She makes *a*coverings for herself;
Her clothing is *b*fine linen and *c*purple.

★23 *aDeut. 16:18; Ruth 4:1, 11*

23 Her husband is known *a*in the gates,
When he sits among the elders of the land.

24 *aJudg. 14:12*

24 She makes *a*linen garments and sells *them,*
And supplies belts to the tradesmen.

★25 *a1 Tim. 2:9, 10*

25 Strength and *a*dignity are her clothing,
And she smiles at the future.

26 *aProv. 10:31*

26 She *a*opens her mouth in wisdom,
And the teaching of kindness is on her tongue.

★27 *aProv. 19:15*

27 She looks well to the ways of her household,
And does not eat the *a*bread of idleness.

28 Her children rise up and bless her;
Her husband *also,* and he praises her, *saying:*

29 "Many daughters have done nobly,
But you excel them all."

★30 *aPs. 112:1; Prov. 22:4*

30 Charm is deceitful and beauty is vain,
But a woman who *a*fears the LORD, she shall be praised.

31 Give her the product of her hands,
And let her works praise her in the gates.

31:17 *makes her arms strong.* I.e., works hard.
31:18 She works late into the night.
31:21 *scarlet.* I.e., the best material.
31:23 *gates.* The place in the city where the elders sat to judge and discuss local affairs (see note on Ruth 4:1).
31:25 She has no anxiety, for her family is well taken care of.
31:27 She is energetic and always occupied.
31:30 The key to her beautiful character is her spiritual life. She is a godly woman who fears the Lord (see note on 1:7). Thus the book ends as it began, stressing the importance of reverence for God.

INTRODUCTION TO
THE BOOK OF ECCLESIASTES

AUTHOR: Solomon   DATE: c. 935 B.C.

Title   *The Hebrew title is Qoheleth, which means "one who convenes and speaks at an assembly" or "an ecclesiastic" or "preacher." The Greek equivalent, ecclesiastes, also means "preacher" and is derived from the word "assembly."*

Authorship   *While not specified as Solomon, the author identifies himself as "the son of David, king in Jerusalem" (1:1). References in the book to the author's unrivaled wisdom (1:16), unequalled wealth (2:7), opportunities for pleasure (2:3), and extensive building activities (2:4-6) all point to Solomon, since no other descendant of David measured up to such specifications. Jewish tradition explicitly stated that Solomon was the author.*
  Following the lead of Martin Luther, many have abandoned the traditional view of the Solomonic authorship of this book, feeling that it was written after the Exile by an unknown author who used Solomon as his central character. Linguistic evidence is said to demand a postexilic date, but such evidence is inconclusive. Fragments of Ecclesiastes found at Qumran rule out any date later than 150 B.C.

Message   *The message of the book may be stated in the form of three propositions. (1) When you look at life with its seemingly aimless cycles (1:4ff.) and inexplicable paradoxes (4:1; 7:15; 8:8), you might conclude that all is futile, since it is impossible to discern any purpose in the ordering of events. (2) Nevertheless, life is to be enjoyed to the fullest, realizing that it is the gift of God (3:12-13; 3:22; 5:18-19; 8:15; 9:7-9). (3) The wise man will live his life in obedience to God, recognizing that God will eventually judge all men (3:16-17; 12:14).*
  Verses frequently quoted from the book include 1:2; 3:1; 4:12b; 11:1; 12:1, 13.

OUTLINE OF ECCLESIASTES

THE BOOK OF ECCLESIASTES

I PROLOGUE: THE AUTHOR AND THESIS, 1:1-3

★ 1 aEccl. 1:12; 7:27; 12:8-10

1 The words of the aPreacher, the son of David, king in Jerusalem.

★ 2 aPs. 39:5, 6; 62:9; 144:4; Eccl. 12:8; Rom. 8:20

2 "aVanity of vanities," says the Preacher, "Vanity of vanities! All is vanity."

★ 3 aEccl. 2:11; 3:9; 5:16

3 aWhat advantage does man have in all his work Which he does under the sun?

II THE THESIS DEMONSTRATED, 1:4-2:26

A The Futility of the Cycles of Life, 1:4-11

★ 4-11

4 aPs. 104:5; 119:90

4 A generation goes and a generation comes, But the aearth remains forever.

5 aPs. 19:6

5 Also, athe sun rises and the sun sets; And hastening to its place it rises there again.

6 aEccl. 11:5; John 3:8

6 aBlowing toward the south, Then turning toward the north, The wind continues swirling along; And on its circular courses the wind returns.

7 All the rivers flow into the sea, Yet the sea is not full.

To the place where the rivers flow, There they flow again.

8 aProv. 27:20; Eccl. 4:8

8 All things are wearisome; Man is not able to tell *it.* aThe eye is not satisfied with seeing, Nor is the ear filled with hearing.

9 aEccl. 1:10; 2:12; 3:15; 6:10

9 aThat which has been is that which will be, And that which has been done is that which will be done. So, there is nothing new under the sun.

10 Is there anything of which one might say, "See this, it is new"? Already it has existed for ages Which were before us.

★11 aEccl. 2:16; 9:5

11 There is ano remembrance of earlier things; And also of the later things which will occur, There will be for them no remembrance Among those who will come later *still.*

B The Futility of Human Wisdom, 1:12-18

12 aEccl. 1:1; 7:27; 12:8-10

12 I, the aPreacher, have been king over Israel in Jerusalem.

13 aEccl. 1:17 bEccl. 3:10, 11; 7:25; 8:17 cEccl. 2:23, 26; 3:10; 4:8

13 And I aset my mind to seek and bexplore by wisdom concerning all that has been done under heaven. *It* is a grievous

---

1:1 *the Preacher.* Solomon repeatedly uses this appellation to refer to himself. It designates him as one who convenes and speaks at an assembly, an assembler. He addresses an assembly of wise men who, in ancient Israel, were one media that God used to communicate His truth to man (Jer. 18:18).

1:2 *Vanity of vanities . . . All is vanity.* The thesis of the utter futility of all things is developed in 1:3-11 and throughout the book. This thesis accords with Rom. 8:20-22 (see note there). Creation is subject to futility because of sin (Gen. 3:17-18).

1:3 *What advantage.* There is no guarantee of positive benefit from man's work. *under the sun.* A figure of speech (metonymy) in which the location is named instead of the thing. Used repeatedly, it simply means the earth where man dwells, which is under the sun.

1:4-11 The endless cycles of God's natural creation illustrate the monotonous futility of all things.

1:11 Even memories of man's past and future efforts to attain worthwhile accomplishments are soon forgotten.

c task *which* God has given to the sons of men to be afflicted with.

14 I have seen all the works which have been done under the sun, and behold, all is a vanity and striving after wind.

15 What is a crooked cannot be straightened, and what is lacking cannot be counted.

16 I said to myself, "Behold, I have magnified and increased a wisdom more than all who were over Jerusalem before me; and my mind has observed a wealth of wisdom and knowledge."

17 And I a set my mind to know wisdom and to b know madness and folly; I realized that this also is c striving after wind.

18 Because a in much wisdom there is much grief, and increasing knowledge *results in* increasing pain.

C   The Futility of Pleasure and Wealth, 2:1-11

2 I said to myself, "Come now, I will test you with a pleasure. So enjoy yourself." And behold, it too was futility.

2 a I said of laughter, "It is madness," and of pleasure, "What does it accomplish?"

3 I explored with my mind *how* to a stimulate my body with wine while my mind was guiding *me* wisely, and how to take hold of b folly, until I could see c what good there is for the sons of men to do under heaven the few years of their lives.

4 I enlarged my works: I a built houses for myself, I planted b vineyards for myself;

5 I made a gardens and b parks for myself, and I planted in them all kinds of fruit trees;

6 I made a ponds of water for myself from which to irrigate a forest of growing trees.

7 I bought male and female slaves, and I had a homeborn slaves. Also I possessed flocks and b herds larger than all who preceded me in Jerusalem.

8 Also, I collected for myself silver and a gold, and the treasure of kings and provinces. I provided for myself b male and female singers and the pleasures of men— many concubines.

9 Then I became a great and increased more than all who preceded me in Jerusalem. My wisdom also stood by me.

10 And a all that my eyes desired I did not refuse them. I did not withhold my heart from any pleasure, for my heart was pleased because of all my labor and this was my b reward for all my labor.

11 Thus I considered all my activities which my hands had done and the labor which I had exerted, and behold all was a vanity and striving after wind and there was b no profit under the sun.

D   The Futility of Materialism, 2:12-23

12 So I turned to a consider wisdom, madness and folly, for what *will* the man *do* who will come after the king *except* b what has already been done?

13 And I saw that a wisdom excels folly as light excels darkness.

Margin references

★14 ^aEccl. 2:11, 17; 4:4; 6:9

★15 ^aEccl. 7:13

16 ^a1 Kin. 3:12; 4:30; 10:23; Eccl. 2:9

★17-18
17 ^aEccl. 1:13; 7:25 ^bEccl. 2:12; 7:25 ^cEccl. 1:14; 2:11, 17, 28; 4:4, 6, 16; 6:9

18 ^aEccl. 2:23; 12:12

★1-11
1 ^aEccl. 7:4; 8:15

2 ^aProv. 14:13; Eccl. 7:3, 6

★ 3 ^aJudg. 9:13; Ps. 104:15; Eccl. 10:19 ^bEccl. 7:25 ^cEccl. 2:24; 3:12, 13; 5:18; 6:12; 8:15; 12:13

4 ^a1 Kin. 7:1-12 ^bSong 8:11

5 ^aSong 4:16; 5:1 ^bNeh. 2:8

6 ^aNeh. 2:14; 3:15, 16

★ 7 ^aGen. 14:14; 15:3 ^b1 Kin. 4:23

8 ^a1 Kin. 9:28; 10:10, 14, 21 ^b2 Sam. 19:35

9 ^a1 Chr. 29:25; Eccl. 1:16

10 ^aEccl. 6:2 ^bEccl. 3:22; 5:18; 9:9

11 ^aEccl. 1:14; 2:22, 23 ^bEccl. 1:3; 3:9; 5:16

★12 ^aEccl. 1:17 ^bEccl. 1:9, 10; 3:15

13 ^aEccl. 7:11, 12, 19; 9:18; 10:10

1:14 *striving after wind.* I.e., futile activity.
1:15 Life is full of paradoxes that cannot be solved.
1:17-18 Solomon found that even great wisdom was ineffective in easing life's frustrations. It simply enabled him more clearly to discern the futility.
2:1-11 Solomon's pursuit of fulfillment through indulgence (2:1-3), achievements (2:4-6), pos-

sessions and wealth (2:7-8), and great fame (2:9) all failed to bring enduring satisfaction (cf. 1 Kings 4:21-28; 2 Chron. 9:13-28).
2:3 *sons of men.* Used repeatedly in Eccles. for human beings in general.
2:7 *flocks and herds.* I.e., oxen, sheep, and goats.
2:12 Solomon's successor may take up the same issues, but will not arrive at any better solutions to the paradoxes of life.

★14 a1 John
2:11 bPs.
49:10; Eccl.
3:19; 6:6;
7:2; 9:2, 3

14   The wise man's eyes are in his head, but the a fool walks in darkness. And yet I know that b one fate befalls them both.

15 aEccl.
2:16 bEccl.
6:8, 11

15   Then I said to myself, "a As is the fate of the fool, it will also befall me. b Why then have I been extremely wise?" So I said to myself, "This too is vanity."

16 aEccl.
1:11; 9:5
bEccl. 2:14

16   For there is a no lasting remembrance of the wise man as with the fool, inasmuch as in the coming days all will be forgotten. And b how the wise man and the fool alike die!

17 aEccl.
4:2, 3

17   So I a hated life, for the work which had been done under the sun was grievous to me; because everything is futility and striving after wind.

18 aEccl.
1:3; 2:11
bPs. 39:6;
49:10

18   Thus I hated a all the fruit of my labor for which I had labored under the sun, for I must b leave it to the man who will come after me.

19 a1 Kin.
12:13
b1 Tim. 6:10

19   And who knows whether he will be a wise man or a a fool? Yet he will have control over all the fruit of my labor for which I have labored by acting wisely under the sun. This too is b vanity.

★20

20   Therefore I completely despaired of all the fruit of my labor for which I had labored under the sun.

21 aEccl. 4:4
bEccl. 2:18

21   When there is a man who has labored with wisdom, knowledge and a skill, then he b gives his legacy to one who has not labored with them. This too is vanity and a great evil.

22 aEccl.
1:3; 2:11

22   For what does a man get in a all his labor and in his striving with which he labors under the sun?

23   Because all his days his task is painful and a grievous; even at night his mind b does not rest. This too is vanity.

23 aJob 5:7;
14:1; Eccl.
1:18; 5:17
bPs. 127:2

E   Conclusion: Enjoy and Be Content with the Providences of God, 2:24-26

24   There is a nothing better for a man than to eat and drink and tell himself that his labor is good. This also I have seen, that it is b from the hand of God.

25   For who can eat and who can have enjoyment without Him?

26   For to a person who is good in His sight a He has given wisdom and knowledge and joy, while to the sinner He has given the task of gathering and collecting so that he may b give to one who is good in God's sight. This too is c vanity and striving after wind.

★24 aEccl.
2:3; 3:12, 13,
22; 5:18;
6:12; 8:15;
9:7; Is.
56:12; Luke
12:19; 1 Cor.
15:32; 1 Tim.
6:17 bEccl.
3:13

★25

26 aJob
32:8; Prov.
2:6 bJob
27:16, 17;
Prov. 13:22
cEccl. 1:14

III   GOD'S DESIGN FOR LIFE, 3:1-22

A   He Gives Life's Order of Events, 3:1-11

3 There is an appointed time for everything. And there is a a time for every event under heaven—

★ 1-8

1 aEccl.
3:17; 8:6

2   A time to give birth, and a a time to die;

★ 2-3
2 aJob
14:5; Heb.
9:27

2:14 Both the wise and foolish man eventually meet death and are forgotten, even though in life the wise man has an advantage.

2:20 *I completely despaired.* I.e., I turned aside to contemplate the futility of my laborious efforts and despaired over the situation. Solomon despaired over leaving the results of his labor to another (2:18-21) and over the absence of gratifying reward for his work (2:22-23).

2:24 Solomon's solution to the paradoxes of life, set forth six times (3:12-13; 3:22; 5:18-19; 8:15; 9:7-9), is to enjoy to the fullest the life that God has given, recognizing it as His gift. God has not revealed the solution to all of life's inconsistencies, but has given man a life to enjoy while living in obedience to Him. This is vastly different from the solution of the Epicurean sensualists, "Let us eat, drink, and be merry, for tomorrow we die." Solomon advises that one's life must be regulated by an awareness of future divine judgment (12:14).

2:25 There is no enjoyment in life apart from God.

3:1-8 Solomon ponders the sovereign design of God (3:1-22) and concludes that all the events of life are divinely appointed.

3:2-3 Giving and taking life are God's prerogatives (Deut. 32:39). He has, however, given man corporate responsibility to carry out capital punishment in the case of murder (Gen. 9:6).

A time to plant, and a time to uproot what is planted.

3   A [a]time to kill, and a time to heal;
A time to tear down, and a time to build up.

4   A time to [a]weep, and a time to [b]laugh;
A time to mourn, and a time to [c]dance.

5   A time to throw stones, and a time to gather stones;
A time to embrace, and a time to shun embracing.

6   A time to search, and a time to give up as lost;
A time to keep, and a time to throw away.

7   A time to tear apart, and a time to sew together;
A time to [a]be silent, and a time to speak.

8   A time to love, and a time to [a]hate;
A time for war, and a time for peace.

9   [a]What profit is there to the worker from that in which he toils?

10 I have seen the [a]task which God has given the sons of men with which to occupy themselves.

11 He has [a]made everything appropriate in its time. He has also set eternity in their heart, yet so that man [b]will not find out the work which God has done from the beginning even to the end.

B He Gives the Good Gifts of Life, 3:12-13

12 I know that there is [a]nothing better for them than to rejoice and to do good in one's lifetime;
13 moreover, that every man who eats and drinks sees good in all his labor—it is the [a]gift of God.

C He Gives the Perspective of Future Judgment, 3:14-21

14 I know that everything God does will remain forever; there is nothing to add to it and there is nothing to take from it, for God has so worked that men should [a]fear Him.
15 That [a]which is has been already, and that which will be has already been, for God seeks what has passed by.
16 Furthermore, I have seen under the sun that in the place of justice there is [a]wickedness, and in the place of righteousness there is wickedness.
17 I said to myself, "[a]God will judge both the righteous man and the wicked man," for a [b]time for every matter and for every deed is there.
18 I said to myself concerning the sons of men, "God has surely tested them in order for them to see that they are but [a]beasts."
19 [a]For the fate of the sons of men and the fate of beasts is the same. As one dies so dies the other; indeed, they all have the same

---

Side references (left column):

3 [a]Gen. 9:6; 1 Sam. 2:6; Hos. 6:1, 2

★ **4** [a]Rom. 12:15 [b]Ps. 126:2 [c]Ex. 15:20

★ **5**

★ **7** [a]Amos 5:13

★ **8** [a]Ps. 101:3; Prov. 13:5

9 [a]Eccl. 1:3; 2:11; 5:16

10 [a]Eccl. 1:13; 2:26

★ **11** [a]Gen. 1:31 [b]Job 5:9; Eccl. 7:23; 8:17; Rom. 11:33

Side references (right column):

★ **12-14**
12 [a]Eccl. 2:24
13 [a]Eccl. 2:24; 5:19

14 [a]Eccl. 5:7; 7:18; 8:12, 13; 12:13

★ **15** [a]Eccl. 1:9; 6:10

★ **16** [a]Eccl. 4:1; 5:8; 8:9

17 [a]Gen. 18:25; Ps. 96:13; 98:9; Eccl. 11:9; Matt. 16:27; Rom. 2:6-10; 2 Thess. 1:6-9 [b]Eccl. 3:1; 8:6

18 [a]Ps. 49:12, 20; 73:22

★ **19-22**
19 [a]Ps. 49:12; Eccl. 9:12

3:4 *dance.* See note on Psalm 149:3.
3:5 *to gather stones.* In order to clear land for planting or in order to build. Though all is under God's control, the accomplishment of His purposes includes man's efforts.
3:7 *tear apart.* Tear clothes as a sign of bereavement (cf. Gen. 37:29), and *sew* them up again when the period of mourning was over.
3:8 *hate.* This is not necessarily an expression of malice, but of preference (see note on Luke 14:26).
3:11 *eternity.* God has given man an eternal perspective so that he can look beyond the routine of life. Nevertheless, He has not revealed all of life's mysteries to man.

3:12-14 Though man cannot understand all of God's plan, there is *nothing better* for him to do than to resolve to do good, to enjoy the gifts of God in life, and to fear Him.
3:15 The meaning is this: God has ordained the continual cycle of the events of life, the same thought as in verse 1.
3:16 *in the place of justice.* I.e., in the courts. Only God judges righteously (v. 17).
3:19-22 Though both man and beast will suffer a common fate and return to *dust,* man will face God in judgment (cf. 12:14). Therefore he should serve God faithfully in this life, enjoying what God gives him.

breath and there is no advantage for man over beast, for all is vanity.

20 ^aGen. 3:19; Ps. 103:14; Eccl. 12:7

20 All go to the same place. All came from the ^adust and all return to the dust.

21 ^aEccl. 12:7

21 Who knows that the ^abreath of man ascends upward and the breath of the beast descends downward to the earth?

D Conclusion, 3:22

22 ^aEccl. 2:24 ^bEccl. 2:18; 6:12; 8:7; 10:14

22 And I have seen that ^anothing is better than that man should be happy in his activities, for that is his lot. For who will bring him to see ^bwhat will occur after him?

IV THE FUTILITY OF THE VARIOUS CIRCUMSTANCES OF LIFE, 4:1–5:20

A Oppression, 4:1–3

★ 1-3

1 ^aJob 35:9; Ps. 12:5; Eccl. 3:16; 5:8; Is. 5:7 ^bJer. 16:7; Lam. 1:9

4 Then I looked again at all the acts of ^aoppression which were being done under the sun. And behold *I saw* the tears of the oppressed and *that* they had ^bno one to comfort *them;* and on the side of their oppressors was power, but they had no one to comfort *them.*

2 ^aJob 3:11-26; Eccl. 2:17; 7:1

2 So ^aI congratulated the dead who are already dead more than the living who are still living.

3 ^aJob 3:11-22; Eccl. 6:3; Luke 23:29

3 But ^abetter *off* than both of them is the one who has never existed, who has never seen the evil activity that is done under the sun.

B Work, 4:4–12

★ 4-6

4 ^aEccl. 2:21 ^bEccl. 1:14

4 And I have seen that every labor and every ^askill which is done is *the result of* rivalry between a man and his neighbor. This too is ^bvanity and striving after wind.

5 ^aProv. 6:10; 24:33 ^bIs. 9:20

5 The fool ^afolds his hands and ^bconsumes his own flesh.

6 ^aProv. 15:16, 17; 16:8

6 One hand full of rest is ^abetter than two fists full of labor and striving after wind.

7 Then I looked again at vanity under the sun.

★ 8 ^aProv. 27:20; Eccl. 1:8; 5:10 ^bEccl. 2:21 ^cEccl. 1:13

8 There was a certain man without a dependent, having neither a son nor a brother, yet there was no end to all his labor. Indeed, ^ahis eyes were not satisfied with riches *and he never asked,* "And ^bfor whom am I laboring and depriving myself of pleasure?" This too is vanity and it is a ^cgrievous task.

★ 9-12

9 Two are better than one because they have a good return for their labor.

10 For if either of them falls, the one will lift up his companion. But woe to the one who falls when there is not another to lift him up.

11 ^a1 Kin. 1:1-4

11 Furthermore, if two lie down together they keep warm, but ^ahow can one be warm *alone?*

12 And if one can overpower him who is alone, two can resist him. A cord of three *strands* is not quickly torn apart.

C Political Success, 4:13–16

★13-16 **13** ^aEccl. 7:19; 9:15

13 A ^apoor, yet wise lad is better than an old and foolish

4:1–3 Solomon, contemplating the lot of the oppressed of this world, concludes that they would be better off dead than alive (cf. Job 3:11).

4:4–6 Verse 4 pictures the skilled worker who, motivated by competition, becomes a workaholic for nothing. On the other hand, verse 5 pictures the opposite extreme—the fool who does not work at all and who, consequently, *consumes his own flesh;* i.e., starves to death. Verse 6 states the happy balance.

4:8 *There was a certain man without a dependent.* Better, a man without a partner. In addition, according to the next clause, he has no family; yet he continues to pile up profits, though he has no one with whom to share the rewards of his labor.

4:9–12 How much better it is to have a partner and friend who can assist (v. 10), warm (v. 11), and protect (v. 12). Three friends together *(A cord of three strands)* form an even stronger bond.

4:13–16 The poor lad who comes to the throne *out of prison* and who forgets how fickle people can be may himself be reduced again to poverty by a *second* usurper.

king who no longer knows *how* to receive instruction.

14 aGen. 41:14, 41-43

14 For he has come aout of prison to become king, even though he was born poor in his kingdom.

15 I have seen all the living under the sun throng to the side of the second lad who replaces him.

16 aEccl. 1:14

16 There is no end to all the people, to all who were before them, and even the ones who will come later will not be happy with him, for this too is avanity and striving after wind.

D False Worship, 5:1-7

★ 1-7
★1 aEx. 3:5;
30:18-20; Is.
1:12 b1 Sam.
15:22; Prov.
15:8; 21:27

5 aGuard your steps as you go to the house of God, and draw near to listen rather than to offer the bsacrifice of fools; for they do not know they are doing evil.

2 aProv.
20:25 bProv.
10:19; Matt.
6:7

2 Do not be ahasty in word or impulsive in thought to bring up a matter in the presence of God. For God is in heaven and you are on the earth; therefore let your bwords be few.

★3 aJob
11:2; Prov.
15:2; Eccl.
10:14

3 For the dream comes through much effort, and the voice of a afool through many words.

4 aNum.
30:2; Ps.
50:14; 76:11
bPs. 66:13,
14

4 When you amake a vow to God, do not be late in paying it, for He takes no delight in fools. bPay what you vow!

5 aProv.
20:25; Acts
5:4

5 It is abetter that you should not vow than that you should vow and not pay.

★6 aLev.
4:2, 22; Num.
15:25

6 Do not let your speech cause you to sin and do not say in the presence of the messenger *of God* that it was a amistake. Why should God be angry on account of your voice and destroy the work of your hands?

7 For in many dreams and in many words there is emptiness. Rather, afear God.

★7 aEccl.
3:14; 7:18;
8:12, 13;
12:13

E Hoarded Riches, 5:8-17

8 If you see aoppression of the poor and bdenial of justice and righteousness in the province, do not be cshocked at the sight, for one official watches over another official, and there are higher officials over them.

★8 aEccl.
4:1 bEzek.
18:18 c1 Pet.
4:12

9 After all, a king who cultivates the field is an advantage to the land.

10 aHe who loves money will not be satisfied with money, nor he who loves abundance *with its* income. This too is vanity.

10 aEccl.
1:8; 2:10, 11;
4:8

11 aWhen good things increase, those who consume them increase. So what is the advantage to their owners except to look on?

11 aEccl. 2:9

12 The sleep of the working man is apleasant, whether he eats little or much. But the full stomach of the rich man does not allow him to sleep.

12 aProv.
3:24

13 There is a grievous evil *which* I have seen under the sun: ariches being hoarded by their owner to his hurt.

13 aEccl. 6:2

14 When those riches were lost through a bad investment and he had fathered a son, then there was nothing to support him.

15 aAs he had come naked from his mother's womb, so will he return as he came. He will btake nothing from the fruit of his labor that he can carry in his hand.

15 aJob 1:21
bPs. 49:17;
1 Tim. 6:7

16 And this also is a grievous evil—exactly as a man is born, thus will he die. So, awhat is the advantage to him who btoils for the wind?

16 aEccl.
1:3; 2:11; 3:9
bProv. 11:29

5:1-7 In light of the futility of careless worship Solomon sets forth an exhortation concerning proper worship.
5:1 *Guard your steps.* I.e., be careful, attentive. *listen.* I.e., with a view to obedience.
5:3 As nighttime dreams often reveal one's preoccupation with his work, so also excessive words in prayer may show a lack of intelligence.

5:6 *messenger.* I.e., the levitical priest.
5:7 There is vanity in preoccupation with one's work and in careless worship (cf. v. 3).
5:8 There is corruption at every level of government, with higher level oppressors plundering the likewise oppressive lower level magistrates.

★17 *a*Ps.
127:2 *b*Eccl.
2:23

17 Throughout his life *ª he* also eats in darkness with *b*great vexation, sickness and anger.

F Conclusion, 5:18-20

★18-20

18 *a*Eccl.
2:24 *b*Eccl.
2:10

18 Here is what I have seen to be *a*good and fitting: to eat, to drink and enjoy oneself in all one's labor in which he toils under the sun *during* the few years of his life which God has given him; for this is his *b*reward.

19 *a*2 Chr.
1:12; Eccl.
6:2 *b*Eccl.
6:2 *c*Eccl.
3:13

19 Furthermore, as for every man to whom *a*God has given riches and wealth, He has also *b*empowered him to eat from them and to receive his reward and rejoice in his labor; this is the *c*gift of God.

20 *a*Ex.
23:25

20 For he will not often consider the years of his life, because *a*God keeps him occupied with the gladness of his heart.

V THE FUTILITY OF RICHES, 6:1-12

★ 1-9

1 *a*Eccl.
5:13

2 *a*1 Kin.
3:13 *b*Ps.
17:14; 73:7;
Eccl. 2:10

6 There is an *a*evil which I have seen under the sun and it is prevalent among men—

2 a man to whom God has *a*given riches and wealth and honor so that his soul *b*lacks nothing of all that he desires, but God has not empowered him to eat from them, for a foreigner enjoys them. This is vanity and a severe affliction.

★ 3-5

3 *a*Is.
14:20; Jer.
8:2; 22:19
*b*Job 3:16;
Eccl. 4:3

3 If a man fathers a hundred *children* and lives many years, however many they be, but his soul is not satisfied with good things, and he does not even have a *proper a*burial, *then* I say, "Better *b*the miscarriage than he,

4 for it comes in futility and goes into obscurity; and its name is covered in obscurity.

5 "It never sees the sun and it never knows *anything;* it is better off than he.

6 "Even if the *other* man lives a thousand years twice and does not enjoy good things—*a*do not all go to one place?"

★ 6 *a*Eccl.
2:14

7 *a*All a man's labor is for his mouth and yet the appetite is not satisfied.

7 *a*Prov.
16:26

8 For *a*what advantage does the wise man have over the fool? What *advantage* does the poor man have, knowing *how* to walk before the living?

★ 8 *a*Eccl.
2:15

9 What the eyes *a*see is better than what the soul desires. This too is *b*futility and a striving after wind.

★ 9 *a*Eccl.
11:9 *b*Eccl.
1:14

10 Whatever *a*exists has already been named, and it is known what man is; for he *b*cannot dispute with him who is stronger than he is.

★10-12

★10 *a*Eccl.
1:9; 3:15
*b*Job 9:32;
40:2; Prov.
21:30; Is.
45:9

11 For there are many words which increase futility. What *then* is the advantage to a man?

12 For who knows what is good for a man during *his* lifetime, *during* the few years of his futile life? He will spend them like a shadow. For who can tell a man *a*what will be after him under the sun?

★12 *a*Eccl.
3:22

5:17 *eats in darkness.* A figure for gloomy existence.

5:18-20 Man may overcome his frustration over the futility of life by enjoying life and being occupied with God's good gifts.

6:1-9 Solomon sets forth the futility of riches, which fail ultimately to satisfy.

6:3-5 Early death appears superior to an unsatisfied life.

6:6 *one place.* I.e., the grave.

6:8 The wise, the foolish, and the poor are all characterized by desire for things, though the poor, *knowing how to walk before the living,* conceals his poverty and desire.

6:9 It is better to enjoy present good than to long for future delights.

6:10-12 Man is unable to control his destiny, which is determined by God. This is contrary to fatalism, which views God as either nonexistent or uninvolved.

6:10 The whole being of man is fully known by God, against whom no man can contend.

6:12 Because of man's finitude he is unable to know what is really to his advantage.

VI COUNSEL FOR LIVING, 7:1–12:8

A Counsel in View of Man's Wickedness, 7:1–29

★ 1-14

1 aProv. 22:1 bEccl. 4:2; 7:8

7 A ^agood name is better than a good ointment,
And the ^bday of one's death is better than the day of one's birth.

★ 2 aEccl. 2:14, 16; 3:19, 20; 6:6; 9:2, 3 bPs. 90:12

2 It is better to go to a house of mourning
Than to go to a house of feasting,
Because that is the ^aend of every man,
And the living ^btakes it to heart.

★ 3 aEccl. 2:2 b2 Cor. 7:10

3 ^aSorrow is better than laughter,
For ^bwhen a face is sad a heart may be happy.

4 The mind of the wise is in the house of mourning,
While the mind of fools is in the house of pleasure.

5 aPs. 141:5; Prov. 6:23; 13:18; 15:31, 32; 25:12; Eccl. 9:17

5 It is better to ^alisten to the rebuke of a wise man
Than for one to listen to the song of fools.

★ 6 aPs. 58:9; 118:12 bEccl. 2:2

6 For as the crackling of ^athorn bushes under a pot,
So is the ^blaughter of the fool,
And this too is futility.

7 aEccl. 4:1; 5:8 bEx. 23:8; Deut. 16:19; Prov. 17:8, 23

8 aEccl. 7:1 bProv. 14:29; 16:32; Gal. 5:22; Eph. 4:2

7 For ^aoppression makes a wise man mad,
And a ^bbribe corrupts the heart.

8 The ^aend of a matter is better than its beginning;

^bPatience of spirit is better than haughtiness of spirit.

9 aProv. 14:17; James 1:19

9 Do not be ^aeager in your heart to be angry,
For anger resides in the bosom of fools.

10 Do not say, "Why is it that the former days were better than these?"
For it is not from wisdom that you ask about this.

★11 aProv. 8:10, 11; Eccl. 2:13

11 Wisdom along with an inheritance is good
And an ^aadvantage to those who see the sun.

12 aEccl. 7:19; 9:18 bProv. 3:18; 8:35

12 For ^awisdom is protection just as money is protection.
But the advantage of knowledge is that ^bwisdom preserves the lives of its possessors.

★13-14

13 aEccl. 3:11; 8:17 bEccl. 1:15

13 Consider the ^awork of God,
For who is ^bable to straighten what He has bent?

14 aDeut. 26:11; Eccl. 3:22; 9:7; 11:9 bDeut. 8:5; Job 2:10 cEccl. 3:22

14 ^aIn the day of prosperity be happy,
But ^bin the day of adversity consider—
God has made the one as well as the other
So that man may ^cnot discover anything that will be after him.

★ 7:15-8:15

15 aEccl. 6:12; 9:9 bEccl. 8:14 cEccl. 8:12, 13

15 I have seen everything during my ^alifetime of futility; there is ^ba righteous man who perishes in his righteousness, and

---

7:1–14 Through a series of proverbial sayings, Solomon offers counsel concerning wisdom and folly.

7:2 A visit to a home stricken by tragedy reminds one of the brevity of life and of the need for wise living. Such a visit is better for a man than a visit to a place of boisterous festivity.

7:3 Sorrow may have a beneficial effect, tempering one's mirth with seriousness.

7:6 Dry thorns set afire yield a snapping, bright

blaze, but like the empty laughter of a fool, the fire quickly dies out.

7:11 Wisdom with wealth is better than wisdom alone.

7:13–14 God brings both prosperity and adversity into our lives for His sovereign purposes, without revealing the key to His plan.

7:15–8:15 Solomon continues to use proverbial sayings to set forth the advantages and limitations of wisdom.

there is ^ca wicked man who prolongs *his life* in his wickedness.

★16-17
★16 ^aProv. 25:16; Phil. 3:6 ^bRom. 12:3

16 Do not be excessively ^arighteous, and do not ^bbe overly wise. Why should you ruin yourself?

17 ^aJob 22:16; Ps. 55:23; Prov. 10:27

17 Do not be excessively wicked, and do not be a fool. Why should you ^adie before your time?

★18 ^aEccl. 3:14; 5:7; 8:12, 13; 12:13

18 It is good that you grasp one thing, and also not let go of the other; for the one who ^afears God comes forth with both of them.

19 ^aEccl. 7:12; 9:13-18

19 ^aWisdom strengthens a wise man more than ten rulers who are in a city.

20 ^a1 Kin. 8:46; 2 Chr. 6:36; Ps. 143:2; Prov. 20:9; Rom. 3:23

20 Indeed, ^athere is not a righteous man on earth who *continually* does good and who never sins.

★21-22

21 ^aProv. 30:10

21 Also, do not take seriously all words which are spoken, lest you hear your servant ^acursing you.

22 For you also have realized that you likewise have many times cursed others.

★23 ^aEccl. 3:11; 8:17

23 I tested all this with wisdom, *and* I said, "I will be wise," ^abut it was far from me.

24 ^aRom. 11:33 ^bJob 11:7; 37:23; Eccl. 8:17

24 What has been is remote and ^aexceedingly mysterious. ^bWho can discover it?

25 ^aEccl. 1:15, 17; 10:13

25 I ^adirected my mind to know, to investigate, and to seek wisdom and an explanation, and to know the evil of folly and the foolishness of madness.

26 ^aProv. 5:4 ^bProv. 7:23 ^cProv. 6:23, 24 ^dProv. 22:14

26 And I discovered more ^abitter than death the woman whose heart is ^bsnares and nets, whose hands are chains. ^cOne who is pleasing to God will escape from her, but ^dthe sinner will be captured by her.

★27-28

27 "Behold, I have discovered this," says the Preacher, "*adding* one thing to another to find an explanation,

28 ^a1 Kin. 11:3

28 which I am still seeking but have not found. I have found one man among a thousand, but I have not found a ^awoman among all these.

★29 ^aGen. 1:27

29 "Behold, I have found only this, that ^aGod made men upright, but they have sought out many devices."

B Counsel in View of God's Inscrutable Providences, 8:1–9:18

★ 1 ^aEx. 34:29, 30 ^bDeut. 28:50

8 Who is like the wise man and who knows the interpretation of a matter? A man's wisdom ^aillumines him and causes his ^bstern face to beam.

★ 2-9
★ 2 ^aEx. 22:11; 2 Sam. 21:7; Ezek. 17:18

2 I say, "Keep the command of the king because of the ^aoath before God.

★ 3 ^aEccl. 10:4

3 "Do not be in a hurry ^ato leave him. Do not join in an evil matter, for he will do whatever he pleases."

4 ^aJob 9:12; Dan. 4:35

4 Since the word of the king is authoritative, ^awho will say to him, "What are you doing?"

★ 5 ^aEccl. 12:13 ^bProv. 12:21

5 He who ^akeeps a *royal*

7:16–17 Living in moderation rather than excess is Solomon's counsel.

7:16 *Do not be excessively righteous.* I.e., Do not exaggerate your righteousness with superficiality. It will be to no avail.

7:18 Solomon's counsel is to hold fast both to wisdom and righteousness (cf. 7:16), for both characterize the man who reveres God.

7:21–22 There is a need for self-restraint in the face of humiliation.

7:23 Though Solomon was the wisest of men (1 Kings 3:12; 3:16–28), his wisdom was insufficient to comprehend all the mysteries of life.

7:27–28 A wise and upright woman is a rare find.

7:29 Though God made men upright, they have been corrupted by their pursuit of foolish pleasures.

8:1 *Who is like the wise man.* I.e., Who is his equal? The incomparable excellence of the wise man is seen in the fact that no one is his equal or understands a matter as well as he does. *illumines him.* I.e., makes him a source of blessing to others (cf. Num. 6:25).

8:2–9 Solomon points to the wisdom of submitting to the king.

8:2 *oath before God.* I.e., an oath of allegiance made to a ruler in the name of God (2 Chron. 36:13).

8:3 *he will do whatever he pleases.* I.e., he is sovereign and will punish rebellion.

8:5 A wise man's confidence is that inequities eventually will terminate and proper judicial decisions will be made for his vindication.

command *b*experiences no trouble, for a wise heart knows the proper time and procedure.

6 For *a*there is a proper time and procedure for every delight, when a man's trouble is heavy upon him.

7 If no one *a*knows what will happen, who can tell him when it will happen?

8 *a*No man has authority to restrain the wind with the wind, or authority over the day of death; and there is no discharge in the time of war, and *b*evil will not deliver those who practice it.

9 All this I have seen and applied my mind to every deed that has been done under the sun wherein a man has exercised *a*authority over *another* man to his hurt.

10 So then, I have seen the wicked buried, those who used to go in and out from the holy place, and they are *a*soon forgotten in the city where they did thus. This too is futility.

11 Because the *a*sentence against an evil deed is not executed quickly, therefore *b*the hearts of the sons of men among them are given fully to do evil.

12 Although a sinner does evil a hundred *times* and may *a*lengthen his *life,* still I know that it will be *b*well for those who fear God, who fear Him openly.

13 But it will *a*not be well for the evil man and he will not lengthen his days like a *b*shadow, because he does not fear God.

14 There is futility which is done on the earth, that is, there are *a*righteous men to whom it happens according to the deeds of the wicked. On the other hand, there are *b*evil men to whom it happens according to the deeds of the righteous. I say that this too is futility.

15 So I commended pleasure, for there is nothing good for *a*a man under the sun except to eat and to drink and to be merry, and this will stand by him in his toils *throughout* the days of his life which God has given him under the sun.

16 When I *a*gave my heart to know wisdom and to see the task which has been done on the earth (even though one should *b*never sleep day or night),

17 and I saw every work of God, *I concluded* that *a*man cannot discover the work which has been done under the sun. Even though man should seek laboriously, he will not discover; and *b*though the wise man should say, "I know," he cannot discover.

9 For I have taken all this to my heart and explain it that righteous men, wise men, and their deeds are *a*in the hand of God. *b*Man does not know whether *it will be* *c*love or hatred; anything awaits him.

2 *a*It is the same for all. There is *b*one fate for the righteous and for the wicked; for the good, for the clean, and for the unclean; for the man who offers a

Margin references:

★ 6-8
6 *a*Eccl. 3:1, 17

7 *a*Eccl. 3:22; 6:12; 7:14; 9:12

8 *a*Ps. 49:7
*b*Eccl. 8:13

★ 9 *a*Eccl. 4:1; 5:8; 7:7

★10-14
★10 *a*Eccl. 1:11; 2:16; 9:5, 15

11 *a*Ex. 34:6; Ps. 86:15; Rom. 2:4; 2 Pet. 3:9
*b*Eccl. 9:3

12 *a*Eccl. 7:15 *b*Deut. 4:40; 12:25; Ps. 37:11; Prov. 1:33; Is. 3:10

13 *a*Eccl. 8:8; Is. 3:11 *b*Job 14:2; Eccl. 6:12

14 *a*Ps. 73:14; Eccl. 7:15 *b*Job 21:7; Ps. 73:3, 12; Jer. 12:1; Mal. 3:15

★ 8:15-9:10

★15 *a*Eccl. 2:24; 3:12, 13; 5:18; 9:7

★16 *a*Eccl. 1:13, 14 *b*Eccl. 2:23

★17 *a*Eccl. 3:11 *b*Ps. 73:16; Eccl. 7:23; Rom. 11:33

★ 1 *a*Deut. 33:3; Job 12:10; Ps. 119:109 *b*Eccl. 10:14 *c*Eccl. 9:6

★ 2-6

2 *a*Job 9:22; Eccl. 9:11 *b*Eccl. 2:14; 3:19; 6:6; 7:2

8:6-8 Solomon sets forth the limitations of a king's power. He, too, is subject to God's sovereign design (v. 6). Temporal wisdom and authority have definite limits (vv. 7-8). The king receives no exemption from war nor will wicked ways avert his punishment.

8:9 *his hurt.* I.e., the injury of the subject being ruled by a tyrant.

8:10-14 Solomon ponders the incongruities of life.

8:10 Solomon bemoans the absence of apparent retribution on the wicked.

8:15-9:10 A summary of Solomon's quest and the discoveries he has made.

8:15 Solomon's oft repeated recommendation in light of the futilities of life.

8:16 A parenthetical comment emphasizing the exhaustive study Solomon made. It occupied him *day* and *night.*

8:17 Man longs to know the intricacies of the divine plan, which even through exhaustive labors cannot be fully known.

9:1 Many events are beyond the control of men. Every possible circumstance can befall man, but whether faced with *love* (happy circumstances) or *hatred* (unhappy circumstances), God has arranged what will take place in one's life.

9:2-6 Regardless of how haphazard the events of life may appear to be, all men face one certain fate—death.

sacrifice and for the one who does not sacrifice. As the good man is, so is the sinner; as the swearer is, so is the one who is afraid to swear.

3 This is an evil in all that is done under the sun, that there is ᵃone fate for all men. Furthermore, ᵇthe hearts of the sons of men are full of evil, and ᶜinsanity is in their hearts throughout their lives. Afterwards they *go* to the dead.

4 For whoever is joined with the living, there is hope; surely a live dog is better than a dead lion.

5 For the living know they will die; but the dead ᵃdo not know anything, nor have they any longer a reward, for their ᵇmemory is forgotten.

6 Indeed their love, their hate, and their zeal have already perished, and they will no longer have a ᵃshare in all that is done under the sun.

7 Go *then,* ᵃeat your bread in happiness, and drink your wine with a cheerful heart; for God has already approved your works.

8 Let your ᵃclothes be white all the time, and let not ᵇoil be lacking on your head.

9 Enjoy life with the woman whom you love all the days of your ᵃfleeting life which He has given to you under the sun; for this is your ᵇreward in life, and in your toil in which you have labored under the sun.

10 Whatever your hand finds to do, verily, ᵃdo *it* with all your might; for there is no ᵇactivity or planning or wisdom in ᶜSheol where you are going.

11 I again saw under the sun that the ᵃrace is not to the swift, and the ᵇbattle is not to the war-riors, and neither is bread to the wise, nor ᶜwealth to the discerning, nor favor to men of ability; for time and ᵈchance overtake them all.

12 Moreover, man does not ᵃknow his time: like fish caught in a treacherous net, and ᵇbirds trapped in a snare, so the sons of men are ᶜensnared at an evil time when it ᵈsuddenly falls on them.

13 Also this I came to see as wisdom under the sun, and it impressed me.

14 There ᵃwas a small city with few men in it and a great king came to it, surrounded it, and constructed large siegeworks against it.

15 But there was found in it a ᵃpoor wise man and he delivered the city ᵇby his wisdom. Yet ᶜno one remembered that poor man.

16 So I said, "ᵃWisdom is better than strength." But the wisdom of the poor man is despised and his words are not heeded.

17 The ᵃwords of the wise heard in quietness are *better* than the shouting of a ruler among fools.

18 ᵃWisdom is better than weapons of war, but ᵇone sinner destroys much good.

C Counsel in View of the Uncertainties of Life, 10:1-20

10 Dead flies make a ᵃperfumer's oil stink, so a little foolishness is weightier than wisdom *and* honor.

2 A wise man's heart *directs* *him* toward the right, but the

---

Cross references (margin):

3 ᵃEccl. 9:2; Jer. 17:10 ᵇEccl. 8:11 ᶜEccl. 1:17

★ 4-6

5 ᵃJob 14:21 ᵇPs. 88:12; Eccl. 1:11; 2:16; 8:10; Is. 26:14

6 ᵃEccl. 2:10; 3:22

7 ᵃEccl. 2:24; 8:15

★ 8 ᵃRev. 3:4 ᵇPs. 23:5

9 ᵃEccl. 6:12; 7:15 ᵇEccl. 2:10

★10 ᵃEccl. 11:6; Rom. 12:11; Col. 3:23 ᵇEccl. 9:5 ᶜGen. 37:35; Job 21:13; Is. 38:10

★11-12 11 ᵃAmos 2:14, 15 ᵇ2 Chr. 20:15; Ps. 76:5; Zech. 4:6 ᶜDeut. 8:17, 18 ᵈ1 Sam. 6:9

12 ᵃEccl. 8:7 ᵇProv. 7:23 ᶜProv. 29:6; Is. 24:18; Hos. 9:8 ᵈLuke 21:34, 35

14 ᵃ2 Sam. 20:16-22

15 ᵃEccl. 4:13 ᵇ2 Sam. 20:22 ᶜEccl. 2:16; 8:10

16 ᵃProv. 21:22; Eccl. 7:12, 19

★ 9:17-11:8

17 ᵃEccl. 7:5; 10:12

18 ᵃEccl. 9:16 ᵇJosh. 7:1-26; 2 Kin. 21:2-17

1 ᵃEx. 30:25

2 ᵃMatt. 6:33; Col. 3:1

9:4-6 The living do have an advantage over the dead (v. 4). The dead have no further opportunities of securing compensation for their labors (v. 5) and they no longer share in life on this earth (v. 6).

9:8 White garments and much oil signify festal joy.

9:10 Solomon adds a new dimension to his counsel concerning life. Though much of life is futile, one must grasp its opportunities and use them to the fullest in serving God. There will be no such opportunities in the grave (cf. John 9:4). Every man has a particular work, which is accomplished in this life or not at all.

9:11-12 The issues and length of life are quite unpredictable. No one can guarantee success or foresee how God will deal with him.

9:17-11:8 A series of proverbs on the subject of wisdom and folly.

foolish [a]man's heart *directs him* toward the left.

3 Even when the fool walks along the road his sense is lacking, and he [a]demonstrates to everyone *that* he is a fool.

4 If the ruler's temper rises against you, [a]do not abandon your position, because [b]composure allays great offenses.

5 There is an evil I have seen under the sun, like an error which goes forth from the ruler—

6 [a]folly is set in many exalted places while rich men sit in humble places.

7 I have seen [a]slaves *riding* [b]on horses and princes walking like slaves on the land.

8 [a]He who digs a pit may fall into it, and a [b]serpent may bite him who breaks through a wall.

9 He who quarries stones may be hurt by them, and he who splits logs may be endangered by them.

10 If the axe is dull and he does not sharpen *its* edge, then he must exert more strength. Wisdom has the advantage of giving success.

11 If the serpent bites [a]before being charmed, there is no profit for the charmer.

12 [a]Words from the mouth of a wise man are gracious, while the lips of a [b]fool consume him;

13 the beginning of his talking is folly, and the end of it is wicked [a]madness.

14 Yet the [a]fool multiplies words. No man knows what will happen, and who can tell him [b]what will come after him?

15 The toil of a fool *so* wearies him that he does not *even* know how to go to a city.

16 Woe to you, O land, whose [a]king is a lad and whose princes feast in the morning.

17 Blessed are you, O land, whose king is of nobility and whose princes eat at the appropriate time—for strength, and not for [a]drunkenness.

18 Through [a]indolence the rafters sag, and through slackness the house leaks.

19 *Men* prepare a meal for enjoyment, and [a]wine makes life merry, and [b]money is the answer to everything.

20 Furthermore, [a]in your bedchamber do not [b]curse a king, and in your sleeping rooms do not curse a rich man, for a bird of the heavens will carry the sound, and the winged creature will make the matter known.

D   Counsel in View of the Aging Processes of Life, 11:1–12:8

11 Cast your bread on the surface of the waters, for you [a]will find it after many days.

2 [a]Divide your portion to seven, or even to eight, for you do not know what [b]misfortune may occur on the earth.

3 If the clouds are full, they pour out rain upon the earth; and whether a tree falls toward the south or toward the north, wherever the tree falls, there it lies.

4 He who watches the wind will not sow and he who looks at the clouds will not reap.

Marginal references:

3 [a]Prov. 13:16; 18:2

★ 4 [a]Eccl. 8:3 [b]1 Sam. 25:24-33; Prov. 25:15

6 [a]Esth. 3:1, 5f.; Prov. 28:12; 29:2

7 [a]Prov. 19:10 [b]Esth. 6:8-10

8 [a]Ps. 7:15; Prov. 26:27 [b]Amos 5:19

11 [a]Ps. 58:4, 5; Jer. 8:17

12 [a]Prov. 10:32; 22:11; Luke 4:22 [b]Prov. 10:14; 18:7; Eccl. 4:5

13 [a]Eccl. 7:25

14 [a]Prov. 15:2; Eccl. 5:3 [b]Eccl. 3:22; 6:12; 7:14; 8:7

★15

★16 [a]Is. 3:4, 12

17 [a]Prov. 31:4; Is. 5:11

18 [a]Prov. 24:30-34

★19 [a]Judg. 9:13; Ps. 104:15; Eccl. 2:3 [b]Eccl. 7:12

★20 [a]2 Kin. 6:12; Luke 12:3 [b]Ex. 22:28; Acts 23:5

★ 1 [a]Deut. 15:10; Prov. 19:17; Matt. 10:42; Gal. 6:9; Heb. 6:10

★ 2 [a]Ps. 112:9; Matt. 5:42; Luke 6:30; 1 Tim. 6:18, 19 [b]Eccl. 11:8; 12:1

★ 3

★ 4

10:4 *allays.* I.e., checks the anger.

10:15 The fool rambles, failing to see the obvious way of accomplishing his purposes.

10:16 *feast in the morning.* I.e., feast when there is work to be done.

10:19 The verse expresses the attitude of the carousing princes (v. 16).

10:20 *bird of the heavens.* The proverbial expression signifies a report or disclosure by an unknown source. Contempt for authority does not go undiscovered.

11:1 *Cast your bread on the surface of the wa-*

ters. A metaphorical expression taken from the grain trade of a seaport town, illustrating the successful prospects of a bold business venture.

11:2 There is wisdom in diversified investment, for no one knows what calamity may befall one enterprise.

11:3 There is an inevitable sequence and finality in many of life's events.

11:4 There is a danger of being overly cautious in light of nature's unpredictability.

5 ^aJohn 3:8
^bPs. 139:13-16 ^cEccl. 1:13; 3:10, 11; 8:17

5 Just as you do not ^aknow the path of the wind and ^bhow bones *are formed* in the womb of the pregnant woman, so you do not ^cknow the activity of God who makes all things.

6 ^aEccl. 9:10

6 Sow your seed ^ain the morning, and do not be idle in the evening, for you do not know whether morning or evening sowing will succeed, or whether both of them alike will be good.

★ 7-8
7 ^aEccl. 6:5; 7:11

7 The light is pleasant, and *it is* good for the eyes to ^asee the sun.

8 ^aEccl. 9:7
^bEccl. 12:1

8 Indeed, if a man should live many years, let him ^arejoice in them all, and let him remember the ^bdays of darkness, for they shall be many. Everything that is to come *will be* futility.

9 ^aNum. 15:39; Job 31:7; Eccl. 2:10 ^bEccl. 3:17; 12:14; Rom. 14:10

9 Rejoice, young man, during your childhood, and let your heart be pleasant during the days of young manhood. And follow the impulses of your heart and the ^adesires of your eyes. Yet know that ^bGod will bring you to judgment for all these things.

10 ^a2 Cor. 7:1; 2 Tim. 2:22

10 So, remove vexation from your heart and put away ^apain from your body, because childhood and the prime of life are fleeting.

★ 1-7
1 ^aDeut. 8:18; Neh. 4:14; Ps. 63:6; 119:55 ^bEccl. 11:8

12 ^aRemember also your Creator in the days of your youth, before the ^bevil days come and the years draw near when you will say, "I have no delight in them";

★ 2-5
2 ^aIs. 5:30; 13:10; Ezek. 32:7, 8; Joel 3:15; Matt. 24:29

2 before the ^asun, the light, the moon, and the stars are darkened, and clouds return after the rain;

★ 3 ^aPs. 35:14; 38:6 ^bGen. 27:1; 48:10; 1 Sam. 3:2

3 in the day that the watchmen of the house tremble, and mighty men ^astoop, the grinding ones stand idle because they are few, and ^bthose who look through windows grow dim;

★ 4 ^aJer. 25:10; Rev. 18:22 ^b2 Sam. 19:35

4 and the doors on the street are shut as the ^asound of the grinding mill is low, and one will arise at the sound of the bird, and all the ^bdaughters of song will sing softly.

★ 5 ^aJob 17:13; 30:23 ^bGen. 50:10; Jer. 9:17

5 Furthermore, men are afraid of a high place and of terrors on the road; the almond tree blossoms, the grasshopper drags himself along, and the caperberry is ineffective. For man goes to his eternal ^ahome while ^bmourners go about in the street.

★ 6 ^aZech. 4:2, 3

6 *Remember Him* before the silver cord is broken and the ^agolden bowl is crushed, the pitcher by the well is shattered and the wheel at the cistern is crushed;

★ 7 ^aGen. 3:19; Job 34:15; Ps. 104:29; Eccl. 3:20 ^bJob 34:14; Eccl. 3:21; Luke 23:46; Acts 7:59 ^cNum. 16:22; 27:16; Is. 57:16; Zech. 12:1

7 then the ^adust will return to the earth as it was, and the

---

11:7-8 *light.* Signifies life in this world. *darkness.* Signifies death. God's gift of life on earth should be enjoyed, since it eventually terminates.

12:1-7 Solomon exhorts young men to remember God in their youth, before old age and poor health overtake them and life's pleasures vanish.

12:2-5 Solomon poetically pictures old age as a gathering storm (v. 2), as an old house (vv. 3-4), and as an old man (v. 5).

12:3 *watchmen of the house.* I.e., arms and hands. *mighty men stoop.* I.e., legs that become weak. *grinding ones.* I.e., a few remaining teeth. *those who look through windows grow dim.* I.e., weak eyes.

12:4 *doors on the street.* I.e., ears that scarcely hear. *one will arise at the sound of the bird.* I.e., he is unable to sleep. *daughters of song will sing softly.* I.e., a decreased appreciation

for music.

12:5 *afraid of a high place.* I.e., signifies the difficulty of ascending a height. *terrors on the road.* I.e., fear of falling when walking. *almond tree blossoms.* I.e., white hair. *grasshopper drags himself along.* I.e., crippled and bent limbs impair mobility. *caperberry is ineffective.* I.e., sexually impotent. *eternal home.* I.e., absence from the earth. *mourners go about.* I.e., wailers at a funeral.

12:6 *silver cord is broken.* I.e., loss of life support. *golden bowl is crushed.* I.e., signifies the crash of death. *pitcher by the well is shattered.* I.e., fragile life is lost. *wheel at the cistern is crushed.* I.e., the apparatus for sustaining life is ruined.

12:7 *dust will return to the earth.* I.e., man's body returns to dust (cf. Gen. 3:19). *spirit will return to God who gave it.* I.e., man's spirit returns to God for judgment.

^bspirit will return to ^cGod who gave it.

★ 8-14   8 "^aVanity of vanities," says the Preacher, "all is vanity!"

8 ^aEccl. 1:2

VII   CONCLUSION, 12:9–14

9 ^a1 Kin. 4:32

9   In addition to being a wise man, the Preacher also taught the people knowledge; and he pondered, searched out and arranged ^amany proverbs.

★10 ^aProv. 10:32 ^bProv. 22:20, 21

10   The Preacher sought to find ^adelightful words and to write ^bwords of truth correctly.

★11 ^aProv. 1:6; 22:17; Eccl. 7:5; 10:12 ^bActs 2:37 ^cEzra 9:8; Is. 22:23

11   The ^awords of wise men are like ^bgoads, and masters of

these collections are like well-driven ^cnails; they are given by one Shepherd.

12   But beyond this, my son, be warned: the writing of ^amany books is endless, and excessive ^bdevotion to books is wearying to the body.

★12 ^a1 Kin. 4:32 ^bEccl. 1:18

13   The conclusion, when all has been heard, is: ^afear God and ^bkeep His commandments, because this applies to ^cevery person.

★13 ^aEccl. 3:14; 5:7; 7:18; 8:12 ^bDeut. 4:2; Eccl. 8:5 ^cDeut. 10:12; Mic. 6:8

14   For ^aGod will bring every act to judgment, everything which is hidden, whether it is good or evil.

★14 ^aEccl. 3:17; 11:9; Matt. 10:26; Rom. 2:16; 1 Cor. 4:5

12:8-14 The epilogue of the book records the thesis (v. 8), Solomon's educational program (vv. 9–10), the value of his instruction (vv. 11–12), and his closing admonition (vv. 13–14).
12:10 delightful words. Pleasing words. Solomon affirms that his writings are upright and true.
12:11 The reference to the one Shepherd confirms the fact that the teaching of Solomon is God-given.
12:12 A warning against excessive devotion to secular literature.
12:13 The command to fear God is coordinate with the command to keep His commandments, indicating that true reverence toward

God is to be manifested by obedience to Him. because this applies to every person. Lit., for this is the whole of man; i.e., for this is what man is all about.
12:14 God has not told man how to comprehend all the frustrating futilities of life, but He has instructed man to enjoy life as His gift (2:24), to make the most of every opportunity (9:10), and to live life with reverence toward God (12:13), accompanied by an awareness of future judgment (12:14). Solomon learned to live with life's paradoxes by maintaining a proper attitude toward life and God.

INTRODUCTION TO
THE SONG OF SOLOMON

AUTHOR: Solomon   DATE: C. 965 B.C.

Title and Authorship   *This book has been titled several ways: the Hebrew title from verse 1, "The Song of Songs," which means the most superlative, or best, of songs; the English title, also from verse 1, "The Song of Solomon," which designates the author; and the "Canticles," meaning simply "songs," derived from the Latin.*

Verse 1 asserts that Solomon wrote this song (among the 1,005 which he wrote, 1 Kings 4:32), although the verse may be translated, "The Song of Songs which is about or concerning Solomon." The contents of the book agree with all that we know about the abilities and wisdom of Solomon, and there is no compelling reason not to regard him as the author.

Interpretations   *(1) Some regard the book purely as an allegory, i.e., fictional characters are employed to teach the truth of God's love for His people. Such a nonhistorical view, however, is contrary to all principles of normal interpretation and must be rejected. (2) Others rightly understand the book to be an historical record of the romance of Solomon with a Shulammite woman. The "snapshots" in the book portray the joys of love in courtship and marriage and counteract both the extremes of asceticism and of lust. The rightful place of physical love, within marriage only, is clearly established and honored. Within the historical framework, some also see illustrations of the love of God (and Christ) for His people. Obviously Solomon does not furnish the best example of marital devotion, since he had many wives and concubines (140 at this time, 6:8; many more later, 1 Kings 11:3). The experiences recorded in this book may reflect the only (or virtually the only) pure romance he had.*

Contents   *A lyric poem in dialogue form, the book describes Solomon's love for a Shulammite girl. The king comes in disguise to her family's vineyard, wins her heart, and ultimately makes her his bride.*

OUTLINE OF THE SONG OF SOLOMON

I. **Title, 1:1**
II.. **The Courtship, 1:2-3:5**
  A. The Shulammite to Herself, 1:2-4a
  B. The Daughters of Jerusalem to the King, 1:4b
  C. The Shulammite, 1:5-7
  D. The Daughters of Jerusalem, 1:8
  E. Solomon to the Shulammite, 1:9-10
  F. Daughters of Jerusalem to the Shulammite, 1:11
  G. The Shulammite, 1:12-14
  H. Solomon to the Shulammite, 1:15
  I. The Shulammite to Solomon, 1:16-2:1
  J. Solomon to the Shulammite, 2:2
  K. The Shulammite to Solomon, 2:3-6
  L. Solomon to the Daughters of Jerusalem, 2:7
  M. The Shulammite to Herself, 2:8-13
  N. Solomon to the Shulammite, 2:14
  O. A Chorus, 2:15
  P. The Shulammite to Herself, 2:16-3:4
  Q. Husband to Daughters of Jerusalem, 3:5
III. **The Procession for the Marriage, 3:6-11**
IV. **The Consummation of the Marriage, 4:1-5:1**
  A. Solomon to his Bride, 4:1-15

  B. The Bride to Solomon, 4:16
  C. Solomon to his Bride, 5:1a
  D. God to the Couple, 5:1b
V. **The Honeymoon Is Over, 5:2-6:13**
  A. Wife to Daughters of Jerusalem: the Wife Rebuffs her Husband, 5:2-8
  B. Daughters of Jerusalem to the Wife: a Reminder about her Husband, 5:9
  C. Wife to the Daughters of Jerusalem: She Remembers How Fine He Is, 5:10-16
  D. Daughters of Jerusalem to Wife, 6:1
  E. Wife to Daughters of Jerusalem, 6:2-3
  F. Husband to Wife, 6:4-10
  G. Wife to Herself, 6:11-12
  H. Daughters of Jerusalem to Wife, 6:13a
  I. King to Daughters of Jerusalem, 6:13b
VI. **The Marriage Deepens, 7:1-8:4**
  A. Husband to Wife, 7:1-9a
  B. Wife to Husband, 7:9b-10
  C. Wife to Husband (in the Morning), 7:11-8:3
  D. Husband to Daughters of Jerusalem, 8:4
VII. **The Maturity of Love, 8:5-14**
  A. The Question, 8:5a

THE SONG OF SOLOMON

I TITLE, 1:1

★ **1** *a*1 Kin.
4:32

1 The Song of *a*Songs, which is Solomon's.

II THE COURTSHIP, 1:2-3:5

A The Shulammite to Herself, 1:2-4a

★ **2-4**

2 aSong
1:4; 4:10

2 "May he kiss me with the kisses of his mouth!
For your *a*love is better than wine.

3 aSong
4:10; John
12:3 *b*Eccl.
7:1 *c*Ps.
45:14

3 "Your *a*oils have a pleasing fragrance,
Your *b*name is *like* purified oil;
Therefore the *c*maidens love you.

★ **4** *a*Ps.
45:14, 15
*b*Song 1:4;
4:10

4 "Draw me after you *and* let us run *together!*
The *a*king has brought me into his chambers."

B The Daughters of Jerusalem to the King, 1:4b

"We will rejoice in you and be glad;
We will extol your *b*love more than wine.
Rightly do they love you."

★ **5** *a*Song
2:14; 4:3; 6:4
*b*Song 2:7;
3:5, 10; 5:8,
16; 8:4 *c*Ps.
120:5 *d*Is.
60:7

C The Shulammite, 1:5-7

5 "I am black but *a*lovely,
O *b*daughters of Jerusalem,

Like the *c*tents of *d*Kedar,
Like the curtains of Solomon.

6 aPs.
69:8 *b*Song
8:11

6 "Do not stare at me because I am swarthy,
For the sun has burned me.
My *a*mother's sons were angry with me;
They made me *b*caretaker of the vineyards,
But I have not taken care of my own vineyard.

★ **7** *a*Song
3:1-4 *b*Song
2:16; 6:3 *c*Is.
13:20; Jer.
33:12 *d*Song
8:13

7 "Tell me, O you *a*whom my soul loves,
Where do you *b*pasture *your flock,*
Where do you make *it* *c*lie down at noon?
For why should I be like one who veils herself
Beside the flocks of your *d*companions?"

D The Daughters of Jerusalem, 1:8

8 aSong
5:9; 6:1

8 "If you yourself do not know,
*a*Most beautiful among women,
Go forth on the trail of the flock,
And pasture your young goats
By the tents of the shepherds.

1:1 See Introduction.
1:2-4a The Shulammite expresses her love for the king, but waits for him to take the initiative (v. 4). *maidens.* Other young women around the palace.
1:4b *We.* The daughters of Jerusalem (v. 5); i.e., the women of Solomon's harem. *Rightly do they love you.* The king's character attracted the love of the women of the court.
1:5 *black.* Swarthy; i.e., tanned from working in the sun. She likens her skin to the *tents of*

Kedar, which were made of black goat hair; but she also likens her natural beauty to the magnificent *curtains of Solomon's* palace.
1:6 *My mother's sons.* Her stepbrothers made her caretaker of the vineyard, with the result that she could not care for her personal appearance *(my own vineyard)* as well as other girls could.
1:7 Though the Shulammite longed to meet Solomon, she did not want to chase him *like one who veils herself;* i.e., like a prostitute.

E Solomon to the Shulammite, 1:9–10

9 "To me, ^amy darling, you are like
My ^bmare among the chariots of Pharaoh.
10 "Your ^acheeks are lovely with ornaments,
Your neck with strings of ^bbeads."

★ **9** ^aSong 1:15; 2:2, 10, 13 ^b2 Chr. 1:16, 17

10 ^aSong 5:13 ^bGen. 24:53; Is. 61:10

F Daughters of Jerusalem to the Shulammite, 1:11

11 "We will make for you ornaments of gold
With beads of silver."

G The Shulammite, 1:12–14

12 "While the king was at his table,
My ^aperfume gave forth its fragrance.
13 "My beloved is to me a pouch of ^amyrrh
Which lies all night between my breasts.
14 "My beloved is to me a cluster of ^ahenna blossoms
In the vineyards of ^bEngedi."

12 ^aSong 4:14; Mark 14:3; John 12:3

★**13** ^aPs. 45:8; John 19:39

★**14** ^aSong 4:13 ^b1 Sam. 23:29

H Solomon to the Shulammite, 1:15

15 "^aHow beautiful you are, my darling,
How beautiful you are!
Your ^beyes are *like* doves."

★ **1:15–2:3**

15 ^aSong 1:16; 2:10, 13; 4:1, 7; 6:4, 10 ^bSong 4:1; 5:12

I The Shulammite to Solomon, 1:16–2:1

16 "How handsome you are, ^amy beloved,
And so pleasant!
Indeed, our couch is luxuriant!
17 "The beams of our houses are ^acedars,
Our rafters, ^bcypresses.
2 "I am the ^arose of ^bSharon,
The ^clily of the valleys."

16 ^aSong 2:3, 9, 17; 5:2, 5, 6, 8

17 ^a1 Kin. 6:9, 10; Jer. 22:14 ^b2 Chr. 3:5

★ **1** ^aIs. 35:1 ^bIs. 33:9; 35:2 ^cSong 5:13; 7:2; Hos. 14:5

J Solomon to the Shulammite, 2:2

2 "Like a lily among the thorns,
So is ^amy darling among the maidens."

2 ^aSong 1:9

K The Shulammite to Solomon, 2:3–6

3 "Like an ^aapple tree among the trees of the forest,
So is my beloved among the young men.
In his shade I took great delight and sat down,
And his ^bfruit was sweet to my taste.
4 "He has ^abrought me to *his* banquet hall,
And his ^bbanner over me is love.
5 "Sustain me with ^araisin cakes,
Refresh me with ^bapples,
Because ^cI am lovesick.

3 ^aSong 8:5 ^bSong 4:13, 16; 8:11, 12

★ **4** ^aSong 1:4 ^bPs. 20:5

5 ^a2 Sam. 6:19; 1 Chr. 16:3; Hos. 3:1 ^bSong 7:8 ^cSong 5:8

1:9 *My mare.* The height of flattery for Solomon, a lover of horses (1 Kings 4:26).
1:13 Women commonly wore a pouch of perfume around their neck.
1:14 *henna blossoms.* A fragrant flower that grew in the oasis of *Engedi,* on the W. shore of the Dead Sea.
1:15–2:3 The courtship has now progressed to the point of intimate conversation in an outdoor setting.
2:1 *rose.* Lit., crocus (as in Isa. 35:1). *Sharon.* In Solomon's time, a fertile coastal area. *lily.* Perhaps the hyacinth or the Easter lily.
2:4 *his banner over me is love.* A large banner was used to regroup troops. In other words, everyone could see that Solomon loved her.

6 aSong
8:3 bProv.
4:8

6 "Let ªhis left hand be under
      my head
   And ªhis right hand bem-
      brace me."

L Solomon to the Daughters of Jerusalem, 2:7

★ 7 aSong
3:5; 5:8, 9;
8:4 bSong
1:5 cProv.
6:5; Song
2:9, 17; 3:5;
8:14 dGen.
49:21; Ps.
18:33; Hab.
3:19

7 "I ªadjure you, O bdaugh-
      ters of Jerusalem,
   By the cgazelles or by the
      dhinds of the field,
   ªThat you will not arouse
      or awaken my love,
   Until she pleases."

M The Shulammite to Herself, 2:8–13

8 aSong
2:17; Is. 52:7

8 "Listen! My beloved!
   Behold, he is coming,
   Climbing ªon the moun-
      tains,
   Leaping on the hills!

9 aProv.
6:5; Song
2:17; 3:5;
8:14 bSong
2:17; 8:14
c Judg. 5:28

9 "My beloved is like a ªga-
      zelle or a byoung stag.
   Behold, he is standing be-
      hind our wall,
   He is looking through the
      windows,
   He is peering cthrough the
      lattice.

10 aSong
2:13

10 "My beloved responded
      and said to me,
   'ªArise, my darling, my
      beautiful one,
   And come along.

11 'For behold, the winter is
      past,
   The rain is over and gone.

★12 aGen.
15:9; Ps.
74:19; Jer.
8:7

12 'The flowers have already
      appeared in the land;
   The time has arrived for
      pruning the vines,
   And the voice of the ªtur-
      tledove has been
      heard in our land.

13 'The ªfig tree has ripened
      its figs,
   And the bvines in blossom
      have given forth their
      fragrance.
   Arise, my darling, my
      beautiful one,
   And come along!' "

13 aMatt.
24:32 bSong
7:12

N Solomon to the Shulammite, 2:14

14 "O ªmy dove, bin the clefts
      of the rock,
   In the secret place of the
      steep pathway,
   Let me see your form,
   cLet me hear your voice;
   For your voice is sweet,
   And your form is dlovely."

★14 aSong
5:2; 6:9 bJer.
48:28 cSong
8:13 dSong
1:5

O A Chorus, 2:15

15 "ªCatch the foxes for us,
   The little foxes that are
      ruining the vineyards,
   While our bvineyards are
      in blossom."

★15 aEzek.
13:4; Luke
13:32 bSong
2:13

P The Shulammite to Herself, 2:16–3:4

16 "ªMy beloved is mine, and I
      am his;
   He bpastures his flock
      among the lilies.

16 aSong
6:3; 7:10
bSong 4:5;
6:2, 3

17 "ªUntil the cool of the day
      when the shadows
      flee away,
   Turn, my beloved, and be
      like a bgazelle
   Or a young stag con the
      mountains of Bether."

17 aSong
4:6 bSong
2:9 cSong
2:8

3 "On my bed night after night
   I sought him
   ªWhom my soul loves;

★ 1-5
1 aSong
1:7 bSong
5:6

2:7 *Until she pleases.* Better, until it (love) pleases. Let love develop naturally; do not force it.

2:12 Solomon is inviting the Shulammite outside to enjoy a beautiful spring day. Similarly, God invites His people to share the delights of His company (v. 13).

2:14 Solomon longs to know everything about his fiancée.

2:15 Both resolve to keep anything from spoiling their relationship.

3:1-5 This section relates a dream the bride-to-be had just before her wedding. Fearing the loss of her fiancé, she seeks him, finds him, and takes him to her mother's house. On waking (v. 5), she again counsels patience (as in 2:7, see note there).

I ^bsought him but did not
find him.

2 aJer. 5:1

2 'I must arise now and go
about the city;
In the ^astreets and in the
squares
I must seek him whom my
soul loves.'
I sought him but did not
find him.

3 aSong
5:7; Is. 21:6-
8, 11, 12

3 "^aThe watchmen who make
the rounds in the city
found me,
And I said, 'Have you seen
him whom my soul
loves?'

4 aProv.
8:17 bProv.
4:13; Rom.
8:35, 39
cSong 8:2

4 "^aScarcely had I left them
When I found him whom
my soul loves;
I ^bheld on to him and
would not let him go,
Until I had ^cbrought him
to my mother's house,
And into the room of her
who conceived me."

Q   Husband to Daughters of
Jerusalem, 3:5

5 aSong
2:7; 5:8; 8:4
bSong 2:7

5 "I ^aadjure you, O daughters
of Jerusalem,
By the ^bgazelles or by the
hinds of the field,
That you will not arouse or
awaken *my* love,
Until she pleases."

III   THE PROCESSION FOR THE
MARRIAGE, 3:6-11

★ **6** aSong
8:5 bEx.
13:21; Joel
2:30 cSong
1:13; 4:6, 14;
Matt. 2:11
dEx. 30:34;
Rev. 18:13

6 "^aWhat is this coming up
from the wilderness
Like ^bcolumns of smoke,
Perfumed with ^cmyrrh and
^dfrankincense,

With all scented powders
of the merchant?

7 "Behold, it is the *traveling*
couch of Solomon;
Sixty mighty men around
it,
Of the mighty men of Is-
rael.

★ **7**

8 aJer. 50:9
bPs. 45:3
cPs. 91:5

8 "All of them are wielders of
the sword,
^aExpert in war;
Each man has his ^bsword
at his side,
Guarding against the ^cter-
rors of the night.

9 "King Solomon has made
for himself a sedan
chair
From the timber of Leba-
non.

★ **9**

10 aSong
1:5

10 "He made its posts of silver,
Its back of gold
And its seat of purple fab-
ric,
With its interior lovingly
fitted out
By the ^adaughters of Jeru-
salem.

11 "Go forth, O ^adaughters of
Zion,
And gaze on King Solo-
mon with the crown
With which his mother has
crowned him
On the ^bday of his wed-
ding,
And on the day of his
gladness of heart."

★**11** aIs.
3:16, 17; 4:4
bIs. 62:5

IV   THE CONSUMMATION OF THE
MARRIAGE, 4:1-5:1
A   Solomon to his Bride, 4:1-15

4 "How beautiful ^ayou are, my
darling,
How beautiful you are!
Your ^beyes are *like* doves
^cbehind your veil;

★ **1** aSong
1:15 bSong
1:15; 5:12
cSong 6:7
dSong 6:5
eMic. 7:14

3:6 *smoke.* Rising from the burning incense
used in the procession which brought Solomon to his bride.
3:7 *traveling couch.* The litter on which Solomon was carried.
3:9 *a sedan chair.* Though a different word from
that used in verse 7, this probably describes
that same enclosed litter or traveling throne.

3:11 *his mother.* Bathsheba. The wedding day
should be a day of shared *gladness,* though
Solomon had too many such days!
4:1 Solomon extols the beauties of his bride. *like
doves* (eyes). Soft, sparkling beauty. Her *hair*
was long and flowing, like a *flock of goats* that
blend together as they make their way down a
mountainside.

Your ^dhair is like a flock of
goats
That have descended from
Mount ^eGilead.

2 "Your ^ateeth are like a flock
of *newly* shorn ewes
Which have come up from
their washing,
All of which bear twins,
And not one among them
has lost her young.

3 "Your lips are like a ^ascarlet
thread,
And your ^bmouth is lovely.
Your ^ctemples are like a
slice of a pomegranate
Behind your veil.

4 "Your ^aneck is like the
tower of David
Built with rows of stones,
On which are ^bhung a
thousand shields,
All the round ^cshields of
the mighty men.

5 "Your ^atwo breasts are like
two fawns,
Twins of a gazelle,
Which ^bfeed among the
lilies.

6 "^aUntil the cool of the day
When the shadows flee
away,
I will go my way to the
mountain of ^bmyrrh
And to the hill of ^bfrankin-
cense.

7 "^aYou are altogether beautiful, my darling,
And there is no blemish in
you.

8 "*Come* with me from ^aLeb-
anon, *my* ^bbride,
May you come with me
from Lebanon.
Journey down from the
summit of ^cAmana,

From the summit of ^dSenir
and Hermon,
From the dens of lions,
From the mountains of
leopards.

9 "You have made my heart
beat faster, ^amy sister,
my bride;
You have made my heart
beat faster with a sin-
gle *glance* of your
eyes,
With a single strand of
your ^bnecklace.

10 "^aHow beautiful is your
love, my sister, *my*
bride!
How much ^bbetter is your
love than wine,
And the ^cfragrance of your
oils
Than all *kinds* of spices!

11 "Your lips, *my* bride, ^adrip
^bhoney;
Honey and milk are under
your tongue,
And the fragrance of your
garments is like the
^cfragrance of Leba-
non.

12 "A garden locked is my sister, *my* bride,
A rock garden locked, a
^aspring ^bsealed up.

13 "Your shoots are an ^aor-
chard of ^bpomegran-
ates
With ^cchoice fruits,
^dhenna with nard
plants,

14 ^aNard and saffron, calamus
and ^bcinnamon,
With all the trees of
^cfrankincense,
^dMyrrh and aloes, along
with all the finest
spices.

★ 2 ^aSong 6:6
★ 3 ^aJosh. 2:18 ^bSong 5:16 ^cSong 6:7
★ 4 ^aSong 7:4 ^bEzek. 27:10, 11 ^c2 Sam. 1:21
★ 5 ^aSong 7:3 ^bSong 2:16; 6:2, 3
6 ^aSong 2:17 ^bSong 4:14
7 ^aSong 1:15; Eph. 5:27
★ 8 ^a1 Kin. 4:33; Ps. 72:16 ^bSong 5:1; Is. 62:5 ^c2 Kin. 5:12 ^dDeut. 3:9; 1 Chr. 5:23; Ezek. 27:5

★ 9 ^aSong 4:10, 12; 5:1, 2 ^bGen. 41:42; Prov. 1:9; Ezek. 16:11; Dan. 5:7
10 ^aSong 7:6 ^bSong 1:2, 4 ^cSong 1:3
11 ^aProv. 5:3 ^bPs. 19:10; Prov. 24:13 ^cGen. 27:27; Hos. 14:6
★ 4:12-5:1
12 ^aProv. 5:15-18 ^bGen. 29:3
13 ^aEccl. 2:5 ^bSong 6:11; 7:12 ^cSong 2:3; 4:16; 7:13 ^dSong 1:14
14 ^aSong 1:12 ^bEx. 30:23 ^cSong 4:6 ^dPs. 45:8; Song 3:6; John 19:39

4:2 She had perfectly regular, white *teeth* and none were missing.
4:3 Her *temples* (including her cheeks) were ruby colored.
4:4 She bore herself regally and with strength of character.
4:5 Her *breasts* were soft and youthful.
4:8 In these figures of speech, Solomon asks that his bride gather her scattered thoughts, allay her fears, and give herself solely to him.
4:9 *my sister.* An affectionate term for one's wife.
4:12-5:1 In this extended metaphor, Solomon expresses his desire to consummate his marriage (using the imagery of coming into a *garden*), is invited to do so (v. 16), and does (5:1a). God then speaks and blesses the union (5:1b).

15 *a*Zech.
14:8; John
4:10

15 "*You are* a garden spring,
A well of *a*fresh water,
And streams *flowing* from
    Lebanon."

B   The Bride to Solomon, 4:16

16 *a*Song
5:1; 6:2
*b*Song 1:13;
2:3, 8; 6:2
*c*Song 4:13

16 "Awake, O north *wind,*
And come, *wind of* the
    south;
Make my *a*garden breathe
    out *fragrance,*
Let its spices be wafted
    abroad.
May *b*my beloved come
    into his garden
And eat its *c*choice fruits!"

C   Solomon to his Bride, 5:1a

1 *a*Song
6:2 *b*Song
4:9 *c*Song
1:13; 4:14
*d*Song 4:11
*e*Prov. 9:5;
Is. 55:1
*f*Judg. 14:11,
20; John
3:29

5 "I have *a*come into my gar-
den, *b*my sister, *my*
bride;
I have gathered my *c*myrrh
    along with my bal-
    sam.
I have eaten my honey-
    comb and my *d*honey;
I have *e*drunk my wine
    and my milk.

D   God to the Couple, 5:1b

Eat, *f*friends;
Drink and imbibe deeply,
    O lovers."

V   THE HONEYMOON IS OVER,
                                5:2–6:13
A   Wife to Daughters of
    Jerusalem: the Wife
    Rebuffs her
    Husband, 5:2–8

★ 2-8
2 *a*Song
4:9 *b*Song
2:14; 6:9
*c*Song 5:11

2 "I was asleep, but my heart
    was awake.

A voice! My beloved was
    knocking:
'Open to me, *a*my sister,
    my darling,
*b*My dove, my perfect one!
For my head is drenched
    with dew,
My *c*locks with the damp
    of the night.'

3 *a*Luke
11:7 *b*Gen.
19:2

3 "I have *a*taken off my dress,
How can I put it on *again?*
I have *b*washed my feet,
How can I dirty them
    again?

4 *a*Jer.
31:20

4 "My beloved extended his
    hand through the
    opening,
And my *a*feelings were
    aroused for him.

5 *a*Song
5:13

5 "I arose to open to my be-
    loved;
And my hands *a*dripped
    with myrrh,
And my fingers with liquid
    myrrh,
On the handles of the bolt.

6 *a*Song
6:1 *b*Song
5:2 *c*Song
3:1 *d*Prov.
1:28

6 "I opened to my beloved,
But my beloved had
    *a*turned away *and* had
    gone!
My heart went out *to him*
    as he *b*spoke.
I *c*searched for him, but I
    did not find him;
I *d*called him, but he did
    not answer me.

7 *a*Song
3:3

7 "The *a*watchmen who make
    the rounds in the city
    found me,
They struck me *and*
    wounded me;
The guardsmen of the
    walls took away my
    shawl from me.

8 *a*Song
2:7; 3:5
*b*Song 2:5

8 "I *a*adjure you, O daughters
    of Jerusalem,
If you find my beloved,
As to what you will tell
    him:
For *b*I am lovesick."

5:2–8 The next scene, sometime after the wedding night, shows the bride refusing to let her
husband in (vv. 2–3), regretting it, finding that
he had left (vv. 5–6), and then searching for
him (vv. 7–8). The king had left *myrrh* on the
door (v. 5) as a reminder that he had been
there. The *watchmen* mistook her for a criminal (v. 7).

B Daughters of Jerusalem to the Wife: a Reminder about her Husband, 5:9

★ **9** *a*Song 1:8; 6:1

9 "What kind of beloved is your beloved, O *a*most beautiful among women? What kind of beloved is your beloved, That thus you adjure us?"

C Wife to the Daughters of Jerusalem: She Remembers How Fine He Is, 5:10-16

10 *a*1 Sam. 16:12 *b*Ps. 45:2

10 "My beloved is dazzling and *a*ruddy, *b*Outstanding among ten thousand.

★**11** *a*Song 5:2

11 "His head is *like* gold, pure gold; His *a*locks are *like* clusters of dates, *And* black as a raven.

12 *a*Song 1:15; 4:1 *b*Ex. 25:7

12 "His *a*eyes are like doves, Beside streams of water, Bathed in milk, *And* reposed in *their* *b*setting.

★**13** *a*Song 6:2 *b*Song 2:1 *c*Song 5:5

13 "His cheeks are like a *a*bed of balsam, Banks of sweet-scented herbs; His lips are *b*lilies, *c*Dripping with liquid myrrh.

14 *a*Ex. 28:20; 39:13; Ezek. 1:16; Dan. 10:6 *b*Ex. 24:10; 28:18; Is. 28:16; Is. 54:11

14 "His hands are rods of gold Set with *a*beryl; His abdomen is carved ivory Inlaid with *b*sapphires.

★**15** *a*Song 7:4 *b*1 Kin. 4:33; Ps. 80:10; Ezek. 17:23; 31:8

15 "His legs are pillars of alabaster Set on pedestals of pure gold;

His appearance is like *a*Lebanon, Choice as the *b*cedars.

16 *a*Song 7:9 *b*2 Sam. 1:23

16 "His *a*mouth is *full of* sweetness. And he is wholly *b*desirable. This is my beloved and this is my friend, O daughters of Jerusalem."

D Daughters of Jerusalem to Wife, 6:1

1 *a*Song 5:6 *b*Song 1:8

6 "*a*Where has your beloved gone, O *b*most beautiful among women? Where has your beloved turned, That we may seek him with you?"

E Wife to Daughters of Jerusalem, 6:2-3

★ **2-3**

2 *a*Song 4:16; 5:1 *b*Song 5:13 *c*Song 1:7 *d*Song 2:1; 5:13

2 "My beloved has gone down to his *a*garden, To the *b*beds of balsam, To *c*pasture *his* flock in the gardens And gather *d*lilies.

3 *a*Song 2:16; 7:10 *b*Song 2:16; 4:5

3 "*a*I am my beloved's and my beloved is mine, He who *b*pastures *his* flock among the lilies."

F Husband to Wife, 6:4-10

★ **4** *a*Song 1:15 *b*1 Kin. 14:17 *c*Song 1:5 *d*Ps. 48:2; 50:2 *e*Song 6:10

4 "*a*You are as beautiful as *b*Tirzah, my darling, As *c*lovely as *d*Jerusalem, As *e*awesome as an army with banners.

5:9 When reminded by the daughters of Jerusalem of how much Solomon meant to her, she bursts into an ecstatic description of him (vv. 10-16).
5:11 *gold.* His bearing was regal.
5:13 His face was perfumed.
5:15 *pillars of alabaster.* He was strong. His entire *appearance* was as impressive as the cedars of Lebanon (see note on Nahum 1:4).

6:2-3 To the question from the daughters of Jerusalem in verse 1, the wife replies that her husband has gone to his favorite *garden* (v. 2), and she affirms the security of their relationship (v. 3).
6:4 *Tirzah* means "pleasantness," and was a city known for its beauty (see note on 1 Kings 14:17).

★ 5-6
5 aSong
4:1

5 "Turn your eyes away from
me,
For they have confused
me;
aYour hair is like a flock of
goats
That have descended from
Gilead.

6 aSong
4:2

6 "aYour teeth are like a flock
of ewes
Which have come up from
their washing,
All of which bear twins,
And not one among them
has lost her young.

7 aSong
4:3

7 "aYour temples are like a
slice of a pomegranate
Behind your veil.

★ 8-9
8 a1 Kin.
11:3 bSong
1:3

8 "There are sixty aqueens
and eighty concu-
bines,
And bmaidens without
number;

9 aSong
2:14; 5:2
bGen. 30:13
c1 Kin. 11:3

9 *But* amy dove, my perfect
one, is unique:
She is her mother's only
daughter;
She is the pure *child* of the
one who bore her.
The bmaidens saw her and
called her blessed,
The cqueens and the con-
cubines *also,* and they
praised her, *saying,*

10 aJob
31:26 bMatt.
17:2; Rev.
1:16 cSong
6:4

10 'Who is this that grows like
the dawn,
As beautiful as the full
amoon,
As pure bas the sun,
As cawesome as an army
with banners?'

G   Wife to Herself, 6:11-12

11 aSong
7:12 bSong
4:13

11 "I went down to the orchard
of nut trees
To see the blossoms of the
valley,

To see whether athe vine
had budded
Or the bpomegranates had
bloomed.

12 "Before I was aware, my
soul set me
Over the chariots of my
noble people."

★12

H   Daughters of Jerusalem to Wife, 6:13a

13 "Come back, come back, O
Shulammite;
Come back, come back,
that we may gaze at
you!"

★13 aJudg.
21:21 bGen.
32:2; 2 Sam.
17:24

I   King to Daughters of Jerusalem, 6:13b

"Why should you gaze at
the Shulammite,
As at the adance of bthe
two companies?

VI   THE MARRIAGE DEEPENS, 7:1-8:4
A   Husband to Wife, 7:1-9a

7 "How beautiful are your feet
in sandals,
O aprince's daughter!
The curves of your hips
are like jewels,
The work of the hands of
an artist.

★ 1-9

1 aPs.
45:13

2 "Your navel is *like* a round
goblet
Which never lacks mixed
wine;
Your belly is like a heap of
wheat
Fenced about with lilies.

3 "Your atwo breasts are like
two fawns,
Twins of a gazelle.

3 aSong
4:5

6:5-6 These are the same compliments Solomon
paid her on their wedding night (see notes on
4:1-2).
6:8-9 The Shulammite stands unique among all
of Solomon's women.
6:12 The meaning seems to be this: Before she
knew it, Solomon had placed his wife in his
own chariot, a sure sign of their reconciliation.

6:13 To the women's request to gaze upon the
Shulammite, Solomon observes that they like
to gaze on her as if they were watching a festive dance.
7:1-9 Solomon now extols the physical beauty
of his wife. Her *eyes* were as sparkling as
pools; her *nose,* apparently prominent (v. 4).
Carmel was noted for its beauty.

4 "Your *neck is *like* a tower
of ivory,
Your eyes *like* the pools in
*Heshbon
By the gate of Bath-
rabbim;
Your nose is like the tower
of Lebanon,
Which faces toward Da-
mascus.

5 "Your head crowns you like
*Carmel,
And the flowing locks of
your head are like
purple threads;
The king is captivated by
your tresses.

6 "How *beautiful and how
delightful you are,
My love, with *all* your
charms!

7 "Your stature is like a palm
tree,
And your breasts are *like*
its clusters.

8 "I said, 'I will climb the
palm tree,
I will take hold of its fruit
stalks.'
Oh, may your breasts be
like clusters of the
vine,
And the fragrance of your
breath like *apples,

9 And your *mouth like the
best wine!"

B Wife to Husband, 7:9b–10

"It *goes *down* smoothly for
my beloved,
Flowing gently *through* the
lips of those who fall
asleep.

10 "*I am my beloved's,
And his *desire is for me.

C Wife to Husband (in the Morning), 7:11–8:3

11 "Come, my beloved, let us
go out into the coun-
try,
Let us spend the night in
the villages.

12 "Let us rise early *and go to
the vineyards;
Let us *see whether the
vine has budded
And its blossoms have
opened,
And whether the pome-
granates have
bloomed.
There I will give you my
love.

13 "The *mandrakes have giv-
en forth fragrance;
And over our doors are all
*choice *fruits,*
Both new and old,
Which I have saved up for
you, my beloved.

8 "Oh that you were like a
brother to me
Who nursed at my moth-
er's breasts.
If I found you outdoors, I
would kiss you;
No one would despise me,
either.

2 "I would lead you *and*
*bring you
Into the house of my
mother, who used to
instruct me;
I would give you spiced
wine to drink from
the juice of my pome-
granates.

3 "Let *his left hand be under
my head,
And his right hand em-
brace me."

Margin references (left column):
4 *Song 4:4 *Num. 21:26
5 *Is. 35:2
6 *Song 1:15, 16; 4:10
8 *Song 2:5
9 *Song 5:16 *Prov. 23:31
10 *Song 2:16; 6:3 *Ps. 45:11; Gal. 2:20

Margin references (right column):
★12 *Song 6:11
13 *Gen. 30:14 *Song 2:3; 4:13, 16; Matt. 13:52
★ 1-3
2 *Song 3:4
3 *Song 2:6

7:12 Apparently a year has elapsed since their
courtship, for it is spring again (2:12).
8:1-3 The Shulammite wishes Solomon were
her natural *brother* so she could express her
affection for him in public, a thing improper
for a married couple to do in that culture.

D Husband to Daughters of Jerusalem, 8:4

★ **4** *a*Song
2:7; 3:5

4 "*a*I want you to swear, O daughters of Jerusalem,
Do not arouse or awaken *my* love,
Until she pleases."

VII THE MATURITY OF LOVE, 8:5-14
A The Question, 8:5a

★ **5** *a*Song
3:6 *b*Song
2:3

5 "*a*Who is this coming up from the wilderness,
Leaning on her beloved?"

B Solomon's Reminiscence, 8:5b

"Beneath the *b*apple tree I awakened you;
There your mother was in labor with you,
There she was in labor *and* gave you birth."

C The Wife to her Husband, 8:6-7

★ **6** *a*Is.
49:16; Jer.
22:24; Hag.
2:23 *b*Prov.
6:34

6 "Put me like a seal over your heart,
Like a *a*seal on your arm.
For love is as strong as death,
*b*Jealousy is as severe as Sheol;
Its flashes are flashes of fire,
The *very* flame of the LORD.

7 "Many waters cannot quench love,
Nor will rivers overflow it;
*a*If a man were to give all the riches of his house for love,
It would be utterly despised."

★ **7** *a*Prov.
6:35

D The Brothers of the Shulammite, 8:8-9

8 "We have a little sister,
And she *a*has no breasts;
What shall we do for our sister
On the day when she is spoken for?
9 "If she is a wall,
We shall build on her a battlement of silver;
But if she is a door,
We shall barricade her with *a*planks of cedar."

★ **8-9**

8 *a*Ezek.
16:7

9 *a*1 Kin.
6:15

E The Wife to Everyone, 8:10-12

10 "I was a wall, and *a*my breasts were like towers;
Then I became in his eyes as one who finds peace.
11 "Solomon had a *a*vineyard at Baal-hamon;
He *b*entrusted the vineyard to *c*caretakers;
Each one was to bring a *d*thousand *shekels* of silver for its *e*fruit.

10 *a*Ezek.
16:7

★**11-12**

11 *a*Eccl. 2:4
*b*Matt. 21:33
*c*Song 1:6
*d*Is. 7:23
*e*Song 2:3;
8:12

8:4 See note on 2:7.
8:5 The question may come from the villagers, with whom the Shulammite grew up, as they see the couple approach. The last part of the verse is Solomon's reminiscence of their first meeting.
8:6 *like a seal.* I.e., like a precious possession (see note on Gen. 38:18). She wants to be her husband's most treasured possession.
8:7 True love cannot be quenched, nor bought. To attempt to buy it is to despise it.
8:8-9 The Shulammite recalls her brothers' atti-

tude toward her when she was young. If she would resist temptation *(a wall)* they would reward her *(silver)*, but if she were loose *(a door)* they would be strict with her *(barricade her with planks of cedar)*. She turned out virtuous (v. 10).
8:11-12 In contrast to Solomon, who had great wealth (v. 11), the Shulammite had only herself to give, which she gladly did, asking only that Solomon remember her stepbrothers *(those who take care of its fruit).*

12 "My very own vineyard is
    at my disposal;
The thousand *shekels* are
    for you, Solomon,
And two hundred are for
    those who take care of
    its fruit."

F The Husband to his Wife,
8:13

^{13 a}Song
1:7 ^bSong
2:14

13 "O you who sit in the gar-
    dens,

My ^acompanions are lis-
    tening   for   your
    voice—
^bLet me hear it!"

G The Wife to her Husband,
8:14

14 "Hurry, my beloved,   ★14 ^aSong
And be ^alike a gazelle or a   2:7, 9, 17
    young stag   ^bSong 4:6
On the ^bmountains of
    spices."

8:14 As separated lovers long to be reunited, so   22:20).
the Church longs to see her Bridegroom (Rev.

INTRODUCTION TO
THE BOOK OF ISAIAH

AUTHOR: Isaiah   DATE: 740–680 B.C.

The Prophet Born into an influential, upper-class family, Isaiah rubbed shoulders with royalty and gave advice concerning the foreign affairs of the nation. Though usually scoffed at, he warned vigorously against foreign alliances and urged Judah to trust the Lord (7:4; 30:1–17). He also attacked the social ills of the day, not because he was a social reformer, but because he saw those abuses as symptoms of spiritual declension (1:3–9; 58:6–10). After living most of his life in Jerusalem, tradition says that Isaiah was martyred during the reign of Manasseh (696–642) by being sawed in two inside a hollow log (cf. Heb. 11:37).

The Times During the latter half of the eighth century Judah seemingly was about to follow the example of apostasy of the ten northern tribes of Israel (who were captured by Assyria in 722). King Ahaz foolishly looked to Assyria for protection, even though Isaiah told him the Northern Kingdom would shortly fall at the hands of the Assyrians (8:3–4). Hezekiah, Ahaz's God-fearing son, instituted spiritual reforms but sought the help of Egypt in foreign affairs. Egypt fell before Sennacherib of Assyria, and only through divine intervention was Judah saved from the same fate (37:36–37). During the reign of Manasseh, idolatrous practices were reinstated, and Isaiah warned of the inevitability of the Babylonian captivity. He also gave assurance of the preservation of the people and restoration of the nation.

Composition Much dispute has arisen over the authorship of chapters 40–66. Some assign the entire section to a "Deutero-Isaiah," who lived around 540 B.C. (after the Babylonian captivity). Others see a "Trito-Isaiah," who wrote chapters 56–66. Still others see insertions and editing as late as the first century B.C., a position difficult to maintain in view of the discovery of the Qumran Isaiah scroll dated in the second century B.C.

These suggestions attempt to eliminate the supernatural element necessary for predictive prophecy. Hence, the Babylonian captivity and the return under a Persian king (specifically named Cyrus) are not viewed as being predicted 150 years in advance, but as happenings recorded after the events. But even if one were to grant such a conclusion, it would not invalidate predictive prophecy. The name of King Josiah was predicted by a prophet three centuries before his time (1 Kings 13:2), and Bethlehem was named as the birthplace of Messiah seven centuries before the event (Mic. 5:2). In addition, there is predictive prophecy in chapters 1–39 of Isaiah (see 7:16; 8:4, 7; 37:33–35; 38:8 for prophecies soon fulfilled and 9:1–2; 13:17–20 for prophecies of the more distant future).

If "Deutero-Isaiah" lived in Babylon, as is claimed, he shows little knowledge of Babylonian geography but great familiarity with Palestine (41:19; 43:14; 44:14). Further, it is asserted that differences in language and style can only be accounted for by assuming different authors, a theory which, if applied to Milton, Goethe, or Shakespeare, would force us to conclude that many of their writings were spurious. On the contrary, one can point out 40 or 50 sentences and phrases that appear in both sections of the book and that therefore argue for single authorship (cf. 1:20 with 40:5 and 58:14; 11:6–9 with 65:25; 35:6 with 41:18, etc.).

To claim two or more authors for this book is also to contradict the evidence of the New Testament. Quotations from chapters 40–66 are found in Matthew 3:3; 12:17–21; Luke 3:4–6; Acts 8:28; Romans 10:16, 20 and all are attributed to Isaiah. Moreover, in John 12:38–41, quotations from Isaiah 6:9–10 and 53:1 appear together and both are ascribed to the Isaiah who saw the Lord in the Temple vision of chapter 6. We must therefore conclude that the same author was responsible for the entire book, and that no part of it was written at the time of the Babylonian captivity.

Contents Isaiah has often been called "the evangelical prophet" because he says so much about the redemptive work of Messiah. More about the person and work of Christ is found here than in any other book of the Old Testament. Consequently, there are many important and favorite passages in the book, some of which are 1:18; 2:4; 6:3, 8; 7:14; 9:6–7; 11:9; 26:3; 35:1; 40:3; 48:16; chapter 53; 55:1; 57:15; 59:1; 61:1–3.

OUTLINE OF ISAIAH

Part 1: Denunciation, 1:1-39:8

I. Denunciation of Judah, 1:1-12:6
A. The Condemnation of Judah, 1:1-5:30
  1. Superscription, 1:1
  2. God's indictment, 1:2-23
  3. God's promise of restoration after judgment, 1:24-31
  4. The glory of the future kingdom, 2:1-4
  5. The purging, 2:5-4:1
  6. The millennial kingdom, 4:2-6
  7. The parable of the vineyard, 5:1-30
B. The Commission of Isaiah, 6:1-13
C. The Coming of Messiah, 7:1-12:6
  1. The sign of Immanuel, 7:1-25
  2. The sign of Maher-shalal-hash-baz, 8:1-22
  3. The sign of Messiah, 9:1-7
  4. Judgment on Samaria, 9:8-10:4
  5. Retribution (on Assyria) and return (of Israel), 10:5-34
  6. The rule of the Branch of Jesse, 11:1-16
  7. A hymn of praise, 12:1-6

II. Denunciations Against Other Nations, 13:1-23:18
A. Against Babylon, 13:1-14:23
B. Against Assyria, 14:24-27
C. Against Philistia, 14:28-32
D. Against Moab, 15:1-16:14
E. Against Damascus (Syria) and Her Ally, Israel, 17:1-14
F. Against Ethiopia, 18:1-7
G. Against Egypt, 19:1-20:6
H. Against Babylon, 21:1-10
I. Against Edom, 21:11-12
J. Against Arabia, 21:13-17
K. Against Jerusalem, 22:1-25
L. Against Tyre, 23:1-18

III. The Future Tribulation and Kingdom (Isaiah's Apocalypse), 24:1-27:13
A. The Judgments of the Tribulation Period, 24:1-23
B. The Triumphs of the Kingdom Age, 25:1-12
C. Praise in the Kingdom, 26:1-21
D. Israel in the Kingdom, 27:1-13

IV. Denunciation of Israel and Judah (Woes and Blessings), 28:1-35:10
A. Woe on Samaria, 28:1-29
B. Woe on Judah, 29:1-31:9
  1. For her hypocrisy, 29:1-24
  2. For her alliance with Egypt, 30:1-31:9
C. Messiah and His Kingdom, 32:1-20
D. Assyria and her Destruction, 33:1-24
E. Armageddon and Its Judgments, 34:1-17
F. The Kingdom and Its Blessings, 35:1-10

V. Denunciation of Sennacherib, 36:1-39:8
A. The Taunt from Assyria, 36:1-22
B. The Truth from God, 37:1-7
C. The Threat from Assyria, 37:8-35
D. The Triumph over Assyria, 37:36-38
E. The Sickness of Hezekiah, 38:1-22
F. The Stupidity of Hezekiah, 39:1-8

Part 2: Consolation, 40:1-66:24

I. The Greatness of God, 40:1-48:22
A. In Releasing Judah from Captivity, 40:1-11
B. In Relation to the Creation, 40:12-31
C. In Comparison to Idols, 41:1-29
D. In Providing His Servant, 42:1-25
E. In Restoring Israel, 43:1-44:28
F. In Using Cyrus, 45:1-25
G. In Judging Babylon, 46:1-47:15
H. In Releasing Judah from Babylon, 48:1-22

II. The Salvation of the Servant-Messiah, 49:1-57:21
A. The Servant Commissioned, 49:1-26
B. The Servant Contrasted with Disobedient Israel, 50:1-11
C. The Remnant Encouraged and Exhorted, 51:1-52:12
D. The Suffering and Triumph of the Servant, 52:13-53:12
E. Salvation through the Servant, 54:1-57:21
  1. The song of salvation, 54:1-17
  2. The invitation of salvation, 55:1-13
  3. Millennial blessings extended to gentiles, 56:1-8
  4. Rebuke to those who refuse salvation, 56:9-57:21

III. The Program of God for Peace, 58:1-66:24
A. The Contrast between Right and Wrong Worship, 58:1-14
B. The Dealing with Sin, 59:1-21
  1. Description of Israel's sins, 59:1-8
  2. Confession of Israel's sins, 59:9-15
  3. Blotting out of Israel's sins, 59:16-21
C. The Glory of Israel in the Millennial Kingdom, 60:1-22
D. The Messiah's Ministry of Peace during Both Advents, 61:1-11
E. The Restoration of Israel, 62:1-12
F. The Prerequisites for Blessing, 63:1-65:16
  1. Judgment of God's enemies, 63:1-6
  2. Confession of God's people, 63:7-64:12
  3. Repentance of sins, 65:1-16
G. The Characteristics of the Kingdom, 65:17-25
H. The Rebuke of Hypocrisy, 66:1-6
I. The Rebirth of Israel, 66:7-9
J. The Rejoicing in the Future, 66:10-24

THE BOOK OF ISAIAH

PART 1   DENUNCIATION, 1:1–39:8
I   DENUNCIATION OF JUDAH, 1:1–12:6
A   The Condemnation of Judah, 1:1–5:30
1   Superscription, 1:1

★ **1** *a*Is. 2:1;
40:9 *b*2 Kin.
15:1-7, 13;
2 Chr. 26:1-
23 *c*2 Kin.
15:32-38;
2 Chr. 27:1-9
*d*2 Kin. 16:1-
20; 2 Chr.
28:1-27; Is.
7:1 *e*2 Kin.
18:1-20:21;
2 Chr. 29:1-
32:33

1 The vision of Isaiah the son of Amoz, concerning *a*Judah and Jerusalem which he saw during the reigns of *b*Uzziah, *c*Jotham, *d*Ahaz, *and* *e*Hezekiah, kings of Judah.

2   God's indictment, 1:2–23

★ **2-4**

2 *a*Deut.
32:1 *b*Mic.
1:2 *c*Jer.
3:22 *d*Is.
30:1, 9; 65:2

2 *a*Listen, O heavens, and
    hear, O *b*earth;
For the LORD speaks,
"*c*Sons I have reared and
    brought up,
But they have *d*revolted
    against Me.

3 *a*Jer. 9:3,
6 *b*Is. 44:18

3 "An ox knows its owner,
And a donkey its master's
    manger,
But Israel *a*does not know,
My people *b*do not under-
    stand."

★ **4** *a*Is.
14:20 *b*Neh.
1:7 *c*Is. 1:28
*d*Is. 5:24

4 Alas, sinful nation,
People weighed down with
    iniquity,
*a*Offspring of evildoers,
Sons who *b*act corruptly!
They have *c*abandoned the
    LORD,
They have *d*despised the
    Holy One of Israel,
They have turned away
    from Him.

5 Where will you be
    stricken again,
As you *a*continue in *your*
    rebellion?
The whole head is *b*sick,
And the whole heart is
    faint.

★ **5-6**

5 *a*Is. 31:6
*b*Is. 33:24;
Ezek. 34:4,
16

6 *a*From the sole of the foot
    even to the head
There is *b*nothing sound in
    it,
Only bruises, welts, and
    raw wounds,
*c*Not pressed out or ban-
    daged,
Nor softened with oil.

6 *a*Job 2:7
*b*Ps. 38:3
*c*Jer. 8:22

7 Your *a*land is desolate,
Your cities are burned
    with fire,
Your fields—strangers are
    devouring them in
    your presence;
It is desolation, as over-
    thrown by strangers.

★ **7** *a*Lev.
26:33; Jer.
44:6

8 And the daughter of Zion
    is left like a shelter in
    a vineyard,
Like a watchman's hut in a
    cucumber field, like a
    besieged city.

★ **8**

9 *a*Unless the LORD of hosts
    Had left us a few *b*surviv-
    ors,
We would be like *c*Sodom,
We would be like Gomor-
    rah.

★ **9** *a*Rom.
9:29 *b*Is.
10:20-22;
11:11, 16;
37:4, 31, 32;
46:3 *c*Gen.
19:24

★ **10-15**

10 Hear *a*the word of the
    LORD,
You rulers of *b*Sodom;

10 *a*Is. 8:20;
28:14 *b*Is.
3:9; Ezek.
16:49; Rom.
9:29; Rev.
11:8

1:1 *Uzziah.* A good king (also known as Azariah), who reigned from 791–740 (cf. 6:1); *Jotham* was also godly (750–736, including a co-regency with Uzziah); *Ahaz,* a wicked and idolatrous king, ruled 736–716; *Hezekiah* (716–687) promoted religious reform.
1:2–4 God's *sons* have turned against the Lord, showing not even the sense of gratitude and ownership that an *ox* or a *donkey* does. *manger.* Feeding trough.
1:4 *sinful.* From a verb meaning "to miss the mark." Israel was a *nation* that had missed God's goal. *iniquity.* A perversion, from a verb meaning "to bend or twist." *evildoers.* From a

verb meaning "to be harmful, injurious." *act corruptly.* Cause to putrefy. The Lord's indictment of Israel is very specific.
1:5–6 The picture is not of a sick man but rather of one who has been flogged.
1:7 In Isaiah's lifetime, Judah was subjected to attacks from Israel, Syria, Edom, Philistia, and Assyria.
1:8 *shelter . . . hut.* A temporary shanty.
1:9 Quoted in Rom. 9:29 with reference to Christian Jews. On the wickedness of *Sodom,* see notes on Gen. 13:10 and 18:20.
1:10–15 The people's sacrifices (v. 11), religious festivals (vv. 13–14), and prayers (v. 15) were

Give ear to the instruction
of our God,
You people of Gomorrah.

11 "ᵃWhat are your multiplied
sacrifices to Me?"
Says the Lᴏʀᴅ.
"I have had enough of
burnt offerings of
rams,
And the fat of fed cattle.
And I take no pleasure in
the blood of bulls,
lambs, or goats.

12 "When you come ᵃto appear before Me,
Who requires of you this
trampling of My
courts?

13 "Bring your worthless offerings no longer,
ᵃIncense is an abomination
to Me.
ᵇNew moon and sabbath,
the ᶜcalling of assem-
blies—
I cannot ᵈendure iniquity
and the solemn as-
sembly.

14 "I hate your new moon festivals and your ᵃap-
pointed feasts,
They have become a bur-
den to Me.
I am ᵇweary of bearing
them.

15 "So when you ᵃspread out
your hands in prayer,
ᵇI will hide My eyes from
you,
Yes, even though you
ᶜmultiply prayers,
I will not listen.
ᵈYour hands are covered
with blood.

16 "ᵃWash yourselves, ᵇmake
yourselves clean;
ᶜRemove the evil of your
deeds from My sight.
ᵈCease to do evil,

17 Learn to do good;
ᵃSeek justice,

Reprove the ruthless;
ᵇDefend the orphan,
Plead for the widow.

18 "Come now, and ᵃlet us
reason together,"
Says the Lᴏʀᴅ,
"ᵇThough your sins are as
scarlet,
They will be as white as
snow;
Though they are red like
crimson,
They will be like wool.

19 "ᵃIf you consent and obey,
You will ᵇeat the best of
the land;

20 "But if you refuse and
rebel,
You will be ᵃdevoured by
the sword."
Truly, ᵇthe mouth of the
Lᴏʀᴅ has spoken.

21 How the faithful city has
become a ᵃharlot,
She who was full of jus-
tice!
Righteousness once lodged
in her,
But now murderers.

22 Your silver has become
dross,
Your drink diluted with
water.

23 Your ᵃrulers are rebels,
And companions of
thieves;
Everyone ᵇloves a bribe,
And chases after rewards.
They ᶜdo not defend the
orphan,
Nor does the widow's plea
come before them.

**3   God's promise of restoration
after judgment, 1:24–31**

24 Therefore the Lord Gᴏᴅ of
hosts,
The ᵃMighty One of Israel
declares,

Marginal references

11 ᵃPs. 50:8; Jer. 6:20; Amos 5:21, 22; Mal. 1:10

12 ᵃEx. 23:17

13 ᵃIs. 66:3 ᵇ1 Chr. 23:31 ᶜEx. 12:16 ᵈJer. 7:9, 10

14 ᵃIs. 29:1, 2 ᵇIs. 7:13; 43:24

15 ᵃ1 Kin. 8:22; Lam. 1:17 ᵇIs. 8:17; 59:2 ᶜMic. 3:4 ᵈIs. 59:3

16 ᵃPs. 26:6 ᵇIs. 52:11 ᶜIs. 55:7 ᵈJer. 25:5

★17 ᵃJer. 22:3; Zeph. 2:3 ᵇPs. 82:3

★18 ᵃIs. 41:1, 21; 43:26; Mic. 6:2 ᵇPs. 51:7; Is. 43:25; 44:22; Rev. 7:14

19 ᵃDeut. 28:1; 30:15, 16 ᵇIs. 55:2

20 ᵃIs. 3:25; 65:12 ᵇIs. 40:5; 58:14; Mic. 4:4; Titus 1:2

21 ᵃIs. 57:3-9; Jer. 2:20

23 ᵃHos. 5:10; Mic. 7:3 ᵇEx. 23:8; Mic. 7:3 ᶜIs. 10:2; Jer. 5:28; Ezek. 22:7; Zech. 7:10

24 ᵃPs. 132:2; Is. 49:26; 60:16 ᵇDeut. 28:63; Is. 35:4; 59:18; 61:2; 63:4

Footnotes

shams. God was not repudiating the sacrificial system (which He Himself had established) but was condemning religious pretense.
1:17 *Defend the orphan.* Better, bring justice to the orphan.
1:18 *scarlet* and *crimson* were both glaring and colorfast.

"Ah, I will be relieved of
   My adversaries,
And ᵇavenge Myself on
   My foes."

25 aEzek.
22:19-22;
Mal. 3:3

25 "I will also turn My hand
   against you,
And will ᵃsmelt away your
   dross as with lye,
And will remove all your
   alloy.

★26 aIs.
60:17 bIs.
33:5; 60:14;
62:1, 2;
Zech. 8:3

26 "Then I will restore your
   ᵃjudges as at the first,
And your counselors as at
   the beginning;
After that you will be
   called the ᵇcity of
   righteousness,
A faithful city."

27 aIs.
35:9f.; 62:12;
63:4

27 Zion will be ᵃredeemed
   with justice,
And her repentant ones
   with righteousness.

28 aPs. 9:5;
Is. 66:24;
2 Thess.
1:8, 9

28 But transgressors and sinners will be ᵃcrushed
   together,
And those who forsake the
   LORD shall come to an
   end.

★29 aIs.
57:5 bIs.
65:3; 66:17

29 Surely, you will be
   ashamed of the ᵃoaks
   which you have de-
   sired,
And you will be embar-
   rassed at the ᵇgardens
   which you have cho-
   sen.

30 aIs. 64:6

30 For you will be like an oak
   whose ᵃleaf fades
   away,
Or as a garden that has no
   water.

31 aIs. 5:24;
9:19; 26:11;
33:11-14 bIs.
66:24; Matt.
3:12; Mark
9:43

31 And the strong man will
   become tinder,
His work also a spark.
Thus they shall both ᵃburn
   together,
And there will be ᵇnone to
   quench *them*.

4   *The glory of the future kingdom,* 2:1-4

1 aIs. 1:1

2 The word which ᵃIsaiah the
  son of Amoz saw concerning
Judah and Jerusalem.

★ 2-4

2 aMic. 4:1-
3 bIs. 27:13;
66:20 cIs.
56:7

2 Now it will come about
   that
  ᵃIn the last days,
The ᵇmountain of the
   house of the LORD
Will be established as the
   chief of the moun-
   tains,
And will be raised above
   the hills;
And ᶜall the nations will
   stream to it.

3 aIs. 51:4,
5; Luke
24:47

3 And many peoples will
   come and say,
"Come, let us go up to the
   mountain of the LORD,
To the house of the God of
   Jacob;
That He may teach us con-
   cerning His ways,
And that we may walk in
   His paths."
For the law will go forth
   ᵃfrom Zion,
And the word of the LORD
   from Jerusalem.

4 aIs.
32:17, 18;
Joel 3:10
bIs. 9:5, 7;
11:6-9; Hos.
2:18; Zech.
9:10

4 And He will judge between the nations,
And will render decisions
   for many peoples;
And ᵃthey will hammer
   their swords into
   plowshares, and their
   spears into pruning
   hooks.
ᵇNation will not lift up
   sword against nation,
And never again will they
   learn war.

5   *The purging,* 2:5-4:1

5 aIs. 58:1
bIs. 60:1, 2,
19, 20;
1 John 1:5

5 Come, ᵃhouse of Jacob,
   and let us walk in the
   ᵇlight of the LORD.

1:26 These prophecies will be fulfilled in the millennial kingdom.
1:29 oaks . . . gardens. Likely a reference to the oak groves and gardens connected with their idolatrous and adulterous heathen worship.
2:2-4 As in Mic. 4:1-5, a description of the mil-

lennial kingdom. God's government *(mountain)* will be established over all the kingdoms of this world; Gentiles *(nations)* and Jews *(peoples)* will do the will of God; justice and peace will reign (Isa. 2:4).

★ 6 ªDeut.
31:17
b2 Kin. 1:2
c2 Kin. 16:7,
8; Prov. 6:1

6 For Thou hast ªabandoned
Thy people, the house
of Jacob,
Because they are filled
with influences from
the east,
And *they are* soothsayers
blike the Philistines,
And they cstrike *bargains*
with the children of
foreigners.

★ 7 ªDeut.
17:16; Is.
30:16; 31:1;
Mic. 5:10

7 Their land has also been
filled with silver and
gold,
And there is no end to
their treasures;
Their land has also been
filled with ªhorses,
And there is no end to
their chariots.

8 ªIs. 10:11
bPs. 115:4-
8; Is. 17:8;
37:19; 40:19;
44:17

8 Their land has also been
ªfilled with idols;
They worship the bwork of
their hands,
That which their fingers
have made.

9 ªPs. 49:2;
62:9; Is. 5:15
bNeh. 4:5

9 So ªthe *common* man has
been humbled,
And the man *of impor-*
tance has been
abased,
But bdo not forgive them.

10 ªIs. 2:19,
21; Rev.
6:15, 16
b2 Thess.
1:9

10 ªEnter the rock and hide in
the dust
bFrom the terror of the
Lord and from the
splendor of His ma-
jesty.

11 ªIs. 5:15;
37:23 bPs.
18:27; Is.
13:11; 23:9;
2 Cor. 10:5

11 The ªproud look of man
will be abased,
And the bloftiness of man
will be humbled,
And the Lord alone will be
exalted in that day.

★12 ªJob
40:11, 12; Is.
24:4, 21;
Mal. 4:1

12 For the Lord of hosts will
have a day of reckon-
ing

Against ªeveryone who is
proud and lofty,
And against everyone who
is lifted up,
That he may be abased.

13 ªZech.
11:2

13 And *it will be* against all
the cedars of Lebanon
that are lofty and
lifted up,
Against all the ªoaks of Bashan,

14 ªIs. 40:4

14 Against all the ªlofty
mountains,
Against all the hills that
are lifted up,

15 ªIs. 25:12

15 Against every ªhigh tower,
Against every fortified
wall,

★16 ª1 Kin.
10:22; Is.
23:1, 14;
60:9

16 Against all the ªships of
Tarshish,
And against all the beauti-
ful craft.

17 And the pride of man will
be humbled,
And the loftiness of men
will be abased,
And the Lord alone will be
exalted in that day.

18 ªIs. 21:9;
Mic. 1:7

18 But the ªidols will completely vanish.

★19 ªIs.
2:10 bPs.
18:7; Is.
2:21; 13:13;
24:1, 19, 20;
Hag. 2:6, 7;
Heb. 12:26

19 And *men* will ªgo into
caves of the rocks,
And into holes of the
ground
Before the terror of the
Lord,
And before the splendor of
His majesty,
When He arises bto make
the earth tremble.

20 ªIs.
30:22; 31:7
bLev. 11:19

20 In that day men will ªcast
away to the moles and
the bbats
Their idols of silver and
their idols of gold,
Which they made for
themselves to wor-
ship,

2:6 *soothsayers like the Philistines.* See 1 Sam.
6:2; 2 Kings 1:2.
2:7 Judah prospered economically under Uzziah.
2:12 *a day of reckoning.* Or, the day of the Lord
(see Introduction to the Book of Joel).
2:16 *ships of Tarshish.* Especially large and sea-
worthy ships which carried smelted metal to
Tarshish. *Tarshish* comes from a word meaning "to melt or be melted" and might refer to

any place that had smelting operations or any
land that contained mineral deposits, though
many identify it with Tartessus near the SW.
coast of Spain (see Jonah 1:3). *beautiful craft.*
Objects of art.
2:19 See Rev. 6:15, which vividly describes the
desperate actions of people in the coming
tribulation days.

21 In order to ᵃgo into the caverns of the rocks and the clefts of the cliffs,
Before the terror of the LORD and the splendor of His majesty,
When He arises to make the earth tremble.

22 ᵃStop regarding man, whose breath *of life* is in his nostrils;
For ᵇwhy should he be esteemed?

3 For behold, the Lord GOD of hosts ᵃis going to remove from Jerusalem and Judah
Both supply and support, the whole supply of bread,
And the whole supply of water;

2 ᵃThe mighty man and the warrior,
The judge and the prophet,
The diviner and the elder,

3 The captain of fifty and the honorable man,
The counselor and the expert artisan,
And the skillful enchanter.

4 And I will make mere ᵃlads their princes
And capricious children will rule over them,

5 And the people will be ᵃoppressed,
Each one by another, and each one by his ᵇneighbor;
The youth will storm against the elder,
And the inferior against the honorable.

6 When a man ᵃlays hold of his brother in his father's house, *saying,*
"You have a cloak, you shall be our ruler,
And these ruins will be under your charge,"

7 On that day will he protest, saying,
"I will not be *your* ᵃhealer,
For in my house there is neither bread nor cloak;
You should not appoint me ruler of the people."

8 For ᵃJerusalem has stumbled, and Judah has fallen,
Because their ᵇspeech and their actions are against the LORD,
To ᶜrebel against His glorious presence.

9 The expression of their faces bears witness against them.
And they display their sin like ᵃSodom;
They do not *even* conceal *it.*
Woe to them!
For they have ᵇbrought evil on themselves.

10 Say to the ᵃrighteous that *it will go* well *with them,*
For they will eat the fruit of their actions.

11 Woe to the wicked! *It will* go badly *with him,*
For ᵃwhat he deserves will be done to him.

12 O My people! Their oppressors are ᵃchildren,
And women rule over them.
O My people! ᵇThose who guide you lead *you* astray,
And confuse the direction of your paths.

13 ᵃThe LORD arises to contend,
And stands to judge the people.

14 The LORD ᵃenters into judgment with the elders and princes of His people,

---

Marginal references

21 ᵃIs. 2:19

22 ᵃPs. 146:3; Jer. 17:5 ᵇPs. 8:4; 144:3, 4; Is. 40:15, 17; James 4:14

★ 1 ᵃLev. 26:26; Is. 5:13; 9:20; Ezek. 4:16

2 ᵃ2 Kin. 24:14; Is. 9:14, 15; Ezek. 17:12, 13

★ 4 ᵃEccl. 10:16

5 ᵃMic. 7:3-6 ᵇIs. 9:19; Jer. 9:3-8

6 ᵃIs. 4:1

★ 7 ᵃEzek. 34:4; Hos. 5:13

8 ᵃIs. 1:7; 6:11 ᵇPs. 73:9-11; Is. 9:17; 59:3 ᶜIs. 65:3

9 ᵃGen. 13:13; Is. 1:10-15 ᵇProv. 8:36; 15:32; Rom. 6:23

10 ᵃDeut. 28:1-14; Eccl. 8:12; Is. 54:17

11 ᵃDeut. 28:15-68; Is. 65:6, 7

12 ᵃIs. 3:4 ᵇIs. 9:16; 28:14, 15

13 ᵃIs. 66:16; Hos. 4:1; Mic. 6:2

14 ᵃJob 22:4; Ps. 143:2; Ezek. 20:35, 36 ᵇPs. 14:4; Mic. 3:3 ᶜJob 24:9, 14; Ps. 10:9; Prov. 30:14; Is. 10:1, 2; Ezek. 18:12; James 2:6

3:1 *supply and support.* Both words indicate something one leans on. *remove.* Through Nebuchadnezzar (see 2 Kings 24:15-16).
3:4 *mere lads.* Immature physically (Manasseh

was 12 when he began to reign) and immature in political ability (e.g., Jehoiakim, Jehoiachin, Zedekiah).
3:7 It would be no honor to rule the nation.

"It is you who have [b]devoured the vineyard;
The [c]plunder of the poor is in your houses.

15 [a]Ps. 94:5

15 "What do you mean by [a]crushing My people,
And grinding the face of the poor?"
Declares the Lord God of hosts.

★16-26

★16 [a]Song 3:11; Is. 3:16-4:1, 4; 32:9-15

16 Moreover, the Lord said, "Because the [a]daughters of Zion are proud,
And walk with heads held high and seductive eyes,
And go along with mincing steps,
And tinkle the bangles on their feet,

17 Therefore the Lord will afflict the scalp of the daughters of Zion with scabs,
And the Lord will make their foreheads bare."

18 [a]Judg. 8:21, 26

18 In that day the Lord will take away the beauty of *their* anklets, headbands, [a]crescent ornaments,

19 dangling earrings, bracelets, veils,

20 [a]Ex. 39:28

20 [a]headdresses, ankle chains, sashes, perfume boxes, amulets,

21 [a]Gen. 24:47; Ezek. 16:12

21 finger rings, [a]nose rings,

22 festal robes, outer tunics, cloaks, money purses,

23 hand mirrors, undergarments, turbans, and veils.

24 [a]Esth. 2:12 [b]1 Pet. 3:3 [c]Is. 22:12; Ezek. 27:31; Amos 8:10 [d]Is. 15:3; Lam. 2:10

24 Now it will come about that instead of sweet [a]perfume there will be putrefaction;
Instead of a belt, a rope;
Instead of [b]well-set hair, a [c]plucked-out scalp;
Instead of fine clothes, a [d]donning of sackcloth;

And branding instead of beauty.

25 [a]Is. 1:20; 65:12

25 Your men will [a]fall by the sword,
And your mighty ones in battle.

26 [a]Jer. 14:2; Lam. 1:4 [b]Lam. 2:10

26 And her [a]gates will lament and mourn;
And deserted she will [b]sit on the ground.

4 For seven women will take hold of [a]one man in that day, saying, "We will eat our own bread and wear our own clothes, only let us be called by your name; [b]take away our reproach!"

★ 1 [a]Is. 13:12 [b]Gen. 30:23; Is. 54:4

6 The millennial kingdom, 4:2-6

2 In that day the [a]Branch of the Lord will be beautiful and glorious, and the [b]fruit of the earth *will* be the pride and the adornment of the [c]survivors of Israel.

★ 2 [a]Is. 11:1; 53:2; Jer. 23:5; 33:15; Zech. 3:8; 6:12 [b]Ps. 72:16 [c]Is. 10:20; 37:31, 32; Joel 2:32; Obad. 17

3 And it will come about that he who is [a]left in Zion and remains in Jerusalem will be called [b]holy—everyone who is [c]recorded for life in Jerusalem.

★ 3-6

3 [a]Is. 28:5; 46:3; Rom. 11:4; 5 [b]Is. 52:1; 62:12 [c]Ex. 32:32; Ps. 69:28; Luke 10:20

4 When the Lord has washed away the filth of the [a]daughters of Zion, and purged the [b]bloodshed of Jerusalem from her midst, by the [c]spirit of judgment and the [d]spirit of burning,

4 [a]Is. 3:16 [b]Is. 1:15 [c]Is. 28:6 [d]Is. 1:31; 9:19; Matt. 3:11

5 then the Lord will create over the whole area of Mount Zion and over her assemblies [a]a cloud by day, even smoke, and the brightness of a flaming fire by night; for over all the [b]glory will be a canopy.

5 [a]Ex. 13:21, 22; 24:16; Num. 9:15-23 [b]Is. 60:1, 2

6 And there will be a [a]shelter to *give* shade from the heat by day, and refuge and protection from the storm and the rain.

6 [a]Ps. 27:5; Is. 25:4; 32:1, 2

3:16-26 The fashionable women, seeking to lure other women's husbands with their imported luxurious dress, would soon be destitute (cf. 1 Pet. 3:3-4).
3:16 *tinkle.* I.e., with small silver bells on their ankles.
4:1 Wars will slaughter so many men that *in that day* (ultimately the tribulation days),

women will be willing to be self-supporting if only they can be married and escape the *reproach* of being childless.
4:2 *Branch of the Lord.* I.e., Messiah; cf. Jer. 23:5; 33:15; Zech. 3:8; 6:12, where the same term is found.
4:3-6 Fulfillment awaits the return of Messiah and establishment of His Kingdom.

7 The parable of the vineyard, 5:1-30

★ 1-12
1 aPs. 80:8;
Jer. 12:10;
Matt. 21:33;
Mark 12:1;
Luke 20:9

5 Let me sing now for my well-beloved
A song of my beloved concerning His vineyard.
My well-beloved had a avineyard on a fertile hill.

2 aJer. 2:21
bMatt. 21:19;
Mark 11:13;
Luke 13:6

2 And He dug it all around, removed its stones,
And planted it with the achoicest vine.
And He built a tower in the middle of it,
And hewed out a wine vat in it;
Then He bexpected it to produce good grapes,
But it produced only worthless ones.

3 aMatt. 21:40

3 "And now, O inhabitants of Jerusalem and men of Judah,
aJudge between Me and My vineyard.

4 a2 Chr. 36:16; Jer. 2:5; 7:25, 26; Mic. 6:3; Matt. 23:37

4 "aWhat more was there to do for My vineyard that I have not done in it?
Why, when I expected it to produce good grapes did it produce worthless ones?

★ 5 aPs. 89:40 bPs. 80:12 cIs. 10:6; 28:18; Lam. 1:15; Luke 21:24; Rev. 11:2

5 "So now let Me tell you what I am going to do to My vineyard:
I will aremove its hedge and it will be consumed;
I will bbreak down its wall and it will become ctrampled ground.

6 "And I will alay it waste;
It will not be pruned or hoed,
But briars and thorns will come up.
I will also charge the clouds to brain no rain on it."

6 a2 Chr. 36:19-21; Is. 7:19-25; 24:1, 3; Jer. 25:11
b1 Kin. 8:35; 17:1; Jer. 14:1-22

7 For the avineyard of the LORD of hosts is the house of Israel,
And the men of Judah His delightful plant.
Thus He looked for justice, but behold, bbloodshed;
For righteousness, but behold, a cry of distress.

★ 7 aPs. 80:8-11 bIs. 3:14, 15; 30:12; 59:13

8 Woe to those who aadd house to house and join field to field,
Until there is no more room,
So that you have to live alone in the midst of the land!

★ 8-25
8 aJer. 22:13-17; Mic. 2:2; Hab. 2:9-12

9 In my ears the LORD of hosts has sworn, "Surely, amany houses shall become bdesolate,
Even great and fine ones, without occupants.

9 aIs. 6:11, 12 bMatt. 23:38

10 "For aten acres of vineyard will yield only one bath of wine,
And a bhomer of seed will yield but an ephah of grain."

10 aLev. 26:26; Is. 7:23; Hag. 1:6; 2:16
bEzek. 45:11

11 Woe to those who rise early in the morning that they may pursue astrong drink;

11 aProv. 23:29, 30; Eccl. 10:16, 17; Is. 5:22; 22:13; 28:1, 3, 7, 8

5:1-12 Israel is elsewhere pictured as a vineyard (Jer. 12:10; Psalm 80:8-19; Matt. 21:33-45) to whom God had given every advantage, but which yielded only evil fruit. **5:5** The inevitable penalty for Israel would be removal of God's protective hedge, which would result in invasion by her enemies. **5:7** a cry. For help. **5:8-25** In these verses there is a six-point indictment of Israel, each point being introduced with "Woe." (1) Woe to land grabbers (vv. 8-10; cf. 1 Kings 21:3, 16), whose mansions will be desolate and whose land will become

unproductive. one bath. Equal to about 8 gallons; 10 acres might be expected to produce 500 baths of wine. ephah. One-tenth of a homer, which was 58 gallons (cf. Ruth 2:17). (2) Woe to the drunkard (Isa. 5:11-17; cf. 5:22; 19:14; 24:20; 28:1, 7). Such dissipation brings temporal punishment to nations (5:13) and eternal punishment to individuals (v. 14). (3) Woe to the blasphemous (vv. 18-19), who pull their idol of sin along, taunting God to act if He can. (4) Woe to those who pervert moral distinctions (v. 20). (5) Woe to the conceited (v. 21). (6) Woe to drunken judges (vv. 22-25).

Who stay up late in the evening that wine may inflame them!

12 And their banquets are *accompanied* by lyre and *a*harp, by tambourine and flute, and by wine;
But they *b*do not pay attention to the deeds of the LORD,
Nor do they consider the work of His hands.

13 Therefore My people go into exile for their *a*lack of knowledge;
And their *b*honorable men are famished,
And their multitude is parched with thirst.

14 Therefore *a*Sheol has enlarged its throat and opened its mouth without measure;
And Jerusalem's splendor, her multitude, her din *of revelry,* and the jubilant within her, descend *into it.*

15 So the *common* man will be humbled, and the man of *importance* abased,
*a*The eyes of the proud also will be abased.

16 But the *a*LORD of hosts will be *b*exalted in judgment,
And the holy God will show Himself *c*holy in righteousness.

17 *a*Then the lambs will graze as in their pasture,
And strangers will eat in the waste places of the wealthy.

18 Woe to those who drag *a*iniquity with the cords of falsehood,
And sin as if with cart ropes;

19 *a*Who say, "Let Him make speed, let Him hasten His work, that we may see *it;*

And let the purpose of the Holy One of Israel draw near
And come to pass, that we may know *it!*"

20 Woe to those who *a*call evil good, and good evil;
Who *b*substitute darkness for light and light for darkness;
Who substitute bitter for sweet, and sweet for bitter!

21 Woe to those who are *a*wise in their own eyes,
And clever in their own sight!

22 *a*Woe to those who are heroes in drinking wine,
And valiant men in mixing strong drink;

23 *a*Who justify the wicked for a bribe,
And *b*take away the rights of the ones who are in the right!

24 Therefore, *a*as a tongue of fire consumes stubble,
And dry grass collapses into the flame,
So their *b*root will become *c*like rot and their blossom blow away as dust;
For they have *d*rejected the law of the LORD of hosts,
And despised the word of the Holy One of Israel.

25 On this account the *a*anger of the LORD has burned against His people,
And He has stretched out His hand against them and struck them down,
And the *b*mountains quaked; and their *c*corpses lay like refuse in the middle of the streets.
*d*For all this His anger is not spent,

12 *a*Amos 6:5, 6 *b*Job 34:27; Ps. 28:5

13 *a*Is. 1:3; 27:11; Hos. 4:6 *b*Is. 3:3

14 *a*Prov. 30:16; Hab. 2:5

15 *a*Is. 2:11; 10:33

16 *a*Is. 28:17; 30:18; 61:8 *b*Is. 2:11, 17; 33:5, 10 *c*Is. 8:13; 29:23; 1 Pet. 3:15

17 *a*Is. 7:25; Mic. 2:12; Zeph. 2:6

18 *a*Is. 59:4-8; Jer. 23:10-14

19 *a*Ezek. 12:22; 2 Pet. 3:4

20 *a*Prov. 17:15; Amos 5:7 *b*Job 17:12; Matt. 6:22, 23; Luke 11:34, 35

21 *a*Prov. 3:7; Rom. 12:16; 1 Cor. 3:18-20

22 *a*Prov. 23:20; Is. 5:11; 56:12; Hab. 2:15

23 *a*Ex. 23:8; Is. 1:23; 10:1, 2; Mic. 3:11; 7:3 *b*Ps. 94:21; James 5:6

24 *a*Is. 9:18, 19; Joel 2:5 *b*Job 18:16 *c*Hos. 5:12 *d*Is. 8:6; 30:9, 12; Acts 13:41

25 *a*2 Kin. 22:13, 17; Is. 66:15 *b*Ps. 18:7; Is. 64:3; Jer. 4:24; Nah. 1:5 *c*2 Kin. 9:37; Is. 14:19; Jer. 16:4 *d*Is. 9:12, 17, 19, 21; 10:4; Jer. 4:8; Dan. 9:16 *e*Ex. 7:19; Is. 23:11

But His *e*hand is still stretched out.

★26-30

26 a Is. 13:2,
3 **b**Is. 7:18;
Zech. 10:8
cDeut. 28:49
dIs. 13:4, 5

26 He will also lift up a *a*standard to the distant nation,
And will *b*whistle for it *c*from the ends of the earth;
And behold, it will *d*come with speed swiftly.

27 a Joel 2:7,
8 **b**Job 12:18

27 *a*No one in it is weary or stumbles,
None slumbers or sleeps;
Nor is the *b*belt at its waist undone,
Nor its sandal strap broken.

28 a Ps. 7:12,
13; 45:5; Is.
13:18 **b**Is.
21:1; Jer.
4:13

28 *a*Its arrows are sharp, and all its bows are bent;
The hoofs of its horses seem like flint, and its *chariot* *b*wheels like a whirlwind.

29 a Jer.
51:38; Zeph.
3:3; Zech.
11:3 **b**Is.
10:6; 49:24,
25; Mic. 5:8
cIs. 42:22

29 Its *a*roaring is like a lioness, and it roars like young lions;
It growls as it *b*seizes the prey,
And carries *it* off with *c*no one to deliver *it*.

30 a Is.
17:12; Jer.
6:23; Luke
21:25 **b**Is.
8:22; Jer.
4:23-28; Joel
2:10; Luke
21:25, 26

30 And it shall *a*growl over it in that day like the roaring of the sea.
If one *b*looks to the land, behold, there is darkness *and* distress;
Even the light is darkened by its clouds.

B The Commission of Isaiah, 6:1-13

★ 1 a2 Kin.
15:7; 2 Chr.
26:23; Is. 1:1
bJohn 12:41;
Rev. 4:2, 3;
20:11

6 In the year of *a*King Uzziah's death, *b*I saw the Lord sitting on a throne, lofty and exalted, with the train of His robe filling the temple.

★ 2 a Rev.
4:8

2 Seraphim stood above Him, *a*each having six wings; with two he covered his face, and with two he covered his feet, and with two he flew.

3 a Rev. 4:8
bNum.
14:21; Ps.
72:19

3 And one called out to another and said,
"*a*Holy, Holy, Holy, is the LORD of hosts,
The *b*whole earth is full of His glory."

4 a Rev.
15:8

4 And the foundations of the thresholds trembled at the voice of him who called out, while the *a*temple was filling with smoke.

★ 5 a Ex.
33:20; Luke
5:8 **b**Ex.
6:12, 30 **c**Is.
59:3; Jer.
9:3-8 **d**Jer.
51:57

5 Then I said,
"*a*Woe is me, for I am ruined!
Because I am a man of *b*unclean lips,
And I live among a *c*people of unclean lips;
For my eyes have seen the *d*King, the LORD of hosts."

★ 6 a Rev.
8:3

6 Then one of the seraphim flew to me, with a burning coal in his hand which he had taken from the *a*altar with tongs.

7 a Jer. 1:9;
Dan. 10:16
bIs. 40:2;
53:5, 6, 11;
1 John 1:7

7 And he *a*touched my mouth *with it* and said, "Behold, this has touched your lips; and *b*your iniquity is taken away, and your sin is forgiven."

★ 8 a Ezek.
10:5; Acts
9:4 **b**Acts
26:19

8 Then I heard the *a*voice of the Lord, saying, "Whom shall I send, and who will go for Us?" Then *b*I said, "Here am I. Send me!"

9 a Is. 43:8;
Matt. 13:14;
Mark 4:12;
Luke 8:10;
John 12:40;
Acts 28:26;
Rom. 11:8

9 And He said, "Go, and tell this people:
'Keep on *a*listening, but do not perceive;
Keep on looking, but do not understand.'

10 a Matt.
13:15 **b**Deut.
31:20; 32:15
cJer. 5:21

10 "*a*Render the hearts of this people *b*insensitive,
Their ears dull,
And their eyes dim,

5:26-30 With *a standard* (banner) and with a *whistle*, Assyria would be summoned to punish Israel.
6:1 *King Uzziah* died in 740.
6:2 *Seraphim.* Used here of heavenly angels and in Num. 21:6 of fiery serpents. Derived from a verb that means "to burn," the seraphim (the Hebrew form is plural) were agents of cleansing; here they are angelic agents. Compare note on Gen. 3:22-24 on cherubim.

6:5 See similar confessions in Job 42:6; Luke 5:8.
6:6 *a burning coal . . . from the altar.* Either the altar of incense or the altar of burnt offering. In either case, the coal stood for the full significance of the Temple ritual of cleansing. God took the initiative in cleansing the prophet.
6:8 *for Us.* God is seen as a king in council. This phrase certainly allows for the fuller N.T. revelation of the Trinity.

*11 aPs.
79:5 bLev.
26:31; Is.
1:7; 3:8, 26

12 aDeut.
28:64 bJer.
4:29

*13 aJob
14:7 bDeut.
7:6; Ezra 9:2

   cLest they see with their
      eyes,
   Hear with their ears,
   Understand with their
      hearts,
   And return and be
      healed."
11 Then I said, "Lord, ahow
      long?" And He an-
      swered,
   "Until bcities are devastated
      and without inhabi-
      tant,
   Houses are without peo-
      ple,
   And the land is utterly
      desolate,
12 "The LORD has aremoved
      men far away,
   And the bforsaken places
      are many in the midst
      of the land.
13 "Yet there will be a tenth
      portion in it,
   And it will again be sub-
      ject to burning,
   Like a terebinth or an aoak
   Whose stump remains
      when it is felled.
   The bholy seed is its
      stump."

C The Coming of Messiah,
             7:1–12:6

1 *The sign of Immanuel,*
             7:1–25

* 1-2
1 a2 Kin.
16:1; Is. 1:1
b2 Kin.
15:37 c2 Kin.
15:25; 2 Chr.
28:6 dIs.
7:6, 7

7 Now it came about in the
   days of aAhaz, the son of Jotham, the son of Uzziah, king
of Judah, that bRezin the king of
Aram and cPekah the son of

Remaliah, king of Israel, went up
to Jerusalem to *wage* war against
it, but dcould not conquer it.
   2 When it was reported to
the ahouse of David, saying, "The
Arameans bhave camped in
cEphraim," his heart and the
hearts of his people shook as
the trees of the forest shake with
the wind.
   3 Then the LORD said to Isaiah, "Go out now to meet Ahaz,
you and your son Shear-jashub,
at the end of the aconduit of the
upper pool, on the highway to the
fuller's field,
   4 and say to him, 'Take care,
and be acalm, have no bfear and
cdo not be fainthearted because
of these two stubs of smoldering
dfirebrands, on account of the
fierce anger of Rezin and Aram,
and the eson of Remaliah.
   5 'Because aAram, *with* E-
phraim and the son of Remaliah,
has planned evil against you, saying,
   6 "Let us go up against Judah
and terrorize it, and make for ourselves a breach in its walls, and
set up the son of Tabeel as king in
the midst of it,"
   7 thus says the Lord GOD,
"aIt shall not stand nor shall it
come to pass.
   8 "For the head of Aram is
aDamascus and the head of Damascus is Rezin (now within another 65 years Ephraim will be
shattered, *so that it is* no longer a
people),
   9 and the head of Ephraim is
Samaria and the head of Samaria

2 aIs. 7:13;
22:22 bIs.
8:12 cIs. 9:9

* 3 a2 Kin.
18:17; Is.
36:2

* 4 aEx.
14:13; Is.
30:15; Lam.
3:26 bIs.
10:24; Matt.
24:6 cDeut.
20:3; 1 Sam.
17:32; Is.
35:4 dAmos
4:11; Zech.
3:2 eIs.
7:1, 9

5 aIs. 7:2

7 aIs. 8:10;
28:18; Acts
4:25, 26

* 8 aGen.
14:15; Is.
17:1-3

* 9 a2 Chr.
20:20; Is.
5:24; 8:6-8;
30:12-14

6:11 Though the people would not pay attention, Isaiah was to continue to prophesy until
the Babylonian deportation.
6:13 After the 70 years in Babylon, *a tenth*
would return. These would, in turn, be subject
again to chastisement *(burning)* but not eradi-
cation. Israel would sprout like the *terebinth*
(an oak-like tree from which, when cut, flows
a fragrant, resinous juice) and *oak* trees.
7:1-2 Second Kings 16:5-18 and 2 Chron.
28:5-21 record the historical background of
this chapter. *Aram* (Syria) and *Ephraim* (the 10
northern tribes of Israel) rebelled against their
overlord, Assyria, and were attempting to
force Judah into their alliance, even if it meant
deposing Ahaz and substituting a puppet king,

the son of Tabeel (Isa. 7:6). Isaiah saw a political crisis also, since Ahaz was trusting man's
power rather than God's.
7:3 *Shear-jashub* means "a remnant shall return."
7:4 *two stubs.* I.e., Aram (Syria, which was
crushed in 732) and Israel (which lost her national existence in 722). These words of Isaiah
were spoken about 735.
7:8 *within another 65 years.* I.e., by 669, when
the resettling of the land of Israel by foreign
colonists would have taken place.
7:9 A literal translation of the last part of the
verse reveals a play on words similar to, "If
you will not be sure, you cannot be secure" or
"unsure—insecure."

is the son of Remaliah. ᵃIf you will not believe, you surely shall not last." ' "

10 Then the LORD spoke again to Ahaz, saying,

11 ᵃ2 Kin. 19:29; Is. 37:30; 38:7, 8; 55:13

11 "Ask a ᵃsign for yourself from the LORD your God; make *it* deep as Sheol or high as heaven."

★12

12 But Ahaz said, "I will not ask, nor will I test the LORD!"

13 ᵃIs. 7:2 ᵇIs. 1:14; 43:24 ᶜIs. 25:1

13 Then he said, "Listen now, O ᵃhouse of David! Is it too slight a thing for you to try the patience of men, that you will ᵇtry the patience of ᶜmy God as well?

★14-16

14 ᵃMatt. 1:23 ᵇIs. 8:8, 10

14 "Therefore the Lord Himself will give you a sign: Behold, ᵃa virgin will be with child and bear a son, and she will call His name ᵇImmanuel.

15 ᵃIs. 7:22

15 "He will eat ᵃcurds and honey at the time He knows *enough* to refuse evil and choose good.

16 ᵃIs. 8:4 ᵇIs. 8:14; 17:3; Jer. 7:15; Hos. 5:3, 9, 14; Amos 1:3-5

16 "ᵃFor before the boy will know *enough* to refuse evil and choose good, ᵇthe land whose two kings you dread will be forsaken.

17 ᵃ1 Kin. 12:16 ᵇ2 Chr. 28:20; Is. 8:7, 8; 10:5, 6

17 "The LORD will bring on you, on your people, and on your father's house such days as have never come since the day that ᵃEphraim separated from Judah, the ᵇking of Assyria."

★18 ᵃIs. 5:26 ᵇIs. 13:5

18 And it will come about in that day, that the LORD will ᵃwhistle for the fly that is in the ᵇremotest part of the rivers of Egypt, and for the bee that is in the land of Assyria.

19 And they will all come and settle on the steep ravines, on the ᵃledges of the cliffs, ᵇon all the thorn bushes, and on all the watering places.

19 ᵃIs. 2:19; Jer. 16:16 ᵇIs. 7:24, 25

20 In that day the Lord will ᵃshave with a ᵇrazor, ᶜhired from regions beyond ᵈthe Euphrates (*that is,* with the king of Assyria), the head and the hair of the legs; and it will also remove the beard.

★20 ᵃ2 Kin. 18:13-16; Is. 24:1 ᵇEzek. 5:1-4 ᶜIs. 10:5, 15 ᵈIs. 8:7; 11:15; Jer. 2:18

21 Now it will come about in that day that a man may keep alive a ᵃheifer and a pair of sheep;

★21-25 21 ᵃIs. 14:30; 27:10; Jer. 39:10

22 and it will happen that because of the abundance of the milk produced he will eat curds, for everyone that is left within the land will eat ᵃcurds and honey.

22 ᵃIs. 8:15

23 And it will come about in that day, ᵃthat every place where there used to be a thousand vines, *valued* at a thousand *shekels* of silver, will become ᵇbriars and thorns.

23 ᵃIs. 5:10; 32:13, 14 ᵇIs. 5:6

24 *People* will come there with bows and arrows because all the land will be briars and thorns.

25 And as for all the hills which used to be cultivated with the hoe, you will not go there for fear of briars and thorns; but they will become a place for ᵃpasturing oxen and for sheep to trample.

25 ᵃIs. 5:17

2 The sign of Maher-shalal-hash-baz, 8:1-22

8 Then the LORD said to me, "Take for yourself a large tablet and ᵃwrite on it in ordinary

★ 1 ᵃIs. 30:8; Hab. 2:2 ᵇIs. 8:3

7:12 In spite of his smooth, pious response (cf. Deut. 6:16), Ahaz all the while intended to put his trust in Assyria (2 Kings 16:7-9). Isaiah foretold the kind of friend Assyria would prove to be (Isa. 7:17-25).

7:14-16 God's sign to Ahaz was that of a virgin (when the prophecy was spoken, it probably referred to the woman, a virgin at that time, whom Isaiah took later as his second wife, 8:1-4) and whose son would not be more than 12 to 14 years old before Syria and Israel would be captured. The virgin of Isaiah's prophecy is a type of the virgin Mary, who, by the Holy Spirit, miraculously conceived Jesus Christ (see Matt. 1:23). The Hebrew word that is here translated *virgin* is found elsewhere in the O.T. in Gen. 24:43; Exod. 2:8; Psalm 68:25;

Prov. 30:19; Song of Sol. 1:3; 6:8, and in these instances refers only to a chaste maiden who is unmarried. *curds and honey.* A food of a nomadic people, indicating that the land of Judah would soon be devastated. *refuse evil and choose good.* An age of moral discrimination. Within 12 years after this prophecy, Damascus was captured by Assyria (732) and Israel had fallen (722).

7:18 *Egypt* and *Assyria* clashed in 701.

7:20 *a razor, hired.* The king of Assyria, see 2 Kings 16:5-9.

7:21-25 The land of Judah would be reduced to poverty and desolation.

8:1 *Swift is the booty, speedy is the prey.* The meaning of the name *Maher-shalal-hash-baz* (v. 3), Isaiah's second son.

letters: [b]Swift is the booty, speedy is the prey.

2 "And I will take to Myself faithful witnesses for testimony, [a]Uriah the priest and Zechariah the son of Jeberechiah."

3 So I approached the prophetess, and she conceived and gave birth to a son. Then the LORD said to me, "Name him [a]Maher-shalal-hash-baz;

4 for [a]before the boy knows how to cry out 'My father' or 'My mother,' the wealth of [b]Damascus and the spoil of Samaria will be carried away before the king of Assyria."

5 And again the LORD spoke to me further, saying,

6 "Inasmuch as these people have [a]rejected the gently flowing waters of Shiloah, And rejoice in [b]Rezin and the son of Remaliah;

7 "Now therefore, behold, the Lord is about to bring on them the [a]strong and abundant waters of the [b]Euphrates, Even the [c]king of Assyria and all his glory; And it will [d]rise up over all its channels and go over all its banks.

8 "Then [a]it will sweep on into Judah, it will overflow and pass through, It will [b]reach even to the neck; And the spread of its wings will fill the breadth of your land, O [c]Immanuel.

9 "[a]Be broken, O peoples, and be [b]shattered; And give ear all remote places of the earth.

Gird yourselves, yet be shattered; Gird yourselves, yet be shattered.

10 "[a]Devise a plan but it will be thwarted, State a proposal, but [b]it will not stand, For [c]God is with us."

11 For thus the LORD spoke to me with [a]mighty power and instructed me [b]not to walk in the way of this people, saying,

12 "You are not to say, 'It is a [a]conspiracy!' In regard to all that this people call a conspiracy, And [b]you are not to fear what they fear or be in dread of it.

13 "It is the [a]LORD of hosts [b]whom you should regard as holy. And He shall be your fear, And He shall be your dread.

14 "Then He shall become a [a]sanctuary; But to both the houses of Israel, a [b]stone to strike and a rock to stumble over, And a snare and a [c]trap for the inhabitants of Jerusalem.

15 "And many [a]will stumble over them, Then they will fall and be broken; They will even be snared and caught."

16 [a]Bind up the testimony, [b]seal the law among [c]my disciples.

17 And I will [a]wait for the LORD [b]who is hiding His face from the house of Jacob; I will even look eagerly for Him.

18 [a]Behold, I and the children whom the LORD has given me are for [b]signs and wonders in Israel

---

Margin references (left column):

2 [a]2 Kin. 16:10, 11, 15, 16

3 [a]Is. 8:1

4 [a]Is. 7:16 [b]Is. 7:8, 9

★ **6** [a]Is. 1:20; 5:24; 7:9; 30:12 [b]Is. 7:1

7 [a]Is. 17:12, 13 [b]Is. 7:20; 11:15 [c]Is. 7:17; 10:5 [d]Amos 8:8; 9:5

8 [a]Is. 10:6 [b]Is. 30:28 [c]Is. 7:14

9 [a]Is. 17:12-14 [b]Dan. 2:34, 35

Margin references (right column):

10 [a]Job 5:12; Is. 28:18 [b]Is. 7:7 [c]Is. 8:8; Rom. 8:31

11 [a]Ezek. 3:14 [b]Ezek. 2:8

★**12** [a]Is. 7:2; 30:1 [b]1 Pet. 3:14, 15

13 [a]Is. 5:16; 29:23 [b]Num. 20:12

14 [a]Is. 4:6; 25:4; Ezek. 11:16 [b]Luke 2:34; Rom. 9:33; 1 Pet. 2:8 [c]Is. 24:17, 18

15 [a]Is. 28:13; 59:10; Luke 20:18; Rom. 9:32

16 [a]Is. 8:1, 2; 29:11, 12 [b]Dan. 12:4 [c]Is. 50:4

17 [a]Is. 25:9; 30:18; Hab. 2:3 [b]Deut. 31:17; Is. 1:15; 45:15; 54:8

18 [a]Heb. 2:13 [b]Luke 2:34 [c]Ps. 9:11; Zech. 8:3

8:6 *waters of Shiloah.* Siloam was a healing spring in Jerusalem (cf. John 9:7) and here typifies God's help, which Judah was not prepared to accept.

8:12 *a conspiracy.* Apparently the charge of the Assyrian alliance party against Isaiah, because he advised the people to trust God alone (v. 13).

from the LORD of hosts, who ^cdwells on Mount Zion.

19 And when they say to you, "^aConsult the mediums and the spiritists who whisper and mutter," should not a people ^bconsult their God? *Should they* ^cconsult the dead on behalf of the living?

20 To the ^alaw and to the testimony! If they do not speak according to this word, it is because ^bthey have no dawn.

21 And they will pass through the land ^ahard-pressed and famished, and it will turn out that when they are hungry, they will be enraged and curse their king and their God as they face upward.

22 Then they will ^alook to the earth, and behold, distress and darkness, the gloom of anguish; and *they will be* ^bdriven away into darkness.

3 The sign of Messiah, 9:1-7

9 But there will be no *more* ^agloom for her who was in anguish; in earlier times He ^btreated the ^cland of Zebulun and the land of Naphtali with contempt, but later on He shall make *it* glorious, by the way of the sea, on the other side of Jordan, Galilee of the Gentiles.

2 ^aThe people who walk in darkness
Will see a great light;
Those who live in a dark land,
The light will shine on them.

3 ^aThou shalt multiply the nation,
Thou ^bshalt increase their gladness;
They will be glad in Thy presence
As with the gladness of harvest,
As ^cmen rejoice when they divide the spoil.

4 For ^aThou shalt break the yoke of their burden and the staff on their shoulders,
The rod of their ^boppressor, as at the battle of ^cMidian.

5 For every boot of the booted warrior in the *battle* tumult,
And cloak rolled in blood, will be for burning, fuel for the fire.

6 For a ^achild will be born to us, a ^bson will be given to us;
And the ^cgovernment will rest ^don His shoulders;
And His name will be called ^eWonderful Counselor, ^fMighty God,
Eternal ^gFather, Prince of ^hPeace.

7 There will be ^ano end to the increase of *His* government or of peace,
On the ^bthrone of David and over his kingdom,

Marginal references (left column):

19 ^aLev. 20:6; 2 Kin. 21:6; 23:24; Is. 19:3; 29:4; 47:12, 13 ^bIs. 30:2; 45:11 ^c1 Sam. 28:8-11
★**20** ^aIs. 1:10; 8:16; Luke 16:29 ^bIs. 8:22; Mic. 3:6
21 ^aIs. 9:20, 21
22 ^aIs. 5:30; 59:9; Jer. 13:16; Amos 5:18, 20; Zeph. 1:14, 15 ^bIs. 8:20

★**1** ^aIs. 8:22 ^b2 Kin. 15:29; 2 Chr. 16:4 ^cMatt. 4:15, 16

2 ^aMatt. 4:16; Luke 1:79; Eph. 5:8

Marginal references (right column):

3 ^aIs. 26:15 ^bIs. 35:10; 65:14, 18, 19; 66:10 ^c1 Sam. 30:16

★ **4** ^aIs. 10:27; 14:25 ^bIs. 14:4; 49:26; 51:13; 54:14 ^cJudg. 7:25; Is. 10:26

★ **6** ^aIs. 7:14; 11:1, 2; 53:2; Luke 2:11 ^bJohn 3:16 ^cMatt. 28:18; 1 Cor. 15:25 ^dIs. 22:22 ^eIs. 28:29 ^fDeut. 10:17; Neh. 9:32; Is. 10:21 ^gIs. 63:16; 64:8 ^hIs. 26:3, 12; 54:10; 66:12

★ **7** ^aDan. 2:44; Luke 1:32, 33 ^bIs. 16:5 ^cIs. 11:4, 5; 32:1; 42:3, 4; 63:1 ^dIs. 37:32; 59:17

8:20 *the law . . . the testimony.* God's Word, the only absolute and trustworthy standard.

9:1 *Zebulun* and *Naphtali* came under the yoke of Assyria (2 Kings 15:29). Because Christ would minister and live in *Galilee* it will be glorious. See Matt. 4:15-16.

9:4 *battle of Midian.* A reference to Gideon's victory over the Midianites, Judg. 8:24-27.

9:6 Messiah will come as a baby who is *born* and as a gift from God to be a ruler (Luke 1:31-33). His perfections are described as follows: *Wonderful Counselor.* "Wonderful" regularly means supernatural (cf. Judg. 13:18), so the phrase refers to Messiah as the supernatural Counselor who, at His first coming, brought words of eternal life, and who, when

He comes again, will rule with perfect wisdom (Isa. 11:2). *Mighty God.* A term applied to Yahweh (see note on Gen. 2:4) in Deut. 10:17; Isa. 10:21; Jer. 32:18, and which predicts the ultimate victory of Messiah over evil. *Eternal Father.* Lit., Father of Eternity; i.e., Messiah is eternally a Father to His people, guarding, supplying and caring for their needs. *Prince of Peace.* The One who brings peace in the fullest sense of wholeness, prosperity and tranquility. Individuals can now know His peace (Eph. 2:13-18), and one day the world will experience it as well (Isa. 2:4).

9:7 The everlasting rule of Messiah on the *throne of David* awaits the second coming of Christ.

To establish it and to uphold it with ^cjustice and righteousness
From then on and forevermore.
^dThe zeal of the Lord of hosts will accomplish this.

4 Judgment on Samaria, 9:8–10:4

★ 9:8–10:4

8 The Lord sends a message against Jacob,
And it falls on Israel.

9 And all the people know *it*,
That is, ^aEphraim and the inhabitants of Samaria,
Asserting in pride and in ^barrogance of heart:

10 "The bricks have fallen down,
But we will ^arebuild with smooth stones;
The sycamores have been cut down,
But we will replace *them* with cedars."

11 Therefore the Lord raises against them adversaries from ^aRezin,
And spurs their enemies on,

12 The Arameans on the east and the ^aPhilistines on the west;
And they ^bdevour Israel with gaping jaws.
^cIn *spite of* all this His anger does not turn away,
And His hand is still stretched out.

13 Yet the people ^ado not turn back to Him who struck them,
Nor do they ^bseek the Lord of hosts.

14 So the Lord cuts off ^ahead and tail from Israel,

Both palm branch and bulrush ^bin a single day.

15 The head is ^athe elder and honorable man,
And the prophet who teaches ^bfalsehood is the tail.

16 ^aFor those who guide this people are leading *them* astray;
And those who are guided by them are brought to confusion.

17 Therefore the Lord does ^anot take pleasure in their young men,
^bNor does He have pity on their orphans or their widows;
For every one of them is ^cgodless and an ^devildoer,
And every ^emouth is speaking foolishness.
^fIn *spite of* all this His anger does not turn away,
And His hand is still stretched out.

18 ^aFor wickedness burns like a fire;
It consumes briars and thorns;
It even sets the thickets of the forest aflame,
And they roll upward in a column of smoke.

19 By the ^afury of the Lord of hosts the ^bland is burned up,
And the ^cpeople are like fuel for the fire;
No ^dman spares his brother.

20 And they slice off *what is* on the right hand but *still* are ^ahungry,
And they eat *what is* on the left hand but they are not satisfied;
Each of them eats the ^bflesh of his own arm.

Cross references (left margin):

9 ^aIs. 7:8, 9; 28:1, 3 ^bIs. 46:12
10 ^aMal. 1:4
11 ^aIs. 7:1, 8
12 ^a2 Chr. 28:18 ^bPs. 79:7; Jer. 10:25 ^cIs. 5:25
13 ^aJer. 5:3; Hos. 7:10 ^bIs. 31:1; Hos. 3:5
14 ^aIs. 19:15 ^bRev. 18:8

Cross references (right margin):

15 ^aIs. 3:2, 3 ^bIs. 28:15; 59:3, 4; Jer. 23:14, 32; Matt. 24:24
16 ^aIs. 3:12; Matt. 15:14; 23:16, 24
17 ^aJer. 18:21; Amos 4:10; 8:13 ^bIs. 27:11 ^cIs. 10:6; 32:6 ^dIs. 1:4; 14:20; 31:2 ^eMatt. 12:34 ^fIs. 5:25
18 ^aPs. 83:14; Is. 1:7; Nah. 1:10; Mal. 4:1
19 ^aIs. 10:6; 13:9, 13; 42:25 ^bJoel 2:3 ^cIs. 1:31; 24:6 ^dMic. 7:2, 6
20 ^aIs. 8:21, 22 ^bIs. 49:26

9:8–10:4 The imminent judgment on the northern tribes of Israel would be deserved (vv. 8–12), sudden (vv. 13–17), cruel (vv. 18–21; note the civil war between *Manasseh* and *Ephraim*, two main tribes of the Northern Kingdom), and complete (10:1–4; exile or death being the only alternatives, v. 4).

21 a2 Chr.
28:6, 8; Is.
11:13 bIs.
5:25

21 Manasseh *devours* Ephraim, and Ephraim Ma-
nasseh,
ᵃAnd together they are
against Judah.
ᵇIn *spite of* all this His anger does not turn
away,
And His hand is still
stretched out.

1 aPs.
94:20; Is.
29:21; 59:4,
13

10 Woe to those who ᵃenact
evil statutes,
And to those who con-
stantly record unjust
decisions,

2 aIs. 5:23
bIs. 1:23;
3:14, 15

2 So as ᵃto deprive the needy
of justice,
And rob the poor of My
people of *their* rights,
In order ᵇthat widows may
be their spoil,
And that they may plun-
der the orphans.

3 aJob
31:14 bIs.
13:6; 26:14,
21; 29:6; Jer.
9:9; Hos. 9:7;
Luke 19:44
cIs. 5:26 dIs.
20:6; 30:5, 7;
31:3

3 Now ᵃwhat will you do in
the ᵇday of punish-
ment,
And in the devastation
which will come
ᶜfrom afar?
ᵈTo whom will you flee for
help?
And where will you leave
your wealth?

4 aIs. 24:22
bIs. 22:2;
34:3; 66:16
cIs. 5:25

4 Nothing *remains* but to
crouch among the
ᵃcaptives
Or fall among the ᵇslain.
ᶜIn *spite of* all this His anger does not turn
away,
And His hand is still
stretched out.

**5 *Retribution (on Assyria) and
return (of Israel)*, 10:5-34**

★ 5-19
5 aIs. 7:17;
8:7; 14:24-
27; Zeph.
2:13-15
bJer. 51:20
cIs. 13:5;
30:30; 34:2;
66:14

5 Woe to ᵃAssyria, the ᵇrod
of My anger
And the staff in whose
hands is ᶜMy indigna-
tion,

6 I send it against a ᵃgodless
nation
And commission it against
the ᵇpeople of My
fury
To capture booty and ᶜto
seize plunder,
And to trample them
down like ᵈmud in the
streets.

6 aIs. 9:17
bIs. 9:19 cIs.
5:29 dIs.
5:25

7 Yet it ᵃdoes not so intend
Nor does it plan so in its
heart,
But rather it is its purpose
to destroy,
And to cut off many na-
tions.

7 aGen.
50:20; Mic.
4:11, 12;
Acts 2:23, 24

8 For it says, "Are not my
princes all kings?
9 "Is not ᵃCalno like ᵇCarche-
mish,
Or ᶜHamath like Arpad,
Or ᵈSamaria like ᵉDamas-
cus?

9 aGen.
10:10; Amos
6:2 b2 Chr.
35:20 cNum.
34:8 d2 Kin.
17:6 e2 Kin.
16:9

10 "As my hand has reached to
the ᵃkingdoms of the
idols,
Whose graven images
were greater than
those of Jerusalem
and Samaria,

10 a2 Kin.
19:17, 18

11 Shall I not do to Jerusalem
and her images
Just as I have done to Samaria and ᵃher idols?"

11 aIs. 2:8

12 So it will be that when the
Lord has completed all His ᵃwork
on Mount Zion and on Jerusalem,
He will say, "I will punish the
fruit of the arrogant heart of the
king of Assyria and ᵇthe pomp of
his haughtiness."

12 a2 Kin.
19:31; Is.
28:21, 22;
29:14; 65:7
bIs. 37:23

13 For ᵃhe has said,
"By the power of my hand
and by my wisdom I
did *this*,
For I have understanding;
And I ᵇremoved the
boundaries of the
peoples,
And plundered their trea-
sures,

13 a2 Kin.
19:22-24; Is.
37:24-27;
Ezek. 28:4;
Dan. 4:30
bHab. 2:6-11

10:5-19 Though boastful Assyria was God's instrument to punish Judah, in turn she would
be judged by God. God, who is called the *light
of Israel* (v. 17), would destroy Assyria (between the fall of Nineveh in 612 and the battle
of Carchemish in 605) so completely that a
child could easily count the number of leaders
remaining (v. 19).

And like a mighty man I brought down *their* inhabitants,

14 And my hand reached to the riches of the peoples like a ᵃnest,
And as one gathers abandoned eggs, I gathered all the earth;
And there was not one that flapped its wing or opened *its* beak or chirped."

15 Is the ᵃaxe to ᵇboast itself over the one who chops with it?
Is the saw to exalt itself over the one who wields it?
That would be like ᶜa club wielding those who lift it,
Or like ᵈa rod lifting *him* who is not wood.

16 Therefore the Lord, the GOD of hosts, will send a ᵃwasting disease among his ᵇstout warriors;
And under his ᶜglory a fire will be kindled like a burning flame.

17 And the ᵃlight of Israel will become a fire and his ᵇHoly One a flame,
And it will ᶜburn and devour his thorns and his briars in a single day.

18 And He will ᵃdestroy the glory of his forest and of his fruitful garden, both soul and body;
And it will be as when a sick man wastes away.

19 And the ᵃrest of the trees of his forest will be so small in number
That a child could write them down.

20 Now it will come about in that day that the ᵃremnant of Israel, and those of the house of Jacob ᵇwho have escaped, will never again rely on the one who struck them, but will truly ᶜrely on the LORD, the Holy One of Israel.

21 A ᵃremnant will return, the remnant of Jacob, to the ᵇmighty God.

22 For ᵃthough your people, O Israel, may be like the sand of the sea,
Only a remnant within them will return;
A ᵇdestruction is determined, overflowing with righteousness.

23 For a complete destruction, one that is decreed, ᵃthe Lord GOD of hosts will execute in the midst of the whole land.

24 Therefore thus says the Lord GOD of hosts, "O My people who dwell in ᵃZion, ᵇdo not fear the Assyrian who ᶜstrikes you with the rod and lifts up his staff against you, the way Egypt *did*.

25 "For in a very ᵃlittle while ᵇMy indignation *against you* will be spent, and My anger *will be directed* to their destruction."

26 And the LORD of hosts will ᵃarouse a scourge against him like the slaughter of ᵇMidian at the rock of Oreb; and His ᶜstaff will be over the sea, and He will lift it up ᵈthe way *He did* in Egypt.

27 So it will be in that day, that his ᵃburden will be removed from your shoulders and his yoke from your neck, and the yoke will be broken because ᵇof fatness.

28 He has come against Aiath,
He has passed through ᵃMigron;
At ᵇMichmash he deposited his ᶜbaggage.

29 They have gone through ᵃthe pass, saying,
"ᵇGeba will be our lodging place."
ᶜRamah is terrified, and ᵈGibeah of Saul has fled away.

Marginal references (left column):

14 ᵃJer. 49:16; Obad. 4

15 ᵃJer. 51:20 ᵇIs. 29:16; 45:9; Rom. 9:20, 21 ᶜIs. 10:5 ᵈIs. 10:5

16 ᵃPs. 106:15 ᵇIs. 17:4 ᶜIs. 8:7; 10:18

17 ᵃIs. 30:33; 31:9 ᵇIs. 37:23 ᶜNum. 11:1-3; Is. 27:4; 33:12; Jer. 4:4; 7:20

18 ᵃIs. 10:33, 34

19 ᵃIs. 21:17

★20-34
20 ᵃIs. 1:9; 11:11, 16; 46:3 ᵇIs. 4:2; 37:31, 32 ᶜ2 Chr. 14:11; Is. 17:7, 8; 50:10

Marginal references (right column):

21 ᵃIs. 7:3 ᵇIs. 9:6

22 ᵃRom. 9:27, 28 ᵇIs. 28:22; Dan. 9:27; Rom. 9:28

23 ᵃIs. 28:22; Dan. 9:27; Rom. 9:28

24 ᵃPs. 87:5, 6 ᵇIs. 7:4; 12:2; 37:6 ᶜEx. 5:14-16

25 ᵃIs. 17:14; Hag. 2:6 ᵇIs. 10:5; 26:20; Dan. 11:36

26 ᵃIs. 37:36-38 ᵇJudg. 7:25; Is. 9:4 ᶜEx. 14:16 ᵈEx. 14:27

27 ᵃIs. 9:4; 14:25 ᵇIs. 30:23; 55:2

28 ᵃ1 Sam. 14:2 ᵇ1 Sam. 13:2, 5 ᶜJudg. 18:21; 1 Sam. 17:22

29 ᵃ1 Sam. 13:23 ᵇJosh. 21:17; 1 Sam. 13:16 ᶜJosh. 18:25; 1 Sam. 7:17 ᵈ1 Sam. 10:26

10:20-34 The theme of this section is found in verse 22b, which literally says, "destruction is decreed, overflowing with righteousness." I.e., a remnant would survive the victory of Assyria over apostate Judah. Verses 28-32 graphically describe the Assyrian advance toward Jerusalem (all cities named are within a three-hour march of Jerusalem).

30 *a*1 Sam.
25:44 *b*Josh.
21:18; Jer.
1:1

30 Cry aloud with your voice,
O daughter of *a*Gal-
lim!
Pay attention, Laishah and
wretched *b*Anathoth!

31 Madmenah has fled.
The inhabitants of Gebim
have sought refuge.

32 *a*1 Sam.
21:1; 22:9
*b*Is. 19:16;
Zech. 2:9
*c*Is. 1:8; Jer.
6:23

32 Yet today he will halt at
*a*Nob;
He *b*shakes his fist at
the mountain of the
*c*daughter of Zion, the
hill of Jerusalem.

33 *a*Is.
37:24, 36-38;
Ezek. 31:3;
Amos 2:9

33 Behold, the Lord, the GOD
of hosts, will lop off
the boughs with a ter-
rible crash;
Those also who are *a*tall in
stature will be cut
down,
And those who are lofty
will be abased.

34 *a*Is. 2:13;
33:9; 37:24

34 And He will cut down the
thickets of the forest
with an iron *axe*,
And *a*Lebanon will fall by
the Mighty One.

**6 The rule of the Branch of
Jesse, 11:1-16**

★ 1-5
1 *a*Is. 4:2;
53:2 *b*Is. 9:7;
11:10; Acts
13:23 *c*Is.
6:13; Jer.
23:5; Zech.
3:8 *d*Rev.
5:5; 22:16
2 *a*Is. 42:1;
48:16; 61:1;
Matt. 3:16;
John 1:32
*b*John 16:13;
1 Cor. 1:30;
Eph. 1:17, 18
*c*2 Tim. 1:7

11 Then a *a*shoot will spring
from the *b*stem of
Jesse,
And a *c*branch from *d*his
roots will bear fruit.

2 And the *a*Spirit of the LORD
will rest on Him,
The spirit of *b*wisdom and
understanding,
The spirit of counsel and
*c*strength,
The spirit of knowledge
and the fear of the
LORD.

3 *a*John
2:25; 7:24

3 And He will delight in the
fear of the LORD,
And He will not judge by
what His eyes *a*see,

Nor make a decision by
what His ears hear;

4 But with *a*righteousness
He will judge the
*b*poor,
And decide with fairness
for the *c*afflicted of the
earth;
And He will strike the
earth with the *d*rod of
His mouth,
And with the *e*breath of
His lips He will slay
the wicked.

4 *a*Is. 9:7;
16:5; 32:1
*b*Ps. 72:2,
13, 14; Is.
3:14 *c*Is.
29:19; 32:7;
61:1 *d*Ps.
2:9; Is. 49:2;
Mal. 4:6
*e*Job 4:9; Is.
30:28, 33;
2 Thess. 2:8

5 Also *a*righteousness will be
the belt about His
loins,
And *b*faithfulness the belt
about His waist.

5 *a*Eph.
6:14 *b*Is.
25:1

6 And the *a*wolf will dwell
with the lamb,
And the leopard will lie
down with the kid,
And the calf and the
young lion and the
fatling together;
And a little boy will lead
them.

★ 6-9

6 *a*Is. 65:25

7 Also the cow and the bear
will graze;
Their young will lie down
together;
And the *a*lion will eat
straw like the ox.

7 *a*Is. 65:25

8 And the nursing child will
play by the hole of the
cobra,
And the weaned child will
put his hand on the
viper's den.

9 They will *a*not hurt or destroy in all My holy
mountain,
For the *b*earth will be full
of the knowledge of
the LORD
As the waters cover the
sea.

9 *a*Job
5:23; Is.
65:25; Ezek.
34:25; Hos.
2:18 *b*Ps.
98:2, 3; Is.
45:6; 52:10;
66:18-23;
Hab. 2:14

10 Then it will come about in
that day

10 *a*Luke
2:32; Acts
11:18 *b*Is.
11:1; Rom.
15:12 *c*Is.
11:12; 49:22;
62:10; John
3:14, 15;
12:32 *d*Is.
14:3; 28:12;
32:17, 18

11:1-5 Though the tree of David is felled (6:13)
a *shoot* or *branch* would grow up from the
stump (the family of David; *Jesse* was David's
father, 1 Sam. 17:12), in the person of Messiah. He would be characterized by the full-

ness of the Holy Spirit (Isa. 11:2) and absolute
integrity (vv. 3-5).
11:6-9 Messiah's reign in the yet future millennial kingdom will be characterized by harmony in the whole creation (Rom. 8:18-22).

That the [a]nations will resort to the [b]root of Jesse,
Who will stand as a [c]signal for the peoples;
And His [d]resting place will be glorious.

11 Then it will happen on that day that the Lord
Will again recover the second time with His hand
The [a]remnant of His people, who will remain,
From [b]Assyria, [c]Egypt, Pathros, Cush, [d]Elam, Shinar, Hamath,
And from the [e]islands of the sea.

12 And He will lift up a [a]standard for the nations,
And will [b]assemble the banished ones of Israel,
And will gather the dispersed of Judah
From the four corners of the earth.

13 Then the [a]jealousy of Ephraim will depart,
And those who harass Judah will be cut off;
Ephraim will not be jealous of Judah,
And Judah will not harass Ephraim.

14 And they will [a]swoop down on the slopes of the Philistines on the [b]west;
Together they will [c]plunder the sons of the east;
They will possess [d]Edom and [e]Moab;
And the sons of Ammon will be subject to them.

15 And the LORD will [a]utterly destroy
The tongue of the Sea of Egypt;
And He will [b]wave His hand over the [c]River
With His scorching wind;
And He will strike it into seven streams,
And make *men* walk over dry-shod.

16 And there will be a [a]highway from Assyria
For the [b]remnant of His people who will be left,
Just as there was for Israel
In [c]the day that they came up out of the land of Egypt.

7 A hymn of praise, 12:1–6

12 Then you will say on that day,
"[a]I will give thanks to Thee, O LORD;
For [b]although Thou wast angry with me,
Thine anger is turned away,
And Thou dost comfort me.

2 "Behold, [a]God is my salvation,
I will [b]trust and not be afraid;
For [c]the LORD GOD is my strength and song,
And He has become my salvation."

3 Therefore you will joyously [a]draw water
From the [b]springs of salvation.

4 And in that day you will [a]say,

★11 [a]Is. 10:20-22; 37:4, 31, 32; 46:3 [b]Is. 19:23-25; Hos. 11:11; Zech. 10:10 [c]Is. 19:21, 22; Mic. 7:12 [d]Gen. 10:22; 14:1 [e]Is. 24:15; 42:4, 10, 12; 49:1; 51:5; 60:9; 66:19

★12 [a]Is. 11:10 [b]Is. 56:8; Zeph. 3:10; Zech. 10:6

13 [a]Is. 9:21; Jer. 3:18; Ezek. 37:16, 17, 22; Hos. 1:11

★14 [a]Jer. 48:40; 49:22; Hab. 1:8 [b]Is. 9:12 [c]Jer. 49:28 [d]Is. 63:1; Dan. 11:41; Joel 3:19; Amos 9:12 [e]Is. 16:14; 25:10

★15 [a]Is. 43:16; 44:27; 50:2; 51:10, 11 [b]Is. 19:16 [c]Is. 7:20; 8:7; Rev. 16:12

16 [a]Is. 19:23; 35:8; 40:3; 62:10 [b]Is. 11:11 [c]Ex. 14:26-29

★ 1-6

1 [a]Ps. 9:1; Is. 25:1 [b]Ps. 30:5; Is. 40:1, 2; 54:7-10

2 [a]Is. 32:2; 45:17; 62:11 [b]Is. 26:3 [c]Ex. 15:2; Ps. 118:14

3 [a]John 4:10; 7:37, 38 [b]Is. 41:18; Jer. 2:13

4 [a]Is. 24:15; 42:12; 48:20 [b]Ps. 105:1 [c]Ps. 145:4

11:11 *the second time.* Refers to a yet future regathering of the Jewish people, the first being the regathering under Zerubbabel in 537 B.C.
11:12 *nations.* Gentiles.
11:14 *the slopes of the Philistines.* The low range of foothills between Philistia and the mountains of Judah.

11:15 *The tongue of the Sea of Egypt.* The northwestern finger of the Red Sea that leads to Suez. *the River* = the Euphrates.
12:1–6 So certain were God's promises of future blessing for Israel *on that* future *day* that Isaiah composed this song of praise in anticipation of the Millennium.

"ᵇGive thanks to the LORD,
call on His name.
ᶜMake known His deeds
among the peoples;
Make *them* remember that
His name is exalted."

<sup>5 ᵃEx. 15:1;
Ps. 98:1; Is.
24:14; 42:10,
11; 44:23</sup>

5 ᵃPraise the LORD in song,
for He has done excel-
lent things;
Let this be known
throughout the earth.

<sup>6 ᵃIs. 52:9;
54:1; Zeph.
3:14 ᵇIs.
1:24; 49:26;
60:16; Zeph.
3:15-17;
Zech. 2:5,
10, 11</sup>

6 ᵃCry aloud and shout for
joy, O inhabitant of
Zion,
For ᵇgreat in your midst is
the Holy One of Is-
rael.

II DENUNCIATIONS AGAINST
OTHER NATIONS,
13:1–23:18

A   Against Babylon, 13:1–14:23

<sup>★ 1 ᵃIs.
14:28; 15:1
ᵇIs. 13:19;
14:4; 47:1-
15; Jer. 24:1;
50:1-51:64;
Matt. 1:11;
Rev. 14:8
ᶜIs. 1:1

2 ᵃIs. 5:26;
Jer. 50:2
ᵇJer. 51:25
ᶜIs. 10:32;
19:16 ᵈIs.
45:1-3; Jer.
51:58
★ 3-5

3 ᵃJoel
3:11

4 ᵃIs. 5:30;
17:12; Joel
3:14</sup>

13 The ᵃoracle concerning
ᵇBabylon which ᶜIsaiah
the son of Amoz saw.
2 ᵃLift up a standard on the
ᵇbare hill,
Raise your voice to them,
ᶜWave the hand that they
may ᵈenter the doors
of the nobles.
3 I have commanded My
consecrated ones,
I have even called My
ᵃmighty warriors,
My proudly exulting ones,
To *execute* My anger.
4 A ᵃsound of tumult on the
mountains,
Like that of many people!
A sound of the uproar of
kingdoms,
Of nations gathered to-
gether!
The LORD of hosts is mus-
tering the army for
battle.

5 They are coming from a
far country
From the ᵃfarthest hori-
zons,
The LORD and His instru-
ments of ᵇindignation,
To ᶜdestroy the whole
land.

<sup>5 ᵃIs. 5:26;
7:18 ᵇIs.
10:5 ᶜIs.
24:1</sup>

6 Wail, for the ᵃday of the
LORD is near!
It will come as ᵇdestruction
from the Almighty.

<sup>★ 6 ᵃIs.
2:12; 10:3;
13:9; 34:2, 8;
61:2; Ezek.
30:3; Amos
5:18; Zeph.
1:7 ᵇIs.
10:25; 14:23;
Joel 1:15</sup>

7 Therefore ᵃall hands will
fall limp,
And every man's ᵇheart
will melt.

<sup>7 ᵃEzek.
7:17 ᵇIs.
19:1; Ezek.
21:7; Nah.
2:10</sup>

8 And they will be ᵃterrified,
Pains and anguish will
take hold of *them*;
They will ᵇwrithe like a
woman in labor,
They will look at one an-
other in astonishment,
Their faces aflame.

<sup>8 ᵃ2 Kin.
19:26; Is.
21:3; Jer.
46:5 ᵇIs.
26:17; Jer.
4:31; John
16:21</sup>

9 Behold, ᵃthe day of the
LORD is coming,
Cruel, with fury and burn-
ing anger,
To make the land a desola-
tion;
And He will exterminate
its sinners from it.

^{9 ᵃIs. 13:6}

10 For the ᵃstars of heaven
and their constella-
tions
Will not flash forth their
light;
The ᵇsun will be dark
when it rises,
And the moon will not
shed its light.

<sup>10 ᵃIs. 5:30;
Ezek. 32:7;
Joel 2:10;
Matt. 24:29;
Mark 13:24;
Luke 21:25;
Rev. 6:13;
8:12 ᵇIs.
24:23; 50:3;
Ezek. 32:7;
Acts 2:20;
Rev. 6:12</sup>

11 Thus I will ᵃpunish the
world for its evil,
And the ᵇwicked for their
iniquity;
I will also put an end to the
ᶜarrogance of the
proud,
And abase the ᵈhaughti-
ness of the ᵉruthless.

<sup>11 ᵃIs. 26:21
ᵇIs. 3:11;
11:4; 14:5
ᶜIs. 2:11;
23:9; Dan.
5:22, 23
ᵈJer. 48:29
ᵉIs. 25:3;
29:5, 20</sup>

13:1 The section (chaps. 13-23) that begins here
deals principally with foreign nations who at
some time had persecuted Judah and teaches
the universal sovereignty of God.
13:3-5 *My consecrated ones.* The Medes (or
Persians, v. 17), whom God ordained to overthrow Babylon in 539 (Dan. 5:30-31). They

came *From the farthest horizons,* about 350
miles east of Babylon.
13:6 *the day of the LORD.* A time of judgment,
here on Babylon and ultimately on the whole
world (v. 11) during the coming days of tribulation (cf. v. 10 with Rev. 6:12-13; for the eschatological Babylon, see note on Rev. 17:5).

12 aIs. 4:1;
6:11, 12
b1 Kin. 9:28;
Job 28:16;
Ps. 45:9

12 I will make mortal man
ascarcer than pure
gold,
And mankind than the
bgold of Ophir.

13 aIs. 34:4;
51:6 bPs.
18:7; Is.
2:19; 24:1,
19, 20; Hag.
2:6 cLam.
1:12

13 Therefore I shall make the
aheavens tremble,
And bthe earth will be
shaken from its place
At the fury of the LORD of
hosts
In cthe day of His burning
anger.

14 a1 Kin.
22:17; Matt.
9:36; Mark
6:34; 1 Pet.
2:25

14 And it will be that like a
hunted gazelle,
Or like asheep with none
to gather them,
They will each turn to his
own people,
And each one flee to his
own land.

15 aIs.
14:19; Jer.
50:25;
51:3, 4

15 Anyone who is found will
be athrust through,
And anyone who is cap-
tured will fall by the
sword.

16 aPs.
137:8, 9; Is.
13:18; 14:21;
Hos. 10:14;
Nah. 3:10

16 Their alittle ones also will
be dashed to pieces
Before their eyes;
Their houses will be plun-
dered
And their wives ravished.

17 aJer.
51:11; Dan.
5:28 bProv.
6:34, 35

17 Behold, I am going to astir
up the Medes against
them,
Who will not value silver
or btake pleasure in
gold,

18 a2 Kin.
8:12; 2 Chr.
36:17 bEzek.
9:5, 10

18 And their bows will mow
down the ayoung
men,
They will not even have
compassion on the
fruit of the womb,
Nor will their beye pity
children.

★19-22

19 aIs. 21:9;
48:14 bDan.
4:30; Rev.
18:11-16, 19,
21 cGen.
19:24; Deut.
29:23; Jer.
49:18; Amos
4:11

19 And aBabylon, the bbeauty
of kingdoms, the glo-
ry of the Chaldeans'
pride,

Will be as when God
coverthrew Sodom
and Gomorrah.

20 aIs.
14:23; 34:10-
15; Jer.
51:37-43
b2 Chr.
17:11

20 It will anever be inhabited
or lived in from gen-
eration to generation;
Nor will the bArab pitch
his tent there,
Nor will shepherds make
their flocks lie down
there.

21 aIs.
34:11-15;
Zeph. 2:14;
Rev. 18:2

21 But adesert creatures will
lie down there,
And their houses will be
full of owls,
Ostriches also will live
there, and shaggy
goats will frolic there.

22 aIs. 25:2;
32:14; 34:13

22 And hyenas will howl in
their fortified towers
And jackals in their luxurious apalaces.
Her fateful time also will
soon come
And her days will not be
prolonged.

14 When the LORD will ahave
compassion on Jacob, and
again bchoose Israel, and settle
them in their own land, then
cstrangers will join them and attach themselves to the house of
Jacob.

★ 1-3
1 aPs.
102:13; Is.
49:13, 15;
54:7, 8 bIs.
41:8, 9; 44:1;
49:7; Zech.
1:17; 2:12
cIs. 56:3, 6;
Eph. 2:12-19

2 And the peoples will take
them along and bring them to
their place, and the ahouse of Israel will possess them as an inheritance in the land of the LORD bas
male servants and female servants; and they will take their
captors captive, and will rule over
their oppressors.

2 aIs.
45:14; 49:23;
54:3 bIs.
60:10; 61:5;
Dan. 7:18, 27

3 And it will be in the day
when the LORD gives you arest
from your pain and turmoil and
harsh service in which you have
been enslaved,

3 aEzra 9:8,
9; Is. 11:10;
40:2; Jer.
30:10; 46:27

4 that you will atake up this
taunt against the king of Babylon,
and say,
"How bthe oppressor has
ceased,

★ 4-11
4 aHab. 2:6
bIs. 9:4;
16:4; 49:26;
51:13; 54:14

13:19-22 The decline of Babylon occurred in
stages. By 20 B.C. Strabo described it as a "vast
desolation." Even the desert wanderer (the
Arab) shunned the site because it became an
omen of ill fortune.
14:1-3 Israel would outlast even the conquerors

of Babylon and would return to her land.
14:4-11 A taunting song against the king (and
system) of Babylon, both historical and eschatological. Even Sheol is pictured as welcoming
him (v. 9).

    And how fury has ceased!

5 "The LORD has broken the
    staff of the wicked,
    The scepter of rulers

6 a Is.
10:14; 47:6

6 a Which used to strike the
    peoples in fury with
    unceasing strokes,
    Which subdued the na-
    tions in anger with
    unrestrained persecu-
    tion.

7 a Ps.
47:1-3; 98:1-
9; 126:1-3

7 "The whole earth is at rest
    and is quiet;
    They a break forth into
    shouts of joy.

8 a Is.
55:12; Ezek.
31:16

8 "Even the a cypress trees re-
    joice over you, *and*
    the cedars of Leba-
    non, *saying,*
    'Since you were laid low,
    no *tree* cutter comes
    up against us.'

9 a Is. 5:14

9 "a Sheol from beneath is ex-
    cited over you to meet
    you when you come;
    It arouses for you the spir-
    its of the dead, all the
    leaders of the earth;
    It raises all the kings of the
    nations from their
    thrones.

10 a Ezek.
32:21

10 "a They will all respond and
    say to you,
    'Even you have been made
    weak as we,
    You have become like *us.*

11 a Is. 5:14

11 'Your a pomp *and* the music
    of your harps
    Have been brought down
    to Sheol;
    Maggots are spread out *as*
    your bed beneath
    you,

    And worms are your cov-
    ering.'

12 "How you have a fallen from
    heaven,
    O b star of the morning,
    son of the dawn!
    You have been cut down
    to the earth,
    You who have weakened
    the nations!

★**12** a Is.
34:4; Luke
10:18; Rev.
8:10; 9:1
b 2 Pet. 1:19;
Rev. 2:28;
22:16

13 "But you said in your heart,
    'I will a ascend to heaven;
    I will b raise my throne
    above the stars of
    God,
    And I will sit on the mount
    of assembly
    In the recesses of the
    north.

★**13-14**

13 a Ezek.
28:2 b Dan.
5:22, 23;
8:10;
2 Thess. 2:4

14 'I will ascend above the
    heights of the clouds;
    a I will make myself like
    the Most High.'

14 a Is. 47:8;
2 Thess. 2:4

15 "Nevertheless you a will be
    thrust down to Sheol,
    To the recesses of the pit.

15 a Ezek.
28:8; Matt.
11:23; Luke
10:15

16 "Those who see you will
    gaze at you,
    They will ponder over you,
    saying,
    'Is this the man who made
    the earth tremble,
    Who shook kingdoms,

17 Who made the world like
    a a wilderness
    And a overthrew its cities,
    Who b did not allow his
    prisoners to *go* home?'

★**17** a Joel
2:3 b Is.
45:13

18 "All the kings of the nations
    lie in glory,
    Each in his own tomb.

19 "But you have been a cast
    out of your tomb
    Like a rejected branch,

19 a Is.
22:16-18
b Jer. 41:7, 9
c Is. 5:25

14:12 *star of the morning.* Lit., the bright one,
evidently a reference to Satan, because of
Christ's similar description (Luke 10:18) and
because of the inappropriateness of the expressions of Isa. 14:13-14 on the lips of any
but Satan (cf. 1 Tim. 3:6). *weakened the nations.* Cf. Rev. 20:3.
14:13-14 Five phrases beginning with *I will* detail Satan's sin. He wished to occupy *heaven,*
the abode of God Himself. To exalt his throne
above the *stars of God* may refer to his desire
to rule all the angelic creatures, or it may sim-

ply be another way to indicate his self-exaltation. *north,* in heathen literature, indicated the
abode of the gods; thus, Satan was ambitious
to govern the universe as the council *(assembly)* of Babylonian gods supposedly did. He
wanted the glory that belonged to God alone
(on *clouds,* see 19:1; Exod. 16:10) and his entire goal was to be *like the Most High* (Heb.,
Elyon; see note on Gen. 14:18).
14:17 *prisoners.* Those whom Satan held captive, Christ came to set free (Luke 4:18).

Clothed with the slain who
are pierced with a
sword,
Who go down to the
stones of the [b]pit,
Like a [c]trampled corpse.
20 "You will not be united
with them in burial,
Because you have ruined
your country,
You have slain your peo-
ple.
May the [a]offspring of evildoers not be men-
tioned forever.
21 "Prepare for his sons a place
of slaughter
Because of the [a]iniquity of
their fathers.
They must not arise and
take possession of the
earth
And fill the face of the
world with cities."
22 "And I will rise up against
them," declares the LORD of hosts,
"and will cut off from Babylon
[a]name and survivors, [b]offspring
and posterity," declares the LORD.
23 "I will also make it a possession for the [a]hedgehog, and
swamps of water, and I will sweep
it with the broom of [b]destruc-
tion," declares the LORD of hosts.

B Against Assyria, 14:24-27

24 The LORD of hosts has
sworn saying, "Surely, [a]just as I
have intended so it has happened,
and just as I have planned so it
will stand,
25 to [a]break Assyria in My
land, and I will trample him on
My mountains. Then his [b]yoke
will be removed from them, and

his burden removed from their
shoulder.
26 "This is the [a]plan devised
against the whole earth; and this
is the [b]hand that is stretched out
against all the nations.
27 "For [a]the LORD of hosts has
planned, and who can frustrate *it*?
And as for His stretched-out
hand, who can turn it back?"

C Against Philistia, 14:28-32

28 In the [a]year that King
Ahaz died this [b]oracle came:
29 "Do not rejoice, O [a]Philis-
tia, all of you,
Because the rod that
[b]struck you is broken;
For from the serpent's root
a [c]viper will come out,
And its fruit will be a
[d]flying serpent.
30 "And those who are most
[a]helpless will eat,
And the needy will lie
down in security;
I will destroy your root
with [b]famine,
And it will kill off your
survivors.
31 "Wail, O [a]gate; cry, O city;
Melt away, O [b]Philistia, all
of you;
For smoke comes from the
[c]north,
And [d]there is no straggler
in his ranks.
32 "How then will one answer
the [a]messengers of
the nation?
That [b]the LORD has
founded Zion,
And [c]the afflicted of His
people will seek ref-
uge in it."

Cross references

20 [a]Job 18:16, 19; Ps. 21:10; 37:28; Is. 1:4; 31:2

21 [a]Ex. 20:5; Lev. 26:39; Is. 13:16; Matt. 23:35

22 [a]Prov. 10:7 [b]Job 18:19; Is. 47:9

★**23** [a]Is. 34:11; Zeph. 2:14 [b]1 Kin. 14:10; Is. 13:6

★**24-27**

24 [a]Job 23:13; Is. 46:11; 55:8, 9; Acts 4:28

25 [a]Is. 10:12; 30:31; 31:8 [b]Is. 9:4; 10:27; Nah. 1:13

26 [a]Is. 23:9; Zeph. 3:6, 8 [b]Ex. 15:12

27 [a]2 Chr. 20:6; Is. 43:13; Dan. 4:31, 35

★**28-32**

28 [a]2 Kin. 16:20; 2 Chr. 28:27 [b]Is. 13:1

29 [a]Is. 2:6; 11:14; Jer. 47:1-7; Ezek. 25:15-17; Joel 3:4-8; Amos 1:6-8; Zeph. 2:4-7; Zech. 9:5-7 [b]2 Chr. 26:6 [c]Is. 11:8 [d]Is. 30:6

30 [a]Is. 3:14, 15; 7:21, 22; 11:4 [b]Is. 8:21; 9:20; 51:19

31 [a]Is. 3:26; 24:12; 45:2 [b]Is. 14:29 [c]Jer. 1:14 [d]Is. 34:16

32 [a]Is. 37:9 [b]Ps. 87:1, 5; 102:16; Is. 28:16; 44:28; 54:11 [c]Is. 4:6; 25:4; 57:13; Zeph. 3:12; Heb. 11:10; James 2:5

14:23 *hedgehog.* A porcupine.
14:24-27 The fulfillment of this prediction of the destruction of Assyria is recorded in 37:21-38.
14:28-32 *Ahaz died* in 715. He was pro-Assyrian, but now Assyria was in difficulty (v. 29a). Messengers from Philistia proposed to King Hezekiah that they join in a revolt against Assyria (v. 32). The Lord told Isaiah that the respite from Assyrian domination was only temporary (v. 29b), that Philistia was doomed (v. 30), and that their trust should be in the Lord (v. 32).

D   Against Moab, 15:1–16:14

★ 1-9

1 a Is.
11:14; 25:10;
Jer. 48:1;
Ezek. 25:8-
11; Amos
2:1-3; Zeph.
2:8-11
b Num. 21:28

2 a Jer.
48:18, 22
b Lev. 21:5;
Jer. 48:37

3 a Jon. 3:6-
8 b Jer. 48:38
c Is. 22:4

4 a Num.
21:28; 32:3;
Jer. 48:34

5 a Jer.
48:34 b Jer.
48:5 c Is.
59:7; Jer.
4:20

6 a Is. 19:5-
7; Jer. 48:34
b Joel 1:10-
12; 2:3

15 The oracle concerning a Moab.
Surely in a night b Ar of
Moab is devastated
and ruined;
Surely in a night Kir of
Moab is devastated
and ruined.

2 They have gone up to the
temple and *to* a Dibon,
even to the high
places to weep.
Moab wails over Nebo and
Medeba;
Everyone's head is b bald
and every beard is cut
off.

3 In their streets they have
girded themselves
with a sackcloth;
b On their housetops and in
their squares
Everyone is wailing, c dissolved in tears.

4 a Heshbon and Elealeh also
cry out,
Their voice is heard all the
way to Jahaz;
Therefore the armed men
of Moab cry aloud;
His soul trembles within
him.

5 My heart cries out for
Moab;
His fugitives are as far as
a Zoar and Eglath-
shelishiyah,
For they go up the b ascent
of Luhith weeping;
Surely on the road to
Horonaim they raise a
cry of distress c over
their ruin.

6 For the a waters of Nimrim
are desolate.
Surely the grass is with-
ered, the tender grass
died out,
There is b no green thing.

7 a Is. 30:6;
Jer. 48:36

9 a 2 Kin.
17:25; Jer.
50:17

★ 1-5

1 a 2 Kin.
3:4; Ezra
7:17 b 2 Kin.
14:7; Is.
42:11 c Is.
10:32

2 a Prov.
27:8 b Jer.
48:20, 46
c Num.
21:13, 14

3 a Is. 25:4;
32:2 b 1 Kin.
18:4

4 a Is. 9:4;
14:4; 49:26;
51:13; 54:14

5 a Is. 9:6,
7; 32:1; 55:4;
Dan. 7:14;
Mic. 4:7;
Luke 1:33
b Is. 9:7

7 Therefore the a abundance
which they have ac-
quired and stored up
They carry off over the
brook of Arabim.

8 For the cry of distress has
gone around the terri-
tory of Moab,
Its wail *goes* as far as Egla-
im and its wailing
even to Beer-elim.

9 For the waters of Dimon
are full of blood;
Surely I will bring added
woes upon Dimon,
A a lion upon the fugitives
of Moab and upon the
remnant of the land.

16 a Send the *tribute* lamb to
the ruler of the land,
From b Sela by way of
the wilderness to the
c mountain of the
daughter of Zion.

2 Then, like a fleeing birds *or*
scattered nestlings,
The daughters of b Moab
will be at the fords of
the c Arnon.

3 "Give *us* advice, make a decision;
Cast your a shadow like
night at high noon;
b Hide the outcasts, do not
betray the fugitive.

4 "Let the outcasts of Moab
stay with you;
Be a hiding place to them
from the destroyer."
For the extortioner has
come to an end, de-
struction has ceased,
a Oppressors have com-
pletely *disappeared*
from the land.

5 A a throne will even be established in loving-
kindness,
And a judge will sit on it in
faithfulness in the
tent of b David;

15:1-9 Judgment on Moab by Assyria is described in this section (see note on Amos 2:1).
It will be swift (*Ar* and *Kir*, Isa. 15:1, though 25
miles apart, would fall in the same night);
refugees would flee as far as *Zoar* at the south
end of the Dead Sea (v. 5). Notice Isaiah's sensitivity to the horrors of war (e.g., v. 8).
16:1-5 From their asylum in Edom (*Sela* is Petra,
the capital), the Moabite refugees sent a request with a *tribute lamb* to Judah, asking that
they might be resettled there.

Moreover, he will seek justice
And be prompt in righteousness.

★ 6-11

6 aJer.
48:29; Amos
2:1; Obad. 3,
4; Zeph. 2:8,
10 bJer.
48:30

6 aWe have heard of the pride of Moab, an excessive pride;
Even of his arrogance, pride, and fury;
bHis idle boasts are false.

7 a1 Chr.
16:3 b2 Kin.
3:25; Jer.
48:31

7 Therefore Moab shall wail; everyone of Moab shall wail.
You shall moan for the araisin cakes of bKir-hareseth
As those who are utterly stricken.

8 aIs. 15:4
bNum. 32:38
cJer. 48:32

8 For the fields of aHeshbon have withered, the vines of bSibmah as well;
The lords of the nations have trampled down its choice clusters
Which reached as far as Jazer and wandered to the deserts;
cIts tendrils spread themselves out and passed over the sea.

9 aJer.
48:32 bIs.
15:4 cJer.
40:10, 12;
48:32

9 Therefore I will aweep bitterly for Jazer, for the vine of Sibmah;
I will drench you with my tears, O bHeshbon and Elealeh;
For the shouting over your csummer fruits and your harvest has fallen away.

10 aIs. 24:8;
Jer. 48:33;
bJudg. 9:27;
Is. 24:7;
Amos 5:11,
17 cJob
24:11; Amos
9:13

10 And agladness and joy are taken away from the fruitful field;
In the bvineyards also there will be no cries of joy or jubilant shouting,

No ctreader treads out wine in the presses,
For I have made the shouting to cease.

11 Therefore my aheart intones like a harp for Moab,
And my inward feelings for Kir-hareseth.

12 So it will come about when Moab apresents himself,
When he bwearies himself upon his chigh place,
And comes to his sanctuary to pray,
That he will not prevail.

13 This is the word which the LORD spoke earlier concerning Moab. .

14 But now the LORD speaks, saying, "Within three years, as aa hired man would count them, the glory of bMoab will be degraded along with all his great population, and his remnant will be very small and impotent."

11 aIs. 15:5;
63:15; Jer.
48:36; Hos.
11:8; Phil.
2:1

12 aNum.
22:39-41;
Jer. 48:35
b1 Kin.
18:29 cIs.
15:2

★14 aJob
7:1; 14:6; Is.
21:16 bIs.
25:10; Jer.
48:42

E   Against Damascus (Syria) and Her Ally, Israel, 17:1-14

17 The aoracle concerning bDamascus.
"Behold, Damascus is about to be cremoved from being a city,
And it will become a dfallen ruin.

2 "The cities of aAroer are forsaken;
They will be for bflocks to lie down in,
And there will be cno one to frighten them.

3 "The afortified city will disappear from Ephraim,
And sovereignty from Damascus

★ 1-6

1 aIs. 13:1
bGen. 14:15;
15:2; 2 Kin.
16:9; Jer.
49:23; Amos
1:3-5; Zech.
9:1; Acts 9:2
cIs. 7:16;
8:4; 10:9 dIs.
25:2; Jer.
49:2; Mic.
1:6

2 aNum.
32:34 bIs.
7:21, 22;
Ezek. 25:5;
Zeph. 2:6
cMic. 4:4

3 aIs. 7:8,
16; 8:4 bIs.
17:4; Hos.
9:11

16:6-11 The request was denied because of Moab's pride. *raisin cakes* (v. 7). Used for offerings.
16:14 *as a hired man would count them.* I.e., shorter, not longer, since a hired man hopes the time will pass more quickly.
17:1-6 Another description (cf. 7:1-9:21) of the

failure of the alliance between Aram (Syria, indicated by its capital *Damascus,* 17:1, 3) and Israel (indicated by *Ephraim* and *Jacob,* vv. 3-4). Tiglath-pileser annexed the northern part of Israel in 732 when he took Damascus, and Sargon took Samaria in 722, deporting much of the populace.

And the remnant of Aram;
They will be like the
    ^bglory of the sons of
    Israel,"
Declares the LORD of hosts.

4 ^aIs. 10:3
^bIs. 10:16

4 Now it will come about in
that day that the ^aglo-
ry of Jacob will fade,
And ^bthe fatness of his
flesh will become
lean.

5 ^aIs.
17:11; Jer.
51:33; Joel
3:13; Matt.
13:30
^b2 Sam.
5:18, 22

5 It will be ^aeven like the
reaper gathering the
standing grain,
As his arm harvests the
ears,
Or it will be like one
gleaning ears of grain
In the ^bvalley of Rephaim.

6 ^aDeut.
4:27; Is.
24:13; 27:12;
Obad. 5

6 Yet ^agleanings will be left
in it like the shaking
of an olive tree,
Two or three olives on the
topmost bough,
Four or five on the
branches of a fruitful
tree,
Declares the LORD, the God
of Israel.

★ **7** ^aIs.
10:20; Hos.
3:5; 6:1; Mic.
7:7

7 In that day man will ^ahave
regard for his Maker,
And his eyes will look to
the Holy One of Is-
rael.

★ **8** ^a2 Chr.
34:7; Is. 27:9
^bIs. 2:8, 20;
30:22; 31:7
^cEx. 34:13;
Deut. 7:5;
Mic. 5:14

8 And he will not have regard for the ^aaltars,
the work of his hands,
Nor will he look to that
which his ^bfingers
have made,
Even the ^cAsherim and incense stands.

9 In that day their strong
cities will be like for-
saken places in the
forest,
Or like branches which
they abandoned be-
fore the sons of Israel;

And the land will be a
desolation.

10 For ^ayou have forgotten
the ^bGod of your salvation
And have not remembered
the ^crock of your refuge.
Therefore you plant de-
lightful plants
And set them with vine
slips of a strange god.

★**10** ^aIs.
51:13 ^bPs.
68:19; Is.
12:2; 33:2;
61:10; 62:11
^cDeut. 32:4,
18, 31; Is.
26:4; 30:29;
44:8

11 In the day that you plant it
you carefully fence it
in,
And in the ^amorning you
bring your seed to
blossom;
But the harvest will ^bbe a
heap
In a day of sickliness and
incurable pain.

11 ^aPs. 90:6
^bJob 4:8;
Hos. 8:7;
10:13

12 Alas, the uproar of many
peoples
^aWho roar like the roaring
of the seas,
And the rumbling of na-
tions
Who rush on like the
^brumbling of mighty
waters!

12 ^aIs. 5:30;
Jer. 6:23;
Ezek. 43:2;
Luke 21:25
^bPs. 18:4

13 The ^anations rumble on
like the rumbling of
many waters,
But He will ^brebuke them
and they will flee far
away,
And be chased ^clike chaff
in the mountains be-
fore the wind,
Or like whirling dust be-
fore a gale.

13 ^aIs. 33:3
^bPs. 9:5; Is.
41:11 ^cJob
21:18; Ps.
1:4; 83:13;
Is. 29:5;
41:15, 16

14 At evening time, behold,
there is terror!
Before morning ^athey are
no more.
Such will be the portion of
those who plunder us,
And the lot of those who
pillage us.

★**14** ^a2 Kin.
19:35; Is.
41:12

17:7 Some would turn to the Lord at that time of deportation.
17:8 *Asherim.* Wooden pillars representing the female goddess in Canaanite religion.
17:10 *plant delightful plants.* Probably a refer-ence to Adonis gardens, whose plants repre-sented the death and resurrection facet of hea-then worship.
17:14 *they are no more.* See 37:36 for the fulfill-ment.

F   Against Ethiopia, 18:1-7

★ 1 *a*2 Kin. 19:9; Is. 20:3-5; Ezek. 30:4, 5, 9; Zeph. 2:12; 3:10
★ 2 *a*Ex. 2:3 *b*Is. 18:7 *c*Gen. 10:8, 9; 2 Chr. 12:2-4; 14:9; 16:8

18 Alas, oh land of whirring
    wings
Which lies beyond the riv-
    ers of *a*Cush,
2 Which sends envoys by
    the sea,
Even in *a*papyrus vessels
    on the surface of the
    waters.
Go, swift messengers, to a
    nation   *b*tall   and
    smooth,
To a people *c*feared far and
    wide,
A powerful and oppressive
    nation
Whose land the rivers di-
    vide.

3 *a*Ps. 49:1; Mic. 1:2 *b*Is. 26:11

3   *a*All you inhabitants of the
    world and dwellers on
    earth,
As soon as a standard is
    raised on the moun-
    tains, *b*you will see *it,*
And as soon as the trum-
    pet is blown, you will
    hear *it.*

4 *a*Is. 26:21; Hos. 5:15 *b*2 Sam. 23:4 *c*Prov. 19:12; Is. 26:19; Hos. 14:5

4 For thus the Lord has told
    me,
"I will look from My
    *a*dwelling place qui-
    etly
Like dazzling heat in the
    *b*sunshine,
Like a cloud of *c*dew in the
    heat of harvest."

5 *a*Is. 17:10, 11; Ezek. 17:6-10

5 For *a*before the harvest, as
    soon as the bud blos-
    soms
And the flower becomes a
    ripening grape,
Then He will cut off the
    sprigs with pruning
    knives
And remove *and* cut away
    the   spreading
    branches.

6 *a*Is. 46:11; 56:9; Jer. 7:33; Ezek. 32:4-6; 39:17-20

6 They will be left together
    for mountain birds *a*of
    prey,
And for the beasts of the
    earth;
And the birds of prey will
    spend the summer
    feeding on them,
And all the beasts of the
    earth will spend har-
    vest time on them.

★ 7 *a*Ps. 68:31; Is. 45:14; Zeph. 3:10; Acts 8:27-38 *b*Zech. 14:16, 17

7 At that time a gift of hom-
    age will be brought to
    the Lord of hosts
From a *a*people tall and
    smooth,
Even from a people feared
    far and wide,
A powerful and oppressive
    nation,
Whose land the rivers di-
    vide—
To the *b*place of the name
    of the Lord of hosts,
    even Mount Zion.

G   Against Egypt, 19:1-20:6

1 *a*Is. 13:1 *b*Joel 3:19 *c*Ps. 18:9, 10; 104:3; Matt. 26:64; Rev. 1:7 *d*Ex. 12:12; Jer. 43:12; 44:8 *e*Josh. 2:11; Is. 13:7

19 The *a*oracle concerning
    *b*Egypt.
Behold, the Lord is *c*riding
    on a swift cloud, and
    is about to come to
    Egypt;
The *d*idols of Egypt will
    tremble at His pres-
    ence,
And the *e*heart of the
    Egyptians will melt
    within them.

★ 2 *a*Judg. 7:22; 1 Sam. 14:20; 2 Chr. 20:23; Matt. 10:21, 36

2 "So I will incite Egyptians
    against Egyptians;
And they will *a*each fight
    against his brother,
    and each against his
    neighbor,
City against city, *and* king-
    dom against kingdom.

18:1 *of whirring wings.* Probably a reference to the insects of the region.
18:2 *tall and smooth.* The appearance of the Ethiopians (see also v. 7). An Ethiopian dynasty established in Egypt about 714 pursued an anti-Assyrian policy similar to Hezekiah's.

Isaiah warns against being involved in any Ethiopian alliance.
18:7 In the millennial kingdom the Ethiopians will do homage to the Lord. The *people* themselves are the *gift* (omit both "froms").
19:2 Egypt would experience civil war.

3 "Then the spirit of the Egyptians will be demoralized within them;
And I will confound their strategy,
So that *they will resort to idols and ghosts of the dead,
And to mediums and spiritists.

4 "Moreover, I will deliver the Egyptians into the hand of a *cruel master,
And a mighty king will rule over them," declares the Lord GOD of hosts.

5 *And the waters from the sea will dry up,
And the river will be parched and dry.

6 And the *canals will emit a stench,
The *streams of Egypt will thin out and dry up;
*The reeds and rushes will rot away.

7 The bulrushes by the *Nile, by the edge of the Nile
And all the sown fields by the Nile
Will become dry, be driven away, and be no more.

8 And the *fishermen will lament,
And all those who cast a line into the Nile will mourn,
And those who spread nets on the waters will pine away.

9 Moreover, the manufacturers of linen made from combed flax

And the weavers of white *cloth will be utterly dejected.

10 And the *pillars of Egypt will be crushed;
All the hired laborers will be grieved in soul.

11 The princes of *Zoan are mere fools;
The advice of Pharaoh's wisest advisers has become stupid.
How can you men say to Pharaoh,
"I am a son of the *wise, a son of ancient kings"?

12 Well then, where are your wise men?
Please let them tell you,
And let them understand what the LORD of hosts
Has *purposed against Egypt.

13 The princes of Zoan have acted foolishly,
The princes of *Memphis are deluded;
Those who are the *cornerstone of her tribes
Have led Egypt astray.

14 The LORD has mixed within her a spirit of *distortion;
*They have led Egypt astray in all that it does,
As a *drunken man staggers in his vomit.

15 And there will be no work for Egypt
*Which its head or tail, its palm branch or bulrush, may do.

16 In that day the Egyptians will become like women, and they will tremble and be in *dread because of the *waving of the

---

Cross references (left column):

3 *a*1 Chr. 10:13; Is. 8:19; Dan. 2:2

★ 4 *a*Is. 20:4; Jer. 46:26; Ezek. 29:19

★ 5-10

5 *a*Is. 50:2; Jer. 51:36; Ezek. 30:12

6 *a*Ex. 7:18 *b*Is. 37:25 *c*Ex. 2:3; Job 8:11; Is. 15:6

7 *a*Is. 23:3, 10

8 *a*Ezek. 47:10; Hab. 1:15

9 *a*Prov. 7:16; Ezek. 27:7

Cross references (right column):

10 *a*Ps. 11:3

★11-14

11 *a*Num. 13:22; Ps. 78:12, 43; Is. 30:4 *b*Gen. 41:38, 39; 1 Kin. 4:30; Acts 7:22

12 *a*Is. 14:24; Rom. 9:17

13 *a*Jer. 2:16; 46:14, 19; Ezek. 30:13 *b*Zech. 10:4

14 *a*Prov. 12:8; Matt. 17:17 *b*Is. 3:12; 9:16 *c*Is. 28:7

15 *a*Is. 9:14, 15

★16-25

16 *a*2 Cor. 5:11; Heb. 10:31 *b*Is. 11:15

19:4 *a cruel master.* I.e., Esarhaddon of Assyria, who conquered Egypt in 671.

19:5-10 Drought would bring economic disaster to Egypt. *the pillars* (v. 10). Better, her weavers.

19:11-14 The internationally famous wise men of Egypt would be unable to avert disaster, because the Lord would confuse them (v. 14).

Zoan (v. 13) or Tanis was a capital city in the NE. section of the Delta.

19:16-25 *In that day* of the future coming of the Lord, Egypt will share in millennial blessings by fearing the Lord (vv. 16-17), by worshiping the Lord (vv. 18-22), and by living in peace with Assyria and Israel (vv. 23-25).

hand of the LORD of hosts, which He is going to wave over them.

17 And the land of Judah will become a terror to Egypt; everyone to whom it is mentioned will be in dread of it, because of the [a]purpose of the LORD of hosts which He is purposing against them.

18 In that day five cities in the land of Egypt will be speaking the language of Canaan and [a]swearing *allegiance* to the LORD of hosts; one will be called the City of Destruction.

19 In that day there will be an [a]altar to the LORD in the midst of the land of Egypt, and a [b]pillar to the LORD near its border.

20 And it will become a sign and a witness to the LORD of hosts in the land of Egypt; for they will cry to the LORD because of oppressors, and He will send them a [a]Savior and a [b]Champion, and He will deliver them.

21 Thus the LORD will make Himself known to Egypt, and the Egyptians will know the LORD in that day. They will even worship with [a]sacrifice and offering, and will make a vow to the LORD and perform it.

22 And the LORD will strike Egypt, striking but [a]healing; so they will [b]return to the LORD, and He will respond to them and will heal them.

23 In that day there will be a [a]highway from Egypt to Assyria, and the Assyrians will come into Egypt and the Egyptians into Assyria, and the Egyptians will [b]worship with the Assyrians.

24 In that day Israel will be the third *party* with Egypt and Assyria, a blessing in the midst of the earth,

25 whom the LORD of hosts has blessed, saying, "Blessed is [a]Egypt My people, and Assyria

[b]the work of My hands, and Israel My inheritance."

20 In the year that the [a]commander came to [b]Ashdod, when Sargon the king of Assyria sent him and he fought against Ashdod and captured it,

2 at that time the LORD spoke through [a]Isaiah the son of Amoz, saying, "Go and loosen the [b]sackcloth from your hips, and take your [c]shoes off your feet." And he did so, going [d]naked and barefoot.

3 And the LORD said, "Even as My servant Isaiah has gone naked and barefoot three years as a [a]sign and token against Egypt and [b]Cush,

4 so the [a]king of Assyria will lead away the captives of Egypt and the exiles of Cush, [b]young and old, naked and barefoot with buttocks uncovered, to the shame of Egypt.

5 "Then they shall be [a]dismayed and ashamed because of Cush their hope and Egypt their [b]boast.

6 "So the inhabitants of this coastland will say in that day, 'Behold, such is our hope, where we fled [a]for help to be delivered from the king of Assyria; and we, [b]how shall we escape?' "

H   Against Babylon, 21:1-10

21 The [a]oracle concerning the [b]wilderness of the sea.
As [c]windstorms in the Negev sweep on,
It comes from the wilderness, from a terrifying land.

2 A [a]harsh vision has been shown to me;
The [b]treacherous one still deals treacherously,
and the destroyer still destroys.

Margin references (left column)

17 [a]Is. 14:24; Dan. 4:35
18 [a]Is. 45:23; 65:16
19 [a]Is. 56:7; 60:7 [b]Gen. 28:18; Ex. 24:4; Josh. 22:10, 26, 27
20 [a]Is. 43:3, 11; 45:15, 21; 49:26; 60:16; 63:8 [b]Is. 49:25
21 [a]Is. 56:7; 60:7; Zech. 14:16-18
22 [a]Deut. 32:39; Is. 30:26; 57:18; Heb. 12:11 [b]Is. 27:13; 45:14; Hos. 14:1
23 [a]Is. 11:16; 35:8; 49:11; 62:10 [b]Is. 27:13
25 [a]Is. 45:14 [b]Ps. 100:3; Is. 29:23; 45:11; 60:21; 64:8; Eph. 2:10

Margin references (right column)

★ **1** [a]2 Kin. 18:17 [b]1 Sam. 5:1
★ **2** [a]Is. 1:1; 13:1 [b]Zech. 13:4; Matt. 3:4 [c]Ezek. 24:17, 23 [d]1 Sam. 19:24; Mic. 1:8
3 [a]Is. 8:18 [b]Is. 37:9; 43:3
4 [a]Is. 19:4 [b]Is. 47:2, 3
5 [a]2 Kin. 18:21; Is. 30:3-5; 31:1; Ezek. 29:6, 7 [b]Jer. 9:23, 24; 17:5; 1 Cor. 3:21
6 [a]Is. 10:3; 30:7; 31:3; Jer. 30:1, 7, 15-17; 31:1-3 [b]Matt. 23:33; 1 Thess. 5:3; Heb. 2:3
★ **1** [a]Is. 13:1 [b]Is. 13:20-22; 14:23; Jer. 51:42 [c]Zech. 9:14
★ **2** [a]Ps. 60:3 [b]Is. 24:16; 33:1; Jer. 22:6; Jer. 49:34

20:1 *In the year.* I.e., 711. *the commander.* Tartan, Sargon's general (2 Kings 18:17). Sargon was king of Assyria from 722-705.
20:2 Isaiah was to dress like a prisoner of war (which the Egyptians would be, v. 4) for three years.

21:1 *the wilderness of the sea.* I.e., the plain on which Babylon was built.
21:2 *Elam.* Persia.

Go up, [c]Elam, lay siege,
Media;
I have made an end of all
the groaning she has
caused.

★ 3-4

3 [a]Is. 13:8;
16:11 [b]Ps.
48:6; Is.
13:8; 26:17;
1 Thess. 5:3

3 For this reason my [a]loins
are full of anguish;
Pains have seized me like
the pains of a [b]woman
in labor.
I am so bewildered I can-
not hear, so terrified I
cannot see.

4 [a]Deut.
28:67

4 My mind reels, horror
overwhelms me;
The twilight I longed for
has been [a]turned for
me into trembling.

★ 5 [a]Jer.
51:39, 57;
Dan. 5:1-4

5 They [a]set the table, they
spread out the cloth,
they eat, they drink;
"Rise up, captains, oil the
shields,"

6 [a]2 Kin.
9:17-20

6 For thus the Lord says to
me,
"Go, station the lookout, let
him [a]report what he
sees.

7 [a]Is. 21:9

7 "When he sees [a]riders,
horsemen in pairs,
A train of donkeys, a train
of camels,
Let him pay close atten-
tion, very close atten-
tion."

8 [a]Hab. 2:1

8 Then the lookout called,
"[a]O Lord, I stand continually by day on the
watchtower,
And I am stationed every
night at my guard
post.

★ 9 [a]Is.
13:19; 47:5,
9; 48:14; Jer.
51:8; Rev.
14:8; 18:2
[b]Is. 46:1;
Jer. 50:2;
51:44

9 "Now behold, here comes a
troop of riders, horse-
men in pairs."
And one answered and
said, "[a]Fallen, fallen is
Babylon;

And all the [b]images of her
gods are shattered on
the ground."

10 O my [a]threshed *people*,
and my afflicted of the
threshing floor!
What I have heard from
the Lord of hosts,
The God of Israel, I make
known to you.

10 [a]Jer.
51:33; Mic.
4:13

I   Against Edom, 21:11-12

11 The oracle concerning
[a]Edom.
One keeps calling to me
from [b]Seir,
"Watchman, how far gone
is the night?
Watchman, how far gone
is the night?"

12 The watchman says,
"Morning comes but also
night.
If you would inquire, in-
quire;
Come back again."

★11 [a]Gen.
25:14 [b]Gen.
32:3

★12

J   Against Arabia, 21:13-17

13 The oracle about [a]Arabia.
In the thickets of Arabia
you must spend the
night,
O caravans of [b]Dedanites.

14 Bring water for the thirsty,
O inhabitants of the land
of [a]Tema,
Meet the fugitive with
bread.

15 For they have [a]fled from
the swords,
From the drawn sword,
and from the bent
bow,
And from the press of battle.

★13 [a]Jer.
25:23, 24;
49:28 [b]Gen.
10:7; Ezek.
27:15

★14 [a]Gen.
25:15; Job
6:19

15 [a]Is.
13:14, 15;
17:13

21:3-4 Notice again Isaiah's sensitivity to the
horrors of war (cf. 15:5-7).
21:5 Details are given in Dan. 5.
21:9 *fallen is Babylon.* Though the Babylonian
Empire was defeated in 539, Babylon, as
standing for all that opposes God, will not be
finally destroyed until the close of the Tribulation period (Rev. 14:8; 18:2).
21:11 *Seir.* The land of Edom.
21:12 The *Morning* of blessing for Israel will
come, as will the *night* of judgment for Edom
(cf. Obad. 1-9).
21:13 *Dedanites.* An Arabian tribe (Ezek. 27:15).
21:14 *Tema.* An oasis in NW. Arabia.

★16 a Is.
16:14 b Ps.
120:5; Song
1:5; Is.
42:11; 60:7;
Ezek. 27:21
17 a Is. 10:19
b Num.
23:19; Zech.
1:6

16 For thus the Lord said to me, "In a ªyear, as a hired man would count it, all the splendor of ᵇKedar will terminate; **17** and the ªremainder of the number of bowmen, the mighty men of the sons of Kedar, will be few; for the LORD God of Israel ᵇhas spoken."

K Against Jerusalem, 22:1-25

★ 1 a Ps.
125:2; Jer.
21:13; Joel
3:12, 14 b Is.
15:3

22 The oracle concerning the ªvalley of vision.

What is the matter with you now, that you have all gone up to the ᵇhousetops?

2 a Is. 23:7;
32:13 b Jer.
14:18; Lam.
2:20

2 You who were full of noise,
You boisterous town, you ªexultant city;
Your slain were ᵇnot slain with the sword,
Nor did they die in battle.

3 a Is. 21:15

3 ªAll your rulers have fled together,
And have been captured without the bow;
All of you who were found were taken captive together,
Though they had fled far away.

4 a Is. 15:3;
Jer. 9:1;
Luke 19:41

4 Therefore I say, "Turn your eyes away from me,
Let me ªweep bitterly,
Do not try to comfort me concerning the destruction of the daughter of my people."

★ 5 a Lam.
1:5; 2:2 b Is.
37:3 c Is.
10:6; 63:3
d Is. 22:1

5 ªFor the Lord GOD of hosts has a ᵇday of panic, ᶜsubjugation, and confusion
ᵈIn the valley of vision,
A breaking down of walls

And a crying to the mountain.

★ 6 a Is.
21:2; Jer.
49:35
b 2 Kin. 16:9;
Amos 1:5;
9:7

6 And ªElam took up the quiver
With the chariots, infantry, *and* horsemen;
And ᵇKir uncovered the shield.

7 Then your choicest valleys were full of chariots,
And the horsemen took up fixed positions at the gate.

★ 8-11
8 a 1 Kin.
7:2; 10:17

8 And He removed the defense of Judah.
In that day you depended on the weapons of the ªhouse of the forest,

9 a 2 Kin.
20:20; Neh.
3:16

9 And you saw that the breaches
In the *wall* of the city of David were many;
And you ªcollected the waters of the lower pool.

10 Then you counted the houses of Jerusalem,
And you tore down houses to fortify the wall.

11 a 2 Kin.
25:4; Jer.
39:4 b 2 Kin.
20:20; 2 Chr.
32:3, 4

11 And you made a reservoir ªbetween the two walls
For the waters of the ᵇold pool.
But you did not depend on Him who made it,
Nor did you take into consideration Him who planned it long ago.

12 a Is.
32:11; Joel
1:13; 2:17
b Mic. 1:16

12 Therefore in that day the Lord GOD of hosts, called *you* to ªweeping, to wailing,
To ᵇshaving the head, and to wearing sackcloth.

13 a Is. 5:11,
22; 28:7, 8;
Luke 17:26-
29 b Is.
56:12; 1 Cor.
15:32

13 Instead, there is ªgaiety and gladness,
Killing of cattle and slaughtering of sheep,

21:16 *Kedar.* A powerful Arabian tribe.
22:1 *the valley of vision.* A reference to Jerusalem, which is surrounded by mountains (cf. Psalm 125:2).
22:5 *day of panic.* Most likely refers to the coming siege of Jerusalem by Babylon (589-587), though there may also be glimpses of the in-

vasion of Sennacherib in 701.
22:6 *Elam.* Persia (cf. 21:2). *Kir.* Not yet identified.
22:8-11 Though the leaders tried to provide adequate water supply and defenses, they refused the greatest help, the Lord Himself.

Eating of meat and drink-
ing of wine:
"ᵇLet us eat and drink, for
tomorrow we may
die."

14 But the Lᴏʀᴅ of hosts revealed Himself to me,
"Surely this ᵃiniquity ᵇshall
not be forgiven you
ᶜUntil you die," says the
Lord Gᴏᴅ of hosts.

15 Thus says the Lord Gᴏᴅ of
hosts,
"Come, go to this steward,
To ᵃShebna, who is in
charge of the *royal*
household,

16 'What right do you have
here,
And whom do you have
here,
That you have ᵃhewn a
tomb for yourself
here,
You who hew a tomb on
the height,
You who carve a resting
place for yourself in
the rock?

17 'Behold, the Lᴏʀᴅ is about
to hurl you headlong,
O man.
And He is about to grasp
you firmly,

18 *And* roll you tightly like a
ball,
To be ᵃcast into a vast
country;
There you will die,
And there your splendid
chariots will be,
You shame of your mas-
ter's house.'

19 "And I will ᵃdepose you
from your office,
And I will pull you down
from your station.

20 "Then it will come about in
that day,

That I will summon My
servant ᵃEliakim the
son of Hilkiah

21 And I will clothe him with
your tunic,
And tie your sash securely
about him,
I will entrust him with
your authority,
And he will become a ᵃfa-
ther to the inhabitants
of Jerusalem and to
the house of Judah.

22 "Then I will set ᵃthe key of
the ᵇhouse of David
on his shoulder,
When he opens no one
will shut,
When he shuts no one will
ᶜopen.

23 "And I will drive him *like* a
ᵃpeg in a firm place,
And he will become a
ᵇthrone of glory to his
father's house.

24 "So they will hang on him
all the glory of his father's house,
offspring and issue, all the least of
vessels, from bowls to all the jars.

25 "In that day," declares the
Lᴏʀᴅ of hosts, "the ᵃpeg driven in
a firm place will give way; it will
even ᵇbreak off and fall, and the
load hanging on it will be cut off,
for the ᶜLᴏʀᴅ has spoken."

L   Against Tyre, 23:1-18

23 The oracle concerning
ᵃTyre.
Wail, O ᵇships of ᶜTar-
shish,
For *Tyre* is destroyed,
without house *or*
ᵈharbor;
It is reported to them from
the land of ᵉCyprus.

2 ᵃBe silent, you inhabitants
of the coastland,

22:15 *Shebna.* A leader of the pro-Egypt party (chaps. 30-31), who ordered a tomb built for himself (22:16), not knowing he would die in captivity (vv. 17-18).
22:20 *Eliakim.* Shebna's replacement (2 Kings 18:18; Isa. 36:3; 37:2).
22:22 *the key.* Depicts the responsible position

and the power to make decisions *(opens . . . shuts)* (cf. Matt. 16:19; Rev. 3:7-8).
23:1 *Tyre.* One of the most famous cities of the ancient world. Her mariners were the explorers and merchants of the world (1 Kings 10:11, 22). *Tarshish.* See Isa. 2:16.

You merchants of Sidon;
Your messengers crossed
the sea

3 And *were* on many waters.
  [a]The grain of the [b]Nile,
  the harvest of the
  River was her rev-
  enue;
  And she was the [c]market
  of nations.

4 Be ashamed, O [a]Sidon;
For the sea speaks, the
  stronghold of the sea,
  saying,
"I have neither travailed nor
  given birth,
I have neither brought up
  young men *nor* reared
  virgins."

5 When the report *reaches*
  Egypt,
They will be in [a]anguish at
  the report of Tyre.

6 Pass over to [a]Tarshish;
Wail, O inhabitants of the
  coastland.

7 Is this your [a]jubilant *city,*
Whose origin is from an-
  tiquity,
Whose feet used to carry
  her to colonize distant
  places?

8 Who has planned this
  against Tyre, [a]the be-
  stower of crowns,
Whose merchants were
  princes, whose traders
  were the honored of
  the earth?

9 [a]The LORD of hosts has
  planned it to [b]defile
  the pride of all
  beauty,
To despise all the [c]hon-
  ored of the earth.

10 Overflow your land like
  the Nile, O daughter
  of Tarshish,
There is no more restraint.

11 He has [a]stretched His hand
  out [b]over the sea,

He has [c]made the king-
  doms tremble;
The LORD has given a com-
  mand concerning Ca-
  naan to [d]demolish its
  strongholds.

12 And He has said, "[a]You
  shall exult no more, O
  crushed virgin daugh-
  ter of Sidon.
Arise, pass over to [b]Cy-
  prus; even there you
  will find no rest."

13 Behold, the land of the
Chaldeans—this is the people
which was not; [a]Assyria appointed it for [b]desert creatures—
they erected their siege towers,
they stripped its palaces, [c]they
made it a ruin.

14 Wail, O [a]ships of Tarshish,
  For your stronghold is destroyed.

15 Now it will come about in
that day that Tyre will be forgotten for [a]seventy years like the
days of one king. At the end of
seventy years it will happen to
Tyre as *in* the song of the harlot:

16 Take *your* harp, walk
  about the city,
O forgotten harlot;
Pluck the strings skillfully,
  sing many songs,
That you may be remem-
  bered.

17 And it will come about at
[a]the end of seventy years that the
LORD will visit Tyre. Then she will
go back to her harlot's wages, and
will [b]play the harlot with all the
kingdoms on the face of the
earth.

18 And her [a]gain and her harlot's wages will be [b]set apart to
the LORD; it will not be stored up
or hoarded, but her gain will become sufficient food and choice
attire for those who dwell in the
presence of the LORD.

3 [a]Is. 19:7-
9 [b]Josh.
13:3; 1 Chr.
13:5; Jer.
2:18 [c]Ezek.
27:3-23

4 [a]Gen.
10:15, 19;
Josh. 11:8;
Judg. 10:6;
Jer. 25:22;
27:3; 47:4;
Ezek. 28:21,
22

5 [a]Ex.
15:14-16;
Josh. 2:9-11

6 [a]Is. 23:1

7 [a]Is. 22:2;
32:13

8 [a]Ezek.
28:2

9 [a]Is. 2:11;
13:11 [b]Job
40:11, 12;
Dan. 4:37
[c]Is. 5:13;
9:15

11 [a]Ex.
14:21; Is.
14:26 [b]Is.
19:5; 50:2
[c]Is. 13:13
[d]Is. 25:2;
Zech. 9:3, 4

12 [a]Ezek.
26:13, 14;
Rev. 18:22
[b]Is. 23:1

★13 [a]Is.
10:5 [b]Is.
13:21; 18:6
[c]Is. 10:7

14 [a]Is. 2:16;
Ezek. 27:25,
26

★15-17

15 [a]Jer.
25:11, 22

17 [a]Is. 23:15
[b]Ezek.
16:25-29;
Nah. 3:4

18 [a]Ps.
72:10, 11; Is.
60:5-9; Mic.
4:13 [b]Ex.
28:36; Zech.
14:20

23:13 The Lord would punish Tyre through the Chaldeans (Babylonians) who did raze all but the island city.
23:15-17 *seventy years.* From Nebuchadnezzar's conquest to the fall of Babylon, Tyre was weak and poor. Under the Persians she re-gained some of her former power, until Alexander the Great demolished the island city in 332.

III THE FUTURE TRIBULATION AND KINGDOM (ISAIAH'S APOCALYPSE), 24:1-27:13

A The Judgments of the Tribulation Period, 24:1-23

★ 1-13
★ 1 aIs. 2:19; 13:13; 24:19, 20; 30:32; 33:9

24 Behold, the Lord alays the earth waste, devastates it, distorts its surface, and scatters its inhabitants.

2 aLev. 25:36, 37; Deut. 23:19, 20

2 And the people will be like the priest, the servant like his master, the maid like her mistress, the buyer like the seller, the lender like the borrower, the acreditor like the debtor.

3 The earth will be completely laid waste and completely despoiled, for the Lord has spoken this word.

4 aIs. 33:9
bIs. 2:12; 24:21

4 The aearth mourns and withers, the world fades and withers, the bexalted of the people of the earth fade away.

5 aGen. 3:17; Num. 35:33; Is. 9:17; 10:6
bIs. 33:8

5 The earth is also apolluted by its inhabitants, for they transgressed laws, violated statutes, bbroke the everlasting covenant.

6 aJosh. 23:15; Is. 34:5; 43:28; Zech. 5:3, 4
bIs. 1:31; 5:24; 9:19

6 Therefore, a acurse devours the earth, and those who live in it are held guilty. Therefore, the binhabitants of the earth are burned, and few men are left.

7 aIs. 16:10; Joel 1:10, 12

7 The anew wine mourns,
The vine decays,
All the merry-hearted sigh.

8 aIs. 5:12, 14; Ezek. 26:13; Hos. 2:11; Rev. 18:22

8 The agaiety of tambourines ceases,
The noise of revelers stops,
The gaiety of the harp ceases.

9 aIs. 5:11, 22 bIs. 5:20

9 They do not drink wine with song;
aStrong drink is bbitter to those who drink it.

★10 aIs. 34:11 bIs. 23:1

10 The acity of chaos is broken down;
bEvery house is shut up so that none may enter.

11 There is an aoutcry in the streets concerning the wine;
bAll joy turns to gloom.
The gaiety of the earth is banished.

11 aJer. 14:2; 46:12
bIs. 16:10; 32:13

12 Desolation is left in the city,
And the agate is battered to ruins.

12 aIs. 14:31; 45:2

13 For athus it will be in the midst of the earth among the peoples,
As the shaking of an olive tree,
As the gleanings when the grape harvest is over.

13 aIs. 17:6; 27:12

14 aThey raise their voices, they shout for joy.
They cry out from the west concerning the majesty of the Lord.

14 aIs. 12:6; 48:20; 52:8; 54:1

15 Therefore aglorify the Lord in the east,
The bname of the Lord, the God of Israel
In the ccoastlands of the sea.

15 aIs. 25:3
bMal. 1:11
cIs. 11:11; 42:4, 10, 12; 49:1; 51:5; 60:9; 66:19

16 From the aends of the earth we hear songs,
"bGlory to the Righteous One,"
But I say, "cWoe to me! Woe to me! Alas for me!
The dtreacherous deal treacherously,
And the treacherous deal very treacherously."

16 aIs. 11:12; 42:10
bIs. 28:5; 60:21 cLev. 26:39 dIs. 21:2; 33:1; Jer. 3:20; 5:11

17 aTerror and pit and snare Confront you, O inhabitant of the earth.

17 aJer. 48:43; Amos 5:19

18 Then it will be that he who flees the report of disaster will fall into the pit,
And he who climbs out of the pit will be caught in the snare;

18 aGen. 7:11 bPs. 18:7; 46:2; Is. 2:19, 21; 13:13

24:1-13 The coming judgment will be on the entire *earth* (vv. 1, 4), on all classes of people (v. 2), and will remove all pleasures (vv. 7-13). Only a small remnant will survive (vv. 6, 13). 24:1 The section (chapters 24-27) which begins here is Isaiah's apocalypse, since it deals with judgments of the Tribulation period and blessings of the millennial age. 24:10 *chaos.* The same Heb. word is used in Gen. 1:2.

For the ªwindows above are opened, and the ᵇfoundations of the earth shake.

19   19 ªThe earth is broken asunder,
als. 24:1
ᵇNum. 16:31, 32;
Deut. 11:6

The earth is ᵇsplit through,
The earth is shaken violently.

20   20 The earth ªreels to and fro like a drunkard,
als. 19:14; 24:1;
28:7 ᵇIs. 1:28; 43:27;
66:24 ᶜDan. 11:19; Amos 8:14

And it totters like a shack,
For its ᵇtransgression is heavy upon it,
And it will fall, ᶜnever to rise again.

★21   21 So it will happen in that day,
als. 10:12; 13:11
ᵇPs. 76:12

That the Lᴏʀᴅ will ªpunish the host of heaven, on high,
And the ᵇkings of the earth, on earth.

22   22 And they will be gathered together
als. 10:4;
42:22 ᵇEzek. 38:8; Zech. 9:11, 12

Like ªprisoners in the dungeon,
And will be confined in prison;
And after many days they will ᵇbe punished.

★23   23 Then the ªmoon will be abashed and the sun ashamed,
als. 13:10 ᵇIs. 60:19, 20;
Zech. 14:6, 7; Rev. 21:23; 22:5
ᶜMic. 4:7;
Heb. 12:22

For the ᵇLᴏʀᴅ of hosts will reign on ᶜMount Zion and in Jerusalem,
And His glory will be before His elders.

B   The Triumphs of the Kingdom Age, 25:1–12

1   **25** O Lᴏʀᴅ, Thou art ªmy God;
aEx. 15:2;
Ps. 118:28;
Is. 7:13;
49:4, 5;
61:10 ᵇPs. 40:5; 98:1
ᶜEph. 1:11

I will exalt Thee, I will give thanks to Thy name;

For Thou hast ᵇworked wonders,
ᶜPlans formed long ago, with perfect faithfulness.

2 For Thou hast made a city into a ªheap,
★ 2 als. 17:1; 26:5;
27:10; 32:19
ᵇIs. 17:3;
25:12 ᶜIs. 13:22; 32:14;
34:13

A ᵇfortified city into a ruin;
A ᶜpalace of strangers is a city no more,
It will never be rebuilt.

3 Therefore a strong people will ªglorify Thee;
3 als. 24:15
ᵇIs. 13:11

ᵇCities of ruthless nations will revere Thee.

4 For Thou hast been a ªdefense for the helpless,
4 als. 14:32; 17:10;
27:5; 33:16
ᵇIs. 4:6; 32:2
ᶜIs. 29:5, 20;
49:25

A defense for the needy in his distress,
A ᵇrefuge from the storm, a shade from the heat;
For the breath of the ᶜruthless
Is like a *rain* storm *against* a wall.

5 Like heat in drought, Thou dost subdue the ªuproar of aliens;
5 aJer. 51:54-56

Like heat by the shadow of a cloud, the song of the ruthless is silenced.

6 And ªthe Lᴏʀᴅ of hosts will prepare a lavish banquet for ᵇall peoples on this mountain;
★ 6 als. 1:19 ᵇIs. 2:2-4; 56:7

A banquet of aged wine, choice pieces with marrow,
And refined, aged wine.

7 And on this mountain He will swallow up the ªcovering which is over all peoples,
7 a2 Cor. 3:15, 16;
Eph. 4:18

Even the veil which is stretched over all nations.

24:21 *the host of heaven.* Probably a reference to rebellious angels who will also be judged (1 Cor. 6:3).

24:23 The *moon* and *sun* will pale when the glory of the Lord is revealed at the second coming of Christ (Rev. 21:23).

25:2 *a city.* Doubtless Babylon, used representatively of all opposition to God.

25:6 *this mountain.* I.e., Zion, the center of millennial government (cf. 2:2-3). *choice pieces . . . refined, aged wine.* The choice luxuries of an Eastern banquet. The wine described is that in which the sediment has been allowed to remain and is particularly good wine up to a certain point of time.

★ 8 aHos.
13:14; 1 Cor.
15:54 bIs.
30:19; 35:10;
51:11; 65:19;
Rev. 7:17;
21:4 cPs.
69:9; 89:50,
51; Is. 51:7;
54:4; Matt.
5:11; 1 Pet.
4:14

8 He will aswallow up death
for all time,
And the Lord God will
bwipe tears away from
all faces,
And He will remove the
creproach of His peo-
ple from all the earth;
For the Lord has spoken.

9 aIs. 35:2;
40:9; 52:10
bIs. 8:17;
30:18; 33:2
cIs. 33:22;
35:4; 49:25;
26; 60:16
dPs. 20:5; Is.
35:1, 2, 10;
65:18; 66:10

9 And it will be said in that
day,
"Behold, athis is our God
for whom we have
bwaited that cHe
might save us.
This is the Lord for whom
we have waited;
dLet us rejoice and be glad
in His salvation."

10 aIs.
16:14; Jer.
48:1-47;
Ezek. 25:8-
11; Amos
2:1-3; Zeph.
2:9

10 For the hand of the Lord
will rest on this
mountain,
And aMoab will be trod-
den down in his place
As straw is trodden down
in the water of a ma-
nure pile.

11 aIs. 5:25;
14:26 bJob
40:11; Is.
2:10-12, 15-
17; 16:6, 14

11 And he will aspread out his
hands in the middle of
it
As a swimmer spreads out
his hands to swim,
But the Lord will blay low
his pride together
with the trickery of
his hands.

12 aIs. 15:1;
25:2; 26:5

12 And the aunassailable fortifications of your
walls He will bring
down,
Lay low, and cast to the
ground, even to the
dust.

C Praise in the Kingdom,
26:1-21

★ 1 aIs. 4:2;
12:1 bIs.
14:31; 31:5,
9; 33:5, 6,
20-24 cIs.
60:18

26 aIn that day this song will
be sung in the land of
Judah:
"We have a bstrong city;
He sets up walls and ram-
parts for csecurity.

2 "Open the agates, that the
brighteous nation may
enter,
The one that remains
faithful.

3 "The steadfast of mind
Thou wilt keep in per-
fect apeace,
Because he trusts in Thee.

4 "aTrust in the Lord forever,
For in God the Lord, we
have an everlasting
bRock.

5 "For He has brought low
those who dwell on
high, the aunassail-
able city;
bHe lays it low, He lays it
low to the ground, He
casts it to the dust.

6 "aThe foot will trample it,
The feet of the bafflicted,
the steps of the help-
less."

7 The away of the righteous
is smooth;
O Upright One, bmake the
path of the righteous
level.

8 Indeed, while following
the way of aThy judg-
ments, O Lord,
We have waited for Thee
eagerly;
bThy name, even Thy
cmemory, is the desire
of our souls.

9 aAt night my soul longs for
Thee,
Indeed, my spirit within
me bseeks Thee dili-
gently;
For when the earth experiences Thy judgments
The inhabitants of the
world clearn right-
eousness.

10 Though the wicked is
shown favor,
He does not alearn right-
eousness;

2 aIs.
60:11, 18;
62:10 bIs.
45:25; 54:14,
17; 58:8;
60:21; 61:3;
62:1, 2

★ 3 aIs.
26:12; 27:5;
57:19; 66:12

★ 4 aIs.
12:2; 50:10;
51:5 bIs.
17:10; 30:29;
44:8

5 aIs. 25:12
bJob 40:11-
13

6 aIs. 28:3
bIs. 3:14, 15;
11:4; 29:19

7 aIs. 57:2
bPs. 25:4, 5;
27:11; Is.
42:16; 52:12

8 aIs. 51:4;
56:1 bIs.
12:4; 24:15;
25:1; 26:13
cEx. 3:15

9 aPs. 63:5,
6; 77:2;
119:62; Is.
50:10; Luke
6:12 bPs.
63:1; 78:34;
Matt. 6:33
cIs. 55:6;
Hos. 5:15

10 aIs.
22:12, 13;
32:6, 7
bHos. 11:7;
John 5:37,
38

25:8 Quoted in 1 Cor. 15:54 and Rev. 21:4.
26:1 The redeemed will sing this song of praise
during the Millennium.

26:3 perfect peace. Lit., peace, peace; i.e., full,
genuine well-being.
26:4 everlasting Rock. Lit., Rock of ages.

He [b]deals unjustly in the land of uprightness,
And does not perceive the majesty of the LORD.

11 [a]Is. 44:9;
18 [b]Is. 9:7;
37:32; 59:17
[c]Is. 5:24;
9:18, 19;
10:17; 66:15,
24; Heb.
10:27

11 O LORD, Thy hand is lifted up yet they [a]do not see it.
They see [b]Thy zeal for the people and are put to shame;
Indeed, [c]fire will devour Thine enemies.

12 [a]Is. 26:3

12 LORD, Thou wilt establish [a]peace for us,
Since Thou hast also performed for us all our works.

13 [a]Is. 2:8;
10:11 [b]Is.
63:7

13 O LORD our God, [a]other masters besides Thee have ruled us;
But through Thee alone we [b]confess Thy name.

★14 [a]Deut.
4:28; Ps.
135:17; Is.
8:19; Hab.
2:19 [b]Is.
10:3

14 [a]The dead will not live, the departed spirits will not rise;
Therefore Thou hast [b]punished and destroyed them,
And Thou hast wiped out all remembrance of them.

15 [a]Is. 9:3
[b]Is. 33:17;
54:2, 3

15 [a]Thou hast increased the nation, O LORD,
Thou hast increased the nation, Thou art glorified;
Thou hast [b]extended all the borders of the land.

16 [a]Is. 37:3;
Hos. 5:15

16 O LORD, they sought Thee [a]in distress;
They could only whisper a prayer,
Your chastening was upon them.

17 [a]Is. 13:8;
21:3; John
16:21

17 [a]As the pregnant woman approaches the time to give birth,
She writhes and cries out in her labor pains,

Thus were we before Thee, O LORD.

18 We were pregnant, we writhed in labor,
We [a]gave birth, as it were, only to wind.
We could not accomplish deliverance for the earth
Nor were [b]inhabitants of the world born.

19 Your [a]dead will live;
Their corpses will rise.
You who lie in the dust, [b]awake and shout for joy,
For your dew is as the dew of the dawn,
And the earth will give birth to the departed spirits.

20 Come, my people, [a]enter into your rooms,
And close your doors behind you;
Hide for a little [b]while,
Until [c]indignation runs its course.

21 For behold, the LORD is about to [a]come out from His place
To [b]punish the inhabitants of the earth for their iniquity;
And the earth will [c]reveal her bloodshed,
And will no longer cover her slain.

18 [a]Is.
33:11; 59:4
[b]Ps. 17:14

★19 [a]Is.
25:8; Ezek.
37:1-14;
Dan. 12:2;
Hos. 13:14
[b]Eph. 5:14

20 [a]Ex.
12:22, 23;
Ps. 91:1, 4
[b]Ps. 30:5; Is.
54:7, 8;
2 Cor. 4:17
[c]Is. 10:5, 25;
13:5; 34:2;
66:14

21 [a]Mic. 1:3;
Jude 14 [b]Is.
13:11; 30:12-
14; 65:6, 7
[c]Job 16:18;
Luke 11:50

D　Israel in the Kingdom,
27:1-13

27 In that day [a]the LORD will punish [b]Leviathan the fleeing serpent,
With His fierce and great and mighty sword,
Even Leviathan the twisted serpent;
And [c]He will kill the dragon who lives in the sea.

★ 1 [a]Is.
66:16 [b]Job
3:8; 41:1; Ps.
74:14;
104:26 [c]Is.
51:9

26:14 The earthly rulers who oppressed Israel are dead and will never rise to power again.
26:19 This verse, along with Job 19:26 and Dan. 12:2, explicitly teaches the bodily resurrection

of believers.
27:1 Leviathan the fleeing serpent. A symbol of the enemies of God.

2 aPs. 80:8;
Is. 5:7; Jer.
2:21

3 aIs. 58:11
b1 Sam. 2:9;
Is. 31:5; John
10:28

★ **4** a2 Sam.
23:6; Is.
10:17 bIs.
33:12; Matt.
3:12; Heb.
6:8

5 aIs. 12:2;
25:4 bJob
22:21; Is.
26:3, 12;
Rom. 5:1;
2 Cor. 5:20

6 aIs. 37:31
bIs. 35:1, 2;
Hos.
14:5, 6 cIs.
4:2

7 aIs.
10:12, 17;
30:31-33;
31:8, 9;
37:36-38

★ **8** aIs.
50:1; 54:7
bJer. 4:11;
Ezek. 19:12;
Hos. 13:15

★ **9** aIs.
1:25; 48:10;
Dan. 11:35
bRom. 11:27
cEx. 34:13;
Deut. 12:3;
2 Kin. 10:26;
Is. 17:8

2 In that day,
"A avineyard of wine, sing of it!

3 "I, the LORD, am its keeper;
aI water it every moment.
Lest anyone damage it,
I bguard it night and day.

4 "I have no wrath.
Should someone give Me
abriars and thorns in battle,
Then I would step on them, bI would burn them completely.

5 "Or let him arely on My protection,
Let him make peace with Me,
Let him bmake peace with Me."

6 In the days to come Jacob
awill take root,
Israel will bblossom and sprout;
And they will fill the whole world with cfruit.

7 Like the striking of Him who has struck them,
has aHe struck them?
Or like the slaughter of His slain, have they been slain?

8 Thou didst contend with them by banishing them, by adriving them away.
With His fierce wind He has expelled them on the day of the beast wind.

9 Therefore through this Jacob's iniquity will be aforgiven;

And this will be the full price of the bpardoning of his sin:
When he makes all the caltar stones like pulverized chalk stones;
When Asherim and incense altars will not stand.

10 For the fortified city is aisolated,
A homestead forlorn and forsaken like the desert;
bThere the calf will graze,
And there it will lie down and feed on its branches.

11 When its alimbs are dry, they are broken off;
Women come and make a fire with them.
For they are not a people of bdiscernment,
Therefore ctheir Maker dwill not have compassion on them.
And their Creator will not be gracious to them.

12 And it will come about in that day, that the LORD awill start His threshing from the flowing stream of the bEuphrates to the brook of Egypt; and you will be cgathered up one by one, O sons of Israel.

13 It will come about also in that day that a great atrumpet will be blown; and those who were perishing in the land of bAssyria and who were scattered in the land of Egypt will come and cworship the LORD in the holy mountain at Jerusalem.

10 aIs.
32:13, 14
bIs. 17:2

11 aIs. 18:5
bDeut.
32:28; Is.
1:3; 5:13;
Jer. 8:7
cDeut.
32:18; Is.
43:1, 7; 44:2,
21, 24 dIs.
9:17

★**12** aIs.
11:11; 17:6;
24:13; 56:8
bGen. 15:18
cDeut. 30:3,
4; Neh. 1:9

13 aLev.
25:9; 1 Chr.
15:24; Matt.
24:31; Rev.
11:15 bIs.
19:24, 25
cIs. 19:21,
23; 49:7;
66:23; Zech.
14:16; Heb.
12:22

27:4 God's wrath is no longer against His vineyard (cf. 5:5-6).
27:8 The Babylonian captivity was for the purpose of chastening Judah.
27:9 *chalk stones.* A soft, powdery limestone, brittle and easily pulverized. Israel will completely abandon her idolatry.
27:12 *the brook of Egypt.* The Wadi el-Arish. *brook.* From a different Hebrew word than that used for the river of Egypt in Gen. 15:18. Isaiah 27:12-13 describes the future regathering of the Jewish people (cf. Matt. 24:31).

IV DENUNCIATION OF ISRAEL AND JUDAH (WOES AND BLESSINGS), 28:1–35:10

A Woe on Samaria, 28:1–29

★ 1 *a*Is. 28:7; Hos. 7:5 *b*Is. 9:9

28 Woe to the proud crown of the *a*drunkards of *b*Ephraim,
And to the fading flower of its glorious beauty,
Which is at the head of the fertile valley
Of those who are overcome with wine!

2 *a*Is. 8:7; 40:10 *b*Is. 28:17; 30:30; 32:19; Ezek. 13:11 *c*Is. 8:6, 7; 30:28; Nah. 1:8

2 Behold, the Lord has a strong and *a*mighty *agent;*
As a storm of *b*hail, a tempest of destruction,
Like a storm of *c*mighty overflowing waters,
He has cast *it* down to the earth with *His* hand.

3 *a*Is. 28:18; 26:6

3 The proud crown of the drunkards of Ephraim is *a*trodden under foot.

4 *a*Hos. 9:10; Mic. 7:1; Nah. 3:12

4 And the fading flower of its glorious beauty,
Which is at the head of the fertile valley,
Will be like the *a*first-ripe fig prior to summer;
Which one sees,
And as soon as it is in his hand,
He swallows it.

5 *a*Is. 41:16; 45:25; 60:1, 19 *b*Is. 62:3

5 In that day the *a*LORD of hosts will become a beautiful *b*crown
And a glorious diadem to the remnant of His people;

6 *a*1 Kin. 3:28; Is. 11:2; 32:15, 16; John 5:30 *b*2 Chr. 32:6-8; Is. 25:4

6 A *a*spirit of justice for him who sits in judgment,
A *b*strength to those who repel the onslaught at the gate.

7 *a*Is. 5:11, 22; 22:13; 56:12; Hos. 4:11 *b*Is. 24:2 *c*Is. 9:15 *d*Hab. 2:15, 16 *e*Is. 29:11

7 And these also *a*reel with wine and stagger from strong drink:

*b*The priest and *c*the prophet reel with strong drink,
They are confused by wine, they stagger from *d*strong drink;
They reel while having *e*visions,
They totter *when rendering* judgment.

8 *a*Jer. 48:26

8 For all the tables are full of filthy *a*vomit, without a *single clean* place.

★ 9-10

9 *a*Is. 2:3; 28:26; 30:20; 48:17; 50:4; 54:13 *b*Ps. 131:2

9 "To *a*whom would He teach knowledge?
And to whom would He interpret the message?
Those *just* *b*weaned from milk?
Those *just* taken from the breast?

10 *a*2 Chr. 36:15; Neh. 9:30

10 "For *He says,*
'*a*Order on order, order on order,
Line on line, line on line,
A little here, a little there.'"

★11 *a*Is. 33:19; 1 Cor. 14:21

11 Indeed, He will speak to this people
Through *a*stammering lips and a foreign tongue,

12 *a*Is. 11:10; 30:15; 32:17, 18; Jer. 6:16; Matt. 11:28, 29

12 He who said to them, "Here is *a*rest, give rest to the weary,"
And, "Here is repose," but they would not listen.

13 *a*Is. 8:15; Matt. 21:44

13 So the word of the LORD to them will be,
"Order on order, order on order,
Line on line, line on line,
A little here, a little there,"
That they may go and *a*stumble backward,
be broken, snared, and taken captive.

14 *a*Is. 1:10; 28:22 *b*Is. 29:20

14 Therefore, *a*hear the word of the LORD, O *b*scoffers,
Who rule this people who are in Jerusalem,

28:1 *Ephraim.* The chief tribe of the Northern Kingdom of Israel.

28:9-10 The leaders were indignant at Isaiah's lecturing them as if they were little children, and they mocked his method (v. 10).

28:11 Soon God would speak to Israel through the unintelligible (to the Israelites) language of the Assyrian conquerors. This verse is quoted by Paul in 1 Cor. 14:21 to show that tongues are a sign of rebuke to unbelievers.

★15 *a*Is.
28:18 *b*Is.
8:8; 28:2;
30:28; Dan.
11:22 *c*Is.
9:15; 30:9;
44:20; 59:3,
4; Ezek.
13:22 *d*Is.
29:15

15 Because you have said, "We have made a ^acovenant with death, And with Sheol we have made a pact. ^bThe overwhelming scourge will not reach us when it passes by, For we have made ^cfalsehood our refuge and we have ^dconcealed ourselves with deception."

★16 *a*Rom.
9:33; 10:11;
1 Pet. 2:6
*b*Ps. 118:22;
Is. 8:14, 15;
Matt. 21:42;
Mark 12:10;
Luke 20:17;
Acts 4:11;
Eph. 2:20

16 Therefore thus says the Lord GOD, "^aBehold, I am laying in Zion a stone, a tested ^bstone, A costly cornerstone *for* the foundation, firmly placed. He who believes *in it* will not be disturbed.

17 *a*2 Kin.
21:13; Is.
5:16; 30:18;
61:8; Amos
7:7-9 *b*Is.
28:2

17 "And I will make ^ajustice the measuring line, And righteousness the level; Then ^bhail shall sweep away the refuge of lies, And the waters shall overflow the secret place.

★18-20

18 *a*Is. 28:15
*b*Is. 7:7; 8:10
*c*Is. 28:15
*d*Is. 28:3;
Dan. 8:13

18 "And your ^acovenant with death shall be ^bcanceled, And your pact with Sheol shall not stand; When the ^coverwhelming scourge passes through, Then you become its ^dtrampling *place*.

19 *a*2 Kin.
24:2 *b*Is.
50:4 *c*Job
6:4; 18:11;
24:17; Ps.
55:4; 88:15;
Lam. 2:22

19 "As ^aoften as it passes through, it will seize you.

For ^bmorning after morning it will pass through, *anytime* during the day or night. And it will be sheer ^cterror to understand what it means."

20 The bed is too short on which to stretch out, And the ^ablanket is too small to wrap oneself in.

20 *a*Is. 59:6

21 For the LORD will rise up as at Mount ^aPerazim, He will be stirred up as in the valley of ^bGibeon; To do His ^ctask, His ^dunusual task, And to work His work, His extraordinary work.

★21 *a*2 Sam.
5:20; 1 Chr.
14:11 *b*Josh.
10:10, 12;
2 Sam. 5:25;
1 Chr. 14:16
*c*Is. 10:12;
29:14; 65:7
*d*Lam. 2:15;
3:33; Luke
19:41-44

22 And now do not carry on as ^ascoffers, Lest your fetters be made stronger; For I have heard from the Lord GOD of hosts, Of decisive ^bdestruction on all the earth.

22 *a*Is. 28:14
*b*Is. 10:22,
23

23 Give ear and hear my voice, Listen and hear my words.

★23-29

24 Does the farmer plow continually to plant seed? Does he *continually* turn and harrow the ground?

25 Does he not level its surface, And sow dill and scatter ^acummin, And plant ^bwheat in rows, Barley in its place, and rye within its area?

25 *a*Matt.
23:23 *b*Ex.
9:32

26 For his God instructs and teaches him properly.

28:15 The pro-Assyrian party preferred to trust their *covenant with death, And with Sheol* (perhaps involving necromancy) rather than God.

28:16 Messiah is a *foundation* stone in His atonement, a *tested stone* in His temptations, and a *costly cornerstone* in His relationship to His people. *See* 8:14; Psalm 118:22; Rom. 9:33; 1 Pet. 2:6.

28:18-20 The alliance would be *canceled* when

Assyria turned against Israel; even help from Egypt would be insufficient (v. 20).

28:21 As David routed the Philistines at *Mount Perazim* (2 Sam. 5:17-25), so God would have to chastise His own people (an *unusual task*).

28:23-29 Just as a farmer uses the proper threshing instruments for each type of grain, God intends to produce righteousness from His people through particular judgments.

27 aAmos
1:3

27 For dill is not threshed
with a athreshing
sledge,
Nor is the cartwheel driven
over cummin;
But dill is beaten out with
a rod, and cummin
with a club.

28 Grain for bread is crushed,
Indeed, he does not con-
tinue to thresh it for-
ever.
Because the wheel of his
cart and his horses
eventually damage it,
He does not thresh it
longer.

29 aIs. 9:6
bIs. 31:2;
Rom. 11:33

29 This also comes from the
LORD of hosts,
Who has made His counsel
awonderful and His
wisdom bgreat.

B Woe on Judah, 29:1–31:9
1 For her hypocrisy, 29:1–24

★ 1 a2 Sam.
5:9 bIs. 1:14;
5:12; 22:12,
13; 29:9, 13

29 Woe, O Ariel, Ariel the
city where David once
acamped!
Add year to year, bobserve
your feasts on sched-
ule.

2 aIs. 3:26;
Lam. 2:5

2 And I will bring distress to
Ariel,
And she shall be a city of
lamenting and
amourning;
And she shall be like an
Ariel to me.

★ 3 aLuke
19:43, 44

3 And I will acamp against
you encircling you,
And I will set siegeworks
against you,
And I will raise up battle
towers against you.

4 aIs. 8:19

4 Then you shall abe
brought low;
From the earth you shall
speak,
And from the dust where
you are prostrate,

Your words shall come.
Your voice shall also be
like that of a spirit
from the ground,
And your speech shall
whisper from the
dust.

5 But the multitude of your
enemies shall become
like fine adust,
And the multitude of the
bruthless ones like the
chaff which blows
away;
And it shall happen cin-
stantly, suddenly.

6 From the LORD of hosts you
will be apunished
with bthunder and
earthquake and loud
noise,
With whirlwind and tem-
pest and the flame of
a consuming fire.

7 And the amultitude of all
the nations who wage
war against Ariel,
Even all who wage war
against her and her
stronghold, and who
distress her,
Shall be like a dream, a
bvision of the night.

8 And it will be as when a
hungry man dreams—
And behold, he is eating;
But when he awakens, his
hunger is not satisfied,
Or as when a thirsty man
dreams—
And behold, he is drink-
ing,
But when he awakens, be-
hold, he is faint,
And his thirst is not
quenched.
aThus the multitude of all
the nations shall be,
Who wage war against
Mount Zion.

5 aIs.
17:13; 41:15,
16 bIs.
13:11; 25:3;
29:20 cIs.
17:14; 30:13;
47:11;
1 Thess. 5:3

6 aIs. 10:3;
26:14, 21
b1 Sam.
2:10; Matt.
24:7; Mark
13:8; Luke
21:11; Rev.
11:13, 19;
16:18

★ 7 aMic.
4:11, 12;
Zech. 12:9
bJob 20:8;
Ps. 73:20; Is.
17:14

8 aIs. 54:17

29:1 Ariel. A name for Jerusalem (v. 8). observe
your feasts. Though still unrepentant, the Jews
were observing feast days.
29:3 siegeworks. Of Sennacherib in 701.
29:7 like a dream, a vision of the night. So the
nations fighting Jerusalem would vanish, as
happened to Sennacherib's forces (37:33–37),
foreshadowing what will happen at the second
coming of Christ (Zech. 14:2–3).

9 aIs. 29:1
bIs. 51:17,
21, 22; 63:6

9 aBe delayed and wait.
Blind yourselves and be
blind.
They bbecome drunk, but
not with wine;
They stagger, but not with
strong drink.

10 aPs.
69:23; Is.
6:9, 10; Mic.
3:6; Rom.
11:8 bIs.
44:18;
2 Thess. 2:9-
12

10 For the LORD has poured
over you a spirit of
deep asleep,
He has bshut your eyes,
the prophets;
And He has covered your
heads, the seers.

11 aIs. 8:16;
Dan. 12:4, 9;
Matt. 13:11

11 And the entire vision shall
be to you like the words of a
sealed abook, which when they
give it to the one who is literate,
saying, "Please read this," he will
say, "I cannot, for it is sealed."
12 Then the book will be giv-
en to the one who is illiterate,
saying, "Please read this." And he
will say, "I cannot read."

13 aEzek.
33:31; Matt.
15:8, 9; Mark
7:6, 7

13 Then the Lord said,
"Because athis people draw
near with their words
And honor Me with their
lip service,
But they remove their
hearts far from Me,
And their reverence for
Me consists of tradi-
tion learned by rote,

14 aIs. 6:9,
10; 28:21;
65:7; Hab.
1:5 bIs.
44:25; Jer.
8:9; 49:7;
1 Cor. 1:19

14 Therefore behold, I will
once again deal amar-
velously with this
people, wondrously
marvelous;
And bthe wisdom of their
wise men shall perish,
And the discernment of
their discerning men
shall be concealed.

★15-16

15 aPs.
10:11, 13; Is.
28:15; 30:1
bJob 22:13;
Is. 57:12;
Ezek. 8:12
cPs. 94:7; Is.
47:10; Mal.
2:17

15 Woe to those who deeply
ahide their plans from
the LORD,
And whose bdeeds are
done in a dark place,
And they say, "cWho sees
us?" or "Who knows
us?"

16 You turn things around!
Shall the potter be considered as equal with the
clay,
That awhat is made should
say to its maker, "He
did not make me";
Or what is formed say to
him who formed it,
"He has no under-
standing"?

16 aIs. 45:9;
64:8; Jer.
18:1-6; Rom.
9:19-21

★17-24

17 aPs. 84:6;
107:33, 35;
Is. 32:15

17 Is it not yet just a little
while
Before Lebanon will be
turned into a afertile
field,
And the fertile field will be
considered as a forest?

18 aIs. 35:5;
42:18, 19;
43:8; Matt.
11:5; Mark
7:37 bIs.
29:11 cPs.
119:18; Prov.
20:12; Is.
32:3

18 And on that day the adeaf
shall hear bwords of a
book,
And out of their gloom
and darkness the
ceyes of the blind
shall see.

19 aPs. 25:9;
37:11; Is.
11:4; 61:1;
Matt. 5:5;
11:29 bIs.
3:14, 15;
11:4; 14:30;
32; 25:4;
26:6; Matt.
11:5; James
1:9; 2:5

19 The aafflicted also shall increase their gladness
in the LORD,
And the bneedy of man-
kind shall rejoice in
the Holy One of Is-
rael.

20 aIs. 29:5
bIs. 28:14
cIs. 59:4;
Mic. 2:1

20 For the aruthless will come
to an end, and the
bscorner will be fin-
ished,
Indeed call who are intent
on doing evil will be
cut off;

21 aAmos
5:10 bIs.
32:7; Amos
5:12

21 Who cause a person to be
indicted by a word,
And aensnare him who ad-
judicates at the gate,
And bdefraud the one in
the right with mean-
ingless arguments.

22 aIs. 41:8;
51:2; 63:16
bIs. 45:17;
49:23; 50:7;
54:4

22 Therefore thus says the
LORD, who redeemed aAbraham,
concerning the house of Jacob,
"Jacob bshall not now be
ashamed, nor shall his
face now turn pale;

29:15-16 They thought the Lord was not aware
of their political intrigues and alliances (see
Rom. 9:19-21).

29:17-24 Another description of millennial
blessing.

23 But when he sees his ᵃchildren, the ᵇwork of My hands, in his midst, They will sanctify My name; Indeed, they will ᶜsanctify the Holy One of Jacob, And will stand in awe of the God of Israel.

24 "And those who ᵃerr in mind will ᵇknow the truth, And those who criticize will ᶜaccept instruction.

2 For her alliance with Egypt, 30:1–31:9

30 "Woe to the ᵃrebellious children," declares the LORD, "Who ᵇexecute a plan, but not Mine, And ᶜmake an alliance, but not of My Spirit, In order to add sin to sin;

2 Who ᵃproceed down to Egypt, Without ᵇconsulting Me, ᶜTo take refuge in the safety of Pharaoh, And to seek shelter in the shadow of Egypt!

3 "Therefore the safety of Pharaoh will be ᵃyour shame, And the shelter in the shadow of Egypt, your humiliation.

4 "For ᵃtheir princes are at Zoan, And their ambassadors arrive at Hanes.

5 "Everyone will be ᵃashamed because of a people who cannot profit them, Who are ᵇnot for help or profit, but for shame and also for reproach."

6 The oracle concerning the ᵃbeasts of the ᵇNegev. Through a land of ᶜdistress and anguish, From where *come* lioness and lion, viper and ᵈflying serpent, They ᵉcarry their riches on the backs of young donkeys And their treasures on ᶠcamels' humps, To a people who cannot profit *them;*

7 Even Egypt, whose ᵃhelp is vain and empty. Therefore, I have called her "ᵇRahab who has been exterminated."

8 Now go, ᵃwrite it on a tablet before them And inscribe it on a scroll, That it may serve in the time to come As a witness forever.

9 For this is a ᵃrebellious people, ᵇfalse sons, Sons who refuse to ᶜlisten To the instruction of the LORD;

10 Who say to the ᵃseers, "You must not see *visions*"; And to the prophets, "You must not ᵇprophesy to us what is right, ᶜSpeak to us pleasant words, Prophesy illusions.

11 "Get out of the way, ᵃturn aside from the path, ᵇLet us hear no more about the Holy One of Israel."

12 Therefore thus says the Holy One of Israel, "ᵃSince you have rejected this word, And have put your trust in ᵇoppression and guile, and have relied on them,

---

30:1-7 A further warning against Hezekiah's seeking *an alliance* with Egypt against Assyria (cf. Exod. 23:32). Ambassadors were negotiating at *Zoan* (Tanis, 19:13) and *Hanes* (Ahnas, 55 miles south of Memphis).

13 *a*Is. 26:21
*b*1 Kin.
20:30; Ps.
62:4; Is.
58:12 *c*Is.
29:5; 47:11

13 Therefore this *a*iniquity will be to you
Like a *b*breach about to fall,
A bulge in a high wall,
Whose collapse comes *c*suddenly in an instant.

14 *a*Ps. 2:9;
Jer. 19:10,
11

14 "And whose collapse is like the smashing of a *a*potter's jar;
So ruthlessly shattered
That a sherd will not be found among its pieces
To take fire from a hearth,
Or to scoop water from a cistern."

15 *a*Ps.
116:7; Is.
28:12 *b*Is.
7:4; 32:17

15 For thus the Lord GOD, the Holy One of Israel, has said,
"In repentance and *a*rest you shall be saved,
In *b*quietness and trust is your strength."
But you were not willing,

16 *a*Is. 2:7;
31:1, 3

16 And you said, "No, for we will flee on *a*horses,"
Therefore you shall flee!
"And we will ride on swift *horses*,"
Therefore those who pursue you shall be swift.

17 *a*Lev.
26:36; Deut.
28:25; 32:30;
Josh. 23:10;
Prov. 28:1

17 *a*One thousand *shall flee* at the threat of one *man*,
You shall flee at the threat of five;
Until you are left as a flag on a mountain top,
And as a signal on a hill.

★**18-26**

18 *a*Is.
42:14, 16;
48:9; Jon.
3:4, 10;
2 Pet. 3:9, 15
*b*Is. 2:11, 17;
33:5 *c*Is.
5:16; 28:17;
61:8 *d*Is.
8:17; 25:9;
26:8; 33:2

18 Therefore the LORD *a*longs to be gracious to you,
And therefore He waits on *b*high to have compassion on you.
For the LORD is a *c*God of justice;
How blessed are all those who *d*long for Him.

19 *a*Is. 65:9;
Ezek. 37:25,
28 *b*Is. 25:8;
60:20; 61:1-3
*c*Ps. 50:15;
Is. 58:9;
65:24; Matt.
7:7-11

19 O people in Zion, *a*inhabitant in Jerusalem, you will *b*weep no longer. He will surely be gracious to you at the sound of your cry; when He hears it, He will *c*answer you.

20 Although the Lord has given you *a*bread of privation and water of oppression, *He*, your Teacher will no longer *b*hide Himself, but your eyes will behold your Teacher.

21 And your ears will hear a word behind you, "This is the *a*way, walk in it," whenever you *b*turn to the right or to the left.

22 And you will defile your graven *a*images, overlaid with silver, and your molten *a*images plated with gold. You will scatter them as an impure thing; *and* say to them, "*b*Be gone!"

23 Then He will *a*give *you* rain for the seed which you will sow in the ground, and bread *from* the yield of the ground, and it will be rich and plenteous; on that day *b*your livestock will graze in a roomy pasture.

24 Also the oxen and the donkeys which work the ground will eat salted fodder, which has been *a*winnowed with shovel and fork.

25 And on every lofty mountain and on *a*every high hill there will be streams running with water on the day of the great *b*slaughter, when the towers fall.

26 And *a*the light of the moon will be as the light of the sun, and the light of the sun will be seven times *brighter*, like the light of seven days, on the day *b*the LORD binds up the *c*fracture of His people and *d*heals the bruise He has inflicted.

27 Behold, *a*the name of the LORD comes from a remote place;
*b*Burning is His anger, and dense is *His* smoke;
His lips are filled with *c*indignation,
And His tongue is like a *d*consuming fire;

20 *a*1 Kin.
22:27; Ps.
80:5 *b*Ps.
74:9; Amos
8:11

21 *a*Ps. 25:8,
9; Prov. 3:6;
Is. 35:8, 9;
42:16 *b*Is.
29:24

22 *a*Ex. 32:2,
4; Judg.
17:3, 4; Is.
46:6 *b*Matt.
4:10

23 *a*Ps.
65:9-13;
104:13, 14
*b*Ps. 144:13;
Is. 32:20;
Hos. 4:16

24 *a*Matt.
3:12; Luke
3:17

25 *a*Is. 35:6,
7; 41:18;
43:19, 20
*b*Is. 34:2

26 *a*Is.
24:23; 60:19,
20; Rev.
21:23; 22:5
*b*Is. 61:1 *c*Is.
1:6; 30:13,
14 *d*Deut.
32:39; Job
5:18; Is.
33:24; Jer.
33:6; Hos.
6:1, 2

27 *a*Is. 59:19
*b*Is. 10:17
*c*Is. 10:5;
13:5; 66:14
*d*Is. 66:15

30:18-26 A description of the glories of the Millennium, though *the day of the great slaughter* (v. 25) refers to Armageddon.

28 *a*Is. 11:4;
30:33;
2 Thess. 2:8
*b*Is. 8:8
*c*Amos 9:9
*d*2 Kin.
19:28; Is.
37:29

28 And His *a*breath is like an
overflowing torrent,
Which *b*reaches to the
neck,
To *c*shake the nations back
and forth in a sieve,
And to *put* in the jaws of
the peoples *d*the bri-
dle which leads to
ruin.

29 You will have songs as in
the night when you
keep the festival;
And gladness of heart as
when one marches to
the sound of the flute,
To go to the mountain of
the LORD, to the Rock
of Israel.

30 And the LORD will cause
His voice of authority
to be heard.
And the descending of His
arm to be seen in
fierce anger,
And *in* the flame of a consuming fire,
In cloudburst, downpour,
and hailstones.

31 *a*Is. 11:4
*b*Is. 10:12;
14:25; 31:8
*c*Is. 10:26;
11:4

31 For *a*at the voice of the
LORD *b*Assyria will be
terrified,
When He strikes with the
*c*rod.

32 *a*Is. 10:24
*b*1 Sam.
18:6; Jer.
31:4 *c*Ezek.
32:10

32 And every blow of the
*a*rod of punishment,
Which the LORD will lay on
him,
Will be with *the music of*
*b*tambourines and
lyres;
And in battles, *c*brandish-
ing weapons, He will
fight them.

★33 *a*2 Kin.
23:10; Jer.
7:31; 19:6
*b*Is. 11:4;
30:28 *c*Gen.
19:24; Is.
34:9

33 For *a*Topheth has long
been ready,
Indeed, it has been pre-
pared for the king.
He has made it deep and
large,
A pyre of fire with plenty
of wood;

The *b*breath of the LORD,
like a torrent of
*c*brimstone, sets it
afire.

31 Woe to those who go
down to *a*Egypt for
help,
And *b*rely on horses,
And trust in chariots be-
cause they are many,
And in horsemen because
they are very strong,
But they do not *c*look to
the *d*Holy One of Is-
rael, nor seek the
LORD!

2 Yet He also is *a*wise and
will *b*bring disaster,
And does *c*not retract His
words,
But will arise against the
house of *d*evildoers,
And against the help of the
*e*workers of iniquity.

3 Now the Egyptians are
*a*men, and not God,
And their *b*horses are flesh
and not spirit;
So the LORD will *c*stretch
out His hand,
And *d*he who helps will
stumble
And he who is helped will
fall,
And all of them will come
to an end together.

4 For thus says the LORD to
me,
"As the *a*lion or the young
lion growls over his
prey,
Against which a band of
shepherds is called
out,
Will not be terrified at
their voice, nor dis-
turbed at their noise,
So will the LORD of hosts
come down to wage
*b*war on Mount Zion
and on its hill."

★ 1-5

1 *a*Is. 30:2,
7; 36:6
*b*Deut.
17:16; Ps.
20:7; 33:17;
Is. 2:7; 30:16
*c*Is. 9:13;
Dan. 9:13;
Amos 5:4-8
*d*Is. 10:17;
43:15; Hos.
11:9; Hab.
1:12; 3:3

2 *a*Is.
28:29; Rom.
16:27 *b*Is.
45:7 *c*Num.
23:19; Jer.
44:29 *d*Is.
1:4; 9:17;
14:20 *e*Is.
22:14; 32:6

3 *a*Ezek.
28:9;
2 Thess. 2:4
*b*Is. 36:9 *c*Is.
9:17; Jer.
15:6; Ezek.
20:33, 34
*d*Is. 30:5, 7;
Matt. 15:14

4 *a*Num.
24:9; Hos.
11:10; Amos
3:8 *b*Is.
42:13; Zech.
12:8

30:33 *Topheth.* The place of burning; the name
of the Valley of Hinnom (outside the SW. corner of Jerusalem), where Molech worship, including infant sacrifice, was carried on. *the*

king. A reference to Molech.
31:1-5 God, not Egypt, will defend His people.
God is *wise* (v. 2); He is like a *lion* (v. 4), and is
like *birds* protecting their nests (v. 5).

5 aDeut.
32:11; Ps.
91:4 bIs.
37:35; 38:6

6 aIs.
44:22; 55:7;
Jer. 3:10, 14,
22; Ezek.
18:31, 32
bIs. 1:2; 5

7 aIs. 2:20;
30:22
b1 Kin.
12:30

8 aIs.
10:12; 14:25;
30:31-33;
37:7, 36-38
bIs. 66:16
cIs. 21:15
dGen. 49:15;
Is. 14:2

★ 9 aDeut.
32:31, 37
bIs. 5:26;
13:2; 18:3
cIs. 10:16,
17; 30:33;
Zech. 2:5

★ 1-8
1 aPs.
72:1-4; Is.
9:6, 7; 11:4,
5; Jer. 23:5;
33:15; Ezek.
37:24; Zech.
9:9

2 aIs. 4:6;
25:4 bIs.
35:6; 41:18;
43:19, 20

5 Like flying abirds so the LORD of hosts will protect Jerusalem.
He will bprotect and deliver it;
He will pass over and rescue it.

6 aReturn to Him from whom you have bdeeply defected, O sons of Israel.

7 For in that day every man will acast away his silver idols and his gold idols, which your hands have made as ba sin.

8 And the aAssyrian will fall by a sword not of man,
And a bsword not of man will devour him.
So he will cnot escape the sword,
And his young men will become dforced laborers.

9 "And his arock will pass away because of panic,
And his princes will be terrified at the bstandard,"
Declares the LORD, whose cfire is in Zion and whose furnace is in Jerusalem.

C   Messiah and His Kingdom, 32:1-20

32 Behold, a aking will reign righteously,
And princes will rule justly.

2 And each will be like a arefuge from the wind,
And a shelter from the storm,
Like bstreams of water in a dry country,
Like the ashade of a huge rock in a parched land.

3 aIs. 29:18

4 aIs. 29:24

5 a1 Sam.
25:25

6 aProv.
19:3; 24:7-9;
Is. 59:7, 13
bIs. 9:17;
10:6 cIs.
3:15; 10:2

7 aJer.
5:26-28; Mic.
7:3 bIs. 11:4;
61:1 cIs.
5:23

8 aProv.
11:25

9 aIs. 47:8;
Amos 6:1;
Zeph. 2:15
bIs. 28:23

★10 aIs. 5:5,
6; 7:23; 24:7

3 Then athe eyes of those who see will not be blinded,
And the ears of those who hear will listen.

4 And the mind of the ahasty will discern the truth,
And the tongue of the stammerers will hasten to speak clearly.

5 No longer will the afool be called noble,
Or the rogue be spoken of as generous.

6 For a fool speaks nonsense,
And his heart ainclines toward wickedness,
To practice bungodliness and to speak error against the LORD,
To ckeep the hungry person unsatisfied
And to withhold drink from the thirsty.

7 As for a rogue, his weapons are evil;
He adevises wicked schemes
To bdestroy the afflicted with slander,
cEven though the needy one speaks what is right.

8 But athe noble man devises noble plans;
And by noble plans he stands.

9 Rise up you awomen who are at ease,
And hear my voice;
bGive ear to my word, You complacent daughters.

10 Within a year and a few days,
You will be troubled, O complacent daughters;
aFor the vintage is ended,
And the fruit gathering will not come.

31:9 *his rock.* Refers to the strength of the Assyrians.
32:1-8 A picture of the ideal king and government, fully realized only in Messiah when He comes again to establish His righteous government on earth.
32:10 The *complacent daughters* (women) of Jerusalem were warned of coming poverty and devastation (v. 14) when Sennacherib invaded the land (cf. 3:16-26).

11 aIs. 22:12
bIs. 47:2

11 Tremble, you *women* who
are at ease;
aBe troubled, you compla-
cent *daughters;*
bStrip, undress, and put
sackcloth on *your*
waist,

12 aNah. 2:7

12 aBeat your breasts for the
pleasant fields, for the
fruitful vine,

13 aIs. 5:6,
10, 17; 27:10
bIs. 22:2;
23:9

13 aFor the land of my people
in which thorns *and*
briars shall come up;
Yea, for all the joyful
houses, *and for* the
bjubilant city.

14 aIs.
13:22; 25:2;
34:13 bIs.
6:11; 22:2;
24:10, 12
cIs. 13:21;
34:13 dPs.
104:11; Jer.
14:6

14 Because athe palace has
been abandoned, the
populated bcity for-
saken.
Hill and watch-tower have
become ccaves for-
ever,
A delight for dwild don-
keys, a pasture for
flocks;

★15-20

15 aIs. 11:2;
44:3; 59:21;
Ezek. 39:29;
Joel 2:28
bPs. 107:35;
Is. 29:17;
35:1, 2

15 Until the aSpirit is poured
out upon us from on
high,
And the wilderness be-
comes a bfertile field
And the fertile field is considered as a forest.

16 aIs. 33:5;
Zech. 8:3

16 Then ajustice will dwell in
the wilderness,
And righteousness will
abide in the fertile
field.

17 aPs. 72:2,
3; 85:8;
119:165; Is.
2:4; Rom.
14:17; James
3:18 bIs.
30:15

17 And the awork of righteousness will be
peace,
And the service of right-
eousness, bquietness
and confidence for-
ever.

18 aIs. 26:3,
12 bIs.
11:10; 14:3;
30:15; Hos.
2:18-23;
Zech. 2:5;
3:10

18 Then my people will live
in a apeaceful habita-
tion,
And in secure dwellings
and in undisturbed
bresting places;

19 aIs. 28:2,
17; 30:30
bIs. 10:18,
19, 34 cIs.
24:10, 12;
26:5; 27:10;
29:4

19 And it will ahail when the
bforest comes down,
And cthe city will be utterly laid low.

20 aEccl.
11:1; Is.
30:23, 24

20 How ablessed will you be,
you who sow beside
all waters,
Who let out freely the ox
and the donkey.

D Assyria and her Destruction, 33:1-24

★ 1 aIs.
10:6; 21:2
bIs. 24:16;
48:8 cIs.
10:12; 31:8;
14:25; Hab.
2:8 dJer.
25:12-14;
Matt. 7:2

33 Woe ato you, O destroyer,
While you were not de-
stroyed;
And he bwho is treacher-
ous, while *others* did
not deal treacherously
with him.
As soon as you shall finish
destroying, cyou shall
be destroyed;
As soon as you shall cease
to deal treacherously,
others shall ddeal
treacherously with
you.

2 aIs.
30:18, 19
bIs. 25:9 cIs.
40:10; 51:5;
59:16 dIs.
37:3

2 O Lord, abe gracious to us;
we have bwaited for
Thee.
Be Thou their cstrength
every morning,
Our salvation also in the
dtime of distress.

3 aIs.
17:13; 21:15
bIs. 10:33;
17:13; 59:16-
18; Jer.
25:30, 31
★ 4

3 At the sound of the tumult
apeoples flee;
At the blifting up of Thyself nations disperse.

4 And your spoil is gathered
as the caterpillar gathers;
As locusts rushing about,
men rush about on it.

5 aPs. 97:9
bIs. 1:26;
28:6; 32:16

5 The Lord is aexalted, for
He dwells on high;
He has bfilled Zion with
justice and righteous-
ness.

32:15-20 Again Isaiah depicts the millennial blessings of the *Spirit* (v. 15), prosperity (v. 15), *righteousness* (v. 16), and peace (when the *forest* of human pride is leveled by *hail*, vv. 18-19).

33:1 *O destroyer.* I.e., Sennacherib, king of Assyria. Chapter 33 concerns the Lord's victory over Assyria, and the background is in 2 Kings 18:13-37.
33:4 *your spoil.* I.e., the Assyrians.

6 *a*Is. 33:20
*b*Is. 45:17;
51:6 *c*Is.
11:9 *d*2 Kin.
18:7; Ps.
112:1-3; Is.
11:3; Matt.
6:33

7 *a*2 Kin.
18:18, 37

8 *a*Is. 35:8
*b*Is. 24:5

9 *a*Is. 3:26;
24:4; 29:2
*b*Is. 2:13;
10:34 *c*Is.
35:2; 65:10

10 *a*Ps. 12:5;
Is. 2:19, 21

11 *a*Ps. 7:14;
Is. 26:18;
59:4; James
1:15 *b*Is.
1:31

★12 *a*2 Sam.
23:6, 7; Is.
10:17; 27:4

13 *a*Ps.
48:10; Is.
49:1

14 *a*Is. 1:28
*b*Is. 32:11
*c*Is. 30:27,
30; Heb.
12:29 *d*Is.
9:18, 19;
10:16; 47:14

6 And He shall be the *a*stability of your times,
A *b*wealth of salvation, wisdom, and *c*knowledge;
The *d*fear of the Lᴏʀᴅ is his treasure.

7 Behold, their brave men cry in the streets,
The *a*ambassadors of peace weep bitterly.

8 The highways are desolate, the *a*traveler has ceased,
He has *b*broken the covenant, he has despised the cities,
He has no regard for man.

9 *a*The land mourns and pines away,
*b*Lebanon is shamed and withers;
*c*Sharon is like a desert plain,
And Bashan and Carmel lose *their foliage.*

10 "Now *a*I will arise," says the Lᴏʀᴅ,
"Now I will be exalted, now I will be lifted up.

11 "You have *a*conceived chaff, you will give birth to stubble;
My *b*breath will consume you like a fire.

12 "And the peoples will be burned to lime,
*a*Like cut thorns which are burned in the fire.

13 "You who are far away, *a*hear what I have done;
And you who are near, acknowledge My might."

14 *a*Sinners in Zion are terrified;
*b*Trembling has seized the godless.

"Who among us can live with *c*the consuming fire?
Who among us can live with continual *d*burning?"

15 He who *a*walks righteously, and speaks with sincerity,
He who rejects unjust gain,
And shakes his hands so that they hold no bribe;
He who stops his ears from hearing about bloodshed,
And *b*shuts his eyes from looking upon evil;

16 He will dwell on the heights;
*a*His refuge will be the impregnable rock;
*b*His bread will be given *him;*
His water will be sure.

17 Your eyes will see *a*the King in His beauty;
They will behold *b*a far-distant land.

18 Your heart will meditate on *a*terror:
"Where is *b*he who counts?
Where is he who weighs?
Where is he who counts the towers?"

19 You will no longer see a fierce people,
A people of *a*unintelligible speech which no one comprehends,
Of a stammering tongue which no one understands.

20 *a*Look upon Zion, the city of our appointed feasts;
Your eyes shall see Jerusalem an *b*undisturbed habitation,

15 *a*Ps. 15:2;
24:4; Is.
58:6-11 *b*Ps.
119:37

16 *a*Is. 25:4
*b*Is. 49:10

★17-24

17 *a*Is. 6:5;
24:23; 33:21,
22 *b*Is. 26:15

★18 *a*Is.
17:14
*b*1 Cor. 1:20

19 *a*Deut.
28:49, 50; Is.
28:11; Jer.
5:15

20 *a*Ps.
48:12 *b*Ps.
46:5; 125:1,
2; Is. 32:18
*c*Is. 54:2

33:12 *burned to lime.* Assyria would be thoroughly destroyed, like the small lump left after lime has been burned.
33:17-24 The Lord's victory over Sennacherib is a foretaste of His universal dominion over the world.

33:18 Every Assyrian official was a terror to the people: *he who counts* the amount of tribute due, *he who weighs* the gold and silver brought, and *he who counts the towers* (the one making plans for a siege).

c A tent which shall not be
folded,
Its stakes shall never be
pulled up
Nor any of its cords be
torn apart.

21 But there the majestic
One, the LORD, shall
be for us
A place of a rivers and wide
canals,
On which no boat with
oars shall go,
And on which no mighty
ship shall pass—

22 For the LORD is our a judge,
The LORD is b our lawgiver,
The LORD is c our king;
d He will save us—

23 Your tackle hangs slack;
It cannot hold the base of
its mast firmly,
Nor spread out the sail.
Then the a prey of an
abundant spoil will be
divided;
b The lame will take the
plunder.

24 And no resident will say,
"I am a sick";
The people who dwell
there will be b forgiven
their iniquity.

**E Armageddon and Its
Judgments, 34:1-17**

34 Draw near, a O nations, to
hear; and listen, O
peoples!
b Let the earth and all it
contains hear, and the
world and all that
springs from it.

2 For the LORD's a indignation
is against all the na-
tions,
And *His* wrath against all
their armies;
He has b utterly destroyed
them,

He has given them over to
c slaughter.

3 So their slain will be
a thrown out,
And their corpses will give
off their b stench,
And the mountains will be
drenched with their
c blood.

4 And a all the host of
heaven will wear
away,
And the b sky will be rolled
up like a scroll;
All their hosts will also
wither away
As a leaf withers from the
vine,
Or as *one* withers from the
fig tree.

5 For a My sword is satiated
in heaven,
Behold it shall descend for
judgment upon
b Edom,
And upon the people
whom I have c devoted
to destruction.

6 The sword of the LORD is
filled with blood,
It is sated with fat, with the
blood of lambs and
goats,
With the fat of the kidneys
of rams.
For the LORD has a sacrifice
in a Bozrah,
And a great slaughter in
the land of b Edom.

7 a Wild oxen shall also fall
with them,
And b young bulls with
strong ones;
Thus their land shall be
c soaked with blood,
And their dust become
greasy with fat.

8 For the LORD has a day of
a vengeance,
A year of recompense for
the cause of Zion.

Cross references (left margin):

21 a Is. 41:18; 43:19, 20; 48:18; 66:12

22 a Is. 2:4; 11:4; 16:5; 51:5 b Is. 1:10; 51:4, 7; James 4:12 c Ps. 89:18; Is. 33:17; Zech. 9:9 d Is. 25:9; 35:4; 49:25, 26; 60:16

★23 a 2 Kin. 7:16 b 2 Kin. 7:8; Is. 35:6

24 a Is. 30:26; 58:8; Jer. 30:17 b Is. 40:2; 44:22; 50:20; Mic. 7:18, 19; 1 John 1:7-9

1 a Ps. 49:1; Is. 41:1; 43:9 b Deut. 32:1; Is. 1:2

★2 a Is. 26:20 b Is. 13:5; 24:1 c Is. 30:25; 63:6; 65:12

Cross references (right margin):

3 a Is. 14:19 b Joel 2:20; Amos 4:10 c Ezek. 14:19; 35:6; 38:22

★4 a Is. 13:13; 51:6; Ezek. 32:7, 8; Joel 2:31; Matt. 24:29; 2 Pet. 3:10 b Rev. 6:12-14

★5 a Deut. 32:41, 42; Jer. 46:10; Ezek. 21:3-5 b Is. 63:1; Jer. 49:7, 8, 20; Ezek. 25:12-14; 35:1-15; Amos 1:11, 12; Obad. 1-14; Mal. 1:4 c Is. 24:6; 43:28

★6 a Is. 63:1; Jer. 49:13 b Is. 63:1

7 a Num. 23:22; Ps. 22:21 b Ps. 68:30; Jer. 50:27 c Is. 63:6

8 a Is. 13:6; 35:4; 47:3; 61:2; 63:4

33:23 The overthrow of the Assyrians is compared to a shipwreck, so complete that even
the *lame* could loot the attacker.
34:2 This prediction anticipates the future judgment of *all the nations* in the Tribulation days.

34:4 Compare the description in Rev. 6:12-14.
34:5 *Edom.* The estranged brother of Israel represents all estranged unbelievers (Heb. 12:16).
34:6 *Bozrah.* A sheep herding center in Edom.

9 And its streams shall be
　turned into pitch,
　And its loose earth into
　　ᵃbrimstone,
　And its land shall become
　　burning pitch.

10 It shall ᵃnot be quenched
　night or day;
　Its ᵇsmoke shall go up for-
　ever;
　From ᶜgeneration to gen-
　　eration it shall be
　　desolate;
　ᵈNone shall pass through it
　　forever and ever.

11 But ᵃpelican and hedgehog
　shall possess it,
　And owl and raven shall
　　dwell in it;
　And He shall stretch over
　　it the ᵇline of desola-
　　tion
　And the plumb line of
　　emptiness.

12 Its nobles—there is ᵃno
　one there
　Whom they may proclaim
　king—
　And all its princes shall be
　　ᵇnothing.

13 And thorns shall come up
　in its ᵃfortified towers,
　Nettles and thistles in its
　　fortified cities;
　It shall also be a haunt of
　　ᵇjackals
　And an abode of ostriches.

14 And the desert ᵃcreatures
　shall meet with the
　wolves,
　The ᵇhairy goat also shall
　cry to its kind;
　Yes, the night monster
　shall settle there
　And shall find herself a
　resting place.

15 The tree snake shall make
　its nest and lay eggs
　there,

And it will hatch and
　gather them under its
　protection.
　Yes, ᵃthe hawks shall be
　gathered there,
　Every one with its kind.

16 Seek from the ᵃbook of
　the Lᴏʀᴅ, and read:
　Not one of these will be
　missing;
　None will lack its mate.
　For ᵇHis mouth has com-
　manded,
　And His Spirit has gath-
　ered them.

17 And He has cast the ᵃlot
　for them,
　And His hand has divided
　it to them by ᵇline.
　They shall possess it for-
　ever;
　From ᶜgeneration to gen-
　eration they shall
　dwell in it.

F　The Kingdom and Its Blessings, 35:1–10

35 The ᵃwilderness and the
　desert will be glad,
　And the ᵇArabah will re-
　joice and blossom;
　Like the crocus

2 It will ᵃblossom profusely
　And ᵇrejoice with rejoicing
　and shout of joy.
　The ᶜglory of Lebanon will
　be given to it,
　The majesty of ᵈCarmel
　and Sharon.
　They will see the ᵉglory of
　the Lᴏʀᴅ,
　The majesty of our God.

3 ᵃEncourage the exhausted,
　and strengthen the
　feeble.

Margin references (left column):

9 ᵃDeut. 29:23; Ps. 11:6; Is. 30:33

10 ᵃIs. 1:31; 66:24 ᵇRev. 14:11; 19:3 ᶜIs. 13:20-22; 24:1; 34:10-15; Mal. 1:3, 4 ᵈEzek. 29:11

★11 ᵃZeph. 2:14 ᵇ2 Kin. 21:13; Is. 24:10; Lam. 2:8

12 ᵃJer. 27:20; 39:6 ᵇIs. 41:11, 12

13 ᵃIs. 13:22; 25:2; 32:13 ᵇPs. 44:19; Jer. 9:11; 10:22

★14 ᵃIs. 13:21 ᵇIs. 30:8

15 ᵃDeut. 14:13

Margin references (right column):

★16 ᵃIs. 30:8 ᵇIs. 1:20; 40:5; 58:14

17 ᵃIs. 17:13, 14; Jer. 13:25 ᵇIs. 34:11 ᶜIs. 34:10

★ 1-10 1 ᵃIs. 6:11; 7:21-25; 27:10; 41:18; 55:12, 13 ᵇIs. 41:19; 51:3

★ 2-7 2 ᵃIs. 27:6; 32:15 ᵇIs. 25:9; 35:10; 55:12, 13; 66:10, 14 ᶜIs. 60:13 ᵈSong 7:5 ᵉIs. 25:9

3 ᵃJob 4:3, 4; Heb. 12:12

34:11 The Hebrew words for *desolation* and *emptiness* are also found together in Gen. 1:2 ("formless and void").

34:14 *night monster.* Possibly a reference to a demon.

34:16 *the book of the Lᴏʀᴅ.* I.e., Isaiah's prophecies concerning these decrees of judgment from the Lord.

35:1-10 This chapter is one of the great descriptions in the Bible of the millennial kingdom, which period follows the judgments described in chapter 34.

35:2-7 The land will become extremely productive; the people will be saved and healed. *scorched land* (v. 7). May be the term for desert mirage.

4 *a*Is. 32:4
*b*Is. 1:24;
47:3; 61:2;
63:4 *c*Is.
34:8; 59:18
*d*Ps. 145:19;
Is. 33:22;
35:4

4 Say to those with *a*anxious heart,
"Take courage, fear not.
Behold, your God will come *with* *b*vengeance;
The *c*recompense of God will come,
But He will *d*save you."

5 *a*Is. 29:18; 32:3, 4; 42:7, 16; 50:4; Matt. 11:5; John 9:6, 7
6 *a*Matt. 15:30; John 5:8, 9; Acts 3:8 *b*Matt. 9:32; Luke 11:14 *c*Is. 35:1; 41:18; 43:19; 49:10; 51:3; John 7:38

5 Then the *a*eyes of the blind will be opened,
And the ears of the deaf will be unstopped.

6 Then the *a*lame will leap like a deer,
And the *b*tongue of the dumb will shout for joy.
For waters will break forth in the *c*wilderness
And streams in the Arabah.

7 *a*Is. 49:10 *b*Is. 13:22; 34:13

7 And the scorched land will become a pool,
And the thirsty ground *a*springs of water;
In the *b*haunt of jackals, its resting place,
Grass *becomes* reeds and rushes.

8 *a*Is. 11:16; 19:23; 40:3; 49:11; 62:10 *b*Is. 30:21; 51:10 *c*Is. 4:3; 52:1; Matt. 7:13, 14; 1 Pet. 1:15, 16 *d*Is. 33:8

8 And *a*a highway will be there, *b*a roadway,
And it will be called the Highway of *c*Holiness.
The unclean will not travel on it,
But it *will* be for him who walks *that* way,
And *d*fools will not wander *on it*.

9 *a*Is. 5:29; 30:6 *b*Is. 51:10; 62:12; 63:4

9 No *a*lion will be there,
Nor will any vicious beast go up on it;
These will not be found there.
But *b*the redeemed will walk *there*,

10 *a*Is. 1:27; 51:11 *b*Is. 25:8; 30:19; 65:19; Rev. 7:17; 21:4

10 And *a*the ransomed of the LORD will return,
And come with joyful shouting to Zion,
With everlasting joy upon their heads.

They will find gladness and joy,
And *b*sorrow and sighing will flee away.

V DENUNCIATION OF SENNACHERIB,
36:1-39:8

A The Taunt from Assyria,
36:1-22

36 *a*Now it came about in the fourteenth year of King Hezekiah, *b*Sennacherib king of Assyria came up against all the fortified cities of Judah and seized them.

★ **1** *a*2 Kin. 18:13 *b*2 Chr. 32:1

2 And the *a*king of Assyria sent Rabshakeh from Lachish to Jerusalem to King Hezekiah with a large army. And he stood by the *b*conduit of the upper pool on the highway of the fuller's field.

★ **2** *a*2 Kin. 18:17-20:11; 2 Chr. 32:9-24; Is. 36:2-38:8 *b*Is. 7:3

3 Then *a*Eliakim the son of Hilkiah, who was over the household, and *b*Shebna the scribe, and Joah the son of Asaph, the recorder, came out to him.

3 *a*Is. 22:20 *b*Is. 22:15

4 Then *a*Rabshakeh said to them, "Say now to Hezekiah, 'Thus says the great king, the king of Assyria, "What is this confidence that you have?

4 *a*2 Kin. 18:19

5 "I say, 'Your counsel and strength for the war are only empty words.' Now on whom do you rely, that *a*you have rebelled against me?

5 *a*2 Kin. 18:7

6 "Behold, you rely on the *a*staff of this crushed reed, *even* on Egypt; on which if a man leans, it will go into his hand and pierce it. *b*So is Pharaoh king of Egypt to all who rely on him.

6 *a*Ezek. 29:6, 7 *b*Ps. 146:3; Is. 30:3, 5, 7

7 "But if you say to me, 'We trust in the LORD our God,' is it not He *a*whose high places and whose altars Hezekiah has taken away, and has said to Judah and to Jerusalem, 'You shall worship before this altar'?

★ **7** *a*Deut. 12:2-5; 2 Kin. 18:4, 5

36:1 Chapters 36–39 contain a recital of the dramatic events of 701 B.C., when arrogant Assyria tried to conquer Judah.
36:2 *Rabshakeh.* Lit., chief wine-pourer, but indicates a high official, an envoy.
36:7 The unenlightened Assyrian considered this an insult to Yahweh, who was falsely worshiped at these LORD *high places.*

8 "Now therefore, come make a bargain with my master the king of Assyria, and I will give you two thousand horses, if you are able on your part to set riders on them.

9 "How then can you repulse one official of the least of my master's servants, and ^arely on Egypt for chariots and for horsemen?

10 "And have I now come up without the LORD's approval against this land to destroy it? ^aThe LORD said to me, 'Go up against this land, and destroy it.' " ' "

11 Then Eliakim and Shebna and Joah said to Rabshakeh, "Speak now to your servants in ^aAramaic, for we understand *it*; and do not speak with us in ^bJudean, in the hearing of the people who are on the wall."

12 But Rabshakeh said, "Has my master sent me only to your master and to you to speak these words, *and* not to the men who sit on the wall, *doomed* to eat their own dung and drink their own urine with you?"

13 Then Rabshakeh stood and ^acried with a loud voice in Judean, and said, "Hear the words of the great king, the king of Assyria.

14 "Thus says the king, 'Do not let Hezekiah ^adeceive you, for he will not be able to deliver you;

15 nor let Hezekiah make you ^atrust in the LORD, saying, "The LORD will surely deliver us, this city shall not be given into the hand of the king of Assyria."

16 'Do not listen to Hezekiah,' for thus says the king of Assyria, 'Make your peace with me and come out to me, and eat each of his ^avine and each of his fig tree and drink each of the ^bwaters of his own cistern,

17 until I come and take you away to a land like your own land, a land of grain and new wine, a land of bread and vineyards.

18 '*Beware* lest Hezekiah misleads you, saying, "^aThe LORD will deliver us." Has any one of the gods of the nations delivered his land from the hand of the king of Assyria?

19 'Where are the gods of ^aHamath and Arpad? Where are the gods of ^aSepharvaim? And when have they ^bdelivered Samaria from my hand?

20 'Who among all the ^agods of these lands have delivered their land from my hand, that the ^bLORD should deliver Jerusalem from my hand?' "

21 But they were silent and ^aanswered him not a word; for the king's commandment was, "Do not answer him."

22 Then ^aEliakim the son of Hilkiah, who was over the household, and ^bShebna the scribe and Joah the son of Asaph, the recorder, came to Hezekiah with their clothes torn and told him the words of Rabshakeh.

B   The Truth from God, 37:1-7

37 And ^awhen King Hezekiah heard *it*, he tore his clothes, covered himself with sackcloth and entered the house of the LORD.

2 Then he sent ^aEliakim who was over the household with ^bShebna the scribe and the elders of the priests, covered with sackcloth, to ^cIsaiah the prophet, the son of Amoz.

3 And they said to him, "Thus says Hezekiah, 'This day is a ^aday of distress, rebuke, and rejection; for ^bchildren have come

---

Marginal references:

9 ^aIs. 20:5; 30:2-5, 7; 31:3

10 ^a1 Kin. 13:18; 22:6, 12

*11 ^aEzra 4:7; Dan. 2:4 ^bIs. 36:13

13 ^a2 Chr. 32:18

14 ^aIs. 37:10

15 ^aIs. 36:18, 20; 37:10, 11

*16-17

16 ^a1 Kin. 4:25; Mic. 4:4; Zech. 3:10 ^bProv. 5:15

18 ^aIs. 36:15

19 ^aIs. 10:9-11; 37:11-13; Jer. 49:23 ^b2 Kin. 17:6

20 ^a1 Kin. 20:23, 28 ^bIs. 36:15

21 ^aProv. 9:7, 8; 26:4

22 ^aIs. 22:20; 36:3 ^bIs. 22:15

* **1** ^a2 Kin. 19:1-37; Is. 37:1-38

2 ^aIs. 22:20 ^bIs. 22:15 ^cIs. 1:1; 20:2

* **3** ^aIs. 22:5; 26:16; 33:2 ^bIs. 26:17, 18; 66:9; Hos. 13:13

36:11 *Aramaic* was becoming the lingua franca, though the average Jew did not yet understand it.

36:16-17 The Jews were offered a better land, but at the awful price of giving up their liberty.

37:1 Tearing one's *clothes* and wearing *sackcloth* (a dark, coarse-textured cloth) were signs of distress and humiliation.

37:3 Judah's situation was similar to that of a child ready, but unable, to be born. Death seemed to be the only prospect.

to birth, and there is no strength to deliver.

4 'Perhaps the LORD your God will hear the words of Rabshakeh, whom his master the king of Assyria has sent to ᵃreproach the living God, and will rebuke the words which the LORD your God has heard. Therefore, offer a prayer for ᵇthe remnant that is left.' "

5 So the servants of King Hezekiah came to Isaiah.

6 And Isaiah said to them, "Thus you shall say to your master, 'Thus says the LORD, "ᵃDo not be afraid because of the words that you have heard, with which the servants of the king of Assyria have blasphemed Me.

7 "Behold, I will put a spirit in him so that he shall ᵃhear a rumor and ᵇreturn to his own land. And I will make him fall by the sword in his own land." ' "

C The Threat from Assyria, 37:8-35

8 Then Rabshakeh returned and found the king of Assyria fighting against ᵃLibnah, for he had heard that the king had left ᵇLachish.

9 When he ᵃheard *them* say concerning Tirhakah king of ᵇCush, "He has come out to fight against you," and when he heard *it* he sent messengers to Hezekiah, saying,

10 "Thus you shall say to Hezekiah king of Judah, 'ᵃDo not let your God in whom you trust deceive you, saying, "Jerusalem shall not be given into the hand of the king of Assyria."

11 'ᵃBehold, you have heard what the kings of Assyria have done to all the lands, destroying them completely. So will you be spared?

12 'Did the gods of those nations which my fathers have destroyed deliver them, *even* ᵃGozan and ᵇHaran and Rezeph and the sons of Eden who *were* in Telassar?

13 'Where is the king of Hamath, the king of Arpad, the king of the city of Sepharvaim, *and of* Hena and Ivvah?' "

14 Then Hezekiah took the letter from the hand of the messengers and read it, and he went up to the house of the LORD and spread it out before the LORD.

15 And Hezekiah prayed to the LORD saying,

16 "O LORD of hosts, the God of Israel, ᵃwho art enthroned *above* the cherubim, Thou art the ᵇGod, Thou alone, of all the kingdoms of the earth. ᶜThou hast made heaven and earth.

17 "ᵃIncline Thine ear, O LORD, and hear; open Thine eyes, O LORD, and see; and ᵇlisten to all the words of Sennacherib, who sent *them* to ᶜreproach the living God.

18 "Truly, O LORD, the ᵃkings of Assyria have devastated all the countries and their lands,

19 and have cast their gods into the fire, for they were not gods but the ᵃwork of men's hands, wood and stone. So they have ᵇdestroyed them.

20 "And now, O LORD our God, ᵃdeliver us from his hand that ᵇall the kingdoms of the earth may know that Thou alone, LORD, art God."

21 Then ᵃIsaiah the son of Amoz sent word to Hezekiah, saying, "Thus says the LORD, the God of Israel, 'Because you have prayed to Me about Sennacherib king of Assyria,

22 this is the word that the LORD has spoken against him:

"She has despised you and mocked you,

Cross references (margin)

4 ᵃIs. 36:13-15, 18, 20 ᵇIs. 1:9; 10:20-22; 37:31, 32; 46:3

6 ᵃIs. 7:4; 35:4

7 ᵃIs. 37:9 ᵇIs. 37:37, 38

★ **8** ᵃNum. 33:20; Josh. 10:29 ᵇJosh. 10:31, 32

9 ᵃIs. 37:7 ᵇIs. 18:1; 20:5

10 ᵃIs. 36:15

11 ᵃIs. 10:9-11; 36:18-20

★**12** ᵃ2 Kin. 17:6; 18:11 ᵇGen. 11:31; 12:1-4; Acts 7:2

★**13**

★**15-20**

16 ᵃEx. 25:22; 1 Sam. 4:4; Ps. 80:1; 99:1 ᵇDeut. 10:17; Ps. 86:10; 136:2, 3 ᶜIs. 42:5; 45:12; Jer. 10:12

17 ᵃ2 Chr. 6:40; Ps. 17:6; Dan. 9:18 ᵇPs. 74:22 ᶜIs. 37:4

18 ᵃ2 Kin. 15:29; 16:9; 17:6, 24; 1 Chr. 5:26

19 ᵃIs. 2:8; 17:8; 41:24, 29 ᵇIs. 26:14

20 ᵃIs. 25:9; 33:22; 35:4 ᵇ1 Kin. 18:36, 37; Ps. 46:10; Is. 37:16; Ezek. 36:23

21 ᵃIs. 37:2

22 ᵃJer. 14:17; Lam. 2:13 ᵇPs. 9:14; Zeph. 3:14; Zech. 2:10 ᶜJob 16:4

37:8 *Libnah.* About 25 miles SW. of Jerusalem.
37:12 These cities were in Mesopotamia.
37:13 These cities were in Syria.
37:15-20 This brief, beautiful prayer shows great faith in God and asks only that His glory be vindicated (v. 20). Compare 2 Chron. 20:5-12; Jer. 32:17-25; Acts 4:24-30 for prayers of those in similar straits.

The ^avirgin ^bdaughter of Zion;
She has ^cshaken *her* head behind you,
The daughter of Jerusalem!

^{23 a}Is. 37:4
^bIs. 2:11;
5:15, 21
^cEzek. 39:7;
Hab. 1:12

23 "Whom have you ^areproached and blasphemed?
And against whom have you raised *your* voice,
And haughtily ^blifted up your eyes?
Against the ^cHoly One of Israel!

^{24 a}Is. 10:33, 34
^bIs. 14:8 ^cIs. 10:18

24 "Through your servants you have reproached the Lord,
And you have said, 'With my many chariots I came up to the heights of the mountains,
To the remotest parts of ^aLebanon;
And I cut down its tall ^bcedars *and* its choice cypresses.
And I will go to its highest peak, its thickest ^cforest.

^{25 a}Deut. 11:10; 1 Kin. 20:10

25 'I dug *wells* and drank waters,
And ^awith the sole of my feet I dried up
All the rivers of Egypt.'

^{26 a}Is. 40:21, 28
^bActs 2:23;
4:27, 28;
1 Pet. 2:8
^cIs. 46:11
^dIs. 10:6 ^eIs. 17:1; 25:2

26 "^aHave you not heard?
Long ago I did it,
From ancient times I ^bplanned it.
Now ^cI have brought it to pass,
That ^dyou should turn fortified cities into ^eruinous heaps.

^{27 a}Is. 40:7
^bPs. 129:6

27 "Therefore their inhabitants were short of strength,
They were dismayed and put to shame;
They were *as* the ^avegetation of the field and *as* the green herb,
As ^bgrass on the housetops is scorched before it is grown up.

^{28 a}Ps. 139:1

28 "But I ^aknow your sitting down,
And your going out and your coming in,
And your raging against Me.

^{29 a}Is. 10:12
^bEzek. 29:4;
38:4 ^cIs. 30:28 ^dIs. 37:34

29 "Because of your raging against Me,
And because your ^aarrogance has come up to My ears,
Therefore I will put My ^bhook in your nose,
And My ^cbridle in your lips,
And I will turn you back ^dby the way which you came.

★30-33

^{30 a}Lev. 25:5, 11

30 "Then this shall be the sign for you: you shall eat this year what ^agrows of itself, in the second year what springs from the same, and in the third year sow, reap, plant vineyards, and eat their fruit.

^{31 a}Is. 4:2;
10:20 ^bIs. 37:4 ^cIs. 27:6

31 "And the ^asurviving ^bremnant of the house of Judah shall again ^ctake root downward and bear fruit upward.

^{32 a}Is. 37:4
^b2 Kin. 19:31; Is. 9:7; 59:17;
Joel 2:18;
Zech. 1:14

32 "For out of Jerusalem shall go forth a ^aremnant, and out of Mount Zion survivors. The ^bzeal of the LORD of hosts shall perform this." '

^{33 a}Jer. 6:6;
32:24

33 "Therefore, thus says the LORD concerning the king of Assyria, 'He shall not come to this city, or shoot an arrow there; neither shall he come before it with a shield, nor throw up a ^amound against it.

^{34 a}Is. 37:29

34 'By the way that he came, by the same he shall return, and he shall not come to this city,' declares the LORD.

^{35 a}2 Kin. 20:6; Is. 31:5; 38:6
^bIs. 43:25;
48:9, 11

35 'For I will ^adefend this city to save it ^bfor My own sake and for My servant David's sake.' "

37:30–33 God promised that after three years, ravaged Judah would be restored to normal and that Jerusalem itself would be spared (v. 33).

D The Triumph over Assyria,
37:36-38

★36 a2 Kin.
19:35; Is.
10:12, 33, 34

36 Then the ªangel of the LORD went out, and struck 185,000 in the camp of the Assyrians; and when men arose early in the morning, behold, all of these were dead.

37 aGen.
10:11; Jon.
1:2; 3:3;
4:11; Zeph.
2:13
★38 aGen.
8:4; Jer.
51:27 bEzra
4:2

37 So Sennacherib, king of Assyria, departed and returned *home*, and lived at ªNineveh.

38 And it came about as he was worshiping in the house of Nisroch his god, that Adrammelech and Sharezer his sons killed him with the sword; and they escaped into the land of ªArarat. And ᵇEsarhaddon his son became king in his place.

E The Sickness of Hezekiah,
38:1-22

1 a2 Kin.
20:1-6, 9-11;
2 Chr. 32:24;
Is. 38:1-8
bIs. 1:1; 37:2
c2 Sam.
17:23

38 ªIn those days Hezekiah became mortally ill. And ᵇIsaiah the prophet the son of Amoz came to him and said to him, "Thus says the LORD, 'ᶜSet your house in order, for you shall die and not live.' "

2 Then Hezekiah turned his face to the wall, and prayed to the LORD,

3 aNeh.
13:14
b2 Kin. 18:5,
6; Ps. 26:3
c1 Chr. 28:9;
29:19 dDeut.
6:18 ePs.
6:6-8

3 and said, "ªRemember now, O LORD, I beseech Thee, how I have ᵇwalked before Thee in truth and with a ᶜwhole heart, and ᵈhave done what is good in Thy sight." And Hezekiah ᵉwept bitterly.

4 Then the word of the LORD came to Isaiah, saying,

5 a2 Kin.
18:2, 13

5 "Go and say to Hezekiah, 'Thus says the LORD, the God of your father David, "I have heard

your prayer, I have seen your tears; behold, I will add ªfifteen years to your life.

6 "And I will ªdeliver you and this city from the hand of the king of Assyria; and I will defend this city." '

6 aIs. 31:5;
37:35

7 "And this shall be the ªsign to you from the LORD, that the LORD will do this thing that He has spoken:

7 aJudg.
6:17, 21, 36-
40; Is. 7:11,
14; 37:30

8 "Behold, I will ªcause the shadow on the stairway, which has gone down with the sun on the stairway of Ahaz, to go back ten steps." So the ᵇsun's *shadow* went back ten steps on the stairway on which it had gone down.

★ 8 a2 Kin.
20:9-11
bJosh.
10:12-14

9 A writing of Hezekiah king of Judah, after his illness and recovery:

10 I said, "ªIn the middle of my life
I am to enter the ᵇgates of Sheol;
I am to be ᶜdeprived of the rest of my years."

10 aPs.
102:24 bPs.
107:18 cJob
17:11, 15;
2 Cor. 1:9

11 I said, "I shall not see the LORD,
The LORD ªin the land of the living;
I shall look on man no more among the inhabitants   of   the world.

11 aPs.
27:13; 116:9

12 "Like a shepherd's ªtent my dwelling is pulled up and removed from me;
As a ᵇweaver I ᶜrolled up my life.
He ᵈcuts me off from the loom;
From ᵉday until night Thou dost make an end of me.

★12 a2 Cor.
5:1, 4; 2 Pet.
1:13, 14
bJob 7:6
cHeb. 1:12
dJob 6:9
eJob 4:20;
Ps. 73:14

13 "I composed *my soul* until morning.
ªLike a lion—so He ᵇbreaks all my bones,

13 aJob
10:16 bPs.
51:8; Dan.
6:24 cPs.
32:4

37:36 The Lord used a sudden outbreak of a particularly virulent plague to slay the Assyrian army. Herodotus records that the army camp was infected with mice (or rats). See 2 Kings 19:35.

37:38 The fulfillment of the prediction of verse 7.

38:8 *the stairway of Ahaz.* A westward facing flight of stairs on which, normally, the declining sun would cause a shadow to move upward. As a confirmatory sign to Hezekiah, the shadow went down ten steps.

38:12 *rolled up.* As a strip of fabric is rolled into a bolt of cloth when completed.

From ^cday until night
Thou dost make an
end of me.

14 "^aLike a swallow, *like* a
crane, so I twitter;
I ^bmoan like a dove;
My ^ceyes look wistfully to
the heights;
O Lord, I am oppressed, be
my ^dsecurity.

15 "^aWhat shall I say?
For He has spoken to me,
and He Himself has
done it;
I shall ^bwander about all
my years because of
the ^cbitterness of my
soul.

16 "O Lord, ^aby *these* things
men live;
And in all these is the life
of my spirit;
^bO restore me to health,
and ^clet me live!

17 "Lo, for *my own* welfare I
had great bitterness;
It is Thou who hast ^akept
my soul from the pit
of nothingness,
For Thou hast ^bcast all my
sins behind Thy back.

18 "For ^aSheol cannot thank
Thee,
Death cannot praise Thee;
Those who go down ^bto
the pit cannot hope
for Thy faithfulness.

19 "It is the ^aliving who give
thanks to Thee, as I
do today;
A ^bfather tells his sons
about Thy faithfulness.

20 "The LORD will surely save
me;
So we will ^aplay my songs
on stringed instruments
^bAll *the* days of our life ^cat
the house of the
LORD."

21 Now ^aIsaiah had said, "Let
them take a cake of figs, and apply it to the boil, that he may recover."

22 Then Hezekiah had said,
"What is the ^asign that I shall go
up to the house of the LORD?"

F　The Stupidity of Hezekiah,
39:1–8

39 ^aAt that time Merodach-baladan son of Baladan,
king of Babylon, sent letters and a
present to Hezekiah, for he heard
that he had been sick and had recovered.

2 And Hezekiah was
^apleased, and showed them all his
treasure house, the ^bsilver and the
gold and the spices and the precious oil and his whole armory
and all that was found in his treasuries. There was nothing in his
house, nor in all his dominion,
that Hezekiah did not show them.

3 Then Isaiah the ^aprophet
came to King Hezekiah and said
to him, "What did these men say,
and from where have they come
to you?" And Hezekiah said,
"They have come to me from a
far ^bcountry, from Babylon."

4 And he said, "What have
they seen in your house?" So
Hezekiah answered, "They have
seen all that is in my house; there
is nothing among my treasuries
that I have not shown them."

5 Then Isaiah said to Hezekiah, "Hear the ^aword of the
LORD of hosts,

6 'Behold, the days are coming when ^aall that is in your
house, and all that your fathers
have laid up in store to this day
shall be carried to Babylon; nothing shall be left,' says the LORD.

7 'And *some* of your sons
who shall issue from you, whom
you shall beget, ^ashall be taken

---

14 ^aJob
30:29; Ps.
102:6 ^bIs.
59:11; Ezek.
7:16; Nah.
2:7 ^cPs.
119:123
^dJob 17:3;
Ps. 119:122

15 ^aPs. 39:9
^b1 Kin.
21:27 ^cJob
7:11; 10:1;
Is. 38:17

16 ^aPs.
119:71, 75
^bPs. 39:13
^cPs. 119:25

17 ^aPs. 30:3;
86:13; Jon.
2:6 ^bIs.
43:25; Jer.
31:34; Mic.
7:19

★**18** ^aPs.
6:5; 30:9;
88:11; Eccl.
9:10 ^bNum.
16:33; Ps.
28:1

19 ^aPs.
118:17;
119:175
^bDeut. 6:7;
11:19; Ps.
78:5-7

20 ^aPs.
33:1-3;
68:24-26
^bPs. 104:33;
116:2; 146:2
^cPs. 116:17-
19

21 ^a2 Kin.
20:7, 8

22 ^aIs. 38:7

★ **1** ^a2 Kin.
20:12-19;
2 Chr. 32:31;
Is. 39:1-8

2 ^a2 Chr.
32:25, 31;
Job 31:25
^b2 Kin.
18:15, 16

3 ^a2 Sam.
12:1; 2 Chr.
16:7 ^bDeut.
28:49; Jer.
5:15

5 ^a1 Sam.
13:13, 14;
15:16

★ **6** ^a2 Kin.
24:13; 25:13-
15; Jer. 20:5

7 ^a2 Kin.
24:10-16;
2 Chr. 36:10
^bDan. 1:1-7

38:18 *Sheol.* Equivalent here to death; i.e., in
death one is cut off from the living who can
praise God.
39:1 *At that time.* I.e., in 712 the king of Babylon, which was then a vassal state of Assyria,
tried to enlist the aid of Hezekiah against Assyria. But two years later Sargon, king of Assyria, captured Babylon. See 2 Kings 20:12ff.
39:6 A prophecy fulfilled in the days of Nebuchadnezzar. See Dan. 1:2; 5:3, 23.

away; and [b]they shall become officials in the palace of the king of Babylon.' "

8 [a]Then Hezekiah said to Isaiah, "The word of the LORD which you have spoken is good." For he thought, "For there will be peace and truth [b]in my days."

PART 2　CONSOLATION, 40:1–66:24
I　THE GREATNESS OF GOD,
40:1–48:22
A　In Releasing Judah from Captivity, 40:1–11

40 "[a]Comfort, O comfort My people," says your God.

2 "[a]Speak kindly to Jerusalem;
And call out to her, that her [b]warfare has ended,
That her [c]iniquity has been removed,
That she has received of the LORD's hand
[d]Double for all her sins."

3 [a]A voice is calling,
"[b]Clear the way for the LORD in the wilderness;
Make smooth in the desert a highway for our God.

4 "Let every valley be lifted up,
And every mountain and hill be made low;
And let the rough ground become a plain,
And the rugged terrain a broad valley;

5 Then the [a]glory of the LORD will be revealed,

And [b]all flesh will see it together;
For the [c]mouth of the LORD has spoken."

6 A voice says, "Call out." Then he answered, "What shall I call out?"
[a]All flesh is grass, and all its loveliness is like the flower of the field.

7 The [a]grass withers, the flower fades,
When the [b]breath of the LORD blows upon it;
Surely the people are grass.

8 The grass withers, the flower fades,
But [a]the word of our God stands forever.

9 Get yourself up on a [a]high mountain,
O Zion, bearer of [b]good news,
Lift up your voice mightily,
O Jerusalem, bearer of good news;
Lift it up, do not fear.
Say to the [c]cities of Judah,
"[d]Here is your God!"

10 Behold, the Lord GOD will come [a]with might,
With His [b]arm ruling for Him.
Behold, His [c]reward is with Him,
And His recompense before Him.

11 Like a shepherd He will [a]tend His flock,
In His arm He will gather the lambs,
And carry them in His bosom;
He will gently lead the nursing ewes.

Cross references (margin)

8 [a]2 Chr. 32:26
[b]2 Chr. 34:28

★1 [a]Is. 12:1; 49:13; 51:3, 12; 52:9; 61:2; 66:13; Jer. 31:10-14; Zeph. 3:14-17; 2 Cor. 1:4

★2 [a]Is. 35:4; Zech. 1:13 [b]Is. 41:11-13; 49:25; 54:15, 17 [c]Is. 33:24; 53:5, 6, 11 [d]Jer. 16:18; Zech. 9:12; Rev. 18:6

★3-5

3 [a]Matt. 3:3; Mark 1:3; Luke 3:4-6; John 1:23 [b]Mal. 3:1; 4:5, 6

5 [a]Is. 6:3; Hab. 2:14 [b]Is. 52:10; Joel 2:28 [c]Is. 1:20; 34:16; 58:14

6 [a]Job 14:2; Ps. 102:11; 103:15; 1 Pet. 1:24, 25

7 [a]Ps. 90:5, 6; James 1:10, 11 [b]Job 4:9; 41:21; Is. 11:4; 40:24

8 [a]Is. 55:11; 59:21; Matt. 5:18

9 [a]Is. 52:7 [b]Is. 61:1 [c]Is. 44:26 [d]Is. 25:9; 35:2

★10 [a]Is. 9:6, 7 [b]Is. 59:16, 18 [c]Is. 62:11; Rev. 22:12

11 [a]Jer. 31:10; Ezek. 34:12-14, 23, 31; Mic. 5:4; John 10:11, 14-16

40:1 Here begins the great second section (chapters 40–66) of the book. In contrast to the dark judgment of the preceding chapters, it shines with the light of the promises of restoration to the land (40–48), of the coming of Messiah (49–57), and of millennial blessings for Israel (58–66). Though the people had not yet gone into exile, Isaiah saw beyond that terrible time to future blessings.

40:2 *Double*. May refer to full and sufficient punishment for Israel's sins, or perhaps to superabundant grace to cover her sins

40:3–5 These verses have immediate reference to the Lord going before the people as they made the 900-mile journey from Babylon to Palestine. They are also applied to the ministry of John the Baptist, who prepared the way for Christ's ministry of eternal salvation (Matt. 3:3).

40:10 *recompense*. I.e., His wages or reward of blessing to the godly and retribution to the wicked.

B   In Relation to the Creation, 40:12–31

★12 aJob 38:8-11; Ps. 102:25, 26; Is 48:13; Heb. 1:10-12

12 Who has ªmeasured the waters in the hollow of His hand, And marked off the heavens by the span, And calculated the dust of the earth by the measure, And weighed the mountains in a balance, And the hills in a pair of scales?

13 aRom. 11:34; 1 Cor. 2:16 bIs. 41:28

13 ªWho has directed the Spirit of the LORD, Or as His ᵇcounselor has informed Him?

14 aJob 38:4 bJob 21:22; Col. 2:3

14 ªWith whom did He consult and *who* ᵇgave Him understanding? And *who* taught Him in the path of justice and taught Him knowledge, And informed Him of the way of understanding?

★15-17

15 aJer. 10:10 bIs. 17:13; 29:5

15 Behold, the ªnations are like a drop from a bucket, And are regarded as a speck of ᵇdust on the scales; Behold, He lifts up the islands like fine dust.

16 aPs. 50:9-11; Mic. 6:6, 7; Heb. 10:5-9

16 Even Lebanon is not enough to burn, Nor its ªbeasts enough for a burnt offering.

17 aIs. 29:7

17 ªAll the nations are as nothing before Him, They are regarded by Him as less than nothing and meaningless.

18 aEx. 8:10; 15:11; 1 Sam. 2:2; Is. 40:25; 46:5; Mic. 7:18; Acts 17:29

18 ªTo whom then will you liken God? Or what likeness will you compare with Him?

19 As *for* the ªidol, a craftsman casts it, A goldsmith ᵇplates it with gold, And a silversmith *fashions* chains of silver.

19 aPs. 115:4-8; Is. 41:7; 44:10; Hab. 2:18, 19 bIs. 2:20; 30:22

20 He who is too impoverished for *such* an offering Selects a ªtree that does not rot; He seeks out for himself a skillful craftsman To prepare an idol that ᵇwill not totter.

20 aIs. 44:14 b1 Sam. 5:3, 4; Is. 41:7; 46:7

21 ªDo you not know? Have you not heard? Has it not been declared to you from the beginning? Have you not understood ᵇfrom the foundations of the earth?

21 aPs. 19:1; 50:6; Is. 37:26; Acts 14:17; Rom. 1:19 bIs. 48:13; 51:13

22 It is He who sits above the ªvault of the earth, And its inhabitants are like ᵇgrasshoppers, Who ᶜstretches out the heavens like a ᵈcurtain And spreads them out like a ᵉtent to dwell in.

★22-24

22 aJob 22:14; Prov. 8:27 bNum. 13:33 cJob 9:8; Is. 37:16; 42:5; 44:24 dPs. 104:2 eJob 36:29; Ps. 18:11; 19:4

23 He *it is* who reduces ªrulers to nothing, Who ᵇmakes the judges of the earth meaningless.

23 aJob 12:21; Ps. 107:40; Is. 34:12 bIs. 5:21; Jer. 25:18-27

24 Scarcely have they been planted, Scarcely have they been sown, Scarcely has their stock taken root in the earth, But He merely blows on them, and they wither, And the ªstorm carries them away like stubble.

24 aIs. 17:13; 41:16

40:12 The entire universe is on a Lilliputian scale when compared to God the mighty Creator. *span.* The distance between the outstretched thumb and the little finger—half a cubit, or about nine inches.

40:15-17 God is sovereign over all the nations. They are as a *drop* which drips from the outside of a bucket when it is drawn from a well.

40:22-24 God is also the Governor of the world, sitting *above the vault* (circle or zenith; the Heb. word allows for the concept that the earth is a sphere) and controlling the rulers of the world.

25 aIs. 40:18

25 "aTo whom then will you liken Me
That I should be *his* equal?" says the Holy One.

★**26** aIs. 51:6 bIs. 42:5; 48:12, 13 cPs. 147:4 dPs. 89:11-13 eIs. 34:16; 48:13

26 aLift up your eyes on high
And see bwho has created these *stars,*
The cOne who leads forth their host by number,
He calls them all by name;
Because of the dgreatness of His might and the strength of *His* power
eNot one *of them* is missing.

★**27-31**

27 aIs. 49:4, 14 bIs. 54:8 cJob 27:2; 34:5; Luke 18:7, 8 dIs. 25:1

27 aWhy do you say, O Jacob, and assert, O Israel,
"My way is bhidden from the LORD,
And the cjustice due me escapes the notice of dmy God"?

28 aIs. 40:21 bGen. 21:33; Ps. 90:2 cPs. 147:5; Rom. 11:33

28 aDo you not know? Have you not heard?
The bEverlasting God, the LORD, the Creator of the ends of the earth
Does not become weary or tired.
His understanding is cinscrutable.

29 aIs. 50:4; Jer. 31:25 bIs. 41:10

29 He gives strength to the aweary,
And to *him who* lacks might He bincreases power.

30 aJer. 6:11; 9:21 bIs. 9:17

30 Though ayouths grow weary and tired,
And vigorous byoung men stumble badly,

31 aJob 17:9; Ps. 103:5; 2 Cor. 4:8-10, 16 bEx. 19:4; Deut. 32:11; Luke 18:1; 2 Cor. 4:1, 16; Gal. 6:9; Heb. 12:3

31 Yet those who wait for the LORD
Will again new strength;
They will bmount up *with* wings like eagles,
They will run and not get tired,
They will walk and not become weary.

C In Comparison to Idols, 41:1-29

41

1 aIs. 11:11 bHab. 2:20; Zech. 2:13 cIs. 40:31 dIs. 34:1; 48:16 eIs. 1:18; 43:26; 50:8

"aCoastlands, listen to Me bin silence,
And let the peoples cgain new strength;
dLet them come forward, then let them speak;
eLet us come together for judgment.

★ **2** aIs. 41:25; 45:1-3; 46:11 bIs. 42:6 c2 Chr. 36:23; Ezra 1:2 d2 Sam. 22:43 eIs. 40:24

2 "aWho has aroused one from the east
Whom He bcalls in righteousness to His feet?
He cdelivers up nations before him,
And subdues kings.
He makes them like ddust with his sword,
As the wind-driven echaff with his bow.

3 "He pursues them, passing on in safety,
By a way he had not been traversing with his feet.

4 aIs. 41:26; 44:7; 46:10 bIs. 43:10; 44:6; Rev. 1:8, 17; 22:13 cIs. 43:13; 46:4; 48:12

4 "aWho has performed and accomplished *it,*
Calling forth the generations from the beginning?
bI, the LORD, am the first, and with the last. cI am He.' "

5 aIs. 41:1; Ezek. 26:15, 16 bJosh. 5:1; Ps. 67:7

5 The acoastlands have seen and are afraid;
The bends of the earth tremble;
They have drawn near and have come.

6 Each one helps his neighbor,
And says to his brother, "Be strong!"

7 aIs. 44:12, 13 bIs. 40:19 cIs. 40:20; 46:7

7 So the acraftsman encourages the bsmelter,
And he who smooths metal with the hammer encourages him who beats the anvil,

---

40:26 God also controls the stars.
40:27-31 God is not too great to care, as Israel complained (v. 27). He gives power to those who wait on or hope in Him (v. 29), and they exchange *(gain)* their strength for His (v. 31).

41:2 *from the east.* A reference to Cyrus the Great of Persia (558-529), a type of Christ because he would liberate God's people from their bondage in Babylon (cf. 44:28).

Saying of the soldering, "It
is good";
And he fastens it with
nails,
^cThat it should not totter.

★ 8 ^aIs.
42:19; 43:10;
44:1, 2, 21
^bIs. 29:22;
51:2; 63:16
^c2 Chr. 20:7;
James 2:23

8 "But you, Israel, ^aMy ser-
vant,
Jacob whom I have chosen,
Descendant of ^bAbraham
My ^cfriend,

9 ^aIs. 11:11
^bIs. 43:5-7
^cIs. 42:1;
44:1 ^dDeut.
7:6; 14:2; Ps.
135:4

9 "You whom I have ^ataken
from the ends of the
earth,
And called from its ^bre-
motest parts,
And said to you, 'You are
^cMy servant,
I have ^dchosen you and not
rejected you.

10 ^aDeut.
20:1; 31:6;
Josh. 1:9;
Ps. 27:1; Is.
41:13, 14;
43:2, 5; Rom.
8:31 ^bIs.
41:14; 44:2;
49:8 ^cPs.
89:13, 14

10 'Do not ^afear, for I am with
you;
Do not anxiously look
about you, for I am
your God.
I will strengthen you,
surely ^bI will help
you,
Surely I will uphold you
with My righteous
^cright hand.'

11 ^aIs. 45:24
^bIs. 17:13;
29:5, 7, 8

11 "Behold, ^aall those who are
angered at you will be
shamed and dishon-
ored;
^bThose who contend with
you will be as noth-
ing, and will perish.

12 ^aJob
20:7-9; Ps.
37:35, 36; Is.
17:14

12 "^aYou will seek those who
quarrel with you, but
will not find them,
Those who war with you
will be as nothing,
and non-existent.

13 ^aIs. 42:6;
45:1 ^bIs.
41:10

13 "For I am the LORD your
God, ^awho upholds
your right hand,
Who says to you, '^bDo not
fear, I will help you.'

★14-15
14 ^aJob
25:6; Ps.
22:6 ^bIs.
35:10; 43:14;
44:6, 22-24

14 "Do not fear, you ^aworm Jacob, you men of Is-
rael;

I will help you," declares
the LORD, "and ^byour
Redeemer is the Holy
One of Israel.

15 "Behold, I have made you a
new, sharp threshing
sledge with double
edges;
^aYou will thresh the
^bmountains, and pul-
verize them,
And will make the hills
like chaff.

15 ^aMic.
4:13; Hab.
3:12 ^bIs.
42:15; 64:1;
Jer. 9:10;
Ezek. 33:28

16 "You will ^awinnow them,
and the wind will car-
ry them away,
And the storm will scatter
them;
But you will ^brejoice in the
LORD,
You will glory in the Holy
One of Israel.

16 ^aJer. 51:2
^bIs. 25:9;
35:10; 51:3;
61:10

17 "The afflicted and needy
are seeking ^awater,
but there is none,
And their tongue is
parched with thirst;
I, the LORD, ^bwill answer
them Myself,
As the God of Israel I ^cwill
not forsake them.

★17-20
17 ^aIs.
43:20; 44:3;
49:10; 55:1
^bIs. 30:19;
65:24 ^cIs.
42:16; 62:12

18 "I will open ^arivers on the
bare heights,
And springs in the midst
of the valleys;
I will make ^bthe wilderness
a pool of water,
And the dry land fountains
of water.

18 ^aIs.
30:25; 43:19
^bPs. 107:35;
Is. 35:6, 7

19 "I will put the cedar in the
wilderness,
The acacia, and the
^amyrtle, and the olive
tree;
I will place the ^ajuniper in
the desert,
Together with the box tree
and the cypress,

19 ^aIs. 35:1;
55:13; 60:13

20 That ^athey may see and
recognize,

20 ^aIs. 40:5;
43:10 ^bJob
12:9; Is.
66:14

41:8 In this passage the *servant* is the nation Israel (as also in 43:1-10; 44:1-8, 21; 45:4; 48:20);
in other passages it is an individual whom the
N.T. identifies as Jesus Christ (42:1-12; chap.
49; 50:4-6; 52:13-53:12; cf. Acts 8:28-35).
41:14-15 Israel is called a *worm* because she is
feeble, despised, and stepped on by the nations of the world. But God will make Israel a
sledge, a solid object made of heavy timbers
and studded with flint.
41:17-20 God promises to supply all their needs
as His people return from Babylon.

And consider and gain in-
sight as well,
That the [b]hand of the LORD
has done this,
And the Holy One of Israel
has created it.

21 "Present your case," the
LORD says.
"Bring forward your strong
arguments,"
The [a]King of Jacob says.

22 [a]Let them bring forth and
declare to us what is
going to take place;
As for the [b]former *events,*
declare what they
were,
That we may consider
them, and know their
outcome;
Or announce to us what is
coming.

23 [a]Declare the things that
are going to come af-
terward,
That we may know that
you are gods;
Indeed, [b]do good or evil,
that we may anxiously
look about us and fear
together.

24 Behold, [a]you are of no account,
And [b]your work amounts
to nothing;
He who chooses you is an
[c]abomination.

25 "I have aroused [a]one from
the north, and he has
come;
From the rising of the sun
he will call on My
name;
And he will come upon
rulers as *upon* [b]mor-
tar,

Even as the potter treads
clay."

26 Who has [a]declared *this*
from the beginning,
that we might know?
Or from former times, that
we may say, "*He is*
right!"?
Surely there was [b]no one
who declared,
Surely there was no one
who proclaimed,
Surely there was no one
who heard your
words.

27 "[a]Formerly *I said* to Zion,
'Behold, here they
are.'
And to Jerusalem, 'I will
give a [b]messenger of
good news.'

28 "But [a]when I look, there is
no one,
And there is no [b]counselor
among them
Who, if I ask, can [c]give an
answer.

29 "Behold, all of them are
false;
Their [a]works are [b]worth-
less,
Their molten images are
[c]wind and emptiness.

D In Providing His Servant,
42:1-25

42 "[a]Behold, My [b]Servant,
whom I uphold;
My [c]chosen one *in whom*
My [d]soul delights.
I have put My [e]Spirit upon
Him;
He will bring forth [f]justice
to the nations.

2 "He will not cry out or raise
His voice,

41:21-26 God challenges the idol-worshiping
heathen to prove the power of their idols by
means of a test of prophecy accurately fulfilled
(v. 22), which, of course, they cannot do. But
God predicts the coming of Cyrus 150 years
later from the *rising of the sun* (the east) to
attack *from the north* (v. 25).
41:27 *here they are.* I.e., the fulfillment of these

prophecies. *a messenger of good news.* Isaiah
himself.
42:1 *Servant.* Here an individual (Jesus Christ
according to Matt. 12:18-20), who would have
an unassuming ministry and who (at His second coming) will bring justice to the whole
world.

Nor make His voice heard
in the street.

3 "A bruised reed He will not
break,
And a dimly burning wick
He will not extin-
guish;
He will faithfully bring
forth ᵃjustice.

4 "He will not be ᵃdisheart-
ened or crushed,
Until He has established
justice in the earth;
And the ᵇcoastlands will
wait expectantly for
His law."

5 Thus says God the LORD,
Who ᵃcreated the heavens
and ᵇstretched them
out,
Who spread out the ᶜearth
and its offspring,
Who ᵈgives breath to the
people on it,
And spirit to those who
walk in it,

6 "I am the LORD, I have
ᵃcalled you in right-
eousness,
I will also ᵇhold you by the
hand and ᶜwatch over
you,
And I will appoint you as a
ᵈcovenant to the peo-
ple,
As a ᵉlight to the nations,

7 To ᵃopen blind eyes,
To ᵇbring out prisoners
from the dungeon,
And those who dwell in
darkness from the
prison.

8 "ᵃI am the LORD, that is ᵇMy
name;
I will not give My ᶜglory to
another,
Nor My praise to graven
images.

9 "Behold, the ᵃformer things
have come to pass,
Now I declare ᵇnew things;

Before they spring forth I
proclaim *them* to
you."

10 Sing to the LORD a ᵃnew
song,
Sing His praise from the
ᵇend of the earth!
ᶜYou who go down to the
sea, and ᵈall that is in
it.
You ᵉislands and those
who dwell on them.

11 Let the ᵃwilderness and its
cities lift up *their*
voices,
The settlements where
ᵇKedar inhabits.
Let the inhabitants of ᶜSela
sing aloud,
Let them shout for joy
from the tops of the
ᵈmountains.

12 Let them ᵃgive glory to the
LORD,
And declare His praise in
the ᵇcoastlands.

13 ᵃThe LORD will go forth
like a warrior,
He will arouse *His* ᵇzeal
like a man of war.
He will utter a shout, yes,
He will raise a war
cry.
He will ᶜprevail against His
enemies.

14 "ᵃI have kept silent for a
long time,
I have kept still and re-
strained Myself.
Now like a woman in labor
I will groan,
I will both gasp and pant.

15 "I will ᵃlay waste the mountains and hills,
And wither all their vegetation;
I will ᵇmake the rivers into
coastlands,
And dry up the ponds.

---

3 ᵃPs. 72:2,
4; 96:13

4 ᵃIs. 40:28
ᵇIs. 11:11;
24:15; 42:10,
12; 49:1;
51:5; 60:9;
66:19

5 ᵃPs.
102:25, 26;
Is. 45:18
ᵇPs. 104:2;
Is. 40:22
ᶜPs. 24:1, 2;
136:6 ᵈJob
12:10; 33:4;
Is. 57:16;
Dan. 5:23;
Acts 17:25

★ **6** ᵃIs.
41:2; Jer.
23:5, 6 ᵇIs.
41:13; 45:1
ᶜIs. 26:3;
27:3 ᵈIs.
49:8 ᵉIs.
49:6; 51:4;
60:1, 3; Luke
2:32; Acts
13:47; 26:23

7 ᵃIs.
29:18; 35:5
ᵇIs. 49:9;
61:1

8 ᵃIs. 43:3,
11, 15 ᵇEx.
3:15; Ps.
83:18 ᶜEx.
20:3-5; Is.
48:11

9 ᵃIs. 48:3
ᵇIs. 43:19;
48:6

10 ᵃPs. 33:3;
40:3; 98:1
ᵇIs. 49:6;
62:11 ᶜPs.
65:5; 107:23
ᵈEx. 20:11;
1 Chr. 16:32;
Ps. 96:11
ᵉIs. 42:4

★**11** ᵃIs.
32:16; 35:1,
6 ᵇIs. 21:16;
60:7 ᶜIs.
16:1 ᵈIs.
52:7; Nah.
1:15

12 ᵃIs. 24:15
ᵇIs. 42:4

★**13** ᵃEx.
15:3 ᵇIs. 9:7;
26:11; 37:32;
59:17 ᶜIs.
66:14-16

14 ᵃPs.
50:21; Is.
57:11

15 ᵃIs. 2:12-
16; Ezek.
38:19, 20
ᵇIs. 44:27;
50:2; Nah.
1:4-6

42:6 The ministry of the Servant would be to
fulfill the *covenant* promises to the *people* of
Israel and to bring *light* to the *nations.*
42:11 *Kedar.* The second son of Ishmael (Gen.

25:13), whose descendants roamed the desert
E. of Palestine.
42:13 The complete fulfillment of this verse will
come at Armageddon.

★16 *a*Is.
29:18; 30:21;
32:3; Jer.
31:8, 9; Luke
1:78, 79 *b*Is.
29:18; Eph.
5:8 *c*Is. 40:4;
Luke 3:5
*d*Josh. 1:5;
Ps. 94:14; Is.
41:17; Heb.
13:5

16 "And I will *a*lead the blind
     by a way they do not
     know,
In paths they do not know
     I will guide them.
I will *b*make darkness into
     light before them
And *c*rugged places into
     plains.
These are the things I will
     do,
And I will *d*not leave them
     undone."

17 *a*Ps. 97:7;
Is. 1:29;
44:9, 11;
45:16

17 They shall be turned back
     and be *a*utterly put to
     shame,
Who trust in idols,
Who say to molten images,
     "You are our gods."

18 *a*Is.
29:18; 35:5

18 *a*Hear, you deaf!
And look, you blind, that
     you may see.

19 *a*Is. 41:8
*b*Is. 44:26
*c*Is. 26:3;
27:5

19 Who is blind but My *a*ser-
     vant,
Or so deaf as My *b*messen-
     ger whom I send?
Who is so blind as he that
     is *c*at peace *with Me,*
Or so blind as the servant
     of the LORD?

20 *a*Rom.
2:21

20 *a*You have seen many
     things, but you do not
     observe *them;*
Your ears are open, but
     none hears.

21 *a*Is. 42:4;
51:4

21 The LORD was pleased for
     His righteousness'
     sake
To make the law *a*great
     and glorious.

22 *a*Is. 24:18
*b*Is. 24:22

22 But this is a people plun-
     dered and despoiled;
All of them are *a*trapped in
     caves,
Or are *b*hidden away in
     prisons;
They have become a prey
     with none to deliver
     them,

And a spoil, with none to
     say, "Give *them*
     back!"

23 Who among you will give
     ear to this?
Who will give heed and
     listen hereafter?

24 *a*Is. 30:15
*b*Is. 48:18;
57:17

24 Who gave Jacob up for
     spoil, and Israel to
     plunderers?
Was it not the LORD,
     against whom we
     have sinned,
And in whose ways they
     *a*were not willing to
     walk,
And whose law they did
     not *b*obey?

25 *a*Is. 5:25;
9:19 *b*Is.
29:13; 47:7;
57:1; Hos.
7:9

25 So He poured out on him
     the heat of His anger
And the *a*fierceness of bat-
     tle;
And it set him aflame all
     around,
Yet he did not recognize *it;*
And it burned him, but he
     *b*paid no attention.

E In Restoring Israel,
     43:1–44:28

★ 1-7

1 *a*Is. 43:15
*b*Is. 43:7, 21;
44:2, 21, 24
*c*Is. 43:5 *d*Is.
44:22, 23;
48:20 *e*Gen.
32:28; Is.
43:7; 45:3, 4
*f*Is. 43:21

43 But now, thus says the
     LORD, your *a*Creator,
     O Jacob,
And He who *b*formed you,
     O Israel,
"Do not *c*fear, for I have
     *d*redeemed you;
I have *e*called you by
     name; you are *f*Mine!

2 *a*Ps.
66:12; Is.
8:7, 8 *b*Deut.
31:6, 8 *c*Is.
29:6; 30:27-
29; Dan.
3:25, 27

2 "When you *a*pass through
     the waters, *b*I will be
     with you;
And through the rivers,
     they will not overflow
     you.
When you *c*walk through
     the fire, you will not
     be scorched,

42:16 *blind.* Backslidden Jews who worshiped
idols. Details are given in verses 17-22.
43:1-7 Even though Israel was unfaithful, God
still loved her and promised release from
Babylon. As a reward for releasing captive Israel, the Persians under Cambyses, son of Cyrus, were given *Egypt* and parts of *Cush* (Ethiopia) and *Seba* (SW. Arabia). Ultimately (at
the second coming of Christ), Israel will return
from all parts of the *earth* (Matt. 24:31).

Nor will the flame burn you.

3 "For ^aI am the LORD your God,
The Holy One of Israel, your ^bSavior;
I have given Egypt as your ransom,
^cCush and Seba in your place.

4 "Since you are ^aprecious in My sight,
Since you are ^bhonored and I ^clove you,
I will give *other* men in your place and *other* peoples in exchange for your life.

5 "Do not fear, for ^aI am with you;
I will bring ^byour offspring from the east,
And ^cgather you from the west.

6 "I will say to the ^anorth, 'Give *them* up!'
And to the south, 'Do not hold *them* back.'
Bring My ^bsons from afar,
And My daughters from the ^cends of the earth,

7 Everyone who is ^acalled by My name,
And whom I have ^bcreated for My ^cglory,
^dWhom I have formed, even whom I have made."

8 Bring out the people who are ^ablind, even though they have eyes,
And the deaf, even though they have ears.

9 All the nations have ^agathered together
In order that the peoples may be assembled.
Who among them can ^bdeclare this
And proclaim to us the former things?

Let them present ^ctheir witnesses ^dthat they may be justified,
Or let them hear and say, "It is true."

10 "You are ^aMy witnesses," declares the LORD,
"And ^bMy servant whom I have chosen,
In order that you may know and believe Me,
And understand that ^cI am He.
^dBefore Me there was no God formed,
And there will be none after Me.

11 "I, even I, am the LORD;
And there is no ^asavior ^bbesides Me.

12 "It is I who have declared and saved and proclaimed,
And there was no ^astrange *god* among you;
So you are My witnesses," declares the LORD,
"And I am God.

13 "Even ^afrom eternity ^bI am He;
And there is ^cnone who can deliver out of My hand;
^dI act and who can reverse it?"

14 Thus says the LORD your ^aRedeemer, the Holy One of Israel,
"For your sake I have sent to Babylon,
And will bring them all down as fugitives,
Even the ^bChaldeans, into the ^cships in which they rejoice.

15 "I am the LORD, your Holy One,
^aThe Creator of Israel, your ^bKing."

16 Thus says the LORD,
Who ^amakes a way through the sea

43:14–21 God would destroy Babylon and bring His people back to Palestine, a new thing which, when compared to most other wonders of Israel's history, would make those seem as nothing.

Cross references (left column):

3 ^aEx. 20:2 ^bIs. 19:20; 43:11; 45:15, 21; 49:26; 60:16; 63:8 ^cIs. 20:3-5

4 ^aEx. 19:5, 6 ^bIs. 49:5 ^cIs. 63:9

5 ^aIs. 8:10; 43:2 ^bIs. 41:8; 49:12; 61:9 ^cIs. 49:12

6 ^aPs. 107:3 ^b2 Cor. 6:18 ^cIs. 45:22

7 ^aIs. 56:5; 62:2; James 2:7 ^bPs. 100:3; Is. 29:23; Eph. 2:10 ^cIs. 44:23; 46:13 ^dIs. 43:1

8 ^aIs. 6:9; 42:19; Ezek. 12:2

9 ^aIs. 34:1; 41:1 ^bIs. 41:22, 23, 26 ^cIs. 44:9 ^dIs. 43:26

Cross references (right column):

10 ^aIs. 44:8 ^bIs. 41:8 ^cIs. 41:4 ^dIs. 45:5, 6

11 ^aIs. 43:3; 45:21; Hos. 13:4 ^bIs. 44:6, 8

12 ^aDeut. 32:16; Ps. 81:9

13 ^aPs. 90:2; Is. 48:16 ^bIs. 41:4 ^cPs. 50:22 ^dJob 9:12; Is. 14:27

★14-21

14 ^aIs. 41:14 ^bIs. 23:13 ^cJer. 51:13

15 ^aIs. 43:1 ^bIs. 41:20; 44:6

16 ^aEx. 14:21, 22; Ps. 77:19; Is. 11:15; 44:27; 50:2; 51:10; 63:11, 12

And a path through the
mighty waters,

17 Who brings forth the
^achariot and the
horse,
The army and the mighty
man
(They will lie down to-
gether *and* not rise
again;
They have been
^bquenched *and* extin-
guished like a wick):

18 "^aDo not call to mind the
former things,
Or ponder things of the
past.

19 "Behold, I will do some-
thing ^anew,
Now it will spring forth;
Will you not be aware of
it?
I will even ^bmake a road-
way in the wilderness,
Rivers in the desert.

20 "The beasts of the field will
glorify Me;
The ^ajackals and the ostriches;
Because I have ^bgiven waters in the wilderness
And rivers in the desert,
To give drink to My cho-
sen people.

21 "The people whom ^aI
formed for Myself,
^bWill declare My praise.

22 "Yet you have not called on
Me, O Jacob;
But you have become
^aweary of Me, O Is-
rael.

23 "You have ^anot brought to
Me the sheep of your
burnt offerings;
Nor have you ^bhonored
Me with your sacri-
fices.
I have not ^cburdened you
with offerings,

Nor wearied you with ^din-
cense.

24 "You have bought Me no
^asweet cane with
money,
Neither have you filled Me
with the fat of your
sacrifices;
Rather you have burdened
Me with your sins,
You have ^bwearied Me
with your iniquities.

25 "I, even I, am the one who
^awipes out your trans-
gressions ^bfor My
own sake;
And I will ^cnot remember
your sins.

26 "Put Me in remembrance;
^alet us argue our case
together,
State your *cause,* ^bthat you
may be proved right.

27 "Your ^afirst forefather
sinned,
And your ^bspokesmen
have transgressed
against Me.

28 "So I will pollute the princes
of the sanctuary;
And I will consign Jacob to
the ^aban, and Israel to
^brevilement.

44 "But now listen, O Jacob,
My ^aservant;
And Israel, whom I have
chosen:

2 Thus says the Lord who
made you
And ^aformed you from the
womb, who ^bwill help
you,
'^cDo not fear, O Jacob My
servant;
And you ^dJeshurun whom
I have chosen.

3 'For ^aI will pour out water
on the thirsty *land*
And streams on the dry
ground;

Cross-reference column (left):

17 ^aEx. 15:19 ^bPs. 118:12; Is. 1:31

18 ^aIs. 65:17; Jer. 23:7

19 ^aIs. 42:9; 48:6; 2 Cor. 5:17 ^bEx. 17:6; Num. 20:11; Deut. 8:15; Ps. 78:16; Is. 35:1, 6; 41:18, 19; 49:10; 51:3

20 ^aIs. 13:22; 35:7 ^bIs. 41:17, 18; 48:21

21 ^aIs. 43:1 ^bPs. 102:18; Is. 42:12; Luke 1:74, 75; 1 Pet. 2:9

22 ^aMic. 6:3; Mal. 1:13; 3:14

23 ^aAmos 5:25 ^bZech. 7:5, 6; Mal. 1:6-8 ^cJer. 7:21-26 ^dEx. 30:34; Lev. 2:1; 24:7

Cross-reference column (right):

★**24** ^aEx. 30:23; Jer. 6:20 ^bPs. 95:10; Is. 1:14; 7:13; Ezek. 6:9; Mal. 2:17

25 ^aIs. 44:22; 55:7; Jer. 50:20 ^bIs. 37:35; 48:9, 11; Ezek. 36:22 ^cIs. 38:17; Jer. 31:34

26 ^aIs. 1:18; 41:1; 50:8 ^bIs. 43:9

★**27** ^aIs. 51:2; Ezek. 16:3 ^bIs. 9:15; 28:7; 29:10; Jer. 5:31

28 ^aIs. 24:6; 34:5; Jer. 24:9; Dan. 9:11; Zech. 8:13 ^bPs. 79:4; Ezek. 5:15

1 ^aIs. 41:8; Jer. 30:10; 46:27, 28

★ **2** ^aIs. 44:21, 24 ^bIs. 41:10 ^cIs. 43:5 ^dDeut. 32:15; 33:5, 26

3 ^aIs. 41:17; Ezek. 34:26; Joel 3:18 ^bIs. 32:15; Joel 2:28 ^cIs. 61:9; 65:23

43:24 *sweet cane.* An ingredient of the anointing
oil (Exod. 30:23).
43:27 *Your first forefather.* Probably a reference
to Jacob, or possibly Abraham. *your spokes-
men.* Including both prophets and priests. Is-

rael's ancestors and spiritual leaders offered
little to boast of.
44:2 *Jeshurun.* Lit., upright one (cf. Deut. 33:5), a
term of endearment.

I will [b]pour out My Spirit
on your [c]offspring,
And My blessing on your
descendants;

4 [a]Lev.
23:40; Job
40:22

4 And they will spring up
among the grass
Like [a]poplars by streams
of water.'

5 [a]Ex. 13:9;
Neh. 9:38

5 "This one will say, 'I am the
LORD's';
And that one will call on
the name of Jacob;
And another will [a]write on
his hand, 'Belonging
to the LORD,'
And will name Israel's
name with honor.

6 [a]Is.
41:21; 43:15
[b]Is. 41:14;
43:1, 14 [c]Is.
41:4; 43:10;
48:12; Rev.
1:8, 17;
22:13 [d]Is.
43:11; 44:8;
45:5, 6, 21

6 "Thus says the LORD, the
[a]King of Israel
And his [b]Redeemer, the
LORD of hosts:
'I am the [c]first and I am the
last,
And there is no God [d]be-
sides Me.

7 [a]Is.
41:22, 26

7 'And who is like Me? [a]Let
him proclaim and de-
clare it;
Yes, let him recount it to
Me in order,
From the time that I established the ancient na-
tion.
And let them declare to
them the things that
are coming
And the events that are
going to take place.

8 [a]Is. 42:9;
48:5 [b]Is.
43:10 [c]Deut.
4:35, 39;
1 Sam. 2:2;
Is. 45:5; Joel
2:27 [d]Is.
17:10; 26:4;
30:29

8 'Do not tremble and do not
be afraid;
[a]Have I not long since announced it to you and
declared it?
And [b]you are My wit-
nesses.
Is there any God [c]besides
Me,
Or is there any other
[d]Rock?
I know of none.' "

★ 9-20
9 [a]Ps. 97:7;
Is. 42:17;
44:11; 45:16

9 Those who fashion a
graven image are all of them futile, and their precious things are
of no profit; even their own witnesses fail to see or know, so that
they will be [a]put to shame.
10 Who has fashioned a god
or cast an idol to [a]no profit?
11 Behold, all his companions
will be [a]put to shame, for the
craftsmen themselves are mere
men. Let them all assemble themselves, let them stand up, let them
tremble, let them together be put
to shame.
12 The [a]man shapes iron into
a cutting tool, and does his work
over the coals, fashioning it with
hammers, and working it with his
strong arm. He also gets hungry
and his strength fails; he drinks
no water and becomes weary.
13 [a]Another shapes wood, he
extends a measuring line; he outlines it with red chalk. He works
it with planes, and outlines it with
a compass, and makes it like the
form of a man, like the beauty of
[b]man, so that it may sit in a
[c]house.
14 Surely he cuts cedars for
himself, and takes a cypress or an
oak, and raises it for himself
among the trees of the forest. He
plants a fir, and the rain makes it
grow.
15 Then it becomes some-
thing for a man to burn, so he
takes one of them and warms
himself; he also makes a fire to
bake bread. He also [a]makes a god
and worships it; he makes it a
graven image, and [b]falls down before it.
16 Half of it he burns in the
fire; over this half he eats meat as
he roasts a roast, and is satisfied.
He also warms himself and says,
"Aha! I am warm, I have seen the
fire."
17 But the rest of it he [a]makes
into a god, his graven image. He
falls down before it and worships;
he also [b]prays to it and says, "Deliver me, for thou art my god."
18 They do not [a]know, nor
do they understand, for He has
[b]smeared over their eyes so that

10 [a]Is.
41:29; Jer.
10:5; Hab.
2:18; Acts
19:26

11 [a]Ps. 97:7;
Is. 42:17;
44:9; 45:16

12 [a]Is.
40:19, 20;
41:6, 7; 46:6,
7; Jer. 10:3-
5; Hab. 2:18

13 [a]Is. 41:7
[b]Ps. 115:5-7
[c]Judg. 17:4,
5; Ezek.
8:10, 11

15 [a]Is. 44:17
[b]2 Chr.
25:14

17 [a]Is. 44:15
[b]1 Kin.
18:26, 28; Is.
45:20

18 [a]Is. 1:3;
Jer. 10:8, 14
[b]Ps. 81:12;
Is. 6:9, 10;
29:10

44:9–20 Another devastating attack on idolatry
(an intended "vaccination" against the coming
exposure to idolatry in Babylon!).

they cannot see and their hearts so that they cannot comprehend.

19 *a*Is. 5:13; 44:18, 19; 45:20 *b*Deut. 27:15; 1 Kin. 11:5, 7; 2 Kin. 23:13, 14

19 And no one recalls, nor is there *a*knowledge or understanding to say, "I have burned half of it in the fire, and also have baked bread over its coals. I roast meat and eat *it*. Then I make the rest of it into an *b*abomination, I fall down before a block of wood!"

20 *a*Ps. 102:9 *b*Job 15:31; Hos. 4:12; Rom. 1:21, 22; 2 Thess. 2:11; 2 Tim. 3:13 *c*Is. 57:11; 59:3, 4, 13; Rom. 1:25

★21-28

21 *a*Is. 46:8; Zech. 10:9 *b*Is. 44:1, 2 *c*Is. 49:15

20 He *a*feeds on ashes; a *b*deceived heart has turned him aside. And he cannot deliver himself, nor say, "*c*Is there not a lie in my right hand?"

21 "*a*Remember these things, O Jacob, And Israel, for you are *b*My servant; I have formed you, you are My servant, O Israel, you will *c*not be forgotten by Me.

22 *a*Ps. 51:1, 9; Is. 43:25; Acts 3:19 *b*Is. 31:6; 55:7 *c*Is. 43:1; 48:20; 1 Cor. 6:20; 1 Pet. 1:18, 19

22 "I have *a*wiped out your transgressions like a thick cloud, And your sins like a heavy mist. *b*Return to Me, for I have *c*redeemed you."

23 *a*Ps. 69:34; 96:11, 12; Is. 42:10; 49:13 *b*Ps. 98:7, 8; 148:7, 9; Is. 55:12 *c*Is. 43:1 *d*Is. 49:3; 61:3

23 *a*Shout for joy, O heavens, for the LORD has done *it!* Shout joyfully, you lower parts of the earth; *b*Break forth into a shout of joy, you mountains, O forest, and every tree in it; For *c*the LORD has redeemed Jacob And in Israel He *d*shows forth His glory.

24 *a*Is. 41:14; 43:14 *b*Is. 44:2 *c*Is. 40:22; 42:5; 45:12, 18; 51:13

24 Thus says the LORD, your *a*Redeemer, and the one who *b*formed you from the womb,

"I, the LORD, am the maker of all things, *c*Stretching out the heavens by Myself, And spreading out the earth all alone,

25 *a*Is. 47:13 *b*2 Sam. 15:31; Job 5:12-14; Ps. 33:10; Is. 29:14; Jer. 51:57; 1 Cor. 1:20, 27

25 *a*Causing the omens of boasters to fail, Making fools out of diviners, *b*Causing wise men to draw back, And turning their knowledge into foolishness,

26 *a*Zech. 1:6; Matt. 5:18 *b*Is. 40:9 *c*Jer. 32:15, 44

26 *a*Confirming the word of His servant, And performing the purpose of His messengers. *It is* I who says of Jerusalem, 'She shall be inhabited!' And of the *b*cities of Judah, '*c*They shall be built.' And I will raise up her ruins *again.*

27 *a*Is. 42:15; 50:2; Jer. 50:38; 51:36

27 "*It is* I who says to the depth of the sea, 'Be dried up!' And I will make your rivers *a*dry.

28 *a*Is. 45:1 *b*2 Chr. 36:22, 23; Ezra 1:1; Is. 14:32; 45:13; 54:11

28 "*It is* I who says of *a*Cyrus, '*He is* My shepherd! And he will perform all My desire.' And he declares of Jerusalem, '*b*She will be built,' And of the temple, 'Your foundation will be laid.' "

F In Using Cyrus, 45:1-25

★ 1 *a*Is. 44:28 *b*Ps. 73:23; Is. 41:13; 42:6 *c*Is. 41:2, 25; Jer. 50:3, 35; 51:11, 20, 24 *d*Job 12:21; Is. 45:5

45 Thus says the LORD to *a*Cyrus His anointed, Whom I have taken by the right *b*hand,

---

44:21-28 Another prediction of release from Babylon, through the decree of *Cyrus* (cf. Ezra 1).

45:1 *anointed.* Lit., messiah (cf. Cyrus' designation as shepherd in 44:28). This is an appropriate title for a heathen king for two reasons: Cyrus, as a temporal deliverer of God's people, serves as an illustration of Jesus Christ, the eternal Redeemer; and since vassal rulers were anointed by their superior rulers, Cyrus, as one who carried out God's purposes, could properly be said to be an anointed vassal. *open doors.* On the night the Persians captured Babylon some of the men entered on the dry river bed and opened the gates to their armies from the inside.

To [c]subdue nations before him,
And to [d]loose the loins of kings;
To open doors before him so that gates will not be shut:

2 "I will go before you and [a]make the rough places smooth;
I will [b]shatter the doors of bronze, and cut through their iron [c]bars.

3 "And I will give you the [a]treasures of darkness,
And hidden wealth of secret places,
In order that you may know that it is I,
The LORD, the God of Israel, who [b]calls you by your name.

4 "For the sake of [a]Jacob My servant,
And Israel My chosen one,
I have also [b]called you by your name;
I have given you a title of honor
Though you have [c]not known Me.

5 "I am the LORD, and [a]there is no other;
[b]Besides Me there is no God.
I will [c]gird you, though you have not known Me;

6 That [a]men may know from the rising to the setting of the sun
That there is [b]no one besides Me.
I am the LORD, and there is no other,

7 The One [a]forming light and [b]creating darkness,
Causing well-being and [c]creating calamity;
I am the LORD who does all these.

8 "[a]Drip down, O heavens, from above,
And let the clouds pour down righteousness;
Let the [b]earth open up and salvation bear fruit,
[c]And righteousness spring up with it.
I, the LORD, have created it.

9 "Woe to *the one* who [a]quarrels with his Maker—
An earthenware vessel among the vessels of earth!
Will the [b]clay say to the potter, 'What are you doing?'
Or the thing you are making *say*, 'He has no hands'?

10 "Woe to him who says to a father, 'What are you begetting?'
Or to a woman, 'To what are you giving birth?' "

11 Thus says the [a]LORD, the Holy One of Israel, and his [b]Maker:
"[c]Ask Me about the things to come concerning My [d]sons,
And you shall commit to Me [e]the work of My hands.

Marginal references

2 [a]Is. 40:4 [b]Ps. 107:16 [c]Jer. 51:30

★ 3 [a]Jer. 41:8; 50:37 [b]Ex. 33:12, 17; Is. 43:1; 49:1

4 [a]Is. 41:8, 9; 44:1 [b]Is. 43:1 [c]Acts 17:23

★ 5 [a]Is. 45:6, 14, 18, 21; 46:9 [b]Is. 44:6, 8 [c]Ps. 18:39

6 [a]Ps. 102:15; Mal. 1:11 [b]Is. 45:5

★ 7 [a]Is. 42:16 [b]Ps. 104:20; 105:28 [c]Is. 31:2; 47:11; Amos 3:6

8 [a]Ps. 72:6; Hos. 10:12; 14:5; Joel 3:18 [b]Ps. 85:11 [c]Is. 60:21; 61:11

★ 9-10

9 [a]Job 15:25; 40:8, 9; Ps. 2:2, 3; Prov. 21:30; Jer. 50:24 [b]Is. 29:16; 64:8; Jer. 18:6; Rom. 9:20, 21

11 [a]Is. 43:15; 48:17; Ezek. 39:7 [b]Is. 44:2; 54:5 [c]Is. 8:19 [d]Jer. 31:9 [e]Is. 19:25; 29:23; 60:21; 64:8

45:3 As conqueror of Croesus (king of Lydia) and Babylon, Cyrus amassed incalculable *treasures.*

45:5 *you have not known Me.* Though used to carry out God's plan, Cyrus did not personally know God, as evidenced in his ascribing his victories to "the great gods" and his defeat of the Babylonians especially to Marduk, head god of the Babylonian pantheon.

45:7 Included in God's plan are all things (Eph. 1:11), though the responsibility for committing sin rests on the creature, not the Creator.

45:9-10 It is folly to question or criticize God's ways.

12 aIs. 42:5;
45:18; Jer.
27:5 bPs.
104:2; Is.
42:5; 44:24
cGen. 2:1;
Neh. 9:6

12 "It is I who ^amade the earth,
　and created man upon
　it.
I ^bstretched out the heav-
　ens with My hands,
And I ordained ^call their
　host.

★13 aIs.
41:2 bIs.
45:2 c2 Chr.
36:22, 23; Is.
44:28 dIs.
52:3

13 "I have aroused him in
　^arighteousness,
And I will ^bmake all his
　ways smooth;
He will ^cbuild My city, and
　will let My exiles go
　^dfree,
Without any payment or
　reward," says the
　Lord of hosts.

14 aPs.
68:31; Is.
19:21 bIs.
18:1; 43:3
cIs. 14:1, 2;
49:23; 54:3
dPs. 149:8
eIs. 49:23;
60:14 fJer.
16:19; Zech.
8:20-23;
1 Cor. 14:25
gIs. 45:5

14 Thus says the Lord,
"The products of ^aEgypt
　and the merchandise
　of ^bCush
And the Sabeans, men of
　stature,
Will ^ccome over to you
　and will be yours;
They will walk behind
　you, they will come
　over in ^dchains
And will ^ebow down to
　you;
They will make supplica-
　tion to you:
'Surely, ^fGod is with you,
　and ^gthere is none
　else,
No other God.' "

★15 aPs.
44:24; Is.
1:15; 8:17;
57:17 bIs.
43:3

15 Truly, Thou art a God who
　^ahides Himself,
O God of Israel, ^bSavior!

16 aIs.
42:17; 44:9
bIs. 44:11

16 They will be ^aput to shame
　and even humiliated,
　all of them;
The ^bmanufacturers of
　idols will go away to-
　gether in humiliation.

17 aIs. 26:4;
51:6; Rom.
11:26 bIs.
49:23; 50:7;
54:4

17 Israel has been saved by
　the Lord
With an ^aeverlasting salva-
　tion;
You ^bwill not be put to
　shame or humiliated
To all eternity.

18 For thus says the Lord,
　who ^acreated the
　heavens
(He is the God who
　^bformed the earth and
　made it,
He established it and did
　not create it a ^cwaste
　place,
But formed it to be ^dinhab-
　ited),
"I am the Lord, and ^ethere
　is none else.

★18 aIs.
42:5 bIs.
45:12 cGen.
1:2 dGen.
1:26; Ps.
115:16 eIs.
45:5

19 "^aI have not spoken in se-
　cret,
In some dark land;
I did not say to the ^boff-
　spring of Jacob,
'^cSeek Me in a waste place';
I, the Lord, ^dspeak right-
　eousness
^eDeclaring things that are
　upright.

19 aIs. 48:16
bIs. 45:25;
65:9 c2 Chr.
15:2; Ps.
78:34; Jer.
29:13, 14
dPs. 19:8; Is.
45:23; 63:1
eIs. 43:12;
44:8

20 "^aGather yourselves and
　come;
Draw near together, you
　fugitives of the na-
　tions;
^bThey have no knowledge,
Who ^ccarry about their
　wooden idol,
And ^dpray to a god who
　cannot save.

20 aIs. 43:9
bIs. 44:18,
19; 48:5-7
cIs. 46:1, 7;
Jer. 10:5 dIs.
44:17;
46:6, 7

21 "^aDeclare and set forth *your*
　case;
Indeed, let them consult
　together.
^bWho has announced this
　from of old?
Who has long since de-
　clared it?
Is it not I, the Lord?
And there is ^cno other God
　besides Me,
A righteous God and a
　^dSavior;
There is none except Me.

21 aIs.
41:23; 43:9
bIs. 41:26;
44:7; 48:14
cIs. 45:5 dIs.
43:3, 11

22 "^aTurn to Me, and ^bbe
　saved, all the ends of
　the earth;
For I am God, and there is
　no other.

22 aNum.
21:8, 9;
2 Chr. 20:12;
Mic. 7:7;
Zech. 12:10
bIs. 30:15;
49:6, 12;
52:10

45:13 *I have aroused him.* I.e., Cyrus.
45:15 *a God who hides Himself.* In contrast to
idols, the true God is invisible.
45:18 *He . . . did not create it a waste place.*

Though the original condition of the earth was
"formless" (Gen. 1:2), God's intention was
that it should be inhabited, so He filled it with
living things, including man.

★23 aGen.
22:16; Is.
62:8; Heb.
6:13 bIs.
55:11 cRom.
14:11; Phil.
2:10 dDeut.
6:13; Ps.
63:11; Is.
19:18; 65:16

23 "aI have sworn by Myself,
The bword has gone forth
from My mouth in
righteousness
And will not turn back,
That to Me cevery knee
will bow, every
tongue will dswear al-
legiance.

24 aJer.
33:16 bIs.
41:11

24 "They will say of Me, 'Only
ain the Lord are right-
eousness and
strength.'
Men will come to Him,
And ball who were angry
at Him shall be put to
shame.

25 a1 Kin.
8:32; Is.
53:11 bIs.
41:16; 60:19

25 "In the Lord all the offspring of Israel
Will be ajustified, and will
bglory."

G   In Judging Babylon,
46:1–47:15

★ 1 aIs.
2:18; 21:9;
Jer. 50:2-4;
51:44

46 aBel has bowed down,
Nebo stoops over;
Their images are con-
signed to the beasts
and the cattle.
The things that you carry
are burdensome,
A load for the weary beast.

2 aJudg.
18:17, 18,
24; 2 Sam.
5:21; Jer.
43:12, 13;
48:7; Hos.
10:5, 6

2 They stooped over, they
have bowed down to-
gether;
They could not rescue the
burden,
But have themselves agone
into captivity.

3 aIs. 46:12
bIs. 10:21,
22 cPs. 71:6;
Is. 49:1

3 "aListen to Me, O house of
Jacob,
And all bthe remnant of
the house of Israel,
You who have been
cborne by Me from
birth,
And have been carried
from the womb;

4 Even to your old age, aI
shall be the same,
And even to your bgraying
years I shall bear you!
I have done it, and I shall
carry you;
And I shall bear you, and I
shall deliver you.

4 aIs. 41:4;
43:13; 48:12
bPs. 71:18

5 "aTo whom would you lik-
en Me,
And make Me equal and
compare Me,
That we should be alike?

5 aIs.
40:18, 25

6 "Those who alavish gold
from the purse
And weigh silver on the
scale
Hire a goldsmith, and he
makes it into a god;
They bbow down, indeed
they worship it.

6 aIs.
40:19; 41:7;
44:12-17;
Jer. 10:4 bIs.
44:15, 17

7 "They alift it upon the
shoulder and carry it;
They set it in its place and
it stands there.
bIt does not move from its
place.
Though one may cry to it,
it ccannot answer;
It dcannot deliver him
from his distress.

7 aIs.
45:20; 46:1;
Jer. 10:5 bIs.
40:20; 41:7
cIs. 41:28
dIs. 45:20

8 "aRemember this, and be
assured;
bRecall it to mind, you
ctransgressors.

★ 8-11

8 aIs. 44:21
bIs. 44:19
cIs. 50:1

9 "Remember the aformer
things long past,
For I am God, and there is
bno other;
I am God, and there is cno
one like Me,

9 aDeut.
32:7; Is.
42:9; 65:17
bIs. 45:5, 21
cIs. 41:26,
27

10 Declaring the end from the
beginning
And from ancient times
things which have not
been done,
Saying, 'aMy purpose will
be established,
And I will accomplish all
My good pleasure';

10 aPs.
33:11; Prov.
19:21; Is.
14:24; 25:1;
40:8; Acts
5:39

45:23 See Phil. 2:10.
46:1 *Bel.* The Babylonian form of Baal. *Nebo.*
The god of learning. The images of these gods
would be loaded on animals when the Babylonians would flee from the conquering Persians.
46:8-11 Only the true God can predict the future and *bring it to pass* (v. 11). *bird of prey.*
I.e., Cyrus.

11 aIs. 18:6
bIs. 41:2
cNum.
23:19; Is.
14:24; 37:26

11 Calling a ᵃbird of prey
from the ᵇeast,
The man of My purpose
from a far country.
Truly I have ᶜspoken; truly
I will bring it to pass.
I have planned *it, surely* I
will do it.

12 aIs. 46:3
bPs. 76:5; Is.
48:4; Zech.
7:11, 12;
Mal. 3:13
cPs.
119:150; Is.
48:1; Jer. 2:5

13 aIs. 51:5;
61:11; Rom.
3:21 bIs.
61:3; 62:11;
Joel 3:17;
1 Pet. 2:6
cIs. 43:7;
44:23

12 "ᵃListen to Me, you ᵇstub-
born-minded,
Who are ᶜfar from right-
eousness.
13 "I ᵃbring near My righteousness, it is not far
off;
And My salvation will not
delay.
And I will grant ᵇsalvation
in Zion,
And My ᶜglory for Israel.

★ **1-15**

47

1 aIs. 3:26;
Jer. 48:18
bIs. 23:12;
37:22; Jer.
46:11 cPs.
137:8; Jer.
50:42; 51:33;
Zech. 2:7
dDeut. 28:56

"ᵃCome down and sit in
the dust,
O ᵇvirgin ᶜdaughter of
Babylon;
Sit on the ground without
a throne,
O daughter of the Chalde-
ans.
For you shall no longer be
called ᵈtender and
delicate.

2 aEx. 11:5;
Jer. 25:10
bJob 31:10;
Eccl. 12:4;
Matt. 24:41
cGen. 24:65;
Is. 3:23;
1 Cor. 11:5
dIs. 32:11

3 aEzek.
16:37; Nah.
3:5 bIs. 34:8;
63:4

2 "Take the ᵃmillstones and
ᵇgrind meal.
Remove your ᶜveil, ᵈstrip
off the skirt,
Uncover the leg, cross the
rivers.
3 "Your ᵃnakedness will be
uncovered,
Your shame also will be
exposed;
I will ᵇtake vengeance and
will not spare a man."

4 aIs. 41:14

4 Our ᵃRedeemer, the LORD
of hosts is His name,
The Holy One of Israel.

5 aIs. 23:2;
Jer. 8:14;
Lam. 2:10
bIs. 13:10
cIs. 47:7 dIs.
13:19; Dan.
2:37

5 "ᵃSit silently, and go into
ᵇdarkness,
O daughter of the Chalde-
ans;

For you will no more be
called
The ᶜqueen of ᵈkingdoms.
6 "I was angry with My people,
I profaned My heritage,
And gave them into your
hand.
You did not show mercy to
them,
On the ᵃaged you made
your yoke very heavy.
7 "Yet you said, 'I shall be a
ᵃqueen forever.'
These things you did not
ᵇconsider,
Nor remember the ᶜout-
come of them.

6 aDeut.
28:50

7 aIs. 47:5
bIs. 42:25;
57:11 cDeut.
32:29; Jer.
5:31; Ezek.
7:2, 3

8 "Now, then, hear this, you
ᵃsensual one,
Who ᵇdwells securely,
Who says in your heart,
'ᶜI am, and there is no one
besides me.
I shall ᵈnot sit as a widow,
Nor shall I know loss of
children.'
9 "But these ᵃtwo things shall
come on you ᵇsud-
denly in one day:
Loss of children and wid-
owhood.
They shall come on you in
full measure
In spite of your many ᶜsor-
ceries,
In spite of the great power
of your spells.
10 "And you felt ᵃsecure in
your wickedness and
said,
'ᵇNo one sees me,'
Your ᶜwisdom and your
knowledge, they have
deluded you;
For you have said in your
heart,
'ᵈI am, and there is no one
besides me.'

8 aIs.
22:13; 32:9;
Jer. 50:11
bIs. 32:9, 11;
Zeph. 2:15
cIs. 45:5, 6,
18; 47:10;
Zeph. 2:15
dRev. 18:7

9 aIs.
13:16, 18;
14:22 bPs.
73:19;
1 Thess. 5:3;
Rev. 18:8, 10
cIs. 47:13;
Nah. 3:4;
Rev. 18:23

10 aPs. 52:7;
62:10; Is.
59:4 bIs.
29:15; Ezek.
8:12; 9:9 cIs.
5:21; 44:20
dIs. 47:8

47:1-15 A song of triumph over Babylon, who is
charged with pride (vv. 5, 7), excessive cruelty
(the elderly were especially mistreated, v. 6),
and practicing sorcery and divination (vv. 9,
12-15; cf. Deut. 18:9-12). Though this chapter
focuses on the Babylonian Empire that was
crushed by Persia, Babylon in the Bible is also
a symbol of organized humanity in rebellion
against God (see note on Rev. 17:5).

11 *a*Is. 57:1
*b*Is. 13:6;
Jer. 51:8, 43;
Luke 17:27;
1 Thess. 5:3
*c*Is. 47:9

11 "But *a*evil will come on you
Which you will not know
how to charm away;
And disaster will fall on
you
For which you cannot
atone,
And *b*destruction about
which you do not
know
Will come on you *c*sud-
denly.

12 *a*Is. 47:9

12 "Stand *fast* now in your
*a*spells
And in your many sorcer-
ies
With which you have la-
bored from your
youth;
Perhaps you will be able to
profit,
Perhaps you may cause
trembling.

13 *a*Jer.
51:58, 64
*b*Is. 8:19;
44:25; 47:9;
Dan. 2:2, 10
*c*Is. 47:15

13 "You are *a*wearied with
your many counsels;
Let now the *b*astrologers,
Those who prophesy by
the stars,
Those who predict by the
new moons,
Stand up and *c*save you
from what will come
upon you.

14 *a*Is. 5:24;
Nah. 1:10;
Mal. 4:1 *b*Is.
10:17; Jer.
51:30, 32, 58
*c*Is. 44:16

14 "Behold, they have become
*a*like stubble,
*b*Fire burns them;
They cannot deliver them-
selves from the power
of the flame;
There will be *c*no coal to
warm by,
Nor a fire to sit before!

15 *a*Rev.
18:11 *b*Is.
5:29; 43:13;
46:7

15 "So have those become to
you with whom you
have labored,
Who have *a*trafficked with
you from your youth;
Each has wandered in his
own way.
There is *b*none to save you.

H In Releasing Judah from Babylon, 48:1-22

48 "*a*Hear this, O house of Jacob, who are named
Israel
And who came forth from
the *b*loins of Judah,
Who *c*swear by the name
of the Lord
And invoke the God of Is-
rael,
But not in truth nor in
*d*righteousness.

★ 1 *a*Is.
46:12 *b*Num.
24:7; Deut.
33:28; Ps.
68:26 *c*Deut.
6:13; Is.
45:23; 65:16
*d*Is. 58:2;
Jer. 4:2

2 "For they call themselves
after the *a*holy city,
And *b*lean on the God of
Israel;
The Lord of hosts is His
name.

2 *a*Is. 52:1;
64:10 *b*Is.
10:20; Jer.
7:4; 21:2;
Mic. 3:11;
Rom. 2:17

3 "I *a*declared the former
things long ago
And they went forth from
My mouth, and I pro-
claimed them.
*b*Suddenly I acted, and
they *c*came to pass.

★ 3 *a*Is.
41:22; 42:9;
43:9; 44:7, 8;
45:21; 46:10
*b*Is. 29:5;
30:13 *c*Josh.
21:45; Is.
42:9

4 "Because I know that you
are *a*obstinate,
And your *b*neck is an iron
sinew,
And your *c*forehead
bronze,

4 *a*Ex. 32:9;
Deut. 31:27;
Ezek. 2:4;
3:7 *b*2 Chr.
36:13; Prov.
29:1; Acts
7:51 *c*Ezek.
3:7-9

5 Therefore I declared *them*
to you long ago,
Before they took place I
proclaimed *them* to
you,
Lest you should say, 'My
*a*idol has done them,
And my graven image and
my molten image
have commanded
them.'

5 *a*Jer.
44:15-18

6 "You have heard; look at all
this.
And you, will you not de-
clare it?
I proclaim to you *a*new
things from this time,
Even hidden things which
you have not known.

★ 6 *a*Is.
42:9; 43:19

48:1 The people talk of the Lord but practice idolatry (v. 5).
48:3 *the former things.* The predictions of the

Babylonian captivity.
48:6 *new things.* The prophecies of the return from Babylon.

7 "They are created now and
not long ago;
And before today you
have not heard them,
Lest you should say, 'Be-
hold, I knew them.'

8 als.
42:25; 47:11;
Hos. 7:9
bDeut. 9:7,
24; Ps. 58:3;
Is. 46:8

8 "You have not ªheard, you
have not known.
Even from long ago your
ear has not been
open,
Because I knew that you
would deal very
treacherously;
And you have been called
a ᵇrebel from birth.

9 als. 48:11
bNeh. 9:30,
31; Ps.
78:38; 103:8-
10; Is. 30:18;
65:8

9 "ªFor the sake of My name I
ᵇdelay My wrath,
And for My praise I re-
strain it for you,
In order not to cut you off.

★10 aJer.
9:7; Ezek.
22:18-22
bDeut. 4:20;
1 Kin. 8:51;
Jer. 11:4

10 "Behold, I have refined you,
but ªnot as silver;
I have tested you in the
ᵇfurnace of affliction.

11 a1 Sam.
12:22; Ps.
25:11; 106:8;
Is. 37:35;
43:25; Jer.
14:7; Ezek.
20:9, 14, 22,
44; Dan.
9:17-19
bDeut.
32:26, 27; Is.
42:8

11 "ªFor My own sake, for My
own sake, I will act;
For how can My name be
profaned?
And My ᵇglory I will not
give to another.

12 als. 41:4;
43:10-13;
46:4 bls.
44:6; Rev.
1:17; 22:13

12 "Listen to Me, O Jacob,
even Israel whom I
called;
ªI am He, ᵇI am the first, I
am also the last.

13 aEx.
20:11; Ps.
102:25; Is.
42:5; 45:12,
18; Heb.
1:10-12 bls.
40:26

13 "Surely My hand ªfounded
the earth,
And My right hand spread
out the heavens;
When I ᵇcall to them, they
stand together.

★14 als.
43:9; 45:20
bls. 45:21
cls. 46:10,
11 dls. 13:4,
5, 17-19; Jer.
50:21-29;
51:24

14 "ªAssemble, all of you, and
listen!
ᵇWho among them has de-
clared these things?
The Lᴏʀᴅ loves him; he
shall ᶜcarry out His
good pleasure on
ᵈBabylon,

And His arm shall be
against the Chaldeans.

15 als. 41:2;
45:1, 2

15 "I, even I, have spoken; indeed I have ªcalled
him,
I have brought him, and
He will make his ways
successful.

★16 als.
34:1; 41:1;
57:3 bls.
45:19 cls.
43:13
dZech. 2:9,
11

16 "ªCome near to Me, listen
to this:
From the first I have ᵇnot
spoken in secret,
ᶜFrom the time it took
place, I was there.
And now ᵈthe Lᴏʀᴅ Gᴏᴅ
has sent Me, and His
Spirit."

17 als.
41:14; 43:14;
49:7, 26;
54:5, 8 bPs.
32:8; Is.
30:21; 49:9,
10

17 Thus says the Lᴏʀᴅ, your
ªRedeemer, the Holy
One of Israel;
"I am the Lᴏʀᴅ your God,
who teaches you to
profit,
Who ᵇleads you in the way
you should go.

18 aDeut.
5:29; 32:29;
Ps. 81:13-16
bPs.
119:165; Is.
32:16-18;
66:12 cls.
45:8; 61:10,
11; 62:1;
Hos. 10:12;
Amos 5:24

18 "If only you had ªpaid attention to My com-
mandments!
Then your ᵇwell-being
would have been like
a river,
And your ᶜrighteousness
like the waves of the
sea.

19 aGen.
22:17; Is.
10:22; 44:3,
4; 54:3; Jer.
33:22 bls.
56:5; 66:22

19 "Your ªdescendants would
have been like the
sand,
And your offspring like its
grains;
ᵇTheir name would never
be cut off or destroyed
from My presence."

★20-22
20 aJer.
50:8; 51:6,
45; Zech.
2:6, 7; Rev.
18:4 bls.
42:10; 49:13;
52:9 cls.
62:11; Jer.
31:10; 50:2
dls. 43:1;
52:9; 63:9

20 ªGo forth from Babylon!
Flee from the Chalde-
ans!
Declare with the sound of
ᵇjoyful shouting, pro-
claim this,

48:10 but not as silver. Or, with silver. If "with,"
the meaning is that the process of melting
(chastisement for the nation) does not produce
silver. If "as," the meaning is that God would
punish them with an even hotter flame than
required to refine silver.
48:14 him. I.e., Cyrus (though apparently Cyrus
was never redeemed, see 45:5).

48:16 Me. A reference to the preincarnate
Christ, who is here associated with the Lord
Gᴏᴅ and the Spirit, giving us an O.T. glimpse
of the Trinity.
48:20-22 The people are urged to seize the opportunity which would be afforded by Cyrus'
decree to leave Babylon; otherwise, they
would know no peace (v. 22).

cSend it out to the end of the earth;
Say, "dThe LORD has redeemed His servant Jacob."

21 And they did not athirst when He led them through the deserts.
He bmade the water flow out of the rock for them;
He split the rock, and cthe water gushed forth.

22 "aThere is no peace for the wicked," says the LORD.

II THE SALVATION OF THE SERVANT-MESSIAH,
49:1–57:21

A The Servant Commissioned, 49:1–26

49 Listen to Me, O aislands,
And pay attention, you peoples from afar.
bThe LORD called Me from the womb;
From the body of My mother He named Me.

2 And He has made My amouth like a sharp sword;
In the bshadow of His hand He has concealed Me,
And He has also made Me a select carrow;
He has hidden Me in His quiver.

3 And He said to Me, "aYou are My Servant, Israel,
bIn Whom I will show My glory."

4 But I said, "I have atoiled in vain,
I have spent My strength for nothing and vanity;
Yet surely the justice *due* to Me is with the LORD,

And My breward with My God."

5 And now says athe LORD, who formed Me from the womb to be His Servant,
To bring Jacob back to Him, in order that bIsrael might be gathered to Him
(For I am chonored in the sight of the LORD,
And My God is My dstrength),

6 He says, "It is too small a thing that You should be My Servant
To raise up the tribes of Jacob, and to restore the apreserved ones of Israel;
I will also make You a blight of the nations
So that My salvation may reach to the cend of the earth."

7 Thus says the LORD, the aRedeemer of Israel, *and* its Holy One,
To the bdespised One,
To the One abhorred by the nation,
To the Servant of rulers,
"cKings shall see and arise, Princes shall also dbow down;
Because of the LORD who is faithful, the Holy One of Israel who has chosen You."

8 Thus says the LORD, "In a afavorable time I have answered You,
And in a day of salvation I have helped You;
And I will bkeep You and cgive You for a covenant of the people,
To drestore the land, to make *them* inherit the desolate heritages;

---

21 aIs. 30:25; 35:6, 7; 41:17, 18; 43:19, 20; 49:10 bEx. 17:6; Ps. 78:15, 16 cPs. 78:20; 105:41

22 aIs. 57:21

★ 1-7

1 aIs. 42:4 bIs. 44:2, 24; 46:3; Jer. 1:5

2 aIs. 11:4; Heb. 4:12; Rev. 1:16; 2:12, 16 bIs. 51:16 cHab. 3:11

3 aZech. 3:8 bIs. 44:23

4 aIs. 65:23 bIs. 35:4; 59:18

5 aIs. 44:2 bIs. 11:12; 27:12 cIs. 43:4 dIs. 12:2

6 aPs. 37:28; 97:10 bIs. 42:6; 51:4; Luke 2:32; Acts 13:47; 26:23 cIs. 48:20

7 aIs. 48:17 bPs. 22:6-8; 69:7-9; Is. 53:3 cIs. 52:15 dIs. 19:21, 23; 27:13; 66:23

8 aPs. 69:13; 2 Cor. 6:2 bIs. 26:3; 27:3; 42:6 cIs. 42:6 dIs. 44:26

49:1-7 *Servant.* Here the Messiah (cf. 41:8; 42:1), called *Israel* because in Him alone all of God's expectations were realized (49:3). His mission is to *restore* Israel to God and to bring *light* to the Gentiles (v. 6). Though *despised* at His first coming, He will be worshiped at His second coming (v. 7).

9 aIs. 42:7;
61:1; Luke
4:18 bIs.
41:18

9 Saying to those who are
 abound, 'Go forth,'
To those who are in dark-
ness, 'Show your-
selves.'
Along the roads they will
feed,
And their pasture will be
on all bbare heights.

10 aIs.
33:16; 48:21;
Rev. 7:16
bPs. 121:6
cIs. 14:1
dPs. 23:2; Is.
40:11 eIs.
35:7; 41:17

10 "They will anot hunger or
thirst,
Neither will the scorching
bheat or sun strike
them down;
For cHe who has compas-
sion on them will
dlead them,
And will guide them to
esprings of water.

11 aIs. 40:4
bIs. 11:16;
19:23; 35:8;
62:10

11 "And I will make all aMy
mountains a road,
And My bhighways will be
raised up.

★12 aIs.
49:1; 60:4
bIs. 43:5, 6

12 "Behold, these shall come
afrom afar;
And lo, these will come
from the bnorth and
from the west,
And these from the land of
Sinim."

13 aIs. 44:23
bIs. 40:1;
51:3, 12 cIs.
54:7, 8, 10

13 aShout for joy, O heavens!
And rejoice, O earth!
Break forth into joyful
shouting, O moun-
tains!
For the bLord has com-
forted His people,
And will chave compassion
on His afflicted.

★14-26

14 But Zion said, "The Lord
has forsaken me,
And the Lord has forgotten
me."

15 aIs. 44:21

15 "Can a woman forget her
nursing child,
And have no compassion
on the son of her
womb?
Even these may forget, but
aI will not forget you.

16 aSong
8:6; Hag.
2:23 bPs.
48:12, 13; Is.
62:6, 7

16 "Behold, I have ainscribed
you on the palms of
My hands;
Your bwalls are continually
before Me.

17 aIs. 10:6;
37:18

17 "Your builders hurry;
Your adestroyers and
devastators
Will depart from you.

18 aIs. 60:4;
John 4:35
bIs. 43:5;
54:7; 60:4
cIs. 49:12
dIs. 45:23;
54:9 eIs.
52:1; 61:10

18 "aLift up your eyes and look
around;
bAll of them gather to-
gether, cthey come to
you.
dAs I live," declares the
Lord,
"You shall surely eput on all
of them as jewels, and
bind them on as a
bride.

19 aIs. 1:7;
3:8; 5:6; 51:3
bIs. 54:1, 2;
Zech. 10:10
cPs. 56:1, 2

19 "For ayour waste and desolate places, and your
destroyed land—
Surely now you will be
btoo cramped for the
inhabitants,
And those who cswallowed
you will be far away.

20 aIs.
54:1-3

20 "The achildren of whom
you were bereaved
will yet say in your
ears,
'The place is too cramped
for me;
Make room for me that I
may live here.'

21 aIs.
29:23; 54:6,
7 bIs. 27:10;
Lam. 1:1 cIs.
5:13 dIs. 1:8
eIs. 60:8

21 "Then you will asay in your
heart,
'Who has begotten these
for me,
Since I have been bereaved
of my children,
And am bbarren, an cexile
and a wanderer?
And who has reared these?
Behold, I was dleft alone;
eFrom where did these
come?'"

22 aIs.
11:10, 12;
18:3; 62:10
bIs. 14:2;
43:6; 60:4

22 Thus says the Lord God,
"Behold, I will lift up My
hand to the nations,

49:12 Sinim. The identification is uncertain, perhaps Aswan in Egypt.
49:14-26 Here the Lord encourages His people
who will be in captivity. He has not forgotten
them (vv. 14-18); He will restore them to their
land (vv. 19-23) and punish their enemies (vv.
24-26).

And set up My ^astandard
to the peoples;
And they will ^bbring your
sons in *their* bosom,
And your daughters will
be carried on *their*
shoulders.

23 "And ^akings will be your
guardians,
And their princesses your
nurses.
They will ^bbow down to
you with their faces to
the earth,
And ^click the dust of your
feet;
And *you* will ^dknow that I
am the LORD;
Those who hopefully ^ewait
for Me will ^fnot be
put to shame.

24 "^aCan the prey be taken
from the mighty man,
Or the captives of a tyrant
be rescued?"

25 Surely, thus says the LORD,
"Even the ^acaptives of the
mighty man will be
taken away,
And the prey of the tyrant
will be rescued;
For I will contend with the
one who contends
with you,
And I will ^bsave your sons.

26 "And I will feed your
^aoppressors with their
^bown flesh,
And they will become
drunk with their own
blood as with sweet
wine;
And ^call flesh will know
that I, the LORD, am
your ^dSavior,
And your ^eRedeemer, the
Mighty One of Ja-
cob."

B   The Servant Contrasted with Disobedient Israel, 50:1-11

50 Thus says the LORD,
"Where is the ^acertificate of
divorce,
By which I have ^bsent your
mother away?
Or to whom of My credi-
tors did I ^csell you?
Behold, you were sold for
your ^diniquities,
And for your ^etransgres-
sions your mother
^fwas sent away.

2 "Why was there ^ano man
when I came?
When I called, *why* was
there none to answer?
Is My ^bhand so short that
it cannot ransom?
Or have I no power to de-
liver?
Behold, I ^cdry up the sea
with My rebuke,
I ^dmake the rivers a wilderness;
Their fish stink for lack of
water,
And die of thirst.

3 "I ^aclothe the heavens with
blackness,
And I make sackcloth their
covering."

4   The Lord GOD has given
Me the tongue of ^adis-
ciples,
That I may know how to
^bsustain the weary
one with a word.
He awakens *Me* ^cmorning
by morning,
He awakens My ear to lis-
ten as a disciple.

5   The Lord GOD has ^aopened
My ear;
And I was ^bnot disobedi-
ent,
Nor did I turn back.

Cross references

23 ^aIs. 14:1, 2; 60:3, 10, 11 ^bIs. 45:14; 60:14 ^cPs. 72:9; Mic. 7:17 ^dIs. 41:20; 43:10; 60:16 ^ePs. 37:9; Is. 25:9; 26:8 ^fPs. 25:3; Is. 45:17; Joel 2:27

24 ^aMatt. 12:29; Luke 11:21

25 ^aIs. 10:6; 14:1, 2; Jer. 50:33, 34 ^bIs. 25:9; 33:22; 35:4

26 ^aIs. 9:4; 14:4; 16:4; 51:13; 54:14 ^bIs. 9:20 ^cIs. 45:6; Ezek. 39:7 ^dIs. 43:3 ^eIs. 49:7

★ 1 ^aDeut. 24:1, 3; Jer. 3:8 ^bIs. 54:6, 7 ^cDeut. 32:30; 2 Kin. 4:1; Neh. 5:5 ^dIs. 52:3; 59:2 ^eIs. 1:28; 43:27 ^fJer. 3:8

2 ^aIs. 41:28; 59:16; 66:4 ^bGen. 18:14; Num. 11:23; Is. 59:1 ^cEx. 14:21; Is. 19:5; 43:16; 44:27 ^dJosh. 3:16; Is. 42:15

3 ^aIs. 13:10; Rev. 6:12

★ 4-9

4 ^aIs. 8:16; 54:13 ^bIs. 57:19; Jer. 31:25 ^cPs. 5:3; 88:13; 119:147; 143:8

5 ^aPs. 40:6; Is. 35:5 ^bMatt. 26:39; John 8:29; 14:31; 15:10; Acts 26:19; Phil. 2:8; Heb. 5:8; 10:7

50:1 The Lord charges Israel with the responsibility for her coming captivity and divorce
from Himself.
50:4-9 By contrast, the true Servant gives total
obedience, especially in the sufferings leading
to His death (v. 6; cf. Matt. 26:67; 27:28-31,

39-44; John 19:1-3). *who pluck out the beard.*
The beard was a sign of respect; to pluck it out
was therefore a gesture of utter contempt.
they (v. 9). The enemies and accusers of the
Lord.

6 *a*Matt.
26:67; 27:30;
Mark 14:65;
15:19; Luke
22:63

6 I *a*gave My back to those
who strike *Me,*
And My cheeks to those
who pluck out the
beard;
I did not cover My face
from humiliation and
spitting.

7 *a*Is. 42:1;
49:8 *b*Is.
45:17; 54:4
*c*Ezek. 3:8, 9

7 For the Lord GOD *a*helps
Me,
Therefore, I am *b*not dis-
graced;
Therefore, I have set My
face like *c*flint,
And I know that I shall not
be ashamed.

8 *a*Is.
45:25; Rom.
8:33, 34 *b*Is.
1:18; 41:1;
43:26

8 He who *a*vindicates Me is
near;
Who will contend with
Me?
Let us *b*stand up to each
other;
Who has a case against
Me?
Let him draw near to Me.

9 *a*Is. 41:10
*b*Is. 54:17
*c*Job 13:28;
Is. 51:8

9 Behold, *a*the Lord GOD
helps Me;
*b*Who is he who condemns
Me?
Behold, *c*they will all wear
out like a garment;
The moth will eat them.

10 *a*Is. 49:2,
3; 50:4 *b*Is.
9:2; 26:9;
Eph. 5:8 *c*Is.
12:2; 26:4

10 Who is among you that
fears the LORD,
That obeys the voice of
His *a*servant,
That *b*walks in darkness
and has no light?
Let him *c*trust in the name
of the LORD and rely
on his God.

★11 *a*Prov.
26:18; Is.
9:18; James
3:6 *b*Is. 8:22;
65:13-15;
Amos 4:9, 10

11 Behold, all you who
*a*kindle a fire,
Who encircle yourselves
with firebrands,
Walk in the light of your
fire
And among the brands
you have set ablaze.
This you will have from
My hand;

And you will *b*lie down in
torment.

C   The Remnant Encouraged and Exhorted, 51:1–52:12

★ 1-3

1 *a*Is. 46:3;
48:12; 51:7
*b*Ps. 94:15;
Prov. 15:9
*c*Gen. 17:15-
17

51 "*a*Listen to me, you who
*b*pursue righteous-
ness,
Who seek the LORD:
Look to the *c*rock from
which you were
hewn,
And to the quarry from
which you were dug.

2 *a*Is.
29:22; 41:8;
63:16 *b*Gen.
12:1; 15:5;
Deut. 1:10;
Ezek. 33:24

2 "Look to *a*Abraham your
father,
And to Sarah who gave
birth to you in pain;
When *he* *b*was one I called
him,
Then I blessed him and
multiplied him."

3 *a*Is. 40:1;
49:13 *b*Is.
52:9 *c*Is.
35:1; 41:19
*d*Gen. 2:8;
Joel 2:3
*e*Gen. 13:10
*f*Is. 25:9;
41:16; 65:18;
66:10

3 Indeed, *a*the LORD will
comfort Zion;
He will comfort all her
*b*waste places.
And her *c*wilderness He
will make like *d*Eden,
And her desert like the
*e*garden of the LORD;
*f*Joy and gladness will be
found in her,
Thanksgiving and sound
of a melody.

4 *a*Ps. 50:7;
78:1 *b*Deut.
18:18; Is.
2:3; Mic. 4:2
*c*Is. 1:27;
42:4 *d*Is.
42:6; 49:6

4 "*a*Pay attention to Me, O
My people;
And give ear to Me, O My
nation;
For a *b*law will go forth
from Me,
And I will set My *c*justice
for a *d*light of the peoples.

5 *a*Is.
46:13; 54:17
*b*Is. 40:10
*c*Is. 42:4;
60:9 *d*Is.
59:16; 63:5

5 "My *a*righteousness is near,
My salvation has gone
forth,
And My *b*arms will judge
the peoples;
The *c*coastlands will wait
for Me,

50:11 The self-reliant, who try to illumine the
darkness by their own light, will only know
sorrow.
51:1-3 The faithful are encouraged to remember
their past (v. 1) and the power of God that

brought forth a great nation from a single couple: an old man, and a woman beyond the age
of childbearing (Gen. 17:17; 18:11). This same
powerful God would restore His people to
their land after the Babylonian captivity.

And for My ^darm they will wait expectantly.

6 ^aIs. 40:26
^bPs. 102:25,
26; Is. 13:13;
34:4; Matt.
24:35; Heb.
1:10-12;
2 Pet. 3:10
^cIs. 45:17;
51:8

6 "^aLift up your eyes to the sky,
Then look to the earth beneath;
For the ^bsky will vanish like smoke,
And the ^bearth will wear out like a garment,
And its inhabitants will die in like manner,
But My ^csalvation shall be forever,
And My righteousness shall not wane.

7 ^aIs. 51:1
^bPs. 37:31
^cIs. 25:8;
54:4; Matt.
5:11; Acts
5:41

7 "^aListen to Me, you who know righteousness,
A people in whose ^bheart is My law;
Do not fear the ^creproach of man,
Neither be dismayed at their revilings.

8 ^aIs. 50:9
^bIs. 14:11;
66:24 ^cIs.
51:6

8 "For the ^amoth will eat them like a garment,
And the ^bgrub will eat them like wool.
But My ^crighteousness shall be forever,
And My salvation to all generations."

★ **9** ^aIs.
51:17; 52:1
^bEx. 6:6;
Deut. 4:34
^cJob 26:12;
Ps. 89:10; Is.
30:7 ^dPs.
74:13; Is.
27:1

9 ^aAwake, awake, put on strength, O arm of the LORD;
Awake as in the ^bdays of old, the generations of long ago.
^cWas it not Thou who cut Rahab in pieces,
Who pierced the ^ddragon?

★**10** ^aIs.
11:15, 16;
50:2; 63:11,
12 ^bEx.
15:13; Ps.
106:10; Is.
63:9

10 Was it not Thou who ^adried up the sea,
The waters of the great deep;
Who made the depths of the sea a pathway
For the ^bredeemed to cross over?

★**11-23**
11 ^aIs.
35:10; Jer.
31:11, 12
^bIs. 60:19;
61:7 ^cIs.
25:8; 60:20;
65:19; Rev.
7:17; 21:1, 4;
22:3

11 So the ^aransomed of the LORD will return,

And come with joyful shouting to Zion;
And ^beverlasting joy *will be* on their heads.
They will obtain gladness and joy,
And ^csorrow and sighing will flee away.

12 ^aIs. 51:3
^bPs. 118:6;
Is. 2:22 ^cIs.
40:6, 7;
1 Pet. 1:24

12 "I, even I, am He who ^acomforts you.
Who are you that you are afraid of ^bman who dies,
And of the son of man who is made ^clike grass;

13 ^aDeut.
6:12; 8:11;
Is. 17:10
^bJob 9:8; Ps.
104:2; Is.
40:22; 45:12,
18; 48:13
^cIs. 7:4;
10:24 ^dIs.
49:26; 54:14

13 That you have ^aforgotten the LORD your Maker,
Who ^bstretched out the heavens,
And laid the foundations of the earth;
That you ^cfear continually all day long because of the fury of the oppressor,
As he makes ready to destroy?
But where is the fury of the ^doppressor?

14 ^aIs.
48:20; 52:2
^bIs. 33:6;
49:10

14 "The ^aexile will soon be set free, and will not die in the dungeon, ^bnor will his bread be lacking.

15 ^aPs.
107:25; Jer.
31:35

15 "For I am the LORD your God, who ^astirs up the sea and its waves roar (the LORD of hosts is His name).

16 ^aDeut.
18:18; Is.
59:21 ^bEx.
33:22; Is.
49:2 ^cIs.
66:22

16 "And I have ^aput My words in your mouth, and have ^bcovered you with the shadow of My hand, to ^cestablish the heavens, to found the earth, and to say to Zion, 'You are My people.' "

17 ^aIs. 51:9;
52:1 ^bJob
21:20; Is.
29:9; 63:6;
Jer. 25:15;
Rev. 14:10;
16:19

17 ^aRouse yourself! Rouse yourself! Arise, O Jerusalem,
You who have ^bdrunk from the LORD's hand the cup of His anger;
The chalice of reeling you have drained to the dregs.

51:9 *Rahab.* The chaos monster of mythology symbolizing Egypt (as in 30:7).
51:10 See the account in Exod. 14.
51:11-23 The exiles are promised comfort and

help on their return journey (vv. 11-16), and Jerusalem would prosper again after the battering and slaughter the Babylonians would inflict (v. 20).

18 aPs.
88:18; 142:4;
Is. 49:21

18 There is ^anone to guide
    her among all the sons
    she has borne;
Nor is there one to take
    her by the hand
    among all the sons
    she has reared.

19 aIs. 8:21;
9:20; 14:30

19 These two things have be-
    fallen you;
Who will mourn for you?
The ^adevastation and de-
    struction, famine and
    sword;
How shall I comfort you?

20 aIs. 5:25;
Jer. 14:16
bDeut. 14:5
cIs. 66:15

20 Your sons have fainted,
They ^alie *helpless* at the
    head of every street,
Like an ^bantelope in a net,
Full of the wrath of the
    LORD,
The ^crebuke of your God.

21 aIs. 54:11
bIs. 29:9;
51:17; 63:6

21 Therefore, please hear
    this, you ^aafflicted,
Who are ^bdrunk, but not
    with wine:

22 aIs. 3:12,
13; 49:25;
Jer. 50:34
bIs. 51:17

22 Thus says your Lord, the
    LORD, even your God
Who ^acontends for His
    people,
"Behold, I have taken out of
    your hand the ^bcup of
    reeling;
The chalice of My anger,
You will never drink it
    again.

23 aIs.
49:26; Jer.
25:15-17, 26,
28; Zech.
12:2 bJosh.
10:24

23 "And I will ^aput it into the
    hand of your tormen-
    tors,
Who have said to you,
    '^bLie down that we
    may walk over you.'
You have even made your
    back like the ground,
And like the street for
    those who walk over
    it."

1 aIs. 51:9,
17 bEx.
28:2, 40;
1 Chr. 16:29;
Ps. 110:3; Is.
49:18; 61:3,
10; Zech. 3:4
cNeh. 11:1;
Is. 48:2;
64:10; Zech.
14:20, 21;
Matt. 4:5;
Rev. 21:2-27
dIs. 35:8

52 ^aAwake, awake,
    Clothe yourself in your
        strength, O Zion;
    Clothe yourself in your
        ^bbeautiful garments,

O Jerusalem, the ^choly
    city.
For the uncircumcised and
    the ^dunclean
Will no more come into
    you.

2 Shake yourself ^afrom the
    dust, ^brise up,
O captive Jerusalem;
^cLoose yourself from the
    chains around your
    neck,
O captive daughter of
    Zion.

2 aIs. 29:4
bIs. 60:1 cIs.
9:4; 10:27;
14:25; Zech.
2:7

3 For thus says the LORD,
"You were ^asold for nothing and
you will be ^bredeemed ^cwithout
money."

★ 3 aPs.
44:12; Jer.
15:13 bIs.
1:27; 62:12;
63:4 cIs.
45:13

4 For thus says the Lord
GOD, "My people ^awent down at
the first into Egypt to reside there,
then the Assyrian oppressed them
without cause.

4 aGen.
46:6

5 "Now therefore, what do I
have here," declares the LORD,
"seeing that My people have been
taken away without cause?"
Again the LORD declares, "Those
who rule over them howl, and My
^aname is continually blasphemed
all day long.

5 aEzek.
36:20, 23;
Rom. 2:24

6 "Therefore My people shall
^aknow My name; therefore in
that day I am the one who is
speaking, 'Here I am.' "

6 aIs. 49:23

7 How lovely on the moun-
    tains
Are the feet of him who
    brings ^agood news,
Who announces peace
And brings good news of
    happiness,
Who announces salvation,
And says to Zion, "Your
    ^bGod reigns!"

★ 7 aIs.
40:9; 61:1;
Nah. 1:15;
Rom. 10:15;
Eph. 6:15
bPs. 93:1; Is.
24:23

8 Listen! Your watchmen lift
    up *their* ^avoices,
They shout joyfully to-
    gether;
For they will see with their
    own eyes

8 aIs. 62:6

52:3 Israel was *sold* into captivity *for nothing* of
value and would be released from Babylon
without paying any ransom. Egypt and Assyria also tyrannized Israel without cause and
God delivered His people (v. 4).

52:7 Here the *good news* is the announcement
of the exiles' return to Jerusalem, but Paul applies this verse to messengers of the Gospel
(Rom. 10:15).

When the LORD restores Zion.

9 aPs. 98:4;
Is. 44:23 bIs.
44:26; 51:3;
61:4 cIs.
43:1; 48:20

9 aBreak forth, shout joyfully together,
You bwaste places of Jerusalem;
For the LORD has comforted His people,
He has credeemed Jerusalem.

10 aPs.
98:1-3; Is.
51:9; 66:18,
19 bIs.
45:22; 48:20

10 The LORD has bared His holy aarm
In the sight of all the nations,
That ball the ends of the earth may see
The salvation of our God.

★11-12

11 aIs.
48:20; Jer.
50:8; Zech.
2:6, 7; 2 Cor.
6:17 bNum.
19:11, 16
cLev. 22:2;
Is. 1:16

11 aDepart, depart, go out from there,
bTouch nothing unclean;
Go out of the midst of her,
cpurify yourselves,
You who carry the vessels of the LORD.

12 aEx.
12:11, 33;
Deut. 16:3
bIs. 26:7;
42:16; 49:10,
11 cEx.
14:19, 20; Is.
58:8

12 But you will not go out in ahaste,
Nor will you go as fugitives;
For the bLORD will go before you,
And cthe God of Israel *will be* your rear guard.

D The Suffering and Triumph of the Servant, 52:13–53:12

★52:13-
53:12
★13-15

13 aIs. 42:1;
49:1-7; 53:11
bIs. 57:15;
Phil. 2:9

14 aIs.
53:2, 3

13 Behold, My aservant will prosper,
He will be high and lifted up, and greatly bexalted.
14 Just as many were astonished at you, *My people,*
So His aappearance was marred more than any man,
And His form more than the sons of men.

15 aNum.
19:18-21;
Ezek. 36:25
bJob 21:5
cRom.
15:21; Eph.
3:5

15 Thus He will asprinkle many nations,
Kings will bshut their mouths on account of Him;
For cwhat had not been told them they will see,
And what they had not heard they will understand.

★ 1-3

1 aJohn
12:38; Rom.
10:16

53 aWho has believed our message?
And to whom has the arm of the LORD been revealed?

52:11-12 This exhortation is addressed to those in Babylon who would have to choose between staying in relative security there or risking the long journey back to Palestine. Those who left would not leave in *haste,* since they would have the protection of Cyrus and, more importantly, the Lord.

52:13-53:12 One of the most treasured and important passages in the O.T. These verses present the Servant suffering vicariously for men's sins. Traditional Jewish interpretation understood the passage to be speaking of Messiah, as, of course, did the early Christians, who believed Jesus to be that Messiah (Acts 8:35). Not until the 12th century did the view emerge that the nation Israel is referred to, a view that has since become dominant in Judaism. But the Servant is distinguished from the "people" (Isa. 53:8), and He is an innocent victim, something that could not be said of the nation (53:9). The passage divides into 5 sections of 3 verses each: (1) 52:13-15, (2) 53:1-3,

(3) 53:4-6, (4) 53:7-9, (5) 53:10-12.
52:13-15 The preeminence of the Servant. *high and lifted up* (v. 13). The same words used of God in 6:1 (cf. Phil. 2:9-11). As a result of the mistreatment done Him by Pilate's soldiers, Messiah's *appearance was marred* (Isa. 52:14) so that He could scarcely be recognized as human. Because of His sacrifice He would be able to *sprinkle* (v. 15) many, as a priest does in order to purify them (cf. 1 Pet. 1:2).
53:1-3 The person of the Servant. The *arm of the LORD* (v. 1) represents the power of the Lord in past miracles and in the future miracles of Messiah. *tender shoot* (v. 2). Lit., a suckling; i.e., frail (contrast 11:1). *root out of parched ground* (53:2). Refers to Messiah's lowly background. There would be nothing in His personal appearance that would especially attract men to Him (v. 2b). He would experience *sorrows* (lit., pains, v. 3) but men would not recognize His worth.

2 ªIs. 11:1
ᵇIs. 52:14

2 For He grew up before Him like a ªtender shoot,
And like a root out of parched ground;
He has ᵇno *stately* form or majesty
That we should look upon Him,
Nor appearance that we should be attracted to Him.

3 ªPs. 22:6;
Is. 49:7; Luke
18:31-33 ᵇIs.
53:10 ᶜMark
10:33, 34
ᵈJohn 1:10,
11

3 He was ªdespised and forsaken of men,
A man of sorrows, and ᵇacquainted with grief;
And like one from whom men hide their face,
He was ᶜdespised, and we did not ᵈesteem Him.

★ **4-6**

4 ªMatt.
8:17 ᵇJohn
19:7

4 Surely our griefs He Himself ªbore,
And our sorrows He carried;
Yet we ourselves esteemed Him stricken,
Smitten of ᵇGod, and afflicted.

5 ªIs. 53:8;
Heb. 9:28
ᵇIs. 53:10;
Rom. 4:25;
1 Cor. 15:3
ᶜDeut. 11:2;
Heb. 5:8
ᵈ1 Pet. 2:24,
25

5 But He was pierced through for ªour transgressions,
He was crushed for ᵇour iniquities;
The ᶜchastening for our well-being *fell* upon Him,
And by ᵈHis scourging we are healed.

6 All of us like sheep have gone astray,
Each of us has turned to his own way;

But the LORD has caused the iniquity of us all
To fall on Him.

7 He was oppressed and He was afflicted,
Yet He did not ªopen His mouth;
ᵇLike a lamb that is led to slaughter,
And like a sheep that is silent before its shearers,
So He did not open His mouth.

★ **7-9**

7 ªMatt.
26:63; 27:12-
14; Mark
14:61; 15:5;
Luke 23:9;
John 19:9
ᵇActs 8:32,
33; Rev. 5:6

8 By oppression and judgment He was taken away;
And as for His generation, who considered
That He was cut off out of the land of the living,
ªFor the transgression of my people to whom the stroke *was due?*

8 ªIs. 53:5,
12

9 His grave was assigned with wicked men,
Yet He was with a ªrich man in His death,
ᵇBecause He had ᶜdone no violence,
Nor was there any deceit in His mouth.

9 ªMatt.
27:57-60 ᵇIs.
42:1-3
ᶜ1 Pet. 2:22

10 But the LORD was pleased To ªcrush Him, ᵇputting *Him* to grief;
If He would render Himself *as* a guilt ᶜoffering,
He will see ᵈHis offspring,
He will prolong His days,
And the good ᵉpleasure of the LORD will prosper in His hand.

★ **10-12**

10 ªIs. 53:5
ᵇIs. 53:3, 4
ᶜIs. 53:6, 12;
John 1:29
ᵈPs. 22:30;
Is. 54:3;
61:9; 66:22
ᵉIs. 46:10

53:4-6 The passion of the Servant. Though men would think that God was causing the Servant to suffer for His own sins, the truth was that He suffered vicariously for theirs. *pierced through* (v. 5). A term appropriate to crucifixion. *chastening for our well-being.* I.e., His punishment which obtained peace or well-being for us.

53:7-9 The passivity of the Servant. *He did not open His mouth* (v. 7). See Matt. 26:63-64; Jesus did affirm His deity when placed under oath. Compare Isa. 53:9 with Matt. 27:57-60.

53:10-12 The portion of the Servant. His whole being, including *His soul* (v. 11), was involved in the *offering* (v. 10) (the word used in Lev. 6-7 of the trespass offering, which required 120% restitution, Lev. 6:5). *His offspring* (Isa. 53:10) are those who would believe on Him. To *prolong His days* after being made an offering would necessitate bodily resurrection. *By His knowledge* (v. 11). I.e., by knowledge of Him (cf. Rom. 3:26). *the great* (Isa. 53:12). Lit., the many, as in Isa. 53:11.

11 aJohn
10:14-18 bIs.
45:25; Rom.
5:18, 19 cIs.
53:5, 6

11 As a result of the anguish
of His soul,
He will asee *it* and be satis-
fied;
By His bknowledge the
Righteous One,
My Servant, will justify
the many,
As He will cbear their iniq-
uities.

12 aIs.
52:13; Phil.
2:9-11
bMatt. 26:38,
39, 42 cMark
15:28; Luke
22:37 dIs.
53:6, 11;
2 Cor. 5:21

12 Therefore, I will allot Him
a aportion with the
great,
And He will divide the
booty with the strong;
Because He poured out
bHimself to death,
And was cnumbered with
the transgressors;
Yet He Himself dbore the
sin of many,
And interceded for the
transgressors.

E **Salvation through the
Servant, 54:1-57:21**

1 *The song of salvation,
54:1-17*

1 aGal.
4:27 bIs.
62:4 c1 Sam.
2:5; Is. 49:20

54 "aShout for joy, O barren
one, you who have
borne no *child;*
Break forth into joyful
shouting and cry
aloud, you who have
not travailed;
For the sons of the bdesolate one *will be* cmore
numerous
Than the sons of the mar-
ried woman," says the
Lord.

★ 2 aIs.
33:20; 49:19,
20 bEx.
35:18; 39:40

2 "aEnlarge the place of your
tent;
Stretch out the curtains of
your dwellings, spare
not;
Lengthen your bcords,
And strengthen your
bpegs.

3 aGen.
28:14; Is.
43:5, 6; 60:3
bIs. 14:1, 2
cIs. 49:19

3 "For you will aspread
abroad to the right
and to the left.

And your descendants will
bpossess nations,
And they will cresettle the
desolate cities.

4 "Fear not, for you will anot
be put to shame;
Neither feel humiliated,
for you will not be
disgraced;
But you will forget the
bshame of your youth,
And the creproach of your
widowhood you will
remember no more.

★ 4-10

4 aIs. 45:17
bJer. 31:19
cIs. 4:1;
25:8; 51:7

5 "For your ahusband is your
Maker,
Whose name is the Lord of
hosts;
And your bRedeemer is
the Holy One of Is-
rael,
Who is called the cGod of
all the earth.

5 aJer.
3:14; Hos.
2:19 bIs.
43:14; 48:17
cIs. 6:3;
11:9; 65:16

6 "For the Lord has called
you,
Like a wife aforsaken and
grieved in spirit,
Even like a wife of *one's*
youth when she is re-
jected,"
Says your God.

6 aIs.
49:14-21;
50:1, 2; 62:4

7 "For a abrief moment I for-
sook you,
But with great compassion
I will bgather you.

7 aIs. 26:20
bIs. 11:12;
43:5; 49:18

8 "In an aoutburst of anger
I hid My face from you for
a moment;
But with everlasting blov-
ingkindness I will
chave compassion on
you,"
Says the Lord your dRe-
deemer.

8 aIs. 60:10
bIs. 54:10;
63:7 cIs.
49:10, 13
dIs. 54:5

9 "For this is like the days of
Noah to Me;
When I swore that the wa-
ters of Noah
Should anot flood the earth
again,

9 aGen.
9:11 bIs.
12:1; Ezek.
39:29

54:2 The illustration of the enlarging of postexilic Israel is that of a bedouin tent, easily
enlarged by adding skins, lengthening *cords,*
and putting down stronger *pegs.*

54:4-10 Judah in exile is viewed as a wife separated from her husband (the Lord) but eventually to be restored (cf. v. 9 with Gen. 9:11).

So I have sworn that I will
    [b]not be angry with
    you,
Nor will I rebuke you.

10 "For the [a]mountains may be
    removed and the hills
    may shake,
But My lovingkindness
    will not be removed
    from you,
And My [b]covenant of
    peace will not be
    shaken,"
Says [c]the Lord who has
    compassion on you.

11 "O [a]afflicted one, storm-
    tossed, and [b]not com-
    forted,
Behold, I will set your
    stones in antimony,
And your foundations I
    will [c]lay in [d]sapphires.
12 "Moreover, I will make
    your battlements of
    rubies,
And your gates of crystal,
And your entire wall of
    precious stones.
13 "And [a]all your sons will be
    taught of the Lord;
And the well-being of
    your sons will be
    [b]great.
14 "In [a]righteousness you will
    be established;
You will be far from [b]op-
    pression, for you will
    [c]not fear;
And from [d]terror, for it
    will not come near
    you.
15 "If anyone fiercely assails
    you it will not be from
    Me.
[a]Whoever assails you will
    fall because of you.
16 "Behold, I Myself have cre-
    ated the smith who
    blows the fire of coals,

And brings out a weapon
    for its work;
And I have created the de-
    stroyer to ruin.
17 "[a]No weapon that is formed
    against you shall pros-
    per;
And [b]every tongue that ac-
    cuses you in judgment
    you will condemn.
This is the heritage of the
    servants of the Lord,
And their [c]vindication is
    from Me," declares
    the Lord.

2 The invitation of salvation, 55:1-13

55 "Ho! Every one who
    [a]thirsts, come to the
    waters;
And you who have [b]no
    money come, buy and
    eat.
Come, buy [c]wine and milk
    [d]Without money and
    without cost.
2 "Why do you spend money
    for what is [a]not bread,
And your wages for what
    does not satisfy?
Listen carefully to Me, and
    [b]eat what is good,
And [c]delight yourself in
    abundance.
3 "[a]Incline your ear and come
    to Me.
Listen, that you may [b]live;
And I will make [c]an ever-
    lasting covenant with
    you,
According to the [d]faithful
    mercies shown to Da-
    vid.
4 "Behold, I have made [a]him
    a witness to the peo-
    ples,
A [b]leader and commander
    for the peoples.

10 [a]Ps.
102:26; Is.
51:6 [b]2 Sam.
23:5; Ps.
89:34; Is.
55:3; 59:21;
61:8 [c]Is.
54:8

★**11-17**
11 [a]Is. 51:21
[b]Is. 51:18,
19 [c]Is.
14:32; 28:16;
44:28 [d]Job
28:16; Rev.
21:19

13 [a]John
6:45 [b]Is.
48:18; 66:12

14 [a]Is. 1:26,
27; 9:7; 62:1
[b]Is. 9:4; 14:4
[c]Is. 54:4 [d]Is.
33:18

15 [a]Is.
41:11-16

17 [a]Is.
17:12-14;
29:8 [b]Is.
50:8, 9 [c]Is.
45:24; 46:13

★ **1-2**
1 [a]Ps. 42:1,
2; 63:1;
143:6; Is.
41:17; 44:3;
John 4:14;
7:37; Rev.
21:6 [b]Lam.
5:4 [c]Song
5:1; Joel
3:18 [d]Hos.
14:4; Matt.
10:8

2 [a]Eccl.
6:2; Hos. 8:7
[b]Ps. 22:26;
Is. 1:19;
62:8, 9 [c]Is.
25:6; Jer.
31:14

★ **3** [a]Is.
51:4 [b]Lev.
18:5; Rom.
10:5 [c]Is.
61:8 [d]Acts
13:34

4 [a]Ps.
18:43; Jer.
30:9; Hos.
3:5 [b]Ezek.
34:24; 37:24,
25; Dan.
9:25; Mic.
5:2

54:11-17 The full accomplishment of what is described here for Israel awaits the millennial
age.
55:1-2 Eternal life cannot be bought, only received as a gift.

55:3 *everlasting covenant.* Also called the new
covenant (Jer. 31:31; 32:40; Heb. 13:20), it is as
enduring as the covenant made with David
(2 Sam. 7).

5 ªIs.
45:14, 22-24;
49:6, 12, 23
ᵇZech. 8:22
ᶜIs. 60:9

5 "Behold, you will call a ªnation you do not know,
And a nation which knows you not will ᵇrun to you,
Because of the LORD your God, even the Holy One of Israel;
For He has ᶜglorified you."

6 ªPs. 32:6;
Is. 45:19, 22;
49:8; Amos
5:6 ᵇIs. 58:9;
65:24

7 ªIs. 1:16,
19; 58:6 ᵇIs.
32:7; 59:7
ᶜIs. 31:6;
44:22 ᵈIs.
14:1; 54:8,
10 ᵉIs. 1:18;
40:2; 43:25;
44:22

6 ªSeek the LORD while He may be found;
ᵇCall upon Him while He is near.

7 ªLet the wicked forsake his way,
And the unrighteous man his ᵇthoughts;
And let him ᶜreturn to the LORD,
And He will have ᵈcompassion on him;
And to our God,
For He will ᵉabundantly pardon.

8 ªIs. 65:2;
66:18 ᵇIs.
53:6

8 "For My thoughts are not ªyour thoughts,
Neither are ᵇyour ways My ways," declares the LORD.

9 ªPs.
103:11

9 "For ªas the heavens are higher than the earth,
So are My ways higher than your ways,
And My thoughts than your thoughts.

10 ªIs. 30:23
ᵇ2 Cor. 9:10

10 "For as the ªrain and the snow come down from heaven,
And do not return there without watering the earth,
And making it bear and sprout,
And furnishing ᵇseed to the sower and bread to the eater;

11 ªIs.
45:23; Matt.
24:35 ᵇIs.
44:26; 59:21
ᶜIs. 46:10;
53:10

11 So shall My ªword be which goes forth from My mouth;
It shall ᵇnot return to Me empty,

Without ᶜaccomplishing what I desire,
And without succeeding in the matter for which I sent it.

12 ªPs.
105:43; Is.
51:11; 52:9,
13; Jer.
29:11 ᶜIs.
44:23; 49:13
ᵈ1 Chr.
16:33

12 "For you will go out with ªjoy,
And be led forth with ᵇpeace;
The ᶜmountains and the hills will break forth into shouts of joy before you,
And all the ᵈtrees of the field will clap their hands.

13 ªIs. 7:19
ᵇIs. 60:13
ᶜIs. 5:6;
7:24; 32:13
ᵈIs. 63:12,
14; Jer. 33:9
ᵉIs. 19:20
ᶠIs. 56:5

13 "Instead of the ªthorn bush the ᵇcypress will come up;
And instead of the ᶜnettle the myrtle will come up;
And it will be a ᵈmemorial to the LORD,
For an everlasting ᵉsign which ᶠwill not be cut off."

3   Millennial blessings extended to gentiles, 56:1-8

56 Thus says the LORD,
"ªPreserve justice, and do righteousness,
For My ᵇsalvation is about to come
And My righteousness to be revealed.

★ 1-2

1 ªIs. 1:17;
33:5; 61:8
ᵇPs. 85:9; Is.
46:13; 51:5

2 "How ªblessed is the man who does this,
And the son of man who ᵇtakes hold of it;
Who ᶜkeeps from profaning the sabbath,
And keeps his hand from doing any evil."

2 ªPs.
112:1; 119:1,
2 ᵇIs. 56:4, 6
ᶜEx. 20:8-
11; 31:13-17;
Is. 56:6;
58:13; Jer.
17:21, 22;
Ezek. 20:12,
20

3 Let not the ªforeigner who has joined himself to the LORD say,
"The LORD will surely separate me from His people."

★ 3-8

3 ªIs. 14:1;
56:6 ᵇDeut.
23:1; Jer.
38:7; Acts
8:27

56:1-2 An admonition for Israel to maintain a good testimony both after the return from Babylon and in the kingdom age.
56:3-8 An assurance that non-Israelites will enjoy the blessings of the kingdom age. Special concern is shown for *eunuchs*, who were then excluded from the congregation (Deut. 23:1).

Neither let the [b]eunuch say, "Behold, I am a dry tree."

4 For thus says the LORD,
"To the eunuchs who [a]keep My sabbaths,
And choose what pleases Me,
And [b]hold fast My covenant,

5 als. 2:2,
3; 56:7;
66:20 bls.
26:1; 60:18
cls. 62:2 dls.
48:19; 55:13

5 To them I will give in My [a]house and within My [b]walls a memorial,
And a name better than that of sons and daughters;
I will give them an everlasting [c]name which [d]will not be cut off.

6 "Also the [a]foreigners who join themselves to the LORD,
To minister to Him, and to love the name of the LORD,
To be His servants, every one who [b]keeps from profaning the sabbath,
And holds fast My covenant;

7 als. 2:2,
3; 60:11;
Mic. 4:1, 2
bls. 11:9;
65:25 cls.
61:10 dls.
60:7 eMatt.
21:13; Mark
11:17; Luke
19:46

7 Even [a]those I will bring to My [b]holy mountain,
And [c]make them joyful in My house of prayer.
Their burnt offerings and their sacrifices will be acceptable on [d]My altar;
For [e]My house will be called a house of prayer for all the peoples."

8 The Lord GOD, who [a]gathers the dispersed of Israel, declares,
"Yet [b]others I will gather to them, to those *already* gathered."

4 *Rebuke to those who refuse salvation,* 56:9–57:21

9 All you [a]beasts of the field,
All you beasts in the forest,
Come to eat.

10 His [a]watchmen are [b]blind,
All of them know nothing.
All of them are dumb dogs unable to bark,
Dreamers lying down, who love to slumber;

11 And the dogs are [a]greedy, they are not satisfied.
And they are shepherds who have [b]no understanding;
They have all [c]turned to their own way,
Each one to his unjust gain, to the last one.

11 als. 28:7;
Ezek. 13:19;
Mic. 3:5, 11
bls. 1:3 cls.
57:17; Jer.
22:17

12 "Come," *they* say, "let us get [a]wine, and let us drink heavily of strong drink;
And [b]tomorrow will be like today, only more so."

57

The righteous man perishes, and no man [a]takes it to heart;
And devout men are taken away, while no one understands.
For the righteous man is taken away from [b]evil,

★ 1-13
1 als.
42:25; 47:7
b2 Kin.
22:20; Is.
47:11; Jer.
18:11

2 He enters into peace;
They rest in their beds,
Each one who [a]walked in his upright way.

3 "But come here, you sons of a [a]sorceress,
[b]Offspring of an adulterer and a [c]prostitute.

4 "Against whom do you jest?
Against whom do you open wide your mouth

56:9-12 These verses rebuke professional prophets for being *watchmen* that are blind (Jer. 6:17; Ezek. 33:7) and *dogs* that do not bark.
57:1-13 The people are no better than their leaders and are rebuked for being insensitive to righteousness (vv. 1-2), for idolatry (including sex orgies and infant sacrifices, vv. 3-8), and for lack of trust in God (vv. 9-13).

And stick out your tongue?
Are you not children of
   ªrebellion,
Offspring of deceit,

5 Who inflame yourselves
   among the ªoaks,
   ᵇUnder every luxuriant
   tree,
Who ᶜslaughter the chil-
   dren in the ravines,
Under the clefts of the
   crags?

6 "Among the ªsmooth *stones*
   of the ravine
Is your portion, they are
   your lot;
Even to them you have
   ᵇpoured out a liba-
   tion,
You have made a grain of-
   fering.
Shall I ᶜrelent concerning
   these things?

7 "Upon a ªhigh and lofty
   mountain
You have ᵇmade your bed.
You also went up there to
   offer sacrifice.

8 "And behind the door and
   the doorpost
You have set up your sign;
Indeed, far removed from
   Me, you have ªuncov-
   ered yourself;
And have gone up and
   made your bed wide.
And you have made an
   agreement for your-
   selves with them,
You have loved their bed,
You have looked on *their*
   manhood.

9 "And you have journeyed
   to the king with oil
And increased your per-
   fumes;
You have ªsent your en-
   voys a great distance,
And made *them* go down
   to Sheol.

10 "You were tired out by the
   length of your road,
Yet you did not say, 'ªIt is
   hopeless.'

You found renewed
   strength,
Therefore you did not
   faint.

11 "Of ªwhom were you wor-
   ried and fearful,
When you lied, and did
   ᵇnot remember Me,
Nor ᶜgive *Me* a thought?
Was I not silent even for a
   long time
So you do not fear Me?

12 "I will ªdeclare your righteousness and your
   ᵇdeeds,
But they will not profit
   you.

13 "When you cry out, ªlet
   your collection *of*
   idols deliver you.
But the wind will carry all
   of them up,
And a breath will take
   them away.
But he who ᵇtakes refuge
   in Me shall ᶜinherit
   the land,
And shall ᵈpossess My
   holy mountain."

14 And it shall be said,
"ªBuild up, build up, prepare the way,
Remove *every* obstacle out
   of the way of My peo-
   ple."

15 For thus says the ªhigh and
   exalted One
Who ᵇlives forever, whose
   name is Holy,
"I ᶜdwell *on* a high and holy
   place,
And *also* with the ᵈcontrite
   and lowly of spirit
In order to ᵉrevive the
   spirit of the lowly
And to revive the heart of
   the contrite.

16 "For I will ªnot contend forever,
ᵇNeither will I always be
   angry;
For the spirit would grow
   faint before Me,

5 ªIs. 1:29
ᵇ2 Kin. 16:4;
Jer. 2:20;
3:13 ᶜ2 Kin.
23:10; Ps.
106:37, 38;
Jer. 7:31

6 ªJer. 3:9;
Hab. 2:19
ᵇJer. 7:18
ᶜJer. 5:9, 29;
9:9

7 ªJer. 3:6;
Ezek. 16:16
ᵇEzek. 23:41

8 ªEzek.
23:18

9 ªEzek.
23:16, 40

10 ªJer.
2:25; 18:12

11 ªProv.
29:25; Is.
51:12, 13
ᵇJer. 2:32;
3:21 ᶜPs.
50:21; Is.
42:14

12 ªIs. 58:1,
2 ᵇIs. 29:15;
59:6; 65:7;
66:18; Mic.
3:2-4

13 ªJer.
22:20; 30:14
ᵇPs. 37:3, 9;
Is. 25:4 ᶜIs.
49:8; 60:21
ᵈIs. 65:9

★**14-21**

14 ªIs.
62:10; Jer.
18:15

15 ªIs. 52:13
ᵇDeut.
33:27; Is.
40:28 ᶜIs.
33:5; 66:1
ᵈPs. 34:18;
51:17; Is.
66:2 ᵉPs.
147:3; Is.
61:1-3

16 ªGen. 6:3
ᵇPs. 85:5;
103:9; Mic.
7:18 ᶜIs.
42:5

57:14-21 God encourages the repentant and humble (notice v. 15 especially) and warns the wicked (vv. 20-21).

And the ^cbreath *of those whom* I have made.

^{17 a}Is. 2:7;
56:11; Jer.
6:13 ^bIs. 1:4;
Jer. 3:14, 22

17 "Because of the iniquity of his ^aunjust gain I was angry and struck him;
I hid *My face* and was angry,
And he went on ^bturning away, in the way of his heart.

^{18 a}Is.
19:22; 30:26;
53:5 ^bIs.
52:12 ^cIs.
61:1-3

18 "I have seen his ways, but I will ^aheal him;
I will ^blead him and ^crestore comfort to him and to his mourners,

^{19 a}Is. 6:7;
51:16; 59:21;
Heb. 13:15
^bIs. 26:12;
32:17 ^cActs
2:39; Eph.
2:17

19 Creating the ^apraise of the lips.
^bPeace, peace to him who is ^cfar and to him who is near,"
Says the LORD, "and I will heal him."

^{20 a}Job
18:5-14; Is.
3:9, 11

20 But the ^awicked are like the tossing sea,
For it cannot be quiet,
And its waters toss up refuse and mud.

^{21 a}Is.
48:22; 59:8
^bIs. 49:4

21 "^aThere is no peace," says ^bmy God, "for the wicked."

III   THE PROGRAM OF GOD FOR PEACE, 58:1—66:24

A   The Contrast between Right and Wrong Worship, 58:1-14

★ 1-7

^{1 a}Is. 40:6
^bIs. 43:27;
50:1; 59:12

58

"^aCry loudly, do not hold back;
Raise your voice like a trumpet,
And declare to My people their ^btransgression,
And to the house of Jacob their sins.

^{2 a}Is. 1:11;
Titus 1:16
^bIs. 48:1;
Jer. 7:9, 10
^cIs. 1:4, 28;
59:13 ^dPs.
119:150; Is.
29:13; 57:3;
James 4:8

2 "Yet they ^aseek Me day by day, and delight to know My ways,
As a nation that has done ^brighteousness,
And ^chas not forsaken the ordinance of their God.

They ask Me *for* just decisions,
They delight ^din the nearness of God.

^{3 a}Mal.
3:14; Luke
18:12 ^bIs.
22:12, 13;
Zech. 7:5, 6

3 'Why have we ^afasted and Thou dost not see?
Why have we humbled ourselves and Thou dost not notice?'
Behold, on the ^bday of your fast you find *your* desire,
And drive hard all your workers.

^{4 a}Is. 3:14,
15; 59:6 ^bIs.
1:15; 59:2;
Joel 2:12-14

4 "Behold, you fast for contention and ^astrife and to strike with a wicked fist.
You do not fast like *you do* today to ^bmake your voice heard on high.

^{5 a}1 Kin.
21:27 ^bIs.
49:8; 61:2

5 "Is it a fast like this which I choose, a day for a man to humble himself?
Is it for bowing one's head like a reed,
And for spreading out ^asackcloth and ashes as a bed?
Will you call this a fast, even an ^bacceptable day to the LORD?

^{6 a}Neh.
5:10-12; Jer.
34:8 ^bIs.
1:17 ^cIs.
58:9

6 "Is this not the fast which I chose,
To ^aloosen the bonds of wickedness,
To undo the bands of the yoke,
And to ^blet the oppressed go free,
And ^cbreak every yoke?

^{7 a}Job
31:19, 20; Is.
58:10; Ezek.
18:7, 16 ^bIs.
16:3, 4; Heb.
13:2 ^cMatt.
25:35, 36;
Luke 3:11
^dDeut. 22:1-
4; Luke
10:31, 32

7 "Is it not to ^adivide your bread with the hungry,
And ^bbring the homeless poor into the house;
When you see the ^cnaked, to cover him;
And not to ^dhide yourself from your own flesh?

^{8 a}Is. 58:10
^bIs. 30:26;
33:24; Jer.
30:17; 33:6
^cPs. 85:13;
Is. 62:1 ^dEx.
14:19; Is.
52:12

8 "Then your ^alight will break out like the dawn,

58:1-7 Going through the motions of fasting is not as important as concern for the poor (cf. 1:10-17; Matt. 23:13-36).

And your [b]recovery will speedily spring forth;
And your [c]righteousness will go before you;
The glory of the [d]LORD will be your rear guard.

9 "Then you will [a]call, and the LORD will answer;
You will cry, and He will say, 'Here I am.'
If you [b]remove the yoke from your midst,
The [c]pointing of the finger, and [d]speaking wickedness,

10 And if you [a]give yourself to the hungry,
And satisfy the desire of the afflicted,
Then your [b]light will rise in darkness,
And your gloom *will become* like midday.

11 "And the [a]LORD will continually guide you,
And [b]satisfy your desire in scorched places,
And [c]give strength to your bones;
And you will be like a [d]watered garden,
And like a [e]spring of water whose waters do not fail.

12 "And those from among you will [a]rebuild the ancient ruins;
You will [b]raise up the age-old foundations;
And you will be called the repairer of the [c]breach,
The restorer of the streets in which to dwell.

13 "If because of the sabbath, you [a]turn your foot
From doing your *own* pleasure on My holy day,
And call the sabbath a [b]delight, the holy *day* of the LORD honorable,

And shall honor it, desisting from your [c]own ways,
From seeking your *own* pleasure,
And [d]speaking *your own* word,

14 Then you will take [a]delight in the LORD,
And I will make you ride [b]on the heights of the earth;
And I will feed you *with* the heritage of Jacob your father,
For the [c]mouth of the LORD has spoken."

B The Dealing with Sin, 59:1–21

1 Description of Israel's sins, 59:1–8

59 Behold, [a]the LORD's hand is not so short
That it cannot save;
[b]Neither is His ear so dull
That it cannot hear.

2 But your [a]iniquities have made a separation between you and your God,
And your sins have hidden *His* face from you, so that He does [b]not hear.

3 For your [a]hands are defiled with blood,
And your fingers with iniquity;
Your lips have spoken [b]falsehood,
Your tongue mutters wickedness.

4 [a]No one sues righteously and [b]no one pleads honestly.
They [c]trust in confusion, and speak lies;
They [d]conceive mischief, and bring forth iniquity.

Margin references

★ **9** [a]Ps. 50:15; Is. 55:6; 65:24 [b]Is. 58:6 [c]Prov. 6:13 [d]Ps. 12:2; Is. 59:13

10 [a]Deut. 15:7; Is. 58:7 [b]Job 11:17; Ps. 37:6; Is. 42:16; 58:8

11 [a]Is. 49:10; 57:18 [b]Ps. 107:9; Is. 41:17 [c]Is. 66:14 [d]Song 4:15; Is. 27:3; Jer. 31:12 [e]John 4:14; 7:38

12 [a]Is. 49:8; 61:4; Ezek. 36:10 [b]Is. 44:28 [c]Is. 30:13; Amos 9:11

★**13** [a]Ex. 31:16, 17; 35:2, 3; Is. 56:2, 4, 6; Jer. 17:21-27 [b]Ps. 27:4; 42:4; 84:2, 10 [c]Is. 55:8 [d]Is. 59:13

14 [a]Job 22:26; Is. 61:10 [b]Deut. 32:13; 33:29; Is. 33:16; Hab. 3:19 [c]Is. 1:20; 40:5

1 [a]Num. 11:23; Is. 50:2; Jer. 32:17 [b]Is. 58:9; 65:24; Ezek. 8:18

2 [a]Is. 1:15; 50:1 [b]Is. 58:4

3 [a]Is. 1:15, 21; Jer. 2:30, 34; Ezek. 7:23; Hos. 4:2 [b]Is. 28:15; 30:9; 59:13

4 [a]Is. 5:7; 59:14 [b]Is. 59:14, 15 [c]Is. 30:12; Jer. 7:4, 8 [d]Job 15:35; Ps. 7:14; Is. 33:11

58:9 *the yoke.* I.e., oppression. *The pointing of the finger.* A gesture of contempt.

58:13 *If . . . you turn your foot.* I.e., if you do not use the Sabbath for work.

★ 5 aJob
8:14

5 They hatch adders' eggs
and aweave the spi-
der's web;
He who eats of their eggs
dies,
And *from* that which is
crushed a snake
breaks forth.

6 aIs. 28:20
bIs. 57:12;
Jer. 6:7 cIs.
58:4; Ezek.
7:11

6 Their webs will not be-
come clothing,
Nor will they acover themselves with their
works;
Their bworks are works of
iniquity,
And an cact of violence is
in their hands.

★ 7 aProv.
1:16; 6:17;
Rom. 3:15-17
bIs. 65:2;
66:18; Mark
7:21, 22

7 aTheir feet run to evil,
And they hasten to shed
innocent blood;
bTheir thoughts are
thoughts of iniquity;
Devastation and destruc-
tion are in their high-
ways.

8 aLuke
1:79 bIs.
59:9, 11;
Hos. 4:1 cIs.
57:20, 21

8 They do not know the
away of peace,
And there is bno justice in
their tracks;
They have made their
paths crooked;
cWhoever treads on them
does not know peace.

2 Confession of Israel's sins,
59:9-15

9 aIs. 59:14
bIs. 5:30;
8:21, 22

9 Therefore, ajustice is far
from us,
And righteousness does
not overtake us;
We bhope for light, but
behold, darkness;
For brightness, but we
walk in gloom.

10 aDeut.
28:29; Job
5:14 bIs.
8:14, 15;
28:13 cLam.
3:6

10 We agrope along the wall
like blind men,
We grope like those who
have no eyes;
We bstumble at midday as
in the twilight,
Among those who are vig-
orous we are clike
dead men.

11 All of us growl like bears,
And amoan sadly like
doves;
We hope for bjustice, but
there is none,
For salvation, *but* it is far
from us.

11 aIs.
38:14; Ezek.
7:16 bIs.
59:9, 14

12 For our atransgressions are
multiplied before
Thee,
And our bsins testify
against us;
For our transgressions are
with us,
And we know our iniqui-
ties:

12 aEzra 9:6;
Is. 58:1 bIs.
3:9; Jer.
14:7; Hos.
5:5

13 Transgressing and adeny-
ing the LORD,
And turning away from
our God,
Speaking boppression and
revolt,
Conceiving *in* and cutter-
ing from the heart
lying words.

13 aJosh.
24:27; Prov.
30:9; Matt.
10:33; Titus
1:16 bIs. 5:7;
30:12; Jer.
9:3, 4 cIs.
59:3, 4; Mark
7:21, 22

14 And ajustice is turned
back,
And brighteousness stands
far away;
For truth has stumbled in
the street,
And uprightness cannot
enter.

14 aIs. 1:21;
5:7 bIs.
46:12; Hab.
1:4

15 Yes, truth is lacking;
And he who turns aside
from evil amakes him-
self a prey.

15 aIs. 5:23;
10:2; 29:21;
32:7 bIs.
1:21-23

Now the LORD saw,
And it was displeasing in
His sight bthat there
was no justice.

3 Blotting out of Israel's sins,
59:16-21

16 And He saw that there was
ano man,
And was astonished that
there was no one to
intercede;
Then His bown arm
brought salvation to
Him;

★16 aIs.
41:28; 63:5;
Ezek. 22:30
bPs. 98:1; Is.
52:10; 63:5

59:5 *adders'*. Poisonous snakes'; i.e., the hypocritical people were like poisonous snakes.
59:7 Compare Rom. 3:15-17.

59:16 Because there was no qualified human
mediator, God *brought salvation* at the first
advent of Jesus Christ.

And His righteousness upheld Him.

★17-21

17 ^aEph.
6:14 ^bEph.
6:17;
1 Thess. 5:8
^cIs. 63:2, 3
^dIs. 9:7;
37:32; Zech.
1:14

17 And He put on ^arighteousness like a breastplate,
And a ^bhelmet of salvation on His head;
And He put on ^cgarments of vengeance for clothing,
And wrapped Himself with ^dzeal as a mantle.

18 ^aJob
34:11; Is.
65:6, 7; 66:6;
Jer. 17:10

18 ^aAccording to *their* deeds,
so He will repay,
Wrath to His adversaries,
recompense to His enemies;
To the coastlands He will make recompense.

19 ^aIs. 49:12
^bPs. 113:3
^cIs. 30:28;
66:12

19 So they will fear the name of the LORD from the ^awest
And His glory from the ^brising of the sun,
For He will ^ccome like a rushing stream,
Which the wind of the LORD drives.

20 ^aRom.
11:26 ^bEzek.
18:30, 31;
Acts 2:38, 39

20 "And a ^aRedeemer will come to Zion,
And to those who ^bturn from transgression in Jacob," declares the LORD.

21 ^aJer.
31:31-34;
Rom. 11:27
^bIs. 11:2;
32:15; 44:3
^cIs. 55:11

21 "And as for Me, this is My ^acovenant with them," says the LORD: "My ^bSpirit which is upon you, and My ^cwords which I have put in your mouth, shall not depart from your mouth, nor from the mouth of your offspring, nor from the mouth of your offspring's offspring," says the LORD, "from now and forever."

C The Glory of Israel in the Millennial Kingdom, 60:1-22

60 "^aArise, shine; for your ^blight has come,
And the ^cglory of the LORD has risen upon you.

2 "For behold, ^adarkness will cover the earth,
And deep darkness the peoples;
But the LORD will rise upon you,
And His ^bglory will appear upon you.

3 "And ^anations will come to your light,
And kings to the brightness of your rising.

4 "^aLift up your eyes round about, and see;
They all gather together, they ^bcome to you.
Your sons will come from afar,
And your ^cdaughters will be carried in the arms.

5 "Then you will see and be ^aradiant,
And your heart will thrill and rejoice;
Because the ^babundance of the sea will be turned to you,
The ^cwealth of the nations will come to you.

6 "A multitude of camels will cover you,
The young camels of Midian and ^aEphah;
All those from ^bSheba will come;

★ 1 ^aIs.
52:2 ^bIs.
60:19, 20
^cIs. 24:23;
35:2; 58:8

2 ^aIs.
58:10; Jer.
13:16; Col.
1:13 ^bIs. 4:5

★ 3 ^aIs. 2:3;
45:14, 22-25;
49:23

4 ^aIs.
11:12; 49:18
^bIs. 49:20-22
^cIs. 43:6;
49:22

★ 5 ^aPs.
34:5 ^bIs.
23:18; 24:14
^cIs. 61:6

★ 6-7

6 ^aGen.
25:4 ^bGen.
25:3; Ps.
72:10 ^cIs.
60:9; Matt.
2:11 ^dIs.
42:10

59:17-21 At His second advent He will judge His enemies (vv. 17-19) and bring salvation to Israel (vv. 20-21; cf. Rom. 11:26-27). The word for *Redeemer* (Isa. 59:20) means kinsman-redeemer; i.e., one who is related by blood to those he redeems, indicating the necessity for the incarnation (Heb. 2:14-16).

60:1 This chapter describes the glory of Jerusalem and Israel in the millennial kingdom (including previews seen in the return from

Babylon). *your . . . you.* Referring to Jerusalem.

60:3 The truth will come to the *nations* (Gentiles) through the preaching of the Gospel of Christ (cf. 42:6).

60:5 The *nations* (Gentiles) will share in the blessings of the millennial kingdom (cf. 11:10).

60:6-7 *Midian, Ephah, Sheba, Kedar* and *Nebaioth* are all associated with the Arabian desert.

They will bring [c]gold and
frankincense,
And will [d]bear good news
of the praises of the
LORD.

7 "All the flocks of [a]Kedar
will be gathered to-
gether to you,
The rams of Nebaioth will
minister to you;
They will go up with ac-
ceptance on My [b]altar,
And I shall [c]glorify My
glorious house.

8 "[a]Who are these who fly
like a cloud,
And like the doves to their
lattices?

9 "Surely the [a]coastlands will
wait for Me;
And the [b]ships of Tarshish
will come first,
To [c]bring your sons from
afar,
Their silver and their gold
with them,
For the name of the LORD
your God,
And for the Holy One of
Israel because He has
[d]glorified you.

10 "And [a]foreigners will build
up your walls,
And their [b]kings will minister to you;
For in My [c]wrath I struck
you,
And in My favor I have
had compassion on
you.

11 "And your [a]gates will be
open continually;
They will not be closed
day or night,
So that *men* may [b]bring to
you the wealth of the
nations,
With [c]their kings led in
procession.

12 "For the [a]nation and the
kingdom which will
not serve you will per-
ish,
And the nations will be utterly ruined.

13 "The [a]glory of Lebanon will
come to you,
The [b]juniper, the box tree,
and the cypress to-
gether,
To beautify the place of
My sanctuary;
And I shall make the
[c]place of My feet glo-
rious.

14 "And the [a]sons of those
who afflicted you will
come bowing to you,
And all those who de-
spised you will bow
themselves at the
soles of your feet;
And they will call you the
[b]city of the LORD,
The [c]Zion of the Holy One
of Israel.

15 "Whereas you have been
[a]forsaken and [b]hated
With no one passing
through,
I will make you an ever-
lasting [c]pride,
A joy from generation to
generation.

16 "You will also [a]suck the
milk of nations,
And will suck the breast of
kings;
Then you will know that I,
the LORD, am your
[b]Savior,
And your [c]Redeemer, the
Mighty One of Jacob.

17 "Instead of bronze I will
bring gold,
And instead of iron I will
bring silver,

Cross references (margin)

7 [a]Gen.
25:13 [b]Is.
19:19; 56:7
[c]Is. 60:13;
Hag. 2:7, 9

8 [a]Is. 49:21

★ **9** [a]Is.
11:11; 24:15;
42:4, 10, 12;
49:1; 51:5;
66:19 [b]Ps.
48:7; Is. 2:16
[c]Is. 14:2;
43:6; 49:22
[d]Is. 55:5

10 [a]Is. 14:1,
2; 61:5;
Zech. 6:15
[b]Is. 49:23;
Rev. 21:24
[c]Is. 54:8

11 [a]Is. 26:2;
60:18; 62:10;
Rev. 21:25,
26 [b]Is. 60:5
[c]Ps. 149:8;
Is. 24:21

12 [a]Is. 14:2;
Zech. 14:17

13 [a]Is. 35:2
[b]Is. 41:19
[c]1 Chr. 28:2;
Ps. 99:5;
132:7

14 [a]Is. 14:1,
2; 45:14, 23;
49:23; Rev.
3:9 [b]Is. 1:26
[c]Heb. 12:22

★**15-22**

15 [a]Is. 1:7-9;
6:11-13; Jer.
30:17 [b]Is.
66:5 [c]Is. 4:2;
65:18

16 [a]Is. 66:11
[b]Is. 19:20;
43:3, 11;
45:15, 21;
63:8 [c]Is.
59:20; 63:16

60:9 *Tarshish.* Probably an area in the south of
Spain (see note on 2:16).
60:15-22 Isaiah contrasts the glories of the millennial kingdom with the inglorious condition

of Israel before the Exile. Verse 16 draws on a
figure in Deut. 33:19 to show the luxuriant
quality of life in that future time.

And instead of wood,
bronze,
And instead of stones,
iron.
And I will make peace
your administrators,
And righteousness your
overseers.

18 *a*Is. 54:14
*b*Is. 51:19
*c*Is. 26:1 *d*Is.
60:11

18 "*a*Violence will not be heard
again in your land,
Nor *b*devastation or de-
struction within your
borders;
But you will call your
*c*walls salvation, and
your *d*gates praise.

19 *a*Rev.
21:23; 22:5
*b*Is. 2:5; 9:2
*c*Is. 41:16;
45:25; Zech.
2:5

19 "No longer will you have
the *a*sun for light by
day,
Nor for brightness will the
moon give you light;
But you will have the
*b*Lord for an ever-
lasting light,
And your *c*God for your
glory.

20 *a*Is. 30:26
*b*Is. 35:10;
65:19; Rev.
21:4

20 "Your *a*sun will set no
more,
Neither will your moon
wane;
For you will have the Lord
for an everlasting
light,
And the days of your
*b*mourning will be fin-
ished.

21 *a*Is.
45:24, 25;
52:1 *b*Ps.
37:11, 22; Is.
57:13; 61:7
*c*Is. 19:25;
29:23; 45:11;
64:8 *d*Is.
61:3

21 "Then all your *a*people *will
be* righteous;
They will *b*possess the land
forever,
The branch of My plant-
ing,
The *c*work of My hands,
That I may be *d*glorified.

22 *a*Is.
10:22; 51:2

22 "The *a*smallest one will become a clan,
And the least one a mighty
nation.
I, the Lord, will hasten it in
its time."

D The Messiah's Ministry of Peace during Both Advents, 61:1–11

61 The *a*Spirit of the Lord
God is upon me,
Because the Lord has
anointed me
To *b*bring good news to
the *c*afflicted;
He has sent me to *d*bind
up the brokenhearted,
To *e*proclaim liberty to
captives,
And freedom to prisoners;

★ 1-3

1 *a*Is. 11:2;
48:16; Luke
4:18 *b*Matt.
11:5; Luke
7:22 *c*Is.
11:4; 29:19;
32:7 *d*Is.
57:15 *e*Is.
42:7; 49:9

2 To *a*proclaim the favorable
year of the Lord,
And the *b*day of vengeance
of our God;
To *c*comfort all who
mourn,

2 *a*Is. 49:8;
60:10 *b*Is.
2:12; 13:6;
34:2, 8 *c*Is.
57:18; Jer.
31:13; Matt.
5:4

3 To *a*grant those who
mourn *in* Zion,
Giving them a garland in-
stead of ashes,
The *b*oil of gladness instead of mourning,
The mantle of praise in-
stead of a spirit of
fainting.
So they will be called
*c*oaks of righteous-
ness,
The planting of the Lord,
that He may be glori-
fied.

3 *a*Is. 60:20
*b*Ps. 23:5;
45:7; 104:15
*c*Is. 60:21;
Jer. 17:7, 8

4 Then they will *a*rebuild
the ancient ruins,
They will raise up the former devastations,
And they will repair the
ruined cities,
The desolations of many
generations.

★ 4-11

4 *a*Is. 49:8;
58:12; Ezek.
36:33; Amos
9:14

5 And *a*strangers will stand
and pasture your
flocks,

5 *a*Is. 14:2;
60:10

61:1–3 The ministry of Messiah at His first coming is described in verses 1–2a and at His second coming in verses 2b–3. In claiming to be
Messiah, Jesus Christ read in the synagogue
only that which applied to His ministry during

His first coming (Luke 4:18–19).
61:4–11 A description of conditions in the millennial kingdom. *double* (v. 7). Refers to double honor.

And foreigners will be
your farmers and your
vinedressers.

6   **6** But you will be called the
ᵃls. 66:21   ᵃpriests of the Lᴏʀᴅ;
ᵇls. 56:6 ᶜls.   You will be spoken of as
60:5, 11   ᵇministers of our God.
You will eat the ᶜwealth of
nations,
And in their riches you
will boast.

7   **7** Instead of your ᵃshame
ᵃls. 54:4   *you will have a*
ᵇls. 40:2;   ᵇdouble *portion,*
Zech. 9:12
ᶜPs. 16:11   And *instead of* humiliation
they will shout for joy
over their portion.
Therefore they will possess
a double *portion* in
their land,
ᶜEverlasting joy will be
theirs.

8   **8** For I, the Lᴏʀᴅ, ᵃlove jus-
ᵃls. 5:16;   tice,
28:17; 30:18   I hate robbery in the burnt
ᵇGen. 17:7;   offering;
Ps. 105:10;
ls. 55:3; Jer.   And I will faithfully give
32:40   them their recom-
pense,
And I will make an ᵇever-
lasting covenant with
them.

9   **9** Then their offspring will
ᵃls. 44:3   be known among the
nations,
And their descendants in
the midst of the peo-
ples.
All who see them will recognize them
Because they are the ᵃoff-
spring *whom* the Lᴏʀᴅ
has blessed.

10   **10** I will ᵃrejoice greatly in the
ᵃls. 12:1,   Lᴏʀᴅ,
2; 25:9;   My soul will exult in ᵇmy
41:16; 51:3
ᵇls. 49:4 ᶜls.   God;
49:18; 52:1   For He has ᶜclothed me
ᵈRev. 21:2   with garments of salvation,
He has wrapped me with a
robe of righteousness,

As a bridegroom decks
himself with a gar-
land,
And ᵈas a bride adorns
herself with her jew-
els.

11 For as the ᵃearth brings   **11** ᵃls. 4:2;
forth its sprouts,   55:10 ᵇls.
And as a garden causes the   45:23, 24;
things sown in it to   60:18, 21
                     ᶜPs. 72:3;
spring up,   85:11
So the Lord Gᴏᴅ will
ᵇcause ᶜrighteousness
and praise
To spring up before all the
nations.

E   **The Restoration of Israel,**
          62:1–12

62 For Zion's sake I will not   **1** ᵃls. 1:26;
keep silent,   58:8; 61:11
And for Jerusalem's sake I   ᵇls. 46:13;
will not keep quiet,   52:10
Until her ᵃrighteousness
goes forth like bright-
ness,
And her ᵇsalvation like a
torch that is burning.

2 And the ᵃnations will see   **2** ᵃls. 60:3
your righteousness,   ᵇls. 56:5;
And all kings your glory;   62:4, 12;
And you will be called by   65:15
a new ᵇname,
Which the mouth of the
Lᴏʀᴅ will designate.

3 You will also be a ᵃcrown   **3** ᵃls. 28:5;
of beauty in the hand   Zech. 9:16;
of the Lᴏʀᴅ,   1 Thess. 2:19
And a royal diadem in the
hand of your God.

4 It will no longer be said to   ★ **4** ᵃls.
you, "ᵃForsaken,"   54:6, 7;
Nor to your land will it any   60:15, 18
longer be said, "Deso-   ᵇHos. 2:19,
late";   20 ᶜJer.
But you will be called,   32:41; Zeph.
"My delight is in her,"   3:17
And your land, "ᵇMar-
ried";
For the ᶜLᴏʀᴅ delights in
you,
And *to Him* your land will
be married.

62:4 *"My delight is in her."* A translation of   "Beulah." The entire chapter relates to the
"Hephzibah." *"Married"* is a translation of   time of the millennial kingdom.

5 For *as* a young man marries a virgin,
So your sons will marry you;
And *as* the bridegroom rejoices over the bride,
So your [a]God will rejoice over you.

6 On your walls, O Jerusalem, I have appointed [a]watchmen;
All day and all night they will never keep silent.
You who [b]remind the LORD, take no rest for yourselves;

7 And [a]give Him no rest until He establishes
And makes [b]Jerusalem a praise in the earth.

8 [a]The LORD has sworn by His right hand and by His strong arm,
"I will [b]never again give your grain *as* food for your enemies;
Nor will foreigners drink your new wine, for which you have labored."

9 But those who [a]garner it will eat it, and praise the LORD;
And those who gather it will drink it in the courts of My sanctuary.

10 Go through, [a]go through the gates;
Clear the way for the people;
[b]Build up, build up the [c]highway;
Remove the stones, lift up a [d]standard over the peoples.

11 Behold, the LORD has proclaimed to the [a]end of the earth,

[b]Say to the daughter of Zion, "Lo, your [c]salvation comes;
[d]Behold His reward is with Him, and His recompense before Him."

12 And they will call them,
"[a]The holy people,
The [b]redeemed of the LORD";
And you will be called,
"Sought out, a city [c]not forsaken."

F   The Prerequisites for Blessing, 63:1—65:16

1   Judgment of God's enemies, 63:1–6

63 Who is this who comes from [a]Edom,
With [b]garments of glowing colors from [c]Bozrah,
This One who is majestic in His apparel,
Marching in the greatness of His strength?
"It is I who speak in righteousness, [d]mighty to save."

2 Why is Your apparel red,
And Your garments like the one who [a]treads in the wine press?

3 "[a]I have trodden the wine trough alone,
And from the peoples there was no man with Me.
I also [b]trod them in My anger,
And [c]trampled them in My wrath;
And [d]their lifeblood is sprinkled on My garments,
And I stained all My raiment.

4 "For the [a]day of vengeance was in My heart,

Cross-references (margin)

5 [a]Is. 65:19

6 [a]Is. 52:8; Jer. 6:17; Ezek. 3:17; 33:7 [b]Ps. 74:2; Jer. 14:21; Lam. 5:1, 20

7 [a]Luke 18:1-8 [b]Is. 60:18; Jer. 33:9; Zeph. 3:19, 20

8 [a]Is. 45:23; 54:9 [b]Lev. 26:16; Deut. 28:31, 33; Judg. 6:3-6; Is. 1:7; Jer. 5:17

9 [a]Is. 65:13, 21-23

10 [a]Is. 26:1; 60:11, 18 [b]Is. 57:14 [c]Is. 11:16; 19:23; 35:8; 49:11 [d]Is. 11:10, 12; 49:22

11 [a]Is. 42:10; 49:6 [b]Matt. 21:5; Zech. 9:9 [c]Is. 51:5 [d]Rev. 40:10; Rev. 22:12

12 [a]Deut. 7:6; Is. 4:3; 1 Pet. 2:9 [b]Is. 35:9; 51:10 [c]Is. 41:17; 42:16; 62:4

★ **1** [a]Ps. 137:7; Is. 34:5, 6; Ezek. 25:12-14; 35:1-15; Obad. 1-14; Mal. 1:2-5 [b]Is. 63:2 [c]Is. 34:6; Jer. 49:13; Amos 1:12 [d]Zeph. 3:17

2 [a]Rev. 19:13, 15

3 [a]Rev. 14:20; 19:15 [b]Is. 22:5; 28:3 [c]Mic. 7:10 [d]Rev. 19:13

4 [a]Is. 34:8; 35:4; 61:2; Jer. 51:6

63:1 *garments of glowing colors.* Better, crimson garments. *Bozrah.* A capital of *Edom.* There is a play on words here, for Edom means red and Bozrah is similar to the word for grape gath-erer. Both figures, along with the crimson garments, highlight the picture of Christ's second coming in judgment (cf. Rev. 14:18–20; 19:13).

And My year of redemption has come.

5 "And I looked, and there was ªno one to help, And I was astonished and there was no one to uphold; So My ᵇown arm brought salvation to Me; And My wrath upheld Me.

6 "And I ªtrod down the peoples in My anger, And made them ᵇdrunk in My wrath, And I poured out their lifeblood on the earth."

2 *Confession of God's people,* 63:7—64:12

7 I shall make mention of the ªlovingkindnesses of the Lᴏʀᴅ, the praises of the Lᴏʀᴅ, According to all that the Lᴏʀᴅ has granted us, And the great ᵇgoodness toward the house of Israel, Which He has granted them according to His ᶜcompassion, And according to the multitude of His lovingkindnesses.

8 For He said, "Surely, they are ªMy people, Sons who will not deal falsely." So He became their ᵇSavior.

9 In all their affliction ªHe was afflicted, And the ᵇangel of His presence saved them; In His ᶜlove and in His mercy He ᵈredeemed them; And He ᵉlifted them and carried them all the days of old.

10 But they ªrebelled And grieved His ᵇHoly Spirit; Therefore, He turned Himself to become their enemy, He fought against them.

11 Then ªHis people remembered the days of old, of Moses. Where is ᵇHe who brought them up out of the sea with the shepherds of His flock? Where is He who ᶜput His Holy Spirit in the midst of them,

12 Who caused His ªglorious arm to go at the right hand of Moses, Who ᵇdivided the waters before them to make for Himself an everlasting name,

13 Who led them through the depths? Like the horse in the wilderness, they did not ªstumble;

14 As the cattle which go down into the valley, The Spirit of the ªLᴏʀᴅ gave them rest. So didst Thou ᵇlead Thy people, To make for Thyself a glorious name.

15 ªLook down from heaven, and see from Thy holy and glorious ᵇhabitation; Where are Thy ᶜzeal and Thy mighty deeds? The ᵈstirrings of Thy heart and Thy compassion are restrained toward me.

16 For Thou art our ªFather, though ᵇAbraham does not know us,

5 ªIs. 59:16
ᵇPs. 44:3; Is. 40:10; 52:10

6 ªIs. 22:5; 34:2; 65:12
ᵇIs. 29:9; 51:17, 21

7 ªPs. 25:6; 92:2; Is. 54:8, 10
ᵇ1 Kin. 8:66; Neh. 9:25, 35
ᶜPs. 51:1; 86:5, 15; Is. 54:7, 8; Eph. 2:4

8 ªEx. 6:7; Is. 3:15; 51:4
ᵇIs. 60:16

★ 9 ªJudg. 10:16 ᵇEx. 23:20-23; 33:14, 15
ᶜDeut. 7:7, 8
ᵈIs. 43:1; 52:9 ᵉDeut. 1:31; 32:10-12; Is. 46:3

10 ªPs. 78:40; 106:33; Acts 7:51; Eph. 4:30 ᵇPs. 51:11; Is. 63:11

★11 ªPs. 106:44, 45
ᵇIs. 51:10
ᶜNum. 11:17, 25, 29; Hag. 2:5

★12 ªEx. 6:6; 15:16
ᵇEx. 14:21, 22; Is. 11:15; 51:10

13 ªJer. 31:9

14 ªJosh. 21:44; 23:1
ᵇDeut. 32:12

15 ªDeut. 26:15; Ps. 80:14 ᵇPs. 68:5; 123:1
ᶜIs. 9:7; 26:11; 37:32; 42:13; 59:17
ᵈJer. 31:20; Hos. 11:8

★16 ªIs. 1:2; 64:8 ᵇIs. 29:22; 41:8; 51:2 ᶜIs. 41:14; 44:6; 60:16

63:9 *the angel of His presence.* The angel of the Lord, who is the Lord Himself (cf. Exod. 33:14 and note on Gen. 16:10).
63:11 *the shepherds.* Moses and Aaron.

63:12 *divided the waters.* See Exod. 14:16.
63:16 The meaning is, Even if *Abraham* and *Israel* (i.e., Jacob) disowned the people, God would still be their Father.

And Israel does not recognize us.
Thou, O Lord, art our Father,
Our ᶜRedeemer from of old is Thy name.

17 Why, O Lord, dost Thou ᵃcause us to stray from Thy ways,
And ᵇharden our heart from fearing Thee?
ᶜReturn for the sake of Thy servants, the tribes of Thy heritage.

18 Thy holy people possessed Thy sanctuary for a little while,
Our adversaries have ᵃtrodden it down.

19 We have become like those over whom Thou hast never ruled,
Like those who were not called by Thy name.

64

Oh, that Thou wouldst rend the heavens and ᵃcome down,
That the mountains might ᵇquake at Thy presence—

2 As fire kindles the brushwood, as fire causes water to boil—
To make Thy name known to Thine adversaries,
That the ᵃnations may tremble at Thy presence!

3 When Thou didst ᵃawesome things which we did not expect,
Thou didst come down, the mountains quaked at Thy presence.

4 For from of old ᵃthey have not heard nor perceived by ear,
Neither has the eye seen a God besides Thee,

Who acts in behalf of the one who ᵇwaits for Him.

5 Thou dost ᵃmeet him who rejoices in ᵇdoing righteousness,
Who ᶜremembers Thee in Thy ways.
Behold, ᵈThou wast angry, for we sinned,
We continued in them a long time;
And shall we be saved?

6 For all of us have become like one who is ᵃunclean,
And all our ᵇrighteous deeds are like a filthy garment;
And all of us ᶜwither like a leaf,
And our ᵈiniquities, like the wind, take us away.

7 And there is ᵃno one who calls on Thy name,
Who arouses himself to take hold of Thee;
For Thou hast ᵇhidden Thy face from us,
And hast delivered us into the power of our iniquities.

8 But now, O Lord, ᵃThou art our Father,
We are the ᵇclay, and Thou our potter;
And all of us are the ᶜwork of Thy hand.

9 Do not be ᵃangry beyond measure, O Lord,
ᵇNeither remember iniquity forever;
Behold, look now, all of us are ᶜThy people.

10 Thy ᵃholy cities have become a ᵇwilderness,
Zion has become a wilderness,
Jerusalem a desolation.

Cross references (margin):

17 ᵃIs. 30:28; Ezek. 14:7-9 ᵇIs. 29:13, 14 ᶜNum. 10:36

18 ᵃPs. 74:3-7; Is. 64:11

★ 1-7
1 ᵃEx. 19:18; Ps. 18:9; 144:5; Mic. 1:3, 4; Hab. 3:13 ᵇJudg. 5:5; Ps. 68:8; Nah. 1:5
2 ᵃPs. 99:1; Jer. 5:22; 33:9

3 ᵃPs. 65:5; 66:3, 5; 106:22

4 ᵃ1 Cor. 2:9 ᵇIs. 25:9; 30:18; 40:31

5 ᵃEx. 20:24 ᵇIs. 56:1 ᶜIs. 26:13; 63:7 ᵈIs. 12:1

6 ᵃIs. 6:5 ᵇIs. 46:12; 48:1 ᶜPs. 90:5, 6; Is. 1:30 ᵈIs. 50:1

7 ᵃIs. 59:4; Ezek. 22:30 ᵇDeut. 31:18; Is. 1:15; 54:8

★ 8 ᵃIs. 63:16 ᵇIs. 29:16; 45:9 ᶜPs. 100:3; Is. 60:21

9 ᵃIs. 57:17; 60:10 ᵇIs. 43:25; Mic. 7:18 ᶜPs. 79:13; Is. 63:8

10 ᵃIs. 48:2; 52:1 ᵇIs. 1:7; 6:11

64:1-7 A prayer for divine intervention as at Mt. Sinai, and the kind of prayer Israel will pray during the Tribulation days. Compare verse 4 with 1 Cor. 2:9. *filthy garment* (v. 6). Lit., garment of times, referring to the woman's menstrual period and illustrating the polluting and disgusting nature of sin.
64:8 *potter*. Lit., the one who forms us; as also in 29:16 and 45:9.

★11 a2 Kin.
25:9; Ps.
74:5-7; Is.
63:18 bLam.
1:7, 10, 11

11 Our holy and beautiful ^ahouse,
Where our fathers praised Thee,
Has been burned *by* fire;
And ^ball our precious things have become a ruin.

12 aPs.
74:10, 11,
18, 19; Is.
42:14; 63:15

12 Wilt Thou ^arestrain Thyself at these things, O LORD?
Wilt Thou keep silent and afflict us beyond measure?

3 Repentance of sins, 65:1-16

★ 1-2

1 aRom.
9:24-26;
10:20 bIs.
63:19; Hos.
1:10

65 "I permitted Myself to be sought by ^athose who did not ask *for Me;*
I permitted Myself to be found by those who did not seek Me.
I said, 'Here am I, here am I,'
To a nation which ^bdid not call on My name.

2 aRom.
10:21 bIs.
1:2, 23; 30:1,
9 cPs. 81:11,
12; Is. 59:7;
66:18

2 "^aI have spread out My hands all day long to a ^brebellious people,
Who walk *in* the way which is not good, following their own ^cthoughts,

★ 3-7

3 aJob
1:11; 2:5; Is.
3:8 bIs. 1:29;
66:17 cIs.
66:3

3 A people who continually ^aprovoke Me to My face,
Offering sacrifices in ^bgardens and ^cburning incense on bricks;

4 aLev.
11:7; Is.
66:3, 17

4 Who sit among graves, and spend the night in secret places;
Who ^aeat swine's flesh,
And the broth of unclean meat is *in* their pots.

5 aMatt.
9:11; Luke
7:39; 18:9-12

5 "Who say, '^aKeep to yourself, do not come near me,

For I am holier than you!'
These are smoke in My nostrils,
A fire that burns all the day.

6 "Behold, it is written before Me,
I will ^anot keep silent, but ^bI will repay;
I will even repay into their bosom,

6 aPs. 50:3,
21; Is. 42:14;
64:12 bJer.
16:18

7 Both their own ^ainiquities and the iniquities of their fathers together," says the LORD.
"Because they have ^bburned incense on the mountains,
And ^cscorned Me on the hills,
Therefore I will ^dmeasure their former work into their bosom."

7 aIs.
13:11; 22:14;
26:21; 30:13,
14 bIs. 57:7;
Hos. 2:13
cEzek.
20:27, 28
dJer. 5:29;
13:25

8 Thus says the LORD,
"As the new wine is found in the cluster,
And one says, 'Do not destroy it, for there is benefit in it,'
So I will act on behalf of My servants
In order ^anot to destroy all of them.

★ 8-9

8 aIs. 1:9;
10:21, 22;
48:9

9 "And I will bring forth ^aoffspring from Jacob,
And an ^bheir of My mountains from Judah;
Even ^cMy chosen ones shall inherit it,
And ^dMy servants shall dwell there.

9 aIs.
45:19, 25;
Jer. 31:36,
37 bIs. 49:8;
60:21; Amos
9:11-15 cIs.
57:13 dIs.
32:18

10 "And ^aSharon shall be a pasture land for flocks,
And the ^bvalley of Achor a resting place for herds,

★10 aIs.
33:9; 35:2
bJosh. 7:24,
26; Hos. 2:15
cIs. 51:1;
55:6

64:11 *Our holy and beautiful house.* The Temple in Jerusalem.

65:1-2 Verse 1 refers to the Gentiles' seeking God, while verse 2 reiterates God's willingness *(spread out My hands)* to receive Israel (Rom. 10:20-21).

65:3-7 The rebellious people of Israel (cf. v. 2)

are indicted for idol worship (vv. 3, 7), consulting with the dead (v. 4), and eating forbidden *swine's flesh* (v. 4; cf. Lev. 11:7).

65:8-9 Like the few good grapes in a *cluster* so there is a godly remnant in Israel.

65:10 *the valley of Achor.* See note on Hos. 2:15.

For My people who ^cseek Me.

★11 ^aDeut. 29:24, 25; Is. 1:4, 28 ^bIs. 2:2, 3; 66:20

11 "But you who ^aforsake the Lord,
Who forget My ^bholy mountain,
Who set a table for Fortune,
And who fill *cups* with mixed wine for Destiny,

12 ^aIs. 27:1; 34:5, 6; 66:16 ^bIs. 63:6 ^c2 Chr. 36:15, 16; Prov. 1:24; Is. 41:28; 50:2; 66:4; Jer. 7:13

12 I will destine you for the ^asword,
And all of you shall bow down to the ^bslaughter.
Because I called, but you ^cdid not answer;
I spoke, but you did not hear.
And you did evil in My sight,
And chose that in which I did not delight."

13 ^aIs. 1:19 ^bIs. 8:21 ^cIs. 41:17, 18; 49:10 ^dIs. 5:13 ^eIs. 61:7; 66:14 ^fIs. 42:17; 44:9, 11; 66:5

13 Therefore, thus says the Lord God,
"Behold, My servants shall ^aeat, but you shall be ^bhungry.
Behold, My servants shall ^cdrink, but you shall be ^dthirsty.
Behold, My servants shall ^erejoice, but you shall be ^fput to shame.

14 ^aPs. 66:4; Is. 51:11; James 5:13 ^bIs. 13:6; Matt. 8:12

14 "Behold, My servants shall ^ashout joyfully with a glad heart,
But you shall ^bcry out with a heavy heart,
And you shall wail with a broken spirit.

15 ^aJer. 24:9; 25:18; Zech. 8:13 ^bIs. 62:2

15 "And you will leave your name for a ^acurse to My chosen ones,
And the Lord God will slay you.
But My servants will be called by ^banother name.

16 "Because he who is blessed in the earth
Shall be blessed by the ^aGod of truth;
And he who swears in the earth
Shall ^bswear by the God of truth;
Because the former troubles are forgotten,
And because they are hidden from My sight!

16 ^aEx. 34:6; Ps. 31:5 ^bIs. 19:18; 45:23

G   The Characteristics of the Kingdom, 65:17-25

17 "For behold, I create ^anew heavens and a new earth;
And the ^bformer things shall not be remembered or come to mind.

★17-25

17 ^aIs. 66:22; 2 Pet. 3:13; Rev. 21:1 ^bIs. 43:18; Jer. 3:16

18 "But be ^aglad and rejoice forever in what I create;
For behold, I create Jerusalem *for* rejoicing,
And her people *for* gladness.

18 ^aPs. 98; Is. 12:1, 2; 25:9; 35:10; 41:16; 51:3; 61:10

19 "I will also ^arejoice in Jerusalem, and be glad in My people;
And there will no longer be heard in her
The voice of ^bweeping and the sound of crying.

19 ^aIs. 62:4, 5; Jer. 32:41 ^bIs. 25:8; 30:19; 35:10; 51:11; Rev. 7:17; 21:4

20 "No longer will there be *in it* an infant *who lives but a few* days,
Or an old man who does ^anot live out his days;
For the youth will die at the age of one hundred
And the ^bone who does not reach the age of one hundred
Shall be *thought* accursed.

20 ^aDeut. 4:40; Job 5:26; Ps. 34:12 ^bEccl. 8:12, 13; Is. 3:11; 22:14

65:11 *Fortune . . . Destiny.* Lit., Gad (the Aramean god of luck) and Meni (god of destiny).
65:17-25 A description of the millennial kingdom, which is preliminary to the *new heavens and a new earth* (v. 17). Characteristics include Jerusalem being a joy instead of a burden (v.

18; cf. Zech. 12:2-3), longevity (Isa. 65:20; notice that sin will be punished in the Millennium), peace and security (vv. 21-23), and removing of the animosity in nature (v. 25; cf. 11:7-9).

21 "And they shall [a]build houses and inhabit *them;*
They shall also [b]plant vineyards and eat their fruit.

22 "They shall not build, and [a]another inhabit,
They shall not plant, and another eat;
For [b]as the lifetime of a tree, *so shall be* the days of My people,
And My chosen ones shall [c]wear out the work of their hands.

23 "They shall [a]not labor in vain,
Or bear *children* for calamity;
For they are the [b]offspring of those blessed by the LORD,
And their descendants with them.

24 "It will also come to pass that before they call, I will [a]answer; and while they are still speaking, I will hear.

25 "The [a]wolf and the lamb shall graze together, and the [b]lion shall eat straw like the ox; and [c]dust shall be the serpent's food. They shall [d]do no evil or harm in all My [e]holy mountain," says the LORD.

H   The Rebuke of Hypocrisy, 66:1–6

66 Thus says the LORD,
"[a]Heaven is My throne, and the earth is My footstool.
Where then is a [b]house you could build for Me?
And where is a place that I may rest?

2 "For [a]My hand made all these things,
Thus all these things came into being," declares the LORD.

"But to this one I will look,
To him who is humble and [b]contrite of spirit, and who [c]trembles at My word.

3 "But he who kills an ox is *like* one who slays a man;
He who sacrifices a lamb is *like* the one who breaks a dog's neck;
He who offers a grain offering *is like one who* offers [a]swine's blood;
He who [b]burns incense is *like* the one who blesses an idol.
As they have chosen their [c]own ways,
And their soul delights in their [d]abominations,

4 So I will [a]choose their punishments,
And I will [b]bring on them what they dread.
Because I called, but [c]no one answered;
I spoke, but they did not listen.
And they did [d]evil in My sight,
And chose that in which I did not delight."

5 Hear the word of the LORD, you who [a]tremble at His word:
"Your brothers who [b]hate you, who [c]exclude you for My name's sake,
Have said, 'Let the LORD be glorified, that we may see your joy.'
But [d]they will be put to shame.

6 "A voice of uproar from the city, a voice from the temple,
The voice of the LORD who is [a]rendering recompense to His enemies.

66:3 The meaning is this: ritualistic offerings apart from a change of heart (v. 2) are as abominable to God as murder or offering unclean animals.

Cross references (left margin):

21 [a]Is. 32:18; Amos 9:14 [b]Is. 30:23; 37:30; Jer. 31:5

22 [a]Is. 62:8, 9 [b]Ps. 92:12-14 [c]Ps. 21:4; 91:16

23 [a]Deut. 28:3-12; Is. 55:2 [b]Is. 61:9; Jer. 32:38, 39; Acts 2:39

24 [a]Ps. 91:15; Is. 55:6; 58:9; Dan. 9:20-23; 10:12

25 [a]Is. 11:6 [b]Is. 11:7 [c]Gen. 3:14; Mic. 7:17 [d]Is. 11:9; Mic. 4:3 [e]Is. 65:11

1 [a]1 Kin. 8:27; Ps. 11:4; Matt. 5:34, 35; 23:22 [b]2 Sam. 7:5-7; Jer. 7:4; John 4:20, 21; Acts 7:48-50

2 [a]Is. 40:26 [b]Ps. 34:18; Is. 57:15; Matt. 5:3, 4; Luke 18:13, 14 [c]Ps. 119:120; Is. 66:5

★ 3 [a]Is. 65:4 [b]Lev. 2:2; Is. 1:13 [c]Is. 57:17; 65:2 [d]Is. 44:19

4 [a]Prov. 1:31, 32; Is. 65:7 [b]Prov. 10:24 [c]Prov. 1:24; Is. 65:12; Jer. 7:13 [d]2 Kin. 21:2, 6; Is. 59:7; 65:12; Jer. 7:30

5 [a]Is. 66:2 [b]Ps. 38:20; Is. 60:15 [c]Matt. 5:10-12; 10:22; John 9:34; 15:18-20 [d]Luke 13:17

6 [a]Is. 59:18; 65:6; Joel 3:7

I   The Rebirth of Israel, 66:7-9

★ **7-9**

7 aIs. 37:3;
54:1 bRev.
12:5

8 aIs. 64:4

7 "Before she travailed, ^ashe brought forth;
Before her pain came, ^bshe gave birth to a boy.

8 "^aWho has heard such a thing? Who has seen such things?
Can a land be born in one day?
Can a nation be brought forth all at once?
As soon as Zion travailed, she also brought forth her sons.

9 aIs. 37:3

9 "Shall I bring to the point of birth, and ^anot give delivery?'' says the LORD.
"Or shall I who gives delivery shut *the womb?''* says your God.

J   The Rejoicing in the Future, 66:10-24

★**10-14**

10 aDeut.
32:43; Is.
65:18; Rom.
15:10 bPs.
26:8; 122:6
cPs. 137:6

11 aIs.
49:23; 60:16;
Joel 3:18
bIs. 60:1, 2;
62:2

12 aPs. 72:3,
7; Is. 48:18
bIs. 60:5;
61:6 cIs.
60:4

10 "Be ^ajoyful with Jerusalem and rejoice for her, all you who ^blove her;
Be exceedingly ^cglad with her, all you who mourn over her,

11 That you may nurse and ^abe satisfied with her comforting breasts,
That you may suck and be delighted with her ^bbountiful bosom.''

12 For thus says the LORD, "Behold, I extend ^apeace to her like a river,
And the ^bglory of the nations like an overflowing stream;
And you shall be nursed, you shall be ^ccarried on the hip and fondled on the knees.

13 "As one whom his mother comforts, so I will ^acomfort you;
And you shall be comforted in Jerusalem.''

13 aIs. 12:1;
40:1, 2;
49:13; 51:3;
2 Cor. 1:3, 4

14 Then you shall ^asee *this,* and your ^bheart shall be glad,
And your ^cbones shall flourish like the new grass;
And the ^dhand of the LORD shall be made known to His servants,
But He shall be ^eindignant toward His enemies.

14 aIs. 33:20
bZech. 10:7
cProv. 3:8;
Is. 58:11
dEzra 7:9;
8:31 eIs.
10:5; 13:5;
34:2

15 For behold, the LORD will come in ^afire
And His ^bchariots like the whirlwind,
To render His anger with fury,
And His rebuke with flames of fire.

★**15-17**

15 aIs.
10:17; 30:27,
33; 31:9
bPs. 68:17;
Is. 5:28; Hab.
3:8

16 For the LORD will execute judgment by ^afire
And by His ^bsword on all flesh,
And those slain by the LORD will be many.

16 aIs.
30:30; Ezek.
38:22 bIs.
65:12; Ezek.
38:21

17 "Those who sanctify and purify themselves *to* go to the ^agardens,
Following one in the center,
Who eat ^bswine's flesh, detestable things, and mice,
Shall ^ccome to an end altogether,'' declares the LORD.

17 aIs. 1:29;
65:3 bLev.
11:7; Is. 65:4
cIs. 1:28, 31

18 "For I know their works and their ^athoughts; the time is coming to ^bgather all nations and tongues. And they shall come and see My glory.

★**18-21**

18 aIs. 59:7;
65:2 bIs.
45:22-25;
Jer. 3:17

19 "And I will set a ^asign among them and will send survivors from them to the nations: ^bTarshish, Put, ^cLud, Meshech,

19 aIs.
11:10, 12;
49:22; 62:10
bIs. 2:16;
60:9 cEzek.
27:10 dGen.
10:2 eIs.
11:11; 24:15;
60:9 f1 Chr.
16:24; Is.
42:12

66:7-9 At the second coming of Christ all living Israelites will be saved (Rom. 11:26; Zech. 12:10; 13:1).
66:10-14 A description of the millennial age.
66:15-17 A vivid picture of the judgments at the return of Christ (2 Thess. 1:7-9).
66:18-21 This section gives details of missionary

witness during the Millennium to *Tarshish* (SW. coast of Spain), *Put* (Libya), *Lud* (Lydia in Asia Minor), *Meshech* and *Rosh* (better translated, those that draw the bow, indicating their warlike character), *Tubal* (NE. Asia Minor), and *Javan* (Greece).

Rosh, ^dTubal, and Javan, to the distant ^ecoastlands that have neither heard My fame nor seen My glory. And they will ^fdeclare My glory among the nations.

20 "Then they shall ^abring all your brethren from all the nations as a grain offering to the LORD, on horses, in chariots, in litters, on mules, and on camels, to My ^bholy mountain Jerusalem," says the LORD, "just as the sons of Israel bring their grain offering in a ^cclean vessel to the house of the LORD.

21 "I will also take some of them for ^apriests *and* for Levites," says the LORD.

22 "For just as the ^anew heavens and the new earth Which I make will endure before Me," declares the LORD,

"So your ^boffspring and your ^cname will endure.

23 "And it shall be from ^anew moon to new moon And from sabbath to sabbath, All mankind will come to ^bbow down before Me," says the LORD.

24 "Then they shall go forth and look On the ^acorpses of the men Who have ^btransgressed against Me. For their ^cworm shall not die, ^dAnd their fire shall not be quenched; And they shall be an ^eabhorrence to all mankind."

20 ^aIs. 43:6;
49:22; 60:4
^bIs. 2:2, 3;
11:9; 56:7;
65:11, 25
^cIs. 52:11

21 ^aEx. 19:6;
Is. 61:6;
1 Pet. 2:5, 9

★22-24
22 ^aIs.
65:17; Heb.
12:26, 27;
2 Pet. 3:13;
Rev. 21:1
^bIs. 61:8, 9;
65:22, 23;
John 10:27-
29; 1 Pet.
1:4, 5 ^cIs.
56:5

23 ^aIs. 1:13,
14; Ezek.
46:1, 6 ^bIs.
19:21, 23;
27:13; 49:7

24 ^aIs. 5:25;
34:3 ^bIs.
1:28; 24:20
^cIs. 14:11;
Mark 9:48
^dIs. 1:31;
Matt. 3:12
^eDan. 12:2

66:22-24 Refers to the eternal state, including the eternal punishment of the wicked (v. 24).

INTRODUCTION TO
THE BOOK OF JEREMIAH

AUTHOR: Jeremiah   DATE: 627–585 B.C.

The Prophet *Often called the "weeping prophet" (9:1; 13:17) or the "prophet of loneliness" (because he was commanded not to marry, 16:2), Jeremiah was also the "reluctant prophet" (1:6). Yet for more than 40 years he faithfully proclaimed God's judgment on apostate Judah, all the while enduring opposition, beatings, and imprisonment (11:18-23; 12:6; 18:18; 20:1-3; 26:1-24; 37:11-38:28).*

Jeremiah began his ministry (at about the age of 20) under good King Josiah, with whom he enjoyed cordial relations. After Josiah's death, opposition to the prophet mounted. He barely escaped arrest, was forbidden to go to the Temple, and had to deputize Baruch, his secretary, to deliver his prophecies. King Jehoiakim destroyed Jeremiah's written predictions (which the prophet rewrote, 36:22ff.). King Zedekiah permitted nationalistic-minded nobles to imprison Jeremiah, then he reduced the punishment. When the forces of Nebuchadnezzar took Jerusalem in 586, Jeremiah was freed and given the choice of going to Babylon or remaining in Jerusalem. He chose the latter, but was soon abducted and taken to Egypt by Jews who fled there rather than face Nebuchadnezzar. In Egypt Jeremiah prophesied a few more years and apparently there he died.

Sensitive and sympathetic by nature, he nevertheless was commanded by God to deliver a stern message of judgment. The opposition he faced was cruel and crushing, so much so that more than once he wanted to resign from his office as prophet; yet, he continued faithfully to proclaim God's Word.

A Chronology of the Times

627	Jeremiah called of God. Judah under tribute to Assyria, whose power was beginning to wane.
612	Nineveh, capital of Assyria, sacked.
609	King Josiah killed at Megiddo by Necho of Egypt, who was fighting to bolster Assyria (2 Kings 23:29-30).
609	Jehoahaz ruled Judah for 3 months before being deposed by Necho and taken to Egypt in chains (2 Kings 23:32-33; cf. Jer. 22:10).
609-598	Jehoiakim reigned over Judah as an Egyptian vassal (Jer. 22:13-17).
605	Battle of Carchemish, where Nebuchadnezzar defeated Egyptian forces (Jer. 46:2). Nebuchadnezzar entered Palestine and took Daniel and others hostage (2 Kings 24:1). Jehoiakim abandoned Egyptian suzerainty and became a vassal of Babylon.
601	Jehoiakim sided with Egypt again against Jeremiah's warnings (Jer. 22:13-19).
597	Jehoiakim died (either late in 598 or early in 597). Nebuchadnezzar captured Jerusalem and deported King Jehoiachin, replacing him with Zedekiah (2 Kings 24:17).
586	Nebuchadnezzar again occupied Jerusalem because Zedekiah had entered into negotiations with Egypt (2 Kings 25:1-7). Gedaliah appointed governor of Judah (2 Kings 25:22-26). Gedaliah assassinated. Jeremiah taken to Egypt.

Archaeological Discoveries *Several important archaeological discoveries have corroborated the historicity of the biblical accounts of the last years of Judah. (1) The Babylonian Chronicle gives information about the campaigns of the Babylonian armies from 626 on, including the capture of Jerusalem in 597. (2) The Lachish letters describe the situation in Judah just prior to Nebuchadnezzar's final siege of Judah in 586. A seal was also found at Lachish bearing the name of Gedaliah. (3) Tablets excavated near the Ishtar Gate of ancient Babylon include the name of "Yaukin [Jehoiachin] king of the land of Yahud [Judah]" as receiving royal bounty (i.e., ration tablets, 2 Kings 25:29-30).*

Contents *The arrangement of the prophecies is not chronological. The following chart attempts to place some of the oracles against their historical background, indicated by the ruling king of Judah.*

Josiah	chapters 1-6
Jehoahaz (Shallum)	22:10-12
Jehoiakim	7-20; 25; 26; 35; 36; 45; 46:1-12; 47-49
Jehoiachin (Coniah)	22-23

Zedekiah   21; 24; 27-34; 37-39
Gedaliah   40-44

Warnings against sin and judgment are paramount throughout the book, but so also is the message of hope and restoration. Important prophecies include the curse on Coniah (Jehoiachin, 22:30), the prediction of the Messiah (23:5-6), the duration of the Babylonian captivity (25:11), and the revelation of the new covenant (31:31-34). Backsliding is a key word (occurring 13 times), and there are more references to Babylon (164) in Jeremiah than in the rest of the Bible together.

OUTLINE OF JEREMIAH

I. Jeremiah's Call and Commission, 1:1-19
A. His Call, 1:1-10
B. The Confirmation of the Call, 1:11-19
II. Prophecies Concerning Judah, 2:1-45:5
A. Judah's Willful Sin, 2:1-3:5
B. Judah's Chastening, 3:6-6:30
  1. Contrast between Israel and Judah, 3:6-11
  2. Call to repentance, 3:12-25
  3. Prediction of judgment, 4:1-31
  4. Reasons for judgment, 5:1-31
  5. Certainty of judgment, 6:1-30
C. Judah's Wrong Religion, 7:1-10:25
  1. The indictment of the people; the Temple sermon, 7:1-8:3
  2. The retribution of God, 8:4-9:26
  3. The folly of idolatry, 10:1-18
  4. The reaction of the prophet, 10:19-25
D. Judah's Breaking of God's Covenant, 11:1-13:27
  1. The fact, 11:1-17
  2. The consequence, 11:18-12:17
  3. The warnings, 13:1-27
E. Judah's Coming Drought, 14:1-15:9
  1. Jeremiah's message, 14:1-6
  2. Jeremiah's intercession, 14:7-15:9
F. Judah's Prophet Recommissioned, 15:10-16:9
  1. Jeremiah's remorse, 15:10-21
  2. Jeremiah's restrictions, 16:1-9
G. Judah's Sins, 16:10-17:27
H. Judah and the Sovereign Potter, 18:1-23
I. Judah as a Broken Flask, 19:1-20:18
  1. The message, 19:1-15
  2. The reaction: Jeremiah persecuted, 20:1-18
J. Judah's Kings, 21:1-23:8
  1. The message to Zedekiah, 21:1-22:9
  2. The message concerning Jehoahaz (Shallum), 22:10-12
  3. The message concerning Jehoiakim, 22:13-19
  4. The message concerning Jehoiachin (Coniah, Jeconiah), 22:20-30
  5. The message concerning Messiah, 23:1-8
K. Judah's False Prophets, 23:9-40
L. Judah's Captivity, 24:1-25:38
  1. The deportees, 24:1-10
  2. The duration, 25:1-11

  3. The disposition of the captor nation, 25:12-38
M. Judah's Reaction to Jeremiah's Ministry, 26:1-24
N. Judah's Advice from Jeremiah: Submit to Nebuchadnezzar, 27:1-29:32
  1. Sign of the yokes, 27:1-22
  2. Opposition of a false prophet, 28:1-17
  3. Letter to Jews in captivity, 29:1-32
O. Judah's Hope of Restoration, 30:1-33:26
  1. The promise declared: restoration after tribulation, 30:1-31:26
  2. The promise covenanted: the new covenant, 31:27-40
  3. The promise illustrated: a field bought, 32:1-44
  4. The promise reaffirmed: the Davidic covenant, 33:1-26
P. Events before the Fall of Jerusalem, 34:1-38:28
  1. Message to Zedekiah, 34:1-7
  2. Message to the people, 34:8-22
  3. Message concerning the Rechabites, 35:1-19
  4. Jehoiakim burns Jeremiah's scroll, 36:1-32
  5. Jeremiah imprisoned, 37:1-38:28
Q. The Fall of Jerusalem, 39:1-18
  1. The fate of the Jews, 39:1-10
  2. The fate of Jeremiah, 39:11-18
R. Events After the Fall of Jerusalem, 40:1-45:5
  1. Jeremiah ministers to Jews in Palestine, 40:1-42:22
  2. Jeremiah ministers to Jews in Egypt, 43:1-44:30
  3. Jeremiah ministers to Baruch, 45:1-5
III. Prophecies Concerning the Nations, 46:1-51:64
A. Prophecies against Egypt, 46:1-28
B. Prophecies against the Philistines, 47:1-7
C. Prophecies against Moab, 48:1-47
D. Prophecies against Ammon, 49:1-6
E. Prophecies against Edom, 49:7-22
F. Prophecies against Damascus, 49:23-27
G. Prophecies against Arabia, 49:28-33
H. Prophecies against Elam, 49:34-39
I. Prophecies against Babylon, 50:1-51:64
IV. Historical Supplement, 52:1-34
A. The Fate of Jerusalem, 52:1-23
B. The Fate of Certain People, 52:24-34

THE BOOK OF JEREMIAH

I JEREMIAH'S CALL AND COMMISSION, 1:1–19
A His Call, 1:1–10

★ **1** *a*2 Chr.
35:25; 36:12,
21, 22; Ezra
1:1; Dan. 9:2;
Matt. 2:17;
16:14; 27:9
*b*Josh.
21:18; 1 Kin.
2:26; 1 Chr.
6:60; Is.
10:30; Jer.
11:21; 32:7
★ **2** *a*1 Kin.
13:2; 2 Kin.
21:24; 22:3;
2 Chr. 34:1;
Jer. 3:6; 36:2
*b*2 Kin.
21:18, 24
*c*Jer. 25:3
★ **3** *a*2 Kin.
23:34; 1 Chr.
3:15; 2 Chr.
36:5–8; Jer.
25:1 *b*2 Kin.
24:17; 1 Chr.
3:15; 2 Chr.
36:11–13;
Jer. 39:2
★ **5** *a*Ps.
139:15, 16
*b*Is. 49:1, 5;
Luke 1:15
*c*Jer. 1:10;
25:15–26

1 The words of *a*Jeremiah, the son of Hilkiah, of the priests who were in *b*Anathoth in the land of Benjamin,

2 to whom the word of the LORD came in the days of *a*Josiah, the son of *b*Amon, king of Judah, in the *c*thirteenth year of his reign.

3 It came also in the days of *a*Jehoiakim, the son of Josiah, king of Judah, until the end of the eleventh year of *b*Zedekiah, the son of Josiah, king of Judah, until the exile of Jerusalem in the fifth month.

4 Now the word of the LORD came to me saying,

5 "Before I *a*formed you in the womb I knew you,
And *b*before you were born I consecrated you;
I have *c*appointed you a prophet to the nations."

6 *a*Ex. 4:10
*b*1 Kin. 3:7

6 Then *a*I said, "Alas, Lord God!
Behold, I do not know how to speak,
Because *b*I am a youth."

★ **7** *a*Ezek.
2:3, 4 *b*Num.
22:20; Jer.
1:17

7 But the LORD said to me, "Do not say, 'I am a youth,' *a*Because everywhere I send you, you shall go,

And *b*all that I command you, you shall speak.

8 "*a*Do not be afraid of them,
For *b*I am with you to deliver you," declares the LORD.

9 Then the LORD stretched out His hand and *a*touched my mouth, and the LORD said to me, "Behold, I have *b*put My words in your mouth.

10 "See, *a*I have appointed you this day over the nations and over the kingdoms,
*b*To pluck up and to break down,
To destroy and to overthrow,
*c*To build and to plant."

★ **8** *a*Ex.
3:12; Deut.
31:6; Josh.
1:5; Jer.
15:20 *b*Ezek.
2:6

9 *a*Is. 6:7;
Mark 7:33–35
*b*Ex. 4:11–
16; Deut.
18:18; Is.
51:16

★**10** *a*Rev.
11:3–6 *b*Jer.
18:7–10;
Ezek. 32:18;
2 Cor. 10:4
*c*Is. 44:26–
28; Jer. 24:6;
31:28, 40

B The Confirmation of the Call, 1:11–19

11 And the word of the LORD came to me saying, "What do you see, *a*Jeremiah?" And I said, "I see a rod of an almond tree."

12 Then the LORD said to me, "You have seen well, for *a*I am watching over My word to perform it."

13 And the word of the LORD came to me a second time saying, "*a*What do you see?" And I said, "I see a boiling *b*pot, facing away from the north."

14 Then the LORD said to me, "*a*Out of the north the evil will

★**11-12**

11 *a*Jer.
24:3; Amos
7:8

12 *a*Jer.
31:28

★**13-16**

13 *a*Zech.
4:2 *b*Ezek.
11:3, 7

14 *a*Is.
41:25; Jer.
4:6; 10:22

1:1 *words.* Also translated "deeds" (5:28) referring both to the prophecies of Jeremiah and events in his career. *Jeremiah* may mean "the Lord exalts" or "the Lord founds." *Anathoth.* Modern Anata, about 3 miles N. of Jerusalem.
1:2 *the thirteenth year.* 627 B.C.
1:3 *the exile of Jerusalem.* In 586. However, Jeremiah continued his ministry a little longer.
1:5 Jeremiah was set apart by God for his prophetic ministry before he was born. Paul was similarly chosen (Gal. 1:15).
1:7 Jeremiah's objection was overruled on the ground that the authority for his message resided in the One who chose him (cf. John 15:16).

1:8 *Do not be afraid.* Similar words were also spoken to Abraham (Gen. 15:1), Moses (Num. 21:34; Deut. 3:2), Daniel (Dan. 10:12, 19), Mary (Luke 1:30), Peter (Luke 5:10), and Paul (Acts 27:24).
1:10 Jeremiah would prophesy both destruction and blessing.
1:11-12 The *almond* (Heb., *shaqed*) *tree* was to reassure Jeremiah that God was not asleep but that He was *watching* (Heb., *shoqed*).
1:13-16 The *pot* (a large vessel used for cooking or washing) about to spill its *boiling* contents *from the north* illustrates the coming invasion of Babylon (3:18).

break forth on all the inhabitants of the land.

15 aJer. 25:9
bIs. 22:7;
Jer. 39:3
cJer. 4:16;
9:11

15 "For, behold, I am calling aall the families of the kingdoms of the north," declares the LORD; "and they will come, and they will bset each one his throne at the entrance of the gates of Jerusalem, and against all its walls round about, and against all the ccities of Judah.

16 aDeut.
28:20 bJer.
7:9; 19:4;
44:17 cIs.
2:8; 37:19;
Jer. 10:3-5

16 "And I will pronounce My judgments on them concerning all their wickedness, whereby they have aforsaken Me and have boffered sacrifices to other gods, and worshiped the cworks of their own hands.

★17-19

17 a1 Kin.
18:46; Job
38:3 bEzek.
2:6; 3:16-18

17 "Now, agird up your loins, and arise, and speak to them all which I command you. bDo not be dismayed before them, lest I dismay you before them.

18 "Now behold, I have made you today as a fortified city, and as a pillar of iron and as walls of bronze against the whole land, to the kings of Judah, to its princes, to its priests and to the people of the land.

19 aNum.
14:9; Jer.
1:8; 20:11

19 "And they will fight against you, but they will not overcome you, for aI am with you to deliver you," declares the LORD.

II PROPHECIES CONCERNING JUDAH, 2:1–45:5

A Judah's Willful Sin, 2:1–3:5

2 Now the word of the LORD came to me saying,

★ 2-3

2 aIs. 58:1;
Jer. 7:2; 11:6
bEzek. 16:8;
Hos. 2:15
cDeut. 2:7;
Jer. 2:6

2 "Go and aproclaim in the ears of Jerusalem, saying, 'Thus says the LORD,
  "I remember concerning
    you the bdevotion of
    your youth,
  The love of your betroth-
    als,
  cYour following after Me
    in the wilderness,
  Through a land not sown.

3 "Israel was aholy to the LORD,
  The bfirst of His harvest;
  cAll who ate of it became
    guilty;
  Evil came upon them," de-
    clares the LORD.' "

3 aEx. 19:5,
6; Deut. 7:6;
14:2 bJames
1:18; Rev.
14:4 cIs.
41:11; Jer.
30:16; 50:7

4 Hear the word of the LORD, O house of Jacob, and all the families of the house of Israel.

5 Thus says the LORD,
  "aWhat injustice did your
    fathers find in Me,
  That they went far from
    Me
  And walked after bempti-
    ness and became
    empty?

★ 5 aIs. 5:4;
Mic. 6:3
b2 Kin.
17:15; Jer.
8:19; Rom.
1:21

6 "And they did not say,
    'Where is the LORD
  Who abrought us up out of
    the land of Egypt,
  Who bled us through the
    wilderness,
  Through a land of deserts
    and of pits,
  Through a land of drought
    and of deep darkness,
  Through a land that no
    one crossed
  And where no man dwelt?'

6 aEx. 20:2;
Is. 63:11
bDeut. 8:15;
32:10

7 "And I brought you into the
    afruitful land,
  To eat its fruit and its good
    things.
  But you came and bdefiled
    My land,
  And My inheritance you
    made an abomination.

7 aDeut.
8:7-9; 11:10-
12 bPs.
106:38; Jer.
3:2; 16:18

8 "The apriests did not say,
    'Where is the LORD?'
  And those who handle the
    law bdid not know
    Me;
  The rulers also trans-
    gressed against Me,
  And the cprophets proph-
    esied by Baal
  And walked after dthings
    that did not profit.

★ 8 aJer.
10:21 bJer.
4:22; Mal.
2:7, 8 cJer.
23:13 dJer.
16:19; Hab.
2:18

1:17-19 Jeremiah is commanded to be strong as a fortified city, which he was for over 40 years and without losing his gentle spirit.
2:2-3 Israel's relation to God at Sinai is likened

to a marriage. devotion. See note on Hos. 2:19.
2:5 walked after. To serve as a vassal.
2:8 priests . . . rulers . . . prophets. These leaders led the way to apostasy.

9 ªJer.
2:35; Ezek.
20:35, 36

★10 ªIs.
23:12 ᵇPs.
120:5; Is.
21:16; Jer.
49:28

11 ªIs.
37:19; Jer.
5:7; 16:20
ᵇPs. 106:20;
Rom. 1:23

12 ªIs. 1:2;
Jer. 4:23

13 ªPs. 36:9;
Jer. 17:13;
John 4:14
ᵇJer. 14:3

★14 ªJer.
5:19; 17:4

★15 ªJer.
50:17 ᵇJer.
4:7

★16 ªIs.
19:13; Jer.
44:1; Hos.
9:6 ᵇDeut.
33:20; Jer.
48:45

9 "Therefore I will yet ªcontend with you," declares the Lᴏʀᴅ,
"And with your sons' sons I will contend.

10 "For ªcross to the coastlands of Kittim and see,
And send to ᵇKedar and observe closely,
And see if there has been such a *thing* as this!

11 "Has a nation changed gods,
When ªthey were not gods?
But My people have ᵇchanged their glory
For that which does not profit.

12 "Be appalled, ªO heavens, at this,
And shudder, be very desolate," declares the Lᴏʀᴅ.

13 "For My people have committed two evils:
They have forsaken Me,
The ªfountain of living waters,
To hew for themselves ᵇcisterns,
Broken cisterns,
That can hold no water.

14 "Is Israel ªa slave? Or is he a homeborn servant?
Why has he become a prey?

15 "The young ªlions have roared at him,
They have roared loudly.
And they have ᵇmade his land a waste;
His cities have been destroyed, without inhabitant.

16 "Also the men of ªMemphis and Tahpanhes

Have shaved the ᵇcrown of your head.

17 "Have you not ªdone this to yourself,
By your forsaking the Lᴏʀᴅ your God,
When He ªled you in the way?

18 "But now what are you doing ªon the road to Egypt,
To drink the waters of the ᵇNile?
Or what are you doing on the road to Assyria,
To drink the waters of the Euphrates?

19 "ªYour own wickedness will correct you,
And your ᵇapostasies will reprove you;
Know therefore and see that it is evil and ᶜbitter
For you to forsake the Lᴏʀᴅ your God,
And ᵈthe dread of Me is not in you," declares the Lord Gᴏᴅ of hosts.

20 "For long ago ªI broke your yoke
And tore off your bonds;
But you said, 'I will not serve!'
For on every ᵇhigh hill
And under every green tree
You have lain down as a harlot.

21 "Yet I ªplanted you a choice vine,
A completely faithful seed.
How then have you turned yourself before Me
Into the ᵇdegenerate shoots of a foreign vine?

17 ªDeut.
32:10; Jer.
4:18

18 ªIs. 30:2
ᵇJosh. 13:3

19 ªIs. 3:9;
Jer. 4:18;
Hos. 5:5
ᵇJer. 3:6, 8,
11, 14; Hos.
11:7 ᶜJob
20:12-16;
Amos 8:10
ᵈPs. 36:1;
Jer. 5:24

20 ªLev.
26:13 ᵇDeut.
12:2; Is.
57:5, 7; Jer.
3:2, 6; 17:2

★21 ªEx.
15:17; Ps.
44:2; 80:8;
Is. 5:2 ᵇIs.
5:4

2:10 *Kittim* (Cyprus) and *Kedar* (Arabia). Search from west to east to try to find a nation that abandons its gods! But Israel had forsaken the living God.
2:14 *homeborn servant.* A slave born in the house of his master, in contrast to one purchased.
2:15 A reference to the capture of the Northern Kingdom in 722 by Assyria.
2:16 Egyptian armies had begun to plague Judah. *Memphis.* The ancient capital of Lower Egypt, located near Cairo. *Tahpanhes.* In NE. Egypt, commanding the road to Palestine (44:1).
2:21 Cf. the vineyard illustration in Isa. 5:1-7.

22 ᵃJer. 4:14
ᵇJob 14:17;
Hos. 13:12

22 "Although you ᵃwash yourself with lye
And use much soap,
The ᵇstain of your iniquity
is before Me," de-
clares the Lord Gᴏᴅ.

★**23** ᵃProv.
30:12 ᵇJer.
9:14 ᶜJer.
7:31 ᵈJer.
2:33, 36;
31:22

23 "ᵃHow can you say, 'I am
not defiled,
I have not gone after the
ᵇBaals'?
Look at your way in the
ᶜvalley!
Know what you have
done!
You are a swift young
camel ᵈentangling her
ways,

24 ᵃJer. 14:6

24 A ᵃwild donkey accus-
tomed to the wilder-
ness,
That sniffs the wind in her
passion.
In the time of her heat
who can turn her
away?
All who seek her will not
become weary;
In her month they will find
her.

25 ᵃJer.
18:12 ᵇDeut.
32:16; Jer.
14:10

25 "Keep your feet from being
unshod
And your throat from
thirst;
But you said, 'ᵃIt is hopeless!
No! For I have ᵇloved
strangers,
And after them I will
walk.'

26 ᵃJer.
48:27

26 "As the ᵃthief is shamed
when he is discovered,
So the house of Israel is
shamed;
They, their kings, their
princes,
And their priests, and their
prophets,

★**27** ᵃJer.
18:17; 32:33
ᵇJudg.
10:10; Is.
26:16

27 Who say to a tree, 'You are
my father,'
And to a stone, 'You gave
me birth.'

For they have turned their
ᵃback to Me,
And not their face;
But in the ᵇtime of their
trouble they will say,
'Arise and save us.'

28 "But where are your ᵃgods
Which you made for your-
self?
Let them arise, if they can
ᵇsave you
In the time of your trou-
ble;
For ᶜaccording to the num-
ber of your cities
Are your gods, O Judah.

28 ᵃDeut.
32:37; Judg.
10:14; Is.
45:20; Jer.
1:16 ᵇJer.
11:12 ᶜ2 Kin.
17:30, 31;
Jer. 11:13

29 "Why do you contend with
Me?
You have ᵃall transgressed
against Me," declares
the Lᴏʀᴅ.

29 ᵃJer. 5:1;
6:13; Dan.
9:11

30 "ᵃIn vain I have struck your
sons;
They accepted no chasten-
ing.
Your ᵇsword has devoured
your prophets
Like a destroying lion.

30 ᵃIs. 1:5;
Jer. 5:3; 7:28
ᵇNeh. 9:26;
Jer. 26:20-
24; Acts
7:52;
1 Thess. 2:15

31 "O generation, heed the
word of the Lᴏʀᴅ.
Have I been a wilderness
to Israel,
Or a ᵃland of thick dark-
ness?
Why do My people say,
'ᵇWe are free to roam;
We will come no more to
Thee'?

31 ᵃIs. 45:19
ᵇDeut.
32:15; Jer.
2:20, 25

32 "Can a virgin forget her or-
naments,
Or a bride her attire?
Yet My people have ᵃfor-
gotten Me
Days without number.

32 ᵃPs.
106:21; Is.
17:10; Jer.
3:21; 13:25;
Hos. 8:14

33 "How well you prepare
your way
To seek love!
Therefore even the wicked
women

2:23 Israel's sexual promiscuity, connected with
her idolatrous worship, is likened to the actions of a swift young camel (lit., a she-camel)
in heat, running every direction looking for a
mate.

2:27 tree. A wooden pole that stood in a Canaanite high place of worship. stone. A pillar
or image used in connection with the worship
of Baal.

You have taught your ways.

34 a2 Kin.
21:16; 24:4;
Ps. 106:38;
Jer. 7:6; 19:4
bEx. 22:2

34 "Also on your skirts is found
The ^alifeblood of the innocent poor;
You did not find them ^bbreaking in.
But in spite of all these things,

35 aJer.
25:31 bProv.
28:13;
1 John 1:8,
10

35 Yet you said, 'I am innocent;
Surely His anger is turned away from me.'
Behold, I will ^aenter into judgment with you
Because you ^bsay, 'I have not sinned.'

★36-37

36 aJer.
2:23; 31:22;
Hos. 12:1
bIs. 30:3
c2 Chr.
28:16, 20, 21

36 "Why do you ^ago around so much
Changing your way?
Also, ^byou shall be put to shame by Egypt
As you were put to shame by ^cAssyria.

37 a2 Sam.
13:19; Jer.
14:3, 4 bJer.
37:7-10

37 "From this *place* also you shall go out
With ^ayour hands on your head;
For the LORD has rejected ^bthose in whom you trust,
And you shall not prosper with them."

★ 1 aDeut.
24:1-4 bJer.
2:20; Ezek.
16:26, 28, 29
cJer. 4:1;
Zech. 1:3

3 God says, "^aIf a husband divorces his wife,
And she goes from him,
And belongs to another man,
Will he still return to her?
Will not that land be completely polluted?
But you ^bare a harlot *with* many lovers;
Yet you ^cturn to Me," declares the LORD.

2 "Lift up your eyes to the ^abare heights and see;
Where have you not been violated?
By the roads you have ^bsat for them
Like an Arab in the desert,
And you have ^cpolluted a land
With your harlotry and with your wickedness.

★ 2 aDeut.
12:2; Jer.
2:20; 3:21;
7:29 bGen.
38:14; Ezek.
16:25 cJer.
2:7

3 "Therefore the ^ashowers have been withheld,
And there has been no spring rain.
Yet you had a ^bharlot's forehead;
You refused to be ashamed.

★ 3 aLev.
26:19; Jer.
14:3-6 bJer.
6:15; 8:12

4 "Have you not just now called to Me,
'^aMy Father, Thou art the ^bfriend of my ^cyouth?

4 aJer.
3:19; 31:9
bPs. 71:17;
Prov. 2:17
cJer. 2:2;
Hos. 2:15

5 '^aWill He be angry forever?
Will He be indignant to the end?'
Behold, you have spoken
And have done evil things,
And you have had your way."

5 aPs.
103:9; Is.
57:16; Jer.
3:12

B Judah's Chastening, 3:6–6:30

1 Contrast between Israel and Judah, 3:6–11

6 Then the LORD said to me in the days of Josiah the king, "Have you seen what faithless Israel did? She ^awent up on every high hill and under every green tree, and she was a harlot there.

★ 6-10

6 aJer.
17:2; Ezek.
23:4-10

7 "And ^aI thought, 'After she has done all these things, she will return to Me'; but she did not re-

7 a2 Kin.
17:13 bJer.
3:11; Ezek.
16:47

2:36-37 Jeremiah bluntly stated that if Israel looked to Egypt for help she would find only misery *(hands on your head)*.
3:1 Deut. 24:1-4 forbade a man divorced from his wife to remarry her if she had been married in the meantime even if her second husband had died or divorced her. Israel's spiritual defilement made divine reconciliation difficult. *Yet you turn to Me.* Better, would you return to me?
3:2 *violated.* Lain with. The meaning is this: Is-

rael by her idolatrous worship in the *bare heights* (high places) was like an *Arab* waiting to plunder a passing caravan or like a harlot soliciting clients (cf. Gen. 38:14).
3:3 Even God's withholding the *showers* (lit., latter rain), which came in March and April and helped bring the crops to fruition, did not bring the people to their senses.
3:6-10 The punishment of *Israel* (here meaning the Northern Kingdom) should have been a warning to *Judah* (the Southern Kingdom).

turn, and her [b]treacherous sister Judah saw it.

8 [a]Deut. 24:1, 3; Is. 50:1 [b]Ezek. 16:46, 47; 23:11

8 "And I saw that for all the adulteries of faithless Israel, I had sent her away and [a]given her a writ of divorce, yet her [b]treacherous sister Judah did not fear; but she went and was a harlot also.

9 [a]Jer. 2:7; 3:2 [b]Is. 57:6; Jer. 2:27; 10:8

9 "And it came about because of the lightness of her harlotry, that she [a]polluted the land and committed adultery with [b]stones and trees.

10 [a]Jer. 12:2; Hos. 7:14

10 "And yet in spite of all this her treacherous sister Judah did not return to Me with all her heart, but rather in [a]deception," declares the LORD.

11 [a]Ezek. 16:51, 52; 23:11

11 And the LORD said to me, "[a]Faithless Israel has proved herself more righteous than treacherous Judah.

2 Call to repentance, 3:12-25

★12 [a]Jer. 3:14, 22; Ezek. 33:11 [b]Jer. 3:5 [c]Ps. 86:15; Jer. 12:15; 31:20; 33:26

12 "Go, and proclaim these words toward the north and say,
'[a]Return, faithless Israel,' declares the LORD;
'[b]I will not look upon you in anger.
For I am [c]gracious,' declares the LORD;
'I will not be angry forever.

13 [a]Deut. 30:1-3; Jer. 3:25; 14:20; 1 John 1:9 [b]Jer. 2:20, 25; 3:2, 6 [c]Deut. 12:2

13 'Only [a]acknowledge your iniquity,
That you have transgressed against the LORD your God
And have [b]scattered your favors to the strangers [c]under every green tree,
And you have not obeyed My voice,' declares the LORD.

14 [a]Jer. 31:32; Hos. 2:19 [b]Jer. 31:6, 12

14 'Return, O faithless sons,' declares the LORD;
'For I am a [a]master to you,
And I will take you one from a city and two from a family,

And [b]I will bring you to Zion.'

15 [a]Jer. 23:4; 31:10; Ezek. 34:23; Eph. 4:11 [b]Acts 20:28

15 "Then I will give you [a]shepherds after My own heart, who will [b]feed you on knowledge and understanding.

★16-17
16 [a]Is. 65:17

16 "And it shall be in those days when you are multiplied and increased in the land," declares the LORD, "they shall [a]say no more, 'The ark of the covenant of the LORD.' And it shall not come to mind, nor shall they remember it, nor shall they miss it, nor shall it be made again.

17 [a]Jer. 17:12; Ezek. 43:7 [b]Jer. 3:19; 4:2; 12:15, 16; 16:19 [c]Is. 60:9 [d]Jer. 11:8

17 "At that time they shall call Jerusalem 'The [a]Throne of the LORD,' and [b]all the nations will be gathered to it, to Jerusalem, for the [c]name of the LORD; nor shall they [d]walk anymore after the stubbornness of their evil heart.

18 [a]Is. 11:13; Jer. 50:4, 5; Hos. 1:11 [b]Jer. 16:15; 31:8 [c]Amos 9:15

18 "[a]In those days the house of Judah will walk with the house of Israel, and they will come together [b]from the land of the north to the [c]land that I gave your fathers as an inheritance.

19 [a]Ps. 16:6 [b]Is. 63:16; Jer. 3:4

19 "Then I said,
'How I would set you among My sons,
And give you a pleasant land,
The most [a]beautiful inheritance of the nations!'
And I said, 'You shall call Me, [b]My Father,
And not turn away from following Me.'

20 [a]Is. 48:8

20 "Surely, as a woman treacherously departs from her lover,
So you have [a]dealt treacherously with Me,
O house of Israel," declares the LORD.

21 [a]Is. 15:2; Jer. 3:2; 7:29 [b]Is. 17:10; Jer. 2:32; 13:25

21 A voice is heard on the [a]bare heights,
The weeping and the supplications of the sons of Israel;

3:12 toward the north. I.e., toward Assyria, which had taken Israel captive. A promise of eventual restoration follows.
3:16-17 When Christ returns, the ark of the covenant will not be the place where God meets His people, but Christ will reign in Jerusalem.

Because they have per-
verted their way,
They have *b*forgotten the
Lord their God.

22 "Return, O faithless sons,
*a*I will heal your faithless-
ness."
"Behold, we come to Thee;
For Thou art the Lord our
God.

23 "Surely, *a*the hills are a de-
ception,
A tumult *on* the moun-
tains.
Surely, in the *b*Lord our
God
Is the salvation of Israel.

24 "But *a*the shameful thing
has consumed the labor of our fathers since our youth, their flocks
and their herds, their sons and
their daughters.

25 "Let us lie down in our
*a*shame, and let our humiliation
cover us; for we have sinned
against the Lord our God, we and
our fathers, *b*since our youth even
to this day. And we have not
obeyed the voice of the Lord our
God."

3 Prediction of judgment, 4:1-31

4 "If you will *a*return, O Is-
rael," declares the
Lord;
"Then you should return to
Me.
And *b*if you will put away
your detested things
from My presence,
And will not waver,

2 And you will *a*swear, 'As
the Lord lives,'
*b*In truth, in justice, and in
righteousness;
Then the *c*nations will
bless themselves in
Him,

And *d*in Him they will
glory."

3 For thus says the Lord to
the men of Judah and to Jerusalem,
"*a*Break up your fallow
ground,
And *b*do not sow among
thorns.

4 "*a*Circumcise yourselves to
the Lord
And remove the foreskins
of your heart,
Men of Judah and inhabi-
tants of Jerusalem,
Lest My *b*wrath go forth
like fire
And burn with *c*none to
quench it,
Because of the evil of your
deeds."

5 Declare in Judah and proclaim in Jerusalem,
and say,
"*a*Blow the trumpet in the
land;
Cry aloud and say,
*b*Assemble yourselves, and
let us go
Into the fortified cities.'

6 "Lift up a *a*standard toward
Zion!
Seek refuge, do not stand
still,
For I am bringing *b*evil
from the north,
And great destruction.

7 "A *a*lion has gone up from
his thicket,
And a *b*destroyer of na-
tions has set out;
He has gone out from his
place
To *c*make your land a
waste.
Your cities will be ruins
Without inhabitant.

3:24 *shameful thing.* A reference to Baal worship.
4:1-2 Apparently Josiah's reforms (3:6) had only
superficial effects on many.
4:3 *fallow ground.* Untilled ground.
4:4 *Circumcise yourselves.* Here the meaning is
figurative and has the idea of purifying, separating from the sins of the flesh (Deut. 10:16;

30:6; Ezek. 44:7).
4:5-18 A vivid description (in the prophetic present tense, which sees the judgment as already
in progress, so certain is its fulfillment) of the
invasion by Babylon. Jeremiah compares this
event to a *lion* seeking prey (v. 7), a *scorching
wind* (the sirocco, v. 11) from the desert, and
threatening *clouds* (v. 13).

8 aIs.
22:12; Jer.
6:26 bIs.
5:25; 10:4;
Jer. 30:24

8 "For this, ᵃput on sackcloth,
Lament and wail;
For the ᵇfierce anger of the
LORD
Has not turned back from
us."

9 aIs. 22:3-
5; Jer. 48:41
bIs. 29:9, 10;
Ezek. 13:9-
16

9 "And it shall come about in
that day," declares the LORD, "that
the ᵃheart of the king and the
heart of the princes will fail; and
the priests will be appalled, and
the ᵇprophets will be astounded."

10 aEzek.
14:9;
2 Thess. 2:11
bJer. 5:12;
14:13

10 Then I said, "Ah, Lord
GOD! Surely Thou hast utterly
ᵃdeceived this people and Jerusalem, saying, 'ᵇYou will have
peace'; whereas a sword touches
the throat."

11 aJer.
13:24; 51:1;
Ezek. 17:10;
Hos. 13:15

11 In that time it will be said
to this people and to Jerusalem,
"A ᵃscorching wind from the bare
heights in the wilderness in the
direction of the daughter of My
people—not to winnow, and not
to cleanse,
12 a wind too strong for
this—will come at My command;
now I will also pronounce judgments against them.

13 aIs. 19:1;
Nah. 1:3 bIs.
5:28; 66:15
cLam. 4:19;
Hab. 1:8 dIs.
:3:8

13 "Behold, he ᵃgoes up like
clouds,
And his ᵇchariots like the
whirlwind;
His horses are ᶜswifter
than eagles.
Woe to us, for ᵈwe are
ruined!"

14 aProv.
1:22; Jer.
6:19; 13:27;
James 4:8

14 Wash your heart from
evil, O Jerusalem,
That you may be saved.
How long will your
ᵃwicked thoughts
Lodge within you?

15 aJer. 8:16

15 For a voice declares from
ᵃDan,
And proclaims wickedness
from Mount Ephraim.

16 aIs. 39:3;
Jer. 5:15
bEzek. 21:22

16 "Report it to the nations,
now!
Proclaim over Jerusalem,
'Besiegers come from a ᵃfar
country,

And ᵇlift their voices
against the cities of
Judah.

17 'Like watchmen of a field
they are ᵃagainst her
round about,
Because she has ᵇrebelled
against Me,' declares
the LORD.

17 a2 Kin.
25:1, 4 bIs.
1:20; 23; Jer.
5:23

18 "Your ᵃways and your
deeds
Have brought these things
to you.
This is your evil. How ᵇbit-
ter!
How it has touched your
heart!"

18 aPs.
107:17; Is.
50:1; Jer.
2:17, 19
bJer. 2:19

19 ᵃMy soul, my soul! I am in
anguish! Oh, my
heart!
My ᵇheart is pounding in
me;
I cannot be silent,
Because you have heard, O
my soul,
The ᶜsound of the trum-
pet,
The alarm of war.

★19-31

19 aIs. 15:5;
16:11; 21:3;
22:4; Jer.
9:1, 10; 20:9
bHab. 3:16
cNum. 10:9

20 ᵃDisaster on disaster is
proclaimed,
For the ᵇwhole land is devastated;
Suddenly my ᶜtents are
devastated,
My curtains in an instant.

20 aPs. 42:7;
Ezek. 7:26
bJer. 4:27
cJer. 10:20

21 How long must I see the
standard,
And hear the sound of the
trumpet?

22 "ᵃFor My people are foolish,
They know Me not;
They are stupid children,
And they have no under-
standing.
They are shrewd to ᵇdo
evil,
But to do good they do not
know."

22 aJer. 5:4,
21; 10:8;
Rom. 1:22
bJer. 9:3;
13:23; Rom.
16:19; 1 Cor.
14:20

23 I looked on the earth, and
behold, it was ᵃform-
less and void;

23 aGen.
1:2; Is. 24:19

4:19-31 Jeremiah is appalled by the extent of the
coming judgment. So devastating will it be
that it is compared with the original state of
the world (formless and void, v. 23; cf. Gen.

1:2). Even in the final hour of destruction
some will try to placate their enemies by allur-
ing them as a harlot does (Jer. 4:29-31).

And to the heavens, and they had no light.

24 *a*Is. 5:25;
Jer. 10:10;
Ezek. 38:20

24 I looked on the mountains, and behold, they were *a*quaking,
And all the hills moved to and fro.

25 *a*Jer.
9:10; 12:4;
Zeph. 1:3

25 I looked, and behold, there was no man,
And all the *a*birds of the heavens had fled.

26 *a*Jer. 9:10

26 I looked, and behold, the *a*fruitful land was a wilderness,
And all its cities were pulled down
Before the Lord, before His fierce anger.

27 *a*Jer.
12:11, 12;
25:11 *b*Jer.
5:10, 18;
30:11; 46:28

27 For thus says the Lord,
"The *a*whole land shall be a desolation,
Yet I will *b*not execute a complete destruction.

28 *a*Jer.
12:4, 11;
14:2; Hos.
4:3 *b*Is. 5:30;
50:3; Joel
2:30, 31
*c*Num.
23:19; Jer.
23:20; 30:24

28 "For this the *a*earth shall mourn,
And the *b*heavens above be dark,
Because I have *c*spoken, I have purposed,
And I will not change My mind, nor will I turn from it."

29 *a*2 Kin.
25:4 *b*Is.
2:19-21; Jer.
16:16 *c*Jer.
4:7

29 At the sound of the horseman and bowman *a*every city flees;
They *b*go into the thickets and climb among the rocks;
*c*Every city is forsaken,
And no man dwells in them.

30 *a*Is. 10:3;
20:6; Jer.
13:21
*b*2 Kin. 9:30;
Ezek. 23:40
*c*Jer. 22:20,
22; Lam. 1:2,
19; Ezek.
23:9, 10, 22

30 And you, O desolate one, *a*what will you do?
Although you dress in scarlet,
Although you decorate *yourself with* ornaments of gold,
Although you *b*enlarge your eyes with paint,
In vain you make yourself beautiful;

Your *c*lovers despise you;
They seek your life.

31 *a*Is. 42:14
*b*Is. 1:15;
Lam. 1:17

31 For I heard a cry as of a woman in labor,
The anguish as of one giving birth to her first child,
The cry of the daughter of Zion *a*gasping for breath,
*b*Stretching out her hands, *saying,*
"Ah, woe is me, for I faint before murderers."

4 Reasons for judgment, 5:1–31

★ 1-9

1 *a*2 Chr.
16:9; Dan.
12:4 *b*Ezek.
22:30 *c*Gen.
18:26, 32

5 "*a*Roam to and fro through the streets of Jerusalem,
And look now, and take note.
And seek in her open squares,
If you can *b*find a man,
*c*If there is one who does justice, who seeks truth,
Then I will pardon her.

2 *a*Is. 48:1;
Titus 1:16

2 "And *a*although they say, 'As the Lord lives,'
Surely they swear falsely."

3 *a*2 Chr.
16:9 *b*Is. 1:5;
9:13; Jer.
2:30 *c*Jer.
7:28; 8:5;
Zeph. 3:2
*d*Jer. 7:26;
19:15; Ezek.
3:8

3 O Lord, do not *a*Thine eyes look for truth?
Thou hast *b*smitten them,
But they did not weaken;
Thou hast consumed them,
But they *c*refused to take correction.
They have *d*made their faces harder than rock;
They have refused to repent.

4 *a*Is.
27:11; Jer.
8:7; Hos. 4:6

4 Then I said, "They are only the poor,
They are foolish;
For they *a*do not know the way of the Lord
Or the ordinance of their God.

5:1-9 Jeremiah is sent to try to find one righteous person among the people (cf. Gen. 18:32). He finds none among the common people (who, even though poor, are without excuse, Jer. 5:4) or among the leaders (v. 5). Therefore, the people must be punished for they are like *well-fed lusty horses* (v. 8).

5 ^aMic. 3:1
^bEx. 32:25;
Ps. 2:3; Jer.
2:20

5 "I will go to the great
    And will speak to them,
    For ^athey know the way of
       the Lord,
    And the ordinance of their
       God."
    But they too, with one ac-
       cord, have ^bbroken
       the yoke
    And burst the bonds.

6 ^aJer. 4:7
^bEzek.
22:27; Hab.
1:8; Zeph.
3:3 ^cHos.
13:7 ^dJer.
30:14, 15

6 Therefore ^aa lion from the
       forest shall slay them,
    A ^bwolf of the deserts shall
       destroy them,
    A ^cleopard is watching
       their cities.
    Everyone who goes out of
       them shall be torn in
       pieces,
    Because their ^dtransgres-
       sions are many,
    Their apostasies are nu-
       merous.

7 ^aJosh.
23:7; Jer.
12:16; Zeph.
1:5 ^bDeut.
32:21; Jer.
2:11; Gal.
4:8 ^cJer. 7:9

7 "Why should I pardon you?
    Your sons have forsaken
       Me
    And ^asworn by those who
       are ^bnot gods.
    When I had fed them to
       the full,
    They ^ccommitted adultery
    And trooped to the harlot's
       house.

8 ^aJer.
13:27; 29:23;
Ezek. 22:11

8 "They were well-fed lusty
       horses,
    Each one neighing after his
       ^aneighbor's wife.

9 ^aJer. 9:9

9 "Shall I not punish these
       people," declares the
       Lord,
    "And on a nation such as
       this
    ^aShall I not avenge My-
       self?

★10

10 "Go up through her vine
       rows and destroy,
    But do not execute a com-
       plete destruction;
    Strip away her branches,
    For they are not the Lord's.

11 "For the ^ahouse of Israel
       and the house of Ju-
       dah
    Have dealt very treacher-
       ously with Me," de-
       clares the Lord.

11 ^aJer. 3:6,
7, 20

12 They have ^alied about the
       Lord
    And said, "^bNot He;
    Misfortune will ^cnot come
       on us;
    And we ^dwill not see
       sword or famine.

12 ^a2 Chr.
36:16 ^bProv.
30:9; Jer.
14:22; 43:1-4
^cJer. 23:17
^dJer. 14:13

13 "And the ^aprophets are as
       wind,
    And the word is not in
       them.
    Thus it will be done to
       them!"

13 ^aJob 8:2;
Jer. 14:13,
15; 22:22

14 Therefore, thus says the
       Lord, the God of
       hosts,
    "Because you have spoken
       this word,
    Behold, I am ^amaking My
       words in your mouth
       fire
    And this people wood, and
       it will consume them.

14 ^aIs. 24:6;
Jer. 1:9;
23:29; Hos.
6:5; Zech.
1:6

15 "Behold, I am ^abringing a
       nation against you
       from afar, O house of
       Israel," declares the
       Lord.
    "It is an enduring nation,
    It is an ancient nation,
    A nation whose ^blanguage
       you do not know,
    Nor can you understand
       what they say.

★15 ^aDeut.
28:49; Is.
5:26; Jer.
4:16 ^bIs.
28:11

16 "Their ^aquiver is like an
       ^bopen grave,
    All of them are mighty
       men.

16 ^aIs. 5:28;
13:18 ^bPs.
5:9

17 "And they will ^adevour
       your harvest and your
       food;
    They will devour your
       sons and your daugh-
       ters;
    They will devour your
       flocks and your herds;

17 ^aLev.
26:16; Deut.
28:31, 33;
Jer. 8:16;
50:7, 17
^bJer. 8:13
^cHos. 8:14

5:10 God's fruitless vineyard will be pillaged (2:21).   **5:15** Quoted from Deut. 28:49.

They will devour your
ᵇvines and your fig
trees;
They will demolish with
the sword your ᶜforti-
fied cities in which
you trust.

+18 18 "Yet even in those days,"
declares the Lᴏʀᴅ, "I will not
make you a complete destruction.

19 "And it shall come about
ᵃwhen they say, 'Why has the
Lᴏʀᴅ our God done all these
things to us?' then you shall say
to them, 'As you have forsaken
Me and served foreign gods in
your land, so you shall ᵇserve
strangers in a land that is not
yours.'

+20-31 20 "Declare this in the house
of Jacob
And proclaim it in Judah,
saying,

21 'Hear this, O foolish and
senseless people,
Who have ᵃeyes, but see
not;
Who have ears, but hear
not.

22 'Do you not ᵃfear Me?' declares the Lᴏʀᴅ.
'Do you not tremble in My
presence?
For I have ᵇplaced the sand
as a boundary for the
sea,
An eternal decree, so it
cannot cross over it.
Though the waves toss, yet
they cannot prevail;
Though they roar, yet they
cannot cross over it.

23 'But this people has a
ᵃstubborn and rebel-
lious heart;
They have turned aside
and departed.

24 'They do not say in their
heart,
"Let us now fear the Lᴏʀᴅ
our God,

Who ᵃgives rain in its season,
Both ᵇthe autumn rain and
the spring rain,
Who keeps for us
The ᶜappointed weeks of
the harvest."

25 'Your ᵃiniquities have
turned these away,
And your sins have with-
held good from you.

26 'For wicked men are found
among My people,
They ᵃwatch like fowlers
lying in wait;
They set a trap,
They catch men.

27 'Like a cage full of birds,
So their houses are full of
ᵃdeceit;
Therefore they have be-
come great and rich.

28 'They are ᵃfat, they are
sleek,
They also excel in deeds of
wickedness;
They do not plead the
cause,
The cause of the ᵇorphan,
that they may pros-
per;
And they do not defend
the rights of the poor.

29 'ᵃShall I not punish these
people?' declares the
Lᴏʀᴅ,
'On a nation such as this
Shall I not avenge Myself?'

30 "An appalling and ᵃhorrible
thing
Has happened in the land:

31 The ᵃprophets prophesy
falsely,
And the priests rule on
their *own* authority;
And My people ᵇlove it so!
But what will you do at the
end of it?

Cross-references (side margins):

19 ᵃDeut.
29:24-26;
1 Kin. 9:8, 9;
Jer. 13:22;
16:10-13
ᵇDeut.
28:48; Jer.
16:13

21 ᵃIs. 6:9;
43:8; Ezek.
12:2; Matt.
13:14; Mark
8:18; John
12:40; Acts
28:26; Rom.
11:8

22 ᵃDeut.
28:58; Ps.
119:120; Jer.
2:19; 10:7;
Rev. 15:4
ᵇJob 38:8-
11; Ps.
104:9; Prov.
8:29

23 ᵃDeut.
21:18; Ps.
78:8; Jer.
4:17; 6:28

24 ᵃPs.
147:8; Jer.
3:3; Matt.
5:45; Acts
14:17 ᵇJoel
2:23 ᶜGen.
8:22

25 ᵃJer.
2:17; 4:18

26 ᵃPs. 10:9;
Prov. 1:11;
Jer. 18:22;
Hab. 1:15

27 ᵃJer. 9:6

28 ᵃDeut.
32:15 ᵇIs.
1:23; Jer.
7:6; 22:3;
Zech. 7:10

29 ᵃJer. 5:9;
Mal. 3:5

30 ᵃJer.
23:14; Hos.
6:10

31 ᵃEzek.
13:6 ᵇMic.
2:11

5:18 Another promise that Israel will not be
eradicated (cf. 4:27).
5:20-31 Reasons for the coming catastrophe include stubbornness (vv. 20-22), rebellion (vv.
23-25), illegal exploitation (vv. 26-28), and
faithless prophets and priests (v. 31).

5 Certainty of judgment,
6:1-30

6 "Flee for safety, O sons of
  *a*Benjamin,
  From the midst of Jerusa-
    lem!
  Now blow a trumpet in
    Tekoa,
  And raise a signal over
    *b*Beth-haccerem;
  For evil looks down from
    the *c*north,
  And a great destruction.
2 "The comely and *a*dainty
    one, *b*the daughter of
    Zion, I will cut off.
3 "*a*Shepherds and their
    flocks will come to
    her,
  They will *b*pitch *their* tents
    around her,
  They will pasture each in
    his place.
4 "*a*Prepare war against her;
  Arise, and let us attack at
    *b*noon.
  Woe to us, for the day de-
    clines,
  For the shadows of the
    evening lengthen!
5 "Arise, and let us attack by
    night
  And *a*destroy her palaces!"
6 For thus says the LORD of
    hosts,
  "*a*Cut down her trees,
  And cast up a *b*siege
    against Jerusalem.
  This is the city to be pun-
    ished,
  In whose midst there is
    only *c*oppression.
7 "*a*As a well keeps its waters
    fresh,
  So she keeps fresh her
    wickedness.
  *b*Violence and destruction
    are heard in her;

  *c*Sickness and wounds are
    ever before Me.
8 "*a*Be warned, O Jerusalem,
  Lest *b*I be alienated from
    you;
  Lest I make you a desola-
    tion,
  A land not inhabited."

9 Thus says the LORD of
    hosts,
  "They will *a*thoroughly
    glean as the vine the
    *b*remnant of Israel;
  Pass your hand again like a
    grape gatherer
  Over the branches."
10 To whom shall I speak and
    give warning,
  That they may hear?
  Behold, their *a*ears are
    closed,
  And they cannot listen.
  Behold, *b*the word of the
    LORD has become a re-
    proach to them;
  They have no delight in it.
11 But I am *a*full of the wrath
    of the LORD;
  I am *b*weary with holding
    it in.
  "*c*Pour *it* out on the chil-
    dren in the street,
  And on the gathering of
    young men together;
  For both husband and wife
    shall be taken,
  The aged and the very old.
12 "And their *a*houses shall be
    turned over to others,
  Their fields and their wives
    together;
  For I will *b*stretch out My
    hand
  Against the inhabitants of
    the land," declares the
    LORD.

Cross references (margin)

★ 1 *a*Josh. 18:28 *b*Neh. 3:14 *c*Jer. 1:14; 4:6; 6:22

2 *a*Deut. 28:56 *b*Is. 1:8; Jer. 4:31

★ 3 *a*Jer. 12:10 *b*2 Kin. 25:1; Jer. 4:17; Luke 19:43

4 *a*Jer. 6:23; Joel 3:9 *b*Jer. 15:8; Zeph. 2:4

5 *a*Is. 32:14; Jer. 52:13

6 *a*Deut. 20:19, 20 *b*Jer. 32:24; 33:4 *c*Jer. 22:17

7 *a*James 3:11f. *b*Jer. 20:8; Ezek. 7:11, 23 *c*Jer. 30:12, 13

8 *a*Jer. 7:28; 17:23 *b*Ezek. 23:18; Hos. 9:12

★ 9 *a*Jer. 16:16; 49:9; Obad. 5, 6 *b*Jer. 8:3; 11:23

★10-21

10 *a*Jer. 5:21; 7:26; Acts 7:51 *b*Jer. 20:8

11 *a*Job 32:18, 19; Mic. 3:8 *b*Jer. 15:6; 20:9 *c*Jer. 7:20; 9:21

12 *a*Deut. 28:30; Jer. 8:10; 38:22, 23 *b*Jer. 15:6

6:1 Jeremiah warns his own tribe *Benjamin* to
flee from Jerusalem. *Tekoa*, a play on the Hebrew word *blow*, was 12 miles S. of Jerusalem.
Beth-haccerem. Modern Ramat Rahel, 2 miles
S. of Jerusalem (Neh. 3:14).
6:3 *Shepherds and their flocks*. A reference to
the Babylonian leaders and their flocks of soldiers, eager to feed on Judah (cf. 12:10).
6:9 Judah would be *thoroughly* devastated, as a

grapevine a gatherer picks clean.
6:10-21 Judah is further condemned for not
hearing the warnings (v. 10), for having no
shame (v. 15), for stubbornness (v. 16), and for
ostentatious though empty worship (v. 20), including *frankincense* from *Sheba* (Yemen) and
sweet cane (an aromatic root probably imported from India).

13 "For ^afrom the least of them
even to the greatest of
them,
Everyone is ^bgreedy for
gain,
And from the prophet
even to the priest
Everyone deals falsely.

14 "And they have ^ahealed the
brokenness of My
people superficially,
Saying, 'Peace, peace,'
But there is no peace.

15 "Were they ^aashamed because of the abomina-
tion they have done?
They were not even
ashamed at all;
They did not even know
how to blush.
Therefore they shall fall
among those who fall;
At the time that I punish
them,
They shall be cast down,"
says the LORD.

16 Thus says the LORD,
"Stand by the ways and see
and ask for the ^aan-
cient paths,
Where the good way is,
and walk in it;
And ^byou shall find rest
for your souls.
But they said, 'We will not
walk in it.'

17 "And I set ^awatchmen over
you, saying,
'Listen to the sound of the
trumpet!'
But they said, 'We will not
listen.'

18 "Therefore hear, O nations,
And know, O congrega-
tion, what is among
them.

19 "^aHear, O earth: behold, I
am bringing disaster
on this people,
The ^bfruit of their plans,
Because they have not listened to My words,
And as for My law, they
have ^crejected it also.

20 "^aFor what purpose does
^bfrankincense come to
Me from Sheba,
And the ^csweet cane from
a distant land?
^dYour burnt offerings are
not acceptable,
And your sacrifices are not
pleasing to Me."

21 Therefore, thus says the
LORD,
"Behold, ^aI am laying stumbling blocks before
this people.
And they will stumble
against them,
^bFathers and sons together;
Neighbor and friend will
perish."

22 Thus says the LORD,
"Behold, ^aa people is coming from the north
land,
And a great nation will be
aroused from the ^bre-
mote parts of the
earth.

23 "They seize ^abow and spear;
They are ^bcruel and have
no mercy;
Their voice ^croars like the
sea,
And they ride on horses,
Arrayed as a man for the
battle
Against you, O daughter
of Zion!"

24 We have ^aheard the report
of it;
Our hands are limp.
^bAnguish has seized us,
Pain as of a woman in
childbirth.

25 ^aDo not go out into the
field,
And ^bdo not walk on the
road,
For the enemy has a
sword,
^cTerror is on every side.

26 O daughter of my people,
^aput on sackcloth
And ^broll in ashes;

13 ^aJer. 8:10
^bIs. 56:11;
57:17; Jer.
8:10; 22:17

14 ^aJer.
8:11; Ezek.
13:10

15 ^aJer. 3:3;
8:12

16 ^aIs. 8:20;
Jer. 12:16;
18:15; 31:21;
Mal. 4:4;
Luke 16:29
^bMatt. 11:29

17 ^aIs.
21:11; 58:1;
Jer. 25:4;
Ezek. 3:17;
Hab. 2:1

19 ^aIs. 1:2;
Jer. 19:3, 15;
22:29 ^bProv.
1:31 ^cJer.
8:9

20 ^aPs.
50:7-9; Is.
1:11; 66:3;
Mic. 6:6 ^bIs.
60:6 ^cEx.
30:23 ^dPs.
40:6; Amos
5:22

21 ^aIs. 8:14;
Jer. 13:16
^bIs. 9:14-17;
Jer. 9:21, 22

★22-26

22 ^aJer.
1:15; 10:22;
50:41-43
^bNeh. 1:9

23 ^aIs.
13:18; Jer.
4:29 ^bJer.
50:42 ^cIs.
5:30

24 ^aIs.
28:19; Jer.
4:19-21 ^bIs.
21:3; Jer.
4:31; 13:21;
30:6; 49:24;
50:43

25 ^aJer.
14:18 ^bJudg.
5:6 ^cJer.
20:10; 46:5;
49:29

26 ^aJer. 4:8
^bJer. 25:34;
Mic. 1:10
^cAmos 8:10;
Zech. 12:10

6:22-26 Jeremiah portrays the cruelty of the Babylonian invaders.

ᶜMourn as for an only son,
A lamentation most bitter.
For suddenly the destroyer
Will come upon us.

★27-31

27 a Jer.
1:18; 15:20

27 "I have ᵃmade you an assayer *and* a tester
among My people,
That you may know and
assay their way."

28 a Jer. 9:4
b Ezek. 22:18

28 All of them are stubbornly
rebellious,
ᵃGoing about as a tale-
bearer.
They are ᵇbronze and iron;
They, all of them, are corrupt.

29 a Jer.
15:19

29 The bellows blow fiercely,
The lead is consumed by
the fire;
In vain the refining goes
on,
But the ᵃwicked are not
separated.

30 a Ps.
119:119; Is.
1:22 **b** Jer.
7:29; Hos.
9:17; Zech.
11:8

30 ᵃThey call them rejected
silver,
Because the ᵇLᴏʀᴅ has re-
jected them.

C Judah's Wrong Religion,
7:1–10:25

1 The indictment of the
people; the Temple
sermon, 7:1–8:3

★ 2 a Jer.
17:19; 26:2

7 The word that came to Jeremiah from the Lᴏʀᴅ, saying,
2 "ᵃStand in the gate of the
Lᴏʀᴅ's house and proclaim there
this word, and say, 'Hear the
word of the Lᴏʀᴅ, all you of Judah, who enter by these gates to
worship the Lᴏʀᴅ!' "

3 a Jer. 4:1;
7:5; 18:11;
26:13

3 Thus says the Lᴏʀᴅ of
hosts, the God of Israel, "ᵃAmend
your ways and your deeds, and I
will let you dwell in this place.

4 "ᵃDo not trust in deceptive
words, saying, 'This is the temple
of the Lᴏʀᴅ, the temple of the
Lᴏʀᴅ, the temple of the Lᴏʀᴅ.'

5 "For ᵃif you truly amend
your ways and your deeds, if you
truly ᵇpractice justice between a
man and his neighbor,

6 *if* you do not oppress the
alien, the ᵃorphan, or the widow,
and do not shed ᵇinnocent blood
in this place, nor ᶜwalk after other
gods to your own ruin,

7 then I will let you ᵃdwell in
this place, in the ᵇland that I gave
to your fathers forever and ever.

8 "Behold, you are trusting in
ᵃdeceptive words to no avail.

9 "Will you steal, murder,
and commit adultery, and swear
falsely, and ᵃoffer sacrifices to
Baal, and walk after ᵇother gods
that you have not known,

10 then ᵃcome and stand before Me in ᵇthis house, which is
called by My name, and say, 'We
are delivered!'—that you may do
all these abominations?

11 "Has ᵃthis house, which is
called by My name, become a
ᵇden of robbers in your sight? Behold, ᶜI, even I, have seen *it*," declares the Lᴏʀᴅ.

12 "But go now to My place
which was in ᵃShiloh, where I
ᵇmade My name dwell at the first,
and ᶜsee what I did to it because
of the wickedness of My people
Israel.

13 "And now, because you
have done all these things," declares the Lᴏʀᴅ, "and I spoke to
you, ᵃrising up early and ᵇspeaking, but you did not hear, and I
ᶜcalled you but you did not answer,

14 therefore, I will do to the
ᵃhouse which is called by My
name, ᵇin which you trust, and to

★ 4 a Jer.
7:8; Mic.
3:11

5 a Is. 1:19;
Jer. 4:1, 2
b 1 Kin. 6:12;
Jer. 21:12;
22:3

6 a Ex.
22:21-24;
Jer. 5:28
b Jer. 2:34;
19:4 **c** Deut.
6:14, 15;
8:19; 11:28;
Jer. 13:10

7 a Deut.
4:40 **b** Jer.
3:18

8 a Jer. 7:4;
28:15

9 a Jer.
11:13, 17
b Ex. 20:3;
Jer. 7:6; 19:4

10 a Ezek.
23:39 **b** Jer.
7:11, 14, 30;
32:34

★11 a Is.
56:7 **b** Matt.
21:13; Mark
11:17; Luke
19:46 **c** Jer.
29:23

★12-14

12 a Judg.
18:31; Jer.
26:6 **b** Josh.
18:1, 10
c 1 Sam.
4:10, 11, 22;
Ps. 78:60-64

13 a Jer. 7:25
b Jer. 35:17
c Prov. 1:24;
Is. 65:12;
66:4

14 a Deut.
12:5; 1 Kin.
9:7 **b** Jer. 7:4
c Jer. 7:12

6:27–31 Jeremiah tests the people as an assayer
tests metal, but all are dross.

7:2 This *word* (7:1–8:3) was delivered before one
of the 7 gates of the Temple courts shortly
after Jehoiakim's accession (about 608, cf.
26:7–24). The theme of this message is stated
in 7:3.

7:4 The miraculous deliverance of Jerusalem
from Sennacherib's army almost a century be-

fore (2 Kings 18:13–19:37) made Judah believe
that Jerusalem, because it was the site of the
temple, was invincible.

7:11 Quoted by the Lord (Mark 11:17; cf. Luke
19:46).

7:12–14 Just as the presence of the tabernacle in
Shiloh during the time of the judges did not
save that city from falling, so the Temple
would not save Jerusalem.

the place which I gave you and your fathers, as I ^cdid to Shiloh.

15 "And I will ^acast you out of My sight, as I have cast out all your brothers, all the offspring of ^bEphraim.

16 "As for you, ^ado not pray for this people, and do not lift up cry or prayer for them, and do not intercede with Me; for I do not hear you.

17 "Do you not see what they are doing in the cities of Judah and in the streets of Jerusalem?

18 "The children gather wood, and the fathers kindle the fire, and the women knead dough to make cakes for the queen of heaven; and *they* ^apour out libations to other gods in order to ^bspite Me.

19 "^aDo they spite Me?" declares the LORD. "Is it not themselves *they spite,* to their own ^bshame?"

20 Therefore thus says the Lord GOD, "Behold, My ^aanger and My wrath will be poured out on this place, on man and on beast and on the ^btrees of the field and on the fruit of the ground; and it will burn and not be quenched."

21 Thus says the LORD of hosts, the God of Israel, "Add your ^aburnt offerings to your sacrifices and ^beat flesh.

22 "For I did not ^aspeak to your fathers, or command them in the day that I brought them out of the land of Egypt, concerning burnt offerings and sacrifices.

23 "But this is what I commanded them, saying, '^aObey My voice, and ^bI will be your God, and you will be My people; and you will walk in all the way which

I command you, that it may ^cbe well with you.'

24 "Yet they ^adid not obey or incline their ear, but walked in *their own* counsels *and* in the stubbornness of their evil heart, and ^bwent backward and not forward.

25 "Since the day that your fathers came out of the land of Egypt until this day, I have ^asent you all My servants the prophets, daily rising early and sending *them.*

26 "Yet they did not listen to Me or incline their ear, but ^astiffened their neck; they ^bdid evil more than their fathers.

27 "And you shall ^aspeak all these words to them, but they will not listen to you; and you shall call to them, but they will ^bnot answer you.

28 "And you shall say to them, 'This is the nation that ^adid not obey the voice of the LORD their God or accept correction; ^btruth has perished and has been cut off from their mouth.

29 '^aCut off your hair and cast
    it away,
And ^btake up a lamenta-
    tion on the bare
    heights;
For the LORD has ^crejected
    and forsaken
The generation of His
    wrath.'

30 "For the sons of Judah have done that which is evil in My sight," declares the LORD, "they have ^aset their detestable things in the house which is called by My name, to defile it.

31 "And they have ^abuilt the high places of Topheth, which is in the valley of the son of Hin-

---

7:18 *the queen of heaven.* The Assyro-Babylonian goddess Ishtar (cf. 44:17).

7:21 *burnt offerings.* Though burned in its entirety on the altar (Lev. 1:9), the people might as well *eat* the offering, since it meant nothing to God in their backslidden condition.

7:22 *concerning.* Better, for the sake of; i.e., the Mosaic legislation was not primarily concerned with offerings *per se* but with a rela-

tionship with the Lord which would show itself in true worship through the offerings.

7:29 *Cut off your hair.* As a sign of mourning (Job 1:20; Mic. 1:16).

7:31 *Topheth.* Probably means "fireplace." *Hinnom.* Gehenna, a valley on the SW. of Jerusalem. Judah was outdoing the heathen, who rarely made child sacrifices.

nom, to ᵇburn their sons and their daughters in the fire, which I ᶜdid not command, and it did not come into My mind.

32 "ᵃTherefore, behold, days are coming," declares the LORD, "when it will no more be called Topheth, or the valley of the son of Hinnom, but the valley of the Slaughter; for they will ᵇbury in Topheth because there is no *other* place.

33 "And the ᵃdead bodies of this people will be food for the birds of the sky, and for the beasts of the earth; and no one will frighten *them* away.

34 "Then I will make to ᵃcease from the cities of Judah and from the streets of Jerusalem the voice of joy and the voice of gladness, the voice of the bridegroom and the voice of the bride; for the ᵇland will become a ruin.

8 "At that time," declares the LORD, "they will ᵃbring out the bones of the kings of Judah, and the bones of its princes, and the bones of the priests, and the bones of the prophets, and the bones of the inhabitants of Jerusalem from their graves.

2 "And they will spread them out to the sun, the moon, and to all the ᵃhost of heaven, which they have loved, and which they have served, and which they have gone after, and which they have sought, and which they have worshiped. They will not be gathered ᵇor buried; ᶜthey will be as dung on the face of the ground.

3 "And ᵃdeath will be chosen rather than life by all the remnant that remains of this evil family, that remains in all the ᵇplaces to which I have driven them," declares the LORD of hosts.

2　The retribution of God,
8:4–9:26

4 "And you shall say to them,
'Thus says the LORD,
"Do *men* ᵃfall and not get up again?
Does one turn away and not repent?

5 "Why then has this people, Jerusalem,
ᵃTurned away in continual apostasy?
They ᵇhold fast to deceit,
They ᶜrefuse to return.

6 "I ᵃhave listened and heard,
They have spoken what is not right;
ᵇNo man repented of his wickedness,
Saying, 'What have I done?'
Everyone turned to his course,
Like a ᶜhorse charging into the battle.

7 "Even the stork in the sky
ᵃKnows her seasons;
And the ᵇturtledove and the swift and the thrush
Observe the time of their migration;
But ᶜMy people do not know
The ordinance of the LORD.

8 "ᵃHow can you say, 'We are wise,
And the law of the LORD is with us'?
But behold, the lying pen of the scribes
Has made *it* into a lie.

9 "The wise men are ᵃput to shame,
They are dismayed and caught;

Marginal references:

32 ᵃJer. 19:6, 11 ᵇ2 Kin. 23:10

33 ᵃDeut. 28:26; Ps. 79:2; Jer. 12:9; 19:7

34 ᵃIs. 24:7, 8; Jer. 16:9; 25:10; Ezek. 26:13; Hos. 2:11; Rev. 18:23 ᵇLev. 26:33; Is. 1:7; Jer. 4:27

★ **1** ᵃEzek. 6:5

2 ᵃ2 Kin. 23:5; Jer. 19:13; Zeph. 1:5; Acts 7:42 ᵇJer. 22:19; 36:30 ᶜ2 Kin. 9:37; Ps. 83:10; Jer. 9:22

3 ᵃJob 3:21, 22; 7:15, 16; Jon. 4:3; Rev. 9:6 ᵇDeut. 30:1, 4; Jer. 23:3, 8; 29:14

4 ᵃProv. 24:16; Amos 5:2; Mic. 7:8

5 ᵃJer. 5:6; 7:24 ᵇJer. 5:27; 9:6 ᶜJer. 5:3

6 ᵃPs. 14:2; Mal. 3:16 ᵇEzek. 22:30; Mic. 7:2; Rev. 9:20 ᶜJob 39:21-25

★ **7** ᵃProv. 6:6-8; Is. 1:3 ᵇSong 2:12 ᶜJer. 5:4

★ **8** ᵃJob 5:12, 13; Jer. 4:22; Rom. 1:22

9 ᵃIs. 19:11; Jer. 6:15; 1 Cor. 1:27 ᵇJer. 6:19

8:1 The desecration of graves was a common practice in warfare, calculated to deliberately insult the conquered people (Amos 2:1). Sometimes it was done in order to uncover valuables thought to be buried with the bodies.

8:7 Israel, in contrast to the birds which follow their instincts in order to survive, behaves unnaturally toward her Creator.

8:8 The first mention of *scribes* as a professional class.

Behold, they have ᵇrejected the word of the
LORD,
And what kind of wisdom
do you have?

10 aDeut.
28:30; Jer.
6:12, 13;
38:22f. ᵇIs.
56:11; 57:17;
Jer. 6:13

10 "Therefore I will ᵃgive their
wives to others,
Their fields to new owners;
Because from the least
even to the greatest
Everyone is ᵇgreedy for
gain;
From the prophet even to
the priest
Everyone practices deceit.

11 aJer.
6:14; 14:13,
14; Lam.
2:14; Ezek.
13:10

11 "And they ᵃheal the brokenness of the daugh-
ter of My people su-
perficially,
Saying, 'Peace, peace,'
But there is no peace.

12 aPs. 52:1,
7; Is. 3:9;
Jer. 3:3;
6:15; Zeph.
3:5 ᵇIs. 9:14;
Jer. 6:21;
Hos. 4:5
cDeut.
32:35; Jer.
10:15

12 "Were they ᵃashamed because of the abomina-
tion they had done?
They certainly were not
ashamed,
And they did not know
how to blush;
Therefore they shall ᵇfall
among those who fall;
At the ᶜtime of their punishment they shall be
brought down,"
Declares the LORD.

13 aJer.
14:12; Ezek.
22:20, 21
ᵇJer. 5:17;
7:20; Joel
1:7 cMatt.
21:19; Luke
13:6

13 "I will ᵃsurely snatch them
away," declares the
LORD;
"There will be ᵇno grapes
on the vine,
And ᶜno figs on the fig
tree,
And the leaf shall wither;
And what I have given
them shall pass
away."'"

14 aJer. 4:5
ᵇ2 Sam.
20:6; Jer.
35:11 cDeut.
29:18; Ps.
69:21; Jer.
9:15; 23:15;
Lam. 3:19;
Matt. 27:34
dJer. 3:25;
14:20

14 Why are we sitting still?
ᵃAssemble yourselves, and
let us ᵇgo into the
fortified cities,
And let us perish there,
Because the LORD our God
has doomed us
And given us ᶜpoisoned
water to drink,

For ᵈwe have sinned
against the LORD.

15 aJer.
8:11; 14:19

15 We ᵃwaited for peace, but
no good came;
For a time of healing, but
behold, terror!

16 aJudg.
18:29; Jer.
4:15 ᵇJudg.
5:22 cJer.
3:24; 10:25

16 From ᵃDan is heard the
snorting of his horses;
At the sound of the neigh-
ing of his ᵇstallions
The whole land quakes;
For they come and ᶜdevour
the land and its ful-
ness,
The city and its inhabi-
tants.

17 aNum.
21:6; Deut.
32:24 ᵇPs.
58:4, 5

17 "For behold, I am ᵃsending
serpents against you,
Adders, for which there is
ᵇno charm,
And they will bite you,"
declares the LORD.

18 aIs. 22:4;
Lam. 1:16,
17 ᵇJer.
23:9; Lam.
5:17

18 My ᵃsorrow is beyond
healing,
My ᵇheart is faint within
me!

19 aIs. 13:5;
39:3; Jer.
4:16; 9:16
ᵇDeut.
32:21; Jer.
7:19 cPs.
31:6

19 Behold, listen! The cry of
the daughter of my
people from a ᵃdistant
land:
"Is the LORD not in Zion? Is
her King not within
her?"
"Why have they ᵇprovoked
Me with their graven
images, with foreign
ᶜidols?"

20 "Harvest is past, summer is
ended,
And we are not saved."

21 aJer.
4:19; 9:1;
14:17 ᵇJer.
14:2; Joel
2:6; Nah.
2:10

21 For the ᵃbrokenness of the
daughter of my peo-
ple I am broken;
I ᵇmourn, dismay has
taken hold of me.

★22 aGen.
37:25; Jer.
46:11 ᵇJer.
14:19; 30:13

22 Is there no ᵃbalm in Gilead?
Is there no physician
there?
ᵇWhy then has not the
health of the daughter
of my people been re-
stored?

8:22 *balm in Gilead.* A resin used medicinally
and available little more than a day's journey
away in Gilead (cf. Gen. 37:25). Though it was
near, the people refused God's help.

★ 1-3
1 aIs. 22:4;
Jer. 8:18;
13:17; Lam.
2:18 bJer.
6:26; 8:21,
22

9 aOh, that my head were waters,
And my eyes a fountain of tears,
That I might weep day and night
For the slain of the bdaughter of my people!

2 aPs. 55:6,
7; 120:5, 6
bJer. 5:7, 8;
23:10; Hos.
4:2 cJer.
5:11; 12:1, 6

2 aOh that I had in the desert
A wayfarers' lodging place;
That I might leave my people,
And go from them!
For all of them are badulterers,
An assembly of ctreacherous men.

3 aPs. 64:3;
Is. 59:4; Jer.
9:8 bJer.
4:22 cJudg.
2:10; 1 Sam.
2:12; Jer.
4:22; 5:4, 5;
Hos. 4:1;
1 Cor. 15:34

3 "And they abend their tongue like their bow;
Lies and not truth prevail in the land;
For they bproceed from evil to evil,
And they cdo not know Me," declares the Lord.

★ 4 aPs.
12:2; Prov.
26:24, 25;
Jer. 9:8; Mic.
7:5, 6 bJer.
12:6 cGen.
27:35 dPs.
15:3; Prov.
10:18; Jer.
6:28

4 "Let everyone abe on guard against his neighbor,
And bdo not trust any brother;
Because every cbrother deals craftily,
And every neighbor dgoes about as a slanderer.

5 aMic.
6:12 bJer.
12:13; 51:58,
64

5 "And everyone adeceives his neighbor,
And does not speak the truth,
They have taught their tongue to speak lies;
They bweary themselves committing iniquity.

6 aPs.
120:5, 6; Jer.
5:27; 8:5
bJob 21:14,
15; Prov.
1:24; Jer.
11:10; 13:10;
John 3:19,
20

6 "Your adwelling is in the midst of deceit;
Through deceit they brefuse to know Me," declares the Lord.

7 aIs. 1:25;
Jer. 6:27;
Mal. 3:3
bHos. 11:8

7 Therefore thus says the Lord of hosts,
"Behold, I will refine them and aassay them;

For bwhat else can I do, because of the daughter of My people?

8 aJer. 9:3
bPs. 28:3
cJer. 5:26

8 "Their atongue is a deadly arrow;
It speaks deceit;
With his mouth one bspeaks peace to his neighbor,
But inwardly he csets an ambush for him.

9 aIs. 1:24;
Jer. 5:9, 29

9 "aShall I not punish them for these things?" declares the Lord.
"On a nation such as this Shall I not avenge Myself?

★10-11
10 aJer.
4:24; 7:29
bJer. 4:26;
Hos. 4:3
cJer. 12:4,
10; Ezek.
14:15; 29:11;
33:28 dJer.
4:25; 12:4;
Hos. 4:3

10 "For the amountains I will take up a weeping and wailing,
And for the pastures of the bwilderness a dirge,
Because they are claid waste, so that no one passes through,
And the lowing of the cattle is not heard;
Both the dbirds of the sky and the beasts have fled; they are gone.

11 aIs. 25:2;
Jer. 51:37
bIs. 13:22;
34:13 cJer.
4:27; 26:9

11 "And I will make Jerusalem a aheap of ruins,
A haunt of bjackals;
And I will make the cities of Judah a cdesolation, without inhabitant."

12 aPs.
107:43; Is.
42:23; Hos.
14:9 bJer.
9:20; 23:16
cPs. 107:34;
Jer. 23:10

12 Who is the awise man that may understand this? And who is he to whom bthe mouth of the Lord has spoken, that he may declare it? cWhy is the land ruined, laid waste like a desert, so that no one passes through?

13 a2 Chr.
7:19; Ps.
89:30; Jer.
5:19; 22:9

13 And the Lord said, "Because they have aforsaken My law which I set before them, and have not obeyed My voice nor walked according to it,

14 aJer.
7:24; 11:8;
Rom. 1:21-24
bJer. 2:8, 23;
23:27 cGal.
1:14; 1 Pet.
1:18

14 but have awalked after the stubbornness of their heart and after the bBaals, as their cfathers taught them,"

9:1-3 Notice Jeremiah's grief over the sin of his people.
9:4 *deals craftily.* A pun, in Hebrew, on the name Jacob, which means supplanter, or one

who deals craftily. Everyone was a Jacob (Gen. 27:36).
9:10-11 The coming desolation of the land of Judah is vividly described.

★15 aPs.
80:5 bDeut.
29:18; Jer.
8:14; 23:15;
Lam. 3:15

15 therefore thus says the Lord of hosts, the God of Israel, "behold, aI will feed them, this people, with wormwood and give them bpoisoned water to drink.

16 aLev.
26:33; Deut.
28:64; Jer.
13:24 bJer.
44:27; Ezek.
5:2, 12

16 "And I will ascatter them among the nations, whom neither they nor their fathers have known; and I will send the bsword after them until I have annihilated them."

★17 a2 Chr.
35:25; Eccl.
12:5 bAmos
5:16

17 Thus says the Lord of hosts,

"Consider and call for the
amourning women,
that they may come;
And send for the bwailing
women, that they may
come!

18 aIs. 22:4;
Jer. 9:1;
14:17

18 "And let them make haste,
and take up a wailing
for us,
That our aeyes may shed
tears,
And our eyelids flow with
water.

19 aJer.
7:29; Ezek.
7:16-18
bDeut.
28:29; Jer.
4:13 cJer.
7:15; 15:1

19 "For a voice of awailing is
heard from Zion,
'bHow are we ruined!
We are put to great shame,
For we have cleft the land,
Because they have cast
down our dwell-
ings.' "

20 aIs. 32:9

20 Now hear the word of the
Lord, O you awomen,
And let your ear receive
the word of His
mouth;
Teach your daughters
wailing,
And everyone her neigh-
bor a dirge.

21 a2 Chr.
36:17; Jer.
15:7; 18:21;
Ezek 9:5, 6;
Amos 6:9, 10
bJer. 6:11

21 For adeath has come up
through our windows;
It has entered our palaces

To cut off the bchildren
from the streets,
The young men from the
town squares.

22 aPs.
83:10; Is.
5:25; Jer.
8:2; 16:4;
25:33

22 Speak, "Thus declares the
Lord,
'The corpses of men will
fall alike dung on the
open field,
And like the sheaf after
the reaper,
But no one will gather
them.' "

23 aEccl.
9:11; Is.
47:10; Ezek.
28:3-7
b1 Kin.
20:10, 11; Is.
10:8-12 cJob
31:24, 25;
Ps. 49:6-9

23 Thus says the Lord, "aLet not a wise man boast of his wisdom, and let not the bmighty man boast of his might, let not a crich man boast of his riches;

★24 aPs.
20:7; 44:8;
Is. 41:16;
Jer. 4:2;
1 Cor. 1:31;
2 Cor. 10:17;
Gal. 6:14
bEx. 34:6, 7;
Ps. 36:5, 7;
51:1 cIs.
61:8; Mic.
7:18

24 but let him who boasts aboast of this, that he understands and knows Me, that I am the Lord who bexercises lovingkindness, justice, and righteousness on earth; for I cdelight in these things," declares the Lord.

25 "Behold, the days are coming," declares the Lord, "that I will punish all who are circumcised and yet auncircumcised—

25 aJer. 4:4;
Rom. 2:28,
29

26 Egypt, and Judah, and Edom, and the sons of Ammon, and Moab, and aall those inhabiting the desert who clip the hair on their temples; for all the nations are uncircumcised, and all the house of Israel are buncircumcised of heart."

★26 aJer.
25:23 bLev.
26:41; Jer.
4:4; 6:10;
Ezek. 44:7;
Rom. 2:28

3 The folly of idolatry, 10:1-18

★ 1-16

10 Hear the word which the Lord speaks to you, O house of Israel.

2 Thus says the Lord,
"aDo not learn the way of
the nations,

2 aLev.
18:3; 20:23;
Deut. 12:30

9:15 *wormwood.* A plant having very bitter juice.

9:17 *mourning women.* Professional mourners (cf. Matt. 9:23). *wailing women.* Those skilled in mourning for the dead.

9:24 *lovingkindness.* God's covenant love was the only hope (on the Heb. word *hesed,* see Hos. 2:19).

9:26 *who clip the hair on their temples.* Better, that cut the corners of their hair; this practice, in honor of the gods of the heathen, was con-

demned in Lev. 19:27.

10:1-16 A scathing denunciation of idolatry, involving a threefold contrast: (1) Heathen worship attached great importance to the sun, moon, and stars (v. 2), though God made the heavens (v. 12); (2) man-made idols have to be stabilized (v. 4), but God even controls the nations (v. 10); (3) idols are *stupid* (without intellectual capacity) because they are inanimate (v. 8), but the living God designed and created all things (vv. 12-13).

And do not be terrified by
the signs of the heav-
ens
Although the nations are
terrified by them;

3 For the customs of the
peoples are ^adelusion;
Because ^bit is wood cut
from the forest,
The work of the hands of a
craftsman with a cut-
ting tool.

4 "They ^adecorate it with silver and with gold;
They ^bfasten it with nails
and with hammers
So that it will not totter.

5 "Like a scarecrow in a cu-
cumber field are they,
And they ^acannot speak;
They must be ^bcarried,
Because they cannot walk!
Do not fear them,
For they ^ccan do no harm,
Nor can they do any
good."

6 ^aThere is none like Thee,
O Lord;
Thou art ^bgreat, and great
is Thy name in might.

7 ^aWho would not fear
Thee, O ^bKing of the
nations?
Indeed it is Thy due!
For among all the ^cwise
men of the nations,
And in all their kingdoms,
There is none like Thee.

8 But they are altogether
^astupid and foolish
In their discipline of delusion—their idol is
wood!

9 Beaten ^asilver is brought
from ^bTarshish,
And ^cgold from Uphaz,
The work of a craftsman
and of the hands of a
goldsmith;
Violet and purple are their
clothing;
They are all the ^dwork of
skilled men.

10 But the Lord is the ^atrue
God;
He is the ^bliving God and
the ^ceverlasting King.
At His wrath the ^dearth
quakes,
And the nations cannot
^eendure His indigna-
tion.

11 Thus you shall say to
them, "The ^agods that did not
make the heavens and the earth
shall ^bperish from the earth and
from under the heavens."

12 It is ^aHe who made the
earth by His power,
Who ^bestablished the
world by His wisdom;
And by His understanding
He has ^cstretched out
the heavens.

13 When He utters His
^avoice, there is a tu-
mult of waters in the
heavens,
And He causes the ^bclouds
to ascend from the
end of the earth;
He makes lightning for the
rain,
And brings out the ^cwind
from His storehouses.

14 Every man is ^astupid, devoid of knowledge;
Every goldsmith is put to
shame by his idols;
For his molten images are
deceitful,
And there is no breath in
them.

15 They are ^aworthless, a
work of mockery;
In the ^btime of their punishment they will per-
ish.

16 The ^aportion of Jacob is
not like these;
For the ^bMaker of all is He,
And ^cIsrael is the tribe of
His inheritance;
The ^dLord of hosts is His
name.

Cross references (left margin):

3 ^aJer. 14:22 ^bIs. 44:9-20

4 ^aIs. 40:19 ^bIs. 40:20; 41:7

5 ^aPs. 115:5; Is. 46:7; Jer. 10:14; 1 Cor. 12:2 ^bPs. 115:7; Is. 46:1, 7 ^cIs. 41:23, 24

6 ^aEx. 15:11; Deut. 33:26; Ps. 86:8, 10; Jer. 10:16 ^bPs. 48:1; 96:4; Is. 12:6; Jer. 32:18

7 ^aRev. 15:4 ^bPs. 22:28 ^cDan. 2:27, 28; 1 Cor. 1:19, 20

8 ^aJer. 4:22; 5:4; 10:8

★ 9 ^aIs. 40:19 ^bPs. 72:10; Is. 23:6 ^cDan. 10:5 ^dPs. 115:4

Cross references (right margin):

10 ^aIs. 65:16 ^bJer. 4:2 ^cPs. 10:16; 29:10 ^dJer. 4:24; 50:46 ^ePs. 76:7

★11 ^aPs. 96:5 ^bIs. 2:18; Zeph. 2:11

12 ^aGen. 1:1, 6; Job 38:4-7; Ps. 136:5; 148:4, 5; Jer. 51:15; 19 ^bPs. 78:69; Is. 45:18 ^cJob 9:8; Is. 40:22

13 ^aPs. 29:3-9 ^bJob 36:27-29 ^cPs. 135:7

14 ^aJer. 10:8; 51:17, 18

15 ^aIs. 41:24; Jer. 8:19; 14:22 ^bJer. 8:12; 51:18

16 ^aPs. 16:5; 73:26; 119:57; Jer. 51:19; Lam. 3:24 ^bIs. 45:7; Jer. 10:12 ^cDeut. 32:9; Ps. 74:2 ^dJer. 31:35; 32:18

10:9 *Tarshish.* See note on Isa. 2:16. *Uphaz.* Unknown as a location; it may be a term for refined gold (cf. Dan. 10:5).

10:11 The only verse in Jeremiah written in Aramaic.

★17-25
★17 ªEzek.
12:3-12

17 ªPick up your bundle from
the ground,
You who dwell under
siege!

18 ª1 Sam.
25:29

18 For thus says the LORD,
"Behold, I am ªslinging out
the inhabitants of the
land
At this time,
And will cause them dis-
tress,
That they may be found."

**4 The reaction of the prophet,
10:19–25**

★19-20
19 ªJer. 4:31
ᵇJer. 14:17
ᶜMic. 7:9

19 ªWoe is me, because of
my injury!
My ᵇwound is incurable.
But I said, "Truly this is a
sickness,
And I ᶜmust bear it."

20 ªJer.
4:20; Lam.
2:4 ᵇJer.
31:15; Lam.
1:5 ᶜIs.
51:18

20 My ªtent is destroyed,
And all my ropes are bro-
ken;
My ᵇsons have gone from
me and are no more.
There is ᶜno one to stretch
out my tent again
Or to set up my curtains.

★21 ªJer.
2:8 ᵇJer.
23:2

21 For the shepherds have be-
come stupid
And ªhave not sought the
LORD;
Therefore they have not
prospered,
And ᵇall their flock is scat-
tered.

22 ªJer. 4:15
ᵇJer. 1:14;
25:9 ᶜJer.
9:11; 49:33

22 The sound of a ªreport! Behold, it comes—
A great commotion ᵇout of
the land of the
north—
To ᶜmake the cities of Judah
A desolation, a haunt of
jackals.

23 I know, O LORD, that ªa
man's way is not in
himself;
ᵇNor is it in a man who
walks to direct his
steps.

23 ªProv.
16:1; 20:24
ᵇIs. 26:7

24 ªCorrect me, O LORD, but
with justice;
Not with Thine anger, lest
Thou bring me to
nothing.

24 ªPs. 6:1;
38:1

25 ªPour out Thy wrath on
the nations that ᵇdo
not know Thee,
And on the families that
ᶜdo not call Thy
name;
For they have devoured Jacob;
They have ᵈdevoured him
and consumed him,
And have laid waste his
habitation.

25 ªPs. 79:6,
7; Zeph. 3:8
ᵇJob 18:21;
1 Thess. 4:5;
2 Thess. 1:8
ᶜZeph. 1:6
ᵈJer. 8:16;
50:7, 17

**D Judah's Breaking of God's
Covenant, 11:1–13:27**

1 The fact, 11:1–17

11 The word which came to
Jeremiah from the LORD,
saying,

2 "ªHear the words of this
ᵇcovenant, and speak to the men
of Judah and to the inhabitants of
Jerusalem;

★ 2 ªJer.
11:6 ᵇEx.
19:5

3 and say to them, 'Thus
says the LORD, the God of Israel,
"ªCursed is the man who does not
heed the words of this covenant

3 ªDeut.
27:26; Jer.
17:5; Gal.
3:10

4 which I commanded your
forefathers in the ªday that I
brought them out of the land of
Egypt, from the ᵇiron furnace,
saying, 'ᶜListen to My voice, and
do according to all which I command you; so you shall be ᵈMy
people, and I will be your God,'

4 ªEx.
24:3-8; Jer.
31:32 ᵇDeut.
4:20; 1 Kin.
8:51 ᶜLev.
26:3; Deut.
11:27; Jer.
7:23; 26:13
ᵈJer. 24:7;
Zech. 8:8

10:17–25 These verses describe the nearness of
the Babylonian Exile.
10:17 *bundle.* Belongings to be gathered for the
long trek into exile.
10:19–20 This section describes, in the language
of nomads, the desolation of Judah.
10:21 *shepherds.* The leaders of the nation who
are responsible for the calamity (2:8; 6:3).

11:2 *this covenant.* The historic agreement between God and Israel made at Mt. Sinai (also
vv. 3, 6, 8). Jeremiah's warning to be faithful to
the Sinaitic covenant was delivered during the
reformation under Josiah (2 Kings 22–23). He
obviously viewed this revival as superficial
and inadequate (Jer. 11:13 shows the people
continued to worship Baal).

5 aEx. 13:5;
Deut. 7:12;
Ps. 105:9;
Jer. 32:22
bJer. 28:6

5 in order to confirm the aoath which I swore to your forefathers, to give them a land flowing with milk and honey, as *it is this day.*" ' " Then I answered and said, "bAmen, O LORD."

6 aJer.
3:12; 7:2
bJer. 11:2
cJohn 13:17;
Rom. 2:13;
James 1:22

6 And the LORD said to me, "aProclaim all these words in the cities of Judah and in the streets of Jerusalem, saying, bHear the words of this covenant and cdo them.

7 a1 Sam.
8:9 bJer.
11:4 cEx.
15:26; 2 Chr.
36:15; Jer.
7:25 dJer.
11:7

7 'For I solemnly awarned your fathers in the bday that I brought them up from the land of Egypt, even to this day, cwarning persistently, saying, "dListen to My voice."

8 aJer.
7:24; 9:14;
35:15; Ezek.
20:8 bLev.
26:14-43

8 'Yet they adid not obey or incline their ear, but walked, each one, in the stubbornness of his evil heart; therefore I brought on them all the bwords of this covenant, which I commanded *them* to do, but they did not.' "

9 aEzek.
22:25; Hos.
6:9

9 Then the LORD said to me, "A aconspiracy has been found among the men of Judah and among the inhabitants of Jerusalem.

10 a1 Sam.
15:11; Jer.
3:10, 11;
Ezek. 20:18
bDeut. 9:7;
Ps. 78:8-10;
Jer. 13:10
cJudg. 2:11-
13 dJer. 3:6-
11; Ezek.
16:59

10 "They have aturned back to the iniquities of their ancestors who brefused to hear My words, and they chave gone after other gods to serve them; the house of Israel and the house of Judah have dbroken My covenant which I made with their fathers."

11 a2 Kin.
22:16; Jer.
6:19; 11:17
bIs. 24:17;
Jer. 25:35
cPs. 18:41;
Prov. 1:28;
Is. 1:15; Jer.
11:14; 14:12;
Ezek. 8:18;
Mic. 3:4;
Zech. 7:13

11 Therefore thus says the LORD, "Behold I am abringing disaster on them which they will bnot be able to escape; though they will ccry to Me, yet I will not listen to them.

12 aDeut.
32:37; Jer.
44:17

12 "Then the cities of Judah and the inhabitants of Jerusalem will ago and cry to the gods to whom they burn incense, but they surely will not save them in the time of their disaster.

★13 a2 Kin.
23:13; Jer.
2:28 bJer.
3:24 cJer.
7:9

13 "For your gods are aas many as your cities, O Judah; and as many as the streets of Jerusalem are the altars you have set up to the bshameful thing, altars to cburn incense to Baal.

14 "Therefore ado not pray for this people, nor lift up a cry or prayer for them; for I will bnot listen when they call to Me because of their disaster.

14 aEx.
32:10; Jer.
7:16; 14:11;
1 John 5:16
bPs. 66:18;
Jer. 11:11;
Hos. 5:6

15 "What right has My abeloved in My house
When bshe has done many vile deeds?
Can the sacrificial flesh take away from you your disaster,
So *that* you can rejoice?"

★15 aJer.
13:27 bEzek.
16:25

16 The LORD called your name,
"A agreen olive tree, beautiful in fruit and form";
With the bnoise of a great tumult
He has ckindled fire on it,
And its branches are worthless.

16 aPs. 52:8;
Rom. 11:17
bPs. 83:2
cPs. 80:16;
Is. 27:11;
Jer. 21:14

17 And the LORD of hosts, who aplanted you, has bpronounced evil against you because of the evil of the house of Israel and of the house of Judah, which they have done to provoke Me by coffering up sacrifices to Baal.

17 aIs. 5:2;
Jer. 2:21;
12:2 bJer.
1:14; 16:10;
19:15 cJer.
7:9; 11:13;
32:29

2 The consequence, 11:18–12:17

18 Moreover, the LORD amade it known to me and I knew it;
Then Thou didst show me their deeds.

★18-23

18 a1 Sam.
23:11, 12;
Ezek. 6:9,
10; Ezek. 8:6

19 But I was like a gentle alamb led to the slaughter;
And I did not know that they had bdevised plots against me, *saying,*
"Let us destroy the tree with its fruit,
And clet us cut him off from the dland of the living,

19 aIs. 53:7
bJer. 18:18;
20:10 cPs.
83:4; Is. 53:8
dJob 28:13;
Ps. 52:5 ePs.
109:13

11:13 *shameful thing.* See 3:24.
11:15 *the sacrificial flesh* of the rituals of sacrifice, when offered in hypocrisy, could not avert the coming disaster.

11:18-23 A description of the hostility which Jeremiah encountered from the people of his home town. They wanted to kill him *(the tree)* and silence his message (*its fruit,* v. 19).

That his ^ename be remembered no more."

20 aGen.
18:25; Ps.
7:8; Jer.
20:12
b1 Sam.
16:7; Ps. 7:9;
Jer. 17:10

20 But, O Lord of hosts, who
^ajudges righteously,
Who ^btries the feelings
and the heart,
Let me see Thy vengeance
on them,
For to Thee have I committed my cause.

21 aJer. 1:1
bJer. 12:5, 6;
20:10 cAmos
2:12 dJer.
26:8; 38:4

21 Therefore thus says the
Lord concerning the men of ^aAnathoth, who ^bseek your life, saying, "^cDo not prophesy in the
name of the Lord, that you might
not ^ddie at our hand";

22 aJer.
21:14
b2 Chr.
36:17; Jer.
18:21

22 therefore, thus says the
Lord of hosts, "Behold, I am
about to ^apunish them! The
^byoung men will die by the
sword, their sons and daughters
will die by famine;

23 aJer. 6:9
bJer. 23:12;
Hos. 9:7;
Mic. 7:4
cLuke 19:44

23 and a remnant ^awill not be
left to them, for I will ^bbring disaster on the men of Anathoth—
^cthe year of their punishment."

★ 1-6
1 aEzra
9:15; Ps.
51:4; 129:4;
Jer. 11:20
bJob 13:3
cJob 12:6;
Jer. 5:27, 28;
Hab. 1:4;
Mal. 3:15
dJer. 3:7, 20;
5:11

12 ^aRighteous art Thou, O
Lord, that I would
plead *my* case with
Thee;
Indeed I would ^bdiscuss
matters of justice with
Thee:
Why has the ^cway of the
wicked prospered?
Why are all those who
^ddeal in treachery at
ease?

2 aJer.
11:17; 45:4;
Ezek. 17:5-
10 bIs.
29:13; Jer.
3:10; Ezek.
33:31; Titus
1:16

2 Thou hast ^aplanted them,
they have also taken
root;
They grow, they have even
produced fruit.
Thou art ^bnear to their lips
But far from their mind.

3 aPs.
139:1-4 bPs.
7:9; 11:5;
Jer. 11:20
cJer. 17:18;
50:27; James
5:5

3 But Thou ^aknowest me, O
Lord;
Thou seest me;
And Thou dost ^bexamine
my heart's *attitude*
toward Thee.

Drag them off like sheep
for the slaughter
And set them apart for a
^cday of carnage!

4 How long is the ^aland to
mourn
And the ^bvegetation of the
countryside to wither?
For the ^cwickedness of
those who dwell in it,
^dAnimals and birds have
been snatched away,
Because *men* have said,
"He will not see our
latter ^eending."

4 aJer.
4:28; 9:10;
23:10 bJoel
1:10-17 cPs.
107:34 dJer.
4:25; 7:20;
9:10; Hos.
4:3; Hab.
3:17 eJer.
5:31; Ezek.
7:2

5 "If you have run with footmen and they have
tired you out,
Then how can you compete with horses?
If you fall down in a land
of peace,
How will you do in the
^athicket of the Jordan?

5 aJer.
49:19; 50:44

6 "For even your ^abrothers
and the household of
your father,
Even they have dealt
treacherously with
you,
Even they have cried aloud
after you.
Do not believe them, although they may say
^bnice things to you."

6 aGen.
37:4-11; Job
6:15; Ps.
69:8; Jer.
9:4, 5 bPs.
12:2; Prov.
26:25

7 "I have ^aforsaken My
house,
I have abandoned My inheritance;
I have given the ^bbeloved
of My soul
Into the hand of her enemies.

★ 7-13
7 aIs. 2:6;
Jer. 7:29;
23:39 bJer.
11:15; Hos.
11:1-8

8 "My inheritance has become to Me
Like a lion in the forest;
She has ^aroared against
Me;
Therefore I have come to
^bhate her.

8 aIs. 59:13
bHos. 9:15;
Amos 6:8

12:1-6 Jeremiah asked the age-old question,
Why do the godless prosper? God's reply is to
warn him of even greater opposition from the
people in Jerusalem (*horses,* v. 5) than he was
experiencing from those in Anathoth (*foot-*

men, v. 5). *the thicket of the Jordan.* The low
luxuriant bottom land of the Jordan inhabited
by wild animals (cf. 49:19).
12:7-13 Jeremiah describes the coming devastation as if it had already occurred.

9 a2 Kin.
24:2; Ezek.
23:22-25 bIs.
56:9; Jer.
7:33; 15:3;
34:20

9 "Is My inheritance like a
speckled bird of prey
to Me?
Are the abirds of prey
against her on every
side?
Go, gather all the bbeasts
of the field,
Bring them to devour!

10 aJer. 6:3;
23:1 bPs.
80:8-16; Is.
5:1-7 cIs.
63:18 dJer.
3:19

10 "Many ashepherds have
ruined My bvineyard,
They have ctrampled
down My field;
They have made My
dpleasant field
A desolate wilderness.

11 aJer.
12:4; 14:2;
23:10 bJer.
4:20, 27;
25:11 cIs.
42:25

11 "It has been made a desolation,
Desolate, it amourns be-
fore Me;
The bwhole land has been
made desolate,
Because no man clays it to
heart.

★12 aJer.
3:2, 21 bIs.
34:6; Jer.
47:6; Amos
9:4 cJer.
16:5; 30:5

12 "On all the abare heights in
the wilderness
Destroyers have come,
For a bsword of the LORD is
devouring
From one end of the land
even to the other;
There is cno peace for anyone.

13 aLev.
26:16; Deut.
28:38; Mic.
6:15; Hag.
1:6 bIs. 55:2;
Jer. 9:5 cJer.
17:10 dJer.
4:26; 25:37,
38

13 "They have asown wheat
and have reaped
thorns,
They have bstrained them-
selves to no profit.
But be ashamed of your
charvest
Because of the dfierce anger of the LORD."

★14 aJer.
49:1, 7;
Zeph. 2:8-10
bJer. 2:3;
50:11, 12;
Zech. 2:8
cDeut. 30:3;
Ps. 106:47;
Is. 11:11-16

14 Thus says the LORD concerning all My awicked neighbors
who bstrike at the inheritance
with which I have endowed My
people Israel, "Behold I am about
to uproot them from their land

and will cuproot the house of Judah from among them.
15 "And it will come about
that after I have uprooted them, I
will aagain have compassion on
them; and I will bbring them
back, each one to his inheritance
and each one to his land.
16 "Then it will come about
that if they will really alearn the
ways of My people, to bswear by
My name, 'As the Lord lives,'
even as they taught My people to
cswear by Baal, then they will be
dbuilt up in the midst of My people.
17 "But if they will not listen,
then I will auproot that nation,
uproot and destroy it," declares
the LORD.

3 The warnings, 13:1-27

13 Thus the LORD said to me,
"Go and abuy yourself a
linen waistband, and put it
around your waist, but do not put
it in water."
2 So I bought the waistband
in accordance with the aword of
the LORD and put it around my
waist.
3 Then the word of the LORD
came to me a second time, saying,
4 "Take the waistband that
you have bought, which is around
your waist, and arise, go to the
aEuphrates and hide it there in a
crevice of the rock."
5 So I went and hid it by the
Euphrates, aas the LORD had commanded me.
6 And it came about after
many days that the LORD said to
me, "Arise, go to the Euphrates
and take from there the waistband which I commanded you to
hide there."

15 aJer.
48:47; 49:6,
39 bAmos
9:14

16 aIs. 42:6;
49:6 bJer.
4:2; Zeph.
1:5 cJosh.
23:7; Jer. 5:7
dJer. 3:17;
4:2; 16:19

17 aPs. 2:8-
12; Is. 60:12

★ 1-11

1 aJer.
13:11

2 aIs. 20:2;
Ezek. 2:8

4 aJer.
51:63

5 aEx.
39:42, 43;
40:16

12:12 *sword of the LORD.* The Babylonian armies
which would be used in God's hands to punish His people.
12:14 *My wicked neighbors.* Syria (Aram),
Moab, and Ammon, who, with Judah, would
be punished by Babylon.
13:1-11 Actions speak louder than words, so
Jeremiah is told to take a *waistband* (a thigh-
length undergarment that clung to the body,

symbolizing the closeness of Israel to God's
heart, v. 11), hide it in a rock, then retrieve it
only to discover that, like the nation, it was
ruined and useless. *Euphrates* (v. 6) may mean
the river (at least 350 miles away) or may refer
to the town of Parah about 3 miles from Anathoth (in the expression "to the Euphrates,"
both names take on an identical form in Hebrew).

7 Then I went to the Euphrates and dug, and I took the waistband from the place where I had hidden it; and lo, the waistband was ruined, it was totally worthless.

8 Then the word of the LORD came to me, saying,

9 "Thus says the LORD, 'Just so will I destroy the ªpride of Judah and the great pride of Jerusalem.

10 'This wicked people, who ªrefuse to listen to My words, who ᵇwalk in the stubbornness of their hearts and have gone after other gods to serve them and to bow down to them, let them be just like this waistband, which is totally worthless.

11 'For as the waistband clings to the waist of a man, so I made the whole household of Israel and the whole household of Judah ªcling to Me,' declares the LORD, 'that they might be for Me a people, for ᵇrenown, for ᶜpraise, and for glory; but they ᵈdid not listen.'

12 "Therefore you are to speak this word to them, 'Thus says the LORD, the God of Israel, "Every jug is to be filled with wine."' And when they say to you, 'Do we not very well know that every jug is to be filled with wine?'

13 then say to them, 'Thus says the LORD, "Behold I am about to fill all the inhabitants of this land—the kings that sit for David on his throne, the priests, the prophets and all the inhabitants of Jerusalem—with ªdrunkenness!

14 "And I will ªdash them against each other, both the ᵇfathers and the sons together," declares the LORD. "I will ᶜnot show pity nor be sorry nor have com-

passion that I should not destroy them."' "

15 Listen and give heed, do not be ªhaughty, For the LORD has spoken.

16 ªGive glory to the LORD your God, Before He brings ᵇdarkness And before your ᶜfeet stumble On the dusky mountains, And while you are hoping for light He makes it into ᵈdeep darkness, *And* turns *it* into gloom.

17 But ªif you will not listen to it, My soul will ᵇsob in secret for *such* pride; And my eyes will bitterly weep And flow down with tears, Because the ᶜflock of the LORD has been taken captive.

18 Say to the ªking and the queen mother, "ᵇTake a lowly seat, For your beautiful ᶜcrown Has come down from your head."

19 The ªcities of the Negev have been locked up, And there is no one to open *them*; All ᵇJudah has been carried into exile, Wholly carried into exile.

20 "Lift up your eyes and see Those coming ªfrom the north. Where is the ᵇflock that was given you, Your beautiful sheep?

Side column references:

9 ªLev. 26:19; Is. 2:10-17; 23:9; Jer. 13:15-17; Zeph. 3:11

10 ªNum. 14:11; 2 Chr. 36:15, 16; Jer. 11:10 ᵇJer. 9:14; 11:8; 16:12

11 ªEx. 19:5, 6; Deut. 32:10, 11 ᵇJer. 32:20 ᶜIs. 43:21; Jer. 33:9 ᵈPs. 81:11; Jer. 7:13, 24, 26

★12-14

13 ªPs. 60:3; 75:8; Is. 51:17; 63:6; Jer. 25:27; 51:7, 57

14 ªIs. 9:20, 21; Jer. 19:9-11 ᵇJer. 6:21; Ezek. 5:10 ᶜDeut. 29:20; Is. 27:11; Jer. 16:5; 21:7

★15-17
15 ªProv. 16:5; Is. 28:14-22

16 ªJosh. 7:19; Ps. 96:8 ᵇIs. 5:30; 8:22; 59:9; Amos 5:18; 8:9 ᶜProv. 4:19; Jer. 23:12 ᵈPs. 44:19; 107:10, 14; Jer. 2:6

17 ªMal. 2:2 ᵇPs. 119:136; Jer. 9:1; 14:17; Luke 19:41, 42 ᶜPs. 80:1; Jer. 23:1, 2

★18-19
18 ª2 Kin. 24:12, 15; Jer. 22:26 ᵇ2 Chr. 33:12, 19 ᶜEx. 39:28; Is. 3:20; Ezek. 24:17, 23; 44:18

19 ªJer. 32:44 ᵇJer. 20:4; 52:27-30

★20-27
20 ªJer. 1:15; 6:22; Hab. 1:6 ᵇJer. 13:17; 23:2

13:12-14 Though the people complacently looked for prosperity (illustrated by the *jug* filled with wine), in reality they would behave in the coming crisis as though inebriated, unable to distinguish friend from foe.

13:15-17 The third warning was against pride and arrogance.

13:18-19 A lament over King Jehoiachin (then

18 years old) and the queen mother (Nehushta, 2 Kings 24:8) who were taken captive into Babylon (Jer. 29:2).

13:20-27 A final warning that punishment (the Babylonian captivity) would be the inevitable consequence of Judah's continuance in sin. Verse 23 shows how impossible it was for Judah to change her ways.

21 "What will you say when
    He appoints over
    you—
And you yourself had
    taught them—
Former ᵃcompanions to be
    head over you?
Will not ᵇpangs take hold
    of you,
Like a woman in child-
    birth?
22 "And if you ᵃsay in your
    heart,
    'ᵇWhy have these things
    happened to me?'
Because of the ᶜmagnitude
    of your iniquity
ᵈYour skirts have been re-
    moved,
And your heels have been
    exposed.
23 "ᵃCan the Ethiopian change
    his skin
Or the leopard his spots?
Then you also can ᵇdo
    good
Who are accustomed to do
    evil.
24 "Therefore I will ᵃscatter
    them like drifting
    straw
To the desert ᵇwind.
25 "This is your ᵃlot, the por-
    tion measured to you
From Me," declares the
    LORD,
"Because you have ᵇforgot-
    ten Me
And trusted in falsehood.
26 "So I Myself have also
    ᵃstripped your skirts
    off over your face,
That your shame may be
    seen.
27 "As for your ᵃadulteries and
    your lustful neigh-
    ings,
The ᵇlewdness of your
    prostitution
On the ᶜhills in the field,
I have seen your abomina-
    tions.

Woe to you, O Jerusalem!
ᵈHow long will you remain
    unclean?"

E Judah's Coming Drought,
14:1–15:9
1 Jeremiah's message, 14:1–6

14 That which came as the
    word of the LORD to Jere-
miah in regard to the ᵃdrought:
2 "Judah mourns,
And ᵃher gates languish
They sit on the ground ᵇin
    mourning,
And the ᶜcry of Jerusalem
    has ascended.
3 "And their nobles have
    ᵃsent their servants
    for water;
They have come to the
    ᵇcisterns and found
    no water.
They have returned with
    their vessels empty;
They have been ᶜput to
    shame and humil-
    iated,
And they ᵈcover their
    heads.
4 "Because the ᵃground is
    cracked,
For there has been ᵇno rain
    on the land;
The ᶜfarmers have been
    put to shame,
They have covered their
    heads.
5 "For even the doe in the
    field has given birth
    only to abandon her
    young,
Because there is ᵃno grass.
6 "And the ᵃwild donkeys
    stand on the bare
    heights;
They pant for air like jack-
    als,
Their eyes fail
For there is ᵇno vegetation.

Marginal references (left column)

21 ᵃJer. 2:25; 38:22 ᵇIs. 13:8; Jer. 4:31
22 ᵃDeut. 7:17 ᵇJer. 5:19; 16:10 ᶜJer. 2:17-19; 9:2-9 ᵈIs. 47:2; Ezek. 16:37; Nah. 3:5
23 ᵃProv. 27:22; Is. 1:5 ᵇJer. 4:22; 9:5
24 ᵃLev. 26:33; Jer. 9:16; Ezek. 5:2, 12 ᵇJer. 4:11; 18:17
25 ᵃJob 20:29; Ps. 11:6; Matt. 24:51 ᵇPs. 9:17; Jer. 2:32; 3:21
26 ᵃLam. 1:8; Ezek. 23:29; Hos. 2:10
27 ᵃJer. 5:7, 8 ᵇJer. 11:15 ᶜIs. 65:7; Jer. 2:20; Ezek. 6:13 ᵈProv. 1:22; Hos. 8:5

Marginal references (right column)

★ 1-6
1 ᵃJer. 17:8
2 ᵃIs. 3:26 ᵇJer. 8:21 ᶜ1 Sam. 5:12; Jer. 11:11; 46:12; Zech. 7:13
3 ᵃ1 Kin. 18:5 ᵇ2 Kin. 18:31; Jer. 2:13 ᶜJob 6:20; Ps. 40:14 ᵈ2 Sam. 15:30
4 ᵃJoel 1:19, 20 ᵇJer. 3:3 ᶜJoel 1:11
5 ᵃIs. 15:6
6 ᵃJob 39:5, 6; Jer. 2:24 ᵇJoel 1:18

14:1–6 A drought which affects city dwellers (vv. 2–3), farmers (v. 4), and even the animals (vv. 5–6), intended as a warning from God, goes unheeded.

2 Jeremiah's intercession,
14:7–15:9

★ 7-22

7 "Although our [a]iniquities
testify against us,
O Lord, act [b]for Thy
name's sake!
Truly our [c]apostasies have
been many,
We have [d]sinned against
Thee.

8 "Thou [a]Hope of Israel,
Its [b]Savior in [c]time of distress,
Why art Thou like a stranger in the land
Or like a traveler who has
pitched his *tent* for
the night?

9 "Why art Thou like a man
dismayed,
Like a mighty man who
[a]cannot save?
Yet [b]Thou art in our midst,
O Lord,
And we are [c]called by Thy
name;
Do not forsake us!"

10　Thus says the Lord to this
people, "Even so they have [a]loved
to wander; they have not [b]kept
their feet in check. Therefore the
Lord does [c]not accept them; now
He will [d]remember their iniquity
and call their sins to account."

11　So the Lord said to me,
"[a]Do not pray for the welfare of
this people.

12　"When they fast, I am [a]not
going to listen to their cry; and
when they offer [b]burnt offering
and grain offering, I am not going
to accept them. Rather I am going
to [c]make an end of them by the
[d]sword, famine and pestilence."

13　But, "Ah, Lord God!" I
said, "Look, the prophets are telling them, 'You [a]will not see the
sword nor will you have famine,
but I will give you lasting [b]peace
in this place.'"

14　Then the Lord said to me,
"The [a]prophets are prophesying
falsehood in My name. [b]I have
neither sent them nor commanded them nor spoken to
them; they are prophesying to
you a [c]false vision, divination, futility and the deception of their
own minds.

15　"Therefore thus says the
Lord concerning the prophets
who are prophesying in My
name, although it was not I who
sent them—yet they keep saying,
'There shall be no sword or famine in this land'—[a]by sword and
famine those prophets shall meet
their end!

16　"The people also to whom
they are prophesying will be
[a]thrown out into the streets of Jerusalem because of the famine
and the sword; and there will be
no one to [b]bury them—*neither*
them, *nor* their wives, nor their
sons, nor their daughters—for I
shall [c]pour out their *own* wickedness on them.

17　"And you will say this word
to them,
'[a]Let my eyes flow down
with tears night and
day,
And let them not cease;
For the virgin [b]daughter of
my people has been
crushed with a mighty
blow,
With a sorely [c]infected
wound.

18　'If I [a]go out to the country,
Behold, those slain with
the sword!
Or if I enter the city,
Behold, diseases of famine!
For [b]both prophet and
priest
Have gone roving about in
the land that they do
not know.'"

Cross references (margin)

7 [a]Is. 59:12; Hos. 5:5 [b]Ps. 25:11; Jer. 14:21 [c]Jer. 5:6; 8:5 [d]Jer. 3:25; 8:14; 14:20

8 [a]Jer. 17:13 [b]Is. 43:3; 63:8 [c]Ps. 9:9; 50:15

9 [a]Num. 11:23; Is. 50:2; 59:1 [b]Ex. 29:45; Ps. 46:5; Jer. 8:19 [c]Is. 63:19; Jer. 15:16

10 [a]Jer. 2:25; 3:13 [b]Ps. 119:101 [c]Jer. 6:20; Amos 5:22 [d]Jer. 44:21-23; Hos. 8:13; 9:9

11 [a]Ex. 32:10; Jer. 7:16; 11:14

12 [a]Prov. 1:28; Is. 1:15; Jer. 11:11; Ezek. 8:18; Mic. 3:4; Zech. 7:13 [b]Jer. 6:20; 7:21 [c]Jer. 8:13 [d]Jer. 21:9

13 [a]Jer. 5:12; 23:17 [b]Jer. 6:14; 8:11

14 [a]Jer. 5:31; 23:25 [b]Jer. 23:21 [c]Jer. 23:16, 26; 27:9, 10; Ezek. 12:24

15 [a]Jer. 23:15; Ezek. 14:10

16 [a]Ps. 79:2, 3; Jer. 7:33; 15:2, 3 [b]Jer. 8:1, 2 [c]Prov. 1:31; Jer. 13:22-25

17 [a]Jer. 9:1; 13:17; Lam. 1:16 [b]Is. 37:22; Jer. 8:21; Lam. 1:15; 2:13 [c]Jer. 10:19; 30:14

18 [a]Jer. 6:25; Lam. 1:20; Ezek. 7:15 [b]Jer. 6:13; 8:10

14:7-22 Jeremiah interceded for the people, confessing sin and pleading the covenant relationship (vv. 7-9), but God told him to stop praying (vv. 11-12), since judgment is certain on
the false prophets and those who listened to
them (vv. 15-16). Still, Jeremiah, in the tradition of Abraham (Gen. 18:22-33), continued to
intercede (vv. 17-22).

19 *a*Jer.
6:30; 7:29;
12:7; Lam.
5:22 *b*Jer.
30:13 *c*Job
30:26; Jer.
8:15;
1 Thess. 5:3

19 Hast Thou completely *a*rejected Judah?
Or hast Thou loathed Zion?
Why hast Thou stricken us so that we *b*are beyond healing?
We *c*waited for peace, but nothing good *came;*
And for a time of healing, but behold, terror!

20 *a*Neh.
9:2; Ps. 32:5;
Jer. 3:25
*b*Jer. 8:14;
14:7; Dan.
9:8

20 We *a*know our wickedness, O LORD,
The iniquity of our fathers, for *b*we have sinned against Thee.

21 *a*Ps.
25:11; Jer.
14:7 *b*Jer.
3:17; 17:12

21 Do not despise *us,* *a*for Thine own name's sake;
Do not disgrace the *b*throne of Thy glory;
Remember *and* do not annul Thy covenant with us.

22 *a*Is.
41:29; Jer.
10:3 *b*1 Kin.
17:1; Jer.
5:24 *c*Lam.
3:26

22 Are there any among the *a*idols of the nations who *b*give rain?
Or can the heavens grant showers?
Is it not Thou, O LORD our God?
Therefore we *c*hope in Thee,
For Thou art the one who hast done all these things.

★ **1** *a*Ps.
99:6; Ezek.
14:14, 20
*b*Ex. 32:11-
14; Num.
14:13-20; Ps.
99:6; 106:23
*c*1 Sam. 7:9;
12:23 *d*Jer.
15:19; 18:20;
35:19 *e*2 Kin.
17:20; Jer.
7:15; 10:18;
52:3

15 Then the LORD said to me, "Even *a*though *b*Moses and *c*Samuel were to *d*stand before Me, My heart would not be with this people; *e*send them away from My presence and let them go!

2 *a*Jer.
14:12; 24:10;
43:11; Ezek.
5:2, 12;
Zech. 11:9;
Rev. 13:10

2 "And it shall be that when they say to you, 'Where should we go?' then you are to tell them, 'Thus says the LORD:
"Those *destined* *a*for death, to death;
And those *destined* for the sword, to the sword;
And those *destined* for famine, to famine;

And those *destined* for captivity, to captivity." '

3 "And I shall *a*appoint over them four kinds *of doom,"* declares the LORD: "the sword to slay, the *b*dogs to drag off, and the *c*birds of the sky and the beasts of the earth to devour and destroy.

3 *a*Lev.
26:16, 22,
25; Ezek.
14:21
*b*1 Kin.
21:23, 24
*c*Deut.
28:26; Is.
18:6; Jer.
7:33

4 "And I shall *a*make them an object of horror among all the kingdoms of the earth because of *b*Manasseh, the son of Hezekiah, the king of Judah, for what he did in Jerusalem.

★ **4** *a*Lev.
26:33; Jer.
24:9; 29:18;
Ezek. 23:46
*b*2 Kin. 21:1-
18; 23:26,
27; 24:3, 4;
2 Chr. 33:1-9

5 "Indeed, who will have *a*pity on you, O Jerusalem,
Or who will *b*mourn for you,
Or who will turn aside to ask about your welfare?

5 *a*Ps.
69:20; Is.
51:19; Jer.
13:14; 21:7
*b*Nah. 3:7

6 "You who have *a*forsaken Me," declares the LORD,
"You keep *b*going backward.
So I will *c*stretch out My hand against you and destroy you;
I am *d*tired of relenting!

6 *a*Jer.
6:19; 8:9 *b*Is.
1:4; Jer. 7:24
*c*Jer. 6:12;
Zeph. 1:4
*d*Jer. 6:11;
7:16

7 "And I will *a*winnow them with a winnowing fork
At the gates of the land;
I will *b*bereave *them* of children, I will destroy My people;
*c*They did not repent of their ways.

7 *a*Ps. 1:4;
Jer. 51:2
*b*Jer. 18:21;
Hos. 9:12-16
*c*Is. 9:13

8 "Their *a*widows will be more numerous before Me
Than the sand of the seas;
I will bring against them, against the mother of a young man,
A *b*destroyer at noonday;
I will suddenly bring down on her
Anguish and dismay.

8 *a*Is. 3:25,
26; 4:1 *b*Jer.
22:7

15:1 Even if *Moses* and *Samuel* were to intercede for Judah (as they successfully did in their own day, Exod. 32:11-14; Num. 14:13-24; Deut. 9:18-20, 25-29; 1 Sam. 7:5-9; 12:19-25),

God would not spare Judah.
15:4 *Manasseh.* Introduced gross idolatry into Judah (2 Kings 23:26; 24:3).

9 "She who ªbore seven *sons*
     pines away;
Her breathing is labored.
Her ᵇsun has set while it
     was yet day;
She has been ᶜshamed and
     humiliated.
So I shall ᵈgive over their
     survivors to the sword
Before their enemies," de-
     clares the LORD.

F Judah's Prophet Recommissioned, 15:10-16:9

1 Jeremiah's remorse, 15:10-21

10 ªWoe to me, my mother,
     that you have borne
     me
As a ᵇman of strife and a
     man of contention to
     all the land!
I have neither ᶜlent, nor
     have men lent money
     to me,
Yet everyone curses me.

11 The LORD said, "Surely I
     will ªset you free for
     purposes of good;
Surely I will cause the
     ᵇenemy to make sup-
     plication to you
In a time of disaster and a
     time of distress.

12 "Can anyone smash iron,
     ªIron from the north, or
     bronze?

13 "Your ªwealth and your
     treasures
I will give for booty ᵇwith-
     out cost,
Even for all your sins
And within all your bor-
     ders.

14 "Then I will cause your en-
     emies to bring *it*
Into a ªland you do not
     know;

For a ᵇfire has been kin-
     dled in My anger,
It will burn upon you."

15 ªThou who knowest, O
     LORD,
Remember me, take notice
     of me,
And ᵇtake vengeance for
     me on my persecu-
     tors.
Do *not,* in view of Thy pa-
     tience, take me away;
Know that ᶜfor Thy sake I
     endure reproach.

16 Thy words were found and
     I ªate them,
And Thy ᵇwords became
     for me a joy and the
     delight of my heart;
For I have been ᶜcalled by
     Thy name,
O LORD God of hosts.

17 I ªdid not sit in the circle of
     merrymakers,
Nor did I exult.
Because of Thy hand *upon*
     me I sat ᵇalone,
For Thou didst ᶜfill me
     with indignation.

18 Why has my pain been
     perpetual
And my ªwound incurable,
     refusing to be healed?
Wilt Thou indeed be to me
     ᵇlike a deceptive
     stream
With water that is unreli-
     able?

19 Therefore, thus says the
     LORD,
"ªIf you return, then I will
     restore you—
ᵇBefore Me you will stand;
And ᶜif you extract the
     precious from the
     worthless,
You will become My
     spokesman.
They for their part may
     turn to you,

15:10-11 Jeremiah rued the day he was born, but God reassured him. *I will set you free for purposes of good.* I will strengthen you for good.
15:12 Judah *(iron)* would not be able to withstand Babylon *(Iron from the north).*

15:18 *like a deceptive stream.* Just as a thirsty traveller is disappointed when he finds a brook dried up, Jeremiah felt God had failed him.
15:19 *you must not turn to them.* Don't sink to the level of the people.

20 aJer.
1:18, 19;
Ezek. 3:9
bPs. 46:7; Is.
41:10; Jer.
1:8, 19;
15:15; 20:11

But as for you, you must not turn to them.

20 "Then I will ᵃmake you to this people
A fortified wall of bronze;
And though they fight against you,
They will not prevail over you;
For ᵇI am with you to save you
And deliver you," declares the LORD.

21 aPs.
37:40; Is.
49:25; Jer.
20:13; 39:11,
12 bGen.
48:16; Is.
49:26; 60:16;
Jer. 31:11;
50:34

21 "So I will ᵃdeliver you from the hand of the wicked,
And I will ᵇredeem you from the grasp of the violent."

2 Jeremiah's restrictions, 16:1-9

★ 1-9

16 The word of the LORD also came to me saying,

2 "You shall not take a wife for yourself nor have sons or daughters in this place."

3 aJer. 15:8
bJer. 6:21

3 For thus says the LORD concerning the sons and daughters born in this place, and concerning their ᵃmothers who bear them, and their ᵇfathers who beget them in this land:

4 aJer. 15:2
bJer. 25:33
cPs. 83:10;
Jer. 9:22;
25:33 dPs.
79:2; Is.
18:6; Jer.
15:3; 34:20

4 "They will ᵃdie of deadly diseases, they ᵇwill not be lamented or buried; they will be as ᶜdung on the surface of the ground and come to an end by sword and famine, and their carcasses will become food for the ᵈbirds of the sky and for the beasts of the earth."

5 aEzek.
24:16-23
bJer. 12:12;
15:1-4 cPs.
25:6; Is.
27:11; Jer.
13:14

5 For thus says the LORD, "Do not enter a house of ᵃmourning, or go to lament or to console them; for I have ᵇwithdrawn My peace from this people," declares the LORD, "My ᶜlovingkindness and compassion.

6 a2 Chr.
36:17; Ezek.
9:6 bDeut.
14:1; Jer.
41:5; 47:5
cIs. 22:12

6 "Both ᵃgreat men and small will die in this land; they will not be buried, they will not be la-

mented, nor will anyone ᵇgash himself or ᶜshave his head for them.

7 "Neither will men ᵃbreak bread in mourning for them, to comfort anyone for the dead, nor give them a cup of consolation to drink for anyone's father or mother.

★ 7 aDeut.
26:14; Ezek.
24:17; Hos.
9:4

8 "Moreover you shall ᵃnot go into a house of feasting to sit with them to eat and drink."

8 aEccl.
7:2-4; Is.
22:12-14;
Jer. 15:17;
Amos 6:4-6

9 For thus says the LORD of hosts, the God of Israel: "Behold, I am going to ᵃeliminate from this place, before your eyes and in your time, the voice of rejoicing and the voice of gladness, the voice of the groom and the voice of the bride.

9 aJer.
7:34; 25:10;
Ezek. 26:13;
Hos. 2:11;
Rev. 18:23

G Judah's Sins, 16:10-17:27

10 "Now it will come about when you tell this people all these words that they will say to you, 'ᵃFor what reason has the LORD declared all this great calamity against us? And what is our iniquity, or what is our sin which we have committed against the LORD our God?'

10 aDeut.
29:24; 1 Kin.
9:8; Jer.
5:19; 13:22;
22:8

11 "Then you are to say to them, 'It is ᵃbecause your forefathers have forsaken Me,' declares the LORD, 'and have followed ᵇother gods and served them and bowed down to them; but Me they have forsaken and have not kept My law.

11 aDeut.
29:25; 1 Kin.
9:9; 2 Chr.
7:22; Neh.
9:26-29; Jer.
22:9 bDeut.
29:26; 1 Kin.
9:9; Ps.
106:35-41;
Jer. 5:7-9;
8:2; Ezek.
11:21; 1 Pet.
4:3

12 'You too have done evil, even ᵃmore than your forefathers; for behold, you are each one walking according to the ᵇstubbornness of his own ᶜevil heart, without listening to Me.

12 aJer. 7:26
b1 Sam.
15:23; Jer.
7:24; 9:14;
13:10 cEccl.
9:3; Mark
7:21

13 'So I will ᵃhurl you out of this land into the ᵇland which you have not known, neither you nor your fathers; and there you will ᶜserve other gods day and night, for I shall grant you no favor.'

13 aDeut.
4:26, 27;
2 Chr. 7:20;
Jer. 15:1
bJer. 15:14;
17:4 cDeut.
4:28; 28:36;
Jer. 5:19

16:1-9 Jeremiah was forbidden to marry (v. 2) and to take part in funeral rites (v. 5) and joyous occasions (v. 8) as vivid warnings of the coming captivity.

16:7 *break bread.* A custom whereby friends provided a meal after the funeral. How these restrictions affected the sensitive prophet can scarcely be imagined.

14 "ᵃTherefore behold, days are coming," declares the Lᴏʀᴅ, "when it will no longer be said, 'As the Lᴏʀᴅ lives, who ᵇbrought up the sons of Israel out of the land of Egypt,'

15 but, 'As the Lᴏʀᴅ lives, who brought up the sons of Israel from the ᵃland of the north and from all the countries where He had banished them.' For I will restore them to their own land which I gave to their fathers.

16 "Behold, I am going to send for many ᵃfishermen," declares the Lᴏʀᴅ, "and they will fish for them; and afterwards I shall send for many hunters, and they will ᵇhunt them ᶜfrom every mountain and every hill, and from the clefts of the rocks.

17 "ᵃFor My eyes are on all their ways; they are not hidden from My face, ᵇnor is their iniquity concealed from My eyes.

18 "And I will first ᵃdoubly repay their iniquity and their sin, because they have ᵇpolluted My land; they have filled My inheritance with the carcasses of their ᶜdetestable idols and with their abominations."

19 O Lᴏʀᴅ, my ᵃstrength and my stronghold,
And my ᵇrefuge in the day of distress,
To Thee the ᶜnations will come
From the ends of the earth and say,
"Our fathers have inherited nothing but ᵈfalsehood,
Futility and ᵉthings of no profit."

20 Can man make gods for himself?
Yet they are ᵃnot gods!

21 "Therefore behold, I am going to make them know—
This time I will ᵃmake them know
My power and My might;
And they shall ᵇknow that My name is the Lᴏʀᴅ."

17 The ᵃsin of Judah is written down with an ᵇiron stylus;
With a diamond point it is ᶜengraved upon the tablet of their heart,
And on the horns of their altars,

2 As they remember their ᵃchildren,
So they *remember* their altars and their ᵇAsherim
By ᶜgreen trees on the high hills.

3 O ᵃmountain of Mine in the countryside,
I will ᵇgive over your wealth and all your treasures for booty,
Your high places for sin throughout your borders.

4 And you will, even of yourself, ᵃlet go of your inheritance
That I gave you;
And I will make you serve your ᵇenemies
In the ᶜland which you do not know;
For you have ᵈkindled a fire in My anger
Which will burn forever.

5 Thus says the Lᴏʀᴅ,
"ᵃCursed is the man who trusts in mankind

Cross references (margin):

14 ᵃIs. 43:18; Jer. 23:7 ᵇEx. 20:2; Deut. 15:15

★15 ᵃPs. 106:47; Is. 11:11-16; 14:1; Jer. 3:18; 23:8; 24:6

★16 ᵃAmos 4:2; Hab. 1:14, 15 ᵇ1 Sam. 26:20; Mic. 7:2 ᶜIs. 2:21; Amos 9:3

17 ᵃ2 Chr. 16:9; Job 34:21; Ps. 90:8; Prov. 5:21; 15:3; Jer. 23:24; 32:19; Zech. 4:10; Luke 12:2; 1 Cor. 4:5; Heb. 4:13 ᵇJer. 2:22

18 ᵃJer. 17:18; Rev. 18:6 ᵇNum. 35:33, 34; Jer. 2:7; 3:9 ᶜJer. 7:30; Ezek. 11:18, 21

19 ᵃPs. 18:1, 2; Is. 25:4 ᵇNah. 1:7 ᶜPs. 22:27; Is. 2:2; Jer. 3:17; 4:2 ᵈIs. 44:20; Hab. 2:18 ᵉIs. 44:10

20 ᵃPs. 115:4-8; Is. 37:19; Jer. 2:11; 5:7; Hos. 8:4-6; Gal. 4:8

21 ᵃPs. 9:16 ᵇPs. 83:18; Is. 43:3; Jer. 33:2; Amos 5:8

1 ᵃJer. 2:22; 4:14 ᵇJob 19:24 ᶜProv. 3:3; 7:3; Is. 49:16; 2 Cor. 3:3

★2 ᵃJer. 7:18 ᵇEx. 34:13; 2 Chr. 24:18; 33:3; Is. 17:8 ᶜJer. 3:6

★3 ᵃJer. 26:18; Mic. 3:12 ᵇ2 Kin. 24:13; Is. 39:4-6; Jer. 15:13; 20:5

4 ᵃJer. 12:7; Lam. 5:2 ᵇDeut. 28:48; Is. 14:3; Jer. 15:14; 27:12, 13 ᶜJer. 16:13 ᵈIs. 5:25; Jer. 7:20; 15:14

★5-8
5 ᵃPs. 146:3; Is. 2:22; 30:1; Ezek. 29:7 ᵇ2 Chr. 32:8; Is. 31:3

16:15 *I will restore them.* A promise of the future regathering of the Jewish people, to be fulfilled at the second coming of Christ (cf. Matt. 24:31).

16:16 *fishermen . . . hunters.* What might slip through a fisherman's net would be hunted down by hunters in the Babylonian captivity.

17:2 *Asherim.* Representations of the Canaanite goddess Asherah set up beside the idol altars (cf. Deut. 16:21).

17:3 *O mountain of Mine.* A poetic reference to Jerusalem (Isa. 2:2).

17:5-8 The background of these verses was Judah's periodic attempts to seek the help of Egypt against Babylon. *bush* (v. 6) refers to the tamarisk, a dwarf juniper which has a stark appearance. On verses 7-8 cf. Psalm 1.

And makes ᵇflesh his
strength,
And whose heart turns
away from the LORD.

6 ᵃJer. 48:6
ᵇDeut.
29:23; Job
39:6

6 "For he will be like a ᵃbush
in the desert
And will not see when
prosperity comes,
But will live in stony
wastes in the wilder-
ness,
A ᵇland of salt without inhabitant.

7 ᵃPs. 2:12;
34:8; 84:12;
Prov. 16:20
ᵇPs. 40:4

7 "ᵃBlessed is the man who
trusts in the LORD
And whose ᵇtrust is the
LORD.

8 ᵃPs. 1:3;
92:12-14;
Ezek. 31:3-9
ᵇJer. 14:1-6

8 "For he will be like a ᵃtree
planted by the water,
That extends its roots by a
stream
And will not fear when the
heat comes;
But its leaves will be green,
And it will not be anxious
in a year of ᵇdrought
Nor cease to yield fruit.

★ 9 ᵃEccl.
9:3; Mark
7:21, 22
ᵇRom. 7:11;
Eph. 4:22
ᶜIs. 1:5, 6;
6:10; Matt.
13:15; Mark
2:17; Rom.
1:21

9 "The ᵃheart is more ᵇde-
ceitful than all else
And is desperately ᶜsick;
Who can understand it?

★10 ᵃ1 Sam.
16:7; 1 Chr.
28:9; Ps.
139:23; Prov.
17:3; Jer.
11:20; 20:12;
Rom. 8:27;
Rev. 2:23
ᵇPs. 62:12;
Jer. 32:19;
Rom. 2:6

10 "I, the LORD, ᵃsearch the
heart,
I test the mind,
Even ᵇto give to each man
according to his ways,
According to the results of
his deeds.

11 ᵃJer.
6:13; 8:10;
22:13, 17
ᵇLuke 12:20

11 "As a partridge that hatches
eggs which it has not
laid,
So is he who ᵃmakes a fortune, but unjustly;
In the midst of his days it
will forsake him,
And in the end he will be a
ᵇfool."

12 ᵃJer.
3:17; 14:21

12 ᵃA glorious throne on high
from the beginning

Is the place of our sanctuary.

13 O LORD, the ᵃhope of Israel,
All who ᵇforsake Thee will
be put to shame.
Those who turn away on
earth will be ᶜwritten
down,
Because they have for-
saken the fountain of
living water, even the
LORD.

14 ᵃHeal me, O LORD, and I
will be healed;
ᵇSave me and I will be
saved,
For Thou art my ᶜpraise.

15 Look, they keep ᵃsaying to
me,
"Where is the word of the
LORD?
Let it come now!"

16 But as for me, I have not
hurried away from
being a shepherd after
Thee,
Nor have I longed for the
woeful day;
ᵃThou Thyself knowest
the utterance of my
lips
Was in Thy presence.

17 Do not be a ᵃterror to me;
Thou art my ᵇrefuge in the
day of disaster.

18 Let those who persecute
me be ᵃput to shame,
but as for me, ᵇlet me
not be put to shame;
Let them be dismayed, but
let me not be dis-
mayed.
ᶜBring on them a day of disaster,
And crush them with two-
fold destruction!

19 Thus the LORD said to me,
"Go and stand in the public gate,
through which the kings of Judah

13 ᵃJer.
14:8; 50:7
ᵇIs. 1:28
ᶜLuke 10:20

★14-18
14 ᵃJer.
30:17; 33:6
ᵇPs. 54:1;
60:5 ᶜDeut.
10:21; Ps.
109:1

15 ᵃIs. 5:19;
2 Pet. 3:4

16 ᵃJer. 12:3

17 ᵃPs.
88:15 ᵇJer.
16:19; Nah.
1:7

18 ᵃPs. 35:4,
26; Jer.
17:13; 20:11
ᵇJer. 1:17
ᶜPs. 35:8

★19-27

17:9 An important verse describing the natural
condition of man.
17:10 mind. Lit., kidneys, once thought to be the
seat of affections.
17:14-18 Jeremiah made an eloquent plea for
vindication.

17:19-27 A call to hallow the Sabbath as a sign
of repentance on the part of the people (cf.
Neh. 10:31; 13:15-22), who were using the
Sabbath to bring their crops and wares into
the city in violation of the Law.

come in and go out, as well as in all the gates of Jerusalem;

20 and say to them, 'ᵃListen to the word of the Lord, ᵇkings of Judah, and all Judah, and all inhabitants of Jerusalem, who come in through these gates:

21 Thus says the Lord, "ᵃTake heed for yourselves, and ᵇdo not carry any load on the sabbath day or bring anything in through the gates of Jerusalem.

22 "And you shall not bring a load out of your houses on the sabbath day ᵃnor do any work, but keep the sabbath day holy, as I ᵇcommanded your forefathers.

23 "Yet they ᵃdid not listen or incline their ears, but ᵇstiffened their necks in order not to listen or take correction.

24 "But it will come about, if you ᵃlisten attentively to Me," declares the Lord, "to ᵇbring no load in through the gates of this city on the sabbath day, ᶜbut to keep the sabbath day holy by doing no work on it,

25 ᵃthen there will come in through the gates of this city kings and princes ᵇsitting on the throne of David, riding in chariots and on horses, they and their princes, the men of Judah, and the inhabitants of Jerusalem; and this ᶜcity will be inhabited forever.

26 "They will come in from the ᵃcities of Judah and from the environs of Jerusalem, from the land of Benjamin, from the ᵇlowland, from the hill country, and from the ᶜNegev, bringing burnt offerings, sacrifices, grain offerings and incense, and ᵈbringing sacrifices of thanksgiving to the house of the Lord.

27 "But ᵃif you do not listen to Me to keep the sabbath day holy by not carrying a load and coming in through the gates of Jerusalem on the sabbath day, then ᵇI shall kindle a fire in its gates, and it will ᶜdevour the palaces of Jerusalem and ᵈnot be quenched." ' "

H Judah and the Sovereign Potter, 18:1-23

18 The word which came to Jeremiah from the Lord saying,

2 "Arise and ᵃgo down to the potter's house, and there I shall announce My words to you."

3 Then I went down to the potter's house, and there he was, making something on the wheel.

4 But the vessel that he was making of clay was spoiled in the hand of the potter; so he remade it into another vessel, as it pleased the potter to make.

5 Then the word of the Lord came to me saying,

6 "Can I not, O house of Israel, deal with you as this potter *does?*" declares the Lord. "Behold, like the ᵃclay in the potter's hand, so are you in My hand, O house of Israel.

7 "At one moment I might speak concerning a nation or concerning a kingdom to ᵃuproot, to pull down, or to destroy *it;*

8 ᵃif that nation against which I have spoken turns from its evil, I will ᵇrelent concerning the calamity I planned to bring on it.

9 "Or at another moment I might speak concerning a nation or concerning a kingdom to ᵃbuild up or to plant *it;*

10 if it does ᵃevil in My sight by not obeying My voice, then I will ᵇthink better of the good with which I had promised to bless it.

11 "So now then, speak to the men of Judah and against the inhabitants of Jerusalem saying, 'Thus says the Lord, "Behold, I am ᵃfashioning calamity against you and devising a plan against

---

Cross references (left margin):

20 ᵃEzek. 2:7 ᵇPs. 49:1, 2; Jer. 19:3, 4

21 ᵃDeut. 4:9, 15, 23; Mark 4:24 ᵇNum. 15:32-36; Neh. 13:15-21; John 5:9-12

22 ᵃEx. 16:23-29; 20:8-10; Deut. 5:12-14; Is. 56:2-6; 58:13 ᵇEx. 31:13-17; Ezek. 20:12; Zech. 1:4

23 ᵃJer. 7:24, 28; 11:10 ᵇProv. 29:1; Jer. 7:26; 19:15

24 ᵃEx. 15:26; Deut. 11:13; Is. 21:7; 55:2 ᵇJer. 17:21, 22 ᶜEx. 20:8-11; Ezek. 20:20

25 ᵃJer. 22:4 ᵇ2 Sam. 7:16; Is. 9:7; Jer. 33:15, 17, 21; Luke 1:32 ᶜPs. 132:13, 14; Heb. 12:22

26 ᵃJer. 32:44; 33:13 ᵇZech. 7:7 ᶜPs. 107:22; Jer. 33:11

27 ᵃIs. 1:20; Jer. 22:5; 26:4; Zech. 7:11-14 ᵇLam. 4:11 ᶜ2 Kin. 25:9; Jer. 39:8; Amos 2:5 ᵈJer. 7:20; Ezek. 20:47

Cross references (right margin):

★ 1-11

2 ᵃJer. 19:1, 2

★ 3

6 ᵃIs. 45:9; 64:8; Matt. 20:15; Rom. 9:21

7 ᵃJer. 1:10

8 ᵃJer. 7:3-7; 12:16; Ezek. 18:21 ᵇPs. 106:45; Jer. 26:3, 13, 19; Hos. 11:8; Joel 2:13, 14; Jon. 3:10

9 ᵃJer. 1:10; 31:28; Amos 9:11-15

10 ᵃPs. 125:5; Jer. 7:24-28; Ezek. 33:18 ᵇ1 Sam. 2:30; 13:13

11 ᵃIs. 5:5; Jer. 4:6; 11:11 ᵇ2 Kin. 17:13; Is. 1:16-19; Jer. 4:1; Acts 26:20

18:1-11 This parable of the potter teaches the absolute sovereignty of God over nations, not capriciously, but with sensitivity to the possibility of their repenting (v. 8).

18:3 *wheel.* On a vertical axis were two circular stones; the lower one was spun by the potter's feet, causing the upper one to rotate also. The clay was placed on the upper wheel.

you. Oh [b]turn back, each of you from his evil way, and reform your ways and your deeds."'

12 a Is. 57:10; Jer. 2:25 **b**Deut. 29:19; Jer. 7:24; 16:12

12 "But [a]they will say, 'It's hopeless! For we are going to follow our own plans, and each of us will act according to the [b]stubbornness of his evil heart.'

★13 a Is. 66:8; Jer. 2:10, 11 **b**Jer. 14:17; 31:4 **c**Jer. 5:30; 23:14; Hos. 6:10

13 "Therefore thus says the LORD,
'[a]Ask now among the nations,
Who ever heard the like of this?
The [b]virgin of Israel
Has done a most [c]appalling thing.

★14

14 'Does the snow of Lebanon forsake the rock of the open country?
Or is the cold flowing water *from* a foreign *land* ever snatched away?

15 a Jer. 2:32; 3:21 **b**Is. 65:7; Jer. 7:9; 10:15; 44:17 **c**Jer. 6:16 **d**Is. 57:14; 62:10

15 'For [a]My people have forgotten Me,
[b]They burn incense to worthless gods
And they have stumbled from their ways,
From the [c]ancient paths,
To walk in bypaths,
Not on a [d]highway,

16 a Jer. 25:9; 49:13; 50:13; Ezek. 33:28, 29 **b**1 Kin. 9:8; Lam. 2:15; Mic. 6:16 **c**Ps. 22:7; Is. 37:22; Jer. 48:27

16 To make their land a [a]desolation,
An *object of* perpetual [b]hissing;
Everyone who passes by it will be astonished
And [c]shake his head.

★17 a Ps. 48:7 **b**Job 27:21; Jer. 13:24 **c**Jer. 2:27; 32:33 **d**Jer. 46:21 **★18-23**

17 'Like an [a]east wind I will [b]scatter them
Before the enemy;
I will show them [c]My back and not *My* face
[d]In the day of their calamity.'"

18 a Jer. 11:19; 18:11 **b**Jer. 2:8; Mal. 2:7 **c**Job 5:13; Jer. 8:8 **d**Jer. 5:13 **e**Ps. 52:2; Jer. 20:10 **f**Jer. 43:2

18 Then they said, "Come and let us [a]devise plans against Jeremiah. Surely the [b]law is not going to be lost to the priest, nor

[c]counsel to the sage, nor the *divine* [d]word to the prophet! Come on and let us [e]strike at him with *our* tongue, and let us [f]give no heed to any of his words."

19 Do give heed to me, O LORD,
And listen to what my opponents are saying!

20 a Ps. 109:4 **b**Ps. 35:7; 57:6; Jer. 5:26; 18:22 **c**Ps. 106:23

20 [a]Should good be repaid with evil?
For they have [b]dug a pit for me.
Remember how I [c]stood before Thee
To speak good on their behalf,
So as to turn away Thy wrath from them.

21 a Ps. 109:9-20; Jer. 11:22; 14:16 **b**1 Sam. 15:33; Is. 13:18 **c**Jer. 15:8; Ezek. 22:25 **d**Jer. 9:21; 11:22

21 Therefore, [a]give their children over to famine,
And deliver them up to the power of the sword;
And let their wives become [b]childless and [c]widowed.
Let their men also be smitten to death,
Their [d]young men struck down by the sword in battle.

22 a Jer. 6:26; 25:34, 36 **b**Jer. 18:20 **c**Ps. 140:5

22 May an [a]outcry be heard from their houses,
When Thou suddenly bringest raiders upon them;
[b]For they have dug a pit to capture me
And [c]hidden snares for my feet.

23 a Neh. 4:5; Ps. 109:14; Is. 2:9 **b**Jer. 6:15, 21 **c**Jer. 7:20; 17:4

23 Yet Thou, O LORD, knowest
All their deadly designs against me;
[a]Do not forgive their iniquity
Or blot out their sin from Thy sight.
But may they be [b]overthrown before Thee;

18:13 *The virgin of Israel.* Who should have kept herself untainted (cf. 14:17).
18:14 The meaning seems to be this: the course of nature is consistent, but Judah has unnaturally changed her course by apostasizing.
18:17 *an east wind.* See 4:11. *My back and not*

My face. Because God would be departing from the nation.
18:18-23 Another conspiracy against Jeremiah, with his reactions (cf. 11:18-23; 12:1-6; 15:10-21).

Deal with them in the
^ctime of Thine anger!

I   Judah as a Broken Flask,
19:1—20:18
1   The message, 19:1-15

19 Thus says the Lord, "Go
and buy a ^apotter's earthenware ^bjar, and *take* some of the
^celders of the people and some of
the ^dsenior priests.

2 "Then go out to the ^avalley
of Ben-hinnom, which is by the
entrance of the potsherd gate; and
^bproclaim there the words that I
shall tell you,

3 and say, 'Hear the word of
the Lord, O ^akings of Judah and
inhabitants of Jerusalem: thus
says the Lord of hosts, the God of
Israel, "Behold I am about to
bring a ^bcalamity upon this place,
at which the ^cears of everyone
that hears of it will tingle.

4 "Because they have ^aforsak-
en Me and have ^bmade this an
alien place and have burned sacrifices in it to ^cother gods that neither they nor their forefathers nor
the kings of Judah had *ever*
known, and *because* they have
filled this place with the ^dblood of
the innocent

5 and have built the ^ahigh
places of Baal to burn their ^bsons
in the fire as burnt offerings to
Baal, a thing which I never commanded or spoke of, nor did it
ever enter My mind;

6 therefore, behold, ^adays
are coming," declares the Lord,
"when this place will no longer be
called ^bTopheth or ^cthe valley of
Ben-hinnom, but rather the valley
of Slaughter.

7 "And I shall ^amake void the
counsel of Judah and Jerusalem in
this place, and ^bI shall cause them
to fall by the sword before their

enemies and by the hand of those
who seek their life; and I shall
give over their ^ccarcasses as food
for the birds of the sky and the
beasts of the earth.

8 "I shall also make this city a
^adesolation and an *object of* hiss-
ing; ^beveryone who passes by it
will be astonished and hiss because of all its disasters.

9 "And I shall make them
^aeat the flesh of their sons and the
flesh of their daughters, and they
will eat one another's flesh in the
siege and in the distress with
which their enemies and those
who seek their life will distress
them."'

10 "Then you are to break the
^ajar in the sight of the men who
accompany you

11 and say to them, 'Thus
says the Lord of hosts, "Just as
shall I ^abreak this people and this
city, even as one breaks a potter's
vessel, which cannot again be repaired; and they will ^bbury in Topheth because there is no *other*
place for burial.

12 "This is how I shall treat
this place and its inhabitants," declares the Lord, "so as to make
this city like Topheth.

13 "And the ^ahouses of Jerusalem and the houses of the kings
of Judah will be ^bdefiled like the
place Topheth, because of all the
^chouses on whose rooftops they
burned sacrifices to ^dall the heavenly host and ^epoured out libations to other gods.' ' "

14 Then Jeremiah came from
Topheth, where the Lord had sent
him to prophesy; and he stood in
the ^acourt of the Lord's house and
said to all the people:

15 "Thus says the Lord of
hosts, the God of Israel, 'Behold, I
am about to bring on this city and
all its towns the entire calamity
that I have declared against it, be-

Cross-reference column

★ **1** ^aJer.
18:2 ^bJer.
19:10 ^cNum.
11:16
^d2 Kin. 19:2;
Ezek. 8:11

★ **2** ^aJosh.
15:8; 2 Kin.
23:10; Jer.
7:31, 32;
32:35 ^bProv.
1:20

3 ^aJer.
17:20 ^bJer.
6:19; 19:15
^c1 Sam. 3:11

★ **4** ^aDeut.
28:20; Is.
65:11; Jer.
2:13, 17, 19;
17:13 ^bEzek.
7:22; Dan.
11:31 ^cJer.
7:9; 11:13
^d2 Kin. 21:6,
16; Jer. 2:34;
7:6

5 ^aNum.
22:41; Jer.
32:35 ^bLev.
18:21; 2 Kin.
17:17; Ps.
106:37, 38

★ **6** ^aJer.
7:32 ^bIs.
30:33 ^cJosh.
15:8

7 ^aPs.
33:10, 11; Is.
28:17, 18;
Jer. 8:8, 9
^bLev. 26:17;
Deut. 28:25;
Jer. 15:2, 9
^cPs. 79:2;
Jer. 16:4

8 ^aJer.
18:16; 49:13;
50:13
^b1 Kin. 9:8;
2 Chr. 7:21

9 ^aLev.
26:29; Deut.
28:53, 55; Is.
9:20; Lam.
4:10; Ezek.
5:10

10 ^aJer. 19:1

11 ^aPs. 2:9;
Is. 30:14;
Lam. 4:2;
Rev. 2:27
^bJer. 7:32

★**13** ^aJer.
52:13
^b2 Kin.
23:10; Ps.
74:7; 79:1;
Ezek. 7:21,
22 ^cJer.
32:29; Zeph.
1:5 ^dDeut.
4:19; 2 Kin.
17:16; Jer.
8:2 ^eJer.
7:18; 44:18;
Ezek. 20:28

14 ^a2 Chr.
20:5; Jer.
26:2

15 ^aNeh.
9:17, 29; Jer.
7:26; 17:23
^bPs. 58:4

19:1 *earthenware jar.* Once hardened, it could
not be remade but had to be broken if unacceptable. Judah had arrived at that stage.
19:2 *the valley of Ben-hinnom.* See note on 7:31.
the potsherd gate. Leading into the valley
where broken pottery was thrown.

19:4 *blood of the innocent.* Infant sacrifice
(7:31).
19:6 *Topheth.* See note on 7:31.
19:13 The flat roofs of the houses were used for
worshiping astral deities (cf. 32:29).

cause they have ^astiffened their necks so ^bas not to heed My words.' "

2 The reaction: Jeremiah persecuted, 20:1-18

★ 1 ^a1 Chr. 24:14; Ezra 2:37, 38
^b2 Kin. 25:18

20 When Pashhur the priest, the son of ^aImmer, who was ^bchief officer in the house of the LORD, heard Jeremiah prophesying these things,

★ 2 ^a1 Kin. 22:27; 2 Chr. 16:10; 24:21; Jer. 1:19; Amos 7:10-13 ^bJob 13:27; 33:11 ^cJer. 37:13; 38:7; Zech. 14:10

2 Pashhur had Jeremiah the prophet ^abeaten, and put him in the ^bstocks that were at the upper ^cBenjamin Gate, which was by the house of the LORD.

★ 3 ^aIs. 8:3; Hos. 1:4, 9 ^bJer. 6:25; 20:10

3 Then it came about on the next day, when Pashhur released Jeremiah from the stocks, that Jeremiah said to him, "Pashhur is not the name the LORD has ^acalled you, but rather ^bMagor-missabib.

4 ^aJob 18:11-21; Jer. 6:25; 46:5; Ezek. 26:21 ^bJer. 29:21; 39:6, 7 ^cJer. 21:4-10; 25:9 ^dJer. 13:10; 52:27

4 "For thus says the LORD, 'Behold, I am going to make you a ^aterror to yourself and to all your friends; and while ^byour eyes look on, they will fall by the sword of their enemies. So I shall ^cgive over all Judah to the hand of the king of Babylon, and he will carry them away as ^dexiles to Babylon and will slay them with the sword.

5 ^aJer. 15:13; 17:3 ^b2 Kin. 20:17, 18; 2 Chr. 36:10; Jer. 27:21, 22

5 'I shall also give over all the ^awealth of this city, all its produce, and all its costly things; even all the treasures of the kings of Judah I shall give over to the ^bhand of their enemies, and they will plunder them, take them away, and bring them to Babylon.

6 ^aJer. 20:1 ^bJer. 20:4; 29:21 ^cJer. 14:14, 15; Lam. 2:14

6 'And you, ^aPashhur, and all who live in your house will go into captivity; and you will enter Babylon, and there you will die, and there you will be buried, you

and all your ^bfriends to whom you have ^cfalsely prophesied.' "

7 O LORD, Thou hast deceived me and I was deceived;
Thou hast ^aovercome me and prevailed.
I have become a ^blaughingstock all day long;
Everyone ^cmocks me.

★ 7-18
7 ^aEzek. 3:14 ^bJob 12:4; Lam. 3:14 ^cPs. 22:7; Jer. 38:19

8 For each time I speak, I cry aloud;
I ^aproclaim violence and destruction,
Because for me the ^bword of the LORD has resulted
In reproach and derision all day long.

8 ^aJer. 6:7 ^b2 Chr. 36:16; Jer. 6:10

9 But if I say, "I will not ^aremember Him
Or speak anymore in His name,"
Then in ^bmy heart it becomes like a burning fire
Shut up in my bones;
And I am weary of holding it in,
And ^cI cannot endure it.

9 ^a1 Kin. 19:3, 4; Jon. 1:2, 3 ^bJob 32:18-20; Ps. 39:3; Jer. 4:19; 23:9; Ezek. 3:14; Acts 4:20 ^cJob 32:18-20

10 For ^aI have heard the whispering of many,
"^bTerror on every side!
^cDenounce him; yes, let us denounce him!"
All my ^dtrusted friends,
Watching for my fall, say:
"Perhaps he will be deceived, so that we may ^eprevail against him
And take our revenge on him."

10 ^aPs. 31:13 ^bJer. 6:25 ^cNeh. 6:6-13; Is. 29:21; Jer. 18:18 ^dPs. 41:9 ^e1 Kin. 19:2

11 But the ^aLORD is with me like a dread champion;
Therefore my ^bpersecutors will stumble and not prevail.

11 ^aJer. 1:8; 15:20; Rom. 8:31 ^bDeut. 32:35, 36; Jer. 15:15, 20; 17:18 ^cJer. 23:40

20:1 *chief officer.* The officer responsible for law and order in the Temple (cf. Luke 22:52; Acts 4:1; 5:24).

20:2 *beaten.* I.e., with 40 lashes across the feet (cf. Deut. 25:3; 2 Cor. 11:24). The *stocks* secured the feet, hands and neck, bending the body almost double (cf. 2 Chron. 16:10; Jer. 29:26).

20:3 *Magor-missabib.* Means "terror on every

side"; i.e., Pashhur's change of name became a symbol of what would happen when the Babylonians came (vv. 4-6).

20:7-18 Jeremiah complained about his lot (vv. 7-8, 14-18), yet was compelled to proclaim God's message (v. 9). *Terror on every side* (v. 10). In Hebrew, *Magor-missabib* (see note on v. 3). A sarcastic nickname for Jeremiah.

They will be utterly
ashamed, because
they have failed,
With an ^ceverlasting disgrace that will not be
forgotten.

12 Yet, O LORD of hosts, Thou
who dost ^atest the
righteous,
Who seest the mind and
the heart;
Let me ^bsee Thy vengeance
on them;
For ^cto Thee I have set
forth my cause.

13 ^aSing to the LORD, praise
the LORD!
For He has ^bdelivered the
soul of the needy one
From the hand of evil-
doers.

14 Cursed be the ^aday when I
was born;
Let the day not be blessed
when my mother bore
me!

15 Cursed be the man who
brought the news
To my father, saying,
"A ^ababy boy has been
born to you!"
And made him very hap-
py.

16 But let that man be like
the cities
Which the LORD ^aover-
threw without relent-
ing,
And let him hear an ^bout-
cry in the morning
And a shout of alarm at
noon;

17 Because he did not ^akill me
before birth,
So that my mother would
have been my grave,
And her womb ever preg-
nant.

18 Why did I ever come forth
from the womb

To ^alook on trouble and
sorrow,
So that my ^bdays have
been spent in ^cshame?

J Judah's Kings, 21:1–23:8
1 The message to Zedekiah,
21:1–22:9

21 The word which came to
Jeremiah from the LORD
when ^aKing Zedekiah sent to him
^bPashhur the son of Malchijah,
and ^cZephaniah the priest, the
son of Maaseiah, saying,
2 "Please ^ainquire of the LORD
on our behalf, for ^bNebuchadnez-
zar king of ^cBabylon is warring
against us; perhaps the LORD will
deal with us ^daccording to all His
wonderful acts, that the enemy
may withdraw from us."
3 Then Jeremiah said to
them, "You shall say to Zedekiah
as follows:
4 'Thus says the LORD God of
Israel, "Behold, I am about to
^aturn back the weapons of war
which are in your hands, with
which you are warring against the
king of Babylon and the Chaldeans who are besieging you out-
side the wall; and I shall ^bgather
them into the center of this city.
5 "And I ^aMyself shall war
against you with an ^boutstretched
hand and a mighty arm, even in
^canger and wrath and great indig-
nation.
6 "I shall also strike down the
inhabitants of this city, both man
and beast; they will die of a great
^apestilence.
7 "Then afterwards," declares
the LORD, "^aI shall give over Zedekiah king of Judah and his ser-
vants and the people, even those
who survive in this city from the
pestilence, the sword, and the
famine, into the hand of Nebu-

21:1 This message to Zedekiah (21:1–22:9), delivered during the latter part of his reign
(597–586), urged him to submit to Nebuchad-

nezzar, in opposition to the nobles who advised a pro-Egyptian policy.

chadnezzar king of Babylon, and into the hand of their foes, and into the hand of those who seek their lives; and he will strike them down with the edge of the sword. He ᵇwill not spare them nor have pity nor compassion." '

★ 8-10

8 aDeut. 30:15, 19; Is. 1:19, 20

8 "You shall also say to this people, 'Thus says the LORD, "Behold, I ᵃset before you the way of life and the way of death.

9 aJer. 38:2, 17-23; 39:18; 45:5
ᵇJer. 14:12; 24:10

9 "He who ᵃdwells in this city will die by the ᵇsword and by famine and by pestilence; but he who goes out and falls away to the Chaldeans who are besieging you will live, and he will have his own life as booty.

10 aLev. 17:10; Jer. 44:11, 27; Amos 9:4
ᵇJer. 32:28, 29; 38:3
c2 Chr. 36:19; Jer. 34:2, 37:10; 38:18; 39:8; 52:13

10 "For I have ᵃset My face against this city for harm and not for good," declares the LORD. "It will be ᵇgiven into the hand of the king of Babylon, and he will cburn it with fire." '

11 aJer. 17:20

11 "Then say to the household of the ᵃking of Judah, 'Hear the word of the LORD,

12 aIs. 7:2,
13 ᵇPs. 72:1; Is. 1:17; Jer. 7:5; 22:3; Zech. 7:9, 10
cPs. 101:8; Zeph. 3:5
dJer. 4:4; 17:4; Ezek. 20:47, 48; Nah. 1:6
eIs. 1:31; Jer. 7:20

12 O ᵃhouse of David, thus says the LORD:
"ᵇAdminister justice every cmorning;
And deliver the person who has been robbed from the power of his oppressor,
ᵈThat My wrath may not go forth like fire
And eburn with none to extinguish it,
Because of the evil of their deeds.

13 aJer. 23:30-32; Ezek. 13:8
ᵇPs. 125:2; Is. 22:1
c2 Sam. 5:6, 7; Jer. 49:4; Lam. 4:12; Obad. 3, 4

13 "Behold, ᵃI am against you, O ᵇvalley dweller, O rocky plain," declares the LORD,
"You men who say, 'cWho will come down against us?
Or who will enter into our habitations?'

14 "But I shall punish you ᵃaccording to the results of your deeds," declares the LORD,
"And I shall ᵇkindle a fire in its forest
That it may devour all its environs." ' "

22 Thus says the LORD, "Go down to the house of the king of Judah, and there speak this word,

14 aIs. 3:10, 11; Jer. 17:10; 32:19
ᵇ2 Chr. 36:19; Is. 10:16, 18; Jer. 11:16; 17:27; 52:13; Ezek. 20:47, 48

2 and say, 'Hear the word of the LORD, O king of Judah, who ᵃsits on David's throne, you and your servants and your people who enter these gates.

2 aIs. 9:7; Jer. 22:4, 30; 17:25; Luke 1:32

3 'Thus says the LORD, "ᵃDo justice and righteousness, and deliver the one who has been robbed from the power of his ᵇoppressor. Also cdo not mistreat or do violence to the stranger, the orphan, or the widow; and do not ᵈshed innocent blood in this place.

3 aIs. 58:6, 7; Jer. 7:5, 23; 21:12; Mic. 6:8; Zech. 7:9; 8:16; Matt. 23:23
ᵇPs. 72:4
cEx. 22:21-24
dJer. 7:6; 19:4; 22:17

4 "For if you men will indeed perform this thing, then ᵃkings will enter the gates of this house, sitting in David's place on his throne, riding in chariots and on horses, even the king himself and his servants and his people.

4 aJer. 17:25

5 "ᵃBut if you will not obey these words, I ᵇswear by Myself," declares the LORD, "that this house will become a desolation." ' "

5 aJer. 17:27; 26:4
ᵇGen. 22:16; Amos 6:8; Heb. 6:13

6 For thus says the LORD concerning the house of the king of Judah:
"You are like ᵃGilead to Me,
Like the summit of Lebanon;
Yet most assuredly I shall make you like a ᵇwilderness,
Like cities which are not inhabited.

★ 6 aGen. 37:25; Num. 32:1; Song 4:1
ᵇPs. 107:34; Is. 6:11; Jer. 7:34; Mic. 3:12

21:8-10 Little wonder Jeremiah was considered a traitor by his fellow countrymen. The *way of life* which he counselled them to accept was to surrender to the Babylonians; otherwise, their lives would be *booty* for the captors.
22:6 *Gilead . . . Lebanon.* Fertile, beautiful regions.

7 aIs. 10:3-
6; Jer. 4:6, 7
bIs. 10:33,
34; 37:24
cJer. 21:14

7 "For I shall set apart adestroyers against you,
Each with his weapons;
And they will bcut down
your choicest cedars
And cthrow *them* on the
fire.

8 aDeut.
29:24-26;
1 Kin. 9:8, 9;
2 Chr. 7:20-
22; Jer.
16:10
9 a2 Kin.
22:17; 2 Chr.
34:25; Jer.
11:3

8 "And many nations will
pass by this city; and they will
asay to one another, 'Why has the
Lord done thus to this great city?'
9 "Then they will answer,
'Because they aforsook the covenant of the Lord their God and
bowed down to other gods and
served them.' "

2 **The message concerning
Jehoahaz (Shallum),
22:10-12**

★10 aEccl.
4:2; Is. 57:1;
Jer. 16:7;
22:18 bJer.
25:27; 44:14

10 aDo not weep for the dead
or mourn for him,
But weep continually for
the one who goes
away;
For bhe will never return
Or see his native land.

11 a2 Kin.
23:30-34;
1 Chr. 3:15;
2 Chr. 36:1-4

11 For thus says the Lord in
regard to aShallum the son of Josiah, king of Judah, who became
king in the place of Josiah his father, who went forth from this
place, "He will never return there;

12 a2 Kin.
23:34; Jer.
22:18

12 but in the place where
they led him captive, there he will
adie and not see this land again.

3 **The message concerning
Jehoiakim, 22:13-19**

★13-19

13 aJer.
17:11; Mic.
3:10; Hab.
2:9 bLev.
19:13; James
5:4

13 "Woe to him who builds
his house awithout
righteousness
And his upper rooms with-
out justice,
Who uses his neighbor's
services without pay

And bdoes not give him his
wages,
14 Who says, 'I will abuild
myself a roomy house
With spacious upper
rooms,
And cut out its windows,
Paneling *it* with bcedar and
painting *it* bright red.'
15 "Do you become a king because you are compet-
ing in cedar?
Did not your father eat
and drink,
And ado justice and righteousness?
Then it was bwell with
him.
16 "He pled the cause of the
aafflicted and needy;
Then it was well.
bIs not that what it means
to know Me?"
Declares the Lord.
17 "But your eyes and your
heart
Are *intent* only upon your
own adishonest gain,
And on bshedding inno-
cent blood
And on practicing oppres-
sion and extortion."
18 Therefore thus says the
Lord in regard to aJehoiakim the
son of Josiah, king of Judah,
"They will not blament for
him:
'cAlas, my brother!' or,
'Alas, sister!'
They will not lament for
him:
'Alas for the master!' or,
'Alas for his splendor!'
19 "He will be aburied with a
donkey's burial,
Dragged off and thrown
out beyond the gates
of Jerusalem.

14 aIs. 5:8
b2 Sam. 7:2;
Hag. 1:4

15 a2 Kin.
23:25; Jer.
7:5; 21:12
bPs. 128:2;
Is. 3:10; Jer.
42:6

16 aPs.
72:1-4, 12,
13 b1 Chr.
28:9; Jer.
9:24

17 aJer.
6:13; 8:10;
Luke 12:15-
20 b2 Kin.
24:4; Jer.
22:3

18 a2 Kin.
23:36-24:6;
2 Chr. 36:5
bJer. 22:10;
34:5 c1 Kin.
13:30

19 a1 Kin.
21:23, 24;
Jer. 36:30

22:10 *for the dead.* I.e., for King Josiah, who had
been killed recently. *the one who goes away.*
I.e., Josiah's son (Shallum, or Jehoahaz;
1 Chron. 3:15), who reigned 3 months before
being deported to Egypt by Necho. He never
returned to Palestine (2 Kings 23:29-35).
22:13-19 A denunciation against Jehoiakim, the
elder brother and successor of Shallum. He

built elaborate royal buildings with forced labor (vv. 13-14). Jeremiah predicted that the
normal form of lament would not be used
when Jehoiakim died and that he would not
be buried, but simply dragged out of the city
and dumped on the garbage heap (the absence
of "and was buried" in 2 Kings 24:6 is significant).

4   The message concerning Jehoiachin (Coniah, Jeconiah), 22:20-30

20 ᵃNum.
27:12; Deut.
32:49 ᵇJer.
2:25; 3:1

20 "Go up to Lebanon and cry
    out,
And lift up your voice in
    Bashan;
Cry out also from ᵃAba-
    rim,
For all your ᵇlovers have
    been crushed.

21 ᵃJer.
13:10; 19:15
ᵇJer. 3:25
ᶜJer. 3:24;
32:30

21 "I spoke to you in your
    prosperity;
But ᵃyou said, 'I will not
    listen!'
ᵇThis has been your prac-
    tice ᶜfrom your youth,
That you have not obeyed
    My voice.

22 ᵃJer. 23:1
ᵇJer. 30:14
ᶜIs. 65:13;
Jer. 20:11

22 "The wind will sweep away
    all your ᵃshepherds,
And your ᵇlovers will go
    into captivity;
Then you will surely be
    ᶜashamed and humil-
    iated
Because of all your wick-
    edness.

★23 ᵃJer.
4:31; 6:24

23 "You who dwell in Leba-
    non,
Nested in the cedars,
How you will groan when
    pangs come upon you,
ᵃPain like a woman in
    childbirth!

★24-30
24 ᵃ2 Kin.
24:6; 1 Chr.
3:16; 2 Chr.
36:9; Jer.
37:1 ᵇSong
8:6; Is.
49:16; Hag.
2:23

24 "As I live," declares the
LORD, "even though ᵃConiah the
son of Jehoiakim king of Judah
were a ᵇsignet *ring* on My right
hand, yet I would pull you off;

25 ᵃ2 Kin.
24:15, 16;
Jer. 21:7;
34:20, 21

25 and I shall ᵃgive you over
into the hand of those who are

seeking your life, yes, into the
hand of those whom you dread,
even into the hand of Nebuchadnezzar king of Babylon, and into
the hand of the Chaldeans.

26 "I shall ᵃhurl you and your
ᵇmother who bore you into another country where you were not
born, and there you will die.

27 "But as for the land to
which they desire to return, they
will not return to it.

28 "Is this man Coniah a de-
    spised, shattered jar?
Or is he an ᵃundesirable
    vessel?
Why have he and his de-
    scendants   been
    ᵇhurled out
And cast into a ᶜland that
    they had not known?

29 "ᵃO land, land, land,
    Hear the word of the LORD!

30 "Thus says the LORD,
'Write this man down
    ᵃchildless,
A man who will ᵇnot pros-
    per in his days;
For no man of his
    ᶜdescendants   will
    prosper
Sitting on the throne of
    David
Or ruling again in Judah.' "

26 ᵃ2 Kin.
24:15; Jer.
10:18; 16:13
ᵇ2 Kin. 24:8

28 ᵃPs.
31:12; Jer.
48:38; Hos.
8:8 ᵇJer.
15:1 ᶜJer.
17:4

29 ᵃDeut.
4:26; Jer.
6:19; Mic.
1:2

★30 ᵃ1 Chr.
3:17; Matt.
1:12 ᵇJer.
2:37; 10:21
ᶜPs. 94:20;
Jer. 36:30

5   The message concerning Messiah, 23:1-8

23 "ᵃWoe to the shepherds
who are ᵇdestroying and
scattering the ᶜsheep of My pasture!" declares the LORD.

2 Therefore thus says the
LORD God of Israel concerning the

★ 1 ᵃEzek.
13:3; 34:2;
Zech. 11:17
ᵇIs. 56:9-12;
Jer. 10:21;
50:6 ᶜEzek.
34:31

2 ᵃEx.
32:34 ᵇJer.
21:12; 44:22

22:23 *You who dwell in Lebanon.* The reference
is to Jerusalem, many of whose buildings were
built with cedars from Lebanon.

22:24-30 These verses describe the fate of Jehoiachin (here and in 37:1 called Coniah; also
called Jeconiah, 24:1; 27:20), son of Jehoiakim.
After a three-month reign, he was taken to
Babylon, never to return (2 Kings 24:8-15;
25:27-30), in spite of Hananiah's false prophecy to the contrary (Jer. 28:4, 15; cf. 52:31-34).

22:30 *childless.* Although Coniah had 7 sons
(perhaps adopted; cf. 1 Chron. 3:17), none occupied the throne. So as far as a continuing
dynasty was concerned, Coniah was to be considered "childless." Although his line of descendants retained the legal throne rights, no

physical descendant would ever prosperously
reign on the Davidic throne. The genealogy of
Matthew traces the descent of Jesus through
Solomon and Jeconiah (Coniah) (Matt. 1:12);
this is the genealogy of Jesus' legal father,
Joseph. Luke traces Jesus' physical descent
back through Mary and Nathan to David, bypassing Jeconiah's line and showing accurately
the fulfillment of this prophecy of Jeremiah. If
Jesus had been born only in the line of Joseph
(and thus of Jeconiah), He would not have
been qualified to reign on the throne of David
in the Millennium. See note on Matt. 1:11.

23:1 *shepherds.* The unrighteous rulers of Judah
(see note on 10:21).

shepherds who are tending My people: "You have scattered My flock and driven them away, and have not attended to them; behold, I am about to ᵃattend to you for the ᵇevil of your deeds," declares the Lᴏʀᴅ.

3 "Then I Myself shall ᵃgather the remnant of My flock out of all the countries where I have driven them and shall bring them back to their pasture; and they will be fruitful and multiply.

4 "I shall also raise up ᵃshepherds over them and they will tend them; and they will ᵇnot be afraid any longer, nor be terrified, ᶜnor will any be missing," declares the Lᴏʀᴅ.

5 "Behold, *the* ᵃdays are coming," declares the Lᴏʀᴅ, "When I shall raise up for David a righteous ᵇBranch; And He will ᶜreign as king and act wisely And ᵈdo justice and righteousness in the land.

6 "In His days Judah will be saved, And ᵃIsrael will dwell securely; And this is His ᵇname by which He will be called, 'The ᶜLᴏʀᴅ our righteousness.'

7 "ᵃTherefore behold, *the* days are coming," declares the Lᴏʀᴅ, "when they will no longer say, 'As the Lᴏʀᴅ lives, who brought up the sons of Israel from the land of Egypt,'

8 ᵃbut, 'As the Lᴏʀᴅ lives, who ᵇbrought up and led back the descendants of the household of Israel from *the* north land and from all the countries where I had driven them.' Then they will live on their own soil."

K Judah's False Prophets, 23:9–40

9 As for the prophets: My ᵃheart is broken within me, All my bones tremble; I have become like a drunken man, Even like a man overcome with wine, Because of the Lᴏʀᴅ And because of His holy words.

10 For the land is full of ᵃadulterers; For the land ᵇmourns because of the curse. The ᶜpastures of the wilderness have dried up. Their course also is evil, And their might is not right.

11 "For ᵃboth prophet and priest are polluted; Even in My house I have found their wickedness," declares the Lᴏʀᴅ.

12 "Therefore their way will be like ᵃslippery paths to them, They will be driven away into the ᵇgloom and fall down in it; For I shall bring ᶜcalamity upon them, The year of their punishment," declares the Lᴏʀᴅ.

13 "Moreover, among the prophets of Samaria I saw an ᵃoffensive thing: They ᵇprophesied by Baal and ᶜled My people Israel astray.

14 "Also among the prophets of Jerusalem I have seen a ᵃhorrible thing:

★ **3** ᵃIs. 11:11, 12, 16; Jer. 31:7, 8; 32:37

4 ᵃJer. 3:15; 31:10; Ezek. 34:23 ᵇJer. 30:10; 46:27, 28 ᶜJohn 6:39; 10:28; 1 Pet. 1:5

★ **5** ᵃJer. 33:14 ᵇIs. 4:2; 11:1-5; 53:2; Jer. 30:9; 33:15, 16; Zech. 3:8; 6:12, 13 ᶜIs. 9:7; 52:13; Luke 1:32, 33 ᵈPs. 72:2; Is. 9:7; 32:1; Dan. 9:24

6 ᵃDeut. 33:28; Jer. 30:10; Zech. 14:11 ᵇIs. 7:14; 9:6; Matt. 1:21-23 ᶜIs. 45:24; Jer. 33:16; Dan. 9:24; Rom. 3:22; 1 Cor. 1:30

7 ᵃIs. 43:18, 19; Jer. 16:14, 15

★ **8** ᵃJer. 16:15 ᵇIs. 43:5, 6; Ezek. 34:13; Amos 9:14, 15

9 ᵃJer. 8:18; Hab. 3:16

★ **10-15**

10 ᵃPs. 9:2; Hos. 4:2, 3; Mal. 3:5 ᵇJer. 12:4 ᶜPs. 107:34; Jer. 9:10

11 ᵃJer. 6:13; Zeph. 3:4

12 ᵃPs. 35:6; Prov. 4:19; Jer. 13:16 ᵇIs. 8:22; John 12:35 ᶜJer. 11:23

13 ᵃHos. 9:7, 8 ᵇ1 Kin. 18:18-21; Jer. 2:8; 23:32 ᶜIs. 9:16

14 ᵃJer. 5:30 ᵇJer. 29:23 ᶜJer. 23:22; Ezek. 13:22, 23 ᵈGen. 18:20; Deut. 32:32; Is. 1:9, 10; Jer. 20:16; 49:18; Matt. 11:24

23:3 The return from Babylonian captivity is promised, as well as a yet future regathering from *all the countries* (cf. Matt. 24:31).
23:5 *Branch.* Lit., shoot, a Messianic title signifying the new life that Messiah will bring. See Isa. 4:2. He will secure *righteousness* for His people.
23:8 See note on 16:15.
23:10-15 A description of the immoral conduct of the false prophets.

The committing of [b]adultery and walking in falsehood;
And they strengthen the hands of [c]evildoers,
So that no one has turned back from his wickedness.
All of them have become to Me like [d]Sodom,
And her inhabitants like Gomorrah.

15 aDeut. 29:18; Jer. 8:14; 9:15

15 "Therefore thus says the LORD of hosts concerning the prophets,
'Behold, I am going to [a]feed them wormwood
And make them drink poisonous water,
For from the prophets of Jerusalem
Pollution has gone forth into all the land.'"

★16-17

16 aJer. 27:9, 10, 14-17; 1 John 4:1 bMatt. 7:15; 2 Cor. 11:13-15; Gal. 1:8, 9 cJer. 14:14; Ezek. 13:3, 6 dJer. 9:12, 20

16 Thus says the LORD of hosts,
"[a]Do not listen to the words of the prophets who are prophesying to you.
They are [b]leading you into futility;
They speak a [c]vision of their own imagination,
Not [d]from the mouth of the LORD.

17 aMic. 2:11 bJer. 8:11; Ezek. 13:10 cJer. 13:10; 18:12 dJer. 5:12; Amos 9:10; Mic. 3:11

17 "They keep saying to those who [a]despise Me,
'The LORD has said, "[b]You will have peace"';
And as for everyone who walks in the [c]stubbornness of his own heart,
They say, '[d]Calamity will not come upon you.'

★18-40

18 aJob 15:8, 9; Jer. 23:22; 1 Cor. 2:16 bJob 33:31

18 "But [a]who has stood in the council of the LORD,
That he should see and hear His word?
Who has given [b]heed to His word and listened?

19 "Behold, the [a]storm of the LORD has gone forth in wrath,
Even a whirling tempest;
It will swirl down on the head of the wicked.

19 aJer. 25:32; 30:23; Amos 1:14

20 "The [a]anger of the LORD will not turn back
Until He has [b]performed and carried out the purposes of His heart;
[c]In the last days you will clearly understand it.

20 a2 Kin. 23:26, 27; Jer. 30:24 bIs. 55:11; Zech. 1:6 cGen. 49:1

21 "[a]I did not send *these* prophets,
But they ran.
I did not speak to them,
But they prophesied.

21 aJer. 14:14; 23:32; 27:15

22 "But if they had [a]stood in My council,
Then they would have [b]announced My words to My people,
And would have turned them back from their evil way
And from the evil of their deeds.

22 aJer. 9:12; 23:18 bJer. 35:15; Zech. 1:4

23 "Am I a God who is [a]near," declares the LORD,
"And not a God far off?

23 aPs. 139:1-10

24 "Can a man [a]hide himself in hiding places,
So I do not see him?" declares the LORD.
"[b]Do I not fill the heavens and the earth?" declares the LORD.

24 aJob 22:13, 14; 34:21, 22; Ps. 139:7-12; Is. 29:15; Jer. 49:10; Heb. 4:13 b1 Kin. 8:27; 2 Chr. 2:6; Is. 66:1

25 "I have [a]heard what the prophets have said who [b]prophesy falsely in My name, saying, 'I had a [c]dream, I had a dream!'

25 aJer. 8:6; 1 Cor. 4:5 bJer. 14:14; Jer. 23:28, 32; 29:8; Joel 2:28

26 "How long? Is there *anything* in the hearts of the prophets who prophesy falsehood, even *these* prophets of the [a]deception of their own heart,

26 a1 Tim. 4:1, 2

27 who intend to [a]make My people forget My name by their dreams which they relate to one another, just as their fathers [b]forgot My name because of Baal?

27 aDeut. 13:1-3; Jer. 29:8 bJudg. 3:7; 8:33, 34

23:16-17 These prophets were preaching a false message of peace.
23:18-40 The life (v. 18) and message (v. 28) of the true prophet are contrasted with those of the false prophet (v. 32).

28 ^aJer.
9:12, 20
^b1 Cor. 3:12,
13

28 "The prophet who has a dream may relate *his* dream, but let him who has ^aMy word speak My word in truth. ^bWhat does straw have *in common* with grain?" declares the LORD.

29 ^aJer.
5:14; 20:9
^b2 Cor.
10:4, 5

29 "Is not My word like ^afire?" declares the LORD, "and like a ^bhammer which shatters a rock?

30 ^aDeut.
18:20; Ps.
34:16; Jer.
14:14, 15;
Ezek. 13:8

30 "Therefore behold, ^aI am against the prophets," declares the LORD, "who steal My words from each other.

31 "Behold, I am against the prophets," declares the LORD, "who use their tongues and declare, *'The Lord declares.'*

32 ^aDeut.
13:1, 2; Jer.
23:25
^bZeph. 3:4
^cJer. 23:21;
Lam. 3:37
^dJer. 7:8;
Lam. 2:14

32 "Behold, I am against those who have prophesied ^afalse dreams," declares the LORD, "and related them, and led My people astray by their falsehoods and ^breckless boasting; yet ^cI did not send them or command them, nor do they ^dfurnish this people the slightest benefit," declares the LORD.

★33 ^aIs.
13:1; Nah.
1:1; Hab.
1:1; Zech.
9:1; Mal. 1:1
^bJer. 12:7;
23:39

33 "Now when this people or the prophet or a priest asks you saying, 'What is the ^aoracle of the LORD?' then you shall say to them, 'What oracle?' The LORD declares, 'I shall ^babandon you.'

34 ^aLam.
2:14; Zech.
13:3

34 "Then as for the prophet or the priest or the people who say, 'The ^aoracle of the LORD,' I shall bring punishment upon that man and his household.

35 ^aJer.
33:3; 42:4

35 "Thus shall each of you say to his neighbor and to his brother, '^aWhat has the LORD answered?' or, 'What has the LORD spoken?'

36 ^aGal. 1:7,
8; 2 Pet. 3:16
^b2 Kin. 19:4;
Jer. 10:10

36 "For you will no longer remember the oracle of the LORD, because every man's own word will become the oracle, and you have ^aperverted the words of the ^bliving God, the LORD of hosts, our God.

37 "Thus you will say to *that* prophet, 'What has the LORD answered you?' and, 'What has the LORD spoken?'

38 "For if you say, 'The oracle of the LORD!' surely thus says the LORD, 'Because you said this word, "The oracle of the LORD!" I have also sent to you, saying, "You shall not say, 'The oracle of the LORD!' " '

39 ^aJer.
7:14, 15;
23:33; Ezek.
8:18

39 "Therefore behold, ^aI shall surely forget you and cast you away from My presence, along with the city which I gave you and your fathers.

40 ^aJer.
20:11; 42:18;
Ezek. 5:14,
15

40 "And I will put an everlasting ^areproach on you and an everlasting humiliation which will not be forgotten."

L Judah's Captivity, 24:1-25:38

1 The deportees, 24:1-10

24 After ^aNebuchadnezzar king of Babylon had carried away captive Jeconiah the son of Jehoiakim, king of Judah, and the officials of Judah with the craftsmen and smiths from Jerusalem and had brought them to Babylon, the LORD showed me: behold, two ^bbaskets of figs set before the temple of the LORD!

★ 1-10

1 ^a2 Kin.
24:10-16;
2 Chr. 36:10;
Jer. 27:20;
29:1, 2
^bAmos 8:1

2 One basket had very good figs, like ^afirst-ripe figs; and the other basket had ^bvery bad figs, which could not be eaten due to rottenness.

2 ^aMic. 7:1;
Nah. 3:12
^bIs. 5:4, 7;
Jer. 29:17

3 Then the LORD said to me, "^aWhat do you see, Jeremiah?" And I said, "Figs, the good figs, very good; and the bad *figs*, very bad, which cannot be eaten due to rottenness."

3 ^aJer.
1:11, 13;
Amos 8:2;
Zech. 4:2

4 Then the word of the LORD came to me, saying,

23:33 *oracle.* A customary word for a weighty, prophetic message (cf. Nah. 1:1; Hab. 1:1). Some of the people were mocking Jeremiah for his sobering words by asking him, "What's the heavy word (burden) from the Lord today?"

24:1-10 This vision occurred after Jeconiah and others were taken to Babylon in 597. The *good figs* represented those who had been deported and promised their return to Palestine. The *bad figs* depicted those who remained in the land of Palestine or who went to Egypt and were not promised restoration. Excavations show the remarkable architectural accomplishments of Nebuchadnezzar, who used the skilled artisans referred to in verse 1.

5 aNah.
1:7; Zech.
13:9

6 aJer.
12:15; 29:10;
32:37; Ezek.
11:17; bJer.
31:4; 32:41;
33:7; 42:10
cJer. 32:41

7 aDeut.
30:6; Jer.
31:33; 32:40;
Ezek. 11:19;
36:26 bIs.
51:16; Jer.
7:23; 30:22;
31:33; 32:38;
Ezek. 14:11;
Zech. 8:8;
Heb. 8:10
c1 Sam. 7:3;
Ps. 119:2;
Jer. 29:13

8 aJer.
29:17 bJer.
39:5; Ezek.
12:12, 13
cJer. 39:9
dJer. 44:1,
26-30

9 aJer.
15:4; 29:18;
34:17
b1 Kin. 9:7;
Ps. 44:13, 14
cIs. 65:15

10 aIs.
51:19; Jer.
21:9; 27:8;
Ezek. 5:12-
17

5 "Thus says the LORD God of Israel, 'Like these good figs, so I will regard *a*as good the captives of Judah, whom I have sent out of this place *into* the land of the Chaldeans.

6 'For I will set My eyes on them for good, and I will *a*bring them again to this land; and I will *b*build them up and not overthrow them, and I will *c*plant them and not pluck *them* up.

7 'And I will give them a *a*heart to know Me, for I am the LORD; and they will be *b*My people, and I will be their God, for they will *c*return to Me with their whole heart.

8 'But like the *a*bad figs which cannot be eaten due to rottenness—indeed, thus says the LORD—so I will abandon *b*Zedekiah king of Judah and his officials, and the *c*remnant of Jerusalem who remain in this land, and the ones who dwell in the land of *d*Egypt.

9 'And I will *a*make them a terror *and an* evil for all the kingdoms of the earth, as a *b*reproach and a proverb, a taunt and a *c*curse in all places where I shall scatter them.

10 'And I will send the *a*sword, the famine, and the pestilence upon them until they are destroyed from the land which I gave to them and their forefathers.' "

2 The duration, 25:1-11

★ 1 aJer.
36:1; 46:2
b2 Kin. 24:1,
2; 2 Chr.
36:4-6; Dan.
1:1, 2 cJer.
32:1

★ 2-7
2 aJer.
18:11

25 The word that came to Jeremiah concerning all the people of Judah, in the *a*fourth year of *b*Jehoiakim the son of Josiah, king of Judah (that was the *c*first year of Nebuchadnezzar king of Babylon),

2 which Jeremiah the prophet spoke to all the *a*people of Judah and to all the inhabitants of Jerusalem, saying,

3 "From the *a*thirteenth year of *b*Josiah the son of Amon, king of Judah, even to this day, these *c*twenty-three years the word of the LORD has come to me, and I have spoken to you *d*again and again, but you have not listened.

4 "And the LORD has sent to you all His *a*servants the prophets again and again, but you have not listened nor inclined your ear to hear,

5 saying, '*a*Turn now everyone from his evil way and from the evil of your deeds, and dwell on the land which the LORD has given to you and your forefathers *b*forever and ever;

6 and *a*do not go after other gods to serve them and to worship them, and do not provoke Me to anger with the work of your hands, and I will do you no harm.'

7 "Yet you have not listened to Me," declares the LORD, "in order that you might *a*provoke Me to anger with the work of your hands to your own harm.

8 "Therefore thus says the LORD of hosts, 'Because you have not obeyed My words,

9 behold, I will *a*send and take all the families of the north,' declares the LORD, 'and *I will send* to Nebuchadnezzar king of Babylon, *b*My servant, and will bring them against this land, and against its inhabitants, and against all these nations round about; and I will utterly destroy them, and *c*make them a horror, and a hissing, and an everlasting desolation.

10 'Moreover, I will *a*take from them the voice of joy and the voice of gladness, the voice of the bridegroom and the voice of

3 aJer. 1:2
b2 Chr. 34:1-
3, 8 cJer.
36:2 dJer.
7:25; 11:7;
26:5

4 a2 Chr.
36:15; Jer.
26:5

5 a2 Kin.
17:13; Is.
55:6, 7; Jer.
4:1; 35:15;
Ezek. 18:30;
Jon. 3:8-10
bGen. 17:8;
Jer. 7:7;
17:25

6 aDeut.
6:14; 8:19;
2 Kin. 17:35;
Jer. 35:15

7 a2 Kin.
17:17; 21:15;
Jer. 7:19;
32:30-33

9 aJer.
1:15; 6:22,
23 bIs. 13:3;
Jer. 27:6;
43:10 c1 Kin.
9:7, 8; Jer.
18:16; 25:18

10 aIs. 24:8-
11; Jer. 7:34;
16:9; Ezek.
26:13; Rev.
18:23 bEccl.
12:4; Is. 47:2

25:1 *the fourth year of Jehoiakim.* I.e., 605. In Palestine the accession year was counted as the first year of the reign, whereas in Babylon it was reckoned separately, so that the next year was considered the first year of the reign.

Daniel, therefore, dates this event from the Babylonian viewpoint, as the third year of Jehoiakim's reign (Dan. 1:1).

25:2-7 For 23 years Jeremiah had urged the people to turn from their evil ways.

the bride, the ^bsound of the mill-stones and the light of the lamp.

11 'And ^athis whole land shall be a desolation and a horror, and these nations shall serve the king of Babylon ^bseventy years.

3 The disposition of the captor nation, 25:12-38

12 'Then it will be ^awhen seventy years are completed I will ^bpunish the king of Babylon and that nation,' declares the LORD, 'for their iniquity, and the land of the Chaldeans; and ^cI will make it an everlasting desolation.

13 'And I will bring upon that land all My words which I have pronounced against it, all that is written in ^athis book, which Jeremiah has prophesied against ^ball the nations.

14 '(For ^amany nations and great kings shall make slaves of them, even them; and I will ^brecompense them according to their deeds, and according to the work of their hands.)' "

15 For thus the LORD, the God of Israel, says to me, "Take this ^acup of the wine of wrath from My hand, and cause all the nations, to whom I send you, to drink it.

16 "And they shall ^adrink and stagger and go mad because of the sword that I will send among them."

17 Then I took the cup from the LORD's hand, and ^amade all the nations drink, to whom the LORD sent me:

18 ^aJerusalem and the cities of Judah, and its kings and its princes, to make them a ruin, a horror, a hissing, and a curse, as it is this day;

19 ^aPharaoh king of Egypt, his servants, his princes, and all his people;

20 and all the ^aforeign people, all the kings of the ^bland of Uz, all the kings of the land of the ^cPhilistines (even Ashkelon, Gaza, Ekron, and the remnant of ^dAshdod);

21 ^aEdom, ^bMoab, and the sons of ^cAmmon;

22 and all the kings of ^aTyre, all the kings of Sidon, and the kings of ^bthe coastlands which are beyond the sea;

23 and ^aDedan, Tema, ^bBuz, and all who ^ccut the corners of their hair;

24 and all the kings of ^aArabia and all the kings of the ^bforeign people who dwell in the desert;

25 and all the kings of Zimri, all the kings of ^aElam, and all the kings of ^bMedia;

26 and all the kings of the north, near and far, one with another; and ^aall the kingdoms of the earth which are upon the face of the ground, and the king of ^bSheshach shall drink after them.

27 "And you shall say to them, 'Thus says the LORD of hosts, the God of Israel, "^aDrink, be drunk, vomit, fall, and rise no more because of the ^bsword which I will send among you.' "

28 "And it will be, if they ^arefuse to take the cup from your hand to drink, then you will say to them, 'Thus says the LORD of hosts: "^bYou shall surely drink!

29 "For behold, I am ^abeginning to work calamity in this city which is ^bcalled by My name, and shall you be completely free from punishment? You will not be free from punishment; for ^cI am summoning a sword against all the inhabitants of the earth," declares the LORD of hosts.'

30 "Therefore you shall prophesy against them all these words, and you shall say to them,
'The ^aLORD will ^broar from on high,
And utter His voice from His holy habitation;
He will roar mightily against His fold.
He will shout like those who tread the grapes,
Against all the inhabitants of the earth.

31 'A clamor has come to the end of the earth,

11 ^aJer. 4:27; 12:11, 12 ^b2 Chr. 36:21; Jer. 29:10; Dan. 9:2; Zech. 7:5

12 ^aEzra 1:1; Jer. 29:10; Dan. 9:2 ^bIs. 13:14; Jer. ch. 50, 51 ^cIs. 13:19

13 ^aJer. 36:4, 29, 32 ^bJer. 1:5, 10; 36:2

14 ^aJer. 27:7; 50:9, 41; 51:27, 28 ^bJer. 51:6, 24, 56

15 ^aJob 21:20; Ps. 75:8; Is. 51:17, 22; Jer. 51:7

16 ^aNah. 3:11

17 ^aJer. 1:10; 25:28

18 ^aPs. 60:3; Is. 51:17

19 ^aJer. 46:2-28; Nah. 3:8-10

20 ^aJer. 25:24; 50:37; Ezek. 30:5 ^bJob 1:1; Lam. 4:21 ^cJer. 47:1-7 ^dIs. 20:1

21 ^aPs. 137:7; Jer. 49:7-22 ^bJer. 48:1-47; Amos 2:1-3 ^cJer. 49:1-6; Amos 1:13-15

22 ^aJer. 47:4; Zech. 9:2-4 ^bJer. 31:10

23 ^aIs. 21:13; Jer. 49:7, 8 ^bGen. 22:21 ^cJer. 9:26;

24 ^a2 Chr. 9:14 ^bJer. 25:20; 50:37; Ezek. 30:5

25 ^aGen. 10:22; Is. 11:11; Jer. 49:34 ^bIs. 13:17; Jer. 51:11, 28

26 ^aJer. 25:9; 50:9 ^bJer. 51:41

27 ^aJer. 25:16; Hab. 2:16 ^bEzek. 21:4, 5

28 ^aJob 34:33 ^bJer. 49:12

29 ^aProv. 11:31; Is. 10:12; Jer. 13:13; Ezek. 9:6; 1 Pet. 4:17 ^b1 Kin. 8:43 ^cEzek. 38:21

30 ^aIs. 42:13; Jer. 25:38 ^bJoel 2:11; 3:16; Amos 1:2

31 ^aHos. 4:1; Mic. 6:2 ^bIs. 66:16; Ezek. 20:35, 36; Joel 3:2

Because the LORD has ᵃa controversy with the nations.

He is entering into ᵇjudgment with all flesh;

As for the wicked, He has given them to the sword,' declares the LORD.''

32 Thus says the LORD of hosts,

"Behold, evil is going forth From ᵃnation to nation,

And a great ᵇstorm is being stirred up From the remotest parts of the earth.

33 "And those ᵃslain by the LORD on that day shall be from one end of the earth to the other. They shall ᵇnot be lamented, gathered, or buried; they shall be like ᶜdung on the face of the ground.

34 "Wail, you shepherds, and cry;

And ᵃwallow in ashes, you masters of the flock;

For the days of your ᵇslaughter and your dispersions have come,

And you shall fall like a choice vessel.

35 "ᵃFlight shall perish from the shepherds,

And escape from the masters of the flock.

36 "Hear the sound of the cry of the shepherds,

And the wailing of the masters of the flock!

For the LORD is destroying their pasture,

37 "And the peaceful ᵃfolds are made silent

Because of the ᵇfierce anger of the LORD.

38 "He has left His hiding place ᵃlike the lion;

For their land has become a horror

Because of the fierceness of the oppressing *sword,*

And because of His fierce anger.''

M Judah's Reaction to Jeremiah's Ministry, 26:1-24

26 In the beginning of the reign of ᵃJehoiakim the son of Josiah, king of Judah, this word came from the LORD, saying,

2 "Thus says the LORD, 'ᵃStand in the court of the LORD's house, and speak to all the cities of Judah, who have ᵇcome to worship *in* the LORD's house, ᶜall the words that I have commanded you to speak to them. ᵈDo not omit a word!

3 'ᵃPerhaps they will listen and everyone will turn from his evil way, that ᵇI may repent of the calamity which I am planning to do to them because of the evil of their deeds.'

4 "And you will say to them, 'Thus says the LORD, "ᵃIf you will not listen to Me, to ᵇwalk in My law, which I have set before you,

5 to listen to the words of ᵃMy servants the prophets, whom I have been sending to you again and again, but you have not listened;

6 then I will make this house like ᵃShiloh, and this city I will make a ᵇcurse to all the nations of the earth." ' "

7 And the ᵃpriests and the prophets and all the people heard Jeremiah speaking these words in the house of the LORD.

8 And when Jeremiah finished speaking all that the LORD had commanded *him* to speak to all the people, the priests and the prophets and all the people seized him, saying, "ᵃYou must die!

9 "Why have you prophesied in the name of the LORD saying, 'This house will be like Shiloh, and this city will be ᵃdesolate, without inhabitant'?" And ᵇall the people gathered about Jeremiah in the house of the LORD.

10 And when the ᵃprinces of Judah heard these things, they came up from the king's house to the house of the LORD and sat in the ᵇentrance of the New Gate of the LORD's *house.*

---

32 ᵃ2 Chr. 15:6; Is. 34:2 ᵇIs. 30:30; Jer. 23:19

33 ᵃIs. 34:2, 3; 66:16 ᵇPs. 79:3; Jer. 16:4; Ezek. 39:4, 17 ᶜIs. 5:25

34 ᵃJer. 6:26; Ezek. 27:30 ᵇIs. 34:6, 7; Jer. 50:27

35 ᵃJob 11:20; Jer. 11:11; Amos 2:14

37 ᵃIs. 27:10, 11; Jer. 5:17; 13:20 ᵇPs. 97:1-3; Is. 66:15; Jer. 12:29

38 ᵃJer. 4:7; 5:6; Hos. 5:14; 13:7, 8

1 ᵃ2 Kin. 23:36; 2 Chr. 36:4, 5

2 ᵃ2 Chr. 24:20, 21; Jer. 7:2; 19:14 ᵇDeut. 12:5 ᶜJer. 1:17; 42:4; Matt. 28:20; Acts 20:20, 27 ᵈDeut. 4:2

3 ᵃIs. 1:16-19; Jer. 36:3-7 ᵇJer. 18:8; Jon. 3:8

4 ᵃLev. 26:14; 1 Kin. 9:6; Is. 1:20; Jer. 17:27; 22:5 ᵇJer. 32:23; 44:10, 23

5 ᵃ2 Kin. 9:7; Ezra 9:11; Jer. 7:13; 25:3, 4

6 ᵃJosh. 18:1; 1 Sam. 4:12; Ps. 78:60, 61; Jer. 7:12, 14 ᵇ2 Kin.

7 ᵃJer. 22:19; Is. 65:15; Jer. 24:9; 25:18

7 ᵃJer. 5:31; Mic. 3:11

8 ᵃJer. 11:19; 18:23; Lam. 4:13, 14; Matt. 21:35, 36; 23:34, 35; 27:20

9 ᵃJer. 9:11; 33:10 ᵇActs 3:11; 5:12

10 ᵃJer. 26:21 ᵇJer. 36:10

11 Then the priests and the prophets ^aspoke to the officials and to all the people, saying, "A ^bdeath sentence for this man! For he has prophesied ^cagainst this city as you have heard in your hearing."

12 Then Jeremiah spoke to all the officials and to all the people, saying, "^aThe LORD sent me to prophesy against this house and against this city all the words that you have heard.

13 "Now therefore ^aamend your ways and your deeds, and obey the voice of the LORD your God; and the LORD will change His mind about the misfortune which He has pronounced against you.

14 "But as for me, behold, ^aI am in your hands; do with me as is good and right in your sight.

15 "Only know for certain that if you put me to death, you will bring ^ainnocent blood on yourselves, and on this city, and on its inhabitants; for truly the LORD has sent me to you to speak all these words in your hearing."

16 Then the officials and all the people ^asaid to the priests and to the prophets, "No ^bdeath sentence for this man! For he has spoken to us in the name of the LORD our God."

17 Then ^asome of the elders of the land rose up and spoke to all the assembly of the people, saying,

18 "^aMicah of Moresheth prophesied in the days of Hezekiah king of Judah; and he spoke to all the people of Judah, saying, 'Thus the LORD of hosts has said,
"^bZion will be plowed as a field,
And Jerusalem will become ruins,
And the ^cmountain of the house as the high places of a forest."'

19 "Did Hezekiah king of Judah and all Judah put him to death? Did he not ^afear the LORD and entreat the favor of the LORD, and ^bthe LORD changed His mind about the misfortune which He had pronounced against them? But we are ^ccommitting a great evil against ourselves."

20 Indeed, there was also a man who prophesied in the name of the LORD, Uriah the son of Shemaiah from ^aKiriath-jearim; and he prophesied against this city and against this land words similar to all those of Jeremiah.

21 When King Jehoiakim and all his mighty men and all the officials heard his words, then the ^aking sought to put him to death; but Uriah heard it, and he was afraid and ^bfled, and went to Egypt.

22 Then King Jehoiakim sent men to Egypt: ^aElnathan the son of Achbor and certain men with him went into Egypt.

23 And they brought Uriah from Egypt and led him to King Jehoiakim, who ^aslew him with a sword, and cast his dead body into the burial place of the common people.

24 But the hand of ^aAhikam the son of Shaphan was with Jeremiah, so that he was ^bnot given into the hands of the people to put him to death.

N Judah's Advice from Jeremiah: Submit to Nebuchadnezzar, 27:1-29:32

1 Sign of the yokes, 27:1-22

27 In the beginning of the reign of ^aZedekiah the son of Josiah, king of Judah, this word came to Jeremiah from the LORD, saying—

26:20-23 Jehoiakim vented his anger on another prophet, *Uriah*, who, though he fled to Egypt, was returned under extradition and put to death.
26:24 *Ahikam.* Associated with Josiah in his re-

form (2 Kings 22:12) and the father of Gedaliah, the ill-fated governor of Judah after the fall of Jerusalem (2 Kings 25:22).
27:1 Ambassadors of the nations mentioned in verse 3 had gathered in Jerusalem to conspire

Marginal references:
11 ^aJer. 18:23 ^bDeut. 18:20; Matt. 26:66 ^cJer. 38:4; Acts 6:11-14
12 ^aJer. 1:17, 18; 26:15; Amos 7:15; Acts 4:19; 5:29
13 ^aJer. 7:3, 5; 18:8, 11; 26:3; 35:15; Joel 2:14; Jon. 3:9; 4:2
14 ^aJer. 38:5
15 ^aNum. 35:33; Prov. 6:16, 17; Jer. 7:6
16 ^aJer. 26:11; 36:19, 25; 38:7, 13 ^bActs 5:34-39; 23:9, 29; 25:25; 26:31
17 ^aActs 5:34
18 ^aMic. 1:1 ^bNeh. 4:2; Ps. 79:1; Jer. 9:11; Mic. 3:12 ^cIs. 2:2, 3; Jer. 17:3; Mic. 4:1; Zech. 8:3
19 ^a2 Chr. 29:6-11; 32:26; Is. 37:1, 4, 15-20 ^bEx. 32:14; 2 Sam. 24:16 ^cJer. 44:7; Hab. 2:10
★20-23
20 ^aJosh. 9:17; 1 Sam. 6:21; 7:2
21 ^a2 Chr. 16:10; 24:21; Jer. 36:26; Matt. 14:5 ^b1 Kin. 19:2-4; Matt. 10:23
22 ^aJer. 36:12
23 ^aJer. 2:30
★24 ^a2 Kin. 22:12-14; Jer. 39:14; 40:5-7 ^b1 Kin. 18:4; Jer. 1:18, 19
★1 ^a2 Kin. 24:18-20; 2 Chr. 36:11-13

2 aJer. 30:8
bJer. 28:10,
13

3 aJer.
25:21, 22

5 aPs. 96:5;
146:5, 6; Is.
42:5; 45:12;
Jer. 10:12;
51:15 bDeut.
9:29; Jer.
32:17; Dan.
4:17 cPs.
115:15, 16;
Acts 17:26
6 aJer.
21:7; 22:25;
Ezek. 29:18-
20 bIs.
44:28; Jer.
25:9; 43:10
cJer. 28:14;
Dan. 2:38
7 a2 Chr.
36:20; Jer.
44:30; 46:13
bDan. 5:26;
Zech. 2:8, 9
cIs. 14:4-6;
Jer. 25:12

8 aJer.
38:17-19;
42:15, 16;
Ezek. 17:19-
21 bJer.
24:10; 27:13;
29:17, 18;
Ezek. 14:21

9 aEx.
22:18; Deut.
18:10; Prov.
19:27; Is.
8:19; Mal.
3:5; Eph. 5:6

2 thus says the LORD to me— "Make for yourself ᵃbonds and ᵇyokes and put them on your neck,

3 and send word to the king of ᵃEdom, to the king of ᵃMoab, to the king of the sons of ᵃAmmon, to the king of ᵃTyre, and to the king of ᵃSidon by the messengers who come to Jerusalem to Zedekiah king of Judah.

4 "And command them *to go* to their masters, saying, 'Thus says the LORD of hosts, the God of Israel, thus you shall say to your masters,

5 "ᵃI have made the earth, the men and the beasts which are on the face of the earth ᵇby My great power and by My outstretched arm, and I will ᶜgive it to the one who is pleasing in My sight.

6 "And now I ᵃhave given all these lands into the hand of Nebuchadnezzar king of Babylon, ᵇMy servant, and I have given him also the ᶜwild animals of the field to serve him.

7 "And ᵃall the nations shall serve him, and his son, and his grandson, ᵇuntil the time of his own land comes; then ᶜmany nations and great kings will make him their servant.

8 "And it will be, *that* the nation or the kingdom which ᵃwill not serve him, Nebuchadnezzar king of Babylon, and which will not put its neck under the yoke of the king of Babylon, I will punish that nation with the ᵇsword, with famine, and with pestilence," declares the LORD, "until I have destroyed it by his hand.

9 "But as for you, ᵃdo not listen to your prophets, your diviners, your dreamers, your soothsayers, or your sorcerers, who speak to you, saying, 'You shall not serve the king of Babylon.'

10 aJer.
23:25 bJer.
8:19; 32:31

11 aJer.
27:2, 8, 12
bJer. 21:9;
38:2; 40:9-
12; 42:10, 11

12 aJer.
27:3; 28:1;
38:17

13 aProv.
8:36; Jer.
27:8; 38:23;
Ezek. 18:31

14 aJer.
27:9; 2 Cor.
11:13-15
bJer. 14:14;
23:21; 27:10;
29:8, 9;
Ezek. 13:22

15 aJer.
23:21; 29:9
bJer. 23:25
c2 Chr.
25:16; Jer.
27:10 dJer.
6:13-15;
14:15, 16

★16 a2 Kin.
24:13; 2 Chr.
36:7, 10; Jer.
28:3; Dan.
1:2 bJer.
27:10

17 aJer. 7:34

18 a1 Kin.
18:24
b1 Sam. 7:8;
12:19, 23;
Jer. 18:20

10 "For they prophesy a ᵃlie to you, in order to ᵇremove you far from your land; and I will drive you out, and you will perish.

11 "But the nation which will ᵃbring its neck under the yoke of the king of Babylon and serve him, I will ᵇlet remain on its land," declares the LORD, "and they will till it and dwell in it." ' "

12 And I spoke words like all these to ᵃZedekiah king of Judah, saying, "Bring your necks under the yoke of the king of Babylon, and serve him and his people, and live!

13 "Why will you ᵃdie, you and your people, by the sword, famine, and pestilence, as the LORD has spoken to that nation which will not serve the king of Babylon?

14 "So ᵃdo not listen to the words of the prophets who speak to you, saying, 'You shall not serve the king of Babylon,' for they prophesy a ᵇlie to you;

15 for ᵃI have not sent them," declares the LORD, "but they ᵇprophesy falsely in My name, in order that I may ᶜdrive you out, and that you may perish, ᵈyou and the prophets who prophesy to you."

16 Then I spoke to the priests and to all this people, saying, "Thus says the LORD: Do not listen to the words of your prophets who prophesy to you, saying, 'Behold, the ᵃvessels of the LORD's house will now shortly be brought again from Babylon'; for they are prophesying a ᵇlie to you.

17 "Do not listen to them; serve the king of Babylon, and live! Why should this city ᵃbecome a ruin?

18 "But ᵃif they are prophets, and if the word of the LORD is

---

with Judah against Nebuchadnezzar. Jeremiah warned them that such conspiracy would result in slavery (symbolized by the *yokes,* v. 2). Only by submitting to Nebuchadnezzar could they hope to survive.
27:16 *vessels.* Taken to Babylon in 597, there was no hope of their soon return, as the false

prophets were predicting. Indeed, what had been left would soon be taken to Babylon by Nebuchadnezzar (v. 22). A conqueror customarily took the idols of a conquered people back to the temple of his own god. Since Judaism was an imageless religion, the vessels of the Temple were taken instead.

with them, let them now [b]entreat
the LORD of hosts, that the vessels
which are left in the house of the
LORD, in the house of the king of
Judah, and in Jerusalem, may not
go to Babylon.

19 [a]1 Kin. 7:15; 2 Kin. 25:13, 17; Jer. 52:17-23

19 "For thus says the LORD of
hosts concerning the [a]pillars, concerning the sea, concerning the
stands, and concerning the rest of
the vessels that are left in this
city,

20 [a]2 Kin. 24:12, 14-16; 2 Chr. 36:10, 18; Jer. 22:28; 24:1

20 which Nebuchadnezzar
king of Babylon did not take
when he [a]carried into exile Jeconiah the son of Jehoiakim, king of
Judah, from Jerusalem to Babylon, and all the nobles of Judah
and Jerusalem.

21 "Yes, thus says the LORD of
hosts, the God of Israel, concerning the vessels that are left in the
house of the LORD, and in the
house of the king of Judah, and in
Jerusalem,

22 [a]Jer. 34:2, 3 [b]Jer. 25:11, 12; 27:7; 29:10; 32:5 [c]Ezra 1:7-11; 5:13-15; 7:19

22 'They shall be [a]carried to
Babylon, and they shall be there
until the [b]day I visit them,' declares the LORD. 'Then I will
[c]bring them back and restore
them to this place.' "

2 *Opposition of a false prophet,* 28:1–17

★ 1-17

1 [a]Jer. 27:1; 49:34 [b]2 Kin. 24:18-20; 2 Chr. 36:11-13; Jer. 27:3, 12 [c]Jer. 28:17 [d]Josh. 9:3; 10:12; 1 Kin. 3:4

28 Now it came about in the
same year, [a]in the beginning of the reign of [b]Zedekiah
king of Judah, in the fourth year,
in the fifth month, that [c]Hanani-
ah the son of Azzur, the prophet,
who was from [d]Gibeon, spoke to
me in the house of the LORD in the
presence of the priests and all the
people, saying,

2 [a]Jer. 27:12; 28:11

2 "[a]Thus says the LORD of
hosts, the God of Israel, 'I have
broken the yoke of the king of
Babylon.

3 [a]2 Kin. 24:13; 2 Chr. 36:10; Jer. 27:16; Dan. 1:2

3 'Within two years I am
going to bring back to this place
[a]all the vessels of the LORD's
house, which Nebuchadnezzar
king of Babylon took away from
this place and carried to Babylon.

4 [a]Jer. 22:26, 27 [b]2 Kin. 25:27; Jer. 22:24; 24:1 [c]Jer. 22:10 [d]Jer. 27:8

4 'I am [a]also going to bring
back to this place [b]Jeconiah the
son of Jehoiakim, king of Judah,
and all the [c]exiles of Judah who
went to Babylon,' declares the
LORD, 'for I will break the [d]yoke
of the king of Babylon.' "

5 [a]Jer. 28:1

5 Then the prophet Jeremiah spoke to the prophet Hananiah
in the presence of the priests and
in the presence of all the people
who were standing in the [a]house
of the LORD,

6 [a]1 Kin. 1:36; Ps. 41:13; Jer. 11:5

6 and the prophet Jeremiah
said, "[a]Amen! May the LORD do
so; may the LORD confirm your
words which you have prophesied
to bring back the vessels of the
LORD's house and all the exiles,
from Babylon to this place.

7 [a]1 Kin. 22:28

7 "Yet [a]hear now this word
which I am about to speak in your
hearing and in the hearing of all
the people!

8 [a]Lev. 26:14-39; 1 Kin. 14:15; 17:1; 22:17; Is. 5:5-7; Joel 1:20; Amos 1:2; Nah. 1:2

8 "The prophets who were
before me and before you from
ancient times [a]prophesied against
many lands and against great
kingdoms, of war and of calamity
and of pestilence.

9 [a]Deut. 18:22

9 "The prophet who proph-
esies of peace, [a]when the word of
the prophet shall come to pass,
then that prophet will be known
as one whom the LORD has truly
sent."

10 [a]Jer. 27:2

10 Then Hananiah the
prophet took the [a]yoke from the
neck of Jeremiah the prophet and
broke it.

11 [a]Jer. 14:14; 27:10; 28:15

11 And Hananiah spoke in
the presence of all the people,
saying, "[a]Thus says the LORD,
'Even so will I break within two
full years, the yoke of Nebuchadnezzar king of Babylon from the
neck of all the nations.' " Then
the prophet Jeremiah went his
way.

12 [a]Jer. 1:2

12 And the [a]word of the LORD
came to Jeremiah, after Hananiah

28:1–17 Hananiah, a false prophet, challenged Jeremiah's prediction of 70 years of captivity and prophesied that within two years the vessels and Jeconiah would be returned to Jerusalem. Jeremiah wished that it would be so (v. 6) but prophesied again that it would not (v. 14). Notice that he was still wearing his "visual aid," the yoke around his neck (v. 10).

the prophet had broken the yoke from off the neck of the prophet Jeremiah, saying,

13 "Go and speak to Hananiah, saying, 'Thus says the LORD, "You have broken the yokes of wood, but you have made instead of them ᵃyokes of iron."

14 'For thus says the LORD of hosts, the God of Israel, "I have put a ᵃyoke of iron on the neck of all these nations, that they may serve Nebuchadnezzar king of Babylon; and they shall ᵇserve him. And ᶜI have also given him the beasts of the field."' "

15 Then Jeremiah the prophet said to Hananiah the prophet, "Listen now, Hananiah, the LORD has not sent you, and ᵃyou have made this people trust in a lie.

16 "Therefore thus says the LORD, 'ᵃBehold, I am about to remove you from the face of the earth. This year you are going to ᵇdie, because you have ᶜcounseled rebellion against the LORD.' "

17 So Hananiah the prophet died in the same year in the seventh month.

3   Letter to Jews in captivity, 29:1–32

29 Now these are the words of the ᵃletter which Jeremiah the prophet sent from Jerusalem to the rest of the elders of the exile, the priests, the prophets, and all the people whom Nebuchadnezzar had taken into exile from Jerusalem to Babylon.

2 (This was after King ᵃJeconiah and the ᵇqueen mother, the court officials, the princes of Judah and Jerusalem, the craftsmen and the smiths had departed from Jerusalem.)

3 *The letter was sent* by the hand of Elasah the son of Shaphan, and Gemariah the son of ᵃHilkiah, whom Zedekiah king of Judah sent to Babylon to Nebu-

chadnezzar king of Babylon, saying,

4 "Thus says the LORD of hosts, the God of Israel, to all the exiles whom I have ᵃsent into exile from Jerusalem to Babylon,

5 'ᵃBuild houses and live *in them;* and plant gardens, and eat their produce.

6 'Take ᵃwives and become the fathers of sons and daughters, and take wives for your sons and give your daughters to husbands, that they may bear sons and daughters; and multiply there and do not decrease.

7 'And ᵃseek the welfare of the city where I have sent you into exile, and ᵇpray to the LORD on its behalf; for in its welfare you will have welfare.'

8 "For thus says the LORD of hosts, the God of Israel, 'Do not let your ᵃprophets who are in your midst and your diviners ᵇdeceive you, and do not listen to ᶜthe dreams which they dream.

9 'For they ᵃprophesy falsely to you in My name; ᵇI have not sent them,' declares the LORD.

10 "For thus says the LORD, 'When ᵃseventy years have been completed for Babylon, I will visit you and fulfill My ᵇgood word to you, to bring you back to this place.

11 'For I know the ᵃplans that I have for you,' declares the LORD, 'plans for ᵇwelfare and not for calamity to give you a future and a ᶜhope.

12 'Then you will ᵃcall upon Me and come and pray to Me, and I will ᵇlisten to you.

13 'And you will ᵃseek Me and find *Me,* when you ᵇsearch for Me with all your heart.

14 'And I will be ᵃfound by you,' declares the LORD, 'and I will ᵇrestore your fortunes and will ᶜgather you from all the nations and from all the places where I have driven you,' declares the

Margin cross-references

13 ᵃPs. 107:16; Is. 45:2

14 ᵃDeut. 28:48; Jer. 27:8 ᵇJer. 25:11 ᶜJer. 27:6

15 ᵃJer. 20:6; 29:31; Lam. 2:14; Ezek. 13:2, 3, 22; 22:28; Zech. 13:3

16 ᵃGen. 7:4; Ex. 32:12; Deut. 6:15; 1 Kin. 13:34 ᵇJer. 20:6 ᶜDeut. 13:5; Jer. 29:32

★ 1-23

1 ᵃ2 Chr. 30:1, 6; Esth. 9:20; Jer. 29:25, 29

2 ᵃ2 Kin. 24:12-16; 2 Chr. 36:9, 10; Jer. 22:24-28; 24:1; 27:20 ᵇ2 Kin. 24:12, 15; Jer. 13:18; 22:26

3 ᵃ1 Chr. 6:13

4 ᵃJer. 24:5

5 ᵃJer. 29:28

6 ᵃJer. 16:2-4

7 ᵃDan. 4:27; 6:4, 5 ᵇEzra 6:10; 7:23; Dan. 4:19; 1 Tim. 2:1, 2

8 ᵃJer. 27:9; 29:1 ᵇJer. 14:14; 23:21; 27:14, 15; 28:15; Eph. 5:6 ᶜJer. 23:25, 27

9 ᵃJer. 27:15; 29:21 ᵇJer. 29:31

10 ᵃ2 Chr. 36:21-23; Jer. 25:12; 27:22; Dan. 9:2; Zech. 7:5 ᵇJer. 24:6, 7; Zeph. 2:7

11 ᵃPs. 40:5; Jer. 23:5, 6; 30:9, 10 ᵇIs. 40:9-11; Jer. 30:18-22 ᶜJer. 31:17; Hos. 2:15

12 ᵃPs. 50:15; Jer. 33:3; Dan. 9:3 ᵇPs. 145:19

13 ᵃDeut. 4:29; Ps. 32:6; Matt. 7:7 ᵇ1 Chr. 22:19; 2 Chr. 22:9; Jer. 24:7

14 ᵃDeut. 30:1-10; Ps. 32:6; Is. 55:6 ᵇJer. 30:3; 32:37-41 ᶜIs. 43:5, 6; Jer. 23:8; 32:37 ᵈJer. 3:14; 12:15; 16:15

29:1-23 *letter.* Sent to the 3,023 Jews who had been taken to Babylon in 597 (cf. 52:28) to exhort them to live as normal a life as possible (29:4-9), to await God's deliverance after 70 years (vv. 10-14), and to disregard false prophets such as *Ahab* and *Zedekiah* (v. 21).

Lord, 'and I will ᵈbring you back to the place from where I sent you into exile.'

15 "Because you have said, 'The Lord has raised up ᵃprophets for us in Babylon'—

16 for thus says the Lord concerning the king who sits on the throne of David, and concerning all the people who dwell in this city, your brothers who did ᵃnot go with you into exile—

17 thus says the Lord of hosts, 'Behold, I am sending upon them the ᵃsword, famine, and pestilence, and I will make them like ᵇsplit-open figs that cannot be eaten due to rottenness.

18 'And I will pursue them with the sword, with famine and with pestilence; and I will ᵃmake them a terror to all the kingdoms of the earth, to be a ᵇcurse, and a horror, and a ᶜhissing, and a reproach among all the nations where I have driven them,

19 because they have ᵃnot listened to My words,' declares the Lord, 'which I sent to them again and again by ᵇMy servants the prophets; but you did not listen,' declares the Lord.

20 "You, therefore, hear the word of the Lord, all you exiles, whom I have ᵃsent away from Jerusalem to Babylon.

21 "Thus says the Lord of hosts, the God of Israel, concerning Ahab the son of Kolaiah and concerning Zedekiah the son of Maaseiah, who are ᵃprophesying to you falsely in My name, 'Behold, I will deliver them into the hand of Nebuchadnezzar king of Babylon, and he shall slay them before your eyes.

22 'And because of them a ᵃcurse shall be used by all the exiles from Judah who are in Babylon, saying, "May the Lord make you like Zedekiah and like Ahab,

whom the king of Babylon ᵇroasted in the fire,

23 because they have ᵃacted foolishly in Israel, and ᵇhave committed adultery with their neighbors' wives, and have ᶜspoken words in My name falsely, which I did not command them; and I am He who ᵈknows, and am a witness," declares the Lord.' "

24 And to ᵃShemaiah the Nehelamite you shall speak, saying,

25 "Thus says the Lord of hosts, the God of Israel, 'Because you have sent ᵃletters in your own name to all the people who are in Jerusalem, and to ᵇZephaniah the son of Maaseiah, the priest, and to all the priests, saying,

26 "The Lord has made you priest instead of Jehoiada the priest, to be the ᵃoverseer in the house of the Lord over every ᵇmadman who ᶜprophesies, to ᵈput him in the stocks and in the iron collar,

27 now then, why have you not rebuked Jeremiah of ᵃAnathoth who prophesies to you?

28 "For he has ᵃsent to us in Babylon, saying, 'The exile will be ᵇlong; ᶜbuild houses and live in them and plant gardens and eat their produce.' " '

29 And ᵃZephaniah the priest read this letter to Jeremiah the prophet.

30 Then came the word of the Lord to Jeremiah, saying,

31 "Send to ᵃall the exiles, saying, 'Thus says the Lord concerning ᵇShemaiah the Nehelamite, "Because Shemaiah has ᶜprophesied to you, although I did not send him, and he has ᵈmade you trust in a lie,"

32 therefore thus says the Lord, "Behold, I am about to ᵃpunish Shemaiah the Nehelamite and his descendants; he

15 ᵃJer. 29:21, 24

16 ᵃJer. 38:2, 3, 17-23

17 ᵃJer. 27:8; 29:18; 32:24 ᵇJer. 24:3, 8-10

18 ᵃDeut. 28:25; 2 Chr. 29:8; Jer. 15:4; 24:9; 34:17; Ezek. 12:15 ᵇIs. 65:15; Jer. 42:18 ᶜJer. 25:9; Lam. 2:15, 16

19 ᵃJer. 6:19 ᵇJer. 25:4; 26:5; 35:15

20 ᵃJer. 24:5; Ezek. 11:9; Mic. 4:10

21 ᵃJer. 14:14, 15; 29:8, 9; Lam. 2:14; 2 Pet. 2:1

22 ᵃIs. 65:15 ᵇDan. 3:6, 21

23 ᵃGen. 34:7; 2 Sam. 13:12 ᵇJer. 5:8; 23:14 ᶜJer. 29:8, 9, 21 ᵈProv. 5:21; Jer. 7:11; 16:17; Mal. 3:5; Heb. 4:13

★24-32
24 ᵃJer. 29:31, 32

25 ᵃJer. 29:1 ᵇ2 Kin. 25:18; Jer. 21:1; 29:29; 37:3; 52:24

26 ᵃJer. 20:1 ᵇ2 Kin. 9:11; Hos. 9:7; Mark 3:21; John 10:20; Acts 26:24, 25; 2 Cor. 5:13 ᶜDeut. 13:1-5; Zech. 13:1-5 ᵈJer. 20:1, 2; Acts 16:24

27 ᵃJer. 1:1

28 ᵃJer. 29:1 ᵇJer. 29:10 ᶜJer. 29:5

29 ᵃJer. 29:25

31 ᵃJer. 29:20 ᵇJer. 29:24 ᶜJer. 14:14, 15; 29:9, 23; Ezek. 13:8-16, 22, 23 ᵈJer. 28:15

32 ᵃJer. 36:31 ᵇ1 Sam. 2:30-34; Jer. 22:30 ᶜ2 Kin. 7:2; 19, 20; Jer. 17:6; 29:10 ᵈDeut. 13:5; Jer. 28:16

29:24-32 Many exiles in Babylon objected to Jeremiah's letter and tried to engineer official reprisals against him by appealing through a false prophet *(Shemaiah)* to *Zephaniah,* a deputy to the high priest in Jerusalem (cf. 52:24), who read Shemaiah's letter to Jeremiah. The true prophet then denounced the false prophet.

shall *b*not have anyone living among this people, *c*and he shall not see the good that I am about to do to My people," declares the Lord, "because he has *d*preached rebellion against the Lord." ' "

O   Judah's Hope of Restoration,
30:1–33:26
1   *The promise declared: restoration after tribulation,*
30:1–31:26

★ 1   **30** The word which came to Jeremiah from the Lord, saying,

2 "Thus says the Lord, the God of Israel, '*a*Write all the words which I have spoken to you in a book.

3 'For, behold, *a*days are coming,' declares the Lord, 'when I will *b*restore the fortunes of My people *c*Israel and Judah.' The Lord says, 'I will also *d*bring them back to the land that I gave to their forefathers, and they shall possess it.' "

4 Now these are the words which the Lord spoke concerning Israel and concerning Judah,

5 "For thus says the Lord,
'I have heard a sound of *a*terror,
Of dread, and there is no peace.

6 'Ask now, and see,
If a male can give birth.
Why do I see every man
With his hands on his loins, *a*as a woman in childbirth?
And *why* have all faces turned pale?

7 'Alas! for that *a*day is great,
There is *b*none like it;
And it is the time of Jacob's *c*distress,
But he will be *d*saved from it.

8 'And it shall come about on that day,' declares the Lord of hosts, 'that I will *a*break his yoke from off their neck, and will tear off their *b*bonds; and strangers shall no longer *c*make them their slaves.

9 'But they shall serve the Lord their God, and *a*David their king, whom I will raise up for them.

10 '*a*And fear not, O Jacob My servant,' declares the Lord,
'And do not be dismayed, O Israel;
For behold, I will save you *b*from afar,
And your offspring from the land of their captivity.
And Jacob shall return,
and shall be *c*quiet and at ease,
And *d*no one shall make him afraid.

11 'For *a*I am with you,' declares the Lord, 'to save you;
For I will *b*destroy completely all the nations where I have scattered you,
Only I will *c*not destroy you completely.
But I will *d*chasten you justly,
And will by no means leave you unpunished.'

12 "For thus says the Lord,
'Your wound is incurable,
And your *a*injury is serious.

13 'There is no one to plead your cause;
No healing for *your* sore,
*a*No recovery for you.

14 'All your *a*lovers have forgotten you,

Cross references (margin)

2 *a*Is. 30:8; Jer. 25:13; 36:4, 28, 32; Hab. 2:2

3 *a*Jer. 29:10 *b*Ps. 53:6; Jer. 29:14; 30:18; 32:44; Ezek. 39:25; Amos 9:14; Zeph. 3:20 *c*Jer. 3:18 *d*Jer. 16:15; 23:7, 8; Ezek. 20:42; 36:24

5 *a*Is. 5:30; Jer. 6:25; 8:16; Amos 5:16-18

6 *a*Jer. 4:31; 6:24; 22:23

★ 7 *a*Is. 2:12; Hos. 1:11; Joel 2:11; Amos 5:18; Zeph. 1:14 *b*Lam. 1:12; Dan. 9:12; 12:1 *c*Jer. 2:27, 28; 14:8 *d*Jer. 30:10; 50:19

★ 8 *a*Is. 9:4; Jer. 2:20; Ezek. 34:27 *b*Jer. 27:2 *c*Ezek. 34:27

9 *a*Is. 55:3-5; Ezek. 34:23, 24; 37:24, 25; Hos. 3:5; Luke 1:69; Acts 2:30; 13:23, 34

10 *a*Is. 41:13; 43:5; 44:2; Jer. 46:27, 28 *b*Is. 60:4; Jer. 23:3, 8; 29:14 Cls. 35:9; Jer. 33:16; Hos. 2:18 *d*Mic. 4:4

11 *a*Jer. 1:8, 19 *b*Jer. 46:28; Amos 9:8 *c*Jer. 4:27; 5:10, 18 *d*Ps. 6:1; Jer. 10:24

12 *a*2 Chr. 36:16; Jer. 15:18; 30:15

13 *a*Jer. 14:19; 46:11

14 *a*Jer. 22:20, 22; Lam. 1:2 *b*Lam. 2:4, 5 *c*Job 30:21 *d*Jer. 6:23; 50:42 *e*Jer. 32:30-35; 44:22 *f*Jer. 5:6

30:1 In this section (through 32:25) Jeremiah looks beyond the immediate judgment to the future day of the Lord, the restoration of Israel and the blessings of the new covenant.
30:7 *the time of Jacob's distress.* The coming

days of tribulation which will come upon all Israel *(Jacob).*
30:8 *that day.* I.e., the day of the Lord, which will also see the restoration of Israel under Messiah, the son of David.

They do not seek you;
For I have [b]wounded you
　with the wound of an
　enemy,
With the [c]punishment of a
　[d]cruel one,
Because your [e]iniquity is
　great
And your [f]sins are numer-
　ous.

15 'Why do you cry out over
　your injury?
Your pain is incurable.
Because your iniquity is
　great
And your sins are numer-
　ous,
I have done these things to
　you.

16 'Therefore all who [a]devour
　you shall be de-
　voured;
And all your adversaries,
　every one of them,
　[b]shall go into captiv-
　ity;
And those who plunder
　you shall be for plun-
　der,
And all who prey upon
　you I will give for
　prey.

17 'For I will restore you to
　[a]health
And I will heal you of your
　wounds,' declares the
　LORD,
'Because they have called
　you an [b]outcast, say-
　ing:
"It is Zion; no one cares for
　her." '

18 "Thus says the LORD,
'Behold, I will [a]restore the
　fortunes of the tents
　of Jacob
And [b]have compassion on
　his dwelling places;
And the [c]city shall be re-
　built on its ruin,

And the [d]palace shall
　stand on its rightful
　place.

19 'And from them shall pro-
　ceed [a]thanksgiving
And the voice of those
　who [b]make merry;
And I will [c]multiply them,
　and they shall not be
　diminished;
I will also [d]honor them,
　and they shall not be
　insignificant.

20 'Their children also shall be
　as formerly,
And their congregation
　shall be [a]established
　before Me;
And I will punish all their
　oppressors.

21 'And their [a]leader shall be
　one of them,
And their ruler shall come
　forth from their
　midst;
And I will [b]bring him near,
　and he shall approach
　Me;
For who would dare to risk
　his life to [c]approach
　Me?' declares the
　LORD.

22 'And you shall be [a]My peo-
　ple,
And I will be your God.' "

23 Behold, the [a]tempest of
　the LORD!
Wrath has gone forth,
A sweeping tempest;
It will burst on the head of
　the wicked.

24 The [a]fierce anger of the
　LORD will not turn
　back,
Until He has performed,
　and until He has ac-
　complished
The intent of His heart;
In the [b]latter days you will
　understand this.

Marginal references (left column):

16 [a]Jer. 2:3;
8:16; 10:25
[b]Is. 14:2;
Joel 3:8

★17-22

17 [a]Ex.
15:26; Ps.
107:20; Is.
30:26; Jer.
8:22; 33:6
[b]Is. 11:12;
56:8; Jer.
33:24

18 [a]Jer.
30:3; 31:23
[b]Ps. 102:13
[c]Jer. 31:4,
38-40
[d]1 Chr. 29:1,
19; Ps. 48:3,
13; 122:7

Marginal references (right column):

19 [a]Is. 12:1;
35:10; 51:3;
Jer. 17:26;
33:11 [b]Ps.
126:1, 2; Is.
51:11; Jer.
31:4; Zeph.
3:14 [c]Jer.
33:22 [d]Is.
55:5; 60:9

20 [a]Is. 54:14

21 [a]Jer.
30:9; Ezek.
34:23, 24;
37:24 [b]Num.
16:5; Ps.
65:4 [c]Ex.
3:5; Jer.
50:44

22 [a]Ex. 6:7;
Jer. 32:38;
Ezek. 36:28;
Hos. 2:23;
Zech. 13:9

23 [a]Jer.
23:19

24 [a]Jer. 4:8
[b]Jer. 23:20

30:17-22 God's future blessings on Israel will include *health* (i.e., physical and spiritual healing, v. 17), restoration of the people and Jerusalem (v. 18), reestablishment of the Davidic
line in the person of King Messiah (v. 21), and
fellowship with God (v. 22).

★ 1 *a*Jer.
30:22 *b*Gen.
17:7, 8; Is.
41:10; Rom.
11:26-28

★ 2 *a*Num.
14:20 *b*Ex.
33:14; Num.
10:33; Deut.
1:33; Josh.
1:13

★ 3 *a*Deut.
4:37; 7:8;
Mal. 1:2 *b*Ps.
25:6

4 *a*Jer.
24:6; 33:7
*b*Is. 30:32
*c*Jer. 30:19

5 *a*Ps.
107:37; Is.
65:21; Ezek.
28:26; Amos
9:14

★ 6 *a*Is. 2:3;
Jer. 31:12;
50:4, 5; Mic.
4:2

7 *a*Ps. 14:7;
Jer. 20:13
*b*Deut.
28:13; Is.
61:9 *c*Ps.
28:9 *d*Is.
37:31; Jer.
23:3

31 "At that time," declares the LORD, "I will be the *a*God of all the *b*families of Israel, and they shall be My people."

2 Thus says the LORD,
"The people who survived the sword
*a*Found grace in the wilderness—
Israel, when it went to *b*find its rest."

3 The LORD appeared to him from afar, *saying,*
"I have *a*loved you with an everlasting love;
Therefore I have drawn you with *b*lovingkindness.

4 "*a*Again I will build you, and you shall be rebuilt,
O virgin of Israel!
Again you shall take up your *b*tambourines,
And go forth to the dances of the *c*merrymakers.

5 "Again you shall *a*plant vineyards
On the hills of Samaria;
The planters shall plant
And shall enjoy *them.*

6 "For there shall be a day when watchmen
On the hills of Ephraim shall call out,
'Arise, and *a*let us go up *to* Zion,
To the LORD our God.' "

7 For thus says the LORD,
"*a*Sing aloud with gladness for Jacob,
And shout among the *b*chiefs of the nations;
Proclaim, give praise, and say,
'O LORD, *c*save Thy people,
The *d*remnant of Israel.'

8 "Behold, I am *a*bringing them from the north country,
And I will *b*gather them from the remote parts of the earth,
Among them the *c*blind and the *d*lame,
The woman with child and she who is in labor with child, together;
A great company, they shall return here.

9 "*a*With weeping they shall come,
And by supplication I will lead them;
I will make them walk by *b*streams of waters,
On a straight path in which they shall *c*not stumble;
For I am a *d*father to Israel,
And Ephraim is *e*My firstborn."

10 Hear the word of the LORD,
O nations,
And declare in the *a*coastlands afar off,
And say, "He who scattered Israel will *b*gather him,
And keep him as a *c*shepherd keeps his flock."

11 For the LORD has *a*ransomed Jacob,
And redeemed him from the hand of him who was *b*stronger than he.

12 "And they shall *a*come and shout for joy on the *b*height of Zion,
And they shall be *c*radiant over the bounty of the LORD—
Over the *d*grain, and the new wine, and the oil,
And over the young of the *e*flock and the herd;

8 *a*Jer.
3:18; 23:8
*b*Deut. 30:4;
Is. 43:6;
Ezek. 34:13
*c*Is. 42:16
*d*Is. 40:11;
Ezek. 34:16;
Mic. 4:6

9 *a*Ps.
126:5; Jer.
50:4 *b*Is.
43:20; 49:10
*c*Is. 63:13
*d*Is. 64:8;
Jer. 3:4, 19
*e*Ex. 4:22

10 *a*Is.
66:19; Jer.
25:22 *b*Jer.
50:19 *c*Is.
40:11; Ezek.
34:12

11 *a*Is.
44:23; 48:20;
Jer. 15:21;
50:34 *b*Ps.
142:6

12 *a*Jer.
31:6, 7
*b*Ezek. 17:23
*c*Is. 2:2; Mic.
4:1 *d*Hos.
2:22; Joel
3:18 *e*Jer.
31:24; 33:12,
13 *f*Is. 58:11
*g*Is. 35:10;
60:20; 65:19;
John 16:22;
Rev. 21:4

31:1 This chapter continues the theme of restoration for Israel. Verses 1-22 concern the Northern Kingdom; verses 23-26, the Southern Kingdom; verses 27-40, both kingdoms.
31:2 *survived the sword.* I.e., those who escaped the cruel treatment by Pharaoh in Egypt.
31:3 *lovingkindness.* Heb., *hesed;* cf. 2:2; 9:24;

note on Hos. 2:19.
31:6 *watchmen.* Those who signaled the first appearance of the crescent moon in connection with Passover or new moon celebrations. In the Millennium the schism between north and south will be healed and all will go *to Zion* (Jerusalem) to worship.

And their life shall be like
a ᶠwatered garden,
And they shall ᵍnever languish again.

13 ᵃJudg.
21:21; Ps.
30:11; Zech.
8:4, 5 ᵇIs.
61:3 ᶜIs.
51:11

13 "Then the virgin shall rejoice in the ᵃdance,
And the young men and
the old, together,
For I will ᵇturn their
mourning into joy,
And will comfort them,
and give them ᶜjoy for
their sorrow.

14 ᵃJer.
50:19

14 "And I will fill the soul of
the priests with abun-
dance,
And My people shall be
ᵃsatisfied with My
goodness," declares
the Lᴏʀᴅ.

★15 ᵃMatt.
2:18 ᵇJosh.
18:25; Judg.
4:5; Is.
10:29; Jer.
40:1 ᶜGen.
37:35; Ps.
77:2 ᵈGen.
5:24; 42:13,
36; Jer.
10:20

15 Thus says the Lᴏʀᴅ,
"ᵃA voice is heard in ᵇRamah,
Lamentation *and* bitter
weeping.
Rachel is weeping for her
children;
She ᶜrefuses to be com-
forted for her chil-
dren,
Because ᵈthey are no
more."

16 ᵃIs. 25:8;
30:19 ᵇRuth
2:12; Heb.
6:10 ᶜJer.
30:3; Ezek.
11:17

16 Thus says the Lᴏʀᴅ,
"ᵃRestrain your voice from
weeping,
And your eyes from tears;
For your ᵇwork shall be rewarded," declares the
Lᴏʀᴅ,
"And they shall ᶜreturn
from the land of the
enemy.

17 ᵃJer.
29:11

17 "And there is ᵃhope for
your future," declares
the Lᴏʀᴅ,

"And *your* children shall return to their own ter-
ritory.

18 "I have surely heard Ephraim ᵃgrieving,
'Thou hast ᵇchastised me,
and I was chastised,
Like an untrained ᶜcalf;
ᵈBring me back that I may
be restored,
For Thou art the Lᴏʀᴅ my
God.

19 'For after I turned back, I
ᵃrepented;
And after I was instructed,
I ᵇsmote on *my* thigh;
I was ᶜashamed, and also
humiliated,
Because I bore the re-
proach of my youth.'

20 "Is ᵃEphraim My dear son?
Is he a delightful child?
Indeed, as often as I have
spoken against him,
I certainly *still* remember
him;
Therefore My ᵇheart
yearns for him;
I will surely ᶜhave mercy
on him," declares the
Lᴏʀᴅ.

21 "Set up for yourself road-
marks,
Place for yourself guide-
posts;
ᵃDirect your mind to the
highway,
The way by which you
went.
ᵇReturn, O virgin of Israel,
Return to these your cities.

22 "How long will you go here
and there,
O ᵃfaithless daughter?

18 ᵃJer. 3:21
ᵇJob 5:17;
Ps. 94:12
ᶜHos. 4:16
ᵈPs. 80:3, 7,
19; Jer.
17:14; Lam.
5:21; Acts
3:26

19 ᵃEzek.
36:31; Zech.
12:10 ᵇEzek.
21:12; Luke
18:13 ᶜJer.
3:25

20 ᵃHos.
11:8 ᵇGen.
43:30; Judg.
10:16; Is.
63:15; Hos.
11:8 ᶜIs.
55:7; 57:18;
Hos. 14:4;
Mic. 7:18

21 ᵃJer. 50:5
ᵇIs. 48:20;
52:11

★22 ᵃJer.
3:6; 49:4

31:15 *Ramah.* A town 5½ miles N. of Jerusalem, used as an assembly point for the captives taken to Babylon (40:1). *Rachel.* The mother of Joseph and Benjamin is seen weeping over the exiles, but is assured that they will return (31:16). This weeping is used as a type in connection with Herod's slaughter of the infants (Matt. 2:18).

31:22 *A woman will encompass a man.* The meaning is uncertain. Some understand it to indicate the security of Israel in the Millennium when a woman can provide all the protection needed. Others take it as a reference to Israel *(A woman)* embracing a man (i.e., God). Still others relate it to the incarnation.

For the Lord has created a
new thing in the
earth—
A woman will encompass a
man."

23 Thus says the Lord of
hosts, the God of Israel, "Once
again they will speak this word in
the land of Judah and in its cities,
when I *restore their fortunes,
The Lord bless you, O
*abode of righteous-
ness,
O *holy hill!'

24 "And Judah and all its cities
will *dwell together in it, the
farmer and they who go about
with flocks.

25 "*For I satisfy the weary
ones and refresh everyone who
languishes."

26 At this I *awoke and
looked, and my *sleep was pleasant to me.

2 The promise covenanted: the
new covenant, 31:27-40

27 "Behold, days are coming,"
declares the Lord, "when I will
*sow the house of Israel and the
house of Judah with the seed of
man and with the seed of beast.

28 "And it will come about
that as I have *watched over them
to *pluck up, to break down, to
overthrow, to destroy, and to
bring disaster, so I will watch over
them to *build and to plant," declares the Lord.

29 "In those days they will not
say again,
'*The fathers have eaten
sour grapes,
And the children's teeth
are set on edge.'

30 "But *everyone will die for
his own iniquity; each man who

eats the sour grapes, his teeth will
be set on edge.

31 "*Behold, days are coming,"
declares the Lord, "when I will
make a *new covenant with the
house of Israel and with the
house of Judah,

32 not like the *covenant
which I made with their fathers in
the day I *took them by the hand
to bring them out of the land of
Egypt, My *covenant which they
broke, although I was a husband
to them," declares the Lord.

33 "But *this is the covenant
which I will make with the house
of Israel after those days," declares the Lord, "*I will put My
law within them, and on their
heart I will write it; and *I will be
their God, and they shall be My
people.

34 "And they shall *not teach
again, each man his neighbor and
each man his brother, saying,
'Know the Lord,' for they shall all
*know Me, from the least of them
to the greatest of them," declares
the Lord, "for I will *forgive their
iniquity, and their *sin I will remember no more."

35 Thus says the Lord,
Who *gives the sun for
light by day,
And the fixed order of the
moon and the stars
for light by night,
Who *stirs up the sea so
that its waves roar;
*The Lord of hosts is His
name:

36 "*If this fixed order departs
From before Me," declares
the Lord,
"Then the offspring of Israel
also shall *cease
From being a nation before
Me forever."

Cross-references (margin)

23 *Jer.
30:18; 32:44
*Is. 1:26;
Jer. 50:7
*Ps. 48:1;
87:1; Zech.
8:3

24 *Jer.
31:12; Ezek.
36:10; Zech.
8:4-8

25 *Ps.
107:9; Jer.
31:12, 14;
Matt. 5:6;
John 4:14

26 *Zech.
4:1 *Prov.
3:24

27 *Ezek.
36:9, 11;
Hos. 2:23

28 *Jer.
44:27; Dan.
9:14 *Jer.
1:10; 18:7
*Jer. 24:6

★29-30
29 *Lam.
5:7; Ezek.
18:2

30 *Deut.
24:16; Is.
3:11; Ezek.
18:4, 20

★31-34
31 *Jer.
31:31-34;
Heb. 8:8-12
*Jer. 32:40;
33:14; Ezek.
37:26; Luke
22:20; 1 Cor.
11:25; 2 Cor.
3:6; Heb.
8:8-12;
10:16, 17
32 *Ex. 19:5;
24:6-8; Deut.
5:2, 3 *Deut.
1:31; Is.
63:12 *Jer.
11:7, 8
33 *Jer.
32:40; Heb.
10:16 *Ps.
40:8; 2 Cor.
3:3 *Jer.
24:7; 30:22;
32:38

34 *1 Thess.
4:9; 1 John
2:27 *Is.
11:9; 54:13;
Jer. 24:7;
Hab. 2:14;
John 6:45;
1 John 2:20
*Jer. 33:8;
50:20; Mic.
7:18; Rom.
11:27 *Is.
43:25; Heb.
10:17

★35-37
35 *Gen.
1:14-18;
Deut. 4:19;
Ps. 19:1-6;
136:7-9 *Is.
51:15 *Jer.
10:16; 32:18;
50:34

36 *Ps.
89:36, 37;
148:6; Is.
54:9, 10; Jer.
33:20-26
*Amos
9:8, 9

31:29-30 The people excused themselves by
saying they were being punished for the sins
of their fathers; in reality each person is punished for his own sins (cf. Deut. 24:16; Ezek.
18:2-4).
31:31-34 The principal O.T. passage on the new
covenant (cf. Isa. 59:20-21; Jer. 32:37-40; Ezek.
16:60-63; 37:21-28; see note on Heb. 8:6). It
will be made in the future with the whole nation of Israel (Jer. 31:31); it will be unlike the

Mosaic covenant in that it will be unconditional (Jer. 31:32); its provisions will include (1)
a change of heart, (2) fellowship with God, (3)
knowledge of the Lord, and (4) forgiveness of
sins. All of this will be fulfilled for Israel when
the Lord returns (Rom. 11:26-27).
31:35-37 The permanence of the cycle of nature
(vv. 35-36) and the immeasurableness of
heaven and earth (v. 37) guarantee the survival
of the Hebrew people.

37 aIs.
40:12; Jer.
33:22 bJer.
33:24-26;
Rom. 11:2-5,
26, 27

37 Thus says the LORD,
"aIf the heavens above can
be measured,
And the foundations of the
earth searched out be-
low,
Then I will also bcast off all
the offspring of Israel
For all that they have
done," declares the
LORD.

★38 aJer.
30:18; 31:4
bNeh. 3:1;
12:39; Zech.
14:10 c2 Kin.
14:13; 2 Chr.
26:9

38 "Behold, days are coming,"
declares the LORD, "when the acity
shall be rebuilt for the LORD from
the bTower of Hananel to the
cCorner Gate.

★39 aZech.
2:1

39 "And the ameasuring line
shall go out farther straight ahead
to the hill Gareb; then it will turn
to Goah.

★40 aJer.
7:32; 8:2
b2 Sam.
15:23; 2 Kin.
23:6, 12;
John 18:1
c2 Kin.
11:16; 2 Chr.
23:15; Neh.
3:28 dJoel
3:17; Zech.
14:20

40 "And athe whole valley of
the dead bodies and of the ashes,
and all the fields as far as the
brook bKidron, to the corner of
the cHorse Gate toward the east,
shall be dholy to the LORD; it shall
not be plucked up, or overthrown
anymore forever."

3   The promise illustrated: a field bought, 32:1-44

★ 1 a2 Kin.
25:1, 2; Jer.
39:1, 2

32 The word that came to Jeremiah from the LORD in
the atenth year of Zedekiah king
of Judah, which was the eighteenth year of Nebuchadnezzar.

2 aNeh.
3:25; Jer.
33:1; 37:21;
38:6; 39:14

2 Now at that time the army
of the king of Babylon was besieging Jerusalem, and Jeremiah
the prophet was shut up in the
acourt of the guard, which was in
the house of the king of Judah,

3 a2 Kin.
6:32 bJer.
26:8, 9 cJer.
21:3-7; 34:2,
3 dJer. 21:4-
7; 32:28, 29;
34:2, 3

3 because Zedekiah king of
Judah had ashut him up, saying,
"Why do you bprophesy, saying,

'cThus says the LORD, "Behold, I
am about to dgive this city into
the hand of the king of Babylon,
and he will take it;

4 and Zedekiah king of Judah shall anot escape out of the
hand of the Chaldeans, but he
shall surely be given into the
hand of the king of Babylon, and
he shall bspeak with him face to
face, and see him eye to eye;

4 a2 Kin.
25:4-7; Jer.
37:17; 38:18,
23; 39:4-7
bJer. 39:5

5 and he shall atake Zedekiah to Babylon, and he shall be
there until I visit him," declares
the LORD. "If you fight against the
Chaldeans, you shall bnot succeed" ' ? "

5 aJer.
27:22; 39:7;
Ezek. 12:12,
13 bEzek.
17:9, 10, 15

6 And Jeremiah said, "The
word of the LORD came to me,
saying,

7 'Behold, Hanamel the son
of Shallum your uncle is coming
to you, saying, "Buy for yourself
my field which is at aAnathoth,
for you have the bright of redemption to buy it." '

★ 7 aJer.
1:1; 11:21
bLev. 25:25;
Ruth 4:3, 4

8 "Then Hanamel my uncle's
son came to me in the acourt of
the guard according to the word
of the LORD, and said to me, 'Buy
my field, please, that is at bAna-
thoth, which is in the land of Benjamin; for you have the right of
possession and the redemption is
yours; buy it for yourself.' Then I
knew that this was the cword of
the LORD.

8 aJer.
32:2; 33:1
bJer. 1:1;
32:7 c1 Sam.
9:16, 17;
10:3-7; 1 Kin.
22:25; Jer.
32:25

9 "And I bought the field
which was at Anathoth from
Hanamel my uncle's son, and I
aweighed out the silver for him,
seventeen bshekels of silver.

10 "And I asigned and bsealed
the deed, and ccalled in witnesses,
and weighed out the silver on the
scales.

★ 9-15
9 aGen.
23:16; Zech.
11:12 bGen.
24:22; Ex.
21:32; Neh.
5:15; Ezek.
4:10

10 aIs. 44:5;
Jer. 32:44
bDeut.
32:34; Job
14:17 cRuth
4:1, 9; Is. 8:2

31:38 the Tower of Hananel. At the NE. corner
of Jerusalem. Corner Gate. At the NW. corner
(Neh. 3:1; 12:39; Zech. 14:10).
31:39 Gareb . . . Goah. The locations are unknown, but the verse seems to indicate that
rebuilt Jerusalem will be extended on the west
side.
31:40 valley of the dead bodies. Hinnom (7:31).
Horse Gate. At the SE. corner (Neh. 3:28).
32:1 The events of this chapter occurred in
587-586, when the Babylonians were besieging Jerusalem and Jeremiah was in custody

(37:11-21).
32:7 the right of redemption. According to Lev.
25:25 a near relative could redeem property so
as to keep it in the family. This particular
property was worthless since it was in Anathoth, which by this time had already been
captured by the Babylonians.
32:9-15 Jeremiah's purchase of the field showed
his trust in the promise of the Lord that one
day his descendants would return to that land.
The deed consisted of both a sealed and an
open copy (v. 11).

11 aLuke
2:27

11 "Then I took the deeds of purchase, both the sealed *copy containing* the ªterms and conditions, and the open *copy;*

12 aJer.
32:16; 36:4,
5, 32; 43:3;
45:1 bJer.
51:59

12 and I gave the deed of purchase to ªBaruch the son of bNeriah, the son of Mahseiah, in the sight of Hanamel my uncle's *son,* and in the sight of the witnesses who signed the deed of purchase, before all the Jews who were sitting in the court of the guard.

13 "And I commanded Baruch in their presence, saying,

15 aJer.
30:18; 31:5,
12, 24;
32:37, 43,
44; 33:12,
13; Amos
9:14, 15;
Zech. 3:10
★16-25
16 aGen.
32:9-12; Jer.
12:1; Phil.
4:6, 7
17 aJer. 1:6;
4:10 b2 Kin.
19:15; Ps.
102:25; Is.
40:26-29;
Jer. 27:5
cGen. 18:14;
Jer. 32:27;
Zech. 8:6;
Matt. 19:26;
Mark 10:27;
Luke 1:37;
18:27
18 aEx. 20:6;
34:6, 7; Deut.
5:9, 10; 7:9,
10 b1 Kin.
14:9, 10;
16:1-3; Matt.
23:32-36
cPs. 145:3
dPs. 50:1; Is.
9:6; Jer.
20:11 eJer.
10:16; 31:35
19 aIs. 9:6;
28:29 bJob
34:21; Jer.
23:24 cPs.
62:12; Jer.
17:10; 21:14;
Matt. 16:27;
John 5:29
20 aPs.
78:43;
105:27 bEx.
9:16; Is.
63:12, 14;
Dan. 9:15
21 aEx. 6:6;
Deut. 4:34;
7:19; 26:8;
2 Sam. 7:23;
1 Chr. 17:21;
Ps. 136:11

14 Thus says the Lord of hosts, the God of Israel, "Take these deeds, this sealed deed of purchase, and this open deed, and put them in an earthenware jar, that they may last a long time."

15 'For thus says the Lord of hosts, the God of Israel, "ªHouses and fields and vineyards shall again be bought in this land." '

16 "After I had given the deed of purchase to Baruch the son of Neriah, then I ªprayed to the Lord, saying,

17 'ªAh Lord God! Behold, Thou hast bmade the heavens and the earth by Thy great power and by Thine outstretched arm! cNothing is too difficult for Thee,

18 who ªshowest lovingkindness to thousands, but brepayest the iniquity of fathers into the bosom of their children after them, O cgreat and dmighty God. The eLord of hosts is His name;

19 ªgreat in counsel and mighty in deed, whose beyes are open to all the ways of the sons of men, cgiving to everyone according to his ways and according to the fruit of his deeds;

20 who hast ªset signs and wonders in the land of Egypt, *and* even to this day both in Israel and among mankind; and Thou hast bmade a name for Thyself, as at this day.

21 'And Thou didst ªbring Thy people Israel out of the land of Egypt with signs and with wonders, and with a strong hand and with an outstretched arm, and with great terror;

22 and gavest them this land, which Thou didst ªswear to their forefathers to give them, a land flowing with milk and honey.

22 aEx. 3:8,
17; 13:5;
Deut. 1:8; Ps.
105:9-11;
Jer. 11:5

23 'And they ªcame in and took possession of it, but they bdid not obey Thy voice or cwalk in Thy law; they have done nothing of all that Thou commandedst them to do; therefore Thou hast made dall this calamity come upon them.

23 aPs. 44:2,
3; 78:54, 55;
Jer. 2:7
bNeh. 9:26;
Jer. 11:8;
Dan. 9:10-14
cEzra 9:7;
Jer. 26:4;
44:10 dLam.
1:18; Dan.
9:11, 12

24 Behold, the ªsiege mounds have reached the city to take it; and the city is bgiven into the hand of the Chaldeans who fight against it, because of the csword, the famine, and the pestilence; and what Thou hast spoken has dcome to pass; and, behold, Thou seest *it.*

24 aJer.
33:4; Ezek.
21:22 bJer.
20:5; 21:4-7;
32:5 cJer.
14:12; 29:17,
18; 32:36;
34:17; Ezek.
14:21 dDeut.
4:26; Josh.
23:15, 16;
Zech. 1:6

25 'And Thou hast said to me, O Lord God, "Buy for yourself the field with money, and call in witnesses"—although the city is given into the hand of the Chaldeans.' "

26 Then the word of the Lord came to Jeremiah, saying,

★26-44

27 "Behold, I am the Lord, the ªGod of all flesh; is anything btoo difficult for Me?"

27 aNum.
16:22; 27:16
bJer. 32:17;
Matt. 19:26

28 Therefore thus says the Lord, "Behold, I am about to ªgive this city into the hand of the Chaldeans and into the hand of Nebuchadnezzar king of Babylon, and he shall take it.

28 a2 Kin.
25:11; 2 Chr.
36:17-21;
Jer. 19:7-12;
32:3, 24, 36;
34:2, 3

29 "And the Chaldeans who are fighting against this city shall enter and ªset this city on fire and burn it, with the bhouses where *people* have offered incense to Baal on their roofs and poured out libations to other gods to provoke Me to anger.

29 a2 Chr.
36:19; Jer.
21:10; 37:8,
10; 39:8
bJer. 19:13;
44:17-19, 25;
52:13

30 "Indeed the sons of Israel and the sons of Judah have been doing only ªevil in My sight from

30 aDeut.
9:7-12; Is.
63:10; Jer.
2:7; 7:22-26
bJer. 8:19;
11:17; 25:7

32:16-25 In view of the advancing armies of Babylon, Jeremiah had second thoughts about the wisdom of buying the property. *siege mounds* (v. 24). Mounds of earth built up over

city walls by the invaders.
32:26-44 God reassured His prophet that after the captivity He would cause His people to prosper again in their land.

their youth; for the sons of Israel have been only [b]provoking Me to anger by the work of their hands," declares the LORD.

31 [a]1 Kin. 11:7, 8; 2 Kin. 21:4-7, 16; Jer. 5:9-11; 6:6, 7; Matt. 23:37 [b]2 Kin. 23:27; 24:3, 4; Jer. 27:10
32 [a]Ezra 9:7; Is. 1:4-6, 23; Jer. 2:26; 44:17, 21; Dan. 9:8

31 "Indeed this city has been to Me a [a]*provocation of* My anger and My wrath from the day that they built it, even to this day, that it should be [b]removed from before My face,

32 because of all the evil of the sons of Israel and the sons of Judah, which they have done to provoke Me to anger—they, their [a]kings, their leaders, their priests, their prophets, the men of Judah, and the inhabitants of Jerusalem.

33 [a]2 Chr. 36:15, 16; Jer. 7:13; 25:3; 26:5; 35:15; John 8:2

33 "And they have turned *their* back to Me, and not *their* face; though *I* taught them, [a]teaching again and again, they would not listen and receive instruction.

34 [a]2 Kin. 21:1-7; Jer. 7:30; 19:4-6; Ezek. 8:5
35 [a]2 Chr. 28:2, 3; 33:6; Jer. 7:31; 19:5 [b]Lev. 18:21; 20:2-5; 1 Kin. 11:7; 2 Kin. 23:10; Acts 7:43

34 "But they [a]put their detestable things in the house which is called by My name, to defile it.

35 "And they built the [a]high places of Baal that are in the valley of Ben-hinnom to cause their sons and their daughters to pass through *the fire* to [b]Molech, which I had not commanded them nor had it entered My mind that they should do this abomination, to cause Judah to sin.

36 [a]Jer. 32:24

36 "Now therefore thus says the LORD God of Israel concerning this city of which you say, 'It is [a]given into the hand of the king of Babylon by sword, by famine, and by pestilence.'

37 [a]Deut. 30:3; Ps. 106:47; Is. 11:11-16; Jer. 16:14, 15; 23:3, 8; Ezek. 11:17; Hos. 1:11; Amos 9:14, 15 [b]Jer. 23:6; Ezek. 34:25, 28; Zech. 14:11
38 [a]Jer. 24:7
39 [a]2 Chr. 30:12; Jer. 31:33; Ezek. 11:19; John 17:21; Acts 4:32 [b]Deut. 11:18-21; Ezek. 37:25

37 "Behold, I will [a]gather them out of all the lands to which I have driven them in My anger, in My wrath, and in great indignation; and I will bring them back to this place and [b]make them dwell in safety.

38 "And they shall be [a]My people, and I will be their God;

39 and I will [a]give them one heart and one way, that they may fear Me always, for their own [b]good, and for *the good of* their children after them.

40 "And I will make an [a]everlasting covenant with them that I will [b]not turn away from them, to do them good; and I will [c]put the fear of Me in their hearts so that they will not turn away from Me.

41 "And I will [a]rejoice over them to do them good, and I will faithfully [b]plant them in this land with [c]all My heart and with all My soul.

42 "For thus says the LORD, '[a]Just as I brought all this great disaster on this people, so I am going to [b]bring on them all the good that I am promising them.

43 'And [a]fields shall be bought in this land of which you say, "[b]It is a desolation, without man or beast; it is given into the hand of the Chaldeans."

44 'Men shall buy fields for money, [a]sign and seal deeds, and call in witnesses in the [b]land of Benjamin, in the environs of Jerusalem, in the cities of Judah, in the cities of the hill country, in the cities of the lowland, and in the cities of the Negev; for I will [c]restore their fortunes,' declares the LORD."

40 [a]Is. 55:3; Jer. 31:33, 34; 50:5; Ezek. 37:26 [b]Deut. 31:6, 8; Ezek. 39:29 [c]Jer. 24:7; 31:33
41 [a]Deut. 30:9; Is. 62:5; 65:19 [b]Jer. 24:6; 31:28; Amos 9:15 [c]Hos. 2:19, 20
42 [a]Jer. 31:28; Zech. 8:14, 15 [b]Jer. 33:14
43 [a]Jer. 32:15, 25; Ezek. 37:11-14 [b]Jer. 33:10
44 [a]Jer. 32:10 [b]Jer. 17:26; 33:13 [c]Jer. 31:23; 33:7, 11, 26

4 The promise reaffirmed: the Davidic covenant, 33:1-26

33 Then the word of the LORD came to Jeremiah the second time, while he was still [a]confined in the court of the guard, saying,

1 [a]Jer. 32:2, 8; 37:21; 38:28

2 "Thus says [a]the LORD who made *the earth*, the LORD who formed it to establish it, the [b]LORD is His name,

2 [a]Jer. 51:19 [b]Ex. 3:15; 6:3; 15:3; Jer. 10:16

3 '[a]Call to Me, and I will answer you, and I will tell you [b]great and mighty things, [c]which you do not know.'

★ 3 [a]Ps. 50:15; 91:15; Is. 55:6, 7; Jer. 29:12 [b]Jer. 32:17, 27 [c]Is. 48:6

4 "For thus says the LORD God of Israel concerning the [a]houses of this city, and concerning the houses of the kings of Judah, which are broken down to *make a defense* against the [b]siege mounds and against the sword,

4 [a]Is. 32:13, 14 [b]Jer. 32:24; Ezek. 4:2; 21:22; Hab. 1:10

33:3 *mighty*. Some texts read "hidden."

5 aJer.
21:4-7; 32:5
bIs. 8:17;
Jer. 21:10;
Mic. 3:4

★ **6-13**

6 aJer.
17:14; 30:17;
Hos. 6:1 bIs.
66:12; Gal.
5:22, 23

7 aPs. 85:1;
Jer. 30:18;
32:44; 33:26;
Amos 9:14
bIs. 1:26;
Jer. 30:18;
31:4, 38;
Amos 9:14,
15

8 aPs. 51:2;
Is. 44:22;
Jer. 50:20;
Ezek. 36:25,
33; Mic.
7:18, 19;
Zech. 13:1;
Heb. 9:11-14

9 aIs. 62:2,
4, 7; Jer.
13:11 bJer.
3:17; 19; 4:2;
16:19 cJer.
24:6; 32:42
dNeh. 6:16;
Ps. 40:3; Is.
60:5; Hos.
3:5

10 aJer.
32:43 bJer.
26:9; 34:22

11 aIs.
35:10; 51:3,
11 b1 Chr.
16:8, 34;
2 Chr. 5:13;
7:3; Ezra
3:11; Ps.
100:4, 5;
106:1; 107:1;
118:1; 136:1
cLev. 7:12,
13; Ps.
107:22;
116:17; Jer.
17:26; Heb.
13:15

5 'While *they* are coming to
ªfight with the Chaldeans, and to
fill them with the corpses of men
whom I have slain in My anger
and in My wrath, and I have ᵇhidden My face from this city because of all their wickedness:

6 'Behold, I will bring to it
ªhealth and healing, and I will
heal them; and I will reveal to
them an ᵇabundance of peace and
truth.

7 'And I will ªrestore the fortunes of Judah and the fortunes of
Israel, and I will ᵇrebuild them as
they were at first.

8 'And I will ªcleanse them
from all their iniquity by which
they have sinned against Me, and
I will pardon all their iniquities by
which they have sinned against
Me, and by which they have
transgressed against Me.

9 'And it shall be to Me a
ªname of joy, praise, and glory
before ᵇall the nations of the
earth, which shall hear of all the
ᶜgood that I do for them, and they
shall ᵈfear and tremble because of
all the good and all the peace that
I make for it.'

10 "Thus says the LORD, 'Yet
again there shall be heard in this
place, of which you say, "It is a
ªwaste, without man and without
beast," *that is,* in the cities of Judah and in the streets of Jerusalem that are ᵇdesolate, without
man and without inhabitant and
without beast,

11 the voice of ªjoy and the
voice of gladness, the voice of
the bridegroom and the voice of
the bride, the voice of those who
say,

> ᵇ"Give thanks to the LORD
>   of hosts,
> For the LORD is good,
> For His lovingkindness is
>   everlasting";

and of those who bring a ᶜthank
offering into the house of the
LORD. For I will restore the fortunes of the land as they were at
first,' says the LORD.

12 "Thus says the LORD of
hosts, 'There shall again be in this
place which is waste, ªwithout
man or beast, and in all its cities,
a habitation of shepherds who
rest their ᵇflocks.

13 'In the ªcities of the hill
country, in the cities of the lowland, in the cities of the Negev, in
the land of Benjamin, in the environs of Jerusalem, and in the
cities of Judah, the flocks shall
again ᵇpass under the hands of
the one who numbers them,' says
the LORD.

14 'Behold, ªdays are coming,'
declares the LORD, 'when I will
ᵇfulfill the good word which I
have spoken concerning the
house of Israel and the house of
Judah.

15 'In those days and at that
time I will cause a ªrighteous
Branch of David to spring forth;
and He shall execute ᵇjustice and
righteousness on the earth.

16 'In those days ªJudah shall
be saved, and Jerusalem shall
dwell in safety; and this is *the
name* by which she shall be
called: the ᵇLORD is our righteousness.'

17 "For thus says the LORD,
'David shall ªnever lack a man to
sit on the throne of the house of
Israel;

18 and the ªLevitical priests
shall never lack a man before Me
to offer burnt offerings, to burn
grain offerings, and to ᵇprepare
sacrifices continually.' "

19 And the word of the LORD
came to Jeremiah, saying,

20 "Thus says the LORD, 'If you
can ªbreak My covenant for the
day, and My covenant for the
night, so that day and night will
not be at their appointed time,

21 then ªMy covenant may
also be broken with David My
servant that he shall not have a
son to reign on his throne, and

12 aJer.
32:43; 36:29;
51:62 bIs.
65:10; Jer.
31:12; Ezek.
34:12-15;
Zeph. 2:6, 7

13 aJer.
17:26; 32:44
bLev. 27:32;
Luke 15:4

★ **14-26**

14 aJer. 23:5
bIs. 32:1, 2;
Jer. 29:10;
32:42; 33:9;
Ezek. 34:23-
25; Hag.
2:6-9

15 aIs. 4:2;
11:1-5; Jer.
23:5, 6; 30:9;
Zech. 3:8;
6:12, 13
bPs.
72:1-5

16 aIs.
45:17, 22;
Jer. 23:6 bIs.
45:24, 25;
Jer. 23:6;
1 Cor. 1:30;
2 Cor. 5:21;
Phil. 3:9

17 a2 Sam.
7:16; 1 Kin.
2:4; 8:25;
1 Chr. 17:11-
14; Ps.
89:29-37

18 aNum.
3:5-10; Deut.
18:1; 24:8;
Josh. 3:3;
Ezek. 44:15
bEzra 3:5;
Heb. 13:15

20 aPs.
89:37;
104:19-23;
Is. 54:9, 10;
Jer. 31:35-
37; 33:25

21 a2 Sam.
23:5; 2 Chr.
7:18; 21:7

33:6-13 God promised again to restore His people and Jerusalem.
33:14-26 The King-Messiah will emerge from

the Davidic dynasty to rule in the millennial
kingdom (see 23:5).

with the Levitical priests, My ministers.

22 'As the [a]host of heaven cannot be counted, and the [b]sand of the sea cannot be measured, so I will [c]multiply the descendants of David My servant and the [d]Levites who minister to Me.' "

23 And the word of the LORD came to Jeremiah, saying,

24 "Have you not observed what this people have spoken, saying, 'The [a]two families which the LORD chose, He has [b]rejected them'? Thus they [c]despise My people, no longer are they as a nation in their sight.

25 "Thus says the LORD, 'If My [a]covenant *for* day and night *stand* not, *and* the fixed patterns of heaven and earth I have [b]not established,

26 then I would [a]reject the descendants of Jacob and David My servant, not taking from his descendants [b]rulers over the descendants of Abraham, Isaac, and Jacob. But I will [c]restore their fortunes and will have [d]mercy on them.' "

P   Events before the Fall of Jerusalem, 34:1–38:28

1   *Message to Zedekiah, 34:1-7*

34 The word which came to Jeremiah from the LORD, when [a]Nebuchadnezzar king of Babylon and all his army, with [b]all the kingdoms of the earth that were under his dominion and all the peoples, were fighting against Jerusalem and against all its cities, saying,

2 "Thus says the LORD God of Israel, '[a]Go and speak to Zede-

kiah king of Judah and say to him: "Thus says the LORD, 'Behold, [b]I am giving this city into the hand of the king of Babylon, and [c]he will burn it with fire.

3 'And [a]you will not escape from his hand, for you will surely be captured and delivered into his hand; and you will [b]see the king of Babylon eye to eye, and he will speak with you face to face, and you will go to Babylon.' " '

4 "Yet hear the word of the LORD, O Zedekiah king of Judah! Thus says the LORD concerning you, 'You will not die by the sword.

5 'You will die in peace; and as spices were burned for your fathers, the former kings who were before you, so they will [a]burn spices for you; and [b]they will lament for you, "Alas, lord!" ' For I have spoken the word," declares the LORD.

6 Then Jeremiah the prophet spoke [a]all these words to Zedekiah king of Judah in Jerusalem

7 when the army of the king of Babylon was fighting against Jerusalem and against all the remaining cities of Judah, *that is,* [a]Lachish and [b]Azekah, for they *alone* remained as [c]fortified cities among the cities of Judah.

2   *Message to the people, 34:8-22*

8 The word which came to Jeremiah from the LORD, after King Zedekiah had [a]made a covenant with all the people who were in Jerusalem to [b]proclaim release to them:

Margin references

22 [a]Gen. 15:5; Jer. 31:37 [b]Gen. 22:17 [c]Ezek. 37:24-27 [d]Is. 66:21; Jer. 33:18

24 [a]Is. 7:17; 11:13; Jer. 3:7, 8, 10, 18; 33:26; Ezek. 37:22 [b]Jer. 30:17 [c]Neh. 4:2-4; Esth. 3:6, 8, 9; Ps. 44:13, 14; 83:4

25 [a]Gen. 8:22; Jer. 31:35, 36; 33:20 [b]Ps. 74:16, 17

26 [a]Jer. 31:37 [b]Gen. 49:10 [c]Jer. 33:7 [d]Is. 14:1; 54:8; Jer. 31:20; Ezek. 39:25; Hos. 1:7; 2:23

★ 1-7
1 [a]2 Kin. 25:1; Jer. 32:2; 39:1; 52:4 [b]Jer. 1:15; 27:7; Dan. 2:37, 38

2 [a]2 Chr. 36:11, 12; Jer. 22:1, 2; 37:1, 2 [b]Jer. 21:10; 32:3; 34:22; 37:8-10 [c]Jer. 32:29

3 [a]2 Kin. 25:4, 5; Jer. 21:7; 32:4; 34:21 [b]2 Kin. 25:6, 7; Jer. 39:6, 7

5 [a]2 Chr. 16:14; 21:19 [b]Jer. 22:18

6 [a]1 Sam. 3:18; 15:16-24

7 [a]Josh. 10:3, 5; 2 Kin. 14:19; 18:14; Is. 36:2 [b]Josh. 10:10; 2 Chr. 11:9 [c]2 Chr. 11:5-10

★ 8-11
8 [a]2 Kin. 11:17; 23:2, 3 [b]Ex. 21:2; Lev. 25:10, 39-46; Neh. 5:1-13; Is. 58:6; Jer. 34:14, 17

34:1-7 The final assault against Jerusalem had begun, provoked by Zedekiah's revolt in 589. Jeremiah again predicted the downfall of Jerusalem (v. 2) and Zedekiah's captivity in Babylon, where he would die in peace (v. 5). His death would be marked by ceremonial incense burning (cf. the burial of Jehoiakim, 22:18-19). *Lachish.* 30 miles SW. of Jerusalem. *Azekah.* 15 miles SW. of Jerusalem. The Lachish letters, written at this time, describe the Babylonian conquest.

34:8-11 Zedekiah convinced the people to release their Hebrew slaves (who were supposed to be given their freedom after six years, Exod. 21:2), hoping thereby to impress God and cause Him to relieve the Babylonian siege against Jerusalem. But when news came that an advancing Egyptian army caused the Babylonians temporarily to lift the siege and regroup against the Egyptians (Jer. 37:5), the slaveowners, feeling that the danger was past, forced their slaves back into service.

9 ^aGen. 14:13; Ex. 2:6 ^bLev. 25:39

10 ^aJer. 26:10, 16

13 ^aEx. 24:3, 7, 8; Deut. 5:2, 3, 27; Jer. 31:32 ^bEx. 20:2

14 ^aEx. 21:2; Deut. 15:12; 1 Kin. 9:22 ^b1 Sam. 8:7, 8; 2 Kin. 17:13, 14

15 ^aJer. 34:8 ^b2 Kin. 23:3; Neh. 10:29 ^cJer. 7:10f.; 32:34

16 ^a1 Sam. 15:11; Jer. 34:11; Ezek. 3:20; 18:24 ^bEx. 20:7; Lev. 19:12

9 that each man should set free his male servant and each man his female servant, a ^aHebrew man or a Hebrew woman; so that ^bno one should keep them, a Jew his brother, in bondage.

10 And all the ^aofficials and all the people obeyed, who had entered into the covenant that each man should set free his male servant and each man his female servant, so that no one should keep them any longer in bondage; they obeyed, and set *them free.*

11 But afterward they turned around and took back the male servants and the female servants, whom they had set free, and brought them into subjection for male servants and for female servants.

12 Then the word of the Lord came to Jeremiah from the Lord, saying,

13 "Thus says the Lord God of Israel, 'I ^amade a covenant with your forefathers in the day that I ^bbrought them out of the land of Egypt, from the house of bondage, saying,

14 "^aAt the end of seven years each of you shall set free his Hebrew brother, who has been sold to you and has served you six years, you shall send him out free from you; but your forefathers ^bdid not obey Me, or incline their ear to Me.

15 "Although recently you *had* turned and ^adone what is right in My sight, each man proclaiming release to his neighbor, and you had ^bmade a covenant before Me ^cin the house which is called by My name.

16 "Yet you ^aturned and ^bprofaned My name, and each man took back his male servant and each man his female servant, whom you had set free according to their desire, and you brought them into subjection to be your male servants and female servants."'

17 "Therefore thus says the Lord, 'You have not obeyed Me in proclaiming release each man to his brother, and each man to his neighbor. Behold, I am ^aproclaiming a release to you,' declares the Lord, 'to the ^bsword, to the pestilence, and to the famine; and I will make you a ^cterror to all the kingdoms of the earth.

18 'And I will give the men who have ^atransgressed My covenant, who have not fulfilled the words of the covenant which they made before Me, *when* they ^bcut the calf in two and passed between its parts—

19 the ^aofficials of Judah, and the officials of Jerusalem, the court officers, and the priests, and all the people of the land, who passed between the parts of the calf—

20 and I will give them into the hand of their enemies and into the hand of those who ^aseek their life. And their ^bdead bodies shall be food for the birds of the sky and the beasts of the earth.

21 'And ^aZedekiah king of Judah and his officials I will give into the hand of their enemies, and into the hand of those who seek their life, and into the hand of the army of the king of Babylon which has ^bgone away from you.

22 'Behold, I am going to command,' declares the Lord, 'and I will bring them back to this city; and they shall fight against it and ^atake it and burn it with fire; and I will make the cities of Judah a ^bdesolation ^cwithout inhabitant.'"

17 ^aLev. 26:34, 35; Esth. 7:10; Dan. 6:24; Matt. 7:2 ^bJer. 32:24; 38:2 ^cDeut. 28:25; Jer. 29:18

★18 ^aDeut. 17:2; Hos. 6:7; 8:1; Rom. 2:8 ^bGen. 15:10

19 ^aJer. 34:10; Ezek. 22:27; Zeph. 3:3, 4

20 ^aJer. 11:21; 21:7; 22:25 ^bDeut. 28:26; 1 Sam. 17:44, 46; 1 Kin. 14:11; 16:4; Ps. 79:2; Jer. 7:33; 16:4; 19:7

21 ^a2 Kin. 25:18-21; Jer. 32:3, 4; 39:6; 52:10; 24:27; Ezek. 17:16 ^bJer. 37:5-11

22 ^aJer. 34:2; 39:1, 2, 8; 52:7, 13 ^bJer. 4:7; 9:11 ^cJer. 33:10; 44:22

3 *Message concerning the Rechabites,* 35:1-19

35 The word which came to Jeremiah from the Lord in

1 ^a2 Kin. 23:34-36; 24:1; 2 Chr. 36:5-7; Jer. 1:3; 27:20; Dan. 1:1

34:18 *when they cut the calf in two.* The ancient method of ratifying a covenant, here used in

the matter of the slaves (v. 8; cf. Gen. 15:9–17).

the days of ªJehoiakim the son of Josiah, king of Judah, saying,

2 "Go to the house of the ªRechabites, and speak to them, and bring them into the house of the LORD, into one of the ᵇchambers, and give them wine to drink."

3 Then I took Jaazaniah the son of Jeremiah, son of Habazziniah, and his brothers, and all his sons, and the whole house of the Rechabites,

4 and I brought them into the house of the LORD, into the chamber of the sons of Hanan the son of Igdaliah, the ªman of God, which was near the chamber of the officials, which was above the chamber of Maaseiah the son of Shallum, ᵇthe doorkeeper.

5 Then I set before the men of the house of the Rechabites pitchers full of wine, and cups; and I said to them, "ªDrink wine!"

6 But they said, "We will not drink wine, for ªJonadab the son of ᵇRechab, our father, commanded us, saying, 'You shall ᶜnot drink wine, you or your sons, forever.

7 'And you shall not build a house, and you shall not sow seed, and you shall not plant a vineyard or own one; but in ªtents you shall dwell all your days, that you may live ᵇmany days in the land where you ᶜsojourn.'

8 "And we have ªobeyed the voice of Jonadab the son of Rechab, our father, in all that he commanded us, not to drink wine all our days, we, our wives, our sons, or our daughters,

9 nor to build ourselves houses to dwell in; and we ªdo not have vineyard or field or seed.

10 "We have only ªdwelt in tents, and have obeyed, and have done according to all that ᵇJonadab our father commanded us.

11 "But it came about, when ªNebuchadnezzar king of Babylon came up against the land, that we said, 'Come and let us ᵇgo to Jerusalem before the army of the Chaldeans and before the army of the Arameans.' So we have dwelt in Jerusalem."

12 Then the word of the LORD came to Jeremiah, saying,

13 "Thus says the LORD of hosts, the God of Israel, 'Go and say to the men of Judah and the inhabitants of Jerusalem, "ªWill you not receive instruction by listening to My words?" declares the LORD.

14 "The ªwords of Jonadab the son of Rechab, which he commanded his sons not to drink wine, are observed. So they do not drink *wine* to this day, for they have obeyed their father's command. But I have spoken to you ᵇagain and again; yet you have ᶜnot listened to Me.

15 "Also I have sent to you all My ªservants the prophets, sending *them* again and again, saying: 'ᵇTurn now every man from his evil way, and amend your deeds, and ᶜdo not go after other gods to worship them, then you shall ᵈdwell in the land which I have given to you and to your forefathers; but you have not ᵉinclined your ear or listened to Me.

16 'Indeed, the sons of Jonadab the son of Rechab have ªobserved the command of their father which he commanded them, but this people has not listened to Me.'

17 "Therefore thus says the LORD, the God of hosts, the God of Israel, 'Behold, ªI am bringing on Judah and on all the inhabitants of Jerusalem all the disaster that I have pronounced against them; because I ᵇspoke to them but they did not listen, and I have

---

Cross references (left column):

★ **2** ª2 Kin. 10:15; 1 Chr. 2:55 ᵇ1 Kin. 6:5, 8; 1 Chr. 9:26, 33

4 ªDeut. 33:1; Josh. 14:6; 1 Kin. 12:22; 2 Kin. 1:9-13 ᵇ1 Chr. 9:18f.

5 ªAmos 2:12

6 ª2 Kin. 10:15, 23 ᵇ1 Chr. 2:55 ᶜLev. 10:9; Num. 6:2-4; Judg. 13:7, 14; Luke 1:15

7 ªGen. 25:27; Heb. 11:9 ᵇEx. 20:12; Eph. 6:2, 3 ᶜGen. 36:7

8 ªProv. 1:8, 9; 4:1, 2, 10; 6:20; Eph. 6:1; Col. 3:20

9 ªPs. 37:16; Jer. 35:7; 1 Tim. 6:6

10 ªJer. 35:7 ᵇJer. 35:6

Cross references (right column):

11 ª2 Kin. 24:1, 2; Dan. 1:1, 2 ᵇJer. 4:5-7; 8:14

★**12-19**

13 ªIs. 28:9-12; Jer. 5:3; 6:8-10; 32:33

14 ªJer. 35:6-10 ᵇ2 Chr. 36:15; Jer. 7:13, 25; 11:7; 25:3, 4 ᶜIs. 30:9; 50:2

15 ªJer. 7:25; 25:4; 26:5; 29:19; 32:33 ᵇIs. 1:16, 17; Jer. 4:1; 18:11; 25:5f.; Ezek. 18:30-32; Acts 26:20 ᶜDeut. 6:14; Jer. 7:6; 13:10; 25:6 ᵈJer. 7:7; 25:5, 6 ᵉJer. 7:24, 26; 11:8; 17:23; 34:14

16 ªJer. 35:14; Mal. 1:6

17 ªJosh. 23:15; Jer. 19:3, 15; 21:4-10; Mic. 3:12 ᵇProv. 1:24, 25; Is. 65:12; 66:4; Jer. 7:13, 26, 27; 26:5; Luke 13:34, 35; Rom. 10:21

35:2 *Rechabites.* A puritan protest group, advocating a nomadic way of life, that originated with Jonadab, son of Rechab, in Israel about 842 B.C. (2 Kings 10:15-23). Jeremiah was commanded to give them wine to drink, which

they refused.

35:12-19 Jeremiah used the fidelity of the Rechabites as an object lesson to Judah, who, by contrast, had broken God's commands.

called them but they did not answer.' "

18 Then Jeremiah said to the house of the Rechabites, "Thus says the LORD of hosts, the God of Israel, 'Because you have *obeyed the command of Jonadab your father, kept all his commands, and done according to all that he commanded you;

19 therefore thus says the LORD of hosts, the God of Israel, "Jonadab the son of Rechab *shall not lack a man to *stand before Me always." ' "

4 Jehoiakim burns Jeremiah's scroll, 36:1-32

36 And it came about in the *fourth year of Jehoiakim the son of Josiah, king of Judah, that this word came to Jeremiah from the LORD, saying,

2 "Take a *scroll and write on it all the *words which I have spoken to you concerning *Israel, and concerning Judah, and concerning all the *nations, from the *day I *first* spoke to you, from the days of Josiah, even to this day.

3 "*Perhaps the house of Judah will hear all the calamity which I plan to bring on them, in order that every man will *turn from his evil way; then I will *forgive their iniquity and their sin."

4 Then Jeremiah called *Baruch the son of Neriah, and Baruch wrote at the dictation of Jeremiah all the words of the LORD, which He had spoken to him, on a *scroll.

5 And Jeremiah commanded Baruch, saying, "I am *restricted; I cannot go into the house of the LORD.

6 "So you go and *read from the scroll which you have *written at my dictation the words of

the LORD to the people in the LORD's house on a *fast day. And also you shall read them to all *the people of* Judah who come from their cities.

7 "*Perhaps their supplication will come before the LORD, and everyone will turn from his evil way, for *great is the anger and the wrath that the LORD has pronounced against this people."

8 And Baruch the son of Neriah did according to all that Jeremiah the prophet commanded him, *reading from the book the words of the LORD in the LORD's house.

9 Now it came about in the *fifth year of Jehoiakim the son of Josiah, king of Judah, in the *ninth month, that all the people in Jerusalem and all the people who *came from the cities of Judah to Jerusalem proclaimed a *fast before the LORD.

10 Then Baruch read from the book the words of Jeremiah in the house of the LORD in the *chamber of *Gemariah the son of Shaphan the *scribe, in the upper court, at the *entry of the New Gate of the LORD's house, to all the people.

11 Now when *Micaiah the son of Gemariah, the son of Shaphan, had heard all the words of the LORD from the book,

12 he went down to the king's house, into the scribe's chamber. And, behold, all the officials were sitting there—*Elishama the scribe, and *Delaiah the son of Shemaiah, and *Elnathan the son of Achbor, and Gemariah the son of Shaphan, and Zedekiah the son of Hananiah, and all the *other* officials.

13 And Micaiah *declared to them all the words that he had

---

18 *aEx. 20:12; Eph. 6:1-3

19 *a1 Chr. 2:55; Jer. 33:17 *bJer. 15:19; Luke 21:36

1 *a2 Kin. 24:1; 2 Chr. 36:5-7; Jer. 25:1, 3; 45:1; 46:2; Dan. 1:1

★ **2** *aEx. 17:14; Is. 8:1; Jer. 36:6, 23, 28; Zech. 5:1, 2 *bJer. 1:9, 10; 30:2; Hab. 2:2 *cJer. 3:3-10; 23:13, 14; 32:30-32 *dJer. 1:5, 10; 25:9-29; chs. 47-51 *eJer. 1:2, 3; 25:3

3 *aJer. 26:3; 36:7; Ezek. 12:3 *bDeut. 30:2, 8; 1 Sam. 7:3; Is. 55:7; Jer. 18:8, 11; 35:15; Jon. 3:8 *cJon. 3:10; Mark 4:12; Acts 3:19

★ **4** *aJer. 32:12; 36:18; 43:3; 45:1 *bJer. 36:14; Ezek. 2:9

★ **5** *aJer. 32:2; 33:1; 2 Cor. 11:23

6 *aJer. 36:8 *bJer. 36:4 *cJer. 36:9; Zech. 8:19

7 *a1 Kin. 8:33; 2 Chr. 33:12, 13; Jer. 26:3; 36:3 *bDeut. 28:15; 31:16, 17; 2 Kin. 22:13, 17; Jer. 4:4; 21:5; Lam. 4:11

8 *aJer. 1:17; 36:6

★ **9** *aJer. 36:1 *bJer. 36:22 *cJer. 36:6 *dJudg. 20:26; 1 Sam. 7:6; 2 Chr. 20:3; Esth. 4:16; Joel 1:14; 2:15; Jon. 3:5

★**10** *aJer. 35:4 *bJer. 36:11, 25 *c2 Sam. *dJer. 52:25 *dJer. 26:10

11 *aJer. 36:13

12 *aJer. 36:20 *bJer. 36:25 *cJer. 26:22

13 *a2 Kin. 22:10

36:2 *a scroll.* Papyrus sheets pasted together (cf. v. 23). It contained Jeremiah's prophecies from 627 to 605.

36:4 *Baruch.* See 32:12-25; 36:10-19, 26; 43:3, 6. He was Jeremiah's attendant and scribe.

36:5 *I am restricted* from going into the Temple, probably because of reaction against his mes-

sages (cf. chapters 7, 26).

36:9 *a fast.* In December 604, probably because the Babylonians had conquered Ashkelon at that time.

36:10 The scroll was read three times: in the Temple court (v. 10), before the princes (v. 15), and before King Jehoiakim (v. 21).

heard, when Baruch read from the book to the people.

14 Then all the officials sent ^aJehudi the son of Nethaniah, the son of Shelemiah, the son of Cushi, to Baruch, saying, "Take in your hand the scroll from which you have read to the people and come." So Baruch the son of Neriah ^btook the scroll in his hand and went to them.

15 And they said to him, "Sit down please, and read it to us." So Baruch ^aread it to them.

16 Now it came about when they had heard all the words, they turned in ^afear one to another and said to Baruch, "We will surely ^breport all these words to the king."

17 And they asked Baruch, saying, "Tell us please, ^ahow did you write all these words? *Was it* at his dictation?"

18 Then Baruch said to them, "He ^adictated all these words to me, and I wrote them with ink on the book."

19 Then the officials said to Baruch, "Go, ^ahide yourself, you and Jeremiah, and do not let anyone know where you are."

20 So they went to the ^aking in the court, but they had deposited the scroll in the chamber of ^aElishama the scribe, and they reported all the words to the king.

21 Then the king sent Jehudi to get the scroll, and he took it out of the chamber of Elishama the scribe. And Jehudi ^aread it to the king as well as to all the officials who stood beside the king.

22 Now the king was sitting in the ^awinter house in the ^bninth month, with a *fire* burning in the brazier before him.

23 And it came about, when Jehudi had read three or four columns, *the king* cut it with a scribe's knife and ^athrew *it* into the fire that was in the brazier, until all the scroll was consumed in the fire that was in the brazier.

24 Yet the king and all his servants who heard all these words were ^anot afraid, nor did they ^brend their garments.

25 Even though Elnathan and Delaiah and Gemariah ^aentreated the king not to burn the scroll, he would not listen to them.

26 And the king commanded Jerahmeel the king's son, Seraiah the son of Azriel, and Shelemiah the son of Abdeel to ^aseize Baruch the scribe and Jeremiah the prophet, but the ^bLORD hid them.

27 Then the word of the LORD came to Jeremiah after the king had ^aburned the scroll and the words which ^bBaruch had written at the dictation of Jeremiah, saying,

28 "^aTake again another scroll and write on it all the former words that were ^bon the first scroll which Jehoiakim the king of Judah burned.

29 "And concerning Jehoiakim king of Judah you shall say, 'Thus says the LORD, "You have ^aburned this scroll, saying, '^bWhy have you written on it that the ^cking of Babylon shall certainly come and destroy this land, and shall make man and beast to cease from it?' "

30 'Therefore thus says the LORD concerning Jehoiakim king of Judah, "He shall have ^ano one to sit on the throne of David, and his ^bdead body shall be cast out to the heat of the day and the frost of the night.

31 "I shall also ^apunish him and his descendants and his servants for their iniquity, and I shall ^bbring on them and the inhabitants of Jerusalem and the men of Judah all the calamity that I have declared to them—but they did not listen." ' "

32 Then Jeremiah took another scroll and gave it to Baruch the son of Neraiah, the scribe, and he ^awrote on it at the dictation of Jeremiah all the words of the book which Jehoiakim king of

---

Cross references (left margin):

14 ^aJer. 36:21 ^bJer. 36:2; Ezek. 2:7-10

15 ^aJer. 36:21

16 ^aJer. 36:24; Acts 24:25 ^bJer. 13:18; Amos 7:10, 11

17 ^aJohn 9:10, 15, 26

18 ^aJer. 36:4

19 ^a1 Kin. 17:3; 18:4, 10; Jer. 26:20-24; 36:26

20 ^aJer. 36:12

21 ^a2 Kin. 22:10; 2 Chr. 34:18; Ezek. 2:4, 5

★22 ^aJudg. 3:20; Amos 3:15 ^bJer. 36:9

23 ^a1 Kin. 22:8, 27; Prov. 1:30; Is. 5:18, 19; 28:14, 22; Jer. 36:29

Cross references (right margin):

24 ^aPs. 36:1; 64:5; Jer. 36:16 ^bGen. 37:29, 34; 2 Sam. 1:11; 1 Kin. 21:27; 2 Kin. 19:1; 2; 22:11, 19; Is. 36:22; 37:1; Jon. 3:6

25 ^aGen. 37:22, 26, 27; Acts 5:34-39

26 ^a1 Kin. 19:1-3, 10, 14; Matt. 23:34, 37 ^bPs. 91:1

27 ^aJer. 36:23 ^bJer. 36:4, 18

28 ^aZech. 1:5, 6 ^bJer. 36:4, 23

29 ^aDeut. 29:19; Job 15:24, 25; Is. 45:9 ^bIs. 29:21; 30:10; Jer. 26:9; 32:3 ^cJer. 25:9-11

30 ^a2 Kin. 24:12-15; Jer. 22:30 ^bJer. 22:19

31 ^aJer. 23:34 ^bDeut. 28:15; Prov. 29:1; Jer. 19:15; 35:17

32 ^aEx. 4:15, 16; 34:1; Jer. 36:4, 18, 23

36:22 *winter house.* Not a separate house, but a warmer part of his residence.

Judah had burned in the fire; and many similar words were added to them.

5　Jeremiah imprisoned,
37:1-38:28

37 Now *a*Zedekiah the son of Josiah whom Nebuchadnezzar king of Babylon had *b*made king in the land of Judah, reigned as king in place of *c*Coniah the son of Jehoiakim.

2 But *a*neither he nor his servants nor the people of the land listened to the words of the LORD which He spoke through Jeremiah the prophet.

3 Yet *a*King Zedekiah sent Jehucal the son of Shelemiah, and *b*Zephaniah the son of Maaseiah, the priest, to Jeremiah the prophet, saying, "*c*Please pray to the LORD our God on our behalf."

4 Now Jeremiah was *still* coming in and going out among the people, for they had not *yet* *a*put him in the prison.

5 Meanwhile, *a*Pharaoh's army had set out from Egypt; and when the Chaldeans who had been besieging Jerusalem heard the report about them, they *b*lifted the *siege* from Jerusalem.

6 Then the word of the LORD came to Jeremiah the prophet, saying,

7 "Thus says the LORD God of Israel, '*a*Thus you are to say to the king of Judah, who sent you to Me to inquire of Me: "Behold, *b*Pharaoh's army which has come out for your assistance is going to return to its own land of Egypt.

8 "The Chaldeans will also *a*return and fight against this city, and they will capture it and burn it with fire." '

9 "Thus says the LORD, 'Do not *a*deceive yourselves, saying,

"The Chaldeans will surely go away from us," for they will not go.

10 'For *a*even if you had defeated the entire army of Chaldeans who were fighting against you, and there were *only* wounded men left among them, each man in his tent, they would rise up and *b*burn this city with fire.' "

11 Now it happened, when the army of the Chaldeans had lifted *the siege* from Jerusalem because of Pharaoh's army,

12 that Jeremiah went out from Jerusalem to go to the land of Benjamin in order to *a*take possession of *some* property there among the people.

13 While he was at the *a*Gate of Benjamin, a captain of the guard whose name was Irijah, the son of Shelemiah the son of Hananiah was there; and he *b*arrested Jeremiah the prophet, saying, "You are going over to the Chaldeans!"

14 But Jeremiah said, "*a*A lie! I am not going over to the Chaldeans"; yet he would not listen to him. So Irijah arrested Jeremiah and brought him to the officials.

15 Then the officials were *a*angry at Jeremiah and beat him, and they *b*put him in jail in the house of Jonathan the scribe, which they had made into the prison.

16 For Jeremiah had come into the *a*dungeon, that is, the vaulted cell; and Jeremiah stayed there many days.

17 Now King Zedekiah sent and took him *out;* and in his palace the king *a*secretly asked him and said, "Is there a *b*word from the LORD?" And Jeremiah said, "There is!" Then he said, "You will be *c*given into the hand of the king of Babylon!"

1 *a*2 Kin. 24:17; 1 Chr. 3:15; 2 Chr. 36:10 *b*Ezek. 17:12-21 *c*2 Kin. 24:12; 1 Chr. 3:16; 2 Chr. 36:9; 10; Jer. 22:24, 28; 24:1; 52:31
2 *a*2 Kin. 24:19, 20; 2 Chr. 36:12-16; Prov. 29:12
3 *a*Jer. 21:1, 2 *b*Jer. 29:25; 52:24 *c*1 Kin. 13:6; Jer. 2:27; 15:11; 21:1, 2, 42:1-4, 20; Acts 8:24
4 *a*Jer. 32:2, 3; 37:15
★ **5** *a*2 Kin. 24:7; Jer. 37:7; Ezek. 17:15 *b*Jer. 37:11
7 *a*2 Kin. 22:18; Jer. 21:1, 2; 37:3 *b*Is. 30:1-3; 31:1-3; Jer. 2:18, 36; Lam. 4:17; Ezek. 17:17
8 *a*Jer. 34:22; 38:23; 39:2-8
9 *a*Jer. 29:8; Obad. 3; Matt. 24:4, 5; Eph. 5:6
10 *a*Lev. 26:36-38; Is. 30:17; Jer. 21:4, 5 *b*Jer. 37:8
12 *a*Jer. 32:8
★ **13** *a*Jer. 38:7; Zech. 14:10 *b*Jer. 18:18; 20:10; Luke 23:2; Acts 6:11; 24:5-9, 13
14 *a*Ps. 27:12; 52:1, 2; Jer. 40:4-6; Matt. 5:11, 12
15 *a*Jer. 18:23; 20:1-3; 26:16; Matt. 21:35 *b*Gen. 39:20; 2 Chr. 16:10; Jer. 18:26; 38:26; Acts 5:18
★ **16** *a*Jer. 38:6
17 *a*1 Kin. 14:1-4; Jer. 38:5, 14-16, 24-27 *b*1 Kin. 22:15, 16; 2 Kin. 3:11, 12; Jer. 15:11; 21:1, 2; 37:3 *c*Jer. 21:7; 24:8; Ezek. 12:12, 13; 17:19, 20

37:5 The Pharaoh was Hophra (44:30), who reigned from 589-570 and who marched to support Zedekiah against Babylon (Jer. 52:3; Ezek. 17:11-21). He retreated before actually engaging in battle and left Jerusalem to fall to the Babylonians in 587.

37:13 He thought Jeremiah was deserting to the enemy, though actually Jeremiah was likely going to inspect the property purchased from Hanamel (32:1-15).
37:16 *dungeon . . . vaulted cell.* Probably a cistern (38:6, 13).

18 Moreover Jeremiah said to King Zedekiah, "*a In* what *way* have I sinned against you, or against your servants, or against this people, that you have put me in prison?

19 "*a* Where then are your prophets who prophesied to you, saying, 'The *b* king of Babylon will not come against you or against this land'?

20 "But now, please listen, O my lord the king; please let my *a* petition come before you, and do not make me return to the house of Jonathan the scribe, that I may not die there."

21 Then King Zedekiah gave commandment, and they committed Jeremiah to the *a* court of the guardhouse and gave him a loaf of *b* bread daily from the bakers' street, until all the bread in the city was *c* gone. So Jeremiah remained in the court of the guardhouse.

38 Now Shephatiah the son of Mattan, and Gedaliah the son of Pashhur, and Jucal the *a* son of Shelemiah, and *b* Pashhur the son of Malchijah heard the words that Jeremiah was speaking to all the people, saying,

2 "Thus says the LORD, 'He who *a* stays in this city will die by the *b* sword and by famine and by pestilence, but he who goes out to the Chaldeans will live and have his *own* *c* life as booty and stay alive.'

3 "Thus says the LORD, 'This city will certainly be *a* given into the hand of the army of the king of Babylon, and he will capture it.'"

4 Then the *a* officials said to the king, "Now let this man be put to death, inasmuch as he is *b* discouraging the men of war who are left in this city and all the people, by speaking such words to them; for this man *c* is not seek-ing the well-being of this people, but rather their harm."

5 So King Zedekiah said, "Behold, he is in your hands; for the king *a* can *do* nothing against you."

6 Then they took Jeremiah and cast him into the *a* cistern *of* Malchijah the king's son, which was in the court of the guard-house; and they let Jeremiah down with ropes. Now in the cis-tern there was no water but only *b* mud, and Jeremiah sank into the mud.

7 But *a* Ebed-melech the Ethiopian, a *b* eunuch, while he was in the king's palace, heard that they had put Jeremiah into the cistern. Now the king was sit-ting in the *c* Gate of Benjamin;

8 and Ebed-melech went out from the king's palace and spoke to the king, saying,

9 "My lord the king, these men have acted wickedly in all that they have done to Jeremiah the prophet whom they have cast into the cistern; and he will die right where he is because of the famine, for there is *a* no more bread in the city."

10 Then the king commanded Ebed-melech the Ethiopian, say-ing, "Take thirty men from here under your authority, and bring up Jeremiah the prophet from the cistern before he dies."

11 So Ebed-melech took the men under his authority and went into the king's palace to *a place* beneath the storeroom and took from there worn-out clothes and worn-out rags and let them down by ropes into the cistern to Jere-miah.

12 Then Ebed-melech the Ethiopian said to Jeremiah, "Now put these worn-out clothes and rags under your armpits under the ropes"; and Jeremiah did so.

---

18 *a* 1 Sam. 24:9; 26:18; Dan. 6:22; John 10:32; Acts 25:8, 11, 25

19 *a* Deut. 32:37, 38; 2 Kin. 3:13; Jer. 2:28 *b* Jer. 27:14; 28:1-4, 10-17

20 *a* Jer. 36:7; 38:26

21 *a* Jer. 32:2; 38:13, 28 *b* 1 Kin. 17:6; Job 5:20; Ps. 33:18, 19; Is. 33:16 *c* 2 Kin. 25:3; Jer. 38:9; 52:6

1 *a* Jer. 37:3 *b* Jer. 21:1

2 *a* Jer. 21:9 *b* Jer. 34:17; 42:17 *c* Jer. 21:9; 39:18; 45:5

3 *a* Jer. 21:10; 32:3-5

4 *a* Jer. 18:23; 26:11, 21; 36:12 *b* Ex. 5:4; 1 Kin. 18:17, 18; 21:20; Neh. 6:9; Amos 7:10; Acts 16:20 *c* Jer. 29:7

5 *a* 2 Sam. 3:39

6 *a* Jer. 37:16, 21; Acts 16:24 *b* Ps. 40:2; 69:2, 14, 15; Jer. 38:22; Zech. 9:11

★ 7 *a* Jer. 39:16 *b* Jer. 29:2; Acts 8:27 *c* Deut. 21:19; Job 29:7; Jer. 37:13; Amos 5:10

9 *a* Jer. 37:21; 52:6

★11

38:7 *eunuch.* I.e., officer or palace official. Only a foreigner cared enough for Jeremiah to risk rescuing him.

38:11 These rags were placed under Jeremiah's emaciated arms so the ropes would not cut into them.

13 aNeh.
3:25; Jer.
32:2; 37:21;
38:6; 39:14,
15; Acts
23:35; 24:27;
28:16, 30

14 aJer.
21:1, 2;
37:17
b1 Sam.
3:17, 18;
1 Kin. 22:16;
Jer. 15:11;
42:2-5, 20

15 aLuke
22:67, 68

16 aJer.
37:17; John
3:2 bNum.
16:22; 27:16;
Is. 42:5;
57:16; Zech.
12:1; Acts
17:25, 28
cJer. 34:20;
38:4-6

17 aPs. 80:7,
14; Amos
5:27 b1 Chr.
17:24; Ezek.
8:4 c2 Kin.
24:12; 25:27-
30; Jer. 21:8-
10; 27:12,
17; 38:2;
39:3

18 aJer. 27:8
b2 Kin. 25:4-
10; Jer. 24:8-
10; 32:3-5;
37:8; 38:3
cJer. 32:4;
34:3

19 aIs.
51:12, 13;
57:11; John
12:42; 19:12,
13 bJer. 39:9
c2 Chr.
30:10; Neh.
4:1; Jer.
38:22

20 a2 Chr.
20:20; Jer.
11:4, 8;
26:13; Dan.
4:27; Acts
26:29 bJer.
7:23 cGen.
19:20; Is.
55:3

13 So they pulled Jeremiah up with the ropes and lifted him out of the cistern, and Jeremiah stayed in the ^acourt of the guardhouse.

14 Then King Zedekiah ^asent and had Jeremiah the prophet brought to him at the third entrance that is in the house of the Lord; and the king said to Jeremiah, "I am going to ^bask you something; do not hide anything from me."

15 Then Jeremiah said to Zedekiah, "^aIf I tell you, will you not certainly put me to death? Besides, if I give you advice, you will not listen to me."

16 But King Zedekiah swore to Jeremiah in ^asecret saying, "As the Lord lives, who made this ^blife for us, surely I will not put you to death nor will I give you over to the hand of ^cthese men who are seeking your life."

17 Then Jeremiah said to Zedekiah, "Thus says the Lord ^aGod of hosts, the ^bGod of Israel, 'If you will indeed ^cgo out to the officers of the king of Babylon, then you will live, this city will not be burned with fire, and you and your household will survive.

18 'But if you will ^anot go out to the officers of the king of Babylon, then this city ^bwill be given over to the hand of the Chaldeans; and they will burn it with fire, and ^cyou yourself will not escape from their hand.' "

19 Then King Zedekiah said to Jeremiah, "I ^adread the Jews who have ^bgone over to the Chaldeans, lest they give me over into their hand and they ^cabuse me."

20 But Jeremiah said, "They will not give you over. Please ^aobey the Lord in what I am saying to you, that it may go ^bwell with you and ^cyou may live.

21 "But if you keep refusing to go out, this is the word which the Lord has shown me:

22 'Then behold, all of the ^awomen who have been left in the palace of the king of Judah are going to be brought out to the officers of the king of Babylon; and those women will say,

"Your close friends
Have misled and overpowered you;
While your feet were sunk
in the mire,
They turned back."

23 'They will also bring out all your wives and your ^asons to the Chaldeans, and ^byou yourself will not escape from their hand, but will be seized by the hand of the king of Babylon, and ^bthis city will be burned with fire.' "

24 Then Zedekiah said to Jeremiah, "Let no man know about these words and you will not die.

25 "But if the ^aofficials hear that I have talked with you and come to you and say to you, 'Tell us now what you said to the king, and what the king said to you; do not hide it from us, and we will not put you to death,'

26 then you are to say to them, 'I was ^apresenting my petition before the king, not to make me return to the house of Jonathan to die there.' "

27 Then all the officials came to Jeremiah and questioned him. So he reported to them in accordance with all these words which the king had commanded; and they ceased speaking with him, since the conversation had not been overheard.

28 So Jeremiah ^astayed in the court of the guardhouse until the day that Jerusalem was captured.

Q The Fall of Jerusalem, 39:1-18

1 The fate of the Jews, 39:1-10

39 Now it came about when Jerusalem was captured

★22 aJer.
6:12; 8:10;
43:6

23 a2 Kin.
25:7; Jer.
39:6; 41:10
bJer. 38:18

25 aJer.
38:4-6, 27

26 aJer.
37:20

28 aPs. 23:4;
Jer. 15:20,
21; 37:20,
21; 38:13;
39:13, 14

★ 1 a2 Kin.
25:1-12; Jer.
52:4; Ezek.
24:1, 2

38:22 the women. The harem.
39:1 The events of this chapter are also described in chapter 52.

ain the ninth year of Zedekiah king of Judah, in the tenth month, Nebuchadnezzar king of Babylon and all his army came to Jerusalem and laid siege to it;

2 in the eleventh year of Zedekiah, in the fourth month, in the ninth *day* of the month, the city *wall* was abreached.

3 Then all the aofficials of the king of Babylon came in and sat down at the bMiddle Gate: Nergal-sar-ezer, Samgar-nebu, Sar-sekim the Rab-saris, Nergal-sar-ezer *the* Rab-mag, and all the rest of the officials of the king of Babylon.

4 And it came about, when Zedekiah the king of Judah and all the men of war saw them, that they afled and went out of the city at night by way of the king's garden through the gate bbetween the two walls; and he went out toward the Arabah.

5 But the army of the aChaldeans pursued them and overtook Zedekiah in the bplains of Jericho; and they seized him and brought him up to Nebuchadnezzar king of Babylon at cRiblah in the land of Hamath, and he passed sentence on him.

6 Then the aking of Babylon slew the sons of Zedekiah bbefore his eyes at Riblah; the king of Babylon also slew all the cnobles of Judah.

7 He then ablinded Zedekiah's eyes and bound him in bfetters of bronze to bring him to cBabylon.

8 The Chaldeans also aburned with fire the king's palace and the houses of the people, and they bbroke down the walls of Jerusalem.

9 And as for the rest of the people who were left in the city, the adeserters who had gone over to him and bthe rest of the people who remained, cNebuzaradan the dcaptain of the bodyguard carried *them* into exile in Babylon.

10 But some of the apoorest people who had nothing, aNebuzaradan the captain of the bodyguard left behind in the land of Judah, and gave them vineyards and fields at that time.

2   *The fate of Jeremiah,* 39:11-18

11 Now Nebuchadnezzar king of Babylon gave orders about aJeremiah through Nebuzaradan the captain of the bodyguard, saying,

12 "Take him and look after him, and ado nothing harmful to him; but rather deal with him just as he tells you."

13 So Nebuzaradan the captain of the bodyguard sent *word,* along with Nebushazban the Rabsaris, and Nergal-sar-ezer *the* Rab-mag, and all the leading officers of the king of Babylon;

14 they even sent and atook Jeremiah out of the court of the guardhouse and entrusted him to bGedaliah, the son of cAhikam, the son of Shaphan, to take him home. So he stayed among the people.

15 Now the word of the LORD had come to Jeremiah while he was aconfined in the court of the guardhouse, saying,

16 "Go and speak to aEbed-melech the Ethiopian, saying, 'Thus says the LORD of hosts, the God of Israel, "Behold, I am about to bring My words on this city bfor disaster and not for prosperity; and they will ctake place before you on that day.

17 "But I will adeliver you on that day," declares the LORD, "and you shall not be given into the hand of the men whom you dread.

18 "For I will certainly rescue you, and you will not fall by the sword; but you will have your *own* alife as booty, because you

Marginal references

2 a2 Kin. 25:4; Jer. 52:7
★ 3 aJer. 38:17 bJer. 21:4
4 a2 Kin. 25:4; Is. 30:16; Jer. 52:7; Amos 2:14 b2 Chr. 32:5
5 aJer. 32:4, 5; 38:18, 23; 52:8 bJosh. 4:13; 5:10 c2 Kin. 23:33; Jer. 52:9, 26, 27
6 a2 Kin. 25:7; Jer. 52:10 bDeut. 28:34 cJer. 21:7; 24:8-10; 34:19-21
7 a2 Kin. 25:7; Jer. 52:11; Ezek. 12:13 bJudg. 16:21 cJer. 32:5
8 a2 Kin. 25:9; Jer. 21:10; 38:18; 52:13 b2 Kin. 25:10; Neh. 1:3; Jer. 52:14
9 aJer. 38:19; 52:15 bJer. 24:8 c2 Kin. 25:11, 20; Jer. 39:13; 40:1; 52:12-16, 26 dGen. 37:36
★10 a2 Kin. 25:12; Jer. 52:16
11 aJob 5:15, 16; Jer. 1:8; 15:20, 21; Acts 24:23
★12 aPs. 105:14, 15; Prov. 16:7; 21:1; 1 Pet. 3:13
14 aJer. 38:28; 40:1-6 bJer. 40:5 c2 Kin. 22:12, 14; 2 Chr. 34:20; Jer. 26:24
15 aJer. 38:28
16 aJer. 38:7 bJer. 21:10; Dan. 9:12; Zech. 1:6 cPs. 91:8
17 aPs. 41:1, 2; 50:15
18 aJer. 21:9; 38:2; 45:5 bPs. 34:22; Jer. 17:7, 8

39:3 *Nergal-sar-ezer.* King Neriglissar, son-in-law of Nebuchadnezzar; he reigned 560–556.
39:10 Only peasants, not likely to cause trouble, were left in Palestine.
39:12 God honored His promise to Jeremiah (1:8).

have ^btrusted in Me," declares the LORD.' "

R   Events After the Fall of Jerusalem, 40:1–45:5

1   Jeremiah ministers to Jews in Palestine, 40:1–42:22

★ 1 ^aJer. 39:9, 11 ^bJer. 31:15 ^cActs 12:6, 7; 21:13; 28:20; Eph. 6:20

40 The word which came to Jeremiah from the LORD after ^aNebuzaradan captain of the bodyguard had released him from ^bRamah, when he had taken him bound in ^cchains, among all the exiles of Jerusalem and Judah, who were being exiled to Babylon.

2 ^aLev. 26:14-38; Deut. 28:15-68; 29:24-28; 31:17; 32:19-25; Jer. 22:8, 9

2 Now the captain of the bodyguard had taken Jeremiah and said to him, "The ^aLORD your God promised this calamity against this place;

3 ^aJer. 50:7; Dan. 9:11; Rom. 2:5

3 and the LORD has brought it on and done just as He promised. Because you *people* ^asinned against the LORD and did not listen to His voice, therefore this thing has happened to you.

4 ^aJer. 39:11, 12 ^bGen. 13:9; 20:15; 47:6

4 "But now, behold, I am ^afreeing you today from the chains which are on your hands. If you would prefer to come with me to Babylon, come *along,* and I will look after you; but if you would prefer not to come with me to Babylon, never mind. Look, the ^bwhole land is before you; go wherever it seems good and right for you to go."

★ 5 ^aJer. 39:14 ^b2 Kin. 25:23 ^cJer. 52:34 ^d2 Kin. 8:7-9

5 As Jeremiah was still not going back, *he said,* "Go on back then to ^aGedaliah the son of Ahikam, the son of Shaphan, whom the king of Babylon has ^bappointed over the cities of Judah, and stay with him among the people; or else go anywhere it seems right for you to go." So the captain of the bodyguard gave

him a ^cration and a ^dgift and let him go.

★ 6 ^aJudg. 20:1; 21:1; 1 Sam. 7:5; 2 Chr. 16:6 ^bJer. 39:14

6 Then Jeremiah went to ^aMizpah to ^bGedaliah the son of Ahikam and stayed with him among the people who were left in the land.

★ 7 ^a2 Kin. 25:23 ^bJer. 39:10; 52:16

7 ^aNow all the commanders of the forces that were in the field, they and their men, heard that the king of Babylon had appointed Gedaliah the son of Ahikam over the land and that he had put him in charge of the men, women and children, those of the ^bpoorest of the land who had not been exiled to Babylon.

8 ^aJer. 40:14; 41:2 ^bJer. 40:13, 15; 42:1; 43:2 ^c2 Sam. 23:28, 29; Ezra 2:22; Neh. 7:26 ^dJer. 42:1 ^eDeut. 3:14; Josh. 12:5; 2 Sam. 10:6, 8

8 So they came to Gedaliah at Mizpah, along with ^aIshmael the son of Nethaniah, and ^bJohanan and Jonathan the sons of Kareah, and Seraiah the son of Tanhumeth, and the sons of Ephai the ^cNetophathite, and ^dJezaniah the son of the ^eMaacathite, *both* they and their men.

9 ^a1 Sam. 20:16, 17; 2 Kin. 25:24 ^bJer. 27:11; 38:17-20

9 Then Gedaliah the son of Ahikam, the son of Shaphan, ^aswore to them and to their men, saying, "^bDo not be afraid of serving the Chaldeans; stay in the land and serve the king of Babylon, that it may go well with you.

10 ^aDeut. 1:38; 1 Kin. 10:8; Jer. 35:19 ^bDeut. 16:13; Jer. 39:10 ^cIs. 16:9; Jer. 40:12; 48:32

10 "Now as for me, behold, I am going to stay at Mizpah to ^astand *for you* before the Chaldeans who come to us; but as for you, ^bgather in wine and ^csummer fruit and oil, and put *them* in your *storage* vessels, and live in your cities that you have taken over."

★11-12

11 ^aNum. 22:1; 25:1, 2; Is. 16:4; Jer. 9:26 ^b1 Sam. 11:1; 12:12 ^cGen. 36:8; Is. 11:14

11 Likewise also all the Jews who were in ^aMoab and among the sons of ^bAmmon and in ^cEdom, and who were in all the *other* countries, heard that the king of Babylon had left a remnant for Judah and that he had appointed

---

40:1 *Ramah.* Five miles N. of Jerusalem, it was the area where deportees were screened before being sent to Babylon. Jeremiah was allowed to choose whether he would go to Babylon or stay in Palestine; he chose to stay.
40:5 Gedaliah, grandson of one of Josiah's nobles, was made puppet governor of denud-

ed Judah.
40:6 *Mizpah.* A city a few miles N. of Jerusalem.
40:7 *forces that were in the field.* Jewish guerilla units that had not been captured. They are urged to obey the Babylonian officials.
40:11-12 Jewish refugees, who had fled before Nebuchadnezzar, returned to farm the land.

over them Gedaliah the son of Ahikam, the son of Shaphan.

12 aJer. 43:5

12 Then all the Jews ªreturned from all the places to which they had been driven away and came to the land of Judah, to Gedaliah at Mizpah, and gathered in wine and summer fruit in great abundance.

★13-16

13 Now Johanan the son of Kareah and all the commanders of the forces that were in the field came to Gedaliah at Mizpah,

14 a1 Sam. 11:1-3; 2 Sam. 10:1- 6; Jer. 25:21; 41:10

14 and said to him, "Are you well aware that Baalis the king of the sons of ªAmmon has sent Ishmael the son of Nethaniah to take your life?" But Gedaliah the son of Ahikam did not believe them.

15 a1 Sam. 26:8 b2 Sam. 21:17 cJer. 42:2

15 Then Johanan the son of Kareah spoke secretly to Gedaliah in Mizpah, saying, "ªLet me go and kill Ishmael the son of Nethaniah, and not a man will know! Why should he btake your life, so that all the Jews who are gathered to you should be scattered and the cremnant of Judah perish?"

16 aMatt. 10:16; 1 Cor. 13:5

16 But Gedaliah the son of Ahikam said to Johanan the son of Kareah, "ªDo not do this thing, for you are telling a lie about Ishmael."

★ 1 a2 Kin. 25:25 bJer. 40:8, 14 cJer. 39:14; 40:5, 6 dPs. 41:9; Jer. 40:13, 14

41 Now it ªcame about in the seventh month that bIshmael the son of Nethaniah, the son of Elishama, of the royal family and one of the chief officers of the king, along with ten men, came to Mizpah to cGedaliah the son of Ahikam. While they dwere eating bread together there in Mizpah,

2 a2 Sam. 3:27; 20:9, 10; 2 Kin. 25:25; Ps. 41:9; 109:5; John 13:18 b2 Kin. 25:25 cJer. 40:5

2 Ishmael the son of Nethaniah and the ten men who were with him arose and ªstruck down Gedaliah the son of Ahikam, the son of Shaphan, with the sword and bput to death the one cwhom the king of Babylon had appointed over the land.

3 Ishmael also struck down all the Jews who were with him, that is with Gedaliah at Mizpah, and the Chaldeans who were found there, the men of war.

4 Now it happened on the next day after the killing of Gedaliah, when no one knew about it,

5 a2 Kin. 10:13, 14 bGen. 33:18; 37:12; Judg. 9:1; 1 Kin. 12:1, 25 cJosh. 18:1; Judg. 18:31; 1 Sam. 3:21; Ps. 78:60 d1 Kin. 16:24, 29 eLev. 19:27; Deut. 14:1 fDeut. 14:1; Jer. 16:6 g1 Sam. 1:7; Jer. 25:9

5 that eighty men ªcame from bShechem, from cShiloh, and from dSamaria with etheir beards shaved off and their clothes torn and their bodies fgashed, having grain offerings and incense in their hands to bring to the ghouse of the LORD.

6 a2 Sam. 3:16; Jer. 50:4

6 Then Ishmael the son of Nethaniah went out from Mizpah to meet them, ªweeping as he went; and it came about as he met them that he said to them, "Come to Gedaliah the son of Ahikam!"

7 aPs. 55:23; Is. 59:7; Ezek. 22:27; 33:24, 26

7 Yet it turned out that as soon as they came inside the city, Ishmael the son of Nethaniah and the men that were with him ªslaughtered them, and cast them into the cistern.

8 aIs. 45:3

8 But ten men who were found among them said to Ishmael, "Do not put us to death; for we have ªstores of wheat, barley, oil and honey hidden in the field." So he refrained and did not put them to death along with their companions.

9 a1 Kin. 15:17-22; 2 Chr. 16:1-6 bJudg. 6:2; 1 Sam. 13:6; 2 Sam. 17:9; Heb. 11:38

9 Now as for the cistern where Ishmael had cast all the corpses of the men whom he had struck down because of Gedaliah, it was the ªone that King Asa had made on baccount of Baasha, king of Israel; Ishmael the son of Nethaniah filled it with the slain.

10 aJer. 40:11, 12 bJer. 43:6 cNeh. 2:10, 19; 4:7; Jer. 40:14

10 Then Ishmael took captive all the ªremnant of the people who were in Mizpah, the bking's daughters and all the people who were left in Mizpah, whom Nebuzaradan the captain of the bodyguard had put under the charge of

---

40:13–16 Gedaliah refused to believe his life was in danger from Ishmael, a would-be assassin.
41:1 of the royal family. Ishmael may have been motivated by jealousy to kill Gedaliah, because he felt slighted in being passed over for

the office of governor.
41:5 shaved . . . torn . . . gashed. Signs of mourning by these pilgrims, probably because of the fall of Jerusalem.
41:9 See 1 Kings 15:22 and 2 Chron. 16:6.

Gedaliah the son of Ahikam; thus Ishmael the son of Nethaniah took them captive and proceeded to cross over to the sons of ᶜAmmon.

11 But Johanan the son of Kareah and all the ᵃcommanders of the forces that were with him heard of all the evil that Ishmael the son of Nethaniah had done.

12 So they took all the men and went to ᵃfight with Ishmael the son of Nethaniah and they found him by the ᵇgreat pool that is in Gibeon.

13 Now it came about, as soon as all the people who were with Ishmael saw Johanan the son of Kareah and the commanders of the forces that were with him, they were glad.

14 So all the people whom Ishmael had taken captive from Mizpah turned around and came back, and went to Johanan the son of Kareah.

15 But Ishmael the son of Nethaniah ᵃescaped from Johanan with eight men and went to the sons of Ammon.

16 Then Johanan the son of Kareah and all the commanders of the forces that were with him took from Mizpah ᵃall the remnant of the people whom he had recovered from Ishmael the son of Nethaniah, after he had struck down Gedaliah the son of Ahikam, *that is,* the men who were soldiers, *the* women, *the* children, and *the* eunuchs, whom he had brought back from Gibeon.

17 And they went and stayed in ᵃGeruth Chimham, which is beside Bethlehem, in order to ᵇproceed into Egypt

18 because of the Chaldeans; for they were ᵃafraid of them, since Ishmael the son of Nethaniah had struck down Gedaliah the son of Ahikam, whom ᵇthe king of Babylon had appointed over the land.

42 Then all the commanders of the forces, ᵃJohanan the son of Kareah, Jezaniah the son of Hoshaiah, and all the people ᵇboth small and great approached

2 and said to Jeremiah the prophet, "Please let our ᵃpetition come before you, and ᵇpray for us to the LORD your God, *that is* for all this remnant; because we are left *but* a ᶜfew out of many, as your own eyes *now* see us,

3 that the LORD your God may tell us the ᵃway in which we should walk and the thing that we should do."

4 Then Jeremiah the prophet said to them, "I have heard *you.* Behold, I am going to ᵃpray to the LORD your God in accordance with your words; and it will come about that the whole message which the ᵇLORD will answer you I will tell you. I will ᶜnot keep back a word from you."

5 Then they said to Jeremiah, "May the ᵃLORD be a true and faithful witness against us, if we do not act in accordance with the whole message with which the LORD your God will send you to us.

6 "Whether *it* is pleasant or unpleasant, we will ᵃlisten to the voice of the LORD our God to whom we are sending you, in order that it may go ᵇwell with us when we listen to the voice of the LORD our God."

7 Now it came about at the ᵃend of ten days that the word of the LORD came to Jeremiah.

8 Then he called for Johanan the son of Kareah, and all the commanders of the forces that were with him, and for all the people both small and great,

9 and said to them, "Thus ᵃsays the LORD the God of Israel,

Cross references (margin)

11 ᵃJer. 40:7, 8, 13-16

12 ᵃGen. 14:14-16; 1 Sam. 30:1-8, 18, 20 ᵇ2 Sam. 2:13

15 ᵃ1 Sam. 30:17; 1 Kin. 20:20; Job 21:30; Prov. 28:17

16 ᵃJer. 42:8; 43:4-7

★17 ᵃ2 Sam. 19:37, 38, 40 ᵇJer. 42:14

18 ᵃIs. 51:12, 13; 57:11; Jer. 42:11, 16; 43:2, 3; Luke 12:4, 5 ᵇJer. 40:5

★ 1-6
1 ᵃJer. 40:8, 13; 41:11, 18 ᵇJer. 6:13; 8:10; 42:8; 44:12; Acts 8:10

2 ᵃJer. 36:7; 37:20 ᵇEx. 8:28; 1 Sam. 7:8; 12:19; 1 Kin. 13:6; Is. 37:4; Jer. 37:3; 42:20; Acts 8:24; James 5:16 ᶜLev. 26:22; Deut. 28:62; Is. 1:9; Lam. 1:1

3 ᵃPs. 86:11; Prov. 3:6; Jer. 6:16; Mic. 4:2

4 ᵃEx. 8:29; 1 Sam. 12:23 ᵇ1 Kin. 22:14; Jer. 23:28 ᶜ1 Sam. 3:17, 18; Ps. 40:10; Acts 20:20

5 ᵃGen. 31:50; Judg. 11:10; Jer. 43:2; Mic. 1:2; Mal. 2:14; 3:5

6 ᵃEx. 24:7; Deut. 5:27; Josh. 24:24 ᵇDeut. 5:29, 33; 6:3; Jer. 7:23

★ 7-22

7 ᵃPs. 27:14; Is. 30:18

9 ᵃ2 Kin. 19:4, 6, 20; 22:15

41:17 *Chimham.* See 2 Sam. 19:37-40. This was part of a grant of land by David. The people thought about going to Egypt because they feared Babylonian reprisals for Gedaliah's murder.

42:1-6 The people inquired of Jeremiah if God would approve their plan to migrate to Egypt.
42:7-22 Jeremiah's warning is clear: stay in Palestine and trust God, who will protect you; or go to Egypt and die.

to whom you sent me to present your petition before Him:

10 'If you will indeed stay in this land, then I will *a*build you up and not tear you down, and I will plant you and not uproot you; for I shall *b*relent concerning the calamity that I have inflicted on you.

11 '*a*Do not be afraid of the king of Babylon, whom you are *now* fearing; do not be afraid of him,' declares the LORD, 'for *b*I am with you to save you and deliver you from his hand.

12 'I will also show you compassion, so that *a*he will have compassion on you and restore you to your own soil.

13 'But if you are going to say, "We will *a*not stay in this land," so as not to listen to the voice of the LORD your God,

14 saying, "No, but we will *a*go to the land of Egypt, where we shall not see war or *b*hear the sound of a trumpet or hunger for bread, and we will stay there";

15 then in that case listen to the word of the LORD, O remnant of Judah. Thus says the LORD of hosts, the God of Israel, "If you really set your mind to enter *a*Egypt, and go in to reside there,

16 then it will come about that the *a*sword, which you are afraid of will overtake you there in the land of Egypt; and the famine, about which you are anxious, will follow closely after you there *in* Egypt; and you will die there.

17 "So all the men who set their mind to go to Egypt to reside there will die by the *a*sword, by famine, and by pestilence; and they will *b*have no survivors or refugees from the calamity that I am going to bring on them." ' "

18 For thus says the LORD of hosts, the God of Israel, "As My *a*anger and wrath have been poured out on the inhabitants of Jerusalem, so My wrath will be poured out on you when you enter Egypt. And you will become a *b*curse, an object of horror, an imprecation, and a reproach; and *c*you will see this place no more."

19 The LORD has spoken to you, O remnant of Judah, "Do not *a*go into Egypt!" You should clearly *b*understand that today I have *c*testified against you.

20 For you have *only* *a*deceived yourselves; for it is you who sent me to the LORD your God, saying, "Pray for us to the LORD our God; and whatever the LORD our God says, tell us so, and we will do it."

21 So, I have *a*told you today, but you have *b*not obeyed the LORD your God, even in whatever He has sent me to *tell* you.

22 Therefore you should now clearly understand that you will *a*die by the sword, by famine, and by pestilence, in the *b*place where you wish to go to reside.

2   *Jeremiah ministers to Jews in Egypt, 43:1-44:30*

43 But it came about, as soon as Jeremiah whom the LORD their God had sent, had *a*finished telling all the people all the words of the LORD their God—that is, all these words—

2 that Azariah the *a*son of Hoshaiah, and Johanan the son of Kareah, and all the arrogant men said to Jeremiah, "You are *b*telling a lie! The LORD our God has not sent you to say, 'You are not to enter Egypt to reside there';

3 but *a*Baruch the son of Neriah is inciting you against us to give us over into the hand of the Chaldeans, so they may put us to death or exile us to Babylon."

4 So *a*Johanan the son of Kareah and all the commanders of the forces, and all the people, *b*did not obey the voice of the LORD, so as to *c*stay in the land of Judah.

5 But Johanan the son of Kareah and all the commanders of the forces took the *a*entire remnant of Judah who had returned from all the nations to which they had been driven away, in order to reside in the land of Judah—

6 the men, the women, the children, the *a*king's daughters

10 *a*Jer. 24:6; 31:28; 33:7; Ezek. 36:36 *b*Jer. 18:7, 8; Hos. 11:8; Joel 2:13; Amos 7:3, 6; Jon. 3:10; 4:2

11 *a*Jer. 1:8; 27:12, 17; 41:18 *b*Num. 14:9; 2 Chr. 32:7, 8; Ps. 46:7, 11; 118:6; Is. 8:9, 10; 43:2, 5; Jer. 1:19; 15:20; Rom. 8:31

12 *a*Neh. 1:11; Ps. 106:46; Prov. 16:7

13 *a*Ex. 5:2; Jer. 44:16

14 *a*Is. 31:1; Jer. 41:17 *b*Ex. 16:3; Num. 11:4; Jer. 4:19, 21

15 *a*Deut. 17:16; Jer. 42:17; 44:12-14

16 *a*Jer. 44:13, 27; Ezek. 11:8; Amos 9:1-4

17 *a*Jer. 24:10; 38:2; 42:22; 44:13 *b*Jer. 44:14, 28

18 *a*2 Chr. 36:16-19; Jer. 7:20; 33:5; 39:1-9 *b*Deut. 29:21; Is. 65:15; Jer. 18:16; 24:9; 29:18; 44:12 *c*Jer. 22:10, 27

19 *a*Deut. 17:16; Is. 30:1-7 *b*Ezek. 2:5 *c*Neh. 9:26, 29, 30

20 *a*Jer. 43:2; Ezek. 14:3

21 *a*Deut. 11:26; Jer. 43:1; Ezek. 2:7; Zech. 7:11; Acts 20:26, 27 *b*Jer. 43:4

22 *a*Jer. 43:11; Ezek. 6:11 *b*Hos. 9:6

1 *a*Jer. 26:8; 51:63

2 *a*Jer. 42:1 *b*2 Chr. 36:13; Is. 7:9; Jer. 5:12, 13; 42:5

3 *a*Jer. 36:4, 10, 26, 32; 43:6; 45:1-3

4 *a*Jer. 42:8 *b*2 Chr. 25:16; Jer. 42:5, 6; 44:5 *c*Ps. 37:3; Jer. 42:10-12

5 *a*Jer. 40:11

6 *a*Jer. 41:10 *b*Jer. 39:10; 40:7 *c*Eccl. 9:1, 2; Lam. 3:1

and *b*every person that Nebuzaradan the captain of the bodyguard had left with Gedaliah the son of Ahikam and grandson of Shaphan, together with *c*Jeremiah the prophet and Baruch the son of Neriah—

7 and they entered the land of Egypt (for they did not obey the voice of the LORD) and went in as far as *a*Tahpanhes.

8 Then the word of the LORD came to Jeremiah in *a*Tahpanhes, saying,

9 "Take *some* large stones in your hands and hide them in the mortar in the brick *terrace* which is at the entrance of Pharaoh's palace in Tahpanhes, in the sight of some *of the* Jews;

10 and say to them, 'Thus says the LORD of hosts, the God of Israel, "Behold, I am going to send and get *a*Nebuchadnezzar the king of Babylon, *b*My servant, and I am going to set his throne *right* over these stones that I have hidden; and he will spread his *c*canopy over them.

11 "He will also come and *a*strike the land of Egypt; those who are *meant* for death *will be given over* to death, and those for captivity to captivity, and *b*those for the sword to the sword.

12 "And I shall set fire to the temples of the *a*gods of Egypt, and he will burn them and take them captive. So he will *b*wrap himself with the land of Egypt as a shepherd wraps himself with his garment, and he will depart from there safely.

13 "He will also shatter the obelisks of Heliopolis, which is in the land of Egypt; and the temples of the gods of Egypt he will burn with fire." ' "

44 The word that came to Jeremiah for all the Jews living in the land of Egypt, those who were living in *a*Migdol, *b*Tahpanhes, *c*Memphis, and the land of *d*Pathros, saying,

2 "Thus says the LORD of hosts, the God of Israel, 'You yourselves have seen all the calamity that I have brought on Jerusalem and all the cities of Judah; and behold, this day they are in *a*ruins and no one lives in them,

3 *a*because of their wickedness which they committed so as to *b*provoke Me to anger by continuing to *c*burn sacrifices *and* to *d*serve other gods whom they had not known, *neither* they, you, nor your fathers.

4 'Yet I *a*sent you all My servants the prophets, again and again, saying, "Oh, do not do this *b*abominable thing which I hate."

5 'But *a*they did not listen or incline their ears to turn from their wickedness, so as not to burn sacrifices to other gods.

6 'Therefore My *a*wrath and My anger were poured out and burned in the *b*cities of Judah and in the streets of Jerusalem, so they have become a ruin and a *c*desolation as it is this day.

7 'Now then thus says the LORD God of hosts, the God of Israel, "Why are you *a*doing great harm to yourselves, so as to *b*cut off from you man and woman, child and infant, from among Judah, leaving yourselves without remnant,

8 *a*provoking Me to anger with the works of your hands, *b*burning sacrifices to other gods in the land of Egypt, where you

---

Marginal references:

★ 7 *a*Jer. 2:16; 44:1

8 *a*Jer. 2:16; 44:1; 46:14; Ezek. 30:18

★ 9

10 *a*Jer. 25:9, 11 *b*Is. 44:28; 45:1; Jer. 25:9; 27:6 *c*Ps. 18:11; 27:5; 31:20

★11 *a*Is. 19:1-25; Jer. 25:15-19; 44:13; 46:1, 2, 13-26; Ezek. 29:19, 20 *b*Jer. 15:2

12 *a*Ex. 12:12; Is. 19:1; Jer. 46:25; Ezek. 30:13 *b*Ps. 104:2; 109:18, 19; Is. 49:18

★13

★ 1-14
1 *a*Ex. 14:2; Jer. 46:14 *b*Jer. 43:7; Ezek. 30:18 *c*Is. 19:13; Jer. 2:16; 46:14; Ezek. 30:13, 16; Hos. 9:6 *d*Is. 11:11; Ezek. 29:14; 30:14

2 *a*Is. 6:11; Jer. 4:7; 9:11; 34:22; Mic. 3:12

3 *a*Neh. 9:33; Jer. 2:17-19; 44:23; Ezek. 8:17, 18; Dan. 9:5 *b*Is. 3:8; Jer. 7:19; 32:30-32; 44:8 *c*Jer. 19:4 *d*Deut. 13:6; 29:26; 32:17
4 *a*Jer. 7:13, 25; 25:4; 26:5; 29:19; 35:15; Zech. 7:7 *b*Jer. 16:18; 32:34, 35; Ezek. 8:10
5 *a*Jer. 11:8, 10; 13:10

6 *a*Is. 51:17-20; Jer. 42:18; Ezek. 8:18; Jer. 7:17, 34 *c*Jer. 4:27; 34:22

7 *a*Num. 16:38; Jer. 26:19; Ezek. 33:11; Hab. 2:10 *b*Jer. 3:24; 9:21; 51:22

8 *a*2 Kin. 17:15-17; Jer. 25:6, 7; 44:3; 1 Cor. 10:21, 22 *b*Jer. 7:9; 11:12, 17; 44:3; Hos. 4:13; Hab. 1:16 *c*1 Kin. 9:7, 8; 2 Chr. 7:20; Jer. 42:18

43:7 *Tahpanhes.* In NE. Egypt. See 2:16.
43:9 *brick terrace.* Such a paved area has been found in front of the entrance to the royal dwelling.
43:11 Nebuchadnezzar did invade Egypt in 568/7.
43:13 *Heliopolis.* Heb., *Beth-shemesh;* lit., House of the Sun; an ancient city near Cairo. *obelisks.* One such obelisk from Heliopolis is

in Central Park in New York City; another is on the bank of the Thames River in London.
44:1-14 This last message of Jeremiah (to the Jews in Egypt) was the same he had preached throughout his ministry: God must punish their sins of idolatry. *Migdol, Tahpanhes* and *Memphis* were in Lower (northern) Egypt, while *Pathros* was the general designation for Upper (southern) Egypt.

are entering to reside, so that you might be cut off and become a ᶜcurse and a reproach among all the nations of the earth?

9 "Have you forgotten the ᵃwickedness of your fathers, the wickedness of the kings of Judah, and the wickedness of their wives, your own wickedness, and the wickedness of your wives, which they committed in the land of Judah and in the streets of Jerusalem?

10 "But they ᵃhave not become contrite even to this day, nor have they feared nor ᵇwalked in My law or My statutes, which I have set before you and before your fathers."'

11 "Therefore thus says the LORD of hosts, the God of Israel, 'Behold, I am going to ᵃset My face against you for woe, even to cut off all Judah.

12 'And I will ᵃtake away the remnant of Judah who have set their mind on entering the land of Egypt to reside there, and they will all ᵇmeet their end in the land of Egypt; they will fall by the sword *and* meet their end by famine. Both small and great will die by the sword and famine; and they will become a ᶜcurse, an object of horror, an imprecation and a reproach.

13 'And I will ᵃpunish those who live in the land of Egypt, as I have punished Jerusalem, with the sword, with famine, and with pestilence.

14 'So there will be ᵃno refugees or survivors for the remnant of Judah who have entered the land of Egypt to reside there and then to return to the land of Judah, to which they are ᵇlonging to return and live; for none will ᶜreturn except *a few* refugees.'"

★15-19

15 Then ᵃall the men who were aware that their wives were burning sacrifices to other gods, along with all the women who were standing by, *as* a large as-

sembly, including all the people who were living in Pathros in the land of Egypt, responded to Jeremiah, saying,

16 "As for the ᵃmessage that you have spoken to us in the name of the LORD, ᵇwe are not going to listen to you!

17 "But rather we will certainly ᵃcarry out every word that has proceeded from our mouths, by burning sacrifices to the ᵇqueen of heaven and pouring out libations to her, just as ᶜwe ourselves, our forefathers, our kings and our princes did in the cities of Judah and in the streets of Jerusalem; for *then* we had ᵈplenty of food, and were well off, and saw no misfortune.

18 "But since we stopped burning sacrifices to the queen of heaven and pouring out libations to her, we have ᵃlacked everything and have met our end by the sword and by famine."

19 "And," *said the women*, "when we were ᵃburning sacrifices to the queen of heaven, and were pouring out libations to her, was it ᵇwithout our husbands that we made for her *sacrificial* cakes in her image and poured out libations to her?"

20 Then Jeremiah said to all the people, to the men and women—even to all the people who were giving him *such* an answer—saying,

21 "As for the ᵃsmoking sacrifices that you burned in the cities of Judah and in the ᵇstreets of Jerusalem, you and your forefathers, your kings and your princes, and the people of the land, did not the LORD ᶜremember them, and did not *all this* come into His mind?

22 "So the LORD was ᵃno longer able to endure *it*, ᵇbecause of the evil of your deeds, because of the abominations which you have committed; thus your land has

9 ᵃJer. 7:9, 10, 17, 18; 44:17, 21

10 ᵃJer. 6:15; 8:12 ᵇJer. 26:4; 32:23; 44:23

11 ᵃLev. 17:10; 20:5, 6; 26:17; Jer. 21:10; Amos 9:4

12 ᵃJer. 42:15-18, 22 ᵇIs. 1:28; Jer. 16:4; 44:7 ᶜIs. 65:15; Jer. 18:16; 24:9; 26:6; 29:18; 42:18; Zech. 8:13

13 ᵃJer. 11:22; 44:27, 28

14 ᵃJer. 22:10; 44:27 ᵇJer. 22:26, 27 ᶜIs. 4:2; 10:20; Jer. 44:28; Rom. 9:27

15 ᵃProv. 11:21; Is. 1:5; Jer. 5:1-5

16 ᵃJer. 43:2 ᵇProv. 1:24-27; Jer. 11:8, 10; 13:10

17 ᵃNum. 30:12; Deut. 23:23 ᵇ2 Kin. 17:16; Jer. 7:18 ᶜNeh. 9:34; Jer. 32:32; 44:21 ᵈEx. 16:3; Hos. 2:5-9; Phil. 3:19

18 ᵃNum. 11:5, 6; Jer. 40:12; Mal. 3:13-15

19 ᵃJer. 7:18 ᵇNum. 30:6, 7; Jer. 44:15

21 ᵃEzek. 8:10, 11 ᵇJer. 11:13; 44:9, 17 ᶜPs. 79:8; Is. 64:9; Jer. 14:10; Hos. 7:2; Amos 8:7

22 ᵃIs. 7:13; 43:24; Mal. 2:17 ᵇJer. 4:4; 21:12; 30:14 ᶜGen. 19:13; Ps. 107:33, 34; Jer. 25:11, 18, 38; 29:18; 42:18; 44:12

44:15-19 The scornful reply of the people shows that they had not learned a lesson from the destruction of Jerusalem. *queen of heaven* (v.

17). See note on 7:18. *cakes* (v. 19). Probably shaped in the form of the goddess.

become a ᶜruin, an object of horror and a curse, without an inhabitant, as *it is* this day.

23 "Because you have burned sacrifices and have sinned against the LORD and ᵃnot obeyed the voice of the LORD or ᵇwalked in His law, His statutes or His testimonies, therefore this ᶜcalamity has befallen you, as *it has* this day."

24 Then Jeremiah said to all the people, including all the women, "ᵃHear the word of the LORD, all Judah who are ᵇin the land of Egypt,

25 thus says the LORD of hosts, the God of Israel, as follows: 'As for you and your wives, you have spoken with your mouths and fulfilled *it* with your hands, saying, "We will ᵃcertainly perform our vows that we have vowed, to burn sacrifices to the queen of heaven and pour out libations to her." ᵇGo ahead and confirm your vows, and certainly perform your vows!'

26 "Nevertheless hear the word of the LORD, all Judah who are living in the land of Egypt, 'Behold, I have ᵃsworn by My great name,' says the LORD, 'ᵇnever shall My name be invoked again by the mouth of any man of Judah in all the land of Egypt, saying, "ᶜAs the Lord GOD lives."

27 'Behold, I am watching over them ᵃfor harm and not for good, and ᵇall the men of Judah who are in the land of Egypt will meet their end by the sword and by famine until they are completely gone.

28 'ᵃAnd those who escape the sword will return out of the land of Egypt to the land of Judah ᵇfew in number. Then all the remnant of Judah who have gone to the land of Egypt to reside there will

know ᶜwhose word will stand, Mine or theirs.

29 'And this will be the ᵃsign to you,' declares the LORD, 'that I am going to punish you in this place, so that you may know that ᵇMy words will surely stand against you for harm.'

30 "Thus says the LORD, 'Behold, I am going to give over ᵃPharaoh Hophra king of Egypt to the hand of his enemies, just as I gave over ᵇZedekiah king of Judah to the hand of Nebuchadnezzar king of Babylon, *who was* his enemy and was seeking his life.' "

3 *Jeremiah ministers to Baruch,*
45:1–5

45 *This is* the message which Jeremiah the prophet spoke to ᵃBaruch the son of Neriah, when he had ᵇwritten down these words in a book at Jeremiah's dictation, in the ᶜfourth year of Jehoiakim the son of Josiah, king of Judah, saying:

2 "Thus says the LORD the God of Israel to you, O Baruch:

3 'You said, "Ah, woe is me! For the LORD has added sorrow to my pain; I am ᵃweary with my groaning and have found no rest." '

4 "Thus you are to say to him, 'Thus says the LORD, "Behold, ᵃwhat I have built I am about to tear down, and what I have planted I am about to uproot, that is, the whole land."

5 'But you, are you ᵃseeking great things for yourself? Do not seek *them;* for behold, I am going to ᵇbring disaster on all flesh,' declares the LORD, 'but I will ᶜgive your life to you as booty in all the places where you may go.' "

---

23 ᵃJer. 7:13-15; 40:3 ᵇJer. 44:10; Ps. 119:136, 150 ᶜ1 Kin. 9:9; Neh. 13:18; Jer. 44:2; Dan. 9:11, 12

24 ᵃJer. 42:15; 44:16 ᵇJer. 43:7; 44:15, 26

25 ᵃJer. 44:17; Matt. 14:9; Acts 23:12 ᵇEzek. 20:39

26 ᵃGen. 22:16; Deut. 32:40, 41; Jer. 22:5; Amos 6:8; Heb. 6:13 ᵇPs. 50:16; Ezek. 20:39 ᶜIs. 48:1, 2; Jer. 5:2

27 ᵃJer. 1:10; 31:28; 39:16 ᵇ2 Kin. 21:14; Jer. 44:14

★**28** ᵃJer. 44:14 ᵇIs. 10:19; 27:12, 13 ᶜPs. 33:11; Is. 14:27; 46:10, 11; Zech. 1:6

29 ᵃIs. 7:11, 14; 8:18; Jer. 44:30; Matt. 24:15, 16, 32 ᵇProv. 19:21; Is. 40:8

★**30** ᵃJer. 43:9-13; 46:25; Ezek. 29:3; 30:21 ᵇ2 Kin. 25:4-7; Jer. 34:21; 39:5-7

★ **1** ᵃJer. 32:12, 16; 43:3, 6 ᵇJer. 36:4, 18, 32 ᶜ2 Kin. 24:1; 2 Chr. 36:5-7; Jer. 25:1; 36:1; 46:2; Dan. 1:1

3 ᵃPs. 6:6; 69:3; 2 Cor. 4:1, 16; Gal. 6:9

4 ᵃIs. 5:5; Jer. 1:10; 11:17; 18:7-10; 31:28

★ **5** ᵃ1 Kin. 3:9, 11; 2 Kin. 5:26; Matt. 6:25, 32; Rom. 12:16 ᵇIs. 66:16; Jer. 25:31 ᶜJer. 21:9; 38:2; 39:18

44:28 *Only a few in number* would return to Palestine from Egypt (cf. v. 14). The future for the nation lay with those who went to Babylon and returned.

44:30 *Pharaoh Hophra.* See note on 37:5. He was slain in a revolt led by Ahmose in 569.

45:1 *fourth year of Jehoiakim.* I.e., 605. This chapter connects with the events of chapter 36.

45:5 Rather than pity himself (v. 3), Baruch is told to consider how much heartache Judah's sins brought to God (v. 4) and not to seek *great things* for himself (v. 5). *as booty.* I.e., his reward would be that his life would be spared.

III PROPHECIES CONCERNING THE NATIONS, 46:1–51:64

A Prophecies against Egypt, 46:1–28

^{1 aJer. 1:10; 25:15–38}

46 That which came as the word of the LORD to Jeremiah the prophet ^aconcerning the nations.

^{★2 aJer. 46:14; Ezek. chs. 29-32 b2 Kin. 18:21; 23:29, 33-35; Jer. 25:19 c2 Chr. 35:20; Is. 10:9 dJer. 45:1}

2 To ^aEgypt, concerning the army of ^bPharaoh Neco king of Egypt, which was by the Euphrates River at ^cCarchemish, which Nebuchadnezzar king of Babylon defeated in the ^dfourth year of Jehoiakim the son of Josiah, king of Judah:

^{3 aIs. 21:5; Jer. 51:11; Joel 3:9; Nah. 2:1; 3:14}

3 "^aLine up the shield and buckler,
And draw near for the battle!

^{★4 aEzek. 21:9-11 b1 Sam. 17:5, 38; 2 Chr. 26:14; Neh. 4:16; Jer. 51:3}

4 "Harness the horses,
And mount the steeds,
And take your stand with helmets on!
^aPolish the spears,
Put on the ^bscale-armor!

^{5 aIs. 42:17; Jer. 46:21 bIs. 5:25; Ezek. 39:18 cJer. 6:25; 20:3; 49:29}

5 "Why have I seen it?
They are terrified,
They are ^adrawing back,
And their ^bmighty men are defeated
And have taken refuge in flight,
Without facing back;
^cTerror is on every side!"
Declares the LORD.

^{6 aIs. 30:16 bJer. 46:12, 16; Dan. 11:19}

6 Let not the ^aswift man flee,
Nor the mighty man escape;
In the north beside the river Euphrates
They have ^bstumbled and fallen.

^{7 aJer. 47:2}

7 Who is this that ^arises like the Nile,
Like the rivers whose waters surge about?

8 Egypt rises like the Nile,
Even like the rivers whose waters surge about;
And He has said, "I will ^arise and cover that land;
I will surely ^bdestroy the city and its inhabitants."

^{8 aIs. 37:24 bIs. 10:13}

9 Go up, you horses, and ^adrive madly, you chariots,
That the mighty men may march forward:
Ethiopia and ^bPut, that handle the shield,
And the ^cLydians, that handle and bend the bow.

^{★9 aJer. 47:3; Nah. 2:4 bNah. 3:9 cIs. 66:19}

10 For ^athat day belongs to the Lord GOD of hosts,
A day of ^bvengeance, so as to avenge Himself on His foes;
And the ^csword will devour and be satiated
And drink its fill of their blood;
For there will be a ^dslaughter for the Lord GOD of hosts,
In the land of the north by the river Euphrates.

^{★10 aJoel 1:15 bJer. 50:15, 18 cDeut. 32:42; Is. 31:8; Jer. 12:12 dIs. 34:6; Zeph. 1:7}

11 Go ^aup to Gilead and obtain balm,
^bO virgin daughter of Egypt!
In vain have you multiplied remedies;
There is ^cno healing for you.

^{★11 aJer. 8:22 bIs. 47:1; Jer. 31:4, 21 cJer. 30:13; Mic. 1:9; Nah. 3:19}

12 The nations have heard of your ^ashame,
And the earth is full of your ^bcry of distress;
For one ^cwarrior has stumbled over another,
And both of them have fallen down together.

^{12 aJer. 2:36; Nah. 3:8-10 bJer. 14:2 cIs. 19:2}

46:2 The battle at *Carchemish* in 605, in which Egypt was defeated, tipped the balance of power in favor of Babylon.
46:4 *scale-armor.* Coat of armor.
46:9 Men from *Ethiopia* (Upper Nile region) and *Put* (N. coast of Africa), and *Lydians* (inhabitants of Asia Minor) were employed as mercenaries by the Egyptians.

46:10 Here the *day of the Lord* is not eschatological (as also in Isa. 13:6), but indicates God's intervention in judging Egypt.
46:11 *balm.* See note on Jer. 8:22. *remedies.* Medical skills developed in Egypt long before this time were unable to heal the wounds of defeat.

13 *This is* the message which the LORD spoke to Jeremiah the prophet about the ªcoming of Nebuchadnezzar king of Babylon to ᵇsmite the land of Egypt:

14 "Declare in Egypt and proclaim in ªMigdol,
Proclaim also in Memphis and ᵇTahpanhes;
Say, 'Take your stand and get yourself ready,
For the ᶜsword has devoured those around you.'

15 "Why have your ªmighty ones become prostrate?
They do not stand because the LORD has ᵇthrust them down.

16 "They have repeatedly ªstumbled;
Indeed, they have fallen one against another.
Then they said, 'Get up! And ᵇlet us go back
To our own people and our native land
Away from the ᶜsword of the oppressor.'

17 "They cried there, 'Pharaoh king of Egypt *is but* ªa big noise;
He has let the appointed time pass by!'

18 "As I live," declares the ªKing
Whose name is the LORD of hosts,
"Surely one shall come *who looms up* like ᵇTabor among the mountains,
Or like ᶜCarmel by the sea.

19 "Make your baggage ready for ªexile,
O ᵇdaughter dwelling in Egypt,
For ᶜMemphis will become a desolation;
It will even be burned down *and* bereft of inhabitants.

20 "Egypt is a pretty ªheifer,
But a horsefly is coming ᵇfrom the north—it is coming!

21 "Also her ªmercenaries in her midst
Are like fattened ᵇcalves,
For even they too have turned back *and* have fled away together;
They did not stand *their* ground.
For the day of their calamity has come upon them,
The time of their ᶜpunishment.

22 "Its sound moves along like a serpent;
For they move on like an army
And come to her as woodcutters with axes.

23 "They have cut down her ªforest," declares the LORD;
"Surely it will no *more* be found,
Even though they are *now* more numerous than ᵇlocusts
And are without number.

24 "The daughter of Egypt has been put to shame,
Given over to the power of the ªpeople of the north."

25 The LORD of hosts, the God of Israel, says, "Behold, I am going to punish Amon of ªThebes, and ᵇPharaoh, and Egypt along with her ᶜgods and her kings, even Pharaoh and those who ᵈtrust in him.

26 "And I shall give them over to the power of those who are ªseeking their lives, even into the hand of Nebuchadnezzar king of Babylon and into the hand of his officers. ᵇAfterwards, however, it

---

46:14 *Migdol . . . Memphis . . . Tahpanhes.* See note on 44:1.
46:18 As *Tabor* and *Carmel* dominate northern Palestine, so Nebuchadnezzar would dominate Egypt.
46:25 *Amon of Thebes.* The chief deity of Upper Egypt.

13 ªJer. 43:10-13 ᵇIs. 19:1
★14 ªJer. 44:1 ᵇJer. 43:8 ᶜIs. 1:20; Jer. 2:30; 46:10; Nah. 2:13
15 ªIs. 66:15, 16; Jer. 46:5 ᵇPs. 18:14; 39; 68:1, 2
16 ªLev. 26:36, 37; Jer. 46:6 ᵇJer. 51:9 ᶜJer. 50:16
17 ªEx. 15:9, 10; 1 Kin. 20:10, 11; Is. 19:11-16
★18 ªJer. 48:15; Mal. 1:14 ᵇJosh. 19:22; Judg. 4:6; Ps. 89:12 ᶜJosh. 12:22; 1 Kin. 18:42
19 ªIs. 20:4 ᵇJer. 48:18 ᶜJer. 46:14; Ezek. 30:13
20 ªHos. 10:11 ᵇJer. 1:14; 47:2
21 ª2 Sam. 10:6; 2 Kin. 7:6; Jer. 46:5 ᵇIs. 34:7 ᶜJer. 48:44; Hos. 9:7; Obad. 13; Mic. 7:4
23 ªJer. 21:14 ᵇJudg. 6:5; 7:12; Joel 2:25
24 ªJer. 1:15
★25 ªEzek. 30:14-16; Nah. 3:8 ᵇJer. 44:30 ᶜEx. 12:12; Jer. 43:12, 13; Ezek. 30:13; Zeph. 2:11 ᵈIs. 20:5
26 ªJer. 44:30; Ezek. 32:11 ᵇEzek. 29:8-14

will be inhabited as in the days of old," declares the LORD.

27 "But as for you, O Jacob My servant, ᵃdo not fear,
Nor be dismayed, O Israel!
For, see, I am going to ᵇsave you from afar,
And your descendants from the land of their captivity;
And Jacob shall return and be ᶜundisturbed
And secure, with no one making *him* tremble.

28 "O Jacob My servant, do not fear," declares the LORD,
"For ᵃI am with you.
For I shall make a full end of all the nations
Where I have driven you,
Yet I shall ᵇnot make a full end of you;
But I shall ᶜcorrect you properly
And by no means leave you unpunished."

B   Prophecies against the Philistines, 47:1-7

47 That which came as the word of the LORD to Jeremiah the prophet concerning the ᵃPhilistines, before Pharaoh conquered ᵇGaza.

2 Thus says the LORD:
"Behold, waters are going to rise from ᵃthe north
And become an overflowing torrent,
And ᵇoverflow the land and all its fulness,
The city and those who live in it;
And the men will ᶜcry out,
And every inhabitant of the land will wail.

3 "Because of the noise of the ᵃgalloping hoofs of his stallions,
The tumult of his chariots, *and* the rumbling of his wheels,
The fathers have not turned back for *their* children,
Because of the limpness of *their* hands,

4 On account of the day that is coming
To ᵃdestroy all the Philistines,
To cut off from ᵇTyre and Sidon
Every ally that is left;
For the LORD is going to destroy the Philistines,
The remnant of the coastland of ᶜCaphtor.

5 "ᵃBaldness has come upon Gaza;
ᵇAshkelon has been ruined.
O remnant of their valley,
How long will you ᶜgash yourself?

6 "Ah, ᵃsword of the LORD,
How long will you not be quiet?
Withdraw into your sheath;
Be at rest and stay still.

7 "How can it be quiet,
When the LORD has ᵃgiven it an order?
Against Ashkelon and against the seacoast—
There He has ᵇassigned it."

C   Prophecies against Moab, 48:1-47

48 Concerning ᵃMoab.
Thus says the LORD of hosts, the God of Israel,

Margin cross-references

27 ᵃIs. 41:13, 14; Jer. 30:10, 11 ᵇIs. 11:11; Jer. 23:3, 4; 29:14; Mic. 7:12 ᶜJer. 23:6; 50:19

28 ᵃPs. 46:7, 11; Is. 8:10; 43:2; Jer. 1:19 ᵇJer. 4:27; Amos 9:8, 9 ᶜJer. 10:24; Hab. 3:2

★ 1 ᵃJer. 25:20; Zech. 9:6 ᵇGen. 10:19; 1 Kin. 4:24; Amos 25:20; Zeph. 1:6; Zeph. 2:4

★ 2 ᵃIs. 14:31; Jer. 1:14; 6:22; 46:20, 24 ᵇIs. 8:7, 8 ᶜIs. 15:2-5; Jer. 46:12

3 ᵃJudg. 5:22; Jer. 8:16; Nah. 3:2

★ 4 ᵃIs. 14:31 ᵇIs. 23:5; Jer. 25:22; Joel 3:4; Amos 1:9, 10; Zech. 9:2-4 ᶜGen. 10:14; Deut. 2:23; Amos 9:7

★ 5 ᵃJer. 48:37; Mic. 1:16 ᵇJudg. 1:18; Jer. 25:20; Amos 2:4, 7; Zeph. 2:4, 7; Zech. 9:5 ᶜJer. 16:6; 41:5

6 ᵃJudg. 7:20; Jer. 12:12; Ezek. 21:3-5

7 ᵃIs. 10:6; Ezek. 14:17 ᵇMic. 6:9

★ 1 ᵃIs. 15:1; Ezek. 25:9 ᵇNum. 32:3, 38; Jer. 48:22 ᶜNum. 32:37; Jer. 48:23; Ezek. 25:9

47:1 *before Pharaoh conquered Gaza.* Pharaoh Necho's campaign in 609 (2 Kings 23:29ff.). Other oracles against the Philistines are in Isa. 14:28-31; Ezek. 25:15-17; Amos 1:6-8; Zeph. 2:4-7.
47:2 *waters are going to rise from the north.* A reference to the Babylonian invasion.
47:4 *Tyre and Sidon.* Though Phoenician cities,

they were apparently allies of the Philistines. *Caphtor.* Crete, the original home of the Philistines (Amos 9:7).
47:5 *Baldness.* Either a sign of mourning or a symbol indicating the complete razing of Gaza.
48:1 *Moab.* See note on Amos 2:1. Other oracles against Moab are in Isa. 15-16; Jer. 9:26; 25:21;

"Woe to ᵇNebo, for it has
been destroyed;
ᶜKiriathaim has been put
to shame, it has been
captured;
The lofty stronghold has
been put to shame
and shattered.

2 "There is praise for Moab
no longer;
In ᵃHeshbon they have de-
vised calamity against
her:
'Come and let us cut her off
from *being* a nation!'
You too, Madmen, will be
silenced;
The sword will follow after
you.

3 "The sound of an outcry
from ᵃHoronaim,
'Devastation and great destruction!'

4 "Moab is broken,
Her little ones have
sounded out a cry *of
distress.*

5 "For by the ascent of ᵃLu-
hith
They will ascend with continual weeping;
For at the descent of Horonaim
They have heard the an-
guished cry of de-
struction.

6 "ᵃFlee, save your lives,
That you may be like a juniper in the wilder-
ness.

7 "For because of your ᵃtrust
in your own achieve-
ments and treasures,
Even you yourself will be
captured;
And ᵇChemosh will go off
into exile
Together with his priests
and his princes.

8 "And a destroyer will come
to every city,
So that no city will escape;
The valley also will be
ruined,
And the ᵃplateau will be
destroyed,
As the LORD has said.

9 "Give ᵃwings to Moab,
For she will flee away;
And her cities will become
a ᵇdesolation,
Without inhabitants in
them.

10 "ᵃCursed be the one who
does the LORD's work
ᵇnegligently,
And cursed be the one
who restrains his
ᶜsword from blood.

11 "Moab has been ᵃat ease
since his youth;
He has also been ᵇundis-
turbed on his lees,
Neither has he been ᶜemp-
tied from vessel to
vessel,
Nor has he gone into exile.
Therefore he retains his
flavor,
And his aroma has not
changed.

12 "Therefore behold, the days
are coming," declares the LORD,
"when I shall send to him those
who tip *vessels,* and they will tip
him over, and they will empty his
vessels and shatter his jars.

13 "And Moab will be
ᵃashamed of ᵇChemosh, as the
house of Israel was ashamed of
ᶜBethel, their confidence.

14 "How can you say, 'We are
ᵃmighty warriors,
And men valiant for bat-
tle'?

15 "Moab has been destroyed,
and men have gone
up to his cities;

Cross references (margin)

2 ᵃNum. 21:25; Jer. 48:34, 45; 49:3

3 ᵃIs. 15:5; Jer. 48:5, 34

5 ᵃIs. 15:5

6 ᵃJer. 51:6

★ 7 ᵃPs. 52:7; Is. 59:4; Jer. 9:23 ᵇNum. 21:29; 1 Kin. 11:33; Jer. 48:13, 46

8 ᵃJosh. 13:9, 17, 21

9 ᵃPs. 11:1; Is. 16:2; Jer. 48:28 ᵇJer. 44:22

10 ᵃJer. 11:3 ᵇ1 Kin. 20:39, 40, 42; 2 Kin. 13:19 ᶜJer. 47:6, 7

★11 ᵃJer. 22:21; Ezek. 16:49; Zech. 1:15 ᵇZeph. 1:12 ᶜNah. 2:2

13 ᵃIs. 45:16; Jer. 48:39 ᵇJudg. 11:24 ᶜ1 Kin. 12:29; Hos. 8:5, 6

14 ᵃPs. 33:16; Is. 10:13-16

15 ᵃIs. 40:30, 31; Jer. 50:27 ᵇJer. 46:18; 51:57; Mal. 1:14

27:3; Ezek. 25:8-11; Zeph. 2:8-11. Concerning the relationship between Moab and Israel see Num. 25:1-3; Judg. 3:12-30; 1 Sam. 14:47; 2 Sam. 8:2, 12. The background of the chapter was apparently the attacks (in 602) against Judah by bands of Moabites under Babylonian orders (2 Kings 24:2).

48:7 *Chemosh.* The chief Moabite deity (Num. 21:29; 2 Kings 23:13).
48:11 *undisturbed on his lees.* Like wine that had been left undisturbed (instead of being poured from flask to flask), the Moabites had not yet known exile.

His choicest ^ayoung men
have also gone down
to the slaughter,"
Declares the ^bKing, whose
name is the Lᴏʀᴅ of
hosts.

16 "The disaster of Moab will
^asoon come,
And his calamity has
swiftly hastened.

17 "Mourn for him, all you
who *live* around him,
Even all of you who know
his name;
Say, 'How has the mighty
^ascepter been broken,
A staff of splendor!'

18 "^aCome down from your
glory
And sit on the parched
ground,
O ^bdaughter dwelling in
^cDibon,
For the destroyer of Moab
has come up against
you,
He has ruined your strongholds.

19 "Stand by the road and
keep watch,
O inhabitant of ^aAroer;
^bAsk him who flees and
her who escapes
And say, 'What has hap-
pened?'

20 "Moab has been put to
shame, for it has been
shattered.
Wail and cry out;
Declare by the ^aArnon
That Moab has been de-
stroyed.

21 "Judgment has also come
upon the plain, upon Holon, ^aJah-
zah, and against ^bMephaath,
22 against Dibon, Nebo, and
Beth-diblathaim,
23 against Kiriathaim, Beth-
gamul, and ^aBeth-meon,
24 against ^aKerioth, Bozrah,
and all the cities of the land of
Moab, far and near.

25 "The ^ahorn of Moab has
been cut off, and his ^barm broken," declares the Lᴏʀᴅ.
26 "^aMake him drunk, for he
has become ^barrogant toward the
Lᴏʀᴅ; so Moab will wallow in his
vomit, and he also will become a
laughingstock.
27 "Now was not Israel a
^alaughingstock to you? Or was he
^bcaught among thieves? For each
time you speak about him you
^cshake *your head in scorn*.

28 "Leave the cities and dwell
among the ^acrags,
O inhabitants of Moab,
And be like a ^bdove that
nests
Beyond the mouth of the
chasm.

29 "^aWe have heard of the
pride of Moab—he *is*
very proud—
Of his haughtiness, his
^bpride, his arrogance
and his self-exalta-
tion.

30 "I know his ^afury," declares
the Lᴏʀᴅ,
"But it is futile;
His idle boasts have ac-
complished nothing.

31 "Therefore I shall ^awail for
Moab,
Even for all Moab shall I
cry out;
I will moan for the men of
^bKir-heres.

32 "More than the ^aweeping
for ^bJazer
I shall weep for you, O
vine of Sibmah!
Your tendrils stretched
across the sea,
They reached to the sea of
Jazer;
Upon your summer fruits
and your grape har-
vest
The destroyer has fallen.

33 "So ^agladness and joy are
taken away

Cross references (left margin):

16 ^aIs. 13:22

17 ^aIs. 9:4;
14:5

★18 ^aIs.
47:1 ^bJer.
46:19 ^cNum.
21:30; Josh.
13:9, 17; Is.
15:2; Jer.
48:22

19 ^aDeut.
2:36; Josh.
12:2 ^b1 Sam.
4:13, 14, 16

20 ^aNum.
21:13

21 ^aNum.
21:23; Is.
15:4; Jer.
48:34 ^bJosh.
13:18

23 ^aJosh.
13:17

24 ^aJer.
48:41; Amos
2:2

Cross references (right margin):

★25 ^aPs.
75:10; Zech.
1:19-21
^bJob 22:9;
Ps. 10:15

★26 ^aJer.
25:15 ^bEx.
5:2; Jer.
48:42; Dan.
5:23

27 ^aLam.
2:15-17; Mic.
7:8-10 ^bJer.
2:26 ^cJob
16:4; Jer.
18:16

28 ^aJudg.
6:2; Is. 2:19;
Jer. 49:16;
Obad. 3 ^bPs.
55:6; Song
2:14

29 ^aIs. 16:6;
Zeph. 2:8
^bJob 40:11,
12; Ps. 138:6

30 ^aIs. 37:28

31 ^aIs. 15:5;
16:7, 11
^b2 Kin. 3:25;
Is. 16:7, 11;
Jer. 48:36

32 ^aIs. 16:8,
9 ^bNum.
21:32

33 ^aIs.
16:10; Jer.
25:10; Joel
1:12 ^bIs.
5:10; Hag.
2:16

48:18 *Dibon.* 13 miles E. of the Dead Sea and the site of the discovery of the famous Moab-ite Stone.

48:25 *The horn.* A symbol of power (cf. v. 14).
48:26 Moab would be *drunk* with terror in the face of God's judgment.

From the fruitful field,
even from the land of
Moab.
And I have made the wine
to ᵇcease from the
wine presses;
No one will tread *them*
with shouting,
The shouting will not be
shouts *of joy.*

34 "ᵃFrom the outcry at Heshbon even to ᵇElealeh, even to Jahaz they have raised their voice, from ᶜZoar even to Horonaim *and to* Eglath-shelishiyah; for even the waters of Nimrim will become desolate.

35 "And I shall make an end of Moab," declares the Lᴏʀᴅ, "the one who offers *sacrifice* on the ᵃhigh place and the one who ᵇburns incense to his gods.

36 "Therefore My ᵃheart wails for Moab like flutes; My heart also wails like flutes for the men of Kir-heres. Therefore they have ᵇlost the abundance it produced.

37 "For ᵃevery head is bald and every beard cut short; there are gashes on all the hands and ᵇsackcloth on the loins.

38 "On all the ᵃhousetops of Moab and in its streets there is lamentation everywhere; for I have broken Moab like an undesirable ᵇvessel," declares the Lᴏʀᴅ.

39 "How shattered it is! *How* they have wailed! How Moab has turned his back—he is ashamed! So Moab will become a laughingstock and an ᵃobject of terror to all around him."

40 For thus says the Lᴏʀᴅ,
"Behold, one will ᵃfly
swiftly like an eagle,
And ᵇspread out his wings
against Moab.
41 "Kerioth has been captured
And the strongholds have
been seized,

So the ᵃhearts of the
mighty men of Moab
in that day
Will be like the heart of a
ᵇwoman in labor.

42 "And Moab will be ᵃdestroyed from *being* a people
Because he has become
ᵇarrogant toward the
Lᴏʀᴅ.

43 "ᵃTerror, pit, and snare are
coming upon you,
O inhabitant of Moab,"
declares the Lᴏʀᴅ.

44 "The one who ᵃflees from
the terror
Will fall into the pit,
And the one who climbs
up out of the pit
Will be caught in the
snare;
For I shall bring upon her,
even upon Moab,
The year of their ᵇpunishment," declares the
Lᴏʀᴅ.

45 "In the shadow of Heshbon
The fugitives stand without strength;
For a fire has gone forth
from Heshbon,
And a ᵃflame from the
midst of ᵇSihon,
And it has devoured the
ᶜforehead of Moab
And the scalps of the riotous revelers.

46 "ᵃWoe to you, Moab!
The people of ᵇChemosh
have perished;
For your sons have been
taken away captive,
And your daughters into
captivity.

47 "Yet I will ᵃrestore the fortunes of Moab
In the latter days," declares
the Lᴏʀᴅ.
Thus far the judgment on
Moab.

---

34 ᵃIs. 15:4-6 ᵇNum. 32:3, 37 ᶜGen. 13:10; 14:2; Is. 15:5, 6

35 ᵃIs. 15:2; 16:12 ᵇJer. 7:9; 11:13

★36 ᵃIs. 15:5; 16:11 ᵇIs. 15:7

37 ᵃIs. 15:2; Jer. 16:6; 41:5; 47:5 ᵇGen. 37:34; Is. 15:3; 20:2

38 ᵃIs. 22:1 ᵇJer. 19:10, 11; 22:28; 25:34

39 ᵃEzek. 26:16

40 ᵃDeut. 28:49; Jer. 49:22; Hos. 8:1; Hab. 1:8 ᵇIs. 8:8

41 ᵃJer. 49:22 ᵇIs. 13:8; 21:3; Jer. 30:6; Mic. 4:9, 10

★42 ᵃPs. 83:4; Jer. 48:2 ᵇIs. 37:23; Jer. 48:26

43 ᵃIs. 24:17, 18; Lam. 3:47

44 ᵃ1 Kin. 19:17; Is. 24:18; Amos 5:19 ᵇJer. 46:21

45 ᵃNum. 21:28, 29 ᵇNum. 21:21, 26; Ps. 135:11 ᶜNum. 24:17

46 ᵃNum. 21:29 ᵇJudg. 11:24; 1 Kin. 11:7; Jer. 48:7

★47 ᵃJer. 12:14-17; 49:6, 39

48:36 *flutes.* Used for funeral dirges.
48:42 The land of Moab was inhabited by the Nabataeans in the first century ʙ.ᴄ. and later by the Arabs.
48:47 Moab will be restored to share in the Messianic kingdom.

D Prophecies against Ammon,
49:1-6

★ 1 ªDeut.
23:3, 4;
2 Chr. 20:1;
Ezek. 21:28-
32; 25:2-10;
Amos 1:13-
15; Zeph.
2:8-11

49 Concerning the sons of
ªAmmon.
Thus says the LORD:
"Does Israel have no sons?
Or has he no heirs?
Why then has Malcam
taken possession of
Gad
And his people settled in
its cities?

★ 2 ªNum.
10:9; Jer.
4:19 ᵇDeut.
3:11; 2 Sam.
11:1; Ezek.
21:20 ᶜJosh.
17:11, 16
ᵈIs. 14:2

2 "Therefore behold, the days
are coming," declares
the LORD,
"That I shall cause a ªtrumpet blast of war to be
heard
Against ᵇRabbah of the
sons of Ammon;
And it will become a desolate heap,
And her ᶜtowns will be set
on fire.
Then Israel will take ᵈpos-
session of his posses-
sors,"
Says the LORD.

3 ªJer. 48:2
ᵇJosh. 7:2-5;
8:1-29; Ezra
2:28 ᶜIs.
32:11; Jer.
48:37 ᵈJer.
46:25; 48:7

3 "Wail, O ªHeshbon, for ᵇAi
has been destroyed!
Cry out, O daughters of
Rabbah,
ᶜGird yourselves with
sackcloth and lament,
And rush back and forth
inside the walls;
For Malcam will ᵈgo into
exile
Together with his priests
and his princes.

4 ªJer. 9:23
ᵇJer. 31:22
ᶜPs. 62:10;
Ezek. 28:4,
5; 1 Tim.
6:17 ᵈJer.
21:13

4 "How ªboastful you are
about the valleys!
Your valley is flowing
away,
O ᵇbacksliding daughter
Who trusts in her ᶜtrea-
sures, saying,

'ᵈWho will come against
me?'

5 ªJer.
48:43f.;
49:29 ᵇJer.
16:16; 46:5
ᶜLam. 4:15

5 "Behold, I am going to bring
ªterror upon you,"
Declares the Lord GOD of
hosts,
"From all directions around
you;
And each of you will be
ᵇdriven out headlong,
With no one to gather the
ᶜfugitives together.

6 ªJer.
48:47; 49:39

6 "But afterward I will ªre-
store
The fortunes of the sons of
Ammon,"
Declares the LORD.

E Prophecies against Edom,
49:7-22

★ 7-8
7 ªGen.
25:30; 32:3;
Is. 34:5, 6;
Jer. 25:21;
Ezek. 25:12;
Amos 1:11;
Obad. 1-21
ᵇJob 2:11;
Jer. 8:9
ᶜGen. 36:11,
15, 34; Jer.
49:20

7 Concerning ªEdom.
Thus says the LORD of
hosts,
"Is there no longer any
ᵇwisdom in ᶜTeman?
Has good counsel been lost
to the prudent?
Has their wisdom decayed?

8 ªIs.
21:13; Jer.
25:23 ᵇJer.
46:21; Mal.
1:3, 4

8 "Flee away, turn back,
dwell in the depths,
O inhabitants of ªDedan,
For I will bring the ᵇdisas-
ter of Esau upon him
At the time I punish him.

★ 9-10

9 ªObad. 5

9 "ªIf grape gatherers came to
you,
Would they not leave
gleanings?
If thieves came by night,
They would destroy only
until they had
enough.

10 ªJer.
13:26 ᵇIs.
17:14

10 "But I have ªstripped Esau
bare,
I have uncovered his hid-
ing places

49:1 *sons of Ammon.* See note on Amos 1:13.
Other oracles are in Ezek. 21:20; 25:1-7; Zeph.
2:8-11. On the relations with Judah see
2 Kings 24:2; Jer. 40:11-14. *Malcam.* The god
of the Ammonites (1 Kings 11:5, 7, 33; 2 Kings
23:13).
49:2 *Rabbah.* The chief city; modern Amman.
49:7-8 *Edom.* See Introduction to Obadiah.

Other oracles are in Ezek. 25:12-14; 35:1-15;
Joel 3:19; Amos 9:12; the Book of Obadiah.
Teman . . . Dedan. See 25:23.
49:9-10 Usually *grape gatherers* and *thieves*
leave something behind, but Edom will be
completely destroyed. In the third century B.C.
Edom was overrun by the Nabataeans.

So that he will not be able
to conceal himself;
His offspring has been destroyed along with his
relatives
And his neighbors, and
[b]he is no more.

11 "Leave your [a]orphans behind, I will keep *them*
alive;
And let your [b]widows trust
in Me."

12 For thus says the LORD,
"Behold, those who were not sen-
tenced to drink the [a]cup will certainly drink *it,* and are you the
one who will be [b]completely acquitted? You will not be acquitted, but you will certainly drink
it.

13 "For I have [a]sworn by Myself," declares the LORD, "that
[b]Bozrah will become an [c]object of
horror, a reproach, a ruin and a
curse; and all its cities will become perpetual ruins."

14 I have [a]heard a message
from the LORD,
And an [b]envoy is sent
among the nations,
saying,
"[c]Gather yourselves to-
gether and come
against her,
And rise up for battle!"

15 "For behold, I have made
you small among the
nations,
Despised among men.

16 "As for the terror of you,
The arrogance of your
heart has deceived
you,
O you who live in the
clefts of the [a]rock,
Who occupy the height of
the hill.
Though you make your
nest as [b]high as an ea-
gle's,

I will [c]bring you down
from there," declares
the LORD.

17 "And Edom will become an
[a]object of horror; everyone who
passes by it will be horrified and
will [b]hiss at all its wounds.

18 "Like the [a]overthrow of
Sodom and Gomorrah with its
neighbors," says the LORD, "[b]no
one will live there, nor will a son
of man reside in it.

19 "[a]Behold, one will come up
like a lion from the [b]thickets of
the Jordan against a perennially
watered pasture; for in an instant
I shall make him run away from
it, and whoever is [c]chosen I shall
appoint over it. For who is [d]like
Me, and who will summon Me
into court? And who then is the
shepherd [e]who can stand against
Me?"

20 Therefore hear the [a]plan
of the LORD which He has planned
against Edom, and His purposes
which He has purposed against
the inhabitants of Teman: surely
they will drag them off, *even* the
little ones of the flock; surely He
will make their pasture [b]desolate
because of them.

21 The [a]earth has quaked at
the noise of their downfall. There
is an outcry! The noise of it has
been heard at the Red Sea.

22 Behold, He will mount up
and [a]swoop like an eagle, and
spread out His wings against Bozrah; and the [b]hearts of the mighty
men of Edom in that day will be
like the heart of a woman in labor.

**F Prophecies against Damascus,
49:23–27**

23 Concerning [a]Damascus.
"[b]Hamath and [c]Arpad are
put to shame,

49:12 For Edom's particular sins, see Obad.
10–14.
49:13 *Bozrah.* See note on Isa. 34:6.
49:16 See Obad. 3.
49:23 *Damascus.* The capital of Syria (Aram).
Hamath. A city on the Orontes River, about

110 miles N. of Damascus. *Arpad.* About 20
miles NW. of Aleppo. Though Damascus had
fallen to Assyria in 732, the background in
these verses must relate to Nebuchadnezzar's
subjugation of the territory.

11 [a]Ps. 68:5;
Hos. 14:3
[b]Ps. 68:5;
Zech. 7:10

★**12** [a]Jer.
25:15 [b]Jer.
25:28, 29;
1 Pet. 4:17

★**13** [a]Gen.
22:16; Is.
45:23; Jer.
44:26; Amos
6:8 [b]Gen.
36:33; 1 Chr.
1:44; Is.
34:6; 63:1;
Amos 1:12
[c]Is. 34:9-15;
Jer. 18:16

14 [a]Obad. 1-
4 [b]Is. 18:2;
30:4 [c]Jer.
50:14

★**16** [a]2 Kin.
14:7; Jer.
48:28 [b]Job
39:27; Is.
14:13-15
[c]Amos 9:2

17 [a]Jer.
18:16; 49:13;
50:13; Ezek.
35:7 [b]1 Kin.
9:8; Jer.
51:37
18 [a]Gen.
19:24, 25;
Deut. 29:23;
Jer. 50:40;
Amos 4:11;
Zeph. 2:9
[b]Job 18:15-
18; Jer.
49:33

19 [a]Jer.
50:44 [b]Josh.
3:15; Jer.
12:5 [c]Num.
16:5 [d]Ex.
15:11; Is.
46:9 [e]Job
41:10

20 [a]Is.
14:24, 27;
Jer. 50:45
[b]Mal. 1:3, 4

21 [a]Jer.
50:46; Ezek.
26:15, 18

22 [a]Jer.
4:13; 48:40;
Hos. 8:1 [b]Is.
13:8; Jer.
30:6; 48:41
★**23** [a]Gen.
14:15; 15:2;
2 Kin. 5:12;
2 Chr. 16:2;
Is. 7:8; 17:1;
Amos 1:3;
Acts 9:2
[b]Num.
13:21; Is.
10:9; Jer.
39:5; Amos
6:2 [c]2 Kin.
18:34; 19:13;
Is. 10:9 [d]Ex.
15:15; Nah.
2:10 [e]Is.
57:20

For they have heard bad
news;
They are ᵈdisheartened.
There is anxiety by the
sea,
It ᵉcannot be calmed.

24 "Damascus has become
helpless;
She has turned away to
flee,
And panic has gripped her;
ᵃDistress and pangs have
taken hold of her
Like a woman in child-
birth.

25 "How the ᵃcity of praise has
not been deserted,
The town of My joy!

26 "Therefore, her ᵃyoung
men will fall in her
streets,
And all the men of war
will be silenced in that
day," declares the
LORD of hosts.

27 "And I shall ᵃset fire to the
wall of Damascus,
And it will devour the
fortified towers of
ᵇBen-hadad."

G   Prophecies against Arabia,
49:28-33

★28-33

28 Concerning ᵃKedar and
the kingdoms of Hazor, which
Nebuchadnezzar king of Babylon
defeated. Thus says the LORD,
"Arise, go up to Kedar
And devastate the ᵇmen of
the east.

29 "They will take away their
tents and their flocks;
They will carry off for
themselves
Their tent ᵃcurtains, all
their goods, and their
ᵇcamels,
And they will call out to
one another, 'ᶜTerror
on every side!'

30 "Run away, flee! Dwell in
the depths,
O inhabitants of Hazor,"
declares the LORD;
"For ᵃNebuchadnezzar king
of Babylon has
formed a plan against
you
And devised a scheme
against you.

31 "Arise, go up against a na-
tion which is ᵃat ease,
Which lives securely," de-
clares the LORD.
"It has ᵇno gates or bars;
They ᶜdwell alone.

32 "And their camels will become plunder,
And the multitude of their
cattle for booty,
And I shall ᵃscatter to all
the winds those who
ᵇcut the corners of
their hair;
And I shall bring their disaster from every
side," declares the
LORD.

33 "And Hazor will become a
ᵃhaunt of jackals,
A desolation forever;
No one will live there,
Nor will a son of man re-
side in it."

H   Prophecies against Elam,
49:34-39

★34

34 That which came as the
word of the LORD to Jeremiah the
prophet concerning ᵃElam, ᵇat the
beginning of the reign of Zedekiah king of Judah, saying,

35 "Thus says the LORD of
hosts,
'Behold, I am going to
ᵃbreak the bow of
Elam,
The finest of their might.

36 'And I shall bring upon
Elam the ᵃfour winds

Cross references (margin):

24 ᵃIs. 13:8

25 ᵃJer. 33:9; 51:41

26 ᵃJer. 11:22; 50:30; Amos 4:10

27 ᵃJer. 43:12; Amos 1:3-5 ᵇ1 Kin. 15:18-20; 2 Kin. 13:3

28 ᵃGen. 25:13; Ps. 120:5; Is. 21:16, 17; Jer. 2:10; Ezek. 27:21 ᵇJob 1:3; Is. 11:14

29 ᵃHab. 3:7 ᵇ1 Chr. 5:21 ᶜJer. 46:5

30 ᵃJer. 25:9; 27:6

31 ᵃJudg. 18:7; Is. 47:8 ᵇIs. 42:11 ᶜNum. 23:9; Deut. 33:28; Mic. 7:14

32 ᵃEzek. 5:10; 12:14, 15 ᵇJer. 9:26; 25:23

33 ᵃIs. 13:20-22; Jer. 9:11; 10:22; 51:37; Zeph. 2:9, 13-15; Mal. 1:3

34 ᵃGen. 10:22; 14:1, 9; Is. 11:11; Jer. 25:25; Ezek. 32:24; Dan. 8:2 ᵇ2 Kin. 24:17, 18; Jer. 28:1

35 ᵃPs. 46:9; Is. 22:6; Jer. 51:56

36 ᵃDan. 7:2; 8:8; Rev. 7:1 ᵇJer. 49:32; Ezek. 5:10; Amos 9:9

49:28-33 These verses relate to nomadic desert
tribes whom Nebuchadnezzar sought to bring
under control in a campaign in 599. *Kedar* was
one of these Arab tribes (2:10; Isa. 21:16; 60:7;
Ezek. 27:21). This *Hazor* was a desert area, not
the city in northern Palestine.
49:34 *Elam.* Located E. of Babylonia. The Elamites had had a long and eventful history but,
by Jeremiah's time, had largely been absorbed
by the Persians.

From the four ends of
heaven,
And shall [b]scatter them to
all these winds;
And there will be no na-
tion
To which the outcasts of
Elam will not go.

37 'So I shall shatter Elam before their enemies
And before those who
seek their lives;
And I shall [a]bring calamity
upon them,
Even My [b]fierce anger,' declares the LORD,
'And I shall [c]send out the
sword after them
Until I have consumed
them.

38 'Then I shall set My throne
in Elam,
And I shall destroy out of
it king and princes,'
Declares the LORD.

39 'But it will come about in
the last days
That I shall [a]restore the
fortunes of Elam,' "
Declares the LORD.

I　Prophecies against Babylon,
50:1—51:64

50 The word which the LORD
spoke concerning [a]Baby-
lon, the land of the Chaldeans,
through Jeremiah the prophet:
2 "[a]Declare and proclaim
among the nations.
Proclaim it and [b]lift up a
standard.
Do not conceal it but say,
'[c]Babylon has been cap-
tured,
[d]Bel has been put to
shame, Marduk has
been shattered;

Her [e]images have been put
to shame, her idols
have been shattered.'
3 "For a nation has come up
against her out of the [a]north; it
will make her land [b]an object of
horror, and there will be [c]no inhabitant in it. Both man and beast
have wandered off, they have
gone away!
4 "In those days and at that
time," declares the LORD, "the
sons of Israel will come, both they
and the sons of Judah [a]as well;
they will go along [b]weeping as
they go, and it will be [c]the LORD
their God they will seek.
5 "They will [a]ask for the way
to Zion, turning their faces in its
direction; they will come that they
may join themselves to the LORD
in an [b]everlasting covenant that
will not be forgotten.
6 "My people have become
[a]lost sheep;
[b]Their shepherds have led
them astray.
They have made them
turn aside on the
[c]mountains;
They have gone along
from mountain to hill
And have forgotten their
[d]resting place.
7 "All who came upon them
have devoured them;
And their adversaries have
said, '[a]We are not
guilty,
Inasmuch as they have
sinned against the
LORD who is the [b]hab-
itation of righteous-
ness,
Even the LORD, the [c]hope
of their fathers.'
8 "Wander away from the
[a]midst of Babylon,
And go forth from the land
of the Chaldeans;

---

37 [a]Jer. 6:19
[b]Jer. 30:24
[c]Jer. 9:16;
48:2

39 [a]Jer.
48:47

1 [a]Gen.
10:10; 11:9;
2 Kin. 17:24;
Is. 13:1;
47:1; Dan.
1:1; Rev.
14:8

★ **2** [a]Jer.
4:16 [b]Jer.
51:27 [c]Jer.
51:31 [d]Is.
46:1 [e]Jer.
51:47

★ **3** [a]Is.
13:17; Jer.
50:9; 51:11,
27 [b]Is.
14:22, 23;
Jer. 50:13
[c]Jer. 9:10,
11; Zeph. 1:3

4 [a]Is.
11:12, 13;
Jer. 3:18;
31:31; 33:7;
Hos. 1:11
[b]Ezra 3:12,
13; Ps.
126:5; Jer.
31:9 [c]Hos.
3:5

5 [a]Is. 35:8;
Jer. 6:16 [b]Is.
55:3; Jer.
32:40; Heb.
8:6-10

6 [a]Is. 53:6;
Ezek. 34:15,
16; Matt.
9:36; 10:6
[b]Jer. 23:11-
14 [c]Jer.
13:16; Ezek.
34:6 [d]Jer.
33:12; 50:19

7 [a]Jer. 2:3;
Zech. 11:5
[b]Jer. 31:23;
40:2, 3 [c]Ps.
22:4; Jer.
14:8; 17:13

★ **8** [a]Is.
48:20; Jer.
51:6; Rev.
18:4

50:2 *Bel.* Means lord and was a title applied at
this time to *Marduk,* the chief god of Babylon
and supposed creator of the world.
50:3 *out of the north.* In Jewish thought, the origin of anything sinister, since most of the
invasions came from this direction. But now
the conquering Persians came from the north

and the east to conquer Babylon in 539 B.C.
and allowed the Jews to return to Palestine
(v. 5).
50:8 *male goats.* Who leave the enclosure first.
So Judah ought to be the first of the captive
peoples to leave Babylon.

Be also like male goats at
the head of the flock.

9 a Jer. 51:1

9 "For behold, I am going to
^aarouse and bring up
against Babylon
A horde of great nations
from the land of the
north,
And they will draw up
their battle lines
against her;
From there she will be
taken captive.
Their arrows will be like
an expert warrior
Who does not return
empty-handed.

10 a Jer.
51:24, 35;
Ezek. 11:24

10 "And ^aChaldea will become
plunder;
All who plunder her will
have enough," de-
clares the LORD.

11 a Jer.
12:14 b Jer.
46:20

11 "Because you are glad, because you are jubilant,
O you who ^apillage My
heritage,
Because you skip about
like a threshing
^bheifer
And neigh like stallions,

12 a Jer. 15:9
b Jer. 22:6;
51:43

12 Your ^amother will be
greatly ashamed,
She who gave you birth
will be humiliated.
Behold, *she will be* the
least of the nations,
A ^bwilderness, a parched
land, and a desert.

★**13** a Jer.
34:22 b Jer.
51:26 c Jer.
18:16; 49:17

13 "Because of the indignation
of the LORD she will
^anot be inhabited,
But she will be ^bcom-
pletely desolate;
Everyone who passes by
Babylon ^cwill be horrified
And will hiss because of all
her wounds.

14 a Hab.
2:8, 17

14 "Draw up your battle lines
against Babylon on
every side,
All you who bend the
bow;

Shoot at her, do not be
sparing with *your* ar-
rows,
For she has ^asinned against
the LORD.

15 "Raise your battle cry
against her on every
side!
She has ^agiven herself up,
her pillars have fallen,
Her ^bwalls have been torn
down.
For this is the ^cvengeance
of the LORD:
Take vengeance on her;
^dAs she has done *to others,*
so do to her.

15 a 1 Chr.
29:24; 2 Chr.
30:8; Lam.
5:6 b Jer.
50:44, 58;
51:58 c Jer.
46:10 d Ps.
137:8; Rev.
18:6

16 "Cut off the ^asower from
Babylon,
And the one who wields
the sickle at the time
of harvest;
From before the ^bsword of
the oppressor
^cThey will each turn back
to his own people,
And they will each flee to
his own land.

16 a Joel
1:11 b Jer.
25:38; 46:16
c Is. 13:14

17 "Israel is a ^ascattered flock,
the ^blions have driven *them* away.
The first one *who* devoured him
was the ^cking of Assyria, and this
last one *who* has broken his
bones is ^dNebuchadnezzar king of
Babylon.

17 a Joel 3:2
b Jer. 2:15;
4:7 c 2 Kin.
15:19; 17:6;
18:9-13
d 2 Kin. 24:1,
10-12; 25:1-7

18 "Therefore thus says the
LORD of hosts, the God of Israel:
'Behold, I am going to punish the
king of Babylon and his land, just
as I ^apunished the king of Assyria.

18 a Is.
10:12; Ezek.
31:3, 11, 12;
Nah. 3:7, 18,
19

19 'And I shall ^abring Israel
back to his pasture, and he will
graze on Carmel and Bashan, and
his desire will be satisfied in the
^bhill country of Ephraim and Gil-
ead.

19 a Is.
65:10; Jer.
31:10; 33:12;
Ezek. 34:13
b Jer. 31:6

20 'In those days and at that
time,' declares the LORD, 'search
will be made for the iniquity of
Israel, but ^athere will be none;
and for the sins of Judah, but they
will not be found; for I shall par-

20 a Is.
43:25; Jer.
31:34; Mic.
7:19 b Is. 1:9

50:13 *desolate.* The Persians captured Babylon
in 539 (Dan. 5:30-31). In 514 Darius Hystaspes
put down a revolt and partially destroyed the

walls. Xerxes demolished the walls and temples of Babylon in 478. Subsequent attempts
to restore the city have been unsuccessful.

don those [b]whom I leave as a
remnant.'

★21 [a]Ezek. 23:23

21 "Against the land of Merathaim, go up against
it,
And against the inhabi-
tants of [a]Pekod.
Slay and utterly destroy
them," declares the
LORD,
"And do according to all
that I have com-
manded you.

22 [a]Jer. 4:19-21; 51:54-56

22 "The [a]noise of battle is in
the land,
And great destruction.

23 [a]Jer. 51:20-24

23 "How the [a]hammer of the
whole earth
Has been cut off and bro-
ken!
How Babylon has become
An object of horror among
the nations!

24 [a]Jer. 48:43, 44 [b]Jer. 51:31; Dan. 5:30, 31 [c]Job 9:4; 40:2, 9

24 "I [a]set a snare for you, and
you were also
[b]caught, O Babylon,
While you yourself were
not aware;
You have been found and
also seized
Because you have engaged
in [c]conflict with the
LORD."

25 [a]Is. 13:5 [b]Jer. 50:15; 51:12, 25, 55

25 The LORD has opened His
armory
And has brought forth the
[a]weapons of His in-
dignation,
For it is a [b]work of the
Lord GOD of hosts
In the land of the Chaldeans.

26 [a]Is. 45:3; Jer. 50:10 [b]Is. 14:23

26 Come to her from the far-
thest border;
[a]Open up her barns,
Pile her up like heaps
And [b]utterly destroy her,
Let nothing be left to her.

27 [a]Is. 34:7 [b]Jer. 48:10 [c]Ps. 37:13; Jer. 46:21; 48:44; Ezek. 7:7

27 [a]Put all her young bulls to
the sword;
Let them [b]go down to the
slaughter!

Woe be upon them, for
their [c]day has come,
The time of their punish-
ment.

28 There is a [a]sound of fugitives and refugees
from the land of
Babylon,
To declare in Zion the
[b]vengeance of the
LORD our God,
Vengeance for His
[c]temple.

★28 [a]Is. 48:20 [b]Ps. 149:6-9; Jer. 50:15; 51:10 [c]Lam. 1:10; 2:6, 7

29 "Summon many against
Babylon,
All those who bend the
bow:
Encamp against her on ev-
ery side,
Let there be no escape.
Repay her according to her
work;
[a]According to all that she
has done, so do to her;
For she has become [b]arro-
gant against the LORD,
Against the Holy One of
Israel.

29 [a]Ps. 137:8; Jer. 50:15; 51:56; 2 Thess. 1:6 [b]Ex. 10:3; Jer. 49:16; Dan. 4:37

30 "Therefore her [a]young men
will fall in her streets,
And all her men of war
will be [b]silenced in
that day," declares the
LORD.

30 [a]Is. 13:17, 18; Jer. 9:21; 18:21; 49:26; 51:57 [b]Jer. 51:57

31 "Behold, [a]I am against you,
O arrogant one,"
Declares the Lord GOD of
hosts,
"For your day has come,
The time when I shall pun-
ish you.

31 [a]Jer. 21:13; Nah. 2:13

32 "And the [a]arrogant one will
stumble and fall
With no one to raise him
up;
And I shall [b]set fire to his
cities,
And it will devour all his
environs."

32 [a]Is. 10:12-15 [b]Jer. 21:14; 49:27

50:21 *Merathaim* (lit., double rebellion) and *Pekod* (lit., visitation) are sarcastic wordplays on
the southern and eastern districts of Babylon.

50:28 *Vengeance for His temple.* See Dan. 5:1-4
for a description of the Babylonians' sin.

33 Thus says the Lord of hosts,

"The sons of Israel are oppressed,

And the sons of Judah as well;

And aall who took them captive have held them fast,

They have refused to let them go.

34 "Their aRedeemer is strong, bthe Lord of hosts is His name;

He will vigorously cplead their case,

So that He may dbring rest to the earth,

But turmoil to the inhabitants of Babylon.

35 "A asword against the Chaldeans," declares the Lord,

"And against the inhabitants of Babylon,

And against her bofficials and her cwise men!

36 "A sword against the aoracle priests, and they will become fools!

A sword against her bmighty men, and they will be cshattered!

37 "A sword against their ahorses and against their chariots,

And against all the bforeigners who are in the midst of her,

And they will become cwomen!

A sword against her treasures, and they will be plundered!

38 "A adrought on her waters, and they will be dried up!

For it is a land of bidols,

And they are mad over fearsome idols.

39 "Therefore the adesert creatures will live there along with the jackals;

The ostriches also will live in it,

And it will bnever again be inhabited

Or dwelt in from generation to generation.

40 "As when God overthrew aSodom

And Gomorrah with its neighbors," declares the Lord,

"No man will live there,

Nor will any son of man reside in it.

41 "Behold, a people is coming afrom the north,

And a great nation and many kings

Will be aroused from the remote parts of the earth.

42 "They aseize their bow and javelin;

They are bcruel and have no mercy.

Their cvoice roars like the sea,

And they ride on dhorses,

eMarshalled like a man for the battle

Against you, O daughter of Babylon.

43 "The aking of Babylon has heard the report about them,

And his hands hang limp;

bDistress has gripped him,

Agony like a woman in childbirth.

44 "aBehold, one will come up like a lion from the thicket of the Jordan to a perennially watered pasture; for in an instant I shall make them run away from it, and whoever is bchosen I shall appoint over it. For who is clike Me, and who will summon Me into court? And who then is the shepherd who can dstand before Me?"

45 Therefore hear the aplan of the Lord which He has planned against Babylon, and His purposes which He has purposed

---

Cross references (margin):

33 aIs. 14:17; 58:6

34 aProv. 23:11; Is. 43:14; Jer. 15:21; 31:11; Rev. 18:8 bIs. 47:4; Jer. 32:18; 51:19 cJer. 51:36; Mic. 7:9 dIs. 14:3-7

35 aJer. 47:6; Hos. 11:6 bDan. 5:1, 2 cDan. 5:7, 8

36 aIs. 44:25 bJer. 49:22 cNah. 3:13

37 aPs. 20:7, 8; Jer. 51:21, 22 bJer. 25:20; Ezek. 30:5 cJer. 48:41; 51:30; Nah. 3:13

38 aIs. 44:27; Jer. 51:32, 36; Rev. 16:12 bIs. 46:1, 6, 7

39 aIs. 13:21; 34:14; Rev. 18:2 bIs. 13:20; Jer. 25:12

40 aGen. 19:24, 25; Is. 13:19; Jer. 49:18; Luke 17:28-30; 2 Pet. 2:6; Jude 7

41 aIs. 13:2-5; Jer. 6:22; 50:3, 9; 51:27, 28

42 aJer. 6:23 bIs. 13:17, 18; 47:6 cIs. 5:30 dJer. 8:16; 47:3; Hab. 1:8 eJer. 50:9, 14; Joel 2:5

43 aJer. 51:31 bJer. 30:6; 49:24

★44 aJer. 49:19-21 bNum. 16:5 cIs. 46:9 dJob 41:10; Jer. 30:21

45 aPs. 33:11; Is. 14:24; Jer. 51:10, 11 bJer. 49:20

50:44 The reference is to Cyrus. *the thicket of the Jordan.* See note on 12:1-6.

against the land of the Chaldeans:
[b]surely they will drag them off,
even the little ones of the flock;
surely He will make their pasture
desolate because of them.

46 At the shout, "Babylon has
been seized!" the [a]earth is
shaken, and an [b]outcry is heard
among the nations.

51 Thus says the LORD:
"Behold, I am going to
arouse against Baby-
lon
And against the inhabi-
tants of Leb-kamai
The [a]spirit of a destroyer.

2 "And I shall dispatch foreigners to Babylon
that they may [a]win-
now her
And may devastate her
land;
For on every side they will
be opposed to her
In the day of *her* calamity.

3 "Let not him who [a]bends
his bow bend *it,*
Nor let him rise up in his
[b]scale-armor;
So do not spare her young
men;
Devote all her army to destruction.

4 "And they will fall down
slain in the land of the
Chaldeans,
And [a]pierced through in
their streets."

5 For [a]neither Israel nor Judah has been forsaken
By his God, the LORD of
hosts,
Although their land is [b]full
of guilt
Before the Holy One of Israel.

6 [a]Flee from the midst of
Babylon,
And each of you save his
life!

Do not be [b]destroyed in
her punishment,
For this is the [c]LORD's time
of vengeance;
He is going to [d]render recompense to her.

7 Babylon has been a golden
[a]cup in the hand of
the LORD,
Intoxicating all the earth.
The [b]nations have drunk
of her wine;
Therefore the nations are
[c]going mad.

8 Suddenly [a]Babylon has
fallen and been bro-
ken;
[b]Wail over her!
[c]Bring balm for her pain;
Perhaps she may be
healed.

9 We applied healing to
Babylon, but she was
not healed;
Forsake her and [a]let us
each go to his own
country,
For her judgment has
[b]reached to heaven
And towers up to the very
skies.

10 The LORD has [a]brought
about our vindication;
Come and let us [b]recount
in Zion
The work of the LORD our
God!

11 [a]Sharpen the arrows, fill
the quivers!
The LORD has aroused the
spirit of the kings of
the Medes,
Because His purpose is
against Babylon to de-
stroy it;
For it is the [b]vengeance of
the LORD, vengeance
for His temple.

12 [a]Lift up a signal against the
walls of Babylon;

---

46 [a]Jer. 10:10; 49:21; Ezek. 26:18; 31:16 [b]Is. 5:7; 15:5; Jer. 46:12; 51:54; Ezek. 27:28

1 [a]Jer. 4:11, 12; 23:19; Hos. 13:15

2 [a]Is. 41:16; Jer. 15:7; Matt. 3:12

★**3** [a]Jer. 50:14, 29 [b]Jer. 46:4

4 [a]Is. 13:15; 14:19; Jer. 49:26; 50:30, 37

5 [a]Is. 54:7, 8; Jer. 33:24-26 [b]Hos. 4:1, 2

6 [a]Jer. 50:8, 28; Rev. 18:4 [b]Num. 16:26 [c]Jer. 50:15 [d]Jer. 25:14

★ **7-8**
7 [a]Jer. 25:15; Hab. 2:16; Rev. 14:8; 17:4 [b]Rev. 14:8; 18:3 [c]Jer. 25:16

8 [a]Is. 21:9; Jer. 50:2; Rev. 14:8; 18:2 [b]Is. 13:6; Rev. 18:9 [c]Jer. 46:11

9 [a]Is. 13:14; Jer. 46:16; 50:16 [b]Ezra 9:6; Rev. 18:5

10 [a]Ps. 37:6; Mic. 7:9 [b]Is. 40:2; Jer. 50:28

★**11** [a]Jer. 46:4, 9; Joel 3:9, 10 [b]Jer. 50:28

12 [a]Is. 13:2; Jer. 50:2; 51:27 [b]Jer. 4:28; 23:20; 51:29

51:3 *scale-armor.* Coat of armor.
51:7-8 *a golden cup.* Outwardly Babylon was splendid, but its "cup" was filled with idolatry. The same figure is used of the eschatological Babylon in Rev. 14:8 and 17:1-6. No *balm* (v. 8) could now heal Babylon.

51:11 *the Medes.* An Aryan people who lived E. of the Tigris River and S. of the Caspian Sea. Here and in Isa. 13:17-19 it is predicted that they would play a part, along with the Persians, in the fall of Babylon—a prophecy confirmed in Dan. 5:30-31.

Post a strong guard,
Station sentries,
Place men in ambush!
For the LORD has both
    [b]purposed and per-
    formed
What He spoke concern-
    ing the inhabitants of
    Babylon.

13 ^aRev.
17:1; ^bIs.
45:3; ^cIs.
57:17; Hab.
2:9-11

13 O you who [a]dwell by
    many waters,
Abundant in [b]treasures,
Your end has come,
The measure of your [c]end.

14 ^aJer.
49:13 ^bJer.
51:27; Nah.
3:15

14 The [a]LORD of hosts has
    sworn by Himself:
"Surely I will fill you with a
    population like [b]lo-
    custs,
And they will cry out with
    shouts of victory over
    you."

15 ^aGen.
1:1; Jer.
10:12-16;
51:15-19
^bJob 9:8; Ps.
146:5, 6; Jer.
32:17; Acts
14:15; Rom.
1:20

15 It is [a]He who made the
    earth by His power,
Who established the world
    by His wisdom,
And by His understanding
    He [b]stretched out the
    heavens.

16 ^aJob
37:2-6; Ps.
18:13 ^bPs.
135:7; Jer.
10:13 ^cJon.
1:4

16 When He utters His
    [a]voice, there is a tu-
    mult of waters in the
    heavens,
And He causes the [b]clouds
    to ascend from the
    end of the earth;
He makes lightning for the
    rain,
And brings forth the [c]wind
    from His storehouses.

★17-18

17 ^aIs.
44:18-20;
Jer. 10:14
^bHab. 2:18,
19

17 [a]All mankind is stupid, de-
    void of knowledge;
Every goldsmith is put to
    shame by his idols,
For his molten images are
    [b]deceitful,
And there is no breath in
    them.

18 ^aJer.
18:15

18 They are [a]worthless, a
    work of mockery;
In the time of their punish-
    ment they will perish.

19 The [a]portion of Jacob is
    not like these;
For the Maker of all is He,
And of the tribe of His in-
    heritance;
The [b]LORD of hosts is His
    name.

19 ^aPs.
73:26; Jer.
10:16 ^bJer.
50:34

20 He says, "You are My
    [a]war-club, My
    weapon of war;
And with you I [b]shatter
    nations,
And with you I destroy
    kingdoms.

★20-23

20 ^aIs. 10:5;
41:15, 16;
Jer. 50:23
^bIs. 8:9;
41:15, 16;
Mic. 4:12, 13

21 "And with you I [a]shatter
    the horse and his
    rider,

21 ^aEx. 15:1

22 And with you I shatter the
    [a]chariot and its rider,
And with you I shatter
    [b]man and woman,
And with you I shatter old
    man and [c]youth,
And with you I shatter
    young man and vir-
    gin,

22 ^aEx. 15:4;
Is. 43:17
^b2 Chr.
36:17; Is.
13:15, 16
^cIs. 13:18

23 And with you I shatter the
    shepherd and his
    flock,
And with you I shatter the
    farmer and his team,
And with you I shatter
    governors and pre-
    fects.

24 "But I will repay Babylon
and all the inhabitants of [a]Chal-
dea for [b]all their evil that they
have done in Zion before your
eyes," declares the LORD.

24 ^aJer.
50:10 ^bJer.
50:15, 29

25 "Behold, [a]I am against you,
    [b]O destroying moun-
    tain,
Who destroy the whole
    earth," declares the
    LORD,
"And I will stretch out My
    hand against you,
And roll you down from
    the crags
And I will make you a
    [c]burnt out mountain.

25 ^aJer.
50:31 ^bIs.
13:2; Zech.
4:7 ^cRev. 8:8

26 "And they will not take
    from you even a stone
    for a corner

26 ^aIs.
13:19-22;
50:13; Jer.
51:29

51:17-18 The idols of Babylon would perish
along with the people.

51:20-23 These verses refer to Cyrus.

Nor a stone for foundations,

But you will be [a]desolate forever," declares the LORD.

★27 [a]Is.
13:2-5; 18:3;
Jer. 50:2;
51:12 [b]Jer.
50:3, 9
[c]Gen. 8:4;
2 Kin. 19:37;
Is. 37:38
[d]Gen. 10:3
[e]Jer. 50:42

27 [a]Lift up a signal in the land,

Blow a trumpet among the nations!

Consecrate the nations against her,

Summon against her the [b]kingdoms of [c]Ararat, Minni and [d]Ashkenaz;

Appoint a marshal against her,

Bring up the [e]horses like bristly locusts.

28 Consecrate the nations against her,

The kings of the Medes,

Their governors and all their prefects,

And every land of their dominion.

29 [a]Jer.
8:16; 10:10;
50:46; Amos
8:8 [b]Is.
13:19, 20;
47:11; Jer.
50:13; 51:26,
43

29 So the [a]land quakes and writhes,

For the purposes of the LORD against Babylon stand,

To make the land of Babylon

A [b]desolation without inhabitants.

30 [a]Ps. 76:5;
Jer. 50:15,
36, 37 [b]Is.
13:7, 8; Nah.
3:13 [c]Is.
45:1, 2; Lam.
2:9; Amos
1:5; Nah.
3:13

30 The [a]mighty men of Babylon have ceased fighting,

They stay in the strongholds;

[b]Their strength is exhausted,

They are becoming [b]like women;

Their dwelling places are set on fire,

The [c]bars of her gates are broken.

31 One [a]courier runs to meet another,

And one [b]messenger to meet another,

To tell the king of Babylon

That his city has been captured from end to end;

★31 [a]2 Chr.
30:6 [b]2 Sam.
18:19-31

32 The fords also have been seized,

And they have burned the marshes with fire,

And the men of war are terrified.

★32

33 For thus says the LORD of hosts, the God of Israel:

"The daughter of Babylon is like a [a]threshing floor

At the time it is stamped firm;

Yet in a little while the time of [b]harvest will come for her."

33 [a]Is.
21:10; 41:15,
16; Mic. 4:13
[b]Is. 17:5;
Hos. 6:11;
Joel 3:13;
Rev. 14:15

34 "Nebuchadnezzar king of Babylon has [a]devoured me and crushed me,

He has set me down like an [b]empty vessel;

He has [c]swallowed me like a monster,

He has filled his stomach with my delicacies;

He has washed me away.

34 [a]Jer.
50:17 [b]Is.
24:1-3 [c]Job
20:15; Jer.
51:44

35 "May the [a]violence done to me and to my flesh be upon Babylon,"

The inhabitant of Zion will say;

And, "May my blood be upon the inhabitants of Chaldea,"

Jerusalem will say.

35 [a]Ps.
137:8

36 Therefore thus says the LORD,

"Behold, I am going to [a]plead your case

★36 [a]Ps.
140:12 [b]Jer.
51:6, 11;
Rom. 12:19
[c]Jer. 50:38

51:27 *the kingdoms of Ararat, Minni, and Ashkenaz.* N. of Babylon; conquered by the Medes in the sixth century and here summoned to help fight against Babylon. *bristly locusts.* A particularly destructive stage in the life of the locust.

51:31 The famous courier system of the Babylonians would announce the destruction.

51:32 *marshes.* Burned to prevent refugees from hiding there.

51:36 *her sea.* The sea-like plain, between the Tigris and Euphrates rivers, that was interlaced with canals. The effect of this drying up is described in 50:16.

And ᵇexact full vengeance for you;
And ᶜI shall dry up her sea
And make her fountain dry.

37 "And ᵃBabylon will become a heap *of ruins*, a haunt of jackals,
An ᵇobject of horror and hissing, without inhabitants.

38 "They will roar together like ᵃyoung lions,
They will growl like lions' cubs.

39 "When they become heated up, I shall serve *them* their banquet
And ᵃmake them drunk, that they may become jubilant
And may ᵇsleep a perpetual sleep
And not wake up," declares the LORD.

40 "I shall bring them down like lambs ᵃto the slaughter,
Like rams together with male goats.

41 "How ᵃSheshak has been captured,
And ᵇthe praise of the whole earth been seized!
How Babylon has become an object of horror among the nations!

42 "The ᵃsea has come up over Babylon;
She has been engulfed with its tumultuous waves.

43 "Her cities have become an ᵃobject of horror,
A parched land and a desert,
A land in which ᵇno man lives,
And through which no son of man passes.

44 "And ᵃI shall punish Bel in Babylon,

And I shall make what he has swallowed ᵇcome out of his mouth;
And the nations will no longer ᶜstream to him.
Even the ᵈwall of Babylon has fallen down!

45 "ᵃCome forth from her midst, My people,
And each of you ᵇsave yourselves
From the fierce anger of the LORD.

46 "Now ᵃlest your heart grow faint,
And you be afraid at the ᵇreport that *will be* heard in the land—
For the report will come one year,
And after that another report in another year,
And violence *will be* in the land
With ᶜruler against ruler—

47 Therefore behold, days are coming
When I shall punish the ᵃidols of Babylon;
And her whole land will be ᵇput to shame,
And all her slain will fall in her midst.

48 "Then ᵃheaven and earth and all that is in them
Will shout for joy over Babylon,
For ᵇthe destroyers will come to her from the north,"
Declares the LORD.

49 ᵃIndeed Babylon is to fall *for* the slain of Israel,
As also for Babylon ᵇthe slain of all the earth have fallen.

50 You ᵃwho have escaped the sword,
Depart! Do not stay!
ᵇRemember the LORD from afar,

51:41 *Sheshak*. A cryptic term for Babylon (25:26).
51:42 *sea . . . waves*. I.e., Persian troops that pour in like a flood.
51:44 *Bel*. See note on 50:2.

---

37 ᵃRev. 18:2 ᵇJer. 25:9

38 ᵃJer. 2:15

39 ᵃJer. 25:27; 48:26; 51:57 ᵇPs. 76:5

40 ᵃJer. 48:15; 50:27

★**41** ᵃJer. 25:26 ᵇJer. 49:25

★**42** ᵃIs. 8:7, 8; Jer. 51:55; Dan. 9:26

43 ᵃJer. 50:12 ᵇIs. 13:20; Jer. 2:6

★**44** ᵃIs. 46:1; Jer. 50:2 ᵇEzra 1:7, 8 ᶜIs. 2:2 ᵈJer. 50:15; 51:58

45 ᵃIs. 48:20; Jer. 50:8, 28; 51:6; Rev. 18:4 ᵇGen. 19:12-16; Acts 2:40

46 ᵃIs. 43:5; Jer. 46:27, 28 ᵇ2 Kin. 19:7; Is. 13:3-5 ᶜIs. 19:2

47 ᵃIs. 21:9; 46:1, 2; Jer. 50:2; 51:52 ᵇJer. 50:12, 35-37

48 ᵃIs. 44:23; 48:20; 49:13; Rev. 18:20 ᵇJer. 50:3

49 ᵃPs. 137:8; Jer. 50:29 ᵇRev. 18:24

50 ᵃJer. 44:28 ᵇDeut. 4:29-31; Ps. 137:6

And let Jerusalem come to your mind.

51 [a]We are ashamed because we have heard reproach;
Disgrace has covered our faces,
For [b]aliens have entered
The holy places of the Lord's house.

52 "Therefore behold, the days are coming," declares the Lord,
"When I shall punish her [a]idols,
And the mortally wounded will groan throughout her land.

53 "Though Babylon should [a]ascend to the heavens,
And though she should fortify her lofty stronghold,
From [b]Me destroyers will come to her," declares the Lord.

54 The [a]sound of an outcry from Babylon,
And of great destruction from the land of the Chaldeans!

55 For the Lord is going to destroy Babylon,
And He will make *her* loud noise vanish from her.
And their [a]waves will roar like many waters;
The tumult of their voices sounds forth.

56 For the [a]destroyer is coming against her, against Babylon,
And her mighty men will be captured,
Their [b]bows are shattered;

For the Lord is a God of [c]recompense,
He will fully repay.

57 "And I shall [a]make her princes and her wise men drunk,
Her governors, her prefects, and her mighty men,
That they may sleep a [b]perpetual sleep and not wake up,"
[c]Declares the King, whose name is the Lord of hosts.

58 Thus says the Lord of hosts,
"The broad [a]wall of Babylon will be completely razed,
And her high [b]gates will be set on fire;
So the peoples will [c]toil for nothing,
And the nations become [d]exhausted *only* for fire."

59 The message which Jeremiah the prophet commanded Seraiah the son of [a]Neriah, the grandson of Mahseiah, when he went with [b]Zedekiah the king of Judah to Babylon in the fourth year of his reign. (Now Seraiah was quartermaster.)

60 So Jeremiah [a]wrote in a single scroll all the calamity which would come upon Babylon, *that is,* all these words which have been written concerning Babylon.

61 Then Jeremiah said to Seraiah, "As soon as you come to Babylon, then see that you read all these words aloud,

62 and say, 'Thou, O Lord, hast promised concerning this place to [a]cut it off, so that there will be [b]nothing dwelling in it, whether man or beast, but it will be a perpetual desolation.'

---

51 [a]Ps. 44:15 [b]Ps. 74:3-8; Lam. 1:10

52 [a]Jer. 50:38

★**53** [a]Gen. 11:4; Job 20:6; Ps. 139:8-10; Is. 14:12-14; Jer. 49:16; Amos 9:2; Obad. 4 [b]Is. 13:3

54 [a]Jer. 48:3-5; 50:22, 46

55 [a]Ps. 18:4; 69:2; 124:2, 4, 5; Jer. 51:42

56 [a]Jer. 51:48, 53; Hab. 2:8 [b]Ps. 46:9; 76:3 [c]Deut. 32:35; Ps. 94:1, 2; Jer. 51:6, 24

57 [a]Jer. 25:27 [b]Ps. 76:5, 6 [c]Jer. 46:18; 48:15

58 [a]Jer. 50:15 [b]Is. 45:1, 2 [c]Hab. 2:13 [d]Jer. 9:5; 51:64; Lam. 5:5

★**59** [a]Jer. 32:12; 36:4; 45:1 [b]Jer. 28:1; 52:1

60 [a]Is. 30:8; Jer. 30:2, 3; 36:2, 4, 32

62 [a]Is. 13:19-22; 14:22, 23; Jer. 50:3, 13, 39, 40 [b]Jer. 51:43; Ezek. 35:9

51:53 The towering ziggurat and beautiful palace of Babylon, though protected by a double wall (v. 58) of defensive fortifications, would fall.

51:59 *Seraiah.* The brother of Baruch (cf. 32:12), to be distinguished from the Seraiahs in 36:26; 40:8; 52:24-27. *quartermaster.* The officer in charge of arrangements when the group stopped to camp. As Jeremiah counselled the people to submit to Babylon (cf. 27:1-15), he predicted the eventual destruction of Babylon. Seraiah's throwing the scroll into the Euphrates River symbolized that destruction (51:63-64).

63 _a_Jer.
19:10, 11;
Rev. 18:21

64 _a_Nah.
1:8, 9 _b_Jer.
51:58 _c_Job
31:40; Ps.
72:20

63 "And it will come about as soon as you finish reading this scroll, you will tie a stone to it and _a_throw it into the middle of the Euphrates,

64 and say, 'Just so shall Babylon sink down and _a_not rise again, because of the calamity that I am going to bring upon her; and they will become _b_exhausted.' " _c_Thus far are the words of Jeremiah.

IV   HISTORICAL SUPPLEMENT, 52:1-34

A   The Fate of Jerusalem, 52:1-23

★ **1** _a_2 Kin.
24:18; 2 Chr.
36:11
_b_2 Kin.
22:31; 24:18
_c_Josh.
10:29; 2 Kin.
8:22; Is. 37:8

2 _a_1 Kin.
14:22; 2 Kin.
24:19; 2 Chr.
36:12 _b_Jer.
36:30, 31

3 _a_2 Kin.
24:20; Is.
3:1, 4, 5
_b_2 Chr.
36:13; Ezek.
17:12-16

★ **4-5**

4 _a_2 Kin.
25:1; Jer.
39:1; Ezek.
24:1, 2;
Zech. 8:19
_b_Jer. 32:24

5 _a_2 Kin.
25:2
6 _a_Jer. 39:2
_b_2 Kin. 25:3;
Is. 3:1; Jer.
38:9; Ezek.
4:16; 5:16;
14:13
7 _a_2 Kin.
25:4; Jer.
39:2 _b_Jer.
39:4-7; 51:32
_c_Ezek. 33:21

52 _a_Zedekiah was twenty-one years old when he became king, and he reigned eleven years in Jerusalem; and his mother's name was _b_Hamutal the daughter of Jeremiah of _c_Libnah.

2 And he did _a_evil in the sight of the Lord like all that _b_Jehoiakim had done.

3 For through the _a_anger of the Lord _this_ came about in Jerusalem and Judah until He cast them out from His presence. And Zedekiah _b_rebelled against the king of Babylon.

4 _a_Now it came about in the ninth year of his reign, on the tenth day of the tenth month, that Nebuchadnezzar king of Babylon came; he and all his army, against Jerusalem, camped against it, and built a _b_siege wall all around it.

5 _a_So the city was under siege until the eleventh year of King Zedekiah.

6 On the ninth day of the _a_fourth month the _b_famine was so severe in the city that there was no food for the people of the land.

7 Then the city was _a_broken into, and all the _b_men of war fled and went forth from the city at night by way of the gate between the two walls which _was_ by the king's garden, though the Chaldeans were _c_all around the city. And they went by way of the Arabah.

8 But the army of the Chaldeans pursued the king and _a_overtook Zedekiah in the plains of Jericho, and all his army was scattered from him.

9 Then they captured the king and _a_brought him up to the king of Babylon at _b_Riblah in the land of _c_Hamath; and he passed sentence on him.

10 And the king of Babylon _a_slaughtered the sons of Zedekiah before his eyes, and he also slaughtered all the princes of Judah in Riblah.

11 Then he _a_blinded the eyes of Zedekiah; and the king of Babylon bound him with bronze fetters and brought him to Babylon, and put him in prison until the day of his death.

12 _a_Now on the tenth day of the fifth month, which was the _b_nineteenth year of King Nebuchadnezzar, king of Babylon, _c_Nebuzaradan the captain of the bodyguard, who was in the service of the king of Babylon, came to Jerusalem.

13 And he _a_burned the house of the Lord, the _b_king's house, and all the houses of Jerusalem; even every large house he burned with fire.

14 So all the army of the Chaldeans who _were_ with the captain of the guard _a_broke down all the walls around Jerusalem.

15 Then Nebuzaradan the captain of the guard _a_carried away into exile some of the poorest of the people, the rest of the people who were left in the city, the _b_deserters who had deserted to the

★ **8-11**

8 _a_Jer.
21:7; 32:4;
34:21; 37:17;
38:23

★ **9** _a_2 Kin.
25:6; Jer.
32:4; 39:5
_b_Num.
34:11; Jer.
39:5 _c_Num.
13:21; Josh.
13:5

10 _a_2 Kin.
25:7; Jer.
22:30; 39:6

11 _a_Jer.
39:7; Ezek.
12:13

★**12** _a_2 Kin.
25:8-21;
Zech. 7:5;
8:19 _b_2 Kin.
24:12; 25:8;
Jer. 52:29
_c_Jer. 39:9

13 _a_1 Kin.
9:8; 2 Kin.
25:9; 2 Chr.
36:19; Ps.
74:6-8; 79:1;
Is. 64:10, 11;
Lam. 2:7;
Mic. 3:12
_b_Jer. 39:8

14 _a_2 Kin.
25:10; Neh.
1:3

15 _a_2 Kin.
25:11 _b_Jer.
39:9

52:1 This historical appendix (through the end of the book) shows how Jeremiah's prophecies were fulfilled and is almost identical with 2 Kings 24:18-25:30.
52:4-5 The siege of Jerusalem began in January 587 and continued until July 586.
52:8-11 See 39:4-7.

52:9 _Riblah._ Situated 36 miles NE. of Baalbek, it was the site of the field headquarters for the Babylonians (cf. 2 Kings 25:6, 20, 21).
52:12 _the nineteenth year._ Includes the accession year of Nebuchadnezzar, whereas the reference in verse 29 does not. See note on 25:1.

king of Babylon, and the rest of the artisans.

16 But ᵃNebuzaradan the captain of the guard left some of the poorest of the land to be vinedressers and plowmen.

17 Now the bronze ᵃpillars which belonged to the house of the LORD and the ᵇstands and the bronze ᶜsea, which were in the house of the LORD, the Chaldeans broke in pieces and carried all their bronze to Babylon.

18 And they also took away the ᵃpots, the shovels, the snuffers, the basins, the pans, and all the bronze vessels which were used in *temple* service.

19 The captain of the guard also took away the ᵃbowls, the firepans, the basins, the pots, the lampstands, the pans and the libation bowls, what was fine gold and what was fine silver.

20 The two pillars, the one sea, and the twelve bronze bulls that were under the sea, *and* the stands, which King Solomon had made for the house of the LORD— the bronze of all these vessels was ᵃbeyond weight.

21 As for the pillars, the ᵃheight of each pillar was eighteen cubits, and it was twelve cubits in ᵃcircumference and four fingers in thickness, *and* hollow.

22 Now a ᵃcapital of bronze was on it; and the height of each capital was five cubits, with network and ᵇpomegranates upon the capital all around, all of bronze. And the second pillar was like these, including pomegranates.

23 And there were ninety-six exposed pomegranates; all ᵃthe pomegranates *numbered* a hundred on the network all around.

B The Fate of Certain People, 52:24-34

24 Then the captain of the guard took ᵃSeraiah the chief priest and ᵇZephaniah the second priest, with the three ᶜofficers of the temple.

25 He also took from the city one official who was overseer of the men of war, and seven of the ᵃking's advisers who were found in the city, and the scribe of the commander of the army who mustered the people of the land, and sixty men of the people of the land who were found in the midst of the city.

26 And Nebuzaradan the captain of the guard took them and ᵃbrought them to the king of Babylon at Riblah.

27 Then the king of Babylon ᵃstruck them down and put them to death at Riblah in the land of Hamath. So Judah was ᵇled away into exile from its land.

28 These are the people whom ᵃNebuchadnezzar carried away into exile: in the seventh year 3,023 Jews;

29 in the eighteenth year of Nebuchadnezzar 832 persons from Jerusalem;

30 in the twenty-third year of Nebuchadnezzar, ᵃNebuzaradan the captain of the guard carried into exile 745 Jewish people; there were 4,600 persons in all.

31 ᵃNow it came about in the thirty-seventh year of the exile of Jehoiachin king of Judah, in the twelfth month, on the twenty-fifth of the month, that Evilmerodach king of Babylon, in the *first* year of his reign, ᵇshowed favor to Jehoiachin king of Judah and brought him out of prison.

Cross references (margin)

16 ᵃ2 Kin. 25:12; Jer. 39:10; 40:2-6
17 ᵃ1 Kin. 7:15-22; 2 Kin. 25:13; Jer. 27:19-22; 52:20-23 ᵇ1 Kin. 7:27-37 ᶜ1 Kin. 7:23-26
18 ᵃEx. 27:3; 1 Kin. 7:40, 45; 2 Kin. 25:14
19 ᵃ1 Kin. 7:49, 50; 2 Kin. 25:15
20 ᵃ1 Kin. 7:47; 2 Kin. 25:16
21 ᵃ1 Kin. 7:15; 2 Kin. 25:17; 2 Chr. 3:15
22 ᵃ1 Kin. 7:16; 2 Kin. 25:17 ᵇ1 Kin. 7:20, 42
23 ᵃ1 Kin. 7:20

24 ᵃ2 Kin. 25:18; 1 Chr. 6:14; Ezra 7:1 ᵇ2 Kin. 25:18; Jer. 21:1; 29:25, 29; 37:3 ᶜ1 Chr. 9:19; Jer. 35:4
25 ᵃ2 Kin. 25:19; Esth. 1:14
26 ᵃ2 Kin. 25:20
27 ᵃ2 Kin. 25:21; Ezek. 8:11-18 ᵇIs. 6:11, 12; 27:10; 32:13, 14; Jer. 13:19; 20:4; 25:9-11; 39:9; Ezek. 33:28; Mic. 4:10
★28 ᵃ2 Kin. 24:2, 3, 12-16; 2 Chr. 36:20; Ezra 2:1; Neh. 7:6; Dan. 1:1-3
★30 ᵃ2 Kin. 25:11; Jer. 39:9
★31-34
31 ᵃ2 Kin. 25:27 ᵇGen. 40:13, 20; Ps. 3:3; 27:6

52:28 The 3,023 mentioned in this verse probably was the number of adult males (cf. 2 Kings 24:12-16).
52:30 This third deportation was probably a punishment for the assassination of Gedaliah (chap. 41).
52:31-34 *Evil-merodach.* Son of Nebuchadnezzar; reigned 562-560. Tablets recovered from the ruined Ishtar Gate in Babylon confirm this account of the kindness shown to Jehoiachin.

32 *a*2 Kin. 25:28

32 *a*Then he spoke kindly to him and set his throne above the thrones of the kings who *were* with him in Babylon.

33 *a*Gen. 41:14, 42; 2 Kin. 25:29 *b*2 Sam. 9:7, 13; 1 Kin. 2:7

33 So Jehoiachin *a*changed his prison clothes, and *b*had his meals in the king's presence regularly all the days of his life.

34 And for his allowance, a *a*regular allowance was given him by the king of Babylon, a daily portion all the days of his life until the day of his death.

34 *a*2 Sam. 9:10; 2 Kin. 25:30

INTRODUCTION TO
THE BOOK OF LAMENTATIONS

AUTHOR: Jeremiah   DATE: 586/5 B.C.

Title *The term Lamentations is from a Greek verb meaning "to cry aloud" and accurately describes the contents of the book, which consists of five melancholy poems of mourning over the utter destruction of Jerusalem and the Temple by the Babylonians.*

Authorship *Though the book itself does not name its author, the consensus of Jewish tradition attributed it to Jeremiah. A superscription to this book in the Septuagint (Greek translation of the O.T.) and Vulgate (Latin Bible) reads in part, "Jeremiah sat weeping and lamented with this lamentation over Jerusalem." Also, there are many similarities between Lamentations and Jeremiah (e.g., the phrase "daughter of" occurs about twenty times in each book). Further, Jeremiah is connected with this type of literature in 2 Chron. 35:25.*

Structure *The book consists of five poems, one for each chapter, the first four being written as acrostics (each verse begins with a word whose first letter is successively one of the twenty-two letters of the Hebrew alphabet—except in chapter 3, where three verses are allotted to each letter). These four chapters are also written in what is called "limping meter," a cadence used in funeral dirges, and thus most appropriate for this lament over the destruction of Jerusalem.*

Use *The Jews read this book publicly on the ninth day of the month of Ab (about mid-July), in commemoration of the destructions of Jerusalem in 586 B.C. (by the Babylonians) and in A.D. 70 (by the Romans). Roman Catholics use it during the last three days of Holy Week. The concern of the book reminds one of Jesus' burden over Jerusalem (Matt. 23:37-38). The best known verses in the book are undoubtedly 1:12a and 3:22-23.*

OUTLINE OF LAMENTATIONS

I. **The Desolation of Jerusalem, 1:1-22**
  A. The Barrenness of the City, 1:1-11
  B. The Anguish of the City, 1:12-22
II. **The Destruction of Jerusalem, 2:1-22**
  A. The Lord's Judgment, 2:1-10
  B. The Author's Lament, 2:11-22
III. **The Distraught Prophet, 3:1-66**
  A. His Lament, 3:1-18
  B. His Hope, 3:19-42

  C. His Suffering, 3:43-54
  D. His Prayer, 3:55-66
IV. **The Defeated People of Jerusalem, 4:1-22**
  A. The Siege of the City, 4:1-12
  B. The Reasons for the Siege, 4:13-20
  C. The Hope for the Future, 4:21-22
V. **The Prayer for the People, 5:1-22**
  A. Confession, 5:1-18
  B. Petition, 5:19-22

THE BOOK OF LAMENTATIONS

I THE DESOLATION OF JERUSALEM, 1:1–22

A The Barrenness of the City, 1:1–11

★ 1 *a*Is. 3:26 *b*Is. 22:2 *c*Is. 54:4 *d*1 Kin. 4:21; Ezra 4:20; Jer. 31:7 *e*2 Kin. 23:35; Jer. 40:9

1 How *a*lonely sits the city
    That was *b*full of peo-
    ple!
She has become like a
    *c*widow
Who was once *d*great
    among the nations!
She who was a princess
    among the provinces
Has become a *e*forced la-
    borer!

★ 2 *a*Ps. 6:6; 77:2-6; Lam. 1:16 *b*Jer. 2:25; 3:1; 22:20-22 *c*Job 19:13, 14; Ps. 31:11; Mic. 7:5

2 She *a*weeps bitterly in the
    night,
And her tears are on her
    cheeks;
She has none to comfort
    her
Among all her *b*lovers.
All her friends have *c*dealt
    treacherously with
    her;
They have become her en-
    emies.

3 *a*Jer. 13:19 *b*Lev. 26:39; Deut. 28:64-67 *c*2 Kin. 25:4, 5

3 *a*Judah has gone into exile
    under affliction,
And under harsh servi-
    tude;
She dwells *b*among the na-
    tions,
But she has found no rest;
All *c*her pursuers have
    overtaken her
In the midst of distress.

★ 4 *a*Is. 24:4-6; Lam. 2:6, 7 *b*Jer. 9:11; 10:22 *c*Lam. 2:10, 21 *d*Joel 1:8-13

4 The roads of Zion are in
    mourning
Because *a*no one comes to
    the appointed feasts.
All her gates are *b*desolate;
Her priests are groaning,
Her *c*virgins are afflicted,
And she herself is *d*bitter.

5 Her adversaries have be-
    come her masters,
Her enemies prosper;
For the LORD has *a*caused
    her grief
Because of the multitude
    of her transgressions;
Her little ones have gone
    away
As captives before the ad-
    versary.

5 *a*Ps. 90:7, 8; Ezek. 8:17, 18; 9:9, 10

6 And all her *a*majesty
Has departed from the
    daughter of Zion;
Her princes have become
    like bucks
That have found no pas-
    ture;
And they have *b*fled with-
    out strength
Before the pursuer.

★ 6 *a*Jer. 13:18 *b*2 Kin. 25:4, 5

7 In the days of her affliction
    and homelessness
*a*Jerusalem remembers all
    her precious things
That were from the days of
    old
When her people fell into
    the hand of the adver-
    sary,
And *b*no one helped her.
The adversaries saw her,
They *c*mocked at her ruin.

7 *a*Ps. 42:4; 77:5-9 *b*Jer. 37:7; Lam. 4:17 *c*Ps. 79:4; Jer. 48:27

8 Jerusalem sinned *a*greatly,
Therefore *b*she has be-
    come an unclean
    thing.
All who honored her de-
    spise her
Because they have seen
    her nakedness;
Even *c*she herself groans
    and turns away.

8 *a*Is. 59:2-13; Lam. 1:5, 20 *b*Lam. 1:17 *c*Lam. 1:11, 21, 22

9 Her *a*uncleanness was in
    her skirts;

9 *a*Jer. 2:34; Ezek. 24:13 *b*Deut. 32:29; Is. 47:7 *c*Is. 3:8; Jer. 13:17, 18 *d*Eccl. 4:1; Jer. 16:7 *e*Ps. 25:18; 119:153 *f*Ps. 74:23; Zeph. 2:10

1:1 The contrast between *princess* and *forced laborer* (vassal) shows the extent of the fall of Jerusalem.
1:2 *her lovers.* I.e., the nations in which Judah trusted, some of whom helped the Babylonians plunder Jerusalem.

1:4 *The roads of Zion.* The roads to Jerusalem, formerly crowded with worshipers travelling to the Temple, were now deserted.
1:6 *princes.* Probably a reference to Zedekiah's sons (Jer. 39:6).

She did not consider her
ᵇfuture;
Therefore she has ᶜfallen
astonishingly;
ᵈShe has no comforter.
"ᵉSee, O LORD, my affliction,
For the enemy has ᶠmagni-
fied himself!"

10 ᵃPs.
74:4-8; Is.
64:10, 11;
Jer. 51:51
ᵇDeut. 23:3

10   The   adversary   has
stretched out his hand
Over   all   her   precious
things,
For she has seen the ᵃna-
tions enter her sanctu-
ary,
The   ones   whom   Thou
didst command
That they should ᵇnot en-
ter into Thy congrega-
tion.

★11 ᵃJer.
38:9; 52:6
ᵇ1 Sam.
30:12 ᶜJer.
15:19

11   All   her   people   groan
ᵃseeking bread;
They have given their pre-
cious things for food
To   ᵇrestore   their   lives
themselves.
"See, O LORD, and look,
For I am ᶜdespised."

B   The Anguish of the City,
1:12–22

12 ᵃJer.
18:16; 48:27
ᵇJer. 30:23,
24 ᶜIs.
13:13; Jer.
4:8

12   "Is ᵃit nothing to all you
who pass this way?
Look and see if there is
any pain like my pain
Which was severely dealt
out to me,
Which the ᵇLORD inflicted
on the day of His
ᶜfierce anger.

★13 ᵃJob
30:30; Ps.
22:14; Hab.
3:16 ᵇJob
19:6; Ps.
66:11 ᶜJer.
44:6

13   "From on high He sent fire
into my ᵃbones,
And   it   prevailed   over
them;
He has spread a ᵇnet for
my feet;
He has turned me back;
He has made me ᶜdesolate,
Faint all day long.

14 ᵃProv.
5:22; Is. 47:6
ᵇJer. 28:13,
14 ᶜJer.
32:3, 5;
Ezek. 25:4, 7

14   "The ᵃyoke of my transgressions is bound;

By His hand they are knit
together;
They have ᵇcome upon my
neck;
He has made my strength
fail;
The Lord ᶜhas given me
into the hands
Of those against whom I
am not able to stand.

15 ᵃIs. 41:2;
Jer. 13:24;
37:10 ᵇJer.
6:11; 18:21
ᶜMal. 4:3

15   "The ᵃLord has rejected all
my strong men
In my midst;
He has called an appointed
time against me
To crush my ᵇyoung men;
The Lord has ᶜtrodden as
in a wine press
The virgin daughter of Ju-
dah.

16 ᵃJer.
14:17; Lam.
2:11, 18;
3:48, 49
ᵇPs. 69:20;
Eccl. 4:1;
Lam. 1:2

16   "For these things I ᵃweep;
My eyes run down with
water;
Because far from me is a
ᵇcomforter,
One who restores my soul;
My children are desolate
Because the enemy has
prevailed."

★17 ᵃIs.
1:15; Jer.
4:31 ᵇ2 Kin.
24:2-4; Jer.
12:9 ᶜLam.
1:8

17   Zion ᵃstretches out her
hands;
There is no one to comfort
her;
The LORD has ᵇcommanded
concerning Jacob
That the ones round about
him should be his ad-
versaries;
ᶜJerusalem has become an
unclean thing among
them.

18 ᵃPs.
119:75; Jer.
12:1 ᵇ1 Sam.
12:14, 15;
Jer. 4:17
ᶜLam. 1:12
ᵈDeut.
28:32, 41

18   "The LORD is ᵃrighteous;
For I have ᵇrebelled against
His command;
Hear now, all peoples,
And ᶜbehold my pain;
ᵈMy virgins and my young
men
Have gone into captivity.

19 ᵃJob
19:13-19;
Lam. 1:2
ᵇJer. 14:15;
Lam. 2:20
ᶜLam. 1:11

19   "I ᵃcalled to my lovers, but
they deceived me;
My ᵇpriests and my elders
perished in the city,

1:11 their precious things. During the siege the
people gladly traded their valuables for food.
1:13 fire . . . net . . . desolate. A description of

the siege of Jerusalem.
1:17 an unclean thing. See Lev. 15:19-27. All Judah's lovers (allies) became her enemies.

While they sought food to
ᶜrestore their strength
themselves.

20 ᵃIs.
16:11; Lam.
2:11 ᵇJer.
14:20

20 "See, O Lᴏʀᴅ, for I am in
distress;
My ᵃspirit is greatly troubled;
My heart is overturned
within me,
For I have been very ᵇre-
bellious.
In the street the sword
slays;
In the house it is like
death.

★21 ᵃLam.
1:4, 8, 22
ᵇPs. 35:15;
Jer. 50:11;
Lam. 2:15
ᶜIs. 14:5, 6;
47:6, 11; Jer.
30:16

21 "They have heard that I
ᵃgroan;
There is no one to comfort
me;
All my enemies have
heard of my calamity;
They are ᵇglad that Thou
hast done it.
Oh, that Thou wouldst
bring the day which
Thou hast proclaimed,
That they may become
ᶜlike me.

22 ᵃNeh.
4:4, 5; Ps.
137:7, 8

22 "Let all their wickedness
come before Thee;
And ᵃdeal with them as
Thou hast dealt with
me
For all my transgressions;
For my groans are many,
and my heart is faint."

II THE DESTRUCTION OF
JERUSALEM, 2:1–22
A The Lord's Judgment, 2:1–10

1 ᵃEzek.
30:18 ᵇIs.
14:12-15;
Ezek. 28:14-
16 ᶜIs. 64:11
ᵈPs. 99:5;
132:7

2 How the Lord has ᵃcovered
the daughter of Zion
With a cloud in His anger!
He has ᵇcast from heaven
to earth
The ᶜglory of Israel,
And has not remembered
His ᵈfootstool
In the day of His anger.

2 ᵃPs. 21:9;
Lam. 3:43
ᵇLam. 2:5;
Mic. 5:11, 14
ᶜIs. 25:12;
26:5 ᵈPs.
89:39, 40; Is.
43:28

2 The Lord has ᵃswallowed
up; He has not spared

All the habitations of Jacob.
In His wrath He has
ᵇthrown down
The strongholds of the
daughter of Judah;
He has ᶜbrought *them*
down to the ground;
He has ᵈprofaned the
kingdom and its
princes.

3 In fierce anger He has cut
off
All the ᵃstrength of Israel;
He has ᵇdrawn back His
right hand
From before the enemy.
And He has ᶜburned in Ja-
cob like a flaming fire
Consuming round about.

3 ᵃPs. 75:5,
10; Jer.
48:25 ᵇPs.
74:11; Jer.
21:4, 5 ᶜIs.
42:25; Jer.
21:14

4 He has bent His ᵃbow like
an enemy,
He has set His right hand
like an adversary
And slain all that were
ᵇpleasant to the eye;
In the tent of the daughter
of Zion
He has ᶜpoured out His
wrath like fire.

4 ᵃJob 6:4;
16:13; Lam.
3:12, 13
ᵇEzek. 24:25
ᶜIs. 42:25;
Jer. 7:20

5 The Lord has become like
an ᵃenemy.
He has ᵇswallowed up Is-
rael;
He has swallowed up all its
ᶜpalaces;
He has destroyed its
strongholds
And ᵈmultiplied in the
daughter of Judah
Mourning and moaning.

5 ᵃJer.
30:14 ᵇLam.
2:2 ᶜJer.
52:13; Lam.
2:2 ᵈJer.
9:17-20

6 And He has violently
treated His tabernacle
like a garden *booth;*
He has ᵃdestroyed His ap-
pointed meeting
place;
The Lᴏʀᴅ has ᵇcaused to
be forgotten
The appointed feast and
sabbath in Zion,
And He has ᶜdespised king
and priest

6 ᵃJer.
52:13 ᵇJer.
17:27; Lam.
1:4; Zeph.
3:18 ᶜLam.
4:16

1:21 *the day.* Of Babylon's punishment, as predicted in Jer. 50–51. *bring.* Or, brought, referring to the day of Judah's captivity.

In the indignation of His anger.

7 The Lord has [a]rejected His altar,
He has abandoned His sanctuary;
He [b]has delivered into the hand of the enemy
The walls of her palaces.
They have made a [c]noise in the house of the LORD
As in the day of an appointed feast.

8 The LORD determined to destroy
The wall of the daughter of Zion.
He has [a]stretched out a line,
He has not restrained His hand from destroying;
And He has [b]caused rampart and wall to lament;
They have languished together.

9 Her [a]gates have sunk into the ground,
He has destroyed and broken her bars.
Her king and her princes are among the nations;
The [b]law is no more;
Also, her prophets find
[c]No vision from the LORD.

10 The elders of the daughter of Zion
[a]Sit on the ground, they [b]are silent.
They have thrown [c]dust on their heads;
They have girded themselves with [d]sackcloth.
The [e]virgins of Jerusalem
Have bowed their heads to the ground.

B The Author's Lament,
2:11-22

11 My [a]eyes fail because of tears,
My [b]spirit is greatly troubled;
My [c]heart is poured out on the earth,
[d]Because of the destruction of the daughter of my people,
When [e]little ones and infants faint
In the streets of the city.

12 They say to their mothers,
"[a]Where is grain and wine?"
As they faint like a wounded man
In the streets of the city,
As their [b]life is poured out
On their mothers' bosom.

13 How shall I admonish you?
To what [a]shall I compare you,
O daughter of Jerusalem?
To what shall I liken you as I comfort you,
O [b]virgin daughter of Zion?
For your ruin is as vast as the sea;
Who can [c]heal you?

14 Your [a]prophets have seen for you
False and foolish visions;
And they have not [b]exposed your iniquity
So as to restore you from captivity,
But they have [c]seen for you false and misleading oracles.

15 All who pass along the way
[a]Clap their hands in derision at you;

Cross references (left column):

7 [a]Ps. 78:59-61; Is. 64:11; Ezek. 7:20-22
[b]Jer. 33:4, 5; 52:13 [c]Ps. 74:3-8

8 [a]2 Kin. 21:13; Is. 34:11; Amos 7:7-9 [b]Is. 3:26; Jer. 14:2

9 [a]Neh. 1:3 [b]Hos. 3:4 [c]Jer. 14:14; 23:16; Ezek. 7:26

★10-12

10 [a]Job 2:13; Is. 3:26; 47:1 [b]Amos 8:3 [c]Job 2:12; Ezek. 27:30 [d]Is. 15:3; Jon. 3:6-8 [e]Lam. 1:4

Cross references (right column):

11 [a]Lam. 1:16; 3:48, 51 [b]Jer. 4:19 [c]Job 16:13 [d]Is. 22:4; Lam. 4:10 [e]Jer. 44:7; Lam. 2:19

12 [a]Jer. 5:17 [b]Job 30:16; Ps. 42:4; 62:8

13 [a]Lam. 1:12 [b]Is. 37:22 [c]Jer. 8:22; 30:12-15

★14 [a]Jer. 23:25-29; 29:8, 9 [b]Is. 58:1; Ezek. 23:36; Mic. 3:8 [c]Jer. 23:36; Ezek. 22:25, 28

15 [a]Job 27:23; Ezek. 25:6 [b]Ps. 22:7; Is. 37:22; Jer. 18:16; 19:8; Zeph. 2:15 [c]Ps. 50:2 [d]Ps. 48:2

2:10-12 The inevitable accompaniments of war: silenced *elders*, shamed *virgins*, and starving *infants*.
2:14 Instead of confronting the people with their

sins, the false prophets had predicted peace and prosperity (Jer. 2:5; 10:15; 14:14-16; 23:9-40).

They [b]hiss and shake their heads
At the daughter of Jerusalem,
"Is this the city of which they said,
'[c]The perfection of beauty,
[d]A joy to all the earth'?"

16 All [a]your enemies
Have opened their mouths wide against you;
They hiss and [b]gnash *their* teeth.
They say, "We have [c]swallowed *her* up!
Surely this is the [d]day for which we waited;
We have reached *it,* we have seen *it.*"

17 The Lord has [a]done what He purposed;
He has accomplished His word
Which He commanded from days of old.
He has thrown down [b]without sparing,
And He has caused the enemy to [c]rejoice over you;
He has [d]exalted the might of your adversaries.

18 Their [a]heart cried out to the Lord,
"O [b]wall of the daughter of Zion,
Let *your* [c]tears run down like a river day and night;
Give yourself no relief;
Let your eyes have no rest.

19 "Arise, cry aloud in the [a]night
At the beginning of the night watches;
[b]Pour out your heart like water
Before the presence of the Lord;
Lift up your hands to Him

For the [c]life of your little ones
Who are [d]faint because of hunger
At the head of every street."

20 See, O Lord, and look!
With [a]whom hast Thou dealt thus?
Should women [b]eat their offspring,
The little ones who were born healthy?
Should [c]priest and prophet be slain
In the sanctuary of the Lord?

21 On the ground in the streets
Lie [a]young and old,
My [b]virgins and my young men
Have fallen by the sword.
Thou hast slain *them* in the day of Thine anger,
Thou hast slaughtered, [c]not sparing.

22 Thou didst call as in the day of an appointed feast
My [a]terrors on every side;
And there was [b]no one who escaped or survived
In the day of the Lord's anger.
Those [c]whom I bore and reared,
My enemy annihilated them.

III   THE DISTRAUGHT PROPHET, 3:1–66

A   His Lament, 3:1–18

3 I am the man who has [a]seen affliction
Because of the rod of His wrath.

Cross references (left margin):

16 [a]Job 16:10; Ps. 22:13; Lam. 3:46 [b]Job 16:9; Ps. 35:16; 37:12 [c]Ps. 56:2; 124:3; Jer. 51:34 [d]Obad. 12-15

17 [a]Jer. 4:28 [b]Lam. 2:1, 2; Ezek. 5:11; 7:8, 9; 8:18 [c]Ps. 35:24, 26; 89:42; Is. 14:29 [d]Deut. 28:43, 44; Lam. 1:5

★18 [a]Ps. 119:145; Hos. 7:14 [b]Lam. 2:8; Hab. 2:11 [c]Ps. 119:136; Jer. 9:1; Lam. 1:2, 16; 3:48, 49

★19 [a]Ps. 42:3; Is. 26:9 [b]1 Sam. 1:15; Ps. 42:4; 62:8 [c]Lam. 2:11 [d]Is. 51:20

Cross references (right margin):

★20-21
20 [a]Ex. 32:11; Deut. 9:26 [b]Jer. 19:9; Lam. 4:10 [c]Ps. 78:64; Jer. 14:15; 23:11, 12

21 [a]2 Chr. 36:17; Jer. 6:11 [b]Ps. 78:62, 63 [c]Jer. 13:14; Zech. 11:6

22 [a]Ps. 31:13; Is. 24:17; Jer. 6:25 [b]Jer. 11:11 [c]Jer. 16:2-4; 44:7

1 [a]Ps. 88:7, 15, 16

2:18 *Let your eyes have no rest.* I.e., continue your weeping.
2:19 *At the beginning of the night watches.* I.e., interrupt your sleep at the beginning of each four-hour period (a watch), into which the twelve-hour night was divided.
2:20-21 The siege drove some mothers to eat their children, saw priests slain in the Temple, and left bodies unburied in the streets.

2 He has driven me and
made me walk
In ªdarkness and not in
light.

3 Surely against me He has
ªturned His hand
Repeatedly all the day.

4 He has caused my ªflesh
and my skin to waste
away,
He has ᵇbroken my bones.

5 He has ªbesieged and encompassed me with
ᵇbitterness and hard-
ship.

6 In ªdark places He has
made me dwell,
Like those who have long
been dead.

7 He has ªwalled *me* in so
that I cannot go out;
He has made my ᵇchain
heavy.

8 Even when I cry out and
call for help,
He ªshuts out my prayer.

9 He has ªblocked my ways
with hewn stone;
He has made my paths
crooked.

10 He is to me like a bear
lying in wait,
Like a lion in secret places.

11 He has turned aside my
ways and ªtorn me to
pieces;
He has made me desolate.

12 He ªbent His bow
And ᵇset me as a target for
the arrow.

13 He made the arrows of His
ªquiver
To enter into my inward
parts.

14 I have become a ªlaughing-
stock to all my people,
Their *mocking* ᵇsong all
the day.

15 He has ªfilled me with bitterness,

He has made me drunk
with wormwood.

16 And He has ªbroken my
teeth with ᵇgravel;
He has made me cower in
the ᶜdust.

17 And my soul has been rejected ªfrom peace;
I have forgotten happiness.

18 So I say, "My strength has
perished,
And *so has* my ªhope from
the LORD."

B His Hope, 3:19–42

19 Remember my affliction
and my wandering,
the ªwormwood and
bitterness.

20 Surely ªmy soul remem-
bers
And is ᵇbowed down
within me.

21 This I recall to my mind,
Therefore I have ªhope.

22 The LORD's ªlovingkindnesses indeed never
cease,
ᵇFor His compassions nev-
er fail.

23 *They* are new ªevery
morning;
Great is ᵇThy faithfulness.

24 "The LORD is my ªportion,"
says my soul,
"Therefore I ᵇhave hope in
Him."

25 The LORD is good to those
who ªwait for Him,
To the person who ᵇseeks
Him.

26 *It is* good that he ªwaits si-
lently
For the salvation of the
LORD.

27 *It is* good for a man that he
should bear
The yoke in his youth.

3:7 *He has walled me in.* The Assyrians popular-
ized the practice of walling up prisoners so
that they would die more quickly. Jeremiah,
using poetic license, feels like he had experienced that torture.
3:13 *inward parts.* Lit., kidneys, thought to be

one of the centers of life and emotions (cf. Job
19:27; Psalm 73:21; Prov. 23:16; Jer. 17:10).
3:14 *a laughingstock.* See Jer. 20:7.
3:22 *lovingkindnesses.* See note at Hos. 2:19.
Some texts read, It is of the Lord's lovingkindness that we are not consumed.

28 ^aJer.
15:17

28 Let him ^asit alone and be
silent
Since He has laid *it* on
him.

★**29** ^aJob
16:15; 40:4
^bJer. 31:17

29 Let him put his mouth in
the ^adust,
Perhaps there is ^bhope.

★**30** ^aJob
16:10; Is.
50:6

30 Let him give his ^acheek to
the smiter;
Let him be filled with reproach.

31 ^aPs. 77:7;
94:14; Is.
54:7-10

31 For the Lord will ^anot reject forever,

32 ^aPs.
78:38;
106:43-45;
Hos. 11:8

32 For if He causes grief,
Then He will have ^acom-
passion
According to His abundant
lovingkindness.

33 ^aPs.
119:67, 71,
75; Ezek.
33:11; Heb.
12:10

33 For He ^adoes not afflict
willingly,
Or grieve the sons of men.

34 To crush under His feet
All the prisoners of the
land,

★**35-36**

35 ^aPs.
140:12; Prov.
17:15

35 To deprive a man of ^ajus-
tice
In the presence of the
Most High

36 ^aJer.
22:3; Hab.
1:13

36 To ^adefraud a man in his
lawsuit—
Of these things the Lord
does not approve.

★**37-38**

37 ^aPs.
33:9-11

37 Who is there who speaks
and it ^acomes to pass,
Unless the Lord has com-
manded *it*?

38 ^aJob
2:10; Is.
45:7; Jer.
32:42

38 *Is it* not from the mouth of
the Most High
That ^aboth good and ill go
forth?

39 ^aJer.
30:15; Mic.
7:9; Heb.
12:5, 6

39 Why should *any* living
mortal, or *any* man,
Offer ^acomplaint in view
of his sins?

40 ^aPs.
119:59;
139:23, 24;
2 Cor. 13:5

40 Let us ^aexamine and probe
our ways,
And let us return to the
LORD.

41 ^aPs. 25:1;
28:2; 141:2

41 We ^alift up our heart and
hands
Toward God in heaven;

42 We have ^atransgressed and
rebelled,
Thou hast ^bnot pardoned.

42 ^aNeh.
9:26; Jer.
14:20; Dan.
9:5 ^b2 Kin.
24:4; Jer.
5:7, 9

C   His Suffering, 3:43-54

43 Thou hast covered *Thyself*
with ^aanger
And ^bpursued us;
Thou hast slain *and* ^chast
not spared.

43 ^aLam.
2:21 ^bPs.
83:15; Lam.
3:66 ^cLam.
2:2, 17, 21

44 Thou hast ^acovered Thyself with a cloud
So that ^bno prayer can pass
through.

44 ^aPs. 97:2
^bLam. 3:8;
Zech. 7:13

45 *Mere* ^aoffscouring and refuse Thou hast made
us
In the midst of the peoples.

★**45** ^a1 Cor.
4:13

46 All our enemies have
^aopened their mouths
against us.

46 ^aJob
30:9, 10; Ps.
22:6-8; Lam.
2:16

47 ^aPanic and pitfall have befallen us,
Devastation and destruc-
tion;

47 ^aIs.
24:17, 18;
Jer. 48:43,
44

48 My ^aeyes run down with
streams of water
Because of the destruction
of the daughter of my
people.

48 ^aPs.
119:136; Jer.
9:1, 18; Lam.
1:16; 2:11,
18

49 My eyes pour down ^aun-
ceasingly,
Without stopping,

49 ^aPs. 77:2;
Jer. 14:17

50 Until the LORD ^alooks
down
And sees from heaven.

50 ^aPs.
80:14; Is.
63:15; Lam.
5:1

51 My eyes bring pain to my
soul
Because of all the daugh-
ters of my city.

52 My enemies ^awithout
cause
Hunted me down ^blike a
bird;

52 ^aPs. 35:7,
19 ^b1 Sam.
26:20; Ps.
11:1; 124:7

53 They have silenced me ^ain
the pit
And have ^bplaced a stone
on me.

★**53** ^aJer.
37:16; 38:6,
9 ^bDan. 6:17

3:29 *his mouth in the dust.* A typical Oriental
way of exacting total submission.
3:30 *give his cheek.* A sign of unconditional surrender (see Mic. 5:1 and Luke 22:64).
3:35-36 God disapproves of any attempt to deprive a person of his rights.

3:37-38 Nothing can happen without God's
knowledge (see Isa. 45:7).
3:45 *offscouring.* Something rejected and unfit
for use. See 1 Cor. 4:13.
3:53 *pit.* See Jer. 38:6.

54 aPs. 69:2;
Jon. 2:3-5

54 Waters flowed ªover my
head;
I said, "I am cut off!"

D His Prayer, 3:55–66

55 aPs.
130:1; Jon.
2:2

55 I ªcalled on Thy name, O
LORD,
Out of the lowest pit.

56 aJob
34:28 bPs.
55:1

56 Thou hast ªheard my
voice,
"ᵇDo not hide Thine ear
from my *prayer for*
relief,
From my cry for help."

57 aPs.
145:18 bIs.
41:10, 14

57 Thou didst ªdraw near
when I called on
Thee;
Thou didst say, "ᵇDo not
fear!"

58 aJer.
50:34 bPs.
34:22

58 O Lord, Thou didst ªplead
my soul's cause;
Thou hast ᵇredeemed my
life.

59 aJer.
18:19, 20
bPs. 26:1;
43:1

59 O LORD, Thou hast ªseen
my oppression;
ᵇJudge my case.

60 aJer.
11:19

60 Thou hast seen all their
vengeance,
All their ªschemes against
me.

61 aPs.
74:18; 89:50;
Lam. 5:1;
Zeph. 2:8

61 Thou hast heard their ªreproach, O LORD,
All their schemes against
me.

62 aPs. 59:7,
12; 140:3;
Ezek. 36:3

62 The ªlips of my assailants
and their whispering
Are against me all day
long.

63 aPs.
139:2 bJob
30:9; Lam.
3:14

63 Look on their ªsitting and
their rising;
ᵇI am their mocking song.

64 aPs. 28:4;
Jer. 51:6, 24,
56

64 Thou wilt ªrecompense
them, O LORD,
According to the work of
their hands.

65 aEx. 14:8;
Deut. 2:30;
Is. 6:10

65 Thou wilt give them
ªhardness of heart,
Thy curse will be on them.

66 Thou wilt ªpursue them in
anger and destroy
them
From under the ᵇheavens
of the LORD!

66 aLam.
3:43 bPs.
8:3

**IV THE DEFEATED PEOPLE OF
JERUSALEM, 4:1–22**

A The Siege of the City, 4:1–12

4 How ªdark the gold has become,
How the pure gold has
changed!
The sacred stones are
poured out
At the corner of every
street.

1 aEzek.
7:19-22

2 The precious sons of Zion,
Weighed against fine gold,
How they are regarded as
ªearthen jars,
The work of a potter's
hands!

★ 2-4

2 aIs.
30:14; Jer.
19:1, 11

3 Even ªjackals offer the
breast,
They nurse their young;
But the daughter of my
people has become
ᵇcruel
Like ᶜostriches in the wilderness.

3 aIs.
13:22; 34:13
bIs. 49:15;
Ezek. 5:10
cJob 39:14-
17

4 The ªtongue of the infant
cleaves
To the roof of its mouth
because of ᵇthirst;
The little ones ᶜask for
bread,
But no one breaks *it* for
them.

4 aPs.
22:15 bJer.
14:3 cLam.
2:12

5 Those who ate ªdelicacies
Are desolate in the streets;
Those reared in purple
Embrace ash pits.

★ 5 aJer.
6:2; Amos
6:3-7

6 For the iniquity of the
daughter of my peo-
ple
Is greater than the ªsin of
Sodom,

★ 6 aGen.
19:24 bGen.
19:25; Jer.
20:16

4:2–4 In the siege of Jerusalem, children received worse treatment than the offspring of
animals (see 2:19).
4:5 *reared in purple.* I.e., the wealthy.
4:6 *no hands were turned toward her.* The
meaning of the phrase is unclear. It may mean

that Sodom's destruction was directly from the
hand of God rather than through human
hands; or it may mean that it was so sudden
that there was no time for anyone to wring his
hands (i.e., no time to panic).

Which was *b*overthrown as
in a moment,
And no hands were turned
toward her.

★ 7 *a*Ps.
51:7 *b*Ex.
24:10; Job
28:16

7 Her consecrated ones were
*a*purer than snow,
They were whiter than
milk;
They were more ruddy *in*
body than corals,
Their polishing *was* like
*b*lapis lazuli.

8 *a*Job
30:30; Lam.
5:10 *b*Job
19:20; Ps.
102:3-5

8 Their appearance is
*a*blacker than soot,
They are not recognized in
the streets;
Their *b*skin is shriveled on
their bones,
It is withered, it has become like wood.

9 *a*Jer. 16:4
*b*Lev. 26:39;
Ezek. 24:23

9 Better are those *a*slain with
the sword
Than those slain with hunger;
For they *b*pine away, being
stricken
For lack of the fruits of the
field.

10 *a*Lev.
26:29; Deut.
28:57; 2 Kin.
6:29; Jer.
19:9; Lam.
2:20; Ezek.
5:10 *b*Deut.
28:53-55

10 The hands of compassionate women
*a*Boiled their own children;
They became *b*food for
them
Because of the destruction
of the daughter of my
people.

11 *a*Jer.
7:20; Lam.
2:17; Ezek.
22:31 *b*Deut.
32:22; Jer.
17:27

11 The LORD has *a*accomplished His wrath,
He has poured out His
fierce anger;
And He has *b*kindled a fire
in Zion
Which has consumed its
foundations.

12 *a*Deut.
29:24 *b*Jer.
21:13

12 The kings of the earth did
not believe,
Nor *did* any of *a*the inhabi-
tants of the world,
That the adversary and the
enemy
Could *b*enter the gates of
Jerusalem.

B The Reasons for the Siege,
4:13-20

13 Because of the sins of her
*a*prophets
And the iniquities of her
priests,
Who have shed in her
midst
The *b*blood of the righteous,

13 *a*Jer.
5:31; 6:13;
Lam. 2:14;
Ezek. 22:26-
28 *b*Jer.
2:30; 26:8, 9;
Matt. 23:31

14 They wandered, *a*blind, in
the streets;
They were defiled with
*b*blood
So that no one could touch
their *c*garments.

14 *a*Deut.
28:28, 29; Is.
29:10; 56:10;
59:9, 10 *b*Is.
1:15 *c*Jer.
2:34

15 "Depart! *a*Unclean!" they
cried of themselves.
"Depart, depart, do not
touch!"
So they *b*fled and wan-
dered;
Men among the nations
said,
"They shall not continue to
dwell *with us.*"

★15 *a*Lev.
13:45, 46
*b*Jer. 49:5

16 The presence of the LORD
has scattered them;
He will not continue to regard them.
They did not *a*honor the
priests,
They did not favor the elders.

16 *a*Is. 9:14-
16; Jer.
52:24-27

17 Yet our eyes failed;
Looking for help was *a*useless.
In our watching we have
watched
For a *b*nation that could
not save.

★17 *a*Jer.
37:7; Lam.
1:7 *b*Ezek.
29:6, 7, 16

18 They *a*hunted our steps
So that we could not walk
in our streets;
Our *b*end drew near,
Our days were finished
For our end had come.

18 *a*Jer.
16:16 *b*Jer.
5:31; Ezek.
7:2-12; Amos
8:2

19 Our pursuers were
*a*swifter
Than the eagles of the sky.
They chased us on the
mountains;

19 *a*Is. 5:26-
28; 30:16,
17; Jer. 4:13;
Hab. 1:8

4:7 *consecrated ones.* Better, her nobles.
4:15 The false prophets and priests of Judah (v.
13), when their true character was recognized,

were treated like lepers (cf. Lev. 13:45-46).
4:17 *a nation that could not save.* Egypt; see Jer.
37:5-7.

They waited in ambush for
us in the wilderness.

20 aGen. 2:7
b2 Sam.
1:14; 19:21
cJer. 39:5;
52:9 dDan.
4:12

20 The ªbreath of our nostrils,
the ᵇLᴏʀᴅ's anointed,
Was ᶜcaptured in their
pits,
Of whom we had said,
"Under his ᵈshadow
We shall live among the
nations."

C The Hope for the Future,
4:21–22

★21 aPs.
137:7; Jer.
25:21
bObad. 16

21 Rejoice and be glad, O
daughter of ªEdom,
Who dwells in the land of
Uz;
But the ᵇcup will come
around to you as well,
You will become drunk
and make yourself
naked.

22 aIs. 40:2;
Jer. 33:7, 8
bJer. 49:10;
Mal. 1:3, 4

22 *The punishment* of your
iniquity has been
ªcompleted, O daugh-
ter of Zion;
He will exile you no
longer.
But He ᵇwill punish your
iniquity, O daughter
of Edom;
He will expose your sins!

V THE PRAYER FOR THE PEOPLE,
5:1–22

A Confession, 5:1–18

★ 1-18
1 aPs.
44:13-16

5 Remember, O Lᴏʀᴅ, what has
befallen us;
Look, and see our ªre-
proach!

2 aIs. 1:7;
Hos. 8:7, 8
bZeph. 1:13

2 Our inheritance has been
turned over to
ªstrangers,
Our ᵇhouses to aliens.

3 aEx.
22:24; Jer.
15:8; 18:21

3 We have become orphans
ªwithout a father,
Our mothers are like wid-
ows.

4 We have to pay for our
drinking ªwater,
Our wood comes *to us* at a
price.

4 aIs. 3:1

5 Our pursuers are at our
necks;
We are worn out, there is
ªno rest for us.

5 aNeh.
9:36, 37

6 We ·have submitted to
ªEgypt *and* Assyria to
get enough bread.

6 aHos.
9:3; 12:1

7 Our ªfathers sinned, *and*
are no more;
It is we who have borne
their iniquities.

7 aJer.
14:20; 16:12

8 ªSlaves rule over us;
There is ᵇno one to deliver
us from their hand.

8 aNeh.
5:15 bPs.
7:2; Zech.
11:6

9 We get our bread at the
ªrisk of our lives
Because of the sword in
the wilderness.

9 aJer.
40:9-12

10 Our skin has become as
ªhot as an oven,
Because of the burning
heat of famine.

10 aJob
30:30; Lam.
4:8

11 They ravished the ªwomen
in Zion,
The virgins in the cities of
Judah.

11 aIs.
13:16; Zech.
14:2

12 Princes were hung by their
hands;
ªElders were not respected.

12 aIs. 47:6;
Lam. 4:16

13 Young men ªworked at the
grinding mill;
And youths ᵇstumbled un-
der *loads* of wood.

★13 aJudg.
16:21 bJer.
7:18

14 Elders are gone from the
gate,
Young men from their
ªmusic.

14 aIs. 24:8;
Jer. 7:34

15 The joy of our hearts has
ªceased;
Our dancing has been
turned into mourning.

15 aJer.
25:10; Amos
8:10

16 The ªcrown has fallen
from our head;
ᵇWoe to us, for we have
sinned!

16 aJob
19:9; Ps.
89:39; Jer.
13:18 bIs.
3:9-11

4:21 Although *Edom* was allotted the rural areas
of Judah by Nebuchadnezzar (Ezek. 25:12–14;
Obad. 11–14), she would eventually drink the
cup of God's wrath.
5:1–18 A description of the affliction, disgrace,

and despondency of the Jews under their
Babylonian captors.
5:13 To grind grain, considered to be women's
work (see Judg. 16:21), was demeaning for
men.

17 als. 1:5
bJob 17:7;
Lam. 2:11

17 Because of this our [a]heart
is faint;
Because of these things
our [b]eyes are dim;

18 aMic.
3:12 bNeh.
4:3

18 Because of [a]Mount Zion
which lies desolate,
[b]Foxes prowl in it.

B Petition, 5:19–22

19 aPs.
102:12, 25-
27 bPs. 45:6

19 [a]Thou, O Lord, dost rule
forever;

Thy [b]throne is from generation to generation.

20 Why dost Thou [a]forget us
forever;
Why dost Thou forsake us
so long?

20 aPs. 13:1;
44:24

21 [a]Restore us to Thee, O
Lord, that we may be
restored;
Renew [b]our days as of old,

21 aPs. 80:3;
Jer. 31:18
bIs. 60:20-22

22 Unless [a]Thou hast utterly
rejected us,
And art exceedingly [b]an-
gry with us.

★**22** aPs.
60:1, 2; Jer.
7:29 bIs.
64:9

5:22 Like Malachi (4:6) this book ends on a negative note; therefore, when it was publicly read, verse 21 was customarily repeated after the reading of verse 22.

INTRODUCTION TO
THE BOOK OF EZEKIEL

AUTHOR: Ezekiel   DATE: 592–570 B.C.

The Prophet *Of a priestly family (1:3), Ezekiel, whose name means "God strengthens," spent his early years in Jerusalem, until he was taken with other hostages by Nebuchadnezzar to Babylon in 597. There he settled in his own house in a village near Nippur, along the river Chebar (Nebuchadnezzar's royal canal), in Babylonia (3:15, 24). He prophesied for at least 22 years (1:2 and 29:17–21). His wife died in 587 (24:16–18).*

The Times *Ezekiel's ministry to the exiles in Babylon was at the same time as that of Jeremiah to the Jews in Palestine, and of the early years of the ministry of Daniel. For the important events of that period see the Introduction to Jeremiah.*

Contents *Ezekiel's ministry was to keep before the exiles the sins which had brought God's judgment on them and to assure them of God's future blessing in keeping with His covenant. Chapters 1–24 were written before the fall of Jerusalem to remind his fellow captives that God's judgment on the city and Temple was surely coming. Chapters 33–48 contain prophecies of the still future restoration of Israel in the millennial kingdom.*
  Important Messianic sections in the book are 17:22–24; 21:26–27; 34:23–24. The overthrow of Gog is described in chapters 38–39, and the millennial Temple and worship in chapters 40–48. Some well-known passages include 1:4–28; 3:16–21; 11:17–20; 14:14; 28:11–19; 36:24–28; 37:1–28.

OUTLINE OF EZEKIEL

THE BOOK OF EZEKIEL

I EZEKIEL'S CALL AND COMMISSIONING, 1:1-3:27

A Ezekiel's Circumstances, 1:1-3

★ 1 aEzek. 3:23; 10:15, 20 bMatt. 3:16; Mark 1:10; Luke 3:21; Acts 7:56; 10:11; Rev. 4:1; 19:11 cEx. 24:10; Num. 12:6; Is. 1:1; 6:1; Ezek. 8:3; 11:24; 40:2; Dan. 8:1, 2

1 Now it came about in the thirtieth year, on the fifth *day* of the fourth month, while I was by the ªriver Chebar among the exiles, the bheavens were opened and I saw cvisions of God.

2 (On the fifth of the month in the ªfifth year of King Jehoiachin's exile,

3 the ªword of the LORD came expressly to Ezekiel the priest, son of Buzi, in the bland of the Chaldeans by the river Chebar; and there cthe hand of the LORD came upon him.)

★ 2 a2 Kin. 24:12-15; Ezek. 8:1; 20:1

3 a2 Pet. 1:21 bEzek. 12:13 c1 Kin. 18:46; 2 Kin. 3:15; Ezek. 3:14, 22

1:1 *the thirtieth year.* Possibly Ezekiel's own age, and the age at which he would have entered the priesthood had he remained in Jerusalem (Num. 4:3).

1:2 *the fifth year.* I.e., 592.

B Ezekiel's Vision of God, 1:4-28

1 The four living creatures and the chariot, 1:4-14

4 And as I looked, behold, a *a*storm wind was coming from the north, a great cloud with fire flashing forth continually and a bright light around it, and in its midst something like *b*glowing metal in the midst of the fire.

5 And within it there were figures resembling *a*four living beings. And this was their appearance: they had human *b*form.

6 Each of them had *a*four faces and *b*four wings.

7 And their legs were straight and their feet were like a calf's hoof, and they gleamed like *a*burnished bronze.

8 Under their wings on their *a*four sides *were* human *b*hands. As for the faces and wings of the four of them,

9 their wings touched one another; their *faces* did *a*not turn when they moved, each *b*went straight forward.

10 As for the *a*form of their faces, *each* had the *b*face of a man, all four had the face of a lion on the right and the face of a bull on the left, and all four had the face of an eagle.

11 Such were their faces. Their wings were spread out above; each had two touching another *being*, and *a*two covering their bodies.

12 And *a*each went straight forward; *b*wherever the spirit was about to go, they would go, without turning as they went.

13 In the midst of the living beings there was something that looked like burning coals of *a*fire, like torches darting back and forth among the living beings. The fire was bright, and lightning was flashing from the fire.

14 And the living beings *a*ran to and fro like bolts of *b*lightning.

2 The four wheels, 1:15-21

15 Now as I looked at the living beings, behold, there was one *a*wheel on the earth beside the living beings, for *each of* the four of them.

16 The *a*appearance of the wheels and their workmanship *was* like sparkling *b*beryl, and all four of them had the same form, their appearance and workmanship *being* as if one wheel were within another.

17 Whenever they moved, they moved in any of their four directions, without *a*turning as they moved.

18 As for their rims they were lofty and awesome, and the rims of all four of them were *a*full of eyes round about.

19 And *a*whenever the living beings moved, the wheels moved with them. And whenever the living beings *b*rose from the earth, the wheels rose *also*.

20 *a*Wherever the spirit was about to go, they would go in that direction. And the wheels rose close beside them; for the spirit of the living beings *was* in the wheels.

21 *a*Whenever those went, these went; and whenever those stood still, these stood still. And whenever those rose from the earth, the wheels rose close beside them; for the spirit of the living beings *was* in the wheels.

★ **4** *a*Is. 21:1; Jer. 23:19; Ezek. 13:11, 13 *b*Ezek. 1:27; 8:2

★ **5** *a*Ezek. 10:15, 17, 20; Rev. 4:6-8 *b*Ezek. 1:26

6 *a*Ezek. 1:10; 10:14, 21 *b*Ezek. 1:23

★ **7** *a*Dan. 10:6; Rev. 1:15

8 *a*Ezek. 1:17; 10:11 *b*Ezek. 10:8, 21

9 *a*Ezek. 1:17 *b*Ezek. 1:12; 10:22

10 *a*Rev. 4:7 *b*Ezek. 10:14

11 *a*Is. 6:2; Ezek. 1:23

12 *a*Ezek. 1:9 *b*Ezek. 1:20

13 *a*Ps. 104:4; Rev. 4:5

14 *a*Zech. 4:10 *b*Matt. 24:27; Luke 17:24

15 *a*Ezek. 1:19-21; 10:9

★**16** *a*Ezek. 10:9-11 *b*Ezek. 10:9; Dan. 10:6

17 *a*Ezek. 1:9, 12; 10:11

18 *a*Ezek. 10:12; Rev. 4:6, 8

19 *a*Ezek. 10:16 *b*Ezek. 10:19

20 *a*Ezek. 1:12

21 *a*Ezek. 10:17

1:4 Ezekiel saw a cloud flashing fire from a center of reflecting metal.

1:5 *four living beings.* Identified as cherubim (10:15, 20; see note on Rev. 4:6). The cherubim are an order of angels, concerned with guarding the holiness of God. They guarded the way to the tree of life (Gen. 3:24), and a representation of them was fastened to the Mercy Seat of the Ark (Exod. 25:18-22). Satan was a cherub (Ezek. 28:14, 16).

1:7 *a calf's hoof.* I.e., rounded.

1:16 *beryl.* The gold color of topaz quartz.

3 The radiant expanse, 1:22-28

22 Now [a]over the heads of the living beings *there was* something like an expanse, like the awesome gleam of crystal, extended over their heads.

23 And under the expanse their wings *were stretched out* straight, one toward the other; each one also had [a]two wings covering their bodies on the one side and on the other.

24 I also heard the sound of their wings like the [a]sound of abundant waters as they went, like the [b]voice of the Almighty, a sound of tumult like the [c]sound of an army camp; whenever they stood still, they dropped their wings.

25 And there came a voice from above the [a]expanse that was over their heads; whenever they stood still, they dropped their wings.

26 Now [a]above the expanse that was over their heads there was something [b]resembling a throne, like [c]lapis lazuli in appearance; and on that which resembled a throne, high up, *was* a figure with the appearance of a [d]man.

27 Then I noticed from the appearance of His loins and upward something [a]like glowing metal that looked like fire all around within it, and from the appearance of His loins and downward I saw something like fire; and *there was* a radiance around Him.

28 As the appearance of the [a]rainbow in the clouds on a rainy day, so *was* the appearance of the surrounding radiance. Such *was* the appearance of the likeness of the [b]glory of the LORD. And when I saw *it,* I [c]fell on my face and heard a voice speaking.

C Ezekiel's Call, 2:1-10

2 Then He said to me, "Son of man, [a]stand on your feet that I may speak with you!"

2 And as He spoke to me the [a]Spirit entered me and set me on my feet; and I heard *Him* speaking to me.

3 Then He said to me, "Son of man, I am sending you to the sons of Israel, to a rebellious people who have [a]rebelled against Me; [b]they and their fathers have transgressed against Me to this very day.

4 "And I am sending you to them who are [a]stubborn and obstinate children; and you shall say to them, 'Thus says the Lord GOD.'

5 "As for them, [a]whether they listen or not—for they are a rebellious house—they will [b]know that a prophet has been among them.

6 "And you, son of man, [a]neither fear them nor fear their words, though [b]thistles and thorns are with you and you sit on scorpions; neither fear their words nor be dismayed at their presence, for they are a rebellious house.

7 "But you shall [a]speak My words to them [b]whether they listen or not, for they are rebellious.

8 "Now you, son of man, listen to what I am speaking to you; do not be rebellious like that rebellious house. Open your mouth and [a]eat what I am giving you."

Marginal references:

★22 [a]Ezek. 10:1

23 [a]Ezek. 1:6, 11

24 [a]Ezek. 43:2; Rev. 1:15; 19:6 [b]Ezek. 10:5 [c]2 Kin. 7:6; Dan. 10:6

25 [a]Ezek. 1:22; 10:1

★26-28

26 [a]Ezek. 1:22; 10:1 [b]Is. 6:1; Ezek. 10:1; Dan. 7:9 [c]Ex. 24:10; Is. 54:11 [d]Ezek. 43:6, 7; Rev. 1:13

27 [a]Ezek. 1:4; 8:2

28 [a]Gen. 9:13; Rev. 4:3; 10:1 [b]Ex. 24:16; Ezek. 8:4; 11:22, 23; 43:4, 5 [c]Gen. 17:3; Ezek. 3:23; Dan. 8:17; Rev. 1:17

★ 1 [a]Dan. 10:11; Acts 9:6

2 [a]Ezek. 3:24; Dan. 8:18

★ 3-5

3 [a]1 Sam. 8:7, 8; Jer. 3:25 [b]Ezek. 20:18, 30

4 [a]Ps. 95:8; Is. 48:4; Jer. 5:3; 6:15; Ezek. 3:7

5 [a]Ezek. 2:7; 3:11, 27; Matt. 10:12-15; Acts 13:46 [b]Ezek. 33:33; Luke 10:10, 11; John 15:22

6 [a]Is. 51:12; Jer. 1:8, 17; Ezek. 3:9 [b]2 Sam. 23:6, 7; Ezek. 28:24; Mic. 7:4

7 [a]Jer. 1:7, 17; Ezek. 3:10, 17 [b]Ezek. 2:5

8 [a]Jer. 15:16; Ezek. 3:3; Rev. 10:9

1:22 *expanse.* Ezekiel saw a "platform" over the heads of the living creatures dazzling like *crystal* (or ice).

1:26-28 The description suggests that Ezekiel saw a fiery brightness that had human shape and which he knew to be living and personal (cf. John 1:18). However illuminating appearances of God were in O.T. times, they could not effect redemption. God, not merely appearing as a man, but becoming man in the incarnation of Jesus Christ so that He could die, was essential for the work of redemption.

2:1 *Son of man.* An emphatic form "man," occurring 93 times in the book to remind Ezekiel that, in contrast to the majestic God, he was merely a mortal man.

2:3-5 As that of Isaiah (6:9-12) and Jeremiah (1:17-19), Ezekiel's ministry to a rebellious people would have discouraging results.

★ **9-10**

9 aEzek.
8:3 bJer.
36:2; Ezek.
3:1; Rev. 5:1-
5; 10:8-11

10 aIs. 3:11;
Rev. 8:13

9 Then I looked, behold, a ahand was extended to me; and lo, a bscroll was in it.

10 When He spread it out before me, it was written on the front and back; and written on it were lamentations, mourning and awoe.

D Ezekiel's Commissioning, 3:1-27

1 aEzek.
2:9

2 aJer.
25:17

★ **3** aJer.
6:11; 20:9
bJer. 15:16
cPs. 19:10;
119:103;
Rev. 10:9, 10

5 aJon. 1:2;
Acts 14:11;
26:17 bIs.
28:11; 33:19

7 a1 Sam.
8:7

3 Then He said to me, "Son of man, eat what you find; aeat this scroll, and go, speak to the house of Israel."

2 So I aopened my mouth, and He fed me this scroll.

3 And He said to me, "Son of man, feed your stomach, and afill your body with this scroll which I am giving you." Then I bate it, and it was sweet as choney in my mouth.

4 Then He said to me, "Son of man, go to the house of Israel and speak with My words to them.

5 "For ayou are not being sent to a people of bunintelligible speech or difficult language, but to the house of Israel,

6 nor to many peoples of unintelligible speech or difficult language, whose words you cannot understand. But I have sent you to them who should listen to you;

7 yet the house of Israel will not be willing to listen to you, since they are anot willing to listen to Me. Surely the whole house of Israel is stubborn and obstinate.

8 "Behold, I have made your face as hard as their faces, and your forehead as hard as their foreheads.

9 "Like emery harder than flint I have made your forehead. Do not be afraid of them or be dismayed before them, though they are a rebellious house."

10 Moreover, He said to me, "Son of man, take into your heart all My awords which I shall speak to you, and listen closely.

11 "And go to the exiles, to the sons of your people, and speak to them and tell them, whether they listen or not, 'Thus says the Lord GOD.'"

12 Then the aSpirit lifted me up, and I heard a great brumbling sound behind me, "Blessed be the glory of the LORD in His place."

13 And I heard the sound of the wings of the living beings touching one another, and the sound of the awheels beside them, even a great rumbling sound.

14 So the Spirit lifted me up and took me away; and I went embittered in the rage of my spirit, and athe hand of the LORD was strong on me.

15 Then I came to the exiles who lived beside the river Chebar at Tel-abib, and I sat there aseven days where they were living, causing consternation among them.

16 Now it came about aat the end of seven days that the word of the LORD came to me, saying,

17 "Son of man, I have appointed you a awatchman to the house of Israel; whenever you hear a word from My mouth, bwarn them from Me.

18 "When I say to the wicked, 'You shall surely die'; and you do not warn him or speak out to warn the wicked from his wicked

★ **9**

10 aJob
22:22; Ezek.
2:8; 3:1-3

12 aEzek.
3:14; 8:3;
Acts 8:39
bActs 2:2

13 aEzek.
1:15; 10:16,
17

★**14** a2 Kin.
3:15

15 aJob 2:13

16 aJer. 42:7

★**17** aIs.
52:8; 56:10;
62:6; Jer.
6:17; Ezek.
33:7-9
b2 Chr.
19:10; Is.
58:1; Hab.
2:1

★**18-21**
18 aEzek.
3:20; 33:6, 8

2:9-10 Scrolls were made of skins sewn together and were usually written on one side only, though this one was written on the front and back.
3:3 In digesting God's message, Ezekiel found it sweet to yield to the will of God (cf. v. 14 and John's experience in Rev. 10:8-11).
3:9 emery. A hard stone.
3:14 Ezekiel was embittered because the obduracy of his people would make his task so dif-

ficult (cf. Matt. 11:21-24; Luke 4:24-27).
3:17 Just as the task of a watchman was to warn the city against impending danger, so Ezekiel was to warn his people of the coming destruction of Jerusalem.
3:18-21 Ezekiel was responsible for warning each of the four kinds of people mentioned in these verses, but each individual was personally responsible for his response to the warning.

way that he may live, that wicked man shall die in his iniquity, but his ªblood I will require at your hand.

19 "Yet if you have ªwarned the wicked, and he does not turn from his wickedness or from his wicked way, he shall die in his iniquity; but you have ᵇdelivered yourself.

20 "Again, ªwhen a righteous man turns away from his righteousness and commits iniquity, and I place an ᵇobstacle before him, he shall die; since you have not warned him, he shall die in his sin, and his righteous deeds which he has done shall not be remembered; but his blood I will require at your hand.

21 "However, if you have ªwarned the righteous man that the righteous should not sin, and he does not sin, he shall surely live because he took warning; and you have delivered yourself."

22 And the hand of the Lᴏʀᴅ was on me there, and He said to me, "Get up, go out to the plain, and there I will ªspeak to you."

23 So I got up and went out to the plain; and behold, the ªglory of the Lᴏʀᴅ was standing there, like the glory which ᵇI saw by the river Chebar, and I fell on my face.

24 The ªSpirit then entered me and made me stand on my feet, and He spoke with me and said to me, "Go, shut yourself up in your house.

25 "As for you, son of man, they will ªput ropes on you and

bind you with them, so that you cannot go out among them.

26 "Moreover, ªI will make your tongue stick to the roof of your mouth so that you will be dumb, and cannot be a man who rebukes them, for they are a rebellious house.

27 "But ªwhen I speak to you, I will open your mouth, and you will say to them, 'Thus says the Lord Gᴏᴅ.' He who hears, let him hear; and he who refuses, let him refuse; ᵇfor they are a rebellious house.

II PROPHECIES AGAINST JUDAH AND JERUSALEM, 4:1-24:27

A Prophecies through Symbols, 4:1-5:17

1 A brick: the siege of Jerusalem, 4:1-3

4 "Now you son of man, ªget yourself a brick, place it before you, and inscribe a city on it, Jerusalem.

2 "Then ªlay siege against it, build a siege wall, raise up a ramp, pitch camps, and place battering rams against it all around.

3 "Then get yourself an iron plate and set it up as an iron wall between you and the city, and set your face toward it so that ªit is under siege, and besiege it. This is a ᵇsign to the house of Israel.

2 A posture: the duration of the Exile, 4:4-8

4 "As for you, lie down on your left side, and lay the iniquity

Marginal references:

19 ª2 Kin. 17:13, 14; Ezek. 33:3, 9
ᵇEzek. 14:14, 20; Acts 18:6; 1 Tim. 4:16

20 ªPs. 125:5; Ezek. 18:24; 33:18; Zeph. 1:6
ᵇIs. 8:14; Jer. 6:21; Ezek. 14:3, 7-9

21 ªActs 20:31

22 ªActs 9:6

23 ªEzek. 1:28; Acts 7:55 ᵇEzek. 1:1

24 ªEzek. 2:2

★25 ªEzek. 4:8

26 ªLuke 1:20, 22

27 ªEzek. 24:27; 33:22
ᵇEzek. 12:2, 3

★ 1-3

1 ªIs. 20:2; Jer. 13:1; 18:2; 19:1

2 ªJer. 6:6; Ezek. 21:22

3 ªJer. 39:1, 2; Ezek. 5:2
ᵇIs. 8:18; 20:3; Ezek. 12:6, 11; 24:24-27

★ 4-8
4 ªLev. 10:17; 16:22; Num. 18:1

3:25 *ropes.* Not physical restraints, but restrictions on Ezekiel's public ministry. He did, however, prophesy in his own house (8:1).

4:1-3 Ezekiel was told to "act out" the coming siege of Jerusalem (in 587; 2 Kings 24:20-25:21; Jer. 52:4-11). On a *brick* of soft clay he drew a picture of Jerusalem, built a *siege wall* (a tower), connected the two with a *ramp,* and arranged *camps* (soldiers) to besiege it. The strength of the besiegers and the impossibility of escape was represented by the *iron plate* which Ezekiel set up (v. 3).

4:4-8 By lying on his left side (not continuously, but during the hours of the day when he was

prophesying), Ezekiel illustrated the sin of the Northern Kingdom, Israel; when lying on his right side, the iniquity of the Southern Kingdom, Judah. The numbers are difficult to understand (the Greek translation of the O.T. has 190 days in vv. 5 and 9, rather than 390). Three hundred ninety years from the division of the kingdom (in 931) comes to 541 (the exiles were free to return in 538). One hundred ninety years from the Assyrian captivity in 722 comes to 532. The 40 years might be reckoned from 586 (the fall of Jerusalem) to 546, when Cyrus was a threatening power to Babylon.

of the house of Israel on it; you shall [a]bear their iniquity for the number of days that you lie on it.

5 "For I have assigned you a number of days corresponding to the years of their iniquity, three hundred and ninety days; thus [a]you shall bear the iniquity of the house of Israel.

6 "When you have completed these, you shall lie down a second time, *but* on your right side, and bear the iniquity of the house of Judah; I have assigned it to you for forty days, a day for [a]each year.

7 "Then you shall set your face toward the siege of Jerusalem with your arm bared, and [a]prophesy against it.

8 "Now behold, I will [a]put ropes on you so that you cannot turn from one side to the other, until you have completed the days of your siege.

3   Bread: scarcity, 4:9–17

9 "But as for you, take wheat, barley, beans, lentils, millet and [a]spelt, put them in one vessel and make them into bread for yourself; you shall eat it according to the number of the days that you lie on your side, three hundred and ninety days.

10 "And your food which you eat *shall be* [a]twenty shekels a day by weight; you shall eat it from time to time.

11 "And the water you drink will be the sixth part of a hin by measure; you shall drink it from time to time.

12 "And you shall eat it as a barley cake, having baked *it* in their sight over human [a]dung."

13 Then the LORD said, "Thus shall the sons of Israel eat their bread [a]unclean among the nations where I shall banish them."

14 But I said, "[a]Ah, Lord GOD! Behold, I have [b]never been defiled; for from my youth until now I have never eaten what [c]died of itself or was torn by beasts, nor has any [d]unclean meat ever entered my mouth."

15 Then He said to me, "See, I shall give you cow's dung in place of human dung over which you will prepare your bread."

16 Moreover, He said to me, "Son of man, behold, I am going to [a]break the staff of bread in Jerusalem, and they will eat bread by [b]weight and with anxiety, and drink water by [c]measure and in horror,

17 because bread and water will be scarce; and they will be appalled with one another and [a]waste away in their iniquity.

4   Shaving: destruction of the people of Jerusalem, 5:1–17

5 "As for you, son of man, take a [a]sharp sword; take and use it *as* a barber's razor on your head and beard. Then take [b]scales for weighing and divide the hair.

2 "One third you shall burn in the fire at the center of the city, when the [a]days of the siege are completed. Then you shall take one third and strike *it* with the sword all around the city, and one third you shall scatter to the wind; and I will [b]unsheathe a sword behind them.

3 "Take also a few in number from them and bind them in the edges of your *robes*.

4 "And take again some of them and throw them into the fire, and burn them in the fire;

Marginal references (left column):

5 [a]Num. 14:34
6 [a]Num. 14:34; Dan. 9:24-26; 12:11, 12; Rev. 11:2, 3
7 [a]Ezek. 21:2
8 [a]Ezek. 3:25
★ 9-17
9 [a]Ex. 9:32; Is. 28:25
10 [a]Ezek. 45:12
12 [a]Is. 36:12
13 [a]Dan. 1:8; Hos. 9:3

Marginal references (right column):

14 [a]Jer. 1:6; Ezek. 9:8; 20:49 [b]Acts 10:14 [c]Lev. 17:15; 22:8; Ezek. 44:31 [d]Deut. 14:3; Is. 65:4; 66:17
16 [a]Lev. 26:26; Is. 3:1; Ezek. 5:16; 14:13 [b]Ezek. 4:10, 11; 12:19 [c]Lam. 5:4; Ezek. 12:18, 19
17 [a]Lev. 26:39; Ezek. 24:23; 33:10
★ 1-4
1 [a]Lev. 21:5; Is. 7:20; Ezek. 44:20 [b]Dan. 5:27
2 [a]Jer. 39:1, 2; Ezek. 4:2-8 [b]Lev. 26:33

4:9-17 Ezekiel now learned the horrors of the coming siege. He was allowed to drink about one quart of water and eat only 8 ounces of coarse bread a day, baking the bread using human excrement for fuel. Ezekiel prayed that he might not have to do the latter lest he defile himself (v. 14; cf. Exod. 22:31; Deut. 23:13), and thus was permitted to substitute *cow's dung* (v. 15).

5:1-4 The hair from Ezekiel's shaved head represented four categories among the people. One part would be destroyed in the city; one part killed in the battle; one part blown into exile; and a faithful remnant (*a few*, v. 3) only subjected to further trials.

from it a fire will spread to all the house of Israel.

5 "Thus says the Lord GOD, 'This is ªJerusalem; I have set her at the ᵇcenter of the nations, with lands around her.

6 'But she has rebelled against My ordinances more wickedly than the nations and against My statutes ªmore than the lands which surround her; for they have ᵇrejected My ordinances and have not walked in My statutes.'

7 "Therefore, thus says the Lord GOD, 'Because you have ªmore turmoil than the nations which surround you, and have not walked in My statutes, nor observed My ordinances, nor observed the ordinances of the nations which surround you,'

8 therefore, thus says the Lord GOD, 'Behold, I, even I, am ªagainst you, and I will ᵇexecute judgments among you in the sight of the nations.

9 'And because of all your abominations, I will do among you what I have ªnot done, and the like of which I will never do again.

10 'Therefore, ªfathers will eat *their* sons among you, and sons will eat their fathers; for I will execute judgments on you, and ᵇscatter all your remnant to every wind.

11 'So as I live,' declares the Lord GOD, 'surely, because you have ªdefiled My sanctuary with all your ᵇdetestable idols and with all your abominations, therefore I will also withdraw, and My eye shall have no pity and I will not spare.

12 'One third of you will die by ªplague or be consumed by famine among you, one third will fall by the sword around you, and one third I will ᵇscatter to every

wind, and I will ᶜunsheathe a sword behind them.

13 'Thus My anger will be spent, and I will satisfy My wrath on them, and I shall be ªappeased; then they will know that I, the LORD, have ᵇspoken in My zeal when I have spent My wrath upon them.

14 'Moreover, I will make you a desolation and a ªreproach among the nations which surround you, in the sight of all who pass by.

15 'So it will be a reproach, a reviling, a ªwarning and an object of horror to the nations who surround you, when I ᵇexecute judgments against you in anger, wrath, and raging rebukes. I, the LORD, have spoken.

16 'When I send against them the deadly arrows of famine which were for the destruction of those whom I shall send to destroy you, then I shall also intensify the famine upon you, and break the staff of bread.

17 'Moreover, ªI will send on you famine and wild beasts, and they will bereave you of children; ᵇplague and bloodshed also will pass through you, and I will bring the sword on you. I, the LORD, have spoken.'"

B　Prophecies through Sermons, 6:1-7:27

1　The cause of coming judgment: idolatry, 6:1-14

6 And the word of the LORD came to me saying,

2 "Son of man, set your face toward the ªmountains of Israel, and prophesy against them,

3 and say, 'Mountains of Israel, listen to the word of the Lord GOD! Thus says the Lord GOD to

---

5 ªJer. 6:6; Ezek. 4:1 ᵇDeut. 4:6; Lam. 1:1; Ezek. 16:14

6 ª2 Kin. 17:8-20; Ezek. 16:47, 48, 51 ᵇNeh. 9:16, 17; Ps. 78:10; Jer. 11:10; Zech. 7:11

7 ª2 Kin. 21:9-11; 2 Chr. 33:9; Jer. 2:10, 11

8 ªJer. 21:5, 13; Ezek. 15:7; 21:3; Zech. 14:2 ᵇJer. 24:9; Ezek. 5:15; 11:9

9 ªDan. 9:12; Amos 3:2; Matt. 24:21

★**10** ªLev. 26:29; Jer. 19:9; Lam. 4:10 ᵇPs. 44:11; Ezek. 5:2, 12; 6:8; 12:14; Amos 9:9; Zech. 2:6; 7:14

11 ªJer. 7:9-11; Ezek. 8:5, 6, 16 ᵇJer. 16:18; Ezek. 7:20

12 ªJer. 15:2; 21:9; Ezek. 5:17; 6:11, 12 ᵇEzek. 5:2, 10; Amos 9:9; Zech. 2:6 ᶜJer. 43:10, 11; 44:27; Ezek. 5:2; 12:14

13 ªIs. 1:24 ᵇIs. 59:17; Ezek. 36:5, 6; 38:19

14 ªPs. 74:3-10; 79:1-4; Ezek. 22:4

15 ªIs. 26:9; Jer. 22:8, 9; 1 Cor. 10:11 ᵇIs. 66:15, 16; Ezek. 5:8; 25:17

17 ªLev. 26:22; Rev. 6:8 ᵇEzek. 38:22

★**2** ªEzek. 36:1

3 ªLev. 26:30

5:10 This cannibalism is also referred to in Lam. 4:10.

6:2 On most of the *mountains* of Palestine at this time would have been some kind of altar to Baal (cf. Jer. 3:6-9; see note on Hos. 2:13).

This worship of idols, which they should have destroyed when they conquered the land (Deut. 7:5), is the reason for God's judgment on them. He would spare only a *remnant* (vv. 8-10).

the mountains, the hills, the ravines and the valleys: "Behold, I Myself am going to bring a sword on you, and [a]I will destroy your high places.

4 "So your [a]altars will become desolate, and your incense altars will be smashed; and I shall make your slain fall in front of your idols.

5 "I shall also lay the dead bodies of the sons of Israel in front of their idols; and I shall scatter your [a]bones around your altars.

6 "In all your dwellings, [a]cities will become waste and the high places will be desolate, that your altars may become waste and desolate, your [b]idols may be broken and brought to an end, your incense altars may be cut down, and your works may be blotted out.

7 "And the slain will fall among you, and you will know that I am the LORD.

8 "However, I shall leave a [a]remnant, for you will have those who [b]escaped the sword among the nations when you are scattered among the countries.

9 "Then those of you who escape will [a]remember Me among the nations to which they will be carried captive, how I have [b]been hurt by their adulterous hearts which turned away from Me, and by their eyes, which played the harlot after their idols; and they will [c]loathe themselves in their own sight for the evils which they have committed, for all their abominations.

10 "Then they will know that I am the LORD; I have not said in vain that I would inflict this disaster on them." '

11 "Thus says the Lord GOD, 'Clap your hand, [a]stamp your foot, and say, "[b]Alas, because of all the evil abominations of the house of Israel, which will fall by [c]sword, famine, and plague!

12 "He who is [a]far off will die by the plague, and he who is near will fall by the sword, and he who remains and is besieged will die by the famine. Thus shall I [b]spend My wrath on them.

13 "Then you will know that I am the LORD, when their [a]slain are among their idols around their altars, on [b]every high hill, on all the tops of the mountains, under every green tree, and under every leafy oak—the places where they offered soothing aroma to all their idols.

14 "So throughout all their habitations I shall [a]stretch out My hand against them and make the land more desolate and waste than the wilderness toward Diblah; thus they will know that I am the LORD." ' "

2 The character of coming judgment: severe, 7:1-27

7 Moreover, the word of the LORD came to me saying,

2 "And you, son of man, thus says the Lord GOD to the land of Israel, 'An [a]end! The end is coming on the four corners of the land.

3 'Now the end is upon you, and I shall send My anger against you; I shall judge you according to your ways, and I shall bring all your abominations upon you.

4 'For My eye will have no pity on you, nor shall I spare you, but I shall [a]bring your ways upon you, and your abominations will be among you; then you will [b]know that I am the LORD!'

5 "Thus says the Lord GOD, 'A [a]disaster, unique disaster, behold it is coming!

4 [a]Lev. 26:30; 2 Chr. 14:5; Is. 27:9; Ezek. 6:6

5 [a]2 Kin. 23:14, 16, 20; Jer. 8:1, 2

6 [a]Lev. 26:31; Is. 6:11; Ezek. 5:14 [b]Ezek. 6:4; Mic. 1:7; Zech. 13:2

8 [a]Is. 6:13; Jer. 30:11 [b]Jer. 44:14, 28; Ezek. 7:16; 14:22

9 [a]Deut. 4:29; 30:2; Jer. 51:50 [b]Ps. 78:40; Is. 7:13; 43:24; Hos. 11:8 [c]Job 42:6; Ezek. 20:43; 36:31

11 [a]Ezek. 25:6 [b]Ezek. 9:4 [c]Ezek. 5:12; 7:15

12 [a]Dan. 9:7 [b]Lam. 4:11, 22; Ezek. 5:13

13 [a]Ezek. 6:4-7 [b]1 Kin. 14:23; 2 Kin. 16:4; Is. 57:5-7; Ezek. 20:28; Hos. 4:13

★14 [a]Is. 5:25; 9:12; Ezek. 14:13; 20:33, 34

★ 2 [a]Ezek. 7:3, 5, 6; 11:13; Amos 8:2, 10

4 [a]Ezek. 11:21; 22:31; Hos. 9:7 [b]Ezek. 6:7, 14; 7:27

5 [a]2 Kin. 21:12, 13; Nah. 1:9

6:14 *the wilderness toward Diblah.* This should probably read, from the wilderness to Riblah (a city in the north near Hamath), which was the same as saying, "from Dan to Beersheba." In other words, the destruction of the land would be complete, from north to south.

7:2 *the four corners of the land.* The coming Babylonian judgment would encompass all the land of Israel.

6 aZech. 13:7

6 'An end is coming; the end has come! It has aawakened against you; behold, it has come!

7 aEzek. 7:12; 12:23-25, 28 bIs. 22:5

7 'Your doom has come to you, O inhabitant of the land. The atime has come, the bday is near—tumult rather than joyful shouting on the mountains.

8 aIs. 42:25; Ezek. 9:8; 14:19; Nah. 1:6 bEzek. 7:3; 33:20; 36:19

8 'Now I will shortly apour out My wrath on you, and spend My anger against you, bjudge you according to your ways, and bring on you all your abominations.

9 'And My eye will show no pity, nor will I spare. I will repay you according to your ways, while your abominations are in your midst; then you will know that I, the LORD, do the smiting.

★10 aPs. 89:32; Is. 10:5

10 'Behold, the day! Behold, it is coming! *Your* doom has gone forth; the arod has budded, arrogance has blossomed.

11 aPs. 73:8; 125:3; Is. 59:6-8 bZeph. 1:18

11 'Violence has grown into a rod of awickedness. None of them *shall remain*, none of their multitude, none of their bwealth, nor anything eminent among them.

★12-13
12 aEzek. 7:5-7, 10; 1 Cor. 7:29-31; James 5:8, 9 bProv. 20:14; 1 Cor. 7:30 cIs. 5:13, 14; Ezek. 6:11, 12; 7:14

12 'The atime has come, the day has arrived. Let not the bbuyer rejoice nor the seller mourn; for cwrath is against all their multitude.

13 aLev. 25:24-28, 31

13 'Indeed, the seller will not aregain what he sold as long as they *both* live; for the vision regarding all their multitude will not be averted, nor will any of them maintain his life by his iniquity.

14 aNum. 10:9; Jer. 4:5

14 'They have ablown the trumpet and made everything ready, but no one is going to the battle; for My wrath is against all their multitude.

15 aJer. 14:18; Ezek. 5:12; 6:11, 12; 12:16

15 'The asword is outside, and the plague and the famine are within. He who is in the field will die by the sword; famine and the plague will also consume those in the city.

16 'Even when their survivors aescape, they will be on the mountains like bdoves of the valleys, all of them cmourning, each over his own iniquity.

★16 aEzra 9:15; Is. 37:31; Ezek. 6:8; 14:22 bIs. 38:14 cIs. 59:11; Nah. 2:7

17 'All ahands will hang limp, and all knees will become like water.

17 aIs. 13:7; Ezek. 21:7; 22:14; Heb. 12:12

18 'And they will agird themselves with sackcloth, and bshuddering will overwhelm them; and shame *will be* on all faces, and cbaldness on all their heads.

★18 aIs. 15:3; Ezek. 27:31; Amos 8:10 bJob 21:6; Ps. 55:5 cEzek. 27:31

19 'They shall afling their silver into the streets, and their gold shall become an abhorrent thing; their bsilver and their gold shall not be able to deliver them in the day of the wrath of the LORD. They cannot satisfy their appetite, nor can they fill their stomachs, for their iniquity has become an occasion of stumbling.

★19 aIs. 2:20; 30:22 bProv. 11:4; Zeph. 1:18

20 'And they transformed the beauty of His ornaments into pride, and athey made the images of their abominations *and* their detestable things with it; therefore I will make it an abhorrent thing to them.

★20 aJer. 7:30

21 'And I shall give it into the hands of the aforeigners as plunder and to the wicked of the earth as spoil, and they will profane it.

21 a2 Kin. 24:13; Ps. 74:2-8; Jer. 52:13

22 'I shall also turn My aface from them, and they will profane My secret place; then robbers will enter and profane it.

★22 aJer. 18:17; Ezek. 39:23, 24

23 'aMake the chain, for the land is full of bbloody crimes, and the city is cfull of violence.

23 aJer. 27:2 bEzek. 9:9; Hos. 4:2 cEzek. 8:17

24 aEzek. 21:31; 28:7 bEzek. 33:28 c2 Chr. 7:20; Ezek. 24:21

24 'Therefore, I shall bring the worst of the anations, and they will possess their houses. I shall

---

7:10 *the rod.* A reference to Babylon, whom God would use to punish Judah (Isa. 10:5).

7:12-13 The meaning is this: since the Exile is imminent, a purchaser of property need not rejoice over getting a bargain, nor the seller sad at having to sell.

7:16 Just as *doves* whose homes are in the valleys can escape by flying to the *mountains,* so some of the people would escape, *mourning* for their sins.

7:18 *sackcloth . . . baldness.* Signs of mourning in the face of disaster or death (cf. Isa. 15:2-3; Jer. 16:6).

7:19 Gold would be more plentiful than food. Cf. Isa. 13:12 in which God said it would be easier to find gold than people.

7:20 *His ornaments.* The Temple, which the people had perverted by worshiping idols.

7:22 *My secret place.* The Temple.

also make the *b*pride of the strong ones cease, and their *c*holy places will be profaned.

25 'When anguish comes, they will seek *a*peace, but there will be none.

26 '*a*Disaster will come upon disaster, and *b*rumor will be added to rumor; then they will seek a *c*vision from a prophet, but the *d*law will be lost from the priest and *e*counsel from the elders.

27 'The king will mourn, the prince will be *a*clothed with horror, and the hands of the people of the land will tremble. According to their conduct I shall deal with them, and by their judgments I shall judge them. And they will know that I am the LORD.' "

C   Prophecies through Visions, 8:1–11:25

1   A vision of wickedness in the Temple, 8:1–18

8 And it came about in the sixth year, on the fifth *day* of the sixth month, as I was sitting in my house with the elders of Judah sitting before me, that the hand of the Lord GOD fell on me there.

2 Then I looked, and behold, a likeness as the appearance of a man; from His loins and downward *there was* the *a*appearance of fire, and from His loins and upward the appearance of brightness, like the appearance *b*of glowing metal.

3 And He stretched out the form of a hand and caught me by a lock of my head; and the *a*Spirit lifted me up between earth and heaven and brought me in the visions of God to Jerusalem, to the entrance of the north gate of the inner *court,* where the seat of the idol of jealousy, which *b*provokes to jealousy, was *located.*

4 And behold, the *a*glory of the God of Israel *was* there, like the appearance which I saw in the plain.

5 Then He said to me, "Son of man, *a*raise your eyes, now, toward the north." So I raised my eyes toward the north, and behold, to the north of the altar gate *was* this *b*idol of jealousy at the entrance.

6 And He said to me, "Son of man, do you see what they are doing, the great *a*abominations which the house of Israel are committing here, that I should be far from My sanctuary? But yet you will see still greater abominations."

7 Then He brought me to the entrance of the court, and when I looked, behold, a hole in the wall.

8 And He said to me, "Son of man, now *a*dig through the wall." So I dug through the wall, and behold, an entrance.

9 And He said to me, "Go in and see the wicked abominations that they are committing here."

10 So I entered and looked, and behold, every form of creeping things and beasts *and* detestable things, with all the idols of the house of Israel, were carved on the wall all around.

11 And standing in front of them were *a*seventy *b*elders of the house of Israel, with Jaazaniah the son of Shaphan standing among them, each man with his *c*censer in his hand, and the fragrance of the cloud of incense rising.

Marginal references:

25 *a*Ezek. 13:10, 16

26 *a*Is. 47:11; Jer. 4:20 *b*Ezek. 21:7 *c*Jer. 21:2; 37:17 *d*Ps. 74:9; Ezek. 22:26; Mic. 3:6 *e*Jer. 18:18; Ezek. 11:2

27 *a*Job 8:22; Ps. 35:26; 109:18, 29; Ezek. 26:16

2 *a*Ezek. 1:27 *b*Ezek. 1:4, 27

★ 3 *a*Ezek. 3:12; 11:1 *b*Ex. 20:4; Deut. 32:16

4 *a*Ezek. 1:28; 3:22, 23

5 *a*Jer. 3:2; Zech. 5:5 *b*Ps. 78:58; Jer. 7:30; 32:34; Ezek. 8:3

6 *a*2 Kin. 23:4, 5; Ezek. 5:11; 8:9, 17

8 *a*Is. 29:15

★10-11

11 *a*Num. 11:16, 25; Luke 10:1 *b*Jer. 19:1 *c*Num. 16:17, 35

8:1 This vision occurred 14 months after Ezekiel's call (time enough for his hair to have grown back, v. 3; cf. 5:1). In it he was transported to Jerusalem to relate to the exiles in Babylon the utter degradation of Jerusalem so they might understand why God would judge the city so severely.

8:3 *the idol of jealousy.* Perhaps a replacement of the image of the goddess Asherah, originally set up by King Manasseh (2 Kings 21:7) and subsequently destroyed by Josiah (2 Kings 23:6).

8:10-11 Ezekiel went into a room frescoed with animal deities where the elders of Judah were worshiping.

12 Then He said to me, "Son of man, do you see what the elders of the house of Israel are committing in the dark, each man in the room of his carved images? For they say, '[a]The LORD does not see us; the LORD has [b]forsaken the land.' "

13 And He said to me, "Yet you will see still greater abominations which they are committing."

14 Then He brought me to the entrance of the [a]gate of the LORD's house which *was* toward the north; and behold, women were sitting there weeping for Tammuz.

15 And He said to me, "Do you see *this,* son of man? Yet you will see still greater abominations than these."

16 Then He brought me into the inner court of the LORD's house. And behold, at the entrance to the temple of the LORD, between the porch and the altar, *were* about twenty-five men with their [a]backs to the temple of the LORD and their faces toward the east; and [b]they were prostrating themselves eastward toward the sun.

17 And He said to me, "Do you see *this,* son of man? Is it too light a thing for the house of Judah to commit the abominations which they have committed here, that they have [a]filled the land with violence and [b]provoked Me repeatedly? For behold, they are putting the twig to their nose.

18 "Therefore, I indeed shall deal in wrath. My eye will have no pity nor shall I spare; and [a]though they cry in My ears with a loud voice, yet I shall not listen to them."

2　*A vision of the slaying of the inhabitants of Jerusalem,*
9:1–11

9 Then He cried out in my hearing with a loud [a]voice saying, "Draw near, O executioners of the city, each with his destroying weapon in his hand."

2 And behold, six men came from the direction of the upper gate which faces north, each with his shattering weapon in his hand; and among them was [a]a certain man clothed in linen with a writing case at his loins. And they went in and stood beside the bronze altar.

3 Then the [a]glory of the God of Israel went up from the cherub on which it had been, to the threshold of the temple. And He called to the man clothed in linen at whose loins was the writing case.

4 And the LORD said to him, "Go through the midst of the city, *even* through the midst of Jerusalem, and put a [a]mark on the foreheads of the men who [b]sigh and groan over all the abominations which are being committed in its midst."

5 But to the others He said in my hearing, "Go through the city after him and strike; do not let your eye have pity, and do not spare.

Marginal references

12 [a]Ps. 14:1; Is. 29:15; Ezek. 9:9 [b]Ps. 10:11

★14 [a]Ezek. 44:4; 46:9

★16 [a]2 Chr. 29:6; Jer. 2:27; Ezek. 23:39 [b]Deut. 4:19; 17:3; Job 31:26–28; Jer. 44:17

★17 [a]Ezek. 7:11, 23; 9:9; Amos 3:10; Mic. 2:2 [b]Jer. 7:18, 19; Ezek. 16:26

18 [a]Is. 1:15; Jer. 11:11; Mic. 3:4; Zech. 7:13

1 [a]Is. 6:8

★ 2 [a]Lev. 16:4

★ 3 [a]Ezek. 10:4; 11:22, 23

★ 4 [a]Ex. 12:7, 13; Ezek. 9:6; 2 Cor. 1:22; 2 Tim. 2:19; Rev. 7:2, 3; 9:4; 14:1 [b]Ps. 119:53, 136; Jer. 13:17; Ezek. 6:11; 21:6

8:14 *Tammuz.* A Babylonian deity, husband of Ishtar, who after his death supposedly became god of the underworld. Some have understood him as a vegetation-deity, dying in the heat of the summer and rising in the spring. Base immorality was connected with his worship.

8:16 On sun worship see 2 Kings 23:5, 11; Rom. 1:25.

8:17 *the abominations.* Ezekiel had seen the people in idol worship (vv. 1–6), spirit worship (vv. 7–13), Tammuz worship (vv. 14–15), and sun worship (v. 16).

9:2 *writing case.* Containing reed pens and ink and carried in the waistband.

9:3 *cherub.* Used collectively for the cherubim (plural of cherub) over the Mercy Seat in the Holy of Holies. The glory of the Lord departed to the threshold of the Temple (also 10:4), then to the east gate of the outer court (10:18–19), and finally to the Mount of Olives (11:23). Ezekiel also envisioned it returning eventually to the millennial Temple (43:2–5).

9:4 *a mark.* Lit., a *taw,* the last letter of the Hebrew alphabet, written at that time like a cross (cf. Gen. 4:15 for another mark). Persons so marked would be spared.

6 "Utterly ^aslay old men, young men, maidens, little children, and women, but do not ^btouch any man on whom is the mark; and you shall ^cstart from My sanctuary." So they started with the elders who *were* before the temple.

7 And He said to them, "^aDefile the temple and fill the courts with the slain. Go out!" Thus they went out and struck down *the people* in the city.

8 Then it came about as they were striking and I *alone* was left, that I ^afell on my face and cried out saying, "^bAlas, Lord God! Art Thou destroying the whole remnant of Israel by pouring out Thy wrath on Jerusalem?"

9 Then He said to me, "The iniquity of the house of Israel and Judah is very, very great, and the land is ^afilled with blood, and the city is ^bfull of perversion; for ^cthey say, 'The LORD has forsaken the land, and the LORD does not see!'

10 "But as for Me, ^aMy eye will have no pity nor shall I spare, but ^bI shall bring their conduct upon their heads."

11 Then behold, the man clothed in linen at whose loins was the writing case reported, saying, "I have done just as Thou hast commanded me."

3 A vision of the burning of Jerusalem, 10:1-22

10 Then I looked, and behold, in the ^aexpanse that was over the heads of the cherubim something like a ^bsapphire stone, in appearance resembling a ^cthrone, appeared above them.

2 And He spoke to the man clothed in linen and said, "Enter between the ^awhirling wheels under the cherubim, and fill your hands with ^bcoals of fire from between the cherubim, and scatter *them* over the city." And he entered in my sight.

3 Now the cherubim were standing on the right side of the temple when the man entered, and the cloud filled the ^ainner court.

4 Then the ^aglory of the LORD went up from the cherub to the threshold of the temple, and the ^btemple was filled with the cloud, and the court was filled with the ^cbrightness of the glory of the LORD.

5 Moreover, the sound of the wings of the cherubim was heard as far as the outer court, like the ^avoice of God Almighty when He speaks.

6 And it came about when He commanded the man clothed in linen, saying, "Take fire from between the whirling wheels, from between the cherubim," he entered and stood beside a wheel.

7 Then the cherub stretched out his hand from between the cherubim to the fire which *was* between the cherubim, took some and put it into the hands of the one clothed in linen, who took *it* and went out.

8 And the cherubim appeared to have the form of a man's hand under their wings.

9 Then I looked, and behold, ^afour wheels beside the cherubim, one wheel beside each cherub; and the appearance of the wheels *was* like the gleam of a ^bTarshish stone.

Cross references (left column):

6 ^a2 Chr. 36:17 ^bEx. 12:23; Rev. 9:4 ^cJer. 25:29; Amos 3:2; Luke 12:47

★ 7 ^a2 Chr. 36:17; Ezek. 7:20-22

8 ^a1 Chr. 21:16 ^bEzek. 11:13; Amos 7:2-6

9 ^a2 Kin. 21:16; Jer. 2:34; Ezek. 7:23; 22:2, 3 ^bEzek. 22:29; Mic. 3:1-3; 7:3 ^cJob 22:13; Ps. 10:11; 94:7; Is. 29:15; Ezek. 8:12

10 ^aIs. 65:6; Ezek. 8:18; 24:14 ^bEzek. 7:4; 11:21; Hos. 9:7

1 ^aEzek. 1:22, 26 ^bEx. 24:10 ^cRev. 4:2, 3

Cross references (right column):

★ 2 ^aEzek. 1:15-21; 10:13 ^bPs. 18:10-13; Is. 6:6; Ezek. 1:13; Rev. 8:5

3 ^aEzek. 8:3, 16

★ 4 ^aEzek. 9:3; 11:22, 23 ^bEx. 40:34, 35; Is. 6:1-4 ^cEzek. 1:28

5 ^aJob 40:9; Ezek. 1:24; Rev. 10:3

★ 8-17

9 ^aEzek. 1:15-17 ^bDan. 10:6; Rev. 21:20

9:7 The Temple would be defiled by the presence of dead bodies (cf. Num. 19:11).

10:2 The same scribe who marked the faithful remnant now scattered coals of destruction on the city.

10:4 *cherub.* In this verse the same one as in 9:3. The other cherubim in this chapter are a different kind and are connected with the throne-chariot vision.

10:8-17 A description of the throne-chariot similar to that given in chapter 1. In 1:10 the four faces of the living creatures are described as that of a man (in front as they moved toward Ezekiel), of a lion (on the right), of a bull (on the left), and of an eagle (in back). Here (10:14) they are south of Ezekiel, moving east, placing the bull face toward Ezekiel, which he calls the cherub face, perhaps because he saw it first.

10 And as for their appearance, all four of them had the same likeness, as if one wheel were within another wheel.

11 *a*Ezek.
1:17

11 When they moved, they went *a*in *any of* their four directions without turning as they went; but they followed in the direction which they faced, without turning as they went.

12 *a*Rev. 4:6,
8 *b*Ezek.
1:18

12 And their *a*whole body, their backs, their hands, their wings, and the *b*wheels were full of eyes all around, the wheels belonging to all four of them.

13 The wheels were called in my hearing, the whirling wheels.

14 *a*1 Kin.
7:29, 36;
Ezek 1:6,
10; 10:21;
Rev. 4:7

14 And *a*each one had four faces. The first face *was* the face of a cherub, the second face *was* the face of a man, the third the face of a lion, and the fourth the face of an eagle.

15 *a*Ezek.
1:3, 5

15 Then the cherubim rose up. They are the *a*living beings that I saw by the river Chebar.

16 Now when the cherubim moved, the wheels would go beside them; also when the cherubim lifted up their wings to rise from the ground, the wheels would not turn from beside them.

17 *a*Ezek.
1:21

17 When the cherubim *a*stood still, the wheels would stand still; and when they rose up, the wheels would rise with them; for the spirit of the living beings *was* in them.

★18-19

18 *a*Ps. 18:10

18 Then the glory of the LORD departed from the threshold of the temple and stood *a*over the cherubim.

19 *a*Ezek.
11:22

19 When *a*the cherubim departed, they lifted their wings and rose up from the earth in my sight with the wheels beside them; and they stood still at the entrance of the east gate of the LORD's house. And the glory of the God of Israel hovered over them.

20 *a*Ezek.
1:5, 22, 26;
10:15 *b*Ezek.
1:1

20 These are the *a*living beings that I saw beneath the God of Israel by *b*the river Chebar; so I knew that they *were* cherubim.

21 *a*Ezek.
1:6, 8; 10:14;
41:18, 19

21 *a*Each one had four faces and each one four wings, and beneath their wings *was* the form of human hands.

22 As for the likeness of their faces, they were the same faces whose appearance I had seen by the river Chebar. Each one went straight ahead.

*4 A vision of wicked princes
and departed glory,*
11:1-25

★ 1 *a*Ezek.
3:12, 14; 8:3;
11:24; 43:5
*b*Ezek. 11:13

11 Moreover, the *a*Spirit lifted me up and brought me to the east gate of the LORD's house which faced eastward. And behold, *there were* twenty-five men at the entrance of the gate, and among them I saw Jaazaniah son of Azzur and *b*Pelatiah son of Benaiah, leaders of the people.

2 *a*Ps. 2:1,
2; 52:2; Is.
30:1; Jer.
5:5; Mic. 2:1

2 And He said to me, "Son of man, these are the men who devise iniquity and *a*give evil advice in this city,

★ 3 *a*Jer.
1:13; Ezek.
11:7, 11;
24:3, 6

3 who say, 'Is not *the time* near to build houses? This *a city* is the pot and we are the flesh.'

4 *a*Ezek.
3:4, 17

4 "Therefore, *a*prophesy against them, son of man, prophesy!"

5 *a*Jer.
11:20; 17:10
*b*Ezek. 38:10

5 Then the Spirit of the LORD fell upon me, and He said to me, "Say, 'Thus says the LORD, "So you think, house of Israel, for *a*I know your *b*thoughts.

6 *a*Is. 1:15;
Ezek. 7:23;
22:2-6, 9, 12,
27
7 *a*Ezek.
24:3-13; Mic.
3:2, 3
*b*2 Kin.
25:18-22;
Jer. 52:24-
27; Ezek.
11:9

6 "You have *a*multiplied your slain in this city, filling its streets with them."

7 Therefore, thus says the Lord GOD, "Your *a*slain whom you have laid in the midst of the

---

10:18-19 The glory of the Lord departed to the *east gate* (cf. 43:4). Had He been accepted as Messiah at His first coming, Jesus Christ presumably would have entered the Temple by the same gate. When rejected, He departed through it (Matt. 21:12-17).

11:1 *twenty-five men.* The civil leaders of Judah.

Jaazaniah. Possibly the brother of Jeremiah's opponent, Hananiah (cf. Jer. 28:1).

11:3 These leaders counselled the people to build houses in Jerusalem which, like a *pot,* would supposedly protect the inhabitants from Nebuchadnezzar. As prophesied by Ezekiel (v. 11), quite the opposite would be true.

city are the flesh, and this *city* is the pot; but I shall ᵇbring you out of it.

8 "You have ªfeared a sword; so I will ᵇbring a sword upon you," the Lord GOD declares.

9 "And I shall bring you out of the midst of the city, and I shall deliver you into the hands of ªstrangers and ᵇexecute judgments against you.

10 "You will ªfall by the sword. I shall judge you to the ᵇborder of Israel; so you shall know that I am the LORD.

11 "This *city* will ªnot be a pot for you, nor will you be flesh in the midst of it, *but* I shall judge you to the border of Israel.

12 "Thus you will know that I am the LORD; for you have not walked in My statutes nor have you ªexecuted My ordinances, but have acted according to the ordinances of the ᵇnations around you." ' "

13 Now it came about as I prophesied, that ªPelatiah son of Benaiah died. Then I fell on my face and cried out with a loud voice and said, "ᵇAlas, Lord GOD! Wilt Thou bring the remnant of Israel to a complete end?"

14 Then the word of the LORD came to me, saying,

15 "Son of man, your brothers, your relatives, your fellow exiles, and the whole house of Israel, all of them, *are those* to whom the inhabitants of Jerusalem have said, 'Go far from the LORD; this land has been given ªus as a possession.'

16 "Therefore say, 'Thus says the Lord GOD, "Though I had removed them far away among the nations, and though I had scattered them among the countries, yet I was a ªsanctuary for them a little while in the countries where they had gone." '

17 "Therefore say, 'Thus says the Lord GOD, "I shall ªgather you from the peoples and assemble you out of the countries among which you have been scattered, and I shall give you the land of Israel." '

18 "When they come there, they will ªremove all its ᵇdetestable things and all its abominations from it.

19 "And I shall ªgive them one heart, and shall put a new spirit within them. And I shall take the ᵇheart of stone out of their flesh and give them a ᶜheart of flesh,

20 that they may ªwalk in My statutes and keep My ordinances, and do them. Then they will be ᵇMy people, and I shall be their God.

21 "But as for those whose hearts go after their ªdetestable things and abominations, I shall ᵇbring their conduct down on their heads," declares the Lord GOD.

22 Then the cherubim ªlifted up their wings with the wheels beside them, and ᵇthe glory of the God of Israel hovered over them.

23 And the ªglory of the LORD went up from the midst of the city, and ᵇstood over the mountain which is east of the city.

24 And the ªSpirit lifted me up and brought me in a vision by the Spirit of God to the exiles in Chaldea. So the vision that I had seen ᵇleft me.

25 Then I ªtold the exiles all the things that the LORD had shown me.

Marginal references (left column):

8 ªProv. 10:24; Is. 66:4 ᵇJob 3:25; Is. 24:17, 18

9 ªDeut. 28:36, 49, 50; Ps. 106:41 ᵇEzek. 5:8; 16:41

10 ªJer. 52:9, 10 ᵇ2 Kin. 14:25

11 ªEzek. 11:3, 7; 24:3, 6

12 ªEzek. 18:8, 9 ᵇEzek. 8:10, 14, 16

★13 ªEzek. 11:1 ᵇEzek. 9:8

★14-21

15 ªEzek. 33:24

16 ªPs. 31:20; 90:1; 91:9; Is. 8:14; Jer. 29:7, 11

Marginal references (right column):

17 ªIs. 11:11-16; Jer. 3:12, 18; 24:5; Ezek. 20:41, 42; 28:25

18 ªEzek. 37:23 ᵇEzek. 5:11; 7:20

19 ªJer. 24:7; 32:39; Ezek. 18:31; 36:26 ᵇZech. 7:12; Rom. 2:4, 5 ᶜ2 Cor. 3:3

20 ªPs. 105:45; Ezek. 36:27 ᵇEzek. 14:11

21 ªJer. 16:18; Ezek. 11:18 ᵇEzek. 9:10; 16:43

22 ªEzek. 10:19 ᵇEzek. 43:2

23 ªEzek. 8:4 ᵇZech. 14:4

24 ªEzek. 8:3; 11:1; 37:1; 2 Cor. 12:2-4 ᵇActs 10:16

25 ªEzek. 2:7; 3:4, 17, 27

11:13 The death of *Pelatiah* was a preview of the coming judgment.
11:14-21 The first promise, in Ezekiel, of restoration. The sneer of those in Jerusalem (against the exiles of Judah and the descendants of the northern tribes which were exiled by Samaria in 722) reflected their belief that God's power was limited to His land. Verse 16 contradicts that idea. Concerning the new covenant (vv. 19–20), see note on Jer. 31:31–34.

D The Certainty and Causes of Judgment through Signs, Messages, and Parables, 12:1–24:27

1 The sign of the prophet's baggage, 12:1–16

★ 1-7

12 Then the word of the LORD came to me saying,

2 "Son of man, you live in the ᵃmidst of the ᵇrebellious house, who ᶜhave eyes to see but do not see, ears to hear but do not hear; for they are a rebellious house.

3 "Therefore, son of man, prepare for yourself baggage for exile and go into exile by day in their sight; even go into exile from your place to another place in their sight. ᵃPerhaps they will understand though they are a rebellious house.

4 "And bring your baggage out by day in their sight, as baggage for exile. Then you will go out ᵃat evening in their sight, as those going into exile.

5 "Dig a hole through the wall in their sight and go out through it.

6 "Load the baggage on your shoulder in their sight, and carry it out in the dark. You shall ᵃcover your face so that you can not see the land, for I have set you as a ᵇsign to the house of Israel."

7 And I ᵃdid so, as I had been commanded. By day I ᵇbrought out my baggage like the baggage of an exile. Then in the evening I dug through the wall with my hands; I went out in the dark and carried the baggage on my shoulder in their sight.

★ 8-16

8 And in the morning the word of the LORD came to me, saying,

9 "Son of man, has not the house of Israel, the ᵃrebellious house, said to you, 'ᵇWhat are you doing?'

10 "Say to them, 'Thus says the Lord GOD, "This ᵃburden concerns the prince in Jerusalem, as well as all the house of Israel who are in it." '

11 "Say, 'I am a ᵃsign to you. As I have done, so it will be done to them; they will ᵇgo into exile, into captivity.'

12 "And the ᵃprince who is among them will load his baggage on his shoulder in the dark and go out. They will dig a hole through the wall to bring it out. He will cover his face so that he can not see the land with his eyes.

13 "I shall also spread My ᵃnet over him, and he will be caught in My snare. And I shall bring him to Babylon in the land of the Chaldeans; yet he will ᵇnot see it, though he will die there.

14 "And I shall ᵃscatter to every wind all who are around him, his helpers and all his troops; and I shall draw out a sword after them.

15 "So they will ᵃknow that I am the LORD when I scatter them among the nations, and spread them among the countries.

16 "But I shall spare a few of them from the ᵃsword, the famine, and the pestilence that they may tell all their abominations among the nations where they go, and may ᵇknow that I am the LORD."

2 The sign of trembling, 12:17–28

★17-20

17 Moreover, the word of the LORD came to me saying,

18 "Son of man, ᵃeat your bread with trembling, and drink

Marginal references:

2 ᵃIs. 6:5
ᵇPs. 78:40; Is. 1:23; Ezek. 2:7, 8
ᶜIs. 6:9f.; 43:8; Jer. 5:21; Matt. 13:13, 14; Mark 4:12; 8:18; Luke 8:10; John 9:39-41; 12:40; Acts 28:26f.; Rom. 11:8
3 ᵃJer. 26:3; 36:3, 7; Luke 20:13; 2 Tim. 2:25
4 ᵃ2 Kin. 25:4; Jer. 39:4; Ezek. 12:12
6 ᵃ1 Sam. 28:8; Ezek. 12:12, 13
ᵇIs. 8:18; 20:3; Ezek. 4:3; 12:11; 24:24
7 ᵃEzek. 24:18; 37:7, 10
ᵇEzek. 12:3-6
9 ᵃEzek. 2:5-8; 12:1-3
ᵇEzek. 17:12; 20:49; 24:19
10 ᵃ2 Kin. 9:25; Is. 13:1; Ezek. 12:3-8
11 ᵃEzek. 12:6
ᵇJer. 15:2; 52:15; 28-30; Ezek. 12:3
12 ᵃ2 Kin. 25:4; Jer. 39:4; 52:7; Ezek. 12:6
13 ᵃIs. 24:17, 18; Ezek. 17:20; 19:8; Hos. 7:12
ᵇJer. 39:7; 52:11
14 ᵃ2 Kin. 25:4, 5; Ezek. 5:2; 17:21
15 ᵃEzek. 6:7, 14; 12:16, 20
16 ᵃEzek. 7:15; 14:21
ᵇJer. 22:8, 9
18 ᵃLam. 5:9; Ezek. 4:16

12:1-7 God told Ezekiel to pack a rucksack with bare necessities and leave his house in broad daylight. He was to do the same at twilight, acting as if he were escaping by crawling through a hole in the wall.
12:8-16 Ezekiel's actions illustrated the plight of many who would flee from Jerusalem, particularly King Zedekiah, who would try to creep out at night but would be captured and taken to Babylon as a blind man (vv. 12-13; 2 Kings 25:4, 7).
12:17-20 By eating his meals in fear and trembling, Ezekiel warned the people of the coming captivity.

your water with quivering and anxiety.

19 aJer. 10:22; Ezek. 6:6, 7, 14; Mic. 7:13; Zech. 7:14

19 "Then say to the people of the land, 'Thus says the Lord GOD concerning the inhabitants of Jerusalem in the land of Israel, "They will eat their bread with anxiety and drink their water with horror, because their land will be ^astripped of its fulness on account of the violence of all who live in it.

20 aIs. 3:26; Jer. 4:7; Ezek. 5:14 bIs. 7:23, 24; Jer. 25:9; Ezek. 36:3

20 "And the inhabited ^acities will be laid waste, and the ^bland will be a desolation. So you will know that I am the LORD." ' "

★21-28

21 Then the word of the LORD came to me saying,

22 aEzek. 16:44; 18:2, 3 bJer. 5:12; Ezek. 11:3; 12:27; Amos 6:3; 2 Pet. 3:4 cEzek. 7:26

22 "Son of man, what is this ^aproverb you *people* have concerning the land of Israel, saying, 'The ^bdays are long and every ^cvision fails'?

23 aPs. 37:13; Joel 2:1; Zeph. 1:14

23 "Therefore say to them, 'Thus says the Lord GOD, "I will make this proverb cease so that they will no longer use it as a proverb in Israel." But tell them, "^aThe days draw near as well as the fulfillment of every vision.

24 aJer. 14:13-16; Ezek. 13:6, 23; Zech. 13:2-4

24 "For there will no longer be any ^afalse vision or flattering divination within the house of Israel.

25 aNum. 14:28-34; Is. 14:24; Ezek. 6:10; 12:28 bJer. 16:9; Hab. 1:5 cEzek. 12:2

25 "For I the LORD shall speak, and whatever ^aword I speak will be performed. It will no longer be delayed, for in ^byour days, O ^crebellious house, I shall speak the word and perform it," declares the Lord GOD.' "

26 Furthermore, the word of the LORD came to me saying,

27 aEzek. 12:22; Dan. 10:14

27 "Son of man, behold, the house of Israel is saying, 'The vision that he sees is for ^amany years *from now,* and he prophesies of times far off.'

28 "Therefore say to them, 'Thus says the Lord GOD, "None of My words will be delayed any longer. Whatever word I speak will be performed," ' " declares the Lord GOD.

3 The message against false prophets and prophetesses, 13:1-23

13 Then the word of the LORD came to me saying,

★ 1-16

2 "Son of man, prophesy against the ^aprophets of Israel who prophesy, and say to those who prophesy from their own inspiration, '^bListen to the word of the LORD!

2 aIs. 9:15; Jer. 37:19; Ezek. 22:25, 28 bIs. 1:10; Amos 7:16

3 'Thus says the Lord GOD, "Woe to the ^afoolish prophets who are following their own spirit and have ^bseen nothing.

3 aLam. 2:14; Hos. 9:7; Zech. 11:15 bJer. 23:28-32

4 "O Israel, your prophets have been like foxes among ruins.

5 "You have not ^agone up into the ^bbreaches, nor did you build the wall around the house of Israel to stand in the battle on the ^cday of the LORD.

5 aPs. 106:23; Jer. 23:22; Ezek. 22:30 bIs. 58:12 cIs. 13:6, 9; Ezek. 7:19

6 "They see ^afalsehood and lying divination who are saying, 'The LORD declares,' when the LORD has not sent them; ^byet they hope for the fulfillment of *their* word.

6 aJer. 29:8; Ezek. 22:28 bJer. 28:15; 37:19

7 "^aDid you not see a false vision and speak a lying divination when you said, 'The LORD declares,' but it is not I who have spoken?" ' "

7 aEzek. 22:28

8 Therefore, thus says the Lord GOD, "Because you have spoken falsehood and seen a lie, therefore behold, ^aI am against you," declares the Lord GOD.

8 aEzek. 5:8; 21:3; Nah. 2:13

9 "So My hand will be against the ^aprophets who see false visions and utter lying divinations. They will have no place in the council of My people, ^bnor will they be written down in the register of the house of Israel, nor will they enter the land of Israel, that

9 aJer. 20:3-6; 28:15-17 bPs. 69:28; 87:6; Jer. 17:13; Dan. 12:1

12:21-28 Since Ezekiel (and Jeremiah) had been prophesying for some months and yet no conquest had occurred, the people were growing skeptical (v. 22), encouraged by false prophets (v. 24).
13:1-16 There were two classes of false prophets: those who represented false gods (the prophets of Baal, 1 Kings 18:19), and those who spoke falsehoods in the name of the Lord (as here; cf. Jer. 23:9-32; 28; 29:15-32). They did not build the moral defenses of the people (v. 5), they lied and saw false visions (vv. 6-8), and they whitewashed sin (v. 11).

you may know that I am the Lord GOD.

10 aJer. 23:32; 50:6 bJer. 6:14; 8:11; 14:13 cEzek. 7:25; 13:16

10 "It is definitely because they have amisled My people by saying, 'bPeace!' when there is cno peace. And when anyone builds a wall, behold, they plaster it over with whitewash;

11 aEzek. 38:22

11 so tell those who plaster it over with whitewash, that it will fall. A aflooding rain will come, and you, O hailstones, will fall; and a violent wind will break out.

12 "Behold, when the wall has fallen, will you not be asked, 'Where is the plaster with which you plastered it?' "

13 aEx. 9:24, 25; Ps. 18:12, 13; Is. 30:30; Rev. 11:19; 16:21

13 Therefore, thus says the Lord GOD, "I will make a violent wind break out in My wrath. There will also be in My anger a flooding rain and ahailstones to consume it in wrath.

14 aMic. 1:6; Hab. 3:13 bJer. 6:15; 14:15 cEzek. 13:9

14 "So I shall tear down the wall which you plastered over with whitewash and bring it down to the ground, so that its afoundation is laid bare; and when it falls, you will be bconsumed in its midst. And you will cknow that I am the LORD.

15 "Thus I shall spend My wrath on the wall and on those who have plastered it over with whitewash; and I shall say to you, 'The wall is gone and its plasterers are gone,

16 aJer. 6:14; 8:11; Ezek. 13:10 bIs. 57:21

16 along with the prophets of Israel who prophesy to Jerusalem, and who asee visions of peace for her when there is bno peace,' declares the Lord GOD.

★17-23
17 aJudg. 4:4; 2 Kin. 22:14; Luke 2:36; Acts 21:9 bEzek. 13:2; Rev. 2:20

17 "Now you, son of man, set your face against the daughters of your people who are aprophesying bfrom their own inspiration. Prophesy against them,

18 a2 Pet. 2:14

18 and say, 'Thus says the Lord GOD, "Woe to the women who sew magic bands on all wrists, and make veils for the heads of persons of every stature to ahunt down lives! Will you hunt down the lives of My people, but preserve the lives of others for yourselves?

19 aProv. 28:21; Mic. 3:5 bJer. 23:14, 17

19 "And afor handfuls of barley and fragments of bread, you have profaned Me to My people to put to death some who should not die and to bkeep others alive who should not live, by your lying to My people who listen to lies." ' "

20 Therefore, thus says the Lord GOD, "Behold, I am against your magic bands by which you hunt lives there as birds, and I will tear them off your arms; and I will let them go, even those lives whom you hunt as birds.

21 aPs. 91:3; 124:7

21 "I will also tear off your veils and adeliver My people from your hands, and they will no longer be in your hands to be hunted; and you will know that I am the LORD.

22 aAmos 5:12 bJer. 23:14; 34:16, 22 cEzek. 18:21, 27, 30-32; 33:14-16

22 "Because you adisheartened the righteous with falsehood when I did not cause him grief, but have bencouraged the wicked not to cturn from his wicked way and preserve his life,

23 aEzek. 12:24; 13:6; Mic. 3:6; Zech. 13:3 bEzek. 13:21; 34:10 cEzek. 13:9, 21

23 therefore, you women will no longer see afalse visions or practice divination, and I will bdeliver My people out of your hand. Thus you will cknow that I am the LORD."

4   The message against the idolatrous elders,
14:1-23

★ 1-5
1 a2 Kin. 6:32; Ezek. 8:1; 20:1 bIs. 29:13; Ezek. 33:31, 32
3 aEzek. 20:16 bEzek. 7:19; 14:4, 7; Zeph. 1:3 cIs. 1:15; Jer. 11:11; Ezek. 20:3, 31

14 Then some aelders of Israel came to me and bsat down before me.

2 And the word of the LORD came to me saying,

3 "Son of man, these men have aset up their idols in their hearts, and have bput right before

---

13:17-23 Sorceresses, using occult powers, were putting curses on the innocent and promising life to wrongdoers (v. 19). The exact nature of these spells is uncertain, but they involved the use of bands and veils (v. 18).
14:1-5 elders. Supposed to be spiritual leaders of the nation in exile, they were anxious about the future of Jerusalem and inquired of Ezekiel about it. God knew their idolatrous hearts and said He would answer by the act of judgment which would come upon Jerusalem.

their faces the stumbling block of their iniquity. Should I be ᶜconsulted by them at all?

4 "Therefore speak to them and tell them, 'Thus says the Lord GOD, "Any man of the house of Israel who sets up his idols in his heart, puts right before his face the stumbling block of his iniquity, and *then* comes to the prophet, I the LORD will be brought to give him an answer in the matter in view of the ᵃmultitude of his idols,

5 in order to lay hold of ᵃthe hearts of the house of Israel who are ᵇestranged from Me through all their idols." '

6 "Therefore say to the house of Israel, 'Thus says the Lord GOD, "ᵃRepent and turn away from your idols, and turn your faces away from all your ᵇabominations.

7 "For anyone of the house of Israel or of the ᵃimmigrants who stay in Israel who separates himself from Me, sets up his idols in his heart, puts right before his face the stumbling block of his iniquity, and *then* comes to the prophet to inquire of Me for himself, ᵇI the LORD will be brought to answer him in My own person.

8 "And I shall ᵃset My face against that man and make him a ᵇsign and a proverb, and I shall cut him off from among My people. So you will know that I am the LORD.

9 "But if the prophet is prevailed upon to speak a word, it is I, the LORD, who have prevailed upon that prophet, and I will stretch out My hand against him and ᵃdestroy him from among My people Israel.

10 "And they will bear *the punishment of* their iniquity; as the iniquity of the inquirer is, so

the iniquity of the prophet will be,

11 in order that the house of Israel may no longer ᵃstray from Me and no longer ᵇdefile themselves with all their transgressions. Thus they will be ᶜMy people, and I shall be their God," ' declares the Lord GOD."

12 Then the word of the LORD came to me saying,

13 "Son of man, if a country sins against Me by ᵃcommitting unfaithfulness, and I stretch out My hand against it, destroy its ᵇsupply of bread, send famine against it, and cut off from it both man and beast,

14 even ᵃ*though* these three men, ᵇNoah, ᶜDaniel, and ᵈJob were in its midst, by their *own* righteousness they could *only* deliver ᵉthemselves," declares the Lord GOD.

15 "If I were to cause ᵃwild beasts to pass through the land, and they depopulated it, and it became desolate so that no one would pass through it because of the beasts,

16 *though* these three men were in its midst, as I live," declares the Lord GOD, "they could not deliver either *their* sons or *their* daughters. ᵃThey alone would be delivered, but the country would be desolate.

17 "Or *if* I should ᵃbring a sword on that country and say, 'Let the sword pass through the country and ᵇcut off man and beast from it,'

18 even *though* these three men were in its midst, as I live," declares the Lord GOD, "they could not deliver either *their* sons or *their* daughters, but they alone would be delivered.

19 "Or *if* I should send a ᵃplague against that country and

Cross references (margin)

4 ᵃ1 Kin. 21:20-24; 2 Kin. 1:16; Is. 66:4

5 ᵃJer. 17:10; Zech. 7:12 ᵇIs. 1:4; Jer. 2:11; Zech. 11:8

6 ᵃ1 Sam. 7:3; Neh. 1:9; Is. 2:20; 30:22; 55:6, 7; Ezek. 18:30 ᵇEzek. 8:6; 14:4

7 ᵃEx. 12:48; 20:10 ᵇEzek. 14:4

8 ᵃJer. 44:11; Ezek. 15:7 ᵇIs. 65:15; Ezek. 5:15

9 ᵃJer. 6:14, 15; 14:15

11 ᵃEzek. 44:10, 15; 48:11 ᵇEzek. 11:18; 37:23 ᶜEzek. 11:20; 34:30; 36:28

13 ᵃEzek. 15:8; 20:27 ᵇLev. 26:26; Is. 3:1; Ezek. 4:16

★14 ᵃJer. 15:1 ᵇGen. 6:8; 7:1; Heb. 11:7 ᶜEzek. 28:3; Dan. 1:6; 9:21; 10:11 ᵈJob 1:1, 5; 42:8, 9 ᵉEzek. 16:18, 20; 18:20

15 ᵃLev. 26:22; Num. 21:6; Ezek. 5:17; 14:21

16 ᵃGen. 19:29; Ezek. 18:20

17 ᵃLev. 26:25; Ezek. 5:12; 21:3, 4 ᵇEzek. 25:13; Zeph. 1:3

19 ᵃJer. 14:12; Ezek. 5:12; 14:21

14:14 Even if such righteous men as *Noah, Daniel, and Job* were then in Palestine, the prolonged sin of the land would forbid its being spared judgment. This may be a reference to the Daniel of the book named after him, a contemporary of Ezekiel, who did escape judgment. Some see it as a reference to a patriarch Daniel (one is mentioned in the Ras Shamra tablets, c. 1400 B.C.). The latter seems unlikely, however, since the patriarch Daniel (though portrayed in these tablets as a righteous and wise man) was a worshiper of Baal and could not therefore be called righteous in the sense that Noah and Job were.

pour out My wrath in blood on it, to cut off man and beast from it,

20 even *though* Noah, Daniel, and Job were in its midst, as I live," declares the Lord God, "they could not deliver either *their* son or *their* daughter. They would deliver only themselves by their righteousness."

21 ªEzek. 5:17; 33:27; Amos 4:6-10; Rev. 6:8

21 For thus says the Lord God, "How much more when ªI send My four severe judgments against Jerusalem: sword, famine, wild beasts, and plague to cut off man and beast from it!

★22 ªEzek. 12:16; 36:20 ᵇEzek. 16:54; 31:16; 32:31

22 "Yet, behold, survivors will be left in it who will be brought out, *both* sons and daughters. Behold, they are going to come forth to you and you will ªsee their conduct and actions; then you will be ᵇcomforted for the calamity which I have brought against Jerusalem for everything which I have brought upon it.

23 ªJer. 22:8, 9

23 "Then they will comfort you when you see their conduct and actions, for you will know that I have not done ªin vain whatever I did to it," declares the Lord God.

5   The parable of the fruitless vine, 15:1-8

★ 2 ªPs. 80:8-16; Is. 5:1-7; Hos. 10:1

15 Then the word of the Lord came to me saying,

2 "Son of man, how is the wood of the ªvine *better* than any wood of a branch which is among the trees of the forest?

3 "Can wood be taken from it to make anything, or can *men* take a peg from it on which to hang any vessel?

4 "If it has been put into the ªfire for fuel, *and* the fire has consumed both of its ends, and its middle part has been charred, is it *then* useful for anything?

5 "Behold, while it is intact, it is not made into anything. How much less, when the fire has consumed it and it is charred, can it still be made into anything!

6 "Therefore, thus says the Lord God, 'As the wood of the vine among the trees of the forest, which I have given to the fire for fuel, so have I given up the inhabitants of Jerusalem;

7 and I ªset My face against them. *Though* they have ᵇcome out of the fire, yet the fire will consume them. Then you will know that I am the Lord, when I set My face against them.

8 Thus I will make the land desolate, because they have ªacted unfaithfully,' " declares the Lord God.

6   The parable of the adulterous woman, 16:1-63

a   Her youth, 16:1-14

16 Then the word of the Lord came to me saying,

2 "Son of man, ªmake known to Jerusalem her abominations,

3 and say, 'Thus says the Lord God to Jerusalem, "Your origin and your birth are from the land of the Canaanite, your father was an Amorite and your mother a Hittite.

4 "As for your birth, ªon the day you were born your navel cord was not cut, nor were you washed with water for cleansing;

4 ªIs. 27:11; Ezek. 15:6; 19:14

7 ªLev. 26:17; Ps. 34:16; Jer. 21:10; Ezek. 14:8 ᵇ1 Kin. 19:17; Is. 24:18; Amos 9:1-4

8 ªEzek. 14:13; 17:20

★ 1

2 ªIs. 58:1; Ezek. 20:4; 22:2

★ 3

★ 4 ªHos. 2:3

14:22 *survivors.* Wicked people who would be exiled to Babylon and be positive proof of the righteousness of God's judgment on Jerusalem.

15:2 Judah is compared to the wild vine of the forest (not the cultivated one of the vineyard, as elsewhere in the O.T.), from which God has been able to make nothing useful (v. 3), which was partly charred by judgment (v. 4), and which would soon be completely burned in judgment (v. 6).

16:1 This chapter depicts Israel as an unfaithful wife (cf. Hos. 1-3; Jer. 2; Isa. 1:21; 50:1). Her sin is described in verses 3-34, her punishment in verses 35-52, and her restoration in verses 53-63.

16:3 Israel's "moral genealogy" included the *Amorite* (Canaanite) and *Hittite* (a non-Semitic pagan people).

16:4 Rubbing the skin with salt was supposed to make it firm and clean.

★ 5-7

5 aDeut.
32:10

you were not rubbed with salt or even wrapped in cloths.

5 "No eye looked with pity on you to do any of these things for you, to have compassion on you. Rather you were thrown out into the aopen field, for you were abhorred on the day you were born.

6 "When I passed by you and saw you squirming in your blood, I said to you *while you were* in your blood, 'Live!' I said to you while you were in your blood, 'Live!'

7 aEx. 1:7;
Deut. 1:10

7 "I amade you numerous like plants of the field. Then you grew up, became tall, and reached the age for fine ornaments; *your* breasts were formed and your hair had grown. Yet you were naked and bare.

★ 8-14

8 aRuth
3:9; Jer. 2:2
bGen. 22:16-
18 cEx. 24:7,
8 dEx. 19:5;
Ezek. 20:5;
Hos. 2:19, 20

8 "Then I passed by you and saw you, and behold, you were at the time for love; so I aspread My skirt over you and covered your nakedness. I also bswore to you and centered into a covenant with you so that you dbecame Mine," declares the Lord God.

9 aRuth 3:3

9 "Then I bathed you with water, washed off your blood from you, and aanointed you with oil.

10 aEx.
26:36; Ezek.
16:13, 18;
26:16; 27:7,
16

10 "I also clothed you with aembroidered cloth, and put sandals of porpoise skin on your feet; and I wrapped you with fine linen and covered you with silk.

11 aGen.
24:22, 47; Is.
3:19; Ezek.
23:42 bGen.
41:42; Prov.
1:9

11 "And I adorned you with ornaments, put abracelets on your hands, and a bnecklace around your neck.

12 aGen.
24:47; Is.
3:21 bIs.
28:5; Jer.
13:18; Ezek.
16:14

12 "I also put a aring in your nostril, earrings in your ears, and a bbeautiful crown on your head.

13 aPs.
45:13, 14;
Ezek. 16:17
b1 Sam.
10:1; 1 Kin.
4:21

13 "Thus you were adorned with agold and silver, and your dress was of fine linen, silk, and embroidered cloth. You ate fine flour, honey, and oil; so you were exceedingly beautiful and advanced to broyalty.

14 "Then your afame went forth among the nations on account of your beauty, for it was bperfect because of My splendor which I bestowed on you," declares the Lord God.

b   Her sins, 16:15-34

15 "But you atrusted in your beauty and bplayed the harlot because of your fame, and you poured out your harlotries on every passer-by who might be *willing.*

16 "And you took some of your clothes, made for yourself high places of various colors, and played the harlot on them, which should never come about nor happen.

17 "You also took your beautiful ajewels *made* of My gold and of My silver, which I had given you, and made for yourself male images that you might play the harlot with them.

18 "Then you took your embroidered cloth and covered them, and offered My oil and My incense before them.

19 "Also aMy bread which I gave you, fine flour, oil, and honey with which I fed you, you would offer before them for a soothing aroma; so it happened," declares the Lord God.

20 "Moreover, you took your sons and daughters whom you had borne to aMe, and you bsacrificed them to idols to be devoured. Were your harlotries so small a matter?

21 "You slaughtered aMy children, and offered them up to idols by bcausing them to pass through *the fire.*

22 "And besides all your abominations and harlotries you

14 a1 Kin.
10:1, 24
bPs. 50:2;
Lam. 2:15

★15-34

15 aEzek.
16:25; 27:3
bIs. 57:8;
Jer. 2:20

17 aEzek.
16:11, 12

19 aHos. 2:8

★20-21

20 aEx. 13:2,
12; Deut.
29:11, 12
bPs. 106:37,
38; Jer. 7:31;
Ezek. 20:31;
23:37

21 aEx. 13:2
b2 Kin.
17:17; Jer.
19:5

22 aJer. 2:2

16:5-7 Israel, a foundling child thrown out and left to die, was rescued by the Lord.
16:8-14 The child, now grown, became the Lord's bride. *I spread My skirt over you.* An act which symbolized marriage (Ruth 3:9).

16:15-34 The wife became unfaithful by practicing idolatry (vv. 15-22) and by entering into alliances with foreign countries (vv. 23-34).
16:20-21 Children were offered in sacrifice to Molech (cf. Jer. 7:30-32; 19:4-5; 32:35).

did not remember the days of [a]your youth, when you were naked and bare and squirming in your blood.

23 "Then it came about after all your wickedness ('Woe, woe to you!' declares the Lord GOD),

24 that you built yourself a [a]shrine and made yourself a [b]high place in every square.

25 "You built yourself a high place at the top of [a]every street, and made your beauty abominable; and you spread your legs to every passer-by to multiply your harlotry.

26 "You also played the harlot with the Egyptians, your lustful neighbors, and multiplied your harlotry to [a]make Me angry.

27 "Behold now, I have stretched out My hand against you and diminished your rations. And I delivered you up to the desire of those who hate you, the [a]daughters of the Philistines, who are ashamed of your lewd conduct.

28 "Moreover, you played the harlot with the [a]Assyrians because you were not satisfied; you even played the harlot with them and still were not satisfied.

29 "You also multiplied your harlotry with the land of merchants, Chaldea, yet even with this you were not satisfied." ' "

30 "How [a]languishing is your heart," declares the Lord GOD, "while you do all these things, the actions of a [b]bold-faced harlot.

31 "When you built your shrine at the beginning of every street and made your high place in every square, in [a]disdaining money, you were not like a harlot.

32 "You adulteress wife, who takes strangers instead of her husband!

33 "Men give gifts to all harlots, but you [a]give your gifts to all your lovers to bribe them to come

to you from every direction for your harlotries.

34 "Thus you are different from those women in your harlotries, in that no one plays the harlot as you do, because you give money and no money is given you; thus you are different."

c   Her condemnation, 16:35–52

35 Therefore, O harlot, hear the word of the LORD.

36 Thus says the Lord GOD, "Because your lewdness was poured out and your nakedness uncovered through your harlotries with your lovers and with all your detestable [a]idols, and because of the blood of your sons which you gave to idols,

37 therefore, behold, I shall [a]gather all your lovers with whom you took pleasure, even all those whom you loved *and* all those whom you [b]hated. So I shall gather them against you from every direction and [c]expose your nakedness to them that they may see all your nakedness.

38 "Thus I shall [a]judge you, like women who commit adultery or shed blood are judged; and I shall bring on you the blood of [b]wrath and jealousy.

39 "I shall also give you into the hands of your lovers, and they will tear down your shrines, demolish your high places, [a]strip you of your clothing, take away your jewels, and will leave you naked and bare.

40 "They will incite a [a]crowd against you, and they will stone you and cut you to pieces with their swords.

41 "And they will [a]burn your houses with fire and execute judgments on you in the sight of many women. Then I shall [b]stop you from playing the harlot, and you will also no longer pay your lovers.

---

24 [a]Jer. 11:13; Ezek. 16:31, 39; 20:28, 29
[b]Ps. 78:58; Is. 57:7

25 [a]Prov. 9:14

26 [a]Jer. 7:18, 19; Ezek. 8:17

27 [a]Is. 9:12; Ezek. 16:57

28 [a]2 Kin. 16:7, 10-18; 2 Chr. 28:16, 20-23; Jer. 2:18, 36; Ezek. 23:12; Hos. 10:6

30 [a]Prov. 9:13; Is. 1:3; Jer. 4:22 [b]Is. 3:9; Jer. 3:3

31 [a]Is. 52:3

33 [a]Is. 57:9; Ezek. 16:41; Hos. 8:9, 10

★35-52

36 [a]Jer. 19:5; Ezek. 20:31; 23:37

37 [a]Jer. 13:22, 26; Ezek. 23:9, 22; Hos. 2:3, 10; Nah. 3:5, 6 [b]Ezek. 23:17, 28 [c]Is. 47:3

38 [a]Ezek. 23:45 [b]Ps. 79:3, 5; Jer. 18:21; Ezek. 23:25; Zeph. 1:17

39 [a]Ezek. 23:26; Hos. 2:3

40 [a]Ezek. 23:47; Hab. 1:6-10

41 [a]2 Kin. 25:9; Jer. 39:8; 52:13 [b]Ezek. 23:48

16:35-52 Israel's punishment is described (vv. 35-43) and justified, because her sin is worse than that of her two sisters, *Sodom* and then *Samaria* (vv. 44-52).

42 a2 Sam.
24:25; Ezek.
5:13; 21:17;
Zech. 6:8
bIs. 40:1, 2;
54:9, 10;
Ezek. 39:29

43 aPs.
78:42;
106:13;
Ezek. 16:22
bIs. 63:10;
Ezek. 6:9
cEzek.
11:21; 22:31

44 a1 Sam.
24:13; Ezek.
12:22, 23;
18:2, 3

45 aEzek.
23:2 bIs. 1:4;
Ezek. 23:37-
39; Zech.
11:8

46 aJer. 3:8-
11; Ezek.
23:4 bGen.
13:10-13;
18:20; Ezek.
16:48, 49,
53-56, 61

47 a1 Kin.
16:31 b2
Kin. 21:9;
Ezek. 5:6;
16:48, 51

48 aMatt.
10:15; 11:23,
24

49 aGen.
19:9; Ps.
138:6; Is.
3:9; Ezek.
28:2, 9, 17
bGen. 13:10;
Is. 22:13;
Amos 6:4-6
cLuke 12:16-
20; 16:19
dEzek. 18:7,
12, 16

50 aGen.
13:13; 18:20;
19:5 bGen.
19:24, 25

51 aJer. 3:8-
11

42 "So I ashall calm My fury against you, and My jealousy will depart from you, and I shall be pacified and angry bno more.

43 "Because you have anot remembered the days of your youth but have benraged Me by all these things, behold, I in turn will cbring your conduct down on your own head," declares the Lord GOD, "so that you will not commit this lewdness on top of all your *other* abominations.

44 "Behold, everyone who quotes aproverbs will quote *this* proverb concerning you, saying, 'Like mother, like daughter.'

45 "You are the daughter of your mother, who loathed her husband and children. You are also the asister of your sisters, who bloathed their husbands and children. Your mother was a Hittite and your father an Amorite.

46 "Now your aolder sister is Samaria, who lives north of you with her daughters; and your younger sister, who lives south of you, is bSodom with her daughters.

47 "Yet you have not merely walked in their ways or done according to their abominations; but, as if that were atoo little, you acted bmore corruptly in all your conduct than they.

48 "As I live," declares the Lord GOD, "Sodom, your sister, and her daughters, have anot done as you and your daughters have done.

49 "Behold, this was the guilt of your sister Sodom: she and her daughters had aarrogance, babundant food, and ccareless ease, but she did not help the dpoor and needy.

50 "Thus they were haughty and committed aabominations before Me. Therefore I bremoved them when I saw *it*.

51 "Furthermore, Samaria did not commit half of your sins, for you have multiplied your abominations more than they. Thus you have made your sisters appear arighteous by all your abominations which you have committed.

52 "Also bear your disgrace in that you have made judgment favorable for your sisters. Because of your sins in which you acted amore abominably than they, they are more in the right than you. Yes, be also ashamed and bear your disgrace, in that you made your sisters appear righteous.

d Her restoration, 16:53-63

53 "Nevertheless, I will restore their captivity, the captivity of Sodom and her daughters, the captivity of Samaria and her daughters, and along with them your own captivity,

54 in order that you may bear your humiliation, and feel aashamed for all that you have done when you become ba consolation to them.

55 "And your sisters, Sodom with her daughters and Samaria with her daughters, will return to their former state, and you with your daughters will *also* return to your former state.

56 "As *the name of* your sister Sodom was not heard from your lips in your day of pride,

57 before your awickedness was uncovered, so now you have become the breproach of the daughters of Edom, and of all who are around her, of the daughters of the Philistines— those surrounding *you* who despise you.

58 "You have aborne *the penalty of* your lewdness and abominations," the LORD declares.

59 For thus says the Lord GOD, "I will also do with you as you have done, you who have

52 aEzek.
16:47, 48, 51

★53-59

54 aJer. 2:26
bEzek.
14:22, 23

57 aEzek.
16:36, 37
b2 Kin. 16:5-
7; 2 Chr.
28:5, 6, 18-
23; Ezek.
5:14, 15;
22:4

58 aEzek.
23:49

59 aIs. 24:5;
Ezek. 17:19

16:53-59 A statement of the hopelessness of the restoration of Israel (just as it was impossible to imagine the restoration of Sodom and Samaria).

^adespised the oath by breaking the covenant.

★60-63

60 ^aIs. 55:3; Jer. 32:38-41; Ezek. 37:26

60 "Nevertheless, I will remember My covenant with you in the days of your youth, and I will establish an ^aeverlasting covenant with you.

61 ^aJer. 50:4, 5; Ezek. 6:9

61 "Then you will ^aremember your ways and be ashamed when you receive your sisters, both your older and your younger; and I will give them to you as daughters, but not because of your covenant.

62 ^aEzek. 20:37; 34:25; 37:26 ^bJer. 24:7; Ezek. 20:43, 44

62 "Thus I will ^aestablish My covenant with you, and you shall ^bknow that I am the Lord.

63 ^aEzek. 36:31, 32; Dan. 9:7, 8 ^bPs. 39:9; Rom. 3:19 ^cPs. 65:3; 78:38; 79:9

63 in order that you may ^aremember and be ashamed, and ^bnever open your mouth anymore because of your humiliation, when I have ^cforgiven you for all that you have done," the Lord God declares.

7   The parable of the two eagles, 17:1-24

★ 2 ^aEzek. 20:49; 24:3

17 Now the word of the Lord came to me saying,

2 "Son of man, propound a riddle, and speak a ^aparable to the house of Israel,

3 ^aJer. 48:40; Ezek. 17:12; Hos. 8:1 ^bDan. 4:22 ^cJer. 22:23

3 saying, 'Thus says the Lord God, "A great ^aeagle with ^bgreat wings, long pinions and a full plumage of many colors, came to ^cLebanon and took away the top of the cedar.

4 "He plucked off the topmost of its young twigs and brought it to a land of merchants; he set it in a city of traders.

5 ^aDeut. 8:7-9 ^bIs. 44:4

5 "He also took some of the seed of the land and planted it in ^afertile soil. He placed it beside abundant waters; he set it like a ^bwillow.

6 "Then it sprouted and became a low, spreading vine with its branches turned toward him, but its roots remained under it. So it became a vine, and yielded shoots and sent out branches.

7 "But there was another great eagle with great wings and much plumage; and behold, this vine bent its roots toward him and sent out its branches toward him from the beds where it was ^aplanted, that he might water it.

7 ^aEzek. 31:4

8 "It was planted in good soil beside abundant waters, that it might yield branches and bear fruit, and become a splendid vine." '

9 "Say, 'Thus says the Lord God, "Will it thrive? Will he not pull up its roots and cut off its fruit, so that it withers—so that all its sprouting leaves wither? And neither by great strength nor by many people can it be raised from its roots again.

10 "Behold, though it is planted, will it thrive? Will it not ^acompletely wither as soon as the east wind strikes it—wither on the beds where it grew?" ' "

10 ^aEzek. 19:14; Hos. 13:15

11 Moreover, the word of the Lord came to me saying,

★11-21

12 "Say now to the ^arebellious house, 'Do you not ^bknow what these things mean?' Say, 'Behold, the ^cking of Babylon came to Jerusalem, took its king and princes, and brought them to him in Babylon.

12 ^aEzek. 2:3-5 ^bEzek. 12:9-11; 24:19 ^c2 Kin. 24:11, 12, 15; Ezek. 1:2; 17:3

13 'And he took one of the royal ^afamily and made a covenant with him, putting him under ^boath. He also took away the ^cmighty of the land,

13 ^a2 Kin. 24:17; Ezek. 17:5 ^b2 Chr. 36:13 ^c2 Kin. 24:15, 16

14 that the kingdom might ^abe in subjection, not exalting it-

14 ^aEzek. 29:14

16:60-63 Nevertheless, God will restore Israel when He brings them into the blessings of the new covenant in the millennial kingdom (cf. 11:19-20; Jer. 31:31).

17:2 A riddle contained an obscure idea requiring interpretation; a parable was an illustration by comparison.

17:11-21 An explanation of the features of the parable. (1) The king of Babylon took King Jehoiachin from Judah to Babylon in 597 (v. 12; cf. vv. 3-4; 2 Kings 24:8-16; 25:27-30). (2) Nebuchadnezzar made Zedekiah a puppet king in Judah (v. 13; cf. vv. 5-6; 2 Kings 24:17). (3) Egypt attracted Zedekiah (v. 7). (4) Zedekiah broke his covenant with Nebuchadnezzar and thus with God (vv. 15-19). (5) Zedekiah would die in Babylon and his troops would be defeated (vv. 20-21).

15 ᵃ2 Kin.
24:20; 2 Chr.
36:13; Jer.
52:3; Ezek.
17:7 ᵇJer.
34:3; 38:18,
23; Ezek.
17:18

self, *but* keeping his covenant, that it might continue.

15 'But he ᵃrebelled against him by sending his envoys to Egypt that they might give him horses and many troops. Will he succeed? Will he who does such things ᵇescape? Can he indeed break the covenant and escape?

16 ᵃ2 Kin.
24:17, 20;
Ezek. 16:59;
17:13, 18, 19
ᵇJer. 52:11;
Ezek. 12:13

16 'As I live,' declares the Lord GOD, 'Surely in the country of the king who put him on the throne, whose oath he ᵃdespised, and whose covenant he broke, ᵇin Babylon he shall die.

17 ᵃIs. 36:6;
Jer. 37:5, 7;
Ezek. 29:6, 7

17 'And ᵃPharaoh with *his* mighty army and great company will not help him in the war, when they cast up mounds and build siege walls to cut off many lives.

18 ᵃ1 Chr.
29:24

18 'Now he despised the oath by breaking the covenant, and behold, he ᵃpledged his allegiance, yet did all these things; he shall not escape.' "

19 Therefore, thus says the Lord GOD, "As I live, surely My oath which he despised and My covenant which he broke, I will inflict on his head.

20 ᵃEzek.
12:13; 32:3
ᵇJer. 39:5-7
ᶜJer. 2:35;
Ezek. 20:35,
36

20 "And I will spread My ᵃnet over him, and he will be ᵇcaught in My snare. Then I will bring him to Babylon and ᶜenter into judgment with him there *regarding* the unfaithful act which he has committed against Me.

21 ᵃ2 Kin.
25:5, 11;
Ezek. 5:2,
10, 12-14

21 "And all the ᵃchoice men in all his troops will fall by the sword, and the survivors will be scattered to every wind; and you will know that I, the LORD, have spoken."

★22 ᵃPs.
72:16; Ezek.
20:40; 37:22

22 Thus says the Lord GOD, "I shall also take *a sprig* from the lofty top of the cedar and set *it* out; I shall pluck from the topmost of its young twigs a tender one, and I shall plant *it* on a ᵃhigh and lofty mountain.

23 ᵃPs.
92:12

23 "On the high mountain of Israel I shall plant it, that it may bring forth boughs and bear fruit, and become a stately ᵃcedar. And birds of every kind will nest under it; they will nest in the shade of its branches.

★24 ᵃPs.
96:12; Is.
55:12 ᵇAmos
9:11

24 "And all the ᵃtrees of the field will know that I am the LORD; I bring down the high tree, exalt the low tree, dry up the green tree, and make the dry tree ᵇflourish. I am the LORD; I have spoken, and I will perform *it.*"

8 The proverb of the sour grapes repudiated,
18:1-32

18 Then the word of the LORD came to me saying,

★ 2 ᵃIs.
3:15 ᵇJer.
31:29; Lam.
5:7

2 "ᵃWhat do you mean by using this proverb concerning the land of Israel saying,

'ᵇThe fathers eat the sour grapes,
But the children's teeth are set on edge'?

3 "As I live," declares the Lord GOD, "you are surely not going to use this proverb in Israel anymore.

4 ᵃNum.
16:22; 27:16;
Is. 42:5;
57:16 ᵇEzek.
18:20; Rom.
6:23

4 "Behold, ᵃall souls are Mine; the soul of the father as well as the soul of the son is Mine. The soul who ᵇsins will die.

5 "But if a man is righteous, and practices justice and righteousness,

★ 6 ᵃEzek.
6:13; 18:15;
22:9 ᵇDeut.
4:19; Ezek.
18:12, 15;
20:24; 33:25
ᶜEzek.
18:15; 22:11

6 and does not ᵃeat at the mountain *shrines* or ᵇlift up his eyes to the idols of the house of Israel, or ᶜdefile his neighbor's wife, or approach a woman during her menstrual period—

★ 7 ᵃDeut.
24:13; Ezek.
33:15; Amos
2:8 ᵇLev.
19:13; Amos
3:10 ᶜDeut.
15:11; Ezek.
18:16; Matt.
25:35-40;
Luke 3:11

7 if a man does not oppress anyone, but ᵃrestores to the debtor his pledge, ᵇdoes not commit robbery, *but* ᶜgives his bread to the hungry, and covers the naked with clothing,

---

17:22 *a tender one.* A sprig; i.e., Messiah (cf. Isa. 11:1; Jer. 23:5; 33:15; Zech. 3:8; 6:12).

17:24 Cf. Luke 1:52.

18:2 A *proverb* was circulating in Jerusalem (Jer. 31:29) and Babylon that the children were suffering for the sins of their fathers. While there are cumulative effects of sin (cf. Exod. 20:5-6;

Matt. 23:35-36), the Lord here declares that each individual is accountable for his own sin (v. 4).

18:6 *does not eat.* Refers to sacrificial meals to idols.

18:7 *pledge.* I.e., items given as a pledge when borrowing money (cf. Exod. 22:26).

8 if he does not lend *money* on ᵃinterest or take ᵇincrease, *if* he keeps his hand from iniquity, *and* ᶜexecutes true justice between man and man,

9 *if* he walks in ᵃMy statutes and My ordinances so as to deal faithfully—ᵇhe is righteous *and* will surely ᶜlive," declares the Lord Goᴅ.

10 "Then he may have a violent son who sheds blood, and who does any of these things to a brother

11 (though he himself did not do any of these things), that is, he even eats at the mountain *shrines,* and ᵃdefiles his neighbor's wife,

12 oppresses the ᵃpoor and needy, ᵇcommits robbery, does not restore a pledge, but lifts up his eyes to the idols, *and* ᶜcommits abomination,

13 he ᵃlends *money* on interest and takes increase; will he live? He will not live! He has committed all these abominations, he will surely be put to death; his ᵇblood will be on his own head.

14 "Now behold, he has a son who has observed all his father's sins which he committed, and ᵃobserving does not do likewise.

15 "He does not eat at the mountain *shrines* or lift up his eyes to the idols of the house of Israel, or defile his neighbor's wife,

16 or oppress anyone, or retain a pledge, or commit robbery, *but* he ᵃgives his bread to the hungry, and covers the naked with clothing,

17 he keeps his hand from the poor, does not take interest or increase, *but* executes My ordinances, and walks in My statutes; ᵃhe will not die for his father's iniquity, he will surely live.

18 "As for his father, because he practiced extortion, robbed *his* brother, and did what was not good among his people, behold, he will die for his iniquity.

19 "Yet you say, 'ᵃWhy should the son not bear the punishment for the father's iniquity?' When the son has practiced ᵇjustice and righteousness, and has observed all My statutes and done them, he shall surely live.

20 "The person who ᵃsins will die. The ᵇson will not bear the punishment for the father's iniquity, nor will the father bear the punishment for the son's iniquity; the ᶜrighteousness of the righteous will be upon himself, and the wickedness of the wicked will be upon himself.

21 "But if the ᵃwicked man turns from all his sins which he has committed and observes all My statutes and practices justice and righteousness, he shall surely live; he shall not die.

22 "ᵃAll his transgressions which he has committed will not be remembered against him; because of his ᵇrighteousness which he has practiced, he will live.

23 "ᵃDo I have any pleasure in the death of the wicked," declares the Lord Goᴅ, "rather than that he should ᵇturn from his ways and live?

24 "But when a righteous man ᵃturns away from his righteousness, commits iniquity, and does according to all the abominations that a wicked man does, will he live? ᵇAll his righteous deeds which he has done will not be remembered for his ᶜtreachery which he has committed and his sin which he has committed; for them he will die.

25 "Yet you say, 'ᵃThe way of the Lord is not right.' Hear now, O house of Israel! Is ᵇMy way not right? Is it not your ways that are not right?

★ **8** ᵃEx. 22:25; Deut. 23:19, 20
ᵇLev. 25:36
ᶜZech. 7:9; 8:16

9 ᵃLev. 18:5 ᵇRom. 8:1 ᶜAmos 5:4; Hab. 2:4; Rom. 1:17

11 ᵃ1 Cor. 6:9

12 ᵃAmos 4:1; Zech. 7:10 ᵇIs. 59:6, 7; Jer. 22:3, 17; Ezek. 7:23; 18:7, 16, 18 ᶜ2 Kin. 21:11; Ezek. 8:6, 17

13 ᵃEx. 22:25 ᵇEzek. 33:4, 5

14 ᵃ2 Chr. 29:6-10; 34:21

16 ᵃJob 31:16, 20; Ps. 41:1; Is. 58:7, 10; Ezek. 18:7

17 ᵃRom. 2:7

★**19-20**
19 ᵃEx. 20:5; Jer. 15:4; Ezek. 18:2 ᵇEzek. 18:9; 20:18-20; Zech. 1:3-6

20 ᵃ2 Kin. 14:6; 22:18-20; Ezek. 18:4 ᵇDeut. 24:16; Jer. 31:30 ᶜ1 Kin. 8:32; Is. 3:10, 11; Matt. 16:27; Rom. 2:6-9

21 ᵃEzek. 18:27, 28; 33:12, 19

22 ᵃIs. 43:25; Jer. 50:20; Ezek. 18:24; 33:16; Mic. 7:19 ᵇPs. 18:20-24

23 ᵃEzek. 18:32; 33:11 ᵇPs. 147:11; Mic. 7:18

24 ᵃ1 Sam. 15:11; 2 Chr. 24:2, 17-22; Ezek. 3:20; 18:26; 33:18 ᵇEzek. 18:22; Gal. 3:3, 4 ᶜProv. 21:16; Ezek. 17:20; 20:27

★**25** ᵃEzek. 18:29; 33:17, 20; Mal. 2:17; 3:13-15 ᵇGen. 18:25; Jer. 12:1; Zeph. 3:5

18:8 Loans to fellow Jews were to be interest-free (Exod. 22:25) though not those to foreigners (Deut. 23:20). *take increase.* To take more than was lent.

18:19-20 The principle of individual accountability is reiterated.

18:25 *right.* Lit., balanced; i.e., they accused the Lord of being unjust. Actually it was the people who were out of balance, and God appeals to them to repent (vv. 30-32).

26 "When a righteous man turns away from his righteousness, commits iniquity, and dies because of it, for his iniquity which he has committed he will die.

27 a Is. 1:18; 55:7

27 "Again, when a wicked man turns away a from his wickedness which he has committed and practices justice and righteousness, he will save his life.

28 "Because he considered and turned away from all his transgressions which he had committed, he shall surely live; he shall not die.

29 "But the house of Israel says, 'The way of the Lord is not right.' Are My ways not right, O house of Israel? Is it not your ways that are not right?

30 a Ezek. 14:6; 33:11; Hos. 12:6

30 "Therefore I will judge you, O house of Israel, each according to his conduct," declares the Lord GOD. "a Repent and turn away from all your transgressions, so that iniquity may not become a stumbling block to you.

31 a Is. 1:16, 17; 55:7
b Ps. 51:10;
Ezek. 11:19;
36:26

31 "a Cast away from you all your transgressions which you have committed, and make yourselves a b new heart and a new spirit! For why will you die, O house of Israel?

32 a Ezek. 18:23; 33:11

32 "For I have a no pleasure in the death of anyone who dies," declares the Lord GOD. "Therefore, repent and live."

9 The lamentation for the princes of Israel, 19:1-14

1 a Ezek. 2:10; 19:14
b 2 Kin. 23:29, 30, 34; 24:6, 12; 25:5-7

★ 2

19 "As for you, take up a a lamentation for the b princes of Israel, 2 and say,
'What was your mother?
A lioness among lions!
She lay down among young lions,
She reared her cubs.

3 'When she brought up one of her cubs,
He became a lion,
And he learned to tear his prey;
He devoured men.

★ 3-4

4 'Then nations heard about him;
He was captured in their pit,
And they a brought him with hooks
To the land of Egypt.

4 a 2 Kin. 23:34; 2 Chr. 36:4, 6

5 'When she saw, as she waited,
That her hope was lost,
She took another of her cubs
And made him a young lion.

★ 5-9

6 'And he a walked about among the lions;
He became a young lion,
He learned to tear his prey;
He devoured men.

6 a 2 Kin. 24:9; 2 Chr. 36:9

7 'And he destroyed their fortified towers
And laid waste their cities;
And the land and its fulness were appalled
Because of the sound of his roaring.

8 'Then a nations set against him
On every side from their provinces,
And they spread their net over him;
He was captured in their pit.

8 a 2 Kin. 24:11

9 'And a they put him in a cage with hooks
And b brought him to the king of Babylon;
They brought him in hunting nets
So that his voice should be heard no more
On the mountains of Israel.

9 a 2 Chr. 36:6 b 2 Kin. 24:15

19:2 Judah is pictured as a *lioness,* the *mother* of mighty kings.
19:3-4 The *lion* (king) referred to here was Jehoahaz, taken as a prisoner to *Egypt* by Pha-

raoh Neco in 609 (2 Kings 23:33-34).
19:5-9 The second *lion* was Jehoiachin, taken to Babylon by Nebuchadnezzar in 597 (2 Kings 24:15).

★10-14
10 aPs.
80:8-11

11 aPs.
80:15 bEzek.
31:3

12 aJer.
31:28 bLam.
2:1; Ezek.
28:17 cEzek.
17:10; Hos.
13:15 dIs.
27:11; Ezek.
19:11

13 a2 Kin.
24:12-16;
Ezek. 19:10;
20:35; Hos.
2:3

14 aEzek.
15:4; 20:47,
48

★ 1-32
1 aEzek.
8:1, 11, 12

10 'Your mother was ªlike a
vine in your vineyard,
Planted by the waters;
It was fruitful and full of
branches
Because of abundant
waters.

11 'And it had ªstrong
branches *fit* for scep-
ters of rulers,
And its bheight was
raised above the
clouds
So that it was seen in its
height with the mass
of its branches.

12 'But it was ªplucked up
in fury;
It was bcast down to the
ground;
And the ceast wind
dried up its fruit.
Its dstrong branch was
torn off
So that it withered;
The fire consumed it.

13 'And now it is planted in
the ªwilderness,
In a dry and thirsty land.

14 'And ªfire has gone out
from *its* branch;
It has consumed its
shoots *and* fruit,
So that there is not in it
a strong branch,
A scepter to rule.' "

This is a lamentation, and has become a lamentation.

10 The message concerning
Israel's unfaithfulness,
20:1-32

20 Now it came about in the
seventh year, in the fifth
month, on the tenth of the
month, that certain of the ªelders
of Israel came to inquire of the
LORD, and sat before me. 2 And the word of the LORD
came to me saying,

3 "Son of man, speak to the
elders of Israel, and say to them,
'Thus says the Lord GOD, "Do you
come to inquire of Me? As I live,"
declares the Lord GOD, "ªI will not
be inquired of by you." '

4 "Will you judge them, will
you judge them, son of man?
ªMake them know the abominations of their fathers;

5 and say to them, 'Thus
says the Lord GOD, "On the day
when I ªchose Israel and swore to
the descendants of the house of
Jacob and made Myself known to
them in the land of Egypt, when I
swore to them, saying, bI am the
LORD your God,

6 on that day I swore to
them, ªto bring them out from the
land of Egypt into a land that I
had selected for them, bflowing
with milk and honey, which is
cthe glory of all lands.

7 "And I said to them, 'ªCast
away, each of you, the detestable
things of his eyes, and bdo not defile yourselves with the idols of
Egypt; cI am the LORD your God.'

8 "But they ªrebelled against
Me and were not willing to listen
to Me; they did not cast away the
detestable things of their eyes,
nor did they forsake the bidols of
Egypt.
Then I resolved to cpour out
My wrath on them, to accomplish
My anger against them in the
midst of the land of Egypt.

9 "But I acted ªfor the sake of
My name, that it should bnot be
profaned in the sight of the nations among whom they *lived*, in
whose sight I made Myself
known to them by bringing them
out of the land of Egypt.

10 "So I took them out of the
land of Egypt and brought them
into the ªwilderness.

3 aEzek.
14:3

4 aEzek.
16:2; 22:2;
Matt. 23:32

5 aEx. 6:6-
8 bEx. 6:2, 3

6 aJer.
32:22 bEx.
13:5; 33:3
cPs. 48:2

7 aEx. 20:4,
5; 22:20
bLev. 18:3;
Deut. 29:16-
18 cEx. 20:2

8 aDeut.
9:7; Is. 63:10
bEx. 32:1-9
cEzek. 5:13;
7:8; 20:13,
21

9 aEx.
32:11-14;
Ezek. 20:14,
22; 36:21, 22
bEzek. 39:7

10 aEx. 19:1

19:10-14 Judah is here compared to a *vine . . .
plucked up in fury* by Nebuchadnezzar in 586
because of the rebellion of Zedekiah (2 Kings
24:20; Jer. 52:3).
20:1-32 Ezekiel reviews the different periods in
the history of Israel and the preservation of
the people for the Lord's name's sake in spite

of their repeated rebellion. They rebelled in
Egypt (vv. 5-9), on the journey from Egypt to
Kadesh-barnea (vv. 10-17), in the wilderness
(vv. 18-26), and even when they came into Canaan (vv. 27-29). Ezekiel's own generation was
equally unfaithful (vv. 30-32).

11 aEx.
20:1-23:33
bLev. 18:5;
Ezek. 20:13

11 "And I gave them My astatutes and informed them of My ordinances, by bwhich, if a man observes them, he will live.

12 aEx.
31:13, 17;
Ezek. 20:20

12 "And also I gave them My sabbaths to be a asign between Me and them, that they might know that I am the LORD who sanctifies them.

13 aNum.
14:11, 12,
22; Ezek.
20:8 bLev.
18:5 cIs.
56:6; Ezek.
20:21 dEx.
32:10; Deut.
9:8; Ezek.
20:8, 21

13 "But the house of Israel are-belled against Me in the wilderness. They did not walk in My statutes, and they rejected My ordinances, bby which, if a man observes them, he will live; and My csabbaths they greatly profaned. Then I resolved to dpour out My wrath on them in the wilderness, to annihilate them.

14 "But I acted for the sake of My name, that it should not be profaned in the sight of the nations, before whose sight I had brought them out.

15 aNum.
14:30; Ps.
95:11;
106:26

15 "And also aI swore to them in the wilderness that I would not bring them into the land which I had given them, flowing with milk and honey, which is the glory of all lands,

16 aEzek.
11:21; 14:3-
7; 20:8

16 because they rejected My ordinances, and as for My statutes, they did not walk in them; they even profaned My sabbaths, for their aheart continually went after their idols.

17 aJer.
4:27; 5:18;
Ezek. 11:13

17 "Yet My eye spared them rather than destroying them, and I did not cause their aannihilation in the wilderness.

18 aNum.
14:31; Deut.
4:3-6 bZech.
1:4

18 "And I said to their achildren in the wilderness, 'bDo not walk in the statutes of your fathers, or keep their ordinances, or defile yourselves with their idols.

19 aEx. 6:7;
20:2 bDeut.
5:32, 33; 6:1,
2; 8:1, 2;
11:1; 12:1

19 'aI am the LORD your God; bwalk in My statutes, and keep My ordinances, and observe them.

20 aJer.
17:22

20 'And asanctify My sabbaths; and they shall be a sign between Me and you, that you may know that I am the LORD your God.'

21 aNum.
21:5; 25:1-3

21 "But the achildren rebelled against Me; they did not walk in My statutes, nor were they careful to observe My ordinances, by which, if a man observes them, he will live; they profaned My sabbaths. So I resolved to pour out My wrath on them, to accomplish My anger against them in the wilderness.

22 aJob
13:21; Ps.
78:38; Ezek.
20:17 bIs.
48:9-11; Jer.
14:7, 21;
Ezek. 20:9,
14

22 "But I awithdrew My hand and acted bfor the sake of My name, that it should not be profaned in the sight of the nations in whose sight I had brought them out.

23 aLev.
26:33; Deut.
4:27; 28:64

23 "Also I swore to them in the wilderness that I would ascatter them among the nations and disperse them among the lands,

24 aEzek.
6:9

24 because they had not observed My ordinances, but had rejected My statutes, and had profaned My sabbaths, and atheir eyes were on the idols of their fathers.

25 aPs.
81:12; Is.
66:4; Rom.
1:21-25, 28

25 "And I also gave them statutes that were anot good and ordinances by which they could not live;

26 aLev.
18:21; 20:2-
5; Is. 63:17;
Ezek. 20:30;
Rom. 11:8
bJer. 7:31;
19:4-9
cEzek. 6:7;
20:12, 20

26 and I pronounced them aunclean because of their gifts, in that they bcaused all their firstborn to pass through the fire so that I might make them desolate, in order that they might cknow that I am the LORD."'

27 aEzek.
2:7; 3:4, 11,
27 bNum.
15:30; Rom.
2:24 cEzek.
18:24; 39:23,
26

27 "Therefore, son of man, aspeak to the house of Israel, and say to them, 'Thus says the Lord GOD, "Yet in this your fathers have bblasphemed Me by cacting treacherously against Me.

28 aJosh.
23:3, 14;
Neh. 9:22-
26; Ps.
78:55; Jer.
2:7 b1 Kin.
14:23; Ps.
78:58; Is.
57:5-7; Jer.
3:6; Ezek.
6:13

28 "When I had abrought them into the land which I swore to give to them, then they saw every bhigh hill and every leafy tree, and they offered there their sacrifices, and there they presented the provocation of their offering. There also they made their soothing aroma, and there they poured out their libations.

29 "Then I said to them, 'What is the high place to which you go?' So its name is called Bamah to this day."'

30 aJudg.
2:19; Jer.
7:26; 16:12

30 "Therefore, say to the house of Israel, 'Thus says the Lord GOD, "Will you defile yourselves after the manner of your

31 aPs.
106:37-39;
Jer. 7:31;
Ezek. 16:20;
20:26

ᵃfathers and play the harlot after their detestable things?

31 "And when you offer your gifts, when you ᵃcause your sons to pass through the fire, you are defiling yourselves with all your idols to this day. And shall I be inquired of by you, O house of Israel? As I live," declares the Lord GOD, "I will not be inquired of by you.

32 aEzek.
11:5 bJer.
2:25; 44:17

32 "And what ᵃcomes into your mind will not come about, when you say: 'We will be like the nations, like the tribes of the lands, ᵇserving wood and stone.'

11 The promise of future restoration, 20:33-44

★33-44
33 aJer. 21:5
bJer. 51:57

33 "As I live," declares the Lord GOD, "surely with a mighty hand and with an ᵃoutstretched arm and with wrath poured out, I shall be ᵇking over you.

34 aIs.
27:12, 13;
Ezek. 20:38;
34:16 bJer.
42:18; 44:6;
Lam. 2:4

34 "And I shall ᵃbring you out from the peoples and gather you from the lands where you are scattered, with a mighty hand and with an outstretched arm and with ᵇwrath poured out;

35 aEzek.
19:13; 20:36;
Hos. 2:14

35 and I shall bring you into the ᵃwilderness of the peoples, and there I shall enter into judgment with you face to face.

36 aNum.
11:1-35; Ps.
106:15;
Ezek. 20:13,
21; 1 Cor.
10:5-10
bDeut. 32:10

36 "As I ᵃentered into judgment with your fathers in the ᵇwilderness of the land of Egypt, so I will enter into judgment with you," declares the Lord GOD.

37 aLev.
27:32; Jer.
33:13

37 "And I shall make you ᵃpass under the rod, and I shall bring you into the bond of the covenant;

38 aEzek.
34:17-22;
Amos 9:9,
10; Zech.
13:8, 9; Mal.
3:3; 4:1-3
bNum.
14:29, 30;
Ps. 95:11;
Ezek. 13:9;
20:15, 16;
Heb. 4:3

38 and I shall ᵃpurge from you the rebels and those who transgress against Me; I shall bring them out of the land where they sojourn, but they will ᵇnot enter the land of Israel. Thus you will know that I am the LORD.

39 "As for you, O house of Israel," thus says the Lord GOD, "ᵃGo, serve everyone his idols; but later, you will surely listen to Me, and My holy name you will ᵇprofane no longer with your gifts and with your idols.

40 "For on My holy mountain, on the high mountain of Israel," declares the Lord GOD, "there the whole house of Israel, ᵃall of them, will serve Me in the land; there I shall ᵇaccept them, and there I shall seek your contributions and the choicest of your gifts, with all your holy things.

41 "As a soothing aroma I shall accept you, when I ᵃbring you out from the peoples and gather you from the lands where you are scattered; and I shall prove Myself ᵇholy among you in the sight of the nations.

42 "And ᵃyou will know that I am the LORD, ᵇwhen I bring you into the land of Israel, into the ᶜland which I swore to give to your forefathers.

43 "And there you will ᵃremember your ways and all your deeds, with which you have defiled yourselves; and you will ᵇloathe yourselves in your own sight for all the evil things that you have done.

44 "Then ᵃyou will know that I am the LORD when I have dealt with you ᵇfor My name's sake, not according to your evil ways or according to your corrupt deeds, O house of Israel," declares the Lord GOD.' "

12 The forest fire, 20:45-49

45 Now the word of the LORD came to me saying,

46 "Son of man, set your face toward Teman, and speak out against the ᵃsouth, and ᵇprophesy

39 aJer.
44:25, 26
bIs. 1:13-15;
Ezek. 23:38,
39; 43:7

40 aIs.
66:23; Ezek.
37:22, 24
bIs. 56:7;
60:7; Ezek.
43:12, 27

41 aIs.
27:12, 13;
Ezek. 11:17;
28:25 bIs.
5:16; Ezek.
28:25; 36:23

42 aEzek.
36:23; 38:23
bEzek.
11:17; 34:13;
36:24 cEzek.
20:6, 15

43 aEzek.
6:9; 16:61,
63; Hos. 5:15
bJer. 31:18;
Ezek. 36:31;
Zech. 12:10

44 aEzek.
24:24 bEzek.
36:22

★45-49
46 aJer.
13:19; Ezek.
21:4 bEzek.
21:2; Amos
7:16 cIs.
30:6-11

20:33-44 This section describes the coming judgment of those Jews who will be living at the conclusion of the Tribulation period when Christ returns to earth. The Chief Shepherd (Christ) will then examine His flock (*pass un-*der the rod; cf. Lev. 27:32), *purge . . . the rebels,* and bring the faithful into the blessings of the new *covenant* in the kingdom.

20:45-49 *south.* Palestine, which was S. of the attackers.

against the cforest land of the Negev,

47 aIs. 9:18, 19; Jer. 21:14 bIs. 13:8

47 and say to the forest of the Negev, 'Hear the word of the LORD: thus says the Lord GOD, "Behold, I am about to akindle a fire in you, and it shall consume every green tree in you, as well as every dry tree; the blazing flame will not be quenched, and bthe whole surface from south to north will be burned by it.

48 aJer. 7:20; 17:27

48 "And all flesh will see that I, the LORD, have kindled it; it shall anot be quenched." ' "

49 aEzek. 17:2; Matt. 13:13; John 16:25

49 Then I said, "Ah Lord GOD! They are saying of me, 'Is he not just speaking aparables?' "

13 The sword, 21:1-32

★ 2 aEzek. 20:46; 25:2; 28:21 bJob 29:22; Ezek. 20:46

21 And the word of the LORD came to me saying, **2** "Son of man, aset your face toward Jerusalem, and bspeak against the sanctuaries, and prophesy against the land of Israel;

3 aJer. 21:13; Ezek. 5:8; Nah. 2:13; 3:5 bIs. 57:1

3 and say to the land of Israel, 'Thus says the LORD, "Behold, aI am against you; and I shall draw My sword out of its sheath and cut off from you the brighteous and the wicked.

4 aJer. 12:12; Ezek. 7:2; 20:47

4 "Because I shall cut off from you the righteous and the wicked, therefore My sword shall go forth from its sheath against aall flesh from south to north.

5 a1 Sam. 3:12; Jer. 23:20; Ezek. 21:30; Nah. 1:9

5 "Thus all flesh will know that I, the LORD, have drawn My sword out of its sheath. It will anot return to its sheath again." '

6 "As for you, son of man, groan with breaking heart and bitter grief, groan in their sight.

7 aEzek. 7:26 bIs. 13:7; Nah. 2:10

7 "And it will come about when they say to you, 'Why do you groan?' that you will say, 'Because of the anews that is coming;

and bevery heart will melt, all hands will be feeble, every spirit will faint, and all knees will be weak as water. Behold, it comes and it will happen,' declares the Lord GOD."

8 Again the word of the LORD came to me saying,

★ 8-17

9 "Son of man, prophesy and say, 'Thus says the LORD.' Say,

9 aDeut. 32:41

  'aA   sword,   a   sword
    sharpened
  And also polished!

10   'Sharpened to make a
    aslaughter,
  Polished to flash like
    lightning!'

★10 aIs. 34:5, 6 bPs. 110:5, 6; Ezek. 20:47

Or shall we rejoice, the rod of My son bdespising every tree?

11 "And it is given to be polished, that it may be handled; the sword is sharpened and polished, to give it into the hand of the slayer.

12 "aCry out and wail, son of man; for it is against My people, it is against all the bofficials of Israel. They are delivered over to the sword with My people, therefore strike your thigh.

★12 aEzek. 21:6; Joel 1:13 bEzek. 21:25; 22:6

13 "For there is a testing; and what if even the rod which despises will be no more?" declares the Lord GOD.

★13

14 "You therefore, son of man, prophesy, and clap your hands together; and let the sword be adoubled the third time, the sword for the slain. It is the sword for the great one slain, which surrounds them,

14 aLev. 26:21, 24; 2 Kin. 24:1, 10-16; 25:1

15 that their ahearts may melt, and many bfall at all their cgates. I have given the glittering sword. Ah! It is made for striking like lightning, it is wrapped up in readiness for slaughter.

15 aJosh. 2:11; 2 Sam. 17:10; Ps. 22:14; Ezek. 21:7 bIs. 59:10; Jer. 13:16; 18:15 cJer. 17:27; Ezek. 21:19

16 "Show yourself sharp, go to the right; set yourself; go to the

---

21:2 against the sanctuaries. The Temple and its precincts.
21:8-17 An ode to the avenging Babylonian sword.
21:10 Or shall we rejoice, the rod of My son despising every tree? The text is unclear, but probably refers to those who found false secu-

rity (against the coming invasion) in the promise of Gen. 49:9-10 that Judah's scepter must triumph over all others.
21:12 strike your thigh. As a sign of despair (cf. Jer. 31:19).
21:13 The verse means: what will happen to Judah if it is left without a ruler?

left, wherever your edge is appointed.

17 "I shall also clap My hands together, and I shall ᵃappease My wrath; I, the Lᴏʀᴅ, have spoken."

18 And the word of the Lᴏʀᴅ came to me saying,

19 "As for you, son of man, ᵃmake two ways for the sword of the king of Babylon to come; both of them will go out of one land. And make a signpost; make it at the head of the way to the city.

20 "You shall mark a way for the sword to come to ᵃRabbah of the sons of Ammon, and to Judah into ᵇfortified Jerusalem.

21 "For the king of Babylon stands at the parting of the way, at the head of the two ways, to use ᵃdivination; he ᵇshakes the arrows, he consults the ᶜhousehold idols, he looks at the liver.

22 "Into his right hand came the divination, 'Jerusalem,' to ᵃset battering rams, to open the mouth for slaughter, to lift up the voice with a battle cry, to set battering rams against the gates, to cast up mounds, to build a siege wall.

23 "And it will be to them like a false divination in their eyes; ᵃthey have *sworn* solemn oaths. But he ᵇbrings iniquity to remembrance, that they may be seized.

24 "Therefore, thus says the Lord Gᴏᴅ, 'Because you have made your iniquity to be remembered, in that your transgressions are uncovered, so that in all your deeds your sins appear—because you have come to remembrance, you will be seized with the hand.

25 'And you, O slain, wicked one, the prince of Israel, whose ᵃday has come, in the time of the punishment of the end,'

26 thus says the Lord Gᴏᴅ, 'Remove the turban, and take off the ᵃcrown; this will *be* no more the same. ᵇExalt that which is low, and abase that which is high.

27 'ᵃA ruin, a ruin, a ruin, I shall make it. This also will be no more, until ᵇHe comes whose right it is; and I shall give it *to Him.*'

28 "And you, son of man, prophesy and say, 'Thus says the Lord Gᴏᴅ concerning the sons of Ammon and concerning their ᵃreproach,' and say: 'A sword, a sword is drawn, polished for the slaughter, to cause it to ᵇconsume, that it may be like lightning—

29 while they see for you ᵃfalse visions, while they divine lies for you—to place you on the necks of the wicked who are slain, whose day has come, in the ᵇtime of the punishment of the end.

30 'ᵃReturn *it* to its sheath. In the ᵇplace where you were created, in the land of your origin, I shall judge you.

31 'And I shall ᵃpour out My indignation on you; I shall ᵇblow on you with the fire of My wrath, and I shall give you into the hand of brutal men, ᶜskilled in destruction.

32 'You will be ᵃfuel for the fire; your blood will be in the midst of the land. You will ᵇnot be remembered, for I, the Lᴏʀᴅ, have spoken.' "

Side reference column:

17 ᵃEzek. 5:13

★19-20

19 ᵃJer. 1:10; Ezek. 4:1-3

20 ᵃDeut. 3:11; Jer. 49:2; Ezek. 25:5; Amos 1:14 ᵇPs. 48:12, 13; 125:1, 2

★21 ᵃNum. 22:7; 23:23 ᵇProv. 16:33 ᶜGen. 31:19, 30; Judg. 17:5; 18:17, 20

22 ᵃEzek. 4:2; 26:9

★23 ᵃEzek. 17:16, 18 ᵇNum. 5:15; Ezek. 21:24; 29:16

★25 ᵃPs. 37:13; Ezek. 7:2, 3, 7

26 ᵃJer. 13:18; Ezek. 16:12 ᵇPs. 75:7; Ezek. 17:24

★27 ᵃHag. 2:21, 22 ᵇPs. 2:6; 72:7, 10; Jer. 23:5, 6; Ezek. 34:24; 37:24

★28-32

28 ᵃEzek. 36:15; Zeph. 2:8-10 ᵇIs. 31:8; Jer. 12:12; 46:10, 14

29 ᵃJer. 27:9; Ezek. 13:6-9; 22:28 ᵇEzek. 21:25; 35:5

30 ᵃJer. 47:6, 7 ᵇEzek. 25:5

31 ᵃEzek. 14:19; 25:7; Nah. 1:6 ᵇPs. 18:15; Is. 30:33; Ezek. 22:20, 21; Hag. 1:9 ᶜJer. 4:7; 6:22, 23; 51:20-23; Hab. 1:6, 10

32 ᵃEzek. 20:47, 48; Mal. 4:1 ᵇEzek. 25:10

21:19-20 Ezekiel drew two roads, both starting from Babylon, but one leading to *Rabbah* (Philadelphia or Amman) and the other to *Jerusalem.*

21:21 Nebuchadnezzar is seen at the crossroads using *divination* to ascertain which road to take. *arrows* (one marked Jerusalem and the other Rabbah) were placed in a quiver, shaken, and one taken out. The king looked at the color and marks on a *liver* from a sacrificed sheep to help decide.

21:23 *to them.* To the Jews who had allegiance

to Nebuchadnezzar the results of the divination would seem false, since they believed an attack on Jerusalem was impossible.

21:25 *prince of Israel.* I.e., Zedekiah.

21:27 Israel would have no king until Messiah comes (Gen. 49:10).

21:28-32 Though Nebuchadnezzar would turn away from *Ammon* and toward Jerusalem, Ammon's doom would be worse, for no promise of restoration is given her (v. 32) as there is for Israel.

14 The smelting furnace of judgment, 22:1-31

a The catalog of sins, 22:1-12

★ 1-12

22 Then the word of the LORD came to me saying,

2 "And you, son of man, will you judge, will you judge the bloody city? Then cause her to know all her abominations.

3 "And you shall say, 'Thus says the Lord GOD, "A city ᵃshedding blood in her midst, so that her time will come, and that makes idols, contrary to her *interest,* for defilement!

4 "You have become ᵃguilty by the blood which you have shed, and defiled by your idols which you have made. Thus you have brought your day near and have come to your years; therefore I have made you a ᵇreproach to the nations, and a mocking to all the lands.

5 "Those who are near and those who are far from you will mock you, you of ill repute, full of ᵃturmoil.

6 "Behold, the ᵃrulers of Israel, each according to his power, have been in you for the purpose of shedding blood.

7 "They have ᵃtreated father and mother lightly within you. The ᵇalien they have oppressed in your midst; the ᶜfatherless and the widow they have wronged in you.

8 "You have ᵃdespised My holy things and ᵇprofaned My sabbaths.

9 "Slanderous men have been in you for the purpose of shedding blood, and in you they have eaten at the mountain *shrines.* In your midst they have ᵃcommitted acts of lewdness.

10 "In you they have ᵃuncovered *their* fathers' nakedness; in you they have humbled her who was ᵇunclean in her menstrual impurity.

11 "And one has committed abomination with his ᵃneighbor's wife, and another has lewdly defiled his ᵇdaughter-in-law. And another in you has ᶜhumbled his sister, his father's daughter.

12 "In you they have ᵃtaken bribes to shed blood; you have taken ᵇinterest and profits, and you have injured your neighbors for gain by ᶜoppression, and you have ᵈforgotten Me," declares the Lord GOD.

b The certainty of judgment, 22:13-22

13 "Behold, then, I smite My hand at your ᵃdishonest gain which you have acquired and at the bloodshed which is among you.

14 "Can ᵃyour heart endure, or can your hands be strong, in the days that I shall deal with you? ᵇI, the LORD, have spoken and shall act.

15 "And I shall ᵃscatter you among the nations, and I shall disperse you through the lands, and I shall ᵇconsume your uncleanness from you.

16 "And you will profane yourself in the sight of the nations, and you will ᵃknow that I am the LORD." '"

17 And the word of the LORD came to me saying,

18 "Son of man, the house of Israel has become ᵃdross to Me; all of them are ᵇbronze and tin and iron and lead in the ᶜfurnace; they are the dross of silver.

19 "Therefore, thus says the Lord GOD, 'Because all of you have become dross, therefore, behold, I am going to gather you into the midst of Jerusalem.

20 'As they gather silver and bronze and iron and lead and tin

Cross references

3 ᵃEzek. 22:6, 27; 23:37, 45

4 ᵃ2 Kin. 21:16; Ezek. 24:7, 8 ᵇPs. 44:13, 14; Ezek. 5:14, 15; 16:57

5 ᵃIs. 22:2

6 ᵃIs. 1:23; Ezek. 22:27

7 ᵃEx. 20:12; Lev. 20:9; Deut. 5:16; 27:16 ᵇEx. 22:21f.; 23:9; Deut. 24:17; Jer. 7:6; Zech. 7:10 ᶜEx. 22:22; Ezek. 22:25; Mal. 3:5

8 ᵃEzek. 22:26 ᵇEzek. 20:13, 21, 24; 23:38, 39

9 ᵃEzek. 23:29; Hos. 4:2, 10, 14

10 ᵃLev. 18:8 ᵇLev. 18:19; Ezek. 18:6

11 ᵃEzek. 18:11; 33:26 ᵇLev. 18:15 ᶜ2 Sam. 13:11-14

12 ᵃEx. 23:8; Deut. 16:19; 27:25; Mic. 7:2, 3 ᵇLev. 25:36; Deut. 23:19 ᶜLev. 19:13 ᵈPs. 106:21; Ezek. 23:35

13 ᵃIs. 33:15; Amos 2:6-8; Mic. 2:2

14 ᵃEzek. 21:7 ᵇEzek. 17:24

15 ᵃDeut. 4:27; Neh. 1:8; Ezek. 20:23; Zech. 7:14 ᵇEzek. 23:27, 48

16 ᵃPs. 83:18; Ezek. 6:7

★18-19

18 ᵃPs. 119:119; Is. 1:22; Lam. 4:1 ᵇJer. 6:28-30 ᶜProv. 17:3; Is. 48:10

20 ᵃIs. 1:25

22:1-12 The catalog of Judah's sins includes idolatry (v. 3), bloodshedding (vv. 2-4, 6, 9, 12), immorality (vv. 10-11, *uncovered their fathers' nakedness* meant to defile their fathers' wives, Lev. 18:7), indecency (v. 7), and extor-tion (v. 12).

22:18-19 Israel is viewed as metal to be refined (in the siege of Jerusalem), but she came out as *dross* (worthless).

into the ªfurnace to blow fire on it in order to melt *it*, so I shall gather *you* in My anger and in My wrath, and I shall lay you *there* and melt you.

21 'And I shall gather you and blow on you with the fire of My wrath, and you will be melted in the midst of it.

22 'As silver is melted in the furnace, so you will be melted in the midst of it; and you will know that I, the Lᴏʀᴅ, have ªpoured out My wrath on you.' "

c The classes of sinners,
22:23-31

23 And the word of the Lᴏʀᴅ came to me saying,

24 "Son of man, say to her, 'You are a land that is ªnot cleansed or rained on in the day of indignation.'

25 "There is a ªconspiracy of her prophets in her midst, like a roaring lion tearing the prey. They have ᵇdevoured lives; they have taken treasure and precious things; they have made many ᶜwidows in the midst of her.

26 "Her ªpriests have done violence to My law and have ᵇprofaned My holy things; they have made no ᶜdistinction between the holy and the profane, and they have not taught the difference between the ᵈunclean and the clean; and they hide their eyes from My sabbaths, and I am profaned among them.

27 "Her princes within her are like wolves tearing the prey, by shedding blood *and* ªdestroying lives in order to get ᵇdishonest gain.

28 "And her prophets have smeared whitewash for them, seeing ªfalse visions and divining lies for them, saying, 'Thus says the Lord Gᴏᴅ,' when the Lᴏʀᴅ has not spoken.

29 "The people of the land have practiced ªoppression and committed robbery, and they have wronged the poor and needy and have ᵇoppressed the sojourner without justice.

30 "And I ªsearched for a man among them who should ᵇbuild up the wall and ᶜstand in the gap before Me for the land, that I should not destroy it; but I found no one.

31 "Thus I have poured out My ªindignation on them; I have consumed them with the fire of My wrath; ᵇtheir way I have brought upon their heads," declares the Lord Gᴏᴅ.

15 The parable of the two sisters, 23:1-49

a Their identification, 23:1-4

23 The word of the Lᴏʀᴅ came to me again saying,

2 "Son of man, there were ªtwo women, the daughters of one mother;

3 and they played the harlot in Egypt. They ªplayed the harlot in their youth; there their breasts were pressed, and there their virgin bosom was handled.

4 "And their names were Oholah the elder and Oholibah her sister. And they became Mine, and they bore sons and daughters. And *as for* their names, Samaria is Oholah, and Jerusalem is Oholibah.

Margin references:

22 ªEzek. 20:8, 33; Hos. 5:10

24 ªIs. 9:13; Jer. 2:30; Ezek. 24:13; Zeph. 3:2

★25-29

25 ªJer. 11:9; Hos. 6:9 ᵇJer. 2:34; Ezek. 13:19; 22:27 ᶜJer. 15:8; Ezek. 22:7

26 ªJer. 2:8, 26; Ezek. 7:26 ᵇ1 Sam. 2:12-17, 22; Ezek. 22:8 ᶜLev. 10:10; Ezek. 44:23 ᵈHag. 2:11-14

27 ªEzek. 22:25 ᵇEzek. 22:13

28 ªJer. 23:25-32; Ezek. 13:6

29 ªIs. 5:7; Ezek. 9:9; 22:7; Amos 3:10 ᵇEx. 23:9

30 ªIs. 59:16; 63:5; Jer. 5:1 ᵇEzek. 13:5 ᶜPs. 106:23; Jer. 15:1

31 ªIs. 10:5; 13:5; 30:27; Ezek. 22:20 ᵇEzek. 7:3, 8, 9; 9:10; 16:43; Rom. 2:8, 9

★ 1ff.

2 ªEzek. 16:46

3 ªLev. 17:7; Jer. 3:9

★ 4

22:25-29 Various groups in Israel's society are indicted for their sins: *prophets* (v. 25), *priests* (v. 26), *princes* (v. 27), *prophets* again (v. 28), and the *people* (v. 29).
23:1ff. Chapter 23 gives an allegory of two sisters, *Samaria* (representing the Northern Kingdom, Israel, v. 4) and *Jerusalem* (representing the Southern Kingdom, Judah, v. 4). Verses 1-10 describe the unfaithfulness and punishment of *Oholah* (Samaria); verses

11-21, the unfaithfulness of *Oholibah* (Jerusalem); verses 22-35, her punishment. Verses 36-49 also describe the punishment of the two sisters.
23:4 *Oholah* means "she who has a tent"; *Oholibah* means "a tent is in her." The reference to tents may symbolize God's dwelling with His people, or it may have in view the tents associated with false worship (cf. 16:16).

b Their infidelities, 23:5-21

5 "And Oholah played the harlot while she was Mine; and she lusted after her lovers, after the ^aAssyrians, *her* neighbors,

6 who were clothed in purple, ^agovernors and officials, all of them desirable young men, horsemen riding on horses.

7 "And she bestowed her harlotries on them, all of whom *were* the choicest men of Assyria; and with all whom she lusted after, with all their idols she ^adefiled herself.

8 "And she did not forsake her harlotries ^afrom the time in Egypt; for in her youth men had lain with her, and they handled her virgin bosom and poured out their lust on her.

9 "Therefore, I gave her into the hand of her ^alovers, into the hand of the Assyrians, after whom she lusted.

10 "They ^auncovered her nakedness; they took her sons and her daughters, but they slew her with the sword. Thus she became a byword among women, and they executed judgments on her.

11 "Now her sister Oholibah saw *this,* yet she was ^amore corrupt in her lust than she, and her harlotries were more than the harlotries of her sister.

12 "She lusted after the ^aAssyrians, governors and officials, the ones near, magnificently dressed, horsemen riding on horses, all of them desirable young men.

13 "And I saw that she had defiled herself; they both took the same way.

14 "So she increased her harlotries. And she saw men ^aportrayed on the wall, images of the ^bChaldeans portrayed with vermilion,

15 girded with belts on their loins, with flowing turbans on their heads, all of them looking like officers, like the Babylonians in Chaldea, the land of their birth.

16 "And when she saw them she ^alusted after them and sent messengers to them in Chaldea.

17 "And the ^aBabylonians came to her to the bed of love, and they defiled her with their harlotry. And when she had been defiled by them, she became disgusted with them.

18 "And she ^auncovered her harlotries and uncovered her nakedness; then I became ^bdisgusted with her, as I had become disgusted with her ^csister.

19 "Yet she multiplied her harlotries, remembering the days of her youth, when she played the harlot in the land of Egypt.

20 "And she ^alusted after their paramours, whose flesh is *like* the flesh of donkeys and whose issue is *like* the issue of horses.

21 "Thus you longed for the ^alewdness of your youth, when the Egyptians handled your bosom because of the breasts of your youth.

c Their punishment, 23:22-49

22 "Therefore, O Oholibah, thus says the Lord God, 'Behold I will arouse your lovers against you, from whom you were alienated, and I will bring them against you from every side:

23 the ^aBabylonians and all the ^bChaldeans, ^cPekod and Shoa and Koa, *and* all the ^dAssyrians with them; desirable young men, governors and officials all of them, officers and men of renown, all of them riding on horses.

24 'And they will come against you with weapons, ^achariots, and

Marginal references (left column)

★ 5-8
5 ^a2 Kin. 15:19; 16:7; 17:3; Ezek. 16:28; Hos. 5:13; 8:9, 10
6 ^aEzek. 23:12, 13

7 ^aEzek. 20:7; 22:3, 4; Hos. 5:3; 6:10

8 ^aEx. 32:4; 1 Kin. 12:28; 2 Kin. 10:29; 17:16; Ezek. 23:3, 19

9 ^aEzek. 16:37; 23:22

★10 ^aEzek. 16:37, 41

★11-21
11 ^aJer. 3:8-11; Ezek. 16:51

12 ^a2 Kin. 16:7

14 ^aEzek. 8:10 ^bEzek. 16:29

Marginal references (right column)

16 ^aEzek. 23:20; Matt. 5:28

17 ^a2 Kin. 24:17

18 ^aJer. 8:12; Ezek. 21:24; 23:10 ^bPs. 78:59; 106:40; Jer. 12:8 ^cEzek. 23:9; Amos 5:21

20 ^aEzek. 16:26; 17:15

21 ^aJer. 3:9; Ezek. 23:3

★23 ^a2 Kin. 20:14-17; Ezek. 21:19; 23:14-17 ^b2 Kin. 24:2; Job 1:17; Is. 23:13 ^cJer. 50:21 ^dGen. 2:14; 25:18; Ezra 6:22
24 ^aJer. 47:3; Ezek. 26:10; Nah. 2:3, 4 ^bJer. 39:5, 6; Ezek. 16:38; 23:45

23:5-8 Israel is condemned for her alliances with Assyria (cf. 2 Kings 15:19-29) and with Egypt (cf. 2 Kings 17:3-6).
23:10 *a byword.* Or, notorious. The captivity of the northern tribes by Assyria had taken place about 130 years before.

23:11-21 Judah is condemned for her alliances with Assyria (cf. Isa. 7:1-25), with Babylon (cf. 2 Kings 24:1), and with Egypt (cf. Isa. 30-31).
23:23 *Pekod and Shoa and Koa.* Tribes E. of the Tigris River and part of the Babylonian Empire.

wagons, and with a company of peoples. They will set themselves against you on every side with buckler and shield and helmet; and I shall commit the ᵇjudgment to them, and they will judge you according to their customs.

25 'And I will set My ᵃjealousy against you, that they may deal with you in wrath. They will remove your nose and your ears; and your survivors will fall by the sword. They will take your ᵇsons and your daughters; and your survivors will be consumed by the fire.

26 They will also ᵃstrip you of your clothes and take away your ᵇbeautiful jewels.

27 Thus ᵃI shall make your lewdness and your harlotry *brought* from the land of Egypt to cease from you, so that you will not lift up your eyes to them or remember Egypt anymore.'

28 "For thus says the Lord GOD, 'Behold, I will give you into the hand of those whom you ᵃhate, into the hand of those from whom you were alienated.

29 'And they will ᵃdeal with you in hatred, take all your property, and leave you naked and bare. And the nakedness of your harlotries shall be uncovered, both your lewdness and your harlotries.

30 'These things will be done to you because you have ᵃplayed the harlot with the nations, because you have defiled yourself with their idols.

31 'You have walked in the way of your sister; therefore I will give ᵃher cup into your hand.'

32 "Thus says the Lord GOD,
'You will ᵃdrink your sister's cup,
Which is deep and wide.
You will be ᵇlaughed at and held in derision;
It contains much.

33 'You will be filled with ᵃdrunkenness and sorrow,
The cup of horror and desolation,
The cup of your sister Samaria.

34 'And you will ᵃdrink it and drain it.
Then you will gnaw its fragments
And tear your breasts;
for I have spoken,' declares the Lord GOD.

35 "Therefore, thus says the Lord GOD, 'Because you have ᵃforgotten Me and ᵇcast Me behind your back, bear now the *punishment* of your lewdness and your harlotries.' "

36 Moreover, the LORD said to me, "Son of man, will you ᵃjudge Oholah and Oholibah? Then ᵇdeclare to them their abominations.

37 "For they have committed adultery, and blood is on their hands. Thus they have committed adultery with their idols and even caused their sons, ᵃwhom they bore to Me, to pass through *the fire* to them as food.

38 "Again, they have done this to Me: they have ᵃdefiled My sanctuary on the same day and have ᵇprofaned My sabbaths.

39 "For when they had slaughtered their children for their idols, they entered My ᵃsanctuary on the same day to profane it; and lo, thus they did within My house.

40 "Furthermore, they have even sent for men who come from afar, to whom a messenger was sent; and lo, they came—for whom you bathed, ᵃpainted your eyes, and ᵇdecorated yourselves with ornaments;

41 and you sat on a splendid ᵃcouch with a ᵇtable arranged before it, on which you had set My ᶜincense and My ᶜoil.

42 "And the sound of a ᵃcarefree multitude was with her; and

---

25 ᵃEx. 34:14; Ezek. 5:13; 8:17, 18; Zeph. 1:18 ᵇEzek. 23:47; Hos. 2:4

26 ᵃJer. 13:22; Ezek. 16:39; 23:29 ᵇIs. 3:18-23

27 ᵃEzek. 16:41

28 ᵃJer. 21:7-10; 34:20; Ezek. 16:37; 23:17, 22

29 ᵃDeut. 28:48; Ezek. 23:25, 26, 45-47

30 ᵃEzek. 6:9

31 ᵃ2 Kin. 21:13; Jer. 7:14, 15; Ezek. 23:33

★32 ᵃPs. 60:3; Is. 51:17; Jer. 25:15 ᵇEzek. 5:14, 15; 16:57; 22:4, 5

33 ᵃJer. 25:15, 16, 27; Hab. 2:16

34 ᵃPs. 75:8; Is. 51:17

35 ᵃIs. 17:10; Jer. 3:21; Ezek. 22:12; Hos. 8:14; 13:6 ᵇ1 Kin. 14:9; Jer. 2:27; 32:33

36 ᵃJer. 1:10; Ezek. 20:4; 22:2 ᵇIs. 58:1; Ezek. 16:2; Mic. 3:8

37 ᵃEzek. 16:20; 20:26

38 ᵃ2 Kin. 21:4, 7; Ezek. 5:11; 7:20 ᵇIs. 17:27; Ezek. 20:13, 24

★39 ᵃJer. 7:9-11

40 ᵃ2 Kin. 9:30; Jer. 4:30 ᵇIs. 3:18-23; Ezek. 16:13-16

41 ᵃEsth. 1:6; Is. 57:7; Amos 6:4 ᵇIs. 65:11; Ezek. 44:16 ᶜJer. 44:17; Hos. 2:8

★42 ᵃEzek. 16:49; Amos 6:3-6 ᵇJer. 51:7 ᶜGen. 24:30; Ezek. 16:11, 12

23:32 *your sister's cup.* Judah would be judged just as Israel was.
23:39 See note on 16:20–21.

23:42 *drunkards.* Referring to Israel's near neighbors, the Edomites and Moabites.

^bdrunkards were brought from the wilderness with men of the common sort. And they put ^cbracelets on the hands of the women and beautiful crowns on their heads.

43 "Then I said concerning her who was ^aworn out by adulteries, 'Will they now commit adultery with her when she is *thus?'*

44 "But they went in to her as they would go in to a harlot. Thus they went in to Oholah and to Oholibah, the lewd women.

45 "But they, righteous men, will ^ajudge them with the judgment of adulteresses, and with the judgment of women who shed blood, because they are adulteresses and blood is on their hands.

46 "For thus says the Lord GOD, 'Bring up a company against them, and give them over to ^aterror and plunder.

47 'And the company will ^astone them with stones and cut them down with their swords; they will slay their sons and their daughters and ^bburn their houses with fire.

48 'Thus I shall make lewdness cease from the land, that all women may be admonished and not commit lewdness as you have done.

49 'And your lewdness will be ^arequited upon you, and you will bear *the penalty of worshiping* your idols; thus you will know that I am the Lord GOD.' "

16 The parable of the boiling pot, 24:1–14

★1 **24** And the word of the LORD came to me in the ninth year, in the tenth month, on the tenth of the month, saying,

2 "Son of man, write the name of the day, this very day. The king of Babylon has ^alaid siege to Jerusalem this very day.

3 "And speak a ^aparable to the ^brebellious house, and say to them, 'Thus says the Lord GOD,
  "Put on the ^cpot, put *it* on, and also pour water in it;

4 ^aPut in it the pieces,
  Every good piece, the thigh, and the shoulder;
  Fill *it* with choice bones.

5 "Take the ^achoicest of the flock,
  And also pile wood under the pot.
  Make it boil vigorously.
  Also seethe its bones in it."

6 'Therefore, thus says the Lord GOD,
  "Woe to the ^abloody city,
  To the pot in which there is rust
  And whose rust has not gone out of it!
  Take out of it piece after piece,
  Without making a choice.

7 "For her blood is in her midst;
  She placed it on the bare rock;
  She did not ^apour it on the ground
  To cover it with dust.

8 "That it may ^acause wrath to come up to take vengeance,
  I have put her blood on the bare rock,
  That it may not be covered."

9 'Therefore, thus says the Lord GOD,
  "^aWoe to the bloody city!
  I also shall make the pile great.

10 "Heap on the wood, kindle the fire,
  Boil the flesh well,

Marginal references:

43 ^aEzek. 23:3

45 ^aEzek. 16:38

46 ^aJer. 15:4; 24:9; 29:18

★47 ^aLev. 20:10; Ezek. 16:40 ^bJer. 39:8

49 ^aIs. 59:18; Ezek. 7:4, 9; 9:10; 23:35

2 ^a2 Kin. 25:1; Jer. 39:1; 52:4

3 ^aPs. 78:2; Ezek. 17:2; 20:49 ^bIs. 1:2; 30:1, 9; Ezek. 2:3, 6, 8 ^cJer. 1:13, 14; Ezek. 11:3, 7, 11; 24:6

4 ^aMic. 3:2, 3

5 ^aJer. 39:6; 52:10, 24-27

6 ^a2 Kin. 24:3, 4; Ezek. 22:2, 3, 27; Mic. 7:2; Nah. 3:1

★ 7-8

7 ^aLev. 17:13; Deut. 12:16

8 ^aIs. 26:21

9 ^aEzek. 24:6; Hab. 2:12

23:47 Stoning was the prescribed punishment for adultery (Deut. 22:22–24).
24:1 Ezekiel's parable was acted out in Babylon on the very day the siege of Jerusalem began (in January 588; cf. 2 Kings 25:1) and illustrates the destruction of the city.
24:7-8 Jerusalem's sin was open; so also would be her judgment.

And mix in the spices,
And let the bones be
burned.

11 "Then ^aset it empty on its
coals,
So that it may be hot,
And its bronze may
glow,
And its ^bfilthiness may
be melted in it,
Its rust consumed.

12 "She has ^awearied *Me*
with toil,
Yet her great rust has
not gone from her;
Let her rust *be* in the
fire!

13 "In your filthiness is
lewdness.
Because I *would* have
cleansed you,
Yet you are ^anot clean,
You will not be cleansed
from your filthiness
again,
Until I have ^bspent My
wrath on you.

14 "I, the Lord, have spoken; it
is ^acoming and I shall act. I shall
not relent, and I shall not ^bpity,
and I shall not be sorry; ^caccord-
ing to your ways and according to
your deeds I shall judge you," declares the Lord God.' "

**17   The sign of the death of
Ezekiel's wife, 24:15–27**

15 And the word of the Lord
came to me saying,

16 "Son of man, behold, I am
about to take from you the ^ade-
sire of your eyes with a ^bblow;
but you shall not ^cmourn, and
you shall not weep, and your
^dtears shall not come.

17 "Groan silently; make ^ano
mourning for the dead. Bind on
your turban, and put your shoes
on your feet, and do not cover

your mustache, and ^bdo not eat
the bread of men."

18 So I spoke to the people in
the morning, and in the evening
my wife died. And in the morning
I did as I was commanded.

19 And the people said to me,
"Will you not tell us what these
things that you are doing mean
for us?"

20 Then I said to them, "The
word of the Lord came to me saying,

21 'Speak to the house of Israel, "Thus says the Lord God,
'Behold, I am about to profane
My sanctuary, the pride of your
power, the ^adesire of your eyes,
and the delight of your soul; and
your ^bsons and your daughters
whom you have left behind will
fall by the sword.

22 'And you will do as I have
done; you will not cover *your*
mustache, and you will not eat
the bread of men.

23 'And your turbans will be
on your heads and your shoes on
your feet. You ^awill not mourn,
and you will not weep; but ^byou
will rot away in your iniquities,
and you will groan to one another.

24 'Thus Ezekiel will be a
^asign to you; according to all that
he has done you will do; when it
comes, then you will know that I
am the Lord God.' "

25 'As for you, son of man,
will *it* not be on the day when I
take from them their ^astronghold,
the joy of their pride, the desire of
their eyes, and their heart's delight, their sons and their daughters,

26 that on that day he who
^aescapes will come to you with in-
formation for *your* ears?

27 'On that day your ^amouth
will be opened to him who es-
caped, and you will speak and be

11 ^aJer.
21:10; Mal.
4:1 ^bEzek.
22:15; 23:27

12 ^aJer. 9:5

13 ^aJer.
6:28-30;
Ezek. 22:24
^bEzek. 5:13;
8:18

14 ^aPs. 33:9;
Is. 55:11
^bJer. 13:14;
Ezek. 9:10
^cIs. 3:11;
Ezek. 18:30;
36:19

★**16** ^aSong
7:10; Ezek.
24:18 ^bJob
23:2 ^cJer.
16:5; 22:10
^dJer. 13:17

★**17** ^aLev.
21:10-12
^bJer. 16:7;
Hos. 9:4

★**21** ^aPs.
27:4; 84:1;
Ezek. 24:16
^bJer. 6:11;
16:3, 4;
Ezek. 23:25,
47

★**22-23**

23 ^aJob
27:15; Ps.
78:64 ^bLev.
26:39; Ezek.
33:10

24 ^aEzek.
4:3; Luke
11:29, 30

★**25-27**

25 ^aPs. 48:2;
50:2; Ezek.
24:21

26 ^a1 Sam.
4:12; Job
1:15-19

27 ^aEzek.
3:26; 33:22

24:16 *the desire of your eyes.* A reference to
Ezekiel's wife, who was about to die *with a
blow;* i.e., suddenly, or by a plague (cf. Num.
14:37).

24:17 Ezekiel employed the normal signs of
mourning.

24:21 *I am about to profane My sanctuary.* The

Temple would be destroyed by heathens.

24:22-23 The people would mourn deeply but
silently over the destruction of Jerusalem (just
as Ezekiel had been commanded to do with
respect to the death of his wife).

24:25-27 When the refugees arrived from Jerusalem, Ezekiel would be free to speak.

dumb no longer. Thus you will be a sign to them, and they will know that I am the LORD.' "

III PROPHECIES AGAINST FOREIGN NATIONS, 25:1-32:32
A Judgment on Ammon, 25:1-7

25 And the word of the LORD came to me saying,

2 "Son of man, set your face toward the ᵃsons of Ammon, and prophesy against them,

3 and say to the sons of Ammon, 'Hear the word of the Lord GOD! Thus says the Lord GOD, "Because you said, 'ᵃAha!' against My sanctuary when it was profaned, and against the land of Israel when it was made desolate, and against the house of Judah when they went into exile,

4 therefore, behold, I am going to give you to the ᵃsons of the east for a possession, and they will set their encampments among you and make their dwellings among you; they will ᵇeat your fruit and drink your milk.

5 "And I shall make ᵃRabbah a pasture for camels and the sons of Ammon a resting place for flocks. Thus you will know that I am the LORD."

6 'For thus says the Lord GOD, "Because you have ᵃclapped your hands and stamped your feet and ᵇrejoiced with all the scorn of your soul against the land of Israel,

7 therefore, behold, I have ᵃstretched out My hand against you, and I shall give you for ᵇspoil to the nations. And I shall ᶜcut you off from the peoples and ᵈmake you perish from the lands;

I shall destroy you. Thus you will ᵉknow that I am the LORD."

B Judgment on Moab, 25:8-11

8 'Thus says the Lord GOD, "Because ᵃMoab and Seir say, 'Behold, the house of Judah is like all the nations,'

9 therefore, behold, I am going to deprive the flank of Moab of its cities, of its cities which are on its frontiers, the glory of the land, ᵃBeth-jeshimoth, ᵇBaal-meon, and ᶜKiriathaim,

10 and I will give it for a possession, along with the sons of Ammon, to the ᵃsons of the east, that the sons of Ammon may not be remembered among the nations.

11 "Thus I will execute judgments on Moab, and they will know that I am the LORD."

C Judgment on Edom, 25:12-14

12 'Thus says the Lord GOD, "Because ᵃEdom has acted against the house of Judah by taking vengeance, and has incurred grievous guilt, and avenged themselves upon them,"

13 therefore, thus says the Lord GOD, "I will also ᵃstretch out My hand against Edom and ᵇcut off man and beast from it. And I will lay it waste; from ᶜTeman even to ᵈDedan they will fall by the sword.

14 "And ᵃI will lay My vengeance on Edom by the hand of My people Israel. Therefore, they will act in Edom ᵇaccording to My

★ **2** ᵃJer. 49:1-6; Amos 1:13-15; Zeph. 2:9
★ **3** ᵃPs. 70:2, 3; Ezek. 21:28; 25:6; 26:2; 36:2
★ **4** ᵃJudg. 6:3, 33; 1 Kin. 4:30 ᵇDeut. 28:33, 51; Is. 1:7
★ **5** ᵃDeut. 3:11; 2 Sam. 12:26; Jer. 49:2; Ezek. 21:20
6 ᵃJob 27:23; Nah. 3:19 ᵇObad. 12; Zeph. 2:8, 10
7 ᵃEzek. 25:13, 16; Zeph. 1:4 ᵇIs. 33:4; Ezek. 26:5 ᶜEzek. 21:32 ᵈAmos 1:14, 15 ᵉEzek. 6:14

★ **8** ᵃIs. 15:1; Jer. 48:1; Amos 2:1, 2
9 ᵃNum. 33:49; Josh. 12:3; 13:20 ᵇNum. 32:3, 38; Josh. 13:17; 1 Chr. 5:8; Jer. 48:23 ᶜNum. 32:37; Josh. 13:19; Jer. 48:1, 23
10 ᵃEzek. 25:4
★**11**
★**12** ᵃ2 Chr. 28:17; Ps. 137:7; Jer. 49:7-22
★**13** ᵃJer. 49:8, 13 ᵇEzek. 29:8; Mal. 1:3, 4 ᶜGen. 36:34; Jer. 49:7; Amos 1:12 ᵈJer. 25:23; 49:8
14 ᵃIs. 11:14 ᵇEzek. 35:11

25:2 *sons of Ammon.* See note on Amos 1:13.
25:3 The Ammonites took advantage of Babylon's victory over Judah and grabbed whatever they could.
25:4 *sons of the east.* The nomadic tribes of Transjordan, or possibly the Babylonians who spoiled Ammon.
25:5 *Rabbah.* The chief city of Ammon (Philadelphia; cf. note on 21:20).
25:8 *Moab.* See note on Amos 2:1. *Seir.* Edom, whose judgment is described in verses 12-14.

Moab denied that Judah had any special relation with the true God.
25:11 Both Moab and Ammon were conquered by Nebuchadnezzar in the fifth year after the destruction of Jerusalem, and were then occupied by Bedouin tribes.
25:12 *Edom.* See Introduction to Obadiah. *by taking vengeance.* See note on Obad. 1-14.
25:13 For her crimes Edom would be destroyed, from *Teman* in the north to *Dedan* in the south (cf. Jer. 25:23).

anger and according to My wrath; thus they will know My vengeance," declares the Lord God.

D   Judgment on Philistia, 25:15-17

*15 ªIs.
14:29-31;
Ezek. 25:6,
12; Joel 3:4

15 'Thus says the Lord God, "Because the Philistines have acted in ªrevenge and have taken vengeance with scorn of soul to destroy with everlasting enmity,"

*16 ªJer.
25:20; 47:1-7
ᵇ1 Sam.
30:14; Zeph.
2:5

16 therefore, thus says the Lord God, "Behold, I will ªstretch out My hand against the Philistines, even cut off the ᵇCherethites and destroy the remnant of the seacoast.

17 ªPs. 9:16

17 "And I will execute great vengeance on them with wrathful rebukes; and they will ªknow that I am the Lord when I lay My vengeance on them." ' "

E   Judgment on Tyre, 26:1-28:19
1   The overthrow of Tyre, 26:1-21

* 2 ª2 Sam.
5:11; Is.
23:1; Jer.
25:22 ᵇIs.
62:10 ᶜEzek.
25:8; 35:10

* 3-14
3 ªMic.
4:11 ᵇIs.
5:30; Jer.
50:42; 51:42

26 Now it came about in the eleventh year, on the first of the month, that the word of the Lord came to me saying,

2 "Son of man, because ªTyre has said concerning Jerusalem, 'Aha, the ᵇgateway of the peoples is broken; it has ᶜopened to me. I shall be filled, *now that* she is laid waste,'

3 therefore, thus says the Lord God, 'Behold, I am against you, O Tyre, and I will bring up ªmany nations against you, as the ᵇsea brings up its waves.

4 'And they will ªdestroy the walls of Tyre and break down her towers; and I will scrape her debris from her and make her a bare rock.

5 'She will be a place for the spreading of nets in the midst of the sea, for I have spoken,' declares the Lord God, 'and she will become ªspoil for the nations.

6 'Also her ªdaughters who are on the mainland will be slain by the sword, and they will know that I am the Lord.' "

7 For thus says the Lord God, "Behold, I will bring upon Tyre from the north Nebuchadnezzar king of Babylon, ªking of kings, with horses, ᵇchariots, cavalry, and a great army.

8 "He will slay your daughters on the mainland with the sword; and he will make ªsiege walls against you, cast up a ᵇmound against you, and raise up a large shield against you.

9 "And the blow of his battering rams he will direct against your walls, and with his axes he will break down your towers.

10 "Because of the multitude of his ªhorses, the dust *raised by* them will cover you; your walls will ᵇshake at the noise of cavalry and wagons and chariots, when he ᶜenters your gates as men enter a city that is breached.

11 "With the hoofs of his ªhorses he will trample all your streets. He will slay your people

4 ªIs.
23:11; Ezek.
26:9; Amos
1:10

5 ªEzek.
25:7; 29:19

6 ªEzek.
16:46, 53;
26:8

7 ªEzra
7:12; Is.
10:8; Jer.
52:32; Dan.
2:37, 47
ᵇEzek.
23:24; Nah.
2:3, 4

8 ªJer.
52:4; Ezek.
21:22 ᵇJer.
32:24

10 ªJer.
4:13; 47:3
ᵇEzek.
26:15; 27:28
ᶜJer. 39:3

11 ªIs. 5:28;
Hab. 1:8 ᵇIs.
26:5; Jer.
43:13

25:15 *Philistines.* Descendants of Mizraim, the son of Ham (Gen. 10:14; 1 Chron. 1:12), they were a constant thorn in the side of Israel (cf. Exod. 13:17; Judg. 3:2-3; 10:6-7; 1 Sam. 4; Judg. 13-16; 1 Sam. 13: 19-22; 17-18; 2 Chron. 17:11; 28:18; Zech. 9:1-8). They worshiped Dagon (the Semitic grain deity; cf. 1 Sam. 5) and other gods, and were finally liquidated under the Maccabees in the second century b.c.
25:16 *Cherethites.* Synonomous with the Philistines (see note on Zeph. 2:5).
26:2 *Tyre.* An ancient Phoenician city-state on the Mediterranean, between Acre and Sidon. She enjoyed great prosperity under King Hiram (980-947), who provided men and materials for the construction of David's palace (2 Sam. 5:11-12) and Solomon's palace and Temple (2 Chron. 2).
26:3-14 *many nations* would be involved in the destruction of Tyre. *Nebuchadnezzar* (v. 7) besieged the mainland city for 13 years (585-572) and destroyed it. In 332 Alexander the Great besieged the island city for six months and finally captured it by building a causeway out to it from the debris of the destroyed mainland city. The city was rebuilt and is mentioned in Matt. 15:21-28; Mark 3:8; Matt. 11:21-22; Acts 21:3-6. The city was almost completely destroyed by the Muslims in a.d. 1291.

with the sword; and your strong pillars will [b]come down to the ground.

12 "Also they will make a spoil of your riches and a prey of your [a]merchandise, [b]break down your walls and destroy your [c]pleasant houses, and throw your stones and your timbers and your debris [d]into the water.

13 "So I will silence the sound of your [a]songs, and the sound of your [b]harps will be heard no more.

14 "And I will make you a bare rock; you will be a place for the spreading of nets. You will be [a]built no more, for I the [b]LORD have spoken," declares the Lord GOD.

15 Thus says the Lord GOD to Tyre, "Shall not the [a]coastlands [b]shake at the sound of your fall when the wounded groan, when the slaughter occurs in your midst?

16 "Then all the princes of the sea will [a]go down from their thrones, remove their robes, and strip off their embroidered garments. They will [b]clothe themselves with trembling; they will sit on the ground, [c]tremble every moment, and be appalled at you.

17 "And they will take up a [a]lamentation over you and say to you,

> '[b]How you have perished, O inhabited one,
> From the seas, O renowned city,
> Which was [c]mighty on the sea,
> She and her inhabitants,
> Who imposed her terror
> On all her inhabitants!

18 'Now the [a]coastlands will tremble
> On the day of your fall;
> Yes, the coastlands which are by the sea
> Will be terrified at your [b]passing.' "

19 For thus says the Lord GOD, "When I shall make you a desolate city, like the cities which are not inhabited, when I shall [a]bring up the deep over you, and the great waters will cover you,

20 then I shall bring you down with those who [a]go down to the pit, to the people of old, and I shall make you dwell in the [b]lower parts of the earth, like the ancient waste places, with those who go down to the pit, so that you will not be inhabited; but I shall set [c]glory in the land of the living.

21 "I shall bring [a]terrors on you, and you will be no more; though you will be sought, [b]you will never be found again," declares the Lord GOD.

2 The lamentation over Tyre, 27:1–36

27 Moreover, the word of the LORD came to me saying,

2 "And you, son of man, [a]take up a lamentation over Tyre;

3 and say to Tyre, [a]who dwells at the entrance to the sea, [b]merchant of the peoples to many coastlands, 'Thus says the Lord GOD,

> "O Tyre, you have said, 'I am perfect in beauty.'

4 "Your borders are in the heart of the seas;
> Your builders have perfected your beauty.

5 "They have made all *your* planks of fir trees from [a]Senir;
> They have taken a cedar from Lebanon to make a mast for you.

6 "Of [a]oaks from [b]Bashan they have made your oars;
> With ivory they have inlaid your deck of boxwood from the coastlands of [c]Cyprus.

Cross references (margin)

12 [a]Is. 23:8, 18; Ezek. 27:3-27; Zech. 9:3 [b]Jer. 52:14 [c]2 Chr. 32:27; Amos 5:11 [d]Ezek. 27:27, 32, 34; 28:8

13 [a]Is. 23:16; 24:8, 9; Amos 6:5 [b]Is. 5:12; Rev. 18:22

14 [a]Deut. 13:16; Job 12:14; Mal. 1:4 [b]Is. 14:27

15 [a]Ezek. 26:18; 27:35 [b]Jer. 49:21; Ezek. 31:16

16 [a]Jon. 3:6 [b]Job 8:22; Ps. 35:26; Ezek. 7:27; 1 Pet. 5:5 [c]Ezek. 32:10; Hos. 11:10

17 [a]Ezek. 19:1, 14; 27:2, 32; 32:2, 16 [b]Is. 14:12; Jer. 48:39; 50:23 [c]Ezek. 27:3, 10, 11; 28:2

18 [a]Is. 41:5; Ezek. 26:15; 27:35 [b]Is. 23:5-7, 10, 11

19 [a]Is. 8:7, 8; Ezek. 26:3

20 [a]Is. 14:9, 10; Ezek. 32:30 [b]Ps. 88:6; Amos 9:2; Jon. 2:2, 6 [c]Jer. 33:9; Zech. 2:8

21 [a]Ezek. 26:15, 16; 27:36 [b]Rev. 18:21

★ 1-9

2 [a]Jer. 9:10, 17-20; Ezek. 28:12

3 [a]Ezek. 28:2 [b]Is. 23:3

5 [a]Deut. 3:9; 1 Chr. 5:23; Song 4:8

6 [a]Is. 2:13; Zech. 11:2 [b]Num. 21:33; Is. 2:13; Jer. 22:20 [c]Gen. 10:4; Is. 23:1, 12; Jer. 2:10

27:1-9 Tyre is depicted as a gallant ship made from the *fir trees from Senir* (Mt. Hermon, v. 5), with a *mast* from the cedars of *Lebanon* and *oars* from *Bashan* (NE. of Galilee).

★ 7 aEx.
25:4; Jer.
10:9 bGen.
10:4

★ 8 aGen.
10:18; 1 Chr.
1:16; Ezek.
27:11
b1 Kin. 9:27

★ 9-25

★9 aJosh.
13:5; 1 Kin.
5:18

10 aEzek.
30:5; 38:5

13 aGen.
10:2; Is.
66:19; Ezek.
27:19 bGen.
10:2; Ezek.
38:2; 39:1
cJoel 3:3;
Rev. 18:13
14 aGen.
10:3; Ezek.
39:6
15 aJer.
25:23; Ezek.
25:13; 27:20
b1 Kin.
10:22; Rev.
18:12

7 "Your sail was of fine embroidered linen from Egypt
So that it became your distinguishing mark;
Your awning was a blue and purple from the coastlands of b Elishah.

8 "The inhabitants of Sidon and a Arvad were your rowers;
Your b wise men, O Tyre, were aboard; they were your pilots.

9 "The elders of a Gebal and her wise men were with you repairing your seams;
All the ships of the sea and their sailors were with you in order to deal in your merchandise.

10 "a Persia and b Lud and a Put were in your army, your men of war. They hung shield and helmet in you; they set forth your splendor.

11 "The sons of Arvad and your army were on your walls, all around, and the Gammadim were in your towers. They hung their shields on your walls, all around; they perfected your beauty.

12 "Tarshish was your customer because of the abundance of all kinds of wealth; with silver, iron, tin, and lead, they paid for your wares.

13 "a Javan, a Tubal, and b Meshech, they were your traders; with the c lives of men and vessels of bronze they paid for your merchandise.

14 "Those from a Beth-togarmah gave horses and war horses and mules for your wares.

15 "The sons of a Dedan were your traders. Many coastlands were your market; b ivory tusks

and ebony they brought as your payment.

16 "a Aram was your customer because of the abundance of your goods; they paid for your wares with b emeralds, purple, c embroidered work, fine linen, coral, and rubies.

17 "Judah and the land of Israel, they were your traders; with the wheat of a Minnith, cakes, honey, oil, and balm they paid for your merchandise.

18 "a Damascus was your customer because of the abundance of your goods, because of the abundance of all kinds of wealth, because of the wine of Helbon and white wool.

19 "Vedan and Javan paid for your wares from Uzal; wrought iron, cassia, and sweet cane were among your merchandise.

20 "a Dedan traded with you in saddlecloths for riding.

21 "a Arabia and all the princes of Kedar, they were your customers for b lambs, rams, and goats; for these they were your customers.

22 "The traders of a Sheba and Raamah, they traded with you; they paid for your wares with the best of all kinds of b spices, and with all kinds of precious stones, and gold.

23 "Haran, Canneh, a Eden, the traders of Sheba, Asshur, and Chilmad traded with you.

24 "They traded with you in choice garments, in clothes of blue and embroidered work, and in carpets of many colors, and tightly wound cords, which were among your merchandise.

25 "The a ships of Tarshish were the carriers for your merchandise.

And you were filled and were very glorious
In the heart of the seas.

16 aJudg.
10:6; Is. 7:1-
8; Ezek.
16:57 bEzek.
28:13 cEzek.
16:13, 18

17 aJudg.
11:33

18 aGen.
14:15; Is.
7:8; Jer.
49:23; Ezek.
47:16-18

20 aGen.
25:3

21 aIs. 21:13
bIs. 60:7

22 aGen.
10:7; Is.
60:6; Ezek.
38:13 bGen.
43:11; 1 Kin.
10:2

23 a2 Kin.
19:12; Is.
37:12; Amos
1:5

25 aIs. 2:16

27:7 Elishah. Probably Cyprus.
27:8 Sidon and Arvad (an island city N. of Tripoli) furnished the oarsmen; Tyre, the pilots.
27:9-25 A description of the richness of the

wares from many nations which were carried on the ships of Tyre.
27:9 Gebal. Ancient Byblos, N. of modern Beirut.

★26-36

26 aEzek.
26:19 bPs.
48:7; Jer.
18:17; Acts
27:14

26 "Your rowers have brought
    you
Into agreat waters;
The beast wind has broken
    you
In the heart of the seas.
27 "Your wealth, your wares,
    your merchandise,
Your sailors, and your pi-
    lots,
Your repairers of seams,
    your dealers in mer-
    chandise,
And all your men of war
    who are in you,
With all your company
    that is in your midst,
Will fall into the heart of
    the seas
On the day of your over-
    throw.

28 aEzek.
26:10, 15, 18

28 "At the sound of the cry of
    your pilots
The pasture lands will
    ashake.

29 aRev.
18:17-19

29 "And all who handle the
    oar,
The asailors, and all the pi-
    lots of the sea
Will come down from
    their ships;
They will stand on the
    land,

30 aIs. 23:1-
6; Ezek.
26:17
b1 Sam.
4:12; 2 Sam.
1:2; Lam.
2:10; Rev.
18:19 cJer.
6:26; Jon.
3:6

30 And they will amake their
    voice heard over you
And will cry bitterly.
They will bcast dust on
    their heads,
They will cwallow in
    ashes.

31 aIs. 15:2;
Ezek. 29:18
bIs. 22:12;
Ezek. 7:18
cIs. 16:9;
22:4

31 "Also they will make them-
    selves abald for you
And bgird themselves with
    sackcloth;
And they will cweep for
    you in bitterness of
    soul
With bitter mourning.

32 aEzek.
26:17; 27:2;
28:12

32 "Moreover, in their wailing
    they will take up a
    alamentation for you
And lament over you:

'Who is like Tyre,
Like her who is silent in
    the midst of the sea?
33 'When your wares went
    out from the seas,
You satisfied many peo-
    ples;
With the aabundance of
    your wealth and your
    merchandise
You enriched the kings of
    earth.
34 'Now that you are abroken
    by the seas
In the depths of the wa-
    ters,
Your bmerchandise and all
    your company
Have fallen in the midst of
    you.
35 'All the ainhabitants of the
    coastlands
Are appalled at you,
And their kings are horri-
    bly afraid;
They are troubled in coun-
    tenance.
36 'The merchants among the
    peoples ahiss at you;
You have become terrified,
And you bwill be no
    more.' " '"

33 aEzek.
27:12, 18;
28:4, 5

34 aEzek.
26:12; 27:26,
27 bZech.
9:3, 4

35 aIs. 23:6;
Ezek. 26:16

36 aJer.
18:16; 19:8;
49:17; 50:13;
Zeph. 2:15
bPs. 37:10,
36

3   The fall of the leader of Tyre, 28:1-10

28 The word of the LORD
came again to me saying,
2 "Son of man, say to the
leader of Tyre, 'Thus says the
Lord GOD,

    "Because your heart is lifted
    up
And you have said, 'aI am
    a god,
I sit in the seat of gods,
In the heart of the seas';
Yet you are a bman and
    not God,
Although you make your
    heart like the heart of
    God—

★ 2 aIs.
14:14; 47:8;
Ezek. 28:9;
2 Thess. 2:4
bPs. 9:20;
82:6, 7; Is.
31:3; Ezek.
28:9

27:26-36 A picture of the shipwreck (ruin) of Tyre and the resulting astonishment of the seafaring men.

28:2 *the leader of Tyre.* The reigning king, Ittobaal II, whose pride is severely denounced.

★ 3 ªDan.
1:20; 2:20-
23, 28; 5:11,
12

4 ªEzek.
27:33; Zech.
9:2, 3

5 ªEzek.
27:12; Hos.
12:7, 8 ªJob
31:24, 25;
Ps. 52:7;
Ezek. 28:2;
Hos. 13:6

6 ªEx. 9:17;
Ezek. 28:2

★ 7 ªEzek.
26:7 ªEzek.
30:11; 31:12;
32:12; Hab.
1:6-8

★ 8 ªEzek.
27:26, 27, 34

3 Behold, you are wiser than
ªDaniel;
There is no secret that is a
match for you.
4 "By your wisdom and un-
derstanding
You have acquired ªriches
for yourself,
And have acquired gold
and silver for your
treasuries.
5 "By your great wisdom, by
your ªtrade
You have increased your
riches,
And your ªheart is lifted
up because of your
riches—
6 Therefore, thus says the
Lord GOD;
'Because you have ªmade
your heart
Like the heart of God,
7 Therefore, behold, I will
bring ªstrangers upon
you,
The ªmost ruthless of the
nations.
And they will draw their
swords
Against the beauty of your
wisdom
And defile your splendor.
8 'They will bring you down
to the pit,
And you will die the
ªdeath of those who
are slain
In the heart of the seas.
9 'Will you still say, "I am a
god,"
In the presence of your
slayer,
Although you are a man
and not God,

★10 ª1 Sam.
17:26, 36;
Ezek. 31:18;
32:30

★12 ªEzek.
19:1; 26:17;
27:2

★13 ªGen.
2:8; Is. 51:3;
Ezek. 31:8,
9, 16; 36:35
ªEzek.
27:16, 22
ªEx. 28:17-
20 ªIs. 24:8;
30:32

★14 ªEx.
25:17-20;
30:26; 40:9;
Ezek. 28:16
ªEzek.
20:40; 28:16
ªEzek.
28:13, 16;
Rev. 18:16

In the hands of those who
wound you?
10 'You will die the death of
the ªuncircumcised
By the hand of strangers,
For I have spoken!' de-
clares the Lord
GOD!' ' "

4 The lamentation over the king of Tyre, 28:11-19

11 Again the word of the
LORD came to me saying,
12 "Son of man, ªtake up a
lamentation over the king of
Tyre, and say to him, 'Thus says
the Lord GOD,
"You had the seal of perfection,
Full of wisdom and perfect
in beauty.
13 "You were in ªEden, the
garden of God;
ªEvery precious stone was
your covering:
The ªruby, the topaz, and
the diamond;
The beryl, the onyx, and
the jasper;
The lapis lazuli, the turquoise, and the emer-
ald;
And the gold, the work-
manship of your ªset-
tings and sockets,
Was in you.
On the day that you were
created
They were prepared.
14 "You were the ªanointed
cherub who covers,
And I placed you there.
You were on the holy
ªmountain of God;

28:3 *Daniel.* Undoubtedly the biblical Daniel
(see note on 14:14).
28:7 *strangers.* I.e., the Babylonians (cf. 26:7).
28:8 *the pit.* Sheol. *the death.* I.e., without burial.
28:10 *the death of the uncircumcised.* I.e., a
shameful death.
28:12 *the king of Tyre.* This section (vv. 11-19),
with its superhuman references, apparently
describes someone other than the human ruler
of Tyre; namely, Satan. If so, Satan's unique

privileges before his fall are described in
verses 12-15 and the judgment on him in
verses 16-19. *You had the seal of perfection.*
I.e., Satan was the consummation of perfection in his original wisdom and beauty.
28:13 *covering.* I.e., dress or robe. *settings and
sockets.* The sockets and grooves used as the
settings for the precious stones.
28:14 Satan had occupied a special place of
prominence in guarding the throne of God (cf.
Exod. 25:20).

You walked in the midst of the ^cstones of fire.

★15 ^aEzek.
27:3, 4; 28:3-
6, 12 ^bEzek.
28:17, 18

15 "You were ^ablameless in your ways
From the day you were created,
Until ^bunrighteousness was found in you.

★16-19

16 ^aEzek.
27:12 ^bEzek.
8:17; Hab.
2:8, 17

16 "By the ^aabundance of your trade
You were internally ^bfilled with violence,
And you sinned;
Therefore I have cast you as profane
From the mountain of God.
And I have destroyed you, O covering cherub,
From the midst of the stones of fire.

17 ^aEzek.
27:3, 4; 28:7
^bIs. 19:11
^cEzek. 26:16

17 "Your heart was lifted up because of your ^abeauty;
You ^bcorrupted your wisdom by reason of your splendor.
I cast you to the ground;
I put you before ^ckings,
That they may see you.

18 ^aAmos
1:9, 10 ^bMal.
4:3

18 "By the multitude of your iniquities,
In the unrighteousness of your trade,
You profaned your sanctuaries.
Therefore I have brought ^afire from the midst of you;
It has consumed you,
And I have turned you to ^bashes on the earth
In the eyes of all who see you.

19 ^aEzek.
26:21; 27:36
^bJer. 51:64

19 "All who know you among the peoples
Are appalled at you;
You have become ^aterrified,

And you will be ^bno more." ' "

F   Judgment on Sidon, 28:20-26

★20-23

20 And the word of the LORD came to me saying,

21 ^aEzek.
6:2; 25:2
^bGen. 10:15,
19; Is. 23:2,
4; Ezek. 27:8

21 "Son of man, ^aset your face toward ^bSidon, prophesy against her,

22 ^aEzek.
28:26; 30:19

22 and say, 'Thus says the Lord GOD,
"Behold, I am against you, O Sidon,
And I shall be glorified in your midst.
Then they will know that I am the LORD, when I ^aexecute judgments in her,
And I shall manifest My holiness in her.

23 ^aEzek.
38:22 ^bJer.
51:52

23 "For ^aI shall send pestilence to her
And blood to her streets,
And the ^bwounded will fall in her midst
By the sword upon her on every side;
Then they will know that I am the LORD.

★24-26

24 "And there will be no more for the house of Israel a ^aprickling brier or a painful thorn from any round about them who scorned them; then they will know that I am the Lord GOD."

24 ^aNum.
33:55; Josh.
23:13; Is.
55:13; Ezek.
2:6

25 Thus says the Lord GOD, "When I ^agather the house of Israel from the peoples among whom they are scattered, and shall manifest My holiness in them in the sight of the nations, then they will ^blive in their land which I gave to My servant Jacob.

25 ^aPs.
106:47; Is.
11:12, 13;
Jer. 32:37;
Ezek. 20:41;
34:13, 27
^bJer. 23:8;
27:11

26 ^aJer.
23:6; Ezek.
34:25-28;
38:8 ^bJer.
32:15, 43,
44; Amos
9:13, 14
^cEzek.
25:11; 28:22

26 "And they will ^alive in it securely; and they will ^bbuild houses, plant vineyards, and live

---

28:15 *blameless.* In the sense of moral soundness and integrity. By creation Satan was perfect; but pride was his downfall (1 Tim. 3:6; Isa. 14:13-14).

28:16-19 Satan's judgment, announced in these verses, will not be consummated until he is cast forever into the lake of fire (Rev. 20:10).

28:20-23 *Sidon,* Tyre's neighbor, will also be punished (see note on Joel 3:4-8).

28:24-26 A promise of the restoration of Israel (at the second coming of Christ) and of peace for that nation (during the millennial kingdom).

securely, when I ^cexecute judgments upon all who scorn them round about them. Then they will know that I am the LORD their God." ' "

G Judgment on Egypt,
29:1–32:32
1 The certainty of judgment,
29:1–21

29 In the ^atenth year, in the tenth *month*, on the twelfth of the month, the word of the LORD came to me saying,

2 "Son of man, set your face against ^aPharaoh, king of Egypt, and prophesy against him and against all ^bEgypt.

3 "Speak and say, 'Thus says the Lord GOD,

"Behold, I am against you, Pharaoh, king of Egypt,

The great ^amonster that lies in the midst of his rivers,

That ^bhas said, 'My Nile is mine, and I myself have made it.'

4 "And I shall put ^ahooks in your jaws,

And I shall make the fish of your rivers cling to your scales.

And I shall bring you up out of the midst of your rivers,

And all the fish of your rivers will cling to your scales.

★ 1 ^aEzek. 26:1; 29:17; 30:20

★ 2 ^aJer. 44:30 ^bIs. 19:1-17; Jer. 46:2-26; Ezek. 30:1-32:32
3 ^aIs. 27:1; Ezek. 32:2 ^bEzek. 29:9; 30:12

4 ^a2 Kin. 19:28; Ezek. 38:4

5 "And I shall ^aabandon you to the wilderness, you and all the fish of your rivers;

You will fall on the open field; you will not be brought together or ^bgathered.

I have given you for ^cfood to the beasts of the earth and to the birds of the sky.

6 "Then all the inhabitants of Egypt will know that I am the LORD,

Because they have been only a ^astaff *made* of reed to the house of Israel.

7 "When they took hold of you with the hand,

You ^abroke and tore all their hands;

And when they leaned on you,

You broke and made all their loins quake."

8 Therefore, thus says the Lord GOD, "Behold, I shall ^abring upon you a sword, and I shall cut off from you man and beast.

9 "And the ^aland of Egypt will become a desolation and waste. Then they will know that I am the LORD.

Because you ^bsaid, 'The Nile is mine, and I have made *it*,'

10 therefore, behold, I am ^aagainst you and against your rivers, and I will make the land of Egypt an utter waste and desolation, from Migdol *to* Syene and even to the border of Ethiopia.

5 ^aEzek. 32:4-6 ^bJer. 8:2; 25:33 ^cJer. 7:33; 34:20; Ezek. 39:4

6 ^a2 Kin. 18:21; Is. 36:6

7 ^a2 Kin. 18:21; Is. 36:6; Ezek. 17:15-17

8 ^aJer. 46:13; Ezek. 14:17

9 ^aEzek. 29:10-12; 30:7, 8, 13-19 ^bProv. 16:18; 18:12; Ezek. 29:3

★10 ^aEzek. 13:8; 21:3; 26:3; 29:3

29:1 This prophecy against Egypt (through v. 17) was given in January 586, seven months before the fall of Jerusalem.

29:2 *Egypt* has played a large role in the history of Israel. Its black, fertile soil deposited by the Nile drew Abraham there in order to escape the famine in Palestine (Gen. 12:10). About 200 years later Joseph was sold into slavery in Egypt and was followed there by his family, who also came to escape famine. From these 70 people grew the nation Israel. Solomon married Pharaoh's daughter and enjoyed cordial relations with Egypt; but this was the exception. Shishak of Egypt sacked the Temple in the fifth year of Rehoboam (926; 1 Kings 14:25-26). Several kings of Judah sought

Egypt's help against Babylon, but in vain (Isa. 36:6). Josiah died in an attempt to stop the Egyptians at Megiddo in 609 (2 Kings 23:29-30). Ironically, the victorious Pharaoh (Neco II) was defeated by Nebuchadnezzar in 605 at Carchemish. After the capture of Jerusalem, some Jews fled to Egypt (Jer. 44). The *Pharaoh* of Ezek. 29:2 was Hophra (588-569), grandson of Neco, and the king to whom Zedekiah looked for help against Nebuchadnezzar (Jer. 37:5-7; 44:30).

29:10 *Migdol* was on the NE. border of Egypt and *Syene* was near Assuan (modern Aswan), the southern boundary. Nebuchadnezzar took numbers of Egyptian captives to Babylon after he conquered the land.

11 ^aJer.
43:11, 12;
46:19; Ezek.
32:13

11 "A man's foot will ^anot pass through it, and the foot of a beast will not pass through it, and it will not be inhabited for forty years.

12 ^aJer.
25:15-19;
27:6-11;
Ezek. 30:7
^bJer. 46:19;
Ezek. 30:23,
26

12 "So I shall make the land of Egypt a desolation in the ^amidst of desolated lands. And her cities, in the midst of cities that are laid waste, will be desolate forty years; and I shall ^bscatter the Egyptians among the nations and disperse them among the lands."

★13 ^aIs.
19:22; Jer.
46:26

13 For thus says the Lord God, "At the end of forty years I shall ^agather the Egyptians from the peoples among whom they were scattered.

14 ^aIs.
11:11; Jer.
44:1, 15;
Ezek. 30:14

14 "And I shall turn the fortunes of Egypt and shall make them return to the land of ^aPathros, to the land of their origin; and there they will be a lowly kingdom.

15 ^aEzek.
17:6, 14;
30:13; Zech.
10:11 ^bEzek.
31:2; 32:2;
Nah. 3:8-10

15 "It will be the ^alowest of the kingdoms; and it will never again lift itself up above the nations. And I shall make them so small that they will not ^brule over the nations.

16 ^aIs. 20:5;
30:1-3; 31:1;
36:6; Ezek.
17:15; 29:6,
7 ^bIs. 64:9;
Jer. 14:10;
Ezek. 21:23;
Hos. 8:13

16 "And it will never again be the ^aconfidence of the house of Israel, ^bbringing to mind the iniquity of their having turned to Egypt. Then they will know that I am the Lord God." ' "

★17 ^aEzek.
24:1; 26:1;
29:1;
30:20;40:1

17 Now in the ^atwenty-seventh year, in the first *month*, on the first of the month, the word of the Lord came to me saying,

★18-20
18 ^aJer.
25:9; 27:6;
Ezek. 26:7-
12 ^bJer.
48:37; Ezek.
27:31

18 "Son of man, ^aNebuchadnezzar king of Babylon made his army labor hard against Tyre; every head was made ^bbald, and every shoulder was rubbed bare. But he and his army had no wages from Tyre for the labor that he had performed against it."

19 ^aEzek.
30:10, 24;
25; 32:11
^bJer. 43:10-
13; Ezek.
30:14

19 Therefore, thus says the Lord God, "Behold, I ^ashall give the land of Egypt to Nebuchadnezzar king of Babylon. And he will carry off her ^bwealth, and capture her spoil and seize her plunder; and it will be wages for his army.

20 ^aIs. 10:6,
7; 45:1-3;
Jer. 25:9

20 "I have given him the land of Egypt *for* his labor which he ^aperformed, because they acted for Me," declares the Lord God.

★21 ^a1 Sam.
2:10; Ps.
92:10;
132:17
^bEzek. 3:27;
24:27; 33:22;
Amos 3:7, 8;
Luke 21:15

21 "On that day I shall make a ^ahorn sprout for the house of Israel, and I shall ^bopen your mouth in their midst. Then they will know that I am the Lord."

2 The description of judgment, 30:1–26

30 The word of the Lord came again to me saying,

2 ^aIs. 13:6;
15:2; Ezek.
21:12; Joel
1:5, 11, 13

2 "Son of man, prophesy and say, 'Thus says the Lord God,

"^aWail, 'Alas for the day!'

★ 3 ^aEzek.
7:19; 13:5;
Joel 1:15;
2:1; Obad.
15 ^bEzek.
30:18; 32:7;
34:12

3 "For the day is near,
Even ^athe day of the
Lord is near;
It will be a day of
^bclouds,
A time *of doom* for the
nations.

4 ^aEzek.
29:19

4 "And a sword will come
upon Egypt,
And anguish will be in
Ethiopia,
When the slain fall in
Egypt,

29:13 *At the end of forty years.* Because of the lenient policy Persia had toward subject nations, the captives were allowed to go home.
29:17 March-April 571.
29:18-20 Though Nebuchadnezzar laid siege to Tyre for 13 years (585-572), the campaign was an economic failure (see note on 26:3-14). Since he had no booty with which to pay his soldiers (it was a simple matter for Tyre to ship her treasures out by sea during the siege), he invaded Egypt and got booty for *wages* for

his army.
29:21 Since *horn* is a symbol of power (cf. Jer. 48:25), this prophecy is of Israel's eventual regaining of power.
30:3 *the day of the Lord.* The time of God's intervention in judgment. Though the phrase is usually used eschatologically, here Egypt is viewed as representative of God's judgment on all godless nations. See the Introduction to Joel.

They ^atake away her
wealth,
And her foundations are
torn down.

★ **5** ^aJer.
25:20, 24

5 "Ethiopia, Put, Lud, all
^aArabia, Libya, and the people of
the land that is in league will fall
with them by the sword."

★ **6** ^aIs.
20:3-6

6 Thus says the Lord,
"Indeed, those who sup-
port ^aEgypt will fall,
And the pride of her
power will come
down;
From Migdol *to* Syene
They will fall within her
by the sword,"
Declares the Lord God.

7 ^aJer.
25:18-26;
Ezek. 29:12

7 "And they will be desolate
In the ^amidst of the
desolated lands;
And her cities will be
In the midst of the dev-
astated cities.

8 ^aPs.
58:11; Ezek.
29:6, 9, 16
^bEzek.
22:31; 30:14,
16; Amos
1:4, 7, 10,
12, 14

8 "And they will ^aknow
that I am the Lord,
When I set a ^bfire in
Egypt
And all her helpers are
broken.

9 ^aIs. 18:1, 2
^bIs. 47:8;
Ezek. 38:11;
39:6 ^cIs.
19:17; 23:5;
Ezek. 32:9,
10

9 "On that day ^amessengers
will go forth from Me in ships to
frighten ^bsecure Ethiopia; and
^canguish will be on them as on
the day of Egypt; for, behold, it
comes!"

★**10** ^aEzek.
29:19

10 Thus says the Lord God,
"^aI will also make the
multitude of Egypt
cease
By the hand of Nebu-
chadnezzar king of
Babylon.

11 "He and his people with
him,
^aThe most ruthless of
the nations,
Will be brought in to
destroy the land;
And they will draw their
swords against Egypt
And fill the land with
the slain.

11 ^aEzek.
28:7

12 "Moreover, I will make
the ^aNile canals dry
And ^bsell the land into
the hands of evil men.
And I will make the land
desolate,
And all that is in it,
By the hand of strang-
ers; I, the Lord, have
spoken."

12 ^aEzek.
29:3, 9 ^bIs.
19:4

13 Thus says the Lord God,
"I will also ^adestroy the
idols
And make the images
cease from ^bMemphis.
And there will no longer
be a prince in the land
of Egypt;
And I will put fear in the
land of Egypt.

★**13-19**

13 ^aIs. 2:18
^bIs. 19:13;
Jer. 2:16;
44:1; 46:14;
Ezek. 30:16

14 "And I will make ^aPath-
ros desolate,
Set a fire in ^bZoan,
And execute judgments
on ^cThebes.

14 ^aIs.
11:11; Jer.
44:1, 15;
Ezek. 29:14
^bPs. 78:12,
43; Is. 19:11,
13 ^cJer.
46:25; Ezek.
30:15, 16;
Nah. 3:8

15 "And I will pour out My
wrath on Sin,
The stronghold of Egypt;
I will also cut off the
multitude of Thebes.

16 "And I will set a fire in
Egypt;
Sin will writhe in an-
guish,

30:5 *Put, Lud.* The former was on the N. coast of
Africa in Libya and the latter was in Asia Minor; see Jer. 46:9. *Arabia.* Lit., the mixed people, probably a reference to foreign mercenaries in the Egyptian army. *Libya.* Lit., Chub
("Libya" is taken from the Septuagint), an unidentified place.
30:6 *From Migdol to Syene.* See note on 29:10.
30:10 Cf. 29:10.
30:13-19 Principal towns are mentioned in this
description of the destruction of Egypt. *Mem-*

phis. Ten miles S. of Cairo. *Pathros.* Upper
(South) Egypt. *Zoan.* The land of Goshen,
where the Israelites had settled. *Thebes.* Capital of Upper Egypt. *Sin.* Or Pelusium, situated
on the NE. frontier of Egypt, 23 miles SE. of
modern Port Said. *On.* Heliopolis, seven miles
NE. of Cairo (see Jer. 43:13). *Pi-beseth.* About
30 miles NE. of Cairo and a center of worship
of the cat-headed goddess. *Tehaphnehes.* Another frontier fortress, SW. of Pelusium.

Thebes will be
breached,
And Memphis *will have*
distresses daily.

17 ^aGen.
41:45; 46:20

17 "The young men of ^aOn
and of Pi-beseth
Will fall by the sword,
And the women will go
into captivity.

18 ^aJer.
43:8-13
^bEzek. 30:3
^cLev. 26:13;
Is. 10:27;
Jer. 27:2;
28:10, 13;
30:8; Ezek.
34:27

18 "And in ^aTehaphnehes
the day will be ^bdark
When I ^cbreak there the
yoke bars of Egypt.
Then the pride of her
power will cease in
her;
A cloud will cover her,
And her daughters will
go into captivity.

19 ^aPs. 9:16;
Ezek. 5:8,
15; 25:11;
30:14

19 "Thus I will ^aexecute
judgments on Egypt,
And they will know that
I am the LORD." ' "

★20 ^aEzek.
26:1; 29:1,
17; 31:1

20 And it came about in the
^aeleventh year, in the first *month,*
on the seventh of the month, that
the word of the LORD came to me
saying,

★21 ^aPs.
10:15; 37:17;
Ezek. 30:24
^bJer. 30:13;
46:11

21 "Son of man, I have ^abro-
ken the arm of Pharaoh king of
Egypt; and, behold, it has not
been ^bbound up for healing or
wrapped with a bandage, that it
may be strong to hold the sword.

22 ^aJer.
46:25; Ezek.
29:3 ^b2 Kin.
24:7; Jer.
37:7 ^cJer.
46:21

22 "Therefore, thus says the
Lord GOD, 'Behold, I am ^aagainst
Pharaoh king of Egypt and will
break his arms, both the strong
and the ^bbroken; and I will make
the sword ^cfall from his hand.

23 ^aEzek.
29:12; 30:17,
18, 26

23 'And I will ^ascatter the
Egyptians among the nations and
disperse them among the lands.

★24-26

24 ^aNeh.
6:9; Is. 45:1,
5; Ezek.
30:10, 25;
Zech. 10:12
^bEzek.
30:11, 25;
Zeph. 2:12

24 'For I will ^astrengthen the
arms of the king of Babylon and
put ^bMy sword in his hand; and I
will break the arms of Pharaoh, so
that he will groan before him
with the groanings of a wounded
man.

25 'Thus I will strengthen the
arms of the king of Babylon, but
the arms of Pharaoh will fall.
Then they will know that I am the
LORD, when I put My sword into
the hand of the king of Babylon
and he ^astretches it out against
the land of Egypt.

25 ^aJosh.
8:18; 1 Chr.
21:16; Is.
5:25

26 'When I scatter the Egyptians among the nations and disperse them among the lands, then
they will know that I am the
LORD.' "

3 The comparison between
Assyria and Egypt,
31:1-18

31 And it came about in the
^aeleventh year, in the third
month, on the first of the month,
that the word of the LORD came to
me saying,

★ 1-18

★ 1 ^aJer.
52:5, 6;
Ezek. 30:20;
32:1

2 "Son of man, say to Pharaoh king of Egypt, and to his
^amultitude,

'Whom are you like in
your greatness?

2 ^aEzek.
29:19; 30:10;
Nah. 3:9

3 'Behold, Assyria *was* a
^acedar in Lebanon
With beautiful branches
and forest shade,
And ^bvery high;
And its top was among
the clouds.

★ 3 ^aIs.
10:33, 34;
Ezek. 17:3,
4, 22; 31:16;
Dan. 4:10,
20-23 ^bIs.
10:33; Ezek.
31:5, 10

4 'The ^awaters made it
grow, the deep made
it high.
With its rivers it con-
tinually extended all
around its planting
place,
And it sent out its chan-
nels to all the trees of
the field.

4 ^aEzek.
17:5, 8; Rev.
17:1, 15

5 'Therefore ^aits height
was loftier than all the
trees of the field
And its boughs became
many and its branches
long

5 ^aDan.
4:11 ^bPs.
1:3; Ezek.
17:5

30:20 March-April 586, three months before the
fall of Jerusalem.
30:21 *Pharaoh.* Hophra (see note on Jer. 37:5).
30:24-26 Nebuchadnezzar was the Lord's instrument to destroy Egypt.
31:1-18 In verses 1-9 Egypt is likened to a lofty
cedar; verses 10-14 describe her destruction;

verses 15-18, the reaction of the nations.
31:1 One month before the fall of Jerusalem.
31:3 *Assyria.* Either the downfall of Assyria is
used as a warning to Egypt (v. 18), or perhaps
the correct reading should be, "a stately cedar
in Lebanon."

Because of [b]many waters as it spread them out.

6 'All the [a]birds of the heavens nested in its boughs,
And under its branches all the beasts of the field gave birth,
And all great nations lived under its shade.

7 'So it was beautiful in its greatness, in the length of its branches;
For its roots extended to many waters.

8 'The [a]cedars in [b]God's garden could not match it;
The cypresses could not compare with its boughs,
And the plane trees could not match its branches.
No tree in [b]God's garden could compare with it in its beauty.

9 'I made it beautiful with the multitude of its branches,
And all the trees of [a]Eden, which were in the [a]garden of God, were jealous of it.

10 'Therefore, thus says the Lord God, "Because it is high in stature, and it has set its top among the clouds, and its [a]heart is haughty in its loftiness,

11 therefore, I will give it into the hand of a [a]despot of the nations; he will thoroughly deal with it. According to its wickedness I have [b]driven it away.

12 "And [a]alien [b]tyrants of the nations have cut it down and left it; on the [c]mountains and in all the valleys its branches have fallen, and its boughs have been broken in all the ravines of the land. And all the peoples of the earth have [d]gone down from its shade and left it.

13 "On its ruin all the [a]birds of the heavens will dwell. And all the beasts of the field will be on its *fallen* branches

14 in order that all the trees by the waters may not be exalted in their stature, nor set their top among the clouds, nor their well-watered mighty ones stand *erect* in their height. For they have all been given over to death, to the [a]earth beneath, among the sons of men, with those who go down to the pit."

15 Thus says the Lord God, "On the day when it went down to Sheol I [a]caused lamentations; I closed the deep over it and held back its rivers. And *its* many waters were stopped up, and I made Lebanon mourn for it, and all the trees of the field wilted away on account of it.

16 "I made the nations [a]quake at the sound of its fall when I made it [b]go down to Sheol with those who go down to the pit; and all the well-watered trees of Eden, the choicest and best of [c]Lebanon, were [d]comforted in the earth beneath.

17 "They also [a]went down with it to Sheol to those who were [b]slain by the sword; and those who were its strength lived [c]under its shade among the nations.

18 "To which among the trees of Eden are you thus equal in glory and greatness? Yet you will be brought down with the trees of Eden to the earth beneath; you will lie in the midst of the [a]uncircumcised, with those who were slain by the sword. [b]So is Pharaoh and all his multitude!" ' declares the Lord God."

31:10 Pharaoh's sin was pride (as was Satan's, **28:6, 17**).
31:11 *a despot of the nations.* Nebuchadnezzar.
31:16–17 Other nations were *comforted* when Egypt fell, but they too would go down (*went down* is a prophetic perfect indicating future time) to *Sheol* eventually.
31:18 *the uncircumcised.* See note on 28:10.

Cross-reference column (left):

6 [a]Ezek. 17:23; 31:13; Dan. 4:12, 21; Matt. 13:32

8 [a]Ps. 80:10; Ezek. 31:3 [b]Gen. 2:8, 9; 13:10; Is. 51:3; Ezek. 28:13; 31:16, 18

9 [a]Gen. 2:8, 9; 13:10; Is. 51:3; Ezek. 28:13; 31:16, 18

★**10** [a]2 Chr. 32:25; Is. 10:12; 14:13, 14; Ezek. 28:17; Dan. 5:20
★**11** [a]Ezek. 30:10, 11; 32:11, 12; Dan. 5:18, 19 [b]Deut. 18:12; Nah. 3:18

12 [a]Ezek. 7:21; 28:7; 30:12; Hab. 1:6 [b]Ezek. 28:7; 30:11; 32:12 [c]Ezek. 32:5; 35:8 [d]Ezek. 31:17; Dan. 4:14; Nah. 3:17, 18

Cross-reference column (right):

13 [a]Is. 18:6; Ezek. 29:5; 31:6; 32:4

14 [a]Num. 16:30, 33; Ps. 63:9; Ezek. 26:20; 31:18; 32:24; Amos 9:2; Jon. 2:2, 6; Eph. 4:9

15 [a]Ezek. 32:7; Nah. 2:10

★**16–17**
16 [a]Ezek. 26:15; 27:28; Hag. 2:7 [b]Is. 14:15; Ezek. 32:18 [c]Is. 14:8; Hab. 2:17 [d]Ezek. 14:22, 23; 32:31

17 [a]Ps. 9:17 [b]Ezek. 32:20f. [c]Ezek. 31:3, 6; Dan. 4:12

★**18** [a]Jer. 9:25, 26; Ezek. 28:10; 32:19, 21 [b]Ps. 52:7; Matt. 13:19

4 The lamentation over Egypt,
32:1-32

★ 1 aEzek.
30:20; 31:1;
32:17; 33:21

32 And it came about in the ªtwelfth year, in the twelfth *month*, on the first of the month, that the word of the LORD came to me saying,

★ 2 aEzek.
19:1; 27:2;
28:12; 32:16
bJer. 4:7;
Ezek. 19:2-6;
Nah. 2:11-13
cIs. 27:1;
Ezek. 29:3
dJer. 46:7, 8

2 "Son of man, take up a ªlamentation over Pharaoh king of Egypt, and say to him,
'You compared yourself to a young ᵇlion of the nations,
Yet you are like the ᶜmonster in the seas;
And you ᵈburst forth in your rivers,
And muddied the waters with your feet,
And fouled their rivers.'"

3 aEzek.
12:13

3 Thus says the Lord GOD, "Now I will ªspread My net over you
With a company of many peoples,
And they shall lift you up in My net.

4 aIs. 18:6

4 "And I will leave you on the land;
I will cast you on the open field.
And I will cause all the ªbirds of the heavens to dwell on you,
And I will satisfy the beasts of the whole earth with you.

5 aEzek.
31:12

5 "And I will lay your flesh ªon the mountains,
And fill the valleys with your refuse.

6 aEx. 7:17;
Is. 34:3, 7;
Ezek. 35:6;
Rev. 14:20
7 aJob
18:5, 6; Prov.
13:9 bEx.
10:21-23; Is.
34:4; Ezek.
30:3, 18;
34:12 cIs.
13:10 dJoel
2:2, 31; 3:15;
Amos 8:9;
Matt. 24:29;
Mark 13:24f.;
Luke 21:25;
Rev. 6:12;
8:12

6 "I will also make the land drink the discharge of your ªblood,
As far as the mountains,
And the ravines shall be full of you.

7 "And when I ªextinguish you,
I will ᵇcover the heavens, and darken their ᶜstars;

I will cover the ᵈsun with a cloud,
And the moon shall not give its light.

8 aGen.
1:14

8 "All the shining ªlights in the heavens
I will darken over you
And will set darkness on your land,"
Declares the Lord GOD.

9 aEzek.
27:29-32;
28:19; Rev.
18:10-15
bEx. 15:14-
16

9 "I will also ªtrouble the hearts of many peoples, when I ᵇbring your destruction among the nations, into lands which you have not known.

10 aEzek.
27:35 bEzek.
26:16

10 "And I will make many peoples ªappalled at you, and their kings shall be horribly afraid of you when I brandish My sword before them; and ᵇthey shall tremble every moment, every man for his own life, on the day of your fall."

11 aJer.
46:26

11 For ªthus says the Lord GOD, "The sword of the king of Babylon shall come upon you.

12 aEzek.
28:7 bEzek.
28:19

12 "By the swords of the mighty ones I will cause your multitude to fall; all of them are ªtyrants of the nations,
And they shall ᵇdevastate the pride of Egypt,
And all its multitude shall be destroyed.

13 aEzek.
29:11

13 "I will also destroy all its cattle from beside many waters;
And ªthe foot of man shall not muddy them anymore,
And the hoofs of beasts shall not muddy them.

14 "Then I will make their waters settle,
And will cause their rivers to run like oil,"
Declares the Lord GOD.

15 aPs.
107:33, 34;
Ezek. 29:12,
19, 20 bEx.
7:5; 14:4, 18;
Ps. 9:16;
83:17, 18;
Ezek. 6:7;
30:19, 26

15 "When I make the land of Egypt a ªdesolation,
And the land is destitute of that which filled it,

32:1 February-March 585, one year and seven months after the fall of Jerusalem.
32:2 *monster*. See 29:3. Egypt's fall is described in verses 2-8; the reactions of the nations in verses 9-10; the instrument (Nebuchadnezzar) in verses 11-16.

When I smite all those
who live in it,
Then they shall [b]know
that I am the LORD.

16 "This is a [a]lamentation and
they shall chant it. The daughters
of the nations shall chant it. Over
Egypt and over all her multitude
they shall chant it," declares the
Lord GOD.

17 And it came about in the
[a]twelfth year, on the [a]fifteenth of
the month, that the word of the
LORD came to me saying,

18 "Son of man, [a]wail for the
multitude of Egypt, and [b]bring it
down, her and the daughters of
the powerful nations, to the
[c]nether world, with those who go
down to the pit;

19 'Whom do you surpass in
beauty?
Go down and make your
bed with the [a]uncir-
cumcised.'

20 "They shall fall in the midst
of those who are slain by the
sword. She is given over to the
sword; they have [a]drawn her and
all her multitudes away.

21 "The [a]strong among the
mighty ones shall speak of him
and his helpers from the midst of
Sheol, 'They have gone down,
they lie still, the uncircumcised,
slain by the sword.'

22 "[a]Assyria is there and all
her company; her graves are
round about her. All of them are
slain, fallen by the sword,

23 whose [a]graves are set in
the remotest parts of the pit, and
her company is round about her
grave. All of them are slain, fallen
by the sword, who spread terror
in the land of the living.

24 "[a]Elam is there and all her
multitude around her grave; all of
them slain, fallen by the sword,
who went down uncircumcised to
the [b]lower parts of the earth, who

instilled their terror in the [c]land
of the living, and [d]bore their disgrace with those who went down
to the pit.

25 "They have made a [a]bed for
her among the slain with all her
multitude. Her graves are around
it, they are all uncircumcised,
slain by the sword (although their
terror was instilled in the land of
the living), and they bore their
disgrace with those who go down
to the pit; they were put in the
midst of the slain.

26 "[a]Meshech, [b]Tubal and all
their multitude are there; their
graves surround them. All of
them were slain by the sword
[c]uncircumcised, though they instilled their terror in the land of
the living.

27 "[a]Nor do they lie beside the
fallen [b]heroes of the uncircumcised, who went down to Sheol
with their weapons of war, and
whose swords were laid under
their heads; but the punishment
for their [c]iniquity rested on their
bones, though the terror of *these*
heroes *was* once in the land of the
living.

28 "But in the midst of the uncircumcised you will be broken
and lie with those slain by the
sword.

29 "There also is [a]Edom, its
kings, and all its princes, who for
all their might are laid with those
slain by the sword; they will lie
with the uncircumcised, and with
those who go down to the pit.

30 "There also are the chiefs of
the [a]north, all of them, and all the
[b]Sidonians, who in spite of the
terror resulting from their might,
in shame went down with the
slain. So they lay down uncircumcised with those slain by the
sword, and bore their disgrace
with those who go down to the
pit.

32:17-32 Two weeks later than verse 1. A
graphic description of Sheol (*the pit*, vv. 18,
24, 25, 29, 30). Other nations are there to greet
Egypt. *Elam*, once a mighty power in SW.
Asia, was absorbed by Persia (vv. 24-25). *Me-*

shech and *Tubal* (v. 26) were powers to the
NW. (see 38:2-3). On *Edom* (v. 29) see Introduction to Obadiah. Pharaoh would find comfort in knowing his is not the only empire that
has gone to Sheol (v. 31)!

Marginal references:

16 [a]2 Sam. 1:17; 3:33, 34; 2 Chr. 35:25; Jer. 9:17; Ezek. 26:17; 32:2

★17-32

17 [a]Ezek. 31:1; 32:1; 33:21

18 [a]Is. 16:9; Ezek. 21:6; 32:2, 16; Mic. 1:8 [b]Jer. 1:10; Ezek. 43:3; Hos. 6:5 [c]Ezek. 31:14, 16, 18; 32:24

19 [a]Jer. 9:25, 26; Ezek. 31:18; 32:21, 24, 29, 30

20 [a]Ps. 28:3

21 [a]Is. 14:9-12; Ezek. 32:27

22 [a]Ezek. 27:23; 31:3, 16

23 [a]Is. 14:15
24 [a]Gen. 10:22; 14:1; Is. 11:11; Jer. 25:25; 49:34-39 [b]Ezek. 26:20; 31:14, 18; 32:18 [c]Job 28:13; Ps. 27:13; 52:5; 142:5; Is. 38:11; Jer. 11:19 [d]Ezek. 16:52, 54; 32:25, 30

25 [a]Ps. 139:8

26 [a]Gen. 10:2; Ezek. 27:13; 38:2, 3; 39:1 [b]Gen. 10:2; Is. 66:19; Ezek. 27:13; 38:2, 3; 39:1 [c]Ezek. 32:19

27 [a]Is. 14:18, 19 [b]Job 3:13-15; Ezek. 32:21 [c]Job 20:11; Ps. 109:18

29 [a]Is. 34:5-15; Jer. 49:7-22; Ezek. 25:13; 35:9, 15

30 [a]Jer. 1:15; 25:26; Ezek. 38:6, 15; 39:2 [b]Jer. 25:22; Ezek. 28:21-23

31 aEzek. 14:22; 31:16

31 "These Pharaoh will see, and he will be acomforted for all his multitude slain by the sword, *even* Pharaoh and all his army," declares the Lord GOD.

32 "Though I instilled a terror of him in the land of the living, yet he will be made to lie down among *the* uncircumcised *along* with those slain by the sword, *even* Pharaoh and all his multitude," declares the Lord GOD.

IV PROPHECIES OF ISRAEL'S RESTORATION, 33:1-39:29

A Ezekiel's Appointment as a Watchman, 33:1-33

★ 1-9

2 aEzek. 3:11; 33:12, 17, 30; 37:18

3 aNeh. 4:18-20; Is. 58:1; Ezek. 33:9; Hos. 8:1; Joel 2:1

4 a2 Chr. 25:16; Jer. 6:17; Zech. 1:4 bEzek. 18:13; 33:5, 9; Acts 18:6

5 aEx. 9:19-21; Heb. 11:7

6 aEzek. 18:20, 24; 33:8, 9 bEzek. 3:18, 20

7 aIs. 62:6; Ezek. 3:17-21 bJer. 1:17; 26:2; Ezek. 2:7, 8; Acts 5:20

33 And the word of the LORD came to me saying,

2 "Son of man, speak to the asons of your people, and say to them, 'If I bring a sword upon a land, and the people of the land take one man from among them and make him their watchman;

3 and he sees the sword coming upon the land, and he ablows on the trumpet and warns the people,

4 then he who hears the sound of the trumpet and adoes not take warning, and a sword comes and takes him away, his bblood will be on his *own* head.

5 'He heard the sound of the trumpet, but did not take warning; his blood will be on himself. But had he taken warning, he would have adelivered his life.

6 'But if the watchman sees the sword coming and does not blow the trumpet, and the people are not warned, and a sword comes and takes a person from them, he is ataken away in his iniquity; but his bblood I will require from the watchman's hand.'

7 "Now as for you, son of man, I have aappointed you a watchman for the house of Israel; so you will hear a message from My mouth, and give them bwarning from Me.

8 aIs. 3:11; Ezek. 18:4, 13, 18, 20; 33:14

8 "When I say to the wicked, 'O wicked man, you shall asurely die,' and you do not speak to warn the wicked from his way, that wicked man shall die in his iniquity, but his blood I will require from your hand.

9 aActs 13:40, 41, 46 bEzek. 3:19, 21; Acts 20:26

9 "But if you on your part warn a wicked man to turn from his way, and he adoes not turn from his way, he will die in his iniquity; but you have bdelivered your life.

★10-11

10 aLev. 26:39; Ezek. 4:17; 24:23 bIs. 49:14; Ezek. 37:11

10 "Now as for you, son of man, say to the house of Israel, 'Thus you have spoken, saying, "Surely our transgressions and our sins are upon us, and we are arotting away in them; bhow then can we survive?"'

11 aIs. 49:18; Ezek. 5:11 bEzek. 18:23, 32; Hos. 11:8 cJer. 31:20; 1 Tim. 2:4; 2 Pet. 3:9 dIs. 55:6, 7; Jer. 3:22; Ezek. 18:30, 31; Hos. 14:1; Acts 3:19

11 "Say to them, 'aAs I live!' declares the Lord GOD, 'I take bno pleasure in the death of the wicked, but rather that the wicked cturn from his way and live. dTurn back, turn back from your evil ways! Why then will you die, O house of Israel?'

12 aEzek. 3:18; 18:24; 33:20 b2 Chr. 7:14; Ezek. 18:21; 33:19

12 "And you, son of man, say to your fellow citizens, 'The arighteousness of a righteous man will not deliver him in the day of his transgression, and as for the wickedness of the wicked, he will bnot stumble because of it in the day when he turns from his wickedness; whereas a righteous man will not be able to live by his righteousness on the day when he commits sin.'

13 aEzek. 18:26; Heb. 10:38; 2 Pet. 2:20, 21

13 "When I say to the righteous he will surely live, and he *so* trusts in his righteousness that he acommits iniquity, none of his righteous deeds will be remembered; but in that same iniquity

---

33:1-9 In these verses Ezekiel is reminded of his call to be a watchman (see notes on 3:17, 18-21).
33:10-11 *we are rotting away in them.* I.e., we are wasting away because of the inevitable consequences of our sins. To those feeling this way God gave two words of comfort: God desires men to live, and sin is forgiveable.

of his which he has committed he will die.

14 "But when I say to the wicked, 'You will surely die,' and he ᵃturns from his sin and practices ᵇjustice and righteousness,

15 if a wicked man restores a pledge, ᵃpays back what he has taken by robbery, walks by the ᵇstatutes which ensure life without committing iniquity, he will surely live; he shall not die.

16 "ᵃNone of his sins that he has committed will be remembered against him. He has practiced justice and righteousness; he will surely live.

17 "Yet your fellow citizens say, 'The way of the Lord is not right', when it is their own way that is not right.

18 "When the righteous turns from his righteousness and ᵃcommits iniquity, then he shall die in it.

19 "But when the wicked turns from his wickedness and practices justice and righteousness, he will live by them.

20 "Yet you say, 'ᵃThe way of the Lord is not right.' O house of Israel, I will judge each of you according to his ways."

21 Now it ᵃcame about in the ᵇtwelfth year of our exile, on the fifth of the tenth month, that the refugees from Jerusalem came to me, saying, "ᶜThe city has been taken."

22 Now the ᵃhand of the Lord had been upon me in the evening, before the refugees came. And He ᵇopened my mouth at the time they came to me in the morning; so my mouth was ᶜopened, and I was no longer speechless.

23 Then the word of the Lord came to me saying,

24 "Son of man, they who ᵃlive in these waste places in the land of Israel are saying, 'ᵇAbraham was only one, yet he possessed the land; so to ᶜus who are many the land has been given as a possession.'

25 "Therefore, say to them, 'Thus says the Lord God, "You eat meat with the ᵃblood in it, lift up your eyes to your idols as you shed blood. ᵇShould you then possess the land?

26 "You ᵃrely on your sword, you commit abominations, and each of you defiles his neighbor's wife. Should you then possess the land?"'

27 "Thus you shall say to them, 'Thus says the Lord God, "As I live, surely those who are in the waste places will ᵃfall by the sword, and whoever is in the open field I will give to the beasts to be devoured, and those who are in the strongholds and in the ᵇcaves will die of pestilence.

28 "And I shall ᵃmake the land a desolation and a waste, and the ᵇpride of her power will cease; and the mountains of Israel will be desolate, so that no one will pass through.

29 "Then they will know that I am the Lord, when I make the land a desolation and a waste because of all their abominations which they have committed."'

30 "But as for you, son of man, your fellow citizens who talk about you by the walls and in the doorways of the houses, speak to one another, each to his brother, saying, 'ᵃCome now, and hear

---

14 ᵃIs. 55:7; Jer. 18:7, 8; Ezek. 18:27; 33:8, 19; Hos. 14:1, 4 ᵇMic. 6:8
15 ᵃEx. 22:1-4; Lev. 6:4, 5; Luke 19:8 ᵇPs. 119:59; 143:8; Ezek. 20:11
16 ᵃIs. 1:18; 43:25; Ezek. 18:22

18 ᵃEzek. 3:20; 18:24; 33:12, 13

20 ᵃEzek. 18:25

★21 ᵃEzek. 31:1; 32:1, 17 ᵇJer. 39:1, 2; 40:1; 52:4-7; Ezek. 24:1, 2 ᶜ2 Kin. 25:10; Jer. 39:8
★22 ᵃEzek. 1:3; 8:1; 37:1 ᵇEzek. 3:26, 27; 24:27 ᶜLuke 1:64

★23-29
24 ᵃJer. 39:10; 40:7; Ezek. 33:27 ᵇIs. 51:2; Luke 3:8; Acts 7:5; Rom. 4:12 ᶜEzek. 11:15
25 ᵃLev. 17:10, 12, 14; Deut. 12:16, 23; 15:23 ᵇJer. 7:9, 10
26 ᵃMic. 2:1, 2; Zeph. 3:3

27 ᵃJer. 15:2, 3; 42:22; Ezek. 5:12 ᵇ1 Sam. 13:6; Is. 2:19

28 ᵃEzek. 5:14; 6:14; Mic. 7:13 ᵇEzek. 7:24; 24:21; 30:6

★30-33
30 ᵃIs. 29:13; 58:2; Ezek. 14:3; 20:3, 31

33:21 A turning point in Ezekiel's ministry. The fall of Jerusalem, for which Ezekiel had waited seven years, has happened. Now his ministry would be one of promise for the nation. *twelfth year.* Some Hebrew manuscripts read "eleventh year," the year Jerusalem fell (cf. Jer. 39:2), which would mean that Ezekiel received the news 6 months after the fall. Some feel two systems of dating are involved (Palestinian and Babylonian), though it is not impossible that half a year passed before Ezekiel received full details.
33:22 See 3:26.
33:23-29 A message for those who evaded the Babylonian conquerors. They were saying that if Abraham, a single individual, was given the land, how much more did they have a right to it. Ezekiel answered by cataloging six sins of which they were guilty (vv. 25-26).
33:30-33 Many of the exiles looked on Ezekiel as merely providing entertainment for them, and they did not heed his message.

31 aPs.
78:36, 37; Is.
29:13;
1 John 3:18
bEzek.
22:13, 27;
Luke 12:15

32 aMark
6:20

33 aJer.
28:9; Ezek.
33:29

what the message is which comes forth from the Lord.'

31 "And they come to you as people come, and sit before you as My people, and hear your words, but they do not do them, for they do the lustful desires expressed by their amouth, and their heart goes after their bgain.

32 "And behold, you are to them like a sensual song by one who has a abeautiful voice and plays well on an instrument; for they hear your words, but they do not practice them.

33 "So when it acomes to pass—as surely it will—then they will know that a prophet has been in their midst."

B Israel's Shepherds, 34:1–31
1 False shepherds, 34:1–10

★ 2 aJer.
2:8; 3:15;
10:21; 12:10
bJer. 23:1;
Ezek. 22:25;
34:8-10; Mic.
3:1-3, 11
cPs. 78:71,
72; Is. 40:11;
Ezek. 34:14,
15; John
10:11; 21:15-
17

3 aZech.
11:16 bEzek.
22:25, 27

4 aZech.
11:16 bMatt.
9:36; 10:6;
18:12, 13;
Luke 15:4

5 aNum.
27:17; 2 Chr.
18:16; Jer.
10:21; 23:2;
50:6, 7; Matt.
9:36; Mark
6:34 bEzek.
34:8, 28

6 aJer.
40:11, 12;
Ezek. 7:16;
1 Pet. 2:25
bJohn 10:16
cPs. 142:4

34 Then the word of the Lord came to me saying,

2 "Son of man, prophesy against the ashepherds of Israel. Prophesy and say to those shepherds, 'Thus says the Lord God, "Woe, shepherds of Israel who have been bfeeding themselves! Should not the shepherds cfeed the flock?

3 "You aeat the fat and clothe yourselves with the wool, you bslaughter the fat sheep without feeding the flock.

4 "Those who are sickly you have not strengthened, the diseased you have not healed, athe broken you have not bound up, the scattered you have not brought back, nor have you bsought for the lost; but with force and with severity you have dominated them.

5 "And they were ascattered for lack of a shepherd, and they became bfood for every beast of the field and were scattered.

6 "My flock awandered through all the mountains and on every high hill, and bMy flock was

scattered over all the surface of the earth; and there was cno one to search or seek for them." ' "

7 Therefore, you shepherds, hear the word of the Lord:

8 "As I live," declares the Lord God, "surely because My flock has become a aprey, My flock has even become food for all the beasts of the field for lack of a shepherd, and My shepherds did not search for My flock, but rather the shepherds fed themselves and did not feed My flock;

9 therefore, you shepherds, hear the word of the Lord:

10 Thus says the Lord God, "Behold, I am aagainst the shepherds, and I shall demand My sheep from them and make them bcease from feeding sheep. So the shepherds will not feed themselves anymore, but I shall cdeliver My flock from their mouth, that they may not be food for them." ' "

2 The true Shepherd, 34:11–31

11 For thus says the Lord God, "Behold, I Myself will asearch for My sheep and seek them out.

12 "aAs a shepherd cares for his herd in the day when he is among his scattered sheep, so I will bcare for My sheep and will deliver them from all the places to which they were scattered on a ccloudy and gloomy day.

13 "And I will bring them out from the peoples and gather them from the countries and bring them to their own land; and I will afeed them on the mountains of Israel, by the bstreams, and in all the inhabited places of the land.

14 "I will feed them in a agood pasture, and their grazing ground will be on the mountain heights of Israel. There they will lie down in good grazing ground, and they will feed in brich pasture on the mountains of Israel.

8 aActs
20:29

10 aJer.
21:13; Ezek.
5:8; 13:8;
34:2; Zech.
10:3 b1 Sam.
2:29, 30; Jer.
52:24-27
cPs. 72:12-
14; Ezek.
13:23

11 aEzek.
11:17; 20:41

12 aJer.
31:10 bIs.
40:11; 56:8;
Jer. 23:3;
31:8; Luke
19:10; John
10:16 cJer.
13:16; Ezek.
30:3; Joel
2:2

★13 aEzek.
34:23; 36:29,
30; Mic. 7:14
bIs. 30:25

14 aPs. 23:2;
Jer. 31:12-
14, 25; John
10:9 bEzek.
28:25, 26;
36:29, 30

34:2 shepherds of Israel. I.e., like Jehoiakim and Zedekiah, who did not protect and provide for the people (see note on Jer. 23:1).

34:13 God, the good Shepherd, will restore the people to their land (to be completely fulfilled in the millennial kingdom).

15 aPs. 23:1,
2; Ezek.
34:23

15 "I will ªfeed My flock and I will lead them to rest," declares the Lord GOD.

16 aIs. 10:16
bIs. 49:26

16 "I will seek the lost, bring back the scattered, bind up the broken, and strengthen the sick; but the ªfat and the strong I will destroy. I will ᵇfeed them with judgment.

★17-22

17 aEzek.
20:38; 34:20-
22; Mal. 4:1;
Matt. 25:32

17 "And as for you, My flock, thus says the Lord GOD, 'Behold, I will ªjudge between one sheep and another, between the rams and the male goats.

18 aNum.
16:9, 13;
2 Sam. 7:19;
Is. 7:13

18 'Is it too ªslight a thing for you that you should feed in the good pasture, that you must tread down with your feet the rest of your pastures? Or that you should drink of the clear waters, that you must foul the rest with your feet?

19 'And as for My flock, they must eat what you tread down with your feet, and they must drink what you foul with your feet!' "

20 Therefore, thus says the Lord GOD to them, "Behold, I, even I, will judge between the fat sheep and the lean sheep.

21 aDeut.
33:17; Dan.
8:4; Luke
13:14-16

21 "Because you push with side and with shoulder, and ªthrust at all the weak with your horns, until you have scattered them abroad,

22 aPs.
72:12-14;
Jer. 23:3;
Ezek. 34:10

22 therefore, I will ªdeliver My flock, and they will no longer be a prey; and I will judge between one sheep and another.

★23 aRev.
7:17 bIs.
40:11; John
10:11 cJer.
30:9; Ezek.
37:24

23 "Then I will ªset over them one ᵇshepherd, My servant ᶜDavid, and he will feed them; he will feed them himself and be their shepherd.

24 aIs. 55:3;
Jer. 30:9;
Ezek. 37:24,
25; Hos. 3:5

24 "And I, the LORD, will be their God, and My servant ªDavid will be prince among them; I, the LORD, have spoken.

★25 aEzek.
16:60; 20:37;
37:26 bJob
5:22, 23; Is.
11:6-9 cJer.
33:16; Ezek.
28:26; 34:27,
28

25 "And I will make a ªcovenant of peace with them and ᵇeliminate harmful beasts from the land, so that they may ᶜlive securely in the wilderness and sleep in the woods.

26 "And I will make them and the places around My hill a ªblessing. And I will cause ᵇshowers to come down in their season; they will be showers of ᶜblessing.

26 aGen.
12:2; Ezek.
34:14 bDeut.
11:13-15;
28:12 cLev.
25:21; Is.
44:3

27 "Also the tree of the field will yield its fruit, and the earth will yield its increase, and they will be ªsecure on their land. Then they will know that I am the LORD, when I have ᵇbroken the bars of their yoke and have delivered them from the hand of those who enslaved them.

27 aEzek.
38:8, 11
bLev. 26:13;
Is. 52:2, 3;
Jer. 30:8

28 "And they will no longer be a prey to the nations, and the beasts of the earth will not devour them; but they will ªlive securely, and no one will make *them* afraid.

28 aJer.
30:10; Ezek.
39:26

29 "And I will establish for them a ªrenowned planting place, and they will ᵇnot again be victims of famine in the land, and they will not ᶜendure the insults of the nations anymore.

29 aIs. 4:2;
60:21; 61:3
bEzek.
34:26, 27;
36:29 cEzek.
36:6, 15

30 "Then they will know that ªI, the LORD their God, am with them, and that they, the house of Israel, are My people," declares the Lord GOD.

30 aPs. 46:7,
11; Ezek.
14:11; 36:28

31 "As for you, My ªsheep, the ᵇsheep of My pasture, you are men, and I am your God," declares the Lord GOD.

31 aPs.
78:52; 80:1;
Ezek. 36:38
bPs. 100:3;
Jer. 23:1

C The Rebirth of the Nation, 35:1–36:38

1 The destruction of Edom, 35:1-15

35 Moreover, the word of the LORD came to me saying,

2 "Son of man, set your face against ªMount Seir, and prophesy against it,

★ 2 aGen.
36:8; Ezek.
25:12; 36:5

34:17-22 God not only judges false leaders, but also those who trample on the poor (v. 18).

34:23 *My servant David.* Not King David resurrected, but David's greatest descendant, the Messiah (see notes on Isa. 55:3 and Jer. 23:5).

34:25 *a covenant of peace.* I.e., the new covenant (see note on Jer. 31:31-34). Its blessings include the taming of nature (Isa. 11:6-9), increased productivity of the land (Isa. 35:1-2), safe occupation of the land of Palestine (Amos 9:14-15), and the knowledge of God (Jer. 31:34).

35:2 *Mount Seir.* The mountainous region SW. of the Dead Sea where the Edomites lived (see

3 ªJer.
6:12; 15:6;
Ezek. 25:13
bJer. 49:13,
17, 18; Ezek.
35:7

3 and say to it, 'Thus says the Lord GOD,
"Behold, I am against you, Mount Seir,
And I will ªstretch out My hand against you,
And I will make you a bdesolation and a waste.

4 ªEzek.
6:6; 35:9;
Mal. 1:3, 4

4 "I will ªlay waste your cities,
And you will become a desolation.
Then you will know that I am the LORD.

5 ªPs.
137:7; Ezek.
25:12, 15;
36:5; Amos
1:11; Obad.
10 bEzek.
7:2; 21:25,
29

5 "Because you have had everlasting ªenmity and have delivered the sons of Israel to the power of the sword at the time of their calamity, at the time of the bpunishment of the end,

6 ªIs. 63:2-
6; Ezek.
16:38; 32:6

6 therefore, as I live," declares the Lord GOD, "I will give you over to ªbloodshed, and bloodshed will pursue you; since you have not hated bloodshed, therefore bloodshed will pursue you.

7 "And I will make Mount Seir a waste and a desolation, and I will cut off from it the one who passes through and returns.

8 ªIs. 34:5,
6; Ezek.
31:12; 32:4,
5; 39:4, 5

8 "And I will ªfill its mountains with its slain; on your hills and in your valleys and in all your ravines those slain by the sword will fall.

9 ªJer.
49:13; Ezek.
25:13

9 "I will make you an everlasting ªdesolation, and your cities will not be inhabited. Then you will know that I am the LORD.

★10 ªPs.
83:4-12;
Ezek. 36:2, 5
bPs. 48:1-3;
132:13, 14;
Is. 12:6;
Ezek. 48:35;
Zeph. 3:15

10 "Because you have ªsaid, 'These two nations and these two lands will be mine, and we will possess them,' although the bLORD was there,

11 ªPs.
137:7; Ezek.
25:14; Amos
1:11 bPs.
9:16;
73:17, 18

11 therefore, as I live," declares the Lord GOD, "I will deal with you ªaccording to your anger and according to your envy which you showed because of your ha-

tred against them; so I will bmake Myself known among them when I judge you.

12 ªJer.
50:7; Ezek.
36:2

12 "Then you will know that I, the LORD, have heard all your revilings which you have spoken against the mountains of Israel saying, 'They are laid desolate; they are ªgiven to us for food.'

13 ªIs.
10:13, 14;
36:20; Jer.
48:26, 42;
Dan. 11:36
bJer. 7:11;
29:23

13 "And you have ªspoken arrogantly against Me and have multiplied your words against Me; bI have heard."

★14-15
14 ªIs.
44:23; 49:13;
Jer. 51:48

14 Thus says the Lord GOD, "As all the ªearth rejoices, I will make you a desolation.

15 ªJer.
50:11; Lam.
4:21 bObad.
15 cIs. 34:5,
6; Ezek.
35:3, 4

15 "As you ªrejoiced over the inheritance of the house of Israel because it was desolate, bso I will do to you. You will be a cdesolation, O Mount Seir, and all Edom, all of it. Then they will know that I am the LORD."'

2 The new covenant with Israel, 36:1-38

★ 1

36 "And you, son of man, prophesy to the mountains of Israel and say, 'O mountains of Israel, hear the word of the LORD.

2 ªDeut.
32:13; Ps.
78:69; Is.
58:14; Hab.
3:19

2 Thus says the Lord GOD, "Because the enemy has spoken against you, 'Aha!' and, 'The everlasting ªheights have become our possession,'

3 ªJer. 2:15
bPs. 44:13,
14; Jer.
18:16; Ezek.
35:13

3 therefore, prophesy and say, 'Thus says the Lord GOD, "For good cause they have made you ªdesolate and crushed you from every side, that you should become a possession of the rest of the nations, and you have been taken up in the btalk and the whispering of the people."' "

4 ªDeut.
11:11; Ezek.
36:1, 6, 8
bEzek. 34:8,
28

4 'Therefore, O ªmountains of Israel, hear the word of the Lord GOD. Thus says the Lord GOD to the mountains and to the hills, to the ravines and to the valleys, to the desolate wastes and to

---

Introduction to Obadiah and Ezek. 25:12-14). Edom joined with the Babylonians in 587 in killing Jewish refugees (v. 5) and grabbing some of the land (v. 10).
35:10 These two nations. Israel and Judah.
35:14-15 As Edom rejoiced over the fall of Ju-

dah, so the nations of the world would rejoice over the fall of Edom.
36:1 the mountains of Israel. I.e., the mountain land of Israel, which is here promised deliverance from all her enemies.

the forsaken cities, which have become a ᵇprey and a derision to the rest of the nations which are round about,

5 therefore, thus says the Lord GOD, "Surely in the fire of My ᵃjealousy I have spoken against the ᵇrest of the nations, and against all Edom, who appropriated My land for themselves as a possession with wholehearted ᶜjoy *and* with scorn of soul, to drive it out for a prey."

6 'Therefore, prophesy concerning the land of Israel, and say to the mountains and to the hills, to the ravines and to the valleys, "Thus says the Lord GOD, 'Behold, I have spoken in My jealousy and in My wrath because you have ᵃendured the insults of the nations.'

7 "Therefore, thus says the Lord GOD, 'I have sworn that surely the nations which are around you will themselves endure their insults.

8 'But you, O mountains of Israel, you will ᵃput forth your branches and bear your fruit for My people Israel; for they will soon come.

9 'For, behold, I am for you, and I will ᵃturn to you, and you shall be ᵇcultivated and sown.

10 'And I will multiply men on you, ᵃall the house of Israel, all of it; and the ᵇcities will be inhabited, and the waste places will be rebuilt.

11 'And I will multiply on you man and beast; and they will increase and be fruitful; and I will cause you to be inhabited as you were ᵃformerly and will treat you ᵇbetter than at the first. Thus you will know that I am the LORD.

12 'Yes, I will cause ᵃmen— My people Israel—to walk on you and possess you, so that you will become their ᵇinheritance and never again ᶜbereave them of children.'

13 "Thus says the Lord GOD, 'Because they say to you, "You are a ᵃdevourer of men and have bereaved your nation of children,"

14 therefore, you will no longer devour men, and no longer bereave your nation of children,' declares the Lord GOD.

15 "And I will not let you hear ᵃinsults from the nations anymore, nor will you bear ᵇdisgrace from the peoples any longer, nor will you cause your nation to ᶜstumble any longer," declares the Lord GOD.' "

16 Then the word of the LORD came to me saying,

17 "Son of man, when the house of Israel was living in their own land, they ᵃdefiled it by their ways and their deeds; their way before Me was like ᵇthe uncleanness of a woman in her impurity.

18 "Therefore, I ᵃpoured out My wrath on them for the blood which they had shed on the land, because they had defiled it with their idols.

19 "Also I ᵃscattered them among the nations, and they were dispersed throughout the lands. ᵇAccording to their ways and their deeds I judged them.

20 "When they came to the nations where they went, they ᵃprofaned My holy name, because it was said of them, 'These are the ᵇpeople of the LORD; yet they have come out of His land.'

21 "But I had concern for My ᵃholy name, which the house of Israel had profaned among the nations where they went.

22 "Therefore, say to the house of Israel, 'Thus says the Lord GOD, "It is ᵃnot for your sake, O house of Israel, that I am about to act, but for My holy name, which you have profaned among the nations where you went.

---

5 ᵃEzek. 5:13; 36:6; 38:19 ᵇJer. 25:9, 15-29; Ezek. 36:3 ᶜJer. 50:11; Ezek. 35:15; Mic. 7:8

6 ᵃPs. 74:10; 123:3, 4; Ezek. 34:29

★ 8-15

8 ᵃIs. 4:2; 27:6; Ezek. 17:23; 34:26-29

9 ᵃLev. 26:9 ᵇEzek. 28:26; 34:14; 36:34

10 ᵃIs. 27:6; 49:17-23; Ezek. 37:21, 22 ᵇJer. 31:27, 28; 33:12; Ezek. 36:33

11 ᵃJer. 30:18; Ezek. 16:55; Mic. 7:14 ᵇJob 42:12; Is. 51:3

12 ᵃEzek. 34:13, 14 ᵇEzek. 47:14 ᶜJer. 15:7; Ezek. 22:12, 27

13 ᵃNum. 13:32

15 ᵃIs. 60:14; Ezek. 34:29; 36:7 ᵇPs. 89:50; Is. 54:4; Ezek. 22:4 ᶜIs. 63:13; Jer. 13:16; 18:15

★17-20

17 ᵃJer. 2:7 ᵇLev. 15:19

18 ᵃ2 Chr. 34:21, 25; Lam. 2:4; 4:11; Ezek. 22:20, 22

19 ᵃDeut. 28:64; Ezek. 5:12; 22:15; Amos 9:9 ᵇEzek. 24:14; 39:24; Rom. 2:6

20 ᵃIs. 52:5; Ezek. 12:16; Rom. 2:24 ᵇJer. 33:24

21 ᵃPs. 74:18; Is. 48:9; Ezek. 20:44

22 ᵃDeut. 7:7, 8; 9:5, 6; Ezek. 36:32

36:8-15 In the kingdom age, the land of Israel will be luxuriantly fruitful (see note on 34:25).
36:17-20 The behavior of the Israelites conveyed the impression that their God was no different from the gods of the heathen. Consequently, the heathen said, sarcastically, *These are the people of the LORD* (v. 20); meaning, They certainly do not act like it.

23 aIs. 5:16;
Ezek. 20:41;
38:23; 39:7,
25 bPs.
102:15;
126:2

23 "And I will avindicate the holiness of My great name which has been profaned among the nations, which you have profaned in their midst. Then the bnations will know that I am the LORD," declares the Lord GOD, "when I prove Myself holy among you in their sight.

*24 aIs.
43:5, 6;
Ezek. 34:13;
37:21

24 "For I will atake you from the nations, gather you from all the lands, and bring you into your own land.

*25-28
25 aNum.
19:17-19; Ps.
51:7; Titus
3:5, 6; Heb.
9:13, 19;
10:22 bIs.
4:4; Zech.
13:1 cIs.
2:18, 20;
Hos. 14:3, 8
26 aPs.
51:10; Ezek.
11:19; 18:31;
John 3:3, 5;
2 Cor. 5:17
bEzek.
11:19; Zech.
7:12

25 "Then I will asprinkle clean water on you, and you will be clean; I will cleanse you from all your bfilthiness and from all your cidols.

26 "Moreover, I will give you a anew heart and put a new spirit within you; and I will remove the bheart of stone from your flesh and give you a heart of flesh.

27 aIs. 44:3;
59:21; Ezek.
37:14; 39:29;
Joel 2:28, 29
*28-32
28 aEzek.
14:11; 37:23,
27

27 "And I will aput My Spirit within you and cause you to walk in My statutes, and you will be careful to observe My ordinances.

28 "And you will live in the land that I gave to your forefathers; so you will be aMy people, and I will be your God.

29 aEzek.
34:27, 29;
Hos. 2:21-23

29 "Moreover, I will save you from all your uncleanness; and I will call for the grain and multiply it, and I awill not bring a famine on you.

30 aLev.
26:4; Ezek.
34:27

30 "And I will amultiply the fruit of the tree and the produce of the field, that you may not receive again the disgrace of famine among the nations.

31 aEzek.
16:61-63;
20:43

31 "Then you will aremember your evil ways and your deeds that were not good, and you will loathe yourselves in your own sight for your iniquities and your abominations.

32 aDeut.
9:5

32 "I am not doing this afor your sake," declares the Lord GOD, "let it be known to you. Be ashamed and confounded for your ways, O house of Israel!"

*33 aEzek.
36:10; Zech.
8:7, 8 bIs.
58:12

33 Thus says the Lord GOD, "On the day that I cleanse you from all your iniquities, I will cause the acities to be inhabited, and the bwaste places will be rebuilt.

34 "And the desolate land will be cultivated instead of being a desolation in the sight of everyone who passed by.

35 aIs. 51:3;
Ezek. 31:9;
Joel 2:3

35 "And they will say, 'This desolate land has become like the agarden of Eden; and the waste, desolate, and ruined cities are fortified and inhabited.'

36 aEzek.
17:24; 22:14;
37:14; Hos.
14:4-9

36 "Then the nations that are left round about you will know that I, the LORD, have rebuilt the ruined places and planted that which was desolate; I, the LORD, have spoken and awill do it."

37 Thus says the Lord GOD, "This also I will let the house of Israel ask Me to do for them: I will increase their men like a flock.

38 a1 Kin.
8:63; 2 Chr.
35:7-9; John
2:14 bPs.
74:1; 100:3;
Jer. 23:1;
John 10:7, 9,
16

38 "Like the aflock for sacrifices, like the flock at Jerusalem during her appointed feasts, so will the waste cities be filled with bflocks of men. Then they will know that I am the LORD.' "

D   The Resuscitation of the Nation, 37:1-14

* 1-2
1 aEzek.
1:3; 33:22;
40:1 bEzek.
8:3; 11:24;
43:5; Acts
8:39 cJer.
7:32-8:2

37 The ahand of the LORD was upon me, and He bbrought

36:24 Here is another promise of the ultimate regathering of scattered Israel from the nations to her own land, a prophecy that will find fulfillment at the end of the Tribulation period (Matt. 24:31; cf. Jer. 16:15).

36:25-28 The new covenant with Israel (to be inaugurated for them at the second coming of Christ, Rom. 11:26-27) provides for the spiritual regeneration of those Jews living at that time (cleansing, new heart, and presence of the Spirit are specifically promised in these verses).

36:28-32 Other results of Israel's regeneration include possession of their land (v. 28a), renewed relationship with God (v. 28b), productivity of the land (vv. 29-30), and repentance of past sins (vv. 31-32).

36:33 Cf. Amos 9:14.

37:1-2 the valley; and it was full of bones . . . very dry. In chapter 37 Ezekiel predicts the political and spiritual revival of his nation (vv. 1-14) and the reuniting of its two divisions (vv. 15-28). The dry bones indicate an army slain in battle, a fitting description of the then hopeless condition of Israel.

me out by the Spirit of the LORD and set me down in the middle of the cvalley; and it was full of bones.

2 And He caused me to pass among them round about, and behold, *there were* very many on the surface of the valley; and lo, *they were* very dry.

3 And He said to me, "Son of man, acan these bones live?" And I answered, "O Lord GOD, bThou knowest."

4 Again He said to me, "aProphesy over these bones, and say to them, 'O dry bones, bhear the word of the LORD.'

5 "Thus says the Lord GOD to these bones, 'Behold, I will cause abreath to enter you that you may come to life.

6 'And I will put sinews on you, make flesh grow back on you, cover you with skin, and put breath in you that you may come alive; and you will aknow that I am the LORD.' "

7 So I prophesied aas I was commanded; and as I prophesied, there was a noise, and behold, a rattling; and the bones came together, bone to its bone.

8 And I looked, and behold, sinews were on them, and flesh grew, and skin covered them; but there was no breath in them.

9 Then He said to me, "Prophesy to the breath, prophesy, son of man, and say to the breath, 'Thus says the Lord GOD, "Come from the four winds, O breath, and abreathe on these slain, that they bcome to life." ' "

10 So I prophesied as He commanded me, and the abreath came into them, and they came to

life, and stood on their feet, an bexceedingly great army.

11 Then He said to me, "Son of man, these bones are the awhole house of Israel; behold, they say, 'Our bbones are dried up, and our hope has perished. We are completely ccut off.'

12 "Therefore prophesy, and say to them, 'Thus says the Lord GOD, "Behold, I will open your graves and acause you to come up out of your graves, My people; and I will bring you into the land of Israel.

13 "Then you will know that I am the LORD, when I have opened your graves and caused you to come up out of your graves, My people.

14 "And I will aput My Spirit within you, and you will come to life, and I will place you on your own land. Then you will know that I, the LORD, have spoken and done it," declares the LORD.' "

E   The Reuniting of the Nation, 37:15–28

15 The word of the LORD came again to me saying,

16 "And you, son of man, take for yourself aone stick and write on it, 'For bJudah and for the sons of Israel, his companions'; then take another stick and write on it, 'For cJoseph, the stick of Ephraim and all the house of Israel, his companions.'

17 "Then ajoin them for yourself one to another into one stick, that they may become one in your hand.

---

3 aEzek. 26:19 bDeut. 32:39; 1 Sam. 2:6

4 aEzek. 37:9, 12 bJer. 22:29; Ezek. 36:1

5 aGen. 2:7; Ps. 104:29, 30; Ezek. 37:9, 10, 14

6 aIs. 49:23; Ezek. 35:9; 38:23; 39:6; Joel 2:27; 3:17

7 aJer. 13:5-7

★ **8**

★ **9** aPs. 104:30 bHos. 13:14

10 aRev. 11:11 bJer. 30:19; 33:22

★**11-14**

11 aJer. 33:24; Ezek. 36:10; 39:25 bPs. 141:7 cPs. 88:5; Lam. 3:54

12 aDeut. 32:39; 1 Sam. 2:6; Is. 26:19; 66:14; Hos. 13:14

14 aIs. 32:15; Ezek. 11:19; 36:27; 37:6, 9; 39:29; Joel 2:28, 29; Zech. 12:10

★**16** aNum. 17:2, 3 b2 Chr. 10:17; 11:11-17; 15:9 c1 Kin. 12:16-20; 2 Chr. 10:19

17 aIs. 11:13; Jer. 50:4; Ezek. 37:22-24; Hos. 1:11; Zeph. 3:9

37:8 *there was no breath in them.* The political revival of Israel in the end time will be spiritually dead until God breathes life into the people (v. 9).
37:9 *Come from the four winds.* I.e., from the four quarters of the globe.
37:11-14 An interpretation of the vision. The *bones* represent hopeless and helpless Israel. The *graves* speak of her political demise. The *Spirit* is the Holy Spirit, who will effect the regeneration of the people. The vision does

not depict the physical resurrection of individuals, but the political (prior to the second coming of Christ) and spiritual (at the second coming of Christ) revivals of Israel.
37:16 *Judah.* The principal tribe of the Southern Kingdom. *his companions.* I.e., Benjamin, Simeon, and Levi. The house of *Joseph* comprised the two powerful tribes of *Ephraim* and Manasseh, the main body of the Northern Kingdom.

18 ^aEzek. 12:9; 17:12; 20:49; 24:19

18 "And when the sons of your people speak to you saying, 'Will you not declare to us ^awhat you mean by these?'

19 say to them, 'Thus says the Lord GOD, "Behold, I will take the stick of Joseph, which is in the hand of Ephraim, and the tribes of Israel, his companions; and I will put them with it, with the stick of Judah, and make them one stick, and they will be one in My hand." '

20 "And the sticks on which you write will be in your hand before their eyes.

★21-28

21 ^aIs. 43:5, 6; Jer. 29:14; Ezek. 36:24; 39:27; Amos 9:14, 15

21 "And say to them, 'Thus says the Lord GOD, "Behold, I will ^atake the sons of Israel from among the nations where they have gone, and I will gather them from every side and bring them into their own land;

22 ^aJer. 3:18; 50:4, 5; Ezek. 36:10 ^bEzek. 34:23, 24; 37:24

22 and I will make them ^aone nation in the land, on the mountains of Israel; and ^bone king will be king for all of them; and they will no longer be two nations, and they will no longer be divided into two kingdoms.

23 ^aEzek. 36:25 ^bEzek. 36:28, 29

23 "And they will ^ano longer defile themselves with their idols, or with their detestable things, or with any of their transgressions; but ^bI will deliver them from all their dwelling places in which they have sinned, and will cleanse

them. And they will be My people, and I will be their God.

24 "And My servant ^aDavid will be king over them, and they will all have ^bone shepherd; and they will walk in My ordinances, and keep My statutes, and observe them.

24 ^aJer. 30:9; Ezek. 34:24; 37:25; Hos. 3:5 ^bPs. 78:71; Is. 40:11; Ezek. 34:23

25 "And they shall live on the land that I gave to Jacob My servant, in which your fathers lived; and they will live on it, they, and their sons, and their sons' sons, forever; and ^aDavid My servant shall be their prince forever.

25 ^aIs. 11:1; Ezek. 37:24; Zech. 6:12

26 "And I will make a ^acovenant of peace with them; it will be an ^beverlasting covenant with them. And I will place them and ^cmultiply them, and will set My ^dsanctuary in their midst forever.

26 ^aEzek. 16:62; 20:37; 34:25 ^bPs. 89:3, 4; Is. 55:3; 59:21; Ezek. 16:60 ^cJer. 30:19; Ezek. 36:10, 11, 37 ^dEzek. 20:40; 43:7

27 "My ^adwelling place also will be with them; and ^bI will be their God, and they will be My people.

27 ^aJohn 1:14; Rev. 21:3 ^bEzek. 37:23; 2 Cor. 6:16

28 "And the nations will know that I am the LORD ^awho sanctifies Israel, when My sanctuary is in their midst forever." ' "

28 ^aEx. 31:13; Ezek. 20:12

F   The Victory of the Nation over Gog and Magog,
38:1–39:29

1   The invasion by Gog, 38:1-16

38 And the word of the LORD came to me saying,   ★ 1

37:21-28 Promises for Israel which will be fulfilled at the second coming of Christ include: restoration to the land of Palestine (v. 21), unification of the two kingdoms (v. 22), purification from all idolatry (v. 23), Messiah ruling over them (v. 24; see note on 34:23), possession of the land forever (v. 25; cf. Gen. 15:18-21), and the presence of God and His sanctuary in their midst (vv. 26-28).

38:1 Chapters 38–39 describe a future attack on Israel and God's deliverance of His people. The invading armies come from "the remote parts of the north" (38:15) to invade Palestine, but are destroyed by supernatural intervention (39:3). Seven months will be required to bury their corpses (39:11-15), and their weapons will supply fuel for Israel for seven years (39:9-10). The time of the battle is unclear. Israel will be living in security, whether real or imagined (38:11-12), which might indicate that the battle takes place before the middle of the Tribulation while Israel feels secure under

a treaty with Antichrist. But the consummation of the battle involves birds and beasts eating the flesh of the warriors, a scene similar to the description of Armageddon at the end of the Tribulation (39:17-20; Rev. 19:17-18). Also at the conclusion of the conflict the nations will understand the judging hand of God, and Israel will know that the LORD (Yahweh) is their God (Ezek. 39:21-22). John envisioned a battle of Gog and Magog at the conclusion of the millennial kingdom (Rev. 20:7-9). Perhaps the first thrust will begin just before the middle of the Tribulation, with successive waves of the invasion continuing throughout the last part of that period and building up to Armageddon. Perhaps, also, this passage in Ezekiel is describing two battles of Gog and Magog, one during the Tribulation and the other at the conclusion of the Millennium. It is not unusual for biblical prophecies to have more than one fulfillment.

★ 2 aEzek.
38:3, 14, 16,
18; 39:1, 11;
Rev. 20:8
bGen. 10:2;
Ezek. 39:6;
Rev. 20:8
cEzek. 38:3;
39:1 dEzek.
27:13; 38:3;
39:1

4 aIs. 43:17
bEzek.
38:15; Dan.
11:40

★ 5-6
5 a2 Chr.
36:20; Ezra
1:1; Ezek.
27:10; Dan.
8:20 bGen.
10:6-8; Ezek.
30:4, 5
cEzek.
27:10; 30:5
6 aGen.
10:2, 3
bGen. 10:3;
Ezek. 27:14
7 aIs. 8:9

8 aIs. 24:22
bIs. 11:11;
Ezek. 36:24;
37:21; 38:12;
39:27, 28
cEzek.
34:13; 36:1-8
dEzek.
38:11, 14;
39:26

9 aIs. 5:28;
21:1; 25:4;
28:2; Jer.
4:13 bEzek.
30:18; 38:16;
Joel 2:2

10 aPs. 36:4;
Mic. 2:1

2 "Son of man, set your face toward aGog of the land of bMagog, the prince of cRosh, dMeshech, and dTubal, and prophesy against him,

3 and say, 'Thus says the Lord GOD, "Behold, I am against you, O Gog, prince of Rosh, Meshech, and Tubal.

4 "And I will turn you about, and put hooks into your jaws, and I will abring you out, and all your army, bhorses and horsemen, all of them splendidly attired, a great company with buckler and shield, all of them wielding swords;

5 aPersia, bEthiopia, and cPut with them, all of them with shield and helmet;

6 aGomer with all its troops; Beth-btogarmah from the remote parts of the north with all its troops—many peoples with you.

7 "aBe prepared, and prepare yourself, you and all your companies that are assembled about you, and be a guard for them.

8 "aAfter many days you will be summoned; in the latter years you will come into the land that is restored from the sword, whose inhabitants have been bgathered from many nations to the cmountains of Israel which had been a continual waste; but its people were brought out from the nations, and they are dliving securely, all of them.

9 "And you will go up, you will come alike a storm; you will be like a bcloud covering the land, you and all your troops, and many peoples with you."

10 'Thus says the Lord GOD, "It will come about on that day, that thoughts will come into your mind, and you will adevise an evil plan,

11 and you will say, 'I will go up against the land of aunwalled villages. I will go against those who are bat rest, that live securely, all of them living without walls, and having no bars or gates,

12 to acapture spoil and to seize plunder, to turn your hand against the waste places which are now inhabited, and against the people who are gathered from the nations, who have acquired cattle and goods, who live at the center of the world.'

13 "aSheba, and bDedan, and the merchants of cTarshish, with all its villages, will say to you, 'Have you come to capture spoil? Have you assembled your company to seize plunder, to carry away silver and gold, to take away cattle and goods, to capture great dspoil?' " '

14 "Therefore, prophesy, son of man, and say to Gog, 'Thus says the Lord GOD, "On that day when My people Israel are aliving securely, will you not know it?

15 "And ayou will come from your place out of the remote parts of the north, you and many peoples with you, all of them riding on horses, a great assembly and a mighty army;

16 and you will come up against My people Israel like a cloud to cover the land. It will come about in the last days that I shall bring you against My land, in order that the nations may aknow Me when I shall be bsanctified through you before their eyes, O Gog."

11 aZech.
2:4 bJer.
49:31

★12 aIs.
10:6; Ezek.
29:19

★13 aEzek.
27:22, 23
bEzek.
25:13; 27:15,
20 cEzek.
27:12 dIs.
10:6; 33:23;
Jer. 15:13

14 aJer.
23:6; Ezek.
38:8, 11;
Zech. 2:5, 8

15 aEzek.
39:2

16 aPs.
83:18; Ezek.
36:23; 38:23
bIs. 5:16;
8:13; 29:23;
Ezek. 28:22

38:2 *Gog.* The derivation of the word is uncertain. It probably refers to the ruler of the people who live in Magog. *Magog* was identified by Josephus as the land of the Scythians, the region N. and NE. of the Black Sea and E. of the Aral Sea (now occupied by Russia). *the prince of Rosh* (better, the chief prince of Meshech and Tubal). The area of modern Turkey.

38:5-6 Other allies will include *Persia* (modern Iran), *Ethiopia* (northern Sudan), *Put* (Libya),

Gomer (probably the eastern part of Turkey and the Ukraine), and *Beth-togarmah* (the part of Turkey near the Syrian border).

38:12 The wealth of Israel is the prize the invaders will seek. *the center of the world.* Lit., the navel of the earth (cf. 5:5).

38:13 *Sheba, and Dedan.* Arab peoples. *Tarshish.* Located in the S. of Spain near Gibraltar (see note on Jonah 1:3). *villages* (or young lions). Greedy rulers.

2   The victory over Gog,
38:17–39:29

17 aIs. 5:26-
29; 34:1-6;
63:1-6;
66:15, 16;
Joel 3:9-14

17 'Thus says the Lord GOD, "Are you the one of whom I spoke in former days through My servants the prophets of Israel, who aprophesied in those days for *many* years that I would bring you against them?

18 aPs. 18:8,
15

18 "And it will come about on that day, when Gog comes against the land of Israel," declares the Lord GOD, "that My fury will mount up in My aanger.

19 aDeut.
32:22; Ps.
18:7, 8;
Ezek. 5:13;
36:5, 6; Nah.
1:2; Heb.
12:29 bJoel
3:16; Hag.
2:6, 7, 21

19 "And in My azeal and in My blazing wrath I declare *that* on that day there will surely be a great bearthquake in the land of Israel.

20 aJer.
4:24, 25;
Hos. 4:3;
Nah. 1:4-6
bZech. 14:4

20 "aAnd the fish of the sea, the birds of the heavens, the beasts of the field, all the creeping things that creep on the earth, and all the men who are on the face of the earth will shake at My presence; the bmountains also will be thrown down, the steep pathways will collapse, and every wall will fall to the ground.

21 aEzek.
14:17 bJudg.
7:22; 1 Sam.
14:20; 2 Chr.
20:23; Hag.
2:22

21 "And I shall call for a asword against him on all My mountains," declares the Lord GOD. "bEvery man's sword will be against his brother.

22 aIs.
66:16; Jer.
25:31 bPs.
11:6; 18:12-
14; Is. 28:17

22 "And with pestilence and with blood I shall enter into ajudgment with him; and I shall rain on him, and on his troops, and on the many peoples who are with him, a torrential rain, with bhailstones, fire, and brimstone.

23 aPs. 9:16;
Ezek. 37:28;
38:16

23 "And I shall magnify Myself, sanctify Myself, and amake Myself known in the sight of many nations; and they will know that I am the LORD." '

1 aEzek.
38:2

39 "And ayou, son of man, prophesy against Gog, and say, 'Thus says the Lord GOD, "Behold, I am against you, O Gog, prince of Rosh, Meshech, and Tubal;

2 and I shall turn you around, drive you on, take you up from the remotest parts of the north, and bring you against the mountains of Israel.

3 "And I shall astrike your bow from your left hand, and dash down your arrows from your right hand.

3 aPs. 76:3;
Ezek. 30:21-
24; Hos. 1:5

4 "You shall afall on the mountains of Israel, you and all your troops, and the peoples who are with you; I shall give you as bfood to every kind of predatory bird and beast of the field.

4 aIs.
14:24, 25;
Ezek. 39:17-
20 bEzek.
29:5; 32:4, 5;
33:27

5 "You will fall on the open field; for it is I who have spoken," declares the Lord GOD.

6 "And I shall send afire upon Magog and those who inhabit the bcoastlands in safety; and they will know that I am the LORD.

6 aEzek.
30:8, 16;
38:19, 22;
Amos 1:4, 7,
10; Nah. 1:6
bPs. 72:10;
Is. 66:19;
Jer. 25:22

7 "And My aholy name I shall make known in the midst of My people Israel; and I shall not let My holy name be bprofaned anymore. And the cnations will know that I am the Lord, the dHoly One in Israel.

7 aEzek.
36:20-22;
39:25 bEx.
20:7; Ezek.
20:9, 14, 39
cEzek.
38:16, 23
dIs. 12:6;
43:3, 14;
55:5; 60:9,
14

8 "Behold, it is coming and it shall be done," declares the Lord GOD. "That is the day of which I have spoken.

9 "Then those who inhabit the cities of Israel will ago out, and make bfires with the weapons and burn *them*, both shields and bucklers, bows and arrows, war clubs and spears and for seven years they will make fires of them.

9 aIs.
66:24; Mal.
1:5 bJosh.
11:6; Ps.
46:9

10 "And they will not take wood from the field or gather firewood from the forests, for they will make fires with the weapons; and they will take the spoil of those who despoiled them, and seize the aplunder of those who plundered them," declares the Lord GOD.

10 aIs. 14:2;
33:1; Mic.
5:8; Hab. 2:8

11 "And it will come about on that day that I shall give Gog a burial ground there in Israel, the

                ★11

39:11 *the valley of those who pass by.* A valley E. of the Dead Sea. *Hamon-gog.* Lit., the multitude of Gog.

valley of those who pass by east of the sea, and it will block off the passers-by. So they will bury Gog there with all his multitude, and they will call *it* the valley of Hamon-gog.

12 "For seven months the house of Israel will be burying them in order to [a]cleanse the land.

13 "Even all the people of the land will bury *them;* and it will be to their [a]renown *on* the day that I [b]glorify Myself," declares the Lord God.

14 "And they will set apart men who will constantly pass through the land, [a]burying those who were passing through, even those left on the surface of the ground, in order to cleanse it. At the end of seven months they will make a search.

15 "And as those who pass through the land pass through and anyone sees a man's bone, then he will set up a marker by it until the buriers have buried it in the valley of Hamon-gog.

16 "And even *the* name of *the* city will be Hamonah. So they will cleanse the land." '

17 "And as for you, son of man, thus says the Lord God, 'Speak to every kind of [a]bird and to every [a]beast of the field, "Assemble and come, gather from every side to My sacrifice which I am going to [b]sacrifice for you, as a great sacrifice on the mountains of Israel, that you may eat flesh and drink blood.

18 "You shall [a]eat the flesh of mighty men, and drink the blood of the princes of the earth, as *though they were* [b]rams, lambs, goats, and [c]bulls, all of them fatlings of [d]Bashan.

19 "So you will eat fat until you are glutted, and drink blood until you are drunk, from My sac-

rifice which I have sacrificed for you.

20 "And you will be glutted at My table with [a]horses and charioteers, with mighty men and all the men of war," declares the Lord God.

21 "And I shall set My [a]glory among the nations; and all the nations will see My judgment which I have executed, and My hand which I have laid on them.

22 "And the house of Israel will [a]know that I am the Lord their God from that day onward.

23 "And the nations will know that the house of Israel went into exile for their [a]iniquity because they acted treacherously against Me, and I [b]hid My face from them; so I gave them into the hand of their adversaries, and all of them fell by the sword.

24 "[a]According to their uncleanness and according to their transgressions I dealt with them, and I hid My face from them." ' "

25 Therefore thus says the Lord God, "Now I shall [a]restore the fortunes of Jacob, and have mercy on the whole [b]house of Israel; and I shall be [c]jealous for My holy name.

26 "And they shall [a]forget their disgrace and all their treachery which they perpetrated against Me, when they [b]live securely on their *own* land with [c]no one to make them afraid.

27 "When I [a]bring them back from the peoples and gather them from the lands of their enemies, then I shall be [b]sanctified through them in the sight of the many nations.

28 "Then they will know that I am the Lord their God because I made them go into exile among the nations, and then gathered them *again* to their own land; and I will leave none of them there any longer.

---

12 [a]Deut. 21:23; Ezek. 39:14, 16

13 [a]Jer. 33:9; Zeph. 3:19, 20 [b]Ezek. 28:22

★14-15

14 [a]Jer. 14:16

★16

17 [a]Is. 56:9; Jer. 12:9; Ezek. 39:4; Rev. 19:17, 18 [b]Is. 34:6, 7; Jer. 46:10; Zeph. 1:7

18 [a]Ezek. 29:5; Rev. 19:18 [b]Jer. 51:40 [c]Jer. 50:27 [d]Ps. 22:12; Amos 4:1

20 [a]Ps. 76:5, 6; Ezek. 38:4; Hag. 2:22; Rev. 19:18

★21-29

21 [a]Ex. 9:16; Is. 37:20; Ezek. 36:23; 38:16, 23; 39:13

22 [a]Jer. 24:7

23 [a]Jer. 22:8, 9; 44:22; Ezek. 36:18, 19 [b]Is. 1:15; 59:2; Ezek. 39:29

24 [a]2 Kin. 17:7; Jer. 2:17, 19; 4:18; Ezek. 36:19

25 [a]Is. 27:12, 13; Jer. 33:7; Ezek. 34:13 [b]Jer. 31:1; Ezek. 36:10; 37:21, 22; Hos. 1:11 [c]Ex. 20:5; Nah. 1:2

26 [a]Is. 16:63; 20:43; 36:31 [b]1 Kin. 4:25; Ezek. 34:25-28 [c]Is. 17:2; Mic. 4:4

27 [a]Ezek. 36:24; 37:21 [b]Ezek. 36:23; 38:16, 23

39:14-15 A group of investigators will be appointed to finish the work of removing the bones (v. 14), and ordinary people will also help (v. 15).

39:16 *Hamonah.* Lit., multitude (cf. note on 39:11).

39:21-29 The twofold purpose of this judgment is that the nations might acknowledge God's glory and that Israel might know God's grace.

29 a Is.
32:15; Ezek.
36:27; 37:14;
Joel 2:28

29 "And I will not hide My face from them any longer, for I shall have ªpoured out My Spirit on the house of Israel," declares the Lord God.

V PROPHECIES CONCERNING ISRAEL IN THE MILLENNIAL KINGDOM, 40:1–48:35

A A New Temple, 40:1–43:27

1 Introduction, 40:1–4

★40-48
★ 1 a Ezek.
32:1, 17;
33:21
b 2 Kin. 25:1-
7; Jer. 39:1-
9; 52:4-11;
Ezek. 33:21
c Ezek. 1:3;
3:14, 22;
37:1

2 a Ezek.
1:1; 8:3; Dan.
7:1, 7 **b** Is.
2:2, 3; Ezek.
17:23; 20:40;
37:22; Mic.
4:1; Rev.
21:10 **c** Ps.
48:2; Is.
14:13
d 1 Chr.
28:12, 19
★ 3 a Ezek.
1:7; Dan.
10:6; Rev.
1:15 **b** Ezek.
47:3; Zech.
2:1, 2 **c** Rev.
11:1; 21:15

4 a Ezek.
2:1, 3, 6, 8;
44:5 **b** Ezek.
2:7, 8; 44:5
c Is. 21:10;
Jer. 26:2;
Acts 20:27

40 In the ªtwenty-fifth year of our exile, at the beginning of the year, on the tenth of the month, in the fourteenth year after the ᵇcity was taken, on that same day the ᶜhand of the Lord was upon me and He brought me there.

2 In the ªvisions of God He brought me into the land of Israel, and set me on a very ᵇhigh mountain; and on it ᶜto the south there was a ᵈstructure like a city.

3 So He brought me there; and behold, there was a man whose appearance was like the appearance of ªbronze, with a ᵇline of flax and a ᶜmeasuring rod in his hand; and he was standing in the gateway.

4 And the man said to me, "ªSon of man, ᵇsee with your eyes, hear with your ears, and give attention to all that I am going to show you; for you have been brought here in order to

show it to you. ᶜDeclare to the house of Israel all that you see."

2 The outer court and its three gates, 40:5–27

5 And behold, there was a ªwall on the outside of the temple all around, and in the man's hand was a measuring rod of six cubits, each of which was a cubit and a handbreadth. So he measured the thickness of the wall, one rod; and the height, one rod.

6 Then he went to the gate which faced ªeast, went up its steps, and measured the threshold of the gate, one rod in width; and the other threshold was one rod in width.

7 And the ªguardroom was one rod long and one rod wide; and there were five cubits between the guardrooms. And the threshold of the gate by the porch of the gate facing inward was one rod.

8 Then he measured the porch of the gate facing inward, one rod.

9 And he measured the porch of the gate, eight cubits; and its side pillars, two cubits. And the porch of the gate was faced inward.

10 And the guardrooms of the gate toward the east numbered three on each side; the three of them had the same measurement. The side pillars also had the same measurement on each side.

★ 5 a Is.
26:1; Ezek.
42:20

★ 6-16

6 a Ezek.
8:16; 11:1;
40:20; 43:1

7 a Ezek.
40:10-16, 21,
29, 33, 36

40-48 These chapters are a complement to the many predictions of judgment announced by Ezekiel. He now foresees the rebuilding of the Temple, the establishment of a right relationship between the Lord (Yahweh) and Israel, and the reorganization of her national life. Detailed instructions are recorded for the building of this future Temple and for the service attached to it. The description is not of Solomon's Temple, the specifications being different and larger. If the description was given to help the exiles on their return from Babylon to rebuild the Temple, it is inexplicable why Ezra, Nehemiah, or Haggai do not refer to it. If it is a description of God's relation to the Church, then it is so symbolic as to be meaningless. If understood plainly, the Temple and

worship here referred to must relate to Israel when she is reestablished in her land (cf. chapters 47–48) during Christ's millennial kingdom.

40:1 The date is March-April 573.

40:3 *a man.* Evidently the Angel of the Lord; i.e., the Lord Himself (44:2, 5). *a line of flax.* For longer measurements. *a measuring rod.* For shorter measurements.

40:5 *a wall* surrounded the entire Temple area. *a cubit and a handbreadth.* 20.679 inches. *one rod.* 10 ⅓ feet.

40:6-16 The massive gateway on the *east* is described in these verses. There were three *guardrooms* on each side of the passageway leading to the outer court of the Temple.

11 And he measured the width of the gateway, ten cubits, and the length of the gate, thirteen cubits.

12 And *there was* a barrier *wall* one cubit *wide* in front of the guardrooms on each side; and the guardrooms *were* six cubits *square* on each side.

13 And he measured the gate from the roof of the one guardroom to the roof of the other, a width of twenty-five cubits from one door to *the* door opposite.

14 And he made the side pillars sixty cubits *high;* the gate *extended* round about to the side pillar of the ^acourtyard.

15 And *from* the front of the entrance gate to the front of the inner porch of the gate *was* fifty cubits.

16 And *there were* ^ashuttered windows *looking* toward the guardrooms, and toward their side pillars within the gate all around, and likewise for the porches. And *there were* windows all around inside; and on *each* side pillar *were* ^bpalm tree ornaments.

17 Then he brought me into the ^aouter court, and behold, *there were* ^bchambers and a pavement, made for the court all around; thirty chambers faced the pavement.

18 And the pavement (*that is,* the lower pavement) *was* by the side of the gates, corresponding to the length of the gates.

19 Then he measured the width from the front of the ^alower gate to the front of the exterior of the inner court, a ^bhundred cubits on the east and on the north.

20 And *as for* the ^agate of the outer court which faced the north, he measured its length and its width.

21 And it had three ^aguardrooms on each side; and its ^bside pillars and its porches had the same measurement as the first gate. Its length *was* ^cfifty cubits, and the width ^dtwenty-five cubits.

22 And its ^awindows, and its porches, and its palm tree ornaments *had* the same measurements as the ^bgate which faced toward the east; and it was reached by seven ^csteps, and its porch *was* in front of them.

23 And the inner court had a gate opposite the gate on the north as well as *the gate* on the east; and he measured a ^ahundred cubits from gate to gate.

24 Then he led me toward the south, and behold, there was a ^agate toward the south; and he measured its ^bside pillars and its porches according to those same measurements.

25 And the gate and its porches had ^awindows all around like those other windows; the length *was* ^bfifty cubits and the width twenty-five cubits.

26 And *there were* seven ^asteps going up to it, and its porches *were* in front of them; and it had ^bpalm tree ornaments on its side pillars, one on each side.

27 And the inner court had a gate toward the ^asouth; and he measured from gate to gate toward the south, a ^bhundred cubits.

3   The inner court and its three gates, 40:28–47

28 Then he brought me to the inner court by the south gate; and he measured the south gate ^aaccording to those same measurements.

29 Its ^aguardrooms also, its side pillars, and its ^bporches *were*

Side references (left column):

14 ^aEx. 27:9; 1 Chr. 28:6; Ps. 100:4; Is. 62:9; Ezek. 8:7; 42:1

16 ^a1 Kin. 6:4; Ezek. 41:16, 26 ^b1 Kin. 6:29, 32, 35; 2 Chr. 3:5; Ezek. 40:22, 26, 31, 34, 37; 41:18-20, 25, 26

★17-19

17 ^aEzek. 10:5; 42:1; 46:21; Rev. 11:2 ^b2 Kin. 23:11; 1 Chr. 9:26; 23:28; 2 Chr. 31:11; Ezek. 40:38

19 ^aEzek. 40:23, 27; 46:1, 2 ^bEzek. 40:23, 27

★20-27

20 ^aEzek. 40:6

Side references (right column):

21 ^aEzek. 40:7 ^bEzek. 40:16, 30 ^cEzek. 40:15 ^dEzek. 40:13

22 ^aEzek. 40:16 ^bEzek. 40:6 ^cEzek. 40:26, 31, 34, 37, 49

23 ^aEzek. 40:19, 27

24 ^aEzek. 40:6, 20, 35; 46:9 ^bEzek. 40:21

25 ^aEzek. 40:16, 22, 29 ^bEzek. 40:21, 33

26 ^aEzek. 40:6, 22 ^bEzek. 40:16

★27-47

27 ^aEzek. 40:23, 32 ^bEzek. 40:19

28 ^aEzek. 40:32, 35

29 ^aEzek. 40:7, 10, 21 ^bEzek. 40:16, 22, 25 ^cEzek. 40:21

40:17-19 In the outer court were *thirty chambers.*

40:20-27 The gateways on the *north* and *south* were similar to the one on the *east.*

40:27-47 Ezekiel walked through another large gateway into the inner court, which was built on a higher level, and he viewed the arrangements for preparing sacrifices (vv. 39-43) and certain rooms set apart for the priests (vv. 45-46). He describes the south (vv. 27-28), east (vv. 32-34) and north (vv. 35-38) gateways to the inner court.

according to those same measurements. And the gate and its porches had [b]windows all around; it was [c]fifty cubits long and twenty-five cubits wide.

30 And *there were* [a]porches all around, twenty-five cubits long and five cubits wide.

31 And its porches *were* toward the outer court; and [a]palm tree ornaments *were* on its side pillars, and its stairway had eight [b]steps.

32 And he brought me into the [a]inner court toward the east. And he measured the gate [b]according to those same measurements.

33 Its [a]guardrooms also, its side pillars, and its porches *were* according to those same measurements. And the gate and its porches had [b]windows all around; it *was* [c]fifty cubits long and twenty-five cubits wide.

34 And its [a]porches *were* toward the outer court; and [a]palm tree ornaments *were* on its side pillars, on each side, and its stairway had eight [b]steps.

35 Then he brought me to the [a]north gate; and he measured *it* according to those same measurements,

36 *with* its [a]guardrooms, its side pillars, and its [b]porches. And the gate had [b]windows all around; the length *was* [c]fifty cubits and the width twenty-five cubits.

37 And its side pillars *were* toward the outer court; and [a]palm tree ornaments *were* on its side pillars on each side, and its stairway had eight [b]steps.

38 And a [a]chamber with its doorway was by the side pillars at the gates; there they [b]rinse the burnt offering.

39 And in the porch of the gate *were* two [a]tables on each

side, on which to slaughter the [b]burnt offering, the sin offering, and the guilt offering.

40 And on the outer side, as one went up to the gateway toward the north, were two tables; and on the other side of the porch of the gate *were* two tables.

41 Four [a]tables *were* on each side next to the gate; *or,* eight tables on which they slaughter *sacrifices.*

42 And for the burnt offering *there were* four [a]tables of [b]hewn stone, a cubit and a half long, a cubit and a half wide, and one cubit high, on which they lay the instruments with which they slaughter the [c]burnt offering and the sacrifice.

43 And the double hooks, one handbreadth in length, were installed in the house all around; and on the tables *was* the flesh of the offering.

44 And from the outside to the [a]inner gate were [b]chambers for the [c]singers in the inner court, *one of* which was at the side of the north gate, with its front toward the south, and one at the side of the east gate facing toward the north.

45 And he said to me, "This is the [a]chamber which faces toward the south, *intended* for the priests who [b]keep charge of the temple;

46 but the [a]chamber which faces toward the north is for the priests who [b]keep charge of the altar. These are the [c]sons of Zadok, who from the sons of Levi [d]come near to the LORD to minister to Him."

47 And he measured the court, a *perfect* square, a [a]hundred cubits long and a hundred cubits wide; and the altar was in front of the temple.

30 [a]Ezek. 40:16, 21

31 [a]Ezek. 40:16 [b]Ezek. 40:22, 26, 34, 37

32 [a]Ezek. 40:28-31, 35 [b]Ezek. 40:28

33 [a]Ezek. 40:29 [b]Ezek. 40:16 [c]Ezek. 40:21

34 [a]Ezek. 40:16 [b]Ezek. 40:22, 37

35 [a]Ezek. 40:27, 32; 44:4; 47:2

36 [a]Ezek. 40:7, 29 [b]Ezek. 40:16 [c]Ezek. 40:21

37 [a]Ezek. 40:16 [b]Ezek. 40:34

38 [a]1 Chr. 28:12; Neh. 13:5, 9; Jer. 35:4; 36:10; Ezek. 40:17; 41:10; 42:13 [b]2 Chr. 4:6

39 [a]Ezek. 40:42 [b]Lev. 1:3-17; Ezek. 46:2

41 [a]Ezek. 40:39, 40

42 [a]Ezek. 40:39 [b]Ex. 20:25 [c]Ezek. 40:39

44 [a]Ezek. 40:23, 27 [b]Ezek. 40:17, 38 [c]1 Chr. 6:31, 32; 16:41-43; 25:1-7

45 [a]Ezek. 40:17, 38 [b]1 Chr. 9:23; Ps. 134:1

46 [a]Ezek. 40:17, 38 [b]Lev. 6:12, 13; Ezek. 44:15 [c]1 Kin. 2:35; Ezek. 43:19; 48:11 [d]Lev. 10:3; Num. 16:5, 40; Ezek. 42:13; 45:4

47 [a]Ezek. 40:19, 23, 27

40:46 *the sons of Zadok.* Charged with offering the sacrifices (43:19; 44:15; 48:11). Solomon set aside the priesthood of the house of Eli when he deposed Abiathar and put Zadok in his place (1 Kings 2:26-27; cf. 1 Sam. 2:30-36).

4 The Temple itself, 40:48–41:26

*40:48-
41:26

48 a1 Kin.
6:3; 2 Chr.
3:4

48 Then he brought me to the ªporch of the temple and measured *each* side pillar of the porch, five cubits on each side; and the width of the gate was three cubits on each side.

49 aEzek.
40:31, 34, 37
b1 Kin. 7:15-
22; 2 Chr.
3:17; Jer.
52:17-23;
Rev. 3:12

49 The length of the porch was twenty cubits, and the width eleven cubits; and at the ªstairway by which it was ascended *were* ᵇcolumns belonging to the side pillars, one on each side.

1 aEzek.
40:2, 3, 17
bEzek.
41:21, 23
cEzek. 40:9;
41:3

41 Then he ªbrought me to the ᵇnave and measured the ᶜside pillars; six cubits wide on each side *was* the width of the side pillar.

2 a1 Kin.
6:2, 17;
2 Chr. 3:3

2 And the width of the entrance *was* ten cubits, and the sides of the entrance were five cubits on each side. And he measured the length of the nave, ªforty cubits, and the width, ªtwenty cubits.

3 aEzek.
40:16 bEzek.
41:1

3 Then he went ªinside and measured each ᵇside pillar of the doorway, two cubits, and the doorway, six cubits *high;* and the width of the doorway, seven cubits.

4 a1 Kin.
6:20 b1 Kin.
6:5 cEx.
26:33, 34;
1 Kin. 6:16;
7:50; 8:6;
2 Chr. 5:7;
Heb. 9:3-8

4 And he measured its length, ªtwenty cubits, and the width, twenty cubits, before the ᵇnave; and he said to me, "This is the ᶜmost holy *place.*"

5 a1 Kin.
6:5; Ezek.
41:6-11

5 Then he measured the wall of the temple, six cubits; and the width of the ªside chambers, four cubits, all around about the house on every side.

6 a1 Kin.
6:5-10
b1 Kin. 6:6,
10

6 And ªthe side chambers were in three stories, one above another, and thirty in each story; and the side chambers ᵇextended to the wall which *stood* on their inward side all around, that they might be fastened, and not be fastened into the wall of the temple *itself.*

7 And the side chambers surrounding the temple were wider at each successive story. Because the ªstructure surrounding the temple went upward by stages on all sides of the temple, therefore the width of the temple increased as it went higher; and thus one went up from the lowest *story* to the highest by way of the second *story.*

7 a1 Kin.
6:8

8 I saw also that the house had a raised platform all around; the foundations of the side chambers were a full rod of ªsix long cubits *in height.*

8 aEzek.
40:5

9 The thickness of the outer wall of the side chambers was five cubits. But the ªfree space between the side chambers belonging to the temple

9 aEzek.
41:11

10 and the *outer* ªchambers *was* twenty cubits in width all around the temple on every side.

10 aEzek.
40:17

11 And the doorways of the side chambers toward the ªfree space *consisted of* one doorway toward the north and another doorway toward the south; and the width of the ªfree space was five cubits all around.

11 aEzek.
41:9

12 And the ªbuilding that *was* in front of the ᵇseparate area at the side toward the west *was* seventy cubits wide; and the wall of the building was five cubits thick all around, and its length *was* ninety cubits.

12 aEzek.
41:13, 15;
42:1 bEzek.
41:14; 42:10,
13

13 Then he measured the temple, a ªhundred cubits long; the ᵇseparate area with the ᶜbuilding and its walls *were* also a ªhundred cubits long.

13 aEzek.
40:47 bEzek.
41:13-15;
42:1, 10, 13
cEzek. 41:12

14 Also the width of the front of the temple and *that of* the separate areas along the east *side* totaled a hundred cubits.

15 And he measured the length of the ªbuilding along the front of the ᵇseparate area behind it, with a ᶜgallery on each side, a hundred cubits; *he* also *measured*

15 aEzek.
41:12, 13;
42:1 bEzek.
41:14; 42:1,
10, 13
cEzek.
41:16;
42:3, 5

40:48–41:26 A description of the Temple itself: first, the porch (40:48-49); then the *nave* or holy place (41:1-2); next, *the most holy place* (vv. 3-4), the *side chambers* (3 floors of rooms, 30 per floor, for storage purposes, vv. 5-11), a large building behind the Temple (v. 12), the total measurements of the Temple and its immediate surroundings (vv. 13-17), and a description of the interior of the Temple (vv. 18-26).

the inner nave and the porches of the court.

16 The ᵃthresholds, the ᵇlatticed windows, and the ᶜgalleries round about their ᵈthree stories, opposite the threshold, were ᵉpaneled with wood all around, and from the ground to the windows (but the windows were covered),

17 over the entrance, and to the inner house, and on the outside, and on all the wall all around inside and outside, by measurement.

18 And it was carved with ᵃcherubim and ᵇpalm trees; and a palm tree was between cherub and cherub, and every cherub had two faces,

19 a ᵃman's face toward the palm tree on one side, and a young ᵃlion's face toward the palm tree on the other side; they were carved on all the house all around.

20 From the ground to above the entrance ᵃcherubim and ᵃpalm trees were carved, as well as on the wall of the nave.

21 The ᵃdoorposts of the ᵇnave were square; as for the front of the sanctuary, the appearance of one doorpost was like that of the other.

22 The ᵃaltar was of wood, three cubits high, and its length two cubits; its corners, its base, and its sides were of wood. And he said to me, "This is the ᵇtable that is before the LORD."

23 And the ᵃnave and the ᵇsanctuary each had a double ᶜdoor.

24 And each of the doors had two leaves, two ᵃswinging leaves; two leaves for one door and two leaves for the other.

25 Also there were carved on them, on the doors of the nave, ᵃcherubim and ᵃpalm trees like those carved on the walls; and

there was a ᵇthreshold of wood on the front of the porch outside.

26 And there were ᵃlatticed windows and ᵇpalm trees on one side and on the other, on the sides of the ᶜporch; thus were the ᵈside chambers of the house and the thresholds.

5 The chambers in the inner court, 42:1–20

42 Then he ᵃbrought me out into the ᵇouter court, the way ᶜtoward the north; and he brought me to the ᵈchamber which was opposite the ᵉseparate area and opposite the ᶠbuilding toward the north.

2 Along the length, which was a ᵃhundred cubits, was the north door; the width was fifty cubits.

3 Opposite the ᵃtwenty cubits which belonged to the inner court, and opposite the ᵇpavement which belonged to the outer court, was ᶜgallery corresponding to gallery in three stories.

4 And before the ᵃchambers was an inner walk ten cubits wide, a way of one hundred cubits; and their openings were on the north.

5 Now the upper chambers were smaller because the ᵃgalleries took more space away from them than from the lower and middle ones in the building.

6 For they were in ᵃthree stories and had no pillars like the pillars of the courts; therefore the upper chambers were set back from the ground upward, more than the lower and middle ones.

7 As for the ᵃouter wall by the side of the chambers, toward the outer court facing the chambers, its length was fifty cubits.

8 For the length of the chambers which were in the outer court was fifty cubits; and behold,

16 ᵃIs. 6:4; Ezek. 10:18; 40:6; 41:25
ᵇ1 Kin. 6:4; Ezek. 40:16, 25; 41:26
ᶜEzek. 41:15
ᵈEzek. 42:3
ᵉ1 Kin. 6:15

18 ᵃ1 Kin. 6:29, 32, 35; 7:36; Ezek. 41:20, 25
ᵇ2 Chr. 3:5; Ezek. 40:16

19 ᵃEzek. 1:10; 10:14

20 ᵃEzek. 41:18

21 ᵃ1 Kin. 6:33; Ezek. 40:9, 14, 16; 41:1
ᵇEzek. 41:1

22 ᵃEx. 30:1-3; 1 Kin. 6:20; Rev. 8:3
ᵇEx. 25:23, 30; Lev. 24:6; Ezek. 23:41; 44:16; Mal. 1:7, 12

23 ᵃEzek. 41:1
ᵇEzek. 41:4
ᶜ1 Kin. 6:31-35

24 ᵃ1 Kin. 6:34

25 ᵃEzek. 41:18
ᵇEzek. 41:16

26 ᵃEzek. 41:16
ᵇEzek. 40:16
ᶜEzek. 40:9, 48
ᵈEzek. 41:5

★ 1-13
1 ᵃEzek. 40:17, 28, 48; 41:1
ᵇEzek. 40:17, 20
ᶜEzek. 40:20
ᵈEzek. 40:17; 42:4
ᵉEzek. 41:12; 42:10, 13
ᶠEzek. 41:12

2 ᵃEzek. 41:13

3 ᵃEzek. 41:10
ᵇEzek. 40:17
ᶜEzek. 41:15, 16; 42:5

4 ᵃEzek. 46:19

5 ᵃEzek. 42:3

6 ᵃEzek. 41:6

7 ᵃEzek. 42:10, 12

8 ᵃEzek. 41:13, 14

42:1-13 North of the Temple in the inner court were two blocks of three-story buildings, one twice the length of the other, used by the priests when eating sacrifices (46:20) and for storing their garments (44:19).

the length of those facing the temple *was* a ᵃhundred cubits.

9 And below these chambers *was* the ᵃentrance on the east side, as one enters them from the outer court.

10 In the thickness of the ᵃwall of the court toward the east, facing the ᵇseparate area and facing the building, *there were* ᶜchambers.

11 And the ᵃway in front of them *was* like the appearance of the chambers which *were* on the north, according to their length so was their width; and all their exits *were* both according to their arrangements and openings.

12 And corresponding to the openings of the chambers which were toward the south was an opening at the head of the way, the way in front of the ᵃwall toward the east, as one enters them.

13 Then he said to me, "The north chambers *and* the south chambers, which are opposite the ᵃseparate area, they are the ᵇholy chambers where the priests who are ᶜnear to the Lᴏʀᴅ shall eat the ᵈmost holy things. There they shall lay the most holy things, the grain offering, the sin offering, and the guilt offering; for the place is holy.

14 "When the priests enter, then they shall not go out into the outer court from the sanctuary without ᵃlaying there their ᵇgarments in which they minister, for they are holy. They shall put on other garments; then they shall approach that which is for the people."

15 Now when he had finished measuring the inner house, he brought me out by the way of the ᵃgate which faced toward the east, and measured it all around.

16 He measured on the east side with the measuring reed five hundred reeds, by the ᵃmeasuring reed.

17 He measured on the north side five hundred reeds by the measuring reed.

18 On the south side he measured five hundred reeds with the measuring reed.

19 He turned to the west side, *and* measured five hundred reeds with the measuring reed.

20 He measured it on the four sides; it had a ᵃwall all around, the ᵇlength five hundred and the ᵇwidth five hundred, to ᶜdivide between the holy and the profane.

6 The return of the glory of the Lord, 43:1–12

43 Then he led me to the ᵃgate, the gate facing toward the east;

2 and behold, the ᵃglory of the God of Israel was coming from the way of the ᵇeast. And His ᶜvoice was like the sound of many waters; and the earth ᵈshone with His glory.

3 And *it was* like the appearance of the vision which I saw, like the ᵃvision which I saw when He came to ᵇdestroy the city. And the visions *were* like the vision which I saw by the ᶜriver Chebar; and I ᵈfell on my face.

4 And the glory of the Lᴏʀᴅ came into the house by the way of the gate facing toward the ᵃeast.

5 And the ᵃSpirit lifted me up and brought me into the inner court; and behold, the ᵇglory of the Lᴏʀᴅ filled the house.

6 Then I heard one speaking to me from the house, while a ᵃman was standing beside me.

42:15–20 The overall measurements of the Temple represented a square of *five hundred reeds* (about one mile) on a side.

43:1–5 Ezekiel saw the Lord returning through the east gate, through which He had earlier departed (see note on 10:19).

43:6–12 The Lord announces that the Temple must be holy and thus free from *harlotry* (temple prostitution) (v. 7), and separated from the graves and palaces of kings (vv. 7–9) which were on the same hill as Solomon's Temple (cf. 2 Kings 23:7; 21:18, 26).

---

9 ᵃEzek. 44:5; 46:19

10 ᵃEzek. 42:7 ᵇEzek. 42:1, 13 ᶜEzek. 40:17

11 ᵃEzek. 42:4

12 ᵃEzek. 42:7

13 ᵃEzek. 42:1, 10 ᵇEx. 29:31; Lev. 7:6; 10:13, 14, 17 ᶜLev. 10:3; Deut. 21:5; Ezek. 40:46 ᵈLev. 6:25, 29; 14:13; Num. 18:9, 10

14 ᵃEzek. 44:19 ᵇEx. 29:4-9; Lev. 8:7, 13; Is. 61:10; Zech. 3:4, 5

★**15-20**

15 ᵃEzek. 40:6; 43:1

16 ᵃEzek. 40:3

20 ᵃIs. 60:18; Ezek. 40:5; Zech. 2:5 ᵇEzek. 45:2; Rev. 21:16 ᶜEzek. 22:26; 44:23; 48:15

★ **1-5**
1 ᵃEzek. 10:19; 40:6; 42:15; 43:4; 44:1; 46:1
2 ᵃIs. 6:3; Ezek. 1:28; 3:23; 10:18, 19 ᵇEzek. 11:23 ᶜEzek. 1:24; Rev. 1:15; 14:2 ᵈEzek. 1:28; 10:4; Rev. 18:1
3 ᵃEzek. 1:4-28 ᵇJer. 1:10; Ezek. 9:1, 5; 32:18 ᶜEzek. 1:3; 10:20 ᵈEzek. 1:28; 3:23

4 ᵃEzek. 10:19; 11:23; 43:2

5 ᵃEzek. 3:14; 8:3; 11:1, 24; 2 Cor. 12:2-4 ᵇEzek. 10:4

★ **6-12**

6 ᵃEzek. 1:26; 40:3

7 *Ps. 47:8;
Ezek. 1:26
*b*Ezek.
37:26, 28
*c*Lev. 26:30;
Ezek. 6:5, 13

7 And He said to me, "Son of man, *this is* the place of My *a*throne and the place of the soles of My feet, where I will *b*dwell among the sons of Israel forever. And the house of Israel will not again defile My holy name, neither they nor their kings, by their harlotry and by the *c*corpses of their kings when they die,

8 *a*Ezek.
8:3, 16

8 by setting their threshold by My threshold, and their door post beside My door post, with *only* the wall between Me and them. And they have *a*defiled My holy name by their abominations which they have committed. So I have consumed them in My anger.

9 *a*Ezek.
18:30, 31
*b*Ezek.
37:26-28;
43:7

9 "Now let them *a*put away their harlotry and the corpses of their kings far from Me; and I will *b*dwell among them forever.

10 *a*Ezek.
40:4 *b*Ezek.
16:61, 63;
43:11 *c*Ezek.
28:12

10 "As for you, son of man, *a*describe the temple to the house of Israel, that they may be *b*ashamed of their iniquities; and let them measure the *c*plan.

11 *a*Ezek.
44:5 *b*Ezek.
12:3 *c*Ezek.
11:20; 36:27

11 "And if they are ashamed of all that they have done, make known to them the design of the house, its structure, its *a*exits, its entrances, all its designs, all its statutes, and all its laws. And write *it* *b*in their sight, so that they may observe its whole design and all its statutes, and *c*do them.

12 *a*Ezek.
40:2

12 "This is the law of the house: its entire area on the top of the *a*mountain all around *shall be* most holy. Behold, this is the law of the house.

7 The altar of burnt offering,
43:13-27

★13-27

13 *a*Ex.
27:1-8;
2 Chr. 4:1
*b*Ezek. 40:5;
41:8

13 "And these are the measurements of the *a*altar by cubits (the *b*cubit being a cubit and a handbreadth): the base *shall be* a cubit, and the width a cubit, and its border on its edge round about one span; and this *shall be* the *height of the* base of the altar.

14 *a*Ezek.
43:17, 20;
45:19

14 "And from the base on the ground to the lower *a*ledge *shall be* two cubits, and the width one cubit; and from the smaller ledge to the larger ledge *shall be* four cubits, and the width one cubit.

15 *a*Ex. 27:2;
Lev. 9:9;
1 Kin. 1:50;
Ps. 118:27

15 "And the altar hearth *shall be* four cubits; and from the altar hearth shall extend upwards four *a*horns.

16 *a*Ex. 27:1

16 "Now the altar hearth *shall be* twelve *cubits* long by twelve wide, *a*square in its four sides.

17 *a*Ex.
20:26 *b*Ezek.
40:6

17 "And the ledge *shall be* fourteen *cubits* long by fourteen wide in its four sides, the border around it *shall be* half a cubit, and its base *shall be* a cubit round about; and its *a*steps shall *b*face the east."

18 *a*Ezek.
2:1 *b*Ex.
40:29 *c*Lev.
1:5, 11; Heb.
9:21, 22

18 And He said to me, "*a*Son of man, thus says the Lord GOD, 'These are the statutes for the altar on the day it is built, to offer *b*burnt offerings on it and to *c*sprinkle blood on it.

★19 *a*1 Kin.
2:35; Ezek.
40:46; 44:15
*b*Num. 16:5;
40 *c*Lev. 4:3;
Ezek. 43:23;
45:18 *d*Ezek.
45:19; Heb.
7:27

19 'And you shall give to the Levitical priests who are from the offspring of *a*Zadok, who draw *b*near to Me to minister to Me,' declares the Lord GOD, 'a *c*young bull for a *d*sin offering.

20 *a*Lev.
8:15; 9:9;
Ezek. 43:15
*b*Ezek.
43:14, 17
*c*Lev. 16:19;
Ezek. 43:22,
26

20 'And you shall take some of its blood, and put it on its four *a*horns, and on the four corners of the *b*ledge, and on the border round about; thus you shall *c*cleanse it and make atonement for it.

21 *a*Ex.
29:14; Lev.
4:12; Heb.
13:11

21 'You shall also take the bull for the sin offering; and it *shall be* *a*burned in the appointed place of the house, outside the sanctuary.

22 *a*Ezek.
43:25 *b*Ezek.
43:20, 26

22 'And on the second day you shall offer a *a*male goat without blemish for a sin offering; and they shall *b*cleanse the altar, as they cleansed *it* with the bull.

23 *a*Ezek. 29:1,
10; Ezek.
45:18 *b*Ex.
29:1

23 'When you have finished cleansing *it*, you shall present a *a*young bull without blemish and a *b*ram without blemish from the flock.

43:13-27 *altar.* Of burnt offering. It is described in verses 13-17, and the procedure for its con-

secration is detailed in verses 18-27.
43:19 *the offspring of Zadok.* See note on **40:46**.

24 aLev.
2:13; Num.
18:19; Mark
9:49, 50; Col.
4:6

25 aEx.
29:35-37;
Lev. 8:33, 35

*26

27 aLev. 9:1
bLev. 3:1;
17:5 cEzek.
20:40

24 'And you shall present them before the LORD, and the priests shall throw ªsalt on them, and they shall offer them up as a burnt offering to the LORD.

25 'ªFor seven days you shall prepare daily a goat for a sin offering; also a young bull and a ram from the flock, without blemish, shall be prepared.

26 'For seven days they shall make atonement for the altar and purify it; so shall they consecrate it.

27 'And when they have completed the days, it shall be that on the ªeighth day and onward, the priests shall offer your burnt offerings on the altar, and your ᵇpeace offerings; and I will ᶜaccept you,' declares the Lord GOD."

B   A New Service of Worship,
44:1-46:24

1   Those who may minister,
44:1-31

* 1-3

1 aEzek.
40:6, 17;
42:14

2 aEzek.
43:2-4

3 aEzek.
34:24; 37:25
bGen. 31:54;
Ex. 24:9-11
cEzek. 46:2,
8-10 dEzek.
40:9

* 4-14
4 aEzek.
40:20, 40
bIs. 6:3, 4;
Ezek. 1:28;
3:23; 43:4, 5;
Hag. 2:7
cEzek. 1:28;
43:3

44 Then He brought me back by the way of the ªouter gate of the sanctuary, which faces the east; and it was shut.

2 And the LORD said to me, "This gate shall be shut; it shall not be opened, and no one shall enter by it, for the ªLORD God of Israel has entered by it; therefore it shall be shut.

3 "As for the ªprince, he shall sit in it as prince to ᵇeat bread before the LORD; he shall ᶜenter by way of the ᵈporch of the gate, and shall go out by the same way."

4 Then He brought me by way of the ªnorth gate to the front of the house; and I looked, and behold, the ᵇglory of the LORD

filled the house of the LORD, and I ᶜfell on my face.

5 And the LORD said to me, "Son of man, ªmark well, see with your eyes, and hear with your ears all that I say to you concerning all the ᵇstatutes of the house of the LORD and concerning all its laws; and mark well the entrance of the house, with all exits of the sanctuary.

6 "And you shall say to the ªrebellious ones, to the house of Israel, 'Thus says the Lord GOD, "ᵇEnough of all your abominations, O house of Israel,

7 when you brought in ªforeigners, ᵇuncircumcised in heart and uncircumcised in flesh, to be in My sanctuary to profane it, even My house, when you ᶜoffered My food, the fat and the blood; for they ᵈmade My covenant void—this in addition to all your abominations.

8 "And you have not ªkept charge of My holy things yourselves, but you have set foreigners to keep charge of My sanctuary."

9 'Thus says the Lord GOD, "ªNo foreigner, uncircumcised in heart and uncircumcised in flesh, of all the foreigners who are among the sons of Israel, shall enter My sanctuary.

10 "But the Levites who went far from Me, when Israel went astray, who ªwent astray from Me after their idols, shall ᵇbear the punishment for their iniquity.

11 "Yet they shall be ªministers in My sanctuary, having ᵇoversight at the gates of the house and ᶜministering in the house; they shall ᵈslaughter the burnt offering and the sacrifice for the people, and they shall

5 aDeut.
32:46; Ezek.
40:4 bDeut.
12:32; Ezek.
43:10, 11

6 aEzek.
2:5-7; 3:9
bEzek. 45:9;
1 Pet. 4:3

7 aEx.
12:43-49
bLev. 26:41;
Deut. 10:16;
Jer. 4:4; 9:26
cLev. 22:25
dGen. 17:14

8 aLev.
22:2; Num.
18:7

9 aEzek.
44:7; Joel
3:17; Zech.
14:21

10 a2 Kin.
23:8, 9;
Ezek. 22:26;
44:12 bNum.
18:23

11 aNum.
3:5-37; 4:1-
33; 18:2-7
b1 Chr. 26:1-
19 cEzek.
40:45; 44:14
d2 Chr.
29:34; 30:17
eNum. 16:9

43:26 *consecrate.* Lit., to fill its hand; i.e., to invest it with office.

44:1-3 The outer, east gate was shut so that no one could use it. Even *the prince* did not use this gate, though he could eat the sacrificial meal there. Though some consider him to be the Messiah, this is impossible, since he needs to offer a sin offering (45:22) and he has sons (46:16). He is evidently a human representa-

tive of Messiah in the government of the kingdom.

44:4-14 Foreigners, probably prisoners of war, had formerly done the menial work of the sanctuary (v. 8). They are to be replaced by Levites, who had been responsible for religious declension and who would be excluded from performing the more important priestly duties (vv. 10-14).

ᵉstand before them to minister to them.

12 a2 Kin. 16:10-16 bEzek. 14:3, 4 cEzek. 20:15, 23 dEzek. 44:10

12 "Because they ministered to them ᵃbefore their idols and became a ᵇstumbling block of iniquity to the house of Israel, therefore I have ᶜsworn against them," declares the Lord GOD, "that they shall ᵈbear the punishment for their iniquity.

13 aNum. 18:3 bEzek. 16:61, 63; 39:26

13 "And they shall ᵃnot come near to Me to serve as a priest to Me, nor come near to any of My holy things, to the things that are most holy; but they shall ᵇbear their shame and their abominations which they have committed.

14 aNum. 18:4; 1 Chr. 23:28-32; Ezek. 44:11

14 "Yet I will appoint them to ᵃkeep charge of the house, of all its service, and of all that shall be done in it.

15 aJer. 33:18-22 bEzek. 40:46; 43:19; 48:11 cNum. 18:7; Ezek. 40:45 dEzek. 44:10; 48:11 eZech. 3:1, 7 fLev. 3:16, 17; 17:5, 6; Ezek. 44:7

15 "But the ᵃLevitical priests, the sons of ᵇZadok, who ᶜkept charge of My sanctuary when the sons of Israel ᵈwent astray from Me, shall come near to Me to minister to Me; and they shall ᵉstand before Me to offer Me the ᶠfat and the blood," declares the Lord GOD.

16 aNum. 18:5, 7, 8 bEzek. 41:22; Mal. 1:7, 12

16 "They shall ᵃenter My sanctuary; they shall come near to My ᵇtable to minister to Me and keep My charge.

17 aEx. 28:42, 43; 39:27-29; Rev. 19:8

17 "And it shall be that when they enter at the gates of the inner court, they shall be clothed with ᵃlinen garments; and wool shall not be on them while they are ministering in the gates of the inner court and in the house.

18 aEx. 28:40; Is. 3:20; Ezek. 24:17, 23 bEx. 28:42; Lev. 16:4

18 "Linen ᵃturbans shall be on their heads, and ᵇlinen undergarments shall be on their loins; they shall not gird themselves with *anything which makes them* sweat.

19 aLev. 6:10; 16:4, 23, 24; Ezek. 42:14 bLev. 6:27; Ezek. 46:20

19 "And when they go out into the outer court, into the outer court to the people, they shall

ᵃput off their garments in which they have been ministering and lay them in the holy chambers; then they shall put on other garments that they may ᵇnot transmit holiness to the people with their garments.

20 "Also they shall ᵃnot shave their heads, yet they shall not ᵇlet their locks grow long; they shall only trim *the hair of* their heads.

★**20** aLev. 21:5 bNum. 6:5

21 "ᵃNor shall any of the priests drink wine when they enter the inner court.

★**21** aLev. 10:9

22 "And they shall not marry a widow or a ᵃdivorced woman but shall ᵇtake virgins from the offspring of the house of Israel, or a widow who is the widow of a priest.

22 aLev. 21:7, 14 bLev. 21:13

23 "Moreover, they shall teach My people the ᵃdifference between the holy and the profane, and cause them to discern between the unclean and the clean.

★**23** aLev. 10:10; Ezek. 22:26; Hos. 4:6; Mic. 3:9-11; Zeph. 3:4; Hag. 2:11-13; Mal. 2:6-8

24 "And in a dispute ᵃthey shall take their stand to judge; they shall judge it according to My ordinances. They shall also keep My laws and My statutes in all My ᵇappointed feasts, and ᶜsanctify My sabbaths.

24 aDeut. 17:8, 9; 19:17; 21:5; 1 Chr. 23:4; 2 Chr. 19:8-10 bLev. 23:2, 4, 44 cEzek. 20:12, 20

25 "And ᵃthey shall not go to a dead person to defile *themselves;* however, for father, for mother, for son, for daughter, for brother, or for a sister who has not had a husband, they may defile themselves.

★**25** aLev. 21:1-4

26 "And after he is ᵃcleansed, seven days shall elapse for him.

26 aNum. 19:13-19

27 "And on the day that he goes into the sanctuary, into the ᵃinner court to minister in the sanctuary, he shall offer his ᵇsin offering," declares the Lord GOD.

27 aEzek. 44:17 bLev. 5:3, 6; Num. 6:9-11

28 "And it shall be with regard to an inheritance for them, *that* ᵃI am their inheritance; and you shall give them no possession in Israel—I am their possession.

28 aNum. 18:20; Deut. 10:9; 18:1, 2; Josh. 13:33

44:20 Shaving the head and letting the hair grow long were both signs of mourning (Lev. 21:5; 10:6). Priests were to avoid extremes and were to *trim* their hair.

44:21 Ministering priests will be forbidden to *drink wine* so as to be in full control of their

faculties (Lev. 10:9; Hos. 4:11).

44:23 One of the principal duties of priests was to *teach* the people (see note on Mal. 2:8-9; cf. Deut. 33:10).

44:25 Mourning was forbidden to the priests except for the closest of relatives.

29 aNum.
18:9, 14;
Josh. 13:14
bLev. 27:21,
28; Num.
18:14
30 aNum.
18:12, 13;
2 Chr. 31:4-
6, 10; Neh.
10:35-37
bNum.
15:20, 21
cMal. 3:10

31 aLev.
22:8; Deut.
14:21; Ezek.
4:14

29 "They shall ªeat the grain offering, the sin offering, and the guilt offering; and every bdevoted thing in Israel shall be theirs.

30 "And the first of all the ªfirst fruits of every kind and every contribution of every kind, from all your contributions, shall be for the priests; you shall also give to the priest the bfirst of your dough to cause a cblessing to rest on your house.

31 "The priests shall not eat any bird or beast that has ªdied a natural death or has been torn to pieces.

2 Support for those who minister, 45:1-17

★ 1-8

1 aNum.
34:13; Josh.
13:7; 14:3;
Ezek. 47:21;
48:29 bEzek.
48:8, 9
cZech.
14:20, 21
dEzek.
42:16; 45:2

2 aEzek.
42:20 bEzek.
27:28

45 "And when you shall ªdivide by lot the land for inheritance, you shall offer an ballotment to the Lord, a choly portion of the land; the length shall be the length of 25,000 dcubits, and the width shall be 10,000. It shall be holy within all its boundary round about.

2 "Out of this there shall be for the holy place a square round about ªfive hundred by five hundred cubits, and fifty cubits for its bopen space round about.

3 "And from this area you shall measure a length of 25,000 cubits, and a width of 10,000 cubits; and in it shall be the sanctuary, the most holy place.

4 aEzek.
48:10, 11
bNum. 16:5;
Ezek. 40:45;
43:19

4 "It shall be the holy portion of the land; it shall be for the ªpriests, the ministers of the sanctuary, who bcome near to minister to the Lord, and it shall be a place for their houses and a holy place for the sanctuary.

5 aEzek.
48:13

5 "And an area ª25,000 cubits in length and 10,000 in width shall be for the Levites, the minis-ters of the house, and for their possession cities to dwell in.

6 "And you shall give the ªcity possession of an area 5,000 cubits wide and 25,000 cubits long, alongside the allotment of the holy portion; it shall be for the whole house of Israel.

7 "And the ªprince shall have land on either side of the holy allotment and the property of the city, adjacent to the holy allotment and the property of the city, on the west side toward the west and on the east side toward the east, and in length comparable to one of the portions, from the west border to the east border.

8 "This shall be his land for a possession in Israel; so My princes shall no longer ªoppress My people, but they shall give the rest of the land to the house of Israel bac-cording to their tribes."

9 Thus says the Lord God, "ªEnough, you princes of Israel; put away bviolence and destruction, and cpractice justice and righteousness. Stop your dexpropriations from My people," declares the Lord God.

10 "You shall have ªjust balances, a just bephah, and a just bbath.

11 "The ephah and the bath shall be the same quantity, so that the bath may contain a tenth of a ªhomer, and the ephah a tenth of a homer; their standard shall be according to the homer.

12 "And the ªshekel shall be twenty ªgerahs; twenty shekels, twenty-five shekels, and fifteen shekels shall be your maneh.

13 "This is the offering that you shall offer: a sixth of an ephah from a homer of wheat; a sixth of an ephah from a homer of barley;

6 aEzek.
48:15-18, 30-
35

★ 7 aEzek.
34:24; 37:24;
46:16-18;
48:21

8 aIs. 11:3-
5; Jer. 23:5;
Ezek. 19:7;
22:27; 46:18
bJosh. 11:23

9 aEzek.
44:6 bJer.
6:7; Ezek.
7:11, 23;
8:17 cJer.
22:3; Zech.
8:16 dNeh.
5:1-5

★10 aLev.
19:36; Deut.
25:15; Prov.
16:11; Amos
8:4-6; Mic.
6:10, 11 bIs.
5:10

11 aIs. 5:10

12 aEx.
30:13; Lev.
27:25; Num.
3:47

★13-17

45:1-8 The Temple was protected from desecration by being situated in the midst of sacred territory (about 8 miles square) surrounded by the priests' quarters.
45:7 The prince's portion of land extended 25,000 cubits (or about 8 miles) beyond the sacred area, both toward the Mediterranean and the Dead Sea.

45:10 The ephah, a dry measure, equaled two-thirds of a bushel, and had the same volume as a bath, which was a liquid measure (about 6 gallons). Falsifying weights and measures was robbery (Prov. 11:1; Amos 8:4-7).
45:13-17 Because of the dues paid him by the people, the prince provided the sacrifices for public worship.

14 and the prescribed portion of oil (*namely,* the bath of oil), a tenth of a bath from *each* kor (*which is* ten baths *or* a homer, for ten baths are a homer);

15 and one sheep from *each* flock of two hundred from the watering places of Israel—for a *a*grain offering, for a burnt offering, and for peace offerings, to *b*make atonement for them," declares the Lord GOD.

16 "*a*All the people of the land shall give to this offering for the *b*prince in Israel.

17 "And it shall be the *a*prince's part *to provide* the *b*burnt offerings, the grain offerings, and the libations, at the *c*feasts, on the *d*new moons, and on the sabbaths, at all the appointed feasts of the house of Israel; he shall provide the sin offering, the grain offering, the burnt offering, and the *e*peace offerings, to make atonement for the house of Israel."

3 Offerings, 45:18–46:24
a Offerings at the feasts, 45:18–25

18 Thus says the Lord GOD, "In the *a*first *month,* on the first of the month, you shall take a young bull *b*without blemish and *c*cleanse the sanctuary.

19 "And the priest shall take some of the blood from the sin offering and put *it* on the door posts of the house, on the *a*four corners of the *b*ledge of the altar, and on the posts of the gate of the inner court.

20 "And thus you shall do on the seventh *day* of the month for everyone who goes *a*astray or is naive; so you shall make *b*atonement for the house.

21 "In the *a*first *month,* on the fourteenth day of the month, you shall have the *b*Passover, a feast of seven days; unleavened bread shall be eaten.

22 "And on that day the prince shall provide for himself and all the people of the land a *a*bull for a sin offering.

23 "And *during* the *a*seven days of the feast he shall provide as a *b*burnt offering to the LORD *c*seven bulls and seven rams without blemish on every day of the seven days, and a male goat daily for a sin offering.

24 "And he shall provide as a *a*grain offering an ephah with a bull, an ephah with a ram, and a hin of oil with an ephah.

25 "In the *a*seventh *month,* on the fifteenth day of the month, at the feast, he shall provide like this, seven days for the sin offering, the burnt offering, the grain offering, and the oil."

b Offerings on sabbaths, new moons, and daily sacrifices, 46:1–15

46 Thus says the Lord GOD, "The *a*gate of the *b*inner court facing east shall be *c*shut the six *d*working days; but it shall be opened on the *e*sabbath day, and opened on the day of the *f*new moon.

2 "And the *a*prince shall enter by way of the porch of the gate from outside and stand by the *b*post of the gate. Then the priests shall provide his burnt offering and his peace offerings, and he shall worship at the threshold of the gate and then go out; but the gate shall not be *c*shut until the evening.

3 "The *a*people of the land shall also worship at the doorway of that gate before the LORD on the sabbaths and on the *b*new moons.

4 "And the *a*burnt offering which the prince shall offer to the

---

Cross references (margin):

15 *a*Ezek. 45:17 *b*Lev. 1:4; 6:30

16 *a*Ex. 30:14, 15 *b*Is. 16:1

17 *a*Ezek. 46:4-12 *b*1 Kin. 8:64; 1 Chr. 16:2; 2 Chr. 31:3 *c*Lev. 23:1-44; 28:1-29:39 *d*Is. 66:23 *e*1 Kin. 8:63; Ezek. 43:27

18 *a*Ex. 12:2 *b*Lev. 22:20; Heb. 9:14 *c*Lev. 16:16, 33; Ezek. 43:22, 26

19 *a*Lev. 16:18-20; Ezek. 43:20 *b*Ezek. 43:14, 17, 20

20 *a*Lev. 4:27; Ps. 19:12 *b*Lev. 16:20; Ezek. 45:15, 18

21 *a*Num. 28:16f. *b*Ex. 12:1-24; Lev. 23:5-8

22 *a*Lev. 4:14

23 *a*Lev. 23:8 *b*Num. 28:16-25 *c*Num. 23:1, 2; Job 42:8

24 *a*Num. 28:12-15; Ezek. 46:5-7

★25 *a*Lev. 23:33-43; Num. 29:12-38; 2 Chr. 5:3; 7:8, 10

★ 1-15 1 *a*Ezek. 45:19 *b*Ezek. 8:16; 10:3 *c*Ezek. 44:1, 2 *d*Ex. 20:9 *e*Is. 66:23; Ezek. 45:17 *f*Ezek. 45:18; 46:3, 6

2 *a*Ezek. 44:3; 46:8 *b*Ezek. 45:19 *c*Ezek. 46:12

3 *a*Luke 1:10 *b*Ezek. 46:1

4 *a*Ezek. 45:17 *b*Num. 28:9

45:25 A reference to the Feast of Tabernacles (cf. Deut. 16:13-15; Zech. 14:16-19).
46:1-15 Here are details of the weekly (sabbath), monthly (new moon), and daily offerings. If the great festivals of Passover and Tabernacles are to be observed during the Millennium, there is no reason why sacrifices would not also be offered. Then, of course, they will be memorials of the finished sacrifice of Christ.

LORD on the sabbath day shall be [b]six lambs without blemish and a ram without blemish;

5 and the [a]grain offering shall be an ephah with the ram, and the grain offering with the lambs as much as he is [b]able to give, and a hin of oil with an ephah.

6 "And on the day of the [a]new moon *he shall offer* a young bull without blemish, also six lambs and a ram, *which* shall be without blemish.

7 "And he shall provide a [a]grain offering, an ephah with the bull, and an ephah with the ram, and with the lambs as much as he is [b]able, and a hin of oil with an ephah.

8 "And when the [a]prince enters, he shall go in by way of the porch of the gate and go out by the same way.

9 "But when the people of the land come [a]before the LORD at the appointed feasts, he who enters by way of the north gate to worship shall go out by way of the south gate. And he who enters by way of the south gate shall go out by way of the north gate. No one shall return by way of the gate by which he entered but shall go straight out.

10 "And when they go in, the prince shall go in [a]among them; and when they go out, he shall go out.

11 "And at the [a]festivals and the appointed feasts the [b]grain offering shall be an ephah with a bull and an ephah with a ram, and with the lambs as much as one is able to give, and a hin of oil with an ephah.

12 "And when the prince provides a [a]freewill offering, a burnt offering, or peace offerings *as a* freewill offering to the LORD, the gate facing east shall be [b]opened for him. And he shall provide his burnt offering and his peace offer-

ings as he does on the [c]sabbath day. Then he shall go out, and the gate shall be shut after he goes out.

13 "And you shall provide a [a]lamb a year old without blemish for a burnt offering to the LORD daily; [b]morning by morning you shall provide it.

14 "Also you shall provide a grain offering with it morning by morning, a [a]sixth of an ephah, and a third of a hin of oil to moisten the fine flour, a grain offering to the LORD continually by a perpetual ordinance.

15 "Thus they shall provide the lamb, the grain offering, and the oil, morning by morning, for a [a]continual burnt offering."

c *Regulations for the prince,*
46:16–18

16 'Thus says the Lord GOD, "If the prince gives a [a]gift *out of* his inheritance to any of his sons, it shall belong to his sons; it is their possession by inheritance.

17 "But if he gives a gift from his inheritance to one of his servants, it shall be his until the [a]year of liberty; then it shall return to the prince. His inheritance *shall be* only his sons'; it shall belong to them.

18 "And the prince shall [a]not take from the people's inheritance, [b]thrusting them out of their possession; he shall give his sons inheritance from his own possession so that My people shall not be scattered, anyone from his possession." ' "

d *Places for preparing the offerings, 46:19–24*

19 Then he brought me through the [a]entrance, which *was* at the side of the gate, into the holy chambers for the priests, which faced north; and behold, there *was* a place at the extreme rear toward the west.

46:17 *the year of liberty.* The fiftieth year, the year of Jubilee (cf. Lev. 25:13–15).
46:19–24 A description of the kitchens for the priests (vv. 19–20; cf. 42:1–14) and the people (vv. 21–24) for cooking the sacrificial meals.

Marginal references:

5 [a]Num. 28:12; Ezek. 45:24; 46:7, 11 [b]Ezek. 46:7
6 [a]Ezek. 46:1
7 [a]Ezek. 46:5 [b]Lev. 14:21; Deut. 16:17; Ezek. 46:5
8 [a]Ezek. 44:3; 46:2
9 [a]Ex. 34:23; Ps. 84:7; Mic. 6:6
10 [a]2 Sam. 6:14, 15; 1 Chr. 29:20, 22; 2 Chr. 6:3; 7:4; Ps. 42:4
11 [a]Ezek. 45:17 [b]Ezek. 46:5, 7
12 [a]Lev. 23:38; 2 Chr. 29:31 [b]Ezek. 44:3; 46:1, 2, 8 [c]Ezek. 45:17

13 [a]Num. 28:3-5 [b]Is. 50:4
14 [a]Num. 28:5
15 [a]Ex. 29:42; Num. 28:6
16 [a]2 Chr. 21:3
★17 [a]Lev. 25:10
18 [a]Ezek. 45:8 [b]1 Kin. 21:19; Ezek. 22:27; Mic. 2:1, 2
★19-24
19 [a]Ezek. 42:9; 44:5

20 a 2 Chr.
35:13; Ezek.
44:29 b Lev.
2:4-7

20 And he said to me, "This is the place where the priests shall boil the ªguilt offering and the sin offering, *and* where they shall ᵇbake the grain offering, in order that they may not bring *them* out into the outer court to transmit holiness to the people."

21 Then he brought me out into the outer court and led me across to the four corners of the court; and behold, in every corner of the court *there was a small* court.

22 In the four corners of the court *there were* enclosed courts, forty *cubits* long and thirty wide; these four in the corners *were* the same size.

23 And *there was* a row *of masonry* round about in them, around the four of them, and boiling places were made under the rows round about.

24 Then he said to me, "These are the boiling places where the ministers of the house shall boil the sacrifices of the people."

C   A New Holy Land,
47:1–48:35
1   The river giving life to the land, 47:1–12

★ 1-12

1 a Ezek.
41:2, 23-25
b Ps. 46:4; Is.
30:25; 55:1;
Jer. 2:13;
Joel 3:18;
Zech. 13:1;
14:8; Rev.
22:1, 17

47 Then he brought me back to the ªdoor of the house; and behold, ᵇwater was flowing from under the threshold of the house toward the east, for the house faced east. And the water was flowing down from under, from the right side of the house, from south of the altar.

2 And he brought me out by way of the north gate and led me around on the outside to the outer gate by way of *the gate* that faces east. And behold, water was trickling from the south side.

3 When the man went out toward the east with a line in his hand, he measured a thousand cubits, and he led me through the water, water *reaching* the ankles.

4 Again he measured a thousand and led me through the water, water *reaching* the knees. Again he measured a thousand and led me through *the water,* water *reaching* the loins.

5 Again he measured a thousand; *and it was* a river that I could not ford, for the water had risen, *enough* water to swim in, a ªriver that could not be forded.

5 a Is. 11:9;
Hab. 2:14

6 And he said to me, "Son of man, have you ªseen *this?*" Then he brought me back to the bank of the river.

6 a Ezek.
8:6; 40:4;
44:5

7 Now when I had returned, behold, on the bank of the river there *were* very many ªtrees on the one side and on the other.

7 a Is.
60:13, 21;
61:3; Ezek.
47:12

8 Then he said to me, "These waters go out toward the eastern region and go down into the ªArabah; then they go toward the sea, being made to flow into the ᵇsea, and the waters of the sea become fresh.

8 a Deut.
3:17; Is.
35:6, 7;
41:17-19;
44:3 b Josh.
3:16

9 "And it will come about that every living creature which swarms in every place where the river goes, will live. And there will be very many fish, for these waters go there, and *the others* become fresh; so ªeverything will live where the river goes.

9 a Is. 12:3;
55:1; John
4:14; 7:37,
38

10 "And it will come about that ªfishermen will stand beside it; from ᵇEngedi to Eneglaim there will be a place for the ᶜspreading of nets. Their fish will be according to their kinds, like the fish of the ᵈGreat Sea, ᵉvery many.

10 a Matt.
4:19; 13:47;
Luke 5:10
b Gen. 14:7;
Josh. 15:62;
1 Sam.
23:29; 24:1;
2 Chr. 20:2
c Ezek. 26:5,
14 d Num.
34:6; Ps.
104:25;
Ezek. 47:15;
48:28 e Luke
5:5-9; John
21:6
11 a Deut.
29:23
12 a Ezek.
47:7; Rev.
22:2 b Gen.
2:9 c Ps. 1:3;
Jer. 17:8
d Rev. 22:2

11 "But its swamps and marshes will not become fresh; they will be left for ªsalt.

12 "And ªby the river on its bank, on one side and on the

47:1–12 Ezekiel saw a river emerging from the Temple flowing eastward, beginning as a trickle (v. 2) and becoming a deep river (v. 5). Trees will grow along its banks (v. 7), and it will even sweeten the waters of the Dead Sea so that fish can live in it (vv. 8–10). *Engedi* (v.

10) is on the middle of the western shore of the Dead Sea, and *Eneglaim* is possibly near the Qumran area, where the Dead Sea scrolls were found. Some salt marshes will be left unsweetened (v. 11).

other, will grow all *kinds of* ^btrees for food. Their ^cleaves will not wither, and their fruit will not fail. They will bear every month because their water flows from the sanctuary, and their fruit will be for food and their ^dleaves for healing."

2 The boundaries of the land, 47:13-23

★13-20

13 ^aNum. 34:2-12
^bGen. 48:5; Ezek. 48:4, 5

13 Thus says the Lord God, "This *shall be* the ^aboundary by which you shall divide the land for an inheritance among the twelve tribes of Israel; Joseph *shall have* two ^bportions.

14 ^aDeut. 1:8; Ezek. 20:6

14 "And you shall divide it for an inheritance, each one equally with the other; for I ^aswore to give it to your forefathers, and this land shall fall to you as an inheritance.

15 ^aNum. 34:7-9
^bNum. 34:8

15 "And this *shall be* the boundary of the land: on the ^anorth side, from the Great Sea *by* the way of Hethlon, to the entrance of ^bZedad;

16 ^aNum. 13:21; Is. 10:9; Ezek. 47:17, 20; 48:1; Zech. 9:2 ^bGen. 14:15; Ezek. 47:17, 18; 48:1

16 ^aHamath, Berothah, Sibraim, which is between the border of ^bDamascus and the border of Hamath; Hazer-hatticon, which is by the border of Hauran.

17 ^aNum. 34:9

17 "And the boundary shall extend from the sea to ^aHazarenan *at* the border of Damascus, and on the north toward the north is the border of Hamath. This is the north side.

18 ^aNum. 34:10-12
^bGen. 37:25; Jer. 50:19 ^cGen. 13:10, 11

18 "And the ^aeast side, from between Hauran, Damascus, ^bGilead, and the land of Israel, *shall be* the ^cJordan; from the *north* border to the eastern sea you shall measure. This is the east side.

19 ^aNum. 34:3-5
^bEzek. 48:28
^cDeut. 32:51
^dNum. 34:5; 1 Kin. 8:65; Is. 27:12
^eEzek. 47:10, 15

19 "And the ^asouth side toward the south *shall extend* from ^bTamar as far as the waters of ^cMeribath-kadesh, to the ^dbrook *of Egypt, and* to the ^eGreat Sea. This is the south side toward the south.

20 ^aNum. 34:6 ^bJudg. 3:3; 2 Chr. 7:8; Ezek. 48:1; Amos 6:14

20 "And the ^awest side *shall be* the Great Sea, from the *south* border to a point opposite ^bLebohamath. This is the west side.

21 "So you shall divide this land among yourselves according to the tribes of Israel.

22 ^aNum. 26:55, 56 ^bIs. 14:1; 56:6, 7 ^cActs 11:18; 15:9; Eph. 2:12-14; 3:6; Col. 3:11

22 "And it will come about that you shall divide it by ^alot for an inheritance among yourselves and among the ^baliens who stay in your midst, who bring forth sons in your midst. And they shall be to you as the native-born among the sons of Israel; they shall be allotted an ^cinheritance with you among the tribes of Israel.

23 "And it will come about that in the tribe with which the alien stays, there you shall give *him* his inheritance," declares the Lord God.

3 The division of the land, 48:1-35

★ 1-7

1 ^aEx. 1:1
^bJosh. 19:40-48

48 "Now ^athese are the names of the tribes: from the northern extremity, beside the way of Hethlon to Lebohamath, *as far as* Hazar-enan *at* the border of Damascus, toward the north beside Hamath, running from east to west, ^bDan, one *portion.*

2 ^aJosh. 19:24-31

2 "And beside the border of Dan, from the east side to the west side, ^aAsher, one *portion.*

3 ^aJosh. 19:32-39

3 "And beside the border of Asher, from the east side to the west side, ^aNaphtali, one *portion.*

47:13-20 The northern border of Israel's land will run from the Mediterranean north of Tyre to a point near Damascus (vv. 15-17); the eastern border will be formed by the Jordan River and the Dead Sea (v. 18); the southern boundary will run from a little below the Dead Sea to the *brook of Egypt* (v. 19; see note on Isa. 27:12); and the western border will be the Mediterranean. This particular area will be allotted to the Israelites for their residences, though apparently they will control all the land from the Nile to the Euphrates (cf. Gen. 15:18).

48:1-7 Seven tribes will be given portions of the land N. of the Temple area: *Dan* (see note on Rev. 7:4), *Asher, Naphtali, Manasseh, Ephraim, Reuben,* and *Judah.*

4 aJosh.
13:29-31;
17:1-11

5 aJosh.
16:5-9; 17:8-
10, 14-18

6 aJosh.
13:15-21

7 aJosh.
15:1-63; 19:9

★ 8-22

8 aIs. 12:6;
33:20-22;
Ezek. 45:3, 4

10 aEzek.
44:28; 45:4

11 aEzek.
40:46; 44:15
bEzek.
44:10, 12

14 aLev.
25:32-34;
27:10, 28, 33

4 "And beside the border of Naphtali, from the east side to the west side, aManasseh, one *portion.*

5 "And beside the border of Manasseh, from the east side to the west side, aEphraim, one *portion.*

6 "And beside the border of Ephraim, from the east side to the west side, aReuben, one *portion.*

7 "And beside the border of Reuben, from the east side to the west side, aJudah, one *portion.*

8 "And beside the border of Judah, from the east side to the west side, shall be the allotment which you shall set apart, 25,000 *cubits* in width, and in length like one of the portions; from the east side to the west side; and the asanctuary shall be in the middle of it.

9 "The allotment that you shall set apart to the LORD *shall be* 25,000 *cubits* in length, and 10,000 in width.

10 "And the holy allotment shall be for these, *namely* for the apriests, toward the north 25,000 *cubits in length,* toward the west 10,000 in width, toward the east 10,000 in width, and toward the south 25,000 in length; and the sanctuary of the LORD shall be in its midst.

11 "*It shall be* for the priests who are sanctified of the asons of Zadok, who have kept My charge, who did not go astray when the sons of Israel went astray, as the bLevites went astray.

12 "And it shall be an allotment to them from the allotment of the land, a most holy place, by the border of the Levites.

13 "And alongside the border of the priests the Levites *shall have* 25,000 *cubits* in length and 10,000 in width. The whole length *shall be* 25,000 *cubits* and the width 10,000.

14 "Moreover, they ashall not

sell or exchange any of it, or alienate this choice *portion* of land; for it is holy to the LORD.

15 "And the remainder, 5,000 *cubits* in width and 25,000 in length, shall be for acommon use for the city, for dwellings and for open spaces; and the city shall be in its midst.

16 "And these *shall be* its measurements: the north side 4,500 *cubits,* the south side a4,500 *cubits,* the east side 4,500 *cubits,* and the west side 4,500 *cubits.*

17 "And the city shall have open spaces: on the north 250 *cubits,* on the south 250 *cubits,* on the east 250 *cubits,* and on the west 250 *cubits.*

18 "And the remainder of the length alongside the holy allotment shall be 10,000 *cubits* toward the east, and 10,000 toward the west; and it shall be alongside the holy allotment. And its produce shall be food for the workers of the city.

19 "And the workers of the city, out of all the tribes of Israel, shall cultivate it.

20 "The whole allotment *shall be* 25,000 by 25,000 *cubits;* you shall set apart the holy allotment, a square, with the property of the city.

21 "And the aremainder *shall be* for the prince, on the one side and on the other of the holy allotment and of the property of the city; in front of the 25,000 *cubits* of the allotment toward the east border and westward in front of the 25,000 toward the west border, alongside the portions, *it shall be* for the prince. And the holy allotment and the sanctuary of the house shall be in the middle of it.

22 "And exclusive of the property of the Levites and the property of the city, *which* are in the middle of that which belongs to

15 aEzek.
42:20; 45:6

16 aRev.
21:16

21 aEzek.
34:24; 45:7;
48:22

48:8-22 A description again (see 45:1-8) of the sacred portion of the land, which included the *sanctuary* (v. 8), the priests' portion (vv. 10-12), the Levites' portion (vv. 13-14), the city (vv. 15-20), and the prince's portion (vv. 21-22).

the prince, *everything* between the border of Judah and the border of Benjamin shall be for the prince.

★23-29
23 a Josh. 18:21-28
23 "As for the rest of the tribes: from the east side to the west side, ^aBenjamin, one *portion.*

24 a Josh. 19:1-9
24 "And beside the border of Benjamin, from the east side to the west side, ^aSimeon, one *portion.*

25 a Josh. 19:17-23
25 "And beside the border of Simeon, from the east side to the west side, ^aIssachar, one *portion.*

26 a Josh. 19:10-16
26 "And beside the border of Issachar, from the east side to the west side, ^aZebulun, one *portion.*

27 a Josh. 13:24-28
27 "And beside the border of Zebulun, from the east side to the west side, ^aGad, one *portion.*

28 a Gen. 14:7; 2 Chr. 20:2; Ezek. 47:19 **b**Ezek. 47:10, 15, 19, 20
28 "And beside the border of Gad, at the south side toward the south, the border shall be from ^aTamar to the waters of Meribath-kadesh, to the brook *of Egypt,* to the ^bGreat Sea.

29 a Ezek. 47:13-20
29 "This is the ^aland which you shall divide by lot to the tribes of Israel for an inheritance,

and these are their *several* portions," declares the Lord God.

30 a Ezek. 48:32-34
30 "And these are the exits of the city: on the ^anorth side, 4,500 *cubits* by measurement,

★31-34
31 a Rev. 21:12, 13
31 shall be the gates of the city, ^anamed for the tribes of Israel, three gates toward the north: the gate of Reuben, one; the gate of Judah, one; the gate of Levi, one.

32 "And on the east side, 4,500 *cubits,* shall be three gates: the gate of Joseph, one; the gate of Benjamin, one; the gate of Dan, one.

33 "And on the south side, 4,500 *cubits* by measurement, shall be three gates: the gate of Simeon, one; the gate of Issachar, one; the gate of Zebulun, one.

34 "On the west side, 4,500 *cubits, shall be* three gates: the gate of Gad, one; the gate of Asher, one; the gate of Naphtali, one.

35 a Jer. 23:6; 33:16 **b**Is. 12:6; 14:32; 24:23; Jer. 3:17; 8:19; 14:9; Ezek. 35:10; Joel 3:21; Zech. 2:10; Rev. 21:3; 22:3
35 *"The city shall be* 18,000 *cubits* round about; and the ^aname of the city from *that day shall be,* 'The ^bLORD is there.' "

48:23-29 Five tribes will be given land S. of the sacred area: *Benjamin, Simeon, Issachar, Zebulun,* and *Gad.* The arrangement is different from the allotment recorded in Josh. 13-17.

48:31-34 There are three gates to each side of the city, each named after a tribe of Israel (*Levi* is included, v. 31, and *Joseph* represents Ephraim and Manasseh, v. 32).

INTRODUCTION TO
THE BOOK OF DANIEL

AUTHOR: Daniel   DATE: 537 B.C.

The Prophet   *Daniel, whose name means "God is my judge," was a statesman in the court of heathen monarchs. Taken captive as a youth to Babylon by Nebuchadnezzar in 605, he spent the rest of his long life there as a governmental official and as a prophet of the true God. He claimed to have written this book (12:4), and Jesus Christ identified him as a prophet (Matt. 24:15; Mark 13:14). Since he did not occupy the prophetic office, the book is found in the third division of the Hebrew Bible, the "Writings," rather than in the second, the Prophets. Throughout his life he was uncompromising and faithful to his God.*

Date   *The first attack on the traditional sixth century B.C. date for the composition of the book came from Porphyry (A.D. 232-303), a vigorous opponent of Christianity, who maintained that the book was written by an unknown Jew who lived at the time of Antiochus Epiphanes (175-163 B.C.). This view was widely promoted by scholars of the 18th and 19th centuries for the following reasons: it is alleged that Daniel could not have made these predictions, since they were accurately fulfilled and could therefore have been written only after the events occurred; Persian and Greek words used in the book would have been unknown to a sixth-century Jewish author; the Aramaic used in 2:4-7:28 belongs to a time after that of Daniel; and certain alleged historical inaccuracies. In answer we observe that predictive prophecy is not only possible but expected from a true prophet of God. Since Daniel lived into the Persian period he would have known Persian words. The presence of Greek words is easily accounted for, since one hundred years before Daniel, Greek mercenaries served in the Assyrian army under Esarhaddon (683) and in the Babylonian army under Nebuchadnezzar. Recent discoveries of fifth century B.C. Aramaic documents have shown that Daniel was written in a form of Imperial Aramaic, an official dialect known in all parts of the Near East at that time. Alleged historical inaccuracies are fast disappearing, with the information provided by the Nabonidus Chronicle as to the identity of Belshazzar (5:1) and with evidence that identifies Darius the Mede with a governor named Gubaru (5:31).*
   In addition, how can the use of relatively few Greek words be explained if the book was written around 170 B.C., when a Greek-speaking government had controlled Palestine for 160 years? One would expect the presence of many Greek terms. Also, the Qumran documents (Dead Sea Scrolls), dated only a few decades before the alleged second-century writing of Daniel, show grammatical differences that indicate they were written centuries, not decades, after that time. Further, the scrolls of Daniel found at Qumran are copies, indicating that the original was written before the Maccabean era.

The Times   *In 605 Nebuchadnezzar took Daniel and others as captives to Babylon (see Introduction to Jeremiah). Because of the events recorded in chapter 2 of the book, Daniel was given a place of prominence and responsibility in Nebuchadnezzar's kingdom. After the king's death, Daniel apparently fell from favor, but was recalled to interpret the writing that appeared at Belshazzar's feast (5:13). He was made one of three presidents under Darius (6:1) and lived until the third year of Cyrus (536). His ministry was to testify, in his personal life and in his prophecies, to the power of God. Though in exile, the people of Israel were not deserted by God, and Daniel revealed many details about His plan for their future. He also traced the course of Gentile world powers from his own day to the second coming of Christ.*

Contents   *Important prophecies in the book include: the course of Gentile kingdoms (the future of Babylon, Persia, Greece and Rome, chaps. 2 and 7), details concerning Medo-Persia and Greece (chap. 8), more details concerning Greece (chap. 11), the prophecy of the seventy weeks of years (9:24-27), and the activities of Antichrist (11:36-45). Among the doctrines mentioned in the book are: personal separation (1:8; 3:12; 6:10; 9:2-3; 10:2-3); angels (8:16; 9:21; 10:13, 20-21; 11:1); resurrection (12:2); Antichrist (7:24-25; 9:27; 11:36). Favorite stories include those of: Shadrach, Meshach, and Abed-nego (chap. 3), and the lions' den (chap. 6).*

OUTLINE OF DANIEL

THE BOOK OF DANIEL

I DANIEL'S DEDICATION, 1:1-21

A Daniel's Circumstances, 1:1-7

★ 1 a2 Kin. 24:1; 2 Chr. 36:5, 6 bJer. 25:1; 52:12; 28-30

1 In the third year of the reign of aJehoiakim king of Judah, bNebuchadnezzar king of Babylon came to Jerusalem and besieged it.

2 And the aLord gave Jehoiakim king of Judah into his hand, along with some of the bvessels of the house of God; and he brought them to the land of cShinar, to the house of his god, and he brought the vessels into the treasury of his dgod.

3 Then the king ordered

★ 2 aIs. 42:24; Dan. 2:37, 38 b2 Chr. 36:7; Jer. 27:19, 20; Dan. 5:2 cGen. 10:10; 11:2; Is. 11:11; Zech. 5:11 dJer. 50:2; 51:44 ★ 3 a2 Kin. 24:15; Is. 39:7

1:1 *In the third year.* I.e., 605. See note on Jer. 25:1. *Jehoiakim.* Jehoiakim was the eldest son of godly Josiah and was made king in place of his younger brother in 609 by Pharaoh Neco. A vassal to Egypt for four years and then to Babylon, Jehoiakim squandered state funds on a new palace (Jer. 22:13-19) and destroyed Jeremiah's writings, which warned him of coming judgment. He died in 598. *came.* May be translated "went" (cf. 2 Kings 24:1). Nebuchadnezzar, whose name means "Nebo, protect my frontier," reigned for 43 years (605-562). Sent by his father, Nabopolassar, to lead the Babylonian army against Egypt (which he defeated at Carchemish in May-

June 605), he was called back home at the death of his father late in July to be crowned king. Thus he was not yet king of Babylon when he invaded Jerusalem in 605 (the title is used prophetically).

1:2 *the vessels of the house of God.* Taken as a prize and as proof of the power of Nebuchadnezzar's gods (see 1 Kings 7:48-51; 2 Kings 24:13; Dan. 5:1-3). *Shinar.* Babylonia (Gen. 10:10; 11:2).

1:3 *officials.* Lit., eunuchs. The word does mean those who were castrated, but it also stood for officials in general. It is uncertain whether Daniel and his friends were emasculated (see 2 Kings 20:18).

Ashpenaz, the chief of his officials, to bring in some of the sons of Israel, including some of the royal ªfamily and of the nobles,

4 youths in whom was ªno defect, who were good-looking, showing ᵇintelligence in every *branch of* wisdom, endowed with understanding, and discerning knowledge, and who had ability for serving in the king's court; and *he ordered him* to teach them the literature and ᶜlanguage of the ᵈChaldeans.

5 And the king appointed for them a daily ration from the ªking's choice food and from the wine which he drank, and *appointed* that they should be educated three years, at the end of which they were to ᵇenter the king's personal service.

6 Now among them from the sons of Judah were ªDaniel, Hananiah, Mishael and Azariah.

7 Then the commander of the officials assigned *new* names to them; and to Daniel he assigned *the name* ªBelteshazzar, to Hananiah ᵇShadrach, to Mishael ᵇMeshach, and to Azariah ᵇAbednego.

B   Daniel's Dedication, 1:8–16

8 But Daniel made up his mind that he would not ªdefile himself with the ᵇking's choice food or with the ᶜwine which he drank; so he sought *permission* from the commander of the officials that he might not defile himself.

9 Now God granted Daniel ªfavor and compassion in the sight of the commander of the officials,

10 and the commander of the officials said to Daniel, "I am afraid of my lord the king, who has appointed your food and your drink; for why should he see your faces looking more haggard than the youths who are your own age? Then you would make me forfeit my head to the king."

11 But Daniel said to the overseer whom the commander of the officials had appointed over Daniel, Hananiah, Mishael and Azariah,

12 "Please test your servants for ten days, and let us be ªgiven some vegetables to eat and water to drink.

13 "Then let our appearance be observed in your presence, and the appearance of the youths who are eating the king's choice food; and deal with your servants according to what you see."

14 So he listened to them in this matter and tested them for ten days.

15 And at the end of ten days their appearance seemed ªbetter and they were fatter than all the youths who had been eating the king's choice food.

16 So the overseer continued to withhold their choice food and the wine they were to drink, and kept ªgiving them vegetables.

C   Daniel's Rise to Favor, 1:17–21

17 And as for these four youths, ªGod gave them

Cross references (margin)

4 ª2 Sam. 14:25 ᵇDan. 1:17 ᶜIs. 36:11; Jer. 5:15; Dan. 2:4 ᵈDan. 2:2, 4, 5, 10; 3:8; 4:7; 5:7, 11, 30; 9:1

★ **5** ªDan. 1:8 ᵇ1 Sam. 16:22; Dan. 1:19

6 ªEzek. 14:14, 20; 28:3; Matt. 24:15

★ **7** ªDan. 2:26; 4:8; 5:12 ᵇDan. 2:49; 3:12

★ **8** ªLev. 11:47; Ezek. 4:13, 14; Hos. 9:3, 4 ᵇPs. 141:4; Dan. 1:5 ᶜDeut. 32:38; Dan. 5:4

9 ªGen. 39:21; 1 Kin. 8:50; Job 5:15, 16; Ps. 106:46; Prov. 16:7

12 ªDan. 1:16

15 ªEx. 23:25; Prov. 10:22

16 ªDan. 1:12

17 ª1 Kin. 3:12, 28; Job 32:8; Dan. 1:20; 2:21, 23; Acts 7:22 ᵇDan. 2:19; 7:1; 8:1

1:5 The accession year of Nebuchadnezzar was the first year of the youths' training; the first full year of Nebuchadnezzar's reign was the second year of training; the second year of his reign was the third year of training.

1:7 In order to make these young men more Babylonian, their names were changed (cf. Joseph, Gen. 41:45; and Esther, in Esther 2:7). *Daniel* means "God is judge." *Belteshazzar* means "May Bel protect his life." *Hananiah* means "Yahweh is gracious." *Shadrach* possibly means "command of Aku" (the moon

god). *Mishael* means "Who is what God is?" *Meshach* may mean "Who is what Aku is?" *Azariah* means "Whom Yahweh helps." *Abed-nego* means "servant of Nebo." In each case the Hebrew name contains a name for the true God (either *el* or *iah*, an abbreviation for Yahweh) and the Babylonian name contains the name of a heathen god.

1:8 *he would not defile himself.* By eating meat that doubtless had not been slain in accordance with the Mosaic Law and had been offered to a pagan god (cf. Exod. 34:15).

knowledge and intelligence in every *branch of* literature and wisdom; Daniel even understood all *kinds of* ᵇvisions and dreams.

18 Then at the end of the days which the king had specified for presenting them, the commander of the officials presented them before Nebuchadnezzar.

19 And the king talked with them, and out of them all not one was found like ᵃDaniel, Hananiah, Mishael and Azariah; so they ᵇentered the king's personal service.

20 And as for every matter of ᵃwisdom and understanding about which the king consulted them, he found them ᵇten times ᶜbetter than all the ᵈmagicians *and* conjurers who *were* in all his realm.

21 And Daniel continued until the ᵃfirst year of Cyrus the king.

II NEBUCHADNEZZAR'S DREAM: THE GREAT IMAGE, 2:1–49
A The Dream Received by Nebuchadnezzar, 2:1–6

2 Now in the second year of the reign of Nebuchadnezzar, Nebuchadnezzar ᵃhad dreams; and his spirit was troubled and his ᵇsleep left him.

2 Then the king gave orders to call in the ᵃmagicians, the conjurers, the sorcerers and the Chaldeans, to tell the king his dreams. So they came in and stood before the king.

3 And the king said to them, "I ᵃhad a dream, and my spirit is anxious to understand the dream."

4 Then the Chaldeans spoke to the king in ᵃAramaic: "ᵇO king, live forever! ᶜTell the dream to your servants, and we will declare the interpretation."

5 The king answered and said to the Chaldeans, "The command from me is firm: if you do not make known to me the dream and its interpretation, you will be ᵃtorn limb from limb, and your houses will be made a rubbish heap.

6 "But if you declare the dream and its interpretation, you will receive from me ᵃgifts and a reward and great honor; therefore declare to me the dream and its interpretation."

B The Dream Revealed to Daniel, 2:7–23

7 They answered a second time and said, "Let the king ᵃtell the dream to his servants, and we will declare the interpretation."

8 The king answered and said, "I know for certain that you are bargaining for time, inasmuch as you have seen that the command from me is firm,

9 that if you do not make the dream known to me, there is only ᵃone decree for you. For you have agreed together to speak lying and corrupt words before me until the situation is changed; therefore tell me the dream, that I may ᵇknow that you can declare to me its interpretation."

10 The Chaldeans answered the king and said, "There is not a man on earth who could declare the matter for the king, inasmuch

Marginal references

19 ᵃDan. 1:6, 7 ᵇGen. 41:46; Dan. 1:5

20 ᵃ1 Kin. 4:30, 31; Dan. 1:17 ᵇGen. 31:7; Num. 14:22; Neh. 4:12; Job 19:3 ᶜDan. 2:27, 28, 46, 48 ᵈIs. 19:3; Dan. 2:2; 4:18; 5:7

★21 ᵃDan. 6:28; 10:1

1 ᵃGen. 40:5-8; 41:1, 8; Job 33:15-17; Dan. 2:3; 4:5 ᵇEsth. 6:1; Dan. 6:18

★ 2 ᵃGen. 41:8; Ex. 7:11; Is. 47:12, 13; Dan. 1:20; 2:10, 27; 4:6; 5:7

3 ᵃGen. 40:8; 41:15; Dan. 4:5

★ 4 ᵃEzra 4:7; Is. 36:11 ᵇDan. 3:9; 5:10 ᶜDan. 2:7

★ 5 ᵃEzra 6:11; Dan. 2:12; 3:29

6 ᵃDan. 2:48; 5:7, 16, 29

7 ᵃDan. 2:4

9 ᵃEsth. 4:11; Dan. 3:15 ᵇIs. 41:23

10 ᵃDan. 2:2, 27

1:21 *continued.* Daniel, who was among the first captives taken, lived to see the official end of the Exile in the "first year of Cyrus the king" (Ezra 1:1). Daniel did not die then but lived a few years longer (10:1).

2:2 *magicians.* Textual scribes of the religious ritual. *conjurers.* Enchanters. *sorcerers.* Those who deal in magic potions; also enchanters. *Chaldeans.* Not all the Babylonians (as in 1:4) but a class of wise men priests.

2:4 Aramaic was the common language of the Assyrian Empire and was used in both the neo-Babylonian and Persian empires as a diplomatic and commercial language. It is used appropriately in the Gentile-related portion of the book (2:4–7:28).

2:5 *The command from me is firm.* Or, the thing is gone; or, the dream is certain to me. It is uncertain whether or not the king had forgotten the dream. If not, he was putting his wise men to the ultimate test.

as no great king or ruler has *ever* asked anything like this of any [a]magician, conjurer or Chaldean.

11 "Moreover, the thing which the king demands is difficult, and there is no one else who could declare it to the king except [a]gods, whose [b]dwelling place is not with *mortal* flesh."

12 Because of this the king became [a]indignant and very furious, and gave orders to destroy all the wise men of Babylon.

13 So the decree went forth that the wise men should be slain; and they looked for [a]Daniel and his friends to kill *them*.

14 Then Daniel replied with discretion and discernment to [a]Arioch, the captain of the king's bodyguard, who had gone forth to slay the wise men of Babylon;

15 he answered and said to Arioch, the king's commander, "For what reason is the decree from the king *so* urgent?" Then Arioch informed Daniel about the matter.

16 So Daniel went in and requested of the king that he would give him time, in order that he might declare the interpretation to the king.

17 Then Daniel went to his house and informed his friends, [a]Hananiah, Mishael and Azariah, about the matter,

18 in order that they might [a]request compassion from the God of heaven concerning this mystery, so that Daniel and his friends might not be [b]destroyed with the rest of the wise men of Babylon.

19 Then the mystery was revealed to Daniel in a night [a]vision. Then Daniel blessed the God of heaven;

20 Daniel answered and said,
"Let the name of God be
   [a]blessed forever and
      ever,
For [b]wisdom and power
   belong to Him.

21 "And it is He who
   [a]changes the times
      and the epochs;
He [b]removes kings and
   establishes kings;
He gives [c]wisdom to
   wise men,
And knowledge to men
   of understanding.

22 "It is He who [a]reveals the
   profound and hidden
      things;
[b]He knows what is in
   the darkness,
And the [c]light dwells
   with Him.

23 "To Thee, O [a]God of my
   fathers, I give thanks
      and praise,
For Thou hast given me
   [b]wisdom and power;
Even now Thou hast
   made known to me
   what we [c]requested of
   Thee,
For Thou hast made
   known to us the
   king's matter."

C The Dream Recited and Interpreted to Nebuchadnezzar, 2:24–45

24 Therefore, Daniel went in to Arioch, whom the king had appointed to destroy the wise men of Babylon; he went and spoke to him as follows: "[a]Do not destroy the wise men of Babylon! Take me into the king's presence, and I will declare the interpretation to the king."

25 Then Arioch hurriedly [a]brought Daniel into the king's presence and spoke to him as follows: "I have found a man among the [b]exiles from Judah who can make the interpretation known to the king!"

26 The king answered and said to Daniel, whose name was [a]Belteshazzar, "Are you able to

Marginal references

11 [a]Gen. 41:39; Dan. 5:11 [b]Ex. 29:45; Is. 57:15

12 [a]Ps. 76:10; Dan. 2:5; 3:13, 19

13 [a]Dan. 1:19, 20

★14-15

14 [a]Dan. 2:24

17 [a]Dan. 1:6

18 [a]Esth. 4:15, 16; Is. 37:4; Jer. 33:3; Ezek. 36:37; Dan. 2:23 [b]Gen. 18:28; Mal. 3:18

19 [a]Num. 12:6; Job 33:15, 16; Dan. 1:17; 7:2, 7, 13
20 [a]Ps. 103:1, 2; 113:1, 2; 115:18; 145:1, 2, 21 [b]1 Chr. 29:11, 12; Job 12:13, 16-22; Dan. 2:21-23

21 [a]Ps. 31:15; Dan. 2:9; 7:25 [b]Job 12:18; Ps. 75:6, 7; Dan. 4:17, 32 [c]1 Kin. 3:9, 10; 4:29; James 1:5

22 [a]Job 12:22; Ps. 25:14; Dan. 2:19, 28 [b]Job 26:6; Ps. 139:12; Is. 45:7; Jer. 23:24; Heb. 4:13 [c]Ps. 36:9; Dan. 5:11, 14; James 1:17; 1 John 1:5

23 [a]Gen. 31:42; Ex. 3:15 [b]Dan. 1:17; 2:21 [c]Ps. 21:2, 4; Dan. 2:18, 29, 30

24 [a]Dan. 2:12, 13; Acts 27:24

25 [a]Gen. 41:14 [b]Dan. 1:6; 5:13; 6:13

26 [a]Dan. 1:7; 4:8; 5:12

2:14-15 Apparently Daniel, keeping himself untainted from the heathen magic, had not gone to the king with the Babylonian wise men.

make known to me the dream which I have seen and its interpretation?"

★27-30

27 aDan. 2:2, 10, 11; 5:7, 8

27 Daniel answered before the king and said, "As for the mystery about which the king has inquired, neither awise men, conjurers, magicians, nor diviners are able to declare it to the king.

28 aGen. 40:8; 41:16; Dan. 2:22, 45 bGen. 49:1; Is. 2:2; Dan. 10:14; Mic. 4:1 cDan. 4:5

28 "However, there is a aGod in heaven who reveals mysteries, and He has made known to King Nebuchadnezzar what will take place in the blatter days. This was your dream and the cvisions in your mind while on your bed.

29 aDan. 2:23, 47

29 "As for you, O king, while on your bed your thoughts turned to what would take place in the future; and aHe who reveals mysteries has made known to you what will take place.

30 aGen. 41:16; Dan. 1:17 bPs. 139:2; Amos 4:13

30 "But as for me, this mystery has not been revealed to me for any awisdom residing in me more than in any other living man, but for the purpose of making the interpretation known to the king, and that you may understand the bthoughts of your mind.

31 aHab. 1:7

31 "You, O king, were looking and behold, there was a single great statue; that statue, which was large and of extraordinary splendor, was standing in front of you, and its appearance was aawesome.

32 aDan. 2:38

32 "The ahead of that statue was made of fine gold, its breast and its arms of silver, its belly and its thighs of bronze,

33 its legs of iron, its feet partly of iron and partly of clay.

34 aDan. 2:45 bDan. 8:25; Zech. 4:6 cPs. 2:9; Is. 60:12

34 "You continued looking until a astone was cut out bwithout hands, and it struck the statue on

its feet of iron and clay, and ccrushed them.

35 "Then the iron, the clay, the bronze, the silver and the gold were crushed all at the same time, and became alike chaff from the summer threshing floors; and the wind carried them away so that bnot a trace of them was found. But the stone that struck the statue became a great cmountain and filled the whole earth.

★35 aPs. 1:4; Is. 17:13; 41:15, 16; Hos. 13:3 bPs. 37:10, 36 cIs. 2:2; Mic. 4:1

36 "This was the dream; now we shall tell aits interpretation before the king.

36 aDan. 2:24

37 "You, O king, are the aking of kings, to whom the God of heaven has given the kingdom, the bpower, the strength, and the glory;

★37-38

37 aIs. 47:5; Jer. 27:6, 7; Ezek. 26:7 bPs. 62:11

38 and wherever the sons of men dwell, or the abeasts of the field, or the birds of the sky, He has given them into your hand and has caused you to rule over them all. You are the head of gold.

38 aPs. 50:10, 11; Dan. 4:21, 22

39 "And after you there will arise another kingdom inferior to you, then another third kingdom of bronze, which will rule over all the earth.

★39

40 "Then there will be a afourth kingdom as strong as iron; inasmuch as iron crushes and shatters all things, so, like iron that breaks in pieces, it will crush and break all these in pieces.

★40 aDan. 7:23

41 "And in that you saw the feet and toes, partly of potter's clay and partly of iron, it will be a divided kingdom; but it will have in it the toughness of iron, inasmuch as you saw the iron mixed with common clay.

★41

2:27-30 Daniel disclaimed any natural or magical ability, but credits the Lord with the revelation of the dream.

2:35 *the stone . . . filled the whole earth.* To refer this to the first coming of Christ and the victory of the Gospel in the whole world is contrary to such verses as Matt. 13:24-30, 36-43 and 2 Tim. 3:1-13. It is a reference to the future millennial kingdom of Christ.

2:37-38 The gold head of the image (v. 32) is interpreted as representing Babylon.

2:39 The breast and arms of silver (v. 32) represented the kingdom that followed Babylon, i.e., the kingdom of the Medes and Persians (538-333). The belly and thighs of brass (v. 32) stood for Greece (333 B.C.-63 B.C.; cf. 8:20-21).

2:40 The *fourth kingdom* (legs and feet, v. 33) was Rome.

2:41 *divided.* Better, composite, since it was composed of strong peoples (*iron*) and weak ones (*clay*).

★42

42 "And *as* the toes of the feet *were* partly of iron and partly of pottery, *so* some of the kingdom will be strong and part of it will be brittle.

43 "And in that you saw the iron mixed with common clay, they will combine with one another in the seed of men; but they will not adhere to one another, even as iron does not combine with pottery.

44 *a*Dan. 2:28, 37 *b*Is. 9:6, 7 *c*Ps. 145:13; Ezek. 37:25; Dan. 4:3, 34; 6:26; 7:14, 27; Mic. 4:7; Luke 1:32, 33 *d*Ps. 2:9; Is. 60:12; Dan. 2:34, 35

44 "And in the days of those kings the *a*God of heaven will *b*set up a *c*kingdom which will never be destroyed, and *that* kingdom will not be left for another people; it will *d*crush and put an end to all these kingdoms, but it will itself endure forever.

45 *a*Dan. 2:34 *b*Deut. 10:17; 2 Sam. 7:22; Ps. 48:1; Jer. 32:18, 19; Dan. 2:29; Mal. 1:11 *c*Gen. 41:28, 32

45 "Inasmuch as you saw that a *a*stone was cut out of the mountain without hands and that it crushed the iron, the bronze, the clay, the silver, and the gold, the *b*great God has made known to the king what *c*will take place in the future; so the dream is true, and its interpretation is trustworthy."

D　The Promotion of Daniel, 2:46-49

46 *a*Dan. 3:5, 7; Acts 10:25; 14:13; Rev. 19:10; 22:8 *b*Lev. 26:31; Ezra 6:10 47 *a*Dan. 3:15; 4:25 *b*Deut. 10:17; Ps. 136:2, 3; Dan. 11:36 *c*Dan. 2:22; 30; Amos 3:7 48 *a*Gen. 41:39-43; Dan. 2:6; 5:16, 29 *b*Dan. 3:1, 12, 30

46 Then King Nebuchadnezzar fell on his face and did *a*homage to Daniel, and gave orders to present to him an offering and *b*fragrant incense.

47 The king answered Daniel and said, "Surely *a*your God is a *b*God of gods and a Lord of kings and a *c*revealer of mysteries, since you have been able to reveal this mystery."

48 Then the king *a*promoted Daniel and gave him many great gifts, and he made him ruler over

the whole *b*province of Babylon and chief prefect over all the wise men of Babylon.

★49 *a*Dan. 3:12, *b*Dan. 1:7 *c*Esth. 2:19, 21; Amos 5:15

49 And Daniel made request of the king, and he *a*appointed *b*Shadrach, Meshach and Abednego over the administration of the province of Babylon, while Daniel *was* at the king's *c*court.

III　THE FIERY FURNACE: A LESSON IN FAITH, 3:1-30

A　The Test of Faith, 3:1-12

★ 1 *a*1 Kin. 12:28; Is. 46:6; Jer. 16:20; Dan. 2:31; Hos. 2:8; 8:4; Hab. 2:19 *b*Dan. 2:48; 3:30

3 Nebuchadnezzar the king made an *a*image of gold, the height of which *was* sixty cubits *and* its width six cubits; he set it up on the plain of Dura in the *b*province of Babylon.

★ 2 *a*Dan. 3:3, 27; 6:1-7

2 Then Nebuchadnezzar the king sent *word* to assemble the *a*satraps, the prefects and the governors, the counselors, the treasurers, the judges, the magistrates and all the rulers of the provinces to come to the dedication of the image that Nebuchadnezzar the king had set up.

3 Then the satraps, the prefects and the governors, the counselors, the treasurers, the judges, the magistrates and all the rulers of the provinces were assembled for the dedication of the image that Nebuchadnezzar the king had set up; and they stood before the image that Nebuchadnezzar had set up.

4 *a*Dan. 3:7; 4:1; 6:25

4 Then the herald loudly proclaimed: "To you the command is given, *a*O peoples, nations and *men of every* language,

★ 5 *a*Dan. 3:7, 10, 15

5 that at the moment you *a*hear the sound of the horn, flute, lyre, trigon, psaltery, bagpipe, and all kinds of music, you are to fall

---

2:42 *the toes.* Explained in verse 44 as ten kings (or kingdoms) that will exist concurrently at the time God sets up His kingdom at the second coming of Christ (7:24). The present age of the church is omitted in the vision (not an unusual phenomenon; cf. Isa. 61:1-2).

2:49 *the king's court.* The royal offices, the chancellory.

3:1 *an image of gold.* Probably the image was in human form (though not necessarily an image

of Nebuchadnezzar) overlaid with gold, rather than solid gold (Isa. 40:19). It was 90 feet by 9 feet, probably including a pedestal.

3:2 *satraps.* Leaders of the various provinces.

3:5 *horn.* A wind instrument. *trigon.* A triangular instrument with four *strings* that played high notes. *psaltery.* Another triangular instrument whose strings were beneath the sounding board.

down and worship the golden image that Nebuchadnezzar the king has set up.

6 "But whoever does not fall down and worship shall immediately be [a]cast into the midst of a [b]furnace of blazing fire."

7 Therefore at that time, when all the peoples heard the sound of the horn, flute, lyre, trigon, psaltery, bagpipe, and all kinds of music, all the peoples, nations and men of every language fell down and worshiped the golden image that Nebuchadnezzar the king had set up.

8 For this reason at that time certain [a]Chaldeans came forward and [b]brought charges against the Jews.

9 They responded and said to Nebuchadnezzar the king: "[a]O king, live forever!

10 You yourself, O king, have [a]made a decree that every man who hears the sound of the horn, flute, lyre, trigon, psaltery, and bagpipe, and all kinds of music, is to [b]fall down and worship the golden image.

11 "But whoever does not fall down and worship shall be cast into the midst of a furnace of blazing fire.

12 "There are certain Jews whom you have [a]appointed over the administration of the province of Babylon, namely Shadrach, Meshach and Abed-nego. These men, O king, have disregarded you; they do not serve your gods or worship the golden image which you have set up."

B The Demonstration of Faith,
3:13–18

13 Then Nebuchadnezzar in [a]rage and anger gave orders to bring Shadrach, Meshach and Abed-nego; then these men were brought before the king.

14 Nebuchadnezzar responded and said to them, "Is it true, Shadrach, Meshach and Abed-nego, that you do not serve [a]my gods or worship the golden image that I have set up?

15 "Now if you are ready, [a]at the moment you hear the sound of the horn, flute, lyre, trigon, psaltery, and bagpipe, and all kinds of music, to fall down and worship the image that I have made, very well. But if you will not worship, you will immediately be [b]cast into the midst of a furnace of blazing fire; and [c]what god is there who can deliver you out of my hands?"

16 [a]Shadrach, Meshach and Abed-nego answered and said to the king, "O Nebuchadnezzar, we do not need to give you an answer concerning this.

17 "If it be so, our [a]God whom we serve is able to deliver us from the furnace of blazing fire; and [b]He will deliver us out of your hand, O king.

18 "[a]But even if He does not, [b]let it be known to you, O king, that we are not going to serve your gods or worship the golden image that you have set up."

C The Vindication of Faith,
3:19–30

19 Then Nebuchadnezzar was filled with [a]wrath, and his facial expression was altered toward Shadrach, Meshach and Abed-nego. He answered by giving orders to heat the furnace seven times more than it was usually heated.

20 And he commanded certain valiant warriors who were in his army to tie up Shadrach, Meshach and Abed-nego, in order to cast them into the furnace of blazing fire.

3:17–18 They do not make any conditions with God; deliverance or martyrdom were equally possible in His plan.

6 [a]Dan. 3:11, 15, 21; 6:7 [b]Jer. 29:22; Ezek. 22:18-22; Matt. 13:42, 50; Rev. 9:2; 14:11

8 [a]Dan. 2:2, 10; 4:7 [b]Ezra 4:12-16; Esth. 3:8, 9; Dan. 6:12, 13

9 [a]Dan. 2:4; 5:10; 6:6, 21

10 [a]Esth. 3:12-14; Dan. 3:4-6; 6:12 [b]Dan. 3:5, 7, 15

12 [a]Dan. 2:49

13 [a]Dan. 2:12; 3:19

14 [a]Is. 46:1; Jer. 50:2; Dan. 3:1; 4:8

15 [a]Dan. 3:5 [b]Dan. 3:6 [c]Ex. 5:2; Is. 36:18-20; Dan. 2:47

16 [a]Dan. 1:7; 3:12.

★17-18
17 [a]Job 5:19; Ps. 27:1, 2; Is. 26:3, 4; Jer. 1:8; 15:20, 21 [b]1 Sam. 17:37; Mic. 7:7; 2 Cor. 1:10

18 [a]Josh. 24:15; 1 Kin. 19:14, 18; Is. 51:12, 13; Dan. 3:28 [b]Heb. 11:25

19 [a]Esth. 7:7; Dan. 3:13

21 aDan.
3:27

22 aEx.
12:33; Dan.
2:15

23 aIs. 43:2

21 Then these men were tied up in their atrousers, their coats, their caps and their *other* clothes, and were cast into the midst of the furnace of blazing fire.

22 For this reason, because the king's command *was* aurgent and the furnace had been made extremely hot, the flame of the fire slew those men who carried up Shadrach, Meshach and Abed-nego.

23 But these three men, Shadrach, Meshach and Abed-nego, afell into the midst of the furnace of blazing fire *still* tied up.

24 Then Nebuchadnezzar the king was astounded and stood up in haste; he responded and said to his high officials, "Was it not three men we cast bound into the midst of the fire?" They answered and said to the king, "Certainly, O king."

★25 aPs.
91:3-9; Is.
43:2 bJer.
1:8, 19;
15:21

25 He answered and said, "Look! I see four men loosed *and* awalking *about* in the midst of the fire without harm, and the appearance of the fourth is like a son of *the* bgods!"

26 aDan.
3:17; 4:2
bDeut. 4:20;
1 Kin. 8:51;
Jer. 11:4

26 Then Nebuchadnezzar came near to the door of the furnace of blazing fire; he responded and said, "Shadrach, Meshach and Abed-nego, come out, you servants of the aMost High God, and come here!" Then Shadrach, Meshach and Abed-nego bcame out of the midst of the fire.

★27-30
27 aDan.
3:2, 3 bIs.
43:2;
Heb.11:34
cDan. 3:21
28 aDan.
2:47; 3:15-17
bPs. 34:7, 8;
Is. 37:36;
Dan. 3:25;
6:22; Acts
5:19; 12:7
cPs. 22:4, 5;
40:4; 84:12;
Is. 12:2;
26:3, 4;
50:10; Jer.
17:7 dDan.
3:16-18

27 And the asatraps, the prefects, the governors and the king's high officials gathered around *and* saw in regard to these men that the bfire had no effect on the bodies of these men nor was the hair of their head singed, nor were their ctrousers damaged, nor had the smell of fire *even* come upon them.

28 Nebuchadnezzar responded and said, "Blessed be the

aGod of Shadrach, Meshach and Abed-nego, who has bsent His angel and delivered His servants who put their ctrust in Him, violating the king's command, and yielded up their bodies so as dnot to serve or worship any god except their own God.

29 "Therefore, I amake a decree that any people, nation or tongue that speaks anything offensive against the God of bShadrach, Meshach and Abed-nego shall be torn limb from limb and their chouses reduced to a rubbish heap, inasmuch as there is dno other god who is able to deliver in this way."

30 Then the king acaused Shadrach, Meshach and Abed-nego to prosper in the province of Babylon.

29 aDan.
6:26 bDan.
1:7, 19; 2:17,
49; 3:12
cEzra 6:11;
Dan. 2:5
dDan. 2:47;
3:15

30 aDan.
2:49; 3:12

IV NEBUCHADNEZZAR'S VISION OF THE HIGH TREE, 4:1-37

A The Vision Narrated by Nebuchadnezzar, 4:1-18

4 Nebuchadnezzar the king to all the peoples, nations, and *men of every* language that live in all the earth: "May your apeace abound!

2 "It has seemed good to me to declare the signs and wonders which the aMost High God has done for me.

3 "How great are His asigns,
And how mighty are His wonders!
His bkingdom is an everlasting kingdom,
And His dominion is from generation to generation.

4 "I, Nebuchadnezzar, was at ease in my house and aflourishing in my palace.

★ 1 aEzra
4:17; Dan.
6:25

2 aDan.
3:26; 4:17,
24, 25, 32,
34

3 aPs.
77:19;
105:27; Is.
25:1; Dan.
6:27 bDan.
2:44; 4:34;
6:26

4 aPs. 30:6;
Is. 47:7, 8

3:25 The fourth form Nebuchadnezzar saw in the furnace was like a divine being. It may have been an angel or possibly a preincarnate appearance of Christ, though the king would not have known who He was.

3:27-30 There can be no natural explanation for

such complete deliverance (cf. v. 22). Their faith brought deliverance, protection, reward, and glory to God (cf. 1 Pet. 4:14).

4:1 This chapter is a public decree or state paper of Nebuchadnezzar.

5 ªDan. 2:3
ᵇDan. 2:1,
28; 4:10, 13

5 "I saw a ªdream and it made me fearful; and *these* fantasies *as I lay* on my bed and the ᵇvisions in my mind kept alarming me.

6 ªGen.
41:8; Dan.
2:2

6 "So I gave orders to ªbring into my presence all the wise men of Babylon, that they might make known to me the interpretation of the dream.

7 ªGen.
41:8; Dan.
2:10, 27; 5:7
ᵇIs. 44:25;
Jer. 27:9, 10;
Dan. 2:7

7 "Then the ªmagicians, the conjurers, the Chaldeans, and the diviners came in, and I related the dream to them; but they could not make its ᵇinterpretation known to me.

★ 8 ªDan.
1:7; 2:26;
5:12 ᵇDan.
4:9, 18; 5:11,
14

8 "But finally Daniel came in before me, whose name is ªBelteshazzar according to the name of my god, and in whom is ᵇa spirit of the holy gods; and I related the dream to him, *saying,*

9 ªDan.
1:20; 2:48;
5:11 ᵇGen.
41:38; Dan.
4:8 ᶜEzek.
28:3; Dan.
2:47 ᵈGen.
41:15; Dan.
2:4, 5

9 'O Belteshazzar, ªchief of the magicians, since I know that ᵇa spirit of the holy gods is in you and ᶜno mystery baffles you, ᵈtell *me* the visions of my dream which I have seen, along with its interpretation.

10 ªDan. 4:5
ᵇEzek.
31:3, 6

10 'Now *these were* the ªvisions in my mind *as I lay* on my bed: I was looking, and behold, *there was* a ᵇtree in the midst of the earth, and its height *was* great.

11 ªDeut.
9:1; Dan.
4:21, 22

11   'The tree grew large and became strong,
And its height ªreached to the sky,
And it *was* visible to the end of the whole earth.

12 ªEzek.
31:7 ᵇJer.
27:6; Ezek.
31:6 ᶜLam.
4:20 ᵈEzek.
17:23; Matt.
13:32; Luke
13:19

12   'Its foliage *was* ªbeautiful and its fruit abundant,
And in it *was* food for all.
The ᵇbeasts of the field found ᶜshade under it,

And the ᵈbirds of the sky dwelt in its branches,
And all living creatures fed themselves from it.

13 'I was looking in the ªvisions in my mind *as I lay* on my bed, and behold, ᵇan *angelic* watcher, a ᶜholy one, descended from heaven.

14 'He shouted out and spoke as follows:

"ªChop down the tree and cut off its branches,
Strip off its foliage and scatter its fruit;
Let the ᵇbeasts flee from under it,
And the birds from its branches.

15   "Yet ªleave the stump with its roots in the ground,
But with a band of iron and bronze *around it*
In the new grass of the field;
And let him be drenched with the dew of heaven,
And let him share with the beasts in the grass of the earth.

16   "Let his mind be changed from *that of* a man,
And let a beast's mind be given to him,
And let ªseven periods of time pass over him.

17   "This sentence is by the decree of the *angelic* watchers,
And the decision is a command of the holy ones,

★13 ªDan.
7:1 ᵇDan.
4:17, 23
ᶜDeut. 33:2;
Ps. 89:7;
Dan. 8:13

14 ªEzek.
31:10-14;
Dan. 4:23;
Matt. 3:10;
7:19; Luke
13:7-9
ᵇEzek.
31:12, 13;
Dan. 4:12

★15 ªJob
14:7-9

★16 ªDan.
4:23, 25, 32

17 ªPs. 9:16;
83:18; Dan.
2:21; 5:21
ᵇJer. 27:5-7;
Dan. 4:25;
5:18, 19
ᶜ1 Sam. 2:8;
Dan. 11:21

4:8 Daniel did not appear immediately, perhaps of his own choosing or perhaps because Nebuchadnezzar did not summon him for fear Daniel might tell him something he did not want to hear. *in whom is a spirit of the holy gods.* The king may only be acknowledging his own gods' supposed work in Daniel's life, or (since *gods* may be properly translated by the singular, God) it may indicate his recognition of the true God of Israel.

4:13 *an angelic watcher, a holy one.* I.e., an angel (see vv. 17 and 23).

4:15 *a band of iron and bronze.* Either for restraint (as for a madman) or for preservation to prevent the stump's being dug up.

4:16 *seven periods of time.* Likely seven years (cf. v. 32b).

In order that the living may [a]know
That the Most High is ruler over the realm of mankind,
And [b]bestows it on whom He wishes,
And sets over it the [c]lowliest of men."

18 aGen. 41:8, 15; Dan. 4:7; 5:8, 15 bDan. 4:8, 9

18 'This is the dream *which* I, King Nebuchadnezzar, have seen. Now you, Belteshazzar, tell *me* its interpretation, inasmuch as none of the [a]wise men of my kingdom is able to make known to me the interpretation; but you are able, for a [b]spirit of the holy gods is in you.'

B The Vision Interpreted by Daniel, 4:19–27

★19 aJer. 4:19; Dan. 7:15, 28; 8:27; 10:16, 17 b1 Sam. 3:17; Dan. 4:4, 5 c2 Sam. 18:31; Dan. 4:24; 10:16 d2 Sam. 18:32

19 "Then Daniel, whose name is Belteshazzar, was appalled for a while as his [a]thoughts alarmed him. The king responded and said, 'Belteshazzar, do not [b]let the dream or its interpretation alarm you.' Belteshazzar answered and said, '[c]My lord, *if only* the dream applied to those who hate you, and its interpretation to [d]your adversaries!

20 aDan. 4:10-12

20 'The [a]tree that you saw, which became large and grew strong, whose height reached to the sky and was visible to all the earth,

21 and whose foliage *was* beautiful and its fruit abundant, and in which *was* food for all, under which the beasts of the field dwelt and in whose branches the birds of the sky lodged—

22 a2 Sam. 12:7; Dan. 2:37, 38 bJer. 27:6, 7

22 it is [a]you, O king; for you have become great and grown strong, and your majesty has become great and reached to the sky and your [b]dominion to the end of the earth.

23 aDan. 4:14, 15 bDan. 4:16

23 'And in that the king saw an *angelic* watcher, a holy one, descending from heaven and saying, "[a]Chop down the tree and destroy it; yet leave the stump with its roots in the ground, but with a band of iron and bronze *around it* in the new grass of the field, and let him be drenched with the dew of heaven, and let him share with the beasts of the field until [b]seven periods of time pass over him";

24 this is the interpretation, O king, and this is the decree of the Most High, which has [a]come upon my lord the king:

24 aJob 40:11, 12; Ps. 107:40

25 that you be [a]driven away from mankind, and your dwelling place be with the beasts of the field, and you be given grass to eat like cattle and be drenched with the dew of heaven; and seven periods of time will pass over you, until you recognize that the [b]Most High is ruler over the realm of mankind, and [c]bestows it on whomever He wishes.

25 aDan. 4:33; 5:21 bPs. 83:18; Jer. 27:5; Dan. 4:2, 17 cDan. 2:37; 4:17; 5:21

26 'And in that it was commanded to [a]leave the stump with the roots of the tree, your kingdom will be assured to you after you recognize that *it is* [b]Heaven *that* rules.

26 aDan. 4:15, 23 bDan. 2:18, 19, 28, 37, 44; 4:31

27 'Therefore, O king, may my [a]advice be pleasing to you: [b]break away now from your sins by *doing* righteousness, and from your iniquities by [c]showing mercy to *the* poor, in case there may be a [d]prolonging of your prosperity.'

★27 aGen. 41:33-37 bProv. 28:13; Is. 55:6, 7; Ezek. 18:7, 21, 22; Acts 8:22 cPs. 41:1-3; Is. 58:6, 7, 10 d1 Kin. 21:29; Jon. 3:9

C The Vision Fulfilled by God, 4:28–37

28 "All *this* [a]happened to Nebuchadnezzar the king.

28 aNum. 23:19; Zech. 1:6

29 "[a]Twelve months later he was walking on the *roof of the* royal palace of Babylon.

★29 a2 Pet. 3:9

30 "The king reflected and said, 'Is this not Babylon the

30 aHab. 2:4

4:19 *Daniel . . . was appalled.* Not because the dream was unintelligible to him, but because of his reluctance to announce God's judgment to the king, whom he apparently had grown to love.

4:27 After interpreting the dream, Daniel counselled the king to abandon his despotic ways and acknowledge the rule of God.

4:29 *the royal palace.* Nebuchadnezzar was admiring the great city he had helped build, possibly from the top terrace of his famous "Hanging Gardens."

^agreat, which I myself have built as a royal residence by the might of my power and for the glory of my majesty?'

31 "While the word *was* in the king's mouth, a voice came from heaven, *saying,* 'King Nebuchadnezzar, to you it is declared: sovereignty has been removed from you,

32 and ^ayou will be driven away from mankind, and your dwelling place *will be* with the beasts of the field. You will be given grass to eat like cattle, and ^bseven periods of time will pass over you, until you recognize that the ^cMost High is ruler over the realm of mankind, and bestows it on whomever He wishes.'

33 "Immediately the word concerning Nebuchadnezzar was fulfilled; and he was ^adriven away from mankind and began eating grass like cattle, and his body was drenched with the dew of heaven, until his hair had grown like eagles' *feathers* and his nails like birds' *claws.*

34 "But at the end of that period I, Nebuchadnezzar, raised my eyes toward heaven, and my reason returned to me, and I blessed the ^aMost High and praised and honored ^bHim who lives forever;

For His dominion is an ^ceverlasting dominion,
And His kingdom *endures* from generation to generation.

Margin references:
32 ^aDan. 4:25 ^bDan. 4:16 ^cDan. 4:17
★33 ^aDan. 4:25; 5:21
★34-37
34 ^aDan. 4:2; 5:18, 21 ^bPs. 102:24-27; Dan. 6:26; 12:7; Rev. 4:10 ^cPs. 145:13; Jer. 10:10; Dan. 4:3; Mic. 4:7; Luke 1:33

35 "And ^aall the inhabitants of the earth are accounted as nothing,
But ^bHe does according to His will in the host of heaven
And *among* the inhabitants of earth;
And ^cno one can ward off His hand
Or say to Him, '^dWhat hast Thou done?'

36 "At that time my ^areason returned to me. And my majesty and ^bsplendor were restored to me for the glory of my kingdom, and my counselors and my nobles began seeking me out; so I was reestablished in my sovereignty, and surpassing ^cgreatness was added to me.

37 "Now I Nebuchadnezzar praise, exalt, and honor the King of ^aheaven, for ^ball His works are true and His ways just, and He is able to humble those who ^cwalk in pride."

Margin references:
35 ^aPs. 39:5; Is. 40:15, 17 ^bPs. 33:11; 115:3; 135:6; Dan. 6:27 ^cJob 42:2; Is. 43:13 ^dJob 9:12; Is. 45:9; Rom. 9:20
36 ^a2 Chr. 33:12, 13; Dan. 4:34 ^bDan. 2:31 ^cProv. 22:4; Dan. 4:22
37 ^aDan. 4:26; 5:23 ^bDeut. 32:4; Ps. 33:4, 5; Is. 5:16 ^cEx. 18:11; Job 40:11, 12; Dan. 5:20

V   BELSHAZZAR'S FEAST, 5:1-31
A   Belshazzar's Contribution to the Feast: Unrestrained Sensuality, 5:1-4

5 Belshazzar the king held a great ^afeast for a thousand of his nobles, and he was drinking wine in the presence of the thousand.

2 When Belshazzar tasted the wine, he gave orders to bring the gold and silver ^avessels which

Margin references:
★1 ^aEsth. 1:3; Is. 22:12-14
★2 ^a2 Kin. 24:13; 25:15; Ezra 1:7-11; Dan. 1:2

4:33 *like cattle.* The king's illness was boanthropy (imagining himself to be an animal and acting accordingly), a condition that has been observed in modern times. Probably the king was kept in one of the royal parks during his insanity.

4:34-37 The king acknowledged God's absolute sovereignty, and his kingdom was restored to him.

5:1 *Belshazzar.* Until recently this king was unknown except for mention in this chapter, but contemporary records have been discovered which report that Nabonidus, the last king of Babylon, "entrusted the kingship to his son, Bel-shar-usus" while he retired to Arabia.

Nebuchadnezzar died in 562 and was succeeded by his son, Amel-marduk (the Evil-merodach of Jer. 52:31). He in turn was murdered by his brother-in-law (the Nergal-sarezer of Jer. 39:3, 13), who was enthroned in August 560. He in turn was succeeded in 556 by his son Labashi-marduk who was assassinated that same year by a group that included Nabonidus, who was made king.

5:2 *vessels.* See note on 1:2. *Nebuchadnezzar his father.* The term "father" can simply mean a predecessor on the throne, or in this case it may indicate that Belshazzar's mother, the wife of Nabonidus, was the daughter of Nebuchadnezzar.

Nebuchadnezzar his father had taken out of the temple which *was* in Jerusalem, in order that the king and his nobles, his wives, and his concubines might drink from them.

3 Then they brought the gold vessels that had been taken out of the temple, the house of God which *was* in Jerusalem; and the king and his nobles, his wives, and his concubines drank from them.

★ 4 ªIs. 42:8; Dan. 5:23; Rev. 9:20 ᵇPs. 115:4; 135:15; Is. 40:19, 20; Dan. 3:1; Hab. 2:19

4 They ªdrank the wine and praised the gods of ᵇgold and silver, of bronze, iron, wood, and stone.

B God's Contribution to the Feast: Handwriting on the Wall, 5:5-6

6 ªDan. 5:9, 10; 7:28 ᵇPs. 69:23 ᶜEzek. 7:17; 21:7; Nah. 2:10

5 Suddenly the fingers of a man's hand emerged and began writing opposite the lampstand on the plaster of the wall of the king's palace, and the king saw the back of the hand that did the writing.

6 Then the king's ªface grew pale, and his thoughts alarmed him; and his ᵇhip joints went slack, and his ᶜknees began knocking together.

C Daniel's Contribution to the Feast: Announcement of Doom, 5:7-29

★ 7 ªIs. 44:25; 47:13; Dan. 4:6, 7; 5:11, 15 ᵇGen. 41:42-44; Dan. 5:16, 29 ᶜEzek. 16:11 ᵈDan. 2:48; 5:16, 29; 6:2, 3

7 The king called aloud to bring in the ªconjurers, the Chaldeans and the diviners. The king spoke and said to the wise men of Babylon, "Any man who can read this inscription and explain its interpretation to me will be ᵇclothed with purple, and *have* a ᶜnecklace of gold around his neck, and have authority as ᵈthird *ruler* in the kingdom."

8 Then all the king's wise men came in, but ªthey could not read the inscription or make known its interpretation to the king.

9 Then King Belshazzar was greatly ªalarmed, his ᵇface grew *even* paler, and his nobles were perplexed.

10 The queen entered the banquet hall because of the words of the king and his nobles; the queen spoke and said, "ªO king, live forever! Do not let your thoughts alarm you or your face be pale.

11 "There is a ªman in your kingdom in whom is a ᵇspirit of the holy gods; and in the days of your father, illumination, insight, and wisdom like the wisdom of the gods were found in him. And King Nebuchadnezzar, your father, your father ᶜthe king, appointed him chief of the magicians, conjurers, Chaldeans, *and* diviners.

12 "*This was* because an ªextraordinary spirit, knowledge and insight, interpretation of dreams, explanation of enigmas, and solving of difficult problems were found in this Daniel, whom the king named ᵇBelteshazzar. Let Daniel now be summoned, and he will declare the interpretation."

13 Then Daniel was brought in before the king. The king spoke and said to Daniel, "Are you that Daniel who is one of the ªexiles from Judah, whom my father the king ᵇbrought from Judah?

14 "Now I have heard about you that a spirit of the gods is in you, and that illumination, insight, and extraordinary wisdom have been found in you.

15 "Just now the ªwise men *and* the conjurers were brought in before me that they might read this inscription and make its

8 ªGen. 41:8; Dan. 2:27; 4:7; 5:15

9 ªJob 18:11; Is. 21:2-4; Jer. 6:24; Dan. 2:1; 5:6 ᵇIs. 13:6-8

★10 ªDan. 3:9; 6:6

11 ªGen. 41:11-15; Dan. 2:47 ᵇDan. 4:8, 9, 18; 5:14 ᶜDan. 2:48

12 ªDan. 5:14; 6:3 ᵇDan. 1:7; 4:8

13 ªEzra 4:1; 6:16, 19, 20; Dan. 2:25; 6:13 ᵇDan. 1:1, 2

15 ªDan. 5:7 ᵇIs. 47:12f.; Dan. 5:8

5:4 Belshazzar was evidently trying to boost morale in the face of the Persian armies already outside the walls of Babylon.

5:7 *third ruler*. After Nabonidus and Belshazzar.
5:10 *The queen*. Belshazzar's mother.

interpretation known to me, but they *b*could not declare the interpretation of the message.

16 *a*Gen. 40:8 *b*Dan. 5:7, 29

16 "But I personally have heard about you, that you are able to give interpretations and solve difficult problems. Now if you are able to read the inscription and make its *a*interpretation known to me, you will be *b*clothed with purple and *wear* a necklace of gold around your neck, and you will have authority as the third *ruler* in the kingdom."

17 *a*2 Kin. 5:16

17 Then Daniel answered and said before the king, "Keep your *a*gifts for yourself, or give your rewards to someone else; however, I will read the inscription to the king and make the interpretation known to him.

18 *a*Dan. 4:2; 5:21 *b*Dan. 2:37, 38; 4:17 *c*Jer. 25:9; 27:5-7

18 "O king, the *a*Most High God *b*granted sovereignty, *c*grandeur, glory, and majesty to Nebuchadnezzar your father.

19 *a*Dan. 2:12, 13; 3:6; 11:3, 16, 36

19 "And because of the grandeur which He bestowed on him, all the peoples, nations, and *men of every* language feared and trembled before him; *a*whomever he wished he killed, and whomever he wished he spared alive; and whomever he wished he elevated, and whomever he wished he humbled.

20 *a*Ex. 9:17; Job 15:25; Is. 14:13-15; Dan. 4:30, 31 *b*2 Kin. 17:14; 2 Chr. 36:13 *c*Job 40:11, 12; Jer. 13:18

20 "But when his heart was *a*lifted up and his spirit became so *b*proud that he behaved arrogantly, he was *c*deposed from his royal throne, and *his* glory was taken away from him.

21 *a*Job 30:3-7; Dan. 4:32, 33 *b*Job 39:5-8 *c*Ex. 9:14-16; Ps. 83:17, 18; Ezek. 17:24; Dan. 4:17, 34, 35

21 "He was also *a*driven away from mankind, and his heart was made like *that of* beasts, and his dwelling place *was* with the *b*wild donkeys. He was given grass to eat like cattle, and his body was drenched with the dew of heaven, until he recognized that the *c*Most High God is ruler over the realm of mankind, and *that* He sets over it whomever He wishes.

22 *a*Ex. 10:3; 2 Chr. 33:23; 36:12

22 "Yet you, his son, Belshazzar, have *a*not humbled your heart, even though you knew all this,

23 *a*2 Kin. 14:10; Is. 2:12; 37:23; Jer. 50:29; Dan. 5:3, 4 *b*Dan. 4:37 *c*Ps. 115:4-8; Is. 37:19; Hab. 2:18, 19 *d*Job 12:10 *e*Job 31:4; Ps. 139:3; Prov. 20:24; Jer. 10:23

23 but you have *a*exalted yourself against the *b*Lord of heaven; and they have brought the vessels of His house before you, and you and your nobles, your wives and your concubines have been drinking wine from them; and you have praised the *c*gods of silver and gold, of bronze, iron, wood and stone, which do not see, hear or understand. But the God *d*in whose hand are your life-breath and your *e*ways, you have not glorified.

24 *a*Dan. 5:5

24 "Then the *a*hand was sent from Him, and this inscription was written out.

★25

25 "Now this is the inscription that was written out: 'MENĒ, MENĒ, TEKĒL, UPHARSIN.'

26 *a*Is. 13:6, 17-19; Jer. 50:41-43

26 "This is the interpretation of the message: 'MENĒ'—God has numbered your kingdom and *a*put an end to it.

27 *a*Job 31:6; Ps. 62:9

27 "'TEKĒL'—you have been *a*weighed on the scales and found deficient.

★28 *a*Is. 13:17; 21:2; 45:1, 2; Dan. 5:31; 6:8, 28; Acts 2:9

28 "'PERĒS'—your kingdom has been divided and given over to the *a*Medes and Persians."

29 *a*Dan. 5:7, 16

29 Then Belshazzar gave orders, and they *a*clothed Daniel with purple and *put* a necklace of gold around his neck, and issued a proclamation concerning him that he *now* had authority as the third *ruler* in the kingdom.

D Darius' Contribution to the Feast: Destruction of Babylon, 5:30-31

★30 *a*Dan. 5:1, 2 *b*Is. 21:4-9; 47:9; Jer. 51:11, 31, 39, 57

30 That same night *a*Belshazzar the Chaldean king was *b*slain.

5:25 The writing was not in an unknown language, though possibly in an unusual script and perhaps also mixed up as an anagram. In any case the meaning was unknown until Daniel interpreted it.

5:28 *PERES*. The singular of *PHARSIN* (v. 25;

the U means "and").

5:30 Herodotus and Xenophon testify that the city was entered by diverting the Euphrates River, and that the enemy entered to find the people in a drunken festival (on Oct. 11 or 12, 539 B.C.).

31 So aDarius the Mede received the kingdom at about the age of sixty-two.

VI DANIEL IN THE LIONS' DEN,
6:1-28
A The Position of Daniel,
6:1-3

6 It seemed good to Darius to appoint 120 satraps over the kingdom, that they should be in charge of the whole kingdom,

2 and over them three commissioners (of whom aDaniel was one), that these satraps might be accountable to them, and that the king might not suffer bloss.

3 Then this Daniel began distinguishing himself among the commissioners and satraps because he possessed an aextraordinary spirit, and the king planned to appoint him over the bentire kingdom.

B The Plot against Daniel,
6:4-9

4 Then the commissioners and satraps began atrying to find a ground of accusation against Daniel in regard to government affairs; but they could find bno ground of accusation or *evidence of corruption*, inasmuch as he was faithful, and no negligence or corruption was *to be* found in him.

5 Then these men said, "We shall not find any ground of accusation against this Daniel unless we find *it* against him with regard to the alaw of his God."

6 Then these commissioners and satraps came by agreement to the king and spoke to him as follows: "King Darius, alive forever!

7 "All the acommissioners of the kingdom, the prefects and the satraps, the high officials and the governors have bconsulted together that the king should establish a statute and enforce an injunction that anyone who makes a petition to any god or man besides you, O king, for thirty days, shall cbe cast into the lions' den.

8 "Now, O king, aestablish the injunction and sign the document so that it may not be changed, according to the blaw of the Medes and Persians, which may not be revoked."

9 Therefore King Darius asigned the document, that is, the injunction.

C The Prayer of Daniel,
6:10-11

10 Now when Daniel knew that the document was signed, he entered his house (now in his roof chamber he had windows open atoward Jerusalem); and he continued bkneeling on his knees three times a day, cpraying and dgiving thanks before his God, as he had been doing previously.

11 Then these men came aby agreement and found Daniel making petition and supplication before his God.

D The Prosecution of Daniel,
6:12-17

12 Then they approached and aspoke before the king about the king's injunction, "Did you not sign an injunction that any man who makes a petition to any god or man besides you, O king, for

---

5:31 *Darius.* His identity is uncertain. He may have been Gubaru, a governor under Cyrus the king of Persia; or Darius may be another name for Cyrus himself; or he may have been Cambyses, son of Cyrus, who served as ruler of Babylon.
6:1 *120 satraps.* 120 assistants to Darius.
6:2 *the king might not suffer loss.* I.e., have no financial loss. That is why he wanted someone

trustworthy like Daniel.
6:8 The unchangeableness of Medo-Persian law is seen in Esther 1:19; 8:8.
6:10 *toward Jerusalem.* A practice suggested by David and Solomon (Psalm 5:7; 1 Kings 8:33). Daniel's example is one of legitimate disobedience to the government (cf. Acts 5:29; Rom. 13:1-2).

thirty days, is to be cast into the lions' den?" The king answered and said, "The statement is true, according to the ᵇlaw of the Medes and Persians, which may not be revoked."

13 Then they answered and spoke before the king, "ᵃDaniel, who is one of the exiles from Judah, pays ᵇno attention to you, O king, or to the injunction which you signed, but keeps making his petition three times a day."

14 Then, as soon as the king heard this statement, he was deeply ᵃdistressed and set *his* mind on delivering Daniel; and even until sunset he kept exerting himself to rescue him.

15 Then these men came by agreement to the king and said to the king, "Recognize, O king, that it is a ᵃlaw of the Medes and Persians that no injunction or statute which the king establishes may be changed."

16 Then the king gave orders, and Daniel was brought in and ᵃcast into the lions' den. The king spoke and said to Daniel, "ᵇYour God whom you constantly serve will Himself deliver you."

17 And a ᵃstone was brought and laid over the mouth of the den; and the king sealed it with his own signet ring and with the signet rings of his nobles, so that nothing might be changed in regard to Daniel.

E The Protection of Daniel,
6:18–28

18 Then the king went off to his palace and spent the night ᵃfasting, and no entertainment was brought before him; and his ᵇsleep fled from him.

19 Then the king arose with the dawn, at the break of day, and went in haste to the lions' den.

20 And when he had come near the den to Daniel, he cried out with a troubled voice. The king spoke and said to Daniel, "Daniel, servant of the living God, has ᵃyour God, whom you constantly serve, been ᵇable to deliver you from the lions?"

21 Then Daniel spoke to the king, "ᵃO king, live forever!

22 "My God ᵃsent His angel and ᵇshut the lions' mouths, and they have not harmed me, inasmuch as I was found innocent before Him; and also toward you, O king, I have committed no crime."

23 Then the king was very pleased and gave orders for Daniel to be taken up out of the den. So Daniel was taken up out of the den, and ᵃno injury whatever was found on him, because he had ᵇtrusted in his God.

24 The king then gave orders, and they brought those men who had maliciously accused Daniel, and they ᵃcast them, their ᵇchildren, and their wives into the lions' den; and they had not reached the bottom of the den before the lions overpowered them and crushed all their bones.

25 Then Darius the king wrote to all the ᵃpeoples, nations, and *men of every* language who were living in all the land: "ᵇMay your peace abound!

26 "I ᵃmake a decree that in all the dominion of my kingdom men are to fear and tremble before the God of Daniel;

For He is the ᵇliving God
   and ᶜenduring for-
   ever,
And ᵈHis kingdom is
   one which will not be
   destroyed,
And His dominion *will*
   be forever.

27 "He delivers and rescues
   and performs ᵃsigns
   and wonders
In heaven and on earth,
Who has *also* delivered
   Daniel   from   the
   power of the lions."

13 ᵃDan. 2:25; 5:13
ᵇEsth. 3:8; Dan. 3:12; Acts 5:29

14 ᵃMark 6:26

15 ᵃEsth. 8:8; Ps. 94:20, 21; Dan. 6:8, 12

★**16** ᵃ2 Sam. 3:39; Jer. 38:5; Dan. 6:7 ᵇJob 5:19; Ps. 37:39, 40; Is. 41:10; Dan. 3:17, 28; 6:20; 2 Cor. 1:10

17 ᵃLam. 3:53; Matt. 27:66

18 ᵃ2 Sam. 12:16, 17 ᵇEsth. 6:1; Ps. 77:4; Dan. 2:1

20 ᵃDan. 6:16, 27 ᵇGen. 18:14; Num. 11:23; Jer. 32:17; Dan. 3:17

21 ᵃDan. 2:4; 6:6

22 ᵃNum. 20:16; Is. 63:9; Dan. 3:28; Acts 12:11; Heb. 1:14 ᵇPs. 91:11-13; 2 Tim. 4:17; Heb. 11:33

23 ᵃDan. 3:25, 27 ᵇ1 Chr. 5:20; 2 Chr. 20:20; Ps. 118:8, 9; Is. 26:3; Dan. 3:17, 28

★**24** ᵃDeut. 19:18, 19; Esth. 7:10 ᵇDeut. 24:16; 2 Kin. 14:6; Esth. 9:10

25 ᵃEzra 1:1, 2; Esth. 3:12; 8:9; Dan. 4:1 ᵇEzra 4:17; 1 Pet. 1:2

26 ᵃEzra 6:8-12; 7:13, 21; Dan. 3:29 ᵇDan. 4:34; 6:20; Hos. 1:10; Rom. 9:26 ᶜPs. 93:1, 2; Mal. 3:6 ᵈDan. 2:44; 4:3; 7:14, 27; Luke 1:33

27 ᵃDan. 4:2, 3

6:16 *the lions' den.* A large (v. 24) underground cave with an opening at the top (v. 23) and probably one at the side.
6:24 This cruel punishment is typically Persian.

28 ^aDan.
1:21 ^b2 Chr.
36:22, 23;
Dan. 10:1

28 So this ^aDaniel enjoyed success in the reign of Darius and in the reign of ^bCyrus the Persian.

VII DANIEL'S VISION OF THE FOUR BEASTS AND THE ANCIENT OF DAYS, 7:1-28

A Historical Data, 7:1-3

★ **1** ^aJob
33:14-16;
Dan. 1:17;
2:1, 26-28;
4:5-9; Joel
2:28 ^bJer.
36:4, 32

7 In the first year of Belshazzar king of Babylon Daniel saw a ^adream and visions in his mind as he lay on his bed; then he ^bwrote the dream down and related the following summary of it.

2 ^aDan.
7:7, 13
^bRev. 7:1

2 Daniel said, "I was ^alooking in my vision by night, and behold, the ^bfour winds of heaven were stirring up the great sea.

★ **3** ^aDan.
7:17; Rev.
13:1; 17:8

3 "And four great ^abeasts were coming up from the sea, different from one another.

B The Vision and the Interpretation, 7:4-28

★ **4** ^aJer.
4:7

4 "The first was ^alike a lion and had the wings of an eagle. I kept looking until its wings were plucked, and it was lifted up from the ground and made to stand on two feet like a man; a human mind also was given to it.

★ **5**

5 "And behold, another beast, a second one, resembling a bear. And it was raised up on one side, and three ribs were in its mouth between its teeth; and thus they said to it, 'Arise, devour much meat!'

★ **6** ^aRev.
13:2 ^bDan.
8:22

6 "After this I kept looking, and behold, another one, ^alike a leopard, which had on its back four wings of a bird; the beast also had ^bfour heads, and dominion was given to it.

7 "After this I kept looking in the night visions, and behold, a ^afourth beast, dreadful and terrifying and extremely strong; and it had large iron teeth. It devoured and crushed, and trampled down the remainder with its feet; and it was different from all the beasts that were before it, and it had ^bten horns.

★ **7-8**

7 ^aDan.
7:19, 20, 23
^bRev. 12:3;
13:1

8 "While I was contemplating the horns, behold, ^aanother horn, a little one, came up among them, and three of the first horns were pulled out by the roots before it; and behold, this horn possessed eyes like the eyes of a man, and ^ba mouth uttering great boasts.

8 ^aDan. 8:9
^bRev.
13:5, 6

9 "I kept looking
Until ^athrones were set up,
And the Ancient of Days took His seat;
His ^bvesture was like white snow,
And the ^chair of His head like pure wool.
His ^dthrone was ablaze with flames,
Its ^ewheels were a burning fire.

★ **9** ^aRev.
20:4 ^bMark
9:3 ^cRev.
1:14 ^dEzek.
1:13, 26
^eEzek.
10:2, 6

10 "A river of ^afire was flowing
And coming out from before Him;
^bThousands upon thousands were attending Him,
And myriads upon myriads were standing before Him;
The ^ccourt sat,
And ^dthe books were opened.

10 ^aPs. 18:8;
50:3; 97:3;
Is. 30:27, 33
^bDeut. 33:2;
1 Kin. 22:19;
Rev. 5:11
^cPs. 96:11-
13; Dan.
7:22, 26
^dDan. 12:1;
Rev. 20:11-
15

7:1 In the first year of Belshazzar. I.e., 553 B.C., 14 years before the fall of Babylon described in chapter 5.

7:3 four great beasts. Representing the rulers of the four world empires previously described in Nebuchadnezzar's dream in chapter 2 (cf. 7:17).

7:4 like a lion . . . eagle. Both symbols (of strength and speed, respectively) were used of Babylon (cf. Jer. 4:7, 13).

7:5 resembling a bear. A symbol of the Medo-Persian Empire, known for its strength and fierceness in battle (cf. Isa. 13:17-18).

7:6 like a leopard. Representing the Greek Empire under Alexander the Great. After his death the empire had four heads; i.e., Asia Minor, Syria, Egypt, and Macedonia (cf. 8:8).

7:7-8 a fourth beast. Rome. The ten horns are explained in verse 24, and the little horn (Antichrist) in verses 24-25.

7:9 Ancient of Days. A reference to God as Judge (cf. Isa. 57:15).

11 aRev.
19:20; 20:10

11 "Then I kept looking because of the sound of the boastful words which the horn was speaking; I kept looking until the beast was slain, and its body was destroyed and given to the ªburning fire.

12 "As for the rest of the beasts, their dominion was taken away, but an extension of life was granted to them for an appointed period of time.

13 aMatt.
24:30; 26:64;
Mark 13:26;
14:62; Luke
21:27; Rev.
1:7, 13;
14:14

13 "I kept looking in the night visions,
And behold, with the clouds of heaven
One like a ªSon of Man was coming,
And He came up to the Ancient of Days
And was presented before Him.

14 aDan.
7:27; John
3:35; 1 Cor.
15:27; Eph.
1:20-22; Phil.
2:9-11; Rev.
1:6; 11:15
bDan. 2:37
cPs. 72:11;
102:22 dMic.
4:7; Luke
1:33 eHeb.
12:28

14 "And to Him was given ªdominion,
Glory and bª kingdom,
cThat all the peoples, nations, and men of every language
Might serve Him.
dHis dominion is an everlasting dominion
Which will not pass away;
eAnd His kingdom is one
Which will not be destroyed.

15 aDan. 7:1
bDan. 4:19;
7:28

15 "As for me, Daniel, my spirit was distressed within me, and the ªvisions in my mind kept bªlarming me.

16 aZech.
1:9, 19; Rev.
5:5; 7:13, 14
bDan. 8:16,
17; 9:22

16 "I approached one of those who were ªstanding by and began asking him the exact meaning of all this. So he btold me and made known to me the interpretation of these things:

18 aDan.
7:22, 25, 27
bPs. 149:5-
9; Is. 60:12-
14; Dan.
7:14; Rev.
2:26, 27;
20:4; 22:5

17 'These great beasts, which are four in number, are four kings who will arise from the earth.

18 'But the ªsaints of the Highest One will breceive the kingdom and possess the kingdom forever, for all ages to come.'

19 "Then I desired to know the exact meaning of the ªfourth beast, which was different from all the others, exceedingly dreadful, with its teeth of iron and its claws of bronze, and which devoured, crushed, and trampled down the remainder with its feet,

19 aDan.
7:7, 8

20 and the meaning of the ten horns that were on its head, and the other horn which came up, and before which three of them fell, namely, that horn which had eyes and a mouth uttering great boasts, and which was larger in appearance than its associates.

21 "I kept looking, and that horn was ªwaging war with the saints and overpowering them

21 aRev.
11:7; 13:7

22 until the Ancient of Days came, and ªjudgment was passed in favor of the saints of the Highest One, and the time arrived when the saints took possession of the kingdom.

22 aDan.
7:10; 1 Cor.
6:2, 3

23 "Thus he said: 'The fourth beast will be a fourth kingdom on the earth, which will be different from all the other kingdoms, and it will devour the whole earth and tread it down and crush it.

24 'As for the ªten horns, out of this kingdom ten kings will arise; and another will arise after them, and he will be different from the previous ones and will subdue three kings.

★24-27

★24 aDan.
7:7; Rev.
17:12

25 'And he will ªspeak out against the bMost High and cwear down the saints of the Highest One, and he will intend to make dalterations in times and in law; and they will be given into his hand for a etime, times, and half a time.

25 aDan.
11:36; Rev.
13:6 bDan.
3:26; 4:2, 17,
34 cRev.
13:7; 18:24
dDan. 2:21
eDan. 12:7;
Rev. 12:14

26 'But the court will sit for judgment, and his dominion will be ªtaken away, annihilated and destroyed forever.

26 aRev.
17:14; 19:2

7:24-27 Antichrist will march to power by subduing three of the 10 nations (v. 24), will blaspheme God (v. 25), will try in some way to change times and laws in order to promote his anti-Christian program (v. 25), and will persecute God's saints (they, v. 25) for the last three and one-half years of the Tribulation period.
7:24 The final form of the Roman world power will be a confederation of 10 nations who will arise simultaneously in the Tribulation days.

27 *a*Is. 54:3;
Dan. 7:14,
18, 22; Rev.
20:4 *b*Ps.
145:13; Is.
9:7; Dan.
2:44; 4:34;
7:14; Luke
1:33; Rev.
11:15; 22:5
*c*Ps. 2:6-12;
22:27; 72:11;
86:9; Is.
60:12; Rev.
11:1

28 *a*Dan.
4:19 *b*Luke
2:19, 51

★ 1

★ 2 *a*Num.
12:6; Dan.
7:2, 15; 8:3
*b*Neh. 1:1;
Esth. 1:2; 2:8
*c*Gen. 10:22;
14:1; Is.
11:11; Jer.
25:25; Ezek.
32:24

★ 3 *a*Dan.
8:20

4 *a*Deut.
33:17; 1 Kin.
22:11; Ezek.
34:21 *b*Dan.
11:3

27 'Then the *a*sovereignty, the dominion, and the greatness of *all* the kingdoms under the whole heaven will be given to the people of the saints of the Highest One; His kingdom *will be* an *b*everlasting kingdom, and all the dominions will *c*serve and obey Him.'

28 "At this point the revelation ended. As for me, Daniel, my thoughts were *a*greatly alarming me and my face grew pale, but I *b*kept the matter to myself."

VIII DANIEL'S VISION OF THE RAM, GOAT, AND LITTLE HORN, 8:1-27

A The Vision, 8:1-14

8 In the third year of the reign of Belshazzar the king a vision appeared to me, Daniel, subsequent to the one which appeared to me previously.

2 And I *a*looked in the vision, and it came about while I was looking, that I was in the citadel of *b*Susa, which is in the province of *c*Elam; and I looked in the vision, and I myself was beside the Ulai Canal.

3 Then I lifted my gaze and looked, and behold, a *a*ram which had two horns was standing in front of the canal. Now the two horns *were* long, but one *was* longer than the other, with the longer one coming up last.

4 I saw the ram *a*butting westward, northward, and southward, and no *other* beasts could

stand before him, nor was there anyone to rescue from his power; but *b*he did as he pleased and magnified *himself*.

5 While I was observing, behold, a male goat was coming from the west over the surface of the whole earth without touching the ground; and the goat *had* a *a*conspicuous horn between his eyes.

6 And he came up to the ram that had the two horns, which I had seen standing in front of the canal, and rushed at him in his mighty wrath.

7 And I saw him come beside the ram, and he was enraged at him; and he struck the ram and shattered his two horns, and the ram had no strength to withstand him. So he hurled him to the ground and trampled on him, and there was none to rescue the ram from his power.

8 Then the male goat magnified *himself* exceedingly. But as soon as *a*he was mighty, the *b*large horn was broken; and in its place there came up four conspicuous *horns* toward the *c*four winds of heaven.

9 And out of one of them came forth a rather *a*small horn which grew exceedingly great toward the south, toward the east, and toward the *b*Beautiful *Land*.

10 And it grew up to the host of heaven and caused some of the host and some of the *a*stars to fall to the earth, and it *b*trampled them down.

★ 5 *a*Dan.
8:8, 21; 11:3

★ 8 *a*2 Chr.
26:16; Dan.
5:20 *b*Dan.
8:22 *c*Dan.
7:2; Rev. 7:1

★ 9 *a*Dan.
8:23 *b*Ps.
48:2; Dan.
11:16, 41

★10-11

10 *a*Is.
14:13; Jer.
48:26; Rev.
12:4 *b*Dan.
7:7; 8:7

8:1 *a vision.* Concerning the second and third world empires, Medo-Persia (vv. 3-4, 20) and Greece (vv. 5-7, 21).

8:2 *Susa.* About 250 miles E. of Babylon.

8:3 *a ram.* Medo-Persia (v. 20). *with the longer one coming up last.* Lit., the higher one. Though Persia was the younger kingdom, under Cyrus it became the dominant one in 550.

8:5 *goat.* Greece. *a conspicuous horn.* Alexander the Great, whose army swept through Asia Minor, Syria, Egypt, and Mesopotamia from 334-331.

8:8 *the large horn was broken.* The death of Alexander, after which his kingdom was divided among his *four* generals. Cassander took

Macedonia; Lysimachus, Thrace and much of Asia Minor; Seleucus, Syria; and Ptolemy, Egypt.

8:9 *a . . . small horn.* Not the same as the horn of 7:8, which will arise out of the restored Roman Empire. This little horn came out of Greece and refers to Antiochus Epiphanes, who came to the throne in 175 B.C. and plundered the Temple in Jerusalem, desecrating it by offering pig's flesh on the altar. *the Beautiful Land.* I.e., Palestine.

8:10-11 *the host of heaven.* God's people, the Jews, who were horribly persecuted by Antiochus. The *Commander* is God.

11 a2 Kin. 19:22, 23; 2 Chr. 32:15-17; Is. 37:23; Dan. 8:25; 11:36, 37 bEzek. 46:14; Dan. 11:31; 12:11

12 aIs. 59:14

11 It even ªmagnified *itself* to be equal with the Commander of the host; and it removed the ᵇregular sacrifice from Him, and the place of His sanctuary was thrown down.

12 And on account of transgression the host will be given over *to the horn* along with the regular sacrifice; and it will ªfling truth to the ground and perform *its will* and prosper.

13 aDan. 4:13, 23; 1 Pet. 1:12 bPs. 74:10; 79:5; Is. 6:11; Dan. 12:6, 8; Rev. 6:10 cIs. 63:18; Jer. 12:10; Luke 21:24; Heb. 10:29; Rev. 11:2

★**14** aDan. 7:25; 12:7, 11; Rev. 11:2, 3; 12:14; 13:5

13 Then I heard a ªholy one speaking, and another holy one said to that particular one who was speaking, "ᵇHow long will the vision *about* the regular sacrifice apply, while the transgression causes horror, so as to allow both the holy place and the host to be ᶜtrampled?"

14 And he said to me, "For ª2,300 evenings *and* mornings; then the holy place will be properly restored."

B The Interpretation, 8:15-27
1 The ram, 8:15-20

15 aDan. 8:1 bDan. 7:13; 10:16, 18

15 And it came about when ªI, Daniel, had seen the vision, that I sought to understand it; and behold, standing before me was one who looked like a ᵇman.

★**16** aDan. 9:21; Luke 1:19, 26

16 And I heard the voice of a man between *the banks of* Ulai, and he called out and said, "ªGabriel, give this *man* an understanding of the vision."

17 aEzek. 1:28; 44:4; Dan. 2:46; Rev. 1:17 bDan. 8:19; 11:35, 40

17 So he came near to where I was standing, and when he came I was frightened and ªfell on my face; but he said to me, "Son of man, understand that the vision pertains to the ᵇtime of the end."

18 aDan. 10:9; Luke 9:32 bEzek. 2:2; Dan. 10:10, 16, 18

18 Now while he was talking with me, I ªsank into a deep sleep with my face to the ground; but

he ᵇtouched me and made me stand upright.

19 And he said, "Behold, I am going to ªlet you know what will occur at the final period of the indignation, for *it* pertains to the appointed time of the end.

19 aDan. 8:15-17

20 "The ªram which you saw with the two horns represents the kings of Media and Persia.

20 aDan. 8:3

2 The goat, 8:21-22

21 "And the shaggy goat *represents* the kingdom of Greece, and the large horn that is between his eyes is the first king.

22 "And the ªbroken *horn* and the four *horns that* arose in its place *represent* four kingdoms *which* will arise from *his* nation, although not with his power.

22 aDan. 8:8

3 The little horn, 8:23-25

23 "And in the latter period of their rule, When the transgressors have run *their course,* A king will arise Insolent and skilled in intrigue.

★**23-25**

24 "And his power will be mighty, but not by his *own* power, And he will ªdestroy to an extraordinary degree And prosper and perform *his will;* He will destroy mighty men and the holy people.

24 aDan. 8:11-13; 11:36; 12:7

25 "And through his shrewdness He will cause deceit to succeed by his influence; And he will magnify *himself* in his heart,

25 aDan. 8:11 bJob 34:20; Dan. 2:34, 45

8:14 Antiochus' persecution of the Jews would last for 2,300 days, the period from 171 B.C. (when peaceful relations between Antiochus and the Jews came to an end) to Dec. 25, 165 B.C. (when Judas Maccabeus restored the Temple for its proper worship).

8:16 *Gabriel.* An angel, whose name means "hero of God" and who often brought impor-

tant messages to various individuals (9:21; Luke 1:19, 26). The only other good angel mentioned by name in the Bible is Michael (see 10:13; Jude 9).

8:23-25 These verses give added details concerning Antiochus and his persecution of the Jews (see 1 Maccabees 1-6).

And he will destroy many while *they are* at ease.
He will even ᵃoppose the Prince of princes,
But he will be broken ᵇwithout human agency.

4 The effect on Daniel, 8:26-27

26ᵃDan. 10:1 ᵇEzek. 12:27; Dan. 12:4, 9; Rev. 22:10 ᶜDan. 10:14

26 "And the vision of the evenings and mornings
Which has been told is ᵃtrue;
But ᵇkeep the vision secret,
For *it* pertains to many ᶜdays *in the future*."

27ᵃDan. 7:28; 8:17; Hab. 3:16 ᵇDan. 2:48

27 Then I, Daniel, was ᵃexhausted and sick for days. Then I got up *again* and ᵇcarried on the king's business; but I was astounded at the vision, and there was none to explain *it*.

IX DANIEL'S PROPHECY OF SEVENTY WEEKS OF YEARS, 9:1-27

A Historical Data, 9:1-2

★ 1 ᵃDan. 5:31; 11:1

9 In the first year of ᵃDarius the son of Ahasuerus, of Median descent, who was made king over the kingdom of the Chaldeans—

★ 2 ᵃ2 Chr. 36:21; Ezra 1:1; Jer. 25:11, 12; 29:10; Zech. 7:5

2 in the first year of his reign I, Daniel, observed in the books the number of the years which was *revealed as* the word of the LORD to ᵃJeremiah the prophet for the completion of the desolations of Jerusalem, *namely*, ᵃseventy years.

B Daniel's Prayer, 9:3-19

★ 3-19

3 So I gave my attention to the Lord God to seek *Him by* prayer and supplications, with fasting, sackcloth, and ashes.

4ᵃDeut. 7:21; Neh. 9:32 ᵇDeut. 7:9

4 And I prayed to the LORD my God and confessed and said, "Alas, O Lord, the ᵃgreat and awesome God, who ᵇkeeps His covenant and lovingkindness for those who love Him and keep His commandments,

5ᵃ1 Kin. 8:48; Neh. 9:33; Ps. 106:6; Is. 64:5-7; Jer. 14:7 ᵇLam. 1:18, 20 ᶜPs. 119:176; Is. 53:6; Dan. 9:11

5 ᵃwe have sinned, committed iniquity, acted wickedly, and ᵇrebelled, even ᶜturning aside from Thy commandments and ordinances.

6ᵃ2 Chr. 36:16; Jer. 44:4, 5

6 "Moreover, we have not ᵃlistened to Thy servants the prophets, who spoke in Thy name to our kings, our princes, our fathers, and all the people of the land.

7ᵃJer. 23:6; 33:16; Dan. 9:18 ᵇPs. 44:15; Jer. 2:26, 27; 3:25 ᶜDeut. 4:27

7 "ᵃRighteousness belongs to Thee, O Lord, but to us ᵇopen shame, as it is this day—to the men of Judah, the inhabitants of Jerusalem, and all Israel, those who are nearby and those who are far away in ᶜall the countries to which Thou hast driven them, because of their unfaithful deeds which they have committed against Thee.

8 "Open shame belongs to us, O Lord, to our kings, our princes, and our fathers, because we have sinned against Thee.

9ᵃNeh. 9:17; Ps. 130:4 ᵇPs. 106:43; Jer. 14:7; Dan. 9:5, 6

9 "To the Lord our God belong ᵃcompassion and forgiveness, for we have ᵇrebelled against Him;

10ᵃ2 Kin. 17:13-15; 18:12

10 nor have we obeyed the voice of the LORD our God, to walk in His teachings which He ᵃset before us through His servants the prophets.

9:1 *In the first year of Darius.* I.e., 538 B.C., 67 years after Daniel had been taken from Palestine. This is the same Darius as in chap. 6.
9:2 *in the books.* Daniel understood, from his knowledge of Jer. 25:11-12, that it was about time for the *desolations of Jerusalem* to be finished.
9:3-19 In this remarkable prayer of confession

(see Ezra 9 and Neh. 9 for similar prayers), Daniel associated himself with the sins of his people 32 times. He approaches God on the basis of His loyal love (see note on Hos. 2:19) in His covenant with Israel (v. 4), confesses their sins (vv. 5-10), acknowledges their deserved judgment (vv. 11-14), and supplicates God for His mercy (vv. 15-19).

11 aIs. 1:3,
4; Jer. 8:5-10
bDeut.
27:15-26

11 "Indeed aall Israel has transgressed Thy law and turned aside, not obeying Thy voice; so the bcurse has been poured out on us, along with the oath which is written in the law of Moses the servant of God, for we have sinned against Him.

12 aIs.
44:26; Jer.
44:2-6; Lam.
2:17; Zech.
1:6 bJob
12:17; Ps.
82:2-7;
148:11
cLam. 1:12;
2:13; Ezek.
5:9

12 "Thus He has aconfirmed His words which He had spoken against us and against our brulers who ruled us, to bring on us great calamity; for under the whole heaven there has cnot been done *anything* like what was done to Jerusalem.

13 aLev.
26:14-45;
Deut. 28:15-
68; Dan. 9:11
bJob 36:13;
Is. 9:13; Jer.
2:30; 5:3
cJer. 31:18

13 "As it is written in the alaw of Moses, all this calamity has come on us; yet we have bnot sought the favor of the LORD our God by cturning from our iniquity and giving attention to Thy truth.

14 aJer.
31:28; 44:27
bPs. 51:14;
Dan. 9:7

14 "Therefore, the LORD has akept the calamity in store and brought it on us; for the LORD our God is brighteous with respect to all His deeds which He has done, but we have not obeyed His voice.

15 aDeut.
5:15 bNeh.
9:10; Jer.
32:20

15 "And now, O Lord our God, who hast abrought Thy people out of the land of Egypt with a mighty hand and hast bmade a name for Thyself, as it is this day—we have sinned, we have been wicked.

16 aJer.
32:31, 32
bPs. 87:1-3;
Dan. 9:20;
Joel 3:17;
Zech. 8:3
cEzek. 5:14

16 "O Lord, in accordance with all Thy righteous acts, let now Thine aanger and Thy wrath turn away from Thy city Jerusalem, Thy bholy mountain; for because of our sins and the iniquities of our fathers, Jerusalem and Thy people *have become* a creproach to all those around us.

17 aNum.
6:24-26; Ps.
80:3, 7, 19
bLam. 5:18

17 "So now, our God, listen to the prayer of Thy servant and to his supplications, and for Thy sake, O Lord, alet Thy face shine on Thy bdesolate sanctuary.

18 aIs. 37:17
bPs. 80:14
cJer. 7:10-12
dJer. 36:7

18 "O my God, aincline Thine ear and hear! Open Thine eyes and bsee our desolations and the city which is ccalled by Thy name; for we are not dpresenting our supplications before Thee on account of any merits of our own, but on account of Thy great compassion.

19 aPs.
44:23; 74:10,
11

19 "O Lord, hear! O Lord, forgive! O Lord, listen and take action! For Thine own sake, O my God, ado not delay, because Thy city and Thy people are called by Thy name."

C   The Prophecy, 9:20-27

20 aPs.
145:18; Is.
58:9; Dan.
9:3; 10:12
bIs. 6:5

20   Now while I was aspeaking and praying, and bconfessing my sin and the sin of my people Israel, and presenting my supplication before the LORD my God in behalf of the holy mountain of my God,

*21 aDan.
8:16; Luke
1:19, 26
bEx. 29:39;
1 Kin. 18:36;
Ezra 9:4

21   while I was still speaking in prayer, then the man aGabriel, whom I had seen in the vision previously, came to me in *my* extreme weariness about the time of the bevening offering.

22 aDan.
8:16; 10:21;
Zech. 1:9

22   And he gave *me* instruction and talked with me, and said, "O Daniel, I have now come forth to give you insight with aunderstanding.

23 aDan.
10:12 bDan.
10:11, 19
cMatt. 24:15

23   "At the abeginning of your supplications the command was issued, and I have come to tell *you,* for you are bhighly esteemed; so give heed to the message and gain cunderstanding of the vision.

*24 aLev.
25:8; Num.
14:34; Ezek.
4:5, 6
b2 Chr.
29:24; Is.
53:10; Rom.
5:10 cIs.
51:6, 8; 56:1;
Jer. 23:5, 6;
Rom. 3:21,
22

24   "Seventy aweeks have been decreed for your people and your holy city, to finish the transgres-

---

9:21 *about the time of the evening offering.* About 3 p.m. (cf. Exod. 29:39).
9:24 *Seventy weeks.* Lit., seventy sevens, but obviously years are meant since Daniel had been thinking of the years of the captivity (9:2). Furthermore, weeks of days are so speci-

fied in 10:2-3, where the Hebrew adds "days." This period of 490 years concerns *your people* (the Jews) and *your holy city* (Jerusalem). *to finish the transgression.* To end the apostasy of the Jews. *to make an end of sin.* May mean either to atone for sin or to seal up sin in the

sion, to make an end of sin, to [b]make atonement for iniquity, to bring in [c]everlasting righteousness, to seal up vision and prophecy, and to anoint the most holy *place.*

★25 [a]Ezra 4:24; 6:1-15; Neh. 2:1-8; 3:1 [b]John 1:41; 4:25 [c]Is. 9:6; Dan. 8:11, 25

25 "So you are to know and discern *that* from the issuing of a [a]decree to restore and rebuild Jerusalem until [b]Messiah the [c]Prince *there will be* seven weeks and sixty-two weeks; it will be built again, with plaza and moat, even in times of distress.

★26 [a]Is. 53:8; Mark 9:12; Luke 24:26 [b]Matt. 24:2; Mark 13:2; Luke 19:43, 44 [c]Nah. 1:8

26 "Then after the sixty-two weeks the Messiah will be [a]cut off and have nothing, and the people of the prince who is to come will [b]destroy the city and the sanctuary. And its end *will come* with a [c]flood; even to the end there will be war; desolations are determined.

★27 [a]Dan. 11:31; Matt. 24:15; Mark 13:14; Luke 21:20 [b]Is. 10:23; 28:22

27 "And he will make a firm covenant with the many for one week, but in the middle of the week he will put a stop to sacrifice and grain offering; and on the wing of [a]abominations *will come* one who makes desolate, even until a [b]complete destruction, one

that is decreed, is poured out on the one who makes desolate."

X DANIEL'S PROPHETIC PANORAMA, 10:1–12:13

A Daniel's Vision, 10:1-9

10 In the third year of [a]Cyrus king of Persia a message was revealed to [b]Daniel, who was named Belteshazzar; and the [c]message was true and *one of* great conflict, but he understood the message and had an [d]understanding of the vision.

★1 [a]Dan. 1:21; 6:28 [b]Dan. 1:7 [c]Dan. 8:26 [d]Dan. 1:17; 2:21

2 In those days I, Daniel, had been [a]mourning for three entire weeks.

★2 [a]Ezra 9:4, 5; Neh. 1:4

3 I [a]did not eat any tasty food, nor did meat or wine enter my mouth, nor did I use any ointment at all, until the entire three weeks were completed.

3 [a]Dan. 6:18

4 And on the twenty-fourth day of the first month, while I was by the bank of the great [a]river, that is, the Tigris,

★4 [a]Ezek. 1:3; Dan. 8:2

5 I lifted my eyes and looked, and behold, there was a certain man [a]dressed in linen,

5 [a]Ezek. 9:2; Dan. 12:6, 7 [b]Rev. 1:13; 15:6 [c]Jer. 10:9

---

sense of judging it finally. *to make atonement for iniquity.* Refers to the death of Christ on the cross, which is the basis for Israel's future forgiveness (Zech. 12:10; Rom. 11:26–27). *to bring in everlasting righteousness.* In the millennial kingdom of Messiah (Jer. 23:5-6). *to seal up vision and prophecy.* To set God's seal of fulfillment on all the prophecies concerning the Jewish people and Jerusalem. *to anoint the most holy place.* The anointing of the Holy of Holies in the millennial Temple.
9:25 The seventy sevens begin with *a decree to restore and rebuild Jerusalem,* the commandment of Artaxerxes Longimanus given in 445 B.C. (Neh. 2:5). Earlier, Cyrus had authorized the rebuilding of the Temple (in 538; 2 Chron. 36:22–23; Ezra 1:1-4). *with plaza and moat.* The public square and moat were rebuilt by the time the first 7 weeks (49 years) were completed.
9:26 Certain important events were to happen *after the sixty-two weeks* (plus the 7 weeks, or a total of 69 weeks): the crucifixion of *Messiah* and the destruction of Jerusalem in A.D. 70 by

the Romans who are *the people of the prince who is to come.* Since these events were to occur after the 69 weeks had run their course and before the seventieth week began, there must be a space of time between the conclusion of the sixty-ninth week and the beginning of the seventieth.
9:27 *he.* The prince of verse 26, the Antichrist previously introduced in 7:8, 24–26, who will make a pact with *many* (of the Jewish people) at the beginning of the Tribulation period. But *in the middle of the week* (i.e., 3½ years later) Antichrist will break his covenant and desecrate the Temple by demanding worship of himself in it (see notes on Matt. 24:15 and 2 Thess. 2:4).
10:1 *the third year of Cyrus.* 536 B.C.
10:2 *three entire weeks.* Lit., weeks of days.
10:4 Obviously Daniel was not among those who returned to build the Temple in Jerusalem in connection with Cyrus' decree (9:25). His age (middle 80's) and governmental duties prevented him.

whose waist was *b*girded with a belt of pure *c*gold of Uphaz.

6 aRev.
1:14; 2:18;
19:12

6 His body also was like beryl, his face had the appearance of lightning, *a*his eyes were like flaming torches, his arms and feet like the gleam of polished bronze, and the sound of his words like the sound of a tumult.

7 a2 Kin.
6:17-20
bActs 9:7
cEzek. 12:18

7 Now I, Daniel, *a*alone saw the vision, while the *b*men who were with me did not see the vision; nevertheless, a great *c*dread fell on them, and they ran away to hide themselves.

8 aGen.
32:24 bDan.
7:28; 8:27;
Hab. 3:16

8 So I was *a*left alone and saw this great vision; yet *b*no strength was left in me, for my natural color turned to a deathly pallor, and I retained no strength.

9 aGen.
15:12; Job
4:13; Dan.
8:18

9 But I heard the sound of his words; and as soon as I heard the sound of his words, I *a*fell into a deep sleep on my face, with my face to the ground.

B Daniel's Strengthening, 10:10–11:1

10 aJer. 1:9;
Dan. 8:18

10 Then behold, a hand *a*touched me and set me trembling on my hands and knees.

11 aDan.
10:19 bDan.
8:16, 17
cEzek. 2:1
dJob 4:14,
15

11 And he said to me, "O *a*Daniel, man of high esteem, *b*understand the words that I am about to tell you and *c*stand upright, for I have now been sent to you." And when he had spoken this word to me, I stood up *d*trembling.

★12 aIs.
41:10, 14;
Dan. 10:19
bDan. 9:20-
23; 10:2, 3
cActs 10:30,
31

12 Then he said to me, "*a*Do not be afraid, Daniel, for from the first day that you set your heart on understanding *this* and on *b*humbling yourself before your God, your words were heard, and

I have come in response *c*to your words.

13 "But the prince of the kingdom of Persia was withstanding me for twenty-one days; then behold, *a*Michael, one of the chief princes, came to help me, for I had been left there with the kings of Persia.

★13 aDan.
10:21; 12:1;
Jude 9; Rev.
12:7

14 "Now I have come to *a*give you an understanding of what will happen to your people in the *b*latter days, for the vision pertains to *c*the days yet *future.*"

★14 aDan.
8:16; 9:22
bDeut.
31:29; Dan.
2:28 cDan.
8:26; 12:4, 9

15 And when he had spoken to me according to these words, I turned my face toward the ground and became *a*speechless.

15 aEzek.
3:26; 24:27;
Luke 1:20

16 And behold, *a*one who resembled a human being was *b*touching my lips; then I opened my mouth and spoke, and said to him who was standing before me, "O my lord, as a result of the vision *c*anguish has come upon me, and I have retained no strength.

16 aDan.
8:15 bIs. 6:7;
Jer. 1:9
cDan. 7:15,
28; 8:17, 27;
10:8, 9

17 "For *a*how can such a servant of my lord talk with such as my lord? As for me, there remains just now *b*no strength in me, nor has any breath been left in me."

17 aEx.
24:10, 11; Is.
6:1-5 bDan.
10:8

18 Then *this* one with human appearance touched me again and *a*strengthened me.

18 aIs.
35:3, 4

19 And he said, "O man of high esteem, *a*do not be afraid. Peace be with you; take *b*courage and be courageous!" Now as soon as he spoke to me, I received strength and said, "May my lord speak, for you have *c*strengthened me."

19 aJudg.
6:23; Is.
43:1; Dan.
10:12 bJosh.
1:6, 7, 9; Is.
35:4 cPs.
138:3; 2 Cor.
12:9

20 Then he said, "Do you understand why I came to you? But I shall now return to fight against the prince of Persia; so I am going forth, and behold, the *a*prince of Greece is about to come.

20 aDan.
8:21; 11:2

10:12 Daniel's prayer was heard on the first day of the three-week period, but the answer was delayed because of angelic warfare.

10:13 *the prince of the kingdom of Persia.* A supernatural creature who tried to direct the human rulers of Persia to oppose God's plan. Evil angels seek to influence the affairs of nations. *Michael*, which means "who is like God?" (v. 21; 12:1; Jude 9; Rev. 12:7), is the special guardian of the affairs of Israel (12:1) and is

designated the archangel (Jude 9). *I had been left there with the kings of Persia.* The good angel (cf. vv. 5–6), with Michael's help, was left in a place of preeminence in influencing Persia. But the battle between good and evil angels over the control of nations continues (see v. 20).

10:14 *the latter days.* Future days culminating in the events surrounding the second coming of Christ (cf. Gen. 49:1; Dan. 2:28).

21 *aDan.
12:4 *bDan.
10:13; Rev.
12:7

21 "However, I will tell you what is inscribed in the writing of *a truth. Yet there is no one who stands firmly with me against these *forces* except *bMichael your prince.

1 *aDan.
5:31; 9:1

11 "And in the *afirst year of Darius the Mede, I arose to be an encouragement and a protection for him.

C Prophecies Concerning the Nations, 11:2-45
1 Persia, 11:2

★ 2 *aDan.
8:26; 10:1,
21 *bDan.
8:21; 10:20

2 "And now I will tell you the *atruth. Behold, three more kings are going to arise in Persia. Then a fourth will gain far more riches than all *of them;* as soon as he becomes strong through his riches, he will arouse the whole *empire* against the realm of *bGreece.

2 Greece, 11:3-4

★ 3-4
3 *aDan.
8:5, 21
*bDan. 5:19;
8:4; 11:16,
36

3 "And a *amighty king will arise, and he will rule with great authority and *bdo as he pleases.

4 *aDan.
8:8, 22 *bJer.
49:36; Ezek.
37:9; Dan.
7:2; 8:8;
Zech. 2:6;
Rev. 7:1
*cJer. 12:15,
17; 18:7

4 "But as soon as he has arisen, his kingdom will be broken up and parceled out *atoward the *bfour points of the compass, though not to his *own* descendants, nor according to his authority which he wielded; for his sovereignty will be *cuprooted and *given* to others besides them.

3 Egypt and Syria, 11:5-20

★ 5 *aDan.
11:9, 11, 14,
25, 40

5 "Then the *aking of the South will grow strong, along with *one* of his princes who will gain ascendancy over him and obtain dominion; his domain *will be* a great dominion *indeed.*

6 "And after some years they will form an alliance, and the daughter of the king of the South will come to the *aking of the North to carry out a peaceful arrangement. But she will not retain her position of power, nor will he remain with his power, but she will be given up, along with those who brought her in, and the one who sired her, as well as he who supported her in *those* times.

★ 6 *aDan.
11:7, 13, 15,
40

7 "But one of the descendants of her line will arise in his place, and he will come against *their* army and enter the *afortress of the king of the North, and he will deal with them and display *great* strength.

★ 7-8

7 *aDan.
11:19, 38, 39

8 "And also their *agods with their metal images *and* their precious vessels of silver and gold he will take into captivity to Egypt, and he on his part will refrain from *attacking* the king of the North for *some* years.

8 *aIs.
37:19; 46:1,
2; Jer.
43:12, 13

9 "Then the latter will enter the realm of the king of the South, but will return to his *own* land.

★ 9-13

10 "And his sons will mobilize and assemble a multitude of great forces; and one of them will keep on coming and *aoverflow and pass through, that he may again wage war up to his *very* fortress.

10 *aIs. 8:8;
Jer. 46:7, 8;
51:42; Dan.
11:26, 40

11 "And the *aking of the South will be enraged and go forth and

11 *aDan.
11:5

11:2 Here begins a remarkable section of detailed prophecy, first about Persia (v. 2), then Alexander the Great (vv. 3-4), the Ptolemies and Seleucids until Antiochus Epiphanes (vv. 5-20), Antiochus Epiphanes (vv. 21-35). All the details of these predictions have since been fulfilled accurately. Next Daniel gives a prophecy about Antichrist yet to be fulfilled (vv. 36-45). *three more kings.* Cambyses (529-522), Pseudo-Smerdis (522-521), Darius I Hystaspes (also called Darius the Great, 521-486; cf. Ezra 5-6). *a fourth.* Xerxes (486-465), known in the book of Esther as Ahasuerus.
11:3-4 *a mighty king.* Alexander the Great (see note on 8:8).

11:5 This section (vv. 5-20) traces the various struggles between the kings of the south (the Ptolemies of Egypt) and the kings of the north (the Seleucids of Syria). The *king of the South* in this verse is Ptolemy I, who ruled Egypt and *one of his princes* was Seleucus I Nicator, whose kingdom eventually stretched from Palestine to India.
11:6 Ptolemy II gave his daughter in marriage to Antiochus I, a Seleucid, but Antiochus deserted her and was later murdered.
11:7-8 *one of the descendants . . . will come.* Ptolemy III invaded Syria in 246.
11:9-13 A description of the seesaw struggles between the Seleucids and the Ptolemies between 223 and 200 B.C.

fight with the king of the North. Then the latter will raise a great multitude, but *that* multitude will be given into the hand of the *former.*

12 "When the multitude is carried away, his heart will be lifted up, and he will cause tens of thousands to fall; yet he will not prevail.

13 "For the king of the North will again raise a greater multitude than the former, and after an [a]interval of some years he will press on with a great army and much equipment.

14 "Now in those times many will rise up against the king of the South; the violent ones among your people will also lift themselves up in order to fulfill the vision, but they will fall down.

15 "Then the king of the North will come, cast up a [a]siege mound, and capture a well-fortified city; and the forces of the South will not stand *their ground,* not even their choicest troops, for there will be no strength to make a stand.

16 "But he who comes against him will [a]do as he pleases, and [b]no one will *be able to* withstand him; he will also stay *for a time* in the [c]Beautiful Land, with destruction in his hand.

17 "And he will [a]set his face to come with the power of his whole kingdom, bringing with him a proposal of peace which he will put into effect; he will also give him the daughter of women to ruin it. But she will not take a stand *for him* or be on his side.

18 "Then he will turn his face to the [a]coastlands and capture many. But a commander will put

a stop to his scorn against him; moreover, he will [b]repay him for his scorn.

19 "So he will turn his face toward the fortresses of his own land, but he will [a]stumble and fall and be [b]found no more.

20 "Then in his place one will arise who will [a]send an oppressor through the Jewel of *his* kingdom; yet within a few days he will be shattered, though neither in anger nor in battle.

4 Antiochus Epiphanes, 11:21–35

21 "And in his place a despicable person will arise, on whom the honor of kingship has not been conferred, but he will come in a time of tranquility and [a]seize the kingdom by intrigue.

22 "And the overflowing [a]forces will be flooded away before him and shattered, and also the prince of the covenant.

23 "And after an alliance is made with him he will practice deception, and he will go up and gain power with a small *force of* people.

24 "In a time of tranquility he will enter the [a]richest *parts* of the realm, and he will accomplish what his fathers never did, nor his ancestors; he will distribute plunder, booty, and possessions among them, and he will devise his schemes against strongholds, but *only* for a time.

25 "And he will stir up his strength and courage against the [a]king of the South with a large army; so the king of the South will mobilize an extremely large

13 [a]Dan. 4:16; 12:7

★15-20

15 [a]Jer. 6:6; Ezek. 4:2; 17:17

16 [a]Dan. 5:19; 11:3, 36 [b]Josh. 1:5 [c]Dan. 8:9; 11:41

17 [a]2 Kin. 12:17; Ezek. 4:3, 7

18 [a]Gen. 10:5; Is. 66:19; Jer. 2:10; 31:10; Zeph. 2:11 [b]Hos. 12:14

19 [a]Ps. 27:2; Jer. 46:6 [b]Job 20:8; Ps. 37:36; Ezek. 26:21

20 [a]Is. 60:17

★21-35

21 [a]2 Sam. 15:6

22 [a]Dan. 9:26; 11:10

24 [a]Num. 13:20; Neh. 9:25; Ezek. 34:14

25 [a]Dan. 11:5

11:15-20 Antiochus III (the Great) defeated the Egyptian army in Sidon (vv. 15–16). He came to terms with Ptolemy V and gave him his daughter in marriage (v. 17). He annexed the coastlands of Asia Minor and unsuccessfully tried to invade Greece (v. 18). He was defeated by the Romans at Magnesia in 190 B.C., was forced to pay tribute, and soon died (v. 19). He was succeeded by his son Seleucus IV (Philopator) who heavily taxed the people of Israel (v. 20).

11:21-35 These verses describe the career of Antiochus IV (Epiphanes, 175–164), who came to the throne by intrigue (v. 21), made several expeditions into Egypt (vv. 24–27), then turned his hatred on Israel (v. 28). The *ships of Kittim* refer to Roman power that came from the west past *Kittim* (Cyprus) to defeat Antiochus in Egypt. Venting his anger on the Jews, Antiochus declared the Mosaic ceremonies illegal and erected in the holy place a statue of Zeus (v. 31). Some Jews resisted and were martyred (vv. 32–33).

and mighty army for war; but he will not stand, for schemes will be devised against him.

26 "And those who eat his choice food will destroy him, and his army will [a]overflow, but many will fall down slain.

27 "As for both kings, their hearts will be *intent* on [a]evil, and they will [b]speak lies *to each other* at the same table; but it will not succeed, for the [c]end is still *to come* at the appointed time.

28 "Then he will return to his land with much plunder; but his heart will be *set* against the holy covenant, and he will take action and *then* return to his *own* land.

29 "At the appointed time he will return and come into the South, but this last time it will not turn out the way it did before.

30 "For ships of [a]Kittim will come against him; therefore he will be disheartened, and will return and become enraged at the holy covenant and take action; so he will come back and show regard for those who forsake the holy covenant.

31 "And forces from him will arise, [a]desecrate the sanctuary fortress, and do away with the regular sacrifice. And they will set up the [b]abomination of desolation.

32 "And by [a]smooth *words* he will turn to godlessness those who act wickedly toward the covenant, but the people who know their God will display [b]strength and take action.

33 "And [a]those who have insight among the people will give understanding to the many; yet

they will [b]fall by sword and by flame, by captivity and by plunder, for *many* days.

34 "Now when they fall they will be granted a little help, and many will [a]join with them in [b]hypocrisy.

35 "And some of those who have insight will fall, in order to [a]refine, [b]purge, and make them [c]pure, until the [d]end time; because *it is* still *to come* at the appointed time.

5 Antichrist, 11:36–45

36 "Then the king will [a]do as he pleases, and he will exalt and [b]magnify himself above every god, and will [c]speak monstrous things against the [d]God of gods; and he will prosper until the [e]indignation is finished, for that which is [f]decreed will be done.

37 "And he will show no regard for the gods of his fathers or for the desire of women, nor will he show regard for any *other* god; for he will magnify himself above *them* all.

38 "But instead he will honor a god of fortresses, a god whom his fathers did not know; he will honor *him* with gold, silver, costly stones, and treasures.

39 "And he will take action against the strongest of fortresses with *the help of* a foreign god; he will give great honor to those who acknowledge *him*, and he will cause them to rule over the many, and will parcel out land for a price.

40 "And at the [a]end time the [b]king of the South will collide with him, and the [c]king of the

---

Cross-references

26 [a]Dan. 11:10, 40

27 [a]Ps. 52:1; 64:6 [b]Ps. 12:2; Jer. 9:3-5; 41:1-3 [c]Dan. 8:19; 11:35, 40; Hab. 2:3

30 [a]Gen. 10:4; Num. 24:24; Is. 23:1, 12; Jer. 2:10

31 [a]Dan. 8:11-13; 12:11 [b]Dan. 9:27; Matt. 24:15; Mark 13:14

32 [a]Dan. 11:21, 34 [b]Mic. 5:7-9; Zech. 9:13-16; 10:3-6

33 [a]Mal. 2:7 [b]Matt. 24:9; John 16:2; Heb. 11:36-38

34 [a]Matt. 7:15; Acts 20:29, 30 [b]Dan. 11:21, 32; Rom. 16:18

35 [a]Deut. 8:16; Prov. 17:3; Dan. 12:10; Zech. 13:9; Mal. 3:2, 3 [b]John 15:2 [c]Rev. 7:14 [d]Dan. 11:27

★36 [a]Dan. 5:19; 11:3, 16 [b]Is. 14:13; Dan. 5:20; 8:11, 25; 2 Thess. 2:4 [c]Rev. 13:5, 6 [d]Deut. 10:17; Ps. 136:2; Dan. 2:47 [e]Is. 10:25; 26:20; Dan. 8:19 [f]Dan. 9:27

★37

★38

★40-45 40 [a]Dan. 11:27, 35; 12:4, 9 [b]Dan. 11:11, 25 [c]Dan. 11:7, 13, 15 [d]Is. 5:28; Jer. 4:13 [e]Dan. 11:10, 26

11:36 This section gives details of Antichrist's future career. Though some refer the section entirely to Antiochus, the scope also requires reference to some details of Israel's last days (10:14 and 12:1–2).

11:37 *the gods of his fathers.* Antichrist will have no respect for religion or religious heritages. He will be unkind, cruel, and inhumane.

11:38 Antichrist's "god" will be military power and activity.

11:40-45 In the Tribulation period *the king of the South* and *the king of the North* will at-

tempt a pincer movement against Antichrist (v. 40). But with Palestine as his base (v. 41), he will first defeat Egypt, then Libya and Ethiopia (Sudan). *follow at his heels.* Be part of his dominion. *rumors from the East and from the North.* May relate to the armies of Rev. 9:13–21; 16:12. The threat of these armies will cause Antichrist to return to Palestine, making his headquarters between Jerusalem and the Mediterranean (v. 45). But he will *come to his end* at the hands of the victorious, returning Christ (Rev. 19:11–21).

North will ^dstorm against him with chariots, with horsemen, and with many ships; and he will enter countries, ^eoverflow *them*, and pass through.

41 aDan.
8:9; 11:16
bJer. 48:47
cJer. 49:6

41 "He will also enter the ^aBeautiful Land, and many *countries* will fall; but these will be rescued out of his hand: Edom, ^bMoab and the foremost of the sons of ^cAmmon.

42 "Then he will stretch out his hand against *other* countries, and the land of Egypt will not escape.

43 a2 Chr.
12:3; Nah.
3:9 b2 Chr.
12:3; Ezek.
30:4, 5; Nah.
3:9

43 "But he will gain control over the hidden treasures of gold and silver, and over all the precious things of Egypt; and ^aLibyans and ^bEthiopians *will follow* at his heels.

44 "But rumors from the East and from the North will disturb him, and he will go forth with great wrath to destroy and annihilate many.

45 aIs. 11:9;
27:13; 65:25;
66:20; Dan.
9:16, 20

45 "And he will pitch the tents of his royal pavilion between the seas and the beautiful ^aHoly Mountain; yet he will come to his end, and no one will help him.

★ 1 aDan.
10:13, 21;
Rev. 12:7
bRev. 7:14;
16:18 cJer.
30:7; Ezek.
5:9; Dan.
9:12; Matt.
24:21; Mark
13:19 dDan.
7:10; 10:21

D   Prophecies Concerning Israel, 12:1-13

12 "Now at that time ^aMichael, the great prince who stands *guard* over the sons of your people, will arise. And there will be a ^btime of distress ^csuch as

never occurred since there was a nation until that time; and at that time your people, everyone who is found written in the ^dbook, will be rescued.

2 "And ^amany of those who sleep in the dust of the ground will awake, ^bthese to everlasting life, but the others to disgrace *and* everlasting contempt.

★ 2 aIs.
26:19; Ezek.
37:12-14
bMatt. 25:46;
John 5:28,
29

3 "And those who have ^ainsight will ^bshine brightly like the brightness of the expanse of heaven, and those who ^clead the many to righteousness, like the stars forever and ever.

★ 3 aDan.
11:33, 35;
12:10 bJohn
5:35 cIs.
53:11; Dan.
11:33

4 "But as for you, Daniel, ^aconceal these words and ^bseal up the book until the ^cend of time; ^dmany will go back and forth, and knowledge will increase."

★ 4 aDan.
8:26; 12:9
bIs. 8:16;
Dan. 12:9;
Rev. 22:10
cDan. 8:17;
12:9, 13 dIs.
11:9; 29:18,
19; Dan.
11:33

5 Then I, Daniel, looked and behold, two others were standing, one on this bank of the river, and the other on that bank of the river.

6 And ^aone said to the man ^bdressed in linen, who was above the waters of the river, "^cHow long *will it be* until the end of these wonders?"

6 aDan.
8:16; Zech.
1:12, 13
bEzek. 9:2;
Dan. 10:5
cDan. 8:13;
12:8; Matt.
24:3; Mark
13:4

7 And I heard the man dressed in linen, who was above the waters of the river, as he ^araised his right hand and his left toward heaven, and swore by ^bHim who lives forever that it would be for a ^ctime, times, and half *a* time; and as soon as they finish ^dshattering the power of

★ 7 aEzek.
20:5; Rev.
10:5, 6
bDan. 4:34
cDan. 7:25;
Rev. 12:14
dDan. 8:24;
Luke 21:24

12:1 *at that time.* The time of the events of 11:36-45, the Great Tribulation. *Michael.* See note on 10:13. *such as never occurred.* Cf. Jesus' words in Matt. 24:21.

12:2 The verse predicts the resurrection of the righteous at the second coming of Christ (Rev. 20:4-6), and also of the wicked (though this resurrection does not occur at the same time, but after the Millennium; Rev. 20:5).

12:3 *those who have insight.* Those who will see through Antichrist's deception. They will also lead others to the truth during the Tribulation period.

12:4 *seal up the book.* Not that its meaning was to be left unexplained, but that the book was to be kept intact so as to help those living in the future Tribulation days. *many will go back and forth.* As the end approaches, people will travel about seeking to discover what the future holds.

12:7 The events of the Tribulation will be consummated when the three and one-half times (the last 3½ years of that 7-year period) come to a close. These last 3½ years constitute the Great Tribulation (cf. Matt. 24:21).

the holy people, all these *events* will be completed.

★ 8   **8** As for me, I heard but could not understand; so I said, "My lord, what *will be* the outcome of these *events?"*

9 ªDan. 12:4   **9** And he said, "Go *your* way, Daniel, for *these* words are concealed and ªsealed up until the end time.

10 ªZech. 13:9 ᵇIs. 32:6, 7; Rev. 22:11 ᶜDan. 12:3; Hos. 14:9; John 7:17; 8:47   **10** "ªMany will be purged, purified and refined; but the ᵇwicked will act wickedly, and none of the wicked will under-

stand, but those who ᶜhave insight will understand.

11 "And from the time that the regular sacrifice is abolished, and the ªabomination of desolation is set up, *there will be* 1,290 days.

12 "How ªblessed is he who keeps waiting and attains to the ᵇ1,335 days!

13 "But as for you, go *your* way to the end; then you will enter into ªrest and rise *again* for your ᵇallotted portion at the end of the age."

★11 ªDan. 9:27; 11:31; Matt. 24:15; Mark 13:14

★12 ªIs. 30:18 ᵇDan. 8:14; Rev. 11:2; 12:6; 13:5

★13 ªIs. 57:2; Rev. 14:13 ᵇPs. 16:5

12:8 Even Daniel did not understand all these prophecies.

12:11 *the abomination of desolation.* At the mid-point of the Tribulation week Antichrist will abolish the Jewish sacrifices (9:27; Matt. 24:15; 2 Thess. 2:4). From that time to the end will be 1,290 days. Normally 3½ years (of 360 days per year) would include only 1,260 days. The extra 30 days mentioned here allow for the judgments which will take place after the

second coming of Christ (see notes at Ezek. 20:33–44; Joel 3:2–3; Matt. 25:32).

12:12 Since the one who lives 75 days after the second advent (1,335 days from the mid-point of the Tribulation) is called *blessed,* this must mark the beginning of the actual functioning of Christ's millennial kingdom.

12:13 *you will enter into rest.* I.e., Daniel would die, but is promised that he will *rise* (be resurrected).

INTRODUCTION TO
THE BOOK OF HOSEA

AUTHOR: Hosea   DATE: c. 710 B.C.

The Prophet and His Times *All that we know about the prophet we discover from the autobiographical sections of the book itself. Like his contemporary, Amos, he prophesied to the Northern Kingdom (Israel; sometimes called Ephraim, after the largest tribe), while Isaiah and Micah were ministering to the Southern Kingdom (Judah). Material prosperity and spiritual bankruptcy characterized the time under Jeroboam II (782-753), when Hosea began his ministry (2 Kings 14:23-17:41). Judgment seemed remote, but by 732 Damascus had fallen to the Assyrians and by 722 Samaria, the capital of Israel, fell and the people were deported. Some of the specific sins Hosea denounces are listed in 4:2, 4, 11, 12, 13; 5:2; 6:8, 9; 7:1, 5; 8:14; 10:1, 4; 13:2.*

Hosea's Marriage *The theme of the book is God's steadfast love for Israel in spite of her continued unfaithfulness, vividly depicted by Hosea's marital experience. Hosea married Gomer only to discover that she was unfaithful. Though separation followed, Hosea's love (like God's for His people) persisted, and reconciliation eventually ensued.*

Three views have been proposed concerning Hosea's marriage: (1) Merely an allegory, the book contains no factual history of an actual marriage. (2) Hosea married a woman who was already a harlot, perhaps a temple prostitute. (3) Gomer became a harlot after her marriage. Though Hosea's tragic experience illustrates God's love for His wayward people, there are no legitimate grounds for rejecting the historicity of the marriage. Whether (2) or (3) is correct is difficult to determine.

Contents *Chapters 1-3 detail the prophet's domestic life, while the remainder of the book records excerpts of his messages delivered during his 50-year career as a prophet. In the prophetic section three themes dominate: the sins of the people, the certainty of judgment, and the assurance of God's loyal love.*

OUTLINE OF HOSEA

I. The Prodigal Wife, 1:1-3:5
A. Her Unfaithfulness, 1:1-11
B. Her Punishment, 2:1-13
C. Her Restoration and Israel's, 2:14-23
D. Her Redemption, 3:1-5
II. The Prodigal People, 4:1-14:9
A. The Message of Judgment, 4:1-10:15
  1. The indictment, 4:1-19
  2. The verdict, 5:1-15
  3. The plea of Israel, 6:1-3

  4. The reply of the Lord, 6:4-11
  5. The crimes of Israel, 7:1-16
  6. The prophecy of judgment, 8:1-10:15
B. The Message of Restoration, 11:1-14:9
  1. God's love for the prodigal people, 11:1-11
  2. God's chastisement of the prodigal people, 11:12-13:16
  3. God's restoration of the prodigal people, 14:1-9

THE BOOK OF HOSEA

I THE PRODIGAL WIFE, 1:1-3:5

★ 1 *a*Rom. 9:25 *b*2 Chr. 26:1-23; Is. 1:1; Amos 1:1 *c*2 Kin. 15:5, 7, 32-38; 2 Chr. 27:1-9 *d*2 Kin. 16:1-

A Her Unfaithfulness, 1:1-11

1 The word of the LORD which came to ªHosea the son of Beeri, during the days of ᵇUzziah, ᶜJotham, ᵈAhaz, *and* ᵉHezekiah, kings of Judah, and during the days of ᶠJeroboam the son of Joash, king of Israel.

20; 2 Chr. 28:1-27; Is. 1:1; 7:1-17; Mic. 1:1 *e*2 Kin. 18:1-20:21; 2 Chr. 29:1-32:33; Mic. 1:1 *f*2 Kin. 13:13; 14:23-29; Amos 1:1

1:1 *Hosea.* The name means salvation. The dates of these kings are as follows: *Uzziah* (also called Azariah), 791-740; *Jotham,* 750-732;

Ahaz, 746-716; *Hezekiah,* 716-687; *Jeroboam* II, 793-753.

★ 2 aHos.
3:1 bDeut.
31:16; Jer.
3:1; Ezek.
23:3-21; Hos.
2:5; 5:3

2 When the Lord first spoke through Hosea, the Lord said to Hosea, "aGo, take to yourself a wife of harlotry, and *have* children of harlotry; for bthe land commits flagrant harlotry, forsaking the Lord."

3 aEzek.
23:4

3 So he went and took Gomer the daughter of Diblaim, and she conceived and abore him a son.

★ 4 aHos.
2:22 b2 Kin.
10:11 c2 Kin.
15:8-10

4 And the Lord said to him, "Name him aJezreel; for yet a little while, and bI will punish the house of Jehu for the bloodshed of Jezreel, and cI will put an end to the kingdom of the house of Israel.

★ 5 aJer.
49:35; Ezek.
39:3 bJosh.
17:16; Judg.
6:33

5 "And it will come about on that day, that I will abreak the bow of Israel in the bvalley of Jezreel."

★ 6 aHos.
2:4

6 Then she conceived again and gave birth to a daughter. And the Lord said to him, "Name her Lo-ruhamah, for I will no longer ahave compassion on the house of Israel, that I should ever forgive them.

★ 7 a2 Kin.
19:29-35; Is.
30:18 bJer.
25:5, 6;
Zech. 9:9, 10
cPs. 44:3-7;
Zech. 4:6

7 "But I will have acompassion on the house of Judah and bdeliver them by the Lord their God, and will not deliver them by cbow, sword, battle, horses, or horsemen."

8 When she had weaned Loruhamah, she conceived and gave birth to a son.

★ 9

9 And the Lord said, "Name him Lo-ammi, for you are not My people and I am not your God."

★10-11

10 Yet the number of the sons of Israel
Will be like the asand of the sea,
Which cannot be measured or numbered;
And bit will come about that, in the place
Where it is said to them,
"You are cnot My people,"
It will be said to them,
"*You are* the dsons of the living God."

10 aGen.
22:17; 32:12;
Jer. 33:22
bRom. 9:26
cIs. 65:1;
Hos. 1:9 dIs.
63:16; 64:8;
John 1:12;
1 Pet. 2:10

11 And the asons of Judah and the sons of Israel will be bgathered together,
And they will appoint for themselves cone leader,
And they will go up from the land,
For great will be the day of Jezreel.

11 aIs. 11:12
bJer. 23:5, 6;
50:4, 5;
Ezek. 37:21-
24 cJer.
30:21; Hos.
3:5

B Her Punishment, 2:1-13

2 Say to your brothers, "Ammi," and to your sisters, "Ruhamah."

★ 1-2

2 "Contend with your mother, acontend,
For she is bnot my wife, and I am not her husband;
And let her put away her charlotry from her face,

2 aEzek.
23:45; Hos.
2:5; 4:5 bIs.
50:1 cJer.
3:1, 9, 13

1:2 *a wife of harlotry.* If proleptic, the phrase indicates Gomer became a harlot after her marriage to Hosea. If not, he married a known prostitute. In either case the marriage was providentially ordained in order to illustrate vividly the infidelity of the people of Israel.

1:4 *Jezreel* means "God sows," and refers to a valley in northern Israel, the scene of Jehu's ill-advised and wrongly motivated murder of the sons of Ahab in order to seize the throne (2 Kings 10:1-11). *put an end to.* . . . Fulfilled by the Assyrian captivity in 722 and prophesied to Jehu (2 Kings 10:30).

1:5 *break the bow.* Break the power.

1:6 *Lo-ruhamah* means "unpitied." This child symbolized the plight of Israel.

1:7 Though Israel fell before the Assyrians, God intervened to save Jerusalem when Sennach-

erib besieged it (2 Kings 19:34-35).

1:9 *Lo-ammi* means "not my people." This child symbolized the rejection of Israel, who, at Sinai, had covenanted to be God's people (Exod. 19:1-8).

1:10-11 Having predicted judgment, Hosea assured the people of their ultimate restoration, numerically and spiritually. Jezreel, a place of judgment in verse 4, is viewed in verse 11 as a place where God will bless Israel during the kingdom age.

2:1-2 *brothers . . . sisters* refer to individual Israelites and *mother* refers to the nation. Gomer's adultery is used as an illustration of Israel's unfaithfulness. The words in verse 2 are similar to those used in the Jewish formula for divorce.

3 aJer.
13:22; Ezek.
16:7, 22, 39
bEzek. 16:4
cIs. 32:13,
14; Hos.
13:15 dJer.
14:3; Amos
8:11-13

4 aJer.
13:14

★ 5 aIs.
1:21; Jer.
2:25; 3:1, 2;
Hos. 3:1
bJer. 44:17,
18; Hos. 2:12
cHos. 2:8

6 aJob
19:8; Lam.
3:7, 9 bHos.
9:6; 10:8
cJer. 18:15

★ 7 aHos.
5:13 bLuke
15:17, 18
cJer. 2:2;
3:1; Ezek.
16:8; 23:4
dJer. 14:22;
Hos. 13:6

8 aIs. 1:3
bEzek. 16:19

3 And her adultery from between her breasts,
Lest I strip her anaked
And expose her as on the bday when she was born.
I will also cmake her like a wilderness,
Make her like desert land,
And slay her with dthirst.

4 "Also, I will have no compassion on her children,
Because they are achildren of harlotry.

5 "For their mother has aplayed the harlot;
She who conceived them has acted shamefully.
For she said, 'aI will go after my lovers,
Who bgive me my bread and my water,
My wool and my flax, my coil and my drink.'

6 "Therefore, behold, I will ahedge up her way with bthorns,
And I will build a wall against her so that she cannot find her cpaths.

7 "And she will apursue her lovers, but she will not overtake them;
And she will seek them, but will not find them.
Then she will say, 'bI will go back to my cfirst husband,
For it was dbetter for me then than now!'

8 "For she does anot know that it was bI who

gave her the grain, the new wine, and the oil,
And lavished on her silver and gold,
Which they used for Baal.

9 "Therefore, I will atake back My grain at harvest time
And My new wine in its season.
I will also take away My wool and My flax
Given to cover her nakedness.

10 "And then I will auncover her lewdness
In the sight of her lovers,
And no one will rescue her out of My hand.

11 "I will also aput an end to all her gaiety,
Her bfeasts, her cnew moons, her sabbaths,
And all her festal assemblies.

12 "And I will adestroy her vines and fig trees,
Of which she said, 'These are my wages
Which my lovers have given me.'
And I will bmake them a forest,
And the cbeasts of the field will devour them.

13 "And I will punish her for the adays of the Baals
When she used to boffer sacrifices to them
And cadorn herself with her earrings and jewelry,
And follow her lovers, so that she dforgot Me," declares the LORD.

9 aHos.
8:7; 9:2

★10 aEzek.
16:37

11 aJer.
7:34; 16:9
bHos. 3:4;
Amos 5:21;
8:10 cIs.
1:13, 14

★12 aJer.
5:17; 8:13
bIs. 5:5; 7:23
cHos. 13:8

★13 aHos.
4:13; 11:2
bJer. 7:9
cEzek.
16:12, 17;
23:40 dHos.
4:6; 8:14;
13:6

2:5 *my lovers.* Just as Gomer went after her paramours, so Israel worshiped Baal and other Canaanite gods.

2:7 Neither Gomer nor God's people could find satisfaction in unfaithfulness.

2:10 *uncover her lewdness.* I.e., reveal her to her lovers as the shameful creature she was.

2:12 *forest.* Jungle.

2:13 *days of the Baals.* The whole period of the worship of Baal (the chief Canaanite deity) by

Israel. Baal means "lord" or "owner" and was often used as a general term for god. Israel's worship of Baal developed in three stages: (1) placing the Canaanite gods in a secondary place to the LORD (Yahweh; see note on Gen. 2:4); (2) considering Yahweh as a super-Baal; (3) Canaanizing or Baalizing Yahweh worship so that the people completely forsook Yahweh.

C Her Restoration and Israel's, 2:14-23

★14 ªEzek. 20:33-38

14 "Therefore, behold, I will allure her,
ªBring her into the wilderness,
And speak kindly to her.

★15 ªEzek. 28:25, 26
ᵇJosh. 7:26
ᶜJer. 2:1-3;
Ezek. 16:8-14 ᵈHos. 11:1; 12:9, 13; 13:4

15 "Then I will give her her ªvineyards from there,
And ᵇthe valley of Achor as a door of hope.
And she will ᶜsing there as in the days of her youth,
As in the ᵈday when she came up from the land of Egypt.

★16 ªIs. 54:5; Hos. 2:7

16 "And it will come about in that day," declares the Lᴏʀᴅ,
"That you will call Me ªIshi
And will no longer call Me Baali.

17 ªEx. 23:13; Josh. 23:7; Ps. 16:4

17 "For ªI will remove the names of the Baals from her mouth,
So that they will be mentioned by their names no more.

★18 ªJob 5:23; Is. 11:6-9; Ezek. 34:25 ᵇIs. 2:4; Ezek. 39:1-10
ᶜLev. 26:5; Jer. 23:6; Ezek. 34:25

18 "In that day I will also make a covenant for them
With the ªbeasts of the field,
The birds of the sky,
And the creeping things of the ground.
And I will ᵇabolish the bow, the sword, and war from the land,
And will make them ᶜlie down in safety.

★19 ªIs. 62:4, 5 ᵇIs. 1:27; 54:6-8

19 "And I will ªbetroth you to Me forever;

Yes, I will betroth you to Me in ᵇrighteousness and in justice,
In lovingkindness and in compassion,

20 ªJer. 31:33, 34; Hos. 6:6; 13:4

20 And I will betroth you to Me in faithfulness.
Then you will ªknow the Lᴏʀᴅ.

★21 ªIs. 55:10; Zech. 8:12; Mal. 3:10, 11

21 "And it will come about in that day that ªI will respond," declares the Lᴏʀᴅ.
"I will respond to the heavens, and they will respond to the earth,

★22-23
22 ªJer. 31:12; Joel 2:19

22 And the ªearth will respond to the grain, to the new wine, and to the oil,
And they will respond to Jezreel.

23 ªJer. 31:27 ᵇHos. 1:6 ᶜRom. 9:25; 1 Pet. 2:10 ᵈHos. 1:9

23 "And I will ªsow her for Myself in the land.
ᵇI will also have compassion on her who had not obtained compassion,
And ᶜI will say to those who were ᵈnot My people,
'You are My people!'
And they will say, 'Thou art my God!' "

D Her Redemption, 3:1-5

★ 1 ªJer. 3:20 ᵇ2 Sam. 6:19; 1 Chr. 16:3; Song 2:5

3 Then the Lᴏʀᴅ said to me, "Go again, love a woman who is loved by her husband, yet an adulteress, even ªas the Lᴏʀᴅ loves the sons of Israel, though

---

2:14 *speak kindly.* Lit., speak to her heart.
2:15 *valley of Achor.* The "valley of trouble," where Achan died (Josh. 7:26). Only through trouble would Israel have hope of restoration.
2:16 *Ishi.* Means my husband. *Baali.* Means my owner.
2:18 *With the beasts of the field.* In the millennial age even the beasts will be tamed (Isa. 11:6-9).
2:19 *lovingkindness.* The Hebrew word is *hesed,* used about 250 times in the O.T. It means loyal, steadfast, or faithful love and stresses the idea of a belonging together of those involved in the love relationship. Here it connotes

God's faithful love for His unfaithful people. See also 4:1; 6:4, 6; 10:12; 12:6; Joel 2:13; Jonah 2:8; 4:2; Mic. 6:8; 7:18, 20; Zech. 7:9. In the O.T., communion, deliverance, enablement, enlightenment, guidance, forgiveness, hope, praise, preservation are all based on God's *hesed.*
2:21 *respond to the heavens.* I.e., answer the prayers that have ascended to heaven.
2:22-23 *Jezreel.* God will sow restored Israel in fertile soil and she will flourish.
3:1 *loved by her husband.* Better, loved by another; i.e., her paramour.

they turn to other gods and love raisin [b]cakes."

★ 2 [a]Ruth 4:10

2 So I [a]bought her for myself for fifteen *shekels* of silver and a homer and a half of barley.

★ 3-5
3 [a]Deut. 21:13
★ 4 [a]Hos. 10:3; 13:10, 11 [b]Dan. 9:27; 11:31; 12:11; Hos. 2:11 [c]Hos. 10:1, 2 [d]Ex. 28:4-12; 1 Sam. 23:9-12 [e]Gen. 31:19, 34; Judg. 17:5; 18:14, 17; 1 Sam. 15:23

5 [a]Jer. 50:4, 5 [b]Jer. 30:9; Ezek. 34:24 [c]Is. 2:2, 3; Jer. 31:9

3 Then I said to her, "You shall [a]stay with me for many days. You shall not play the harlot, nor shall you have a man; so I will also be toward you."

4 For the sons of Israel will remain for many days [a]without king or prince, [b]without sacrifice or *sacred* [c]pillar, and without [d]ephod or [e]household idols.

5 Afterward the sons of Israel will [a]return and seek the Lord their God and [b]David their king; and [c]they will come trembling to the Lord and to His goodness in the last days.

II THE PRODIGAL PEOPLE, 4:1-14:9

A The Message of Judgment,
4:1-10:15

1 *The indictment,* 4:1-19

1 [a]Hos. 5:1 [b]Hos. 12:2; Mic. 6:2 [c]Is. 59:4; Jer. 7:28 [d]Jer. 4:22

4 [a]Listen to the word of the Lord, O sons of Israel, For the Lord has a [b]case against the inhabitants of the land, Because there is [c]no faithfulness or kindness Or [d]knowledge of God in the land.

★ 2 [a]Deut. 5:11; Hos. 10:4 [b]Hos. 7:3; 10:13; 11:12 [c]Gen. 4:8; Hos. 6:9 [d]Deut. 5:19; Hos. 7:1 [e]Deut. 5:18; Hos. 7:4 [f]Hos. 6:8; 12:14

3 [a]Is. 24:4; 33:9; Amos 5:16; Zeph. 1:3

2 *There is* [a]swearing, [b]deception, [c]murder, [d]stealing, and [e]adultery. They employ violence, so that [f]bloodshed follows bloodshed.

3 Therefore the land [a]mourns,

And everyone who lives in it languishes Along with the beasts of the field and the birds of the sky; And also the fish of the sea disappear.

4 [a]Ezek. 3:26; Amos 5:10, 13 [b]Deut. 17:12

4 Yet let no one [a]find fault, and let none offer reproof; For your people are like those who [b]contend with the priest.

★ 5 [a]Ezek. 14:3, 7; Hos. 5:5 [b]Jer. 15:8; Hos. 2:2, 5

5 So you will [a]stumble by day, And the prophet also will stumble with you by night; And I will destroy your [b]mother.

★ 6 [a]Is. 5:13 [b]Hos. 4:14; Mal. 2:7, 8 [c]Zech. 11:8, 9, 15-17 [d]Hos. 2:13; 8:14; 13:6 [e]Hos. 8:1, 12

6 [a]My people are destroyed for lack of knowledge. Because you have [b]rejected knowledge, I also will [c]reject you from being My priest. Since you have [d]forgotten the [e]law of your God, I also will forget your children.

7 [a]Hos. 10:1; 13:6 [b]Hab. 2:16

7 The more they [a]multiplied, the more they sinned against Me; I will [b]change their glory into shame.

★ 8 [a]Hos. 10:13 [b]Is. 56:11; Mic. 3:11

8 They [a]feed on the sin of My people, And [b]direct their desire toward their iniquity.

9 [a]Is. 24:2; Jer. 5:31 [b]Hos. 8:13; 9:9

9 And it will be, like people, [a]like priest; So I will [b]punish them for their ways, And repay them for their deeds.

3:2 *I bought her.* Gomer, no longer considered Hosea's wife, had to be restored to that position through the customary practice of purchase. The price of a slave was 30 shekels of silver. Hosea apparently paid half in money and half in grain.
3:3-5 Gomer was placed in forced seclusion for some days, symbolizing Israel's exile.
3:4 *ephod.* Part of the high priest's attire (see note on Exod. 28:6-14).

4:2 *bloodshed follows bloodshed.* I.e., one murder follows another, leaving a trail of blood.
4:5 *mother.* The nation itself.
4:6 The nation will be rejected from her priestly position before God (Exod. 19:6).
4:8 *the sin.* May refer to the sin offering (the same Hebrew word is used), indicating that the priests grew wealthy by seizing the offerings the people brought.

10 aLev.
26:26; Is.
65:13; Mic.
6:14 bHos.
7:4 cHos.
9:17

10 And ªthey will eat, but not
have enough;
They will ᵇplay the harlot,
but not increase,
Because they have
ᶜstopped giving heed
to the LORD.

11 aProv.
20:1; Is.
5:12; 28:7

11 Harlotry, ªwine, and new
wine take away the
understanding.

12 aIs.
44:19; Jer.
2:27

12 My people ªconsult their
wooden idol, and their
diviner's wand in-
forms them;
For a spirit of harlotry has
led *them* astray,
And they have played the
harlot, *departing* from
their God.

★13 aJer.
3:6 bHos.
2:13; 11:2
cIs. 1:29;
Jer. 2:20

13 They offer sacrifices on the
ªtops of the moun-
tains
And ᵇburn incense on the
hills,
ᶜUnder oak, poplar, and
terebinth,
Because their shade is
pleasant.
Therefore your daughters
play the harlot,
And your brides commit
adultery.

★14 aDeut.
23:17

14 I will not punish your
daughters when they
play the harlot
Or your brides when they
commit adultery,
For *the men* themselves go
apart with harlots
And offer sacrifices with
ªtemple prostitutes;
So the people without
understanding are
ruined.

★15 aHos.
9:15; 12:11
bJer. 5:2;
44:26; Amos
8:14

15 Though you, Israel, play
the harlot,

Do not let Judah become
guilty;
Also do not go to ªGilgal,
Or go up to Beth-aven,
ᵇAnd take the oath:
"As the LORD lives!"

16 Since Israel is ªstubborn
Like a stubborn heifer,
Can the LORD now ᵇpasture
them
Like a lamb in a large
field?

16 aPs. 78:8
bIs. 5:17;
7:25

17 Ephraim is joined to ªidols;
ᵇLet him alone.

★17 aHos.
13:2 bPs.
81:12; Hos.
4:4

18 Their liquor gone,
They play the harlot con-
tinually;
ªTheir rulers dearly love
shame.

18 aMic.
3:11

19 ªThe wind wraps them in
its wings,
And they will be ashamed
because of their sacri-
fices.

★19 aHos.
12:1; 13:15

2 The verdict, 5:1-15

5 Hear this, O priests!
Give heed, O house of
Israel!
Listen, O house of the
king!
For the judgment applies
to you,
For you have been a ªsnare
at Mizpah,
And a net spread out on
Tabor.

★ 1 aHos.
9:8

2 And the ªrevolters have
ᵇgone deep in deprav-
ity,
But I will chastise all of
them.

2 aHos.
9:15 bIs.
29:15; Hos.
4:2; 6:9

3 I ªknow Ephraim, and Israel is not hidden
from Me;

3 aAmos
3:2; 5:12

4:13 Sacrifices to the heathen gods were offered
on the *tops of the mountains* and were accompanied by immoral ceremonies.
4:14 *brides.* Better, daughters-in-law.
4:15 The people were told not to worship at
what were formerly holy cities, *Gilgal* and
Beth-aven (which means House of Wickedness and was Hosea's name for Bethel, which
means House of God).

4:17 *Let him alone.* Judah was warned to stay
away from the Northern Kingdom (see Matt.
15:14).
4:19 *The wind* of judgment will come suddenly
and violently.
5:1 The priests and kings are condemned for
snaring the people with idolatrous practices at
Mizpah, on the E. of Jordan, and at *Tabor* on
the W.

For now, O Ephraim, you have played the harlot,
Israel has defiled itself.

4 ^aHos. 4:12 ^bHos. 4:6, 14

4 Their deeds will not allow them
To return to their God.
For a ^aspirit of harlotry is within them,
And they ^bdo not know the LORD.

5 ^aHos. 7:10 ^bEzek. 23:31-35

5 Moreover, the ^apride of Israel testifies against him,
And Israel and Ephraim stumble in their iniquity;
^bJudah also has stumbled with them.

6 ^aHos. 8:13; Mic. 6:6, 7 ^bProv. 1:28; Is. 1:15; Jer. 14:12 ^cEzek. 8:6

6 They will ^ago with their flocks and herds
To seek the LORD, but they will ^bnot find *Him*;
He has ^cwithdrawn from them.

7 ^aIs. 48:8; Jer. 3:20; Hos. 6:7 ^bHos. 2:4 ^cIs. 1:14; Hos. 2:11

7 They have ^adealt treacherously against the LORD,
For they have borne ^billegitimate children.
Now the ^cnew moon will devour them with their land.

★ **8** ^aJoel 2:1 ^bHos. 9:9; 10:9 ^cJudg. 5:14

8 ^aBlow the horn in ^bGibeah,
The trumpet in Ramah.
Sound an alarm at Beth-aven:
"^cBehind you, Benjamin!"

★ **9** ^aIs. 28:1-4; Hos. 9:11-17 ^bIs. 37:3 ^cIs. 46:10; Zech. 1:6

9 Ephraim will become a ^adesolation in the ^bday of rebuke;
Among the tribes of Israel I ^cdeclare what is sure.

★ **10** ^aDeut. 19:14; 27:17 ^bEzek. 7:8 ^cPs. 32:6; 93:3, 4

10 The princes of Judah have become like those

who ^amove a boundary;
On them I will ^bpour out My wrath ^clike water.

★ **11** ^aDeut. 28:33 ^bMic. 6:16

11 Ephraim is ^aoppressed, crushed in judgment,
^bBecause he was determined to follow *man's* command.

12 ^aPs. 39:11; Is. 51:8

12 Therefore I am like a ^amoth to Ephraim,
And like rottenness to the house of Judah.

★ **13** ^aHos. 7:11; 8:9; 12:1 ^bHos. 10:6 ^cJer. 30:12-15

13 When Ephraim saw his sickness,
And Judah his wound,
Then Ephraim went to ^aAssyria
And sent to ^bKing Jareb.
But he is ^cunable to heal you,
Or to cure you of your wound.

14 ^aPs. 7:2; Hos. 13:7, 8; Amos 3:4 ^bPs. 50:22 ^cMic. 5:8

14 For I *will be* ^alike a lion to Ephraim,
And like a young lion to the house of Judah.
^bI, even I, will tear to pieces and go away,
I will carry away, and there will be ^cnone to deliver.

15 ^aIs. 64:7-9; Jer. 3:13, 14 ^bPs. 50:15; 78:34; Jer. 2:27; Hos. 3:5

15 I will go away *and* return to My place
Until they ^aacknowledge their guilt and seek My face;
In their affliction they will earnestly ^bseek Me.

3 The plea of Israel, 6:1-3

1 ^aJer. 50:4, 5 ^bDeut. 32:39; Hos. 5:14 ^cJer. 30:17; Hos. 14:4 ^dIs. 30:26

6 "^aCome, let us return to the LORD.
For ^bHe has torn *us*, but ^cHe will heal us;

5:8 *horn.* Heb., *shophar;* usually a simple ram's horn. *Gibeah* and *Ramah* were high mountains in central Palestine, excellent places for sounding an alarm.
5:9 *the day of rebuke.* I.e., the day of God's judgment against the people.
5:10 To move a boundary was a crime (Deut.

19:14; 27:17).
5:11 *command.* Of Jeroboam, who led Israel into sin (1 Kings 12:28).
5:13 *King Jareb.* Probably Tiglath-pileser III. In her troubles, Israel sought help from the Assyrian.

He has wounded *us,* but
He will ᵈbandage us.

★ 2 ᵃPs.
30:5 ᵇ1 Cor.
15:4

2 "He will ᵃrevive us after two
days;
He will ᵇraise us up on the
third day
That we may live before
Him.

3 ᵃIs. 2:3;
Mic. 4:2 ᵇPs.
19:6; Mic.
5:2 ᶜJob
29:23; Ps.
72:6; Joel
2:23

3 "So let us ᵃknow, let us
press on to know the
LORD.
His ᵇgoing forth is as certain as the dawn;
And He will come to us
like the ᶜrain,
Like the spring rain watering the earth."

4 The reply of the Lord, 6:4–11

★ 4 ᵃHos.
7:1; 11:8
ᵇPs. 78:34-
37; Hos. 13:3

4 What shall I do with you,
O ᵃEphraim?
What shall I do with you,
O Judah?
For your loyalty is like a
ᵇmorning cloud,
And like the dew which
goes away early.

5 ᵃ1 Sam.
15:32, 33;
Jer. 1:10;
5:14 ᵇJer.
23:29

5 Therefore I have ᵃhewn
them in pieces by the
prophets;
I have slain them by the
ᵇwords of My mouth;
And the judgments on you
are *like* the light that
goes forth.

★ 6 ᵃMatt.
9:13; 12:7
ᵇIs. 1:11

6 For ᵃI delight in loyalty
ᵇrather than sacrifice,
And in the knowledge of
God rather than burnt
offerings.

★ 7 ᵃJob
31:33 ᵇHos.
8:1 ᶜHos.
5:7

7 But ᵃlike Adam they have
ᵇtransgressed the cov-
enant;
There they have ᶜdealt
treacherously against
Me.

8 ᵃGilead is a city of wrongdoers,
Tracked with ᵇbloody
footprints.

8 ᵃHos.
12:11 ᵇHos.
4:2

9 And as ᵃraiders wait for a
man,
So a band of priests ᵇmur-
der on the way to
Shechem;
Surely they have commit-
ted ᶜcrime.

9 ᵃHos. 7:1
ᵇJer. 7:9, 10;
Hos. 4:2
ᶜEzek. 22:9;
23:27; Hos.
2:10

10 In the house of Israel I
have seen a ᵃhorrible
thing;
Ephraim's ᵇharlotry is
there, Israel has de-
filed itself.

10 ᵃJer.
5:30, 31;
23:14 ᵇHos.
5:3

11 Also, O Judah, there is a
ᵃharvest appointed for
you,
When I ᵇrestore the for-
tunes of My people.

11 ᵃJer.
51:33; Joel
3:13 ᵇZeph.
2:7

5 The crimes of Israel, 7:1–16

7 When I ᵃwould heal Israel,
The iniquity of Ephra-
im is uncovered,
And the evil deeds of Sa-
maria,
For they deal ᵇfalsely;
The thief enters in,
ᶜBandits raid outside,

★ 1 ᵃEzek.
24:13; Hos.
6:4; 7:13;
11:8 ᵇHos.
4:2 ᶜHos.
6:9

2 And they do not consider
in their hearts
That I ᵃremember all their
wickedness.
Now their ᵇdeeds are all
around them;
They are before My face.

2 ᵃPs. 25:7;
Jer. 14:10;
17:1; Hos.
8:13; 9:9;
Amos 8:7
ᵇJer. 2:19;
4:18; Hos.
4:9

3 ᵃWith their wickedness
they make the ᵇking
glad,
And the princes with their
ᶜlies.

3 ᵃRom.
1:32 ᵇJer.
28:1-4; Hos.
7:5; Mic. 7:3
ᶜHos. 4:2;
11:12

4 They are ᵃall adulterers
Like an oven heated by the
baker,

★ 4-5
4 ᵃJer. 9:2;
23:10

6:2 *after two days . . . the third day.* I.e., in a
short period of time (see Luke 13:32–33; 2 Pet.
3:8). The restoration of Israel will occur at the
second coming of Christ (Rom. 11:26).
6:4 Israel's attempts at self-reformation were deceptive like the *morning cloud,* which looms
large but is soon dissipated.
6:6 *loyalty.* Heb., *hesed;* see note on 2:19.
6:7 *Adam.* May refer to men in general, trans-

gressing God's commandments, or specifically
to Adam's original sin.
7:1 *Samaria.* The capital of Ephraim (Israel), the
Northern Kingdom.
7:4-5 Hosea describes a particularly despicable
time of revelry (perhaps a coronation or a
royal birthday). The lusts of the leaders
burned like an oven.

Who ceases to stir up *the* fire
From the kneading of the dough until it is leavened.

5 [a]Is. 28:1, 7 [b]Is. 28:14

5 On the day of our king, the princes [a]became sick with the heat of wine;
He stretched out his hand with [b]scoffers,

6 [a]Ps. 21:9

6 For their hearts are like an [a]oven
As they approach their plotting;
Their anger smolders all night,
In the morning it burns like a flaming fire.

★ 7 [a]Hos. 13:10 [b]Is. 64:7

7 All of them are hot like an oven,
And they consume their [a]rulers;
All their kings have fallen.
[b]None of them calls on Me.

★ 8-9

8 [a]Ps. 106:35

8 Ephraim [a]mixes himself with the nations;
Ephraim has become a cake not turned.

9 [a]Is. 1:7; Hos. 8:7 [b]Hos. 4:6

9 [a]Strangers devour his strength,
Yet he [b]does not know *it;*
Gray hairs also are sprinkled on him,
Yet he does not know *it.*

10 [a]Hos. 5:5 [b]Is. 9:13

10 Though the [a]pride of Israel testifies against him,
Yet [b]they have neither returned to the LORD their God,
Nor have they sought Him, for all this.

11 [a]Hos. 11:11 [b]Hos. 4:6, 11, 14; 5:4 [c]Hos. 8:13; 9:3, 6 [d]Hos. 5:13; 8:9; 12:1

11 So [a]Ephraim has become like a silly dove, [b]without sense;
They call to [c]Egypt, they go to [d]Assyria.

12 [a]Ezek. 12:13 [b]Lev. 26:14-39; Deut. 28:15

12 When they go, I will [a]spread My net over them;
I will bring them down like the birds of the sky.
I will [b]chastise them in accordance with the proclamation to their assembly.

13 [a]Hos. 9:12 [b]Jer. 14:10; Ezek. 34:6; Hos. 9:17 [c]Jer. 51:9; Hos. 7:1; Matt. 23:37

13 [a]Woe to them, for they have [b]strayed from Me!
Destruction is theirs, for they have rebelled against Me!
I [c]would redeem them, but they speak lies against Me.

14 [a]Job 35:9-11; Hos. 8:2; Zech. 7:5 [b]Judg. 9:27; Amos 2:8; Mic. 2:11 [c]Hos. 13:16

14 And [a]they do not cry to Me from their heart
When they wail on their beds;
For the sake of grain and new wine they [b]assemble themselves,
They [c]turn away from Me.

15 [a]Nah. 1:9

15 Although I trained *and* strengthened their arms,
Yet they [a]devise evil against Me.

16 [a]Ps. 78:57 [b]Ps. 12:3, 4; 17:10; 73:9; Dan. 7:25; Mal. 3:13, 14 [c]Ezek. 23:32; Hos. 9:3, 6

16 They turn, *but* not upward,
They are like a [a]deceitful bow;
Their princes will fall by the sword
Because of the [b]insolence of their tongue.
This *will be* their [c]derision in the land of Egypt.

6 *The prophecy of judgment,* 8:1–10:15

★ 1 [a]Jer. 4:13; Hos. 5:8 [b]Hab. 1:8 [c]Deut. 28:49 [d]Hos. 6:7 [e]Hos. 4:6

8 [a]*Put* the trumpet to your lips!
[b]Like an eagle *the enemy comes* [c]against the house of the LORD,
Because they have [d]transgressed My covenant,
And rebelled against My [e]law.

7:7 *All their kings have fallen.* Four of Israel's last six kings were murdered.

7:8–9 Foreign alliances made Israel weak (*a cake not turned*) and decrepit (as evidenced by her *Gray hairs*).

8:1 Assyria would come against Israel like an *eagle* or, literally, a vulture.

2 They cry out to Me,
"My God, we of Israel
know Thee!"

3 Israel has rejected the
good;
The enemy will pursue
him.

4 They have set up kings,
but not by Me;
They have appointed
princes, but I did not
know it.
With their silver and gold
they have made idols
for themselves,
That they might be cut off.

5 He has rejected your calf,
O Samaria, saying,
"My anger burns against
them!"
How long will they be in-
capable of inno-
cence?

6 For from Israel is even this!
A craftsman made it, so it
is not God;
Surely the calf of Samaria
will be broken to
pieces.

7 For they sow the wind,
And they reap the whirl-
wind.
The standing grain has no
heads;
It yields no grain.
Should it yield, strangers
would swallow it up.

8 Israel is swallowed up;
They are now among the
nations
Like a vessel in which no
one delights.

9 For they have gone up to
Assyria,
Like a wild donkey all
alone;
Ephraim has hired lovers.

10 Even though they hire allies among the na-
tions,

Now I will gather them
up;
And they will begin to diminish
Because of the burden of
the king of princes.

11 Since Ephraim has multiplied altars for sin,
They have become altars
of sinning for him.

12 Though I wrote for him
ten thousand precepts
of My law,
They are regarded as a
strange thing.

13 As for My sacrificial gifts,
They sacrifice the flesh
and eat it,
But the LORD has taken no
delight in them.
Now He will remember
their iniquity,
And punish them for
their sins;
They will return to Egypt.

14 For Israel has forgotten
his Maker and built
palaces;
And Judah has multiplied
fortified cities,
But I will send a fire on its
cities that it may con-
sume its palatial
dwellings.

9 Do not rejoice, O Israel, with
exultation like the na-
tions!
For you have played the
harlot, forsaking your
God.
You have loved harlots'
earnings on every
threshing floor.

2 Threshing floor and wine
press will not feed
them,
And the new wine will fail
them.

3 They will not remain in
the LORD's land,

Cross-reference column (left):
2 aPs. 78:34; Hos. 7:14 bTitus 1:16
4 a2 Kin. 15:13, 17, 25; Hos. 13:10, 11 bHos. 2:8; 13:1, 2
★ 5 aHos. 10:5; 13:2 bPs. 19:13; Jer. 13:27
6 aHos. 13:2
7 aProv. 22:8 bIs. 66:15; Nah. 1:3 cHos. 2:9
8 a2 Kin. 17:6; Jer. 51:34 bJer. 22:28; 25:34
9 aHos. 7:11 bJer. 2:24 cEzek. 16:33, 34
★10 aEzek. 16:37; 22:20 bJer. 42:2 cIs. 10:8

Cross-reference column (right):
11 aHos. 10:1
12 aDeut. 4:6, 8 bHos. 4:6
★13 aHos. 5:6 bJer. 6:20; 7:21 cJer. 14:10; Hos. 7:2; Luke 12:2; 1 Cor. 4:5 dHos. 4:9; 9:7 eHos. 9:3, 6
14 aDeut. 32:18; Hos. 2:13; 4:6; 13:6 bIs. 9:9, 10 cJer. 17:27
★ 1 aIs. 22:12, 13; Hos. 10:5 bHos. 4:12
2 aHos. 2:9
★ 3 aLev. 25:23; Jer. 2:7 bHos. 7:16; 8:13 cHos. 7:11 dEzek. 4:13

8:5 The calf was worshiped (cf. Exod. 32:4; 1 Kings 12:28).
8:10 burden. The tribute imposed on Israel by the king of princes, the Assyrian monarch.
8:13 They will return to Egypt. God would re- verse their deliverance from Egypt and send

them back into captivity (this time to Assyria).
9:1 Israel had followed her heathen neighbors in practicing licentious fertility rites.
9:3 Some did actually go to Egypt (2 Kings 25:26).

But Ephraim will return to
ᵇEgypt,
And in ᶜAssyria they will
eat ᵈunclean food.

4 ᵃEx.
29:40 ᵇJer.
6:20; Hos.
8:13 ᶜHag.
2:13, 14

4 They will not pour out libations of ᵃwine to
the Lᴏʀᴅ,
ᵇTheir sacrifices will not
please Him.
Their bread will be like
mourners' bread;
All who eat of it will be
ᶜdefiled,
For their bread will be for
themselves *alone;*
It will not enter the house
of the Lᴏʀᴅ.

5 ᵃIs. 10:3;
Jer. 5:31
ᵇHos. 2:11;
Joel 1:13

5 ᵃWhat will you do on the
day of the appointed
festival
And on the day of the
ᵇfeast of the Lᴏʀᴅ?

6 ᵃIs.
19:13; Jer.
2:16; 44:1;
46:14, 19;
Ezek. 30:13,
16 ᵇIs. 5:6;
7:23; Hos.
10:8

6 For behold, they will go
because of destruc-
tion;
Egypt will gather them up,
ᵃMemphis will bury
them.
Weeds will take over their
treasures of silver;
ᵇThorns *will be* in their
tents.

★ 7-8

7 ᵃIs. 10:3;
Jer. 10:15;
Mic. 7:4;
Luke 21:22
ᵇIs. 34:8;
Jer. 16:18;
25:14 ᶜLam.
2:14; Ezek.
13:3, 10 ᵈIs.
44:25 ᵉEzek.
14:9, 10

7 The days of ᵃpunishment
have come,
The days of ᵇretribution
have come;
Let Israel know *this!*
The prophet is a ᶜfool,
The inspired man is ᵈde-
mented,
Because of the grossness of
your ᵉiniquity,
And *because* your hostility
is *so* great.

8 Ephraim *was* a watchman
with my God, a
prophet;

Yet the snare of a bird
catcher is in all his
ways,
And there is *only* hostility
in the house of his
God.

★ 9 ᵃIs.
31:6 ᵇJudg.
19:12, 16-30;
Hos. 10:9
ᶜHos. 7:2;
8:13

9 They have gone ᵃdeep in
depravity
As in the days of ᵇGibeah;
He will ᶜremember their
iniquity,
He will punish their sins.

★10-17

10 ᵃMic. 7:1
ᵇJer. 24:2
ᶜNum. 25:1-
5; Ps.
106:28, 29
ᵈJer. 11:13;
Hos. 4:18
ᵉPs. 115:8;
Ezek. 20:8

10 I found Israel like ᵃgrapes
in the wilderness;
I saw your forefathers as
the ᵇearliest fruit on
the fig tree in its first
season.
But they came to ᶜBaal-
peor and devoted
themselves to ᵈshame,
And they became as ᵉde-
testable as that which
they loved.

11 ᵃHos.
4:7; 10:5

11 As for Ephraim, their ᵃglory will fly away like a
bird—
No birth, no pregnancy,
and no conception!

12 ᵃDeut.
31:17; Hos.
7:13

12 Though they bring up
their children,
Yet I will bereave them
until not a man is left.
Yes, ᵃwoe to them indeed
when I depart from
them!

13 ᵃEzek.
26:1-21

13 Ephraim, as I have seen,
Is planted in a pleasant
meadow like ᵃTyre;
But Ephraim will bring out
his children for
slaughter.

14 ᵃHos.
9:11

14 Give them, O Lᴏʀᴅ—what
wilt Thou give?
Give them a ᵃmiscarrying
womb and dry
breasts.

9:7-8 The people reacted to Hosea's somber
warnings by declaring him a *fool,* whereas in
reality he was the nation's *watchman.*
9:9 The evil of Hosea's day is compared to the
days of Gibeah (cf. Judg. 19-21), when the
tribe of Benjamin was almost annihilated.
9:10-17 Though at the beginning of the nation
God found His people to be like refreshing

grapes in the wilderness, they turned to immorality at *Baal-peor* (cf. Num. 25) and defection at *Gilgal* (v. 15), where they proclaimed
Saul king (1 Sam. 11:15). This combination of
Baal worship and the desire for human kings
instead of God destined the people to become
wanderers among the nations (v. 17).

15 aHos.
4:15; 12:11
bHos. 4:9;
7:2; 12:2 cIs.
1:23; Hos.
5:2

15 All their evil is at aGilgal;
Indeed, I came to hate
them there!
Because of the bwicked-
ness of their deeds
I will drive them out of My
house!
I will love them no more;
All their princes are
crebels.

16 aHos.
5:11 bHos.
8:7 cEzek.
24:21

16 aEphraim is stricken, their
root is dried up,
They will bear bno fruit.
Even though they bear
children,
I will slay the cprecious
ones of their womb.

17 aHos.
4:10 bHos.
7:13

17 My God will cast them
away
Because they have anot listened to Him;
And they will be bwander-
ers among the na-
tions.

★ **1** aIs. 5:1-
7; Ezek.
15:1-6 bJer.
2:28; Hos.
8:11; 12:11
c1 Kin.
14:23; Hos.
3:4

10 Israel is a luxuriant avine;
He produces fruit for him-
self.
The more his fruit,
The more altars he bmade;
The richer his land,
The better he made the sa-
cred cpillars.

2 a1 Kin.
18:21; Zeph.
1:5 bHos.
13:16 cHos.
10:8; Mic.
5:13

2 Their heart is afaithless;
Now they must bear their
bguilt.
The LORD will cbreak down
their altars
And destroy their sacred
pillars.

★ **3** aPs.
12:4; Is. 5:19

3 Surely now they will say,
"We have ano king,
For we do not revere the
LORD.
As for the king, what can
he do for us?"

4 aEzek.
17:13-19;
Hos. 4:2
bDeut.
31:16, 17;
2 Kin.
17:3, 4;
Amos 5:7

4 They speak mere words,
With aworthless oaths
they make covenants;

And bjudgment sprouts
like poisonous weeds
in the furrows of the
field.

5 The inhabitants of Samaria
will fear
For the acalf of bBeth-
aven.
Indeed, its people will
mourn for it,
And its cidolatrous priests
will cry out over it,
Over its dglory, since it has
departed from it.

★ **5** aHos.
8:5, 6 bHos.
4:15; 5:8
c2 Kin. 23:5
dHos. 9:11

6 The thing itself will be carried to aAssyria
As tribute to bKing Jareb;
Ephraim will be cseized
with shame,
And Israel will be ashamed
of its down counsel.

★ **6** aHos.
11:5 bHos.
5:13 cHos.
4:7 dIs. 30:3;
Jer. 7:24

7 Samaria will be acut off
with her king,
Like a stick on the surface
of the water.

7 aHos.
13:11

8 Also the ahigh places of
Aven, the bsin of Is-
rael, will be de-
stroyed;
cThorn and thistle will
grow on their altars,
Then they will dsay to the
mountains,
"Cover us!" And to the
hills, "Fall on us!"

★ **8** aHos.
4:13 b1 Kin.
12:28-30;
13:34 cIs.
32:13; Hos.
9:6; 10:2 dIs.
2:19; Luke
23:30; Rev.
6:16

9 From the days of Gibeah
you have sinned, O Is-
rael;
There they stand!
Will not the battle against
the sons of iniquity
overtake them in Gib-
eah?

★ **9**

10 When it is My adesire, I
will bchastise them;
And cthe peoples will be
gathered against them
When they are bound for
their double guilt.

10 aEzek.
5:13 bHos.
4:9 cJer.
16:16

10:1 The richer the people became, the more idols they made (see 8:11).
10:3 We have no king. I.e., none worthy of the name, because their kings made worthless covenants.
10:5 Beth-aven. Hosea's contemptuous name for Bethel (see note on 4:15).
10:6 King Jareb. See note on 5:13.

10:8 the high places. Canaanite in origin, these were used as local sanctuaries and settings for fertility rites. Aven. Short for Beth-aven. say to the mountains. See Rev. 6:16 for the ulti-mate fulfillment of these words during the Tribulation.
10:9 Gibeah. Emblematic of gross and cruel sen-suality (Judg. 19).

★11 ªJer.
50:11; Hos.
4:16; Mic.
4:13 ᵇJer.
28:14

11 And Ephraim is a trained ªheifer that loves to thresh,
But I will ᵇcome over her fair neck *with a yoke*;
I will harness Ephraim, Judah will plow, Jacob will harrow for himself.

12 ªProv.
11:18 ᵇJer.
4:3 ᶜHos.
12:6 ᵈHos.
6:3 ᵉls. 44:3;
45:8

12 ªSow with a view to righteousness,
Reap in accordance with kindness;
ᵇBreak up your fallow ground,
For it is time to ᶜseek the LORD
Until He ᵈcomes to ᵉrain righteousness on you.

13 ªJob 4:8;
Prov. 22:8;
Gal. 6:7, 8
ᵇHos. 4:2;
7:3; 11:12
ᶜPs. 33:16

13 You have ªplowed wickedness, you have reaped injustice,
You have eaten the fruit of ᵇlies.
Because you have trusted in your way, in your ᶜnumerous warriors,

★14 ªls.
17:3 ᵇHos.
13:16

14 Therefore, a tumult will arise among your people,
And all your ªfortresses will be destroyed,
As Shalman destroyed Beth-arbel on the day of battle,
When ᵇmothers were dashed in pieces with *their* children.

15 Thus it will be done to you at Bethel because of your great wickedness.
At dawn the king of Israel will be completely cut off.

B   The Message of Restoration, 11:1-14:9

1   *God's love for the prodigal people*, 11:1-11

11 When Israel *was* a youth I loved him,
And ªout of Egypt I ᵇcalled My son.

★ 1 ªHos.
2:15; 12:9,
13; 13:4
ᵇEx. 4:22,
23; Matt.
2:15

2 The more ªthey called them,
The more they went from them;
They kept ᵇsacrificing to the Baals
And ᶜburning incense to idols.

★ 2 ª2 Kin.
17:13-15
ᵇHos. 2:13;
4:13 ᶜls.
65:7; Jer.
18:15

3 Yet it is I who taught Ephraim to walk,
I ªtook them in My arms;
But they did not know that I ᵇhealed them.

3 ªDeut.
1:31; 32:10,
11 ᵇPs.
107:20; Jer.
30:17

4 I ªled them with cords of a man, with bonds of love,
And ᵇI became to them as one who lifts the yoke from their jaws;
And I bent down *and* ᶜfed them.

4 ªJer.
31:2, 3 ᵇLev.
26:13 ᶜEx.
16:32; Ps.
78:25

5 They will not return to the land of Egypt;
But Assyria—he will be their king,
Because they ªrefused to return *to Me*.

5 ªHos.
7:16

6 And the ªsword will whirl against their cities,
And will demolish their gate bars
And ᵇconsume *them* because of their ᶜcounsels.

6 ªHos.
13:16 ᵇLam.
2:9 ᶜHos.
4:16, 17

10:11 God placed no heavy yoke over Ephraim's (Israel's) *fair neck*, but since she abused God's kindness, He would cause her to draw a heavy load.

10:14 *Shalman.* Perhaps Shalmaneser V, king of Assyria; the battle at *Beth-arbel* is otherwise unknown.

11:1 *Israel.* The nation, who was taken from Egypt and cared for by God (Exod. 4:22), though subsequently she proved to be unfaithful. Here Israel also refers to Christ (cf. Matt. 2:15) who, by contrast, always did that which pleased God.

11:2 *they* (the prophets) *called them* (the people).

7 *a*Jer. 3:6,
7; 8:5

7 So My people are bent on
  *a*turning from Me.
Though they call them to
  the One on high,
None at all exalts *Him*.

★ 8 *a*Hos.
6:4; 7:1
*b*Gen. 14:8;
Deut. 29:23

8 *a*How can I give you up, O
  Ephraim?
How can I surrender you,
  O Israel?
How can I make you like
  *b*Admah?
How can I treat you like
  *b*Zeboiim?
My heart is turned over
  within Me,
All my compassions are
  kindled.

9 *a*Deut.
13:17 *b*Jer.
26:3; 30:11
*c*Num. 23:19
*d*Is. 5:24;
12:6; 41:14,
16

9 I will *a*not execute My
  fierce anger;
I will not destroy Ephraim
  *b*again.
For *c*I am God and not
  man, the *d*Holy One
  in your midst,
And I will not come in
  wrath.

★10 *a*Hos.
3:5; 6:1-3
*b*Is. 31:4;
Joel 3:16;
Amos 1:2
*c*Is. 66:2, 5

10 They will *a*walk after the
  LORD,
He will *b*roar like a lion;
Indeed He will roar,
And His sons will come
  *c*trembling from the
  west.

11 *a*Is. 11:11
*b*Is. 60:8;
Hos. 7:11
*c*Ezek.
28:25, 26;
34:27, 28

11 They will come trembling
  like   birds   from
  *a*Egypt,
And like *b*doves from the
  land of *a*Assyria;
And I will *c*settle them in
  their houses, declares
  the LORD.

2 God's chastisement of the
prodigal people,
11:12–13:16

12 *a*Hos.
4:2; 7:3

12 Ephraim surrounds Me
  with *a*lies,

And the house of Israel
  with deceit;
Judah is also unruly
  against God,
Even against the Holy One
  who is faithful.

12 Ephraim feeds on *a*wind,
And pursues the *b*east
  wind continually;
He multiplies lies and vio-
  lence.
Moreover, he makes a cov-
  enant with Assyria,
And oil is carried to Egypt.

★ 1 *a*Jer.
22:22 *b*Gen.
41:6; Ezek.
17:10

2 The LORD also has a *a*dispute with Judah,
And will punish Jacob *b*according to his ways;
He will repay him accord-
  ing to his deeds.

★ 2 *a*Hos.
4:1; Mic. 6:2
*b*Hos. 4:9;
7:2

3 In the womb he *a*took his
  brother by the heel,
And in his maturity he
  *b*contended with God.

★ 3-4

3 *a*Gen.
25:26 *b*Gen.
32:28

4 Yes, he wrestled with the
  angel and prevailed;
He wept and *a*sought His
  favor.
He found Him at *b*Bethel,
And there He spoke with
  us,

4 *a*Gen.
32:26 *b*Gen.
28:13-19;
35:10-15

5 Even the LORD, the God of
  hosts;
The LORD is His *a*name.

5 *a*Ex. 3:15

6 Therefore, *a*return to your
  God,
*b*Observe kindness and
  justice,
And *c*wait for your God
  continually.

6 *a*Hos.
6:1-3; 10:12
*b*Mic. 6:8
*c*Mic. 7:7

7 A merchant, in whose
  hands are false *a*bal-
  ances,
He loves to oppress.

★ 7 *a*Prov.
11:1; Amos
8:5; Mic.
6:11

8 And Ephraim said, "Surely
  I have become *a*rich,

8 *a*Ps.
62:10; Hos.
13:6; Rev.
3:17 *b*Hos.
4:8; 14:1

11:8 *Admah* and *Zeboiim*. Destroyed with Sodom and Gomorrah (Deut. 29:23).
11:10 Though judgment was imminent, God
would one day *roar* like a lion summoning its
young, and Israel, trembling with eagerness,
would be restored and regathered to her land.
12:1 *feeds on wind.* Lit., shepherds the wind;
i.e., runs in vain to Egypt and Assyria for help.
At the same time she makes a *covenant* with

Assyria, she exports *oil* to Assyria's rival,
Egypt. Israel played both ends against the
middle and would herself soon be trapped.
12:2 *Jacob.* Frequently in Scripture, the name
stands for all his descendants.
12:3-4 See Gen. 25:26; 32:24-28.
12:7 *merchant.* Lit., Canaanite. Israel entered
Canaan and Canaan's ways entered Israel.

I have found wealth for myself;
In all my labors they will find in me
[b]No iniquity, which *would be* sin."

9 But I *have been* the LORD your God since the land of Egypt;
I will make you [a]live in tents again,
As in the days of the appointed festival.

10 I have also spoken to the [a]prophets,
And I gave numerous visions;
And through the prophets I gave [b]parables.

11 Is there iniquity *in* Gilead?
Surely they are worthless.
In Gilgal they sacrifice bulls,
Yes, [a]their altars are like the stone heaps
Beside the furrows of the field.

12 Now [a]Jacob fled to the land of Aram,
And [b]Israel worked for a wife,
And for a wife he kept *sheep.*

13 But by a [a]prophet the LORD brought Israel from Egypt,
And by a prophet he was kept.

14 [a]Ephraim has provoked to bitter anger;
So his Lord will leave his [b]bloodguilt on him,
And bring back his [c]reproach to him.

13 [a]When Ephraim spoke, *there was* trembling.
He [b]exalted himself in Israel,

But through [c]Baal he did wrong and died.

2 And now they sin more and more,
And make for themselves [a]molten images,
Idols [b]skillfully made from their silver,
All of them the [c]work of craftsmen.
They say of them, "Let the men who sacrifice kiss the [d]calves!"

3 Therefore, they will be like the [a]morning cloud,
And like dew which soon disappears,
Like [b]chaff which is blown away from the threshing floor,
And like [c]smoke from a chimney.

4 Yet I *have been* the [a]LORD your God
Since the land of Egypt;
And you were not to know [b]any god except Me,
For there is no savior [c]besides Me.

5 I [a]cared for you in the wilderness,
[b]In the land of drought.

6 As *they had* their pasture, they became [a]satisfied,
And being satisfied, their [b]heart became proud;
Therefore, they [c]forgot Me.

7 So I will be [a]like a lion to them;
Like a [b]leopard I will lie in wait by the wayside.

8 I will encounter them [a]like a bear robbed of her cubs,
And I will tear open their chests;

Marginal references (left column):

★ **9** [a]Lev. 23:42

10 [a]2 Kin. 17:13; Jer. 7:25 [b]Ezek. 17:2; 20:49

11 [a]Hos. 8:11; 10:1, 2

★**12** [a]Gen. 28:5 [b]Gen. 29:20

★**13** [a]Ex. 14:19-22; Is. 63:11-14

★**14** [a]2 Kin. 17:7-18 [b]Ezek. 18:10-13 [c]Dan. 11:18; Mic. 6:16

★ **1** [a]Job 29:21, 22 [b]Judg. 8:1; 12:1 [c]Hos. 2:8-17; 11:2

Marginal references (right column):

2 [a]Is. 46:6; Jer. 10:4; Hos. 2:8 [b]Is. 44:17-20 [c]Hos. 8:6 [d]Hos. 8:5, 6; 10:5

3 [a]Hos. 6:4 [b]Ps. 1:4; Is. 17:13; Dan. 2:35 [c]Ps. 68:2

4 [a]Hos. 12:9 [b]Ex. 20:3; 2 Kin. 18:35 [c]Is. 43:11; 45:21, 22

5 [a]Deut. 2:7; 32:10 [b]Deut. 8:15

6 [a]Deut. 8:12, 14; 32:13-15; Jer. 5:7 [b]Hos. 7:14 [c]Hos. 2:13; 4:6; 8:14

★ **7-8**
7 [a]Lam. 3:10; Hos. 5:14 [b]Jer. 5:6

8 [a]2 Sam. 17:8 [b]Ps. 50:22

12:9 Israel would once again live in *tents*, because her cities would be destroyed.
12:12 The account of this story is in Gen. 29.
12:13 *prophet.* Moses.
12:14 *leave his bloodguilt on him.* Israel would have to bear the consequences of sin.
13:1 *he . . . died.* I.e., spiritually.

13:7-8 God, who had been the protector of Israel in the wilderness (vv. 5-6), would become her destroyer. Like a *lion* He would devour; like a *leopard* He would *lie in wait* or lurk, suddenly springing on an unprepared people; and like a *bear* His judgment would be ferocious.

There I will also ᵇdevour
them like a lioness,
As a wild beast would tear
them.

9 *It is* your destruction, O Israel,
That *you are* ᵃagainst Me,
against your ᵇhelp.

10 Where now is your ᵃking
That he may save you in
all your cities,
And your ᵇjudges of whom
you requested,
"Give me a king and
princes"?

11 I ᵃgave you a king in My
anger,
And ᵇtook him away in
My wrath.

12 The iniquity of Ephraim is
bound up;
His sin is ᵃstored up.

13 The pains of ᵃchildbirth
come upon him;
He is ᵇnot a wise son,
For it is not the time that
he should ᶜdelay at
the opening of the
womb.

14 I will ᵃransom them from
the power of Sheol;
I will redeem them from
death.
ᵇO Death, where are your
thorns?
O Sheol, where is your
sting?
ᶜCompassion will be hid-
den from My sight.

15 Though he ᵃflourishes
among the reeds,
An ᵇeast wind will come,
The wind of the LORD com-
ing up from the wil-
derness;
And his fountain will ᶜbe-
come dry,

And his spring will be
dried up;
It will ᵈplunder *his* treasury of every precious
article.

16 Samaria will be held
ᵃguilty,
For she has ᵇrebelled
against her God.
ᶜThey will fall by the
ᵈsword,
Their little ones will be
ᵉdashed in pieces,
And their pregnant ᶠwom-
en will be ripped
open.

3   *God's restoration of the prodigal people,* 14:1–9

14 ᵃReturn, O Israel, to the
LORD your God,
For you have stumbled be-
cause of your ᵇiniq-
uity.

2 Take words with you and
return to the LORD.
Say to Him, "ᵃTake away
all iniquity,
And receive *us* graciously,
That we may ᵇpresent the
fruit of our lips.

3 "Assyria will not save us,
We will ᵃnot ride on
horses;
Nor will we say again,
'ᵇOur god,'
To the ᶜwork of our hands;
For in ᵈThee the orphan
finds mercy."

4 I will ᵃheal their apostasy,
I will ᵇlove them freely,
For My anger has ᶜturned
away from them.

5 I will be like the ᵃdew to
Israel;
He will blossom like the
ᵇlily,

Cross-references (margin)

9 ᵃJer. 2:17, 19; Mal. 1:12, 13 ᵇDeut. 33:26, 29

10 ᵃ2 Kin. 17:4; Hos. 8:4 ᵇ1 Sam. 8:5, 6

11 ᵃ1 Sam. 8:7; 10:17-24 ᵇ1 Sam. 15:26; 1 Kin. 14:7-10; Hos. 10:7

12 ᵃDeut. 32:34, 35; Job 14:17; Rom. 2:5

★**13** ᵃIs. 13:8; Mic. 4:9, 10 ᵇDeut. 32:6; Hos. 5:4 ᶜIs. 37:3; 66:9

★**14** ᵃPs. 49:15; Ezek. 37:12, 13 ᵇ1 Cor. 15:55 ᶜJer. 20:16; 31:35-37

15 ᵃGen. 49:22; Hos. 10:1 ᵇGen. 41:6; Jer. 4:11, 12; Ezek. 17:10; 19:12 ᶜJer. 51:36 ᵈJer. 20:5

★**16** ᵃHos. 10:2 ᵇHos. 7:14 ᶜ2 Kin. 8:12 ᵈHos. 11:6 ᵉHos. 10:14 ᶠ2 Kin. 15:16

1 ᵃHos. 6:1; 10:12; 12:6; Joel 2:13 ᵇHos. 4:8; 5:5; 9:7

★**2** ᵃMic. 7:18, 19 ᵇPs. 51:16, 17; Hos. 6:6; Heb. 13:15

★**3** ᵃPs. 33:17; Is. 31:1 ᵇHos. 8:6; 13:2 ᶜHos. 4:12 ᵈPs. 10:14; 68:5

★**4-8**
4 ᵃIs. 57:18; Hos. 6:1 ᵇZeph. 3:17 ᶜIs. 12:1

5 ᵃProv. 19:12; Is. 26:19 ᵇSong 2:1; Matt. 6:28 ᶜIs. 35:2

13:13 An unwise Israel delayed coming out of
the womb into a new life (of obedience).
13:14 See 1 Cor. 15:55.
13:16 Israel would suffer these terrible atrocities
(see also 2 Kings 15:16).
14:2 *the fruit of our lips.* I.e., the praise of our

lips.
14:3 *Assyria* will not save Israel nor will the
horses of the Egyptian cavalry.
14:4-8 These verses speak of the future blessing
of Israel in the Millennium.

And he will take root like
the cedars of cLeba-
non.

6 aJer.
11:16 bSong
4:11

6   His shoots will sprout,
And his beauty will be like
the aolive tree,
And his fragrance like *the*
cedars of bLebanon.

7 aEzek.
17:23 bHos.
2:21, 22

7   Those who alive in his
shadow
Will again raise bgrain,
And they will blossom like
the vine.
His renown *will be* like the
wine of Lebanon.

8 aJob
34:32; Hos.
14:3 bIs.
41:19 cEzek.
17:23

8   O Ephraim, what more
have I to do with ai-
dols?

It is I who answer and look
after you.
I am like a luxuriant bcy-
press;
From cMe comes your
fruit.

9   aWhoever is wise, let him
understand   these
things;
Whoever is discerning, let
him know them.
For the bways of the Lord
are right,
And the crighteous will
walk in them,
But dtransgressors will
stumble in them.

9 aPs.
107:43; Jer.
9:12 bPs.
111:7, 8;
Prov. 10:29;
Zeph. 3:5
cIs. 26:7 dIs.
1:28

INTRODUCTION TO
THE BOOK OF JOEL

AUTHOR: Joel   DATE: 835 B.C.

The Prophet and His Times   *Joel, whose name means "Yahweh is God," apparently wrote during the days of young King Joash (835-796), who was under the regency of priests when he ascended the throne of Judah at the age of 7 (2 Kings 11:21). Though some date the book after the Exile, the enemies of Judah are not identified in the prophecy as Syrians, Assyrians, or Babylonians, as would be the case if the book were written after the captivity (see 3:4, 19).*

The prophecy was occasioned by a severe drought and an invasion of locusts, which Joel saw as a punishment for the sins of the people. He also depicted this invasion of locusts as an army, a harbinger of a future military campaign in the Day of the LORD.

The Day of the LORD   *The Day of the LORD, the major theme of this prophecy, involves God's special intervention in the affairs of human history. Three facets of the Day of the LORD are discernible: (1) the historical, God's intervention in the affairs of Israel (Zeph. 1:14-18; Joel 1:15) and heathen nations (Isa. 13:6; Jer. 46:10; Ezek. 30:3); (2) the illustrative, whereby an historical incident represents a partial fulfillment of the eschatological Day of the LORD (Joel 2:1-11; Isa. 13:6-13); (3) the eschatological. This eschatological "day" includes the time of the Great Tribulation (Isa. 2:12-19; 4:1), the second coming of Christ (Joel 2:30-32), and the Millennium (Isa. 4:2; 12; 19:23-25; Jer. 30:7-9).*

OUTLINE OF JOEL

I. Title Verse: the Author, 1:1
II. Desolation, 1:2-2:17
  A. The Character of the Desolation, 1:2-12
  B. The Reactions to the Desolation, 1:13-14
  C. The Picture of the Desolation, 1:15-20
  D. The Prophecy of Future Desolation, 2:1-11
  E. The Exhortation in View of Desolation,
    2:12-17

III. Deliverance, 2:18-3:21
  A. The Promise of Immediate Deliverance,
    2:18-27
  B. The Promise of Future Deliverance,
    2:28-3:21
    1. Its initiation, 2:28-32
    2. Its judgments, 3:1-17
    3. Its consummation, 3:18-21

THE BOOK OF JOEL

I   TITLE VERSE: THE AUTHOR, 1:1

1 *a*Jer. 1:2;
Ezek. 1:3;
Hos. 1:1
*b*Acts 2:16

1 The *a*word of the LORD that came to *b*Joel, the son of Pethuel.

II   DESOLATION, 1:2-2:17
A   The Character of the Desolation, 1:2-12

★ 2 *a*Hos.
4:1; 5:1 *b*Job
8:8; Joel
1:14 *c*Jer.
30:7; Joel
2:2

2 *a*Hear this, O *b*elders,
And listen, all inhabitants
of the land.

*c*Has *anything like* this
happened in your
days
Or in your fathers' days?

3 *a*Tell your sons about it,
And *let* your sons *tell* their
sons,
And their sons the next
generation.

3 *a*Ex. 10:2;
Ps. 78:4

4 What the *a*gnawing locust
has left, the swarming
locust has eaten;

★ 4 *a*Deut.
28:38; Joel
2:25; Amos
4:9 *b*Nah.
3:15, 16 *c*Is.
33:4

1:2 The reply to the question could only be an emphatic NO. This plague was unique.
1:4 Four varieties of locust (out of a total of more than 80) are mentioned. Literally, the

Heb. words mean shearer, swarmer, lapper, and devourer. Locust swarms commonly number in the millions, if not billions.

And what the ^bswarming
locust has left, the
creeping locust has
eaten;
And what the creeping lo-
cust has left, the
^cstripping locust has
eaten.

5 Awake, ^adrunkards, and
weep;
And wail, all you wine
drinkers,
On account of the sweet
wine
That is ^bcut off from your
mouth.

6 For a ^anation has invaded
my land,
Mighty and without num-
ber;
^bIts teeth are the teeth of a
lion,
And it has the fangs of a
lioness.

7 It has ^amade my vine a
waste,
And my fig tree splinters.
It has stripped them bare
and cast *them* away;
Their branches have be-
come white.

8 ^aWail like a virgin ^bgirded
with sackcloth
For the bridegroom of her
youth.

9 The ^agrain offering and the
libation are cut off
From the house of the
LORD.
The ^bpriests mourn,
The ministers of the LORD.

10 The field is ^aruined,
^bThe land mourns,
For the grain is ruined,
The new wine dries up,
Fresh oil fails.

11 ^aBe ashamed, O farmers,
Wail, O vinedressers,

For the wheat and the barley;
Because the ^bharvest of the
field is destroyed.

12 The ^avine dries up,
And the fig tree fails;
The ^bpomegranate, the
^cpalm also, and the
^dapple tree,
All the trees of the field
dry up.
Indeed, ^erejoicing dries up
From the sons of men.

**B   The Reactions to the
Desolation, 1:13–14**

13 ^aGird   yourselves   *with*
sackcloth,
And lament, O priests;
^bWail, O ministers of the
altar!
Come, ^cspend the night in
sackcloth,
O ministers of my God,
For the grain offering and
the libation
Are withheld from the
house of your God.

14 ^aConsecrate a fast,
Proclaim a ^bsolemn assem-
bly;
Gather the elders
And all the inhabitants of
the land
To the house of the LORD
your God,
And ^ccry out to the LORD.

**C   The Picture of the
Desolation,
1:15–20**

15 ^aAlas for the day!
For the ^bday of the LORD is
near,

5 ^aJoel 3:3
^bIs. 32:10

6 ^aJoel 2:2,
11, 25 ^bRev.
9:8

★ 7 ^aIs. 5:6;
Amos 4:9

8 ^aIs. 22:12
^bJoel 1:13;
Amos 8:10

★ 9 ^aHos.
9:4; Joel
1:13; 2:14
^bJoel 2:17

10 ^aIs. 24:4,
7 ^bJer. 12:11

11 ^aJer.
14:4; Amos
5:16 ^bIs.
17:11; Jer.
9:12

★12 ^aJoel
1:10; Hab.
3:17 ^bHag.
2:19 ^cSong
7:8 ^dSong
2:3 ^eIs.
16:10; 24:11;
Jer. 48:33

★13-14

13 ^aJer. 4:8;
Ezek. 7:18
^bJer. 9:10
^c1 Kin. 21:27

14 ^aJoel
2:15, 16
^bLev. 23:36
^cJon. 3:8

★15 ^aIs.
13:9; Jer.
30:7; Amos
5:16 ^bJoel
2:1, 11, 31
^cIs. 13:6;
Ezek. 7:2-12

1:7 The branches were *white* because they were
stripped.
1:9 *The grain offering and the libation* could no
longer be offered because the locusts had
wiped out the raw materials for these offerings.
1:12 *the apple tree.* Likely an apricot tree (see

Song 2:5; 7:8).
1:13–14 *priests.* Called upon to lead the people
in a *fast* and *solemn* public gathering of national repentance.
1:15 *destruction.* Heb., *shod;* a play on words related to the word *Almighty* (Heb., *Shaddai*).

And it will come as ᶜdestruction from the Almighty.

16 ᵃIs. 3:7;
Amos 4:6
ᵇDeut. 12:7;
Ps. 43:4

16 Has not ᵃfood been cut off before our eyes,
Gladness and ᵇjoy from the house of our God?

17 ᵃIs. 17:10, 11

17 The ᵃseeds shrivel under their clods;
The storehouses are desolate,
The barns are torn down,
For the grain is dried up.

18 ᵃ1 Kin. 8:5; Jer. 12:4; 14:5, 6; Hos. 4:3

18 How ᵃthe beasts groan!
The herds of cattle wander aimlessly
Because there is no pasture for them;
Even the flocks of sheep suffer.

★19-20

19 ᵃPs. 50:15; Mic. 7:7 ᵇJer. 9:10; Amos 7:4

19 ᵃTo Thee, O Lord, I cry;
For ᵇfire has devoured the pastures of the wilderness,
And the flame has burned up all the trees of the field.

20 ᵃPs. 104:21; 147:9; Joel 1:18 ᵇ1 Kin. 17:7; 18:5

20 Even the beasts of the field ᵃpant for Thee;
For the ᵇwater brooks are dried up,
And fire has devoured the pastures of the wilderness.

D The Prophecy of Future Desolation, 2:1-11

★ 1-11
1 ᵃJer. 4:5; Joel 2:15; Zeph. 1:16
ᵇJoel 1:15; 2:11, 31; 3:14; Obad. 15; Zeph. 1:14
2 ᵃJoel 2:10, 31; Amos 5:18; Zeph. 1:15
ᵇJoel 1:6; 2:11, 25
ᶜLam. 1:12; Dan. 9:12; 12:1; Joel 1:2

2 ᵃBlow a trumpet in Zion,
And sound an alarm on My holy mountain!
Let all the inhabitants of the land tremble,
For the ᵇday of the Lord is coming;
Surely it is near,

2 A day of ᵃdarkness and gloom,

A day of clouds and thick darkness.
As the dawn is spread over the mountains,
So there is a ᵇgreat and mighty people;
There has ᶜnever been anything like it,
Nor will there be again after it
To the years of many generations.

3 ᵃPs. 97:3; Is. 9:18, 19
ᵇIs. 51:3; Ezek. 36:35, 15; Ps. 105:34, 35; Zech. 7:14

3 A ᵃfire consumes before them,
And behind them a flame burns.
The land is ᵇlike the garden of Eden before them,
But a ᶜdesolate wilderness behind them,
And nothing at all escapes them.

4 ᵃRev. 9:7

4 Their ᵃappearance is like the appearance of horses;
And like war horses, so they run.

5 ᵃRev. 9:9
ᵇIs. 5:24; 30:30

5 With a ᵃnoise as of chariots
They leap on the tops of the mountains,
Like the crackling of a ᵇflame of fire consuming the stubble,
Like a mighty people arranged for battle.

6 ᵃIs. 13:8; Nah. 2:10
ᵇJer. 30:6

6 Before them the people are in ᵃanguish;
All ᵇfaces turn pale.

7 ᵃProv. 30:27

7 They run like mighty men;
They climb the wall like soldiers;
And they each ᵃmarch in line,
Nor do they deviate from their paths.

8 They do not crowd each other;

1:19-20 Even the animals suffer because of man's sin, and they too cry to God.

2:1-11 The locust army is regarded as a foretaste of an invading army in the *day of the Lord;* i.e., in the Tribulation period. The future reference may be to the demon-locusts described in Rev. 9:1-12 and/or to the invasion of the king of the North (Ezek. 38:15; Dan. 11:40). Resembling the Garden of Eden before the invasion, the land of Palestine will be reduced to a wilderness afterward (v. 3). The same (or similar) disturbances described in verse 10 are predicted in Rev. 6:12-13; 8:12.

They march everyone in
his path.
When they burst through
the defenses,
They do not break ranks.

9 [a]Ex. 10:6 [b]Jer. 9:21; John 10:1

9 They rush on the city,
They run on the wall;
They climb into the
[a]houses,
They [b]enter through the
windows like a thief.

10 [a]Ps. 18:7; Joel 3:16; Nah. 1:5 [b]Is. 13:10; 34:4; Jer. 4:23; Ezek. 32:7, 8; Joel 2:31; 3:15; Matt. 24:29; Rev. 8:12

10 Before them the earth
[a]quakes,
The heavens tremble,
The [b]sun and the moon
grow dark,
And the stars lose their
brightness.

11 [a]Ps. 46:6; Is. 13:4; Jer. 25:30; Joel 3:16 [b]Joel 2:25 [c]Jer. 50:34; Rev. 18:8 [d]Jer. 30:7; Joel 1:15; 2:1, 31; 3:14; Zeph. 1:14, 15; Rev. 6:17 [e]Ezek. 22:14; Mal. 3:2

11 And the LORD [a]utters His
voice before [b]His
army;
Surely His camp is very
great,
For [c]strong is He who carries out His word.
The [d]day of the LORD is indeed great and very
awesome,
And [e]who can endure it?

E The Exhortation in View of Desolation, 2:12–17

★12-14

12 [a]Deut. 4:29; Jer. 4:1, 2; Ezek. 33:11; Hos. 12:6 [b]Dan. 9:3

12 "Yet even now," declares
the LORD,
"[a]Return to Me with all
your heart,
And with [b]fasting, weeping, and mourning;

13 [a]Ps. 34:18; 51:17; Is. 57:15 [b]Gen. 37:34; 2 Sam. 1:11; Job 1:20; Jer. 41:5 [c]Ex. 34:6 [d]Jer. 18:8; 42:10; Amos 7:3, 6

13 And [a]rend your heart and
not [b]your garments."
Now return to the LORD
your God,
For He is [c]gracious and
compassionate,
Slow to anger, abounding
in lovingkindness,
And [d]relenting of evil.

14 [a]Jer. 26:3; Jon. 3:9 [b]Hag. 2:19 [c]Joel 1:9, 13

14 Who knows [a]whether He
will *not* turn and re-
lent,
And leave a [b]blessing behind Him,
Even [c]a grain offering and
a libation
For the LORD your God?

★15-17
15 [a]Num. 10:3; 2 Kin. 10:20 [b]Joel 1:14

15 [a]Blow a trumpet in Zion,
[b]Consecrate a fast, proclaim a solemn assem-
bly,

16 [a]1 Sam. 16:5; 2 Chr. 29:5 [b]Ps. 19:5

16 Gather the people, [a]sancti-
fy the congregation,
Assemble the elders,
Gather the children and
the nursing infants.
Let the [b]bridegroom come
out of his room
And the bride out of her
bridal chamber.

17 [a]2 Chr. 8:12; Ezek. 8:16 [b]Ex. 32:11, 12; Is. 37:20; Amos 7:2, 5 [c]Ps. 44:13; 74:10 [d]Ps. 42:10; 79:10; 115:2

17 Let the priests, the LORD's
ministers,
Weep [a]between the porch
and the altar,
And let them say, "[b]Spare
Thy people, O LORD,
And do not make Thine
inheritance a [c]re-
proach,
A byword among the na-
tions.
Why should they among
the peoples say,
'[d]Where is their God?' "

III DELIVERANCE, 2:18–3:21

A The Promise of Immediate Deliverance, 2:18–27

18 [a]Zech. 1:14; 8:2 [b]Is. 60:10; 63:9, 15

18 Then the LORD will be
[a]zealous for His land,
And will have [b]pity on His
people.

19 [a]Jer. 31:12; Hos. 2:21, 22; Joel 1:10; Mal. 3:10 [b]Ezek. 34:29; 36:15

19 And the LORD will answer
and say to His people,
"Behold, I am going to
[a]send you grain, new
wine, and oil,
And you will be satisfied
in full with them;
And I will [b]never again
make you a reproach
among the nations.

2:12–14 A call to personal repentance that comes from the *heart.* The heart was considered to include the intellect as well as the emotions.

2:15–17 A call to national repentance in a *solemn assembly* from which no one, not even babies or newlyweds, would be exempt (see Deut. 24:5).

★20 aJer.
1:14, 15
bZech. 14:8
cDeut. 11:24
dIs. 34:3;
Amos 4:10

20 "But I will remove the
    ªnorthern *army* far
    from you,
And I will drive it into a
    parched and desolate
    land,
And its vanguard into the
    ᵇeastern sea,
And its rear guard into the
    ᶜwestern sea.
And its ᵈstench will arise
    and its foul smell will
    come up,
For it has done great
    things."

21 aIs. 54:4;
Jer. 30:10;
Zeph. 3:16,
17 bPs.
126:3; Joel
2:26

21 ªDo not fear, O land, re-
    joice and be glad,
For the LORD has done
    ᵇgreat things.

22 aPs.
65:12, 13

22 Do not fear, beasts of the
    field,
For the ªpastures of the
    wilderness have
    turned green,
For the tree has borne its
    fruit,
The fig tree and the vine
    have yielded in full.

★23 aPs.
149:2 bIs.
12:2-6
cDeut.
11:14; Is.
41:16; Jer.
5:24; Hab
3:18; Zech.
10:7 dLev.
26:4; Hos.
6:3; Zech.
10:1

23 So rejoice, O ªsons of Zion,
    And ᵇbe glad in the LORD
    your God;
For He has ᶜgiven you the
    early rain for *your*
    vindication.
And He has poured down
    for you the rain,
The early and ᵈlatter rain
    as before.

24 aLev.
26:10; Amos
9:13; Mal.
3:10

24 And the threshing floors
    will be full of grain,
And the vats will ªoverflow
    with the new wine
    and oil.

25 aJoel 1:4-
7; 2:2-11

25 "Then I will make up to you
    for the years
That the swarming ªlocust
    has eaten,

The creeping locust, the
    stripping locust, and
    the gnawing locust,
My great army which I
    sent among you.

26 "And you shall have plenty
    to ªeat and be satis-
    fied,
And ᵇpraise the name of
    the LORD your God,
Who has ᶜdealt won-
    drously with you;
Then My people will ᵈnev-
    er be put to shame.

27 "Thus you will ªknow that I
    am in the midst of Is-
    rael,
And that I am the LORD
    your God
And there is ᵇno other;
And My people will never
    be ᶜput to shame.

26 aLev.
26:5; Deut.
11:15; Is.
62:9 bDeut.
12:7; Ps.
67:5-7 cPs.
126:2, 3; Is.
25:1 dIs.
45:17

27 aLev.
26:11, 12;
Joel 3:17, 21
bIs. 45:5, 6
cIs. 49:23

**B The Promise of Future
Deliverance, 2:28-3:21**

1 Its initiation, 2:28-32

28 "ªAnd it will come about
    after this
That I will ᵇpour out My
    Spirit on all ᶜman-
    kind;
And your sons and daugh-
    ters will prophesy,
Your old men will dream
    dreams,
Your young men will see
    visions.

29 "And even on the ªmale
    and female servants
I will pour out My Spirit in
    those days.

30 "And I will ªdisplay won-
    ders in the sky and on
    the earth,
Blood, fire, and columns of
    smoke.

★28 aActs
2:17-21 bIs.
32:15; 44:3;
Ezek. 39:29;
Zech. 12:10
cIs. 40:5;
49:26

29 a1 Cor.
12:13; Gal.
3:28

30 aMatt.
24:29, Mark
13:24, 25;
Luke 21:11,
25, 26; Acts
2:19

2:20 *northern army.* Would be scattered in the desert, the *eastern sea* (the Dead Sea), and the *western sea* (the Mediterranean). See Ezek. 39:2 for the destruction of the army from the north during the Tribulation period.
2:23 *early* and *latter rain.* In March-April and Sept.-Oct. respectively.

2:28 *after this.* I.e., after Israel's future repentance and restoration (Zech. 12:10; 13:1) in connection with the second advent of Christ, as witnessed by the portents of verse 30 (see note on Acts 2:16-21). The Holy Spirit will then be poured out on all classes in Israel who belong to the believing remnant (v. 32).

31 a Is.
13:10; 34:4;
Joel 2:10;
3:15; Matt.
24:29; Mark
13:24; Luke
21:25; Acts
2:20; Rev.
6:12, 13 b Is.
13:9; Zeph.
1:14-16; Mal.
4:1, 5

32 a Jer.
33:3; Acts
2:21; Rom.
10:13 b Is.
46:13; Rom.
11:26 c Is.
4:2; Obad.
17 d Is.
11:11; Jer.
31:7; Mic.
4:7; Rom.
9:27

31 "The ᵃsun will be turned
  into darkness,
And the moon into blood,
  Before the ᵇgreat and awesome day of the LORD
  comes.
32 "And it will come about
  that ᵃwhoever calls on
  the name of the LORD
Will be delivered;
For ᵇon Mount Zion and in
  Jerusalem
There will be those who
  ᶜescape,
As the LORD has said,
Even among the ᵈsurvivors
  whom the LORD calls.

2 Its judgments, 3:1-17

★ 1 a Jer.
30:3; Ezek.
38:14 b Jer.
16:15

3 "For behold, ᵃin those days
  and at that time,
  When I ᵇrestore the fortunes of Judah and Je-
  rusalem,

★ 2-3

2 a Is.
66:18; Mic.
4:12; Zech.
14:2 b Joel
3:12, 14 c Is.
66:16; Jer.
25:31; Ezek.
38:22 d Jer.
50:17; Ezek.
34:6 e Ezek.
35:10; 36:1-5

2 I will ᵃgather all the nations,
And bring them down to
  the ᵇvalley of Jehosha-
  phat.
Then I will ᶜenter into
  judgment with them
  there
On behalf of My people
  and My inheritance,
  Israel,
Whom they have ᵈscat-
  tered among the na-
  tions;
And they have ᵉdivided up
  My land.

3 a Obad.
11; Nah. 3:10
b Amos 2:6

3 "They have also ᵃcast lots
  for My people,
ᵇTraded a boy for a harlot,
And sold a girl for wine
  that they may drink.

4 "Moreover, what are you to
Me, O ᵃTyre, Sidon, and all the
regions of ᵇPhilistia? Are you rendering Me a recompense? But if
you do recompense Me, swiftly
and speedily I will ᶜreturn your
recompense on your head.
5 "Since you have ᵃtaken My
silver and My gold, brought My
precious treasures to your temples,
6   and sold the ᵃsons of Judah
and Jerusalem to the Greeks in
order to remove them far from
their territory,
7   behold, I am going to
ᵃarouse them from the place
where you have sold them, and
return your recompense on your
head.
8 "Also I will ᵃsell your sons
and your daughters into the hand
of the sons of Judah, and they will
sell them to the ᵇSabeans, to a
distant nation," for the LORD has
spoken.
9   ᵃProclaim this among the
  nations:
ᵇPrepare a war; ᶜrouse the
  mighty men!
Let all the soldiers draw
  near, let them come
  up!
10   ᵃBeat your plowshares into
  swords,
And your pruning hooks
  into spears;
ᵇLet the weak say, "I am a
  mighty man."
11   ᵃHasten and come, all you
  surrounding nations,
And gather yourselves
  there.
Bring down, O LORD, Thy
  ᵇmighty ones.

★ 4-8

4 a Is. 23:1-
18; Amos
1:9, 10;
Zech. 9:2-4;
Matt. 11:21,
22; Luke
10:13, 14
b Is. 14:29-
31; Jer. 47:1-
7; Ezek.
25:15-17;
Amos 1:6-8;
Zech. 9:5-7
c Is. 34:8;
59:18

5 a 2 Kin.
12:18; 2 Chr.
21:16, 17

6 a Ezek.
27:13

7 a Is. 43:5,
6; Jer. 23:8;
Zech. 9:13

8 a Is. 14:2;
60:14 b Job
1:15; Ps.
72:10; Ezek.
38:13

★ 9-17

9 a Jer.
51:27 b Jer.
6:4; Ezek.
38:7; Mic.
3:5 c Is. 8:9,
10; Jer. 46:3,
4; Zech.
14:2, 3

10 a Is. 2:4;
Mic. 4:3
b Zech. 12:8

11 a Ezek.
38:15, 16
b Is. 13:3

3:1 At the second coming of Christ, Israel will be
regathered to Palestine (Matt. 24:31).
3:2-3 Also at the second coming the Gentiles
will be judged for their treatment of Israel
(Matt. 25:40, 45) in the valley of Jehoshaphat
(which means "Yahweh judges," and may refer to the Kidron Valley on the E. of Jerusalem).
3:4-8 More immediate judgment was announced on the Phoenicians and Philistines,
who were notorious slave-traders. Verse 8 was

fulfilled in 345 B.C., when Artaxerxes III sold
the Sidonians into slavery, and in 332 B.C.,
when Alexander the Great did the same to the
people of Tyre and Gaza. *Sabeans.* A trading
people who lived in Arabia.
3:9-17 A description of the campaign of Armageddon (Rev. 16:14). Mic. 4:3, the reverse of
verse 10, cannot be fulfilled until after Armageddon. *Thy mighty ones* (v. 11). The Lord's
armies (Rev. 19:14). The wicked are a harvest
ripe (v. 13) for judgment (cf. Rev. 14:18-19).

12 aJoel 3:2,
14 bPs. 7:6;
96:13; 98:9;
Is. 2:4; 3:13

12 Let the nations be aroused
And come up to the avalley of Jehoshaphat,
For there I will sit to bjudge
All the surrounding nations.

13 aRev.
14:14-19
bJer. 51:33;
Hos. 6:11
cRev. 14:19,
20; 19:15
dIs. 63:3;
Lam. 1:15
eGen. 18:20

13 aPut in the sickle, for the bharvest is ripe.
Come, ctread, for the dwine press is full;
The vats overflow, for their ewickedness is great.

★14 aIs.
34:2-8 bJoel
3:2, 12 cJoel
1:15; 2:1, 11,
31

14 aMultitudes, multitudes in the bvalley of decision!
For the cday of the Lord is near in the valley of decision.

15 aJoel
2:10, 31

15 The asun and moon grow dark,
And the stars lose their brightness.

16 aHos.
11:10; Amos
1:2 bJoel
2:11 cEzek.
38:19; Joel
2:10; Hag.
2:6 dPs.
61:3; Is.
33:16; Jer.
17:17 eJer.
16:19; Nah.
1:7

16 And the Lord aroars from Zion
And butters His voice from Jerusalem,
And the cheavens and the earth tremble.
But the Lord is a drefuge for His people
And a estronghold to the sons of Israel.

17 aJoel
2:27 bIs.
11:9; 56:7;
Ezek. 20:40
cIs. 4:3;
Obad. 17
dIs. 52:1;
Nah. 1:15

17 Then you will aknow that I am the Lord your God,
Dwelling in Zion My bholy mountain.

So Jerusalem will be choly,
And dstrangers will pass through it no more.

3 Its consummation, 3:18-21

18 And it will come about in that day
That the amountains will drip with sweet wine,
And the hills will bflow with milk,
And all the cbrooks of Judah will flow with water;
And a dspring will go out from the house of the Lord,
To water the valley of Shittim.

19 Egypt will become a waste,
And Edom will become a desolate wilderness,
Because of the aviolence done to the sons of Judah,
In whose land they have shed innocent blood.

20 But Judah will be ainhabited forever,
And Jerusalem for all generations.

21 And I will aavenge their blood which I have not avenged,
For the Lord dwells in Zion.

★18 aAmos
9:13 bEx.
3:8 cIs.
30:25; 35:6
dEzek. 47:1-
12

★19 aObad.
10

20 aEzek.
37:25; Amos
9:15

21 aIs. 4:4

3:14 *the valley of decision.* The same as the valley of Jehoshaphat (v. 2), where God will decide about men, not where men decide about God.

3:18 *in that day.* The day of Messiah's reign in His earthly millennial kingdom. *valley of Shittim.* A dry valley near the N. end of the Dead Sea.

3:19 *Edom.* See Introduction to Obadiah.

INTRODUCTION TO
THE BOOK OF AMOS

AUTHOR: Amos   DATE: 755 B.C.

The Prophet *Amos was a southerner of Tekoa (a village 10 miles S. of Jerusalem), who travelled north to Bethel to preach on what was virtually foreign soil. Though a layman, not a professional prophet, he had a direct call of God to his work (7:15). By occupation he was a sheep breeder, perhaps a master shepherd with others in his employ. The same Hebrew word is used to describe the occupation of Mesha (2 Kings 3:4). Amos' preaching in Bethel, a center of idol worship and the residence of the reigning king, Jeroboam II, aroused such opposition that he returned to Judah, where he committed his message to writing. That writing shows that he was a man of affairs, not an untutored rustic.*

The Times *Uzziah, king of Judah (791-740), reigned over a prosperous nation, but was under the influence of Jeroboam II, king of Israel (793-753), whose kingdom then was outwardly at the zenith of power but inwardly was idolatrous and corrupt (cf. 2 Kings 14:24-25). Material prosperity and social evils further characterized the times (2:6-8; 3:10; 4:1; 5:10-12; 8:4-6).*

Theme *Attacking the social evils of the people as well as their paganized worship, Amos issued an urgent call to repentance as the only escape from imminent judgment. Israel's privileged position, he declared, should have been an incentive to righteous living, certainly not an excuse for sinning. Some favorite and important verses include 3:2; 3:3; 5:24; 9:11.*

OUTLINE OF AMOS

THE BOOK OF AMOS

I THE AUTHOR AND THEME OF THE BOOK, 1:1-2

★ 1 *a*Amos 7:14 *b*2 Sam. 14:2; Jer. 6:1 *c*2 Chr. 26:1-23; Is. 1:1 *d*2 Kin. 14:23-29; Hos. 1:1; Amos 7:10.

1 The words of Amos, who was among the *a*sheepherders from *b*Tekoa, which he envisioned in visions concerning Israel in the days of *c*Uzziah king of Judah, and in the days of *d*Jeroboam son of Joash, king of Israel, two years before the *e*earthquake.

2 And he said,
"The *a*LORD roars from Zion,

11 *e*Zech. 14:5
★ 2 *a*Is. 42:13; Jer. 25:30; Joel 3:16 *b*Jer. 12:4; Joel 1:18, 19 *c*Amos 9:3

1:1 *the earthquake.* Referred to by Zechariah (14:5) and Josephus, who relates it to Uzziah's sin in acting as a priest (2 Chron. 26:16).
1:2 God *roars* as a lion leaping on his prey. *Car-* *mel,* meaning garden land, epitomizes the prosperity Israel was enjoying and which would soon be brought to nothing.

And from Jerusalem He
   utters His voice;
And the shepherds' [b]pas-
   ture grounds mourn,
And the [c]summit of Car-
   mel dries up."

II THE PROPHECIES OF AMOS,
1:3–2:16
A Concerning Damascus, 1:3–5

★ **3** [a]Amos
2:1, 4, 6 [b]Is.
8:4; 17:1-3;
Jer. 49:23-
27; Zech. 9:1

3 Thus says the LORD,
  "For [a]three transgressions
    of [b]Damascus and for
    four
  I will not revoke its *pun-
    ishment*,
  Because they threshed Gil-
    ead with *implements*
    of sharp iron.

★ **4** [a]1 Kin.
20:1; 2 Kin.
6:24

4 "So I will send fire upon the
    house of Hazael,
  And it will consume the
    citadels of [a]Ben-
    hadad.

★ **5** [a]Jer.
51:30; Lam.
2:9 [b]2 Kin.
16:9; Amos
9:7

5 "I will also [a]break the *gate*
    bar of Damascus,
  And cut off the inhabitant
    from the valley of
    Aven,
  And him who holds the
    scepter, from Beth-
    eden;
  So the people of Aram will
    go exiled to [b]Kir,"
  Says the LORD.

B Concerning Philistia, 1:6–8

6 [a]1 Sam.
6:17; Jer.
47:1, 5;
Zeph. 2:4
[b]Ezek. 35:5;
Obad. 11

6 Thus says the LORD,
  "For three transgressions of
    [a]Gaza and for four
  I will not revoke its *pun-
    ishment*,

Because they deported an
   entire population
To [b]deliver *it* up to Edom.

★ **7**

7 "So I will send fire upon the
    wall of Gaza,
  And it will consume her
    citadels.

8 [a]2 Chr.
26:6; Amos
3:9; Zech.
9:6 [b]Jer.
47:5; Zeph.
2:4 [c]Is.
14:29-31;
Jer. 47:1-7;
Ezek. 25:16;
Joel 3:4-8;
Zeph. 2:4-7;
Zech. 9:5-7

8 "I will also cut off the in-
    habitant from [a]Ash-
    dod,
  And him who holds the
    scepter, from [b]Ashke-
    lon;
  I will even unleash My
    power upon Ekron,
  And the remnant of the
    [c]Philistines will per-
    ish,"
  Says the Lord GOD.

C Concerning Tyre, 1:9–10

★ **9** [a]Is.
23:1-18; Jer.
25:22; Ezek.
26:2-4; Joel
3:4-8; Zech.
9:1-4; Matt.
11:21, 22;
Luke 10:13,
14 [b]1 Kin.
9:11-14

9 Thus says the LORD,
  "For three transgressions of
    [a]Tyre and for four
  I will not revoke its *pun-
    ishment*,
  Because they delivered up
    an entire population
    to Edom
  And did not remember *the*
    covenant of [b]brother-
    hood.

10 [a]Zech.
9:4

10 "So I will [a]send fire upon
    the wall of Tyre,
  And it will consume her
    citadels."

11 [a]Is. 34:5,
6; 63:1-6;
Jer. 49:7-22;
Ezek. 25:12-
14; 35:1-15;
Obad. 1-14;
Mal. 1:2-5
[b]Num.
20:14-21;
2 Chr. 28:17;
Obad. 10-12
[c]Is. 57:16;
Mic. 7:18

D Concerning Edom, 1:11–12

11 Thus says the LORD,
  "For three transgressions of
    [a]Edom and for four

1:3 *For three transgressions . . . and for four.* I.e.,
for repeated and innumerable acts of rebellion
(also vv. 6, 9, 11, 13; 2:1, 4, 6). The Syrians
(Arameans) of Damascus literally *threshed*
and mangled the bodies of prisoners under
heavily studded threshing sledges.
1:4 *house of Hazael.* The palace of Hazael,
founder of the Syrian (Aramean) dynasty and
ruler in Amos' time. *Ben-hadad.* Hazael's son
and successor.
1:5 *bar.* Used to lock the gates of cities. *Aven.*
Probably Baalbeck, near Damascus, a center

of heathen worship. *Beth-eden.* The summer
residence of the king of Damascus. Though
the site of *Kir* is yet unidentified, it was the
place to which Tiglath-pileser exiled the Syrians (Arameans; 2 Kings 16:9).
1:7 *Gaza.* A trade city, trafficking in slaves,
where many Israelites were sold into slavery
by Edom, their bitterest enemy.
1:9 *covenant.* Between Hiram, king of Tyre, and
David and Solomon, apparently including a
prohibition against selling Hebrews into slavery (2 Sam. 5:11; 1 Kings 5:1-12; 9:13).

I will not revoke its *punishment,*
Because he *b*pursued his
brother with the
sword,
While he stifled his com-
passion;
His anger also *c*tore continually,
And he maintained his
fury forever.

★12 *a*Jer.
49:7; 20;
Obad. 9

12 "So I will send fire upon
*a*Teman,
And it will consume the
citadels of Bozrah."

E Concerning Ammon, 1:13-15

★13 *a*Jer.
49:1-6; Ezek.
21:28-32;
25:2-7; Zeph.
2:8, 9
*b*2 Kin.
15:16; Hos.
13:16 *c*Is.
5:8; Ezek.
35:10

13 Thus says the LORD,
"For three transgressions of
the sons of *a*Ammon
and for four
I will not revoke its *punishment,*
Because they *b*ripped open
the pregnant women
of Gilead
In order to *c*enlarge their
borders.

★14 *a*Deut.
3:11; 1 Chr.
20:1; Jer.
49:2 *b*Ezek.
21:22; Amos
2:2 *c*Is. 29:6;
30:30

14 "So I will kindle a fire on
the wall of *a*Rabbah,
And it will consume her
citadels
Amid *b*war cries on the
day of battle
And a *c*storm on the day of
tempest.

15 *a*Jer. 49:3

15 "Their *a*king will go into
exile,
He and his princes to-
gether," says the
LORD.

F Concerning Moab, 2:1-3

2 Thus says the LORD,
"For three transgressions of
*a*Moab and for four
I will not revoke its *pun-
ishment,*
Because he *b*burned the
bones of the king of
Edom to lime.

★ 1 *a*Is.
15:1-16:14;
25:10-12;
Jer. 48:1-47;
Ezek. 25:8-
11; Zeph.
2:8, 9
*b*2 Kin. 3:26,
27

2 "So I will send fire upon
Moab,
And it will consume the
citadels of *a*Kerioth;
And Moab will die amid
*b*tumult,
With war cries and the
sound of a trumpet.

★ 2 *a*Jer.
48:24, 41
*b*Jer. 48:45

3 "I will also cut off the
*a*judge from her
midst,
And slay all her *b*princes
with him," says the
LORD.

★ 3 *a*Ps.
2:10; 141:6;
Amos 5:7,
12; 6:12
*b*Job 12:21;
Is. 40:23

G Concerning Judah, 2:4-5

4 Thus says the LORD,
"For three transgressions of
*a*Judah and for four
I will not revoke its *punishment,*
Because they *b*rejected the
law of the LORD
And have not kept His
statutes;
Their *c*lies also have led
them astray,
Those after which their
*d*fathers walked.

4 *a*2 Kin.
17:19; Hos.
12:2; Amos
2:17-20;
2 Kin. 22:11-
17; Jer. 6:19;
8:9 *c*Is. 9:15,
16; 28:15;
Jer. 16:19;
Hab. 2:18
*d*Jer. 9:14;
16:11, 12;
Ezek. 20:18,
24, 30

5 "So I will *a*send fire upon
Judah,
And it will consume the
citadels of Jerusalem."

5 *a*Jer.
17:27; 21:10;
Hos. 8:14

1:12 *Teman.* Edom (Jer. 49:7; Obad. 9). *Bozrah.*
One of the principal cities of Edom (Jer. 49:22).
1:13 The Ammonites were descendants of Lot
through Ben-ammi, Lot's son by his younger
daughter (Gen. 19:38). Concerning the inhumane incident referred to, see 2 Kings 8:12;
15:16.
1:14 *Rabbah.* The capital city of the Ammonites

(Jer. 49:2).
2:1 Moab was the nation descended from the
son of Lot by his elder daughter (Gen. 19:37).
to lime. To powder.
2:2 *Kerioth.* Possibly the capital of Moab (Isa.
15:1).
2:3 *judge.* A term sometimes used of a king,
who frequently functioned as judge (Mic. 5:1).

H Concerning Israel, 2:6-16

6 [a]2 Kin. 18:11, 12 [b]Joel 3:3; Amos 5:11, 12; 8:6

6 Thus says the LORD,
"For three transgressions of
[a]Israel and for four
I will not revoke its *punishment,*
Because they [b]sell the
righteous for money
And the needy for a pair of
sandals.

★ **7** [a]Amos 8:4; Mic. 2:2, 9 [b]Amos 5:12 [c]Hos. 4:14

7 "These who pant after the
very dust of the earth
on the head of the
[a]helpless
Also [b]turn aside the way of
the humble;
And a [c]man and his father
resort to the same girl
In order to profane My
holy name.

★ **8** [a]Ex. 22:26 [b]Amos 3:14 [c]Amos 4:1; 6:6

8 "And on garments [a]taken as
pledges they stretch
out beside [b]every al-
tar,
And in the house of their
God they [c]drink the
wine of those who
have been fined.

★ **9** [a]Num. 21:23-25; Josh. 10:12 [b]Num. 13:32 [c]Ezek. 17:9; Mal. 4:1

9 "Yet it was I who destroyed
the [a]Amorite before
them,
Though his [b]height *was*
like the height of ce-
dars
And he *was* strong as the
oaks;
I even destroyed his [c]fruit
above and his root be-
low.

10 [a]Ex. 12:51; 20:2; Amos 3:1; 9:7 [b]Deut. 2:7 [c]Ex. 3:8

10 "And it was I who [a]brought
you up from the land
of Egypt,
And I led you in the wil-
derness [b]forty years
That you might take pos-
session of the land of
the [c]Amorite.

11 "Then I [a]raised up some of
your sons to be
prophets
And some of your young
men to be [b]Nazirites.
Is this not so, O sons of Israel?" declares the
LORD.

★**11-12**

11 [a]Deut. 18:18; Jer. 7:25 [b]Num. 6:2, 3; Judg. 13:5

12 "But you made the Nazirites
drink wine,
And you commanded the
prophets saying, 'You
[a]shall not prophesy!'

12 [a]Is. 30:10; Jer. 11:21; Amos 7:13, 16; Mic. 2:6

13 "Behold, I am [a]weighted
down beneath you
As a wagon is weighted
down when filled with
sheaves.

13 [a]Is. 1:14

14 "[a]Flight will perish from the
swift,
And the stalwart will not
strengthen his power,
Nor the [b]mighty man save
his life.

14 [a]Is. 30:16, 17 [b]Ps. 33:16; Jer. 9:23

15 "He who [a]grasps the bow
will not stand *his
ground,*
The swift of foot will not
escape,
Nor will he who rides the
[b]horse save his life.

15 [a]Jer. 51:56; Ezek. 39:3 [b]Is. 31:3

16 "Even the bravest among
the warriors will [a]flee
naked in that day,"
declares the LORD.

16 [a]Judg. 4:17

III THE SERMONS OF AMOS, 3:1-6:14

A The Doom of Israel, 3:1-15

3 Hear this word which the
LORD has spoken against you,
sons of Israel, against the entire
[a]family which He brought up
from the land of Egypt,

★ **1** [a]Jer. 8:3; 13:11

2:7 The rich long to see (*pant after*) the poor
reduced to the place where dust is thrown on
their heads as a sign of grief. *girl.* Likely a
temple prostitute. How degraded family life
must have been!
2:8 *garments.* When taken as security for loans,
they were to be returned at night because the
poor needed them for covering (Exod.

22:25-26). The picture is of ruthless foreclo-
sure because of debts.
2:9 *Amorite.* The preconquest inhabitants of
Canaan.
2:11-12 *Nazirites.* Were forbidden to drink
wine (see Num. 6:1-21).
3:1 *the entire family.* I.e., all 12 tribes, not just
the northern 10 tribes of Israel.

★ 2 aGen.
18:19; Ex.
19:5, 6; Deut.
4:32-37; 7:6
bJer. 14:10;
Ezek. 20:36;
Dan. 9:12;
Rom. 2:9

★ 3

4 aPs.
104:21; Hos.
5:14; 11:10

★ 5

6 aJer. 4:5,
19, 21; 6:1;
Hos. 5:8;
Zeph. 1:16
bIs. 14:24-
27; 45:7

★ 7 aGen.
6:13; 18:17;
Jer. 23:22;
Dan. 9:22;
John 15:15

8 aAmos
1:2 bJon.
1:1-3; 3:1-3
cJer. 20:9;
Acts 4:20

★ 9 a1 Sam.
5:1 bAmos
4:1; 6:1
cAmos 5:11;
8:6

2 "ªYou only have I chosen
among all the families
of the earth;
Therefore, I will ᵇpunish
you for all your iniq-
uities."

3 Do two men walk together
unless they have
made an appoint-
ment?

4 Does a ªlion roar in the
forest when he has no
prey?
Does a young lion growl
from his den unless
he has captured some-
thing?

5 Does a bird fall into a trap
on the ground when
there is no bait in it?
Does a trap spring up from
the earth when it cap-
tures nothing at all?

6 If a ªtrumpet is blown in a
city will not the peo-
ple tremble?
If a ᵇcalamity occurs in a
city has not the LORD
done it?

7 Surely the LORD God does
nothing
Unless He ªreveals His secret counsel
To His servants the prophets.

8 A ªlion has roared! Who
will not fear?
The ᵇLord GOD has spo-
ken! ᶜWho can but
prophesy?

9 Proclaim on the citadels in
ªAshdod and on the citadels in
the land of Egypt and say, "Assemble yourselves on the ᵇmountains of Samaria and see the great

tumults within her and the ᶜop-
pressions in her midst.

10 "But they ªdo not know
how to do what is right," declares
the LORD, "these who ᵇhoard up
violence and devastation in their
citadels."

11 Therefore, thus says the
Lord GOD,
"An ªenemy, even one sur-
rounding the land,
Will pull down your
strength from you
And your ᵇcitadels will be
looted."

12 Thus says the LORD,
"Just as the shepherd
ªsnatches from the
lion's mouth a couple
of legs or a piece of an
ear,
So will the sons of Israel
dwelling in Samaria
be snatched away—
With the ᵇcorner of a bed
and the ᶜcover of a
couch!

13 "Hear and ªtestify against
the house of Jacob,"
Declares the Lord GOD, the
God of hosts.

14 "For on the day that I punish Israel's transgres-
sions,
I will also punish the altars
of ªBethel;
The horns of the altar will
be cut off,
And they will fall to the
ground.

15 "I will also smite the ªwin-
ter house together
with the ᵇsummer
house;

10 aPs. 14:4;
Jer. 4:22;
Amos 5:7;
6:12 bHab.
2:8-10; Zeph.
1:9; Zech.
5:3, 4

★11-12

11 aAmos
6:14 bAmos
2:5

12 a1 Sam.
17:34-37
bPs. 132:3
cEsth. 1:6;
7:8; Amos
6:4

13 aEzek.
2:7

★14 a2 Kin.
23:15; Hos.
10:5-8, 14,
15; Amos
4:4; 5:5, 6;
7:10, 13

15 aJer.
36:22 bJudg.
3:20 c1 Kin.
22:39; Ps.
45:8 dAmos
2:5; 6:11

3:2 The special privileges God bestowed on Israel by choosing them increased their ethical
responsibilities and did not exempt them from
judgment as some thought.
3:3 The questions in verses 3-6 are calculated to
show Israel how her sin had separated her
from God.
3:5 when there is no bait. I.e., where there is no
mechanism that releases the trap.
3:7 God had warned the people through His
prophets (including Amos), but the people
told the prophets to keep quiet (2:12).
3:9 Ashod and Egypt, representing the heathen,

are summoned to witness the punishment of
Israel.
3:11-12 An enemy. I.e., the Assyrians, who will
sack Israel, leaving only remnants of her former prosperity, like the few pieces of the carcass a shepherd would snatch out of the
mouth of a lion that had killed one of his
sheep. In the meantime the leaders in Samaria
lived in luxury on a cushioned corner of a bed.
3:14 Bethel. The principal center of idol worship. horns of the altar. Sacred because the
blood of the sacrifice was applied there (Lev.
4:30).

The houses of ^civory will also perish
And the ^dgreat houses will come to an end,"
Declares the LORD.

B The Depravity of Israel, 4:1-13

★ 1 aPs. 22:12; Ezek. 39:18 bAmos 3:9; 6:1 cAmos 5:11; 8:6 dAmos 2:8; 6:6

4 Hear this word, you cows of ^aBashan who are on the ^bmountain of Samaria,
Who ^coppress the poor, who crush the needy,
Who say to your husbands, "Bring now, that we may ^ddrink!"

★ 2-3

2 aAmos 6:8; 8:7 bPs. 89:35 cIs. 37:29; Ezek. 38:4 dJer. 16:16; Ezek. 29:4; Hab. 1:15

2 The Lord GOD has ^asworn by His ^bholiness,
"Behold, the days are coming upon you
When they will take you away with ^cmeat hooks,
And the last of you with ^dfish hooks.

3 aJer. 52:7

3 "You will ^ago out through breaches in the walls,
Each one straight before her,
And you will be cast to Harmon," declares the LORD.

★ 4-5

4 aNum. 28:3; Amos 5:21, 22

4 "Enter Bethel and transgress;
In Gilgal multiply transgression!
^aBring your sacrifices every morning,
Your tithes every three days.

5 aLev. 7:13 bLev. 22:18-21 cJer. 7:9, 10; Hos. 9:1, 10

5 "Offer a ^athank offering also from that which is leavened,

And proclaim ^bfreewill offerings, make them known.
For so you ^clove to do, you sons of Israel,"
Declares the Lord GOD.

6 "But I gave you also ^acleanness of teeth in all your cities
And lack of bread in all your places,
Yet you have ^bnot returned to Me," declares the LORD.

★ 6 aIs. 3:1; Jer. 14:18 bIs. 9:13; Jer. 5:3; Hag. 2:17

7 "And furthermore, I ^awithheld the rain from you
While there were still three months until harvest.
Then I would send rain on one city
And on ^banother city I would not send rain;
One part would be rained on,
While the part not rained on would dry up.

7 aDeut. 11:17; 2 Chr. 7:13; Is. 5:6 bEx. 9:4, 26; 10:22, 23

8 "So two or three cities would stagger to another city to drink ^awater,
But would ^bnot be satisfied;
Yet you have ^cnot returned to Me," declares the LORD.

8 a1 Kin. 18:5; Jer. 14:4 bEzek. 4:16, 17; Hag. 1:6 cJer. 3:7

9 "I ^asmote you with scorching wind and mildew;
And the ^bcaterpillar was devouring
Your many gardens and vineyards, fig trees and olive trees;

9 aDeut. 28:22; Hag. 2:17 bJoel 1:4, 7; Amos 7:1, 2 cJer. 3:10

4:1 *cows of Bashan.* The well-fed women of Samaria (Bashan was known for its fat cattle; cf. Psalm 22:12). These women were insatiable (v. 1), pretentiously religious (vv. 4-5), and calloused in the face of warnings (vv. 6-11).
4:2-3 The people will be led into captivity through *breaches* or gaps in the walls of their cities, just as animals are led by using *meat hooks. fish hooks.* Used when the other hooks run out, because of the number of Israelites

who will be taken.
4:4-5 This sarcastic call to false worship was intended to show the people how far they were from God. *thank offering.* See Lev. 7:12. *freewill offerings.* See Deut. 12:6.
4:6 *cleanness of teeth.* I.e., nothing to eat, because of famine. These "natural" catastrophes (vv. 6-11) were God's warnings, which Israel did not heed (*Yet you have not returned to Me,* vv. 6, 8, 9, 10, 11).

Yet you have ^cnot returned to Me," declares the LORD.

10 "I sent a ^aplague among you
after the manner of
Egypt;
I ^bslew your young men by
the sword along with
your ^ccaptured horses,
And I made the ^dstench of
your camp rise up in
your nostrils;
Yet you have ^enot returned to Me," declares the LORD.

11 "I overthrew you as ^aGod
overthrew Sodom and
Gomorrah,
And you were like a ^bfirebrand snatched from
a blaze;
Yet you have ^cnot returned to Me," declares the LORD.

12 "Therefore, thus I will do to
you, O Israel;
Because I shall do this to
you,
Prepare to ^ameet your
God, O Israel."

13 For behold, He who ^aforms
mountains and
^bcreates the wind
And ^cdeclares to man what
are His thoughts,
He who ^dmakes dawn into
darkness
And ^etreads on the high
places of the earth,
^fThe LORD God of hosts is
His name.

C A Dirge over Israel, 5:1-6:14
1 The ruin of Israel in coming judgment, 5:1-17

5 Hear this word which I take
up for you as a ^adirge, O
house of Israel.
2 She has fallen, she will
^anot rise again—
The ^bvirgin Israel.

She *lies* neglected on her
land;
There is ^cnone to raise her
up.

3 For thus says the Lord
GOD,
"The city which goes forth a
thousand *strong*
Will have a ^ahundred left,
And the *one* which goes
forth a hundred
strong
Will have ^bten left to the
house of Israel."

4 For thus says the LORD to
the house of Israel,
"^aSeek Me ^bthat you may
live.

5 "But do not resort to ^aBethel,
And do not come to ^bGilgal,
Nor cross over to ^cBeersheba;
For Gilgal will certainly go
into captivity,
And Bethel will come to
trouble.

6 "^aSeek the LORD that you
may live,
Lest He break forth like a
^bfire, O house of
Joseph,
And it consume with none
to quench *it* for
Bethel,

7 *For* those who turn ^ajustice
into wormwood
And cast righteousness
down to the earth."

8 He who made the ^aPleiades and Orion
And ^bchanges deep darkness into morning,
Who also ^cdarkens day
into night,
Who ^dcalls for the waters
of the sea
And pours them out on
the surface of the
earth,
The ^eLORD is His name.

Side references (left column)
10 ^aEx. 9:3;
Lev. 26:25;
Deut. 28:27,
60; Ps. 78:50
^bJer. 11:22;
18:21; 48:15
^c2 Kin. 13:3,
7 ^dJoel 2:20
^eIs. 9:13

11 ^aGen.
19:24, 25;
Deut. 29:23;
Is. 13:19
^bZech. 3:2
^cJer. 23:14

★12 ^aIs.
32:11; 64:2;
Jer. 5:22

13 ^aJob
38:4-7; Ps.
65:6; Is.
40:12 ^bPs.
135:7; Jer.
10:13 ^cDan.
2:28, 30
^dJer. 13:16;
Joel 2:2;
Amos 5:8
^eMic. 1:3 ^fIs.
47:4; Jer.
10:16; Amos
5:8; 27; 9:6

1 ^aJer.
7:29; 9:10,
17; Ezek.
19:1
★ 2 ^aAmos
8:14 ^bJer.
14:17 ^cIs.
51:18; Jer.
50:32

Side references (right column)
★ 3 ^aIs.
6:13 ^bAmos
6:9

4 ^aDeut.
4:29; 32:46,
47; Jer.
29:13 ^bIs.
55:3

5 ^a1 Kin.
12:28, 29;
Amos 3:14;
4:4; 7:10, 13
^b1 Sam.
7:16; 11:14
^cGen.
21:31-33;
Amos 8:14

6 ^aIs. 55:3,
6, 7; Amos
5:14 ^bDeut.
4:24

★ 7 ^aAmos
2:3; 5:12;
6:12

8 ^aJob 9:9;
38:31 ^bJob
12:22; 38:12;
Is. 42:16
^cPs. 104:20
^dPs. 104:6-
9; Amos 9:6
^eAmos 4:13

4:12 *Prepare* to repent and thus be acquitted
when you *meet your God.*
5:2 *The virgin Israel.* Up to this time Israel had
been unconquered.

5:3 Israel would be 90% destroyed (cf. 3:12).
5:7 Those who were responsible for justice
turned it to *wormwood;* i.e., bitterness (cf.
Rev. 8:11) of injustice.

9 aIs. 29:5;
Amos 2:14
bMic. 5:11

9 It is He who aflashes forth
with destruction upon
the strong,
So that bdestruction comes
upon the fortress.

★10-12
10 aIs.
29:21; Amos
5:15 b1 Kin.
22:8; Is.
59:15; Jer.
17:16-18

10 They hate him who are-
proves in the gate,
And they babhor him who
speaks *with* integrity.

11 aAmos
3:15; 6:11
bMic. 6:15

11 Therefore, because you
impose heavy rent on
the poor
And exact a tribute of
grain from them,
Though you have built
ahouses of well-hewn
stone,
Yet you will not live in
them;
You have planted pleasant
vineyards, yet you
will bnot drink their
wine.

12 aIs. 1:23;
5:23; Amos
2:6

12 For I know your transgressions are maný and
your sins are great,
You who adistress the
righteous *and* accept
bribes,
And turn aside the poor in
the gate.

13 aEccl.
3:7; Hos. 4:4

13 Therefore, at such a time
the prudent person
akeeps silent, for it is
an evil time.

14 aMic.
3:11

14 Seek good and not evil,
that you may live;
And thus may the Lord
God of hosts be with
you,
aJust as you have said!

15 aPs.
97:10; Rom.
12:9 bJoel
2:14 cMic.
5:3, 7, 8

15 aHate evil, love good,
And establish justice in the
gate!
Perhaps the Lord God of
hosts
bMay be gracious to the
cremnant of Joseph.

16 Therefore, thus says the
Lord God of hosts, the
Lord,
"There is awailing in all the
plazas,
And in all the streets they
say, 'Alas! Alas!'
They also call the bfarmer
to mourning
And cprofessional mourn-
ers to lamentation

★16 aJer.
9:10, 18-20;
Amos 8:3
bJoel 1:11
c2 Chr.
35:25; Jer.
9:17

17 "And in all the avineyards
there is wailing,
Because I shall pass
through the midst of
you," says the Lord. .

17 aIs.
16:10; Jer.
48:33

**2 The rebuke of religious
people, 5:18-27**

18 Alas, you who are longing
for the aday of the
Lord,
For what purpose *will* the
day of the Lord *be* to
you?
It *will be* bdarkness and
not light;

18 aIs. 5:19;
Jer. 30:7;
Joel 1:15;
2:1, 11, 31
bIs. 5:30;
Joel 2:2

19 As when a man aflees from
a lion,
And a bear meets him,
Or goes home, leans his
hand against the wall,
And a snake bites him.

19 aJob
20:24; Is.
24:17, 18;
Jer. 15:2, 3;
48:44

20 *Will* not the day of the
Lord *be* adarkness in-
stead of light,
Even gloom with no
brightness in it?

20 aIs.
13:10; Zeph.
1:15

21 "I hate, I areject your festivals,
Nor do I bdelight in your
solemn assemblies.

21 aIs. 1:11-
16; 66:3;
Amos 4:4, 5;
8:10 bLev.
26:31; Jer.
14:12; Hos.
5:6

22 "Even though you aoffer up
to Me burnt offerings
and your grain offer-
ings,
I will not accept *them;*

22 aIs. 66:3;
Mic. 6:6, 7
bLev. 7:11-
15; Amos 4:5

5:10-12 The people are indicted for (1) hating
honest judges (the *gate* of the city was where
justice was administered, v. 15; cf. Deut. 22:15;
Ruth 4:1-2), (2) robbing the poor, and (3) tak-

ing bribes.
5:16 Professional mourners, usually women (cf.
Jer. 9:17).

And I will not *even* look at
the *b*peace offerings of
your fatlings.

23 "Take away from Me the
noise of your songs;
I will not even listen to the
sound of your harps.

24 *a*Jer.
22:3; Ezek.
45:9; Mic.
6:8

24 "But let *a*justice roll down
like waters
And righteousness like an
ever-flowing stream.

★25-26
25 *a*Deut.
32:17; Josh.
24:14; Neh.
9:18-21;
Acts 7:42, 43

25 "*a*Did you present Me with
sacrifices and grain offerings in
the wilderness for forty years, O
house of Israel?

26 *a*Acts
7:43

26 "*a*You also carried along
Sikkuth your king and Kiyyun,
your images, the star of your gods
which you made for yourselves.

★27

27 "Therefore, I will make you
go into exile beyond Damascus,"
says the LORD, whose name is the
God of hosts.

**3   The reprimand of the entire
nation, 6:1–14**

1 *a*Is. 32:9-
11; Zeph.
1:12; Luke
6:24 *b*Ex.
19:5; Amos
3:2

6 *a*Woe to those who are at ease
in Zion,
And to those who *feel* secure in the mountain
of Samaria,
The *b*distinguished men of
the foremost of na-
tions,
To whom the house of Is-
rael comes.

★ 2 *a*Gen.
10:10; Is.
10:9 *b*1 Kin.
8:65; 2 Kin.
18:34; Is.
10:9 *c*1 Sam.
5:8; 2 Chr.
26:6

2 Go over to *a*Calneh and
look,
And go from there to *b*Hamath the great,
Then go down to *c*Gath of
the Philistines.
Are they better than these
kingdoms,

Or is their territory greater
than yours?

3 Do you *a*put off the day of
calamity,
And would you *b*bring
near the seat of vio-
lence?

3 *a*Is.
56:12; Amos
9:10 *b*Amos
3:10

4 Those who recline on beds
of ivory
And sprawl on their
*a*couches,
And *b*eat lambs from the
flock
And calves from the midst
of the stall,

4 *a*Amos
3:12 *b*Ezek.
34:2, 3

5 Who improvise to the
sound of the harp,
And like David have composed *a*songs for
themselves,

5 *a*1 Chr.
15:16; 23:5;
Is. 5:12

6 Who *a*drink wine from
sacrificial bowls
While they anoint them-
selves with the finest
of oils,
Yet they have not *b*grieved
over the ruin of
Joseph.

6 *a*Amos
2:8; 4:1
*b*Ezek. 9:4

7 Therefore, they will now
*a*go into exile at the
head of the exiles,
And the *b*sprawlers' ban-
queting will pass
away.

7 *a*Amos
7:11, 17
*b*1 Kin.
20:16-21;
Dan. 5:4-6,
30

8 The Lord GOD has *a*sworn
by Himself, the LORD
God of hosts has de-
clared:
"I *b*loathe the arrogance of
Jacob,
And I detest his *c*citadels;
Therefore, I will *d*deliver
up *the* city and all it
contains."

★ 8 *a*Gen.
22:16; Jer.
22:5; 51:14;
Amos 4:2;
8:7 *b*Lev.
26:30; Deut.
32:19; Ps.
106:40;
Amos 5:21
*c*Amos 3:10,
11 *d*Hos.
11:6

★ 9-10
9 *a*Amos
5:3

9 And it will be, if *a*ten men

5:25-26 During the 40 years of wilderness wanderings the people were not always able to
bring offerings, yet God cared for them. Their
hearts were now set on the false gods of verse
26.
5:27 See 2 Kings 17:6 for the fulfillment.
6:2 Since *Gath* had fallen to Uzziah in 760
(2 Chron. 26:6) and since *Calneh* and *Hamath*
would soon be captured by Assyria (Isa. 10:9),
how could Israel expect to escape the coming
judgment?
6:8 *the arrogance of Jacob.* In boasting about her

great cities and palaces.
6:9-10 Many not killed in battle would die from
resulting pestilences, and those who would
bury the bodies would fear to mention *the
name of the LORD,* lest additional judgment fall
on them. *his undertaker.* Lit., the one who
burns him, perhaps referring to cremation
made necessary by the excessive number of
dead or to the burning of spices (cf. 2 Chron.
16:14). The Hebrews did not usually cremate
(but see 1 Sam. 31:12).

are left in one house, they will die.

10 Then one's uncle, or his ᵃundertaker, will lift him up to carry out *his* bones from the house, and he will say to the one who is in the innermost part of the house, "Is anyone else with you?" And that one will say, "No one." Then he will answer, "ᵇKeep quiet. For the name of the LORD is ᶜnot to be mentioned."

11 For behold, the LORD is going to ᵃcommand that the ᵇgreat house be smashed to pieces and the small house to fragments.

12 Do horses run on rocks?
　　Or does one plow them
　　　　with oxen?
　　Yet you have turned ᵃjus-
　　　　tice into poison,
　　And the fruit of righteous-
　　　　ness into wormwood,

13 You who rejoice in ᵃLo-
　　debar,
　　And say, "Have we not
　　　ᵇby our *own* strength
　　　taken Karnaim for
　　　ourselves?"

14 "For behold, ᵃI am going to
　　raise up a nation
　　against you,
　　O house of Israel," de-
　　clares the LORD God of
　　hosts,
　　"And they will afflict you
　　from the ᵇentrance of
　　Hamath
　　To the ᵇbrook of the Ara-
　　bah."

IV THE VISIONS OF AMOS, 7:1-9:15
A A Vision of Devouring Locusts, 7:1-3

7 Thus the Lord GOD showed me, and behold, He was forming a ᵃlocust-swarm when the spring crop began to sprout.

And behold, the spring crop *was* after the king's mowing.

2 And it came about, when it had ᵃfinished eating the vegeta-tion of the land, that I said,
　　"ᵇLord GOD, please pardon!
　　How can Jacob stand,
　　For he is ᶜsmall?"

3 The LORD ᵃchanged His
　　mind about this.
　　"It shall not be," said the
　　LORD.

B A Vision of Fire, 7:4-6

4 Thus the Lord GOD showed me, and behold, the Lord GOD was calling to contend *with them* by ᵃfire, and it consumed the great deep and began to con-sume the farm land.

5 Then I said,
　　"ᵃLord GOD, please stop!
　　ᵇHow can Jacob stand, for
　　　he is small?"

6 The LORD ᵃchanged His
　　mind about this.
　　"This too shall not be," said
　　the Lord GOD.

C A Vision of a Plumbline, 7:7-9

7 Thus He showed me, and behold, the Lord was standing by a vertical wall, with a plumb line in His hand.

8 And the LORD said to me, "ᵃWhat do you see, Amos?" And I said, "A plumb line." Then the LORD said,
　　"Behold I am about to put a
　　　ᵇplumb line
　　In the midst of My people
　　　Israel.
　　I will ᶜspare them no
　　　longer.

6:12 Israel's mixed-up moral standards were as ridiculous as *horses* trying to *run on rocks.*
6:14 *Hamath.* A city on the northern boundary of Israel (Num. 13:21). *the brook of the Ara-bah.* A stream that flows into the Dead Sea, marking the southern boundary of the king-dom of Jeroboam II.

7:1-3 Amos envisioned a swarm of locusts de-stroying the second mowing of grass that went to the people after the king had taken the first mowing to feed his animals.
7:4 The fire *consumed the great deep;* i.e., the sources of water.

---

10 ᵃ1 Sam. 31:12 ᵇAmos 5:13; 8:3 ᶜJer. 44:26; Ezek. 20:39

11 ᵃIs. 55:11 ᵇ2 Kin. 25:9; Amos 3:15; 5:11

★**12** ᵃ1 Kin. 21:7-13; Is. 59:13, 14; Hos. 10:4; Amos 5:7, 11, 12

13 ᵃJob 8:14, 15; Ps. 2:2-4; Luke 12:19, 20 ᵇPs. 75:4, 5; Is. 28:14, 15

★**14** ᵃJer. 5:15 ᵇNum. 34:7, 8; 1 Kin. 8:65; 2 Kin. 14:25

★ **1-3**
1 ᵃJoel 1:4; Amos 4:9; Nah. 3:15

2 ᵃEx. 10:15 ᵇJer. 14:7, 20, 21; Ezek. 9:8; 11:13 ᶜIs. 37:4; Jer. 42:2

3 ᵃDeut. 32:36; Jer. 26:19; Hos. 11:8; Amos 5:15; Jon. 3:10

★ **4** ᵃDeut. 32:22; Is. 66:15, 16; Amos 2:5

5 ᵃPs. 85:4; Joel 2:17 ᵇAmos 7:2

6 ᵃPs. 106:45; Amos 7:3; Jon. 3:10

8 ᵃJer. 1:11; Amos 8:2 ᵇ2 Kin. 21:13; Is. 28:17; 34:11; Lam. 2:8 ᶜJer. 15:6; Ezek. 7:4-9; Amos 8:2

★ **9** aGen.
46:1; Hos.
10:8; Mic.
1:5 bLev.
26:31; Is.
63:18; Jer.
51:51; Amos
7:13 c2 Kin.
15:8-10;
Amos 7:11

9 "The ahigh places of Isaac
will be desolated
And the bsanctuaries of Israel laid waste.
Then shall I crise up
against the house of
Jeroboam with the
sword."

D An Historical Interlude: Opposition from the Priest of Bethel, 7:10-17

★**10-13**

10 a1 Kin.
12:31, 32;
13:33
b2 Kin.
14:23, 24
cJer. 26:8-
11; 38:4

10 Then Amaziah, the apriest
of Bethel, sent *word* to bJerobo-
am, king of Israel, saying, "Amos
has cconspired against you in the
midst of the house of Israel; the
land is unable to endure all his
words.

11 "For thus Amos says, 'Jeroboam will die by the sword and
Israel will certainly go from its
land into exile.' "

12 aMatt.
8:34

12 Then Amaziah said to
Amos, "aGo, you seer, flee away
to the land of Judah, and there eat
bread and there do your prophesying!

13 aAmos
2:12; Acts
4:18 b1 Kin.
12:29, 32;
Amos 7:9

13 "But ano longer prophesy at
Bethel, for it is a bsanctuary of the
king and a royal residence."

★**14** a1 Kin.
20:35; 2 Kin.
2:3, 5; 4:38;
2 Chr. 19:2

14 Then Amos answered and
said to Amaziah, "I am not a
prophet, nor am I the ason of a
prophet; for I am a herdsman and
a grower of sycamore figs.

15 aJer. 1:7;
Ezek. 2:3, 4

15 "But the LORD took me from
following the flock and the LORD
said to me, 'Go aprophesy to My
people Israel.'

16 aAmos
2:12; 7:13
bDeut. 32:2;
Ezek. 20:46;
21:2

16 "And now hear the word of
the LORD: you are saying, 'You

ashall not prophesy against Israel
bnor shall you speak against the
house of Isaac.'

17 "Therefore, thus says the
LORD, 'Your awife will become a
harlot in the city, your bsons and
your daughters will fall by the
sword, your land will be parceled
up by a *measuring* line, and you
yourself will die upon cunclean
soil. Moreover, Israel will certainly go from its land into
exile.' "

17 aHos.
4:13, 14
bJer. 14:16
c2 Kin. 17:6;
Ezek. 4:13;
Hos. 9:3

E A Vision of a Basket of Ripe Fruit, 8:1-14

8 Thus the Lord GOD showed
me, and behold, *there was* a
basket of summer fruit.

★ **1**

2 And He said, "What do
you see, Amos?" And aI said, "A
basket of summer fruit." Then
the LORD said to me, "The bend
has come for My people Israel. I
will cspare them no longer.

2 aJer. 24:3
bEzek. 7:2,
3, 6 cAmos
7:8

3 "The asongs of the palace
will turn to bwailing in that day,"
declares the Lord GOD. "Many
will be the ccorpses; in every
place they will cast them forth in
silence."

3 aAmos
5:23; 6:4, 5;
8:10 bAmos
5:16 cAmos
6:8-10

4 Hear this, you who atram-
ple the needy, to do away with
the humble of the land,

4 aPs. 14:4;
Prov. 30:14;
Amos 2:7;
5:11, 12

5 saying,
"When will the anew moon
be over,
So that we may buy grain,
And the bsabbath, that we
may open the wheat
market,
To make the bushel
smaller and the shekel
bigger,

★ **5** aNum.
28:11; 2 Kin.
4:23 bEx.
31:13-17;
Neh. 13:15
cHos. 12:7;
Mic. 6:11

7:9 *high places.* Altars built on hills or artificial
mounds where Israel carried on her idolatrous
worship (cf. Hos. 4:13).
7:10-13 Amaziah, the royal chaplain of the king,
accused Amos of conspiracy against the king
(vv. 10-11), of being a "visionary" (*seer*, v. 12),
of being a foreign intruder (v. 12), and of tres-
passing on the sacred precincts of Bethel (v.
13). He twisted the prophecy of Amos (cf. v.
11a with v. 9) in order to try to evoke a more
violent reaction from Jeroboam.
7:14 *a grower of sycamore figs.* A pincher or
nipper of these figs, a necessary procedure in

order for the fruit to ripen.
8:1 *summer fruit.* End-of-the-season fruit, fully
ripe, whose edible life was short.
8:5 Though the people observed the holidays of
new moon (at the beginning of each month;
cf. 2 Kings 4:23; Isa. 1:13) and *sabbath,* the
merchants could scarcely wait until these days
were over to get back to their business of
cheating people. An undersized container
(*bushel*) plus a heavy *shekel* weight (against
which the customer weighed his money) gave
the merchant an illegal double profit.

And to ^ccheat with dishonest scales,

6 So as to ^abuy the helpless for money
And the needy for a pair of sandals,
And *that* we may sell the refuse of the wheat?"

7 The LORD has ^asworn by the ^bpride of Jacob,
"Indeed, I will ^cnever forget any of their deeds.

8 "Because of this will not the land ^aquake
And everyone who dwells in it ^bmourn?
Indeed, all of it will ^crise up like the Nile,
And it will be tossed about,
And subside like the Nile of Egypt.

9 "And it will come about in that day," declares the Lord GOD,
"That I shall make the ^asun go down at noon
And ^bmake the earth dark in broad daylight.

10 "Then I shall ^aturn your festivals into mourning
And all your songs into lamentation;
And I will bring ^bsackcloth on everyone's loins
And baldness on every head.
And I will make it ^clike *a time of* mourning for an only son,
And the end of it will be like a bitter day.

11 "Behold, days are coming," declares the Lord GOD,
"When I will send a famine on the land,

Not a famine for bread or a thirst for water,
But rather ^afor hearing the words of the LORD.

12 "And people will stagger from sea to sea,
And from the north even to the east;
They will go to and fro to ^aseek the word of the LORD,
But they will not find *it*.

13 "In that day the beautiful ^avirgins
And the young men will ^bfaint from thirst.

14 "*As for* those who swear by the ^aguilt of Samaria,
Who say, 'As your god lives, O ^bDan,'
And, 'As the way of ^cBeersheba lives,'
They will fall and ^dnot rise again."

F A Vision of the Lord Judging, 9:1–10

9 I saw the Lord standing beside the ^aaltar, and He said,
"Smite the capitals so that the ^bthresholds will shake,
And ^cbreak them on the heads of them all!
Then I will ^dslay the rest of them with the sword;
They will ^enot have a fugitive who will flee,
Or a refugee who will escape.

2 "Though they dig into ^aSheol,
From there shall My hand take them;
And though they ^bascend to heaven,
From there will I bring them down.

8:6 *the refuse of the wheat.* The thin, unfilled grain that could fall through the sieve.
8:7 *the pride of Jacob.* Here, unlike its use in 6:8, means God Himself.
8:9 Amos used a total eclipse of the sun, which occurred in Asia Minor in June 763, as imagery for God's coming judgment on Israel.

8:11 The day would come, in captivity, when the people would long for the *words of the LORD,* which they had ignored in prosperity.
9:1 Judgment begins at the center of idolatry.
9:2–4 Neither *Sheol* nor *heaven* nor any other place will conceal the people so that they escape God's judgment.

★ 6 ^aAmos 2:6

★ 7 ^aAmos 4:2 ^bDeut. 33:26, 29; Ps. 68:34; Amos 6:8 ^cPs. 10:11; Hos. 7:2; 8:13

8 ^aPs. 18:7; 60:2; Is. 5:25 ^bHos. 4:3 ^cJer. 46:7, 8; Amos 9:5

★ 9 ^aJob 5:14; Is. 13:10; Jer. 15:9; Mic. 3:6 ^bIs. 59:9, 10; Amos 4:13; 5:8

10 ^aJob 20:23; Amos 5:21 ^bIs. 15:2, 3; Jer. 48:37; Ezek. 7:18; 27:31 ^cJer. 6:26; Zech. 12:10

★11 ^a1 Sam. 3:1; 2 Chr. 15:3; Ps. 74:9; Ezek. 7:26; Mic. 3:6

12 ^aEzek. 20:3, 31

13 ^aLam. 1:18; 2:21 ^bIs. 41:17; Hos. 2:3

14 ^aHos. 8:5 ^b1 Kin. 12:28, 29 ^cAmos 5:5 ^dAmos 5:2

★ 1 ^aAmos 3:14 ^bZeph. 2:14 ^cPs. 68:21; Hab. 3:13 ^dAmos 7:17 ^eJer. 11:11

★ 2-4

2 ^aPs. 139:8 ^bJer. 51:53; Obad. 4

3 "And though they hide on the summit of Carmel, I will ^asearch them out and take them from there; And though they ^bconceal themselves from My sight on the floor of the sea, From there I will command the ^cserpent and it will bite them.

4 "And though they go into ^acaptivity before their enemies, From there I will command the sword that it slay them, And I will ^bset My eyes against them for evil and not for good."

5 And the Lord God of hosts, The One who ^atouches the land so that it melts, And ^ball those who dwell in it mourn, And all of it rises up like the Nile And subsides like the Nile of Egypt;

6 The One who builds His ^aupper chambers in the heavens, And has founded His vaulted dome over the earth, He who ^bcalls for the waters of the sea And ^cpours them out on the face of the earth, ^dThe Lord is His name.

7 "Are you not as the sons of ^aEthiopia to Me, O sons of Israel?" declares the Lord.

"Have I not brought up Israel from the land of Egypt, And the ^bPhilistines from Caphtor and the ^cArameans from ^dKir?

8 "Behold, the ^aeyes of the Lord God are on the sinful kingdom, And I will ^bdestroy it from the face of the earth; Nevertheless, I will ^cnot totally destroy the house of Jacob," Declares the Lord.

9 "For behold, I am commanding, And I will ^ashake the house of Israel among all nations As *grain* is shaken in a sieve, But not a kernel will fall to the ground.

10 "All the ^asinners of My people will die by the sword, Those who say, '^bThe calamity will not overtake or confront us.'

G A Vision of Future Blessing, 9:11-15

11 "In that day I will ^araise up the fallen ^bbooth of David, And wall up its ^cbreaches; I will also raise up its ruins, And rebuild it as in the ^ddays of old;

12 ^aThat they may possess the remnant of ^bEdom And all the nations who are ^ccalled by My name," Declares the Lord who does this.

9:7 All nations are under God's control; so the Israelites should not think that they are the only people God has an interest in.
9:11 *In that day.* The aspect of the Day of the Lord known as the Millennium. *booth of David.* The dynasty of David, though humbled for a time, will be reinstated to rule over all the world (v. 12; see Acts 15:15-17).

Cross-reference column (left):
3 ^aJer. 16:16 ^bJob 34:22; Ps. 139:9, 10 ^cIs. 27:1
4 ^aLev. 26:33 ^bLev. 17:10; Jer. 21:10; 39:16; 44:11
5 ^aPs. 104:32; 144:5; Is. 64:1; Mic. 1:4 ^bAmos 8:8
6 ^aPs. 104:3, 13 ^bAmos 5:8 ^cPs. 104:6 ^dAmos 4:13
★ **7** ^a2 Chr. 14:9, 12; Is. 20:4; 43:3 ^bDeut. 2:23; Jer. 47:4 ^cAmos 1:5 ^d2 Kin. 16:9; Is. 22:6

Cross-reference column (right):
8 ^aJer. 44:27; Amos 9:4 ^bAmos 7:17; 9:10 ^cJer. 5:10; 30:11; 31:35, 36; Joel 2:32; Amos 3:12; Obad. 17
9 ^aIs. 30:28; Luke 22:31
10 ^aIs. 33:14; Zech. 13:8 ^bAmos 6:3
★**11** ^aActs 15:16-18 ^bIs. 16:5 ^cPs. 80:12 ^dIs. 63:11; Jer. 46:26
12 ^aObad. 19 ^bNum. 24:18; Is. 11:14 ^cIs. 43:7

★13-15

13 ªLev.
26:5 ᵇJoel
3:18 ᶜGen.
49:11

14 ªPs. 53:6;
Is. 60:4; Jer.
30:3, 18 ᵇIs.
61:4; 65:21
ᶜJer. 24:6;
31:28

13 "Behold, days are coming,"
    declares the Lᴏʀᴅ,
"When the ªplowman will
    overtake the reaper
And the treader of grapes
    him who sows seed;
When the ᵇmountains will
    drip sweet ᶜwine,
And all the hills will be
    dissolved.
14 "Also I will ªrestore the cap-
    tivity of My people Is-
    rael,
    And they will ᵇrebuild the

ruined cities and live
    in them,
They will also ᶜplant vine-
    yards and drink their
    wine,
And make gardens and eat
    their fruit.
15 "I will also plant them on
    their land,
And ªthey will not again
    be rooted out from
    their land
Which I have given them,"
Says the Lᴏʀᴅ your God.

15 ªIs.
60:21; Ezek.
34:28; 37:25

9:13-15 The millennial kingdom will be characterized by fertility (v. 13), prosperity (v. 14),
and security (v. 15), with Israel permanently
possessing the land promised in Gen.
15:18-21.

INTRODUCTION TO
THE BOOK OF OBADIAH

AUTHOR: Obadiah   DATE: 840 or 586 B.C.

Theme *Edom stands judged, and her doom is certain, because of her pride in rejoicing over the misfortunes that befell Jerusalem.*

The Edomites *Descendants of Esau, Jacob's twin, the Edomites were in constant conflict with Israel, the descendants of Jacob. They rejected Moses' request to pass through their land (Num. 20:14-20), they opposed King Saul (1 Sam. 14:47), they fought against David (1 Kings 11:14-17), opposed Solomon (1 Kings 11:14-25) and Jehoshaphat (2 Chron. 20:22), and rebelled against Jehoram (2 Chron. 21:8). From the 13th to the 6th centuries B.C. they settled in Mt. Seir, a mountainous region S. of the Dead Sea, of which Sela (Petra) was the capital. So rugged is the terrain that the valley in which Petra is located can only be reached through a narrow canyon guarded by towering mountain walls 200-250 feet high (see Obad. 3-4). During the 5th century B.C., the Nabataeans dislodged the Edomites from their territory, causing them to withdraw to Idumea in southern Palestine. Herod the Great was an Edomite.*

Date *The question of date relates to which battle against Jerusalem the Edomites were associated with (vv. 11-14). There were four significant invasions of Jerusalem in O.T. times: (1) by Shishak, king of Egypt, during Rehoboam's reign, in 926 (1 Kings 14:25-26); (2) by the Philistines and Arabians during the reign of Jehoram, from 848-841 (2 Chron. 21:16-17); (3) by King Joash of Israel during the reign of Amaziah, in 790 (2 Kings 14:13-14); (4) by Babylon during the years 605-586 (2 Kings 24-25). Obadiah prophesied against Edom either in connection with invasion #2 or #4. If the first, this book is the earliest of the writing prophets (see 2 Kings 8:20 and 2 Chron. 21:16-17; then see Joel 3:3-6 compared with Obad. 11-12 and the use of Obad. 1-9 in the extended passage in Jer. 49:7-22 as support for the earlier date).*

OUTLINE OF OBADIAH

I. The Doom of Edom, 1-9
  A. The Certainty of It, 1-4
  B. The Completeness of It, 5-9
II. The Denunciation of Edom, 10-14
  A. For Unbrotherliness, 10

B. For Aloofness, 11-12
C. For Aggressiveness, 13-14
III. The Destruction of Edom, 15-21
  A. The Time of the Destruction, 15
  B. The Nature of the Destruction, 16-21

THE BOOK OF OBADIAH

I THE DOOM OF EDOM, 1-9

A The Certainty of It, 1-4

★ 1 aPs. 137:7; Is. 21:11, 12; 34:1-17; 63:1-6; Jer. 49:7-22; Ezek. 25:12-14; 35:15; Joel 3:19; Amos 1:11, 12; Mal. 1:4

1 The vision of Obadiah.
Thus says the Lord GOD
concerning aEdom—
bWe have heard a report
from the LORD,

And an cenvoy has been
sent among the na-
tions saying,
"dArise and let us go against
her for battle"—
2 "Behold, I will make you
asmall among the na-
tions;
You are greatly despised.

b Jer. 49:14-16; Obad. 1-4 c Is. 18:2; 30:4 d Jer. 6:4, 5

2 aNum. 24:18; Is. 23:9

---

1 *Obadiah.* One of 12 men in the O.T. with this name. We know nothing about him except that his name means "servant of the Lord."

★ 3 aIs.
16:6; Jer.
49:16
b2 Kin. 14:7;
2 Chr.
25:11f. cIs.
14:13-15;
Rev. 18:7

3 "The ªarrogance of your heart has deceived you,
You who live in the clefts of the ᵇrock,
In the loftiness of your dwelling place,
Who say in your heart,
'ᶜWho will bring me down to earth?'

4 aJob
20:6, 7; Hab.
2:9 bIs.
14:12-15

4 "Though you ªbuild high like the eagle,
Though you set your nest among the ᵇstars,
From there I will bring you down," declares the LORD.

B   The Completeness of It, 5-9

★ 5-6
5 aJer. 49:9
bDeut. 24:21

5 "If ªthieves came to you,
If robbers by night—
O how you will be ruined!—
Would they not steal only until they had enough?
If grape gatherers came to you,
ᵇWould they not leave some gleanings?

6 aJer.
49:10

6 "O how Esau will be ªransacked,
And his hidden treasures searched out!

★ 7 aJer.
30:14 bPs.
41:9 cIs.
19:11; Jer.
49:7

7 "All the ªmen allied with you
Will send you forth to the border,
And the men at peace with you
Will deceive you and overpower you.
They who eat your ᵇbread

Will set an ambush for you.
(There is ᶜno understanding in him.)

8 "Will I not on that day," declares the LORD,
"ªDestroy wise men from Edom
And understanding from the mountain of Esau?

8 aJob
5:12-14; Is.
29:14

9 "Then your ªmighty men will be dismayed, O ᵇTeman,
In order that everyone may be ᶜcut off from the mountain of Esau by slaughter.

★ 9 aJer.
49:22 bGen.
36:11; 1 Chr.
1:45; Job
2:11; Jer.
49:7; Ezek.
25:13; Amos
1:12; Hab.
3:3 cIs. 34:5-
8; 63:1-3;
Obad. 5

II   THE DENUNCIATION OF EDOM, 10-14

A   For Unbrotherliness, 10

10 "Because of ªviolence to your brother Jacob,
You will be covered with shame,
ᵇAnd you will be cut off forever.

★10 aGen.
27:41; Ezek.
25:12; Joel
3:19; Amos
1:11 bEzek.
35:9

B   For Aloofness, 11-12

11 "On the day that you ªstood aloof,
On the day that strangers carried off his wealth,
And foreigners entered his gate
And ᵇcast lots for Jerusalem—
ᶜYou too were as one of them.

★11-14
11 aPs. 83:5,
6; 137:7;
Amos 1:6, 9
bJoel 3:3;
Nah. 3:10
cEzek. 35:10

12 "ªDo not gloat over your brother's day,
The day of his misfortune.

12 aMic.
4:11; 7:10
bProv. 17:5;
Ezek. 35:15;
36:5 cPs.
31:18; Ezek.
35:12

---

3 A reference to the almost impregnable fortress city of Petra. Some of the surrounding cliffs are 2000 feet high.

5-6 The meaning of these verses is this: while thieves usually take only that which is valuable and grape gatherers leave gleanings, Edom will be completely devastated.

7 Even Edom's allies would lay an ambush against her.

9 Teman. One of the chief settlements of Edom and home of one of Job's friends, Eliphaz.

10 brother. See Gen. 25:33; 27:36; 33:4; Deut. 2:4-5; 23:7.

11-14 The progression in Edom's crimes is detailed in these verses: first, Edom stood by while Jerusalem was invaded (v. 11); second, she rejoiced over the captivity of the sons of Judah (v. 12); third, Edom actively participated in the sacking of the city (v. 13); and, finally, she helped set up roadblocks to prevent the escape of the Jewish people (v. 14).

And [b]do not rejoice over
the sons of Judah
In the day of their destruc-
tion;
Yes, [c]do not boast
In the day of *their* distress.

C   For Aggressiveness, 13-14

13 "Do not enter the gate of
My people
In the [a]day of their disas-
ter.
Yes, you, do not gloat over
their calamity
In the day of their disaster.
And do not [b]loot their
wealth
In the day of their disaster.
14 "And do not [a]stand at the
fork of the road
To cut down their fugi-
tives;
And do not imprison their
survivors
In the day of their distress.

III   THE DESTRUCTION OF EDOM,
15-21

A   The Time of the
Destruction, 15

15 "For the [a]day of the LORD
draws near on all the
nations.
[b]As you have done, it will
be done to you.
Your [c]dealings will return
on your own head.

13 [a]Ezek.
35:5 [b]Ezek.
35:10;
36:2, 3

14 [a]Is.
16:3, 4

★**15** [a]Ezek.
30:3; Joel
1:15; 2:1, 11,
31; Amos
5:18, 20
[b]Jer. 50:29;
51:56; Hab.
2:8 [c]Ezek.
35:11

B   The Nature of the
Destruction,
16-21

16 "Because just as you [a]drank
on [b]My holy moun-
tain,
All the nations [c]will drink
continually.
They will drink and swal-
low,
And become as if they had
never existed.
17 "But on Mount [a]Zion there
will be those who es-
cape,
And it will be holy.
And the house of Jacob
will [b]possess their
possessions.
18 "Then the house of Jacob
will be a [a]fire
And the house of Joseph a
flame;
But the house of Esau *will
be* as stubble.
And they will set them on
fire and consume
them,
So that there will be [b]no
survivor of the house
of Esau,"
For the LORD has spoken.
19 Then *those of* the Negev
will [a]possess the
mountain of Esau,
And *those of* the Shephelah the [b]Philistine
plain;

16 [a]Jer.
49:12 [b]Joel
3:17 [c]Is.
51:22, 23;
Jer. 25:15,
16

17 [a]Is. 4:2, 3
[b]Is. 14:1, 2;
Amos 9:11-
15

★**18** [a]Is.
5:24; 9:18,
19; Zech.
12:6 [b]Jer.
11:23; Amos
1:8

★**19-20**

19 [a]Is.
11:14; Amos
9:12 [b]Is.
11:14 [c]Jer.
31:5; 32:44

---

15 *day of the LORD.* See Introduction to Joel. The
aspect referred to here is the time of Christ's
second coming and the judgments on all the
nations that accompany that event (Joel 3:2).
Edom's punishment, however, does not await
that future time but has already been carried
out.
18 There is *no survivor* today of the once
mighty Edomites. See Isa. 34:5-17.
19-20 Better, they (i.e., my people, Israel) shall
possess the Negev, that is, Mount Esau, etc. In

other words, the boundaries of the Davidic
kingdom will include the territory formerly
occupied by Edom in the south, *the Philistine
plain* (Gath, Ekron, Ashdod, Ashkelon, Gaza),
the territory of *Ephraim* and *Samaria, Gilead*
across the Jordan River, and as far north as
Zarephath (between Tyre and Sidon). *Sepharad* is not mentioned elsewhere in the Bible
and is unidentified (some say it is Sardis in
Asia Minor), but Obadiah is referring to a particular group of Jewish exiles.

Also, they will ^cpossess the territory of Ephraim and the territory of Samaria,
And Benjamin *will possess* Gilead.

20 And the exiles of this host of the sons of Israel,
Who are *among* the Canaanites as far as ^aZarephath,

And the exiles of Jerusalem who are in Sepharad
Will possess the ^bcities of the Negev.

21 The ^adeliverers will ascend Mount Zion
To judge the mountain of Esau,
And the ^bkingdom will be the Lord's.

20 ^a1 Kin. 17:9; Luke 4:26 ^bJer. 32:44; 33:13

★21 ^aNeh. 9:27 ^bPs. 22:28; 47:7-9; 67:4; Zech. 14:9; Rev. 11:15

---

21 *deliverers.* Most likely judges who will help rule in the millennial kingdom.

INTRODUCTION TO
THE BOOK OF JONAH

AUTHOR: Jonah   DATE: 760 B.C.

History or Allegory? *Some regard this book as an allegory, written about 430 B.C. to counter the exclusivism of Ezra and Nehemiah. In this view, Jonah represents disobedient Israel; the sea represents the Gentiles; the great fish, Babylon; and the three days in the fish's belly, the Babylonian captivity of the Jews.*

According to 2 Kings 14:25, however, Jonah was not only a real person but an accredited prophet from Gath-hepher near Nazareth. Further, Jesus Christ treated Jonah's experience in the belly of the fish as factual (Matt. 12:39-41). And, of course, the book reads as a straightforward historical account. This does not rule out the presence of typical lessons illustrated by the historical incidents.

The Times *In 2 Kings 14:27 Jonah is connected with the reign of Jeroboam II of Israel (793-753 B.C.), who had succeeded in reestablishing the power of Israel over most of the territory N. of Judah previously controlled by David and Solomon. No Assyrian inscription mentions a religious awakening such as that described in this book. However, during the reign of Adad-nirari III (810-783) there was a swing toward monotheism, which may have been the result of Jonah's preaching. The awakening may have occurred in the days of Ashurdan III (771-754). The plague of 765, the eclipse of the sun in 763, and a second plague in 759 were events of the type regarded by ancients as evidence of divine judgment, and could have prepared the people to receive Jonah's message.*

Miracles *A number of miracles are recorded in the book: the calming of the sea before the crew lost their lives (1:15); the provision of the great fish and the preservation of Jonah in the fish (1:17); the disgorging of Jonah on land (2:10); the preparing of the gourd (4:6), the worm (4:7), and the wind (4:8); and the salvation of many Ninevites.*

Theme *The book shows that the God of the Hebrews has concern for the whole world.*

OUTLINE OF JONAH

I. **Jonah Fleeing, 1:1-17**
  A. The Reason for his Flight, 1:1-2
  B. The Route of his Flight, 1:3
  C. The Results of his Flight, 1:4-17
    1. To the sailors, 1:4-11
    2. To Jonah, 1:12-17
II. **Jonah Praying, 2:1-10**
  A. The Characteristics of his Prayer, 2:1-9
  B. The Answer to his Prayer, 2:10

III. **Jonah Preaching, 3:1-10**
  A. God's Command to Preach, 3:1-3
  B. The Content of Jonah's Preaching, 3:4
  C. The Consequences of Jonah's Preaching, 3:5-10
IV. **Jonah Learning, 4:1-11**
  A. Jonah's Complaint to God, 4:1-3
  B. God's Curriculum for Jonah, 4:4-11

THE BOOK OF JONAH

I JONAH FLEEING, 1:1-17

A The Reason for his Flight, 1:1-2

★ **1** a2 Kin.
14:25; Matt.
12:39-41;
16:4; Luke
11:29, 30, 32

★ **2** a Gen.
10:11; 2 Kin.
19:36; Is.
37:37; Nah.
1:1; Zeph.
2:13 b Is.
58:1 c Gen.
18:20; Hos.
7:2

1 The word of the LORD came to aJonah the son of Amittai saying,

2 "Arise, go to aNineveh the great city, and bcry against it, for their cwickedness has come up before Me."

B The Route of his Flight, 1:3

★ **3** a Is.
23:1, 6, 10;
Jer. 10:9
b Gen. 4:16;
Ps. 139:7, 9,
10 c Josh.
19:46; 2 Chr.
2:16; Ezra
3:7; Acts
9:36, 43

3 But Jonah rose up to flee to aTarshish bfrom the presence of the LORD. So he went down to cJoppa, found a ship which was going to Tarshish, paid the fare, and went down into it to go with them to Tarshish from the presence of the LORD.

C The Results of his Flight, 1:4-17

1 To the sailors, 1:4-11

4 a Ps.
107:23-28;
135:6, 7

4 And the aLORD hurled a great wind on the sea and there was a great storm on the sea so that the ship was about to break up.

5 a1 Kin.
18:26 b Acts
27:18, 19, 38

5 Then the sailors became afraid, and every man cried to ahis god, and they bthrew the cargo which was in the ship into the sea to lighten it for them. But Jonah had gone below into the hold of the ship, lain down, and fallen sound asleep.

6 a Ps.
107:28
b 2 Sam.
12:22; Amos
5:15; Jon.
3:9

6 So the captain approached him and said, "How is it that you are sleeping? Get up, acall on your god. Perhaps your bgod will be concerned about us so that we will not perish."

7 And each man said to his mate, "Come, let us acast lots so we may learn on whose account this calamity has struck us." So they cast lots and the blot fell on Jonah.

8 Then they said to him, "aTell us, now! On whose account has this calamity struck us? What is your boccupation? And where do you come from? What is your country? From what people are you?"

9 And he said to them, "I am a aHebrew, and I bfear the LORD cGod of heaven who dmade the sea and the dry land."

10 Then the men became extremely frightened and they said to him, "How could you do this?" For the men knew that he was afleeing from the presence of the LORD, because he had told them.

11 So they said to him, "What should we do to you that the sea may become calm for us?"—for the sea was becoming increasingly stormy.

2 To Jonah, 1:12-17

12 And he said to them, "Pick me up and throw me into the sea. Then the sea will become calm for you, for I know that aon account of me this great storm has come upon you."

13 However, the men rowed desperately to return to land but they could not, for the sea was

★ **7** a Josh.
7:14-18;
1 Sam.
10:20, 21;
14:41, 42;
Acts 1:23-26
b Num.
32:23; Prov.
16:33

8 a Josh.
7:19; 1 Sam.
14:43 b Gen.
47:3; 1 Sam.
30:13

9 a Gen.
14:13; Ex.
1:15; 2:13
b 2 Kin.
17:25, 28,
32, 33 c Ezra
1:2; Neh. 1:4;
Ps. 136:26;
Dan. 2:18
d Neh. 9:6;
Ps. 95:5;
146:6

10 a Job
27:22; Jon.
1:3

12 a2 Sam.
24:17; 1 Chr.
21:17

1:1 The name *Jonah* means "dove."
1:2 *Nineveh.* Located on the E. bank of the Tigris River, more than 500 miles from Palestine. Sennacherib made it the capital of Assyria about 700 B.C. Calah, however, about 20 miles S. of Nineveh and part of a city-state complex that included Nineveh, was the capital in Jonah's time (see Gen. 10:11-12). *wickedness.* Included idolatrous worship and extreme cruelty to prisoners of war.

1:3 *Tarshish.* Located in the S. of Spain near Gibraltar, 2000 miles W. of Palestine. But no one can escape *from the presence of the LORD* (Psalm 139:7-12).
1:7 Casting *lots* by mixing small stones in a container, then taking one out, was a popular form of divination used both by pagans and the Hebrews (Lev. 16:8; Josh. 18:6; 1 Sam. 14:42; Neh. 10:34; Acts 1:23-26).

becoming *even* stormier against them.

14aPs.
107:28; Jon.
1:16 bPs.
115:3; 135:6;
Dan. 4:34, 35

14 Then they called on the aLORD and said, "We earnestly pray, O LORD, do not let us perish on account of this man's life and do not put innocent blood on us; for bThou, O LORD, hast done as Thou hast pleased."

15aPs. 65:7;
93:3, 4;
107:29

15 So they picked up Jonah, threw him into the sea, and the sea astopped its raging.

★16aPs.
50:14; 66:13,
14

16 Then the men feared the LORD greatly, and they offered a sacrifice to the LORD and made avows.

★17aMatt.
12:40; 16:4

17 And the LORD appointed a great fish to swallow Jonah, and Jonah was in the astomach of the fish three days and three nights.

II JONAH PRAYING, 2:1-10
A The Characteristics of his Prayer, 2:1-9

1aJob
13:15; Ps.
130:1, 2;
Lam. 3:53-56

2 Then Jonah prayed to the LORD his God afrom the stomach of the fish,

★2a1 Sam.
30:6; Ps.
18:4-6;
22:24; 120:1
bPs. 18:5, 6;
86:13;
88:1-7

2 and he said,
"I acalled out of my distress
   to the LORD,
And He answered me.
I cried for help from the
   depth of bSheol;
Thou didst hear my voice.

★3aPs.
69:1, 2, 14,
15; Lam.
3:54 bPs.
42:7

3 "For Thou hadst acast me
   into the deep,
Into the heart of the seas,
And the current engulfed
   me.
All Thy bbreakers and billows passed over me.

4aPs.
31:22; Jer.
7:15 b1 Kin.
8:38; 2 Chr.
6:38; Ps. 5:7

4 "So I said, 'I have been aex-
   pelled from Thy sight.
Nevertheless I will look
   again btoward Thy
   holy temple.'

5aLam.
3:54 bPs.
69:1, 2

5 "aWater encompassed me
   to the point of death.
The great bdeep engulfed
   me,
Weeds were wrapped
   around my head.

6aPs. 18:5;
116:3 bIs.
38:10; Matt.
16:18 cJob
16:10; 30:3;
Is. 38:17

6 "I adescended to the roots
   of the mountains.
The earth with its bbars
   was around me for-
   ever,
But Thou hast cbrought up
   my life from the pit,
O LORD my God.

7aPs.
142:3 bPs.
77:10, 11;
143:5
c2 Chr.
30:27; Ps.
18:6 dPs.
11:4; 65:4;
Jon. 2:4; Mic.
1:2; Hab.
2:20

7 "While I was afainting
   away,
I bremembered the LORD;
And my cprayer came to
   Thee,
Into dThy holy temple.

★8a2 Kin.
17:15; Ps.
31:6; Jer.
10:8

8 "Those who aregard vain
   idols
Forsake their faithfulness,

★9aPs.
50:14, 23;
Jer. 33:11;
Hos. 14:2
bJob 22:27;
Eccl. 5:4, 5
cPs. 3:8; Is.
45:17

9 But I will asacrifice to Thee
With the voice of thanks-
   giving.
That which I have vowed I
   will bpay.
cSalvation is from the
   LORD."

B The Answer to his Prayer, 2:10

10aJon.
1:17

10 Then the LORD com-
manded the afish, and it vomited
Jonah up onto the dry land.

III JONAH PREACHING, 3:1-10
A God's Command to Preach, 3:1-3

3 Now the word of the LORD
came to Jonah the second
time, saying,

1:16 Apparently the sailors were convinced that Yahweh (see note on Gen. 2:4) was the true God; thus they *offered a sacrifice* to Him.

1:17 We do not know what kind of *great fish* God prepared, though there are whales and sharks capable of swallowing a man. On the expression *three days and three nights* see note on Matt. 12:40.

2:2 *from the depth of Sheol.* Although Sheol re-fers to the place of the dead, the expression

here means "from death's door" and does not necessarily indicate that Jonah actually died (cf. Psalm 30:3).

2:3 *Thy breakers.* Jonah acknowledged that his punishment came from God.

2:8 Jonah includes himself among those who forsake God's *faithfulness* for lies.

2:9 *That which I have vowed I will pay.* I.e., I will keep my promise to God and obey Him.

2 aZeph.
2:13 bJer.
1:17; Ezek.
2:7

★ 3 aJon.
1:2; 4:11

2 "Arise, go to aNineveh the great city and bproclaim to it the proclamation which I am going to tell you."

3 So Jonah arose and went to Nineveh according to the word of the Lord. Now Nineveh was an aexceedingly great city, a three days' walk.

B The Content of Jonah's Preaching, 3:4

4 aMatt.
12:41; Luke
11:32

4 Then Jonah began to go through the city one day's walk; and he acried out and said, "Yet forty days and Nineveh will be overthrown."

C The Consequences of Jonah's Preaching, 3:5-10

5 aDan.
9:3; Joel
1:14

5 Then the people of Nineveh believed in God; and they called a afast and put on sackcloth from the greatest to the least of them.

★ 6 aEsth.
4:1-4; Jer.
6:26; Ezek.
27:30, 31

6 When the word reached the king of Nineveh, he arose from his throne, laid aside his robe from him, acovered himself with sackcloth, and sat on the ashes.

7 a2 Chr.
20:3; Ezra
8:21; Jon.
3:5

7 And he issued a aproclamation and it said, "In Nineveh by the decree of the king and his nobles: Do not let man, beast, herd, or flock taste a thing. Do not let them eat or drink water.

8 aPs.
130:1; Jon.
1:6, 14 bIs.
1:16-19;
55:6, 7; Jer.
18:11

8 "But both man and beast must be covered with sackcloth; and let men acall on God earnestly that each may bturn from his wicked way and from the violence which is in his hands.

9 a2 Sam.
12:22; Joel
2:14

9 "aWho knows, God may turn and relent, and withdraw His burning anger so that we shall not perish?"

★10 a1 Kin.
21:27-29;
Jer. 31:18
bEx. 32:14;
Jer. 18:8;
Amos 7:3, 6

10 When God saw their deeds, that they aturned from their wicked way, then bGod relented concerning the calamity which He had declared He would bring upon them. And He did not do it.

IV JONAH LEARNING, 4:1-11
A Jonah's Complaint to God, 4:1-3

★ 1-3
1 aJon. 4:4,
9; Matt.
20:15; Luke
15:28

4 But it greatly displeased Jonah, and he became aangry.

2 aJer. 20:7
bJon. 1:3
cEx. 34:6;
Num. 14:18;
Ps. 86:5, 15;
Joel 2:13

2 And he aprayed to the Lord and said, "Please Lord, was not this what I said while I was still in my own country? Therefore, in order to forestall this I bfled to Tarshish, for I knew that Thou art a cgracious and compassionate God, slow to anger and abundant in lovingkindness, and one who relents concerning calamity.

3 a1 Kin.
19:4; Job
6:8, 9 bJob
7:15, 16;
Eccl. 7:1

3 "Therefore now, O Lord, please atake my life from me, for death is bbetter to me than life."

B God's Curriculum for Jonah, 4:4-11

4 And the Lord said, "Do you have good reason to be angry?"

★ 5 a1 Kin.
19:9, 13

5 Then Jonah went out from the city and sat east of it. There he made a shelter for himself and asat under it in the shade until he could see what would happen in the city.

3:3 great city. Lit., a great city before God, because of the people in it who needed Him. a three days' walk. The circumference of the city, including some surrounding land, was about 60 miles.
3:6 the king of Nineveh. Either Adad-nirari III (810-783) or Ashurdan III (771-754). sackcloth. A symbol of sorrow and repentance, it was coarse, dark cloth unfit for normal wear (cf. Rev. 6:12). Sitting in ashes was a sign of helplessness and despair (cf. Job 2:8; Mic.

1:10).
3:10 God relented. See Gen. 6:6.
4:1-3 angry. Lit., hot; because he knew that God would spare the Ninevites if they repented, and he did not want these enemies of Israel to be spared. lovingkindness. See note on Hos. 2:19. Jonah preferred death to being reconciled to the gracious will of God.
4:5 a shelter. Of branches under which Jonah would wait the forty days, hoping for the destruction of Nineveh.

★ 6

6 So the Lord God appointed a plant and it grew up over Jonah to be a shade over his head to deliver him from his discomfort. And Jonah was extremely happy about the plant.

7 aJoel
1:12

7 But God appointed a worm when dawn came the next day, and it attacked the plant and it awithered.

★ 8 aEzek.
19:12; Hos.
13:15 bPs.
121:6; Is.
49:10 cJon.
4:3

8 And it came about when the sun came up that God appointed a scorching aeast wind, and the bsun beat down on Jonah's head so that he became faint and begged with *all* his soul to die, saying, "cDeath is better to me than life."

9 Then God said to Jonah, "Do you have good reason to be angry about the plant?" And he said, "I have good reason to be angry, even to death."

★10-11

10 Then the Lord said, "You had compassion on the plant for which you did not work, and *which* you did not cause to grow, which *came up* overnight and perished overnight.

11 "And should I not ahave compassion on Nineveh, the great city in which there are more than 120,000 persons who do not bknow *the difference* between their right and left hand, as well as many canimals?"

11 aJon.
3:10 bDeut.
1:39; Is. 7:16
cPs. 36:6

4:6 *a plant.* Probably the castor oil plant, whose large leaves provided welcome shade from the sun's heat. Its swift growth was an act of God.
4:8 *east wind.* Known for its scorching heat.
4:10–11 God used the *plant* as an object lesson to teach Jonah this important truth: if Jonah was justified in being so upset about the loss of a plant to whose existence he had contributed nothing, was not God justified in show-

ing love and concern for the people of Nineveh, whom He had created? The population must have been around 600,000 if there were 120,000 children. *as well as many animals.* A final touch of irony, as if to say, "Jonah, even if you approve of the destruction of hundreds of thousands of people, think of the waste of livestock that would be involved!"

INTRODUCTION TO
THE BOOK OF MICAH

AUTHOR: Micah   DATE: 700 B.C.

The Prophet   *While Hosea prophesied to the northern tribes of Israel and Isaiah to the court in Jerusalem, Micah, a Judean from Moresheth in the SW. of Palestine, preached to the common people of Judah. His name means "who is like Yahweh?"*

His Times   *Micah ministered during the reigns of Jotham (750-732), Ahaz (736-716), and Hezekiah (716-687) (1:1). Though for the most part a good king, Jotham did not remove the idolatrous high places from his kingdom. Ahaz, a wicked king (see 2 Kings 16:2-4), adopted a pro-Assyrian foreign policy, and during his reign the captivity of the northern tribes took place. Hezekiah, one of Judah's best kings, was anti-Assyrian and withstood the siege of Jerusalem which Sennacherib led in 701 (2 Kings 18:13-19:36). For peasants and villagers, these were days of harassment from enemy armies, of hardship because of exploitation by the wealthy (2:1-13), and of oppression by the rulers (3:1-4) and false prophets (3:5-8). Micah, as Amos, cried for social justice.*

Contents   *Three important quotations from Micah are found elsewhere in the Bible. One saved the prophet Jeremiah's life (Jer. 26:18, a quote of Mic. 3:12). The priests and scribes quoted Micah 5:2 in answer to Herod's question about the birthplace of Messiah (Matt. 2:5-6). Christ quoted Micah 7:6 when He commissioned the disciples the first time (Matt. 10:35-36). Micah chapter 4, is one of the most important descriptions in the Bible of the future glory of Israel and Micah 6:8 is one of the favorite verses. The major sections of the book are introduced with the word "Hear" (1:2; 3:1; 6:1).*

OUTLINE OF MICAH

I. **The Superscription, 1:1**
II. **A Message of Destruction for Samaria and Judah, 1:2-2:13**
  A. The Revelation of the Coming Judgment, 1:2-16
  B. The Reasons for the Coming Judgment, 2:1-13
III. **A Message of Doom and Deliverance, 3:1-5:15**
  A. Doom: The Coming Judgment, 3:1-12
    1. Judgment on the rulers, 3:1-4
    2. Judgment on the false prophets, 3:5-8
    3. Judgment on Jerusalem, 3:9-12

  B. Deliverance: the Coming Kingdom, 4:1-5:1
    1. The glories of the kingdom, 4:1-8
    2. The suffering that precedes the kingdom, 4:9-5:1
  C. Deliverance: the Coming King, 5:2-15
    1. His first coming, 5:2-3
    2. His second coming, 5:4-15
IV. **A Message of Denunciation, 6:1-7:10**
  A. God's First Indictment, 6:1-5
  B. Israel's First Reply, 6:6-8
  C. God's Second Indictment, 6:9-16
  D. Israel's Second Reply, 7:1-10
V. **Epilogue: Blessings for Israel, 7:11-20**

THE BOOK OF MICAH

I THE SUPERSCRIPTION, 1:1

1 *a* 2 Pet.
1:21 *b* Jer.
26:18 *c* 2 Kin.
15:5, 32-38;
2 Chr.
27:1-9; Is.
1:1; Hos. 1:1
d 2 Kin.
16:1-20;
2 Chr.
28:1-27; Is.
7:1-12
e 2 Kin.
18:1-20;
2 Chr. 29:1-31

1 The *a*word of the LORD which
came to *b*Micah of Moresheth
in the days of *c*Jotham, *d*Ahaz,
and *e*Hezekiah, kings of Judah,
which he saw concerning Samaria
and Jerusalem.

II A MESSAGE OF DESTRUCTION FOR SAMARIA AND JUDAH, 1:2-2:13

A The Revelation of the Coming Judgment, 1:2-16

★ 2-9

2 *a* Jer.
6:19; 22:29
b Is. 50:7

2 Hear, O peoples, all of
   you;
*a*Listen, O earth and all it
   contains,
And let the Lord GOD be a
   *b*witness against you,
The Lord from His holy
   temple.

3 *a* Is. 26:21
b Amos 4:13

3 For behold, the LORD is
   *a*coming forth from
   His place.
He will come down and
   *b*tread on the high
   places of the earth.

4 *a* Ps. 97:5;
Is. 64:1, 2;
Nah. 1:5

4 *a*The mountains will melt
   under Him,
And the valleys will be
   split,
Like wax before the fire,
Like water poured down a
   steep place.

5 *a* Jer. 2:19
b Is. 7:9;
Amos 8:14
c 2 Chr.
34:3, 4

5 All this is for the rebellion
   of Jacob
And for the sins of the
   house of Israel.

What is the *a*rebellion of
   Jacob?
Is it not *b*Samaria?
What is the *c*high place of
   Judah?
Is it not Jerusalem?

6 *a* 2 Kin.
19:25; Mic.
3:12 *b* Jer.
31:5; Amos
5:11 *c* Lam.
4:1 *d* Ezek.
13:14

6 For I will make Samaria a
   *a*heap of ruins in the
   open country,
*b*Planting places for a vineyard.
I will *c*pour her stones
   down into the valley,
And will *d*lay bare her
   foundations.

7 *a* Deut.
9:21; 2 Chr.
34:7 *b* Deut.
23:18; Is.
23:17

7 All of her *a*idols will be
   smashed,
All of her earnings will be
   burned with fire,
And all of her images I will
   make desolate,
For she collected *them*
   from a *b*harlot's earnings,
And to the earnings of a
   harlot they will re-
   turn.

8 *a* Is. 32:11
b Is. 13:21,
22

8 Because of this I must lament and wail,
I must go *a*barefoot and
   naked;
I must make a lament like
   the *b*jackals
And a mourning like the
   ostriches.

9 *a* Is. 3:26;
Jer. 30:12,
15 *b* 2 Kin.
18:13; Is.
8:7, 8 *c* Mic.
1:12

9 For her *a*wound is incur-
   able,
For *b*it has come to Judah;
It has reached the *c*gate of
   my people,
Even to Jerusalem.

★10-16

10 *a* 2 Sam.
1:20

10 *a*Tell it not in Gath,
   Weep not at all.

1:2-9 These verses describe the Lord descending in judgment against Israel (and its capital *Samaria*, v. 6) and against Judah (and its capital *Jerusalem*, vv. 5b, 9, 12) because of idolatry. Samaria was captured by Assyria in 722; Jerusalem was besieged by Sennacherib in 701 (2 Kings 18:13-16) and by Nebuchadnezzar in 605 and later. *earnings* (v. 7). I.e., wages paid to harlots.

1:10-16 Micah traces the route of the invading army from the Philistine coastal plain through the Judean hills to Jerusalem. *Tell it not in*

Gath. A proverbial expression for disaster (2 Sam. 1:20). Micah foresaw the women being taken captive first (the word for *inhabitant* in vv. 11 and 12 is feminine). Micah uses puns in denouncing these cities; e.g., *Shaphir* (v. 11) sounds like the Hebrew word for beauty and is contrasted with their shame; *Zaanan* (v. 11) sounds like a verb meaning "to go out" and is contrasted with the fear of the people to go outside their houses; *Beth-ezel* (v. 11) sounds like a word meaning "foundation," and they had none; *Maroth* (v. 12), like a word meaning

11 aEzek.
23:29 bJosh.
15:37

11 Go on your way, inhabitant of Shaphir, in
ashameful nakedness.
The inhabitant of bZaanan
does not escape.
The lamentation of
Beth-ezel: "He will
take from you its sup-
port."

12 aIs. 59:9-
11; Jer.
14:19 bMic.
1:9

12 For the inhabitant of Ma-
roth
Becomes weak awaiting for
good,
Because a calamity has
come down from the
LORD
To the bgate of Jerusalem.

13 aJosh.
10:3; 2 Kin.
14:19; Is.
36:2 bMic.
1:5

13 Harness the chariot to the
team of horses,
O inhabitant of aLachish—
She was the beginning of
sin
To the daughter of Zion—
Because in you were found
The brebellious acts of Is-
rael.

14 a2 Kin.
16:8 bJosh.
15:44 cJer.
15:18

14 Therefore, you will give
parting agifts
On behalf of Moresheth-
gath;
The houses of bAchzib will
become a cdeception
To the kings of Israel.

15 aJosh.
15:44 bJosh.
12:15; 15:35;
2 Sam. 23:13

15 Moreover, I will bring on
you
The one who takes posses-
sion,
O inhabitant of aMare-
shah.
The glory of Israel will enter bAdullam.

★16 aIs.
22:12
b2 Kin. 17:6;
Amos 7:11,
17

16 Make yourself abald and
cut off your hair,
Because of the children of
your delight;
Extend your baldness like
the eagle,

For they will bgo from you
into exile.

B   The Reasons for the Coming Judgment, 2:1-13

2 Woe to those who ascheme
iniquity,
Who work out evil on
their beds!
bWhen morning comes,
they do it,
For it is in the cpower of
their hands.

2 They acovet fields and
then bseize them,
And houses, and take
them away.
They crob a man and his
house,
A man and his inheritance.

3 Therefore, thus says the
LORD,
"Behold, I am aplanning
against this bfamily a
calamity
From which you ccannot
remove your necks;
And you will not walk
dhaughtily,
For it will be an eevil time.

4 "On that day they will atake
up against you a taunt
And butter a bitter lamentation and say,
'We are completely cde-
stroyed!
He exchanges the portion
of my people;
How He removes it from
me!
To the apostate He dappor-
tions our fields.'

5 "Therefore, you will have
no one astretching a
measuring line

★ 1-2
1 aPs. 36:4;
Is. 32:7; Nah.
1:11 bHos.
7:6, 7 cGen.
31:29; Deut.
28:32; Prov.
3:27

2 aJer.
22:17; Amos
8:4 bIs. 5:8
c1 Kin. 21:1-
15

★ 3-5
3 aDeut.
28:48; Jer.
18:11 bJer.
8:3; Amos
3:1, 2 cLam.
1:14; 5:5 dIs.
2:11, 12
eAmos 5:13

4 aHab. 2:6
bJer. 9:10,
17-21; Mic.
1:8 cIs. 6:11;
24:3; Jer.
4:13 dJer.
6:12; 8:10

5 aNum.
34:13, 16-29;
Deut. 32:8;
Josh. 18:4,
10

"to wait for good," whereas they were waiting
for evil. *The glory of Israel.* The nobility, who
would flee to *Adullam,* where there were
caves (cf. 1 Sam. 22:1).
1:16 *Make yourself bald and cut off your hair.*
As a sign of deep mourning.
2:1-2 *it is in the power of their hands.* The land-

grabbing upper classes thought that "might
makes right." They unjustly took away the
land (*inheritance,* v. 2) of the poor, a most serious matter in an agricultural community.
2:3-5 God would punish Judah by allowing foreigners to take away their land.

For you by lot in the assembly of the LORD.

★ 6-7

6 a Is. 30:10; Amos 2:12; 7:16 b Is. 29:10; Mic. 3:6 c Mic. 6:16

6 'a Do not speak out,' *so* they speak out.
But if they do b not speak out concerning these things,
c Reproaches will not be turned back.

7 a Is. 50:2; 59:1 b Ps. 119:65, 68, 116; Jer. 15:16 c Ps. 15:2; 84:11

7 "Is it being said, O house of Jacob:
'Is the Spirit of the LORD a impatient?
Are these His doings?'
Do not My words b do good
To the one c walking uprightly?

8 a Jer. 12:8 b Mic. 3:2, 3; 7:2, 3 c Ps. 120:6, 7

8 "Recently My people have arisen as an a enemy—
You b strip the robe off a fellow Israelite,
From c unsuspecting passers-by,
From those returned from war.

9 a Jer. 10:20 b Ezek. 39:21; Hab. 2:14

9 "The women of My people you a evict,
Each *one* from her pleasant house.
From her children you take My b splendor forever.

10 a Deut. 12:9 b Ps. 106:38

10 "Arise and go,
For this is no place a of rest
Because of the b uncleanness that brings on destruction,
A painful destruction.

★11 a Jer. 5:31 b Is. 28:7 c Is. 30:10, 11

11 "If a man walking after wind and a falsehood
Had told lies *and said,*
'I will speak out to you concerning b wine and liquor,'
He would be spokesman to c this people.

12 "I will surely a assemble all of you, Jacob,
I will surely gather the b remnant of Israel.
I will put them together like sheep in the fold;
Like a flock in the midst of its pasture
They will be noisy with men.

★12-13

12 a Mic. 4:6, 7 b Mic. 5:7, 8; 7:18

13 "The breaker goes up before them;
They break out, pass through the gate, and go out by it.
So their king goes on before them,
And the LORD at their head."

III   A MESSAGE OF DOOM AND DELIVERANCE, 3:1-5:15

A   Doom: the Coming Judgment, 3:1-12

1   *Judgment on the rulers*, 3:1-4

3 And I said,
"a Hear now, heads of Jacob
And rulers of the house of Israel.
Is it not for you to b know justice?

★ 1-4

1 a Is. 1:10; Mic. 3:9 b Ps. 82:1-5; Jer. 5:5

2 "You who hate good and love evil,
Who a tear off their skin from them
And their flesh from their bones,

2 a Ps. 53:4; Ezek. 22:27; Mic. 2:8; 7:2, 3

3 And who a eat the flesh of my people,
Strip off their skin from them,
Break their bones,
And b chop *them* up as for the pot
And as meat in a kettle."

3 a Ps. 14:4; 27:2; Zeph. 3:3 b Ezek. 11:3, 6, 7

2:6-7 Verse 6 is likely a listener's enraged reply to Micah, and verse 7, Micah's answer. To one living *uprightly* God's words are good.
2:11 The people preferred to listen to false prophets under the influence of alcohol rather than to Micah under the influence of the Holy Spirit (cf. Acts 2:15-16; Eph. 5:18).
2:12-13 A prediction of the regathering and de-

liverance of Israel in connection with the second coming of Messiah, who is called *The breaker;* i.e., the one who goes ahead to remove obstacles in the path.
3:1-4 The unjust leaders showed about as much consideration for the people as butchers do for carcasses!

4 *a*Ps.
18:41; Prov.
1:28; Is.
1:15; Jer.
11:11 *b*Deut.
31:17; Is.
59:2 *c*Is.
3:11; Mic.
7:13

4 Then they will *a*cry out to
the Lord,
But He will not answer
them.
Instead, He will *b*hide His
face from them at that
time,
Because they have *c*practiced evil deeds.

2   Judgment on the false prophets, 3:5-8

★ 5 *a*Is.
3:12; 9:15,
16; Jer.
14:14, 15
*b*Jer. 6:14

5 Thus says the Lord con-
cerning the prophets
Who *a*lead my people
astray;
When they have *some-
thing* to bite with
their teeth,
They *b*cry, "Peace,"
But against him who puts
nothing in their
mouths,
They declare holy war.

6 *a*Is. 8:20-
22; 29:10-12
*b*Is. 59:10

6 Therefore *it will be* *a*night
for you—without vi-
sion,
And darkness for you—
without divination.
The *b*sun will go down on
the prophets,
And the day will become
dark over them.

7 *a*Zech.
13:4 *b*Is.
44:25; 47:12-
14 *c*Mic.
7:16 *d*1 Sam.
28:6; Mic.
3:4

7 The seers will be *a*ashamed
And the *b*diviners will be
embarrassed.
Indeed, they will all *c*cover
their mouths
Because there is *d*no answer from God.

8 *a*Is. 61:1,
2; Jer. 1:18
*b*Is. 58:1

8 On the other hand *a*I am
filled with power—
With the Spirit of the
Lord—
And with justice and cour-
age
To *b*make known to Jacob
his rebellious act,
Even to Israel his sin.

3   Judgment on Jerusalem, 3:9-12

9 *a*Mic. 1:1
*b*Ps. 58:1, 2;
Is. 1:23

9 Now hear this, *a*heads of
the house of Jacob
And rulers of the house of
Israel,
Who *b*abhor justice
And twist everything that
is straight,

10 *a*Jer.
22:13, 17;
Hab. 2:12

10 Who *a*build Zion with
bloodshed
And Jerusalem with vio-
lent injustice.

★11 *a*Is.
1:23; Mic.
7:3 *b*Jer.
6:13 *c*Is.
48:2

11 Her leaders pronounce
*a*judgment for a bribe,
Her *b*priests instruct for a
price,
And her prophets divine
for money.
Yet they lean on the Lord
saying,
"*c*Is not the Lord in our
midst?
Calamity will not come
upon us."

12 *a*Jer.
26:18 *b*Ps.
79:1; Jer.
9:11 *c*Mic.
4:1

12 Therefore, on account of
you,
*a*Zion will be plowed as a
field,
*b*Jerusalem will become a
heap of ruins,
And the *c*mountain of the
temple *will become*
high places of a forest.

B   Deliverance: the Coming Kingdom, 4:1-5:1

1   The glories of the kingdom, 4:1-8

★ 1-3

1 *a*Is.
2:2-4; Dan.
2:28; 10:14;
Hos. 3:5
*b*Ezek.
43:12; Mic.
3:12; Zech.
8:3 *c*Ps.
22:27; 86:9;
Jer. 3:17

4 And it will come about in the
*a*last days
That the *b*mountain of the
house of the Lord
Will be established as the
chief of the moun-
tains.
It will be raised above the
hills,

3:5 When the false prophets had plenty to eat
(*bite with their teeth*) they predicted *Peace.*
3:11 Everyone had his price because mammon
was his god.
4:1-3 Almost identical to Isa. 2:2-4, this passage
describes the glories of the millennial king-

dom. *the mountain of the house of the Lord.*
Jerusalem and the Temple on Mt. Zion, which
will be the center of the government of the
kingdom. *as the chief.* Lit., at the head (of
lesser governmental divisions). *render decisions.* Arbitrate.

And the ^cpeoples will stream to it.

2 And ^amany nations will come and say,
"^bCome and let us go up to the mountain of the LORD
And to the house of the God of Jacob,
That ^cHe may teach us about His ways
And that we may walk in His paths."
For ^dfrom Zion will go forth the law,
Even the word of the LORD from Jerusalem.

3 And He will ^ajudge between many peoples
And render decisions for mighty, distant nations.
Then they will hammer their swords ^binto plowshares
And their spears into pruning hooks;
Nation will not lift up sword against nation,
And never again will they train for war.

4 And each of them will ^asit under his vine
And under his fig tree,
With ^bno one to make *them* afraid,
For the ^cmouth of the LORD of hosts has spoken.

5 Though all the peoples walk
Each in the ^aname of his god,
As for us, ^bwe will walk
In the name of the ^cLORD our God forever and ever.

6 "In that day," declares the LORD,
"I will assemble the ^alame,

And ^bgather the outcasts,
Even those whom I have afflicted.

7 "I will make the lame a ^aremnant,
And the outcasts a strong nation,
And the ^bLORD will reign over them in Mount Zion
From now on and forever.

8 "And as for you, ^atower of the flock,
Hill of the daughter of Zion,
To you it will come—
Even the ^bformer dominion will come,
The kingdom of the daughter of Jerusalem.

2   *The suffering that precedes the kingdom, 4:9—5:1*

9 "Now, why do you ^acry out loudly?
Is there no king among you,
Or has your ^bcounselor perished,
That agony has gripped you like a woman in childbirth?

10 "^aWrithe and labor to give birth,
Daughter of Zion,
Like a woman in childbirth,
For now you will ^bgo out of the city,
Dwell in the field,
And go to Babylon.
^cThere you will be rescued;
^dThere the LORD will redeem you
From the hand of your enemies.

2 ^aZech. 2:11; 14:16 ^bIs. 2:3; Jer. 31:6 ^cPs. 25:8, 9, 12; Is. 54:13 ^dIs. 42:1-4; Zech. 14:8, 9

3 ^aIs. 2:4; 11:3-5 ^bJoel 3:10

4 ^a1 Kin. 4:25; Zech. 3:10 ^bLev. 26:6; Jer. 30:10 ^cIs. 1:20; 40:5

5 ^a2 Kin. 17:29 ^bZech. 10:12 ^cJosh. 24:15; Is. 26:8, 13

6 ^aZeph. 3:19 ^bPs. 147:2; Ezek. 34:13, 16; 37:21

7 ^aMic. 5:7, 8; 7:18 ^bIs. 24:23

★ **8** ^aPs. 48:3, 12; 61:3; Mic. 2:12 ^bIs. 1:26; Zech. 9:10

★ **9-10**

9 ^aJer. 8:19 ^bIs. 3:1-3

10 ^aMic. 5:3 ^b2 Kin. 20:18; Hos. 2:14 ^cIs. 43:14; 45:13; Mic. 7:8-12 ^dIs. 48:20; 52:9-12

4:8 *tower of the flock.* I.e., Jerusalem, which, in the figure, watches over Israel as a shepherd watches his sheep from a tower. The millennial kingdom will be greater in extent than David's or Solomon's, *the former dominion.*

4:9-10 Refers to the Babylonian captivity and later return to Palestine under Cyrus. In Micah's time Babylon was only a vassal of powerful Assyria, making this an even more startling prophecy.

★11-13

11 als. 5:25-30; 17:12-14

11 "And now [a]many nations have been assembled against you
Who say, 'Let her be polluted,
And let our eyes gloat over Zion.'

12 aPs. 147:19, 20

12 "But they do not [a]know the thoughts of the LORD,
And they do not understand His purpose;
For He has gathered them like sheaves to the threshing floor.

13 als. 41:15
bJer. 51:20-23 cls. 60:9

13 "Arise and [a]thresh, daughter of Zion,
For your horn I will make iron
And your hoofs I will make bronze,
That you may [b]pulverize many peoples,
That you may [c]devote to the LORD their unjust gain
And their wealth to the Lord of all the earth.

★ 1 a1 Kin. 22:24; Job 16:10; Lam. 3:30

5 "Now muster yourselves in troops, daughter of troops;
They have laid siege against us;
With a rod they will [a]smite the judge of Israel on the cheek.

C   Deliverance: the Coming King, 5:2-15

1   His first coming, 5:2-3

★ 2 aGen. 35:19; 48:7; Ruth 4:11; Matt. 2:6 bls. 11:1; Luke 2:4; John 7:42 cJer. 30:21; Zech. 9:9 dPs. 102:25; Prov. 8:22, 23

2 "But as for [a]you, Bethlehem Ephrathah,
Too little to be among the clans of Judah,
From [b]you One will go forth for Me to be [c]ruler in Israel.
His goings forth are [d]from long ago,
From the days of eternity."

★ 3 aHos. 11:8; Mic. 4:10; 7:13 bMic. 4:9, 10 cls. 10:20-22; Mic. 5:7, 8

3 Therefore, He will [a]give them up until the time
When she [b]who is in labor has borne a child.
Then the [c]remainder of His brethren
Will return to the sons of Israel.

2   His second coming, 5:4-15

★ 4-15

4 als. 40:11; 49:9; Ezek. 34:13-15, 23, 24; Mic. 7:14 bls. 45:22; 52:10

4 And He will arise and [a]shepherd His flock
In the strength of the LORD,
In the majesty of the name of the LORD His God.
And they will remain,

4:11-13 This passage looks further ahead, to the great campaign of Armageddon immediately preceding the second coming of Christ and the millennial kingdom. There the world will be lined up against Israel but God will give Israel victory, using a *horn* of iron and *hoofs* of brass.

5:1 *the judge of Israel.* The puppet King Zedekiah, who was taken captive to Babylon (2 Kings 24:17-25:7).

5:2 *Ephrathah.* The ancient name for Bethlehem and also apparently the name of the district (cf. Gen. 35:19; Ruth 4:11). Both names indicate the fertility of the area, Bethlehem meaning "House of Bread" and Ephrathah, "fruitful." This was the birthplace of King David (1 Sam. 16:1) as well as of his most eminent descendant, Jesus Christ, the Messiah. *for Me.* I.e., to do My will. *goings forth.* Refers primarily to Christ's preincarnate appearances as the Angel of the Lord, thus affirming the existence of Christ before His birth in Bethlehem. *from long ago.* May mean "from days of old" or it may mean "from eternity," indicating the eternal existence of Messiah (cf. Hab. 1:12).

5:3 *give them up.* To their enemies until *she* (the virgin Mary, Isa. 7:14) gives birth to Messiah, who will reunite Israel (a work in connection with His second coming).

5:4-15 In this section Micah again describes the glories of the Messianic kingdom. King Jesus, who is greater than Shepherd-King David, will *shepherd* His people (v. 4). They will be safe from the Assyrian, used here as typical of all Israel's enemies (vv. 5-6). Regathered Israel will be strong as a *lion* (vv. 7-9) and purified from all idolatrous practices (vv. 10-15).

Because at that time He will be great
To the ᵇends of the earth.

5 And this One ᵃwill be *our* peace.

When the ᵇAssyrian invades our land,
When he tramples on our citadels,
Then we will raise against him
Seven shepherds and eight leaders of men.

6 And they will ᵃshepherd the land of Assyria with the sword,
The land of ᵇNimrod at its entrances;
And He will ᶜdeliver *us* from the Assyrian
When he attacks our land
And when he tramples our territory.

7 Then the ᵃremnant of Jacob
Will be among many peoples
Like ᵇdew from the Lᴏʀᴅ,
Like ᶜshowers on vegetation
Which do not wait for man
Or delay for the sons of men.

8 And the remnant of Jacob
Will be among the nations,
Among many peoples
ᵃLike a lion among the beasts of the forest,
Like a young lion among flocks of sheep,
Which, if he passes through,
ᵇTramples down and ᶜtears,
And there is ᵈnone to rescue.

9 Your hand will be ᵃlifted up against your adversaries,
And all your enemies will be cut off.

10 "And it will be in that day," declares the Lᴏʀᴅ,

"ᵃThat I will cut off your ᵇhorses from among you
And destroy your chariots.

11 "I will also cut off the ᵃcities of your land
And tear down all your ᵇfortifications.

12 "I will cut off ᵃsorceries from your hand,
And you will have fortunetellers no more.

13 "ᵃI will cut off your carved images
And your *sacred* pillars from among you,
So that you will no longer bow down
To the work of your hands.

14 "I will root out your ᵃAsherim from among you
And destroy your cities.

15 "And I will ᵃexecute vengeance in anger and wrath
On the nations which have not obeyed."

IV A MESSAGE OF DENUNCIATION, 6:1–7:10

A God's First Indictment, 6:1–5

6 Hear now what the Lᴏʀᴅ is saying,
"Arise, plead your case before the mountains,
And let the hills hear your voice.

2 "Listen, you mountains, to the indictment of the Lᴏʀᴅ,
And you enduring ᵃfoundations of the earth,
Because the ᵇLᴏʀᴅ has a case against His people;
Even with Israel He will dispute.

3 "ᵃMy people, ᵇwhat have I done to you,
And ᶜhow have I wearied you? Answer Me.

Cross references (left margin):

5 ᵃIs. 9:6;
Luke 2:14;
Eph. 2:14;
Col. 1:20
ᵇIs. 8:7, 8;
10:24-27

6 ᵃNah.
2:11-13;
Zeph. 2:13
ᵇGen. 10:8-
11 ᶜIs.
14:25; 37:36,
37

7 ᵃMic.
2:12; 4:7;
5:3; 7:18
ᵇDeut. 32:2;
Ps. 110:3;
Hos. 14:5
ᶜPs. 72:6; Is.
44:3

8 ᵃGen.
49:9; Num.
24:9 ᵇPs.
44:5; Is.
41:15, 16;
Mic. 4:13;
Zech. 10:5
ᶜHos. 5:14
ᵈPs. 50:22

9 ᵃPs.
10:12; 21:8;
Is. 26:11

10 ᵃZech.
9:10 ᵇDeut.
17:16; Is.
2:7; Hos.
14:3

Cross references (right margin):

11 ᵃIs. 1:7;
6:11 ᵇIs.
2:12-17; Hos.
10:14; Amos
5:9

12 ᵃDeut.
18:10-12; Is.
2:6; 8:19

13 ᵃIs. 2:18;
17:8; Ezek.
6:9

14 ᵃEx.
34:13; Is.
17:8; 27:9

15 ᵃIs. 1:24;
65:12

2 ᵃ2 Sam.
22:16; Ps.
104:5 ᵇIs.
1:18; Hos.
4:1; 12:2

3 ᵃPs. 50:7
ᵇJer. 2:5 ᶜIs.
43:22, 23

★ 4-5

4 aEx.
12:51; 20:2
bDeut. 7:8
cEx.
4:10-16; Ps.
77:20 dEx.
15:20

5 aNum.
22:5, 6
bNum. 25:1;
Josh. 2:1;
3:1 cJosh.
4:19; 5:9, 10
d1 Sam.
12:7; Is. 1:27

4 "Indeed, I abrought you up from the land of Egypt
And bransomed you from the house of slavery,
And I sent before you cMoses, Aaron, and dMiriam.

5 "My people, remember now What aBalak king of Moab counseled
And what Balaam son of Beor answered him,
And from bShittim to cGilgal,
In order that you might know the drighteous acts of the LORD."

B　Israel's First Reply, 6:6-8

★ 6-8

6 aPs.
40:6-8 bPs.
51:16, 17

7 aPs. 50:9;
Is. 1:1; 40:16
bLev. 18:21;
20:1-5; 2 Kin.
16:3; Jer.
7:31

8 aDeut.
30:15 bDeut.
10:12 cIs.
56:1; Jer.
22:3 dHos.
6:6 eIs.
57:15; 66:2

6 aWith what shall I come to the LORD
And bow myself before the God on high?
Shall I come to Him with bburnt offerings,
With yearling calves?

7 Does the LORD take delight in athousands of rams,
In ten thousand rivers of oil?
Shall I present my bfirstborn for my rebellious acts,
The fruit of my body for the sin of my soul?

8 He has atold you, O man, what is good;
And bwhat does the LORD require of you
But to cdo justice, to dlove kindness,
And to walk ehumbly with your God?

C　God's Second Indictment, 6:9-16

9 The voice of the LORD will call to the city—
And it is sound wisdom to fear Thy name:
"Hear, O tribe. Who has appointed its time?

10 "Is there yet a man in the wicked house,
Along with treasures of awickedness,
And a bshort measure that is cursed?

11 "Can I justify wicked ascales
And a bag of deceptive weights?

12 "For the rich men of the city are full of aviolence,
Her residents speak blies,
And their ctongue is deceitful in their mouth.

13 "So also I will make you asick, striking you down,
bDesolating you because of your sins.

14 "You will eat, but you will anot be satisfied,
And your vileness will be in your midst.
You will try to remove for safekeeping,
But you will bnot preserve anything,
And what you do preserve I will give to the sword.

15 "You will sow but you will anot reap.
You will tread the olive but will not anoint yourself with oil;
And the grapes, but you will bnot drink wine.

10 aJer.
5:26, 27;
Amos 3:10
bEzek. 45:9,
10; Amos 8:5

11 aLev.
19:36; Hos.
12:7

12 aIs. 1:23;
5:7; Amos
6:3, 4; Mic.
2:1, 2 bJer.
9:2-6, 8;
Hos. 7:13;
Amos 2:4
cIs. 3:8

13 aMic. 1:9
bIs. 1:7; 6:11

★14 aIs.
9:20 bIs.
30:6

15 aDeut.
28:38-40;
Jer. 12:13
bAmos 5:11;
Zeph. 1:13

6:4-5 God, as prosecutor in this cosmic courtroom (vv. 1-2), states His case: (1) He rescued Israel from Egypt; (2) He gave as leaders Moses, Aaron, and Miriam; (3) He reversed the intended curse of Balaam (Num. 23-24); and (4) He brought His people into the promised land (Shittim being the last encampment E. of the Jordan River and Gilgal the first on the W. bank).

6:6-8 In reply to God, Israel proposes to make up for her sin by offering sacrifices. But God replies that He had previously told them (Deut. 10:12) that He prefers obedient, spiritual people (v. 8). to do justice. In contrast to 3:2. kindness. See note on Hos. 2:19.

6:14 vileness. Probably means "emptiness" (in their stomachs).

16 "The statutes of ᵃOmri
And all the works of the
　　house of ᵇAhab are
　　observed;
And in their devices you
　　ᶜwalk.
Therefore, I will give you
　　up for ᵈdestruction
And your inhabitants for
　　ᵉderision,
And you will bear the ᶠre-
　　proach of My people."

D Israel's Second Reply, 7:1-10

7 Woe is me! For I am
Like the fruit pickers and
　　the ᵃgrape gatherers.
There is not a cluster of
　　grapes to eat,
Or a ᵇfirst-ripe fig *which* I
　　crave.

2 The godly person has ᵃper-
　　ished from the land,
And there is no upright
　　person among men.
All of them lie in wait for
　　ᵇbloodshed;
Each of them hunts the
　　other with a ᶜnet.

3 Concerning evil, both
　　hands do it ᵃwell.
The prince asks, also the
　　judge, for a ᵇbribe,
And a great man speaks
　　the desire of his soul;
So they weave it together.

4 The best of them is like a
　　ᵃbriar,
The most upright like a
　　ᵇthorn hedge.
The day when you post a
　　watchman,
Your ᶜpunishment will
　　come.
Then their ᵈconfusion will
　　occur.

5 Do not ᵃtrust in a neigh-
　　bor;
Do not have confidence in
　　a friend.
From her who lies in your
　　bosom
Guard your lips.

6 For ᵃson treats father con-
　　temptuously,
Daughter rises up against
　　her mother,
Daughter-in-law　against
　　her mother-in-law;
ᵇA man's enemies are the
　　men of his own
　　household.

7 But as for me, I will ᵃwatch
　　expectantly for the
　　LORD;
I will ᵇwait for the God of
　　my salvation.
My ᶜGod will hear me.

8 ᵃDo not rejoice over me, O
　　ᵇmy enemy.
Though I fall I will ᶜrise;
Though I dwell in dark-
　　ness, the LORD is a
　　ᵈlight for me.

9 I will bear the indignation
　　of the LORD
Because I have sinned
　　against Him,
Until He ᵃpleads my case
　　and executes justice
　　for me.
He will bring me out to the
　　ᵇlight,
And I will see His ᶜright-
　　eousness.

10 Then my enemy will see,
And shame will cover her
　　who ᵃsaid to me,
"Where is the LORD your
　　God?"
My eyes will look on her;
At that time she will be
　　ᵇtrampled down,
Like mire of the streets.

6:16 The people had degenerated to the low level that characterized the days of *Omri* and
Ahab, a period that had become a byword for
apostasy (cf. 1 Kings 16–22).
7:1-10 Micah bemoaned the sinfulness of Israel.

It is universal (v. 1), unrestrained (vv. 2–3), involves the leaders (v. 3), and exhibits itself in
perverse (v. 4) and unnatural (vv. 5–6) ways.
But God is merciful and in Him there is hope
(vv. 7–10).

★16 ᵃ1 Kin.
16:25, 26
ᵇ1 Kin.
16:29-33
ᶜJer. 7:24
ᵈJer. 18:16;
Mic. 6:13
ᵉJer. 19:8;
25:9, 18;
29:18 ᶠPs.
44:13; Jer.
51:51; Hos.
12:14

★ 1-10
1 ᵃIs. 24:13
ᵇIs. 28:4;
Hos. 9:10

2 ᵃIs. 57:1
ᵇIs. 59:7;
Mic. 3:10
ᶜJer. 5:26;
Hos. 5:1

3 ᵃProv.
4:16, 17
ᵇAmos 5:12;
Mic. 3:11

4 ᵃEzek.
2:6; 28:24
ᵇNah. 1:10
ᶜIs. 10:3;
Hos. 9:7 ᵈIs.
22:5

5 ᵃJer. 9:4

6 ᵃMatt.
10:21, 35;
Luke 12:53
ᵇMatt. 10:36

7 ᵃHab. 2:1
ᵇPs. 130:5;
Is. 25:9 ᶜPs.
4:3

8 ᵃProv.
24:17; Obad.
12 ᵇMic.
7:10 ᶜAmos
9:11 ᵈIs. 9:2

9 ᵃJer.
50:34 ᵇPs.
37:6; Is.
42:7, 16 ᶜIs.
46:13; 56:1

10 ᵃJoel
2:17 ᵇIs.
51:23; Zech.
10:5

V EPILOGUE: BLESSINGS FOR ISRAEL, 7:11-20

★11-20
11 als. 54:11; Amos 9:11

11 It *will be* a day for [a]building your walls.
On that day will your boundary be extended.

12 als. 19:23-25; 60:4, 9

12 It *will be* a day when they will [a]come to you
From Assyria and the cities of Egypt,
From Egypt even to the Euphrates,
Even from sea to sea and mountain to mountain.

13 aJer. 25:11; Mic. 6:13 bls. 3:10, 11; Mic. 3:4

13 And the earth will become [a]desolate because of her inhabitants,
On account of the [b]fruit of their deeds.

14 aPs. 95:7; Is. 40:11; 49:10; Mic. 5:4 bLev. 27:32; Ps. 23:4 cJer. 50:19 dAmos 9:11

14 [a]Shepherd Thy people with Thy [b]scepter,
The flock of Thy possession
Which dwells by itself in the woodland,
In the midst of a fruitful field.
Let them feed in [c]Bashan and Gilead
[d]As in the days of old.

15 aEx. 3:20; 34:10; Ps. 78:12

15 "As in the days when you came out from the land of Egypt,
I will show [a]you miracles."

16 als. 26:11 bMic. 3:7

16 Nations [a]will see and be ashamed
Of all their might.
They will [b]put *their* hand on *their* mouth,
Their ears will be deaf.

17 aPs. 72:9; Is. 49:23 bDeut. 32:24 cPs. 18:45 dls. 25:3; 59:19

17 They will [a]lick the dust like a serpent,
Like [b]reptiles of the earth.
They will come [c]trembling out of their fortresses;
To the LORD our God they will come in [d]dread,
And they will be afraid before Thee.

18 aEx. 34:7, 9; Is. 43:25 bMic. 2:12; 4:7; 5:7, 8 cPs. 103:8, 9, 13 dJer. 32:41

18 Who is a God like Thee, who [a]pardons iniquity
And passes over the rebellious act of the [b]remnant of His possession?
He does not [c]retain His anger forever,
Because He [d]delights in unchanging love.

19 aJer. 50:20 bls. 38:17; 43:25; Jer. 31:34

19 He will again have compassion on us;
[a]He will tread our iniquities under foot.
Yes, Thou wilt [b]cast all their sins
Into the depths of the sea.

20 aGen. 24:27; 32:10 bDeut. 7:8, 12

20 Thou wilt give [a]truth to Jacob
And unchanging love to Abraham,
Which Thou didst [b]swear to our forefathers
From the days of old.

7:11-20 The promised millennial blessing for Israel will include her restoration (vv. 11-13), her blessing (vv. 14-15), her exaltation over the other nations (vv. 16-17), and forgiveness (vv. 18-19)—all on the basis of the covenant God made with Abraham (Gen. 12:1-3; 15:18-21).

INTRODUCTION TO
THE BOOK OF NAHUM

AUTHOR: Nahum   DATE: 663–612 B.C.

The Prophet *Nothing is known of Nahum (whose name means "consolation") except that he came from Elkosh, which was possibly Capernaum. His message against Nineveh was given to Judah, since the Northern Kingdom, Israel, had already been taken captive.*

Theme *Nineveh will be destroyed! Almost every verse from 1:15–3:19 describes that event, which took place in 612 B.C. The Ninevites (Assyrians) converted through the preaching of Jonah (more than one hundred years before Nahum wrote) had not transmitted their knowledge of the true God to their children, and the people had quickly reverted to their cruel and heathen practices. They had destroyed Samaria (the Northern Kingdom, Israel) in 722 and nearly captured Jerusalem in 701. Nahum briefly describes Nineveh's wickedness in 3:1, 4. God had to destroy such an apostate people.*

Contents *Chapter 1 contains a magnificent description of the character of God (see especially vv. 2–8). Reading chapter 2, one can almost hear the noise of the battle of Nineveh.*

OUTLINE OF NAHUM

THE BOOK OF NAHUM

I THE THEME AND AUTHOR, 1:1

★ **1-8**

★ **1** aIs. 13:1; 19:1; Jer. 23:33, 34; Hab. 1:1; Zech. 9:1; Mal. 1:1 b2 Kin. 19:36; Jon. 1:2; Nah. 2:8; Zeph. 2:13

1 The ^aoracle of ^bNineveh. The book of the vision of Nahum the Elkoshite.

II THE MAJESTY OF GOD, 1:2–14

A The Attributes of God, 1:2–8

2 aEx. 20:5; Josh. 24:19 bDeut. 32:35, 41 cPs. 94:1

2 A ^ajealous and avenging God is the LORD; The LORD is ^bavenging and wrathful.

The LORD takes ^cvengeance on His adversaries, And He reserves wrath for His enemies.

3 aEx. 34:6, 7; Neh. 9:17; Ps. 103:8 bEx. 19:16; Is. 29:6 cPs. 104:3; Is. 19:1

3 The LORD is ^aslow to anger and great in power, And the LORD will by no means leave *the guilty* unpunished. In ^bwhirlwind and storm is His way, And ^cclouds are the dust beneath His feet.

★ **4** aJosh. 3:15, 16; Ps. 106:9; Is. 50:2; Matt. 8:26 bIs. 33:9

4 He ^arebukes the sea and makes it dry; He dries up all the rivers.

1:1-8 In this section God is characterized as all-knowing (v. 1), righteous (v. 2), longsuffering (v. 3a), all-powerful (vv. 3b–6), good (v. 7), and holy (v. 8).
1:1 *oracle.* I.e., judicial sentence against Nine-veh.
1:4 *Bashan* was known for its lush pastures (Amos 4:1); *Carmel* for its vineyards (Amos 1:2); *Lebanon* for its choice trees (Ezek. 31:16).

ᵇBashan and Carmel
  wither;
The blossoms of Lebanon
  wither.

5 Mountains ᵃquake because
  of Him,
And the hills ᵇdissolve;
Indeed the earth is ᶜup-
  heaved by His pres-
  ence,
The ᵈworld and all the inhabitants in it.

6 ᵃWho can stand before His
  indignation?
Who can endure the
  ᵇburning of His an-
  ger?
His ᶜwrath is poured out
  like fire,
And the ᵈrocks are broken
  up by Him.

7 The LORD is ᵃgood,
A stronghold in the day of
  trouble,
And ᵇHe knows those who
  take refuge in Him.

8 But with an ᵃoverflowing
  flood
He will make a complete
  end of its site,
And will pursue His en-
  emies into ᵇdarkness.

B The Anger of God, 1:9-14

9 Whatever you ᵃdevise
  against the LORD,
He will make a ᵇcomplete
  end of it.
Distress will not rise up
  twice.

10 Like tangled ᵃthorns,
And like those who are
  ᵇdrunken with their
  drink,
They are ᶜconsumed
As stubble completely
  withered.

11 From you has gone forth
  One who ᵃplotted evil
  against the LORD,
A ᵇwicked counselor.

12 Thus says the LORD,
"Though they are at full
  strength and likewise
  many,
Even so, they will be ᵃcut
  off and pass away.
Though I have afflicted
  you,
I will afflict you ᵇno longer.

13 "So now, I will ᵃbreak his
  yoke bar from upon
  you,
And I will tear off your
  shackles."

14 The LORD has issued a
  command concerning
  you:
"Your name will ᵃno longer
  be perpetuated.
I will cut off ᵇidol and
  image
From the house of your
  gods.
I will prepare your ᶜgrave,
For you are contemptible."

III THE JUDGMENT OF GOD, 1:15-3:19

A Judgment Proclaimed, 1:15

15 Behold, ᵃon the mountains
  the feet of him who
  brings good news,
Who announces peace!
  ᵇCelebrate your feasts, O
  Judah;
Pay your vows.
For ᶜnever again will the
  wicked one pass
  through you;
He is ᵈcut off completely.

---

5 ᵃEx. 19:18; 2 Sam. 22:8; Ps. 18:7 ᵇMic. 1:4 ᶜIs. 24:1, 20 ᵈPs. 98:7

6 ᵃJer. 10:10; Mal. 3:2 ᵇIs. 13:13 ᶜIs. 66:15 ᵈ1 Kin. 19:11

7 ᵃPs. 25:8; 37:39, 40; Jer. 33:11 ᵇPs. 1:6; John 10:14; 2 Tim. 2:19

8 ᵃIs. 28:2, 17f.; Amos 8:8 ᵇIs. 13:9, 10

★ **9** ᵃPs. 2:1; Nah. 1:11 ᵇIs. 28:22

10 ᵃ2 Sam. 23:6; Mic. 7:4 ᵇIs. 56:12; Nah. 3:11 ᶜIs. 5:24; 10:17; Mal. 4:1

★**11** ᵃIs. 10:7-11; Nah. 1:9 ᵇEzek. 11:2

12 ᵃIs. 10:16-19, 33, 34 ᵇLam. 3:31, 32

13 ᵃIs. 9:4; 10:27; Jer. 2:20

★**14** ᵃJob 18:17; Ps. 109:13; Is. 14:22 ᵇIs. 46:1, 2; Mic. 5:13, 14 ᶜEzek. 32:22, 23

★**15** ᵃIs. 40:9; 52:7; Rom. 10:15 ᵇLev. 23:2, 4 ᶜIs. 52:1; Joel 3:17 ᵈIs. 29:7, 8

1:9 So complete would be God's judgment of Nineveh that He would not need to do it *twice.*
1:11 The verse refers to Sennacherib of Assyria (see the story in 2 Kings 19).
1:14 The *house* of Sennacherib's *gods* would

witness his death (the fulfillment is recorded in 2 Kings 19:37).
1:15 The sacking of Nineveh by the Babylonians and Medes would be *good news* for Judah. This occurred in 612.

B Judgment Predicted, 2:1-2

★ 1 aJer.
51:20-23

2 The one who ªscatters has come up against you. Man the fortress, watch the road; Strengthen your back, summon all *your* strength.

★ 2 aIs.
60:15 bEzek.
37:21-23
cPs. 80:12,
13

2 For the LORD will restore the ªsplendor of Jacob bLike the splendor of Israel, Even though devastators have devastated them And cdestroyed their vine branches.

C Judgment Described, 2:3-10

★ 3 aEzek.
23:14, 15
bJob 39:23

3 The shields of his mighty men are *colored* red, The warriors are dressed in ªscarlet, The chariots are *enveloped* in flashing steel When he is prepared *to march*, And the cypress bspears are brandished.

4 aIs.
66:15; Jer.
4:13; Ezek.
26:10; Nah.
3:2, 3

4 The ªchariots race madly in the streets, They rush wildly in the squares, Their appearance is like torches, They dash to and fro like lightning flashes.

5 aNah.
3:18 bJer.
46:12

5 He remembers his ªnobles; They bstumble in their march, They hurry to her wall, And the mantelet is set up.

★ 6

6 The gates of the rivers are opened,

And the palace is dissolved.

7 als.
38:14; 59:11
bIs. 32:12

7 And it is fixed: She is stripped, she is carried away, And her handmaids are ªmoaning like the sound of doves, bBeating on their breasts.

8 aJer.
46:5; 47:3

8 Though Nineveh *was* like a pool of water throughout her days, Now they are fleeing; "Stop, stop," But ªno one turns back.

★ 9 aRev.
18:12, 16

9 Plunder the silver! Plunder the ªgold! For there is no limit to the treasure— Wealth from every kind of desirable object.

10 als. 24:1;
34:10-13;
Nah. 2:2
bPs. 22:14;
Is. 13:7, 8;
Ezek. 21:7
cJoel 2:6

10 She is ªemptied! Yes, she is desolate and waste! bHearts are melting and knees knocking! Also anguish is in the whole body, And all their cfaces are grown pale!

D Judgment Vindicated, 2:11-3:7

★11-12

11 als. 5:29

11 Where is the den of the lions And the feeding place of the ªyoung lions, Where the lion, lioness, and lion's cub prowled, With nothing to disturb *them*?

12 The lion tore enough for his cubs,

2:1 *The one who scatters.* Cyaxares the Mede and Nabopolassar the Babylonian, who conquered Nineveh.
2:2 Judah is viewed as God's heritage (*vine branches*) whom Assyria had plundered.
2:3 The Medes and Babylonians made their *shields* red by painting them or overlaying them with copper (Ezek. 23:14); their tunics were *scarlet;* their chariots flashed with steel because they attached scythes at right angles to the axles.

2:6 When the river gates were breached, the *palace* (better, temple of Ishtar) was flooded by the Tigris.
2:9 There was much looting in Nineveh because Assyria had plundered countries she had captured.
2:11-12 Assyria is pictured as a lion soon to be captured (v. 11), though once fierce in conquest (v. 12). The illustration is particularly appropriate, since lions in various forms are found on Assyrian sculptures.

Killed *enough* for his lion-
    esses,
And filled his lairs with
    prey
And his dens with torn
    flesh.

13 "Behold, [a]I am against
you," declares the LORD of hosts.
"I will [b]burn up her chariots in
smoke, a sword will devour your
young lions, I will [c]cut off your
prey from the land, and no longer
will the voice of your messengers
be heard."

3 [a]Woe to the bloody city, com-
    pletely full of lies *and*
    pillage;
Her prey never departs.

2 The [a]noise of the whip,
The noise of the rattling of
    the wheel,
Galloping horses,
And bounding chariots!

3 Horsemen charging,
Swords flashing, [a]spears
    gleaming,
[b]Many slain, a mass of
    corpses,
And [c]countless dead bod-
    ies—
They stumble over the
    dead bodies!

4 *All* because of the [a]many
    harlotries of the har-
    lot,
The charming one, the
    [b]mistress of sorceries,
Who [c]sells nations by her
    harlotries
And families by her sor-
    ceries.

5 "Behold, [a]I am against
    you," declares the
    LORD of hosts;
"And I will [b]lift up your
    skirts over your face,

And [c]show to the nations
    your nakedness
And to the kingdoms your
    disgrace.

6 "I will [a]throw filth on you
    And [b]make you vile,
And set you up as a [c]spec-
    tacle.

7 "And it will come about
    that all who see you
Will shrink from you and
    say,
'Nineveh is devastated!
[a]Who will grieve for her?'
Where will I seek comfort-
    ers for you?"

E   Judgment Forewarned, 3:8–10

8 Are you better than
    [a]No-amon,
Which was situated by the
    [b]waters of the Nile,
With water surrounding
    her,
Whose rampart *was* the
    sea,
Whose wall *consisted* of
    the sea?

9 [a]Ethiopia was *her* might,
And Egypt too, without
    limits.
[b]Put and [c]Lubim were
    among her helpers.

10 Yet she [a]became an exile,
She went into captivity;
Also her [b]small children
    were dashed to pieces
[c]At the head of every
    street;
They [d]cast lots for her
    honorable men,
And all her great men
    were bound with fet-
    ters.

Marginal references (left column):

★13 [a]Jer. 21:13; Ezek. 5:8; Nah. 3:5
[b]Josh. 11:6, 9; Ps. 46:9
[c]Is. 49:24, 25; Nah. 3:1

★ 1 [a]Ezek. 24:6, 9

★ 2 [a]Job 39:22-25; Jer. 47:3; Nah. 2:3, 4

3 [a]Hab. 3:11 [b]Is. 34:3; 66:16 [c]Is. 37:36; Ezek. 39:4

4 [a]Is. 23:17; Ezek. 16:25-29; Rev. 17:1, 2 [b]Is. 47:9, 12, 13 [c]Rev. 18:3

5 [a]Jer. 50:31; Ezek. 26:3; Nah. 2:13 [b]Is. 47:2, 3; Jer. 13:26 [c]Ezek. 16:37

Marginal references (right column):

6 [a]Job 9:31 [b]Job 30:8; Mal. 2:9 [c]Is. 14:16; Jer. 51:37

7 [a]Is. 51:19; Jer. 15:5

★ 8 [a]Jer. 46:25; Ezek. 30:14-16 [b]Is. 19:6-8

★ 9 [a]Is. 20:5 [b]Jer. 46:9; Ezek. 27:10; 30:5; 38:5 [c]2 Chr. 12:3; 16:8

10 [a]Is. 19:4; 20:4 [b]Ps. 137:9; Is. 13:16; Hos. 13:16 [c]Lam. 2:19 [d]Joel 3:3; Obad. 11

2:13 *your messengers.* I.e., Assyrian officials who demanded tribute from conquered nations.

3:1 *Her prey never departs.* Assyria lived by plundering others.

3:2 *The noise of the whip.* Urging the horses of the Medes and Babylonians.

3:8 *No-amon.* Thebes, capital of Upper Egypt, which was sacked by the Assyrians in 663 B.C. Like Nineveh, Thebes was located on a river. In Thebes' case, the river was the Nile.

3:9 Thebes, like Nineveh, turned to her vassal territories for support, but to no avail. *Put* is probably Somaliland and *Lubim*, Libya.

F   Judgment Inevitable, 3:11-19

★11 aIs. 49:26; Jer. 25:27; Nah. 1:10 bIs. 2:10, 19; Hos. 10:8

11 You too will become
   ^adrunk,
   You will be ^bhidden.
   You too will search for a
      refuge from the
      enemy.

12 aRev. 6:13 bIs. 28:4

12 All your fortifications are
   ^afig trees with ^bripe
   fruit—
   When shaken, they fall
      into the eater's
      mouth.

13 aIs. 19:16; Jer. 50:37; 51:30 bIs. 45:1, 2; Nah. 2:6

13 Behold, your people are
   ^awomen in your
   midst!
   The gates of your land are
      ^bopened wide to your
      enemies;
   Fire consumes your gate
      bars.

14 a2 Chr. 32:3, 4 bNah. 2:1

14 ^aDraw for yourself water
      for the siege!
   ^bStrengthen your fortifica-
      tions!
   Go into the clay and tread
      the mortar!
   Take hold of the brick
      mold!

15 aIs. 66:15, 16; Nah. 2:13; 3:13 bJoel 1:4

15 There ^afire will consume
      you,
   The sword will cut you
      down;
   It will ^bconsume you as the
      locust *does*.

   Multiply yourself like the
      creeping locust,
   Multiply yourself like the
      swarming locust.

16 aIs. 23:8

16 You have increased your
   ^atraders more than
      the stars of heaven—
   The creeping locust strips
      and flies away.

17 aRev. 9:7 bJer. 51:27

17 Your ^aguardsmen are like
      the swarming locust.
   Your ^bmarshals are like
      hordes of grasshop-
      pers
   Settling in the stone walls
      on a cold day.
   The sun rises and they
      flee,
   And the place where they
      are is not known.

★18 aPs. 76:5, 6; Is. 56:10; Jer. 51:57 bJer. 50:18 cNah. 2:5 d1 Kin. 22:17; Is. 13:14

18 Your shepherds are ^asleep-
      ing, O ^bking of As-
      syria;
   Your ^cnobles are lying
      down.
   Your people are ^dscattered
      on the mountains,
   And there is no one to re-
      gather *them*.

★19 aJer. 46:11; Mic. 1:9 bJer. 30:12 cJob 27:23; Lam. 2:15

19 There is ^ano relief for your
      breakdown,
   Your ^bwound is incurable.
   All who hear about you
   Will ^cclap *their* hands over
      you,
   For on whom has not your
      evil passed continu-
      ally?

3:11 *become drunk.* I.e., with the wrath of God in judgment. Even the site of Nineveh was *hidden* until its discovery in 1842.

3:18 *Your shepherds.* Political officials.
3:19 Nineveh's destruction would be greeted with delight by all.

INTRODUCTION TO
THE BOOK OF HABAKKUK

AUTHOR: Habakkuk   DATE: 607 B.C.

The Times *Though nothing is known of the prophet himself (whose name means "embracer," because of his love for God), we know something of his times. Prophesying just before Nebuchadnezzar first invaded Judah in 605 (and took Daniel and others as captives to Babylon), Habakkuk was commissioned to announce the Lord's intention to punish Judah by this coming deportation into Babylon. The reigning king in Judah, Jehoiakim, is described by the prophet Jeremiah this way: "your eyes and your heart are intent only upon your own dishonest gain, and on shedding innocent blood and on practicing oppression and extortion" (Jer. 22:17; cf. Hab. 1:2-4 and 2 Kings 23:34-24:5).*

Habakkuk's Questions *The book presents a picture of a man who trusted God, yet was perplexed. Habakkuk's questions were two: (1) Why did God permit the increasing evil in Judah to go unpunished (1:2-4)? (2) How could a holy God justify using the Babylonians, a people more wicked than the Jews, to punish the Jews (1:12-2:1)? The answer to the first question is recorded in 1:5-11 and to the second, in 2:2-20. Thus the book is a theodicy, a defense of God's goodness and power in view of the existence of evil.*

Contents *The best known verse in Habakkuk is 2:4 (quoted in Rom. 1:17; Gal. 3:11; Heb. 10:38), not only because it was the heart of God's answer to Habakkuk's questions, but because the N.T. shows that its truth is central to the doctrine of justification by faith. Another favorite verse is 2:20. Chapter 3 is a great psalm of praise, scarcely equaled anywhere else in the O.T.*

OUTLINE OF HABAKKUK

I. **Introduction, 1:1**
II. **Habakkuk's Problems, 1:2-2:20**
   A. Problem #1: Why Does God Allow Wicked Practices to Continue in Judah? 1:2-4
   B. Answer #1, 1:5-11
   C. Problem #2: Why Will God Use Wicked People to Punish Judah? 1:12-2:1
   D. Answer #2, 2:2-20
III. **Habakkuk's Praise, 3:1-19**
   A. Praise for the Person of God, 3:1-3
   B. Praise for the Power of God, 3:4-7
   C. Praise for the Purpose of God, 3:8-16
   D. Praise because of Faith in God, 3:17-19

THE BOOK OF HABAKKUK

I INTRODUCTION, 1:1

★ 1 *a*Is. 13:1; Nah. 1:1

1 The *a*oracle which Habakkuk the prophet saw.

II HABAKKUK'S PROBLEMS, 1:2–2:20

A Problem #1: Why Does God Allow Wicked Practices to Continue in Judah? 1:2–4

2 *a*Ps. 13:1, 2; 22:1, 2 *b*Jer. 14:9

2 *a*How long, O Lord, will I call for help,
And Thou wilt not hear?
I cry out to Thee, "Violence!"
Yet Thou dost *b*not save.

★ 3 *a*Ps. 55:9–11; Jer. 20:18 *b*Jer. 20:8 *c*Jer. 15:10

3 Why dost Thou make me *a*see iniquity,
And cause *me* to look on wickedness?
Yes, *b*destruction and violence are before me;
*c*Strife exists and contention arises.

★ 4 *a*Ps. 58:1, 2; 119:126; Is. 59:12–14 *b*Ps. 22:12; Is. 1:21–23 *c*Is. 5:20; Ezek. 9:9

4 Therefore, the *a*law is ignored
And justice is never upheld.
For the wicked *b*surround the righteous;
Therefore, justice comes out *c*perverted.

B Answer #1, 1:5–11

5 *a*Acts 13:41 *b*Is. 29:9 *c*Is. 29:14; Ezek. 12:22–28

5 "*a*Look among the nations! Observe!
Be astonished! *b*Wonder!
Because *I* am doing *c*something in your days—
You would not believe if you were told.

6 "For behold, I am *a*raising up the Chaldeans,
That fierce and impetuous people
Who march throughout the earth
To *b*seize dwelling places which are not theirs.

★ 6 *a*2 Kin. 24:2; Jer. 4:11–13 *b*Jer. 8:10

7 "They are dreaded and *a*feared.
Their *b*justice and authority originate with themselves.

★ 7 *a*Is. 18:2, 7 *b*Jer. 39:5–9

8 "Their *a*horses are swifter than leopards
And keener than *b*wolves in the evening.
Their horsemen come galloping,
Their horsemen come from afar;
They fly like an *c*eagle swooping *down* to devour.

★ 8 *a*Jer. 4:13 *b*Zeph. 3:3 *c*Ezek. 17:3; Hos. 8:1

9 "All of them come for violence.
Their horde of *a*faces *moves* forward.
They collect captives like sand.

9 *a*2 Kin. 12:17; Dan. 11:17

10 "They *a*mock at kings,
And rulers are a laughing matter to them.
They *b*laugh at every fortress,
And *c*heap up rubble to capture it.

★10 *a*2 Chr. 36:6, 10; Is. 37:13 *b*Is. 10:9; 14:16 *c*Jer. 32:24; Ezek. 26:8

11 "Then they will sweep through *like* the *a*wind and pass on.
But they will be held *b*guilty,
They whose *c*strength is their god."

11 *a*Jer. 4:11, 12 *b*Jer. 2:3 *c*Dan. 4:30; Hab. 1:16

1:1 *oracle.* Or, sentence, implying an ominous announcement (see Nah. 1:1).
1:3 *Strife* and *contention.* Between the Jewish people themselves, not with their enemies. Notice the extreme sensitivity of the prophet about sin.
1:4 *ignored.* Paralyzed.
1:6 *Chaldeans.* A Semitic people who became dominant in the Babylonian Empire.

1:7 *Their justice and authority originate with themselves.* The Babylonians were a law to themselves.
1:8 *wolves in the evening.* Ravenous because they had found no prey all day (cf. Gen. 49:27; Jer. 5:6; Zeph. 3:3).
1:10 *heap up rubble.* A reference to the common practice of building mounds in order to besiege or bridge the wall of a city.

C Problem #2: Why Will God Use Wicked People to Punish Judah? 1:12–2:1

12 ªDeut.
33:27; Ps.
90:2; Mal.
3:6 ᵇIs. 10:5,
6; Mal. 3:5
ᶜDeut. 32:4

12 Art Thou not from ªever-lasting,
O LORD, my God, my Holy One?
We will not die.
Thou, O LORD, hast ᵇap-pointed them to judge;
And Thou, O ᶜRock, hast established them to correct.

13 ªPs.
11:4-6;
34:15, 16
ᵇJer. 12:1, 2
ᶜIs. 24:16
ᵈPs. 50:21
ᵉPs. 35:25

13 *Thine* eyes are too ªpure to approve evil,
And Thou canst not look on wickedness *with favor.*
Why dost Thou ᵇlook with favor
On those who deal ᶜtreacherously?
Why art Thou ᵈsilent when the wicked ᵉswallow up
Those more righteous than they?

★14-17

14 *Why* hast Thou made men like the fish of the sea,
Like creeping things with-out a ruler over them?

15 ªJer.
16:16; Amos
4:2 ᵇPs.
10:9

15 *The* Chaldeans ªbring all of them up with a hook,
ᵇDrag them away with their net,
And gather them together in their fishing net.
Therefore, they rejoice and are glad.

16 ªJer.
44:17

16 Therefore, they offer a sac-rifice to their net,

And burn incense to their fishing net;
Because through ªthese things their catch is large,
And their food is plentiful.

17 Will they therefore empty their ªnet
And continually ᵇslay na-tions without sparing?

17 ªIs. 19:8
ᵇIs. 14:5, 6

2 I will ªstand on my guard post
And station myself on the rampart;
And I will ᵇkeep watch to see ᶜwhat He will speak to me,
And how I may reply when I am reproved.

★ 1 ªIs.
21:8 ᵇPs.
5:3 ᶜPs. 85:8

D Answer #2, 2:2–20

2 Then the LORD answered me and said,
"ªRecord the vision
And inscribe *it* on tablets,
That the one who reads it may run.

★ 2 ªDeut.
27:8; Rom.
15:4; Rev.
1:19

3 "For the vision is yet for the ªappointed time;
It hastens toward the goal, and it will not fail.
Though it tarries, ᵇwait for it;
For it will certainly come, it ᶜwill not delay.

★ 3 ªDan.
8:17, 19;
10:14 ᵇPs.
27:14 ᶜEzek.
12:25; Heb.
10:37

4 "Behold, as for the ªproud one,
His soul is not right within him;
But the ᵇrighteous will live by his faith.

★ 4 ªPs.
49:18; Is.
13:11 ᵇRom.
1:17; Gal.
3:11; Heb.
10:38

1:14-17 The Chaldeans would treat the He-brews like fish, using every means to capture them. They would worship their weapons of war (v. 16). *empty their net* (v. 17). I.e., con-sume their prey and continually take others captive. In this section Habakkuk asked God three questions: (1) Would He tolerate the sin of Babylon (v. 13)? (2) Would He allow Judah to be caught as fish (vv. 14-16)? (3) Would He keep silent forever (v. 17)?

2:1 *when I am reproved.* I.e., when God argues with (answers) me.

2:2 Habakkuk was instructed to write God's an-swer on *tablets* so that whoever *reads it may run* to proclaim what he has read. However, the last phrase may mean "write it plainly," so that anyone who "runs his eye" over the tab-let will read it easily.

2:3 The fulfillment would come in God's ap-pointed time.

2:4 *His soul* = the Chaldean's soul. In contrast, the *righteous* shall *live* (enjoy deliverance and abundance of life) *by his faith,* or better, faith-fulness; i.e., moral steadfastness. A person who has faith is a person who trusts and who can be trusted. See note on Heb. 10:38.

★ **5** aProv.
20:1 bProv.
21:24 c2 Kin.
14:10 dProv.
27:20; 30:16;
Is. 5:11-15

5 "Furthermore, awine betrays the bhaughty man,
So that he does not cstay at home.
He denlarges his appetite like Sheol,
And he is like death, never satisfied.
He also gathers to himself all nations
And collects to himself all peoples.

★ **6** aIs.
14:4-10; Jer.
50:13 bJob
20:15-29;
Hab. 2:12

6 "Will not all of these atake up a taunt-song against him,
Even mockery and insinuations against him,
And say, 'bWoe to him who increases what is not his—
For how long—
And makes himself rich with loans?'

7 aProv.
29:1

7 "Will not your creditors arise up suddenly,
And those who collect from you awaken?
Indeed, you will become plunder for them.

8 aIs. 33:1;
Jer. 27:7;
Zech. 2:8

8 "Because you have alooted many nations,
All the remainder of the peoples will loot you—
Because of human bloodshed and violence done to the land,
To the town and all its inhabitants.

9 "Woe to him who gets aevil gain for his house
To bput his nest on high
To be delivered from the hand of calamity!

9 aJer.
22:13; Ezek.
22:27 bJer.
49:16

10 "You have devised a ashameful thing for your house
By cutting off many peoples;
So you are bsinning against yourself.

10 a2 Kin.
9:26; Nah.
1:14; Hab.
2:16 bJer.
26:19

11 "Surely the astone will cry out from the wall,
And the rafter will answer it from the framework.

11 aJosh.
24:27; Luke
19:40

12 "Woe to him who abuilds a city with bloodshed
And founds a town with violence!

12 aMic.
3:10; Nah.
3:1

13 "Is it not indeed from the Lord of hosts
That peoples atoil for fire,
And nations grow weary for nothing?

★**13** aIs.
50:11; Jer.
51:58

14 "For the earth will be afilled
With the knowledge of the glory of the Lord,
As the waters cover the sea.

★**14** aPs.
22:27; Is.
11:9; Zech.
14:9

15 "Woe to you who make your neighbors drink,
Who mix in your venom even to make them drunk
So as to look on their nakedness!

★**15**

2:5 To the charge that the Chaldeans were arrogant (v. 4), Habakkuk adds that they are drunk with *wine* and as insatiable as *Sheol* and *death*.

2:6 *all of these.* All the victims of the injustices described in the song of verses 6-20. The "woes" are addressed to five different classes of evildoers: greedy usurers (vv. 6-8); extortioners who think they are secure (vv. 9-11); rulers who build cities with the blood and sweat of others less fortunate (vv. 12-14; Jehoiakim squandered state funds and used forced labor to build a new palace for himself); lascivious people who use alcohol as a prelude to perversion (vv. 15-17); and idolaters who worship inanimate objects (vv. 18-20). These woes are not pronounced against the Babylonians only, but also against Israelites who practiced these evils.

2:13 God causes plans and peoples who are opposed to Him to fail.

2:14 This great prophecy, to be fulfilled in the millennial kingdom, is given five times in the O.T.: Num. 14:21; Psalm 72:19; Isa. 6:3; 11:9; and here.

2:15 *your venom.* I.e., poisonous wrath or poisonous wine.

16 aLam.
4:21 bJer.
25:15, 17
cNah. 3:6

16 "You will be filled with disgrace rather than honor.

Now you yourself ᵃdrink and expose your *own* nakedness.

The ᵇcup in the Lord's right hand will come around to you,

And ᶜutter disgrace *will come* upon your glory.

★**17** aJoel
3:19; Zech.
11:1 bPs.
55:23; Hab.
2:8 cJer.
51:35; Hab.
2:8

17 "For the ᵃviolence done to Lebanon will overwhelm you,

And the devastation of *its* beasts by which you terrified them,

ᵇBecause of human bloodshed and ᶜviolence *done* to the land,

To the town and all its inhabitants.

18 aIs.
42:17; 44:9;
Jer. 2:27, 28
bJer. 10:8,
14; Zech.
10:2 cPs.
115:4, 8

18 "What ᵃprofit is the idol when its maker has carved it,

Or an image, a ᵇteacher of falsehood?

For *its* maker ᶜtrusts in his *own* handiwork

When he fashions speechless idols.

19 aJer.
2:27, 28;
10:3 b1 Kin.
18:26-29
cPs. 135:15-
18; Jer. 10:4,
9, 14 dPs.
135:17

19 "Woe to him who ᵃsays to a *piece of* wood, 'ᵇAwake!'

To a dumb stone, 'Arise!'

And that is *your* teacher?

Behold, it is overlaid with ᶜgold and silver,

And there is ᵈno breath at all inside it.

20 "But the ᵃLord is in His holy temple.

Let all the earth ᵇbe silent before Him."

★**20** aMic.
1:2 bZeph.
1:7; Zech.
2:13

III HABAKKUK'S PRAISE, 3:1-19

A Praise for the Person of God, 3:1-3

3 A prayer of Habakkuk the prophet, according to Shigionoth.

★ **1**

2 Lord, I have ᵃheard the report about Thee *and* I ᵇfear.

O Lord, ᶜrevive ᵈThy work in the midst of the years,

In the midst of the years make it known;

In wrath remember ᵉmercy.

★ **2** aJob
42:5 bPs.
119:120; Jer.
10:7 cPs.
71:20; 85:6
dPs. 44:1-8;
Hab. 1:5
eNum.
14:19;
2 Sam.
24:15-17; Is.
54:8

3 God comes from ᵃTeman,

And the Holy One from Mount ᵇParan. [Selah.

His ᶜsplendor covers the heavens,

And the ᵈearth is full of His praise.

★ **3** aJer.
49:7; Amos
1:12; Obad.
9 bGen.
21:21; Deut.
33:2 cPs.
113:4;
148:13 dPs.
48:10

B Praise for the Power of God, 3:4-7

4 *His* ᵃradiance is like the sunlight;

He has rays *flashing* from His hand,

And there is the hiding of His ᵇpower.

4 aPs.
18:12 bJob
26:14

5 Before Him goes ᵃpestilence,

★ **5-11**
5 aEx.
12:29, 30;
Num. 16:46-
49 bNum.
11:1-3; Ps.
18:12, 13

2:17 *violence done to Lebanon* by several rulers in cutting down its great forests and killing its cattle would be done to Judah (see Isa. 14:7-8).

2:20 *His holy temple.* Heaven (Psalm 11:4). *be silent.* A very strong command, like Hush! or Be Quiet!

3:1 *Shigionoth.* Obscure, though it may indicate something about the liturgical use of this psalm (see Psalm 7 for the singular of the word).

3:2 *revive Thy work.* Lit., preserve or make alive Thy work; i.e., God's declared program of judgment on Judah and then on Babylon (1:5-11). Habakkuk was satisfied that God's ways, though not fully comprehensible, are best.

3:3 Verses 3-15 relate a theophany (an appearance of God) accompanied by the awesome features of a violent storm. *Teman.* One of the chief settlements in Edom. *Paran.* The mountainous area between Edom and Sinai.

3:5-11 God's judgments in days past had included many of the features mentioned here. Compare *pestilence* (v. 5) with Exod. 7-12; judgment on the *rivers* with Exod. 7:20-25 and the *sea* (v. 8) with Exod. 14:13-31; the *Sun and moon stood in their places* (v. 11) with Josh. 10:12-13. These past events form the background for God's future judgment on His enemies (v. 12) and deliverance of His people (v. 13).

And ^bplague comes after Him.

6   He stood and surveyed the earth;
He looked and ^astartled the nations.
Yes, the perpetual mountains were shattered,
The ancient hills collapsed.
His ways are ^beverlasting.

7   I saw the tents of Cushan under ^adistress,
The tent curtains of the land of ^bMidian were trembling.

C   Praise for the Purpose of God, 3:8–16

8   Did the LORD rage against the ^arivers,
Or *was* Thine anger against the rivers,
Or *was* Thy wrath against the ^bsea,
That Thou didst ^cride on Thy horses,
On Thy ^dchariots of salvation?

9   Thy ^abow was made bare,
The rods of chastisement were sworn.   [Selah.
Thou didst ^bcleave the earth with rivers.

10   The mountains saw Thee *and* quaked;
The downpour of waters swept by.
The deep ^auttered forth its voice,
It lifted high its hands.

11   ^aSun *and* moon stood in their places;
They went away at the ^blight of Thine arrows,
At the radiance of Thy gleaming spear.

12   In indignation Thou didst ^amarch through the earth;
In anger Thou didst ^btrample the nations.

13   Thou didst go forth for the ^asalvation of Thy people,
For the salvation of Thine ^banointed.
Thou didst strike the ^chead of the house of the evil
To lay him open from thigh to neck.   [Selah.

14   Thou didst pierce with his ^aown spears
The head of his throngs.
They ^bstormed in to scatter us;
Their exultation *was* like those
Who ^cdevour the oppressed in secret.

15   Thou didst ^atread on the sea with Thy horses,
On the ^bsurge of many waters.

16   I heard and my inward parts ^atrembled,
At the sound my lips quivered.
Decay enters my ^bbones,
And in my place I tremble.
Because I must ^cwait quietly for the day of distress,
For the ^dpeople to arise *who* will invade us.

D   Praise because of Faith in God, 3:17–19

17   Though the ^afig tree should not blossom,
And there be no fruit on the vines,
Though the yield of the ^bolive should fail,

---

6 ^aJob 21:18; Ps. 35:5 ^bHab. 1:12

★ **7** ^aEx. 15:14-16 ^bNum. 31:7, 8; Judg. 7:24, 25; 8:12

8 ^aEx. 7:19, 20; Josh. 3:16; Is. 50:2 ^bEx. 14:16, 21; Ps. 114:3, 5 ^cDeut. 33:26; Ps. 18:10; Hab. 3:15 ^dPs. 68:17

9 ^aPs. 7:12, 13; Hab. 3:11 ^bPs. 78:16; 105:41

10 ^aPs. 93:3; 98:7, 8

11 ^aJosh. 10:12-14 ^bPs. 18:14

12 ^aPs. 68:7 ^bIs. 41:15; Jer. 51:33; Mic. 4:13

13 ^aEx. 15:2; 2 Sam. 5:20; Ps. 68:19, 20 ^bPs. 20:6; 28:8 ^cPs. 68:21; 110:6

14 ^aJudg. 7:22 ^bDan. 11:40; Zech. 9:14 ^cPs. 10:8; 64:2-5

15 ^aPs. 77:19; Hab. 3:8 ^bEx. 15:8

★ **16** ^aDan. 10:8; Hab. 3:2 ^bJob 30:17, 30; Jer. 23:9 ^cLuke 21:19 ^dJer. 5:15

★ **17-19**

17 ^aJoel 1:10-12; Amos 4:9; 2 Cor. 4:8, 9 ^bMic. 6:15 ^cJoel 1:18 ^dJer. 5:17

3:7 *Cushan.* Part of the territory of the Midianites.

3:16 Habakkuk was astonished at this vision of God. The last part of the verse should probably be translated "that I should be resting quietly in the day of trouble when He comes up against the people who will invade us."

3:17-19 Though the Chaldean invasion would strip the land (v. 17), Habakkuk would rejoice in the Lord (v. 18), who makes his feet *like hinds' feet* (lit., gazelles' feet), signifying surefooted confidence). This prayer was sung to the accompaniment of *stringed instruments.*

And the fields produce no
   food,
Though the ^cflock should
   be cut off from the
   fold,
And there be ^dno cattle in
   the stalls,

18 Yet I will ^aexult in the
   LORD,
I will ^brejoice in the ^cGod
   of my salvation.

19 The Lord GOD is my
   ^astrength,
And ^bHe has made my feet
   like hinds' *feet,*
And makes me walk on
   my ^chigh places.

For the choir director, on my
stringed instruments.

18 *a*Ex. 15:1, 2; Job 13:15; Is. 61:10; Rom. 5:2, 3 *b*Ps. 46:1-5; Phil. 4:4 *c*Ps. 25:5; 27:1; Is. 12:2

19 *a*Ps. 18:32, 33; 27:1; 46:1; Is. 45:24 *b*2 Sam. 22:34 *c*Deut. 33:29

INTRODUCTION TO
THE BOOK OF ZEPHANIAH

AUTHOR: Zephaniah   DATE: c. 625 B.C.

The Prophet and His Times   *Zephaniah, of noble birth (1:1), apparently helped prepare Judah for the revival which took place under good King Josiah in 621 B.C. (2 Chron. 34:3). For more than half a century, times had been evil under kings Manasseh and Amon, and Zephaniah called his people to repentance. Reform came, but, after Josiah, the leaders and many of the people reverted to their old ways.*

Theme   *Judgment is the central theme of Zephaniah's message. The immediate fulfillment occurred when Babylon, under Nebuchadnezzar, captured Judah. The ultimate fulfillment will yet occur in the Day of the Lord, during the coming Tribulation years. Zephaniah also predicted the doom of heathen nations, both immediately (as Nineveh, which fell in 612; see 2:13) and in the future (3:8). The book closes with a glorious description of the future Millennium (also an aspect of the Day of the Lord).*

OUTLINE OF ZEPHANIAH

I. The Author and Time of the Prophecy, 1:1
II. The Prophecies of Judgment, 1:2–3:8
  A. Judgment on Judah, 1:2–18
  B. An Exhortation to Repent, 2:1–3
  C. Judgments on Gentile Nations, 2:4–15
    1. Philistia (to the west), 2:4–7
    2. Moab and Ammon (to the east), 2:8–11

    3. Ethiopia (to the south), 2:12
    4. Assyria (to the north), 2:13–15
  D. Judgment on Jerusalem, 3:1–7
  E. Judgment on the Nations, 3:8
III. The Prophecies of Blessing, 3:9–20
  A. Future Blessings for Gentiles, 3:9–10
  B. Future Blessings for Jews, 3:11–20

THE BOOK OF ZEPHANIAH

I THE AUTHOR AND TIME OF THE PROPHECY, 1:1

★ **1** ᵃ2 Kin. 22:1, 2; 2 Chr. 34:1-33; Jer. 1:2; 22:11 ᵇ2 Kin. 21:18-26; 2 Chr. 33:20-25

1 The word of the LORD which came to Zephaniah son of Cushi, son of Gedaliah, son of Amariah, son of Hezekiah, in the days of ᵃJosiah son of ᵇAmon, king of Judah,

II THE PROPHECIES OF JUDGMENT, 1:2–3:8

A Judgment on Judah, 1:2–18

2 ᵃGen. 6:7; Jer. 7:20; Ezek. 33:27, 28

2 "I will completely ᵃremove all *things*

From the face of the earth," declares the LORD.

3 "I will remove ᵃman and beast;
I will remove the ᵇbirds of the sky
And the fish of the sea,
And the ᶜruins along with the wicked;
And I will cut off man from the face of the earth," declares the LORD.

★ **3** ᵃIs. 6:11, 12 ᵇJer. 4:25; 9:10 ᶜEzek. 7:19; 14:3, 4, 8

4 "So I will ᵃstretch out My hand against Judah
And against all the inhabitants of Jerusalem.

★ **4** ᵃJer. 6:12; Ezek. 6:14 ᵇMic. 5:13 ᶜ2 Kin. 23:5; Hos. 10:5

1:1 Zephaniah means "the Lord hides." The long genealogy suggests noble birth, his great-great-grandfather being good King *Hezekiah.*

1:3 *ruins.* I.e., things that entice a man to sin.
1:4 Regarding *Baal* worship see note on Hos. 2:13.

And I will [b]cut off the remnant of Baal from this place,

And the names of the [c]idolatrous priests along with the priests.

★ 5 [a]2 Kin.
23:12; Jer.
19:13 [b]Jer.
5:2, 7; 7:9,
10 [c]1 Kin.
11:5, 33; Jer.
49:1

5 "And those who bow down on the [a]housetops to the host of heaven,

And those who bow down *and* [b]swear to the LORD and *yet* swear by [c]Milcom,

6 [a]Is. 1:4;
Hos. 7:10
[b]Is. 9:13

6 And those who have [a]turned back from following the LORD,

And those who have [b]not sought the LORD or inquired of Him."

★ 7 [a]Hab.
2:20; Zech.
2:13 [b]Zeph.
1:14 [c]Is.
34:6; Jer.
46:10
[d]1 Sam.
16:5; Is. 13:3

7 [a]Be silent before the Lord GOD!

For the [b]day of the LORD is near,

For the LORD has prepared a [c]sacrifice,

He has [d]consecrated His guests.

★ 8 [a]Is.
24:21; Hab.
1:10 [b]Is. 2:6

8 "Then it will come about on the day of the LORD's sacrifice,

That I will [a]punish the princes, the king's sons,

And all who clothe themselves with [b]foreign garments.

★ 9 [a]Jer.
5:27; Amos
3:10

9 "And I will punish on that day all who leap on the *temple* threshold,

Who fill the house of their lord with [a]violence and deceit.

10 "And on that day," declares the LORD,

"There will be the sound of a cry from the [a]Fish Gate,

A wail from the [b]Second Quarter,

And a loud crash from the [c]hills.

★10 [a]2 Chr.
33:14; Neh.
3:3; 12:39
[b]2 Chr.
34:22 [c]Ezek.
6:13

11 "Wail, O inhabitants of the Mortar,

For all the people of [a]Canaan will be silenced;

All who weigh out [b]silver will be cut off.

★11 [a]Zeph.
2:5; Zech.
14:21 [b]Job
27:16, 17;
Hos. 9:6

12 "And it will come about at that time

That I will [a]search Jerusalem with lamps,

And I will punish the men Who are [b]stagnant in spirit,

Who say in their hearts, 'The LORD will [c]not do good or evil!'

★12 [a]Jer.
16:16, 17;
Ezek. 9:4-11;
Amos 9:1-3
[b]Jer. 48:11;
Amos 6:1
[c]Ezek. 8:12;
9:9

13 "Moreover, their wealth will become [a]plunder,

And their houses desolate;

Yes, [b]they will build houses but not inhabit *them*,

And plant vineyards but not drink their wine."

13 [a]Jer.
15:13; 17:3
[b]Amos 5:11;
Mic. 6:15

14 Near is the [a]great [b]day of the LORD,

Near and coming very quickly;

14 [a]Jer.
30:7; Joel
2:11; Mal.
4:5 [b]Ezek.
7:7, 12; 30:3;
Joel 1:15;
3:14; Zeph.
1:7 [c]Ezek.
7:16-18

1:5 *host of heaven.* Astrology was common among the idolaters of Judah (Jer. 19:13). *Milcom.* Or Molech, an Ammonite deity worshiped with human sacrifice (cf. Jer. 32:35). Solomon built a sanctuary for Molech (1 Kings 11:7) which, soon after Zephaniah gave this warning, was desecrated by Josiah (2 Kings 23:13). Israel's was a syncretistic worship, for they swore by the Lord and Molech.
1:7 *day of the LORD.* See Introduction to Joel. The soon-coming captivity, in which Judah would be the *sacrifice* and the nations *guests* in Babylon, was but a preview of the much worse punishment of the still future Day of the Lord (cf. Matt. 6:24).
1:8 *foreign garments.* A mark of apostasy, for

the Jews' clothing with its blue ribbon had spiritual significance (cf. Num. 15:38-39).
1:9 *leap on the temple threshold.* I.e., rush into peoples' houses to steal, avoiding the threshold in order to avoid provoking the gods who supposedly guarded the house.
1:10 *Fish Gate.* Opened into the northern end of the Tyrophoeon Valley (cf. 2 Chron. 33:14; Neh. 3:3). *Second Quarter.* The new or lower city (cf. 2 Kings 22:14).
1:11 *Mortar.* A district of Jerusalem lying in a hollow. The word likely contains an allusion to the way the inhabitants would be beaten and ground down.
1:12 The idea is that the people had become complacent.

Listen, the day of the LORD!
In it the warrior [c]cries out
  bitterly.

15 A day of wrath is that day,
A day of [a]trouble and distress,
A day of destruction and
  desolation,
A day of [b]darkness and
  gloom,
A day of clouds and thick
  darkness,

16 A day of [a]trumpet and battle cry,
Against the [b]fortified cities
And the high corner tow-
  ers.

17 And I will bring [a]distress
  on men,
So that they will walk [b]like
  the blind,
Because they have sinned
  against the LORD;
And their [c]blood will be
  poured out like dust,
And their [d]flesh like dung.

18 Neither their [a]silver nor
  their gold
Will be able to deliver
  them
On the day of the LORD's
  wrath;
And [b]all the earth will be
  devoured
In the fire of His jealousy,
For He will [c]make a com-
  plete end,
Indeed a terrifying one,
Of all the inhabitants of
  the earth.

B   An Exhortation to Repent,
2:1-3

2 Gather yourselves together,
  yes, [a]gather,
O nation [b]without shame,

2 Before the decree takes effect—
The day passes [a]like the
  chaff—

Before the [b]burning anger
  of the LORD comes
  upon you,
Before the [c]day of the
  LORD's anger comes
  upon you.

3 [a]Seek the LORD,
All you [b]humble of the
  earth
Who have carried out His
  ordinances;
[c]Seek righteousness, seek
  humility.
Perhaps you will be [d]hid-
  den
In the day of the LORD's anger.

C   Judgments on Gentile
Nations, 2:4-15

1   Philistia (to the west), 2:4-7

4 For [a]Gaza will be abandoned,
And Ashkelon a desola-
  tion;
[a]Ashdod will be driven out
  at noon,
And [a]Ekron will be up-
  rooted.

5 Woe to the inhabitants of
  the seacoast,
The nation of the [a]Cher-
  ethites!
The word of the LORD is
[b]against you,
O [c]Canaan, land of the
  Philistines;
And I will [d]destroy you,
So that there will be [e]no
  inhabitant.

6 So the seacoast will be
[a]pastures,
With caves for shepherds
  and folds for flocks.

7 And the coast will be
For the [a]remnant of the
  house of Judah,
They will [b]pasture on it.

Side reference notes:

15 [a]Is. 22:5
[b]Joel 2:2,
31; Amos
5:18-20

16 [a]Is.
27:13; Jer.
4:19 [b]Is.
2:12-15

17 [a]Jer.
10:18 [b]Deut.
28:29 [c]Ezek.
24:7, 8 [d]Jer.
8:2; 9:22

18 [a]Ezek.
7:19 [b]Zeph.
3:8 [c]Gen.
6:7; Ezek.
7:5-7

★ 1 [a]2 Chr.
20:4; Joel
1:14 [b]Jer.
3:3; 6:15
★ 2 [a]Is.
17:13; Hos.
13:3 [b]Lam.
4:11; Nah.
1:6 [c]Zeph.
1:18

3 [a]Ps.
105:4; Amos
5:6 [b]Ps.
22:26; Is.
11:4 [c]Amos
5:14, 15
[d]Ps. 57:1; Is.
26:20

4 [a]Amos
1:7, 8; Zech.
9:5-7

★ 5 [a]Ezek.
25:16 [b]Amos
3:1 [c]Zeph.
1:11 [d]Is.
14:29, 30
[e]Zeph. 3:6

6 [a]Is. 5:17;
7:25

★ 7 [a]Is.
11:16 [b]Is.
32:14 [c]Ex.
4:31; Ps.
80:14 [d]Jer.
32:44; Zeph.
3:20

2:1 *O nation without shame.* I.e., Judah.
2:2 The judgment described in chapter 1.
2:5 *Cherethites.* Occupants of the southern coast
of the Philistine country who had roots in
Crete.
2:7 A small *remnant* of Jews would be restored
after the Babylonian captivity.

In the houses of Ashkelon
they will lie down at
evening;
For the LORD their God will
^ccare for them
And ^drestore their fortune.

2 Moab and Ammon (to the east), 2:8-11

★ 8 ^aEzek.
25:8 ^bEzek.
25:3 ^cAmos
1:13

8 "I have heard the ^ataunting
of Moab
And the ^brevilings of the
sons of Ammon,
With which they have
taunted My people
And ^cbecome arrogant
against their territory.

★ 9 ^aIs.
15:1-9; Jer.
48:1-47;
Amos 2:1-3
^bGen. 19:24
^cJer. 49:1-6;
Ezek. 25:1-
10 ^dDeut.
29:23 ^eIs.
11:14

9 "Therefore, as I live," declares the LORD of
hosts,
The God of Israel,
"Surely ^aMoab will be like
^bSodom,
And the sons of ^cAmmon
like ^dGomorrah—
A place possessed by net-
tles and salt pits,
And a perpetual desola-
tion.
The remnant of My people
will ^eplunder them,
And the remainder of My
nation will inherit
them."

10 ^aIs. 16:6
^bZeph. 2:8

10 This they will have in re-
turn for their ^apride, because they
have ^btaunted and become arrogant against the people of the
LORD of hosts.

11 ^aJoel
2:11 ^bZeph.
1:4 ^cIs.
24:15 ^dPs.
72:8-11;
Zeph. 3:9

11 The LORD will be ^aterrify-
ing to them, for He will starve ^ball
the gods of the earth; and all the
^ccoastlands of the nations will
^dbow down to Him, everyone
from his own place.

3 Ethiopia (to the south), 2:12

12 ^aIs. 18:1-
7; 20:4, 5;
Ezek. 30:4-9

12 "You also, O ^aEthiopians,
will be slain by My
sword."

4 Assyria (to the north), 2:13-15

13 And He will ^astretch out
His hand against the
north
And destroy ^bAssyria,
And He will make ^cNine-
veh a desolation,
Parched like the wilder-
ness.

13 ^aIs.
14:26; Zeph.
1:4 ^bIs.
10:16; Mic.
5:6 ^cNah.
3:7

14 And flocks will lie down in
her midst,
All beasts which range in
herds;
Both the ^apelican and the
hedgehog
Will lodge in the tops of
her pillars;
Birds will sing in the window,
Desolation will be on the
threshold;
For He has laid bare the
cedar work.

14 ^aIs.
14:23; 34:11

15 This is the ^aexultant city
Which ^bdwells securely,
Who says in her heart,
"^cI am, and there is no one
besides me."
How she has become a
^ddesolation,
A resting place for beasts!
^eEveryone who passes by
her will hiss
And wave his hand in con-
tempt.

15 ^aIs. 22:2
^bIs. 32:9, 11;
47:8 ^cIs.
47:8; Ezek.
28:2, 9 ^dIs.
32:14 ^eJer.
18:16; 19:8

D Judgment on Jerusalem, 3:1-7

3 Woe to her who is ^arebellious
and ^bdefiled,
The ^ctyrannical city!

★ 1 ^aJer.
5:23 ^bEzek.
23:30 ^cJer.
6:6

2 She ^aheeded no voice;
She ^baccepted no instruc-
tion.
She did not ^ctrust in the
LORD;
She did not ^ddraw near to
her God.

2 ^aJer.
7:23-28
^bJer. 2:30;
5:3; 2 Tim.
3:16 ^cPs.
78:22; Jer.
13:25 ^dPs.
73:28

2:8 Moab. See note on Amos 2:1. Ammon. See
note on Amos 1:13.
2:9 nettles. Plants with strong, stinging hairs.

3:1 to her. Jerusalem. To see how defiled Jerusalem was, read Jer. 5:1; 19:5; 23:13-14; 32:35.

★ 3 aEzek.
22:27 bJer.
5:6; Hab. 1:8

3　Her aprinces within her are
　　roaring lions,
　Her judges are bwolves at
　　evening;
　They leave nothing for the
　　morning.

4 aJudg.
9:4 bEzek.
22:26; Mal.
2:7, 8

4　Her prophets are areckless,
　　treacherous men;
　Her bpriests have profaned
　　the sanctuary.
　They have done violence
　　to the law.

5 aDeut.
32:4 bZeph.
3:15, 17 cPs.
92:15 dJob
7:18 eZeph.
2:1

5　The Lord is arighteous
　　bwithin her;
　He will cdo no injustice.
　dEvery morning He brings
　　His justice to light;
　He does not fail.
　But the unjust eknows no
　　shame.

6 aJer.
9:12; Zech.
7:14; Matt.
23:38 bLev.
26:31; Is.
6:11 cZeph.
2:5

6　"I have cut off nations;
　Their corner towers are in
　　ruins.
　I have made their streets
　　adesolate,
　With no one passing by;
　Their bcities are laid waste,
　Without a man, cwithout
　　an inhabitant.

7 aJob
36:10; Ps.
32:8; 1 Tim.
1:5 bJer. 7:7
cHos. 9:9

7　"I said, 'Surely you will re-
　　vere Me,
　aAccept instruction.'
　So her dwelling will bnot
　　be cut off
　According to all that I have
　　appointed concerning
　　her.
　But they were eager to
　　ccorrupt all their
　　deeds.

E　Judgment on the Nations, 3:8

★ 8 aPs.
27:14; Is.
30:18; Hab.
2:3 bEzek.
38:14-23;
Joel 3:2
cZeph. 1:18

8　"Therefore, await for Me,"
　　declares the Lord,
　"For the day when I rise up
　　to the prey.

Indeed, My decision is to
　bgather nations,
To assemble kingdoms,
To pour out on them My
　indignation,
All My burning anger;
For call the earth will be
　devoured
By the fire of My zeal.

III　THE PROPHECIES OF BLESSING,
3:9–20

A　Future Blessings for Gentiles, 3:9–10

9　"For then I will give to the
　　peoples apurified lips,
　That all of them may bcall
　　on the name of the
　　Lord,
　To serve Him shoulder to
　　shoulder.
10　"From beyond the rivers of
　　aEthiopia
　My worshipers, My dis-
　　persed ones,
　Will bbring My offerings.

B　Future Blessings for Jews,
3:11–20

11　"In that day you will afeel
　　no shame
　Because of all your deeds
　By which you have re-
　　belled against Me;
　For then I will remove
　　from your midst
　Your bproud, exulting
　　ones,
　And you will never again
　　be haughty
　On My choly mountain.
12　"But I will leave among you
　　A ahumble and lowly peo-
　　ple,

★ 9-20

9 aIs.
19:18; 57:19
bPs. 22:27;
86:9, Hab.
2:14; Zeph.
2:11

10 aPs.
68:31; Is.
18:1 bIs.
60:6, 7

11 aIs.
45:17; 54:4;
Joel 2:26, 27
bIs. 2:12;
5:15 cIs.
11:9; 56:7;
Ezek. 20:40

12 aIs. 14:30
bIs. 14:32;
50:10; Nah.
1:7; Zech.
13:8, 9

3:3 They leave not a bone for the morning, so greedy are they.
3:8 This verse will be fulfilled in the Tribulation period, climaxing at Armageddon (Rev. 16:14), after which will be judgment on the *nations* (Joel 3:2; Matt. 25:31–32).
3:9–20 Zephaniah here describes the millennial age and some of its blessings: pure worship (v.

9; this is apparently the meaning of *purified lips*, in contrast to the blasphemy of idolatrous worship); the Jewish nation regathered and purified (vv. 10–13); Christ personally reigning *in your midst* (v. 15); security (v. 16); enemies punished (v. 19); and Israel restored to her land (v. 20).

And they will *b*take refuge in the name of the LORD.

13 "The *a*remnant of Israel will *b*do no wrong
And *c*tell no lies,
Nor will a deceitful tongue
Be found in their mouths;
For they shall *d*feed and lie down
With no one to make them tremble."

14 Shout for joy, O daughter of Zion!
*a*Shout *in triumph,* O Israel!
Rejoice and exult with all *your* heart,
O daughter of Jerusalem!

15 The LORD has taken away *a*His judgments against you,
He has cleared away your enemies.
The King of Israel, the LORD, is *b*in your midst;
You will *c*fear disaster no more.

16 *a*In that day it will be said to Jerusalem:
"*b*Do not be afraid, O Zion;
*c*Do not let your hands fall limp.

17 "The LORD your God is *a*in your midst,
A *b*victorious warrior.
He will *c*exult over you with joy,
He will be quiet in His love,
He will rejoice over you with shouts of joy.

18 "I will gather those who *a*grieve about the appointed feasts—
They came from you, O Zion;
The reproach *of exile* is a burden on them.

19 "Behold, I am going to deal at that time
With all your *a*oppressors,
I will save the *b*lame
And gather the outcast,
And I will turn their *c*shame into *d*praise and renown
In all the earth.

20 "At that time I will *a*bring you in,
Even at the time when I gather you together;
Indeed, I will give you *b*renown and praise
Among all the peoples of the earth,
When I *c*restore your fortunes before your eyes,"
Says the LORD.

13 *a*Is. 10:20-22; Mic. 4:7; Zeph. 2:7 *b*Ps. 119:3; Jer. 31:33; Zeph. 3:5 *c*Zech. 8:3, 16; Rev. 14:5 *d*Ezek. 34:13-15

14 *a*Zech. 9:9

15 *a*Ps. 19:9; John 5:30; Rev. 18:20 *b*Ezek. 37:26-28; Zeph. 3:5 *c*Is. 54:14

16 *a*Is. 25:9 *b*Is. 35:3, 4 *c*Job 4:3; Heb. 12:12

17 *a*Zeph. 3:5, 15 *b*Is. 63:1 *c*Is. 62:5

18 *a*Ps. 42:2-4; Ezek. 9:4

19 *a*Is. 60:14 *b*Ezek. 34:16; Mic. 4:6 *c*Ezek. 16:27, 57 *d*Is. 60:18; 62:7; Zech. 8:23

20 *a*Ezek. 37:12, 21 *b*Deut. 26:18, 19; Is. 56:5; 66:22 *c*Jer. 29:14; Joel 3:1; Zeph. 2:7

INTRODUCTION TO
THE BOOK OF HAGGAI

AUTHOR: Haggai   DATE: 520 B.C.

The Prophet *Haggai (whose name means "my feast") was the first prophetic voice to be heard after the Babylonian Exile. He was a contemporary of Zechariah (and of Confucius) and his ministry was to call the people to finish the Temple, whose completion had been delayed for 15 years. These prophecies were given between August and December 520, and the Temple was completed 4 years later. Haggai likely returned to Jerusalem from Babylon with Zerubbabel.*

Recipients *The book is addressed to all the people (1:13; 2:2), to encourage them to rebuild the Temple. But it is also particularly addressed to Zerubbabel, the governor, and to Joshua, the high priest (1:1; 2:2, 21).*

Contents *The book contains four appeals, each introduced by "the word of the LORD came."*

OUTLINE OF HAGGAI

I. **A Call to Construction of the Temple,**
   1:1–15
   A. Introduction, 1:1–2
   B. The Reprimand, 1:3–6
   C. The Remedy, 1:7–8
   D. The Rebuke from God, 1:9–11

E. The Reaction of the People, 1:12–15
II. **A Call to Courage in the Lord, 2:1–9**
III. **A Call to Cleanness of Life, 2:10–19**
IV. **A Call to Confidence in the Future,**
   2:20–23

THE BOOK OF HAGGAI

I A CALL TO CONSTRUCTION OF THE TEMPLE, 1:1–15

A Introduction, 1:1–2

★ 1 aEzra
4:24 bEzra
5:1; 6:14;
Hag. 1:3, 12,
13; 2:1, 10,
20 cEzra 2:2;
Neh. 7:7;
Hag. 1:12,
14; Zech.
4:6; Matt.
1:12, 13
d1 Kin.
10:15; Ezra
5:3 eZech.
6:11

1 In the ªsecond year of Darius the king, on the first day of the sixth month, the word of the LORD came by the prophet ᵇHaggai to ᶜZerubbabel the son of Shealtiel, ᵈgovernor of Judah, and to ᵉJoshua the son of Jehozadak, the high priest saying,

2 "Thus says the LORD of hosts, 'This people says, "The time has not come, *even* the time for the house of the LORD to be rebuilt." ' "

B The Reprimand, 1:3–6

3 Then the word of the LORD came by Haggai the prophet saying,

4 "Is it time for you yourselves to dwell in your paneled houses while this house ªlies desolate?"

5 Now therefore, thus says the LORD of hosts, "Consider your ways!

6 "You have ªsown much, but harvest little; *you* eat, but *there is* not *enough* to be satisfied; *you* drink, but *there is* not *enough* to become drunk; *you* put on clothing, but no one is warm *enough*;

★ 4 aJer.
33:10, 12;
Hag. 1:9

★ 6 aDeut.
28:38-40;
Hos. 8:7;
Hag. 1:9, 10;
2:16, 17

1:1 *Darius* I (Hystaspes) ascended to the throne of Persia in 522 and appointed *Zerubbabel*, grandson of Jehoiachin, king of Judah (1 Chron. 3:17, 19), as governor of the newly constituted province of Judah. *sixth month*. Elul (September). *Jehozadak*. High priest at the time of the Babylonian invasion (1 Chron.

6:15).
1:4 *paneled houses*. A sign of luxury, since expensive timber had to be imported. *this house*. The Temple, which had been started about 16 years earlier (Ezra 3:2–4:5).
1:6 This verse illustrates the truth of Matt. 6:19, 33.

and he who earns, earns wages *to put* into a purse with holes."

C The Remedy, 1:7-8

7 Thus says the LORD of hosts, "Consider your ways!

8 "Go up to the mountains, bring wood and ªrebuild the temple, that I may be ᵇpleased with it and be ᶜglorified," says the LORD.

D The Rebuke from God, 1:9-11

9 "ªYou look for much, but behold, *it comes* to little; when you bring *it* home, I ᵇblow it *away*. Why?" declares the LORD of hosts, "Because of My house which ᶜlies desolate, while each of you runs to his own house.

10 "Therefore, because of you the ªsky has withheld its dew, and the earth has withheld its produce.

11 "And I called for a ªdrought on the land, on the mountains, on the grain, on the new wine, on the oil, on what the ground produces, on ᵇmen, on cattle, and on ᶜall the labor of your hands."

E The Reaction of the People, 1:12-15

12 Then ªZerubbabel the son of Shealtiel, and ᵇJoshua the son of Jehozadak, the high priest, with all the remnant of the people, ᶜobeyed the voice of the LORD their God and the words of Haggai the prophet, as the LORD their

God had sent him. And the people ᵈshowed reverence for the LORD.

13 Then Haggai, the ªmessenger of the LORD, spoke by the commission of the LORD to the people saying, " ᵇI am with you,' declares the LORD."

14 So the LORD stirred up the spirit of ªZerubbabel the son of Shealtiel, ªgovernor of Judah, and the spirit of Joshua the son of Jehozadak, the high priest, and the spirit of all the ᵇremnant of the people; and they came and ᶜworked on the house of the LORD of hosts, their God,

15 on the twenty-fourth day of the sixth month in the second year of Darius the king.

II A CALL TO COURAGE IN THE LORD, 2:1-9

2 On the twenty-first of the seventh month, the word of the LORD came by ªHaggai the prophet saying,

2 "Speak now to ªZerubbabel the son of Shealtiel, ªgovernor of Judah, and to ªJoshua the son of Jehozadak, the high priest, and to the ᵇremnant of the people saying,

3 'Who is ªleft among you who saw this temple in its ᵇformer glory? And how do you see it now? Does it not seem to you like nothing in comparison?

4 'But now ªtake courage, Zerubbabel,' declares the LORD, 'take courage also, Joshua son of Jehozadak, the high priest, and all you people of the land take courage,' declares the LORD, 'and work;

---

8 ª1 Kin. 6:1 ᵇPs. 132:13, 14 ᶜHag. 2:7, 9

★ **9** ªProv. 27:20; Eccl. 1:8 ᵇIs. 40:7 ᶜHag. 1:4

10 ªDeut. 28:23, 24; 1 Kin. 17:1; Joel 1:18-20

11 ªJer. 14:2-6; Mal. 3:9, 11 ᵇDeut. 28:22 ᶜHag. 2:17

★**12-15** **12** ªHag. 1:1 ᵇHag. 1:14; 2:2 ᶜIs. 1:19; 1 Thess. 2:13 ᵈDeut. 31:12, 13; Ps. 112:1; Is. 50:10

13 ªIs. 44:26; Ezek. 3:17; Mal. 2:7; 3:1 ᵇPs. 46:11; Is. 41:10; 43:2

14 ªHag. 1:1; 2:2, 21 ᵇHag. 1:12 ᶜEzra 5:2; Neh. 4:6

★ **1** ªHag. 1:1

2 ªHag. 1:1 ᵇHag. 1:12

★ **3** ªEzra 3:12 ᵇHag. 2:9

4 ªDeut. 31:23; 1 Chr. 22:13; 28:20; Zech. 8:9; Eph. 6:10 ᵇ2 Sam. 5:10; Acts 7:9

1:9 Even the little they were able to reap, God would *blow it away,* dispersing it in order to chastise the people for their disobedience in not finishing the Temple.

1:12-15 Seldom has a sermon had such immediate practical impact (though Haggai realized it was the Lord's doing, v. 14). Only 23 days elapsed between the events recorded in verse 1 and those recorded in verse 15.

2:1 The 21st day of the *seventh month* was the 7th and last day of the Feast of Tabernacles

(Lev. 23:39-44), usually a joyous occasion of thanksgiving for the harvest. That year, however, the harvest was scanty (1:6, 11).

2:3 The background for this question is in Ezra 3:8-13. A few septuagenarians and older ones, who could remember the larger and more beautiful Temple of Solomon, wept when they saw the smaller, plainer Temple of Zerubbabel. Coupled with the slim harvest, this sight also infected others with discouragement.

for ᵇI am with you,' says the Lᴏʀᴅ of hosts.

★ 5 ᵃEx.
19:4-6;
29:45, 46;
33:12-14;
34:8-10
ᵇNeh. 9:20;
Is. 63:11, 14
ᶜIs. 41:10,
13; Zech.
8:13

5 'As for the ᵃpromise which I made you when you came out of Egypt, My ᵇSpirit is abiding in your midst; ᶜdo not fear!'

★ 6 ᵃHeb.
12:26 ᵇIs.
10:25; 29:17
ᶜHag. 2:21

6 "For thus says the Lᴏʀᴅ of hosts, 'ᵃOnce more in a ᵇlittle while, I am going to ᶜshake the heavens and the earth, the sea also and the dry land.

★ 7 ᵃDan.
2:44; Joel
3:9, 16 ᵇIs.
60:4-9
ᶜ1 Kin. 8:11;
Is. 60:7

7 'And I will shake ᵃall the nations; and they will come with the ᵇwealth of all nations; and I will ᶜfill this house with glory,' says the Lᴏʀᴅ of hosts.

8 ᵃ1 Chr.
29:14, 16; Is.
60:17

8 'The ᵃsilver is Mine, and the gold is Mine,' declares the Lᴏʀᴅ of hosts.

★ 9 ᵃZech.
2:5 ᵇHag.
2:3 ᶜIs. 9:6,
7; 66:12

9 'The latter ᵃglory of this house will be greater than the ᵇformer,' says the Lᴏʀᴅ of hosts, 'and in this place I shall give ᶜpeace,' declares the Lᴏʀᴅ of hosts."

III   A CALL TO CLEANNESS OF LIFE,
2:10-19

★10 ᵃHag.
2:20

10 On the ᵃtwenty-fourth of the ninth month, in the second year of Darius, the word of the Lᴏʀᴅ came to Haggai the prophet saying,

11 ᵃDeut.
17:8-11; Mal.
2:7

11 "Thus says the Lᴏʀᴅ of hosts, 'ᵃAsk now the priests for a ruling:

12 'If a man carries ᵃholy meat in the fold of his garment, and touches bread with this fold, or cooked food, wine, oil, or any other food, will it become holy?' " And the priests answered and said, "No."

★12 ᵃEx.
29:37; Lev.
6:27, 29; 7:6;
Ezek. 44:19;
Matt. 23:19

13 Then Haggai said, "ᵃIf one who is unclean from a corpse touches any of these, will the latter become unclean?" And the priests answered and said, "It will become unclean."

★13 ᵃLev.
22:4-6; Num.
19:22

14 Then Haggai answered and said, " 'ᵃSo is this people. And so is this nation before Me,' declares the Lᴏʀᴅ, 'and so is every work of their hands; and what they offer there is unclean.

14 ᵃProv.
15:8; Is.
1:11-15

15 'But now, do ᵃconsider from this day onward: before one ᵇstone was placed on another in the temple of the Lᴏʀᴅ,

★15 ᵃHag.
1:5, 7; 2:18
ᵇEzra 3:10;
4:24

16 from that time when one came to a grain heap of twenty measures, there would be only ten; and when one came to the wine vat to draw fifty measures, there would be only twenty.

17 'I smote you and every work of your hands with ᵃblasting wind, mildew, and hail; yet you did not come back to Me,' declares the Lᴏʀᴅ.

17 ᵃDeut.
28:22; 1 Kin.
8:37; Amos
4:9

18 'Do ᵃconsider from this day onward, from the ᵇtwenty-fourth day of the ninth month; from the

★18 ᵃDeut.
32:29; Hag.
2:15 ᵇHag.
2:10 ᶜEzra
5:1, 2; Zech.
8:9, 12

2:5 See Exod. 19:5; 29:45-46; 33:14.

2:6 The scope of these words points to a yet future fulfillment at the time of the second coming of Christ.

2:7 The well-known translation "the desire of all nations" (KJV) makes this a reference to Messiah and is in accord with Jewish tradition. However, many feel that the phrase is more properly translated, as here, the wealth (precious things) of all nations, referring to the offerings the nations will bring to the millennial Temple.

2:9 this house. This may refer to Zerubbabel's Temple (and its successor Temple built by Herod) and to the peace made by Christ on the cross at His first coming, or it may refer to the millennial Temple (Ezek. 40-48) and the world peace which He will bring at His second coming.

2:10 the ninth month. Chislev (Nov.-Dec.), when they looked for the early rain to water

the new crop.

2:12 The first question is: Since a man who is carrying holy meat, that is, meat for a sacrifice, is sanctified (cf. Lev. 6:27), can he transfer that sanctification to things he touches? The answer is, No.

2:13 The second question is: Since a man who touches a corpse is defiled, does he transfer that defilement to other things he touches (cf. Num. 19:11-13)? The answer is, Yes. The point of these two questions is: sanctification or cleanness cannot be transferred, but defilement can; just as health is not contagious, but disease can be. The disobedience of the people was like a dead thing in their midst, contaminating all of them (v. 14).

2:15 onward. Better, backward; their past history was characterized by scarcity.

2:18 onward. Their future would be one of blessing.

day when the temple of the LORD was ^cfounded, consider:

19 'Is the seed still in the barn? Even including the vine, the fig tree, the pomegranate, and the olive tree, it has not borne fruit. Yet from this day on I will ^abless you.' "

IV A CALL TO CONFIDENCE IN THE FUTURE, 2:20-23

20 Then the word of the LORD came a second time to Haggai on the ^atwenty-fourth *day* of the month saying,

21 "Speak to ^aZerubbabel gov-ernor of Judah saying, 'I am going to ^bshake the heavens and the earth.

22 'And I will ^aoverthrow the thrones of kingdoms and destroy the ^bpower of the kingdoms of the nations; and I will ^coverthrow the chariots and their riders, and the ^dhorses and their riders will go down, ^eeveryone by the sword of another.'

23 'On that day,' declares the LORD of hosts, 'I will take you, Zerubbabel, son of Shealtiel, my servant,' declares the LORD, 'and I will make you like a ^asignet *ring,* for ^bI have chosen you,' " declares the LORD of hosts.

Marginal references:

19 ^aPs. 128:1-6; Jer. 31:12, 14; Mal. 3:10

20 ^aHag. 2:10

★21-22

21 ^aEzra 5:2; Hag. 1:1; Zech. 4:6-10 ^bHag. 2:6; Heb. 12:26, 27

22 ^aEzek. 26:16; Zeph. 3:8 ^bMic. 7:16 ^cPs. 46:9; Ezek. 39:20; Mic. 5:10 ^dAmos 2:15 ^eJudg. 7:22; 2 Chr. 20:23

★23 ^aSong 8:6; Jer. 22:24 ^bIs. 42:1; 43:10

2:21-22 The prophecy looks ahead to the time when Christ will rule the nations of the world. In Haggai's time Persia ruled more than 2 million square miles of territory.

2:23 *signet ring.* An indication of the honor God gave to Zerubbabel, who, perhaps because of this and the suspicion it created in the minds of the Persian rulers, shortly afterward disappeared from the scene.

INTRODUCTION TO
THE BOOK OF ZECHARIAH

AUTHOR: Zechariah   DATE: 520-518 B.C.

Author   Zechariah's father, Berechiah, probably died when his son was young, making Zechariah the immediate successor of his grandfather, Iddo (Neh. 12:4). Iddo was a priest who returned from Babylon with Zerubbabel and Joshua and was, according to tradition, a member of the Great Synagogue (the governing body of the Jews before the Sanhedrin). The name Zechariah (used in the O.T. of 27 other people) means "Yahweh remembers." This Zechariah was a contemporary of the prophet Haggai (Ezra 5:1; 6:14).

Background and Purpose   During the reign of Cyrus, more than 50,000 Jews returned to Palestine from Babylon in 538. They laid the foundation of the Temple in 536, but opposition stalled the work for about 15 years (Ezra 1:1-4; 4:1-5). Darius Hystaspes (1:1), who came to the throne in 521, confirmed Cyrus' decree, and Zechariah, like Haggai, encouraged the people to finish the Temple (which they did in 516).

Christology of the Book   Zechariah predicted more about Messiah than any other prophet except Isaiah. Prophecies concerning His first coming include 3:8; 9:9, 16; 11:11-13; 12:10; 13:1, 6; and prophecies to be fulfilled at His second coming include 6:12; 14:1-21.

Contents   The book is one of consolation and hope, beginning with a call to repentance and concluding with prophecies concerning the return and reign of Christ.

OUTLINE OF ZECHARIAH

THE BOOK OF ZECHARIAH

I THE CALL TO REPENTANCE, 1:1-6

★ 1 ᵃEzra
4:24; 6:15;
Hag. 1:15;
2:10; Zech.
1:7; 7:1
ᵇEzra 5:1;
6:14; Zech.
7:1; Matt.
23:35; Luke
11:51 ᶜNeh.
12:4, 16
2 ᵃ2 Chr.
36:16; Jer.
44:6; Ezek.
8:18; Zech.
1:15
3 ᵃIs. 31:6;
44:22; Mal.
3:7
★ 4 ᵃPs.
78:8; 106:6.
7 ᵇ2 Chr.
24:19; 36:15
ᶜIs. 1:16-19;
Jer. 4:1;
Ezek. 33:11
ᵈJer. 6:17;
11:7, 8

★ 5-6
5 ᵃLam. 5:7
ᵇJohn 8:52

6 ᵃJer.
12:16, 17;
44:28, 29;
Amos 9:10
ᵇLam. 2:17

1 In the eighth month of the second year of ᵃDarius, the word of the Lord came to ᵇZechariah the prophet, the son of Berechiah, the son of ᶜIddo saying,

2 "The Lord was very ᵃangry with your fathers.

3 "Therefore say to them, 'Thus says the Lord of hosts, "ᵃReturn to Me," declares the Lord of hosts, "that I may return to you," says the Lord of hosts.

4 "Do not be ᵃlike your fathers, to whom the ᵇformer prophets proclaimed, saying, 'Thus says the Lord of hosts, "ᶜReturn now from your evil ways and from your evil deeds."' But they did ᵈnot listen or give heed to Me," declares the Lord.

5 "Your ᵃfathers, where are they? And the ᵇprophets, do they live forever?

6 "But did not My words and My statutes, which I commanded My servants the prophets, ᵃovertake your fathers? Then they repented and said, 'ᵇAs the Lord of hosts purposed to do to us in accordance with our ways and our deeds, so He has dealt with us.'"'"

II THE VISIONS OF ZECHARIAH, 1:7-6:15

A The Vision of the Horses and Riders, 1:7-17

★ 7

7 On the twenty-fourth day of the eleventh month, which is the month Shebat, in the second year of Darius, the word of the Lord came to Zechariah the prophet, the son of Berechiah, the son of Iddo, as follows:

8 I saw at night, and behold, a man was riding on a ᵃred horse, and he was standing among the ᵇmyrtle trees which were in the ravine, with red, sorrel, and ᶜwhite horses behind him.

9 Then I said, "My ᵃlord, what are these?" And the ᵇangel who was speaking with me said to me, "I will show you what these are."

10 And the man who was standing among the myrtle trees answered and said, "These are those whom the Lord has sent to ᵃpatrol the earth."

11 So they answered the angel of the Lord who was ᵃstanding among the myrtle trees, and said, "We have patrolled the earth, and behold, ᵇall the earth is peaceful and quiet."

12 Then the angel of the Lord answered and said, "O Lord of hosts, ᵃhow long wilt Thou ᵇhave no compassion for Jerusalem and the cities of Judah, with which Thou hast been ᶜindignant these ᵈseventy years?"

13 And the Lord answered the ᵃangel who was speaking with me with gracious words, ᵇcomforting words.

14 So the angel who was speaking with me said to me, "ᵃProclaim, saying, 'Thus says the Lord of hosts, "I am ᵇexceedingly jealous for Jerusalem and Zion.

★ 8-17
★ 8 ᵃZech.
6:2; Rev. 6:4
ᵇNeh. 8:15;
Is. 41:19;
55:13; Zech.
6:3;
ᶜZech. 6:3;
Rev. 6:2
9 ᵃZech.
1:19; 4:4, 5,
13; 6:4
ᵇZech. 2:3;
5:5

10 ᵃJob 1:7;
Zech. 1:11;
4:10; 6:5-8

★11 ᵃZech.
1:8, 10 ᵇIs.
14:7

★12 ᵃPs.
74:10; Jer.
12:4; Hab.
1:2 ᵇPs.
102:13; Jer.
30:18 ᶜPs.
102:10; Jer.
15:17 ᵈJer.
25:11; 29:10;
Dan. 9:2;
Zech. 7:5

13 ᵃZech.
1:9; 4:1 ᵇIs.
40:1, 2;
57:18

14 ᵃIs. 40:2,
6; Zech. 1:17
ᵇZech. 8:2

1:1 eighth month . . . second year. Oct.-Nov. 520.

1:4 the former prophets. Such as Isaiah and Jeremiah, who warned of the Babylonian captivity.

1:5-6 The idea is: pay attention to the Word of God because, though prophets die, it endures, and the proof that it endures is that its warnings come true (overtake).

1:7 eleventh month. Three months after the call to repentance of 1:1-6 and after Hag. 2:10-23 had been spoken, the people had repented.

1:8-17 The meaning of the vision is: though Israel is oppressed, God is still greatly concerned for His people and will restore them.

1:8 myrtle trees. Evergreens that grow about 30 feet high. sorrel. A reddish-brown color.

1:11 God's patrols report that the earth is peaceful and quiet; i.e., the heathen nations still flourished and were self-confidently secure, while Israel was downtrodden.

1:12 these seventy years. The years the Temple lay in ruins (586-516).

15 "But I am very ^aangry with the nations who are ^bat ease; for while I was only a little angry, they ^cfurthered the disaster."

16 'Therefore, thus says the Lord, "I will ^areturn to Jerusalem with compassion; My ^bhouse will be built in it," declares the Lord of hosts, "and a measuring ^cline will be stretched over Jerusalem." '

17 "Again, proclaim, saying, 'Thus says the Lord of hosts, "My ^acities will again overflow with prosperity, and the Lord will again ^bcomfort Zion and again ^cchoose Jerusalem." ' "

B The Vision of the Four Horns and Four Workmen, 1:18-21

18 Then I lifted up my eyes and looked, and behold, *there were* four horns.

19 So I said to the angel who was speaking with me, "What are these?" And he answered me, "These are the ^ahorns which have scattered Judah, Israel, and Jerusalem."

20 Then the Lord showed me four ^acraftsmen.

21 And I said, "What are these coming to do?" And he said, "These are the ^ahorns which have scattered Judah, so that no man lifts up his head; but these *craftsmen* have come to terrify them, to ^bthrow down the horns of the nations who have lifted up *their* horns against the land of Judah in order to scatter it."

C The Vision of the Surveyor, 2:1-13

2 Then I lifted up my eyes and looked, and behold, *there was* a man with a ^ameasuring line in his hand.

2 So I said, "Where are you going?" And he said to me, "To ^ameasure Jerusalem, to see how wide it is and how long it is."

3 And behold, the ^aangel who was speaking with me was going out, and another angel was coming out to meet him,

4 and said to him, "Run, speak to that ^ayoung man, saying, '^bJerusalem will be inhabited ^cwithout walls, because of the ^dmultitude of men and cattle within it.

5 'For I,' declares the Lord, 'will be a ^awall of fire around her, and I will be the ^bglory in her midst.' "

6 "Ho there! ^aFlee from the land of the north," declares the Lord, "for I have ^bdispersed you as the four winds of the heavens," declares the Lord.

7 "Ho, Zion! ^aEscape, you who are living with the daughter of Babylon."

8 For thus says the Lord of hosts, "After ^aglory He has sent me against the nations which plunder you, for he who touches you, touches the ^bapple of His eye.

9 "For behold, I will ^awave My hand over them, so that they will be ^bplunder for their slaves.

Cross references (margin)

★15 ^aZech. 1:2 ^bPs. 123:4; Jer. 48:11 ^cAmos 1:11

★16 ^aIs. 54:8-10; Zech. 2:10, 11 ^bEzra 6:14, 15; Zech. 4:9 ^cJer. 31:39; Zech. 2:2, 4

17 ^aIs. 44:26; 61:4 ^bIs. 51:3 ^cZech. 2:12

★18-21

19 ^a1 Kin. 22:11; Ps. 75:4, 5; Amos 6:13 mg.

20 ^aIs. 44:12; 54:16

21 ^aZech. 1:19 ^bPs. 75:10

★ 1-13

1 ^aJer. 31:39; Ezek. 40:3; 47:3; Zech. 1:16

2 ^aJer. 31:39; Ezek. 40:3; Rev. 21:15-17

3 ^aZech. 1:9

4 ^aJer. 1:6; Dan. 1:4; 1 Tim. 4:12 ^bZech. 1:17; 8:4 ^cEzek. 38:11 ^dIs. 49:20; Jer. 30:19; 33:22

5 ^aIs. 4:5; 26:1; 60:18 ^bHag. 2:9; Zech. 2:10, 11

6 ^aJer. 3:18 ^bJer. 31:10; Ezek. 11:16

7 ^aIs. 48:20; Jer. 51:6

8 ^aIs. 60:7-9 ^bDeut. 32:10; Ps. 17:8

9 ^aIs. 19:16 ^bIs. 14:2

1:15 *they furthered the disaster.* Lit., they helped for evil. Though the heathen nations were used of God to punish Israel, they went too far in trying to annihilate her.

1:16 The Temple (*My house*) was finished in 516 (cf. Ezra 6:15). A *line* was used to measure before destruction or construction (in this case, the latter).

1:18-21 *four horns.* The power of Gentile nations (perhaps Assyria, Egypt, Babylonia, and Medo-Persia specifically) which afflicted and *scattered* Israel. *craftsmen.* Those peoples and nations whom God used to overthrow the enemies of Israel. The vision reinforces the warning and promise of Gen. 12:3.

2:1-13 This vision signifies the assured restoration and blessing of Israel and Jerusalem. In the future Jerusalem will expand beyond its walls (v. 4), yet the inhabitants will live in it safely because of the personal presence of the Lord (v. 5) during the Millennium. Those who had not yet returned from Babylon (*the land of the north,* Jer. 1:14) are called on to return (vv. 6-7; only about 50,000 had returned under Cyrus' decree in 538), because Babylon would soon be taken (as happened 3 years later). *apple* (v. 8). Pupil. Verses 10-13 describe millennial blessings for the nations, Israel, and Jerusalem. *the holy land* (v. 12). Palestine; used only here in the O.T.

Then you will know that the LORD of hosts has sent Me.

10 "^aSing for joy and be glad, O daughter of Zion; for behold I am coming and I will ^bdwell in your midst," declares the LORD.

11 "And ^amany nations will join themselves to the LORD in that day and will become My people. Then I will ^bdwell in your midst; and you will ^cknow that the LORD of hosts has sent Me to you.

12 "And the LORD will ^apossess Judah as His portion in the holy land, and will again ^bchoose Jerusalem.

13 "^aBe silent, all flesh, before the LORD; for He is ^baroused from His holy habitation."

D The Vision of Joshua the High Priest, 3:1-10

3 Then he showed me ^aJoshua the high priest standing before the angel of the LORD, and ^bSatan standing at his right hand to accuse him.

2 And the LORD said to Satan, "^aThe LORD rebuke you, Satan! Indeed, the LORD who has ^bchosen Jerusalem rebuke you! Is this not a ^cbrand plucked from the fire?"

3 Now Joshua was clothed with ^afilthy garments and standing before the angel.

4 And he spoke and said to those who were standing before

him saying, "^aRemove the filthy garments from him." Again he said to him, "See, I have ^btaken your iniquity away from you and will ^cclothe you with festal robes."

5 Then I said, "Let them put a clean ^aturban on his head." So they put a clean turban on his head and clothed him with garments, while the angel of the LORD was standing by.

6 And the angel of the LORD admonished Joshua saying,

7 "Thus says the LORD of hosts, 'If you will ^awalk in My ways, and if you will perform My service, then you will also ^bgovern My house and also have charge of My ^ccourts, and I will grant you free access among these who are standing *here*.

8 'Now listen, Joshua the high priest, you and your friends who are sitting in front of you— indeed they are men who are a ^asymbol, for behold, I am going to bring in My servant the ^bBranch.

9 'For behold, the stone that I have set before Joshua; on one stone are ^aseven eyes. Behold, I will engrave an inscription on it,' declares the LORD of hosts, 'and I will ^bremove the iniquity of that land in one day.

10 'In that day,' declares the LORD of hosts, 'every one of you will invite his neighbor to *sit* under *his* ^avine and under *his* fig tree.' "

Cross references (left margin):

10 ^aIs. 65:18, 19; Zech. 9:9 ^bZech. 2:5; 8:3

11 ^aMic. 4:2 ^bZech. 2:5, 10 ^cZech. 2:9

12 ^aDeut. 32:9; Ps. 33:12; Jer. 10:16 ^b2 Chr. 6:6; Ps. 132:13, 14; Zech. 1:17

13 ^aHab. 2:20; Zeph. 1:7 ^bPs. 78:65; Is. 51:9

★ 1-10
★ 1 ^aEzra 5:2; Hag. 1:1; Zech. 6:11 ^b1 Chr. 21:1; Job 1:6; Ps. 109:6; Rev. 12:10

2 ^aMark 9:25; Jude 9 ^bZech. 2:12 ^cAmos 4:11; Jude 23

3 ^aEzra 9:15; Is. 4:4; 64:6

4 ^aIs. 43:25; Ezek. 36:25 ^bMic. 7:18, 19; Zech. 3:9 ^cIs. 52:1; 61:10

Cross references (right margin):

★ 5 ^aJob 29:14; Is. 3:23

★ 7 ^a1 Kin. 3:14 ^bDeut. 17:9, 12 ^cIs. 62:9

★ 8 ^aIs. 8:18; 20:3; Ezek. 12:11 ^bIs. 11:1; 53:2; Jer. 23:5; 33:15; Zech. 6:12

★ 9 ^aZech. 4:10 ^bJer. 31:34; 50:20; Zech. 3:4

★ 10 ^a1 Kin. 4:25; Is. 36:16; Mic. 4:4

3:1-10 Joshua the high priest is cleansed in this vision. This had personal significance in that it answered the charge some had made that Joshua was unfit to serve in that office. It had priestly significance for the nation, picturing their restoration to a priestly position before God. It also had prophetic significance, illustrating the future cleansing of the nation at the return of Christ.

3:1 *Satan . . . to accuse.* See Rev. 12:10. *Is this not a brand plucked from the fire?* (v. 2) Israel had been saved out of the fire of the Babylonian captivity.

3:5 On the turban was a plate on which was engraved "Holy to the Lord" (Exod. 28:36-38).

3:7 *I will grant you free access.* I.e., Joshua would have access to God along with the angels.

3:8 *your friends who are sitting in front of you.* The other priests, men who were a sign or symbol pointing to another, namely, Messiah, who is here designated as *My servant the Branch* (humble and human; cf. Isa. 42:1; 52:13; Ezek. 34:23-24; Isa. 4:2; Jer. 23:5).

3:9 *the stone.* Also a reference to Messiah (cf. Psalm 118:22; Matt. 21:42; 1 Pet. 2:6). At His second coming He will cleanse Israel (Rom. 11:25-26).

3:10 See Micah 4:4.

E The Vision of the Golden Lampstand, 4:1-14

4 Then ᵃthe angel who was speaking with me returned, and ᵇroused me as a man who is awakened from his sleep.

2 And he said to me, "ᵃWhat do you see?" And I said, "I see, and behold, a ᵇlampstand all of gold with its bowl on the top of it, and its ᶜseven lamps on it with seven spouts belonging to each of the lamps which are on the top of it;

3 also ᵃtwo olive trees by it, one on the right side of the bowl and the other on its left side."

4 Then I answered and said to the angel who was speaking with me saying, "What are these, ᵃmy lord?"

5 So ᵃthe angel who was speaking with me answered and said to me, "ᵇDo you not know what these are?" And I said, "No, my lord."

6 Then he answered and said to me, "This is the word of the Lord to ᵃZerubbabel saying, ᵇNot by might nor by power, but by My ᶜSpirit,' says the Lord of hosts.

7 'What are you, O great ᵃmountain? Before Zerubbabel you will become a plain; and he will bring forth the top stone with ᵇshouts of "Grace, grace to it!" ' "

8 Also the word of the Lord came to me saying,

9 "The hands of Zerubbabel have ᵃlaid the foundation of this house, and his hands will ᵇfinish it. Then you will know that the Lord of hosts has sent me to you.

10 "For who has despised the day of ᵃsmall things? But these ᵇseven will be glad when they see the ᶜplumb line in the hand of Zerubbabel—these are the ᵈeyes of the Lord which ᵉrange to and fro throughout the earth."

11 Then I answered and said to him, "What are these ᵃtwo olive trees on the right of the lampstand and on its left?"

12 And I answered the second time and said to him, "What are the two olive branches which are beside the two golden pipes, which empty the golden oil from themselves?"

13 So he answered me saying, "ᵃDo you not know what these are?" And I said, "No, ᵇmy lord."

14 Then he said, "These are the two ᵃanointed ones, who are ᵇstanding by the ᶜLord of the whole earth."

F The Vision of the Flying Scroll, 5:1-4

5 Then I lifted up my eyes again and looked, and behold, there was a flying ᵃscroll.

2 And he said to me, "ᵃWhat do you see?" And I answered, "I see a flying scroll; its length is

---

Marginal references (left column):

1 ᵃZech. 1:9 ᵇ1 Kin. 19:5-7; Jer. 31:26

★ 2 ᵃJer. 1:13; Zech. 5:2 ᵇEx. 25:31, 37; Jer. 52:19 ᶜRev. 4:5

3 ᵃZech. 4:11; Rev. 11:4

4 ᵃZech. 1:9; 4:5, 13; 6:4

5 ᵃZech. 1:9; 4:1 ᵇZech. 4:13

★ 6-7
6 ᵃEzra 5:2; Hag. 2:4, 5 ᵇIs. 11:2-4; 30:1; Hos. 1:7 ᶜ2 Chr. 32:7, 8; Eph. 6:17

7 ᵃPs. 114:4, 6; Is. 40:4; Jer. 51:25; Nah. 1:5; Zech. 14:4, 5 ᵇEzra 3:10, 11; Ps. 84:11

Marginal references (right column):

9 ᵃEzra 3:8-10; 5:16; Hag. 2:18 ᵇEzra 6:14, 15; Zech. 6:12, 13

★10 ᵃNeh. 4:2-4; Amos 7:2, 5; Hag. 2:3 ᵇZech. 3:9; Rev. 5:6 ᶜAmos 7:7, 8 ᵈ2 Chr. 16:9; Prov. 15:3; Jer. 16:17 ᵉZech. 1:10; Rev. 5:6

11 ᵃZech. 4:3; Rev. 11:4

★12

13 ᵃZech. 4:5 ᵇZech. 4:4, 5

★14 ᵃEx. 29:7; 40:15; 1 Sam. 16:1, 12, 13; Is. 61:1-3; Dan. 9:24-26 ᵇZech. 3:1-7 ᶜMic. 4:13

★ 1-4
1 ᵃJer. 36:2; Ezek. 2:9; Rev. 5:1

2 ᵃZech. 4:2

4:2 Seven pipes to each of the seven lamps; i.e., 49 conduits in all.

4:6-7 Just as Joshua, the religious leader, was cleansed in the preceding vision, now Zerubbabel, the civil leader, is encouraged by this vision. The Temple would be finished by the power of the Holy Spirit; every *mountain* (obstacle) would be removed. When the *top stone* was put in place, the people would beseech God for grace upon the Temple.

4:10 *the day of small things.* A reference to the unfavorable comparison some were making between Solomon's glorious Temple and Zerubbabel's smaller structure (cf. Ezra 3:12-13; Hag. 2:3).

4:12 *two olive branches.* Better, clusters. On each olive tree (v. 11) was a bunch or cluster of olives. Also, on the sides of the golden bowl on top of the lampstand (v. 2) were *two golden*

pipes (v. 12) turned upward, into which the two clusters of olives poured their oil (a symbol of the Holy Spirit's power, v. 6), which then flowed into the bowls and through the 49 pipes to the seven lamps.

4:14 *the two anointed ones.* Lit., the two sons of oil, namely, Joshua and Zerubbabel. The point of the vision is that of light bearing or witness. Israel is God's witness; Joshua and Zerubbabel witnessed to His power in seeing to the completion of the Temple; and in the Tribulation days two mighty witnesses will yet arise (Rev. 11:4). All true witness must be done in the power of the Spirit.

5:1-4 The large flying *scroll,* unrolled because it was able to be measured (30 feet by 15 feet, a cubit being 18 inches), symbolized God's judgment against sinners.

twenty cubits and its width ten cubits."

3 Then he said to me, "This is the ^acurse that is going forth over the face of the whole land; surely everyone who ^bsteals will be purged away according to the writing on one side, and everyone who ^cswears will be purged away according to the writing on the other side.

4 "I will ^amake it go forth," declares the LORD of hosts, "and it will ^benter the house of the ^cthief and the house of the one who swears falsely by My name; and it will spend the night within that house and ^dconsume it with its timber and stones."

G The Vision of the Woman in the Ephah, 5:5-11

5 Then ^athe angel who was speaking with me went out, and said to me, "Lift up now your eyes, and see what this is, going forth."

6 And I said, "What is it?" And he said, "This is the ^aephah going forth." Again he said, "This is their appearance in all the land

7 (and behold, a lead cover was lifted up); and this is a woman sitting inside the ephah."

8 Then he said, "This is ^aWickedness!" And he threw her down into the middle of the ephah and cast the lead weight on its opening.

9 Then I lifted up my eyes and looked, and there two women were coming out with the wind in their wings; and they had wings like the wings of a ^astork, and they lifted up the ephah between the earth and the heavens.

10 And I said to the angel who was speaking with me, "Where are they taking the ephah?"

11 Then he said to me, "To build a temple for her in the land of ^aShinar; and when it is prepared, she will be set there on her own pedestal."

H The Vision of the Four Chariots, 6:1-8

6 Now I lifted up my eyes again and looked, and behold, ^afour chariots were coming forth from between the two mountains; and the mountains *were* bronze mountains.

2 With the first chariot *were* ^ared horses, with the second chariot ^bblack horses,

3 with the third chariot ^awhite horses, and with the fourth chariot strong ^bdappled horses.

4 Then I spoke and said to the angel who was speaking with me, "^aWhat are these, my lord?"

5 And the angel answered and said to me, "These are the ^afour spirits of heaven, going forth after standing before the Lord of all the earth,

6 with one of which the black horses are going forth to the ^anorth country; and the white ones go forth after them, while the dappled ones go forth to the ^bsouth country.

7 "When the strong ones went out, they were eager to go to ^apatrol the earth." And He said, "Go, patrol the earth." So they patrolled the earth.

Marginal references:

★ **3** ^aIs. 24:6; 43:28; Jer. 26:6
^bEx. 20:15; Lev. 19:11; Mal. 3:8, 9
^cLev. 19:12; Is. 48:1; Jer. 5:2; Zech. 5:4

★ **4** ^aMal. 3:5 ^bHos. 4:2, 3 ^cJer. 2:26 ^dLev. 14:34, 35; Job 18:15

★ **5-11**

5 ^aZech. 1:9

6 ^aLev. 19:36; Amos 8:5

8 ^aHos. 12:7; Amos 8:5; Mic. 6:11

9 ^aLev. 11:13, 19; Ps. 104:17; Jer. 8:7

11 ^aGen. 10:10; 11:2; 14:1; Is. 11:11; Dan. 1:2

★ **1-8**

1 ^aDan. 7:3; 8:22; Zech. 1:18; 6:5

2 ^aZech. 1:8; Rev. 6:4 ^bRev. 6:5

3 ^aRev. 6:2 ^bRev. 6:8

4 ^aZech. 1:9

5 ^aJer. 49:36; Ezek. 37:9; Dan. 7:2; 11:4; Matt. 24:31; Rev. 7:1

6 ^aJer. 1:14, 15; 4:6; 6:1; 25:9; 46:10; Ezek. 1:4 ^bIs. 43:6; Dan. 11:5

7 ^aZech. 1:10

5:3 God's law, written on each side of the scroll, judged specific sins.
5:4 *it.* I.e., the curse (for violating the law).
5:5-11 In this vision a woman sitting in an ephah (like a barrel, larger than a bushel) with a *lead cover* represents *wickedness*. She is banished appropriately to *Shinar* (Babylon; cf. Gen. 11:2; Rev. 17:3-5).

6:1-8 A vision of God's judgment on the nations of the world, especially focusing on Babylon (*the land of the north*, v. 8) which revolted 3 years later and was devastated and depopulated by the Persians (cf. 2:6-7). The vision may also depict the final subjugation of the world, especially "Babylon," during the Tribulation days (cf. Rev. 11:15; 18:21).

8 a Ezek. 5:13; 24:13; Zech. 1:15

8 Then He cried out to me and spoke to me saying, "See, those who are going to the land of the north have ªappeased My wrath in the land of the north."

I The Crowning of Joshua, 6:9-15

9 a Zech. 1:1; 7:1; 8:1

9 The ªword of the LORD also came to me saying,

★**10** a Ezra 7:14-16; 8:26-30; Jer. 28:6

10 "ªTake an offering from the exiles, from Heldai, Tobijah, and Jedaiah; and you go the same day and enter the house of Josiah the son of Zephaniah, where they have arrived from Babylon.

★**11** a 2 Sam. 12:30; Ps. 21:3; Song 3:11 b Ezra 3:2; Hag. 1:1; Zech. 3:1

11 "And take silver and gold, make an ornate ªcrown, and set it on the head of bJoshua the son of Jehozadak, the high priest.

★**12-13** **12** a Is. 4:2; 11:1; Jer. 23:5; 33:15; Zech. 3:8 b Is. 53:2 c Ezra 3:8, 10; Amos 9:11; Zech. 4:6-9

12 "Then say to him, 'Thus says the LORD of hosts, "Behold, a man whose name is ªBranch, for He will bbranch out from where He is; and He will cbuild the temple of the LORD.

13 a Is. 9:6; 11:10; 22:24; 49:5, 6 b Is. 9:7 c Ps. 110:1, 4

13 "Yes, it is He who will build the temple of the LORD, and He who will ªbear the honor and sit and brule on His throne. Thus, He will be a cpriest on His throne, and the counsel of peace will be between the two offices." '

14 a Zech. 6:11

14 "Now the ªcrown will become a reminder in the temple of the LORD to Helem, Tobijah, Jedaiah, and Hen the son of Zephaniah.

★**15** a Is. 56:6-8; 60:10 b Zech. 2:9-11; 4:9 c Is. 58:10-14; Jer. 7:23; Zech. 3:7

15 "And ªthose who are far off will come and build the temple of the LORD." Then you will bknow that the LORD of hosts has sent me to you. And it will take place, if you completely cobey the LORD your God.

III THE QUESTIONS CONCERNING FASTS, 7:1-8:23

A The Fasts, 7:1-3

★**1** a Neh. 1:1

7 Then it came about in the fourth year of King Darius, that the word of the LORD came to Zechariah on the fourth day of the ninth month, which is ªChislev.

★**2** a 1 Kin. 13:6; Jer. 26:19; Zech. 8:21

2 Now the town of Bethel had sent Sharezer and Regemmelech and their men to ªseek the favor of the LORD,

★**3** a Ezra 3:10-12 b Zech. 8:19

3 speaking to the ªpriests who belong to the house of the LORD of hosts, and to the prophets saying, "Shall I weep in the bfifth month and abstain, as I have done these many years?"

B The Failure of the People, 7:4-14

4 Then the word of the LORD of hosts came to me saying,

★**5-7** **5** a Zech. 1:12 b Is. 1:11, 12; 58:5

5 "Say to all the people of the land and to the priests, 'When you fasted and mourned in the fifth and seventh months these ªseventy years, was it actually for bMe that you fasted?

6:10 exiles. Jews whose residence continued to be in Babylon, but who had come to Jerusalem on a visit to bring an offering for the building of the Temple.
6:11 an ornate crown. A composite crown made up of several circles. The crown was placed on Joshua; no crown was placed on Zerubbabel.
6:12-13 The crowning of Joshua foreshadowed the crowning of Messiah, who at His second coming will build the (millennial) temple and unite the offices of King and Priest in one Person.
6:15 In the Millennium Gentiles will join in building that Temple (Hag. 2:7).
7:1 fourth year. 518 B.C.
7:2 The people of the town of Bethel sent this delegation to Jerusalem to worship and ask

about the national fasts.
7:3 The question was: since the Temple was being rebuilt, was it now necessary to keep the fast in the fifth month, which commemorated the burning of the first Temple by Nebuchadnezzar in 586 (Jer. 52:12-13)?
7:5-7 The fast in the seventh month commemorated the assassination of Gedaliah, the Jewish governor of Judah (2 Kings 25:23-25). Though done from good motives, these fasts were nevertheless man-made, were not commanded by God, and were observed self-righteously (v. 6). Had the people heeded God's word through the prophets, they would not have experienced captivity and would have had no need for the fasts (v. 7).

6 'And when you eat and drink, do you not eat for yourselves and do you not drink for yourselves?

7 'Are not *these* the words which the LORD ^aproclaimed by the former prophets, when Jerusalem was inhabited and ^bprosperous with its cities around it, and the ^cNegev and the foothills were inhabited?' "

8 Then the word of the LORD came to Zechariah saying,

9 "Thus has the LORD of hosts said, '^aDispense true justice, and practice ^bkindness and compassion each to his brother;

10 and ^ado not oppress the widow or the orphan, the stranger or the poor; and do ^bnot devise evil in your hearts against one another.'

11 "But they ^arefused to pay attention, and ^bturned a stubborn shoulder and ^cstopped their ears from hearing.

12 "And they made their ^ahearts like ^bflint so that they could not hear the law and the ^cwords which the LORD of hosts had sent by His Spirit through the ^dformer prophets; therefore great ^ewrath came from the LORD of hosts.

13 "And it came about that just as ^aHe called and they would not listen, so ^bthey called and I would not listen," says the LORD of hosts;

14 "but I ^ascattered them with a ^bstorm wind among all the nations whom they have not known. Thus the land is ^cdesolated behind them, so that ^dno one went back and forth, for they ^emade the pleasant land desolate."

C The Future for Jerusalem, 8:1-23

8 Then the word of the LORD of hosts came saying,

2 "Thus says the LORD of hosts, 'I am ^aexceedingly jealous for Zion, yes, with great wrath I am jealous for her.'

3 "Thus says the LORD, 'I will return to Zion and will ^adwell in the midst of Jerusalem. Then Jerusalem will be called the City of ^bTruth, and the mountain of the LORD of hosts *will be called* the Holy Mountain.'

4 "Thus says the LORD of hosts, '^aOld men and old women will again sit in the streets of Jerusalem, each man with his staff in his hand because of age.

5 'And the streets of the city will be filled with ^aboys and girls playing in its streets.'

6 "Thus says the LORD of hosts, 'If it is ^atoo difficult in the sight of the remnant of this people in those days, will it also be ^btoo difficult in My sight?' declares the LORD of hosts.

7 "Thus says the LORD of hosts, 'Behold, I am going to save My people from the land of the ^aeast and from the land of the west;

8 and I will ^abring them *back*, and they will ^blive in the midst of Jerusalem, and they will be ^cMy people and I will be their God in truth and in righteousness.'

9 "Thus says the LORD of hosts, 'Let your hands be ^astrong, you who are listening in these days to these words from the mouth of the ^bprophets, *those* who *spoke* in the day that the foundation of the house of the LORD of hosts was laid, to the end that the temple might be built.

10 'For before those days there was ^ano wage for man or any wage for animal; and for him who went out or came in there was no ^bpeace because of his enemies, and I ^cset all men one against another.

11 'But now I will ^anot treat the remnant of this people as in

Marginal references

7 ^aIs. 1:16-20; Jer. 7:5, 23; Zech. 1:4 ^bJer. 22:21 ^cJer. 13:19; 32:44

9 ^aEzek. 18:8; 45:9; Zech. 8:16 ^b2 Sam. 9:7; Job 6:14; Mic. 6:8

10 ^aEx. 22:22; Ps. 72:4; Jer. 7:6 ^bPs. 21:11; Mic. 2:1; Zech. 8:17

11 ^aJer. 5:3; 8:5; 11:10 ^bJer. 7:26; 17:23 ^cPs. 58:4; Jer. 5:21

★12 ^a2 Chr. 36:13; Ezek. 2:4; 3:7-9 ^bJer. 17:1; Ezek. 3:9 ^cZech. 7:7 ^dNeh. 9:30 ^e2 Chr. 36:16; Dan. 9:11, 12

13 ^aJer. 11:10, 14; 14:12 ^bProv. 1:24-28; Is. 1:15

14 ^aDeut. 4:27; 28:64 ^bJer. 23:19 ^cJer. 44:6 ^dIs. 60:15 ^eJer. 12:10

★ 1-8

2 ^aZech. 1:14

3 ^aZech. 2:10, 11 ^bZech. 8:16, 19

4 ^aIs. 65:20

5 ^aJer. 30:19, 20; 31:12, 13

6 ^aPs. 118:23; 126:1-3 ^bJer. 32:17, 27

7 ^aPs. 107:3; Is. 11:11; 27:12, 13; 43:5

8 ^aZeph. 3:20; Zech. 10:10 ^bJer. 3:17; Ezek. 37:25 ^cEzek. 11:20; 36:28; Zech. 2:11

9 ^a1 Chr. 22:13; Is. 35:4; Hag. 2:4 ^bEzra 5:1; 6:14

10 ^aHag. 2:15-19 ^b2 Chr. 15:5 ^cIs. 19:2; Amos 3:6; 9:4

11 ^aPs. 103:9; Is. 12:1; Hag. 2:19

7:12 *like flint.* A very hard stone.
8:1-8 Some features of this glorious picture of Jerusalem were evident in the Maccabean times (2nd century B.C.), but the complete ful-

fillment awaits the establishment of the millennial kingdom. Jerusalem will be secure (vv. 4-5) and the people will be regathered from all parts of the world (v. 8).

the former days,' declares the LORD of hosts.

12 'For *there will be* [a]peace for the seed: the vine will yield its fruit, the land will yield its produce, and the heavens will give their [b]dew; and I will cause the remnant of this people to inherit [c]all these *things*.

13 'And it will come about that just as you were a [a]curse among the nations, O house of Judah and house of Israel, so I will save you that you may become a [b]blessing. Do not fear; let your [c]hands be strong.'

14 "For thus says the LORD of hosts, 'Just as I [a]purposed to do harm to you when your fathers provoked Me to wrath,' says the LORD of hosts, 'and I have not [b]relented,

15 so I have again purposed in these days to [a]do good to Jerusalem and to the house of Judah. [b]Do not fear!

16 'These are the things which you should do: speak the [a]truth to one another; [b]judge with truth and judgment for peace in your gates.

17 'Also let none of you [a]devise evil in your heart against another, and do not love [b]perjury; for all these are what I [c]hate,' declares the LORD."

18 Then the word of the LORD of hosts came to me saying,

19 "Thus says the LORD of hosts, 'The fast of the [a]fourth, the fast of the [b]fifth, the fast of the [c]seventh, and the fast of the [d]tenth *months* will become [e]joy, gladness, and cheerful feasts for

the house of Judah; so [f]love truth and peace.'

20 "Thus says the LORD of hosts, 'It will yet *be* that [a]peoples will come, even the inhabitants of many cities.

21 And the inhabitants of one will go to another saying, "Let us go at once to [a]entreat the favor of the LORD, and to seek the LORD of hosts; I will also go."

22 'So [a]many peoples and mighty nations will come to seek the LORD of hosts in Jerusalem and to [b]entreat the favor of the LORD.'

23 "Thus says the LORD of hosts, 'In those days ten men from all the nations will [a]grasp the garment of a Jew saying, "Let us go with you, for we have heard that God is with you." ' "

IV THE BURDENS CONCERNING THE FUTURE, 9:1–14:21

A The First Burden, 9:1–11:17

1 The victories of Alexander the Great, 9:1–8

9 The burden of the word of the LORD is against the land of Hadrach, with [a]Damascus as its resting place (for the eyes of men, especially of all the tribes of Israel, are toward the LORD),

2 And [a]Hamath also, which borders on it; [b]Tyre and [c]Sidon, though they are [b]very wise.

3 For Tyre built herself a [a]fortress And [b]piled up silver like dust,

---

Margin references (left column):

12 [a]Lev. 26:3-6 [b]Gen. 27:28; Deut. 33:13, 28; Hos. 13:3 [c]Is. 61:7; Obad. 17

13 [a]Jer. 29:18; Dan. 9:11 [b]Ps. 72:17; Is. 19:24, 25; Ezek. 34:26; Zech. 14:11 [c]Zech. 8:9

14 [a]Jer. 31:28 [b]Jer. 4:28; Ezek. 24:14

15 [a]Jer. 29:11; Mic. 7:18-20 [b]Zech. 8:13

16 [a]Ps. 15:2; Prov. 12:17-19; Zech. 8:3; Eph. 4:25 [b]Is. 9:7; 11:4, 5; Zech. 7:9

17 [a]Prov. 3:29; Jer. 4:14; Zech. 7:10 [b]Zech. 5:4; Mal. 3:5 [c]Prov. 6:16-19; Hab. 1:13

★19 [a]2 Kin. 25:3, 4; Jer. 39:2 [b]Zech. 7:3, 5 [c]2 Kin. 25:25; Zech. 7:5 [d]Ps. 52:4 [e]Ps. 30:11; Is. 12:1 [f]Zech. 8:16; Luke 1:74, 75

Margin references (right column):

20 [a]Ps. 117:1; Jer. 16:19; Mic. 4:2, 3; Zech. 2:11; 14:16

21 [a]Zech. 7:2

22 [a]Is. 2:2, 3; 25:7; 49:6, 22, 23; 60:3-12 [b]Zech. 8:21

★23 [a]Is. 45:14, 24; 60:14

★ 1-8

★ 1 [a]Is. 17:1; Jer. 49:23-27; Amos 1:3-5

2 [a]Jer. 49:23 [b]Ezek. 28:2-5, 12 [c]Ezek. 28:21

3 [a]Josh. 19:29; 2 Sam. 24:7 [b]Job 27:16; Ezek. 27:33; 28:4, 5 [c]1 Kin. 10:21, 27

8:19 *The fast of the fourth.* Commemorated Nebuchadnezzar's entering Jerusalem in 586 (2 Kings 25:3-4). *the fast of the tenth.* The beginning of the siege of Jerusalem in 588 (2 Kings 25:1). All these fasts (see 7:3 and 7:5-7) will be turned into feast days when Israel is restored. On fasting, see notes on Matt. 9:14 and Acts 27:9.

8:23 Gentiles, too, will seek the blessings and knowledge of God in the Millennium.

9:1-8 *the land of Hadrach.* Hattarika, near Hamath. *its resting place.* I.e., of the prophecy. The section sketches the march of Alexander

the Great through Syria (Aram; vv. 1-2a), then Phoenicia (vv. 2b-4), and finally Philistia (vv. 5-8). But Jerusalem would be spared (*I will camp around My house,* v. 8).

9:1 Some hold that chapters 9-14 are not to be ascribed to Zechariah. However, many similarities exist between chapters 1-8 and 9-14, and difference of style is never a conclusive argument for different authorship. The reference to Greece as a future dominant power (9:13) is no problem if one accepts the validity of predictive prophecy.

And ^cgold like the mire
of the streets.

4 ^aEzek.
26:3-5
^bEzek. 28:18

4 Behold, the Lord will
^adispossess her
And cast her wealth into
the sea;
And she will be ^bcon-
sumed with fire.

5 Ashkelon will see it and
be afraid.
Gaza too will writhe in
great pain;
Also Ekron, for her ex-
pectation has been
confounded.
Moreover, the king will
perish from Gaza,
And Ashkelon will not
be inhabited.

6 ^aAmos
1:8; Zeph.
2:4

6 And a mongrel race will
dwell in ^aAshdod,
And I will cut off the
pride of the Philis-
tines.

7 And I will remove their
blood from their
mouth,
And their detestable
things from between
their teeth.
Then they also will be a
remnant for our God,
And be like a clan in Ju-
dah,
And Ekron like a Jebu-
site.

8 ^aIs. 52:1
^bIs. 54:14;
60:18

8 But I will camp around
My house because of
an army,
Because of ^ahim who
passes by and returns;
And ^bno oppressor will
pass over them any-
more,
For now I have seen
with My eyes.

2 The comings of the King,
9:9-10

9 ^aRejoice greatly, O
daughter of Zion!
Shout in triumph, O
daughter of Jerusa-
lem!
Behold, your ^bking is
coming to you;
He is ^cjust and ^den-
dowed with salvation,
^eHumble, and mounted
on a donkey,
Even on a ^fcolt, the foal
of a donkey.

10 And I will ^acut off the
chariot from Ephraim,
And the ^bhorse from Jerusalem;
And the ^cbow of war
will be cut off.
And He will speak
^dpeace to the nations;
And His ^edominion will
be from sea to sea,
And from the River to
the ends of the earth.

3 The victories of the
Maccabees, 9:11-17

11 As for you also, because
of the ^ablood of My
covenant with you,
I have set your ^bprison-
ers free from the wa-
terless pit.

12 Return to the ^astrong-
hold, O prisoners who
have the ^bhope;
This very day I am de-
claring that I will re-
store ^cdouble to you.

13 For I will ^abend Judah as
My bow,

★ 9 ^aZeph.
3:14, 15;
Zech. 2:10
^bPs. 110:1;
Is. 9:6, 7;
Jer. 23:5, 6;
Matt. 21:5;
John 12:15
^cZeph. 3:5
^dIs. 43:3, 11
^eIs. 57:15
^fJudg. 10:4;
Is. 30:6

★10 ^aHos.
1:7 ^bMic.
5:10 ^cHos.
2:18 ^dIs.
57:19; Mic.
4:2-4 ^ePs.
72:8; Is.
60:12

★11-12

11 ^aEx. 24:8;
Heb. 10:2
^bIs. 24:22;
51:14

12 ^aJer.
16:19; Joel
3:16 ^bJer.
14:8; 17:13;
Heb. 6:18,
19 ^cIs. 61:7

★13-17
13 ^aJer.
51:20 ^bJoel
3:6 ^cPs. 45:3

9:9 This great prophecy was fulfilled completely at the first advent of Jesus Christ (Matt. 21:4-5). In sharp contrast to Alexander, Messiah is just, brings salvation, and is humble. the foal of a donkey. Lit., the son of a she-ass.
9:10 The fulfillment of this prophecy of universal peace awaits the second advent of Christ.

9:11-12 Restoration and blessing for those still in Babylon is promised. waterless pit. Cisterns used as dungeons.
9:13-17 These verses predict the defeat of Greece (particularly of Antiochus Epiphanes) by the Jewish people during the Maccabean era (2nd century B.C.).

I will fill the bow with E-
phraim.
And I will stir up your
sons, O Zion, against
your sons, O [b]Greece;
And I will make you like
a [c]warrior's sword.

14 Then the LORD will ap-
pear [a]over them,
And His [b]arrow will go
forth like lightning,
And the Lord GOD will
blow the [c]trumpet,
And will march in the
[d]storm winds of the
south.

15 [a]The LORD of hosts will
defend them.
And they will [b]devour,
and trample on the
[c]sling stones;
And they will drink, and
be [d]boisterous as with
wine;
And they will be filled
like a sacrificial basin,
Drenched like the [e]cor-
ners of the altar.

16 And the LORD their God
will [a]save them in that
day
As the flock of His peo-
ple;
For they are as the
stones of a [b]crown,
Sparkling in His land.

17 For what [a]comeliness
and [b]beauty will be
theirs!
Grain will make the
young men flourish,
and new wine the vir-
gins.

4 The blessings from Messiah,
10:1–12

10 Ask [a]rain from the LORD at
the time of the spring
rain—
The LORD who [b]makes
the storm clouds;

And He will give them
[c]showers of rain,
vegetation in the field
to each man.

2 For the [a]teraphim speak
iniquity,
And the [b]diviners see
lying visions,
And tell [c]false dreams;
They comfort in vain.
Therefore the people
wander like [d]sheep,
They are afflicted, be-
cause there is no
shepherd.

3 "My [a]anger is kindled
against the shepherds,
And I will punish the
male goats;
For the LORD of hosts has
[b]visited His flock, the
house of Judah,
And will make them like
His majestic horse in
battle.

4 "From them will come
the [a]cornerstone,
From them the tent peg,
From them the bow of
[b]battle,
From them every ruler,
all of them together.

5 "And they will be as
mighty men,
[a]Treading down the
enemy in the mire of
the streets in battle;
And they will fight, for
the LORD will be with
them;
And the [b]riders on
horses will be put to
shame.

6 "And I shall [a]strengthen
the house of Judah,
And I shall [b]save the
house of Joseph,
And I shall [c]bring them
back,
Because I have had
[d]compassion on them;

Cross references (left column):
14 [a]Is. 31:5;
Zech. 2:5
[b]Ps. 18:14;
Hab. 3:11
[c]Is. 27:13
[d]Is. 21:1;
66:15

15 [a]Is.
37:35; Zech.
12:8 [b]Zech.
12:6 [c]Job
41:28 [d]Ps.
78:65 [e]Ex.
27:2

16 [a]Jer.
31:10, 11
[b]Is. 62:3

17 [a]Jer.
31:12, 14
[b]Ps. 27:4; Is.
33:17

1 [a]Joel
2:23 [b]Jer.
10:13 [c]Is.
30:23

Cross references (right column):
★ 2 [a]Ezek.
21:21; Hos.
3:4 [b]Jer.
27:9 [c]Jer.
23:32 [d]Ezek.
34:5, 8; Matt.
9:36; Mark
6:34

★ 3 [a]Jer.
25:34-36
[b]Ezek. 34:12

★ 4 [a]Luke
20:17; Eph.
2:20; 1 Pet.
2:6 [b]Jer.
51:20; Zech.
9:10

5 [a]2 Sam.
22:43 [b]Amos
2:15; Hag.
2:22

6 [a]Zech.
10:12
[b]Zech. 8:7;
9:16 [c]Zech.
8:8 [d]Is. 54:8;
Zech. 1:16
[e]Is. 54:4
[f]Zech. 13:9

10:2 *teraphim.* Household gods frequently associated with divination (cf. Gen. 31:19; 2 Kings
23:24; Ezek. 21:21).
10:3 *shepherds . . . goats.* Foreign overlords who
would be destroyed (v. 11).

10:4 *From them.* I.e., from Judah. Messiah is
designated as the *cornerstone,* the *tent peg,*
the *bow of battle,* and the *ruler* (suppressor of
the wicked).

And they will be as
though I had *not re-
jected them,
For I am the LORD their
God, and I will *an-
swer them.

7 "And Ephraim will be
like a mighty man,
And their heart will be
glad as if *from* wine;
Indeed, their *children
will see *it* and be glad,
Their heart will rejoice
in the LORD.

8 "I will *whistle for them
to gather them to-
gether,
For I have redeemed
them;
And they will be as *nu-
merous as they *were
before.

9 "When I scatter them
among the peoples,
They will *remember
Me in far countries,
And they with their chil-
dren will live and
come back.

10 "I will *bring them back
from the land of
Egypt,
And gather them from
Assyria;
And I will bring them
into the land of *Gile-
ad and Lebanon,
Until *no *room* can be
found for them.

11 "And He will pass
through the *sea *of*
distress,
And strike the waves in
the sea,
So that all the depths of
the *Nile will dry up;
And the pride of *Assyr-
ia will be brought
down,
And the scepter of *E-
gypt will depart.

12 "And I shall *strengthen
them in the LORD,

And in His name *they
will walk," declares
the LORD.

5 The rejection of the Shepherd, 11:1-17

11 Open your doors, O Lebanon,
That a *fire may feed on
your *cedars.

2 Wail, O cypress, for the
cedar has fallen,
Because the glorious
trees have been de-
stroyed;
Wail, O oaks of Bashan,
For the impenetrable
forest has come down.

3 There is a sound of the
shepherds' *wail,
For their glory is ruined;
There is a *sound of the
young lions' roar,
For the pride of the Jor-
dan is ruined.

4 Thus says the LORD my
God, "Pasture the flock *doomed*
to *slaughter.

5 "Those who buy them slay
them and go *unpunished, and
each of those who sell them says,
'Blessed be the LORD, for *I have
become rich!' And their *own
shepherds have no pity on them.

6 "For I shall *no longer have
pity on the inhabitants of the
land," declares the LORD; "but behold, I shall *cause the men to
fall, each into another's power
and into the power of his king;
and they will strike the land, and I
shall *not deliver *them* from their
power."

7 So I *pastured the flock
doomed to slaughter, hence the
*afflicted of the flock. And I took
for myself two *staffs: the one I
called *Favor, and the other I
called *Union; so I pastured the
flock.

8 Then I annihilated the
three shepherds in *one month,

Marginal references (left column):

7 *Is. 54:13; Ezek. 37:25

8 *Is. 5:26; 7:18, 19 *Jer. 33:22; Rev. 7:9 *Jer. 30:20; Ezek. 36:11

9 *1 Kin. 8:47, 48; Ezek. 6:9

10 *Is. 11:11 *Jer. 50:19 *Is. 49:19, 20

11 *Is. 51:9, 10 *Is. 19:5-7 *Zeph. 2:13 *Ezek. 30:13

12 *Zech. 10:6 *Mic. 4:5

Marginal references (right column):

★ 1-3

1 *Jer. 22:6, 7 *Ezek. 31:3

3 *Jer. 25:34-36 *Jer. 2:15; 50:44

4 *Ps. 44:22; Zech. 11:7

5 *Jer. 50:7 *Hos. 12:8; 1 Tim. 6:9 *Ezek. 34:2, 3

6 *Jer. 13:14 *Is. 9:19-21; Mic. 7:2-6; Zech. 14:13 *Ps. 50:22; Mic. 5:8

★ 7 *Zech. 11:4 *Jer. 39:10; Zeph. 3:12 *Ezek. 37:16 *Ps. 27:4; 90:17; Zech. 11:10 *Ps. 133:1; Ezek. 37:16-23; Zech. 11:14

8 *Hos. 5:7

11:1-3 A continuation of the mock lamentation over the fall of unidentified powers (*cedars . . . oaks*; cf. Isa. 2:13) who attack Israel.
11:7 The two staffs symbolized the good inten-

tions of Zechariah acting the part of a good shepherd; i.e., in bringing *Favor* and *Union* to Israel and Judah.

for my soul was impatient with them, and their soul also was weary of me.

9 Then I said, "I will not pasture you. What is to [a]die, let it die, and what is to be annihilated, let it be annihilated; and let those who are left eat one another's flesh."

10 And I took my staff, [a]Favor, and cut it in pieces, to [b]break my covenant which I had made with all the peoples.

11 So it was broken on that day, and thus the [a]afflicted of the flock who were watching me realized that it was the word of the Lord.

12 And I said to them, "If it is good in your sight, give *me* my [a]wages; but if not, never mind!" So they weighed out [b]thirty *shekels* of silver as my wages.

13 Then the Lord said to me, "Throw it to the [a]potter, *that* magnificent price at which I was valued by them." So I took the thirty *shekels* of silver and threw them to the potter in the house of the Lord.

14 Then I cut my second staff, [a]Union, in pieces, to [b]break the brotherhood between Judah and Israel.

15 And the Lord said to me, "Take again for yourself the equipment of a [a]foolish shepherd.

16 "For behold, I am going to raise up a shepherd in the land who will [a]not care for the perishing, seek the scattered, heal the broken, or sustain the one standing, but will [b]devour the flesh of the fat *sheep* and tear off their hoofs.

17 "[a]Woe to the worthless shepherd
Who leaves the flock!
A [b]sword will be on his arm

And on his right eye!
His [c]arm will be totally withered,
And his right eye will be blind."

B The Second Burden, 12:1–14:21

1 *The Lord's care for Jerusalem,* 12:1–14

12 The burden of the word of the Lord concerning Israel. *Thus* declares the Lord who [a]stretches out the heavens, [b]lays the foundation of the earth, and [c]forms the spirit of man within him,

2 "Behold, I am going to make Jerusalem a [a]cup that causes reeling to all the peoples around; and when the siege is against Jerusalem, it will also be against [b]Judah.

3 "And it will come about in that day that I will make Jerusalem a heavy [a]stone for all the peoples; all who lift it will be [b]severely injured. And all the [c]nations of the earth will be gathered against it.

4 "In that day," declares the Lord, "I will strike every horse with bewilderment, and his rider with madness. But I will watch over the house of Judah, while I strike every horse of the peoples with blindness.

5 "Then the clans of Judah will say in their hearts, 'A strong support for us are the inhabitants of Jerusalem through the Lord of hosts, their God.'

6 "In that day I will make the clans of Judah like a [a]firepot among pieces of wood and a flaming torch among sheaves, so they will consume on the right hand and on the left all the surrounding peoples, while the [b]inhabi-

---

Cross references (left column margin):

9 [a]Jer. 15:2

10 [a]Zech. 11:7 [b]Ps. 89:39; Jer. 14:21

11 [a]Zeph. 3:12

★12 [a]1 Kin. 5:6; Mal. 3:5 [b]Gen. 37:28; Ex. 21:32; Matt. 26:15; 27:9, 10

13 [a]Matt. 27:3-10; Acts 1:18, 19

14 [a]Zech. 11:7 [b]Is. 9:21; Zech. 11:6

15 [a]Is. 6:10-12; Zech. 11:17

16 [a]Jer. 23:2 [b]Ezek. 34:2-6

17 [a]Jer. 23:1; Zech. 10:2; 11:15 [b]Jer. 50:35-37 [c]Ezek. 30:21, 22

Cross references (right column margin):

1 [a]Is. 42:5; 44:24; Jer. 51:15 [b]Job 26:7; Ps. 102:25, 26; Heb. 1:10-12 [c]Is. 57:16; Heb. 12:9

2 [a]Ps. 75:8; Is. 51:22, 23 [b]Zech. 14:14

★ 3 [a]Dan. 2:34, 35, 44, 45 [b]Matt. 21:44 [c]Zech. 14:2

★ 4

★ 6 [a]Is. 10:17, 18; Obad. 18; Zech. 11:1 [b]Zech. 2:4; 8:3-5

11:12 Because the people rejected the good shepherd's ministry, he asked as his wages only the price of a slave (cf. Exod. 21:32; Matt. 27:3-7). Zechariah was acting the role of the coming Messiah.

12:3 This prophecy will be fulfilled during the campaign of Armageddon.

12:4 *bewilderment.* Supernatural confusion and panic will overtake the armies attacking Jerusalem.

12:6 The *clans* (chiefs, leaders) of Judah will be like a *firepot* on which their enemies are consumed.

tants of Jerusalem again dwell on their own sites in Jerusalem.

7 "The LORD also will [a]save the tents of Judah first in order that the glory of the house of [b]David and the glory of the inhabitants of Jerusalem may not be magnified above Judah.

8 "In that day the LORD will [a]defend the inhabitants of Jerusalem, and the one who [b]is feeble among them in that day will be like David, and the house of David *will be* like [c]God, like the [d]angel of the LORD before them.

9 "And it will come about in that day that I will [a]set about to destroy all the nations that come against Jerusalem.

10 "And I will [a]pour out on the house of David and on the inhabitants of Jerusalem, the Spirit of grace and of supplication, so that they will look on Me whom they have [b]pierced; and they will mourn for Him, as one [c]mourns for an only son, and they will weep bitterly over Him, like the bitter weeping over a first-born.

11 "In that day there will be great [a]mourning in Jerusalem, like the mourning of Hadadrimmon in the plain of Megiddo.

12 "And the land will mourn, every family by itself; the family of the house of David by itself, and their wives by themselves; the family of the house of Nathan by itself, and their wives by themselves;

13 the family of the house of Levi by itself, and their wives by themselves; the family of the

Shimeites by itself, and their wives by themselves;

14 all the families that remain, every family by itself, and their wives by themselves.

2 The Lord's cleansing of Jerusalem, 13:1-9

13 "In that day a [a]fountain will be opened for the house of David and for the inhabitants of Jerusalem, for [b]sin and for [c]impurity.

2 "And it will come about in that day," declares the LORD of hosts, "that I will [a]cut off the names of the idols from the land, and they will no longer be remembered; and I will also remove the [b]prophets and the [c]unclean spirit from the land.

3 "And it will come about that if anyone still [a]prophesies, then his father and mother who gave birth to him will say to him, 'You shall [b]not live, for you have spoken [c]falsely in the name of the LORD'; and his [d]father and mother who gave birth to him will pierce him through when he prophesies.

4 "Also it will come about in that day that the prophets will each be [a]ashamed of his vision when he prophesies, and they will not put on a [b]hairy robe in order to deceive;

5 but he will say, 'I am [a]not a prophet; I am a tiller of the ground, for a man sold me as a slave in my youth.'

6 "And one will say to him, 'What are these wounds [a]between your arms?' Then he will

Cross references (margin)

7 [a]Jer. 30:18 [b]Amos 9:11

8 [a]Joel 3:16; Zech. 9:14, 15 [b]Lev. 26:8; Josh. 23:10; Mic. 7:8 [c]Ps. 8:5; 82:6 [d]Ex. 14:19; 33:2

9 [a]Zech. 14:2, 3

★10 [a]Is. 44:3; Ezek. 39:29; Joel 2:28, 29 [b]John 19:37; Rev. 1:7 [c]Jer. 6:26; Amos 8:10

★11 [a]Matt. 24:30; Rev. 1:7

★12-14

★ 1 [a]Jer. 2:13; 17:13 [b]Ps. 51:2, 7; Is. 1:16-18; John 1:29 [c]Num. 19:17; Is. 4:4; Ezek. 36:25

★ 2-6 2 [a]Ex. 23:13; Hos. 2:17 [b]Jer. 23:14, 15 [c]1 Kin. 22:22; Ezek. 36:25, 29

3 [a]Jer. 23:34 [b]Deut. 18:20; Ezek. 14:9 [c]Jer. 23:25 [d]Deut. 13:6-11; Matt. 10:37

4 [a]Jer. 6:15; 8:9; Mic. 3:7 [b]2 Kin. 1:8; Is. 20:2; Matt. 3:4

5 [a]Amos 7:14

6 [a]2 Kin. 9:24

12:10 At the second coming of Christ, Israel will recognize Jesus as her Messiah, acknowledging with deep contrition that He was the One whom their forefathers *pierced.*

12:11 The reference is to the slaying of good King Josiah by Pharaoh Neco (2 Kings 23:29).

12:12-14 All, both high and low, shall mourn individually when they see the rejected Messiah. *Nathan,* son of David, illustrates prominent families, while *Shimeites* represents all ordinary families (cf. Num. 3:18).

13:1 Cleansing from sin follows the mourning mentioned in the preceding chapter. *fountain.* Calvary, now opened for the salvation of all

living at the time of the return of Christ (Rom. 11:26-27).

13:2-6 All idolatry will be uprooted and all false prophesying will cease. In their zeal to obey the law of God, parents will put to death any child who is involved in false prophesying (v. 3; cf. Deut. 13:6-10). False prophets will not wear a *hairy robe* (v. 4), which true prophets often did (cf. 2 Kings 1:8; Matt. 3:4). Instead, they will pretend to be farmers (v. 5) and lie concerning *wounds* received in ecstatic frenzy (cf. 1 Kings 18:28), pretending they were received as part of parental punishment or from friendly fighting.

say, 'Those with which I was wounded in the house of my friends.'

★ 7 ªJer. 47:6; Ezek. 21:3-5 ᵇIs. 40:11; Ezek. 34:23, 24; 37:24; Mic. 5:2, 4 ᶜPs. 2:2; Jer. 23:5, 6 ᵈIs. 53:4, 5, 10; Matt. 26:31; Mark 14:27 ᵉIs. 1:25

7 "Awake, O ªsword,
    against My ᵇShep-
    herd,
And against the man,
    My ᶜAssociate,"
Declares the LORD of
    hosts.
"ᵈStrike the Shepherd
    that the sheep may be
    scattered;
And I will ᵉturn My
    hand against the little
    ones.

★ 8-9

8 ªIs. 6:13; Ezek. 5:2-4, 12

8 "And it will come about
    in all the land,"
Declares the LORD,
"That ªtwo parts in it will
    be cut off and perish;
But the third will be left
    in it.

9 ªIs. 48:10; Mal. 3:3 ᵇPs. 34:15-17; 50:15; Zech. 12:10 ᶜIs. 58:9; 65:24; Jer. 29:11-13, Zech. 10:6 ᵈHos. 2:23

9 "And I will bring the
    third part through the
    ªfire,
Refine them as silver is
    refined,
And test them as gold is
    tested.
They will ᵇcall on My
    name,
And I will ᶜanswer
    them;
I will say, 'They are ᵈMy
    people,'
And they will say, 'The
    LORD is my God.' "

3 The Lord's second coming to Jerusalem, 14:1-21

★ 1-5
1 ªIs. 13:6, 9; Joel 2:1; Mal. 4:1 ᵇZech. 14:14

14 Behold, a ªday is coming for the LORD when ᵇthe spoil taken from you will be divided among you.

2 aZech. 12:2, 3 bIs. 13:16

2 For I will ªgather all the nations against Jerusalem to battle, and the city will be captured, the ᵇhouses plundered, and the women ravished, and half of the city exiled, but the rest of the people will not be cut off from the city.

3 ªZech. 9:14, 15

3 Then the LORD will go forth and ªfight against those nations, as when He fights on a day of battle.

4 ªEzek. 11:23 bIs. 64:1, 2; Ezek. 47:1-10; Mic. 1:3, 4; Hab. 3:6; Zech. 4:7; 14:8

4 And in that day His feet will ªstand on the Mount of Olives, which is in front of Jerusalem on the east; and the Mount of Olives will be ᵇsplit in its middle from east to west by a very large valley, so that half of the mountain will move toward the north and the other half toward the south.

5 aIs. 29:6; Amos 1:1 bPs. 96:13; Is. 66:15, 16; Matt. 16:27; 25:31

5 And you will flee by the valley of My mountains, for the valley of the mountains will reach to Azel; yes, you will flee just as you fled before the ªearthquake in the days of Uzziah king of Judah. ᵇThen the LORD, my God, will come, and all the holy ones with Him!

★ 6 aIs. 13:10; Jer. 4:23; Ezek. 32:7, 8; Joel 2:30, 31; Acts 2:16, 19

6 And it will come about in that day that there will be ªno light; the luminaries will dwindle.

7 aJer. 30:7; Amos 8:9 bIs. 45:21; Acts 15:18 cIs. 58:10; Rev. 22:5

7 For it will be ªa unique day which is ᵇknown to the LORD, neither day nor night, but it will come about that at ᶜevening time there will be light.

★ 8 ªEzek. 47:1-12; Joel 3:18; John 7:38; Rev. 22:1, 2

8 And it will come about in that day that ªliving waters will flow out of Jerusalem, half of them toward the eastern sea and the other half toward the western

---

13:7 A reference to the death of Christ and the scattering of the disciples (cf. Matt. 26:31).

13:8-9 God's judgment of Israel at the return of Christ will weed out all but one-third of them. These will constitute the "all Israel" that will then be saved.

14:1-5 A description of one of the last battles of the campaign of Armageddon (see note on Rev. 16:14). Jerusalem will be taken and the spoil divided. Just when the armies of the nations seem undefeatable, Jesus Christ personally and visibly will return to the Mount of Olives, causing it to split and provide a valley

through which survivors may flee. The location of Azel is uncertain, perhaps being a village near Jerusalem. the earthquake. See Amos 1:1. holy ones. Perhaps believers who, having been previously taken to heaven, return with Christ, or angels who accompany Him, or both.

14:6 Cosmic disturbances will affect day and night when Christ returns (cf. Acts 2:19-20).

14:8 living waters. Both natural (for the land) and spiritual (for the people) refreshment. eastern sea. The Dead Sea. western sea. The Mediterranean.

sea; it will be in summer as well as in winter.

9 And the LORD will be ^aking over all the earth; in that day the LORD will be *the only* ^bone, and His name *the only* one.

10 All the land will be changed into a plain from ^aGeba to ^bRimmon south of Jerusalem; but Jerusalem will ^crise and ^dremain on its site from ^eBenjamin's Gate as far as the place of the First Gate to the ^fCorner Gate, and from the ^gTower of Hananel to the king's wine presses.

11 And people will live in it, and there will be ^ano more curse, for Jerusalem will ^bdwell in security.

12 Now this will be the plague with which the LORD will strike all the peoples who have gone to war against Jerusalem; their flesh will ^arot while they stand on their feet, and their eyes will rot in their sockets, and their tongue will rot in their mouth.

13 And it will come about in that day that a great panic from the LORD will fall on them; and they will ^aseize one another's hand, and the hand of one will be lifted against the hand of another.

14 And ^aJudah also will fight at Jerusalem; and the ^bwealth of all the surrounding nations will be gathered, gold and silver and garments in great abundance.

15 So also like this ^aplague, will be the plague on the horse, the mule, the camel, the donkey,

and all the cattle that will be in those camps.

16 Then it will come about that any who are left of all the nations that went against Jerusalem will ^ago up from year to year to worship the King, the LORD of hosts, and to celebrate the ^bFeast of Booths.

17 And it will be that whichever of the families of the earth does not go up to Jerusalem to worship the ^aKing, the LORD of hosts, there will be ^bno rain on them.

18 And if the family of Egypt does not go up or enter, then no *rain will fall* on them; it will be the ^aplague with which the LORD smites the nations who do not go up to celebrate the Feast of Booths.

19 This will be the punishment of Egypt, and the punishment of all the nations who do not go up to celebrate the Feast of Booths.

20 In that day there will be *inscribed* on the bells of the horses, "^aHOLY TO THE LORD." And the ^bcooking pots in the LORD's house will be like the bowls before the altar.

21 And every cooking pot in Jerusalem and in Judah will be ^aholy to the LORD of hosts; and all who sacrifice will come and take of them and boil in them. And there will no longer be a ^bCanaanite in the house of the LORD of hosts in that day.

Cross references (margin):

9 ^aIs. 2:2-4; 45:23; Zech. 9:9; 14:16, 17 ^bDeut. 6:4; Is. 45:21-24

★10 ^a1 Kin. 15:22 ^bJosh. 15:32; Judg. 20:45, 47 ^cIs. 2:2; Amos 9:11 ^dJer. 30:18; Zech. 12:6 ^eJer. 37:13; 38:7 ^f2 Kin. 14:13 ^gJer. 31:38

11 ^aZech. 8:13; Rev. 22:3 ^bJer. 23:5, 6; Ezek. 34:25-28

★12-16 12 ^aLev. 26:16; Deut. 28:21, 22

13 ^aZech. 11:6

14 ^aZech. 12:2, 5 ^bIs. 23:18; Zech. 14:1

15 ^aZech. 14:12

★16-19 16 ^aIs. 60:6-9; 66:18-21, 23 ^bLev. 23:34-44

17 ^aZech. 14:9, 16 ^bJer. 14:3-6; Amos 4:7

18 ^aZech. 14:12, 15

★20-21 20 ^aEx. 28:36-38 ^bEzek. 46:20

21 ^aNeh. 8:10; Rom. 14:6, 7; 1 Cor. 10:31 ^bZeph. 1:11

14:10 *Geba.* 10 miles N. of Jerusalem. *Rimmon.* 35 miles SW. of Jerusalem (see Isa. 2:2). *Benjamin's Gate* was in the northern wall of Jerusalem; the *First Gate* at the northeastern corner; the *Corner Gate* at the northwestern corner; the *Tower of Hananel* at the N. corner; the king's winepresses at the S. end (Neh. 3:15).

14:12-16 As Israel's enemies (v. 12) and the enemies' animals (v. 15) are struck with a plague, Israel will resume the fight in Jerusalem and

take the spoil (v. 14).

14:16-19 *Feast of Booths.* See Lev. 23:33-43. During this millennial period, God, in Christ the King, will live among men. Those who do not keep the feast will experience drought, except Egypt, which will experience *plague.*

14:20-21 In the Millennium everything (down to the bells on the horses' harnesses) will be holy. *Canaanite.* Symbol of all unscrupulous unbelievers.

INTRODUCTION TO
THE BOOK OF MALACHI

Author: Malachi   Date: 450–400 b.c.

The Prophet *Malachi means "my messenger" and could simply be a designation of an anonymous writer. More likely, however, it is a proper name. He is not mentioned elsewhere in the O.T.*

The Times *About 100 years had passed since the return of the Jews to Palestine. The city of Jerusalem and the second Temple had been built, but initial enthusiasm had worn off. Following a period of revival under Nehemiah (Neh. 10:28–39), the people and priests had backslidden and become mechanical in their observance of the Law. Though lax in their worship (1:7) and delinquent in their tithing (3:8), they could not understand why God was dissatisfied with them.*

Purpose and Theme *Malachi rebuked the people for their neglect of the true worship of the Lord, and called them to repentance (1:6; 3:7).*

Contents *Malachi used a question-and-answer method, there being no fewer than 23 questions in the book.*

OUTLINE OF MALACHI

THE BOOK OF MALACHI

I GOD'S COMPASSION FOR ISRAEL, 1:1-5

A His Compassion Declared, 1:1-2a

1 ^aIs. 13:1;
Nah. 1:1;
Hab. 1:1;
Zech. 9:1
^bMal. 2:11

1 The ^aoracle of the word of the LORD to ^bIsrael through Malachi.

★ 2-3
★ 2 ^aDeut.
4:37; 7:8;
23:5; Is.
41:8, 9; Jer.
31:3; John
15:12 ^bRom.
9:13

2 "I have ^aloved you," says the LORD.

B His Compassion Doubted, 1:2b

But you say, "How hast Thou loved us?" "Was not Esau Jacob's brother?" declares the LORD. "Yet I ^bhave loved Jacob;

C His Compassion Demonstrated, 1:3-5

3 ^aJer.
49:10, 16-18;
Ezek. 35:3,
4, 7, 8, 15

3 but I have hated Esau, and I have ^amade his mountains a desolation, and appointed his inheritance for the jackals of the wilderness."

★ 4 ^aJer.
5:17 ^bIs. 9:9,
10 ^cAmos
3:15; 5:11;
6:11 ^dEzek.
35:9; Obad.
10

4 Though Edom says, "We have been ^abeaten down, but we will ^breturn and build up the ruins"; thus says the LORD of hosts, "They may ^cbuild, but I will tear down; and men will call them the wicked territory, and the people toward whom the LORD is indignant ^dforever."

5 ^aPs.
35:27; Mic.
5:4

5 And your eyes will see this and you will say, "^aThe LORD be magnified beyond the border of Israel!"

II GOD'S COMPLAINT AGAINST ISRAEL, 1:6-3:15

A Cheating, 1:6-14

★ 6-8

6 ^aEx.
20:12; Prov.
30:11, 17
^bDeut. 1:31;
Is. 1:2; Jer.
3:4; Mal.
2:10 ^cZeph.
3:4; Mal.
2:1-9

6 "'A son ^ahonors his father, and a servant his master. Then if I am a ^bfather, where is My honor? And if I am a master, where is My respect?' says the LORD of hosts to you, O ^cpriests who despise My name. But you say, 'How have we despised Thy name?'

7 ^aMal. 1:8,
13 ^bLev.
3:11; 21:6, 8
^cMal. 1:12

7 "You are presenting ^adefiled ^bfood upon My altar. But you say, 'How have we defiled Thee?' In that you say, 'The ^ctable of the LORD is to be despised.'

8 ^aLev.
22:22; Deut.
15:21 ^bHag.
1:1

8 "But when you present the ^ablind for sacrifice, is it not evil? And when you present the lame and sick, is it not evil? Why not offer it to your ^bgovernor? Would he be pleased with you? Or would he receive you kindly?" says the LORD of hosts.

9 ^aJer.
27:18; Joel
2:12-14
^bAmos 5:22

9 "But now will you not ^aentreat God's favor, that He may be gracious to us? With such an offering on your part, will He ^breceive any of you kindly?" says the LORD of hosts.

★10 ^aIs.
1:13 ^bJer.
14:10, 12;
Hos. 5:6

10 "Oh that there were one among you who would ^ashut the gates, that you might not uselessly kindle fire on My altar! I am not pleased with you," says the LORD of hosts, "^bnor will I accept an offering from you.

11 ^aIs. 45:6
^bPs. 111:9
^cIs. 66:18,
19 ^dIs. 60:6
^eIs. 12:4, 5;
54:5; Jer.
10:6, 7

11 "For from the ^arising of the sun, even to its setting, ^bMy name will be ^cgreat among the nations, and in every place ^dincense is going to be offered to My name, and a grain offering that is pure; for My name will be ^egreat

---

1:2-3 I have loved Jacob . . . I have hated Esau. Since the love is an elected love, the hate is the opposite; i.e., rejection from a chosen position (cf. Gen. 25:23; Rom. 9:10-13). his mountains. The land of Edom, for the Edomites were descendants of Esau (see Introduction to Obadiah). Nebuchadnezzar invaded Edom in 586 (Jer. 25:9, 21), and later the Nabataeans drove the Edomites from their territory.
1:2 How. Occurs in 1:6, 7; 2:17; 3:7, 8, 13 as an expression of "injured innocence" on the part

of the people!
1:4 Regarding how wicked Edom was, read Gen. 26:34; 27:41; Obad. 10-14.
1:6-8 defiled food. Including meat. They offered defective animals (strictly forbidden by the Law, Lev. 22:20-25 and Deut. 15:21), an act insulting even to an earthly governor, and much more so to the heavenly Ruler.
1:10 God prefers no worship to contemptible worship.

among the nations," says the LORD of hosts.

12 aMal. 1:7

12 "But you are aprofaning it, in that you say, 'The table of the LORD is defiled, and as for its fruit, its food is to be despised.'

★13 aIs. 43:22 bLev. 6:4; Is. 61:8 cMal. 1:8 dMal. 1:10

13 "You also say, 'My, how atiresome it is!' And you disdainfully sniff at it," says the LORD of hosts, "and you bring what was taken by brobbery, and what is clame or sick; so you bring the offering! Should I dreceive that from your hand?" says the LORD.

★14 aActs 5:1-4 bLev. 22:18-20 cZech. 14:9 dZeph. 2:11

14 "But cursed be the aswindler who has a male in his flock, and vows it, but sacrifices a bblemished animal to the Lord, for I am a great cKing," says the LORD of hosts, "and My name is dfeared among the nations."

B   Unfaithfulness, 2:1-9

2 "And now, this commandment is for you, O priests.

★ 2 aLev. 26:14, 15; Deut. 28:15 bDeut. 28:16-20 cMal. 3:9

2 "If you do anot listen, and if you do not take it to heart to give honor to My name," says the LORD of hosts, "then I will send the bcurse upon you, and I will curse your blessings; and indeed, I have ccursed them already, because you are not taking it to heart.

★ 3 aLev. 26:16; Deut. 28:38 bNah. 3:6 cEx. 29:14

3 "Behold, I am going to arebuke your offspring, and I will bspread refuse on your faces, the refuse of your cfeasts; and you will be taken away with it.

★ 4 aNum. 3:11-13, 45; 18:21; Neh. 13:29; Mal. 3:1

4 "Then you will know that I have sent this commandment to you, that My acovenant may con-

tinue with Levi," says the LORD of hosts.

5 aNum. 25:12 bNum. 25:7, 8, 13

5 "My covenant with him was one of life and apeace, and I gave them to him as an object of reverence; so he brevered Me, and stood in awe of My name.

6 aPs. 119:142, 151, 160 bDeut. 33:8, 9; Ps. 37:37 cJer. 23:22

6 "aTrue instruction was in his mouth, and unrighteousness was not found on his lips; he walked bwith Me in peace and uprightness, and he cturned many back from iniquity.

7 aLev. 10:11; Neh. 8:7 bNum. 27:21; Deut. 17:8-11; Jer. 18:18; Ezek. 7:26 cHag. 1:13

7 "For the lips of a priest should preserve aknowledge, and men should bseek instruction from his mouth; for he is the cmessenger of the LORD of hosts.

★ 8-9
8 aJer. 18:15 bNum. 25:12, 13; Neh. 13:29; Ezek. 44:10

8 "But as for you, you have turned aside from the way; you have caused many to astumble by the instruction; you have bcorrupted the covenant of Levi," says the LORD of hosts.

9 aNah. 3:6 bEzek. 7:26 cDeut. 1:17; Mic. 3:11

9 "So aI also have made you despised and babased before all the people, just as you are not keeping My ways, but are showing cpartiality in the instruction.

C   Spiritually Mixed Marriages, 2:10-12

★10 aIs. 63:16; 64:8; Jer. 31:9; 1 Cor. 8:6; Eph. 4:6 bActs 17:24f. cJer. 9:4, 5 dEx. 19:4-6; 24:3, 7, 8

10 "Do we not all have aone father? bHas not one God created us? Why do we deal ctreacherously each against his brother so as to profane the dcovenant of our fathers?

★11 aJer. 3:7-9 bEzra 9:1, 2

11 "Judah has dealt atreacherously, and an abomination has been committed in Israel and in Jerusalem; for Judah has bpro-

---

1:13 sniff at. Belittle.
1:14 a blemished animal. Lit., a blemished female animal, in place of the more valuable male animal vowed to be offered.
2:2 I will curse your blessings. I.e., dry up the supply from which the priests received their portions of meat, grain, etc.
2:3 offspring. Better, seed for the crops.
2:4 covenant . . . with Levi. The arrangement with Levi and his descendants setting up the priesthood (Num. 1:50).
2:8-9 One of the principal functions of the Lev-

ites was to teach the people (Deut. 33:10), but they were showing partiality or favoritism in applying the law (cf. James 2:1).
2:10 Marriages with non-Israelites violated the special relationship God had with the Jews as the father of that people (Exod. 4:22). Marriages with the heathen were prohibited in Exod. 34:14-16 and Deut. 7:3.
2:11 the daughter of a foreign god. I.e., heathen girls brought foreign gods into Jewish homes and said, in effect, Marry me, marry my religion. See Neh. 13:23-28.

faned the sanctuary of the LORD which He loves, and has married the daughter of a foreign god.

★12 *a*Ezek. 24:21; Hos. 9:12 *b*Mal. 1:10, 13

12 "As for the man who does this, may the *a*LORD cut off from the tents of Jacob *everyone* who awakes and answers, or who *b*presents an offering to the LORD of hosts.

D Divorce, 2:13-16

★13-15

13 *a*Jer. 11:14; 14:12

13 "And this is another thing you do: you cover the altar of the LORD with tears, with weeping and with groaning, because He *a*no longer regards the offering or accepts *it with* favor from your hand.

14 *a*Is. 54:6 *b*Jer. 9:2; Mal. 3:5

14 "Yet you say, 'For what reason?' Because the LORD has been a witness between you and the *a*wife of your youth, against whom you have dealt *b*treacherously, though she is your companion and your wife by covenant.

15 *a*Gen. 2:24; Matt. 19:4, 5 *b*Ruth 4:12; 1 Sam. 2:20 *c*Ex. 20:14; Lev. 20:10

15 "But not one has *a*done *so* who has a remnant of the Spirit. And what did *that* one *do* while he was seeking a *b*godly offspring? Take heed then, to your spirit, and let no one deal *c*treacherously against the wife of your youth.

★16 *a*Deut. 24:1; Matt. 5:31; 19:6-8 *b*Ps. 73:6; Is. 59:6

16 "For I hate *a*divorce," says the LORD, the God of Israel, "and him who covers his garment with *b*wrong," says the LORD of hosts. "So take heed to your spirit, that you do not deal treacherously."

E Impiety and Impertinence, 2:17

★17 *a*Is. 43:22, 24 *b*Is. 5:20; Zeph. 1:12 *c*Job 9:24 *d*2 Pet. 3:4 *e*Is. 5:19; Jer. 17:15

17 You have *a*wearied the LORD with your words. Yet you say, "How have we wearied *Him?*" In that you say, "*b*Everyone who does evil is good in the sight of the LORD, and He *c*delights in them," or, "*d*Where is the God of *e*justice?"

F Parenthesis: The Coming of John the Baptist, 3:1-6

★ 1 *a*Matt. 11:10; 14; Mark 1:2; Luke 1:76; 7:27 *b*Hag. 1:13; John 1:6, 7 *c*Is. 40:3 *d*Is. 63:9

3 "*a*Behold, I am going to send *b*My messenger, and he will *c*clear the way before Me. And the Lord, whom you seek, will suddenly come to His temple; and the *d*messenger of the covenant, in whom you delight, behold, He is coming," says the LORD of hosts.

★ 2 *a*Is. 33:14; Ezek. 22:14; Rev. 6:17 *b*Zech. 13:9; Matt. 3:10-12; 1 Cor. 3:13-15

2 "But who can *a*endure the day of His coming? And who can stand when He appears? For He is like a *b*refiner's fire and like fullers' soap.

3 *a*Is. 1:25; Dan. 12:10 *b*Ps. 4:5; 51:19

3 "And He will sit as a smelter and purifier of silver, and He will *a*purify the sons of Levi and refine them like gold and silver, so that they may *b*present to the LORD offerings in righteousness.

4 *a*Ps. 51:17-19 *b*2 Chr. 7:1-3, 12

4 "Then the offering of Judah and Jerusalem will be *a*pleasing to the LORD, as in the *b*days of old and as in former years.

★ 5 *a*Deut. 18:10; Jer. 27:9, 10 *b*Ezek. 22:9-11 *c*Jer. 5:2; 7:9; Zech. 5:4 *d*Lev. 19:13 *e*Ex. 22:22-24 *f*Deut. 27:19

5 "Then I will draw near to you for judgment; and I will be a

---

2:12 *everyone who awakes and answers.* A proverbial expression for all living people.

2:13-15 Though distressed that God no longer accepted their *offering,* the people refused to face up to the seriousness of divorce. Some divorced wives were taken in *youth.* All divorce breaks the *covenant* (promise) made at the time of marriage, and remarriage violates the pattern God established at creation when He made only one wife for Adam (v. 15).

2:16 *covers his garment with wrong.* Better, violence covers his garment (a symbol of protection). Divorce removed the wife's protection and treated her cruelly.

2:17 Not only had they tried to make *evil . . .*

good, but they implied that God delighted in evil because He did not dispense immediate *justice.*

3:1 *messenger.* John the Baptist (Matt. 11:10). The *Lord* and *the messenger of the* (new) *covenant* (Matt. 26:28) is Jesus Christ.

3:2 *a refiner's fire* purifies, and *fullers'* (laundrymen's) *soap* cleanses.

3:5 Specific violations of the law included sorcery (cf. Exod. 22:18), adultery (cf. Exod. 20:14), false swearing (cf. Lev. 19:12), withholding wages (cf. Lev. 19:13), oppressing the widow and orphan (cf. Exod. 22:22-24), and injustice to a stranger (cf. Deut. 24:17).

swift witness against the *sorcer-ers and against the *adulterers and against those who *swear falsely, and against those who op-press the *wage earner in his wages, the *widow and the or-phan, and those who turn aside the *alien, and do not fear Me," says the LORD of hosts.

6 aNum. 23:19; James 1:17

6 "For I, the LORD, *do not change; therefore you, O sons of Jacob, are not consumed.

G Robbery, 3:7-12

7 aJer. 7:25, 26; 16:11, 12 bZech. 1:3

7 "From the *days of your fa-thers you have turned aside from My statutes, and have not kept *them.* *Return to Me, and I will return to you," says the LORD of hosts. "But you say, 'How shall we return?'

★ **8** aNeh. 13:11, 12

8 "Will a man rob God? Yet you are robbing Me! But you say, 'How have we robbed Thee?' In *tithes and offerings.

9 aMal. 2:2

9 "You are *cursed with a curse, for you are robbing Me, the whole nation *of you!*

★**10** aLev. 27:30; Num. 18:21-24; Deut. 12:6; 14:22-29; Neh. 13:12 bPs. 78:23-29 cEzek. 34:26 dLev. 26:3-5

10 "*Bring the whole tithe into the storehouse, so that there may be food in My house, and test Me now in this," says the LORD of hosts, "if I will not *open for you the windows of heaven, and *pour out for you a blessing until *it overflows.

★**11** aJoel 1:4; 2:25

11 "Then I will rebuke the *de-vourer for you, so that it may not destroy the fruits of the ground; nor will your vine in the field cast *its grapes,"* says the LORD of hosts.

12 aIs. 61:9 bIs. 62:4

12 "And *all the nations will call you blessed, for you shall be a *delightful land," says the LORD of hosts.

H Arrogance, 3:13-15

13 "Your words have been ar-rogant against Me," says the LORD. "Yet you say, 'What have we spoken against Thee?'

★**14** aJer. 2:25; 18:12 bIs. 58:3

14 "You have said, 'It is *vain to serve God; and what *profit is it that we have kept His charge, and that we have walked in mourning before the LORD of hosts?

15 aIs. 2:22; Mal. 4:1 bJer. 7:10

15 "So now we *call the arro-gant blessed; not only are the doers of wickedness built up, but they also test God and *escape.' "

III GOD'S CONDEMNATION OF THE PEOPLE, 3:16-4:6

A The Ungodly People, 3:16-18

★**16** aPs. 34:15; Jer. 31:18-20 bIs. 4:3; Dan. 12:1

16 Then those who feared the LORD spoke to one another, and the LORD *gave attention and heard *it,* and a *book of remem-brance was written before Him for those who fear the LORD and who esteem His name.

★**17** aIs. 43:1 bIs. 4:2 cEx. 19:5; Deut. 7:6; Is. 43:21; 1 Pet. 2:9 dPs. 103:13

17 "And they will be *Mine," says the LORD of hosts, "on the *day that I prepare *My *own pos-session, and I will spare them as a man *spares his own son who serves him."

18 aGen. 18:25; Amos 5:15

18 So you will again *distin-guish between the righteous and the wicked, between one who serves God and one who does not serve Him.

3:8 Two *tithes* were required: an annual tithe for the maintenance of the Levites (Lev. 27:30; Num. 18:21) and a second tithe brought to Je-rusalem for the Lord's feast (Deut. 14:22). Eve-ry third year, however, the second tithe was kept at home and used for the poor (Deut. 14:28). One's use of money is often a barom-eter of his spirituality (cf. 1 John 3:17).
3:10 From the time of King Hezekiah on (2 Chron. 31:11), special *storehouses* held grain brought in payment of tithes. These may have been special rooms in the Temple or a kind of lean-to against a side of the Temple.
3:11 *the devourer.* Any pest that destroys crops.
3:14 Some wrongly maintained that if material prosperity did not result, there was no point in serving the Lord.
3:16 Not all had defected, and God remembered their faithfulness to Him.
3:17 *My own possession.* I.e., a special, valued treasure.

B The Nature of God's Judgment, 4:1-6

★ **1** aPs. 21:9; Nah. 1:5, 6; Mal. 3:2, 3; 2 Pet. 3:7 bIs. 5:24; Obad. 18 cIs. 9:18, 19

4 "For behold, the day is coming, aburning like a furnace; and all the arrogant and every evildoer will be bchaff; and the day that is coming will cset them ablaze," says the LORD of hosts, "so that it will leave them neither root nor branch."

★ **2** a2 Sam. 23:4; Is. 30:26; 60:1 bJer. 30:17; 33:6 cIs. 35:6 **3** aJob 40:12; Is. 26:6; Mic. 5:8 bEzek. 28:18 cMal. 3:17

2 "But for you who fear My name the asun of righteousness will rise with bhealing in its wings; and you will go forth and cskip about like calves from the stall.

3 "And you will atread down the wicked, for they shall be bashes under the soles of your feet con the day which I am preparing," says the LORD of hosts.

★ **4** aDeut. 4:23; 8:11, 19

4 "aRemember the law of Moses My servant, *even the* statutes and ordinances which I commanded him in Horeb for all Israel.

★ **5** aMatt. 11:14; 17:10-13; Mark 9:11-13; Luke 1:17; John 1:21

5 "Behold, I am going to send you aElijah the prophet before the coming of the great and terrible day of the LORD.

6 aLuke 1:17 bIs. 11:4; Rev. 19:15

6 "And he will arestore the hearts of the fathers to *their* children, and the hearts of the children to their fathers, lest I come and bsmite the land with a curse."

4:1 *the day.* The Day of the Lord (Zeph. 1:14-18).

4:2 *sun of righteousness.* An impersonal reference to the display of righteousness throughout the entire earth (as the sun sends its rays everywhere) in the coming millennial kingdom. *skip about.* Like calves set free from their stalls.

4:4 *Horeb.* Sinai (Deut. 5:2).

4:5 *Elijah.* See note on Matt. 17:11-12.

The New Testament
Annotated

INTRODUCTION TO
THE NEW TESTAMENT

The name given to the second half of the English Bible is "the New Testament," which literally means "the New Covenant" (see Luke 22:20). The word *covenant* meant an arrangement made by one party which the other party involved could accept or reject but could not alter. The Old Testament primarily records God's dealings with Israel on the basis of the covenant given through Moses at Mt. Sinai, while the New Testament describes the new arrangement of God with men through Christ on the basis of the New Covenant (see Ex. 24:1-8; Luke 22:14-20; 2 Cor. 3:6-11). The Old Covenant revealed the holiness of God in the righteous standard of the Law and promised a coming Redeemer; the New Covenant shows the holiness of God in His righteous Son. The New Testament, then, contains those writings which reveal the content of this New Covenant.

The message of the New Testament centers around (1) the Person who gave Himself for the remission of sins (Matt. 26:28) and (2) the people (the church) who have received His salvation. Thus the central theme of the New Testament is salvation. The Gospels introduce the Savior. The book called the Acts of the Apostles describes the spread of the good news about His salvation through a large part of the Mediterranean world of the first century A.D. The Epistles give details of the blessings of that salvation, and the Revelation previews the culmination of salvation.

The Arrangement of the Books of the New Testament The New Testament includes 27 books written by nine different authors (unless Paul wrote Hebrews, then only eight) over about 50 years' time. These books fall naturally into four divisions:

(1) The Four Gospels. These describe the life and ministry of Jesus Christ. Although they were written later than many other books of the New Testament, it was natural that, in the order of the books, a priority position should be given to these accounts of Jesus' earthly life and ministry.

(2) The book of Acts. This is the history of the beginning of the church and the spread of Christianity throughout the Greco-Roman world.

(3) The 21 letters (Romans through Jude). Since archaeological discoveries have shown that letter writing was a common means of communication in the first Christian centuries, it is not surprising to find that most of the books of the New Testament were in the form of letters. The apostle Paul, the great missionary and theologian of the early church, wrote 13 or 14 of these letters. They were addressed to churches as well as to individuals, and they teach Christian doctrine both in a formal way (as in Romans) and in application to life situations (as in 1 Corinthians and Philemon).

(4) The Revelation. This last book describes the ultimate triumph of Jesus Christ and His people in the future.

The Order of the Books of the New Testament As already suggested, the order of the books of the New Testament is logical. First come the Gospels, which record the life of Christ; then Acts, which gives the history of the spread of Christianity; then the letters, which show the development of the doctrines of the church along with its problems; and finally the vision of the second coming of Christ in the Revelation.

The order of the writing of the books, however, was approximately like this:

James	A.D. 45–50	Matthew	60's
Galatians	49	1 Timothy	63
1 and 2 Thessalonians	51	1 Peter	63
Mark	50's	Titus	65
1 Corinthians	56	2 Timothy	66
2 Corinthians	57	2 Peter	66
Romans	58	Hebrews	64–68
Luke	60	Jude	70–80
Colossians, Ephesians, Phi-		John	85–90
lippians, Philemon	61	1, 2, 3 John	90
Acts	61	Revelation	90's

The Collection of the Books After they were written, the individual books were not immediately gathered together into the canon, or collection of 27 which comprise the New Testament. Groups of books like Paul's letters and the Gospels were preserved at first by the churches or people to whom they were sent, and gradually all 27 books were collected and formally acknowledged by the church as a whole.

This process took about 350 years. In the second century the circulation of books that promoted heresy accentuated the need for distinguishing valid scripture from other Christian literature. Certain tests were developed to determine which books should be included. (1) Was the book written or approved by an apostle? (2) Were its contents of a spiritual nature? (3) Did it give evidence of being inspired by God? (4) Was it widely received by the churches?

Not all of the 27 books that were eventually recognized as canonical were accepted by all the churches in the early centuries, but this does not mean that those that were not immediately or universally accepted were spurious. Letters addressed to individuals (Philemon, 2 and 3 John) would not have been circulated as widely as those sent to churches. The books most disputed were James, Jude, 2 Peter, 2 and 3 John, and Philemon, but ultimately these were included and the canon was certified at the Council of Carthage in A.D. 397.

Although no original copy of any of the writings which comprise the New Testament has survived, there exist more than 4,500 Greek manuscripts of all or part of the text, plus some 8,000 Latin manuscripts and at least 1,000 other versions into which the original books were translated. Careful study and comparison of these many copies has given us an accurate and trustworthy New Testament.

INTRODUCTION TO THE GOSPELS

What Are the Gospels? Gospel means "good news." The Gospels are so called because they record the good news that a way of salvation has been opened to all mankind through the death and resurrection of Jesus Christ (Mark 1:1; 1 Cor. 15:3-4).

Biography as we know it was unknown when the Gospels were written, and they are not really biographies as we understand that literary form today. They were written that people might know who Jesus was and believe in Him (John 20:31).

Why Did the Gospels Need to Be Written? The rapid spread of Christianity precipitated the need for written accounts of the life of Christ. Too, as major figures in the stories and eyewitnesses began to die, there was an increasing need for written accounts of what they had seen and heard. These written Gospels were used to evangelize, to catechize new converts, and probably were part of early Christian worship (Luke 1:1-4). In the Introduction to each Gospel we shall try to show its distinctive quality.

Why Four Gospels? Although there were numerous other gospel accounts written, only four were deemed worthy to be included in the New Testament. The other gospels were written later and are of doubtful reliability. Although they contain some of the information that is in the four canonical Gospels, they also add much that is obviously fanciful and legendary (like the story of Jesus' condemning a boy to die because he had knocked Him down, as reported in an apocryphal Gnostic writing known as 1 Infancy). They also often tried to bolster heretical or sectarian viewpoints.

The early church distinguished these gospels from the true ones and regarded the apocryphal ones as of much lesser importance. One of the reasons was that the Four Gospels were written by apostles or by a close associate. Later church councils confirmed the authenticity of these books and included only the four in the canon, or collection of books recognized as inspired and authoritative.

The Gospels were written to the four general groups of people in the first century. Matthew was written for the Jews; Mark, for the Romans; Luke, for the other pagan Gentiles; and John, for Christians.

What Are the Synoptic Gospels? Matthew, Mark, and Luke present much similar material about the life of Christ, as even a quick examination of a harmony of His life will show. They have a more or less common view of His activities and teachings and of the chronology of events. They are therefore called the Synoptic Gospels (from *synopsis,* a viewing together). For example, all but 31 verses in Mark have parallels in either Matthew or Luke. On the other hand, much of the material in John's Gospel is unique, and it is organized according to long discourses. The differences in the four Gospels supplement each other without contradiction and the similarities complement each other. The result is a comprehensive fourfold record of the redemptive ministry of Jesus Christ.

INTRODUCTION TO
THE GOSPEL ACCORDING TO MATTHEW

Author: Matthew   Date: 60's

Authorship   *Matthew, who was surnamed Levi (Mark 2:14), was a Jewish tax collector (publican) for the Roman government (Matt. 9:9). Because he collaborated with the Romans, who were hated by the Jews as overlords of their country, Matthew (and all publicans) was despised by fellow Jews. Nevertheless, Matthew responded to Christ's simple call to follow Him. After the account of the banquet he gave for his colleagues so they too could meet Jesus, he is not mentioned again except in the list of the Twelve (Matt. 10:3; see also Acts 1:13). Tradition says that he preached in Palestine for a dozen years after the resurrection of Christ and then went to other lands, but there is no certainty of this.*

Distinctive Approach of Matthew   *Matthew was written to Jews to answer their questions about Jesus of Nazareth who claimed to be their Messiah. Was He in fact the Messiah predicted in the Old Testament? If He was, why did He fail to establish the promised kingdom? Will it ever be established? What is God's purpose in the meantime? Thus, in this Gospel, Jesus is often spoken of as the Son of David and the One who fulfills the Old Testament prophecies of Messiah; and the kingdom of heaven is the subject of much of His recorded teaching.*

    Matthew is also characterized by its inclusion of people outside of Judaism. The closing verses record the commission to go into all the world, and only in Matthew does the word church appear in the Gospels (16:18; 18:17). Jesus is also designated as the Son of Abraham (1:1), for in Abraham "all the families of the earth shall be blessed" (Gen. 12:3).

Date   *Although the Gospel has sometimes been dated in the 80's or 90's, the fact that the destruction of Jerusalem in A.D. 70 is viewed as an event yet future (24:2) seems to require an earlier date. Some feel that this was the first of the Gospels to be written (about 50), while others think it was not the first and that it was written in the 60's.*

Contents   *Important sections in Matthew are the Sermon on the Mount (chapters 5-7), including the Beatitudes (5:3-12) and the Lord's Prayer (6:9-13); the parables of the kingdom (chapter 13); and the Olivet Discourse concerning future events (chapters 24-25). The theme of the book is Christ the King, and the outline reflects that theme.*

OUTLINE OF THE GOSPEL OF MATTHEW

I. **The Person of the King, 1:1-4:25**
  A. His Background, 1:1-17
  B. His Birth, 1:18-2:23
   1. The announcement of the birth, 1:18-25
   2. The adoration of the baby, 2:1-12
   3. The advancement of the boy, 2:13-23
  C. His Baptism, 3:1-17
  D. His Temptation, 4:1-11
  E. His Inauguration, 4:12-25
II. **The Preaching of the King, 5:1-7:29**
  A. The Picture of Kingdom Life, 5:1-16
  B. The Precepts for Kingdom Life, 5:17-48
   1. The law of Moses, 5:17-20
   2. The law of murder, 5:21-22
   3. The law of reconciliation, 5:23-26
   4. The law of adultery, 5:27-30
   5. The law of divorce, 5:31-32
   6. The law of oaths, 5:33-37
   7. The law of nonresistance, 5:38-42
   8. The law of love, 5:43-48
  C. The Practice of Kingdom Life, 6:1-7:12
   1. In relation to almsgiving, 6:1-4

   2. In relation to prayer, 6:5-15
   3. In relation to fasting, 6:16-18
   4. In relation to money, 6:19-24
   5. In relation to anxiety, 6:25-34
   6. In relation to judging, 7:1-5
   7. In relation to prudence, 7:6
   8. In relation to prayer, 7:7-11
   9. In relation to others, 7:12
  D. The Proof of Kingdom Life, 7:13-29
III. **The Proof of the King, 8:1-9:38**
  A. Exhibit 1: Power, 8:1-34
   1. Power over defilement, 8:1-4
   2. Power over distance, 8:5-13
   3. Power over disease, 8:14-17
   4. Power over disciples, 8:18-22
   5. Power over the deep, 8:23-27
   6. Power over demons, 8:28-34
  B. Exhibit 2: Pardon, 9:1-17
   1. Pardon of a paralytic, 9:1-8
   2. Pardon of a publican, 9:9-13
   3. Problem concerning fasting, 9:14-17

THE GOSPEL ACCORDING TO MATTHEW

I THE PERSON OF THE KING, 1:1-4:25
A His Background, 1:1-17

★ 1 *a*2 Sam. 7:12-16; Ps. 89:3f.; 132:11; Is. 9:6f.; 11:1; Matt. 9:27; Luke 1:32, 69; John 7:42; Acts 13:23; Rom. 1:3; Rev. 22:16 *b*Gen. 22:18; Matt. 1:1-6; *Luke* 3:32-34; Gal. 3:16

1 The book of the genealogy of Jesus Christ, *a*the son of David, *b*the son of Abraham.

3 *a*Ruth 4:18-22; 1 Chr. 2:1-15; Matt. 1:3-6

2 To Abraham was born Isaac; and to Isaac, Jacob; and to Jacob, Judah and his brothers;

3 and to Judah were born Perez and Zerah by Tamar; and to *a*Perez was born Hezron; and to Hezron, Ram;

4 and to Ram was born Amminadab; and to Amminadab, Nahshon; and to Nahshon, Salmon;

5 and to Salmon was born Boaz by Rahab; and to Boaz was born Obed by Ruth; and to Obed, Jesse;

6 *a*2 Sam. 11:27; 12:24

6 and to Jesse was born David the king.

And to David *a*was born Solomon by her *who had been the wife* of Uriah;

7 *a*1 Chr. 3:10ff.

7 and to Solomon *a*was born Rehoboam; and to Rehoboam, Abijah; and to Abijah, Asa;

8 and to Asa was born Jehoshaphat; and to Jehoshaphat, Joram; and to Joram, Uzziah;

9 and to Uzziah was born Jotham; and to Jotham, Ahaz; and to Ahaz, Hezekiah;

10 and to Hezekiah was born Manasseh; and to Manasseh, Amon; and to Amon, Josiah;

11 and to Josiah were born Jeconiah and his brothers, at the time of the *a*deportation to Babylon.

★11 *a*2 Kin. 24:14f.; Jer. 27:20; Matt. 1:17

12 And after the *a*deportation to Babylon, to Jeconiah was born Shealtiel; and to Shealtiel, Zerubbabel;

12 *a*2 Kin. 24:14f.; Jer. 27:20; Matt. 1:17

13 and to Zerubbabel was born Abiud; and to Abiud, Eliakim; and to Eliakim, Azor;

14 and to Azor was born Zadok; and to Zadok, Achim; and to Achim, Eliud;

15 and to Eliud was born Eleazar; and to Eleazar, Matthan; and to Matthan, Jacob;

16 and to Jacob was born Joseph the husband of Mary, by whom was born Jesus, *a*who is called Christ.

★16 *a*Matt. 27:17, 22; Luke 2:11; John 4:25

17 Therefore all the generations from Abraham to David are fourteen generations; and from David to the *a*deportation to Babylon fourteen generations; and from Babylon to the *time of* Christ fourteen generations.

17 *a*2 Kin. 24:14f.; Jer. 27:20; Matt. 1:11, 12

B His Birth, 1:18-2:23
1 The announcement of the birth, 1:18-25

18 Now the birth of Jesus Christ was as follows. When His *a*mother Mary had been

18 *a*Matt. 12:46; Luke 1:27 *b*Luke 1:35

1:1 *Jesus Christ.* The name "Jesus" is from the Greek (and Latin) for the Hebrew "Jeshua" (Joshua), which means "the Lord is salvation." "Christ" is from the Greek for the Hebrew *Meshiah* (Messiah), meaning "anointed one." *Son of David* was a highly popular Messianic title of the times. The genealogy is here traced through Joseph, Jesus' legal (though not natural) father, and it establishes His claim and right to the throne of David (1:6). The genealogy in Luke 3:23-38 is evidently that of Mary, though some believe it is also Joseph's, by assuming that Matthan (Matt. 1:15) and Matthat (Luke 3:24) were the same person and Jacob (Matt. 1:16) and Eli (Luke 3:23) were brothers (one being Joseph's father and the other his

uncle). See note at Luke 3:23.
1:11 *Jeconiah.* Jehoiachin, king of Judah, who was taken into captivity by Nebuchadnezzar in 597 B.C. Jeremiah contracted "Jeconiah" to "Coniah" (Jer. 22:24, 28; 37:1). A curse was pronounced on Coniah that none of his descendants would prosper sitting on the throne of David. Had our Lord been the natural son of Joseph, He could not have been successful on the throne of David because of this curse. But since He came through Mary's lineage, He was not affected by this curse.
1:16 *by whom.* The word is feminine singular, indicating clearly that Jesus was born of Mary only and not of Mary and Joseph. It is one of the strongest evidences for Jesus' virgin birth.

betrothed to Joseph, before they came together she was ᵇfound to be with child by the Holy Spirit.

★19   **19** And Joseph her husband, being a righteous man, and not wanting to disgrace her, desired to put her away secretly.

20 But when he had considered this, behold, an angel of the Lord appeared to him in a dream, saying, "Joseph, son of David, do not be afraid to take Mary as your wife; for that which has been conceived in her is of the Holy Spirit.

21 ᵃLuke 1:31; 2:21 ᵇLuke 2:11; John 1:29; Acts 13:23

21 "And she will bear a Son; and ᵃyou shall call His name Jesus, for it is He who ᵇwill save His people from their sins."

22 Now all this took place that what was spoken by the Lord through the prophet might be fulfilled, saying,

23 ᵃIs. 7:14

23 "ᵃBEHOLD, THE VIRGIN SHALL BE WITH CHILD, AND SHALL BEAR A SON, AND THEY SHALL CALL HIS NAME IMMANUEL," which translated means, "GOD WITH US."

24 And Joseph arose from his sleep, and did as the angel of the Lord commanded him, and took her as his wife,

25 ᵃMatt. 1:21

25 and kept her a virgin until she gave birth to a Son; and ᵃhe called His name Jesus.

2 The adoration of the baby, 2:1-12

★ 1 ᵃLuke 2:4-7 ᵇLuke 1:5

2 Now after Jesus was ᵃborn in Bethlehem of Judea in the days of ᵇHerod the king, behold, magi from the east arrived in Jerusalem, saying,

2 "Where is He who has been born ᵃKing of the Jews? For we saw ᵇHis star in the east, and have come to worship Him."

2 ᵃJer. 23:5; 30:9; Zech. 9:9; Matt. 27:11; Luke 19:38; 23:38; John 1:49 ᵇNum. 24:17; Rev. 22:16

3 And when Herod the king heard it, he was troubled, and all Jerusalem with him.

4 And gathering together all the chief priests and scribes of the people, he *began* to inquire of them where the Christ was to be born.

★ 4

5 And they said to him, "ᵃIn Bethlehem of Judea, for so it has been written by the prophet,

5 ᵃJohn 7:42

6 'ᵃAND YOU, BETHLEHEM, LAND OF JUDAH,
ARE BY NO MEANS LEAST AMONG THE LEADERS OF JUDAH;
FOR OUT OF YOU SHALL COME FORTH A RULER,
WHO WILL ᵇSHEPHERD MY PEOPLE ISRAEL.' "

★ 6 ᵃMic. 5:2 ᵇJohn 21:16

7 Then Herod secretly called the magi, and ascertained from them the time the star appeared.

8 And he sent them to Bethlehem, and said, "Go and make careful search for the Child; and when you have found *Him*, report to me, that I too may come and worship Him."

9 And having heard the king, they went their way; and lo, the star, which they had seen in the east, went on before them, until it came and stood over where the Child was.

1:19 *her husband.* Although Joseph and Mary were not yet married, so sacred was the period of engagement, or betrothal, that they were by custom considered as if married (cf. Gen. 29:21; Deut. 22:23-30). Consequently, Joseph's only recourse seemed to be to "put her away," which meant to give her a bill of divorcement, a certificate saying, in effect, "This woman is not my wife; I am not her husband" (see Hos. 2:2).

2:1 *Bethlehem.* The town is five miles S. of Jerusalem. *Herod the king.* This was Herod the Great, whose family, though nominally Jewish, were in reality Edomite, and who was king, with Roman help, from 40-4 B.C. He built the temple in Jerusalem which Christ knew. *magi.* These wise men from the east were experts in the study of the stars. Tradition says that there were three and that they were kings, but we do not know for certain.

2:4 *scribes.* Scribes, who belonged mainly to the party of the Pharisees, functioned as members of a highly honored profession. They were professional students and defenders of the law (scriptural and traditional), gathering around them pupils whom they instructed in the law. They were also referred to as lawyers because they were entrusted with the administration of the law as judges in the Sanhedrin (cf. Matt. 22:35).

2:6 *a Ruler.* See Micah 5:2. An earthly king, though a supernatural one, is meant.

10 And when they saw the star, they rejoiced exceedingly with great joy.

★11 *a*Matt. 1:18; 12:46

11 And they came into the house and saw the Child with *a*Mary His mother; and they fell down and worshiped Him; and opening their treasures they presented to Him gifts of gold and frankincense and myrrh.

12 *a*Matt. 2:13, 19, 22; Luke 2:26; Acts 10:22; Heb. 8:5; 11:7

12 And having been *a*warned by God in a dream not to return to Herod, they departed for their own country by another way.

3 The advancement of the boy, 2:13-23

13 *a*Matt. 2:12, 19

13 Now when they had departed, behold, an angel of the Lord *★a*appeared to Joseph in a dream, saying, "Arise and take the Child and His mother, and flee to Egypt, and remain there until I tell you; for Herod is going to search for the Child to destroy Him."

14 And he arose and took the Child and His mother by night, and departed for Egypt;

★15 *a*Hos. 11:1 *b*Ex. 4:22f.

15 and was there until the death of Herod, that what was spoken by the Lord through the prophet might be fulfilled, saying, "*a*OUT OF EGYPT DID I CALL *b*MY SON."

16 Then when Herod saw that he had been tricked by the magi, he became very enraged, and sent and slew all the male children who were in Bethlehem and in all its environs, from two years old and under, according to the time which he had ascertained from the magi.

17 Then that which was spoken through Jeremiah the prophet was fulfilled, saying,

★17-18

18 "*a*A VOICE WAS HEARD IN RAMAH,
WEEPING AND GREAT MOURNING,
RACHEL WEEPING FOR HER CHILDREN;
AND SHE REFUSED TO BE COMFORTED,
BECAUSE THEY WERE NO MORE."

18 *a*Jer. 31:15

19 But when Herod was dead, behold, an angel of the Lord *★a*appeared in a dream to Joseph in Egypt, saying,

19 *a*Matt. 2:12, 13, 22

20 "Arise and take the Child and His mother, and go into the land of Israel; for those who sought the Child's life are dead."

21 And he arose and took the Child and His mother, and came into the land of Israel.

22 But when he heard that Archelaus was reigning over Judea in place of his father Herod, he was afraid to go there. And being *a*warned by God in a dream, he departed for the regions of Galilee,

★22 *a*Matt. 2:12

23 and came and resided in a city called *a*Nazareth, that what was spoken through the prophets

★23 *a*Luke 1:26 *b*Is. 11:1 *c*Mark 1:24

2:11 *into the house . . . the Child.* These words need not indicate that the wise men came some time after the birth of Christ. The family would naturally have moved into a house as quickly as possible after Jesus was born, and "child" can mean a newborn (John 16:21). We do not know how many wise men there were. *gold and frankincense and myrrh.* These were gifts worthy of a king. The early church fathers understood the gold to be symbolic of Christ's deity; the frankincense, of His purity; and the myrrh, of His death (since it was used for embalming).

2:15 See Hosea 11:1.

2:17-18 A quotation of Jer. 31:15, which depicts the wailing at the time of Israel's exile. That calamity and Herod's new atrocity are viewed as part of the same broad picture. Since Mat-

thew was writing to those with Jewish background, he used more quotations from the O.T. than the other Gospel writers. There are 93 such quotations in Matthew, 49 in Mark, 80 in Luke, and 33 in John.

2:22 *Archelaus.* On the death of Herod the Great, the Romans divided his kingdom among his sons: Archelaus (Judah and Samaria), Antipas (Galilee and Perea), Philip (NE. Palestine). Archelaus was a bloody king and, worse in the eyes of Rome, ineffective. He was removed by Caesar Augustus in A.D. 6 and banished to Gaul.

2:23 *He shall be called a Nazarene.* Probably a synonym for "contemptible" or "despised" since Nazareth was a most unlikely place for the residence of the Messiah (cf. Isa. 53:3; Ps. 22:6).

might be fulfilled, "[b]He shall be called a [c]Nazarene."

C His Baptism, 3:1-17

★ 1 [a]Matt. 3:1-12; Mark 1:3-8; Luke 3:2-17; John 1:6-8, 19-28 [b]Josh. 15:61 Judg. 1:16
★ 2 [a]Matt. 4:17 [b]Dan. 2:44; Matt. 4:17, 23; 6:10; 10:7; Mark 1:15; Luke 10:9f.; 11:20; 21:31
3 [a]Is. 40:3 [b]John 1:23

3 Now [a]in those days John the Baptist *came, preaching in the [b]wilderness of Judea, saying, 2 "[a]Repent, for [b]the kingdom of heaven is at hand." 3 For this is the one referred to by Isaiah the prophet, saying,

"[a]THE VOICE OF ONE CRYING IN THE WILDERNESS, [b]MAKE READY THE WAY OF THE LORD, MAKE HIS PATHS STRAIGHT!' "

4 [a]2 Kin. 1:8; Zech. 13:4 [b]Lev. 11:22

4 Now John himself had [a]a garment of camel's hair, and a leather belt about his waist; and his food was [b]locusts and wild honey.

5 [a]Luke 3:3

5 Then Jerusalem was going out to him, and all Judea, and all [a]the district around the Jordan;

6 and they were being baptized by him in the Jordan River, as they confessed their sins.

★ 7 [a]Matt. 16:1ff.; 23:13, 15 [b]Matt. 16:1ff.; 22:23; Acts 4:1; 5:17; 23:6ff. [c]Matt. 12:34; 23:33 [d]1 Thess. 1:10
8 [a]Acts 26:20
★ 9 [a]John 8:33, 39

7 But when he saw many of the [a]Pharisees and [b]Sadducees coming for baptism, he said to them, "You [c]brood of vipers, who warned you to flee from [d]the wrath to come? 8 "Therefore bring forth fruit [a]in keeping with repentance; 9 and do not suppose that you can say to yourselves, '[a]We have Abraham for our father'; for I say to you, that God is able from these stones to raise up children to Abraham.

10 [a]Matt. 7:19

10 "And the axe is already laid at the root of the trees; [a]every tree therefore that does not bear good fruit is cut down and thrown into the fire.

★11 [a]John 1:26 [b]John 1:33

11 "As for me, [a]I baptize you with water for repentance, but He who is coming after me is mightier than I, and I am not fit to re-

---

3:1 *the wilderness of Judea.* A barren wasteland extending along the W. shore of the Dead Sea.

3:2 *Repent.* Repentance is a change of mind that bears fruit in a changed life (see v. 8). *kingdom of heaven.* This is the rule of heaven over the earth. The Jewish people of Christ's day were looking for this Messianic or Davidic kingdom to be established on the earth, and this is what John proclaimed as being "at hand." The rejection of Christ by the people delayed its establishment until the second coming of Christ (Matt. 25:31). The character of the kingdom today is described in the parables of Matt. 13.

3:7 *Pharisees.* The Pharisees were the most influential of the Jewish sects at the time of Christ. Though holding orthodox doctrines, their zeal for the Mosaic law led them to a degenerate, though strict, outward observance of both the law and their equally authoritative (in their own eyes) interpretations of it. They knew the Scriptures (Matt. 23:2), tithed (Luke 18:12), fasted (Matt. 9:14), prayed (Mark 12:40); but they were also hypocritical (Matt. 23:15), self-righteous (Luke 18:9), and the foremost persecutors of the Lord (Matt. 9:3). *Sadducees.* The Sadducees, whose membership came largely from the priesthood and upper classes, were the anti-supernaturalists of Christ's day. They denied the truth of bodily resurrection, of future punishment and reward, and of the existence of angels (Acts 23:8). Though they upheld the written law of

Moses, they were opposed to the oral traditions observed by the Pharisees. They were the party of the high-priestly families of Jerusalem with direct interests in the apparatus of temple worship and generally collaborated with the Roman rulers. They opposed Christ as vigorously as the Pharisees and were condemned by Him as severely, though not so frequently (Matt. 16:1-4, 6).

3:9 *We have Abraham for our father.* The common teaching of that day said that the Jews participated in the merits of Abraham, which made their prayers acceptable, helped in war, expiated sins, appeased the wrath of God, and assured a share in God's eternal kingdom. Consequently the people were startled when John and Jesus preached the necessity of personal repentance.

3:11 *baptize.* Baptism is a form of identification. John's baptism was a sign of an individual's acknowledgment of his need of repentance for the remission of his sins. When Jesus was baptized by John (v. 15) He identified Himself with John's message of righteousness (though, being sinless, He Himself needed no cleansing from sin). The baptism with the Holy Spirit, predicted here, identifies members of the body of Christ with Christ, the risen Head of that body (1 Cor. 12:13). Christian baptism is identification with the Christian message and the Christian group. *and fire.* Probably a reference to the judgments associated with the return of Christ (v. 12; Mal. 3:1-5; 4:1-3).

move His sandals; [b]He will baptize you with the Holy Spirit and fire.

★12 [a]Is. 30:24; Luke 3:17 [b]Matt. 13:30 [c]Mark 9:43, 48

12 "And His [a]winnowing fork is in His hand, and He will thoroughly clear His threshing floor; and He will [b]gather His wheat into the barn, but He will burn up the chaff with [c]unquenchable fire."

13 [a]Matt. 3:13-17; Mark 1:9-11; Luke 3:21, 22; John 1:31-34 [b]Matt. 2:22

13 [a]Then Jesus *arrived [b]from Galilee at the Jordan coming to John, to be baptized by him.

14 But John tried to prevent Him, saying, "I have need to be baptized by You, and do You come to me?"

15 But Jesus answering said to him, "Permit it at this time; for in this way it is fitting for us to fulfill all righteousness." Then he *permitted Him.

★16-17

16 [a]John 1:32

16 And after being baptized, Jesus went up immediately from the water; and behold, the heavens were opened, and [a]he saw the Spirit of God descending as a dove, and coming upon Him,

17 [a]Is. 42:1; Matt. 12:18; 17:5; Mark 9:7; Luke 9:35

17 and behold, a voice out of the heavens, saying, "[a]This is My beloved Son, in whom I am well-pleased."

D His Temptation, 4:1-11

★ 1 [a]Matt. 4:1-11; Mark 1:12, 13; Luke 4:1-13
2 [a]Ex. 34:28; 1 Kin. 19:8

4 [a]Then Jesus was led up by the Spirit into the wilderness to be tempted by the devil.

2 And after He had [a]fasted forty days and forty nights, He then became hungry.

3 [a]1 Thess. 3:5

3 And [a]the tempter came and said to Him, "If You are the Son of God, command that these stones become bread."

★ 4 [a]Deut. 8:3

4 But He answered and said, "It is written, '[a]MAN SHALL NOT LIVE ON BREAD ALONE, BUT ON EVERY WORD THAT PROCEEDS OUT OF THE MOUTH OF GOD.' "

5 [a]Neh. 11:1, 18; Dan. 9:24; Matt. 27:53

5 Then the devil *took Him into [a]the holy city; and he had Him stand on the pinnacle of the temple,

★ 6 [a]Ps. 91:11-12

6 and *said to Him, "If You are the Son of God throw Yourself down; for it is written,

'[a]HE WILL GIVE HIS ANGELS
    CHARGE CONCERNING YOU';
and
'ON their HANDS THEY WILL
    BEAR YOU UP,
LEST YOU STRIKE YOUR FOOT
    AGAINST A STONE.' "

★ 7 [a]Deut. 6:16

7 Jesus said to him, "On the other hand, it is written, '[a]YOU SHALL NOT PUT THE LORD YOUR GOD TO THE TEST.' "

8 Again, the devil *took Him to a very high mountain, and *showed Him all the kingdoms of the world, and their glory;

★ 9

9 and he said to Him, "All these things will I give You, if You fall down and worship me."

★10 [a]Deut. 6:13

10 Then Jesus *said to him, "Begone, Satan! For it is written, '[a]YOU SHALL WORSHIP THE LORD YOUR GOD, AND SERVE HIM ONLY.' "

11 [a]Matt. 26:53; Luke 22:43

11 Then the devil *left Him; and behold, [a]angels came and began to minister to Him.

3:12 *His winnowing fork is in His hand.* A wooden shovel used for tossing grain against the wind after threshing so that the lighter chaff would be blown away, leaving the kernels to settle in a pile.

3:16-17 This is the first clear expression of the concept of the Trinity. The descent of the Spirit upon Christ was for special power at the beginning of His public ministry.

4:1 Satan's intention in the temptation was to make Christ sin so as to thwart God's plan for man's redemption by disqualifying the Savior. God's purpose (note that the Spirit led Jesus to the test) was to prove His Son to be sinless and

thus a worthy Savior. It is clear that He was actually tempted; it is equally clear that He was sinless (2 Cor. 5:21). See note on Heb. 4:15.

4:4 See Deut. 8:3.

4:6 Satan, as well as Jesus, quotes the Bible (in this instance, Ps. 91:11-12). But Satan did not quote accurately, for he omitted a phrase which was not suited to his purpose.

4:7 See Deut. 6:16.

4:9 *will I give You.* Satan, as prince of this world, was within his rights to make this offer (John 12:31; see note at 1 John 2:15).

4:10 See Deut. 6:13; 10:20.

E His Inauguration, 4:12-25

12 Now when He heard that *a*John had been taken into custody, *b*He withdrew into Galilee;

13 and leaving Nazareth, He came and *a*settled in Capernaum, which is by the sea, in the region of Zebulun and Naphtali,

14 *This was* to fulfill what was spoken through Isaiah the prophet, saying,

15 "*a*THE LAND OF ZEBULUN AND THE LAND OF NAPHTALI,
BY THE WAY OF THE SEA, BEYOND THE JORDAN, GALILEE OF THE GENTILES—

16 "*a*THE PEOPLE WHO WERE SITTING IN DARKNESS SAW A GREAT LIGHT,
AND TO THOSE WHO WERE SITTING IN THE LAND AND SHADOW OF DEATH,
UPON THEM A LIGHT DAWNED."

17 *a*From that time Jesus began to preach and say, "*b*Repent, for the kingdom of heaven is at hand."

18 *a*And walking by *b*the Sea of Galilee, He saw two brothers, *c*Simon who was called Peter, and Andrew his brother, casting a net into the sea; for they were fishermen.

19 And He *said to them,

"Follow Me, and I will make you fishers of men."

20 And they immediately left the nets, and followed Him.

21 And going on from there He saw two other brothers, *a*James the *son* of Zebedee, and John his brother, in the boat with Zebedee their father, mending their nets; and He called them.

22 And they immediately left the boat and their father, and followed Him.

23 And *Jesus* was going about *a*in all Galilee, *b*teaching in their synagogues, and *c*proclaiming the gospel of the kingdom, and *d*healing every kind of disease and every kind of sickness among the people.

24 And the news about Him went out *a*into all Syria; and they brought to Him all who were ill, taken with various diseases and pains, *b*demoniacs, *c*epileptics, *d*paralytics; and He healed them.

25 And great multitudes *a*followed Him from Galilee and *b*Decapolis and Jerusalem and Judea and *from* *c*beyond the Jordan.

II THE PREACHING OF THE KING, 5:1-7:29

A The Picture of Kingdom Life, 5:1-16

5 *a*And when He saw the multitudes, He went up on *b*the

4:13 *leaving Nazareth.* According to Luke 4:16-30, He left because of what had happened there.

4:14 See Isa. 9:1-2; 42:6-7.

4:19 *Follow Me.* This was their call to service and illustrates the directness, profundity, and power of Christ's commands ("Go . . . ," 28:19; "love one another," John 13:34).

4:21 *James the son of Zebedee.* This is the apostle James, the brother of John, who was martyred under Herod Agrippa I (Acts 12:2). Other men named James in the N.T. are: James the son of Alphaeus, "the less" (Mark 15:40), also one of The Twelve (Matt. 10:3); James, the half brother of Christ and writer of the epistle of James; James, the father or, less probably, brother of the apostle Judas, to be distinguished from Judas Iscariot (Luke 6:16; Acts 1:13).

4:23 *the gospel of the kingdom.* This is the good news that the presence of the King caused the rule of God on the earth (in fulfill-

ment of many O.T. prophecies) to be "at hand." Prerequisites for entrance into the kingdom included repentance (Matt. 4:17), righteousness (Matt. 5:20), childlike faith (Matt. 18:3), or, in summary, being born again (John 3:3). Because the people rejected these requirements, Christ taught that His earthly reign would not immediately come (Luke 19:11). However, this gospel of the kingdom will be preached again during the tribulation period (Matt. 24:14), just prior to the return of Christ to establish His kingdom on earth (Matt. 25:31, 34).

4:25 *Decapolis.* A district, originally containing ten cities, S. of the Sea of Galilee, mainly to the E. of the Jordan river. These were cities with Gentile populations and typical Greco-Roman structures—pagan temples, hippodromes, etc.

5:1 *on the mountain.* Chapters 5-7 contain the widely known and loved Sermon on the Mount. It is one of 5 long discourses by Christ

12 *a*Matt. 14:3; Mark 1:14; Luke 3:20; John 3:24 *b*Mark 1:14; Luke 4:14; John 1:43; 2:11
★13 *a*Matt. 11:23; Mark 1:21; 2:1; Luke 4:23, 31; John 2:12; 4:46f.
★14

15 *a*Is. 9:1

16 *a*Is. 9:2

17 *a*Mark 1:14, 15 *b*Matt. 3:2
18 *a*Matt. 4:18-22; Mark 1:16-20; Luke 5:2-11; John 1:40-42 *b*Matt. 15:29; Mark 7:31; Luke 5:1; John 6:1 *c*Matt. 10:2; 16:18; John 1:40, 42
★19

★21 *a*Matt. 10:2; 20:20
★23 *a*Mark 1:39; Luke 4:15, 44 *b*Matt. 9:35; 13:54; Mark 1:21; 6:2; 10:1; Luke 4:15; 6:6; 13:10; John 6:59; 18:20 *c*Matt. 3:2; 9:35; 24:14; Mark 1:14; Acts 20:25; 28:31 *d*Matt. 8:16; 9:35; 14:14; 15:30; 19:2; 21:14; Acts 10:38
24 *a*Mark 7:26; Luke 2:2; Acts 15:23; 18:18; 20:3; 21:3; Gal. 1:21 *b*Matt. 8:16, 28, 33; 9:32; 12:22; 15:22; Mark 1:32; 5:15, 16, 18; Luke 8:36; John 10:21 *c*Matt. 17:15 *d*Matt. 8:6; 9:2, 6; Mark 2:3, 4, 5, 9;
★25 *a*Mark 3:7, 8; Luke 6:17 *b*Mark 5:20; 7:31 *c*Matt. 4:15

★ 1 *a*Matt. 5-7; Luke 6:20-49 *b*Mark 3:13;

mountain; and after He sat down, His disciples came to Him. **2** And [a]opening His mouth He *began* to teach them, saying, **3** "[a]Blessed are the poor in spirit, for [b]theirs is the kingdom of heaven.

4 "Blessed are [a]those who mourn, for they shall be comforted.

5 "Blessed are [a]the gentle, for they shall inherit the earth.

6 "Blessed are [a]those who hunger and thirst for righteousness, for they shall be satisfied.

7 "Blessed are the merciful, for they shall receive mercy.

8 "Blessed are [a]the pure in heart, for [b]they shall see God.

9 "Blessed are the peacemakers, for [a]they shall be called sons of God.

10 "Blessed are those who have been [a]persecuted for the sake of righteousness, for [b]theirs is the kingdom of heaven.

11 "Blessed are you when *men* [a]cast insults at you, and persecute you, and say all kinds of evil against you falsely, on account of Me.

12 "Rejoice, and be glad, for your reward in heaven is great, for [a]so they persecuted the prophets who were before you.

13 "You are the salt of the earth; but [a]if the salt has become tasteless, how will it be made salty *again?* It is good for nothing anymore, except to be thrown out and trampled under foot by men.

14 "You are [a]the light of the world. A city set on a hill cannot be hidden.

15 "[a]Nor do *men* light a lamp, and put it under the peck-measure, but on the lampstand; and it gives light to all who are in the house.

16 "Let your light shine before men in such a way that they may [a]see your good works, and [b]glorify your Father who is in heaven.

B The Precepts for Kingdom Life, 5:17–48

1 The law of Moses, 5:17–20

17 "Do not think that I came to abolish the Law or the Prophets; I did not come to abolish, but to fulfill.

18 "For truly I say to you, [a]until heaven and earth pass away, not the smallest letter or stroke shall pass away from the Law, until all is accomplished.

19 "Whoever then annuls one of the least of these commandments, and so teaches others, shall be called least in the kingdom of heaven; but whoever keeps and teaches *them,* he shall be called great in the kingdom of heaven.

20 "For I say to you, that unless your righteousness surpasses *that* of the scribes and Pharisees, you shall not enter the kingdom of heaven.

2 The law of murder, 5:21–22

21 "[a]You have heard that the ancients were told, '[b]You shall not commit murder' and 'Whoever commits murder shall be liable to [c]the court.'

Marginal references:

2 [a]Matt. 13:35; Acts 8:35; 10:34; 18:14
★ **3-12**
3 [a]Matt. 5:3-12; Luke 6:20-23 [b]Matt. 5:10; 19:14; 25:34; Mark 10:14; Luke 6:20; 22:29f.
4 [a]Is. 61:2; John 16:20; Rev. 7:17
5 [a]Ps. 37:11
6 [a]Is. 55:1, 2; John 4:14; 6:48ff.; 7:37
8 [a]Ps. 24:4 [b]Heb. 12:14; 1 John 3:2; Rev. 22:4
9 [a]Matt. 5:45; Luke 6:35; Rom. 8:14
10 [a]1 Pet. 3:14 [b]Matt. 5:3; 19:14; 25:34; Mark 10:14; Luke 6:20; 22:29f.
11 [a]1 Pet. 4:14
12 [a]2 Chr. 36:16; Matt. 23:37; Acts 7:52; 1 Thess. 2:15; Heb. 11:33ff.; James 5:10
13 [a]Mark 9:50; Luke 14:34f.
14 [a]John 8:12
15 [a]Mark 4:21; Luke 8:16; 11:33
16 [a]1 Pet. 2:12 [b]Matt. 9:8
★ **18** [a]Matt. 24:35; Luke 16:17
★ **20**
21 [a]Matt. 5:27, 33, 38, 43 [b]Ex. 20:13; Deut. 5:17 [c]Deut. 16:18; 2 Chr. 19:5f.

---

found in Matthew, the others being 9:35–10:42; 13:1–52; 17:24–18:35; and 23:1–25:46. The Sermon on the Mount does not present the way of salvation but the way of righteous living for those who are in God's family, contrasting the new Way with the "old one" of the scribes and the Pharisees. For the Jews of Christ's day this message was a detailed explanation of "repent" (3:2; 4:17). It was also an elaboration of the spirit of the law (5:17, 21–22, 27–28). For all of us it is a detailed revelation of the righteousness of God, and its principles are applicable to the children of God today.

5:3-12 The Beatitudes (*blessed* means happy) describe the inner condition of a follower of Christ and promise him blessings in the future.

5:18 *smallest letter or stroke.* The smallest Hebrew letter is *yodh,* which looks like an apostrophe ('). A stroke is a very small extension or protrusion on several Hebrew letters which distinguish these letters from similar ones. The Lord's point is that every letter of every word of the O.T. is vital and will be fulfilled.

5:20 *your righteousness.* We may understand this as "your practice of religion."

22 "But I say to you that everyone who is angry with his brother shall be guilty before ᵃthe court; and whoever shall say to his brother, 'Raca,' shall be guilty before ᵇthe supreme court; and whoever shall say, 'You fool,' shall be guilty *enough to go* into the ᶜfiery hell.

3 The law of reconciliation, 5:23-26

23 "If therefore you are presenting your offering at the altar, and there remember that your brother has something against you,

24 leave your offering there before the altar, and go your way; first be reconciled to your brother, and then come and present your offering.

25 "ᵃMake friends quickly with your opponent at law while you are with him on the way, in order that your opponent may not deliver you to the judge, and the judge to the officer, and you be thrown into prison.

26 "Truly I say to you, you shall not come out of there, until you have paid up the last cent.

4 The law of adultery, 5:27-30

27 "ᵃYou have heard that it was said, 'ᵇYou shall not commit adultery';

28 but I say to you, that everyone who looks on a woman to lust for her has committed adultery with her already in his heart.

29 "And ᵃif your right eye makes you stumble, tear it out, and throw it from you; for it is better for you that one of the parts of your body perish, than for your whole body to be thrown into ᵇhell.

30 "And ᵃif your right hand makes you stumble, cut it off, and throw it from you; for it is better for you that one of the parts of your body perish, than for your whole body to go into ᵇhell.

5 The law of divorce, 5:31-32

31 "And it was said, 'ᵃWHOEVER DIVORCES HIS WIFE, LET HIM GIVE HER A CERTIFICATE OF DISMISSAL';

32 ᵃbut I say to you that everyone who divorces his wife, except for *the* cause of unchastity, makes her commit adultery; and whoever marries a divorced woman commits adultery.

6 The law of oaths, 5:33-37

33 "Again, ᵃyou have heard that the ancients were told, 'ᵇYou SHALL NOT MAKE FALSE VOWS, BUT SHALL FULFILL YOUR VOWS TO THE LORD.'

34 "But I say to you, ᵃmake no oath at all, either by heaven, for it is ᵇthe throne of God,

★22 ᵃDeut. 16:18; 2 Chr. 19:5f. ᵇMatt. 10:17; 26:59; Mark 13:9; 14:55; 15:1; Luke 22:66; John 11:47; Acts 4:15; 5:21; 6:12; 22:30; 23:1; 24:20 ᶜMatt. 5:29f.; 10:28; 18:9; 23:15, 33; Mark 9:43ff.; Luke 12:5; James 3:6

25 ᵃLuke 12:58

27 ᵃMatt. 5:21, 33, 38, 43 ᵇEx. 20:14; Deut. 5:18

★28

★29-30

29 ᵃMatt. 17:27; 18:9; Mark 9:47 ᵇMatt. 5:22

30 ᵃMatt. 17:27; 18:8; Mark 9:43 ᵇMatt. 5:22

31 ᵃDeut. 24:1, 3

★32 ᵃMatt. 19:9; Mark 10:11f.; Luke 16:18; 1 Cor. 7:11f.

★33 ᵃMatt. 5:21, 27, 38, 43; 23:16ff. ᵇLev. 19:12; Num. 30:2; Deut. 23:21

34 ᵃJames 5:12 ᵇIs. 66:1; Matt. 23:22

5:22 *Raca.* Probably means "empty-head." *fiery hell.* The word translated "hell" is *Geenna,* or *Gehenna,* a place in the valley of Hinnom where human sacrifices had been offered (cf. Jer. 7:31) and where the continuous burning of rubbish made it an apt illustration of the lake of fire (Mark 9:44; Jas. 3:6; Rev. 20:14).
5:28 The desire itself is sinful, and wrong desire leads to a sinful act.
5:29-30 This is strong language, used to emphasize the comparison; i.e., sin is so dangerous, because it leads to eternal condemnation, that it would be better to lose hands or eyes temporarily than to lose life eternally.
5:32 *except for the cause of unchastity.* See Matt. 19:3-9; Mark 10:2-12; and Luke 16:18 for Jesus' teaching on divorce (cf. 1 Cor. 7:10-11). It is disallowed except for unchastity,

which may mean (1) adultery, (2) unfaithfulness during the period of betrothal (see Matt. 1:19), or (3) marriage between near relatives (Lev. 18).
5:33 *make false vows.* Or, "perjure yourself." Oaths taken in the name of the Lord were binding, and perjury was strongly condemned in the law (Ex. 20:7; Lev. 19:12; Deut. 19:16-19). Every oath contained an affirmation or promise and an appeal to God as the omniscient punisher of falsehoods, which made the oath binding. Thus we find phrases like "as the Lord lives" (1 Sam. 14:39). The emphasis on the sanctity of oaths led to the feeling that ordinary phrasing need not be truthful or binding. Jesus, however, taught (Matt. 5:37) that we should say and mean yes or no and never equivocate.

35 ªIs. 66:1;
Acts 7:49
ᵇPs. 48:2

35 or by the earth, for it is the ªfootstool of His feet, or by Jerusalem, for it is ᵇTHE CITY OF THE GREAT KING.

36 "Nor shall you make an oath by your head, for you cannot make one hair white or black.

37 ªMatt.
6:13; 13:19,
38; John
17:15;
2 Thess. 3:3;
1 John
2:13f.; 3:12;
5:18f.

37 "But let your statement be, 'Yes, yes' or 'No, no'; and anything beyond these is of ªevil.

7 The law of nonresistance, 5:38–42

★38 ªMatt.
5:21, 27, 33,
43 ᵇEx.
21:24; Lev.
19:21

38 "ªYou have heard that it was said, ᵇAN EYE FOR AN EYE, AND A TOOTH FOR A TOOTH.'

39 ªMatt.
5:39-42;
Luke 6:29,
30; 1 Cor.
6:7

39 "But I say to you, do not resist him who is evil; but ªwhoever slaps you on your right cheek, turn to him the other also.

40 "And if anyone wants to sue you, and take your shirt, let him have your coat also.

41 "And whoever shall force you to go one mile, go with him two.

42 ªLuke
6:34f.

42 "ªGive to him who asks of you, and do not turn away from him who wants to borrow from you.

8 The law of love, 5:43–48

★43 ªMatt.
5:21, 27, 33,
38 ᵇLev.
19:18

43 "ªYou have heard that it was said, ᵇYOU SHALL LOVE YOUR NEIGHBOR, and hate your enemy.'

★44 ªLuke
6:27f.; 23:34;
Acts 7:60

44 "But I say to you, ªlove your enemies, and pray for those who persecute you

45 ªMatt. 5:9

45 in order that you may be ªsons of your Father who is in heaven; for He causes His sun to rise on the evil and the good, and sends rain on the righteous and the unrighteous.

46 ªLuke
6:32

46 "For ªif you love those who love you, what reward have you?

Do not even the tax-gatherers do the same?

47 "And if you greet your brothers only, what do you do more than others? Do not even the Gentiles do the same?

48 "Therefore ªyou are to be perfect, as your heavenly Father is perfect.

★48 ªLev.
19:2

C The Practice of Kingdom Life, 6:1–7:12

1 In relation to almsgiving, 6:1–4

6 "Beware of practicing your righteousness before men ªto be noticed by them; otherwise you have no reward with your Father who is in heaven.

1 ªMatt.
6:5, 16; 23:5

2 "When therefore you give alms, do not sound a trumpet before you, as the hypocrites do in the synagogues and in the streets, that they ªmay be honored by men. ᵇTruly I say to you, they have their reward in full.

2 ªMatt.
6:5, 16; 23:5
ᵇMatt. 6:5,
16; Luke
6:24

3 "But when you give alms, do not let your left hand know what your right hand is doing

4 that your alms may be in secret; and ªyour Father who sees in secret will repay you.

★ 4 ªMatt.
6:6, 18

2 In relation to prayer, 6:5–15

5 "And when you pray, you are not to be as the hypocrites; for they love to ªstand and pray in the synagogues and on the street corners, ᵇin order to be seen by men. ᶜTruly I say to you, they have their reward in full.

5 ªMark
11:25; Luke
18:11, 13
ᵇMatt. 6:1,
16 ᶜMatt.
6:2, 16; Luke
6:24

6 "But you, when you pray, ªgo into your inner room, and when you have shut your door, pray to your Father who is in

6 ªIs. 26:20
ᵇMatt. 6:4,
18

5:38 See Ex. 21:24. The *lex talionis* (law of retaliation) did provide for the ending of feuds, but Christ showed another way to do the same (Matt. 5:39–42). See note on Lev. 24:20.
5:43 See Lev. 19:16–18.
5:44 A new teaching, found nowhere in the O.T.
5:48 *perfect.* Not necessarily without sin, but mature and complete in the likeness of God.

6:1–18 Christ discusses three pharisaic practices of piety: almsgiving, prayer, and fasting.
6:4 *that your alms may be in secret.* Jewish tradition said that there was in the temple a "chamber of secrets" into which the devout used to put their gifts in secret so that the poor could receive support therefrom in secret.

secret, and ^byour Father who sees in secret will repay you.

7 "And when you are praying, do not use meaningless repetition, as the Gentiles do, for they suppose that they will be heard for their ^amany words.

8 "Therefore do not be like them; for ^ayour Father knows what you need, before you ask Him.

9 "^aPray, then, in this way:

'Our Father who art in heaven,
Hallowed be Thy name.
10 '^aThy kingdom come.
Thy will be done,
On earth as it is in heaven.
11 '^aGive us this day our daily bread.
12 'And forgive us our debts,
as we also have forgiven our debtors.
13 'And do not lead us into temptation, but deliver us from ^aevil. [For Thine is the kingdom, and the power, and the glory, forever. Amen.]'

14 "^aFor if you forgive men for their transgressions, your heavenly Father will also forgive you. **15** "But if you do not forgive men, then your Father will not forgive your transgressions.

3 In relation to fasting, 6:16-18

16 "And ^awhenever you fast, do not put on a gloomy face as the hypocrites *do*, for they neglect their appearance in order to be seen fasting by men. ^bTruly I say to you, they have their reward in full.

17 "But you, when you fast,

anoint your head, and wash your face

18 so that you may not be seen fasting by men, but by your Father who is in secret; and your ^aFather who sees in secret will repay you.

4 In relation to money, 6:19-24

19 "Do not lay up for yourselves treasures upon earth, where moth and rust destroy, and where thieves break in and steal.

20 "But lay up for yourselves ^atreasures in heaven, where neither moth nor rust destroys, and where thieves do not break in or steal;

21 for ^awhere your treasure is, there will your heart be also.

22 "^aThe lamp of the body is the eye; if therefore your eye is clear, your whole body will be full of light.

23 "But if ^ayour eye is bad, your whole body will be full of darkness. If therefore the light that is in you is darkness, how great is the darkness!

24 "^aNo one can serve two masters; for either he will hate the one and love the other, or he will hold to one and despise the other. You cannot serve God and ^bmammon.

5 In relation to anxiety, 6:25-34

25 "^aFor this reason I say to you, do not be ^banxious for your life, *as to* what you shall eat, or what you shall drink; nor for your body, *as to* what you shall put on. Is not life more than food, and the body than clothing?

Cross references (left column):
7 ^a1 Kin. 18:26f.
8 ^aMatt. 6:32
★ 9 ^aMatt. 6:9-13; Luke 11:2-4
10 ^aMatt. 3:2
★11 ^aProv. 30:8
★12
13 ^aMatt. 5:37
★14-15
14 ^aMatt. 18:35; Mark 11:25f.
16 ^aIs. 58:5 ^bMatt. 6:2

Cross references (right column):
18 ^aMatt. 6:4, 6
20 ^aMatt. 19:21; Luke 12:33; 1 Tim. 6:19
21 ^aLuke 12:34
22 ^aMatt. 6:22, 23; Luke 11:34, 35
23 ^aMatt. 20:15; Mark 7:22
★24 ^aLuke 16:13 ^bLuke 16:9, 11, 13
25 ^aMatt. 6:25-33; Luke 12:22-31 ^bMatt. 6:27, 28, 31, 34; Luke 10:41; 12:11, 22; Phil. 4:6; 1 Pet. 5:7

6:9 *in this way.* The Lord's Prayer is a model for our prayers. It begins with adoration of God (v. 9), acknowledges subjection to His will (v. 10), asks petitions of Him (vv. 11-13a), and ends with an ascription of praise (v. 13b, though this may have been added later).

6:11 *bread.* All necessary food.

6:12 *debts.* These are obligations incurred; i.e., sins of omission and commission. Forgiveness means cancellation of these debts or obliga-

tions.

6:14-15 Notice that the only point the Lord emphasizes in the prayer is the necessity for forgiving one another. Forgiveness with the Father depends on forgiveness among the members of the family of God. This is the forgiveness that affects fellowship within the family of God, not the forgiveness that leads to salvation.

6:24 *mammon* = money.

★26 aMatt.
10:29ff.

26 "aLook at the birds of the air, that they do not sow, neither do they reap, nor gather into barns, and *yet* your heavenly Father feeds them. Are you not worth much more than they?

★27 aMatt.
6:25, 28, 31,
34; Luke
10:41; 12:11,
22; Phil. 4:6;
1 Pet. 5:7
bPs. 39:5
28 aMatt.
6:25, 27, 31,
34; Luke
10:41; 12:11,
22; Phil. 4:6;
1 Pet. 5:7
29 a1 Kin.
10:4-7
30 aMatt.
8:26; 14:31;
16:8

27 "And which of you by being ªanxious can ᵇadd a *single* cubit to his life's span?

28 "And why are you ªanxious about clothing? Observe how the lilies of the field grow; they do not toil nor do they spin,

29 yet I say to you that even ªSolomon in all his glory did not clothe himself like one of these.

30 "But if God so arrays the grass of the field, which is *alive* today and tomorrow is thrown into the furnace, *will* He not much more *do so for* you, ªO men of little faith?

31 aMatt.
6:25, 27, 28,
34; Luke
10:41; 12:11,
22; Phil. 4:6;
1 Pet. 5:7
32 aMatt. 6:8

31 "Do not be ªanxious then, saying, 'What shall we eat?' or 'What shall we drink?' or 'With what shall we clothe ourselves?'

32 "For all these things the Gentiles eagerly seek; for ªyour heavenly Father knows that you need all these things.

33 aMatt.
19:28; Mark
10:29f.; Luke
18:29f.
1 Tim. 4:8

33 "But seek first His kingdom and His righteousness; and ªall these things shall be added to you.

★34 aMatt.
6:25, 27, 28,
31; Luke
10:41; 12:11,
22; Phil. 4:6;
1 Pet. 5:7

34 "Therefore do not be ªanxious for tomorrow; for tomorrow will care for itself. *Each* day has enough trouble of its own.

6   In relation to judging, 7:1-5

★ 1 aMatt.
7:1-5; Luke
6:37f., 41f.
2 aMark
4:24; Luke
6:38

7 "ªDo not judge lest you be judged.

2 "For in the way you judge, you will be judged; and ªby your standard of measure, it will be measured to you.

3 "And why do you look at the speck that is in your brother's eye, but do not notice the log that is in your own eye?

4 "Or how can you say to your brother, 'Let me take the speck out of your eye,' and behold, the log is in your own eye?

5 "You hypocrite, first take the log out of your own eye, and then you will see clearly to take the speck out of your brother's eye.

7   In relation to prudence, 7:6

6 "Do not give what is holy to dogs, and do not throw your pearls before swine, lest they trample them under their feet, and turn and tear you to pieces.   ★ 6

8   In relation to prayer, 7:7-11

7 aMatt.
7:7-11; Luke
11:9-13
bMatt. 18:19,
21:22; Mark
11:24; John
14:13; 15:7,
16; 16:23f.;
James 1:5f.;
1 John 3:22;
5:14f.

7 "ªAsk, and ᵇit shall be given to you; seek, and you shall find; knock, and it shall be opened to you.

8 "For everyone who asks receives, and he who seeks finds, and to him who knocks it shall be opened.

9 "Or what man is there among you, when his son shall ask him for a loaf, will give him a stone?

10 "Or if he shall ask for a fish, he will not give him a snake, will he?

11 "If you then, being evil, know how to give good gifts to your children, how much more shall your Father who is in heaven give what is good to those who ask Him?

6:26 *your heavenly Father feeds them.* God feeds the birds not by miraculous supply of food but through natural processes involving the earth and the birds' use of their faculties. Likewise, the child of God, though sometimes the recipient of a miracle, is usually cared for by normal means.

6:27 *cubit.* About 18 inches.

6:34 *trouble.* Let each day's trouble be enough for that day. This saying is like a proverb.

7:1 *Do not judge.* This does not mean that one is never, in any sense or to any extent, to judge another, for v. 5 indicates that when one's own life is pure he should "take the speck out" of the brother's eye. It does mean, however, that a follower of Christ is not to be censorious.

7:6 The disciples were expected to make moral distinctions and not allow those who reject the invitation of Christ to treat precious things as cheap.

9 In relation to others, 7:12

★12 aLuke 6:31 bMatt. 22:40; Rom. 13:8ff.; Gal. 5:14

12 "aTherefore, however you want people to treat you, so treat them, for bthis is the Law and the Prophets.

D The Proof of Kingdom Life, 7:13–29

★13-29

13 aLuke 13:24

13 "aEnter by the narrow gate; for the gate is wide, and the way is broad that leads to destruction, and many are those who enter by it.

14 "For the gate is small, and the way is narrow that leads to life, and few are those who find it.

15 aMatt. 24:11, 24; Mark 13:22; Luke 6:26; Acts 13:6; 2 Pet. 2:1; 1 John 4:1; Rev. 16:13; 19:20; 20:10 bEzek. 22:27; John 10:12; Acts 20:29

15 "Beware of the afalse prophets, who come to you in sheep's clothing, but inwardly are bravenous wolves.

16 aMatt. 7:20; 12:33; Luke 6:44; James 3:12

16 "You will know them aby their fruits. Grapes are not gathered from thorn *bushes*, nor figs from thistles, are they?

17 "Even so, every good tree bears good fruit; but the bad tree bears bad fruit.

18 "A good tree cannot produce bad fruit, nor can a bad tree produce good fruit.

19 aMatt. 3:10; Luke 13:7

19 "aEvery tree that does not bear good fruit is cut down and thrown into the fire.

20 aMatt. 7:16; 12:33; Luke 6:44; James 3:12

20 "So then, you will know them aby their fruits.

★21 aLuke 6:46

21 "aNot everyone who says to Me, 'Lord, Lord,' will enter the kingdom of heaven; but he who does the will of My Father who is in heaven.

★22 aMatt. 25:11f.; Luke 13:25ff. bMatt. 10:15

22 "aMany will say to Me on bthat day, 'Lord, Lord, did we not prophesy in Your name, and in Your name cast out demons, and in Your name perform many miracles?'

23 "And then I will declare to them, 'I never knew you; aDEPART FROM ME, YOU WHO PRACTICE LAWLESSNESS.'

23 aPs. 6:8; Matt. 25:41; Luke 13:27

24 "Therefore aeveryone who hears these words of Mine, and acts upon them, may be compared to a wise man, who built his house upon the rock.

24 aMatt. 7:24-27; Luke 6:47-49; James 1:22-25

25 "And the rain descended, and the floods came, and the winds blew, and burst against that house; and *yet* it did not fall, for it had been founded upon the rock.

26 "And everyone who hears these words of Mine, and does not act upon them, will be like a foolish man, who built his house upon the sand.

27 "And the rain descended, and the floods came, and the winds blew, and burst against that house; and it fell, and great was its fall."

28 "aThe result was that when Jesus had finished these words, bthe multitudes were amazed at His teaching;

28 aMatt. 11:1; 13:53; 19:1; 26:1 bMatt. 13:54; 22:33; Mark 1:22; 6:2; 11:18; Luke 4:32; John 7:46

29 for He was teaching them as *one* having authority, and not as their scribes.

★29

III THE PROOF OF THE KING, 8:1–9:38

A Exhibit 1: Power, 8:1–34

1 Power over defilement, 8:1–4

8 And when He had come down from the mountain, great multitudes followed Him.

7:12 The well-known Golden Rule. It was also taught by the great Jewish rabbis, such as Rabbi Hillel.

7:13–29 In these verses notice the two ways (13–14), two trees (15–20), two professions (21–23), and two builders (24–29). The "two ways" was a common teaching method in Judaism and Greco-Roman philosophy.

7:21 Obedience to the will of God comes first.

7:22 *demons.* There is only one devil (Satan) but there are many demons. The demons are those angels who sinned with Satan by following him when he revolted against God. Some are confined (2 Pet. 2:4), but many are active in the world (Matt. 12:43-45). They seek to thwart the purposes of God (Eph. 6:11-12); they promote their own system of doctrine (1 Tim. 4:1); they can inflict diseases (Matt. 9:33) and possess the bodies of men and of animals (Matt. 4:24; Mark 5:13).

7:29 The scribes had to rely on tradition for authority; Christ's authority was His own. It disturbed the Pharisees that He had no "credentials" as an official teacher in their system.

★ 2 aMatt.
8:2-4; Mark
1:40-44;
Luke 5:12-14
bMatt. 9:18;
15:25; 18:26;
20:20; John
9:38; Acts
10:25

2 And behold, a leper acame to Him, and bbowed down to Him, saying, "Lord, if You are willing, You can make me clean."

3 And He stretched out His hand and touched him, saying, "I am willing; be cleansed." And immediately his leprosy was cleansed.

★ 4 aMatt.
9:30; 12:16;
17:9; Mark
1:44; 3:12;
5:43; 7:36;
8:30; 9:9;
Luke 4:41;
8:56; 9:21
bMark 1:44;
Luke 5:14;
17:14 cLev.
13:49; 14:2ff.

4 And Jesus *said to him, "aSee that you tell no one; but bgo, cshow yourself to the priest, and present the offering that Moses commanded, for a testimony to them."

2 Power over distance, 8:5-13

★ 5 aMatt.
8:5-13; Luke
7:1-10

5 And awhen He had entered Capernaum, a centurion came to Him, entreating Him,

6 aMatt.
4:24

6 and saying, "Lord, my servant is lying aparalyzed at home, suffering great pain."

7 And He *said to him, "I will come and heal him."

8 But the centurion answered and said, "Lord, I am not worthy for You to come under my roof, but just say the word, and my servant will be healed.

★9

9 "For I, too, am a man under authority, with soldiers under me; and I say to this one, 'Go!' and he goes, and to another, 'Come!' and he comes, and to my slave, 'Do this!' and he does it."

10 Now when Jesus heard this, He marveled, and said to those who were following, "Truly I say to you, I have not found such great faith with anyone in Israel.

★11 aIs.
49:12; 59:19;
Mal. 1:11;
Luke 13:29

11 "And I say to you, that many ashall come from east and west, and recline at the table with Abraham, and Isaac, and Jacob, in the kingdom of heaven;

12 but athe sons of the kingdom shall be cast out into bthe outer darkness; in that place cthere shall be weeping and gnashing of teeth."

★12 aMatt.
13:38 bMatt.
22:13; 25:30
cMatt. 13:42,
50; 22:13;
24:51; 25:30;
Luke 13:28

13 And Jesus said to the centurion, "Go your way; let it be done to you aas you have believed." And the servant was healed that very hour.

13 aMatt.
9:22, 29

3 Power over disease, 8:14-17

14 aAnd when Jesus had come to Peter's home, He saw his mother-in-law lying sick in bed with a fever.

★14 aMatt.
8:14-16;
Mark 1:29-
34; Luke
4:38-41

15 And He touched her hand, and the fever left her; and she arose, and waited on Him.

★15

16 And when evening had come, they brought to Him many awho were demon-possessed; and He cast out the spirits with a word, and bhealed all who were ill

16 aMatt.
4:24 bMatt.
4:23; 8:33

17 in order that what was spoken through Isaiah the prophet might be fulfilled, saying, "aHE HIMSELF TOOK OUR INFIRMITIES, AND CARRIED AWAY OUR DISEASES."

★17 aIs.
53:4

18 aMark
4:35; Luke
8:22

4 Power over disciples, 8:18-22

18 Now when Jesus saw a crowd around Him, aHe gave orders to depart to the other side.

19 aAnd a certain scribe came and said to Him, "Teacher, I will follow You wherever You go."

19 aMatt.
8:19-22;
Luke 9:57-60

20 And Jesus *said to him, "The foxes have holes, and the birds of the air have nests; but

★20 aDan.
7:13; Matt.
9:6; 12:8, 32,
40; 13:41;
16:13, 27f.;
17:9; 19:28;
26:64; Mark
8:38; Luke
12:8; 18:8;
21:36; John
1:51; 3:13f.;
6:27; 12:34;
Acts 7:56

8:2 a leper. See note on Luke 5:12.

8:4 the offering that Moses commanded. See Lev. 14:4-32.

8:5 centurion. A Roman army officer who commanded 100 men.

8:9 a man under authority. If a lesser officer can give orders, certainly Christ, who possesses all authority, can.

8:11 Gentiles will be included in the blessings of the millennial reign of Christ on this earth.

8:12 sons = heirs = Jews.

8:14 his mother-in-law. Peter was married (see 1 Cor. 9:5).

8:15 waited on Him = served Him food.

8:17 See Isa. 53:4.

8:20 Son of Man. The title "Son of God" is Jesus' divine name (Matt. 8:29); "Son of David," His Jewish name (Matt. 9:27); but "Son of Man," the name that links Him to the earth and to His mission. It was His favorite designation of Himself (used over 80 times) and was based on Dan. 7:13-14. It emphasizes: (1) His lowliness and humanity (Matt. 8:20); (2) His suffering and death (Luke 19:10); and (3) His future reign as King (Matt. 24:27).

^athe Son of Man has nowhere to lay His head."

21 And another of the disciples said to Him, "Lord, permit me first to go and bury my father."

22 But Jesus *said to him, "^aFollow Me; and allow the dead to bury their own dead."

22 ^aMatt.
9:9; Mark
2:14; Luke
9:59; John
1:43; 21:19

5 *Power over the deep, 8:23-27*

23 ^aMatt.
8:23-27;
Mark 4:36-
41; Luke
8:22-25

23 ^aAnd when He got into the boat, His disciples followed Him.

24 And behold, there arose a great storm in the sea, so that the boat was covered with the waves; but He Himself was asleep.

25 And they came to *Him*, and awoke Him, saying, "Save *us*, Lord; we are perishing!"

26 ^aMatt.
6:30; 14:31;
16:8

26 And He *said to them, "Why are you timid, ^ayou men of little faith?" Then He arose, and rebuked the winds and the sea; and it became perfectly calm.

27 And the men marveled, saying, "What kind of a man is this, that even the winds and the sea obey Him?"

6 *Power over demons, 8:28-34*

★28 ^aMatt.
8:28-34;
Mark 5:1-17;
Luke 8:26-37
^bMatt. 4:24

28 ^aAnd when He had come to the other side into the country of the Gadarenes, two men who were ^bdemon-possessed met Him as they were coming out of the tombs; *they were* so exceedingly violent that no one could pass by that road.

29 ^aJudg.
11:12;
2 Sam.
16:10; 19:22;
1 Kin. 17:18;
2 Kin. 3:13;
2 Chr. 35:21;
Mark 1:24;
5:7; Luke
4:34; 8:28;
John 2:4

29 And behold, they cried out, saying, "^aWhat do we have to do with You, Son of God? Have You come here to torment us before the time?"

30 Now there was at a distance from them a herd of many swine feeding.

31 And the demons *began* to entreat Him, saying, "If You are *going to* cast us out, send us into the herd of swine."

32 And He said to them, "Begone!" And they came out, and went into the swine, and behold, the whole herd rushed down the steep bank into the sea and perished in the waters.

33 ^aMatt.
4:24

33 And the herdsmen ran away; and went to the city, and reported everything, including the *incident* of the ^ademoniacs.

34 And behold, the whole city came out to meet Jesus; and when they saw Him, they entreated *Him* to depart from their region.

B Exhibit 2: Pardon, 9:1-17

1 *Pardon of a paralytic, 9:1-8*

★ 1 ^aMatt.
4:13; Mark
5:21

9 And getting into a boat, He crossed over, and came to ^aHis own city.

★ 2 ^aMatt.
9:2-8; Mark
2:3-12; Luke
5:18-26
^bMatt. 4:24;
9:6 ^cMatt.
9:22; 14:27;
Mark 6:50;
10:49; John
16:33; Acts
23:11 ^dMark
2:5, 9; Luke
5:20, 23;
7:48

2 ^aAnd behold, they were bringing to Him a ^bparalytic, lying on a bed; and Jesus seeing their faith said to the paralytic, "^cTake courage, My son, ^dyour sins are forgiven."

3 And behold, some of the scribes said to themselves, "This *fellow blasphemes*."

4 ^aMatt.
12:25; Luke
6:8; 9:47

4 And Jesus ^aknowing their thoughts said, "Why are you thinking evil in your hearts?

★ 5 ^aMark
2:5, 9; Luke
5:20, 23;
7:48

5 "For which is easier, to say, '^aYour sins are forgiven,' or to say, 'Rise, and walk'?

6 ^aMatt.
8:20 ^bMatt.
4:24; 9:2

6 "But in order that you may know that ^athe Son of Man has authority on earth to forgive sins"—then He *said to the ^bparalytic—"Rise, take up your bed, and go home."

7 And he rose, and went home.

8:28 *Gadarenes.* Lived on the E. shore of the Lake of Galilee.

9:1 *His own city.* Capernaum.

9:2 *your sins are forgiven.* This may indicate that the man's sickness was the direct result of sin. Some Jews speculated that such was always the case, but see John 9:2 and note at

Phil. 2:30.

9:5 It is obviously easier to *say,* "Your sins are forgiven," since the validity of the statement cannot be tested so easily as "Rise." By making the statement, Christ was asserting a prerogative of God, who alone can forgive sins.

8 aMatt.
5:16; 15:31;
Mark 2:12;
Luke 2:20;
5:25, 26;
7:16; 13:13;
17:15; 23:47;
John 15:8;
Acts 4:21;
11:18; 21:20;
2 Cor. 9:13;
Gal. 1:24
9 aMatt.
9:9-17; Mark
2:14-22;
Luke 5:27-38
bMatt. 10:3;
Mark 2:14;
3:18; Luke
6:15; Acts
1:13 cMatt.
8:22
★10

8 But when the multitudes saw *this*, they were filled with awe, and ^aglorified God, who had given such authority to men.

2 Pardon of a publican, 9:9-13

9 ^aAnd as Jesus passed on from there, He saw a man, called ^bMatthew, sitting in the tax office; and He *said to him, "^cFollow Me!" And he rose, and followed Him.

10 And it happened that as He was reclining *at the table* in the house, behold many tax-gatherers and sinners came and were dining with Jesus and His disciples.

11 aMatt.
11:19; Mark
2:16; Luke
5:30; 15:2

11 And when the Pharisees saw *this*, they said to His disciples, "^aWhy is your Teacher eating with the tax-gatherers and sinners?"

12 aMark
2:17; Luke
5:31

12 But when He heard this, He said, "*It is* not ^athose who are healthy who need a physician, but those who are sick.

★13 aMatt.
12:7 bHos.
6:6 cMark
2:17; Luke
5:32; 1 Tim.
1:15

13 "But go and learn ^awhat *this* means, '^bI DESIRE COMPASSION, AND NOT SACRIFICE,' for ^cI did not come to call the righteous, but sinners."

3 Problem concerning fasting, 9:14-17

★14 aLuke
18:12

14 Then the disciples of John *came to Him, saying, "Why do we and ^athe Pharisees fast, but Your disciples do not fast?"

15 And Jesus said to them, "The attendants of the bridegroom cannot mourn as long as the bridegroom is with them, can they? But the days will come when the bridegroom is taken away from them, and then they will fast.

16 "But no one puts a patch of unshrunk cloth on an old garment; for the patch pulls away from the garment, and a worse tear results.

17 "Nor do *men* put new wine into old wineskins; otherwise the wineskins burst, and the wine pours out, and the wineskins are ruined; but they put new wine into fresh wineskins, and both are preserved."

★16-17

C Exhibit 3: Power, 9:18-38
1 Power over death, 9:18-26

18 ^aWhile He was saying these things to them, behold, there came a *synagogue* official, and ^bbowed down before Him, saying, "My daughter has just died; but come and lay Your hand on her, and she will live."

19 And Jesus rose and *began* to follow him, and *so did* His disciples.

20 And behold, a woman who had been suffering from a hemorrhage for twelve years, came up behind Him and touched ^athe fringe of His cloak;

21 for she was saying to herself, "If I only ^atouch His garment, I shall get well."

22 But Jesus turning and seeing her said, "Daughter, ^atake courage; ^byour faith has made you well." And at once the woman was made well.

23 And when Jesus came into the official's house, and saw ^athe flute-players, and the crowd in noisy disorder,

24 He *began* to say, "Depart; for the girl ^ahas not died, but is

18 aMatt.
9:18-26;
Mark 5:22-
43; Luke
8:41-56
bMatt. 8:2

★20 aNum.
15:38; Deut.
22:12; Matt.
14:36; 23:5

21 aMatt.
14:36; Mark
3:10; Luke
6:19

22 aMatt. 9:2
bMatt. 9:29;
15:28; Mark
5:34; 10:52;
Luke 7:50;
8:48; 17:19;
18:42

★23 a2 Chr.
35:25; Jer.
9:17; 16:6;
Ezek. 24:17

24 aJohn
11:13; Acts
20:10

9:10 *tax-gatherers and sinners*. Men who collected taxes for the Romans had a bad reputation for extortion and malpractice. "Sinners" were those whose daily occupations rendered them ceremonially unclean and not, in Pharisaic eyes, to be associated with.

9:13 See Hos. 6:6.

9:14 The Pharisees fasted twice a week—conspicuous piety. John's followers were probably fasting in mourning for him. The required public fasts were only 3 in number: the Day of Atonement; the day before Purim; and the 9th

of Ab, commemorating the fall of Jerusalem.

9:16-17 The old and new cannot be combined. See note at Luke 5:37.

9:20 *the fringe of His cloak*. Probably the fringes or tassels at the corners of Christ's mantle. These were religious reminders to the wearer to observe the commandments (Num. 15:37-39).

9:23 *flute-players*. It was customary, even among the very poor, to hire two or more flute-players at times of mourning.

asleep." And they *began* laughing at Him.

25 But when the crowd had been put out, He entered and took her by the hand; and the girl arose.

26 And [a]this news went out into all that land.

26 [a]Matt.
4:24; 9:31;
14:1; Mark
1:28, 45;
Luke 4:14,
37; 5:15;
7:17

2 Power over darkness, 9:27-31

27 And as Jesus passed on from there, two blind men followed Him, crying out, and saying, "Have mercy on us, [a]Son of David!"

28 And after He had come into the house, the blind men came up to Him, and Jesus *said to them, "Do you believe that I am able to do this?" They *said to Him, "Yes, Lord."

29 Then He touched their eyes, saying, "Be it done to you [a]according to your faith."

30 And their eyes were opened. And Jesus [a]sternly warned them, saying, "See *here*, let no one know *about this!*"

31 But they went out, and [a]spread the news about Him in all that land.

27 [a]Matt.
1:1; 12:23;
15:22; 20:30,
31; 21:9, 15;
22:42; Mark
10:47, 48;
12:35; Luke
18:38, 39;
20:41f.

29 [a]Matt.
8:13; 9:22

30 [a]Matt. 8:4

31 [a]Matt.
4:24; 9:26;
14:1; Mark
1:28, 45;
Luke 4:14,
37; 5:15;
7:17

3 Power over dumbness, 9:32-34

32 And as they were going out, behold, [a]a dumb man, [b]demon-possessed, was brought to Him.

33 And after the demon was cast out, the dumb man spoke; and the multitudes marveled, saying, "[a]Nothing like this was ever seen in Israel."

34 But the Pharisees were saying, "He casts out the demons [a]by the ruler of the demons."

32 [a]Matt.
12:22, 24
[b]Matt. 4:24

33 [a]Mark
2:12

34 [a]Matt.
12:24; Mark
3:22; Luke
11:15; John
7:20f.

4 Power over disease, 9:35

35 And Jesus was going about all the cities and the villages, [a]teaching in their synagogues, and proclaiming the gospel of the kingdom, and [b]healing every kind of disease and every kind of sickness.

35 [a]Matt.
4:23 [b]Matt.
4:23; Mark
1:14

5 Pity on the people, 9:36-38

36 And [a]seeing the multitudes, He felt compassion for them, [b]because they were distressed and downcast like sheep without a shepherd.

37 Then He *said to His disciples, "[a]The harvest is plentiful, but the workers are few.

38 "[a]Therefore beseech the Lord of the harvest to send out workers into His harvest."

36 [a]Matt.
14:14; 15:32;
Mark 6:34;
8:2 [b]Num.
27:17; Ezek.
34:5; Zech.
10:2; Mark
6:34
37 [a]Luke
10:2

38 [a]Luke
10:2

IV THE PROGRAM OF THE KING, 10:1-16:12

A The Program Announced, 10:1-11:1

10 And [a]having summoned His twelve disciples, He gave them authority over unclean spirits, to cast them out, and to [b]heal every kind of disease and every kind of sickness.

2 [a]Now the names of the twelve apostles are these: The first, [b]Simon, who is called Peter; and [c]Andrew his brother; and [d]James the *son* of Zebedee, and John his brother;

3 [a]Philip and Bartholomew; [b]Thomas and [c]Matthew the tax-gatherer; [d]James the *son* of Alphaeus, and [e]Thaddaeus;

★ 1 [a]Mark
3:13-15; 6:7
[b]Matt. 9:35;
Luke 9:1

★ 2 [a]Matt.
10:2-4; Mark
3:16-19;
Luke 6:14-
16; Acts 1:13
[b]Matt. 4:18
[c]Matt. 4:18
[d]Matt. 4:21

3 [a]John
1:45ff. [b]John
11:16; 14:5;
20:24ff.; 21:2
[c]Matt. 9:9
[d]Mark 15:40
[e]Mark 3:18;
Luke 6:16;
Acts 1:13

10:1 *disciples.* A disciple is one who is taught by another; he is a learner. In the Gospels the word is frequently used—of disciples of Moses (John 9:28), of John the Baptist (John 3:25), and of Christ. Judas is an example of an unsaved disciple of Christ and there were others who deserted Him as well (John 6:66). The word is used in Acts as a synonym for believer. It does not appear at all in the rest of the N.T.

10:2 *apostles.* The word "apostle" means "one sent forth" as an ambassador who bears a message and who represents the one who sent him. The qualifications included: (1) seeing the Lord and being an eyewitness to His resurrection (Acts 1:22; 1 Cor. 9:1); (2) being invested with miraculous sign-gifts (Acts 5:15-16; Heb. 2:3-4); and (3) being chosen by the Lord or the Holy Spirit (Matt. 10:1-2; Acts 1:26).

★ **4** aMatt.
26:14; Luke
22:3; John
6:71; 13:2,
26
5 aMark
6:7; Luke 9:2
b2 Kin.
17:24ff.;
Luke 9:52;
10:33; 17:16;
John 4:9,
39.; 8:48;
Acts 8:25
6 aMatt.
15:24
7 aMatt. 3:2

9 aMatt.
10:9-15;
Mark 6:8-11;
Luke 9:3-5;
10:4-12;
Luke 22:35
★**10** a1 Cor.
9:14; 1 Tim.
5:18

12 a1 Sam.
25:6; Ps.
122:7, 8

14 aActs
13:51
15 aMatt.
11:22, 24
bMatt. 11:24;
2 Pet. 2:6;
Jude 7
cMatt. 7:22;
11:22, 24;
12:36; Acts
17:31;
1 Thess. 5:4;
Heb. 10:25;
2 Pet. 2:9;
3:7; 1 John
4:17; Jude 6

4 Simon the Zealot, and aJudas Iscariot, the one who betrayed Him.

5 aThese twelve Jesus sent out after instructing them, saying, "Do not go in the way of the Gentiles, and do not enter any city of the bSamaritans;

6 but rather go to athe lost sheep of the house of Israel.

7 "And as you go, preach, saying, 'aThe kingdom of heaven is at hand.'

8 "Heal the sick, raise the dead, cleanse the lepers, cast out demons; freely you received, freely give.

9 "aDo not acquire gold, or silver, or copper for your money belts,

10 or a bag for your journey, or even two tunics, or sandals, or a staff; for athe worker is worthy of his support.

11 "And into whatever city or village you enter, inquire who is worthy in it; and abide there until you go away.

12 "And as you enter the house, agive it your greeting.

13 "And if the house is worthy, let your greeting of peace come upon it; but if it is not worthy, let your greeting of peace return to you.

14 "And whoever does not receive you, nor heed your words, as you go out of that house or that city, ashake off the dust of your feet.

15 "Truly I say to you, ait will be more tolerable for the land of bSodom and Gomorrah in cthe day of judgment, than for that city.

16 "aBehold, I send you out as sheep in the midst of wolves; therefore be bshrewd as serpents, and cinnocent as doves.

17 "But beware of men; for they will deliver you up to the acourts, and scourge you bin their synagogues;

18 and you shall even be brought before governors and kings for My sake, as a testimony to them and to the Gentiles.

19 "aBut when they deliver you up, bdo not become anxious about how or what you will speak; for it shall be given you in that hour what you are to speak.

20 "For ait is not you who speak, but it is the Spirit of your Father who speaks in you.

21 "aAnd brother will deliver up brother to death, and a father his child; and bchildren will rise up against parents, and cause them to be put to death.

22 "And ayou will be hated by all on account of My name, but bit is the one who has endured to the end who will be saved.

23 "But whenever they apersecute you in this city, flee to the next; for truly I say to you, you shall not finish going through the cities of Israel, buntil the Son of Man comes.

24 "aA disciple is not above his teacher, nor a slave above his master.

25 "It is enough for the disciple that he become as his teacher, and the slave as his master. aIf

16 aLuke
10:3 bGen.
3:1; Matt.
24:25; Rom.
16:19 cHos.
7:11
★**17** aMatt.
5:22 bMatt.
23:34; Mark
13:9; Luke
12:11; Acts
5:40; 22:19;
26:11

19 aMatt.
10:19-22;
Mark 13:11-
13; Luke
21:12-17
bMatt. 6:25

20 aLuke
12:12; Acts
4:8; 13:9;
2 Cor. 13:3
★**21-23**

21 aMatt.
10:35, 36
bMic. 7:6

22 aMatt.
24:9; John
15:18ff.
bMatt. 24:13

23 aMatt.
23:34 bMatt.
16:27f.

24 aLuke
6:40; John
13:16; 15:20
★**25** aMatt.
9:34 b2 Kin.
1:2; Matt.
12:24, 27;
Mark 3:22;
Luke 11:15,
18, 19

10:4 *Zealot.* As in Luke 6:15 and Acts 1:13 Simon is called "Zelotes" (the Zealot) (the equivalent Greek term for Cananaean, a resident of Cana). He likely belonged, before following the Lord, to the extremist party of Zealots who advocated the overthrow of Rome by force.

10:10 *or a bag for your journey.* They are to travel light; perhaps it was a quick journey. They could count on traditional hospitality at the hands of many devout Jewish householders. Notice the later change of instructions in Luke 22:36.

10:17 *scourge* = to flog with a bastinado (stick or club), a painful punishment.

10:21-23 These verses are a prediction of persecution in the tribulation days and at the second coming of Christ (Matt. 24:9-14). Such unnatural acts against members of one's own family have taken place under totalitarian regimes in the past and in modern times.

10:25 *Beelzebul.* Means "lord of flies," a guardian deity of the Ekronites (2 Kings 1:2), but used by the Jews as an epithet for Satan. The name may have been a mocking Hebrew alteration of Baal-zebul, a local arch-demon of N. Palestine and Syria. For Jesus' enemies to allege that He was possessed by Beelzebul was the worst kind of blasphemy (Mark 3:22).

they have called the head of the house ᵇBeelzebul, how much more the members of his household!

26 "Therefore do not ᵃfear them, ᵇfor there is nothing covered that will not be revealed, and hidden that will not be known.

27 "ᵃWhat I tell you in the darkness, speak in the light; and what you hear *whispered* in *your* ear, proclaim ᵇupon the housetops.

28 "And do not fear those who kill the body, but are unable to kill the soul; but rather ᵃfear Him who is able to destroy both soul and body in ᵇhell.

29 "ᵃAre not two sparrows sold for a cent? And *yet* not one of them will fall to the ground apart from your Father.

30 "But ᵃthe very hairs of your head are all numbered.

31 "Therefore do not fear; ᵃyou are of more value than many sparrows.

32 "Everyone therefore who shall confess Me before men, I will also confess ᵃhim before My Father who is in heaven.

33 "But ᵃwhoever shall deny Me before men, I will also deny him before My Father who is in heaven.

34 "ᵃDo not think that I came to bring peace on the earth; I did not come to bring peace, but a sword.

35 "For I came to ᵃSET A MAN AGAINST HIS FATHER, AND A DAUGHTER AGAINST HER MOTHER, AND A DAUGHTER-IN-LAW AGAINST HER MOTHER-IN-LAW;

36 and ᵃA MAN'S ENEMIES WILL BE THE MEMBERS OF HIS HOUSEHOLD.

37 "ᵃHe who loves father or mother more than Me is not wor-

thy of Me; and he who loves son or daughter more than Me is not worthy of Me.

38 "And ᵃhe who does not take his cross and follow after Me is not worthy of Me.

39 "ᵃHe who has found his life shall lose it, and he who has lost his life for My sake shall find it.

40 "ᵃHe who receives you receives Me, and ᵇhe who receives Me receives Him who sent Me.

41 "He who receives a prophet in *the* name of a prophet shall receive a prophet's reward; and he who receives a righteous man in the name of a righteous man shall receive a righteous man's reward.

42 "And ᵃwhoever in the name of a disciple gives to one of these little ones even a cup of cold water to drink, truly I say to you he shall not lose his reward."

11 ᵃAnd it came about that when Jesus had finished giving instructions to His twelve disciples, He departed from there ᵇto teach and preach in their cities.

B The Program Attested, 11:2–12:50

1 By comforting John's disciples, 11:2–19

2 ᵃNow when ᵇJohn in prison heard of the works of Christ, he sent *word* by his disciples,

3 and said to Him, "Are You ᵃthe Expected One, or shall we look for someone else?"

4 And Jesus answered and said to them, "Go and report to John what you hear and see:

Side references (left column)
26 ᵃMatt. 10:26-33; Luke 12:2-9 ᵇMark 4:22; Luke 8:17; 12:2
27 ᵃLuke 12:3 ᵇMatt. 24:17
★**28** ᵃHeb. 10:31 ᵇMatt. 5:22
★**29** ᵃLuke 12:6
30 ᵃ1 Sam. 14:45; 2 Sam. 14:11; 1 Kin. 1:52; Luke 21:18; Acts 27:34
31 ᵃMatt. 12:12
32 ᵃLuke 12:8; Rev. 3:5
33 ᵃMark 8:38; Luke 9:26; 2 Tim. 2:12
★**34** ᵃMatt. 10:34, 35; Luke 12:51-53
35 ᵃMic. 7:6; Matt. 10:21
36 ᵃMic. 7:6; Matt. 10:21
37 ᵃLuke 14:26

Side references (right column)
★**38** ᵃMatt. 16:24; Mark 8:34; Luke 9:23; 14:27
39 ᵃMatt. 16:25; Mark 8:35; Luke 9:24; 17:33; John 12:25
40 ᵃMatt. 18:5; Luke 10:16; John 13:20; Gal. 4:14 ᵇMark 9:37; Luke 9:48; John 12:44
★**41**
42 ᵃMatt. 25:40; Mark 9:41
1 ᵃMatt. 7:28 ᵇMatt. 9:35
2 ᵃMatt. 11:2-19; Luke 7:18-35 ᵇMatt. 14:3; Mark 6:17; Luke 9:7ff.
3 ᵃPs. 118:26; Matt. 11:10; John 6:14; 11:27; Heb. 10:37

10:28 *Him.* i.e., God, not Satan.
10:29 *a cent.* This small copper coin is called, in the Greek of this verse, *assarion.* Its value was 1/16 of a denarius, the basic unit in Roman coinage. One denarius was the day's wage of a rural worker. *apart from your Father.* Without His knowledge.
10:34 Christ's mission involves tension, persecution, death. The gospel divides families (cf.

Mic. 7:6). The world will experience true peace only when the King returns again to rule (Isa. 2:4).
10:38 *cross.* This reference to a cross needed no explanation, for the Jews had seen thousands of their countrymen crucified by the Romans. Allegiance even to death is demanded of Christ's followers.
10:41 *in the name of* = because he is.

5 a Is.
35:5f.; 61:1

5 *a the* BLIND RECEIVE SIGHT and *the* lame walk, *the* lepers are cleansed and *the* deaf hear, and *the* dead are raised up, and *the* POOR HAVE THE GOSPEL PREACHED TO THEM.

★ 6 a Matt.
5:29; 13:21,
57; 24:10;
26:31; Mark
6:3; John
6:61; 16:1
★ 7-8

6 "And blessed is he who a keeps from stumbling over Me."

7 And as these were going away, Jesus began to speak to the multitudes about John, "What did you go out into a the wilderness to look at? A reed shaken by the wind?

7 a Matt. 3:1

8 "But what did you go out to see? A man dressed in soft *clothing?* Behold, those who wear soft *clothing* are in kings' palaces.

9 a Matt.
14:5; 21:26;
Luke 1:76;
20:6

9 "But why did you go out? To see a a prophet? Yes, I say to you, and one who is more than a prophet.

★10 a Mal.
3:1; Mark 1:2

10 "This is the one about whom it is written,

'a BEHOLD, I SEND MY MESSEN-GER BEFORE YOUR FACE,
WHO WILL PREPARE YOUR WAY BEFORE YOU.'

★11

11 "Truly, I say to you, among those born of women there has not arisen *anyone* greater than John the Baptist; yet he who is least in the kingdom of heaven is greater than he.

★12 a Luke
16:16

12 "And a from the days of John the Baptist until now the kingdom of heaven suffers violence, and violent men take it by force.

13 a Luke
16:16
★14 a Mal.
4:5; Mark
17:10-13;
Mark 9:11-
13; Luke
1:17; John
1:21

13 "For a all the prophets and the Law prophesied until John.

14 "And if you care to accept *it,* he himself is a Elijah, who was to come.

15 "a He who has ears to hear, let him hear.

16 "But to what shall I compare this generation? It is like children sitting in the market places, who call out to the other *children,*

17 and say, 'We played the flute for you, and you did not dance; we sang a dirge, and you did not mourn.'

18 "For John came neither a eating nor b drinking, and they say, 'c He has a demon!'

19 "The Son of Man came eating and drinking, and they say, 'Behold, a gluttonous man and a drunkard, a a friend of tax-gatherers and sinners!' Yet wisdom is vindicated by her deeds."

15 a Matt.
13:9, 43;
Mark 4:9, 23;
Luke 8:8;
14:35; Rev.
2:7, 11, 17,
29; 3:6, 13,
22; 13:9

18 a Matt. 3:4
b Luke 1:15
c Matt. 9:34;
John 7:20;
8:48f., 52;
10:20

★19 a Matt.
9:11; Luke
15:2

2 By condemning the cities,
11:20-24

20 Then He began to reproach the cities in which most of His miracles were done, because they did not repent.

21 "a Woe to you, Chorazin! Woe to you, b Bethsaida! For if the miracles had occurred in c Tyre and c Sidon which occurred in you, they would have repented long ago in d sackcloth and ashes.

22 "Nevertheless I say to you, a it shall be more tolerable for Tyre and Sidon in b the day of judgment, than for you.

23 "And you, a Capernaum, will not be exalted to heaven, will you? You shall b descend to c Hades; for if the miracles had occurred in d Sodom which occurred in you, it would have remained to this day.

★21 a Matt.
11:21-23;
Luke 10:13-
15 b Mark
6:45; 8:22;
Luke 9:10;
John 1:44;
12:21 c Matt.
11:22; 15:21;
Mark 3:8;
7:24, 31;
Luke 4:26;
6:17; Acts
12:20; 27:3
d Rev. 11:3

22 a Matt.
10:15; 11:24
b Matt. 10:15
23 a Matt.
4:13 b Is.
14:13, 15;
Ezek. 26:20;
31:14; 32:18,
24 c Matt.
16:18; Luke
10:15; 16:23;
Acts 2:27,
31; Rev.
1:18; 6:8;
20:13f.
d Matt. 10:15

11:6 *who keeps from stumbling over Me.* I.e., he who can in full faith acknowledge and accept My "mighty work" as evidence of My Messiahship.

11:7-8 These are rhetorical questions expecting negative answers.

11:10 See Isa. 40:3; Mal. 3:1.

11:11 *is greater than he.* The greatness of John the Baptist in the old dispensation before the Cross fades in comparison to the high position every believer has had since Jesus' crucifixion and resurrection, and the descent of the Spirit.

11:12 Since the time John began preaching, the

response had been violent, whether by vicious opponents or enthusiastic supporters.

11:14 *he himself is Elijah.* Jesus is saying that if the Jews had received Him, they would also have understood that John fulfilled the O.T. prediction of the coming of Elijah before the day of the Lord (Mal. 4:5; see Matt. 17:12).

11:19 One can always find a reason to carp at prophets rather than repent at their urging.

11:21 *Chorazin* was about 2½ miles N. of Capernaum. *Bethsaida* was at the N. end of the Sea of Galilee. *Tyre and Sidon* were pagan cities in Phoenicia.

24 *a*Matt.
10:15; 11:22
*b*Matt. 10:15

24 "Nevertheless I say to you that *a*it shall be more tolerable for the land of *b*Sodom in *b*the day of judgment, than for you."

3   By calling all to Himself, 11:25-30

25 *a*Matt.
11:25-27;
Luke 10:21,
22 *b*Acts
3:12 *c*Luke
22:42; 23:34;
John 11:41;
12:27, 28
*d*1 Cor.
1:26ff.

26 *a*Luke
22:42; 23:34;
John 11:41;
12:27, 28
27 *a*Matt.
28:18; John
3:35; 13:3;
17:2 *b*John
7:29; 10:15;
17:25

★**28-30**
28 *a*Jer.
31:25; John
7:37
29 *a*John
13:15; Eph.
4:20; Phil.
2:5; 1 Pet.
2:21; 1 John
2:6 *b*Jer.
6:16

25 *a*At that time Jesus *b*answered and said, "I praise Thee, O *c*Father, Lord of heaven and earth, that *d*Thou didst hide these things from *the* wise and intelligent and didst reveal them to babes.

26 "Yes, *a*Father, for thus it was well-pleasing in Thy sight.

27 "*a*All things have been handed over to Me by My Father; and no one knows the Son, except the Father; nor does anyone know the Father, *b*except the Son, and anyone to whom the Son wills to reveal *Him*.

28 "*a*Come to Me, all who are weary and heavy-laden, and I will give you rest.

29 "Take My yoke upon you, and *a*learn from Me, for I am gentle and humble in heart; and *b*YOU SHALL FIND REST FOR YOUR SOULS.

30 "For My yoke is easy, and My load is light."

4   By controversies over the Sabbath, 12:1-13

1 *a*Matt.
12:1-8; Mark
2:23-28;
Luke 6:1-5
*b*Deut. 23:25

★ **2** *a*Matt.
12:10; Luke
13:14; 14:3;
John 5:10;
7:23; 9:16

12 *a*At that time Jesus went on the Sabbath through the grainfields, and His disciples became hungry and began to *b*pick the heads *of grain* and eat.

2 But when the Pharisees saw it, they said to Him, "Behold, Your disciples do what *a*is not lawful to do on a Sabbath."

3 But He said to them, "Have you not read what David did, when he became hungry, he and his companions;

4 how he entered the house of God, and *a*they ate the consecrated bread, which was not lawful for him to eat, nor for those with him, but for the priests alone?

5 "Or have you not read in the Law, that on the Sabbath the priests in the temple break the Sabbath, and are innocent?

6 "But I say to you, that something *a*greater than the temple is here.

7 "But if you had known what this means, '*a*I DESIRE COMPASSION, AND NOT A SACRIFICE,' you would not have condemned the innocent.

8 "For *a*the Son of Man is Lord of the Sabbath."

9 *a*And departing from there, He went into their synagogue.

10 And behold, *there was a* man with a withered hand. And they questioned Him, saying, "*a*Is it lawful to heal on the Sabbath?"—in order that they might accuse Him.

11 And He said to them, "What man shall there be among you, who shall have one sheep, and if it falls into a pit on the Sabbath, will he not take hold of it, and lift it out?

12 "Of *a*how much more value then is a man than a sheep! So then, it is lawful to do good on the Sabbath."

13 Then He *said to the man, "Stretch out your hand!" And he

★ **3**

★ **4** *a*1 Sam.
21:6

★ **6** *a*Matt.
12:41, 42

7 *a*Hos. 6:6

8 *a*Matt.
8:20; 12:32,
40
9 *a*Matt.
12:9-14;
Mark 3:1-6;
Luke 6:6-11
10 *a*Matt.
12:2; Luke
13:14; 14:3;
John 5:10;
7:23; 9:16

12 *a*Matt.
10:31

11:28-30 This great invitation, extended to all, is threefold: (1) to come and receive salvation; (2) to learn in discipleship; and (3) to serve in yoke with the Lord. The yoke involves instruction under discipline. Yet, in contrast to the teaching of the scribes, Jesus' yoke is easy. Through the ages these verses have been among the most beloved in the N.T.

12:2 *not lawful to do on a Sabbath.* It was lawful for persons to pick grain from another's field to satisfy a hunger (Deut. 23:25) but not to do regular work on the Sabbath (Ex. 20:10).

The latter was the charge of the Pharisees.
12:3 *what David did.* See 1 Sam. 21:1-6.
12:4 *the consecrated bread.* Better, bread of the Presence. Twelve cakes, made of fine flour, were placed in the Holy Place in the tabernacle each day on the table which stood opposite the candlestick. The old bread was eaten by the priests. It was this bread that David requested of Ahimelech, the priest, for himself and his men.
12:6 *something.* I.e., the kingdom of God.

stretched it out, and it was restored to normal, like the other.

5 By condemnation of the Pharisees (the unpardonable sin), 12:14-37

14 aMatt.
26:4; Mark
14:1; Luke
22:2; John
7:30, 44;
8:59; 10:31,
39; 11:53
15 aMatt.
4:23

14 But the Pharisees went out, and acounseled together against Him, as to how they might destroy Him.

15 But Jesus, aware of this, withdrew from there. And many followed Him, and aHe healed them all,

★16 aMatt.
8:4

16 and awarned them not to make Him known,

17 in order that what was spoken through Isaiah the prophet, might be fulfilled, saying,

★18-21

18 aIs. 42:1
bMatt. 3:17;
17:5 cLuke
4:18; John
3:34

18 "aBEHOLD, MY SERVANT WHOM I HAVE CHOSEN;
bMY BELOVED IN WHOM MY SOUL IS WELL-PLEASED;
cI WILL PUT MY SPIRIT UPON HIM,
aAND HE SHALL PROCLAIM JUSTICE TO THE GENTILES.

19 aIs. 42:2

19 "aHE WILL NOT QUARREL, NOR CRY OUT;
NOR WILL ANYONE HEAR HIS VOICE IN THE STREETS.

20 aIs. 42:3

20 "aA BATTERED REED HE WILL NOT BREAK OFF,
AND A SMOLDERING WICK HE WILL NOT PUT OUT,
UNTIL HE LEADS JUSTICE TO VICTORY.

21 aIs. 42:4;
Rom. 15:12

21 "aAND IN HIS NAME THE GENTILES WILL HOPE."

22 aMatt.
12:22, 24;
Luke 11:14,
15; Matt.
9:32, 34
bMatt. 4:24

22 aThen there was brought to Him a bdemon-possessed man who was blind and dumb, and He healed him, so that the dumb man spoke and saw.

23 And all the multitudes were amazed, and began to say, "This man cannot be the aSon of David, can he?"

23 aMatt.
9:27

24 But when the Pharisees heard it, they said, "This man casts out demons only aby Beelzebul the ruler of the demons."

24 aMatt.
9:34

25 aAnd bknowing their thoughts He said to them, "Any kingdom divided against itself is laid waste; and any city or house divided against itself shall not stand.

25 aMatt.
12:25-29;
Mark 3:23-
27; Luke
11:17-22
bMatt. 9:4

26 "And if aSatan casts out aSatan, he is divided against himself; how then shall his kingdom stand?

26 aMatt.
4:10

27 "And if I aby Beelzebul cast out demons, bby whom do your sons cast them out? Consequently they shall be your judges.

27 aMatt.
9:34 bActs
19:13

28 "But if I cast out demons by the Spirit of God, then the kingdom of God has come upon you.

29 "Or how can anyone enter the strong man's house and carry off his property, unless he first binds the strong man? And then he will plunder his house.

30 "aHe who is not with Me is against Me; and he who does not gather with Me scatters.

30 aMark
9:40; Luke
9:50; 11:23

31 "aTherefore I say to you, any sin and blasphemy shall be forgiven men, but blasphemy against the Spirit shall not be forgiven.

★31 aMatt.
12:31, 32;
Mark 3:28-
30; Luke
12:10

32 "And whoever shall speak a word against the Son of Man, it shall be forgiven him; but whoever shall speak against the Holy Spirit, it shall not be forgiven him, either in athis age, or in the age to come.

32 aMatt.
13:22, 39;
Mark 10:30;
Luke 16:8;
18:30; 20:34,
35; Eph.
1:21; 1 Tim.
6:17; 2 Tim.
4:10; Titus
2:12; Heb.
6:5

33 "Either make the tree good, and its fruit good; or make the tree bad, and its fruit bad; for athe tree is known by its fruit.

33 aMatt.
7:16

12:16 not to make Him known. Many were drawn to Christ because of His reputation as a healer, which may have been diverting attention from His primary role as Messiah.
12:18-21 See Isa. 42:1-4. Here is one of Matthew's descriptive gems, highlighting Jesus' graciousness and gentleness.
12:31 blasphemy against the Spirit. Techni-

cally, according to the scribes, blasphemy involved direct and explicit abuse of the divine name. Jesus here teaches that it also may be the reviling of God by attributing the Spirit's work to Satan. The special circumstances involved in this blasphemy cannot be duplicated today.

34 aMatt.
3:7; 23:33
b1 Sam.
24:13; Matt.
12:34, 35;
15:18; Luke
6:45; Eph.
4:29; James
3:2-12

34 "ªYou brood of vipers, how can you, being evil, speak what is good? ᵇFor the mouth speaks out of that which fills the heart.

35 "The good man out of *his* good treasure brings forth what is good; and the evil man out of *his* evil treasure brings forth what is evil.

★36 aMatt.
10:15

36 "And I say to you, that every careless word that men shall speak, they shall render account for it in ªthe day of judgment.

37 "For by your words you shall be justified, and by your words you shall be condemned."

6 By certain signs, 12:38-45

38 aMatt.
16:1; Mark
8:11, 12;
Luke 11:16;
John 2:18;
6:30; 1 Cor.
1:22

38 Then some of the scribes and Pharisees answered Him, saying, "Teacher, ªwe want to see a sign from You."

★39 aMatt.
12:39-42;
Luke 11:29-
32; Matt.
16:4

39 But He answered and said to them, "ªAn evil and adulterous generation craves for a sign; and *yet* no sign shall be given to it but the sign of Jonah the prophet;

★40 aJon.
1:17 bMatt.
8:20 cMatt.
16:21

40 for just as ªJONAH WAS THREE DAYS AND THREE NIGHTS IN THE BELLY OF THE SEA MONSTER, so shall ᵇthe Son of Man be ᶜthree days and three nights in the heart of the earth.

★41 aJon.
1:2 bJon. 3:5
cMatt. 12:6,
42

41 "ªThe men of Nineveh shall stand up with this generation at the judgment, and shall condemn it because ᵇthey repented at the preaching of Jonah; and behold, ᶜsomething greater than Jonah is here.

42 a1 Kin.
10:1; 2 Chr.
9:1 bMatt.
12:6, 41

42 "ªThe Queen of *the* South shall rise up with this generation at the judgment and shall condemn it, because she came from the ends of the earth to hear the wisdom of Solomon; and behold, ᵇsomething greater than Solomon is here.

43 "ªNow when the unclean spirit goes out of a man, it passes through waterless places, seeking rest, and does not find *it.*

★43 aMatt.
12:43-45;
Luke 11:24-
26

44 "Then it says, 'I will return to my house from which I came'; and when it comes, it finds it unoccupied, swept, and put in order.

45 "Then it goes, and takes along with it seven other spirits more wicked than itself, and they go in and live there; and ªthe last state of that man becomes worse than the first. That is the way it will also be with this evil generation."

45 a2 Pet.
2:20

7 By changed relationships, 12:46-50

46 ªWhile He was still speaking to the multitudes, behold, His ᵇmother and ᶜbrothers were standing outside, seeking to speak to Him.

46 aMatt.
12:46-50;
Mark 3:31-
35; Luke
8:19-21
bMatt. 1:18;
2:11ff.;
13:55; Luke
1:43; 2:33f.,
48, 51; John
2:1, 5, 12;
19:25f.; Acts
1:14 cMatt.
13:55; Mark
6:3; John
2:12; 7:3, 5,
10; Acts
1:14; 1 Cor.
9:5; Gal.
1:19

47 And someone said to Him, "Behold, Your mother and Your brothers are standing outside seeking to speak to You."

48 But He answered the one who was telling Him and said, "Who is My mother and who are My brothers?"

49 And stretching out His hand toward His disciples, He said, "Behold, My mother and My brothers!

50 "For whoever does the will of My Father who is in heaven, he is My brother and sister and mother."

★50

12:36 *careless* = useless.
12:39 *adulterous.* The nation was unfaithful in its vows to the Lord. *the sign of Jonah the prophet.* In Matt. 16:4 and Luke 11:29-32 the sign is the warning of judgment to come (cf. Jonah 1:2; 3:4). Here the sign is related to the death and resurrection of the Son of Man.
12:40 *three days and three nights.* This phrase does not necessarily require that 72 hours elapse between Christ's death and resurrection, for the Jews reckoned part of a day to be as a whole day. Thus this prophecy can be properly fulfilled if the crucifixion occurred on Friday. However, the statement does require an historical Jonah who was actually swallowed by a great fish.
12:41 *something greater.* The Greek word is neuter here and in v. 42 and refers to the kingdom of God.
12:43 *unclean spirit* = a demon. See note at Matt. 7:22.
12:50 This means that the spiritual relation between Christ and believers is closer than the closest of blood ties. Obedience to God takes precedence over responsibilities to family.

C The Program Altered,
13:1-52
1 The sower, 13:1-23

1 *a*Matt.
9:28; 13:36;
Mark 3:19
*b*Matt. 13:1-
15; Mark 4:1-
12; Luke 8:4-
10
2 *a*Luke 5:3

13 On that day Jesus went out of *a*the house, and was sitting *b*by the sea.

2 And great multitudes gathered to Him, so that *a*He got into a boat and sat down, and the whole multitude was standing on the beach.

★ **3** *a*Matt.
13:10ff.
Mark 4:2ff.

3 And He spoke many things to them in *a*parables, saying, "Behold, the sower went out to sow;

4 and as he sowed, some *seeds* fell beside the road, and the birds came and ate them up.

5 "And others fell upon the rocky places, where they did not have much soil; and immediately they sprang up, because they had no depth of soil.

6 "But when the sun had risen, they were scorched; and because they had no root, they withered away.

7 "And others fell among the thorns, and the thorns came up and choked them out.

8 *a*Gen.
26:12; Matt.
13:23

8 "And others fell on the good soil, and *yielded a crop, some a *a*hundredfold, some sixty, and some thirty.

9 *a*Matt.
11:15

9 "*a*He who has ears, let him hear."

10 And the disciples came and said to Him, "Why do You speak to them in parables?"

11 *a*Matt.
19:11; 20:23;
John 6:65;
1 Cor. 2:10;
Col. 1:27;
1 John 2:20,
27

11 And He answered and said to them, "*a*To you it has been granted to know the mysteries of the kingdom of heaven, but to them it has not been granted.

12 *a*Matt.
25:29; Mark
4:25; Luke
8:18; 19:26

12 "*a*For whoever has, to him shall *more* be given, and he shall have an abundance; but whoever does not have, even what he has shall be taken away from him.

13 *a*Deut.
29:4; Is.
42:19, 20;
Jer. 5:21;
Ezek. 12:2

13 "Therefore I speak to them in parables; because while *a*seeing

they do not see, and while hearing they do not hear, nor do they understand.

14 "And in their case the prophecy of Isaiah is being fulfilled, which says,

> '*a*YOU WILL KEEP ON HEARING,
> BUT WILL NOT UNDERSTAND;
> AND YOU WILL KEEP ON SEEING, BUT WILL NOT PERCEIVE;

15 *a*FOR THE HEART OF THIS PEOPLE HAS BECOME DULL,
> AND WITH THEIR EARS THEY SCARCELY HEAR,
> AND THEY HAVE CLOSED THEIR EYES
> LEST THEY SHOULD SEE WITH THEIR EYES,
> AND HEAR WITH THEIR EARS,
> AND UNDERSTAND WITH THEIR HEART AND RETURN,
> AND I SHOULD HEAL THEM.'

★ **14** *a*Is. 6:9,
Mark 4:12;
Luke 8:10;
John 12:40;
Acts 28:26,
27; Rom.
10:16; 11:8

15 *a*Is. 6:10

16 "*a*But blessed are your eyes, because they see; and your ears, because they hear.

16 *a*Matt.
13:16, 17;
Luke 10:23,
24

17 "For truly I say to you, that *a*many prophets and righteous men desired to see what you see, and did not see *it*; and to hear what you hear, and did not hear *it*.

17 *a*John
8:56; Heb.
11:13; 1 Pet.
1:10-12

18 "*a*Hear then the parable of the sower.

18 *a*Matt.
13:18-23;
Mark 4:13-
20; Luke
8:11-15
19 *a*Matt.
4:23 *b*Matt.
5:37

19 "When anyone hears *a*the word of the kingdom, and does not understand it, *b*the evil *one* comes and snatches away what has been sown in his heart. This is the one on whom seed was sown beside the road.

20 "And the one on whom seed was sown on the rocky places, this is the man who hears the word, and immediately receives it with joy;

21 yet he has no *firm* root in himself, but is *only* temporary, and when affliction or persecution arises because of the word, immediately he *a*falls away.

21 *a*Matt.
11:6

13:3 *parables.* A parable is a figure of speech in which a moral or spiritual truth is illustrated by an analogy drawn from everyday experiences. These parables present truths about the kingdom in this present day. These truths are called "mysteries" (v. 11) because they were not revealed in the O.T., and they are revealed by Christ only to those who are properly related to Him (vv. 11-13 and Mark 4:11-12).
13:14 See Isa. 6:9-10.

22 "And the one on whom seed was sown among the thorns, this is the man who hears the word, and the worry of [a]the world, and the [b]deceitfulness of riches choke the word, and it becomes unfruitful.

23 "And the one on whom seed was sown on the good soil, this is the man who hears the word and understands it; who indeed bears fruit, and brings forth, some [a]a hundredfold, some sixty, and some thirty."

2   The wheat and the tares, 13:24-30

24 He presented another parable to them, saying, "[a]The kingdom of heaven may be compared to [b]a man who sowed good seed in his field.

25 "But while men were sleeping, his enemy came and sowed tares also among the wheat, and went away.

26 "But when the wheat sprang up and bore grain, then the tares became evident also.

27 "And the slaves of the landowner came and said to him, 'Sir, did you not sow good seed in your field? How then does it have tares?'

28 "And he said to them, 'An enemy has done this!' And the slaves *said to him, 'Do you want us, then, to go and gather them up?'

29 "But he *said, 'No; lest while you are gathering up the tares, you may root up the wheat with them.

30 'Allow both to grow together until the harvest; and in the time of the harvest I will say to the reapers, "First gather up the tares and bind them in bundles to burn

them up; but [a]gather the wheat into my barn." '"

3   The mustard seed, 13:31-32

31 He presented another parable to them, saying, "[a]The kingdom of heaven is like [b]a mustard seed, which a man took and sowed in his field;

32 and this is smaller than all *other* seeds; but when it is full grown, it is larger than the garden plants, and becomes a tree, so that [a]THE BIRDS OF THE AIR come and NEST IN ITS BRANCHES."

4   The leaven, 13:33

33 He spoke another parable to them, "[a]The kingdom of heaven is like leaven, which a woman took, and hid in [b]three pecks of meal, until it was all leavened."

5   The wheat and the tares, 13:34-43

34 All these things Jesus spoke to the multitudes in parables, and He did not speak to them [a]without a parable,

35 so that what was spoken through the prophet might be fulfilled, saying,

"[a]I WILL OPEN MY MOUTH IN
      PARABLES;

I WILL UTTER THINGS HIDDEN
      SINCE THE FOUNDATION OF
      THE WORLD."

36 Then He left the multitudes, and went into [a]the house. And His disciples came to Him, saying, "[b]Explain to us the parable of the tares of the field."

37 And He answered and

Cross-references (margin)

22 [a]Matt. 12:32; 13:39; Mark 4:19; Rom. 12:2; 1 Cor. 1:20; 2:6, 8; 3:18; 2 Cor. 4:4; Gal. 1:4; Eph. 2:2 [b]Matt. 19:23; 1 Tim. 6:9, 10, 17 **23** [a]Matt. 13:8

24 [a]Matt. 13:31, 33, 45, 47; 18:23; 20:1; 22:2; 25:1; Mark 4:30; Luke 13:18, 20 [b]Mark 4:26-29 ★**25**

30 [a]Matt. 3:12

★**31** [a]Matt. 13:31, 32; Mark 4:30-32; Luke 13:18, 19; Matt. 13:24 [b]Matt. 17:20; Luke 17:6 **32** [a]Ps. 104:12; Ezek. 17:23; 31:6; Dan. 4:12

★**33** [a]Matt. 13:33; Luke 13:21; Matt. 13:24 [b]Gen. 18:6; Judg. 6:19; 1 Sam. 1:24

34 [a]Mark 4:34; John 10:6; 16:25

★**35** [a]Ps. 78:2

36 [a]Matt. 13:1 [b]Matt. 15:15

37 [a]Matt. 8:20

13:25 *tares.* Weeds, in this case probably darnel, which in the blade resembles wheat but which can be distinguished from wheat when fully ripe.
13:31 See note on Luke 13:19.
13:33 *leaven.* Since leaven is everywhere else in the Bible regarded as typifying the presence of impurity or evil, some understand it here to indicate the presence of evil within Christendom (Ex. 12:15; Lev. 2:11; Matt. 16:6; 1 Cor. 5:6-9; Gal. 5:9; cf. 1 Tim. 4:1; Jude 12). Others regard the meaning of leaven in this parable in a good sense, as indicating the growth of the kingdom of heaven by means of the penetrating power of the gospel.
13:35 See Ps. 78:2-3.

said, "The one who sows the good seed is [a]the Son of Man,

38 and the field is the world; and as for the good seed, these are [a]the sons of the kingdom; and the tares are [b]the sons of [c]the evil one;

39 and the enemy who sowed them is the devil, and the harvest is [a]the end of the age; and the reapers are angels.

40 "Therefore just as the tares are gathered up and burned with fire, so shall it be at [a]the end of the age.

41 "[a]The Son of Man [b]will send forth His angels, and they will gather out of His kingdom all [c]stumbling blocks, and those who commit lawlessness,

42 and [a]will cast them into the furnace of fire; in that place [b]there shall be weeping and gnashing of teeth.

43 "[a]Then THE RIGHTEOUS WILL SHINE FORTH AS THE SUN in the kingdom of their Father. [b]He who has ears, let him hear.

6   *The hidden treasure,* 13:44

44 "[a]The kingdom of heaven is like a treasure hidden in the field, which a man found and hid; and from joy over it he goes and [b]sells all that he has, and buys that field.

7   *The pearl of great price,* 13:45-46

45 "Again, [a]the kingdom of heaven is like a merchant seeking fine pearls,

46 and upon finding one pearl of great value, he went and sold all that he had, and bought it.

8   *The dragnet,* 13:47-50

47 "Again, [a]the kingdom of heaven is like a dragnet cast into the sea, and gathering fish of every kind;

48 and when it was filled, they drew it up on the beach; and they sat down, and gathered the good fish into containers, but the bad they threw away.

49 "So it will be at [a]the end of the age; the angels shall come forth, and take out the wicked from among the righteous,

50 and [a]will cast them into the furnace of fire; [b]there shall be weeping and gnashing of teeth.

9   *The householder,* 13:51-52

51 "Have you understood all these things?" They *said to Him, "Yes."

52 And He said to them, "Therefore every scribe who has become a disciple of the kingdom of heaven is like a head of a household, who brings forth out of his treasure things new and old."

D   The Program Attacked, 13:53-16:12
1   *Attack by His own townspeople,* 13:53-58

53 [a]And it came about that when Jesus had finished these parables, He departed from there.

54 [a]And coming to His home town He [b]began teaching them in their synagogue, so that [c]they became astonished, and said, "Where did this man get this wisdom, and these miraculous powers?

55 "Is not this the carpenter's

Marginal references (left column):

38 [a]Matt. 8:12 [b]John 8:44; Acts 13:10; 1 John 3:10 [c]Matt. 5:37

39 [a]Matt. 12:32; 13:22, 40, 49; 24:3; 28:20; 1 Cor. 10:11; Heb. 9:26

40 [a]Matt. 12:32; 13:22, 39, 49; 24:3; 28:20; 1 Cor. 10:11; Heb. 9:26

41 [a]Matt. 8:20 [b]Matt. 24:31 [c]Zeph. 1:3

42 [a]Matt. 13:50 [b]Matt. 8:12

43 [a]Dan. 12:3 [b]Matt. 11:15

★**44-46**

44 [a]Matt. 13:24 [b]Matt. 13:46

45 [a]Matt. 13:24

Marginal references (right column):

47 [a]Matt. 13:44

49 [a]Matt. 13:39, 40

50 [a]Matt. 13:42 [b]Matt. 8:12

53 [a]Matt. 7:28

54 [a]Matt. 13:54-58; Mark 6:1-6 [b]Matt. 4:23 [c]Matt. 7:28

★**55** [a]Matt. 12:46

13:44-46 The parables of the treasure and pearl indicate the incomparable value of the kingdom, which will cause a man to do everything possible to possess it. Another possible interpretation equates the man with Christ (as in v. 37) who sacrifices His all to purchase His people.

13:55 *His brothers.* These were the sons of Joseph and Mary born subsequent to the birth of Jesus from Mary alone. To understand them as sons of Joseph by a former marriage or cousins of Jesus is contrary to the usual sense of brothers.

son? Is not ªHis mother called Mary, and His ªbrothers, James and Joseph and Simon and Judas? **56** "And ªHis sisters, are they not all with us? Where then *did* this man *get* all these things?"

57 And they took ªoffense at Him. But Jesus said to them, "ᵇA prophet is not without honor except in his home town, and in his *own* household."

58 And He did not do many miracles there because of their unbelief.

2 Attack by Herod, followed by miracles (5000 fed and Jesus walks on water), 14:1-36

14 ªAt that time ᵇHerod the tetrarch heard the news about Jesus,

2 and said to his servants, "ªThis is John the Baptist; he has risen from the dead; and that is why miraculous powers are at work in him."

3 For when ªHerod had John arrested, he bound him, and put him ᵇin prison on account of ᶜHerodias, the wife of his brother Philip.

4 For John had been saying to him, "ªIt is not lawful for you to have her."

5 And although he wanted to put him to death, he feared the multitude, because they regarded him as ªa prophet.

6 But when Herod's birthday came, the daughter of ªHerodias danced before *them* and pleased ᵇHerod.

7 Thereupon he promised with an oath to give her whatever she asked.

8 And having been prompted by her mother, she *said, "Give me here on a platter the head of John the Baptist."

9 And although he was grieved, the king commanded *it* to be given because of his oaths, and because of his dinner guests.

10 And he sent and had John beheaded in the prison.

11 And his head was brought on a platter and given to the girl; and she brought *it* to her mother.

12 And his disciples came and took away the body and buried it; and they went and reported to Jesus.

13 ªNow when Jesus heard *it*, He withdrew from there in a boat, to a lonely place by Himself; and when the multitudes heard of *this*, they followed Him on foot from the cities.

14 And when He went ashore, He ªsaw a great multitude, and felt compassion for them, and ᵇhealed their sick.

15 And when it was evening, the disciples came to Him, saying, "The place is desolate, and the time is already past; so send the multitudes away, that they may go into the villages and buy food for themselves."

16 But Jesus said to them, "They do not need to go away; you give them *something* to eat!"

17 And they *said to Him, "We have here only ªfive loaves and two fish."

18 And He said, "Bring them here to Me."

19 And ordering the multitudes to recline on the grass, He took the five loaves and the two fish, and looking up toward heaven, He ªblessed *the food*, and

56 ªMark 6:3

57 ªMatt. 11:6 ᵇMark 6:4; Luke 4:24; John 4:44

★ 1 ªMatt. 14:1-12; Mark 6:14-29; Matt. 14:1, 2; Luke 9:7-9 ᵇMark 8:15; Luke 3:1, 19; 8:3; 13:31; 23:7f., 11f., 15; Acts 4:27; 12:1 2 ªMatt. 16:14; Mark 6:14; Luke 9:7

★ 3 ªMatt. 14:1-12; Mark 6:14-29; Matt. 14:1, 2; Luke 9:7-9; Mark 8:15; Luke 3:1, 19; 8:3; 13:31; 23:7f., 11f., 15; Acts 4:27; 12:1 ᵇMatt. 4:12; 11:2 ᶜMatt. 14:6; Mark 6:17, 19, 22; Luke 3:19 4 ªLev. 18:16; 20:21 5 ªMatt. 11:9 6 ªMatt. 14:3; Mark 6:17, 19, 22; Luke 3:19 ᵇMatt. 14:1-12; Mark 6:14-29; Matt. 14:1, 2; Luke 9:7-9; Mark 8:15; Luke 3:1, 19; 8:3; 13:31; 23:7f., 11f., 15; Acts 4:27; 12:1

13 ªMatt. 14:13-21; Mark 6:32-44; Luke 9:10-17; John 6:1-13; Matt. 15:32-38

14 ªMatt. 9:36 ᵇMatt. 4:23

★15

17 ªMatt. 16:9

19 ª1 Sam. 9:13; Matt. 15:36; 26:26; Mark 6:41; 8:7; 14:22; Luke 24:30; Acts 27:35; Rom. 14:6

14:1 *Herod the tetrarch.* Herod Antipas, who ruled from 4 B.C.–A.D. 39, son of Herod the Great and brother of Archelaus (see Matt. 2:1, 22).

14:3 *Herodias.* The former wife of Herod's half brother Philip, her uncle. She had been persuaded to leave her husband and marry Herod Antipas, thus committing incest (Lev. 18:16). John condemned him for this, and Antipas knew that John spoke the truth. See Mark 6:20.

14:15 *when it was evening.* The Hebrew day, that is, the interval between dawn and darkness, was divided into three parts: morning, noon, and evening (Ps. 55:17). The Jews distinguished two evenings in the day: the first began about 3 p.m., and the second, at sundown (see Ex. 12:6, lit., "between the evenings.") In this verse the first evening is meant; in v. 23, the second.

breaking the loaves He gave them to the disciples, and the disciples *gave* to the multitudes,

20 and they all ate, and were satisfied. And they picked up what was left over of the broken pieces, twelve full ᵃbaskets.

21 And there were about five thousand men who ate, aside from women and children.

22 ᵃAnd immediately He made the disciples get into the boat, and go ahead of Him to the other side, while He sent the multitudes away.

23 And after He had sent the multitudes away, ᵃHe went up to the mountain by Himself to pray; and when it was evening, He was there alone.

24 But the boat was already many stadia away from the land, battered by the waves; for the wind was contrary.

25 And in ᵃthe fourth watch of the night He came to them, walking on the sea.

26 And when the disciples saw Him walking on the sea, they were frightened, saying, "It is ᵃa ghost!" And they cried out for fear.

27 But immediately Jesus spoke to them, saying, "ᵃTake courage, it is I; ᵇdo not be afraid."

28 And Peter answered Him and said, "Lord, if it is You, command me to come to You on the water."

29 And He said, "Come!" And Peter got out of the boat, and walked on the water and came toward Jesus.

30 But seeing the wind, he became afraid, and beginning to sink, he cried out, saying, "Lord, save me!"

31 And immediately Jesus stretched out His hand and took hold of him, and *said to him,

"ᵃO you of little faith, why did you doubt?"

32 And when they got into the boat, the wind stopped.

33 And those who were in the boat worshiped Him, saying, "You are certainly ᵃGod's Son!"

34 ᵃAnd when they had crossed over, they came to land at ᵇGennesaret.

35 And when the men of that place recognized Him, they sent into all that surrounding district and brought to Him all who were sick;

36 and they *began* to entreat Him that they might just touch ᵃthe fringe of His cloak; and as many as ᵇtouched *it* were cured.

3   Attack by the scribes and Pharisees, followed by miracles (Syrophoenician woman's daughter healed and 4000 fed), 15:1-39

15 ᵃThen some Pharisees and scribes *came to Jesus ᵇfrom Jerusalem, saying,

2 "Why do Your disciples transgress the tradition of the elders? For they ᵃdo not wash their hands when they eat bread."

3 And He answered and said to them, "And why do you yourselves transgress the commandment of God for the sake of your tradition?

4 "For God said, 'ᵃHONOR YOUR FATHER AND MOTHER,' and, 'ᵇHE WHO SPEAKS EVIL OF FATHER OR MOTHER, LET HIM BE PUT TO DEATH.'

5 "But you say, 'Whoever shall say to *his* father or mother, "Anything of mine you might have been helped by has been given *to God*,"

6 he is not to honor his father or his mother.' And *thus* you

Margin references

20 ᵃMatt. 16:9; Mark 6:43; 8:19; Luke 9:17; John 6:13

22 ᵃMatt. 14:22-33; Mark 6:45-51; John 6:15-21

23 ᵃMark 6:46; Luke 6:12; 9:28; John 6:15

★25 ᵃMatt. 24:43; Mark 13:35

26 ᵃLuke 24:37

27 ᵃMatt. 9:2 ᵇMatt. 17:7; 28:5, 10; Mark 6:50; Luke 1:13; 30; 2:10; 5:10; 12:32; John 6:20; Rev. 1:17

31 ᵃMatt. 6:30; 8:26; 16:8

33 ᵃMatt. 4:3

★34 ᵃMatt. 14:34-36; Mark 6:53-56; John 6:24, 25 ᵇMark 6:53; Luke 5:1

36 ᵃMatt. 9:20 ᵇMatt. 9:21; Mark 3:10; 6:56; 8:22; Luke 6:19

1 ᵃMatt. 15:1-20; Mark 7:1-23 ᵇMark 3:22; 7:1; John 1:19; Acts 25:7

★ 2 ᵃLuke 11:38

4 ᵃEx. 20:12; Deut. 5:16 ᵇEx. 21:17; Lev. 20:9

14:25 *fourth watch* = 3-6 a.m.
14:34 *land at Gennesaret.* NW. of the Sea of Galilee.
15:2 Only traditional interpretation and expansion of the law required this. The written law did not (Lev. 22:1-16). Only priests needed to

make an ablution before eating to cleanse themselves from anything unclean. Christ accused them of also expanding (and negating) the commandment about honoring parents (vv. 4-6).

invalidated the word of God for the sake of your tradition.

★7   7 "You hypocrites, rightly did Isaiah prophesy of you, saying,

8 aIs. 29:13

8 'aTHIS PEOPLE HONORS ME
     WITH THEIR LIPS,
BUT THEIR HEART IS FAR AWAY
     FROM ME.

9 aIs. 29:13
bCol. 2:22

9 'aBUT IN VAIN DO THEY WOR-
     SHIP ME,
TEACHING AS bDOCTRINES THE
     PRECEPTS OF MEN.' "

10 And after He called the multitude to Him, He said to them, "Hear, and understand.

11 aMatt.
15:18; Acts
10:14, 15;
1 Tim. 4:3

11 "aNot what enters into the mouth defiles the man, but what proceeds out of the mouth, this defiles the man."

12 Then the disciples *came and *said to Him, "Do You know that the Pharisees were offended when they heard this statement?"

13 aIs.
60:21; 61:3;
John 15:2;
1 Cor. 3:9

13 But He answered and said, "aEvery plant which My heavenly Father did not plant shall be rooted up.

14 aMatt.
23:16, 24
bLuke 6:39

14 "Let them alone; athey are blind guides of the blind. And bif a blind man guides a blind man, both will fall into a pit."

★15 aMatt.
13:36

15 And Peter answered and said to Him, "aExplain the parable to us."

16 And He said, "Are you still lacking in understanding also?

17 "Do you not understand that everything that goes into the mouth passes into the stomach, and is eliminated?

18 aMatt.
12:34; Mark
7:20

18 "But athe things that proceed out of the mouth come from the heart, and those defile the man.

19 aGal.
5:19ff.

19 "aFor out of the heart come evil thoughts, murders, adulteries, fornications, thefts, false witness, slanders.

20 "These are the things which defile the man; but to eat with unwashed hands does not defile the man."

21 aAnd Jesus went away from there, and withdrew into the district of bTyre and bSidon.

21 aMatt.
15:21-28;
Mark 7:24-30
bMatt. 11:21

22 And behold, a Canaanite woman came out from that region, and began to cry out, saying, "Have mercy on me, O Lord, aSon of David; my daughter is cruelly bdemon-possessed."

22 aMatt.
9:27 bMatt.
4:24

23 But He did not answer her a word. And His disciples came to Him and kept asking Him, saying, "Send her away, for she is shouting out after us."

24 But He answered and said, "I was sent only to athe lost sheep of the house of Israel."

24 aMatt.
10:6

25 But she came and a began to bow down before Him, saying, "Lord, help me!"

25 aMatt. 8:2

26 And He answered and said, "It is not good to take the children's bread and throw it to the dogs."

★26

27 But she said, "Yes, Lord; but even the dogs feed on the crumbs which fall from their master's table."

28 Then Jesus answered and said to her, "O woman, ayour faith is great; be it done for you as you wish." And her daughter was healed at once.

28 aMatt.
9:22

29 aAnd departing from there, Jesus went along by bthe Sea of Galilee, and having gone up to the mountain, He was sitting there.

29 aMatt.
15:29-31;
Mark 7:31-37
bMatt. 4:18

30 And great multitudes came to Him, bringing with them *those who were* lame, crippled, blind, dumb, and many others, and they laid them down at His feet; and aHe healed them,

30 aMatt.
4:23

31 so that the multitude marveled as they saw the dumb speaking, the crippled restored, and the lame walking, and the blind seeing; and they aglorified the God of Israel.

31 aMatt. 9:8

15:7 See Isa. 29:13.
15:15 *the parable.* The reference is to v. 11.
15:26 *to the dogs.* Children ("the lost sheep of the house of Israel") must be fed before dogs.

This Gentile woman, like the centurion, showed great faith (v. 28) and was rewarded for it.

32 *a*Matt.
15:32-39;
Mark 8:1-10;
Matt. 14:13-
21 *b*Matt.
9:36
32 *a*And Jesus called His disciples to Him, and said, "*b*I feel compassion for the multitude, because they have remained with Me now three days and have nothing to eat; and I do not wish to send them away hungry, lest they faint on the way."

33 And the disciples *said to Him, "Where would we get so many loaves in a desolate place to satisfy such a great multitude?"

34 And Jesus *said to them, "How many loaves do you have?" And they said, "Seven, and a few small fish."

35 And He directed the multitude to sit down on the ground;

36 *a*Matt.
14:19
36 and He took the seven loaves and the fish; and *a*giving thanks, He broke them and started giving them to the disciples, and the disciples *in turn*, to the multitudes.

37 *a*Matt.
16:10; Mark
8:8, 20; Acts
9:25
37 And they all ate, and were satisfied, and they picked up what was left over of the broken pieces, seven large *a*baskets full.

38 And those who ate were four thousand men, besides women and children.

39 *a*Mark 3:9
*b*Mark 8:10
39 And sending away the multitudes, He got into *a*the boat, and came to the region of *b*Magadan.

4 Attack by the Pharisees and Sadducees, 16:1-12

1 *a*Matt.
16:1-12;
Mark 8:11-21
*b*Matt. 3:7;
16:6, 11, 12
*c*Matt. 12:38
2 *a*Luke
12:54f.
16 *a*And the *b*Pharisees and Sadducees came up, and testing Him *c*asked Him to show them a sign from heaven.

2 But He answered and said to them, "*a*When it is evening, you say, '*It will be* fair weather, for the sky is red.'

3 "And in the morning, 'There *will be* a storm today, for the sky is red and threatening.' Do you know how to discern the appearance of the sky, but cannot *discern* the signs of the times?

4 "*a*An evil and adulterous generation seeks after a sign; and a sign will not be given it, except the sign of Jonah." And He left them, and went away.

★ 4 *a*Matt.
12:39

5 And the disciples came to the other side and had forgotten to take bread.

6 *a*Matt.
16:11; Mark
8:15; Luke
12:1 *b*Matt.
3:7; 16:1, 11,
12
6 And Jesus said to them, "Watch out and *a*beware of the leaven of the *b*Pharisees and Sadducees."

7 And they began to discuss among themselves, saying, "It is because we took no bread."

★ 8 *a*Matt.
6:30; 8:26;
14:31
8 But Jesus, aware of this, said, "*a*You men of little faith, why do you discuss among yourselves that you have no bread?

9 *a*Matt.
14:17-21
*b*Matt. 14:20
9 "Do you not yet understand or remember *a*the five loaves of the five thousand, and how many *b*baskets you took up?

10 *a*Matt.
15:34-38
*b*Matt. 15:37
10 "Or *a*the seven loaves of the four thousand, and how many large *b*baskets you took up?

11 *a*Matt.
16:6, Mark
8:15; Luke
12:1 *b*Matt.
3:7; 16:6, 12
11 "How is it that you do not understand that I did not speak to you concerning bread? But *a*beware of the leaven of the *b*Pharisees and Sadducees."

12 *a*Matt.
3:7; 16:6, 11
12 Then they understood that He did not say to beware of the leaven of bread, but of the teaching of the *a*Pharisees and Sadducees.

V THE PEDAGOGY OF THE KING, 16:13-20:28

A Concerning His Church (Peter's Confession of Faith), 16:13-20

★13 *a*Matt.
16:13-16;
Mark 8:27-
29; Luke
9:18-20
*b*Mark 8:27
*c*Matt. 8:20;
16:27, 28
★14 *a*Matt.
14:2 *b*Matt.
17:10; Mark
6:15; Luke
9:8; John
1:21
13 *a*Now when Jesus came into the district of *b*Caesarea Philippi, He *began* asking His disciples, saying, "Who do people say that *c*the Son of Man is?"

14 And they said, "Some *say a*John the Baptist; and others,

16:4 See note on Matt. 12:39.
16:8 *discuss among yourselves.* Arguing over the fact that they had no bread.
16:13 *district.* This Caesarea was in Herod Philip's tetrarchy, about 25 miles N. of the Sea of

Galilee.
16:14 *Elijah . . . Jeremiah.* Some must have seen resemblances between Christ's teachings and those of these two great prophets.

^bElijah; but still others, Jeremiah, or one of the prophets."

15 He *said to them, "But who do you say that I am?"

16 And Simon Peter answered and said, "Thou art ^athe Christ, ^bthe Son of ^cthe living God."

17 And Jesus answered and said to him, "Blessed are you, ^aSimon Barjona, because ^bflesh and blood did not reveal *this* to you, but My Father who is in heaven.

18 "And I also say to you that you are ^aPeter, and upon this rock I will build My church; and the gates of ^bHades shall not overpower it.

19 "I will give you ^athe keys of the kingdom of heaven; and ^bwhatever you shall bind on earth shall be bound in heaven, and whatever you shall loose on earth shall be loosed in heaven."

20 ^aThen He warned the disciples that they should tell no one that He was ^bthe Christ.

B Concerning His Death, 16:21-28

21 ^aFrom that time Jesus Christ began to show His disciples that He must go to Jerusalem, and

^bsuffer many things from the elders and chief priests and scribes, and be killed, and be raised up on the third day.

22 And Peter took Him aside and began to rebuke Him, saying, "God forbid *it*, Lord! This shall never happen to You."

23 But He turned and said to Peter, "Get behind Me, ^aSatan! You are a stumbling block to Me; for you are not setting your mind on God's interests, but man's."

24 Then Jesus said to His disciples, "If anyone wishes to come after Me, let him deny himself, and ^atake up his cross, and follow Me.

25 "For ^awhoever wishes to save his life shall lose it; but whoever loses his life for My sake shall find it.

26 "For what will a man be profited, if he gains the whole world, and forfeits his soul? Or what will a man give in exchange for his soul?

27 "For the ^aSon of Man ^bis going to come in the glory of His Father with His angels; and ^cWILL THEN RECOMPENSE EVERY MAN ACCORDING TO HIS DEEDS.

28 "Truly I say to you, there are some of those who are standing here who shall not taste death

Marginal references

16 ^aMatt. 1:16; 16:20; John 11:27
^bMatt. 4:3
^cPs. 42:2; Matt. 26:63; Acts 14:15; Rom. 9:26; 2 Cor. 3:3; 6:16; 1 Thess. 1:9; 1 Tim. 3:15; 4:10; Heb. 3:12; 9:14; 10:31; 12:22; Rev. 7:2
★17 ^aJohn 1:42; 21:15-17 ^b1 Cor. 15:50; Gal. 1:16; Eph. 6:12; Heb. 2:14
★18 ^aMatt. 4:18 ^bMatt. 11:23
★19 ^aIs. 22:22; Rev. 1:18; 3:7
^bMatt. 18:18; John 20:23
20 ^aMatt. 8:4; Mark 8:30; Luke 9:21 ^bMatt. 1:16; 16:16; John 11:27
★21 ^aMatt. 16:21-28; Mark 8:31-9:1; Luke 9:22-27
^bMatt. 12:40; 17:9, 12, 22f.; 20:18f.; 27:63; Mark 9:12, 31; Luke 17:25; 18:32; 24:7; John 2:19

★23 ^aMatt. 4:10
★24-28
★24 ^aMatt. 10:38
★25 ^aMatt. 10:39
27 ^aMatt. 8:20 ^bMatt. 10:23; 24:3, 27, 37, 39; 26:64; Mark 8:38; 13:26; Luke 21:27; John 21:22; Acts 1:11; 1 Cor. 15:23; 1 Thess. 1:10; 4:16; 2 Thess. 1:7, 10; 2:1, 8; James 5:7f.; 2 Pet. 1:16; 3:4, 12; 1 John 2:28; Rev. 1:7 ^cPs. 62:12; Prov. 24:12; Rom. 2:6; 14:12; 1 Cor. 3:13; 2 Cor. 5:10; Eph. 6:8; Col. 3:25; Rev. 2:23; 20:12; 22:12
★28 ^aMatt. 8:20 ^bMatt. 10:23; 24:3, 27, 37, 39; 26:64; Mark 8:38; 13:26; Luke 21:27; John 21:22; Acts 1:11; 1 Cor. 15:23; 1 Thess. 1:10; 4:16; 2 Thess. 1:7, 10; 2:1, 8; James 5:7f.; 2 Pet. 1:16; 3:4, 12; 1 John 2:28; Rev. 1:7

Study notes

16:17 *Blessed are you.* Because he had received this insight through divine revelation and not through human influences.

16:18 *you are Peter.* The name Peter (Greek, *Petros*) means rock or rock-man. In the next phrase Christ used *petra* ("upon this rock"), a feminine form for "rock," not a name. Christ used a play on words. He does not say "upon you, Peter" or "upon your successors," but "upon this rock"—upon this divine revelation and profession of faith in Christ. *I will build* shows that the formation of the church is still in the future. It began on the day of Pentecost (Acts 2). The word "church" appears in the Gospels only here and in 18:17.

16:19 *the keys.* The authority to open the doors of Christendom was given to Peter, who used that authority for Jews on the day of Pentecost and for Gentiles in the house of Cornelius (Acts 10). *shall be bound . . . shall be loosed.* Heaven, not the apostles, initiates all binding and loosing, while the apostles announce these things. In John 20:22-23 sins are in view; here, things (i.e., practices). An example of the

apostles' binding practices on people is found in Acts 15:20.

16:21 This is Matthew's first prediction of the Passion (see also 17:22; 20:18). Notice the number of specific details in this prediction.

16:23 *Satan.* Peter is sharply rebuked for aligning himself with Satan's plan to deter Jesus from fulfilling His mission. The harshness of the rebuke stems from Christ's fierce realism about the principal purpose of His coming to earth, which was to die. *a stumbling block.* Or "rock of offence" (Rom. 9:33), perhaps a further play on the word "rock" in v. 18.

16:24-28 This passage is on discipleship. Verses 13-20 are on Messiahship; 21-23 are on the atonement; 17:1-8 concern eschatology. These four passages together deal with the foundational truths of N.T. theology.

16:24 *cross.* See note on 10:38.

16:25 *whoever wishes to save his life.* By renouncing the Gospel. *shall find it.* Shall find eternal life.

16:28 *see the Son of Man coming in His kingdom.* This was fulfilled when the disciples wit-

until they see the [a]Son of Man [b]coming in His kingdom.''

C Concerning His Glory (the Transfiguration), 17:1-21

17 [a]And six days later Jesus *took with Him [b]Peter and James and John his brother, and *brought them up to a high mountain by themselves.

2 And He was transfigured before them; and His face shone like the sun, and His garments became as white as light.

3 And behold, Moses and Elijah appeared to them, talking with Him.

4 And Peter [a]answered and said to Jesus, ''Lord, it is good for us to be here; if You wish, [b]I will make three tabernacles here, one for You, and one for Moses, and one for Elijah.''

5 While he was still speaking, behold, a bright cloud overshadowed them; and behold, [a]a voice out of the cloud, saying, ''[b]This is My beloved Son, with whom I am well-pleased; listen to Him!''

6 And when the disciples heard *this,* they fell on their faces and were much afraid.

7 And Jesus came to *them* and touched them and said, ''Arise, and [a]do not be afraid.''

8 And lifting up their eyes, they saw no one, except Jesus Himself alone.

9 [a]And as they were coming down from the mountain, Jesus commanded them, saying, ''[b]Tell the vision to no one until [c]the Son of Man has [d]risen from the dead.''

10 And His disciples asked Him, saying, ''Why then do the scribes say that [a]Elijah must come first?''

11 And He answered and said, ''Elijah is coming and will restore all things;

12 but I say to you, that Elijah already came, and they did not recognize him, but did to him whatever they wished. So also [a]the Son of Man is going to suffer at their hands.''

13 Then the disciples understood that He had spoken to them about John the Baptist.

14 [a]And when they came to the multitude, a man came up to Him, falling on his knees before Him, and saying,

15 ''Lord, have mercy on my son, for he is a [a]lunatic, and is very ill; for he often falls into the fire, and often into the water.

16 ''And I brought him to Your disciples, and they could not cure him.''

17 And Jesus answered and said, ''O unbelieving and perverted generation, how long shall I be with you? How long shall I put up with you? Bring him here to Me.''

18 And Jesus rebuked him, and the demon came out of him, and the boy was cured at once.

19 Then the disciples came to Jesus privately and said, ''Why could we not cast it out?''

---

nessed the transfiguration (17:1-8), which was, in miniature, a preview of the kingdom, with the Lord appearing in a state of glory (Dan. 7:9-14).
17:1 *six days later.* Luke's ''some eight days'' includes the beginning and ending days as well as the interval between. *Peter and James and John.* The inner circle of the disciples.
17:2 *transfigured.* Lit., transformed. The transfiguration gave the three disciples a preview of Jesus' future exaltation and the coming kingdom. The Lord was seen in His body of glory; Moses and Elijah illustrated those whom Christ will bring with Him (either through death or translation, 1 Thess. 4:13-18); the disciples represented those who will behold His coming (Rev. 1:7).
17:4 *tabernacles.* Booths or shelters, for temporary residence.
17:10 *scribes.* I.e., the accredited expounders of Hebrew scriptures.
17:11-12 The sequence of thought is as follows: (1) Elijah is coming as the restorer (Mal. 4:5); (2) he came, unrecognized, in the person of John the Baptist, and was killed; (3) the Son of Man faces a like fate. The disciples seem to grasp only the first two points.

Marginal references:

★1 [a]Matt. 17:1-8; Mark 9:2-8; Luke 9:28-36 [b]Matt. 26:37; Mark 5:37; 13:3
★2
★4 [a]Acts 3:12 [b]Mark 9:5; Luke 9:33
5 [a]2 Pet. 1:17f; [b]Matt. 3:17
7 [a]Matt. 14:27
9 [a]Matt. 17:9-13; Mark 9:9-13 [b]Matt. 8:4 [c]Matt. 8:20; 17:12, 22 [d]Matt. 16:21
★10 [a]Matt. 11:14; 16:14
★11-12
12 [a]Matt. 8:20; 17:9, 22
14 [a]Matt. 17:14-19; Mark 9:14-28; Matt. 17:14-18; Luke 9:37-42
15 [a]Matt. 4:24

20 And He *said to them, "Because of the littleness of your faith; for truly I say to you, ^aif you have faith as ^ba mustard seed, you shall say to ^cthis mountain, 'Move from here to there,' and it shall move; and ^dnothing shall be impossible to you. **21** ["^aBut this kind does not go out except by prayer and fasting."]

D Concerning His Betrayal, 17:22–23

22 ^aAnd while they were gathering together in Galilee, Jesus said to them, "The Son of Man is going to be delivered into the hands of men; **23** and ^athey will kill Him, and He will be raised on the third day." And they were deeply grieved.

E Concerning Taxes, 17:24–27

24 And when they had come to Capernaum, those who collected ^athe two-drachma *tax* came to Peter, and said, "Does your teacher not pay ^athe two-drachma *tax*?" **25** He *said, "Yes." And when he came into the house, Jesus spoke to him first, saying, "What do you think, Simon? From whom do the kings of the earth collect ^acustoms or ^bpoll-tax, from their sons or from strangers?"

26 And upon his saying, "From strangers," Jesus said to him, "Consequently the sons are exempt. **27** "But, lest we ^agive them offense, go to the sea, and throw in a hook, and take the first fish that comes up; and when you open its mouth, you will find a stater. Take that and give it to them for you and Me."

F Concerning Humility, 18:1–35

1 Illustrated in childlike faith, 18:1–6

18 ^aAt that time the disciples came to Jesus, saying, "Who then is greatest in the kingdom of heaven?" **2** And He called a child to Himself and set him before them, **3** and said, "Truly I say to you, unless you are converted and ^abecome like children, you shall not enter the kingdom of heaven. **4** "Whoever then humbles himself as this child, he is the greatest in the kingdom of heaven. **5** "And whoever receives one such child in My name receives Me; **6** but ^awhoever ^bcauses one of these little ones who believe in Me to stumble, it is better for him that a heavy millstone be hung around his neck, and that he be drowned in the depth of the sea.

★20 ^aMatt. 21:21f.; Mark 11:23f.; Luke 17:6 ^bMatt. 13:31; Luke 17:6 ^cMatt. 17:9; 1 Cor. 13:2 ^dMark 9:23; John 11:40

★21 ^aMark 9:29

22 ^aMatt. 17:22, 23; Mark 9:30-32; Luke 9:44, 45

23 ^aMatt. 16:21; 17:9

★24-27

24 ^aEx. 30:13; 38:26

25 ^aRom. 13:7 ^bMatt. 22:17, 19

27 ^aMatt. 5:29, 30; 18:6, 8, 9; Mark 9:42, 43, 45, 47; Luke 17:2; John 6:61; 1 Cor. 8:13

1 ^aMatt. 18:1-5; Mark 9:33-37; Luke 9:46-48

★ 3 ^aMatt. 19:14; Mark 10:15; Luke 18:17; 1 Cor. 14:20; 1 Pet. 2:2

★ 4

★ 6-7

6 ^aMark 9:42; Luke 17:2; 1 Cor. 8:12 ^bMatt. 17:27

17:20 *nothing shall be impossible.* The will of God, of course, governs all things, including this promise.

17:21 Many manuscripts do not contain this verse.

17:24–27 This assessment of a half-stater, or half-shekel (2 drachmas), was collected annually for the support of the temple. Jesus anticipated Peter's confusion by trying to show him that members of the royal family are exempt from the tax. Thus, Jesus, the Son of God, was not personally obligated to pay for the support of God's house. Nevertheless, to avoid offense, He would pay. The miraculously caught fish yielded a stater, or shekel, which was equal to two half-shekels, sufficient for Jesus and Peter.

18:3 *are converted* = turn, an active and voluntary turning from sin.

18:4 *humbles himself.* The sense is, whoever humbles himself until he becomes as this little child—exhibiting trust, openness, and eagerness to learn. These are the childlike qualities that constitute greatness.

18:6-7 *causes . . . to stumble.* I.e., leads into sin. *stumbling blocks* (v. 7) are occasions for stumbling or temptations to sin. *millstone* (v. 6). The milling of grain was done by grinding it between 2 stones, each about 18 inches in diameter and 3 or 4 inches thick. The upper millstone was turned by a donkey walking in a circle.

2 Illustrated in concern for the lost, 18:7-14

7 aLuke 17:1; 1 Cor. 11:19; 1 Tim. 4:1

7 "Woe to the world because of its stumbling blocks! For ^ait is inevitable that stumbling blocks come; but woe to that man through whom the stumbling block comes!

★ 8 aMatt. 5:30; 17:27; Mark 9:43 bMatt. 17:27

8 "And ^aif your hand or your foot ^bcauses you to stumble, cut it off and throw it from you; it is better for you to enter life crippled or lame, than having two hands or two feet, to be cast into the eternal fire.

9 aMatt. 5:29; 17:27; Mark 9:47 bMatt. 17:27 cMatt. 5:22

9 "And ^aif your eye ^bcauses you to stumble, pluck it out, and throw it from you. It is better for you to enter life with one eye, than having two eyes, to be cast into the ^cfiery hell.

★10 a1 Kin. 10:8; 2 Kin. 25:19; Luke 1:19; Acts 12:15; Rev. 8:2

10 "See that you do not despise one of these little ones, for I say to you, that ^atheir angels in heaven continually behold the face of My Father who is in heaven.

11 aLuke 19:10

11 ["^aFor the Son of Man has come to save that which was lost.]

12 aMatt. 18:12-14; Luke 15:4-7

12 "What do you think? ^aIf any man has a hundred sheep, and one of them has gone astray, does he not leave the ninety-nine on the mountains and go and search for the one that is straying?

13 "And if it turns out that he finds it, truly I say to you, he rejoices over it more than over the ninety-nine which have not gone astray.

14 "Thus it is not the will of your Father who is in heaven that one of these little ones perish.

15 aLev. 19:17; Luke 17:3; Gal. 6:1; 2 Thess. 3:15; James 5:19

3 Illustrated in church discipline, 18:15-20

15 "And ^aif your brother sins, go and reprove him in private; if

he listens to you, you have won your brother.

16 "But if he does not listen to you, take one or two more with you, so that ^aBY THE MOUTH OF TWO OR THREE WITNESSES EVERY FACT MAY BE CONFIRMED.

★16 aDeut. 19:15; John 8:17; 2 Cor. 13:1; 1 Tim. 5:19; Heb. 10:28

17 "And if he refuses to listen to them, ^atell it to the church; and if he refuses to listen even to the church, ^blet him be to you as a Gentile and a tax-gatherer.

★17 a1 Cor. 6:1ff. b2 Thess. 3:6, 14f.

18 "Truly I say to you, ^awhatever you shall bind on earth shall be bound in heaven; and whatever you loose on earth shall be loosed in heaven.

★18 aMatt. 16:19; John 20:23

19 "Again I say to you, that if two of you agree on earth about anything that they may ask, ^ait shall be done for them by My Father who is in heaven.

19 aMatt. 7:7

20 "For where two or three have gathered together in My name, there I am in their midst."

4 Illustrated in continual forgiveness, 18:21-35

21 Then Peter came and said to Him, "Lord, ^ahow often shall my brother sin against me and I forgive him? Up to ^bseven times?"

★21 aMatt. 18:15 bLuke 17:4

22 Jesus *said to him, "I do not say to you, up to seven times, but up to ^aseventy times seven.

22 aGen. 4:24

23 "For this reason ^athe kingdom of heaven may be compared to a certain king who wished to ^bsettle accounts with his slaves.

23 aMatt. 13:24 bMatt. 25:19

24 "And when he had begun to settle them, there was brought to him one who owed him ten thousand talents.

★24

25 "But since he ^adid not have the means to repay, his lord commanded him ^bto be sold, along with his wife and children and all

25 aLuke 7:42 bEx. 21:2; Lev. 25:39; 2 Kin. 4:1; Neh. 5:5

18:8 cut it off. See note on Matt. 5:29-30.
18:10 their angels. Apparently children have guardian angels (Ps. 91:11; Acts 12:15). behold the face = are in the immediate presence.
18:16 two or three witnesses. An ancient law (Deut. 19:15) for the purpose of reconciliation.
18:17 church. Here and in 16:18 are the only mention of the church in the Gospels. A local congregation is meant here; in 16:18, all the

followers of Christ.
18:18 See notes on Matt. 16:19 and John 20:23.
18:21 Up to seven times? The rabbis said to forgive 3 times, so Peter thought he was being exceptionally worthy by suggesting 7 times.
18:24 talents. A talent was a measure of weight varying in size from about 58-80 lbs. It was used to weigh precious metals.

that he had, and repayment to be made.

26 aMatt. 8:2   **26** "The slave therefore falling down, aprostrated himself before him, saying, 'Have patience with me, and I will repay you everything.'

27 "And the lord of that slave felt compassion and released him and forgave him the debt.

★28   **28** "But that slave went out and found one of his fellow slaves who owed him a hundred denarii; and he seized him and *began* to choke *him,* saying, 'Pay back what you owe.'

29 "So his fellow slave fell down and *began* to entreat him, saying, 'Have patience with me and I will repay you.'

30 "He was unwilling however, but went and threw him in prison until he should pay back what was owed.

31 "So when his fellow slaves saw what had happened, they were deeply grieved and came and reported to their lord all that had happened.

32 "Then summoning him, his lord *said to him, 'You wicked slave, I forgave you all that debt because you entreated me.

33 'Should you not also have had mercy on your fellow slave, even as I had mercy on you?'

34 "And his lord, moved with anger, handed him over to the torturers until he should repay all that was owed him.

35 aMatt. 6:14   **35** "aSo shall My heavenly Father also do to you, if each of you does not forgive his brother from your heart."

G Concerning Human Problems, 19:1-26

1 Physical problems, 19:1-2

19 aAnd it came about that when Jesus had finished these words, He departed from Galilee, and bcame into the region of Judea beyond the Jordan;

2 and great multitudes followed Him, and aHe healed them there.

★1 aMatt. 7:28 bMatt. 19:1-9; Mark 10:1-12

2 aMatt. 4:23

2 Divorce and remarriage, 19:3-12

3 And *some* Pharisees came to Him, testing Him, and saying, "aIs it lawful *for* a man to divorce his wife for any cause at all?"

4 And He answered and said, "Have you not read, athat He who created *them* from the beginning MADE THEM MALE AND FEMALE,

5 and said, 'aFOR THIS CAUSE A MAN SHALL LEAVE HIS FATHER AND MOTHER, AND SHALL CLEAVE TO HIS WIFE; AND bTHE TWO SHALL BECOME ONE FLESH'?

6 "Consequently they are no longer two, but one flesh. What therefore God has joined together, let no man separate."

7 They *said to Him, "aWhy then did Moses command to GIVE HER A CERTIFICATE AND DIVORCE HER?"

8 He *said to them, "Because of your hardness of heart, Moses permitted you to divorce your wives; but from the beginning it has not been this way.

9 "And I say to you, awhoever divorces his wife, except for im-

★3 aMatt. 5:31

★4-5

4 aGen. 1:27; 5:2

5 aGen. 2:24; Eph. 5:31 b1 Cor. 6:16

★7 aDeut. 24:1-4

★8

9 aMatt. 5:32

18:28 *a hundred denarii.* A 100 days' wages, a trifling sum in comparison.

19:1 *beyond the Jordan* = Perea, not part of Judea but within the tetrarchy of Herod Antipas. Perea was a region east of the Jordan, extending from the Sea of Galilee almost to the Dead Sea.

19:3 *for any cause at all.* The rabbis were divided on what were legitimate grounds for divorce. The followers of Shammai held that a man could not divorce his wife unless he found her guilty of sexual immorality. The followers of Hillel were more lax, allowing di-

vorce for many, including trivial, reasons.

19:4-5 See Gen. 1:27; 2:23-24. Rather than aligning Himself with either rabbinical position, Jesus cites the purpose of God in creation that husband and wife should be one flesh—the oneness of kinship or fellowship with the body as the medium, causing marriage to be the deepest physical and spiritual unity.

19:7 *a certificate.* See note on Matt. 5:32.

19:8 *permitted.* Moses made a concession with regard to God's intention that marriage be lifelong and monogamous (Deut. 24:1-4).

morality, and marries another woman commits adultery."

★10   **10** The disciples *said to Him, "If the relationship of the man with his wife is like this, it is better not to marry."

11 But He said to them, "^aNot all men *can* accept this statement, but ^b*only* those to whom it has been given.

12 "For there are eunuchs who were born that way from their mother's womb; and there are eunuchs who were made eunuchs by men; and there are *also* eunuchs who made themselves eunuchs for the sake of the kingdom of heaven. He who is able to accept *this,* let him accept *it.*"

3   Children, 19:13-15

13 ^aThen *some* children were brought to Him so that He might lay His hands on them and pray; and the disciples rebuked them.

14 But Jesus said, "^aLet the children alone, and do not hinder them from coming to Me; for ^bthe kingdom of heaven belongs to such as these."

15 And after laying His hands on them, He departed from there.

4   Wealth, 19:16-26

16 ^aAnd behold, one came to Him and said, "Teacher, what good thing shall I do that I may obtain ^beternal life?"

17 And He said to him, "Why are you asking Me about what is good? There is *only* One who is good; but ^aif you wish to enter into life, keep the commandments."

18 He *said to Him, "Which ones?" And Jesus said, "^aYOU SHALL NOT COMMIT MURDER; YOU SHALL NOT COMMIT ADULTERY; YOU SHALL NOT STEAL; YOU SHALL NOT BEAR FALSE WITNESS;

19 ^aHONOR YOUR FATHER AND MOTHER; and ^bYOU SHALL LOVE YOUR NEIGHBOR AS YOURSELF."

20 The young man *said to Him, "All these things I have kept; what am I still lacking?"

21 Jesus said to him, "If you wish to be complete, go and ^asell your possessions and give to the poor, and you shall have ^btreasure in heaven; and come, follow Me."

22 But when the young man heard this statement, he went away grieved; for he was one who owned much property.

23 And Jesus said to His disciples, "Truly I say to you, ^ait is hard for a rich man to enter the kingdom of heaven.

24 "And again I say to you, ^ait is easier for a camel to go through the eye of a needle, than for a rich man to enter the kingdom of God."

25 And when the disciples heard *this,* they were very astonished and said, "Then who can be saved?"

26 And looking upon *them* Jesus said to them, "^aWith men this is impossible, but with God all things are possible."

Marginal references:

11 ^a1 Cor. 7:7ff. ^bMatt. 13:11

13 ^aMatt. 19:13-15; Mark 10:13-16; Luke 18:15-17

14 ^aMatt. 18:3; Mark 10:15; Luke 18:17; 1 Cor. 14:20; 1 Pet. 2:2 ^bMatt. 5:3

★16 ^aMatt. 19:16-29; Mark 10:17-30; Luke 18:18-30; Luke 10:25-28 ^bMatt. 25:46

17 ^aLev. 18:5; Neh. 9:29; Ezek. 20:21

18 ^aEx. 20:13-16; Deut. 5:17-20

19 ^aEx. 20:12; Deut. 5:16 ^bLev. 19:18

★21 ^aLuke 12:33; 16:9; Acts 2:45; 4:34f. ^bMatt. 6:20

23 ^aMatt. 13:22; Mark 10:23f.; Luke 18:24

★24 ^aMark 10:25; Luke 18:25

26 ^aGen. 18:14; Job 42:2; Jer. 32:17; Zech. 8:6; Mark 10:27; Luke 1:37; 18:27

19:10 *it is better not to marry.* The disciples seemed to have understood that Christ was teaching a very restricted meaning to "immorality" and that He completely disallowed divorce of married persons (see note on Matt. 5:32). In turn, Christ acknowledges that the saying "it is better not to marry" is valid in some cases, and these are enumerated in v. 12—those congenitally incapable, those made incapable, and those who wish to devote themselves more completely to the service of God (1 Cor. 7:7, 8, 26, 32-35). Celibacy is an acceptable option.
19:16 Jews of the time believed that performing some single act would guarantee salvation.

19:21 *complete.* I.e., genuinely pleasing to God. *go and sell.* The man was being asked to prove his claim to have kept the commandments, especially the one that says "thou shalt love thy neighbor as thyself." His unwillingness to do so belied his claim (v. 20) and showed him as a sinner in need of salvation.
19:24 *needle.* This means a sewing needle. In this proverbial expression, Christ does not say that a rich man could not be saved (v. 26), but only that, for him, it is more difficult, since such a person seldom senses his personal need as readily as a poorer man does.

H Concerning the Kingdom,
19:27–20:28

1 Rewards in the kingdom,
19:27-30

★27 **27** Then Peter answered and said to Him, "Behold, we have left everything and followed You; what then will there be for us?"

★28 *a*Matt. 25:31 *b*Luke 22:30; Rev. 3:21; 4:4; 11:16; 20:4 **28** And Jesus said to them, "Truly I say to you, that you who have followed Me, in the regeneration when *a*the Son of Man will sit on His glorious throne, *b*you also shall sit upon twelve thrones, judging the twelve tribes of Israel.

29 *a*Matt. 6:33; Mark 10:29f.; Luke 18:29f. **29** "And *a*everyone who has left houses or brothers or sisters or father or mother or children or farms for My name's sake, shall receive many times as much, and shall inherit eternal life.

30 *a*Matt. 20:16; Mark 10:31; Luke 13:30 **30** "*a*But many *who are* first will be last; and *the* last, first.

2 Recognition in the kingdom,
20:1-16

★ 1-16 **20** "For *a*the kingdom of heaven is like a landowner who went out early in the morning to hire laborers for his *b*vineyard.

1 *a*Matt. 13:24 *b*Matt. 21:28, 33

★ 2 **2** "And when he had agreed with the laborers for a denarius for the day, he sent them into his vineyard.

3 "And he went out about the third hour and saw others standing idle in the market place;

4 and to those he said, 'You too go into the vineyard, and whatever is right I will give you.' And *so* they went.

5 "Again he went out about the sixth and the ninth hour, and did the same thing.

6 "And about the eleventh *hour* he went out, and found others standing; and he *said to them, 'Why have you been standing here idle all day long?'

7 "They *said to him, 'Because no one hired us.' He *said to them, 'You too go into the vineyard.'

8 *a*Lev. 19:13 *b*Luke 8:3 **8** "And when *a*evening had come, the owner of the vineyard *said to his *b*foreman, 'Call the laborers and pay them their wages, beginning with the last *group* to the first.'

9 "And when those *hired* about the eleventh hour came, each one received a denarius.

10 "And when those *hired* first came, they thought that they would receive more; and they also received each one a denarius.

11 "And when they received it, they grumbled at the landowner,

12 *a*Jon. 4:8; Luke 12:55; James 1:11 **12** saying, 'These last men have worked *only* one hour, and you have made them equal to us who have borne the burden and the *a*scorching heat of the day.'

13 *a*Matt. 22:12; 26:50 **13** "But he answered and said to one of them, '*a*Friend, I am doing you no wrong; did you not agree with me for a denarius?

14 'Take what is yours and go your way, but I wish to give to this last man the same as to you.

★14

15 *a*Deut. 15:9; Matt. 6:23; Mark 7:22 **15** 'Is it not lawful for me to do what I wish with what is my own? Or is your *a*eye envious because I am generous?'

16 *a*Matt. 19:30 **16** "Thus *a*the last shall be first, and the first last."

3 Rank in the kingdom,
20:17-28

17 *a*Matt. 20:17-19; Mark 10:32-34; Luke 18:31-33 **17** *a*And as Jesus was about to go up to Jerusalem, He took the

---

19:27 Peter must have been thinking, "Well, we disciples certainly don't have any such hindrances of wealth!"

19:28 *in the regeneration* = in the New Age, the millennium, when the earth will be made new. The only other use of the word "regeneration" in the N.T. speaks of people being made new (Titus 3:5). *on His glorious throne.* See Matt. 25:31.

20:1-16 The subject is the reward of willingness to serve, whether one comes early or late. Christ is not teaching economics.

20:2 *a denarius for the day.* A good and normal wage for a rural worker. Additional workers were hired at about 9 a.m., noon, 3 p.m., and 5 p.m.

20:14 *I wish to give.* This is the point of the parable: God's grace and generosity know no bounds, and man's ideas of merit and earned rewards are irrelevant.

twelve *disciples* aside by themselves, and on the way He said to them,

18 "Behold, we are going up to Jerusalem; and the Son of Man ^awill be delivered to the chief priests and scribes, and they will condemn Him to death,

19 and ^awill deliver Him to the Gentiles to mock and scourge and crucify *Him*, and on ^bthe third day He will be raised up."

20 ^aThen the mother of ^bthe sons of Zebedee came to Him with her sons, ^cbowing down, and making a request of Him.

21 And He said to her, "What do you wish?" She *said to Him, "Command that in Your kingdom these two sons of mine ^amay sit, one on Your right and one on Your left."

22 But Jesus answered and said, "You do not know what you are asking for. Are you able ^ato drink the cup that I am about to drink?" They *said to Him, "We are able."

23 He *said to them, "^aMy cup you shall drink; but to sit on My right and on *My* left, this is not Mine to give, ^bbut it is for those for whom it has been ^cprepared by My Father."

24 And hearing *this,* the ten became indignant with the two brothers.

25 ^aBut Jesus called them to Himself, and said, "You know that the rulers of the Gentiles lord it over them, and *their* great men exercise authority over them.

26 "It is not so among you, ^abut whoever wishes to become

great among you shall be your servant,

27 and whoever wishes to be first among you shall be your slave;

28 just as ^athe Son of Man ^bdid not come to be served, but to serve, and to give His life a ransom for many."

VI THE PRESENTATION OF THE KING, 20:29–23:39
A The Power of the King, 20:29–34

29 ^aAnd as they were going out from Jericho, a great multitude followed Him.

30 And behold, two blind men sitting by the road, hearing that Jesus was passing by, cried out, saying, "Lord, ^ahave mercy on us, ^bSon of David!"

31 And the multitude sternly told them to be quiet; but they cried out all the more, saying, "Lord, have mercy on us, ^aSon of David!"

32 And Jesus stopped and called them, and said, "What do you want Me to do for you?"

33 They *said to Him, "Lord, *we want* our eyes to be opened."

34 And moved with compassion, Jesus touched their eyes; and immediately they regained their sight and followed Him.

B The Presentation of the King, 21:1–11

21 ^aAnd when they had approached Jerusalem and

20:22 *the cup that I am about to drink?* I.e., the cup of suffering. *We are able.* James was the first of the apostles to be martyred (Acts 12:2).

20:28 *ransom for many.* The word "for" undebatably means "in the place of" many. Christ here clearly interprets the meaning of His sacrifice as a substitution for sinners.

20:29-34 The differences in this account (which speaks of 2 blind men and of the miracle being done as Jesus left Jericho) and the accounts in Mark 10:46-52 and Luke 18:35-43 (which mention only 1 blind man and the miracle performed as they entered Jericho) are ex-

plained thus: (1) there were actually 2 men involved, but Bartimaeus, being more aggressive, takes the place of prominence; and (2) the men pled with Jesus as He entered Jericho but were not healed until He was leaving. It is also possible that the healing took place after Jesus left old Jericho and was nearing new Jericho.

20:30 *Son of David.* The specific Messianic title (Ps. 72; Isa. 9:7).

21:1 *Bethphage.* A village ½ mile E. of Jerusalem, on the S. side of the Mount of Olives.

had come to Bethphage, to *b*the Mount of Olives, then Jesus sent two disciples,

2 saying to them, "Go into the village opposite you, and immediately you will find a donkey tied *there* and a colt with her; untie *them*, and bring *them* to Me.

★ 3

3 "And if anyone says something to you, you shall say, 'The Lord has need of them,' and immediately he will send them."

4 *a*Matt.
21:4-9; John
12:12-15

4 *a*Now this took place that what was spoken through the prophet might be fulfilled, saying,

★ 5 *a*Is.
62:11; Zech.
9:9

5 "*a*SAY TO THE DAUGHTER OF ZION,

'BEHOLD YOUR KING IS COMING TO YOU,

GENTLE, AND MOUNTED ON A DONKEY,

EVEN ON A COLT, THE FOAL OF A BEAST OF BURDEN.'"

6 And the disciples went and did just as Jesus had directed them,

7 and brought the donkey and the colt, and laid on them their garments, on which He sat.

8 *a*2 Kin.
9:13

8 And most of the multitude *a*spread their garments in the road, and others were cutting branches from the trees, and spreading them in the road.

★ 9 *a*Ps.
118:26f.
*b*Matt. 9:27
*c*Luke 2:14

9 And the multitudes going before Him, and those who followed after were crying out, saying,

"*a*Hosanna to the *b*Son of David;

*a*BLESSED IS HE WHO COMES IN THE NAME OF THE LORD;

Hosanna *c*in the highest!"

10 And when He had entered Jerusalem, all the city was stirred, saying, "Who is this?"

11 And the multitudes were saying, "This is *a*the prophet Jesus, from *b*Nazareth in Galilee."

11 *a*Matt.
21:26; Mark
6:15; Luke
7:16, 39;
13:33; 24:19;
John 1:21,
25; 4:19;
6:14; 7:40;
9:17; Acts
3:22f.; 7:37
*b*Matt. 2:23

C The Purification by the King, 21:12-17

12 *a*And Jesus entered the temple and cast out all those who were buying and selling in the temple, and overturned the tables of the *b*moneychangers and the seats of those who were selling *c*doves.

★12 *a*Matt.
21:12-16;
Mark 11:15-
18; Luke
19:45-47;
Matt. 21:12,
13; John
2:13-16 *b*Ex.
30:13 *c*Lev.
1:14; 5:7;
12:8

13 And He *said to them, "It is written, '*a*MY HOUSE SHALL BE CALLED A HOUSE OF PRAYER'; but you are making it a ROBBERS' DEN."

★13 *a*Is.
56:7; Jer.
7:11

14 And *the* blind and *the* lame came to Him in the temple, and *a*He healed them.

★14 *a*Matt.
4:23

15 But when the chief priests and the scribes saw the wonderful things that He had done, and the children who were crying out in the temple and saying, "Hosanna to the *a*Son of David," they became indignant,

15 *a*Matt.
9:27

16 and said to Him, "Do You hear what these are saying?" And Jesus *said to them, "Yes; have you never read, '*a*OUT OF THE MOUTH OF INFANTS AND NURSING BABES THOU HAST PREPARED PRAISE FOR THYSELF'?"

★16 *a*Ps. 8:2

17 And He left them and went out of the city to *a*Bethany, and lodged there.

17 *a*Matt.
26:6; Mark
11:1, 11, 12;
14:3; Luke
19:29; 24:50;
John 11:1,
18; 12:1

21:3 *he will send them.* I.e., the owner will.
21:5 See Zech. 9:9.
21:9 *Hosanna* = save now. The acclamation is a quotation based upon Ps. 118:25-27, sung at the Feast of Tabernacles. The crowd wanted salvation from the oppression of Rome, not the spiritual salvation which Christ offered.
21:12 *moneychangers.* Ordinary coinage had to be exchanged for ancient Hebrew or Tyrian shekels, which were of standard weight and without blemish, as an offering to God.

21:13 Jesus here combines parts of 2 O.T. verses, Isa. 56:7 and Jer. 7:11.
21:14 *in the temple.* Doubtless at the gate or in the temple court, for *the blind and the lame* were not permitted into the temple (2 Sam. 5:8).
21:16 Jesus is apparently quoting Ps. 8:2, though *prepared praise* comes from the Septuagint version of the Psalm and may be translated "provided thyself with praise."

D The Cursing of the Fig Tree,
21:18-22

★18 *a*Matt.
21:18-22;
Mark 11:12-
14, 20-24

18 *a*Now in the morning, when He returned to the city, He became hungry.

★19

19 And seeing a lone fig tree by the road, He came to it, and found nothing on it except leaves only; and He *said to it, "No longer shall there ever be *any* fruit from you." And at once the fig tree withered.

20 And seeing *this*, the disciples marveled, saying, "How did the fig tree wither at once?"

21 *a*Matt.
17:20; Mark
11:23; Luke
17:6; James
1:6

21 And Jesus answered and said to them, "Truly I say to you, *a*if you have faith, and do not doubt, you shall not only do what was done to the fig tree, but even if you say to this mountain, 'Be taken up and cast into the sea,' it shall happen.

22 *a*Matt. 7:7

22 "And *a*all things you ask in prayer, believing, you shall receive."

E The Challenge to the King,
21:23-27

★23-27

★23 *a*Matt.
21:23-27;
Mark 11:27-
33; Luke
20:1-8

23 *a*And when He had come into the temple, the chief priests and the elders of the people came to Him as He was teaching, and said, "By what authority are You doing these things, and who gave You this authority?"

24 And Jesus answered and said to them, "I will ask you one thing too, which if you tell Me, I will also tell you by what authority I do these things.

★25

25 "The baptism of John was from what *source*, from heaven or from men?" And they *began* reasoning among themselves, saying, "If we say, 'From heaven,' He will say to us, 'Then why did you not believe him?'

26 "But if we say, 'From men,' we fear the multitude; for they all hold John to be *a*a prophet."

26 *a*Matt.
11:9; Mark
6:20

27 And answering Jesus, they said, "We do not know." He also said to them, "Neither will I tell you by what authority I do these things.

F The Parables of the King,
21:28-22:14
1 The rebellion of the nation,
21:28-32

28 "But what do you think? A man had two sons, and he came to the first and said, 'Son, go work today in the *a*vineyard.'

28 *a*Matt.
20:1; 21:33

29 "And he answered and said, 'I will, sir'; and he did not go.

30 "And he came to the second and said the same thing. But he answered and said, 'I will not'; *yet* he afterward regretted *it* and went.

31 "Which of the two did the will of his father?" They *said, "The latter." Jesus *said to them, "Truly I say to you that *a*the taxgatherers and harlots will get into the kingdom of God before you.

31 *a*Luke
7:29, 37-50

32 "For John came to you in the way of righteousness and you did not believe him; but *a*the taxgatherers and harlots did believe him; and you, seeing this, did not even feel remorse afterward so as to believe him.

32 *a*Luke
3:12

2 The retribution on the
nation, 21:33-46

33 "Listen to another parable. *a*There was a landowner who *b*PLANTED A *c*VINEYARD AND PUT A WALL AROUND IT AND DUG A *d*WINE PRESS IN IT, AND *d*BUILT A TOWER, and

33 *a*Matt.
21:33-46;
Mark 12:1-
12; Luke
20:9-19 *b*Ps.
80:8; Is.
5:1ff. *c*Matt.
20:1; 21:28
*d*Is. 5:2
*e*Matt. 25:14

21:18 *in the morning.* I.e., on Monday of Holy Week.

21:19 *except leaves only.* Normally the fruit and leaves appear at the same time. The curse on the tree is illustrative of the rejection of Israel, a nation unfruitful despite every advantage.

21:23-27 In effect, Jesus refuses to accept their claim of a right to examine Him.

21:23 This begins Tuesday of Holy Week.

21:25 *from what source.* Christ placed these men on the horns of a dilemma by asking them what test they would apply in the case of John.

rented it out to vine-growers, and *e*went on a journey.

34 "And when the harvest time approached, he *a*sent his slaves to the vine-growers to receive his produce.

35 "And the vine-growers took his slaves and beat one, and killed another, and stoned a third.

36 "Again he *a*sent another group of slaves larger than the first; and they did the same thing to them.

37 "But afterward he sent his son to them, saying, 'They will respect my son.'

38 "But when the vine-growers saw the son, they said among themselves, 'This is the heir; come, let us kill him, and seize his inheritance.'

39 "And they took him, and threw him out of the vineyard, and killed him.

40 "Therefore when the owner of the vineyard comes, what will he do to those vine-growers?"

41 They *said to Him, "He will bring those wretches to a wretched end, and *a*will rent out the vineyard to other vine-growers, who will pay him the proceeds at the *proper* seasons."

42 Jesus *said to them, "Did you never read in the Scriptures,

'*a*THE STONE WHICH THE BUILDERS REJECTED,
THIS BECAME THE CHIEF CORNER *stone*;
THIS CAME ABOUT FROM THE LORD,
AND IT IS MARVELOUS IN OUR EYES'?

43 "Therefore I say to you, the kingdom of God will be taken away from you, and be given to a nation producing the fruit of it.

44 "And he who falls on this stone will be broken to pieces; but on whomever it falls, it will scatter him like dust."

45 And when the chief priests and the Pharisees heard His parables, they understood that He was speaking about them.

46 And when they sought to seize Him, they *a*feared the multitudes, because they held Him to be a *b*prophet.

3 The rejection of the nation, 22:1-14

22 And Jesus *a*answered and spoke to them again in parables, saying,

2 "*a*The kingdom of heaven may be compared to a king, who gave a wedding feast for his son.

3 "And he *a*sent out his slaves to call those who had been invited to the wedding feast, and they were unwilling to come.

4 "Again he *a*sent out other slaves saying, 'Tell those who have been invited, "Behold, I have prepared my dinner; my oxen and my fattened livestock are *all* butchered and everything is ready; come to the wedding feast." '

5 "But they paid no attention and went their way, one to his own farm, another to his business,

6 and the rest seized his slaves and mistreated them and killed them.

7 "But the king was enraged and sent his armies, and destroyed those murderers, and set their city on fire.

8 "Then he *said to his slaves, 'The wedding is ready, but those who were invited were not worthy.

9 'Go therefore to *a*the main highways, and as many as you find *there*, invite to the wedding feast.'

10 "And those slaves went out into the streets, and gathered together all they found, both evil

Margin references

34 *a*Matt. 22:3

36 *a*Matt. 22:4

41 *a*Matt. 8:11f.; Acts 13:46; 18:6; 28:28

★**42** *a*Ps. 118:22; Acts 4:11; Rom. 9:33; 1 Pet. 2:7

★**43**

46 *a*Matt. 21:26 *b*Matt. 21:11

1 *a*Acts 3:12

2 *a*Matt. 13:24; 22:2-14; Luke 14:16-24

3 *a*Matt. 21:34

4 *a*Matt. 21:36

★**7**

★**9** *a*Ezek. 21:21; Obad. 14

21:42 See Ps. 118:22-23. The cornerstone figure was popular with N.T. writers (Acts 4:11; Eph. 2:20; 1 Pet. 2:7).
21:43 *taken away from you . . . given to a nation.* I.e., taken from the Jews and given to the

Church (1 Pet. 2:9).
22:7 *set their city on fire.* A prediction of the destruction of Jerusalem in A.D. 70.
22:9 *highways.* Better, broad places or plazas.

and good; and the wedding hall was filled with dinner guests.

11 a2 Kin. 10:22

11 "But when the king came in to look over the dinner guests, he saw there ᵃa man not dressed in wedding clothes,

★12 aMatt. 20:13; 26:50

12 and he *said to him, 'ᵃFriend, how did you come in here without wedding clothes?' And he was speechless.

13 aMatt. 8:12

13 "Then the king said to the servants, 'Bind him hand and foot, and cast him into ᵃthe outer darkness; in that place ᵃthere shall be weeping and gnashing of teeth.'

★14 aMatt. 24:22; 2 Pet. 1:10; Rev. 17:14

14 "For many are ᵃcalled, but few are ᵃchosen."

G The Pronouncements of the King, 22:15-23:39

1 In answer to the Herodians, 22:15-22

15 aMatt. 22:15-22; Mark 12:13-17; Luke 20:20-26
★16 aMark 3:6; 8:15; 12:13

15 ᵃThen the Pharisees went and counseled together how they might trap Him in what He said.

16 And they *sent their disciples to Him, along with the ᵃHerodians, saying, "Teacher, we know that You are truthful and teach the way of God in truth, and defer to no one; for You are not partial to any.

★17 aMatt. 17:25 bLuke 2:1; 3:1

17 "Tell us therefore, what do You think? Is it lawful to give a ᵃpoll-tax to ᵇCaesar, or not?"

18 But when Jesus perceived their malice, and said, "Why are you testing Me, you hypocrites?

19 aMatt. 17:25

19 "Show Me the ᵃcoin used for the poll-tax." And they brought Him a denarius.

20 And He *said to them, "Whose likeness and inscription is this?"

★21 aMark 12:17; Luke 20:25; Rom. 13:7

21 They *said to Him, "Caesar's." Then He *said to them, "ᵃThen render to Caesar the things that are Caesar's; and to God the things that are God's."

22 aMark 12:12

22 And hearing this, they marveled, and ᵃleaving Him, they went away.

2 In answer to the Sadducees, 22:23-33

23 aMatt. 22:23-33; Mark 12:18-27; Luke 20:27-40 bMatt. 3:7 cActs 23:8
★24 aDeut. 25:5

23 ᵃOn that day some ᵇSadducees (who say ᶜthere is no resurrection) came to Him and questioned Him,

24 saying, "Teacher, Moses said, 'ᵃIF A MAN DIES, HAVING NO CHILDREN, HIS BROTHER AS NEXT OF KIN SHALL MARRY HIS WIFE, AND RAISE UP AN OFFSPRING TO HIS BROTHER.'

25 "Now there were seven brothers with us; and the first married and died, and having no offspring left his wife to his brother;

22:12 *without wedding clothes.* This assumes that the guests would have been supplied with robes by the king's servants, since all the guests came in a hurry and most were unsuitably attired.

22:14 An ancient proverb, used 3 times in the apocryphal 4 Ezra. Here it indicates that there is a general call of God to sinners inviting them to receive His salvation, and there is also a specific election that brings some to Him. At the same time, man is held responsible for his rejecting Christ, whether it be because of indifference (Matt. 22:5), rebellion (v. 6), or self-righteousness (v. 12).

22:16 *Herodians.* A Jewish party who favored the Herodian dynasty, the party of "peace at any price" and appeasement of Rome.

22:17 *Is it lawful.* I.e., is it in accordance with the Torah, the sacred law? *to give a poll-tax to Caesar.* The poll-tax was imposed by Rome on every Jew. The burning question in the minds of many Jews of that day was simply this: If God gave the land of Israel to the Hebrews, and if God meant them to live there, and if He received their sacrifices and offerings in acknowledgment of His relationship to them, how could they pay tribute to any other power, king, god, or person? If Christ said that they should pay, they could then charge Him with disloyalty to Judaism; if He said no, they could denounce Him to the Romans.

22:21 Christ recognized the distinction between political and spiritual responsibilities. Caesar should be given taxes and all rightful political obedience; God should be given worship, obedience, service, and the dedication of one's whole life.

22:24 *children.* See Deut. 25:5-6; Gen. 38:8. The object of such a marriage law was to perpetuate the line of the dead brother and to keep his property within the family.

26 so also the second, and the third, down to the seventh.

27 "And last of all, the woman died.

28 "In the resurrection therefore whose wife of the seven shall she be? For they all had her."

29 But Jesus answered and said to them, "You are mistaken, [a]not understanding the Scriptures, or the power of God.

30 "For in the resurrection they neither [a]marry, nor are given in marriage, but are like angels in heaven.

31 "But regarding the resurrection of the dead, have you not read that which was spoken to you by God, saying,

32 '[a]I AM THE GOD OF ABRAHAM, AND THE GOD OF ISAAC, AND THE GOD OF JACOB'? God is not *the God* of *the* dead but of *the* living."

33 And when the multitudes heard *this*, [a]they were astonished at His teaching.

3 In answer to the Pharisees, 22:34-40

34 [a]But when the Pharisees heard that He had put [b]the Sadducees to silence, they gathered themselves together.

35 And one of them, [a]a lawyer, asked Him a question, testing Him,

36 "Teacher, which is the great commandment in the Law?"

37 And He said to him, "'[a]YOU SHALL LOVE THE LORD YOUR GOD WITH ALL YOUR HEART, AND WITH ALL YOUR SOUL, AND WITH ALL YOUR MIND.'

38 "This is the great and foremost commandment.

39 "And a second is like it, '[a]YOU SHALL LOVE YOUR NEIGHBOR AS YOURSELF.'

40 "[a]On these two commandments depend the whole Law and the Prophets."

4 In questioning the Pharisees, 22:41-46

41 [a]Now while the Pharisees were gathered together, Jesus asked them a question,

42 saying, "What do you think about the Christ, whose son is He?" They *said to Him, "[a]The son of David."

43 He *said to them, "Then how does David [a]in the Spirit call Him 'Lord,' saying,

44 '[a]THE LORD SAID TO MY LORD,

"SIT AT MY RIGHT HAND,
UNTIL I PUT THINE ENEMIES
BENEATH THY FEET?"'

45 "If David then calls Him 'Lord', how is He his son?"

46 And [a]no one was able to answer Him a word, nor did anyone dare from that day on to ask Him another question.

5 Concerning the Pharisees, 23:1-36

23 [a]Then Jesus spoke to the multitudes and to His disciples,

2 saying, "[a]The scribes and the Pharisees have seated themselves in the chair of Moses;

3 therefore all that they tell

Marginal references:

29 [a]John 20:9
★30 [a]Matt. 24:38; Luke 17:27
★32 [a]Ex. 3:6
33 [a]Matt. 7:28
34 [a]Matt. 22:34-40; Mark 12:28-31; Luke 10:25-37 [b]Matt. 3:7
★35 [a]Luke 7:30; 10:25; 11:45, 46, 52; 14:3; Titus 3:13
★36
★37 [a]Deut. 6:5
★39 [a]Lev. 19:18; Matt. 19:19; Gal. 5:14
40 [a]Matt. 7:12
41 [a]Matt. 22:41-46; Mark 12:35-37; Luke 20:41-44
42 [a]Matt. 9:27
★43 [a]2 Sam. 23:2; Rev. 1:10; 4:2
★44 [a]Ps. 110:1; Matt. 26:64; Mark 16:19; Acts 2:34; 1 Cor. 15:25; Heb. 1:13; 10:13
46 [a]Mark 12:34; Luke 14:6; 20:40
1 [a]Matt. 23:1-7; Mark 12:38, 39; Luke 20:45, 46
★ 2 [a]Deut. 33:3f; Ezra 7:6, 25; Neh. 8:4

22:30 *like angels in heaven.* Christ's argument is: In the resurrection men will not marry and women will not be given in marriage. There is no married state in that life. Thus the whole case cited is irrelevant and immaterial. Resurrected saints will be as angels who do not produce offspring.

22:32 See Ex. 3:6. For believers, there is life after death, a truth rooted in the character of God.

22:35 *lawyer* = scribe.

22:36 Other answers to this question are found in Isa. 33:15; Amos 5:4; Mic. 6:8; Hab. 2:4.

22:37 Christ quotes Deut. 6:5, part of the Shema, used by all Jews in their daily prayers.

22:39-40 See Lev. 19:18. Christ was the first to combine these two texts into a summary of the law.

22:43 *in the Spirit.* I.e., inspired by the Holy Spirit.

22:44 *The Lord said to my Lord.* Christ was trying to make the Pharisees see that the Son of David was also the Lord of David (Ps. 110:1); i.e., the Messiah was David's human descendant and divine Lord.

23:2 *seated . . . in the chair of Moses.* I.e., act as teachers of the law.

you, do and observe, but do not do according to their deeds; for they say *things,* and do not do them.

4 "And ^athey tie up heavy loads, and lay them on men's shoulders; but they themselves are unwilling to move them with *so much as* a finger.

5 "But they do all their deeds ^ato be noticed by men; for they ^bbroaden their phylacteries, and lengthen ^cthe tassels *of their garments.*

6 "And they ^alove the place of honor at banquets, and the chief seats in the synagogues,

7 and respectful greetings in the market places, and being called by men, ^aRabbi.

8 "But ^ado not be called ^bRabbi; for One is your Teacher, and you are all brothers.

9 "And do not call *anyone* on earth your father; for ^aOne is your Father, He who is in heaven.

10 "And do not be called leaders; for One is your Leader, *that is,* Christ.

11 "^aBut the greatest among you shall be your servant.

12 "And ^awhoever exalts himself shall be humbled; and whoever humbles himself shall be exalted.

13 "^aBut woe to you, scribes and Pharisees, hypocrites, ^bbecause you shut off the kingdom of heaven from men; for you do not enter in yourselves, nor do you al-low those who are entering to go in.

14 ["Woe to you, scribes and Pharisees, hypocrites, because ^ayou devour widows' houses, even while for a pretense you make long prayers; therefore you shall receive greater condemnation.]

15 "Woe to you, scribes and Pharisees, hypocrites, because you travel about on sea and land to make one ^aproselyte; and when he becomes one, you make him twice as much a son of ^bhell as yourselves.

16 "Woe to you, ^ablind guides, who say, '^bWhoever swears by the temple, that is nothing; but whoever swears by the gold of the temple, he is obligated.'

17 "You fools and blind men; ^awhich is more important, the gold, or the temple that sanctified the gold?

18 "And, 'Whoever swears by the altar, *that* is nothing, but whoever swears by the offering upon it, he is obligated.'

19 "You blind men, ^awhich is more important, the offering or the altar that sanctifies the offering?

20 "Therefore he who swears, swears *both* by the altar and by everything on it.

21 "And he who swears by the temple, swears *both* by the temple and by Him who ^adwells within it.

Cross references:

4 ^aLuke 11:46; Acts 15:10

★ 5 ^aMatt. 6:1, 5, 16 ^bEx. 13:9; Deut. 6:8; 11:18 ^cMatt. 9:20

6 ^aLuke 11:43; 14:7; 20:46

7 ^aMatt. 23:8; 26:25, 49; Mark 9:5; 10:51; 11:21; John 1:38, 49; 3:2, 26; 4:31; 6:25; 9:2; 11:8; 20:16

8 ^aJames 3:1 ^bMatt. 23:7; 26:25, 49; Mark 9:5; 10:51; 11:21; 14:45; John 1:38, 49; 3:2, 26; 4:31; 6:25; 9:2; 11:8; 20:16

9 ^aMatt. 6:9; 7:11

11 ^aMatt. 20:26

12 ^aLuke 14:11; 18:14

★13-33

13 ^aMatt. 23:15, (16), 23, 25, 27, 29 ^bLuke 11:52

★14 ^aMark 12:40; Luke 20:47

★15 ^aActs 2:10; 6:5; 13:43 ^bMatt. 5:22

★16 ^aMatt. 15:14; 23:24; ^bMatt. 5:33-35

17 ^aEx. 30:29

★18

19 ^aEx. 29:37

21 ^a1 Kin. 8:13; Ps. 26:8; 132:14

23:5 *phylacteries.* A phylactery was a square leather box which contained four strips of parchment on which were written Deut. 11:13-21, Deut. 6:4-9, Ex. 13:11-16, and Ex. 13:1-10. During prayer one was worn on the forehead between the eyebrows and another on the left arm close to the elbow. They were held in place by leather bands, which the Pharisees made broad to attract more attention to themselves. The custom was based on Ex. 13:9, 16; Deut. 6:8; 11:18, though phylacteries had only begun to be used by the ultra-pious in Christ's day. Christ criticizes not the custom itself but the spirit that corrupted it. *lengthen the tassels of their garments.* A hem or fringe on a garment was placed there in accordance with Num. 15:38, but the Pharisees made theirs unnecessarily wide.

23:13-33 This passage is often called "the seven woes," each beginning with the same phrase. (There are 8 if v. 14, omitted in many manuscripts, is included).

23:14 *devour widows' houses.* They used their position as jurists to adjust claims against wealthy widows or to get them to bestow on them their estates.

23:15 *proselyte.* Converts from paganism to Judaism.

23:16 *swears.* Here Christ argues with the Pharisees on their own grounds. *he is obligated.* I.e., his oath is binding. See Matt. 5:33-37.

23:18 *obligated.* I.e., guilty if he fails to carry out his oath.

22 ^aMatt. 5:34

22 "And he who swears by heaven, ^aswears *both* by the throne of God and by Him who sits upon it.

★23 ^aMatt. 23:13; Luke 11:42

23 "^aWoe to you, scribes and Pharisees, hypocrites! For you tithe mint and dill and cummin, and have neglected the weightier provisions of the law: justice and mercy and faithfulness; but these are the things you should have done without neglecting the others.

24 ^aMatt. 23:16

24 "You ^ablind guides, who strain out a gnat and swallow a camel!

25 ^aMark 7:4; Luke 11:39f.

25 "^aWoe to you, scribes and Pharisees, hypocrites! For ^ayou clean the outside of the cup and of the dish, but inside they are full of robbery and self-indulgence.

26 ^aMark 7:4; Luke 11:39f.

26 "You blind Pharisee, first ^aclean the inside of the cup and of the dish, so that the outside of it may become clean also.

★27 ^aLuke 11:44; Acts 23:3

27 "^aWoe to you, scribes and Pharisees, hypocrites! For you are like whitewashed tombs which on the outside appear beautiful, but inside they are full of dead men's bones and all uncleanness.

28 "Even so you too outwardly appear righteous to men, but inwardly you are full of hypocrisy and lawlessness.

29 ^aLuke 11:47f.

29 "^aWoe to you, scribes and Pharisees, hypocrites! For you build the tombs of the prophets and adorn the monuments of the righteous,

30 and say, 'If we had been *living* in the days of our fathers,

we would not have been partners with them in *shedding* the blood of the prophets.'

31 "Consequently you bear witness against yourselves, that you ^aare sons of those who murdered the prophets.

★31 ^aMatt. 23:34, 37; Acts 7:51f.

32 "Fill up then the measure *of the guilt* of your fathers.

★32

33 "You serpents, ^ayou brood of vipers, how shall you escape the sentence of ^bhell?

33 ^aMatt. 3:7 ^bMatt. 5:22

34 "^aTherefore, behold, ^bI am sending you prophets and wise men and scribes; some of them you will kill and crucify, and some of them you will ^cscourge in your synagogues, and ^dpersecute from city to city,

★34 ^aMatt. 23:34-36; Luke 11:49-51 ^b2 Chr. 36:15, 16 ^cMatt. 10:17 ^dMatt. 10:23

35 that upon you may fall *the guilt of* all the righteous blood shed on earth, from the blood of righteous ^aAbel to the blood of Zechariah, the ^bson of Berechiah, whom ^cyou murdered between the temple and the altar.

★35 ^aGen. 4:8ff.; Heb. 11:4 ^bZech. 1:1 ^c2 Chr. 24:21

36 "Truly I say to you, all these things shall come upon ^athis generation.

36 ^aMatt. 10:23; 24:34

6   Concerning Jerusalem, 23:37–39

37 "^aO Jerusalem, Jerusalem, who ^bkills the prophets and stones those who are sent to her! How often I wanted to gather your children together, ^cthe way a hen gathers her chicks under her wings, and you were unwilling.

37 ^aMatt. 23:37-39; Luke 13:34 ^bMatt. 5:12 ^cRuth 2:12

38 "Behold, ^ayour house is being left to you desolate!

★38 ^a1 Kin. 9:7f.; Jer. 22:5

23:23 *tithe.* The tithing of various herbs was based on Lev. 27:30. Though tithing of grain, fruit, wine, and oil was demanded (see also Num. 18:12; Deut. 14:22-23), the scribes had expanded the items required to be tithed to include even the smallest of herbs. *cummin* = a seed resembling the caraway. *without neglecting the others.* I.e., without neglecting the proper normal tithing.

23:27 *whitewashed tombs.* The outsides of tombs were often whitewashed to make them attractive and easily seen, while inside were death and decay.

23:31 The idea is: "like father, like son."

23:32 *the measure.* I.e., add to the iniquity of your fathers and bring down divine judgment

on yourselves.

23:34 The last part of the verse refers to the apostles (see Matt. 10:17, 23).

23:35 *Zechariah, the son of Berechiah.* This murder is recorded in 2 Chron. 24:20-22. Berechiah was likely the father of Zechariah, while the famous Jehoiada was his grandfather. This is not the prophet Zechariah (though his father was also named Berechiah). Since Abel's death is recorded in Genesis, and since 2 Chronicles is the last book in the Hebrew Bible, Christ was saying, in effect, "from the first to the last murder in the Bible." See Luke 11:51.

23:38 *your house* = the temple and the city of Jerusalem.

★39 *a*Ps.
118:26; Matt.
   21:9

39 "For I say to you, from now on you shall not see Me until you say, '*a*BLESSED IS HE WHO COMES IN THE NAME OF THE LORD!' "

VII THE PREDICTIONS OF THE KING, 24:1-25:46

A The Destruction of the Temple, 24:1-2

★ 1 *a*Matt.
24:1-51;
Mark 13;
Luke 21:5-36
*b*Matt. 21:23

24 *a*And Jesus *b*came out from the temple and was going away when His disciples came up to point out the temple buildings to Him.

2 *a*Luke
19:44

2 And He answered and said to them, "Do you not see all these things? Truly I say to you, *a*not one stone here shall be left upon another, which will not be torn down."

B The Disciples' Questions, 24:3

★ 3 *a*Matt.
21:1 *b*Matt.
16:27 f.;
24:27, 37, 39

3 And as He was sitting on *a*the Mount of Olives, the disciples came to Him privately, saying, "Tell us, when will these things be, and what *will be* the sign of *b*Your coming, and of the end of the age?"

C The Signs of the End of the Age, 24:4-28

4 *a*Jer. 29:8

4 And Jesus answered and said to them, "*a*See to it that no one misleads you.

5 *a*Matt.
24:11, 24;
Acts 5:36 f.;
1 John 2:18;
4:3
★ 6-7

5 "For *a*many will come in My name, saying, 'I am the Christ,' and will mislead many.

6 "And you will be hearing of wars and rumors of wars; see that you are not frightened, for *those things* must take place, but *that* is not yet the end.

7 *a*2 Chr.
15:6; Is. 19:2
*b*Acts 11:28

7 "For *a*nation will rise against nation, and kingdom against kingdom, and in various places there will be *b*famines and earthquakes.

8 "But all these things are *merely* the beginning of birth pangs.

★ 9 *a*Matt.
10:17; John
16:2 *b*Matt.
10:22; John
15:18 ff.

9 "*a*Then they will deliver you to tribulation, and will kill you, and *b*you will be hated by all nations on account of My name.

10 *a*Matt.
11:6

10 "And at that time many will *a*fall away and will deliver up one another and hate one another.

11 *a*Matt.
7:15; 24:24
13 *a*Matt.
10:22

11 "And many *a*false prophets will arise, and will mislead many.

★14 *a*Matt.
4:23 *b*Rom.
10:18; Col.
1:6, 23
*c*Luke 2:1;
4:5; Acts
11:28; 17:6,
31; 19:27;
Rom. 10:18;
Heb. 1:6;
2:5; Rev.
3:10; 16:14
★15 *a*Dan.
9:27; 11:31;
12:11 *b*Mark
13:14; Luke
21:20; John
11:48; Acts
6:13 f.; 21:28
*c*Mark 13:14;
Rev. 1:3

12 "And because lawlessness is increased, most people's love will grow cold.

13 "*a*But the one who endures to the end, he shall be saved.

14 "And this *a*gospel of the kingdom *b*shall be preached in the whole *c*world for a witness to all the nations, and then the end shall come.

15 "Therefore when you see the *a*ABOMINATION OF DESOLATION which was spoken of through

---

23:39 *from now on you shall not see me.* I.e., I will no longer teach publicly. *until you say.* At the second coming of Christ Israel will recognize and welcome their rejected Messiah (Zech. 12:10).

24:1 *the temple buildings.* Herod the Great began the building of this temple in 20 B.C., and it was finished in A.D. 64. The stones, 10-12 feet in length, would have been plainly visible.

24:3 *the Mount of Olives,* just E. of Jerusalem across the Kidron Valley. In this discourse Jesus answered two of the three questions the disciples asked. He does not answer *"when will these things be?".* He answers *"what will be the sign of Your coming?"* in vv. 29-31 and He speaks of the signs of the end of the age in vv. 4-28. Verses 4-14 list characteristics of the first half of the tribulation period, while vv. 15-28 deal with the second half.

24:6-7 See the same judgments outlined in Rev. 6:1-8.

24:9 *on account of My name.* I.e., because they are His followers.

24:14 *this gospel of the kingdom.* This is the good news that will be preached during the tribulation days concerning the coming of Messiah and the setting up of His kingdom.

24:15 *abomination of desolation.* This is the man of sin (2 Thess. 2:4), the Antichrist, who at this midpoint in the tribulation breaks his covenant which he made at the beginning of the tribulation with the Jewish people (Dan. 9:27), and demands that they and the world worship him. Those who resist will be persecuted and many will be martyred; that is the reason for the urgency of the instructions in vv. 16-22.

Daniel the prophet, standing in [b]the holy place ([c]let the reader understand),

16 then let those who are in Judea flee to the mountains;

17 let him who is on [a]the housetop not go down to get the things out that are in his house;

18 and let him who is in the field not turn back to get his cloak.

19 "But [a]woe to those who are with child and to those who nurse babes in those days!

20 "But pray that your flight may not be in the winter, or on a Sabbath;

21 for then there will be a [a]great tribulation, such as has not occurred since the beginning of the world until now, nor ever shall.

22 "And unless those days had been cut short, no life would have been saved; but for [a]the sake of the elect those days shall be cut short.

23 "[a]Then if anyone says to you, 'Behold, here is the Christ,' or 'There He is,' do not believe him.

24 "For false Christs and [a]false prophets will arise and will show great [b]signs and wonders, so as to mislead, if possible, even [c]the elect.

25 "Behold, I have told you in advance.

26 "If therefore they say to you, 'Behold, He is in the wilderness,' do not go forth, or, 'Behold, He is in the inner rooms,' do not believe them.

27 "[a]For just as the lightning comes from the east, and flashes

even to the west, so shall the [b]coming of the [c]Son of Man be.

28 "[a]Wherever the corpse is, there the vultures will gather.

D The Sign of His Coming, 24:29-31

29 "But immediately after the [a]tribulation of those days [b]THE SUN WILL BE DARKENED, AND THE MOON WILL NOT GIVE ITS LIGHT, AND [c]THE STARS WILL FALL from the sky, and the powers of the heavens will be shaken,

30 and then [a]the sign of the Son of Man will appear in the sky, and then all the tribes of the earth will mourn, and they will see [b]the SON OF MAN COMING ON THE CLOUDS OF THE SKY with power and great glory.

31 "And [a]He will send forth His angels with [b]A GREAT TRUMPET and THEY WILL GATHER TOGETHER His [c]elect from [d]the four winds, [e]from one end of the sky to the other.

E The Illustrations, 24:32-25:46
1 The fig tree, 24:32-35

32 "Now learn the parable from the fig tree: when its branch has already become tender, and puts forth its leaves, you know that summer is near;

33 even so you too, when you see all these things, recognize that He is near, right [a]at the door.

34 "Truly I say to you, [a]this generation will not pass away until all these things take place.

Margin references

17 [a]1 Sam. 9:25; 2 Sam. 11:2; Matt. 10:27; Luke 5:19; 12:3; Acts 10:9

19 [a]Luke 23:29

21 [a]Dan. 12:1; Joel 2:2; Matt. 24:29

★**22** [a]Matt. 22:14; 24:24, 31; Luke 18:7

23 [a]Luke 17:23f.

24 [a]Matt. 7:15; 24:11 [b]John 4:48; 2 Thess. 2:9 [c]Matt. 22:14 [Gr.]; 24:22, 31; Luke 18:7 ★**25**

27 [a]Luke 17:23f. [b]Matt. 24:3, 37, 39 [c]Matt. 8:20

28 [a]Job 39:30; Ezek. 39:17; Hab. 1:8; Luke 17:37

★**29** [a]Matt. 24:21 [b]Is. 13:10; 13:23; Ezek. 32:7; Joel 2:10, 31; 3:15; Amos 5:20; 8:9; Zeph. 1:15; Acts 2:20; Rev. 6:12; 8:12 [c]Is. 34:4; Rev. 6:13 ★**30** [a]Matt. 24:3; Rev. 1:7 [b]Dan. 7:13; Matt. 16:27; 24:3, 37, 39

31 [a]Matt. 13:41 [b]Ex. 19:16; Is. 27:13; Zech. 9:14; 1 Cor. 15:52; 1 Thess. 4:16; Heb. 12:19; Rev. 8:2; 11:15 [c]Matt. 24:22 [d]Dan. 7:2; Zech. 2:6; Rev. 7:1 [e]Deut. 4:32

★**33** [a]James 5:9; Rev. 3:20

★**34** [a]Matt. 10:23; 16:28; 23:36

24:22 *no life* = no human being. *the elect.* Those redeemed during the tribulation days. The elect of this age (the Church) will have been translated before that time begins.

24:25 *in advance.* This is a warning as well as a prediction.

24:29 *the sun . . . darkened.* These astral phenomena which will accompany the return of the Son of Man are foretold in Isa. 13:9-10 and Joel 2:31, 3:15.

24:30 *the sign.* Some think this is the lightning of v. 27; others, the Shekinah, or glory, of Christ; still others leave it unspecified. At any

rate, *the Son of Man* Himself will come visibly (Rev. 1:7). There seems to be no reason for not taking this part of Jesus' teaching as plainly as other parts.

24:33 *all these things.* The signs described in vv. 4-28.

24:34 *this generation.* No one living when Jesus spoke these words lived to see "all these things" come to pass. However, the Greek word can mean "race" or "family," which makes good sense here; i.e., the Jewish race will be preserved, in spite of terrible persecution, until the Lord comes.

35 aMatt.
5:18; Mark
13:31; Luke
21:33

35 "aHeaven and earth will pass away, but My words shall not pass away.

2 The days of Noah, 24:36-39

36 aMark
13:32; Acts
1:7

36 "But aof that day and hour no one knows, not even the angels of heaven, nor the Son, but the Father alone.

37 aMatt.
16:27; 24:3,
30, 39 bGen.
6:5; 7:6-23;
Luke 17:26f.
38 aMatt.
22:30 bGen.
7:7

37 "For the acoming of the Son of Man will be bjust like the days of Noah.

38 "For as in those days which were before the flood they were eating and drinking, they were amarrying and giving in marriage, until the day that bNoah entered the ark,

39 aMatt.
16:27; 24:3,
30, 37

39 and they did not understand until the flood came and took them all away, so shall the acoming of the Son of Man be.

3 The two, 24:40-41

40 "Then there shall be two men in the field; one will be taken, and one will be left.

41 aLuke
17:35 bEx.
11:5; Deut.
24:6; Is. 47:2

41 "aTwo women will be grinding at the bmill; one will be taken, and one will be left.

4 The faithful householder, 24:42-44

42 aMatt.
24:43, 44;
25:10, 13;
Luke 12:39f.;
21:36
43 aMatt.
24:42, 44;
25:10, 13;
Luke 12:39f.;
21:36 bMatt.
14:25; Mark
6:48; 13:35;
Luke 12:38
44 aMatt.
24:42, 43;
25:10, 13;
Luke 12:39f.;
21:36 bMatt.
24:27

42 "Therefore abe on the alert, for you do not know which day your Lord is coming.

43 "But be sure of this, that aif the head of the house had known bat what time of the night the thief was coming, he would have been on the alert and would not have allowed his house to be broken into.

44 "For this reason ayou be ready too; for bthe Son of Man is coming at an hour when you do not think He will.

5 The wise servant, 24:45-51

45 aMatt.
24:45-51;
Luke 12:42-
46 bMatt.
25:21, 23;
Luke 16:10
cMatt. 7:24;
10:16; 25:2ff.
dMatt. 25:21,
23

45 "aWho then is the bfaithful and csensible slave whom his master dput in charge of his household to give them their food at the proper time?

46 "Blessed is that slave whom his master finds so doing when he comes.

47 aMatt.
25:21, 23

47 "Truly I say to you, that ahe will put him in charge of all his possessions.

48 "But if that evil slave says in his heart, 'My master is not coming for a long time,'

49 and shall begin to beat his fellow slaves and eat and drink with drunkards;

50 the master of that slave will come on a day when he does not expect him and at an hour which he does not know,

51 aMatt.
8:12

51 and shall cut him in pieces and assign him a place with the hypocrites; aweeping shall be there and the gnashing of teeth.

6 The ten virgins, 25:1-13

★ **1-13**

★ **1** aMatt.
13:24 bJohn
18:3; Acts
20:8; Rev.
4:5; 8:10
[Gr.]
2 aMatt.
7:24; 10:16;
25:2ff.

25 "Then athe kingdom of heaven will be comparable to ten virgins, who took their blamps, and went out to meet the bridegroom.

2 "And five of them were foolish, and five were aprudent.

3 "For when the foolish took their lamps, they took no oil with them,

4 aMatt.
7:24; 10:16;
25:2ff.

4 but the aprudent took oil in flasks along with their lamps.

5 "Now while the bridegroom was delaying, they all got drowsy and began to sleep.

6 "But at midnight there was

25:1-13 The story clearly teaches watchfulness (v. 13); i.e., only those who are prepared for His coming will enter the kingdom.
25:1 to meet the bridegroom. There were two phases to Jewish weddings. First the bridegroom went to the bride's home to obtain his bride and observe certain religious ceremonies. Then he took his bride to his own home

for a resumption of the festivities. Christ will take His bride, the church, to heaven before the tribulation period begins; then He will return with His bride at His second coming to the marriage supper on earth. The virgins represent the professing Jewish remnant on earth at His return.

a shout, 'Behold, the bridegroom! Come out to meet *him*.'

7 "Then all those virgins arose, and trimmed their lamps.

8 "And the foolish said to the prudent, 'Give us some of your oil, for our lamps are going out.'

9 "But the ᵃprudent answered, saying, 'No, there will not be enough for us and you *too*; go instead to the dealers and buy *some* for yourselves.'

10 "And while they were going away to make the purchase, the bridegroom came, and those who were ᵃready went in with him to ᵇthe wedding feast; and ᶜthe door was shut.

11 "And later the other virgins also came, saying, 'ᵃLord, lord, open up for us.'

12 "But he answered and said, 'Truly I say to you, I do not know you.'

13 "ᵃBe on the alert then, for you do not know the day nor the hour.

7   The talents, 25:14–30

14 "ᵃFor *it is* just like a man ᵇabout to go on a journey, who called his own slaves, and entrusted his possessions to them.

15 "And to one he gave five ᵃtalents, to another, two, and to another, one, each according to his own ability; and he ᵇwent on his journey.

16 "Immediately the one who had received the five ᵃtalents went and traded with them, and gained five more talents.

17 "In the same manner the one who had *received* the two *talents* gained two more.

18 "But he who received the one *talent* went away and dug in the ground, and hid his master's money.

19 "Now after a long time the master of those slaves *came and *ᵃsettled accounts with them.

20 "And the one who had received the five ᵃtalents came up and brought five more talents, saying, 'Master, you entrusted five talents to me; see, I have gained five more talents.'

21 "His master said to him, 'Well done, good and ᵃfaithful slave; you were faithful with a few things, I will put you in charge of many things, enter into the joy of your master.'

22 "The one also who had *received* the two ᵃtalents came up and said, 'Master, you entrusted to me two talents; see, I have gained two more talents.'

23 "His master said to him, 'Well done, good and ᵃfaithful slave; you were faithful with a few things, I will put you in charge of many things; enter into the joy of your master.'

24 "And the one also who had received the one ᵃtalent came up and said, 'Master, I knew you to be a hard man, reaping where you did not sow, and gathering where you scattered no *seed*.

25 'And I was afraid, and went away and hid your talent in the ground; see, you have what is yours.'

26 "But his master answered and said to him, 'You wicked, lazy slave, you knew that I reap where I did not sow, and gather where I scattered no *seed*.

27 'Then you ought to have put my money in the bank, and on my arrival I would have received my *money* back with interest.

28 'Therefore take away the talent from him, and give it to the one who has the ten talents.'

29 "ᵃFor to everyone who has shall *more* be given, and he shall have an abundance; but from the

Cross references (margin)

9 ᵃMatt. 7:24; 10:16; 25:2ff.

10 ᵃMatt. 24:42ff.; ᵇLuke 12:35f.; ᶜMatt. 7:21ff.; Luke 13:25

11 ᵃMatt. 7:21ff.; Luke 13:25

13 ᵃMatt. 24:42ff.

★**14** ᵃMatt. l. 25:14–30; Luke 19:12-27 ᵇMatt. 21:33

★**15** ᵃMatt. 18:24; Luke 19:13 ᵇMatt. 21:33

16 ᵃMatt. 18:24; Luke 19:13

19 ᵃMatt. 18:23

20 ᵃMatt. 18:24; Luke 19:13

★**21** ᵃMatt. 24:45, 47; 25:23

22 ᵃMatt. 18:24; Luke 19:13

★**23** ᵃMatt. 24:45, 47; 25:21

24 ᵃMatt. 18:24; Luke 19:13

★**26**

29 ᵃMatt. 13:12

25:14–30 The contrast here is between those who make use of God's gifts and those who do not.

25:15 *talents*. See note on 18:24. These were silver (the word "money" in v. 18 means silver).

25:21, 23, 26 Two of the men received the same reward, indicating that faithfulness in the use of the different abilities given to each of us is what is required. The third is condemned for his sloth and indifference.

one who does not have, even what he does have shall be taken away.

30 "And cast out the worthless slave into ᵃthe outer darkness; in that place there shall be weeping and gnashing of teeth.

8　The judgment of Gentiles, 25:31-46

31 "But when ᵃthe Son of Man comes in His glory, and all the angels with Him, then ᵇHe will sit on His glorious throne.

32 "And all the nations will be gathered before Him; and He will separate them from one another, ᵃas the shepherd separates the sheep from the goats;

33 and He will put the sheep ᵃon His right, and the goats ᵇon the left.

34 "Then the King will say to those on His right, 'Come, you who are blessed of My Father, ᵃinherit the kingdom prepared for you ᵇfrom the foundation of the world.

35 'For ᵃI was hungry, and you gave Me *something* to eat; I was thirsty, and you gave Me drink; ᵇI was a stranger, and you invited Me in;

36 ᵃnaked, and you clothed Me; I was sick, and you ᵇvisited Me; ᶜI was in prison, and you came to Me.'

37 "Then the righteous will answer Him, saying, 'Lord, when did we see You hungry, and feed You, or thirsty, and give You drink?

38 'And when did we see You a stranger, and invite You in, or naked, and clothe You?

39 'And when did we see You

sick, or in prison, and come to You?'

40 "And ᵃthe King will answer and say to them, 'Truly I say to you, ᵇto the extent that you did it to one of these brothers of Mine, *even* the least *of them*, you did it to Me.'

41 "Then He will also say to those on His left, 'ᵃDepart from Me, accursed ones, into the ᵇeternal fire which has been prepared for ᶜthe devil and his angels;

42 for I was hungry, and you gave Me *nothing* to eat; I was thirsty, and you gave Me nothing to drink;

43 I was a stranger, and you did not invite Me in; naked, and you did not clothe Me; sick, and in prison, and you did not visit Me.'

44 "Then they themselves also will answer, saying, 'Lord, when did we see You hungry, or thirsty, or a stranger, or naked, or sick, or in prison, and did not take care of You?'

45 "Then He will answer them, saying, 'Truly I say to you, to the extent that you did not do it to one of the least of these, you did not do it to Me.'

46 "And these will go away into ᵃeternal punishment, but the righteous into ᵇeternal life."

VIII　THE PASSION OF THE KING, 26:1-27:66
A　The Preparation, 26:1-16

26 ᵃAnd it came about that when Jesus had finished all these words, He said to His disciples,

2 "ᵃYou know that after two days ᵇthe Passover is coming, and

---

Margin references (left column):
30 ᵃMatt. 8:12
31 ᵃMatt. 16:27f. ᵇMatt. 19:28
★32 ᵃEzek. 34:17, 20
★33 ᵃ1 Kin. 2:19; Ps. 45:9 ᵇEccles. 10:2
34 ᵃMatt. 5:3; 19:29; Luke 12:32; 1 Cor. 6:9; 15:50; Gal. 5:21; James 2:5 ᵇMatt. 13:35; Luke 11:50; John 17:24; Eph. 1:4; Heb. 4:3; 9:26; 1 Pet. 1:20; Rev. 13:8; 17:8
35 ᵃIs. 58:7; Ezek. 18:7, 16; James 2:15, 16 ᵇJob 31:32; Heb. 13:2
36 ᵃIs. 58:7; Ezek. 18:7, 16; James 2:15, 16 ᵇJames 1:27 ᶜ2 Tim. 1:16f.
★37

Margin references (right column):
40 ᵃMatt. 25:34; Luke 19:38; Rev. 17:14; 19:16 ᵇProv. 19:17; Matt. 10:42; Heb. 6:10
41 ᵃMatt. 7:23 ᵇMark 9:48; Luke 16:24; Jude 7 ᶜMatt. 4:10; Rev. 12:9
46 ᵃDan. 12:2; John 5:29; Acts 24:15 ᵇMatt. 19:29; John 3:15f., 36; 5:24; 6:27, 40, 47, 54; 17:2f.; Acts 13:46, 48; Rom. 2:7; 5:21; 6:23; Gal. 6:8; 1 John 5:11
1 ᵃMatt. 7:28
★2 ᵃMatt. 26:2-5; Mark 14:1-2; Luke 22:1-2 ᵇJohn 11:55; 13:1 ᶜMatt. 10:4

25:32 *all the nations.* Lit., all the Gentiles. This is a judgment of those Gentiles who survive the tribulation and whose heart relation to God is evidenced by their treatment of the Jews (Christ's brethren, v. 40), especially during that time. Surviving Jews will also be judged at this same time (Ezek. 20:33-38).
25:33 *on His right.* The place of honor.
25:37 *when.* They are unconscious of their goodness, in contrast to the ostentation of the

Pharisees. In v. 44 we see the opposite, the unconscious neglect of duty.
26:2 *after two days* = two days from now. The events recorded in 26:1-5 occurred on Wednesday. *Passover.* This was the ancient Jewish festival commemorating the deliverance from Egypt. It was followed immediately by the seven days' Feast of Unleavened Bread, and the entire festival was often called "Passover." See note on Acts 2:1.

the Son of Man is *to be* ^cdelivered up for crucifixion."

3 ^aThen the chief priests and the elders of the people were gathered together in ^bthe court of the high priest, named ^cCaiaphas;

4 and they ^aplotted together to seize Jesus by stealth, and kill *Him.*

5 But they were saying, "Not during the festival, ^alest a riot occur among the people."

6 ^aNow when Jesus was in ^bBethany, at the home of Simon the leper,

7 a woman came to Him with an alabaster vial of very costly perfume, and she poured it upon His head as He reclined *at the table.*

8 But the disciples were indignant when they saw *this,* and said, "Why this waste?

9 "For this *perfume* might have been sold for a high price and *the money* given to the poor."

10 But Jesus, aware of this, said to them, "Why do you bother the woman? For she has done a good deed to Me.

11 "For ^athe poor you have with you always; but you do not always have Me.

12 "For when she poured this perfume upon My body, she did it ^ato prepare Me for burial.

13 "Truly I say to you, ^awherever this gospel is preached in the whole world, what this woman has done shall also be spoken of in memory of her."

14 ^aThen one of the twelve, named ^bJudas Iscariot, went to the chief priests,

15 and said, "What are you willing to give me to ^adeliver Him up to you?" And ^bthey weighed out to him thirty pieces of silver.

16 And from then on he *began* looking for a good opportunity to betray Him.

B   The Passover, 26:17-30

17 ^aNow on the first *day* of ^bUnleavened Bread the disciples came to Jesus, saying, "Where do You want us to prepare for You to eat the Passover?"

18 And He said, "Go into the city to ^aa certain man, and say to him, 'The Teacher says, "^bMy time is at hand; I *am to* keep the Passover at your house with My disciples." ' "

19 And the disciples did as Jesus had directed them; and they prepared the Passover.

20 ^aNow when evening had come, He was reclining *at the table* with the twelve disciples.

21 And as they were eating, He said, "^aTruly I say to you that one of you will betray Me."

22 And being deeply grieved, they each one began to say to Him, "Surely not I, Lord?"

Marginal references:

★ **3** ^aJohn 11:47. ^bMatt. 26:58, 69; 27:27; Mark 14:54, 66; 15:16; Luke 11:21; 22:55; John 18:15. ^cMatt. 26:57; Luke 3:2; John 11:49; 18:13, 14, 24, 28; Acts 4:6

4 ^aMatt. 12:14

5 ^aMatt. 27:24

★ **6** ^aMatt. 26:6-13; Mark 14:3-9; Luke 7:37-39; John 12:1-8. ^bMatt. 21:17

★ **7**

★**11** ^aDeut. 15:11; Mark 14:7; John 12:8

★**12** ^aJohn 19:40

13 ^aMark 14:9

14 ^aMatt. 26:14-16; Mark 14:10, 11; Luke 22:3-6. ^bMatt. 10:4; 26:25, 47; 27:3; John 6:71; 12:4; 13:26; Acts 1:16

★**15** ^aMatt. 10:4. ^bEx. 21:32; Zech. 11:12

★**17** ^aMatt. 26:17-19; Mark 14:12-16; Luke 22:7-13. ^bEx. 12:18-20

★**18** ^aMark 14:13; Luke 22:10. ^bJohn 7:6, 8

★**20** ^aMatt. 26:20-24; Mark 14:17-21

21 ^aLuke 22:21-23; John 13:21f.

26:3 *Caiaphas,* high priest A.D. 18-36 and son-in-law and successor of Annas.

26:6 *Simon the leper.* Nothing more of him is known. Perhaps Christ had healed him.

26:7 *very costly perfume.* Mark (14:5) says it was worth 300 denarii or approximately a year's salary for a rural worker.

26:11 *For the poor you have with you always.* This should not be understood callously. Christ says, in effect, that there will be other opportunities to do good to the poor, but not another opportunity to do what had just been done to Him.

26:12 *she did it to prepare Me for burial.* Though the disciples ignored Christ's many predictions of His approaching death, apparently this woman believed them (16:21; 17:22; 20:18). John identifies her as Mary (John 12:3).

26:15 *thirty pieces of silver.* The coin is uniden-

tified. If it was a denarius, this sum represented approximately five weeks' wages. It could have amounted to much more.

26:17 *eat the Passover.* I.e., the Passover lamb (Ex. 12:3-10), meaning the whole sacred meal.

26:18 *My time* (of death) *is at hand.*

26:20 *He was reclining at table.* The order of events that night was: eating the Passover; washing the disciples' feet (John 13:1-20); identifying Judas as the betrayer (Matt. 26:21-25), after which he left (John 13:30); the institution of the Lord's Supper (Matt. 26:26-29); messages in the Upper Room (John 14) and on the way to Gethsemane (John 15-16); Christ's great prayer for His people (John 17); His anguish in Gethsemane (Matt. 26:36-46); the betrayal and arrest (Matt. 26:47-56).

23 *a*John
13:18, 26

23 And He answered and said, "*a*He who dipped his hand with Me in the bowl is the one who will betray Me.

24 *a*Matt.
26:31, 54,
56; Mark
9:12; Luke
24:25-27, 46;
Acts 17:2f.
26:22f.
1 Cor. 15:3;
1 Pet. 1:10f.
*b*Matt. 18:7;
Mark 14:21

24 "The Son of Man *is to* go, *a*just as it is written of Him; but woe to that man by whom the Son of Man is betrayed! *b*It would have been good for that man if he had not been born."

25 *a*Matt.
26:14 *b*Matt.
23:7; 26:49
*c*Matt. 26:64;
27:11; Luke
22:70

25 And *a*Judas, who was betraying Him, answered and said, "Surely it is not I, *b*Rabbi?" He *said to him, "*c*You have said *it* yourself."

26 *a*Matt.
26:26-29;
Mark 14:22-
25; Luke
22:17-20;
1 Cor. 11:23-
25; 1 Cor.
10:16 *b*Matt.
14:19

26 *a*And while they were eating, Jesus took *some* bread, and *b*after a blessing, He broke *it* and gave *it* to the disciples, and said, "Take, eat; this is My body."

27 And when He had taken a cup and given thanks, He gave *it* to them, saying, "Drink from it, all of you;

★28 *a*Heb.
9:20 *b*Matt.
20:28

28 for *a*this is My blood of the covenant, which is poured out for *b*many for forgiveness of sins.

★29

29 "But I say to you, I will not drink of this fruit of the vine from now on until that day when I drink it new with you in My Father's kingdom."

★30 *a*Matt.
26:30-35;
Mark 14:26-
31; Luke
22:31-34
*b*Matt. 21:1

30 *a*And after singing a hymn, they went out to *b*the Mount of Olives.

C The Betrayal, 26:31-56

★31 *a*Matt.
11:6 *b*Zech.
13:7 *c*John
16:32

31 Then Jesus *said to them, "You will all *a*fall away because of Me this night, for it is written, '*b*I WILL STRIKE DOWN THE SHEPHERD, AND THE SHEEP OF THE FLOCK SHALL BE *c*SCATTERED.'

32 *a*Matt.
28:7, 10, 16;
Mark 16:7

32 "But after I have been raised, *a*I will go before you to Galilee."

33 But Peter answered and said to Him, "*Even* though all may fall away because of You, I will never fall away."

34 *a*Matt.
26:75; John
13:38 *b*Mark
14:30

34 Jesus said to him, "*a*Truly I say to you that *b*this *very* night, before a cock crows, you shall deny Me three times."

35 *a*John
13:37

35 Peter *said to Him, "*a*Even if I have to die with You, I will not deny You." All the disciples said the same thing too.

★36 *a*Matt.
26:36-46;
Mark 14:32-
42; Luke
22:40-46
*b*Mark 14:32;
Luke 22:39;
John 18:1
★37 *a*Matt.
4:21; 17:1;
Mark 5:37

36 *a*Then Jesus *came with them to a place called *b*Gethsemane, and *said to His disciples, "Sit here while I go over there and pray."

37 And He took with Him *a*Peter and the two sons of Zebedee, and began to be grieved and distressed.

★38 *a*John
12:27 *b*Matt.
26:40, 41

38 Then He *said to them, "*a*My soul is deeply grieved, to the point of death; remain here and *b*keep watch with Me."

★39 *a*Matt.
20:22 *b*Matt.
26:42; Mark
14:36; Luke
22:42; John
6:38

39 And He went a little beyond *them*, and fell on His face and prayed, saying, "My Father, if it is possible, let *a*this cup pass from Me; *b*yet not as I will, but as Thou wilt."

40 *a*Matt.
26:38

40 And He *came to the disciples and *found them sleeping, and *said to Peter, "So, you *men* could not *a*keep watch with Me for one hour?

41 *a*Matt.
26:38 *b*Mark
14:38

41 "*a*Keep watching and praying, that you may not enter into

---

26:28 *the covenant*. The new testament, or new covenant, is God's new arrangement with men based on the death of Christ. See Introduction to the New Testament.

26:29 *until that day when I drink it new with you in My Father's kingdom*. The disciples' attention is directed toward their eventual reunion in the future millennial kingdom with its joy and fellowship.

26:30 *hymn*. Probably all or part of Pss. 115–118, the traditional Passover Hallel.

26:31 *You will all fall away*. All the disciples would "fall away" before the night was over (v. 56), not only Peter. See Zech. 13:7.

26:36 *Gethsemane*. The name means "oil press." It was a garden, doubtless containing olive trees, on the side of the Mount of Olives.

26:37 *the two sons of Zebedee*. I.e., James and John.

26:38 *keep watch* = stay awake, be alert. So also in vv. 40, 41.

26:39 *this cup*. The cup was all the suffering involved in the sinless Son of God taking upon Himself the sin of mankind including the necessary, though temporary, separation from God (27:46). He naturally shrank from this, though He willingly submitted to it.

temptation; [b]the spirit is willing, but the flesh is weak."

42 He went away again a second time and prayed, saying, "My Father, if this [a]cannot pass away unless I drink it, [b]Thy will be done."

43 And again He came and found them sleeping, for their eyes were heavy.

44 And He left them again, and went away and prayed a third time, saying the same thing once more.

45 Then He *came to the disciples, and *said to them, "Are you still sleeping and taking your rest? Behold, [a]the hour is at hand and the Son of Man is being betrayed into the hands of sinners.

46 "Arise, let us be going; behold, the one who betrays Me is at hand!"

47 [a]And while He was still speaking, behold, [b]Judas, one of the twelve, came up, accompanied by a great multitude with swords and clubs, from the chief priests and elders of the people.

48 Now he who was betraying Him gave them a sign, saying, "Whomever I shall kiss, He is the one; seize Him."

49 And immediately he went to Jesus and said, "Hail, [a]Rabbi!" and kissed Him.

50 And Jesus said to him, "[a]Friend, *do* what you have come for." Then they came and laid hands on Jesus and seized Him.

51 And behold, [a]one of those who were with Jesus reached and drew out his [b]sword, and struck the [c]slave of the high priest, and cut off his ear.

52 Then Jesus *said to him, "Put your sword back into its place; for [a]all those who take up

the sword shall perish by the sword.

53 "Or do you think that I cannot appeal to My Father, and He will at once put at My disposal more than twelve [a]legions of [b]angels?

54 "How then shall [a]the Scriptures be fulfilled, that it must happen this way?"

55 At that time Jesus said to the multitudes, "Have you come out with swords and clubs to arrest Me as against a robber? [a]Every day I used to sit in the temple teaching and you did not seize Me.

56 "But all this has taken place that [a]the Scriptures of the prophets may be fulfilled." Then all the disciples left Him and fled.

D   The Hearings, 26:57-27:26
1   Before the high priest,
          26:57-75

57 [a]And those who had seized Jesus led Him away to [b]Caiaphas, the high priest, where the scribes and the elders were gathered together.

58 But [a]Peter also was following Him at a distance as far as the [b]courtyard of the high priest, and entered in, and sat down with the [c]officers to see the outcome.

59 Now the chief priests and the whole [a]Council kept trying to obtain false testimony against Jesus, in order that they might put Him to death;

60 and they did not find *any*, even though many false witnesses came forward. But later on [a]two came forward,

61 and said, "This man stated, '[a]I am able to destroy the temple

42 [a]Matt. 20:22 [b]Matt. 26:39; Mark 14:36; Luke 22:42; John 6:38
45 [a]Mark 14:41; John 12:27, 13:1
47 [a]Matt. 26:47-56; Mark 14:43-50; Luke 22:47-53; John 18:3-11 [b]Matt. 26:14
49 [a]Matt. 23:7; 26:25
*50 [a]Matt. 20:13; 22:12
*51 [a]Mark 14:47; Luke 22:50; John 18:10 [b]Luke 22:38 [c]Mark 14:47; Luke 22:50; John 18:10
52 [a]Gen. 9:6; Rev. 13:10
*53 [a]Mark 5:9, 15; Luke 8:30 [b]Matt. 4:11
54 [a]Matt. 26:24
55 [a]Mark 12:35; 14:49; Luke 4:20; 19:47; 20:1; 21:37; John 7:14, 28; 8:2, 20; 18:20
56 [a]Matt. 26:24
*57 [a]Matt. 26:57-68; Mark 14:53-65; John 18:12f., 19-24 [b]Matt. 26:3
58 [a]John 18:15 [b]Matt. 26:3 [c]Matt. 5:25; John 7:32; 19:6; Acts 5:22, 26
59 [a]Matt. 5:22
*60 [a]Deut. 19:15
61 [a]Matt. 27:40; Mark 14:58; 15:29; John 2:19; Acts 6:14

26:50 *Friend* = comrade or companion.
26:51 *one of those.* This was Peter (John 18:10).
26:53 *twelve legions.* Christ meant simply a very large, not an exact, number. A Roman legion varied in number from 3000 to 6000.
26:57 The order of Jesus' trials was as follows: (1) the hearing before Annas (John 18:12-14, 19-23); (2) the trial before Caiaphas and the

Sanhedrin (Matt. 26:57-68; 27:1); (3) the first appearance before Pilate (Matt. 27:2, 11-14); (4) an appearance before Herod (Luke 23:6-12); (5) a second trial before Pilate (Matt. 27:15-26).
26:60 *false witnesses.* To establish a charge, two witnesses were required under Jewish law, and their testimony had to be in agreement.

of God and to rebuild it in three days.' "

62 And the high priest stood up and said to Him, "Do You make no answer? What is it that these men are testifying against You?"

63 But ªJesus kept silent. ᵇAnd the high priest said to Him, "I ᶜadjure You by ᵈthe living God, that You tell us whether You are the Christ, ᵉthe Son of God."

64 Jesus *said to him, "ªYou have said it *yourself*; nevertheless I tell you, hereafter you shall see ᵇTHE SON OF MAN SITTING AT THE RIGHT HAND OF POWER, and ᶜCOMING ON THE CLOUDS OF HEAVEN."

65 Then the high priest ªtore his robes, saying, "He has blasphemed! What further need do we have of witnesses? Behold, you have now heard the blasphemy;

66 what do you think?" They answered and said, "ªHe is deserving of death!"

67 ªThen they ᵇspat in His face and beat Him with their fists; and others slapped Him,

68 and said, "ªProphesy to us, You Christ; who is the one who hit You?"

69 ªNow Peter was sitting outside in the ᵇcourtyard, and a certain servant-girl came to him and said, "You too were with Jesus the Galilean."

70 But he denied *it* before them all, saying, "I do not know what you are talking about."

71 And when he had gone out to the gateway, another *servant-girl* saw him and *said to those who were there, "This man was with Jesus of Nazareth."

72 And again he denied *it* with an oath, "I do not know the man."

73 And a little later the bystanders came up and said to Peter, "Surely you too are *one* of them; ªfor the way you talk gives you away."

74 Then he began to curse and swear, "I do not know the man!" And immediately a cock crowed.

75 And Peter remembered the word which Jesus had said, "ªBefore a cock crows, you will deny Me three times." And he went out and wept bitterly.

2 Before the Sanhedrin, 27:1–10

27 ªNow when morning had come, all the chief priests and the elders of the people took counsel against Jesus to put Him to death;

2 and they bound Him, and led Him away, and ªdelivered Him up to ᵇPilate the governor.

3 Then when ªJudas, who had betrayed Him, saw that He had been condemned, he felt remorse and returned ᵇthe thirty pieces of silver to the chief priests and elders,

4 saying, "I have sinned by betraying innocent blood." But they said, "What is that to us? ªSee *to that* yourself!"

5 And he threw the pieces of silver into ªthe sanctuary and departed; and ᵇhe went away and hanged himself.

6 And the chief priests took

Marginal references

★63 ªMatt. 27:12, 14; John 19:9 ᵇMatt. 26:63-66; Luke 22:67-71 ᶜLev. 5:1 ᵈMatt. 16:16 ᵉMatt. 4:3
64 ªMatt. 26:25 ᵇPs. 110:1 ᶜDan. 7:13; Matt. 16:27f.
★65 ªNum. 14:6; Mark 14:63; Acts 14:14
66 ªLev. 24:16; John 19:7
★67 ªMatt. 26:67, 68; Luke 22:63-65; John 18:22 ᵇMatt. 27:30; Mark 10:34
★68 ªMark 14:65; Luke 22:64
69 ªMatt. 26:69-75; Mark 14:66-72; Luke 22:55-62; John 18:16-18, 25-27 ᵇMatt. 26:3

★73 ªMark 14:70; Luke 22:59; John 18:26
★74
75 ªMatt. 26:34

1 ªMark 15:1; Luke 22:66; John 18:28
★ 2 ªMatt. 20:19 ᵇLuke 3:1; 13:1; 23:12; Acts 3:13; 4:27; 1 Tim. 6:13
★ 3-10
★ 3 ªMatt. 26:14 ᵇMatt. 26:15
4 ªMatt. 27:24
5 ªMatt. 26:61 marg.; Luke 1:9, 21 ᵇActs 1:18
★ 6

26:63 *Jesus kept silent.* See Isa. 53:7. *I adjure You* = I command You.
26:65 *the high priest tore his robes.* An action expressive of grief, obligatory on hearing blasphemy.
26:67 *spat.* See Isa. 50:6. *slapped.* See Isa. 52:14.
26:68 *Prophesy to us.* Having blindfolded Him, they suggest He name His taunters (Luke 22:64).
26:73 *the way you talk.* Galilean pronunciation differed from Judean.
26:74 *to curse.* Peter began to call down a curse on himself if he were lying.

27:2 *Pilate.* See note on Mark 15:1. His headquarters were in Caesarea, the city Herod built on the Mediterranean in hónor of Caesar Augustus. He had a palace in Jerusalem and was in the city at Passover time, when crowds would be huge and trouble always possible.
27:3-10 Compare Acts 1:16-19.
27:3 *saw that He had been condemned.* Perhaps Judas had only wanted to force Jesus to do something to confound His enemies, not to get Himself condemned.
27:6 *the price of blood.* I.e., "blood money," and thus impure and defiling to the temple.

the pieces of silver and said, "It is not lawful to put them into the temple treasury, since it is the price of blood."

★ 7   7   And they counseled together and with the money bought the Potter's Field as a burial place for strangers.

8 ªActs 1:19   8   ªFor this reason that field has been called the Field of Blood to this day.

★ 9 ªZech. 11:12, 13; cf., Jer. 18:2; 19:2, 11; 32:6-9   9   Then that which was spoken through Jeremiah the prophet was fulfilled, saying, "ªAND THEY TOOK THE THIRTY PIECES OF SILVER, THE PRICE OF THE ONE WHOSE PRICE HAD BEEN SET by the sons of Israel;

10   AND THEY GAVE THEM FOR THE POTTER'S FIELD, AS THE LORD DIRECTED ME."

3 Before Pilate, 27:11-26

11 ªMatt. 27:11-14; Mark 15:2-5; Luke 23:2-3; John 18:29-38 ᵇMatt. 2:2 ᶜMatt. 26:25   11   ªNow Jesus stood before the governor, and the governor questioned Him, saying, "Are You the ᵇKing of the Jews?" And Jesus said to him, "ᶜIt is as you say."

12 ªMatt. 26:63; John 19:9   12   And while He was being accused by the chief priests and elders, ªHe made no answer.

13   Then Pilate *said to Him, "Do You not hear how many things they testify against You?"

14 ªMatt. 27:12; Mark 15:5; Luke 23:9; John 19:9   14   And ªHe did not answer him with regard to even a single charge, so that the governor was quite amazed.

15 ªMatt. 27:15-26; Mark 15:6-15; Luke 23:[17]-25; John 18:39-19:16   15   ªNow at the feast the governor was accustomed to release for the multitude any one prisoner whom they wanted.

16   And they were holding at that time a notorious prisoner, called Barabbas.

17 ªMatt. 1:16; 27:22   17   When therefore they were gathered together, Pilate said to them, "Whom do you want me to release for you? Barabbas, or Jesus ªwho is called Christ?"

18   For he knew that because of envy they had delivered Him up.

19 ªJohn 19:13; Acts 12:21 marg., 18:12, 16f.; ᵇMatt. 27:24 ᶜGen. 20:6; 31:11; Num. 12:6; Job 33:15; Matt. 1:20; 2:12f., 19, 22   19   And ªwhile he was sitting on the judgment seat, his wife sent to him, saying, "Have nothing to do with that ᵇrighteous Man; for last night I suffered greatly ᶜin a dream because of Him."

20 ªActs 3:14   20   But the chief priests and the elders persuaded the multitudes to ªask for Barabbas, and to put Jesus to death.

21   But the governor answered and said to them, "Which of the two do you want me to release for you?" And they said, "Barabbas."

22 ªMatt. 1:16   22   Pilate *said to them, "Then what shall I do with Jesus ªwho is called Christ?" They all *said, "Let Him be crucified!"

23   And he said, "Why, what evil has He done?" But they kept shouting all the more, saying, "Let Him be crucified!"

★24 ªMatt. 26:5 ᵇDeut. 21:6-8 ᶜMatt. 27:19 ᵈMatt. 27:4   24   And when Pilate saw that he was accomplishing nothing, but rather that ªa riot was starting, he took water and ᵇwashed his hands in front of the multitude, saying, "I am innocent of ᶜthis Man's blood; ᵈsee to that yourselves."

★25 ªJosh. 2:19; Acts 5:28   25   And all the people answered and said, "ªHis blood be on us and on our children!"

27:7 *Potter's Field.* A field where potters dug clay for making pottery vessels. It may have been full of holes so as to make it easy to bury people there who had no family tombs.

27:9 *spoken through Jeremiah.* These words are found in Zech. 11:12-13 with allusions to Jer. 18:1-4; 19:1-3. They are ascribed to Jeremiah since, in Jesus' day, the books of the prophets were headed by Jeremiah, not Isaiah as now, and the quotation is identified by the name of the first book of the group, rather than by the name of the specific book within the group. Similarly in Luke 24:44, "Psalms" includes all the books known as the "Writ-

ings," because it is the first book of the group.

27:24 *and washed his hands in front of the multitude.* A Jewish custom which when used legitimately (though not so in Pilate's case) was a symbol of absolution of an innocent man from implication in a wrongful death. *this Man's blood.* Pilate found no political or military threat to Rome in Christ, and this was his only concern.

27:25 *all the people.* I.e., all those present, which was only a fractional part of the nation. Some of the leaders opposed the crucifixion (Luke 23:51). See also Luke 23:34; Acts 5:28; 1 Cor. 2:8.

★26 aMark
15:15; Luke
23:16; John
19:1
26 Then he released Barabbas for them; but after having Jesus ascourged, he delivered Him to be crucified.

E The Crucifixion, 27:27–66
1 The preliminaries, 27:27–44

★27 aMatt.
27:27-31;
Mark 15:16-
20 bMatt.
26:3; John
18:28, 33;
19:9 cActs
10:1
28 aMark
15:17; John
19:2
29 aMark
15:17; John
19:2 bMark
15:18; John
19:1
30 aMatt.
26:67; Mark
10:34; 14:65;
15:19
★31 aMark
15:20
★32 aMatt.
27:32; Mark
15:21; Luke
23:26; John
19:17 bActs
2:10; 6:9;
11:20; 13:1
★33 aMatt.
27:34-44;
Mark 15:22-
32; Luke
23:33-43;
John 19:17-
24 bLuke
23:33 and
marg.; John
19:17
27 aThen the soldiers of the governor took Jesus into bthe Praetorium and gathered the whole Roman ccohort around Him.
28 And they stripped Him, and aput a scarlet robe on Him.
29 aAnd after weaving a crown of thorns, they put it on His head, and a reed in His right hand; and they kneeled down before Him and mocked Him, saying, "bHail, King of the Jews!"
30 And athey spat on Him, and took the reed and began to beat Him on the head.
31 aAnd after they had mocked Him, they took His robe off and put His garments on Him, and led Him away to crucify Him.
32 aAnd as they were coming out, they found a man of bCyrene named Simon, whom they pressed into service to bear His cross.
33 aAnd when they had come

to a place called bGolgotha, which means Place of a Skull,
34 athey gave Him bwine to drink mingled with gall; and after tasting it, He was unwilling to drink.
35 And when they had crucified Him, athey divided up His garments among themselves, casting lots;
36 and sitting down, they began to akeep watch over Him there.
37 And they put up above His head the charge against Him which read, "aTHIS IS JESUS THE KING OF THE JEWS."
38 At that time two robbers *were crucified with Him, one on the right and one on the left.
39 And those passing by were hurling abuse at Him, awagging their heads,
40 and saying, "aYou who are going to destroy the temple and rebuild it in three days, save Yourself! bIf You are the Son of God, come down from the cross."
41 In the same way the chief priests also, along with the scribes and elders, were mocking Him, and saying,
42 "aHe saved others; He cannot save Himself. bHe is the King of Israel; let Him now come down

★34 aPs.
69:21 bMark
15:23
★35 aPs.
22:18
36 aMatt.
27:54
★37 aMark
15:26; Luke
23:38; John
19:19
★39 aJob
16:4; Ps.
22:7; 109:25;
Lam. 2:15;
Mark 15:29
★40 aMatt.
26:61 bMatt.
27:42
★42 aMark
15:31; Luke
23:35 bMatt.
27:37; Luke
23:37; John
1:49; 12:13

27:26 scourged. Better, flogged by means of a leather whip that had pieces of bone or metal imbedded in its thongs. It was used by the Romans only on murderers and traitors.
27:27 Praetorium. Pilate's residence in Jerusalem. This was probably in the Castle of Antonia, near the temple, though it may have been located near Herod's palace. cohort. One-tenth of a legion, about 300–600 men.
27:31 to crucify Him. A painful and slow means of execution which the Romans adopted from the Phoenicians. The victim usually died after 2 or 3 days, of thirst, exhaustion, and exposure. The hands were often nailed to the crossbeam, which was then hoisted up and affixed to the upright, to which the feet were then nailed. A peg, astride which the victim sat, supported the main weight of the body. Death was sometimes hastened by breaking the legs, but not in Christ's case (John 19:33).
27:32 of Cyrene. From Cyrene, the capital of Cyrenaica in N. Africa. Many Jews lived there. to bear His cross. The crossbeam was carried

to the place of execution usually by the victim, but Jesus was too weakened by the tortures that had already been inflicted on Him.
27:33 Golgotha. Aramaic for "skull," indicating either that the place of crucifixion looked like a skull or that it was a place of execution where skulls accumulated. Its location is uncertain.
27:34 wine . . . mingled with gall. A drink given to victims to help deaden their pain. Jesus refused it, preferring to meet His death with all His faculties unimpaired.
27:35 divided. The victim's clothes were spoils for his executioners.
27:37 above His head. To the soldiers, the charge would be considered insurrection. His cross was in the traditional shape pictured in Christian art, with room over the crossbeam for this sign.
27:39 wagging their heads. A Near Eastern gesture of scorn.
27:40 See 26:61.
27:42 See 12:38; 16:1.

from the cross, and we shall believe in Him.

43 "*a*He trusts in God; let Him deliver *Him* now, if He takes pleasure in Him; for He said, 'I am the Son of God.'"

44 *a*And the robbers also who had been crucified with Him were casting the same insult at Him.

2 The death, 27:45–56

45 *a*Now from the sixth hour darkness fell upon all the land until the ninth hour.

46 And about the ninth hour Jesus cried out with a loud voice, saying, "Eli, Eli, lama sabachthani?" that is, "*a*My God, My God, why hast Thou forsaken Me?"

47 And some of those who were standing there, when they heard it, *began* saying, "This man is calling for Elijah."

48 And *a*immediately one of them ran, and taking a sponge, he filled it with sour wine, and put it on a reed, and gave Him a drink.

49 But the rest *of them* said, "Let us see whether Elijah will come to save Him."

50 And Jesus *a*cried out again with a loud voice, and yielded up *His* spirit.

51 *a*And behold, *b*the veil of the temple was torn in two from top to bottom, and *c*the earth shook; and the rocks were split,

52 and the tombs were opened; and the many bodies of the saints who had *a*fallen asleep were raised;

53 and coming out of the tombs after His resurrection they entered *a*the holy city and appeared to many.

54 *a*Now the centurion, and those who were with him *b*keeping guard over Jesus, when they saw *c*the earthquake and the things that were happening, became very frightened and said, "Truly this was *d*the Son of God!"

55 *a*And many women were there looking on from a distance, who had followed Jesus from Galilee, *b*ministering to Him,

56 among whom was *a*Mary Magdalene, *along with* Mary the mother of James and Joseph, and *b*the mother of the sons of Zebedee.

3 The burial, 27:57–66

57 *a*And when it was evening, there came a rich man from Arimathea, named Joseph, who himself had also become a disciple of Jesus.

58 This man went to Pilate and asked for the body of Jesus. Then Pilate ordered *it* to be given over *to him.*

59 And Joseph took the body and wrapped it in a clean linen cloth,

60 and laid it in his own new tomb, which he had hewn out in the rock; and he rolled *a*a large stone against the entrance of the tomb and went away.

61 And *a*Mary Magdalene was there, and the other Mary, sitting opposite the grave.

Marginal references

43 *a*Ps. 22:8
44 *a*Luke 23:39–43
★45 *a*Matt. 27:45–56; Mark 15:33–41; Luke 23:44–49
★46 *a*Ps. 22:1
★47
★48 *a*Mark 15:36; Luke 23:36; John 19:29
★50 *a*Mark 15:37; Luke 23:46; John 19:30
★51 *a*Matt. 27:51–56; Mark 15:38–41; Luke 23:47–49 *b*Ex. 26:31ff.; Mark 15:38; Luke 23:45; Heb. 9:3 *c*Matt. 27:54
★52–53
52 *a*Acts 7:60
53 *a*Matt. 4:5
54 *a*Mark 15:39; Luke 23:47 *b*Matt. 27:36 *c*Matt. 27:51 *d*Matt. 4:3; 27:43
55 *a*Mark 15:40f.; Luke 23:49; John 19:25 *b*Mark 15:41; Luke 8:2, 3
56 *a*Matt. 28:1; Mark 15:40, 47; 16:9; Luke 8:2; John 19:25; 20:1, 18 *b*Matt. 20:20
★57 *a*Matt. 27:57–61; Mark 15:42–47; Luke 23:50–56; John 19:38–42
★60 *a*Matt. 27:66; 28:2; Mark 16:4
61 *a*Matt. 27:56; 28:1

27:45 *sixth . . . until the ninth hour.* From noon to 3 p.m.

27:46 *Eli, Eli, lama sabachthani.* Quoting Ps. 22:1 in its Aramaic form, except that *Eloi* (Mark 15:34) has been reconverted to the Hebrew *Eli.* This cry may reflect the desertion Jesus felt as He was bearing the sins of the world (2 Cor. 5:21).

27:47 *Elijah.* Some listeners made a poor guess as to what Christ was saying and mistook "Eli" for "Elijah."

27:48 *put it on a reed.* To raise it to His lips.

27:50 *His spirit.* Christ was not directly killed by anyone nor was He overcome by natural processes; He released His spirit (John 10:18).

27:51 *veil.* I.e., the curtain separating the Holy of Holies from the rest of the temple (Ex. 26:37; 38:18; Heb. 9:3). *from top to bottom.* Showing that God did it, not man. It signified that the new and living way was now open into the presence of God (Heb. 10:20; Eph. 2:11–22). One probable result of this supernatural tearing of the veil is recorded in Acts 6:7b.

27:52–53 *out of the tombs.* These people may have been restored to earthly bodies to die again, or resurrected with glorified bodies.

27:57 *Arimathea.* A town N. of Lydda and E. of Joppa.

27:60 *the tomb.* See Isa. 53:9.

★62 aMark
15:42; Luke
23:54; John
19:14, 31, 42

62 Now on the next day, which is *the one* after athe preparation, the chief priests and the Pharisees gathered together with Pilate,

63 aMatt.
16:21

63 and said, "Sir, we remember that when He was still alive that deceiver said, 'aAfter three days I *am to* rise again.'

64 "Therefore, give orders for the grave to be made secure until the third day, lest the disciples come and steal Him away and say to the people, 'He has risen from the dead,' and the last deception will be worse than the first."

65 aMatt.
27:66; 28:11

65 Pilate said to them, "You have a aguard; go, make it *as* secure as you know how."

★66 aMatt.
27:65; 28:11
bDan. 6:17
cMatt. 27:60;
28:2; Mark
16:4

66 And they went and made the grave secure, and along with athe guard they set a bseal on cthe stone.

IX THE POWER OF THE KING, 28:1-20
A The Conquest, 28:1-10

★ 1 aMatt.
28:1-8; Mark
16:1-8; Luke
24:1-10;
John 20:1-8
bMatt. 27:56,
61

28 aNow after the Sabbath, as it began to dawn toward the first *day* of the week, bMary Magdalene and the other Mary came to look at the grave.

2 aLuke
24:4; John
20:12 bMatt.
27:66; 28:2;
Mark 16:4

2 And behold, a severe earthquake had occurred, for aan angel of the Lord descended from heaven and came and rolled away bthe stone and sat upon it.

3 aDan.
7:9; 10:6;
Mark 9:3;
John 20:12;
Acts 1:10

3 And ahis appearance was like lightning, and his garment as white as snow;

4 and the guards shook for fear of him, and became like dead men.

5 aMatt.
14:27; 28:10

5 And the angel answered and said to the women, "aDo not be afraid; for I know that you are

looking for Jesus who has been crucified.

6 "He is not here, for He has risen, ajust as He said. Come, see the place where He was lying.

7 "And go quickly and tell His disciples that He has risen from the dead; and behold, He is going before you ainto Galilee, there you will see Him; behold, I have told you."

8 And they departed quickly from the tomb with fear and great joy and ran to report it to His disciples.

9 And behold, Jesus met them and greeted them. And they came up and took hold of His feet and worshiped Him.

10 Then Jesus *said to them, "aDo not be afraid; go and take word to bMy brethren to leave cfor Galilee, and there they shall see Me."

★ 6 aMatt.
12:40; 16:21;
27:63

7 aMatt.
26:32; 28:10,
16

10 aMatt.
14:27; 28:5
bJohn 20:17;
Rom. 8:29,
Heb. 2:11f.,
17 cMatt.
26:32; 28:7,
16

B The Conspiracy, 28:11-15

11 Now while they were on their way, behold, some of athe guard came into the city and reported to the chief priests all that had happened.

12 And when they had assembled with the elders and counseled together, they gave a large sum of money to the soldiers,

13 and said, "You are to say, 'His disciples came by night and stole Him away while we were asleep.'

14 "And if this should come to athe governor's ears, we will win him over and keep you out of trouble."

15 And they took the money and did as they had been instructed; and this story was

11 aMatt.
27:65, 66

★13

14 aMatt.
27:2

15 aMatt.
9:31; Mark
1:45 bMatt.
27:8

27:62 *the next day.* The Sabbath.
27:66 *set a seal on the stone.* This was likely done by connecting the stone to the tomb with a cord and wax so that any tampering could easily be detected.
28:1 *after the Sabbath.* It was now Sunday morning, and the work of preparing Christ's body for permanent burial could be done.
28:6 *He has risen.* This simply stated fact is the

basis of our Christian faith. *as He said.* See Matt. 16:21; 17:23; 20:19.
28:13 *while we were asleep.* How would sleeping people know what had happened? Would it be likely that all the soldiers were sleeping at the same time? Why would Roman soldiers risk incriminating themselves even for a large bribe? The story was self-contradictory!

widely ᵃspread among the Jews, and is ᵇto this day.

C The Commission, 28:16-20

★16 ᵃMatt.
26:32; 28:7,
10

16 But the eleven disciples proceeded ᵃto Galilee, to the mountain which Jesus had designated.

17 ᵃMark
16:11

17 And when they saw Him, they worshiped *Him*; but ᵃsome were doubtful.

18 And Jesus came up and spoke to them, saying, "ᵃAll authority has been given to Me in heaven and on earth.

19 "ᵃGo therefore and ᵇmake disciples of ᶜall the nations, ᵈbaptizing them in the name of the Father and the Son and the Holy Spirit,

20 teaching them to observe all that I commanded you; and lo, ᵃI am with you always, even to ᵇthe end of the age."

★18 ᵃDan.
7:13f.; Matt.
11:27; 26:64;
Rom. 14:9;
Eph. 1:20-22;
Phil. 2:9f.;
Col. 2:10
★19 ᵃMark
16:15f.
ᵇMatt. 13:52;
Acts 14:21
ᶜMatt. 25:32
ᵈActs 2:38;
8:16; Rom.
6:3
★20 ᵃMatt.
18:20; Acts
18:10 ᵇMatt.
13:39

28:16 *designated* = commanded, see 26:32; 28:7.

28:18 *All authority.* The Great Commission which follows is based upon and backed by the authority of the risen and exalted Lord who promises to be ever-present with His people.

28:19 *make disciples of all the nations.* This is the one command in the Commission. It is surrounded by three participles: *go* (lit., going), *baptizing* and *teaching* (v. 20). This is the missionary task of the church. *in the name of the Father and the Son and the Holy Spirit.* Here is evidence for the trinity of God: one

God (*the name*) who subsists in three persons (Father, Son and Holy Spirit). Each of the three is distinguished from the others; each possesses all the divine attributes; yet the three are one. This is a mystery which no analogy can illustrate satisfactorily. The sun, sunlight, and the power of the sun may come close to a suitable illustration.

28:20 *end of the age.* The personal and empowering presence of the One vividly portrayed in this Gospel is promised to His followers. In His power the commission can be performed.

INTRODUCTION TO
THE GOSPEL ACCORDING TO MARK

AUTHOR: Mark   DATE: 50's

Authorship   *John Mark was the son of Mary, a woman of wealth and position in Jerusalem (Acts 12:12). Barnabas was his cousin (Col. 4:10). Mark was a close friend (and possibly a convert) of the apostle Peter (1 Pet. 5:13). He had the rare privilege of accompanying Paul and Barnabas on the first missionary journey but failed to stay with them through the entire trip. Because of this, Paul refused to take him on the second journey, so he went with Barnabas to Cyprus (Acts 15:38-40). About a dozen years later he was again with Paul (Col. 4:10; Philem. 24), and just before Paul's execution he was sent for by the apostle (2 Tim. 4:11). His biography proves that one failure in life does not mean the end of usefulness.*

Distinctive Approach of Mark   *(1) Mark wrote for Gentile readers in general and Roman readers in particular. For this reason the genealogy of Christ is not included (for it would have meant little to Gentiles), the Sermon on the Mount is not reported, and the condemnations of the Jewish sects receive little attention. As a further indication of his Gentile readership, Mark felt it necessary to interpret Aramaic words (5:41; 7:34; 15:22) and he used Latin words not found in the other Gospels ("executioner," 6:27; "cent," 12:42). (2) There are only about 63 quotations or allusions from the Old Testament in Mark as compared with about 128 in Matthew and between 90 and 100 in Luke. (3) This Gospel emphasizes what Jesus did rather than what He said. It is a book of action (the word "immediately" occurs more than 40 times).*

Mark and Peter   *It is generally agreed that Mark received much of the information in his Gospel from Peter. With Peter's apostolic authority behind the Gospel, there was never any challenge to its inclusion in the canon of Scripture.*

Date   *If one denies the phenomenon of predictive prophecy, then the book must be dated after A.D. 70 because of 13:2, but since our Lord could predict the future, this late date is unnecessary. In fact, if Acts must be dated about 61, and if Luke, the companion volume, preceded it, then Mark must be even earlier, since Luke apparently used Mark in writing his Gospel. This points to a date in the 50's for Mark. However, many scholars believe that Mark was not written until after Peter died; i.e., after 67 but before 70.*

Contents   *The theme of the book is Christ the Servant. The key verse is 10:45, which divides the Gospel into two major divisions: the service of the Servant (1:1-10:52) and the sacrifice of the Servant (11:1-16:20).*

OUTLINE OF THE GOSPEL OF MARK

I. **The Service of the Servant, 1:1-10:52**
  A. His Preparation, 1:1-13
    1. By the ministry of John the Baptist, 1:1-8
    2. By His baptism, 1:9-11
    3. By His temptation, 1:12-13
  B. His Preaching, 1:14-20
  C. His Power, 1:21-3:12
    1. Over a demon, 1:21-28
    2. Over disease, 1:29-39
    3. Over leprosy, 1:40-45
    4. Over paralysis, 2:1-12
    5. Over a publican, 2:13-20
    6. Over the old religion, 2:21-22
    7. Over the Sabbath, 2:23-28
    8. Over deformity, 3:1-6
    9. Over demons, 3:7-12

  D. His Personnel, 3:13-35
    1. The call of The Twelve, 3:13-21
    2. The condemnation of rejectors, 3:22-30
    3. The call to be in Jesus' spiritual family, 3:31-35
  E. His Parables, 4:1-34
    1. The sower, 4:1-20
    2. The lamp, 4:21-25
    3. The seed growing gradually, 4:26-29
    4. The mustard seed, 4:30-34
  F. His Prerogatives, 4:35-9:1
    1. Over the storm, 4:35-41
    2. Over demons, 5:1-20
    3. Over sickness and death, 5:21-43
    4. Rejected by His own townspeople, 6:1-6
    5. In commissioning The Twelve, 6:7-13

THE GOSPEL ACCORDING TO MARK

I THE SERVICE OF THE SERVANT, 1:1-10:52

A His Preparation, 1:1-13

1 By the ministry of John the Baptist, 1:1-8

★ 1 aMatt. 4:3
★ 2 aMark 1:2-8; Matt. 3:1-11; Luke 3:2-16 bMal. 3:1; Matt. 11:10; Luke 7:27

1 The beginning of the gospel of Jesus Christ, athe Son of God.

2 aAs it is written in Isaiah the prophet,

"bBEHOLD, I SEND MY MESSENGER BEFORE YOUR FACE, WHO WILL PREPARE YOUR WAY;

3 "aTHE VOICE OF ONE CRYING IN THE WILDERNESS,

'MAKE READY THE WAY OF THE LORD, MAKE HIS PATHS STRAIGHT.' "

3 aIs. 40:3; Matt. 3:3; Luke 3:4; John 1:23

★ 4 aActs 13:24 bLuke 1:77

4 John the Baptist appeared

1:1 *The beginning of the gospel.* Here begins the good news—i.e., that Jesus Christ is the Savior.
1:2 *in Isaiah the prophet.* See Isa. 40:3; Mal. 3:1.
1:4 *baptism of repentance for the forgiveness of sins.* The Jews practiced self-immersion as a form of baptism, but John immersed others as a witness to their repentance. Christian baptism is performed in the name of the Trinity as a witness to one's faith in Christ. Some who followed John and who later believed in Christ were rebaptized (Acts 19:5).

in the wilderness *preaching a baptism of repentance for the *forgiveness of sins.

5 And all the country of Judea was going out to him, and all the people of Jerusalem; and they were being baptized by him in the Jordan River, confessing their sins.

6 And John was clothed with camel's hair and *wore* a leather belt around his waist, and his diet was locusts and wild honey.

★ 7   **7** And he was preaching, and saying, "After me One is coming who is mightier than I, and I am not fit to stoop down and untie the thong of His sandals.

★ 8   **8** "I baptized you with water; but He will baptize you with the Holy Spirit."

2 *By His baptism,* 1:9-11

9 *a*Mark
1:9-11; Matt.
3:13-17;
Luke 3:21,
22 *b*Matt.
2:23; Luke
2:51
★10

9 *a*And it came about in those days that Jesus *b*came from Nazareth in Galilee, and was baptized by John in the Jordan.

10 And immediately coming up out of the water, He saw the heavens opening, and the Spirit like a dove descending upon Him;

11 *a*Matt.
3:17; Luke
3:22

11 and a voice came out of the heavens: "*a*Thou art My beloved Son, in Thee I am well-pleased."

3 *By His temptation,* 1:12-13

★12 *a*Mark
1:12, 13;
Matt. 4:1-11;
Luke 4:1-13
13 *a*Matt.
4:10

12 *a*And immediately the Spirit *impelled Him *to go* out into the wilderness.

13 And He was in the wilderness forty days being tempted by *a*Satan; and He was with the wild beasts, and the angels were ministering to Him.

B His Preaching, 1:14-20

14 *a*And after John had been taken into custody, Jesus came into Galilee, *b*preaching the gospel of God,

15 and saying, "*a*The time is fulfilled, and the kingdom of God is at hand; *b*repent and believe in the gospel."

16 *a*And as He was going along by the Sea of Galilee, He saw Simon and Andrew, the brother of Simon, casting a net in the sea; for they were fishermen.

17 And Jesus said to them, "Follow Me, and I will make you become fishers of men."

18 And they immediately left the nets and followed Him.

19 And going on a little farther, He saw James the *son* of Zebedee, and John his brother, who were also in the boat mending the nets.

20 And immediately He called them; and they left their father Zebedee in the boat with the hired servants, and went away to follow Him.

C His Power, 1:21-3:12
1 *Over a demon,* 1:21-28

21 *a*And they *went into Capernaum; and immediately on the

★14 *a*Matt.
4:12 *b*Matt.
4:23

★15 *a*Gal.
4:4; Eph.
1:10; 1 Tim.
2:6; Titus 1:3
*b*Acts 20:21

16 *a*Mark
1:16-20;
Matt. 4:18-
22; Luke 5:2-
11; John
1:40-42

★21 *a*Mark
1:21-28;
Luke 4:31-37
*b*Matt. 4:23;
Mark 1:39;
10:1

1:7 *thong of His sandals.* It was usually loosened by a slave as a guest entered a home.
1:8 See note on Matt. 3:11.
1:10 See note on Matt. 3:16-17.
1:12 *the Spirit impelled Him. impelled* reflects Mark's forceful style (the other Gospel writers use "led").
1:14 Between the temptation of Jesus and the imprisonment of John the Baptist occurred the events recorded in John 1:19-4:54. How he came to be imprisoned is told in Mark 6:17-20.
1:15 *the kingdom of God is at hand.* The rule of Messiah on earth, promised in the Old Testament and earnestly longed for by the Jewish

people, was near, for the Messiah had now come. However, the people rejected rather than accepted Him, and the fulfillment of the kingdom promises had to be delayed until God's purpose in saving Jews and Gentiles and forming His church was completed. Then Christ will return and set up God's kingdom on this earth (Acts 15:14-16; Rev. 19:15).
1:21 *Capernaum.* Situated on the NW. shore of the Sea of Galilee, this was an important town on the caravan route to Damascus. It was the site of a customs station (2:14), had a Roman garrison (Matt. 8:5-13), and was the home of Peter, Andrew, James, and John.

Sabbath ᵇHe entered the synagogue and *began* to teach.

★22 ᵃMatt.
7:28

22 And ᵃthey were amazed at His teaching; for He was teaching them as *one* having authority, and not as the scribes.

23 And just then there was in their synagogue a man with an unclean spirit; and he cried out,

24 ᵃMatt.
8:29, ᵇMatt.
2:23; Mark
10:47; 14:67;
16:6; Luke
4:34; 24:19;
Acts 24:5
ᶜLuke 1:35;
4:34; John
6:69; Acts
3:14

24 saying, "ᵃWhat do we have to do with You, Jesus of ᵇNazareth? Have You come to destroy us? I know who You are—ᶜthe Holy One of God!"

25 And Jesus rebuked him, saying, "Be quiet, and come out of him!"

26 And throwing him into convulsions, the unclean spirit cried out with a loud voice, and came out of him.

27 ᵃMark
10:24, 32;
14:33; 16:5,
6

27 And they were all ᵃamazed, so that they debated among themselves, saying, "What is this? A new teaching with authority! He commands even the unclean spirits, and they obey Him."

28 And immediately the news about Him went out everywhere into all the surrounding district of Galilee.

2 Over disease, 1:29-39

29 ᵃMark
1:29-31;
Matt. 8:14,
15; Luke
4:38, 39
ᵇMark 1:21,
23

29 ᵃAnd immediately after they had come ᵇout of the synagogue, they came into the house of Simon and Andrew, with James and John.

30 Now Simon's mother-in-law was lying sick with a fever; and immediately they *spoke to Him about her.

31 And He came to her and raised her up, taking her by the hand, and the fever left her, and she waited on them.

★32 ᵃMark
1:32-34;
Matt. 8:16,
17; Luke
4:40, 41
ᵇMark 8:16;
Luke 4:40
ᶜLuke 4:24

32 ᵃAnd ᵇwhen evening had

come, ᵇafter the sun had set, they *began* bringing to Him all who were ill and those who were ᶜdemon-possessed.

33 And the whole ᵃcity had gathered at the door.

33 ᵃMark
1:21

34 And He ᵃhealed many who were ill with various diseases, and cast out many demons; and He was not permitting the demons to speak, because they knew who He was.

34 ᵃMatt.
4:23

35 ᵃAnd in the early morning, while it was still dark, He arose and went out and departed to a lonely place, and ᵇwas praying there.

35 ᵃMark
1:35-38;
Luke 4:42,
43 ᵇMatt.
14:23; Luke
5:16

36 And Simon and his companions hunted for Him;

37 and they found Him, and *said to Him, "Everyone is looking for You."

38 And He *said to them, "Let us go somewhere else to the towns nearby, in order that I may preach there also; for that is what I came out for."

★38

39 ᵃAnd He went into their synagogues throughout all Galilee, preaching and casting out the demons.

39 ᵃMatt.
4:23; Mark
1:23; 3:1

3 Over leprosy, 1:40-45

40 ᵃAnd a leper *came to Him, beseeching Him and ᵇfalling on his knees before Him, and saying to Him, "If You are willing, You can make me clean."

★40 ᵃMark
1:40-44;
Matt. 8:2-4;
Luke 5:12-14
ᵇMatt. 8:2;
Mark 10:17;
Luke 5:12

41 And moved with compassion, He stretched out His hand, and touched him, and *said to him, "I am willing; be cleansed."

42 And immediately the leprosy left him and he was cleansed.

43 And He sternly warned him and immediately sent him away,

★44 ᵃMatt.
8:4 ᵇMatt.
8:4

44 and He *said to him, "ᵃSee

1:22 *authority.* Jesus' teaching was based on His own personal authority in contrast to that of the scribes, whose manner of teaching was to quote the authoritative statements of scribes who had gone before.

1:32 *after the sun had set.* Burdens could not be carried on the Sabbath (v. 21), but the next day, when they could be, began at sundown.

1:38 *that is what I came out for.* I.e., that is why I left Capernaum.

1:40 *leper.* See note on Luke 5:12. The laws concerning leprosy are found in Lev. 13–14.

1:44 *say nothing to anyone.* Jesus did not want people coming to Him merely to receive physical benefits. The result of the leper's failure to obey is seen in v. 45.

that you say nothing to anyone; but [b]go, show yourself to the priest and offer for your cleansing what Moses commanded, for a testimony to them."

45 But he went out and began to [a]proclaim it freely and to [a]spread the news about, to such an extent that Jesus could no longer publicly enter a city, but stayed out in unpopulated areas; and [b]they were coming to Him from everywhere.

4 Over paralysis, 2:1-12

2 And when He had come back to Capernaum several days afterward, it was heard that He was at home.

2 And [a]many were gathered together, so that there was no longer room, even near the door; and He was speaking the word to them.

3 [a]And they *came, bringing to Him a [b]paralytic, carried by four men.

4 And being unable to get to Him because of the crowd, they [a]removed the roof above Him; and when they had dug an opening, they let down the pallet on which the [b]paralytic was lying.

5 And Jesus seeing their faith *said to the paralytic, "My son, [a]your sins are forgiven."

6 But there were some of the scribes sitting there and reasoning in their hearts,

7 "Why does this man speak that way? He is blaspheming; [a]who can forgive sins but God alone?"

8 And immediately Jesus, aware in His spirit that they were reasoning that way within themselves, *said to them, "Why are you reasoning about these things in your hearts?

9 "Which is easier, to say to the [a]paralytic, 'Your sins are forgiven'; or to say, 'Arise, and take up your pallet and walk'?

10 "But in order that you may know that the Son of Man has authority on earth to forgive sins" —He *said to the paralytic—

11 "I say to you, rise, take up your pallet and go home."

12 And he rose and immediately took up the pallet and went out in the sight of all; so that they were all amazed and [a]were glorifying God, saying, "[b]We have never seen anything like this."

5 Over a publican, 2:13-20

13 And He went out again by the seashore; and [a]all the multitude were coming to Him, and He was teaching them.

14 [a]And as He passed by, He saw [b]Levi the *son* of Alpheus sitting in the tax office, and He *said to him, "[c]Follow Me!" And he rose and followed Him.

15 And it came about that He was reclining *at the table* in his house, and many tax-gatherers and sinners were dining with Jesus and His disciples; for there were many of them, and they were following Him.

16 And when [a]the scribes of the Pharisees saw that He was eating with the sinners and tax-gatherers, they [b]began saying to His disciples, "[b]Why is He eating and drinking with tax-gatherers and sinners?"

17 And hearing this, Jesus *said to them, "[a]It *is* not those who are healthy who need a physician, but those who are sick; I did not come to call the righteous, but sinners."

18 [a]And John's disciples and the Pharisees were fasting; and they *came and *said to Him,

Margin references

45 [a]Matt. 28:15; Luke 5:15 [b]Mark 2:2, 13; 3:7; Luke 5:17; John 6:2

2 [a]Mark 1:45; 2:13

3 [a]Mark 2:3-12; Matt. 9:2-8; Luke 5:18-26 [b]Matt. 4:24

4 [a]Luke 5:19 [b]Matt. 4:24

★ 5 [a]Matt. 9:2

7 [a]Is. 43:25

★ 8

9 [a]Matt. 4:24

★10

12 [a]Matt. 9:8 [b]Matt. 9:33

13 [a]Mark 1:45

14 [a]Mark 2:14-17; Matt. 9:9-13; Luke 5:27-32 [b]Matt. 9:9 [c]Matt. 8:22

16 [a]Luke 5:30; Acts 23:9 [b]Matt. 9:11

17 [a]Matt. 9:12, 13; Luke 5:31, 32

★18 [a]Mark 2:18-22; Matt. 9:14-17; Luke 5:33-38

2:5 See note on Matt. 9:2.
2:8 *in His spirit.* I.e., intuitively.
2:10 *the Son of Man.* A favorite title of Christ, used 14 times in Mark. See note on Matt. 8:20 for its significance.
2:18 Jesus' disciples did not fast because it was incompatible with the joy they had in being

with Him. On the Jews' fasting see note on Matt. 9:14. The N.T. church did not fast regularly as a prescribed rite, though it was done on occasion (Acts 13:2-3; 14:23). Whenever practiced, it is never to be done ostentatiously (Matt. 6:16-18).

"Why do John's disciples and the disciples of the Pharisees fast, but Your disciples do not fast?"

19 And Jesus said to them, "While the bridegroom is with them, the attendants of the bridegroom do not fast, do they? So long as they have the bridegroom with them, they cannot fast.

20 "But the ^adays will come when the bridegroom is taken away from them, and then they will fast in that day.

20 ªMatt. 9:15; Luke 17:22

6 Over the old religion, 2:21-22

21 "No one sews a patch of unshrunk cloth on an old garment; otherwise the patch pulls away from it, the new from the old, and a worse tear results.

22 "And no one puts new wine into old wineskins; otherwise the wine will burst the skins, and the wine is lost, and the skins *as well;* but *one puts* new wine into fresh wineskins."

★22

7 Over the Sabbath, 2:23-28

23 ^aAnd it came about that He was passing through the grainfields on the Sabbath, and His disciples began to make their way along while ^bpicking the heads *of grain.*

23 ªMark 2:23-28; Matt. 12:1-8; Luke 6:1-5 ᵇDeut. 23:25

24 And the Pharisees were saying to Him, "See here, ^awhy are they doing what is not lawful on the Sabbath?"

24 ªMatt. 12:2

25 And He *said to them, "Have you never read what David did when he was in need and became hungry, he and his companions:

★25

26 how he entered the house of God in the time of ^aAbiathar the high priest, and ate the conse-

26 ª1 Sam. 21:1; 2 Sam. 8:17; 1 Chr. 24:6

crated bread, which is not lawful for *anyone* to eat except the priests, and he gave *it* also to those who were with him?"

27 And He was saying to them, "^aThe Sabbath was made for man, and ^bnot man for the Sabbath.

27 ªEx. 23:12; Deut. 5:14 ᵇCol. 2:16

28 "Consequently, the Son of Man is Lord even of the Sabbath."

8 Over deformity, 3:1-6

3 ^aAnd He ^bentered again into a synagogue; and a man was there with a withered hand.

1 ªMark 3:1-6; Matt. 12:9-14; Luke 6:6-11 ᵇMark 1:21, 39

2 And ^athey were watching Him *to see* if He would heal him on the Sabbath, ^bin order that they might accuse Him.

★ 2 ªLuke 6:7; 14:1; 20:20 ᵇMatt. 12:10; Luke 6:7; 11:54

3 And He *said to the man with the withered hand, "Rise and *come* forward!"

4 And He *said to them, "Is it lawful on the Sabbath to do good or to do harm, to save a life or to kill?" But they kept silent.

★ 4

5 And after ^alooking around at them with anger, grieved at their hardness of heart, He *said to the man, "Stretch out your hand." And he stretched it out, and his hand was restored.

5 ªLuke 6:10

6 And the Pharisees went out and immediately *began* taking counsel with the ^aHerodians against Him, *as to* how they might destroy Him.

★ 6 ªMatt. 22:16; Mark 12:13

9 Over demons, 3:7-12

7 ^aAnd Jesus withdrew to the sea with His disciples; and ^ba great multitude from Galilee followed; and *also* from Judea,

7 ªMark 3:7-12; Matt. 12:15, 16; Luke 6:17-19 ᵇMatt. 4:25; Luke 6:17

8 and from Jerusalem, and from ^aIdumea, and beyond the Jordan, and the vicinity of ^bTyre

★ 8 ªJosh. 15:1, 21; Ezek. 35:15; 36:5 ᵇMatt. 11:21

2:22 *wineskins.* See note on Luke 5:37.

2:25 *what David did.* See 1 Sam. 21:1-6. See note on Matt. 12:2.

3:2 *on the Sabbath.* Rabbinic tradition, not the O.T. law, forbade practicing medicine on the Sabbath unless the person were on the verge of death. Christ's critics were simply determined somehow to stop His activities.

3:4 Christ's argument is: To be able to do good and refuse to do it is evil; not to heal this man would have been evil.

3:6 *Pharisees.* See note on Matt. 3:7. *Herodians.* See note on Matt. 22:16.

3:8 *Idumea.* The former country of Edom, which in the time of Christ included the region around Hebron.

and Sidon, a great multitude heard of all that He was doing and came to Him.

9 And He told His disciples that a boat should stand ready for Him because of the multitude, in order that they might not crowd Him;

10 aMatt.
4:23 bMark
5:29, 34;
Luke 7:21
cMatt. 9:21;
14:36; Mark
6:56; 8:22

10 for He had ªhealed many, with the result that all those who had ᵇafflictions pressed about Him in order to ᶜtouch Him.

11 aMatt. 4:3

11 And whenever the unclean spirits beheld Him, they would fall down before Him and cry out, saying, "You are ªthe Son of God!"

12 aMatt. 8:4

12 And He ªearnestly warned them not to make Him known.

D His Personnel, 3:13-35
1 The call of The Twelve, 3:13-21

13 aMatt.
5:1; Luke
6:12 bMatt.
10:1; Mark
6:7; Luke
9:1-6

13 And He *went up to ªthe mountain and *ᵇsummoned those whom He Himself wanted, and they came to Him.

14 And He appointed twelve, that they might be with Him, and that He might send them out to preach,

15 and to have authority to cast out the demons.

*16-19
16 aMark
3:16-19;
Matt. 10:2-4;
Luke 6:14-
16; Acts 1:13
*17

16 And He appointed the twelve: ªSimon (to whom He gave the name Peter),

17 and James, the son of Zebedee, and John the brother of James (to them He gave the name Boanerges, which means, "Sons of Thunder");

18 and Andrew, and Philip, and Bartholomew, and Matthew, and Thomas, and James the son of Alphaeus, and Thaddaeus, and Simon the Zealot;

19 and Judas Iscariot, who also betrayed Him.

20 And He *came ªhome, and the ᵇmultitude *gathered again, ᶜto such an extent that they could not even eat a meal.

20 aMark
2:1; 7:17;
9:28 bMark
1:45; 3:7
cMark 6:31

21 And when ªHis own people heard of this, they went out to take custody of Him; for they were saying, "ᵇHe has lost His senses."

21 aMark
3:31f. bJohn
10:20; Acts
26:24

2 The condemnation of rejectors, 3:22-30

22 And the scribes who came down ªfrom Jerusalem were saying, "He is possessed by ᵇBeelzebul," and "ᶜHe casts out the demons by the ruler of the demons."

*22 aMatt.
15:1 bMatt.
10:25; 11:18
cMatt. 9:34

23 ªAnd He called them to Himself and began speaking to them in ᵇparables, "How can ᶜSatan cast out Satan?

23 aMark
3:23-27;
Matt. 12:25-
29; Luke
11:17-22
bMatt.
13:3ff.; Mark
4:2ff. cMatt.
4:10

24 "And if a kingdom is divided against itself, that kingdom cannot stand.

25 "And if a house is divided against itself, that house will not be able to stand.

26 "And if ªSatan has risen up against himself and is divided, he cannot stand, but he is finished!

26 aMatt.
4:10

27 "ªBut no one can enter the strong man's house and plunder his property unless he first binds the strong man, and then he will plunder his house.

27 aIs.
49:24, 25

28 "ªTruly I say to you, all sins shall be forgiven the sons of men, and whatever blasphemies they utter;

28 aMatt.
12:31, 32;
Mark 3:28-
30; Luke
12:10

29 but whoever blasphemes against the Holy Spirit never has forgiveness, but is guilty of an eternal sin"—

*29

30 because they were saying, "He has an unclean spirit."

3:16-19 There are 4 lists of the apostles given in the N.T. (Matt. 10:1-4; Luke 6:13-16; Acts 1:13 are the others). Thaddaeus (Matt. 10:3; Mark 3:18) is apparently the same as Judas the son or brother of James (Thaddaeus may represent a corruption of *Yaddai*, a form of Judas).

3:17 *Sons of Thunder.* Probably indicating the fiery zeal and energy of James and John.
3:22 *Beelzebul.* See note on Matt. 10:25.
3:29 *blasphemes against the Holy Spirit.* See note on Matt. 12:31.

3 The call to be in Jesus' spiritual family,
3:31-35

31 [a]Mark 3:31-35; Matt. 12:46-50; Luke 8:19-21

31 [a]And His mother and His brothers *arrived, and standing outside they sent *word* to Him, and called Him.

32 And a multitude was sitting around Him, and they *said to Him, "Behold, Your mother and Your brothers are outside looking for You."

33 And answering them, He *said, "Who are My mother and My brothers?"

34 And looking about on those who were sitting around Him, He *said, "Behold, My mother and My brothers!

★**35** **35** "For whoever does the will of God, he is My brother and sister and mother."

E His Parables, 4:1-34
1 The sower, 4:1-20

1 [a]Mark 4:1-12; Matt. 13:1-15; Luke 8:4-10 [b]Mark 2:13; 3:7

4 [a]And He began to teach again [b]by the sea. And such a very great multitude gathered to Him that He got into a boat in the sea and sat down; and the whole multitude was by the sea on the land.

★ **2** [a]Matt. 13:3ff.; Mark 3:23; 4:2ff.

2 And He was teaching them many things in [a]parables, and was saying to them in His teaching,

3 "Listen *to this!* Behold, the sower went out to sow;

4 and it came about that as he was sowing, some *seed* fell beside the road, and the birds came and ate it up.

5 "And other *seed* fell on the rocky *ground* where it did not have much soil; and immediately it sprang up because it had no depth of soil.

★ **5-8**

6 "And after the sun had risen, it was scorched; and because it had no root, it withered away.

7 "And other *seed* fell among the thorns, and the thorns came up and choked it, and it yielded no crop.

8 "And other *seeds* fell into the good soil and as they grew up and increased, they yielded a crop and produced thirty, sixty, and a hundredfold."

9 And He was saying, "[a]He who has ears to hear, let him hear."

9 [a]Matt. 11:15; Mark 4:23

10 And as soon as He was alone, His followers, along with the twelve, *began* asking Him *about* the parables.

11 And He was saying to them, "To you has been given the mystery of the kingdom of God; but [a]those who are outside get everything [b]in parables,

★**11** [a]1 Cor. 5:12f.; Col. 4:5; 1 Thess. 4:12; 1 Tim. 3:7 [b]Mark 3:23; 4:2

12 [a]in order that WHILE SEEING, THEY MAY SEE AND NOT PERCEIVE; AND WHILE HEARING, THEY MAY HEAR AND NOT UNDERSTAND LEST THEY RETURN AND BE FORGIVEN."

12 [a]Is. 6:9; Matt. 13:14

13 [a]And He *said to them, "Do you not understand this parable? And how will you understand all the parables?

13 [a]Mark 4:13-20; Matt. 13:18-23; Luke 8:11-15

14 "The sower sows the word.

15 "And these are the ones who are beside the road where the word is sown; and when they hear, immediately [a]Satan comes and takes away the word which has been sown in them.

15 [a]Matt. 4:10

3:35 Those who belong to God's family are closer to Jesus than His natural family.

4:2 *parables.* A parable is a short discourse that makes a comparison; it is usually designed to inculcate a single truth. Some parables, however, like those of the sower and of the tares, are given detailed interpretations. Also, the Greek word "parable" is used in Luke 4:23 for what we would normally call a proverb. Parables were used by Christ for opposite effects: on the one hand, to make the truth more engaging and clear to those who were willing to hear (Luke 15:3) and, on the other, to make the truth obscure to those who lacked spiritual

concern (Mark 4:11-12).

4:5-8 Jesus wanted the people to examine their hearts' responses to His message. Though some of the soils proved barren, nevertheless how great was the harvest.

4:11 *the mystery.* Just as in pagan mystery religions the initiate was instructed in the teaching of the cult, which was not revealed to outsiders, so the purpose of parables was to instruct the disciples without revealing truths to *those who are outside.* Parables test the spiritual responsiveness of those who hear them.

16 "And in a similar way these are the ones on whom seed was sown on the rocky *places*, who, when they hear the word, immediately receive it with joy;

17 and they have no *firm* root in themselves, but are *only* temporary; then, when affliction or persecution arises because of the word, immediately they fall away.

18 "And others are the ones on whom seed was sown among the thorns; these are the ones who have heard the word,

19 and the worries of ᵃthe world, and the deceitfulness of riches, and the desires for other things enter in and choke the word, and it becomes unfruitful.

20 "And those are the ones on whom seed was sown on the good soil; and they hear the word and accept it, and bear fruit, thirty, sixty, and a hundredfold."

2 The lamp, 4:21-25

21 And He was saying to them, "ᵃA lamp is not brought to be put under a peck-measure, is it, or under a bed? Is it not *brought* to be put on the lampstand?

22 "ᵃFor nothing is hidden, except to be revealed; nor has *anything* been secret, but that it should come to light.

23 "ᵃIf any man has ears to hear, let him hear."

24 And He was saying to them, "Take care what you listen to. ᵃBy your standard of measure it shall be measured to you; and more shall be given you besides.

25 "ᵃFor whoever has, to him shall *more* be given; and whoever does not have, even what he has shall be taken away from him."

3 The seed growing gradually, 4:26-29

26 And He was saying, "ᵃThe kingdom of God is like a man who casts seed upon the soil;

27 and goes to bed at night and gets up by day, and the seed sprouts up and grows—how, he himself does not know.

28 "The soil produces crops by itself; first the blade, then the head, then the mature grain in the head.

29 "But when the crop permits, he immediately puts in the sickle, because the harvest has come."

4 The mustard seed, 4:30-34

30 ᵃAnd He said, "How shall we ᵇpicture the kingdom of God, or by what parable shall we present it?

31 "*It is* like a mustard seed, which, when sown upon the soil, though it is smaller than all the seeds that are upon the soil,

32 yet when it is sown, grows up and becomes larger than all the garden plants and forms large branches; so that THE BIRDS OF THE AIR CAN NEST UNDER ITS SHADE."

33 And with many such parables He was speaking the word to them as they were able to hear it;

34 and He did not speak to them ᵃwithout a parable; but He was explaining everything privately to His own disciples.

F His Prerogatives, 4:35-9:1

1 Over the storm, 4:35-41

35 ᵃAnd on that day, when evening had come, He *said to

Margin references

★19 ᵃMatt. 13:22

21 ᵃMatt. 5:15; Luke 8:16; 11:33

22 ᵃMatt. 10:26; Luke 8:17; 12:2

23 ᵃMatt. 11:15; Mark 4:9

24 ᵃMatt. 7:2; Luke 6:38

25 ᵃMatt. 13:12

★26-29
26 ᵃMatt. 13:24-30; Mark 4:26-29

30 ᵃMark 4:30-32; Matt. 13:31, 32; Luke 13:18, 19
ᵇMatt. 13:24
★31

34 ᵃMatt. 13:34; John 10:6; 16:25

35 ᵃMark 4:35-41; Matt. 8:18, 23-27; Luke 8:22, 25

4:19 *desires for other things.* I.e., desire for things other than the gospel.

4:26-29 The Word of God, when sown in men's hearts, produces fruit sometimes slowly but always surely (see 1 Pet. 1:23-25).

4:31 *a mustard seed.* Though it has one of the smallest seeds and is an herb, the Palestinian mustard plant grows to a height of 10 or 12 feet. It pictures the phenomenally rapid spread of Christianity from a small beginning.

them, "Let us go over to the other side."

36 aMark 3:9; 4:1; 5:2, 21

36 And leaving the multitude, they *took Him along with them, just as He was, ain the boat; and other boats were with Him.

37 And there *arose a fierce gale of wind, and the waves were breaking over the boat so much that the boat was already filling up.

38 And He Himself was in the stern, asleep on the cushion; and they *awoke Him and *said to Him, "Teacher, do You not care that we are perishing?"

39 And being aroused, He rebuked the wind and said to the sea, "Hush, be still." And the wind died down and it became perfectly calm.

40 And He said to them, "Why are you so timid? How is it that you have no faith?"

★**41**

41 And they became very much afraid and said to one another, "Who then is this, that even the wind and the sea obey Him?"

2 Over demons, 5:1-20

1 aMark 5:1-17; Matt. 8:28-34; Luke 8:26-37

2 aMark 3:9; 4:1, 36; 5:21 bMark 1:23

5 aAnd they came to the other side of the sea, into the country of the Gerasenes.

2 And when He had come out of athe boat, immediately a man from the tombs bwith an unclean spirit met Him,

3 and he had his dwelling among the tombs. And no one was able to bind him anymore, even with a chain;

4 because he had often been bound with shackles and chains, and the chains had been torn apart by him, and the shackles broken in pieces, and no one was strong enough to subdue him.

5 And constantly night and day, among the tombs and in the mountains, he was crying out and gashing himself with stones.

6 And seeing Jesus from a distance, he ran up and bowed down before Him;

★ **7** aMatt. 8:29 bMatt. 4:3 cLuke 8:28; Acts 16:17; Heb. 7:1

7 and crying out with a loud voice, he *said, "aWhat do I have to do with You, Jesus, bSon of cthe Most High God? I implore You by God, do not torment me!"

8 For He had been saying to him, "Come out of the man, you unclean spirit!"

★ **9** aMatt. 26:53; Mark 5:15; Luke 8:30

9 And He was asking him, "What is your name?" And he *said to Him, "My name is aLegion; for we are many."

10 And he *began* to entreat Him earnestly not to send them out of the country.

11 Now there was a big herd of swine feeding there on the mountain.

12 And *the* demons entreated Him, saying, "Send us into the swine so that we may enter them."

13 And He gave them permission. And coming out, the unclean spirits entered the swine; and the herd rushed down the steep bank into the sea, about two thousand *of them*; and they were drowned in the sea.

14 And their herdsmen ran away and reported it in the city and *out* in the country. And *the people* came to see what it was that had happened.

15 aMatt. 4:24; Mark 5:16, 18 bLuke 8:27 cLuke 8:35 dMark 5:9

15 And they *came to Jesus and *observed the man who had been ademon-possessed sitting down, bclothed and cin his right mind, the very man who had had the "dlegion"; and they became frightened.

4:41 *they became very much afraid.* The disciples were rebuked (v. 40) for being *timid*, literally, "cowardly." In v. 41 the word *afraid* refers to reverential, respectful awe for the Lord. In exclaiming, *Who then is this*, they acknowledged that He was greater than they thought.

5:7 *What do I have to do with You.* Today we would say instead, "What have you to do with me?" *Jesus, Son of the Most High God.*

Though this apparently was his first encounter with Jesus, this man knew who He was, such knowledge coming to him from the demons who indwelt him.

5:9 *Legion.* The largest unit of the Roman army, 3000-6000 strong, indicating that many demons possessed the man (see Matt. 12:45 and Luke 8:2).

16 aMatt. 4:24; Mark 5:15

16 And those who had seen it described to them how it had happened to the ademon-possessed man, and *all* about the swine.

17 And they began to entreat Him to depart from their region.

18 aMark 5:18-20; Luke 8:38, 39 bMatt. 4:24; Mark 5:15, 16

18 aAnd as He was getting into the boat, the man who had been bdemon-possessed was entreating Him that he might accompany Him.

19 And He did not let him, but He *said to him, "Go home to your people and report to them what great things the Lord has done for you, and *how* He had mercy on you."

★**20** aMatt. 4:25; Mark 7:31

20 And he went away and began to proclaim in aDecapolis what great things Jesus had done for him; and everyone marveled.

3 Over sickness and death, 5:21-43

21 aMatt. 9:1; Luke 8:40 bMark 4:36 cMark 4:1

21 aAnd when Jesus had crossed over again in bthe boat to the other side, a great multitude gathered about Him; and He stayed cby the seashore.

★**22** aMark 5:22-43; Matt. 9:18-26; Luke 8:41-56 bMatt. 9:18; Mark 5:35, 36, 38; Luke 8:49; 13:14; Acts 13:15; 18:8, 17 **23** aMark 6:5; 7:32; 8:23; 16:18; Luke 4:40; 13:13; Acts 6:6; 9:17; 28:8

22 aAnd one of bthe synagogue officials named Jairus *came up, and upon seeing Him, *fell at His feet,

23 and *entreated Him earnestly, saying, "My little daughter is at the point of death; *please* come and alay Your hands on her, that she may get well and live."

24 And He went off with him; and a great multitude was following Him and pressing in on Him.

25 And a woman who had had a hemorrhage for twelve years,

26 and had endured much at the hands of many physicians, and had spent all that she had and

was not helped at all, but rather had grown worse,

27 after hearing about Jesus, came up in the crowd behind *Him*, and touched His cloak.

28 For she thought, "If I just touch His garments, I shall get well."

29 aMark 3:10; 5:34

29 And immediately the flow of her blood was dried up; and she felt in her body that she was healed of her aaffliction.

30 aLuke 5:17

30 And immediately Jesus, perceiving in Himself that athe power *proceeding* from Him had gone forth, turned around in the crowd and said, "Who touched My garments?"

31 And His disciples said to Him, "You see the multitude pressing in on You, and You say, 'Who touched Me?'"

32 And He looked around to see the woman who had done this.

33 But the woman fearing and trembling, aware of what had happened to her, came and fell down before Him, and told Him the whole truth.

★**34** aMatt. 9:22 bLuke 7:50; 8:48; Acts 16:36; James 2:16 cMark 3:10; 5:29 **35** aMark 5:22

34 And He said to her, "Daughter, ayour faith has made you well; bgo in peace, and be healed of your caffliction."

35 While He was still speaking, they *came from the *house of* the asynagogue official, saying, "Your daughter has died; why trouble the Teacher anymore?"

★**36** aMark 5:22 bLuke 8:50

36 But Jesus, overhearing what was being spoken, *said to the asynagogue official, "bDo not be afraid *any longer*, only believe."

37 aMatt. 17:1; 26:37

37 And He allowed no one to follow with Him, except aPeter and James and John the brother of James.

★**38** aMark 5:22

38 And they *came to the

5:20 *Decapolis*, the region SE. of the Sea of Galilee, in which were located 10 cities originally, although the number varied from time to time. They were Greek in organization and culture.

5:22 *one of the synagogue officials*. Jairus was an elder in the synagogue at Capernaum which Jesus attended.

5:34 *your faith has made you well*. I.e., your faith has made possible your recovery.

5:36 *only believe*. Lit., just keep on believing! There are no limits, Christ says, to what faith in the power of God can do.

5:38 *loudly weeping and wailing*. These professional mourners were hired by the family.

house of the [a]synagogue official; and He *beheld a commotion, and *people* loudly weeping and wailing.

★39   **39** And entering in, He *said to them, "Why make a commotion and weep? The child has not died, but is asleep."

40 And they *began* laughing at Him. But putting them all out, He *took along the child's father and mother and His own companions, and *entered the *room* where the child was.

41 [a]Luke 7:14; Acts 9:40   **41** And taking the child by the hand, He *said to her, "Talitha kum!" (which translated means, "Little girl, [a]I say to you, arise!")

42 And immediately the girl rose and *began* to walk; for she was twelve years old. And immediately they were completely astounded.

43 [a]Matt. 8:4   **43** And He [a]gave them strict orders that no one should know about this; and He said that *something* should be given her to eat.

4   Rejected by His own townspeople, 6:1–6

★ 1 [a]Mark 6:1-6; Matt. 13:54-58 [b]Matt. 13:54, 57; Luke 4:16, 23   **6** [a]And He went out from there, and He *came into [b]His home town; and His disciples *followed Him.

2 [a]Matt. 4:23; Mark 10:1 [b]Matt. 7:28   **2** And when the Sabbath had come, He began [a]to teach in the synagogue; and the [b]many listeners were astonished, saying, "Where did this man *get* these things, and what is *this* wisdom given to Him, and such miracles as these performed by His hands?

★ 3 [a]Matt. 13:55 [b]Matt. 12:46 [c]Matt. 13:56 [d]Matt. 11:6   **3** "Is not this [a]the carpenter, [b]the son of Mary, and brother of James, and Joses, and Judas, and

Simon? Are not [c]His sisters here with us?" And they took [d]offense at Him.

4 And Jesus said to them, "[a]A prophet is not without honor except in [b]his home town and among his *own* relatives and in his *own* household."

4 [a]Matt. 13:57 [b]Mark 6:1

5 And He could do no miracle there except that He [a]laid His hands upon a few sick people and healed them.

5 [a]Mark 5:23

6 And He wondered at their unbelief.

[a]And He was going around the villages teaching.

6 [a]Matt. 9:35; Mark 1:39; 10:1; Luke 13:22

5   In commissioning The Twelve, 6:7–13

7 [a]And [b]He *summoned the twelve and began to send them out [c]in pairs; and He was giving them authority over the unclean spirits;

7 [a]Mark 6:7-11; Matt. 10:1, 9-14; Luke 9:1, 3-5; Luke 10:4-11 [b]Matt. 10:1, 5; Mark 3:13; Luke 9:1 [c]Luke 10:1

8 [a]and He instructed them that they should take nothing for *their* journey, except a mere staff; no bread, no bag, no money in their belt;

8 [a]Matt. 10:10

9 but *to* wear sandals; and He added, "Do not put on two tunics."

10 And He said to them, "Wherever you enter a house, stay there until you leave town.

11 "And any place that does not receive you or listen to you, as you go out from there, [a]shake off the dust from the soles of your feet for a testimony against them."

★11 [a]Matt. 10:14

12 [a]And they went out and preached that *men* should repent.

12 [a]Matt. 11:1; Luke 9:6

13 And they were casting out many demons and [a]were anointing with oil many sick people and healing them.

13 [a]James 5:14

5:39   *is asleep.* The girl had been pronounced dead (Luke 8:53). Christ's reference to death as sleep was intended to suggest that her condition was temporary and that she would come back to life again.

6:1   *His home town.* Lit., His native place; i.e., Nazareth.

6:3   *brother of.* The four half brothers and two or more half sisters were children of Joseph and Mary born after Jesus (Matt. 1:25). James

became the leader of the church in Jerusalem and author of the Epistle of James. Jude wrote the letter that bears his name. *they took offense.* Something stood in the way of their believing in Him.

6:11   *shake off the dust.* An action that symbolized a complete break in fellowship and renunciation of all further responsibility. See Acts 13:51; 18:6.

6 As affecting Herod, who killed John the Baptist, 6:14-29

★14 aMark
6:14-29;
Matt. 14:1-
12; Mark
6:14-16;
Luke 9:7-9
bMatt. 14:2

14 aAnd King Herod heard of it, for His name had become well known; and *people* were saying, "bJohn the Baptist has risen from the dead, and that is why these miraculous powers are at work in Him."

15 aMatt.
16:14; Mark
8:28 bMatt.
21:11

15 But others were saying, "He is aElijah." And others were saying, "He is ba prophet, like one of the prophets of old."

16 But when Herod heard of it, he kept saying, "John, whom I beheaded, has risen!"

★17 aMatt.
14:3

17 For Herod himself had sent and had John arrested and bound in prison on account of aHerodias, the wife of his brother Philip, because he had married her.

★18 aMatt.
14:4

18 For John had been saying to Herod, "aIt is not lawful for you to have your brother's wife."

19 aMatt.
14:3

19 And aHerodias had a grudge against him and wanted to put him to death and could not do so;

20 aMatt.
21:26

20 for aHerod was afraid of John, knowing that he was a righteous and holy man, and kept him safe. And when he heard him, he was very perplexed; but he used to enjoy listening to him.

21 aEsther
1:3, 2:18
bLuke 3:1

21 And a strategic day came when Herod on his birthday agave a banquet for his lords and military commanders and the leading men bof Galilee;

22 aMatt.
14:3

22 and when the daughter of aHerodias herself came in and danced, she pleased Herod and his dinner guests; and the king said to the girl, "Ask me for whatever you want and I will give it to you."

23 aEsther
5:3, 6; 7:2

23 And he swore to her, "Whatever you ask of me, I will give it to you; up to ahalf of my kingdom."

24 And she went out and said to her mother, "What shall I ask for?" And she said, "The head of John the Baptist."

25 And immediately she came in haste before the king and asked, saying, "I want you to give me right away the head of John the Baptist on a platter."

26 And although the king was very sorry, *yet* because of his oaths and because of his dinner guests, he was unwilling to refuse her. ★26

27 And immediately the king sent an executioner and commanded *him* to bring *back* his head. And he went and had him beheaded in the prison,

28 and brought his head on a platter, and gave it to the girl; and the girl gave it to her mother.

29 And when his disciples heard *about this,* they came and took away his body and laid it in a tomb.

7 In feeding 5000 men, 6:30-44

30 aLuke
9:10 bMatt.
10:2 [Mark
3:14 in Gr.];
Luke 6:13;
9:10; 17:5;
22:14; 24:10;
Acts 1:2, 26
31 aMark
3:20

30 aAnd the bapostles *gathered together with Jesus; and they reported to Him all that they had done and taught.

31 And He *said to them, "Come away by yourselves to a lonely place and rest a while." (For there were many *people* coming and going, and athey did not even have time to eat.)

32 aMark
6:32-44;
Matt. 14:13-
21; Luke
9:10-17;
John 6:5-13;
Mark 8:2-9
bMark 3:9;
4:36; 6:45

32 aAnd they went away in bthe boat to a lonely place by themselves.

33 And the people saw them going, and many recognized *them,* and they ran there together on foot from all the cities, and got there ahead of them.

★34 aMatt.
9:36

34 And when He went ashore, He asaw a great

6:14　*King Herod.* Herod Antipas, tetrarch of Galilee and Perea from 4 B.C.–A.D. 39. Officially he was not a king, but this title for him was popularly used.

6:17　*Philip.* Herod's brother, but not the same Philip mentioned in Luke 3:1. Herodias, who was married to Herod Philip, left him to live with another uncle, Herod Antipas.

6:18　*not lawful.* See Mark 10:11; Lev. 18:16.

6:26　*because of his oaths.* In the ancient Near East an oath was considered to be irrevocable.

6:34　*a shepherd.* See Num. 27:17; 1 Kings 22:17; Ezek. 34:5.

multitude, and He felt compassion for them because ªthey were like sheep without a shepherd; and He began to teach them many things.

35 And when it was already quite late, His disciples came up to Him and *began* saying, "The place is desolate and it is already quite late;

36 send them away so that they may go into the surrounding countryside and villages and buy themselves something to eat."

★37 ªJohn 6:7 ᵇMatt. 18:28; Luke 7:41

37 But He answered and said to them, "You give them *something* to eat!" ªAnd they *said to Him, "Shall we go and spend two hundred ᵇdenarii on bread and give them *something* to eat?"

38 And He *said to them, "How many loaves do you have? Go look!" And when they found out, they *said, "Five and two fish."

39 And He commanded them all to recline by groups on the green grass.

40 And they reclined in companies of hundreds and of fifties.

41 ªMatt. 14:19

41 And He took the five loaves and the two fish, and looking up toward heaven, He ªblessed *the food* and broke the loaves and He kept giving *them* to the disciples to set before them; and He divided up the two fish among them all.

42 And they all ate and were satisfied.

43 ªMatt. 14:20

43 And they picked up twelve full ªbaskets of the broken pieces, and also of the fish.

★44 ªMatt. 14:21

44 And there were ªfive thousand men who ate the loaves.

8 *In walking on water,* 6:45-52

★45 ªMark 6:45-51; Matt. 14:22-32; John 6:15-21 ᵇMark 6:32 ᶜMatt. 11:21; Mark 8:22

45 ªAnd immediately He made His disciples get into ᵇthe boat and go ahead of *Him* to the

other side to ᶜBethsaida, while He Himself was sending the multitude away.

46 And after ªbidding them farewell, He departed ᵇto the mountain to pray.

46 ªActs 18:18, 21; 2 Cor. 2:13 ᵇMatt. 14:23

47 And when it was evening, the boat was in the midst of the sea, and He *was* alone on the land.

48 And seeing them straining at the oars, for the wind was against them, at about the ªfourth watch of the night, He *came to them, walking on the sea; and He intended to pass by them.

★48 ªMatt. 24:43; Mark 13:35

49 But when they saw Him walking on the sea, they supposed that it was a ghost, and cried out;

50 for they all saw Him and were frightened. But immediately He spoke with them and *said to them, "ªTake courage; it is I, ᵇdo not be afraid."

50 ªMatt. 9:2 ᵇMatt. 14:27

51 And He got into ªthe boat with them, and the wind stopped; and they were greatly astonished.

51 ªMark 6:32

52 for ªthey had not gained any insight from the *incident of* the loaves, but their heart ᵇwas hardened.

★52 ªMark 8:17ff. ᵇRom. 11:7

9 *Over sickness,* 6:53-56

53 ªAnd when they had crossed over they came to land at Gennesaret, and moored to the shore.

★53 ªMark 6:53-56; Matt. 14:34-36; John 6:24, 25

54 And when they had come out of the boat, immediately *the people* recognized Him,

55 and ran about that whole country and began to carry about on their pallets those who were sick, to the place they heard He was.

56 And wherever He entered villages, or cities, or countryside, they were laying the sick in the

56 ªMark 3:10 ᵇMatt. 9:20

6:37 *two hundred denarii.* The basic Roman silver coin used in Palestine, the denarius was a rural worker's average daily wage.

6:44 *five thousand men.* The count did not include women and children.

6:45 *Bethsaida.* About 2 miles N. of the Sea of Galilee.

6:48 *the fourth watch.* From 3 to 6 a.m.

6:52 *their heart was hardened.* I.e., they were spiritually insensitive to the truth concerning the deity of Christ which His miracles were continually demonstrating.

6:53 *land at Gennesaret.* On the NE. shore of the Sea of Galilee.

market places, and entreating Him that they might just [a]touch [b]the fringe of His cloak; and as many as touched it were being cured.

10　Over the Pharisees' traditions, 7:1–23

★ 1 [a]Mark 7:1-23; Matt. 15:1-20
[b]Matt. 15:1

7 [a]And the Pharisees and some of the scribes gathered together around Him when they had come [b]from Jerusalem,

2 [a]Matt. 15:2; Mark 7:5; Luke 11:38; Acts 10:14, 28; 11:8; Rom. 14:14; Heb. 10:29; Rev. 21:27

2 and had seen that some of His disciples were eating their bread with [a]impure hands, that is, unwashed.

★ 3 [a]Mark 7:5, 8, 9, 13; Gal. 1:14

3 (For the Pharisees and all the Jews do not eat unless they carefully wash their hands, *thus* observing the [a]traditions of the elders;

4 [a]Matt. 23:25

4 and *when they come* from the market place, they do not eat unless they cleanse themselves; and there are many other things which they have received in order to observe, such as the washing of [a]cups and pitchers and copper pots.)

★ 5 [a]Mark 7:3, 8, 9, 13; Gal. 1:14
[b]Mark 7:2

5 And the Pharisees and the scribes *asked Him, "Why do Your disciples not walk according to the [a]tradition of the elders, but eat their bread with [b]impure hands?"

6 [a]Is. 29:13

6 And He said to them, "Rightly did Isaiah prophesy of you hypocrites, as it is written,

'[a]THIS PEOPLE HONORS ME WITH THEIR LIPS,
BUT THEIR HEART IS FAR AWAY FROM ME.

7 '[a]BUT IN VAIN DO THEY WORSHIP ME,
TEACHING AS DOCTRINES THE PRECEPTS OF MEN.'

7 [a]Is. 29:13

8 "Neglecting the commandment of God, you hold to the [a]tradition of men."

★ 8 [a]Mark 7:3, 5, 9, 13; Gal. 1:14

9 He was also saying to them, "You nicely set aside the commandment of God in order to keep your [a]tradition.

9 [a]Mark 7:3, 5, 8, 13; Gal. 1:14

10 "For Moses said, '[a]HONOR YOUR FATHER AND YOUR MOTHER'; and, '[b]HE WHO SPEAKS EVIL OF FATHER OR MOTHER, LET HIM BE PUT TO DEATH';

★10 [a]Ex. 20:12; Deut. 5:16 [b]Ex. 21:17; Lev. 20:9

11 but you say, 'If a man says to *his* father or *his* mother, anything of mine you might have been helped by is [a]Corban (that is to say, given *to God*),'

★11 [a]Lev. 1:2; Matt. 27:6

12 you no longer permit him to do anything for *his* father or *his* mother;

13 *thus* invalidating the word of God by your [a]tradition which you have handed down; and you do many things such as that."

13 [a]Mark 7:3, 5, 8, 9; Gal. 1:14

14 And after He called the multitude to Him again, He *began saying to them, "Listen to Me, all of you, and understand:

15 there is nothing outside the man which going into him can defile him; but the things which proceed out of the man are what defile the man.

16 ["If any man has ears to hear, let him hear."]

★16

17 And when leaving the multitude, He had entered [a]the house, [b]His disciples questioned Him about the parable.

17 [a]Mark 2:1; 3:19; 9:28 [b]Matt. 15:15

7:1 *scribes.* See note on Matt. 2:4.
7:3 *the traditions of the elders.* The unwritten body of commands and teachings of honored rabbis of the past, the authoritative source of scribal teachings.
7:5 *impure hands.* This does not mean dirty hands but hands not washed according to the rules of the elders, and therefore not free of ceremonial defilement.
7:8 Christ is here criticizing the reinterpretation and debasement of the law by the scribes and Pharisees who viewed oral tradition as more authoritative than the written law of the O.T.

He then illustrated the point (vv. 9–13).
7:10 *Moses said.* See Ex. 20:12; Deut. 5:16. For *who speaks evil* see Ex. 21:17.
7:11 *Corban.* The transliteration of a Hebrew word meaning a "gift." The word referred to something devoted to God by an inviolable vow. If a son declared that the amount needed to support his parents was Corban, the scribes said that he was exempt from his duty to care for his parents as prescribed in the law. Evidently, too, he was not really obliged to devote that sum to the temple.
7:16 Most manuscripts do not contain this verse.

18 And He *said to them, "Are you so lacking in understanding also? Do you not understand that whatever goes into the man from outside cannot defile him;

19 because it does not go into his heart, but into his stomach, and is eliminated?" (*Thus He* declared a all foods b clean.)

20 And He was saying, "a That which proceeds out of the man, that is what defiles the man.

21 "For from within, out of the heart of men, proceed the evil thoughts, fornications, thefts, murders, adulteries,

22 deeds of coveting *and* wickedness, *as well as* deceit, sensuality, a envy, slander, pride *and* foolishness.

23 "All these evil things proceed from within and defile the man."

11 Over a Syrophoenician woman, 7:24–30

24 a And from there He arose and went away to the region of b Tyre. And when He had entered a house, He wanted no one to know *of it;* yet He could not escape notice.

25 But after hearing of Him, a woman whose little daughter had an unclean spirit, immediately came and fell at His feet.

26 Now the woman was a Gentile, of the Syrophoenician race. And she kept asking Him to cast the demon out of her daughter.

27 And He was saying to her, "Let the children be satisfied first, for it is not good to take the children's bread and throw it to the dogs."

28 But she answered and *said to Him, "Yes, Lord, *but*

even the dogs under the table feed on the children's crumbs."

29 And He said to her, "Because of this answer go your way; the demon has gone out of your daughter."

30 And going back to her home, she found the child lying on the bed, the demon having departed.

12 Over a deaf mute, 7:31–37

31 a And again He went out from the region of b Tyre, and came through Sidon to c the Sea of Galilee, within the region of d Decapolis.

32 And they *brought to Him one who was deaf and spoke with difficulty, and they *entreated Him to a lay His hand upon him.

33 And a He took him aside from the multitude by himself, and put His fingers into his ears, and after a spitting, He touched his tongue *with the saliva;*

34 and looking up to heaven with a deep a sigh, He *said to him, "Ephphatha!" that is, "Be opened!"

35 And his ears were opened, and the impediment of his tongue was removed, and he *began* speaking plainly.

36 And a He gave them orders not to tell anyone; but the more He ordered them, the more widely they b continued to proclaim it.

37 And they were utterly astonished, saying, "He has done all things well; He makes even the deaf to hear, and the dumb to speak."

13 In feeding 4000, 8:1–9

8 In those days again, when there was a great multitude

---

19 a Rom. 14:1-12; Col. 2:16 b Luke 11:41; Acts 10:15; 11:9

20 a Matt. 15:18; Mark 7:23

22 a Matt. 6:23; 20:15

24 a Mark 7:24-30; Matt. 15:21-28 b Matt. 11:21; Mark 7:31

31 a Mark 7:31-37; Matt. 15:29-31 b Matt. 11:21; Mark 7:24 c Matt. 4:18 d Matt. 4:25; Mark 5:20

32 a Mark 5:23

33 a Mark 8:23

34 a Mark 8:12

36 a Matt. 8:4 b Mark 1:45

1 a Mark 8:1-9; Matt. 15:32-39; [Mark 6:34-44]

7:18 *cannot defile him.* Foods declared to be "unclean" are specified in Lev. 11. Jesus is here not abrogating the law but making the point that sin comes from the heart. Thus the defilement that came to a Jew who ate "unclean" food was caused not by the food itself but by the rebellious heart that acted in disobedience to God.

7:26 *Syrophoenician.* By birth this Gentile woman was a Syrian from the region of Phoenicia.

7:27 *the dogs.* See note on Matt. 15:26.

7:30 This miracle was performed from a distance, without any vocal command from Christ.

and they had nothing to eat, [a]He called His disciples and *said to them,

2 [a] Matt. 9:36; Mark 6:34

2 "[a]I feel compassion for the multitude because they have remained with Me now three days, and have nothing to eat;

3 and if I send them away hungry to their home, they will faint on the way; and some of them have come from a distance."

4 And His disciples answered Him, "Where will anyone be able to *find enough to* satisfy these men with bread here in a desolate place?"

5 And He was asking them, "How many loaves do you have?" And they said, "Seven."

6 And He *directed the multitude to sit down on the ground; and taking the seven loaves, He gave thanks and broke them, and started giving them to His disciples to serve to them, and they served the multitude.

7 [a] Matt. 14:19

7 They also had a few small fish; and [a]after He had blessed them, He ordered these to be served as well.

★ **8** [a] Matt. 15:37; Mark 8:20

8 And they ate and were satisfied; and they picked up seven large [a]baskets full of what was left over of the broken pieces.

9 And about four thousand were *there;* and He sent them away.

14 **In condemning the Pharisees,** 8:10-13

★**10** [a] Matt. 15:39

10 And immediately He entered the boat with His disciples, and came to the district of [a]Dalmanutha.

★**11** [a] Mark 8:11-21; Matt. 16:1-12 [b] Matt. 12:38

11 [a]And the Pharisees came out and began to argue with Him,

[b]seeking from Him a sign from heaven, to test Him.

12 And [a]sighing deeply in His spirit, He *said, "Why does this generation seek for a sign? Truly I say to you, no sign shall be given to this generation."

12 [a] Mark 7:34

13 And leaving them, He again embarked and went away to the other side.

15 **In His teaching on leaven,** 8:14-21

14 And they had forgotten to take bread; and did not have more than one loaf in the boat with them.

15 And He was giving orders to them, saying, "[a]Watch out! Beware of the leaven of the Pharisees and the leaven of [b]Herod."

★**15** [a] Matt. 16:6; Luke 12:1 [b] Matt. 14:1; 22:16

16 And they *began* to discuss with one another *the fact* that they had no bread.

17 And Jesus, aware of this, *said to them, "Why do you discuss *the fact* that you have no bread? [a]Do you not yet see or understand? Do you have a hardened heart?

★**17** [a] Mark 6:52

18 "[a]Having eyes, do you not see? And having ears, do you not hear? And do you not remember,

18 [a] Ezek. 12:2

19 when I broke [a]the five loaves for the five thousand, how many [b]baskets full of broken pieces you picked up?" They *said to Him, "Twelve."

19 [a] Mark 6:41-44 [b] Matt. 14:20

20 "And when I broke [a]the seven for the four thousand, how many large [b]baskets full of broken pieces did you pick up?" And they *said to Him, "Seven."

20 [a] Mark 8:6-9 [b] Mark 8:8

21 And He was saying to them, "[a]Do you not yet understand?"

21 [a] Mark 6:52

8:8 *seven large baskets.* The word *basket* itself (in the Greek) denotes larger baskets than the word used of the twelve baskets in which the leftovers were collected from the feeding of the 5,000 (6:43). The larger basket was the kind used to let Paul down over the wall of Damascus (Acts 9:25).
8:10 *Dalmanutha.* An unknown location.
8:11 *a sign from heaven.* The Pharisees wanted

a startling miracle or celestial portent which would prove that Jesus was the Messiah. They did not believe, however, that He could provide such a sign.
8:15 *the leaven of the Pharisees* was hypocrisy (Luke 12:1) and *the leaven of Herod* was secularism and worldliness.
8:17 *Why do you discuss.* See note on Matt. 16:8.

16 Over blindness, 8:22-26

22 ᵃMatt.
11:21; Mark
6:45 ᵇMark
3:10

22 And they *came to ᵃBeth-saida. And they *brought a blind man to Him, and *entreated Him to ᵇtouch him.

23 ᵃMark
7:33 ᵇMark
5:23

23 And taking the blind man by the hand, He ᵃbrought him out of the village; and after ᵃspitting on his eyes, and ᵇlaying His hands upon him, He asked him, "Do you see anything?"

24 And he looked up and said, "I see men, for I am seeing *them* like trees, walking about."

★25

25 Then again He laid His hands upon his eyes; and he looked intently and was restored, and *began* to see everything clearly.

26 ᵃMatt. 8:4
ᵇMark 8:23

26 And He sent him to his home, saying, "ᵃDo not even enter ᵇthe village."

17 Over Peter, 8:27-33

★27-30

★27 ᵃMark
8:27-29;
Matt. 16:13-16; Luke
9:18-20
ᵇMatt. 16:13

27 ᵃAnd Jesus went out, along with His disciples, to the villages of ᵇCaesarea Philippi; and on the way He questioned His disciples, saying to them, "Who do people say that I am?"

28 ᵃMark
6:14

28 ᵃAnd they told Him, saying, "John the Baptist; and others *say* Elijah; but others, one of the prophets."

29 And He *continued* by questioning them, "But who do you say that I am?" Peter *answered and *said to Him, "Thou art the Christ."

30 ᵃMatt.
8:4; 16:20;
Luke 9:21
★31 ᵃMark
8:31-9:1;
Matt. 16:21-28; Luke
9:22-27
ᵇMatt. 16:21

30 And ᵃHe warned them to tell no one about Him.

31 ᵃAnd He began to teach them that ᵇthe Son of Man must suffer many things and be rejected by the elders and the chief priests and the scribes, and be killed, and after three days rise again.

32 ᵃJohn
10:24; 11:14;
16:25, 29;
18:20

32 And He was stating the matter ᵃplainly. And Peter took Him aside and began to rebuke Him.

★33 ᵃMatt.
4:10

33 But turning around and seeing His disciples, He rebuked Peter, and *said, "Get behind Me, ᵃSatan; for you are not setting your mind on God's interests, but man's."

18 Over the lives of His disciples, 8:34-9:1

★34 ᵃMatt.
10:38

34 And He summoned the multitude with His disciples, and said to them, "If anyone wishes to come after Me, let him deny himself, and ᵃtake up his cross, and follow Me.

★35 ᵃMatt.
10:39

35 "For ᵃwhoever wishes to save his life shall lose it; but whoever loses his life for My sake and the gospel's shall save it.

36 "For what does it profit a man to gain the whole world, and forfeit his soul?

37 "For what shall a man give in exchange for his soul?

38 ᵃMatt.
10:33; Luke
9:26; Heb.
11:16 ᵇMatt.
8:20 ᶜMatt.
16:27; Mark
13:26; Luke
9:27

38 "For ᵃwhoever is ashamed of Me and My words in this adulterous and sinful generation, ᵇthe Son of Man will also be ashamed of him when He ᶜcomes in the glory of His Father with the holy angels."

★1 ᵃMatt.
16:27; Mark
13:26; Luke
9:27

9 And He was saying to them, "ᵃTruly I say to you, there

8:25 This miracle was performed in stages.

8:27-30 See notes on Matt. 16:13, 14.

8:27 *Caesarea Philippi.* A city about 25 miles N. of the Sea of Galilee, built by Herod Philip in honor of Caesar Augustus.

8:31 *the Son of Man must suffer.* Christ expanded, for the disciples, the concept of Son of Man, who, in Daniel's vision (Dan. 7:13-14) and in the apocryphal book of Enoch, is not described as suffering and dying. The idea was unthinkable, as Peter declared (Mark 8:32). This was Jesus' first prediction of His death (see 9:31; 10:33-34).

8:33 *Get behind Me, Satan.* Peter was used by Satan to try to dissuade Christ from going to the cross.

8:34 *take up his cross.* See notes on Matt. 10:38 and Luke 9:23.

8:35 The verse means: Whoever would save his life (by renouncing the gospel and thus avoiding the risk of martyrdom) will lose it (eternally because he has not believed the gospel); but whoever is willing to lose his life (as a martyr for Christ) will save it (i.e., will prove that he is a follower of Christ and an heir of eternal life).

9:1 *until they see the kingdom of God after it has come with power.* See note on Matt. 16:28.

are some of those who are standing here who shall not taste death until they see the kingdom of God after it has come with power."

G His Previews, 9:2-50
1 Of His glory, 9:2-29

2 ^aAnd six days later, Jesus *took with Him ^bPeter and James and John, and *brought them up to a high mountain by themselves. And He was transfigured before them;

3 and ^aHis garments became radiant and exceedingly white, as no launderer on earth can whiten them.

4 And Elijah appeared to them along with Moses; and they were talking with Jesus.

5 And Peter answered and *said to Jesus, "^aRabbi, it is good for us to be here; and ^blet us make three tabernacles, one for You, and one for Moses, and one for Elijah."

6 For he did not know what to answer; for they became terrified.

7 Then a cloud formed, overshadowing them, and ^aa voice came out of the cloud, "^bThis is My beloved Son, listen to Him!"

8 And all at once they looked around and saw no one with them anymore, except Jesus alone.

9 ^aAnd as they were coming down from the mountain, He ^bgave them orders not to relate to anyone what they had seen, until the Son of Man should rise from the dead.

10 And they seized upon that statement, discussing with one another what rising from the dead might mean.

11 And they asked Him, saying, *"Why is it* that the scribes say that ^aElijah must come first?"

12 And He said to them, "Elijah does first come and restore all things. And *yet* how is it written of ^athe Son of Man that ^bHe should suffer many things and be treated with contempt?

13 "But I say to you, that Elijah has indeed come, and they did to him whatever they wished, just as it is written of him."

14 ^aAnd when they came *back* to the disciples, they saw a large crowd around them, and *some* scribes arguing with them.

15 And immediately, when the entire crowd saw Him, they were ^aamazed, and *began* running up to greet Him.

16 And He asked them, "What are you discussing with them?"

17 And one of the crowd answered Him, "Teacher, I brought You my son, possessed with a spirit which makes him mute;

18 and whenever it seizes him, it dashes him *to the ground* and he foams *at the mouth,* and grinds his teeth, and stiffens out.

9:2 *six days later.* Luke 9:28 says "some eight days" which includes the beginning and ending days as well as the interval between of six full days. *up to a high mountain.* Either Mt. Tabor, 10 miles SW. of the Sea of Galilee, or Mt. Hermon, 40 miles NE. of the Sea of Galilee. *transfigured = transformed.*
9:4 *Elijah.* Elijah's return was expected (Mal. 4:5-6). *talking with Jesus.* Luke tells what they were talking about (9:31).
9:5 *and let us make three tabernacles.* Booths of intertwined branches. Peter thought they would be there a while so they might as well get settled down! His suggestion also implied that he viewed Jesus, Moses, and Elijah as being equal. God's answer was to remove Moses and Elijah from view (v. 8) and to declare the uniqueness of His Son (v. 7).
9:10 *rising from the dead.* I.e., Christ's resurrection from the dead, not resurrection in general.
9:11-13 The progression of thought is this: If Elijah is to come before the last day and "restore the hearts" (Mal. 4:5-6), why should the Son of Man have to die? Christ replied that they are correct about Elijah but that their concept of the Son of Man was deficient, since it did not include the truths of His suffering and death (Ps. 22:6; Isa. 53). Then Christ adds (Mark 9:13) that Elijah already had come, and been unrecognized, in John the Baptist. See also the note on Matt. 17:11-12.

Marginal references:

★ 2 ^aMark 9:2-8; Matt. 17:1-8; Luke 9:28-36 ^bMark 5:37

3 ^aMatt. 28:3

★ 4

★ 5 ^aMatt. 23:7 ^bMatt. 17:4; Luke 9:33

7 ^a2 Pet. 1:17f. ^bMatt. 3:17; Mark 1:11

9 ^aMark 9:9-13; Matt. 17:9-13 ^bMatt. 8:4; Mark 5:43; 7:36; 8:30

★10

★11-13

11 ^aMatt. 11:14

12 ^aMark 9:31 ^bMatt. 16:21; 26:24

14 ^aMark 9:14-28; Matt. 17:14-19; Luke 9:37-42

15 ^aMark 14:33; 16:5, 6

And I told Your disciples to cast it out, and they could not *do it.*"

19 And He *answered them and *said, "O unbelieving generation, how long shall I be with you? How long shall I put up with you? Bring him to Me!"

20 And they brought the boy to Him. And when he saw Him, immediately the spirit threw him into a convulsion, and falling to the ground, he *began* rolling about and foaming *at the mouth.*

21 And He asked his father, "How long has this been happening to him?" And he said, "From childhood.

22 "And it has often thrown him both into the fire and into the water to destroy him. But if You can do anything, take pity on us and help us!"

★23 *a*Matt. 17:20; John 11:40
23 And Jesus said to him, " 'If You can!' *a*All things are possible to him who believes."

★24
24 Immediately the boy's father cried out and *began* saying, "I do believe; help my unbelief."

25 *a*Mark 9:15
25 And when Jesus saw that *a*a crowd was rapidly gathering, He rebuked the unclean spirit, saying to it, "You deaf and dumb spirit, I command you, come out of him and do not enter him again."

26 And after crying out and throwing him into terrible convulsions, it came out; and *the boy* became so much like a corpse that most *of them* said, "He is dead!"

27 But Jesus took him by the hand and raised him; and he got up.

28 *a*Mark 2:1; 7:17
28 And when He had come *a*into *the* house, His disciples *began* questioning Him privately, "Why could we not cast it out?"

★29
29 And He said to them, "This kind cannot come out by anything but prayer."

2 Of His death, 9:30–32

30 *a*Mark 9:30-32; Matt. 17:22-23; Luke 9:43-45
30 *a*And from there they went out and *began* to go through Galilee, and He was unwilling for anyone to know *about it.*

★31 *a*Matt. 16:21; Mark 8:31; 9:12
31 For He was teaching His disciples and telling them, "*a*The Son of Man is to be delivered into the hands of men, and they will kill Him; and when He has been killed, He will rise three days later."

★32 *a*Luke 2:50; 9:45; 18:34; John 12:16
32 But *a*they did not understand *this* statement, and they were afraid to ask Him.

3 Of rewards, 9:33–41

33 *a*Mark 9:33-37; Matt. [17:24] 18:1-5; Luke 9:46-48
*b*Mark 3:19
33 *a*And they came to Capernaum; and when He was in *b*the house, He *began* to question them, "What were you discussing on the way?"

34 *a*Mark 9:50; Luke 22:24
34 But they kept silent, for on the way *a*they had discussed with one another which *of them was* the greatest.

35 *a*Matt. 20:26
35 And sitting down, He called the twelve and *said to them, "*a*If anyone wants to be first, he shall be last of all, and servant of all."

36 And taking a child, He set him before them, and taking him in His arms, He said to them,

37 *a*Matt. 10:40
37 "*a*Whoever receives one child like this in My name receives Me; and whoever receives Me does not receive Me, but Him who sent Me."

38 *a*Mark 9:38-40; Luke 9:49-50
*b*Num. 11:27-29
38 *a*John said to Him, "Teacher, we saw someone casting out demons in Your name, and *b*we tried to hinder him because he was not following us."

39 But Jesus said, "Do not hinder him, for there is no one who shall perform a miracle in

---

9:23 *All things are possible.* See note on Matt. 17:20.

9:24 *help my unbelief.* The man cried for help for his own weak faith.

9:29 *This kind.* I.e., this kind of demon can be conquered only by prayer. Some manuscripts add the words, "and fasting."

9:31 *they will kill Him.* The second prediction of His death (see 8:31; 10:33–34).

9:32 *and they were afraid to ask Him.* Perhaps because of the rebuke to Peter (8:32–33).

My name, and be able soon afterward to speak evil of Me.

40 "[a]For he who is not against us is for us.

41 "For [a]whoever gives you a cup of water to drink because of your name as *followers* of Christ, truly I say to you, he shall not lose his reward.

4 Of hell, 9:42-50

42 "And [a]whoever causes one of these little ones who believe to stumble, it would be better for him if, with a heavy millstone hung around his neck, he had been cast into the sea.

43 "And [a]if your hand causes you to stumble, cut it off; it is better for you to enter life crippled, than having your two hands, to go into [b]hell, into the [c]unquenchable fire,

44 [where THEIR WORM DOES NOT DIE, AND THE FIRE IS NOT QUENCHED.]

45 "And if your foot causes you to stumble, cut it off; it is better for you to enter life lame, than having your two feet, to be cast into [a]hell,

46 [where THEIR WORM DOES NOT DIE, AND THE FIRE IS NOT QUENCHED.]

47 "And [a]if your eye causes you to stumble, cast it out; it is better for you to enter the kingdom of God with one eye, than having two eyes, to be cast into [b]hell,

48 [a]where THEIR WORM DOES NOT DIE, AND [b]THE FIRE IS NOT QUENCHED.

49 "For everyone will be salted with fire.

50 "Salt is good; but [a]if the salt becomes unsalty, with what will you make it salty *again*? [b]Have

salt in yourselves, and [c]be at peace with one another."

H His Preaching in Perea, 10:1-52

1 Concerning divorce, 10:1-12

10 [a]And rising up, He *went from there to the region of Judea, and beyond the Jordan; and crowds *gathered around Him again, and, [b]according to His custom, He once more *began* to teach them.

2 And *some* Pharisees came up to Him, testing Him, and *began* to question Him whether it was lawful for a man to divorce a wife.

3 And He answered and said to them, "What did Moses command you?"

4 And they said, "[a]Moses permitted *a man* TO WRITE A CERTIFICATE OF DIVORCE AND SEND *her* AWAY."

5 But Jesus said to them, "[a]Because of your hardness of heart he wrote you this commandment.

6 "But [a]from the beginning of creation, God [b]MADE THEM MALE AND FEMALE.

7 "[a]FOR THIS CAUSE A MAN SHALL LEAVE HIS FATHER AND MOTHER,

8 [a]AND THE TWO SHALL BECOME ONE FLESH; consequently they are no longer two, but one flesh.

9 "What therefore God has joined together, let no man separate."

10 And in the house the disciples *began* questioning Him about this again.

11 And He *said to them, "[a]Whoever divorces his wife and marries another woman commits adultery against her;

Margin references:

40 [a]Matt. 12:30
41 [a]Matt. 10:42
*42 [a]Matt. 18:6; Luke 17:2; 1 Cor. 8:12
43 [a]Matt. 5:30; 17:27; 18:8 [b]Matt. 5:22 [c]Matt. 3:12; 25:41
*44
45 [a]Matt. 5:22
47 [a]Matt. 5:29; 17:27; 18:9 [b]Matt. 5:22
48 [a]Is. 66:24 [b]Matt. 3:12; 25:41
*49
*50 [a]Matt. 5:13; Luke 14:34f. [b]Col. 4:6 [c]Mark 9:34; Rom. 12:18; 2 Cor. 13:11; 1 Thess. 5:13

1 [a]Mark 10:1-12; Matt. 19:1-9 [b]Matt. 4:23; 26:55; Mark 1:21; 2:13; 4:2; 6:2, 6, 34; 12:35; 14:49
4 [a]Deut. 24:1, 3
5 [a]Matt. 19:8
* 6 [a]Mark 13:19; 2 Pet. 3:4 [b]Gen. 1:27; 5:2
7 [a]Gen. 2:24
8 [a]Gen. 2:24
*11-12
11 [a]Matt. 5:32

9:42 *causes . . . to stumble.* I.e., causes to fall into sin. So also in vv. 43, 45, 47.

9:44 Many manuscripts do not contain verses 44 and 46, which are identical to verse 48.

9:49 *salted with fire.* Just as salt preserves, everyone who enters hell will be preserved through an eternity of torment.

9:50 *Have salt in yourselves.* Christ's followers

are to be permeated with this preserving power, which influences the world for good.

10:6 *male and female.* See Gen. 2:21-25; it presupposes and enjoins monogamy. The Mosaic law concerning divorce was a concession to the people, not a part of God's original purpose.

10:11-12 See notes on Matt. 5:32 and 19:4-5.

12 *a*1 Cor. 7:11, 13

12 and *a*if she herself divorces her husband and marries another man, she is committing adultery."

2 Concerning children,
10:13-16

13 *a*Mark 10:13-16; Matt. 19:13-15; Luke 18:15-17

13 *a*And they were bringing children to Him so that He might touch them; and the disciples rebuked them.

★14 *a*Matt. 5:3

14 But when Jesus saw this, He was indignant and said to them, "Permit the children to come to Me; do not hinder them; *a*for the kingdom of God belongs to such as these.

15 *a*Matt. 18:3; 19:14; Luke 18:17; 1 Cor. 14:20; 1 Pet. 2:2

15 "Truly I say to you, *a*whoever does not receive the kingdom of God like a child shall not enter it *at all.*"

16 *a*Mark 9:36

16 And He *a*took them in His arms and *began* blessing them, laying His hands upon them.

3 Concerning eternal life,
10:17-31

17 *a*Mark 10:17-31; Matt. 19:16-30; Luke 18:18-30; *b*Mark 1:40; *c*Matt. 25:34; Luke 10:25; 18:18; Acts 20:32; Eph. 1:18; 1 Pet. 1:4
★18

17 *a*And as He was setting out on a journey, a man ran up to Him and *b*knelt before Him, and *began* asking Him, "Good Teacher, what shall I do to *c*inherit eternal life?"

18 And Jesus said to him, "Why do you call Me good? No one is good except God alone.

19 *a*Ex. 20:12-16; Deut. 5:16-20

19 "You know the commandments, '*a*Do not murder, Do not commit adultery, Do not steal, Do not bear false witness, Do not defraud, Honor your father and mother.'"

20 *a*Matt. 19:20

20 And he said to Him, "Teacher, I have kept *a*all these things from my youth up."

★21 *a*Matt. 6:20

21 And looking at him, Jesus felt a love for him, and said to

him, "One thing you lack: go and sell all you possess, and give to the poor, and you shall have *a*treasure in heaven; and come, follow Me."

22 But at these words his face fell, and he went away grieved, for he was one who owned much property.

23 And Jesus, looking around, *said to His disciples, "*a*How hard it will be for those who are wealthy to enter the kingdom of God!"

23 *a*Matt. 19:23

24 And the disciples *a*were amazed at His words. But Jesus *answered again and *said to them, "Children, how hard it is to enter the kingdom of God!

24 *a*Mark 1:27

25 "*a*It is easier for a camel to go through the eye of a needle than for a rich man to enter the kingdom of God."

★25 *a*Matt. 19:24

26 And they were even more astonished and said to Him, "Then who can be saved?"

27 Looking upon them, Jesus *said, "*a*With men it is impossible, but not with God; for all things are possible with God."

★27 *a*Matt. 19:26

28 *a*Peter began to say to Him, "Behold, we have left everything and followed You."

28 *a*Matt. 4:20-22

29 Jesus said, "Truly I say to you, *a*there is no one who has left house or brothers or sisters or mother or father or children or farms, for My sake and for the gospel's sake,

29 *a*Matt. 6:33; 19:29; Luke 18:29f.

30 but that he shall receive a hundred times as much now in the present age, houses and brothers and sisters and mothers and children and farms, along with persecutions; and in *a*the age to come, eternal life.

30 *a*Matt. 12:32

31 "But *a*many *who are* first, will be last; and the last, first."

31 *a*Matt. 19:30

10:14 *the kingdom of God belongs to such as these.* In order to enter the kingdom we must come to Christ in childlike faith.

10:18 *Why do you call Me good?* "Good" was a designation reserved, in the absolute sense, for God. Jesus was reacting to being addressed thus by someone who had no awareness of His divine nature.

10:21 Christ was trying to show the man that, in reality, his love of money violated the law and made him a sinner.

10:25 *eye of a needle.* See note on Matt. 19:24.

10:27 *all things are possible with God.* Also taught in the O.T. (Gen. 18:14; Job 42:2).

4 Concerning His own death and resurrection, 10:32-34

★32 aMark
10:32-34;
Matt. 20:17-
19; Luke
18:31-33
bMark 1:27
32 ^aAnd they were on the road, going up to Jerusalem, and Jesus was walking on ahead of them; and they ^bwere amazed, and those who followed were fearful. And again He took the twelve aside and began to tell them what was going to happen to Him,

★33-34

33 aMark
8:31; 9:12
33 saying, "Behold, we are going up to Jerusalem, and ^athe Son of Man will be delivered to the chief priests and the scribes; and they will condemn Him to death, and will deliver Him to the Gentiles.

34 aMatt.
16:21; 26:67;
27:30; Mark
9:31; 14:65
34 "And they will mock Him and ^aspit upon Him, and scourge Him, and kill Him, and three days later He will rise again."

5 Concerning ambition, 10:35-45

35 aMark
10:35-45;
Matt. 20:20-
28
35 ^aAnd James and John, the two sons of Zebedee, *came up to Him, saying to Him, "Teacher, we want You to do for us whatever we ask of You."

36 And He said to them, "What do you want Me to do for you?"

★37 aMatt.
19:28
37 And they said to Him, "Grant that we ^amay sit in Your glory, one on Your right, and one on Your left."

★38 aMatt.
20:22 bLuke
12:50
38 But Jesus said to them, "You do not know what you are asking for. Are you able ^ato drink the cup that I drink, or ^bto be baptized with the baptism with which I am baptized?"

★39 aActs
12:2; Rev.
1:9
39 And they said to Him, "We are able." And Jesus said to them, "The cup that I drink ^ayou shall drink; and you shall be baptized with the baptism with which I am baptized.

40 aMatt.
13:11
40 "But to sit on My right or on My left, this is not Mine to give; ^abut it is for those for whom it has been prepared."

41 aMark
10:42-45;
Luke 22:25-
27
41 ^aAnd hearing this, the ten began to feel indignant with James and John.

42 And calling them to Himself, Jesus *said to them, "You know that those who are recognized as rulers of the Gentiles lord it over them; and their great men exercise authority over them.

43 aMatt.
20:26; Mark
9:35
43 "But it is not so among you, ^abut whoever wishes to become great among you shall be your servant;

44 and whoever wishes to be first among you shall be slave of all.

45 aMatt.
20:28
45 "For even the Son of Man ^adid not come to be served, but to serve, and to give His life a ransom for many."

6 To blind Bartimaeus, 10:46-52

★46-52

46 aMark
10:46-52;
Matt. 20:29-
34; Luke
18:35-43
bLuke 18:35;
19:1
46 ^aAnd they *came to Jericho. And ^bas He was going out from Jericho with His disciples and a great multitude, a blind beggar named Bartimaeus, the son of Timaeus, was sitting by the road.

47 aMark
1:24 bMatt.
9:27
47 And when he heard that it was Jesus the ^aNazarene, he began to cry out and say, "Jesus, ^bSon of David, have mercy on me!"

48 aMatt.
9:27
48 And many were sternly telling him to be quiet, but he kept crying out all the more, "^aSon of David, have mercy on me!"

10:32 going up. Jerusalem is over 2500 feet above sea level. Their probable route was down the Jordan Valley, below sea level, then up to Jerusalem. amazed. At Jesus' determination to go on to Jerusalem.

10:33-34 The third prediction of His death (see 8:31; 9:31).

10:37 in Your glory. I.e., in the Messianic kingdom (see Matt. 20:21).

10:38 the cup . . . the baptism. Figures of speech for Christ's coming sufferings (see Mark 14:36 and Luke 12:50).

10:39 James did die as a martyr (Acts 12:2) and John suffered exile (Rev. 1:9).

10:46-52 For a comparison of the different accounts of this miracle, see the note on Matt. 20:29-34.

49 *a*Matt. 9:2   **49** And Jesus stopped and said, "Call him *here*." And they *called the blind man, saying to him, "*a*Take courage, arise! He is calling for you."

50 And casting aside his cloak, he jumped up, and came to Jesus.

51 *a*Matt. 23:7; John 20:16   **51** And answering him, Jesus said, "What do you want Me to do for you?" And the blind man said to Him, "*a*Rabboni, *I want* to regain my sight!"

★**52** *a*Matt. 9:22   **52** And Jesus said to him, "Go your way; *a*your faith has made you well." And immediately he regained his sight and *began* following Him on the road.

II THE SACRIFICE OF THE SERVANT, 11:1-15:47

A Triumphal Entry into Jerusalem on Sunday, 11:1-11

1 *a*Mark 11:1-10; Matt. 21:1-9; Luke 19:29-38 *b*Matt. 21:17 *c*Matt. 21:1

11 *a*And as they *approached Jerusalem, at Bethphage and *b*Bethany, near *c*the Mount of Olives, He *sent two of His disciples,

★**2**   **2** and *said to them, "Go into the village opposite you, and immediately as you enter it, you will find a colt tied *there*, on which no one yet has ever sat; untie it and bring it *here*.

3 "And if anyone says to you, 'Why are you doing this?' you say, 'The Lord has need of it'; and immediately he will send it back here."

4 And they went away and found a colt tied at the door outside in the street; and they *untied it.

5 And some of the bystanders were saying to them, "What are you doing, untying the colt?"

6 And they spoke to them just as Jesus had told *them*, and they gave them permission.

7 *a*And they *brought the colt to Jesus and put their garments on it; and He sat upon it.

7 *a*Mark 11:7-10; John 12:12-15

8 And many spread their garments in the road, and others *spread* leafy branches which they had cut from the fields.

9 And those who went before, and those who followed after, were crying out,

★**9** *a*Ps. 118:26; Matt. 21:9

"*a*Hosanna!
Blessed is He who comes in
the name of the Lord;

10 Blessed *is* the coming kingdom of our father David;
Hosanna *a*in the highest!"

★**10** *a*Matt. 21:9

11 And *a*He entered Jerusalem *and came* into the temple; and after looking all around, *b*He departed for Bethany with the twelve, since it was already late.

11 *a*Matt. 21:12 *b*Matt. 21:17

B Cursing of the Fig Tree and Cleansing of the Temple on Monday, 11:12-19

12 *a*And on the next day, when they had departed from Bethany, He became hungry.

12 *a*Mark 11:12-14 [20-24]; Matt. 21:18-22 ★**13**

13 And seeing at a distance a fig tree in leaf, He went *to see* if perhaps He would find anything on it; and when He came to it, He found nothing but leaves, for it was not the season for figs.

14 And He answered and said to it, "May no one ever eat fruit from you again!" And His disciples were listening.

15 *a*And they *came to Jerusalem. And He entered the temple and began to cast out those who were buying and selling in the temple, and overturned the

★**15** *a*Mark 11:15-18; Matt. 21:12-16; Luke 19:45-47; John 2:13-16

10:52 *your faith has made you well.* Cf. 5:34.
11:2 *the village opposite you.* Bethphage, on the S. side of the Mount of Olives.
11:9 *Hosanna* = Save now! This occasion was the fulfillment of Zech. 9:9. In a few days the same crowd who now hailed Him would desert Him.
11:10 *kingdom of our father David.* I.e., the

Messianic kingdom.
11:13 *fig tree.* See note on Matt. 21:19.
11:15 *cast out those who were buying and selling.* This is the second time Christ purged the temple (see John 2:13-17, the beginning of His ministry). The animals, guaranteed to be without blemish, were sold for sacrificial purposes,

tables of the moneychangers and the seats of those who were selling doves;

16 and He would not permit anyone to carry goods through the temple.

17 And He *began* to teach and say to them, "Is it not written, '*a*MY HOUSE SHALL BE CALLED A HOUSE OF PRAYER FOR ALL THE NATIONS'? *b*But you have made it a ROBBERS' DEN.'

18 And the chief priests and the scribes heard *this*, and *a*began seeking how to destroy Him; for they were afraid of Him, for *b*all the multitude was astonished at His teaching.

19 And *a*whenever evening came, they would go out of the city.

C   Teaching on Tuesday, 11:20–13:37

1   Concerning faith, 11:20–26

20 *a*And as they were passing by in the morning, they saw the fig tree withered from the roots up.

21 And being reminded, Peter *said to Him, "*a*Rabbi, behold, the fig tree which You cursed has withered."

22 And Jesus *answered saying to them, "*a*Have faith in God.

23 "Truly I say to you, whoever says to this mountain, 'Be taken up and cast into the sea,' and does not doubt in his heart, but believes that what he says is going to happen, it shall be *granted* him.

24 "Therefore I say to you, *a*all things for which you pray and ask, believe that you have received them, and they shall be *granted* you.

25 "And whenever you *a*stand praying, *b*forgive, if you have anything against anyone; so that your Father also who is in heaven may forgive you your transgressions.

26 ["*a*But if you do not forgive, neither will your Father who is in heaven forgive your transgressions."]

2   Concerning His authority, 11:27–33

27 And they *came again to Jerusalem. *a*And as He was walking in the temple, the chief priests, and scribes, and elders *came to Him,

28 and *began* saying to Him, "By what authority are You doing these things, or who gave You this authority to do these things?"

29 And Jesus said to them, "I will ask you one question, and you answer Me, and *then* I will tell you by what authority I do these things.

30 "Was the baptism of John from heaven, or from men? Answer Me."

31 And they *began* reasoning among themselves, saying, "If we say, 'From heaven,' He will say, 'Then why did you not believe him?'

32 "But shall we say, 'From men'?"—they were afraid of the multitude, for all considered John to have been a prophet indeed.

33 And answering Jesus, they *said, "We do not know." And Jesus *said to them, "Neither will I tell you by what authority I do these things."

---

and Greek and Roman coinage was changed into the standard half-shekel required for the temple tax. The merchants were guilty of profanation of the temple and of excess profiteering.

11:17 See Isa. 56:7 and Jer. 7:11.

11:24 *all things for which you pray.* This principle is qualified by Christ in other teaching (Matt. 6:10) and in His own life (Mark 14:36).

11:25 *stand praying.* In ancient worship this was the normal position of prayer.

11:26 Many manuscripts do not contain this verse.

11:28 *these things.* I.e., the cleansing of the temple (vv. 15–18).

11:30 *Answer Me.* Christ placed these Jewish leaders on the horns of a dilemma. Whichever answer they gave would have condemned them.

3 Concerning the Jewish nation, 12:1-12

★ 1-12

1 aMark
3:23; 4:2ff.
bMark 12:1-
12; Matt.
21:33-46;
Luke 20:9-19
cIs. 5:2

12 *a*And He began to speak to them in parables: "*b*A man *c*PLANTED A VINEYARD, AND PUT A WALL AROUND IT, AND DUG A VAT UNDER THE WINE PRESS, AND BUILT A TOWER, and rented it out to vine-growers and went on a journey.

2 "And at the *harvest* time he sent a slave to the vine-growers, in order to receive *some* of the produce of the vineyard from the vine-growers.

3 "And they took him, and beat him, and sent him away empty-handed.

4 "And again he sent them another slave, and they wounded him in the head, and treated him shamefully.

5 "And he sent another, and that one they killed; and *so with* many others, beating some, and killing others.

6 "He had one more *to send*, a beloved son; he sent him last *of all* to them, saying, 'They will respect my son.'

7 "But those vine-growers said to one another, 'This is the heir; come, let us kill him, and the inheritance will be ours!'

8 "And they took him, and killed him, and threw him out of the vineyard.

9 "What will the owner of the vineyard do? He will come and destroy the vine-growers, and will give the vineyard to others.

★10 aPs.
118:22

10 "Have you not even read this Scripture:

'*a*THE STONE WHICH THE BUILDERS REJECTED, THIS BECAME THE CHIEF CORNER *stone*;

11 aPs.
118:23

11 '*a*THIS CAME ABOUT FROM THE LORD, AND IT IS MARVELOUS IN OUR EYES'?"

12 aMark
11:18 bMatt.
22:22

12 And *a*they were seeking to seize Him; and *yet* they feared the multitude; for they understood that He spoke the parable against them. And so *b*they left Him, and went away.

4 Concerning taxes, 12:13-17

13 aMark
12:13-17;
Matt. 22:15-
22; Luke
20:20-26
bMatt. 22:16
cLuke 11:54

13 *a*And they *sent some of the Pharisees and *b*Herodians to Him, in order to *c*trap Him in a statement.

★14

14 And they *came and *said to Him, "Teacher, we know that You are truthful, and defer to no one; for You are not partial to any, but teach the way of God in truth. Is it lawful to pay a poll-tax to Caesar, or not?

★15

15 "Shall we pay, or shall we not pay?" But He, knowing their hypocrisy, said to them, "Why are you testing Me? Bring Me a denarius to look at."

16 And they brought *one*. And He *said to them, "Whose likeness and inscription is this?" And they said to Him, "Caesar's."

17 aMatt.
22:21

17 And Jesus said to them, "*a*Render to Caesar the things that are Caesar's, and to God the things that are God's." And they were amazed at Him.

5 Concerning resurrection, 12:18-27

★18 aMark
12:18-27;
Matt. 22:23-
33; Luke
20:27-38

18 *a*And *some* Sadducees (who say that there is no resurrection) *came to Him, and *began questioning Him, saying,

---

12:1-12 This parable, addressed to the obdurate religious leaders of Israel, illustrates God's dealings with that people. The man (v. 1) is God. The vineyard (v. 1) is Israel. The servants (vv. 2-5) are the O.T. prophets and John the Baptist. The son whom they killed is Jesus (vv. 6-8). The prediction of the destruction of the vine-growers (v. 9) was fulfilled when Jerusalem was destroyed in A.D. 70.

12:10 *The stone.* See Ps. 118:22-23 and the use of the cornerstone figure in Acts 4:11; 1 Pet. 2:6-7.
12:14 *defer to no one.* I.e., you're no flatterer, you play up to no one. Yet their own opening remark employs flattery. *poll-tax to Caesar.* See note on Matt. 22:17.
12:15 *a denarius.* See note on Mark 6:37.
12:18 *Sadducees.* See note on Matt. 3:7.

★19 aDeut.
25:5

19 "Teacher, Moses wrote for us that ªIF A MAN'S BROTHER DIES, and leaves behind a wife, AND LEAVES NO CHILD, HIS BROTHER SHOULD TAKE THE WIFE, AND RAISE UP OFFSPRING TO HIS BROTHER. **20** "There were seven brothers; and the first took a wife, and died, leaving no offspring. **21** "And the second one took her, and died, leaving behind no offspring; and the third likewise; **22** and so all seven left no offspring. Last of all the woman died also. **23** "In the resurrection, when they rise again, which one's wife will she be? For all seven had her as wife." **24** Jesus said to them, "Is this not the reason you are mistaken, that you do not understand the Scriptures, or the power of God?

★25

25 "For when they rise from the dead, they neither marry, nor are given in marriage, but are like angels in heaven.

★26 aLuke
20:37; Rom.
11:2 bEx.
3:6

26 "But regarding the fact that the dead rise again, have you not read in the book of Moses, ªin the *passage about the burning* bush, how God spoke to him, saying, ᵇI AM THE GOD OF ABRAHAM, AND THE GOD OF ISAAC, AND THE GOD OF JACOB'?

27 aMatt.
22:32; Luke
20:38

27 "ªHe is not the God of the dead, but of the living; you are greatly mistaken."

6 Concerning the greatest commandments,
12:28-34

28 aMark
12:28-34;
Matt. 22:34-
40; Luke
10:25-28;
20:39f.
bMatt. 22:34;
Luke 20:39

28 ªAnd one of the scribes came and heard them arguing, and ᵇrecognizing that He had answered them well, asked Him, "What commandment is the foremost of all?"

29 Jesus answered, "The foremost is, ªHEAR, O ISRAEL! THE LORD OUR GOD IS ONE LORD; **30** ªAND YOU SHALL LOVE THE LORD YOUR GOD WITH ALL YOUR HEART, AND WITH ALL YOUR SOUL, AND WITH ALL YOUR MIND, AND WITH ALL YOUR STRENGTH.' **31** "The second is this, ªYOU SHALL LOVE YOUR NEIGHBOR AS YOURSELF.' There is no other commandment greater than these." **32** And the scribe said to Him, "Right, Teacher, You have truly stated that ªHE IS ONE; AND THERE IS NO ONE ELSE BESIDES HIM; **33** ªAND TO LOVE HIM WITH ALL THE HEART AND WITH ALL THE UNDERSTANDING AND WITH ALL THE STRENGTH, AND TO LOVE ONE'S NEIGHBOR AS HIMSELF, ᵇis much more than all burnt offerings and sacrifices." **34** And when Jesus saw that he had answered intelligently, He said to him, "You are not far from the kingdom of God." ªAnd after that, no one would venture to ask Him any more questions.

7 Concerning His deity,
12:35-37

35 ªAnd Jesus answering *began* to say, as He ᵇtaught in the temple, "How *is it that* the scribes say that the Christ is the ᶜson of David? **36** "David himself said in the Holy Spirit,

'ªTHE LORD SAID TO MY LORD,
"SIT AT MY RIGHT HAND,
UNTIL I PUT THINE ENEMIES
BENEATH THY FEET." '

37 "David himself calls Him 'Lord'; and so in what sense is He his son?" And ªthe great crowd enjoyed listening to Him.

★29 aDeut.
6:4

30 aDeut.
6:5

★31 aLev.
19:18

32 aDeut.
4:35

★33 aDeut.
6:5 b1 Sam.
15:22; Hos.
6:6; Mic. 6:6-
8; Matt. 9:13;
12:7

34 aMatt.
22:46

★35 aMark
12:35-37;
Matt. 22:41-
46; Luke
20:41-44
bMatt. 26:55;
Mark 10:1
cMatt. 9:27
36 aPs.
110:1

37 aJohn
12:9

12:19 See Deut. 25:5.
12:25 *like angels.* In the resurrection state there will be no conjugal union nor reproduction of children.
12:26 See Ex. 3:6. When God spoke to Moses, He was still associated with the patriarchs, though they had died many years before.

Thus there is life after death.
12:29 See Deut. 6:4.
12:31 See Lev. 19:18.
12:33 So taught the prophets (Isa. 1:11-17; Mic. 6:6-8).
12:35 See note on Matt. 22:44.

8 Concerning pride, 12:38-40

38 [a]And in His teaching He was saying: "Beware of the scribes who like to walk around in long robes, and *like* [b]respectful greetings in the market places,

39 and chief seats in the synagogues, and places of honor at banquets,

40 [a]who devour widows' houses, and for appearance's sake offer long prayers; these will receive greater condemnation."

9 Concerning giving, 12:41-44

41 [a]And He sat down opposite [b]the treasury, and *began* observing how the multitude were [c]putting money into the treasury; and many rich people were putting in large sums.

42 And a poor widow came and put in two small copper coins, which amount to a cent.

43 And calling His disciples to Him, He said to them, "Truly I say to you, this poor widow put in more than all the contributors to the treasury;

44 for they all put in out of their surplus, but she, out of her poverty, put in all she owned, all she had [a]to live on."

10 Concerning the future, 13:1-37

13 [a]And as He was going out of the temple, one of His disciples *said to Him, "Teacher, behold what wonderful stones and what wonderful buildings!"

2 And Jesus said to him, "Do you see these great buildings? [a]Not one stone shall be left upon another which will not be torn down."

3 And as He was sitting on [a]the Mount of Olives opposite the temple, [b]Peter and James and John and Andrew were questioning Him privately,

4 "Tell us, when will these things be, and what *will be* the sign when all these things are going to be fulfilled?"

5 And Jesus began to say to them, "See to it that no one misleads you.

6 "Many will come in My name, saying, '[a]I am *He!*' and will mislead many.

7 "And when you hear of wars and rumors of wars, do not be frightened; *those things* must take place; but *that is* not yet the end.

8 "For nation will arise against nation, and kingdom against kingdom; there will be earthquakes in various places; there will *also* be famines. These things are *merely* the beginning of birth pangs.

9 "But be on your guard; for they will [a]deliver you to the courts, and you will be flogged [b]in the synagogues, and you will stand before governors and kings for My sake, as a testimony to them.

10 "[a]And the gospel must first be preached to all the nations.

11 "[a]And when they arrest you and deliver you up, do not be anxious beforehand about what

---

★38 [a]Mark 12:38-40; Matt. 23:1-7; Luke 20:45-47 [b]Matt. 23:6; Luke 11:43

★39

★40 [a]Luke 20:47

★41 [a]Mark 12:41-44; Luke 21:1-4 [b]John 8:20 [c]2 Kin. 12:9

★42

44 [a]Luke 8:43; 15:12, 30; 21:4

★1 [a]Mark 13:1-37; Matt. 24; Luke 21:5-36

2 [a]Luke 19:44

3 [a]Matt. 21:1 [b]Matt. 17:1

★4

6 [a]John 8:24

★9 [a]Matt. 10:17 [b]Matt. 10:17

10 [a]Matt. 24:14

★11 [a]Mark 13:11-13; Matt. 10:19-22; Luke 21:12-17

12:38 *long robes.* The long flowing robe of a dignitary or wealthy man.

12:39 *chief seats.* Seats in the front row.

12:40 *devour widows' houses.* See note on Matt. 23:14.

12:41 *treasury.* A chest located in the temple area, designed to receive coins dropped in a spout.

12:42 *two small copper coins.* The smallest of copper coins, worth very little.

13:1 See note on Matt. 24:1.

13:4 *when will these things be?* There is a double perspective in Christ's answer: some of the events described were to be fulfilled in the destruction of Jerusalem in A.D. 70 and some are yet to be fulfilled during the tribulation days that precede His second coming.

13:9 *synagogues.* They were used as places of assembly and as courtrooms. Floggings were therefore administered in them (2 Cor. 11:24). These predictions began to be fulfilled in the book of Acts (see Acts 4:5ff.; 5:27ff.; 12:1ff.; 24:1ff.; 25:1ff.).

13:11 *deliver you up.* I.e., denounce you to the authorities.

you are to say, but say whatever is given you in that hour; for it is not you who speak, but *it is* the Holy Spirit.

12 "And brother will deliver brother to death, and a father *his* child; and children will rise up against parents and have them put to death.

★**13** aJohn 15:21

13 "And ªyou will be hated by all on account of My name, but the one who endures to the end, he shall be saved.

★**14** aMatt. 24:15 bDan. 9:27; 11:31; 12:11

14 "But ªwhen you see the bA-BOMINATION OF DESOLATION standing where it should not be (let the reader understand), then let those who are in Judea flee to the mountains.

15 "And let him who is on the housetop not go down, or enter in, to get anything out of his house;

16 and let him who is in the field not turn back to get his cloak.

17 "But woe to those who are with child and to those who nurse babes in those days!

18 "But pray that it may not happen in the winter.

19 aMark 10:6

19 "For those days will be a *time of* tribulation such as has not occurred ªsince the beginning of the creation which God created, until now, and never shall.

★**20**

20 "And unless the Lord had shortened *those* days, no life would have been saved; but for the sake of the elect whom He chose, He shortened the days.

21 "And then if anyone says to you, 'Behold, here is the Christ'; or, 'Behold, *He is* there'; do not believe *him;*

22 aMatt. 7:15 bMatt. 24:24; John 4:48

22 for false Christs and ªfalse prophets will arise, and will show

bsigns and bwonders, in order, if possible, to lead the elect astray.

23 "But take heed; behold, I have told you everything in advance.

★**23**

24 "But in those days, after that tribulation, ªTHE SUN WILL BE DARKENED, AND THE MOON WILL NOT GIVE ITS LIGHT,

24 aIs. 13:10

25 ªAND THE STARS WILL BE FALL-ING from heaven, and the powers that are in the heavens will be shaken.

25 aIs. 34:4

26 "ªAnd then they will see THE SON OF MAN bCOMING IN CLOUDS with great power and glory.

26 aDan. 7:13 bMatt. 16:27; Mark 8:38

27 "And then He will send forth the angels, and ªwill gather together His elect from the four winds, bfrom the farthest end of the earth, to the farthest end of heaven.

27 aDeut. 30:4 bZech. 2:6

28 "Now learn the parable from the fig tree: when its branch has already become tender, and puts forth its leaves, you know that summer is near.

★**28**

29 "Even so, you too, when you see these things happening, recognize that He is near, *right* at the door.

★**29**

30 "Truly I say to you, this generation will not pass away until all these things take place.

★**30**

31 "Heaven and earth will pass away, but My words will not pass away.

32 "ªBut of that day or hour no one knows, not even the angels in heaven, nor the Son, but the Father *alone.*

★**32** aMatt. 24:36; Acts 1:7

33 "Take heed, ªkeep on the alert; for you do not know when the *appointed* time is.

★**33** aEph. 6:18; Col. 4:2

34 "*It is* like a man, away on a journey, *who* upon leaving his house and putting his slaves in charge, *assigning* to each one his

---

13:13 *endures.* I.e., remains loyal.
13:14 *abomination of desolation.* See note on Matt. 24:15.
13:20 *the elect.* The elect (saved) remnant of Israel during the tribulation days. At the second coming, these people will be restored to Palestine (v. 27).
13:23 The third warning to be prepared; the others are in v. 5 and v. 9.

13:28 *the parable.* I.e., the principle illustrated by the fig tree.
13:29 *He.* The Son of Man (v. 26).
13:30 *this generation.* See note on Matt. 24:34.
13:32 *nor the Son.* In His humanity, Jesus did not know. See note on Phil. 2:7 on the self-limitation of Christ.
13:33 The fourth and final warning of this chapter.

task, also commanded the door-keeper to stay on the alert.

35 aMatt.
24:42; Mark
13:37 bMark
14:30 cMatt.
14:25; Mark
6:48

35 "Therefore, abe on the alert —for you do not know when the master of the house is coming, whether in the evening, at midnight, at bcockcrowing, or cin the morning—

36 aRom.
13:11

36 lest he come suddenly and find you aasleep.

37 aMatt.
24:42; Mark
13:35

37 "And what I say to you I say to all, 'aBe on the alert!' "

D Anointing by Mary and Agreement to Betray by Judas, on Wednesday, 14:1-11

★ **1** aMark
14:1, 2; Matt.
26:2-5; Luke
22:1, 2
bMark 14:12;
John 11:55;
13:1 cMatt.
12:14

14 aNow bthe Passover and Unleavened Bread was two days off; and the chief priests and the scribes cwere seeking how to seize Him by stealth, and kill *Him*;

2 for they were saying, "Not during the festival, lest there be a riot of the people."

★ **3** aMark
14:3-9; Matt.
26:6-13;
Luke 7:37-
39; John
12:1-8
bMatt. 21:17
cMatt. 26:61;
John 12:3

3 aAnd while He was in bBethany at the home of Simon the leper, and reclining *at the table*, there came a woman with an alabaster vial of very ccostly perfume of pure nard; *and* she broke the vial and poured it over His head.

★ **4**

4 But some were indignantly *remarking* to one another, "Why has this perfume been wasted?

★ **5**

5 "For this perfume might have been sold for over three hundred denarii, and *the money* given to the poor." And they were scolding her.

6 But Jesus said, "Let her alone; why do you bother her? She has done a good deed to Me.

7 "For athe poor you always have with you, and whenever you wish, you can do them good; but you do not always have Me.

★ **7** aDeut.
15:11; Matt.
26:11; John
12:8

8 "She has done what she could; ashe has anointed My body beforehand for the burial.

8 aJohn
19:40

9 "And truly I say to you, awherever the gospel is preached in the whole world, that also which this woman has done shall be spoken of in memory of her."

9 aMatt.
26:13

10 aAnd Judas Iscariot, bwho was one of the twelve, went off to the chief priests, in order to betray Him to them.

★**10-11**
10 aMark
14:10, 11;
Matt. 26:14-
16; Luke
22:3-6 bJohn
6:71
★**11**

11 And they were glad when they heard *this*, and promised to give him money. And he *began* seeking how to betray Him at an opportune time.

E Supper and Betrayal on Thursday, 14:12-52

1 Preparation for the Last Supper, 14:12-16

12 aAnd on the first day of bUnleavened Bread, when the Passover *lamb* was being csacrificed, His disciples *said to Him, "Where do You want us to go and prepare for You to eat the Passover?"

12 aMark
14:12-16;
Matt. 26:17-
19; Luke
22:7-13
bMatt. 26:17
cDeut. 16:5;
Mark 14:1;
Luke 22:7;
1 Cor. 5:7

13 And He *sent two of His disciples, and *said to them, "Go into the city, and a man will meet you carrying a pitcher of water; follow him;

★**13**

14:1 The feast of *the Passover*. One of Israel's three great yearly festivals (the other two were Pentecost and Tabernacles), commemorating their deliverance from Egypt on the night when God "passed over" the homes of the Israelites during the slaughter of the firstborn. It was celebrated on the 14th of Nisan (March–April) and was followed immediately by the Feast of Unleavened Bread, which continued from the 15th to the 21st. See Ex. 12.

14:3 *a woman*. Mary of Bethany (John 12:3). *nard*. A costly aromatic anointing oil extracted from an East Indian plant.

14:4 *wasted*. Judas had instigated the murmuring (John 12:4-6).

14:5 *three hundred denarii*. In purchasing power equivalent to 300 days' wages for a rural worker.

14:7 *the poor*. See note on Matt. 26:11.

14:10-11 Judas' motive in betraying Jesus was, in part, avarice (Matt. 26:15), though it may also have been related to his bitterness at Jesus' failure to be a political Messiah. Basically, however, Judas' act was inspired by Satan (John 12:6; 13:2, 27).

14:11 *opportune time*. I.e., in the absence of the multitude (Luke 22:6).

14:13 *a man . . . carrying a pitcher of water*. Since women usually performed this task, they would easily notice a man carrying water.

14 aLuke 2:7;
22:11

14 and wherever he enters, say to the owner of the house, 'The Teacher says, "Where is My ªguest room in which I may eat the Passover with My disciples?" '

15 "And he himself will show you a large upper room furnished *and* ready; and prepare for us there."

16 And the disciples went out, and came to the city, and found *it* just as He had told them; and they prepared the Passover.

2 Partaking of the Last Supper, 14:17-21

17 aMark
14:17-21;
Matt. 26:20-
24; Luke
22:14, 21-23;
John 13:18ff.

17 ªAnd when it was evening He *came with the twelve.

18 And as they were reclining *at table* and eating, Jesus said, "Truly I say to you that one of you will betray Me—one who is eating with Me."

19 They began to be grieved and to say to Him one by one, "Surely not I?"

20 And He said to them, *"It is* one of the twelve, one who dips with Me in the bowl.

★21

21 "For the Son of Man *is to* go, just as it is written of Him; but woe to that man by whom the Son of Man is betrayed! *It would have been* good for that man if he had not been born."

3 Institution of the Lord's Supper, 14:22-25

22 aMark
14:22-25;
Matt. 26:26-
29; Luke
22:17-20;
1 Cor. 11:23-
25; Mark
10:16 bMatt.
14:19

22 ªAnd while they were eating, He took *some* bread, and after a ᵇblessing He broke *it;* and gave *it* to them, and said, "Take *it;* this is My body."

23 And He took a cup, and when He had given thanks, He gave *it* to them; and they all drank from it.

★24

24 And He said to them, "This is My blood of the cov-

enant, which is *to be* shed on behalf of many.

25 "Truly I say to you, I shall never again drink of the fruit of the vine until that day when I drink it new in the kingdom of God."

★25

4 Walk to Gethsemane, 14:26-31

26 ªAnd after singing a hymn, they went out to ᵇthe Mount of Olives.

★26 aMatt.
26:30 bMatt.
21:1

27 ªAnd Jesus *said to them, "You will all fall away, because it is written, 'ᵇI WILL STRIKE DOWN THE SHEPHERD, AND THE SHEEP SHALL BE SCATTERED.'

27 aMark
14:27-31;
Matt. 26:31-
35 bZech.
13:7

28 "But after I have been raised, I will go before you to Galilee."

29 But Peter said to Him, *"Even* though all may fall away, yet I will not."

30 And Jesus *said to him, "Truly I say to you, that you yourself ªthis very night, before ᵇa cock crows twice, shall three times deny Me."

30 aMatt.
26:34 bMark
14:68, 72;
John 13:38

31 But *Peter* kept saying insistently, *"Even* if I have to die with You, I will not deny You!" And they all were saying the same thing, too.

5 Prayer in Gethsemane, 14:32-42

32 ªAnd they *came to a place named Gethsemane; and He *said to His disciples, "Sit here until I have prayed."

★32 aMark
14:32-42;
Matt. 26:36-
46; Luke
22:40-46

33 And He *took with Him Peter and James and John, and began to be very ªdistressed and troubled.

33 aMark
9:15; 16:5, 6

34 And He *said to them, "ªMy soul is deeply grieved to the point of death; remain here and keep watch."

34 aMatt.
26:38; John
12:27

35 And He went a little beyond *them,* and fell to the

★35 aMatt.
26:45; Mark
14:41

14:21 See Ps. 22 and Isa. 53.
14:24 *the covenant.* See Introduction to the New Testament. *shed* = poured out.
14:25 *until that day.* See note on Matt. 26:29.
14:26 *a hymn.* This would have been a portion

of Ps. 115-118, traditionally sung at this season.
14:32 *Gethsemane.* See note on Matt. 26:36.
14:35 *if it were possible.* I.e., in accordance with God's will.

ground, and *began* to pray that if it were possible, [a]the hour might pass Him by.

36 And He was saying, "[a]Abba! Father! All things are possible for Thee; remove this cup from Me; [b]yet not what I will, but what Thou wilt."

37 And He *came and *found them sleeping, and *said to Peter, "Simon, are you asleep? Could you not keep watch for one hour?

38 "[a]Keep watching and praying, that you may not come into temptation; the spirit is willing, but the flesh is weak."

39 And again He went away and prayed, saying the same words.

40 And again He came and found them sleeping, for their eyes were very heavy; and they did not know what to answer Him.

41 And He *came the third time, and *said to them, "Are you still sleeping and taking your rest? It is enough; [a]the hour has come; behold, the Son of Man is being betrayed into the hands of sinners.

42 "Arise, let us be going; behold, the one who betrays Me is at hand!"

6 Betrayal and arrest in Gethsemane, 14:43–52

43 [a]And immediately while He was still speaking, Judas, one of the twelve, *came up, accompanied by a multitude with swords and clubs, from the chief priests and the scribes and the elders.

44 Now he who was betraying Him had given them a signal, saying, "Whomever I shall kiss,

He is the one; seize Him, and lead Him away under guard."

45 And after coming, he immediately went to Him, saying, "[a]Rabbi!" and kissed Him.

46 And they laid hands on Him, and seized Him.

47 But a certain one of those who stood by drew his sword, and struck the slave of the high priest, and cut off his ear.

48 And Jesus answered and said to them, "Have you come out with swords and clubs to arrest Me, as against a robber?

49 "Every day I was with you [a]in the temple teaching, and you did not seize Me; but *this has happened* that the Scriptures might be fulfilled."

50 And they all left Him and fled.

51 And a certain young man was following Him, wearing *nothing but* a linen sheet over *his* naked *body*; and they *seized him.

52 But he left the linen sheet behind, and escaped naked.

F Trials and Crucifixion, on Friday, 14:53–15:47

1 Christ before Caiaphas, 14:53–65

53 [a]And they led Jesus away to the high priest; and all the chief priests and the elders and the scribes *gathered together.

54 And Peter had followed Him at a distance, [a]right into [b]the courtyard of the high priest; and he was sitting with the officers, and [c]warming himself at the fire.

55 Now the chief priests and the whole [a]Council kept trying to obtain testimony against Jesus to

Margin refs: ★36 [a]Rom. 8:15; Gal. 4:6 [b]Matt. 26:39 · 38 [a]Matt. 26:41 · ★41 [a]Mark 14:35 · 43 [a]Mark 14:43-50; Matt. 26:47-56; Luke 22:47-53; John 18:3-11 · 45 [a]Matt. 23:7 · ★47 · 49 [a]Mark 12:35 · ★53 [a]Mark 14:53-65; Matt. 26:57-68; John 18:12f., 19-24 · 54 [a]Mark 14:68 [b]Matt. 26:3 [c]Mark 14:67; John 18:18 · 55 [a]Matt. 5:22

14:36 *this cup.* See note on Matt. 26:39.
14:41 *Sleep on now, and take your rest.* Some understand this as a statement of reproach; others translate it as a question: Are you still sleeping . . .?
14:47 *one of those.* Peter (John 18:10).
14:53 *to the high priest.* The examination before Caiaphas and the Sanhedrin. See note on Matt. 26:57 for the order of Jesus' trials.

put Him to death; and they were not finding any.

56 For many were giving false testimony against Him, and *yet* their testimony was not consistent.

57 And some stood up and *began* to give false testimony against Him, saying,

58 "We heard Him say, '[a]I will destroy this temple made with hands, and in three days I will build another made without hands.' "

59 And not even in this respect was their testimony consistent.

60 And the high priest stood up *and came* forward and questioned Jesus, saying, "Do You make no answer? What is it that these men are testifying against You?"

61 [a]But He kept silent, and made no answer. [b]Again the high priest was questioning Him, and saying to Him, "Are You the Christ, the Son of the Blessed One?"

62 And Jesus said, "I am; and you shall see [a]THE SON OF MAN SITTING AT THE RIGHT HAND OF POWER, and [b]COMING WITH THE CLOUDS OF HEAVEN."

63 And [a]tearing his clothes, the high priest *said*, "What further need do we have of witnesses?

64 "You have heard the blasphemy; how does it seem to you?" And they all condemned Him to be deserving of death.

65 And some began to [a]spit at Him, and [b]to blindfold Him, and to beat Him with their fists, and to say to Him, "[c]Prophesy!" And the officers received Him with slaps *in the face.*

2 Peter's denial of Jesus, 14:66–72

66 [a]And as Peter was below in [b]the courtyard, one of the servant-girls of the high priest *came,

67 and seeing Peter [a]warming himself, she looked at him, and *said, "You, too, were with Jesus the [b]Nazarene."

68 But he denied *it,* saying, "I neither know nor understand what you are talking about." And he [a]went out onto the porch.

69 And the maid saw him, and began once more to say to the bystanders, "This is *one* of them!"

70 But again [a]he was denying it. And after a little while the bystanders were again saying to Peter, "Surely you are *one* of them, [b]for you are a Galilean too."

71 But he began to curse and swear, "I do not know this man you are talking about!"

72 And immediately a cock crowed a second time. And Peter remembered how Jesus had made the remark to him, "Before [a]a cock crows twice, you will deny Me three times." And he began to weep.

Marginal references

★56

★58 [a]Matt. 26:61; Mark 15:29

★60

★61 [a]Matt. 26:63 [b]Mark 14:61-63; Matt. 26:63ff.; Luke 22:67-71

★62 [a]Ps. 110:1; Mark 13:26 [b]Dan. 7:13

★63 [a]Num. 14:6; Matt. 26:65; Acts 14:14

★64

★65 [a]Matt. 26:67; Mark 10:34 [b]Esther 7:8 [c]Matt. 26:68; Luke 22:64

66 [a]Mark 14:66-72; Matt. 26:69-75; Luke 22:56-62; John 18:16-18, 25-27 [b]Mark 14:54

67 [a]Mark 14:54 [b]Mark 1:24

★68 [a]Mark 14:54

★70 [a]Mark 14:68 [b]Matt. 26:73; Luke 22:59

72 [a]Mark 14:30, 68

14:56 Jewish law required two agreeing witnesses to establish a charge (Deut. 19:15).

14:58 This seems to be another version of 13:2.

14:60 The high priest suggested Christ incriminate Himself.

14:61 *kept silent.* Defense seemed irrelevant to Christ.

14:62 *I am.* Christ affirmed that He was the Messiah and assured His judges that He was also the coming Judge of all mankind. *right hand of Power.* The right hand of God.

14:63 *tearing his clothes.* The proper gesture for the high priest to make upon hearing blasphemy.

14:64 *the blasphemy.* The members of the council understood clearly that in Christ's answer (v. 62) He claimed to be equal with God. Since they viewed Him as a mere man, this claim was blasphemy in their minds, and the penalty was death (Lev. 24:16).

14:65 *spit at Him.* See Isa. 50:6. *Prophesy!* Said in mockery. Perhaps they meant: Tell us who is hitting you (as each blow is given).

14:68 *porch.* Better, gateway or forecourt.

14:70 *Galilean.* Galileans spoke a dialect of Aramaic, with noticeable pronunciation differences.

3 Christ before Pilate, 15:1-15

15 ^aAnd early in the morning the chief priests with the elders and scribes, and the whole ^bCouncil, immediately held a consultation; and binding Jesus, they led Him away, and delivered Him up to Pilate.

2 ^aAnd Pilate questioned Him, "Are You the King of the Jews?" And answering He *said to him, "It is as you say."

3 And the chief priests *began* to accuse Him harshly.

4 And Pilate was questioning Him again, saying, "Do You make no answer? See how many charges they bring against You!"

5 But Jesus ^amade no further answer; so that Pilate was amazed.

6 ^aNow at *the* feast he used to release for them *any* one prisoner whom they requested.

7 And the man named Barabbas had been imprisoned with the insurrectionists who had committed murder in the insurrection.

8 And the multitude went up and began asking him *to do* as he had been accustomed to do for them.

9 And Pilate answered them, saying, "Do you want me to release for you the King of the Jews?"

10 For he was aware that the chief priests had delivered Him up because of envy.

11 But the chief priests stirred up the multitude ^ato ask him to release Barabbas for them instead.

12 And answering again, Pilate was saying to them, "Then what shall I do with Him whom you call the King of the Jews?"

13 And they shouted back, "Crucify Him!"

14 But Pilate was saying to them, "Why, what evil has He done?" But they shouted all the more, "Crucify Him!"

15 And wishing to satisfy the multitude, Pilate released Barabbas for them, and after having Jesus ^ascourged, he delivered *Him* to be crucified.

4 Abuse by the soldiers, 15:16-20

16 ^aAnd the soldiers took Him away into ^bthe palace (that is, the Praetorium), and they *called together the whole *Roman* ^ccohort.

17 And they *dressed Him up in purple, and after weaving a crown of thorns, they put it on Him;

18 and they began to acclaim Him, "Hail, King of the Jews!"

19 And they kept beating His head with a reed, and spitting at Him, and kneeling and bowing before Him.

20 And after they had mocked Him, they took the purple off Him, and put His garments on Him. And they *led Him out to crucify Him.

15:1 *in the morning.* See note on Luke 22:66. *Pilate.* Pilate was the Roman prefect or governor of Judea (usually referred to as procurator), to which position he was appointed by Tiberius in A.D. 26. He was in charge of the army of occupation, kept the taxes flowing to Rome, had power of life and death over his subjects, appointed the high priests, and decided cases involving capital punishment. He was a capricious, weak governor who let personal and political considerations outweigh his awareness that justice was not being done in Jesus' case. He did not want another report to get to Rome that he had offended Jewish customs or could not control a situation—charges against him made to Tiberius earlier.
15:2 *King of the Jews.* The Jews knew that Pilate would be concerned only with a charge of a political nature, which this was. *It is as you say.* This affirmative answer, according to John 18:34-38, was accompanied by an explanation as to what kind of king Jesus claimed to be.
15:6 *at the feast.* I.e., at Passover.
15:15 *scourged.* See note on Matt. 27:26. *crucified.* See note on Matt. 27:31.
15:16 *Praetorium.* The residence of the governor, perhaps in the fortress of Antonia, where the Roman troops were quartered. *whole . . . cohort.* A company or battalion.

5 Crucifixion of Jesus, 15:21-32

21 ^aAnd they *pressed into service a passer-by coming from the country, Simon of Cyrene (the father of Alexander and Rufus), to bear His cross.

22 ^aAnd they *brought Him to the place ^bGolgotha, which is translated, Place of a Skull.

23 And they tried to give Him ^awine mixed with myrrh; but He did not take it.

24 And they *crucified Him, and *^adivided up His garments among themselves, casting lots for them, to decide what each should take.

25 And it was the ^athird hour when they crucified Him.

26 And the inscription of the charge against Him read, "^aTHE KING OF THE JEWS."

27 And they *crucified two robbers with Him, one on His right and one on His left.

28 [And the Scripture was fulfilled which says, "And He was numbered with transgressors."]

29 And those passing by were hurling abuse at Him, ^awagging their heads, and saying, "Ha! You who are going to ^bdestroy the temple and rebuild it in three days,

30 save Yourself, and come down from the cross!"

31 In the same way the chief priests also, along with the scribes, were mocking Him among themselves and saying, "^aHe saved others; He cannot save Himself.

32 "Let this Christ, ^athe King of Israel, now come down from the cross, so that we may see and believe!" And ^bthose who were crucified with Him were casting the same insult at Him.

6 Death of Jesus, 15:33-41

33 ^aAnd when the ^bsixth hour had come, darkness fell over the whole land until the ^bninth hour.

34 And at the ^aninth hour Jesus cried out with a loud voice, "^bELOI, ELOI, LAMA SABACHTHANI?" which is translated, "MY GOD, MY GOD, WHY HAST THOU FORSAKEN ME?"

35 And when some of the bystanders heard it, they began saying, "Behold, He is calling for Elijah."

36 And someone ran and filled a sponge with sour wine, put it on a reed, and gave Him a drink, saying, "Let us see whether Elijah will come to take Him down."

37 ^aAnd Jesus uttered a loud cry, and breathed His last.

38 ^aAnd the veil of the temple was torn in two from top to bottom.

39 ^aAnd when the centurion, who was standing right in front of Him, saw the way He breathed His last, he said, "Truly this man was the Son of God!"

40 ^aAnd there were also some women looking on from a distance, among whom were Mary Magdalene, and Mary the mother of James ^bthe Less and Joses, and ^cSalome.

41 And when He was in Galilee, they used to follow Him and ^aminister to Him; and there were

Cross-references (margin)

★21 ^aMark 15:21; Matt. 27:32; Luke 23:26
★22 ^aMark 15:22-32; Matt. 27:33-44; Luke 23:33-43; John 19:17-24 ^bLuke 23:33; John 19:17
★23 ^aMatt. 27:34
★24 ^aPs. 22:18; John 19:24
★25 ^aMark 15:33; John 19:14
26 ^aMatt. 27:37
★28
29 ^aPs. 22:8; Matt. 27:39 ^bMark 14:58
31 ^aMatt. 27:42; Luke 23:35
★32 ^aMatt. 27:42; Mark 15:26 ^bMatt. 27:44; Mark 15:27; Luke 23:39-43
33 ^aMark 15:33-41; Matt. 27:45-56; Luke 23:44-49 ^bMatt. 27:45f.; Mark 15:25; Luke 23:44
★34 ^aMatt. 27:45f.; Mark 15:25; Luke 23:44 ^bPs. 22:1; Matt. 27:46
★35
★36
37 ^aMatt. 27:50; Luke 23:46; John 19:30
★38 ^aMatt. 27:51; Luke 23:45
39 ^aMatt. 27:54; Mark 15:45; Luke 23:47
★40 ^aMark 15:40, 41; Matt. 27:55f.; Luke 23:49; John 19:25 ^bLuke 19:3 ^cMark 16:1
41 ^aMatt. 27:55f.

15:21 coming from the country. I.e., coming from the country into the city, probably as another pilgrim to Jerusalem at Passover. Simon of Cyrene. Cyrene was a port in N. Africa and had a Jewish community.

15:22 Golgotha. See note on Matt. 27:33.

15:23 wine mixed with myrrh. A sedative.

15:24 divided up His garments. The garments of a victim were customarily taken by his executioners. See Ps. 22:18.

15:25 it was the third hour. 9 a.m.

15:28 This quotation, from Isa. 53:12, is not contained in many manuscripts.

15:32 Let this Christ. I.e., Let the (to them) false Christ.

15:34 why hast Thou forsaken Me? See note on Matt. 27:46.

15:35 Elijah. See note on Matt. 27:47.

15:36 sour wine. See Ps. 69:21.

15:38 the veil. See note on Matt. 27:51.

15:40 A list of trustworthy witnesses (the apostles having fled) is given. Compare 16:1.

many other women who had come up with Him to Jerusalem.

7 Burial of Jesus, 15:42-47

^{42 aMark 15:42-47; Matt. 27:57-61; Luke 23:50-56; John 19:38-42 bMatt. 27:62}

42 ^aAnd when evening had already come, because it was ^bthe preparation day, that is, the day before the Sabbath,

^{★43 aMatt. 27:57; Luke 23:51; Acts 13:50; 17:12 bMatt. 27:57; Luke 2:25, 38; 23:51; John 19:38 cJohn 19:38 ★44}

43 Joseph of Arimathea came, a ^aprominent member of the Council, who himself was ^bwaiting for the kingdom of God; and he ^cgathered up courage and went in before Pilate, and asked for the body of Jesus.

44 And Pilate wondered if He was dead by this time, and summoning the centurion, he questioned him as to whether He was already dead.

^{45 aMark 15:39}

45 And ascertaining this from ^athe centurion, he granted the body to Joseph.

^{★46}

46 And *Joseph* bought a linen cloth, took Him down, and wrapped Him in the linen cloth, and laid Him in a tomb which had been hewn out in the rock; and he rolled a stone against the entrance of the tomb.

^{47 aMatt. 27:56; Mark 15:40; 16:1}

47 And ^aMary Magdalene and Mary the *mother* of Joses were looking on *to see* where He was laid.

III THE SUCCESS OF THE SERVANT, 16:1-20

^{★ 1 aMark 16:1-8; Matt. 28:1-8; Luke 24:1-10; John 20:1-8 bMark 15:47 cLuke 23:56; John 19:39f.}

A His Resurrection, 16:1-8

16 ^aAnd when the Sabbath was over, ^bMary Magda-

lene, and Mary the *mother* of James, and Salome, ^cbought spices, that they might come and anoint Him.

2 And very early on the first day of the week, they *came to the tomb when the sun had risen.

^{★ 3 aMatt. 27:60; Mark 15:46; 16:3, 4}

3 And they were saying to one another, "Who will roll away ^athe stone for us from the entrance of the tomb?"

4 And looking up, they *saw that the stone had been rolled away, although it was extremely large.

^{★ 5 aJohn 20:11, 12 bMark 9:15}

5 And ^aentering the tomb, they saw a young man sitting at the right, wearing a white robe; and they ^bwere amazed.

^{★ 6 aMark 9:15 bMark 1:24 cMatt. 28:6; Luke 24:6}

6 And he *said to them, "^aDo not be amazed; you are looking for Jesus the ^bNazarene, who has been crucified. ^cHe has risen; He is not here; behold, *here is* the place where they laid Him.

^{7 aMatt. 26:32; Mark 14:28}

7 "But go, tell His disciples and Peter, '^aHe is going before you into Galilee; there you will see Him, just as He said to you.' "

8 And they went out and fled from the tomb, for trembling and astonishment had gripped them; and they said nothing to anyone, for they were afraid.

B His Appearances, 16:9-18

^{★ 9-20}

^{9 aMatt. 27:56; John 20:14}

9 [Now after He had risen early on the first day of the week, He first appeared to ^aMary Magdalene, from whom He had cast out seven demons.

15:43 *Joseph.* See Matt. 27:57; Luke 23:50; and John 19:38.

15:44 *wondered if He was dead by this time.* Pilate wondered because several days of agony on a cross before death came was common. Christ's death after only 6 hours was very unusual. *centurion.* The one who had been in charge of the crucifixion.

15:46 *wrapped Him in the linen.* The linen was wrapped around the body in strips (John 19:40). *tomb.* See Isa. 53:9.

16:1 *when the Sabbath was over.* Work could now be done to prepare the body for permanent burial.

16:3 *the stone.* See note on Luke 24:2.

16:5 *a young man.* Evidently the angel who rolled away the stone (Matt. 28:2).

16:6 *He has risen.* This simply stated fact is the foundation of the Christian faith.

16:9-20 These verses do not appear in two of the most truthworthy manuscripts of the N.T., though they are part of many other manuscripts and versions. If they are not a part of the genuine text of Mark, the abrupt ending at verse 8 is probably because the original closing verses were lost. The doubtful genuineness of verses 9-20 makes it unwise to build a doctrine or base an experience on them (especially vv. 16-18).

10 aJohn
20:18

11 aMatt.
28:17; Mark
16:13, 14;
Luke 24:11,
41; John
20:25
12 aMark
16:14; John
21:1, 14
bLuke 24:13-
35
13 aMatt.
28:17; Mark
16:11, 14;
Luke 24:11,
41; John
20:25
14 aMark
16:12; John
21:1, 14
bLuke 24:36;
John 20:19,
26; 1 Cor.
15:5 cMatt
28:17; Mark
16:11, 13;
Luke 24:11,
41; John
20:25
15 aMatt.
28:19
★16 aJohn
3:18, 36;
Acts 16:31
17 aMark
9:38; Luke
10:17; Acts
5:16; 8:7;
16:18; 19:12
bActs 2:4;
10:46; 19:6;
1 Cor. 12:10

10 aShe went and reported to those who had been with Him, while they were mourning and weeping.

11 And when they heard that He was alive, and had been seen by her, athey refused to believe it.

12 And after that, aHe appeared in a different form bto two of them, while they were walking along on their way to the country.

13 And they went away and reported it to the others, but they adid not believe them either.

14 And afterward aHe appeared bto the eleven themselves as they were reclining at the table; and He reproached them for their cunbelief and hardness of heart, because they had not believed those who had seen Him after He had risen.

15 And He said to them, "aGo into all the world and preach the gospel to all creation.

16 "aHe who has believed and has been baptized shall be saved; but he who has disbelieved shall be condemned.

17 "And these signs will ac-

company those who have believed: ain My name they will cast out demons, they will bspeak with new tongues;

18 they will apick up serpents, and if they drink any deadly poison, it shall not hurt them; they will blay hands on the sick, and they will recover."

C His Ascension, 16:19-20

19 So then, when the Lord Jesus had aspoken to them, He bwas received up into heaven, and csat down at the right hand of God.

20 And they went out and preached everywhere, while the Lord worked with them, and confirmed the word by the signs that followed.]

[And they promptly reported all these instructions to Peter and his companions. And after that, Jesus Himself sent out through them from east to west the sacred and imperishable proclamation of eternal salvation.]

18 aLuke
10:19; Acts
28:3-5

19 aActs 1:3
bLuke 9:51;
24:51; John
6:62; 20:17;
Acts 1:2;
1 Tim 3:16
cPs. 110:1;
Luke 22:69;
Acts 7:55f.
Rom. 8:34;
Eph. 1:20;
Col. 3:1;
Heb. 1:3;
8:1; 10:12;
12:2; 1 Pet.
3:22

16:16 baptized. This may be a reference to the baptism of the Holy Spirit (1 Cor. 12:13). Water baptism does not save (see notes on Acts 2:38; 1 Pet. 3:21).

INTRODUCTION TO
THE GOSPEL ACCORDING TO LUKE

AUTHOR: Luke   DATE: 60

Authorship   Luke, the "beloved physician" (Col. 4:14), close friend and companion of Paul, was probably the only Gentile author of any part of the New Testament. We know nothing about his early life or conversion except that he was not an eyewitness of the life of Jesus Christ (Luke 1:2). Though a physician by profession, he was primarily an evangelist, writing this Gospel and the book of Acts and accompanying Paul in missionary work (see the Introduction to Acts). He was with Paul at the time of the apostle's martyrdom (2 Tim. 4:11), but of his later life we have no certain facts.

Methodology   In his prologue, Luke states that his own work was stimulated by the work of others (1:1), that he consulted eyewitnesses (1:2), and that he sifted and arranged the information (1:3) under the guidance of the Holy Spirit to instruct Theophilus in the historical reliability of the faith (1:4). This is a carefully researched and documented writing.

Distinctive Approach   Though specifically dedicated to Theophilus, the Gospel is slanted toward all Gentiles. (1) The author displays an unusual interest in medical matters (4:38; 7:15; 8:55; 14:2; 18:15; 22:50). (2) Much attention is given to recounting of the events surrounding the birth of Christ. Only Luke records the annunciation to Zacharias and Mary, the songs of Elizabeth and Mary, the birth and childhood of John the Baptist, the birth of Jesus, the visit of the shepherds, the circumcision, presentation in the Temple, details of Christ's childhood, and the inner thoughts of Mary. (3) Luke shows an uncommon interest in individuals, as seen in his accounts of Zaccheus (19:1-10) and the penitent thief (23:39-43) and in the parables of the prodigal son (15:11-32) and the penitent publican (18:9-14). It is Luke who gives us the story of the good Samaritan (10:29-37) and the one thankful ex-leper (17:11-19). (4) There is in this Gospel a special emphasis on prayer (3:21; 5:16; 6:12; 9:18, 28-29; 10:21; 11:1; 22:39-46; 23:34, 46). (5) The prominent place given to women is another distinctive feature of this Gospel (chapters 1, 2; 7:11-13; 8:1-3; 10:38-42; 21:1-4; 23:27-31, 49). (6) The writer also shows interest in poverty and wealth (1:52-53; 4:16-22; 6:20, 24-25; 12:13-21; 14:12-13; 16:19-31). (7) The book preserves four beautiful hymns: the Magnificat of Mary (1:46-55), the Benedictus of Zechariah (1:67-79), the Gloria in Excelsis of the angels (2:14), and the Nunc Dimittis of Simeon (2:29-32). This is a Gospel of the compassionate Son of Man offering salvation to the whole world (19:10).

Date   Since the conclusion of Acts shows Paul in Rome, and since the Gospel of Luke was written before Acts (Acts 1:1), Luke's Gospel was probably written about A.D. 60, possibly in Caesarea during Paul's two-year imprisonment there (Acts 24:27).

Contents   The theme of Luke's Gospel is Christ, the Son of Man, and it narrates many of those events which demonstrated Christ's humanity (see Distinctive Approach for a listing of favorite passages).

OUTLINE OF THE GOSPEL OF LUKE

THE GOSPEL ACCORDING TO LUKE

I PREFACE: THE METHOD AND PURPOSE OF WRITING, 1:1-4

1 Inasmuch as many have undertaken to compile an account of the things ªaccomplished among us,

2 just as those who ªfrom the beginning were ᵇeyewitnesses and ᶜservants of ᵈthe word have handed them down to us,

3 it seemed fitting for me as well, ªhaving investigated everything carefully from the beginning, to write it out for you ᵇin consecutive order, ᶜmost excellent ᵈTheophilus;

4 so that you might know the exact truth about the things you have been ªtaught.

II THE IDENTIFICATION OF THE SON OF MAN WITH MEN, 1:5-4:13

A The Announcement of the Birth of John the Baptist, 1:5-25

5 ªIn the days of Herod, king of Judea, there was a certain priest named Zacharias, of the ᵇdivision of Abijah; and he had a wife from the daughters of Aaron, and her name was Elizabeth.

6 And they were both ªrighteous in the sight of God, walking ᵇblamelessly in all the commandments and requirements of the Lord.

7 And they had no child, because Elizabeth was barren, and they were both advanced in years.

8 Now it came about, while ªhe was performing his priestly service before God in the appointed order of his division,

9 according to the custom of the priestly office, he was chosen by lot ªto enter the temple of the Lord and burn incense.

10 And the whole multitude of the people were in prayer ªoutside at the hour of the incense offering.

11 And ªan angel of the Lord appeared to him, standing to the right of the altar of incense.

12 And Zacharias was troubled when he saw him, and fear gripped him.

13 But the angel said to him, "ªDo not be afraid, Zacharias, for your petition has been heard, and your wife Elizabeth will bear you a son, and ᵇyou will give him the name John.

14 "And you will have joy and gladness, and many will rejoice at his birth.

15 "For he will be great in the sight of the Lord, and he will ªdrink no wine or liquor; and he will be filled with the Holy Spirit, while yet in his mother's womb.

16 "And he will turn back many of the sons of Israel to the Lord their God.

17 "And it is he who will ªgo as a forerunner before Him in the spirit and power of ᵇElijah, ᶜTO

Cross-references

1 ª[Gr., in] Rom. 4:21; 14:5; Col. 2:2; 4:12; 1 Thess. 1:5; 2 Tim. 4:5, 17; Heb. 6:11; 10:22 **2** ªJohn 15:27; Acts 1:21f. ᵇ2 Pet. 1:16; 1 John 1:1 ᶜActs 26:16; 1 Cor. 4:1; Heb. 2:3 ᵈMark 4:14; 16:20; Acts 8:4; 14:25; 16:6; 17:11 ★ **3** ª1 Tim. 4:6; 2 Tim. 3:10 [in Gr.] ᵇActs 11:4; 18:23 ᶜActs 23:26; 24:3; 26:25 ᵈActs 1:1

4 ªActs 18:25; Rom. 2:18; 1 Cor. 14:19; Gal. 6:6 [Gr.]

★ **5** ªMatt. 2:1 ᵇ1 Chr. 24:10

★ **6** ªGen. 7:1; Acts 2:25; 8:21 ᵇPhil. 2:15; 1 Thess. 3:6; 1 Thess. 3:13 [Gr.]

8 ª1 Chr. 24:19; 2 Chr. 8:14; 31:2

★ **9** ªEx. 30:7f.

10 ªLev. 16:17

★ **11** ªLuke 2:9; Acts 5:19

13 ªMatt. 14:27; Luke 1:30 ᵇLuke 1:60, 63

15 ªNum. 6:3; Judg. 13:4; Matt. 11:18; Luke 7:33

★ **17** ªLuke 1:76 ᵇMatt. 11:14 ᶜMal. 4:6

1:3 *from the beginning* of the Gospel story; i.e., the birth of John the Baptist. The word "beginning" in some instances is translated "from above"; e.g., John 3:31; Jas. 1:17). *most excellent Theophilus.* His name means "dear to God," or "friend of God." He is unknown otherwise, but the form of the address shows that he was a person of high rank.

1:5 *Herod.* Herod the Great. See note on Matt. 2:1. *the division of Abijah.* Work in the temple was divided among "divisions" of priests, each division named for its leader (1 Chron. 24:10). *daughters of Aaron.* Elizabeth, like Zacharias, was of a priestly family.

1:6 *they were both righteous in the sight of God.* In a godless age this couple lived lives that were fully pleasing to God, yet they were without the much-cherished blessing of children.

1:9 *chosen by lot.* The privilege of burning incense was permitted only once in the lifetime of any priest.

1:11 *an angel.* Gabriel (see v. 19).

1:17 *in the spirit and power of Elijah.* The stern prophet who rebuked the idolatrous King Ahab (1 Kings 21:17-24). He preached repentance, as John the Baptist would also do (Luke 3:8). See notes on Matt. 11:14; 17:11-12.

TURN THE HEARTS OF THE FATHERS BACK TO THE CHILDREN, and the disobedient to the attitude of the righteous; so as to ^amake ready a people prepared for the Lord."

18 And Zacharias said to the angel, "How shall I know this *for certain*? For I am an old man, and my wife is advanced in years."

19 And the angel answered and said to him, "I am ^aGabriel, who ^bstands in the presence of God; and I have been sent to speak to you, and to bring you this good news.

20 "And behold, you shall be silent and unable to speak until the day when these things take place, because you did not believe my words, which shall be fulfilled in their proper time."

21 And the people were waiting for Zacharias, and were wondering at his delay in the temple.

22 But when he came out, he was unable to speak to them; and they realized that he had seen a vision in the temple; and he ^akept making signs to them, and remained mute.

23 And it came about, when the days of his priestly service were ended, that he went back home.

24 And after these days Elizabeth his wife became pregnant; and she kept herself in seclusion for five months, saying,

25 "This is the way the Lord has dealt with me in the days when He looked *with favor* upon

me, to ^atake away my disgrace among men."

B The Announcement of the Birth of the Son of Man, 1:26-56

26 Now in the sixth month the angel ^aGabriel was sent from God to a city in Galilee, called ^bNazareth,

27 to ^aa virgin engaged to a man whose name was Joseph, ^bof the descendants of David; and the virgin's name was Mary.

28 And coming in, he said to her, "Hail, favored one! The Lord *is* with you."

29 But she ^awas greatly troubled at *this* statement, and kept pondering what kind of salutation this might be.

30 And the angel said to her, "^aDo not be afraid, Mary; for you have found favor with God.

31 "And behold, you will conceive in your womb, and bear a son, and you ^ashall name Him Jesus.

32 "He will be great, and will be called the Son of ^athe Most High; and the Lord God will give Him the throne of His father David;

33 ^aand He will reign over the house of Jacob forever; ^band His kingdom will have no end."

34 And Mary said to the angel, "How can this be, since I am a virgin?"

35 And the angel answered

★19 ^aDan. 8:16; 9:21; Luke 1:26 ^bMatt. 18:10

★21

22 ^aLuke 1:62

★23

25 ^aGen. 30:23; Is. 4:1

26 ^aLuke 1:19 ^bMatt. 2:23

★27 ^aMatt. 1:18 ^bMatt. 1:16, 20; Luke 2:4

★28

29 ^aLuke 1:12

30 ^aMatt. 14:27; Luke 1:13

★31 ^aMatt. 1:21, 25; Luke 2:21

★32 ^aMark 5:7; Luke 1:35, 76; 6:35; Acts 7:48

★33 ^aMatt. 1:1 ^bDan. 2:44; 7:14, 18, 27; Matt. 28:18

★35 ^aMatt. 1:18 ^bLuke 1:32 ^cMark 1:24 ^dMatt. 4:3

1:19 *Gabriel.* The angel's name means "man of God," and his ministry involves making special announcements concerning God's plans (Dan. 8:16; 9:21). He and Michael, the archangel, are the only angels named in the Bible.
1:21 *wondering at his delay.* The people probably wondered if Zacharias had died.
1:23 *he went back home.* After serving in his division for a limited time, Zacharias was free to return to his home in the hill country, probably not far from Jerusalem (cf. 1:39).
1:27 *a virgin engaged.* According to Jewish law, espousal or engagement was as binding as marriage. See note on Matt. 1:19.
1:28 *favored one!* = filled with grace. The term is used in the N.T. elsewhere only in Eph. 1:6, where all believers in Christ also are said to be filled with grace.
1:31 *Jesus.* The name means "the Lord is salva-

tion." See note on Matt. 1:1.
1:32 *His father David.* See 3:31 and note on Matt. 1:1.
1:33 *He will reign.* Jesus is the Davidic Messiah, and though He reigns always, the ultimate fulfillment of this promise in relation to the *house of Jacob* begins in the millennial kingdom. See 2 Sam. 7:16.
1:35 *The Holy Spirit will come upon you.* The incarnation was accomplished by this creative act of the Holy Spirit in the body of Mary. The virgin birth was a special miracle performed by the Third Person of the Trinity, the Holy Spirit, whereby the Second Person of the Trinity, the eternal Son of God, took to Himself a genuine, though sinless, human nature and was born as a man, without surrendering in any aspect His deity.

and said to her, "[a]The Holy Spirit will come upon you, and the power of [b]the Most High will overshadow you; and for that reason [c]the holy offspring shall be called [d]the Son of God.

36 "And behold, even your relative Elizabeth has also conceived a son in her old age; and she who was called barren is now in her sixth month.

37 "For [a]nothing will be impossible with God."

38 And Mary said, "Behold, the bondslave of the Lord; be it done to me according to your word." And the angel departed from her.

39 Now at this time Mary arose and went with haste to [a]the hill country, to a city of Judah,

40 and entered the house of Zacharias and greeted Elizabeth.

41 And it came about that when Elizabeth heard Mary's greeting, the baby leaped in her womb; and Elizabeth was [a]filled with the Holy Spirit.

42 And she cried out with a loud voice, and said, "Blessed among women *are* you, and blessed *is* the fruit of your womb!

43 "And how has it *happened* to me, that the mother of [a]my Lord should come to me?

44 "For behold, when the sound of your greeting reached my ears, the baby leaped in my womb for joy.

45 "And [a]blessed *is* she who believed that there would be a fulfillment of what had been spoken to her by the Lord."

46 And Mary said:

"[a]My soul [b]exalts the Lord,

47 "And [a]my spirit has rejoiced in [b]God my Savior.

48 "For He has had regard for the humble state of His bondslave;

For behold, from this time on all generations will count me [a]blessed.

49 "For the Mighty One has done great things for me;

And holy is His name.

50 "[a]AND HIS MERCY IS UPON GENERATION AFTER GENERATION

TOWARD THOSE WHO FEAR HIM.

51 "[a]He has done mighty deeds with His arm;

He has scattered *those who were* proud in the thoughts of their heart.

52 "He has brought down rulers from *their* thrones,

And has exalted those who were humble.

53 "[a]HE HAS FILLED THE HUNGRY WITH GOOD THINGS;

And sent away the rich empty-handed.

54 "He has given help to Israel His servant,

In remembrance of His mercy,

55 [a]As He spoke to our fathers,

To Abraham and his offspring forever."

56 And Mary stayed with her about three months, and *then* returned to her home.

C The Advent of John the Baptist, 1:57–80

57 Now the time had come for Elizabeth to give birth, and she brought forth a son.

58 And her neighbors and her relatives heard that the Lord had [a]displayed His great mercy toward her; and they were rejoicing with her.

59 And it came about that on [a]the eighth day they came to cir-

---

Cross references (margin):

37 [a]Matt. 19:26

39 [a]Josh. 20:7; 21:11; Luke 1:65

41 [a]Luke 1:67

43 [a]Luke 2:11

45 [a]Luke 1:20, 48

★46–56
46 [a]Luke 1:46-53; 1 Sam. 2:1-10 [b]Ps. 34:2f.

47 [a]Ps. 35:9 [b]1 Tim. 1:1; 2:3; Titus 1:3; 2:10; 3:4; Jude 25

48 [a]Luke 1:45

50 [a]Ps. 103:17

51 [a]Ps. 98:1; 118:15

53 [a]Ps. 107:9

55 [a]Gen. 17:19; Ps. 132:11; Gal. 3:16

58 [a]Gen. 19:19

★59 [a]Gen. 17:12; Lev. 12:3; Luke 2:21; Phil. 3:5

1:46–56 Often called "the Magnificat," from the first word of the Latin translation. There are 15 discernible quotations from the O.T. in this poem, showing how much the O.T. was known and loved in the home in which Jesus was reared.

1:59 *to circumcise the child.* This ritual act was performed 8 days after birth, and the name was given at this time.

cumcise the child, and they were going to call him Zacharias, after his father.

60 And his mother answered and said, "No indeed; but *a*he shall be called John."

61 And they said to her, "There is no one among your relatives who is called by that name."

62 And they *a*made signs to his father, as to what he wanted him called.

63 And he asked for a tablet, and wrote as follows, "*a*His name is John." And they were all astonished.

64 *a*And at once his mouth was opened and his tongue *loosed,* and he *began* to speak in praise of God.

65 And fear came on all those living around them; and all these matters were being talked about in all *a*the hill country of Judea.

66 And all who heard them kept them in mind, saying, "What then will this child *turn out to be?"* For *a*the hand of the Lord was certainly with him.

67 And his father Zacharias *a*was filled with the Holy Spirit, and *b*prophesied, saying:

68 "Blessed *be* the Lord God of Israel,
For He has visited us and accomplished *a*redemption for His people,

69 And has raised up a *a*horn of salvation for us In the house of David *b*His servant—

70 *a*As He spoke by the mouth of His holy prophets *b*from of old—

71 *a*Salvation *b*FROM OUR EN-EMIES,
And FROM THE HAND OF ALL WHO HATE US;

72 *a*To show mercy toward our fathers,

*b*And to remember His holy covenant,

73 *a*The oath which He swore to Abraham our father,

74 To grant us that we, being delivered from the hand of our enemies, Might serve Him without fear,

75 In holiness and righteousness before Him all our days.

76 "And you, child, will be called the *a*prophet of *b*the Most High;
For you will go on *c*BEFORE THE LORD TO *d*PREPARE HIS WAYS;

77 To give to His people *the* knowledge of salvation By *a*the forgiveness of their sins,

78 Because of the tender mercy of our God, With which *a*the Sunrise from on high shall visit us,

79 *a*TO SHINE UPON THOSE WHO SIT IN DARKNESS AND THE SHADOW OF DEATH, To guide our feet into the way of peace."

80 *a*And the child continued to grow, and to become strong in spirit, and he lived in the deserts until the day of his public appearance to Israel.

D   The Advent of the Son of Man, 2:1-20

2 Now it came about in those days that a decree went out from *a*Caesar Augustus, that a census be taken of *b*all the inhabited earth.

2 This was the first census taken while Quirinius was governor of *a*Syria.

★60 *a*Luke 1:13, 63
62 *a*Luke 1:22
63 *a*Luke 1:13, 60
64 *a*Luke 1:20
65 *a*Luke 1:39
66 *a*Acts 11:21
67 *a*Luke 1:41 *b*Joel 2:28
68 *a*Luke 1:71; 2:38; Acts 1:6; Heb. 9:12
★69 *a*1 Sam. 2:1, 10; Ps. 18:2; 89:17; 132:17; Ezek. 29:21 *b*Matt. 1:1
70 *a*Rom. 1:2 *b*Acts 3:21
71 *a*Luke 1:68 *b*Ps. 106:10
72 *a*Mic. 7:20 *b*Ps. 105:8f; 106:45
★73 *a*Gen. 22:16ff.
76 *a*Matt. 11:9 *b*Luke 1:32 *c*Mal. 3:1 *d*Luke 1:17
77 *a*Jer. 31:34; Mark 1:4
78 *a*Mal. 4:2; Eph. 5:14; 2 Pet. 1:19
79 *a*Is. 9:1, 2; 59:8; Matt. 4:16
80 *a*Luke 2:40
★ 1 *a*Matt. 22:17; Luke 3:1 *b*Matt. 24:14
★ 2 *a*Matt. 4:24

1:60 *John.* The name means "God is gracious."

1:69 *horn of salvation.* Horn is often used as a metaphor for power (cf. 2 Sam. 22:3); thus this phrase means "a powerful Savior."

1:73 *The oath.* The covenant which God made with Abraham, recorded in Gen. 22:16-18.

2:1 *Caesar Augustus* reigned from 27 B.C. to A.D. 14.

2:2 *Quirinius was governor of Syria.* Apparently he was governor of Syria twice: from 4 B.C. to A.D. 1, when this census was taken, and again in A.D. 6.

3 And all were proceeding to register for the census, everyone to his own city.

★ **4** *a*Luke 1:27
4 And Joseph also went up from Galilee, from the city of Nazareth, to Judea, to the city of David, which is called Bethlehem, because *a*he was of the house and family of David,

5 in order to register, along with Mary, who was engaged to him, and was with child.

6 And it came about that while they were there, the days were completed for her to give birth.

★ **7**
7 And she gave birth to her first-born son; and she wrapped Him in cloths, and laid Him in a manger, because there was no room for them in the inn.

8 And in the same region there were *some* shepherds staying out in the fields, and keeping watch over their flock by night.

9 *a*Luke 1:11; Acts 5:19 *b*Luke 24:4; Acts 12:7
9 And *a*an angel of the Lord suddenly *b*stood before them, and the glory of the Lord shone around them; and they were terribly frightened.

10 *a*Matt. 14:27
10 And the angel said to them, "*a*Do not be afraid; for behold, I bring you good news of a great joy which shall be for all the people;

★**11** *a*Matt. 1:21; John 4:42; Acts 5:31 *b*Matt. 1:16; 16:16, 20; John 11:27 *c*Luke 1:43; Acts 2:36; 10:36
11 for today in the city of David there has been born for you a *a*Savior, who is *b*Christ *c*the Lord.

12 *a*1 Sam. 2:34; 2 Kin. 19:29; 20:8f.; Is. 7:11, 14
12 "And *a*this *will be* a sign for you: you will find a baby wrapped in cloths, and lying in a manger."

13 And suddenly there appeared with the angel a multitude of the heavenly host praising God, and saying,

14 *a*Matt. 21:9; Luke 19:38 *b*Luke 3:22; Eph. 1:9; Phil. 2:13
14 "*a*Glory to God in the highest,
And on earth peace among men *b*with whom He is pleased."

15 And it came about when the angels had gone away from them into heaven, that the shepherds *began* saying to one another, "Let us go straight to Bethlehem then, and see this thing that has happened which the Lord has made known to us."

16 And they came in haste and found their way to Mary and Joseph, and the baby as He lay in the manger.

17 And when they had seen this, they made known the statement which had been told them about this Child.

18 And all who heard it wondered at the things which were told them by the shepherds.

19 *a*Luke 2:51
19 But Mary *a*treasured up all these things, pondering them in her heart.

20 *a*Matt. 9:8
20 And the shepherds went back, *a*glorifying and praising God for all that they had heard and seen, just as had been told them.

E The Adoration of the Babe, 2:21-38

★**21** *a*Luke 1:59 *b*Luke 1:31
21 And when *a*eight days were completed before His circumcision, *b*His name was *then* called Jesus, the name given by the angel before He was conceived in the womb.

★**22**
22 And when the days for their purification according to the

2:4 *to . . . Bethlehem.* To fulfill the prophecy of Mic. 5:2.

2:7 *cloths.* Wrapped around an infant in the Near East in Bible times. *manger.* A feeding trough for animals in a stall or stable. Tradition says that Jesus was born in a cave, in which case the manger may have been cut out of a rock wall.

2:11 Three titles were given to Jesus in the angel's announcement: *Savior, Christ* (Messiah, anointed One), and *Lord* (Yahweh, or God).

He was both God and man.

2:21 *before His circumcision.* In accordance with Lev. 12:3.

2:22 *the days for their purification.* According to the Mosaic law the mother of a male child was unclean. On the eighth day the boy was circumcised but she remained unclean for 33 more days, after which she presented a burnt offering and a sin offering for her cleansing (Lev. 12:4-6).

law of Moses were completed, they brought Him up to Jerusalem to present Him to the Lord

23 ᵃEx. 13:2, 12

23 (as it is written in the Law of the Lord, "ᵃEVERY first-born MALE THAT OPENS THE WOMB SHALL BE CALLED HOLY TO THE LORD"),

★24 ᵃLev. 5:11; 12:8

24 and to offer a sacrifice according to what was said in the Law of the Lord, "ᵃA PAIR OF TURTLEDOVES, OR TWO YOUNG PIGEONS."

★25 ᵃLuke 1:6 ᵇMark 15:43; Luke 2:38; 23:51

25 And behold, there was a man in Jerusalem whose name was Simeon; and this man was ᵃrighteous and devout, ᵇlooking for the consolation of Israel; and the Holy Spirit was upon him.

26 ᵃMatt. 2:12 ᵇPs. 89:48; John 8:51; Heb. 11:5

26 And ᵃit had been revealed to him by the Holy Spirit that he would not ᵇsee death before he had seen the Lord's Christ.

27 ᵃLuke 2:22

27 And he came in the Spirit into the temple; and when the parents brought in the child Jesus, ᵃto carry out for Him the custom of the Law,

28 then he took Him into his arms, and blessed God, and said,

29 ᵃLuke 2:26

29 "Now Lord, Thou dost let
Thy bond-servant depart
In peace, ᵃaccording to Thy word;

30 ᵃIs. 52:10; Luke 3:6

30 For my eyes have ᵃseen
Thy salvation,

31 Which Thou hast prepared in the presence of all peoples,

★32 ᵃIs. 42:6; 49:6; Acts 13:47; 26:23

32 ᵃA LIGHT OF REVELATION TO
THE GENTILES,
And the glory of Thy people Israel."

33 ᵃMatt. 12:46

33 And His father and ᵃmother were amazed at the things which were being said about Him.

34 ᵃMatt. 12:46 ᵇMatt. 21:44; 1 Cor. 1:23; 2 Cor. 2:16; 1 Pet. 2:8

34 And Simeon blessed them, and said to Mary ᵃHis mother, "Behold, this Child is appointed

for ᵇthe fall and rise of many in Israel, and for a sign to be opposed—

35 and a sword will pierce even your own soul—to the end that thoughts from many hearts may be revealed."

★35

36 And there was a ᵃprophetess, Anna the daughter of Phanuel, of ᵇthe tribe of Asher. She was advanced in years, ᶜhaving lived with a husband seven years after her marriage,

36 ᵃLuke 2:38; Acts 21:9 ᵇJosh. 19:24 ᶜ1 Tim. 5:9

37 and then as a widow to the age of eighty-four. And she never left the temple, serving night and day with ᵃfastings and prayers.

37 ᵃLuke 5:33; Acts 13:3; 14:23; 1 Tim. 5:5

38 And at that very moment she came up and began giving thanks to God, and continued to speak of Him to all those who were ᵃlooking for the redemption of Jerusalem.

38 ᵃLuke 1:68; 2:25

F The Advancement of the Boy, 2:39–52

39 And when they had performed everything according to the Law of the Lord, they returned to Galilee, to ᵃtheir own city of Nazareth.

39 ᵃMatt. 2:23; Luke 1:26; 2:51; 4:16

40 ᵃAnd the Child continued to grow and become strong, increasing in wisdom; and the grace of God was upon Him.

40 ᵃLuke 1:80; 2:52

41 And His parents used to go to Jerusalem every year at ᵃthe Feast of the Passover.

41 ᵃEx. 23:15; Deut. 16:1-6

42 And when He became twelve, they went up there according to the custom of the Feast;

★42

43 and as they were returning, after spending the ᵃfull number of days, the boy Jesus stayed behind in Jerusalem. And His parents were unaware of it,

43 ᵃEx. 12:15

2:24 *A pair of turtledoves.* This shows the poverty of Christ's family, since they could not afford a lamb for the offering.
2:25 *Simeon.* All we know of Simeon is what Luke tells us here. *the consolation of Israel* is the promised Messiah.
2:32 Christ's salvation was offered to Gentile and Jew alike.

2:35 *a sword.* Refers to the agony which Mary would have to bear.
2:42 *when He became twelve.* At 13 a Jewish boy became a "son of the commandment" and a full member of the religious community. This age was often anticipated by one or two years in the matter of going to the temple.

44 but supposed Him to be in the caravan, and went a day's journey; and they *began* looking for Him among their relatives and acquaintances.

45 And when they did not find Him, they returned to Jerusalem, looking for Him.

46 And it came about that after three days they found Him in the temple, sitting in the midst of the teachers, both listening to them, and asking them questions.

47 And all who heard Him were amazed at His understanding and His answers.

48 And when they saw Him, they were astonished; and [a]His mother said to Him, "Son, why have You treated us this way? Behold, [b]Your father and I have been anxiously looking for You."

49 And He said to them, "Why is it that you were looking for Me? Did you not know that I had to be in My Father's *house*?"

50 And [a]they did not understand the statement which He had made to them.

51 And He went down with them, and came to [a]Nazareth; and He continued in subjection to them; and [b]His mother [c]treasured all *these* things in her heart.

52 And Jesus kept increasing in wisdom and stature, and in [a]favor with God and men.

G The Baptism of the Son of Man, 3:1-22

3 Now in the fifteenth year of the reign of Tiberius Caesar, when [a]Pontius Pilate was governor of Judea, and [b]Herod was tetrarch of Galilee, and his brother Philip was tetrarch of the region of Ituraea and Trachonitis, and Lysanias was tetrarch of Abilene,

2 in the high priesthood of [a]Annas and [b]Caiaphas, [c]the word of God came to John, the son of Zacharias, in the wilderness.

3 And he came into all [a]the district around the Jordan, preaching a baptism of repentance for the forgiveness of sins;

4 as it is written in the book of the words of Isaiah the prophet,

"[a]THE VOICE OF ONE CRYING IN
　　THE WILDERNESS,
'MAKE READY THE WAY OF THE
　　LORD,
MAKE HIS PATHS STRAIGHT.

5 '[a]EVERY RAVINE SHALL BE
　　FILLED UP,
AND EVERY MOUNTAIN AND
　　HILL SHALL BE BROUGHT
　　LOW;
AND THE CROOKED SHALL BE-
　　COME STRAIGHT,
AND THE ROUGH ROADS
　　SMOOTH;

6 [a]AND ALL FLESH SHALL [b]SEE
　　THE SALVATION OF GOD.'"

7 He therefore *began* saying to the multitudes who were going out to be baptized by him, "You brood of vipers, who warned you to flee from the wrath to come?

8 "Therefore bring forth fruits in keeping with repentance, and [a]do not begin to say to yourselves, 'We have Abraham for our father,' for I say to you that God is able from these stones to raise up children to Abraham.

2:48 *Your father.* As Mary's husband, Joseph was Jesus' legal, though not His natural, father.

2:51 *came to Nazareth.* A veil is drawn over the life of Jesus until the beginning of His public ministry 18 years later.

3:1 *Tiberius Caesar* was the adopted son of Augustus Caesar (2:1) and reigned from A.D. 14–37. *Pilate.* See note on Mark 15:1. *Herod.* Antipas, the son of Herod the Great (Matt. 2:1) ruled over Galilee (*tetrarch* = ruler of one quarter of a given territory). *Philip.* Another son of Herod the Great, he ruled over Ituraea, NE. of Galilee and E. of Mt. Hermon. *Abilene.* A small kingdom on the E. slope of the Lebanon mountains, NE. of Damascus.

3:2 *Annas and Caiaphas.* Caiaphas was the ruling high priest (A.D. 18–36), though Annas, high priest A.D. 6–15, continued to exercise weighty influence (cf. John 18:13; Acts 4:6).

3:8 The meaning is: Do not trust in your religious ancestry, however good it may be; you must personally have a right relation with God.

★**48** [a]Matt. 12:46 [b]Luke 2:49; 3:23; 4:22

50 [a]Mark 9:32

★**51** [a]Luke 2:39 [b]Matt. 12:46 [c]Luke 2:19

52 [a]Luke 2:40

★ **1** [a]Matt. 27:2 [b]Matt. 14:1

★ **2** [a]John 18:13; 24; Acts 4:6 [b]Matt. 26:3 [c]Luke 3:3-10; Matt. 3:1-10; Mark 1:3-5

3 [a]Matt. 3:5

4 [a]Is. 40:3

5 [a]Is. 40:4

6 [a]Is. 40:5 [b]Luke 2:30

★ **8** [a]Luke 5:21; 13:25, 26; 14:9

★ 9   9 "And also the axe is already laid at the root of the trees; every tree therefore that does not bear good fruit is cut down and thrown into the fire."

10 And the multitudes were questioning him, saying, "Then what shall we do?"

11 And he would answer and say to them, "Let the man who has two tunics share with him who has none; and let him who has food do likewise."

★12   12 And *some* tax-gatherers also came to be baptized, and they said to him, "Teacher, what shall we do?"

13 And he said to them, "Collect no more than what you have been ordered to."

★14   14 And *some* soldiers were questioning him, saying, "And *what about* us, what shall we do?" And he said to them, "Do not take money from anyone by force, or accuse *anyone* falsely, and be content with your wages."

★15 aJohn 1:19f.
15 Now while the people were in a state of expectation and all were wondering in their hearts about John, aas to whether he might be the Christ,

★16 aLuke 3:16, 17; Matt. 3:11, 12; Mark 1:7, 8
16 aJohn answered and said to them all, "As for me, I baptize you with water; but One is coming who is mightier than I, and I am not fit to untie the thong of His sandals; He will baptize you with the Holy Spirit and fire.

17 aIs. 30:24 bMark 9:43, 48
17 "And His awinnowing fork is in His hand to thoroughly clear His threshing floor, and to gather the wheat into His barn; but He will burn up the chaff with bunquenchable fire."

18 So with many other exhortations also he preached the gospel to the people.

★19 aMatt. 14:3; Mark 6:17 bMatt. 14:1; Luke 3:1
19 But when aHerod the tetrarch was reproved by him on account of aHerodias, his brother's wife, and on account of all the wicked things which bHerod had done,

20 aJohn 3:24
20 he added this also to them all, that ahe locked John up in prison.

21 aLuke 3:21, 22; Matt. 3:13-17; Mark 1:9-11 bMatt. 14:23; Luke 5:16; 9:18, 28f.
21 aNow it came about when all the people were baptized, that Jesus also was baptized, and while He was bpraying, heaven was opened,

★22 aMatt. 3:17
22 and the Holy Spirit descended upon Him in bodily form like a dove, and a voice came out of heaven, "aThou art My beloved Son, in Thee I am well-pleased."

H   The Genealogy of the Son of Man, 3:23-38

★23 aMatt. 4:17; Acts 1:1 bMatt. 1:16; Luke 3:23-27
23 And awhen He began His ministry, Jesus Himself was about thirty years of age, being supposedly *the* son of bJoseph, the *son of* Eli,

24 the *son* of Matthat, the *son* of Levi, the *son* of Melchi, the *son* of Jannai, the *son* of Joseph,

25 the *son* of Mattathias, the *son* of Amos, the *son* of Nahum, the *son* of Hesli, the *son* of Naggai,

26 the *son* of Maath, the *son* of Mattathias, the *son* of Semein, the *son* of Josech, the *son* of Joda,

27 aMatt. 1:12
27 the *son* of Joanan, the *son*

3:9 *the axe is already laid at the root of the trees.* Just as unproductive trees are cut down, so the unfruitful nation of Israel could expect judgment.

3:12 *tax-gatherers.* See notes on Matt. 9:10 and Luke 19:2.

3:14 *soldiers* were often brutal to civilians and practiced extortion.

3:15 *in a state of expectation* of the Messiah's coming.

3:16 *baptize.* See note on Matt. 3:11. *in the Holy Spirit and fire.* The baptism with the Holy Spirit occurred on the day of Pentecost, while the baptism with fire refers to the judgments accompanying the second coming of Christ.

3:19 *Herodias.* See note on Matt. 14:3.

3:22 *like a dove.* The dove was used as a symbol for all kinds of virtues in those days (see Matt. 10:16). All persons of the Trinity were present at Christ's baptism.

3:23 *son of Eli.* Joseph was Jacob's son by birth (Matt. 1:16) and Eli's son by marriage. This is apparently the genealogy of Jesus through His mother, Mary. See note at Matt. 1:1.

of Rhesa, [a]the son of Zerubbabel, the son of Shealtiel, the son of Neri,

28 the son of Melchi, the son of Addi, the son of Cosam, the son of Elmadam, the son of Er,

29 the son of Joshua, the son of Eliezer, the son of Jorim, the son of Matthat, the son of Levi,

30 the son of Simeon, the son of Judah, the son of Joseph, the son of Jonam, the son of Eliakim,

31 the son of Melea, the son of Menna, the son of Mattatha, the son of Nathan, the son of David,

32 [a]the son of Jesse, the son of Obed, the son of Boaz, the son of Salmon, the son of Nahshon,

33 the son of Amminadab, the son of Admin, the son of Ram, the son of Hezron, the son of Perez, the son of Judah,

34 the son of Jacob, the son of Isaac, [a]the son of Abraham, the son of Terah, the son of Nahor,

35 the son of Serug, the son of Reu, the son of Peleg, the son of Heber, the son of Shelah,

36 the son of Cainan, the son of Arphaxad, the son of Shem, [a]the son of Noah, the son of Lamech,

37 the son of Methuselah, the son of Enoch, the son of Jared, the son of Mahalaleel, the son of Cainan,

38 the son of Enosh, the son of Seth, the son of Adam, the son of God.

I The Temptation of the Son of Man, 4:1-13

4 [a]And Jesus, full of the Holy Spirit, [b]returned from the Jordan and was led about by the Spirit in the wilderness

2 for forty days, being tempted by the devil. And He ate nothing during those days; and when they had ended, He became hungry.

3 And the devil said to Him, "If You are the Son of God, tell this stone to become bread."

4 And Jesus answered him, "It is written, '[a]MAN SHALL NOT LIVE ON BREAD ALONE.'"

5 [a]And he led Him up and showed Him all the kingdoms of [b]the world in a moment of time.

6 And the devil said to Him, "I will give You all this domain and its glory; [a]for it has been handed over to me, and I give it to whomever I wish.

7 "Therefore if You worship before me, it shall all be Yours."

8 And Jesus answered and said to him, "It is written, '[a]YOU SHALL WORSHIP THE LORD YOUR GOD AND SERVE HIM ONLY.'"

9 [a]And he led Him to Jerusalem and had Him stand on the pinnacle of the temple, and said to Him, "If You are the Son of God, throw Yourself down from here;

10 for it is written,

'[a]HE WILL GIVE HIS ANGELS
    CHARGE CONCERNING YOU
    TO GUARD YOU,'

11 and,

'[a]ON *their* HANDS THEY WILL
    BEAR YOU UP,
    LEST YOU STRIKE YOUR FOOT
    AGAINST A STONE.'"

12 And Jesus answered and said to him, "It is said, '[a]YOU SHALL

Margin references

32 [a]Luke 3.32-34. Matt. 1.1-6

34 [a]Luke 3.34-36. Gen. 11.26-30; 1 Chr. 1.24-27

36 [a]Luke 3.36-38. Gen. 5.3-32. 1 Chr. 1.1-4

★ **1** [a]Luke 4.1-13. Matt. 4.1-11. Mark 1.12, 13 [b]Luke 3.3, 21

★ **2**

★ **3**

★ **4** [a]Deut. 8.3

5 [a]Matt. 4.8-10 [b]Matt. 24.14

6 [a]1 John 5.19

★ **8** [a]Deut. 6.13

★ **9** [a]Matt. 4.5-7

★**10** [a]Ps. 91.11

11 [a]Ps. 91.12

★**12** [a]Deut. 6.16

4:1 *the wilderness.* The traditional site of the temptation is NW. of the Dead Sea, near Jericho.

4:2 *tempted by the devil.* See note on Matt. 4:1.

4:3 *If You are the Son of God.* The particular Greek construction used here indicates that the devil did not doubt that Jesus was the Son of God.

4:4 See Deut. 8:3.

4:8 See Deut. 6:13; 10:20.

4:9 *pinnacle of the temple.* One of the battlements or towers that overlooked the courtyard of the temple. If Jesus had cast Himself off and landed unharmed among the crowds below, He surely would have been acclaimed the Messiah.

4:10 See Ps. 91:11-12. Satan omits from the quotation the phrase, "in all your ways," in an attempt to apply the promise to something which was contrary to God's will.

4:12 See Deut. 6:16. The temptations were designed to offer Christ the glory of ruling without the suffering of dying for sin.

NOT PUT THE LORD YOUR GOD TO THE TEST.' "

13 And when the devil had finished every temptation, he departed from Him until an opportune time.

III THE MINISTRY OF THE SON OF MAN TO MEN, 4:14–9:50
A The Announcement of His Ministry, 4:14–30

14 And ^aJesus returned to Galilee in the power of the Spirit; and ^bnews about Him spread through all the surrounding district.

15 And He *began* ^ateaching in their synagogues and was praised by all.

16 And He came to ^aNazareth, where He had been brought up; and as was His custom, ^bHe entered the synagogue on the Sabbath, and ^cstood up to read.

17 And the book of the prophet Isaiah was handed to Him. And He opened the book, and found the place where it was written,

18   "^aTHE SPIRIT OF THE LORD IS UPON ME,

BECAUSE HE ANOINTED ME TO PREACH THE GOSPEL TO THE POOR.

HE HAS SENT ME TO PROCLAIM RELEASE TO THE CAPTIVES,

AND RECOVERY OF SIGHT TO THE BLIND,

TO SET FREE THOSE WHO ARE DOWNTRODDEN,

19   ^aTO PROCLAIM THE FAVORABLE YEAR OF THE LORD."

20 And He ^aclosed the book, and gave it back to the attendant,

and ^bsat down; and the eyes of all in the synagogue were fixed upon Him.

21 And He began to say to them, "Today this Scripture has been fulfilled in your hearing."

22 And all were speaking well of Him, and wondering at the gracious words which were falling from His lips; and they were saying, "^aIs this not Joseph's son?"

23 And He said to them, "No doubt you will quote this proverb to Me, 'Physician, heal yourself! Whatever we heard was done ^aat Capernaum, do here in ^byour home town as well.' "

24 And He said, "Truly I say to you, ^ano prophet is welcome in his home town.

25 "But I say to you in truth, there were many widows in Israel ^ain the days of Elijah, when the sky was shut up for three years and six months, when a great famine came over all the land;

26 and yet Elijah was sent to none of them, but ^aonly to Zarephath, in the land of ^bSidon, to a woman who was a widow.

27 "And there were many lepers in Israel in the time of Elisha the prophet; and none of them was cleansed, but ^aonly Naaman the Syrian."

28 And all in the synagogue were filled with rage as they heard these things;

29 and they rose up and ^acast Him out of the city, and led Him to the brow of the hill on which their city had been built, in order to throw Him down the cliff.

30 But ^apassing through their midst, He went His way.

Cross-references (margin)

14 ^aMatt. 4:12 ^bMatt. 9:26; Luke 4:37
15 ^aMatt. 4:23
16 ^aLuke 2:39, 51 ^bMatt. 13:54; Mark 6:1f ^cActs 13:14-16
★17
★18 ^aIs. 61:1; Matt. 11:5; 12:18; John 3:34
19 ^aLev. 25:10; Is. 61:2
★20 ^aLuke 4:17 ^bMatt. 26:55
22 ^aMatt. 13:55; Mark 6:3; John 6:42
23 ^aMatt. 4:13; Mark 1:21ff.; 2:1ff.; John 4:46ff. ^bMark 6:1; Luke 2:39, 51; 4:16
24 ^aMatt. 13:57; Mark 6:4; John 4:44
★25-26
25 ^a1 Kin. 17:1, 18:1; James 5:17
26 ^a1 Kin. 17:9 ^bMatt. 11:21
27 ^a2 Kin. 5:1-14
29 ^aNum. 15:35; Acts 7:58; Heb. 13:12
★30 ^aJohn 10:39

4:17 *book.* More correctly, the scroll.
4:18 See Isa. 61:1–2a. Christ stopped reading in the middle of 61:2, since at His first coming He preached only the "favorable year of the Lord" (v. 19). The "day of vengeance of our God" (Isa. 61:2b) was reserved for His second coming. Long-suffering and the cross are associated with His first coming; judgment and a crown, with His second.

4:20 *the attendant* had charge of the scrolls of Scriptures.
4:25-26 The story is in 1 Kings 17:8-24.
4:30 *passing through their midst.* These words do not necessarily imply a miraculous deliverance. Rather, His commanding presence and righteousness had power to thwart the crowd's plan.

**B The Authority of His
Ministry, 4:31–6:11**

1 Over demons, 4:31–37

*★31 ᵃLuke
4:31-37;
Mark 1:21-28
ᵇMatt. 4:13;
Luke 4:23*

31 And ᵃHe came down to ᵇCapernaum, a city of Galilee. And He was teaching them on the Sabbath;

*32 ᵃMatt.
7:28 ᵇLuke
4:36; John
7:46*

32 and ᵃthey were amazed at His teaching, for ᵇHis message was with authority.

★33

33 And there was a man in the synagogue possessed by the spirit of an unclean demon, and he cried out with a loud voice,

*34 ᵃMatt.
8:29 ᵇMark
1:24*

34 "Ha! ᵃWhat do we have to do with You, Jesus of ᵇNazareth? Have You come to destroy us? I know You are—ᵇthe Holy One of God!"

*35 ᵃMatt.
8:26; Mark
4:39; Luke
4:39, 41;
8:24*

35 And Jesus ᵃrebuked him, saying, "Be quiet and come out of him!" And when the demon had thrown him down in *their* midst, he came out of him without doing him any harm.

*36 ᵃLuke
4:32*

36 And amazement came upon them all, and they *began* discussing with one another, saying, "What is this message? For ᵃwith authority and power He commands the unclean spirits, and they come out."

*37 ᵃLuke
4:14*

37 And ᵃthe report about Him was getting out into every locality in the surrounding district.

2 Over disease, 4:38–44

*★38 ᵃLuke
4:38, 39;
Matt. 8:14,
15; Mark
1:29-31
ᵇMatt. 4:24*

38 ᵃAnd He arose and *left* the synagogue, and entered Simon's home. Now Simon's mother-in-law was ᵇsuffering from a high fever; and they made request of Him on her behalf.

*39 ᵃLuke
4:35, 41
40 ᵃLuke
4:40, 41;
Matt. 8:16,
17; Mark
1:32-34
ᵇMark 1:32
ᶜMark 5:23
ᵈMatt. 4:23*

39 And standing over her, He ᵃrebuked the fever, and it left her; and she immediately arose and waited on them.

40 ᵃAnd while ᵇthe sun was setting, all who had any sick with various diseases brought them to

Him; and ᶜlaying His hands on every one of them, He was ᵈhealing them.

*41 ᵃMatt. 4:3
ᵇLuke 4:35
ᶜMatt. 8:4;
Mark 1:34*

41 And demons also were coming out of many, crying out and saying, "You are ᵃthe Son of God!" And ᵇrebuking them, He would ᶜnot allow them to speak, because they knew Him to be the Christ.

*42 ᵃLuke
4:42, 43;
Mark 1:35-38*

42 ᵃAnd when day came, He departed and went to a lonely place; and the multitudes were searching for Him, and came to Him, and tried to keep Him from going away from them.

*43 ᵃMark
1:38*

43 But He said to them, "I must preach the kingdom of God to the other cities also, ᵃfor I was sent for this purpose."

*44 ᵃMatt.
4:23*

44 And He kept on preaching in the synagogues ᵃof Judea.

3 Over the disciples, 5:1–11

*★ 1 ᵃMatt.
4:18-22;
Mark 1:16-
20; Luke 5:1-
11; John
1:40-42
ᵇNum.
34:11; Deut.
3:17; Josh.
12:3; 13:27;
Matt. 4:18*

5 ᵃNow it came about that while the multitude were pressing around Him and listening to the word of God, He was standing by ᵇthe lake of Gennesaret;

2 and He saw two boats lying at the edge of the lake; but the fishermen had gotten out of them, and were washing their nets.

*3 ᵃMatt.
13:2; Mark
4:1*

3 And ᵃHe got into one of the boats, which was Simon's, and asked him to put out a little way from the land. And He sat down and *began* teaching the multitudes from the boat.

*4 ᵃJohn
21:6*

4 And when He had finished speaking, He said to Simon, "Put out into the deep water and ᵃlet down your nets for a catch."

*5 ᵃGr. as in
Luke 8:24;
9:33, 49;
17:13*

5 And Simon answered and said, "ᵃMaster, we worked hard all night and caught nothing, but at Your bidding I will let down the nets."

6 And when they had done this, they enclosed a great quan-

4:31 *Capernaum.* A city on the shore of the Lake of Galilee, about 25 miles NE. of Nazareth. Jesus carried on an extensive ministry there.

4:33 *demon.* See note on Matt. 7:22.

4:38 *a high fever.* Only Luke, a physician, recorded this fact.

5:1 *the lake of Gennesaret.* The Lake, or Sea, of Galilee.

tity of fish; and their nets *began* to break;

7 and they signaled to their partners in the other boat, for them to come and help them. And they came, and filled both of the boats, so that they began to sink.

★ 8   **8** But when Simon Peter saw *that,* he fell down at Jesus' feet, saying, "Depart from me, for I am a sinful man, O Lord!"

9 For amazement had seized him and all his companions because of the catch of fish which they had taken;

10 aMatt.
14:27
b2 Tim. 2:26

10 and so also James and John, sons of Zebedee, who were partners with Simon. And Jesus said to Simon, "ᵃDo not fear, from now on you will be ᵇcatching men."

11 aMatt.
4:20, 22;
19:29; Mark
1:18, 20;
Luke 5:28

11 And when they had brought their boats to land, ᵃthey left everything and followed Him.

4   *Over defilement (a leper healed),* 5:12-16

★12 aLuke
5:12-14;
Matt. 8:2-4;
Mark 1:40-44

12 ᵃAnd it came about that while He was in one of the cities, behold, *there was* a man full of leprosy; and when he saw Jesus, he fell on his face and implored Him, saying, "Lord, if You are willing, You can make me clean."

13 And He stretched out His hand, and touched him, saying, "I am willing; be cleansed." And immediately the leprosy left him.

14 aLev.
13:49; 14:2ff.

14 And He ordered him to tell no one, "But go and ᵃshow yourself to the priest, and make an offering for your cleansing, just as Moses commanded, for a testimony to them."

15 aMatt.
9:26

15 But ᵃthe news about Him was spreading even farther, and great multitudes were gathering to hear *Him* and to be healed of their sicknesses.

16 But He Himself would *often* slip away to the wilderness and ᵃpray.

★16 aMatt.
14:23; Mark
1:35; Luke
6:12

5   *Over defectiveness (a paralytic healed),* 5:17-26

17 And it came about one day that He was teaching; and ᵃthere were *some* Pharisees and ᵇteachers of the law sitting *there,* who had ᶜcome from every village of Galilee and Judea and *from* Jerusalem; and ᵈthe power of the Lord was *present* for Him to perform healing.

★17 aMatt.
15:1 bLuke
2:46 cMark
1:45 dMark
5:30; Luke
6:19; 8:46

18 ᵃAnd behold, *some* men *were* carrying on a bed a man who was paralyzed; and they were trying to bring him in, and to set him down in front of Him.

18 aLuke
5:18-26;
Matt. 9:2-8;
Mark 2:3-12

19 And not finding any *way* to bring him in because of the crowd, they went up on ᵃthe roof and let him down ᵇthrough the tiles with his stretcher, right in the center, in front of Jesus.

19 aMatt.
24:17 bMark
2:4

20 And seeing their faith, He said, "Friend, ᵃyour sins are forgiven you."

★20 aMatt.
9:2

21 And the scribes and the Pharisees ᵃbegan to reason, saying, "Who is this *man* who speaks blasphemies? ᵇWho can forgive sins, but God alone?"

21 aLuke 3:8
bIs. 43:25

22 But Jesus, aware of their reasonings, answered and said to them, "Why are you reasoning in your hearts?

23 "Which is easier, to say, 'Your sins have been forgiven you,' or to say, 'Rise and walk'?

5:8 The miracle demonstrated to Peter his own sinfulness and Jesus' deity.

5:12 *leprosy.* See Lev. 13 for 7 forms of this skin disease, generally regarded not to be the leprosy we know today. A leper was ceremonially unclean, had to live outside of the towns, and had to cry "unclean" when other people came near. Leprosy serves as an illustration of sin.

5:16 *pray.* See Introduction, under "Distinctive Approach."

5:17 Only Luke mentions the presence of religious leaders from all parts of the land, listening critically to the claims of Jesus.

5:20 *Friend, your sins are forgiven you.* The Lord began with the man's greater problem, his spiritual need, rather than his physical one. Jesus' statement was considered blasphemy, since it was clearly understood to be a claim of being equal with God. See notes on Matt. 9:2 and 9:5.

24 "But in order that you may know that the Son of Man has authority on earth to forgive sins,"—He said to the [a]paralytic—"I say to you, rise, and take up your stretcher and go home."

25 And at once he rose up before them, and took up what he had been lying on, and went home, [a]glorifying God.

26 And they were all seized with astonishment and *began* [a]glorifying God; and they were filled [b]with fear, saying, "We have seen remarkable things today."

6 Over the despised (the call of Matthew and parables), 5:27-39

27 [a]And after that He went out, and noticed a tax-gatherer named [b]Levi, sitting in the tax office, and He said to him, "Follow Me."

28 And he [a]left everything behind, and rose and *began* to follow Him.

29 And [a]Levi gave a big reception for Him in his house; and there was a great crowd of [b]tax-gatherers and other *people* who were reclining *at the table* with them.

30 And the Pharisees and [a]their scribes *began* grumbling at His disciples, saying, "Why do you eat and drink with the tax-gatherers and sinners?"

31 And Jesus answered and said to them, "[a]*It is* not those who are well who need a physician, but those who are sick.

32 "I have not come to call the righteous but sinners to repentance."

33 And they said to Him, "[a]The disciples of John often fast and offer prayers; the *disciples* of the Pharisees also do the same; but Yours eat and drink."

34 And Jesus said to them, "You cannot make the attendants of the bridegroom fast while the bridegroom is with them, can you?

35 "[a]But *the* days will come; and when the bridegroom is taken away from them, then they will fast in those days."

36 And He was also telling them a parable: "No one tears a piece from a new garment and puts it on an old garment; otherwise he will both tear the new, and the piece from the new will not match the old.

37 "And no one puts new wine into old wineskins; otherwise the new wine will burst the skins, and it will be spilled out, and the skins will be ruined.

38 "But new wine must be put into fresh wineskins.

39 "And no one, after drinking old *wine* wishes for new; for he says, 'The old is good *enough.*'"

7 Over days, 6:1-5

6 [a]Now it came about that on a certain Sabbath He was passing through *some* grainfields; and His disciples [b]were picking and eating the heads *of grain*, rubbing them in their hands.

2 But some of the Pharisees said, "Why do you do what [a]is not lawful on the Sabbath?"

3 And Jesus answering them said, "Have you not even read [a]what David did when he was hungry, he and those who were with him,

4 how he entered the house of God, and took and ate the con-

Margin references:

24 [a]Matt. 4:24
25 [a]Matt. 9:8
26 [a]Matt. 9:8 [b]Luke 1:65; 7:16
★27 [a]Luke 5:27-39; Matt. 9:9-17; Mark 2:14-22 [b]Matt. 9:9
28 [a]Luke 5:11
29 [a]Matt. 9:9 [b]Luke 15:1
30 [a]Mark 2:16; Acts 23:9
31 [a]Matt. 9:12, 13; Mark 2:17
33 [a]Matt. 9:14; Mark 2:18
35 [a]Matt. 9:15; Mark 2:20; Luke 17:22
★37
1 [a]Luke 5:1-5; Matt. 12:1-8; Mark 2:23-28 [b]Deut. 23:25
★ 2 [a]Matt. 12:2
★ 3 [a]1 Sam. 21:6

5:27 *Levi.* Matthew. See Introduction to Matthew and note on Matt. 9:10.

5:37 *wineskins.* Used as containers for liquid. If filled with new wine, old skins lost elasticity and burst when it fermented. The point is that the new teaching of the grace of Christ cannot be contained within the old forms of the law (John 1:17).

6:2 *not lawful on the Sabbath.* Jesus was being charged with working on the Sabbath, though it was lawful to pick grain from another's field to satisfy hunger (Deut. 23:25).

6:3 *what David did.* See 1 Sam. 21:1-6. To the Pharisees' objections Jesus quoted an O.T. example of the spirit of the law taking priority over the letter of the law. See note on Matt. 12:2.

secrated bread which is not lawful for any to eat except the priests alone, and gave it to his companions?"

★ 5   **5** And He was saying to them, "The Son of Man is Lord of the Sabbath."

8 Over deformity, 6:6-11

6 aLuke 5:6-11; Matt. 12:9-14; Mark 3:1-6 bLuke 6:1 cMatt. 4:23

6 aAnd it came about bon another Sabbath, that He entered cthe synagogue and was teaching; and there was a man there whose right hand was withered.

★ 7 aMark 3:2

7 And the scribes and the Pharisees awere watching Him closely, to see if He healed on the Sabbath, in order that they might find reason to accuse Him.

8 aMatt. 9:4

8 But He aknew what they were thinking, and He said to the man with the withered hand, "Rise and come forward!" And he rose and came forward.

9 And Jesus said to them, "I ask you, is it lawful on the Sabbath to do good, or to do harm, to save a life, or to destroy it?"

10 aMark 3:5

10 And after alooking around at them all, He said to him, "Stretch out your hand!" And he did so; and his hand was restored.

11 But they themselves were filled with rage, and discussed together what they might do to Jesus.

C The Associates of His Ministry, 6:12-49

1 The call of the disciples, 6:12-16

12 aMatt. 5:1 bMatt. 14:23; Luke 5:16; 9:18, 28

12 And it was at this time that He went off to athe mountain to bpray, and He spent the whole night in prayer to God.

13 And when day came, aHe called His disciples to Him; and chose twelve of them, whom He also named as bapostles:

14 Simon, whom He also named Peter, and Andrew his brother; and James and John; and Philip and Bartholomew;

15 and aMatthew and Thomas; James the son of Alphaeus, and Simon who was called the Zealot;

16 Judas the son of James, and Judas Iscariot, who became a traitor.

2 The characteristics of disciples (The Great Sermon), 6:17-49

17 And He adescended with them, and stood on a level place; and there was ba great multitude of His disciples, and a great throng of people from all Judea and Jerusalem and the coastal region of cTyre and Sidon,

18 who had come to hear Him, and to be healed of their diseases; and those who were troubled with unclean spirits were being cured.

19 And all the multitude were trying to atouch Him, for bpower was coming from Him and healing them all.

20 And turning His gaze on His disciples, He began to say, "aBlessed are you who are poor, for byours is the kingdom of God.

21 "Blessed are you who hunger now, for you shall be satisfied. Blessed are you who weep now, for you shall laugh.

22 "Blessed are you when men hate you, and aostracize you, and cast insults at you, and spurn

★13 aLuke 6:13-16; Matt. 10:2-4; Mark 3:16-19; Acts 1:13 bMark 6:30

15 aMatt. 9:9

★17-26

17 aLuke 6:12 bMatt. 4:25; Mark 3:7, 8 cMatt. 11:21

19 aMatt. 9:21; 14:36; Mark 3:10 bLuke 5:17

20 aMatt. 5:3-12; Luke 6:20-23 bMatt. 5:3

22 aJohn 9:22; 16:2

6:5 *Lord of the Sabbath.* Not only had Christ claimed deity (5:20), but now He claimed sovereignty over the Sabbath day and its laws, and asserted His right to interpret its laws without reference to the traditions of the Pharisees.

6:7 *reason to accuse Him.* To heal on the Sabbath would have been a violation, according to the traditions of the Pharisees, of the prohibition against work on that day; but not to heal,

as Christ tried to point out, would have been to do evil and to destroy life (v. 9). To heal, and therefore to do a good work, would be no violation of Sabbath laws.

6:13 *apostles.* See note on Matt. 10:2.

6:17-26 This may be Luke's account of the same occasion and teaching recorded in Matt. 5-7 (the Sermon on the Mount) or it may simply be similar teaching given on a different occasion.

your name as evil, for the sake of the Son of Man.

23 "Be glad in that day, and [a]leap for joy, for behold, your reward is great in heaven; for in the same way their fathers used to treat the prophets.

24 "But woe to [a]you who are rich, for [b]you are receiving your comfort in full.

25 "Woe to you who are well-fed now, for you shall be hungry. Woe to you who laugh now, for you shall mourn and weep.

26 "Woe to you when all men speak well of you, for in the same way their fathers used to treat the [a]false prophets.

27 "But I say to you who hear, [a]love your enemies, do good to those who hate you,

28 bless those who curse you, [a]pray for those who mistreat you.

29 "[a]Whoever hits you on the cheek, offer him the other also; and whoever takes away your coat, do not withhold your shirt from him either.

30 "Give to everyone who asks of you, and whoever takes away what is yours, do not demand it back.

31 "[a]And just as you want people to treat you, treat them in the same way.

32 "And [a]if you love those who love you, what credit is that to you? For even sinners love those who love them.

33 "And if you do good to those who do good to you, what credit is that to you? For even sinners do the same.

34 "[a]And if you lend to those from whom you expect to receive, what credit is that to you? Even sinners lend to sinners, in order to receive back the same amount.

35 "But [a]love your enemies, and do good, and lend, expecting nothing in return; and your reward will be great, and you will be [b]sons of [c]the Most High; for

He Himself is kind to ungrateful and evil men.

36 "Be merciful, just as your Father is merciful.

37 "[a]And do not judge and you will not be judged; and do not condemn, and you will not be condemned; [b]pardon, and you will be pardoned.

38 "Give, and it will be given to you; [a]good measure, pressed down, shaken together, running over, they will pour [b]into your lap. For by your standard of measure it will be measured to you in return."

39 And He also spoke a parable to them: "[a]A blind man cannot guide a blind man, can he? Will they not both fall into a pit?

40 "[a]A pupil is not above his teacher; but everyone, after he has been fully trained, will be like his teacher.

41 "And why do you look at the speck that is in your brother's eye, but do not notice the log that is in your own eye?

42 "Or how can you say to your brother, 'Brother, let me take out the speck that is in your eye,' when you yourself do not see the log that is in your own eye? You hypocrite, first take the log out of your own eye, and then you will see clearly to take out the speck that is in your brother's eye.

43 "[a]For there is no good tree which produces bad fruit; nor, on the other hand, a bad tree which produces good fruit.

44 "[a]For each tree is known by its own fruit. For men do not gather figs from thorns, nor do they pick grapes from a briar bush.

45 "[a]The good man out of the good treasure of his heart brings forth what is good; and the evil man out of the evil treasure brings forth what is evil; [b]for his

Cross references

23 [a]Mal. 4

24 [a]Luke 16:25; James 5:1 [b]Matt. 6:2

26 [a]Matt. 7:15

27 [a]Matt. 5:44; Luke 6:35

28 [a]Matt. 5:44; Luke 6:35

29 [a]Luke 6:29, 30; Matt. 5:39-42

31 [a]Matt. 7:12

32 [a]Matt. 5:46

34 [a]Matt. 5:42

35 [a]Luke 6:27 [b]Matt. 5:9 [c]Luke 1:32

37 [a]Luke 6:37-42; Matt. 7:1-5 [b]Matt. 6:14; Luke 23:16; Acts 3:13

★38 [a]Mark 4:24 [b]Ps. 79:12; Is. 65:6, 7; Jer. 32:18

39 [a]Matt. 15:14

40 [a]Matt. 10:24

★41

43 [a]Luke 6:43, 44; Matt. 7:16, 18, 20

44 [a]Matt. 7:16

45 [a]Matt. 12:35 [b]Matt. 12:34

6:38 *pressed down, shaken together, running over.* The imagery is of a container of grain filled to the brim and running over the edge. Our liberality should be like that.

6:41 *speck . . . . log.* A speck is something tiny like a bit of sawdust, while a log, of course, is large. Perhaps Jesus was drawing on His experience as a carpenter.

mouth speaks from that which fills his heart.

46 ᵃMal. 1:6;
Matt. 7:21

46 "And ᵃwhy do you call Me, 'Lord, Lord,' and do not do what I say?

47 ᵃLuke
6:47-49;
Matt. 7:24-27

47 "ᵃEveryone who comes to Me, and hears My words, and acts upon them, I will show you whom he is like:

48 he is like a man building a house, who dug deep and laid a foundation upon the rock; and when a flood rose, the torrent burst against that house and could not shake it, because it had been well built.

49 "But the one who has heard, and has not acted *accordingly,* is like a man who built a house upon the ground without any foundation; and the torrent burst against it and immediately it collapsed, and the ruin of that house was great."

D The Activities of His Ministry, 7:1-9:50

1 Ministry in sickness, 7:1-10

1 ᵃMatt.
7:28 ᵇLuke
7:1-10; Matt.
8:5-13

7 ᵃWhen He had completed all His discourse in the hearing of the people, ᵇHe went to Capernaum.

★ 2

2 And a certain centurion's slave, who was highly regarded by him, was sick and about to die.

3 ᵃMatt. 8:5

3 And when he heard about Jesus, ᵃhe sent some Jewish elders asking Him to come and save the life of his slave.

4 And when they had come to Jesus, they earnestly entreated Him, saying, "He is worthy for You to grant this to him;

★ 5

5 for he loves our nation, and it was he who built us our synagogue."

6 Now Jesus *started* on His way with them; and when He was already not far from the house, the centurion sent friends, saying to Him, "Lord, do not trouble Yourself further, for I am not worthy for You to come under my roof;

7 for this reason I did not even consider myself worthy to come to You, but just say the word, and my servant will be healed.

8 "For I, too, am a man under authority, with soldiers under me; and I say to this one, 'Go!' and he goes; and to another, 'Come!' and he comes; and to my slave, 'Do this!' and he does it."

9 Now when Jesus heard this, He marveled at him, and turned and said to the multitude that was following Him, "I say to you, ᵃnot even in Israel have I found such great faith."

★ 9 ᵃMatt.
8:10; Luke
7:50

10 And when those who had been sent returned to the house, they found the slave in good health.

2 Ministry in death, 7:11-17

11 And it came about soon afterwards, that He went to a city called Nain; and His disciples were going along with Him, accompanied by a large multitude.

★11

12 Now as He approached the gate of the city, behold, a dead man was being carried out, the only son of his mother, and she was a widow; and a sizeable crowd from the city was with her.

13 And when ᵃthe Lord saw her, He felt compassion for her, and said to her, "Do not weep."

13 ᵃLuke
7:19; 10:1;
11:1, 39;
12:42; 13:15;
17:5, 6; 18:6;
19:8; 22:61;
24:34; John
4:1; 6:23;
11:2

14 And He came up and touched the coffin; and the bearers came to a halt. And He said, "Young man, I say to you, arise!"

7:2 *centurion.* Here was an atypical Roman officer who loved his servant and the Jewish people.

7:5 *synagogue.* A Jewish house of worship, first established during the Babylonian captivity but also used after the temple was rebuilt by Jews wherever they settled. Services included

prescribed readings, prayer, and a sermon (4:20). Any competent teacher might be asked to speak (Acts 13:15). Ruins of a later synagogue can be seen in Capernaum today.

7:9 *such great faith.* This Gentile's faith was a welcome contrast to the unbelief of the Jews.

7:11 *Nain.* About 10 miles SE. of Nazareth.

★15

15 And the dead man sat up, and began to speak. And *Jesus* gave him back to his mother.

16 aLuke 5:26 bMatt. 9:8 cMatt. 21:11; Luke 7:39

16 And ªfear gripped them all, and they *began* ᵇglorifying God, saying, "A great ᶜprophet has arisen among us!" and, "God has visited His people!"

17 aMatt. 9:26

17 ªAnd this report concerning Him went out all over Judea, and in all the surrounding district.

3 Ministry in doubt, 7:18-35

18 aLuke 7:18-35; Matt. 11:2-19

18 ªAnd the disciples of John reported to him about all these things.

19 aLuke 7:13; 10:1; 11:1, 39; 12:42; 13:15; 17:5, 6; 18:6; 19:8; 22:61; 24:34; John 4:1; 6:23; 11:2

19 And summoning two of his disciples, John sent them to ªthe Lord, saying, "Are You the Expected One, or do we look for someone else?"

20 And when the men had come to Him, they said, "John the Baptist has sent us to You, saying, 'Are You the Expected One, or do we look for someone else?'"

21 aMatt. 4:23 bMark 3:10

21 At that very time He ªcured many *people* of diseases and ᵇafflictions and evil spirits; and He granted sight to many *who were* blind.

★22 aIs. 61:1

22 And He answered and said to them, "Go and report to John what you have seen and heard: *the* ªBLIND RECEIVE SIGHT, *the* lame walk, *the* lepers are cleansed, and *the* deaf hear, *the* dead are raised up, *the* ªPOOR HAVE THE GOSPEL PREACHED TO THEM.

23 "And blessed is he who keeps from stumbling over Me."

★24-25

24 And when the messengers of John had left, He began to speak to the multitudes about John, "What did you go out into the wilderness to look at? A reed shaken by the wind?

25 "But what did you go out to see? A man dressed in soft clothing? Behold, those who are splendidly clothed and live in luxury are *found* in royal palaces.

26 "But what did you go out to see? A prophet? Yes, I say to you, and one who is more than a prophet.

27 aMal. 3:1; Matt. 11:10; Mark 1:2

27 "This is the one about whom it is written,

'ªBEHOLD, I SEND MY MESSEN-
GER BEFORE YOUR FACE,
WHO WILL PREPARE YOUR
WAY BEFORE YOU.'

★28

28 "I say to you, among those born of women, there is no one greater than John; yet he who is least in the kingdom of God is greater than he."

29 aLuke 7:35 bMatt. 21:32; Luke 3:12 cActs 18:25; 19:3

29 And when all the people and the tax-gatherers heard *this*, they acknowledged ªGod's justice, ᵇhaving been baptized with ᶜthe baptism of John.

30 aMatt. 22:35

30 But the Pharisees and the ªlawyers rejected God's purpose for themselves, not having been baptized by John.

31 "To what then shall I compare the men of this generation, and what are they like?

32 "They are like children who sit in the market place and call to one another; and they say, 'We played the flute for you, and you did not dance; we sang a dirge, and you did not weep.'

33 aLuke 1:15

33 "For John the Baptist has come ªeating no bread and drinking no wine; and you say, 'He has a demon!'

34 "The Son of Man has come eating and drinking; and you say, 'Behold, a gluttonous man, and a drunkard, a friend of tax-gatherers and sinners!'

7:15 *And the dead man sat up.* One of three resurrections recorded in the Gospels that Christ effected, the others being those of Jairus' daughter (Mark 5:41) and Lazarus (John 11:44).

7:22 *report to John what you have seen and heard.* These were things the O.T. predicted the Messiah would do, and Jesus had done

them; the men, therefore, had their answer.

7:24-25 John the Baptist was not like a reed that bends in whatever direction the wind blows it, but was a man of conviction. Neither was he given to soft living.

7:28 *no one greater than John.* See note on Matt. 11:11.

35 ᵃLuke
7:29

35 "Yet wisdom ᵃis vindicated by all her children."

4 Ministry to sinners, 7:36–50

★36-50

36 Now one of the Pharisees was requesting Him to dine with him. And He entered the Pharisee's house, and reclined *at the table.*

★37 ᵃMatt.
26:6-13;
Mark 14:3-9;
Luke 7:37-
39; John
12:1-8

37 ᵃAnd behold, there was a woman in the city who was a sinner; and when she learned that He was reclining *at the table* in the Pharisee's house, she brought an alabaster vial of perfume,

38 and standing behind *Him* at His feet, weeping, she began to wet His feet with her tears, and kept wiping them with the hair of her head, and kissing His feet, and anointing them with the perfume.

39 ᵃLuke
7:16; John
4:19

39 Now when the Pharisee who had invited Him saw this, he said to himself, "If this man were ᵃa prophet He would know who and what sort of person this woman is who is touching Him, that she is a sinner."

40 And Jesus answered and said to him, "Simon, I have something to say to you." And he replied, "Say it, Teacher."

★41 ᵃMatt.
18:28; Mark
6:37

41 "A certain moneylender had two debtors: one owed five hundred ᵃdenarii, and the other fifty.

42 ᵃMatt.
18:25

42 "When they ᵃwere unable to repay, he graciously forgave them both. Which of them therefore will love him more?"

43 Simon answered and said, "I suppose the one whom he forgave more." And He said to him, "You have judged correctly."

44 ᵃGen.
18:4; 19:2;
43:24; Judg.
19:21; 1 Tim.
5:10

44 And turning toward the woman, He said to Simon, "Do you see this woman? I entered your house; you ᵃgave Me no water for My feet, but she has wet My feet with her tears, and wiped them with her hair.

45 ᵃ2 Sam.
15:5

45 "You ᵃgave Me no kiss; but she, since the time I came in, has not ceased to kiss My feet.

46 ᵃ2 Sam.
12:20; Ps.
23:5; Eccles.
9:8; Dan.
10:3

46 "ᵃYou did not anoint My head with oil, but she anointed My feet with perfume.

47 "For this reason I say to you, her sins, which are many, have been forgiven, for she loved much; but he who is forgiven little, loves little."

48 ᵃMatt. 9:2

48 And He said to her, "ᵃYour sins have been forgiven."

49 And those who were reclining *at the table* with Him began to say to themselves, "Who is this *man* who even forgives sins?"

50 ᵃMatt.
9:22 ᵇMark
5:34; Luke
8:48

50 And He said to the woman, "ᵃYour faith has saved you; ᵇgo in peace."

5 Ministry financed, 8:1–3

1 ᵃMatt.
4:23

8 And it came about soon afterwards, that He *began* going about from one city and village to another, ᵃproclaiming and preaching the kingdom of God; and the twelve were with Him,

★ 2 ᵃMatt.
27:55f.; Luke
23:49

2 and *also* ᵃsome women who had been healed of evil spirits and sicknesses: ᵃMary who was called Magdalene, from whom seven demons had gone out,

★ 3 ᵃMatt.
14:1 ᵇMatt.
20:8

3 and Joanna the wife of Chuza, ᵃHerod's ᵇsteward, and Susanna, and many others who were contributing to their support out of their private means.

7:36-50 This is not the same as a similar incident which occurred in Bethany of Judea during the last week of Christ's life (Matt. 26:6-31; Mark 14:3-9; John 12:1-8).
7:37 *an alabaster vial of perfume.* A long-necked flask of fine translucent material, used for storing perfume.
7:41 *denarii.* A Roman silver coin (singular, denarius), a day's wage for ordinary workers.
8:2 *Mary who was called Magdalene.* From Magdala, a small town between Capernaum and Tiberius. Other Marys in the N.T. are: (1)

the mother of Jesus (1:27); (2) the mother of James and wife of Alphaeus, or Clopas (6:15; John 19:25)—these two Marys were evidently cousins; (3) the sister of Martha and Lazarus (Luke 10:39); (4) the mother of John Mark (Acts 12:12); and (5) a Christian woman in Rome (Rom. 16:6).
8:3 *Herod's steward.* A position of some rank involving the management of Herod's finances. *were contributing to their support.* These women helped finance the ministry of the twelve.

6 Ministry illustrated through parables, 8:4-21

4 aLuke
8:4-8; Matt.
13:2-9; Mark
4:1-9

4 aAnd when a great multitude were coming together, and those from the various cities were journeying to Him, He spoke by way of a parable:

5 "The sower went out to sow his seed; and as he sowed, some fell beside the road; and it was trampled under foot, and the birds of the air ate it up.

★ 6

6 "And other seed fell on rocky soil, and as soon as it grew up, it withered away, because it had no moisture.

7 "And other seed fell among the thorns; and the thorns grew up with it, and choked it out.

8 aMatt.
11:15

8 "And other seed fell into the good soil, and grew up, and produced a crop a hundred times as great." As He said these things, He would call out, "aHe who has ears to hear, let him hear."

9 aLuke
8:9-15; Matt.
13:10-23;
Mark 4:10-20

9 aAnd His disciples began questioning Him as to what this parable might be.

10 aMatt.
13:11 bIs.
6:9; Matt.
13:14

10 And He said, "aTo you it has been granted to know the mysteries of the kingdom of God, but to the rest it is in parables, in order that bSEEING THEY MAY NOT SEE, AND HEARING THEY MAY NOT UNDERSTAND.

11 a1 Pet.
1:23

11 "Now the parable is this: athe seed is the word of God.

12 "And those beside the road are those who have heard; then the devil comes and takes away the word from their heart, so that they may not believe and be saved.

13 "And those on the rocky soil are those who, when they hear, receive the word with joy; and these have no firm root; they believe for a while, and in time of temptation fall away.

14 "And the seed which fell among the thorns, these are the ones who have heard, and as they go on their way they are choked with worries and riches and pleasures of this life, and bring no fruit to maturity.

15 "And the seed in the good soil, these are the ones who have heard the word in an honest and good heart, and hold it fast, and bear fruit with perseverance.

16 "Now ano one after lighting a lamp covers it over with a container, or puts it under a bed; but he puts it on a lampstand, in order that those who come in may see the light.

★16 aMatt.
5:15; Mark
4:21; Luke
11:33

17 "aFor nothing is hidden that shall not become evident, nor anything secret that shall not be known and come to light.

17 aMatt.
10:26; Mark
4:22; Luke
12:2

18 "Therefore take care how you listen; afor whoever has, to him shall more be given; and whoever does not have, even what he thinks he has shall be taken away from him."

18 aMatt.
13:12; Luke
19:26

19 aAnd His mother and brothers came to Him, and they were unable to get to Him because of the crowd.

19 aLuke
8:19-21;
Matt. 12:46-
50; Mark
3:31-35

20 And it was reported to Him, "Your mother and Your brothers are standing outside, wishing to see You."

21 But He answered and said to them, "My mother and My brothers are these awho hear the word of God and do it."

★21 aLuke
11:28

7 Ministry in storms, 8:22-25

22 aNow it came about on one of those days, that He and His disciples got into a boat, and He said to them, "Let us go over to the other side of bthe lake." And they launched out.

22 aLuke
8:22-25;
Matt. 8:23-
27; Mark
4:36-41
bLuke 5:1f.;
8:23

23 But as they were sailing along He fell asleep; and a fierce gale of wind descended upon athe

23 aLuke
5:1f.; 8:22

8:6 on rocky soil. Or on thin soil covering rock. Palestine is a stony land.

8:16 lamp. A small clay vessel in which olive oil and a wick were placed. It gave feeble light at best (when placed on a lampstand).

8:21 My mother and My brothers. Those who belong to God's spiritual family are closer to Christ than those related to Him by natural birth.

lake, and they *began* to be swamped and to be in danger.

24 And they came to Him and woke Him up, saying, "[a]Master, Master, we are perishing!" And being aroused, He [b]rebuked the wind and the surging waves, and they stopped, and it became calm. **25** And He said to them, "Where is your faith?" And they were fearful and amazed, saying to one another, "Who then is this, that He commands even the winds and the water, and they obey Him?"

8 Ministry over demons, 8:26–39

26 [a]And they sailed to the country of the Gerasenes, which is opposite Galilee. **27** And when He had come out onto the land, He was met by a certain man from the city who was possessed with demons; and who had not put on any clothing for a long time, and was not living in a house, but in the tombs. **28** And seeing Jesus, he cried out and fell before Him, and said in a loud voice, "[a]What do I have to do with You, Jesus, Son of [b]the Most High God? I beg You, do not torment me." **29** For He had been commanding the unclean spirit to come out of the man. For it had seized him many times; and he was bound with chains and shackles and kept under guard; and *yet* he would burst his fetters and be driven by the demon into the desert. **30** And Jesus asked him, "What is your name?" And he said, "[a]Legion"; for many demons had entered him. **31** And they were entreating Him not to command them to depart into [a]the abyss. **32** Now there was a herd of many swine feeding there on the mountain; and *the demons* en-treated Him to permit them to enter the swine. And He gave them permission.

33 And the demons came out from the man and entered the swine; and the herd rushed down the steep bank into [a]the lake, and were drowned.

34 And when the herdsmen saw what had happened, they ran away and reported it in the city and *out* in the country. **35** And *the people* went out to see what had happened; and they came to Jesus, and found the man from whom the demons had gone out, sitting down [a]at the feet of Jesus, clothed and in his right mind; and they became frightened. **36** And those who had seen it reported to them how the man who was [a]demon-possessed had been made well. **37** And all the people of the country of the Gerasenes and the surrounding district asked Him to depart from them; for they were gripped with great fear; and He got into a boat, and returned. **38** [a]But the man from whom the demons had gone out was begging Him that he might accompany Him; but He sent him away, saying, **39** "Return to your house and describe what great things God has done for you." And he went away, proclaiming throughout the whole city what great things Jesus had done for him.

9 Ministry in death and despair, 8:40–56

40 [a]And as Jesus returned, the multitude welcomed Him, for they had all been waiting for Him. **41** [a]And behold, there came a man named Jairus, and he was an [b]official of the synagogue; and he

---

Marginal references:

24 [a]Luke 5:5 [b]Luke 4:39

★26 [a]Luke 8:26-37; Matt. 8:28-34; Mark 5:1-17

28 [a]Matt. 8:29 [b]Mark 5:7

★30 [a]Matt. 26:53

★31 [a]Rom. 10:7; Rev. 9:1f., 11; 11:7, 17:8; 20:1, 3

33 [a]Luke 5:1f.; 8:22

35 [a]Luke 10:39

36 [a]Matt. 4:24

38 [a]Luke 8:38, 39; Mark 5:18-20

40 [a]Matt. 9:1; Mark 5:21

41 [a]Luke 8:41-56; Matt. 9:18-26; Mark 5:22-43 [b]Mark 5:22; Luke 8:49

8:26 *Gerasenes.* Lived on the E. shore of the Lake of Galilee.

8:30 *Legion.* See note on Mark 5:9.

8:31 *the abyss.* The place to which all evil spirits will ultimately be consigned (Rev. 9:1; 20:1, 3).

fell at Jesus' feet, and *began* to entreat Him to come to his house;

42 for he had an only daughter, about twelve years old, and she was dying. But as He went, the multitudes were pressing against Him.

*43 43 And a woman who had a hemorrhage for twelve years, and could not be healed by anyone,

*44 44 came up behind Him, and touched the fringe of His cloak; and immediately her hemorrhage stopped.

45 ªLuke 5:5   45 And Jesus said, "Who is the one who touched Me?" And while they were all denying it, Peter said, "ªMaster, the multitudes are crowding and pressing upon You."

46 ªLuke 5:17   46 But Jesus said, "Someone did touch Me, for I was aware that ªpower had gone out of Me."

47 And when the woman saw that she had not escaped notice, she came trembling and fell down before Him, and declared in the presence of all the people the reason why she had touched Him, and how she had been immediately healed.

48 ªMatt. 9:22 ᵇMark 5:34; Luke 7:50   48 And He said to her, "Daughter, ªyour faith has made you well; ᵇgo in peace."

49 ªLuke 8:41   49 While He was still speaking, someone *came from *the house of* ªthe synagogue official, saying, "Your daughter has died; do not trouble the Teacher anymore."

50 ªMark 5:36   50 But when Jesus heard *this*, He answered him, "ªDo not be afraid *any longer*; only believe, and she shall be made well."

51 And when He had come to the house, He did not allow anyone to enter with Him, except Peter and John and James, and the girl's father and mother.

52 Now they were all weeping and ªlamenting for her; but He said, "Stop weeping, for she has not died, but ᵇis asleep."

53 And they *began* laughing at Him, knowing that she had died.

54 He, however, took her by the hand and called, saying, "Child, arise!"

55 And her spirit returned, and she rose immediately; and He gave orders for *something* to be given her to eat.

56 And her parents were amazed; but He ªinstructed them to tell no one what had happened.

10 Ministry through the disciples, 9:1-9

9 ªAnd He called the twelve together, and gave them power and authority over all the demons, and to heal diseases.

2 And He sent them out to ªproclaim the kingdom of God, and to perform healing.

3 And He said to them, "ªTake nothing for *your* journey, ᵇneither a staff, nor a bag, nor bread, nor money; and do not *even* have two tunics apiece.

4 "And whatever house you enter, stay there, and take your leave from there.

5 "And as for those who do not receive you, as you go out from that city, ªshake off the dust from your feet as a testimony against them."

6 And departing, they *began* going about among the villages, ªpreaching the gospel, and healing everywhere.

7 ªNow ᵇHerod the tetrarch heard of all that was happening; and he was greatly perplexed, because it was said by some that ᶜJohn had risen from the dead,

*52 ªMatt. 11:17; Luke 23:27 ᵇJohn 11:13

56 ªMatt. 8:4

1 ªMatt. 10:5; Mark 6:7

2 ªMatt. 10:7

★ 3 ªLuke 9:3-5; Matt. 10:9-15; Mark 6:8-11; Luke 10:4-12; 22:35 ᵇMatt. 10:10; Mark 6:8; Luke 22:35f.

★ 5 ªLuke 10:11; Acts 13:51

6 ªMark 6:12; Luke 8:1

★ 7 ªLuke 9:7-9; Matt. 14:1, 2; Mark 6:14f. ᵇMatt. 14:1; Luke 3:1; 13:31; 23:7 ᶜMatt. 14:2

8:43 Luke makes clear that this chronic *hemorrhage* was an incurable condition.
8:44 *the fringe of His cloak*. A tassel which a rabbi wore on his outer garment. The garment was draped over the back so that the tassel of one corner hung between the shoulder blades.
8:52 *she has not died, but is asleep*. The mourners looked on death as irreversible, so

Christ called it sleep, since (though the girl was actually dead) she would be awakened to life once again.
9:3 See Luke 22:35-36 for a change of orders. See note on Matt. 10:10.
9:5 *shake off the dust*. See note on Mark 6:11.
9:7 *Herod the tetrarch*. Herod Antipas, tetrarch of Galilee and Perea, 4 B.C.-A.D. 39.

8 aMatt.
16:14

9 aLuke
23:8

8 and by some that aElijah had appeared, and by others, that one of the prophets of old had risen again.

9 And Herod said, "I myself had John beheaded; but who is this man about whom I hear such things?" And ahe kept trying to see Him.

11 Ministry to physical needs,
9:10-17

★10 aMark
6:30 bMark
6:30 cLuke
9:10-17;
Matt. 14:13-
21; Mark
6:32-44;
John 6:5-13
dMatt. 11:21

10 aAnd when the bapostles returned, they gave an account to Him of all that they had done. cAnd taking them with Him, He withdrew by Himself to a city called dBethsaida.

11 But the multitudes were aware of this and followed Him; and welcoming them, He began speaking to them about the kingdom of God and curing those who had need of healing.

12 And the day began to decline, and the twelve came and said to Him, "Send the multitude away, that they may go into the surrounding villages and countryside and find lodging and get something to eat; for here we are in a desolate place."

★13

13 But He said to them, "You give them something to eat!" And they said, "We have no more than five loaves and two fish, unless perhaps we go and buy food for all these people."

14 aMark
6:39

14 (For there were about five thousand men.) And He said to His disciples, "Have them recline to eat ain groups of about fifty each."

15 And they did so, and had them all recline.

16 And He took the five loaves and the two fish, and looking up to heaven, He blessed them, and broke them, and kept

giving them to the disciples to set before the multitude.

17 And they all ate and were satisfied; and the broken pieces which they had left over were picked up, twelve abaskets full.

17 aMatt.
14:20

12 Ministry of prediction,
9:18-50

★18-21

18 aLuke
9:18-20;
Matt. 16:13-
16; Mark
8:27-29
bMatt. 14:23;
Luke 6:12;
9:28

18 aAnd it came about that while He was bpraying alone, the disciples were with Him, and He questioned them, saying, "Who do the multitudes say that I am?"

19 And they answered and said, "John the Baptist, and others say Elijah; but others, that one of the prophets of old has risen again."

20 And He said to them, "But who do you say that I am?" And Peter answered and said, "aThe Christ of God."

20 aJohn
6:68f.

21 But He awarned them, and instructed them not to tell this to anyone,

21 aMatt.
8:4; 16:20;
Mark 8:30

22 asaying, "bThe Son of Man must suffer many things, and be rejected by the elders and chief priests and scribes, and be killed, and be raised up on the third day."

22 aLuke
9:22-27;
Matt. 16:21-
28; Mark
8:31-9:1
bMatt. 16:21;
Luke 9:44

23 And He was saying to them all, "If anyone wishes to come after Me, let him deny himself, and atake up his cross daily, and follow Me.

★23 aMatt.
10:38

24 "For awhoever wishes to save his life shall lose it, but whoever loses his life for My sake, he is the one who will save it.

24 aMatt.
10:39

25 "For what is a man profited if he gains the whole world, and aloses or forfeits himself?

25 aHeb.
10:34

26 "aFor whoever is ashamed of Me and My words, of him will the Son of Man be ashamed when He comes in His glory, and the

26 aMatt.
10:33; Luke
12:9

9:10 Bethsaida. A small town on the N. shore of the Lake of Galilee.
9:13 loaves . . . fish. The loaves were round cakes (like biscuits) and the fish were small smoked or pickled fish, typical food of the poor in Palestine.

9:18-21 See notes on Matt. 16:13-14.
9:23 cross. The first mention of a cross in Luke. The cross was well-known as an instrument of death, so it represents here the death or separation from the old life that must mark a disciple (Rom. 8:13). See note on Matt. 10:38.

glory of the Father and of the holy angels.

27 "But I say to you truthfully, [a]there are some of those standing here who shall not taste death until they see the kingdom of God."

28 [a]And some eight days after these sayings, it came about that He took along [b]Peter and John and James, and [c]went up to the mountain [d]to pray.

29 And while He was [a]praying, the appearance of His face [b]became different, and His clothing became white and gleaming.

30 And behold, two men were talking with Him; and they were Moses and Elijah,

31 who, appearing in glory, were speaking of His [a]departure which He was about to accomplish at Jerusalem.

32 Now Peter and his companions [a]had been overcome with sleep; but when they were fully awake, they saw His glory and the two men standing with Him.

33 And it came about, as these were parting from Him, Peter said to Jesus, "[a]Master, it is good for us to be here; and [b]let us make three tabernacles: one for You, and one for Moses, and one for Elijah"—[c]not realizing what he was saying.

34 And while he was saying this, a cloud formed and began to overshadow them; and they were afraid as they entered the cloud.

35 And [a]a voice came out of the cloud, saying, "[b]This is My Son, My Chosen One; listen to Him!"

36 And when the voice had spoken, Jesus was found alone. And [a]they kept silent, and reported to no one in those days any of the things which they had seen.

37 [a]And it came about on the next day, that when they had come down from the mountain, a great multitude met Him.

38 And behold, a man from the multitude shouted out, saying, "Teacher, I beg You to look at my son, for he is my only boy,

39 and behold, a spirit seizes him, and he suddenly screams, and it throws him into a convulsion with foaming at the mouth, and as it mauls him, it scarcely leaves him.

40 "And I begged Your disciples to cast it out, and they could not."

41 And Jesus answered and said, "O unbelieving and perverted generation, how long shall I be with you, and put up with you? Bring your son here."

42 And while he was still approaching, the demon dashed him to the ground, and threw him into a convulsion. But Jesus rebuked the unclean spirit, and healed the boy, and gave him back to his father.

43 And they were all amazed at the [a]greatness of God.

[b]But while everyone was marveling at all that He was doing, He said to His disciples,

44 "Let these words sink into your ears; [a]for the Son of Man is going to be delivered into the hands of men."

45 But [a]they did not understand this statement, and it was concealed from them so that they might not perceive it; and they were afraid to ask Him about this statement.

46 [a]And an argument arose among them as to which of them might be the greatest.

47 But Jesus, [a]knowing what they were thinking in their heart, took a child and stood him by His side,

48 and said to them, "[a]Whoever receives this child in My name receives Me; and whoever receives Me receives Him who sent Me; [b]for he who is least among you, this is the one who is great."

Marginal references:

★27-36

27 [a]Matt. 16:28

28 [a]Luke 9:28-36; Matt. 17:1-8; Mark 9:2-8 [b]Matt. 17:1 [c]Matt. 5:1 [d]Luke 3:21; 5:16; 6:12; 9:18

29 [a]Luke 3:21; 5:16; 6:12; 9:18 [b]Mark 16:12

31 [a]2 Pet. 1:15

32 [a]Matt. 26:43; Mark 14:40

33 [a]Luke 5:5; 9:49 [b]Matt. 17:4; Mark 9:5 [c]Mark 9:6

35 [a]2 Pet. 1:17f. [b]Matt. 3:17; Luke 3:22

36 [a]Matt. 17:9; Mark 9:9f.

37 [a]Luke 9:37-42; Matt. 17:14-18; Mark 9:14-27

★40

43 [a]2 Pet. 1:16 [b]Luke 9:43-45; Matt. 17:22f.; Mark 9:30-32

44 [a]Luke 9:22

45 [a]Mark 9:32

46 [a]Luke 9:46-48; Matt. 18:1-5; Mark 9:33-37

47 [a]Matt. 9:4

48 [a]Matt. 10:40 [b]Luke 22:26

9:27-36 See notes on Matt. 16:28; 17:1, 2, 4; Mark 9:5.

9:40 they could not. The reason was that the disciples failed to pray (Mark 9:29).

49 *a*And John answered and said, "*b*Master, we saw someone casting out demons in Your name; and we tried to hinder him because he does not follow along with us."

50 But Jesus said to him, "Do not hinder *him;* *a*for he who is not against you is for you."

IV THE REPUDIATION OF THE SON OF MAN BY MEN, 9:51–19:27
A Rejection by Samaritans, 9:51–56

51 And it came about, when the days were approaching for *a*His ascension, that He resolutely set His face *b*to go to Jerusalem;

52 and He sent messengers on ahead of Him. And they went, and entered a village of the *a*Samaritans, to make arrangements for Him.

53 And they did not receive Him, *a*because He was journeying with His face toward Jerusalem.

54 And when His disciples *a*James and John saw *this,* they said, "Lord, do You want us to command fire to come down from heaven and consume them?"

55 But He turned and rebuked them, [and said, "You do not know what kind of spirit you are of;

56 for the Son of Man did not come to destroy men's lives, but to save them."] And they went on to another village.

B Rejection by Worldly Men, 9:57–62

57 And *a*as they were going along the road, *b*someone said to Him, "I will follow You wherever You go."

58 And Jesus said to him, "The foxes have holes, and the birds of the air *have* nests, but *a*the Son of Man has nowhere to lay His head."

59 And He said to another, "*a*Follow Me." But he said, "Permit me first to go and bury my father."

60 But He said to him, "Allow the dead to bury their own dead; but as for you, go and *a*proclaim everywhere the kingdom of God."

61 And another also said, "I will follow You, Lord; but *a*first permit me to say good-bye to those at home."

62 But Jesus said to him, "*a*No one, after putting his hand to the plow and looking back, is fit for the kingdom of God."

C Commissioning of the Seventy, 10:1–24

10 Now after this *a*the Lord appointed seventy *b*others, and sent them *c*two and two ahead of Him to every city and place where He Himself was going to come.

2 And He was saying to them, "*a*The harvest is plentiful, but the laborers are few; therefore beseech the Lord of the harvest to send out laborers into His harvest.

3 "Go your ways; *a*behold, I send you out as lambs in the midst of wolves.

4 "*a*Carry no purse, no bag, no shoes; and greet no one on the way.

5 "And whatever house you

9:50 *he who is not against you is for you.* The test by which others are tried. In 11:23 is a test by which one tries himself.
9:54 *fire . . . from heaven.* See 2 Kings 1:10-12.
9:58 *Son of Man.* For the meaning of this title see note on Matt. 8:20.
9:59 *bury my father.* The father had not died; the speaker meant that he was obligated to care for him until he died.
9:60 *Allow the dead to bury their own dead.* I.e., let those who are spiritually dead bury

those who die physically. The claims of the kingdom are paramount.
9:62 *looking back.* This will make the furrow crooked.
10:1 *seventy.* Only Luke records this mission. The fact that 70 people could be sent out shows that Jesus must have had a large following.
10:4 *greet no one on the way.* The urgency of the mission did not allow for the usual elaborate greetings.

Marginal references:
49 *a*Luke 9:49, 50; Mark 9:38-40 *b*Luke 5:5; 9:33
★50 *a*Matt. 12:30; Luke 11:23
51 *a*Mark 16:19 *b*Luke 13:22; 17:11; 18:31; 19:11, 28
52 *a*Matt. 10:5; Luke 10:33; 17:16; John 4:4
53 *a*John 4:9
★54 *a*Mark 3:17
57 *a*Luke 9:51 *b*Luke 9:57-60; Matt. 8:19-22
★58 *a*Matt. 8:20
★59 *a*Matt. 8:22
★60 *a*Matt. 4:23
61 *a*1 Kin. 19:20
★62 *a*Phil. 3:13
★ 1 *a*Luke 7:13 *b*Luke 9:1ff., 52 *c*Mark 6:7
2 *a*Matt. 9:37, 38; John 4:35
3 *a*Matt. 10:16
★ 4 *a*Matt. 10:9-14; Mark 6:8-11; Luke 9:3-5; 10:4-12

enter, first say, 'Peace *be* to this house.'

★6　6 "And if a man of peace is there, your peace will rest upon him; but if not, it will return to you.

7 *a*Matt. 10:10; 1 Cor. 9:14; 1 Tim. 5:18
7 "And stay in that house, eating and drinking what they give you; for *a*the laborer is worthy of his wages. Do not keep moving from house to house.

8 *a*1 Cor. 10:27
8 "And whatever city you enter, and they receive you, *a*eat what is set before you;

9 *a*Matt. 3:2; 10:7; Luke 10:11
9 and heal those in it who are sick, and say to them, '*a*The kingdom of God has come near to you.'

10 "But whatever city you enter and they do not receive you, go out into its streets and say,

11 *a*Matt. 10:14; Mark 6:11; Luke 9:5 *b*Matt. 3:2; 10:7; Luke 10:9
11 '*a*Even the dust of your city which clings to our feet, we wipe off *in protest* against you; yet be sure of this, that *b*the kingdom of God has come near.'

★12 *a*Matt. 10:15; 11:24 *b*Matt. 10:15
12 "I say to you, *a*it will be more tolerable in that day for *b*Sodom, than for that city.

13 *a*Luke 10:13-15; Matt. 11:21-23 *b*Matt. 11:21 *c*Rev. 11:3
13 "*a*Woe to you, *b*Chorazin! Woe to you, *b*Bethsaida! For if the miracles had been performed in *b*Tyre and Sidon which occurred in you, they would have repented long ago, sitting in *c*sackcloth and ashes.

14 *a*Matt. 11:21
14 "But it will be more tolerable for *a*Tyre and Sidon in the judgment, than for you.

15 *a*Matt. 4:13 *b*Matt. 11:23
15 "And you, *a*Capernaum, will not be exalted to heaven, will you? You will be brought down to *b*Hades!

16 *a*Matt. 10:40; John 13:20; Gal. 4:14 *b*John 12:48; 1 Thess. 4:8
16 "*a*The one who listens to you listens to Me, and *b*the one who rejects you rejects Me; and he who rejects Me rejects the One who sent Me."

17 *a*Mark 16:17
17 And the seventy returned with joy, saying, "Lord, even *a*the demons are subject to us in Your name."

★18 *a*Matt. 4:10
18 And He said to them, "I was watching *a*Satan fall from heaven like lightning.

19 *a*Mark 16:18
19 "Behold, I have given you authority to *a*tread upon serpents and scorpions, and over all the power of the enemy, and nothing shall injure you.

20 *a*Ex. 32:32; Ps. 69:28; Is. 4:3; Ezek. 13:9; Dan. 12:1; Phil. 4:3; Heb. 12:23; Rev. 3:5; 13:8; 17:8; 20:12, 15; 21:27 21 *a*Luke 10:21, 22; Matt. 11:25-27
20 "Nevertheless do not rejoice in this, that the spirits are subject to you, but rejoice that *a*your names are recorded in heaven."

21 *a*At that very time He rejoiced greatly in the Holy Spirit, and said, "I praise Thee, O Father, Lord of heaven and earth, that Thou didst hide these things from *the* wise and intelligent and didst reveal them to babes. Yes, Father, for thus it was well-pleasing in Thy sight.

22 "All things have been handed over to Me by My Father, and no one knows who the Son is except the Father, and who the Father is except the Son, and anyone to whom the Son wills to reveal *Him*."

23 *a*Luke 10:23, 24; Matt. 13:16, 17
23 *a*And turning to the disciples, He said privately, "Blessed *are* the eyes which see the things you see,

24 for I say to you, that many prophets and kings wished to see the things which you see, and did not see *them*, and to hear the things which you hear, and did not hear *them*."

D Rejection by a Lawyer (Parable of the Good Samaritan), 10:25-37

★25 *a*Luke 10:25-28; Matt. 22:34-40; Mark 12:28-31; Matt. 19:16-19 *b*Matt. 22:35
25 *a*And behold, a certain *b*lawyer stood up and put Him to the test, saying, "Teacher, what shall I do to inherit eternal life?"

26 And He said to him, "What is written in the Law? How does it read to you?"

★27 *a*Lev. 19:18; Deut. 6:5
27 And he answered and said, "*a*YOU SHALL LOVE THE LORD YOUR

10:6 *a man of peace.* A Hebrew idiom meaning "a peaceful man."

10:12 *in that day.* I.e., the day of judgment. The judgment on Sodom is recorded in Gen. 19.

10:18 *Satan fall from heaven.* The power of Sa-

tan was broken, and the success of the seventy over demons was proof of it (v. 17).

10:25 *a certain lawyer.* I.e., a scribe. See note on Matt. 2:4.

10:27 See Deut. 6:5; Lev. 19:18.

GOD WITH ALL YOUR HEART, AND WITH ALL YOUR SOUL, AND WITH ALL YOUR STRENGTH, AND WITH ALL YOUR MIND; AND YOUR NEIGHBOR AS YOUR- SELF."

28 And He said to him, "You have answered correctly; [a]DO THIS, AND YOU WILL LIVE."

29 But wishing [a]to justify himself, he said to Jesus, "And who is my neighbor?"

30 Jesus replied and said, "A certain man was [a]going down from Jerusalem to Jericho; and he fell among robbers, and they stripped him and beat him, and went off leaving him half dead.

31 "And by chance a certain priest was going down on that road, and when he saw him, he passed by on the other side.

32 "And likewise a Levite also, when he came to the place and saw him, passed by on the other side.

33 "But a certain [a]Samaritan, who was on a journey, came upon him; and when he saw him, he felt compassion,

34 and came to him, and ban- daged up his wounds, pouring oil and wine on *them;* and he put him on his own beast, and brought him to an inn, and took care of him.

35 "And on the next day he took out two denarii and gave them to the innkeeper and said, 'Take care of him; and whatever more you spend, when I return, I will repay you.'

36 "Which of these three do you think proved to be a neigh- bor to the man who fell into the robbers' *hands?"*

37 And he said, "The one who showed mercy toward him." And Jesus said to him, "Go and do the same."

Margin references:
28 [a]Lev. 18:5; Matt. 19:17
29 [a]Luke 16:15
★30 [a]Luke 18:31; 19:28
★33 [a]Matt. 10:5; Luke 9:52

E Reception at Bethany, 10:38–42

38 Now as they were travel- ing along, He entered a certain village; and a woman named [a]Martha welcomed Him into her home.

39 And she had a sister called [a]Mary, who moreover was listen- ing to the Lord's word, [b]seated at His feet.

40 But [a]Martha was distracted with all her preparations; and she came up *to Him,* and said, "Lord, do You not care that my sister has left me to do all the serving alone? Then tell her to help me."

41 But the Lord answered and said to her, "[a]Martha, Martha, you are [b]worried and bothered about so many things;

42 [a]but *only* a few things are necessary, really *only* one, for [b]Mary has chosen the good part, which shall not be taken away from her."

Margin references:
★38 [a]Luke 10:40f.; John 11:1, 5, 19ff., 30, 39; 12:2
39 [a]Luke 10:42; John 11:1f., 19f., 28, 31f., 45; 12:3 [b]Luke 8:35; Acts 22:3
40 [a]Luke 10:38, 41; John 11:1, 5, 19ff., 30, 39; 12:2
41 [a]Luke 10:38, 40; John 11:1, 5, 19ff., 30, 39; 12:2 [b]Matt. 6:25
★42 [a]Ps. 27:4; John 6:27 [b]Luke 10:39; John 11:1f., 19f., 28, 31f., 45; 12:3

F Instruction on Prayer, 11:1–13

11 And it came about that while He was praying in a certain place, after He had fin- ished, one of His disciples said to Him, "[a]Lord, teach us to pray just as John also taught his disciples."

2 And He said to them, "[a]When you pray, say:

'Father, hallowed be Thy name.
Thy kingdom come.

3 'Give us [a]each day our dai- ly bread.

4 'And forgive us our sins,

For we ourselves also for- give everyone who [a]is indebted to us.

Margin references:
★1 [a]Luke 7:13
★2-4
2 [a]Luke 11:2-4; Matt. 6:9-13
3 [a]Acts 17:11
4 [a]Luke 13:4 marg.

10:30 *was going down from Jerusalem to Jeri- cho.* The steeply descending road winds through rocky places that easily hide robbers.
10:33 *a certain Samaritan.* The Samaritans were descendants of colonists whom the As- syrian kings planted in Palestine after the fall of the Northern Kingdom in 721 B.C. They were despised by the Jews because of their mixed Gentile blood and their different wor- ship, which centered at Mt. Gerizim (John 4:20-22).
10:38 *a certain village.* I.e., Bethany (John 12:1).
10:42 *really only one.* One simple dish for the meal is all that is necessary, rather than the elaborate preparations Martha had made.
11:1 *teach us to pray.* It was customary for fa- mous rabbis to compose special prayers.
11:2-4 See notes on Matt. 6:9, 11, 12.

And lead us not into temptation.' "

5 And He said to them, "Suppose one of you shall have a friend, and shall go to him at midnight, and say to him, 'Friend, lend me three loaves;

6 for a friend of mine has come to me from a journey, and I have nothing to set before him';

7 and from inside he shall answer and say, 'Do not bother me; the door has already been shut and my children and I are in bed; I cannot get up and give you *anything*.'

8 "I tell you, even though he will not get up and give him *anything* because he is his friend, yet *a*because of his persistence he will get up and give him as much as he needs.

9 "And I say to you, *a*ask, and it shall be given to you; seek, and you shall find; knock, and it shall be opened to you.

10 "For everyone who asks, receives; and he who seeks, finds; and to him who knocks, it shall be opened.

11 "Now suppose one of you fathers is asked by his son for a fish; he will not give him a snake instead of a fish, will he?

12 "Or *if* he is asked for an egg, he will not give him a scorpion, will he?

13 "*a*If you then, being evil, know how to give good gifts to your children, how much more shall *your* heavenly Father give the *b*Holy Spirit to those who ask Him?"

G Rejection by the Nation, 11:14-36

14 *a*And He was casting out a demon, *and it was* dumb; and it came about that when the demon had gone out, the dumb man spoke; and the multitudes marveled.

15 But some of them said, "He casts out demons *a*by *b*Beelzebul, the ruler of the demons."

16 And others, to test *Him*, *a*were demanding of Him a sign from heaven.

17 *a*But He knew their thoughts, and said to them, "Any kingdom divided against itself is laid waste; and a house *divided* against itself falls.

18 "And if *a*Satan also is divided against himself, how shall his kingdom stand? For you say that I cast out demons by *b*Beelzebul.

19 "And if I by *a*Beelzebul cast out demons, by whom do your sons cast them out? Consequently they shall be your judges.

20 "But if I cast out demons by the *a*finger of God, then *b*the kingdom of God has come upon you.

21 "When a strong *man*, fully armed, guards his own *a*homestead, his possessions are undisturbed;

22 but when someone stronger than he attacks him and overpowers him, he takes away from him all his armor on which he had relied, and distributes his plunder.

23 "*a*He who is not with Me is against Me; and he who does not gather with Me, scatters.

24 "*a*When the unclean spirit goes out of a man, it passes through waterless places seeking rest, and not finding any, it says, 'I will return to my house from which I came.'

25 "And when it comes, it finds it swept and put in order.

26 "Then it goes and takes along seven other spirits more evil

---

8 *a*Luke 18:1-6

9 *a*Luke 11:9-13; Matt. 7:7-11

★**13** *a*Luke 18:7f. *b*Matt. 7:11

14 *a*Luke 11:14, 15; Matt. 12:22, 24; Matt. 9:32-34

★**15** *a*Matt. 9:34 *b*Matt. 10:25

16 *a*Matt. 12:38

17 *a*Luke 11:17-22; Matt. 12:25-29; Mark 3:23-27

18 *a*Matt. 4:10 *b*Matt. 10:25

19 *a*Matt. 10:25

20 *a*Ex. 8:19 *b*Matt. 3:2

★**21-22**

21 *a*Matt. 26:3

23 *a*Matt. 12:30

★**24** *a*Luke 11:24-26; Matt. 12:43-45

★**26**

11:13 *give the Holy Spirit.* Since the day of Pentecost, the gift of the Spirit is given to all believers (Acts 10:45; Rom. 8:9).
11:15 *Beelzebul.* See note on Matt. 10:25.
11:21-22 *a strong man* (v. 21) is Satan; the *stronger* (v. 22) is Christ (4:18).

11:24 *my house.* The life of the person the demon indwelt.
11:26 *worse.* See 2 Pet. 2:20-21. Notice also that some demons are more wicked than others.

than itself, and they go in and live there; and the last state of that man becomes worse than the first."

27 *a*Luke 23:29

27 And it came about while He said these things, one of the women in the crowd raised her voice, and said to Him, "*a*Blessed is the womb that bore You, and the breasts at which You nursed."

28 *a*Luke 8:21

28 But He said, "On the contrary, blessed are *a*those who hear the word of God, and observe it."

29 *a*Luke 11:29-32; Matt. 12:39-42 *b*Matt. 12:38; Luke 11:16

29 And as the crowds were increasing, He began to say, "*a*This generation is a wicked generation; it *b*seeks for a sign, and *yet* no sign shall be given to it but the sign of Jonah.

★30

30 "For just as Jonah became a sign to the Ninevites, so shall the Son of Man be to this generation.

31 "The Queen of the South shall rise up with the men of this generation at the judgment and condemn them, because she came from the ends of the earth to hear the wisdom of Solomon; and behold, something greater than Solomon is here.

★32

32 "The men of Nineveh shall stand up with this generation at the judgment and condemn it, because they repented at the preaching of Jonah; and behold, something greater than Jonah is here.

33 *a*Matt. 5:15; Mark 4:21; Luke 8:16

33 "No *a*one, after lighting a lamp, puts it away in a cellar, nor under a peck-measure, but on the lampstand, in order that those who enter may see the light.

34 *a*Luke 11:34, 35; Matt. 6:22, 23

34 "*a*The lamp of your body is your eye; when your eye is clear, your whole body also is full of light; but when it is bad, your body also is full of darkness.

35 "Then watch out that the light in you may not be darkness.

36 "If therefore your whole body is full of light, with no dark part in it, it shall be wholly illumined, as when the lamp illumines you with its rays."

H Rejection by Pharisees and Lawyers, 11:37-54

★37

37 Now when He had spoken, a Pharisee *asked Him to have lunch with him; and He went in, and reclined *at the table.*

38 *a*Matt. 15:2; Mark 7:3f.

38 And when the Pharisee saw it, he was surprised that He had not first *a*ceremonially washed before the meal.

39 *a*Luke 7:13 *b*Matt. 23:25f.

39 But *a*the Lord said to him, "Now *b*you Pharisees clean the outside of the cup and of the platter; but inside of you, you are full of robbery and wickedness.

40 *a*Luke 12:20; 1 Cor. 15:36

40 "*a*You foolish ones, did not He who made the outside make the inside also?

41 *a*Luke 12:33; 16:9 *b*Mark 7:19; Titus 1:15

41 "But *a*give that which is within as charity, and then all things are *b*clean for you.

★42 *a*Matt. 23:23 *b*Luke 18:12

42 "*a*But woe to you Pharisees! For you *b*pay tithe of mint and rue and every *kind of* garden herb, and *yet* disregard justice and the love of God; but these are the things you should have done without neglecting the others.

★43 *a*Matt. 23:6f.; Mark 12:38f.; Luke 14:7; 20:46

43 "Woe to you Pharisees! For you *a*love the front seats in the synagogues, and the respectful greetings in the market places.

★44 *a*Matt. 23:27

44 "*a*Woe to you! For you are like concealed tombs, and the people who walk over *them* are unaware *of it.*"

45 *a*Matt. 22:35; Luke 11:46, 52

45 And one of the *a*lawyers *said to Him in reply, "Teacher, when You say this, You insult us too."

46 *a*Matt. 22:35; Luke 11:45, 52 *b*Matt. 23:4

46 But He said, "Woe to you *a*lawyers as well! For *b*you weigh men down with burdens hard to bear, while you yourselves will

---

11:30 *Jonah became a sign* of judgment. See note on Matt. 12:39.

11:32 *they repented.* See Jonah 3:5-9; 4:11.

11:37 *reclined at table.* Christ often used dinner invitations as opportunities to reach people (Luke 5:29; 7:36; 14:1; 19:5; John 2:1-12; 12:1-2).

11:42 *pay tithe.* See note on Matt. 23:23.

11:43 *the front seats.* Usually reserved for the most important members.

11:44 *concealed tombs.* To step on a grave, even unknowingly, defiled a man (Num. 19:16). Jesus says that the Pharisees cause men to break the law and defile themselves.

not even touch the burdens with one of your fingers.

47 "^aWoe to you! For you build the tombs of the prophets, and it was your fathers who killed them.

48 "Consequently, you are witnesses and approve the deeds of your fathers; because it was they who killed them, and you build their tombs.

49 "For this reason also ^athe wisdom of God said, '^bI will send to them prophets and apostles, and some of them they will kill and some they will persecute,

50 in order that the blood of all the prophets, shed ^asince the foundation of the world, may be charged against this generation,

51 from the blood of Abel to the blood of Zechariah, who perished between the altar and the house of God; yes, I tell you, it shall be charged against this generation.'

52 "Woe to you ^alawyers! For you have taken away the key of knowledge; ^byou did not enter in yourselves, and those who were entering in you hindered."

53 And when He left there, the scribes and the Pharisees began to be very hostile and to question Him closely on many subjects,

54 ^aplotting against Him, ^bto catch Him in something He might say.

I Instruction in the Light of Rejection, 12:1–19:27

1 Concerning hypocrisy, 12:1–12

12 Under these circumstances, after so many thousands of the multitude had gathered together that they were stepping on one another, He began saying to His disciples first of all, "^aBeware of the leaven of the Pharisees, which is hypocrisy.

2 "^aBut there is nothing covered up that will not be revealed, and hidden that will not be known.

3 "Accordingly, whatever you have said in the dark shall be heard in the light, and what you have whispered in the inner rooms shall be proclaimed upon ^athe housetops.

4 "And I say to you, ^aMy friends, do not be afraid of those who kill the body, and after that have no more that they can do.

5 "But I will warn you whom to fear: ^afear the One who after He has killed has authority to cast into ^bhell; yes, I tell you, fear Him!

6 "Are not ^afive sparrows sold for two cents? And yet not one of them is forgotten before God.

7 "^aIndeed, the very hairs of your head are all numbered. Do not fear; you are of more value than many sparrows.

8 "And I say to you, everyone who confesses Me before men, the Son of Man shall confess him also ^abefore the angels of God;

9 but ^ahe who denies Me before men shall be denied ^bbefore the angels of God.

10 "^aAnd everyone who will speak a word against the Son of Man, it shall be forgiven him; but he who blasphemes against the Holy Spirit, it shall not be forgiven him.

11 "And when they bring you before ^athe synagogues and the rulers and the authorities, do not become ^banxious about how or what you should speak in your defense, or what you should say;

12 for ^athe Holy Spirit will

11:51 to the blood of Zechariah. See note on Matt. 23:35.
12:5 fear Him. I.e., God, who alone has the power to cast into hell (Rev. 20:10).
12:6 five sparrows. Sparrows were so cheap that, though they sold two for a cent (Matt.

10:29), a fifth one was thrown in for the price of four. Yet the infinite God is concerned for each one.
12:10 blasphemes against the Holy Spirit. See note on Matt. 12:31.

Marginal references:

47 ^aMatt. 23:29ff.

49 ^a1 Cor. 1:24, 30; Col. 2:3 ^bMatt. 23:34-36; Luke 11:49-51

50 ^aMatt. 25:34

★51

52 ^aMatt. 22:35; Luke 11:45, 46 ^bMatt. 23:13

54 ^aMark 3:2; Luke 20:20; Acts 23:21 ^bMark 12:13

1 ^aMatt. 16:6, 11ff.; Mark 8:15

2 ^aLuke 12:2-9; Matt. 10:26-33; Matt. 10:26; Mark 4:22; Luke 8:17

3 ^aMatt. 10:27; 24:17

4 ^aJohn 15:13-15

★ 5 ^aHeb. 10:31 ^bMatt. 5:22

★ 6 ^aMatt. 10:29

7 ^aMatt. 10:30

8 ^aMatt. 10:32; Luke 15:10; Rom. 10:9

9 ^aMatt. 10:33; Luke 9:26 ^bMatt. 10:32; Luke 15:10; Rom. 10:9

★10 ^aMatt. 12:31, 32; Mark 3:28-30

11 ^aMatt. 10:17 ^bMatt. 6:25; 10:19; Mark 13:11; Luke 12:22; 21:14

12 ^aMatt. 10:20; Luke 21:15

teach you in that very hour what you ought to say."

2 Concerning covetousness, 12:13-34

13 And someone in the crowd said to Him, "Teacher, tell my brother to divide the *family* inheritance with me."

★**14** *a*Mic. 6:8; Rom. 2:1, 3; 9:20

14 But He said to him, "*a*Man, who appointed Me a judge or arbiter over you?"

15 *a*1 Tim. 6:6-10

15 And He said to them, "*a*Beware, and be on your guard against every form of greed; for not *even* when one has an abundance does his life consist of his possessions."

16 And He told them a parable, saying, "The land of a certain rich man was very productive.

17 "And he began reasoning to himself, saying, 'What shall I do, since I have no place to store my crops?'

18 "And he said, 'This is what I will do: I will tear down my barns and build larger ones, and there I will store all my grain and my goods.

★**19-20**

19 *a*Eccles. 11:9

19 'And I will say to my soul, "Soul, *a*you have many goods laid up for many years *to come*; take your ease, eat, drink *and* be merry."'

20 *a*Jer. 17:11; Luke 11:40 *b*Job 27:8 *c*Ps. 39:6

20 "But God said to him, '*a*You fool! This *very* night *b*your soul is required of you; and *c*now who will own what you have prepared?'

21 *a*Luke 12:33

21 "So is the man who *a*lays up treasure for himself, and is not rich toward God."

22 *a*Luke 12:22-31; Matt. 6:25-33

22 And He said to His disciples, "*a*For this reason I say to you, do not be anxious for *your* life, *as to* what you shall eat; nor for your body, *as to* what you shall put on.

23 "For life is more than food, and the body than clothing.

24 *a*Job 38:41 *b*Luke 12:18

24 "Consider the *a*ravens, for they neither sow nor reap; and they have no storeroom nor *b*barn; and *yet* God feeds them; how much more valuable you are than the birds!

25 *a*Ps. 39:5

25 "And which of you by being anxious can add a *single* *a*cubit to his life's span?

26 "If then you cannot do even a very little thing, why are you anxious about other matters?

★**27** *a*1 Kin. 10:4-7

27 "Consider the lilies, how they grow; they neither toil nor spin; but I tell you, even *a*Solomon in all his glory did not clothe himself like one of these.

28 *a*Matt. 6:30

28 "But if God so *arrays* the grass in the field, which is *alive* today and tomorrow is thrown into the furnace, how much more *will He clothe* you, *a*O men of little faith!

29 *a*Matt. 6:31

29 "And do not seek what you shall eat, and what you shall drink, and do not *a*keep worrying.

30 "For all these things the nations of the world eagerly seek; but your Father knows that you need these things.

31 *a*Matt. 6:33

31 "But seek for His kingdom, and *a*these things shall be added to you.

32 *a*Matt. 14:27 *b*John 21:15-17 *c*Eph. 1:5, 9

32 "*a*Do not be afraid, *b*little flock, for *c*your Father has chosen gladly to give you the kingdom.

33 *a*Matt. 19:21; Luke 11:41; 18:22 *b*Matt. 6:20; Luke 12:21

33 "*a*Sell your possessions and give to charity; make yourselves purses which do not wear out, *b*an unfailing treasure in heaven, where no thief comes near, nor moth destroys.

34 *a*Matt. 6:21

34 "For *a*where your treasure is, there will your heart be also.

3 Concerning faithfulness, 12:35-48

★**35** *a*Matt. 25:1ff.; Luke 12:35, 36 *b*Eph. 6:14; 1 Pet. 1:13

35 "*a*Be dressed in *b*readiness, and *keep* your lamps alight.

12:14 *who appointed Me a judge?* Christ refused to assume the position of judge in this secular matter.

12:19-20 Man proposes; God disposes.

12:27 *lilies.* Probably anemones.

12:35 *Be dressed in readiness.* The long, flowing outer robe had to be tucked into a belt before traveling or working. The idea is: "be ready."

★36

36 "And be like men who are waiting for their master when he returns from the wedding feast, so that they may immediately open *the door* to him when he comes and knocks.

37 aMatt
24 42 bLuke
17 8. John
13 4

37 "Blessed are those slaves whom the master shall find ªon the alert when he comes; truly I say to you, that ᵇhe will gird himself *to serve,* and have them recline *at table,* and will come up and wait on them.

38 aMatt
24.43

38 "Whether he comes in the ªsecond watch, or even in the ªthird, and finds *them* so, blessed are those *slaves.*

39 aLuke
12 39. 40
Matt. 24 43.
44 bMatt
6 19

39 "ªAnd be sure of this, that if the head of the house had known at what hour the thief was coming, he would not have allowed his house to be ᵇbroken into.

40 aMark
13 33. Luke
21 36

40 "ªYou too, be ready; for the Son of Man is coming at an hour that you do not expect."

41 aLuke
12 47. 48

41 And Peter said, "Lord, are You addressing this parable to us, or ªto everyone *else* as well?"

42 aLuke
7 13 bLuke
12 42-46.
Matt. 24 45-
51 cMatt
24 45. Luke
16 1ff

42 And ªthe Lord said, "ᵇWho then is the faithful and sensible ᶜsteward, whom his master will put in charge of his servants, to give them their rations at the proper time?

43 aLuke
12 42

43 "Blessed is that ªslave whom his master finds so doing when he comes.

44 "Truly I say to you, that he will put him in charge of all his possessions.

45 "But if that slave says in his heart, 'My master will be a long time in coming,' and begins to beat the slaves, *both* men and women, and to eat and drink and get drunk;

46 the master of that slave will come on a day when he does not expect *him,* and at an hour he does not know, and will cut him in pieces, and assign him a place with the unbelievers.

47 aDeut
25 2

47 "And that slave who knew his master's will and did not get ready or act in accord with his will, shall ªreceive many lashes.

48 aLev
5 17. Num
15 29f
bMatt 13 12

48 but the one who did not ªknow *it,* and committed deeds worthy of a flogging, will receive but few. ᵇAnd from everyone who has been given much shall much be required; and to whom they entrusted much, of him they will ask all the more.

4   *Concerning division and signs,* 12:49–59

★49

49 "I have come to cast fire upon the earth; and how I wish it were already kindled!

★50 aMark
10 38

50 "But I have a ªbaptism to undergo, and how distressed I am until it is accomplished!

51 aLuke
12 51-53
Matt 10 34-
36

51 "ªDo you suppose that I came to grant peace on earth? I tell you, no, but rather division;

52 for from now on five *members* in one household will be divided, three against two, and two against three.

53 aMic 7 6.
Matt 10 21

53 "They will be divided, ªfather against son, and son against father; mother against daughter, and daughter against mother; mother-in-law against daughter-in-law, and daughter-in-law against mother-in-law."

54 aMatt
16 2f

54 And He was also saying to the multitudes, "ªWhen you see a cloud rising in the west, immediately you say, 'A shower is coming,' and so it turns out.

55 aMatt
20 12

55 "And when *you see* a south wind blowing, you say, 'It will be a ªhot day,' and it turns out *that way.*

56 aMatt
16 3

56 "You hypocrites! ªYou know how to analyze the appearance of the earth and the sky, but

---

12:36 *when he returns from the wedding feast.* The groom first had supper with his friends, then went to the house of his bride to claim her, then returned to his own house. Although it might be quite late, he expected his servants to be waiting and ready for him (the second watch was from 9 p.m. to midnight, v. 38). There is no place for slothful ease in the life of a believer while waiting for the return of the Lord.

12:49 *fire.* I.e., judgment.
12:50 *baptism.* I.e., His death.

why do you not analyze this present time?

57 "And [a]why do you not even on your own initiative judge what is right?

58 "For [a]while you are going with your opponent to appear before the magistrate, on *your* way *there* make an effort to settle with him, in order that he may not drag you before the judge, and the judge turn you over to the constable, and the constable throw you into prison.

59 "I say to you, you shall not get out of there until you have paid the very last [a]cent."

5 Concerning repentance,
13:1-9

13 Now on the same occasion there were some present who reported to Him about the Galileans, whose blood [a]Pilate had mingled with their sacrifices.

2 And He answered and said to them, "[a]Do you suppose that these Galileans were *greater* sinners than all *other* Galileans, because they suffered this *fate*?

3 "I tell you, no, but, unless you repent, you will all likewise perish.

4 "Or do you suppose that those eighteen on whom the tower in [a]Siloam fell and killed them, were *worse* [b]culprits than all the men who live in Jerusalem?

5 "I tell you, no, but, unless you repent, you will all likewise perish."

6 And He *began* telling this parable: "A certain man had [a]a fig tree which had been planted in his vineyard; and he came looking for fruit on it, and did not find any.

7 "And he said to the vine-

yard-keeper, 'Behold, for three years I have come looking for fruit on this fig tree without finding any. [a]Cut it down! Why does it even use up the ground?'

8 "And he answered and said to him, 'Let it alone, sir, for this year too, until I dig around it and put in fertilizer;

9 and if it bears fruit next year, *fine*; but if not, cut it down.' "

6 Concerning hypocrisy,
13:10-17

10 And He was [a]teaching in one of the synagogues on the Sabbath.

11 And behold, there was a woman who for eighteen years had had [a]a sickness caused by a spirit; and she was bent double, and could not straighten up at all.

12 And when Jesus saw her, He called her over and said to her, "Woman, you are freed from your sickness."

13 And He [a]laid His hands upon her; and immediately she was made erect again, and *began* [b]glorifying God.

14 And [a]the synagogue official, indignant because Jesus [b]had healed on the Sabbath, *began* saying to the multitude in response, "[c]There are six days in which work should be done; therefore come during them and get healed, and not on the Sabbath day."

15 But [a]the Lord answered him and said, "You hypocrites, [b]does not each of you on the Sabbath untie his ox or his donkey from the stall, and lead him away to water *him*?

16 "And this woman, [a]a daughter of Abraham as she is,

57 [a]Luke 21:30

58 [a]Luke 12:58, 59; Matt. 5:25, 26

★59 [a]Mark 12:42

★ 1 [a]Matt. 27

2 [a]John 9:2f.

4 [a]Is. 8:6 [Neh. 3:15]; John 9:7, 11 [b]Matt. 6:12; Luke 11:4

★ 6 [a]Matt. 21:19

7 [a]Matt. 3:10; 7:19; Luke 3:9

★ 8-9

10 [a]Matt. 4:23

11 [a]Luke 13:16

13 [a]Mark 5:23 [b]Matt. 9:8

14 [a]Mark 5:22 [b]Matt. 12:2; Luke 14:3 [c]Ex. 20:9; Deut. 5:13

15 [a]Luke 7:13 [b]Luke 14:5

★16 [a]Luke 19:9 [b]Matt. 4:10; Luke 13:11

12:59 *cent*. The smallest of copper coins, worth very little (see 21:2).

13:1 Though there is no other record of this incident, apparently some Galileans were slain by Pilate's soldiers while offering sacrifices at the temple, so that their blood and the blood of the sacrifices were mixed. The point Christ makes is that this did not happen to them because they were worse sinners than other Gal-

ileans, but that all need to repent (vv. 2-3).

13:6 *a fig tree*. The fruitless fig tree was symbolic of the Jewish people.

13:8-9 God's judgment is sure, and His patience is great.

13:16 *should she not have been released*. Her healing was obligatory, especially since animals could be watered on the Sabbath (v. 15).

whom [b]Satan has bound for eighteen long years, should she not have been released from this bond on the Sabbath day?"

17 [a]Luke 18:43

17 And as He said this, all His opponents were being humiliated; and [a]the entire multitude was rejoicing over all the glorious things being done by Him.

7 Concerning the kingdom, 13:18-35

18 [a]Luke 13:18, 19; Matt. 13:31, 32; Mark 4:30-32 [b]Matt. 13:24; Luke 13:20 ★**19**

18 Therefore [a]He was saying, "[b]What is the kingdom of God like, and to what shall I compare it?

19 "It is like a mustard seed, which a man took and threw into his own garden; and it grew and became a tree; and THE BIRDS OF THE AIR NESTED IN ITS BRANCHES."

20 [a]Matt. 13:24; Luke 13:18

20 And again He said, "[a]To what shall I compare the kingdom of God?

★**21** [a]Luke 13:20, 21; Matt. 13:33 [b]Matt. 13:33

21 "It is like leaven, which a woman took and hid in [b]three pecks of meal, until it was all leavened."

22 [a]Luke 9:51

22 And He was passing through from one city and village to another, teaching, and [a]proceeding on His way to Jerusalem.

23 And someone said to Him, "Lord, are there just a few who are being saved?" And He said to them,

★**24** [a]Matt. 7:13

24 "[a]Strive to enter by the narrow door; for many, I tell you, will seek to enter and will not be able.

25 [a]Matt. 25:10 [b]Luke 3:8 [c]Matt. 7:22; 25:11 [d]Matt. 7:23; 25:12; Luke 13:27

25 "Once the head of the house gets up and [a]shuts the door, and you [b]begin to stand outside and knock on the door, saying, '[c]Lord, open up to us!' then He will answer and say to you, '[d]I do not know where you are from.'

26 "Then you will [a]begin to say, 'We ate and drank in Your presence, and You taught in our streets';

26 [a]Luke 3:8

27 and He will say, 'I tell you, [a]I do not know where you are from; [b]DEPART FROM ME, ALL YOU EVILDOERS.'

27 [a]Luke 13:25 [b]Ps. 6:8; Matt. 25:41

28 "[a]There will be weeping and gnashing of teeth there when you see Abraham and Isaac and Jacob and all the prophets in the kingdom of God, but yourselves being cast out.

28 [a]Matt. 8:12

29 "And they [a]will come from east and west, and from north and south, and will recline at the table in the kingdom of God.

29 [a]Matt. 8:11

30 "And behold, [a]some are last who will be first and some are first who will be last."

30 [a]Matt. 19:30

31 Just at that time some Pharisees came up, saying to Him, "Go away and depart from here, for [a]Herod wants to kill You."

31 [a]Matt. 14:1; Luke 3:1; 9:7; 23:7

32 And He said to them, "Go and tell that fox, 'Behold, I cast out demons and perform cures today and tomorrow, and the third day I [a]reach My goal.'

★**32** [a]Heb. 2:10; 5:9; 7:28

33 "Nevertheless [a]I must journey on today and tomorrow and the next day; for it cannot be that a [b]prophet should perish outside of Jerusalem.

33 [a]John 11:9 [b]Matt. 21:11

34 "[a]O Jerusalem, Jerusalem, the city that kills the prophets and stones those sent to her! How often I wanted to gather your children together, [b]just as a hen gathers her brood under her wings, and you would not have it!

34 [a]Luke 13:34, 35; Matt. 23:37-39; Luke 19:41 [b]Matt. 23:37

35 "Behold, your house is left to you desolate; and I say to you, you shall not see Me until the time comes when you say, '[a]BLESSED IS HE WHO COMES IN THE NAME OF THE LORD!'"

★**35** [a]Ps. 118:26; Matt. 21:9; Luke 19:38

13:19 *mustard seed.* From the smallest of seeds the Palestinian mustard plant grows in one season to a shrub the size of a small tree.

13:21 *leaven.* See note on Matt. 13:33.

13:24 *narrow door.* Christ Himself, apart from Whom there is no other way to heaven (John 14:6).

13:32 *that fox.* Herod Antipas is described as a fox, known for its use of cunning deceit to achieve its aims.

13:35 *your house is left to you desolate.* This was fulfilled when the temple was destroyed in A.D. 70 and the Jews were expelled under Hadrian in A.D. 135. *Blessed is He who comes.* See Ps. 118:26. This will be fulfilled at the second coming of Christ.

8 Concerning inflexible people,
14:1-6

1 aMark 3:2

14 And it came about when He went into the house of one of the leaders of the Pharisees on *the* Sabbath to eat bread, that ªthey were watching Him closely.

★ 2

2 And there, in front of Him was a certain man suffering from dropsy.

3 aActs
3:12 bMatt.
22:35 cMatt.
12:2; Luke
13:14

3 And Jesus ªanswered and spoke to the ᵇlawyers and Pharisees, saying, "ᶜIs it lawful to heal on the Sabbath, or not?"

4 But they kept silent. And He took hold of him, and healed him, and sent him away.

5 aLuke
13:15

5 And He said to them, "ªWhich one of you shall have a son or an ox fall into a well, and will not immediately pull him out on a Sabbath day?"

6 aMatt.
22:46; Luke
20:40

6 ªAnd they could make no reply to this.

9 Concerning inflated people,
14:7-11

7 aMatt.
23:6

7 And He *began* speaking a parable to the invited guests when He noticed how ªthey had been picking out the places of honor *at the table;* saying to them,

8 aProv.
25:6, 7

8 "When you are invited by someone to a wedding feast, ªdo not take the place of honor, lest someone more distinguished than you may have been invited by him,

9 aLuke 3:8

9 and he who invited you both shall come and say to you, 'Give place to this man,' and then ªin disgrace you proceed to occupy the last place.

10 aProv.
25:6, 7

10 "But when you are invited, go and recline at the last place, so that when the one who has invited you comes, he may say to you, 'Friend, ªmove up higher'; then you will have honor in the sight of all who are at the table with you.

★11 aMatt
23:12; Luke
18:14

11 "ªFor everyone who exalts himself shall be humbled, and he who humbles himself shall be exalted."

10 Concerning invited people,
14:12-14

12 And He also went on to say to the one who had invited Him, "When you give a luncheon or a dinner, do not invite your friends or your brothers or your relatives or rich neighbors, lest they also invite you in return, and repayment come to you.

13 "But when you give a reception, invite *the* poor, *the* crippled, *the* lame, *the* blind,

14 aJohn
5:29; Acts
24:15; Rev
20:4, 5 [?]

14 and you will be blessed, since they do not have *the means* to repay you; for you will be repaid at ªthe resurrection of the righteous."

*11 Concerning indifferent
people,* 14:15-24

★15 aRev
19:9

15 And when one of those who were reclining *at the table* with Him heard this, he said to Him, "ªBlessed is everyone who shall eat bread in the kingdom of God!"

16 aMatt
22:2-14;
Luke 14:16-
24

16 But He said to him, "ªA certain man was giving a big dinner, and he invited many;

17 and at the dinner hour he sent his slave to say to those who had been invited, 'Come; for everything is ready now.'

18 "But they all alike began to make excuses. The first one said to him, 'I have bought a piece of land and I need to go out and look at it; please consider me excused.'

19 "And another one said, 'I have bought five yoke of oxen, and I am going to try them out; please consider me excused.'

14:2 *dropsy.* A swelling of the body due to retention of excessive liquid.
14:11 Humility is the path to promotion in the kingdom of God.

14:15 *Blessed is everyone.* A seemingly pious remark made for the purpose of dulling the point of Christ's teaching.

20 ᵃDeut.
24.5, 1 Cor.
7:33

20 "And another one said, 'ᵃI have married a wife, and for that reason I cannot come.'

21 "And the slave came *back* and reported this to his master. Then the head of the household became angry and said to his slave, 'Go out at once into the streets and lanes of the city and bring in here the poor and crippled and blind and lame.'

22 "And the slave said, 'Master, what you commanded has been done, and still there is room.'

23 "And the master said to the slave, 'Go out into the highways and along the hedges, and compel *them* to come in, that my house may be filled.

24 'For I tell you, none of those men who were invited shall taste of my dinner.'"

12   Concerning indulgent people, 14:25–35

★25-33

25 Now great multitudes were going along with Him; and He turned and said to them,

★26 ᵃMatt.
10:37f.

26 "ᵃIf anyone comes to Me, and does not hate his own father and mother and wife and children and brothers and sisters, yes, and even his own life, he cannot be My disciple.

27 ᵃMatt.
10:38

27 "Whoever does not ᵃcarry his own cross and come after Me cannot be My disciple.

28 "For which one of you, when he wants to build a tower, does not first sit down and calculate the cost, to see if he has enough to complete it?

29 "Otherwise, when he has laid a foundation, and is not able to finish, all who observe it begin to ridicule him,

30 saying, 'This man began to build and was not able to finish.'

31 "Or what king, when he sets out to meet another king in battle, will not first sit down and take counsel whether he is strong enough with ten thousand *men* to encounter the one coming against him with twenty thousand?

32 "Or else, while the other is still far away, he sends a delegation and asks terms of peace.

33 ᵃPhil. 3:7;
Heb. 11:26

33 "So therefore, no one of you can be My disciple who ᵃdoes not give up all his own possessions.

34 ᵃMatt.
5:13; Mark
9:50

34 "Therefore, salt is good; but ᵃif even salt has become tasteless, with what will it be seasoned?

35 ᵃMatt.
11:15

35 "It is useless either for the soil or for the manure pile; it is thrown out. ᵃHe who has ears to hear, let him hear."

13   Concerning God's love for sinners, 15:1–32

1 ᵃLuke
5:29

15 Now all the ᵃtax-gatherers and the sinners were coming near Him to listen to Him.

★ 2 ᵃMatt.
9:11

2 And both the Pharisees and the scribes *began* to grumble, saying, "This man receives sinners and ᵃeats with them."

3 And He told them this parable, saying,

★ 4 ᵃMatt.
18:12-14;
Luke 15:4-7

4 "ᵃWhat man among you, if he has a hundred sheep and has lost one of them, does not leave the ninety-nine in the open pasture, and go after the one which is lost, until he finds it?

5 "And when he has found it, he lays it on his shoulders, rejoicing.

6 "And when he comes home, he calls together his friends and his neighbors, saying to them,

---

14:25-33 The parable that precedes in vv. 16–24 expresses the open, compelling invitation to come to Christ for salvation. The teaching of vv. 25–33 cautions His followers to consider carefully the cost of full commitment to Christ in a life of service.

14:26 *hate.* This saying does not justify malice or ill will toward one's family, but it means that devotion to family must take second place

to one's devotion to Christ.

15:2 *This man receives sinners.* Since the Pharisees disdained publicans and sinners, Christ told three parables (15:4–32) to show God's interest in them.

15:4 *lost.* Eight times in this chapter the lostness of man is emphasized (vv. 4 [twice], 6, 8, 9, 17, 24, 32).

'Rejoice with me, for I have found my sheep which was lost!'

7 "I tell you that in the same way, there will be *more* joy in heaven over one sinner who repents, than over ninety-nine righteous persons who need no repentance.

★ 8   8 "Or what woman, if she has ten silver coins and loses one coin, does not light a lamp and sweep the house and search carefully until she finds it?

9 "And when she has found it, she calls together her friends and neighbors, saying, 'Rejoice with me, for I have found the coin which I had lost!'

10 aMatt
10:32; Luke
15:7
   10 "In the same way, I tell you, there is joy ain the presence of the angels of God over one sinner who repents."

11 And He said, "A certain man had two sons;

12 aDeut
21:17 bMark
12:44; Luke
15:30
   12 and the younger of them said to his father, 'Father, give me athe share of the estate that falls to me.' And he divided his bwealth between them.

13 "And not many days later, the younger son gathered everything together and went on a journey into a distant country, and there he squandered his estate with loose living.

14 "Now when he had spent everything, a severe famine occurred in that country, and he began to be in need.

★15   15 "And he went and attached himself to one of the citizens of that country, and he sent him into his fields to feed swine.

16 "And he was longing to fill his stomach with the pods that the swine were eating, and no one was giving *anything* to him.

17 "But when he came to his senses, he said, 'How many of my father's hired men have more

than enough bread, but I am dying here with hunger!

18 'I will get up and go to my father, and will say to him, "Father, I have sinned against heaven, and in your sight;   ★18

19 "I am no longer worthy to be called your son; make me as one of your hired men."'

20 "And he got up and came to his father. But while he was still a long way off, his father saw him, and felt compassion *for him*, and ran and aembraced him, and kissed him.

20 aGen
45:14; 46:29;
Acts 20:37

21 "And the son said to him, 'Father, I have sinned against heaven and in your sight; I am no longer worthy to be called your son.'

22 "But the father said to his slaves, 'Quickly bring out athe best robe and put it on him, and bput a ring on his hand and sandals on his feet;

22 aZech
3:4; Rev
6:11 bGen
41:42

23 and bring the fattened calf, kill it, and let us eat and be merry;

24 for this son of mine was adead, and has come to life again; he was lost, and has been found.' And they began to be merry.

24 aMatt
8:22; Luke
9:60; 15:32;
Rom. 11:15;
Eph. 2:1, 5;
5:14; Col
2:13; 1 Tim.
5:6

25 "Now his older son was in the field, and when he came and approached the house, he heard music and dancing.

26 "And he summoned one of the servants and *began* inquiring what these things might be.

27 "And he said to him, 'Your brother has come, and your father has killed the fattened calf, because he has received him back safe and sound.'

28 "But he became angry, and was not willing to go in; and his father came out and *began* entreating him.   ★28

29 "But he answered and said to his father, 'Look! For so many years I have been serving you,

---

15:8 *what woman.* The second parable using a woman suggests that many women followed Christ and heard Him teach.

15:15 *to feed swine.* The lowest possible humiliation for a Jew.

15:18 *I have sinned.* Acknowledging one's per-

sonal responsibility for sin is the first step toward reconciliation with God.

15:28 *he became angry.* The elder son's attitude is the same as the Pharisees' (v. 2; 18:11-12). The words reflect self-righteousness.

and I have never neglected a command of yours; and *yet* you have never given me a kid, that I might be merry with my friends;

30 but when this son of yours came, who has devoured your ªwealth with harlots, you killed the fattened calf for him.'

30 ªProv.
29:3; Luke
15:12

31 "And he said to him, *'My* child, you have always been with me, and all that is mine is yours.

32 'But we had to be merry and rejoice, for this brother of yours was ªdead and *has begun* to live, and *was* lost and has been found.'"

32 ªLuke
15:24

14 Concerning wealth, 16:1-31

1 ªLuke
15:13

16 Now He was also saying to the disciples, "There was a certain rich man who had a steward, and this *steward* was reported to him as ªsquandering his possessions.

2 "And he called him and said to him, 'What is this I hear about you? Give an account of your stewardship, for you can no longer be steward.'

3 "And the steward said to himself, 'What shall I do, since my master is taking the stewardship away from me? I am not strong enough to dig; I am ashamed to beg.

4 'I know what I shall do, so that when I am removed from the stewardship, they will receive me into their homes.'

5 "And he summoned each one of his master's debtors, and he *began* saying to the first, 'How much do you owe my master?'

6 "And he said, 'A hundred measures of oil.' And he said to him, 'Take your bill, and sit down quickly and write fifty.'

7 "Then he said to another,

'And how much do you owe?' And he said, 'A hundred measures of wheat.' He *said to him, 'Take your bill, and write eighty.'

8 "And his master praised the unrighteous steward because he had acted shrewdly; for the sons of ªthis age are more shrewd in relation to their own kind than the ᵇsons of light.

★ 8 ªMatt.
12:32; Luke
20:34 ᵇJohn
12:36; Eph.
5:8; 1 Thess.
5:5

9 "And I say to you, ªmake friends for yourselves by means of the ᵇmammon of unrighteousness; that when it fails, ᶜthey may receive you into the eternal dwellings.

★ 9 ªMatt.
19:21; Luke
11:41; 12:33
ᵇMatt. 6:24;
Luke 16:11,
13 ᶜLuke
16:4

10 "ªHe who is faithful in a very little thing is faithful also in much; and he who is unrighteous in a very little thing is unrighteous also in much.

10 ªMatt.
25:21, 23

11 "If therefore you have not been faithful in the *use of* unrighteous ªmammon, who will entrust the true *riches* to you?

★11 ªLuke
16:9

12 "And if you have not been faithful in *the use of* that which is another's, who will give you that which is your own?

★12

13 "ªNo servant can serve two masters; for either he will hate the one, and love the other, or else he will hold to one, and despise the other. You cannot serve God and ᵇmammon."

13 ªMatt.
6:24 ᵇLuke
16:9

14 Now the Pharisees, who were ªlovers of money, were listening to all these things, and they ᵇwere scoffing at Him.

14 ª2 Tim.
3:2 ᵇLuke
23:35

15 And He said to them, "You are those who ªjustify yourselves in the sight of men, but ᵇGod knows your hearts; for that which is highly esteemed among men is detestable in the sight of God.

15 ªLuke
10:29; 18:9,
14 ᵇ1 Sam.
16:7; Prov.
21:2; Acts
1:24; Rom.
8:27

16 "ªThe Law and the Prophets *were* proclaimed until John; since

★16 ªMatt.
11:12f.
ᵇMatt. 4:23

16:8 *acted shrewdly.* What is commended is the ingenuity, not the dishonesty, of the steward in using his present opportunities to prepare for the future. Likewise, the believer should use what he has in this life in the service of God in order to assure rewards in heaven (v. 9).

16:9 *mammon* = money and other material

possessions.

16:11 *the true riches.* I.e., spiritual responsibilities.

16:12 Unfaithfulness in managing another's goods proves one unworthy to be given much for himself.

16:16 *everyone is forcing his way into it.* Men were crowding to enter the kingdom.

then [b]the gospel of the kingdom of God is preached, and everyone is forcing his way into it.

★17 [a]Matt. 5:18

17 "[a]But it is easier for heaven and earth to pass away than for one stroke of a letter of the Law to fail.

★18 [a]Matt. 5:32

18 "[a]Everyone who divorces his wife and marries another commits adultery; and he who marries one who is divorced from a husband commits adultery.

★19

19 "Now there was a certain rich man, and he habitually dressed in purple and fine linen, gaily living in splendor every day.

20 [a]Acts 3:2

20 "And a certain poor man named Lazarus [a]was laid at his gate, covered with sores,

21 and longing to be fed with the *crumbs* which were falling from the rich man's table; besides, even the dogs were coming and licking his sores.

★22 [a]John 1:18; 13:23

22 "Now it came about that the poor man died and he was carried away by the angels to [a]Abraham's bosom; and the rich man also died and was buried.

★23 [a]Matt. 11:23

23 "And in [a]Hades he lifted up his eyes, being in torment, and *saw Abraham far away, and Lazarus in his bosom.

24 [a]Luke 3:8; 16:30; 19:9 [b]Matt. 25:41

24 "And he cried out and said, '[a]Father Abraham, have mercy on me, and send Lazarus, that he may dip the tip of his finger in water and cool off my tongue; for I am in agony in [b]this flame.'

25 [a]Luke 6:24

25 "But Abraham said, 'Child, remember that [a]during your life you received your good things, and likewise Lazarus bad things; but now he is being comforted here, and you are in agony.

26 'And besides all this, between us and you there is a great

chasm fixed, in order that those who wish to come over from here to you may not be able, and *that* none may cross over from there to us.'

27 "And he said, 'Then I beg you, Father, that you send him to my father's house—

28 [a]Acts 2:40; 8:25; 10:42; 18:5; 20:21ff.; 23:11; 28:23; Gal. 5:3; Eph. 4:17; 1 Thess. 2:11; 4:6

28 for I have five brothers— that he may [a]warn them, lest they also come to this place of torment.'

29 [a]Luke 4:17; John 5:45-47; Acts 15:21

29 "But Abraham *said, 'They have [a]Moses and the Prophets; let them hear them.'

30 [a]Luke 3:8; 16:24; 19:9

30 "But he said, 'No, [a]Father Abraham, but if someone goes to them from the dead, they will repent!'

31 "But he said to him, 'If they do not listen to Moses and the Prophets, neither will they be persuaded if someone rises from the dead.'"

15 Concerning forgiveness, 17:1-6

1 [a]Matt. 18:7; 1 Cor. 11:19; 1 Tim. 4:1

17 And He said to His disciples, "[a]It is inevitable that stumbling blocks should come, but woe to him through whom they come!

★ 2 [a]Matt. 18:6; Mark 9:42; 1 Cor. 8:12

2 "[a]It would be better for him if a millstone were hung around his neck and he were thrown into the sea, than that he should cause one of these little ones to stumble.

3 [a]Matt. 18:15

3 "Be on your guard! [a]If your brother sins, rebuke him; and if he repents, forgive him.

4 [a]Matt. 18:21f.

4 "And if he sins against you [a]seven times a day, and returns to you seven times, saying, 'I repent,' forgive him."

16:17 *stroke.* See note on Matt. 5:18.

16:18 *divorces.* See notes on Matt. 5:32; 19:10.

16:19 *rich man.* His name is not given. Dives, sometimes said to be his name, is simply Latin for "rich man." Life was one continual party for him.

16:22 *Abraham's bosom.* Figurative speech for paradise, or the presence of God (Luke 23:43; 2 Cor. 12:4).

16:23 *in Hades.* The unseen world in general, but specifically here the abode of the unsaved

dead between death and judgment at the great white throne (Rev. 20:11-15). See note on Eph. 4:9. In this saying the Lord taught: (1) conscious existence after death; (2) the reality and torment of hell; (3) no second chance after death; and (4) the impossibility of the dead communicating with the living (v. 26). The two men in this story illustrate two different lives, two different deaths, and two different destinies.

17:2 *a millstone.* See note on Matt. 18:6.

5 And ^athe apostles said to ^bthe Lord, "Increase our faith!"

6 And ^athe Lord said, "If you had faith like ^ba mustard seed, you would say to this ^cmulberry tree, 'Be uprooted and be planted in the sea'; and it would obey you.

16 Concerning service, 17:7-10

7 "But which of you, having a slave plowing or tending sheep, will say to him when he has come in from the field, 'Come immediately and sit down to eat'?

8 "But will he not say to him, '^aPrepare something for me to eat, and *properly* clothe yourself and serve me until I have eaten and drunk; and afterward you will eat and drink'?

9 "He does not thank the slave because he did the things which were commanded, does he?

10 "So you too, when you do all the things which are commanded you, say, 'We are unworthy slaves; we have done *only* that which we ought to have done.' "

17 Concerning gratitude, 17:11-19

11 And it came about while He was ^aon the way to Jerusalem, that ^bHe was passing between Samaria and Galilee.

12 And as He entered a certain village, ten leprous men who ^astood at a distance met Him;

13 and they raised their voices, saying, "Jesus, ^aMaster, have mercy on us!"

14 And when He saw them, He said to them, "^aGo and show yourselves to the priests." And it came about that as they were going, they were cleansed.

15 Now one of them, when he saw that he had been healed, turned back, ^aglorifying God with a loud voice,

16 and he fell on his face at His feet, giving thanks to Him. And he was a ^aSamaritan.

17 And Jesus answered and said, "Were there not ten cleansed? But the nine—where are they?

18 "Was no one found who turned back to ^agive glory to God, except this foreigner?"

19 And He said to him, "Rise, and go your way; ^ayour faith has made you well."

18 Concerning the kingdom, 17:20-37

20 Now having been questioned by the Pharisees ^aas to when the kingdom of God was coming, He answered them and said, "The kingdom of God is not coming with ^bsigns to be observed;

21 nor will ^athey say, 'Look, here it is!' or, 'There it is!' For behold, the kingdom of God is in your midst."

22 And He said to the disciples, "^aThe days shall come when you will long to see one of the days of the Son of Man, and you will not see it.

23 "^aAnd they will say to you, 'Look there! Look here!' Do not go away, and do not run after them.

24 "^aFor just as the lightning, when it flashes out of one part of the sky, shines to the other part of the sky, so will the Son of Man be in His day.

Marginal references:

5 ^aMark 6:30 ^bLuke 7:13
★ 6 ^aLuke 7:13 ^bMatt 13:31; 17:20; Mark 4:31; Luke 13:19 ^cLuke 19:4
8 ^aLuke 12:37
11 ^aLuke 9:51 ^bLuke 9:52ff; John 4:3f
★12 ^aLev 13:45f
13 ^aLuke 5:5
★14 ^aMatt 8:4; Luke 5:14
15 ^aMatt 9:8
16 ^aMatt 10:5
18 ^aMatt 9:8
19 ^aMatt 9:22; Luke 18:42
20 ^aLuke 19:11; Acts 1:6 ^bLuke 14:1 [Gr]
★21 ^aLuke 17:23
22 ^aMatt 9:15; Mark 2:20; Luke 5:35
23 ^aMatt 24:23; Mark 13:21; Luke 21:8
24 ^aMatt 24:27

17:6 *mulberry tree.* A tree whose roots were regarded as being particularly strong, making it virtually impossible to uproot.

17:12 *leprous men.* See note on Luke 5:12.

17:14 *Go and show yourselves to the priests.* The priest had to certify the cleansing of a leper (Lev. 14:1-32). The men exhibited faith by starting on their way to the priest before being cleansed.

17:21 *the kingdom of God is in your midst.* The necessary elements of the kingdom were there present and needed only to be recognized. It cannot mean "within you," for the kingdom certainly was completely unconnected with the Pharisees to whom Jesus was speaking (v. 20).

25 "^aBut first He must suffer many things and be rejected by this generation.

26 "^aAnd just as it happened ^bin the days of Noah, so it shall be also in the days of the Son of Man:

27 they were eating, they were drinking, they were marrying, they were being given in marriage, until the day that Noah entered the ark, and the flood came and destroyed them all.

28 "It was the same as happened in ^athe days of Lot: they were eating, they were drinking, they were buying, they were selling, they were planting, they were building;

29 but on the day that Lot went out from Sodom it rained fire and brimstone from heaven and destroyed them all.

30 "It will be just the same on the day that the Son of Man ^ais revealed.

31 "On that day, let not the one who is ^aon the housetop and whose goods are in the house go down to take them away; and likewise let not the one who is in the field turn back.

32 "^aRemember Lot's wife.

33 "^aWhoever seeks to keep his life shall lose it, and whoever loses *his* life shall preserve it.

34 "I tell you, on that night there will be two men in one bed; one will be taken, and the other will be left.

35 "^aThere will be two women grinding at the same place; one will be taken, and the other will be left.

36 ["^aTwo men will be in the field; one will be taken and the other will be left."]

37 And answering they *said to Him, "Where, Lord?" And He said to them, "^aWhere the body *is*, there also will the vultures be gathered."

19   *Concerning prayer,* 18:1-14

18 Now He was telling them a parable to show that at all times they ^aought to pray and not to ^blose heart,

2 saying, "There was in a certain city a judge who did not fear God, and did not ^arespect man.

3 "And there was a widow in that city, and she kept coming to him, saying, 'Give me legal protection from my opponent.'

4 "And for a while he was unwilling; but afterward he said to himself, 'Even though I do not fear God nor ^arespect man,

5 yet ^abecause this ' widow bothers me, I will give her legal protection, lest by continually coming she ^bwear me out.' "

6 And ^athe Lord said, "Hear what the unrighteous judge *said,

7 now shall not God ^abring about justice for His ^belect, who cry to Him day and night, and will He ^cdelay long over them?

8 "I tell you that He will bring about justice for them speedily. However, when the Son of Man comes, ^awill He find faith on the earth?"

9 And He also told this parable to certain ones who ^atrusted in themselves that they were

---

Marginal references

25 ^aMatt. 16:21; Luke 9:22

★**26-27**
26 ^aLuke 17:26, 27; Matt. 24:37-39 ^bGen. 7

★**28** ^aGen. 19

★**30** ^aMatt. 16:27; 1 Cor. 1:7; Col. 3:4; 2 Thess. 1:7; 1 Pet. 1:7; 4:13; 1 John 2:28
31 ^aMatt. 24:17, 18; Mark 13:15f.; Luke 21:21

32 ^aGen. 19:26
33 ^aMatt. 10:39

35 ^aMatt. 24:41

★**36** ^aMatt. 24:40

★**37** ^aMatt. 24:28

★ **1** ^aLuke 11:5-10 ^b2 Cor. 4:1

2 ^aLuke 18:4; 20:13; Heb. 12:9

4 ^aLuke 18:2; 20:13; Heb. 12:9

5 ^aLuke 11:8 ^b1 Cor. 9:27

6 ^aLuke 7:13

7 ^aRev. 6:10 ^bMatt. 24:22; Rom. 8:33; Col. 3:12; 2 Tim. 1:1 ^c2 Pet. 3:9
★ **8** ^aLuke 17:26ff.

9 ^aLuke 16:15 ^bRom. 14:3, 10

17:26-27 *in the days of Noah.* See Gen. 6. The activities mentioned in v. 27 are not wrong; the people were unprepared for the judgment of the flood because they did not heed God's warnings through Noah.
17:28 *in the days of Lot.* See Gen. 19.
17:30 *It will be just the same.* Until the time of Christ's return, many people will be prosperous, feel secure and be unprepared for His return (as in the days of Noah and Lot).
17:36 Many manuscripts do not contain this verse.

17:37 *body.* I.e., a corpse. *vultures.* A reference to the carnage of Armageddon (Rev. 19:17-19).
18:1 *lose heart.* I.e., be discouraged because answers do not come immediately.
18:8 *speedily.* Not necessarily immediately, but quickly when the answer begins to come. For other uses of the term see Rom. 16:20; Rev. 1:1. *will He find faith on the earth?* This does not augur for improved spiritual conditions in the world before Christ's return.

righteous, and ^bviewed others with contempt:

10 "Two men ^awent up into the temple to pray, one a Pharisee, and the other a tax-gatherer.

11 "The Pharisee ^astood and was praying thus to himself, 'God, I thank Thee that I am not like other people: swindlers, unjust, adulterers, or even like this tax-gatherer.

12 'I ^afast twice a week; I ^bpay tithes of all that I get.'

13 "But the tax-gatherer, ^astanding some distance away, ^bwas even unwilling to lift up his eyes to heaven, but ^cwas beating his breast, saying, 'God, be merciful to me, the sinner!'

14 "I tell you, this man went down to his house justified rather than the other; ^afor everyone who exalts himself shall be humbled, but he who humbles himself shall be exalted."

20 Concerning entrance into the kingdom, 18:15-30

15 ^aAnd they were bringing even their babies to Him so that He might touch them, but when the disciples saw it, they *began* rebuking them.

16 But Jesus called for them, saying, "Permit the children to come to Me, and do not hinder them, for the kingdom of God belongs to such as these.

17 "Truly I say to you, ^awhoever does not receive the kingdom of God like a child shall not enter it *at all.*"

18 ^aAnd a certain ruler questioned Him, saying, "Good Teacher, what shall I do to inherit eternal life?"

19 And Jesus said to him, "Why do you call Me good? No one is good except God alone.

20 "You know the commandments, '^aDo not commit adultery, Do not murder, Do not steal, Do not bear false witness, Honor your father and mother.'"

21 And he said, "All these things I have kept from *my* youth."

22 And when Jesus heard *this,* He said to him, "One thing you still lack; ^asell all that you possess, and distribute it to the poor, and you shall have ^btreasure in heaven; and come, follow Me."

23 But when he had heard these things, he became very sad; for he was extremely rich.

24 And Jesus looked at him and said, "^aHow hard it is for those who are wealthy to enter the kingdom of God!

25 "For ^ait is easier for a camel to go through the eye of a needle, than for a rich man to enter the kingdom of God."

26 And they who heard it said, "Then who can be saved?"

27 But He said, "^aThe things impossible with men are possible with God."

28 And Peter said, "Behold, ^awe have left our own *homes,* and followed You."

29 And He said to them, "Truly I say to you, ^athere is no one who has left house or wife or brothers or parents or children, for the sake of the kingdom of God,

30 who shall not receive many times as much at this time and in ^athe age to come, eternal life."

10 ^a1 Kin. 10:5; 2 Kin. 20:5, 8; Acts 3:1
11 ^aMatt. 6:5; Mark 11:25; Luke 22:41
★**12** ^aMatt. 9:14 ^bLuke 11:42
★**13** ^aMatt. 6:5; Mark 11:25; Luke 22:41 ^bEzra 9:6 ^cLuke 23:48
★**14** ^aMatt. 23:12; Luke 14:11
15 ^aLuke 18:15-17; Matt. 19:13-15; Mark 10:13-16
17 ^aMatt. 18:3; 19:14; Mark 10:15; 1 Cor. 14:20; 1 Pet. 2:2
18 ^aLuke 18:18-30; Matt. 19:16-29; Mark 10:17-30; Luke 10:25-28
20 ^aEx. 20:12-16; Deut. 5:16-20
★**22** ^aMatt. 19:21; Luke 12:33 ^bMatt. 6:20
24 ^aMatt. 19:23; Mark 10:23f.
★**25** ^aMatt. 19:24; Mark 10:25
27 ^aMatt. 19:26
28 ^aLuke 5:11
29 ^aMatt. 6:33; 19:29; Mark 10:29f.
30 ^aMatt. 12:32

18:12 *I fast.* See note on Matt. 9:14. *I pay tithes.* See note on Matt. 23:23.
18:13 *God, be merciful.* Lit., God be propitiated or satisfied. Now Christ is the propitiation or satisfaction for our sins (1 John 2:1).
18:14 The Pharisee thought God operated on a merit system, and thus could be put in man's debt through good works. The publican knew

God was merciful and was worthy of trust.
18:22 *One thing you still lack.* Apparently the man had kept the laws of v. 20, but Jesus saw his attachment to material things. Rather than admit this, the man turned his back on Christ's help.
18:25 *the eye of a needle.* See note on Matt. 19:24.

21   Concerning His death,
18:31-34

31 aLuke 18:31-33; Matt. 20:17-19; Mark 10:32-34
bLuke 9:51
cPs. 22; Is. 53

31 ªAnd He took the twelve aside and said to them, "Behold, bwe are going up to Jerusalem, and call things which are written through the prophets about the Son of Man will be accomplished.

32 aMatt. 16:21

32 "ªFor He will be delivered to the Gentiles, and will be mocked and mistreated and spit upon, **33** and after they have scourged Him, they will kill Him; and the third day He will rise again."

34 aMark 9:32; Luke 9:45

34 And ªthey understood none of these things, and this saying was hidden from them, and they did not comprehend the things that were said.

22   Concerning salvation,
18:35-19:10

★35 aLuke 18:35-43; Matt. 20:29-34; Mark 10:46-52
bMatt. 20:29; Mark 10:46; Luke 19:1

35 ªAnd it came about that bas He was approaching Jericho, a certain blind man was sitting by the road, begging. **36** Now hearing a multitude going by, he began to inquire what this might be. **37** And they told him that Jesus of Nazareth was passing by.

38 aMatt. 9:27; Luke 18:39

38 And he called out, saying, "Jesus, ªSon of David, have mercy on me!"

39 aLuke 18:38

39 And those who led the way were sternly telling him to be quiet; but he kept crying out all the more, "ªSon of David, have mercy on me!" **40** And Jesus stopped and commanded that he be brought to Him; and when he had come near, He questioned him, **41** "What do you want Me to

do for you?" And he said, "Lord, I want to regain my sight!" **42** And Jesus said to him, "Receive your sight; ªyour faith has made you well." **43** And immediately he regained his sight, and began following Him, ªglorifying God; and when ball the people saw it, they gave praise to God.

42 aMatt. 9:22

43 aMatt. 9:8
bLuke 9:43; 13:17; 19:37

19 And He ªentered and was passing through Jericho. **2** And behold, there was a man called by the name of Zaccheus; and he was a chief tax-gatherer, and he was rich. **3** And he was trying to see who Jesus was, and he was unable because of the crowd, for he was small in stature. **4** And he ran on ahead and climbed up into a ªsycamore tree in order to see Him, for He was about to pass through that way. **5** And when Jesus came to the place, He looked up and said to him, "Zaccheus, hurry and come down, for today I must stay at your house." **6** And he hurried and came down, and received Him gladly. **7** And when they saw it, they all began to grumble, saying, "He has gone to be the guest of a man who is a sinner." **8** And Zaccheus stopped and said to ªthe Lord, "Behold, Lord, half of my possessions I will give to the poor, and if I have bdefrauded anyone of anything, I will give back cfour times as much." **9** And Jesus said to him, "Today salvation has come to this house, because he, too, is ªa son of Abraham. **10** "For ªthe Son of Man has come to seek and to save that which was lost."

1 aLuke 18:35

★2

4 a1 Kin. 10:27; 1 Chr. 27:28; 2 Chr. 1:15; 9:27; Ps. 78:47; Is. 9:10; Luke 17:6 [?]

★8 aLuke 7:13 bLuke 3:14 cEx. 22:1; Lev. 6:5; Num. 5:7; 2 Sam. 12:6

9 aLuke 3:8; 13:16; Rom. 4:16; Gal. 3:7

10 aMatt. 18:11

18:35   *a certain blind man.* Concerning the differences in the accounts in the Gospels see note on Matt. 20:29-34.

19:2   *tax-gatherer.* As a tax collector for the Romans, he therefore had a bad reputation, since the system was open to abuse and extortion

was common. The word *chief* implies that Zaccheus was responsible for all the taxes of Jericho and had other collectors under him.

19:8 Zaccheus' declaration of what he intended to do from then on, now that his life had been changed by Christ.

23 Concerning faithfulness,
19:11-27

★11 ᵃLuke
9:51 ᵇLuke
17:20

11 And while they were listening to these things, He went on to tell a parable, because ᵃHe was near Jerusalem, and they supposed that ᵇthe kingdom of God was going to appear immediately.

12 ᵃMatt.
25:14-30;
Luke 19:12-
27

12 He said therefore, "ᵃA certain nobleman went to a distant country to receive a kingdom for himself, and then return.

★13

13 "And he called ten of his slaves, and gave them ten minas, and said to them, 'Do business with this until I come back.'

14 "But his citizens hated him, and sent a delegation after him, saying, 'We do not want this man to reign over us.'

15 "And it came about that when he returned, after receiving the kingdom, he ordered that these slaves, to whom he had given the money, be called to him in order that he might know what business they had done.

16 "And the first appeared, saying, 'Master, your mina has made ten minas more.'

17 ᵃLuke
16:10

17 "And he said to him, 'Well done, good slave, because you have been ᵃfaithful in a very little thing, be in authority over ten cities.'

18 "And the second came, saying, 'Your mina, master, has made five minas.'

19 "And he said to him also, 'And you are to be over five cities.'

20 "And another came, saying, 'Master, behold your mina, which I kept put away in a handkerchief;

21 for I was afraid of you, because you are an exacting man;

you take up what you did not lay down, and reap what you did not sow.'

22 "He *said to him, 'By your own words I will judge you, you worthless slave. Did you know that I am an exacting man, taking up what I did not lay down, and reaping what I did not sow?

23 'Then why did you not put the money in the bank, and having come, I would have collected it with interest?'

24 "And he said to the bystanders, 'Take the mina away from him, and give it to the one who has the ten minas.'

25 "And they said to him, 'Master, he has ten minas already.'

26 ᵃMatt.
13:12; Luke
8:18

26 "ᵃI tell you, that to everyone who has shall more be given, but from the one who does not have, even what he does have shall be taken away.

27 ᵃLuke
19:14 ᵇMatt.
22:7; Luke
20:16

27 "But ᵃthese enemies of mine, who did not want me to reign over them, bring them here and ᵇslay them in my presence."

V THE CONDEMNATION OF THE SON OF MAN FOR MEN,
19:28-23:56

A Sunday, 19:28-44

28 ᵃMark
10:32 ᵇLuke
9:51

28 And after He had said these things, He ᵃwas going on ahead, ᵇascending to Jerusalem.

★29 ᵃLuke
19:29-38;
Matt. 21:1-9;
Mark 11:1-10
ᵇMatt. 21:17
ᶜLuke 21:37;
Acts 1:12

29 And it came about that ᵃwhen He approached Bethphage and ᵇBethany, near the mount that is called ᶜOlivet, He sent two of the disciples,

30 saying, "Go into the village opposite you, in which as you enter you will find a colt tied, on which no one yet has ever sat; untie it, and bring it here.

19:11 *they supposed.* The disciples still could not understand why they should not expect the political triumph of the Messianic kingdom immediately (and without the cross).
19:13 *minas.* A mina was a measure of money worth 100 drachmas or denarii. Notice that each servant received the same amount (in contrast to the parable of the talents in which

each received according to his ability, Matt. 25:15). The minas represent the equal opportunity of life itself; the talents, the different gifts God gives each individual.
19:29 *Bethphage.* Its site is unknown though it was near *Bethany* which was on the SE. side of the Mount of Olives.

31 "And if anyone asks you, 'Why are you untying it?' thus shall you speak, 'The Lord has need of it.' "

32 And those who were sent went away and found it just as He had told them.

33 And as they were untying the colt, its owners said to them, "Why are you untying the colt?"

34 And they said, "The Lord has need of it."

35 And they brought it to Jesus, ^aand they threw their garments on the colt, and put Jesus on it.

36 And as He was going, they were spreading their garments in the road.

37 And as He was now approaching, near the descent of ^athe Mount of Olives, the whole multitude of the disciples began to ^bpraise God joyfully with a loud voice for all the miracles which they had seen,

38 saying,

"^aBLESSED IS THE ^bKING WHO COMES IN THE NAME OF THE LORD;
Peace in heaven and ^cglory in the highest!"

39 ^aAnd some of the Pharisees in the multitude said to Him, "Teacher, rebuke Your disciples."

40 And He answered and said, "I tell you, if these become silent, ^athe stones will cry out!"

41 And when He approached, He saw the city and ^awept over it,

42 saying, "If you had known in this day, even you, the things which make for peace! But now they have been hidden from your eyes.

43 "For the days shall come upon you when your enemies will ^athrow up a bank before you, and ^bsurround you, and hem you in on every side,

44 and will level you to the ground and your children within

you, and ^athey will not leave in you one stone upon another, because you did not recognize ^bthe time of your visitation."

B Monday, 19:45-48

45 ^aAnd He entered the temple and began to cast out those who were selling,

46 saying to them, "It is written, '^aAND MY HOUSE SHALL BE A HOUSE OF PRAYER,' but you have made it a ROBBERS' DEN."

47 And ^aHe was teaching daily in the temple; but the chief priests and the scribes and the leading men among the people ^bwere trying to destroy Him,

48 and they could not find anything that they might do, for all the people were hanging upon His words.

C Tuesday, 20:1-21:38
1 Authority requested, 20:1-8

20 ^aAnd it came about on one of the days while ^bHe was teaching the people in the temple and ^cpreaching the gospel, that the chief priests and the scribes with the elders ^dconfronted Him,

2 and they spoke, saying to Him, "Tell us by what authority You are doing these things, or who is the one who gave You this authority?"

3 And He answered and said to them, "I shall also ask you a question, and you tell Me:

4 "Was the baptism of John from heaven or from men?"

5 And they reasoned among themselves, saying, "If we say, 'From heaven,' He will say, 'Why did you not believe him?'

6 "But if we say, 'From men,' all the people will stone us to death, for they are convinced that John was a ^aprophet."

Margin references

35 ^aLuke 19:35-38; John 12:12-15

37 ^aMatt. 21:1; Luke 19:29 ^bLuke 18:43

★38 ^aPs. 118:26 ^bMatt. 2:2; 25:34 ^cMatt. 21:9; Luke 2:14

39 ^aMatt. 21:15f.

40 ^aHab. 2:11

41 ^aLuke 13:34, 35

★43 ^aEccles. 9:14; Is. 29:3; 37:33; Jer. 6:6; Ezek. 4:2; 26:8 ^bLuke 21:20

44 ^aMatt. 24:2; Mark 13:2; Luke 21:6 ^b1 Pet. 2:12

★45 ^aLuke 19:45, 46; Matt. 21:12-16; Mark 11:15-18; John 2:13-16

46 ^aIs. 56:7; Jer. 7:11; Matt. 21:13; Mark 11:17

47 ^aMatt. 26:55 ^bLuke 20:19

★ 1-8

1 ^aLuke 20:1-8; Matt. 21:23-27; Mark 11:27-33 ^bMatt. 26:55 ^cLuke 8:1 ^dActs 4:1; 6:12

6 ^aMatt. 11:9; Luke 7:29, 30

19:38 This quotation from Ps. 118:26 was sung as the pilgrims made their way into Jerusalem.
19:43 *your enemies.* The Romans under Titus in A.D. 70.
19:45 *to cast out.* See note on Mark 11:15.
20:1-8 See note on Mark 11:30.

7 And they answered that they did not know where *it came* from.

8 And Jesus said to them, "Neither will I tell you by what authority I do these things."

2 Authority revealed, 20:9-18

★ **9** aLuke 20:9-19; Matt. 21:33-46; Mark 12:1-12

9 aAnd He began to tell the people this parable: "A man planted a vineyard and rented it out to vine-growers, and went on a journey for a long time.

10 "And at the *harvest* time he sent a slave to the vine-growers, in order that they might give him *some* of the produce of the vineyard; but the vine-growers beat him and sent him away empty-handed.

11 "And he proceeded to send another slave; and they beat him also and treated him shamefully, and sent him away empty-handed.

12 "And he proceeded to send a third; and this one also they wounded and cast out.

13 aLuke 18:2

13 "And the owner of the vineyard said, 'What shall I do? I will send my beloved son; perhaps they will arespect him.'

14 "But when the vine-growers saw him, they reasoned with one another, saying, 'This is the heir; let us kill him that the inheritance may be ours.'

15 "And they threw him out of the vineyard and killed him. What, therefore, will the owner of the vineyard do to them?

16 aMatt. 21:41; Mark 12:9; Luke 19:27 bRom. 3:4, 6, 31; 6:2, 15; 7:7, 13; 9:14; 11:1, 11; 1 Cor. 6:15; Gal. 2:17; 3:21; 6:14

16 "He will come and adestroy these vine-growers and will give the vineyard to others." And when they heard it, they said, "bMay it never be!"

★ **17** aPs. 118:22 bEph. 2:20; 1 Pet. 2:6

17 But He looked at them and said, "What then is this that is written,

'aThe stone which the builders rejected, This became bthe chief corner stone'?

18 aMatt. 21:44

18 "aEveryone who falls on that stone will be broken to pieces; but on whomever it falls, it will scatter him like dust."

3 Authority resisted, 20:19-40

19 aLuke 19:47

19 And the scribes and the chief priests atried to lay hands on Him that very hour, and they feared the people; for they understood that He spoke this parable against them.

20 aLuke 20:20-26; Matt. 22:15-22; Mark 12:13-17; Mark 3:2 bLuke 11:54; 20:26 cMatt. 27:2

20 aAnd they watched Him, and sent spies who pretended to be righteous, in order bthat they might catch Him in some statement, so as to deliver Him up to the rule and the authority of cthe governor.

21 And they questioned Him, saying, "Teacher, we know that You speak and teach correctly, and You are not partial to any, but teach the way of God in truth.

22 aMatt. 17:25; Luke 23:2

22 "Is it lawful for us ato pay taxes to Caesar, or not?"

23 But He detected their trickery and said to them,

★ **24**

24 "Show Me a denarius. Whose likeness and inscription does it have?" And they said, "Caesar's."

★ **25** aMatt. 22:21; Mark 12:17

25 And He said to them, "Then arender to Caesar the things that are Caesar's, and to God the things that are God's."

26 aLuke 11:54; 20:26

26 And they were unable to acatch Him in a saying in the presence of the people; and marveling at His answer, they became silent.

27 aLuke 20:27-40; Matt. 22:23-33; Mark 12:18-27

27 aNow there came to Him some of the Sadducees (who say that there is no resurrection),

---

20:9 *a vineyard.* The parable explains God's dealings with Israel (see Isa. 5:1-7 for a similar story). The O.T. prophets are called slaves (vv. 10-12); Jesus Himself is the beloved son (v. 13).

20:17 See Ps. 118:22.

20:24 *a denarius.* A Roman silver coin, bearing

Caesar's image. See notes on Matt. 20:2; 22:17, 21.

20:25 A follower of Christ has dual citizenship and responsibility. Of course, God's due takes precedence over Caesar's when there is conflict between them.

★28 ᵃDeut. 25:5

28 and they questioned Him, saying, "Teacher, Moses wrote for us that ᵃIF A MAN'S BROTHER DIES, having a wife, AND HE IS CHILDLESS, HIS BROTHER SHOULD TAKE THE WIFE AND RAISE UP OFFSPRING TO HIS BROTHER.

29 "Now there were seven brothers; and the first took a wife, and died childless;

30 and the second

31 and the third took her; and in the same way all seven died, leaving no children.

32 "Finally the woman died also.

33 "In the resurrection therefore, which one's wife will she be? For all seven had her as wife."

34 ᵃMatt. 12:32; Luke 16:8

34 And Jesus said to them, "The sons of ᵃthis age marry and are given in marriage,

35 ᵃMatt. 12:32; Luke 16:8

35 but those who are considered worthy to attain to ᵃthat age and the resurrection from the dead, neither marry, nor are given in marriage;

★36 ᵃRom. 8:16f.; 1 John 3:1, 2

36 for neither can they die anymore, for they are like angels, and are ᵃsons of God, being sons of the resurrection.

★37 ᵃMark 12:26 ᵇEx. 3:6

37 "But that the dead are raised, even Moses showed, in ᵃthe *passage about the burning* bush, where he calls the Lord ᵇTHE GOD OF ABRAHAM, AND THE GOD OF ISAAC, AND THE GOD OF JACOB.

38 ᵃMatt. 22:32; Mark 12:27 ᵇRom. 14:8

38 "ᵃNow He is not the God of the dead, but of the living; for ᵇall live to Him."

39 And some of the scribes answered and said, "Teacher, You have spoken well."

40 ᵃMatt. 22:46; Luke 14:6

40 For ᵃthey did not have courage to question Him any longer about anything.

4 Authority reiterated, 20:41–21:4

41 ᵃLuke 20:41-44 Matt. 22:41-46; Mark 12:35-37 ᵇMatt. 9:27

41 ᵃAnd He said to them, "How *is it that* they say the Christ is ᵇDavid's son?

42 ᵃPs. 110:1

42 "For David himself says in the book of Psalms,

'ᵃTHE LORD SAID TO MY LORD,
"SIT AT MY RIGHT HAND,

43 ᵃPs. 110:1

43 ᵃUNTIL I MAKE THINE ENEMIES A FOOTSTOOL FOR THY FEET."'

★44

44 "David therefore calls Him 'Lord,' and how is He his son?"

45 ᵃLuke 20:45-47 Matt. 23:1-7; Mark 12:38-40

45 ᵃAnd while all the people were listening, He said to the disciples,

46 ᵃLuke 11:43; 14:7

46 "Beware of the scribes, ᵃwho like to walk around in long robes, and love respectful greetings in the market places, and chief seats in the synagogues, and places of honor at banquets,

47 who devour widows' houses, and for appearance's sake offer long prayers; these will receive greater condemnation."

21

★ 1 ᵃLuke 21:1-4; Mark 12:41-44

1 ᵃAnd He looked up and saw the rich putting their gifts into the treasury.

★ 2 ᵃMark 12:42

2 And He saw a certain poor widow putting in ᵃtwo small copper coins.

3 And He said, "Truly I say to you, this poor widow put in more than all *of them*;

4 ᵃMark 12:44

4 for they all out of their surplus put into the offering; but she out of her poverty put in all that she had ᵃto live on."

5 The apocalyptic discourse, 21:5–38

5 ᵃLuke 21:5-36; Matt. 24; Mark 13

5 ᵃAnd while some were talking about the temple, that it

20:28 See Deut. 25:5-10. According to the law, if a man died without an heir, any unmarried brother was obliged to marry the man's widow.

20:36 *like angels.* I.e., in the resurrection state there is no marriage or procreation. See note on Matt. 22:30.

20:37 See Ex. 3:6. God acknowledged a continu-

ing relationship with Abraham, Isaac, and Jacob, though they had died long before.

20:44 *how is He his son?* See note on Matt. 22:44.

21:1 *treasury.* Chests in the court of the temple where gifts were deposited.

21:2 *small copper coins.* See note on Luke 12:59.

was adorned with beautiful stones and votive gifts, He said,

6 *a*Luke 19:44

6 *"As for* these things which you are looking at, the days will come in which *a*there will not be left one stone upon another which will not be torn down."

★ 7

7 And they questioned Him, saying, "Teacher, when therefore will these things be? And what *will be* the sign when these things are about to take place?"

8 *a*John 8:24 *b*Luke 17:23

8 And He said, "See to it that you be not misled; for many will come in My name, saying, '*a*I am *He*,' and, 'The time is at hand'; *b*do not go after them.

9 "And when you hear of wars and disturbances, do not be terrified; for these things must take place first, but the end *does* not *follow* immediately."

10 Then He continued by saying to them, "Nation will rise against nation, and kingdom against kingdom,

11 and there will be great earthquakes, and in various places plagues and famines; and there will be terrors and great signs from heaven.

12 *a*Luke 21:12-17; Matt. 10:19-22; Mark 13:11-13

12 "But before all these things, *a*they will lay their hands on you and will persecute you, delivering you to the synagogues and prisons, bringing you before kings and governors for My name's sake.

13 *a*Phil. 1:12

13 "*a*It will lead to an opportunity for your testimony.

14 *a*Luke 12:11

14 "*a*So make up your minds not to prepare beforehand to defend yourselves;

15 *a*Luke 12:12

15 for *a*I will give you utterance and wisdom which none of your opponents will be able to resist or refute.

16 "But you will be delivered up even by parents and brothers

and relatives and friends, and they will put *some* of you to death,

17 and you will be hated by all on account of My name.

18 *a*Matt. 10:30; Luke 12:7

18 "Yet *a*not a hair of your head will perish.

19 *a*Matt. 10:22; 24:13; Rom. 2:7; 5:3f.; Heb. 10:36; James 1:3; 2 Pet. 1:6

19 "*a*By your endurance you will gain your lives.

20 *a*Luke 19:43

20 "But when you see Jerusalem *a*surrounded by armies, then recognize that her desolation is at hand.

21 *a*Luke 17:31

21 "Then let those who are in Judea flee to the mountains, and let those who are in the midst of the city depart, and *a*let not those who are in the country enter the city;

22 *a*Is. 63:4; Dan. 9:24-27; Hos. 9:7

22 because these are *a*days of vengeance, in order that all things which are written may be fulfilled.

23 *a*Dan. 8:19; 1 Cor. 7:26

23 "Woe to those who are with child and to those who nurse babes in those days; for *a*there will be great distress upon the land, and wrath to this people,

★24 *a*Gen. 34:26; Ex. 17:13; Heb. 11:34 *b*Is. 63:18; Dan. 8:13; Rev. 11:2 *c*Rev. 11:2 *d*Rom. 11:25

24 and they will fall by *a*the edge of the sword, and will be led captive into all the nations; and *b*Jerusalem will be *c*trampled underfoot by the Gentiles until *d*the times of the Gentiles be fulfilled.

25 "And there will be signs in sun and moon and stars, and upon the earth dismay among nations, in perplexity at the roaring of the sea and the waves,

26 men fainting from fear and the expectation of the things which are coming upon the world; for the powers of the heavens will be shaken.

27 *a*Matt. 16:27; 24:30; 26:64; Mark 13:26 *b*Dan. 7:13

27 "And *a*then they will see *b*THE SON OF MAN COMING IN A CLOUD with power and great glory.

28 *a*Luke 18:7

28 "But when these things begin to take place, straighten up and lift up your heads, because

---

21:7 *when . . . will these things be?* There is a double perspective in Christ's answer—the destruction of Jerusalem in A.D. 70 and the tribulation days just prior to His second coming. Verses 8-19 and 25-28 relate particularly to the latter time while vv. 20-24 refer to the former.

21:24 *the times of the Gentiles.* The period of Gentile domination of Jerusalem, which began probably under Nebuchadnezzar (587 B.C.), was certainly in effect in A.D. 70, and which continues into the tribulation days (cf. Rev. 11:2).

[a]your redemption is drawing near."

29 And He told them a parable: "Behold the fig tree and all the trees;

30 [a]Luke 12:57

30 as soon as they put forth *leaves*, you see it and [a]know for yourselves that summer is now near.

31 [a]Matt 3:2

31 "Even so you, too, when you see these things happening, recognize that [a]the kingdom of God is near.

★32

32 "Truly I say to you, this generation will not pass away until all things take place.

33 [a]Matt 5:18; Luke 16:17

33 "[a]Heaven and earth will pass away, but My words will not pass away.

34 [a]Matt 24:42-44; Mark 4:19; Luke 12:40, 45; 1 Thess 5:2ff

34 "[a]Be on guard, that your hearts may not be weighted down with dissipation and drunkenness and the worries of life, and that day come on you suddenly like a trap;

35 for it will come upon all those who dwell on the face of all the earth.

36 [a]Mark 13:33; Luke 12:40 [b]Luke 1:19; Rev. 7:9; 8:2; 11:4

36 "But [a]keep on the alert at all times, praying in order that you may have strength to escape all these things that are about to take place, and to [b]stand before the Son of Man."

37 [a]Matt 26:55 [b]Mark 11:19 [c]Matt 21:1

37 Now during the day He was [a]teaching in the temple, but [b]at evening He would go out and spend the night on [c]the mount that is called Olivet.

38 [a]John 8:2

38 And all the people would get up [a]early in the morning *to come* to Him in the temple to listen to Him.

D Wednesday, 22:1-6

★ 1 [a]Luke 22:1, 2; Matt 26:2-5; Mark 14:1, 2 [b]John 11:55; 13:1

2 [a]Matt 12:14

22 [a]Now the Feast of Unleavened Bread, which is called the [b]Passover, was approaching.

2 And the chief priests and the scribes [a]were seeking how they might put Him to death; for they were afraid of the people.

3 [a]And [b]Satan entered into Judas who was called Iscariot, belonging to the number of the twelve.

4 And he went away and discussed with the chief priests and [a]officers how he might betray Him to them.

5 And they were glad, and agreed to give him money.

6 And he consented, and *began* seeking a good opportunity to betray Him to them apart from the multitude.

★ 3 [a]Luke 22:3-6; Matt 26:14-16; Mark 14:10, 11 [b]Matt 4:10; John 13:2, 27

4 [a]1 Chr 9:11; Neh 11:11; Luke 22:52; Acts 4:1, 5:24, 26

E Thursday, 22:7-53

1 The Lord's Supper, 22:7-38

7 [a]Then came the *first* day of Unleavened Bread on which [b]the Passover *lamb* had to be sacrificed.

8 And He sent [a]Peter and John, saying, "Go and prepare the Passover for us, that we may eat it."

9 And they said to Him, "Where do You want us to prepare it?"

10 And He said to them, "Behold, when you have entered the city, a man will meet you carrying a pitcher of water; follow him into the house that he enters.

11 "And you shall say to the owner of the house, 'The Teacher says to you, "Where is the guest room in which I may eat the Passover with My disciples?"'

12 "And he will show you a large, furnished, upper room; prepare it there."

13 And they departed and found *everything* just as He had told them; and they prepared the Passover.

14 [a]And when the hour had come He reclined *at the table*, and [b]the apostles with Him.

7 [a]Luke 22:7-13; Matt 26:17-19; Mark 14:12-16 [b]Mark 14:12

8 [a]Acts 3:1, 11, 4:13, 19; 8:14; Gal 2:9

★10

14 [a]Matt 26:20; Mark 14:17 [b]Mark 6:30

21:32 *this generation.* See note on Matt. 24:34.
22:1 *Passover.* See Ex. 12:1-28 and Lev. 23:5-6 and note on Matt. 26:2.
22:3 *And Satan entered into Judas.* Satan did

this twice (see John 13:27).
22:10 *a man . . . carrying a pitcher of water.* He would be easily identifiable, since women usually performed this task.

15 And He said to them, "I have earnestly desired to eat this Passover with you before I suffer;

★16 aLuke 14:15; 22:18, 30; Rev. 19:9

16 for I say to you, I shall never again eat it auntil it is fulfilled in the kingdom of God."

17 aLuke 22:17-20; Matt. 26:26-29; Mark 14:22-25; 1 Cor. 11:23-25; 10:16 bMatt. 14:19 18 aMatt. 26:29; Mark 14:25

17 aAnd when He had taken a cup and bgiven thanks, He said, "Take this and share it among yourselves;

18 for aI say to you, I will not drink of the fruit of the vine from now on until the kingdom of God comes."

★19 aMatt. 14:19

19 And when He had taken some bread and agiven thanks, He broke it, and gave it to them, saying, "This is My body which is given for you; do this in remembrance of Me."

★20 aMatt. 26:28; Mark 14:24 bEx. 24:8; Jer. 31:31; 1 Cor. 11:25; 2 Cor. 3:6; Heb. 8:8, [13]; 9:15 21 aLuke 22:21-23; Matt. 26:21-24; Mark 14:18-21; John 13:18, 21, 22, 26 22 aActs 2:23; 4:28; 10:42; 17:31

20 And in the same way He took the cup after they had eaten, saying, "This cup which is apoured out for you is the bnew covenant in My blood.

21 "aBut behold, the hand of the one betraying Me is with Me on the table.

22 "For indeed, the Son of Man is going aas it has been determined; but woe to that man by whom He is betrayed!"

23 And they began to discuss among themselves which one of them it might be who was going to do this thing.

24 aMark 9:34; Luke 9:46

24 And there arose also aa dispute among them as to which one of them was regarded to be greatest.

★25 aLuke 22:25-27; Matt. 20:25-28; Mark 10:42-45

25 aAnd He said to them, "The kings of the Gentiles lord it over them; and those who have authority over them are called 'Benefactors.'

26 aLuke 9:48 b1 Pet. 5:5

26 "But not so with you, abut let him who is the greatest among you become as bthe youngest, and the leader as the servant.

27 aLuke 12:37 bMatt. 20:28

27 "For awho is greater, the one who reclines at the table, or the one who serves? Is it not the one who reclines at the table? But bI am among you as the one who serves.

28 aHeb. 2:18; 4:15

28 "And you are those who have stood by Me in My atrials;

29 aMatt. 5:3; 2 Tim. 2:12

29 and just as My Father has granted Me a akingdom, I grant you

★30 aLuke 22:16 bMatt. 5:3; 2 Tim. 2:12 cMatt. 19:28

30 that you may aeat and drink at My table in My bkingdom, and cyou will sit on thrones judging the twelve tribes of Israel.

31 aJob 1:6-12; 2:1-6; Matt. 4:10 bAmos 9:9

31 "Simon, Simon, behold, aSatan has demanded permission to bsift you like wheat;

★32 aJohn 17:9, 15 bJohn 21:15-17

32 but I ahave prayed for you, that your faith may not fail; and you, when once you have turned again, bstrengthen your brothers."

33 aLuke 22:33, 34; Matt. 26:33-35; Mark 14:29-31; John 13:37, 38

33 aAnd he said to Him, "Lord, with You I am ready to go both to prison and to death!"

34 And He said, "I say to you, Peter, the cock will not crow today until you have denied three times that you know Me."

35 aMatt. 10:9f.; Mark 6:8; Luke 9:3ff.; 10:4

35 And He said to them, "aWhen I sent you out without purse and bag and sandals, you did not lack anything, did you?" And they said, "No, nothing."

36 And He said to them, "But now, let him who has a purse take it along, likewise also a bag, and let him who has no sword sell his robe and buy one.

37 aIs. 53:12 bJohn 17:4; 19:30

37 "For I tell you, that this which is written must be fulfilled in Me, 'aAND HE WAS NUMBERED WITH TRANSGRESSORS'; for bthat which refers to Me has its fulfillment."

38 aLuke 22:36, 49

38 And they said, "Lord, look, here are two aswords." And He said to them, "It is enough."

2 The garden of Gethsemane, 22:39-46

39 aMatt. 26:30; Mark 14:26; John 18:1 bLuke 21:37 cMatt. 21:1

39 aAnd He came out and proceeded bas was His custom to

22:16 until it is fulfilled in the kingdom of God. See note on Matt. 26:29.
22:19 This is My body. The bread remains bread but represents His body. It is an illustration, like "I am the door" (John 10:7).
22:20 the new covenant. See note on Matt.

26:28.
22:25 Benefactors. A favorite title used by the Greek kings of Egypt and Syria.
22:30 See note on Matt. 19:28.
22:32 I have prayed for you. An illustration of Heb. 7:25.

cthe Mount of Olives; and the disciples also followed Him.

40 ᵃAnd when He arrived at the place, He said to them, "ᵇPray that you may not enter into temptation."

41 And He withdrew from them about a stone's throw, and He ᵃknelt down and *began* to pray,

42 saying, "Father, if Thou art willing, remove this ᵃcup from Me; ᵇyet not My will, but Thine be done."

43 Now an ᵃangel from heaven appeared to Him, strengthening Him.

44 And ᵃbeing in agony He was praying very fervently; and His sweat became like drops of blood, falling down upon the ground.

45 And when He rose from prayer, He came to the disciples and found them sleeping from sorrow,

46 and said to them, "Why are you sleeping? Rise and ᵃpray that you may not enter into temptation."

3 The arrest, 22:47-53

47 ᵃWhile He was still speaking, behold, a multitude *came,* and the one called Judas, one of the twelve, was preceding them; and he approached Jesus to kiss Him.

48 But Jesus said to him, "Judas, are you betraying the Son of Man with a kiss?"

49 And when those who were around Him saw what was going to happen, they said, "Lord, shall we strike with the ᵃsword?"

50 And a certain one of them struck the slave of the high priest and cut off his right ear.

51 But Jesus answered and said, "Stop! No more of this." And He touched his ear and healed him.

52 And Jesus said to the chief priests and ᵃofficers of the temple and elders who had come against Him, "Have you come out with swords and clubs ᵇas against a robber?

53 "While I was with you daily in the temple, you did not lay hands on Me; but this hour and the power of darkness are yours."

F Friday, 22:54-23:55
1 Peter's denial, 22:54-62

54 ᵃAnd having arrested Him, they led Him *away,* and brought Him to the house of the high priest; but ᵇPeter was following at a distance.

55 ᵃAnd after they had kindled a fire in the middle of ᵇthe courtyard and had sat down together, Peter was sitting among them.

56 And a certain servant-girl, seeing him as he sat in the firelight, and looking intently at him, said, "This man was with Him too."

57 But he denied *it,* saying, "Woman, I do not know Him."

58 And a little later, ᵃanother saw him and said, "You are *one* of them too!" But Peter said, "Man, I am not!"

59 And after about an hour had passed, another man *began* to insist, saying, "Certainly this man also was with Him, ᵃfor he is a Galilean too."

60 But Peter said, "Man, I do not know what you are talking about." And immediately, while he was still speaking, a cock crowed.

61 And ᵃthe Lord turned and looked at Peter. And Peter remembered the word of the Lord, how He had told him, "ᵇBefore a cock crows today, you will deny Me three times."

62 And he went out and wept bitterly.

40 ᵃLuke 22:40-46; Matt. 26:36-46; Mark 14:32-42 ᵇMatt. 6:13; Luke 22:46
41 ᵃMatt. 26:39; Mark 14:35; Luke 18:11
★**42** ᵇMatt. 20:22 ᵇMatt. 26:39
★**43-44**
43 ᵃMatt. 4:11
44 ᵃHeb. 5:7
46 ᵃLuke 22:40
47 ᵃLuke 22:47-53; Matt. 26:47-56; Mark 14:43-50; John 18:3-11
49 ᵃLuke 22:38
★**50**
52 ᵃLuke 22:4 ᵇLuke 22:37
54 ᵃMatt. 26:57; Mark 14:53 ᵇMatt. 26:58; Mark 14:54; John 18:15
55 ᵃLuke 22:55-62; Matt. 26:69-75; Mark 14:66-72; John 18:16-18, 25-27 ᵇMatt. 26:3
58 ᵃJohn 18:26
★**59** ᵃMatt. 26:73; Mark 14:70
★**61** ᵃLuke 7:13 ᵇLuke 22:34

22:42 *this cup.* See note on Matt. 26:39.
22:43-44 These verses are not in certain important manuscripts.
22:50 *one of them.* This was Peter (John 18:10).

22:59 *he is a Galilean.* See note on Mark 14:70.
22:61 *Before a cock crows.* A Roman term for the end of the third watch at 3 a.m.

2   Christ derided, beaten,
22:63-65

63 aMatt.
26:67f.; Mark
14:65; John
18:22f.

64 aMatt.
26:68; Mark
14:65

65 aMatt.
27:39

63 [a]And the men who were holding Jesus in custody were mocking Him, and beating Him, **64** and they blindfolded Him and were asking Him, saying, "[a]Prophesy, who is the one who hit You?" **65** And they were saying many other things against Him, [a]blaspheming.

3   Christ before the Sanhedrin,
22:66-71

*66 aMatt.
27:11; Mark
15:1; John
18:28 bActs
22:5 cMatt.
5:22

67 aMatt.
26:63-66;
Mark 14:61-
63; Luke
22:67-71;
John 18:19-
21

69 aMatt.
26:64; Mark
14:62; 16:19
bPs. 110:1

70 aMatt. 4:3
bMatt. 26:64;
27:11; Luke
23:3

1 aMatt.
27:2; Mark
15:1; John
18:28

* 2 aLuke
23:2, 3; Matt.
27:11-14;
Mark 15:2-5;
John 18:29-
37 bLuke
23:14 cJohn
20:22; John
18:33ff.;
19:12; Acts
17:7

66 [a]And when it was day, [b]the Council of elders of the people assembled, both chief priests and scribes, and they led Him away to their [c]council chamber, saying, **67** "[a]If You are the Christ, tell us." But He said to them, "If I tell you, you will not believe; **68** and if I ask a question, you will not answer. **69** "[a]But from now on [b]THE SON OF MAN WILL BE SEATED AT THE RIGHT HAND of the power of GOD." **70** And they all said, "Are You [a]the Son of God, then?" And He said to them, "[b]Yes, I am." **71** And they said, "What further need do we have of testimony? For we have heard it ourselves from His own mouth."

4   Christ before Pilate, 23:1-5

23 Then the whole body of them arose and [a]brought Him before Pilate. **2** [a]And they began to accuse Him, saying, "We found this man [b]misleading our nation and [c]forbidding to pay taxes to Caesar, and saying that He Himself is Christ, a King." **3** And Pilate asked Him, saying, "Are You the King of the Jews?" And He answered him and said, "[a]It is as you say." **4** And Pilate said to the chief priests and the multitudes, "[a]I find no guilt in this man." **5** But they kept on insisting, saying, "He stirs up the people, teaching all over Judea, [a]starting from Galilee, even as far as this place."

3 aLuke
22:70

4 aMatt.
27:23; Mark
15:14; Luke
23:14, 22;
John 18:38;
19:4, 6.
5 aMatt.
4:12

5   Christ before Herod, 23:6-12

6 But when Pilate heard it, he asked whether the man was a Galilean. **7** And when he learned that He belonged to Herod's jurisdiction, he sent Him to [a]Herod, who himself also was in Jerusalem at that time. **8** Now Herod was very glad when he saw Jesus; for [a]he had wanted to see Him for a long time, because he had been hearing about Him and was hoping to see some sign performed by Him. **9** And he questioned Him at some length; but [a]He answered him nothing. **10** And the chief priests and the scribes were standing there, accusing Him vehemently. **11** And Herod with his soldiers, after treating Him with contempt and mocking Him, [a]dressed Him in a gorgeous robe and sent Him back to Pilate.

* 7 aMatt.
14:1; Mark
6:14; Luke
3:1; 9:7;
13:31

8 aLuke 9:9

9 aMatt.
27:12, 14;
Mark 15:5;
John 19:9

*11 aMatt.
27:28

22:66 *when it was day.* Matthew (26:57-58) and Mark (14:53, 55) mention a preliminary hearing held at night, but the Sanhedrin (70 or 72 elders and teachers of the nation) could not legally convene at night, so this verdict was made official as soon as it was day. Since, however, the Sanhedrin had no power to carry out a capital sentence, the case had to be remanded to Pilate, senior representative of the Roman government in Judea.

23:2 *Christ, a King.* The charge against Jesus made before Pilate was political—that He was a rival "king." Insurrection against Rome was implied. The Jews knew that blasphemy would not be regarded by Rome as sufficient ground for the death penalty.

23:7 *he sent Him to Herod.* Pilate was not required to send Jesus to Herod Antipas but did so hoping to find a way out of his own dilemma and perhaps also as a diplomatic gesture (see v. 12).

23:11 *sent Him back to Pilate.* To Herod the whole matter seemed to be a joke, since he treated the incident as an occasion for amusement and then returned Jesus to Pilate.

12 Now [a]Herod and Pilate became friends with one another that very day; for before they had been at enmity with each other.

6 Christ again before Pilate, 23:13-25

13 And Pilate summoned the chief priests and the [a]rulers and the people,

14 and said to them, "You brought this man to me as one who [a]incites the people to rebellion, and behold, having examined Him before you, I [b]have found no guilt in this man regarding the charges which you make against Him.

15 "No, nor has [a]Herod, for he sent Him back to us; and behold, nothing deserving death has been done by Him.

16 "I will therefore [a]punish Him and release Him."

17 [Now he was obliged to release to them at the feast one prisoner.]

18 But they cried out all together, saying, "[a]Away with this man, and release for us Barabbas!"

19 (He was one who had been thrown into prison for a certain insurrection made in the city, and for murder.)

20 And Pilate, wanting to release Jesus, addressed them again,

21 but they kept on calling out, saying, "Crucify, crucify Him!"

22 And he said to them the third time, "Why, what evil has this man done? I have found in Him no guilt *demanding* death; I will therefore [a]punish Him and release Him."

23 But they were insistent, with loud voices asking that He be crucified. And their voices *began* to prevail.

24 And Pilate pronounced sentence that their demand should be granted.

25 And he released the man they were asking for who had been thrown into prison for insurrection and murder, but he delivered Jesus to their will.

7 The crucifixion, 23:26-49

26 [a]And when they led Him away, they laid hold of one Simon of [b]Cyrene, coming in from the country, and placed on him the cross to carry behind Jesus.

27 And there were following Him a great multitude of the people, and of women who were [a]mourning and lamenting Him.

28 But Jesus turning to them said, "Daughters of Jerusalem, stop weeping for Me, but weep for yourselves and for your children.

29 "For behold, the days are coming when they will say, '[a]Blessed are the barren, and the wombs that never bore, and the breasts that never nursed.'

30 "Then they will begin to [a]SAY TO THE MOUNTAINS, 'FALL ON US,' AND TO THE HILLS, 'COVER US.'

31 "For if they do these things in the green tree, what will happen in the dry?"

32 [a]And two others also, who were criminals, were being led away to be put to death with Him.

33 [a]And when they came to the place called The Skull, there they crucified Him and the criminals, one on the right and the other on the left.

34 But Jesus was saying, "[a]Father, forgive them; for they do not know what they are doing." [b]And

---

Marginal references:

12 [a]Acts 4:27

13 [a]Luke 23:35; John 7:26, 48; 12:42; Acts 3:17; 4:5, 8; 13:27

14 [a]Luke 23:2 [b]Luke 23:4

15 [a]Luke 9:9

16 [a]Matt. 27:26; Mark 15:15; Luke 23:22; John 19:1; Acts 16:37

★17

18 [a]Luke 23:18-25; Matt. 27:15-26; Mark 15:6-15; John 18:39-19:16

★22 [a]Luke 23:16

★26 [a]Luke 23:26; Matt. 27:32; Mark 15:21; John 19:17 [b]Matt. 27:32

27 [a]Luke 8:52

★28

★29 [a]Matt. 24:19; Luke 11:27; 21:23

★30 [a]Is. 2:19, 20; Hos. 10:8; Rev. 6:16

★31

32 [a]Matt. 27:38; Mark 15:27; John 19:18

★33 [a]Luke 23:33-43; Matt. 27:33-44; Mark 15:22-32; John 19:17-24

★34 [a]Matt. 11:25; Luke 22:42 [b]Ps. 22:18; John 19:24

23:17 Many manuscripts do not contain this verse. See John 18:39.

23:22 *I will therefore punish Him.* Done by scourging (Mark 15:15), i.e., whipping (see note on Matt. 27:26).

23:26 *of Cyrene.* See note on Matt. 27:32.

23:28 *weep for yourselves and for your children.* The Lord foresaw the destruction of Jerusalem, with its attendant miseries, in A.D. 70.

23:29 See Luke 21:23.

23:30 See Hos. 10:8; Rev. 6:16.

23:31 The meaning is this: If such injustice can be done to an innocent man, as was being done then to Jesus, what would befall the Jews in time of war?

23:33 *The Skull.* See note on Matt. 27:33.

23:34 *dividing up His garments.* See Ps. 22:18 and note on Matt. 27:35.

they cast lots, dividing up His garments among themselves.

35 And the people stood by, looking on. And even the [a]rulers were sneering at Him, saying, "He saved others; [b]let Him save Himself if this is the Christ of God, His Chosen One."

36 And the soldiers also mocked Him, coming up to Him, [a]offering Him sour wine,

37 and saying, "[a]If You are the King of the Jews, save Yourself!"

38 Now there was also an inscription above Him, "[a]THIS IS THE KING OF THE JEWS."

39 [a]And one of the criminals who were hanged *there* was hurling abuse at Him, saying, "Are You not the Christ? [b]Save Yourself and us!"

40 But the other answered, and rebuking him said, "Do you not even fear God, since you are under the same sentence of condemnation?

41 "And we indeed justly, for we are receiving what we deserve for our deeds; but this man has done nothing wrong."

42 And he was saying, "Jesus, remember me when You come in Your kingdom!"

43 And He said to him, "Truly I say to you, today you shall be with Me in [a]Paradise."

44 [a]And it was now about [b]the sixth hour, and darkness fell over the whole land until the ninth hour,

45 the sun being obscured; and [a]the veil of the temple was torn in two.

46 And Jesus, [a]crying out with a loud voice, said, "Father, [b]INTO THY HANDS I COMMIT MY SPIRIT." And having said this, He breathed His last.

47 [a]Now when the centurion saw what had happened, he *began* [b]praising God, saying, "Certainly this man was innocent."

48 And all the multitudes who came together for this spectacle, when they observed what had happened, *began* to return, [a]beating their breasts.

49 [a]And all His acquaintances and [a]the women who accompanied Him from Galilee, were standing at a distance, seeing these things.

8 The burial, 23:50-55

50 [a]And behold, a man named Joseph, who was a [b]member of the Council, a good and righteous man

51 (he had not consented to their plan and action), *a man* from Arimathea, a city of the Jews, who was [a]waiting for the kingdom of God;

52 this man went to Pilate and asked for the body of Jesus.

53 And he took it down and wrapped it in a linen cloth, and laid Him in a tomb cut into the rock, where no one had ever lain.

54 And it was [a]the preparation day, and the Sabbath was about to begin.

55 Now [a]the women who had come with Him out of Galilee followed after, and saw the tomb and how His body was laid.

G Saturday, 23:56

56 And they returned and [a]prepared spices and perfumes.
And on the Sabbath they rested according to [b]the commandment.

23:38 *an inscription.* See note on Matt. 27:37.
23:42 *when You come in Your kingdom.* Seeing Jesus dying on a cross but believing that He would come into His kingdom shows the amazing faith of the thief.
23:43 *Paradise.* Heaven, the abode of God (Luke 16:22; 2 Cor. 12:4).
23:44 *the sixth hour* = noon.
23:45 *the veil of the temple.* See note on Matt. 27:51.

23:50 *the Council.* I.e., the Sanhedrin.
23:51 *Arimathea.* A town north of Lydda.
23:53 *wrapped it.* The word means "wrap by winding tightly," referring to the linen around the body. See also Isa. 53:9.
23:54 *it was the preparation day.* Friday, the day Jesus died, was the time of the preparation for the Sabbath, which began Friday at sunset.
23:56 *according to the commandment.* I.e., not to work on the Sabbath (Ex. 20:10).

35 [a]Luke 23:13 [b]Matt. 27:43
36 [a]Matt. 27:48
37 [a]Matt. 27:43
★**38** [a]Matt. 27:37; Mark 15:26; John 19:19
39 [a]Matt. 27:44; Mark 15:32; Luke 23:39-43 [b]Luke 23:35, 37
★**42**
★**43** [a]Gen. 2:8 [Septuagint]; 2 Cor. 12:4; Rev. 2:7
★**44** [a]Luke 23:44-49; Matt. 27:45-56; Mark 15:33-41 [b]John 19:14
★**45** [a]Matt. 27:51
46 [a]Matt. 27:50; Mark 15:37; John 19:30 [b]Ps. 31:5
47 [a]Matt. 27:54; Mark 15:39 [b]Matt. 9:8
48 [a]Luke 8:52; 18:13
49 [a]Matt. 27:55f.; Mark 15:40f.; Luke 8:2; John 19:25
★**50** [a]Luke 23:50-56; Matt. 27:57-61; Mark 15:42-47; John 19:38-42 [b]Mark 15:43
★**51** [a]Mark 15:43; Luke 2:25
★**53**
★**54** [a]Matt. 27:62; Mark 15:42
55 [a]Luke 23:49
★**56** [a]Mark 16:1; Luke 24:1 [b]Ex. 20:10

VI THE VINDICATION OF THE SON OF MAN BEFORE MEN, 24:1-53

A The Victor over Death, 24:1-12

1 aLuke 24:1-10; Matt. 28:1-8; Mark 16:1-8; John 20:1-8

24 aBut on the first day of the week, at early dawn, they came to the tomb, bringing the spices which they had prepared.

★ 2   2 And they found the stone rolled away from the tomb,

3 aLuke 7:13; Acts 1:21

3 but when they entered, they did not find the body of athe Lord Jesus.

4 aJohn 20:12 bLuke 2:9; Acts 12:7

4 And it happened that while they were perplexed about this, behold, atwo men suddenly bstood near them in dazzling apparel;

5 and as the women were terrified and bowed their faces to the ground, the men said to them, "Why do you seek the living One among the dead?

★ 6-7
6 aMark 16:6 bMatt. 17:22f.; Mark 9:30f.; Luke 9:44; 24:44
7 aMatt. 16:21; Luke 24:46

6 "He is not here, but He ahas risen. Remember how He spoke to you bwhile He was still in Galilee,

7 saying that athe Son of Man must be delivered into the hands of sinful men, and be crucified, and the third day rise again."

8 aJohn 2:22

8 And athey remembered His words,

9 and returned from the tomb and reported all these things to the eleven and to all the rest.

10 aMatt. 27:56 bMark 6:30

10 Now they were aMary Magdalene and Joanna and Mary the mother of James; also the other women with them were telling these things to bthe apostles.

11 aMark 16:11

11 And these words appeared to them as nonsense, and they awould not believe them.

★12 aJohn 20:3-6 bJohn 20:10

12 [But Peter arose and aran to the tomb; astooping and looking in, he *saw the linen wrappings only; and he went away bto his home, marveling at that which had happened.]

B The Fulfiller of the Prophecies (the Emmaus Disciples), 24:13-35

★13 aMark 16:12

13 And behold, atwo of them were going that very day to a village named Emmaus, which was about seven miles from Jerusalem.

14 And they were conversing with each other about all these things which had taken place.

15 And it came about that while they were conversing and discussing, Jesus Himself approached, and began traveling with them.

16 aLuke 24:31; John 20:14; 21:4

16 But atheir eyes were prevented from recognizing Him.

17 And He said to them, "What are these words that you are exchanging with one another as you are walking?" And they stood still, looking sad.

18 And one of them, named Cleopas, answered and said to Him, "Are You the only one visiting Jerusalem and unaware of the things which have happened here in these days?"

19 aMark 1:24 bMatt. 21:11

19 And He said to them, "What things?" And they said to Him, "The things about aJesus the Nazarene, who was a bprophet mighty in deed and word in the sight of God and all the people,

20 aLuke 23:13

20 and how the chief priests and our arulers delivered Him up to the sentence of death, and crucified Him.

24:2 the stone rolled away. A circular stone like a solid wheel rolled in front of the entrance to the tomb-cave to keep out intruders.
24:6-7 Remember. See 9:31; 18:31-34.
24:12 the linen wrappings. The wide bandage-like strips that were wound around the body (23:53). only. Or, by themselves. Despite the absence of the body, the clothes retained the same shape and position they had when it was there. If someone had stolen the body but left

the clothes, he would have had to unwrap it and the clothes would not have been in this position. See John 20:6-7.
24:13 two of them. One is identified as Cleopas (v. 18); the other may have been his wife (v. 32: "our hearts"). Many identify Cleopas as the person mentioned in John 19:25, in which case his wife's name was Mary. Emmaus. The location is uncertain, though it was less than 7 miles from Jerusalem.

21 "But we were hoping that it was He who was going to ^aredeem Israel. Indeed, besides all this, it is the third day since these things happened.

22 "But also some women among us amazed us. ^aWhen they were at the tomb early in the morning,

23 and did not find His body, they came, saying that they had also seen a vision of angels, who said that He was alive.

24 "And some of those who were with us went to the tomb and found it just exactly as the women also had said; but Him they did not see."

25 And He said to them, "O foolish men and slow of heart to believe in all that ^athe prophets have spoken!

26 "^aWas it not necessary for the Christ to suffer these things and to enter into His glory?"

27 And beginning with ^aMoses and with all the ^bprophets, He explained to them the things concerning Himself in all the Scriptures.

28 And they approached the village where they were going, and ^aHe acted as though He would go farther.

29 And they urged Him, saying, "Stay with us, for it is *getting* toward evening, and the day is now nearly over." And He went in to stay with them.

30 And it came about that when He had reclined *at the table* with them, He took the bread and ^ablessed *it*, and breaking *it*, He *began* giving *it* to them.

31 And their ^aeyes were opened and they recognized Him; and He vanished from their sight.

32 And they said to one another, "Were not our hearts burning within us while He was speaking to us on the road, while He ^awas explaining the Scriptures to us?"

33 And they arose that very hour and returned to Jerusalem, and ^afound gathered together the eleven and ^bthose who were with them,

34 saying, "^aThe Lord has really risen, and ^bhas appeared to Simon."

35 And they *began* to relate their experiences on the road and how ^aHe was recognized by them in the breaking of the bread.

C The Pattern of Resurrection Life, 24:36-43

36 And while they were telling these things, ^aHe Himself stood in their midst.

37 But they were startled and frightened and thought that they were seeing ^aa spirit.

38 And He said to them, "Why are you troubled, and why do doubts arise in your hearts?

39 "^aSee My hands and My feet, that it is I Myself; ^btouch Me and see, for a spirit does not have flesh and bones as you see that I have."

40 [And when He had said this, He showed them His hands and His feet.]

41 And while they still ^acould not believe *it* for joy and were marveling, He said to them, "^bHave you anything here to eat?"

42 And they gave Him a piece of a broiled fish;

43 and He took it and ^aate *it* before them.

Margin references

21 ^aLuke 1:68
22 ^aLuke 24:1ff.
25 ^aMatt. 26:24
26 ^aLuke 24:7, 44ff.; Heb. 2:10; 1 Pet. 1:11
★27 ^aGen. 3:15; 12:3; Num. 21:9 [John 3:14]; Deut. 18:15 [John 1:45]; John 5:46 ^b2 Sam. 7:12-16; Is. 7:14 [Matt. 1:23]; 9:1f. [Matt. 4:15f.]; 42:1 [Matt. 12:18ff.]; 53:4 [Matt. 8:17]; Luke 22:37]; Dan. 7:13 [Matt. 24:30]; Mic. 5:2 [Matt. 2:6]; Zech. 9:9 [Matt. 21:5]; Acts 13:27
28 ^aMark 6:48
★30 ^aMatt. 14:19
★31 ^aLuke 24:16
32 ^aLuke 24:45
33 ^aMark 16:13 ^bActs 1:14
★34 ^aLuke 24:6 ^b1 Cor. 15:5
35 ^aLuke 24:30f.
36 ^aMark 16:14
37 ^aMatt. 14:26; Mark 6:49
★39 ^aJohn 20:20, 27 ^bJohn 20:27; 1 John 1:1
★40
41 ^aLuke 24:11 ^bJohn 21:5
43 ^aActs 10:41

24:27 *in all the Scriptures.* E.g., passages like Pss. 16; 22; Isa. 53.

24:30 *He took the bread.* Christ's assuming the position as host, and perhaps something in His gestures, made them recognize Him.

24:31 He vanished from their sight. Lit., He became invisible.

24:34 *appeared to Simon.* There is no other record of this event except the mention in 1 Cor. 15:5.

24:39 The evidences that Jesus' appearance was not as a spirit are: (1) the scars in His hands and feet; (2) His tangibleness in being handled; and (3) His ability to eat (v. 43; Acts 10:41). *touch.* The same word is used in 1 John 1:1.

24:40 Many manuscripts do not contain this verse.

D The Head of the Church, 24:44-48

★44 aLuke
9:22, 44f.;
18:31-34;
22:37 bLuke
24:27 cPs. 2
[Acts 13:33];
Ps. 16 [Acts
2:27]; Ps. 22
[Matt. 27:34-
46]; Ps. 69
[John
19:28ff.]; Ps.
72; 110
[Matt.
22:43f.]; Ps.
118 [Matt.
21:42]
45 aLuke
24:32; Acts
16:14;
1 John 5:20
46 aLuke
24:26, 44
bLuke 24:7
47 aActs
5:31; 10:43;
13:38; 26:18
bMatt. 28:19
48 aActs 1:8,
22; 2:32;
3:15; 4:33;
5:32; 10:39,
41; 13:31;
1 Pet. 5:1

44 Now He said to them, "aThese are My words which I spoke to you while I was still with you, that all things which are written about Me in the bLaw of Moses and bthe Prophets and cthe Psalms must be fulfilled."

45 Then He aopened their minds to understand the Scriptures,

46 and He said to them, "aThus it is written, that the Christ should suffer and brise again from the dead the third day;

47 and that arepentance for forgiveness of sins should be proclaimed in His name to ball the nations, beginning from Jerusalem.

48 "You are awitnesses of these things.

E The Giver of the Holy Spirit, 24:49

49 "And behold, aI am sending forth the promise of My Father upon you; but byou are to stay in the city until you are clothed with power from on high."

★49 aJohn
14:26 bActs
1:4

F The Ascended Lord, 24:50-53

50 And He led them out as far as aBethany, and He lifted up His hands and blessed them.

★50 aMatt.
21:17; Acts
1:12

51 And it came about that while He was blessing them, He parted from them.

★51

52 And they returned to Jerusalem with great joy,

53 and were continually in the temple, praising God.

24:44 A common Jewish division of the O.T. The *Prophets* included most of the historical books, and the *Psalms* included the "writings."

24:49 *the promise of My Father.* The coming of the Holy Spirit on the day of Pentecost.

24:50 *as far as Bethany.* Or, toward Bethany.

24:51 Luke gives details of the ascension of Christ in his other book; see Acts 1:9.

INTRODUCTION TO
THE GOSPEL ACCORDING TO JOHN

AUTHOR: The Apostle John   —   DATE: 85-90

Authorship   The writer of this Gospel is identified in the book only as "the disciple whom Jesus loved" (21:20, 24). He obviously was a Palestinian Jew who was an eyewitness of the events of Christ's life, for he displays knowledge of Jewish customs (7:37-39; 18:28) and of the land of Palestine (1:44, 46; 5:2) and he includes details of an eyewitness (2:6; 13:26; 21:8, 11). Eliminating the other disciples that belonged to the "inner circle" (because James had been martyred before this time, Acts 12:1-5, and because Peter is named in close association with the disciple whom Jesus loved (13:23-24; 20:2-10), one concludes that John was the author. Whether this was the apostle John or a different John (the Elder) is discussed in the Introduction to 1 John.

John the apostle was the son of Zebedee and Salome and was the younger brother of James. He was a Galilean who apparently came from a fairly well-to-do home (Mark 15:40-41). Though often painted centuries later as effeminate, his real character was such that he was known as a "son of thunder" (Mark 3:17). He played a leading role in the work of the early church in Jerusalem (Acts 3:1; 8:14; Gal. 2:9). Later he went to Ephesus and for an unknown reason was exiled to the island of Patmos (Rev. 1:9).

Distinctive Approach   This is the most theological of the four Gospels. It deals with the nature and person of Christ and the meaning of faith in Him. John's presentation of Christ as the divine Son of God is seen in the titles given Him in the book: "the Word was God" (1:1), "the Lamb of God" (1:29), "the Messiah" (1:41), "the Son of God" and "the King of Israel" (1:49), the "Savior of the world" (4:42), "Lord and . . . God" (20:28). His deity is also asserted in the series of "I am . . ." claims (6:35; 8:12; 10:7, 9, 11, 14; 11:25; 14:6; 15:1, 5). In other "I am" statements Christ made implicit and explicit claim to be the I AM-Yahweh of the Old Testament (4:24, 26; 8:24, 28, 58; 13:19). These are the strongest claims to deity that Jesus could have made.

The structure and style of the Gospel are different from those of the synoptics. It contains no parables, only seven miracles (five of which are not recorded elsewhere), and many personal interviews. The author emphasizes the physical actuality of Jesus' hunger, thirst, weariness, pain, and death as a defense against the Gnostic denial of Jesus' true human nature.

Date   Though the Gospel of John used to be dated by some extreme critics as being written in the middle of the second century, the discovery of the Rylands papyrus fragment (a few verses from John 18 dated about A.D. 135) forced an earlier date. Several decades would have been required between the original writing of the Gospel and its being copied and circulated as far as the Egyptian hinterland where the fragment was found. The Gospel was apparently being circulated between 89 and 90, though it may have been written from Ephesus earlier (a pre-70 date has been suggested on the basis of 5:2 which may indicate that Jerusalem had not yet been destroyed). Discoveries at Qumran have attested to the genuineness of the Jewish background and thought patterns seen in the book.

Contents   John's statement of purpose is clearly spelled out in 20:30-31. The Gospel is sometimes called The Book of the Seven Signs, since the author chose seven sign-miracles to reveal the person and mission of Jesus. These are: (1) the turning of water into wine (2:1-11); (2) the cure of the nobleman's son (4:46-54); (3) the cure of the paralytic (5:1-18); (4) the feeding of the multitude (6:6-13); (5) the walking on the water (6:16-21); (6) the giving of sight to the blind (9:1-7); and (7) the raising of Lazarus (11:1-45). Other important themes in the book include the Holy Spirit (14:26; 15:26; 16:7-14), Satan and the world (8:44; 12:31; 17:15), the Word (1:1-14), and the new birth (3:1-12).

OUTLINE OF THE GOSPEL OF JOHN

THE GOSPEL ACCORDING TO JOHN

I INCARNATION OF THE SON OF GOD, 1:1-18

★ 1 ªGen. 1:1; Col. 1:17; 1 John 1:1 ᵇJohn 1:14; Rev. 19:13 ᶜJohn 17:5; 1 John 1:2 ᵈPhil. 2:6

1 In the beginning was ᵇthe Word, and the Word was ᶜwith God, and ᵈthe Word was God.

2 He was in the beginning with God.

3 ªAll things came into being by Him, and apart from Him nothing came into being that has come into being.

★ 3 ªJohn 1:10; 1 Cor. 8:6; Col. 1:16; Heb. 1:2

4 ªIn Him was life, and the life was ᵇthe light of men.

★ 4-5 4 ªJohn 5:26; 11:25; 14:6 ᵇJohn 8:12; 9:5; 12:46 5 ªJohn 3:19

5 And ªthe light shines in the darkness, and the darkness did not comprehend it.

1:1 *In the beginning.* Before time began, Christ was already in existence with God. This is what is meant by the term "the pre-existent Christ." See Gen. 1:1 and 1 John 1:1. *Word* (Greek: *logos*). *Logos* means word, thought, concept, and the expressions thereof. In the O.T. the concept conveyed activity and revelation, and the word or wisdom of God is often personified (Ps. 33:6; Prov. 8). In the Targums (Aramaic paraphrases of the O.T.) it was a designation of God. To the Greek mind it expressed the ideas of reason and creative control. Revelation is the keynote idea in the *logos* concept. Here it is applied to Jesus, who is all that God is and the expression of Him (1:1,

14). In this verse the Word (Christ) is said to be *with God* (i.e., in communion with and yet distinct from God) and to be *God* (i.e., identical in essence with God).
1:3 *came into being by Him.* Christ was active in the work of creation (cf. Col. 1:16).
1:4-5 *life . . . light.* These are two words especially associated with John (8:12; 9:5; 11:25; 14:6). "Light" in John implies revelation which reveals the "life" that is in Christ and which brings into judgment those who refuse it (3:19). "Life" denotes salvation and deliverance, based on Christ's atonement. *the darkness did not comprehend it.* I.e., the darkness did not overcome the light.

★ 6 ªMatt.
3:1
7 ªJohn
1:15, 19, 32;
3:26; 5:33
ᵇJohn 1:12;
Acts 19:4;
Gal. 3:26
8 ªJohn
1:20
★ 9 ª1 John
2:8
★10 ª1 Cor.
8:6; Col.
1:16; Heb.
1:2
★11
★12 ªJohn
11:52; Gal.
3:26 ᵇJohn
1:7; 3:18;
1 John 3:23
★13 ªJohn
3:5f.; James
1:18; 1 Pet.
1:23; 1 John
2:29; 3:9
★14 ªRev.
19:13 ᵇRom.
1:3; Gal. 4:4;
Phil. 2:7f.;
1 Tim. 3:16;
1 John 1:1f.;
4:2; 2 John 7
cRev. 21:3
dLuke 9:32;
John 2:11;
17:22, 24;
2 Pet. 1:16f.;
1 John 1:1
eJohn 1:17;
Rom. 5:21;
6:14 fJohn
8:32; 14:6;
18:37

6 There came a man, sent from God, whose name was ªJohn.

7 He came ªfor a witness, that he might bear witness of the light, ᵇthat all might believe through him.

8 ªHe was not the light, but came that he might bear witness of the light.

9 There was ªthe true light which, coming into the world, enlightens every man.

10 He was in the world, and ªthe world was made through Him, and the world did not know Him.

11 He came to His own, and those who were His own did not receive Him.

12 But as many as received Him, to them He gave the right to become ªchildren of God, even ᵇto those who believe in His name,

13 ªwho were born not of blood, nor of the will of the flesh, nor of the will of man, but of God.

14 And ªthe Word ᵇbecame

flesh, and cdwelt among us, and dwe beheld His glory, glory as of the only begotten from the Father, full of ªgrace and ftruth.

15 John *ªbore witness of Him, and cried out, saying, "This was He of whom I said, 'ᵇHe who comes after me has a higher rank than I, cfor He existed before me.'"

16 For of His ªfulness we have all received, and grace upon grace.

17 For ªthe Law was given through Moses; ᵇgrace and ctruth were realized through Jesus Christ.

18 ªNo man has seen God at any time; ᵇthe only begotten God, who is cin the bosom of the Father, dHe has explained *Him.*

15 ªJohn 1:7
ᵇMatt. 3:11;
John 1:27;
30 cJohn
1:30
★16 ªEph.
1:23; 3:19;
4:13; Col.
1:19; 2:9
★17 ªJohn
7:19 ᵇJohn
1:14; Rom.
5:21; 6:14
cJohn 8:32;
14:6; 18:37
★18 ªEx.
33:20; John
6:46; Col.
1:15; 1 Tim.
6:16; 1 John
4:12 ᵇJohn
3:16, 18;
1 John 4:9
cLuke 16:22;
John 13:23
dJohn 3:11
★19 ªJohn
1:7 ᵇJohn
2:18, 20;
5:10, 15f.;
18; 6:41, 52:

II PRESENTATION OF THE SON OF GOD, 1:19–4:54

A By John the Baptizer, 1:19–34

19 And this is ªthe witness of John, when ᵇthe Jews sent to him

7:1, 11, 13,
15, 35; 8:22,
48, 52, 57;
9:18, 22;
10:24, 31, 33
cMatt. 15:1

1:6 *John* (the Baptist). His role, it is made clear in v. 8, was simply as a witness to the Light.

1:9 *enlightens every man.* Not that every man is redeemed automatically, for redemption comes through faith in the Savior (1:12). But this light is available to all men.

1:10 *did not know Him.* The world did not recognize Jesus as the Christ, God's Son, Creator, Savior, etc.

1:11 *He came to His own* (thing or place—i.e., the world which He made). *His own* (people— the Jews) *did not receive Him.*

1:12 *even to those who believe in His name.* An explanation of what it means to "receive" Him.

1:13 The new birth is supernatural and therefore completely distinct from natural birth. It is *not of blood* (lit., bloods), i.e., contains no human element; nor does it lie within the scope of human achievement (it is not *of the will of the flesh* or *man*).

1:14 *the Word became flesh.* Jesus Christ was unique, for He was God from all eternity and yet joined Himself to sinful humanity in the incarnation. The God-man possessed all the attributes of deity (Phil. 2:6) and the attributes common to humanity (apart from sin), and He will *exist forever* as the God-man in His resurrected body (Acts 1:11; Rev. 5:6). Only the God-man could be an adequate Savior; for He

must be human in order to be able to suffer and die, and He must be God to make that death effective as a payment for sin. The use of the word *flesh* contradicts the Gnostic teaching that pure deity could not be united with flesh, which was regarded as entirely evil. *glory.* In the O.T., glory expressed the splendor of divine manifestation and attested the divine presence. Here it means the visible manifestation of God in Christ.

1:16 *grace upon grace.* I.e., grace piled upon grace in the experiences of the Christian life.

1:17 *grace.* Though grace was manifest in the O.T. (Gen. 6:8; Ex. 34:6; Jer. 31:3), it was but a candle compared with the brightness of grace that appeared at the incarnation (Titus 2:11). Grace is the unmerited favor of God and is the basis of our salvation, justification, election, faith, and spiritual gifts (Eph. 1:7; Rom. 3:24; 11:5–6; Eph. 2:8–9; Rom. 12:6).

1:18 *No man has seen God at any time.* I.e., since God is Spirit (John 4:24), no man has ever seen God in His essence, His Spirit-being. Yet He assumed visible form which men saw in O.T. times (Gen. 32:30; Ex. 24:9–10; Judg. 13:22; Isa. 6:1; Dan. 7:9) and is Jesus men could see God (John 14:8–9). Christ gives life (1:12); He reveals (vv. 14, 18); He gives grace and truth (vv. 16–17).

1:19 *the Jews.* I.e., probably the chief priests.

priests and Levites ᶜfrom Jerusalem to ask him, "Who are you?"

20 And he confessed, and did not deny, and he confessed, "ᵃI am not the Christ."

21 And they asked him, "What then? Are you ᵃElijah?" And he *said, "I am not." "Are you ᵇthe Prophet?" And he answered, "No."

22 They said then to him, "Who are you, so that we may give an answer to those who sent us? What do you say about yourself?"

23 He said, "ᵃI am A VOICE OF ONE CRYING IN THE WILDERNESS, 'ᵇMAKE STRAIGHT THE WAY OF THE LORD,' as Isaiah the prophet said."

24 Now they had been sent from the Pharisees.

25 And they asked him, and said to him, "Why then are you baptizing, if you are not the Christ, nor Elijah, nor ᵃthe Prophet?"

26 John answered them saying, "ᵃI baptize in water, *but* among you stands One whom you do not know.

27 "*It is* ᵃHe who comes after me, the ᵇthong of whose sandal I am not worthy to untie."

28 These things took place in Bethany ᵃbeyond the Jordan, where John was baptizing.

29 The next day he *saw Jesus coming to him, and *said, "Behold, ᵃthe Lamb of God who ᵇtakes away the sin of the world!

30 "This is He on behalf of whom I said, 'ᵃAfter me comes a Man who has a higher rank than I, ᵇfor He existed before me.'

31 "And I did not recognize Him, but in order that He might be manifested to Israel, I came baptizing in water."

32 And John ᵃbore witness saying, "ᵇI have beheld the Spirit descending as a dove out of heaven, and He remained upon Him.

33 "And I did not recognize Him, but He who sent me to baptize in water said to me, 'He upon whom you see the Spirit descending and remaining upon Him, ᵃthis is the one who baptizes in the Holy Spirit.'

34 "And I have seen, and have borne witness that this is ᵃthe Son of God."

B To John's Disciples, 1:35-51

35 Again ᵃthe next day John was standing with two of his disciples,

36 and he looked upon Jesus as He walked, and *said, "Behold, ᵃthe Lamb of God!"

37 And the two disciples heard him speak, and they followed Jesus.

38 And Jesus turned, and beheld them following, and *said to them, "What do you seek?" And they said to Him, "ᵃRabbi (which translated means Teacher), where are You staying?"

39 He *said to them, "Come, and you will see." They came therefore and saw where He was staying; and they stayed with Him that day, for it was about the tenth hour.

40 ᵃOne of the two who heard John *speak,* and followed Him, was Andrew, Simon Peter's brother.

41 He *found first his own

Marginal references

20 ᵃJohn 3:28; cf. Luke 3:15f.
★21 ᵃMatt. 11:14; 16:14 ᵇDeut. 18:15, 18; Matt. 21:11; John 1:25
23 ᵃMatt. 3:3; Mark 1:3; Luke 3:4 ᵇIs. 40:3
★24
★25 ᵃDeut. 18:15, 18; Matt. 21:11; John 1:21
26 ᵃMatt. 3:11; Mark 1:8; Luke 3:16; Acts 1:5
27 ᵃMatt. 3:11; John 1:30 ᵇMatt. 3:11; Mark 1:7; Luke 3:16
28 ᵃJohn 3:26; 10:40
★29 ᵃIs. 53:7; John 1:36; Acts 8:32; 1 Pet. 1:19; Rev. 5:6, 8, 12f.; 6:1 ᵇMatt. 1:21; 1 John 3:5
30 ᵃMatt. 3:11; John 1:27 ᵇJohn 1:15
32 ᵃJohn 1:7 ᵇMatt. 3:16; Mark 1:10; Luke 3:22
33 ᵃMatt. 3:11; Mark 1:8; Luke 3:16; Acts 1:5
34 ᵃMatt. 4:3; John 1:49
35 ᵃJohn 1:29
36 ᵃJohn 1:29
38 ᵃMatt. 23:7f.; John 1:49
★39
40 ᵃMatt. 4:18-22; Mark 1:16-20; Luke 5:2-11; John 1:40-42
★41 ᵃDan. 9:25; John 4:25

1:21 *Elijah.* See Mal. 4:5. He was supposed to return to earth before the time of judgment (see note on Matt. 11:14). *the Prophet.* The prophecy referred to (Deut. 18:15) is of Christ, though the Jews did not understand it correctly, since (John 1:25) they distinguished Christ and the Prophet (Acts 3:22-23).
1:24 *Pharisees.* See note on Matt. 3:7.
1:25 They seem to be saying: Since you have no authority, what are you doing baptizing and thus gathering followers?
1:29 *Lamb.* History (the Passover lamb, Ex. 12:3) and prophecy (the Messiah, Isa. 53:7) are linked in this metaphor. *the sin of the world.* No longer just the sins of Israel (Isa. 53:4-12; 1 John 2:2).
1:39 *the tenth hour.* 10 a.m. by Roman time; 4 p.m. by Jewish time.
1:41 *Messiah.* See note on Matt. 1:1.

42 aJohn
21:15-17
b1 Cor. 1:12;
3:22; 9:5;
15:5; Gal.
1:18; 2:9, 11,
14 cMatt.
16:18
43 aJohn
1:29, 35
bMatt. 4:12;
John 1:28;
2:11 cMatt.
10:3; John
1:44-48; 6:5,
7; 12:21f.;
14:8f. dMatt.
8:22
44 aMatt.
10:3; John
1:44-48; 6:5,
7; 12:21f.;
14:8f. bMatt.
11:21
45 aMatt.
10:3; John
1:44-48; 6:5,
7; 12:21f.;
14:8f. bJohn
1:46-49; 21:2
cLuke 24:27
dMatt. 2:23
eLuke 2:48;
3:23; 4:22;
John 6:42
★46 aJohn
7:41, 52
bMatt. 10:3;
John 1:44-
48; 6:5, 7;
12:21f.;
14:8f.
47 aRom.
9:4
★48 aMatt.
10:3; John
1:44-48; 6:5,
7; 12:21f.;
14:8f.
★49 aJohn
1:38 bJohn
1:34 cMatt.
2:2; 27:42;
Mark 15:32;
John 12:13
★50
★51 aEzek.
1:1; Matt.
3:16; Luke
3:21; Acts
7:56; 10:11;
Rev. 19:11
bGen. 28:12
cMatt. 8:20

brother Simon, and *said to him, "We have found the aMessiah" (which translated means Christ).

42 He brought him to Jesus. Jesus looked at him, and said, "You are Simon the son of aJohn; you shall be called bCephas" (which translated means cPeter).

43 aThe next day He purposed to go forth into bGalilee, and He *found cPhilip, and Jesus *said to him, "dFollow Me."

44 Now aPhilip was from bBethsaida, of the city of Andrew and Peter.

45 aPhilip *found bNathanael and *said to him, "We have found Him of whom cMoses in the Law and also cthe Prophets wrote, Jesus of dNazareth, ethe son of Joseph."

46 And Nathanael *said to him, "aCan any good thing come out of Nazareth?" bPhilip *said to him, "Come and see."

47 Jesus saw Nathanael coming to Him, and *said of him, "Behold, an aIsraelite indeed, in whom is no guile!"

48 Nathanael *said to Him, "How do You know me?" Jesus answered and said to him, "Before aPhilip called you, when you were under the fig tree, I saw you."

49 Nathanael answered Him, "aRabbi, You are bthe Son of God; You are the cKing of Israel."

50 Jesus answered and said to him, "Because I said to you that I saw you under the fig tree, do you believe? You shall see greater things than these."

51 And He *said to him,

"Truly, truly, I say to you, you shall see athe heavens opened, and bthe angels of God ascending and descending on cthe Son of Man."

C At a Wedding in Cana, 2:1-11

2 And on athe third day there was a wedding in bCana of Galilee, and the cmother of Jesus was there;

2 and Jesus also was invited, and His adisciples, to the wedding.

3 And when the wine gave out, the mother of Jesus *said to Him, "They have no wine."

4 And Jesus *said to her, "aWoman, bwhat do I have to do with you? cMy hour has not yet come."

5 His amother *said to the servants, "Whatever He says to you, do it."

6 Now there were six stone waterpots set there afor the Jewish custom of purification, containing twenty or thirty gallons each.

7 Jesus *said to them, "Fill the waterpots with water." And they filled them up to the brim.

8 And He *said to them, "Draw some out now, and take it to the headwaiter." And they took it to him.

9 And when the headwaiter tasted the water awhich had become wine, and did not know

1 aJohn
1:29, 35, 43
bJohn 2:11;
4:46; 21:2
cMatt. 12:46
2 aJohn
1:40-49;
2:12, 17, 22;
3:22; 4:2, 8,
27ff.; 6:8, 12,
16, 22, 24,
60f., 66; 7:3;
8:31
★4 aJohn
19:26 bMatt.
8:29 cJohn
7:6, 8, 30;
8:20
5 aMatt.
12:46
6 aMark
7:3f.; John
3:25
9 aJohn
4:46

1:46 *Nazareth.* The town had a negative reputation at this period (see 7:52).

1:48 *when you were under the fig tree, I saw you.* Though bodily removed from Philip, the omnipresent Lord was with him under the fig tree.

1:49 *Son of God.* A Messianic title for the One in whom the true destiny of Israel is to be fulfilled; also a claim of deity (5:18). The title *King of Israel* stated the Jewish political Messianic hope.

1:50 *greater things.* I.e., greater proofs of who I am as revealed in the seven great "signs" that comprise chapters 2-12.

1:51 *the heavens opened.* A symbol of the fellowship open to followers of Christ. *Son of Man.* See note on Matt. 8:20. Notice the titles given to Jesus in chapter 1: Word (v. 1), God (v. 1), Creator (v. 3), Light (v. 7), only begotten God (v. 18), Lamb of God (vv. 29, 36), Son of God (vv. 34, 49), Messiah (v. 41), King of Israel (v. 49), and Son of Man (v. 51).

2:4 *Woman, what do I have to do with you?* "Woman" was a term of respectful address (see 19:26). Christ's remark meant: "that concerns you, leave Me alone." The *hour* for manifesting Himself as Messiah had *not yet come* (see 8:20).

where it came from (but the servants who had drawn the water knew), the headwaiter *called the bridegroom,

10 and *said to him, "Every man serves the good wine first, and when *men* ᵃhave drunk freely, *then* that which is poorer; you have kept the good wine until now."

11 This beginning of *His* ᵃsigns Jesus did in Cana of ᵇGalilee, and manifested His ᶜglory, and His disciples believed in Him.

D At the Temple in Jerusalem, 2:12-25

12 After this He went down to ᵃCapernaum, He and His ᵇmother, and *His* ᵇbrothers, and His ᶜdisciples; and there they stayed a few days.

13 And ᵃthe Passover of the Jews was at hand, and Jesus ᵇwent up to Jerusalem.

14 ᵃAnd He found in the temple those who were selling oxen and sheep and doves, and the moneychangers seated.

15 And He made a scourge of cords, and drove *them* all out of the temple, with the sheep and the oxen; and He poured out the coins of the moneychangers, and overturned their tables;

16 and to those who were selling ᵃthe doves He said, "Take these things away; stop making ᵇMy Father's house a house of merchandise."

17 His ᵃdisciples remembered

that it was written, "ᵇZeal for Thy house will consume me."

18 ᵃThe Jews therefore answered and said to Him, "ᵇWhat sign do You show to us, seeing that You do these things?"

19 Jesus answered and said to them, "ᵃDestroy this temple, and in three days I will raise it up."

20 ᵃThe Jews therefore said, "It took ᵇforty-six years to build this temple, and will You raise it up in three days?"

21 But He was speaking of ᵃthe temple of His body.

22 When therefore He was raised from the dead, His ᵃdisciples ᵇremembered that He said this; and they believed ᶜthe Scripture, and the word which Jesus had spoken.

23 Now when He was in Jerusalem at ᵃthe Passover, during the feast, many believed in His name, ᵇbeholding His signs which He was doing.

24 But Jesus, on His part, was not entrusting Himself to them, for He knew all men,

25 and because He did not need anyone to bear witness concerning man ᵃfor He Himself knew what was in man.

E To Nicodemus, 3:1-21

3 Now there was a man of the Pharisees, named ᵃNicodemus, a ᵇruler of the Jews;

2 this man came to Him by night, and said to Him, "ᵃRabbi, we know that You have come from God *as* a teacher; for no one

Cross references (margin)

10 ᵃMatt. 24:49; Luke 12:45; Acts 2:15; 1 Cor. 11:21; Eph. 5:18; 1 Thess. 5:7; Rev. 17:2, 6

★11 ᵃJohn 2:23; 3:2; 4:54; 6:2, 14; 26, 30; 7:31; 9:16; 10:41; 11:47; 12:18, 37; 20:30 ᵇJohn 1:43 ᶜJohn 1:14

12 ᵃMatt. 4:13 ᵇMatt. 12:46 ᶜJohn 2:2

★13 ᵃJohn 5:1 marg.; 6:4; 11:55 ᵇDeut. 16:1-6; Luke 2:41; John 2:23 ★14 ᵃJohn 2:14-16; Matt. 21:12ff.; Mark 11:15, 17; Luke 19:45f.; Mal. 3:1ff.

16 ᵃMatt. 21:12 ᵇLuke 2:49

★17 ᵃJohn 2:2 ᵇPs. 69:9

18 ᵃJohn 1:19 ᵇMatt. 12:38

★19 ᵃMatt. 26:61; 27:40; Mark 14:58; 15:29; Acts 6:14 20 ᵃJohn 1:19 ᵇEzra 5:16

21 ᵃ1 Cor. 6:19

22 ᵃJohn 2:2 ᵇLuke 24:8; John 2:17; 12:16; 14:26 ᶜPs. 16:10; Luke 24:26f.; John 20:9; Acts 13:33

23 ᵃJohn 2:13 ᵇJohn 2:11

25 ᵃMatt. 9:4; John 1:42, 47; 6:61, 64; 13:11

★ 1 ᵃJohn 7:50; 19:39 ᵇLuke 23:13; John 7:26, 48 2 ᵃMatt. 23:7; John 3:26 ᵇJohn 2:11 ᶜJohn 9:33; 10:38; 14:10f.; Acts 2:22; 10:38

Footnotes

2:11 *beginning of His signs.* The miracles of Jesus are called signs by John in order to emphasize the significance of the miracles rather than the miracles themselves. They revealed various aspects of the person or work of Christ (here His *glory*), and their purpose was to encourage faith in His followers. For the specific signs in this book see Introduction, under "Contents."

2:13 *Passover.* See note on Mark 14:1.

2:14 The many pilgrims that came to Jerusalem for Passover brought a variety of currency and no animals for sacrifice. The outer courts of the temple became a noisy market for chang-

ing money and selling animals.

2:17 See Ps. 69:9. Christ was jealous for the holiness of God's house. The offense of the money-changers was in their defiling it.

2:19 *in three days I will raise it up.* This cryptic expression is explained in v. 21, after a verse which shows how the Jews characteristically misunderstood Jesus.

3:1 *Nicodemus, a ruler of the Jews.* A member of the Sanhedrin (see note on Luke 22:66). He perfectly represents the aristocratic, well-intentioned but unenlightened Judaism of his day. For additional information on Nicodemus see John 7:50-51 and 19:39.

★ 3 ᵃ2 Cor. 5:17; 1 Pet. 1:23 ᵇMatt. 19:24; 21:31; Mark 9:47; 10:14f.; John 3:5

can do these ᵇsigns that You do unless ᶜGod is with him."

3 Jesus answered and said to him, "Truly, truly, I say to you, unless one ᵃis born again, he cannot see ᵇthe kingdom of God."

4 Nicodemus *said to Him, "How can a man be born when he is old? He cannot enter a second time into his mother's womb and be born, can he?"

★ 5 ᵃEzek. 36:25-27; Eph. 5:26; Titus 3:5 ᵇMatt. 19:24; 21:31; Mark 9:47; 10:14f.; John 3:5 6 ᵃJohn 1:13; 1 Cor. 15:50

5 Jesus answered, "Truly, truly, I say to you, unless one is born of ᵃwater and the Spirit, he cannot enter into ᵇthe kingdom of God.

6 "ᵃThat which is born of the flesh is flesh, and that which is born of the Spirit is spirit.

7 "Do not marvel that I said to you, 'You must be born again.'

★ 8 ᵃPs. 135:7; Eccles. 11:5; Ezek. 37:9

8 "ᵃThe wind blows where it wishes and you hear the sound of it, but do not know where it comes from and where it is going; so is everyone who is born of the Spirit."

9 Nicodemus answered and said to Him, "How can these things be?"

10 ᵃLuke 2:46; 5:17; Acts 5:34

10 Jesus answered and said to him, "Are you ᵃthe teacher of Israel, and do not understand these things?

★11 ᵃJohn 1:18; 7:16f.; 8:26, 28; 12:49; 14:24 ᵇJohn 3:32

11 "Truly, truly, I say to you, ᵃwe speak that which we know, and ᵇbear witness of that which we have seen; and ᵇyou do not receive our witness.

12 "If I told you earthly things and you do not believe, how shall you believe if I tell you heavenly things?

13 "And ᵃno one has ascended into heaven, but ᵇHe who descended from heaven, *even* ᶜthe Son of Man.

14 "And as ᵃMoses lifted up the serpent in the wilderness, even so must ᵇthe Son of Man ᶜbe lifted up;

15 that whoever believes may ᵃin Him have eternal life.

16 "For God so ᵃloved the world, that He ᵇgave His ᶜonly begotten Son, that whoever ᵈbelieves in Him should not perish, but have eternal life.

17 "For God ᵃdid not send the Son into the world ᵇto judge the world, but that the world should be saved through Him.

18 "ᵃHe who believes in Him is not judged; he who does not believe has been judged already, because he has not believed in the name of ᵇthe only begotten Son of God.

19 "And this is the judgment, that ᵃthe light is come into the world, and men loved the darkness rather than the light; for ᵇtheir deeds were evil.

20 "ᵃFor everyone who does evil hates the light, and does not come to the light, lest his deeds should be exposed.

13 ᵃDeut. 30:12; Prov. 30:4; Acts 2:34; Rom. 10:6; Eph. 4:9 ᵇJohn 3:31; 6:38, 42 ᶜMatt. 8:20
★14 ᵃNum. 21:9 ᵇMatt. 8:20 ᶜJohn 8:28; 12:34
15 ᵃJohn 20:31; 1 John 5:11-13
★16 ᵃRom. 5:8; Eph. 2:4; 2 Thess. 2:16; 1 John 4:10; Rev. 1:5 ᵇRom. 8:32; 1 John 4:9 ᶜJohn 1:18; 3:18; 1 John 4:9 ᵈJohn 3:36; 6:40; 11:25f.
17 ᵃJohn 3:34; 5:36, 38; 6:29, 38, 57; 7:29; 8:42; 10:36; 11:42; 17:3, 8, 18, 21, 23, 25; 20:21 ᵇLuke 19:10; John 8:15; 12:47; 1 John 4:14
18 ᵃMark 16:16; John 5:24 ᵇJohn 1:18; 1 John 4:9
19 ᵃJohn 1:4; 8:12; 9:5; 12:46 ᵇJohn 7:7
20 ᵃJohn 3:20, 21; Eph. 5:11, 13

3:3 *born again.* Lit., "from above" (as in 3:31; 19:11), though the word also means "again" (Gal. 4:9). Both ideas (merged in John's Gospel) are combined in the translation "be born anew." The new birth or regeneration (Titus 3:5) is the act of God which gives eternal life to the one who believes in Christ. As a result, he becomes a member of God's family (1 Pet. 1:23) with a new capacity and desire to please his heavenly Father (2 Cor. 5:17).

3:5 *born of water and the Spirit.* Various interpretations have been suggested for the meaning here of "water": (1) It refers to baptism as a requirement for salvation. However, this would contradict many other N.T. passages (Eph. 2:8–9). (2) It stands for the act of repentance which John the Baptist's baptism signified. (3) It refers to natural birth; thus it means "except a man be born the first time by water and the second time by the Spirit . . ." (4) It

means the Word of God, as in John 15:3. (5) It is a synonym for the Holy Spirit and may be translated, "by water, even the Spirit." One truth is clear: the new birth is from God through the Spirit.

3:8 *wind.* The Greek word, *pneuma,* means both *wind* and *spirit.*

3:11 *witness.* Or testimony. The witness theme is found throughout John (3:31-36; 5:31-47; 8:12-20).

3:14 *Moses.* The reference is to Num. 21:5-9.

3:16 *eternal life.* A new quality of life, not an everlasting "this-life." Here begins another major theme of John: the dual one of redemption and judgment. It reappears at 5:22; 8:15; 9:39; 12:47. Here the emphasis is on the fact that men judge themselves. The acquitted are those who have believed in Him; the condemned, those who have rejected Him.

21 "But he who ªpractices the truth comes to the light, that his deeds may be manifested as having been wrought in God."

F   By John the Baptizer, 3:22–36

22 ªJohn 2:2
ᵇJohn 4:1, 2

22 After these things Jesus and His ªdisciples came into the land of Judea, and there He was spending time with them and ᵇbaptizing.

★23

23 And John also was baptizing in Aenon near Salim, because there was much water there; and they were coming and were being baptized.

24 ªMatt.
4:12

24 For ªJohn had not yet been thrown into prison.

25 ªJohn 2:6

25 There arose therefore a discussion on the part of John's disciples with a Jew about ªpurification.

26 ªMatt.
23:7; John
3:2 ᵇJohn
1:28 ᶜJohn
1:7

26 And they came to John and said to him, "ªRabbi, He who was with you ᵇbeyond the Jordan, to whom you ᶜhave borne witness, behold, He is baptizing, and all are coming to Him."

27 ª1 Cor.
4:7; Heb. 5:4

27 John answered and said, "ªA man can receive nothing, unless it has been given him from heaven.

28 ªJohn
1:20, 23

28 "You yourselves bear me witness, that I said, 'ªI am not the Christ,' but, 'I have been sent before Him.'

★29 ªMatt.
9:15; 25:1
ᵇJohn 15:11;
16:24; 17:13;
Phil. 2:2;
1 John 1:4;
2 John 12

29 "He who has the bride is ªthe bridegroom; but the friend of the bridegroom, who stands and hears him, rejoices greatly because of the bridegroom's voice. And so this ᵇjoy of mine has been made full.

★31 ªJohn
3:13; 8:23
ᵇ1 John 4:5

30 "He must increase, but I must decrease.

31 "ªHe who comes from

above is above all, he who is of the earth is from the earth and speaks ᵇof the earth. ªHe who comes from heaven is above all.

32 "What He has seen and heard, of that He ªbears witness; and ªno man receives His witness.

32 ªJohn
3:11

33 "He who has received His witness ªhas set his seal to *this*, that God is true.

33 ªJohn
6:27; Rom.
4:11; 15:28;
1 Cor. 9:2;
2 Cor. 1:22;
Eph. 1:13;
4:30; 2 Tim.
2:19; Rev.
7:3-8

34 "For He whom God has ªsent speaks the words of God; ᵇfor He gives the Spirit without measure.

34 ªJohn
3:17 ᵇMatt.
12:18; Luke
4:18; Acts
1:2; 10:38

35 "ªThe Father loves the Son, and has given all things into His hand.

35 ªMatt.
28:18; John
5:20; 17:2

36 "He who ªbelieves in the Son has eternal life; but he who ᵇdoes not obey the Son shall not see life, but the wrath of God abides on him."

36 ªJohn
3:16 ᵇActs
14:2; Heb.
3:18

G   To the Samaritan Woman, 4:1–42

4 When therefore ªthe Lord knew that the Pharisees had heard that Jesus was making and ᵇbaptizing more disciples than John

★ 1-3

1 ªLuke
7:13 ᵇJohn
3:22, 26;
1 Cor. 1:17

2 (although ªJesus Himself was not baptizing, but His ᵇdisciples were),

2 ªJohn
3:22, 26;
1 Cor. 1:17
ᵇJohn 2:2

3 He left ªJudea, and departed ᵇagain into Galilee.

3 ªJohn
3:22 ᵇJohn
2:11f.

4 And He had to pass through ªSamaria.

4 ªLuke
9:52

5 So He *came to a city of ªSamaria, called Sychar, near the parcel of ground that ᵇJacob gave to his son Joseph;

5 ªLuke
9:52 ᵇGen.
33:19; 48:22;
Josh. 24:32;
John 4:12

6 and Jacob's well was there. Jesus therefore, being wearied from His journey, was sitting thus by the well. It was about the sixth hour.

★ 6

3:21 *truth.* I.e., what is true or right.
3:23 *Aenon . . . Salim.* Though not positively identified, they are thought to be in Samaria.
3:29 *the friend of the bridegroom.* As the bridegroom, Christ must occupy the prominent place, though John the Baptist's place as the friend was unique, and he vicariously participated in the joy of the bridegroom.
3:31 This verse picks up where 3:13 left off. *He who comes* is the Son of Man.

4:1–3 The meaning is this: When the Lord knew that the Pharisees had heard that He was making and baptizing more disciples than John (though actually Jesus' disciples did the baptizing, not Jesus Himself), He determined to leave the area and go into Galilee to avoid trouble with the Pharisees.
4:6 *the sixth hour.* 6 p.m. by Roman time and 12 noon by Jewish. The latter, at the sun's zenith, seems indicated.

★ 7

7 There *came a woman of Samaria to draw water. Jesus *said to her, "Give Me a drink."

8 aJohn 2:2
bJohn 4:5, 39
9 aLuke 9:52 bEzra 4:3-6, 11ff.; Matt. 10:5; John 8:48

8 For His adisciples had gone away into bthe city to buy food.

9 The aSamaritan woman therefore *said to Him, "How is it that You, being a Jew, ask me for a drink since I am a Samaritan woman?" (For bJews have no dealings with Samaritans.)

★10 aJohn 7:37f.; Rev. 21:6; 22:17

10 Jesus answered and said to her, "If you knew the gift of God, and who it is who says to you, 'Give Me a drink,' you would have asked Him, and He would have given you aliving water."

11 aJohn 7:37f.; Rev. 21:6; 22:17

11 She *said to Him, "Sir, You have nothing to draw with and the well is deep; where then do You get that aliving water?

12 aJohn 4:6

12 "You are not greater than our father Jacob, are You, who agave us the well, and drank of it himself, and his sons, and his cattle?"

13 Jesus answered and said to her, "Everyone who drinks of this water shall thirst again;

14 aJohn 6:35; 7:38
bMatt. 25:46; John 6:27

14 but whoever drinks of the water that I shall give him ashall never thirst; but the water that I shall give him shall become in him a well of water springing up to beternal life."

15 aJohn 6:34

15 The woman *said to Him, "Sir, agive me this water, so I will not be thirsty, nor come all the way here to draw."

16 He *said to her, "Go, call your husband, and come here."

17 The woman answered and said, "I have no husband." Jesus *said to her, "You have well said, 'I have no husband';

18 for you have had five husbands, and the one whom you now have is not your husband; this you have said truly."

19 aMatt. 21:11; Luke 7:39

19 The woman *said to Him, "Sir, I perceive that You are aa prophet.

★20 aGen. 33:20 [John 4:12] bDeut. 11:29; Josh. 8:33 cLuke 9:53

20 "aOur fathers worshiped in bthis mountain, and you *people* say that cin Jerusalem is the place where men ought to worship."

21 aJohn 4:23; 5:25, 28; 16:2, 32
bMal. 1:11; 1 Tim. 2:8

21 Jesus *said to her, "Woman, believe Me, aan hour is coming when bneither in this mountain, nor in Jerusalem, shall you worship the Father.

★22 a2 Kin. 17:28-41 bIs. 2:3; Rom. 3:1f.; 9:4f.

22 "aYou worship that which you do not know; we worship that which we know, for bsalvation is from the Jews.

23 aJohn 4:21; 5:25, 28; 16:2, 32
bPhil. 3:3

23 "But aan hour is coming, and now is, when the true worshipers shall worship the Father bin spirit and truth; for such people the Father seeks to be His worshipers.

★24 aPhil.

24 "God is spirit, and those who worship Him must worship ain spirit and truth."

★25 aJohn 1:41 bMatt. 1:16

25 The woman *said to Him, "I know that aMessiah is coming (bHe who is called Christ); when that One comes, He will declare all things to us."

26 aJohn 8:24; 9:35-37

26 Jesus *said to her, "aI who speak to you am He."

27 aJohn 4:8
bJohn 2:2

27 And at this point His adisciples bcame, and they marveled that He had been speaking with a woman; yet no one said, "What do You seek?" or, "Why do You speak with her?"

28 So the woman left her waterpot, and went into the city, and *said to the men,

---

4:7 *a woman of Samaria.* On the Samaritans, see note on Luke 10:33.

4:10 *living water.* New life through the Spirit (see Jer. 2:13; Zech. 14:8; John 7:37-39). Salvation is a gift from Jesus Christ, the Son of God and Messiah. Notice that Christ asked the woman to receive Him and His gift without any prerequisite change in her life. After she believed, and because she believed, her way of living would be changed.

4:20 *in this mountain.* On Mt. Gerizim the Samaritans had built a temple to rival the one in Jerusalem, from which they had long been

separated politically and religiously.

4:22 *salvation is from the Jews.* The Savior was a Jew and the Jews were the first messengers of the good news.

4:24 *must worship in spirit and truth.* The English word "worship" was originally spelled "worthship" and means to acknowledge the worth of the object worshiped. We should acknowledge God's worth *in spirit* (in contrast to material ways) and *in truth* (in contrast to falsehood).

4:25 The Samaritans also believed in a coming Messiah.

29 *John
4:17f. *Matt.
12:23; John
7:26, 31

29 "Come, see a man *who told me all the things that I *have* done; *this is not the Christ, is it?"

30 They went out of the city, and were coming to Him.

31 *Matt.
23:7

31 In the meanwhile the disciples were requesting Him, saying, "*Rabbi, eat."

32 But He said to them, "I have food to eat that you do not know about."

33 *John 2:2

33 The *disciples therefore were saying to one another, "No one brought Him *anything* to eat, did he?"

34 *John
5:30; 6:38
*John 5:36;
17:4; 19:28,
30

34 Jesus *said to them, "My food is to *do the will of Him who sent Me, and to *accomplish His work.

★35 *Luke
10:2

35 "Do you not say, 'There are yet four months, and *then* comes the harvest'? Behold, I say to you, lift up your eyes, and look on the fields, that they are white *for harvest.

36 *1 Cor.
9:17f. *Rom.
1:13 *John
4:14

36 "Already he who reaps is receiving *wages, and is gathering *fruit for *life eternal; that he who sows and he who reaps may rejoice together.

37 *Job
31:8; Mic.
6:15

37 "For in this *case* the saying is true, '*One sows, and another reaps.'

38 "I sent you to reap that for which you have not labored; others have labored, and you have entered into their labor."

39 *John
4:5, 30
*John 4:29

39 And from *that city many of the Samaritans believed in Him because of the word of the woman who testified, "*He told me all the things that I *have* done."

40 So when the Samaritans came to Him, they were asking Him to stay there two days.

41 And many more believed because of His word;

42 *Luke
2:11; Acts
5:31; 13:23;
1 Tim. 4:10;
1 John 4:14

42 and they were saying to the woman, "It is no longer because of what you said that we believe, for we have heard for ourselves and know that this One is indeed *the Savior of the world."

H To an Official of Capernaum,
4:43-54

43 *John
4:40

43 And after *the two days He went forth from there into Galilee.

44 *Matt.
13:57

44 For Jesus Himself testified that *a prophet has no honor in his own country.

45 *John
2:23

45 So when He came to Galilee, the Galileans received Him, *having seen all the things that He did in Jerusalem at the feast; for they themselves also went to the feast.

46 *John 2:1
*John 2:9
*Luke 4:23;
John 2:12

46 He came therefore again to *Cana of Galilee *where He had made the water wine. And there was a certain royal official, whose son was sick at *Capernaum.

47 *John
4:3, 54

47 When he heard that Jesus had come *out of Judea into Galilee, he went to Him, and was requesting *Him* to come down and heal his son; for he was at the point of death.

48 *Dan.
4:2f.; 6:27;
Matt. 24:24;
Mark 13:22;
Acts 2:19,
22, 43; 4:30;
5:12; 6:8;
7:36; 14:3;
15:12; Rom.
15:19; 1 Cor.
1:22; 2 Cor.
12:12;
2 Thess. 2:9;
Heb. 2:4

48 Jesus therefore said to him, "Unless you *people* see *signs and *wonders, you *simply* will not believe."

49 The royal official *said to Him, "Sir, come down before my child dies."

50 Jesus *said to him, "Go your way; your son lives." The man believed the word that Jesus spoke to him, and he started off.

51 And as he was now going down, *his* slaves met him, saying that his son was living.

52 So he inquired of them the hour when he began to get better. They said therefore to him, "Yesterday at the seventh hour the fever left him."

53 *Acts
11:14

53 So the father knew that *it was* at that hour in which Jesus

---

4:35 *they are white for harvest.* The mission fields, Christ says, are ripe and waiting for harvesters.

said to him, "Your son lives"; and he himself believed, and [a]his whole household.

54 a John 2:11 b John 4:45f.

54 This is again a [a]second sign that Jesus performed, when He had [b]come out of Judea into Galilee.

III CONFRONTATIONS WITH THE SON OF GOD, 5:1-12:50
A At a Feast in Jerusalem, 5:1-47
1 The miraculous sign, 5:1-9

★ 2 a Neh. 3:1, 32; 12:39 b John 19:13, 17, 20; 20:16; Acts 21:40; Rev. 9:11; 16:16
★ 3

5 After these things there was a feast of the Jews, and Jesus went up to Jerusalem.

2 Now there is in Jerusalem by [a]the sheep gate a pool, which is called [b]in Hebrew Bethesda, having five porticoes.

3 In these lay a multitude of those who were sick, blind, lame, and withered, [waiting for the moving of the waters;

4 for an angel of the Lord went down at certain seasons into the pool, and stirred up the water; whoever then first, after the stirring up of the water, stepped in was made well from whatever disease with which he was afflicted.]

5 And a certain man was there, who had been thirty-eight years in his sickness.

6 When Jesus saw him lying there, and knew that he had already been a long time in that condition, He *said to him, "Do you wish to get well?"

7 a John 5:4

7 The sick man answered Him, "Sir, I have no man to put me into the pool when [a]the water is stirred up, but while I am coming, another steps down before me."

8 Jesus *said to him, "[a]Arise, take up your pallet, and walk."

★ 8 a Matt. 9:6; Mark 2:11; Luke 5:24
9 a John 9:14

9 And immediately the man became well, and took up his pallet and began to walk.

[a]Now it was the Sabbath on that day.

2 The reaction, 5:10-18

★10 a John 1:19; 5:15, 16, 18 b Neh. 13:19; Jer. 17:21f.; Matt. 12:2; John 7:23; 9:16

10 Therefore [a]the Jews were saying to him who was cured, "It is the Sabbath, and [b]it is not permissible for you to carry your pallet."

11 But he answered them, "He who made me well was the one who said to me, 'Take up your pallet and walk.'"

12 They asked him, "Who is the man who said to you, 'Take up your pallet, and walk'?"

13 But he who was healed did not know who it was; for Jesus had slipped away while there was a crowd in that place.

14 a Mark 2:5; John 8:11 b Ezra 9:14

14 Afterward Jesus *found him in the temple, and said to him, "Behold, you have become well; do not [a]sin anymore, [b]so that nothing worse may befall you."

★15 a John 1:19; 5:16, 18

15 The man went away, and told [a]the Jews that it was Jesus who had made him well.

16 a John 1:19; 5:10, 15, 18

16 And for this reason [a]the Jews were persecuting Jesus, because He was doing these things on the Sabbath.

★17-47

17 But He answered them, "My Father is working until now, and I Myself am working."

18 a John 1:19; 5:15, 16 b John 5:16; 7:1 c John 10:33; 19:7

18 For this cause therefore [a]the Jews [b]were seeking all the more to kill Him, because He not only was breaking the Sabbath,

---

5:2 *the sheep gate.* See Neh. 3:1; 12:39. *five porticoes.* I.e., colonnades or cloisters to shelter the sick.

5:3 *waiting for the moving of the waters.* This phrase and all of v. 4 are not found in some manuscripts.

5:8 *pallet.* The bed of the very poor.

5:10 *it is not permissible for you to carry your pallet.* Carrying furniture on the Sabbath was a kind of work which the rabbis taught that the fourth commandment prohibited.

5:15 *the Jews.* I.e., the Jewish authorities; here as in vv. 10, 16, 18.

5:17-47 In this important Christological passage, Jesus asserts His authority, which He bases on His special relation to the Father. The Jews were perfectly aware that Jesus was claiming full deity—equality with God (v. 18).

but also was calling God His own Father, ^cmaking Himself equal with God.

3 The discourse, 5:19-47

¹⁹ ^aJohn 5:30; 8:28; 12:49; 14:10

19 Jesus therefore answered and was saying to them, "Truly, truly, I say to you, ^athe Son can do nothing of Himself, unless *it is* something He sees the Father doing; for whatever *the Father* does, these things the Son also does in like manner.

²⁰ ^aJohn 3:35 ^bJohn 14:12

20 "^aFor the Father loves the Son, and shows Him all things that He Himself is doing; and ^bgreater works than these will He show Him, that you may marvel.

★21-27

²¹ ^aRom. 4:17; 8:11 ^bJohn 11:25

21 "For just as the Father raises the dead and ^agives them life, even so ^bthe Son also gives life to whom He wishes.

²² ^aJohn 5:27; 9:39; Acts 10:42; 17:31

22 "For not even the Father judges anyone, but ^aHe has given all judgment to the Son,

²³ ^aLuke 10:16; 1 John 2:23

23 in order that all may honor the Son, even as they honor the Father. ^aHe who does not honor the Son does not honor the Father who sent Him.

²⁴ ^aJohn 3:18; 12:44; 20:31; 1 John 5:13 ^bJohn 3:18 ^c1 John 3:14

24 "Truly, truly, I say to you, he who hears My word, and ^abelieves Him who sent Me, has eternal life, and ^bdoes not come into judgment, but has ^cpassed out of death into life.

²⁵ ^aJohn 4:21, 23; 5:28 ^bLuke 15:24 ^cJohn 6:60; 8:43, 47; 9:27

25 "Truly, truly, I say to you, ^aan hour is coming and now is, when ^bthe dead shall hear the voice of the Son of God; and those who ^chear shall live.

²⁶ ^aJohn 1:4; 6:57

26 "For just as the Father has life in Himself, even so He ^agave to the Son also to have life in Himself;

²⁷ ^aJohn 9:39; Acts 10:42; 17:31

27 and He gave Him authority to ^aexecute judgment, because He is *the* Son of Man.

²⁸ ^aJohn 4:21 ^bJohn 11:24; 1 Cor. 15:52

28 "Do not marvel at this; for ^aan hour is coming, in which ^ball who are in the tombs shall hear His voice,

²⁹ ^aDan. 12:2; Matt. 25:46; Acts 24:15

29 and shall come forth; ^athose who did the good *deeds* to a resurrection of life, those who committed the evil *deeds* to a resurrection of judgment.

³⁰ ^aJohn 5:19 ^bJohn 8:16 ^cJohn 4:34; 6:38

30 "^aI can do nothing on My own initiative. As I hear, I judge; and ^bMy judgment is just, because I do not seek My own will, but ^cthe will of Him who sent Me.

★31 ^aJohn 8:14

31 "^aIf I *alone* bear witness of Myself, My testimony is not true.

³² ^aJohn 5:37

32 "There is ^aanother who bears witness of Me, and I know that the testimony which He bears of Me is true.

³³ ^aJohn 1:7

33 "You have sent to John, and he ^ahas borne witness to the truth.

³⁴ ^aJohn 5:32; 1 John 5:9

34 "But ^athe witness which I receive is not from man, but I say these things that you may be saved.

³⁵ ^a2 Sam. 21:17; 2 Pet. 1:19 ^bMark 1:5

35 "He was ^athe lamp that was burning and was shining and you ^bwere willing to rejoice for a while in his light.

³⁶ ^aMatt. 11:4; John 2:23; 10:25, 38; 14:11; 15:24 ^bJohn 4:34 ^cJohn 3:17

36 "But the witness which I have is greater than *that of* John; for ^athe works which the Father has given Me ^bto accomplish, the very works that I do, bear witness of Me, that the Father ^chas sent Me.

³⁷ ^aLuke 24:27; John 8:18

37 "And the Father who sent Me, ^aHe has borne witness of Me. You have neither heard His voice at any time, nor seen His form.

³⁸ ^a1 John 2:14 ^bJohn 3:17

38 "And you do not have ^aHis word abiding in you, for you do not believe Him whom He ^bsent.

★39 ^aJohn 7:52; Rom. 2:17ff. ^bLuke 24:25, 27; Acts 13:27

39 "^aYou search the Scriptures because you think that in them you have eternal life; and it is ^bthese that bear witness of Me;

5:21-27 Christ's authority is seen in the spheres of resurrection (vv. 21, 25, 26) and judgment (vv. 22-23, 27). God will make Christ the judge in order that the Son may be honored. Those who believe will escape judgment (v. 24).

5:31 Here Christ acquiesces to the arguments of His opponents that His witness alone (without other witnesses) is not true. But He goes on to remind them that *another*, His Father, wit-

nesses to the validity of His claims (vv. 32, 37). Other witnesses cited are John the Baptist (v. 33), His miracles (v. 36), the Scriptures (v. 39), and Moses (v. 46). In 8:14 He claims that His witness is indeed true.

5:39 *search the Scriptures*. This may be either a command or a statement of fact, probably the latter.

40 and you are unwilling to come to Me, that you may have life.

41 a John 5:44; 7:18

41 "aI do not receive glory from men;

42 but I know you, that you do not have the love of God in yourselves.

★43 aMatt. 24:5

43 "I have come in My Father's name, and you do not receive Me; aif another shall come in his own name, you will receive him.

44 aJohn 5:41 bRom. 2:29 cJohn 17:3; 1 Tim. 1:17

44 "How can you believe, when you areceive glory from one another, and you do not seek bthe glory that is from cthe one and only God?

45 aJohn 9:28; Rom. 2:17ff.

45 "Do not think that I will accuse you before the Father; the one who accuses you•is aMoses, in whom you have set your hope.

46 aLuke 24:27

46 "For if you believed Moses, you would believe Me; for ahe wrote of Me.

47 aLuke 16:29, 31

47 "But aif you do not believe his writings, how will you believe My words?"

B   At Passover Time in Galilee, 6:1-71

1   The miraculous sign, 6:1-21

★1 aJohn 6:1-13; Matt. 14:13-21; Mark 6:32-44; Luke 9:10-17 bMatt. 4:18; Luke 5:1 cJohn 6:23; 21:1

6 After these things aJesus went away to the other side of bthe Sea of Galilee (or cTiberias).

2 aJohn 2:11

2 And a great multitude was following Him, because they were seeing the asigns which He was performing on those who were sick.

3 aMatt. 5:1; John 6:15

3 And Jesus went up on athe mountain, and there He sat with His disciples.

4 aJohn 2:13

4 Now athe Passover, the feast of the Jews, was at hand.

5 Jesus therefore lifting up His eyes, and seeing that a great multitude was coming to Him, *said to aPhilip, "Where are we to buy bread, that these may eat?"

5 aJohn 1:43

6 And this He was saying to atest him; for He Himself knew what He was intending to do.

6 aCompare 2 Cor. 13:5 and Rev. 2:2 in Gr.

7 aPhilip answered Him, "bTwo hundred denarii worth of bread is not sufficient for them, for everyone to receive a little."

★7 aJohn 1:43 bMark 6:37

8 One of His adisciples, bAndrew, Simon Peter's brother, *said to Him,

8 aJohn 2:2 bJohn 1:40

9 "There is a lad here who has five barley loaves and two afish, but what are these for so many people?"

★9 aJohn 6:11; 21:9, 10, 13

10 Jesus said, "Have the people sit down." Now there was amuch grass in the place. So the men sat down, in number about bfive thousand.

10 aMark 6:39; John 6:4 bMatt. 14:21

11 Jesus therefore took the loaves; and ahaving given thanks, He distributed to those who were seated; likewise also of the bfish as much as they wanted.

11 aMatt. 15:36; John 6:23 bJohn 6:9; 21:9, 10, 13

12 And when they were filled, He *said to aHis disciples, "Gather up the leftover fragments that nothing may be lost."

12 aJohn 2:2

13 And so they gathered them up, and filled twelve abaskets with fragments from the five barley loaves, which were left over by those who had eaten.

13 aMatt. 14:20

14 When therefore the people saw the sign which He had performed, they said, "This is of a truth the aProphet who is to come into the world."

★14 aMatt. 11:3; 21:11; John 1:21

15 Jesus therefore perceiving that they were intending to come and take Him by force, ato make

★15 aJohn 18:36f. bJohn 6:15-21; Matt. 14:22-33; Mark 6:45-51 cJohn 6:3

5:43 *in My Father's name.* I.e., as His representative. Though you won't follow Me, Christ says, you will, ironically, follow false Messiahs—which the Jews did periodically until finally crushed by Rome in A.D. 135.

6:1 *Sea of Galilee.* An earlier name for this lake was Gennesaret; later it was called *Galilee,* and finally *Tiberias,* after the city built on its shore by Herod Antipas in honor of the Roman emperor Tiberius.

6:7 *Two hundred denarii.* For the denarius, see

note on Matt. 20:2.

6:9 *barley loaves.* The cheap food of the common people.

6:14 *the Prophet.* See Deut. 18:15 and John 1:21.

6:15 *to make Him king.* Jesus had to escape from the enthusiasm of the crowd, which would have forced Him to lead them in revolt against the Roman government. Jesus refused to become a political revolutionist.

Him king, [b]withdrew again to [c]the mountain by Himself alone.

16 Now when evening came, His [a]disciples went down to the sea,

17 and after getting into a boat, they *started to* cross the sea [a]to Capernaum. And it had already become dark, and Jesus had not yet come to them.

18 And the sea *began* to be stirred up because a strong wind was blowing.

19 When therefore they had rowed about three or four miles, they *beheld Jesus walking on the sea and drawing near to the boat; and they were frightened.

20 But He *said to them, "It is I; [a]do not be afraid."

21 They were willing therefore to receive Him into the boat; and immediately the boat was at the land to which they were going.

2 The discourse, 6:22-40

22 The next day [a]the multitude that stood on the other side of the sea saw that there was no other small boat there, except one, and that Jesus [b]had not entered with His disciples into the boat, but *that* His disciples had gone away alone.

23 There came other small boats from [a]Tiberias near to the place where they ate the bread after the [b]Lord [c]had given thanks.

24 When the multitude therefore saw that Jesus was not there, nor His disciples, they themselves got into the small boats, and [a]came to Capernaum, seeking Jesus.

25 And when they found Him on the other side of the sea, they said to Him, "[a]Rabbi, when did You get here?"

26 Jesus answered them and said, "Truly, truly, I say to you, you [a]seek Me, not because you saw [b]signs, but because you ate of the loaves, and were filled.

27 "Do not [a]work for the food which perishes, but for the food which endures to [b]eternal life, which [c]the Son of Man shall give to you, for on Him the Father, *even* God, [d]has set His seal."

28 They said therefore to Him, "What shall we do, that we may work the works of God?"

29 Jesus answered and said to them, "This is [a]the work of God, that you believe in Him whom He [b]has sent."

30 They said therefore to Him, "[a]What then do You do for a [b]sign, that we may see, and believe You? What work do You perform?

31 "[a]Our fathers ate the manna in the wilderness; as it is written, '[b]HE GAVE THEM BREAD OUT OF HEAVEN TO EAT.' "

32 Jesus therefore said to them, "Truly, truly, I say to you, it is not Moses who has given you the bread out of heaven, but it is My Father who gives you the true bread out of heaven.

33 "For the bread of God is that which [a]comes down out of heaven, and gives life to the world."

34 They said therefore to Him, "Lord, evermore [a]give us this bread."

35 Jesus said to them, "[a]I am the bread of life; he who comes to Me shall not hunger, and he who believes in Me [b]shall never thirst.

36 "But [a]I said to you, that you have seen Me, and yet do not believe.

37 "[a]All that the Father gives Me shall come to Me, and the one who comes to Me I will certainly not cast out.

38 "For [a]I have come down from heaven, [b]not to do My own will, but [c]the will of Him who [d]sent Me.

39 "And this is the will of Him

16 [a]John 2:2

17 [a]Mark 6:45; John 6:24, 59

20 [a]Matt. 14:27

22 [a]John 6:2
[b]John 6:15ff.

23 [a]John 6:1
[b]Luke 7:13
[c]John 6:11

24 [a]Matt. 14:34; Mark 6:53; John 6:17, 59

25 [a]Matt. 23:7

26 [a]John 6:24 [b]John 6:2, 14, 30

27 [a]Is. 55:2
[b]John 3:15f.; 4:14; 6:40, 47, 54; 10:28; 17:2f.
[c]Matt. 8:20; John 6:53, 62 [d]John 3:33

★29
[a]1 Thess. 1:3; James 2:22; 1 John 3:23; Rev. 2:26 [b]John 3:17

30 [a]Matt. 12:38 [b]John 6:2, 14, 26

★31 [a]Ex. 16:21; Num. 11:8; John 6:49, 58
[b]Ex. 16:4, 15; Neh. 9:15; Ps. 78:24; 105:40

33 [a]John 6:41, 50

34 [a]John 4:15

35 [a]John 6:48, 51
[b]John 4:14

36 [a]John 6:26

37 [a]John 6:39; 17:2, 24

38 [a]John 3:13 [b]Matt. 26:39 [c]John 4:34; 5:30 [d]John 6:29

★39 [a]John 6:37; 17:2, 24 [b]John 17:12; 18:9 [c]Matt. 10:15; John 6:40, 44, 54; 11:24

6:29 The only "work" that a man can do that is acceptable to God is to believe in Christ (cf. 1 John 3:23).

6:31 *manna.* See Ex. 16:15; Num. 11:8; Neh.

9:15.

6:39 It is the Father's will to preserve those who come to Christ.

who sent Me, that of [a]all that He has given Me I [b]lose nothing, but [c]raise it up on the last day.

40 "For this is the will of My Father, that everyone who [a]beholds the Son and [b]believes in Him, may have eternal life; and I Myself will [c]raise him up on the last day."

3 The reactions, 6:41-71

41 [a]The Jews therefore were grumbling about Him, because He said, "I am the bread that [b]came down out of heaven."

42 And they were saying, "[a]Is not this Jesus, the son of Joseph, whose father and mother [b]we know? How does He now say, '[c]I have come down out of heaven'?"

43 Jesus answered and said to them, "Do not grumble among yourselves.

44 "No one can come to Me, unless the Father who sent Me [a]draws him; and I will [b]raise him up on the last day.

45 "It is written [a]in the prophets, '[b]AND THEY SHALL ALL BE [c]TAUGHT OF GOD.' Everyone who has heard and learned from the Father, comes to Me.

46 "[a]Not that any man has seen the Father, except the One who is from God; He has seen the Father.

47 "Truly, truly, I say to you, he who believes [a]has eternal life.

48 "[a]I am the bread of life.

49 "[a]Your fathers ate the manna in the wilderness, and they died.

50 "This is the bread which [a]comes down out of heaven, so that one may eat of it and [b]not die.

51 "[a]I am the living bread that [b]came down out of heaven; if anyone eats of this bread, [c]he shall live forever; and the bread

also which I shall give [d]for the life of the world is [e]My flesh."

52 [a]The Jews therefore [b]began to argue with one another, saying, "How can this man give us [His] flesh to eat?"

53 Jesus therefore said to them, "Truly, truly, I say to you, unless you eat the flesh of [a]the Son of Man and drink His blood, you have no life in yourselves.

54 "He who eats My flesh and drinks My blood has eternal life, and I will [a]raise him up on the last day.

55 "For My flesh is true food, and My blood is true drink.

56 "He who eats My flesh and drinks My blood [a]abides in Me, and I in him.

57 "As the [a]living Father [b]sent Me, and I live because of the Father, so he who eats Me, he also shall live because of Me.

58 "This is the bread which [a]came down out of heaven; not as [b]the fathers ate, and died, he who eats this bread [c]shall live forever."

59 These things He said [a]in the synagogue, as He taught [b]in Capernaum.

60 Many therefore of His [a]disciples, when they heard *this* said, "[b]This is a difficult statement; who can listen to it?"

61 But Jesus, [a]conscious that His disciples grumbled at this, said to them, "Does this [b]cause you to stumble?

62 "[What] then if you should behold [a]the Son of Man [b]ascending where He was before?

63 "[a]It is the Spirit who gives life; the flesh profits nothing; [b]the words that I have spoken to you are spirit and are life.

64 "But there are [a]some of you who do not believe." For Jesus [b]knew from the beginning who they were who did not believe,

---

40 [a]John 12:45; 14:17, 19 [b]John 3:16 [c]Matt. 10:15; John 6:39, 44, 54; 11:24

41 [a]John 1:19; 6:52 [b]John 6:33, 51, 58

42 [a]Luke 4:22 [b]John 7:27f. [c]John 6:38, 62

44 [a]Jer. 31:3; Hos. 11:4; John 6:65; 12:32 [b]John 6:39
★**45** [a]Acts 7:42; 13:40; Heb. 8:11 [b]Is. 54:13; Jer. 31:34 [c]Phil. 3:15; 1 Thess. 4:9; 1 John 2:27
★**46** [a]John 1:18
47 [a]John 3:36; 5:24; 6:51, 58; 11:26
48 [a]John 6:35, 51
49 [a]John 6:31, 58
50 [a]John 6:33 [b]John 3:36; 5:24; 6:47, 51, 58; 11:26
★**51** [a]John 6:35, 48 [b]John 6:41, 58 [c]John 3:36; 5:24; 6:47, 58; 11:26 [d]John 1:29; 3:14f.; Heb. 10:10; 1 John 4:10 [e]John 6:53-56

52 [a]John 1:19; 6:41 [b]John 9:16; 10:19
★**53-56**
53 [a]Matt. 8:20; John 6:27, 62
★**54** [a]John 6:39
56 [a]John 15:4f.; 17:23; 1 John 2:24; 3:24; 4:15f.
57 [a]Matt. 16:16; John 5:26 [b]John 3:17; 6:29, 38
58 [a]John 6:33, 41, 51 [b]John 6:31, 49 [c]John 3:36; 5:24; 6:47, 51; 11:26
59 [a]Matt. 4:23 [b]John 6:24
★**60** [a]John 2:2; 6:66; 7:3 [b]John 6:52
61 [a]John 6:64 [b]Matt. 11:6
62 [a]Matt. 8:20; John 6:27, 53 [b]Mark 16:19; John 3:13
★**63** [a]2 Cor. 3:6 [b]John 6:68
64 [a]John 6:60, 66 [b]John 2:25 [c]Matt. 10:4; John 6:71; 13:11

6:45 See Isa. 54:13.
6:46 On seeing God, see note on 1:18.
6:51 *the bread . . . which I shall give.* A reference to His sacrificial death on the cross.
6:53-56 Just as one eats and drinks in order to have physical life, so it is necessary to appro-

priate Christ in order to have eternal life.
6:54 *has eternal life.* I.e., already has it, and so can count on being raised.
6:60 *listen to it.* I.e., accept it.
6:63 *profits nothing.* I.e., is of no account.

and cwho it was that would betray Him.

65 And He was saying, "For this reason I have asaid to you, that no one can come to Me, unless bit has been granted him from the Father."

66 As a result of this many of His adisciples bwithdrew, and were not walking with Him anymore.

67 Jesus said therefore to athe twelve, "You do not want to go away also, do you?"

68 aSimon Peter answered Him, "Lord, to whom shall we go? You have bwords of eternal life.

69 "And we have believed and have come to know that You are athe Holy One of God."

70 Jesus answered them, "aDid I Myself not choose you, bthe twelve, and yet one of you is ca devil?"

71 Now He meant Judas athe son of Simon Iscariot, for he, bone of cthe twelve, was going to betray Him.

C At the Feast of Booths in Jerusalem, 7:1–10:21

1 Debate #1—the discourse, 7:1–29

7 And after these things Jesus awas walking in Galilee; for He was unwilling to walk in Judea, because bthe Jews cwere seeking to kill Him.

2 Now the feast of the Jews, athe Feast of Booths, was at hand.

3 His abrothers therefore said to Him, "Depart from here, and go into Judea, that Your bdisciples also may behold Your works which You are doing.

4 "For no one does anything in secret, when he himself seeks to be *known* publicly. If You do these things, show Yourself to the world."

5 For not even His abrothers were believing in Him.

6 Jesus therefore *said to them, "aMy time is not yet at hand, but your time is always opportune.

7 "aThe world cannot hate you; but it hates Me because I testify of it, that bits deeds are evil.

8 "Go up to the feast yourselves; I do not go up to this feast because aMy time has not yet fully come."

9 And having said these things to them, He stayed in Galilee.

10 But when His abrothers had gone up to the feast, then He Himself also went up, not publicly, but as it were, in secret.

11 aThe Jews therefore bwere seeking Him at the feast, and were saying, "Where is He?"

12 And there was much grumbling among the multitudes concerning Him; asome were saying, "He is a good man"; others were saying, "No, on the contrary, He leads the multitude astray."

13 Yet no one was speaking openly of Him for afear of the Jews.

14 But when it was now the midst of the feast Jesus went up into the temple, and *began to ateach.

15 aThe Jews therefore were marveling, saying, "How has this man bbecome learned, having never been educated?"

16 Jesus therefore answered them, and said, "aMy teaching is not Mine, but His who sent Me.

17 "aIf any man is willing to do

7:2 *Feast of Booths.* This was one of the three pilgrimage festivals of the Jewish year, occurring in the autumn after harvest. The Jews dwelt in booths made of the boughs of trees for the seven days of the festival.

7:6 *your time is always opportune.* I.e., it doesn't make any difference when you go.

7:7 The world rejected Jesus because His words and acts were a witness against its evil deeds.

7:13 *the Jews.* Since *the multitude* (v. 12) were all Jews, here the Jewish authorities must be meant.

7:15 *having never been educated.* Jesus was not trained in the rabbinical schools (Acts 4:13).

7:17 The thought is: Anyone who does God's will will be able to judge the authority of My teaching.

---

65 aJohn 6:37, 44 bMatt. 13:11; John 3:27

66 aJohn 2:2; 7:3 bJohn 6:60, 64

67 aMatt. 10:2; John 2:2; 6:70f.; 20:24

68 aMatt. 16:16 bJohn 6:63; 12:49f.; 17:8

69 aMark 1:24

70 aJohn 15:16, 19 bMatt. 10:2; John 2:2; 6:71; 20:24 cJohn 8:44; 13:2, 27; 17:12

71 aJohn 12:4; 13:2, 26 bMark 14:10 cMatt. 10:2; John 2:2; 6:70f.; 20:24

1 aJohn 4:3; 6:1; 11:54 bJohn 1:19; 7:11, 13, 15, 35 cJohn 5:18; 7:19; 8:37, 40; 11:53

★ **2** aLev. 23:34; Deut. 16:16; Zech. 14:16-19

3 aMatt. 12:46; Mark 3:21; John 7:5, 10 bJohn 6:60

5 aMatt. 12:46; Mark 3:21; John 7:3, 10

★ **6** aMatt. 26:18; John 2:4; 7:8, 30

★ **7** aJohn 15:18f. bJohn 3:19f.

8 aJohn 7:6

10 aMatt. 12:46; Mark 3:21; John 7:3, 5

11 aJohn 7:13, 15, 35 bJohn 11:56

12 aJohn 7:40-43

★ **13** aJohn 9:22; 12:42; 19:38; 20:19

14 aMatt. 26:55; John 7:28

★ **15** aJohn 1:19; 7:11, 13, 35 bActs 26:24 [Gr.]

16 aJohn 3:11

★ **17** aPs. 25:9, 14; Prov. 3:32; Dan. 12:10; John 3:21; 8:43f.

His will, he shall know of the teaching, whether it is of God, or *whether* I speak from Myself.

18 "He who speaks from himself [a]seeks his own glory; but He who is seeking the glory of the one who sent Him, He is true, and there is no unrighteousness in Him.

19 "[a]Did not Moses give you the law, and *yet* none of you carries out the law? Why do you [b]seek to kill Me?"

20 The multitude answered, "[a]You have a demon! Who seeks to kill You?"

21 Jesus answered and said to them, "I did [a]one deed, and you all marvel.

22 "On this account [a]Moses has given you circumcision (not because it is from Moses, but from [b]the fathers), and on *the* Sabbath you circumcise a man.

23 "[a]If a man receives circumcision on *the* Sabbath that the Law of Moses may not be broken, are you angry with Me because I made an entire man well on *the* Sabbath?

24 "Do not [a]judge according to appearance, but judge with righteous judgment."

25 Therefore some of the people of Jerusalem were saying, "Is this not the man whom they are seeking to kill?

26 "And look, He is speaking publicly, and they are saying nothing to Him. [a]The rulers do not really know that this is the Christ, do they?

27 "However, [a]we know where this man is from; but whenever the Christ may come, no one knows where He is from."

28 Jesus therefore cried out in the temple, [a]teaching and saying,

"[b]You both know Me and know where I am from; and [c]I have not come of Myself, but He who sent Me is true, whom you do not know.

29 "[a]I know Him; because [b]I am from Him, and [c]He sent Me."

2 The reactions, 7:30-36

30 They [a]were seeking therefore to seize Him; and no man laid his hand on Him, because His [b]hour had not yet come.

31 But [a]many of the multitude believed in Him; and they were saying, "[b]When the Christ shall come, He will not perform more [c]signs than those which this man has, will He?"

32 The Pharisees heard the multitude muttering these things about Him; and the chief priests and the Pharisees sent [a]officers to [b]seize Him.

33 Jesus therefore said, "[a]For a little while longer I am with you, then [b]I go to Him who sent Me.

34 "[a]You shall seek Me, and shall not find Me; and where I am, you cannot come."

35 [a]The Jews therefore said to one another, "[b]Where does this man intend to go that we shall not find Him? He is not intending to go to [c]the Dispersion among [d]the Greeks, and teach the Greeks, is He?

36 "What is this statement that He said, '[a]You will seek Me, and will not find Me; and where I am, you cannot come'?"

3 Debate #2—the discourse, 7:37-39

37 Now on [a]the last day, the great *day* of the feast, Jesus stood

---

Reference column (left):

18 [a]John 5.41; 8.50, 54; 12.43

19 [a]John 1.17 [b]Mark 11.18; John 7.1

★20 [a]Matt 11.18; John 8.48f.; 52; 10.20

★21 [a]John 5.2-9, 16; 7.23

22 [a]Lev. 12.3 [b]Gen. 17.10ff.; 21.4; Acts 7.8

★23 [a]Matt 12.2; John 5.10

24 [a]Lev. 19.15; Is 11.3; Zech. 7.9; John 8.15

26 [a]Luke 23.13; John 3.1

★27 [a]John 6.42; 7.41; 9.29

★28 [a]John 7.14 [b]John 6.42; 7.14f.; 9.29 [c]John 8.42

Reference column (right):

29 [a]Matt 11.27; John 8.55; 17.25 [b]John 6.46 [c]John 3.17

30 [a]Matt 21.46; John 7.32; 44; 10.39 [b]John 7.6; 8.20

31 [a]John 2.23; 8.30; 10.42; 11.45; 12.11; 42 [b]John 7.26 [c]John 2.11

32 [a]Matt 26.58; John 7.45f. [b]Matt 12.14

33 [a]John 12.35; 13.33; 14.19; 16.16-19 [b]John 14.12; 28; 16.5; 10; 17; 28; 20.17

★34 [a]John 7.36; 8.21; 13.33

35 [a]John 7.1 [b]John 8.22 [c]Ps. 147.2; Is. 11.12; 56.8; Zeph 3.10; James 1.1; 1 Pet. 1.1 [d]John 12.20; Acts 14.1; 17.4; 18.4; Rom 1.16

36 [a]John 7.34; 8.21; 13.33

★37-39

37 [a]Lev. 23.36; Num. 29.35; Neh. 8.18 [b]John 4.10; 14; 6.35

7:20 *a demon.* See Mark 3:22. The question of the last half of this verse seems strange in light of 5:18.

7:21 The *one deed* which, at this time, most turned the authorities against Him was the healing of the man on the Sabbath day (5:1-9).

7:23 If circumcision be allowed on the Sabbath (Lev. 12:3), should not also a deed of mercy like the complete healing of a man (John 5:5-9)?

7:27 A popular idea associated with the coming

of Messiah was that He would be a man of mystery, coming out of nowhere. Jesus was known to have come from Nazareth and so did not fulfill the requirement.

7:28 Christ says, in effect, If you knew God, you would recognize Me.

7:34 The Jewish authorities would die in their sins (8:24) and so could not come to be with Him in heaven.

7:37-39 Though it is not mentioned in the O.T.,

and cried out, saying, "[b]If any man is thirsty, let him come to Me and drink.

38 "He who believes in Me, [a]as the Scripture said, 'From his innermost being shall flow rivers of [b]living water.'"

39 But this He spoke [a]of the Spirit, whom those who believed in Him were to receive; for [b]the Spirit was not yet *given*, because Jesus was not yet [c]glorified.

4　The reactions, 7:40-53

40 *Some* of the multitude therefore, when they heard these words, were saying, "This certainly is [a]the Prophet."

41 Others were saying, "This is the Christ." Still others were saying, "[a]Surely the Christ is not going to come from Galilee, is He?

42 "Has not the Scripture said that the Christ comes from [a]the offspring of David, and from Bethlehem, the village where David was?"

43 So [a]there arose a division in the multitude because of Him.

44 And [a]some of them wanted to seize Him, but no one laid hands on Him.

45 The [a]officers therefore came to the chief priests and Pharisees, and they said to them, "Why did you not bring Him?"

46 The [a]officers answered, "[b]Never did a man speak the way this man speaks."

47 The Pharisees therefore answered them, "[a]You have not also been led astray, have you?

48 "[a]No one of [b]the rulers or Pharisees has believed in Him, has he?

49 "But this multitude which does not know the Law is accursed."

50 [a]Nicodemus *said to them (he who came to Him before, being one of them),

51 "[a]Our Law does not judge a man, unless it first hears from him and knows what he is doing, does it?"

52 They answered and said to him, "[a]You are not also from Galilee, are you? Search, and see that no prophet arises out of Galilee."

53 [And everyone went to his home.

5　Debate #3—the discourses, 8:1-58

8 But Jesus went to [a]the Mount of Olives.

2 And early in the morning He came again into the temple, and all the people were coming to Him; and [a]He sat down and *began* to teach them.

3 And the scribes and the Pharisees *brought a woman caught in adultery, and having set her in the midst,

4 they *said to Him, "Teacher, this woman has been caught in adultery, in the very act.

5 "Now in the Law [a]Moses commanded us to stone such women; what then do You say?"

6 And they were saying this, [a]testing Him, [b]in order that they might have grounds for accusing

Side references (left column):
- **★38** [a]Is. 44:3; 55:1; 58:11 [b]John 4:10
- **★39** [a]Joel 2:28; John 1:33 [b]John 20:22; Acts 1:4f.; 2:4, 33; 19:2 [c]John 12:16, 23; 13:31; 16:14; 17:1
- **40** [a]Matt. 21:11; John 1:21
- **41** [a]John 1:46; 7:52
- **★42** [a]Ps. 89:4; Mic. 5:2; Matt. 1:1, 2:5f.; Luke 2:4ff.
- **★43** [a]John 9:16; 10:19
- **44** [a]John 7:30
- **45** [a]John 7:32
- **46** [a]John 7:32 [b]Matt. 7:28
- **47** [a]John 7:12
- **48** [a]John 12:42 [b]Luke 23:13; John 7:26

Side references (right column):
- **★49**
- **50** [a]John 3:1; 19:39
- **51** [a]Ex. 23:1; Deut. 17:6; 19:15; Prov. 18:13; Acts 23:3
- **52** [a]John 1:46; 7:41
- **★7:53-8:11**
- **1** [a]Matt. 21:1
- **2** [a]Matt. 26:55; John 8:20
- **★ 5** [a]Lev. 20:10; Deut. 22:22f.
- **6** [a]Matt. 16:1; 19:3; 22:18, 35; Mark 8:11; 10:2; 12:15; Luke 10:25; 11:16 [b]Mark 3:2

---

the Jews had a ceremony of carrying water from the Pool of Siloam and pouring it into a silver basin by the altar of burnt offering each day for the first seven days of the Feast of Tabernacles. On the eighth day this was not done, making Christ's offer of the water of eternal life from Himself even more startling.

7:38 *innermost being.* The O.T. reference is probably to Isa. 55:1.

7:39 *was not yet given.* Though the Spirit had been active in the world from the beginning (Gen. 1:2), the epoch of the Spirit, in which He would indwell God's people, empowering and energizing them, would not begin until the day of Pentecost (see 14:26; 15:26; 16:7).

7:42 *offspring of David.* See 2 Sam. 7:12. *Bethlehem.* See Mic. 5:2.

7:43 *So there arose a division.* John records three occasions of division regarding Christ: here concerning His person; in 9:16 concerning His power; and in 10:19 concerning His passion.

7:49 *this multitude.* I.e., the crowd, the *am haarez*, the people of the land, whom the Pharisees despised because they no longer observed the minutiae of the Jewish law.

7:53-8:11 This story, though probably authentic, is omitted in many manuscripts and may not have been originally a part of this Gospel.

8:5 See Lev. 20:10; Deut. 22:22-24.

Him. But Jesus stooped down, and with His finger wrote on the ground.

7 aJohn
8:10 bMatt.
7:1; Rom. 2:1
cDeut. 17:7

7   But when they persisted in asking Him, aHe straightened up, and said to them, "bHe who is without sin among you, let him be the cfirst to throw a stone at her."

8   And again He stooped down, and wrote on the ground.

9   And when they heard it, they began to go out one by one, beginning with the older ones, and He was left alone, and the woman, where she had been, in the midst.

10 aJohn 8:7

10   And astraightening up, Jesus said to her, "Woman, where are they? Did no one condemn you?"

11 aJohn
3:17 bJohn
5:14

11   And she said, "No one, Lord." And Jesus said, "aNeither do I condemn you; go your way. From now on bsin no more."]

★12 aJohn
1:4; 12:35
bMatt. 5:14

12   Again therefore Jesus spoke to them, saying, "aI am the light of the world; bhe who follows Me shall not walk in the darkness, but shall have the light of life."

13 aJohn
5:31

13   The Pharisees therefore said to Him, "aYou are bearing witness of Yourself; Your witness is not true."

★14 aJohn
18:37; Rev.
1:5; 3:14
bJohn 8:42;
13:3; 16:28
cJohn 7:28;
9:29

14   Jesus answered and said to them, "aEven if I bear witness of Myself, My witness is true; for I know bwhere I came from, and where I am going; but cyou do not know where I come from, or where I am going.

15 a1 Sam.
16:7; John
7:24 bJohn
3:17

15   "aYou people judge according to the flesh; bI am not judging anyone.

16 aJohn
5:30

16   "But even aif I do judge, My judgment is true; for I am not alone in it, but I and He who sent Me.

17 aDeut.
17:6; 19:15
bMatt. 18:16

17   "Even in ayour law it has been written, that the testimony of btwo men is true.

18 aJohn
5:37; 1 John
5:9

18   "I am He who bears witness of Myself, and athe Father who sent Me bears witness of Me."

19 aJohn
7:28; 8:55;
14:7, 9; 16:3

19   And so they were saying to Him, "Where is Your Father?" Jesus answered, "You know neither Me, nor My Father; aif you knew Me, you would know My Father also."

20 aMark
12:41, 43;
Luke 21:1
bJohn 7:14;
8:2 cJohn
7:30

20   These words He spoke in athe treasury, as bHe taught in the temple; and no one seized Him, because cHis hour had not yet come.

21 aJohn
7:34 bJohn
8:24

21   He said therefore again to them, "I go away, and ayou shall seek Me, and bshall die in your sin; where I am going, you cannot come."

22 aJohn
1:19; 8:48,
52, 57 bJohn
7:35

22   Therefore athe Jews were saying, "Surely He will not kill Himself, will He, since He says, 'bWhere I am going, you cannot come'?"

23 aJohn
3:31 b1 John
4:5 cJohn
17:14, 16

23   And He was saying to them, "aYou are from below, I am from above; byou are of this world, cI am not of this world.

★24 aJohn
8:21 bMark
13:6; Luke
21:8 [Matt.
24:5]; John
4:26; 8:28;
13:19

24   "I said therefore to you, that you ashall die in your sins; for unless you believe that bI am He, ayou shall die in your sins."

25   And so they were saying to Him, "Who are You?" Jesus said to them, "What have I been saying to you from the beginning?

26 aJohn
3:33; 7:28
bJohn 8:40;
12:49; 15:15

26   "I have many things to speak and to judge concerning you, but aHe who sent Me is true; and bthe things which I heard from Him, these I speak to the world."

27   They did not realize that He had been speaking to them about the Father.

28 aJohn
3:14; 12:32
bMark 13:6;
Luke 21:8
[Matt. 24:5];
John 4:26;
8:24; 13:19
cJohn 3:11;
5:19

28   Jesus therefore said, "When you alift up the Son of Man, then you will know that bI am He, and cI do nothing on My

---

8:12 I am the light of the world. Our Lord here draws an analogy between the sun as the physical light of the world and Himself as the spiritual light of the world (see 9:4–5; 11:9–10). This theme also permeates chapter 9.

8:14 Even if. Even, Christ says, if I am testify-

ing about Myself, My testimony is to be believed and trusted. Furthermore, My testimony is attested to by the Father (v. 18).

8:24 This remark doubtlessly infuriated the Jewish authorities, since it ranked them with sinners.

own initiative, but I speak these things as the Father taught Me.

29 "And He who sent Me is with Me; ^aHe has not left Me alone, for ^bI always do the things that are pleasing to Him."

30 As He spoke these things, ^amany came to believe in Him.

31 Jesus therefore was saying to those Jews who had believed Him, "^aIf you abide in My word, *then* you are truly ^bdisciples of Mine;

32 and ^ayou shall know the truth, and ^bthe truth shall make you free."

33 They answered Him, "^aWe are Abraham's offspring, and have never yet been enslaved to anyone; how is it that You say, 'You shall become free'?"

34 Jesus answered them, "Truly, truly, I say to you, ^aeveryone who commits sin is the slave of sin.

35 "And ^athe slave does not remain in the house forever; ^bthe son does remain forever.

36 "If therefore the Son ^ashall make you free, you shall be free indeed.

37 "I know that you are ^aAbraham's offspring; yet ^byou seek to kill Me, because My word has no place in you.

38 "I speak the things which I have seen with *My* Father; therefore you also do the things which you heard from ^ayour father."

39 They answered and said to Him, "Abraham is ^aour father." Jesus *said to them, "^bIf you are Abraham's children, do the deeds of Abraham.

40 "But as it is, ^ayou are seeking to kill Me, a man who has ^btold you the truth, which I heard

from God; this Abraham did not do.

41 "You are doing the deeds of ^ayour father." They said to Him, "We were not born of fornication; ^bwe have one Father, *even* God."

42 Jesus said to them, "If God were your Father, ^ayou would love Me; ^bfor I proceeded forth and have come from God, for I have ^cnot even come on My own initiative, but ^dHe sent Me.

43 "Why do you not understand ^awhat I am saying? *It is* because you cannot ^bhear My word.

44 "^aYou are of ^byour father the devil, and ^cyou want to do the desires of your father. ^dHe was a murderer from the beginning, and does not stand in the truth, because ^ethere is no truth in him. Whenever he speaks a lie, he ^fspeaks from his own *nature;* for he is a liar, and the father of lies.

45 "But because ^aI speak the truth, you do not believe Me.

46 "Which one of you convicts Me of sin? If ^aI speak truth, why do you not believe Me?

47 "^aHe who is of God hears the words of God; for this reason you do not hear *them,* because you are not of God."

48 ^aThe Jews answered and said to Him, "Do we not say rightly that You are a ^bSamaritan and ^chave a demon?"

49 Jesus answered, "I do not ^ahave a demon; but I honor My Father, and you dishonor Me.

50 "But ^aI do not seek My glory; there is One who seeks and judges.

51 "Truly, truly, I say to you, if anyone ^akeeps My word he shall never ^bsee death."

29 ^aJohn 8:16; 16:32 ^bJohn 4:34

30 ^aJohn 7:31

31 ^aJohn 15:7; 2 John 9 ^bJohn 2:2

★32 ^aJohn 1:14, 17 ^bJohn 8:36; Rom. 8:2; 2 Cor. 3:17; Gal. 5:1, 13; James 2:12; 1 Pet. 2:16 **33** ^aMatt. 3:9; John 8:37, 39

34 ^aRom. 6:16; 2 Pet. 2:19

35 ^aGen. 21:10; Gal. 4:30 ^bLuke 15:31

36 ^aJohn 8:32

37 ^aMatt. 3:9; John 8:39 ^bJohn 7:1; 8:40

38 ^aJohn 8:41, 44

★39 ^aMatt. 3:9; John 8:37 ^bRom. 9:7; Gal. 3:7

40 ^aJohn 7:1; 8:37 ^bJohn 8:26

41 ^aJohn 8:38, 44 ^bDeut. 32:6; Is. 63:16; 64:8

42 ^a1 John 5:1 ^bJohn 13:3; 16:28, 30; 17:8 ^cJohn 7:28 ^dJohn 3:17

★43 ^aJohn 8:33, 39, 41 ^bJohn 5:25

★44 ^a1 John 3:8 ^bJohn 8:38, 41 ^cJohn 7:17 ^dGen. 3:4; 1 John 3:8, 15 ^e1 John 2:4 ^fMatt. 12:34

45 ^aJohn 18:37

46 ^aJohn 18:37

47 ^a1 John 4:6

48 ^aJohn 1:19 ^bMatt. 10:5; John 4:9 ^cJohn 7:20

49 ^aJohn 7:20

50 ^aJohn 5:41; 8:54

★51 ^aJohn 8:55; 14:23; 15:20; 17:6 ^bMatt. 16:28; Luke 2:26; John 8:52; Heb. 2:9; 11:5

8:32 *the truth.* I.e., of the divine revelation, not some current Gnostic truth about the cosmos, the soul, its relation to the body, etc.

8:39 *If you are Abraham's children.* The Jews were the natural descendants of Abraham (vv. 33, 37) but, because of their unbelief, not all were spiritual descendants. The father of all unbelievers is the devil (v. 44; see also Eph. 2:2–3; 1 John 3:8–10).

8:43 *cannot hear.* I.e., do not wish to, cannot bear to, accept His teaching. It is not a matter of intellectual capacity but of inner response.

8:44 The true reason for their failure to receive Christ was their relationship to the devil. Notice a similar harsh condemnation in Matt. 23:15.

8:51 *he shall never see death.* The believer shall not see spiritual death (separation from God), because through faith he possesses spiritual life (5:24). It may also have the meaning that he shall not see death forever; that is, though the believer dies physically, this death is only temporary, being eventually overcome by the resurrection of the body.

52 a John 1:19 b John 7:20 c John 8:55; 14:23; 15:20; 17:6 d John 8:51

52 ^aThe Jews said to Him, "Now we know that You ^bhave a demon. Abraham died, and the prophets *also*; and You say, 'If anyone ^ckeeps My word, he shall never ^dtaste of death.'

53 a John 4:12

53 "Surely You ^aare not greater than our father Abraham, who died? The prophets died too; whom do You make Yourself out to be?"

54 a John 8:50 b John 7:39

54 Jesus answered, "^aIf I glorify Myself, My glory is nothing; ^bit is My Father who glorifies Me, of whom you say, 'He is our God';

55 a John 8:19; 15:21 b John 7:29 c John 8:44 d John 8:51; 15:10

55 and ^ayou have not come to know Him, ^bbut I know Him; and if I say that I do not know Him, I shall be ^ca liar like you, ^bbut I do know Him, and ^dkeep His word.

56 a John 8:37, 39 b Matt. 13:17; Heb. 11:13

56 "^aYour father Abraham ^brejoiced to see My day, and he saw *it* and was glad."

57 a John 1:19

57 ^aThe Jews therefore said to Him, "You are not yet fifty years old, and have You seen Abraham?"

★**58** a John 1:1; 17:5, 24

58 Jesus said to them, "Truly, truly, I say to you, before Abraham was born, ^aI am."

6   The reaction, 8:59

59 a Matt. 12:14; John 10:31; 11:8 b John 12:36

59 Therefore they ^apicked up stones to throw at Him; but Jesus ^bhid Himself, and went out of the temple.

7   Debate #4—the miraculous sign, 9:1-12

★ **2** a Matt. 23:7 b Luke 13:2; John 9:34; Acts 28:4 c Ex. 20:5

3 a John 11:4

9 And as He passed by, He saw a man blind from birth.

2 And His disciples asked Him, saying, "^aRabbi, who sinned, ^bthis man or his ^cparents, that he should be born blind?"

3 Jesus answered, "It was

neither *that* this man sinned, nor his parents; but *it was* in order ^athat the works of God might be displayed in him.

4 a John 7:33; 11:9; 12:35; Gal. 6:10

4 "We must work the works of Him who sent Me, ^aas long as it is day; night is coming, when no man can work.

5 a John 1:4; 8:12; 12:46

5 "While I am in the world, I am ^athe light of the world."

6 a Mark 7:33; 8:23

6 When He had said this, He ^aspat on the ground, and made clay of the spittle, and applied the clay to his eyes,

★ **7** a Luke 13:4; John 9:11 b John 11:37

7 and said to him, "Go, wash in ^athe pool of Siloam" (which is translated, Sent). And so he went away and washed, and ^bcame back seeing.

8 a Acts 3:2, 10

8 The neighbors therefore, and those who previously saw him as a beggar, were saying, "Is not this the one who used to ^asit and beg?"

9 Others were saying, "This is he," *still* others were saying, "No, but he is like him." He kept saying, "I am the one."

10 Therefore they were saying to him, "How then were your eyes opened?"

11 a John 9:7

11 He answered, "The man who is called Jesus made clay, and anointed my eyes, and said to me, 'Go to ^aSiloam, and wash'; so I went away and washed, and I received sight."

12 And they said to him, "Where is He?" He *said, "I do not know."

8   The reactions, 9:13-41

13 They *brought to the Pharisees him who was formerly blind.

14 a John 5:9

14 ^aNow it was a Sabbath on the day when Jesus made the clay, and opened his eyes.

8:58 *before Abraham was born, I am.* The "I AM" denotes absolute eternal existence, not simply existence prior to Abraham. It is a claim to be Yahweh of the O.T. That the Jews understood the significance of this claim is clear from their reaction (v. 59) to the supposed blasphemy.
9:2 Sickness and suffering were commonly held to be the consequences of one's sin. The reli-

gious problem became troublesome, however, when the victim was *born* with a handicap such as blindness. Jesus first corrected this false idea and then focused on the purpose of this particular suffering, which provided an occasion for revealing God's glory.
9:7 *pool of Siloam.* This lay at the southern extremity of the Tyropoeon Valley, at the southern end of Hezekiah's tunnel.

15 aJohn 9:10

15 ^aAgain, therefore, the Pharisees also were asking him how he received his sight. And he said to them, "He applied clay to my eyes, and I washed, and I see."

★16 aMatt. 12:2 bJohn 2:11 cJohn 6:52; 7:43; 10:19

16 Therefore some of the Pharisees were saying, "^aThis man is not from God, because He does not keep the Sabbath." But others were saying, "How can a man who is a sinner perform such ^bsigns?" And ^cthere was a division among them.

17 aJohn 9:15 bMatt. 21:11

17 They *said therefore to the blind man ^aagain, "What do you say about Him, since He opened your eyes?" And he said, "He is a ^bprophet."

18 aJohn 1:19; 9:22

18 ^aThe Jews therefore did not believe *it* of him, that he had been blind, and had received sight, until they called the parents of the very one who had received his sight,

19 and questioned them, saying, "Is this your son, who you say was born blind? Then how does he now see?"

20 His parents answered them and said, "We know that this is our son, and that he was born blind;

21 but how he now sees, we do not know; or who opened his eyes, we do not know. Ask him; he is of age, he shall speak for himself."

★22 aJohn 7:13 bJohn 7:45-52 cLuke 6:22; John 12:42; 16:2

22 His parents said this because they ^awere afraid of the Jews; for the Jews ^bhad already agreed, that if anyone should confess Him to be Christ, ^che should be put out of the synagogue.

23 aJohn 9:21

23 For this reason his parents said, "^aHe is of age; ask him."

24 aJosh. 7:19; Ezra 10:11; Rev. 11:13 bJohn 9:16

24 So a second time they called the man who had been blind, and said to him, "^aGive glory to God; we know that ^bthis man is a sinner."

25 He therefore answered, "Whether He is a sinner, I do not know; one thing I do know, that, whereas I was blind, now I see."

26 They said therefore to him, "What did He do to you? How did He open your eyes?"

27 aJohn 9:15 bJohn 5:25

27 He answered them, "^aI told you already, and you did not ^blisten; why do you want to hear *it* again? You do not want to become His disciples too, do you?"

28 aJohn 5:45; Rom. 2:17

28 And they reviled him, and said, "You are His disciple, but ^awe are disciples of Moses.

★29 aJohn 8:14

29 "We know that God has spoken to Moses; but as for this man, ^awe do not know where He is from."

30 The man answered and said to them, "Well, here is an amazing thing, that you do not know where He is from, and *yet* He opened my eyes.

31 aJob 27:8f.; 35:13; Ps. 34:15f.; 66:18; 145:19; Prov. 15:29; 28:9; Is. 1:15; James 5:16ff.

31 "We know that ^aGod does not hear sinners; but if anyone is God-fearing, and does His will, He hears him.

32 "Since the beginning of time it has never been heard that anyone opened the eyes of a person born blind.

33 aJohn 3:2; 9:16

33 "^aIf this man were not from God, He could do nothing."

★34 aJohn 9:2 bJohn 9:22, 35; 3 John 10

34 They answered and said to him, "^aYou were born entirely in sins, and are you teaching us?" And they ^bput him out.

35 aJohn 9:22, 34; 3; John 10 bMatt. 4:3

35 Jesus heard that they had ^aput him out; and finding him, He said, "Do you believe in the ^bSon of Man?"

36 aRom. 10:14

36 He answered and said, "And ^awho is He, Lord, that I may believe in Him?"

37 aJohn 4:26

37 Jesus said to him, "You have both seen Him, and ^aHe is the one who is talking with you."

38 aMatt. 8:2

38 And he said, "Lord, I believe." And he ^aworshiped Him.

9:16 *He does not keep the Sabbath.* The Pharisees considered the making of clay (v. 14) a work that violated the Sabbath (see 5:10).

9:22 *be put out of the synagogue.* I.e., excommunicated from worship and fellowship.

9:29 A typical statement of Pharisaic orthodoxy. But the man refused to be coerced away from the plain fact that he had been cured (vv. 25, 30).

9:34 Their hostility now bordered on fanaticism.

★39 aJohn
3:19; 5:22,
27 bLuke
4:18 cMatt.
13:13; 15:14

39 And Jesus said, "aFor judgment I came into this world, that bthose who do not see may see; and that cthose who see may become blind."

40 aRom.
2:19

40 Those of the Pharisees who were with Him heard these things, and said to Him, "aWe are not blind too, are we?"

★41 aJohn
15:22, 24
bProv. 26:12

41 Jesus said to them, "aIf you were blind, you would have no sin; but since you say, 'bWe see,' your sin remains.

9   Debate #5—the discourse on the Good Shepherd, 10:1-18

1 aJohn
10:8

10 "Truly, truly, I say to you, he who does not enter by the door into the fold of the sheep, but climbs up some other way, he is aa thief and a robber.

2 aJohn
10:11f.

2 "But he who enters by the door is aa shepherd of the sheep.

3 aJohn
10:4f., 16, 27
bJohn 10:9

3 "To him the doorkeeper opens, and the sheep hear ahis voice, and he calls his own sheep by name, and bleads them out.

4 aJohn
10:5, 16, 27

4 "When he puts forth all his own, he goes before them, and the sheep follow him because they know ahis voice.

5 aJohn
10:4f., 16, 27

5 "And a stranger they simply will not follow, but will flee from him, because they do not know athe voice of strangers."

6 aJohn
16:25, 29;
2 Pet. 2:22

6 This afigure of speech Jesus spoke to them, but they did not understand what those things were which He had been saying to them.

7 aJohn
10:1f., 9

7 Jesus therefore said to them again, "Truly, truly, I say to you, I am athe door of the sheep.

★ 8 aJer.
23:1f.; Ezek.
34:2ff.; John
10:1
9 aJohn
10:1f., 9

8 "All who came before Me are athieves and robbers, but the sheep did not hear them.

9 "aI am the door; if anyone enters through Me, he shall be saved, and shall go in and out, and find pasture.

10 aJohn
5:40

10 "The thief comes only to steal, and kill, and destroy; I came that they amight have life, and might have it abundantly.

★11 aIs.
40:11; Ezek.
34:11-16, 23;
John 10:14;
Heb. 13:20;
1 Pet. 5:4;
Rev. 7:17
bJohn 10:15,
17, 18;
15:13;
1 John 3:16
12 aJohn
10:2

11 "aI am the good shepherd; the good shepherd blays down His life for the sheep.

12 "He who is a hireling, and not a ashepherd, who is not the owner of the sheep, beholds the wolf coming, and leaves the sheep, and flees, and the wolf snatches them, and scatters them.

13 "He flees because he is a hireling, and is not concerned about the sheep.

14 aJohn
10:11 bJohn
10:27

14 "aI am the good shepherd; and bI know My own, and My own know Me,

15 aMatt.
11:27 bJohn
10:11, 17, 18

15 even as athe Father knows Me and I know the Father; and bI lay down My life for the sheep.

★16 aIs.
56:8 bJohn
11:52;
17:20f.; Eph.
2:13-18;
1 Pet. 2:25
cEzek.
34:23, 37:24

16 "And I have aother sheep, which are not of this fold; I must bring them also, and they shall hear My voice; and they shall become bone flock with cone shepherd.

17 aJohn
10:11, 15, 18

17 "For this reason the Father loves Me, because I alay down My life that I may take it again.

18 aMatt.
26:53; John
2:19; 5:26
bJohn 10:11,
15, 17 cJohn
14:31; 15:10;
Phil. 2:8;
Heb. 5:8

18 "aNo one has taken it away from Me, but I blay it down on My own initiative. I have authority to lay it down, and I have authority to take it up again. cThis commandment I received from My Father."

10   The reactions, 10:19-21

19 aJohn
7:43, 9:16
20 aJohn
7:20 bMark
3:21

19 aThere arose a division again among the Jews because of these words.

20 And many of them were

9:39 *For judgment I came into this world.* Jesus' coming was not for the purpose of judgment (3:17), but it inevitably resulted in judgment, because some decided against Him. Compare Mark 4:12 and Isa. 6:9.
9:41 The Pharisees' insistence that they could see made their sin willful.
10:8 *thieves and robbers.* I.e., false Messiahs, false teachers, of whom Palestine knew many in the first century A.D.

10:11 *I am the good shepherd.* As Good Shepherd, Christ gave His life for His sheep and became the door to God's fold (v. 7); as the Great Shepherd (Heb. 13:20-21), He rose from the dead to care for His sheep; as Chief Shepherd (1 Pet. 5:4) He will come again for His sheep.
10:16 *I have other sheep.* These are the Gentiles who would believe and, with converted Jews, form one spiritual body (Eph. 2:16).

saying, "He ^ahas a demon and ^bis insane. Why do you listen to Him?"

21 Others were saying, "These are not the sayings of one ^ademon-possessed. ^bA demon cannot open the eyes of the blind, can he?"

D At the Feast of Dedication in Jerusalem, 10:22-42

1 The discourse, 10:22-30

22 At that time the Feast of the Dedication took place at Jerusalem;

23 it was winter, and Jesus was walking in the temple in the portico of ^aSolomon.

24 ^aThe Jews therefore gathered around Him, and were saying to Him, "How long will You keep us in suspense? If You are the Christ, tell us ^bplainly."

25 Jesus answered them, "^aI told you, and you do not believe; ^bthe works that I do in My Father's name, these bear witness of Me.

26 "But you do not believe, because ^ayou are not of My sheep.

27 "My sheep ^ahear My voice, and ^bI know them, and they follow Me;

28 and I give ^aeternal life to them, and they shall never perish; and ^bno one shall snatch them out of My hand.

29 "My Father, who has given *them* to Me, is greater than all; and no one is able to snatch *them* out of the Father's hand.

30 "^aI and the Father are one."

2 The rejection, 10:31-42

31 The Jews ^atook up stones again to stone Him.

32 Jesus answered them, "I showed you many good works from the Father; for which of them are you stoning Me?"

33 The Jews answered Him, "For a good work we do not stone You, but for ^ablasphemy; and because You, being a man, ^bmake Yourself out *to be* God."

34 Jesus answered them, "Has it not been written in ^ayour ^bLaw, 'I SAID, ^cYOU ARE GODS'?

35 "If he called them gods, to whom the word of God came (and the Scripture cannot be broken),

36 do you say of Him, whom the Father ^asanctified and ^bsent into the world, 'You are blaspheming,' because I said, '^cI am the Son of God'?

37 "^aIf I do not do the works of My Father, do not believe Me;

38 but if I do them, though you do not believe Me, believe ^athe works, that you may know and understand that ^bthe Father is in Me, and I in the Father."

39 Therefore ^athey were seeking again to seize Him, and ^bHe eluded their grasp.

40 And He went away ^aagain beyond the Jordan to the place where John was first baptizing, and He was staying there.

41 And many came to Him and were saying, "While John

Marginal references (left column):

21 ^aMatt. 4:24 ^bEx. 4:11; John 9:32f.

★22

23 ^aActs 3:11; 5:12

24 ^aJohn 1:19; 10:31, 33 ^bLuke 22:67; John 16:25

25 ^aJohn 8:56, 58 ^bJohn 5:36; 10:38

26 ^aJohn 8:47

27 ^aJohn 10:4, 16 ^bJohn 10:14

28 ^aJohn 17:2f.; 1 John 2:25; 5:11 ^bJohn 6:37, 39

Marginal references (right column):

★30 ^aJohn 17:21ff.

31 ^aJohn 8:59

★33 ^aLev. 24:16 ^bJohn 5:18

★34 ^aJohn 8:17 ^bJohn 12:34; 15:25; Rom. 3:19; 1 Cor. 14:21 ^cPs. 82:6

★35

36 ^aJer. 1:5; John 6:69 ^bJohn 3:17 ^cJohn 5:17f.; 10:30

37 ^aJohn 10:25; 15:24

★38 ^aJohn 10:25; 14:11 ^bJohn 14:10f., 20; 17:21, 23

★39 ^aJohn 7:30 ^bLuke 4:30; John 8:59

40 ^aJohn 1:28

41 ^aJohn 2:11 ^bJohn 1:27, 30, 34; 3:27-30

10:22 *the Feast of the Dedication.* This was instituted in 165 B.C. by Judas Maccabeus in commemoration of the cleansing and reopening of the temple after its desecration by the Syrian ruler Antiochus Epiphanes in 168 B.C. (Dan. 11:31; 1 Macc. 4:52-59). It is also called the Feast of Lights or Hanukkah. The date falls near the winter solstice, Dec. 22.

10:30 *one.* The Father and Son are in perfect unity in their natures and actions, but the neuter form of "one" rules out the meaning that they are one person.

10:33 *blasphemy.* See note on Mark 14:64.

10:34 *written in your Law.* I.e., in Ps. 82:6. The term "law" was sometimes applied to the entire O.T. Christ's point is that if the O.T. uses the word "God" (Elohim) of men who were representative of God, then the Jews should not oppose Him for calling Himself the Son of God.

10:35 *the Scripture cannot be broken.* I.e., deprived of its binding authority. Jesus here employs rather technical exegesis of the O.T.

10:38 *believe the works.* Even if the leaders could not test Jesus' verbal claims, they could see His works, and these miracles should have led them to acknowledge the truth of His claims.

10:39 *He eluded their grasp.* Apparently He moved without walking, another supernatural phenomenon.

performed no ªsign, yet ᵇeverything John said about this man was true."

42 And ªmany believed in Him there.

42 ªJohn 7:31

E   At Bethany, 11:1–12:11

1   The miraculous sign, 11:1–44

11 Now a certain man was sick, Lazarus of ªBethany, the village of Mary and her sister ᵇMartha.

2 And it was the Mary who ªanointed ᵇthe Lord with ointment, and wiped His feet with her hair, whose brother Lazarus was sick.

3 The sisters therefore sent to Him, saying, "ªLord, behold, ᵇhe whom You love is sick."

4 But when Jesus heard it, He said, "This sickness is not unto death, but for ªthe glory of God, that the Son of God may be glorified by it."

5 Now Jesus loved ªMartha, and her sister, and Lazarus.

6 When therefore He heard that he was sick, He stayed then two days longer in the place where He was.

7 Then after this He *said to the disciples, "ªLet us go to Judea again."

8 The disciples *said to Him, "ªRabbi, the Jews were just now seeking ᵇto stone You, and are You going there again?"

9 Jesus answered, "ªAre there not twelve hours in the day? If anyone walks in the day, he does not stumble, because he sees the light of this world.

10 "But if anyone walks in the night, he stumbles, because the light is not in him."

1 ªMatt. 21:17; John 11:18 ᵇLuke 10:38; John 11:5, 19ff.

★ 2 ªLuke 7:38; John 12:3 ᵇLuke 7:13; John 11:3, 21, 32; 13:13f.

3 ªLuke 7:13; John 11:2, 21, 32; 13:13f. ᵇJohn 11:5, 11, 36

★ 4 ªJohn 9:3; 10:38; 11:40

5 ªJohn 11:1

7 ªJohn 10:40

★ 8–10

8 ªMatt. 23:7 ᵇJohn 8:59; 10:31

9 ªLuke 13:33; John 9:4; 12:35

11 This He said, and after that He *said to them, "Our ªfriend Lazarus ᵇhas fallen asleep; but I go, that I may awaken him out of sleep."

12 The disciples therefore said to Him, "Lord, if he has fallen asleep, he will recover."

13 Now ªJesus had spoken of his death, but they thought that He was speaking of literal sleep.

14 Then Jesus therefore said to them plainly, "Lazarus is dead,

15 and I am glad for your sakes that I was not there, so that you may believe; but let us go to him."

16 ªThomas therefore, who is called ᵇDidymus, said to his fellow disciples, "Let us also go, that we may die with Him."

17 So when Jesus came, He found that he had already been in the tomb ªfour days.

18 Now ªBethany was near Jerusalem, about two miles off;

19 and many of ªthe Jews had come to ᵇMartha and Mary, ᶜto console them concerning their brother.

20 ªMartha therefore, when she heard that Jesus was coming, went to meet Him; but ªMary still sat in the house.

21 Martha therefore said to Jesus, "ªLord, ᵇif You had been here, my brother would not have died.

22 "Even now I know that ªwhatever You ask of God, God will give You."

23 Jesus *said to her, "Your brother shall rise again."

24 Martha *said to Him, "ªI know that he will rise again in the resurrection on the last day."

25 Jesus said to her, "ªI am the resurrection and the life; he

★11 ªJohn 11:3 ᵇMatt. 27:52; Mark 5:39; John 11:13; Acts 7:60

13 ªMatt. 9:24; Luke 8:52

★16 ªMatt. 10:3; Mark 3:18; Luke 6:15; John 14:5; 20:26-28; Acts 1:13 ᵇJohn 20:24; 21:2
17 ªJohn 11:39
18 ªJohn 11:1
19 ªJohn 1:19; 11:8 ᵇJohn 11:1 ᶜ1 Sam. 31:13; 1 Chr. 10:12; Job 2:11; John 11:31
20 ªLuke 10:38-42
21 ªJohn 11:2 ᵇJohn 11:32, 37

22 ªJohn 9:31; 11:41f.

24 ªDan. 12:2; John 5:28f.; Acts 24:15
★25–26
25 ªJohn 1:4; 5:26; 6:39f.; Rev. 1:18

11:2 Mary. See John 12:3; Matt. 26:7; Mark 14:3.

11:4 for the glory of God. The resurrection of Lazarus would demonstrate the glory of God even more than restoration from a sick bed.

11:8-10 Jesus states that He could safely go back to Judea, where an attempt had been made to stone Him (11:8), as long as He was walking in the light of His Father's will.

11:11 fallen asleep. Though the disciples understood this to mean natural sleep (v. 12), Jesus used it as a metaphor to denote death (Mark 5:39; cf. Acts 7:60; 1 Thess. 4:13).

11:16 Didymus = twin. Possibly Thomas was a twin of Matthew, with whose name his own is coupled in Matt. 10:3, Mark 3:18, and Luke 6:15.

11:25-26 he who believes in Me, even if he

who believes in Me shall live even if he dies,

26 and everyone who lives and believes in Me ^ashall never die. Do you believe this?"

27 She *said to Him, "Yes, Lord; I have believed that You are ^athe Christ, the Son of God, even ^bHe who comes into the world."

28 And when she had said this, she ^awent away, and called Mary her sister, saying secretly, "^bThe Teacher is here, and is calling for you."

29 And when she heard it, she *arose quickly, and was coming to Him.

30 Now Jesus had not yet come into the village, but ^awas still in the place where Martha met Him.

31 ^aThe Jews then who were with her in the house, and ^bconsoling her, when they saw that Mary rose up quickly and went out, followed her, supposing that she was going to the tomb to weep there.

32 Therefore, when Mary came where Jesus was, she saw Him, and fell at His feet, saying to Him, "^aLord, ^bif You had been here, my brother would not have died."

33 When Jesus therefore saw her weeping, and ^athe Jews who came with her, also weeping, He ^bwas deeply moved in spirit, and ^cwas troubled,

34 and said, "Where have you laid him?" They *said to Him, "Lord, come and see."

35 Jesus ^awept.

36 And so ^athe Jews were saying, "Behold how He ^bloved him!"

37 But some of them said, "Could not this man, who ^aopened the eyes of him who was blind, have kept this man also from dying?"

38 Jesus therefore again being deeply moved within, *came to

the tomb. Now it was a ^acave, and a stone was lying against it.

39 Jesus *said, "Remove the stone." Martha, the sister of the deceased, *said to Him, "Lord, by this time there will be a stench, for he *has been dead ^afour days."

40 Jesus *said to her, "^aDid I not say to you, if you believe, you will see the glory of God?"

41 And so they removed the ^astone. And Jesus ^braised His eyes, and said, "^cFather, I thank Thee that Thou heardest Me.

42 "And I knew that Thou hearest Me always; but ^abecause of the people standing around I said it, that they may believe that ^bThou didst send Me."

43 And when He had said these things, He cried out with a loud voice, "Lazarus, come forth."

44 He who had died came forth, ^abound hand and foot with wrappings; and ^bhis face was wrapped around with a cloth. Jesus *said to them, "Unbind him, and let him go."

2   The reactions, 11:45-57

45 ^aMany therefore of the Jews, ^bwho had come to Mary and ^cbeheld what He had done, believed in Him.

46 But some of them went away to the ^aPharisees, and told them the things which Jesus had done.

47 Therefore ^athe chief priests and the Pharisees ^bconvened a ^ccouncil, and were saying, "What are we doing? For this man is performing many ^dsigns.

48 "If we let Him go on like this, all men will believe in Him, and the Romans will come and take away both our ^aplace and our nation."

49 But a certain one of them, ^aCaiaphas, ^bwho was high priest

26 ^aJohn 6:47, 50, 51; 8:51

27 ^aMatt. 16:16; Luke 2:11 ^bJohn 6:14

28 ^aJohn 11:30 ^bMatt. 26:18; Mark 14:14; Luke 22:11; John 13:13

30 ^aJohn 11:20

31 ^aJohn 11:19, 33 ^bJohn 11:19

32 ^aJohn 11:2 ^bJohn 11:21

★**33** ^aJohn 11:19 ^bJohn 11:38 ^cJohn 12:27; 13:21

35 ^aLuke 19:41; John 11:33

36 ^aJohn 11:19 ^bJohn 11:3

37 ^aJohn 9:7

38 ^aMatt. 27:60; Mark 15:46; Luke 24:2; John 20:1

39 ^aJohn 11:17

40 ^aJohn 11:4, 23ff.

41 ^aMatt. 27:60; Mark 15:46; Luke 24:2; John 20:1 ^bJohn 17:1; Acts 7:55 ^cMatt. 11:25

42 ^aJohn 12:30; 17:21 ^bJohn 3:17

★**43**

44 ^aJohn 19:40 ^bJohn 20:7

45 ^aJohn 7:31 ^bJohn 11:19; 12:17f. ^cJohn 2:23

46 ^aJohn 7:32, 45; 11:57

47 ^aJohn 7:32, 45; 11:57 ^bMatt. 26:3 ^cMatt. 5:22 ^dJohn 2:11

★**48** ^aMatt. 24:15

49 ^aMatt. 26:3 ^bJohn 11:51; 18:13

---

dies physically shall live spiritually and eternally. *everyone who lives* physically *and believes in Me shall never die* spiritually and eternally.

11:33 *deeply moved.* Because of the sorrow

that sickness and death brought.

11:43 *Lazarus, come forth.* Only Jesus can call the dead to life (5:25); others could move the stone (11:39) and grave clothes (v. 44).

11:48 *our place.* I.e., the holy place, the temple.

that year, said to them, "You know nothing at all,

★50 nor do you take into account that it is expedient for you that one man should die for the people, and that the whole nation should not perish."

51 Now this he did not say on his own initiative; but being high priest that year, he prophesied that Jesus was going to die for the nation,

52 and not for the nation only, but that He might also gather together into one the children of God who are scattered abroad.

53 So from that day on they planned together to kill Him.

54 Jesus therefore no longer continued to walk publicly among the Jews, but went away from there to the country near the wilderness, into a city called Ephraim; and there He stayed with the disciples.

55 Now the Passover of the Jews was at hand, and many went up to Jerusalem out of the country before the Passover, to purify themselves.

56 Therefore they were seeking for Jesus, and were saying to one another, as they stood in the temple, "What do you think; that He will not come to the feast at all?"

57 Now the chief priests and the Pharisees had given orders that if anyone knew where He was, he should report it, that they might seize Him.

3 The anointing by Mary, 12:1-8

12 Jesus, therefore, six days before the Passover, came to Bethany where Lazarus was, whom Jesus had raised from the dead.

2 So they made Him a supper there, and Martha was serving; but Lazarus was one of those reclining at the table with Him.

3 Mary therefore took a pound of very costly perfume of pure nard, and anointed the feet of Jesus, and wiped His feet with her hair; and the house was filled with the fragrance of the perfume.

4 But Judas Iscariot, one of His disciples, who was intending to betray Him, *said,

5 "Why was this perfume not sold for three hundred denarii, and given to poor people?"

6 Now he said this, not because he was concerned about the poor, but because he was a thief, and as he had the money box, he used to pilfer what was put into it.

7 Jesus therefore said, "Let her alone, in order that she may keep it for the day of My burial.

8 "For the poor you always have with you, but you do not always have Me."

4 The reactions, 12:9-11

9 The great multitude therefore of the Jews learned that He was there; and they came, not for Jesus' sake only, but that they might also see Lazarus, whom He raised from the dead.

10 But the chief priests took counsel that they might put Lazarus to death also;

11 because on account of him many of the Jews were going away, and were believing in Jesus.

F At Jerusalem, 12:12-50

1 The triumphal entry, 12:12-19

12 On the next day the great multitude who had come to the

11:50 Caiaphas could hardly realize the full meaning of his own words (18:14). He was simply expressing the thought of a political collaborator with Rome; and yet those words express the central doctrine of the Christian faith, the substitutionary atonement of Christ.

11:56 stood in the temple, after undergoing the purification rites (v. 55).
12:5 three hundred denarii, approximately what a rural worker would earn in one year.
12:6 had the money box. Judas was evidently the treasurer of the group.

feast, when they heard that Jesus was coming to Jerusalem,

13 took the branches of the palm trees, and went out to meet Him, and *began* to cry out, "[a]Hosanna! BLESSED IS HE WHO COMES IN THE NAME OF THE LORD, even the [b]King of Israel."

14 And Jesus, finding a young donkey, sat on it; as it is written,

15 "[a]FEAR NOT, DAUGHTER OF ZION; BEHOLD, YOUR KING IS COMING, SEATED ON A DONKEY'S COLT."

16 [a]These things His disciples did not understand at the first; but when Jesus [b]was glorified, then they remembered that these things were written of Him, and that they had done these things to Him.

17 And so [a]the multitude who were with Him when He called Lazarus out of the tomb, and raised him from the dead, were bearing Him witness.

18 [a]For this cause also the multitude went and met Him, [b]because they heard that He had performed this sign.

19 The Pharisees therefore said to one another, "You see that you are not doing any good; look, the world has gone after Him."

2   The teaching, 12:20–50

20 Now there were certain [a]Greeks among those who were going up to worship at [b]the feast;

21 these therefore came to [a]Philip, who was from [b]Bethsaida of Galilee, and *began to* ask him, saying, "Sir, we wish to see Jesus."

22 Philip *came and *told [a]Andrew; Andrew and Philip *came, and they *told Jesus.

23 And Jesus *answered them, saying, "[a]The hour has come for the Son of Man to [b]be glorified.

24 "Truly, truly, I say to you, [a]unless a grain of wheat falls into the earth and dies, it remains by itself alone; but if it dies, it bears much fruit.

25 "[a]He who loves his life loses it; and he who [b]hates his life in this world shall keep it to life eternal.

26 "If anyone serves Me, let him follow Me; and [a]where I am, there shall My servant also be; if anyone serves Me, the Father will [b]honor him.

27 "[a]Now My soul has become troubled; and what shall I say, '[b]Father, save Me from [c]this hour'? But for this purpose I came to this hour.

28 "[a]Father, glorify Thy name." There came therefore a [b]voice out of heaven: "I have both glorified it, and will glorify it again."

29 The multitude therefore, who stood by and heard it, were saying that it had thundered; others were saying, "[a]An angel has spoken to Him."

30 Jesus answered and said, "[a]This voice has not come for My sake, but for your sakes.

31 "[a]Now judgment is upon this world; now [b]the ruler of this world shall be cast out.

32 "And I, if I [a]be lifted up from the earth, will [b]draw all men to Myself."

33 But He was saying this [a]to indicate the kind of death by which He was to die.

34 The multitude therefore answered Him, "We have heard out of [a]the Law that [b]the Christ is to remain forever; and how can

---

Margin references (left column):
- **13** [a]Ps. 118:25f. [b]John 1:49
- **15** [a]Zech. 9:9
- **★16** [a]Mark 9:32; John 2:22; 14:26 [b]John 7:39; 12:23
- **17** [a]John 11:42
- **18** [a]Luke 19:37; John 12:12 [b]John 12:11
- **20** [a]John 7:35 [b]John 12:1
- **21** [a]John 1:44 [b]Matt. 11:21
- **22** [a]John 1:44
- **★23** [a]Matt. 26:45; Mark 14:35, 41; John 13:1, 32; 17:1 [b]John 7:39; 12:16

Margin references (right column):
- **24** [a]Rom. 14:9; 1 Cor. 15:36
- **25** [a]Matt. 10:39 [b]Luke 14:26
- **26** [a]John 14:3; 17:24; 2 Cor. 5:8; Phil. 1:23; 1 Thess. 4:17 [b]1 Sam. 2:30; Ps. 91:15; Luke 12:37
- **27** [a]Matt. 26:38; Mark 14:34; John 11:33 [b]Matt. 11:25 [c]John 12:23
- **28** [a]Matt. 11:25 [b]Matt. 3:17; 17:5; Mark 1:11; 9:7; Luke 3:22; 9:35
- **29** [a]Acts 23:9
- **30** [a]John 11:42
- **★31** [a]John 3:19; 9:39; 16:11 [b]John 14:30; 16:11; 2 Cor. 4:4; Eph. 2:2; 6:12; 1 John 4:4; 5:19
- **★32** [a]John 3:14; 8:28; 12:34 [b]John 6:44
- **33** [a]John 18:32; 21:19
- **★34** [a]John 10:34 [b]Ps. 110:4; Is. 9:7; Ezek. 37:25; Dan. 7:14 [c]Matt. 8:20 [d]John 3:14; 8:28; 12:32

12:16 *that these things were written of Him.* I.e., in the Hebrew Scriptures, which Christ's followers searched carefully after His death.

12:23 *The hour has come.* The time had come for which He had been working throughout His ministry; namely, the time of His death and resurrection. This is the beginning of the climax of His ministry.

12:31 *judgment is upon this world.* The cross is the condemnation of, the judgment upon, those who reject it; it is also the basis for the ultimate victory over Satan.

12:32 *lifted up* on the cross. *will draw all men.* His saving grace will be available to Greeks (like those present, v. 20) as well as to Jews.

12:34 They could not conceive of the heavenly Son of Man being lifted up to die.

You say, 'The [c]Son of Man must be [d]lifted up'? Who is this [c]Son of Man?''

35 *a*John 7:33; 9:4; 1 John 2:10 *b*John 12:46 *c*Gal. 6:10; Eph. 5:8 *d*1 John 1:6; 2:11

35 Jesus therefore said to them, "[a]For a little while longer [b]the light is among you. [c]Walk while you have the light, that darkness may not overtake you; he who [d]walks in the darkness does not know where he goes.

36 *a*John 12:46 *b*Luke 16:8; John 8:12 *c*John 8:59

36 "While you have the light, [a]believe in the light, in order that you may become [b]sons of light."

These things Jesus spoke, and He departed and [c]hid Himself from them.

★37-50

37 But though He had performed so many signs before them, *yet* they were not believing in Him;

★38-41

38 *a*Is. 53:1; Rom. 10:16

38 that the word of Isaiah the prophet might be fulfilled, which he spoke, "[a]Lord, who has believed our report? And to whom has the arm of the Lord been revealed?''

39 For this cause they could not believe, for Isaiah said again,

40 *a*Is. 6:10; Matt. 13:14f. *b*Mark 6:52

40 "[a]He has blinded their eyes, and He [b]hardened their heart; lest they see with their eyes, and perceive with their heart, and be converted, and I heal them."

41 *a*Is. 6:1ff. *b*Luke 24:27

41 These things Isaiah said, because [a]he saw His glory, and [b]he spoke of Him.

42 *a*John 7:48; 12:11 *b*Luke 23:13 *c*John 7:13 *d*John 9:22

42 Nevertheless [a]many even of [b]the rulers believed in Him, but [c]because of the Pharisees they were not confessing *Him*, lest they should be [d]put out of the synagogue;

43 *a*John 5:41, 44

43 [a]for they loved the approval of men rather than the approval of God.

44 *a*Matt. 10:40; John 5:24

44 And Jesus cried out and said, "[a]He who believes in Me does not believe in Me, but in Him who sent Me.

45 *a*John 14:9

45 "And [a]he who beholds Me beholds the One who sent Me.

46 *a*John 1:4; 3:19; 8:12; 9:5; 12:35f.

46 "[a]I have come *as* light into the world, that everyone who believes in Me may not remain in darkness.

★47 *a*John 3:17; 8:15f.

47 "And if anyone hears My sayings, and does not keep them, I do not judge him; for [a]I did not come to judge the world, but to save the world.

48 *a*Luke 10:16 *b*Deut. 18:18f.; John 5:45ff.; 8:47 *c*Matt. 10:15

48 "[a]He who rejects Me, and does not receive My sayings, has one who judges him; [b]the word I spoke is what will judge him at [c]the last day.

49 *a*John 3:11 *b*John 14:31; 17:8

49 "[a]For I did not speak on My own initiative, but the Father Himself who sent Me [b]has given Me commandment, what to say, and what to speak.

50 *a*John 6:68 *b*John 8:28

50 "And I know that [a]His commandment is eternal life; therefore the things I speak, I speak [b]just as the Father has told Me."

IV INSTRUCTION BY THE SON OF GOD, 13:1-16:33

A Concerning Forgiveness, 13:1-20

★ 1 *a*John 2:13; 11:55 *b*John 12:23 *c*John 13:3; 16:28

13 Now before the Feast of [a]the Passover, Jesus knowing that [b]His hour had come that He should depart out of this world [c]to the Father, having loved His own who were in the world, He loved them to the end.

2 *a*John 6:70; 13:27 *b*John 6:71

2 And during supper, [a]the devil having already put into the heart of [b]Judas Iscariot, *the son* of Simon, to betray Him,

★ 3-11

3 *a*John 3:35 *b*John 8:42

3 *Jesus,* [a]knowing that the Father had given all things into His hands, and that [b]He had come forth from God, and was going back to God,

4 *a*Luke 12:37

4 *rose from supper, and *laid aside His garments; and taking a towel, He [a]girded Himself about.

5 *a*Luke 7:44

5 Then He *poured water into the basin, and began to

12:37-50 These verses summarize the public ministry of Jesus Christ, and explain the rejections which are equated with the rejection of God.
12:38-41 See Isa. 6:10; 53:1.

12:47 See note on 9:39.
13:1 *to the end.* Lit., to the fullest extent.
13:3-11 This dramatic scene of the foot-washing is an acted parable, a lesson in humility, and a vivid portrayal of Christ's self-humiliation.

ᵃwash the disciples' feet, and to wipe them with the towel with which He was girded.

6   And so He *came to Simon Peter. He *said to Him, "Lord, do You wash my feet?"

7   Jesus answered and said to him, "What I do you do not realize now, but you shall understand ᵃhereafter."

8   Peter *said to Him, "Never shall You wash my feet!" Jesus answered him, "If I do not wash you, ᵃyou have no part with Me."

9   Simon Peter *said to Him, "Lord, not my feet only, but also my hands and my head."

10   Jesus *said to him, "He who has bathed needs only to wash his feet, but is completely clean; and ᵃyou are clean, but not all of you."

11   For ᵃHe knew the one who was betraying Him; for this reason He said, "Not all of you are clean."

12   And so when He had washed their feet, and ᵃtaken His garments, and reclined at the table again, He said to them, "Do you know what I have done to you?

13   "You call Me ᵃTeacher and ᵇLord; and you are right, for so I am.

14   "If I then, ᵃthe Lord and the Teacher, washed your feet, you also ought to wash one another's feet.

15   "For I gave you ᵃan example that you also should do as I did to you.

16   "Truly, truly, I say to you, ᵃa slave is not greater than his master; neither is ᵇone who is sent greater than the one who sent him.

17   "If you know these things, you are ᵃblessed if you do them.

18   "ᵃI do not speak of all of you. I know the ones I have ᵇchosen; but it is ᶜthat the Scripture may be fulfilled, 'ᵈHE WHO EATS MY BREAD HAS LIFTED UP HIS HEEL AGAINST ME.'

19   "From now on ᵃI am telling you before it comes to pass, so that when it does occur, you may believe that ᵇI am He.

20   "Truly, truly, I say to you, ᵃhe who receives whomever I send receives Me; and he who receives Me receives Him who sent Me."

B   Concerning His Betrayal
13:21-30

21   When Jesus had said this, He ᵃbecame troubled in spirit, and testified, and said, "Truly, truly, I say to you, that ᵇone of you will betray Me."

22   The disciples began looking at one another, ᵃat a loss to know of which one He was speaking.

23   There was reclining on ᵃJesus' breast one of His disciples, ᵇwhom Jesus loved.

24   Simon Peter therefore *gestured to him, and *said to him, "Tell us who it is of whom He is speaking."

25   He, ᵃleaning back thus on Jesus' breast, *said to Him, "Lord, who is it?"

26   Jesus therefore *answered, "That is the one for whom I shall

---

Cross-references (margin):

7 ᵃJohn 13:12ff.

8 ᵃDeut. 12:12; 2 Sam. 20:1; 1 Kin. 12:16

★10 ᵃJohn 15:3

11 ᵃJohn 6:64; 13:2

12 ᵃJohn 13:4

13 ᵃJohn 11:28 ᵇJohn 11:2; 1 Cor. 12:3; Phil. 2:11

★14 ᵃJohn 11:2; 1 Cor. 12:3; Phil. 2:11

15 ᵃ1 Pet. 5:3

16 ᵃMatt. 10:24 ᵇ2 Cor. 8:23; Phil. 2:25

17 ᵃMatt. 7:24ff.; Luke 11:28; James 1:25
★18 ᵃJohn 13:10f. ᵇJohn 6:70; 15:16, 19 ᶜJohn 15:25; 17:12; 18:32; 19:24, 36; ᵈPs. 41:9; Matt. 26:21ff.; Mark 14:18f.; Luke 22:21ff.; John 13:18, 21, 22, 26
★19 ᵃJohn 14:29; 16:4 ᵇJohn 8:24
★20 ᵃMatt. 10:40; Luke 10:16; Gal. 4:14

21 ᵃJohn 11:33 ᵇMatt. 26:21f.; Mark 14:18ff.; Luke 22:21ff.; John 13:18, 21, 22, 26
22 ᵃMatt. 26:21ff.; Mark 14:18ff.; Luke 22:21ff.; John 13:18, 21, 22, 26
★23 ᵃJohn 1:18 ᵇJohn 19:26; 20:2; 21:7, 20

25 ᵃJohn 21:20

★26 ᵃJohn 6:71

13:10 *He who has bathed needs only to wash his feet.* Just as in the natural life a man who has bathed needs only to wash the dust off his sandaled feet when he returns home, so in the spiritual life a man who has been cleansed from sin need not think that all is lost when he sins in his walk through life. He need only confess these sins to be entirely clean again (1 John 1:9).

13:14 *you also ought to wash one another's feet.* Since the illustration has to do with forgiveness, this phrase means that believers ought to forgive one another (Matt. 5:23-24; Eph. 4:32).

13:18 *Scripture.* Ps. 41:9 is referred to.

13:19 *I am He.* I.e., the one to whom Ps. 41:9 refers.

13:20 Those who are sent are the apostles, as in v. 16.

13:23 *one of His disciples, whom Jesus loved.* I.e., John.

13:26 *the morsel.* At Eastern meals it was customary for the host to offer one of the guests a morsel of bread as a gesture of special friendship. By this Jesus was showing His love for the betrayer.

dip the morsel and give it to him." So when He had dipped the morsel, He *took and *gave it to Judas, *a the son* of Simon Iscariot.

27 And after the morsel, aSatan then bentered into him. Jesus therefore *said to him, "What you do, do quickly."

28 Now no one of those reclining *at the table* knew for what purpose He had said this to him.

29 For some were supposing, because Judas ahad the money box, that Jesus was saying to him, "Buy the things we have need of bfor the feast"; or else, that he should cgive something to the poor.

30 And so after receiving the morsel he went out immediately; and ait was night.

C   Concerning His Departure, 13:31-38

31 When therefore he had gone out, Jesus *said, "Now is athe Son of Man bglorified, and cGod is glorified in Him;

32 if God is glorified in Him, aGod will also glorify Him in Himself, and will glorify Him immediately.

33 "aLittle children, I am with you ba little while longer. cYou shall seek Me; and as I said to the Jews, I now say to you also, 'Where I am going, you cannot come.'

34 "A anew commandment I give to you, bthat you love one another, ceven as I have loved you, that you also love one another.

35 "aBy this all men will know that you are My disciples, if you have love for one another."

36 Simon Peter *said to Him, "Lord, where are You going?" Jesus answered, "aWhere I go, you cannot follow Me now; but byou shall follow later."

37 Peter *said to Him, "Lord, why can I not follow You right now? aI will lay down my life for You."

38 Jesus *answered, "Will you lay down your life for Me? Truly, truly, I say to you, aa cock shall not crow, until you deny Me three times.

D   Concerning Heaven, 14:1-14

14 "aLet not your heart be troubled; believe in God, believe also in Me.

2 "In My Father's house are many dwelling places; if it were not so, I would have told you; for aI go to prepare a place for you.

3 "And if I go and prepare a place for you, aI will come again, and receive you to Myself; that bwhere I am, *there* you may be also.

4 "And you know the way where I am going."

5 aThomas *said to Him, "Lord, we do not know where You are going, how do we know the way?"

6 Jesus *said to him, "I am athe way, and bthe truth, and cthe life; no one comes to the Father, but through Me.

7 "aIf you had known Me, you would have known My Father also; from now on you

---

13:30 *and it was night.* The "hour" for which Christ, the light of the world, had been waiting, when the powers of darkness would engulf Him, begins in darkness.

13:31-32 In His death Christ and the Father will be glorified (v. 31). In the resurrection and exaltation the Father will glorify Christ and validate all His claims (v. 32).

13:35 I.e., their mutual love would be the strongest possible argument for the Christian faith.

14:1 In view of His departure from them, Christ gave the disciples (in this chapter) specific encouragements. These include the provision in the Father's house (v. 2), the promise to return (v. 3), the prospect of doing greater works (v. 12), the promise of answered prayer (v. 14), the coming of the Holy Spirit (v. 16), and the legacy of peace (v. 27).

14:2 *dwelling places.* The same word is used elsewhere in the N.T. only in v. 23, where it is translated "abode."

14:3 *I will come again.* See 1 Thess. 4:13-18. This is not the coming of the Spirit nor the believer's death, but Christ's personal return.

bknow Him, and have cseen Him."

8 *a*John 1:43

8 *a*Philip *said to Him, "Lord, show us the Father, and it is enough for us."

★ 9 *a*John 1:14; 12:45; Col. 1:15; Heb. 1:3

9 Jesus *said to him, "Have I been so long with you, and yet you have not come to know Me, Philip? *a*He who has seen Me has seen the Father; how do you say, 'Show us the Father'?

10 *a*John 10:38; 14:11, 20 *b*John 5:19; 14:24

10 "Do you not believe that *a*I am in the Father, and the Father is in Me? *b*The words that I say to you I do not speak on My own initiative, but the Father abiding in Me does His works.

11 *a*John 10:38; 14:10, 20 *b*John 5:36

11 "Believe Me that *a*I am in the Father, and the Father in Me; otherwise *b*believe on account of the works themselves.

★12 *a*John 4:37f.; 5:20 *b*John 7:33; 14:28

12 "Truly, truly, I say to you, he who believes in Me, the works that I do shall he do also; and *a*greater *works* than these shall he do; because *b*I go to the Father.

★13 *a*Matt. 7:7 *b*John 13:31

13 "And *a*whatever you ask in My name, that will I do, that *b*the Father may be glorified in the Son.

14 *a*John 15:16; 16:23f.

14 "If you ask Me anything *a*in My name, I will do *it*.

15 *a*John 14:21, 23; 15:10; 1 John 5:3; 2 John 6

16 *a*John 7:39; 14:26; 15:26; 16:7; Rom. 8:26; 1 John 2:1 marg.

E   Concerning the Holy Spirit, 14:15-26

15 "*a*If you love Me, you will keep My commandments.

16 "And I will ask the Father,

and He will give you another *a*Helper, that He may be with you forever;

★17 *a*John 15:26; 16:13; 1 John 4:6; 5:7 *b*1 Cor. 2:14

17 *that is* *a*the Spirit of truth, *b*whom the world cannot receive, because it does not behold Him or know Him, *but* you know Him because He abides with you, and will be in you.

18 *a*John 14:3, 28

18 "I will not leave you as orphans; *a*I will come to you.

19 *a*John 7:33 *b*John 16:16, 22 *c*John 6:57

19 "*a*After a little while *b*the world will behold Me no more; but you *will* behold Me; *c*because I live, you shall live also.

20 *a*John 16:23, 26 *b*John 10:38; 14:11

20 "*a*In that day you shall know that *b*I am in My Father, and you in Me, and I in you.

★21 *a*John 14:15, 23; 15:10; 1 John 5:3; 2 John 6 *b*John 14:23; 16:27 *c*Ex. 33:18f.; Prov. 8:17

21 "*a*He who has My commandments and keeps them, he it is who loves Me; and *b*he who loves Me shall be loved by My Father, and I will love him, and will *c*disclose Myself to him."

22 *a*Matt. 10:3; Luke 6:16; Acts 1:13 *b*Acts 10:40, 41

22 *a*Judas (not Iscariot) *said to Him, "Lord, what then has happened *b*that You are going to disclose Yourself to us, and not to the world?"

23 *a*John 14:15, 21; 15:10; 1 John 5:3; 2 John 6 *b*John 8:51; 1 John 2:5 *c*John 14:21 *d*2 Cor. 6:16 for O.T.; Eph. 3:17; 1 John 2:24; Rev. 3:20; 21:3

23 Jesus answered and said to him, "*a*If anyone loves Me, he will *b*keep My word; and *c*My Father will love him, and We *d*will come to him, and make Our abode with him.

24 *a*John 14:23 *b*John 7:16; 14:10

24 "He who does not love Me *a*does not keep My words; and *b*the word which you hear is not Mine, but the Father's who sent Me.

14:9 *He who has seen Me has seen the Father.* See note on 1:18.

14:12 *greater works than these shall he do.* Greater in extent (through the worldwide preaching of the gospel) and effect (the spiritual redemption and placing in the body of Christ multitudes of people since the day of Pentecost). These will be done through prayer in His name (v. 13).

14:13 *in My name.* This is not a formula to be tacked on to the end of prayers, but means praying for the same things which Christ would desire to see accomplished. It is like using a power of attorney which a very dear loved one has given you.

14:16 *another Helper.* The Holy Spirit is called the Helper (Greek: *paraclete,* as also in 14:26; 15:26; 16:7). In the root of this word are the ideas of advising, exhorting, comforting,

strengthening, interceding, and encouraging. The only other occurrence of the word outside this discourse in the N.T. is in 1 John 2:1 applied to Christ and translated "Advocate." Here and in the other passages in John cited above, Christ teaches that the Holy Spirit (1) will indwell Christians (vv. 16-17); (2) will help the disciples recall the events of His life (14:26); (3) will convince the world of sin, righteousness and judgment (16:7-11); (4) will teach believers the truth (15:26; 16:13-15).

14:17 *He abides with you, and will be in you.* The Holy Spirit was active in O.T. times, but His dwelling in the lives of believers after Pentecost is different in that (1) it is permanent and (2) it is true of every individual believer.

14:21 The Christian faith works through love, and the measure of one's love is the extent to which one keeps Christ's commandments.

25 "These things I have spoken to you, while abiding with you.

26 "But the [a]Helper, the Holy Spirit, [b]whom the Father will send in My name, [c]He will teach you all things, and [d]bring to your remembrance all that I said to you.

F Concerning Peace, 14:27-31

27 "[a]Peace I leave with you; My peace I give to you; not as the world gives, do I give to you. [b]Let not your heart be troubled, nor let it be fearful.

28 "[a]You heard that I said to you, 'I go away, and [b]I will come to you.' If you loved Me, you would have rejoiced, because [c]I go to the Father; for [d]the Father is greater than I.

29 "And now [a]I have told you before it comes to pass, that when it comes to pass, you may believe.

30 "I will not speak much more with you, for [a]the ruler of the world is coming, and [b]he has nothing in Me;

31 but that the world may know that I love the Father, and as [a]the Father gave Me commandment, even so I do. Arise, [b]let us go from here.

G Concerning Fruitfulness, 15:1-17

15 "[a]I am the true vine, and My Father is the [b]vinedresser.

2 "Every branch in Me that does not bear fruit, He takes away; and every *branch* that bears fruit, He prunes it, that it may bear more fruit.

3 "[a]You are already clean because of the word which I have spoken to you.

4 "[a]Abide in Me, and I in you. As the branch cannot bear fruit of itself, unless it abides in the vine, so neither *can* you, unless you abide in Me.

5 "I am the vine, you are the branches; he who abides in Me, and I in him, he [a]bears much fruit; for apart from Me you can do nothing.

6 "If anyone does not abide in Me, he is [a]thrown away as a branch, and dries up; and they gather them, and cast them into the fire, and they are burned.

7 "If you abide in Me, and My words abide in you, [a]ask whatever you wish, and it shall be done for you.

8 "[a]By this is My Father glorified, that you bear much fruit, and so [b]prove to be My disciples.

9 "Just as [a]the Father has loved Me, I have also loved you; abide in My love.

10 "[a]If you keep My commandments, you will abide in My love; just as [b]I have kept My Father's commandments, and abide in His love.

11 "[a]These things I have spoken to you, that My joy may be in

---

Side references (left column):

26 [a]John 14:16 [b]Luke 24:49; John 1:33; 15:26; 16:7; Acts 2:33 [c]John 16:13f; 1 John 2:20, 27 [d]John 2:22

27 [a]John 16:33; 20:19; Phil. 4:7; Col. 3:15 [b]John 14:1

28 [a]John 14:2-4 [b]John 14:3, 18 [c]John 14:12 [d]John 10:29; Phil. 2:6

29 [a]John 13:19

★30 [a]John 12:31 [b]Heb. 4:15

31 [a]John 10:18; 12:49 [b]John 13:1; 18:1

★ 1 [a]Ps. 80:8ff.; Is. 5:1ff.; Ezek. 19:10ff.; Matt. 21:33ff. [b]Matt. 15:13; Rom. 11:17; 1 Cor. 3:9

Side references (right column):

★ 2

3 [a]John 13:10; 17:17; Eph. 5:26

★ 4 [a]John 6:56; 15:4-7; 1 John 2:6

5 [a]John 15:16

★ 6 [a]John 15:2

7 [a]Matt. 7:7; John 15:16

★ 8 [a]Matt. 5:16 [b]John 8:31

9 [a]John 3:35; 17:23, 24, 26

10 [a]John 14:15 [b]John 8:29

11 [a]John 17:13 [b]John 3:29

14:30 *and he has nothing in Me.* Satan (*the ruler of the world*) possesses nothing in the person of Christ and has no power over Him whatsoever. This is another evidence of Christ's sinlessness.

15:1 Chapters 15 and 16 contain the second Farewell Discourse. In 15 are the themes of fruit-bearing and the hatred of the world for Christ's disciples. The theme of persecution is continued in chapter 16 along with teaching concerning the ministry of the Holy Spirit.

15:2 *takes away.* The word may mean this literally (as "Remove" in 11:39) and would therefore be a reference to the physical death of fruitless Christians (1 Cor. 11:30); or it may mean lift up (as "picked up" in 8:59) which would indicate that the vinedresser encour-

ages and makes it easier for the fruitless believer, hoping he will respond and begin to bear fruit. *prunes.* This is done through the Word of God, which cleans the life (same root word as *clean* in v. 3).

15:4 *Abide in Me.* John explains what this means when he uses the same word in 1 John 3:24. Abiding depends on keeping Christ's commandments (15:10).

15:6 *they are burned.* This refers to the works of the believer. The Christian who does not abide in Christ cannot do what pleases God; therefore, his works will be burned at the judgment seat of Christ, though he himself will be saved (1 Cor. 3:11-15).

15:8 *By this.* I.e., by answered prayer. Note the progression: the step from fruit to more fruit

you, and *that* your ^bjoy may be made full.

12 "This is ^aMy commandment, that you love one another, just as I have loved you.

13 "^aGreater love has no one than this, that one ^blay down his life for his friends.

14 "You are My ^afriends, if ^byou do what I command you.

15 "No longer do I call you slaves, for the slave does not know what his master is doing; but I have called you friends, for ^aall things that I have heard from My Father I have made known to you.

16 "^aYou did not choose Me, but I chose you, and appointed you, that you should go and ^bbear fruit, and *that* your fruit should remain, that ^cwhatever you ask of the Father in My name, He may give to you.

17 "This ^aI command you, that you love one another.

H Concerning the World, 15:18–16:6

18 "^aIf the world hates you, you know that it has hated Me before *it hated* you.

19 "^aIf you were of the world, the world would love its own; but because you are not of the world, but ^bI chose you out of the world, ^ctherefore the world hates you.

20 "Remember the word that I said to you, '^aA slave is not greater than his master.' If they persecuted Me, ^bthey will also persecute you; if they ^ckept My

word, they will keep yours also.

21 "But all these things they will do to you ^afor My name's sake, ^bbecause they do not know the One who sent Me.

22 "^aIf I had not come and spoken to them, they would not have sin, but now they have no excuse for their sin.

23 "He who hates Me hates My Father also.

24 "^aIf I had not done among them ^bthe works which no one else did, they would not have sin; but now they have both seen and hated Me and My Father as well.

25 "But *they have done this* in order that the word may be fulfilled that is written in their ^aLaw, '^bThey hated Me without a cause.'

26 "When the ^aHelper comes, ^bwhom I will send to you from the Father, *that is* ^cthe Spirit of truth, who proceeds from the Father, ^dHe will bear witness of Me,

27 and ^ayou *will* bear witness also, because you have been with Me ^bfrom the beginning.

16 "^aThese things I have spoken to you, that you may be kept from ^bstumbling.

2 "They will ^amake you outcasts from the synagogue, but ^ban hour is coming for everyone ^cwho kills you to think that he is offering service to God.

3 "And these things they will do, ^abecause they have not known the Father, or Me.

4 "But these things I have spoken to you, ^athat when their hour comes, you may remember that I told you of them. And these things I did not say to you ^bat the

Cross references (margin)

12 ^aJohn 13:34; 15:17

★**13** ^aRom. 5:7f. ^bJohn 10:11

14 ^aLuke 12:4 ^bMatt. 12:50

15 ^aJohn 8:26; 16:12

16 ^aJohn 6:70; 13:18; 15:19 ^bJohn 15:5 ^cJohn 14:13; 15:7; 16:23

17 ^aJohn 15:12

18 ^aJohn 7:7; 1 John 3:13

19 ^aMatt. 10:22; 24:9 ^bJohn 15:16 ^cJohn 17:14

20 ^aJohn 13:16 ^b1 Cor. 4:12; 2 Cor. 4:9; 2 Tim. 3:12 ^cJohn 8:51

★**21** ^aMatt. 10:22; 24:9; Mark 13:13; Luke 21:12, 17; Acts 4:17; 5:41; 9:14; 26:9; 1 Pet. 4:14; Rev. 2:3 ^bJohn 8:19, 55; 16:3; 17:25; Acts 3:17; 1 John 3:1

22 ^aJohn 9:41; 15:24

24 ^aJohn 9:41; 15:21 ^bJohn 5:36; 10:37

★**25** ^aJohn 10:34 ^bPs. 35:19; 69:4

★**26** ^aJohn 14:16 ^bJohn 14:26 ^cJohn 14:17 ^d1 John 5:7

27 ^aLuke 24:48; John 19:35; 21:24; 1 John 1:2; 4:14 ^bLuke 1:2

★ **1** ^aJohn 15:18-27 ^bMatt. 11:6

★ **2** ^aJohn 9:22 ^bJohn 4:21; 16:25 ^cIs. 66:5; Acts 26:9-11; Rev. 6:9

3 ^aJohn 8:19, 55; 15:21; 17:25; Acts 3:17; 1 John 3:1

4 ^aJohn 13:19 ^bLuke 1:2

---

involves pruning (cleansing) through the Word of God (v. 2), and the step from more fruit to much fruit involves a life of answered prayer.

15:13 The highest expression of love is a self-sacrifice which spares not life itself (see 1 John 3:16).

15:21 *for My name's sake.* Better, on My account, i.e., because you are My followers.

15:25 The reference is to Ps. 35:19; 69:4. In this section Christ states: (1) the world hates Me (v. 18); (2) My followers are aliens in the world (v. 19); (3) the world will persecute you because you are My followers (v. 20); (4) the persecu

tors do not know God (v. 21); (5) My words (v. 22) and My works (v. 24) rebuke them. These arguments are found in many early Christian writings, as instruction to the faithful and as warning to pagans and Jews.

15:26 *Helper.* See note on 14:16. *who proceeds from the Father.* The mission of the Spirit is from the Father; the Spirit's witness, therefore, is also that of the Father Himself.

16:1 *stumbling.* Or, falling away.

16:2 *everyone who kills you* (will) *think that he is offering service to God.* The history of religious persecution clearly portrays the fulfillment of this prophecy (e.g., Acts 7:57-60).

beginning, because I was with you.

5 "But now [a]I am going to Him who sent Me; and none of you asks Me, [b]'Where are You going?'

6 "But because I have said these things to you, [a]sorrow has filled your heart.

I Concerning the Holy Spirit, 16:7–15

7 "But I tell you the truth, it is to your advantage that I go away; for if I do not go away, the [a]Helper shall not come to you; but if I go, [b]I will send Him to you.

8 "And He, when He comes, will convict the world concerning sin, and righteousness, and judgment;

9 concerning sin, [a]because they do not believe in Me;

10 and concerning [a]righteousness, because [b]I go to the Father, and you no longer behold Me;

11 [a]and concerning judgment, because the ruler of this world has been judged.

12 "I have many more things to say to you, but you cannot bear *them* now.

13 "But when He, [a]the Spirit of truth, comes, He will [b]guide you into all the truth; for He will not speak on His own initiative, but whatever He hears, He will speak;

and He will disclose to you what is to come.

14 "He shall [a]glorify Me; for He shall take of Mine, and shall disclose *it* to you.

15 "[a]All things that the Father has are Mine; therefore I said, that He takes of Mine, and will disclose *it* to you.

J Concerning His Return, 16:16–33

16 "[a]A little while, and [b]you will no longer behold Me; and again a little while, and [c]you will see Me."

17 *Some* of His disciples therefore said to one another, "What is this thing He is telling us, '[a]A little while, and you will not behold Me; and again a little while, and you will see Me'; and, 'because [b]I go to the Father'?"

18 And so they were saying, "What is this that He says, 'A little while'? We do not know what He is talking about."

19 [a]Jesus knew that they wished to question Him, and He said to them, "Are you deliberating together about this, that I said, 'A little while, and you will not behold Me, and again a little while, and you will see Me'?

20 "Truly, truly, I say to you, that [a]you will weep and lament, but the world will rejoice; you

Marginal references

5 [a]John 7:33; 16:10, 17, 28 [b]John 13:36; 14:5
6 [a]John 14:1; 16:22
7 [a]John 14:16 [b]John 14:26
★ **8-11**
★ **9** [a]John 15:22, 24
10 [a]Acts 3:14; 7:52; 17:31; 1 Pet. 3:18 [b]John 16:5
★**11** [a]John 12:31
★**12**
★**13** [a]John 14:17 [b]John 14:26
★**14** [a]John 7:39
★**15** [a]John 17:10
16 [a]John 7:33 [b]John 14:18-24; 16:16-24 [c]John 16:22
17 [a]John 16:16 [b]John 16:5
19 [a]Mark 9:32; John 6:61
20 [a]Mark 16:10; Luke 23:27 [b]John 20:20

16:8-11 The Spirit, through apostles, evangelists, and preachers, will *convict* the world. To convict means to set forth the truth of the Gospel in such a clear light that men are able to accept or reject it intelligently; i.e., to convince men of the truthfulness of the Gospel. The Spirit will help break down the indifference of the typical pagan who has no conviction of sin, who holds a low regard for righteousness, and who pays no heed to warnings of the coming judgment.

16:9 *because they do not believe in Me.* The greatest, and basic, sin is unbelief. Jesus' return to the Father will vindicate His righteous life and the truthfulness of all He said (v. 10).

16:11 *the ruler of this world has been judged.* At the cross, Christ triumphed over Satan, serving notice on unbelievers of their judgment to come.

16:12 *many more things . . . but you cannot bear them now.* These things would become clear after the resurrection.

16:13 *He will disclose to you what is to come.* These things include the meaning of Christ's death and resurrection (which the disciples did not fully understand) as well as things yet in the future concerning the return of Christ. See Paul's statement in 1 Cor. 2:10.

16:14 *take of Mine.* I.e., My teachings and whatever relates to Me.

16:15 The teaching ministry of the Holy Spirit has guided the church since the Spirit's coming. Doctrine, therefore, does not have to be traced back to the earthly ministry of Jesus to be authoritative, because He (the Spirit) *takes of Mine* (Christ's), *and will disclose it to you* (the apostles). These truths were then recorded in the New Testament.

will be sorrowful, but [b]your sorrow will be turned to joy.

²¹ ^aIs. 13:8;
21:3; 26:17;
66:7; Hos.
13:13; Mic.
4:9; 1 Thess.
5:3

21 "[a]Whenever a woman is in travail she has sorrow, because her hour has come; but when she gives birth to the child, she remembers the anguish no more, for joy that a child has been born into the world.

²² ^aJohn
16:6 ^bJohn
16:16

22 "Therefore [a]you too now have sorrow; but [b]I will see you again, and your heart will rejoice, and no one takes your joy away from you.

★²³ ^aJohn
14:20; 16:26
^bJohn 16:19,
30 ^cJohn
15:16

23 "And [a]in that day [b]you will ask Me no question. Truly, truly, I say to you, [c]if you shall ask the Father for anything, He will give it to you in My name.

²⁴ ^aJohn
14:14 ^bJohn
3:29; 15:11

24 "[a]Until now you have asked for nothing in My name; ask, and you will receive, that your [b]joy may be made full.

★²⁵ ^aMatt.
13:34; John
10:6; 16:29
^bJohn 16:2

25 "These things I have spoken to you in [a]figurative language; [b]an hour is coming when I will speak no more to you in figurative language, but will tell you plainly of the Father.

★²⁶ ^aJohn
14:20; 16:23
^bJohn 16:19,
30

26 "[a]In that day [b]you will ask in My name, and I do not say to you that I will request the Father on your behalf;

²⁷ ^aJohn
14:21, 23
^bJohn 2:11;
16:30 ^cJohn
8:42; 16:30

27 for [a]the Father Himself loves you, because you have loved Me, and [b]have believed that [c]I came forth from the Father.

²⁸ ^aJohn
8:42; 16:30
^bJohn 13:1,
3; 16:5, 10,
17

28 "[a]I came forth from the Father, and have come into the world; I am leaving the world again, and [b]going to the Father."

²⁹ ^aMatt.
13:34; John
10:6; 16:25

29 His disciples *said, "Lo, now You are speaking plainly,

and are not using [a]a figure of speech.

³⁰ ^aJohn
2:11; 16:27
^bJohn 8:42;
16:28

30 "Now we know that You know all things, and have no need for anyone to question You; by this we [a]believe that You [b]came from God."

31 Jesus answered them, "Do you now believe?

³² ^aJohn
4:23; 16:2,
25 ^bZech.
13:7; Matt.
26:31 ^cJohn
19:27 ^dJohn
8:29

32 "Behold, [a]an hour is coming, and has *already* come, for [b]you to be scattered, each to [c]his own *home*, and to leave Me alone; and *yet* [d]I am not alone, because the Father is with Me.

★³³ ^aJohn
14:27 ^bJohn
15:18ff.
^cMatt. 9:2
^dRom. 8:37;
2 Cor. 2:14;
4:7ff.; 6:4ff.;
Rev. 3:21;
12:11

33 "These things I have spoken to you, that [a]in Me you may have peace. [b]In the world you have tribulation, but [c]take courage; [d]I have overcome the world."

V INTERCESSION OF THE SON OF GOD, 17:1–26

★ ¹ ^aJohn
11:41 ^bJohn
7:39; 13:31f.

17 These things Jesus spoke; and [a]lifting up His eyes to heaven, He said, "Father, the hour has come; [b]glorify Thy Son, that the Son may glorify Thee,

² ^aJohn
3:35 ^bJohn
6:37, 39;
17:6, 9, 24
^cJohn 10:28

2 even as [a]Thou gavest Him authority over all mankind, that [b]to all whom Thou hast given Him, [c]He may give eternal life.

★ ³ ^aJohn
5:44 ^bJohn
3:17; 17:8,
21, 23, 25

3 "And this is eternal life, that they may know Thee, [a]the only true God, and Jesus Christ whom [b]Thou hast sent.

⁴ ^aJohn
13:31 ^bLuke
22:37; John
4:34

4 "[a]I glorified Thee on the earth, [b]having accomplished the work which Thou hast given Me to do.

★ ⁵ ^aJohn
17:1 ^bJohn
1:1; 8:58;
17:24; Phil.
2:6

5 "And now, [a]glorify Thou Me together with Thyself, Father,

---

16:23 *in that day.* I.e., after His ascension.

16:25 *in figurative language* (see v. 29).

16:26 *ask in My name.* To address the Father through the Son has been the normal Christian practice ever since. See also note on 14:13.

16:33 *In the world you have tribulation.* There are three aspects of this: (1) general trials which come simply because we live in a sinful world (Rom. 8:35-36); (2) afflictions which God allows to come into our lives (2 Cor. 12:7); and (3) chastisement which comes more directly from God (Heb. 12:6). *I have overcome the world.* See Rom. 8:37; 1 John 5:4.

17:1 In this great so-called "high-priestly"

prayer the Lord prays for: (1) His own glorification (vv. 1, 5); (2) believers' protection (v. 11); (3) believers' sanctification (v. 17); (4) the unity of believers (vv. 21-23); (5) the ultimate glorification of believers (v. 24). It is essentially an intercession for those who will form the church (vv. 6-26).

17:3 This is Christ's definition of salvation, especially if we add what is clearly understood: *sent* to be the Savior of the world (3:16; 4:42; 6:33; 1 John 4:14; 5:20).

17:5 *with Thyself.* I.e., in thy presence, "at the right hand of God."

with the glory which I had *b*with Thee before the world was.

6 "*a*I manifested Thy name to the men whom *b*Thou gavest Me out of the world; *c*Thine they were, and Thou gavest them to Me, and they have *d*kept Thy word.

7 "Now they have come to know that everything Thou hast given Me is from Thee;

8 for *a*the words which *a*Thou gavest Me *b*I have given to them; and they received *them*, and truly understood that *c*I came forth from Thee, and they believed that *d*Thou didst send Me.

9 "*a*I ask on their behalf; *b*I do not ask on behalf of the world, but of those whom *c*Thou hast given Me; for *d*they are Thine;

10 and *a*all things that are Mine are Thine, and Thine are Mine; and I have been glorified in them.

11 "And I am no more in the world; and *yet* *a*they themselves are in the world, and *b*I come to Thee. *c*Holy Father, keep them in Thy name, *the name* *d*which Thou hast given Me, that *e*they may be one, even as We *are*.

12 "While I was with them, I was keeping them in Thy name *a*which Thou hast given Me; and I guarded them, and *b*not one of them perished but *c*the son of perdition, that the *d*Scripture might be fulfilled.

13 "But now *a*I come to Thee; and *b*these things I speak in the world, that they may have My *c*joy made full in themselves.

14 "I have given them Thy word; and *a*the world has hated them, because *b*they are not of

the world, even as I am not of the world.

15 "I do not ask Thee to take them out of the world, but to keep them from *a*the evil *one*.

16 "*a*They are not of the world, even as I am not of the world.

17 "*a*Sanctify them in the truth; Thy word is truth.

18 "As *a*Thou didst send Me into the world, *b*I also have sent them into the world.

19 "And for their sakes I *a*sanctify Myself, that they themselves also may be *b*sanctified *c*in truth.

20 "I do not ask in behalf of these alone, but for those also who believe in Me through their word;

21 that they may all be one; *a*even as Thou, Father, *art* in Me, and I in Thee, that they also may be in Us; *b*that the world may believe that *c*Thou didst send Me.

22 "And the *a*glory which Thou hast given Me I have given to them; that they may be one, just as We are one;

23 *a*I in them, and Thou in Me, that they may be perfected in unity, that the world may know that *b*Thou didst send Me, and didst *c*love them, even as Thou didst love Me.

24 "Father, I desire that *a*they also, whom Thou hast given Me, *b*be with Me where I am, in order that they may behold My *c*glory, which Thou hast given Me; for Thou didst love Me before *d*the foundation of the world.

25 "O *a*righteous Father, although *b*the world has not known Thee, yet I have known Thee; and

---

★ 6 *a*John 17:26 *b*John 6:37, 39, 17:2, 9, 24 *c*John 17:9 *d*John 8:51

★ 8 *a*John 6:68, 12:49 *b*John 15:15, 17:14, 26 *c*John 8:42, 16:27, 30 *d*John 3:17, 17:18, 21, 23, 25

9 *a*Luke 22:32; John 14:16 *b*Luke 23:34; John 17:20f *c*John 6:37, 39, 17:2, 6, 24 *d*John 17:6

10 *a*John 16:15

11 *a*John 13:1 *b*John 7:33, 17:13 *c*John 17:25 *d*John 17:6, Phil. 2:9, Rev. 19:12 *e*John 17:21f; Rom. 12:5; Gal. 3:28

★12 *a*John 17:6, Phil. 2:9, Rev. 19:12 *b*John 6:39, 18:9 *c*John 6:70 *d*Ps. 41:9

13 *a*John 7:33, 17:11 *b*John 15:11 *c*John 3:29

14 *a*John 15:19 *b*John 8:23, 17:16

★15 *a*Matt. 5:37

16 *a*John 17:14

★17 *a*John 15:3

★18 *a*John 3:17, 17:3, 8, 21, 23, 25 *b*Matt. 10:5; John 4:38; 20:21

19 *a*John 15:13 *b*John 15:3 *c*2 Cor. 7:14; Col. 1:6; 1 John 3:18

★21 *a*John 10:38; 17:11, 23 *b*John 17:8 *c*John 3:17, 17:3, 8, 18, 23, 25

22 *a*John 1:14, 17:24

23 *a*John 10:38, 17:11, 21 *b*John 3:17, 17:3, 8, 18, 21, 25 *c*John 16:27

24 *a*John 17:2 *b*John 12:26 *c*John 1:14, 17:22 *d*Matt. 25:34; John 17:5

25 *a*John 17:11, 1 John 1:9 *b*John 7:29, 15:21 *c*John 3:17, 17:3, 8, 18, 21, 23

17:6 *manifested Thy name.* I.e., revealed your true nature. This divine revelation is the basis on which the church is established.
17:8 *the words.* I.e., the divine message.
17:12 *the son of perdition.* Judas. See Ps. 41:9.
17:15 *from the evil one.* The word can be neuter *(from evil)* or masculine *(from the evil one,* Satan). It should be noted that Christ does not teach withdrawal from the world but that Christians should be in the world but not of it (vv. 14–16).

17:17 *Sanctify* means to set apart for God and His holy purposes, so also v. 19.
17:18 A great text for the mission of the church.
17:21 *that they may all be one.* All believers belong to the one body of Christ (1 Cor. 12:13) and to the same household of God (Eph. 2:19). This spiritual unity should be visibly expressed in the exercise of spiritual gifts (Eph. 4:3–16), prayer, and exhortation (2 Cor. 1:11; Heb. 10:25).

these have known that cThou didst send Me;

26 and aI have made Thy name known to them, and will make it known; that bthe love wherewith Thou didst love Me may be in them, and I in them."

VI CRUCIFIXION OF THE SON OF GOD, 18:1–19:42
A The Arrest, 18:1–11

18 When Jesus had spoken these words, aHe went forth with His disciples over bthe ravine of the Kidron, where there was ca garden, into which He Himself entered, and His disciples.

2 Now Judas also, who was betraying Him, knew the place; for Jesus had aoften met there with His disciples.

3 aJudas then, having received bthe *Roman* cohort, and cofficers from the chief priests and the Pharisees, *came there with lanterns and dtorches and weapons.

4 Jesus therefore, aknowing all the things that were coming upon Him, went forth, and *said to them, "bWhom do you seek?"

5 They answered Him, "Jesus the Nazarene." He *said to them, "I am *He."* And Judas also who was betraying Him, was standing with them.

6 When therefore He said to them, "I am *He,"* they drew back, and fell to the ground.

7 Again therefore He asked them, "aWhom do you seek?" And they said, "Jesus the Nazarene."

8 Jesus answered, "I told you that I am *He;* if therefore you seek Me, let these go their way,"

9 that the word might be

fulfilled which He spoke, "aOf those whom Thou hast given Me I lost not one."

10 Simon Peter therefore ahaving a sword, drew it, and struck the high priest's slave, and cut off his right ear; and the slave's name was Malchus.

11 Jesus therefore said to Peter, "Put the sword into the sheath; athe cup which the Father has given Me, shall I not drink it?"

B The Trials, 18:12–19:15
1 *Before Annas,* 18:12–23

12 aSo bthe *Roman* cohort and the commander, and the bofficers of the Jews, arrested Jesus and bound Him,

13 and led Him to aAnnas first; for he was father-in-law of bCaiaphas, who was high priest that year.

14 Now Caiaphas was the one who had advised the Jews that ait was expedient for one man to die on behalf of the people.

15 And aSimon Peter was following Jesus, and *so was* another disciple. Now that disciple was known to the high priest, and entered with Jesus into bthe court of the high priest,

16 abut Peter was standing at the door outside. So the other disciple, who was known to the high priest, went out and spoke to the doorkeeper, and brought in Peter.

17 aThe slave-girl therefore who kept the door *said to Peter, "bYou are not also *one* of this man's disciples, are you?" He *said, "I am not."

18 Now the slaves and the aofficers were standing *there,* bhaving made ca charcoal fire, for it was cold and they were

---

Marginal references (left column):

26 aJohn 17:6 bJohn 15:9

★ 1 aMatt. 26:30, 36; Mark 14:26, 32; Luke 22:39 b2 Sam. 15:23; 1 Kin. 2:37; 15:13; 2 Kin. 23:4, 6, 12; 2 Chr. 15:16; 29:16; 30:14; Jer. 31:40 cMatt. 26:36; Mark 14:32; John 18:26

2 aLuke 21:37; 22:39 ★ 3 aJohn 18:3-11; Matt. 26:47-56; Mark 14:43-50; Luke 22:47-53 bJohn 18:12; Acts 10:1 cJohn 7:32; 18:12, 18 dMatt. 25:1 and marg. 4 aJohn 6:64; 13:1, 11 bJohn 18:7

7 aJohn 18:4

9 aJohn 17:12

Marginal references (right column):

★10 aMatt. 26:51; Mark 14:47

11 aMatt. 20:22

★12 aJohn 18:12f.; Matt. 26:57ff. bJohn 18:3

★13 aLuke 3:2; John 18:24 bMatt. 26:3; John 11:49, 51

14 aJohn 11:50

★15 aMatt. 26:58; Mark 14:54; Luke 22:54 bMatt. 26:3; John 18:24, 28

16 aJohn 18:16-18; Matt. 26:69f.; Mark 14:66-68; Luke 22:55-57

17 aActs 12:13 bJohn 18:25

18 aJohn 18:3 bMark 14:54, 67 cJohn 21:9

18:1 *ravine of the Kidron.* A ravine E. of Jerusalem, between the city and the Mount of Olives.

18:3 *Roman cohort.* A group of 300–600 Roman soldiers.

18:10 *cut off his right ear.* For the sequel see Luke 22:51.

18:12 *officers of the Jews.* Better, servants of the Jewish authorities (high priests).

18:13 A small inner circle of high priests, headed by Annas and Caiaphas, ruled Jerusalem regardless of who was officially *the* high priest. See note on Luke 3:2.

18:15 *another disciple.* John.

warming themselves; and Peter also was with them, standing and warming himself.

19 ^aThe high priest therefore questioned Jesus about His disciples, and about His teaching.

20 Jesus answered him, "I ^ahave spoken openly to the world; I always ^btaught in synagogues, and ^cin the temple, where all the Jews come together; and I spoke nothing in secret.

21 "Why do you question Me? Question those who have heard what I spoke to them; behold, these know what I said."

22 And when He had said this, one of the ^aofficers standing by ^bgave Jesus a blow, saying, "Is that the way You answer the high priest?"

23 ^aJesus answered him, "If I have spoken wrongly, bear witness of the wrong; but if rightly, why do you strike Me?"

2   Before Caiaphas, 18:24-27

24 ^aAnnas therefore sent Him bound to ^aCaiaphas the high priest.

25 ^aNow ^bSimon Peter was standing and warming himself. They said therefore to him, "^cYou are not also *one* of His disciples, are you?" He denied *it*, and said, "I am not."

26 One of the slaves of the high priest, being a relative of the one ^awhose ear Peter cut off, *said, "Did I not see you in ^bthe garden with Him?"

27 Peter therefore denied *it* again; and immediately ^aa cock crowed.

3   Before Pilate, 18:28-19:16

28 ^aThey *led Jesus therefore from ^bCaiaphas into ^cthe Praetorium, and it was early; and they themselves did not enter into ^cthe Praetorium in order that ^dthey might not be defiled, but might eat the Passover.

29 ^aPilate therefore went out to them, and *said, "What accusation do you bring against this Man?"

30 They answered and said to him, "If this Man were not an evildoer, we would not have delivered Him up to you."

31 Pilate therefore said to them, "Take Him yourselves, and judge Him according to your law." The Jews said to him, "We are not permitted to put anyone to death,"

32 that ^athe word of Jesus might be fulfilled, which He spoke, signifying by what kind of death He was about to die.

33 Pilate therefore ^aentered again into the Praetorium, and summoned Jesus, and said to Him, "^bAre You the King of the Jews?"

34 Jesus answered, "Are you saying this on your own initiative, or did others tell you about Me?"

35 Pilate answered, "I am not a Jew, am I? Your own nation and the chief priests delivered You up to me; what have You done?"

36 Jesus answered, "^aMy kingdom is not of this world. If

Reference column notes:

19 ^aJohn 18:19-24; Matt. 26:59-68; Mark 14:55-65; Luke 22:63-71
20 ^aJohn 7:26; 8:26 ^bMatt. 4:23; John 6:59 ^cMatt. 26:55

22 ^aJohn 18:3 ^bJohn 19:3

23 ^aMatt. 5:39; Acts 23:2-5

★24 ^aJohn 18:13

25 ^aJohn 18:25-27; Matt. 26:71-75; Mark 14:69-72; Luke 22:58-62 ^bJohn 18:18 ^cJohn 18:17
26 ^aJohn 18:10 ^bJohn 18:1

27 ^aJohn 13:38

★28 ^aMatt. 27:2; Mark 15:1; Luke 23:1 ^bJohn 18:13 ^cMatt. 27:27; John 18:33; 19:9 ^dJohn 11:55; Acts 11:3

29 ^aJohn 18:29-38; Matt. 27:11-14; Mark 15:2-5; Luke 23:2, 3

★31

32 ^aMatt. 20:19; 26:2; Mark 10:33f.; Luke 18:32f.; John 3:14; 8:28; 12:32f. 33 ^aJohn 18:28, 29; 19:9 ^bLuke 23:3; John 19:12

★34

★36 ^aMatt. 26:53; Luke 17:21; John 6:15

18:24 No examination before *Caiaphas* is reported by John. See note on Matt. 26:57. Under Roman law, as in free societies today, a prisoner was assumed to be innocent until proved guilty.

18:28 *they themselves did not enter into the Praetorium.* The Roman headquarters, the barracks (also in v. 33). As a dwelling place of Gentiles it was unclean. Thus the Jewish authorities would not enter, lest they be defiled for the Passover. They were willing, however, to see the murder of Jesus committed without fearing defilement! See note on Matt. 27:27.

18:31 *We are not permitted.* The Sanhedrin could condemn a man to death, but the Roman government had to approve and execute the sentence. See note on Luke 22:66.

18:34 Jesus asked whether Pilate's question arose from his own Roman viewpoint *(Are you saying this on your own initiative)* or from a Jewish viewpoint *(or did others tell you about Me?).*

18:36 Because Pilate's answer indicated that he was concerned only about a rival political kingdom to Rome (v. 35), our Lord replied as He did in this verse, indicating that His was not such a kingdom. Pilate was then satisfied that Jesus was not a political threat and there-

My kingdom were of this world, then My servants would be fighting, that I might not be delivered up to the Jews; but as it is, My kingdom is not of this realm."

37 Pilate therefore said to Him, "So You are a king?" Jesus answered, "*a*You say *correctly* that I am a king. For this I have been born, and for this I have come into the world, *b*to bear witness to the truth. *c*Everyone who is of the truth hears My voice."

38 Pilate *said to Him, "What is truth?"

And when he had said this, he *a*went out again to the Jews, and *said to them, "*b*I find no guilt in Him.

39 "*a*But you have a custom, that I should release someone for you at the Passover; do you wish then that I release for you the King of the Jews?"

40 Therefore they cried out again, saying, "*a*Not this Man, but Barabbas." Now Barabbas was a robber.

19 Then Pilate therefore took Jesus, and *a*scourged Him.

2 *a*And the soldiers wove a crown of thorns and put it on His head, and arrayed Him in a purple robe;

3 and they *began* to come up to Him, and say, "*a*Hail, King of the Jews!" and to *b*give Him blows in the face.

4 And Pilate *a*came out again, and *said to them, "Behold, I am bringing Him out to you, that you may know that *b*I find no guilt in Him."

5 Jesus therefore came out, *a*wearing the crown of thorns and the purple robe. And *Pilate* *said to them, "Behold, the Man!"

6 When therefore the chief priests and the *a*officers saw Him, they cried out, saying, "Crucify, crucify!" Pilate *said to them, "Take Him yourselves, and crucify Him, for *b*I find no guilt in Him."

7 The Jews answered him, "*a*We have a law, and by that law He ought to die because He *b*made Himself out *to be* the Son of God."

8 When Pilate therefore heard this statement, he was the more afraid;

9 and he *a*entered into the Praetorium again, and *said to Jesus, "Where are You from?" But *b*Jesus gave him no answer.

10 Pilate therefore *said to Him, "You do not speak to me? Do You not know that I have authority to release You, and I have authority to crucify You?"

11 Jesus answered, "*a*You would have no authority over Me, unless it had been given you from above; for this reason *b*he who delivered Me up to you has *the* greater sin."

12 As a result of this Pilate made efforts to release Him, but the Jews cried out, saying, "*a*If you release this Man, you are no friend of Caesar; everyone who makes himself out *to be* a king opposes Caesar."

Margin references (left column):

37 *a*Matt. 27:11; Mark 15:2; Luke 22:70; 23:3 *b*John 1:14; 3:32; 8:14 *c*John 8:47; 1 John 4:6

★**38** *a*John 18:33; 19:4 *b*Luke 23:4; John 19:4

39 *a*John 18:39-19:16; Matt. 27:15-18, 20-23; Mark 15:6-15; Luke 23:18-25

40 *a*Acts 3:14

★ **1** *a*Matt. 27:26

2 *a*Matt. 27:27-30; Mark 15:16-19

3 *a*Matt. 27:29; Mark 15:18 *b*John 18:22

★ **4** *a*John 18:33, 38 *b*Luke 23:4; John 18:38; 19:6

Margin references (right column):

★ **5** *a*John 19:2

6 *a*Matt. 26:58; John 18:3 *b*Luke 23:4; John 18:38; 19:4

★ **7** *a*Lev. 24:16; Matt. 26:63-66 *b*John 5:18; 10:33

★ **8**

★ **9** *a*John 18:33; 26:63; 27:12, 14; John 18:34-37

★**11** *a*Rom. 13:1 *b*John 18:13f., 28ff.; Acts 3:13

★**12** *a*Luke 23:2; John 18:33ff.

---

fore wished to release Him. *kingdom.* Better, kingship; i.e., My authority is not of human origin.
18:38 *What is truth?* Pilate was not being philosophical but was simply expressing frustration and irritation at Jesus' avoidance of a direct answer to what seemed to him to be a simple question. He did not really understand the charges (18:31, 35, 38; 19:4, 12).
19:1 *scourged.* See note on Matt. 27:26.
19:4 Perhaps Pilate now sought a compromise.
19:5 *Behold, the Man!* Pilate's remark was sarcastic: "Look at your so-called king now!"
19:7 *by that law He ought to die.* A reference to Jesus' alleged blasphemy because He claimed to be God.

19:8 *afraid.* Perhaps of several things: of possible violence; of loss of favor in Rome for his inability to control the turbulent Jews (v. 15); of some sense of Jesus' true nature (this may be indicated by the question in v. 9).
19:9 *no answer.* See Isa. 53:7.
19:11 *he who delivered Me.* Evidently a reference to Caiaphas (18:28).
19:12 The Jewish authorities reverted to the political charge against Jesus, suggesting a potent threat to a provincial governor who served at the whim of the emperor (Tiberius). The Jews had already protested to Rome Pilate's actions in other matters where he was insensitive to their customs (see note on Mark 15:1).

★13 aMatt.
27:19 bJohn
5:2; 19:17,
20

13 When Pilate therefore heard these words, he brought Jesus out, and asat down on the judgment seat at a place called The Pavement, but bin Hebrew, Gabbatha.

★14-15
★14 aMatt.
27:62; John
19:31, 42
bMatt. 27:45;
Mark 15:25
cJohn 19:19,
21

14 Now it was athe day of preparation for the Passover; it was about the bsixth hour. And he *said to the Jews, "Behold, cyour King!"

15 aLuke
23:18

15 They therefore cried out, "aAway with *Him*, away with *Him*, crucify Him!" Pilate *said to them, "Shall I crucify your King?" The chief priests answered, "We have no king but Caesar."

★16 aMatt.
27:26; Mark
15:15; Luke
23:25

16 So he then adelivered Him to them to be crucified.

C The Crucifixion, 19:17-37

★17 aJohn
19:17-24;
Matt. 27:33-
44; Mark
15:22-32;
Luke 23:33-
43 bMatt.
27:32; Mark
15:21; Luke
14:27; 23:26
cLuke 23:33
and marg.
dJohn 19:13

17 aThey took Jesus therefore, and He went out, bbearing His own cross, to the place called cthe Place of a Skull, which is called din Hebrew, Golgotha.

18 aLuke
23:32

18 There they crucified Him, and with Him atwo other men, one on either side, and Jesus in between.

19 aMatt.
27:37; Mark
15:26; Luke
23:38 bJohn
19:14, 21

19 And Pilate wrote an inscription also, and put it on the cross. And it was written, "aJESUS THE NAZARENE, bTHE KING OF THE JEWS."

20 aJohn
19:13

20 Therefore this inscription many of the Jews read, for the place where Jesus was crucified was near the city; and it was written ain Hebrew, Latin, *and* in Greek.

21 aJohn
19:14, 19

21 And so the chief priests of the Jews were saying to Pilate, "Do not write, 'aThe King of the Jews'; but that He said, 'I am aKing of the Jews.'"

22 Pilate answered, "aWhat I have written I have written."

22 aGen.
43:14; Esth.
4:16

23 aThe soldiers therefore, when they had crucified Jesus, took His outer garments and made bfour parts, a part to every soldier and *also* the tunic; now the tunic was seamless, woven in one piece.

23 aMatt.
27:35; Mark
15:24; Luke
23:34 bActs
12:4

24 They said therefore to one another, "aLet us not tear it, but cast lots for it, *to decide* whose it shall be"; bthat the Scripture might be fulfilled, "THEY cDIVIDED MY OUTER GARMENTS AMONG THEM, AND FOR MY CLOTHING THEY CAST LOTS."

★24 aEx.
28:32; Matt.
27:35; Mark
15:24; Luke
23:34 bJohn
19:28, 36f.
cPs. 22:18

25 Therefore the soldiers did these things. aBut there were standing by the cross of Jesus bHis mother, and His mother's sister, Mary the *wife* of cClopas, and dMary Magdalene.

★25 aMatt.
27:55f.; Mark
15:40f.; Luke
23:49 bMatt.
12:46 cLuke
24:18 dLuke
8:2; John
20:1, 18

26 When Jesus therefore saw His mother, and athe disciple whom He loved standing nearby, He *said to His mother, "bWoman, behold, your son!"

26 aJohn
13:23 bJohn
2:4

27 Then He *said to the disciple, "Behold, your mother!" And from that hour the disciple took her into ahis own *household*.

27 aLuke
18:28; John
1:11; 16:32;
Acts 21:6
[Gr.]

28 After this, Jesus, aknowing that all things had already been accomplished, bin order that the Scripture might be fulfilled, *said, "cI am thirsty."

28 aJohn
13:1; 17:4
bJohn 19:24,
36f. cPs.
69:21

29 A jar full of sour wine was standing there; so athey put a sponge full of the sour wine upon a branch of hyssop, and brought it up to His mouth.

★29 aJohn
19:29, 30;
Matt. 27:48,
50; Mark
15:36f.; Luke
23:36
30 aJohn
17:4 bMatt.
27:50; Mark
15:37; Luke
23:46

30 When Jesus therefore had received the sour wine, He said,

19:13 *Pavement.* Almost certainly the large paved area that was part of the Castle of Antonia at the NW. corner of the temple area beneath Ecce Homo Arch.

19:14-15 Pilate's sarcasm was directed to the chief priests (whom he hates and mistrusts) and to their clique. He draws from them the response, *"We have no king but Caesar,"* a blasphemous denial of the kingship of God over their nation.

19:14 *preparation for the Passover.* Friday of Passover week. In v. 31 *preparation* refers to Friday as the day of preparation for the Sabbath (see note on Luke 23:54).

19:16 *to be crucified.* See note on Matt. 27:31.

19:17 *Golgotha.* See note on Matt. 27:33.

19:24 See note on Matt. 27:35.

19:25 *Mary.* On the Marys of the N.T. see note on Luke 8:2.

19:29 *sour wine . . . hyssop.* The vinegar was a sour, cheap wine. Hyssop was likely the caper plant, which has stems 2-3 feet long.

"*a*It is finished!" And He bowed His head, and *b*gave up His spirit.

31 The Jews therefore, because it was *a*the day of preparation, so that *b*the bodies should not remain on the cross on the Sabbath (for that Sabbath was a *c*high *day)*, asked Pilate that their legs might be broken, and *that* they might be taken away.

32 The soldiers therefore came, and broke the legs of the first man, and of the other man who was *a*crucified with Him;

33 but coming to Jesus, when they saw that He was already dead, they did not break His legs;

34 but one of the soldiers pierced His side with a spear, and immediately there came out *a*blood and water.

35 And he who has seen has *a*borne witness, and his witness is true; and he knows that he is telling the truth, so that you also may believe.

36 For these things came to pass, *a*that the Scripture might be fulfilled, "*b*Not a bone of Him shall be broken."

37 And again another Scripture says, "*a*They shall look on Him whom they pierced."

D The Burial, 19:38-42

38 *a*And after these things Joseph of Arimathea, being a disciple of Jesus, but a *b*secret *one*, for *c*fear of the Jews, asked Pilate

that he might take away the body of Jesus; and Pilate granted permission. He came therefore, and took away His body.

39 And *a*Nicodemus came also, who had first come to Him by night; *b*bringing a mixture of *c*myrrh and aloes, about a *d*hundred pounds *weight*.

40 And so they took the body of Jesus, and *a*bound it in *b*linen wrappings with the spices, as is the burial custom of the Jews.

41 Now in the place where He was crucified there was a garden; and in the garden a *a*new tomb, *b*in which no one had yet been laid.

42 Therefore on account of the Jewish day of *a*preparation, because the tomb was *b*nearby, they laid Jesus there.

VII RESURRECTION OF THE SON OF GOD, 20:1-21:25
A The Empty Tomb, 20:1-10

20 *a*Now on the first *day* of the week *b*Mary Magdalene *came early to the tomb, while it *was still dark, and *saw *c*the stone *already* taken away from the tomb.

2 And so she *ran and *came to Simon Peter, and to the other *a*disciple whom Jesus loved, and *said to them, "*b*They have taken away the Lord out of the tomb, and we do not know where they have laid Him."

★31 *a*John 19:14, 42; *b*Deut. 21:23; Josh. 8:29; 10:26f; *c*Ex. 12:16

32 *a*John 19:18

34 *a*1 John 5:6, 8

35 *a*John 15:27; 21:24

★36 *a*John 19:24, 28; *b*Ex. 12:46; Num. 9:12; Ps. 34:20

★37 *a*Zech. 12:10

★38 *a*John 19:38-42; Matt. 27:57-61; Mark 15:42-47; Luke 23:50-56; *b*Mark 15:43; *c*John 7:13

★39 *a*John 3:1; *b*Mark 16:1; *c*Ps. 45:8; Prov. 7:17; Song of Sol. 4:14; Matt. 2:11; *d*John 12:3

★40 *a*Matt. 26:12; Mark 14:8; John 11:44; *b*Luke 24:12; John 20:5, 7

★41 *a*Matt. 27:60; *b*Luke 23:53

42 *a*John 19:14, 31; *b*John 19:20, 41

★1 *a*John 20:1-8; Matt. 28:1-8; Mark 16:1-8; Luke 24:1-10; *b*John 19:25; 20:18; *c*Matt. 27:60, 66; 28:2; Mark 15:46; 16:3f; Luke 24:2; John 11:38

2 *a*John 13:23; *b*John 20:13

19:31 *for that Sabbath was a high day.* I.e., the first day of the Feast of Unleavened Bread fell that year on a Sabbath, making it a "high" festival (Ex. 12:16; Lev. 23:7). They were anxious that the body not remain on the cross (see Deut. 21:22-23). *their legs might be broken.* This was done to hasten death, since the victim could no longer raise himself up on the nail through his feet in order to allow himself to breathe.

19:36 See Ex. 12:46; Num. 9:12; Ps. 34:20.

19:37 See Zech. 12:10.

19:38 *Arimathea.* A town 20 miles NW. of Jerusalem.

19:39 *Nicodemus* apparently became a secret follower of Christ.

19:40 *linen wrappings.* I.e., long strips of linen.

19:41 See Isa. 53:9.

20:1 The order of Christ's appearances after His resurrection seems to be as follows: (1) To Mary Magdalene and the other women (Matt. 28:8-10; John 20:11-18; Mark 16:9-10); (2) to Peter, probably in the afternoon (Luke 24:34; 1 Cor. 15:5); (3) to the disciples on the Emmaus road toward evening (Luke 24:13-32; Mark 16:12); (4) to the disciples, except Thomas, in the upper room (Luke 24:36-43; John 20:19-25); (5) to the disciples, including Thomas, on the next Sunday night (Mark 16:14; John 20:26-29); (6) to seven disciples beside the Sea of Galilee (John 21:1-24); (7) to the apostles and more than 500 brethren and James, the Lord's half brother (1 Cor. 15:6-7); (8) to those who witnessed the ascension (Matt. 28:18-20; Mark 16:19; Luke 24:44-53; Acts 1:3-12).

3 ^aPeter therefore went forth, and the other disciple, and they were going to the tomb.

4 And the two were running together; and the other disciple ran ahead faster than Peter, and came to the tomb first;

5 and ^astooping and looking in, he *saw the ^blinen wrappings lying *there*; but he did not go in.

6 Simon Peter therefore also *came, following him, and entered the tomb; and he *beheld the linen wrappings lying *there*,

7 and ^athe face-cloth, which had been on His head, not lying with the ^blinen wrappings, but rolled up in a place by itself.

8 So the other disciple who ^ahad first come to the tomb entered then also, and he saw and believed.

9 For as yet ^athey did not understand the Scripture, ^bthat He must rise again from the dead.

10 So the disciples went away again ^ato their own homes.

B   The Appearances of the Risen Lord, 20:11-21:25

1   To Mary Magdalene, 20:11-18

11 ^aBut Mary was standing outside the tomb weeping; and so, as she wept, she ^bstooped and looked into the tomb;

12 and she *beheld ^atwo angels in white sitting, one at the head, and one at the feet, where the body of Jesus had been lying.

13 And they *said to her, "^aWoman, why are you weeping?" She *said to them, "Because ^bthey have taken away my Lord, and I do not know where they have laid Him."

14 When she had said this, she turned around, and *^abeheld Jesus standing *there*, and ^bdid not know that it was Jesus.

15 Jesus *said to her, "^aWoman, why are you weeping? Whom are you seeking?" Supposing Him to be the gardener, she *said to Him, "Sir, if you have carried Him away, tell me where you have laid Him, and I will take Him away."

16 Jesus *said to her, "Mary!" She *turned and *said to Him ^ain Hebrew, "^bRabboni!" (which means, Teacher).

17 Jesus *said to her, "Stop clinging to Me, for I have not yet ascended to the Father; but go to ^aMy brethren, and say to them, 'I ^bascend to My Father and your Father, and My God and your God.' "

18 ^aMary Magdalene *came, ^bannouncing to the disciples, "I have seen the Lord," and *that* He had said these things to her.

2   To the disciples, Thomas absent, 20:19-25

19 When therefore it was evening, on that day, the first *day* of the week, and when the doors were shut where the disciples were, for ^afear of the Jews, Jesus came and stood in their midst, and *said to them, "^bPeace *be* with you."

20 And when He had said this, ^aHe showed them both His hands and His side. The disciples therefore ^brejoiced when they saw the Lord.

21 Jesus therefore said to them again, "^aPeace *be* with you; ^bas the Father has sent Me, I also send you."

22 And when He had said this, He breathed on them, and

---

3 ^aLuke 24:12; John 20:3-10

5 ^aJohn 20:11 ^bJohn 19:40

★ **6**

7 ^aJohn 11:44 ^bJohn 19:40

8 ^aJohn 20:4

9 ^aMatt. 22:29; John 2:22 ^bLuke 24:26ff., 46

10 ^aLuke 24:12

11 ^aMark 16:5 ^bJohn 20:5

12 ^aMatt. 28:2f.; Mark 16:5; Luke 24:4

13 ^aJohn 20:15 ^bJohn 20:2

14 ^aMatt. 28:9; Mark 16:9 ^bJohn 21:4

15 ^aJohn 20:13

16 ^aJohn 5:2 ^bMatt. 23:7; Mark 10:51

★**17** ^aMatt. 28:10 ^bMark 12:26; 16:19; John 7:33

18 ^aJohn 20:1 ^bMark 16:10; Luke 24:10, 23

★**19** ^aJohn 7:13 ^bLuke 24:36; John 14:27; 20:21, 26

20 ^aLuke 24:39, 40; John 19:34 ^bJohn 16:20, 22

★**21** ^aLuke 24:36; John 14:27; 20:19, 26 ^bJohn 17:18

★**22**

20:6 *beheld the linen wrappings lying.* If the body had been stolen, the thieves would not have taken time to unwrap it; but even if they had, the wrappings would have been strewn around the tomb, not lying in perfect order as they were. See note on Luke 24:12.

20:17 *Stop clinging to Me.* I.e., in order to restrain Him. Inappropriate because of His new relationship as resurrected Lord.

20:19 *the Jews.* I.e., the Jewish authorities.

20:21 Another great verse on the mission of the church (see also 17:18).

20:22 *Receive the Holy Spirit.* This was a filling with the Spirit for power until the regularized relationship of the Spirit began at Pentecost.

*said to them, "Receive the Holy Spirit.

23 "aIf you forgive the sins of any, *their sins* have been forgiven them; if you retain the sins of any, they have been retained."

24 But aThomas, one of bthe twelve, called aDidymus, was not with them when Jesus came.

25 The other disciples therefore were saying to him, "We have seen the Lord!" But he said to them, "Unless I shall see in aHis hands the imprint of the nails, and put my finger into the place of the nails, and put my hand into His side, bI will not believe."

3 To the disciples, Thomas present, 20:26-31

26 And after eight days again His disciples were inside, and Thomas with them. Jesus *came, the doors having been shut, and stood in their midst, and said, "aPeace *be* with you."

27 Then He *said to Thomas, "aReach here your finger, and see My hands; and reach here your hand, and put it into My side; and be not unbelieving, but believing."

28 Thomas answered and said to Him, "My Lord and my God!"

29 Jesus *said to him, "Because you have seen Me, have you believed? aBlessed *are* they who did not see, and *yet* believed."

30 aMany other bsigns therefore Jesus also performed in the presence of the disciples, which are not written in this book;

31 but these have been writ-
ten athat you may believe that Jesus is the Christ, bthe Son of God; and that cbelieving you may have life in His name.

4 To seven disciples, 21:1-14

21 After these things Jesus amanifested Himself bagain to the disciples at the cSea of Tiberias, and He manifested *Himself* in this way.

2 There were together Simon Peter, and aThomas called Didymus, and bNathanael of cCana in Galilee, and dthe *sons* of Zebedee, and two others of His disciples.

3 Simon Peter *said to them, "I am going fishing." They *said to him, "We will also come with you." They went out, and got into the boat; and athat night they caught nothing.

4 But when the day was now breaking, Jesus stood on the beach; yet the disciples did not aknow that it was Jesus.

5 Jesus therefore *said to them, "Children, ayou do not have any fish, do you?" They answered Him, "No."

6 And He said to them, "aCast the net on the right-hand side of the boat, and you will find *a catch.*" They cast therefore, and then they were not able to haul it in because of the great number of fish.

7 aThat disciple therefore whom Jesus loved *said to Peter, "It is the Lord." And so when Simon Peter heard that it was the Lord, he put his outer garment on (for he was stripped *for work),* and threw himself into the sea.

20:23 *have been forgiven . . . have been retained.* Since only God can forgive sins (Mark 2:7), the disciples and the church are here given the authority to declare what God does when a man either accepts or rejects His Son. See note on Matt. 16:19.

20:28 *My Lord and my God.* Thomas, the doubter, finally recognized the full deity of Jesus Christ. This marks the climax of John's Gospel. The Lord had claimed deity throughout His ministry. Note: (1) the names of deity which He uses (Matt. 22:42-45; John 8:58); (2) the attributes of deity which He claimed (holiness, John 8:46; omnipotence and omnipresence, Matt. 28:20; omniscience, John 11:11-14); (3) the things He claimed to be able to do which only God can do (forgive sins, Mark 2:5-7; raise the dead, John 5:28-30; 11:43; judge all men, John 5:22, 27).

21:3 *boat.* A Galilean fishing boat was about 15 feet long.

21:5 *Children* = boys or lads.

21:7 *stripped for work.* I.e., not completely dressed. Peter swam ashore, while others followed in the boat, dragging the net behind them as they rowed ashore.

8 But the other disciples came in the little boat, for they were not far from the land, but about one hundred yards away, dragging the net *full* of fish.

9 And so when they got out upon the land, they *saw a char-coal ᵃfire *already* laid, and ᵇfish placed on it, and bread.

10 Jesus *said to them, "Bring some of the ᵃfish which you have now caught."

11 Simon Peter went up, and drew the net to land, full of large fish, a hundred and fifty-three; and although there were so many, the net was not torn.

12 Jesus *said to them, "Come *and* have ᵃbreakfast." None of the disciples ventured to question Him, "Who are You?" knowing that it was the Lord.

13 Jesus *came and *took ᵃthe bread, and *gave them, and the ᵇfish likewise.

14 This is now the ᵃthird time that Jesus was manifested to the disciples, after He was raised from the dead.

5   To Peter and the beloved disciple, 21:15-25

15 So when they had ᵃfinished breakfast, Jesus *said to Simon Peter, "Simon, *son* of John, do you ᵇlove Me more than these?" He *said to Him, "Yes, Lord; You know that I love You." He *said to him, "Tend ᶜMy lambs."

16 He *said to him again a second time, "Simon, *son* of John, do you love Me?" He *said to Him, "Yes, Lord; You know that I love You." He *said to him, "ᵃShepherd My sheep."

17 He *said to him the third time, "Simon, *son* of John, do you love Me?" Peter was grieved be-cause He said to him ᵃthe third time, "Do you love Me?" And he said to Him, "Lord, ᵇYou know all things; You know that I love You." Jesus *said to him, "ᶜTend My sheep.

18 "Truly, truly, I say to you, when you were younger, you used to gird yourself, and walk wherever you wished; but when you grow old, you will stretch out your hands, and someone else will gird you, and bring you where you do not wish to *go*."

19 Now this He said, ᵃsignify-ing by ᵇwhat kind of death he would glorify God. And when He had spoken this, He *said to him, "ᶜFollow Me!"

20 Peter, turning around, *saw the ᵃdisciple whom Jesus loved following *them*; the one who also had ᵇleaned back on His breast at the supper, and said, "Lord, who is the one who be-trays You?"

21 Peter therefore seeing him *said to Jesus, "Lord, and what about this man?"

22 Jesus *said to him, "If I want him to remain ᵃuntil I come, what *is that* to you? You ᵇfollow Me!"

23 This saying therefore went out among ᵃthe brethren that that disciple would not die; yet Jesus did not say to him that he would not die, but *only*, "If I want him to remain ᵇuntil I come, what *is that* to you?"

24 This is the disciple who ᵃbears witness of these things, and wrote these things; and we know that his witness is true.

25 And there are also ᵃmany other things which Jesus did, which if they *were written in de-tail, I suppose that even the world itself *would not contain the books which *were written.

Cross references (margin):

9 ᵃJohn 18:18 ᵇJohn 6:9, 11; 21:10, 13

10 ᵃJohn 6:9, 11; 21:10, 13

12 ᵃJohn 21:15

13 ᵃJohn 21:9 ᵇJohn 6:9, 11; 21:9, 10

★**14** ᵃJohn 20:19, 26

★**15-17**

15 ᵃJohn 21:12 ᵇMatt. 26:33; Mark 14:29; John 13:37 ᶜLuke 12:32

16 ᵃMatt. 2:6; Acts 20:28; 1 Pet. 5:2; Rev. 7:17

17 ᵃJohn 13:38 ᵇJohn 16:30 ᶜJohn 21:16

★**18-19**

19 ᵃJohn 12:33; 18:32 ᵇ2 Pet. 1:14 ᶜMatt. 8:22; 16:24; John 21:22

20 ᵃJohn 21:7 ᵇJohn 13:25

★**22** ᵃMatt. 16:27f.; 1 Cor. 4:5; 11:26; James 5:7; Rev. 2:25 ᵇMatt. 8:22; 16:24; John 21:19

23 ᵃActs 1:15 ᵇMatt. 16:27f.; 1 Cor. 4:5; 11:26; James 5:7; Rev. 2:25

24 ᵃJohn 15:27

★**25** ᵃJohn 20:30

21:14 *the third time.* See 20:19 and 20:26 for the other two occasions.

21:15-17 Peter's three denials are here offset by three protestations of his love for Christ. John probably used the two different words for love in these verses synonymously (compare 3:35, *agapao*, with 5:20, *phileo*). *more than these* (v. 15) means "more than the other disciples" (see

Matt. 26:33; Mark 14:29).

21:18-19 A prophecy of the martyrdom of Peter.

21:22 The Lord rebuked Peter for being dis-tracted over John's future. Peter's only respon-sibility was to *follow* Christ.

21:25 The Gospels were not intended to be com-plete accounts of the life of Christ.

INTRODUCTION TO
THE ACTS OF THE APOSTLES

AUTHOR: Luke   DATE: 61

Authorship   *That the author of Acts was a companion of Paul is clear from the passages in the book in which "we" and "us" are used (16:10–17; 20:5–21:18; 27:1–28:16). These sections themselves eliminate known companions of Paul other than Luke, and Colossians 4:14 and Philemon 24 point affirmatively to Luke, who was a physician. The frequent use of medical terms also substantiates this conclusion (1:3; 3:7ff.; 9:18, 33; 13:11; 28:1–10). Luke answered the Macedonian call with Paul, was in charge of the work at Philippi for about six years, and later was with Paul in Rome during the time of Paul's house arrest. It was probably during this last period that the book was written. If it were written later it would be very difficult to explain the absence of mention of such momentous events as the burning of Rome, the martyrdom of Paul, or the destruction of Jerusalem.*

Importance of the Book   *(1) Acts gives us the record of the spread of Christianity from the coming of the Spirit on the day of Pentecost to Paul's arrival in Rome to preach the gospel in the world's capital. In this regard, then, it is the record of the continuation of those things which Jesus began while on earth and which He continued as the risen Head of the Church and the One who sent the Holy Spirit (1:2; 2:33). The book is sometimes called The Acts of the Holy Spirit.*
   (2) The thirty years covered by the book were important years of transition. The gospel was preached first only to Jews, and the early church was composed largely of Jewish believers. As more and more Gentiles were included, the Church became distinct from Judaism.
   (3) Doctrines which are later developed in the epistles appear in seed form in Acts (the Spirit, 1:8; the kingdom, 3:21; 15:16; elders, 11:30; Gentile salvation, 15:14). However, the book emphasizes the practice of doctrine more than the statement of doctrine.
   (4) Acts furnishes principles for missionary work. (5) The book reveals patterns for church life. (6) Archaeological discoveries confirm in a remarkable way the historical accuracy of Luke's writing.

Contents   *In the first twelve chapters of the book the important figures are Peter, Stephen, Philip, Barnabas, and James. From chapter 13 to the end, the dominant person is Paul. The book may also be divided according to the geographical divisions mentioned in the Great Commission (1:8).*

OUTLINE OF THE ACTS

I. **Christianity in Jerusalem, 1:1–8:3**
   A. The Risen Lord, 1:1–26
      1. The Lord confirming, 1:1–5
      2. The Lord commissioning, 1:6–11
      3. The Lord choosing, 1:12–26
   B. Pentecost: Birthday of the Church, 2:1–47
      1. The power of Pentecost, 2:1–13
      2. The preaching of Pentecost, 2:14–36
      3. The results of Pentecost, 2:37–47
   C. The Healing of a Lame Man, 3:1–26
      1. The miracle, 3:1–11
      2. The message, 3:12–26
   D. The Beginning of Persecution, 4:1–37
      1. The persecution, 4:1–22
      2. The prayer, 4:23–31
      3. The provision, 4:32–37
   E. Purging and Persecution, 5:1–42
      1. Purging from within, 5:1–11
      2. Purging from without, 5:12–42
   F. Choosing Colaborers, 6:1–7
   G. Stephen, the First Martyr, 6:8–8:3
      1. The stirring of the people, 6:8–15
      2. The sermon of Stephen, 7:1–53
      3. The stoning of Stephen, 7:54–8:3

II. **Christianity in Palestine and Syria, 8:4–12:25**
   A. The Christians Scattered, 8:4–40
      1. The preaching in Samaria, 8:4–25
      2. The preaching on the Gaza road, 8:26–40
   B. The Conversion of Paul, 9:1–31
      1. The account of Paul's conversion, 9:1–19
      2. The aftermath of Paul's conversion, 9:20–31
   C. The Conversion of Gentiles, 9:32–11:30
      1. The preparation of Peter, 9:32–10:22
      2. The preaching of Peter, 10:23–48
      3. The plea of Peter, 11:1–18
      4. The church at Antioch, 11:19–30
   D. The Christians Persecuted by Herod, 12:1–25
      1. The death of James, 12:1–2
      2. The deliverance of Peter, 12:3–19
      3. The death of Herod, 12:20–23
      4. The dissemination of the Word, 12:24–25

THE ACTS OF THE APOSTLES

I CHRISTIANITY IN JERUSALEM, 1:1-8:3

A The Risen Lord, 1:1-26

1 *The Lord confirming,* 1:1-5

1 The first account I composed, *a*Theophilus, about all that Jesus *b*began to do and teach,

2 until the day when He *a*was taken up, after He *b*had by the Holy Spirit given orders to *c*the apostles whom He had *d*chosen.

3 To these *a*He also presented Himself alive, after His suffering, by many convincing proofs, appearing to them over a *period of* forty days, and speaking of *b*the things concerning the kingdom of God.

4 And gathering them together, He commanded them *a*not to leave Jerusalem, but to wait for *b*what the Father had promised, "Which," *He said,* "you have heard of from Me;

5 for *a*John baptized with water, but you shall be baptized with the Holy Spirit *b*not many days from now."

2 *The Lord commissioning,* 1:6-11

6 And so when they had come together, they were asking Him, saying, "Lord, *a*is it at this time You are restoring the kingdom to Israel?"

7 He said to them, "It is not for you to know times or epochs which *a*the Father has fixed by His own authority;

8 but you shall receive power *a*when the Holy Spirit has

Side references (left column):
★ **1** *a*Luke 1:3 *b*Luke 3:23
2 *a*Mark 16:19; Acts 1:9, 11, 22 *b*Matt. 28:19f.; Mark 16:15; John 20:21f.; Acts 10:42 *c*Mark 6:30 *d*John 13:18; Acts 10:41
★ **3** *a*Matt. 28:17; Mark 16:12, 14; Luke 24:34, 36; John 20:19, 26; 21:1, 14; 1 Cor. 15:5-7 *b*Acts 8:12; 19:8; 28:23, 31
4 *a*Luke 24:49 *b*John 14:16, 26; 15:26; 2:33

Side references (right column):
★ **5** *a*Matt. 3:11; Acts 11:16 *b*Acts 2:1-4
★ **6** *a*Matt. 17:11; Mark 9:12; Luke 17:20; 19:11
★ **7** *a*Matt. 24:36; Mark 13:32
8 *a*Acts 2:1-4 *b*Luke 24:48; John 15:27 *c*Acts 8:1, 5, 14 *d*Matt. 28:19; Mark 16:15; Rom. 10:18; Col. 1:23

1:1 *The first account.* I.e., the Gospel of Luke. *Theophilus* means "dear to God" or "friend of God." He was probably a Roman official, since the title "most excellent" (Luke 1:3) indicates an official position in Acts 23:26; 24:3; 26:25.
1:3 *forty days.* The only reference to the length of Christ's ministry on earth between His resurrection and His ascension.
1:5 *baptized with the Holy Spirit.* This promise was first fulfilled on the day of Pentecost (see 11:15-16) and affects every believer by joining

him to the body of Christ (1 Cor. 12:13). See notes on Matt. 3:11.
1:6 *the kingdom to Israel.* The Messianic, Davidic, millennial kingdom on earth. The time of its coming is unrevealed (Matt. 24:36, 42).
1:7 There is no rebuke in Christ's answer, for God is not through with Israel and the kingdom will eventually come (Rom. 11:26). In the meantime, the gospel must be preached throughout the whole world (Acts 1:8).

come upon you; and you shall be
[b]My witnesses both in Jerusalem,
and in all Judea and [c]Samaria,
and even to [d]the remotest part of
the earth."

9　And after He had said
these things, [a]He was lifted up
while they were looking on, and a
cloud received Him out of their
sight.

10　And as they were gazing
intently into the sky while He was
departing, behold, [a]two men in
white clothing stood beside them;

11　and they also said, "[a]Men
of Galilee, why do you stand
looking into the sky? This Jesus,
who [b]has been taken up from you
into heaven, will [c]come in just the
same way as you have watched
Him go into heaven."

3　The Lord choosing, 1:12-26

12　Then they [a]returned to Je-
rusalem from the [b]mount called
Olivet, which is near Jerusalem, a
Sabbath day's journey away.

13　And when they had en-
tered, they went up to [a]the upper
room, where they were staying;
[b]that is, Peter and John and James
and Andrew, Philip and Thomas,
Bartholomew and Matthew,
James the son of Alphaeus, and
Simon the Zealot, and [c]Judas the
son of James.

14　These all with one mind
[a]were continually devoting themselves to prayer, along with [b]the
women, and Mary the [c]mother of
Jesus, and with His [c]brothers.

15　And at this time Peter
stood up in the midst of [a]the
brethren (a gathering of about
one hundred and twenty persons
was there together), and said,

16　"Brethren, [a]the Scripture
had to be fulfilled, which the

Holy Spirit foretold by the mouth
of David concerning Judas, [b]who
became a guide to those who arrested Jesus.

17　"For he was [a]counted
among us, and received his portion in [b]this ministry."

18　(Now this man [a]acquired a
field with [b]the price of his wickedness; and falling headlong, he
burst open in the middle and all
his bowels gushed out.

19　And it became known to
all who were living in Jerusalem;
so that in [a]their own language
that field was called Hakeldama,
that is, Field of Blood.)

20　"For it is written in the
book of Psalms,

'[a]LET HIS HOMESTEAD BE MADE
　　DESOLATE,
AND LET NO MAN DWELL IN
　　IT';

and,

'[b]HIS OFFICE LET ANOTHER MAN
　　TAKE.'

21　"It is therefore necessary
that of the men who have accompanied us all the time that [a]the
Lord Jesus went in and out among
us—

22　[a]beginning with the baptism of John, until the day that He
[b]was taken up from us—one of
these should become a [c]witness
with us of His resurrection."

23　And they put forward two
men, Joseph called Barsabbas
(who was also called Justus), and
[a]Matthias.

24　And they [a]prayed, and
said, "Thou, Lord, [b]who knowest
the hearts of all men, show which
one of these two Thou hast chosen

Marginal references (left column):

9 [a]Acts 1:2

10 [a]Luke 24:4; John 20:12

★11 [a]Acts 2:7; 13:31 [b]Mark 16:19; Acts 1:9, 22 [c]Matt. 16:27f.; Acts 3:21

★12 [a]Luke 24:50, 52 [b]Matt. 21:1

★13 [a]Mark 14:15; Luke 22:12; Acts 9:37, 39; 20:8 [b]Acts 1:13; Matt. 1:2-4; Mark 3:16-19; Luke 6:14-16 [c]John 14:22

14 [a]Acts 2:42; 6:4; Rom. 12:12; Eph. 6:18; Col. 4:2 [b]Luke 8:2f. [c]Matt. 12:46

★15 [a]John 21:23; Acts 6:3; 9:30; 10:23; 11:1, 12, 26, 29; 12:17; 14:2; 15:1, 3, 22, 23, 32f., 40; 16:2, 40; 17:6, 10; 14; 18:18; 27:21,7, 17; 22:5; 28:14f.; Rom. 1:13

★16 [a]John 13:18; 17:12; Acts 1:20 [b]Matt. 26:47; Mark 14:43; Luke 22:47; John 18:3

Marginal references (right column):

17 [a]John 6:70f. [b]Acts 1:25; 20:24; 21:19

★18 [a]Matt. 27:3-10 [b]Matt. 26:14f.

19 [a]Matt. 27:8; Acts 21:40

★20 [a]Ps. 69:25 [b]Ps. 109:8

21 [a]Luke 24:3

22 [a]Mark 1:1-4 [b]Acts 1:8; 2:32 [c]Acts 1:26

23 [a]Acts 1:26

24 [a]Acts 6:6; 13:3; 14:23 [b]1 Sam. 16:7; Jer. 17:10; Acts 15:8; Rom. 8:27

Footnotes:

1:11　in just the same way. The second coming of Christ, like the ascension, will be personal and visible (Rev. 1:8; 19:11-16).

1:12　a Sabbath day's journey. About 2000 cubits, or a little more than half a mile—the distance the rabbis allowed Jews to journey on the Sabbath. This limitation was apparently arrived at on the basis of Ex. 16:29 interpreted by Num. 35:5.

1:13　Simon the Zealot. See note on Matt. 10:4.

1:15　Peter had made a full recovery of confidence and authority from the night of his denial and was now fulfilling Matt. 16:19.

1:16　See Ps. 41:9.

1:18　burst open in the middle. Probably due to Judas' ineptness in trying to hang himself (Matt. 27:5).

1:20　See Ps. 69:25; 109:8.

25 aActs
1:17 bRom.
1:5; 1 Cor.
9:2; Gal. 2:8

25 to occupy ᵃthis ministry and ᵇapostleship from which Judas turned aside to go to his own place."

26 And they ᵃdrew lots for them, and the lot fell to ᵇMatthias; and he was numbered with ᶜthe eleven apostles.

★26 aLev.
16:8; Josh.
14:2; 1 Sam.
14:41f.; Neh.
10:34; 11:1;
Prov. 16:33
bActs 1:23
cActs 2:14

B Pentecost: Birthday of the Church, 2:1-47

1 The power of Pentecost, 2:1-13

★ 1 aLev.
23:15f.; Acts
20:16; 1 Cor.
16:8

2 And when ᵃthe day of Pentecost had come, they were all together in one place.

★ 2 aActs
4:31

2 And suddenly there came from heaven a noise like a violent, rushing wind, and it filled ᵃthe whole house where they were sitting.

★ 3

3 And there appeared to them tongues as of fire distributing themselves, and they rested on each one of them.

★ 4 aMatt.
10:20; Acts
1:5, 8; 4:8,
31; 6:3, 5;
7:55; 8:17;
9:17; 11:15;
13:9, 52
bMark 16:17;
1 Cor.
12:10f.;
14:21
5 aLuke
2:25; Acts
8:2
6 aActs 2:2

7 aActs
2:12 bMatt.
26:73; Acts
1:11

4 And they were all ᵃfilled with the Holy Spirit and began to ᵇspeak with other tongues, as the Spirit was giving them utterance.

5 Now there were Jews living in Jerusalem, ᵃdevout men, from every nation under heaven.

6 And when ᵃthis sound occurred, the multitude came together, and were bewildered, because they were each one hearing them speak in his own language.

7 And ᵃthey were amazed and marveled, saying, "Why, are not all these who are speaking ᵇGalileans?

8 "And how is it that we each hear them in our own language to which we were born?

9 "Parthians and Medes and Elamites, and residents of Mesopotamia, Judea and ᵃCappadocia, ᵇPontus and ᶜAsia,

10 ᵃPhrygia and ᵇPamphylia, Egypt and the districts of Libya around ᶜCyrene, and ᵈvisitors from Rome, both Jews and ᵉproselytes,

11 Cretans and Arabs—we hear them in our own tongues speaking of the mighty deeds of God."

12 And ᵃthey continued in amazement and great perplexity, saying to one another, "What does this mean?"

13 But others were mocking and saying, "ᵃThey are full of sweet wine."

★ 9-11
9 a1 Pet.
1:1 bActs
18:2; 1 Pet.
1:1 cActs
6:9; 16:6;
19:10; 20:4;
21:27; 24:18;
27:2; Rom.
16:5; 1 Cor.
16:19; 2 Cor.
1:8; 2 Tim.
1:15; Rev.
1:4
10 aActs
16:6; 18:23
bActs 13:13;
14:24; 15:38;
27:5 cMatt.
27:32 dActs
17:21 eMatt.
23:15
12 aActs 2:7

13 a1 Cor.
14:23

2 The preaching of Pentecost, 2:14-36

14 But Peter, taking his stand with ᵃthe eleven, raised his voice and declared to them: "Men of Judea, and all you who live in Jerusalem, let this be known to you, and give heed to my words.

15 "For these men are not drunk, as you suppose, ᵃfor it is only the third hour of the day;

16 but this is what was spoken of through the prophet Joel:

★14 aActs
1:26

★15
a1 Thess.
5:7

★16-21

1:26 *drew lots.* Two names were written on stones and placed in an urn. The one that fell out first was taken to be the Lord's choice (cf. Prov. 16:33; Jon. 1:7). The occasion was unique, for the Lord was not there in person to appoint and the Spirit had not been given in the special way of Pentecost.

2:1 *the day of Pentecost.* The fourth of the annual feasts of the Jews (after Passover, Unleavened Bread, and Firstfruits), it came 50 days after Firstfruits (a type of the resurrection of Christ, 1 Cor. 15:23). Pentecost was the Greek name for the Jewish Feast of Weeks, so called because it fell seven (a week of) weeks after Firstfruits. It celebrated the wheat harvest (Ex. 23:16). This day of Pentecost in Acts 2 marked the beginning of the Church (Matt. 16:18).

2:2 *a noise.* It was like a wind but was not wind.

2:3 Possibly at this point the group left the house and went to the temple.

2:4 *with other tongues.* Actual languages unknown to the speakers but understood by the hearers (v. 8).

2:9-11 These countries form a circuit around the Mediterranean Sea.

2:14 Here begins Peter's great sermon, with an explanation of the phenomena they were witnessing (vv. 14-21). He then proclaimed the gospel (vv. 22-35) and applied the message (v. 36).

2:15 *the third hour* = 9 a.m. Jews engaged in the exercises of the synagogue on feast days abstained from eating and drinking until 10 a.m. or noon; therefore, this could not be drunkenness.

2:16-21 The fulfillment of this prophecy will be in the last days, immediately preceding the re-

17 ^aAnd it shall be in the last days,' God says,

'That I will pour forth of My Spirit upon all mankind;

And your sons and your daughters shall prophesy,

And your young men shall see visions,

And your old men shall dream dreams;

18 Even upon My bondslaves, both men and women,

I will in those days pour forth of My Spirit

And they shall prophesy.

19 'And I will grant wonders in the sky above,

And signs on the earth beneath,

Blood, and fire, and vapor of smoke.

20 'The sun shall be turned into darkness,

And the moon into blood, Before the great and glorious day of the Lord shall come.

21 'And it shall be, that ^aeveryone who calls on the name of the Lord shall be saved.'

22 "Men of Israel, listen to these words: ^aJesus the Nazarene, ^ba man attested to you by God with miracles and ^cwonders and signs which God performed through Him in your midst, just as you yourselves know—

23 this *Man*, delivered up by the ^apredetermined plan and foreknowledge of God, ^byou nailed to a cross by the hands of godless men and put *Him* to death.

24 "And ^aGod raised Him up again, putting an end to the agony of death, since it ^bwas impossible for Him to be held in its power.

25 "For David says of Him,

'^aI was always beholding the Lord in my presence;

For He is at my right hand, that I may not be shaken.

26 'Therefore my heart was glad and my tongue exulted;

Moreover my flesh also will abide in hope;

27 Because Thou wilt not abandon my soul to ^aHades,

^bNor allow Thy Holy One to undergo decay.

28 'Thou hast made known to me the ways of life;

Thou wilt make me full of gladness with Thy presence.'

29 "Brethren, I may confidently say to you regarding the ^apatriarch David that he both ^bdied and ^cwas buried, and ^dhis tomb is with us to this day.

30 "And so, because he was ^aa prophet, and knew that ^bGod had sworn to him with an oath to seat *one* of his descendants upon his throne,

31 he looked ahead and spoke of the resurrection of the Christ, that He was neither abandoned to ^aHades, nor did His flesh suffer decay.

32 "This Jesus ^aGod raised up again, to which we are all ^bwitnesses.

33 "Therefore having been

---

17 ^aJoel 2.28-32

21 ^aRom. 10.13

★**22-36**

22 ^aActs 3.6, 4.10; 10.38 ^bJohn 3.2 ^cJohn 4.48; Acts 2.19, 43

23 ^aLuke 22.22; Acts 3.18; 4.28; 1.Pet. 1.20 ^bLuke 24.20; Acts 3.13

24 ^aActs 2.32, 3.15, 26; 4.10, 5.30, 10.40, 13.30, 33, 34, 37, 17.31; Rom. 4.24, 6.4, 8.11, 10.9; 1.Cor. 6.14, 15.15; 2.Cor. 4.14; Gal. 1.1; Eph. 1.20; Col. 2.12; 1.Thess. 1.10; Heb. 13.20, 1.Pet. 1.21 ^bJohn 20.9

25 ^aPs. 16.8-11

★**27** ^aMatt. 11.23; Acts 2.31 ^bActs 13.35

29 ^aActs 7.8f.; Heb. 7.4 ^bActs 13.36 ^c1.Kin. 2.10 ^dNeh. 3.16

30 ^aMatt. 22.43 ^b2.Sam. 7.12f.; Ps. 89.3f., 132.11

31 ^aMatt. 11.23; Acts 2.27

32 ^aActs 2.24, 3.15, 26; 4.10, 5.30, 10.40, 13.30, 33, 34, 37, 17.31; Rom. 4.24, 6.4, 8.11, 10.9; 1.Cor. 6.14, 15.15; 2.Cor. 4.14; Gal. 1.1; Col. 1.20, 2.12; 1.Thess. 1.10; Heb. 13.20, 1.Pet. 1.21 ^bActs 1.8

★**33** ^aMark 16.19; Acts 5.31 ^bActs 1.4 ^cJohn 7.39; Gal. 3.14 ^dActs 2.17, 10.45

---

turn of Christ, when all the particulars (e.g., v. 20 and Rev. 6:12) of the prophecy will come to pass. Peter reminded his hearers that, knowing Joel's prophecy, they should have recognized what they were seeing as a work of the Spirit, not a result of drunkenness.

2:22-36 Peter reviewed the life and death of Jesus of Nazareth (vv. 22-24) and then recited the prophecy of the resurrection, (vv. 25-31), quoting Ps. 16:8-11. Since David was speaking of the Messiah (v. 31), Peter continued, and

since Jesus was raised from the dead (v. 32), Jesus must be the Messiah (v. 36).

2:27 *Hades.* The unseen world, sometimes specifically a place of torment (see note on Luke 16:23) and sometimes merely the grave, as here. The meaning is that Christ's body and spirit would not be allowed to remain separated (v. 31).

2:33 Returning to the original point, Peter declared that it is the exalted Jesus who sent the Holy Spirit.

exalted ᵃto the right hand of God, and ᵇhaving received from the Father ᶜthe promise of the Holy Spirit, He has ᵈpoured forth this which you both see and hear.

34 ᵃPs. 110:1; Matt. 22:44f.

34 "For it was not David who ascended into heaven, but he himself says:

'ᵃTHE LORD SAID TO MY LORD, "SIT AT MY RIGHT HAND,

35 UNTIL I MAKE THINE ENEMIES A FOOTSTOOL FOR THY FEET." '

36 ᵃEzek. 36:22, 32, 37; 45:6 ᵇLuke 2:11 ᶜActs 2:23

36 "Therefore let all the ᵃhouse of Israel know for certain that God has made Him both ᵇLord and Christ—this Jesus ᶜwhom you crucified."

3 The results of Pentecost, 2:37-47

37 ᵃLuke 3:10, 12, 14

37 Now when they heard *this*, they were pierced to the heart, and said to Peter and the rest of the apostles, "Brethren, ᵃwhat shall we do?"

★38 ᵃMark 1:15; Luke 24:47; Acts 3:19; 5:31; 20:21 ᵇMark 16:16; Acts 8:12, 16; 22:16

38 And Peter *said* to them, "ᵃRepent, and let each of you be ᵇbaptized in the name of Jesus Christ for the forgiveness of your sins; and you shall receive the gift of the Holy Spirit.

39 ᵃIs. 44:3; 54:13; 57:19; Joel 2:32; Rom. 9:4; Eph. 2:12 ᵇEph. 2:13, 17

39 "For ᵃthe promise is for you and your children, and for all who are ᵇfar off, as many as the Lord our God shall call to Himself."

40 ᵃLuke 16:28 ᵇDeut. 32:5; Matt. 17:17; Phil. 2:15

40 And with many other words he solemnly ᵃtestified and kept on exhorting them, saying, "Be saved from this ᵇperverse generation!"

41 So then, those who had received his word were baptized; and there were added that day about three thousand ᵃsouls.

42 And they were ᵃcontinually devoting themselves to the apostles' teaching and to fellowship, to ᵇthe breaking of bread and ᵃto prayer.

43 And everyone kept feeling a sense of awe; and many ᵃwonders and signs were taking place through the apostles.

44 And all those who had believed were together, and ᵃhad all things in common;

45 and they ᵃbegan selling their property and possessions, and were sharing them with all, as anyone might have need.

46 ᵃAnd day by day continuing with one mind in the temple, and ᵇbreaking bread from house to house, they were taking their meals together with gladness and sincerity of heart,

47 praising God, and ᵃhaving favor with all the people. And the Lord ᵇwas adding to their number day by day ᶜthose who were being saved.

41 ᵃActs 3:23; 7:14; 27:37; Rom. 13:1; 1 Pet. 3:20; Rev. 16:3
★42 ᵃActs 1:14 ᵇLuke 24:30; Acts 2:46; 20:7; 1 Cor. 10:16
43 ᵃActs 2:22
★44 ᵃActs 4:32, 37; 5:2
45 ᵃMatt. 19:21; Acts 4:34
46 ᵃActs 5:42 ᵇLuke 24:30; Acts 2:42; 20:7; 1 Cor. 10:16
47 ᵃActs 5:13 ᵇActs 2:41; 4:4; 5:14; 6:1, 7; 9:31, 35, 42; 11:21, 24; 14:1, 21; 16:5; 17:12 ᶜ1 Cor. 1:18

C The Healing of a Lame Man, 3:1-26

1 The miracle, 3:1-11

3 Now ᵃPeter and John were going up to the temple at the ninth *hour*, ᵇthe hour of prayer.

2 And ᵃa certain man who had been lame from his mother's

★ 1 ᵃLuke 22:8; Acts 3:3, 4, 11 ᵇPs. 55:17; Matt. 27:45; Acts 10:30
★ 2 ᵃActs 14:8 ᵇLuke 16:20 ᶜJohn 9:8; Acts 3:10

2:38 *Repent.* To change one's mind; specifically, here, about Jesus of Nazareth, and to acknowledge Him as Lord (= God) and Christ (= Messiah). Such repentance brings salvation. There is also a repentance needed in the Christian life in relation to specific sins (2 Cor. 7:9; Rev. 2:5). *be baptized . . . for the forgiveness of your sins.* On baptism see note on Matt. 3:11. Water baptism is the outward sign of repentance and forgiveness of sins. Forgiveness is through faith in Christ, not through the act of baptism (*for* may here mean "because of," as in Matt. 12:41). *the gift of the Holy Spirit.* The Spirit is a gift to all who believe, not a reward to some.

2:42 *breaking of bread.* I.e., celebrating the Lord's Supper.

2:44 *had all things in common.* This community of goods seems to have been limited to the early years of the Jerusalem church only. It may have been necessitated by the many pilgrims who lingered in Jerusalem to learn more of their new Christian faith.

3:1 *the ninth hour.* = 3 p.m., the hour of prayer associated with the evening sacrifice.

3:2 *the gate . . . Beautiful.* Probably the Nicanor Gate, the eastern gate of the temple buildings, leading from the Court of the Gentiles into the Women's Court.

womb was being carried along, whom they [b]used to set down every day at the gate of the temple which is called Beautiful, [c]in order to beg alms of those who were entering the temple.

3 And when he saw [a]Peter and John about to go into the temple, he *began* asking to receive alms.

4 And Peter, along with John, [a]fixed his gaze upon him and said, "Look at us!"

5 And he *began* to give them his attention, expecting to receive something from them.

6 But Peter said, "I do not possess silver and gold, but what I do have I give to you: [a]In the name of Jesus Christ the Nazarene—walk!"

7 And seizing him by the right hand, he raised him up; and immediately his feet and his ankles were strengthened.

8 [a]And with a leap, he stood upright and *began* to walk; and he entered the temple with them, walking and leaping and praising God.

9 And [a]all the people saw him walking and praising God;

10 and they were taking note of him as being the one who used to [a]sit at the Beautiful Gate of the temple to *beg* alms, and they were filled with wonder and amazement at what had happened to him.

11 And while he was clinging to [a]Peter and John, all the people ran together to them at the so-called [b]portico of Solomon, full of amazement.

2   The message, 3:12-26

12 But when Peter saw *this*, he [a]replied to the people, "Men of Israel, why do you marvel at this, or why do you gaze at us, as if by our own power or piety we had made him walk?

13 "[a]The God of Abraham, Isaac, and Jacob, [b]the God of our fathers, has glorified His [c]servant Jesus, *the one* whom [d]you delivered up, and disowned in the presence of [e]Pilate, when he had [f]decided to release Him.

14 "But you disowned [a]the Holy and Righteous One, and [b]asked for a murderer to be granted to you,

15 but put to death the [a]Prince of life, *the one* whom [b]God raised from the dead, *a fact* to which we are [c]witnesses.

16 "And on the basis of faith [a]in His name, *it is* the name of Jesus which has strengthened this man whom you see and know; and the faith which *comes* through Him has given him this perfect health in the presence of you all.

17 "And now, brethren, I know that you acted [a]in ignorance, just as your [b]rulers did also.

18 "But the things which [a]God announced beforehand by the mouth of all the prophets, [b]that His Christ should suffer, He has thus fulfilled.

19 "[a]Repent therefore and return, that your sins may be wiped away, in order that [b]times of refreshing may come from the presence of the Lord;

20 and that He may send Jesus, the Christ appointed for you,

21 [a]whom heaven must receive until *the* period of [b]restoration of all things about which [c]God spoke by the mouth of His holy prophets from ancient time.

Cross references

3 [a]Luke 22:8; Acts 3:1, 4, 11

4 [a]Acts 10:4

★ **6** [a]Acts 2:22; 3:16; 4:10

8 [a]Acts 14:10

9 [a]Acts 4:16, 21

10 [a]John 9:8; Acts 3:2

★**11** [a]Luke 22:8; Acts 3:3, 4 [b]John 10:23; Acts 5:12

12 [a]Matt. 11:25; 17:4; 22:1; Luke 14:3; Acts 5:8; 10:46

★**13** [a]Matt. 22:32 [b]Ex. 3:13, 15; Acts 5:30; 7:32; 22:14 [c]Acts 3:26; 4:27, 30 [d]Matt. 20:19; John 19:11; Acts 2:23 [e]Matt. 27:2 [f]Luke 23:4

14 [a]Mark 1:24; Acts 4:27; 7:52; 2 Cor. 5:21 [b]Matt. 27:20; Mark 15:11; Luke 23:18-25

★**15** [a]Acts 5:31; Heb. 2:10; 12:2 [b]Acts 2:24 [c]Luke 24:48

★**16** [a]Acts 3:6

17 [a]Luke 23:34; John 15:21; Acts 13:27; 26:9; Eph. 4:18 [b]Luke 23:13

18 [a]Acts 2:23 [b]Luke 24:27; Acts 17:3; 26:23

★**19** [a]Acts 2:38; 26:20 [b]2 Thess. 1:7; Heb. 4:1ff.

21 [a]Acts 1:11 [b]Matt. 17:11; Rom. 8:21 [c]Luke 1:70

Footnotes

3:6 *In the name of Jesus Christ.* His power and authority are invoked.

3:11 *the . . . portico of Solomon.* A colonnade running the length of the E. side of the outer court of the temple.

3:13 *His servant.* I.e., the "servant" of Isa. 42:1-9; 49:1-13; 52:13-53:12.

3:15 *Prince of life.* Lit., Author of life; i.e., originator.

3:16 *on the basis of faith.* I.e., through the apostles' faith or possibly the lame man's faith.

3:19 *return.* I.e., turn from sin to God by reversing their verdict about Jesus and confessing Him as the Messiah. *times of refreshing* and *restoration of all things* (v. 21) refer to the millennial kingdom.

★22 aDeut.
18:15; Acts
7:37
22 "Moses said, '*a*THE LORD GOD SHALL RAISE UP FOR YOU A PROPHET LIKE ME FROM YOUR BRETHREN; TO HIM YOU SHALL GIVE HEED in everything He says to you.

★23 aDeut.
18:19 bActs
2:41
23 '*a*And it shall be that every *b*soul that does not heed that prophet shall be utterly destroyed from among the people.'

24 aLuke
24:27; Acts
17:3; 26:23
24 "And likewise, *a*all the prophets who have spoken, from Samuel and *his* successors onward, also announced these days.

25 aActs
2:39 bRom.
9:4f. cGen.
22:18
25 "It is you who are *a*the sons of the prophets, and of the *b*covenant which God made with your fathers, saying to Abraham, '*c*AND IN YOUR SEED ALL THE FAMILIES OF THE EARTH SHALL BE BLESSED.'

★26 aMatt.
15:24; John
4:22; Acts
13:46; Rom.
1:16; 2:9f.
bActs 2:24
26 "For you *a*first, God *b*raised up His Servant, and sent Him to bless you by turning every one *of you* from your wicked ways."

D　The Beginning of Persecution, 4:1-37

1　The persecution, 4:1-22

★1 aLuke
22:4 bMatt.
3:7 cLuke
20:1; Acts
6:12
4 And as they were speaking to the people, the priests and *a*the captain of the temple *guard,* and *b*the Sadducees, *c*came upon them,

2 aActs
3:15; 17:18
2 being greatly disturbed because they were teaching the people and proclaiming *a*in Jesus the resurrection from the dead.

3 aActs
5:18
3 And they laid hands on them, and *a*put them in jail until the next day, for it was already evening.

4 aActs
2:41
4 But many of those who had heard the message believed; and *a*the number of the men came to be about five thousand.

5 aLuke
23:13; Acts
4:8
5 And it came about on the next day, that their *a*rulers and elders and scribes were gathered together in Jerusalem;

★6 aLuke
3:2 bMatt.
26:3
6 and *a*Annas the high priest *was there,* and *b*Caiaphas and John and Alexander, and all who were of high-priestly descent.

7 And when they had placed them in the center, they *began to* inquire, "By what power, or in what name, have you done this?"

★8-12
8 aActs
2:4; 13:9.
bLuke 23:13;
Acts 4:5
8 Then Peter, *a*filled with the Holy Spirit, said to them, "*b*Rulers and elders of the people,

9 aActs
3:7f.
9 if we are on trial today for *a*a benefit done to a sick man, as to how this man has been made well,

10 aActs
2:22; 3:6
bActs 2:24
10 let it be known to all of you, and to all the people of Israel, that *a*by the name of Jesus Christ the Nazarene, whom you crucified, whom *b*God raised from the dead—by this *name* this man stands here before you in good health.

11 aMatt.
21:42 bPs.
118:22
cMark 9:12
11 "*a*He is the *b*STONE WHICH WAS *c*REJECTED by you, THE BUILDERS, *but* WHICH BECAME THE VERY CORNER *stone.*

12 aMatt.
1:21; Acts
10:43; 1 Tim.
2:5
12 "And there is salvation in *a*no one else; for there is no other name under heaven that has been given among men, by which we must be saved."

★13 aActs
4:31 bLuke
22:8; Acts
4:19 cJohn
7:15
13 Now as they observed the *a*confidence of *b*Peter and John, and understood that they were uneducated and untrained men,

---

3:22 The Jews expected a *prophet* and the Messiah—two distinct persons (John 1:20-21; 7:40-41). The Christian view united them in the one person of Jesus Christ (cf. Deut. 18:15).

3:23 See Lev. 23:29; Deut. 18:19.

3:26 *His Servant* (see note on 3:13).

4:1 *the captain of the temple guard.* An official second only to the high priest. He was responsible for order in the temple. The *Sadducees* hated the idea of resurrection which the apostles were preaching (v. 2).

4:6 *Annas . . . and Caiaphas.* See note on Luke 3:2. We know nothing about *John and Alex-*

ander.

4:8-12 In his answer, Peter actually puts his hearers on trial. He calls attention to the fact that the miracle was a good deed, not a crime (v. 9) and that it was performed by the power of Jesus whom they had crucified (v. 10). Jesus' rejection was predicted in the O.T. (v. 11; Ps. 118:22) and salvation is only through Him (v. 12).

4:13 *uneducated and untrained men.* This means that Peter and John were not formally trained in the rabbinic schools; they were not professional scholars or ordained teachers (see also John 7:15).

they were marveling, and ᶜ*began* to recognize them as having been with Jesus.

14 And seeing the man who had been healed standing with them, they had nothing to say in reply.

15 But when they had ordered them to go aside out of the ᵃCouncil, they *began* to confer with one another,

16 saying, "ᵃWhat shall we do with these men? For the fact that a ᵇnoteworthy miracle has taken place through them is apparent to all who live in Jerusalem, and we cannot deny it.

17 "But in order that it may not spread any further among the people, let us warn them to speak no more to any man ᵃin this name."

18 And when they had summoned them, they ᵃcommanded them not to speak or teach at all in the name of Jesus.

19 But ᵃPeter and John answered and said to them, "ᵇWhether it is right in the sight of God to give heed to you rather than to God, you be the judge;

20 for ᵃwe cannot stop speaking what we have seen and heard."

21 And when they had threatened them further, they let them go (finding no basis on which they might punish them) ᵃon account of the people, because they were all ᵇglorifying God for what had happened;

22 for the man was more than forty years old on whom this miracle of healing had been performed.

2   The prayer, 4:23-31

23 And when they had been released, they went to their own *companions,* and reported all that the chief priests and the elders had said to them.

24 And when they heard *this,* they lifted their voices to God with one accord and said, "O Lord, it is Thou who ᵃDIDST MAKE THE HEAVEN AND THE EARTH AND THE SEA, AND ALL THAT IS IN THEM,

25 who ᵃby the Holy Spirit, *through* the mouth of our father David Thy servant, didst say,

'ᵇWHY DID THE GENTILES RAGE,
AND THE PEOPLES DEVISE FUTILE THINGS?

26 'ᵃTHE KINGS OF THE EARTH TOOK THEIR STAND,
AND THE RULERS WERE GATHERED TOGETHER
AGAINST THE LORD, AND AGAINST HIS ᵇCHRIST.'

27 "For truly in this city there were gathered together against Thy holy ᵃservant Jesus, whom Thou didst anoint, both ᵇHerod and ᶜPontius Pilate, along with ᵈthe Gentiles and the peoples of Israel,

28 to do whatever Thy hand and ᵃThy purpose predestined to occur.

29 "And now, Lord, take note of their threats, and grant that Thy bond-servants may ᵃspeak Thy word with all ᵇconfidence,

30 while Thou dost extend Thy hand to heal, and ᵃsigns and wonders take place through the name of Thy holy ᵇservant Jesus."

31 And when they had prayed, the ᵃplace where they had

Cross references (margin)

★15-17
15 ᵃMatt. 5:22

16 ᵃJohn 11:47 ᵇActs 3:7-10

17 ᵃJohn 15:21

18 ᵃActs 5:28f.

19 ᵃActs 4:13 ᵇActs 5:28f.

20 ᵃ1 Cor. 9:16

21 ᵃActs 5:26 ᵇMatt. 9:8

★24-30
24 ᵃEx. 20:11; Ps. 146:6

25 ᵃActs 1:16 ᵇPs. 2:1

26 ᵃPs. 2:2 ᵇDan. 9:24f.; Luke 4:18; Acts 10:38; Heb. 1:9

★27 ᵃActs 3:13; 4:30 ᵇMatt. 14:1 ᶜMatt. 27:2; Luke 23:12 ᵈMatt. 20:19

28 ᵃActs 2:23

29 ᵃPhil. 1:14 ᵇActs 4:13, 31; 14:3

30 ᵃJohn 4:48 ᵇActs 3:13; 4:27

★31 ᵃActs 2:1 ᵇActs 2:4 ᶜPhil. 1:14 ᵈActs 4:13; 14:3

4:15-17 Though the Sanhedrin forbade further preaching, they did not try to disprove the resurrection of Jesus, which would have been the simplest way to discredit the apostles.

4:24-30 A prayer of thanksgiving for the sovereign power of God, not a prayer for deliverance from further opposition. The only petition in the prayer is for boldness (v. 29-31).

4:27 Responsibility for the death of Christ is laid upon both Jews and Gentiles.

4:31 *the Holy Spirit.* There are a number of references to the activity of the Holy Spirit in Acts: (1) He baptizes believers into the body of Christ, thus forming the Church (1:5; 11:15-16). (2) His presence in the believer is evidence of the new birth (2:38; 5:32; 10:44; 15:8). (3) He fills believers for witnessing (4:8), for leadership (6:3), for strength (7:55), and for special discernment (13:9). (4) He leads (13:4; 16:7).

gathered together was shaken, and they were all [b]filled with the Holy Spirit, and *began* to [c]speak the word of God with [d]boldness.

3 The provision, 4:32-37

[*32 [a]Acts 2:44]

32 And the congregation of those who believed were of one heart and soul; and not one *of them* claimed that anything belonging to him was his own; but [a]all things were common property to them.

[33 [a]Acts 1:8
[b]Luke 24:48]

33 And [a]with great power the apostles were giving [b]witness to the resurrection of the Lord Jesus, and abundant grace was upon them all.

[34 [a]Matt. 19:21; Acts 2:45]

34 For there was not a needy person among them, for all who were owners of land or houses [a]would sell them and bring the proceeds of the sales,

[35 [a]Acts 4:37; 5:2
[b]Acts 2:45; 6:1]

35 and [a]lay them at the apostles' feet; and they would be [b]distributed to each, as any had need.

[36 [a]Acts 11:19f.; 13:4; 15:39; 21:3, 16; 27:4
[b]Acts 9:27; 11:22, 30; 12:25; 13:15; 1 Cor. 9:6; Gal. 2:1, 9, 13; Col. 4:10
[c]Acts 2:40; 11:23; 13:15; 1 Cor. 14:3; 1 Thess. 2:3]

36 And Joseph, a Levite of [a]Cyprian birth, who was also called [b]Barnabas by the apostles (which translated means, Son of [c]Encouragement),

[37 [a]Acts 4:35; 5:2]

37 and who owned a tract of land, sold it and brought the money and [a]laid it at the apostles' feet.

E Purging and Persecution, 5:1-42

1 Purging from within, 5:1-11

[2 [a]Acts 5:3
[b]Acts 4:35, 37]

5 But a certain man named Ananias, with his wife Sapphira, sold a piece of property,

2 and [a]kept back *some* of the price for himself, with his wife's full knowledge, and bringing a portion of it, he [b]laid it at the apostles' feet.

3 But Peter said, "Ananias, why has [a]Satan filled your heart to lie [b]to the Holy Spirit, and to [c]keep back *some* of the price of the land?

4 "While it remained *unsold*, did it not remain your own? And after it was sold, was it not under your control? Why is it that you have conceived this deed in your heart? You have not lied to men, but [a]to God."

5 And as he heard these words, Ananias [a]fell down and breathed his last; and [b]great fear came upon all who heard of it.

6 And the young men arose and [a]covered him up, and after carrying him out, they buried him.

7 Now there elapsed an interval of about three hours, and his wife came in, not knowing what had happened.

8 And Peter [a]responded to her, "Tell me whether you sold the land [b]for such and such a price?" And she said, "Yes, that was the price."

9 Then Peter *said* to her, "Why is it that you have agreed together to [a]put [b]the Spirit of the Lord to the test? Behold, the feet of those who have buried your husband are at the door, and they shall carry you out *as well*."

10 And she [a]fell immediately at his feet, and breathed her last; and the young men came in and found her dead, and they carried her out and buried her beside her husband.

11 And [a]great fear came upon the whole church, and upon all who heard of these things.

[*3 [a]Matt. 4:10; Luke 22:3; John 13:2, 27
[b]Acts 5:4, 9
[c]Acts 5:2]

[4 [a]Acts 5:3, 9]

[5 [a]Ezek. 11:13; Acts 5:10 [b]Acts 2:43; 5:11]

[6 [a]John 19:40]

[8 [a]Acts 3:12 [b]Acts 5:2]

[*9 [a]Acts 15:10 [b]Acts 5:3, 4]

[10 [a]Ezek. 11:13; Acts 5:5]

[11 [a]Acts 2:43; 5:5]

4:32 *all things were common property to them.* This display of Christian charity did not abolish the right of personal property. Such community of goods was not compulsory but voluntary, as a way of eliminating need among them.

5:3 *to lie.* The sin of Ananias and Sapphira was not in not selling all their property, or in keeping part of the proceeds of the sale, but in lying about how much they had received. Lying to the Spirit is lying to God, because the Holy Spirit is God (v. 4).

5:9 *to put . . . to the test.* I.e., to see how far they could go in presuming on God's goodness.

2 Purging from without,
5:12-42

★12 aJohn 4:48 bJohn 10:23; Acts 3:11

12 And at the hands of the apostles many ^asigns and wonders were taking place among the people; and they were all with one accord in ^bSolomon's portico.

13 aActs 2:47; 4:21

13 But none of the rest dared to associate with them; however, ^athe people held them in high esteem.

14 a2 Cor. 6:15 bActs 2:47; 11:24

14 And all the more ^abelievers in the Lord, multitudes of men and women, were constantly ^badded to their number;

15 aActs 19:12

15 to such an extent that they even carried the sick out into the streets, and laid them on cots and pallets, so that when Peter came by, ^aat least his shadow might fall on any one of them.

16 And also the people from the cities in the vicinity of Jerusalem were coming together, bringing people who were sick or afflicted with unclean spirits; and they were all being healed.

★17 aActs 15:5 bMatt. 3:7; Acts 4:1

17 But the high priest rose up, along with all his associates (that is ^athe sect of ^bthe Sadducees), and they were filled with jealousy;

18 aActs 4:3

18 and they laid hands on the apostles, and ^aput them in a public jail.

19 aMatt. 1:20, 24; 2:13, 19; 28:2; Luke 1:11; 2:9; Acts 10:3; 12:7, 23; 27:23 **20** aJohn 6:63, 68

19 But ^aan angel of the Lord during the night opened the gates of the prison, and taking them out he said,

20 "Go your way, stand and speak to the people in the temple ^athe whole message of this Life."

★21 aJohn 8:2 bActs 4:6 cMatt. 5:22; Acts 5:27, 34, 41

21 And upon hearing this, they entered into the temple ^aabout daybreak, and began to teach. Now when ^bthe high priest and his associates had come, they called ^cthe Council together, even all the Senate of the sons of Israel,

and sent orders to the prison house for them to be brought.

22 aMatt. 26:58; Acts 5:26

22 But ^athe officers who came did not find them in the prison; and they returned, and reported back,

23 saying, "We found the prison house locked quite securely and the guards standing at the doors; but when we had opened up, we found no one inside."

24 aActs 4:1; 5:26

24 Now when ^athe captain of the temple guard and the chief priests heard these words, they were greatly perplexed about them as to what would come of this.

25 But someone came and reported to them, "Behold, the men whom you put in prison are standing in the temple and teaching the people!"

26 aActs 5:24 bActs 5:22 cActs 4:21; 5:13

26 Then ^athe captain went along with ^bthe officers and proceeded to bring them back without violence (for ^cthey were afraid of the people, lest they should be stoned).

27 aMatt. 5:22; Acts 5:21, 34, 41

27 And when they had brought them, they stood them before ^athe Council. And the high priest questioned them,

28 aActs 4:18 bMatt. 23:35; 27:25; Acts 2:23, 36; 3:14f.; 7:52

28 saying, "We gave you ^astrict orders not to continue teaching in this name, and behold, you have filled Jerusalem with your teaching, and ^bintend to bring this man's blood upon us."

29 aActs 4:19

29 But Peter and the apostles answered and said, "^aWe must obey God rather than men.

30 aActs 3:13 bActs 2:24 cActs 10:39; 13:29; Gal. 3:13; 1 Pet. 2:24

30 "^aThe God of our fathers ^braised up Jesus, whom you had ^cput to death by hanging Him on a cross.

★31 aActs 2:33 bActs 3:15 cLuke 2:11 dLuke 24:47; Acts 2:38

31 "^aHe is the one whom God exalted to His right hand as a ^bPrince and a ^cSavior, to grant ^drepentance to Israel, and forgiveness of sins.

5:12 *Solomon's portico.* See note on 3:11.
5:17 Again the *Sadducees,* who did not believe in resurrection (23:8), were particularly riled at the disciples' preaching the resurrection of Christ (4:33).

5:21 *Council . . . Senate.* These are the same body, the Jewish Sanhedrin.
5:31 *Prince* = Author (Heb. 12:2), or Leader (cf. Acts 3:15).

32 aLuke 24:48 bJohn 15:26; Acts 15:28; Rom. 8:16; Heb. 2:4

33 aActs 2:37; 7:54

★34 aActs 22:3 bLuke 2:46; 5:17 cActs 5:21

★36 aActs 8:9; Gal. 2:6; 6:3

★37 aLuke 2:2

38 aMark 11:30

39 aProv. 21:30; Acts 11:17

40 aMatt. 10:17

32 "And we are awitnesses of these things; and bso is the Holy Spirit, whom God has given to those who obey Him."

33 But when they heard this, they were acut to the quick and were intending to slay them.

34 But a certain Pharisee named aGamaliel, a bteacher of the Law, respected by all the people, stood up in cthe Council and gave orders to put the men outside for a short time.

35 And he said to them, "Men of Israel, take care what you propose to do with these men.

36 "For some time ago Theudas rose up, aclaiming to be somebody; and a group of about four hundred men joined up with him. And he was slain; and all who followed him were dispersed and came to nothing.

37 "After this man Judas of Galilee rose up in the days of athe census, and drew away some people after him, he too perished, and all those who followed him were scattered.

38 "And so in the present case, I say to you, stay away from these men and let them alone, for if this plan or action should abe of men, it will be overthrown;

39 but if it is of God, you will not be able to overthrow them; or else you may even be found afighting against God."

40 And they took his advice; and after calling the apostles in, they aflogged them and ordered them to speak no more in the name of Jesus, and then released them.

41 So they went on their way from the presence of the aCouncil, brejoicing that they had been considered worthy to suffer shame cfor His name.

42 aAnd every day, in the temple and from house to house, they kept right on teaching and bpreaching Jesus as the Christ.

F Choosing Colaborers, 6:1-7

6 Now at this time while the adisciples were increasing bin number, a complaint arose on the part of the cHellenistic Jews against the native dHebrews, because their ewidows were being overlooked in fthe daily serving of food.

2 And the twelve summoned the congregation of the disciples and said, "It is not desirable for us to neglect the word of God in order to serve tables.

3 "But select from among you, abrethren, seven men of good reputation, bfull of the Spirit and of wisdom, whom we may put in charge of this task.

4 "But we will adevote ourselves to prayer, and to the ministry of the word."

5 And the statement found approval with the whole congregation; and they chose aStephen, a man bfull of faith and of the Holy Spirit, and cPhilip, Prochorus, Nicanor, Timon, Parmenas and Nicolas, a dproselyte from eAntioch.

41 aActs 5:21 b1 Pet. 4:14, 16 cJohn 15:21

42 aActs 2:46 bActs 8:35; 11:20; 17:18; Gal. 1:16

★ 1 aActs 11:26 bActs 2:47; 6:7 cActs 9:29; 11:20 marg. d2 Cor. 11:22; Phil. 3:5 eActs 9:39, 41; 1 Tim. 5:3 fActs 4:35; 11:29

★ 2

3 aJohn 21:23; Acts 1:15 bActs 2:4

4 aActs 1:14

★ 5 aActs 6:8ff.; 11:19; 22:20 bActs 6:3; 11:24 cActs 8:5ff.; 21:8 dMatt. 23:15 eActs 11:19

5:34 *Gamaliel.* A respected rabbi who followed the liberal interpretations of Hillel, another rabbi who lived shortly before the time of Christ. His popularity demanded that the Sanhedrin listen to him. Paul was a student of Gamaliel (22:3).

5:36 *Theudas.* This is the only historical reference to him.

5:37 *Judas . . . rose up.* This revolt (in A.D. 6) is described by the historian Josephus. The followers of this Judas became the "Zealots."

6:1 *Hellenistic Jews . . . Hebrews.* The former were Greek-speaking Jewish Christians and the latter, Aramaic-speaking Jewish Christians.

6:2 *serve tables.* I.e., tables of food for the widows or of money (as in John 2:15). The Greek word for "serve" is the one from which we derive "deacon," but these men were "deacons" only in the sense of being servants. They were not yet deacons in the later sense of officers in the church (see note on 1 Tim. 3:8).

6:5 All seven had Greek, not Jewish, names; two, Stephen and Philip, quickly achieved prominence for their vigorous evangelism.

6 And these they brought before the apostles; and after apraying, they blaid their hands on them.

7 And athe word of God kept on spreading; and bthe number of the disciples continued to increase greatly in Jerusalem, and a great many of the priests were becoming obedient to cthe faith.

G Stephen, the First Martyr, 6:8–8:3

1 The stirring of the people, 6:8–15

8 And Stephen, full of grace and power, was performing great awonders and signs among the people.

9 But some men from what was called the Synagogue of the Freedmen, including both aCyrenians and bAlexandrians, and some from cCilicia and dAsia, rose up and argued with Stephen.

10 And yet they were unable to cope with the wisdom and the Spirit with which he was speaking.

11 Then they secretly induced men to say, "We have heard him speak blasphemous words against Moses and against God."

12 And they stirred up the people, the elders and the scribes, and they acame upon him and dragged him away, and brought him before bthe Council.

13 And they put forward afalse witnesses who said, "This man incessantly speaks against this bholy place, and the Law;

14 for we have heard him say that athis Nazarene, Jesus, will destroy this place and alter bthe customs which Moses handed down to us."

15 And fixing their gaze on him, all who were sitting in the aCouncil saw his face like the face of an angel.

2 The sermon of Stephen, 7:1–53

7 And the high priest said, "Are these things so?"

2 And he said, "Hear me, abrethren and fathers! bThe God of glory cappeared to our father Abraham when he was in Mesopotamia, before he lived in Haran,

3 and said to him, 'aDEPART FROM YOUR COUNTRY AND YOUR RELATIVES, AND COME INTO THE LAND THAT I WILL SHOW YOU.'

4 "aThen he departed from the land of the Chaldeans, and settled in Haran. And bfrom there, after his father died, God removed him into this country in which you are now living.

5 "And He gave him no inheritance in it, not even a foot of ground; and yet, even when he had no child, aHe promised that HE WOULD GIVE IT TO HIM AS A POSSESSION, AND TO HIS OFFSPRING AFTER HIM.

6 "But aGod spoke to this effect, that his OFFSPRING WOULD BE ALIENS IN A FOREIGN LAND, AND THAT THEY WOULD BE ENSLAVED AND MISTREATED FOR FOUR HUNDRED YEARS.

7 " 'AND WHATEVER NATION TO WHICH THEY SHALL BE IN BONDAGE I

6:6 *laid their hands on them.* The laying on of hands was a formal sign of appointment to this service. The rite indicates a link or association between the parties involved. Sometimes it was related to healing (Mark 5:23) or to the impartation of the Spirit (Acts 8:17; 9:17; 19:6) or, as here, was a sign of ordination for special service (13:3; 1 Tim. 4:14).

6:9 *Freedmen.* These were Jewish freedmen, or descendants of freedmen, from the various places mentioned in the verse. They had their own synagogue in Jerusalem.

6:12 *the Council.* The Sanhedrin. See note on

Luke 22:66.

7:1 *the high priest.* Caiaphas.

7:2-53 Stephen's sermon is the longest recorded in Acts. The text is: "you are doing just as your fathers did" (v. 51). Stephen recited the privileges of the nation Israel and their rejection of God's messengers; then he laid blame for the slaying of Jesus squarely on his hearers (v. 52).

7:2 God's call to *Abraham* came first when he was in *Mesopotamia* (Gen. 15:7; Neh. 9:7). Later he went to Haran (Gen. 11:31-32) and later to Palestine.

MYSELF WILL JUDGE,' said God, 'AND ^aAFTER THAT THEY WILL COME OUT AND SERVE ME IN THIS PLACE.'

8 "And He ^agave him the covenant of circumcision; and so ^bAbraham became the father of Isaac, and circumcised him on the eighth day; and ^cIsaac *became the father of* Jacob, and ^dJacob *of the* twelve ^epatriarchs.

9 "And the patriarchs ^abecame jealous of Joseph and sold him into Egypt. And *yet* God was with him,

10 and rescued him from all his afflictions, and ^agranted him favor and wisdom in the sight of Pharaoh, king of Egypt; and he made him governor over Egypt and all his household.

11 "Now ^aa famine came over all Egypt and Canaan, and great affliction *with it*; and our fathers could find no food.

12 "But ^awhen Jacob heard that there was grain in Egypt, he sent our fathers *there* the first time.

13 "And on the second *visit* ^aJoseph made himself known to his brothers, and Joseph's family was disclosed to Pharaoh.

14 "And ^aJoseph sent *word* and invited Jacob his father and all his relatives to come to him, ^bseventy-five ^cpersons *in all.*

15 "And ^aJacob went down to Egypt and *there* passed away, he and our fathers.

16 "And *from there* they were removed to ^aShechem, and laid in the tomb which Abraham had purchased for a sum of money from the sons of Hamor in Shechem.

17 "But as the time of the promise was approaching which God had assured to Abraham,

^athe people increased and multiplied in Egypt,

18 until ^aTHERE AROSE ANOTHER KING OVER EGYPT WHO KNEW NOTHING ABOUT JOSEPH.

19 "It was he who took ^ashrewd advantage of our race, and mistreated our fathers so that they would expose their infants and they would not survive.

20 "And it was at this time that ^aMoses was born; and he was lovely in the sight of God; and he was nurtured three months in his father's home.

21 "And after he had been exposed, ^aPharaoh's daughter took him away, and nurtured him as her own son.

22 "And Moses was educated in all ^athe learning of the Egyptians, and he was a man of power in words and deeds.

23 "But when he was approaching the age of forty, ^ait entered his mind to visit his brethren, the sons of Israel.

24 "And when he saw one *of them* being treated unjustly, he defended him and took vengeance for the oppressed by striking down the Egyptian.

25 "And he supposed that his brethren understood that God was granting them deliverance through him; but they did not understand.

26 "^aAnd on the following day he appeared to them as they were fighting together, and he tried to reconcile them in peace, saying, 'Men, you are brethren, why do you injure one another?'

27 "^aBut the one who was injuring his neighbor pushed him away, saying, 'WHO MADE YOU A RULER AND JUDGE OVER US?

28 '^aYOU DO NOT MEAN TO KILL

Cross-references (left column margin):

★ **8** ^aGen. 17:10ff.; ^bGen. 21:2-4; ^cGen. 25:26; ^dGen. 29:31ff.; 30:5ff.; 35:23ff.; ^eActs 2:29

★ **9** ^aGen. 37:11, 28; 39:2, 21f.; 45:4

10 ^aGen. 39:21; 41:40-46; Ps. 105:21

11 ^aGen. 41:54f.; 42:5

12 ^aGen. 42:2

13 ^aGen. 45:1-4

★**14** ^aGen. 45:9f.; ^bGen. 46:26f.; Ex. 1:5; Deut. 10:22; ^cActs 2:41

★**15-16** **15** ^aGen. 46:5; 49:33; Ex. 1:6

16 ^aGen. 23:16; 33:19; 50:13; Josh. 24:32

17 ^aEx. 1:7f.

Cross-references (right column margin):

18 ^aEx. 1:8

19 ^aEx. 1:10f., 16ff.

★**20** ^aEx. 2:2

21 ^aEx. 2:5f., 10

22 ^a1 Kin. 4:30; Is. 19:11

23 ^aEx. 2:11f.

26 ^aEx. 2:13f.

27 ^aEx. 2:14; Acts 7:35

28 ^aEx. 2:14

7:8 *circumcision.* See Gen. 17:9-14.

7:9 *Joseph.* See Gen. 37:11.

7:14 *seventy-five persons.* This number follows the Septuagint (Greek translation of the O.T.), which arrived at 75 by including the son and grandson of Manasseh and two sons and a grandson of Ephraim. See Gen. 46:27, which reflects a different way of numbering Jacob's family, totaling 70.

7:15-16 Jacob was buried at Hebron in the Cave of Machpelah, which Abraham bought from Ephron the Hittite (Gen. 23:16). Joseph was buried at Shechem in a piece of ground Jacob bought from the sons of Hamor (Josh. 24:32). The two transactions are simply telescoped in these verses because of the pressure of Stephen's circumstances and need for brevity.

7:20 *Moses.* See Ex. 2 and Heb. 11:24-26.

ME AS YOU KILLED THE EGYPTIAN YES-
TERDAY, DO YOU?'

29 "And at this remark ^aMOSES
FLED, AND BECAME AN ALIEN IN THE
LAND OF MIDIAN, where he became
the father of two sons.

30 "And after forty years had
passed, ^aAN ANGEL APPEARED TO HIM
IN THE WILDERNESS OF MOUNT SINAI,
IN THE FLAME OF A BURNING THORN
BUSH.

31 "And when Moses saw it,
he *began* to marvel at the sight;
and as he approached to look
more closely, there came the voice
of the Lord:

32 '^aI AM THE GOD OF YOUR FA-
THERS, THE GOD OF ABRAHAM AND
ISAAC AND JACOB.' And Moses
shook with fear and would not
venture to look.

33 "BUT THE LORD SAID TO HIM,
'^aTAKE OFF THE SANDALS FROM YOUR
FEET, FOR THE PLACE ON WHICH YOU
ARE STANDING IS HOLY GROUND.

34 '^aI HAVE CERTAINLY SEEN THE
OPPRESSION OF MY PEOPLE IN EGYPT,
AND HAVE HEARD THEIR GROANS, AND I
HAVE COME DOWN TO DELIVER THEM;
^bCOME NOW, AND I WILL SEND YOU TO
EGYPT.'

35 "This Moses whom they
^adisowned, saying, 'WHO MADE
YOU A RULER AND A JUDGE?' is the
one whom God sent *to be* both a
ruler and a deliverer with the help
of the angel who appeared to him
in the thorn bush.

36 "^aThis man led them out,
performing ^bwonders and signs in
the land of Egypt and in the Red
Sea and in the ^cwilderness for
forty years.

37 "This is the Moses who said
to the sons of Israel, 'GOD SHALL
RAISE UP FOR YOU ^aA PROPHET LIKE ME
FROM YOUR BRETHREN.'

38 "This is the one who was in
^athe congregation in the wilder-
ness together with ^bthe angel who
was speaking to him on Mount
Sinai, and *who was* with our fa-
thers; and he received ^cliving ^dor-
acles to pass on to you.

39 "And our fathers were unwilling to be obedient to him, but
^arepudiated him and in their
hearts turned back to Egypt,

40 SAYING TO AARON, '^aMAKE
FOR US GODS WHO WILL GO BEFORE US;
FOR THIS MOSES WHO LED US OUT OF
THE LAND OF EGYPT—WE DO NOT
KNOW WHAT HAPPENED TO HIM.'

41 "And at that time ^athey
made a calf and brought a sacrifice to the idol, and were rejoicing
in ^bthe works of their hands.

42 "But God ^aturned away and
delivered them up to serve the
host of heaven; as it is written in
the book of the prophets, '^bIT WAS
NOT TO ME THAT YOU OFFERED VIC-
TIMS AND SACRIFICES ^cFORTY YEARS IN
THE WILDERNESS, WAS IT, O HOUSE OF
ISRAEL?

43 '^aYOU ALSO TOOK ALONG THE
TABERNACLE OF MOLOCH AND THE
STAR OF THE GOD ROMPHA, THE IM-
AGES WHICH YOU MADE TO WORSHIP
THEM. I ALSO WILL REMOVE YOU BE-
YOND BABYLON.'

44 "Our fathers had ^athe tabernacle of testimony in the wilderness, just as He who spoke to
Moses directed *him* to make it according to the pattern which he
had seen.

45 "And having received it in
their turn, our fathers ^abrought it
in with Joshua upon dispossessing
the nations whom God drove out

Cross references (left margin):

29 ^aEx. 2:15, 22
30 ^aEx. 3:1f.
32 ^aEx. 3:6
33 ^aEx. 3:5
34 ^aEx. 3:7 ^bEx. 3:10
35 ^aActs 7:27
36 ^aEx. 12:41; 33:1; Heb. 8:9 ^bEx. 7:3; John 4:48 ^cEx. 16:35; Num. 14:33; Ps. 95:8-10; Acts 7:42; 13:18; Heb. 3:8f.
37 ^aDeut. 18:15; Acts 3:22

Cross references (right margin):

★38 ^aEx. 19:17 ^bActs 7:53 ^cDeut. 32:47; Heb. 4:12 ^dRom. 3:2; Heb. 5:12; 1 Pet. 4:11
39 ^aNum. 14:3f.
40 ^aEx. 32:1, 23
41 ^aEx. 32:4, 6 ^bRev. 9:20
42 ^aJosh. 24:20; Is. 63:10; Jer. 19:13; Ezek. 20:39 ^bAmos 5:25 ^cActs 7:36
★43 ^aAmos 5:26, 27
★44 ^aEx. 25:8, 9; 38:21
45 ^aDeut. 32:49; Josh. 3:14ff.; 18:1; 23:9; 24:18; Ps. 44:2f.

7:38 *the congregation in the wilderness.* Lit.,
the assembly in the wilderness; i.e., the gathering of the people to receive the law. The
word translated "church" (or congregation, assembly, gathering) is used in the N.T. of four
kinds of groups: (1) the children of Israel gathered as a nation; (2) in Acts 19:32, 39, 41, a
group of townspeople assembled in a town
meeting; (3) in a technical sense, all believers
who are gathered together in the one body of
Christ, the Church universal (Col. 1:18); and

(4) most frequently, in reference to a local
group of professing Christians; e.g., the church
at Antioch (Acts 13:1).
7:43 *Moloch . . . Rompha.* Moloch was a title
for various Canaanite deities to whom human
sacrifices were offered. Rompha, (better, Re-
phan) was the name of a god connected with
the planet Saturn.
7:44 *tabernacle of testimony.* I.e., the tabernacle was a testimony to the presence of God in
their midst.

before our fathers, until the time of David.

46 "And ᵃ*David* found favor in God's sight, and asked that he might find a dwelling place for the God of Jacob.

47 "But it was ᵃSolomon who built a house for Him.

48 "However, ᵃthe Most High does not dwell in *houses* made by *human* hands; as the prophet says:

49 'ᵃHᴇᴀᴠᴇɴ ɪs Mʏ ᴛʜʀoɴᴇ,
ᴀɴᴅ ᴇᴀʀᴛʜ ɪs ᴛʜᴇ ғooᴛsᴛooʟ
ᴏғ Mʏ ғᴇᴇᴛ;
Wʜᴀᴛ ᴋɪɴᴅ ᴏғ ʜᴏᴜsᴇ ᴡɪʟʟ
ʏᴏᴜ ʙᴜɪʟᴅ ғᴏʀ Mᴇ?' says
the Lord;
'Oʀ ᴡʜᴀᴛ ᴘʟᴀᴄᴇ ɪs ᴛʜᴇʀᴇ ғoʀ
Mʏ ʀᴇᴘᴏsᴇ?

50 'ᵃWᴀs ɪᴛ ɴᴏᴛ Mʏ ʜᴀɴᴅ
ᴡʜɪᴄʜ ᴍᴀᴅᴇ ᴀʟʟ ᴛʜᴇsᴇ
ᴛʜɪɴɢs?'

51 "You men who are ᵃstiff-necked and uncircumcised in heart and ears are always resisting the Holy Spirit; you are doing just as your fathers did.

52 "ᵃWhich one of the prophets did your fathers not persecute? And they killed those who had previously announced the coming of ᵇthe Righteous One, whose betrayers and murderers ᶜyou have now become;

53 you who received the law as ᵃordained by angels, and *yet* did not keep it."

3 *The stoning of Stephen,*
7:54-8:3

54 Now when they heard this, they were ᵃcut to the quick,

and they *began* gnashing their teeth at him.

55 But being ᵃfull of the Holy Spirit, he ᵇgazed intently into heaven and saw the glory of God, and Jesus standing ᶜat the right hand of God;

56 and he said, "Behold, I see the ᵃheavens opened up and ᵇthe Son of Man standing at the right hand of God."

57 But they cried out with a loud voice, and covered their ears, and they rushed upon him with one impulse.

58 And when they had ᵃdriven him out of the city, they *began* stoning *him,* and ᵇthe witnesses ᶜlaid aside their robes at the feet of ᵈa young man named Saul.

59 And they went on stoning Stephen as he ᵃcalled upon *the Lord* and said, "Lord Jesus, receive my spirit!"

60 And ᵃfalling on his knees, he cried out with a loud voice, "Lord, ᵇdo not hold this sin against them!" And having said this, he ᶜfell asleep.

8 And ᵃSaul was in hearty agreement with putting him to death.

And on that day a great persecution arose against ᵇthe church in Jerusalem; and they were all ᶜscattered throughout the regions of Judea and ᵈSamaria, except the apostles.

2 And *some* devout men buried Stephen, and made loud lamentation over him.

3 But ᵃSaul *began* ravaging the church, entering house after house; and ᵇdragging off men and women, he would put them in prison.

46 ᵃ2 Sam. 7:8ff.; Ps. 132:1-5; Acts 13:22
47 ᵃ1 Kin. 8:20
48 ᵃLuke 1:32
49 ᵃIs. 66:1; Matt. 5:34f.
50 ᵃIs. 66:2
★**51-53**
51 ᵃEx. 32:9; 33:3, 5; Lev. 26:41; Num. 27:14; Is. 63:10; Jer. 6:10; 9:26
52 ᵃ2 Chr. 36:15f.; Matt. 5:12; 23:31, 37 ᵇActs 3:14; 22:14; 1 John 2:1 ᶜActs 3:14; 5:28
53 ᵃDeut. 33:2 [Septuagint]; Acts 7:38; Gal. 3:19; Heb. 2:2
54 ᵃActs 5:33

★**55** ᵃActs 2:4 ᵇJohn 11:41 ᶜMark 16:19
56 ᵃJohn 1:51 ᵇMatt. 8:20
★**58** ᵃLev. 24:14, 16; Luke 4:29 ᵇDeut. 13:9f.; 17:7; Acts 6:13 ᶜActs 22:20 ᵈActs 8:1; 22:20; 26:10
59 ᵃActs 9:14, 21; 22:16; Rom. 10:12, 13f.; 1 Cor. 1:2; 2 Tim. 2:22
★**60** ᵃLuke 22:41 ᵇMatt. 5:44; Luke 23:34 ᶜDan. 12:2; Matt. 27:52; John 11:11f.; Acts 13:36; 1 Cor. 15:6, 18, 20; 1 Thess. 4:13ff.; 2 Pet. 3:4
1 ᵃActs 7:58; 22:20; 26:10 ᵇActs 8:4; 11:19 ᶜActs 9:31 ᵈActs 1:8; 8:5, 14; 9:31
3 ᵃActs 9:1, 13, 21; 22:4, 19; 26:10f.; 1 Cor. 15:9; Gal. 1:13; Phil. 3:6; 1 Tim. 1:13 ᵇJames 2:6

7:51-53 Stephen's indictment of unbelieving Jews, amply illustrated in the previously cited history of Israel.
7:55 *Jesus standing at the right hand of God.* Jesus' priestly work of offering a sacrifice for sin was finished on the cross; He is therefore sometimes pictured as seated at the right hand of God (Heb. 1:3). But His priestly work of sustaining His people continues (as here with

Stephen); therefore, He is portrayed as standing to minister (cf. Rev. 2:1).
7:58 The mention of *witnesses* suggests that they went through the motions of a legal execution (Lev. 24:14), though probably without securing the official approval of Pilate.
7:60 *he fell asleep.* This expression is used of the physical death of believers (John 11:11; 1 Thess. 4:13, 15).

II CHRISTIANITY IN PALESTINE AND SYRIA, 8:4–12:25

A The Christians Scattered, 8:4–40

1 The preaching in Samaria, 8:4–25

★ **4** *a*Acts 8:1 *b*Acts 8:12; 15:35

4 Therefore, those *a*who had been scattered went about *b*preaching the word.

★ **5** *a*Acts 6:5; 8:26, 30

5 And *a*Philip went down to the city of Samaria and *began* proclaiming Christ to them.

6 And the multitudes with one accord were giving attention to what was said by Philip, as they heard and saw the signs which he was performing.

7 *a*Mark 16:17 *b*Matt. 4:24

7 For *in the case of* many who had *a*unclean spirits, they were coming out *of them* shouting with a loud voice; and many who had been *b*paralyzed and lame were healed.

8 *a*John 4:40-42; Acts 8:39

8 And there was *a*much rejoicing in that city.

★ **9** *a*Acts 8:11; 13:6 *b*Acts 5:36

9 Now there was a certain man named Simon, who formerly was practicing *a*magic in the city, and astonishing the people of Samaria, *b*claiming to be someone great;

10 *a*Acts 14:11; 28:6

10 and they all, from smallest to greatest, were giving attention to him, saying, "*a*This man is what is called the Great Power of God."

11 *a*Acts 8:9; 13:6

11 And they were giving him attention because he had for a long time astonished them with his *a*magic arts.

12 But when they believed Philip *a*preaching the good news about the kingdom of God and the name of Jesus Christ, they were being *b*baptized, men and women alike.

12 *a*Acts 1:3; 8:4 *b*Acts 2:38

13 And even Simon himself believed; and after being baptized, he continued on with Philip; and as he observed *a*signs and *b*great miracles taking place, he was constantly amazed.

★ **13** *a*Acts 8:6 *b*Acts 19:11

14 Now when *a*the apostles in Jerusalem heard that Samaria had received the word of God, they sent them *b*Peter and John,

14 *a*Acts 8:1 *b*Luke 22:8

★ **14-17**

15 who came down and prayed for them, *a*that they might receive the Holy Spirit.

15 *a*Acts 2:38; 19:2

16 For He had not yet fallen upon any of them; they had simply been *a*baptized in the name of the Lord Jesus.

16 *a*Matt. 28:19

17 Then they *a*began laying their hands on them, and they were *b*receiving the Holy Spirit.

17 *a*Mark 5:23; Acts 6:6 *b*Acts 2:4

18 Now when Simon saw that the Spirit was bestowed through the laying on of the apostles' hands, he offered them money,

★ **18-24**

19 saying, "Give this authority to me as well, so that everyone on whom I lay my hands may receive the Holy Spirit."

20 But Peter said to him, "May your silver perish with you, because you thought you could *a*obtain the gift of God with money!

20 *a*2 Kin. 5:16; Is. 55:1; Dan. 5:17; Matt. 10:8; Acts 2:38

21 "You have *a*no part or portion in this matter, for your heart is not *b*right before God.

21 *a*Deut. 10:9; 12:12; Eph. 5:5 *b*Ps. 78:37

22 "Therefore repent of this wickedness of yours, and pray the

---

8:4 *went about.* See 11:19 for details.

8:5 *Philip.* See 6:5. *the city of Samaria* was then called Sebaste. Some texts read "a city of Samaria," which would mean some smaller city in Samaria. On the Samaritans see the note on Luke 10:33.

8:9 *magic.* Simon was a practitioner of magic, quackery, and various kinds of sorcery. He may also have made Messianic claims.

8:13 *Simon himself believed.* Peter's denunciation (vv. 20–23) indicates that Simon's faith was not unto salvation (Jas. 2:14-20).

8:14–17 Though the Samaritans had been baptized in water (v. 12), the gift of the Holy Spirit

was delayed until Peter and John came and laid their hands on them. Normally the Spirit is given at the moment of faith (10:44; 19:2; Eph. 1:13). In this instance, however, it was imperative that the Samaritans be identified with the apostles and the Jerusalem church so that there would be no rival Samaritan Christian church.

8:18–24 Simon thought he could buy the gift of God (v. 20). When Peter urged him to repent, Simon replied, in effect, "Pray for me that I may escape punishment" (v. 24). He was still thinking in terms of magical powers rather than repentance of heart.

Lord that if possible, the intention of your heart may be forgiven you.

23 *a*Is. 58:6

23 "For I see that you are in the gall of bitterness and in *a*the bondage of iniquity."

24 But Simon answered and said, "Pray to the Lord for me yourselves, so that nothing of what you have said may come upon me."

25 *a*Luke 16:28 *b*Acts 13:12 *c*Acts 8:40 *d*Matt. 10:5

25 And so, when they had solemnly *a*testified and spoken *b*the word of the Lord, they started back to Jerusalem, and were *c*preaching the gospel to many villages of the *d*Samaritans.

2　The preaching on the Gaza road, 8:26-40

★26 *a*Acts 5:19; 8:29 *b*Acts 8:5 *c*Gen. 10:19

26 But *a*an angel of the Lord spoke to *b*Philip saying, "Arise and go south to the road that descends from Jerusalem to *c*Gaza." (This is a desert *road*.)

★27 *a*Ps. 68:31; 87:4; Is. 56:3ff. *b*1 Kin. 8:41f.; John 12:20

27 And he arose and went; and behold, *a*there was an Ethiopian eunuch, a court official of Candace, queen of the Ethiopians, who was in charge of all her treasure; and he *b*had come to Jerusalem to worship.

28 And he was returning and sitting in his chariot, and was reading the prophet Isaiah.

29 *a*Acts 8:39; 10:19; 11:12; 13:2; 16:6, 7; 20:23; 21:11; 28:25; Heb. 3:7

29 And *a*the Spirit said to Philip, "Go up and join this chariot."

30 And when Philip had run up, he heard him reading Isaiah the prophet, and said, "Do you understand what you are reading?"

31 And he said, "Well, how could I, unless someone guides

me?" And he invited Philip to come up and sit with him.

32 Now the passage of Scripture which he was reading was this:

32 *a*Is. 53:7

"*a*HE WAS LED AS A SHEEP TO SLAUGHTER;
AND AS A LAMB BEFORE ITS SHEARER IS SILENT,
SO HE DOES NOT OPEN HIS MOUTH.

33 *a*Is. 53:8f.

33 "*a*IN HUMILIATION HIS JUDGMENT WAS TAKEN AWAY;
WHO SHALL RELATE HIS GENERATION?
FOR HIS LIFE IS REMOVED FROM THE EARTH."

34 And the eunuch answered Philip and said, "Please *tell me*, of whom does the prophet say this? Of himself, or of someone else?"

★35 *a*Matt. 5:2 *b*Luke 24:27; Acts 17:2; 18:28; 28:23 *c*Acts 5:42

35 And Philip *a*opened his mouth, and *b*beginning from this Scripture he *c*preached Jesus to him.

36 *a*Acts 10:47

36 And as they went along the road they came to some water; and the eunuch *said, "Look! Water! *a*What prevents me from being baptized?"

★37

37 [And Philip said, "If you believe with all your heart, you may." And he answered and said, "I believe that Jesus Christ is the Son of God."]

39 *a*1 Kin. 18:12; 2 Kin. 2:16; Ezek. 3:12, 14; 8:3; 11:1, 24; 43:5; 2 Cor. 12:2
★40 *a*Josh. 11:22; 1 Sam. 5:1 *b*Acts 8:25 *c*Acts 9:30; 10:1, 24; 11:11; 12:19; 18:22; 21:8, 16; 23:23, 33; 25:1, 4, 6, 13

38 And he ordered the chariot to stop; and they both went down into the water, Philip as well as the eunuch; and he baptized him.

39 And when they came up out of the water, *a*the Spirit of the Lord snatched Philip away; and the eunuch saw him no more, but went on his way rejoicing.

40 But Philip found himself at *a*Azotus; and as he passed through he *b*kept preaching the

---

8:26 *a desert road.* Possibly the road to Desert Gaza, the old city which had been destroyed in 93 B.C. and which was inland from the Gaza of N.T. times.

8:27 *Ethiopian.* Not from present-day Abyssinia but ancient Nubia, south of Aswan. The story shows how far the gospel was spreading. *Candace.* The hereditary title of Ethiopian queens.

8:35 *preached Jesus to him.* Before the coming

of Jesus, the Jews understood Isa. 53 as referring to the Messiah. This interpretation was abandoned as Christians applied the prophecy to Jesus of Nazareth, and Isa. 53 was then considered by the Jews to be referring either to Isaiah himself or to the people of Israel, who would be a light to the nations, etc.

8:37 Most manuscripts do not contain this verse.

8:40 *Azotus* = O.T. Ashdod, 20 miles N. of Gaza.

gospel to all the cities, until he came to ^{c}Caesarea.

B   The Conversion of Paul,
9:1-31
1 The account of Paul's conversion, 9:1-19

★ **1-19**
1 ^{a}Acts 9:1-22; 22:3-16; 26:9-18
^{b}Acts 8:3; 9:13-21

★ **2** ^{a}Acts 9:14, 21; 22:5; 26:10
^{b}Matt. 10:17
^{c}Gen. 14:15; 2 Cor. 11:32; Gal. 1:17
^{d}John 14:6; Acts 18:25f.; 19:9, 23; 22:4; 24:14, 22

3 ^{a}1 Cor. 15:8

4 ^{a}Acts 22:7; 26:14

★**5**

6 ^{a}Acts 9:16

7 ^{a}Acts 26:14 ^{b}Acts 22:9 [John 12:29f.]

8 ^{a}Acts 9:18; 22:11 ^{b}Gen. 14:15; 2 Cor. 11:32; Gal. 1:17

9 ^{a}Now Saul, still ^{b}breathing threats and murder against the disciples of the Lord, went to the high priest,
2 and asked for ^{a}letters from him to ^{b}the synagogues at ^{c}Damascus, so that if he found any belonging to ^{d}the Way, both men and women, he might bring them bound to Jerusalem.
3 And it came about that as he journeyed, he was approaching Damascus, and ^{a}suddenly a light from heaven flashed around him;
4 and ^{a}he fell to the ground, and heard a voice saying to him, "Saul, Saul, why are you persecuting Me?"
5 And he said, "Who art Thou, Lord?" And He $said,$ "I am Jesus whom you are persecuting,
6 but rise, and enter the city, and ^{a}it shall be told you what you must do."
7 And the men who traveled with him ^{a}stood speechless, ^{b}hearing the voice, but seeing no one.
8 And Saul got up from the ground, and ^{a}though his eyes were open, he could see nothing; and leading him by the hand, they brought him into ^{b}Damascus.

9 And he was three days without sight, and neither ate nor drank.
10 Now there was a certain disciple at ^{a}Damascus, named ^{b}Ananias; and the Lord said to him in ^{c}a vision, "Ananias." And he said, "Behold, $here am$ I, Lord."
11 And the Lord $said$ to him, "Arise and go to the street called Straight, and inquire at the house of Judas for a man from ^{a}Tarsus named Saul, for behold, he is praying,
12 and he has seen in a vision a man named Ananias come in and ^{a}lay his hands on him, so that he might regain his sight."
13 But Ananias answered, "Lord, I have heard from many about this man, ^{a}how much harm he did to ^{b}Thy saints at Jerusalem;
14 and here he ^{a}has authority from the chief priests to bind all who ^{b}call upon Thy name."
15 But the Lord said to him, "Go, for ^{a}he is a chosen instrument of Mine, to bear My name before ^{b}the Gentiles and ^{c}kings and the sons of Israel;
16 for ^{a}I will show him how much he must suffer for My name's sake."
17 And Ananias departed and entered the house, and after ^{a}laying his hands on him said, "^{b}Brother Saul, the Lord Jesus, who appeared to you on the road by which you were coming, has sent me so that you may regain

★**10** ^{a}Gen. 14:15; 2 Cor. 11:32; Gal. 1:17 ^{b}Acts 22:12 ^{c}Acts 10:3, 17, 19; 11:5; 12:9; 16:9f.; 18:9

11 ^{a}Acts 9:30; 11:25; 21:39; 22:3

12 ^{a}Mark 5:23; Acts 6:6; 9:17

13 ^{a}Acts 8:3 ^{b}Acts 9:32, 41; 26:10; Rom 1:7; 15:25f., 31; 16:2, 15; 1 Cor. 1:2

14 ^{a}Acts 9:2, 21 ^{b}Acts 7:59

15 ^{a}Acts 13:2; Rom. 1:1; 9:23; Gal. 1:15; Eph. 3:7 ^{b}Acts 22:21; 26:17; Rom. 1:5; 11:13; 15:16; Gal. 1:16; 2:7ff.; Eph. 3:2, 8; 1 Tim. 2:7; 2 Tim. 4:17 ^{c}Acts 25:22f.; 26:1, 32; 2 Tim. 4:16

16 ^{a}Acts 20:23; 21:11 [4 and 13]; 1 Thess. 3:3; 2 Cor. 6:4f.; 11:23-27

★**17** ^{a}Mark 5:23; Acts 6:6; 9:12 ^{b}Acts 22:13 ^{c}Acts 2:4

9:1-19 Luke here records Paul's conversion (22:4 ff. and 26:12ff. also give accounts of it, to the crowd in Jerusalem and to Herod Agrippa II). In his own writings, Paul refers to it only a few times. He related it to the supernatural purposes of God (Gal. 1:15); he spoke of its suddenness (1 Cor. 15:8; Phil. 3:12); he called it an act of new creation by God (2 Cor. 4:6); he acknowledged the merciful character of it (1 Tim. 1:13); and he claimed that during it he saw the Lord (1 Cor. 9:1). He was, therefore, just as qualified as the other apostles, for his conversion experience was just as objective a reality as their meetings with the risen Christ before the ascension.

9:2 $belonging to the Way.$ I.e., Christians.
9:5 $I am Jesus.$ In this moment Paul identified the Lord Yahweh (or Jehovah) of the O.T., whom he had attempted so zealously to serve, with Jesus of Nazareth, whom he had so ferociously persecuted through His saints. The phrase, "$it is hard for thee to kick against the pricks$" (AV), is not found in most manuscripts.
9:10 $Ananias.$ According to 22:12 Ananias was an unimpeachable witness to the reality of Paul's conversion.
9:17 Through Ananias' $laying his hands on him,$ Paul is identified with the people he had been persecuting.

your sight, and be ^cfilled with the Holy Spirit."

18 And immediately there fell from his eyes something like scales, and he regained his sight, and he arose and was baptized;

19 and he took food and was strengthened.

Now ^afor several days he was with ^bthe disciples who were at Damascus,

2 The aftermath of Paul's conversion, 9:20-31

20 and immediately he *began* to proclaim Jesus ^ain the synagogues, saying, "He is ^bthe Son of God."

21 And all those hearing him continued to be amazed, and were saying, "Is this not he who in Jerusalem ^adestroyed those who ^bcalled on this name, and *who* had come here for the purpose of bringing them bound before the chief priests?"

22 But Saul kept increasing in strength and confounding the Jews who lived at Damascus by proving that this *Jesus* is the Christ.

23 And when ^amany days had elapsed, ^bthe Jews plotted together to do away with him,

24 but ^atheir plot became known to Saul. And ^bthey were also watching the gates day and night so that they might put him to death;

25 but his disciples took him by night, and let him down through *an* opening in the wall, lowering him in a large basket.

26 And ^awhen he had come to Jerusalem, he was trying to associate with the disciples; and they were all afraid of him, not believing that he was a disciple.

27 But ^aBarnabas took hold of him and brought him to the apostles and described to them how he had ^bseen the Lord on the road, and that He had talked to him, and how ^cat Damascus he had ^dspoken out boldly in the name of Jesus.

28 And he was with them moving about freely in Jerusalem, ^aspeaking out boldly in the name of the Lord.

29 And he was talking and arguing with the ^aHellenistic *Jews*; but they were attempting to put him to death.

30 But when ^athe brethren learned *of it*, they brought him down to ^bCaesarea and ^csent him away to ^dTarsus.

31 So ^athe church throughout all Judea and Galilee and Samaria enjoyed peace, being built up; and, going on in the fear of the Lord and in the comfort of the Holy Spirit, it continued to increase.

C The Conversion of Gentiles, 9:32-11:30

1 The preparation of Peter, 9:32-10:22

32 Now it came about that as Peter was traveling through all *those parts,* he came down also to ^athe saints who lived at ^bLydda.

33 And there he found a certain man named Aeneas, who had been bedridden eight years, for he was paralyzed.

34 And Peter said to him, "Aeneas, Jesus Christ heals you; arise, and make your bed." And immediately he arose.

35 And all who lived at ^aLydda and ^bSharon saw him, and they ^cturned to the Lord.

36 Now in ^aJoppa there was a certain disciple named Tabitha (which translated *in Greek* is

Cross-references (margin)

19 ^aActs 26:20 ^bActs 9:26, 38; 11:26

20 ^aActs 13:5, 14; 14:1; 16:13; 17:2, 10; 18:4, 19; 19:8; 28:17 ^bMatt. 4:3; Acts 9:22; 13:33

21 ^aActs 8:3; 9:13; Gal. 1:13, 23 ^bActs 9:14

★23 ^aGal. 1:17, 18 ^b1 Thess. 2:16

24 ^aActs 20:3, 19; 23:12, 30; 25:3 ^b2 Cor. 11:32f.

26 ^aActs 22:17-20; 26:20

27 ^aActs 4:36 ^bActs 9:3-6 ^cActs 9:20, 22 ^dActs 4:13, 29; 9:29

28 ^aActs 4:13, 29; 9:29

★29 ^aActs 6:1

30 ^aActs 1:15 ^bActs 8:40 ^cGal. 1:21 ^dActs 9:11

31 ^aActs 5:11; 8:1; 16:5

★32 ^aActs 9:13 ^b1 Chr. 8:12; Ezra 2:33; Neh. 7:37; 11:35

★35 ^a1 Chr. 8:12; Ezra 2:33; Neh. 7:37; 11:35 ^b1 Chr. 5:16; 27:29; Is. 33:9; 35:2; 65:10 ^cActs 2:47; 9:42; 11:21

★36 ^aJosh. 19:46; 2 Chr. 2:16; Ezra 3:7; Jon. 1:3; Acts 9:38, 42f; 10:5, 8, 23, 32; 11:5, 13

9:23 *when many days had elapsed.* During this time Paul went to Arabia (see note on Gal. 1:17), so that three years elapsed between his conversion and his going to Jerusalem (Acts 9:26).

9:29 *Hellenistic Jews* = Greek-speaking Jews.

9:32 *Lydda* = Lod, 11 miles SE of Joppa.

9:35 *Sharon.* The plain extending southward for 50 miles along the Mediterranean Sea from modern Haifa, which stands on Mt. Carmel.

9:36 *Tabitha* means "gazelle" (*Dorcas* is Greek for the same).

called Dorcas); this woman was abounding with deeds of kindness and charity, which she continually did.

37 And it came about at that time that she fell sick and died; and when they had washed her body, they laid it in an ᵃupper room.

38 And since Lydda was near ᵃJoppa, ᵇthe disciples, having heard that Peter was there, sent two men to him, entreating him, "Do not delay to come to us."

39 And Peter arose and went with them. And when he had come, they brought him into the ᵃupper room; and all the ᵇwidows stood beside him weeping, and showing all the tunics and garments that Dorcas used to make while she was with them.

40 But Peter ᵃsent them all out and ᵇknelt down and prayed, and turning to the body, he said, "ᶜTabitha, arise." And she opened her eyes, and when she saw Peter, she sat up.

41 And he gave her his hand and raised her up; and calling ᵃthe saints and ᵇwidows, he presented her alive.

42 And it became known all over ᵃJoppa, and ᵇmany believed in the Lord.

43 And it came about that he stayed many days in ᵃJoppa with ᵇa certain tanner, Simon.

10 Now *there was* a certain man at ᵃCaesarea named Cornelius, a centurion of what was ᵇcalled the Italian cohort,

2 a devout man, and ᵃone who feared God with all his household, and ᵇgave many alms to the *Jewish* people, and prayed to God continually.

3 About ᵃthe ninth hour of the day he clearly saw ᵇin a vision ᶜan angel of God who had *just*

come in to him, and said to him, "Cornelius!"

4 And ᵃfixing his gaze upon him and being much alarmed, he said, "What is it, Lord?" And he said to him, "Your prayers and alms ᵇhave ascended ᶜas a memorial before God.

5 "And now dispatch *some* men to ᵃJoppa, and send for a man *named* Simon, who is also called Peter;

6 he is staying with a certain tanner *named* ᵃSimon, whose house is by the sea."

7 And when the angel who was speaking to him had departed, he summoned two of his servants and a devout soldier of those who were in constant attendance upon him,

8 and after he had explained everything to them, he sent them to ᵃJoppa.

9 And on the next day, as they were on their way, and approaching the city, ᵃPeter went up on ᵇthe housetop about ᶜthe sixth hour to pray.

10 And he became hungry, and was desiring to eat; but while they were making preparations, he ᵃfell into a trance;

11 and he *beheld ᵃthe sky opened up, and a certain object like a great sheet coming down, lowered by four corners to the ground,

12 and there were in it all *kinds of* four-footed animals and crawling creatures of the earth and birds of the air.

13 And a voice came to him, "Arise, Peter, kill and eat!"

14 But Peter said, "By no means, ᵃLord, for ᵇI have never eaten anything unholy and unclean."

15 And again a voice *came* to him a second time, "ᵃWhat God

37 ᵃActs 1:13; 9:39

38 ᵃJosh. 19:46; 2 Chr. 2:16; Ezra 3:7; Jon. 1:3; Acts 9:36, 42f.; 10:5, 8, 23, 32; 11:5, 13 ᵇActs 11:26

39 ᵃActs 1:13; 9:37 ᵇActs 6:1

40 ᵃMatt. 9:25 ᵇLuke 22:41; Acts 7:60 ᶜMark 5:41

41 ᵃActs 9:13 ᵇActs 6:1

42 ᵃJosh. 19:46; 2 Chr. 2:16; Jon. 1:3; Acts 9:38, 42f.; 10:5, 8, 23, 32; 11:5, 13 ᵇActs 9:35

43 ᵃJosh. 19:46; 2 Chr. 2:16; Ezra 3:7; Jon. 1:3; Acts 9:38, 42f.; 10:5, 8, 23, 32; 11:13, 15 ᵇActs 10:6

★ **1** ᵃActs 8:40; 10:24 ᵇMatt. 27:27; Mark 15:16; John 18:3, 12; Acts 21:31; 27:1

★ **2** ᵃActs 10:22, 35; 13:16, 26 ᵇLuke 7:4f.

3 ᵃActs 3:1 ᵇActs 9:10; 10:17, 19 ᶜActs 5:19

4 ᵃActs 3:4 ᵇRev. 8:4 ᶜMatt. 26:13; Phil. 4:18; Heb. 6:10

5 ᵃActs 9:36

6 ᵃActs 9:43

8 ᵃActs 9:36

9 ᵃActs 10:9-32; 11:5-14 ᵇJer. 19:13; 32:29; Zeph. 1:5; Matt. 24:17 ᶜPs. 55:17; Acts 10:3

10 ᵃActs 11:5; 22:17

11 ᵃJohn 1:51

★**14** ᵃMatt. 8:2ff.; John 4:11ff.; Acts 9:5; 22:8 ᵇLev. 11:20-25; Deut. 14:4-20; Ezek. 4:14; Dan. 1:8; Acts 10:28 **15** ᵃMatt. 15:11; Mark 7:19; Rom. 14:14; 1 Cor. 10:25ff.; 1 Tim. 4:4f.; Titus 1:15

10:1 *a centurion* was a noncommissioned officer who was in command of 100 men. Cornelius was a commander in the *Italian* cohort (see note on John 18:3).

10:2 Cornelius was a semi-proselyte to Judaism, accepting Jewish beliefs and practices but

stopping short of circumcision.

10:14 *unholy and unclean.* The Mosaic law prohibited the eating of certain unclean animals (Lev. 11). God was teaching Peter a lesson about people (see v. 28).

has cleansed, no *longer* consider unholy."

16 And this happened three times; and immediately the object was taken up into the sky.

17 *a*Acts
10:3 *b*Acts
10:8

17 Now while Peter was greatly perplexed in mind as to what *a*the vision which he had seen might be, behold, *b*the men who had been sent by Cornelius, having asked directions for Simon's house, appeared at the gate;

18 and calling out, they were asking whether Simon, who was also called Peter, was staying there.

19 *a*Acts
10:3 *b*Acts
8:29

19 And while Peter was reflecting on *a*the vision, *b*the Spirit said to him, "Behold, three men are looking for you.

20 *a*Acts
15:7-9

20 "But arise, go downstairs, and *a*accompany them without misgivings; for I have sent them Myself."

21 And Peter went down to the men and said, "Behold, I am the one you are looking for; what is the reason for which you have come?"

22 *a*Acts
10:2 *b*Matt.
2:12 *c*Mark
8:38; Luke
9:26; Rev.
14:10 *d*Acts
11:14

22 And they said, "Cornelius, a centurion, a righteous and *a*God-fearing man well spoken of by the entire nation of the Jews, *b*was *divinely* directed by a *c*holy angel to send for you *to come* to his house and hear *d*a message from you."

2   The preaching of Peter, 10:23-48

★23 *a*Acts
10:45; 11:12
*b*Acts 1:15
*c*Acts 9:36

23 And so he invited them in and gave them lodging.
And on the next day he arose and went away with them, and *a*some of *b*the brethren from *c*Joppa accompanied him.

24 *a*Acts
8:40; 10:1

24 And on the following day he entered *a*Caesarea. Now Cornelius was waiting for them,

and had called together his relatives and close friends.

25 And when it came about that Peter entered, Cornelius met him, and fell at his feet and *a*worshiped *him*.

25 *a*Matt. 8:2

26 But Peter raised him up, saying, "*a*Stand up; I too am *just* a man."

26 *a*Acts
14:15; Rev.
19:10; 22:8f.

27 And as he talked with him, he entered, and found *a*many people assembled.

27 *a*Acts
10:24

28 And he said to them, "You yourselves know how *a*unlawful it is for a man who is a Jew to associate with a foreigner or to visit him; and *yet* *b*God has shown me that I should not call any man unholy or unclean.

★28 *a*John
4:9; 18:28;
Acts 11:3
*b*Acts
10:14f., 35;
15:9

29 "That is why I came without even raising any objection when I was sent for. And so I ask for what reason you have sent for me."

30 And Cornelius said, "*a*Four days ago to this hour, I was praying in my house during *b*the ninth hour; and behold, *c*a man stood before me in shining garments,

30 *a*Acts
10:9, 22f.
*b*Acts 3:1;
10:3 *c*Acts
10:3-6, 30-32

31 and he *said, 'Cornelius, your prayer has been heard and your alms have been remembered before God.

32 'Send therefore to *a*Joppa and invite Simon, who is also called Peter, to come to you; he is staying at the house of Simon the tanner by the sea.'

32 *a*John
4:9; 18:28;
Acts 11:3

33 "And so I sent to you immediately, and you have been kind enough to come. Now then, we are all here present before God to hear all that you have been commanded by the Lord."

34 And *a*opening his mouth, Peter said:
"I most certainly understand *now* that *b*God is not one to show partiality,

★34 *a*Matt.
5:2 *b*Deut.
10:17; 2 Chr.
19:7; Rom.
2:11; Gal.
2:6; Eph. 6:9;
Col. 3:25;
1 Pet. 1:17

35 but *a*in every nation the

35 *a*Acts
10:28 *b*Acts
10:2

10:23 *some of the brethren.* There were six of them (11:12).

10:28 The case of Cornelius was the first of its kind and crucial to the spread of Christianity. It answered the question, "Can the new faith (still so closely associated with Judaism) admit

into fellowship an uncircumcised Gentile?" The issue, however, would not be completely resolved for some time.

10:34 *God is not one to show partiality.* This fact was taught in the O.T. (Deut. 10:17; 2 Chron. 19:7).

man who ᵇfears Him and does what is right, is welcome to Him.

36 ᵃActs 13:32 ᵇLuke 1:79; 2:14; Rom. 5:1; Eph. 2:17 ᶜMatt. 28:18; Acts 2:36; Rom. 10:12

36 "The word which He sent to the sons of Israel, ᵃpreaching ᵇpeace through Jesus Christ (He is ᶜLord of all)—

37 you yourselves know the thing which took place throughout all Judea, starting from Galilee, after the baptism which John proclaimed.

38 ᵃActs 2:22 ᵇActs 4:26 ᶜMatt. 4:23 ᵈJohn 3:2

38 "You know of ᵃJesus of Nazareth, how God ᵇanointed Him with the Holy Spirit and with power, ᶜand how He went about doing good, and healing all who were oppressed by the devil; for ᵈGod was with Him.

39 ᵃLuke 24:48; Acts 10:41 ᵇActs 5:30

39 "And we are ᵃwitnesses of all the things He did both in the land of the Jews and in Jerusalem. And they also ᵇput Him to death by hanging Him on a cross.

40 ᵃActs 2:24

40 "ᵃGod raised Him up on the third day, and granted that He should become visible,

41 ᵃJohn 14:19, 22; 15:27 ᵇLuke 24:48; Acts 10:39 ᶜLuke 24:43; Acts 1:4 marg.

41 ᵃnot to all the people, but to ᵇwitnesses who were chosen beforehand by God, that is, to us, ᶜwho ate and drank with Him after He arose from the dead.

42 ᵃActs 1:2 ᵇLuke 16:28 ᶜLuke 22:22 ᵈJohn 5:22, 27; Acts 17:31; 2 Tim. 4:1; 1 Pet. 4:5

42 "And He ᵃordered us to preach to the people, and solemnly to ᵇtestify that this is the One who has been ᶜappointed by God as ᵈJudge of the living and the dead.

43 ᵃActs 3:18 ᵇLuke 24:47; Acts 2:38; 4:12

43 "Of Him ᵃall the prophets bear witness that through ᵇHis name everyone who believes in Him receives forgiveness of sins."

★44 ᵃActs 11:15; 15:8

44 While Peter was still speaking these words, ᵃthe Holy Spirit fell upon all those who were listening to the message.

45 ᵃActs 10:23 ᵇActs 2:33, 38

45 And ᵃall the circumcised believers who had come with Peter were amazed, because the gift of the Holy Spirit had been ᵇpoured out upon the Gentiles also.

46 ᵃMark 16:17; Acts 2:4; 19:6 ᵇActs 3:12

46 For they were hearing them ᵃspeaking with tongues and exalting God. Then Peter ᵇanswered,

47 ᵃActs 8:36 ᵇActs 2:4; 10:44f.; 11:17; 15:8

47 "ᵃSurely no one can refuse the water for these to be baptized who ᵇhave received the Holy Spirit just as we did, can he?"

48 ᵃ1 Cor. 1:14-17 ᵇActs 2:38; 8:16; 19:5

48 And he ᵃordered them to be baptized ᵇin the name of Jesus Christ. Then they asked him to stay on for a few days.

3 The plea of Peter, 11:1-18

1 ᵃActs 1:15

11 Now the apostles and ᵃthe brethren who were throughout Judea heard that the Gentiles also had received the word of God.

★ 2 ᵃActs 10:45

2 And when Peter came up to Jerusalem, ᵃthose who were circumcised took issue with him,

3 ᵃMatt. 9:11; Acts 10:28; Gal. 2:12

3 saying, "ᵃYou went to uncircumcised men and ate with them."

4 ᵃLuke 1:3

4 But Peter began speaking and proceeded to explain to them ᵃin orderly sequence, saying,

5 ᵃActs 10:9-32; 11:5-14 ᵇActs 9:10

5 "ᵃI was in the city of Joppa praying; and in a trance I saw ᵇa vision, a certain object coming down like a great sheet lowered by four corners from the sky; and it came right down to me,

6 and when I had fixed my gaze upon it and was observing it I saw the four-footed animals of the earth and the wild beasts and the crawling creatures and the birds of the air.

7 "And I also heard a voice saying to me, 'Arise, Peter; kill and eat.'

8 "But I said, 'By no means, Lord, for nothing unholy or

10:44 *the Holy Spirit fell upon all.* In the case of these Gentile converts, the gift of the Spirit came before they were baptized in water (v. 48). The authentication of the gift was the speaking in tongues (v. 46), entirely apart from the laying on of hands. All this demonstrated, especially to the Jewish brethren who accompanied Peter, that God had received these Gentiles into the Church on an equal basis with Jewish believers because they had believed in Christ (v. 43).

11:2 *those who were circumcised.* Jewish Christians, the so-called "circumcision party," who were unhappy at the report that Gentiles were being saved without ritual induction into Judaism. After Peter's review of what happened, they were satisfied that this was God's doing (v. 18).

unclean has ever entered my mouth.'

9 aActs 10:15

9 "But a voice from heaven answered a second time, 'aWhat God has cleansed, no longer consider unholy.'

10 "And this happened three times, and everything was drawn back up into the sky.

11 aActs 8:40

11 "And behold, at that moment three men appeared before the house in which we were staying, having been sent to me from aCaesarea.

12 aActs 8:29 bActs 15:9; Rom. 3:22 cActs 10:23

12 "And athe Spirit told me to go with them bwithout misgivings. And cthese six brethren also went with me, and we entered the man's house.

13 "And he reported to us how he had seen the angel standing in his house, and saying, 'Send to Joppa, and have Simon, who is also called Peter, brought here;

14 aActs 10:22 bJohn 4:53; Acts 10:2; 16:15, 31-34; 18:8; 1 Cor. 1:16

14 and he shall speak awords to you by which you will be saved, you and ball your household.'

★15 aActs 10:44 bActs 2:4

15 "And as I began to speak, athe Holy Spirit fell upon them, just bas He did upon us at the beginning.

16 aActs 1:5

16 "And I remembered the word of the Lord, how He used to say, 'aJohn baptized with water, but you shall be baptized with the Holy Spirit.'

17 aActs 10:45, 47 bActs 5:39

17 "If aGod therefore gave to them the same gift as He gave to us also after believing in the Lord Jesus Christ, bwho was I that I could stand in God's way?"

18 aMatt. 9:8 b2 Cor. 7:10

18 And when they heard this, they quieted down, and aglorified God, saying, "Well then, God has granted to the Gentiles also the brepentance that leads to life."

4 The church at Antioch, 11:19-30

★19 aActs 8:1, 4 bActs 15:3; 21:2 cActs 4:36 dActs 6:5; 11:20, 22, 27; 13:1; 14:26; 15:22f., 30, 35; 18:22; Gal. 2:11

19 aSo then those who were scattered because of the persecution that arose in connection with Stephen made their way to bPhoenicia and cCyprus and dAntioch, speaking the word to no one except to Jews alone.

20 aActs 4:36 bMatt. 27:32; Acts 2:10; 6:9; 13:1 cActs 6:5; 11:19, 22, 27; 13:1; 14:26; 15:22f., 30, 35; 18:22; Gal. 2:11 dJohn 7:35 eActs 5:42

20 But there were some of them, men of aCyprus and bCyrene, who came to cAntioch and began speaking to the dGreeks also, epreaching the Lord Jesus.

21 aLuke 1:66 bActs 2:47

21 And athe hand of the Lord was with them, and ba large number who believed turned to the Lord.

★22 aActs 4:36 bActs 6:5; 11:19, 20, 27; 13:1; 14:26; 15:22f., 30, 35; 18:22; Gal. 2:11

22 And the news about them reached the ears of the church at Jerusalem, and they sent aBarnabas off to bAntioch.

23 aActs 13:43; 14:26; 15:40; 20:24, 32

23 Then when he had come and witnessed athe grace of God, he rejoiced and began to encourage them all with resolute heart to remain true to the Lord;

24 aActs 2:4 bActs 2:47; 5:14; 11:21

24 for he was a good man, and afull of the Holy Spirit and of faith. And bconsiderable numbers were brought to the Lord.

★25 aActs 9:11

25 And he left for aTarsus to look for Saul;

11:15 at the beginning. I.e., on the day of Pentecost. Since God had done for the Gentiles in Cornelius' house the same as He had done for the Jews at Pentecost, to refuse to accept these Gentile converts would be to resist the work of God (v. 17).

11:19 Antioch on the Orontes River about 300 miles from Jerusalem was the capital of the Roman province of Syria. It was the third largest city in the empire, with a population of about 500,000. It was one of the cosmopolitan centers of the world of that day and a center of commerce, Seleucia (16 miles away) being its seaport (13:4). Replacing Jerusalem as the number one Christian city, it was the center of the early missionary activity of the Church (6:5; 13:1; 14:26; 15:35; 18:22).

11:22 Barnabas. Described by Luke as one who consoles or encourages (4:36). a good man who was full of the Holy Spirit (11:24), he played an important role in the early life of the church on four occasions: (1) he convinced the apostles of the genuineness of Paul's conversion (Acts 9:27); (2) he represented the apostles at Antioch and recognized that the movement there was the work of God (11:22-24); (3) he and Paul were sent by the Spirit on the first missionary journey (13:2); and (4) he defended the work among Gentiles at the Jerusalem council (15:12, 22, 25).

11:25 to look for Saul. Paul had been in Tarsus, his home city, and in Syria and Cilicia (Gal. 1:21) about 9 years since going there from Jerusalem (Acts 9:30).

★26 *a*Acts
6:5; 11:20,
22, 27; 13:1;
14:26;
15:22f., 30,
35; 18:22;
Gal. 2:11
*b*John 2:2;
Acts 1:15;
6:11; 9:19,
25, 26, 38;
11:29; 13:52;
14:20, 22, 28
*c*Acts 26:28;
1 Pet. 4:16
27 *a*Luke
11:49; Acts
2:17; 13:1;
1 Cor. 12:10,
28f. *b*Acts
18:22 *c*Acts
6:5; 11:20,
22, 26; 13:1;
14:26;
15:22f., 30,
35; 18:22;
Gal. 2:11
★28 *a*Acts
21:10 *b*Matt.
24:14 *c*Acts
18:2
29 *a*John
2:2;
1:15; 6:1f.;
9:19, 25, 26,
38; 11:26;
13:52; 14:20,
22, 28 *b*Acts
11:1
★30 *a*Acts
12:25 *b*Acts
4:36 *c*Acts
14:23; 15:2,
4, 6, 22f.;
16:4; 20:17;
21:18; 1 Tim.
5:17, 19; Ti-
tus 1:5;
James 5:14;
1 Pet. 5:1;
2 John 1;
3 John 1

26 and when he had found him, he brought him to *a*Antioch. And it came about that for an entire year they met with the church, and taught considerable numbers; and *b*the disciples were first called *c*Christians in *a*Antioch.

27 Now at this time *a*some prophets *b*came down from Jerusalem to *c*Antioch.

28 And one of them named *a*Agabus stood up and *began* to indicate by the Spirit that there would certainly be a great famine *b*all over the world. And this took place in the *reign* of *c*Claudius.

29 And in the proportion that any of *a*the disciples had means, each of them determined to send a *contribution* for the relief of *b*the brethren living in Judea.

30 *a*And this they did, sending it in charge of *b*Barnabas and Saul to the *c*elders.

D The Christians Persecuted by Herod, 12:1-25
1 The death of James, 12:1-2

★ 1
★ 2 *a*Matt.
4:21; 20:23
*b*Mark 10:39

12 Now about that time Herod the king laid hands on some who belonged to the church, in order to mistreat them.

2 And he *a*had James the brother of John *b*put to death with a sword.

2 The deliverance of Peter, 12:3-19

3 *a*Acts
24:27; 25:9
*b*Ex. 12:15;
23:15; Acts
20:6
★ 4 *a*John
19:23 *b*Mark
14:1; Acts
12:3

3 And when he saw that it *a*pleased the Jews, he proceeded to arrest Peter also. Now it was during *b*the days of Unleavened Bread.

4 And when he had seized him, he put him in prison, delivering him to four *a*squads of soldiers to guard him, intending after *b*the Passover to bring him out before the people.

5 So Peter was kept in the prison, but prayer for him was being made fervently by the church to God.

6 And on the very night when Herod was about to bring him forward, Peter was sleeping between two soldiers, *a*bound with two chains; and guards in front of the door were watching over the prison.

7 And behold, *a*an angel of the Lord suddenly *b*appeared, and a light shone in the cell; and he struck Peter's side and roused him, saying, "Get up quickly." And *c*his chains fell off his hands.

8 And the angel said to him, "Gird yourself and put on your sandals." And he did so. And he *said to him, "Wrap your cloak around you and follow me."

9 And he went out and continued to follow, and he did not know that what was being done by the angel was real, but thought he was seeing *a*a vision.

10 And when they had passed the first and second guard, they came to the iron gate that leads into the city, which *a*opened for them by itself; and they went out and went along one street; and immediately the angel departed from him.

11 And when Peter *a*came to himself, he said, "Now I know for sure that *b*the Lord has sent forth His angel and rescued me from the hand of Herod and from all that the Jewish people were expecting."

★ 6 *a*Acts
21:33

7 *a*Acts
5:19 *b*Luke
2:9; 24:4
*c*Acts 16:26

9 *a*Acts
9:10

10 *a*Acts
5:19; 16:26

★11 *a*Luke
15:17 *b*Dan.
3:28; 6:22

11:26 *Christians.* The word appears only here, in 26:28, and in 1 Pet. 4:16. It means partisans or followers of Christ, "Christ's men."

11:28 *great famine.* Josephus reports that a famine occurred in about A.D. 46.

11:30 *elders.* See note on 1 Tim. 3:1.

12:1 *Herod.* Herod Agrippa I, grandson of the Herod the Great who ruled at the birth of Jesus. Agrippa, at least on the surface, was a zealous practicer of Jewish rites and a religious patriot.

12:2 *James.* The first of the Twelve to be martyred.

12:4 *Passover.* See note on Mark 14:1.

12:6 *Peter was sleeping.* He had Christ's promise that he would live to an old age (John 21:18).

12:11 *rescued me.* God's ways are inscrutable—Peter was delivered, but James was killed (v. 2).

★12 aActs
12:25; 13:5,
13; 15:37,
39; Col. 4:10;
2 Tim. 4:11;
Philem. 24;
1 Pet. 5:13
bActs 12:5

12 And when he realized *this*, he went to the house of Mary, the mother of [a]John who was also called Mark, where many were gathered together and [b]were praying.

13 aJohn
18:16f.

13 And when he knocked at the door of the gate, [a]a servant-girl named Rhoda came to answer.

14 aLuke
24:41

14 And when she recognized Peter's voice, [a]because of her joy she did not open the gate, but ran in and announced that Peter was standing in front of the gate.

★15 aMatt.
18:10

15 And they said to her, "You are out of your mind!" But she kept insisting that it was so. And they kept saying, "It is [a]his angel."

16 But Peter continued knocking; and when they had opened *the door*, they saw him and were amazed.

17 aActs
13:16; 19:33;
21:40 bMark
6:3; Acts
15:13; 21:18;
1 Cor. 15:7;
Gal. 1:19;
2:9, 12 cActs
1:15

17 But [a]motioning to them with his hand to be silent, he described to them how the Lord had led him out of the prison. And he said, "Report these things to [b]James and [c]the brethren." And he departed and went to another place.

18 Now when day came, there was no small disturbance among the soldiers *as to* what could have become of Peter.

19 aActs
16:27; 27:42
bActs 8:40

19 And when Herod had searched for him and had not found him, he examined that they [a]be led away *to execution*. And he went down from Judea to [b]Caesarea and was spending time there.

3　The death of Herod, 12:20-23

20 Now he was very angry with the people of [a]Tyre and Sidon; and with one accord they came to him, and having won over Blastus the king's chamberlain, they were asking for peace, because [b]their country was fed by the king's country.

★20 aMatt.
11:21
b1 Kin. 5:11;
Ezra 3:7;
Ezek. 27:17

21 And on an appointed day Herod, having put on his royal apparel, took his seat on the rostrum and *began* delivering an address to them.

22 And the people kept crying out, "The voice of a god and not of a man!"

23 And immediately [a]an angel of the Lord struck him because he did not give God the glory, and he was eaten by worms and died.

★23 a2 Sam.
24:16; 2 Kin.
19:35; Acts
5:19

4　The dissemination of the Word, 12:24-25

24 But [a]the word of the Lord continued to grow and to be multiplied.

24 aActs 6:7;
19:20

25 And [a]Barnabas and [a]Saul returned from Jerusalem [b]when they had fulfilled their mission, taking along with *them* [c]John, who was also called Mark.

25 aActs
4:36; 13:1ff.
bActs 11:30
cActs 12:12

III　CHRISTIANITY TO THE UTTERMOST PART OF THE WORLD, 13:1-28:31
A　The First Missionary Journey, 13:1-14:28
1　Events in Antioch, 13:1-3

13 Now there were at [a]Antioch, in the [b]church that

★ 1 aActs
11:19 bActs
11:26 cActs
11:27; 15:32;
19:6; 21:9;
1 Cor. 11:4f.;
13:2, 8f.;
14:29, 32, 37
dRom.
12:6f.; 1 Cor.
12:28f.; Eph.
4:11; James
3:1 eActs
4:36;
fMatt. 27:32;
Acts 11:20
gMatt. 14:1

12:12 *the house of Mary.* Traditionally it was here that the Last Supper was held and here now was the nerve center of the church in Jerusalem.

12:15 *his angel.* For other guardian angels in Scripture, see Gen. 48:16; Dan. 10:20-21; 12:1; Matt. 18:10; Heb. 1:14.

12:20 *Tyre and Sidon* had to import grain; the fields of Galilee produced large supplies (1 Kings 5:9).

12:23 Josephus states that Herod was struck down while delivering his oration and, after

five days of suffering, died (A.D. 44).

13:1 Here begins what has been called "The Acts of Paul," because Paul becomes the dominant figure. *Simeon who was called Niger.* Niger was his Latin name and probably indicates that he was an African. *who had been brought up with.* Lit., foster brother, a designation given to boys of the same age as royal children with whom they were brought up. *Herod the tetrarch.* Herod Antipas, who ruled Galilee during the public ministry of Christ.

was *there,* ^cprophets and ^dteachers: ^eBarnabas, and Simeon who was called Niger, and Lucius of ^fCyrene, and Manaen who had been brought up with ^gHerod the tetrarch, and ^eSaul.

2 And while they were ministering to the Lord and fasting, ^athe Holy Spirit said, "Set apart for Me ^bBarnabas and Saul for ^cthe work to which I have called them."

3 Then, when they had fasted and ^aprayed and ^blaid their hands on them, ^cthey sent them away.

2 Events in Cyprus, 13:4-12

4 So, being ^asent out by the Holy Spirit, they went down to Seleucia and from there they sailed to ^bCyprus.

5 And when they reached Salamis, they *began* to proclaim the word of God in ^athe synagogues of the Jews; and they also had ^bJohn as their helper.

6 And when they had gone through the whole island as far as Paphos, they found a certain ^amagician, a Jewish ^bfalse prophet whose name was Bar-Jesus,

7 who was with the ^aproconsul, Sergius Paulus, a man of intelligence. This man summoned Barnabas and Saul and sought to hear the word of God.

8 But Elymas the ^amagician (for thus his name is translated) was opposing them, seeking to turn the ^bproconsul away from ^cthe faith.

9 But Saul, who was also *known as* Paul, ^afilled with the Holy Spirit, fixed his gaze upon him,

10 and said, "You who are full of all deceit and fraud, you ^ason of the devil, you enemy of all righteousness, will you not cease to make crooked ^bthe straight ways of the Lord?

11 "And now, behold, ^athe hand of the Lord is upon you, and you will be blind and not see the sun for a time." And immediately a mist and a darkness fell upon him, and he went about seeking those who would lead him by the hand.

12 Then the ^aproconsul believed when he saw what had happened, being amazed at ^bthe teaching of the Lord.

3 Events in Galatian cities, 13:13-14:20

13 Now Paul and his companions put out to sea from ^aPaphos and came to ^bPerga in ^cPamphylia; and ^dJohn left them and returned to Jerusalem.

14 But going on from Perga, they arrived at ^aPisidian ^bAntioch, and on ^cthe Sabbath day they went into ^dthe synagogue and sat down.

15 And after ^athe reading of the Law and ^bthe Prophets ^cthe synagogue officials sent to them, saying, "Brethren, if you have any word of exhortation for the people, say it."

16 And Paul stood up, and ^amotioning with his hand, he said,

"Men of Israel, and ^byou who fear God, listen:

17 "The God of this people Israel ^achose our fathers, and made the people great during their stay in the land of Egypt, and with an uplifted arm He led them out from it.

Marginal references:

2 ^aActs 8:29; 13:4 ^bActs 4:36; 13:1ff. ^cActs 9:15

★ 3 ^aActs 1:24 ^bActs 6:6 ^cActs 13:4; 14:26

4 ^aActs 13:2f. ^bActs 4:36

★ 5 ^aActs 9:20; 13:14 ^bActs 12:12

6 ^aActs 8:9 ^bMatt. 7:15

★ 7 ^aActs 13:8, 12; 18:12; 19:38

★ 8 ^aActs 8:9 ^bActs 13:7, 12; 18:12; 19:38 ^cActs 6:7

★ 9 ^aActs 2:4; 4:8 10 ^aMatt. 13:38; John 8:44 ^bHos. 14:9; 2 Pet. 2:15

11 ^aEx. 9:3; 1 Sam. 5:6f.; Job 19:21; Ps. 32:4; Heb. 10:31

12 ^aActs 13:7, 8; 18:12; 19:38 ^bActs 8:25; 13:49; 15:35f.; 19:10, 20

13 ^aActs 13:6 ^bActs 14:25 ^cActs 2:10; 14:24; 15:38; 27:5 ^dActs 12:12

★14 ^aActs 14:24 ^bActs 14:19, 21; 2 Tim. 3:11 ^cActs 13:42, 44; 16:13; 17:2; 18:4 ^dActs 9:20; 13:5

15 ^aActs 15:21; 2 Cor. 3:14f. ^bActs 13:27 ^cMark 5:22

16 ^aActs 12:17 ^bActs 10:2; 13:26

17 ^aEx. 6:1, 6; 13:14, 16; Deut. 7:6-8; Acts 7:17ff.

13:3 *laid their hands on them.* See note on 6:6.

13:5 *John as their helper.* This was John Mark, son of Mary (12:12) and cousin to Barnabas (Col. 4:10). See 13:13; 15:38-40; 2 Tim. 4:11.

13:7 *who was with the proconsul.* Cyprus was a Roman senatorial province.

13:8 *Elymas* the name given to Bar-Jesus by Greek-speaking acquaintances.

13:9 *Saul, who was also known as Paul.* Saul was his Jewish name and Paul his Roman or Gentile name. Both were given him at the time of his birth, but he now begins to use his Gentile name in this Gentile environment.

13:14 *Pisidian Antioch.* Actually it was in Phrygia, but near the border of Pisidia. This Antioch was so called to distinguish it from the larger Antioch in Syria.

18 *a*Acts
7:36 *b*Deut.
1:31

18 "And for *a*a period of about forty years *b*He put up with them in the wilderness.

★19 *a*Acts
7:45 *b*Deut.
7:1 *c*Josh.
19:51; Ps.
78:55 *d*Judg.
11:26; 1 Kin.
6:1

19 "And *a*when He had destroyed *b*seven nations in the land of Canaan, He *c*distributed their land as an inheritance—*all of which took *d*about four hundred and fifty years.

20 *a*Judg.
2:16 *b*Acts
3:24

20 "And after these things He *a*gave *them* judges until *b*Samuel the prophet.

21 *a*1 Sam.
8:5 *b*1 Sam.
9:1f.; 10:1

21 "And then they *a*asked for a king, and God gave them *b*Saul the son of Kish, a man of the tribe of Benjamin, for forty years.

22 *a*1 Sam.
15:23, 26,
28; 16:1, 13
*b*1 Sam.
13:14; Ps.
89:20; Acts
7:46

22 "And after He had *a*removed him, He raised up David to be their king, concerning whom He also testified and said, 'I HAVE FOUND *b*DAVID the son of Jesse, A MAN AFTER MY HEART, who will do all My will.'

23 *a*Matt. 1:1
*b*Acts 13:32f.
*c*Luke 2:11;
John 4:42

23 "*a*From the offspring of this man, *b*according to promise, God has brought to Israel *c*a Savior, Jesus,

24 *a*Mark
1:1-4; Acts
1:22; 19:4

24 after *a*John had proclaimed before His coming a baptism of repentance to all the people of Israel.

25 *a*Acts
20:24 *b*Matt.
3:11; Mark
1:7; Luke
3:16; John
1:20, 27

25 "And while John *a*was completing his course, *b*he kept saying, 'What do you suppose that I am? I am not *He*. But behold, one is coming after me the sandals of whose feet I am not worthy to untie.'

26 *a*John
6:68; Acts
4:12; 5:20;
13:46; 28:28

26 "Brethren, sons of Abraham's family, and those among you who fear God, to us the word of *a*this salvation is sent out.

27 *a*Luke
23:13 *b*Luke
3:17 *c*Luke
24:27 *d*Acts
13:15

27 "For those who live in Jerusalem, and their *a*rulers, *b*recognizing neither Him nor the utterances of *c*the prophets which are *d*read every Sabbath, fulfilled *these* by condemning *Him*.

28 *a*Acts
3:14

28 "And though they found no ground for *putting Him to* death, they *a*asked Pilate that He be executed.

29 *a*Acts
26:22 *b*Luke
23:53 *c*Acts
5:30

29 "And when they had *a*carried out all that was written concerning Him, *b*they took Him down from *c*the cross and laid Him in a tomb.

30 *a*Acts
2:24; 13:33,
34, 37

30 "But God *a*raised Him from the dead;

31 *a*Acts
1:11 *b*Luke
24:48

31 and for many days He appeared to those who came up with Him *a*from Galilee to Jerusalem, the very ones who are now *b*His witnesses to the people.

32 *a*Acts
5:42; 14:15
*b*Acts 13:23;
26:6; Rom.
1:2; 4:13; 9:4

32 "And we *a*preach to you the good news of *b*the promise made to the fathers,

33 *a*Acts
2:24; 13:30,
34, 37 *b*Ps.
2:7

33 that God has fulfilled this *promise* to our children in that He *a*raised up Jesus, as it is also written in the second Psalm, '*b*THOU ART MY SON; TODAY I HAVE BEGOTTEN THEE.'

34 *a*Acts
2:24; 13:30,
33, 37 *b*Is.
55:3

34 "*And as for the fact* that He *a*raised Him up from the dead, no more to return to decay, He has spoken in this way: '*b*I WILL GIVE YOU THE HOLY *and* SURE *blessings* OF DAVID.'

35 *a*Ps.
16:10; Acts
2:27

35 "Therefore He also says in another *Psalm*, '*a*THOU WILT NOT ALLOW THY HOLY ONE TO UNDERGO DECAY.'

36 *a*Acts
2:29 *b*Acts
13:22; 20:27
*c*1 Kin. 2:10;
Acts 8:1

36 "For *a*David, after he had served *b*the purpose of God in his own generation, *c*fell asleep, and was laid among his fathers, and underwent decay;

37 *a*Acts
2:24; 13:30,
33, 34

37 but He whom God *a*raised did not undergo decay.

38 *a*Luke
24:47; Acts
2:38

38 "Therefore let it be known to you, brethren, that *a*through Him forgiveness of sins is proclaimed to you,

39 *a*Acts
10:43; Rom.
3:28; 10:4

39 and through Him *a*everyone who believes is freed from all things, from which you could not be freed through the Law of Moses.

40 *a*Luke
24:44; John
6:45; Acts
7:42

40 "Take heed therefore, so that the thing spoken of *a*in the Prophets may not come upon *you*:

41 *a*Hab. 1:5

41 '*a*BEHOLD, YOU SCOFFERS, AND MARVEL, AND PERISH; FOR I AM ACCOMPLISHING A WORK IN YOUR DAYS, A WORK WHICH YOU WILL NEVER BELIEVE, THOUGH SOMEONE SHOULD DESCRIBE IT TO YOU.'"

13:19 The *four hundred and fifty years* extends from the Patriarchs to the Judges.

42 *a*Acts
13:14

42 And as Paul and Barnabas were going out, the people kept begging that these things might be spoken to them the next *a*Sabbath.

43 *a*Acts
13:50; 16:14;
17:4, 17;
18:7 *b*Matt.
23:15 *c*Acts
11:23

43 Now when *the meeting of* the synagogue had broken up, many of the Jews and of the *a*God-fearing *b*proselytes followed Paul and Barnabas, who, speaking to them, were urging them to continue in *c*the grace of God.

44 *a*Acts
13:14

44 And the next *a*Sabbath nearly the whole city assembled to hear the word of God.

45 *a*Acts
13:50; 14:2,
4, 5, 19;
1 Thess. 2:16

45 But when *a*the Jews saw the crowds, they were filled with jealousy, and *began* contradicting the things spoken by Paul, and were blaspheming.

46 *a*Acts
3:26; 9:20;
13:5, 14
*b*Acts 18:6;
19:9, 15;
22:21; 26:20;
28:28

46 And Paul and Barnabas spoke out boldly and said, "It was necessary that the word of God should be spoken to you *a*first; since you repudiate it, and judge yourselves unworthy of eternal life, behold, *b*we are turning to the Gentiles.

47 *a*Is. 49:6
*b*Luke 2:32

47 "For thus the Lord has commanded us,

'*a*I HAVE PLACED YOU AS A
*b*LIGHT FOR THE GENTILES,
THAT YOU SHOULD BRING
SALVATION TO THE END OF
THE EARTH.'"

★48 *a*Acts
13:12 *b*Rom.
8:28ff.; Eph.
1:4f., 11

48 And when the Gentiles heard this, they *began* rejoicing and glorifying *a*the word of the Lord; and as many as *b*had been appointed to eternal life believed.

49 *a*Acts
13:12

49 And *a*the word of the Lord was being spread through the whole region.

50 *a*Acts
13:45; 14:2,
4, 5, 19;
1 Thess. 2:16
*b*Acts 13:43;
16:14; 17:4,
17; 18:7
*c*Mark 15:43

50 But *a*the Jews aroused the *b*devout women *c*of prominence and the leading men of the city, and instigated a persecution against Paul and Barnabas, and drove them out of their district.

51 But *a*they shook off the dust of their feet *in protest* against them and went to *b*Iconium.

52 And the disciples were continually *a*filled with joy and with the Holy Spirit.

14 And it came about that in *a*Iconium *b*they entered the synagogue of the Jews together, and spoke in such a manner *c*that a great multitude believed, both of Jews and of *d*Greeks.

★51 *a*Matt.
10:14; Acts
18:6 *b*Acts
14:1, 19, 21;
16:2; 2 Tim.
3:11
52 *a*Acts 2:4

1 *a*Acts
13:51; 14:19,
21; 16:2;
2 Tim. 3:11
*b*Acts 13:5
*c*Acts 2:47
*d*John 7:35;
Acts 18:4

2 But *a*the Jews who *b*disbelieved stirred up the minds of the Gentiles, and embittered them against *c*the brethren.

2 *a*Acts
13:45, 50;
14:4, 5, 19;
1 Thess. 2:16
*b*John 3:36
*c*Acts 1:15

3 Therefore they spent a long time *there* *a*speaking boldly *with reliance* upon the Lord, who was bearing witness to the word of His grace, granting that *b*signs and wonders be done by their hands.

3 *a*Acts
4:29f.; 20:32;
Heb. 2:4
*b*John 4:48

4 *a*But the multitude of the city was divided; and some sided with *b*the Jews, and some with *c*the apostles.

4 *a*Acts
17:4f.; 19:9;
28:24 *b*Acts
13:45, 50;
14:2, 5, 19;
1 Thess. 2:16
*c*Acts 14:14

5 And when an attempt was made by both the Gentiles and *a*the Jews with their rulers, to mistreat and to *b*stone them,

5 *a*Acts
13:45, 50;
14:2, 4, 19;
1 Thess. 2:16
*b*Acts 14:19

6 they became aware of it and fled to the cities of *a*Lycaonia, *b*Lystra and *c*Derbe, and the surrounding region;

★ 6 *a*Acts
14:11 *b*Acts
14:8, 21;
16:11; 2 Tim.
3:11 *c*Acts
14:20; 16:1;
20:4

7 and there they continued to *a*preach the gospel.

7 *a*Acts
14:15, 21;
16:10

8 And at *a*Lystra there was sitting *b*a certain man, without strength in his feet, lame from his mother's womb, who had never walked.

8 *a*Acts
14:6, 21;
16:11; 2 Tim.
3:11 *b*Acts
3:2

9 This man was listening to Paul as he spoke, who, *a*when he had fixed his gaze upon him, and had seen that he had *b*faith to be made well,

9 *a*Acts 3:4;
10:4 *b*Matt.
9:28

13:48 *they began rejoicing.* The Gentiles' reception and the Jews' rejection (v. 50) of the gospel is, from here on, a recurring theme in Acts.

13:51 *they shook off the dust.* A good Jew took pains not to carry back into Palestine any dust from non-Jewish countries. To "shake off the

dust" was a vivid gesture of complete break of fellowship and renunciation of responsibility for the person or community gestured at. See Christ's command at Luke 9:5; 10:11; and note on Mark 6:11.

14:6 *Lystra.* About 20 miles from Iconium.

10 ^aActs 3:8

10 said with a loud voice, "Stand upright on your feet." ^aAnd he leaped up and *began* to walk.

11 ^aActs 14:6 ^bActs 8:10; 28:6

11 And when the multitudes saw what Paul had done, they raised their voice, saying in the ^aLycaonian language, "^bThe gods have become like men and have come down to us."

★**12**

12 And they *began* calling Barnabas, Zeus, and Paul, Hermes, because he was the chief speaker.

13 ^aDan. 2:46

13 And the priest of Zeus, whose *temple* was just outside the city, brought oxen and garlands to the gates, and ^awanted to offer sacrifice with the crowds.

14 ^aActs 14:4 ^bNum. 14:6; Matt. 26:65; Mark 14:63

14 But when ^athe apostles, Barnabas and Paul, heard of it, they ^btore their robes and rushed out into the crowd, crying out

15 ^aActs 10:26; James 5:17 ^bActs 13:32; 14:7, 21 ^cDeut. 32:21; 1 Sam. 12:21; Jer. 8:19; 14:22; 1 Cor. 8:4 ^dMatt. 16:16 ^eEx. 20:11; Ps. 146:6; Acts 4:24; 17:24; Rev. 14:7

15 and saying, "Men, why are you doing these things? We are also ^amen of the same nature as you, and ^bpreach the gospel to you in order that you should turn from these ^cvain things to a ^dliving God, ^eWHO MADE THE HEAVEN AND THE EARTH AND THE SEA, AND ALL THAT IS IN THEM.

16 ^aActs 17:30 ^bPs. 81:12; Mic. 4:5

16 "And in the generations gone by He ^apermitted all the nations to ^bgo their own ways;

17 ^aActs 17:26f.; Rom. 1:19f. ^bDeut. 11:14; Job 5:10; Ps. 65:10f.; Ezek. 34:26f.; Joel 2:23

17 and yet ^aHe did not leave Himself without witness, in that He did good and ^bgave you rains from heaven and fruitful seasons, satisfying your hearts with food and gladness."

★**19** ^aActs 13:45, 50; 14:2, 4, 5; 1 Thess. 2:16 ^bActs 13:14; 14:21, 26 ^cActs 13:51; 14:1, 21 ^dActs 14:5; 2 Cor. 11:25; 2 Tim. 3:11

18 And *even* saying these things, they with difficulty restrained the crowds from offering sacrifice to them.

19 But ^aJews came from ^bAntioch and ^cIconium, and having won over the multitudes, they ^dstoned Paul and dragged him out

of the city, supposing him to be dead.

20 But while ^athe disciples stood around him, he arose and entered the city. And the next day he went away with Barnabas to ^bDerbe.

20 ^aActs 11:26; 14:22, 28 ^bActs 14:6

4 Events on the return to Antioch, 14:21-28

21 And after they had ^apreached the gospel to that city and had ^bmade many disciples, they returned to ^cLystra and to ^dIconium and to ^eAntioch,

21 ^aActs 14:7 ^bActs 2:47 ^cActs 14:6 ^dActs 13:51; 14:1, 19 ^eActs 13:14; 14:19, 26

22 strengthening the souls of ^athe disciples, encouraging them to continue in ^bthe faith, and *saying,* "^cThrough many tribulations we must enter the kingdom of God."

22 ^aActs 11:26; 14:28 ^bActs 6:7 ^cMark 10:30; John 15:18, 20; 16:33; 1 Thess. 3:3; 2 Tim. 3:12; 1 Pet. 2:21; Rev. 1:9

★**23** ^a2 Cor. 8:19; Titus 1:5 ^bActs 11:30 ^cActs 1:24; 13:3 ^dActs 20:32

23 And when ^athey had appointed ^belders for them in every church, having ^cprayed with fasting, they ^dcommended them to the Lord in whom they had believed.

24 And they passed through ^aPisidia and came into ^bPamphylia.

24 ^aActs 13:14 ^bActs 13:13

25 And when they had spoken the word in ^aPerga, they went down to Attalia;

25 ^aActs 13:13

26 and from there they sailed to ^aAntioch, from ^bwhich they had been ^ccommended to the grace of God for the work that they had accomplished.

26 ^aActs 11:19 ^bActs 13:3 ^cActs 11:23; 15:40

27 And when they had arrived and gathered the church together, they *began* to ^areport all things that God had done with them and how He had opened a ^bdoor of faith to the Gentiles.

27 ^aActs 15:3, 4, 12; 21:19 ^b1 Cor. 16:9; 2 Cor. 2:12; Col. 4:3; Rev. 3:8

28 And they spent a long time with ^athe disciples.

28 ^aActs 11:26; 14:22

14:12 *Zeus.* The chief god of the Greek Pantheon. *Hermes.* The patron god of orators. In two Greek legends connected with Lystra (and familiar to Paul's listeners) Zeus and Hermes had come down and had "become like men" (v. 11).

14:19 *they stoned Paul.* After suffering the crushing blows of the stones, the victim was

dragged outside the city and left to the dogs and beasts. It was a miracle that Paul could get up and leave the next day. Some think the vision mentioned in 2 Cor. 12:1-5 occurred at this time, and it is also possible that he received the marks spoken of in Gal. 6:17 during this stoning.

14:23 *appointed elders.* See note on 1 Tim. 3:1.

B The Council at Jerusalem,
15:1-35

1 The dissension, 15:1-5

★ 1 aActs
15:24 bActs
1:15; 15:3,
22, 32 cActs
15:5; 1 Cor.
7:18; Gal.
2:11, 14;
5:2f. dActs
6:14

15 And ^asome men came down from Judea and *began* teaching ^bthe brethren, "Unless you are ^ccircumcised according to ^dthe custom of Moses, you cannot be saved."

2 aActs
15:7 bGal.
2:2 cActs
11:30; 15:4,
6, 22, 23;
16:4

2 And when Paul and Barnabas had great dissension and ^adebate with them, ^b*the brethren* determined that Paul and Barnabas and certain others of them should go up to Jerusalem to the ^capostles and elders concerning this issue.

3 aActs
20:38; 21:5;
Rom. 15:24;
1 Cor. 16:6,
11; 2 Cor.
1:16; Titus
3:13; 3 John
6 bActs
11:19 cActs
14:27; 15:4,
12 dActs
1:15; 15:22,
32

3 Therefore, being ^asent on their way by the church, they were passing through both ^bPhoenicia and Samaria, ^cdescribing in detail the conversion of the Gentiles, and were bringing great joy to all ^dthe brethren.

4 aActs
11:30; 15:6,
22, 23; 16:4
bActs 14:27;
15:12

4 And when they arrived at Jerusalem, they were received by the church and ^athe apostles and the elders, and they ^breported all that God had done with them.

5 aActs
5:17; 24:5,
14; 26:5;
28:22 bMatt.
3:7; Acts
26:5 c1 Cor.
7:18; Gal.
2:11, 14;
5:2f.

5 But certain ones of ^athe sect of the ^bPharisees who had believed, stood up, saying, "It is necessary to ^ccircumcise them, and to direct them to observe the Law of Moses."

2 The discussion, 15:6-18

6 aActs
11:30; 15:4,
22, 23; 16:4

6 And ^athe apostles and the elders came together to look into this matter.

7 And after there had been much ^adebate, Peter stood up and said to them, "Brethren, you know that in the early days ^bGod made a choice among you, that by my mouth the Gentiles should hear the word of ^cthe gospel and believe.

★ 7 aActs
15:2 bActs
10:19f. cActs
20:24

8 "And God, ^awho knows the heart, bore witness to them, ^bgiving them the Holy Spirit, just as He also did to us;

8 aActs
1:24 bActs
10:47

9 and ^aHe made no distinction between us and them, ^bcleansing their hearts by faith.

9 aActs
10:28, 34;
11:12 bActs
10:43

10 "Now therefore why do you ^aput God to the test by placing upon the neck of the disciples a yoke which ^bneither our fathers nor we have been able to bear?

★10 aActs
5:9 bMatt.
23:4; Gal.
5:1

11 "But we believe that we are saved through ^athe grace of the Lord Jesus, in the same way as they also are."

★11 aRom.
3:24; 5:15;
2 Cor. 13:14;
Eph.
2:5-8

12 And all the multitude kept silent, and they were listening to Barnabas and Paul as they were ^arelating what ^bsigns and wonders God had done through them among the Gentiles.

12 aActs
14:27; 15:3,
4 bJohn 4:48

13 And after they had stopped speaking, ^aJames answered, saying, "Brethren, listen to me.

★13 aActs
12:17

14 "^aSimeon has related how God first concerned Himself about taking from among the Gentiles a people for His name.

14 aActs
15:7; 2 Pet.
1:1

15:1 *Unless you are circumcised . . . you cannot be saved.* The problems raised by the presence of Gentiles in the Church now came to a head. Peter had learned that no man should be called unclean—not even Gentiles (10:34), and the Jerusalem church had accepted the first Gentile converts on an equal basis with Jewish converts and without the necessity of being circumcised. However, the ultra-Judaistic party went on the offensive and insisted that Gentile converts be circumcised. A parallel question was also being raised: Should there be unrestricted social contact between Jewish and Gentile Christians? The Judaistic party separated themselves from those who did not follow the dietary laws and would not partake

of the common meals. Chapter 15 is concerned with these two questions: circumcision and foods (socializing). Had the division over these questions prevailed, the unity of the Church would have been shattered from the start.

15:7 *by my mouth the Gentiles.* A reference to Peter's ministry in the house of Cornelius (10:44).

15:10 *a yoke.* I.e., that of the law, which in its complexities had become a burden, almost literally impossible to keep.

15:11 Peter means that both Jew and Gentile will be saved through grace without the yoke of the law.

15:13 *James.* See notes on Matt. 4:21 and the Introduction to James.

★15-17
15 aActs
13.40

16 aAmos
9.11 bJer
12.15

17 aAmos
9.12 bDeut.
28.10; Is
63.19; Jer
14.9; Dan
9.19; James
2.7

18 aAmos
9.12 b Is
45.21

★19 aActs
15.28; 21.25
★20 aDan.
1.8; Acts
15.29; 1 Cor.
8.7, 13;
10.7f; 14.28;
Rev. 2.14, 20
bGen. 9.4;
Lev. 3.17;
7.26; 17.10,
14; 19.26;
Deut. 12.16,
23; 15.23;
1 Sam. 14.33
21 aActs
13.15; 2 Cor.
3.14f
22 aActs
15.2 bActs
11.20 cActs
15.27, 32,
40; 16.19;
25.29; 17.4,
10; 14f;
18.5; 2 Cor.
1.19;
1 Thess. 1.1;
2 Thess. 1.1;
1 Pet. 5.12
dActs 15.1

15 "And with this the words of athe Prophets agree, just as it is written,

16 'aAFTER THESE THINGS bI will return,
AND I WILL REBUILD THE TAB-ERNACLE OF DAVID WHICH HAS FALLEN,
AND I WILL REBUILD ITS RUINS,
AND I WILL RESTORE IT,

17 aIN ORDER THAT THE REST OF MANKIND MAY SEEK THE LORD,
AND ALL THE GENTILES bWHO ARE CALLED BY MY NAME,'

18 aSAYS THE LORD, WHO bMAKES THESE THINGS KNOWN FROM OF OLD.

3 The decision, 15:19-29

19 "Therefore it is amy judg-ment that we do not trouble those who are turning to God from among the Gentiles,

20 but that we write to them that they abstain from athings contaminated by idols and from fornication and from bwhat is strangled and from blood.

21 "For aMoses from ancient generations has in every city those who preach him, since he is read in the synagogues every Sab-bath."

22 Then it seemed good to athe apostles and the elders, with the whole church, to choose men from among them to send to bAn-tioch with Paul and Barnabas—Judas called Barsabbas, and cSilas,

leading men among dthe breth-ren,

23 and they sent this letter by them,

"aThe apostles and the brethren who are el-ders, to bthe brethren in cAntioch and dSyria and eCilicia who are from the Gentiles, fgreetings.

24 "Since we have heard that asome of our num-ber to whom we gave no instruction have bdisturbed you with their words, unsettling your souls,

25 ait seemed good to us, having become of one mind, to select men to send to you with our beloved Barnabas and Paul,

26 men who have arisked their lives for the name of our Lord Jesus Christ.

27 "Therefore we have sent aJudas and bSilas, who themselves will also re-port the same things by word of mouth.

28 "For ait seemed good to bthe Holy Spirit and to cus to lay upon you no greater burden than these essentials:

29 that you abstain from athings sacrificed to idols and from ablood

23 aActs
15.2 bActs
15.1 cActs
11.20 dMatt.
4.24; Acts
15.41; Gal.
1.21 eActs
6.9 fActs
23.26; James
1.1; 2 John
10f.

24 aActs
15.1 bGal.
1.7; 5.10

25 aActs
15.28

★26 aActs
9.23ff; 14.19

27 aActs
15.22, 32
bActs 15.22

28 aActs
15.25 bActs
5.32; 15.8
cActs 15.19,
25

★29 aActs
15.20

15:15-17 The quotation is from the Septuagint (Greek) version of Amos 9:11-12. James speci-fies that the prophecy of Amos will be fulfilled "after these things," i.e., after the present worldwide witness. Then, after the return of Christ, the tabernacle of David (in the millen-nial kingdom) will be established, and Jew and Gentile will know the Lord. James assured the council that God's program for Israel had not been abandoned by the coming of Gentiles into the Church.

15:19 we do not trouble those. The clear ver-dict of James, as president of the council, was that Gentile converts need not be circumcised.

15:20 In order to promote peace between Jewish

and Gentile believers, the Gentiles were asked to abstain from any practice abhorrent to Jew-ish Christians. The Jewish Christians would then socialize with them (cf. 1 Cor. 8:13). for-nication. It does not seem likely that the word means illicit sexual relations in this instance (though it does elsewhere), for this would be wrong for any Christian, Gentile or Jew. It evi-dently has the special meaning here of mar-riages contracted between too-near relatives, as forbidden in Lev. 18.

15:26 risked their lives. For some of the risks incurred see 13:50; 14:5, 19.

15:29 do well. I.e., act rightly.

and from ªthings strangled and from ªfornication; if you keep yourselves free from such things, you will do well. Farewell."

4   The letter delivered to Antioch, 15:30–35

30 Acts 15:22f

30 So, when they were sent away, ªthey went down to Antioch; and having gathered the congregation together, they delivered the letter.

31 And when they had read it, they rejoiced because of its encouragement.

32 Acts 15:22, 27 bActs 15:22 cActs 13:1 dActs 15:1

32 And ªJudas and bSilas, also being cprophets themselves, encouraged and strengthened dthe brethren with a lengthy message.

33 Mark 5:34; Acts 16:36; 1 Cor 16:11; Heb. 11:31 bActs 15:22

33 And after they had spent time there, they were sent away from the brethren ªin peace to those who had bsent them out.

★34

34 [But it seemed good to Silas to remain there.]

35 Acts 12:25 bActs 8:4 cActs 13:12

35 But ªPaul and Barnabas stayed in Antioch, teaching and bpreaching, with many others also, cthe word of the Lord.

C The Second Missionary Journey, 15:36–18:22
1 The personnel chosen, 15:36–40

36 Acts 13:4, 13, 14, 51; 14:6, 24f bActs 13:12

36 And after some days Paul said to Barnabas, "Let us return and visit the brethren in ªevery city in which we proclaimed bthe word of the Lord, and see how they are."

37 And Barnabas was desirous of taking ªJohn, called Mark, along with them also.

37 Acts 12:12

38 But Paul kept insisting that they should not take him along who had ªdeserted them in Pamphylia and had not gone with them to the work.

38 Acts 13:13

39 And there arose such a sharp disagreement that they separated from one another, and Barnabas took ªMark with him and sailed away to bCyprus.

★39 Acts 12:12; 15:37; Col. 4:10 bActs 4:36

40 But Paul chose ªSilas and departed, being bcommitted by the brethren to the grace of the Lord.

40 Acts 15:22 bActs 11:23; 14:26

2 The churches revisited, 15:41–16:5

41 And he was traveling through ªSyria and bCilicia, strengthening the churches.

41 Matt 4:24; Acts 15:23 bActs 6:9

16 And he came also to ªDerbe and to ªLystra. And behold, a certain disciple was there, named bTimothy, the son of a cJewish woman who was a believer, but his father was a Greek,

★ 1 Acts 14:6 bActs 17:14f; 18:5; 19:22; 20:4; Rom. 16:21; 1 Cor. 4:17; 16:10; 2 Cor. 1:1, 19; Phil. 1:1; 2:19; Col. 1:1; 1 Thess. 1:1; 3:2, 6; 2 Thess. 1:1; 1 Tim. 1:2, 18; 6:20; 2 Tim. 1:2; Philem. 1; Heb. 13:23 c2 Tim. 1:5; 3:15

2 and he was well spoken of by ªthe brethren who were in bLystra and cIconium.

2 Acts 16:40 bActs 14:6 cActs 13:51

3 Paul wanted this man to go with him; and he ªtook him and circumcised him because of the Jews who were in those parts, for they all knew that his father was a Greek.

★ 3 Gal. 2:3

4 Now while they were passing through the cities, they were delivering ªthe decrees, which

★ 4 Acts 15:28f, bActs 15:2 cActs 11:30

15:34 Some manuscripts do not contain this verse.

15:39 they separated from one another. Here is an example of separation because of personality or practicality, not doctrine, and it seemed to be the only solution to the problem. God brought good out of it in that two missionary teams were sent out, and Barnabas' continued interest in John Mark rescued him from possible uselessness. (For separation on doctrinal grounds see Gal. 1:8; 2 Thess. 3:14; 2 Tim. 2:18; 1 John 2:18; 2 John 10.)

16:1 Timothy. See Introduction to 1 Timothy.

16:3 circumcised him. The Jerusalem council had declared that circumcision was not necessary for salvation or for acceptance into the Christian Church (15:19), but because of Timothy's part-Jewish background it seemed expedient in his case, in order to enlarge his local usefulness in witnessing. In the case of Gentile Titus, Paul insisted that he not be circumcised (Gal. 2:3).

16:4 the decrees. The decisions arrived at in Jerusalem, 15:23–29.

had been decided upon by *b*the apostles and *c*elders who were in Jerusalem, for them to observe.

5 So *a*the churches were being strengthened in the faith, and were *b*increasing in number daily.

3   The call to Europe, 16:6-10

6 And they passed through the *a*Phrygian and *b*Galatian region, having been forbidden by the Holy Spirit to speak the word in *c*Asia;

7 and when they had come to *a*Mysia, they were trying to go into *b*Bithynia, and the *c*Spirit of Jesus did not permit them;

8 and passing by *a*Mysia, they came down to *b*Troas.

9 And *a*a vision appeared to Paul in the night: a certain man of *b*Macedonia was standing and appealing to him, and saying, "Come over to Macedonia and help us."

10 And when he had seen *a*the vision, immediately *b*we sought to go into Macedonia, concluding that God had called us to *c*preach the gospel to them.

4   The work at Philippi, 16:11-40

11 Therefore putting out to sea from *a*Troas, we ran *b*a straight course to Samothrace, and on the day following to Neapolis;

12 and from there to *a*Philippi, which is a leading city of the district of *b*Macedonia, *c*a *Roman* colony; and we were staying in this city for some days.

13 And on *a*the Sabbath day we went outside the gate to a riverside, where we were supposing that there would be a place of prayer; and we sat down and began speaking to the women who had assembled.

14 And a certain woman named Lydia, from the city of *a*Thyatira, a seller of purple fabrics, *b*a worshiper of God, was listening; and the Lord *c*opened her heart to respond to the things spoken by Paul.

15 And when she and *a*her household had been baptized, she urged us, saying, "If you have judged me to be faithful to the Lord, come into my house and stay." And she prevailed upon us.

16 And it happened that as we were going to *a*the place of prayer, a certain slave-girl having *b*a spirit of divination met us, who was bringing her masters much profit by fortunetelling.

17 Following after Paul and us, she kept crying out, saying, "These men are bond-servants of *a*the Most High God, who are proclaiming to you the way of salvation."

18 And she continued doing this for many days. But Paul was greatly annoyed, and turned and said to the spirit, "I command you *a*in the name of Jesus Christ to come out of her!" And it came out at that very moment.

19 But when her masters saw that their hope of *a*profit was gone, they seized *b*Paul and Silas and *c*dragged them into the market place before the authorities,

---

5 *a*Acts 9:31 *b*Acts 2:47

★ 6 *a*Acts 2:10; 18:23 *b*Acts 18:23; 1 Cor. 16:1; Gal. 1:2; 3:1; 2 Tim. 4:10; 1 Pet. 1:1 *c*Acts 2:9

7 *a*Acts 16:8 *b*1 Pet. 1:1 *c*Luke 24:49; Acts 8:29; Rom. 8:9; Gal. 4:6; Phil. 1:19; 1 Pet. 1:11

8 *a*Acts 16:7 *b*Acts 16:11; 20:5f.; 2 Cor. 2:12; 2 Tim. 4:13

9 *a*Acts 9:10 *b*Acts 16:10, 12; 18:5; 19:21f., 29; 20:1, 3; 27:2; Rom. 15:26

★10 *a*Acts 9:10 *b*[we] Acts 16:10-17; 20:5-15; 21:1-18; 27:1-28:16 *c*Acts 14:7

11 *a*Acts 16:8; 20:5f.; 2 Cor. 2:12; 2 Tim. 4:13 *b*Acts 21:1

★12 *a*Acts 20:6; Phil. 1:1; 1 Thess. 2:2 *b*Acts 16:9, 10; 18:5; 19:21f., 29; 20:1, 3; 27:2; Rom. 15:26 *c*Acts 16:21

★13 *a*Acts 13:14

★14 *a*Rev. 1:11; 2:18, 24 *b*Acts 13:43; 18:7 *c*Luke 24:45

15 *a*Acts 11:14

★16 *a*Acts 16:13 *b*Lev. 19:31; 20:6, 27; Deut. 18:11; 1 Sam. 28:3, 7; 2 Kin. 21:6; 1 Chr. 10:13; Is. 8:19 **17** *a*Mark 5:7

18 *a*Mark 16:17

19 *a*Acts 16:16; 19:25f. *b*Acts 15:22, 40; 16:25, 29 *c*Acts 8:3; 17:6f.; 21:30; James 2:6

16:6 Paul traveled in a northwesterly direction around Asia, to Troas and on to Greece. On the *Galatian region,* see the Introduction to Galatians.

16:10 *we.* Luke joined Paul and his group at Troas and went with them to Philippi, where he remained when the others left (v. 40). Six or seven years later he rejoined Paul (20:5) and remained with him until the end of the narrative.

16:12 *Philippi.* See the Introduction to Philippians. *a Roman colony* was like a piece of Rome transplanted abroad, so that those who held

citizenship in a colony enjoyed the same rights they would have had if they had lived in Italy. Other colonies mentioned in Acts are Antioch in Pisidia, Lystra, Troas, Ptolemais, and Corinth.

16:13 *outside the gate to a riverside.* Apparently there was no synagogue in Philippi; it required at least ten men to organize one.

16:14 *seller of purple fabrics.* Thyatira in Asia Minor was famous for its purple dye.

16:16 *a spirit of divination.* The girl was demon-possessed and was being exploited by her masters (v. 19).

★20 20 and when they had brought them to the chief magistrates, they said, "These men are throwing our city into confusion, being Jews,

21 aEsther 3:8 bActs 16:12
21 and aare proclaiming customs which it is not lawful for us to accept or to observe, being bRomans."

22 a2 Cor. 11:25; 1 Thess. 2:2
22 And the crowd rose up together against them, and the chief magistrates tore their robes off them, and proceeded to order them to be abeaten with rods.

23 aActs 16:27, 36
23 And when they had inflicted many blows upon them, they threw them into prison, commanding athe jailer to guard them securely;

24 aJob 13:27, 33:11; Jer. 20:2f.; 29:26
24 and he, having received such a command, threw them into the inner prison, and fastened their feet in athe stocks.

25 aActs 16:19 bEph. 5:19
25 But about midnight aPaul and Silas were praying and bsinging hymns of praise to God, and the prisoners were listening to them;

26 aActs 4:31 bActs 12:10 cActs 12:7
26 and suddenly athere came a great earthquake, so that the foundations of the prison house were shaken; and immediately ball the doors were opened, and everyone's cchains were unfastened.

27 aActs 16:23, 36 bActs 12:19
27 And when athe jailer had been roused out of sleep and had seen the prison doors opened, he drew his sword and was about bto kill himself, supposing that the prisoners had escaped.

28 But Paul cried out with a loud voice, saying, "Do yourself no harm, for we are all here!"

29 aActs 16:19
29 And he called for lights and rushed in and, trembling with fear, he fell down before aPaul and Silas,

30 and after he brought them out, he said, "Sirs, awhat must I do to be saved?"

30 aActs 2:37; 22:10
31 And they said, "aBelieve in the Lord Jesus, and you shall be saved, you and byour household."

★31 aMark 16:16 bActs 11:14; 16:15
32 And they spoke the word of the Lord to him together with all who were in his house.

33 And he took them athat very hour of the night and washed their wounds, and immediately he was baptized, he and all his household.

33 aActs 16:25
34 And he brought them into his house and set food before them, and rejoiced greatly, having believed in God with ahis whole household.

34 aActs 11:14; 16:15
35 Now when day came, the chief magistrates sent their policemen, saying, "Release those men."

36 And athe jailer reported these words to Paul, saying, "The chief magistrates have sent to release you. Now therefore, come out and go bin peace."

36 aActs 16:27 bActs 15:33
37 But Paul said to them, "They have beaten us in public without trial, amen who are Romans, and have thrown us into prison; and now are they sending us away secretly? No indeed! But let them come themselves and bring us out."

★37 aActs 22:25-29
38 And the policemen reported these words to the chief magistrates. And athey were afraid when they heard that they were Romans,

38 aActs 22:29
39 and they came and appealed to them, and when they had brought them out, they kept begging them ato leave the city.

39 aMatt. 8:34
40 And they went out of the prison and entered the house of aLydia, and when they saw bthe

40 aActs 16:14 bActs 1:15; 16:2

16:20 *throwing our city into confusion, being Jews.* Judaism was not a prohibited religion (the cult of the emperor being the official religion), but propagating it was regarded as a menace. Paul and Silas were regarded as Jews, since, at this time, the Romans considered Christianity to be a Jewish sect. See also note on 18:14-16.

16:31 *and your household.* These words must

be connected with "believe" as well as "be saved." Each member of the household must believe in order to be saved.

16:37 *Romans.* Paul was born a Roman citizen (22:28), which gave him certain rights, including a public hearing. Scourging of any Roman citizen was prohibited by law; the rights of Paul and Silas, therefore, had already been violated.

brethren, they encouraged them and departed.

5 The work at Thessalonica, Berea, and Athens, 17:1-34

★ 1 aActs 17:11, 13; 20:4; 27:2; Phil. 4:16; 1 Thess. 1:1; 2 Thess. 1:1; 2 Tim. 4:10

17 Now when they had traveled through Amphipolis and Apollonia, they came to aThessalonica, where there was a synagogue of the Jews.

2 aActs 9:20; 17:10, 17 bActs 13:14 cActs 8:35

2 And aaccording to Paul's custom, he went to them, and for three bSabbaths reasoned with them from cthe Scriptures,

3 aActs 3:18 bJohn 20:9 cActs 9:22; 18:5, 28

3 explaining and giving evidence that the Christ ahad to suffer and brise again from the dead, and saying, "cThis Jesus whom I am proclaiming to you is the Christ."

4 aActs 14:4 bActs 15:22, 40; 17:10, 14f. cActs 13:43; 17:17 dJohn 7:35 eActs 13:50

4 aAnd some of them were persuaded and joined bPaul and Silas, along with a great multitude of the cGod-fearing dGreeks and a number of the eleading women.

5 aActs 17:13; 1 Thess. 2:16 bActs 17:6, 7, 9; Rom. 16:21

5 But athe Jews, becoming jealous and taking along some wicked men from the market place, formed a mob and set the city in an uproar; and coming upon the house of bJason, they were seeking to bring them out to the people.

6 aActs 16:19f. bMatt. 24:14; Acts 17:31

6 And when they did not find them, they began adragging Jason and some brethren before the city authorities, shouting, "These men who have upset bthe world have come here also;

7 aLuke 10:38; James 2:25 bLuke 23:2

7 and Jason ahas welcomed them, and they all act bcontrary to the decrees of Caesar, saying that there is another king, Jesus."

8 And they stirred up the crowd and the city authorities who heard these things.

9 And when they had received a pledge from aJason and the others, they released them.

★ 9 aActs 17:5

10 And athe brethren immediately sent bPaul and Silas away by night to cBerea; and when they arrived, they went into dthe synagogue of the Jews.

10 aActs 1:15; 17:6, 14f. bActs 17:4 cActs 17:13; 20:4 dActs 17:2

11 Now these were more noble-minded than those in aThessalonica, for they received the word with great eagerness, examining the Scriptures daily, to see whether these things were so.

11 aActs 17:1

12 aMany of them therefore believed, along with a number of bprominent Greek cwomen and men.

12 aActs 2:47 bMark 15:43 cActs 13:50

13 But when the Jews of aThessalonica found out that the word of God had been proclaimed by Paul in bBerea also, they came there likewise, agitating and stirring up the crowds.

13 aActs 17:1 bActs 17:10; 20:4

14 And then immediately athe brethren sent Paul out to go as far as the sea; and bSilas and cTimothy remained there.

14 aActs 1:15; 17:6, 10 bActs 15:22; 17:4, 10 cActs 16:1

15 Now athose who conducted Paul brought him as far as bAthens; and receiving a command for cSilas and Timothy to dcome to him as soon as possible, they departed.

15 aActs 15:3 bActs 17:16, 21f.; 18:1; 1 Thess. 3:1 cActs 17:14 dActs 18:5

16 Now while Paul was waiting for them at aAthens, his spirit was being provoked within him as he was beholding the city full of idols.

16 aActs 17:15, 21f.; 18:1; 1 Thess. 3:1

17 So he was reasoning ain the synagogue with the Jews and bthe God-fearing Gentiles, and in the market place every day with those who happened to be present.

17 aActs 9:20; 17:2 bActs 17:4

18 And also some of the Epicurean and Stoic philosophers were conversing with him. And some were saying, "What would athis idle babbler wish to say?"

★18 a1 Cor. 1:20; 4:10 bActs 4:2; 17:31f.

17:1 Thessalonica. See the Introduction to 1 Thessalonians.
17:9 received a pledge from Jason. I.e., made Jason put up a bond, forfeitable if there was further trouble.
17:18 Epicurean . . . philosophers. Followers of Epicurus (341-270 b.c.), who believed that happiness was the chief end of life. The Stoic

philosophers, who regarded Zeno (340-265 b.c.) as their founder and whose name came from Stoa Poikile (Painted Porch) where he taught in Athens, emphasized the rational over the emotional. They were pantheistic. Their ethics were characterized by moral earnestness and a high sense of duty, advocating conduct "according to nature."

Others, "He seems to be a proclaimer of strange deities,"—because he was preaching [b]Jesus and the resurrection.

19 And they [a]took him and brought him to the [b]Areopagus, saying, "May we know what [c]this new teaching is which you are proclaiming?

20 "For you are bringing some strange things to our ears; we want to know therefore what these things mean."

21 (Now all the Athenians and the strangers [a]visiting there used to spend their time in nothing other than telling or hearing something new.)

22 And Paul stood in the midst of the Areopagus and said, "Men of [a]Athens, I observe that you are very [b]religious in all respects.

23 "For while I was passing through and examining the [a]objects of your worship, I also found an altar with this inscription, 'TO AN UNKNOWN GOD.' What therefore [b]you worship in ignorance, this I proclaim to you.

24 "[a]The God who made the world and all things in it, since He is [b]Lord of heaven and earth, does not [c]dwell in temples made with hands;

25 neither is He served by human hands, [a]as though He needed anything, since He Himself gives to all life and breath and all things;

26 and [a]He made from one, every nation of mankind to live on all the face of the earth, having [b]determined *their* appointed times, and the boundaries of their habitation,

27 that they should seek God,

if perhaps they might grope for Him and find Him, [a]though He is not far from each one of us;

28 for [a]in Him we live and move and exist, as even some of your own poets have said, 'For we also are His offspring.'

29 "Being then the offspring of God, we [a]ought not to think that the Divine Nature is like gold or silver or stone, an image formed by the art and thought of man.

30 "Therefore having [a]overlooked [b]the times of ignorance, God is [c]now declaring to men that all everywhere should repent,

31 because He has fixed [a]a day in which [b]He will judge [c]the world in righteousness through a Man whom He has [d]appointed, having furnished proof to all men by [e]raising Him from the dead."

32 Now when they heard of [a]the resurrection of the dead, some *began* to sneer, but others said, "We shall hear you again concerning this."

33 So Paul went out of their midst.

34 But some men joined him and believed, among whom also was Dionysius the [a]Areopagite and a woman named Damaris and others with them.

6 *The ministry at Corinth,* 18:1–17

18 After these things he left [a]Athens and went to [b]Corinth.

2 And he found a certain Jew named [a]Aquila, a native of [b]Pontus, having recently come from [c]Italy with his wife [a]Priscilla, because [d]Claudius had com-

---

Marginal references (left column):

★19 [a]Acts 23:19 [b]Acts 17:22 [c]Mark 1:27

21 [a]Acts 2:10

22 [a]Acts 17:15 [b]Acts 25:19

23 [a]2 Thess. 2:4 [b]John 4:22

★24 [a]Is. 42:5; Acts 14:15 [b]Deut. 10:14; Ps. 115:16; Matt. 11:25 [c]Acts 7:48

25 [a]Job 22:2; Ps. 50:10-12

26 [a]Mal. 2:10 [b]Deut. 32:8; Job 12:23

27 [a]Deut. 4:7; Jer. 23:23f.; Acts 14:17

Marginal references (right column):

28 [a]Job 12:10; Dan. 5:23

★29 [a]Is. 40:18ff.; Rom. 1:23

30 [a]Acts 14:16; Rom. 3:25 [b]Acts 17:23 [c]Luke 24:47; Acts 26:20; Titus 2:11f.

31 [a]Matt. 10:15 [b]Ps. 9:8; 96:13; 98:9; John 5:22, 27; Acts 10:42 [c]Matt. 24:14; Acts 17:6 [d]Luke 22:22 [e]Acts 2:24

32 [a]Acts 17:18, 31

★34 [a]Acts 17:19, 22

★ 1 [a]Acts 17:15 [b]Acts 18:8; 19:1; 1 Cor. 1:2; 2 Cor. 1:1; 23; 6:11; 2 Tim. 4:20

★ 2 [a]Acts 18:18, 26; Rom. 16:3; 1 Cor. 16:19; 2 Tim. 4:19 [b]Acts 2:9 [c]Acts 27:1, 6; Heb. 13:24 [d]Acts 11:28

17:19 *Areopagus.* The venerable council that had charge of religious and educational matters in Athens. It met on the Hill of Ares W. of the Acropolis, the hill also being known as the Areopagus.

17:24. Notice this echo of Stephen's words which Paul had heard years before (7:48-50).

17:29 *Being then the offspring of God.* Because God is the Creator of all.

17:34 *Dionysius the Areopagite.* Membership in the Areopagus was a high distinction. There

is no record of a church in Athens. Paul calls certain Corinthians the first converts on mainland Greece (1 Cor. 16:15).

18:1 *Corinth.* See the Introduction to 1 Corinthians.

18:2 *Aquila . . . his wife Priscilla.* See Rom. 16:3; 1 Cor. 16:19; 2 Tim. 4:19, where Priscilla is called Prisca. *because Claudius had commanded all the Jews to leave Rome.* This imperial edict was issued in A.D. 49 or 50.

manded all the Jews to leave Rome. He came to them,

3 and because he was of the same trade, he stayed with them and [a]they were working; for by trade they were tent-makers.

4 And he was reasoning [a]in the synagogue every [b]Sabbath and trying to persuade [c]Jews and Greeks.

5 But when [a]Silas and Timothy [b]came down from [c]Macedonia, Paul *began* devoting himself completely to the word, solemnly [d]testifying to the Jews that [e]Jesus was the Christ.

6 And when they resisted and blasphemed, he [a]shook out his garments and said to them, "[b]Your blood *be* upon your own heads! I am clean. From now on I shall go [c]to the Gentiles."

7 And he departed from there and went to the house of a certain man named Titius Justus, [a]a worshiper of God, whose house was next to the synagogue.

8 And [a]Crispus, [b]the leader of the synagogue, believed in the Lord [c]with all his household, and many of the [d]Corinthians when they heard were believing and being baptized.

9 And the Lord said to Paul in the night by [a]a vision, "Do not be afraid *any longer*, but go on speaking and do not be silent;

10 for I am with you, and no man will attack you in order to harm you, for I have many people in this city."

11 And he settled *there* a year and six months, teaching the word of God among them.

12 But while Gallio was [a]proconsul of [b]Achaia, [c]the Jews with one accord rose up against Paul and brought him before [d]the judgment seat,

13 saying, "This man persuades men to worship God contrary to [a]the law."

14 But when Paul was about to [a]open his mouth, Gallio said to the Jews, "If it were a matter of wrong or of vicious crime, O Jews, it would be reasonable for me to put up with you;

15 but if there are [a]questions about words and names and your own law, look after it yourselves; I am unwilling to be a judge of these matters."

16 And he drove them away from [a]the judgment seat.

17 And they all took hold of [a]Sosthenes, [b]the leader of the synagogue, and *began* beating him in front of [c]the judgment seat. And Gallio was not concerned about any of these things.

7 The journey completed, 18:18–22

18 And Paul, having remained many days longer, [a]took leave of [b]the brethren and put out to sea for [c]Syria, and with him were [d]Priscilla and [d]Aquila. In [e]Cenchrea he [f]had his hair cut, for he was keeping a vow.

19 And they came to [a]Ephesus, and he left them there. Now he himself entered [b]the synagogue and reasoned with the Jews.

Marginal references

★ 3 [a]Acts 20:34; 1 Cor. 4:12; 9:15; 2 Cor. 11:7; 12:13; 1 Thess. 2:9; 4:11; 2 Thess. 3:8
4 [a]Acts 9:20; 18:19 [b]Acts 13:14 [c]Acts 14:1
5 [a]Acts 15:22; 16:1; 17:14 [b]Acts 17:15 [c]Acts 16:9 [d]Luke 16:28; Acts 20:21 [e]Acts 17:3; 18:28
6 [a]Neh. 5:13; Acts 13:51 [b]2 Sam. 1:16; 1 Kin. 2:33; Ezek. 18:13; 33:4, 6, 8; Matt. 27:25; Acts 20:26 [c]Acts 13:46
7 [a]Acts 13:43; 16:14
8 [a]1 Cor. 1:14 [b]Mark 5:22 [c]Acts 11:14 [d]Acts 18:1; 19:1; 1 Cor. 1:2; 2 Cor. 1:1, 23; 6:11; 2 Tim. 4:20
9 [a]Acts 9:10
★12 [a]Acts 13:7 [b]Acts 18:27; 19:21; Rom. 15:26; 1 Cor. 16:15; 2 Cor. 1:1; 9:2; 11:10; 1 Thess. 1:7f. [c]1 Thess. 2:16 [d]Matt. 27:19
13 [a]John 19:7; Acts 18:15
★14–16
14 [a]Matt. 5:2
15 [a]Acts 23:29; 25:19
16 [a]Matt. 27:19
★17 [a]1 Cor. 1:1 [b]Acts 18:8 [c]Matt. 27:19
★18 [a]Mark 6:46 [b]Acts 1:15; 18:27 [c]Matt. 4:24 [d]Acts 18:2, 26 [e]Rom. 16:1 [f]Num. 6:2, 5, 9, 18; Acts 21:24
19 [a]Acts 18:21, 24; 19:1, 17, 26 [28, 34f.]; 20:16f.; [21:29]; 1 Cor. 15:32; 16:8; Eph. 1:1; 1 Tim. 1:3; 2 Tim. 1:18; 4:12; Rev. 1:11; 2:1 [b]Acts 18:4

18:3 *tent-makers.* Jewish fathers were urged to teach their sons a trade, and Paul learned tent-making, an important industry in Tarsus.
18:12 *proconsul.* Gallio was proconsul of Achaia in 51. He was characterized by contemporaries as an amiable, witty, and lovable person.
18:14–16 Judaism was a "licensed religion" under Roman law. Christianity could take advantage of this protection as long as it sheltered itself under the tent of Judaism. The Jews must have complained that these Christians were not a division or sect of Judaism, and Gallio refuses to see it their way. He says, in effect, "Settle your own religious squabbles yourselves." This ruling was probably important for the spread of the gospel. See also note on 16:20.
18:17 *Sosthenes* became the victim of the Greeks' anti-Jewish feelings. Obviously he was the head of the anti-Pauline faction in the synagogue and a Jew. If this is the same Sosthenes mentioned in 1 Cor. 1:1, perhaps the beating helped him to become a Christian!
18:18 *he had his hair cut.* The sign of the conclusion of a Nazirite vow (Num. 6:18; Acts 21:24). Just why he took the vow is not known. *Cenchrea.* The eastern port of Corinth.

20 And when they asked him to stay for a longer time, he did not consent,

21 but ᵃtaking leave of them and saying, "I will return to you again ᵇif God wills," he set sail from ᶜEphesus.

22 And when he had landed at ᵃCaesarea, he went up and greeted the church, and went down to ᵇAntioch.

D The Third Missionary Journey, 18:23-21:26

1 Ephesus: The power of the Word, 18:23-19:41

23 And having spent some time *there*, he departed and passed successively through the ᵃGalatian region and Phrygia, strengthening all the disciples.

24 Now a certain Jew named ᵃApollos, an ᵇAlexandrian by birth, an eloquent man, came to ᶜEphesus; and he was mighty in the Scriptures.

25 This man had been instructed in ᵃthe way of the Lord; and being fervent in spirit, he was speaking and teaching accurately the things concerning Jesus, being acquainted only with ᵇthe baptism of John;

26 and he began to speak out boldly in the synagogue. But when ᵃPriscilla and Aquila heard him, they took him aside and explained to him ᵇthe way of God more accurately.

27 And when he wanted to go across to ᵃAchaia, ᵇthe brethren encouraged him and wrote to ᶜthe disciples to welcome him; and when he had arrived, he helped greatly those who had believed through grace;

28 for he powerfully refuted the Jews in public, demonstrating ᵃby the Scriptures that ᵇJesus was the Christ.

19 And it came about that while ᵃApollos was at ᵇCorinth, Paul having passed through the ᶜupper country came to ᵈEphesus, and found some disciples,

2 and he said to them, "ᵃDid you receive the Holy Spirit when you believed?" And they *said* to him, "No, ᵇwe have not even heard whether there is a Holy Spirit."

3 And he said, "Into what then were you baptized?" And they said, "ᵃInto John's baptism."

4 And Paul said, "ᵃJohn baptized with the baptism of repentance, telling the people ᵇto believe in Him who was coming after him, that is, in Jesus."

5 And when they heard this, they were ᵃbaptized in the name of the Lord Jesus.

6 And when Paul had ᵃlaid his hands upon them, the Holy Spirit came on them, and they *began* ᵇspeaking with tongues and ᶜprophesying.

7 And there were in all about twelve men.

8 And he entered ᵃthe synagogue and continued speaking out boldly for three months, reasoning and persuading *them* ᵇabout the kingdom of God.

9 But when ᵃsome were becoming hardened and disobedient, speaking evil of ᵇthe Way before the multitude, he withdrew from them and took away ᶜthe disciples, reasoning daily in the school of Tyrannus.

10 And this took place for ᵃtwo years, so that all who lived

---

21 ᵃMark 6:46; ᵇRom. 1:10; 15:32; 1 Cor. 4:19; 16:7; Heb. 6:3; James 4:15; 1 Pet. 3:17; ᶜActs 18:19, 24; 19:1, 17, 26 [28, 34f.]; 20:16f.; [21:29]; 1 Cor. 15:32; 16:8; Eph. 1:1; 1 Tim. 1:3; 2 Tim. 1:18; 4:12; Rev. 1:11; 2:1

22 ᵃActs 8:40; ᵇActs 11:19

23 ᵃActs 16:6

★**24** ᵃActs 19:1; 1 Cor. 1:12; 3:5, 6, 22; 4:6; 16:12; Titus 3:13; ᵇActs 6:9; ᶜActs 18:19

25 ᵃActs 9:2; 18:26; ᵇLuke 7:29; Acts 19:3

26 ᵃActs 18:2, 18; ᵇActs 18:25

27 ᵃActs 18:12; 19:1; ᵇActs 18:18; ᶜActs 11:26

28 ᵃActs 8:35; ᵇActs 18:5

★**1** ᵃActs 18:24; 1 Cor. 1:12; 3:5, 6, 22; 4:6; 16:12; Titus 3:13; ᵇActs 18:1; ᶜActs 18:23; ᵈActs 18:21, 24; 19:1, 17, 26 [28, 34f.]; 20:16f.; [21:29]; 1 Cor. 15:32; 16:8; Eph. 1:1; 1 Tim. 1:3; 2 Tim. 1:18; 4:12; Rev. 1:11; 2:1

★**2** ᵃActs 8:15f.; 11:16f.; ᵇJohn 7:39

3 ᵃLuke 7:29; Acts 18:25

4 ᵃActs 13:24; ᵇJohn 1:7

★**5** ᵃActs 8:12, 16; 10:48

6 ᵃActs 6:6; 8:17; ᵇMark 16:17; Acts 2:4; 10:46; ᶜActs 13:1

★**8** ᵃActs 9:20; 18:26; ᵇActs 1:3

★**9** ᵃActs 14:4; ᵇActs 9:2; 19:23; ᶜActs 11:26; 19:30

10 ᵃActs 19:8; 20:31; ᵇActs 16:6; 19:22, 26, 27; ᶜActs 13:12; 19:20

18:24 *Apollos.* See note on 1 Cor. 1:12.

19:1 *Ephesus.* See the Introduction to Ephesians and note on Rev. 2:1.

19:2 *Did you receive the Holy Spirit when you believed?* The gift of the Spirit is given at the time of believing (10:44).

19:5 *they were baptized in the name of the Lord Jesus.* Though these men had been baptized by John the Baptist, baptism in the name

of Christ was in order as a testimony to their new faith in Christ.

19:8 *synagogue.* Again Paul, on arriving at a city, used the synagogue as his center of witness.

19:9 *school.* I.e., lecture hall owned by Tyrannus, probably used by him to teach students of rhetoric, and made available by him to traveling philosophers or teachers.

in ᵇAsia heard ᶜthe word of the Lord, both Jews and Greeks.

11 And God was performing ᵃextraordinary miracles by the hands of Paul,

12 ᵃso that handkerchiefs or aprons were even carried from his body to the sick, and the diseases left them and ᵇthe evil spirits went out.

13 But also some of the Jewish ᵃexorcists, who went from place to place, attempted to name over those who had the evil spirits the name of the Lord Jesus, saying, "I adjure you by Jesus whom Paul preaches."

14 And seven sons of one Sceva, a Jewish chief priest, were doing this.

15 And the evil spirit answered and said to them, "I recognize Jesus, and I know about Paul, but who are you?"

16 And the man, in whom was the evil spirit, leaped on them and subdued all of them and overpowered them, so that they fled out of that house naked and wounded.

17 And this became known to all, both Jews and Greeks, who lived in ᵃEphesus; and fear fell upon them all and the name of the Lord Jesus was being magnified.

18 Many also of those who had believed kept coming, confessing and disclosing their practices.

19 And many of those who practiced magic brought their books together and *began* burning them in the sight of all; and

they counted up the price of them and found it fifty thousand ᵃpieces of silver.

20 So ᵃthe word of the Lord ᵇwas growing mightily and prevailing.

21 Now after these things were finished, Paul purposed in the spirit to ᵃgo to Jerusalem ᵇafter he had passed through ᶜMacedonia and ᵈAchaia, saying, "After I have been there, ᵉI must also see Rome."

22 And having sent into ᵃMacedonia two of ᵇthose who ministered to him, ᶜTimothy and ᵈErastus, he himself stayed in ᵉAsia for a while.

23 And about that time there arose no small disturbance concerning ᵃthe Way.

24 For a certain man named Demetrius, a silversmith, who made silver shrines of Artemis, ᵃwas bringing no little business to the craftsmen;

25 these he gathered together with the workmen of similar *trades,* and said, "Men, you know that our prosperity depends upon this business.

26 "And you see and hear that not only in ᵃEphesus, but in almost all of ᵇAsia, this Paul has persuaded and turned away a considerable number of people, saying that ᶜgods made with hands are no gods *at all.*

27 "And not only is there danger that this trade of ours fall into disrepute, but also that the temple of the great goddess Artemis be regarded as worthless and that she whom all of ᵃAsia and ᵇthe

---

19:11 *extraordinary miracles.* On other occasions Paul did not have this power (2 Cor. 12:8; Phil. 2:27; 1 Tim. 5:23; 2 Tim. 4:20).

19:13 *exorcists.* Magicians who could cast out demons. The lesson of this story (vv. 13-17) is that to use the name of Jesus effectively in exorcism one must be totally devoted to Him. Contrary to theories of magic of the time, the name by itself could do nothing; this misuse, in fact, backfired (v. 16).

19:19 *magic.* Magical spells written on scrolls. *pieces of silver.* If the silver drachma is meant, the value would have been more than $10,000.

19:24 *silver shrines.* Small shrines in a niche,

representing Artemis (Latin, Diana), for worshipers to dedicate in the temple. No silver ones have been found, only some in terra-cotta. *bringing no little business.* Big profits are clearly implied.

19:27 The gospel was endangering the business of these idol-makers. In order to stir up opposition against the Christians, the craftsmen appealed to the civic pride of the Ephesians. The temple of Artemis was one of the Seven Wonders of the ancient world—a magnificent structure with 127 columns 60 feet high standing on an area 425 feet long and 220 feet wide.

★11 ᵃActs 8:13

12 ᵃActs 5:15 ᵇMark 16:17

★13 ᵃMatt. 12:27; Luke 11:19

17 ᵃActs 18:19

★19 ᵃLuke 15:8

20 ᵃActs 19:10 ᵇActs 6:7; 12:24

21 ᵃActs 20:16, 22; 21:15; Rom. 15:25; 2 Cor. 1:16 ᵇActs 20:1; 1 Cor. 16:5 ᶜActs 16:9; 19:22, 29; Rom. 15:26; 1 Thess. 1:7f. ᵈActs 18:12 ᵉActs 23:11; Rom. 15:24, 28

22 ᵃActs 16:9; 19:21, 29 ᵇActs 13:5; 19:29; 20:34; 2 Cor. 8:19 ᶜActs 16:1 ᵈRom. 16:23; 2 Tim. 4:20 ᵉActs 19:10

23 ᵃActs 19:9

★24 ᵃActs 16:16, 19f.

26 ᵃActs 18:19 ᵇActs 19:10 ᶜDeut. 4:28; Ps. 115:4; Is. 44:10-20; Jer. 10:3ff.; Acts 17:29; 1 Cor. 8:4; 10:19; Rev. 9:20

★27 ᵃActs 19:10 ᵇMatt. 24:14

world worship should even be dethroned from her magnificence."

28 And when they heard *this* and were filled with rage, they *began* crying out, saying, "Great is Artemis of the ᵃEphesians!"

29 And the city was filled with the confusion, and they rushed with one accord into the theater, dragging along ᵃGaius and ᵇAristarchus, Paul's traveling ᶜcompanions from ᵈMacedonia.

30 And when Paul wanted to go into the assembly, ᵃthe disciples would not let him.

31 And also some of the Asiarchs who were friends of his sent to him and repeatedly urged him not to venture into the theater.

32 ᵃSo then, some were shouting one thing and some another, for the assembly was in confusion, and the majority did not know for what cause they had come together.

33 And some of the crowd concluded *it was* Alexander, since the Jews had put him forward; and having ᵃmotioned with his hand, Alexander was intending to make a defense to the assembly.

34 But when they recognized that he was a Jew, a *single* outcry arose from them all as they shouted for about two hours, "Great is Artemis of the Ephesians!"

35 And after quieting the multitude, the town clerk *said, "Men of ᵃEphesus, what man is there after all who does not know that the city of the Ephesians is guardian of the temple of the great Artemis, and of the *image* which fell down from heaven?

36 "Since then these are undeniable facts, you ought to keep calm and to do nothing rash.

37 "For you have brought these men *here* who are neither

ᵃrobbers of temples nor blasphemers of our goddess.

38 "So then, if Demetrius and the craftsmen who are with him have a complaint against any man, the courts are in session and ᵃproconsuls are *available*; let them bring charges against one another.

39 "But if you want anything beyond this, it shall be settled in the lawful assembly.

40 "For indeed we are in danger of being accused of a riot in connection with today's affair, since there is no *real* cause *for it*; and in this connection we shall be unable to account for this disorderly gathering."

41 And after saying this he dismissed the assembly.

2 Greece, 20:1–5

20 And after the uproar had ceased, Paul sent for ᵃthe disciples and when he had exhorted them and taken his leave of them, he departed ᵇto go to ᶜMacedonia.

2 And when he had gone through those districts and had given them much exhortation, he came to Greece.

3 And *there* he spent three months, and when ᵃa plot was formed against him by the Jews as he was about to set sail for ᵇSyria, he determined to return through ᶜMacedonia.

4 And he was accompanied by Sopater of ᵃBerea, *the son of* Pyrrhus; and by ᵇAristarchus and Secundus of the ᶜThessalonians; and ᵈGaius of ᵉDerbe, and ᶠTimothy; and ᵍTychicus and ʰTrophimus of ⁱAsia.

5 But these had gone on ahead and were waiting for ᵃus at ᵇTroas.

Side references (left column):

28 ᵃActs 18:19

29 ᵃActs 20:4; ᵇActs 20:4; 27:2; Col. 4:10; Philem. 24 ᶜActs 13:5; 19:22; 20:34; 2 Cor. 8:19 ᵈActs 16:9; 19:22

30 ᵃActs 19:9

★32 ᵃActs 21:34

33 ᵃActs 12:17

35 ᵃActs 18:19

37 ᵃRom. 2:22

Side references (right column):

38 ᵃActs 13:7

★39

★41

★ 1-4
1 ᵃActs 11:26 ᵇActs 19:21 ᶜActs 16:9; 20:3

3 ᵃActs 9:24; 20:19 ᵇMatt. 4:24 ᶜActs 16:9; 20:1
4 ᵃActs 17:10 ᵇActs 19:29 ᶜActs 17:1 ᵈActs 19:29 ᵉActs 14:6 ᶠActs 16:1 ᵍEph. 6:21; Col. 4:7; 2 Tim. 4:12; Titus 3:12 ʰActs 21:29; 2 Tim. 4:20 ⁱActs 16:6; 20:16, 18
5 ᵃActs 16:10; 20:5-15 ᵇActs 16:8

19:32, 39, 41 *assembly.* The people of Ephesus had the right to meet in a legislative assembly, though this particular gathering was an unlawful one. See note on 7:38.

20:1-4 Luke's brevity here, a mere mention of

the missionary team and a journey through Macedonia revisiting established communities, suggests that Acts could have been a much longer book.

3 Asia Minor: Troas and the elders of Ephesus, 20:6-38

6 aActs 16:10; 20:5-15 bActs 16:12 cActs 12:3 dActs 16:8

6 And ªwe sailed from ᵇPhilippi after ᶜthe days of Unleavened Bread, and came to them at ᵈTroas within five days; and there we stayed seven days.

★ **7** a1 Cor. 16:2; Rev. 1:10 bActs 16:10; 20:5-15 cActs 2:42; 20:11

7 And on ªthe first day of the week, when ᵇwe were gathered together to ᶜbreak bread, Paul *began* talking to them, intending to depart the next day, and he prolonged his message until midnight.

8 aMatt. 25:1 bActs 1:13

8 And there were many ªlamps in the ᵇupper room where we were gathered together.

9 And there was a certain young man named Eutychus sitting on the window sill, sinking into a deep sleep; and as Paul kept on talking, he was overcome by sleep and fell down from the third floor, and was picked up dead.

10 a1 Kin. 17:21; 2 Kin. 4:34 bMatt. 9:23f.; Mark 5:39

10 But Paul went down and ªfell upon him and after embracing him, he ᵇsaid, "Do not be troubled, for his life is in him."

11 aActs 2:42; 20:7

11 And when he had gone *back* up, and had ªbroken the bread and eaten, he talked with them a long while, until daybreak, and so departed.

12 And they took away the boy alive, and were greatly comforted.

13 aActs 16:10; 20:5-15

13 But ªwe, going ahead to the ship, set sail for Assos, intending from there to take Paul on board; for thus he had arranged it, intending himself to go by land.

14 And when he met us at Assos, we took him on board and came to Mitylene.

15 aActs 20:17; 2 Tim. 4:20

15 And sailing from there, we arrived the following day opposite Chios; and the next day we crossed over to Samos; and the day following we came to ªMiletus.

16 For Paul had decided to sail past ªEphesus in order that he might not have to spend time in ᵇAsia; for he was hurrying ᶜto be in Jerusalem, if possible, ᵈon the day of Pentecost.

★**16** aActs 18:19 bActs 16:6; 20:4, 18 cActs 19:21; 20:6, 22; 1 Cor. 16:8 dActs 2:1

17 And from Miletus he sent to ªEphesus and called to him ᵇthe elders of the church.

★**17** aActs 18:19 bActs 11:30

18 And when they had come to him, he said to them,

"You yourselves know, ªfrom the first day that I set foot in Asia, how I was with you the whole time,

18 aActs 18:19; 19:1, 10; 20:4, 16

19 serving the Lord with all humility and with tears and with trials which came upon me through ªthe plots of the Jews;

19 aActs 20:3

20 how I ªdid not shrink from declaring to you anything that was profitable, and teaching you publicly and from house to house,

20 aActs 20:27

21 solemnly ªtestifying to both Jews and Greeks of ᵇrepentance toward God and ᶜfaith in our Lord Jesus Christ.

21 aLuke 16:28; Acts 18:5; 20:23, 24 bActs 2:38; 11:18; 26:20 cActs 24:24; 26:18; Eph. 1:15; Col. 2:5; Philem. 5

22 "And now, behold, bound in spirit, ªI am on my way to Jerusalem, not knowing what will happen to me there,

22 aActs 17:16; 20:16

23 except that ªthe Holy Spirit solemnly ᵇtestifies to me in every city, saying that ᶜbonds and afflictions await me.

23 aActs 8:29 bLuke 16:28; Acts 18:5; 20:21, 24 cActs 9:16; 21:33

24 "But ªI do not consider my life of any account as dear to myself, in order that I may ᵇfinish my course, and ᶜthe ministry which I received from the Lord Jesus, to ᵈtestify solemnly of the gospel of ᵉthe grace of God.

★**24** aActs 21:13 bActs 13:25 cActs 1:17 dLuke 16:28; Acts 18:5; 20:21 eActs 11:23; 20:32

25 "And now, behold, I know that all of you, among whom I went about ªpreaching the kingdom, will see my face no more.

25 aMatt. 4:23; Acts 28:31

26 "Therefore I testify to you

26 aActs 18:6

20:7 *on the first day of the week.* This became the regular day of worship for Christians in remembrance of Christ's resurrection on Sunday.

20:16 If Paul had stopped at Ephesus, friends would surely have delayed him. He *decided* to take a boat that would not stop at Ephesus.

20:17 *elders.* These leaders of the group were recognized by all, since the church knew whom to send when Paul *called to him the elders.* See note on 1 Tim. 3:1.

20:24 Compare Paul's words in 2 Tim. 4:7.

this day, that ªI am innocent of the blood of all men.

27 "For I ªdid not shrink from declaring to you the whole ᵇpurpose of God.

28 "Be on guard for yourselves and for all ªthe flock, among which the Holy Spirit has made you overseers, to shepherd ᵇthe church of God which ᶜHe purchased with His own blood.

29 "I know that after my departure ªsavage wolves will come in among you, not sparing ᵇthe flock;

30 and from among your own selves men will arise, speaking perverse things, to draw away ªthe disciples after them.

31 "Therefore be on the alert, remembering that night and day for a period of ªthree years I did not cease to admonish each one ᵇwith tears.

32 "And now I ªcommend you to God and to ᵇthe word of His grace, which is able to ᶜbuild you up and to give you ᵈthe inheritance among all those who are sanctified.

33 "ªI have coveted no one's silver or gold or clothes.

34 "You yourselves know that ªthese hands ministered to my own needs and to the ᵇmen who were with me.

35 "In everything I showed you that by working hard in this manner you must help the weak and remember the words of the Lord Jesus, that He Himself said, 'It is more blessed to give than to receive.'"

36 And when he had said these things, he ªknelt down and prayed with them all.

37 And they *began* to weep aloud and ªembraced Paul, and repeatedly kissed him,

38 grieving especially over ªthe word which he had spoken,

that they should see his face no more. And they were ᵇaccompanying him to the ship.

4 From Miletus to Caesarea, 21:1-14

21 And when it came about that ªwe had parted from them and had set sail, we ran ᵇa straight course to Cos and the next day to Rhodes and from there to Patara;

2 and having found a ship crossing over to ªPhoenicia, we went aboard and set sail.

3 And when we had come in sight of ªCyprus, leaving it on the left, we kept sailing to ᵇSyria and landed at ᶜTyre; for ᵈthere the ship was to unload its cargo.

4 And after looking up ªthe disciples, we stayed there seven days; and they kept telling Paul ᵇthrough the Spirit not to set foot in Jerusalem.

5 And when it came about that our days there were ended, we departed and started on our journey, while they all, with wives and children, ªescorted us until *we were* out of the city. And after ᵇkneeling down on the beach and praying, we said farewell to one another.

6 Then we went on board the ship, and they returned ªhome again.

7 And when we had finished the voyage from ªTyre, we arrived at Ptolemais; and after greeting ᵇthe brethren, we stayed with them for a day.

8 And on the next day we departed and came to ªCaesarea; and entering the house of ᵇPhilip the ᶜevangelist, who was ᵇone of the seven, we stayed with him.

9 Now this man had four virgin daughters who were ªprophetesses.

---

27 ªActs 20:20 ᵇActs 13:36

★**28-30**
★**28** ªLuke 12:32; John 21:15-17; Acts 20:29; 1 Pet. 5:2f. ᵇMatt. 16:18; Rom. 16:16; 1 Cor. 10:32 ᶜEph. 1:7, 14; Titus 2:14; 1 Pet. 1:19; 2:9; Rev. 5:9
29 ªEzek. 22:27; Matt. 7:15 ᵇLuke 12:32; John 21:15-17; Acts 20:28; 1 Pet. 5:2f.
30 ªActs 11:26
31 ªActs 19:1, 8, 10; 24:17 ᵇActs 20:19

32 ªActs 14:23 ᵇActs 14:3; 20:24 ᶜActs 9:31 ᵈActs 26:18; Eph. 1:14; :5; Col. 1:12; 3:24; Heb. 9:15; 1 Pet. 1:4
33 ª1 Cor. 9:4-18; 2 Cor. 11:7-12; 12:14-18; 1 Thess. 2:5f.
34 ªActs 18:3 ᵇActs 19:22

★**35**

36 ªActs 9:40; 21:5; Luke 22:41

37 ªLuke 15:20

38 ªActs 20:25 ᵇActs 15:3

★ **1** ª[we] Acts 16:10; 21:1-18 ᵇActs 16:11

2 ªActs 11:19; 21:3

3 ªActs 4:36; 21:16 ᵇMatt. 4:24 ᶜActs 12:20; 21:7 ᵈActs 21:2

4 ªActs 11:26; 21:16 ᵇActs 20:23; 21:11

5 ªActs 15:3 ᵇLuke 22:41; Acts 9:40; 20:36

6 ªJohn 19:27

7 ªActs 12:20; 21:3 ᵇActs 1:15; 21:17

★ **8** ªActs 8:40; 21:16 ᵇActs 6:5 ᶜEph. 4:11; 2 Tim. 4:5

9 ªLuke 2:36; Acts 13:1; 1 Cor. 11:5

20:28-30 For what happened at Ephesus later, see 1 Tim. 1:3-7.
20:28 *with His own blood.* Lit., with the blood of His own (Son).
20:35 *remember the words of the Lord Jesus.* This saying is not recorded in the Gospels.

21:1 Luke obviously enjoyed describing a sea voyage. His masterpiece comes later (chap. 27).
21:8 *Philip the evangelist.* He was previously mentioned in 6:5 and 8:5.

10 And as we were staying there for some days, a certain prophet named ªAgabus came down from Judea.

11 And coming to us, he ªtook Paul's belt and bound his own feet and hands, and said, "This bis what the Holy Spirit says: 'In this way the Jews at Jerusalem will cbind the man who owns this belt and ddeliver him into the hands of the Gentiles.'"

12 And when we had heard this, we as well as the local residents began begging him ªnot to go up to Jerusalem.

13 Then Paul answered, "What are you doing, weeping and breaking my heart? For ªI am ready not only to be bound, but even to die at Jerusalem for bthe name of the Lord Jesus."

14 And since he would not be persuaded, we fell silent, remarking, "ªThe will of the Lord be done!"

5 Paul with the Jerusalem church, 21:15-26

15 And after these days we got ready and ªstarted on our way up to Jerusalem.

16 And some of ªthe disciples from bCaesarea also came with us, taking us to Mnason of cCyprus, a ddisciple of long standing with whom we were to lodge.

17 And when we had come to Jerusalem, ªthe brethren received us gladly.

18 And now the following day Paul went in with us to ªJames, and all bthe elders were present.

19 And after he had greeted them, he ªbegan to relate one by one the things which God had done among the Gentiles through his bministry.

20 And when they heard it they began ªglorifying God; and they said to him, "You see, brother, how many thousands there are among the Jews of those who have believed, and they are all bzealous for the Law;

21 and they have been told about you, that you are ªteaching all the Jews who are among the Gentiles to forsake Moses, telling them bnot to circumcise their children nor to walk according to cthe customs.

22 "What, then, is to be done? They will certainly hear that you have come.

23 "Therefore do this that we tell you. We have four men who ªare under a vow;

24 take them and ªpurify yourself along with them, and pay their expenses in order that they may bshave their heads; and all will know that there is nothing to the things which they have been told about you, but that you yourself also walk orderly, keeping the Law.

25 "But concerning the Gentiles who have believed, we wrote, ªhaving decided that they should abstain from meat sacrificed to idols and from blood and from what is strangled and from fornication."

26 Then Paul took the men, and the next day, ªpurifying himself along with them, bwent into the temple, giving notice of the completion of the days of purification, until the sacrifice was offered for each one of them.

E The Journey to Rome, 21:27-28:31

1 Paul's arrest and defense, 21:27-22:29

27 And when ªthe seven days were almost over, bthe Jews from

21:10 *Agabus.* Presumably the same one who prophesied (11:28).

21:20 The old division reappears (see note on 15:1).

21:24 *pay their expenses.* Paul was being asked to pay the expenses involved in the offerings required at the completion of the Nazirite vow these four men had taken (cf. Num. 6:13-21). He was being urged to take actions that would indicate that he was, after all, a "middle-of-the-road" Jewish-Christian.

21:25 See note on 15:19.

^cAsia, upon seeing him in the temple, *began* to stir up all the multitude and laid hands on him,

28 crying out, "Men of Israel, come to our aid! ^aThis is the man who preaches to all men everywhere against our people, and the Law, and this place; and besides he has even brought Greeks into the temple and has ^bdefiled this ^aholy place."

29 For they had previously seen ^aTrophimus the ^bEphesian in the city with him, and they supposed that Paul had brought him into the temple.

30 And all the city was aroused, and the people rushed together; and taking hold of Paul, they ^adragged him out of the temple; and immediately the doors were shut.

31 And while they were seeking to kill him, a report came up to the commander of the ^a*Roman* cohort that all Jerusalem was in confusion.

32 And at once he ^atook along *some* soldiers and centurions, and ran down to them; and when they saw the commander and the soldiers, they stopped beating Paul.

33 Then the commander came up and took hold of him, and ordered him to be ^abound with ^btwo chains; and he *began* asking who he was and what he had done.

34 But among the crowd ^asome were shouting one thing *and* some another, and when he could not find out the facts on account of the uproar, he ordered him to be brought into ^bthe barracks.

35 And when he got to ^athe stairs, it so happened that he was carried by the soldiers because of the violence of the mob;

36 for the multitude of the people kept following behind, crying out, "^aAway with him!"

37 And as Paul was about to be brought into ^athe barracks, he said to the commander, "May I say something to you?" And he *said, "Do you know Greek?

38 "Then you are not ^athe Egyptian who some time ago stirred up a revolt and led the four thousand men of the Assassins out ^binto the wilderness?"

39 But Paul said, "^aI am a Jew of Tarsus in ^bCilicia, a citizen of no insignificant city; and I beg you, allow me to speak to the people."

40 And when he had given him permission, Paul, standing on ^athe stairs, ^bmotioned to the people with his hand; and when there was a great hush, he spoke to them in the ^cHebrew dialect, saying,

22 "^aBrethren and fathers, hear my defense which I now *offer* to you."

2 And when they heard that he was addressing them in the ^aHebrew dialect, they became even more quiet; and he *said,

3 "^aI am ^ba Jew, born in ^cTarsus of ^dCilicia, but brought up in this city, ^eeducated under ^fGamaliel, ^gstrictly according to the law of our fathers, being zealous for God, just as ^hyou all are today.

4 "And ^aI persecuted this ^bWay to the death, binding and putting both men and women into prisons,

5 as also ^athe high priest and all ^bthe Council of the elders can testify. From them I also ^creceived letters to ^dthe brethren, and started off for ^eDamascus in order to bring even those who were there to Jerusalem as prisoners to be punished.

6 "^aAnd it came about that as I was on my way, approaching

Cross references (left margin)

★28 ^aActs 6:13 ^bMatt. 24:15; Acts 6:13f.; 24:6

29 ^aActs 20:4 ^bActs 18:19

30 ^a2 Kin. 11:15; Acts 16:19; 26:21

31 ^aActs 10:1

32 ^aActs 23:27

33 ^aActs 20:23; 21:11; 22:29, 26:29; 28:20; Eph. 6:20; 2 Tim. 1:16; 2:9 ^bActs 12:6

34 ^aActs 19:32 ^bActs 21:37; 22:24; 23:10, 16, 32

35 ^aActs 21:40

36 ^aLuke 23:18; John 19:15; Acts 22:22

Cross references (right margin)

37 ^aActs 21:34; 22:24; 23:10, 16, 32

★38 ^aActs 5:36 ^bMatt. 24:26

39 ^aActs 9:11; 22:3 ^bActs 6:9

40 ^aActs 21:35 ^bActs 12:17 ^cJohn 5:2; Acts 1:19; 22:2; 26:14

1 ^aActs 7:2

2 ^aActs 21:40

3 ^aActs 9:1-22; 22:3-16; 26:9-18 ^bActs 21:39 ^cActs 9:11 ^dActs 6:9 ^eDeut. 33:3; 2 Kin. 4:38; Luke 10:39 ^fActs 5:34 ^gActs 23:6; 26:5; Phil. 3:6 ^hActs 21:20

4 ^aActs 8:3; 22:19f. ^bActs 9:2

5 ^aActs 9:1 ^bLuke 22:66 [Gr.]; Acts 5:21 [Gr.]; 1 Tim. 4:14 [Gr.] ^cActs 9:2 ^dActs 2:29; 3:17; 13:26; 23:1; 28:17, 21; Rom. 9:3 ^eActs 9:2

6 ^aActs 22:6-11; Acts 9:3-8; 26:12-18

21:28 *brought Greeks into the temple.* Verse 29 explains that the crowd assumed (though it was untrue) that Paul had taken Trophimus, a Gentile, into the inner courts of the temple, which were reserved for Jews only. This was an offense punishable by death.

21:38 *the Egyptian.* The historian Josephus records such an event in A.D. 54. The leader disappeared. The tribune jumps to the conclusion that Paul is he.

Damascus about noontime, a very bright light suddenly flashed from heaven all around me,

7 and I fell to the ground and heard a voice saying to me, 'Saul, Saul, why are you persecuting Me?'

8 "And I answered, 'Who art Thou, Lord?' And He said to me, 'I am [a]Jesus the Nazarene, whom you are persecuting.'

9 "And those who were with me [a]beheld the light, to be sure, but [b]did not understand the voice of the One who was speaking to me.

10 "And I said, '[a]What shall I do, Lord?' And the Lord said to me, 'Arise and go on into Damascus; and there you will be told of all that has been appointed for you to do.'

11 "But since I [a]could not see because of the brightness of that light, I was led by the hand by those who were with me, and came into Damascus.

12 "And a certain [a]Ananias, a man who was devout by the standard of the Law, and [b]well spoken of by all the Jews who lived there,

13 came to me, and standing near said to me, '[a]Brother Saul, receive your sight!' And [b]at that very time I looked up at him.

14 "And he said, '[a]The God of our fathers has [b]appointed you to know His will, and to [c]see the [d]Righteous One, and to hear an utterance from His mouth.

15 'For you will be [a]a witness for Him to all men of [b]what you have seen and heard.

16 'And now why do you delay? [a]Arise, and be baptized, and [b]wash away your sins, [c]calling on His name.'

17 "And it came about when I [a]returned to Jerusalem and was praying in the temple, that I [b]fell into a trance,

18 and I saw Him saying to me, '[a]Make haste, and get out of Jerusalem quickly, because they will not accept your testimony about Me.'

19 "And I said, 'Lord, they themselves understand that in one synagogue after another [a]I used to imprison and [b]beat those who believed in Thee.

20 'And [a]when the blood of Thy witness Stephen was being shed, I also was standing by approving, and watching out for the cloaks of those who were slaying him.'

21 "And He said to me, 'Go! For I will send you far away [a]to the Gentiles.' "

22 And they listened to him up to this statement, and then they raised their voices and said, "[a]Away with such a fellow from the earth, for [b]he should not be allowed to live!"

23 And as they were crying out and [a]throwing off their cloaks and [b]tossing dust into the air,

24 the commander ordered him to be brought into [a]the barracks, stating that he should be [b]examined by scourging so that he might find out the reason why they were shouting against him that way.

25 And when they stretched him out with thongs, Paul said to the centurion who was standing by, "Is it lawful for you to scourge [a]a man who is a Roman and uncondemned?"

26 And when the centurion heard this, he went to the commander and told him, saying, "What are you about to do? For this man is a Roman."

27 And the commander came and said to him, "Tell me, are you a Roman?" And he said, "Yes."

28 And the commander an- ★28

8 [a]Acts 26:9

9 [a]Acts 26:13 [b]Acts 9:7

10 [a]Acts 16:30

11 [a]Acts 9:8

12 [a]Acts 9:10 [b]Acts 6:3; 10:22

13 [a]Acts 9:17 [b]Acts 9:18

14 [a]Acts 3:13 [b]Acts 9:15; 26:16 [c]Acts 9:17; 26:16; 1 Cor. 9:1; 15:8 [d]Acts 7:52

15 [a]Acts 23:11; 26:16 [b]Acts 22:14

★16 [a]Acts 9:18 [b]Acts 2:38; 1 Cor. 6:11; Eph. 5:26; Heb. 10:22 [c]Acts 7:59

17 [a]Acts 9:26; 26:20 [b]Acts 10:10

18 [a]Acts 9:29

19 [a]Acts 8:3; 22:4 [b]Matt. 10:17; Acts 26:11

20 [a]Acts 7:58; 8:1; 26:10

★21-23
21 [a]Acts 9:15

22 [a]Acts 21:36; 1 Thess. 2:16 [b]Acts 25:24

23 [a]Acts 7:58 [b]2 Sam. 16:13

24 [a]Acts 21:34 [b]Acts 22:29

25 [a]Acts 16:37

22:16 Lit., "Having arisen, be baptized; and wash away your sins, having called on the name of the Lord." Baptism does not wash away sins.

22:21-23 The reference to the Gentiles, joined with Paul's claiming a divine commission, set off the mob again.

22:28 *with a large sum.* In the reign of Claudius, contemporaneous with these events, Roman citizenship could be purchased for what would be a princely sum for a soldier. Somehow Paul's parents had earned Roman citizenship before Paul's birth. See note on 16:37.

swered, "I acquired this citizenship with a large sum of money." And Paul said, "But I was actually born *a citizen.*"

29 ᵃActs 22:24 ᵇActs 16:38 ᶜActs 22:24f.

29 Therefore those who were about to ᵃexamine him immediately let go of him; and the commander also ᵇwas afraid when he found out that he was a Roman, and because he had ᶜput him in chains.

2 *Paul brought before the Sanhedrin,* 22:30–23:10

★30 ᵃActs 23:28 ᵇActs 21:33 ᶜMatt. 5:22

30 But on the next day, ᵃwishing to know for certain why he had been accused by the Jews, he ᵇreleased him and ordered the chief priests and all ᶜthe Council to assemble, and brought Paul down and set him before them.

1 ᵃActs 22:30; 23:6, 15, 20, 28 ᵇActs 22:5 ᶜActs 24:16; 2 Cor. 1:12; 2 Tim. 1:3

23 And Paul, looking intently at ᵃthe Council, said, "ᵇBrethren, ᶜI have lived my life with a perfectly good conscience before God up to this day."

★ 2 ᵃActs 24:1 ᵇJohn 18:22

2 And the high priest ᵃAnanias commanded those standing beside him ᵇto strike him on the mouth.

3 ᵃMatt. 23:27 ᵇLev. 19:15; Deut. 25:2; John 7:51

3 Then Paul said to him, "God is going to strike you, ᵃyou whitewashed wall! And do you ᵇsit to try me according to the Law, and in violation of the Law order me to be struck?"

4 But the bystanders said, "Do you revile God's high priest?"

★ 5 ᵃEx. 22:28

5 And Paul said, "I was not aware, brethren, that he was high priest; for it is written, 'ᵃYou SHALL NOT SPEAK EVIL OF A RULER OF YOUR PEOPLE.'"

6 But perceiving that one part were ᵃSadducees and the other Pharisees, Paul *began* crying out in ᵇthe Council, "ᶜBrethren, ᵈI am a Pharisee, a son of Pharisees; I am on trial for ᵉthe hope and resurrection of the dead!"

★ 6 ᵃMatt. 3:7; 22:23 ᵇActs 22:30; 23:1, 15, 20, 28 ᶜActs 22:5 ᵈActs 26:5; Phil. 3:5 ᵉActs 24:15, 21; 26:8

7 And as he said this, there arose a dissension between the Pharisees and Sadducees; and the assembly was divided.

8 For ᵃthe Sadducees say that there is no resurrection, nor an angel, nor a spirit; but the Pharisees acknowledge them all.

8 ᵃMatt. 22:23; Acts 3:7

9 And there arose a great uproar; and some of ᵃthe scribes of the Pharisaic party stood up and *began* to argue heatedly, saying, "ᵇWe find nothing wrong with this man; ᶜsuppose a spirit or an angel has spoken to him?"

9 ᵃMark 2:16; Luke 5:30 ᵇActs 23:29 ᶜJohn 12:29; Acts 22:6ff.

10 And as a great dissension was developing, the commander was afraid Paul would be torn to pieces by them and ordered the troops to go down and take him away from them by force, and bring him into ᵃthe barracks.

10 ᵃActs 21:34; 23:16, 32

3 *Paul escorted to Caesarea,* 23:11–35

11 But on ᵃthe night *immediately* following, the Lord stood at his side and said, "ᵇTake courage; for ᶜas you have ᵈsolemnly witnessed to My cause at Jerusalem, so you must witness at Rome also."

★11 ᵃActs 18:9 ᵇMatt. 9:2 ᶜActs 19:21 ᵈLuke 16:28; Acts 28:23

12 And when it was day, ᵃthe Jews formed a conspiracy and ᵇbound themselves under an oath, saying that they would

12 ᵃActs 9:23; 23:30; 1 Thess. 2:16 ᵇActs 23:14, 21

22:30 *the Council* = the Sanhedrin. See note on Luke 22:66. Somehow the Sanhedrin had interposed itself so that Paul's case did not get directly and immediately referred to the Roman governor in Caesarea.

23:2 *commanded . . . to strike him.* Ananias (high priest about A.D. 48–58) was reportedly insolent and overbearing. He was probably angered at Paul's bold claims and ordered him struck.

23:5 *I was not aware, brethren, that he was high priest.* Some think Paul's weak eyes

caused him to fail to recognize the high priest; however, the remark may have been sarcasm—"I didn't think the high priest would ever speak like that!"

23:6 In effect Paul said, "I, a Pharisee by inheritance and training, can hardly be regarded as a subversive teacher!" He then proceeded to split the Sanhedrin into its two factions.

23:11 Christ appeared to Paul four times: at his conversion (9:5), in Corinth (18:9–10), on his first visit to Jerusalem (22:17–18), and here during his last visit to Jerusalem.

neither eat nor drink until they had killed Paul.

13 And there were more than forty who formed this plot.

14 And they came to the chief priests and the elders, and said, "We have ᵃbound ourselves under a solemn oath to taste nothing until we have killed Paul.

15 "Now, therefore, you and ᵃthe Council notify the commander to bring him down to you, as though you were going to determine his case by a more thorough investigation; and we for our part are ready to slay him before he comes near *the place.*"

16 But the son of Paul's sister heard of their ambush, and he came and entered ᵃthe barracks and told Paul.

17 And Paul called one of the centurions to him and said, "Lead this young man to the commander, for he has something to report to him."

18 So he took him and led him to the commander and *said, "Paul ᵃthe prisoner called me to him and asked me to lead this young man to you since he has something to tell you."

19 And the commander took him by the hand and stepping aside, *began* to inquire of him privately, "What is it that you have to report to me?"

20 And he said, "ᵃThe Jews have agreed to ask you to bring Paul down tomorrow to ᵇthe Council, as though they were going to inquire somewhat more thoroughly about him.

21 "So do not listen to them, for more than forty of them are ᵃlying in wait for him who have ᵇbound themselves under a curse not to eat or drink until they slay him; and now they are ready and waiting for the promise from you."

22 Therefore the commander let the young man go, instructing

him, "Tell no one that you have notified me of these things."

23 And he called to him two of the centurions, and said, "Get two hundred soldiers ready by the third hour of the night to proceed to ᵃCaesarea, with seventy horsemen and two hundred spearmen."

24 *They were* also to provide mounts to put Paul on and bring him safely to ᵃFelix the governor.

25 And he wrote a letter having this form:

26 "Claudius Lysias, to the ᵃmost excellent governor Felix, ᵇgreetings.

27 "When this man was arrested by the Jews and was about to be slain by them, I came upon them with the troops and rescued him, ᵇhaving learned that he was a Roman.

28 "And ᵃwanting to ascertain the charge for which they were accusing him, I ᵇbrought him down to their ᶜCouncil;

29 and I found him to be accused over ᵃquestions about their Law, but under ᵇno accusation deserving death or imprisonment.

30 "And when I was ᵃinformed that there would be ᵇa plot against the man, I sent him to you at once, also instructing ᶜhis accusers to bring charges against him before you."

31 So the soldiers, in accordance with their orders, took Paul and brought him by night to Antipatris.

32 But the next day, leaving

---

14 ᵃActs 23:12, 21

15 ᵃActs 22:30; 23:1, 6, 20, 28

★16 ᵃActs 21:34; 23:10, 32

18 ᵃEph. 3:1

20 ᵃActs 23:14f. ᵇActs 22:30; 23:1, 6, 15, 28

21 ᵃLuke 11:54 ᵇActs 23:12, 14

23 ᵃActs 8:40; 23:33

★24 ᵃActs 23:26, 33; 24:1, 3, 10; 25:14

26 ᵃLuke 1:3; Acts 24:3; 26:25 ᵇActs 15:23

27 ᵃActs 21:32f. ᵇActs 22:25-29

28 ᵃActs 22:30 ᵇActs 23:10 ᶜActs 23:1

29 ᵃActs 18:15; 25:19 ᵇActs 23:9; 25:25; 26:31; 28:18

30 ᵃActs 23:20f. ᵇActs 9:24; 23:12 ᶜActs 23:35; 24:19; 25:16

32 ᵃActs 23:23 ᵇActs 23:10

23:16 *son of Paul's sister.* Only here is any mention made of Paul's immediate relatives.
23:24 *Felix the governor.* Roman procurator of Judea (A.D. 52 to probably 58) with headquarters in Caesarea.

^athe horsemen to go on with him, they returned to ^bthe barracks.

33 And when these had come to ^aCaesarea and delivered the letter to ^bthe governor, they also presented Paul to him.

34 And when he had read it, he asked from what ^aprovince he was; and when he learned that ^bhe was from Cilicia,

35 he said, "I will give you a hearing after your ^aaccusers arrive also," giving orders for him to be ^bkept in Herod's Praetorium.

4 Paul's defense before Felix, 24:1-27

24 And after ^afive days the high priest ^bAnanias came down with some elders, with a certain attorney named Tertullus; and they brought charges to ^cthe governor against Paul.

2 And after Paul had been summoned, Tertullus began to accuse him, saying to the governor,

"Since we have through you attained much peace, and since by your providence reforms are being carried out for this nation,

3 we acknowledge this in every way and everywhere, ^amost excellent Felix, with all thankfulness.

4 "But, that I may not weary you any further, I beg you to grant us, by your kindness, a brief hearing.

5 "For we have found this man a real pest and a fellow who stirs up dissension among all the Jews throughout the world, and a ringleader of the ^asect of the Nazarenes.

6 "And he even tried to ^adesecrate the temple; and then we arrested him. [And we wanted to judge him according to our own Law.

7 "But Lysias the commander came along, and with much violence took him out of our hands,

8 ordering his accusers to come before you.] And by examining him yourself concerning all these matters, you will be able to ascertain the things of which we accuse him."

9 And ^athe Jews also joined in the attack, asserting that these things were so.

10 And when ^athe governor had nodded for him to speak, Paul responded:

"Knowing that for many years you have been a judge to this nation, I cheerfully make my defense,

11 since you can take note of the fact that no more than ^atwelve days ago I went up to Jerusalem to worship.

12 "And ^aneither in the temple, nor in the synagogues, nor in the city itself did they find me carrying on a discussion with anyone or ^bcausing a riot.

13 "^aNor can they prove to you the charges of which they now accuse me.

14 "But this I admit to you, that according to ^athe Way which they call a ^bsect I do serve ^cthe God of our fathers, ^dbelieving everything that is in accordance

---

23:34 *from what province he was.* Roman law required that this question be asked at the opening of a hearing, for Paul had the right to be tried in his home province or in the province where the alleged crime was committed. Tarsus was in Cilicia. Felix was a deputy of the legate of Syria and Cilicia, and so claimed the right to conduct the hearing, whichever choice Paul made. Such a detail is strong proof that Luke was with Paul at the hearing.

24:1 *Ananias* headed the group that presented the complaint against Paul. *Tertullus* (Roman name) was probably a lawyer hired by the Jews in Caesarea to present their case.

24:5 Tertullus broadened the charge, and made it more serious in Roman eyes by, for the first time, accusing Paul of being an insurrectionist *(stirs up dissension).*

24:6-8 Most manuscripts do not contain a concluding sentence in verse 6, verse 7, or an opening phrase in verse 8.

24:8 Tertullus now argued that Lysias had exceeded his authority in removing Paul from trial by Jewish authorities on the charge of profaning the temple.

Marginal references:

33 ^aActs 8:40; 23:23 ^bActs 23:24, 26; 24:1, 3, 10; 25:14

★**34** ^aActs 25:1 ^bActs 6:9; 21:39

35 ^aActs 23:30; 24:19; 25:16 ^bActs 24:27

★ **1** ^aActs 24:11 ^bActs 23:2 ^cActs 23:24

3 ^aActs 23:26; 26:25

★ **5** ^aActs 15:5; 24:14

★ **6-8**
6 ^aActs 21:28

★**8**

9 ^a1 Thess. 2:16

10 ^aActs 23:24

11 ^aActs 21:18, 27; 24:1

12 ^aActs 25:8 ^bActs 24:18

13 ^aActs 25:7

14 ^aActs 9:2; 24:22 ^bActs 15:5; 24:5 ^cActs 3:13 ^dActs 25:8; 26:4ff., 22f.; 28:23

with the Law, and that is written in the Prophets;

15 a Dan. 12:2; John 5:28f.; 11:24; Acts 23:6

15 having a hope in God, which ^athese men cherish themselves, that there shall certainly be a resurrection of both the righteous and the wicked.

16 a Acts 23:1

16 "In view of this, ^aI also do my best to maintain always a blameless conscience *both* before God and before men.

17 a Acts 20:31 **b**Acts 11:29f.; Rom. 15:25-28; 1 Cor. 16:1-4; 2 Cor. 8:1-4; 9:1, 2, 12; Gal. 2:10 **18 a**Acts 21:26 **b**Acts 24:12 **c**Acts 21:27

17 "Now ^aafter several years I ^bcame to bring alms to my nation and to present offerings;

18 in which they found me *occupied* in the temple, having been ^apurified, without *any* ^bcrowd or uproar. But *there were* certain ^cJews from Asia—

★19 a Acts 23:30

19 who ought to have been present before you, and to ^amake accusation, if they should have anything against me.

20 a Matt. 5:22

20 "Or else let these men themselves tell what misdeed they found when I stood before ^athe Council,

21 a Acts 23:6; 24:15

21 other than for this one statement which ^aI shouted out while standing among them, 'For the resurrection of the dead I am on trial before you today.' "

★22 a Acts 24:14

22 But Felix, having a more exact knowledge about ^athe Way, put them off, saying, "When Lysias the commander comes down, I will decide your case."

★23 a Acts 23:35 **b**Acts 28:16 **c**Acts 23:16; 27:3

23 And he gave orders to the centurion for him to be ^akept in custody and *yet* ^bhave *some* freedom, and not to prevent any of ^chis friends from ministering to him.

24 a Acts 20:21

24 But some days later, Felix arrived with Drusilla, his wife who was a Jewess, and sent for

Paul, and heard him *speak* about ^afaith in Christ Jesus.

25 And as he was discussing ^arighteousness, ^bself-control and ^cthe judgment to come, Felix became frightened and said, "Go away for the present, and when I find time, I will summon you."

26 At the same time too, he was hoping that ^amoney would be given him by Paul; therefore he also used to send for him quite often and converse with him.

27 But after two years had passed, Felix was succeeded by Porcius ^aFestus; and ^bwishing to do the Jews a favor, Felix left Paul ^cimprisoned.

★25 a Titus 2:12 **b**Gal. 5:23; Titus 1:8; 2 Pet. 1:6 **c**Acts 10:42

26 a Acts 24:17

★27 a Acts 25:1, 4, 9, 12; 26:24f.; 32 **b**Acts 12:3; 25:9 **c**Acts 23:35; 25:14

5 Paul's defense before Festus, 25:1-27

25 Festus therefore, having arrived in ^athe province, three days later went up to Jerusalem from ^bCaesarea.

★ 1 a Acts 23:34 **b**Acts 8:40; 25:4, 6, 13

2 And the chief priests and the leading men of the Jews ^abrought charges against Paul; and they were urging him,

2 a Acts 24:1; 25:15

3 requesting a concession against Paul, that he might have him brought to Jerusalem (*at the same time,* ^asetting an ambush to kill him on the way).

3 a Acts 9:24

4 Festus then ^aanswered that Paul ^bwas being kept in custody at ^cCaesarea and that he himself was about to leave shortly.

4 a Acts 25:16 **b**Acts 24:23 **c**Acts 8:40; 25:1, 6, 13

5 "Therefore," he *said, "let the influential men among you go there with me, and if there is anything wrong about the man, let them prosecute him."

6 a Acts 8:40; 25:1, 4, 13 **b**Matt. 27:19; Acts 25:10, 17

6 And after he had spent not more than eight or ten days

24:19 *who.* I.e., the Jews from Asia. They were not there as witnesses, Paul points out.

24:22 *put them off.* Because Lysias wasn't there to be heard from.

24:23 *have some freedom.* Paul was under a relatively loose military confinement.

24:25 *Felix became frightened.* Felix had stolen Drusilla from her first husband. He also was corrupt as a governor (v. 26), and Paul may have challenged him concerning his low morality.

24:27 *Porcius Festus* was Felix's successor. The change came about A.D. 58. A Roman magistrate could decide when a case would be called; often the delays were long, as here.

25:1 *to Jerusalem.* Since there was much unrest, Festus thought it prudent to make an early visit to the religious capital, Jerusalem. The Jews saw in this an opportunity to ask that Paul be returned there. If the request were granted they would try to kill him on the way (v. 3).

among them, he went down to ^aCaesarea; and on the next day he took his seat on ^bthe tribunal and ordered Paul to be brought.

^{7 a}Acts 24:5f. ^bActs 24:13

7 And after he had arrived, the Jews who had come down from Jerusalem stood around him, bringing ^amany and serious charges against him ^bwhich they could not prove;

^{8 a}Acts 6:13; 24:12; 28:17

8 while Paul said in his own defense, "^aI have committed no offense either against the Law of the Jews or against the temple or against Caesar."

^{9 a}Acts 12:3; 24:27 ^bActs 25:20

9 But Festus, ^awishing to do the Jews a favor, answered Paul and said, "^bAre you willing to go up to Jerusalem and stand trial before me on these charges?"

^{10 a}Matt. 27:19; Acts 25:10, 17

10 But Paul said, "I am standing before Caesar's ^atribunal, where I ought to be tried. I have done no wrong to *the* Jews, as you also very well know.

★^{11 a}Acts 25:21, 25; 26:32; 28:19

11 "If then I am a wrongdoer, and have committed anything worthy of death, I do not refuse to die; but if none of those things is *true* of which these men accuse me, no one can hand me over to them. I ^aappeal to Caesar."

12 Then when Festus had conferred with his council, he answered, "You have appealed to Caesar, to Caesar you shall go."

★^{13 a}Acts 8:40; 25:1, 4, 6

13 Now when several days had elapsed, King Agrippa and Bernice arrived at ^aCaesarea, and paid their respects to Festus.

^{14 a}Acts 24:27

14 And while they were spending many days there, Festus laid Paul's case before the king, saying, "There is a certain man ^aleft a prisoner by Felix;

^{15 a}Acts 24:1; 25:2

15 and when I was at Jerusalem, the chief priests and the elders of the Jews ^abrought charges against him, asking for a sentence of condemnation upon him.

16 "And I ^aanswered them that it is not the custom of the Romans to hand over any man before ^bthe accused meets his accusers face to face, and has an opportunity to make his defense against the charges.

^{16 a}Acts 25:4f. ^bActs 23:30

17 "And so after they had assembled here, I made no delay, but on the next day took my seat on ^athe tribunal, and ordered the man to be brought.

^{17 a}Matt. 27:19; Acts 25:6, 10

18 "And when the accusers stood up, they *began* bringing charges against him not of such crimes as I was expecting;

19 but they *simply* had some ^apoints of disagreement with him about their own ^breligion and about a certain dead man, Jesus, whom Paul asserted to be alive.

^{19 a}Acts 18:15; 23:29 ^bActs 17:22

20 "And ^abeing at a loss how to investigate such matters, I asked whether he was willing to go to Jerusalem and there stand trial on these matters.

^{20 a}Acts 25:9

21 "But when Paul ^aappealed to be held in custody for the Emperor's decision, I ordered him to be kept in custody until I send him to Caesar."

^{21 a}Acts 25:11f.

22 And ^aAgrippa *said* to Festus, "I also would like to hear the man myself." "Tomorrow," he *said, "you shall hear him."

^{22 a}Acts 9:15

23 And so, on the next day when ^aAgrippa had come together with ^aBernice, amid great pomp, and had entered the auditorium accompanied by the commanders and the prominent men of the city, at the command of Festus, Paul was brought in.

^{23 a}Acts 25:13; 26:30

24 And Festus *said, "King Agrippa, and all you gentlemen here present with us, you behold

^{24 a}Acts 25:2, 7 ^bActs 22:22

25:11 *I appeal to Caesar.* Festus' suggestion that Paul appear in Jerusalem for trial (v. 9) provoked this appeal to Caesar. Paul realized that the trial would not be impartial if conducted by Festus, especially if the case were transferred to Jerusalem, and that he would be in great danger if he was returned to the jurisdiction of the Sanhedrin. The right of appeal was one of the most ancient and cherished rights of a Roman citizen. Nero was emperor at this time (A.D. 54–68).

25:13 *Agrippa.* Herod Agrippa II, son of Herod Agrippa I (12:1) and great-grandson of Herod the Great (Matt. 2:1), both of whose territories he ultimately ruled under Rome's jurisdiction. *Bernice* was his sister, with whom he was living incestuously. Paul was not required to defend himself before them, since he had already appealed to Caesar, but he took this opportunity to witness to the Jewish king.

this man about whom ^aall the people of the Jews appealed to me, both at Jerusalem and here, loudly declaring that ^bhe ought not to live any longer.

25 "But I found that he had committed ^anothing worthy of death; and since he himself ^bappealed to the Emperor, I decided to send him.

26 "Yet I have nothing definite about him to write to my lord. Therefore I have brought him before you all and especially before you, King Agrippa, so that after the investigation has taken place, I may have something to write.

27 "For it seems absurd to me in sending a prisoner, not to indicate also the charges against him."

6 Paul's defense before Agrippa, 26:1–32

26 And ^aAgrippa said to Paul, "You are permitted to speak for yourself." Then Paul stretched out his hand and *proceeded* to make his defense:

2 "In regard to all the things of which I am accused by the Jews, I consider myself fortunate, King Agrippa, that I am about to make my defense before you today;

3 especially because you are an expert in all ^acustoms and questions among the Jews; therefore I beg you to listen to me patiently.

4 "So then, all Jews know ^amy manner of life from my youth up, which from the beginning was spent among my *own* nation and at Jerusalem;

5 since they have known about me for a long time previously, if they are willing to testify, that I lived *as* a ^aPharisee ^baccording to the strictest ^csect of our religion.

6 "And now I am standing trial ^afor the hope of ^bthe promise made by God to our fathers;

7 *the promise* ^ato which our twelve tribes hope to attain, as they earnestly serve *God* night and day. And for this ^bhope, O King, I am being ^caccused by Jews.

8 "Why is it considered incredible among you *people* ^aif God does raise the dead?

9 "So then, ^aI thought to myself that I had to do many things hostile to ^bthe name of Jesus of Nazareth.

10 "And this is just what I ^adid in Jerusalem; not only did I lock up many of the saints in prisons, having ^breceived authority from the chief priests, but also when they were being put to death I ^ccast my vote against them.

11 "And ^aas I punished them often in all the synagogues, I tried to force them to blaspheme; and being ^bfuriously enraged at them, I kept pursuing them ^ceven to foreign cities.

12 "While thus engaged ^aas I was journeying to Damascus with the authority and commission of the chief priests,

13 at midday, O King, I saw on the way a light from heaven, brighter than the sun, shining all around me and those who were journeying with me.

14 "And when we had ^aall fallen to the ground, I heard a voice saying to me in the ^bHebrew dialect, 'Saul, Saul, why are you persecuting Me? It is hard for you to kick against the goads.'

15 "And I said, 'Who art Thou, Lord?' And the Lord said, 'I am Jesus whom you are persecuting.

16 'But arise, and ^astand on your feet; for this purpose I have appeared to you, to ^bappoint you a ^cminister and ^da witness not only to the things which you have seen, but also to the things in which I will appear to you;

Marginal references (left column):

25 ^aActs 23:29 ^bActs 25:11f.

1 ^aActs 9:15

3 ^aActs 6:14; 25:19; 26:7

4 ^aGal. 1:13f.; Phil. 3:5

5 ^aActs 23:6 ^bActs 22:3 ^cActs 15:5

★ 6 ^aActs 24:15; 28:20 ^bActs 13:32

Marginal references (right column):

7 ^aJames 1:1 ^bActs 24:15; 28:20 ^cActs 26:2

★ 8 ^aActs 23:6

9 ^aJohn 16:2; 1 Tim. 1:13 ^bJohn 16:2

10 ^aActs 8:3; 9:13 ^bActs 9:1f. ^cActs 22:20

★11 ^aMatt. 10:17; Acts 22:19 ^bActs 9:1 ^cActs 22:5

12 ^aActs 26:12-18; 9:3-8; 22:6-11

14 ^aActs 9:7 ^bActs 21:40

16 ^aEzek. 2:1; Dan. 10:11 ^bActs 22:14 ^cLuke 1:2 ^dActs 22:15

26:6 *the promise.* I.e., of the Messiah (Gen. 22:18; 49:10).
26:8 That Paul preached the resurrection of Jesus Christ was the heart of the complaint of the Jewish authorities.
26:11 *force them to blaspheme.* I.e., to blaspheme against Christ, which would not have been blasphemy to the Jews.

17 a Jer. 1:8,
19 b 1 Chr.
16:35; Acts
9:15

18 a Is. 35:5;
42:7, 16;
Eph. 5:8;
Col. 1:13;
1 Pet. 2:9
b John 1:5;
Eph. 5:8;
Col. 1:12f.;
1 Thess. 5:5;
1 Pet. 2:9
c Matt. 4:10
d Luke 24:47;
Acts 2:38
e Acts 20:32
f Acts 20:21

20 a Acts
9:19ff. b Acts
9:26-29;
22:17-20
c Acts 9:15;
13:46 d Acts
3:19 e Matt.
3:8; Luke 3:8

21 a Acts
21:27, 30
b Acts 21:31

22 a Luke
16:28 b Acts
10:43; 24:14

23 a Matt.
26:24; Acts
3:18 b 1 Cor.
15:20, 23;
Col. 1:18;
Rev. 1:5
c Luke 2:32;
2 Cor. 4:4

★24 a John
7:15; 2 Tim.
3:15

25 a Acts
23:26; 24:3

26 a Acts
26:3

17 ᵃdelivering you ᵇfrom the *Jewish* people and from the Gentiles, to whom I am sending you, **18** to ᵃopen their eyes so that they may turn from ᵇdarkness to light and from the dominion of ᶜSatan to God, in order that they may receive ᵈforgiveness of sins and an ᵉinheritance among those who have been sanctified by ᶠfaith in Me.'

19 "Consequently, King Agrippa, I did not prove disobedient to the heavenly vision,

20 but *kept* declaring both ᵃto those of Damascus first, and *also* ᵇat Jerusalem and *then* throughout all the region of Judea, and *even* ᶜto the Gentiles, that they should ᵈrepent and turn to God, performing deeds ᵉappropriate to repentance.

21 "For this reason *some* Jews ᵃseized me in the temple and tried ᵇto put me to death.

22 "And so, having obtained help from God, I stand to this day ᵃtestifying both to small and great, stating nothing but what ᵇthe Prophets and Moses said was going to take place;

23 ᵃthat the Christ was to suffer, *and* that ᵇby reason of *His* resurrection from the dead He should be the first to proclaim ᶜlight both to the *Jewish* people and to the Gentiles."

24 And while *Paul* was saying this in his defense, Festus *said in a loud voice, "Paul, you are out of your mind! *Your* great ᵃlearning is driving you mad."

25 But Paul *said, "I am not out of my mind, ᵃmost excellent Festus, but I utter words of sober truth.

26 "For the king ᵃknows about these matters, and I speak to him also with confidence, since I am persuaded that none of these things escape his notice; for this has not been done in a corner.

27 "King Agrippa, do you believe the Prophets? I know that you do."

28 And Agrippa *replied* to Paul, "In a short time you will persuade me to become a ᵃChristian."

29 And Paul *said, "I would to God, that whether in a short or long time, not only you, but also all who hear me this day, might become such as I am, except for these ᵃchains."

30 And ᵃthe king arose and the governor and Bernice, and those who were sitting with them,

31 and when they had drawn aside, they *began* talking to one another, saying, "ᵃThis man is not doing anything worthy of death or imprisonment."

32 And Agrippa said to Festus, "This man might have been ᵃset free if he had not ᵇappealed to Caesar."

★28 a Acts
11:26

29 a Acts
21:33

30 a Acts
25:23

31 a Acts
23:29

32 a Acts
28:18 b Acts
25:11

7 Paul's voyage and shipwreck, 27:1–44

27 And when it was decided that ᵃwe ᵇshould sail for ᶜItaly, they proceeded to deliver Paul and some other prisoners to a centurion of the Augustan ᵈcohort named Julius.

2 And embarking in an Adramyttian ship, which was about to sail to the regions along the coast of ᵃAsia, we put out to sea, accompanied by ᵇAristarchus, a ᶜMacedonian of ᵈThessalonica.

3 And the next day we put in at ᵃSidon; and Julius ᵇtreated Paul with consideration and ᶜallowed him to go to his friends and receive care.

★ 1 a[we]
Acts 16:10;
27:1-28
b Acts 25:12,
25 c Acts
18:2; 27:6
d Acts 10:1

★ 2 a Acts
2:9 b Acts
19:29 c Acts
16:9 d Acts
17:1

3 a Matt.
11:21 b Acts
27:43 c Acts
24:23

26:24 *Paul, you are out of your mind!* Festus, a Roman, simply could not comprehend Paul's line of thought and language. Agrippa, a Jew, had no such semantic problems.

26:28 *In a short time.* Lit., In a little . . . This enigmatic statement may mean: "In such a short time are you trying to make a Christian of me?" or "With so few words you are persuading me to be a Christian."

27:1 *centurion.* A commander of 100 Roman soldiers.

27:2 *Adramyttian.* From Adramyttium, a port on the west coast of Asia Minor (modern Turkey), just south of Troas.

★ 4 aActs
4:36 bActs
27:7

4 And from there we put out to sea and sailed under the shelter of aCyprus because bthe winds were contrary.

5 aActs 6:9
bActs 13:13

5 And when we had sailed through the sea along the coast of aCilicia and bPamphylia, we landed at Myra in Lycia.

6 aActs
28:11 bActs
18:2; 27:1

6 And there the centurion found an aAlexandrian ship sailing for bItaly, and he put us aboard it.

7 aActs
27:4 bActs
2:11; 27:12f.,
21; Titus 1:5,
12

7 And when we had sailed slowly for a good many days, and with difficulty had arrived off Cnidus, asince the wind did not permit us to go farther, we sailed under the shelter of bCrete, off Salmone;

8 aActs
27:13 [Gr.]

8 and with difficulty asailing past it we came to a certain place called Fair Havens, near which was the city of Lasea.

★ 9 aLev.
16:29-31;
23:27-29;
Num. 29:7

9 And when considerable time had passed and the voyage was now dangerous, since even athe fast was already over, Paul began to admonish them,

10 aActs
27:21

10 and said to them, "Men, I perceive that the voyage will certainly be attended with adamage and great loss, not only of the cargo and the ship, but also of our lives."

11 aRev.
18:17

11 But the centurion was more persuaded by the apilot and the captain of the ship, than by what was being said by Paul.

12 aActs
2:11; 27:13,
21; Titus 1:5,
12

12 And because the harbor was not suitable for wintering, the majority reached a decision to put out to sea from there, if somehow they could reach Phoenix, a harbor of aCrete, facing southwest and northwest, and spend the winter there.

13 And when a moderate south wind came up, supposing that they had gained their purpose, they weighed anchor and began asailing along bCrete, close inshore.

13 aActs
27:8 [Gr.]
bActs 2:11;
27:12f., 21;
Titus 1:5, 12

14 But before very long there arushed down from the land a violent wind, called Euraquilo;

★14 aMark
4:37

15 and when the ship was caught in it, and could not face the wind, we gave way to it, and let ourselves be driven along.

16 And running under the shelter of a small island called Clauda, we were scarcely able to get the ship's boat under control.

★16

17 And after they had hoisted it up, they used supporting cables in undergirding the ship; and fearing that they might arun aground on the shallows of Syrtis, they let down the sea anchor, and so let themselves be driven along.

★17 aActs
27:26, 29

18 The next day as we were being violently storm-tossed, they began to ajettison the cargo;

18 aJon. 1:5;
Acts 27:38

19 and on the third day they threw the ship's tackle overboard with their own hands.

20 And since neither sun nor stars appeared for many days, and no small storm was assailing us, from then on all hope of our being saved was gradually abandoned.

21 And when they had gone a long time without food, then Paul stood up in their midst and said, "aMen, you ought to have followed my advice and not to have set sail from bCrete, and incurred this adamage and loss.

21 aActs
27:10 bActs
27:7

27:4 *under the shelter of Cyprus.* The prevailing early autumn winds came from the northwest, making headwinds difficult for a coastal vessel to handle in open ocean. So the ship sailed around the east end of Cyprus, the lee side, and headed north for the coast of Cilicia, where it would then head west, close to shore for many miles.

27:9 *the fast was already over.* Only one fast was prescribed by the law and that was on the Day of Atonement (Lev. 16:29-34). If this was the year 59, the fast was on Oct. 5. This means Paul left Caesarea in August or September and did not arrive in Rome until the following March.

27:14 *Euraquilo.* A hybrid word, half Greek, half Latin, meaning east-north and standing for a treacherous east-northeast wind.

27:16 *to get the ship's boat under control.* I.e., the dinghy, probably being towed and starting to fill up.

27:17 *supporting cables in undergirding the ship.* Some sort of rope truss to stiffen the timbers seems indicated.

22 aActs
27:25, 36

22 "And *yet* now I urge you to akeep up your courage, for there shall be no loss of life among you, but *only* of the ship.

23 aActs
5:19 bRom.
1:9 cActs
18:9; 23:11;
2 Tim. 4:17

23 "For this very night aan angel of the God to whom I belong and bwhom I serve cstood before me,

24 aActs
23:11 bActs
27:31, 42, 44

24 saying, 'Do not be afraid, Paul; ayou must stand before Caesar; and behold, God has granted you ball those who are sailing with you.'

25 aActs
27:22, 36

25 "Therefore, akeep up your courage, men, for I believe God, that it will turn out exactly as I have been told.

26 aActs
27:17, 29
bActs 28:1

26 "But we must arun aground on a certain bisland."

★27

27 But when the fourteenth night had come, as we were being driven about in the Adriatic Sea, about midnight the sailors *began* to surmise that they were approaching some land.

★28

28 And they took soundings, and found *it to be* twenty fathoms; and a little farther on they took another sounding and found *it to be* fifteen fathoms.

29 aActs
27:17, 26

29 And fearing that we might arun aground somewhere on the rocks, they cast four anchors from the stern and wished for daybreak.

30 aActs
27:16

30 And as the sailors were trying to escape from the ship, and had let down athe *ship's* boat into the sea, on the pretense of intending to lay out anchors from the bow,

★31-36

31 Paul said to the centurion and to the soldiers, "Unless these men remain in the ship, you yourselves cannot be saved."

32 aJohn
2:15 [Gr.]

32 Then the soldiers cut away the aropes of the *ship's* boat, and let it fall away.

33 And until the day was about to dawn, Paul was encouraging them all to take some food, saying, "Today is the fourteenth day that you have been constantly watching and going without eating, having taken nothing.

34 "Therefore I encourage you to take some food, for this is for your preservation; for anot a hair from the head of any of you shall perish."

34 aMatt.
10:30

35 And having said this, he took bread and agave thanks to God in the presence of all; and he broke it and began to eat.

35 aMatt.
14:19

36 And all aof them were encouraged, and they themselves also took food.

36 aActs
27:22, 25

37 And all of us in the ship were two hundred and seventy-six apersons.

37 aActs
2:41

38 And when they had eaten enough, they *began* to lighten the ship by athrowing out the wheat into the sea.

★**38** aJon.
1:5; Acts
27:18

39 And when day came, athey could not recognize the land; but they did observe a certain bay with a beach, and they resolved to drive the ship onto it if they could.

39 aActs
28:1

40 And casting off athe anchors, they left them in the sea while at the same time they were loosening the ropes of the rudders, and hoisting the foresail to the wind, they were heading for the beach.

40 aActs
27:29

41 But striking a reef where two seas met, they ran the vessel aground; and the prow stuck fast and remained immovable, but the stern *began* to be broken up by the force *of the waves.*

★41

42 And the soldiers' plan was to akill the prisoners, that none *of them* should swim away and escape;

42 aActs
12:19

43 but the centurion, awanting to bring Paul safely through, kept them from their intention,

43 aActs
27:3

27:27 *the Adriatic Sea.* In this period the Adriatic Sea was a name applied to the Mediterranean E. of Sicily, and not merely to the present Adriatic Sea.

27:28 *fathoms.* A fathom is about 6 feet.

27:31-36 Paul the prisoner has risen to a place of commanding leadership.

27:38 The purpose of lightening the ship was to raise her in the water and let her run as far up the beach as possible before grounding.

27:41 *a reef where two seas met.* They did not reach the shore but ran aground on a shoal.

and commanded that those who could swim should jump overboard first and get to land,

44 and the rest *should follow*, some on planks, and others on various things from the ship. And thus it happened that ᵃthey all were brought safely to land.

44 *a*Acts
27:22, 31

8 Paul in Malta and on to Rome, 28:1-16

1 *a*[we]
Acts 16:10;
27:1; *b*Acts
27:39 *c*Acts
27:26

28 And when ᵃthey had been brought safely through, ᵇthen we found out that ᶜthe island was called Malta.

2 And ᵃthe natives showed us extraordinary kindness; for because of the rain that had set in and because of the cold, they kindled a fire and ᵇreceived us all.

★ 2 *a*Acts
28:4; Rom.
1:14; 1 Cor.
14:11; Col.
3:11 *b*Rom.
14:1

3 But when Paul had gathered a bundle of sticks and laid them on the fire, a viper came out because of the heat, and fastened on his hand.

4 And when ᵃthe natives saw the creature hanging from his hand, they *began* saying to one another, "ᵇUndoubtedly this man is a murderer, and though he has been saved from the sea, justice has not allowed him to live."

4 *a*Acts
28:2 *b*Luke
13:2, 4

5 However ᵃhe shook the creature off into the fire and suffered no harm.

5 *a*Mark
16:18

6 But they were expecting that he was about to swell up or suddenly fall down dead. But after they had waited a long time and had seen nothing unusual happen to him, they changed their minds and ᵃ*began* to say that he was a god.

6 *a*Acts
14:11

7 Now in the neighborhood of that place were lands belonging to the leading man of the island, named Publius, who welcomed us and entertained us courteously three days.

8 *a*Acts
9:40; James
5:14f. *b*Mark
5:23

8 And it came about that the father of Publius was lying *in bed* afflicted with *recurrent* fever and dysentery; and Paul went in *to see* him and after he had ᵃprayed, he ᵇlaid his hands on him and healed him.

9 And after this had happened, the rest of the people on the island who had diseases were coming to him and getting cured.

10 And they also honored us with many marks of respect; and when we were setting sail, they supplied *us* with all we needed.

11 And at the end of three months we set sail on ᵃan Alexandrian ship which had wintered at the island, and which had the Twin Brothers for its figurehead.

★11 *a*Acts
27:6

12 And after we put in at Syracuse, we stayed there for three days.

13 And from there we sailed around and arrived at Rhegium, and a day later a south wind sprang up, and on the second day we came to Puteoli.

★13

14 There we found *some* ᵃbrethren, and were invited to stay with them for seven days; and thus we came to Rome.

14 *a*Acts
1:15

15 And the ᵃbrethren, when they heard about us, came from there as far as the Market of Appius and Three Inns to meet us; and when Paul saw them, he thanked God and took courage.

15 *a*Acts
1:15

16 And when we entered Rome, Paul was ᵃallowed to stay by himself, with the soldier who was guarding him.

16 *a*Acts
24:23

9 Paul in Rome, 28:17-31

17 And it happened that after three days he called together those who were ᵃthe leading men of the Jews, and when they had come together, he *began* saying to them, "ᵇBrethren, ᶜthough I had done nothing against our people,

★17 *a*Acts
13:50; 25:2
*b*Acts 22:5
*c*Acts 25:8
*d*Acts 6:14

28:2 *natives.* The primary meaning of the Greek word is "people who speak a foreign tongue," i.e., non-Greeks.
28:11 *at the end of three months.* I.e., in the middle of February.
28:13 *Rhegium.* A town on the "toe" of Italy,

modern Reggio di Calabria. *Puteoli.* A port on the bay of Naples. Ostia, Rome's harbor, wasn't a deep enough harbor at this time to receive Alexandrian grain ships.
28:17 Paul wanted to prevent any derogatory report from his Jewish enemies in Jerusalem.

or ᵈthe customs of our fathers, yet I was delivered prisoner from Jerusalem into the hands of the Romans.

18 *Acts 26:32* *ᵇActs 23:29*   **18** "And when they had examined me, they ᵃwere willing to release me because there was ᵇno ground for putting me to death.

19 *ᵃActs 25:11*   **19** "But when the Jews objected, I was forced to ᵃappeal to Caesar; not that I had any accusation against my nation.

★20 *ᵃActs 21:33* *ᵇActs 26:6f.*   **20** "For this reason therefore, I requested to see you and to speak with you, for I am wearing ᵃthis chain for ᵇthe sake of the hope of Israel."

21 *ᵃActs 22:5*   **21** And they said to him, "We have neither received letters from Judea concerning you, nor have any of ᵃthe brethren come here and reported or spoken anything bad about you.

22 *ᵃActs 24:14* *ᵇ1 Pet. 2:12; 3:16; 4:14, 16*   **22** "But we desire to hear from you what your views are; for concerning this ᵃsect, it is known to us that ᵇit is spoken against everywhere."

★23 *ᵃPhilem. 22* *ᵇLuke 16:28; Acts 1:3; 23:11* *ᶜActs 8:35*   **23** And when they had set a day for him, they came to him at ᵃhis lodging in large numbers; and he was explaining to them by solemnly ᵇtestifying about the kingdom of God, and trying to persuade them concerning Jesus, ᶜfrom both the Law of Moses and from the Prophets, from morning until evening.

24 *ᵃActs 14:4*   **24** And ᵃsome were being persuaded by the things spoken, but others would not believe.

25 And when they did not agree with one another, they *began* leaving after Paul had spoken one parting word, "The Holy Spirit rightly spoke through Isaiah the prophet to your fathers, **26** saying,

  'ᵃGO TO THIS PEOPLE AND SAY,
  "ᵇYOU WILL KEEP ON HEARING,
    BUT WILL NOT UNDERSTAND;
  AND YOU WILL KEEP ON SEE-
    ING, BUT WILL NOT PER-
    CEIVE;

27 ᵃFOR THE HEART OF THIS PEO-
    PLE HAS BECOME DULL,
  AND WITH THEIR EARS THEY
    SCARCELY HEAR,
  AND THEY HAVE CLOSED THEIR
    EYES;
  LEST THEY SHOULD SEE WITH
    THEIR EYES,
  AND HEAR WITH THEIR EARS,
  AND UNDERSTAND WITH THEIR
    HEART AND RETURN,
  AND I SHOULD HEAL THEM." '

28 "Let it be known to you therefore, that ᵃthis salvation of God has been sent ᵇto the Gentiles; they will also listen."

29 [And when he had spoken these words, the Jews departed, having a great dispute among themselves.]

30 And he stayed two full years in his own rented quarters, and was welcoming all who came to him,

31 ᵃpreaching the kingdom of God, and teaching concerning the Lord Jesus Christ ᵇwith all openness, unhindered.

★25-27

26 ᵃIs. 6:9 ᵇMatt. 13:14f.; Acts 28:26, 27

27 ᵃIs. 6:10

28 ᵃPs. 98:3; Luke 2:30; Acts 13:26 ᵇActs 9:15; 13:46

★29

★30

31 ᵃMatt. 4:23; Acts 20:25; 28:23 ᵇ2 Tim. 2:9

28:20 *the hope of Israel.* The Messianic hope, incarnate in Jesus Christ and climaxed in His resurrection.

28:23 *trying to persuade* the Jews meant proving to them from Scripture and His resurrection that Jesus was the Messiah (see 13:30-39).

28:25-27 Paul's citation of this passage (Isa. 6:9-10) has been regarded as a parting shot at their obtuseness. He followed with a declaration that henceforth salvation will be preached to the Gentiles, the Jews having refused it.

28:29 Many manuscripts do not contain this verse.

28:30 *two full years in his own rented quarters.* During this time of confinement Paul wrote Ephesians, Philippians, Colossians, and Philemon. See the Introduction to Ephesians. Knowing that they could not get a verdict of guilty, his accusers probably never showed up and therefore lost the case by default. Paul would then have been released and become free to engage in the ministry reflected in the Pastoral Epistles before being rearrested and finally martyred. See the Introduction to Titus.

INTRODUCTION TO
THE LETTER OF PAUL TO THE ROMANS

AUTHOR: Paul   DATE: 58

The Church at Rome   *Though both Paul and Peter were apparently martyred in Rome, it is unlikely that either was the founder of the church in that city. Possibly some who were converted on the day of Pentecost (Acts 2:10) carried the gospel back to the imperial city; or it may be that converts of Paul or of other apostles founded the church there. The membership was predominantly Gentile (1:13; 11:13; 15:15-16).*

Occasion of the Letter   *Paul was anxious to minister in this church which was already widely known (1:8), so he wrote the letter to prepare the way for his visit (15:14-17). It was written from Corinth, where Paul was completing the collection for the poor in Palestine. From there he went to Jerusalem to deliver the money, intending to continue on to Rome and Spain (15:24). These plans were, of course, changed by his arrest in Jerusalem, though Paul did eventually get to Rome as a prisoner. Phoebe, who belonged to the church at Cenchrea near Corinth (16:1), probably carried the letter to Rome.*

The Question about Chapter 16   *The mention by name of 26 people in a church Paul had never visited (and particularly Priscilla and Aquila, who were most recently associated with Ephesus, Acts 18:18-19) has caused some scholars to consider chapter 16 as part of an epistle sent to Ephesus. It would be natural, however, for Paul to mention to a church to which he was a stranger his acquaintance with mutual friends. Paul's only other long series of greetings is in Colossians—a letter also sent to a church he had not visited.*

Contents   *More formal than Paul's other letters, Romans sets forth the doctrine of justification by faith (and its ramifications) in a systematic way. The theme of the epistle is the righteousness of God (1:16-17). A number of basic Christian doctrines are discussed: natural revelation (1:19-20), universality of sin (3:9-20), justification (3:24), propitiation (3:25), faith (chap. 4), original sin (5:12), union with Christ (chap. 6), the election and rejection of Israel (chaps. 9-11), spiritual gifts (12:3-8), and respect for government (13:1-7).*

OUTLINE OF ROMANS

THE LETTER OF PAUL TO THE ROMANS

I SALUTATION AND STATEMENT OF THEME, 1:1-17

A Greeting, 1:1-7

1 Paul, a bond-servant of Christ Jesus, *called as an apostle, *set apart for *the gospel of God,

2 which He *promised beforehand through His *prophets in the holy Scriptures,

3 concerning His Son, who was born *of a descendant of David *according to the flesh,

4 who was declared *the Son of God with power by the resurrection from the dead, according to the spirit of holiness, Jesus Christ our Lord,

5 through whom we have received grace and *apostleship to bring about *the *obedience* of faith among *all the Gentiles, for His name's sake,

6 among whom you also are the *called of Jesus Christ;

7 to all who are *beloved of God in Rome, called *as *saints: *Grace to you and peace from God our Father and the Lord Jesus Christ.

B Paul's Interest, 1:8-15

8 First, *I thank my God through Jesus Christ for you all, because *your faith is being proclaimed throughout the whole world.

9 For *God, whom I *serve in my spirit in the *preaching of the* gospel of His Son, is my witness *as to* how unceasingly *I make mention of you,

★ 1 *1 Cor. 1:1; 9:1; 2 Cor. 1:1 *Acts 9:15; 13:2; Gal. 1:15 *Mark 1:14; Rom. 15:16; 2 Cor. 2:12; 11:7; 1 Thess. 2:2, 8, 9; 1 Pet. 4:17
2 *Titus 1:2 *Luke 1:70; Rom. 3:21; 16:26
★ 3 *Matt. 1:1 *John 1:14; Rom. 4:1; 9:3, 5; 1 Cor. 10:18
★ 4 *Matt. 4:3
5 *Acts 1:25; Gal. 1:16 *Acts 6:7; Rom. 16:26 *Acts 9:15

★ 6 *Jude 1; Rev. 17:14
★ 7 *Rom. 5:5ff.; 8:39; 1 Thess. 1:4 *Acts 9:13; Rom. 8:28ff.; 1 Cor. 1:2, 24 *Num. 6:25f.; 1 Cor. 1:3; 2 Cor. 1:2; Gal. 1:3;
8 *1 Cor. 1:4; Eph. 1:15f.; Phil. 1:3f.; Col. 1:3f.; 1 Thess. 1:2; 2:13; 2 Thess. 1:3; 2:13; 2 Tim. 1:3; Philem. 4 *Acts 28:22; Rom. 16:19
9 *Rom. 9:1; 2 Cor. 1:23; 11:31; Phil. 1:8; 1 Thess. 2:5, 10 *Acts 24:14; 2 Tim. 1:3 *Eph. 1:16; Phil. 1:3f

1:1 *bond-servant.* Lit., slave, from a word that means "to bind." The believer who voluntarily takes the position of slave to Christ has no rights or will of his own. He does always and only the will of his Master. For His part, the Lord binds Himself to care for His servant (cf. Deut. 15:12-18). *the gospel* is the good news that the death of Jesus Christ provided the full payment for the penalty of sin, and that anyone who trusts that living Christ is forgiven and has eternal life.

1:3 *born of a descendant of David according to the flesh.* Jesus was descended from David. See notes on Matt. 1:1, 1:11; John 1:14.

1:4 *declared.* Better, designated; i.e., Jesus was designated or proved to be the Son of God by His own *resurrection from the dead.* Some understand *according to the Spirit of holiness* to refer to the Holy Spirit, while others consider it a reference to Christ's own holy being. Thus the verse may be understood this way: the resurrection of Jesus is the mighty proof of His deity, and this is declared by the Holy Spirit.

1:6 *the called.* I.e., those who have been summoned by God to salvation (8:30).

1:7 *saints.* The word means "holy ones" or "set-apart ones." The N.T. designates all believers as "saints" because they are by position holy and set apart to God (Phil. 4:21; Col. 1:2).

★10 aActs
18:21; Rom.
15:32
10 always in my prayers making request, if perhaps now at last by athe will of God I may succeed in coming to you.

★11 aActs
19:21; Rom.
15:23
11 For aI long to see you in order that I may impart some spiritual gift to you, that you may be established;

12 that is, that I may be encouraged together with you while among you, each of us by the other's faith, both yours and mine.

13 aRom.
11:25; 1 Cor.
10:1; 12:1;.
2 Cor. 1:8;
1 Thess. 4:13
bActs 1:15;
Rom. 7:1;
1 Cor. 1:10;
14:20, 26;
Gal. 3:15
cActs 19:21;
Rom. 15:22f.
dJohn 4:36;
15:16; Phil.
1:22; Col. 1:6
★14 a1 Cor.
9:16 bActs
28:2
15 aRom.
12:18 bRom.
15:20
13 And aI do not want you to be unaware, bbrethren, that often I chave planned to come to you (and have been prevented thus far) in order that I might obtain some dfruit among you also, even as among the rest of the Gentiles.

14 aI am under obligation both to Greeks and to bbarbarians, both to the wise and to the foolish.

15 Thus, afor my part, I am eager to bpreach the gospel to you also who are in Rome.

★16 a2 Tim.
1:8, 12, 16
b1 Cor. 1:18,
24 cActs
3:26; Rom.
2:9 dJohn
7:35
★17 aRom.
3:21; 9:30;
Phil. 3:9
bHab. 2:4;
Gal. 3:11;
Heb. 10:38
C   Theme, 1:16-17

16 For I am not aashamed of the gospel, for bit is the power of God for salvation to everyone who believes, to the cJew first and also to dthe Greek.

17 For in it athe righteousness of God is revealed from faith to faith; as it is written, "bBut the righteous man shall live by faith."

II   RIGHTEOUSNESS NEEDED; CONDEMNATION, SIN, 1:18-3:20

A   The Condemnation of the Gentile, 1:18-32

1   The cause of the condemnation: willful ignorance, 1:18-23

18 For athe wrath of God is revealed from heaven against all ungodliness and unrighteousness of men, who bsuppress the truth in unrighteousness,

★18 aRom.
5:9; Eph. 5:6;
Col. 3:6
b2 Thess.
2:6f. [Gr.]

19 because athat which is known about God is evident within them; for God made it evident to them.

19 aActs
14:17;
17:24ff.

20 For asince the creation of the world His invisible attributes, His eternal power and divine nature, have been clearly seen, bbeing understood through what has been made, so that they are without excuse.

★20 aMark
10:6 bJob
12:7-9; Ps.
19:1-6; Jer.
5:21f.

21 For even though they knew God, they did not honor Him as God, or give thanks; but they became afutile in their speculations, and their foolish heart was darkened.

21 a2 Kin.
17:15; Jer.
2:5; Eph.
4:17f.

1:10 *making request.* Arrest, trial, two years' languishing in prison (Acts 24:27), and shipwreck intervened before Paul's prayer was answered.

1:11 *impart.* I.e., exercise his gifts for their benefit (as explained in v. 12).

1:14 *Greeks.* Those who spoke Greek and who had adopted Hellenistic culture, in contrast to *barbarians* who had not. However, in v. 16 *Greek* means "Gentile," *wise* = educated.

1:16 *salvation* has three facets: past salvation from the penalties of sin (Luke 7:50); present salvation from the power of sin in the daily life (Rom. 5:10); and future salvation from the actual presence of sin (in heaven) (1 Cor. 3:15; 5:5). This salvation comes *to every one who believes*. We receive and experience it through faith, which is both assent to the truths of the gospel and genuine confidence in the Savior Himself.

1:17 *the righteousness of God.* I.e., the restoration of right relations between man and God

which proceeds from God's gift through His Son (see note on 3:21). *from faith to faith.* I.e., faith from start to finish. *The righteous man shall live by faith.* Quoting Hab. 2:4, Paul is emphasizing that one can be righteous in God's sight only through faith; i.e., he who is just through faith shall live now and forever by faith. See notes on Gal. 3:11 and Heb. 10:38. In vv. 16-17 is the essence of Paul's theology: Believe in the Lord Jesus, and you will be saved.

1:18 From here to 3:20 is God's indictment of the world, showing why man needs the righteousness of God. *suppress.* Man is condemned because truth was given to him (vv. 19-20) and because he by his actions rejected it (vv. 21-32).

1:20 *they are without excuse.* The things that are made (creation) reveal to all men the *power and divine nature* of the true God, so that the rejection of this truth makes a man without excuse before God.

22 ^aJer. 10:14; 1 Cor. 1:20

23 ^aPs. 106:20; Jer. 2:11; Acts 17:29

22 ^aProfessing to be wise, they became fools,

23 and ^aexchanged the glory of the incorruptible God for an image in the form of corruptible man and of birds and four-footed animals and crawling creatures.

2 The consequences of the condemnation: divine abandonment, 1:24-32

★**24** ^aRom. 1:26, 28; Eph. 4:19 ^bEph. 2:3

24 Therefore ^aGod gave them over in the lusts of their hearts to impurity, that their bodies might be ^bdishonored among them.

25 ^aIs. 44:20; Jer. 10:14; 13:25; 16:19 ^bRom. 9:5; 2 Cor. 11:31

25 For they exchanged the truth of God for a ^alie, and worshiped and served the creature rather than the Creator, ^bwho is blessed forever. Amen.

26 ^aRom. 1:24 ^b1 Thess. 4:5

26 For this reason ^aGod gave them over to ^bdegrading passions; for their women exchanged the natural function for that which is unnatural,

27 ^aLev. 18:22; 20:13; 1 Cor. 6:9

27 and in the same way also the men abandoned the natural function of the woman and burned in their desire toward one another, ^amen with men committing indecent acts and receiving in their own persons the due penalty of their error.

28 ^aRom. 1:24

28 And just as they did not see fit to acknowledge God any longer, ^aGod gave them over to a depraved mind, to do those things which are not proper,

29 ^a2 Cor. 12:20

29 being filled with all unrighteousness, wickedness, greed, evil; full of envy, murder, strife, deceit, malice; they are ^agossips,

30 ^aPs. 5:5 ^b2 Tim. 3:2

30 slanderers, ^ahaters of God, insolent, arrogant, boastful, inventors of evil, ^bdisobedient to parents,

31 ^a2 Tim. 3:3

31 without understanding,

untrustworthy, ^aunloving, unmerciful;

32 and, although they know the ordinance of God, that those who practice such things are worthy of ^adeath, they not only do the same, but also ^bgive hearty approval to those who practice them.

★**32** ^aRom. 6:21 ^bLuke 11:48; Acts 8:1; 22:20

B The Condemnation of the Moralist, 2:1-16

2 Therefore you are ^awithout excuse, ^bevery man of you who passes judgment, for in that ^cyou judge another, you condemn yourself; for you who judge practice the same things.

★ **1** ^aRom. 1:20 ^bLuke 12:14; Rom. 2:3; 9:20 ^c2 Sam. 12:5-7; Matt. 7:1; Rom. 14:22

2 And we know that the judgment of God rightly falls upon those who practice such things.

3 ^aLuke 12:14; Rom. 2:1; 9:20

3 And do you suppose this, ^aO man, when you pass judgment upon those who practice such things and do the same yourself, that you will escape the judgment of God?

4 ^aRom. 9:23; 11:33; 2 Cor. 8:2; Eph. 1:7, 18; 2:7; Phil. 4:19; Col. 1:27; 2:2; Titus 3:6 ^bRom. 11:22 ^cRom. 3:25 ^dEx. 34:6; Rom. 9:22; 1 Tim. 1:16; 1 Pet. 3:20; 2 Pet. 3:15 ^e2 Pet. 3:9

4 Or do you think lightly of ^athe riches of His ^bkindness and ^cforbearance and ^dpatience, not knowing that ^ethe kindness of God leads you to repentance?

5 But because of your stubbornness and unrepentant heart ^ayou are storing up wrath for yourself ^bin the day of wrath and revelation of the righteous judgment of God,

★ **5** ^aDeut. 32:34f.; Prov. 1:18 ^bPs. 110:5; 2 Cor. 5:10; 2 Thess. 1:5; Jude 6

6 ^aPs. 62:12; Matt. 16:27

6 ^awho WILL RENDER TO EVERY MAN ACCORDING TO HIS DEEDS:

★ **7** ^aLuke 8:15; Heb. 10:36 ^bRom. 2:10; Heb. 2:7; 1 Pet. 1:7 ^c1 Cor. 15:42, 50, 53f.; Eph. 6:24; 2 Tim. 1:10 ^dMatt. 25:46

7 to those who by ^aperseverance in doing good seek for ^bglory and honor and ^cimmortality, ^deternal life;

1:24 *God gave them over.* Note the repetition of this phrase in vv. 26 and 28. Paul is attacking the frank idolatry of most of the Gentile world, in which animals were considered gods (v. 23), sexual perversion was prevalent (vv. 26-27), and sin in general was rampant (vv. 29-32).

1:32 *give hearty approval to those who practice them.* Not only did the people themselves sin

but they encouraged and vicariously enjoyed the sins of others.

2:1 Paul now shows, first subtly (vv. 1-16), then openly, that the Jews are defenseless.

2:5 *wrath* results when grace is rejected.

2:7 *eternal life.* Good works do not save (Eph. 2:8-9) but are evidence of a changed life. Much of Romans is devoted to this extremely important thesis.

8 ª2 Cor.
12:20; Gal.
5:20; Phil.
1:17; 2:3;
James 3:14,
16 ᵇ2 Thess.
2:12
★ 9-10
9 ªRom.
8:35 ᵇActs
3:26; Rom.
1:16; 1 Pet.
4:17
10 ªRom.
2:7; Heb.
2:7; 1 Pet.
1:7 ᵇRom.
2:9
11 ªActs
10:34
★12 ªActs
2:23; 1 Cor.
9:21
13 ªMatt.
7:21, 24ff.;
John 13:17;
James 1:22f.,
25
★14 ªActs
10:35; Rom.
1:19; 2:15
15 ªRom.
2:14, 27
16 ªRom.
16:25; 1 Cor.
15:1; Gal.
1:11; 1 Tim.
1:11; 2 Tim.
2:8 ᵇActs
10:42; 17:31;
Rom. 3:6;
14:10
★17 ªMic.
3:11; John
5:45; Rom.
2:23; 9:4

8 but to those who are ªselfishly ambitious and ᵇdo not obey the truth, but obey unrighteousness, wrath and indignation.

9 There will be ªtribulation and distress for every soul of man who does evil, of the Jew ᵇfirst and also of the Greek,

10 but ªglory and honor and peace to every man who does good, to the Jew ᵇfirst and also to the Greek.

11 For ªthere is no partiality with God.

12 For all who have sinned ªwithout the Law will also perish without the Law; and all who have sinned under the Law will be judged by the Law;

13 for ªnot the hearers of the Law are just before God, but the doers of the Law will be justified.

14 For when Gentiles who do not have the Law do ªinstinctively the things of the Law, these, not having the Law, are a law to themselves,

15 in that they show ªthe work of the Law written in their hearts, their conscience bearing witness, and their thoughts alternately accusing or else defending them,

16 on the day when, ªaccording to my gospel, ᵇGod will judge the secrets of men through Christ Jesus.

C The Condemnation of the Jew, 2:17-3:8

1 He did not keep the law of God, 2:17-29

17 But if you bear the name "Jew," and ªrely upon the Law, and boast in God,

18 and know His will, and ªapprove the things that are essential, being instructed out of the Law,

19 and are confident that you yourself are a guide to the blind, a light to those who are in darkness,

20 a corrector of the foolish, a teacher of the immature, having in the Law ªthe embodiment of knowledge and of the truth,

21 you, therefore, ªwho teach another, do you not teach yourself? You who preach that one should not steal, do you steal?

22 You who say that one should not commit adultery, do you commit adultery? You who abhor idols, do you ªrob temples?

23 You who ªboast in the Law, through your breaking the Law, do you dishonor God?

24 For "ªTHE NAME OF GOD IS BLASPHEMED AMONG THE GENTILES ᵇBECAUSE OF YOU," just as it is written.

25 For indeed circumcision is of value, if you ªpractice the Law; but if you are a transgressor of the Law, ᵇyour circumcision has become uncircumcision.

26 ªIf therefore ᵇthe uncircumcised man ᶜkeeps the requirements of the Law, will not his uncircumcision be regarded as circumcision?

27 And will not ªhe who is physically uncircumcised, if he keeps the Law, will he not ᵇjudge you who though having the letter of the Law and circumcision are a transgressor of the Law?

28 For ªhe is not a Jew who is one outwardly; neither is circum-

18 ªPhil.
1:10

20 ªRom.
3:31; 2 Tim.
1:13

21 ªMatt.
23:3ff.

22 ªActs
19:37

23 ªMic.
3:11; John
5:45; Rom.
2:17; 9:4

24 ªIs.
52:5 ᵇEzek.
36:20ff.;
2 Pet. 2:2

★25 ªRom.
2:13f., 27
ᵇJer. 4:4;
9:25f.

26 ª1 Cor.
7:19 ᵇRom.
3:30; Eph.
2:11 ᶜRom.
2:25, 27; 8:4

27 ªRom.
3:30; Eph.
2:11 ᵇMatt.
12:41

28 ªJohn
8:39; Rom.
2:17; 9:6;
Gal. 6:15

2:9-10 the Jew first. The Jews' priority of privilege was also one of responsibility, and the principles of God's judgment are the same for all (v. 11).

2:12 without the Law. I.e., Gentiles, to whom the Mosaic law had not been given (9:4).

2:14 instinctively. The interaction of conscience and innate morality may result in a good life. To such persons God sends the gospel (Acts 4:12; Rom. 10:4).

2:17 you bear the name "Jew." The failure of the Jew makes him culpable because of privileges he had in the law and the promises of God. He could and should have become a guide and light to those in darkness (v. 19).

2:25 your circumcision has become uncircumcision. I.e., a Jewish lawbreaker stands before God in the same place as a pagan. Paul emphasizes that the Jewish law was impossible to keep perfectly.

cision that which is outward in the flesh.

29 But ªhe is a Jew who is one inwardly; and circumcision is that which is of the heart, by the ᵇSpirit, not by the letter; ᶜand his praise is not from men, but from God.

2 He did not believe the promises of God,
3:1-8

3 Then what advantage has the Jew? Or what is the benefit of circumcision?

2 Great in every respect. First of all, that ªthey were entrusted with the ᵇoracles of God.

3 What then? If ªsome did not believe, their unbelief will not nullify the faithfulness of God, will it?

4 ªMay it never be! Rather, let God be found true, though every man *be found* ᵇa liar, as it is written,

"ᶜTHAT THOU MIGHTEST BE JUSTIFIED IN THY WORDS, AND MIGHTEST PREVAIL WHEN THOU ART JUDGED."

5 But if our unrighteousness ªdemonstrates the righteousness of God, ᵇwhat shall we say? The God who inflicts wrath is not unrighteous, is He? (ᶜI am speaking in human terms.)

6 ªMay it never be! For otherwise how will ᵇGod judge the world?

7 But if through my lie ªthe truth of God abounded to His glo-

ry, ᵇwhy am I also still being judged as a sinner?

8 And why not *say* (as we are slanderously reported and as some affirm that we say), "ªLet us do evil that good may come"? Their condemnation is just.

D The Condemnation of All Men, 3:9-20

9 What then? ªAre we better than they? Not at all; for we have already charged that both ᵇJews and ᶜGreeks are ᵈall under sin;

10 as it is written,

"ªTHERE IS NONE RIGHTEOUS, NOT EVEN ONE;

11 THERE IS NONE WHO UNDERSTANDS, THERE IS NONE WHO SEEKS FOR GOD;

12 ALL HAVE TURNED ASIDE, TOGETHER THEY HAVE BECOME USELESS; THERE IS NONE WHO DOES GOOD, THERE IS NOT EVEN ONE."

13 "ªTHEIR THROAT IS AN OPEN GRAVE, WITH THEIR TONGUES THEY KEEP DECEIVING," "THE POISON OF ASPS IS UNDER THEIR LIPS";

14 "ªWHOSE MOUTH IS FULL OF CURSING AND BITTERNESS";

15 "ªTHEIR FEET ARE SWIFT TO SHED BLOOD,

16 DESTRUCTION AND MISERY ARE IN THEIR PATHS,

17 AND THE PATH OF PEACE HAVE THEY NOT KNOWN."

Marginal references

★29 ªPhil. 3:3; Col. 2:11; ᵇRom. 2:27; 7:6; 2 Cor. 3:6 ᶜJohn 5:44; 12:43; 1 Cor. 4:5; 2 Cor. 10:18

★1

★2 ªDeut. 4:8; Ps. 147:19; Rom. 9:4 ᵇActs 7:38 3 ªRom. 10:16; Heb. 4:2

★4 ªLuke 20:16; Rom. 3:6, 31 ᵇPs. 116:11; Rom. 3:7 ᶜPs. 51:4

★5 ªRom. 5:8; 2 Cor. 6:4; 7:11 [Gr.]; Gal. 2:18 [Gr.] ᵇRom. 4:1; 7:7; 8:31; 9:14, 30 ᶜRom. 6:19; 1 Cor. 9:8; 15:32; Gal. 3:15 6 ªLuke 20:16; Rom. 3:4, 31 ᵇRom. 2:16 7 ªRom. 3:4 ᵇRom. 9:19

8 ªRom. 6:1

★9 ªRom. 3:1 ᵇRom. 2:1-29 ᶜRom. 1:18-32 ᵈRom. 3:19, 23; 11:32; Gal. 3:22 ★10-18 10 ªPs. 14:1-3; 53:1-4

13 ªPs. 5:9; 140:3

14 ªPs. 10:7

15 ªIs. 59:7f.

2:29 *circumcision is that which is of the heart.* Circumcision is used in three senses in this passage: (1) it stands for the Jews (note that *uncircumcised* in v. 27 means Gentiles; see also Gen. 17:10); (2) it indicates the physical rite commanded in the law (v. 25a and Lev. 12:3); (3) it represents a life that is separated from the flesh and unto God (v. 27 and Deut. 10:16). See note on Acts 16:3.

3:1 *advantage.* A Jew had the advantage of special revelation of God's law. Yet this could not save him, for he was not able to keep it. The law increased his responsibility, but demonstrated his inability to live up to God's standards.

3:2 *the oracles of God.* The promises of God to

the Jews, found in the Scriptures.

3:4 *though every man be found a liar.* Men should believe that they all have broken their word rather than that God has broken His. See Ps. 51:4.

3:5 Does God use man's sin to glorify Himself? No, otherwise He would have to abandon all judgment.

3:9 *Are we better than they?* Possibly this should be translated, "Are we Jews disadvantaged?" i.e., in a worse position than Gentiles.

3:10-18 In these verses Paul quotes and paraphrases a number of O.T. passages, Ps. 5:9; 10:7; 14:1-3; 36:1; 140:3; Isa. 59:7-8. His indictment of the Jews has the authority of Scripture behind it.

18 aPs. 36:1   **18** "ᵃTHERE IS NO FEAR OF GOD BEFORE THEIR EYES."

19 aJohn 10:34 bRom. 2:12 cRom. 3:9   **19** Now we know that whatever the ᵃLaw says, it speaks to ᵇthose who are under the Law, that every mouth may be closed, and ᶜall the world may become accountable to God;

★20 aPs. 143:2; Acts 13:39; Gal. 2:16 bRom. 4:15; 5:13, 20; 7:7   **20** because ᵃby the works of the Law no flesh will be justified in His sight; for ᵇthrough the Law comes the knowledge of sin.

III RIGHTEOUSNESS IMPUTED; JUSTIFICATION, SALVATION, 3:21–5:21
A The Description of Righteousness, 3:21–31

★21 aRom. 1:17; 9:30 bActs 10:43   **21** But now apart from the Law ᵃthe righteousness of God has been manifested, being ᵇwitnessed by the Law and the Prophets,

22 aRom. 1:17; 9:30 bRom. 4:5 cActs 3:16; Gal. 2:16 dRom. 4:11, 16; 10:4 eRom. 10:12; Gal. 3:28   **22** even the ᵃrighteousness of God through ᵇfaith ᶜin Jesus Christ for ᵈall those who believe; for ᵉthere is no distinction;

★23 aRom. 3:9   **23** for all ᵃhave sinned and fall short of the glory of God,

★24 aRom. 4:4f., 16; Eph. 2:8 b1 Cor. 1:30; Eph. 1:7; Col. 1:14   **24** being justified as a gift ᵃby His grace through ᵇthe redemption which is in Christ Jesus;

★25 a1 John 2:2; 4:10 b1 Cor. 5:7; Rev. 1:5 cRom. 2:4 dActs 14:16; 17:30   **25** whom God displayed publicly as ᵃa propitiation ᵇin His blood through faith. This was to demonstrate His righteousness, because in the ᶜforbearance of God He ᵈpassed over the sins previously committed;

★26   **26** for the demonstration, I say, of His righteousness at the present time, that He might be just and the justifier of the one who has faith in Jesus.

27 aRom. 2:17, 23; 4:2; 1 Cor. 1:29ff. bRom. 9:31   **27** Where then is ᵃboasting? It is excluded. By ᵇwhat kind of law? Of works? No, but by a law of faith.

28 aActs 13:39; Rom. 3:20, 21; Eph. 2:9; James 2:20, 24, 26   **28** For ᵃwe maintain that a man is justified by faith apart from works of the Law.

29 aActs 10:34f.; Rom. 9:24; 10:12; 15:9; Gal. 3:28   **29** Or ᵃis God the God of Jews only? Is He not the God of Gentiles also? Yes, of Gentiles also,

30 aRom. 10:12 bRom. 3:22; 4:11f., 16; Gal. 3:8 cDeut. 6:4   **30** since indeed ᵃGod ᵇwho will justify the circumcised by faith and the uncircumcised through faith ᶜis one.

★31 aLuke 20:16; Rom. 3:4 bMatt. 5:17; Rom. 4:3; 8:4   **31** Do we then ᵃnullify the Law through faith? ᵃMay it never be! On the contrary, we ᵇestablish the Law.

B The Illustration of Righteousness, 4:1–25
1 Abraham's faith was apart from works, 4:1–8

★ 1ff 1 aRom. 1:3   **4** What then shall we say that Abraham, our forefather ᵃaccording to the flesh, has found?

3:20 The function of the law, Paul says, is to give knowledge of or about sin, not to save from sin (Acts 13:39; 1 Tim. 1:9–10).

3:21 *righteousness.* Used in various ways in the Bible, righteousness refers: (1) to God's character (John 17:25); (2) to the gift which is given to everyone who receives Christ (here and 5:17); and (3) to standards of right living (6:18; 2 Tim. 2:22).

3:23 *all have sinned.* Sin is defined in 1 John 3:4 as lawlessness, and here as lack of conformity to the *glory of God.* These are complementary ideas, since the law of God is an expression of His character.

3:24 *justified.* To justify was a legal term meaning to secure a favorable verdict, to acquit, to vindicate, to declare righteous (Deut. 25:1). It is an act of God (Rom. 8:33), who takes the initiative and provides the means *through the redemption which is in Christ Jesus.* The sinner who believes in Christ receives God's gift of righteousness (5:17), which then enables

God to pronounce him righteous. On *redemption* see note on Eph. 1:7.

3:25 *propitiation.* Here this may mean the "place of propitiation"; i.e., the mercy seat (as in Heb. 9:5). Christ is pictured as the mercy seat where God's holy demands were satisfied (cf. Lev. 16:14). See note on Heb. 2:17. *sins previously committed.* The death of Christ also paid fully for sins committed before He died.

3:26 *that He might be just and the justifier of the one who has faith in Jesus.* Because of the death of Christ, God can remain just when declaring righteous the one who believes in Jesus and who is thus forgiven of his sins.

3:31 *we establish the Law.* The role of the law in making men conscious of sin (v. 20) is confirmed by everyone who acknowledges sin and turns to Christ in faith.

4:1ff. Paul's point in this chapter is that the faith-righteousness principle is not new, and he uses Abraham as proof.

2 For if Abraham was justified by works, he has something to boast about; but ^anot before God.

3 For what does the Scripture say? "^aAND ABRAHAM BELIEVED GOD, AND IT WAS RECKONED TO HIM AS RIGHTEOUSNESS."

4 Now to the one who ^aworks, his wage is not reckoned as a favor, but as what is due.

5 But to the one who does not work, but ^abelieves in Him who justifies the ungodly, his faith is reckoned as righteousness,

6 just as David also speaks of the blessing upon the man to whom God reckons righteousness apart from works:

7 "^aBLESSED ARE THOSE WHOSE LAWLESS DEEDS HAVE BEEN FORGIVEN, AND WHOSE SINS HAVE BEEN COVERED.

8 "^aBLESSED IS THE MAN WHOSE SIN THE LORD WILL NOT ^bTAKE INTO ACCOUNT."

2 Abraham's faith was apart from circumcision, 4:9-12

9 Is this blessing then upon ^athe circumcised, or upon the uncircumcised also? For ^bwe say, "^cFAITH WAS RECKONED TO ABRAHAM AS RIGHTEOUSNESS."

10 How then was it reckoned? While he was circumcised, or uncircumcised? Not while circumcised, but while uncircumcised;

11 and he ^areceived the sign of circumcision, ^ba seal of the righteousness of the faith which he had while uncircumcised, that he might be ^cthe father of ^dall who believe without being circumcised, that righteousness might be reckoned to them,

12 and the father of circumcision to those who not only are of the circumcision, but who also follow in the steps of the faith of our father Abraham which he had while uncircumcised.

3 Abraham's faith was apart from the law, 4:13-15

13 For ^athe promise to Abraham or to his descendants ^bthat he would be heir of the world was not through the Law, but through the righteousness of faith.

14 For ^aif those who are of the Law are heirs, faith is made void and the promise is nullified;

15 for ^athe Law brings about wrath, but ^bwhere there is no law, neither is there violation.

4 Abraham's faith was in God, 4:16-25

16 For this reason *it is* by faith, that *it might be* in accordance with ^agrace, in order that the promise may be certain to ^ball the descendants, not only to those who are of the Law, but also to those who are of the faith of Abraham, who is ^cthe father of us all,

17 (as it is written, "^aA FATHER OF MANY NATIONS HAVE I MADE YOU") in the sight of Him whom he believed, *even* God, ^bwho gives life to the dead and ^ccalls into being ^dthat which does not exist.

18 In hope against hope he believed, in order that he might become ^aa father of many nations, according to that which had been spoken, "^bSo SHALL YOUR DESCENDANTS BE."

19 And without becoming weak in faith he contemplated his

Marginal references

2 ^a1 Cor. 1:31
★ 3 ^aGen. 15:6; Rom. 4:9, 22; Gal. 3:6; James 2:23
★ 4 ^aRom. 11:6
5 ^aJohn 6:29; Rom. 3:22
★ 7 ^aPs. 32:1
8 ^aPs. 32:2 ^b2 Cor. 5:19
★ 9-25
9 ^aRom. 3:30 ^bRom. 4:3 ^cGen. 15:6
★10
11 ^aGen. 17:10f. ^bJohn 3:33 ^cLuke 19:9; Rom. 4:16f. ^dRom. 3:22; 4:16
13 ^aRom. 9:8; Gal. 3:16 ^bGen. 17:4-6; 22:17f.
14 ^aGal. 3:18
15 ^aRom. 7:7, 10-25; 1 Cor. 15:56; Gal. 3:10 ^bRom. 3:20
16 ^aRom. 3:24 ^bRom. 4:11; 9:8; 15:8 ^cLuke 19:9; Rom. 4:11
★17 ^aGen. 17:5 ^bJohn 5:21 ^cIs. 48:13; 51:2 ^d1 Cor. 1:28
★18 ^aRom. 4:17 ^bGen. 15:5
★19 ^aHeb. 11:12 ^bGen. 17:17 ^cGen. 18:11

4:3 *Abraham* was justified by faith, not by works (Gen. 15:6).

4:4 Wages have nothing to do with grace (unmerited favor) but with what is due.

4:7 See Ps. 32:1-2.

4:9-25 The points Paul makes from the illustrations are these: (1) justification did not come to Abraham by faith plus circumcision (vv. 9-12); (2) justification was not by faith plus keeping the law (vv. 13-17); (3) justification was by faith alone (vv. 18-25).

4:10 Abraham's acceptance by God on the basis of faith preceded his circumcision (Gen. 15 is before Gen. 17).

4:17 See Gen. 17:5.

4:18 See Gen. 15:5.

4:19 Abraham fully faced the difficulty, yet he believed God.

own body, now *as good as dead since *he was about a hundred years old, and *the deadness of Sarah's womb;

20 yet, with respect to the promise of God, he did not waver in unbelief, but grew strong in faith, *giving glory to God,

21 and *being fully assured that *what He had promised, He was able also to perform.

22 Therefore also *IT WAS RECKONED TO HIM AS RIGHTEOUSNESS.

23 Now *not for his sake only was it written, that it was reckoned to him,

24 but for our sake also, to whom it will be reckoned, as those *who believe in Him who *raised Jesus our Lord from the dead,

25 *He who was *delivered up because of our transgressions, and was *raised because of our justification.

C The Benefits of Righteousness, 5:1-11

5 *Therefore having been justified by faith, *we have peace with God through our Lord Jesus Christ,

2 through whom also we have *obtained our introduction by faith into this grace *in which we stand; and we exult in hope of the glory of God.

3 *And not only this, but we also *exult in our tribulations, knowing that tribulation brings about *perseverance;

4 and *perseverance, *proven character; and proven character, hope;

5 and hope *does not disappoint, because the love of God has been *poured out within our hearts through the Holy Spirit who was given to us.

6 For while we were still *helpless, *at the right time *Christ died for the ungodly.

7 For one will hardly die for a righteous man; though perhaps for the good man someone would dare even to die.

8 But God *demonstrates *His own love toward us, in that while we were yet sinners, *Christ died for us.

9 Much more then, having now been justified *by His blood, we shall be saved *from the wrath of God through Him.

10 For if while we were *enemies, we were reconciled to God through the death of His Son, much more, having been reconciled, we shall be saved *by His life.

11 *And not only this, but we also exult in God through our Lord Jesus Christ, through whom we have now received *the reconciliation.

D The Applicability of Righteousness, 5:12-21

12 Therefore, just as through *one man sin entered into the world, and *death through sin, and *so death spread to all men, because all sinned—

Marginal references

20 *Matt. 9:8

21 *Rom. 14:5 *Gen. 18:14; Heb. 11:19

22 *Rom. 4:3

23 *Rom. 15:4; 1 Cor. 9:9f.; 10:11; 2 Tim. 3:16f.

★24 *Rom. 10:9; 1 Pet. 1:21 *Acts 2:24

★25 *Rom. 5:6, 8; 8:32; Gal. 2:20; Eph. 5:2 *Rom. 5:18; 1 Cor. 15:17; 2 Cor. 5:15

★ 1-11 1 *Rom. 3:28 *Rom. 5:11

★ 2 *Eph. 2:18; 3:12; Heb. 10:19f.; 1 Pet. 3:18 *1 Cor. 15:1

3 *Rom. 5:11; 8:23; 9:10; 2 Cor. 8:19 *Matt. 5:12; James 1:2f. *Luke 21:19

4 *Luke 21:19 *Phil. 2:22; James 1:12

5 *Ps. 119:116; Rom. 9:33; Heb. 6:18f. *Acts 2:33; 10:45; Gal. 4:6; Titus 3:6

★ 6-8 6 *Rom. 5:8, 10 *Gal. 4:4 *Rom. 4:25; 5:8; 8:32; Gal. 2:20; Eph. 5:2

8 *Rom. 3:5 *John 3:16; 15:13; Rom. 8:39 *Rom. 4:25; 5:6; 8:32; Gal. 2:20; Eph. 5:2

★ 9 *Rom. 3:25 *Rom. 1:18; 1 Thess. 1:10

★10 *Rom. 11:28; 2 Cor. 5:18f.; Eph. 2:3; Col. 1:21f. *Rom. 8:34; Heb. 7:25; 1 John 2:1

★11 *Rom. 5:3; 8:23; 9:10; 2 Cor. 8:19 *Rom. 5:10; 11:15; 2 Cor. 5:18f.

★12-21 ★12 *Gen. 2:17; 3:6, 19; Rom. 5:15, 16, 17 *Rom. 6:23; 1 Cor. 15:56; James 1:15 *Rom. 5:14, 19, 21; 1 Cor. 15:22

4:24 Saving faith is faith in the Giver of miraculous life, demonstrated in the resurrection of Jesus.

4:25 *because of our justification.* Christ's resurrection was because of our justification; i.e., as a proof of God's acceptance of His Son's sacrifice.

5:1-11 For Paul, justification is not sterile doctrine, but a source of blessing in one's life. *we have* (v. 1). Some manuscripts read "let us have."

5:2 *exult in hope of the glory of God.* Better, we boast in the hope of the glory which God will manifest.

5:6-8 The extent of God's love is shown in the fact that Christ died for men in whom there was nothing that evoked that love.

5:9 *Much more.* Note the repetition of this emphasis in vv. 10, 15, 17, 20. Paul is teaching the vicarious, sacrificial significance of Christ's death.

5:10 *we shall be saved by His life.* Christ's present resurrection ministry in heaven keeps us saved (Heb. 7:25).

5:11 *the reconciliation.* See note on 2 Cor. 5:18.

5:12-21 In the closely worded argument of this section Paul contrasts death in Adam with life in Christ. Just as Adam's sin brought certain

★13 *a*Rom.
4:15

13 for until the Law sin was in the world; but *a*sin is not imputed when there is no law.

14 *a*Hos. 6:7
*b*1 Cor.
15:45

14 Nevertheless death reigned from Adam until Moses, even over those who had not sinned *a*in the likeness of the offense of Adam, who is a *b*type of Him who was to come.

15 *a*Rom.
5:12, 18
*b*Rom. 5:18,
19 *c*Acts
15:11

15 But the free gift is not like the transgression. For if by the transgression of *a*the one *b*the many died, much more did the grace of God and the gift by *c*the grace of the one Man, Jesus Christ, abound to *b*the many.

16 *a*1 Cor.
11:32 [Gr.]

16 And the gift is not like *that which came* through the one who sinned; for on the one hand *a*the judgment *arose* from one *transgression* resulting in condemnation, but on the other hand the free gift *arose* from many transgressions resulting in justification.

17 *a*Gen.
2:17; 3:6, 19;
Rom. 5:12,
15, 16;
1 Cor.
15:21f.
*b*2 Tim. 2:12;
Rev. 22:5

17 For if by the transgression of the one, death reigned *a*through the one, much more those who receive the abundance of grace and of the gift of righteousness will *b*reign in life through the One, Jesus Christ.

★18 *a*Rom.
5:12, 15
*b*Rom. 3:25
*c*Rom. 4:25

18 So then as through *a*one transgression there resulted condemnation to all men, even so through one *b*act of righteousness there resulted *c*justification of life to all men.

19 *a*Rom.
5:15, 18
*b*Rom. 5:12;
11:32 *c*Phil.
2:8

19 For as through the one man's disobedience *a*the many *b*were made sinners, even so through *c*the obedience of the One *a*the many will be made righteous.

20 *a*Rom.
3:20; 7:7f.;
Gal. 3:19
*b*Rom. 6:1;
1 Tim. 1:14

20 And *a*the Law came in that the transgression might increase; but where sin increased, *b*grace abounded all the more,

21 *a*Rom.
5:12, 14
*b*John 1:17;
Rom. 6:23

21 that, as *a*sin reigned in death, even so *b*grace might reign through righteousness to eternal life through Jesus Christ our Lord.

IV   RIGHTEOUSNESS IMPARTED; SANCTIFICATION, SEPARATION, 6:1–8:39

A   The Principles of Sanctification; The Question of License, 6:1–23

1 *Shall we continue in sin?* 6:1–14

★ 1 *a*Rom.
3:5 *b*Rom.
3:8; 6:15
★ 2 *a*Luke
20:16; Rom.
6:15 *b*Rom.
6:11; 7:4, 6;
Gal. 2:19;
Col. 2:20;
3:3; 1 Pet.
2:24
★ 3 *a*Matt.
28:19 *b*Acts
2:38; 8:16;
19:5; Gal.
3:27

6 *a*What shall we say then? Are we to *b*continue in sin that grace might increase?

2 *a*May it never be! How shall we who *b*died to sin still live in it?

3 Or do you not know that all of us who have been *a*baptized

---

results, so did the death of Christ. Yet this does not mean automatic salvation, for men must receive the *grace* God offers (v. 17).

5:12 *as through one man sin entered into the world.* After Adam sinned, he and his descendants could only beget sinners, so that all men are under the sentence of death, the penalty of sin. *all sinned.* True because of the solidarity of the race just explained (see Heb. 7:9–10).

5:13 *sin is not imputed.* I.e., sin is not charged as a specific violation of a particular command *when there is no law.* However, this does not mean that sin was not sin during the period from Adam to Moses, as proved by the fact of death during that period (v. 14). Sin could never be anything but evil.

5:18 Notice here, and often in this passage, the contrasts between Adam and Christ—between their deeds and the results of those deeds. The contrasts would lose meaning if Adam had not been an historical person.

6:1 If grace abounds in the presence of sin

(5:20), then *Are we to continue in sin that grace might increase?*

6:2 *May it never be!* Grace cannot be exploited for evil ends! Because of our union with Christ we *died to sin* and are *alive to God* (v. 11). The new moral life is based on: (1) our union with Christ (6:1–14); (2) our being slaves to righteousness (6:15–23); and (3) the new marriage union we have with Christ (7:1–6). *died to sin.* Death is separation, not extinction: (1) Physical death is the separation of body from spirit (Jas. 2:26). (2) Spiritual death is the separation of a person from God (Eph. 2:1). (3) The second death is eternal separation from God (Rev. 20:14). (4) Death to sin is separation from the ruling power of sin in one's own life (Rom. 6:14).

6:3 *baptized into Christ Jesus.* Baptism with the Holy Spirit joins the believer to Christ, separating him from the old life and associating him with the new. He is no longer "in Adam" but is "in Christ." Water baptism is a reminder of this truth.

into ^bChrist Jesus have been baptized into His death?

4 Therefore we have been ^aburied with Him through baptism into death, in order that as Christ was ^braised from the dead through the ^cglory of the Father, so we too might walk in ^dnewness of life.

5 For ^aif we have become united with *Him* in the likeness of His death, certainly we shall be also *in the likeness* of His resurrection,

6 knowing this, that our ^aold self was ^bcrucified with *Him*, that our ^cbody of sin might be done away with, that we should no longer be slaves to sin;

7 for ^ahe who has died is freed from sin.

8 Now ^aif we have died with Christ, we believe that we shall also live with Him,

9 knowing that Christ, having been ^araised from the dead, is never to die again; ^bdeath no longer is master over Him.

10 For the death that He died, He died to sin, once for all; but the life that He lives, He lives to God.

11 Even so consider yourselves to be ^adead to sin, but alive to God in Christ Jesus.

12 Therefore do not let sin ^areign in your mortal body that you should obey its lusts,

13 and do not go on ^apresenting the members of your body to sin *as* instruments of unrighteousness; but ^bpresent yourselves to God as those alive from the dead, and your members *as* instruments of righteousness to God.

14 For ^asin shall not ^bbe master over you, for ^cyou are not under law, but ^dunder grace.

2   Shall we continue to sin?
6:15–23

15 What then? ^aShall we sin because we are not under law but under grace? ^bMay it never be!

16 Do you not ^aknow that when you present yourselves to someone as ^bslaves for obedience, you are slaves of the one whom you obey, either of ^csin resulting in death, or of obedience resulting in righteousness?

17 But ^athanks be to God that though you were slaves of sin, you became obedient from the heart to that ^bform of teaching to which you were committed,

18 and having been ^afreed from sin, you became slaves of righteousness.

19 ^aI am speaking in human terms because of the weakness of your flesh. For just ^bas you presented your members *as* slaves to impurity and to lawlessness, resulting in *further* lawlessness, so now present your members *as* slaves to righteousness, resulting in sanctification.

20 For ^awhen you were slaves of sin, you were free in regard to righteousness.

21 Therefore what ^abenefit were you then deriving from the things of which you are now ashamed? For the outcome of those things is ^bdeath.

22 But now having been ^afreed from sin and ^benslaved to God, you derive your ^cbenefit, re-

Cross references (margin)

4 ^aCol. 2:12 ^bActs 2:24; Rom. 6:9 ^cJohn 11:40; 2 Cor. 13:4 ^dRom. 7:6; 2 Cor. 5:17; Gal. 6:15; Eph. 4:23f.; Col. 3:10
5 ^a2 Cor. 4:10; Phil. 3:10f.; Col. 2:12; 3:1
★**6** ^aEph. 4:22; Col. 3:9 ^bGal. 2:20; 5:24; 6:14 ^cRom. 7:24
7 ^a1 Pet. 4:1
8 ^aRom. 6:4; 2 Cor. 4:10; 2 Tim. 2:11
9 ^aActs 2:24; Rom. 6:4 ^bRev. 1:18
★**11** ^aRom. 6:2; 7:4, 6; Gal. 2:19; Col. 2:20; 3:3; 1 Pet. 2:24
★**12** ^aRom. 6:14
★**13** ^aRom. 6:16, 19; 7:5; Col. 3:5 ^bRom. 12:1; 2 Cor. 5:14f.; 1 Pet. 2:24

14 ^aRom. 8:2, 12 ^bRom. 6:12 ^cRom. 5:18; 7:4, 6; Gal. 4:21 ^dRom. 5:17, 21
★**15-23**
15 ^aRom. 6:1 ^bLuke 20:16; Rom. 6:2
16 ^aRom. 11:2; 1 Cor. 3:16; 5:6; 6:2, 3, 9, 15, 16, 19; 9:13, 24 ^bJohn 8:34; 2 Pet. 2:19 ^cRom. 6:21, 23
★**17** ^aRom. 1:8; 2 Cor. 2:14 ^b2 Tim. 1:13
18 ^aJohn 8:32; Rom. 6:22; 8:2
★**19** ^aRom. 3:5 ^bRom. 6:13
20 ^aMatt. 6:24; Rom. 6:16
★**21** ^aJer. 12:13; Ezek. 16:63; Rom. 7:5 ^bRom. 1:32; 5:12; 6:16, 23; 8:6, 13; Gal. 6:8
22 ^aJohn 8:32; Rom. 6:18; 8:2 ^b1 Cor. 7:22; 1 Pet. 2:16 ^cRom. 7:4 ^d1 Pet. 1:9

6:6 *old self.* I.e., all that a person is before salvation which is made "old" by reason of the presence of the new life in Christ. *done away.* I.e., made ineffective or impotent (as in 2 Thess. 2:8).

6:11 *consider.* This means "calculate," i.e., by adding up the facts presented in vv. 1-10 and then acting accordingly.

6:12 We must either dethrone sin or obey its evil desires.

6:13 *do not go on presenting the members of your body . . . but present yourselves to God.* The tenses may imply "stop presenting your members . . . but present yourselves once for all unto God."

6:15-23 This passage is the ethical application of 5:12–21. When we were in Adam sin was master, demanding shameful living and repaying with death. In Christ we can be slaves of righteousness.

6:17 *that form of teaching.* I.e., Christian truth.

6:19 Paul uses the illustration of slaves and masters because of the dullness of understanding of those to whom he wrote.

6:21 *then.* I.e., when you were slaves to sin what benefit did you have?

sulting in sanctification, and ᵈthe outcome, eternal life.

★23 ᵃRom. 1:32; 5:12; 6:16, 21; 8:6, 13; Gal. 6:8 ᵇMatt. 25:46; Rom. 5:21; 8:39

23 For the wages of ᵃsin is death, but the free gift of God is ᵇeternal life in Christ Jesus our Lord.

B The Practice of Sanctification; The Question of Law, 7:1-25

1 Is the believer under law? 7:1-6

★ 1-6
★ 1 ᵃRom. 1:13

7 Or do you not know, ᵃbrethren (for I am speaking to those who know the law), that the law has jurisdiction over a person as long as he lives?

2 ᵃ1 Cor. 7:39

2 For ᵃthe married woman is bound by law to her husband while he is living; but if her husband dies, she is released from the law concerning the husband.

3 So then if, while her husband is living, she is joined to another man, she shall be called an adulteress; but if her husband dies, she is free from the law, so that she is not an adulteress, though she is joined to another man.

★ 4 ᵃRom. 6:2; 7:6 ᵇRom. 8:2; Gal. 2:19; 5:18 ᶜCol. 1:22

4 Therefore, my brethren, you also were ᵃmade to die ᵇto the Law ᶜthrough the body of Christ, that you might be joined to another, to Him who was raised from the dead, that we might bear fruit for God.

★ 5 ᵃRom. 8:8f.; 2 Cor. 10:3 ᵇRom. 7:7f. ᶜRom. 6:13, 21, 23
6 ᵃRom. 7:2 ᵇRom. 6:2 ᶜRom. 6:4 ᵈRom. 2:29

5 For while we were ᵃin the flesh, the sinful passions, which were ᵇaroused by the Law, were at work ᶜin the members of our body to bear fruit for death.

6 But now we have been ᵃre-

leased from the Law, having ᵇdied to that by which we were bound, so that we serve in ᶜnewness of ᵈthe Spirit and not in oldness of the letter.

2 Is the law evil? 7:7-12

7 ᵃRom. 3:5 ᵇLuke 20:16 ᶜRom. 3:20; 4:15; 5:20 ᵈEx. 20:17; Deut. 5:21

7 ᵃWhat shall we say then? Is the Law sin? ᵇMay it never be! On the contrary, ᶜI would not have come to know sin except through the Law; for I would not have known about coveting if the Law had not said, "ᵈYou shall not covet."

8 ᵃRom. 7:11 ᵇRom. 3:20; 7:11 ᶜ1 Cor. 15:56

8 But sin, ᵃtaking opportunity ᵇthrough the commandment, produced in me coveting of every kind; for ᶜapart from the Law sin is dead.

★ 9

9 And I was once alive apart from the Law; but when the commandment came, sin became alive, and I died;

10 ᵃLev. 18:5; Luke 10:28; Rom. 10:5; Gal. 3:12
11 ᵃRom. 7:8 ᵇRom. 3:20; 7:8 ᶜGen. 3:13

10 and this commandment, which was ᵃto result in life, proved to result in death for me;

11 for sin, ᵃtaking opportunity ᵇthrough the commandment, ᶜdeceived me, and through it killed me.

★12 ᵃRom. 7:16; 1 Tim. 1:8

12 ᵃSo then, the Law is holy, and the commandment is holy and righteous and good.

3 Is the law a cause of death? 7:13-14

13 ᵃLuke 20:16

13 Therefore did that which is good become a cause of death for me? ᵃMay it never be! Rather it was sin, in order that it might be shown to be sin by effecting my death through that which is good,

---

6:23 *the free gift of God.* Sanctification of life does not earn eternal life; it is still God's gracious gift.

7:1-6 Paul here introduces a new metaphor, that of a fruitful marriage. The Christian, because of his death with Christ, is free from his marriage to the law and is brought into a new marriage with Christ. The new union demands good living as its progeny.

7:1 *know the law.* Legal principles, not the Mosaic law here.

7:4 The believer who has died with Christ is re-

leased from bondage to the law and hence from bondage to sin, and is free to experience the abundant life of Christ.

7:5 *while we were in the flesh.* I.e., before we were saved.

7:9 When Paul came to understand the true meaning of the Law, he realized that he was a sinner and worthy of death.

7:12 The law is fundamentally good, but the result of the law is to bring into the open the power of sin. It is sin, not the law which exposes it, that deceives and kills (v. 11).

that through the commandment sin might become utterly sinful.

14 *a*1 Cor.
3:1 *b*1 Kin.
21:20, 25;
2 Kin. 17:17;
Rom. 6:6;
Gal. 4:3
*c*Rom. 3:9

14 For we know that the Law is *a*spiritual; but I am *a*of flesh, *b*sold *c*into bondage to sin.

4 How can I resolve the struggle within myself? 7:15-25

★15-25
15 *a*John
15:15 *b*Rom.
7:19; Gal.
5:17

15 For that which I am doing, *a*I do not understand; for I am not practicing *b*what I *would* like to do, but I am doing the very thing I hate.

16 *a*Rom.
7:12; 1 Tim.
1:8

16 But if I do the very thing I do not wish *to do,* I agree with *a*the Law, *confessing* that it is good.

★17 *a*Rom.
7:20

17 So now, *a*no longer am I the one doing it, but sin which indwells me.

★18 *a*John
3:6; Rom.
7:25; 8:3

18 For I know that nothing good dwells in me, that is, in my *a*flesh; for the wishing is present in me, but the doing of the good *is* not.

19 *a*Rom.
7:15

19 For *a*the good that I wish, I do not do; but I practice the very evil that I do not wish.

20 *a*Rom.
7:17

20 But if I am doing the very thing I do not wish, *a*I am no longer the one doing it, but sin which dwells in me.

21 *a*Rom.
7:23, 25; 8:2

21 I find then *a*the principle that evil is present in me, the one who wishes to do good.

22 *a*2 Cor.
4:16; Eph.
3:16; 1 Pet.
3:4

22 For I joyfully concur with the law of God in *a*the inner man,

23 *a*Rom.
6:19; Gal.
5:17; James
4:1; 1 Pet.
2:11 *b*Rom.
7:25 *c*Rom.
7:21, 25; 8:2

23 but I see *a*a different law in the members of my body, waging

war against the *b*law of my mind, and making me a prisoner of *c*the law of sin which is in my members.

24 Wretched man that I am! Who will set me free from *a*the body of this *b*death?

★24 *a*Rom.
6:6; Col. 2:11
*b*Rom. 8:2

25 *a*Thanks be to God through Jesus Christ our Lord! So then, on the one hand I myself with my mind am serving the law of God, but on the other, with my flesh *b*the law of sin.

25 *a*1 Cor.
15:57 *b*Rom.
7:21, 23; 8:2

C The Power of Sanctification; The Question of Living, 8:1-39

1 Emancipated living, 8:1-11

8 There is therefore now no *a*condemnation for those who are *b*in *c*Christ Jesus.

1 *a*Rom.
5:16; 8:34
*b*Rom. 8:9f.
*c*Rom. 8:2,
11, 39; 16:3

2 For *a*the law of the Spirit of life in *b*Christ Jesus *c*has set you free from the law of sin and of death.

★ 2 *a*1 Cor.
15:45 *b*Rom.
8:1, 11, 39;
16:3 *c*John
8:32, 36;
Rom. 6:14,
18; 7:4

3 For *a*what the Law could not do, *b*weak as it was through the flesh, God *did*: sending His own Son in *c*the likeness of sinful flesh and *as an offering* for sin, He condemned sin in the flesh,

★ 3 *a*Acts
13:39; Heb.
10:1ff.
*b*Rom. 7:18f;
Heb. 7:18
*c*Phil. 2:7;
Heb. 2:14,
17; 4:15

4 in order that the *a*requirement of the Law might be fulfilled in us, who *b*do not walk according to the flesh, but according to the Spirit.

★ 4-8
4 *a*Luke
1:6; Rom.
2:26 *b*Gal.
5:16, 25

5 For those who are according to the flesh set their minds on *a*the things of the flesh, but those who are according to the Spirit, *b*the things of the Spirit.

5 *a*Gal.
5:19-21
*b*Gal. 5:22-
25

7:15-25 The intensely personal character of these verses seems to indicate that this was Paul's own experience as a believer. This is his diagnosis of what happens when one tries to be sanctified by keeping the law.

7:17 *sin which indwells me.* Though Paul has written of acts of sin (1:21-32), here he speaks of sin as a disposition deep in a man's life which produces those acts.

7:18 *flesh.* Paul uses flesh in several ways. (1) It denotes the personality of man controlled by sin and directed to selfish pursuits rather than the service of God (here; v. 25; 8:5-7; Gal. 5:17). (2) It sometimes refers simply to physical descent (1:3; 9:3). (3) It also stands for the physical existence of a person, i.e., being in

the body (Eph. 2:15; Philem. 16). There is no blame attached to the last two meanings of the word.

7:24 The *body* dominated by sin endures a "living" *death*.

8:2 *the law of the Spirit of life.* The working of the Holy Spirit in the life of a believer is regular (like a *law*) but not mechanical (for it is *life*).

8:3 *in the likeness of sinful flesh.* The word "likeness" is crucial, for it indicates that Jesus was a true man but not a sinful man. *flesh* = body.

8:4-8 The contrast here is between a life dominated by the flesh (= sinful nature within) and one controlled by the Holy Spirit.

6 aGal. 6:8
bRom. 6:21;
8:13

7 aJames
4:4

8 aRom.
7:5

★ 9 aRom.
7:5 bJohn
14:23; Rom.
8:11; 1 Cor.
3:16; 6:19;
2 Cor. 6:16;
·2 Tim. 1:14
cJohn 14:17;
Gal. 4:6; Phil.
1:19; 1 John
4:13
10 aJohn
·17:23; Gal.
2:20; Eph.
3:17; Col.
1:27
11 aActs
2:24; Rom.
6:4 bJohn
5:21 cRom.
8:1, 2, 39;
16:3

6 aFor the mind set on the flesh is bdeath, but the mind set on the Spirit is life and peace,

7 because the mind set on the flesh is ahostile toward God; for it does not subject itself to the law of God, for it is not even able *to do so*;

8 and those who are ain the flesh cannot please God.

9 However, you are not ain the flesh but in the Spirit, if indeed the Spirit of God bdwells in you. But cif anyone does not have the Spirit of Christ, he does not belong to Him.

10 And aif Christ is in you, though the body is dead because of sin, yet the spirit is alive because of righteousness.

11 But if the Spirit of Him who araised Jesus from the dead dwells in you, bHe who raised cChrist Jesus from the dead will also give life to your mortal bodies through His Spirit who indwells you.

2 Exalted living, 8:12–17

★13 aRom.
8:6 bCol. 3:5
14 aGal.
5:18 bHos.
1:10; [Rom.
9:26]; Matt.
5:9; John
1:12; Rom.
8:16, 19; 9:8
2 Cor. 6:18;
Gal. 3:26;
1 John 3:1;
Rev. 21:7
★15 a2 Tim.
1:7; Heb.
2:15 bRom.
8:23; Gal.
4:5f. cMark
14:36; Gal.
4:6

12 So then, brethren, we are under obligation, not to the flesh, to live according to the flesh—

13 for aif you are living according to the flesh, you must die; but if by the Spirit you are bputting to death the deeds of the body, you will live.

14 For all who are abeing led by the Spirit of God, these are bsons of God.

15 For you ahave not received a spirit of slavery leading to fear again, but you bhave received a spirit of adoption as sons by which we cry out, "cAbba! Father!"

16 The Spirit Himself abears witness with our spirit that we are bchildren of God,

17 and if children, aheirs also, heirs of God and fellow heirs with Christ, bif indeed we suffer with *Him* in order that we may also be glorified with *Him*.

3 Expectant living, 8:18–30

18 For I consider that the sufferings of this present time aare not worthy to be compared with the bglory that is to be revealed to us.

19 For the aanxious longing of the creation waits eagerly for bthe revealing of the csons of God.

20 For the creation awas subjected to bfutility, not of its own will, but cbecause of Him who subjected it, in hope

21 that athe creation itself also will be set free from its slavery to corruption into the freedom of the glory of the children of God.

22 For we know that the whole creation agroans and suffers the pains of childbirth together until now.

23 aAnd not only this, but also we ourselves, having bthe first fruits of the Spirit, even we ourselves cgroan within ourselves, dwaiting eagerly for *our* adoption as sons, ethe redemption of our body.

24 For ain hope we have been saved, but bhope that is seen is

16 aActs
5:32 bHos.
1:10; [Rom.
9:26]; Matt.
5:9; John
1:12; Rom.
8:14, 19; 9:8
17 aActs
20:32; Gal.
3:29; 4:7;
Eph. 3:6; Titus 3:7; Heb.
1:14; Rev.
21:7 b2 Cor.
1:5, 7; Phil.
3:10; Col.
1:24
★18-25
18 a2 Cor.
4:17; 1 Pet.
4:13 bCol.
3:4; Titus
2:13
19 aPhil.
1:20 bRom.
8:18; 1 Cor.
1:7f.; Col.
3:4; 1 Pet.
1:7, 13
cHos. 1:10;
Matt. 5:9;
John 1:12;
2 Cor. 6:18;
Gal. 3:26
★20 aGen.
3:17-19 bPs.
39:5f.; Eccl.
1:2 cGen.
3:17; 5:29
21 aActs
3:21; 2 Pet.
3:13; Rev.
21:1

22 aJer.
12:4, 11

★23 aRom.
5:3 bRom.
8:16; 2 Cor.
1:22 c2 Cor.
5:2, 4 dRom.
8:15, 19, 25;
eRom. 7:24
★24 aRom.
8:20;
1 Thess. 5:8;
Titus 3:7
bRom. 4:18;
2 Cor. 5:7

8:9 *if indeed* = since. There is no doubt in the statement; those who belong to Christ have the Holy Spirit.

8:13 *putting to death.* I.e., separating from the deeds of the body (see Col. 3:5).

8:15 *adoption.* The act of God which places the believer in His family as an adult son (v. 23; 9:4; Gal. 4:5; Eph. 1:5). At the same time he is born into the family of God as a child who needs to grow and develop. His position is one of full privilege; his practice involves growth in grace. *Abba.* Aramaic for father.

8:18–25 A statement of the Christian hope as it affects the individual (v. 18) and the entire cre-

ation (vv. 19-25). Compare 2 Cor. 4:17.

8:20 *was subjected to futility.* After Adam sinned, God was obliged to subject the creation to futility so that man in his sinful state might retain some measure of dominion over creation. Nature was involved for evil in man's fall; she will be emancipated when man receives the adoption as sons (v. 23).

8:23 The culmination of our position as adopted sons is the resurrection state.

8:24 *in hope.* I.e., in the just-expressed hope (vv. 21-23) of the future redemption of the body.

not hope; for why does one also hope for what he sees?

25 But ᵃif we hope for what we do not see, with perseverance we wait eagerly for it.

26 And in the same way the Spirit also helps our weakness; for ᵃwe do not know how to pray as we should, but ᵇthe Spirit Himself intercedes for *us* with groanings too deep for words;

27 and ᵃHe who searches the hearts knows what ᵇthe mind of the Spirit is, because He ᶜintercedes for the saints according to *the will* of God.

28 And we know that God causes ᵃall things to work together for good to those who love God, to those who are ᵇcalled according to *His* purpose.

29 For whom He ᵃforeknew, He also ᵇpredestined *to become* ᶜconformed to the image of His Son, that He might be the ᵈfirstborn among many brethren;

30 and whom He ᵃpredestined, these He also ᵇcalled; and whom He called, these He also ᶜjustified; and whom He justified, these He also ᵈglorified.

4 Exultant living, 8:31-39

31 ᵃWhat then shall we say to these things? ᵇIf God *is* for us, who *is* against us?

32 He who ᵃdid not spare His own Son, but ᵇdelivered Him up for us all, how will He not also with Him freely give us all things?

33 Who will bring a charge

against ᵃGod's elect? ᵇGod is the one who justifies;

34 who is the one who ᵃcondemns? Christ Jesus is He who ᵇdied, yes, rather who was ᶜraised, who is ᵈat the right hand of God, who also ᵉintercedes for us.

35 Who shall separate us from ᵃthe love of Christ? Shall ᵇtribulation, or distress, or ᶜpersecution, or ᶜfamine, or ᶜnakedness, or ᶜperil, or sword?

36 Just as it is written,

"ᵃFOR THY SAKE WE ARE BEING
     PUT TO DEATH ALL DAY
     LONG;
WE WERE CONSIDERED AS
     SHEEP TO BE SLAUGHTERED."

37 But in all these things we overwhelmingly ᵃconquer through ᵇHim who loved us.

38 For I am convinced that neither ᵃdeath, nor life, nor ᵇangels, nor principalities, nor ᶜthings present, nor things to come, nor powers,

39 nor height, nor depth, nor any other created thing, shall be able to separate us from ᵃthe love of God, which is ᵇin Christ Jesus our Lord.

V RIGHTEOUSNESS VINDICATED; DISPENSATION, SOVEREIGNTY, 9:1-11:36

A Israel's Past; Election, 9:1-29
1 Paul's sorrow, 9:1-5

9 ᵃI am telling the truth in Christ, I am not lying, my

Marginal references (left column):

25 ᵃ1 Thess. 1:3

★26 ᵃMatt. 20:22; 2 Cor. 12:8 ᵇJohn 14:16; Rom. 8:15f.

27 ᵃPs. 139:1f.; Luke 16:15; Acts 1:24; Rev. 2:23 ᵇRom. 8:6 ᶜRom. 8:34

★28 ᵃRom. 8:32 ᵇRom. 8:30; 9:24; 11:29; 1 Cor. 1:9; Gal. 1:6

★29 ᵃRom. 11:2; 1 Cor. 8:3; 2 Tim. 1:9 ᵇRom. 9:23; 1 Cor. 2:7; ᶜ1 Cor. 15:49; Phil. 3:21; Col. 3:10; 1 John 3:2 ᵈCol. 1:18

★30 ᵃRom. 9:23; 11:29; 1 Cor. 2:7; Eph. 1:5, 11 ᵇRom. 8:28; 9:24; 1 Cor. 1:9; Gal. 1:6 ᶜ1 Cor. 6:11 ᵈJohn 17:22; Rom. 8:21

31 ᵃRom. 3:5; 4:1 ᵇPs. 118:6; Matt. 1:23

32 ᵃJohn 3:16; Rom. 5:8 ᵇRom. 4:25

★33-34

33 ᵃLuke 18:7 ᵇIs. 50:8f.

Marginal references (right column):

34 ᵃRom. 8:1 ᵇRom. 5:6f. ᶜActs 2:24 ᵈMark 16:19 ᵉRom. 8:27; Heb. 7:25; 9:24; 1 John 2:1

35 ᵃRom. 8:37f. ᵇRom. 2:9; 2 Cor. 4:8 ᶜ1 Cor. 4:11; 2 Cor. 11:26f.

★36 ᵃPs. 44:22; Acts 20:24; 1 Cor. 4:9; 15:30f.; 2 Cor. 1:9; 4:10f.; 6:9; 11:23

37 ᵃJohn 16:33; 1 Cor. 15:57 ᵇGal. 2:20; Eph. 5:2; Rev. 1:5

38 ᵃ1 Cor. 3:22 ᵇ1 Cor. 15:24; Eph. 1:21; 1 Pet. 3:22 ᶜ1 Cor. 3:22

★39 ᵃRom. 5:8 ᵇRom. 8:1

★ 1 ᵃRom. 1:9; 2 Cor. 11:10; Gal. 1:20; 1 Tim. 2:7

8:26 The Holy Spirit helps our *weakness* (our inability to pray intelligently about situations) by praying with unutterable *groanings* (= sighs). Such intercession is in accord with God's will (v. 27).

8:28 A promise only for *those who love God.*

8:29 *predestined.* See note on Eph. 1:5. The destiny of the elect is to be conformed to Christ.

8:30 *called.* See note on 1:6. *justified.* See note on 3:24. *glorified.* The tense of this word shows that our future glorification is so certain that it can be said to be accomplished. Those who were foreknown will all be glorified without loss of a single one.

8:33-34 The Father has declared us righteous;

therefore, He will not condemn us. Christ died, rose, and lives for us; therefore neither will He condemn us.

8:36 Difficulties are not necessarily obstacles for God's children, but His appointed way.

8:39 *nor any other created thing.* Nothing in the universe is outside God's control; therefore, nothing can separate us from His eternal love.

9:1 Here begins Paul's discussion of perplexing questions about the Jewish people. Why were they refusing the gospel? How does this new scheme of righteousness apart from the law relate to the privileged position of the Jews? Have the promises contained in their covenants failed?

conscience bearing me witness in
the Holy Spirit,
2 that I have great sorrow
and unceasing grief in my heart.
3 For [a]I could wish that I
myself were [b]accursed, *separated*
from Christ for the sake of my
brethren, my kinsmen [c]according
to the flesh,
4 who are [a]Israelites, to
whom belongs [b]the adoption as
sons and [c]the glory and [d]the covenants and [e]the giving of the Law
and [f]the *temple* service and [g]the
promises,
5 whose are [a]the fathers, and
[b]from whom is the Christ according to the flesh, [c]who is over all,
[d]God [e]blessed forever. Amen.

3 [a]Ex. 32:32 [b]1 Cor. 12:3; 16:22; Gal. 1:8f. [c]Rom. 1:3; 11:14; Eph. 6:5
★ 4-5
4 [a]Rom. 9:6 [b]Ex. 4:22; Rom. 8:15 [c]Ex. 40:34; 1 Kin. 8:11; Ezek. 1:28; Heb. 9:5 [d]Gen. 17:2; Deut. 29:14; Luke 1:72; Acts 3:25; Eph. 2:12 [e]Deut. 4:13f.; Ps. 147:19 [f]Deut. 7:6; 14:1f.; Heb. 9:1, 6 [g]Acts 2:39; 13:32; Eph. 2:12
★ 5 [a]Acts 3:13; Rom. 11:28 [b]Matt. 1:1-16; Rom. 1:3 [c]Col. 1:16-19 [d]John 1:1; Col. 2:9 [e]Rom. 1:25

2 *God's sovereignty,* 9:6–29

6 But *it is* not as though [a]the
word of God has failed. [b]For they
are not all Israel who are *descended* from Israel;
7 neither are they all children [a]because they are Abraham's descendants, but:
"[b]THROUGH ISAAC YOUR DESCENDANTS
WILL BE NAMED."
8 That is, it is not the children of the flesh who are [a]chil-
dren of God, but the [b]children of
the promise are regarded as descendants.
9 For this is a word of promise: "[a]AT THIS TIME I WILL COME, AND
SARAH SHALL HAVE A SON."
10 [a]And not only this, but
there was [b]Rebekah also, when
she had conceived *twins* by one
man, our father Isaac;

6 [a]Num. 23:19 [b]John 1:47; Rom. 2:28f.; Gal. 6:16
7 [a]John 8:33, 39; Gal. 4:23 [b]Gen. 21:12; Heb. 11:18
8 [a]Rom. 8:14 [b]Rom. 4:13, 16; Gal. 3:29; 4:28; Heb. 11:11
★ 9 [a]Gen. 18:10
10 [a]Rom. 5:3 [b]Gen. 25:21

11 for though *the twins* were
not yet born, and had not done
anything good or bad, in order
that [a]God's purpose according to
His choice might stand, not because of works, but because of
Him who calls,
12 it was said to her, "[a]THE
OLDER WILL SERVE THE YOUNGER."
13 Just as it is written, "[a]JACOB
I LOVED, BUT ESAU I HATED."
14 [a]What shall we say then?
[b]There is no injustice with God, is
there? [c]May it never be!
15 For He says to Moses, "[a]I
WILL HAVE MERCY ON WHOM I HAVE
MERCY, AND I WILL HAVE COMPASSION
ON WHOM I HAVE COMPASSION."
16 So then it *does* not *depend*
on the man who wills or the man
who [a]runs, but on [b]God who has
mercy.
17 For the Scripture says to
Pharaoh, "[a]FOR THIS VERY PURPOSE I
RAISED YOU UP, TO DEMONSTRATE MY
POWER IN YOU, AND THAT MY NAME
MIGHT BE PROCLAIMED THROUGHOUT
THE WHOLE EARTH."
18 So then He has mercy on
whom He desires, and He [a]hard-
ens whom He desires.
19 [a]You will say to me then,
"[b]Why does He still find fault?
For [c]who resists His will?"
20 On the contrary, who are
you, [a]O man, who [b]answers back
to God? [c]The thing molded will
not say to the molder, "Why did
you make me like this," will it?
21 Or does not the potter
have a right over the clay, to
make from the same lump one

11 [a]Rom. 4:17; 8:28
★12 [a]Gen. 25:23
★13 [a]Mal. 1:2f.
14 [a]Rom. 3:5 [b]2 Chr. 19:7; Rom. 2:11 [c]Luke 20:16
★15 [a]Ex. 33:19
16 [a]Gal. 2:2 [b]Eph. 2:8
★17 [a]Ex. 9:16
18 [a]Ex. 4:21; 7:3; 9:12; 10:20, 27; 11:10; 14:4, 17; Deut. 2:30; Josh. 11:20; John 12:40; Rom. 11:7, 25
★19 [a]Rom. 11:19; 1 Cor. 15:35; James 2:18 [b]Rom. 3:7 [c]2 Chr. 20:6; Job 9:12; Dan. 4:35
20 [a]Rom. 2:1 [b]Job 33:13 [c]Is. 29:16; 45:9; 64:8; Jer. 18:6; Rom. 9:22f.; 2 Tim. 2:20

9:4-5 The privileges of the Jewish people included adoption as a nation (Ex. 4:22), glory (Ex. 16:10), covenants (Eph. 2:12), the Mosaic Law, service in the tabernacle and temple, thousands of promises, the patriarchs, and Christ.

9:5 *who is over all . . . Amen.* Some regard these words as comprising a grammatically separate sentence, a doxology. Although early manuscripts were not punctuated, the punctuation in the present text seems correct. Paul's anguish over the Jews' rejection of Christ drives him to avow his own recognition of Him as God. A doxology does not fit the train of thought here.

9:9 See Gen. 18:10.

9:12 See Gen. 25:23.

9:13 See Mal. 1:2–3.

9:15 See Ex. 33:19. If God were not free to show His mercy, no one would be blessed, for no one deserves His grace, and it cannot be earned.

9:19 An opponent might say that Paul's conclusion in v. 18 leads to fatalism. Paul, however, does not give an analytical answer but rebukes the questioner for such a preposterous conclusion. If a potter can do what he wishes with his vessels, certainly God can with His.

vessel for honorable use, and another for common use?

22 **22** What if God, although willing to demonstrate His wrath and to make His power known, endured with much *a*patience vessels of wrath *b*prepared for destruction?

23 **23** And *He did so* in order that He might make known *a*the riches of His glory upon *b*vessels of mercy, which He *c*prepared beforehand for glory,

24 **24** *even* us, whom He also *a*called, *b*not from among Jews only, but also from among Gentiles.

★25 **25** As He says also in Hosea,

"*a*I WILL CALL THOSE WHO WERE NOT MY PEOPLE, 'MY PEOPLE,'
AND HER WHO WAS NOT BELOVED, 'BELOVED.' "

26 **26** "*a*AND IT SHALL BE THAT IN THE PLACE WHERE IT WAS SAID TO THEM, 'YOU ARE NOT MY PEOPLE,'
THERE THEY SHALL BE CALLED SONS OF *b*THE LIVING GOD."

★27 **27** And Isaiah cries out concerning Israel, "*a*THOUGH THE NUMBER OF THE SONS OF ISRAEL BE *b*AS THE SAND OF THE SEA, IT IS *c*THE REMNANT THAT WILL BE SAVED;

28 **28** *a*FOR THE LORD WILL EXECUTE HIS WORD UPON THE EARTH, THOROUGHLY AND QUICKLY."

★29 **29** And just as Isaiah foretold,

"*a*EXCEPT *b*THE LORD OF SABAOTH HAD LEFT TO US A POSTERITY,
*c*WE WOULD HAVE BECOME AS SODOM, AND WOULD HAVE RESEMBLED GOMORRAH."

B Israel's Present; Rejection, 9:30-10:21

30 **30** *a*What shall we say then? That Gentiles, who did not pursue righteousness, attained righteousness, even *b*the righteousness which is by faith;

31 **31** but Israel, *a*pursuing a law of righteousness, did not *b*arrive at *that* law.

32 **32** Why? Because *they did* not *pursue it* by faith, but as though *it were* by works. They stumbled over *a*the stumbling stone,

33 **33** just as it is written,

"*a*BEHOLD, I LAY IN ZION A STONE OF STUMBLING AND A ROCK OF OFFENSE,
*b*AND HE WHO BELIEVES IN HIM *c*WILL NOT BE DISAPPOINTED."

10 Brethren, my heart's desire and my prayer to God for them is for *their* salvation.

2 For I bear them witness that they have *a*a zeal for God, but not in accordance with knowledge.

3 For not knowing about *a*God's righteousness, and *b*seeking to establish their own, they did not subject themselves to the righteousness of God.

4 For *a*Christ is the end of the law for righteousness to *b*everyone who believes.

5 For Moses writes that the man who practices the righteousness which is based on law *a*shall live by that righteousness.

6 But *a*the righteousness based on faith speaks thus, "*b*Do NOT SAY IN YOUR HEART, 'WHO WILL

Marginal references (left column):

22 *a*Rom. 2:4; *b*Prov. 16:4; 1 Pet. 2:8

23 *a*Rom. 2:4; Eph. 3:16; *b*Acts 9:15; *c*Rom. 8:29f.

24 *a*Rom. 8:28; *b*Rom. 3:29

★25 *a*Hos. 2:23; 1 Pet. 2:10

26 *a*Hos. 1:10; *b*Matt. 16:16

★27 *a*Is. 10:22; *b*Gen. 22:17; Hos. 1:10; *c*Rom. 11:5

28 *a*Is. 10:23

★29 *a*Is. 1:9; *b*James 5:4; *c*Deut. 29:23; Is. 13:19; Jer. 49:18; 50:40; Amos 4:11

Marginal references (right column):

30 *a*Rom. 9:14; *b*Rom. 1:17; 3:21f.; 10:6; Gal. 2:16; 3:24; Phil. 3:9; Heb. 11:7

31 *a*Is. 51:1; Rom. 9:30; 10:2f.; 20; 11:7; *b*Gal. 5:4

32 *a*Is. 8:14; 1 Pet. 2:6, 8

★33 *a*Is. 28:16; *b*Rom. 10:11; *c*Rom. 5:5

★ 1-21

2 *a*Acts 21:20

3 *a*Rom. 1:17; *b*Is. 51:1; Rom. 8:30; 10:2f.; 20; 11:7

★ 4 *a*Rom. 7:1-4; Gal. 3:24; 4:5; *b*Rom. 3:22

5 *a*Lev. 18:5; Neh. 9:29; Ezek. 20:11, 13, 21; Rom. 7:10

★ 6-8

6 *a*Rom. 9:30; *b*Deut. 30:12f.

9:25 See Hos. 1:9-10.
9:27 See Isa. 10:22-23.
9:29 See Isa. 1:9.
9:33 See Isa. 28:16. The stumbling-stone was Christ (1 Pet. 2:8).
10:1-21 Paul expresses his deep longing for the salvation of Israel (v. 1), who tried to substitute law-righteousness for faith-righteousness (vv. 2-4), though the latter was universally available (vv. 5-13). God gave the Jews every opportunity to receive the gospel but they had

not responded in faith (vv. 14-21).
10:4 Christ is the termination of the law. It could not provide righteousness based on merit, but Christ provides righteousness based on God's grace in response to faith (3:20; Acts 13:39).
10:6-8 Quoting Deut. 30:12-14, which emphasizes the initiative of divine grace and humble reception of God's word, Paul applies this truth to the gospel, which is *near*, ready for a man to take on his lips and into his heart (Rom. 10:9).

ASCEND INTO HEAVEN?' (that is, to bring Christ down),

7 or 'WHO WILL DESCEND INTO THE [a]ABYSS?' (that is, to [b]bring Christ up from the dead)."

8 But what does it say? "[a]THE WORD IS NEAR YOU, IN YOUR MOUTH AND IN YOUR HEART"—that is, the word of faith which we are preaching,

9 that [a]if you confess with your mouth Jesus as Lord, and [b]believe in your heart that [c]God raised Him from the dead, you shall be saved;

10 for with the heart man believes, resulting in righteousness, and with the mouth he confesses, resulting in salvation.

11 For the Scripture says, "[a]WHOEVER BELIEVES IN HIM WILL NOT BE DISAPPOINTED."

12 For [a]there is no distinction between Jew and Greek; for the same Lord is [b]Lord of [c]all, abounding in riches for all who call upon Him;

13 for "[a]WHOEVER WILL CALL UPON THE NAME OF THE LORD WILL BE SAVED."

14 How then shall they call upon Him in whom they have not believed? And how shall they believe in Him [a]whom they have not heard? And how shall they hear without [b]a preacher?

15 And how shall they preach unless they are sent? Just as it is written, "[a]How BEAUTIFUL ARE THE FEET OF THOSE WHO [b]BRING GLAD TIDINGS OF GOOD THINGS!"

16 However, they [a]did not all heed the glad tidings; for Isaiah says, "[b]LORD, WHO HAS BELIEVED OUR REPORT?"

17 So faith comes from [a]hearing, and hearing by [b]the word of Christ.

18 But I say, surely they have never heard, have they? Indeed they have;

"[a]THEIR VOICE HAS GONE OUT
   INTO ALL THE EARTH,
AND THEIR WORDS TO THE
   ENDS OF THE WORLD."

19 But I say, surely Israel did not know, did they? At the first Moses says,

"[a]I WILL [b]MAKE YOU JEALOUS
   BY THAT WHICH IS NOT A
   NATION,
BY A NATION WITHOUT UN-
   DERSTANDING WILL I ANGER
   YOU."

20 And Isaiah is very bold and says,

"[a]I WAS FOUND BY THOSE WHO
   SOUGHT ME NOT,
I BECAME MANIFEST TO THOSE
   WHO DID NOT ASK FOR
   ME."

21 But as for Israel He says, "[a]ALL THE DAY LONG I HAVE STRETCHED OUT MY HANDS TO A DISOBEDIENT AND OBSTINATE PEOPLE."

C   Israel's Future; Salvation, 11:1-36

1   The extent of Israel's rejection (partial), 11:1-10

11 I say then, God has not [a]rejected His people, has He? [b]May it never be! For [c]I too

Marginal references

7 [a]Luke 8:31 [b]Heb. 13:20

8 [a]Deut. 30:14

★ 9 [a]Matt. 10:32; Luke 12:8; Rom. 14:9; 1 Cor. 12:3; Phil. 2:11 [b]Acts 16:31; Rom. 4:24 [c]Acts 2:24

★11 [a]Is. 28:16; Rom. 9:33

12 [a]Rom. 3:22, 29 [b]Acts 10:36 [c]Rom. 3:29

★13 [a]Joel 2:32; Acts 2:21

★14-15
14 [a]Eph. 2:17; 4:21 [b]Acts 8:31; Titus 1:3

15 [a]Is. 52:7 [b]Rom. 1:15; 15:20

★16 [a]Rom. 3:3 [b]Is. 53:1; John 12:38

★17 [a]Gal. 3:2, 5 [b]Col. 3:16

★18 [a]Ps. 19:4; Rom. 1:8; Col. 1:6, 23; 1 Thess. 1:8

★19 [a]Deut. 32:21 [b]Rom. 11:11, 14

★20 [a]Is. 65:1; Rom. 9:30

21 [a]Is. 65:2

★ 1-36
1 [a]1 Sam. 12:22; Jer. 31:37; 33:24-26 [b]Luke 20:16 [c]2 Cor. 11:22; Phil. 3:5

Notes

10:9 *Jesus as Lord.* Lord, or Yahweh, is the O.T. name for God; thus he who confesses that Jesus is Lord affirms His deity.
10:11 See Isa. 28:16; 49:23.
10:13 See Joel 2:32.
10:14-15 Though God's election of His people is of His own free choice and not based on human merit (9:11, 23), the elect are not saved without believing the message which is preached by those who are sent (Isa. 52:7).
10:16 See Isa. 53:1.
10:17 *by the word of Christ.* The spoken word rather than the written Word (Bible). Our oral

testimony (our preaching of Christ) is, of course, based on the Bible.
10:18 See Ps. 19:4.
10:19 See Deut. 32:21.
10:20 See Isa. 65:1-2.
11:1-36 In this chapter Paul assures us that God has not forgotten His people, the Jews, and His promises to them. After the full number of Gentiles have been incorporated into the Church, all Jews will turn to the Lord, not a mere handful as now. Paul does not assert that the O.T. promises to Israel have been transferred to the largely Gentile Church.

am an Israelite, a descendant of Abraham, of the tribe of Benjamin.

2 God [a]has not rejected His people whom He [b]foreknew. [c]Or do you not know what the Scripture says in *the passage about* Elijah, how he pleads with God against Israel?

3 "Lord, [a]THEY HAVE KILLED THY PROPHETS, THEY HAVE TORN DOWN THINE ALTARS, AND I ALONE AM LEFT, AND THEY ARE SEEKING MY LIFE."

4 But what is the divine response to him? "[a]I HAVE KEPT for Myself SEVEN THOUSAND MEN WHO HAVE NOT BOWED THE KNEE TO BAAL."

5 In the same way then, there has also come to be at the present time [a]a remnant according to *God's* gracious choice.

6 But [a]if it is by grace, it is no longer on the basis of works, otherwise grace is no longer grace.

7 What then? That which [a]Israel is seeking for, it has not obtained, but those who were chosen obtained it, and the rest were [b]hardened;

8 just as it is written,

"[a]GOD GAVE THEM A SPIRIT OF
    STUPOR,
EYES TO SEE NOT AND EARS TO
    HEAR NOT,
DOWN TO THIS VERY DAY."

9 And David says,

"[a]LET THEIR TABLE BECOME A
    SNARE AND A TRAP,
AND A STUMBLING BLOCK AND
    A RETRIBUTION TO THEM.

10 "[a]LET THEIR EYES BE DARKENED
    TO SEE NOT,
AND BEND THEIR BACKS FOR-
    EVER."

2 The purpose of Israel's rejection, 11:11-24

11 [a]I say then, they did not stumble so as to fall, did they? [b]May it never be! But by their transgression [c]salvation *has come* to the Gentiles, to [d]make them jealous.

12 Now if their transgression be riches for the world and their failure be riches for the Gentiles, how much more will their [a]fulfillment be!

13 But I am speaking to you who are Gentiles. Inasmuch then as [a]I am an apostle of Gentiles, I magnify my ministry,

14 if somehow I might [a]move to jealousy [b]my fellow countrymen and [c]save some of them.

15 For if their rejection be the [a]reconciliation of the world, what will *their* acceptance be but [b]life from the dead?

16 And if the [a]first piece *of dough* be holy, the lump is also; and if the root be holy, the branches are too.

17 But if some of the [a]branches were broken off, and [b]you, being a wild olive, were grafted in among them and became partaker with them of the rich root of the olive tree,

18 do not be arrogant toward the branches; but if you are arrogant, *remember that* [a]it is not you who supports the root, but the root *supports* you.

19 [a]You will say then, "Branches were broken off so that I might be grafted in."

20 Quite right, they were broken off for their unbelief, but you

---

Marginal references

2 [a]Ps. 94:14 [b]Rom. 8:29 [c]Rom. 6:16
★ 3 [a]1 Kin. 19:10
4 [a]1 Kin. 19:18
5 [a]2 Kin. 19:4; Rom. 9:27
6 [a]Rom. 4:4
★ 7 [a]Rom. 9:31 [b]Mark 6:52; Rom. 9:18; 11:25; 2 Cor. 3:14
8 [a]Deut. 29:4; Is. 29:10, Matt. 13:13f.
★ 9 [a]Ps. 69:22f.
10 [a]Ps. 69:23

11 [a]Rom. 11:1 [b]Luke 20:16 [c]Acts 28:28 [d]Rom. 11:14
12 [a]Rom. 11:25
13 [a]Acts 9:15
14 [a]Rom. 11:11 [b]Gen. 29:14; 2 Sam. 19:12f.; Rom. 9:3 [c]1 Cor. 1:21; 7:16; 9:22; 1 Tim. 1:15; 2:4; 2 Tim. 1:9; Titus 3:5
★ 15 [a]Rom. 5:11 [b]Luke 15:24, 32
16 [a]Num. 15:18ff.; Neh. 10:37; Ezek. 44:30
★ 17-24
17 [a]Jer. 11:16; John 15:2 [b]Eph. 2:11ff.
18 [a]John 4:22
19 [a]Rom. 9:19
20 [a]Rom. 5:2; 1 Cor. 10:12; 2 Cor. 1:24 [b]Rom. 12:16; 1 Tim. 6:17; 1 Pet. 1:17

11:3 See 1 Kings 19:10-18.
11:7 *those who were chosen.* I.e., the elect minority of Jews who are being saved today.
11:9 See Ps. 69:22-23.
11:15 When Israel rejected Jesus Christ, the nation lost her favored position before God, and the gospel was then preached also to Gentiles. Hopefully the Jews would become jealous and be saved (v. 11). But the casting off is only temporary. When the Lord returns, the Jewish

people will be regathered, judged, restored to favor, and redeemed (v. 26).
11:17-24 The olive tree is the place of privilege which was first occupied by the natural branches (the Jews). The wild branches are Gentiles who, because of the unbelief of Israel, now occupy the place of privilege. The root of the tree is the Abrahamic covenant which promised blessing to both Jew and Gentile through Christ.

^astand by your faith. ^bDo not be conceited, but fear;

21 for if God did not spare the natural branches, neither will He spare you.

22 Behold then the kindness and severity of God; to those who fell, severity, but to you, God's ^akindness, ^bif you continue in His kindness; otherwise you also ^cwill be cut off.

23 And they also, ^aif they do not continue in their unbelief, will be grafted in; for God is able to graft them in again.

24 For if you were cut off from what is by nature a wild olive tree, and were grafted contrary to nature into a cultivated olive tree, how much more shall these who are the natural *branches* be grafted into their own olive tree?

3 The duration of Israel's rejection (temporary), 11:25-32

25 For ^aI do not want you, brethren, to be uninformed of this ^bmystery, lest you be ^cwise in your own estimation, that a partial ^dhardening has happened to Israel until the ^efulness of the Gentiles has come in;

26 and thus all Israel will be saved; just as it is written,

    "^aTHE DELIVERER WILL COME
      FROM ZION,
    HE WILL REMOVE UNGODLINESS
      FROM JACOB."

27 "^aAND THIS IS MY COVENANT
    WITH THEM,
    WHEN I TAKE AWAY THEIR
      SINS."

28 From the standpoint of the gospel they are ^aenemies for your sake, but from the standpoint of

God's choice they are beloved for ^bthe sake of the fathers;

29 for the gifts and the ^acalling of God ^bare irrevocable.

30 For just as you once were disobedient to God, but now have been shown mercy because of their disobedience,

31 so these also now have been disobedient, in order that because of the mercy shown to you they also may now be shown mercy.

32 For ^aGod has shut up all in disobedience that He might show mercy to all.

4 Discourse on God's wisdom, 11:33-36

33 Oh, the depth of ^athe riches both of the ^bwisdom and knowledge of God! ^cHow unsearchable are His judgments and unfathomable His ways!

34 For ^aWHO HAS KNOWN THE MIND OF THE LORD, OR WHO BECAME HIS COUNSELOR?

35 Or ^aWHO HAS FIRST GIVEN TO HIM THAT IT MIGHT BE PAID BACK TO HIM AGAIN?

36 For ^afrom Him and through Him and to Him are all things. ^bTo Him be the glory forever. Amen.

VI RIGHTEOUSNESS PRACTICED; APPLICATION, SERVICE, 12:1-15:13

A In Relation to Ourselves, 12:1-2

12 ^aI urge you therefore, brethren, by the mercies of God, to ^bpresent your bodies a living and holy sacrifice, acceptable to God, *which is* your spiritual service of worship.

2 And do not ^abe conformed

Marginal references

22 ^aRom. 2:4 ^b1 Cor. 15:2; Heb. 3:6, 14 ^cJohn 15:2

23 ^a2 Cor. 3:16

★25 ^aRom. 1:13 ^bMatt. 13:11; Rom. 16:25; 1 Cor. 2:7-10; Eph. 3:3-5, 9 ^cRom. 12:16 ^dRom. 11:7 ^eLuke 21:24; John 10:16; Rom. 11:12
★26 ^aIs. 59:20, 21

27 ^aIs. 27:9; Heb. 8:10, 12

28 ^aRom. 5:10 ^bDeut. 7:8; 10:15; Rom. 9:5

29 ^aRom. 8:28; 1 Cor. 1:26; Eph. 1:18; 4:1, 4; Phil. 3:14; 2 Thess. 1:11; 2 Tim. 1:9; Heb. 3:1; 2 Pet. 1:10 ^bHeb. 7:21

★32 ^aRom. 3:9; Gal. 3:22f.

33 ^aRom. 2:4; Eph. 3:8 ^bEph. 3:10; Col. 2:3 ^cJob 5:9; 11:7; 15:8
34 ^aIs. 40:13f; 1 Cor. 2:16
35 ^aJob 35:7; 41:11
★36 ^a1 Cor. 8:6; 11:12; Col. 1:16; Heb. 2:10 ^bRom. 16:27; Eph. 3:21; Phil. 4:20; 1 Tim. 1:17; 2 Tim. 4:18; 1 Pet. 4:11; 5:11; 2 Pet. 3:18; Jude 25; Rev. 1:6; 5:13; 7:12

★ 1 ^a1 Cor. 1:10; 2 Cor. 10:2; Eph. 4:1; 1 Pet. 2:11 ^bRom. 6:13, 16, 19
★ 2 ^a1 Pet. 1:14 ^bMatt. 13:22 ^cEph. 4:23; Titus 3:5 ^dEph. 5:10, 17

11:25 *the fulness of the Gentiles.* I.e., the full number of Gentiles who will be saved (Acts 15:14). After this, God will turn again to the Jews and will save "all Israel" at the Lord's return (v. 26).
11:26 See Isa. 59:20-21.
11:32 *all . . . all.* I.e., Jews and Gentiles alike.
11:36 God is the source *(from Him)*, sustainer

(through Him), and goal *(to Him)* of all things.
12:1 *by the mercies of God*, which have been described in the preceding chapters.
12:2 *do not be conformed.* I.e., do not live according to the style or manner of this present age, but live as if the new age had already arrived. The only other occurrence of this Greek word in the N.T. is in 1 Pet. 1:14.

to ^bthis world, but be transformed by the ^crenewing of your mind, that you may ^dprove what the will of God is, that which is good and acceptable and perfect.

B   In Relation to the Church, 12:3–8

3 For through ^athe grace given to me I say to every man among you ^bnot to think more highly of himself than he ought to think; but to think so as to have sound judgment, as God has allotted to ^ceach a measure of faith.

4 For ^ajust as we have many members in one body and all the members do not have the same function,

5 so we, ^awho are many, are ^bone body in Christ, and individually members one of another.

6 And since we have gifts that ^adiffer according to the grace given to us, *let each exercise them accordingly:* if ^bprophecy, according to the proportion of his faith;

7 if ^aservice, in his serving; or he who ^bteaches, in his teaching;

8 or he who ^aexhorts, in his exhortation; he who gives, with ^bliberality; ^che who leads, with diligence; he who shows mercy, with ^dcheerfulness.

C   In Relation to Society, 12:9–21

9 Let ^alove be without hypocrisy. ^bAbhor what is evil; cling to what is good.

10 Be ^adevoted to one another in brotherly love; give preference to one another ^bin honor;

11 not lagging behind in diligence, ^afervent in spirit, ^bserving the Lord;

12 ^arejoicing in hope, ^bpersevering in tribulation, ^cdevoted to prayer,

13 ^acontributing to the needs of the saints, ^bpracticing hospitality.

14 ^aBless those who persecute you; bless and curse not.

15 ^aRejoice with those who rejoice, and weep with those who weep.

16 ^aBe of the same mind toward one another; do not be haughty in mind, ^bbut associate with the lowly. ^cDo not be wise in your own estimation.

17 ^aNever pay back evil for evil to anyone. ^bRespect what is right in the sight of all men.

18 If possible, ^aso far as it depends on you, ^bbe at peace with all men.

19 ^aNever take your own revenge, beloved, but leave room for the wrath *of God,* for it is written, "^bVengeance is Mine, I will repay," says the Lord.

20 "^aBut if your enemy is hungry, feed him, and if he is thirsty, give him a drink; for ^bin so doing you will heap burning coals upon his head."

21 Do not be overcome by evil, but overcome evil with good.

D   In Relation to Government, 13:1–14

13 Let every ^aperson be in ^bsubjection to the governing authorities. For ^cthere is no authority except from God, and those which exist are established by God.

12:3 In introducing the subject of the use of spiritual gifts, Paul warns against high-mindedness and exhorts sober-mindedness, based on the *measure of faith* to work for God which has been given each one.

12:4 *one body.* For this concept see the note on 1 Cor. 12:12–31.

12:6 *gifts.* On spiritual gifts see note on 1 Cor. 1:7. *according to the proportion of his faith;*

i.e., the revelations that come through the prophet must be in agreement with the body of truth already revealed.

12:11 *not lagging behind in diligence* = Do not let your zeal slacken. *fervent in* = boiling with.

12:19 See Deut. 32:35.

13:1 *be in subjection.* From the same Greek verb used by Paul in Tit. 3:1 and by Peter in 1

★ 3 ^aRom. 1:5; 15:15; 1 Cor. 3:10; 15:10; Gal. 2:9; Eph. 3:7f. ^bRom. 11:20; 12:16 ^c1 Cor. 7:17; 2 Cor. 10:13; Eph. 4:7; 1 Pet. 4:11
★ 4 ^a1 Cor. 12:12-14; Eph. 4:4, 16
5 ^a1 Cor. 10:17, 33 ^b1 Cor. 12:20, 27; Eph. 4:12, 25
★ 6 ^aRom. 12:3; 1 Cor. 7:7; 12:4; 1 Pet. 4:10f. ^bActs 13:1; 1 Cor. 12:10
7 ^aActs 6:1; 1 Cor. 12:5, 28 ^bActs 13:1; 1 Cor. 12:28; 14:26
8 ^aActs 4:36; 11:23; 13:15 ^b2 Cor. 8:2; 9:11, 13 ^c1 Cor. 12:28; 1 Tim. 5:17 ^d2 Cor. 9:7
9 ^a2 Cor. 6:6; 1 Tim. 1:5 ^b1 Thess. 5:21f.
10 ^aJohn 13:34; 1 Thess. 4:9; Heb. 13:1; 2 Pet. 1:7 ^bRom. 13:7; Phil. 2:3; 1 Pet. 2:17

★11 ^aActs 18:25 ^bActs 20:19
12 ^aRom. 5:2 ^bHeb. 10:32, 36 ^cActs 1:14
13 ^aRom. 15:25; 1 Cor. 16:15; 2 Cor. 9:1; Heb. 6:10 ^bMatt. 25:35; 1 Tim. 3:2
14 ^aMatt. 5:44; Luke 6:28; 1 Cor. 4:12
15 ^aJob 30:25; Heb. 13:3
16 ^aRom. 15:5; 2 Cor. 13:11; Phil. 2:2; 4:2; 1 Pet. 3:8 ^bRom. 11:20; 12:3 ^cProv. 3:7; Rom. 11:25
17 ^aProv. 20:22; 24:29; Rom. 12:19 ^b2 Cor. 8:21
18 ^aRom. 1:15 ^bMark 9:50; Rom. 14:19
★19 ^aProv. 20:22; 24:29; Rom. 12:17 ^bDeut. 32:35; Ps. 94:1; 1 Thess. 4:6; Heb. 10:30
20 ^aProv. 25:21f.; Matt. 5:44; Luke 6:27 ^b2 Kin. 6:22

★ 1 ^aActs 2:41 ^bTitus 3:1; 1 Pet. 2:13f. ^cDan. 2:21; 4:17; John 19:11

2 Therefore he who resists authority has opposed the ordinance of God; and they who have opposed will receive condemnation upon themselves.

3 *a*1 Pet. 2:14

3 For *a*rulers are not a cause of fear for good behavior, but for evil. Do you want to have no fear of authority? Do what is good, and you will have praise from the same;

★ 4 *a*1 Thess. 4:6

4 for it is a minister of God to you for good. But if you do what is evil, be afraid; for it does not bear the sword for nothing; for it is a minister of God, an *a*avenger who brings wrath upon the one who practices evil.

5 *a*Eccl. 8; 1 Pet. 2:13, 19

5 Wherefore it is necessary to be in subjection, not only because of wrath, but also *a*for conscience' sake.

6 For because of this you also pay taxes, for *rulers* are servants of God, devoting themselves to this very thing.

7 *a*Matt. 22:21 *b*Luke 20:22; 23:2 *c*Matt. 17:25

7 *a*Render to all what is due them: *b*tax to whom tax *is due*; *c*custom to whom custom; fear to whom fear; honor to whom honor.

★ 8 *a*Matt. 7:12; 22:39f.; John 13:34; Rom. 13:10; Gal. 5:14; James 2:8

8 Owe nothing to anyone except to love one another; for *a*he who loves his neighbor has fulfilled *the* law.

★ 9 *a*Ex. 20:13ff.; Deut. 5:17ff. *b*Lev. 19:18; Matt. 19:19

9 For this, *"a*YOU SHALL NOT COMMIT ADULTERY, YOU SHALL NOT MURDER, YOU SHALL NOT STEAL, YOU SHALL NOT COVET," and if there is any other commandment, it is

summed up in this saying, *"b*YOU SHALL LOVE YOUR NEIGHBOR AS YOURSELF."

10 *a*Matt. 7:12; 22:39f.; John 13:34; Rom. 13:8; Gal. 5:14; James 2:8

10 Love does no wrong to a neighbor; *a*love therefore is the fulfillment of *the* law.

★11 *a*1 Cor. 7:29f.; 10:11; James 5:8; 1 Pet. 4:7 *b*Mark 13:37; 1 Cor. 15:34

11 And this *do,* knowing the time, that it is *a*already the hour for you to *b*awaken from sleep; for now salvation is nearer to us than when we believed.

12 *a*1 Cor. 7:29f.; 10:11; James 5:8; 1 Pet. 4:7; 2 Pet. 3:9, 11; 1 John 2:18; Rev. 1:3; 22:10 *b*Heb. 10:25; 1 John 2:8; Rev. 1:3; 22:10 *c*Eph. 5:11 *d*2 Cor. 6:7; 10:4

12 *a*The night is almost gone, and *b*the day is at hand. Let us therefore lay aside *c*the deeds of darkness and put on *d*the armor of light.

13 *a*1 Thess. 4:12 *b*Luke 21:34; Gal. 5:21

13 Let us *a*behave properly as in the day, *b*not in carousing and drunkenness, not in sexual promiscuity and sensuality, not in strife and jealousy.

★14 *a*Job 29:14; Gal. 3:27; Eph. 4:24 *b*Gal. 5:16; 1 Pet. 2:11

14 But *d*put on the Lord Jesus Christ, and make no provision for the flesh *b*in regard to *its* lusts.

E In Relation to Other Believers,
14:1–15:13
1 Do not judge one another,
14:1–12

★ 1-12
★ 1 *a*Acts. 28:2; Rom. 11:15; 14:3; 15:7 *b*Rom. 14:2; 15:1

14 Now *a*accept the one who is *b*weak in faith, *but not* for *the purpose of* passing judgment on his opinions.

2 *a*Rom. 14:14 *b*Rom. 14:1; 15:1

2 *a*One man has faith that he may eat all things, but he who is *b*weak eats vegetables *only.*

3 *a*Luke 18:9; Rom. 14:10 *b*Rom. 14:10, 13 *c*Acts 28:2; Rom. 11:15

3 Let not him who eats *a*regard with contempt him who does

Pet. 2:13, where essentially the same view of the individual's proper attitude to the state is set forth. *there is no authority except from God.* This does not say that only certain forms of government are ordained of God. God established and upholds the principle of government even though some governments do not fulfill His desires.

13:4 *it does not bear the sword for nothing.* God has given the state the power of life and death over its subjects in order to maintain order. Therefore, one should hold government in healthy respect.

13:8 Love is a debt one can never fully discharge.

13:9 See Ex. 20:13–17; Lev. 19:18.

13:11 *from sleep.* I.e., out of insensitivity to sin. *salvation.*The future culmination of our salva-

tion at the return of the Lord is nearer every day.

13:14 An illustration of obedience to this command is in Acts 19:19.

14:1-12 Paul here discusses the proper attitude Christians should have toward each other in debatable areas of conduct (things which are not clearly stated to be wrong). He says that we are not to judge one another, in such matters, because God has received both the weaker and stronger believer (vv. 1-3), because we can differ in good conscience (vv. 4-6), and because we shall all be judged by the Lord (vv. 7-12).

14:1 *weak in faith.* I.e., one who does not yet have full knowledge of how to live as a Christian. In this case it is one who eats only *vegetables,* v. 2, and not meat.

not eat, and let not him who does not eat ^bjudge him who eats, for God has ^caccepted him.

4 ^aRom. 9:20; James 4:12

4 ^aWho are you to judge the servant of another? To his own master he stands or falls; and stand he will, for the Lord is able to make him stand.

5 ^aGal. 4:10 ^bLuke 1:1; Rom. 4:21; 14:23

5 ^aOne man regards one day above another, another regards every day *alike*. Let each man be ^bfully convinced in his own mind.

6 ^aMatt. 14:19; 1 Cor. 10:30; 1 Tim. 4:3f.

6 He who observes the day, observes it for the Lord, and he who eats, does so for the Lord, for he ^agives thanks to God; and he who eats not, for the Lord he does not eat, and gives thanks to God.

7 ^aRom. 8:38; 2 Cor. 5:15; Gal. 2:20; Phil. 1:20f.

7 For not one of us ^alives for himself, and not one dies for himself;

8 ^aLuke 20:38; Phil. 1:20; 1 Thess. 5:10; Rev. 14:13

8 for if we live, we live for the Lord, or if we die, we die for the Lord; therefore ^awhether we live or die, we are the Lord's.

9 ^aRev. 1:18; 2:8 ^bMatt. 28:18; John 12:24; Phil. 2:11; 1 Thess. 5:10

9 For to this end ^aChrist died and lived *again*, that He might be ^bLord both of the dead and of the living.

★**10** ^aLuke 18:9; Rom. 14:3 ^bRom. 2:16; 2 Cor. 5:10

10 But you, why do you judge your brother? Or you again, why do you ^aregard your brother with contempt? For ^bwe shall all stand before the judgment seat of God.

11 ^aIs. 45:23 ^bPhil. 2:10f.

11 For it is written,

"^aAs I live, says the Lord,
  ^bevery knee shall bow to
  Me,
And every tongue shall
  give praise to God."

12 ^aMatt. 12:36; 16:27; 1 Pet. 4:5

12 So then ^aeach one of us shall give account of himself to God.

2 Do not hinder one another, 14:13-23

★**13** ^aMatt. 7:1; Rom. 14:3 ^b1 Cor. 8:13

13 Therefore let us not ^ajudge one another anymore, but rather

determine this—^bnot to put an obstacle or a stumbling block in a brother's way.

14 I know and am convinced in the Lord Jesus that ^anothing is unclean in itself; but to him who ^bthinks anything to be unclean, to him it is unclean.

★**14** ^aActs 10:15; Rom. 14:2, 20 ^b1 Cor. 8:7

15 For if because of food your brother is hurt, you are no longer ^awalking according to love. ^bDo not destroy with your food him for whom Christ died.

15 ^aEph. 5:2 ^bRom. 14:20; 1 Cor. 8:11

16 Therefore ^ado not let what is for you a good thing be spoken of as evil.

16 ^a1 Cor. 10:30; Titus 2:5

17 for the kingdom of God ^ais not eating and drinking, but righteousness and ^bpeace and ^bjoy in the Holy Spirit.

17 ^a1 Cor. 8:8 ^bRom. 15:13; Gal. 5:22

18 For he who in this *way* ^aserves Christ is ^bacceptable to God and approved by men.

18 ^aRom. 16:18 ^b2 Cor. 8:21; Phil. 4:8; 1 Pet. 2:12

19 So then let us ^apursue the things which make for peace and the ^bbuilding up of one another.

19 ^aPs. 34:14; Rom. 12:18; 1 Cor. 7:15; 2 Tim. 2:22; Heb. 12:14 ^bRom. 15:2; 1 Cor. 10:23; 14:3f., 26; 2 Cor. 12:19; Eph. 4:12, 29

20 ^aDo not tear down the work of God for the sake of food. ^bAll things indeed are clean, but ^cthey are evil for the man who eats and gives offense.

20 ^aRom. 14:15 ^bActs 10:15; Rom. 14:2, 14 ^c1 Cor. 8:9-12

21 ^aIt is good not to eat meat or to drink wine, or *to do anything* by which your brother stumbles.

21 ^a1 Cor. 8:13

22 The faith which you have, have as your own conviction before God. Happy is he who ^adoes not condemn himself in what he approves.

★**22** ^a1 John 3:21

23 But ^ahe who doubts is condemned if he eats, because *his eating is* not from faith; and whatever is not from faith is sin.

23 ^aRom. 14:5

3 Do imitate Christ, 15:1-13

15 Now we who are strong ought to bear the weak-

1 ^aRom. 14:1; Gal. 6:2; 1 Thess. 5:14

14:10 *the judgment seat of God.* See 1 Cor. 3:10-15; 2 Cor. 5:10.

14:13 *stumbling block.* I.e., temptation to sin.

14:14 *unclean.* This refers to foods not permitted by the law (Lev. 11). Though these restrictions no longer applied (Rom. 14:20), some immature believers still applied them to their own lives. The mature brother is exhorted to abstain from those foods and also from wine,

so as not to be a hindrance to his less mature brothers (v. 21). Abstention, though one may personally think it unnecessary, is better than placing temptation in a brother's way.

14:22 *faith.* I.e., a conviction or standard in regard to these matters. Every believer should have standards, but should see that they are used to help others, never to hinder them (15:2).

nesses of ªthose without strength and not *just* please ourselves.

2 Let each of us ªplease his neighbor for his good, to his ᵇedification.

3 For even ªChrist did not please Himself; but as it is written, "ᵇTHE REPROACHES OF THOSE WHO REPROACHED THEE FELL UPON ME."

4 For ªwhatever was written in earlier times was written for our instruction, that through perseverance and the encouragement of the Scriptures we might have hope.

5 Now may the ªGod who gives perseverance and encouragement grant you ᵇto be of the same mind with one another according to Christ Jesus;

6 that with one accord you may with one voice glorify ªthe God and Father of our Lord Jesus Christ.

7 Wherefore, ªaccept one another, just as Christ also accepted us to the glory of God.

8 For I say that Christ has become a servant to ªthe circumcision on behalf of the truth of God to confirm ᵇthe promises *given* to the fathers,

9 and for ªthe Gentiles to ᵇglorify God for His mercy; as it is written,

"ᶜTHEREFORE I WILL GIVE
    PRAISE TO THEE AMONG THE
    GENTILES,
AND I WILL SING TO THY
    NAME."

10 And again he says,

"ªREJOICE, O GENTILES, WITH
    HIS PEOPLE."

11 And again,

"ªPRAISE THE LORD ALL YOU
    GENTILES,
AND LET ALL THE PEOPLES
    PRAISE HIM."

12 And again Isaiah says,

"ªTHERE SHALL COME ᵇTHE
    ROOT OF JESSE,
AND HE WHO ARISES TO RULE
    OVER THE GENTILES,
ᶜIN HIM SHALL THE GENTILES
    HOPE."

13 Now may the God of hope fill you with all ªjoy and peace in believing, that you may abound in hope ᵇby the power of the Holy Spirit.

VII PERSONAL MESSAGES AND BENEDICTION, 15:14-16:27
A Paul's Plans, 15:14-33

14 And concerning you, my brethren, I myself also am convinced that you yourselves are full of ªgoodness, filled with ᵇall knowledge, and able also to admonish one another.

15 But I have written very boldly to you on some points, so as to remind you again, because of ªthe grace that was given me from God,

16 to be ªa minister of Christ Jesus to the Gentiles, ministering as a priest the ᵇgospel of God, that *my* ᶜoffering of the Gentiles might become acceptable, sanctified by the Holy Spirit.

17 Therefore in Christ Jesus I have found ªreason for boasting in ᵇthings pertaining to God.

18 For I will not presume to speak of anything except what ªChrist has accomplished through me, resulting in the obedience of the Gentiles by word and deed,

19 in the power of ªsigns and ªwonders, ᵇin the power of the Spirit; so that ᶜfrom Jerusalem and round about as ᵈfar as Illyricum I have fully preached the gospel of Christ.

15:3 By pointing to the example of Christ and quoting from Psalm 69:9, Paul answers the question, Why should I restrict myself?
15:8 *a servant to the circumcision.* Jesus ministered to his fellow-Jews.
15:9-12 All the quotations in these verses (see marg. refs.) are from the Greek version of the O.T.
15:16 *to the Gentiles.* See Gal. 2:9.
15:19 *Illyricum.* The eastern shore of the Adriatic (present-day Yugoslavia).

Margin references (left column):

2 ª1 Cor. 9:22; 10:24, 33; 2 Cor. 13:9 ᵇRom. 14:19; 1 Cor. 10:23; 14:3f., 26; 2 Cor. 12:19; Eph. 4:12, 29
★ **3** ª2 Cor. 8:9 ᵇPs. 69:9
4 ªRom. 4:23f.; 2 Tim. 3:16
5 ª2 Cor. 1:3 ᵇRom. 12:16
6 ªRev. 1:6
7 ªRom. 14:1
★ **8** ªMatt. 15:24; Acts 3:26 ᵇRom. 4:16; 2 Cor. 1:20
★ **9-12**
9 ªRom. 3:29; 11:30 ᵇMatt. 9:8 ᶜ2 Sam. 22:50; Ps. 18:49
10 ªDeut. 32:43
11 ªPs. 117:1

Margin references (right column):

12 ªIs. 11:10 ᵇRev. 5:5; 22:16 ᶜMatt. 12:21
13 ªRom. 14:17 ᵇRom. 15:19; 1 Cor. 2:4; 1 Thess. 1:5
14 ªEph. 5:9; 2 Thess. 1:11 ᵇ1 Cor. 1:5; 8:1, 7, 10; 12:8; 13:2
15 ªRom. 12:3
★**16** ªActs 9:15; Rom. 11:13 ᵇRom. 1:1; 15:19, 20 ᶜRom. 12:1; Eph. 5:2; Phil. 2:17
17 ªPhil. 3:3 ᵇHeb. 2:17; 5:1
18 ªActs 15:12; 21:19; Rom. 1:5; 2 Cor. 3:5
★**19** ªJohn 4:48 ᵇRom. 15:13; 1 Cor. 2:4; 1 Thess. 1:5 ᶜActs 22:17-21 ᵈActs 20:1f.

★**20** aRom.
1:15; 10:15;
15:16
b1 Cor. 3:10;
2 Cor.
10:15f.

21 aIs.
52:15

22 aRom.
1:13;
1 Thess. 2:18

★**23** aActs
19:21; Rom.
1:10f.; 15:29,
32

24 aRom.
15:28 bActs
15:3 cRom.
1:12

★**25** aActs
19:21 bActs
24:17
26 aActs
16:9; 1 Cor.
16:5; 2 Cor.
1:16; 2:13;
7:5; 8:1; 9:2,
4; 11:9; Phil.
4:15;
1 Thess.
1:7f.; 4:10;
1 Tim. 1:3
bActs 18:12;
19:21
27 a1 Cor.
9:11

★**28** aJohn
3:33 bRom.
15:24

29 aActs
19:21; Rom.
1:10f.; 15:23,
32

20 And thus I aspired to apreach the gospel, not where Christ was *already* named, bthat I might not build upon another man's foundation;

21 but as it is written,

"aTHEY WHO HAD NO NEWS OF HIM SHALL SEE,
AND THEY WHO HAVE NOT HEARD SHALL UNDERSTAND."

22 For this reason aI have often been hindered from coming to you;

23 but now, with no further place for me in these regions, and since I ahave had for many years a longing to come to you

24 whenever I ago to Spain— for I hope to see you in passing, and to be bhelped on my way there by you, when I have first cenjoyed your company for a while—

25 but now, aI am going to Jerusalem bserving the saints.

26 For aMacedonia and bAchaia have been pleased to make a contribution for the poor among the saints in Jerusalem.

27 Yes, they were pleased *to do so,* and they are indebted to them. For aif the Gentiles have shared in their spiritual things, they are indebted to minister to them also in material things.

28 Therefore, when I have finished this, and ahave put my seal on this fruit of theirs, I will bgo on by way of you to Spain.

29 And I know that when aI come to you, I will come in the fulness of the blessing of Christ.

30 Now I urge you, brethren, by our Lord Jesus Christ and by athe love of the Spirit, to bstrive together with me in your prayers to God for me,

31 that I may be adelivered from those who are disobedient in Judea, and *that* my bservice for Jerusalem may prove acceptable to the csaints;

32 so that aI may come to you in joy by bthe will of God and find *refreshing* rest in your company.

33 Now athe God of peace be with you all. Amen.

B Paul's Personal Greetings, 16:1–16

16 I acommend to you our sister Phoebe, who is a servant of the church which is at bCenchrea;

2 that you areceive her in the Lord in a manner worthy of the bsaints, and that you help her in whatever matter she may have need of you; for she herself has also been a helper of many, and of myself as well.

3 Greet aPrisca and aAquila, my fellow workers bin cChrist Jesus,

4 who for my life risked their own necks, to whom not only do I give thanks, but also all the churches of the Gentiles;

5 also *greet* athe church that is in their house. Greet Epaenetus, my beloved, who is the bfirst convert to Christ from cAsia.

6 Greet Mary, who has worked hard for you.

30 aGal.
5:22; Col. 1:8
b2 Cor. 1:11;
Col. 4:12
31 a2 Cor.
1:10;
2 Thess. 3:2;
2 Tim. 3:11;
4:17 bRom.
15:25f.;
2 Cor. 8:4;
9:1 cActs
9:13, 15
32 aRom.
15:23 bActs
18:21; Rom.
1:10
33 aRom.
16:20; 2 Cor.
13:11; Phil.
4:9; 1 Thess.
5:23

★ **1** a2 Cor.
3:1 bActs
18:18

2 aPhil.
2:29 bActs
9:13, 15

★ **3** aActs
18:2 bRom.
8:11ff.; 16:7,
9, 10; 2 Cor.
5:17; 12:2;
Gal. 1:22
cRom. 8:1

★ **5** a1 Cor.
16:19; Col.
4:15; Philem.
2 b1 Cor.
16:15 cActs
16:6

15:20 *not where Christ was already named.* I.e., where Christ was unknown.

15:23 *no further place.* I.e., no more opportunity to preach Christ where He was unknown. Therefore, Paul proposed to go to Spain, stopping off in Rome on his way (v. 24).

15:25 *serving.* I.e., taking the money that had been collected in Greece (see 2 Cor. 8–9).

15:28 *this fruit.* I.e., the money he was collecting.

16:1 *Phoebe. . . a servant of the church.* The word here translated "servant" is often translated "deacon," which leads some to believe

that Phoebe was a deaconess. However, the word is more likely used here in an unofficial sense of helper. *Cenchrea.* The eastern port of Corinth.

16:3 *Prisca and Aquila.* See Acts 18:2, 26; 1 Cor. 16:19; 2 Tim 4:19. Just how they risked their lives for Paul (Rom. 16:4), he does not say.

16:5 *the church that is in their house.* Early congregations met in homes (1 Cor. 16:19; Col. 4:15; Philem. 2). The several house churches in one city would constitute the church in that city (1 Cor. 1:2).

★ **7** aRom.
9:3; 16:11,
21 bCol.
4:10; Philem.
23 cRom.
8:11ff.; 16:3,
9, 10; 2 Cor.
5:17; 12:2;
Gal. 1:22

9 aRom.
8:11ff.; 16:3,
7, 10; 2 Cor.
5:17; 12:2;
Gal. 1:22
10 aRom.
8:11ff.; 16:3,
7, 9; 2 Cor.
5:17; 12:2;
Gal. 1:22
b1 Cor. 1:11
11 aRom.
9:3; 16:7, 21
b1 Cor. 1:11

13 aMark
15:21

15 aRom.
16:2, 14

16 a1 Cor.
16:20; 2 Cor.
13:12;
1 Thess.
5:26; 1 Pet.
5:14

17 a1 Tim.
1:3; 6:3
bMatt. 7:15;
Gal. 1:8f.;
2 Thess. 3:6,
14; Titus
3:10; 2 John
10

7 Greet Andronicus and Junias, my ^akinsmen, and my ^bfellow prisoners, who are outstanding among the apostles, who also were ^cin Christ before me.

8 Greet Ampliatus, my beloved in the Lord.

9 Greet Urbanus, our fellow worker ^ain Christ, and Stachys my beloved.

10 Greet Apelles, the approved ^ain Christ. Greet ^bthose who are of the *household* of Aristobulus.

11 Greet Herodion, my ^akinsman. ^bGreet those of the *household* of Narcissus, who are in the Lord.

12 Greet Tryphaena and Tryphosa, workers in the Lord. Greet Persis the beloved, who has worked hard in the Lord.

13 Greet ^aRufus, a choice man in the Lord, also his mother and mine.

14 Greet Asyncritus, Phlegon, Hermes, Patrobas, Hermas and the brethren with them.

15 Greet Philologus and Julia, Nereus and his sister, and Olympas, and all ^athe saints who are with them.

16 ^aGreet one another with a holy kiss. All the churches of Christ greet you.

C Paul's Concluding Admonition and Benediction,
16:17–27

17 Now I urge you, brethren, keep your eye on those who cause dissensions and hindrances ^acontrary to the teaching which you learned, and ^bturn away from them.

18 For such men are ^aslaves, not of our Lord Christ but of ^btheir own appetites; and by their ^csmooth and flattering speech they deceive the hearts of the unsuspecting.

19 For the report of your obedience ^ahas reached to all; therefore I am rejoicing over you, but ^bI want you to be wise in what is good, and innocent in what is evil.

20 And ^athe God of peace will soon crush ^bSatan under your feet.

^cThe grace of our Lord Jesus be with you.

21 ^aTimothy my fellow worker greets you, and *so do* ^bLucius and ^cJason and ^dSosipater, my ^ekinsmen.

22 I, Tertius, who ^awrite this letter, greet you in the Lord.

23 ^aGaius, host to me and to the whole church, greets you. ^bErastus, the city treasurer greets you, and Quartus, the brother.

24 [The grace of our Lord Jesus Christ be with you all. Amen.]

25 ^aNow to Him who is able to establish you ^baccording to my gospel and the preaching of Jesus Christ, according to the revelation of ^cthe mystery which has been kept secret for ^dlong ages past,

26 but now is manifested, and by ^athe Scriptures of the prophets, according to the commandment of the eternal God, has been made known to all the nations, *leading* to ^bobedience of faith;

27 to the only wise God, through Jesus Christ, ^abe the glory forever. Amen.

18 aRom.
14:18 bPhil.
3:19 cCol.
2:4; 2 Pet.
2:3

★**19** aRom.
1:8 bJer.
4:22; Matt.
10:16; 1 Cor.
14:20

20 aRom.
15:33 bMatt.
4:10 c1 Cor.
16:23; 2 Cor.
13:14; Gal.
6:18; Phil.
4:23;
1 Thess.
5:28;
2 Thess.
3:18; Rev.
22:21
★**21** aActs
16:1 bActs
13:1 [?]
cActs 17:5
[?] dActs
20:4 [?]
eRom. 9:3;
16:7; 11
★**22** a1 Cor.
16:21; Gal.
6:11; Col.
4:18;
2 Thess.
3:17; Philem.
19
★**23** aActs
20:4 [?];
1 Cor. 1:14
bActs 19:22
★**24**
★**25** aEph.
3:20; Jude
24 bRom.
2:16 cMatt.
13:35; Rom.
11:25; 1 Cor.
2:1, 7; 4:1;
Eph. 1:9; 3:3,
9; 6:19; Col.
1:26f., 2:2;
4:3; 1 Tim.
3:16 d2 Tim.
1:9; Titus 1:2
26 aRom.
1:5
27 aRom.
11:36

16:7 *outstanding among the apostles.* Better, well-known to the apostles.

16:19 *innocent in what is evil.* I.e., guileless. The believer should not mix with evil; rather, he should be knowledgeable about good things.

16:21 *my kinsmen.* Not relatives, but fellow countrymen (also v. 7).

16:22 *Tertius.* Paul's stenographer.

16:23 *Gaius.* Presumably the Gaius of 1 Cor. 1:14, whom Paul had baptized. *Erastus'* name has been found on a pavement which he donated to Corinth.

16:24 Many manuscripts do not contain this verse.

16:25 *the mystery.* A definition of a scriptural mystery: something unknown in times past but revealed in the N.T. See note on Eph. 3:3.

INTRODUCTION TO
THE FIRST LETTER OF PAUL TO THE CORINTHIANS

AUTHOR: Paul   DATE: 56

The City of Corinth   *Located on the narrow isthmus between the Aegean and Adriatic Seas, Corinth was a port city and wealthy commercial center. Ships wanting to avoid the dangerous trip around the southern tip of Greece were dragged across that isthmus. The city boasted an outdoor theater that accommodated 20,000 people; athletic games second only to the Olympics; a Greek, Roman, and Oriental population; and the great temple of Aphrodite with its 1,000 prostitutes. The immoral condition of Corinth is vividly seen in the fact that the Greek term Korinthiazomai (literally, to act the Corinthian) came to mean "to practice fornication." There were taverns on the south side of the marketplace, and many drinking vessels have been dug up from those liquor lockers. Corinth was noted for everything sinful.*

The Church in Corinth   *The gospel was first preached in Corinth by Paul on his second missionary journey (A.D. 50). While living and working with Aquila and Priscilla, he preached in the synagogue until opposition forced him to move next door, to the house of Titius Justus. The Jews accused him before the Roman governor Gallio but the charge was dismissed, and Paul remained 18 months in the city (Acts 18:1-17; 1 Cor. 2:3). After leaving, Paul wrote the church a letter which has been lost (5:9), but disturbing news about the believers and questions they asked Paul in a letter they sent to him (7:1) prompted the writing of 1 Corinthians. Problems there included divisions in the church (1:11), immorality (chap. 5; 6:9-20), and the questions concerning marriage, food, worship, and the resurrection. Aberrant beliefs and practices of an astonishing variety characterized this church.*

Place of Writing   *This letter was written from Ephesus (16:8).*

Contents   *The letter is largely practical in emphasis, dealing with spiritual and moral problems and questions. It is a casebook of pastoral theology. Important emphases include: the judgment seat of Christ (3:11-15), the temple of the Holy Spirit (6:19-20), the glory of God (10:31), the Lord's Supper (11:23-34), love (chap. 13), the exercise of gifts (chaps. 12-14), and resurrection (chap. 15).*

OUTLINE OF 1 CORINTHIANS

THE FIRST LETTER OF PAUL TO THE CORINTHIANS

I INTRODUCTION, 1:1-9

A The Salutation, 1:1-3

★ **1** aRom. 1:1 bRom. 1:10; 15:32; 2 Cor. 1:1; 8:5; Eph. 1:1; Col. 1:1; 2 Tim. 1:1 cActs 18:17 dActs 1:15
★ **2** a1 Cor. 10:32 bActs 18:1 cRom. 1:7; 8:28 dActs 7:59

1 Paul, acalled as an apostle of Jesus Christ by bthe will of God, and cSosthenes our dbrother,

2 to athe church of God which is at bCorinth, to those who have been sanctified in Christ Jesus, saints cby calling, with all who in every place dcall upon the name of our Lord Jesus Christ, their *Lord* and ours:

3 aRom. 1:7

3 aGrace to you and peace from God our Father and the Lord Jesus Christ.

B The Expression of Thanks, 1:4-9

4 aRom. 1:8
5 a2 Cor. 9:11 bRom. 15:14; 2 Cor. 8:7

4 aI thank my God always concerning you, for the grace of God which was given you in Christ Jesus,

5 that in everything you

were aenriched in Him, in all bspeech and ball knowledge,

6 even as athe testimony concerning Christ was confirmed in you,

7 so that you are not lacking in any gift, aawaiting eagerly the revelation of our Lord Jesus Christ,

8 awho shall also confirm you to the end, blameless in bthe day of our Lord Jesus Christ.

9 aGod is faithful, through whom you were bcalled into cfellowship with His Son, Jesus Christ our Lord.

6 a2 Thess. 1:10; 1 Tim. 2:6; 2 Tim. 1:8; Rev. 1:2
★ **7** aLuke 17:30; Rom. 8:19, 23; Phil. 3:20; 2 Pet. 3:12
★ **8** aRom. 8:19; Phil. 1:6; Col. 2:7; 1 Thess. 3:13; 5:23 bLuke 17:24, 30; 1 Cor. 5:5; 2 Cor. 1:14; Phil. 1:6, 10; 2:16; 1 Thess. 5:2; 2 Thess. 2:2
9 aDeut. 7:9; Is. 49:7; 1 Cor. 10:13; 2 Cor. 1:18; 1 Thess. 5:24; 2 Thess. 3:3 bRom. 8:28 c1 John 1:3

II DIVISIONS IN THE CHURCH, 1:10-4:21

A The Fact of Divisions, 1:10-17

10 Now aI exhort you, bbrethren, by the name of our Lord Jesus Christ, that you all agree, and there be no cdivisions among

★**10** aRom. 12:1 bRom. 1:13 c1 Cor. 11:18 dRom. 12:16; Phil. 1:27

1:1 *Sosthenes.* Possibly the ruler of the synagogue mentioned in Acts 18:17.
1:2 *sanctified.* I.e., set apart for God's possession and use. See note on 6:11. This was true of the Corinthians because of their position in Christ (1 Cor. 12:13), in spite of their blatant imperfections.
1:7 *gift.* I.e., spiritual gift (cf. 12:4-11). Spiritual gifts are abilities which God gives believers in order that they may serve Him. Every Christian has at least one gift (1 Pet. 4:10). At Corinth all the various gifts were found within the group. Spiritual gifts are discussed in Rom. 12:3-8; 1 Cor. 12:1-14:40 and Eph. 4:7-16.
1:8 *confirm* = guarantee. The Corinthians had God's guarantee that they would be in Christ's presence when He returns and that they

would then be *blameless.* This assurance is based on the wonderful fact that *God is faithful* (v. 9).
1:10 *divisions.* Or, "schisms," "parties." This letter was written to a church divided over personalities (v. 12). Though severely condemned, these factions were allowed to exist in order that "approved" believers could be recognized (11:19). *made complete.* Paul appeals for adjustments to be made in these personality divisions so that there might be unity in the church. Other issues that divided the church included libertinism (6:13), the relation of men and women in the church (11:2-16), food laws (8:10; 10:25), speaking in tongues (chap. 14), and resurrection of the dead (chap. 15).

you, but you be made complete in ᵈthe same mind and in the same judgment.

11 For I have been informed concerning you, my brethren, by ᵃChloe's *people,* that there are quarrels among you.

12 Now I mean this, that ᵃeach one of you is saying, "I am of Paul," and "I of ᵇApollos," and "I of ᶜCephas," and "I of Christ."

13 Has Christ been divided? Paul was not crucified for you, was he? Or were you ᵃbaptized in the name of Paul?

14 I thank God that I ᵃbaptized none of you except ᵃCrispus and ᵇGaius,

15 that no man should say you were baptized in my name.

16 Now I did baptize also the ᵃhousehold of Stephanas; beyond that, I do not know whether I baptized any other.

17 ᵃFor Christ did not send me to baptize, but to preach the gospel, ᵇnot in cleverness of speech, that the cross of Christ should not be made void.

B The Causes of Divisions, 1:18–2:16

1 The misunderstanding of God's message of the cross, 1:18–2:5

18 For the word of the cross is to ᵃthose who are perishing ᵇfoolishness, but to us who are being saved it is ᶜthe power of God.

19 For it is written,

"ᵃI will destroy the wisdom of the wise,
And the cleverness of the clever I will set aside."

20 ᵃWhere is the wise man? Where is the scribe? Where is the debater of ᵇthis age? Has not God ᶜmade foolish the wisdom of ᵈthe world?

21 For since in the wisdom of God ᵃthe world through its wisdom did not *come to* know God, ᵇGod was well-pleased through the ᶜfoolishness of the message preached to ᵈsave those who believe.

22 For indeed ᵃJews ask for signs, and Greeks search for wisdom;

23 but we preach ᵃChrist crucified, ᵇto Jews a stumbling block, and to Gentiles ᶜfoolishness,

24 but to those who are ᵃthe called, both Jews and Greeks, Christ ᵇthe power of God and ᶜthe wisdom of God.

25 Because the ᵃfoolishness of God is wiser than men, and ᵇthe weakness of God is stronger than men.

26 For consider your ᵃcalling, brethren, that there were ᵇnot many wise according to the flesh, not many mighty, not many noble;

27 but ᵃGod has chosen the foolish things of ᵇthe world to shame the wise, and God has chosen the weak things of ᵇthe world to shame the things which are strong,

Cross references (margin)

★11 ᵃRom. 16:10f.

★12 ᵃMatt. 23:8-10; 1 Cor. 3:4
ᵇActs 18:24; 1 Cor. 3:22
ᶜJohn 1:42; 1 Cor. 3:22; 9:5; 15:5
★13 ᵃMatt. 28:19; Acts 2:38

14 ᵃActs 18:8 ᵇRom. 16:23

16 ᵃ1 Cor. 16:15, 17

★17 ᵃJohn 4:2; Acts 10:48
ᵇ1 Cor. 2:1, 4, 13; 2 Cor. 10:10; 11:6

★18-25
18 ᵃActs 2:47; 2 Cor. 2:15; 4:3; 2 Thess. 2:10
ᵇ1 Cor. 1:21, 23, 25; 2:14; 4:10 ᶜRom. 1:16; 1 Cor. 1:24
19 ᵃIs. 29:14

20 ᵃJob 12:17; Is. 19:11f.; 33:18 ᵇMatt. 13:22; 1 Cor. 2:6, 8; 3:18, 19 ᶜRom. 1:20ff. ᵈJohn 1:27f.; 1 Cor. 11:32; James 4:4
21 ᵃJohn 1:27f.; 6:2; 11:32; James 4:4 ᵇLuke 12:32; Gal. 1:15; Col. 1:19 ᶜ1 Cor. 1:18, 23, 25; 2:14; 4:10 ᵈRom. 11:14; 1 Tim. 4:16; 2 Tim. 2:10; 3:15; 4:18; Heb. 7:25; James 5:20
22 ᵃMatt. 12:38
23 ᵃ1 Cor. 2:2; Gal. 3:1; 5:11 ᵇLuke 2:34; 1 Pet. 2:8 ᶜ1 Cor. 1:18, 21, 25; 2:14; 4:10
24 ᵃRom. 8:28 ᵇRom. 1:16; 1 Cor. 1:18 ᶜLuke 11:49; 1 Cor. 1:30
25 ᵃ1 Cor. 1:18, 21, 23; 2:14; 4:10 ᵇ2 Cor. 13:4
★26-31
26 ᵃRom. 11:29 ᵇMatt. 11:25; 1 Cor. 1:20; 2:8
27 ᵃJames 2:5 ᵇ1 Cor. 1:20

1:11 *quarrels.* Or strife, which, according to Gal. 5:20, is a work of the flesh, or old nature.

1:12 The party of *Apollos* apparently preferred a polished style in preaching (Acts 18:24). The party of *Cephas* (Peter) appealed to the traditionalists, who wanted a leader who had walked with Christ. The party of *Christ* included those who disdained attachment to any group and flaunted their liberty in Christ (6:12).

1:13 The impossibility of these things being true demonstrates the fallacies of these factions.

1:17 *For Christ did not send me to baptize, but to preach the gospel.* Though Paul did baptize some (vv. 14, 16), it is clear from this state-ment that he did not consider baptism necessary for salvation.

1:18-25 In these verses Paul shows that worldly wisdom, which the Corinthians prized so highly, is the very antithesis of the wisdom of God.

1:26-31 Not only is the message of the cross foolishness to the perishing (v. 18), but God uses those who would commonly be considered foolish, weak, and of no consequence to convey that message. An illustration of this truth was their own church group, which did not include many *wise, mighty,* or *noble* (v. 26). God's purpose is to exclude all boasting in self (v. 29).

28 *a*1 Cor.
1:20 *b*Rom.
4:17 *c*Job
34:19; 1 Cor.
2:6; 2 Thess.
2:8; Heb.
2:14
29 *a*Eph. 2:9

30 *a*Rom.
8:1; 1 Cor.
4:15 *b*1 Cor.
1:24 *c*Jer.
23:5f.; 33:16;
2 Cor. 5:21;
Phil. 3:9
*d*1 Cor. 1:2;
6:11;
1 Thess. 5:23
*e*Rom. 3:24;
Eph. 1:7, 14;
Col. 1:4
31 *a*Jer.
9:23f.; 2 Cor.
10:17
1 *a*1 Cor.
1:17; 2:4, 13
*b*1 Cor. 2:7

2 *a*1 Cor.
1:23; Gal.
6:14

★ 3 *a*Acts
18:1, 6, 12
*b*1 Cor. 4:10;
2 Cor. 11:30;
12:5, 9f.;
13:9 *c*Is.
19:16; 2 Cor.
7:15; Eph.
6:5
4 *a*1 Cor.
1:17; 2:1, 13
*b*Rom.
15:19; 1 Cor.
4:20
★ 5 *a*2 Cor.
4:7; 6:7; 12:9

6 *a*Eph.
4:13; Phil.
3:15 marg.;
Heb. 5:14;
6:1 *b*Matt.
13:22; 1 Cor.
1:20 *c*1 Cor.
1:28
7 *a*Rom.
11:25;
16:25f.;
1 Cor. 2:1
*b*Rom. 8:29f.
*c*Heb. 1:2;
11:3

28 and the base things of *a*the world and the despised, God has chosen, *b*the things that are not, that He might *c*nullify the things that are,

29 that *a*no man should boast before God.

30 But by His doing you are in *a*Christ Jesus, who became to us *b*wisdom from God, and *c*righteousness and *d*sanctification, and *e*redemption,

31 that, just as it is written, "*a*LET HIM WHO BOASTS, BOAST IN THE LORD."

2 And when I came to you, brethren, I *a*did not come with superiority of speech or of wisdom, proclaiming to you *b*the testimony of God.

2 For I determined to know nothing among you except *a*Jesus Christ, and Him crucified.

3 And I *a*was with you in *b*weakness and in *c*fear and in much trembling.

4 And my message and my preaching were *a*not in persuasive words of wisdom, but in demonstration of *b*the Spirit and of power,

5 that your faith should not rest on the wisdom of men, but on *a*the power of God.

2 The misunderstanding of the Spirit's ministry of revealing, 2:6–16

6 Yet we do speak wisdom among those who are *a*mature; a wisdom, however, not of *b*this age, nor of the rulers of *b*this age, who are *c*passing away;

7 but we speak God's wis-

dom in a *a*mystery, the hidden *wisdom*, which God *b*predestined before the *c*ages to our glory;

8 *the wisdom* *a*which none of the rulers of *b*this age has understood; for if they had understood it, they would not have crucified *c*the Lord of glory;

9 but just as it is written,

"*a*THINGS WHICH EYE HAS NOT SEEN AND EAR HAS NOT HEARD, AND *which* HAVE NOT ENTERED THE HEART OF MAN, ALL THAT GOD HAS PREPARED FOR THOSE WHO LOVE HIM."

10 *a*For to us God revealed *them* *b*through the Spirit; for the Spirit searches all things, even the *c*depths of God.

11 For who among men knows the *thoughts* of a man except the *a*spirit of the man, which is in him? Even so the *thoughts* of God no one knows except the Spirit of God.

12 Now we *a*have received, not the spirit of *b*the world, but the Spirit who is from God, that we might know the things freely given to us by God,

13 which things we also speak, *a*not in words taught by human wisdom, but in those taught by the Spirit, combining spiritual *thoughts* with spiritual words.

14 But a *a*natural man *b*does not accept the things of the Spirit of God; for they are *c*foolishness to him, and he cannot understand them, because they are spiritually appraised.

★ 8 *a*1 Cor.
1:26; 2:6
*b*Matt. 13:22;
1 Cor. 1:20
*c*Acts 7:2;
James 2:1

★ 9 *a*Is.
64:4; 65:17

10 *a*Matt.
11:25; 13:11;
16:17; Gal.
1:12; Eph.
3:3, 5 *b*John
14:26 *c*Rom.
11:33ff.
11 *a*Prov.
20:27

12 *a*Rom.
8:15 *b*1 Cor.
1:27

★13 *a*1 Cor.
1:17; 2:1, 4

★14 *a*1 Cor.
15:44, 46;
James 3:15;
Jude 19
marg. *b*John
14:17
*c*1 Cor. 1:18

2:3 Paul arrived in Corinth after a discouraging experience in Athens and was anxious about the believers he had just left in Thessalonica (Acts 17). The overwhelming wickedness of Corinth undoubtedly added to his anxiety.

2:5 *wisdom of men.* Paul did not want their faith to be placed in clever arguments but in *the power of God.*

2:8 *the rulers of this age.* I.e., those who crucified Christ.

2:9 A free quotation of Isa. 64:4. These things,

long hidden, are now revealed by the Spirit (1 Cor. 2:10).

2:13 *combining spiritual thoughts with spiritual words.* This difficult phrase may perhaps mean, "interpreting spiritual truths to spiritual minds."

2:14 *a natural man.* I.e., an unsaved man. See Jude 19, where the same word is used (translated "worldly-minded") and explained as indicating a person who does not have the Spirit (see also Rom. 8:9).

★15 *a*1 Cor.
3:1; 14:37;
Gal. 6:1

15 But he who is *a*spiritual appraises all things, yet he himself is appraised by no man.

16 *a*Is.
40:13; Rom.
11:34 *b*John
15:15

16 For *a*WHO HAS KNOWN THE MIND OF THE LORD, THAT HE SHOULD INSTRUCT HIM? But *b*we have the mind of Christ.

C   The Consequences of Divisions, 3:1–4:5

1   *Spiritual growth is stunted,*
3:1–9

★ 1 *a*1 Cor.
2:15; 14:37;
Gal. 6:1
*b*Rom. 7:14;
1 Cor. 2:14
*c*1 Cor. 2:6;
Eph. 4:14;
Heb. 5:13
2 *a*Heb.
5:12f.; 1 Pet.
2:2 *b*John
16:12
★ 3 *a*Rom.
13:13; 1 Cor.
1:10f.; 11:18
*b*1 Cor. 3:4
4 *a*1 Cor.
1:12 *b*1 Cor.
3:3
5 *a*Rom.
15:16; 2 Cor.
3:3, 6; 4:1;
5:18; 6:4;
Eph. 3:7;
Col. 1:25;
1 Tim. 1:12
*b*Rom. 12:6;
1 Cor. 3:10
6 *a*Acts
18:4-11, 18;
1 Cor. 4:15;
9:1; 15:1;
2 Cor.
10:14f. *b*Acts
18:27; 1 Cor.
1:12 *c*1 Cor.
15:10

3 And I, brethren, could not speak to you as to *a*spiritual men, but as to *b*men of flesh, as to *c*babes in Christ.

2 I gave you *a*milk to drink, not solid food; for you *b*were not yet able *to receive it.* Indeed, even now you are not yet able,

3 for you are still fleshly. For since there is *a*jealousy and strife among you, are you not fleshly, and are you not walking *b*like mere men?

4 For when *a*one says, "I am of Paul," and another, "I am of Apollos," are you not *mere* *b*men?

5 What then is Apollos? And what is Paul? *a*Servants through whom you believed, even *b*as the Lord gave *opportunity* to each one.

6 *a*I planted, *b*Apollos watered, but *c*God was causing the growth.

7 So then neither the one who plants nor the one who waters is anything, but God who causes the growth.

8 Now he who plants and he who waters are one; but each will *a*receive his own reward according to his own labor.

9 For we are God's *a*fellow workers; you are God's *b*field, God's *c*building.

★ 8 *a*1 Cor.
3:14; 4:5;
9:17; Gal.
6:4

9 *a*Mark
16:20; 2 Cor.
6:1 *b*Is. 61:3;
Matt. 15:13
*c*1 Cor. 3:16;
Eph. 2:20-22;
Col. 2:7;
1 Pet. 2:5

2   *Rewards will be lost,* 3:10–4:5

10 According to *a*the grace of God which was given to me, as a wise master builder *b*I laid a foundation, and *c*another is building upon it. But let each man be careful how he builds upon it.

11 For no man can lay a *a*foundation other than the one which is laid, which is Jesus Christ.

12 Now if any man builds upon the foundation with gold, silver, precious stones, wood, hay, straw,

13 *a*each man's work will become evident; for *b*the day will show it, because it is *to be* revealed with fire; and the fire itself will test the quality of each man's work.

14 If any man's work which he has built upon it remains, he shall *a*receive a reward.

15 If any man's work is burned up, he shall suffer loss;

★10-15

10 *a*Rom.
12:3; 1 Cor.
15:10 *b*Rom.
15:20; 1 Cor.
3:11f.
*c*1 Thess.
3:2

11 *a*Is.
28:16; Eph.
2:20; 1 Pet.
2:4ff.

★12

13 *a*1 Cor.
4:5 *b*Matt.
10:15; 1 Cor.
1:8; 4:3
marg.;
2 Thess. 1:7-
10; 2 Tim.
1:12, 18; 4:8

★14 *a*1 Cor.
3:8; 4:5;
9:17; Gal.
6:4

★15 *a*Job
23:10; Ps.
66:10, 12;
Jude 23

2:15 *he who is spiritual.* The mature Christian, who is led and taught by the Spirit, *appraises all things,* i.e., he can scrutinize, sift, and thereby understand all things; but unbelievers and even carnally-minded Christians cannot appraise (understand) him.

3:1 *men of flesh.* The Greek word *sarkinos* means "fleshly" or "of the flesh," with the idea of weakness; in v. 3 *fleshly* has the overtone of willfulness. Fleshly Christians (brethren) are *babes in Christ* (i.e., undeveloped) who cannot understand the deeper truths of the Word of God (v. 2) and who are characterized by strife (v. 3).

3:3 *still.* Their condition was inexcusable, for they had been saved long enough to have grown up. *walking like mere men.* Carnal Christians are scarcely distinguishable from

natural or unsaved men.

3:8 *are one.* I.e., in harmony, not competition.

3:10-15 This passage refers to the judgment seat of Christ (cf. 2 Cor. 5:10). The works discussed here have nothing to do with earning or losing salvation. The rewards (or loss of them) pertain only to Christians.

3:12 *gold.* Those works which are valuable and enduring. *wood.* Those which are ultimately worthless.

3:14 *reward.* Salvation is a free gift, but rewards, for those who are saved, are earned. The *quality* of our service (v. 13) is the criterion. Rewards are often spoken of as crowns (cf. 9:25; 1 Thess. 2:19; 2 Tim. 4:8; Jas. 1:12; 1 Pet. 5:4; Rev. 2:10; 3:11; 4:4, 10).

3:15 *suffer loss.* I.e., of reward not salvation, as is made clear in the latter part of the verse.

but he himself shall be saved, yet [a]so as through fire.

16 [a]Do you not know that [b]you are a temple of God, and *that* the Spirit of God dwells in you?

17 If any man destroys the temple of God, God will destroy him, for the temple of God is holy, and that is what you are.

18 [a]Let no man deceive himself. [b]If any man among you thinks that he is wise in [c]this age, let him become foolish that he may become wise.

19 For [a]the wisdom of this world is foolishness before God. For it is written, *"He is* [b]THE ONE WHO CATCHES THE WISE IN THEIR CRAFTINESS"*;

20 and again, *"[a]THE LORD KNOWS THE REASONINGS of the wise, THAT THEY ARE USELESS."*

21 So then [a]let no one boast in men. For [b]all things belong to you,

22 [a]whether Paul or Apollos or Cephas or the world or [b]life or death or things present or things to come; all things belong to you,

23 and [a]you belong to Christ; and [b]Christ belongs to God.

4 Let a man regard us in this manner, as [a]servants of Christ, and [b]stewards of [c]the mysteries of God.

2 In this case, moreover, it is required of stewards that one be found trustworthy.

3 But to me it is a very small thing that I should be examined by you, or by *any* human court; in fact, I do not even examine myself.

4 I [a]am conscious of nothing against myself, yet I am not by this [b]acquitted; but the one who examines me is the Lord.

5 Therefore [a]do not go on passing judgment before the time, *but wait* [b]until the Lord comes who will both [c]bring to light the things hidden in the darkness and disclose the motives of *men's* hearts; and then each man's [d]praise will come to him from God.

D The Example of Paul, 4:6–21

6 Now these things, brethren, I have figuratively applied to myself and Apollos for your sakes, that in us you might learn not to exceed [a]what is written, in order that no one of you might [b]become arrogant [c]in behalf of one against the other.

7 For who regards you as superior? And [a]what do you have that you did not receive? But if you did receive it, why do you boast as if you had not received it?

8 You are [a]already filled, you have already become rich, you have become kings without us; and *I* would indeed that you had become kings so that we also might reign with you.

9 For, I think, God has exhibited us apostles last of all, as men [a]condemned to death; because we [b]have become a spectacle to the world, both to angels and to men.

★16 [a]Rom. 6:16 [b]Rom. 8:9; 1 Cor. 6:19; 2 Cor. 6:16; Eph. 2:21f.

★18 [a]Is. 5:21 [b]1 Cor. 8:2; Gal. 6:3 [c]1 Cor. 1:20

19 [a]1 Cor. 1:20 [b]Job 5:13

20 [a]Ps. 94:11

21 [a]1 Cor. 4:6 [b]Rom. 8:32

22 [a]1 Cor. 1:12; 3:5, 6 [b]Rom. 8:38

23 [a]1 Cor. 15:23; 2 Cor. 10:7; Gal. 3:29 [b]1 Cor. 11:3; 15:28 ★1 [a]Luke 1:2 [b]1 Cor. 9:17; Titus 1:7; 1 Pet. 4:10 [c]Rom. 11:25; 16:25 ★2

★4 [a]Acts 23:1; 2 Cor. 1:12 [b]Ps. 143:2; Rom. 2:13

5 [a]Matt. 7:1; Rom. 2:1 [b]John 21:22; Rom. 2:16 [c]1 Cor. 3:13 [d]Rom. 2:29; 1 Cor. 3:8; 2 Cor. 10:18

★6 [a]1 Cor. 1:19, 31; 3:19f. [b]1 Cor. 4:18f.; 8:1; 13:4 [c]1 Cor. 1:12; 3:4

7 [a]John 3:27; Rom. 12:3, 6; 1 Pet. 4:10

★8-13

8 [a]Rev. 3:17f.

9 [a]Rom. 8:36; 1 Cor. 15:31; 2 Cor. 11:23 [b]Heb. 10:33

3:16 *a temple of God.* Here the local church is viewed as a temple of God inhabited by the Spirit; in 6:19 the individual is a temple of God.

3:18 *let him become foolish* by accepting God's wisdom, which the world regards as folly.

4:1 *servants.* The word denotes subordination (originally an under-rower in a trireme, a ship with 3 banks of oars) and is different from the "servants" used in 3:5. *mysteries.* See note on Eph. 3:3.

4:2 *trustworthy.* Reliability was the one necessary virtue for stewards, who were managers or administrators of large estates.

4:4 *against myself.* Paul is saying, I have a clear conscience, but my final judgment rests with God.

4:6 *I have figuratively applied.* I.e., though Paul had been speaking of himself and Apollos (3:5–4:5), others, whom he did not name, were the real culprits. *that in us you might learn not to exceed what is written.* I.e., that you might learn by us to live faithfully according to the Scriptures.

4:8-13 With biting irony, Paul contrasts the imagined exaltation of the Corinthians with the degradation and distress which were the apostles' daily lot.

10 aActs
17:18; 26:24;
1 Cor. 1:18
b1 Cor.
1:19f.; 3:18;
2 Cor. 11:19
c1 Cor. 2:3;
2 Cor. 13:9
11 aRom.
8:35; 2 Cor.
11:23-27

10 We are ªfools for Christ's sake, but ᵇyou are prudent in Christ; ᶜwe are weak, but you are strong; you are distinguished, but we are without honor.

11 To this present hour we are both ªhungry and thirsty, and are poorly clothed, and are roughly treated, and are homeless;

12 aActs
18:3 b1 Pet.
3:9 cJohn
15:20; Rom.
8:35
13 aLam.
3:45
14 a1 Cor.
6:5; 15:34
b2 Cor. 6:13;
12:14;
1 Thess.
2:11; 1 John
2:1; 3 John 4
*15 aGal.
3:24f.
b1 Cor. 1:30;
cNum.
11:12; 1 Cor.
3:8; Gal.
4:19; Philem.
10 d1 Cor.
9:12, 14, 18,
23; 15:1
16 a1 Cor.
11:1; Phil.
3:17; 4:9;
1 Thess. 1:6;
2 Thess. 3:9
17 a1 Cor.
16:10 bActs
16:1 c1 Cor.
4:14; 1 Tim.
1:2, 18;
2 Tim. 1:2
d1 Cor. 7:17;
11:34; 14:33;
16:1; Titus
1:5
18 a1 Cor.
4:6 b1 Cor.
4:21
19 aActs
19:21; 20:2;
1 Cor. 11:34;
16:5f.; 16:8;
2 Cor. 1:15f.
bActs 18:21
c1 Cor. 4:6
20 a1 Cor.
2:4

12 and we toil, ªworking with our own hands; when we are ᵇreviled, we bless; when we are ᶜpersecuted, we endure;

13 when we are slandered, we try to conciliate; we have ªbecome as the scum of the world, the dregs of all things, *even* until now.

14 I do not write these things to ªshame you, but to admonish you as my beloved ᵇchildren.

15 For if you were to have countless ªtutors in Christ, yet *you would* not *have* many fathers; for in ᵇChrist Jesus I ᶜbecame your father through the ᵈgospel.

16 I exhort you therefore, be ªimitators of me.

17 For this reason I ªhave sent to you ᵇTimothy, who is my ᶜbeloved and faithful child in the Lord, and he will remind you of my ways which are in Christ, ᵈjust as I teach everywhere in every church.

18 Now some have become ªarrogant, as though I were not ᵇcoming to you.

19 But I ªwill come to you soon, ᵇif the Lord wills, and I shall find out, not the words of those who are ᶜarrogant, but their power.

20 For the kingdom of God does ªnot consist in words, but in power.

21 What do you desire? ªShall I come to you with a rod or with love and a spirit of gentleness?

21 a2 Cor.
1:23; 2:1, 3;
12:20; 13:2,
10

III MORAL DISORDERS IN THE CHURCH, 5:1-6:20

A The Case of Incest, 5:1-13

1 *The problem stated, 5:1-2*

5 It is actually reported that there is immorality among you, and immorality of such a kind as does not exist even among the Gentiles, that someone has ªhis father's wife.

★ 1 aLev.
18:8; Deut.
22:30; 27:20

2 And you ªhave become arrogant, and have not ᵇmourned instead, in order that the one who had done this deed might be ᶜremoved from your midst.

★ 2 a1 Cor.
4:6 b2 Cor.
7:7-10
c1 Cor. 5:13

2 *The punishment prescribed, 5:3-13*

3 For I, on my part, though ªabsent in body but present in spirit, have already judged him who has so committed this, as though I were present.

3 aCol. 2:5;
1 Thess. 2:17

4 ªIn the name of our Lord Jesus, when you are assembled, and I with you in spirit, ᵇwith the power of our Lord Jesus,

4 a2 Thess.
3:6; bJohn
20:23; 2 Cor.
2:6, 10; 13:3,
10; 1 Tim.
5:20

5 *I have decided* to ªdeliver such a one to ᵇSatan for the destruction of his flesh, that his spirit may be saved in ᶜthe day of the Lord Jesus.

★ 5 aProv.
23:14; Luke
22:31; 1 Tim.
1:20 bMatt.
4:10 c1 Cor.
1:8

6 ªYour boasting is not good. ᵇDo you not know that ᶜa little leaven leavens the whole lump *of dough?*

6 a1 Cor.
5:2; James
4:16 bRom.
6:16 cHos.
7:4; Matt.
16:6, 12;
Gal. 5:9

7 Clean out the old leaven, that you may be a new lump, just

★ 7 aMark
14:12; 1 Pet.
1:19

4:15 *tutors.* The same word is used in Gal. 3:24 (see the note there). The Corinthians had many tutors but only one spiritual father, Paul.

5:1 *immorality.* I.e., incest, forbidden by the law (Lev. 18:8; Deut. 22:22). *has.* Suggesting some sort of permanent relationship. *his father's wife.* Not the offender's mother, but a stepmother, possibly divorced from his father.

5:2 *removed* refers to church discipline and excommunication.

5:5 *to deliver such a one to Satan for the destruction of his flesh.* This evidently means that the church was to discipline this sinning brother by committing him to Satan's domain, the world (1 John 5:19) and to Satan's chastisement, the destruction or ruin of his body (*flesh* means "body" here) through sickness or even death. *destruction* does not mean annihilation, but ruin. Persistent sin often leads to physical punishment (1 Cor. 11:30; 1 John 5:16-17).

5:7 *leaven.* A symbol of impurity (see note on

as you are *in fact* unleavened. For Christ our [a]Passover also has been sacrificed.

★ 8 [a]Ex. 12:19; 13:7; Deut. 16:3

8 Let us therefore celebrate the feast, [a]not with old leaven, nor with the leaven of malice and wickedness, but with the unleavened bread of sincerity and truth.

★ 9 [a]2 Cor. 6:14; Eph. 5:11; 2 Thess. 3:6

9 I wrote you in my letter [a]not to associate with immoral people;

10 [a]1 Cor. 10:27

10 I *did* not at all *mean* with the immoral people of this world, or with the covetous and swindlers, or with [a]idolaters; for then you would have to go out of the world.

11 [a]Acts 1:15; 2 Thess. 3:6 [b]1 Cor. 10:7, 14, 20f.

11 But actually, I wrote to you not to associate with any so-called [a]brother if he should be an immoral person, or covetous, or [b]an idolater, or a reviler, or a drunkard, or a swindler—not even to eat with such a one.

★12-13
12 [a]Mark 4:11 [b]1 Cor. 5:3-5; 6:1-4

12 For what have I to do with judging [a]outsiders? [b]Do you not judge those who are within *the* church?

13 [a]Deut. 13:5; 17:7, 12; 21:21; 22:21; 1 Cor. 5:2

13 But those who are outside, God judges. [a]REMOVE THE WICKED MAN FROM AMONG YOURSELVES.

B   The Problem of Litigation in Heathen Courts, 6:1-8

1 [a]Matt. 18:17

6 Does any one of you, when he has a case against his neighbor, dare to go to law before the unrighteous, and [a]not before the saints?

2 Or [a]do you not know that [b]the saints will judge [c]the world? And if the world is judged by you, are you not competent *to* constitute the smallest law courts?

★ 2 [a]Rom. 6:16 [b]Dan. 7:18, 22, 27; Matt. 19:28 [c]1 Cor. 1:20

3 [a]Do you not know that we shall judge angels? How much more, matters of this life?

3 [a]Rom. 6:16

4 If then you have law courts dealing with matters of this life, do you appoint them as judges who are of no account in the church?

★ 4

5 [a]I say *this* to your shame. *Is it* so, *that* there is not among you one wise man who will be able to decide between his [b]brethren,

5 [a]1 Cor. 4:14; 15:34 [b]Acts 1:15; 9:13; 1 Cor. 6:1

6 but brother goes to law with brother, and that before [a]unbelievers?

6 [a]2 Cor. 6:14f.; 1 Tim. 5:8

7 Actually, then, it is already a defeat for you, that you have lawsuits with one another. [a]Why not rather be wronged? Why not rather be defrauded?

★ 7 [a]Matt. 5:39f.

8 On the contrary, you yourselves wrong and defraud, and that *your* [a]brethren.

8 [a]1 Thess. 4:6

C   The Warning against Moral Laxity, 6:9-20

9 Or [a]do you not know that the unrighteous shall not [b]inherit

★ 9 [a]Rom. 6:16 [b]Acts 20:32; 1 Cor. 15:50; Gal. 5:21; Eph. 5:5 [c]Luke 21:8; 1 Cor. 15:33; Gal. 6:7; James 1:16; 1 John 3:7 [d]Rom. 13:13; 1 Cor. 5:11; Gal. 5:19-21; Eph. 5:5; 1 Tim. 1:10; Rev. 21:8; 22:15

Matt. 13:33). By position they were *unleavened;* Paul urges that their practice correspond. *Passover.* See Ex. 12:1-28. Christ was already sacrificed, and, just as Passover was followed by the Feast of Unleavened Bread, so should the Corinthians, who were already cleansed, now walk in holiness.

5:8 *the feast.* I.e., of Unleavened Bread (cf. Ex. 12:15-20; 13:1-10).

5:9 *to associate.* I.e., have familiar fellowship. It is impossible not to have some contact with the evil people of the world in the daily pursuits of life (v. 10). But, Paul says, it is improper to have fellowship with a Christian who is under discipline (v. 11).

5:12-13 The church should leave the judgment of unbelievers to God and concentrate on setting its own house in order.

6:2 *the saints will judge the world.* Because of

our union with Christ, we will be associated with Him in this judgment (during the millennium, see Matt. 19:28). We will also *judge angels* (v. 3). See 2 Pet. 2:4, 9; Jude 6.

6:4 *appoint them . . .* Better, are you appointing them . . .?

6:7 *a defeat.* Going to court against a brother brings defeat before the case is even heard. It is better to be wronged and take a loss.

6:9 *effeminate, nor homosexuals.* Both expressions refer to homosexuals, the first to those who allow themselves to be used unnaturally, and the second to active homosexuals. Paul's warning is given against the background of incest, homosexuality, pederasty, and other unnatural sexual vices which were prevalent among the Greeks and Romans. Paul did not want Christianity confused with sects that permitted such things.

the kingdom of God? ^cDo not be deceived; ^dneither fornicators, nor idolaters, nor adulterers, nor effeminate, nor homosexuals,

10 nor thieves, nor *the* covetous, nor drunkards, nor revilers, nor swindlers, shall ^ainherit the kingdom of God.

11 And ^asuch were some of you; but you were ^bwashed, but you were ^csanctified, but you were ^djustified in the name of the Lord Jesus Christ, and in the Spirit of our God.

12 ^aAll things are lawful for me, but not all things are profitable. All things are lawful for me, but I will not be mastered by anything.

13 ^aFood is for the stomach, and the stomach is for food; but God will ^bdo away with both of them. Yet the body is not for immorality, but ^cfor the Lord; and ^dthe Lord is for the body.

14 Now God has not only ^araised the Lord, but ^bwill also raise us up through His power.

15 ^aDo you not know that ^byour bodies are members of Christ? Shall I then take away the members of Christ and make them members of a harlot? ^cMay it never be!

16 Or ^ado you not know that the one who joins himself to a harlot is one body *with her?* For He says, "^bThe two will become one flesh."

17 But the one who joins himself to the Lord is ^aone spirit *with Him.*

18 ^aFlee immorality. Every *other* sin that a man commits is outside the body, but the immoral man sins against his own body.

19 Or ^ado you not know that ^byour body is a temple of the Holy Spirit who is in you, whom you have from God, and that ^cyou are not your own?

20 For ^ayou have been bought with a price: therefore glorify God in ^byour body.

IV DISCUSSION CONCERNING MARRIAGE, 7:1-40
A Marriage and Celibacy, 7:1-9

7 Now concerning the things about which you wrote, it is ^agood for a man not to touch a woman.

2 But because of immoralities, let each man have his own wife, and let each woman have her own husband.

3 Let the husband fulfill his duty to his wife, and likewise also the wife to her husband.

Cross references (margin)

10 ^aActs 20:32; 1 Cor. 15:50; Gal. 5:21; Eph. 5:5

★11 ^a1 Cor. 12:2; Eph. 2:21; Col. 3:5-7; Titus 3:3-7 ^bActs 22:16; Eph. 5:26 ^c1:2, 30 ^dRom. 8:30

★12 ^a1 Cor. 10:23

★13 ^aMatt. 15:17 ^bCol. 2:22 ^c1 Cor. 6:15, 19 ^dGal. 5:24; Eph. 5:23

14 ^aActs 2:24 ^bJohn 6:39f.; 1 Cor. 15:23

15 ^a1 Cor. 6:3 ^bRom. 12:5, 27; 1 Cor. 6:13; Eph. 5:30 ^cLuke 20:16

16 ^a1 Cor. 6:3 ^bGen. 2:24; Matt. 19:5; Mark 10:8; Eph. 5:31

17 ^aJohn 17:21-23; Rom. 8:9-11; 1 Cor. 6:15; Gal. 2:20

★18 ^a1 Cor. 6:9; 2 Cor. 5:3; Col. 3:5; Heb. 13:4

★19 ^a1 Cor. 6:3 ^bJohn 2:21 ^cRom. 14:7f.

20 ^aActs 20:28; 1 Cor. 7:23; 1 Pet. 1:18f.; 2 Pet. 2:1; Rev. 5:9 ^bRom. 12:1; Phil. 1:20

★ 1 ^a1 Cor. 7:8, 26

★ 2-5

Study notes

6:11 *washed.* I.e., regenerated (Tit. 3:5). *sanctified.* I.e., set apart for God's use. There are three aspects to sanctification: (1) positional sanctification, possessed by every believer from the moment of his conversion (his perfect standing in holiness, Acts 20:32; 1 Cor. 1:2); (2) progressive sanctification, the daily growth in grace, becoming in practice more and more set apart for God's use (John 17:17; Eph. 5:26); and (3) ultimate sanctification, attained only when we are fully and completely set apart to God in heaven (1 Thess. 5:23). *justified.* See note on Rom. 3:24.

6:12 *are lawful.* Apparently some of the Corinthians were trying to use their Christian freedom to justify their sins. Paul here insists that Christian liberty is limited by two considerations: Is the practice expedient (helpful) and will it enslave?

6:13 Some were saying that just as *food* and the belly necessarily go together, so the body and sexual indulgence go together. Not so, says Paul. Rather, the body should always glorify the Lord.

6:18 *Flee immorality.* I.e., make it your habit to flee immorality. Joseph's reaction to the advances of Potiphar's wife (Gen. 39:12) literally illustrates this principle.

6:19 *your body is a temple.* A sharp contrast to the temple of Aphrodite in Corinth where the priestesses were prostitutes.

7:1 *you wrote.* In this chapter Paul is not writing a treatise on marriage but answering questions which had been sent to him. We have only one side of the correspondence. It is clear that Paul favored celibacy (vv. 1, 7, 8, 9, 27, 38), though he approved marriage (vv. 2, 27, 28). For more complete N.T. teaching concerning marriage, see John 2:1-11; Eph. 5:21-33; 1 Tim. 5:14; Heb. 13:4; 1 Pet. 3:1-7. *it is good . . .* Probably a position taken by some at Corinth. Paul grants its validity but states that marriage is better for those who might be overcome by the practices of the evil society in which they live (v. 2).

7:2-5 In the mutuality of marriage, each partner has rights of his or her own and debts to the other.

4 The wife does not have authority over her own body, but the husband *does*; and likewise also the husband does not have authority over his own body, but the wife *does*.

5 ^aStop depriving one another, except by agreement for a time that you may devote yourselves to prayer, and come together again lest ^bSatan tempt you because of your lack of self-control.

6 But this I say by way of concession, ^anot of command.

7 Yet I wish that all men were ^aeven as I myself am. However, ^beach man has his own gift from God, one in this manner, and another in that.

8 But I say to the unmarried and to widows that it is ^agood for them if they remain ^beven as I.

9 But if they do not have self-control, ^alet them marry; for it is better to marry than to burn.

B Marriage and Divorce, 7:10-24

10 But to the married I give instructions, ^anot I, but the Lord, that the wife should not leave her husband

11 (but if she does leave, let her remain unmarried, or else be reconciled to her husband), and

that the husband should not send his wife away.

12 But to the rest ^aI say, not the Lord, that if any brother has a wife who is an unbeliever, and she consents to live with him, let him not send her away.

13 And a woman who has an unbelieving husband, and he consents to live with her, let her not send her husband away.

14 For the unbelieving husband is sanctified through his wife, and the unbelieving wife is sanctified through her believing husband; for otherwise your children are unclean, but now they are ^aholy.

15 Yet if the unbelieving one leaves, let him leave; the brother or the sister is not under bondage in such *cases*, but God has called us ^ato peace.

16 For how do you know, O wife, whether you will ^asave your husband? Or how do you know, O husband, whether you will save your wife?

17 Only, ^aas the Lord has assigned to each one, as God has called each, in this manner let him walk. And ^bthus I direct in ^call the churches.

18 Was any man called *already* circumcised? Let him not become uncircumcised. Has anyone been called in uncircumcision? ^aLet him not be circumcised.

Marginal references:

5 ^aEx. 19:15; 1 Sam. 21:5 ^bMatt. 4:10

6 ^a2 Cor. 8:8

★ 7 ^a1 Cor. 7:8; 9:5 ^bMatt. 19:11f.; Rom. 12:6; 1 Cor. 12:4, 11

★ 8 ^a1 Cor. 7:1, 26 ^b1 Cor. 7:7; 9:5

★ 9 ^a1 Tim. 5:14

★10-11
10 ^aMal. 2:16; Matt. 5:32; 19:3-9; Mark 10:2-12; Luke 16:18; 1 Cor. 7:6

★12-13
12 ^a1 Cor. 7:6; 2 Cor. 11:17

★14 ^aEzra 9:2; Mal. 2:15

★15 ^aRom. 14:19

16 ^aRom. 11:14; 1 Pet. 3:1

★17-24
17 ^aRom. 12:3 ^b1 Cor. 4:17 ^c1 Cor. 11:16; 14:33; 2 Cor. 8:18; 11:28; Gal. 1:22; 1 Thess. 2:14; 2 Thess. 1:4

18 ^aActs 15:1ff.

7:7 *one in this manner* (i.e., celibate), *and another in that* (i.e., married).

7:8 *even as I.* Paul was obviously unmarried when he wrote these words. He might have been a widower. It is difficult, however, to substantiate that he had been married on the basis that he was a member of the Sanhedrin (Acts 26:10). It is uncertain that he was a member and also uncertain that members had to be married in the period before A.D. 70.

7:9 *burn.* I.e., with passion.

7:10-11 According to both Paul's and Christ's teachings (Mark 10:1-12), believers should not divorce. If separation does occur, the believer must either remain unmarried permanently or be reconciled permanently.

7:12-13 These verses deal with marriages in which one partner becomes a believer after the marriage. *I say, not the Lord.* I.e., Christ did not give any teaching concerning spiritu-

ally mixed marriages, but Paul does, and his teaching is authoritative.

7:14 *sanctified.* The presence of a believer in the home sets the home apart and gives it a Christian influence it would not otherwise have. A believing partner, therefore, should stay with the unbeliever. However, this does not mean that children born into such a home are automatically Christians. They are *holy* in the sense of being set apart by the presence of one believing parent.

7:15 *leaves.* If the unbelieving partner chooses to separate, the believer must accept it, though everything should be done to prevent the separation. Nothing is said about a second marriage for the believer.

7:17-24 The principle of remaining in one's marital relationship is part of a more general principle: in everything the Christian is to remain in his calling, unless it is immoral (v. 24).

19 ᵃCircumcision is nothing, and uncircumcision is nothing, but *what matters is* ᵇthe keeping of the commandments of God.

20 ᵃLet each man remain in that condition in which he was called.

21 Were you called while a slave? Do not worry about it; but if you are able also to become free, rather do that.

22 For he who was called in the Lord while a slave, is ᵃthe Lord's freedman; likewise he who was called while free, is ᵇChrist's slave.

23 ᵃYou were bought with a price; do not become slaves of men.

24 Brethren, ᵃlet each man remain with God in that *condition* in which he was called.

C Marriage and Christian Service, 7:25-38

25 Now concerning virgins I have ᵃno command of the Lord, but I give an opinion as one who ᵇby the mercy of the Lord is trustworthy.

26 I think then that this is good in view of the present ᵃdistress, that ᵇit is good for a man to remain as he is.

27 Are you bound to a wife? Do not seek to be released. Are you released from a wife? Do not seek a wife.

28 But if you should marry, you have not sinned; and if a virgin should marry, she has not sinned. Yet such will have trouble in this life, and I am trying to spare you.

29 But this I say, brethren, ᵃthe time has been shortened, so that from now on those who have wives should be as though they had none;

30 and those who weep, as though they did not weep; and those who rejoice, as though they did not rejoice; and those who buy, as though they did not possess;

31 and those who use the world, as though they did not ᵃmake full use of it; for ᵇthe form of this world is passing away.

32 But I want you to be free from concern. One who is ᵃunmarried is concerned about the things of the Lord, how he may please the Lord;

33 but one who is married is concerned about the things of the world, how he may please his wife,

34 and *his interests* are divided. And the woman who is unmarried, and the virgin, is concerned about the things of the Lord, that she may be holy both in body and spirit; but one who is married is concerned about the things of the world, how she may please her husband.

35 And this I say for your own benefit; not to put a restraint upon you, but to promote what is seemly, and *to secure* undistracted devotion to the Lord.

36 But if any man thinks that he is acting unbecomingly toward his virgin *daughter*, if she should be of full age, and if it must be so, let him do what he wishes, he does not sin; let her marry.

37 But he who stands firm in his heart, being under no constraint, but has authority over his own will, and has decided this in his own heart, to keep his own virgin *daughter*, he will do well.

38 So then both he who gives his own virgin *daughter* in marriage does well, and he who does not give her in marriage will do better.

7:25-35 Celibacy is presented as desirable, though not necessary.

7:26 *the present distress.* Probably a particularly difficult circumstance through which the Corinthian Christians were passing.

7:36 *if she should be of full age.* I.e., if a virgin daughter is getting beyond marriageable age, then her father may arrange a marriage *if it must be so.*

---

19 ᵃRom. 2:27, 29; Gal. 3:28; 5:6; 6:15; Col. 3:11 ᵇRom. 2:25
20 ᵃ1 Cor. 7:24
22 ᵃJohn 8:32, 36; Philem. 16 ᵇEph. 6:6; Col. 3:24; 1 Pet. 2:16
23 ᵃ1 Cor. 6:20
24 ᵃ1 Cor. 7:20
★**25-35**
25 ᵃ1 Cor. 7:6 ᵇ2 Cor. 4:1; 1 Tim. 1:13, 16
★**26** ᵃLuke 21:23; 2 Thess. 2:2 ᵇ1 Cor. 7:1, 8
29 ᵃRom. 13:11f.; 1 Cor. 7:31
31 ᵃ1 Cor. 9:18 ᵇ1 Cor. 7:29; 1 John 2:17
32 ᵃ1 Tim. 5:5
★**36**

D Marriage and Remarriage, 7:39-40

★39 aRom.
7:2 b2 Cor.
6:14

39 ᵃA wife is bound as long as her husband lives; but if her husband is dead, she is free to be married to whom she wishes, only ᵇin the Lord.

40 a1 Cor.
7:6, 25

40 But ᵃin my opinion she is happier if she remains as she is; and I think that I also have the Spirit of God.

V DISCUSSION CONCERNING FOOD OFFERED TO IDOLS, 8:1-11:1

A Enquiry: May a Christian Eat Food Consecrated to a Pagan God? 8:1-13

★ 1 aActs
15:20; 1 Cor.
8:4, 7, 10
bRom.
15:14; 1 Cor.
8:7, 10;
10:15
c1 Cor. 4:6
dRom. 14:19
2 a1 Cor.
3:18 b1 Cor.
13:8, 9, 12;
1 Tim. 6:4
3 aPs. 1:6;
Jer. 1:5;
Amos 3:2;
Rom. 8:29;
11:2; Gal.
4:9
★ 4 aActs
15:20; 1 Cor.
8:1, 7, 10
bActs 14:15;
1 Cor. 10:19;
Gal. 4:8
cDeut. 4:35,
39; 6:4;
1 Cor. 8:6
5 a2 Thess.
2:4
6 aDeut.
4:35, 39; 6:4;
1 Cor. 8:4
bMal. 2:10;
Eph. 4:6
cRom. 11:36
dJohn 13:13;
1 Cor. 1:2;
Eph. 4:5;
1 Tim. 2:5
eJohn 1:3;
Col. 1:16

8 Now concerning ᵃthings sacrificed to idols, we know that we all have ᵇknowledge. Knowledge ᶜmakes arrogant, but love ᵈedifies.

2 ᵃIf anyone supposes that he knows anything, he has not yet ᵇknown as he ought to know;

3 but if anyone loves God, he ᵃis known by Him.

4 Therefore concerning the eating of ᵃthings sacrificed to idols, we know that there is ᵇno such thing as an idol in the world, and that ᶜthere is no God but one.

5 For even if ᵃthere are so-called gods whether in heaven or on earth, as indeed there are many gods and many lords,

6 yet for us ᵃthere is *but* one God, ᵇthe Father, ᶜfrom whom are all things, and we *exist* for Him; and ᵈone Lord, Jesus Christ, ᵉby whom are all things, and we *exist* through Him.

7 However not all men ᵃhave this knowledge; but ᵇsome, being accustomed to the idol until now, eat food as if it were sacrificed to an idol; and their conscience being weak is defiled.

7 a1 Cor.
8:4ff. bRom.
14:14, 22f.

8 But ᵃfood will not commend us to God; we are neither the worse if we do not eat, nor the better if we do eat.

8 aRom.
14:17

9 But ᵃtake care lest this liberty of yours somehow become a stumbling block to the ᵇweak.

9 aRom.
14:13, 21;
1 Cor. 10:28;
Gal. 5:13
bRom. 14:1;
1 Cor. 8:10f.
★10 a1 Cor.
8:4ff. bActs
15:20; 1 Cor.
8:1, 4, 7

10 For if someone sees you, who have ᵃknowledge, dining in an idol's temple, will not his conscience, if he is weak, be strengthened to eat ᵇthings sacrificed to idols?

11 For through ᵃyour knowledge he who is weak ᵇis ruined, the brother for whose sake Christ died.

★11 a1 Cor.
8:4ff. bRom.
14:15, 20

12 ᵃAnd thus, by sinning against the brethren and wounding their conscience when it is weak, you sin ᵇagainst Christ.

12 aMatt.
18:6; Rom.
14:20 bMatt.
25:45

13 Therefore, ᵃif food causes my brother to stumble, I will never eat meat again, that I might not cause my brother to stumble.

★13 aRom.
14:21; 1 Cor.
10:32; 2 Cor.
6:3; 11:29

B Example of Paul, 9:1-27

1 Paul's rights, 9:1-14

9 Am I not ᵃfree? Am I not an ᵇapostle? Have I not ᶜseen Jesus our Lord? Are you not ᵈmy work in the Lord?

2 If to others I am not an apostle, at least I am to you; for you are the ᵃseal of my ᵇapostleship in the Lord.

3 My defense to those who examine me is this:

★ 1 a1 Cor.
9:19; 10:29
bActs 14:14;
Rom. 1:1;
2 Cor. 12:12;
1 Thess. 2:6;
1 Tim. 2:7;
2 Tim. 1:11
cActs 9:3,
17; 18:9;
22:14, 18;
23:11; 1 Cor.
15:8 d1 Cor.
3:6; 4:15
2 aJohn
3:33; 2 Cor.
3:2f. bActs
1:25

7:39 *only in the Lord.* I.e., only to another Christian.

8:1 *things sacrificed to idols.* The remainders of animals which had been sacrificed to heathen idols. If the offering was private, the remainders were claimed by the offerer; if public, they were sold in the market. The question discussed here concerned what a Christian should do about buying such meat or eating it when served to him at a banquet.

8:4 *there is no such thing as an idol in the world.* Yet Paul recognizes (v. 5) that *there are so-called gods.*

8:10 *in an idol's temple.* Probably refers to some official function or festival.

8:11 *ruined,* not eternally, but in his spiritual life.

8:13 Here is the great principle that regulates conduct in morally indifferent matters. It is the principle of love voluntarily regulating liberty (Gal. 5:13).

9:1 This chapter gives an illustration from Paul's own life of the principle of 8:13. He did not take advantage of the rightful privileges he had as an apostle.

4 *a*1 Cor.
9:14;
1 Thess. 2:6,
9; 2 Thess.
3:8f.
★ 5 *a*1 Cor.
7:7f. *b*Matt.
12:46 *c*Matt.
8:14; John
1:42
★ 6 *a*Acts
4:36

4   *a*Do we not have a right to eat and drink?

5   *a*Do we not have a right to take along a believing wife, even as the rest of the apostles, and the *b*brothers of the Lord, and *c*Cephas?

6   Or do only *a*Barnabas and I not have a right to refrain from working?

7 *a*2 Cor.
10:4; 1 Tim.
1:18; 2 Tim.
2:3f. *b*Deut.
20:6; Prov.
27:18; 1 Cor.
3:6, 8

7   Who at any time serves *a*as a soldier at his own expense? Who *b*plants a vineyard, and does not eat the fruit of it? Or who tends a flock and does not use the milk of the flock?

8 *a*Rom.
3:5

8   I am not speaking these things *a*according to human judgment, am I? Or does not the Law also say these things?

★ 9 *a*Deut.
25:4; 1 Tim.
5:18 *b*Deut.
22:1-4; Prov.
12:10

9   For it is written in the Law of Moses, "*a*YOU SHALL NOT MUZZLE THE OX WHILE HE IS THRESHING." God is not concerned about *b*oxen, is He?

10 *a*Rom.
4:23f.
*b*2 Tim. 2:6

10   Or is He speaking altogether for our sake? Yes, *a*for our sake it was written, because *b*the plowman ought to plow in hope, and the thresher *to thresh* in hope of sharing *the crops.*

★11 *a*Rom.
15:27; 1 Cor.
9:14

11   *a*If we sowed spiritual things in you, is it too much if we should reap material things from you?

12 *a*Acts
18:3; 20:33;
1 Cor. 9:15,
18 *b*2 Cor.
6:3; 11:12
*c*1 Cor. 4:15;
9:14, 16, 18,
23; 2 Cor.
2:12
★13 *a*Rom.
6:16 *b*Lev.
6:16, 26; 7:6,
31ff.; Num.
5:9f.; 18:8-
20, 31; Deut.
18:1

12   If others share the right over you, do we not more? Nevertheless, we *a*did not use this right, but we endure all things, *b*that we may cause no hindrance to the *c*gospel of Christ.

13   *a*Do you not know that those who *b*perform sacred services eat the *food* of the temple, and those who attend regularly to the altar have their share with the altar?

14   So also *a*the Lord directed those who proclaim the *b*gospel to *c*get their living from the gospel.

2   Paul's restrictions, 9:15-27

15   But I have *a*used none of these things. And I am not writing these things that it may be done so in my case; for it would be better for me to die than have any man make *b*my boast an empty one.

16   For if I preach the gospel, I have nothing to boast of, for *a*I am under compulsion; for woe is me if I do not preach *b*the gospel.

17   For if I do this voluntarily, I have a *a*reward; but if against my will, I have a *b*stewardship entrusted to me.

18   What then is my *a*reward? That, when I preach the gospel, I may offer the gospel *b*without charge, so as *c*not to make full use of my right in the gospel.

19   For though I am *a*free from all *men,* I have made myself *b*a slave to all, that I might *c*win the more.

20   And *a*to the Jews I became as a Jew, that I might win Jews; to those who are under the Law, as under the Law, though *b*not being myself under the Law, that I might win those who are under the Law;

21   to those who are *a*without law, *b*as without law, though not being without the law of God but *c*under the law of Christ, that I might win those who are without law.

14 *a*Matt.
10:10; Luke
10:7; 1 Tim.
5:18 *b*1 Cor.
4:15; 9:12,
16, 18, 23;
2 Cor. 2:12
*c*Luke 10:8;
1 Cor. 9:4
15 *a*Acts
18:3; 20:33;
1 Cor. 9:12,
18 *b*2 Cor.
11:10
16 *a*Acts
9:15; Rom.
1:14 *b*1 Cor.
4:15; 9:12,
14, 18, 23;
2 Cor. 2:12
★17 *a*John
4:36 [Gr.];
1 Cor. 3:8;
9:18 *b*1 Cor.
4:1; Gal. 2:7;
Eph. 3:2;
Phil. 1:16;
Col. 1:25
18 *a*John
4:36 [Gr.];
1 Cor. 3:8;
9:17 *b*Acts
18:3; 2 Cor.
11:7; 12:13
*c*1 Cor. 7:31;
9:12
19 *a*1 Cor.
9:1 *b*2 Cor.
4:5; Gal.
5:13 *c*Matt.
18:15; 1 Pet.
3:1
★20 *a*Acts
16:3; 21:23-
26; Rom.
11:14 *b*Gal.
2:19
21 *a*Rom.
2:12, 14
*b*Gal. 2:3;
3:2 *c*1 Cor.
7:22; Gal.
6:2

9:5 *to take along a believing wife.* I.e., to be married. Peter was married (Matt. 8:14), as were *the rest of the apostles* and Christ's brothers.

9:6 *to refrain from working.* I.e., Is it only Barnabas and I who must work for a living? Paul had the right to be supported by those to whom he ministered, but he did not insist on this right (1 Thess. 2:9).

9:9 *the Law* (Deut. 25:4) vindicates Paul's claim.

9:11 *material things.* I.e., your material support.

9:13 The priests were supported by the people (Num. 18:8-24).

9:17 Willingly or unwillingly, Paul could not escape his responsibility to preach the gospel, because a *stewardship* (responsibility) had been committed to him and he was under orders to preach even though he was never paid (cf. Luke 17:10).

9:20 *as under the Law.* I.e., I became as one under the Law. Though Paul had broken with the law of Moses, he adds (v. 21) that he was not lawless, *but under the law of Christ.*

22 aRom.
14:1; 15:1;
2 Cor. 11:29
b1 Cor.
10:33 cRom.
11:14

★24 a1 Cor.
9:13 bPhil.
3:14; Col.
2:18 cGal.
2:2; 2 Tim.
4:7; Heb.
12:1

★25 aEph.
6:12; 1 Tim.
6:12; 2 Tim.
2:5; 4:7
b2 Tim. 4:8;
James 1:12;
1 Pet. 5:4;
Rev. 2:10;
3:11

★26 aGal.
2:2; 2 Tim.
4:7; Heb.
12:1 b1 Cor.
14:9

★27 aRom.
8:13

★ **1** aRom.
1:13 bEx.
13:21; Ps.
105:39 cEx.
14:22, 29;
Ps. 66:6

★ **2** aRom.
6:3; 1 Cor.
1:13; Gal.
3:27

22 To the aweak I became weak, that I might win the weak; I have become ball things to all men, cthat I may by all means save some.

23 And I do all things for the sake of the gospel, that I may become a fellow partaker of it.

24 aDo you not know that those who run in a race all run, but only one receives bthe prize? cRun in such a way that you may win.

25 And everyone who acompetes in the games exercises self-control in all things. They then do it to receive a perishable bwreath, but we an imperishable.

26 Therefore I arun in such a way, as not without aim; I box in such a way, as not bbeating the air;

27 but I buffet amy body and make it my slave, lest possibly, after I have preached to others, I myself should be disqualified.

C Exhortations, 10:1-11:1
1 Avoid self-indulgence,
10:1-13

10 For aI do not want you to be unaware, brethren, that our fathers were all bunder the cloud, and all cpassed through the sea;

2 and all were abaptized into Moses in the cloud and in the sea;

3 and all aate the same spiritual food;

4 and all adrank the same spiritual drink, for they were drinking from a spiritual rock which followed them; and the rock was Christ.

5 Nevertheless, with most of them God was not well-pleased; for athey were laid low in the wilderness.

6 Now these things happened as aexamples for us, that we should not crave evil things, as bthey also craved.

7 And do not be aidolaters, as some of them were; as it is written, "bTHE PEOPLE SAT DOWN TO EAT AND DRINK, AND STOOD UP TO cPLAY."

8 Nor let us act immorally, as asome of them did, and btwenty-three thousand fell in one day.

9 Nor let us try the Lord, as asome of them did, and were destroyed by the serpents.

10 Nor grumble, aas some of them did, and bwere destroyed by the cdestroyer.

11 Now these things happened to them as an aexample, and bthey were written for our instruction, upon whom cthe ends of the ages have come.

12 Therefore let him who athinks he stands take heed lest he fall.

★ **3** aEx.
16:4, 35;
Deut. 8:3;
Neh. 9:15,
20; Ps.
78:24f.; John
6:31

★ **4** aEx.
17:6; Num.
20:11; Ps.
78:15

5 aNum.
14:29ff., 37;
26:65; Heb.
3:17; Jude 5

★ **6** a1 Cor.
10:11 bNum.
11:4, 34; Ps.
106:14

★ **7** aEx.
32:4; 1 Cor.
5:11; 10:14
bEx. 32:6
cEx. 32:19

★ **8** aNum.
25:1ff.
bNum. 25:9

★ **9** aNum.
21:5f.

★10 aNum.
16:41; 17:5,
10 bNum.
16:49 cEx.
12:23;
2 Sam.
24:16; 1 Chr.
21:15; Heb.
11:28

11 a1 Cor.
10:6 bRom.
4:23 cRom.
13:11

12 aRom.
11:20; 2 Pet.
3:17

9:24 *race.* Paul draws on his readers' knowledge of the Isthmian games, which were held every two years near Corinth.

9:25 *exercises self-control.* To be a winner one must train diligently. *a perishable wreath.* In the Isthmian games it was a wreath of pine.

9:26 *as not beating the air.* This does not refer to shadowboxing but to wild misses during an actual boxing match.

9:27 *I buffet my body.* Paul changes the metaphor: his opponent is now his own body. By self-discipline he gives it knockout blows. *disqualified.* A reference to the possible loss of reward (see note on 3:14; cf. 2 John 8).

10:1 *our fathers.* The nation Israel is now used as an illustration of some who were disqualified (9:27). *under the cloud* that guided them (Ex. 13:21-22; 14:19). *through the sea.* See Ex. 14:15-22.

10:2 *baptized into Moses.* I.e., united to Moses as their leader.

10:3 *spiritual food.* I.e., the manna (Ex. 16:1-36; Ps. 78:25).

10:4 *from a spiritual rock* which provided water (Ex. 17:1-9; Num. 20:1-13). Since the rock is mentioned twice, and is in different settings, a rabbinic legend held that a material rock actually followed the Israelites. Paul, however, says that it was Christ who was with Israel all the way.

10:6 *craved.* I.e., desired, when they preferred the food of Egypt to God's manna (Num. 11:4).

10:7 *idolaters.* See Ex. 32:1-14 for the making of the golden calf.

10:8 *twenty-three thousand* was the number killed in one day. Num. 25:9 indicates that there were additional deaths afterwards.

10:9 *try the Lord . . . destroyed by the serpents.* See Num. 21:6.

10:10 *grumble,* as some did after the judgment on the rebels who were led by Korah (Num. 16:41-50).

★13 *a*1 Cor.
1:9 *b*2 Pet.
2:9

13 No temptation has overtaken you but such as is common to man; and *a*God is faithful, who will not allow you to be *b*tempted beyond what you are able, but with the temptation will provide the way of escape also, that you may be able to endure it.

2 Do not participate in idol feasts, 10:14-22

★14-22
14 *a*Heb.
6:9 *b*1 Cor.
10:7, 19f.;
1 John 5:21

16 *a*Matt.
26:27f.;
1 Cor. 11:25
*b*Matt. 26:26;
1 Cor.
11:32f.

17 *a*Rom.
12:5; 1 Cor.
12:12f., 27;
Eph. 4:4, 16;
Col. 3:15

18 *a*Rom.
1:3 *b*Lev.
7:6, 14f.;
Deut. 12:17f.

19 *a*1 Cor.
8:4

20 *a*Deut.
32:17; Ps.
106:37; Gal.
4:8; Rev.
9:20

21 *a*2 Cor.
6:16 *b*Is.
65:11

22 *a*Deut.
32:21 *b*Eccl.
6:10; Is. 45:9

14 Therefore, my *a*beloved, flee from *b*idolatry.
15 I speak as to wise men; you judge what I say.
16 Is not the *a*cup of blessing which we bless a sharing in the blood of Christ? Is not the *b*bread which we break a sharing in the body of Christ?
17 Since there is one bread, we *a*who are many are one body; for we all partake of the one bread.
18 Look at the nation *a*Israel; are not those who *b*eat the sacrifices sharers in the altar?
19 What do I mean then? That a thing sacrificed to idols is anything, or *a*that an idol is anything?
20 No, but *I say* that the things which the Gentiles sacrifice, they *a*sacrifice to demons, and not to God; and I do not want you to become sharers in demons.
21 *a*You cannot drink the cup of the Lord and the cup of demons; you cannot partake of the table of the Lord and *b*the table of demons.
22 Or do we *a*provoke the

Lord to jealousy? We are not *b*stronger than He, are we?

3 Glorify God by seeking the welfare of your brother, 10:23-11:1

23 *a*All things are lawful, but not all things are profitable. All things are lawful, but not all things *b*edify.
24 Let no one *a*seek his own good, but that of his neighbor.
25 *a*Eat anything that is sold in the meat market, without asking questions for conscience' sake;
26 *a*FOR THE EARTH IS THE LORD'S, AND ALL IT CONTAINS.
27 If *a*one of the unbelievers invites you, and you wish to go, *b*eat anything that is set before you, without asking questions for conscience' sake;
28 But *a*if anyone should say to you, "This is meat sacrificed to idols," do not eat *it,* for the sake of the one who informed *you,* and for conscience' sake;
29 I mean not your own conscience, but the other *man's;* for *a*why is my freedom judged by another's conscience?
30 If I partake with thankfulness, *a*why am I slandered concerning that for which I *b*give thanks?
31 Whether, then, you eat or drink or *a*whatever you do, do all to the glory of God.
32 *a*Give no offense either to Jews or to Greeks or to *b*the church of God;

23 *a*1 Cor.
6:12 *b*Rom.
14:19

★24 *a*Rom.
15:2; 1 Cor.
10:33; 13:5;
2 Cor. 12:14;
Phil. 2:21
★25 *a*Acts
10:15; 1 Cor.
8:7

26 *a*Ps. 24:1;
50:12; 1 Tim.
4:4
27 *a*1 Cor.
5:10 *b*Luke
10:8

28 *a*1 Cor.
8:7, 10-12

29 *a*Rom.
14:16; 1 Cor.
9:19
30 *a*1 Cor.
9:1 *b*Rom.
14:6
★31 *a*Col.
3:17; 1 Pet.
4:11
32 *a*Acts
24:16; 1 Cor.
8:13 *b*Acts
20:28; 1 Cor.
1:2; 7:17;
11:22; 15:9;
2 Cor. 1:1;
Gal. 1:13;
Phil. 3:6;
1 Tim. 3:5,
15

10:13 *the way of escape.* Lit., the way out. Not necessarily relief, but power to be able to bear the testing.
10:14-22 Paul's point is that partaking in a religious feast means fellowshipping with the one worshiped at that feast. This is true of the Lord's Supper (vv. 16-17), it was true of Israel in O.T. times (v. 18), and it is true of a pagan feast (vv. 19-22). Therefore, believers must not fellowship at pagan feasts since they may thereby open themselves up to demonic attacks (v. 20).
10:24 *good* = welfare.
10:25 *the meat market.* The subject now

changes from meat sacrificed to idols and served at pagan feasts to meat sacrificed to idols that is bought in the market and served at private dinner parties (v. 27). Again, liberty should be voluntarily restricted.
10:31 *do all to the glory of God.* This is the all-inclusive principle concluding the discussion that began in 8:1. It is: Test all conduct by whether or not it manifests the characteristics of God. Other principles for guiding the believer's conduct in this book are: (1) is it beneficial (6:12)? (2) is it enslaving (6:12)? (3) will it hinder the spiritual growth of a brother (8:13)? (4) does it edify (build up, 10:23)?

33 aRom.
15:2; 1 Cor.
9:22; Gal.
1:10 bRom.
15:2; 2 Cor.
12:14; Phil.
2:21cRom.
11:14
★ 1 a1 Cor.
4:16

33 just as I also aplease all men in all things, bnot seeking my own profit, but the *profit* of the many, cthat they may be saved.

11 aBe imitators of me, just as I also am of Christ.

VI DISCUSSION CONCERNING PUBLIC WORSHIP,
11:2–14:40
A The Veiling of Women,
11:2–16

★ 2 a1 Cor.
11:17, 22
b1 Cor. 4:17;
15:2;
1 Thess. 1:6;
3:6
c2 Thess.
2:15; 3:6
★ 3 aEph.
1:22; 4:15;
5:23; Col.
1:18; 2:19
bGen. 3:16;
Eph. 5:23
c1 Cor. 3:23
4 aActs
13:1;
1 Thess. 5:20

★ 5 aLuke
2:36; Acts
21:9; 1 Cor.
14:34 bDeut.
21:12

7 aGen.
1:26; 5:1;
9:6; James
3:9

2 Now aI praise you because you bremember me in everything, and chold firmly to the traditions, just as I delivered them to you.

3 But I want you to understand that Christ is the ahead of every man, and bthe man is the head of a woman, and God is the chead of Christ.

4 Every man who has *something* on his head while praying or aprophesying, disgraces his head.

5 But every awoman who has her head uncovered while praying or prophesying, disgraces her head; for she is one and the same with her whose head is bshaved.

6 For if a woman does not cover her head, let her also have her hair cut off; but if it is disgraceful for a woman to have her hair cut off or her head shaved, let her cover her head.

7 For a man ought not to have his head covered, since he is the aimage and glory of God; but the woman is the glory of man.

8 For aman does not originate from woman, but woman from man;

9 for indeed man was not created for the woman's sake, but awoman for the man's sake.

10 Therefore the woman ought to have a *symbol of* authority on her head, because of the angels.

11 However, in the Lord, neither is woman independent of man, nor is man independent of woman.

12 For as the woman originates from the man, so also the man has his birth through the woman; and aall things originate bfrom God.

13 aJudge for yourselves: is it proper for a woman to pray to God *with head* uncovered?

14 Does not even nature itself teach you that if a man has long hair, it is a dishonor to him,

15 but if a woman has long hair, it is a glory to her? For her hair is given to her for a covering.

16 But if one is inclined to be contentious, awe have no other practice, nor have bthe churches of God.

8 aGen.
2:21-23;
1 Tim. 2:13

9 aGen.
2:18

★10

12 a2 Cor.
5:18 bRom.
11:36

13 aLuke
12:57

★15

★16 a1 Cor.
4:5; 9:1-3, 6
b1 Cor. 7:17

B The Lord's Supper, 11:17–34

17 But in giving this instruction, aI do not praise you, because

17 a1 Cor.
11:2, 22

11:1 This verse belongs in thought with chapter 10. The Corinthians are urged to imitate the self-sacrificing example of Paul and Christ.

11:2 *traditions.* I.e., oral teaching.

11:3 *the man is the head of a woman.* This teaching is based on Gen. 3:16, and Paul makes it the basis for the wearing of a covering.

11:5 *who has her head uncovered.* Women should be veiled or covered in the meeting of the church, and men should not. Paul's reasons were based on theology (headship, v. 3), the order in creation (vv. 7–9), and the presence of angels in the meeting (v. 10). None of these reasons was based on contemporary social custom. *praying or prophesying.* In the light of what he says in 14:34-35, it is doubtful that Paul approved of those activities by the

women at Corinth. He simply acknowledges that these were unauthorized practices.

11:10 *a symbol.* I.e., the covering is the sign of man's authority over the woman. *because of the angels.* The insubordination of an uncovered woman (signifying her refusal to recognize the authority of her husband) would offend the angels who observe the conduct of believers in their church gatherings (1 Pet. 1:12).

11:15 *her hair is given to her for a covering.* This is not the same word as that used in vv. 5–6. The point here is that as the hair represents the proper covering in the natural realm, so the veil is the proper covering in the religious.

11:16 *no other practice.* I.e., no custom of women worshiping without some form of a covering.

you come together not for the better but for the worse.

18 For, in the first place, when you come together as a church, I hear that [a]divisions exist among you; and in part, I believe it.

19 For there [a]must also be factions among you, [b]in order that those who are approved may have become evident among you.

20 Therefore when you meet together, it is not to eat the Lord's Supper,

21 for in your eating each one takes his own supper first; and one is hungry and [a]another is drunk.

22 What! Do you not have houses in which to eat and drink? Or do you despise the [a]church of God, and [b]shame those who have nothing? What shall I say to you? Shall [c]I praise you? In this I will not praise you.

23 For [a]I received from the Lord that which I also delivered to you, that [b]the Lord Jesus in the night in which He was betrayed took bread;

24 and when He had given thanks, He broke it, and said, "This is My body, which is for you; do this in remembrance of Me."

25 In the same way He took [a]the cup also, after supper, saying, "This cup is the [b]new covenant in My blood; do this, as often as you drink it, in remembrance of Me."

26 For as often as you eat this bread and drink the cup, you pro-

claim the Lord's death [a]until He comes.

27 Therefore whoever eats the bread or drinks the cup of the Lord in an unworthy manner, shall be [a]guilty of the body and the blood of the Lord.

28 But let a man [a]examine himself, and so let him eat of the bread and drink of the cup.

29 For he who eats and drinks, eats and drinks judgment to himself, if he does not judge the body rightly.

30 For this reason many among you are weak and sick, and a number [a]sleep.

31 But if we judged ourselves rightly, we should not be judged.

32 But when we are judged, we are [a]disciplined by the Lord in order that we may not be condemned along with [b]the world.

33 So then, my brethren, when you come together to eat, wait for one another.

34 If anyone is [a]hungry, let him eat [b]at home, so that you may not come together for judgment. And the remaining matters I shall [c]arrange [d]when I come.

C The Use of Spiritual Gifts, 12:1–14:40

1 The varieties of gifts, 12:1–11

12 Now concerning [a]spiritual gifts, brethren, [b]I do not want you to be unaware.

2 [a]You know that when you were pagans, you were [b]led astray

---

Cross-references (left margin)

18 [a]1 Cor. 1:10; 3:3

19 [a]Matt. 18:7; Luke 17:1; 1 Tim. 4:1; 2 Pet. 2:1 [b]Deut. 13:3; 1 John 2:19
★**20**

21 [a]Jude 12

22 [a]1 Cor. 10:32 [b]James 2:6 [c]1 Cor. 11:2, 17

23 [a]1 Cor. 15:3; Gal. 1:12; Col. 3:24 [b]1 Cor. 11:23-25; Matt. 26:26-28; Mark 14:22-24; Luke 22:17-20; 1 Cor. 10:16
★**24**

★**25** [a]1 Cor. 10:16 [b]Luke 22:20; 2 Cor. 3:6

★**26** [a]John 21:22; 1 Cor. 4:5

Cross-references (right margin)

★**27** [a]Heb. 10:29

28 [a]Matt. 26:22; 2 Cor. 13:5; Gal. 6:4

30 [a]Acts 7:60

32 [a]2 Sam. 7:14; Ps. 94:12; Heb. 12:7-10; Rev. 3:19 [b]1 Cor. 1:20

34 [a]1 Cor. 11:21 [b]1 Cor. 11:22 [c]1 Cor. 4:17; 7:17; 16:1 [d]1 Cor. 4:19

★ **1** [a]1 Cor. 12:4; 14:1 [b]Rom. 1:13 **2** [a]1 Cor. 6:11; Eph. 2:11f.; 1 Pet. 4:3 [b]1 Thess. 1:9 [c]Ps. 115:5; Is. 46:7; Jer. 10:5; Hab. 2:18f.

11:20 *when you meet together.* The early Christians held a love feast in connection with the Lord's Supper, during which they gathered for a fellowship meal, sent and received communications from other churches, and collected money for widows and orphans. Apparently some of the wealthier members were not sharing their food but greedily consumed it before the poor showed up (v. 21). If the purposes of the love feast were not being realized, it was better to eat at home (v. 22).

11:24 *This is My body.* The bread represents Christ's body and the *cup* (v. 25) His blood. See note on Luke 22:19.

11:25 *the new covenant.* See note on Matt. 26:28.

11:26 *you proclaim the Lord's death until He*

comes. The Lord's Supper is an acted sermon (proclaim), looking back on Christ's life and death and looking forward to His second coming.

11:27 *in an unworthy manner.* I.e., with unconfessed sin. This may result in judgment, even sickness or physical death (v. 30). Therefore, each one is to examine himself before partaking (vv. 28, 31).

12:1 In chapters 12–14 Paul deals with the subject of *spiritual gifts*, against the background of divisions and moral laxity in a church that lacked no gift (1:7, see note). Chapter 12 deals with the unity and diversity of the gifts, chap. 13 with the power of love, and chap. 14 with the specific gifts of prophecy and tongues.

to the [c]dumb idols, however you were led.

3 [a]Matt. 22:43; 1 John 4:2f.; Rev. 1:10 [b]Rom. 9:3 [c]John 13:13; Rom. 10:9

3 Therefore I make known to you, that no one speaking [a]by the Spirit of God says, "Jesus is [b]accursed"; and no one can say, "Jesus is [c]Lord," except [a]by the Holy Spirit.

4 [a]Rom. 12:6f.; 1 Cor. 12:11; Eph. 4:4ff., 11; Heb. 2:4

4 Now there are [a]varieties of gifts, but the same Spirit.

5 And there are varieties of ministries, and the same Lord.

6 [a]1 Cor. 15:28; Eph. 1:23; 4:6

6 And there are varieties of effects, but the same [a]God who works all things in all *persons.*

7 [a]1 Cor. 12:12-30; 14:26; Eph. 4:12

7 But to each one is given the manifestation of the Spirit [a]for the common good.

★ 8-10
8 [a]1 Cor. 2:6; 2 Cor. 1:12 [b]Rom. 15:14; 1 Cor. 2:11, 16; 2 Cor. 2:14; 4:6; 8:7; 11:6
9 [a]1 Cor. 13:2; 2 Cor. 4:13 [b]1 Cor. 12:28, 30
10 [a]1 Cor. 12:28f.; Gal. 3:5 [b]1 Cor. 11:4; 13:2, 8 [c]1 Cor. 14:29; 1 John 4:1 [d]Mark 16:17; 1 Cor. 12:28, 30; 13:1; 14:2ff. [e]1 Cor. 12:30; 14:26
11 [a]1 Cor. 12:4 and ref.

8 For to one is given the word of [a]wisdom through the Spirit, and to another the word of [b]knowledge according to the same Spirit;

9 to another [a]faith by the same Spirit, and to another [b]gifts of healing by the one Spirit,

10 and to another the effecting of [a]miracles, and to another [b]prophecy, and to another the [c]distinguishing of spirits, to another *various* [d]kinds of tongues, and to another the [e]interpretation of tongues.

11 But one and the same Spirit works all these things, [a]distributing to each one individually just as He wills.

2 *The purpose of gifts: unity in diversity,* 12:12–31

★12-31
12 [a]Rom. 12:4; 1 Cor. 10:17 [b]1 Cor. 12:27

12 For even [a]as the body is one and *yet* has many members, and all the members of the body, though they are many, are one body, [b]so also is Christ.

★13 [a]Eph. 2:18 [b]Rom. 3:22; Gal. 3:28; Eph. 2:13-18; Col. 3:11 [c]John 7:37-39

13 For [a]by one Spirit we were all baptized into one body, whether [b]Jews or Greeks, whether slaves or free, and we were all made to [c]drink of one Spirit.

14 [a]1 Cor. 12:20

14 For [a]the body is not one member, but many.

15 If the foot should say, "Because I am not a hand, I am not *a part* of the body," it is not for this reason any the less *a part* of the body.

16 And if the ear should say, "Because I am not an eye, I am not *a part* of the body," it is not for this reason any the less *a part* of the body.

17 If the whole body were an eye, where would the hearing be? If the whole were hearing, where would the sense of smell be?

18 [a]1 Cor. 12:28 [b]Rom. 12:6; 1 Cor. 12:11

18 But now God has [a]placed the members, each one of them, in the body, [b]just as He desired.

19 And if they were all one member, where would the body be?

20 [a]1 Cor. 12:12, 14

20 But now [a]there are many members, but one body.

21 And the eye cannot say to the hand, "I have no need of you"; or again the head to the feet, "I have no need of you."

22 On the contrary, it is much truer that the members of the body which seem to be weaker are necessary;

★23

23 and those *members* of the body, which we deem less honorable, on these we bestow more

---

12:8–10 *the word of wisdom* (v. 8). I.e., the communication of spiritual wisdom. *the word of knowledge* (v. 8). I.e., the communication of practical truth. *faith* (v. 9). I.e., unusual reliance on God. *gifts of healing* (v. 9). Included restoration of life (Acts 9:40; 20:12). *prophecy* (v. 10). The ability to proclaim new revelation from God. *tongues* and *interpretation of tongues* (v. 10). Ability to speak and interpret languages unknown to the speaker or the interpreter. These gifts were necessary before the Word of God was written.

12:12–31 Here Paul describes the relationship of gifted believers to each other, using the analogy of the human body. The Spirit has formed a spiritual organic unity of the many dissimilar members of the body of Christ (vv. 12–13). The constitutions both of the human body and of the body of Christ demand that all members (even those which seem unimportant) function in harmony (vv. 14–20). Finally, the need for mutual dependence, respect, and care for each other is emphasized (vv. 21–31).

12:13 *we were all baptized.* The Spirit joins all believers to the body of Christ. The tense of the verb indicates a past action, and it is something all believers (even carnal ones) have experienced.

12:23 *we bestow more abundant honor.* I.e., by way of clothing.

abundant honor, and our unseemly *members come to* have more abundant seemliness,

24 whereas our seemly *members* have no need *of it.* But God has *so* composed the body, giving more abundant honor to that *member* which lacked,

25 that there should be no division in the body, but *that* the members should have the same care for one another.

26 And if one member suffers, all the members suffer with it; if *one* member is honored, all the members rejoice with it.

27 Now you are ªChrist's body, and ᵇindividually members of it.

28 And God has ªappointed in ᵇthe church, first ᶜapostles, second ᵈprophets, third ᵉteachers, then ᶠmiracles, then ᵍgifts of healings, helps, ʰadministrations, *various* ⁱkinds of tongues.

29 All are not apostles, are they? All are not prophets, are they? All are not teachers, are they? All are not *workers of* miracles, are they?

30 All do not have gifts of healings, do they? All do not speak with tongues, do they? All do not ªinterpret, do they?

31 But ªearnestly desire the greater gifts.

And I show you a still more excellent way.

3　The supremacy of love over gifts, 13:1-13

13 If I speak with the ªtongues of men and of ᵇangels, but do not have love, I have become a noisy gong or a ᶜclanging cymbal.

2 And if I have *the gift of* ªprophecy, and know all ᵇmysteries and all ᶜknowledge; and if I have ᵈall faith, so as to ᵉremove mountains, but do not have love, I am nothing.

3 And if I ªgive all my possessions to feed *the poor,* and if I ᵇdeliver my body to be burned, but do not have love, it profits me nothing.

4 Love ªis patient, love is kind, *and* ᵇis not jealous; love does not brag *and* is not ᶜarrogant,

5 does not act unbecomingly; it ªdoes not seek its own, is not provoked, ᵇdoes not take into account a wrong *suffered,*

6 ªdoes not rejoice in unrighteousness, but ᵇrejoices with the truth;

7 ªbears all things, believes all things, hopes all things, endures all things.

8 Love never fails; but if *there are gifts of* ªprophecy, they will be done away; if *there are* ᵇtongues, they will cease; if *there is* knowledge, it will be done away.

9 For we ªknow in part, and we prophesy in part;

10 but when the perfect comes, the partial will be done away.

11 When I was a child, I used to speak as a child, think as a child, reason as a child; when I

27 ª1 Cor.
1:2; 12:12;
Eph. 1:23;
4:12; Col.
1:18, 24;
2:19 ᵇRom.
12:5; Eph.
5:30
★**28** ª1 Cor.
12:18
ᵇ1 Cor.
10:32 ᶜEph.
4:11 ᵈActs
13:1; Eph.
2:20; 3:5
ᵉActs 13:1
ᶠ1 Cor.
12:10, 29
ᵍ1 Cor. 12:9,
30 ʰRom.
12:8 ⁱ1 Cor.
12:10
★**29-30**
30 ª1 Cor.
12:10

★**31** ª1 Cor.
14:1, 39

★ **1** ª1 Cor.
12:10
ᵇ2 Cor. 12:4;
Rev. 14:2
ᶜPs. 150:5
[Septuagint]

2 ªMatt.
7:22; Acts
13:1; 1 Cor.
11:4; 13:8;
14:1, 39
ᵇ1 Cor. 14:2;
15:51 ᶜRom.
15:14
ᵈ1 Cor. 12:9
ᵉMatt. 17:20;
21:21
3 ªMatt. 6:2
ᵇDan. 3:28

4 ªProv.
10:12; 17:9;
1 Thess.
5:14; 1 Pet.
4:8 ᵇActs
7:9 ᶜ1 Cor.
4:6
★ **5** ª1 Cor.
10:24; Phil.
2:21 ᵇ2 Cor.
5:19

6 ª2 Thess.
2:12 ᵇ2 John
4; 3 John 3f.

7 ª1 Cor.
9:12

8 ª1 Cor.
13:2 ᵇ1 Cor.
13:1

9 ª1 Cor.
8:2; 13:12

★**10**

★**11**

12:28 *first . . .* The gifts are ranked in order of honor.

12:29-30 The answer expected to all of these questions is "No."

12:31 *the greater gifts* (as ranked in v. 28).

13:1 *love.* The Greek word is *agape.* The Greek word for love of an adorable object, especially for love between man and woman, is *eros.* Another Greek word, *phileo,* refers to the love of friendship. *Agape* characterizes God (1 John 4:8) and what He manifested in the gift of His Son (John 3:16). It is more than mutual affection; it expresses unselfish esteem of the object loved. Christ's love for us is undeserved and without thought of return. The love which

His followers show, Paul now says, should be the same. *a noisy gong* and *a clanging cymbal.* Associated with pagan worship.

13:5 *unbecomingly* (see 7:36; 11:5-6, 21). *does not seek its own.* See 6:7.

13:10 *the perfect.* A reference to Christ's second coming.

13:11 There are stages of growth within the present imperfect time before Christ's return. After the church began, there was a period of immaturity, during which spectacular gifts were needed for growth and authentication (Heb. 2:3-4). With the completion of the N.T. and the growing maturity of the church, the need for such gifts disappeared.

became a man, I did away with childish things.

12 For now we *see in a mirror dimly, but then *b*face to face; now I know in part, but then I shall know fully just as I also *c*have been fully known.

13 But now abide faith, hope, love, these three; but the greatest of these is *a*love.

4 The superiority of prophecy over tongues, 14:1-25

14 *a*Pursue love, yet *b*desire earnestly *c*spiritual *gifts*, but especially that you may *d*prophesy.

2 For one who *a*speaks in a tongue does not speak to men, but to God; for no one understands, but in *his* spirit he speaks *b*mysteries.

3 But one who prophesies speaks to men for *a*edification and *b*exhortation and consolation.

4 One who *a*speaks in a tongue *b*edifies himself; but one who *c*prophesies *b*edifies the church.

5 Now I wish that you all *a*spoke in tongues, but *b*even more that you would prophesy; and greater is one who prophesies than one who *a*speaks in tongues, unless he interprets, so that the church may receive *c*edifying.

6 But now, brethren, if I come to you speaking in tongues, what shall I profit you, unless I speak to you either by way of *a*revelation or of *b*knowledge or of *c*prophecy or of *d*teaching?

7 Yet *even* lifeless things, either flute or harp, in producing a sound, if they do not produce a distinction in the tones, how will it be known what is played on the flute or on the harp?

8 For if *a*the bugle produces an indistinct sound, who will prepare himself for battle?

9 So also you, unless you utter by the tongue speech that is clear, how will it be known what is spoken? For you will be *a*speaking into the air.

10 There are, perhaps, a great many kinds of languages in the world, and no *kind* is without meaning.

11 If then I do not know the meaning of the language, I shall be to the one who speaks a *a*barbarian, and the one who speaks will be a barbarian to me.

12 So also you, since you are zealous of spiritual *gifts*, seek to abound for the *a*edification of the church.

13 Therefore let one who speaks in a tongue pray that he may interpret.

14 For if I pray in a tongue, my spirit prays, but my mind is unfruitful.

15 *a*What is *the outcome* then? I shall pray with the spirit and I shall pray with the mind also; I shall *b*sing with the spirit and I shall sing with the mind also.

16 Otherwise if you bless in the spirit *only,* how will the one who fills the place of the ungifted say *a*the "Amen" at your *b*giving of thanks, since he does not know what you are saying?

17 For you are giving thanks well enough, but the other man is not *a*edified.

18 I thank God, I speak in tongues more than you all;

19 however, in the church I desire to speak five words with my mind, that I may instruct others also, rather than ten thousand words in a tongue.

---

12 *a*2 Cor. 5:7; Phil. 3:12; James 1:23 *b*Gen. 32:30; Num. 12:8; 1 John 3:2 *c*1 Cor. 8:3
★13 *a*Gal. 5:6

★ 1 *a*1 Cor. 16:14 *b*1 Cor. 12:31; 14:39 *c*1 Cor. 12:1 *d*1 Cor. 13:2
★ 2 *a*Mark 16:17; 1 Cor. 12:10, 28, 30; 13:1; 14:18ff. *b*1 Cor. 13:2

3 *a*Rom. 14:19; 1 Cor. 14:5, 12, 17, 26 *b*Acts 4:36
4 *a*Mark 16:17; 1 Cor. 12:10, 28, 30; 13:1; 14:18ff., 26f. *b*Rom. 14:19; 1 Cor. 14:5, 12, 17, 26 *c*1 Cor. 13:2
5 *a*Mark 16:17; 1 Cor. 12:10, 28, 30; 13:1; 14:18ff., 26f. *b*Num. 11:29 *c*Rom. 14:19; 1 Cor. 14:4, 12, 17, 26
★ 6-15
6 *a*1 Cor. 14:26; Eph. 1:17 *b*1 Cor. 12:8 *c*1 Cor. 13:2 *d*Acts 2:42; Rom. 6:17; 1 Cor. 14:26

8 *a*Num. 10:9; Jer. 4:19; Ezek. 33:3-6; Joel 2:1
9 *a*1 Cor. 9:26

11 *a*Acts 28:2

12 *a*Rom. 14:19; 1 Cor. 14:4, 5, 17, 26

15 *a*Acts 21:22; 1 Cor. 14:26 *b*Eph. 5:19; Col. 3:16

★16 *a*Deut. 27:15-26; 1 Chr. 16:36; Neh. 5:13; 8:6; Ps. 106:48; Jer. 11:5; 28:6; Rev. 5:14; 7:12 *b*Matt. 15:36
17 *a*Rom. 14:19; 1 Cor. 14:4, 5, 12, 26

13:13 *abide.* Since these three virtues remain after all the gifts have ceased, they should be cultivated. Love is the *greatest,* since it expressed God and Calvary.

14:1 *especially that you may prophesy.* Prophecy is preferred over tongues because it is clear (v. 2) and it edifies the church (v. 4).

14:2 *a tongue.* Though many understand these tongues to be ecstatic speech, it may well be that they were languages, as in Acts 2:4, 6, 8, 11.

14:6-15 *tongues* are useless without interpretation.

14:16 *the place of the ungifted.* I.e., the untaught believer, or perhaps the outsider.

★20-25
20 *a*Rom.
1:13 *b*Eph.
4:14; Heb.
5:12f. *c*Ps.
131:2; Matt.
18:3; Rom.
16:19; 1 Pet.
2:2
★21 *a*John
10:34; 1 Cor.
14:34 *b*Is.
28:11f.

22 *a*1 Cor.
14:1

23 *a*Acts
2:13

24 *a*1 Cor.
14:1 *b*John
16:8

25 *a*John
4:19 *b*Luke
17:16 *c*Is.
45:14; Dan.
2:47; Zech.
8:23; Acts
4:13

★26 *a*1 Cor.
14:15 *b*Rom.
1:13 *c*1 Cor.
12:8-10
*d*Eph. 5:19
*e*1 Cor. 14:6
*f*1 Cor. 14:2
*g*1 Cor.
12:10; 14:5,
13, 27f.
*h*Rom. 14:19
★27 *a*1 Cor.
14:2 *b*1 Cor.
12:10; 14:5,
13, 26ff.

20 *a*Brethren, *b*do not be children in your thinking; yet in evil *c*be babes, but in your thinking be mature.

21 In *a*the Law it is written, "*b*By men of strange tongues and by the lips of strangers I will speak to this people, and even so they will not listen to Me," says the Lord.

22 So then tongues are for a sign, not to those who believe, but to unbelievers; but *a*prophecy *is for a sign,* not to unbelievers, but to those who believe.

23 If therefore the whole church should assemble together and all speak in tongues, and ungifted men or unbelievers enter, will they not say that *a*you are mad?

24 But if all *a*prophesy, and an unbeliever or an ungifted man enters, he is *b*convicted by all, he is called to account by all;

25 *a*the secrets of his heart are disclosed; and so he will *b*fall on his face and worship God, *c*declaring that God is certainly among you.

5　The regulations for the use of gifts, 14:26-40

26 *a*What is *the outcome* then, *b*brethren? When you assemble, *c*each one has a *d*psalm, has a *e*teaching, has a *e*revelation, has a *f*tongue, has an *g*interpretation. Let *h*all things be done for edification.

27 If anyone speaks in a

*a*tongue, *it should be* by two or at the most three, and *each* in turn, and let one *b*interpret;

28 but if there is no interpreter, let him keep silent in the church; and let him speak to himself and to God.

29 And let two or three *a*prophets speak, and let the others *b*pass judgment.

30 But if a revelation is made to another who is seated, let the first keep silent.

31 For you can all prophesy one by one, so that all may learn and all may be exhorted;

32 and the spirits of prophets are subject to prophets;

33 for God is not *a* God of *a*confusion but of peace, as in *b*all the churches of the *c*saints.

34 Let the women *a*keep silent in the churches; for they are not permitted to speak, but *b*let them subject themselves, just as *c*the Law also says.

35 And if they desire to learn anything, let them ask their own husbands at home; for it is improper for a woman to speak in church.

36 Was it from you that the word of God *first* went forth? Or has it come to you only?

37 *a*If anyone thinks he is a prophet or *b*spiritual, let him recognize that the things which I write to you *c*are the Lord's commandment.

38 But if anyone does not recognize *this,* he is not recognized.

★29 *a*1 Cor.
13:2; 14:32,
37 *b*1 Cor.
12:10

★32

33 *a*1 Cor.
14:40 *b*1
Cor. 4:17;
7:17 *c*Acts
9:13
★34 *a*1 Cor.
11:5, 13
*b*1 Tim.
2:11f.; 1 Pet.
3:1 *c*1 Cor.
14:21

★36

37 *a*2 Cor.
10:7 *b*1 Cor.
2:15 *c*1 John
7:40; 1 John
4:6

★38

14:20-25 Prophecy is not only more profitable for those within the church, but also for outsiders.

14:21 See Isa. 28:11-12. Tongues were given as a sign to provoke the Jews to consider the truth of the Christian message.

14:26 Free participation in the service is indicated by this verse, but not to the point of disorder.

14:27 *in turn.* Only *two* or *three* should speak in tongues in a service; never at the same time, but in turn; and not at all if no interpreter is present (v. 28).

14:29 *Two* or *three* prophets can be heard profitably during a meeting.

14:32 I.e., the spiritual activities of the prophets

are under the full control of the prophets. No true prophet can claim a hearing on the ground that he is under a power over which he has no control.

14:34 *Let the women keep silent in the churches.* Whatever this restriction means, it must include tongues and prophecy (see vv. 27, 29, where the same Greek verb for *speak* is used). See also 1 Tim. 2:12.

14:36 I.e., Is Corinth the sole repository of the truth?

14:38 *he is not recognized.* One who does not respect and accept Paul's words should not have his own words respected or accepted. A variant translation is, "he is ignored" (i.e., by God).

39 a1 Cor.
12:31
b1 Cor. 13:2;
14:1

40 a1 Cor.
14:33

39 Therefore, my brethren, [a]desire earnestly to [b]prophesy, and do not forbid to speak in tongues.

40 But [a]let all things be done properly and in an orderly manner.

VII THE DOCTRINE OF THE RESURRECTION, 15:1–58

A The Importance of the Resurrection, 15:1–11

1 aRom.
2:16; Gal.
1:11 bRom.
2:16; 1 Cor.
3:6; 4:15
cRom. 5:2;
11:20; 2 Cor.
1:24
★ 2 aRom.
11:22 bGal.
3:4
3 a1 Cor.
11:23 bJohn
1:29; Gal.
1:4; Heb.
5:1, 3; 1 Pet.
2:24 cls.
53:5-12;
Matt. 26:24;
Luke 24:25-
27; Acts
8:32f.; 17:2f.;
26:22
★ 4 aMatt.
16:21; John
2:21f.; Acts
2:24 bPs.
16:8ff.; Acts
2:31; 26:22f.
5 aLuke
24:34
b1 Cor. 1:12
cMark 16:14
★ 6 aActs
7:60; 1 Cor.
15:18, 20

15 Now [a]I make known to you, brethren, the [b]gospel which I preached to you, which also you received, [c]in which also you stand,

2 by which also you are saved, [a]if you hold fast the word which I preached to you, [b]unless you believed in vain.

3 For [a]I delivered to you as of first importance what I also received, that Christ died [b]for our sins [c]according to the Scriptures,

4 and that He was buried, and that He was [a]raised on the third day [b]according to the Scriptures,

5 and that [a]He appeared to [b]Cephas, then [c]to the twelve.

6 After that He appeared to more than five hundred brethren at one time, most of whom remain until now, but some [a]have fallen asleep;

7 then He appeared to [a]James, then to [b]all the apostles;

8 and last of all, as it were to one untimely born, [a]He appeared to me also.

9 For I am [a]the least of the apostles, who am not fit to be called an apostle, because I [b]persecuted the church of God.

10 But by [a]the grace of God I am what I am, and His grace toward me did not prove vain; but I [b]labored even more than all of them, yet [c]not I, but the grace of God with me.

11 Whether then *it was* I or they, so we preach and so you believed.

B The Consequences of Denying the Resurrection, 15:12–19

12 Now if Christ is preached, that He has been raised from the dead, how do some among you say that there [a]is no resurrection of the dead?

13 But if there is no resurrection of the dead, not even Christ has been raised;

14 and [a]if Christ has not been raised, then our preaching is vain, your faith also is vain.

15 Moreover we are even found *to be* false witnesses of

★ 7 aActs
12:17 bLuke
24:33, 36f.;
Acts 1:3f.
★ 8 aActs
9:3-8; 22:6-
11; 26:12-18;
1 Cor. 9:1
9 a2 Cor.
12:11; Eph.
3:8; 1 Tim.
1:15 bActs
8:3
10 aRom.
12:3 b2 Cor.
11:23; Col.
1:29; 1 Tim.
4:10 c1 Cor.
3:6; 2 Cor.
3:5; Phil.
2:13

★12 aActs
17:32; 23:8;
2 Tim. 2:18

★13-19

14 a1 Thess.
4:14

15 aActs
2:24

15:2 *unless you believed in vain.* That would be the case if the resurrection of Christ were not true.

15:4 *and that He was buried.* Certain proof that Christ actually died. *and that He was raised.* The perfect tense indicates that He is still alive.

15:6 *five hundred brethren.* The citation of these and other witnesses to Christ's resurrection is of great apologetic value, especially in view of the fact that the resurrection was still being attested to by living witnesses 25 years after the event.

15:7 *He appeared to James.* Our Lord's half brother, the author of the letter of James (see John 7:5; Acts 1:14). This appearance is nowhere else recorded in the N.T.

15:8 *one untimely born.* Paul may be referring to his own conversion as premature when viewed in relation to Israel's future conversion (Rom. 11:26); or, more likely, he is regarding

himself as a miscarried infant when compared to the other apostles; that is, one thrust suddenly into apostleship without the nurture of Christ's friendship and direct teaching.

15:12 *no resurrection of the dead.* Nothing in the Greek background of the Gentile converts at Corinth led them to believe in the resurrection of the dead. In general, they believed in the immortality of the soul, but not the resurrection of the body. To them, the body was the source of man's weakness and sin; death, therefore, was the welcome means by which the soul was liberated from the body. Resurrection, in their thinking, would only enslave the soul again.

15:13-19 If the bodily resurrection of Christ is untrue, then preaching the Gospel is a lie (v. 15), Christian faith is without meaningful content (v. 17), and Christians are hopeless concerning their prospects for the future (vv. 18-19).

God, because we witnessed against God that He [a]raised Christ, whom He did not raise, if in fact the dead are not raised.

16 For if the dead are not raised, not even Christ has been raised;

17 and if Christ has not been raised, your faith is worthless; [a]you are still in your sins.

18 Then those also who [a]have fallen asleep in Christ have perished.

19 If we have hoped in Christ in this life only, we are [a]of all men most to be pitied.

C The Christian Hope, 15:20-34

20 But now Christ [a]has been raised from the dead, the [b]first fruits of those who [c]are asleep.

21 For since [a]by a man *came* death, by a man also *came* the resurrection of the dead.

22 For [a]as in Adam all die, so also in Christ all shall be made alive.

23 But each in his own order: Christ [a]the first fruits, after that [b]those who are Christ's at [c]His coming,

24 then *comes* the end, when He delivers up [a]the kingdom to the [b]God and Father, when He has abolished [c]all rule and all authority and power.

25 For He must reign [a]until He has put all His enemies under His feet.

26 The last enemy that will be [a]abolished is death.

27 For [a]HE HAS PUT ALL THINGS IN SUBJECTION UNDER HIS FEET. But when He says, "[b]All things are put in subjection," it is evident that He is excepted who put all things in subjection to Him.

28 And when [a]all things are subjected to Him, then the Son Himself also will be subjected to the One who subjected all things to Him, that [b]God may be all in all.

29 Otherwise, what will those do who are baptized for the dead? If the dead are not raised at all, why then are they baptized for them?

30 Why are we also [a]in danger every hour?

31 I protest, brethren, by the boasting in you, which I have in Christ Jesus our Lord, [a]I die daily.

32 If from human motives I [a]fought with wild beasts at [b]Ephesus, what does it profit me? If the dead are not raised, [c]LET US EAT AND DRINK, FOR TOMORROW WE DIE.

33 [a]Do not be deceived: "Bad company corrupts good morals."

34 [a]Become sober-minded as you ought, and stop sinning; for some have [b]no knowledge of God. [c]I speak *this* to your shame.

D The Resurrection Body, 15:35-50

35 But [a]someone will say, "How are [b]the dead raised? And

Marginal references

17 [a]Rom. 4:25

18 [a]1 Cor. 15:6; 1 Thess. 4:16; Rev. 14:13
19 [a]1 Cor. 4:9; 2 Tim. 3:12

★20 [a]Acts 2:24; 1 Pet. 1:3 [b]Acts 26:23; 1 Cor. 15:23; Rev. 1:5 [c]1 Cor. 15:6; 1 Thess. 4:16; Rev. 14:13
21 [a]Rom. 5:12
★22 [a]Rom. 5:14-18
★23-24
23 [a]Acts 26:23; 1 Cor. 15:20; Rev. 1:5 [b]1 Cor. 6:14; 15:52; 1 Thess. 4:16 [c]1 Thess. 2:19
24 [a]Dan. 2:44; 7:14, 27; 2 Pet. 1:11 [b]Eph. 5:20 [c]Rom. 8:38
25 [a]Ps. 110:1; Matt. 22:44

26 [a]2 Tim. 1:10; Rev. 20:14; 21:4
27 [a]Ps. 8:6 [b]Matt. 11:27; 28:18; Eph. 1:22; Heb. 2:8

28 [a]Phil. 3:21 [b]1 Cor. 3:23; 12:6

★29

30 [a]2 Cor. 11:26

★31 [a]Rom. 8:36

32 [a]2 Cor. 1:8 [b]Acts 18:19; 1 Cor. 16:8f. [c]Is. 22:13; 56:12; Luke 12:19

★33 [a]1 Cor. 6:9

34 [a]Rom. 13:11 [b]Matt. 22:29; Acts 26:8 [c]1 Cor. 6:5

★35-50
35 [a]Rom. 9:19 [b]Ezek. 37:3

15:20 *the first fruits.* Christ's resurrection is an earnest or prototype of resurrections to come (see Lev. 23:9-14).

15:22 *in Christ all shall be made alive.* This refers only to the resurrection of believers (those *in Christ*).

15:23-24 The order of resurrections is as follows: first, Christ's; then that of believers at His coming (1 Thess. 4:13-18); and finally, the resurrection at the end of the millennial kingdom.

15:29 *baptized for the dead.* Various interpretations have been given for this difficult expression. (1) It sanctions being baptized vicariously for another in order to assure him a place in heaven—a view which is heretical. (2) It refers to those who were baptized because

of the testimony of those who had died. (3) Most likely it means being baptized in the place of those who had died; i.e., new converts taking the place of older ones who had died. Paul's point is: unless one believes in the resurrection of the dead (rather than the Greek idea of "immortality") what's the point of such a practice?

15:31 *I die daily.* Paul was exposed to so many physical dangers and to such violent attacks on himself and on his teachings that "daily" cannot be an exaggeration.

15:33 *Do not be deceived.* The same Greek phrase occurs in 6:9; Gal. 6:7; Jas. 1:16. The verse is a Greek proverb, first appearing in a play by Menander.

15:35-50 Here Paul deals with two common er-with what kind of body do they come?"

36 ᵃLuke 11:40 ᵇJohn 12:24

36 ᵃYou fool! That which you ᵇsow does not come to life unless it dies;

37 and that which you sow, you do not sow the body which is to be, but a bare grain, perhaps of wheat or of something else.

38 ᵃGen. 1:11

38 But God gives it a body just as He wished, and ᵃto each of the seeds a body of its own.

39 All flesh is not the same flesh, but there is *one flesh* of men, and another flesh of beasts, and another flesh of birds, and another of fish.

40 There are also heavenly bodies and earthly bodies, but the glory of the heavenly is one, and the *glory* of the earthly is another.

41 There is one glory of the sun, and another glory of the moon, and another glory of the stars; for star differs from star in glory.

★42 ᵃDan. 12:3; Matt. 13:43 ᵇRom. 8:21; 1 Cor. 15:50; Gal. 6:8 ᶜRom. 2:7

42 ᵃSo also is the resurrection of the dead. It is sown ᵇa perishable *body*, it is raised ᶜan imperishable *body*;

43 ᵃPhil. 3:21; Col. 3:4

43 it is sown in dishonor, it is raised in ᵃglory; it is sown in weakness, it is raised in power;

44 ᵃ1 Cor. 2:14 ᵇ1 Cor. 15:50

44 it is sown a ᵃnatural body, it is raised a ᵇspiritual body. If there is a natural body, there is also a spiritual *body.*

45 ᵃGen. 2:7 ᵇRom. 5:14 ᶜJohn 5:21; 6:57; Rom.

45 So also it is written, "The first ᵃMAN, Adam, BECAME A LIVING SOUL." The ᵇlast Adam *became* a ᶜlife-giving spirit.

46 However, the spiritual is not first, but the natural; then the spiritual.

47 ᵃJohn 3:31 ᵇGen. 2:7; 3:19

47 The first man is ᵃfrom the earth, ᵇearthy; the second man is from heaven.

48 As is the earthy, so also are those who are earthy; and as is the heavenly, ᵃso also are those who are heavenly.

48 ᵃPhil. 3:20f.

49 And just as we have ᵃborne the image of the earthy, we ᵇshall also bear the image of the heavenly.

★49 ᵃGen. 5:3 ᵇRom. 8:29

50 Now I say this, brethren, that ᵃflesh and blood cannot ᵇinherit the kingdom of God; nor does the perishable inherit ᶜthe imperishable.

50 ᵃMatt. 16:17; John 3:5f. ᵇ1 Cor. 6:9 ᶜRom. 2:7

E The Christian's Victory through Christ, 15:51-58

51 Behold, I tell you a ᵃmystery; we shall not all sleep, but we shall all be ᵇchanged,

★51-58
51 ᵃ1 Cor. 13:2 ᵇ2 Cor. 5:2, 4

52 in a moment, in the twinkling of an eye, at the last trumpet; for ᵃthe trumpet will sound, and ᵇthe dead will be raised imperishable, and ᶜwe shall be changed.

52 ᵃMatt. 24:31 ᵇJohn 5:28 ᶜ1 Thess. 4:15, 17

53 For this perishable must put on ᵃthe imperishable, and this ᵇmortal must put on immortality.

★53 ᵃRom. 2:7 ᵇ2 Cor. 5:4

54 But when this perishable will have put on the imperishable, and this mortal will have put on immortality, then will come about the saying that is written, "ᵃDEATH IS SWALLOWED UP in victory.

54 ᵃIs. 25:8

55 "ᵃO DEATH, WHERE IS YOUR VICTORY? O DEATH, WHERE IS YOUR STING?"

55 ᵃHos. 13:14

56 The sting of ᵃdeath is sin, and ᵇthe power of sin is the law;

★56 ᵃRom. 5:12 ᵇRom. 3:20; 4:15; 7:8

---

rors in regard to the nature of the resurrection body: (1) that it is the same body that was laid in the grave, simply reconstituted; and (2) that the new body is unrelated to the original one. Paul here explains that it is the body God has chosen (v. 38), related to the former (v. 36) yet different (vv. 39-41).

15:42 *raised an imperishable body.* With no possibility of decay.

15:49 *the image of the heavenly.* I.e., the resurrection body will be like Christ's.

15:51-58 Here Paul answers the question, What happens to those who do not die?

15:51 *we shall not all sleep.* I.e., not all die (1 Thess. 4:15). Some will be alive when the Lord returns, but all will *be changed.*

15:53 *perishable.* I.e., those who have died. *mortal.* I.e., those who are living.

15:56 *The sting of death is sin* because it is by sin that death gains authority over man, *and the power of sin is the law,* because the law stirs up sin (Rom. 5:12; 7:8-11).

57 aRom.
7:25; 2 Cor.
2:14 bRom.
8:37; Heb.
2:14f.;
1 John 5:4;
Rev. 21:4
★**58** a2 Pet.
3:14 b1 Cor.
16:10

57 but athanks be to God, who gives us the bvictory through our Lord Jesus Christ.

58 aTherefore, my beloved brethren, be steadfast, immovable, always abounding in bthe work of the Lord, knowing that your toil is not in vain in the Lord.

VIII PRACTICAL AND PERSONAL MATTERS, 16:1-24
A The Collection for the Saints in Jerusalem, 16:1-4

★ **1** aActs
24:17 bActs
9:13 c1 Cor.
4:17 dActs
16:6

16 Now concerning athe collection for bthe saints, as cI directed the churches of dGalatia, so do you also.

★ **2** aActs
20:7 b2 Cor.
9:4f.

2 On athe first day of every week let each one of you put aside and save, as he may prosper, that bno collections be made when I come.

★ **3** a2 Cor.
3:1; 8:18f.

3 And when I arrive, awhomever you may approve, I shall send them with letters to carry your gift to Jerusalem;

4 and if it is fitting for me to go also, they will go with me.

B The Planned Visit of Paul, 16:5-9

5 a1 Cor.
4:19 bRom.
15:26 cActs
19:21

5 But I ashall come to you after I go through bMacedonia, for I cam going through Macedonia;

6 aActs
15:3; 1 Cor.
16:11

6 and perhaps I shall stay with you, or even spend the winter, that you may asend me on my way wherever I may go.

7 a2 Cor.
1:15f. bActs
18:21

7 For I do not wish to see you now ajust in passing; for I hope to remain with you for some time, bif the Lord permits.

8 aActs
18:19 bActs
2:1

8 But I shall remain in aEphesus until bPentecost;

9 for a awide door for effective service has opened to me, and bthere are many adversaries.

★ **9** aActs
14:27 bActs
19:9

C Exhortations, Greetings, and Benediction, 16:10-24

10 aActs
16:1; 1 Cor.
4:17; 2 Cor.
1:1 b1 Cor.
15:58

10 Now if aTimothy comes, see that he is with you without cause to be afraid; for he is doing bthe Lord's work, as I also am.

11 a1 Tim.
4:12; Titus
2:15 bActs
15:3; 1 Cor.
16:6 cActs
15:33

11 aLet no one therefore despise him. But bsend him on his way cin peace, so that he may come to me; for I expect him with the brethren.

★**12** aActs
18:24 [1 Cor.
1:12; 3:5f.]

12 But concerning aApollos our brother, I encouraged him greatly to come to you with the brethren; and it was not at all his desire to come now, but he will come when he has opportunity.

13 aMatt.
24:42
b1 Cor. 15:1;
Gal. 5:1; Phil.
1:27; 4:1;
1 Thess. 3:8;
2 Thess. 2:15
c1 Sam. 4:9;
2 Sam.
10:12; Is.
46:8 dPs.
31:24; Eph.
3:16; 6:10;
Col. 1:11

13 aBe on the alert, bstand firm in the faith, cact like men, dbe strong.

14 a1 Cor.
14:1

14 Let all that you do be done ain love.

★**15** a1 Cor.
1:16 bRom.
16:5 cActs
18:12 dRom.
15:31
e1 Cor. 16:1

15 Now I urge you, brethren (you know the ahousehold of Stephanas, that they were the bfirst fruits of cAchaia, and that they have devoted themselves for dministry to ethe saints),

16 a1 Thess.
5:12; Heb.
13:17

16 that ayou also be in subjection to such men and to everyone who helps in the work and labors.

★**17** a2 Cor.
7:6f. b2 Cor.
11:9; Phil.
2:30

17 And I rejoice over the acoming of Stephanas and Fortunatus and Achaicus; because they have supplied bwhat was lacking on your part.

18 a2 Cor.
7:13; Philem.
7, 20 bPhil.
2:29;
1 Thess. 5:12

18 For they ahave refreshed my spirit and yours. Therefore backnowledge such men.

19 aActs
16:6 bActs
18:2 cRom.
16:5

19 The churches of aAsia greet you. bAquila and Prisca greet you heartily in the Lord,

---

15:58 A firm belief in the resurrection and a solid hope for the future gives incentive for service in the present.

16:1 the saints. I.e., those in Jerusalem.

16:2 The Christian's giving is to be done (1) regularly on Sunday; (2) into a private fund ("put aside") at home from which fund he makes distributions; and (3) in proportion to

God's prospering.

16:3 Paul would let others handle the money.

16:9 door. I.e., of opportunity.

16:12 his desire. I.e., Apollos'.

16:15 first fruits. I.e., first converts.

16:17 Stephanas and Fortunatus and Achaicus probably brought Paul the letter from the Corinthians mentioned in 7:1.

with ᶜthe church that is in their house.

20 All the brethren greet you. ᵃGreet one another with a holy kiss.

21 The greeting is in ᵃmy own hand—Paul.

22 If anyone does not love the Lord, let him be ᵃaccursed. ᵇMaranatha.

23 ᵃThe grace of the Lord Jesus be with you.

24 My love be with you all in Christ Jesus. Amen.

★20 ᵃRom. 16:16
21 ᵃRom. 16:22; Gal. 6:11; Col. 4:18; 2 Thess. 3:17; Philem. 19
★22 ᵃRom. 9:3 ᵇPhil. 4:5; Rev. 22:20
23 ᵃRom. 16:20

16:20 *a holy kiss.* See note on 1 Pet. 5:14.
16:22 *accursed* (cf. 12:3; Rom. 9:3; Gal. 1:8–9).

Maranatha = our Lord, come! See also Rev. 22:20.

INTRODUCTION TO
THE SECOND EPISTLE OF PAUL TO THE CORINTHIANS

AUTHOR: Paul   DATE: 57

Occasion *After writing 1 Corinthians, Paul found it necessary to make a hurried, painful visit to Corinth, since the problems that occasioned the first letter had not been resolved (2 Cor. 2:1; 12:14; 13:1-2). Following this visit, he wrote the church a severe and sorrowful letter, to which he refers in 2:4 but which has been lost to us. Titus delivered that letter. Paul, unable to wait to meet Titus on his return to Troas, hurried on to Macedonia where Titus related the good news that the church finally had repented of their rebelliousness against Paul. From Macedonia Paul wrote 2 Corinthians and followed it up with his final recorded visit to the church (Acts 20:1-4).*

A popular theory claims that chapters 10-13 are part of that lost "sorrowful letter." Although some features of those chapters correspond to what must have been the contents of the lost letter, the principal subject of that letter (the offender of 2 Corinthians 2:5) is nowhere mentioned in these chapters. Further, there is no evidence for so partitioning 2 Corinthians.

Purpose *The purpose of this letter was threefold: (1) to express joy at the favorable response of the church to Paul's ministry (1-7); (2) to remind the believers of their commitment to the offering for the Christians in Judea (8-9); and (3) to defend Paul's apostolic authority (10-13).*

Contents *The letter contains many personal and autobiographical glimpses into Paul's life (4:8-18; 11:22-33). The longest discussion of giving in the New Testament is in chapters 8 and 9. Important verses include 5:10, 20-21; 6:14; 8:9; 10:5; 11:14; 12:9; and 13:14.*

OUTLINE OF 2 CORINTHIANS

THE SECOND LETTER OF PAUL TO THE CORINTHIANS

I INTRODUCTION, 1:1-11
A Salutation, 1:1-2

1 Paul, ᵃan apostle of ᵇChrist Jesus ᶜby the will of God, and ᵈTimothy our brother, to ᵉthe church of God which is at ʄCorinth with all the saints who are throughout ᵍAchaia:

2 ᵃGrace to you and peace from God our Father and the Lord Jesus Christ.

B Paul's Gratitude for God's Goodness, 1:3-11

3 ᵃBlessed be the God and Father of our Lord Jesus Christ, the Father of mercies and ᵇGod of all comfort;

4 who ᵃcomforts us in all our affliction so that we may be able to comfort those who are in any affliction with the comfort with which we ourselves are comforted by God.

5 For just ᵃas the sufferings of Christ are ours in abundance, so also our comfort is abundant through Christ.

6 But if we are afflicted, it is ᵃfor your comfort and salvation; or if we are comforted, it is for your comfort, which is effective in the patient enduring of the same sufferings which we also suffer;

7 and our hope for you is firmly grounded, knowing that ᵃas you are sharers of our sufferings, so also you are sharers of our comfort.

8 For ᵃwe do not want you to be unaware, brethren, of our ᵇaffliction which came to us in ᶜAsia, that we were burdened excessively, beyond our strength, so that we despaired even of life;

9 indeed, we had the sentence of death within ourselves in order that we should not trust in ourselves, but in God who raises the dead;

10 who ᵃdelivered us from so great a peril of death, and will deliver us, He ᵇon whom we have set our hope. And He will yet deliver us,

11 you also joining in ᵃhelping us through your prayers, that thanks may be given by ᵇmany persons on our behalf for the favor bestowed upon us through the prayers of many.

II THE APOSTLE'S CONCILIATION WITH RESPECT TO THE PROBLEM AT CORINTH, 1:12-2:13
A The Change in Paul's Plans, 1:12-2:4

12 For our proud confidence is this, the testimony of ᵃour

Cross-reference column notes

★ 1 ᵃRom. 1:1; Gal. 1:1; Eph. 1:1; Col. 1:1; 2 Tim. 1:1; Titus 1:1 ᵇGal. 3:26 ᶜ1 Cor. 1:1 ᵈActs 16:1; 1 Cor. 16:10; 2 Cor. 1:19 ᵉ1 Cor. 10:32 ʄActs 18:1 ᵍActs 18:12
★ 2 ᵃRom. 1:7
3 ᵃEph. 1:3; 1 Pet. 1:3 ᵇRom. 15:5
4 ᵃIs. 51:12; 66:13; 2 Cor. 7:6, 7, 13
★ 5 ᵃ2 Cor. 4:10; Phil. 3:10; Col. 1:24
6 ᵃ2 Cor. 4:15; 12:15; Eph. 3:1, 13; 2 Tim. 2:10
7 ᵃRom. 8:17
★ 8 ᵃRom. 1:13 ᵇActs 19:23; 1 Cor. 15:32 ᶜActs 16:6
10 ᵃRom. 15:31 ᵇ1 Tim. 4:10
★11 ᵃRom. 15:30; Phil. 1:19; Philem. 22 ᵇ2 Cor. 4:15; 9:11f.
12 ᵃActs 23:1; 1 Thess. 2:10; Heb. 13:18 ᵇ2 Cor. 2:17 ᶜ1 Cor. 1:17

1:1 *Achaia.* The Roman province comprising all of southern Greece below Macedonia, including Athens and Corinth, the capital.

1:2 *God our Father.* Paul teaches a number of truths about God the Father in this epistle: (1) He is the living God (3:3; 6:16); (2) He is the God of grace, mercy, and comfort (1:2-3); (3) He is faithful (1:18); (4) His power is available to His people (4:7; 6:7; 13:4); and (5) He is the Father of Christ (1:3) and of His people (6:18). Concerning *the Lord Jesus Christ* Paul says: (1) He is the Son of God (1:19); (2) He is the image of God (4:4); and (3) He is sinless (5:21). But Paul seems to be most interested in explaining what Christ does: (1) He gives victory (2:14); (2) He judges (5:10); (3) He reconciles (5:19; 8:9); (4) He appoints and motivates His ambassadors (5:20); and (5) He makes men new creatures (5:17).

1:5 *the sufferings of Christ are ours in abundance.* Paul's own sufferings are identified as Christ's sufferings (see 4:10; Phil. 3:10; Col. 1:24). What Paul suffered was intended to encourage others (2 Cor. 1:6).

1:8 *our affliction which came to us in Asia.* Since Paul offers no details, it seems probable the Corinthians knew what the trouble was. It may have been one of the dangers described in 11:23-26, the mob violence of Acts 19:23-41, or some serious illness (*we despaired even of life*).

1:11 *your prayers.* The good report of the church brought by Titus encouraged Paul to exhort the Corinthians to prayer. Paul's great confidence in intercessory prayer is seen also in Rom. 15:30-31; Phil. 1:9; Col. 4:12.

conscience, that in holiness and ᵇgodly sincerity, ᶜnot in fleshly wisdom but in the grace of God, we have conducted ourselves in the world, and especially toward you.

13 For we write nothing else to you than what you read and understand, and I hope you will understand ᵃuntil the end;

14 just as you also partially did understand us, that we are your reason to be proud as you also are ours, in ᵃthe day of our Lord Jesus.

15 And in this confidence I intended at first to ᵃcome to you, that you might twice receive a ᵇblessing;

16 that is, to ᵃpass your way into ᵇMacedonia, and again from Macedonia to come to you, and by you to be ᶜhelped on my journey ᵈto Judea.

17 Therefore, I was not vacillating when I intended to do this, was I? Or that which I purpose, do I purpose ᵃaccording to the flesh, that with me there should be yes, yes and no, no *at the same time?*

18 But as ᵃGod is faithful, ᵇour word to you is not yes and no.

19 For ᵃthe Son of God, Christ Jesus, who was preached among you by us—by me and ᵇSilvanus and ᶜTimothy—was not yes and no, but is yes ᵈin Him.

20 For ᵃas many as may be the promises of God, ᵇin Him they are yes; wherefore also by

Him is ᶜour Amen to the glory of God through us.

21 Now He who ᵃestablishes us with you in Christ and ᵇanointed us is God,

22 who also ᵃsealed us and ᵇgave *us* the Spirit in our hearts as a pledge.

23 But ᵃI call God as witness to my soul, that ᵇto spare you I came no more to ᶜCorinth.

24 Not that we ᵃlord it over your faith, but are workers with you for your joy; for in your faith you are ᵇstanding firm.

2 But I determined this for my own sake, that I ᵃwould not come to you in sorrow again.

2 For if I ᵃcause you sorrow, who then makes me glad but the one whom I made sorrowful?

3 And this is the very thing I ᵃwrote you, lest, ᵇwhen I came, I should have sorrow from those who ought to make me rejoice; having ᶜconfidence in you all, that my joy would be *the joy* of you all.

4 For out of much affliction and anguish of heart I ᵃwrote to you with many tears; not that you should be made sorrowful, but that you might know the love which I have especially for you.

B   The Change in the Offender's Punishment, 2:5-11

5 But ᵃif any has caused sorrow, he has caused sorrow not to

Cross references (left margin):
13 ᵃ1 Cor. 1:8
14 ᵃ1 Cor. 1:8
15 ᵃ1 Cor. 4:19 ᵇRom. 1:11; 15:29
★16 ᵃActs 13:21; 1 Cor. 16:5-7 ᵇRom. 15:26 ᶜActs 15:3; 1 Cor. 16:6, 11 ᵈActs 19:21
★17 ᵃ2 Cor. 10:2f.; 11:18
18 ᵃ1 Cor. 1:9 ᵇ2 Cor. 2:17
19 ᵃMatt. 4:3; 16:16; 26:63 ᵇActs 15:22; 1 Thess. 1:1; 2 Thess. 1:1; 1 Pet. 5:12 ᶜ2 Cor. 1:1 ᵈHeb. 13:8
★20 ᵃRom. 15:8 ᵇHeb. 13:8 ᶜ1 Cor. 14:16; Rev. 3:14

Cross references (right margin):
21 ᵃ1 Cor. 1:8 ᵇ1 John 2:20, 27
★22 ᵃJohn 3:33 ᵇRom. 8:16; 2 Cor. 5:5; Eph. 1:14
23 ᵃRom. 1:9; Gal. 1:20 ᵇ1 Cor. 4:21; 2 Cor. 2:1, 3 ᶜ2 Cor. 1:1
★24 ᵃ2 Cor. 4:5; 11:20; 1 Pet. 5:3 ᵇRom 11:20; 1 Cor. 15:1
1 ᵃ1 Cor. 4:21; 2 Cor. 12:21
★2 ᵃ2 Cor. 7:8
3 ᵃ2 Cor. 2:9; 7:8, 12 ᵇ1 Cor. 4:21; 2 Cor. 12:21 ᶜGal. 5:10; 2 Thess 3:4; Philem. 21
★4 ᵃ2 Cor. 2:9; 7:8, 12
5 ᵃ1 Cor. 5:1f.

1:16 Paul intended to visit them twice, going to and returning from Macedonia, but he changed his plans. This change was dubbed vacillation and unspirituality (*according to the flesh,* v. 17) by his opponents, charges he denies.

1:17 The verse may be paraphrased like this: Did my change of plans indicate that I couldn't make up my mind? Am I like a worldly man who says "Yes" and "No" at the same time? In 1 Cor. 16:5 Paul had promised to go to Corinth. In the second (lost) letter (between 1 and 2 Cor.) he may have said something different, which seemed to make him say yes and no at the same time. His present itinerary was Ephesus to Troas to Macedonia to Corinth.

1:20 *in Him they are yes.* I.e., the promises of God find their certain fulfillment, their Yes, in Christ. *by Him is our Amen.* I.e., we give our concurrence through saying Amen.

1:22 The seal indicates security, and the *pledge* is a guarantee that God will fulfill His promises. See notes on Eph. 1:13 and 1:14.

1:24 *Not that we lord it over your faith.* Apostolic authority did not give Paul any such right (see 1 Pet. 5:1-3). They stand *in . . . faith,* i.e., their own faith, not by Paul's control.

2:2 The meaning is this: If I hurt you, who will be left to make me glad but sad people? That wouldn't be any comfort!

2:4 *I wrote to you.* See the Introduction to 2 Corinthians for a discussion of this "sorrowful letter."

me, but in some degree—in order not to say too much—to all of you.

6 Sufficient for such a one is *a*this punishment which was *inflicted by* the majority,

7 so that on the contrary you should rather *a*forgive and comfort *him,* lest somehow such a one be overwhelmed by excessive sorrow.

8 Wherefore I urge you to reaffirm *your* love for him.

9 For to this end also *a*I wrote that I might *b*put you to the test, whether you are *c*obedient in all things.

10 But whom you forgive anything, I *forgive* also; for indeed what I have forgiven, if I have forgiven anything, *I did it* for your sakes *a*in the presence of Christ,

11 in order that no advantage be taken of us by *a*Satan; for *b*we are not ignorant of his schemes.

C The Meeting with Titus, 2:12-13

12 Now when I came to *a*Troas for the *b*gospel of Christ and when a *c*door was opened for me in the Lord,

13 I *a*had no rest for my spirit, not finding *b*Titus my brother; but *c*taking my leave of them, I went on to *d*Macedonia.

Margin references (left column)
★ **6** *a* 1 Cor. 5:4f.; 2 Cor. 7:11

7 *a* Gal. 6:1; Eph. 4:32

★ **9** *a* 2 Cor. 2:3f. *b* 2 Cor. 8:2; Phil. 2:22 *c* 2 Cor. 7:15; 10:6

10 *a* 1 Cor. 5:4; 2 Cor. 4:6

★**11** *a* Matt. 4:10 *b* Luke 22:31; 2 Cor. 4:4; 1 Pet. 5:8

12 *a* Acts 16:8 *b* Rom. 1:1; 2 Cor. 4:3, 4; 8:18; 9:13; 10:14; 11:4, 7; 1 Thess. 3:2 *c* Acts 14:27
★**13** *a* 2 Cor. 7:5 *b* 2 Cor. 7:6, 13f.; 8:6, 16, 23; 12:18; Gal. 2:1, 3; 2 Tim. 4:10; Titus 1:4 *c* Mark 6:46 *d* Rom. 15:26

III THE APOSTOLIC MINISTRY, 2:14-6:10

A The Confidence of the Ministry: Victory, 2:14-17

14 *a*But thanks be to God, who always *b*leads us in His triumph in Christ, and manifests through us the *c*sweet aroma of the *d*knowledge of Him in every place.

15 For we are a *a*fragrance of Christ to God among *b*those who are being saved and among those who are perishing;

16 *a*to the one an aroma from death to death, to the other an aroma from life to life. And who is *b*adequate for these things?

17 For we are not like many, *a*peddling the word of God, but *b*as from sincerity, but as from God, we speak in Christ *c*in the sight of God.

B The Commendation of the Ministry: Changed Lives, 3:1-3

3 Are we beginning to *a*commend ourselves again? Or do we need, as some, *b*letters of commendation to you or from you?

2 *a*You are our letter, written in our hearts, known and read by all men;

3 being manifested that you are a letter of Christ, *a*cared for by us, written not with ink, but with

Margin references (right column)
★**14** *a* Rom. 1:8; 6:17; 1 Cor. 15:57; 2 Cor. 8:16; 9:15 *b* Col. 2:15 [Gr.] *c* Song of Sol. 1:3; Ezek. 20:41; Eph. 5:2; Phil. 4:18 *d* 1 Cor. 12:8

★**15-16**
15 *a* Song of Sol. 1:3; Ezek. 20:41; Eph. 5:2; Phil. 4:18 *b* 1 Cor. 1:18

16 *a* Luke 2:34; John 9:39; 1 Pet. 2:7f. *b* 2 Cor. 3:5f.

17 *a* 2 Cor. 4:2; Gal. 1:6-9 *b* 1 Cor. 5:8; 2 Cor. 1:12; 1 Thess. 2:4; 1 Pet. 4:11 *c* 2 Cor. 12:19

★ **1-3**
1 *a* 2 Cor. 5:12; 10:12, 18; 12:11 *b* Acts 18:27; Rom. 16:1; 1 Cor. 16:3
2 *a* 1 Cor. 9:2
3 *a* 2 Cor. 3:6 *b* Matt. 16:16 *c* Ex. 24:12; 31:18; 32:15f.; 2 Cor. 3:7 *d* Prov. 3:3; 7:3; Jer. 17:1 *e* Jer. 31:33; Ezek. 11:19

2:6 *by the majority.* The rebel had been punished sufficiently and had repented. Apparently some wanted a severer penalty (vv. 6-8).

2:9 *whether you are obedient.* Though they had accepted Paul's authority in the case of the rebel, they had yet to prove that they accepted it *in all things* (cf. 10:6).

2:11 *that no advantage be taken of us by Satan.* The forgiven brother needed to be restored to fellowship, lest Satan put him under the pressure of continued self-accusation and introspection. Also, as long as the matter was not settled, Satan kept Paul and the church estranged.

2:13 *I had no rest.* Because of wondering how his severe letter had been received.

2:14 *who always leads us in His triumph in Christ.* The picture is of a Roman conqueror leading his captives in triumph. Paul gladly considered himself one of Christ's captives being led in triumph, to the glory of Christ.

2:15-16 The same gospel brings life to the believer and death to the rejector.

3:1-3 The work of the Spirit in the lives of the Corinthians was sufficient recommendation of Paul's ministry.

the Spirit of ᵇthe living God, not on ᶜtablets of stone, but on ᵈtablets of ᵉhuman hearts.

C The Covenant for the Ministry: The New Covenant, 3:4-18

4 aEph. 3:12

4 And such ᵃconfidence we have through Christ toward God.

★ 5 a1 Cor. 15:10

5 Not that we are adequate in ourselves to consider anything as *coming* from ourselves, but ᵃour adequacy is from God,

★ 6 a1 Cor. 3:5 bLuke 22:20 cRom. 2:29 dJohn 6:63; Rom. 7:6

6 who also made us adequate as ᵃservants of a ᵇnew covenant, not of ᶜthe letter, but of the Spirit; for the letter kills, but ᵈthe Spirit gives life.

★ 7 aRom. 4:15; 5:20; 7:5f.; 2 Cor. 3:9; Gal. 3:10, 21f. bEx. 24:12, 31:18; 32:15f.; 2 Cor. 3:3 cEx. 34:29-35; 2 Cor. 3:13

7 But if the ᵃministry of death, ᵇin letters engraved on stones, came with glory, ᶜso that the sons of Israel could not look intently at the face of Moses because of the glory of his face, fading as it was,

★8

8 how shall the ministry of the Spirit fail to be even more with glory?

9 aDeut. 27:26; 2 Cor. 3:7; Heb. 12:18-21 bRom. 1:17; 3:21f.

9 For if ᵃthe ministry of condemnation has glory, much more does the ᵇministry of righteousness abound in glory.

10 For indeed what had glory,

in this case has no glory on account of the glory that surpasses it.

★11

11 For if that which fades away *was* with glory, much more that which remains *is* in glory.

12 a2 Cor. 7:4 bActs 4:13, 29; 2 Cor. 7:4; Eph. 6:19; 1 Thess. 2:2

12 ᵃHaving therefore such a hope, ᵇwe use great boldness in *our* speech,

★13 a2 Cor. 3:7

13 and *are* not as Moses, ᵃwho used to put a veil over his face that the sons of Israel might not look intently at the end of what was fading away.

14 aRom. 11:7; 2 Cor. 4:4 bActs 13:15 c2 Cor. 3:6

14 But their minds were ᵃhardened; for until this very day at the ᵇreading of ᶜthe old covenant the same veil remains unlifted, because it is removed in Christ.

★15

15 But to this day whenever Moses is read, a veil lies over their heart;

16 aEx. 34:34; Rom. 11:23

16 ᵃbut whenever a man turns to the Lord, the veil is taken away.

★17 aIs. 61:11; Gal. 4:6 bJohn 8:32; Gal. 5:1, 13

17 Now the Lord is the Spirit; and where ᵃthe Spirit of the Lord is, ᵇ*there* is liberty.

★18 a1 Cor. 13:12 b2 Cor. 4:4, 6; John 17:22, 24 cRom. 8:29 d2 Cor. 3:17

18 But we all, with unveiled face ᵃbeholding as in a mirror the ᵇglory of the Lord, are being ᶜtransformed into the same image from glory to glory, just as from ᵈthe Lord, the Spirit.

3:5 *our adequacy is from God.* This answers the question raised in 2:16.

3:6 *a new covenant.* The message of the grace of Christ (Matt. 26:28). *the letter kills, but the Spirit gives life.* The *letter* stands for the whole Mosaic law. It kills because, of itself, it could not give life (Acts 13:39). The work of the law was to make men conscious of sin (Gal. 3:21-25; 1 Tim. 1:9). The Spirit, by contrast, gives life to believers.

3:7 *the ministry of death.* Refers to the law and particularly to the Ten Commandments, which were *engraved on stones* (Deut. 9:10). Since the law showed man his sinfulness and gave him no power to break out of it, it ministered death. Note that the law *fades away* (2 Cor. 3:11). Moses stood before God with unveiled face (see Ex. 34:29-35).

3:8 *even more with glory.* I.e., more glorious than the old order.

3:11 There is no question that the law was glorious for its time and purpose, but its temporariness and limited purpose caused that glory

to fade in the blazing light of the grace of Christ, which has as its eternal purpose the bringing of many sons into glory (John 1:17; Heb. 2:10).

3:13 Paul means here that Moses veiled his face that the Israelites might not see the fading away of the transitory glory reflected in his countenance.

3:15 *a veil lies over their heart.* I.e., as long as they consider the law as permanent and do not turn to Christ, who takes away the veil (v. 14).

3:17 *Now the Lord is the Spirit.* A strong statement that Christ and the Holy Spirit are one in essence, though Paul also recognized the distinctions between them (13:14).

3:18 *with unveiled face beholding.* Paul builds on the experience of Moses in Ex. 34:29-35. We Christians, he says, behold constantly Christ's divine glory; and this beholding changes or transforms us *from glory to glory;* i.e., from one degree of glory to another.

D The Character of the Ministry: Supernatural, 4:1-7

4 Therefore, since we have this ᵃministry, as we ᵇreceived mercy, we ᶜdo not lose heart,

2 but we have renounced the ᵃthings hidden because of shame, not walking in craftiness or ᵇadulterating the word of God, but by the manifestation of truth ᶜcommending ourselves to every man's conscience in the sight of God.

3 And even if our ᵃgospel is ᵇveiled, it is veiled to ᶜthose who are perishing,

4 in whose case ᵃthe god of ᵇthis world has ᶜblinded the minds of the unbelieving, that they might not see the ᵈlight of the gospel of the ᵉglory of Christ, who is the ᶠimage of God.

5 For we ᵃdo not preach ourselves but Christ Jesus as Lord, and ourselves as your bondservants for Jesus' sake,

6 For God, who said, "ᵃLight shall shine out of darkness," is the One who has ᵇshone in our hearts to give the ᶜlight of the knowledge of the glory of God in the face of Christ.

7 But we have this treasure in ᵃearthen vessels, that the surpassing greatness of ᵇthe power may be of God and not from ourselves;

E The Circumstances of the Ministry, 4:8-18

8 we are ᵃafflicted in every way, but not ᵇcrushed; ᶜperplexed, but not despairing;

9 ᵃpersecuted, but not ᵇforsaken; ᶜstruck down, but not destroyed;

10 ᵃalways carrying about in the body the dying of Jesus, that ᵇthe life of Jesus also may be manifested in our body.

11 For we who live are constantly being delivered over to death for Jesus' sake, that the life of Jesus also may be manifested in our mortal flesh.

12 So death works in us, but life in you.

13 But having the same ᵃspirit of faith, according to what is written, "ᵇI BELIEVED, THEREFORE I SPOKE," we also believe, therefore also we speak;

14 knowing that He who ᵃraised the Lord Jesus ᵇwill raise us also with Jesus and will ᶜpresent us with you.

15 For all things are ᵃfor your sakes, that the grace which is ᵇspreading to more and more people may cause the giving of thanks to abound to the glory of God.

16 Therefore we ᵃdo not lose heart, but though our outer man is decaying, yet our ᵇinner man is ᶜbeing renewed day by day.

17 For momentary, ᵃlight affliction is producing for us an eternal weight of glory far beyond all comparison,

18 while we ᵃlook not at the things which are seen, but at the things which are not seen; for the things which are seen are temporal, but the things which are not seen are eternal.

4:1 *we do not lose heart.* (Cf. Luke 18:1; 2 Cor. 4:16; Gal. 6:9; Eph. 3:13; 2 Thess. 3:13.) Paul credits his effectiveness to the *mercy* of God.
4:4 *the god of this world.* I.e., Satan.
4:7 *this treasure.* I.e., the glorious gospel of Jesus Christ. *in earthen vessels.* I.e., in our frail human bodies. *the surpassing greatness of the power.* Paul makes clear that this power belongs to God, not to any leader within the church (see 1 Cor. 1:12).
4:10-11 Paul here compares his own constant persecution and suffering with that of Jesus, in Whose dying and resurrection life the apostle will consequently share (Gal. 2:20; Col. 1:24).
4:12 Paul's physical sufferings *(death works in us)* are the means by which spiritual *life* comes to the Corinthians.
4:13-18 Though he is oppressed, Paul's outlook is one of hope (v. 14). Therefore, he does not lose heart (v. 16), though his *outer man is decaying,* for this *affliction* is *light* and temporary.

Marginal references:

★ **1** ᵃ1 Cor. 3:5 ᵇ1 Cor. 7:25 ᶜLuke 18:1; 2 Cor. 4:16; Gal. 6:9; Eph. 3:13; 2 Thess. 3:13
2 ᵃRom. 6:21; 1 Cor. 4:5 ᵇ2 Cor. 2:17 ᶜ2 Cor. 5:11f.
3 ᵃ2 Cor. 2:12 ᵇ1 Cor. 2:6ff.; 2 Cor. 3:14 ᶜ1 Cor. 1:18; 2 Cor. 2:15
★ **4** ᵃJohn 12:31 ᵇMatt. 13:22 ᶜ2 Cor. 3:14 ᵈActs 26:18; 2 Cor. 4:6 ᵉ2 Cor. 3:18; 4:6 ᶠJohn 1:18; Phil. 2:6; Col. 1:15; Heb. 1:3
5 ᵃ1 Cor. 4:15f.; 1 Thess. 2:6f.
6 ᵃGen. 1:3 ᵇ2 Pet. 1:19 ᶜActs 26:18; 2 Cor. 4:4
★ **7** ᵃJob 4:19; 10:9; 33:6; Lam. 4:2; 2 Cor. 5:1; 2 Tim. 2:20 ᵇJudg. 7:2; 1 Cor. 2:5
8 ᵃ2 Cor. 1:8; 7:5 ᵇ2 Cor. 6:12 ᶜGal. 4:20
9 ᵃJohn 15:20; Rom. 8:35f. ᵇPs. 129:2; Heb. 13:5 ᶜPs. 37:24; Prov. 24:16; Mic. 7:8
★ **10-11**
10 ᵃRom. 6:5; 8:36; Gal. 6:17 ᵇRom. 6:8
★ **12**
★ **13-18**
13 ᵃ1 Cor. 12:9 ᵇPs. 116:10
14 ᵃActs 2:24 ᵇ1 Thess. 4:14 ᶜLuke 21:36; Eph. 5:27; Col. 1:22; Jude 24
15 ᵃRom. 8:28; 2 Cor. 1:6 ᵇ1 Cor. 9:19; 2 Cor. 1:11
16 ᵃ2 Cor. 4:1 ᵇRom. 7:22 ᶜIs. 40:29, 31; Col. 3:10
17 ᵃRom. 8:18
18 ᵃRom. 8:24; 2 Cor. 5:7; Heb. 11:1, 13

F The Compulsions of the Ministry, 5:1-21

1 The assurance of resurrection, 5:1-9

1 aJob 4:19; 1 Cor. 15:47; 2 Cor. 4:7 b2 Pet. 1:13f. cMark 14:58; Acts 7:48; Heb. 9:11, 24

5 For we know that if the aearthly btent which is our house is torn down, we have a building from God, a house cnot made with hands, eternal in the heavens.

2 aRom. 8:23; 2 Cor. 5:4 b1 Cor. 15:53f.; 2 Cor. 5:4 ★3

2 For indeed in this *house* we agroan, longing to be bclothed with our dwelling from heaven;

3 inasmuch as we, having put it on, shall not be found naked.

4 a2 Cor. 5:2 b1 Cor. 15:53f.; 2 Cor. 5:2 c1 Cor. 15:54

4 For indeed while we are in this tent, we agroan, being burdened, because we do not want to be unclothed, but to be bclothed, in order that what is cmortal may be swallowed up by life.

5 aRom. 8:23; 2 Cor. 1:22

5 Now He who prepared us for this very purpose is God, who agave to us the Spirit as a pledge.

6 aHeb. 11:13f.

6 Therefore, being always of good courage, and knowing that awhile we are at home in the body we are absent from the Lord—

7 a1 Cor. 13:12; 2 Cor. 4:18

7 for awe walk by faith, not by sight—

8 aPhil. 1:23 bJohn 12:26; Phil. 1:23

8 we are of good courage, I say, and aprefer rather to be absent from the body and bto be at home with the Lord.

9 aRom. 14:18; Col. 1:10; 1 Thess. 4:1

9 Therefore also we have as our ambition, whether at home or absent, to be apleasing to Him.

2 The judgment seat of Christ, 5:10-13

★10 aMatt. 16:27; Acts 10:42; Rom. 2:16; 14:10, 12; Eph. 6:8

10 For we must all appear before athe judgment seat of Christ, that each one may be recompensed for his deeds in the body, according to what he has done, whether good or bad.

★11 aHeb. 10:31; 12:29; Jude 23 b2 Cor. 4:2

11 Therefore knowing the afear of the Lord, we persuade men, but we are made manifest to God; and I hope that we are bmade manifest also in your consciences.

12 a2 Cor. 3:1 b2 Cor. 1:14; Phil. 1:26

12 We are not aagain commending ourselves to you but *are* giving you an boccasion to be proud of us, that you may have an answer for those who take pride in appearance, and not in heart.

★13 aMark 3:21; 2 Cor. 11:1, 16ff.; 12:11

13 For if we are abeside ourselves, it is for God; if we are of sound mind, it is for you.

3 The love of Christ, 5:14-21

★14 aActs 18:5 bRom. 5:15; 6:6f.; Gal. 2:20; Col. 3:3

14 For the love of Christ acontrols us, having concluded this, that bone died for all, therefore all died;

★15 aRom. 14:7-9

15 and He died for all, that they who live should no longer alive for themselves, but for Him who died and rose again on their behalf.

5:1 *the earthly tent . . . a house not made with hands.* The present earthly body is contrasted with the resurrection body.

5:2 *in this* earthly *body we groan* because of the burdens of life (cf. Rom. 8:23). *our dwelling from heaven.* Lit., dwelling place which is from heaven.

5:3 *shall not be found naked.* We shall not be bodiless after resurrection.

5:4 While in this body we are burdened; so we do not long to be disembodied but to have the resurrection body God will give us (v. 5).

5:9 *we have as our ambition.* The Greek word is found elsewhere only in Rom. 15:20 and 1 Thess. 4:11.

5:10 *the judgment seat of Christ.* The *bema* (judgment seat) was well-known to the Corinthians (see Acts 18:12). Believers will be judged in a review of their works for the purpose of rewards (see note on 1 Cor. 3:14). *bad* = worthless.

5:11 *fear.* Or awe of the Lord (Christ) in view of His judging us.

5:13 *beside ourselves.* Lit., "we went mad," probably referring to some specific occasion when Paul's critics charged him with madness. (For a similar charge against Jesus, see Mark 3:21; see also Acts 26:24.)

5:14 *For the love of Christ controls us.* Christ's love for us (and possibly it may also mean our love for Christ) controls us; i.e., keeps us within bounds. *therefore all died.* Believers are regarded by God as having died in Christ so that they may be able to live to please Him (Rom. 6:8).

5:15 Christ's death was, in part, for the purpose of bringing His followers into the experience of unselfish living for others.

★16 aJohn
8:15; 2 Cor.
11:18; Phil.
3:4

★17 aRom.
16:7 bJohn
3:3; Rom.
6:4; Gal.
6:15 cIs.
43:18f.;
65:17; Eph.
4:24; Rev.
21:4f.
★18 a1 Cor.
11:12 bRom.
5:10; Col.
1:20 c1 Cor.
3:5
★19 aCol.
2:9 bRom.
4:8; 1 Cor.
13:5

20 aMal. 2:7;
Eph. 6:20
b2 Cor. 6:1
cRom. 5:10;
Col. 1:20

★21 aActs
3:14; Heb.
4:15; 7:26;
1 Pet. 2:22;
1 John 3:5
bRom. 3:25;
4:25; 8:3;
Gal. 3:13
cRom. 1:17;
3:21f.; 1 Cor.
1:30

1 a1 Cor.
3:9 b2 Cor.
5:20 cActs
11:23

★ 2 aIs.
49:8

16 Therefore from now on we recognize no man ^aaccording to the flesh; even though we have known Christ according to the flesh, yet now we know *Him* thus no longer.

17 Therefore if any man is ^ain Christ, *he is* ^ba new creature; ^cthe old things passed away; behold, new things have come.

18 Now ^aall *these* things are from God, ^bwho reconciled us to Himself through Christ, and gave us the ^cministry of reconciliation,

19 namely, that ^aGod was in Christ reconciling the world to Himself, ^bnot counting their trespasses against them, and He has committed to us the word of reconciliation.

20 Therefore, we are ^aambassadors for Christ, ^bas though God were entreating through us; we beg you on behalf of Christ, be ^creconciled to God.

21 He made Him who ^aknew no sin *to be* ^bsin on our behalf, that we might become the ^crighteousness of God in Him.

G The Conduct of the Ministry, 6:1-10

6 And ^aworking together *with* Him, ^bwe also urge you not to receive ^cthe grace of God in vain—

2 for He says,

"^aAT THE ACCEPTABLE TIME I LISTENED TO YOU,

AND ON THE DAY OF SALVATION I HELPED YOU";

behold, now is "THE ACCEPTABLE TIME," behold, now is "THE DAY OF SALVATION"—

3 ^agiving no cause for offense in anything, in order that the ministry be not discredited,

4 but in everything ^acommending ourselves as ^bservants of God, ^cin much endurance, in afflictions, in hardships, in distresses,

5 in ^abeatings, in ^aimprisonments, in ^btumults, in labors, in sleeplessness, in ^chunger,

6 in purity, in ^aknowledge, in ^bpatience, in kindness, in the ^cHoly Spirit, in ^dgenuine love,

7 in ^athe word of truth, in ^bthe power of God; by ^cthe weapons of righteousness for the right hand and the left,

8 by glory and ^adishonor, by ^bevil report and good report; *regarded* as ^cdeceivers and yet ^dtrue;

9 as unknown yet well-known, as ^adying yet behold, ^bwe live; as punished yet not put to death,

10 as ^asorrowful yet always ^arejoicing, as ^bpoor yet making many rich, as ^chaving nothing yet possessing ^dall things.

★ 3-10
3 a1 Cor.
8:9, 13; 9:12
4 aRom.
3:5; 1 Cor.
3:5; 2 Tim.
2:24f. cActs
9:16; 2 Cor.
4:8-11; 6:4ff.;
11:23-27;
12:10
★ 5 aActs
16:23 bActs
19:23ff.
c1 Cor. 4:11
★ 6 a1 Cor.
12:8; 2 Cor.
11:6 b2 Cor.
1:23; 2:10;
13:10
c1 Cor. 2:4;
1 Thess. 1:5
dRom. 12:9
7 a2 Cor.
2:17; 4:2
b1 Cor. 2:5
cRom.
13:12; 2 Cor.
10:4; Eph.
6:11ff.
★ 8 a1 Cor.
4:10 bRom.
3:8; 1 Cor.
4:13; 2 Cor.
12:16 cMatt.
27:63
d2 Cor. 1:18;
4:2; 1 Thess.
2:3f.
★ 9 aRom.
8:36 b2 Cor.
1:8, 10; 4:11
10 aJohn
16:22; 2 Cor.
7:4; Phil.
2:17; 4:4;
Col. 1:24;
1 Thess. 1:6
b1 Cor. 1:5;
2 Cor. 8:9
cActs 3:6
dRom. 8:32;
1 Cor. 3:21

5:16 Before his conversion, Paul regarded Christ as merely another man.

5:17 *a new creature.* Lit., a new creation. Old things are passed away (aorist tense indicating the decisive change salvation brings); *behold, new things have come.* (Perfect tense indicating abiding results of the new life in Christ.) The grace of God not only justifies but also makes "a new creation" which results in a changed style of life (v. 15).

5:18 *reconciliation* involves a changed relationship because our trespasses are not counted against us (v. 19). We are now to announce to others this message of God's grace.

5:19 *namely.* Paul here restates v. 18.

5:21 Here is the heart of the gospel: the sinless Savior has taken our sins that we might have God's righteousness.

6:2 The quotation is from Isa. 49:8, Greek version (Septuagint). Paul's emphasis is on the *now*.

6:3-10 The theme of the apostolic ministry, first introduced in 2:14, is here recapitulated.

6:5 See 11:23-24.

6:6 God-given qualities of character are proof of Paul's integrity.

6:8 *as deceivers.* Paul was hardly a deceiver, but apparently was called one by his enemies (cf. Matt. 27:63). Paul says he fights his way through the slanders and faithfully carries on for Christ.

6:9 *as unknown.* His opponents said Paul was an insignificant teacher, a "nobody."

IV THE APOSTLE'S EXHORTATIONS TO THE CORINTHIANS, 6:11-7:16
A Be Open toward Him, 6:11-13

11 ^aOur mouth has spoken freely to you, O Corinthians, our ^bheart is opened wide.

12 You are not restrained by us, but ^ayou are restrained in your own affections.

13 Now in a like ^aexchange— I speak as to ^bchildren—open wide *to us* also.

B Be Separated from Evil, 6:14-7:1

14 ^aDo not be bound together with ^bunbelievers; for what ^cpartnership have righteousness and lawlessness, or what fellowship has light with darkness?

15 Or what ^aharmony has Christ with Belial, or what has a ^bbeliever in common with an ^cunbeliever?

16 Or ^awhat agreement has the temple of God with idols? For we are ^bthe temple of ^cthe living God; just as God said,

"^dI WILL ^eDWELL IN THEM AND ^fWALK AMONG THEM;

AND I WILL BE THEIR GOD, AND THEY SHALL BE MY PEOPLE.

17 "^aTherefore, ^bCOME OUT FROM THEIR MIDST AND BE SEPARATE," says the Lord.

"AND DO NOT TOUCH WHAT IS UNCLEAN;

And I will welcome you.

18 "^aAnd I will be a father to you,

And you shall be ^bsons and daughters to Me,"

Says the Lord Almighty.

7 Therefore, having these promises, ^abeloved, ^blet us cleanse ourselves from all defilement of flesh and spirit, perfecting holiness in the fear of God.

C Be Assured of His Joy over Their Repentance, 7:2-16

2 ^aMake room for us *in your hearts*; we wronged no one, we corrupted no one, we took advantage of no one.

3 I do not speak to condemn you; for I have said ^abefore that you are ^bin our hearts to die together and to live together.

4 Great is my ^aconfidence in you, great is my ^bboasting on your behalf; I am filled with ^ccomfort. I am overflowing with ^djoy in all our affliction.

5 For even when we came into ^aMacedonia our flesh had no rest, but we were ^bafflicted on every side: ^cconflicts without, fears within.

6 But ^aGod, who comforts the depressed, ^bcomforted us by the coming of ^cTitus;

7 and not only by his coming, but also by the comfort with which he was comforted in you, as he reported to us your longing, your mourning, your zeal for me; so that I rejoiced even more.

8 For though I ^acaused you sorrow by my letter, I do not regret it; though I did regret it—*for* I see that that letter caused you sorrow, though only for a while—

Cross references (left margin):

★11 ^aEzek. 33:22; Eph. 6:19 ^bIs. 60:5; 2 Cor. 7:3
12 ^a2 Cor. 7:2
13 ^aGal. 4:12 ^b1 Cor. 4:14
★14 ^aDeut. 22:10; 1 Cor. 5:9f. ^b1 Cor. 6:6 ^cEph. 5:7, 11; 1 John 1:6
★15 ^a1 Cor. 10:21 ^bActs 5:14; 1 Pet. 1:21 ^c1 Cor. 6:6
16 ^a1 Cor. 10:21 ^b1 Cor. 3:16 ^cMatt. 16:16 ^dEx. 29:45; Lev. 26:12; Jer. 31:1; Ezek. 37:27 ^eEx. 25:8; John 14:23 ^fRev. 2:1
★17 ^aIs. 52:11 ^bRev. 18:4
18 ^aIs. 43:6; Hos. 1:10 ^bRom. 8:14

Cross references (right margin):

1 ^aHeb. 6:9 ^b1 Pet. 1:15f.
2 ^a2 Cor. 6:12f.; 12:15
3 ^a2 Cor. 6:11f. ^bPhil. 1:7
4 ^a2 Cor. 3:12 ^b2 Cor. 7:14; 8:24; 9:2f.; 10:8; Phil. 1:26; 2 Thess. 1:4 ^c2 Cor. 1:4 ^d2 Cor. 6:10
★ 5–13a
5 ^aRom. 15:26; 2 Cor. 2:13 ^b2 Cor. 4:8 ^cDeut. 32:25
★ 6 ^a2 Cor. 1:3f. ^b2 Cor. 7:13 ^c2 Cor. 2:13; 7:13f.
8 ^a2 Cor. 2:2

6:11 I.e., our speech is frank and our heart is ready to take you in.

6:14 *Do not be bound together with unbelievers.* This injunction applies to marriage, business, and to ecclesiastical and intimate personal relationships.

6:15 *Belial* = Satan.

6:17 *separate.* Personal separation involves not being unequally yoked (v. 14); not loving the world (1 John 2:15-17), though using it (1 Cor. 7:31); not having fellowship with sinning brethren (1 Cor. 5:11); and, on the positive side, exhibiting Christlikeness. See note on Acts 15:39.

7:5-13a resumes the discussion of Paul's journey to Macedonia introduced in 2:13. He describes his relief because of the good news Titus brought (vv. 5-7) and his reflections on the severe letter he had written and its consequences.

7:6 *the coming of Titus.* I.e., from Corinth, with the news that the church had accepted the severe letter.

9 I now rejoice, not that you were made sorrowful, but that you were made sorrowful to *the point of* repentance; for you were made sorrowful according to *the will of* God, in order that you might not suffer loss in anything through us.

10 For the sorrow that is according to *the will of* God produces a ªrepentance without regret, *leading* to salvation; but the sorrow of the world produces death.

11 For behold what earnestness this very thing, this godly sorrow, has produced in you: what vindication of yourselves, what indignation, what fear, what ªlonging, what zeal, what ᵇavenging of wrong! In everything you ᶜdemonstrated yourselves to be innocent in the matter.

12 So although ªI wrote to you *it was* not for the sake of ᵇthe offender, nor for the sake of the one offended, but that your earnestness on our behalf might be made known to you in the sight of God.

13 For this reason we have been ªcomforted.

And besides our comfort, we rejoiced even much more for the joy of ᵇTitus, because his ᶜspirit has been refreshed by you all.

14 For if in anything I have ªboasted to him about you, I was not put to shame; but as we spoke all things to you in truth, so also our boasting before ᵇTitus proved to be *the* truth.

15 And his affection abounds all the more toward you, as he remembers the ªobedience of you all, how you received him with ᵇfear and trembling.

16 I rejoice that in everything ªI have confidence in you.

V THE APOSTLE'S SOLICITATION (OR COLLECTION) FOR THE JUDEAN SAINTS, 8:1–9:15
A Principles for Giving, 8:1-6

8 Now, brethren, we *wish to* make known to you the grace of God which has been ªgiven in the churches of ᵇMacedonia,

2 that in a great ordeal of affliction their abundance of joy and their deep poverty overflowed in the ªwealth of their liberality.

3 For I testify that ªaccording to their ability, and beyond their ability *they gave* of their own accord,

4 begging us with much entreaty for the ªfavor of participation in the ᵇsupport of the saints,

5 and *this*, not as we had expected, but they first ªgave themselves to the Lord and to us by ᵇthe will of God.

6 Consequently we ªurged ᵇTitus that as he had previously ᶜmade a beginning, so he would also complete in you ᵈthis gracious work as well.

B Purposes for Giving, 8:7-15

7 But just as you ªabound ᵇin everything, in faith and utterance and knowledge and in all earnestness and in the love we inspired in you, *see* that you ªabound in this gracious work also.

8 I ªam not speaking *this* as a command, but as proving through the earnestness of others the sincerity of your love also.

Cross references
10 ªActs 11:18
★11 ª2 Cor. 7:7 ᵇ2 Cor. 2:6 ᶜRom. 3:5
★12 ª2 Cor. 2:3; 9; 7:8 ᵇ1 Cor. 5:1f.
13 ª2 Cor. 7:6 ᵇ2 Cor. 2:13; 7:6, 14 ᶜ1 Cor. 16:18
14 ª2 Cor. 7:4; 8:24; 9:2f.; 10:8; Phil. 1:26; 2 Thess. 1:4 ᵇ2 Cor. 2:13; 7:6, 13
15 ª2 Cor. 2:9 ᵇ1 Cor. 2:3; Phil. 2:12
16 ª2 Cor. 2:3
★ 1-6
1 ª2 Cor. 8:5 ᵇActs 16:9
2 ªRom. 2:4
3 ª1 Cor. 16:2; 2 Cor. 8:11
4 ªActs 24:17; Rom. 15:25f. ᵇRom. 15:31; 2 Cor. 8:19f.; 9:1, 12f.
5 ª2 Cor. 8:1 ᵇ1 Cor. 1:1
6 ª2 Cor. 8:17; 12:18 ᵇ2 Cor. 2:13; 8:16, 23 ᶜ2 Cor. 8:10 ᵈActs 24:17; Rom. 15:25f.
★ 7-15
7 ª2 Cor. 9:8 ᵇRom. 15:14; 1 Cor. 1:5; 12:8
8 ª1 Cor. 7:6

7:11 *vindication of yourselves.* I.e., with regard to Paul's accusations by their change of behavior. Their sorrow had worked the right kind of repentance.

7:12 *the offender.* See 2:6. *the one offended.* I.e., Paul.

8:1-6 Truths about N.T. giving presented here are: (1) it is a grace (vv. 1, 6); (2) it can be exercised even during poverty (v. 2); (3) it is a form of fellowship (v. 4); and (4) it should be

preceded by the dedication of self (v. 5). Apparently the church at Corinth had never, up to this time at least, supported Paul financially (see 11:8-9; 12:13; 1 Cor. 9:11-12).

8:7-15 Some purposes in giving are: (1) to abound in all aspects of Christian experience (v. 7); (2) to prove the reality of one's love (v. 8); (3) to imitate Christ (v. 9); and (4) to help meet the needs of others (v. 14).

9 For you know ^athe grace of our Lord Jesus Christ, that ^bthough He was rich, yet for your sake He became poor, that you through His poverty might become rich.

10 And I ^agive *my* opinion in this matter, for this is to your advantage, who were the first to begin ^ba year ago not only to do *this,* but also to desire *to do it.*

11 But now finish doing it also; that just as *there was* the ^areadiness to desire it, so *there may be* also the completion of it by your ability.

12 For if the readiness is present, it is acceptable ^aaccording to what *a man* has, not according to what he does not have.

13 For *this* is not for the ease of others *and* for your affliction, but by way of equality—

14 at this present time your abundance *being a supply* for ^atheir want, that their abundance also may become *a supply* for ^ayour want, that there may be equality;

15 as it is written, "^aHe who gathered MUCH DID NOT HAVE TOO MUCH, AND HE WHO gathered LITTLE HAD NO LACK."

C Policies in Giving, 8:16-9:5

16 But ^athanks be to God, who ^bputs the same earnestness on your behalf in the heart of ^cTitus.

17 For he not only accepted our ^aappeal, but being himself very earnest, he has gone to you of his own accord.

18 And we have sent along with him ^athe brother whose fame in *the things of* the ^bgospel *has spread* through ^call the churches;

19 ^aand not only *this,* but he has also been ^bappointed by the churches to travel with us in ^cthis gracious work, which is being administered by us for the glory of the Lord Himself, and *to show* our ^dreadiness,

20 taking precaution that no one should discredit us in our administration of this generous gift;

21 for we ^ahave regard for what is honorable, not only in ^bthe sight of the Lord, but also in the sight of men.

22 And we have sent with them our brother, whom we have often tested and found diligent in many things, but now even more diligent, because of *his* great confidence in you.

23 As for ^aTitus, *he is* my ^bpartner and fellow worker among you; as for our ^cbrethren, *they are* ^dmessengers of the churches, ^ea glory to Christ.

24 Therefore openly before the churches show them the proof of your love and of our ^areason for boasting about you.

9 For ^ait is superfluous for me to write to you about this ^bministry to the saints;

2 for I know your readiness, of which I ^aboast about you to the ^bMacedonians, *namely,* that ^cAchaia has been prepared since ^dlast year, and your zeal has stirred up most of them.

3 But I have sent the brethren, that our ^aboasting about you may not be made empty in this case, that, ^bas I was saying, you may be prepared;

4 lest if any ^aMacedonians come with me and find you unprepared, we (not to speak of you) should be put to shame by this confidence.

5 So I thought it necessary to urge the ^abrethren that they

Marginal references:

9 ^a2 Cor. 13:14 ^bMatt. 20:28; 2 Cor. 6:10; Phil. 2:6f.

10 ^a1 Cor. 7:25, 40 ^b1 Cor. 16:2f.; 2 Cor. 9:2

11 ^a2 Cor. 8:12, 19; 9:2

12 ^aMark 12:43f.; Luke 21:3; 2 Cor. 9:7

14 ^aActs 4:34; 2 Cor. 9:12

15 ^aEx. 16:18

16 ^a2 Cor. 2:14 ^bRev. 17:17 ^c2 Cor. 2:13; 8:6, 23

17 ^a2 Cor. 8:6; 12:18

★18 ^a1 Cor. 16:3; 2 Cor. 12:18 ^b2 Cor. 2:12 ^c1 Cor. 4:17; 7:17

19 ^aRom. 5:3 ^bActs 14:23, 1 Cor. 16:3f. ^c2 Cor. 8:4, 6 ^d2 Cor. 8:11, 12; 9:2

21 ^aRom. 12:17 ^bRom. 14:18

23 ^a2 Cor. 8:6 ^bPhilem. 17 ^c2 Cor. 8:18, 22 ^dJohn 13:16; Phil. 2:25 ^e1 Cor. 11:7

24 ^a2 Cor. 7:4

1 ^a1 Thess. 4:9 ^b2 Cor. 8:4

★ 2 ^a2 Cor. 7:4 ^bRom. 15:26 ^cActs 18:12 ^d2 Cor. 8:10

3 ^a2 Cor. 7:4 ^b1 Cor. 16:2

4 ^aRom. 15:26

5 ^a2 Cor. 9:3 ^bGen. 33:11; Judg. 1:15; 2 Cor. 9:6 ^cPhil. 4:17 ^d2 Cor. 12:17f.

8:18 *the brother.* I.e., fellow Christian. Although we do not know who he was (perhaps Luke or Trophimus), this man was obviously well-known for preaching the gospel. Titus, this unnamed brother and a third brother (also unnamed, v. 22), acted as trustees of the money to insure complete propriety in the handling of it (v. 21).

9:2 *readiness* = eagerness (8:10). The Corinthians' *zeal* had been an example and incentive to others to give also. If they did not now fulfill their promise, it would be a disgrace to them and to Paul (v. 4).

would go on ahead to you and arrange beforehand your previously promised *b*bountiful gift, that the same might be ready as a *c*bountiful gift, and not *d*affected by covetousness.

D Promises in Giving, 9:6-15

6 Now this *I say,* *a*he who sows sparingly shall also reap sparingly; and he who sows bountifully shall also reap bountifully.

7 Let each one *do* just as he has purposed in his heart; not *a*grudgingly or under compulsion; for *b*God loves a cheerful giver.

8 And *a*God is able to make all grace abound to you, that always having all sufficiency in everything, you may have an abundance for every good deed;

9 as it is written,

"*a*HE SCATTERED ABROAD, HE
    GAVE TO THE POOR,
HIS RIGHTEOUSNESS ABIDES
    FOREVER."

10 Now He who supplies *a*seed to the sower and bread for food, will supply and multiply your seed for sowing and *b*increase the harvest of your righteousness;

11 you will be *a*enriched in everything for all liberality, which through us is producing *b*thanksgiving to God.

12 For the ministry of this service is not only fully supplying *a*the needs of the saints, but is also overflowing *b*through many thanksgivings to God.

13 Because of the proof given by this *a*ministry they will *b*glorify God for *your* obedience to your *c*confession of the *d*gospel of Christ, and for the liberality of your contribution to them and to all,

14 while they also, by prayer on your behalf, yearn for you because of the surpassing grace of God in you.

15 *a*Thanks be to God for His indescribable *b*gift!

VI THE APOSTLE'S VINDICATION OF HIMSELF, 10:1-12:18
A The Authority of His Apostleship, 10:1-18

10 Now *a*I, Paul, myself *b*urge you by the *c*meekness and gentleness of Christ—I who *d*am meek when face to face with you, but bold toward you when absent!

2 I ask that *a*when I am present I may not be bold with the confidence with which I propose to be courageous against *b*some, who regard us as if we walked *c*according to the flesh.

3 For though we walk in the flesh, we do not war *a*according to the flesh,

4 for the *a*weapons of our warfare are not of the flesh, but *b*divinely powerful *c*for the destruction of fortresses.

5 *We are* destroying speculations and every *a*lofty thing raised up against the knowledge of God, and *we are* taking every thought captive to the *b*obedience of Christ,

6 and we are ready to punish all disobedience, whenever *a*your obedience is complete.

Cross references (left margin):

★ **6** *a*Prov. 11:24f.; 22:9; Gal. 6:7, 9

7 *a*Deut. 15:10; 1 Chr. 29:17; Rom. 12:8; 2 Cor. 8:12 *b*Ex. 25:2; Prov. 22:8 [Septuagint];2 Cor. 8:12
★ **8** *a*Eph. 3:20

★ **9** *a*Ps. 112:9

★**10** *a*Is. 55:10 *b*Hos. 10:12

11 *a*1 Cor. 1:5 *b*2 Cor. 1:11
★**12-14**
12 *a*2 Cor. 8:14 *b*2 Cor. 1:11
13 *a*Rom. 15:31; 2 Cor. 8:4 *b*Matt. 9:8 *c*1 Tim. 6:12f.; Heb. 3:1; 4:14; 10:23 *d*2 Cor. 2:12

15 *a*2 Cor. 2:14 *b*Rom. 5:15f.

★ **1** *a*Gal. 5:2; Eph. 3:1; Col. 1:23 *b*Rom. 12:1 *c*Matt. 11:29; 1 Cor. 4:21; Phil. 4:5 *d*1 Cor. 2:3f.; 2 Cor. 10:10
2 *a*1 Cor. 4:21; 2 Cor. 13:2, 10 *b*1 Cor. 4:18f. *c*Rom. 8:4; 2 Cor. 1:17

★ **3** *a*Rom. 8:4; 2 Cor. 1:17

4 *a*1 Cor. 9:7; 2 Cor. 6:7; 1 Tim. 1:18 *b*Acts 7:20 *c*Jer. 1:10; 2 Cor. 10:8; 13:10
5 *a*Is. 2:11f. *b*2 Cor. 9:13

6 *a*2 Cor. 2:9

9:6 See Prov. 11:24; 19:17; Luke 6:38.
9:8 God will supply the generous giver with enough to meet his own needs and enough to give for *every good deed.*
9:9 The same thought as in v. 8.
9:10 The generous giver will be given increasing means to give *(multiply your seed for sowing)* and increasing fruit. See Hos. 10:12.
9:12-14 The gift of money will (1) supply need (v. 12); (2) be a cause for thanksgiving (v. 12); (3) prove their obedience (v. 13); (4) draw the Jerusalem Christians to them (v. 14, *yearn for*

you).
10:1 In spite of Paul's general satisfaction with the Corinthian church, there were still some there who challenged his apostolic authority and followed certain leaders whom Paul calls "false apostles" (11:13). These leaders were apparently Jewish Christians (11:22) who claimed higher authority than Paul's (10:7) and who lorded over the church (11:20).
10:3 *in the flesh.* I.e., in a human body (with its limitations). *according to the flesh.* I.e., after the impulses of the sinful nature.

7 [a]You are looking at things as they are outwardly. [b]If anyone is confident in himself that he is Christ's, let him consider this again within himself, that just as he is Christ's, [c]so also are we.

8 For even if [a]I should boast somewhat further about our [b]authority, which the Lord gave for building you up and not for destroying you, I shall not be put to shame,

9 for I do not wish to seem as if I would terrify you by my letters.

10 For they say, "His letters are weighty and strong, but his personal presence is [a]unimpressive, and [b]his speech contemptible."

11 Let such a person consider this, that what we are in word by letters when absent, such persons we are also in deed when present.

12 For we are not bold to class or compare ourselves with some of those who [a]commend themselves; but when they measure themselves by themselves, and compare themselves with themselves, they are without understanding.

13 But we will not boast [a]beyond our measure, but [b]within the measure of the sphere which God apportioned to us as a measure, to reach even as far as you.

14 For we are not overextending ourselves, as if we did not reach to you, for [a]we were the first to come even as far as you in the [b]gospel of Christ;

15 not boasting [a]beyond our measure, that is, in [b]other men's labors, but with the hope that as [c]your faith grows, we shall be, within our sphere, [d]enlarged even more by you,

16 so as to [a]preach the gospel even to [b]the regions beyond you, and not to boast [c]in what has been accomplished in the sphere of another.

17 But [a]HE WHO BOASTS, LET HIM BOAST IN THE LORD.

18 For not he who [a]commends himself is approved, but [b]whom the Lord commends.

B The Marks of His Apostleship, 11:1-12:18

1 Paul's conduct, 11:1-15

11 I wish that you would [a]bear with me in a little [b]foolishness; but indeed you are bearing with me.

2 For I am jealous for you with a godly jealousy; for I [a]betrothed you to one husband, that to Christ I might [b]present you as a pure virgin.

3 But I am afraid, lest as the [a]serpent deceived Eve by his craftiness, your minds should be led astray from the simplicity and purity of devotion to Christ.

4 For if one comes and preaches [a]another Jesus whom we have not preached, or you receive a [b]different spirit which you have not received, or a [c]different gospel which you have not accepted, you [d]bear this [e]beautifully.

5 For I consider myself [a]not in the least inferior to the most eminent apostles.

6 But even if I am [a]unskilled in speech, yet I am not so in [b]knowledge; in fact, in every way

★ 7-9
7 [a]John 7:24; 2 Cor. 5:12 [b]1 Cor. 1:12; 14:37 [c]1 Cor. 9:1; 2 Cor. 11:23; Gal. 1:12
8 [a]2 Cor. 7:4 [b]2 Cor. 13:10

★10 [a]1 Cor. 2:3; 2 Cor. 12:7; Gal. 4:13f. [b]1 Cor. 1:17; 2 Cor. 11:6

12 [a]2 Cor. 3:1; 10:18

★13 [a]2 Cor. 10:15 [b]Rom. 12:3; 2 Cor. 10:15f.

14 [a]1 Cor. 3:6 [b]2 Cor. 2:12

★15-16
15 [a]2 Cor. 10:13 [b]Rom. 15:20 [c]2 Thess. 1:3 [d]Acts 5:13

16 [a]2 Cor. 11:7 [b]Acts 19:21 [c]Rom. 15:20

17 [a]Jer. 9:24; 1 Cor. 1:31
18 [a]2 Cor. 10:12 [b]Rom. 2:29; 1 Cor. 4:5

★ 1 [a]Matt. 17:17; 2 Cor. 11:4, 16, 19f. [b]2 Cor. 5:13; 11:17, 21

2 [a]Hos. 2:19f.; Eph. 5:26f. [b]2 Cor. 4:14

★ 3 [a]Gen. 3:4, 13; John 8:44; 1 Thess. 3:5; 1 Tim. 2:14; Rev. 12:9, 15

★ 4 [a]1 Cor. 3:11 [b]Rom. 8:15 [c]Gal. 1:6 [d]2 Cor. 11:1 [e]Mark 7:9

5 [a]2 Cor. 12:11; Gal. 2:6

★ 6 [a]1 Cor. 1:17 [b]1 Cor. 12:8; Eph. 3:4 [c]2 Cor. 4:2

10:7-9 You look, Paul says, only at what lies before your eyes. I belong to Christ as much as they do (v. 7). As a matter of fact, I could claim higher authority (v. 8), but that might frighten you (v. 9)!

10:10 contemptible = of no account.

10:13 beyond our measure. I.e., beyond his limits or assigned region, the territory God had assigned to Paul. In that territory, which included Corinth, he would boast, but not in areas in which others had labored.

10:15-16 As their faith grows and his presence is no longer necessary, Paul could turn to other fields.

11:1 a little foolishness. I.e., the boasting of vv. 21-33. But Paul knows he must do it to make the false apostles appear in their true colors.

11:3 Some texts read, "from the simplicity and purity which is in Christ."

11:4 Paul here and in v. 5 is speaking sarcastically. Of course he did not want them to submit to false teachers, nor did he regard these smooth talkers as "apostles" in any sense.

11:6 unskilled in speech. I.e., not an orator.

we have ᶜmade *this* evident to you in all things.

7 Or ᵃdid I commit a sin in humbling myself that you might be exalted, because I preached the ᵇgospel of God to you ᶜwithout charge?

8 I robbed other churches, ᵃtaking wages *from them* to serve you;

9 and when I was present with you and was in need, I was ᵃnot a burden to anyone; for when ᵇthe brethren came from ᶜMacedonia, they fully supplied my need, and in everything I kept myself from ᵈbeing a burden to you, and will continue to do so.

10 ᵃAs the truth of Christ is in me, ᵇthis boasting of mine will not be stopped in the regions of ᶜAchaia.

11 Why? ᵃBecause I do not love you? ᵇGod knows I do!

12 But what I am doing, I will continue to do, ᵃthat I may cut off opportunity from those who desire an opportunity to be regarded just as we are in the matter about which they are boasting.

13 For such men are ᵃfalse apostles, ᵇdeceitful workers, disguising themselves as apostles of Christ.

14 And no wonder, for even ᵃSatan disguises himself as an ᵇangel of light.

15 Therefore it is not surprising if his servants also disguise themselves as servants of righteousness; ᵃwhose end shall be according to their deeds.

2 Paul's sufferings, 11:16-33

16 ᵃAgain I say, let no one think me foolish; but if *you do,* receive me even as foolish, that I also may boast a little.

17 That which I am speaking, I am not speaking ᵃas the Lord would, but as ᵇin foolishness, in this confidence of boasting.

18 Since ᵃmany boast ᵇaccording to the flesh, I will boast also.

19 For you, ᵃbeing *so* wise, bear with the foolish gladly.

20 For you bear with anyone if he ᵃenslaves you, if he ᵇdevours you, if he ᶜtakes advantage of you, if he ᵈexalts himself, if he ᵉhits you in the face.

21 To *my* ᵃshame I *must* say that we have been ᵇweak *by comparison.* But in whatever respect anyone *else* ᶜis bold (I ᵈspeak in foolishness), I am just as bold myself.

22 Are they ᵃHebrews? ᵇSo am I. Are they ᶜIsraelites? ᶜSo am I. Are they ᵈdescendants of Abraham? ᵉSo am I.

23 Are they ᵃservants of Christ? (I speak as if insane) I more so; in ᵇfar more labors, in ᶜfar more imprisonments, ᵈbeaten times without number, often in ᵉdanger of death.

24 Five times I received from the Jews ᵃthirty-nine *lashes.*

25 Three times I was ᵃbeaten with rods, once I was ᵇstoned, three times I was shipwrecked, a night and a day I have spent in the deep.

Marginal references (left column):
7 ᵃ2 Cor. 12:13 ᵇRom. 1:1; 2 Cor. 2:12 ᶜActs 18:3; 1 Cor. 9:18
★ 8 ᵃ1 Cor. 4:12; 9:6; Phil. 4:15, 18
9 ᵃ2 Cor. 12:13f., 16 ᵇActs 18:5 ᶜRom. 15:26
10 ᵃRom. 1:9; 9:1; 2 Cor. 1:23; Gal. 2:20 ᵇ1 Cor. 9:15 ᶜActs 18:12
11 ᵃ2 Cor. 12:15 ᵇRom. 1:9; 2 Cor. 2:17; 11:31; 12:2f.
★12 ᵃ1 Cor. 9:12
13 ᵃActs 20:30; Gal. 1:7; 2:4; Phil. 1:15; Titus 1:10f.; 2 Pet. 2:1; Rev. 2:2 ᵇPhil. 3:2
★14-15
14 ᵃMatt. 4:10; Eph. 6:12; Col. 1:13 ᵇCol. 1:12
15 ᵃRom. 2:6; 3:8

Marginal references (right column):
16 ᵃ2 Cor. 11:1
★17 ᵃ1 Cor. 7:12, 25 ᵇ2 Cor. 11:21
18 ᵃPhil. 3:3f. ᵇ2 Cor. 5:16
19 ᵃ1 Cor. 4:10
★20 ᵃ2 Cor. 1:24; Gal. 2:4; 4:3, 9; 5:1 ᵇMark 12:40 ᶜLuke 5:5; 2 Cor. 11:3; 12:16 ᵈ2 Cor. 10:5 ᵉ1 Cor. 4:11
21 ᵃ2 Cor. 6:8 ᵇ2 Cor. 10:10 ᶜ2 Cor. 10:2 ᵈ2 Cor. 11:17
22 ᵃActs 6:1 ᵇPhil. 3:5 ᶜRom. 9:4 ᵈGal. 3:16 ᵉRom. 11:1
23 ᵃ1 Cor. 3:5; 2 Cor. 3:6; 10:7 ᵇ1 Cor. 15:10 ᶜ2 Cor. 6:5 ᵈActs 16:23; 2 Cor. 6:5 ᵉRom. 8:36
★24 ᵃDeut. 25:3
★25 ᵃActs 16:22 ᵇActs 14:19

11:8 *robbed.* In the sense of having accepted gifts from other churches who could ill afford to give them, in order not to be a financial burden to the Corinthians.

11:12 By not accepting support, Paul cut off his opponents' *opportunity,* or opening, for attacking him.

11:14-15 Satan's masterful deception is to appear in the guise of an angel of light. These teachers, Satan's servants, appeared as preachers of righteousness.

11:17 *as the Lord would.* Paul means that his forced boasting finds no example in the life of Christ. He had to indulge in it, he says, against his natural instincts, so that he could call some significant facts to their attention.

11:20 *devours.* I.e., by exacting money (cf. Mark 12:40).

11:24 *thirty-nine lashes.* This refers to beatings administered in the synagogue. The law prescribed forty lashes (Deut. 25:1-3), but only 39 were given in order to be certain of not exceeding the limit.

11:25 *beaten with rods.* A Roman punishment, administered to Paul at Philippi (Acts 16:23). *stoned.* At Lystra (Acts 14:11-19).

26 I have been on frequent journeys, in dangers from rivers, dangers from robbers, dangers from my ^acountrymen, dangers from the ^bGentiles, dangers in the ^ccity, dangers in the wilderness, dangers on the sea, dangers among ^dfalse brethren;

26 ^aActs 9:23; 13:45, 50; 14:5; 17:5, 13; 18:12; 20:3, 19; 21:27; 23:10, 12; 25:3; 1 Thess. 2:15 ^bActs 14:5, 19; 19:23ff.; 27:42 ^cActs 21:31 ^dGal. 2:4

27 I have been in ^alabor and hardship, through many sleepless nights, in ^bhunger and thirst, often ^cwithout food, in cold and ^dexposure.

27 ^a1 Thess. 2:9; 2 Thess. 3:8 ^b1 Cor. 4:11; Phil. 4:12 ^c2 Cor. 6:5 ^d1 Cor. 4:11

28 Apart from such external things, there is the daily pressure upon me of concern for ^aall the churches.

28 ^a1 Cor. 7:17

29 Who is ^aweak without my being weak? Who is led into sin without my intense concern?

29 ^a1 Cor. 8:9, 13; 9:22

30 If I have to boast, I will boast of what pertains to my ^aweakness.

30 ^a1 Cor. 2:3

31 The God and Father of the Lord Jesus, ^aHe who is blessed forever, ^bknows that I am not lying.

31 ^aRom. 1:25 ^b2 Cor. 11:11

32 In ^aDamascus the ethnarch under Aretas the king was ^bguarding the city of the Damascenes in order to seize me,

★**32** ^aActs 9:2 ^bActs 9:24

33 and I was let down in a basket ^athrough a window in the wall, and so escaped his hands.

33 ^aActs 9:25

3 Paul's vision, 12:1-10

12 ^aBoasting is necessary, though it is not profitable; but I will go on to visions and ^brevelations of the Lord.

1 ^a2 Cor. 11:16, 18, 30; 12:5, 9 ^b1 Cor. 14:6; 2 Cor. 12:7; Gal. 1:12; 2:2; Eph. 3:3

2 I know a man ^ain Christ who fourteen years ago—whether in the body I do not know, or out of the body I do not know, ^bGod knows—such a man was ^ccaught up to the ^dthird heaven.

★ **2-4**
2 ^aRom. 16:7 ^b2 Cor. 11:11 ^cEzek. 8:3; Acts 8:39; 2 Cor. 12:4; 1 Thess. 4:17; Rev. 12:5 ^dDeut. 10:14; Ps. 148:4; Eph. 4:10; Heb. 4:14

3 And I know how such a man—whether in the body or apart from the body I do not know, ^aGod knows—

3 ^a2 Cor. 11:11

4 was ^acaught up into ^bParadise, and heard inexpressible words, which a man is not permitted to speak.

4 ^aEzek. 8:3; Acts 8:39; 2 Cor. 12:2; 1 Thess. 4:17; Rev. 12:5 ^bLuke 23:43

5 ^aOn behalf of such a man will I boast; but on my own behalf I will not boast, except in regard to my ^bweaknesses.

5 ^a2 Cor. 12:1 ^b1 Cor. 2:3; 2 Cor. 12:9f.

6 For if I do wish to boast I shall not be ^afoolish, ^bfor I shall be speaking the truth; but I refrain from this, so that no one may credit me with more than he sees in me or hears from me.

★ **6** ^a2 Cor. 5:13; 11:16f.; 12:11 ^b2 Cor. 7:14

7 And because of the surpassing greatness of the ^arevelations, for this reason, to keep me from exalting myself, there was given me a ^bthorn in the flesh, a ^cmessenger of Satan to buffet me—to keep me from exalting myself!

★ **7** ^a2 Cor. 12:1 ^bNum. 33:55; Ezek. 28:24; Hos. 2:6 ^cJob 2:6; Matt. 4:10; 1 Cor. 5:5

8 Concerning this I entreated the Lord ^athree times that it might depart from me.

8 ^aMatt. 26:44

9 And He has said to me, "My grace is sufficient for you, for ^apower is perfected in weakness." Most gladly, therefore, I will rather ^bboast about my weaknesses, that the power of Christ may dwell in me.

★ **9** ^a1 Cor. 2:5; Eph. 3:16; Phil. 4:13 ^b1 Cor. 2:3; 2 Cor. 12:5

10 Therefore ^aI am well content with weaknesses, with insults, with ^bdistresses, with ^cpersecutions, with ^bdifficulties, ^dfor Christ's sake; for ^ewhen I am weak, then I am strong.

10 ^aRom. 5:3; 8:35 ^b2 Cor. 6:4 ^c2 Thess. 1:4; 2 Tim. 3:11 ^d2 Cor. 5:15, 20 ^e2 Cor. 13:4

4 Paul's unselfishness, 12:11-18

11 I have become ^afoolish; you yourselves compelled me. Actually I should have been com-

11 ^a2 Cor. 5:13; 11:16f.; 12:6 ^b1 Cor. 15:10; 2 Cor. 11:5 ^c1 Cor. 3:7; 13:2; 15:9

11:32 The record of the events in Damascus is found in Acts 9:24-25.

12:2-4 Paul here speaks of a personal and actual experience when he was caught up into heaven and given revelations he could not speak about. Some think this occurred when he was stoned (Acts 14:19).

12:6 Paul wanted to be judged only on the evidence before their eyes.

12:7 a thorn in the flesh. This seems to have

been some recurrent physical affliction. Migraine headaches, eye trouble (ophthalmia?), malaria, and epilepsy have all been seriously suggested (but see note on Gal. 4:12-15). Paul views it as the work of Satan, permitted by God for a good purpose (keeping him humble). It could not be relieved through prayer (2 Cor. 12:8).

12:9 the power of Christ in him was more important than freedom from pain.

mended by you, for [b]in no respect was I inferior to the most eminent apostles, even though [c]I am a nobody.

12   The [a]signs of a true apostle were performed among you with all perseverance, by signs and wonders and miracles.

13   For in what respect were you treated as inferior to the rest of the churches, except that [a]I myself did not become a burden to you? Forgive me [b]this wrong!

14   Here [a]for this third time I am ready to come to you, and I [b]will not be a burden to you; for I [c]do not seek what is yours, but [d]you; for [e]children are not responsible to save up for *their* parents, but [f]parents for *their* children.

15   And I will [a]most gladly spend and be expended for your souls. If [b]I love you the more, am I to be loved the less?

16   But be that as it may, I [a]did not burden you myself; nevertheless, crafty fellow that I am, I [b]took you in by deceit.

17   [a]Certainly I have not taken advantage of you through any of those whom I have sent to you, have I?

18   I [a]urged [b]Titus *to go,* and sent [c]the brother with him. Titus did not take any advantage of you, did he? Did we not conduct ourselves in the same [d]spirit *and* walk [e]in the same steps?

VII   CONCLUDING REMARKS, 12:19–13:14

A   Appeal for Repentance, 12:19–21

19   All this time you have been thinking that we are defend-

ing ourselves to you. *Actually,* [a]it is in the sight of God that we have been speaking in Christ; and [b]all for your upbuilding, [c]beloved.

20   For I am afraid that perhaps [a]when I come I may find you to be not what I wish and may be found by you to be not what you wish; that perhaps *there may be* [b]strife, jealousy, [c]angry tempers, [d]disputes, [e]slanders, [f]gossip, [g]arrogance, [h]disturbances;

21   I am afraid that when I come again my God may humiliate me before you, and I may mourn over many of those who have [a]sinned in the past and not repented of the [b]impurity, immorality and sensuality which they have practiced.

B   Statement of Plans, 13:1–10

13   [a]This is the third time I am coming to you. [b]EVERY FACT IS TO BE CONFIRMED BY THE TESTIMONY OF TWO OR THREE WITNESSES.

2   I have previously said when present the second time, and though now absent I say in advance to those who have [a]sinned in the past and to all the rest as well, that [b]if I come again, I will not [c]spare *anyone,*

3   since you are [a]seeking for proof of the [b]Christ who speaks in me, and who is not weak toward you, but [c]mighty in you.

4   For indeed He was [a]crucified because of weakness, yet He lives [b]because of the power of God. For we also are [c]weak in Him, yet [d]we shall live with Him because of the power of God directed toward you.

Marginal references:

12 [a]John 4:48; Rom. 15:19; 1 Cor. 9:1

★**13** [a]1 Cor. 9:12, 18; 2 Cor. 11:9; 12:14 [b]2 Cor. 11:7

14 [a]2 Cor. 1:15; 13:1, 2 [b]1 Cor. 9:12, 18; 2 Cor. 11:9; 12:13 [c]1 Cor. 10:24, 33 [d]1 Cor. 9:19 [e]1 Cor. 4:14f.; Gal. 4:19 [f]Prov. 19:14; Ezek. 34:2

★**15** [a]Rom. 9:3; 2 Cor. 1:6; Phil. 2:17; Col. 1:24; 1 Thess. 2:8; 2 Tim. 2:10 [b]2 Cor. 11:11

★**16** [a]2 Cor. 11:9 [b]2 Cor. 11:20

17 [a]2 Cor. 9:5

18 [a]2 Cor. 8:6 [b]2 Cor. 2:13 [c]2 Cor. 8:18 [d]1 Cor. 4:21 [e]Rom. 4:12

19 [a]Rom. 9:1; 2 Cor. 2:17 [b]Rom. 14:19; 2 Cor. 10:8; 1 Thess. 5:11 [c]Heb. 6:9

20 [a]1 Cor. 4:21; 2 Cor. 2:1-4 [b]1 Cor. 1:11; 3:3 [c]Gal. 5:20 [d]Rom. 2:8; 1 Cor. 11:19 [e]Rom. 1:30; James 4:11; 1 Pet. 2:1 [f]Rom. 1:29 [g]1 Cor. 4:6, 18; 5:2 [h]1 Cor. 14:33

★**21** [a]2 Cor. 13:2 [b]1 Cor. 6:9, 18; Gal. 5:19; Col. 3:5

★ **1** [a]2 Cor. 12:14 [b]Deut. 19:15; Matt. 18:16

2 [a]2 Cor. 12:21 [b]1 Cor. 4:21; 2 Cor. 13:10 [c]2 Cor. 1:23; 10:11

3 [a]2 Cor. 10:1, 10 [b]Matt. 10:20; 1 Cor. 5:4; 7:40 [c]2 Cor. 9:8; 10:4

4 [a]Phil. 2:7f.; 1 Pet. 3:18 [b]Rom. 1:4; 6:4; 1 Cor. 6:14 [c]1 Cor. 2:3; 2 Cor. 13:9 [d]Rom. 6:8

12:13 Do you think I made you *inferior to the rest of the churches* because I didn't sponge off you?

12:15 *for your souls.* I.e., for your spiritual good.

12:16 After *nevertheless* add, "they say." To be sure, they said, he didn't take any money while he was here, but what about that collection for the saints? Who knows in whose pockets that will go?

12:21 *God may humiliate me before you.* I.e., if

when Paul comes he finds them still acting like pagans (v. 20).

13:1 *This is the third time I am coming to you.* Acts 18:1 records the first visit; the second was likely the "painful visit" (2 Cor. 2:1); and the third is the one he is about to undertake. *by the testimony of two or three witnesses.* Paul warned that, if necessary, trials were going to be held when he came, in which Jewish rules of evidence-giving would be applied (Deut. 19:15).

★ 5 aJohn
6:6 b1 Cor.
11:28
c1 Cor. 9:27

5 aTest yourselves *to see* if you are in the faith; bexamine yourselves! Or do you not recognize this about yourselves, that Jesus Christ is in you—unless indeed you cfail the test?

6 But I trust that you will realize that we ourselves do not fail the test.

7 Now we pray to God that you do no wrong; not that we ourselves may appear approved, but that you may do what is right, even though we should appear unapproved.

★ 9 a2 Cor.
12:10; 13:4
b1 Cor. 1:10;
2 Cor. 13:11;
Eph. 4:12;
1 Thess. 3:10
10 a2 Cor.
2:3 bTitus
1:13 c1 Cor.
5:4; 2 Cor.
10:8

8 For we can do nothing against the truth, but *only* for the truth.

9 For we rejoice when we ourselves are aweak but you are strong; this we also pray for, that you be bmade complete.

10 For this reason I am writ-

ing these things while absent, in order that when present aI may not use bseverity, in accordance with the cauthority which the Lord gave me, for building up and not for tearing down.

C   Greetings and Benediction, 13:11–14

11   aFinally, brethren, rejoice, bbe made complete, be comforted, cbe like-minded, dlive in peace; and ethe God of love and peace shall be with you.

12   aGreet one another with a holy kiss.

13   aAll the saints greet you.

14   aThe grace of the Lord Jesus Christ, and the blove of God, and the cfellowship of the Holy Spirit, be with you all.

11 a1 Thess.
4:1; 2 Thess.
3:1 b1 Cor.
1:10; 2 Cor.
13:9; Eph.
4:12;
1 Thess. 3:10
cRom. 12:16
dMark 9:50
eRom.
15:33; Eph.
6:23
★12 aRom.
16:16
13 aPhil.
4:22
★14 aRom.
16:20; 2 Cor.
8:9 bRom.
5:5; Jude 21
cPhil. 2:1

13:5   *yourselves* is emphatic; i.e., it is yourselves, not I, whom you should examine. *fail the test.* I.e., they failed to pass the test and were not members of the household of faith (also cf. v. 6).

13:9   *that you be made complete.* I.e., be fully restored to spiritual health (also v. 11).
13:12   *a holy kiss.* See note on 1 Pet. 5:14.
13:14 An early and clear witness to belief in the Trinity.

INTRODUCTION TO
THE LETTER OF PAUL TO THE GALATIANS

AUTHOR: Paul   DATE: 49 or 55

Galatia   At the time of the writing of this letter the term "Galatia" was used both in a geographical and a political sense. The former referred to north central Asia Minor, north of the cities of Pisidian Antioch, Iconium, Lystra, and Derbe; the latter referred to the Roman province (organized in 25 B.C.) which included southern districts and those cities just mentioned. If the letter was written to Christians in North Galatia, the churches were founded on the second missionary journey and the epistle was written on the third missionary journey, either early from Ephesus (about 53) or later (about 55) from Macedonia. In favor of this is the fact that Luke seems to use "Galatia" only to describe North Galatia (Acts 16:6; 18:23).

If the letter was written to Christians in South Galatia, the churches were founded on the first missionary journey, the letter was written after the end of the journey (probably from Antioch, about 49, making it the earliest of Paul's epistles), and the Jerusalem council (Acts 15) convened shortly afterward. In favor of this dating is the fact that Paul does not mention the decision of the Jerusalem council which bore directly on his Galatian argument concerning the Judaizers, indicating that the council had not yet taken place.

The Problem   How can men (sinful by nature) come to God (holy by nature)? Paul's answer is: There is only one way—accept the salvation God's grace makes available through Christ's death and resurrection. Forget about merit-salvation through obedience to the law of Moses. Man is too weak by nature to accomplish self-salvation or self-sanctification. Certain Jewish Christians (the Judaizers) were teaching that such works are necessary, that Paul's gospel was not correct, and that he was not a genuine apostle. Paul's answer was to proclaim the doctrine of justification by faith plus nothing, and of sanctification by the Holy Spirit, not the Mosaic law. This answer was given in the full apostolic authority received from Christ. All theologies that teach salvation by faith plus human effort are forcefully negated by this great letter.

Contents   The theme, justification by faith, is defended, explained, and applied. Other significant subjects include Paul's three years in Arabia (1:17), his correcting Peter (2:11), the law as a tutor (3:24), and the fruit of the Spirit (5:22-23).

OUTLINE OF GALATIANS

I. **Introduction: The Rightness of Paul's Gospel Asserted, 1:1-10**
II. **Justification by Faith Defended: Paul's Authority, 1:11-2:21**
  A. His Authority Acquired through Revelation, 1:11-24
  B. His Authority Approved by the Church in Jerusalem, 2:1-10
  C. His Authority Acknowledged in the Rebuke of Peter, 2:11-21
III. **Justification by Faith Explained: Paul's Gospel, 3:1-4:31**
  A. The Argument from Experience, 3:1-5
  B. The Argument from Abraham, 3:6-9

  C. The Argument from the Law, 3:10-4:11
  D. The Argument from Personal Testimony, 4:12-20
  E. The Argument from an Allegory, 4:21-31
IV. **Justification by Faith Applied: Paul's Ethics, 5:1-6:10**
  A. In Relation to Christian Liberty, 5:1-12
  B. In Relation to License and Love, 5:13-15
  C. In Relation to the Flesh and the Spirit, 5:16-26
  D. In Relation to a Sinning Brother, 6:1-5
  E. In Relation to Giving, 6:6-10
V. **Conclusion: The Substance of Paul's Instruction, 6:11-18**

THE LETTER OF PAUL TO THE GALATIANS

I INTRODUCTION: THE RIGHTNESS OF PAUL'S GOSPEL ASSERTED, 1:1-10

★ 1 *a*2 Cor. 1:1 *b*Gal. 1:11f. *c*Acts 9:15; 20:24; Gal. 1:15f. *d*Acts 2:24

1 Paul, *a*an apostle (*b*not *sent* from men, nor through the agency of man, but *c*through Jesus Christ, and God the Father, who *d*raised Him from the dead),

2 *a*Phil. 4:21 *b*Acts 16:6; 1 Cor. 16:1

2 and all *a*the brethren who are with me, to *b*the churches of Galatia:

★ 3-5

3 *a*Rom. 1:7

3 *a*Grace to you and peace from God our Father, and the Lord Jesus Christ,

4 *a*Matt. 20:28; Rom. 4:25; 1 Cor. 15:3; Gal. 2:20 *b*Matt. 13:22; Rom. 12:2; 2 Cor. 4:4 *c*Phil. 4:20; 1 Thess. 1:3; 3:11, 13

4 who *a*gave Himself for our sins, that He might deliver us out of *b*this present evil age, according to the will of *c*our God and Father,

5 *a*Rom. 11:36

5 *a*to whom *be* the glory forevermore. Amen.

★ 6 *a*Acts 16:6; 18:23; Gal. 4:13 *b*Rom. 8:28; Gal. 1:15; 5:8 *c*2 Cor. 11:4; Gal. 1:7, 11; 2:2; 7; 5:14; 1 Tim. 1:3

6 I am amazed that you are *a*so quickly deserting *b*Him who called you by the grace of Christ, for a *c*different gospel;

★ 7 *a*Acts 15:24; Gal. 5:10

7 which is *really* not another; only there are some who are *a*disturbing you, and want to distort the gospel of Christ.

★ 8 *a*2 Cor. 11:14 *b*Rom. 9:3

8 But even though we, or *a*an angel from heaven, should preach to you a gospel contrary to that which we have preached to you, let him be *b*accursed.

9 *a*Acts 18:23 *b*Rom. 16:17 *c*Rom. 9:3

9 As we *a*have said before, so I say again now, *b*if any man is preaching to you a gospel contrary to that which you received, let him be *c*accursed.

★10 *a*1 Cor. 10:33; 1 Thess. 2:4 *b*Rom. 1:1; Phil. 1:1

10 For am I now *a*seeking the favor of men, or of God? Or am I striving to please men? If I were still trying to please men, I would not be a *b*bond-servant of Christ.

II JUSTIFICATION BY FAITH DEFENDED: PAUL'S AUTHORITY, 1:11-2:21
A His Authority Acquired through Revelation, 1:11-24

★11-17

11 *a*Rom. 2:16; 1 Cor. 15:1 *b*1 Cor. 3:4; 9:8

11 For *a*I would have you know, brethren, that the gospel which was preached by me is *b*not according to man.

12 *a*1 Cor. 11:23; Gal. 1:1 *b*1 Cor. 2:10; 2 Cor. 12:1; Gal. 1:16; 2:2

12 For *a*I neither received it from man, nor was I taught it, but *I received it* through a *b*revelation of Jesus Christ.

13 *a*Acts 26:4f. *b*Acts 8:3 *c*1 Cor. 10:32 *d*Acts 9:21

13 For you have heard of *a*my former manner of life in Judaism, how I *b*used to persecute *c*the church of God beyond measure, and *d*tried to destroy it;

14 *a*Acts 22:3 *b*Jer. 9:14; Matt. 15:2; Mark 7:3; Col. 2:8

14 and I *a*was advancing in Judaism beyond many of my contemporaries among my countrymen, being more extremely zealous for my *b*ancestral traditions.

★15 *a*Gal. 1:6 *b*Is. 49:1, 5; Jer. 1:5; Acts 9:15; Rom. 1:1

15 But when He who had set

1:1 Paul's apostleship was *not . . . from men.* I.e., it did not originate from any man, but God. *nor through the agency of man.* I.e., it was not mediated through any man, but came directly from *Jesus Christ.*

1:3-5 In this greeting Paul neatly summarizes his whole preaching message.

1:6 *deserting Him who called you.* I.e., God the Father. They were deserting grace to retreat into law, and they bore the responsibility for their defection.

1:7 *the gospel of Christ.* The good news of God's grace in Christ, who gave Himself for our sins (v. 4). Those who taught any other way threatened the true gospel.

1:8 *accursed.* Lit., anathema, or devoted to destruction. Ecclesiastically, it was accompanied by excommunication.

1:10 *seeking the favor of men.* I.e., by toning down his message. Paul was being accused of preaching a cheap form of admission to God's kingdom. He counters by saying that he is a *bond-servant of Christ* (lit., slave). How can this cross-centered way be viewed as seeking to please men?

1:11-17 In these verses Paul defends his authority as an apostle. On the one hand, he shows that his teaching was not derived from any human agency; on the other, that it was acknowledged by the other apostles as truly from God.

1:15 Paul was set apart from birth for his work (as was Jeremiah, 1:5).

me apart, *even* from my mother's womb, and ªcalled me through His grace, was ᵇpleased

★16 ªActs
9:15; Gal.
2:9 ᵇActs
9:20 ᶜMatt.
16:17

16 to reveal His Son in me, that I might ªpreach Him among the Gentiles, ᵇI did not immediately consult with ᶜflesh and blood,

★17 ªActs
9:19-22
ᵇActs 9:2

17 ªnor did I go up to Jerusalem to those who were apostles before me; but I went away to Arabia, and returned once more to ᵇDamascus.

★1:18-2:21
★18 ªActs
9:22f. ᵇActs
9:26f. ᶜJohn
1:42; Gal.
2:9, 11, 14
19 ªMatt.
12:46; Acts
12:17

18 Then ªthree years later I went up ᵇto Jerusalem to become acquainted with ᶜCephas, and stayed with him fifteen days.

19 But I did not see any other of the apostles except ªJames, the Lord's brother.

20 ªRom.
9:1; 2 Cor.
1:23; 11:31

20 (Now in what I am writing to you, I assure you ªbefore God *that* I am not lying.)

21 ªActs
9:30 ᵇActs
15:23, 41
ᶜActs 6:9
22 ª1 Cor.
7:17;
1 Thess. 2:14
ᵇRom. 16:7
23 ªActs 6:7;
Gal. 6:10
ᵇActs 9:21

21 Then ªI went into the regions of ᵇSyria and ᶜCilicia.

22 And I was *still* unknown by sight to ªthe churches of Judea which were ᵇin Christ;

23 but only, they kept hearing, "He who once persecuted us is now preaching ªthe faith which he once ᵇtried to destroy."

24 ªMatt. 9:8

24 And they ªwere glorifying God because of me.

B His Authority Approved by the Church in Jerusalem, 2:1-10

2 Then after an interval of fourteen years I ªwent up again to Jerusalem with ᵇBarnabas, taking ᶜTitus along also.

2 And it was because of a ªrevelation that I went up; and I submitted to them the ᵇgospel which I preach among the Gentiles, but I did so in private to those who were of reputation, for fear that I might be ᶜrunning, or had run, in vain.

3 But not even ªTitus who was with me, though he was a Greek, was ᵇcompelled to be circumcised.

4 But *it was* because of the ªfalse brethren who ᵇhad sneaked in to spy out our ᶜliberty which we have in Christ Jesus, in order to ᵈbring us into bondage.

5 But we did not yield in subjection to them for even an hour, so that ªthe truth of the gospel might remain with you.

6 But from those who were of high ªreputation (what they were makes no difference to me; ᵇGod shows no partiality)—well, those who were of reputation contributed nothing to me.

7 But on the contrary, seeing

★ 1-10
1 ªActs
15:2 ᵇActs
4:36; Gal.
2:9, 13
ᶜ2 Cor. 2:13;
Gal. 2:3
2 ªActs
15:2; Gal.
1:12 ᵇGal.
1:6 ᶜRom.
9:16; 1 Cor.
9:24ff.; Gal.
5:7; Phil.
2:16; 2 Tim.
4:7; Heb.
12:1
★ 3 ª2 Cor.
2:13; Gal.
2:1 ᵇActs
16:3; 1 Cor.
9:21
4 ªActs
15:1, 24;
2 Cor. 11:13,
26; Gal. 1:7
ᵇ2 Pet. 2:1;
Jude 4 ᶜGal.
5:1, 13;
James 1:25
ᵈRom. 8:15;
2 Cor. 11:20
★ 5 ªGal.
1:6, 2:14;
Col. 1:5
6 ª2 Cor.
11:5; 12:11;
Gal. 2:9, 6:3
ᵇActs 10:34
★ 7 ª1 Cor.
9:17;
1 Thess. 2:4;
1 Tim. 1:11
ᵇActs 9:15;
Gal. 1:16
ᶜGal. 1:18;
2:9, 11, 14

1:16 *with flesh and blood.* I.e., with other people.

1:17 *Arabia.* This may mean anywhere in the kingdom of the Nabataeans, from near Damascus down to the Sinaitic peninsula. Paul's point is not to pinpoint the location but to emphasize that it was a place, in contrast to Jerusalem, where there was no apostle to instruct him. In Arabia he was alone with God, thinking through the implications of his encounter with the risen Christ on the Damascus road. Though not mentioned in Acts, this period in Paul's life would probably fit between Acts 9:21 and 9:22.

1:18-2:21 Paul's account of his relations with the Jerusalem apostles. Though independent of men, Paul makes it clear that he is within the stream of apostolic tradition represented by James, Peter, and John.

1:18 *become acquainted.* The purpose of Paul's visit to Cephas (Peter) was to become acquainted with him rather than to confer with him. He also saw James, the Lord's half brother (v. 19), but did not visit the Judean churches (v. 22).

2:1-10 Paul's account of the events recorded in Acts 11 (if the letter was written to the churches in South Galatia) or Acts 15 (if written to North Galatia).

2:3 *Titus.* A test case: if he were compelled to be circumcised, then other Gentile believers could be too; if not, then freedom from the law was confirmed.

2:5 *the truth of the gospel.* I.e., grace is everything, and for everyone; to compromise these truths was unthinkable.

2:7 *the gospel to the uncircumcised.* I.e., the gospel to the Gentiles. Paul was especially responsible for spreading the gospel to Gentiles (Rom. 1:5) and Peter *to the circumcised,* the Jews.

that I had been ^aentrusted with the ^bgospel to the uncircumcised, just as ^cPeter *had been* to the circumcised

8 (for He who effectually worked for Peter in *his* ^aapostleship to the circumcised effectually worked for me also to the Gentiles),

9 and recognizing ^athe grace that had been given to me, ^bJames and ^cCephas and John, who were ^dreputed to be ^epillars, gave to me and ^fBarnabas the ^gright hand of fellowship, that we might ^hgo to the Gentiles, and they to the circumcised.

10 *They* only *asked* us to remember the poor—^athe very thing I also was eager to do.

C His Authority Acknowledged in the Rebuke of Peter, 2:11–21

11 But when ^aCephas came to ^bAntioch, I opposed him to his face, because he stood condemned.

12 For prior to the coming of certain men from ^aJames, he used to ^beat with the Gentiles; but when they came, he *began* to withdraw and hold himself aloof, ^cfearing the party of the circumcision.

13 And the rest of the Jews joined him in hypocrisy, with the result that even ^aBarnabas was carried away by their hypocrisy.

14 But when I saw that they ^awere not straightforward about ^bthe truth of the gospel, I said to ^cCephas in the presence of all, "If you, being a Jew, ^dlive like the Gentiles and not like the Jews, how *is it that* you compel the Gentiles to live like Jews?

15 "We *are* ^aJews by nature, and not ^bsinners from among the Gentiles;

16 nevertheless knowing that ^aa man is not justified by the works of the Law but through faith in Christ Jesus, even we have believed in Christ Jesus, that we may be justified by ^bfaith in Christ, and not by the works of the Law; since ^cby the works of the Law shall no flesh be justified.

17 "But if, while seeking to be justified in Christ, we ourselves have also been found ^asinners, is Christ then a minister of sin? ^bMay it never be!

18 "For if I rebuild what I have once destroyed, I ^aprove myself to be a transgressor.

19 "For through the Law I ^adied to the Law, that I might live to God.

20 "I have been ^acrucified with Christ; and it is no longer I who live, but ^bChrist lives in me; and the *life* which I now live in the flesh I live by faith in ^cthe Son of God, who ^dloved me, and ^edelivered Himself up for me.

21 "I do not nullify the grace of God; for ^aif righteousness *comes* through the Law, then Christ died needlessly."

8 ^aActs 1:25
9 ^aRom. 12:3 ^bActs 12:17; Gal. 2:12 ^cLuke 22:8; Gal. 1:18; 2:7, 11, 14 ^d2 Cor. 11:5; 12:11; Gal. 2:2, 6; 6:3 ^e1 Tim. 3:15; Rev. 3:12 ^fActs 4:36; Gal. 2:1, 13 ^g2 Kin. 10:15; Ezra 10:19 ^hGal. 1:16
★10 ^aActs 24:17

★11-13
11 ^aGal. 1:18; 2:6, 9, 14 ^bActs 11:19; 15:1

12 ^aActs 12:17; Gal. 2:9 ^bActs 11:3 ^cActs 11:2

13 ^aActs 4:36; Gal. 2:1, 9

14 ^aHeb. 12:13 ^bGal. 1:6; 2:5; Col. 1:5 ^cGal. 1:18; 2:7, 9, 11 ^dActs 10:28; Gal. 2:12

15 ^aPhil. 3:4f. ^b1 Sam. 15:18; Luke 24:7; 1 Cor. 6:1
★16 ^aActs 13:39; Gal. 3:11 ^bRom. 9:30 ^cPs. 143:2; Rom. 3:20

17 ^aGal. 2:15 ^bLuke 20:16; Gal. 3:21

18 ^aRom. 3:5 [Gr.]

★19 ^aRom. 6:2; 7:4; 1 Cor. 9:20

★20 ^aRom. 6:6; Gal. 5:24; 6:14 ^bRom. 8:10 ^cMatt. 4:3 ^dRom. 8:37 ^eGal. 1:4

★21 ^aGal. 3:21

2:10 *the poor.* The saints in Jerusalem were notoriously poor (Rom. 15:26; see also 1 Cor. 16:1-4).

2:11-13 *Cephas* (Peter) was not preaching heresy but neither was he consistently practicing the gospel of grace. He withdrew from eating with uncircumcised Gentile believers when pressured to do so by some of the Hebrew Christians.

2:16 *justified.* I.e., to be declared righteous in God's sight and to be vindicated of any charge of sin in connection with failure to keep God's law.

2:19 *died to the Law,* because Christ paid the penalty for sin that the Law demanded. Paul could cease giving further thought to legal obedience as a means of winning God's acceptance.

2:20 *I have been crucified with Christ.* Crucifixion with Christ means death to or separation from the reigning power of the old sinful life and freedom to experience the power of the resurrection life of Christ by faith (see Rom. 6:6). *it is no longer I who live, but Christ . . .* Christ had taken up His abode in Paul, yet He did so without submerging Paul's own personality.

2:21 *nullify* = set aside. It was the Galatians, not Paul, who nullified the grace of God by wanting to retain law. If God wanted obedience through law, why would He send His Son to suffer and die on a cross?

III JUSTIFICATION BY FAITH EXPLAINED: PAUL'S GOSPEL, 3:1-4:31

A The Argument from Experience, 3:1-5

1 *a*Gal. 1:2
*b*1 Cor. 1:23;
  Gal. 5:11

3 You foolish *a*Galatians, who has bewitched you, before whose eyes Jesus Christ *b*was publicly portrayed *as* crucified?

2 *a*Rom.
10:17

2 This is the only thing I want to find out from you: did you receive the Spirit by the works of the Law, or by *a*hearing with faith?

★ 3

3 Are you so foolish? Having begun by the Spirit, are you now being perfected by the flesh?

4 *a*1 Cor.
15:2

4 Did you suffer so many things in vain—*a*if indeed it was in vain?

5 *a*2 Cor.
9:10; Phil.
1:19 *b*1 Cor.
12:10 *c*Rom.
10:17

5 Does He then, who *a*provides you with the Spirit and *b*works miracles among you, do it by the works of the Law, or by *c*hearing with faith?

B The Argument from Abraham, 3:6-9

★ 6 *a*Rom.
4:3 *b*Gen.
15:6

6 Even so *a*Abraham *b*BELIEVED GOD, AND IT WAS RECKONED TO HIM AS RIGHTEOUSNESS.

★ 7 *a*Gal.
3:9 *b*Luke
19:9; Gal.
  6:16

7 Therefore, be sure that *a*it is those who are of faith who are *b*sons of Abraham.

8 *a*Gen.
12:3

8 And the Scripture, foreseeing that God would justify the Gentiles by faith, preached the gospel beforehand to Abraham, *saying,* "*a*ALL THE NATIONS SHALL BE BLESSED IN YOU."

9 So then *a*those who are of faith are blessed with Abraham, the believer.

9 *a*Gal. 3:7

C The Argument from the Law, 3:10-4:11

10 For as many as are of the works of the Law are under a curse; for it is written, "*a*CURSED IS EVERYONE WHO DOES NOT ABIDE BY ALL THINGS WRITTEN IN THE BOOK OF THE LAW, TO PERFORM THEM."

★10 *a*Deut.
27:26

11 Now that *a*no one is justified by the Law before God is evident; for, "*b*THE RIGHTEOUS MAN SHALL LIVE BY FAITH."

★11 *a*Gal.
2:16 *b*Hab.
2:4; Rom.
1:17; Heb.
10:38

12 However, the Law is not of faith; on the contrary, "*a*HE WHO PRACTICES THEM SHALL LIVE BY THEM."

12 *a*Lev.
18:5; Rom.
10:5

13 Christ *a*redeemed us from the curse of the Law, having become a curse for us—for it is written, "*b*CURSED IS EVERYONE WHO HANGS ON *c*A TREE"—

★13 *a*Gal.
4:5 *b*Deut.
21:23 *c*Acts
5:30

14 in order that *a*in Christ Jesus the blessing of Abraham might come to the Gentiles, so that we *b*might receive *c*the promise of the Spirit through faith.

14 *a*Rom.
4:9, 16; Gal.
3:28 *b*Gal.
3:2 *c*Acts
2:33; Eph.
1:13

15 *a*Brethren, *b*I speak in terms of human relations: *c*even though it is *only* a man's covenant, yet when it has been ratified, no one sets it aside or adds conditions to it.

15 *a*Acts
1:15; Rom.
1:13; Gal.
6:18 *b*Rom.
3:5 *c*Heb.
6:16

16 Now the promises were

★16 *a*Luke
1:55; Rom.
4:13, 16; 9:4
*b*Acts 3:25

3:3 Paul brought the gospel to them and the *Spirit* worked in them. Yet now they were reverting to flesh-works in the hope that a combination of faith (Spirit) and works (flesh) would work more easily or better.

3:6 Paul now appealed to Scripture (Gen. 15:6) to show that the patriarch Abraham depended on faith for *righteousness.*

3:7 *sons of Abraham.* Abraham's physical descendants through Isaac and Jacob are the Jewish people, but his spiritual descendants those who believe in God for salvation, men of faith, as contrasted with men of works or men of circumcision.

3:10 Having shattered the Jews' confidence in their physical relation to Abraham, Paul now shows that the law brings a curse. Paul quotes Deut. 27:26 (from the Greek O.T.) and argues

that man cannot possibly keep all the laws, hence his bondage (cf. Jas. 2:10).

3:11 *The righteous man shall live by faith.* Paul's use of this quotation from Hab. 2:4 is to stress that one can become justified in God's sight only by faith; i.e., he who is righteous by faith (rather than works) shall live. See note on Heb. 10:38.

3:13 The law brings a curse. The believer is delivered from that curse through Christ, who became a *curse for us.* The crucifixion brought Him under the curse of the law, as explained in the last half of the verse (quoted from Deut. 21:23).

3:16 *seed.* Since Paul's argument here is based on the singular form of the word in the O.T. (Gen. 22:17, 18), he must have believed in the accuracy of the very words of Scripture.

spoken [a]to Abraham and to his seed. He does not say, "And to seeds," as referring to many, but rather to one, "[b]And to your seed," that is, Christ.

17 What I am saying is this: the Law, which came [a]four hundred and thirty years later, does not invalidate a covenant previously ratified by God, so as to nullify the promise.

18 For [a]if the inheritance is based on law, it is no longer based on a promise; but [b]God has granted it to Abraham by means of a promise.

19 [a]Why the Law then? It was added because of transgressions, having been [b]ordained through angels [c]by the agency of a mediator, until [d]the seed should come to whom the promise had been made.

20 Now [a]a mediator is not for one party only; whereas God is only one.

21 Is the Law then contrary to the promises of God? [a]May it never be! For [b]if a law had been given which was able to impart life, then righteousness would indeed have been based on law.

22 But the Scripture has [a]shut up all [b]men under sin, that the promise by faith in Jesus Christ might be given to those who believe.

23 But before faith came, we were kept in custody under the law, [a]being shut up to the faith which was later to be revealed.

24 Therefore the Law has become our [a]tutor to lead us to Christ, that [b]we may be justified by faith.

25 But now that faith has come, we are no longer under a [a]tutor.

26 For you are all [a]sons of God through faith in [b]Christ Jesus.

27 For all of you who were [a]baptized into Christ have [b]clothed yourselves with Christ.

28 [a]There is neither Jew nor Greek, there is neither slave nor free man, there is neither male nor female; for [b]you are all one in [c]Christ Jesus.

29 And if [a]you belong to Christ, then you are Abraham's offspring, heirs according to [b]promise.

4 Now I say, as long as the heir is a child, he does not differ at all from a slave although he is owner of everything,

2 but he is under guardians and managers until the date set by the father.

3 So also we, while we were children, were held [a]in bondage under the [b]elemental things of the world.

4 But when [a]the fulness of the time came, God sent forth His Son, [b]born of a woman, born [c]under the Law,

5 in order that He might redeem those who were under the Law, that we might receive the adoption as [a]sons.

6 And because you are sons, [a]God has sent forth the Spirit of His Son into our hearts, crying, "[b]Abba! Father!"

Marginal references:

★17 [a]Gen. 15:13f.; Ex. 12:40; Acts 7:6

18 [a]Rom. 4:14 [b]Heb. 6:14

★19-20

19 [a]Rom. 5:20 [b]Acts 7:53 [c]Ex. 20:19; Deut. 5:5 [d]Gal. 3:16

20 [a]1 Tim. 2:5; Heb. 8:6; 9:15; 12:24

21 [a]Luke 20:16; Gal. 2:17 [b]Gal. 2:21

22 [a]Rom. 11:32 [b]1 Cor. 1:27

23 [a]Rom. 11:32

★24 [a]1 Cor. 4:15 [b]Gal. 2:16

25 [a]1 Cor. 4:15

26 [a]Rom. 8:14; Gal. 4:5 [b]Rom. 8:1; Gal. 3:28; 4:14; 5:6, 24; Eph. 1:1; Phil. 1:1; Col. 1:4; 1 Tim. 1:12; 2 Tim. 1:1; Titus 1:4

★27 [a]Matt. 28:19; Rom. 6:3; 1 Cor. 10:2 [b]Rom. 13:14

28 [a]Rom. 3:22; 1 Cor. 12:13; Col. 3:11 [b]John 17:11; Eph. 2:15 [c]Rom. 8:1; Gal. 3:26; 4:14; 5:6, 24; Eph. 1:1; Phil. 1:1; Col. 1:4; 1 Tim. 1:12; 2 Tim. 1:1; Titus 1:4

29 [a]1 Cor. 3:23 [b]Rom. 9:8; Gal. 3:18; 4:28

★ 3 [a]Gal. 2:4; 4:8f., 24f. [b]Gal. 4:9; Col. 2:8, 20; Heb. 5:12

★ 4 [a]Mark 1:15 [b]John 1:14; Rom. 1:3; 8:3; Phil. 2:7 [c]Luke 2:21f., 27

★ 5 [a]Rom. 8:14; Gal. 3:26

★ 6 [a]Acts 16:7; Rom. 5:5; 8:9, 16; 2 Cor. 3:17 [b]Mark 14:36; Rom. 8:15

3:17 The Mosaic law did not set aside the promises made to Abraham. And, during those hundreds of years before the law, God had also justified men only by faith.

3:19-20 The law was mediated through angels and Moses, whereas the covenant with Abraham was given directly by God (Gen. 15:18). The presence of a *mediator* assumes two parties, and the need of a mediator shows the inferiority of the law.

3:24 *tutor.* The Greek word here means not a "teacher" but an attendant, a custodian, usually a slave whose job it was to insure the safe arrival of the child at school. Christ is the true teacher.

3:27 *baptized into Christ.* Not water baptism but Spirit baptism, which brings believers into a living union with Christ (cf. 1 Cor. 12:13). *have clothed yourselves with Christ.* A responsible act of appropriating all that Jesus Christ is.

4:3 *the elemental things of the world.* I.e., the bondage of a legalistic practice of Judaism (also v. 9).

4:4 *born under the Law.* Christ was reared in conformity to the Mosaic law.

4:5 *the adoption as sons.* See note on Rom. 8:15.

4:6 The Holy *Spirit* in the heart of the believer shows his acceptance with God as a son and heir (v. 7). *Abba* is the Aramaic word for father.

7 aRom.
8:17

★ 8-11
8 a1 Cor.
1:21; Eph.
2:12;
1 Thess. 4:5;
2 Thess. 1:8
bGal. 4:3
c2 Chr. 13:9;
Is. 37:19;
Jer. 2:11;
1 Cor. 8:4f.;
10:20
9 a1 Cor.
8:3 bCol.
2:20 cGal.
4:3

10 aRom.
14:5; Col.
2:16

7 Therefore you are no longer a slave, but a son; and *a* if a son, then an heir through God.

8 However at that time, *a* when you did not know God, you were *b* slaves to *c* those which by nature are no gods.

9 But now that you have come to know God, or rather to be *a* known by God, *b* how is it that you turn back again to the weak and worthless *c* elemental things, to which you desire to be enslaved all over again?

10 You *a* observe days and months and seasons and years.

11 I fear for you, that perhaps I have labored over you in vain.

D The Argument from Personal Testimony, 4:12-20

★12-15
12 aGal.
6:18 b2 Cor.
6:11, 13

12 I beg of you, *a* brethren, *b* become as I *am,* for I also *have become* as you *are.* You have done me no wrong;

13 but you know that it was because of a bodily illness that I preached the gospel to you the first time;

14 aMatt.
10:40;
1 Thess. 2:13
bGal. 3:26

14 and that which was a trial to you in my bodily condition you did not despise or loathe, but *a* you received me as an angel of God, as *b* Christ Jesus *Himself.*

15 Where then is that sense of blessing you had? For I bear you witness, that if possible, you would have plucked out your eyes and given them to me.

16 aAmos
5:10

16 Have I therefore become your enemy *a* by telling you the truth?

★17

17 They eagerly seek you, not commendably, but they wish to shut you out, in order that you may seek them.

18 But it is good always to be eagerly sought in a commendable manner, and *a* not only when I am present with you.

19 *a* My children, with whom *b* I am again in labor until *c* Christ is formed in you—

20 but I could wish to be present with you now and to change my tone, for *a* I am perplexed about you.

★18 aGal.
4:13f.

19 a1 John
2:1 b1 Cor.
4:15 cEph.
4:13
20 a2 Cor.
4:8

E The Argument from an Allegory, 4:21-31

21 aLuke
16:29

21 Tell me, you who want to be under law, do you not *a* listen to the law?

22 For it is written that Abraham had two sons, one by the bondwoman and one by the free woman.

23 But *a* the son by the bondwoman was born according to the flesh, and *b* the son by the free woman through the promise.

24 *a* This is allegorically speaking: for these *women* are two covenants, one *proceeding* from *b* Mount Sinai bearing children who are to be *c* slaves; she is Hagar.

25 Now this Hagar is Mount Sinai in Arabia, and corresponds to the present Jerusalem, for she is in slavery with her children.

26 But *a* the Jerusalem above is free; she is our mother.

27 For it is written,

23 aRom.
9:7; Gal.
4:29 bGen.
17:16ff.;
18:10ff.;
21:1; Gal.
4:28; Heb.
11:11
★24 a1 Cor.
10:11 bDeut.
33:2 cGal.
4:3

26 aHeb.
12:22; Rev.
3:12; 21:2,
10

27 aIs. 54:1

"*a* REJOICE, BARREN WOMAN WHO DOES NOT BEAR;

4:8-11 Paul tells the Galatians they are not acting like heirs of God!

4:12-15 Paul is saying that he has had a good relationship with the Galatians: you have in the past been ready to "pluck out your eyes for me" (a common expression of the time for giving up everything for another), not an indication of eye trouble. Though he was ill on his former visit, they had not scorned him but had treated him as Christ had treated them. Now he wanted them to hold firm to the truth he had taught them.

4:17 The Judaizers were apparently using flattery and threats on the Galatians.

4:18 *not only when I am present with you.* I.e., Paul was not averse to having others minister to them, as long as it was done sincerely in the truth.

4:24 The allegory Paul offers here—of Ishmael and Isaac (Gen. 16:15; 21:3, 9)—expresses truth in addition to the simple facts of the case, in this instance that the Judaizers (related to Hagar, Sinai, and the law) did not have the authority or blessing of God.

BREAK FORTH AND SHOUT, YOU
WHO ARE NOT IN LABOR;
FOR MORE ARE THE CHILDREN
OF THE DESOLATE
THAN OF THE ONE WHO HAS A
HUSBAND."

28 And you brethren, [a]like Isaac, are [b]children of promise.

29 But as at that time [a]he who was born according to the flesh [b]persecuted him *who was born* according to the Spirit, [c]so it is now also.

30 But what does the Scripture say?

"[a]CAST OUT THE BONDWOMAN
AND HER SON,
FOR [b]THE SON OF THE BOND-
WOMAN SHALL NOT BE AN
HEIR WITH THE SON OF THE
FREE WOMAN."

31 So then, brethren, we are not children of a bondwoman, but of the free woman.

IV JUSTIFICATION BY FAITH APPLIED: PAUL'S ETHICS, 5:1-6:10

A In Relation to Christian Liberty, 5:1-12

5 [a]It was for freedom that Christ set us free; therefore [b]keep standing firm and do not be subject again to a [c]yoke of slavery.

2 Behold I, [a]Paul, say to you that if you receive [b]circumcision, Christ will be of no benefit to you.

3 And I [a]testify again to every man who receives [b]circumcision, that he is under obligation to [c]keep the whole Law.

4 You have been severed from Christ, you who are seeking to be justified by law; you have [a]fallen from grace.

5 For we through the Spirit,

by faith, are [a]waiting for the hope of righteousness.

6 For in [a]Christ Jesus [b]neither circumcision nor uncircumcision means anything, but [c]faith working through love.

7 You were [a]running well; who hindered you from obeying the truth?

8 This persuasion *did* not *come* from [a]Him who calls you.

9 [a]A little leaven leavens the whole lump *of dough.*

10 [a]I have confidence in you in the Lord, that you [b]will adopt no other view; but the one who is [c]disturbing you shall bear his judgment, whoever he is.

11 But I, brethren, if I still preach circumcision, why am I still [a]persecuted? Then [b]the stumbling block of the cross has been abolished.

12 Would that [a]those who are troubling you would even [b]mutilate themselves.

B In Relation to License and Love, 5:13-15

13 For you were called to [a]freedom, brethren; [b]only *do* not turn your freedom into an opportunity for the flesh, but through love [c]serve one another.

14 For [a]the whole Law is fulfilled in one word, in the *statement,* "[b]YOU SHALL LOVE YOUR NEIGHBOR AS YOURSELF."

15 But if you [a]bite and devour one another, take care lest you be consumed by one another.

C In Relation to the Flesh and the Spirit, 5:16-26

16 But I say, [a]walk by the Spirit, and you will not carry out [b]the desire of the flesh.

Marginal references:

28 [a]Gal. 4:23 [b]Rom. 9:7ff.; Gal. 3:29
29 [a]Gal. 4:23 [b]Gen. 21:9 [c]Gal. 5:11
30 [a]Gen. 21:10, 12 [b]John 8:35

1 [a]John 8:32, 36; Rom. 8:15; 2 Cor. 3:17; Gal. 2:4; 5:13 [b]1 Cor. 16:13 [c]Acts 15:10; Gal. 2:4
★ 2 [a]2 Cor. 10:1 [b]Acts 15:1; Gal. 5:3, 6, 11
3 [a]Luke 16:28 [b]Acts 15:1; Gal. 5:2, 6, 11 [c]Rom. 2:25
★ 4 [a]Heb. 12:15; 2 Pet. 3:17
5 [a]Rom. 8:23; 1 Cor. 1:7

6 [a]Gal. 3:26 [b]1 Cor. 7:19; Gal. 6:15 [c]Col. 1:4f.; 1 Thess. 1:3; James 2:18, 20, 22
7 [a]Gal. 2:2
8 [a]Rom. 8:28; Gal. 1:6
9 [a]1 Cor. 5:6
10 [a]2 Cor. 2:3 [b]Gal. 5:7; Phil. 3:15 [c]Gal. 1:7; 5:12
★11 [a]Gal. 4:29; 6:12 [b]Rom. 9:33; 1 Cor. 1:23
12 [a]Gal. 2:4; 5:10 [b]Deut. 23:1

13 [a]Gal. 5:1 [b]1 Cor. 8:9; 1 Pet. 2:16 [c]1 Cor. 9:19; Eph. 5:21
★14 [a]Matt. 7:12; 22:40; Rom. 13:8, 10; Gal. 6:2 [b]Lev. 19:18; Matt. 19:19; John 13:34
15 [a]Gal. 5:20; Phil. 3:2

★16 [a]Rom. 8:4; 13:14; Gal. 5:24f. [b]Rom. 13:14; Eph. 2:3

5:2 Law (circumcision) and grace (Christ) simply do not mix, Paul says.
5:4 *fallen from grace.* To use the impossible ground of justification by law is to leave, abandon, fall from the way of grace as the only basis for justification.

5:11 *the stumbling block of the cross.* That a man can be saved only by faith is an offense to his pride.
5:14 Compare Rom. 13:8-10.
5:16 *by the Spirit,* which will give victory over the flesh and its works.

17 *a*Rom.
7:18, 23;
8:5ff. *b*Rom.
7:15ff.

17 For *a*the flesh sets its desire against the Spirit, and the Spirit against the flesh; for these are in opposition to one another, *b*so that you may not do the things that you please.

18 *a*Rom.
8:14 *b*Rom.
6:14; 7:4;
1 Tim. 1:9

18 But if you are *a*led by the Spirit, *b*you are not under the Law.

★19 *a*1 Cor.
6:9, 18;
2 Cor. 12:21

19 Now the deeds of the flesh are evident, which are: *a*immorality, impurity, sensuality,

★20 *a*Rev.
21:8 *b*2 Cor.
12:20 *c*Rom.
2:8; James
3:14ff.
*d*1 Cor.
11:19

20 idolatry, *a*sorcery, enmities, *b*strife, jealousy, outbursts of anger, *c*disputes, dissensions, *d*factions,

21 *a*Rom.
13:13
*b*1 Cor. 6:9

21 envying, *a*drunkenness, carousing, and things like these, of which I forewarn you just as I have forewarned you that those who practice such things shall not *b*inherit the kingdom of God.

★22 *a*Matt.
7:16ff.; Rom.
6:21; Eph.
5:9 *b*Rom.
5:1-5; 1 Cor.
13:4; Col.
3:12-15
23 *a*Acts
24:25 *b*Gal.
5:18

22 But *a*the fruit of the Spirit is *b*love, joy, peace, patience, kindness, goodness, faithfulness, **23** gentleness, *a*self-control; against such things *b*there is no law.

★24 *a*Gal.
3:26 *b*Rom.
6:6; Gal.
2:20; 6:14
*c*Gal. 5:16f.
25 *a*Gal.
5:16

24 Now those who belong to *a*Christ Jesus have *b*crucified the flesh with its passions and *c*desires. **25** If we live by the Spirit, let us also walk *a*by the Spirit.

26 *a*Phil. 2:3

26 Let us not become *a*boastful, challenging one another, envying one another.

D In Relation to a Sinning Brother, 6:1-5

★ 1 *a*Gal.
6:18;
1 Thess. 4:1
*b*1 Cor. 2:15
*c*2 Cor. 2:7;
2 Thess.
3:15; Heb.
12:13; James
5:19f.
*d*1 Cor. 4:21

6 *a*Brethren, even if a man is caught in any trespass, you who are *b*spiritual, *c*restore such a one *d*in a spirit of gentleness; *each one* looking to yourself, lest you too be tempted.

2 *a*Bear one another's burdens, and thus fulfill *b*the law of Christ.

3 For *a*if anyone thinks he is something when he is nothing, he deceives himself.

4 But let each one *a*examine his own work, and then he will have *reason for* *b*boasting in regard to himself alone, and not in regard to another.

5 For *a*each one shall bear his own load.

★ 2 *a*Rom.
15:1 *b*Rom.
8:2; 1 Cor.
9:21; James
1:25; 2:12;
2 Pet. 3:2
3 *a*Acts
5:36; 1 Cor.
3:18; 2 Cor.
12:11
4 *a*1 Cor.
11:28 *b*Phil.
1:26

5 *a*Prov.
9:12; Rom.
14:12; 1 Cor.
3:8

E In Relation to Giving, 6:6-10

6 And *a*let the one who is taught *b*the word share all good things with him who teaches.

7 *a*Do not be deceived, *b*God is not mocked; for *c*whatever a man sows, this he will also reap.

8 *a*For the one who sows to his own flesh shall from the flesh reap *b*corruption, but *c*the one who sows to the Spirit shall from the Spirit reap eternal life.

9 And *a*let us not lose heart in doing good, for in due time we shall reap if we *b*do not grow weary.

10 So then, *a*while we have opportunity, let us do good to all men, and especially to those who are of the *b*household of *c*the faith.

★ 6 *a*1 Cor.
9:11, 14
*b*2 Tim. 4:2

7 *a*1 Cor.
6:9 *b*Job
13:9 *c*2 Cor.
9:6

8 *a*Job 4:8;
Hos. 8:7;
Rom. 6:21
*b*1 Cor.
15:42 *c*Rom.
8:11; James
3:18

9 *a*1 Cor.
15:58; 2 Cor.
4:1 *b*Matt.
10:22; Heb.
12:3, 5;
James 5:7f.

★10 *a*Prov.
3:27; John
12:35 *b*Eph.
2:19; Heb.
3:6; 1 Pet.
2:5; 4:17
*c*Acts 6:7;
Gal. 1:23

5:19 *evident* = plain, or open, with overtones of being unashamed and blatant.
5:20 *sorcery.* The use of drugs and magical potions (see also Rev. 9:21; 18:23; 21:8; 22:15).
5:22 *faithfulness* in word and deed.
5:24 *crucified.* See note on 2:20.
6:1 *caught* = apprehended, taken by surprise, caught red-handed.
6:2 *burdens.* I.e., the excess burdens which we need to share with one another, in contrast to the *load* (different Greek word) in v. 5 which

means the normal amount each must carry for himself. *the law of Christ.* I.e., the commands of Christ, especially the new commandment to love one another (John 13:34). Living under grace is not license; it is a life of love and service (Gal. 5:6, 13).
6:6 *all good things.* I.e., material things.
6:10 *the household of the faith* = believers. Concern for this group is a special obligation of the children of God.

V CONCLUSION: THE SUBSTANCE OF PAUL'S INSTRUCTION, 6:11–18

★11 *a*1 Cor. 16:21

11 See with what large letters I am writing to you *a*with my own hand.

12 *a*Matt. 23:27; *b*Acts 15:1 *c*Gal. 5:11

12 Those who desire *a*to make a good showing in the flesh try to *b*compel you to be circumcised, simply that they *c*may not be persecuted for the cross of Christ.

13 *a*Rom. 2:25 *b*Phil. 3:3

13 For those who are circumcised do not even *a*keep the Law themselves, but they desire to have you circumcised, that they may *b*boast in your flesh.

14 But *a*may it never be that I should boast, *b*except in the cross of our Lord Jesus Christ, *c*through which the world has been crucified to me, and *d*I to the world.

15 For *a*neither is circumcision anything, nor uncircumcision, but a *b*new creation.

16 And those who will walk by this rule, peace and mercy *be* upon them, and upon the *a*Israel of God.

17 From now on let no one cause trouble for me, for I bear on my body the *a*brand-marks of Jesus.

18 *a*The grace of our Lord Jesus Christ be *b*with your spirit, *c*brethren. Amen.

14 *a*Luke 20:16 [in the Gr.]; Gal. 2:17; 3:21 *b*1 Cor. 2:2 *c*Gal. 2:20 *d*Rom. 6:2, 6; Gal. 2:19f.; 5:24
15 *a*Rom. 2:26, 28; 1 Cor. 7:19 *b*2 Cor. 5:17; Eph. 2:10, 15; 4:24
★16 *a*Rom. 9:6; Gal. 3:7, 29; Phil. 3:3
★17 *a*Is. 44:5; Ezek. 9:4; 2 Cor. 4:10; 11:23; Rev. 13:16
18 *a*Rom. 16:20 *b*2 Tim. 4:22 *c*Acts 1:15; Rom. 1:13

6:11 *with what large letters.* Paul took the pen from his scribe to write this closing section in large letters for emphasis (though some think this indicates that his illness was in his eyes, 4:15).

6:16 *the Israel of God.* I.e., Christian Jews, those who are both the physical and spiritual seed of Abraham.

6:17 *brand-marks.* I.e., scars suffered in persecution, which spoke more eloquently than the mark of circumcision, which the Judaizers sought to impose.

INTRODUCTION TO
THE LETTER OF PAUL TO THE EPHESIANS

AUTHOR: Paul   DATE: 61

The Prison Epistles *Ephesians, Philippians, Colossians, and Philemon are sometimes referred to as the Prison Epistles, since they were all written during Paul's Roman imprisonment (Eph. 3:1; Phil. 1:7; Col. 4:10; Philem. 9). Whether he was imprisoned once or twice in Rome is debated, though two imprisonments seem to fit the facts better. During the first, Paul was kept in or near the barracks of the Praetorian Guard or in rental quarters at his own expense for two years (Acts 28:30), during which these epistles were written. He anticipated being released (Philem. 22) and following his release he made several trips, wrote 1 Timothy and Titus, was rearrested, wrote 2 Timothy, and was martyred (see the Introduction to Titus). These, then, are the first Roman imprisonment letters, while 2 Timothy is the second Roman imprisonment letter.*

An Encyclical *Several things indicate that Ephesians was a circular letter, a doctrinal treatise in the form of a letter, to the churches in Asia Minor. Some good Greek manuscripts omit the words "at Ephesus" in 1:1. There is an absence of controversy in this epistle, and it does not deal with problems of particular churches. Since Paul had worked at Ephesus for about three years, and since he normally mentioned many friends in the churches to whom he wrote, the absence of personal names in this letter strongly supports the idea of its encyclical character. It was likely sent first to Ephesus by Tychicus (Eph. 6:21-22; Col. 4:7-8) and is probably the same letter that is called "my letter . . . from Laodicea" in Colossians 4:16.*

The City of Ephesus *Christianity probably came first to Ephesus with Aquila and Priscilla when Paul made a brief stop there on his second missionary journey (Acts 18:18-19). On his third journey he stayed in the city for about three years and the gospel spread throughout all of Asia Minor (Acts 19:10). The city was a commercial, political, and religious center, the great temple of Artemis (Diana) being there. As a major trading center, it ranked with Alexandria and Antioch. After Paul, Timothy had charge of the church in Ephesus for a time (1 Tim. 1:3) and later the apostle John made the city his headquarters.*

Contents *The great theme of this letter is God's eternal purpose to establish and complete His body, the church of Christ. In developing this theme, Paul discusses predestination (1:3-14), Christ's headship over the body (1:22-23; 4:15-16), the church as the building and temple of God (2:21-22), the mystery of Christ (3:1-21), spiritual gifts (4:7-16), and the Church as the bride of Christ.*

OUTLINE OF EPHESIANS

THE LETTER OF PAUL TO THE EPHESIANS

I GREETINGS, 1:1–2

1 ᵃan apostle of ᵇChrist Jesus ᶜby the will of God, to the ᵈsaints who are at ᵉEphesus, and ᶠwho are faithful in ᵇChrist Jesus:

2 ᵃGrace to you and peace from God our Father and the Lord Jesus Christ.

II THE POSITION OF BELIEVERS, 1:3–3:21

A Chosen and Sealed, 1:3–23

3 ᵃBlessed be the God and Father of our Lord Jesus Christ, who has blessed us with every spiritual blessing in ᵇthe heavenly places in Christ,

4 just as ᵃHe chose us in Him before ᵇthe foundation of the world, that we should be ᶜholy and blameless before Him. ᵈIn love

5 He ᵃpredestined us to ᵇadoption as sons through Jesus Christ to Himself, ᶜaccording to the kind intention of His will,

6 ᵃto the praise of the glory of His grace, which He freely bestowed on us in ᵇthe Beloved.

7 ᵃIn Him we have ᵇredemption ᶜthrough His blood, the ᵈforgiveness of our trespasses, according to ᵉthe riches of His grace,

8 which He lavished upon us. In all wisdom and insight

9 He ᵃmade known to us the mystery of His will, ᵇaccording to His kind intention which He ᶜpurposed in Him

10 with a view to an administration suitable to ᵃthe fulness of the times, that is, ᵇthe summing up of all things in Christ, things in the heavens and things upon the earth. In Him

11 also we ᵃhave obtained an inheritance, having been ᵇpredestined ᶜaccording to His purpose who works all things ᵈafter the counsel of His will,

12 to the end that we who were the first to hope in Christ should be ᵃto the praise of His glory.

13 In Him, you also, after listening to ᵃthe message of truth, the gospel of your salvation— having also believed, you were ᵇsealed in Him with ᶜthe Holy Spirit of promise,

14 who is ᵃgiven as a pledge of ᵇour inheritance, with a view to

Cross references (margin)

1 ᵃ2 Cor. 1:1 ᵇRom. 8:1; Gal. 3:26; Eph. 2:6, 7, 10, 13, 20; 3:1, 6, 11, 21; Col. 1:4; 2:6; 4:12 ᶜ1 Cor. 1:1 ᵈActs 9:13; Phil. 1:1; Col. 1:1 ᵉActs 18:19 ᶠCol. 1:2
2 ᵃRom. 1:7
★ 3 ᵃ2 Cor. 1:3 ᵇEph. 1:20; 2:6; 3:10; 6:12; Phil. 3:20 4 ᵃEph. 2:10; 2 Thess. 2:13f. ᵇMatt. 25:34 ᶜEph. 5:27; Col. 1:22; 2 Tim. 1:9 ᵈEph. 4:2, 15, 16; 5:2
★ 5 ᵃActs 13:48; Rom. 8:29f.; Eph. 1:11 ᵇRom. 8:14ff.; Gal. 4:5 ᶜLuke 12:32; 1 Cor. 1:21; Gal. 1:15; Phil. 2:13; Col. 1:19
★ 6 ᵃEph. 1:12, 14 ᵇMatt. 3:17
★ 7 ᵃCol. 1:14 ᵇRom. 3:24; 1 Cor. 1:30; Eph. 1:14 ᶜActs 20:28; Rom. 3:25 ᵈActs 2:38 ᵉRom. 2:4; Eph. 1:18; 2:7; 3:8, 16
★ 9 ᵃRom. 11:25; 16:25; Eph. 3:3 ᵇLuke 12:32; 1 Cor. 1:21; Gal. 1:15; Phil. 2:13; Col. 1:19 ᶜRom. 8:28; Eph. 1:11
★10 ᵃMark 1:15 ᵇEph. 3:15; Phil. 2:9f.
★11 ᵃDeut. 4:20; 9:26, 29; 32:9; Eph. 1:14, 18; Titus 2:14 ᵇEph. 1:5 ᶜRom. 8:28f.; Eph. 3:11 ᵈRom. 9:11; Heb. 6:17
12 ᵃEph. 1:6, 14
★13 ᵃActs 13:26; Eph. 4:21; Col. 1:5 ᵇJohn 3:33; Eph. 4:30 ᶜActs 1:4f.; 2:33
★14 ᵃ2 Cor. 1:22 ᵇActs 20:32 ᶜEph. 1:7 ᵈEph. 1:11 ᵉEph. 1:6, 12

1:3 *in the heavenly places.* Lit., in the heavenlies, i.e., in the realm of heavenly possessions and experiences into which the Christian is brought because of his association with the risen Christ. The term also occurs in 1:20; 2:6; 3:10; 6:12; cf. John 3:12.

1:5 *predestined.* God has determined beforehand that those who believe in Christ will be adopted into His family and conformed to His Son (cf. Rom. 8:29). It involves a choice on His part (Eph. 1:4); it is done in love (v. 4); it is based on the good pleasure of His perfect will (vv. 5, 9, 11); its purpose is to glorify God (v. 14); but it does not relieve man of his responsibility to believe the gospel in order to bring to pass personally God's predestination (v. 13). *adoption as sons.* See note on Rom. 8:15.

1:6 *in the Beloved.* I.e., in Christ.

1:7 *redemption.* Three ideas are involved in the doctrine of redemption: (1) paying the ransom with the blood of Christ (1 Cor. 6:20; Rev. 5:9); (2) removal from the curse of the law (Gal. 3:13; 4:5); and (3) release from the bondage of

sin into the freedom of grace (1 Pet. 1:18). Redemption is always *through His blood;* i.e., through the death of Christ (Col. 1:14).

1:9 *mystery.* See note on 3:3.

1:10 *an administration suitable to the fulness of the times.* I.e., the plan, the arrangement, of the millennial kingdom. *The summing up of all things in Christ.* I.e., that God might head up everything in Christ and bring everything into harmony (Col. 1:16).

1:11 *we have obtained an inheritance.* May be translated "we were made His inheritance." Both ideas are true: we are Christ's inheritance as He is ours.

1:13 *having also believed.* The time of sealing coincides with the time of believing. *sealed . . . with the Holy Spirit.* A seal indicates possession and security. The presence of the Holy Spirit, the seal, is the believer's guarantee of the security of his salvation.

1:14 *pledge* = deposit, down payment. The presence of the Spirit is God's pledge that our salvation will be consummated.

the ᶜredemption of ᵈGod's own possession, ᵉto the praise of His glory.

15 For this reason I too, ᵃhaving heard of the faith in the Lord Jesus which *exists* among you, and your love for ᵇall the saints,

16 ᵃdo not cease giving thanks for you, ᵇwhile making mention *of you* in my prayers;

17 that the ᵃGod of our Lord Jesus Christ, ᵇthe Father of glory, may give to you a spirit of ᶜwisdom and of ᵈrevelation in the knowledge of Him.

18 *I pray that* ᵃthe eyes of your heart may be enlightened, so that you may know what is the ᵇhope of His ᶜcalling, what are ᵈthe riches of the glory of ᵉHis inheritance in ᶠthe saints,

19 and what is the surpassing greatness of His power toward us who believe. ᵃ*These are* in accordance with the working of the ᵇstrength of His might

20 which He brought about in Christ, when He ᵃraised Him from the dead, and ᵇseated Him at His right hand in ᶜthe heavenly *places,*

21 far above ᵃall rule and authority and power and dominion, and every ᵇname that is named, not only in ᶜthis age, but also in the one to come.

22 And He ᵃput all things in subjection under His feet, and gave Him as ᵇhead over all things to the church,

23 which is His ᵃbody, the ᵇfulness of Him who ᶜfills ᵈall in all.

B Saved by Grace, 2:1-10

2 And you were ᵃdead in your trespasses and sins,

2 in which you ᵃformerly walked according to the course of ᵇthis world, according to ᶜthe prince of the power of the air, of the spirit that is now working in ᵈthe sons of disobedience.

3 Among them we too all ᵃformerly lived in ᵇthe lusts of our flesh, indulging the desires of the flesh and of the mind, and were ᶜby nature ᵈchildren of wrath, ᵉeven as the rest.

4 But God, being ᵃrich in mercy, because of ᵇHis great love with which He loved us,

5 even when we were ᵃdead in our transgressions, made us alive together with Christ (ᵇby grace you have been saved),

6 and ᵃraised us up with Him, and ᵇseated us with Him in ᶜthe heavenly *places,* in ᵈChrist Jesus,

7 in order that in the ages to come He might show the surpassing ᵃriches of His grace in ᵇkindness toward us in Christ Jesus.

8 For ᵃby grace you have

Cross references

15 ᵃRom. 1:8; Col. 1:4; Philem. 5
ᵇEph. 1:1; 3:18

16 ᵃRom. 1:8⨾ Col. 1:9
ᵇRom. 1:9

17 ᵃJohn 20:17; Rom. 15:6 ᵇActs 7:2; 1 Cor. 2:8 ᶜCol. 1:9 ᵈ1 Cor. 14:6
★**18** ᵃActs 26:18; 2 Cor. 4:6; Heb. 6:4 ᵇEph. 4:4 ᶜRom. 11:29 ᵈEph. 1:7 ᵉEph. 1:11 ᶠActs 9:13; Col. 1:12
19 ᵃEph. 3:7; Phil. 3:21; Col. 1:29 ᵇEph. 6:10
★**20** ᵃActs 2:24 ᵇMark 16:19 ᶜEph. 1:3
★**21** ᵃMatt. 28:18; Rom. 8:38; Eph. 3:10; Col. 1:16 ᵇJohn 17:11; Phil. 2:9; Heb. 1:4; Rev. 19:12 ᶜMatt. 12:32; Eph. 2:2
★**22-23**
22 ᵃ1 Cor. 15:27 [Ps. 8:6] ᵇ1 Cor. 11:3; Eph. 4:15; 5:23; Col. 1:18; 2:19

23 ᵃ1 Cor. 12:27; Eph. 4:12; 5:30; Col. 1:18, 24; 2:19 ᵇJohn 1:16; Eph. 3:19 ᶜEph. 4:10 ᵈCol. 3:11
★**1** ᵃLuke 15:24, 32; Eph. 2:5; Col. 2:13
★**2** ᵃRom. 13:13; 1 Cor. 6:11; Eph. 2:3, 11, 13; 5:8; Col. 3:7; 1 Pet. 4:3 ᵇEph. 1:21 ᶜJohn 12:31; Eph. 6:12 ᵈEph. 5:6
★**3** ᵃEph. 2:2 ᵇGal. 5:16f. ᶜRom. 2:14; Gal. 2:15 ᵈRom. 5:10; Col. 1:21; 2 Pet. 2:14 ᵉRom. 5:12, 19; 1 Thess. 4:13; 5:6
4 ᵃEph. 1:7 ᵇJohn 3:16
★**5** ᵃEph. 2:1 ᵇActs 15:11; Eph. 2:8
6 ᵃCol. 2:12 ᵇEph. 1:20 ᶜEph. 1:3 ᵈEph. 1:1; 2:10, 13
★**7** ᵃRom. 2:4; Eph. 1:7 ᵇTitus 3:4
★**8** ᵃActs 15:11; Eph. 1:5 ᶜJohn 4:10; Heb. 6:4

1:18 *of your heart.* "Heart" in scripture is considered the very center and core of life.

1:20 *at His right hand.* See Ps. 110:1. The right hand is a figure for the place of honor and sovereign power.

1:21 *rule and authority and power and dominion.* These words, in rabbinic thought of the time, described different orders of angels (see Rom. 8:38; Eph. 3:10; 6:12; Col. 1:16; 2:10, 15; Titus 3:1).

1:22-23 *the church, which is His body.* The universal church to which every true believer belongs, regardless of local church affiliation. It is a spiritual organism entered by means of the baptism of the Spirit (1 Cor. 12:13). Christ is the risen Head of the church and its members are subject to Him (Eph. 5:24). Local churches should be miniatures of the body of Christ, though it is possible to have unbelieving members in local churches who are not, therefore, members of the body of Christ.

2:1 *dead.* I.e., separated from God because of sins. This is spiritual death. If a man continues in this state, by continuing to reject Christ, spiritual death becomes the second death, eternal separation from God (Rev. 20:14).

2:2 *prince . . . spirit.* Both words refer to Satan. *sons of disobedience.* A Hebraism for "disobedient people."

2:3 Man's basic *nature* has been affected by sin. *children of wrath.* A Hebraism, difficult to translate, but meaning "deserving of wrath."

2:5 *grace.* See note on 1:17.

2:7 Believers will be an eternal display of the grace of God.

2:8 Salvation is *by grace . . . through faith.* Faith involves knowledge of the gospel (Rom. 10:14), acknowledgment of the truth of its message, and personal reception of the Savior (John 1:12). Works cannot save (Eph. 2:9), but good works always accompany salvation (v. 10; Jas. 2:17).

been saved ᵇthrough faith; and that not of yourselves, *it is* ᶜthe gift of God;

9 ᵃnot as a result of works, that ᵇno one should boast.

10 For we are His workmanship, ᵃcreated in ᵇChrist Jesus for ᶜgood works, which God ᵈprepared beforehand, that we should ᵉwalk in them.

C United in One Body, 2:11–22

11 Therefore remember, that ᵃformerly ᵇyou, the Gentiles in the flesh, who are called "ᶜUncircumcision" by the so-called "ᶜCircumcision," *which is* performed in the flesh by human hands—

12 *remember* that you were at that time separate from Christ, ᵃexcluded from the commonwealth of Israel, and strangers to ᵇthe covenants of promise, having ᶜno hope and ᵈwithout God in the world.

13 But now in ᵃChrist Jesus you who ᵇformerly were ᶜfar off have ᶜbeen brought near ᵈby the blood of Christ.

14 For He Himself is ᵃour peace, ᵇwho made both *groups into* one, and broke down the barrier of the dividing wall,

15 by ᵃabolishing in His flesh the enmity, *which is* ᵇthe Law of commandments *contained* in ordinances, that in Himself He might ᶜmake the two into ᵈone

new man, *thus* establishing ᵉpeace,

16 and might ᵃreconcile them both in ᵇone body to God through the cross, by it having ᶜput to death the enmity.

17 AND ᵃHE CAME AND PREACHED ᵇPEACE TO YOU WHO WERE ᶜFAR AWAY, AND PEACE TO THOSE WHO WERE ᶜNEAR;

18 for through Him we both have ᵃour access in ᵇone Spirit to ᶜthe Father.

19 So then you are no longer ᵃstrangers and aliens, but you are ᵇfellow citizens with the saints, and are of ᶜGod's household,

20 having been ᵃbuilt upon ᵇthe foundation of ᶜthe apostles and prophets, ᵈChrist Jesus Himself being the ᵉcorner *stone,*

21 ᵃin whom the whole building, being fitted together is growing into ᵇa holy temple in the Lord;

22 in whom you also are being ᵃbuilt together into a ᵇdwelling of God in the Spirit.

D Equal in the Body (the Mystery), 3:1–21

3 For this reason I, Paul, ᵃthe prisoner of ᵇChrist Jesus ᶜfor the sake of you ᵈGentiles—

2 if indeed you have heard of the ᵃstewardship of God's grace which was given to me for you;

3 ᵃthat ᵇby revelation there was ᶜmade known to me ᵈthe mystery, ᵉas I wrote before in brief.

---

9 ᵃRom. 3:28; 2 Tim. 1:9; Titus 3:5 ᵇ1 Cor. 1:29
10 ᵃEph. 2:15; 4:24; Col. 3:10 ᵇEph. 1:1; 2:6, 13 ᶜTitus 2:14 ᵈEph. 1:4 ᵉEph. 4:1 ★11–22
11 ᵃRom. 13:13; 1 Cor. 6:11; Eph. 2:2, 3, 13; 5:8; Col. 3:7; 1 Pet. 4:3 ᵇ1 Cor. 12:2; Eph. 5:8 ᶜRom. 2:28f.; Col. 2:11, 13
12 ᵃRom. 9:4; Col. 1:21 ᵇGal. 3:17; Heb. 8:6 ᶜ1 Thess. 4:13 ᵈGal. 4:8; Eph. 4:18 ★13 ᵃEph. 1:1; 2:6, 10 ᵇRom. 13:13; 1 Cor. 6:11; Eph. 2:2, 3, 11; 5:8; Col. 3:7; 1 Pet. 4:3 ᶜIs. 57:19; Acts 2:39; Eph. 2:17 ᵈRom. 3:25 ★14 ᵃIs. 9:6; Gal. 3:28; Eph. 2:15; Col. 3:11, 15 ᵇ1 Cor. 12:13 ★15 ᵃEph. 2:16; Col. 1:21f. ᵇCol. 2:14, 20 ᶜEph. 2:10; 4:24; Col. 3:10 ᵈGal. 3:28; Col. 3:10f. ᵉIs. 9:6; Gal. 3:28

16 ᵃ2 Cor. 5:18 ᵇ1 Cor. 10:17; Eph. 4:4 ᶜEph. 2:15
17 ᵃIs. 57:19; Rom. 10:14; Eph. 4:21 ᵇActs 10:36; Eph. 2:14 ᶜIs. 57:19
18 ᵃRom. 5:2; Eph. 3:12 ᵇ1 Cor. 12:13; 4:4 ᶜCol. 1:12
19 ᵃEph. 2:12; Heb. 11:13; 1 Pet. 2:11 ᵇPhil. 3:20; Heb. 12:22f. ᶜGal. 6:10 ★20–21
20 ᵃ1 Cor. 3:9 ᵇMatt. 16:18 ᶜ1 Cor. 12:28; Eph. 3:5 ᵈ1 Cor. 3:11 ᵉLuke 20:17
21 ᵃEph. 4:15f.; Col. 2:19 ᵇ1 Cor. 3:16f.
22 ᵃ1 Cor. 3:9, 16; 2 Cor. 6:16 ᵇEph. 3:17
1 ᵃActs 23:18; Eph. 4:1 ᵇGal. 5:24 ᶜ2 Cor. 1:6; Eph. 3:13 ᵈEph. 3:8 ★2 ᵃEph. 1:10; 3:9 ★3 ᵃActs 22:17, 21; 26:16ff. ᵇGal. 1:12 ᶜEph. 1:9; 3:4, 9 ᵈRom. 11:25; 16:25 ᵉEph. 1:9f.

2:11–22 Paul now expands the concept of the body of Christ put forward in 1:23.

2:13 *near* (to God).

2:14 *the barrier of the dividing wall.* An allusion to the wall which separated the Court of the Gentiles from the Court of the Jews in the temple. An inscription warned Gentiles of the death penalty for going beyond it.

2:15 *in His flesh.* For an explanation of Paul's understanding of this "shorthand" phrase, see Gal. 4:4 and Heb. 2:14. *the Law.* The whole Jewish legal system. *the two.* I.e., Jew and Gentile.

2:20–21 In the figure of the church as a temple, Christ is the *corner stone,* the *apostles and* N.T. *prophets* are the *foundation,* and each Christian is a stone in the building (1 Pet. 2:4–8). In 1 Cor. 3:11 Paul speaks of Christ as

the sole foundation.

3:2 *stewardship.* Paul was entrusted with the message of the grace of God as the apostle to the Gentiles (v. 1; Gal. 2:7).

3:3 *the mystery.* A mystery was not something mysterious (in the modern sense) but something unknown until revealed to the initiated (cf. Rom. 16:25). The mystery spoken of here is not that Gentiles would be blessed (for that was predicted in the O.T.), but that Jews and Gentiles would be equal heirs in the one body of Christ (Eph. 3:6). This was unknown in O.T. prophecy but was revealed by the N.T. apostles and prophets (v. 5). Other mysteries revealed in the N.T. are found in Matt. 13:11; Rom. 11:25; 1 Cor. 15:51–52; Eph. 5:32; 6:19; Col. 1:27; 2:2; 4:3; 2 Thess. 2:7; 1 Tim. 3:16; Rev. 1:20; 17:5, 7.

4 a2 Cor.
11:6 bRom.
11:25; 16:25;
Eph. 3:3, 9;
6:19; Col.
1:26 f.; 4:3
5 a1 Cor.
12:28; Eph.
2:20

4 And by referring to this, when you read you can understand ^amy insight into the ^bmystery of Christ,

5 which in other generations was not made known to the sons of men, as it has now been revealed to His holy ^aapostles and prophets in the Spirit;

6 aGal.
3:29 bEph.
2:16 cEph.
5:7 dGal.
5:24

6 to be specific, that the Gentiles are ^afellow heirs and ^bfellow members of the body, and ^cfellow partakers of the promise in ^dChrist Jesus through the gospel,

★ 7-10
7 aCol.
1:23, 25
b1 Cor. 3:5
cActs 9:15;
Rom. 12:3;
Eph. 3:2
dEph. 1:19;
3:20
8 a1 Cor.
15:9 bActs
9:15; Eph.
3:1 f. cRom.
2:4; Eph. 1:7;
3:16
9 aRom.
11:25; 16:25;
Eph. 3:3, 4;
6:19; Col.
1:26 f.; 4:3
bCol. 3:3
cRev. 4:11
10 aRom.
11:33; 1 Cor.
2:7 bEph.
1:23; 1 Pet.
1:12 cEph.
1:21; 6:12;
Col. 2:10, 15
dEph. 1:3
11 aEph.
1:11 bGal.
5:24; Eph.
3:1
12 aHeb.
4:16; 10:19
35; 1 John
2:28; 3:21
b2 Cor. 3:4
cEph. 2:18
13 a2 Cor.
4:1 bEph.
3:1
★14 aPhil.
2:10

7 ^aof which I was made a ^bminister, according to the gift of ^cGod's grace which was given to me ^daccording to the working of His power.

8 To me, ^athe very least of all saints, this grace was given, to ^bpreach to the Gentiles the unfathomable ^criches of Christ,

9 and to bring to light what is the administration of the ^amystery which for ages has been ^bhidden in God, ^cwho created all things;

10 in order that the manifold ^awisdom of God might now be ^bmade known through the church to the ^crulers and the authorities in ^dthe heavenly places.

11 This was in ^aaccordance with the eternal purpose which He carried out in ^bChrist Jesus our Lord,

12 in whom we have ^aboldness and ^bconfident ^caccess through faith in Him.

13 Therefore I ask you not ^ato lose heart at my tribulations ^bon your behalf, for they are your glory.

14 For this reason, I ^abow my knees before the Father,

15 from whom every family in heaven and on earth derives its name,

16 that He would grant you, according to ^athe riches of His glory, to be ^bstrengthened with power through His Spirit in ^cthe inner man;

16 aEph.
1:18; 3:8
b1 Cor.
16:13; Phil.
4:13; Col.
1:11 cRom.
7:22
★17 aJohn
14:23; Rom.
8:9 f.; 2 Cor.
13:5; Eph.
2:22 b1 Cor.
3:6; Col. 2:7
cCol. 1:23
18 aEph.
1:15 bJob
11:8 f.
19 aRom.
8:35, 39
bPhil. 4:7
cCol. 2:10
dEph. 1:23
★20 aRom.
16:25
b2 Cor. 9:8
cEph. 3:7
21 aRom.
11:36

17 so that ^aChrist may dwell in your hearts through faith; and that you, being ^brooted and ^cgrounded in love,

18 may be able to comprehend with ^aall the saints what is ^bthe breadth and length and height and depth,

19 and to know ^athe love of Christ which ^bsurpasses knowledge, that you may be ^cfilled up to all the ^dfulness of God.

20 ^aNow to Him who is ^bable to do exceeding abundantly beyond all that we ask or think, ^caccording to the power that works within us,

21 ^ato Him be the glory in the church and in Christ Jesus to all generations forever and ever. Amen.

III   THE PRACTICE OF BELIEVERS, 4:1-6:9

A   In Relation to Other Believers, 4:1-6

★ 1 aEph.
3:1 bRom.
12:1 cEph.
2:10; Col.
1:10; 2:6;
1 Thess. 2:12
dRom. 11:29
eRom. 8:28 f.
2 aCol.
3:12 f. bEph.
1:4
3 aCol.
3:14 f.

4 I, therefore, ^athe prisoner of the Lord, ^bentreat you to ^cwalk in a manner worthy of the ^dcalling with which you have been ^ecalled,

2 with all ^ahumility and gentleness, with patience, showing forbearance to one another ^bin love,

3 being diligent to preserve the unity of the Spirit in the ^abond of peace.

3:7-10 Paul here gives his concept of his own mission. Note that this was God's doing (v. 7); that he was to make available to all mankind Israel's hope for a Messiah (v. 8); that he was to be a theologian-teacher as well as a missionary (v. 9); that his ministry would even bring angelic beings to see the wisdom of God in His plan for the church (v. 10). On rulers and . . . . authorities see note on 1:21.

3:14 For this reason. Here Paul resumes the thought begun in 3:1.

3:17 dwell = be completely at home.

3:20 the power that works within us. I.e., the Holy Spirit.

4:1 Here begins Paul's exhortation for his readers to promote the unity of the church through godly living (vv. 1-6) and, through a diversity of gifts, contribute to the common welfare (vv. 7-16).

4 a1 Cor.
12:4ff.; Eph.
2:16, 18
bEph. 1:18

★ 5 a1 Cor.
8:6

★ 6 aRom.
11:36; Col.
1:16

★ 7 a1 Cor.
12:7, 11
bEph. 3:2
cRom. 12:3

★ 8 aPs.
68:18 bJudg.
5:12; Col.
2:15

★ 9-10
★9 aJohn
3:13 bPs.
63:9; Is.
44:23
10 aEph.
1:20f.; Heb.
4:14; 7:26;
9:24 bEph.
1:23

★11 aEph.
4:8 bActs
13:1; 1 Cor.
12:28 cActs
21:8 dActs
13:1
12 a2 Cor.
13:9 b1 Cor.
12:27; Eph.
1:23

4 *There is* ᵃone body and one Spirit, just as also you were called in one ᵇhope of your calling;

5 ᵃone Lord, one faith, one baptism,

6 one God and Father of all ᵃwho is over all and through all and in all.

B In Relation to Spiritual Gifts, 4:7-16

7 But ᵃto each one of us ᵇgrace was given ᶜaccording to the measure of Christ's gift.

8 Therefore it says,

"ᵃWHEN HE ASCENDED ON
   HIGH,
HE ᵇLED CAPTIVE A HOST OF
   CAPTIVES,
AND HE GAVE GIFTS TO MEN."

9 (Now this *expression*, "He ᵃascended," what does it mean except that He also had descended into ᵇthe lower parts of the earth?

10 He who descended is Himself also He who ascended ᵃfar above all the heavens, that He might ᵇfill all things.)

11 And He ᵃgave ᵇsome *as* apostles, and some *as* prophets, and some *as* ᶜevangelists, and some *as* pastors and ᵈteachers,

12 ᵃfor the equipping of the saints for the work of service, to

the building up of ᵇthe body of Christ;

13 until we all attain to ᵃthe unity of the faith, and of the ᵇknowledge of the Son of God, to a ᶜmature man, to the measure of the stature which belongs to the ᵈfulness of Christ.

14 As a result, we are ᵃno longer to be children, ᵇtossed here and there by waves, and carried about by every wind of doctrine, by the trickery of men, by ᶜcraftiness in ᵈdeceitful scheming;

15 but speaking the truth ᵃin love, we are to ᵇgrow up in all *aspects* into Him, who is the ᶜhead, *even* Christ,

16 from whom ᵃthe whole body, being fitted and held together by that which every joint supplies, according to the proper working of each individual part, causes the growth of the body for the building up of itself ᵇin love.

C In Relation to the Former Life, 4:17-32

17 ᵃThis I say therefore, and ᵇaffirm together with the Lord, ᶜthat you walk no longer just as the Gentiles also walk, in the ᵈfutility of their mind,

18 being ᵃdarkened in their understanding, excluded from ᵇthe life of God, because of the ᶜignorance that is in them, be-

13 aEph.
4:3, 5 bJohn
6:69; Eph.
1:17; Phil.
3:10 c1 Cor.
14:20; Col.
1:28; Heb.
5:14 dJohn
1:16; Gal.
4:19; Eph.
1:23
14 a1 Cor.
14:20
bJames 1:6;
Jude 12
c1 Cor. 3:19;
2 Cor. 4:2;
11:3 dEph.
6:11
15 aEph. 1:4
bEph. 2:21
cEph. 1:22

16 aRom.
12:4f.; 1 Cor.
10:17; Col.
2:19 bEph.
1:4

★17 aCol.
2:4 bLuke
16:28 cEph.
2:2; 4:22
dRom. 1:21;
Col. 2:18;
1 Pet. 1:18;
2 Pet. 2:18
18 aRom.
1:21 bEph.
2:1, 12 cActs
3:17; 17:30;
1 Cor. 2:8;
Heb. 5:2;
9:7; 1 Pet.
1:14 dMark
3:5; Rom.
11:7, 25;
2 Cor. 3:14

4:5 *one baptism.* I.e., the baptism of the Spirit, which brings us into the unity of the body of Christ.

4:6 God is *Father* in four relationships: (1) here, of all men by virtue of being their Creator; (2) of the Lord Jesus Christ (Matt. 3:17); (3) of Israel (Ex. 4:22); and (4) of believers in the Lord Jesus Christ (Gal. 3:26).

4:7 In 1 Cor. 12:7-11 Paul attributes the giving of spiritual gifts to the Spirit; here to the ascended Christ.

4:8 *He led captive a host of captives.* Paul uses an illustration from Ps. 68:18, in which the triumphant warrior is elevated when he returns with hosts of prisoners, receiving gifts from the conquered people, and distributing gifts to his followers. Christ conquered Satan and all that had conquered us.

4:9-10 These verses are a parenthetical aside, to

comment on *He ascended* (v. 8) and to prove that only Christ fits the description.

4:9 *lower parts of the earth.* May mean that Christ descended into Hades between His death and resurrection, or "of the earth" may be an appositional phrase, meaning that He descended (at His incarnation) into the lower parts (of the universe), namely, the earth.

4:11 *apostles.* See note on Matt. 10:2. *prophets.* Strictly speaking, those who were given direct revelation by God to communicate to men. *evangelists.* I.e., preachers of the gospel. *pastors and teachers.* The two ministries are linked together here, though separated elsewhere (Rom. 12:7; 1 Pet. 5:2).

4:17 Here begins a long passage (ending at 6:9) in which Paul draws the logical conclusions, in terms of life and morals, that follow from membership in Christ's body.

cause of the ᵈhardness of their heart;

19 and they, having ᵃbecome callous, ᵇhave given themselves over to ᶜsensuality, for the practice of every kind of impurity with greediness.

20 But you did not ᵃlearn Christ in this way,

21 if indeed you ᵃhave heard Him and have ᵇbeen taught in Him, just as truth is in Jesus,

22 that, in reference to your former manner of life, you ᵃlay aside the ᵇold self, which is being corrupted in accordance with the ᶜlusts of deceit,

23 and that you be ᵃrenewed in the spirit of your mind,

24 and ᵃput on the ᵇnew self, which ᶜin the likeness of God has been created in righteousness and holiness of the truth.

25 Therefore, ᵃlaying aside falsehood, ᵇSPEAK TRUTH, EACH ONE OF YOU, WITH HIS NEIGHBOR, for we are ᶜmembers of one another.

26 ᵃBE ANGRY, AND yet DO NOT SIN; do not let ᵇthe sun go down on your anger,

27 and do not ᵃgive the devil an opportunity.

28 Let him who steals steal no longer; but rather ᵃlet him labor, ᵇperforming with his own hands what is good, ᶜin order that he may have something to share with him who has need.

29 Let no ᵃunwholesome word proceed from your mouth, but only such a word as is good for ᵇedification according to the need of the moment, that it may give grace to those who hear.

30 And ᵃdo not grieve the Holy Spirit of God, by whom you were ᵇsealed for the day of redemption.

31 ᵃLet all bitterness and wrath and anger and clamor and slander be ᵇput away from you, along with all ᶜmalice.

32 And ᵃbe kind to one another, tender-hearted, forgiving each other, ᵇjust as God in Christ also has forgiven you.

D In Relation to Evil, 5:1-17

5 ᵃTherefore be imitators of God, as beloved children;

2 and ᵃwalk in love, just as Christ also ᵇloved you, and ᶜgave Himself up for us, an ᵈoffering and a sacrifice to God as a ᵉfragrant aroma.

3 But do not let ᵃimmorality or any impurity or greed even be named among you, as is proper among saints;

4 and there must be no ᵃfilthiness and silly talk, or coarse jesting, which ᵇare not fitting, but rather ᶜgiving of thanks.

5 For this you know with certainty, that ᵃno immoral or impure person or covetous man, who is an idolater, has an inheritance in the kingdom ᵇof Christ and God.

6 ᵃLet no one deceive you with empty words, for because of these things ᵇthe wrath of God comes upon ᶜthe sons of disobedience.

7 Therefore do not be ᵃpartakers with them;

8 for ᵃyou were formerly ᵇdarkness, but now you are light in the Lord; walk as ᶜchildren of light

9 (for ᵃthe fruit of the light consists in all ᵇgoodness and righteousness and truth),

10 ᵃtrying to learn what is pleasing to the Lord.

4:22-24 the old self . . . the new self. The old is what we were before we were saved, and the new is the new life we have in Christ. See 2 Cor. 5:17; Gal. 2:20.

4:26 There is an anger which is not sinful, but even this must not be allowed to stay and fester and give the devil an opportunity.

4:30 the Holy Spirit is grieved or pained by sin,

especially the sins of the tongue (vv. 29, 31). sealed. See note on 1:13.

5:2 a fragrant aroma. The soothing aroma offerings of Lev. 1-3 prefigured the voluntary character of Christ's sacrifice.

5:4 silly talk, or coarse jesting. I.e., unclean speech, often veiled in innuendo or double meaning.

19 ᵃ1 Tim. 4:2 ᵇRom. 1:24 ᶜCol. 3:5
20 ᵃMatt. 11:29
21 ᵃRom. 10:14; Eph. 1:13; 2:17; Col. 1:5 ᵇCol. 2:7
★**22-24**
22 ᵃEph. 4:25, 31; Col. 3:8; Heb. 12:1 [Gr.]; James 1:21; 1 Pet. 2:1 ᵇRom. 6:6 ᶜ2 Cor. 11:3; Heb. 3:13
23 ᵃRom. 12:2
24 ᵃRom. 13:14 ᵇRom. 6:4; 7:6; 12:2; 2 Cor. 5:17; Col. 3:10 ᶜEph. 2:10
25 ᵃEph. 4:22, 31; Col. 3:8; Heb. 12:1 [Gr.]; James 1:21; 1 Pet. 2:1 ᵇZech. 8:16; Eph. 4:15; Col. 3:9 ᶜRom. 12:5
★**26** ᵃPs. 4:4 ᵇDeut. 24:15
27 ᵃRom. 12:19; James 4:7
28 ᵃActs 20:35; 1 Cor. 4:12; Gal. 6:10 ᵇ1 Thess. 4:11; 2 Thess. 3:8, 11f.; Titus 3:8, 14 ᶜLuke 3:11; 1 Thess. 4:12
29 ᵃMatt. 12:34; Eph. 5:4; Col. 3:8 ᵇEccl. 10:12; Rom. 14:19; Col. 4:6
★**30** ᵃIs. 63:10; 1 Thess. 5:19 ᵇJohn 3:33; Eph. 1:13
31 ᵃRom. 3:14; Col. 3:8, 19 ᵇEph. 4:22 ᶜ1 Pet. 2:1

32 ᵃ1 Cor. 13:4; Col. 3:12f.; 1 Pet. 3:8 ᵇMatt. 6:14f.; 2 Cor. 2:10

1 ᵃMatt. 5:48; Luke 6:36; Eph. 4:32
★**2** ᵃRom. 14:15; Col. 3:14 ᵇJohn 13:34; Rom. 8:37 ᶜJohn 6:51; Rom. 4:25; Gal. 2:20; Eph. 5:25 ᵈHeb. 7:27; 9:14; 10:10, 12 ᵉEx. 29:18, 25; 2 Cor. 2:14
3 ᵃCol. 3:5
★**4** ᵃMatt. 12:34; Eph. 4:29; Col. 3:8 ᵇRom. 1:28 ᶜEph. 5:20
5 ᵃ1 Cor. 6:9; Col. 3:5 ᵇCol. 1:13
6 ᵃCol. 2:8 ᵇRom. 1:18; Col. 3:6 ᶜEph. 2:2; Col. 3:6
7 ᵃEph. 3:6
8 ᵃEph. 2:2 ᵇActs 26:18; Col. 1:12f. ᶜLuke 16:8; John 12:36; Rom. 13:12
9 ᵃGal. 5:22 ᵇRom. 15:14
10 ᵃRom. 12:2

11 a1 Cor.
5:9; 2 Cor.
6:14 bRom.
13:12 cActs
26:18; Col.
1:12f.
d1 Tim. 5:20

11 And ªdo not participate in the unfruitful ᵇdeeds of ᶜdarkness, but instead even ᵈexpose them;

12 for it is disgraceful even to speak of the things which are done by them in secret.

13 aJohn
3:20f.

13 But all things become visible ªwhen they are exposed by the light, for everything that becomes visible is light.

14 aIs.
26:19; 51:17;
52:1; 60:1
bRom. 13:11
cEph. 2:1
dLuke 1:78f.

14 For this reason ªit says,

"ᵇAwake, sleeper,
And arise from ᶜthe dead,
And Christ ᵈwill shine on
you."

15 aEph. 5:2
bCol. 4:5

15 Therefore be careful how you ªwalk, not ᵇas unwise men, but as wise,

16 aCol. 4:5
bGal. 1:4;
Eph. 6:13
17 aRom.
12:2; Col.
1:9; 1 Thess.
4:3

16 ªmaking the most of your time, because ᵇthe days are evil.

17 So then do not be foolish, but ªunderstand what the will of the Lord is.

E In Relation to the Holy Spirit, 5:18–21

★18 aProv.
20:1; 23:31f.;
Rom. 13:13;
1 Cor. 5:11;
1 Thess. 5:7
bTitus 1:6;
1 Pet. 4:4
cLuke 1:15
★19 aCol.
3:16; James
5:13 b1 Cor.
14:26 cActs
16:25 dRev.
5:9 e1 Cor.
14:15
20 aRom.
1:8; Eph. 5:4;
Col. 3:17
b1 Cor.
15:24

18 And ªdo not get drunk with wine, for that is ᵇdissipation, but be ᶜfilled with the Spirit,

19 ªspeaking to one another in ᵇpsalms and ᶜhymns and spiritual ᵈsongs, ᵉsinging and making melody with your heart to the Lord;

20 ªalways giving thanks for all things in the name of our Lord Jesus Christ to ᵇGod, even the Father;

21 ªand be subject to one another in the ᵇfear of Christ.

F In Relation to Home Life, 5:22–6:4

22 ªWives, ᵇ*be subject* to your own husbands, ᶜas to the Lord.

23 For ªthe husband is the head of the wife, as Christ also is the ᵇhead of the church, He Himself ᶜ*being* the Savior of the body.

24 But as the church is subject to Christ, so also the wives *ought to be* to their husbands in everything.

25 ªHusbands, love your wives, just as Christ also loved the church and ᵇgave Himself up for her;

26 ªthat He might sanctify her, having ᵇcleansed her by the ᶜwashing of water with ᵈthe word,

27 that He might ªpresent to Himself the church in all her glory, having no spot or wrinkle or any such thing; but that she should be ᵇholy and blameless.

28 So husbands ought also to ªlove their own wives as their own bodies. He who loves his own wife loves himself;

29 for no one ever hated his own flesh, but nourishes and cherishes it, just as Christ also *does* the church,

30 because we are ªmembers of His ᵇbody.

31 ªFOR THIS CAUSE A MAN SHALL LEAVE HIS FATHER AND MOTHER, AND

★21 aGal.
5:13; Phil.
2:3; 1 Pet.
5:5 b2 Cor.
5:11

★22 aEph.
5:22-6:9;
Col. 3:18-4:1
b1 Cor.
14:34f.; Titus
2:5; 1 Pet.
3:1 cEph.
6:5
23 a1 Cor.
11:3 bEph.
1:22 c1 Cor.
6:13

★25 aEph.
5:28, 33;
1 Pet. 3:7
bEph. 5:2

26 aHeb.
10:10, 14,
29; 13:12; Ti-
tus 2:14
b2 Pet. 1:9
cActs 22:16;
1 Cor. 6:11;
Titus 3:5
dJohn 15:3;
17:17; Rom.
10:8f.; Eph.
6:17
27 a2 Cor.
4:14; 11:2;
Col. 1:22
bEph. 1:4
28 aEph.
5:25, 33;
1 Pet. 3:7

30 a1 Cor.
6:15; 12:27
bEph. 1:23
★31 aGen.
2:24; Matt.
19:5; Mark
10:7f.

5:18 *be filled with the Spirit.* Paul has taught in this epistle that all believers are sealed with the Spirit when they believe (1:13–14; 4:30), but not all are filled, since this depends on yieldedness to God's will (5:17). "Filling" describes an experience that can be repeated (Acts 2:4; 4:31), and here, as in Acts, it is connected with joy, courage, spirituality, and Christian character.

5:19 *to one another.* Making music in one's heart is mentioned at the end of this verse.

5:21 *be subject.* The key thought for understanding Paul's view of proper personal rela-

tionships in a Christian household; the subjection is to be mutual and based on reverence for God.

5:22 *Wives* are to submit to the leadership of their husbands in the home (vv. 22, 24); they are to respect their husbands (v. 33); they are to love their husbands (Tit. 2:4), and live with them until death (Rom. 7:2–3).

5:25 *Husbands* are to love their wives, lead them (v. 23), nurture them in the things of Christ (v. 29), and live with them faithfully for life (Matt. 19:3–9).

5:31 See Gen. 2:24.

SHALL CLEAVE TO HIS WIFE; AND THE TWO SHALL BECOME ONE FLESH.

★32　　**32** This mystery is great; but I am speaking with reference to Christ and the church.

33 Nevertheless let each individual among you also [a]love his own wife even as himself; and *let* the wife *see to it* that she [b]respect her husband.

6 [a]Children, obey your parents in the Lord, for this is right.

2 [a]HONOR YOUR FATHER AND MOTHER (which is the first commandment with a promise),

3 [a]THAT IT MAY BE WELL WITH YOU, AND THAT YOU MAY LIVE LONG ON THE EARTH.

4 And, [a]fathers, do not provoke your children to anger; but [b]bring them up in the discipline and instruction of the Lord.

G　In Relation to Slaves and Masters, 6:5-9

5 [a]Slaves, be obedient to those who are your masters according to the flesh, with [b]fear and trembling, in the sincerity of your heart, [c]as to Christ;

6 [a]not by way of eyeservice, as [b]men-pleasers, but as [c]slaves of Christ, doing the will of God from the heart.

7 With good will render service, [a]as to the Lord, and not to men,

8 [a]knowing that [b]whatever good thing each one does, this he will receive back from the Lord, [c]whether slave or free.

9 And, masters, do the same things to them, and [a]give up threatening, knowing that [b]both their Master and yours is in

heaven, and there is [c]no partiality with Him.

IV　THE PROTECTION FOR BELIEVERS, 6:10-20
A　Against Whom? 6:10-12

10 Finally, [a]be strong in the Lord, and in [b]the strength of His might.

11 [a]Put on the full armor of God, that you may be able to stand firm against the [b]schemes of the devil.

12 For our [a]struggle is not against [b]flesh and blood, but [c]against the rulers, against the powers, against the [d]world forces of this [e]darkness, against the [f]spiritual *forces* of wickedness in [g]the heavenly *places*.

B　With What? 6:13-20

13 Therefore, take up [a]the full armor of God, that you may be able to [b]resist in [c]the evil day, and having done everything, to stand firm.

14 Stand firm therefore, [a]HAVING GIRDED YOUR LOINS WITH TRUTH, and HAVING [b]PUT ON THE [c]BREASTPLATE OF RIGHTEOUSNESS,

15 and having [a]shod YOUR FEET WITH THE PREPARATION OF THE GOSPEL OF PEACE;

16 in addition to all, taking up the [a]shield of faith with which you will be able to extinguish all the [b]flaming missiles of [c]the evil one.

17 And take the [a]HELMET OF SALVATION, and the [b]sword of the Spirit, which is [c]the word of God.

18 With all [a]prayer and petition [b]pray at all times [c]in the Spirit, and with this in view, [d]be

★32
33 [a]Eph. 5:25, 28; 1 Pet. 3:7
[b]1 Pet. 3:2, 5f.

★ 1 [a]Prov. 6:20; 23:22; Col. 3:20
★ 2 [a]Ex. 20:12; Deut. 5:16

3 [a]Ex. 20:12; Deut. 5:16

★ 4 [a]Col. 3:21 [b]Gen. 18:19; Deut. 6:7; 11:19; Ps. 78:4; Prov. 22:6; 2 Tim. 3:15

5 [a]Col. 3:22; 1 Tim. 6:1; Titus 2:9
[b]1 Cor. 2:3
[c]Eph. 5:22

6 [a]Col. 3:22 [b]Gal. 1:10 [c]1 Cor. 7:22

7 [a]Col. 3:23

8 [a]Col. 3:24 [b]Matt. 16:27; 2 Cor. 5:10; Col. 3:24f. [c]1 Cor. 12:13; Col. 3:11

9 [a]Lev. 25:43 [b]Job 31:13ff.; John 13:13 [c]Acts 10:34; Col. 3:25

10 [a]1 Cor. 16:13; 2 Tim. 2:1 [b]Eph. 1:19

★11 [a]Rom. 13:12; Eph. 6:13 [b]Eph. 4:14

★12 [a]1 Cor. 9:25 [b]Matt. 16:17 [c]Eph. 1:21; 2:2; 3:10 [d]John 12:31 [e]Acts 26:18; Col. 1:13 [f]Eph. 3:10 [g]Eph. 1:3

13 [a]Eph. 6:11 [b]James 4:7 [c]Eph. 5:16

14 [a]Is. 11:5; Luke 12:35; 1 Pet. 1:13 [b]Rom. 13:12; Eph. 6:13 [c]Is. 59:17; 1 Thess. 5:8

15 [a]Is. 52:7; Rom. 10:15

16 [a]1 Thess. 5:8 [b]Ps. 7:13; 120:4 [c]Matt. 5:37

★17 [a]Is. 59:17 [b]Is. 49:2; Hos. 6:5; Heb. 4:12 [c]Eph. 5:26; Heb. 6:5

18 [a]Phil. 4:6 [b]Luke 18:1; Col. 1:3; 4:2; 1 Thess. 5:17 [c]Rom. 8:26f. [d]Mark 13:33 [e]Acts 1:14 [Gr.] [f]1 Tim. 2:1

5:32 The relationship between believing husbands and wives illustrates that which exists between Christ (the bridegroom) and the church (His bride). See also Matt. 25:1-13; Rev. 19:7-8; 21:2.

6:1 *in the Lord.* I.e., obedience to parents is part of a child's obligation to Christ. See the example of Christ in Luke 2:51 and Heb. 5:8.

6:2 When a child marries, his relationship to his parents changes (5:31), but not his responsibil-

ity to provide for them (1 Tim. 5:4).

6:4 *do not provoke.* I.e., do not nag or arbitrarily assert authority.

6:11 *schemes* = craftiness.

6:12 The believer's enemies are the demonic hosts of Satan, always assembled for mortal combat.

6:17 *take.* Lit., receive, a different word from that in v. 16. Salvation is a gift. *sword.* The only offensive weapon mentioned.

★19 *a*Col.
4:3; 1 Thess.
5:25 *b*2 Cor.
6:11 *c*2 Cor.
3:12 *d*Eph.
3:3
20 *a*2 Cor.
5:20; Philem.
9 marg.
*b*Acts 21:33;
28:20; Eph.
3:1; Phil. 1:7;
Col. 4:3
*c*2 Cor. 3:12
*d*Col. 4:4

on the alert with all *e*perseverance and *f*petition for all the saints,

19 and *a*pray on my behalf, that utterance may be given to me *b*in the opening of my mouth, to make known with *c*boldness *d*the mystery of the gospel,

20 for which I am an *a*ambassador *b*in chains; that in *proclaiming* it I may speak *c*boldly, *d*as I ought to speak.

V CONCLUDING WORDS, 6:21-24

21 *a*Eph.
6:21, 22
*b*Acts 20:4
*c*Col. 4:7

21 *a*But that you also may know about my circumstances,

how I am doing, *b*Tychicus, *c*the beloved brother and faithful minister in the Lord, will make everything known to you.

22 And *a*I have sent him to you for this very purpose, so that you may know about us, and that he may *b*comfort your hearts.

23 *a*Peace be to the brethren, and *b*love with faith, from God the Father and the Lord Jesus Christ.

24 Grace be with all those who love our Lord Jesus Christ with *a love* incorruptible.

22 *a*Col. 4:8
*b*Col. 2:2;
4:8

23 *a*Rom.
15:33; Gal.
6:16; 2
Thess. 3:16;
1 Pet. 5:14
*b*Gal. 5:6;
1 Thess. 5:8

6:19 Even in prison Paul was not thinking of his own welfare but of his testimony for Christ.

INTRODUCTION TO
THE LETTER OF PAUL TO THE PHILIPPIANS

AUTHOR: Paul   DATE: 61

The Church at Philippi   *Founded by Paul on his second missionary journey, this was the first church to be established by him in Europe (Acts 16). Philippi was a small city, founded by King Philip of Macedonia, father of Alexander the Great. Its greatest fame came from the battle fought nearby, in 42 B.C., between the forces of Brutus and Cassius and those of Antony and Octavian (later Caesar Augustus). It became a Roman "colony," a military outpost city with special privileges.*
   Paul's relationship with the church at Philippi was always close and cordial. Having helped him financially at least two times before this letter was written (4:16), and having heard of his confinement in Rome, the church sent Epaphroditus with another gift. Philippians is a thank-you letter for that gift, and it is the most personal letter Paul wrote to a church. Epaphroditus had become almost fatally ill while with Paul (2:27) and on his recovery Paul sent him back with this letter. Though somewhat obscured by Paul's gentleness in this letter, some of the problems in the church are seen beneath the surface. These included: rivalries and personal ambition (2:3-4; 4:2), the teaching of the Judaizers (3:1-3), perfectionism (3:12-14), and the influence of antinomian libertines (3:18-19).

Place of Writing   *Paul was imprisoned when this letter was written, but there is disagreement as to where. Some think he was in Caesarea, others Ephesus; yet he must undoubtedly have been in Rome. In 1:13 (see note there) he mentions the praetorium, a Roman body of troops assigned to the emperor in Rome (see also 4:22). It is also clear that, in the trial facing Paul, his life was at stake, indicating that the trial was before Caesar in Rome (1:20). Although Paul was confined in Caesarea for two years, no final decision of his case was even in prospect there (Acts 24). Ephesus has been suggested as the place of writing on the basis of 1 Corinthians 15:32, but there is no clear reference in that verse to an imprisonment.*

Contents   *One of the most important doctrinal passages in the New Testament is Philippians 2:5-8, in which Paul presents the doctrine of the kenosis—the self-humiliating, or self-emptying, of Christ. Important verses on prayer are 4:6-7. Other favorite verses include 1:21, 23b; 3:10, 20; 4:8, 13. A significant autobiographical sketch appears in 3:4-14.*

OUTLINE OF PHILIPPIANS

I. **Greetings and Expressions of Gratitude,**
   1:1–11
II. **Paul's Personal Circumstances: The**
   Preaching of Christ, 1:12–30
III. **The Pattern of the Christian Life: The**
   Humility of Christ, 2:1–30
   A. The Exhortation to Humility, 2:1–4
   B. The Epitome of Humility, 2:5–11
   C. The Exercise of Humility, 2:12–18
   D. The Examples of Timothy and
      Epaphroditus, 2:19–30

IV. **The Prize of the Christian Life: The**
   Knowledge of Christ, 3:1–21
   A. The Warning against Judaizers, 3:1–3
   B. The Example of Paul, 3:4–14
   C. The Exhortation to Others, 3:15–21
V. **The Peace of the Christian Life: The**
   Presence of Christ, 4:1–23
   A. Peace with Others, 4:1–4
   B. Peace with Self, 4:5–9
   C. Peace with Circumstances, 4:10–23

THE LETTER OF PAUL TO THE PHILIPPIANS

I GREETINGS AND EXPRESSIONS OF GRATITUDE, 1:1-11

1 [a]Paul and [b]Timothy, [c]bond-servants of [d]Christ Jesus, to [e]all the [f]saints in Christ Jesus who are in [g]Philippi, including the [h]overseers and [i]deacons:

2 [a]Grace to you and peace from God our Father and the Lord Jesus Christ.

3 [a]I thank my God in all my remembrance of you,

4 always offering prayer with joy in [a]my every prayer for you all,

5 in view of your [a]participation in the [b]gospel [c]from the first day until now.

6 *For I am* confident of this very thing, that He who began a good work in you will perfect it until [a]the day of Christ Jesus.

7 For [a]it is only right for me to feel this way about you all, because I [b]have you in my heart, since both in my [c]imprisonment and in the [d]defense and confirmation of the [e]gospel, you all are partakers of grace with me.

8 For [a]God is my witness, how I long for you all with the affection of [b]Christ Jesus.

9 And this I pray, that [a]your love may abound still more and

more in [b]real knowledge and all discernment,

10 so that you may [a]approve the things that are excellent, in order to be sincere and blameless until [b]the day of Christ;

11 having been filled with the [a]fruit of righteousness which *comes* through Jesus Christ, to the glory and praise of God.

II PAUL'S PERSONAL CIRCUMSTANCES: THE PREACHING OF CHRIST, 1:12-30

12 Now I want you to know, brethren, that my circumstances [a]have turned out for the greater progress of the [b]gospel,

13 so that my [a]imprisonment in *the cause of* Christ has become well known throughout the whole praetorian guard and to [b]everyone else,

14 and that most of the brethren, trusting in the Lord because of my [a]imprisonment, have [b]far more courage to speak the word of God without fear.

15 [a]Some, to be sure, are preaching Christ even from envy

Marginal references (left column):
★ 1 [a]2 Cor. 1:1; Col. 1:1; 1 Thess. 1:1 [b]Acts 16:1 [c]Rom. 1:1; Gal. 1:10 [d]Gal. 3:26; Phil. 1:8; 2:5, [e]2 Cor. 1:1; Col. 1:2 [f]Acts 9:13 [g]Acts 16:12 [h]Acts 20:28; 1 Tim. 3:1f. [i]1 Tim. 3:8ff.
2 [a]Rom. 1:7
3 [a]Rom. 1:8
4 [a]Rom. 1:9
★ 5 [a]Acts 2:42; Phil. 4:15 [b]Phil. 1:7, 12, 16, 27; 2:22; 4:3, 15 [c]Acts 16:12-40
★ 6 [a]1 Cor. 1:8; Phil. 1:10; 2:16
★ 7 [a]2 Pet. 1:13 [b]2 Cor. 7:3 [c]Acts 21:33; Eph. 6:20 [d]Phil. 1:16 [e]Phil. 1:5
8 [a]Rom. 1:9 [b]Gal. 3:26; Phil. 1:1; 2:5; 3:3, 8, 12, 14; 4:7, 19, 21
9 [a]1 Thess. 3:12 [b]Col. 1:9

Marginal references (right column):
★10 [a]Rom. 2:18 [b]1 Cor. 1:8; Phil. 1:6; 2:16
11 [a]James 3:18
★12-30 12 [a]Luke 21:13 [b]Phil. 1:5, 7, 16, 27; 2:22; 4:3, 15
★13 [a]Phil. 1:7; 2 Tim. 2:9 [b]Acts 28:30
14 [a]Phil. 1:7; 2 Tim. 2:9 [b]Acts 4:31; 2 Cor. 3:12; 7:4; Phil. 1:20
15 [a]2 Cor. 11:13

1:1 *Timothy* had helped Paul found this church. *saints.* See note on Rom. 1:7. *overseers.* Or bishops. See note on 1 Tim. 3:1. *deacons.* See note on 1 Tim. 3:8. Both bishops and deacons were recognizable groups within the church at this time.

1:5 Paul is here complimenting them on their having cooperated with him from the beginning (see Acts 16:40; Phil. 4:15-16).

1:6 *He* (God) *who began.* God will continue His good work of grace in them until the consummation at *the day of Christ Jesus* (the day when Christ returns).

1:7 *right.* The Greek words underlying *imprisonment, defense,* and *confirmation* were courtroom terms. Paul is saying that the Philippian believers shared with him in his courageous witness in the court of law. Whether Paul had already appeared at trial or whether he was still anticipating it is unclear.

1:10 *approve the things that are excellent.* I.e.,

to differentiate between highest matters and side issues.

1:12-30 This passage tells us about all we know of this imprisonment. Paul knew he was facing a great ordeal, but took great pains not to alarm his friends. His all-consuming concern was for the advancement of the gospel. People were beginning to talk about his bonds and his Christ, the church in Rome was becoming more confident, and he intended to follow his course. He existed only to help forward the cause of Christ (v. 21).

1:13 *praetorian guard.* This group of imperial guards, distinct from the army or Roman police, was about 9000 strong in Rome. They had heard the gospel through their various members who had been assigned the duty of guarding Paul. Guard and prisoner were chained together, making a captive audience for the gospel (see Eph. 6:20).

and strife, but some also from good will;

16 the latter *do it* out of love, knowing that I am [a]appointed for the defense of the [b]gospel;

17 the former proclaim Christ [a]out of selfish ambition, rather than from pure motives, thinking to cause me distress in my [b]imprisonment.

18 What then? Only that in every way, whether in pretense or in truth, Christ is proclaimed; and in this I rejoice, yes, and I will rejoice.

19 For I know that this shall turn out for my deliverance [a]through your prayers and the provision of [b]the Spirit of Jesus Christ,

20 according to my [a]earnest expectation and [b]hope, that I shall not be put to shame in anything, but *that* with [c]all boldness, Christ shall even now, as always, be [d]exalted in my body, [e]whether by life or by death.

21 For to me, [a]to live is Christ, and to die is gain.

22 But if *I am* to live *on* in the flesh, this *will mean* [a]fruitful labor for me; and I do not know which to choose.

23 But I am hard-pressed from both *directions*, having the [a]desire to depart and [b]be with Christ, for *that* is very much better;

24 yet to remain on in the flesh is more necessary for your sake.

25 And [a]convinced of this, I know that I shall remain and continue with you all for your progress and joy in the faith,

26 so that your [a]proud confidence in me may abound in Christ Jesus through my coming to you again.

27 Only conduct yourselves in a manner [a]worthy of the [b]gospel of Christ; so that whether I come and see you or remain absent, I may hear of you that you are [c]standing firm in [d]one spirit, with one mind [e]striving together for the faith of the gospel;

28 in no way alarmed by *your* opponents—which is a [a]sign of destruction for them, but of salvation for you, and that *too,* from God.

29 For to you [a]it has been granted for Christ's sake, not only to believe in Him, but also to [b]suffer for His sake,

30 experiencing the same [a]conflict which [b]you saw in me, and now hear *to be* in me.

III THE PATTERN OF THE CHRISTIAN LIFE: THE HUMILITY OF CHRIST, 2:1-30

A The Exhortation to Humility, 2:1-4

2 If therefore there is any encouragement in Christ, if there is any consolation of love, if there is any [a]fellowship of the Spirit, if any [b]affection and compassion,

2 [a]make my joy complete by [b]being of the same mind, maintaining the same love, united in spirit, intent on one purpose.

3 Do nothing from [a]selfishness or [b]empty conceit, but with

---

Cross references (left margin):

16 [a]1 Cor. 9:17 [b]Phil. 1:5, 7, 12, 27; 2:22; 4:3, 15

17 [a]Rom. 2:8; Phil. 2:3 [b]Phil. 1:7; 2 Tim. 2:9

★18

★19 [a]2 Cor. 1:11 [b]Acts 16:7

20 [a]Rom. 8:19 [b]Rom. 5:5; 1 Pet. 4:16 [c]Acts 4:31; 2 Cor. 3:12; 7:4; Phil. 1:14 [d]1 Cor. 6:20 [e]Rom. 14:8

★21 [a]Gal. 2:20

22 [a]Rom. 1:13

23 [a]2 Cor. 5:8; 2 Tim. 4:6 [b]John 12:26

★25 [a]Phil. 2:24

Cross references (right margin):

26 [a]2 Cor. 5:12; 7:4; Phil. 2:16

27 [a]Eph. 4:1 [b]Phil. 1:5 [c]1 Cor. 16:13; Phil. 4:1 [d]Acts 4:32 [e]Jude 3

28 [a]2 Thess. 1:5

29 [a]Matt. 5:12 [b]Acts 14:22

★30 [a]Col. 1:29; 2:1; 1 Thess. 2:2; 1 Tim. 6:12; 2 Tim. 4:7; Heb. 10:32; 12:1 [Gr.] [b]Acts 16:19-40; Phil. 1:13

★1 [a]2 Cor. 13:14 [Gr.] [b]Col. 3:12

★2 [a]John 3:29 [b]Rom. 12:16; Phil. 4:2

3 [a]Rom. 2:8; Phil. 1:17 [b]Gal. 5:26 [c]Rom. 12:10; Eph. 5:21

1:18 Regardless of the motive (cf. v. 15), if Christ is preached, Paul rejoiced.

1:19 *my deliverance.* Paul's trial had probably begun. He was confident that either release or death would advance the cause of Christ (v. 20).

1:21 *to me, to live is Christ.* I.e., his life found all its meaning in Christ. *to die is gain.* Because then there will be union with Christ, without the limitations of this life.

1:25 Here Paul seems certain that he will be acquitted, but the only reason one can see for his momentary confidence is that he believed

that he was still needed on earth in the Lord's service.

1:30 The Philippians were in the same basic *conflict* he was in.

2:1 If men will count on Christ, they can do the things described in the following verses.

2:2 *make my joy complete.* I.e., they would cap off his pleasure if they would work together harmoniously and clear up their petty quarrels. Paul particularly had in mind the division caused by two women, Euodia and Syntyche (4:2).

humility of mind let ^ceach of you regard one another as more important than himself;

★ 4 ^aRom. 15:1f.

4 ^ado not *merely* look out for your own personal interests, but also for the interests of others.

B The Epitome of Humility, 2:5-11

★ **5-11**
5 ^aMatt. 11:29; Rom. 15:3 ^bPhil. 1:1

5 ^aHave this attitude in yourselves which was also in ^bChrist Jesus,

★ **6** ^aJohn 1:1 ^b2 Cor. 4:4 ^cJohn 5:18; 10:33; 14:28

6 who, although He ^aexisted in the ^bform of God, ^cdid not regard equality with God a thing to be grasped,

★ **7** ^a2 Cor. 8:9 ^bMatt. 20:28 ^cJohn 1:14; Rom. 8:3; Gal. 4:4; Heb. 2:17

7 but ^aemptied Himself, taking the form of a ^bbond-servant, *and* ^cbeing made in the likeness of men.

8 ^a2 Cor. 8:9 ^bMatt. 26:39; John 10:18; Rom. 5:19; Heb. 5:8 ^cHeb. 12:2

8 And being found in appearance as a man, ^aHe humbled Himself by becoming ^bobedient to the point of death, even ^cdeath on a cross.

★ **9** ^aHeb. 1:9 ^bMatt. 28:18; Acts 2:33; Heb. 2:9 ^cEph. 1:21

9 ^aTherefore also God ^bhighly exalted Him, and bestowed on Him ^cthe name which is above every name,

10 ^aRom. 14:11 ^bEph. 1:10

10 that at the name of Jesus ^aEVERY KNEE SHOULD BOW, of ^bthose who are in heaven, and on earth, and under the earth,

11 and that every tongue should confess that Jesus Christ is ^aLord, to the glory of God the Father.

11 ^aJohn 13:13; Rom. 10:9; 14:9

C The Exercise of Humility, 2:12-18

★**12-18**
12 ^aPhil. 1:5, 6; 4:15 ^bHeb. 5:9 ^c2 Cor. 7:15

12 So then, my beloved, ^ajust as you have always obeyed, not as in my presence only, but now much more in my absence, work out your ^bsalvation with ^cfear and trembling;

13 ^aRom. 12:3; 1 Cor. 12:6; 15:10; Heb. 13:21 ^bEph. 1:5

13 for it is ^aGod who is at work in you, both to will and to work ^bfor *His* good pleasure.

14 ^a1 Cor. 10:10; 1 Pet. 4:9

14 Do all things without ^agrumbling or disputing;

15 ^aLuke 1:6; Phil. 3:6 ^bMatt. 5:45; Eph. 5:1 ^cActs 2:40 ^dMatt. 24:27 ^eGen. 1:16

15 that you may prove yourselves to be ^ablameless and innocent, ^bchildren of God above reproach in the midst of a ^ccrooked and perverse generation, among whom you ^dappear as ^elights in the world,

16 ^aPhil. 1:6 ^bGal. 2:2 ^cIs. 49:4; Gal. 4:11; 1 Thess. 3:5

16 holding fast the word of life, so that in ^athe day of Christ I may have cause to glory because I did not ^brun in vain nor ^ctoil in vain.

17 ^a2 Cor. 12:15; 2 Tim. 4:6 ^bNum. 28:6, 7; Rom. 15:16

17 But even if I am being ^apoured out as a drink offering upon ^bthe sacrifice and service of

---

2:4 The church was apparently evidencing petty jealousies among members over honors and rewards. Paul commends humility and the right disposition that Christ Himself demonstrated and wants to give to His followers (v. 5).

2:5-11 This passage on the humility of Christ is the high mark of the epistle. Unlike the informal, conversational style of the rest of the letter, vv. 5-11 are highly polished. It is also noteworthy in that they convey in a few verses Paul's conception of the uniqueness of the person and work of Christ. Paul's point is that the disposition, the temper, of church members ought always to be that of Christ.

2:6 *the form of God.* Christ is the same nature and essence as God. *to be grasped.* The verse may be paraphrased: Who, though of the same nature as God, did not think this something to be exploited to His own advantage.

2:7 *emptied Himself.* The *kenosis* (emptying) of Christ during His incarnation does not mean that He surrendered any attributes of deity, but that He took on the limitations of

humanity. This involved a veiling of His preincarnate glory (John 17:5) and the voluntary waiving of some of His divine prerogatives during the time He was on earth (Matt. 24:36).

2:9 Through self-denial and obedience Christ won sovereignty over all peoples and things (v. 10).

2:12-18 Paul now turns to the obligations that the example of Christ lays on the Philippian Christians. They must learn to stand on their own feet, with a sense of human frailty, but knowing that God was behind them (v. 13). They should so live in corrupt human society that they would reflect the light that comes from a heavenly source (vv. 14-15), constantly proclaiming the gospel of the new life (v. 16a). Thus at Christ's coming Paul would have reason to rejoice in them (v. 16b). In vv. 17-18 Paul employed the language of the Jewish offerings and compares his death to a drink-offering which accompanied the Philippians' presentation of themselves as a burnt-offering (cf. Num. 15:10; 28:7).

your faith, I rejoice and share my joy with you all.

18 And you too, *I urge you,* rejoice in the same way and share your joy with me.

D The Examples of Timothy and Epaphroditus, 2:19-30

★19-30
19 *a*Phil. 2:23 *b*Phil. 1:1

19 But I hope in the Lord Jesus to *a*send *b*Timothy to you shortly, so that I also may be encouraged when I learn of your condition.

20 *a*1 Cor. 16:10; 2 Tim. 3:10

20 For I have no one *else* *a*of kindred spirit who will genuinely be concerned for your welfare.

21 *a*1 Cor. 10:24; 13:5; Phil. 2:4

21 For they all *a*seek after their own interests, not those of Christ Jesus.

22 *a*Rom. 5:4 [Gr.] *b*1 Cor. 16:10; 2 Tim. 3:10 *c*1 Cor. 4:17

22 But you know *a*of his proven worth that *b*he served with me in the furtherance of the gospel *c*like a child *serving* his father.

23 *a*Phil. 2:19

23 *a*Therefore I hope to send him immediately, as soon as I see how things *go* with me;

24 *a*Phil. 1:25

24 and *a*I trust in the Lord that I myself also shall be coming shortly.

25 *a*Phil. 4:18 *b*Rom. 16:3, 9, 21; Phil. 4:3; Philem. 1, 24 *c*Philem. 2 *d*John 13:16; 2 Cor. 8:23 *e*Phil. 4:18

25 But I thought it necessary to send to you *a*Epaphroditus, my brother and *b*fellow worker and *c*fellow soldier, who is also your *d*messenger and *e*minister to my need;

26 because he was longing for you all and was distressed because you had heard that he was sick.

27 For indeed he was sick to the point of death, but God had mercy on him, and not on him only but also on me, lest I should have sorrow upon sorrow.

28 Therefore I have sent him all the more eagerly in order that when you see him again you may rejoice and I may be less concerned *about you.*

29 *a*Rom. 16:2 *b*1 Cor. 16:18

29 Therefore *a*receive him in the Lord with all joy, and *b*hold men like him in high regard;

★30 *a*Acts 20:24 *b*1 Cor. 16:17; Phil. 4:10

30 because he came close to death *a*for the work of Christ, risking his life to *b*complete what was deficient in your service to me.

IV THE PRIZE OF THE CHRISTIAN LIFE: THE KNOWLEDGE OF CHRIST, 3:1-21

A The Warning against Judaizers, 3:1-3

★ 1 *a*Phil. 2:18; 4:4

3 Finally, my brethren, *a*rejoice in the Lord. To write the same things *again* is no trouble to me, and it is a safeguard for you.

★ 2 *a*Ps. 22:16, 20; Gal. 5:15; Rev. 22:15 *b*2 Cor. 11:13

2 Beware of the *a*dogs, beware of the *b*evil workers, beware of the false circumcision;

3 *a*Rom. 2:29; 9:6; Gal. 6:15 *b*Gal. 5:25 *c*Rom. 15:17; Gal. 6:14 *d*Rom. 8:39; Phil. 1:1; 3:12

3 for *a*we are the *true* circumcision, who *b*worship in the Spirit of God and *c*glory in *d*Christ Jesus and put no confidence in the flesh,

B The Example of Paul, 3:4-14

★ 4-14
4 *a*2 Cor. 5:16; 11:18

4 although *a*I myself might have confidence even in the flesh.

2:19-30 The letter now returns to personal matters. Paul was going to send Timothy later and send Epaphroditus then; and he wanted them to be accepted as his representative with his authority. No one *else* with him then, except Timothy, had the interest of Christ at heart (v. 21). Epaphroditus was a leader in the Philippian church whom Paul sent home with this letter (v. 25).

2:30 *close to death.* Epaphroditus was dangerously ill from overwork.

3:1 *the same things.* I.e., the content of vv. 2-3, a basic lesson which Paul as their teacher had undoubtedly gone over with them many times

while with them: Do not let Christianity be debased into some form of the Jewish ritualistic religion, obviously a danger then in Philippi.

3:2 Paul here becomes polemical. He labels the Judaizers (who taught that circumcision was necessary for salvation) *dogs* (a term they used to describe Gentiles), *evil workers,* and *false circumcision,* (which meant mutilators). All three epithets are directed at the same people.

3:4-14 Paul reflected on the whole course of his life, which gave him the right to criticize false Judaism.

If anyone else has a mind to put confidence in the flesh, I far more:

5 ^acircumcised the eighth day, of the ^bnation of Israel, of the ^ctribe of Benjamin, a ^bHebrew of Hebrews; as to the Law, ^da Pharisee;

6 as to zeal, ^aa persecutor of the church; as to the ^brighteousness which is in the Law, found ^cblameless.

7 But ^awhatever things were gain to me, those things I have counted as loss for the sake of Christ.

8 More than that, I count all things to be loss in view of the surpassing value of ^aknowing ^bChrist Jesus my Lord, for whom I have suffered the loss of all things, and count them but rubbish in order that I may gain Christ,

9 and may be found in Him, not having ^aa righteousness of my own derived from the Law, but that which is through faith in Christ, ^bthe righteousness which comes from God on the basis of faith,

10 that I may ^aknow Him, and ^bthe power of His resurrection and ^cthe fellowship of His sufferings, being ^dconformed to His death;

11 in order that I may ^aattain to the resurrection from the dead.

12 Not that I have already ^aobtained it, or have already ^bbecome perfect, but I press on in order that I may ^clay hold of that for which also I ^dwas laid hold of by ^eChrist Jesus.

13 Brethren, I do not regard myself as having laid hold of it yet; but one thing I do: ^aforgetting what lies behind and reaching forward to what lies ahead,

14 I ^apress on toward the goal for the prize of the ^bupward call of God in ^cChrist Jesus.

C The Exhortation to Others, 3:15–21

15 Let us therefore, as many as are ^aperfect, have this attitude; and if in anything you have a ^bdifferent attitude, ^cGod will reveal that also to you;

16 however, let us keep ^aliving by that same standard to which we have attained.

17 Brethren, ^ajoin in following my example, and observe those who walk according to the ^bpattern you have in us.

18 For ^amany walk, of whom I often told you, and now tell you even ^bweeping, that they are enemies of ^cthe cross of Christ,

19 whose end is destruction, whose god is their ^aappetite, and whose ^bglory is in their shame, who ^cset their minds on earthly things.

20 For ^aour citizenship is in heaven, from which also we eagerly ^bwait for a Savior, the Lord Jesus Christ;

21 who will ^atransform the body of our humble state into ^bconformity with the ^cbody of His glory, ^dby the exertion of the power that He has even to ^esubject all things to Himself.

Cross-reference column (left)

5 ^aLuke 1:59 ^bRom. 11:1; 2 Cor. 11:22 ^cRom. 11:1 ^dActs 22:3; 23:6; 26:5

6 ^aActs 8:3 ^bPhil. 3:9 ^cPhil. 2:15

7 ^aLuke 14:33

8 ^aJer. 9:23f.; John 17:3; Eph. 4:13; Phil. 3:10; 2 Pet. 1:3 ^bRom. 8:39; Phil. 1:1; 3:12

★ 9 ^aRom. 10:5; Phil. 3:6 ^bRom. 9:30; 1 Cor. 1:30

★10 ^aJer. 9:23f.; John 17:3; Eph. 4:13; Phil. 3:8; 2 Pet. 1:13 ^bRom. 6:5 ^cRom. 8:17 ^dRom. 6:5; 8:36; Gal. 6:17

11 ^aActs 26:7; 1 Cor. 15:23; Rev. 20:5f.

★12 ^a1 Cor. 9:24f.; 1 Tim. 6:12, 19 ^b1 Cor. 13:10 ^c1 Tim. 6:12, 19 ^dActs 9:5f.; ^eRom. 8:39; Phil. 1:1; 3:3, 8

13 ^aLuke 9:62

Cross-reference column (right)

14 ^a1 Cor. 9:24; Heb. 6:1 ^bRom. 8:28; 11:29; 2 Tim. 1:9 ^cPhil. 3:3

★15 ^aMatt. 5:48; 1 Cor. 2:6 ^bGal. 5:10 ^cJohn 6:45; Eph. 1:17; 1 Thess. 4:9

16 ^aGal. 6:16

17 ^a1 Cor. 4:16; Phil. 4:9 ^b1 Pet. 5:3

★18 ^a2 Cor. 11:13 ^bActs 20:31 ^cGal. 6:14

19 ^aRom. 16:18; Titus 1:12 ^bRom. 6:21; Jude 13 ^cRom. 8:5f.; Col. 3:2

★20 ^aEph. 2:19; Phil. 1:27; Col. 3:1; Heb. 12:22 ^b1 Cor. 1:7

★21 ^a1 Cor. 15:43-53 ^bRom. 8:29; Col. 3:4 ^c1 Cor. 15:43, 49 ^dEph. 1:19 ^e1 Cor. 15:28

3:9 Here Paul contrasts works-righteousness, which is based on the law, with faith-righteousness, which is from God through faith in Christ. Rom. 3:21–5:21 is a commentary on this truth.

3:10 *being conformed to His death* means becoming like Him in His death—passing through death into a new life, dying and rising with Christ (cf. Rom. 6).

3:12 Paul makes it clear that he had not "arrived" but was still very much in the race of life.

3:15 *perfect* = mature. In the latter half of the verse Paul says, in effect, "If you don't agree, God will give you light on the subject."

3:18 *enemies of the cross of Christ.* Evil living (by the libertines) is in view. Their principal concern was their *appetite* (v. 19); i.e., all sensual indulgences.

3:20 *citizenship.* This figure would have been particularly appreciated by the Philippians in view of their city's status as a Roman colony, whose inhabitants were Roman citizens.

3:21 *body of our humble state.* Our present state of mortality is a lowly one.

V THE PEACE OF THE CHRISTIAN LIFE: THE PRESENCE OF CHRIST, 4:1-23

A Peace with Others, 4:1-4

★ 1 *a*Phil. 1:8 *b*1 Cor. 16:13; Phil. 1:27

4 Therefore, my beloved brethren whom I *a*long *to see,* my joy and crown, so *b*stand firm in the Lord, my beloved.

2 *a*Phil. 2:2

2 I urge Euodia and I urge Syntyche to *a*live in harmony in the Lord.

★ 3 *a*Phil. 2:25 *b*Luke 10:20

3 Indeed, true comrade, I ask you also to help these women who have shared my struggle in *the cause of* the gospel, together with Clement also, and the rest of my *a*fellow workers, whose *b*names are in the book of life.

4 *a*Phil. 3:1

4 *a*Rejoice in the Lord always; again I will say, rejoice!

B Peace with Self, 4:5-9

5 *a*1 Cor. 16:22 marg.; Heb. 10:37; James 5:8f.

5 Let your forbearing *spirit* be known to all men. *a*The Lord is near.

6 *a*Matt. 6:25 *b*Eph. 6:18; 1 Tim. 2:1; 5:5

6 *a*Be anxious for nothing, but in everything by *b*prayer and supplication with thanksgiving let your requests be made known to God.

7 *a*Is. 26:3; John 14:27; Phil. 4:9; Col. 3:15 *b*Phil. 3:19 *c*1 Pet. 1:5 *d*2 Cor. 10:5 *e*Phil. 1:1; 4:19, 21

7 And *a*the peace of God, which *b*surpasses all comprehension, shall *c*guard your hearts and your *d*minds in *e*Christ Jesus.

★ 8 *a*Rom. 14:18; 1 Pet. 2:12

8 Finally, brethren, *a*whatever is true, whatever is honorable, whatever is right, whatever is pure, whatever is lovely, whatever is of good repute, if there is any excellence and if anything worthy of praise, let your mind dwell on these things.

9 *a*Phil. 3:17 *b*Rom. 15:33

9 The things you have learned and received and heard and seen *a*in me, practice these things; and *b*the God of peace shall be with you.

C Peace with Circumstances, 4:10-23

10 *a*2 Cor. 11:9; Phil. 2:30

10 But I rejoiced in the Lord greatly, that now at last *a*you have revived your concern for me; indeed, you were concerned *before,* but you lacked opportunity.

★11 *a*2 Cor. 9:8; 1 Tim. 6:6, 8; Heb. 13:5

11 Not that I speak from want; for I have learned to be *a*content in whatever circumstances I am.

12 *a*1 Cor. 4:11 *b*2 Cor. 11:9

12 I know how to get along with humble means, and I also know how to live in prosperity; in any and every circumstance I have learned the secret of being filled and going *a*hungry, both of having abundance and *b*suffering need.

13 *a*2 Cor. 12:9; Eph. 3:16; Col. 1:11

13 I can do all things through Him who *a*strengthens me.

★14 *a*Heb. 10:33; Rev. 1:9, [in Gr.]

14 Nevertheless, you have done well to *a*share *with me* in my affliction.

15 *a*Phil. 1:5 *b*Rom. 15:26 *c*2 Cor. 11:9

15 And you yourselves also know, Philippians, that at the *a*first preaching of the gospel, after I departed from *b*Macedonia, no church *c*shared with me in the matter of giving and receiving but you alone;

16 *a*Acts 17:1; 1 Thess. 2:9

16 for even in *a*Thessalonica you sent *a gift* more than once for my needs.

17 *a*1 Cor. 9:11f.; 2 Cor. 9:5

17 *a*Not that I seek the gift itself, but I seek for the profit which increases to your account.

18 *a*Phil. 2:25 *b*2 Cor. 2:14; Eph. 5:2

18 But I have received everything in full, and have an abundance; I am amply supplied, having received from *a*Epaphroditus what you have sent, *b*a fragrant aroma, an acceptable sacrifice, well-pleasing to God.

★19 *a*2 Cor. 9:8 *b*Rom. 2:4

19 And *a*my God shall supply all your needs according to His *b*riches in glory in Christ Jesus.

4:1 Here begins Paul's closing section, consisting first of practical advice followed by personal messages.

4:3 The identity of the *true comrade* is not revealed.

4:8 *honorable* = worthy of respect. *lovely* = winsome.

4:11 *content.* Lit., self-sufficient, independent of external circumstances. The secret of such contentment is found in v. 13.

4:14 *to share with me.* Paul refers to the sending of monetary gifts (vv. 10, 16).

4:19 The church that gives to missionaries will have its own needs supplied.

20 aGal. 1:4
bRom. 11:36

20 Now to aour God and Father bbe the glory forever and ever. Amen.

21 aGal. 1:2

21 Greet every saint in Christ Jesus. aThe brethren who are with me greet you.

22 aAll the bsaints greet you, especially those of Caesar's household.

23 aThe grace of the Lord Jesus Christ bbe with your spirit.

★22 a2 Cor. 13:13 bActs 9:13

23 aRom. 16:20
b2 Tim. 4:22

4:22 *Caesar's household.* Probably employees in the emperor's palace. There is no evidence of the conversion of a member of the imperial family until a generation later.

INTRODUCTION TO
THE EPISTLE OF PAUL TO THE COLOSSIANS

AUTHOR: Paul DATE: 61

The Church at Colossae *About 100 miles east of Ephesus, and near Laodicea and Hierapolis (4:13), Colossae was an ancient but declining commercial center. The gospel may have been taken there during Paul's ministry at Ephesus (Acts 19:10), though it was Epaphras who played the major role in the evangelism and growth of the Colossians. Paul was personally unacquainted with the believers there (2:1), but Epaphras either visited Paul in prison or was imprisoned with him (Philem. 23) and reported on conditions in this church.*

Place of Writing *Like Ephesians, Philippians, and Philemon, Colossians was written during Paul's first imprisonment in Rome (see the Introduction to Titus and the Introduction to Philippians for other suggestions as to the place of writing). The many personal references common to Colossians and Philemon and the many similarities of ideas in Colossians and Ephesians link these letters. Tychicus was apparently the bearer of the letter (Eph. 6:21; Col. 4:7).*

The Colossian Heresy *From Paul's counteremphases in the epistle, we can discern some of the features of the false teaching at Colossae. It was a syncretistic, fusing Jewish legalism, Greek philosophic speculation, and Oriental mysticism. Specifics included dietary and Sabbath observances and circumcision rites (2:11, 16), the worship of angels (2:18), and the practice of asceticism, which stemmed from the belief that the body was inherently evil (2:21-23). In combating this heresy, Paul emphasizes the cosmic significance of Christ as Lord of creation and Head of the Church. Any teaching, practice, or intermediary that detracts from the uniqueness and centrality of Christ, is against the faith.*

Contents *The theme is the supremacy and all-sufficiency of Christ. Important subjects include Christ's person and work (1:15-23), heresy (2:8-23), and believers' union with Christ (3:1-4).*

OUTLINE OF COLOSSIANS

THE LETTER OF PAUL TO THE COLOSSIANS

I INTRODUCTION, 1:1-14
A Greetings, 1:1-2

1 aPaul, ban apostle of Jesus Christ cby the will of God, and dTimothy our brother,

2 to the asaints and faithful brethren in Christ *who are* at Colossae: bGrace to you and peace from God our Father.

B Gratitude for the Colossians' Faith, 1:3-8

3 aWe give thanks to God, bthe Father of our Lord Jesus Christ, praying always for you,

4 asince we heard of your faith in Christ Jesus and the blove which you have for call the saints;

5 because of the ahope blaid up for you in heaven, of which you previously cheard in the word of truth, the gospel,

6 which has come to you, just as ain all the world also it is constantly bearing bfruit and increasing, even as *it has been doing* in you also since the day you cheard *of it* and understood the grace of God in truth;

7 just as you learned *it* from aEpaphras, our bbeloved fellow bond-servant, who is a faithful servant of Christ on our behalf,

8 and he also informed us of your alove in the Spirit.

C Prayer for the Colossians' Growth, 1:9-14

9 For this reason also, asince the day we heard *of it,* bwe have not ceased to pray for you and to ask that you may be filled with the cknowledge of His will in all spiritual dwisdom and understanding,

10 so that you may awalk in a manner worthy of the Lord, bto please *Him* in all respects, cbearing fruit in every good work and increasing in the knowledge of God;

11 astrengthened with all power, according to His glorious might, for the attaining of all steadfastness and patience; bjoyously

12 giving thanks to athe Father, who has qualified us to share in bthe inheritance of the saints in clight.

13 For He delivered us from the adomain of darkness, and transferred us to the kingdom of bHis beloved Son,

14 ain whom we have redemption, the forgiveness of sins.

II THE EXALTED CHRIST, 1:15-29
A Christ's Character, 1:15-23

15 And He is the aimage of the binvisible God, the cfirst-born of all creation.

16 For aby Him all things were created, a*both* in the heavens and on earth, visible and invisible, whether bthrones or dominions or rulers or authorities— call things have been created by Him and for Him.

17 And He ais before all

---

1 aPhil. 1:1
b2 Cor. 1:1
c1 Cor. 1:1
d2 Cor. 1:1
1 Thess. 3:2;
Philem. 1;
Heb. 13:23
2 aActs
9:13; Eph.
1:1; Phil. 1:1
bRom. 1:7;
Col. 4:18

3 aRom.
1:8 bRom.
15:6; 2 Cor.
1:3
★**4-5**
4 aEph.
1:15 bGal.
5:6 cEph.
6:18
5 aActs
23:6; Rom.
5:2; Col.
1:23;
1 Thess. 5:8;
Titus 1:2
b2 Tim. 4:8;
1 Pet. 1:4
cEph. 1:13;
Col. 1:6, 23
6 aRom.
10:18; Col.
1:23; 1 Tim.
3:16 bRom.
1:13 cEph.
4:21; Col. 1:5
★**7** aCol.
4:12; Philem.
23 bCol. 4:7

8 aRom.
15:30

9 aCol. 1:4
bEph. 1:16
cEph. 5:17;
Phil. 1:9
dEph. 1:17

★**10** aEph.
4:1; Col. 2:6
b2 Cor. 5:9;
Eph. 5:10
cRom. 1:13

★**11** a1 Cor.
16:13; Eph.
3:16 bEph.
4:2

12 aEph.
2:18 bActs
20:32 cActs
26:18; Eph.
6:12

★**13** aActs
26:18; Eph.
6:12 bMatt.
3:17; Eph.
1:6

★**14** aRom.
3:24; Eph.
1:7

★**15** a2 Cor.
4:4 bJohn
1:18; 1 Tim.
1:17; Heb.
11:27 cRom.
8:29; Col.
1:17f.
★**16** aEph.
1:10 bEph.
1:20f.; Col.
2:15 cJohn
1:3; Rom.
11:36; 1 Cor.
8:6
17 aJohn
1:1; 8:58

1:4-5 Notice the Colossian believers' triad of Christian graces: *faith, love,* and *hope* (cf. 1 Cor. 13:13).

1:7 *Epaphras* (see 4:12; Philem. 23). Apparently the man who evangelized the cities of the Lycus Valley and founded the churches of Colossae, Hierapolis, and Laodicea. It was his report, brought to Paul in Rome, about the condition of these churches that prompted the writing of this letter. The Epaphroditus of Phil. 2:25 and 4:18 is evidently a different individual.

1:10 *walk in a manner worthy of the Lord* = live a life worthy of the Lord.

1:11 *joyously.* This is what distinguishes the Christian's *steadfastness and patience* from the Stoic's.

1:13 *the kingdom of His beloved Son.* Lit., the kingdom of the Son of His love. Christians are already within the sphere of the new age.

1:14 *redemption.* See note on Eph. 1:7.

1:15 *the first-born of all creation.* I.e., the Son has all the rights belonging to the first-born, because of His preeminent position over all creation (v. 16).

1:16 *rulers or authorities.* See note on Eph. 1:21.

things, and in Him all things hold together.

★18 ᵃEph.
1:22 ᵇEph.
1:23; Col.
1:24; 2:19
ᶜRev. 3:14
ᵈActs 26:23

18 He is also ᵃhead of ᵇthe body, the church; and He is ᶜthe beginning, ᵈthe first-born from the dead; so that He Himself might come to have first place in everything.

★19 ᵃEph.
1:5 ᵇJohn
1:16

19 For it was ᵃthe *Father's* good pleasure for all ᵇthe fulness to dwell in Him,

★20 ᵃ2 Cor.
5:18; Eph.
2:16 ᵇRom.
5:1; Eph.
2:14 ᶜEph.
2:13 ᵈCol.
1:16

20 and through Him to ᵃreconcile all things to Himself, having made ᵇpeace through ᶜthe blood of His cross; through Him, *I say,* ᵈwhether things on earth or things in heaven.

21 ᵃRom.
5:10; Eph.
2:3, 12

21 And although you were ᵃformerly alienated and hostile in mind, *engaged* in evil deeds,

22 ᵃ2 Cor.
5:18; Eph.
2:16 ᵇRom.
7:4 ᶜEph.
5:27; Col.
1:28 ᵈEph.
1:4

22 yet He has now ᵃreconciled you in His fleshly ᵇbody through death, in order to ᶜpresent you before Him ᵈholy and blameless and beyond reproach—

23 ᵃEph.
3:17; Col. 2:7
ᵇCol. 1:5
ᶜMark 16:15;
Acts 2:5; Col.
1:6 ᵈEph.
3:7; Col. 1:25
ᵉ1 Cor. 3:5

23 if indeed you continue in the faith firmly ᵃestablished and steadfast, and not moved away from the ᵇhope of the gospel that you have heard, which was proclaimed ᶜin all creation under heaven, ᵈand of which I, Paul, was made a ᵉminister.

B   Christ's Commission to Paul, 1:24-29

★24 ᵃRom.
8:17; 2 Cor.
1:5; 12:15;
Phil. 2:17
ᵇ2 Tim. 1:8;
2:10 ᶜCol.
1:18

24 ᵃNow I rejoice in my sufferings for your sake, and in my flesh ᵇI do my share on behalf of ᶜHis body (which is the church) in filling up that which is lacking in Christ's afflictions.

★25 ᵃCol.
1:23 ᵇEph.
3:2

25 ᵃOf *this church* I was made a minister according to the ᵇstewardship from God bestowed on me for your benefit, that I might

fully carry out the *preaching of* the word of God,

★26 ᵃRom.
16:25f.; Eph.
3:3f.; Col.
2:2, 4:3

26 *that is,* ᵃthe mystery which has been hidden from the *past* ages and generations; but has now been manifested to His saints,

27 ᵃMatt.
13:11 ᵇEph.
1:7, 18; 3:16
ᶜRom. 8:10
ᵈ1 Tim. 1:1

27 to whom ᵃGod willed to make known what is ᵇthe riches of the glory of this mystery among the Gentiles, which is ᶜChrist in you, the ᵈhope of glory.

28 ᵃActs
20:31; Col.
3:16 ᵇ1 Cor.
2:6f.; Col. 2:3
ᶜCol. 1:22
ᵈMatt. 5:48;
Eph. 4:13

28 And we proclaim Him, ᵃadmonishing every man and teaching every man with all ᵇwisdom, that we may ᶜpresent every man ᵈcomplete in Christ.

29 ᵃ1 Cor.
15:10 ᵇCol.
2:1; 4:12
ᶜEph. 1:19;
Col. 2:12

29 And for this purpose also I ᵃlabor, ᵇstriving ᶜaccording to His power, which mightily works within me.

III   THE EXALTED CHRISTIANITY, 2:1-23

A   Exalted over Philosophy, 2:1-10

1 ᵃCol.
1:29; 4:12
ᵇCol. 4:13,
15f.; Rev.
1:11

2 For I want you to know how great a ᵃstruggle I have on your behalf, and for those who are at ᵇLaodicea, and for all those who have not personally seen my face,

2 ᵃ1 Cor.
14:31; Eph.
6:22; Col. 4:8
ᵇCol. 2:19
ᶜEph. 1:7,
18; 3:16
ᵈLuke 1:1
[Gr.] ᵉMatt.
13:11 ᶠRom.
16:25f.; Col.
3:3f.; Col.
1:26; 4:3

2 that their ᵃhearts may be encouraged, having been ᵇknit together in love, and *attaining* to all ᶜthe wealth that comes from the ᵈfull assurance of understanding, *resulting* in a ᵉtrue knowledge of ᶠGod's mystery, *that is,* Christ Himself,

3 ᵃIs. 11:2;
Rom. 11:33

3 in whom are hidden all ᵃthe treasures of wisdom and knowledge.

4 ᵃEph.
4:17 ᵇRom.
16:18

4 ᵃI say this in order that no one may delude you with ᵇpersuasive argument.

1:18 *the church.* See note on Eph. 1:22-23. *the first-born from the dead.* I.e., the first one to rise from the dead with a resurrection body (Rev. 1:5).

1:19 *all the fulness.* The full essence (powers and attributes) of deity dwells in Christ (see 2:9).

1:20 *to reconcile all things to Himself.* Christ is the remedy for alienation from God, and eventually all things will be changed and

brought into a unity in Him, even though this will involve judgment (1 Cor. 15:24-28).

1:24 Because of the union of believers with Christ, Paul's *sufferings* for the sake of the church can be called Christ's *afflictions* as well.

1:25 *the stewardship,* assignment, office (1 Cor. 4:1).

1:26 *the mystery.* The secret known only by divine revelation of the indwelling of Christ (see note on Eph. 3:3).

5 a1 Cor.
5:3 b1 Cor.
14:40 c1 Pet.
5:9

5 For even though I am *absent in body, nevertheless I am with you in spirit, rejoicing to see your *good discipline and the *stability of your faith in Christ.

★ 6 aGal.
3:26 bCol.
1:10

6 As you therefore have received *Christ Jesus the Lord, so *walk in Him,

7 aEph.
3:17 b1 Cor.
3:9; Eph.
2:20 c1 Cor.
1:8 dEph.
4:21

7 having been firmly *rooted *and now being *built up in Him and *established in your faith, just as you *were instructed, *and overflowing with gratitude.

★ 8 a1 Cor.
8:9; 10:12;
Gal. 5:15;
Heb. 3:12
bEph. 5:6;
Col. 2:23;
1 Tim. 6:20
cGal. 4:3;
Col. 2:20

8 *See to it that no one takes you captive through *philosophy and empty deception, according to the tradition of men, according to the *elementary principles of the world, rather than according to Christ.

★ 9 a2 Cor.
5:19; Col.
1:19
10 aEph.
3:19 bEph.
1:21f.
c1 Cor.
15:24; Eph.
3:10; Col.
2:15

9 For in Him all the *fulness of Deity dwells in bodily form,

10 and in Him you have been *made complete, and *He is the head over all *rule and authority;

★11-12
11 aRom.
2:29; Eph.
2:11 bRom.
6:6; 7:24;
Gal. 5:24;
Col. 3:5
12 aRom.
6:4f. bRom.
6:5; Eph. 2:6;
Col. 2:13; 3:1
cActs 2:24

B Exalted over Legalism, 2:11-17

11 and in Him *you were also circumcised with a circumcision made without hands, in the removal of *the body of the flesh by the circumcision of Christ;

12 having been *buried with Him in baptism, in which you

were also *raised up with Him through faith in the working of God, who *raised Him from the dead.

13 And when you were *dead in your transgressions and the uncircumcision of your flesh, He *made you alive together with Him, having forgiven us all our transgressions,

14 having canceled out *the certificate of debt consisting of decrees against us *and which was hostile to us; and *He has taken it out of the way, having nailed it to the cross.

15 When He had *disarmed the *rulers and authorities, He *made a public display of them, having *triumphed over them through Him.

16 Therefore let no one *act as your judge in regard to *food or *drink or in respect to a *festival or a *new moon or a *Sabbath day—

17 things which are *a *mere* shadow of what is to come; but the substance belongs to Christ.

C Exalted over Mystical Teaching, 2:18-19

18 Let no one keep *defrauding you of your prize by *delighting in self-abasement and the

13 aEph. 2:1
bEph. 2:1, 5;
Col. 2:12

★14 aEph.
2:15; Col.
2:20 b1 Pet.
2:24

★15 aEph.
4:8 b1 Cor.
15:24; Eph.
3:10; Col.
2:10 cIs.
53:12; Matt.
12:29; Luke
10:18; John
12:31; Eph.
4:8 d2 Cor.
2:14 [Gr.]
★16 aRom.
14:3 bMark
7:19; Rom.
14:17; Heb.
9:10 cLev.
23:2; Rom.
14:5 d1 Chr.
23:31; 2 Chr.
31:3; Neh.
10:33 eMark
2:27f.; Gal.
4:10f.
17 aHeb.
8:5; 10:1

★18 a1 Cor.
9:24; Phil.
3:14 bCol.
2:23 c1 Cor.
4:6 dRom.
8:7

2:6 *As . . . so.* Just as Christ is received by faith, the believer is also to walk (live) by faith, acknowledging the Lordship of Christ over his life (2 Cor. 5:7).

2:8 *empty deception.* Paul's belittlement of the Colossian "philosophy." *according to the elementary principles* after the elemental spirits of the universe; i.e., the cosmic spirits of Hellenistic syncretism. Apparently their philosophy involved regulating their religious life by observing the movements of the stars, which they associated with the powers of the angels who were worshiped by some (v. 18). In this passage Paul uses the vocabulary of the heretics, giving the words their proper meaning. He confutes them with their own terms (e.g., *complete*, 1:28; *mystery*, 2:2; *wisdom and knowledge*, 2:3; *elementary principles of the world*, 2:8; *head*, 2:10).

2:9 In Jesus Christ, deity (the divine attributes and nature) dwelt in His earthly body—a strong statement of the deity and humanity of

the God-man.

2:11-12 *removal of the body of the flesh* (the old nature, which is corrupt in its unregenerate state of rebellion against God) is illustrated in the rite of circumcision and the ordinance of baptism, but is accomplished by a spiritual circumcision and Spirit baptism.

2:14 *certificate of debt* = an acknowledgment of debt in the handwriting of the debtor. The Mosaic law (which Paul's phrase symbolizes) put us in debt to God with sin; this debt He has canceled by nailing it to the cross of Christ. Christ has made full payment.

2:15 *disarmed.* Lit., stripped (as was done to enemies).

2:16 False teachers were evidently insisting on abstinence from certain foods and observance of certain days. These, Paul says, are shadows which have been dispersed by the coming of Christ (v. 17).

2:18 Some were also teaching a false humility and the worship of angels as proper, claiming

worship of the angels, taking his stand on *visions* he has seen, ^cinflated without cause by his ^dfleshly mind,

19 and not holding fast to ^athe head, from whom ^bthe entire body, being supplied and held together by the joints and ligaments, grows with a growth which is from God.

19 ^aEph. 1:22 ^bEph. 1:23; 4:16

D Exalted over Asceticism, 2:20-23

★**20-23**
20 ^aRom. 6:2 ^bCol. 2:8 ^cGal. 4:9 ^dCol. 2:14, 16

20 ^aIf you have died with Christ to the ^belementary principles of the world, ^cwhy, as if you were living in the world, do you submit yourself to ^ddecrees, such as,

21 "Do not handle, do not taste, do not touch!"

22 ^a1 Cor. 6:13 ^bIs. 29:13; Matt. 15:9; Titus 1:14

22 (which all *refer* ^a*to* things destined to perish with the using)—in accordance with the ^bcommandments and teachings of men?

23 ^aCol. 2:18 ^b1 Tim. 4:3 ^cRom. 13:14; 1 Tim. 4:8

23 These are matters which have, to be sure, the appearance of wisdom in ^aself-made religion and self-abasement and ^bsevere treatment of the body, *but are* of no value against ^cfleshly indulgence.

IV THE EXALTED CALLING, 3:1-4:6
A The Certainties of Our Calling, 3:1-4

★ **1** ^aCol. 2:12 ^bMark 16:19

3 If then you have been ^araised up with Christ, keep seeking

the things above, where Christ is, ^bseated at the right hand of God.

2 ^aSet your mind on the things above, not on the things that are on earth.

2 ^aMatt. 16:23; Phil. 3:19, 20

3 For you have ^adied and your life is hidden with Christ in God.

3 ^aRom. 6:2; 2 Cor. 5:14; Col. 2:20

4 When Christ, ^awho is our life, is revealed, ^bthen you also will be revealed with Him in glory.

4 ^aJohn 11:25; Gal. 2:20 ^b1 Cor. 1:7; Phil. 3:21; 1 Pet. 1:13; 1 John 2:28; 3:2

B The Characteristics of Our Calling, 3:5-4:6
1 In everyday life, 3:5-17

5 ^aTherefore consider ^bthe members of your earthly body as dead to ^cimmorality, impurity, passion, evil desire, and greed, which amounts to idolatry.

5 ^aRom. 8:13 ^bCol. 2:11 ^cMark 7:21f.; 1 Cor. 6:9f., 18; 2 Cor. 12:21; Gal. 5:19; Eph. 4:19; 5:3, 5

6 For it is on account of these things that ^athe wrath of God will come,

6 ^aRom. 1:18; Eph. 5:6

7 and ^ain them you also once walked, when you were living in them.

7 ^aEph. 2:2

8 But now you also, ^aput them all aside: ^banger, wrath, malice, slander, *and* ^cabusive speech from your mouth.

8 ^aEph. 4:22 ^bEph. 4:31 ^cEph. 4:29

9 ^aDo not lie to one another, since you ^blaid aside the old self with its *evil* practices,

★ **9** ^aEph. 4:25 ^bEph. 4:22

10 and have ^aput on the new self who is being ^brenewed to a true knowledge ^caccording to the image of the One who ^dcreated him

★**10** ^aEph. 4:24 ^bRom. 12:2; 2 Cor. 4:16; Eph. 4:23 ^cRom. 8:29 ^dEph. 2:10

11 —a *renewal* in which ^athere is no *distinction between*

★**11** ^aRom. 10:12; 1 Cor. 12:13; Gal. 3:28 ^b1 Cor. 7:19; Gal. 5:6 ^cActs 28:2 ^dEph. 6:8 ^eEph. 1:23

---

special mystic insights by way of visions *(taking his stand on visions he has seen).* The basic problem was their egoistic or *fleshly mind.*
2:20-23 Christ had freed them from the taboos of asceticism, which can only give a pretense of wisdom, promote a self-made religion, and deal severely with the body. Yet it cannot succeed in combating the desires of the flesh.
3:1 Here begins the ethical section of the letter. Paul's appeal is simple: Become in experience what you already are by God's grace. The Christian is risen with Christ; let him exhibit that new life.
3:9 *the old self.* I.e., the old nature, the predisposition to leave God out of one's life and ac-

tions, which characterized the unregenerate state.
3:10 *the new self.* I.e., the new nature, or disposition, received when one is saved, with which one may serve God and righteousness (Rom. 6:18). Continual renewing is necessary, however, in order that the new life may have full dominion over moral conduct.
3:11 *barbarian.* At this time the word was applied to those who did not speak Greek or had not adopted Greek culture. *Scythian* represents the lowest type of uncouth barbarian nomads of southern Russia. In Christ, distinctions of race, class, and culture are transcended.

Greek and Jew, [b]circumcised and uncircumcised, [c]barbarian, Scythian, [d]slave and freeman, but [e]Christ is all, and in all.

12 And so, as those who have been [a]chosen of God, holy and beloved, [b]put on a [c]heart of compassion, kindness, [d]humility, gentleness and [e]patience;

13 [a]bearing with one another, and [b]forgiving each other, whoever has a complaint against anyone; [b]just as the Lord forgave you, so also should you.

14 And beyond all these things *put on* love, which is [a]the perfect bond of [b]unity.

15 And let [a]the peace of Christ rule in your hearts, to which indeed you were called in [b]one body; and be thankful.

16 Let [a]the word of Christ richly dwell within you, with all wisdom [b]teaching and admonishing one another [c]with psalms *and* hymns *and* spiritual songs, [d]singing with thankfulness in your hearts to God.

17 And [a]whatever you do in word or deed, *do* all in the name of the Lord Jesus, [b]giving thanks through Him to God the Father.

2 In the home, 3:18-21

18 [a]Wives, [b]be subject to your husbands, as is fitting in the Lord.

19 [a]Husbands, love your wives, and do not be embittered against them.

20 [a]Children, be obedient to your parents in all things, for this is well-pleasing to the Lord.

21 [a]Fathers, do not exasperate your children, that they may not lose heart.

3 In servant-master relationships, 3:22-4:1

22 [a]Slaves, in all things obey those who are your masters on earth, [b]not with external service, as those who *merely* please men, but with sincerity of heart, fearing the Lord.

23 Whatever you do, do your work heartily, [a]as for the Lord rather than for men;

24 [a]knowing that from the Lord you will receive the reward of [b]the inheritance. It is the Lord Christ whom you [c]serve.

25 For [a]he who does wrong will receive the consequences of the wrong which he has done, and [b]that without partiality.

4 Masters, grant to your slaves justice and fairness, knowing that you too have a Master in heaven.

4 In prayer, 4:2-4

2 [a]Devote yourselves to prayer, keeping alert in it with *an attitude of* thanksgiving;

3 praying at the same time [a]for us as well, that God may open up to us a [b]door for [c]the word, so that we may speak forth [d]the mystery of Christ, for which I have also [e]been imprisoned;

4 in order that I may make it clear [a]in the way I ought to speak.

5 In witness and speech, 4:5-6

5 [a]Conduct yourselves with wisdom toward [b]outsiders, [c]making the most of the opportunity.

6 [a]Let your speech always be with grace, seasoned, *as it were,* with [b]salt, so that you may know

---

Reference column (left):

12 [a]Luke 18:7 [b]Eph. 4:24 [c]Luke 1:78; Gal. 5:22f.; Phil. 2:1 [d]Eph. 4:2; Phil. 2:3 [e]1 Cor. 13:4; 2 Cor. 6:6
13 [a]Eph. 4:2 [b]Rom. 15:7; Eph. 4:32
14 [a]Eph. 4:3 [b]John 17:23; Heb. 6:1
15 [a]John 14:27 [b]Eph. 2:16
★16 [a]Rom. 10:17; Eph. 5:26; 1 Thess. 1:8 [b]Eph. 5:19; Col. 1:28 [c]Eph. 5:19 [d]1 Cor. 14:15
17 [a]1 Cor. 10:31 [b]Eph. 5:20; Col. 3:15
18 [a]Col. 3:18-4:1; Eph. 5:22-6:9 [b]Eph. 5:22
★19 [a]Eph. 5:25
20 [a]Eph. 6:1
21 [a]Eph. 6:4

Reference column (right):

22 [a]Eph. 6:5 [b]Eph. 6:6
23 [a]Eph. 6:7
24 [a]Eph. 6:8 [b]Acts 20:32; 1 Pet. 1:4 [c]1 Cor. 7:22
★25 [a]Eph. 6:8 [b]Acts 10:34; Eph. 6:9
2 [a]Acts 1:14; Eph. 6:18
★ 3 [a]Eph. 6:19 [b]Acts 14:27 [c]2 Tim. 4:2 [d]Eph. 3:3, 4; 6:19 [e]Eph. 6:20
4 [a]Eph. 6:20
★ 5 [a]Eph. 5:15 [b]Mark 4:11 [c]Eph. 5:16
★ 6 [a]Eph. 4:29 [b]Mark 9:50 [c]1 Pet. 3:15

3:16 The *psalms and hymns and spiritual songs* must be those which teach and admonish.
3:19 *Husbands.* See note on Eph. 5:25.
3:25 *without partiality.* God will show no favoritism, either for the unfaithful slave or for the unjust master (4:1).
4:3 *a door for the word.* I.e., an opportunity to *speak . . . the mystery.*
4:5 *outsiders.* I.e., those who are not Christians,

but pagans. The division between them was sharp; the church was the community and all others were shut-out unbelievers.
4:6 *seasoned . . . with salt.* Salt is a preservative that retards spoilage. Our speech should be tempered so as never to be insipid, corrupt, or obscene. *each person.* I.e., those that are without.

how you should ᶜrespond to each person.

V CONCLUDING PERSONAL REMARKS, 4:7-18

★ 7 ᵃCol.
4:7-9. Eph.
6:21, 22
ᵇActs 20:4
ᶜEph. 6:21.
Col. 1:7

7 ᵃAs to all my affairs, ᵇTychicus, *our* ᶜbeloved brother and faithful servant and fellow bond-servant in the Lord, will bring you information.

8 ᵃFor I have sent him to you for this very purpose, that you may know *about* our circumstances and that he may ᵇencourage your hearts;

9 and with him ᵃOnesimus, *our* faithful and ᵇbeloved brother, ᶜwho is one of your *number.* They will inform you about the whole situation here.

★10 ᵃActs
19:29 ᵇRom.
16:7 ᶜActs
4:36, 12:12;
15:37, 39
ᵈ2 Tim. 4:11

10 ᵃAristarchus, my ᵇfellow prisoner, sends you his greetings; and *also* ᶜBarnabas' cousin Mark (about whom you received instructions: ᵈif he comes to you, welcome him);

11 and *also* Jesus who is called Justus; these are the only ᵃfellow workers for the kingdom of God ᵇwho are from the circumcision; and they have proved to be an encouragement to me.

12 ᵃEpaphras, ᵇwho is one of your number, a bondslave of Jesus Christ, sends you his greetings, always ᶜlaboring earnestly for you in his prayers, that you may stand ᵈperfect and ᵉfully assured in all the will of God.

12 ᵃCol. 1:7
ᵇCol. 4:9
ᶜRom. 15:30
ᵈCol. 1:28
ᵉLuke 1:1
and marg.

13 For I bear him witness that he has a deep concern for you and for those who are in ᵃLaodicea and Hierapolis.

14 ᵃLuke, the beloved physician, sends you his greetings, and *also* ᵇDemas.

15 Greet the brethren who are in ᵃLaodicea and also Nympha and ᵇthe church that is in her house.

16 And ᵃwhen this letter is read among you, have it also read in the church of the Laodiceans; and you, for your part ᵃread my letter *that is coming* from ᵇLaodicea.

★16
ᵃ1 Thess.
5:27;
2 Thess. 3:14
ᵇCol. 2:1;
4:13, 15

17 And say to ᵃArchippus, "Take heed to the ᵇministry which you have received in the Lord, that you may fulfill it."

18 I, Paul, ᵃwrite this greeting with my own hand. ᵇRemember my ᶜimprisonment. ᵈGrace be with you.

18 ᵃ1 Cor.
16:21 ᵇHeb.
13:3 ᶜPhil.
1:7; Col. 4:3
ᵈ1 Tim. 6:21;
2 Tim. 4:22;
Titus 3:15;
Heb. 13:25

4:7 *Tychicus.* One of the bearers of this letter (Acts 20:4).

4:9 *Onesimus.* See the Introduction to Philemon.

4:10 *Aristarchus.* See Acts 19:29; 20:4; 27:2. *Mark,* the author of the second Gospel. He had been restored to Paul's favor after his lapse on the first missionary journey (Acts 15:36-39).

4:11 *Jesus who is called Justus.* Nothing else is known of him.

4:14 *Luke.* The author of the third Gospel. *Demas.* A helper who later defected (2 Tim. 4:10).

4:15 *the church that is in her house.* See note on Rom. 16:5.

4:16 *my letter . . . from Laodicea.* Some think this is the circular letter Ephesians.

4:17 *Archippus.* See Philem. 2.

INTRODUCTION TO
THE FIRST LETTER OF PAUL TO THE THESSALONIANS

Author: Paul   Date: 51

The Work at Thessalonica *Paul, Silas, and Timothy first went to the Macedonian port city of Thessalonica on the second missionary journey (Acts 17:1-14). This was the second place the gospel was preached in Europe, Philippi being the first. Because the preaching of the gospel depleted the ranks of the synagogue, the Jews charged Paul's host, Jason, with harboring traitors to Caesar. The rulers of the city took Jason as security (like a peace bond) and let the missionaries leave the city. When they arrived in Athens, Paul sent Timothy back to Thessalonica (1 Thess. 3:1-2, 5) to encourage the believers and then to report back on the condition of the church there. Timothy rejoined Paul in Corinth (3:6), where the two Thessalonian letters were written.*

Some feel that Paul was in Thessalonica less than a month (only three Sabbaths are mentioned in Acts 17:2). He must, however, have had an extended ministry outside the synagogue and the Jewish community, since the church was largely Gentile (see under 1 Thess. 1:9). In any case, he was concerned about his departing under pressure and about having to leave the church without experienced leadership. Timothy's report gave Paul cause only for praise for the healthy state of the church. This is a letter from a relieved and grateful pastor to his growing flock.

Purpose *In addition (1) to expressing his thankfulness, Paul (2) defended himself against a campaign to slander his ministry which asserted that it was done only for profit (2:9-10); (3) encouraged the new converts to stand not only against persecution but also against the pressure to revert to their former pagan standards (3:2-3; 4:1-12); (4) answered the question about what happens to Christians who die before the return of the Lord (4:13-18); and finally (5) discussed some problems in their church life which needed to be dealt with (5:12-13, 19-20).*

Contents *The key passages in this letter are eschatological; that is, related to events of the last days, such as the rapture of the Church (4:13-18) and the day of the Lord (5:1-11).*

OUTLINE OF 1 THESSALONIANS

THE FIRST LETTER OF PAUL TO THE THESSALONIANS

I PERSONAL AND HISTORICAL, 1:1–3:13

A Paul's Greeting, 1:1

1 [a]Paul and [b]Silvanus and [c]Timothy to the [d]church of the Thessalonians in God the Father and the Lord Jesus Christ: [e]Grace to you and peace.

B Paul's Commendation of the Thessalonians, 1:2–10

2 [a]We give thanks to God always for all of you, [b]making mention of you in our prayers;
3 constantly bearing in mind your [a]work of faith and labor of [b]love and [c]steadfastness of hope in our Lord Jesus Christ in the presence of [d]our God and Father,
4 knowing, [a]brethren beloved by God, [b]His choice of you;
5 for our [a]gospel did not come to you in word only, but also [b]in power and in the Holy Spirit and with [c]full conviction; just as you know [d]what kind of men we proved to be among you for your sake.
6 You also became [a]imitators of us and of the Lord, [b]having received [c]the word in much tribulation with the [d]joy of the Holy Spirit,

7 so that you became an example to all the believers in [a]Macedonia and in [b]Achaia.
8 For [a]the word of the Lord has [b]sounded forth from you, not only in [c]Macedonia and [d]Achaia, but also [e]in every place your faith toward God has gone forth, so that we have no need to say anything.
9 For they themselves report about us what kind of a [a]reception we had with you, and how you [b]turned to God [c]from idols to serve [d]a living and true God,
10 and to [a]wait for His Son from heaven, whom He [b]raised from the dead, that is Jesus, who [c]delivers us from [d]the wrath to come.

C Paul's Conduct among the Thessalonians, 2:1–12

1 His uprightness, 2:1–4

2 For you yourselves know, brethren, that our [a]coming to you [b]was not in vain,
2 but after we had already suffered and been [a]mistreated in [b]Philippi, as you know, we had the boldness in our God [c]to speak to you the [d]gospel of God amid much [e]opposition.

★ 1 [a]2 Thess. 1:1 [b]2 Cor. 1:19 [c]Acts 16:1 [2 Thess. 1:1] [d]Acts 17:1; 2 Thess. 1:1 [e]Rom. 1:7 **2** [a]Rom. 1:8; Eph. 5:20; 1 Thess. 2:13; 2 Thess. 1:3 [b]Rom. 1:9 **3** [a]John 6:29; Gal. 5:6; 2 Thess. 1:11 [b]1 Cor. 13:13; 1 Thess. 3:6; 2 Thess. 1:3f. [c]Rom. 8:25; 15:4 [d]Gal. 1:4 **★ 4** [a]Rom. 1:7; 2 Thess. 2:13 [b]Rom. 9:11; 2 Pet. 1:10 **★ 5** [a]1 Cor. 9:14; 2 Cor. 2:12; 1 Thess. 2:2, 4, 8f.; 3:2; 2 Thess. 2:14 [b]Rom. 15:19; 1 Cor. 2:4; 2 Cor. 6:6 [c]Luke 1:1 [Gr.]; Col. 2:2 [d]1 Thess. 2:10 **★ 6** [a]1 Cor. 4:16; 11:1f. [b]Acts 17:5-10 [c]2 Tim. 4:2 [d]Acts 13:52; 2 Cor. 6:10; Gal. 5:22

★ 7 [a]Rom. 15:26 [b]Acts 18:12 **8** [a]Col. 3:16; 2 Thess. 3:1 [b]Rom. 10:18 [c]Rom. 15:26 [d]Acts 18:12 [e]Rom. 1:8; 16:19; 2 Cor. 2:14 **★ 9** [a]1 Thess. 2:1 [b]Acts 14:15 [c]1 Cor. 12:2 [d]Matt. 16:16 **★10** [a]Matt. 16:27f.; 1 Cor. 1:7 [b]Acts 2:24 [c]Rom. 5:9 [d]Matt. 3:7; 1 Thess. 2:16; 5:9

★ 1 [a]1 Thess. 1:9 [b]2 Thess. 1:10 **★ 2** [a]Acts 14:5; Phil. 1:30 [b]Acts 16:22-24 [c]Acts 17:1-9 [d]Rom. 1:1 [e]Phil. 1:30

1:1 *Silvanus* = Silas, who replaced Barnabas on the second missionary journey (Acts 15:22–18:5).

1:4 *His choice.* In relation to believers, God's choosing is sovereign (Rom. 9:11), it is pretemporal (Eph. 1:4), it is for salvation (2 Thess. 2:13), and it is proved by the fruits which accompany salvation (1 Thess. 1:5; Col. 3:12).

1:5 *what kind of men.* Paul elaborates on this in 2:3–12.

1:6 *imitators* (see 1 Cor. 4:16; 11:1). The Thessalonian Christians imitated the Lord and the apostles in that they responded to the gospel in spite of affliction.

1:7 *an example* = pattern or model. *Macedonia* was the northern province of Greece; *Achaia*, the southern.

1:9 *they themselves.* I.e., people everywhere

gave testimony to the conversion of the Thessalonians. *turned to God from idols.* This church was comprised largely of converts from pagan religions and not from Judaism (see also 2:14–16). The last part of this verse and v. 10 summarize the message Paul, Silvanus, and Timothy preached. *to serve,* as bond-slaves. *a living* (in contrast to lifeless idols) *and true God* (not false gods).

1:10 *to wait.* The Christian's hope of the return of Christ is rooted in the fact that He was *raised from the dead. who delivers* = the Deliverer. *the wrath to come.* I.e., the judgments to come (5:9; Rev. 6:16).

2:1 This verse builds on 1:5. *not in vain* = not without results. Paul returns to this subject in v. 13, after reviewing his ministry (vv. 1–12).

2:2 *in Philippi.* The account is in Acts 16:12–40.

★ 3 aActs
13:15
b2 Thess.
2:11
c1 Thess.
4:7 d2 Cor.
4:2
4 a2 Cor.
2:17 bGal.
2:7 cGal.
1:10 dRom.
8:27

3 For our aexhortation does not *come* from berror or cimpurity or by way of ddeceit;

4 abut just as we have been approved by God to be bentrusted with the gospel, so we speak, cnot as pleasing men but God, who dexamines our hearts.

2   His industry, 2:5-9

★ 5 aActs
20:33; 2 Pet.
2:3 bRom.
1:9; 1 Thess.
2:10

5 For we never came with flattering speech, as you know, nor with aa pretext for greed— bGod is witness—

★ 6 aJohn
5:41, 44;
2 Cor. 4:5
b1 Cor. 9:1f.

6 nor did we aseek glory from men, either from you or from others, even though as bapostles of Christ we might have asserted our authority.

7 a2 Tim.
2:24 bGal.
4:19;
1 Thess. 2:11

7 But we proved to be agentle among you, bas a nursing *mother* tenderly cares for her own children.

★ 8 a2 Cor.
12:15;
1 John 3:16
bRom. 1:1

8 Having thus a fond affection for you, we were wellpleased to aimpart to you not only the bgospel of God but also our own lives, because you had become very dear to us.

9 aPhil.
4:16;
2 Thess. 3:8
bActs 18:3
c1 Cor. 9:4f.;
2 Cor. 11:9
dRom. 1:1

9 For you recall, brethren, our alabor and hardship, *how* bworking night and day so as not to be a cburden to any of you, we proclaimed to you the dgospel of God.

3   His blameless behavior, 2:10-12

10 a1 Thess.
2:5 b2 Cor.
1:12;
1 Thess. 1:5

10 You are witnesses, and *so is* aGod, bhow devoutly and uprightly and blamelessly we behaved toward you believers;

11 just as you know how we *were* aexhorting and encouraging and bimploring each one of you as ca father *would* his own children,

12 so that you may awalk in a manner worthy of the God who bcalls you into His own kingdom and cglory.

D   Paul's Concern for the Thessalonians, 2:13-3:13

1   For their sufferings, 2:13-20

13 And for this reason we also constantly athank God that when you received from us the bword of God's message, you accepted *it* cnot *as* the word of men, but *for* what it really is, the word of God, dwhich also performs its work in you who believe.

14 For you, brethren, became aimitators of bthe churches of God in Christ Jesus that are cin Judea, for dyou also endured the same sufferings at the hands of your own countrymen, eeven as they *did* from the Jews,

15 awho both killed the Lord Jesus and bthe prophets, and drove us out. They are not pleasing to God, but hostile to all men,

16 ahindering us from speaking to the Gentiles bthat they might be saved; with the result that they always cfill up the measure of their sins. But dwrath has come upon them to the utmost.

17 But we, brethren, having been bereft of you for a short while—ain person, not in spirit—

11 a1 Thess.
5:14 bLuke
16:28;
1 Thess. 4:6
c1 Cor. 4:14;
1 Thess. 2:7
★12 aEph.
4:1 bRom.
8:28;
1 Thess.
5:24;
2 Thess. 2:14
c2 Cor. 4:6;
1 Pet. 5:10

13 aRom.
1:8; 1 Thess.
1:2 bRom.
10:17; Heb.
4:2 cMatt.
10:20; Gal.
4:14 dHeb.
4:12
★14
a1 Thess.
1:6 b1 Cor.
7:17; 10:32
cGal. 1:22
dActs 17:5;
1 Thess. 3:4;
2 Thess. 1:4f.
eHeb.
10:33f.
15 aLuke
24:20; Acts
2:23 bMatt.
5:12; Acts
7:52
★16 aActs
9:23; 13:45,
50; 14:2, 5,
19; 17:5, 13;
18:12;
21:21f., 27;
25:2; 7
b1 Cor.
10:33 cGen.
15:16; Dan.
8:23; Matt.
23:32
d1 Thess.
1:10
★17-18
17 a1 Cor.
5:3
b1 Thess.
3:10

2:3 Paul attacks what must have been charges against him: of *error* (i.e., that the gospel he preached was based on error), of *impurity* (that Christianity encouraged sexual immorality), and of *deceit* (that his methods were underhanded).

2:5 *flattering speech* = cajolery, i.e., an attempt to persuade by use of insincere speech.

2:6 *asserted our authority*. Better, made demands (on you), i.e., for support. Paul makes clear his right as an apostle to financial support, but says he behaved as selflessly as a nursing mother (v. 7).

2:8 *fond affection*. An unusual word indicating the yearning love of a mother for her children.

Paul's pastoral heart is laid bare in these verses.

2:12 *walk* = live.

2:14 *imitators*. Paul compared the problems of the Christians at Thessalonica among their fellow Greeks with those of the Christians in Judea, persecuted by Jews.

2:16 *fill up the measure of their sins*. God sometimes allows His people to be persecuted in order to show the evil nature of men and the rightness of His judgment when it falls (cf. Gen. 15:16). These persecutors were heaping sin upon sin.

2:17-18 Paul had several times planned to return to Thessalonica. *Satan thwarted us.*

were all the more eager with great desire *b*to see your face.

18   For *a*we wanted to come to you—I, Paul, *b*more than once—and *yet* *c*Satan *d*thwarted us.

19   For who is our hope or *a*joy or crown of exultation? Is it not even you, in the presence of our Lord Jesus at His *b*coming?

20   For you are *a*our glory and joy.

2   For their testings (Timothy's visit), 3:1-8

3 Therefore *a*when we could endure *it* no longer, we thought it best to be left behind at *b*Athens alone;

2   and we sent *a*Timothy, our brother and God's fellow worker in the gospel of Christ, to strengthen and encourage you as to your faith,

3   so that no man may be disturbed by these afflictions; for you yourselves know that *a*we have been destined for this.

4   For indeed when we were with you, we *kept* telling you in advance that we were going to suffer affliction; *a*and so it came to pass, as you know.

5   For this reason, *a*when I could endure *it* no longer, I also *b*sent to find out about your faith, for fear that *c*the tempter might have tempted you, and *d*our labor should be in vain.

6   But now that *a*Timothy has come to us from you, and has brought us good news of *b*your faith and love, and that you always *c*think kindly of us, longing to see us just as we also long to see you,

7   for this reason, brethren, in all our distress and affliction we were comforted about you through your faith;

8   for now we *really* live, if you *a*stand firm in the Lord.

3   For their continued growth, 3:9-13

9   For *a*what thanks can we render to God for you in return for all the joy with which we rejoice before our God on your account,

10   as we *a*night and day keep praying most earnestly that we may *b*see your face, and may *c*complete what is lacking in your faith?

11   *a*Now may *b*our God and Father *c*Himself and Jesus our Lord *d*direct our way to you;

12   and may the Lord cause you to increase and *a*abound in love for one another, and for all men, just as we also *do* for you;

13   so that He may *a*establish your hearts *b*unblamable in holiness before *c*our God and Father at the *d*coming of our Lord Jesus *e*with all His saints.

II   PRACTICAL AND HORTATORY, 4:1-5:28

A   Teaching Concerning Development, 4:1-12

1   In sexual relations, 4:1-8

4 *a*Finally then, *b*brethren, we request and exhort you in the Lord Jesus, that, as you received from us *instruction* as to how you ought to *c*walk and *d*please God

---

Marginal references (left column):

18 *a*Rom. 15:22 *b*Phil. 4:16 *c*Matt. 4:10 *d*Rom. 1:13; 15:22
19 *a*Phil. 4:1 *b*Matt. 16:27; Mark 8:38; John 21:22; 1 Thess. 3:13; 4:15; 5:23
20 *a*2 Cor. 1:14

1 *a*Phil. 2:19; 1 Thess. 3:5 *b*Acts 17:15f.

2 *a*2 Cor. 1:1; Col. 1:1

★ 3 *a*Acts 9:16; 14:22

★ 4 *a*1 Thess. 2:14

★ 5 *a*Phil. 2:19; 1 Thess. 3:1 *b*1 Thess. 3:2 *c*Matt. 4:3 *d*2 Cor. 6:1; Phil. 2:16

6 *a*Acts 18:5 *b*1 Thess. 1:3 *c*1 Cor. 11:2

Marginal references (right column):

★ 8 *a*1 Cor. 6:13

9 *a*1 Thess. 1:2
★10 *a*2 Tim. 1:3 *b*1 Thess. 2:17 *c*2 Cor. 13:9
★11-13
11 *a*2 Thess. 2:16 *b*Gal. 1:4; 1 Thess. 3:13 *c*1 Thess. 4:16; 5:23; 2 Thess. 2:16; 3:16; Rev. 21:3 *d*2 Thess. 3:5
12 *a*Phil. 1:9; 1 Thess. 4:1, 10; 2 Thess. 1:3
★13 *a*1 Cor. 1:8; 1 Thess. 3:2 *b*Luke 1:6 *c*Gal. 1:4; 1 Thess. 3:11 *d*1 Thess. 2:19 *e*Matt. 25:31; Mark 8:38; 1 Thess. 4:17; 2 Thess. 1:7

1 *a*2 Cor. 13:11; 2 Thess. 3:1 *b*Gal. 6:1; 1 Thess. 5:12; 2 Thess. 1:3; 2:1; 3:1, 13 *c*Eph. 4:1 *d*2 Cor. 5:9 *e*Phil. 1:9; 1 Thess. 3:12; 4:10

Likely refers to the security taken of Jason (Acts 17:9), which probably included a guarantee that Paul would not return to the city.
3:3 *disturbed.* I.e., that they be not seduced away from the faith by the heathen who were urging them to reject their faith.
3:4 *suffer affliction.* To endure the normal afflictions that come to a believer in this life. Paul had told them these would come (v. 3).
3:5 *the tempter.* Again (as in 2:18) Paul traces events to Satan's working.

3:8 The good news of their spiritual well-being was a breath of life to Paul.
3:10 *complete.* I.e., to make complete as one might repair fishing nets (Matt. 4:21) or restore saints (cf. Gal. 6:1; Eph. 4:12).
3:11-13 The thanksgiving portion of the letter ends in a three-verse prayer.
3:13 *saints.* Lit., holy ones. Probably refers here to angels who will accompany the return of Christ (Mark 8:38), or possibly also holy men (cf. 1 Thess. 4:14).

(just as you actually do walk), that you may *excel still more.

2 For you know what commandments we gave you by *the authority of* the Lord Jesus.

★ 3 *a*1 Cor. 6:18

3 For this is the will of God, your sanctification; *that is,* that you *a*abstain from sexual immorality;

★ 4 *a*1 Cor. 7:2, 9
*b*2 Cor. 4:7;
1 Pet. 3:7
*c*Rom. 1:24
5 *a*Rom. 1:26 *b*Gal. 4:8

4 that *a*each of you know how to possess his own *b*vessel in sanctification and *c*honor,

5 not in *a*lustful passion, like the Gentiles who *b*do not know God;

★ 6 *a*1 Cor. 6:8 *b*2 Cor. 7:11 *c*Rom. 12:19; 13:4;
Heb. 13:4
*d*Luke 16:28;
1 Thess. 2:11; Heb. 2:6
7 *a*1 Pet. 1:15
*b*1 Thess. 2:3

6 *and* that no man transgress and *a*defraud his brother *b*in the matter because *c*the Lord is *the* avenger in all these things, just as we also *d*told you before and solemnly warned *you.*

7 For *a*God has not called us for *b*the purpose of impurity, but in sanctification.

★ 8 *a*Rom. 5:5; 2 Cor. 1:22; Gal. 4:6; 1 John 3:24

8 Consequently, he who rejects *this* is not rejecting man but the God who *a*gives His Holy Spirit to you.

2 In brotherly love, 4:9-10

9 *a*John 13:34; Rom. 12:10
*b*2 Cor. 9:1; 1 Thess. 5:1
*c*Jer. 31:33f.;
John 6:45;
1 John 2:27

9 Now as to the *a*love of the brethren, you *b*have no need for *anyone* to write to you, for you yourselves are *c*taught by God to love one another;

10 for indeed *a*you do practice it toward all the brethren who are in all Macedonia. But we urge you, brethren, to *b*excel still more,

3 In orderly living, 4:11-12

11 and to make it your ambition *a*to lead a quiet life and *b*attend to your own business and *c*work with your own hands, just as we commanded you;

12 so that you may *a*behave properly toward *b*outsiders and *c*not be in any need.

B Teaching Concerning the Dead, 4:13-18

13 But *a*we do not want you to be uninformed, brethren, about those who *b*are asleep, that you may not grieve, as do *c*the rest who have *d*no hope.

14 For if we believe that Jesus died and rose again, *a*even so God will bring with Him *b*those who have fallen asleep in Jesus.

15 For this we say to you *a*by the word of the Lord, that *b*we who are alive, and remain until *c*the coming of the Lord, shall not precede *d*those who have fallen asleep.

16 For the Lord *a*Himself *b*will descend from heaven with a

★10
*a*1 Thess. 1:7
*b*1 Thess. 3:12

★11
*a*2 Thess. 3:12 *b*1 Pet. 4:15 *c*Acts 18:3; Eph. 4:28
★12 *a*Rom. 13:13; Col. 4:5 *b*Mark 4:11 *c*Eph. 4:28
★13-18
★13 *a*Rom. 1:13 *b*Acts 7:60 *c*Eph. 2:3; 1 Thess. 5:6 *d*Eph 2:12
★14 *a*Rom. 14:9; 2 Cor. 4:14 *b*1 Cor. 15:18
15 *a*1 Kin. 13:17f.;
20:35; 2 Cor. 12:1; Gal. 1:12 *b*1 Cor. 15:52;
1 Thess. 5:10
*c*1 Thess. 2:19 *d*1 Cor. 15:18;
1 Thess. 4:13
★16-17
16 *a*1 Thess. 3:11
*b*1 Thess. 1:10;
2 Thess. 1:7
*c*Joel 2:11
*d*Jude 9
*e*Matt. 24:31
*f*1 Cor. 15:23;
2 Thess. 2:1;
Rev. 14:13

4:3 *will of God.* I.e., His desire or purpose. *sanctification* (holiness) is viewed in three aspects in the N.T.: (1) a position of being set apart to God, which every believer has at the moment of his salvation (1 Cor. 6:11); (2) a progressive holiness of life that ought to be true of every believer (1 Thess. 4:3); and (3) our condition in heaven, in which we shall be "unblamable in holiness" (3:13). *immorality.* The Greek word means all kinds of illicit or unnatural sexual indulgence. Greek cities like Thessalonica were wide open to all kinds of sexual looseness, even in connection with religious rites.

4:4 *possess his own vessel.* This means either mastery over one's body, keeping it pure (1 Cor. 9:24-27), or refers to an honorable marriage (*vessel* = wife, as 1 Pet. 3:7).

4:6 *transgress.* In this context (vv. 3-8), the reference is to sexual conduct.

4:8 *rejects.* Treats lightly these commands for sexual purity.

4:10 *excel still more.* I.e., practice brotherly

love more and more with your fellow Macedonian Christians.

4:11 *make it your ambition.* Or, aspire. The Greek word is used only here, in Rom. 15:20, and in 2 Cor. 5:9. The problems mentioned in 2 Thess. 3:11-12 gave rise to these exhortations.

4:12 *outsiders.* I.e., non-Christians.

4:13-18 The question is this: Does the death of a believer before the Lord comes cause him to lose all hope of sharing in the glorious reign of Christ? Paul's answer is the reassuring affirmation that the dead will be raised and will share in the kingdom.

4:13 *are asleep.* The body (not the soul) of the believer who dies is said to sleep during the time between death and resurrection.

4:14 *if we believe.* Better, since we do believe. The certainty of the Christian's resurrection is based on the fact of Christ's resurrection.

4:16-17 *the trumpet of God.* See 1 Cor. 15:52. *the dead in Christ shall rise first,* when the Lord comes for His people (v. 17). Then living

*c*shout, with the voice of *d*the archangel, and with the *e*trumpet of God; and *f*the dead in Christ shall rise first.

17 Then *a*we who are alive and remain shall be *b*caught up together with them *c*in the clouds to meet the Lord in the air, and thus we shall always *d*be with the Lord.

18 Therefore comfort one another with these words.

C Teaching Concerning the Day of the Lord, 5:1-11

5 Now as to the *a*times and the epochs, brethren, you *b*have no need of anything to be written to you.

2 For you yourselves know full well that *a*the day of the Lord will come *b*just like a thief in the night.

3 While they are saying, "*a*Peace and safety!" then *b*destruction will come upon them suddenly like *c*birth pangs upon a woman with child; and they shall not escape.

4 But you, brethren, are not in *a*darkness, that the day should overtake you *b*like a thief;

5 for you are all *a*sons of light and sons of day. We are not of night nor of *b*darkness;

6 so then let us not *a*sleep as *b*others do, but let us be alert and *c*sober.

7 For those who sleep do their sleeping at night, and those who get drunk get *a*drunk at night.

8 But since *a*we are of the day, let us *b*be sober, having put on the *c*breastplate of *d*faith and love, and as a *e*helmet, the *f*hope of salvation.

9 For God has not destined us for *a*wrath, but for *b*obtaining salvation through our Lord Jesus Christ,

10 *a*who died for us, that whether we are awake or asleep, we may live together with Him.

11 Therefore encourage one another, and *a*build up one another, just as you also are doing.

D Teaching Concerning Various Duties, 5:12-28

12 But we request of you, brethren, that you *a*appreciate those *b*who diligently labor among you, and *c*have charge over you in the Lord and give you instruction,

13 and that you esteem them very highly in love because of their work. *a*Live in peace with one another.

14 And we urge you, brethren, admonish *a*the unruly, encourage *b*the fainthearted, help *c*the weak, be *d*patient with all men.

15 See that *a*no one repays another with evil for evil, but always *b*seek after that which is good for one another and for all men.

16 *a*Rejoice always;

---

believers will be *caught up.* From the Latin for "caught up" comes the term "rapture." The rapture or catching up of believers described here involves both those who have died and those who are living when the Lord comes. His coming here is *in the air,* not to the earth, and will occur just prior to the beginning of the tribulation period (see Rev. 3:10). That period will end with His coming to the earth (see Matt. 24:29-30; Rev. 19:11-16).

4:18 The *comfort* of the Christian's hope in resurrection is in sharp contrast to the hopelessness of the heathen in the face of death.

5:2 *the day of the Lord.* An extended period of time, beginning with the tribulation and including the events of the second coming of Christ and the millennial kingdom on earth. It will begin *(come)* unexpectedly *(like a thief in the night).*

5:4 *darkness.* A figure of the unbeliever's moral state and separation from God.

5:6 *sleep.* Not physical but moral (as in Mark 13:36; Eph. 5:14).

5:9 *wrath.* I.e., the anguish and tribulation associated with the beginning of the day of the Lord (v. 3), from which the believer is to be delivered (1:10).

5:16-22 Verses 16-18 are closely related; vv. 19-22 form another paragraph.

★17 ªEph.
6:18
18 ªEph.
5:20
★19 ªEph.
4:30
20 ªActs
13:1; 1 Cor.
14:31
21 ª1 Cor.
14:29 ªRom.
12:9; Gal.
6:10
★23-24
23 ªRom.
15:33
ª1 Thess.
3:11 ªLuke
1:46f.; Heb.
4:12 ªJames
1:4 ª1 Thess.
2:19

17 ªpray without ceasing;

18 in everything ªgive thanks; for this is God's will for you in Christ Jesus.

19 ªDo not quench the Spirit;

20 do not despise ªprophetic utterances.

21 But ªexamine everything *carefully;* ªhold fast to that which is good;

22 abstain from every form of evil.

23 Now ªmay the God of peace ªHimself sanctify you entirely; and may your ªspirit and

soul and body be preserved complete, ªwithout blame at ªthe coming of our Lord Jesus Christ.

24 ªFaithful is He who ªcalls you, and He also will bring it to pass.

25 Brethren, ªpray for us.

26 ªGreet all the brethren with a holy kiss.

27 I adjure you by the Lord to ªhave this letter read to all the ªbrethren.

28 ªThe grace of our Lord Jesus Christ be with you.

24 ª1 Cor.
1:9; 2 Thess.
3:3
ª1 Thess.
2:12
25 ªEph.
6:19;
2 Thess. 3:1;
Heb. 13:18
★26 ªRom.
16:16
27 ªCol.
4:16 ªActs
1:15
28 ªRom.
16:20;
2 Thess. 3:18

5:17 *without ceasing.* Paul prayed thus for the Thessalonians (1:3; 2:13).

5:19 *quench. the Spirit* is often likened to fire (Matt. 3:11; Luke 3:16; Acts 2:3). The Spirit is quenched whenever His ministry is stifled in an individual or in the church.

5:23-24 A two-verse prayer that closes the section of instruction and exhortation begun at

4:1. *spirit and soul and body* should not be understood as defining the parts of man, but as representing the whole man.

5:26 *holy kiss.* For the kiss as a symbol of welcome in Jewish life see Luke 7:45; 22:48. As a symbol of Christian fellowship see note on 1 Pet. 5:14. Paul uses the phrase in Rom. 16:16; 1 Cor. 16:20; and 2 Cor. 13:12.

INTRODUCTION TO
THE SECOND LETTER OF PAUL TO THE THESSALONIANS

AUTHOR: Paul   DATE: 51

Purpose   This letter was sent by Paul to the church at Thessalonica, not long after 1 Thessalonians, to meet a new situation. Word had reached Paul that somehow there had been misunderstanding, if not misrepresentation (2:2), of his teaching concerning the coming of the day of the Lord (1 Thess. 5:1-11). Some thought that its judgments had already begun; yet they understood Paul to have taught that they would be exempt from those judgments. The practical ramification of this doctrinal confusion was that some, thinking the end of the world was at hand, had stopped working and were creating an embarrassing situation (3:6, 11). Paul corrects the teaching and reprimands the idlers.

Contents   The major section on the man of sin (2:1-12) should be compared with other passages which tell of this Antichrist (Dan. 9:27; Matt. 24:15; Rev. 11:7, 13:1-10).

OUTLINE OF 2 THESSALONIANS

I. Salutation, 1:1-2
II. Thanksgiving and Encouragement in
    Persecution, 1:3-12
III. Correction Concerning the Day of the
    Lord, 2:1-17
  A. Its Relation to the Present, 2:1-2
  B. Its Relation to the Apostasy, 2:3a
  C. Its Relation to the Man of Lawlessness,
    2:3b-5

D. Its Relation to the Restrainer, 2:6-9
E. Its Relation to Unbelievers, 2:10-12
F. Its Relation to Believers, 2:13-17
IV. Exhortations to Prayer and Discipline,
    3:1-15
  A. Paul's Confidence, 3:1-5
  B. Paul's Commands, 3:6-15
V. Concluding Benediction and Greeting,
    3:16-18.

THE SECOND LETTER OF PAUL TO THE THESSALONIANS

I SALUTATION, 1:1-2

1 ᵃThess.
1:1 ᵇ2 Cor.
1:19 ᶜActs
16:1
[1 Thess.
1:1] ᵈActs
17:1;
1 Thess. 1:1
2 ᵃRom.
1:7

1 ᵃPaul and ᵇSilvanus and ᶜTimothy to the ᵈchurch of the Thessalonians in God our Father and the Lord Jesus Christ:
    2 ᵃGrace to you and peace from God the Father and the Lord Jesus Christ.

II THANKSGIVING AND ENCOURAGEMENT IN PERSECUTION, 1:3-12

★ 3-4
3 ᵃRom.
1:8; Eph. 6:20
ᵇ1 Thess. 4:1
ᶜ1 Thess.
3:12

    3 We ought always ᵃto give thanks to God for you, ᵇbrethren,

as is *only* fitting, because your faith is greatly enlarged, and the ᶜlove of each one of you toward one another grows *ever* greater;
    4 therefore, we ourselves ᵃspeak proudly of you among ᵇthe churches of God for your perseverance and faith ᵇin the midst of all your persecutions and afflictions which you endure.
    5 *This is* a ᵃplain indication of God's righteous judgment so that you may be ᵇconsidered worthy of the kingdom of God, for which indeed you are suffering.
    6 For after all ᵃit is *only* just for God to repay with affliction those who afflict you,

4 ᵃ2 Cor.
7:4; 1 Thess.
2:19 ᵇ1 Cor.
7:17;
1 Thess. 2:14

5 ᵃPhil.
1:28 ᵇLuke
20:35;
2 Thess. 1:11

6 ᵃEx.
23:22; Col.
3:25; Heb.
6:10

1:3-4 *your faith is greatly enlarged.* Paul's earlier fears about their faith (1 Thess. 3:5, 10)

have disappeared in the light of their exceptional growth. *love* (see 1 Thess. 3:12).

★ 7 *a*Luke
17:30
*b*1 Thess.
4:16 *c*Jude
14 *d*Ex. 3:2;
19:18; Is.
66:15; Ezek.
1:13f.; Dan.
7:9; Matt.
25:41; 1 Cor.
3:13; Heb.
10:27; 12:29;
2 Pet. 3:7;
Jude 7; Rev.
14:10

7 and *to give* relief to you who are afflicted and to us as well *a*when the Lord Jesus shall be revealed *b*from heaven *c*with His mighty angels *d*in flaming fire,

8 dealing out retribution to those who *a*do not know God and to those who *b*do not obey the gospel of our Lord Jesus.

8 *a*Gal. 4:8
*b*Rom 2:8

★ 9 *a*Phil.
3:19;
1 Thess. 5:3
*b*Is. 2:10, 19,
21; 2 Thess.
2:8

9 And these will pay the penalty of *a*eternal destruction, *b*away from the presence of the Lord and from the glory of His power,

★10 *a*Is.
49:3; John
17:10;
1 Thess. 2:12
*b*Is. 2:11ff.;
1 Cor. 3:13
*c*1 Cor. 1:6;
1 Thess. 2:1

10 when He comes to be *a*glorified in His saints on that *b*day, and to be marveled at among all who have believed—for our *c*testimony to you was believed.

11 *a*Col. 1:9
*b*2 Thess.
1:5 *c*Rom.
11:29 *d*Rom.
15:14
*e*1 Thess.
1:3

11 To this end also we *a*pray for you always that our God may *b*count you worthy of your *c*calling, and fulfill every desire for *d*goodness and the *e*work of faith with power;

12 *a*Is.
24:15; 66:5;
Mal. 1:11;
Phil. 2:9ff.

12 in order that the *a*name of our Lord Jesus may be glorified in you, and you in Him, according to the grace of our God and the Lord Jesus Christ.

III CORRECTION CONCERNING THE DAY OF THE LORD, 2:1-17

A Its Relation to the Present, 2:1-2

2 Now we request you, *a*brethren, with regard to the *b*coming of our Lord Jesus Christ, and our *c*gathering together to Him,

2 that you may not be quickly shaken from your composure or be disturbed either by a *a*spirit or a *b*message or a *c*letter as if from us, to the effect that *d*the day of the Lord *e*has come.

★ 1
*a*2 Thess.
1:3
*b*1 Thess.
2:19 *c*Mark
13:27;
1 Thess.
4:15-17
★ 2 *a*1 Cor.
14:32;
1 John 4:1
*b*1 Thess.
5:2; 2 Thess.
2:15
*c*2 Thess.
3:17 *d*1 Cor.
1:8 *e*1 Cor.
7:26.

B Its Relation to the Apostasy, 2:3a

3 *a*Let no one in any way deceive you, for *it will not come* unless the *b*apostasy comes first,

★ 3 *a*Eph.
5:6 *b*1 Tim.
4:1 *c*Dan.
7:25; 8:25;
11:36;
2 Thess. 2:8;
Rev. 13:5ff.
*d*John 17:12

C Its Relation to the Man of Lawlessness, 2:3b-5

and the *c*man of lawlessness is revealed, the *d*son of destruction,

4 who opposes and exalts himself above *a*every so-called

★ 4 *a*1 Cor.
8:5 *b*Is.
14:14; Ezek.
28:2

1:7 *relief . . . to us.* I.e., to Paul, Silvanus, and Timothy who knew what it was to be under persecution and pressure for their faith (1 Thess. 1:6; 2:14-18). *Relief* is promised at the return of Christ, who will then judge those who afflict His people (v. 6).

1:9 *eternal destruction.* Not annihilation, but ruin by reason of separation from the presence of the Lord. In 1 Thess. 5:3 the destruction is said to be sudden; here, eternal.

1:10 *on that day.* I.e., the day when the Lord Jesus shall be revealed (v. 7) at His return.

2:1 *with regard to the coming of our Lord Jesus.* I.e., concerning, or in the interest of the truth concerning, the Lord's coming. Paul denies the teaching, ascribed to him, that the day of the Lord had already begun. *our gathering together.* A reference to the rapture of the church (1 Thess. 4:13-18).

2:2 *shaken* = excited, violently disturbed. The Thessalonians were being greatly disturbed by false teaching concerning future events, and Paul seeks to bring them back to true doctrine (2:1-12) and proper living (3:6-16). The false teaching was *by a spirit* (some prophetic utterance), *by a message* (some spoken teaching),

and *by a letter as if from us* (some written communication purporting to be from Paul). The source of these teachings is not given. *day of the Lord* (see note on 1 Thess. 5:2).

2:3 *the apostasy.* An aggressive and climactic revolt against God which will prepare the way for the appearance of the man of sin (see 1 Tim. 4:1-5; 2 Tim. 3:1-5). *man of lawlessness.* While it is true that the forces of lawlessness were at work in Paul's time and are at work today (note v. 7, *the mystery of lawlessness is already at work),* the man of lawlessness (also called *that lawless one,* v. 8) is an individual of the future who will come to power during the tribulation days. John also recognized the presence of many antichrists in his time (1 John 2:18) as well as the coming of one great Antichrist in the future (Rev. 11:7; 13:1-10).

2:4 *takes his seat in the temple of God.* At the midpoint of the tribulation period the Antichrist will desecrate the rebuilt Jewish temple in Jerusalem by placing himself there to be worshiped (see note on Matt. 24:15). This will be the climax of man's great sin of self-deification, in open defiance of God.

god or object of worship, so that he takes his seat in the temple of God, [b]displaying himself as being God.

5 Do you not remember that [a]while I was still with you, I was telling you these things?

5 [a]1 Thess.
3:4

D　Its Relation to the Restrainer, 2:6–9

6 [a]2 Thess.
2:7

6 And you know [a]what restrains him now, so that in his time he may be revealed.

★ 7 [a]Rev.
17:5, 7
[b]2 Thess.
2:6

7 For [a]the mystery of lawlessness is already at work; only [b]he who now restrains *will do so* until he is taken out of the way.

★ 8 [a]Dan.
7:25; 8:25;
11:36;
2 Thess. 2:3;
Rev. 13:5ff.
[b]Is. 11:4;
Rev. 2:16;
19:15
[c]1 Tim. 6:14;
2 Tim. 1:10;
4:1, 8; Titus
2:13
9 [a]Matt.
4:10 [b]Matt.
24:24; John
4:48

8 And then that lawless one [a]will be revealed whom the Lord will slay [b]with the breath of His mouth and bring to an end by the [c]appearance of His coming;

9 *that is,* the one whose coming is in accord with the activity of [a]Satan, with all power and [b]signs and false wonders,

E　Its Relation to Unbelievers, 2:10–12

10 [a]1 Cor.
1:18
[b]2 Thess.
2:12, 13

10 and with all the deception of wickedness for [a]those who perish, because they did not receive the love of [b]the truth so as to be saved.

11 And for this reason [a]God will send upon them a [b]deluding influence so that they might believe what is false,

12 in order that they all may be judged who [a]did not believe the truth, but [b]took pleasure in wickedness.

★11-12
11 [a]1 Kin.
22:22; Rom.
1:28
[b]1 Thess.
2:3; 2 Tim.
4:4
12 [a]Rom.
2:8 [b]Rom.
1:32; 1 Cor.
13:6

F　Its Relation to Believers, 2:13–17

13 [a]But we should always give thanks to God for you, [b]brethren beloved by the Lord, because [c]God has chosen you from the beginning [d]for salvation [e]through sanctification by the Spirit and faith in the truth.

14 And it was for this He [a]called you through [b]our gospel, that you may gain the glory of our Lord Jesus Christ.

15 So then, brethren, [a]stand firm and [b]hold to the traditions which you were taught, whether [c]by word *of mouth* or [c]by letter from us.

16 [a]Now may our Lord Jesus Christ [b]Himself and God our Father, who has [c]loved us and given us eternal comfort and [d]good hope by grace,

17 [a]comfort and [b]strengthen your hearts in every good work and word.

★13
[a]2 Thess.
1:3
[b]1 Thess.
1:4 [c]Eph.
1:4ff. [d]1 Cor.
1:21;
1 Thess.
2:12; 5:9;
1 Pet. 1:5
[e]1 Thess.
4:7; 1 Pet.
1:2
14 [a]1 Thess.
2:12
[b]1 Thess.
1:5
★15 [a]1 Cor.
16:13
[b]1 Cor. 11:2;
2 Thess. 3:6
[c]2 Thess.
2:2
★16-17
16
[a]1 Thess.
3:11
[b]1 Thess.
3:11 [c]John
3:16 [d]Titus
3:7; 1 Pet.
1:3
17 [a]1 Thess.
3:2, 13
[b]2 Thess.
3:3

2:7 *he who now restrains will do so until.* Antichrist is now being held back by a restrainer. Some understand this to be God indwelling His church by the Holy Spirit, while others see human government as the restraint. According to the former view, the removal will be at the rapture of the church (1 Thess. 4:13–18); according to the latter, at the overthrow of human government by Antichrist.

2:8 *then that lawless one will be revealed.* Paul's argument is: The day of the Lord will not begin until the Antichrist is revealed (v. 3); the Antichrist cannot begin to act until the restrainer is removed (v. 7); since the restrainer has not yet been removed, the Thessalonians could be certain that the day of the Lord had not yet begun, regardless of what the false teachers were saying.

2:11–12 The *deluding influence* comes from God; it is both a punishment and a moral result of their rejection of the truth (vv. 10, 12).

These verses reflect the O.T. concept that God is sovereign even in the activities of the powers of evil (cf. Ex. 4:21; Josh. 11:20; 1 Kings 22:19–23; 1 Chron. 21:1; cf. 2 Sam. 24:1). The result will be that men will believe *what is false,* as Satan works through Antichrist.

2:13 *through sanctification by the Spirit and faith in the truth.* God's activity (the Holy Spirit's work of regeneration) and man's responsibility (faith) are equally necessary in salvation.

2:15 *the traditions.* I.e., all the teachings Paul had shared with the Thessalonians.

2:16–17 Paul's prayer for steadfastness on the part of the Thessalonians closes this crucial section. Notice the closing prayers of this letter: for their lives to be such as could be commended by the Lord (1:11-12), for their love and steadfastness (3:5), and for their peace (3:16).

IV EXHORTATIONS TO PRAYER AND DISCIPLINE, 3:1-15

A Paul's Confidence, 3:1-5

1 a1 Thess. 4:1
b1 Thess. 5:25
c1 Thess. 1:8

3 *a*Finally, brethren, *b*pray for us that *c*the word of the Lord may spread rapidly and be glorified, just as *it did* also with you;

★ 2 aRom. 15:31

2   and that we may be *a*delivered from perverse and evil men; for not all have faith.

★ 3 a1 Cor. 1:9; 1 Thess. 5:24 bMatt. 5:37

3   But *a*the Lord is faithful, and He will strengthen and protect you from *b*the evil *one*.

4 a2 Cor. 2:3
b1 Thess. 4:10

4   And we have *a*confidence in the Lord concerning *you*, that you *b*are doing and will continue to do what we command.

★ 5 a1 Thess. 3:11

5   And may the Lord *a*direct your hearts into the love of God and into the steadfastness of Christ.

B Paul's Commands, 3:6-15

★ 6 a1 Cor. 5:4 bRom. 16:17; 1 Cor. 5:11; 2 Thess. 3:14
c1 Thess. 5:14; 2 Thess. 3:7, 11 d1 Cor. 11:2; 2 Thess. 2:15

6   Now we command you, brethren, *a*in the name of our Lord Jesus Christ, that you *b*keep aloof from every brother who leads an *c*unruly life and not according to *d*the tradition which you received from us.

7 a1 Thess. 1:6; 2 Thess. 3:9

7   For you yourselves know how you ought to *a*follow our example, because we did not act in an undisciplined manner among you,

8 a1 Cor. 9:4
b1 Thess. 2:9 cActs 18:3; Eph. 4:28

8   nor did we *a*eat anyone's bread without paying for it, but with *b*labor and hardship we *kept* *c*working night and day so that we might not be a burden to any of you;

9   not because we do not have *a*the right *to this,* but in order to offer ourselves *b*as a model for you, that you might follow our example.

9 a1 Cor. 9:4ff.
b2 Thess. 3:7

10   For even *a*when we were with you, we used to give you this order: *b*if anyone will not work, neither let him eat.

10 a1 Thess. 3:4
b1 Thess. 4:11

11   For we hear that some among you are *a*leading an undisciplined life, doing no work at all, but acting like *b*busybodies.

11 a2 Thess. 3:6 b1 Tim. 5:13; 1 Pet. 4:15

12   Now such persons we command and *a*exhort in the Lord Jesus Christ to *b*work in quiet fashion and eat their own bread.

12 a1 Thess. 4:1
b1 Thess. 4:11

13   But as for you, *a*brethren, *b*do not grow weary of doing good.

13 a1 Thess. 4:1 b2 Thess. 4:1; Gal. 6:9

14   And if anyone does not obey our instruction *a*in this letter, take special note of that man *b*and do not associate with him, so that he may be *c*put to shame.

★14 aCol. 4:16
b2 Thess. 3:6 c1 Cor. 4:14

15   And *yet* *a*do not regard him as an enemy, but *b*admonish him as a *c*brother.

★15 aGal. 6:1
b1 Thess. 5:14
c2 Thess. 3:6, 13

V CONCLUDING BENEDICTION AND GREETING, 3:16-18

16   Now *a*may the Lord of peace *b*Himself continually grant you peace in every circumstance. *c*The Lord be with you all!

16 aRom. 15:33
b1 Thess. 3:11 cRuth 2:4

17   I, Paul, write this greeting *a*with my own hand, and this is a distinguishing mark in every letter; this is the way I write.

17 a1 Cor. 16:21

18   *a*The grace of our Lord Jesus Christ be with you all.

18 aRom. 16:20; 1 Thess. 5:28

3:2 *perverse and evil men.* Those "who did not believe the truth" (2:10-12), Jews and Gentiles, whom Paul encountered in virtually every city he visited. His experiences at Thessalonica are recorded in Acts 17:5-10 and those at Corinth (where he wrote this letter) in Acts 18:6-17.

3:3 *But.* I.e., in contrast to this wickedness of men.

3:5 *steadfastness of Christ.* This may refer to our expectation of Christ's coming or it may mean that the endurance or steadfastness of Christ during His life on earth should be our example.

3:6 *who leads an unruly life.* Paul had instructed them on this point earlier (1 Thess. 4:1; 5:14).

3:14 *do not associate with him.* Idlers were to be ostracized from the company of believers in order to shame them into changing their ways. This was not formal excommunication but group disapproval and social ostracism, a serious thing for a believer in a heathen society at that time.

3:15 *admonish him.* The aim of the discipline was reformation and restoration of the offender.

INTRODUCTION TO
THE FIRST LETTER OF PAUL TO TIMOTHY

AUTHOR: Paul   DATE: 63

The Pastoral Epistles *The two letters to Timothy and the one to Titus are called the "Pastoral Epistles" because they contain principles for the pastoral care of churches and qualifications for ministers.*

Authorship *Some have questioned whether Paul himself wrote these letters, on the grounds that: (1) Paul's travels described in the Pastorals do not fit anywhere into the historical account of the book of Acts; (2) the church organization described in them is that of the second century; (3) the vocabulary and style are significantly different from that of the other Pauline letters. Those who hold to the Pauline authorship reply that: (1) there is no compelling reason to believe that Acts contains the complete history of the life of Paul. Since his death is not recorded in Acts, he was apparently released from his first imprisonment in Rome, traveled over the empire for several years (perhaps even to Spain), was rearrested, imprisoned a second time in Rome, and martyred under Nero. (2) Nothing in the church organization reflected in the Pastorals requires a later date (see Acts 14:23; Phil. 1:1). (3) The question of authorship cannot be decided solely on the basis of vocabulary, without considering how subject matter affects a writer's choice of words. Vocabulary used to describe church organization, for instance, would be expected to be different from that used to teach the doctrine of the Holy Spirit. There is no argument against Pauline authorship that does not have a reasonable answer. And, of course, the letters themselves claim to have been written by Paul.*

Background *Timothy, the son of a Greek Gentile father and a devout Jewish mother named Eunice, was intimately associated with Paul from the time of the second missionary journey, on (2 Tim. 1:5; Acts 16:1-3). When Paul wrote 1 Timothy, probably from Macedonia (1:3), he was on his way to Nicopolis (Tit. 3:12), but Timothy had been left in charge of the work in Ephesus and Asia Minor. Though Paul desired to visit Timothy (3:14; 4:13), this letter, in the meantime, would guide Timothy in the conduct of his pastoral responsibilities.*

Contents *In relation to Timothy personally, the theme is "fighting the good fight" (1:18). In relation to the church corporately, the theme is behaving in the house of God (3:15). Important subjects discussed in the epistle include the law (1:7-11), prayer (2:1-8), appearance and activity of women (2:9-15), qualifications for bishops or elders and for deacons (3:1-13), the last days (4:1-3), care of widows (5:3-16), and use of money (6:6-19).*

OUTLINE OF 1 TIMOTHY

I. **Opening Greetings, 1:1-2**
II. **Instruction Concerning Doctrine, 1:3-20**
  A. Paul's Warning against False Doctrines, 1:3-11
  B. Paul's Testimony Concerning the Grace of God, 1:12-17
  C. Paul's Charge to Timothy, 1:18-20
III. **Instruction Concerning Worship, 2:1-15**
  A. Prayer in the Church, 2:1-8
  B. Women in the Church, 2:9-15
IV. **Instruction Concerning Leaders, 3:1-16**
  A. Bishops, 3:1-7
  B. Deacons, 3:8-16

V. **Instruction Concerning Dangers, 4:1-16**
  A. Description of the Dangers, 4:1-5
  B. Defenses against the Dangers, 4:6-16
VI. **Instruction Concerning Various Duties, 5:1-6:21**
  A. Toward those Older and Younger, 5:1-2
  B. Toward Widows, 5:3-16
  C. Toward Elders, 5:17-25
  D. Toward Masters and Slaves, 6:1-2
  E. Toward False Teachers, 6:3-5
  F. Toward Money and Godliness, 6:6-19
  G. Toward One's Trust, 6:20-21

THE FIRST LETTER OF PAUL TO TIMOTHY

I OPENING GREETINGS, 1:1-2

★ **1** a2 Cor.
1:1; 2 Tim.
1:1 b1 Tim.
1:12 cTitus
1:3 dLuke
1:47; Titus
1:3 eCol.
1:27.

2 aActs
16:1; 2 Tim.
1:2 b2 Tim.
1:2; Titus 1:4
cRom. 1:7
d1 Tim. 1:12

1 Paul, aan apostle of bChrist Jesus caccording to the commandment of dGod our Savior, and of bChrist Jesus, *who is* our ehope;

2 to aTimothy, bmy true child in *the* faith: cGrace, mercy *and* peace from God the Father and dChrist Jesus our Lord.

II INSTRUCTION CONCERNING DOCTRINE, 1:3-20

A Paul's Warning against False Doctrines, 1:3-11

★ **3** aRom.
15:26 bActs
18:19 cRom.
16:17; 2 Cor.
11:4; Gal.
1:6f.; 1 Tim.
6:3

★ **4** a1 Tim.
4:7; 2 Tim.
4:4; Titus
1:14; 2 Pet.
1:16 bTitus
3:9 c1 Tim.
6:4; 2 Tim.
2:23; Titus
3:9 dEph.
3:2

5 a1 Tim.
1:18 b2 Tim.
2:22 c1 Tim.
1:19; 3:9;
2 Tim. 1:3;
1 Pet. 3:16,
21 d2 Tim.
1:5

6 aTitus
1:10

7 aJames
3:1 bLuke
2:46

3 As I urged you upon my departure for aMacedonia, remain on at bEphesus, in order that you may instruct certain men not to cteach strange doctrines,

4 nor to pay attention to amyths and endless bgenealogies, which give rise to mere cspeculation rather than dfurthering the administration of God which is by faith.

5 But the goal of our ainstruction is love bfrom a pure heart and a cgood conscience and a sincere dfaith.

6 For some men, straying from these things, have turned aside to afruitless discussion,

7 awanting to be bteachers of the Law, even though they do not understand either what they are saying or the matters about which they make confident assertions.

8 But we know that athe Law is good, if one uses it lawfully,

9 realizing the fact that alaw is not made for a righteous man, but for those who are lawless and brebellious, for the cungodly and sinners, for the unholy and dprofane, for those who kill their fathers or mothers, for murderers

10 and aimmoral men and bhomosexuals and ckidnappers and dliars and eperjurers, and whatever else is contrary to fsound teaching,

11 according to athe glorious gospel of bthe blessed God, with which I have been centrusted.

B Paul's Testimony Concerning the Grace of God, 1:12-17

12 I thank aChrist Jesus our Lord, who has bstrengthened me, because He considered me faithful, cputting me into service;

13 even though I was formerly a blasphemer and a apersecutor and a violent aggressor. And yet I was bshown mercy, because cI acted ignorantly in unbelief;

14 and the agrace of our Lord was more than abundant, with the bfaith and love which are *found* in Christ Jesus.

15 aIt is a trustworthy statement, deserving full acceptance, that bChrist Jesus came into the world to csave sinners, among whom dI am foremost *of all.*

★ **8** aRom.
7:12, 16
9 aGal.
5:23 bTitus
1:6, 10
c1 Pet. 4:18;
Jude 15
d1 Tim. 4:7
★**10** a1 Cor.
6:9 bLev.
18:22 cEx.
21:16; Rev.
18:13 dRev.
21:8, 27;
22:15 eMatt.
5:33; 23:16
f1 Tim. 4:6;
6:3; 2 Tim.
1:13; 4:3; Titus 1:9, 13

11 a2 Cor.
4:4 b1 Tim.
6:15 cGal.
2:7

12 aGal.
3:26; 1 Tim.
1:1, 2, 15;
2:5; 6:13; Titus 1:4 bActs
9:22; Phil.
4:13; 2 Tim.
4:17 cActs
9:15
13 aActs 8:3;
Phil. 3:6
b1 Cor. 7:25;
1 Tim. 1:16
cActs 26:9
14 aRom.
5:20; 1 Cor.
1:13-16;
3:10; 2 Cor.
4:15
b1 Thess.
1:3; 1 Tim.
2:15; 4:12;
6:11; 2 Tim.
1:13; 2:22;
Titus 2:2
★**15** a1 Tim.
3:1; 4:9;
2 Tim. 2:11;
Titus 3:8
bMark 2:17;
Luke 15:2ff.;
19:10 cRom.
11:14
d1 Cor. 15:9

1:1 *apostle.* Paul's title of authority, indicating his status above elders and deacons. An apostle had the right to expect obedience from the churches. *God our Savior.* 1 Timothy (here; 2:3; 4:10) and Titus (1:3; 2:10; 3:4) especially among N.T. books continue the O.T. title "Savior" applied to God, so frequent in the Psalms (106:21) and in Isaiah (45:21). The title also came to be ascribed to Christ (Phil. 3:20; Tit. 1:4).

1:3 *my departure for Macedonia.* This journey evidently occurred after the close of Acts (see the Introduction to Titus). *strange doctrines.* I.e., doctrines different from what Paul taught.

1:4 *myths and endless genealogies.* Mythical legends added to O.T. history which may have

led to Gnostic teachings concerning emanations extending from God to the creation (see discussion of Gnosticism in the Introduction to 1 John).

1:8 *the Law is good.* When used lawfully, it restrains evil people.

1:10 *sound teaching.* Lit., healthy or wholesome doctrine in contrast to false, which is diseased. See also 6:3; 2 Tim. 1:13; 4:3; Tit. 1:9, 13; 2:1, 2.

1:15 *It is a trustworthy statement.* This formula, which introduces an axiomatic truth, appears only in the pastoral letters (here; 3:1; 4:9; 2 Tim. 2:11; Tit. 3:8). *I am foremost.* Paul considered himself the foremost of sinners even at the end of his illustrious life.

16 a1 Cor.
7:25; 1 Tim.
1:13 bEph.
2:7

17 aRev.
15:3 [Gr.]
b1 Tim. 6:16
cCol. 1:15
dJohn 5:44;
1 Tim. 6:15;
Jude 25
eRom. 2:7,
10; 11:36;
Heb. 2:7

16 And yet for this reason I ^afound mercy, in order that in me as the foremost, Jesus Christ might ^bdemonstrate His perfect patience, as an example for those who would believe in Him for eternal life.

17 Now to the ^aKing eternal, ^bimmortal, ^cinvisible, the ^donly God, ^ebe honor and glory forever and ever. Amen.

C　Paul's Charge to Timothy, 1:18–20

18 a1 Tim.
1:5 b1 Tim.
1:2 c1 Tim.
4:14 d2 Cor.
10:4; 1 Tim.
6:12; 2 Tim.
2:3f.; 4:7

19 a1 Tim.
1:5 b1 Tim.
6:12, 21;
2 Tim. 2:18

★20 a2 Tim.
2:17 b2 Tim.
4:14 c1 Cor.
5:5 d1 Cor.
11:32; Heb.
12:5ff.

18 This ^acommand I entrust to you, Timothy, ^bmy son, in accordance with the ^cprophecies previously made concerning you, that by them you may ^dfight the good fight,

19 keeping ^afaith and a good conscience, which some have rejected and suffered shipwreck in regard to ^btheir faith.

20 Among these are ^aHymenaeus and ^bAlexander, whom I have ^cdelivered over to Satan, so that they may be ^dtaught not to blaspheme.

III　INSTRUCTION CONCERNING WORSHIP, 2:1–15
A　Prayer in the Church, 2:1–8

1 aEph.
6:18

2 aEzra
6:10; Rom.
13:1

2 First of all, then, I urge that ^aentreaties *and* prayers, petitions *and* thanksgivings, be made on behalf of all men,

2 ^afor kings and all who are in authority, in order that we may lead a tranquil and quiet life in all godliness and dignity.

3 This is good and acceptable in the sight of ^aGod our Savior,

4 ^awho desires all men to be ^bsaved and to ^ccome to the knowledge of the truth.

5 For there is ^aone God, *and* ^bone mediator also between God and men, *the* ^cman Christ Jesus,

6 who ^agave Himself as a ransom for all, the ^btestimony *borne* at ^cthe proper time.

7 ^aAnd for this I was appointed a preacher and ^ban apostle (^cI am telling the truth, I am not lying) as a teacher of ^dthe Gentiles in faith and truth.

8 Therefore ^aI want the men ^bin every place to pray, ^clifting up ^dholy hands, without wrath and dissension.

B　Women in the Church, 2:9–15

9 Likewise, *I want* ^awomen to adorn themselves with proper clothing, modestly and discreetly, not with braided hair and gold or pearls or costly garments;

10 but rather by means of good works, as befits women making a claim to godliness.

11 ^aLet a woman quietly receive instruction with entire submissiveness.

12 ^aBut I do not allow a

3 aLuke
1:47; 1 Tim.
1:1; 4:10

★ 4 aEzek.
18:23, 32;
John 3:17;
1 Tim. 4:10;
Titus 2:11;
2 Pet. 3:9
bRom. 11:14
c2 Tim. 2:25;
3:7; Titus
1:1; Heb.
10:26
★ 5 aRom.
3:30; 10:12;
1 Cor. 8:4
b1 Cor. 8:6;
Gal. 3:20
cMatt. 1:1;
Rom. 1:3
6 aMatt.
20:28; Gal.
1:4 b1 Cor.
1:6 cMark
1:15; Gal.
4:4; 1 Tim.
6:15; Titus
1:3
7 aEph.
3:8; 1 Tim.
1:11; 2 Tim.
1:11 b1 Cor.
9:1 cRom.
9:1 dActs
9:15
★ 8 aPhil.
1:12; 1 Tim.
5:14; Titus
3:8; [in Gr.]
bJohn 4:21;
1 Cor. 1:2;
2 Cor. 2:14;
1 Thess. 1:8
cPs. 63:4;
Luke 24:50
dPs. 24:4;
James 4:8
★ 9 a1 Pet.
3:3
11 a1 Cor.
14:34; Titus
2:5
★12 a1 Cor.
14:34; Titus
2:5

1:20 *Hymenaeus and Alexander.* How they made shipwreck of their faith (v. 19) is not stated, though the false teaching of Hymenaeus is described in 2 Tim. 2:17–18. *I have delivered over to Satan.* A remedial discipline (as in 1 Cor. 5:5), which excluded such persons from the help and fellowship of the church—a kind of last-resort punishment.
2:4 *who desires.* An expression of God's wish, not His decree.
2:5 *one mediator.* All other mediators are ruled out in bringing God and man together; Jesus mediates through His death on the cross (Heb. 9:15; 12:24).
2:8 *men.* I.e., males who are to lead in public prayer. *lifting up holy hands.* A common posture for prayer, and representative of the purity of life which is necessary for proper fel-

lowship in prayer. *without wrath and dissension.* When these attitudes are present, prayer is impossible.
2:9 *proper clothing.* Respectable and honorable apparel reflects a godly woman's inner life. Elaborate interweaving of the hair with gold and pearls was discouraged; and orderliness, not ostentation, was the standard. *good works* (v. 10) will be their ornament.
2:12 *I do not allow a woman to teach.* Women are not to assume the office of teacher in the church (see 1 Cor. 14:34). Women may teach as long as they do not usurp the place of leadership and authority of men in the church. The injunction is based on the relationship of man and woman in the original creation (Gen. 2:18; 3:6).

woman to teach or exercise authority over a man, but to remain quiet.

13 ^aFor it was Adam who was first created, *and* then Eve.

14 And *it was* not Adam *who* was deceived, but ^athe woman being quite deceived, fell into transgression.

15 But women shall be preserved through the bearing of children if they continue in ^afaith and love and sanctity with self-restraint.

13 ^aGen. 2:7, 22; 3:16; 1 Cor. 11:8ff.
14 ^aGen. 3:6, 13; 2 Cor. 11:3

★**15** ^a1 Tim. 1:14

IV INSTRUCTION CONCERNING LEADERS, 3:1-16
A Bishops, 3:1-7

3 ^aIt is a trustworthy statement: if any man aspires to the ^boffice of overseer, it is a fine work he desires *to do.*

2 ^aAn overseer, then, must be above reproach, ^bthe husband of one wife, ^ctemperate, prudent, respectable, ^dhospitable, ^eable to teach,

3 ^anot addicted to wine or pugnacious, but gentle, uncontentious, ^bfree from the love of money.

4 *He must be* one who ^amanages his own household

★**1** ^a1 Tim. 1:15 ^bActs 20:28; Phil. 1:1
★**2** ^a1 Tim. 3:2-4; Titus 1:6-8 ^bLuke 2:36f.; 1 Tim. 5:9; Titus 1:6 ^c1 Tim. 3:8. ^dRom. 12:13 ^e2 Tim. 2:24
3 ^aTitus 1:7 ^b1 Tim. 3:8; 6:10; Titus 1:7; Heb. 13:5

★**4-5**
4 ^a1 Tim. 3:12

well, keeping his children under control with all dignity

5 (but if a man does not know how to manage his own household, how will he take care of ^athe church of God?);

6 *and* not a new convert, lest he become ^aconceited and fall into the ^bcondemnation incurred by the devil.

7 And he must ^ahave a good reputation with ^bthose outside *the church,* so that he may not fall into reproach and ^cthe snare of the devil.

5 ^a1 Cor. 10:32; 1 Tim. 3:15

★**6** ^a1 Tim. 6:4; 2 Tim. 3:4 ^b1 Tim. 3:7

7 ^a2 Cor. 8:21 ^bMark 4:11 ^c1 Tim. 6:9; 2 Tim. 2:26

B Deacons, 3:8-16

8 ^aDeacons likewise *must be* men of dignity, not double-tongued, ^bor addicted to much wine ^cor fond of sordid gain,

9 ^abut holding to the mystery of the faith with a clear conscience.

10 And ^alet these also first be tested; then let them serve as deacons if they are beyond reproach.

11 Women *must* likewise *be* dignified, ^anot malicious gossips, but ^btemperate, faithful in all things.

12 Let ^adeacons be ^bhusbands of *only* one wife, *and* ^cgood man-

★**8** ^aPhil. 1:1; 1 Tim. 3:12 ^b1 Tim. 5:23; Titus 2:3 ^c1 Tim. 3:3; Titus 1:7; 1 Pet. 5:2
★**9** ^a1 Tim. 1:5, 19
10 ^a1 Tim. 5:22

★**11** ^a2 Tim. 3:3; Titus 2:3 ^b1 Tim. 3:2

12 ^aPhil. 1:1; 1 Tim. 3:8 ^b1 Tim. 3:2 ^c1 Tim. 3:4

2:15 *preserved through.* This may mean: (1) brought safely through childbirth; (2) saved through the birth of a Child, Jesus the Savior; or (3) that a woman's greatest achievement is found in her devotion to her divinely ordained role: to help her husband, to bear children, and to follow a faithful, chaste way of life.

3:1 *overseer.* Or bishop. Also referred to as an elder in the N.T. (see Tit. 1:5, 7, where the terms are used interchangeably). The elder, the principal official in a local church, was called by the Holy Spirit (Acts 20:28), recognized by other elders (1 Tim. 4:14), and qualified according to the standards listed in this passage. His duties included ruling (5:17), pastoring or shepherding the flock (Acts 20:28; 1 Pet. 5:2), guarding the truth (Tit. 1:9), and general oversight of the work, including finances (Acts 11:30).

3:2 *the husband of one wife* = married only once (see note on Tit. 1:6).

3:4-5 The elder's home provides him with a training-ground for the exercise of his leadership duties in the church.

3:6 *not a new convert.* Lest rapid advancement into a place of leadership cause him to become proud.

3:8 *Deacons.* The word means "minister" or "servant." Deacons were originally the helpers of the elders. Thus their qualifications were practically the same as those for the elders. The office had its beginnings in Jerusalem (Acts 6:1-6). However, the word deacon is used in an unofficial sense throughout the N.T. of anyone who serves (cf. Eph. 6:21), as well as in an official sense, designating those who occupy the office of deacon (cf. Phil. 1:1).

3:9 *the mystery of the faith.* I.e., the body of revealed doctrine. Truth must be united to a life lived with *a clear conscience.*

3:11 *Women.* Most likely a reference to the wives of the deacons, rather than to a separate office of deaconess; since the qualifications for deacons are continued in v. 12. If he had a different group in mind, it would seem more natural for Paul to have finished the qualifications for deacons before introducing the office of deaconess.

agers of *their* children and their own households.

13 For those who have served well as deacons [a]obtain for themselves a high standing and great confidence in the faith that is in Christ Jesus.

14 I am writing these things to you, hoping to come to you before long;

15 but in case I am delayed, *I write* so that you may know how one ought to conduct himself in [a]the household of God, which is the [b]church of [c]the living God, the [d]pillar and support of the truth.

16 And by common confession great is [a]the mystery of godliness:

He who was [b]revealed in the flesh,
Was [c]vindicated in the Spirit,
[d]Beheld by angels,
[e]Proclaimed among the nations,
[f]Believed on in the world,
[g]Taken up in glory.

V INSTRUCTION CONCERNING DANGERS, 4:1-16

A Description of the Dangers, 4:1-5

4 But [a]the Spirit explicitly says that [b]in later times some will fall away from the faith, paying attention to [c]deceitful spirits and [d]doctrines of demons,

2 by means of the hypocrisy of liars [a]seared in their own conscience as with a branding iron,

3 *men* who [a]forbid marriage and *advocate* [b]abstaining from foods, which [c]God has created to be [d]gratefully shared in by those who believe and know the truth.

4 For [a]everything created by God is good, and nothing is to be rejected, if it is [b]received with gratitude;

5 for it is sanctified by means of [a]the word of God and prayer.

B Defenses against the Dangers, 4:6-16

6 In pointing out these things to [a]the brethren, you will be a good [b]servant of Christ Jesus, *constantly* nourished on the words of the faith and of the [c]sound doctrine which you [d]have been following.

7 But have nothing to do with [a]worldly [b]fables fit only for old women. On the other hand, discipline yourself for the purpose of [c]godliness;

8 for [a]bodily discipline is only of little profit, but [b]godliness is profitable for all things, since it [c]holds promise for the [d]present life and *also* for the *life* to come.

9 [a]It is a trustworthy statement deserving full acceptance.

10 For it is for this we labor and strive, because we have fixed [a]our hope on [b]the living God, who is [c]the Savior of all men, especially of believers.

11 [a]Prescribe and teach these things.

12 [a]Let no one look down on your youthfulness, but *rather* in speech, conduct, [b]love, faith *and* purity, show yourself [c]an example of those who believe.

Cross references (left margin):

13 [a]Matt. 25:21

★15 [a]1 Cor. 3:16; 2 Cor. 6:16; Eph. 2:21f.; 1 Pet. 2:5; 4:17 [b]1 Tim. 3:5 [c]Matt. 16:16; 1 Tim. 4:10 [d]Gal. 2:9; 2 Tim. 2:19

★16 [a]Rom. 16:25 [b]John 1:14; 1 Pet. 1:20; 1 John 3:5, 8 [c]Rom. 3:4 [d]Luke 2:13; 24:4; 1 Pet. 1:12 [e]Rom. 16:26; 2 Cor. 1:19; Col. 1:23 [f]2 Thess. 1:10 [g]Mark 16:19; Acts 1:9

★ 1-5 1 [a]John 16:13; Acts 20:23; 21:11; [b]2 Thess. 2:3ff.; 2 Tim. 3:1; 2 Pet. 3:3; Jude 18 [c]1 John 4:6 [d]James 3:15 2 [a]Eph. 4:19 3 [a]Heb. 13:4 [b]Col. 2:16, 23 [c]Gen. 1:29; 9:3 [d]Rom. 14:6; 1 Cor. 10:30f.; 1 Tim. 4:4

Cross references (right margin):

4 [a]1 Cor. 10:26 [b]Rom. 14:6; 1 Cor. 10:30f.; 1 Tim. 4:3

5 [a]Gen. 1:25, 31; Heb. 11:3

6 [a]Acts 1:15 [b]2 Cor. 11:23 [c]1 Tim. 1:10 [d]Luke 1:3 [Gr.]; Phil. 2:20, 22; 2 Tim. 3:10

★ 7 [a]1 Tim. 1:9 [b]1 Tim. 1:4 [c]1 Tim. 4:8; 6:3, 5f.; 2 Tim. 3:5

★ 8 [a]Col. 2:23 [b]1 Tim. 4:7; 6:3, 5f.; 2 Tim. 3:5 [c]Ps. 37:9, 11; Prov. 19:23; 22:4; Matt. 6:33 [d]Matt. 6:33; 12:32; Mark 10:30

9 [a]1 Tim. 1:15

10 [a]2 Cor. 1:10; 1 Tim. 6:17 [b]1 Tim. 3:15 [c]John 4:42; 1 Tim. 2:4

11 [a]1 Tim. 5:7; 6:2

12 [a]1 Cor. 16:11; Titus 2:15 [b]1 Tim. 1:14 [c]Titus 2:7; 1 Pet. 5:3

3:15 *the truth.* I.e., the Christian faith.

3:16 This seems to be a summary of the truth contained in what was likely a part of an early Christian hymn. *He who was revealed in the flesh* refers to the incarnation of Christ (cf. 2 Tim. 1:10; Tit. 2:11). *vindicated in the Spirit.* The vindication of Christ by the Spirit in His resurrection. *Taken up in glory.* Christ's ascension into heaven.

4:1-5 Paul returns to his attack on heresy. False teaching is inspired by *demons* and promulgated by means of *the hypocrisy of liars.* The Christian should live affirmatively, neither renouncing the world for a life of self-denial nor plunging into indulgence (vv. 3-5).

4:7 *fables . . . for old women.* See note on 1:4.

4:8 *little.* The benefits of bodily training are limited and transient when contrasted with the extensive and permanent benefits of godliness.

13 aUntil I come, give attention to the *public* breading *of Scripture,* to exhortation and teaching.

14 Do not neglect the spiritual gift within you, which was bestowed upon you through aprophetic utterance with bthe laying on of hands by the cpresbytery.

15 Take pains with these things; be *absorbed* in them, so that your progress may be evident to all.

16 aPay close attention to yourself and to your teaching; persevere in these things; for as you do this you will binsure salvation both for yourself and for those who hear you.

VI INSTRUCTION CONCERNING VARIOUS DUTIES, 5:1-6:21
A Toward those Older and Younger, 5:1-2

5 aDo not sharply rebuke an bolder man, *but rather* appeal to him as a father, *to* cthe younger men as brothers,

2 the older women as mothers, *and* the younger women as sisters, in all purity.

B Toward Widows, 5:3-16

3 Honor widows who are awidows indeed;

4 but if any widow has children or grandchildren, alet them first learn to practice piety in regard to their own family, and to make some return to their parents; for this is bacceptable in the sight of God.

5 Now she who is a awidow indeed, and who has been left alone bhas fixed her hope on God, and continues in centreaties and prayers night and day.

6 But she who agives herself to wanton pleasure is bdead even while she lives.

7 aPrescribe these things as well, so that they may be above reproach.

8 But if anyone does not provide for his own, and especially for those of his household, he has adenied the faith, and is worse than an unbeliever.

9 Let a widow be aput on the list only if she is not less than sixty years old, *having been* bthe wife of one man,

10 having a reputation for agood works; *and* if she has brought up children, if she has bshown hospitality to strangers, if she chas washed the saints' feet, if she has dassisted those in distress, *and* if she has devoted herself to every good work.

11 But refuse *to put* younger widows *on the list,* for when they feel asensual desires in disregard of Christ, they want to get married,

12 *thus* incurring condemnation, because they have set aside their previous pledge.

13 And at the same time they also learn *to be* idle, as they go around from house to house; and not merely idle, but also agossips and bbusybodies, talking about cthings not proper *to mention.*

14 Therefore, aI want younger *widows* to get bmarried, bear children, ckeep house, *and* dgive the enemy no occasion for reproach;

4:13 *reading.* The public reading of the Scriptures, to be accompanied by *exhortation* (preaching) and *teaching.*

4:14 *the presbytery.* The body of elders.

5:3-16 Widows, who ordinarily would have no financial means of support, were to be cared for by their families, if possible (v. 4). If support were not available from that source, the church should care for them (in such cases the women were called *widows indeed,* v. 3). Younger widows were encouraged to remarry (v. 14), but those over 60 and destitute could be placed on the official relief roll of the church (v. 9). These "enrolled widows" constituted a kind of "order of widows," who were expected to devote themselves to prayer and good works (vv. 5, 10).

5:7 The meaning is: See that these regulations are followed so that both widows and their families will be above criticism in their conduct.

15 a 1 Tim.
1:20 b Matt.
4:10
★16 a 1 Tim.
5:4 b 1 Tim.
5:10 c 1 Tim.
5:3

15 for some ^ahave already turned aside to follow ^bSatan.

16 If any woman who is a believer ^ahas *dependent* widows, let her ^bassist them, and let not the church be burdened, so that it may assist those who are ^cwidows indeed.

C Toward Elders, 5:17-25

★17 a Acts
11:30; 1 Tim.
4:14 [Gr.];
5:19 b Rom.
12:8
c 1 Thess.
5:12
18 a Deut.
25:4; 1 Cor.
9:9 b Lev.
19:13; Deut.
24:15; Matt.
10:10; Luke
10:7; 1 Cor.
9:14
19 a Acts
11:30; 1 Tim.
4:14 [Gr.];
5:17 b Matt.
18:16
★20 a Gal.
2:14; Eph.
5:11; 2 Tim.
4:2 b 2 Cor.
7:11
21 a Luke
9:26; 1 Tim.
6:13; 2 Tim.
2:14; 4:1

17 Let ^athe elders who ^brule well be considered worthy of double honor, especially those who ^cwork hard at preaching and teaching.

18 For the Scripture says, "^aYOU SHALL NOT MUZZLE THE OX WHILE HE IS THRESHING," and "^bThe laborer is worthy of his wages."

19 Do not receive an accusation against an ^aelder except on the basis of ^btwo or three witnesses.

20 Those who continue in sin, ^arebuke in the presence of all, ^bso that the rest also may be fearful *of sinning.*

21 ^aI solemnly charge you in the presence of God and of Christ Jesus and of *His* chosen angels, to maintain these *principles* without bias, doing nothing in a *spirit of partiality.*

★22 a 1 Tim.
3:10; 4:14
b Eph. 5:11;
1 Tim. 3:2-7

22 ^aDo not lay hands upon anyone *too* hastily and thus share ^b*responsibility for* the sins of others; keep yourself free from sin.

★23 a 1 Tim.
3:8

23 No longer drink water *exclusively,* but ^ause a little wine for the sake of your stomach and your frequent ailments.

24 a Rev.
14:13

24 The sins of some men are quite evident, going before them to judgment; for others, their *sins* ^afollow after.

25 Likewise also, deeds that are good are quite evident, and ^athose which are otherwise cannot be concealed.

25 a Prov.
10:9

D Toward Masters and Slaves, 6:1-2

6 ^aLet all who are under the yoke as slaves regard their own masters as worthy of all honor so ^bthat the name of God and *our* doctrine may not be spoken against.

2 And let those who have believers as their masters not be disrespectful to them because they are ^abrethren, but let them serve them all the more, because those who partake of the benefit are believers and beloved. ^bTeach and preach these *principles.*

★ 1-2
1 a Eph.
6:5; Titus
2:9; 1 Pet.
2:18 b Titus
2:5

2 a Acts
1:15; Gal.
3:28; Philem.
16 b 1 Tim.
4:11

E Toward False Teachers, 6:3-5

3 If anyone ^aadvocates a different doctrine, and does not agree with ^bsound words, those of our Lord Jesus Christ, and with the doctrine ^cconforming to godliness,

4 he is ^aconceited *and* understands nothing; but he has a morbid interest in ^bcontroversial questions and ^cdisputes about words, out of which arise envy, strife, abusive language, evil suspicions,

3 a 1 Tim.
1:3 b 1 Tim.
1:10 c Titus
1:1

★ 4-5
4 a 1 Tim.
3:6 b 1 Tim.
1:4 c Acts
18:15; 2 Tim.
2:14

5:16 Relatives should assume the support of widows in their family (cf. vv. 4, 8).

5:17 *double honor.* Respect and remuneration (v. 18). The church was beginning to face the problem of financial support of its workers.

5:20 *Those who continue in sin.* I.e., elders who sin.

5:22 *lay hands . . . too hastily.* Often understood as forbidding hasty ordination, it may well refer to over-hasty receiving of a penitent backslider back into full fellowship.

5:23 *use a little wine.* The words imply that Timothy was a total abstainer and that the advice is given in relation to a medical problem.

6:1-2 The problems of the master-slave relationship are discussed in 1 Cor. 7:21; Eph. 6:5-9; Col. 3:22-4:1; Tit. 2:9-10; and Philem. 10-17. The N.T. writers do not question the institution of slavery, but try to mitigate it through improved attitudes of both masters and slaves. In the church, they met on equal terms as members of the fellowship, though there may have been instances when slaves were elders and thus, in the church, were over masters whom they served all week.

6:4-5 Again heretical teachers are excoriated. Perhaps they charged fees (v. 5).

5 a2 Tim.
3:8; Titus
1:15 bTitus
1:11; 2 Pet.
2:3

5 and constant friction between amen of depraved mind and deprived of the truth, who bsuppose that godliness is a means of gain.

F Toward Money and Godliness, 6:6-19

★ 6 aLuke
12:15-21;
1 Tim. 6:6-10
b1 Tim. 4:8
cPhil. 4:11;
Heb. 13:5
7 aJob
1:21; Eccl.
5:15
8 aProv.
30:8

6 aBut godliness *actually* is a means of bgreat gain, when accompanied by ccontentment.

7 For awe have brought nothing into the world, so we cannot take anything out of it either.

8 And if we ahave food and covering, with these we shall be content.

9 aProv.
15:27; 23:4;
28:20; Luke
12:21; 1 Tim.
6:17 b1 Tim.
3:7

9 aBut those who want to get rich fall into temptation and ba snare and many foolish and harmful desires which plunge men into ruin and destruction.

10 aCol. 3:5;
1 Tim. 3:3;
6:9 bRom.
11:16ff.
cJames 5:19

10 For athe love of money is a broot of all sorts of evil, and some by longing for it have cwandered away from the faith, and pierced themselves with many a pang.

11 a2 Tim.
2:22 b2 Tim.
3:17 c1 Tim.
1:14 d2 Tim.
3:10

11 But aflee from these things, you bman of God; and pursue righteousness, godliness, cfaith, dlove, perseverance *and* gentleness.

★12 a1 Cor.
9:25f.; Phil.
1:30; 1 Tim.
1:18 b1 Tim.
1:19 cPhil.
3:12; 1 Tim.
6:19 dCol.
3:15 e2 Cor.
9:13; 1 Tim.
6:13 f1 Tim.
4:14; 2 Tim.
2:2

12 aFight the good fight of bfaith; ctake hold of the eternal life dto which you were called, and you made the good econfession in the presence of fmany witnesses.

13 a1 Tim.
5:21 bGal.
3:26; 1 Tim.
1:12, 15; 2:5
c2 Cor. 9:13;
1 Tim. 6:12
dMatt. 27:2;
John 18:37

13 aI charge you in the presence of God, who gives life to all things, and of bChrist Jesus, who testified the cgood confession dbefore Pontius Pilate,

14 that you keep the commandment without stain or reproach until the aappearing of our Lord Jesus Christ,

14 a2 Thess.
2:8

15 which He will bring about at athe proper time—He who is bthe blessed and conly Sovereign, dthe King of kings and eLord of lords;

★15 a1 Tim.
2:6 b1 Tim.
1:11 c1 Tim.
1:17 dDeut.
10:17; Rev.
17:14; 19:16
ePs. 136:3

16 awho alone possesses immortality and bdwells in unapproachable light; cwhom no man has seen or can see. dTo Him *be* honor and eternal dominion! Amen.

16 a1 Tim.
1:17 bPs.
104:2; James
1:17; 1 John
1:5 cJohn
1:18 d1 Tim.
1:17

17 Instruct those who are rich in athis present world bnot to be conceited or to cfix their hope on the uncertainty of riches, but on God, dwho richly supplies us with all things to enjoy.

17 aMatt.
12:32; 2 Tim.
4:10; Titus
2:12 bPs.
62:10; Luke
12:20; Rom.
11:20; 1 Tim.
6:9 c1 Tim.
4:10 dActs
14:17

18 *Instruct them* to do good, to be rich in agood works, bto be generous and ready to share,

18 a1 Tim.
5:10 bRom.
12:8; Eph.
4:28

19 astoring up for themselves the treasure of a good foundation for the future, so that they may btake hold of that which is life indeed.

19 aMatt.
6:20 b1 Tim.
6:12

G Toward One's Trust, 6:20-21

20 O aTimothy, guard bwhat has been entrusted to you, avoiding cworldly *and* empty chatter *and* the opposing arguments of what is falsely called "knowledge"—

20 a1 Tim.
1:2 b2 Tim.
1:12, 14
c1 Tim. 1:9;
2 Tim. 2:16

21 which some have professed and thus agone astray from bthe faith.

cGrace be with you.

21 a2 Tim.
2:18 b1 Tim.
1:19 cCol.
4:18

6:6 In contrast to the material gain of the heretics (v. 5), the Christian finds his gain of a nonfinancial sort, *godliness* and *contentment,* or self-sufficiency, which results from an inner satisfaction with the situation that God has ordained for him.

6:12 *made the good confession.* Timothy's

public confession of Christ at his baptism.

6:15 This (His appearing, v. 14) will be manifest at the proper time by *the blessed and only Sovereign.* In other words, the return of Christ (v. 14) will occur at the time ordered and appointed by God.

INTRODUCTION TO
THE SECOND LETTER OF PAUL TO TIMOTHY

AUTHOR: Paul   DATE: 66

Authorship   *See Introduction to 1 Timothy.*

Background   *See* Probable Order of Events *under the Introduction to Titus. Paul, imprisoned in Rome as the result of persecution under Nero, realized, when he wrote this letter, that his death was near (1:8, 16; 4:6–8). Alone and cold in his dungeon (4:10–12), the veteran missionary wrote his young son in the faith this intensely personal letter. Soon afterward, according to tradition, he was beheaded on the Ostian Way, west of Rome.*

Contents   *The theme may be taken from 2:3, "a good soldier of Christ Jesus." Important subjects mentioned include the apostasy of the last days (3:1–9, cf. 1 Tim. 4:1–3), the inspiration of the Scriptures (3:16), and the crown of righteousness (4:8).*

OUTLINE OF 2 TIMOTHY

I. **The Salutation, 1:1–2**
II. **The Expression of Thanks for Timothy, 1:3–7**
III. **The Call of a Soldier of Christ, 1:8–18**
  A. A Call to Courage, 1:8–12
  B. A Call to Faithfulness, 1:13–18
IV. **The Character of a Soldier of Christ, 2:1–26**
  A. He Is Strong, 2:1–2
  B. He Is Single-minded, 2:3–4
  C. He Is Strict, 2:5–10
  D. He Is Secure, 2:11–13
  E. He Is Sound of Faith, 2:14–19
  F. He Is Sanctified, 2:20–23
  G. He Is a Servant, 2:24–26
V. **The Caution for a Soldier of Christ, 3:1–17**
  A. The Peril of Apostasy, 3:1–9
  B. The Protection from Apostasy, 3:10–17
VI. **The Charge to a Soldier of Christ, 4:1–5**
VII. **The Comfort of a Soldier of Christ, 4:6–18**
  A. A Good Finish to Life, 4:6–7
  B. A Good Future after Life, 4:8
  C. Good Friends in Life, 4:9–18
VIII. **Concluding Greetings, 4:19–22**

THE SECOND LETTER OF PAUL TO TIMOTHY

I THE SALUTATION, 1:1–2

★ 1 a2 Cor.
1:1 bGal.
3:26; 1 Tim.
1:12; 2 Tim.
1:2, 9, 13
c1 Cor. 1:1
d1 Tim. 6:19

1 Paul, ᵃan apostle of ᵇChrist Jesus ᶜby the will of God, according to the promise of ᵈlife in Christ Jesus,

2 aActs
16:1; 1 Tim.
1:2 b1 Tim.
1:2; 2 Tim.
2:1; Titus 1:4
c1 Tim. 1:2

2 to ᵃTimothy, my beloved ᵇson: ᶜGrace, mercy *and* peace from God the Father and Christ Jesus our Lord.

II THE EXPRESSION OF THANKS FOR TIMOTHY, 1:3–7

3 aRom.
1:8 bActs
24:14 cActs
23:1; 24:16;
1 Tim. 1:5
dRom. 1:9

3 ᵃI thank God, whom I ᵇserve with a ᶜclear conscience the way my forefathers did, ᵈas I constantly remember you in my prayers night and day,

★ 4 a2 Tim.
4:9, 21
bActs 20:37

4 ᵃlonging to see you, ᵇeven as I recall your tears, so that I may be filled with joy.

1:1 *life in Christ Jesus.* I.e., in union with Christ Jesus.
1:4 *your tears.* Possibly those shed at some

parting, such as in Acts 20:37; or perhaps a reference to tears Paul knows Timothy has shed in the course of his service for Christ.

★ 5 *a*1 Tim.
1:5 *b*Acts
16:1; 2 Tim.
3:15

5 For I am mindful of the *a*sincere faith within you, which first dwelt in your grandmother Lois, and *b*your mother Eunice, and I am sure that *it is* in you as well.

6 *a*1 Tim.
4:14

6 And for this reason I remind you to kindle afresh *a*the gift of God which is in you through *a*the laying on of my hands.

★ 7 *a*John
14:27; Rom.
8:15

7 For God has not given us a *a*spirit of timidity, but of power and love and discipline.

III THE CALL OF A SOLDIER OF CHRIST, 1:8–18
A A Call to Courage, 1:8–12

★ 8 *a*Mark
8:38; Rom.
1:16; 2 Tim.
1:12, 16
*b*1 Cor. 1:6
*c*Eph. 3:1;
2 Tim. 1:16
*d*2 Tim. 2:3,
9; 4:5
*e*2 Tim. 1:10;
2:8

8 Therefore *a*do not be ashamed of the *b*testimony of our Lord, or of me *c*His prisoner; but join with me in *d*suffering for the *e*gospel according to the power of God,

9 *a*Rom.
11:14 *b*Rom.
8:28f. *c*Rom.
11:29 *d*Eph.
2:9 *e*2 Tim.
1:1 *f*Rom.
16:25; Eph.
1:4; Titus 1:2
★10 *a*Rom.
16:26
*b*2 Thess.
2:8; 2 Tim.
4:1, 8; Titus
2:11 *c*2 Tim.
1:1 *d*1 Cor.
15:26; Heb.
2:14f.

9 who has *a*saved us, and *b*called us with a holy *c*calling, *d*not according to our works, but according to His own *b*purpose and grace which was granted us in *e*Christ Jesus from *f*all eternity,

10 but *a*now has been revealed by the *b*appearing of our Savior *c*Christ Jesus, who *d*abolished death, and brought life and immortality to light through the gospel;

11 *a*for which I was appointed a preacher and an apostle and a teacher.

11 *a*1 Tim.
2:7

12 For this reason I also suffer these things, but *a*I am not ashamed; for I know *b*whom I have believed and I am convinced that He is able to *c*guard what I have entrusted to Him until *d*that day.

★12 *a*2 Tim.
1:8, 16 *b*Ti-
tus 3:8
*c*1 Tim. 6:20;
2 Tim. 1:14
*d*1 Cor. 1:8;
3:13; 2 Tim.
1:18; 4:8

B A Call to Faithfulness, 1:13–18

13 *a*Retain the *b*standard of *c*sound words *d*which you have heard from me, in the *e*faith and love which are in *f*Christ Jesus.

13 *a*2 Tim.
3:14; Titus
1:9 *b*Rom.
2:20; 6:17
*c*1 Tim. 1:10
*d*2 Tim. 2:2
*e*1 Tim. 1:14
*f*2 Tim. 1:1

14 Guard, through the Holy Spirit who *a*dwells in us, the *b*treasure which has been entrusted to *you.*

★14 *a*Rom.
8:9 *b*1 Tim.
6:20; 2 Tim.
1:12

15 You are aware of the fact that all who are in *a*Asia *b*turned away from me, among whom are Phygelus and Hermogenes.

★15 *a*Acts
2:9 *b*2 Tim.
4:10, 11, 16

16 The Lord grant mercy to *a*the house of Onesiphorus for he often refreshed me, and *b*was not ashamed of my *c*chains;

★16–18
16 *a*2 Tim.
4:19 *b*2 Tim.
1:8 *c*Eph.
6:20

17 but when he was in Rome, he eagerly searched for me, and found me—

18 the Lord grant to him to find mercy from the Lord on *a*that day—and you know very well what services he rendered at *b*Ephesus.

18 *a*1 Cor.
1:8; 3:13;
2 Tim. 1:12;
4:8 *b*Acts
18:19; 1 Tim.
1:3

1:5 *Lois* is mentioned nowhere else. *your mother Eunice.* See Acts 16:1. Apparently both women had been converted under Paul's ministry.

1:7 *timidity.* cf. John 14:27 and Rev. 21:8. The believer is to have fear in the sense of awe (1 Pet. 1:17; 2:17) but not cowardice.

1:8 *the testimony of our Lord.* I.e., testifying, including by suffering, to our Lord.

1:10 *immortality* = deathlessness, imperishability.

1:12 *whom I have believed.* I.e., on whose trustworthiness I have staked my faith. *what I have entrusted.* Lit., the deposit. Paul's trust is well-founded, for God will preserve this deposit of faith in Christ until the day of judg-

ment, when all dangers will be past. Some understand this to refer to God's deposit of gifts in Paul's life (as in v. 14 and 1 Tim. 6:20).

1:14 *the treasure.* Lit., the good deposit. I.e., the gospel.

1:15 *all who are in Asia.* I.e., all who are now in Asia who had formerly been with Paul in Rome. Asia was the Roman province embracing the western part of what is now called Asia Minor (Turkey). *Phygelus and Hermogenes* were a special disappointment to Paul and were known to Timothy.

1:16–18 *Onesiphorus,* who had ministered to Paul in Ephesus, sought him out in the dungeon where Paul was confined in Rome and ministered to him.

IV　THE CHARACTER OF A SOLDIER OF CHRIST, 2:1–26

A　He Is Strong, 2:1–2

★ **1** *a*2 Tim.
1:2 *b*Eph.
6:10 *c*2 Tim.
1:1

2 You therefore, my *a*son, *b*be strong in the grace that is in *c*Christ Jesus.

★ **2** *a*2 Tim.
1:13 *b*1 Tim.
6:12 *c*1 Tim.
1:18 *d*1 Tim.
1:12 *e*[in
Gr.] 2 Cor.
2:16; 3:5

2 And the things *a*which you have heard from me in the presence of *b*many witnesses, these *c*entrust to *d*faithful men, who will be *e*able to teach others also.

B　He Is Single-minded, 2:3–4

3 *a*2 Tim.
1:8 *b*1 Cor.
9:7; 1 Tim.
1:18 *c*2 Tim.
1:1
★ **4** *a*2 Pet.
2:20

3 *a*Suffer hardship with *me,* as a good *b*soldier of *c*Christ Jesus.
4 No soldier in active service *a*entangles himself in the affairs of everyday life, so that he may please the one who enlisted him as a soldier.

C　He Is Strict, 2:5–10

★ **5** *a*1 Cor.
9:25

5 And also if anyone *a*competes as an athlete, he does not win the prize unless he competes according to the rules.

6 *a*1 Cor.
9:10

6 *a*The hard-working farmer ought to be the first to receive his share of the crops.

★**7**

7 Consider what I say, for the Lord will give you understanding in everything.

8 *a*Acts
2:24 *b*Matt.
1:1 *c*Rom.
2:16

8 Remember Jesus Christ, *a*risen from the dead, *b*descendant of David, *c*according to my gospel,

9 *a*2 Tim.
1:8; 2:3
*b*Phil. 1:7
*c*Luke 23:32
*d*1 Thess.
1:8 *e*Acts
28:31; 2 Tim.
4:17

9 for which I *a*suffer hardship even to *b*imprisonment as a *c*criminal; but *d*the word of God *e*is not imprisoned.

★**10** *a*Col.
1:24 *b*Luke
18:7; Titus
1:1 *c*2 Cor.
1:6; 1 Thess.
5:9 *d*1 Cor.
1:21 *e*2 Tim.
1:1; 2:1, 3
*f*2 Cor. 4:17;
1 Pet. 5:10

10 For this reason *a*I endure all things for *b*the sake of those who are chosen, *c*that they also may obtain the *d*salvation which is in *e*Christ Jesus *and* with *it* *f*eternal glory.

D　He Is Secure, 2:11–13

★**11** *a*1 Tim.
1:15 *b*Rom.
6:8; 1 Thess.
5:10

11 *a*It is a trustworthy statement:

For *b*if we died with Him,
　　we shall also live with
　　Him;

12 *a*Matt.
19:28; Luke
22:29; Rom.
5:17; 8:17
*b*Matt. 10:33;
1 Tim. 5:8

12 If we endure, *a*we shall
　　also reign with Him;
If we *b*deny Him, He also
　　will deny us;

★**13** *a*Rom.
3:3; 1 Cor.
1:9 *b*Num.
23:19; Titus
1:2

13 If we are faithless, *a*He remains faithful; for *b*He cannot deny Himself.

E　He Is Sound of Faith, 2:14–19

★**14** *a*1 Tim.
5:21; 2 Tim.
4:1 *b*1 Tim.
6:4; 2 Tim.
2:23; Titus
3:9

14 Remind *them* of these things, and solemnly *a*charge *them* in the presence of God not to *b*wrangle about words, which is useless, *and* leads to the ruin of the hearers.

2:1 This verse seems to sum up the teaching of chapter 1: Timothy, you have the gift of power from God through Christ (1:7); now find your strength in this gift of grace.

2:2 *heard from me.* The content of Paul's teaching is not stated but was clearly understood by Timothy. *many witnesses.* Perhaps the elders at Timothy's ordination, or more likely the many who had at different times heard Paul's preaching.

2:4 *entangles.* A minister must put priority on his calling and be completely dedicated to his task and his Commander.

2:5 The picture in this verse is of an athlete who must play *according to the rules.* A minister must adhere to the requirements of his calling, making the Word and will of God his standard in all things.

2:7 *Consider.* If they would reflect on his teachings (in the previous verses), Christ would open up for them depths of meaning.

2:10 *For this reason.* I.e., because the Word of God remains unimprisoned (v. 9).

2:11 *died.* Perhaps a reference to the crucifixion of the sin nature, as in Gal. 2:20, but more likely a reference to physical death. I.e., if we die physically, we shall be raised physically.

2:13 *If we are faithless, He remains faithful.* A statement of the consistency of God's character, a strong promise to the believer of the security of his salvation even though he may lose all rewards (see 1 Cor. 3:15).

2:14 *wrangle about words.* I.e., indulge in word battles, wordy controversies, and quibbling about words. These are not only profitless but harmful to those who hear them.

15 Be diligent to ^apresent yourself approved to God as a workman who does not need to be ashamed, handling accurately ^bthe word of truth.

16 But ^aavoid ^bworldly and empty chatter, for it will lead to further ungodliness,

17 and their talk will spread like gangrene. Among them are ^aHymenaeus and Philetus,

18 men who have gone astray from the truth saying that ^athe resurrection has already taken place, and thus they upset ^bthe faith of some.

19 Nevertheless, the ^afirm foundation of God stands, having this ^bseal, "^cThe Lord knows those who are His," and, "^dLet everyone who names the name of the Lord abstain from wickedness."

F   He Is Sanctified, 2:20-23

20 Now in a large house there are not only gold and silver vessels, but also vessels of wood and of earthenware, and ^asome to honor and some to dishonor.

21 Therefore, if a man cleanses himself from ^athese things, he will be a vessel for honor, sanctified, useful to the Master, ^bprepared for every good work.

22 Now ^aflee from youthful lusts, and ^bpursue righteousness, ^bfaith, love and peace, with those

who ^ccall on the Lord ^dfrom a pure heart.

23 But refuse foolish and ignorant ^aspeculations, knowing that they ^bproduce quarrels.

G   He Is a Servant, 2:24-26

24 And ^athe Lord's bond-servant must not be quarrelsome, but be kind to all, ^bable to teach, patient when wronged,

25 ^awith gentleness correcting those who are in opposition, ^bif perhaps God may grant them repentance leading to ^cthe knowledge of the truth,

26 and they may come to their senses and escape from ^athe snare of the devil, having been ^bheld captive by him to do his will.

V   THE CAUTION FOR A SOLDIER OF CHRIST, 3:1-17
A   The Peril of Apostasy, 3:1-9

3 But realize this, that ^ain the last days difficult times will come.

2 For men will be ^alovers of self, ^blovers of money, ^cboastful, ^carrogant, ^drevilers, ^cdisobedient to parents, ^eungrateful, ^funholy,

3 ^aunloving, irreconcilable, ^bmalicious gossips, without self-control, brutal, ^chaters of good,

4 ^atreacherous, ^breckless, ^cconceited, ^dlovers of pleasure rather than lovers of God;

★15 ^aRom. 6:13; James 1:12 ^bEph. 1:13; James 1:18

16 ^aTitus 3:9 ^b1 Tim. 1:9; 6:20

★17 ^a1 Tim. 1:20

18 ^a1 Cor. 15:12 ^b1 Tim. 1:19; Titus 1:11

★19 ^aIs. 28:16f.; 1 Tim. 3:15 ^bJohn 3:33 ^cJohn 10:14; 1 Cor. 8:3 ^dLuke 13:27; 1 Cor. 1:2

★20-21
20 ^aRom. 9:21

21 ^a1 Tim. 6:11; 2 Tim. 2:16-18 ^b2 Cor. 9:8; Eph. 2:10; 2 Tim. 3:17

★22 ^a1 Tim. 6:11 ^b1 Tim. 1:14 ^cActs 7:59 ^d1 Tim. 1:5

23 ^a1 Tim. 6:4; 2 Tim. 2:14; Titus 3:9 ^bTitus 3:9; James 4:1

24 ^a1 Tim. 3:3; Titus 1:7 ^b1 Tim. 3:2

25 ^aGal. 6:1; Titus 3:2; 1 Pet. 3:15 ^bActs 8:22 ^c1 Tim. 2:4

★26 ^a1 Tim. 3:7 ^bLuke 5:10

★ 1 ^a1 Tim. 4:1
2 ^aPhil. 2:21 ^bLuke 16:14; 1 Tim. 3:3; 6:10 ^cRom. 1:30 ^d2 Pet. 2:10-12 ^eLuke 6:35 ^f1 Tim. 1:9
3 ^aRom. 1:31 ^b1 Tim. 3:11 ^cTitus 1:8
4 ^aActs 7:52 [Gr.] ^bActs 19:36 [Gr.] ^c1 Tim. 3:6 ^dPhil. 3:19

2:15 handling accurately. I.e., correctly handling the Word of God, in both analysis and presentation—in contrast to the inane interpretations of false teachers.

2:17 Hymenaeus and Philetus. These troublemakers (Hymenaeus is also mentioned in 1 Tim. 1:20) were probably teaching that the doctrine of resurrection had only an allegorical or spiritual meaning. Gnostic teaching conceived of resurrection allegorically, as referring to acquaintance with truth and as occurring at baptism.

2:19 seal. A mark of authentication and ownership.

2:20-21 There will be some wicked persons

(wood and earthenware) in every church, but (v. 21) no one need remain wicked.

2:22 lusts. Not only for immoral but also foolish things. Temptation is to be avoided by fleeing what hinders, by following what helps, and by seeking the company of spiritual people.

2:26 held captive. I.e., by Satan at Satan's will (see Eph. 2:3).

3:1 in the last days. The whole period between the writing of this letter and the Lord's return. As His return draws near, these characteristics will intensify (see 1 Tim. 4:1-5). The description that follows (vv. 2-9) is of mass corruption, of a breakdown of law and tradition.

★ 5 aRom.
2:20 b1 Tim.
4:7 c1 Tim.
5:8 dMatt.
7:15;
2 Thess. 3:6
★ 6 aJude 4
b1 Tim. 5:6;
Titus 3:3 cTi-
tus 3:3

7 a2 Tim.
2:25

★ 8 aEx.
7:11 bActs
13:8 c1 Tim.
6:5

9 aLuke
6:11 [Gr.]
bEx. 7:12;
8:18; 9:11

10 aLuke 1:3
[Gr.]; Phil.
2:20, 22;
1 Tim. 4:6
b1 Tim 6:11
★11 a2 Tim.
12:10
b2 Cor. 1:5,
7 cActs
13:14, 45, 50
dActs 14:5
eActs 14:19
f2 Cor.
11:23-27
gRom. 15:31
★12 aJohn
15:20; Acts
14:22; 2 Cor.
4:9f.

5 holding to a [a]form of [b]godliness, although they have [c]denied its power; and [d]avoid such men as these.

6 For among them are those who [a]enter into households and captivate [b]weak women weighed down with sins, led on by [c]various impulses,

7 always learning and never able to [a]come to the knowledge of the truth.

8 And just as [a]Jannes and Jambres [b]opposed Moses, so these *men* also oppose the truth, [c]men of depraved mind, rejected as regards the faith.

9 But they will not make further progress; for their [a]folly will be obvious to all, [b]as also that of those *two* came to be.

B The Protection from Apostasy, 3:10-17

10 But you [a]followed my teaching, conduct, purpose, faith, patience, [b]love, perseverance,

11 [a]persecutions, *and* [b]sufferings, such as happened to me at [c]Antioch, at [d]Iconium *and* at [e]Lystra; what [f]persecutions I endured, and out of them all [g]the Lord delivered me!

12 And indeed, all who desire to live godly in Christ Jesus [a]will be persecuted.

13 But evil men and impostors [a]will proceed *from bad to* worse, [b]deceiving and being deceived.

14 You, however, [a]continue in the things you have learned and become convinced of, knowing from whom you have learned *them*;

15 and that [a]from childhood you have known [b]the sacred writings which are able to [c]give you the wisdom that leads to [d]salvation through faith which is in [e]Christ Jesus.

16 [a]All Scripture is inspired by God and profitable for teaching, for reproof, for correction, for training in righteousness;

17 that [a]the man of God may be adequate, [b]equipped for every good work.

VI THE CHARGE TO A SOLDIER OF CHRIST, 4:1-5

4 [a]I solemnly charge *you* in the presence of God and of Christ Jesus, who is to [b]judge the living and the dead, and by His [c]appearing and His kingdom:

2 preach [a]the word; be ready in season *and* out of season; [b]reprove, rebuke, exhort, with great [c]patience and instruction.

13 a2 Tim.
2:16 bTitus
3:3

14 a2 Tim.
1:13; Titus
1:9

15 a2 Tim.
1:5 bJohn
5:47; Rom.
2:27 cPs.
119:98f.
d1 Cor. 1:21
e2 Tim. 1:1

★16 aRom.
4:23f.; 15:4;
2 Pet. 1:20f.

17 a1 Tim.
6:11 b2 Tim.
2:21; Heb.
13:21

★ 1 a1 Tim.
5:21; 2 Tim.
2:14 bActs
10:42
c2 Thess.
2:8
★ 2 aGal.
6:6; Col. 4:3;
1 Thess. 1:6
b1 Tim. 5:20;
Titus 1:13;
2:15 c2 Tim.
3:10

3:5 *holding to a form of godliness.* Having the outer semblance of it without its spiritual dynamic.

3:6 *weak women.* These women, apparently because of sin, were changeable of mind, prone to accept new ideas and swayed by impulses.

3:8 *Jannes and Jambres.* Though these names do not appear in the O.T., in late Jewish, pagan, and certain early Christian writings they are applied to the Egyptian magicians who performed counterfeit miracles in opposition to Moses (Ex. 7:11, 22). They are symbols of the folly of opposing the truth.

3:11 *persecutions.* See Acts 13-14.

3:12 *to live godly.* Apparently involves an aggressive witness such as that Paul gave at the places listed in v. 11.

3:16 *All Scripture is inspired.* Lit., God-breathed; i.e., the Bible came from God through the men who wrote it (see 2 Pet. 1:21).

God superintended these human authors so that, using their individual personalities, they composed and recorded without error God's Word to man. Christ attested to the fact that inspiration extends to the very words (Matt. 5:18; John 10:35). In the same verse, Paul quoted Deuteronomy and Luke as Scripture (1 Tim. 5:18), and Peter declared Paul's epistles to be Scripture (2 Pet. 3:16). Inspiration does not involve mechanical dictation but the accurate recording of God's words. Inspiration does not extend beyond the original manuscripts, though the texts we possess today have been transmitted with high accuracy.

4:1 *by His appearing and His kingdom.* When Christ appears, He will inaugurate the judgment and His faithful will be gathered into His kingdom.

4:2 *be ready in season.* I.e., always be ready, whether the time is opportune for preaching the gospel or not.

★ 3-4
3 a 2 Tim.
3:1 b 1 Tim.
1:10; 2 Tim.
1:13

3 For athe time will come when they will not endure bsound doctrine; but *wanting* to have their ears tickled, they will accumulate for themselves teachers in accordance to their own desires;

4 a 2 Thess.
2:11; Titus
1:14 b 1 Tim.
1:4

4 and awill turn away their ears from the truth, and bwill turn aside to myths.

5 a 1 Pet.
1:13 b 2 Tim.
1:8 cActs
21:8 dLuke
1:1 eEph.
4:12; Col.
4:17

5 But you, abe sober in all things, bendure hardship, do the work of an cevangelist, dfulfill your eministry.

VII THE COMFORT OF A SOLDIER OF CHRIST, 4:6-18
A A Good Finish to Life, 4:6-7

★ 6 aPhil.
2:17 bPhil.
1:23; 2 Pet.
1:14

6 For I am already being apoured out as a drink offering, and the time of bmy departure has come.

★ 7 a 1 Cor.
9:25f.; Phil.
1:30; 1 Tim.
1:18, 6:12
bActs 20:24;
1 Cor. 9:24
c 2 Tim. 3:10

7 aI have fought the good fight, I have finished bthe course, I have kept cthe faith;

B A Good Future after Life, 4:8

★ 8 aCol.
1:5; 1 Pet.
1:4 b 1 Cor.
9:25; 2 Tim.
2:5 c 2 Tim.
1:12 dPhil.
3:11 e 2 Tim.
4:1

8 in the future there ais laid up for me bthe crown of righteousness, which the Lord, the righteous Judge, will award to me on cthat day; and not only to me, but also to dall who have loved His eappearing.

C Good Friends in Life, 4:9-18

9 aMake every effort to come to me soon;

10 for aDemas, having loved bthis present world, has deserted me and gone to cThessalonica; Crescens *has gone* to dGalatia, eTitus to Dalmatia.

11 aOnly bLuke is with me. Pick up cMark and bring him with you, dfor he is useful to me for service.

12 But aTychicus I have sent to bEphesus.

13 When you come bring the cloak which I left at aTroas with Carpus, and the books, especially the parchments.

14 aAlexander the coppersmith did me much harm; bthe Lord will repay him according to his deeds.

15 Be on guard against him yourself, for he vigorously opposed our teaching.

16 At my first defense no one supported me, but all deserted me; amay it not be counted against them.

17 But the Lord stood with me, and astrengthened me, in order that through me bthe proclamation might be cfully accomplished, and that all dthe Gentiles might hear; and I was edelivered out of fthe lion's mouth.

18 The Lord will deliver me

★ 9-22
9 a 2 Tim.
1:4; 4:21; Ti-
tus 3:12
★ 10 aCol.
4:14 b 1 Tim.
6:17 cActs
17:1 dActs
16:6 e 2 Cor.
2:13
★ 11 a 2 Tim.
1:15 bCol.
4:14 cActs
12:12 dCol.
4:10; 2 Tim.
2:21
12 aActs
20:4 bActs
18:19
★ 13 aActs
16:8

★ 14 aActs
19:33; 1 Tim.
1:20 bRom.
2:6; 12:19

★ 16 aActs
7:60; 1 Cor.
13:5
★ 17 a 1 Tim.
1:12; 2 Tim.
2:1 bTitus
1:3 c 2 Tim.
4:5 dActs
9:15; Phil.
1:12ff.
eRom.
15:31; 2 Tim.
3:11 f 1 Sam.
17:37; Ps.
22:21
18 a 1 Cor.
1:21 b 1 Cor.
15:50; 2 Tim.
4:1; Heb.
11:16; 12:22
cRom.
11:36; 2 Pet.
3:18

4:3-4 A description of people who were no longer content to hear the sound teaching of Paul, but who were impelled to turn to many different teachers of novelty and untruth.

4:6 *departure* = release. I.e., his death.

4:7 *the faith.* I.e., the recognized body of Christian doctrine (cf. Jude 3). Paul *kept* the faith in two senses: he was obedient to it, and he passed it on as he received it.

4:8 *laid up.* I.e., safely kept. *crown of righteousness.* One of the rewards (prizes) offered Christians, in this case for loving the coming of Christ. See note on 1 Cor. 3:14.

4:9-22 After a climactic testimony (vv. 6-8), Paul returns to treat worrisome, immediate personnel affairs.

4:10 Why *Demas* deserted Paul is not known.

4:11 *Mark* and Paul had overcome the differences that caused their earlier separation (Acts 15:36-41).

4:13 *the books.* Papyrus rolls. *the parchments.* Skins of vellum, used for more precious documents, in this case probably Paul's personal copies of portions of the O.T. This missionary-prisoner still wanted to study!

4:14 *Alexander.* Probably not the same as the one mentioned in 1 Tim. 1:20, since he is here identified as the coppersmith or metalworker. We may infer from v. 15 that he may have caused the arrest of Paul in some city, that he was still active, and that he was hostile to Paul's teachings.

4:16 *my first defense.* I.e., the preliminary hearing with which Paul's final trial opened (though some take this to mean Paul's first trial in Rome three years before).

4:17 *delivered out of the lion's mouth.* Paul was not immediately condemned and was spared from execution.

from every evil deed, and will
^abring me safely to His ^bheavenly
kingdom; ^cto Him *be* the glory
forever and ever. Amen.

VIII CONCLUDING GREETINGS, 4:19–22

★**19** ^aActs
18:2 ^b2 Tim.
    1:16

19 Greet Prisca and ^aAquila,

and ^bthe household of Onesiphorus.

20 ^aErastus remained at ^bCor-
inth, but Trophimus I left sick at
^cMiletus.

21 ^aMake every effort to
come before ^bwinter. Eubulus
greets you, also Pudens and Linus
and Claudia and all the brethren.

22 ^aThe Lord be with your
spirit. ^bGrace be with you.

★**20** ^aActs
19:22 ^bActs
18:1 ^cActs
20:15

★**21** ^a2 Tim.
4:9 ^bTitus
3:12

22 ^aGal.
6:18; Phil.
4:23; Philem.
25 ^bCol.
4:18

4:19 *Prisca and Aquila.* Devoted friends of Paul
(Acts 18:2, 26; Rom. 16:3; 1 Cor. 16:19). *Onesiphorus.* See note on 1:16–18.

4:20 *Trophimus I left sick.* This happening cannot be fitted into Acts and thus indicates two

imprisonments in Rome for Paul. Trophimus
was an Ephesian (Acts 20:4; 21:29).

4:21 At least the four persons named here had
not deserted Paul (v. 16). Nothing more is
known of them.

INTRODUCTION TO
THE LETTER OF PAUL TO TITUS

AUTHOR: Paul   DATE: 65

Authorship   *See the Introduction to 1 Timothy.*

Historical Background   *The probable order of significant events is: (1) Paul was released from his house arrest in Rome (where we find him at the end of Acts), probably because his accusers did not choose to press their charges against him before Caesar (Acts 24:1; 28:30). Their case, therefore, was lost by default, and Paul was freed. (2) Paul visited Ephesus, left Timothy there to supervise the churches, and went on to Macedonia (northern Greece). (3) From there he wrote 1 Timothy (1 Tim. 1:3). (4) He visited Crete, left Titus there to supervise those churches, and went to Nicopolis in Achaia (southern Greece, Tit. 3:12). (5) Either from Macedonia or Nicopolis, he wrote this letter to encourage Titus. (6) He visited Troas (2 Tim. 4:13), where he was suddenly arrested, taken to Rome, imprisoned, and finally beheaded. (7) From Rome, during this second imprisonment, he wrote 2 Timothy.*

Titus   *A Gentile by birth (Gal. 2:3), Titus was converted through the ministry of Paul (Tit. 1:4). He accompanied Paul to Jerusalem at the time of the apostolic council (Acts 15:2; Gal. 2:1-3). He was Paul's emissary to the church at Corinth during the third missionary journey (2 Cor. 7:6-7; 8:6, 16). Titus and two others took the letter we call 2 Corinthians to Corinth and urged the Corinthians to make good their promise to give to the poor in Jerusalem. Paul left Titus in Crete to use his administrative gifts to consolidate the work there. Artemas or Tychicus probably relieved Titus in Crete so he could join Paul in Nicopolis (Tit. 3:12), from where Paul sent him to Dalmatia (Yugoslavia) (2 Tim. 4:10). Tradition says he returned to Crete and died there.*

Contents   *Important topics discussed in the letter include: qualifications for elders (1:5-9), instructions to various age groups (2:1-8), relationship to government (3:1-2), and the relation of regeneration to human works and to the Spirit (3:5).*

OUTLINE OF TITUS

I. **Opening Greetings, 1:1-4**
II. **Elders in the Church, 1:5-9**
  A. Their Desirability, 1:5
  B. Their Qualifications, 1:6-9
III. **Offenders in the Church, 1:10-16**
IV. **Operation of the Church, 2:1-3:11**
  A. Duties of the Minister, 2:1-10

  B. Living in Response to God's Grace, 2:11-15
  C. Demonstration of Good Works, 3:1-11
    1. In relation to governments, 3:1
    2. In relation to all people, 3:2-7
    3. In relation to false teachers, 3:8-11
V. **Personal Messages and Greetings, 3:12-15**

THE LETTER OF PAUL TO TITUS

I　OPENING GREETINGS, 1:1-4

★ 1 aRom.
1:1; James
1:1; Rev. 1:1
b2 Cor. 1:1
cLuke 18:7
d1 Tim. 2:4
e1 Tim. 6:3

1 Paul, [a]a bond-servant of God, and an [b]apostle of Jesus Christ, for the faith of those [c]chosen of God and [d]the knowledge of the truth which is [e]according to godliness,

2 a2 Tim.
1:1; Titus 3:7
b2 Tim. 2:13
cRom. 1:2
d2 Tim. 1:9
3 a1 Tim.
2:6 bRom.
16:25; 2 Tim.
4:17 c1 Tim.
1:11 d1 Tim.
1:1 eLuke
1:47; 1 Tim.
1:1; Titus
2:10; 3:4
★ 4 a2 Cor.
2:13 b2 Tim.
1:2 c2 Pet.
1:1 dRom.
1:7 e1 Tim.
1:12; 2 Tim.
1:1

2 in [a]the hope of eternal life, which God, [b]who cannot lie, [c]promised [d]long ages ago,

3 but [a]at the proper time manifested, even His word, in [b]the proclamation [c]with which I was entrusted [d]according to the commandment of [e]God our Savior;

4 to [a]Titus, [b]my true child in a [c]common faith: [d]Grace and peace from God the Father and [e]Christ Jesus our Savior.

II　ELDERS IN THE CHURCH, 1:5-9
A　Their Desirability, 1:5

★ 5 aActs
27:7; Titus
1:12 bActs
14:23 cActs
11:30

5 For this reason I left you in [a]Crete, that you might set in order what remains, and [b]appoint [c]elders in every city as I directed you,

B　Their Qualifications, 1:6-9

★ 6 a1 Tim.
3:2-4; Titus
1:6-8 b1 Tim.
3:2 cEph.
5:18 dTitus
1:10

6 namely, [a]if any man be above reproach, the [b]husband of one wife, having children who believe, not accused of [c]dissipation or [d]rebellion.

7 For the [a]overseer must be above reproach as [b]God's steward, not [c]self-willed, not quick-tempered, not [d]addicted to wine, not pugnacious, [e]not fond of sordid gain,

★ 7 a1 Tim.
3:2 b1 Cor.
4:1 c2 Pet.
2:10 d1 Tim.
3:3 e1 Tim.
3:3, 8

8 but [a]hospitable, [b]loving what is good, sensible, just, devout, self-controlled,

8 a1 Tim.
3:2 b2 Tim.
3:3

9 [a]holding fast the faithful word which is in accordance with the teaching, that he may be able both to exhort in [b]sound doctrine and to refute those who contradict.

9 a2 Thess.
2:15; 1 Tim.
1:19; 2 Tim.
1:13 b1 Tim.
1:10; Titus
2:1

III　OFFENDERS IN THE CHURCH, 1:10-16

10 [a]For there are many [b]rebellious men, [c]empty talkers and deceivers, especially [d]those of the circumcision,

10 a2 Cor.
11:13 bTitus
1:6 c1 Tim.
1:6 dActs
11:2

11 who must be silenced because they are upsetting [a]whole families, teaching [b]things they should not teach, [c]for the sake of sordid gain.

11 a1 Tim.
5:4 [in Gr.];
2 Tim. 3:6
b1 Tim. 5:13
c1 Tim. 6:5

12 [a]One of themselves, a prophet of their own, said, "[b]Cretans are always liars, evil beasts, lazy gluttons."

★12 aActs
17:28 bActs
2:11; 27:7

13 This testimony is true. For this cause [a]reprove them [b]severely that they may be [c]sound in the faith,

13 a1 Tim.
5:20; 2 Tim.
4:2; Titus
2:15 b2 Cor.
13:10 cTitus
2:2

14 not paying attention to Jewish [a]myths and [b]command-

★14 a1 Tim.
1:4 bCol.
2:22 c2 Tim.
4:4

1:1　*for the faith . . . according to godliness.* Paul was commissioned to further the faith of God's elect so that they might acquire full knowledge of Christian truth.

1:4　*Titus.* He is not mentioned in Acts, but N.T. references to Titus' activities are found in 2 Cor. 2:13; 7:5-7, 13-14; 8:6, 16-17, 23; 12:18; Gal. 2:1, 3; 2 Tim. 4:10. *child.* A term of affection used also by Paul of Timothy and Onesimus.

1:5　*what remains.* A church is defective unless it has constituted leaders. In Crete these were appointed (= ordained) by Titus. See note on the elders at 1 Tim. 3:1.

1:6　*husband of one wife.* Wherever mentioned in the N.T., elders are seen as being married and as having children. This phrase may mean having only one wife at a time or it may mean being married only once (see 1 Tim. 5:9, where the similar phrase can only mean the latter). See also 1 Cor. 7:39 and 1 Tim. 5:14, where remarriage of a widow is permitted.

1:7　In Greek cities of the first century A.D. the vices described here were common.

1:12　Quoted from the Cretan poet Epimenides, who exaggerated for effect. To Cretanize was to lie.

1:14　*Jewish myths.* Speculations, of a Gnostic sort, supposedly based on O.T. scripture. For Gnosticism, see the Introduction to 1 John.

ments of men who ^cturn away from the truth.

★15 ^aLuke 11:41; Rom. 14:20 ^bRom. 14:14, 23 ^c1 Tim. 6:5

15 ^aTo the pure, all things are pure; but ^bto those who are defiled and unbelieving, nothing is pure, but both their ^cmind and their conscience are defiled.

16 ^a1 John 2:4 ^b1 Tim. 5:8 ^cRev. 21:8 ^dTitus 3:3 ^e2 Tim. 3:8 ^f2 Tim. 3:17; Titus 3:1

16 ^aThey profess to know God, but by *their* deeds they ^bdeny *Him*, being ^cdetestable and ^ddisobedient, and ^eworthless ^ffor any good deed.

IV OPERATION OF THE CHURCH, 2:1–3:11

A Duties of the Minister, 2:1–10

★ 1 ^aTitus 1:9

2 But as for you, speak the things which are fitting for ^asound doctrine.

2 ^aPhilem. 9 ^b1 Tim. 3:2 ^cTitus 1:13 ^d1 Tim. 1:2, 14

2 ^aOlder men are to be ^btemperate, dignified, ^bsensible, ^csound ^din faith, in love, in perseverance.

★ 3 ^a1 Tim. 3:11 ^b1 Tim. 3:8

3 Older women likewise are to be reverent in their behavior, ^anot malicious gossips, nor ^benslaved to much wine, teaching what is good,

4 that they may encourage the young women to love their husbands, to love their children,

★ 5 ^a1 Tim. 5:14 ^bEph. 5:22 ^c1 Tim. 6:1

5 *to be* sensible, pure, ^aworkers at home, kind, being ^bsubject to their own husbands, ^cthat the word of God may not be dishonored.

6 ^a1 Tim. 5:1 ^b1 Tim. 3:2

6 Likewise urge ^athe young men to be ^bsensible;

7 ^a1 Tim. 4:12

7 in all things show yourself to be ^aan example of good deeds, *with* purity in doctrine, dignified,

8 ^a2 Thess. 3:14; 1 Pet. 2:12

8 sound *in* speech which is beyond reproach, in order ^athat

the opponent may be put to shame, having nothing bad to say about us.

9 ^aEph. 6:5; 1 Tim. 6:1

9 Urge ^abondslaves to be subject to their own masters in everything, to be well-pleasing, not argumentative,

10 ^aTitus 1:3

10 not pilfering, but showing all good faith that they may adorn the doctrine of ^aGod our Savior in every respect.

B Living in Response to God's Grace, 2:11–15

★11 ^a2 Tim. 1:10; Titus 3:4 ^b1 Tim. 2:4

11 For the grace of God has ^aappeared, ^bbringing salvation to all men,

★12 ^a1 Tim. 6:9; Titus 3:3 ^b2 Tim. 3:12 ^c1 Tim. 6:17

12 instructing us to deny ungodliness and ^aworldly desires and ^bto live sensibly, righteously and godly ^cin the present age,

13 ^a2 Thess. 2:8 ^b1 Tim. 1:1; 2 Tim. 1:2; Titus 1:4; 2 Pet. 1:1

13 looking for the blessed hope and the ^aappearing of the glory of ^bour great God and Savior, Christ Jesus;

★14 ^a1 Tim. 2:6 ^bPs. 130:8; 1 Pet. 1:18 ^cEzek. 37:23; Heb. 1:3; 9:14; 1 John 1:7 ^dEx. 19:5; Deut. 14:2; Eph. 1:11; 1 Pet. 2:9 ^eEph. 2:10; Titus 3:8; 1 Pet. 3:13

14 who ^agave Himself for us, ^bthat He might redeem us from every lawless deed and ^cpurify for Himself a ^dpeople for His own possession, ^ezealous for good deeds.

15 ^a1 Tim. 4:13; 5:20; 2 Tim. 4:2 ^b1 Tim. 4:12

15 These things speak and ^aexhort and ^areprove with all authority. ^bLet no one disregard you.

C Demonstration of Good Works, 3:1–11

1 In relation to governments, 3:1

★ 1 ^a2 Tim. 2:14 ^bRom. 13:1 ^c2 Tim. 2:21

3 ^aRemind them ^bto be subject to rulers, to authorities, to be obedient, to be ^cready for every good deed,

---

1:15 Purity is an interior matter, of the mind and conscience, not external. See Luke 11:41.

2:1 *But.* I.e., in contrast to false teachers. *sound doctrine.* Lit., healthy teaching (as in 1:9, 13; 2:2). That which causes behavior to be in accord with belief.

2:3 *malicious gossips.* Apparently some of the older women were given to gossiping and drinking.

2:5 *that the word of God may not be dishonored.* Failure to observe the matters mentioned in this verse would expose the Word of

God to contempt by the world.

2:11 *appeared.* The tense of the verb indicates a reference to the incarnation, Christ's first appearing.

2:12 *ungodliness* = irreverence. *worldly desires* = passions, overpowering attractions for the secular world.

2:14 *redeem us from every lawless deed.* I.e., release us from the bondage of sin. See note on redemption at Eph. 1:7.

3:1 *be subject* = to submit or subject oneself. The same Greek word is used in Rom. 13:1

2 In relation to all people, 3:2-7

★ **2** a1 Tim.
3:3; 1 Pet.
2:18 b2 Tim.
2:25

3 aRom.
11:30; 1 Cor.
6:11; Col. 3:7
bTitus 1:16
c2 Tim. 3:13
dRom. 6:6,
12 e2 Tim.
3:6; Titus
2:12 fRom.
1:29
4 aRom.
2:4; Eph. 2:7;
1 Pet. 2:3
bTitus 2:10
cTitus 2:11
★ **5** aRom.
11:14; 2 Tim.
1:9 bEph.
2:9 cEph.
2:4; 1 Pet.
1:3 dJohn
3:5; Eph.
5:26; 1 Pet.
3:21 eRom.
12:2
6 aRom.
5:5 bRom.
2:4; 1 Tim.
6:17
7 aMatt.
25:34; Mark
10:17; Rom.
8:17, 24; Ti-
tus 1:2

2 to malign no one, ato be uncontentious, agentle, bshowing every consideration for all men.

3 aFor we also once were foolish ourselves, bdisobedient, cdeceived, denslaved to evarious lusts and pleasures, spending our life in fmalice and fenvy, hateful, hating one another.

4 But when the akindness of bGod our Savior and His love for mankind cappeared,

5 aHe saved us, bnot on the basis of deeds which we have done in righteousness, but caccording to His mercy, by the dwashing of regeneration and erenewing by the Holy Spirit,

6 awhom He poured out upon us brichly through Jesus Christ our Savior,

7 that being justified by His grace we might be made aheirs according to the hope of eternal life.

3 In relation to false teachers, 3:8-11

★ **8** a1 Tim.
1:15 b1 Tim.
2:8 c2 Tim.
1:12 dTitus
2:7, 14; 3:14

8 aThis is a trustworthy statement; and concerning these things I bwant you to speak confidently, so that those who have

cbelieved God may be careful to dengage in good deeds. These things are good and profitable for men.

9 But ashun bfoolish controversies and cgenealogies and strife and ddisputes about the Law; for they are eunprofitable and worthless.

10 aReject a bfactious man cafter a first and second warning,

11 knowing that such a man is aperverted and is sinning, being self-condemned.

9 a2 Tim.
2:16 b1 Tim.
1:4; 2 Tim.
2:23 c1 Tim.
1:4 dJames
4:1 e2 Tim.
2:14
★ **10** a2 John
10 bRom.
16:17 cMatt.
18:15f.
★ **11** aTitus
1:14

V PERSONAL MESSAGES AND GREETINGS, 3:12-15

12 When I send Artemas or aTychicus to you, bmake every effort to come to me at cNicopolis, for I have decided to dspend the winter there.

13 aDiligently help Zenas the blawyer and cApollos on their way so that nothing is lacking for them.

14 And let aour people also learn to bengage in good deeds to meet cpressing needs, that they may not be dunfruitful.

15 aAll who are with me greet you. Greet those who love us bin the faith.

cGrace be with you all.

★ **12** aActs
20:4; 2 Tim.
4:12 b2 Tim.
4:9 c2 Tim.
4:10 d2 Tim.
4:21
★ **13** aActs
15:3 bMatt.
22:35 cActs
18:24
14 aTitus 2:8
bTitus 3:8
cRom.
12:13; Phil.
4:16 dMatt.
7:19; Phil.
1:11; Col.
1:10
15 aActs
20:34
b1 Tim. 1:2
cCol. 4:18

and 1 Pet 2:13. *rulers . . . authorities* usually refer to angels (good angels as in Eph. 3:10 or evil angels as in Eph. 6:12), but here the reference is to human, governmental rulers. Though Christians are a "special" people elected by God, redeemed from the world and no longer dependent upon it, they are not above the necessity of getting along with the civil authorities who govern them.

3:2 *uncontentious.* Quarreling only arouses the hostility of non-Christians. Christian virtues are of an opposite sort.

3:5 *not on the basis of deeds . . . by the washing of regeneration.* Personal salvation is not achieved through good deeds but through the cleansing of the new birth. *renewing by the Holy Spirit* means either the initial act of conversion or, more probably, continual renewing by the Spirit throughout the life of the be

liever. In any case, salvation is God's gracious work, not a reward for man's worthwhile acts.

3:8 *these things.* I.e., the counsels of vv. 1-7. *engage in good deeds* probably has the general meaning of "apply oneself to good deeds," though the phrase may have the technical meaning of "enter honorable occupations."

3:10 *factious* —one who willfully chooses for himself and sets up a faction (see 1 Cor. 11:19; Gal. 5:20). Our responsibility is to reprimand such a person twice, then avoid him if he does not change.

3:11 *perverted.* Turned aside, and hence, self-condemned.

3:12 *Artemas.* Nothing more is known of him. *Tychicus.* See Acts 20:4; Eph. 6:21; Col. 4:7; 2 Tim. 4:12.

3:13 *Zenas.* Nothing more is known of him. *Apollos.* The well-known associate of Paul.

INTRODUCTION TO
THE LETTER OF PAUL TO PHILEMON

AUTHOR: Paul   DATE: 61

Background *Like Ephesians, Philippians, and Colossians, Philemon is one of the Prison Epistles, written during Paul's first confinement in Rome. Onesimus, one of the millions of slaves in the Roman Empire, had stolen from his master, Philemon, and had run away. Eventually, he made his way to Rome, where he crossed the path of the apostle Paul, who led him to faith in Christ (v. 10). Now Onesimus was faced with doing his Christian duty toward his master by returning to him. Since death would normally have been his punishment, Paul wrote this wonderful letter of intercession on Onesimus' behalf.*

Philemon was not the only slaveholder in the Colossian church (see Col. 4:1), so this letter gave guidelines for other Christian masters in their relationships to their slave-brothers. Paul did not deny the rights of Philemon over his slave, but he asked Philemon to relate the principle of Christian brotherhood to the situation with Onesimus (v. 16). At the same time, Paul offered to pay personally whatever Onesimus owed. This letter is not an attack against slavery as such, but a suggestion as to how Christian masters and slaves could live their faith within that evil system. It is possible that Philemon did free Onesimus and send him back to Paul (v. 14). It has also been suggested that Onesimus became a minister and later bishop of the church at Ephesus (Ignatius, To the Ephesians, 1).

This is the most personal of all Paul's letters.

OUTLINE OF PHILEMON

I. Greetings, 1-3
II. Praise of Philemon, 4-7
III. Plea to Philemon, 8-17

IV. Pledge to Philemon, 18-21
V. Personal Matters, 22-25

THE LETTER OF PAUL TO PHILEMON

I GREETINGS, 1-3

1 *a*Paul, *b*a prisoner of *c*Christ Jesus, and *d*Timothy our brother, to Philemon our beloved *brother* and *e*fellow worker,

2 and to Apphia *a*our sister, and to *b*Archippus our *c*fellow soldier, and to *d*the church in your house:

3 *a*Grace to you and peace from God our Father and the Lord Jesus Christ.

★ 1 *a*Phil. 1:1 *b*Eph. 3:1; Philem. 9, 23 *c*Gal. 3:26; 1 Tim. 1:12; Philem. 9, 23 *d*2 Cor. 1:1 *e*Phil. 2:25
★ 2 *a*Rom. 16:1 *b*Col. 4:17 *c*Phil. 2:25; 2 Tim. 2:3 *d*Rom. 16:5
3 *a*Rom. 1:7

II PRAISE OF PHILEMON, 4-7

4 *a*I thank my God always, *b*making mention of you in my prayers,

5 because I *a*hear of your love, and of the faith which you have toward the Lord Jesus, and toward all the saints;

6 *and I pray* that the fellowship of your faith may become effective through the *a*knowledge of every good thing which is in you for Christ's sake.

4 *a*Rom. 1:8 *b*Rom. 1:9
5 *a*Eph. 1:15; Col. 1:4; 1 Thess. 3:6
★ 6 *a*Phil. 1:9; Col. 1:9; 3:10

---

1 *a prisoner of Christ Jesus.* Better, *for Jesus Christ;* i.e., for His sake, in His service.
2 *Apphia* was likely Philemon's wife; and Ar-

chippus, his son.
6 *fellowship* = sharing.

7 a2 Cor.
7:4, 13
b1 Cor.
16:18; 2 Cor.
7:13; Philem.
20

7 For I have come to have much [a]joy and comfort in your love, because the hearts of the saints have been [b]refreshed through you, brother.

III   PLEA TO PHILEMON, 8–17

★ 8-10
8 a2 Cor.
3:12;
1 Thess. 2:6
bEph. 5:4

9 aRom.
12:1 bTitus
2:2 cPhilem.
1 dGal. 3:26;
1 Tim. 1:12;
Philem. 23

10 aRom.
12:1 b1 Cor.
4:14f. cCol.
4:9

8 Therefore, [a]though I have enough confidence in Christ to order you *to do* that which is [b]proper,

9 yet for love's sake I rather [a]appeal *to you*—since I am such a person as Paul, the [b]aged, and now also [c]a prisoner of [d]Christ Jesus—

10 I [a]appeal to you for my [b]child, whom I have begotten in my imprisonment, [c]Onesimus,

11 who formerly was useless to you, but now is useful both to you and to me.

12 And I have sent him back to you in person, that is, *sending my very heart,*

13 aPhil. 1:7;
Philem. 10

13 whom I wished to keep with me, that in your behalf he might minister to me in my [a]imprisonment for the gospel;

★14 a2 Cor.
9:7; 1 Pet.
5:2

14 but without your consent I did not want to do anything, that your goodness should [a]not be as it were by compulsion, but of your own free will.

★15 aGen.
45:5, 8

15 For perhaps [a]he was for this reason parted *from you* for a while, that you should have him back forever,

★16 a1 Cor.
7:22 bMatt.
23:8; 1 Tim.
6:2 cEph.
6:5; Col. 3:22

16 [a]no longer as a slave, but more than a slave, [b]a beloved brother, especially to me, but how much more to you, both [c]in the flesh and in the Lord.

17 a2 Cor.
8:23; Philem.
6

17 If then you regard me a [a]partner, accept him as *you would* me.

IV   PLEDGE TO PHILEMON, 18–21

★18

18 But if he has wronged you in any way, or owes you anything, charge that to my account;

★19 a1 Cor.
16:21; 2 Cor.
10:1; Gal.
5:2 b2 Cor.
9:4

19 [a]I, Paul, am writing this with my own hand, I will repay it ([b]lest I should mention to you that you owe to me even your own self as well).

20 aPhilem.
7

20 Yes, brother, let me benefit from you in the Lord; [a]refresh my heart in Christ.

21 a2 Cor.
2:3

21 [a]Having confidence in your obedience, I write to you, since I know that you will do even more than what I say.

V   PERSONAL MATTERS, 22–25

★22 aActs
28:23 bPhil.
1:25; 2:24
c2 Cor. 1:11
dActs 27:24;
Heb. 13:19

22 And at the same time also prepare me a [a]lodging; for [b]I hope that through [c]your prayers [d]I shall be given to you.

23 aCol. 1:7
bRom. 16:7
cPhilem. 1
24 aActs
12:12 bActs
19:29; Col.
4:10 cCol.
4:14
dPhilem. 1
25 aGal.
6:18 b2 Tim.
4:22

23 [a]Epaphras, my [b]fellow prisoner in [c]Christ Jesus, greets you,

24 as do [a]Mark, [b]Aristarchus, [c]Demas, [c]Luke, my [d]fellow workers.

25 [a]The grace of the Lord Jesus Christ be [b]with your spirit.

8-10 Paul could use his authority as an apostle to *order* Philemon. Instead Paul used the persuasions of love, age, and his imprisoned state, and simply appealed to Philemon (v. 10). The name *Onesimus* means useful, beneficial.

14 *your goodness.* I.e., Philemon's goodness, if he decided to send Onesimus back to serve Paul.

15 *perhaps.* A suggestion of a deeper purpose of God's providence in Onesimus' running away.

16 *a beloved brother.* Not legal emancipation for Onesimus, but a practical emancipation because of Philemon's changed attitude toward his slave, who was now also his brother in Christ.

18 *charge that to my account.* This Greek phrase is translated "imputed" in Rom. 5:13. It seems that Onesimus' offense included monetary loss to Philemon in addition to loss caused by the slave's running away. Paul asked Philemon to impute or reckon Onesimus' debt against Paul's account and to *accept him as you would me* (v. 17), a beautiful illustration of our sin imputed to Christ, wherein God receives us in the merit of His Son (2 Cor. 5:21).

19 *you owe to me even your own self.* Philemon was apparently converted under Paul's ministry.

22 *I shall be given to you.* Paul expected to be released from prison soon (see Phil. 1:25-26).

INTRODUCTION TO
THE LETTER TO THE HEBREWS

AUTHOR: Uncertain   DATE: 64-68

Authorship   *Many suggestions have been made for the author of this anonymous book—Paul, Barnabas, Apollos, Silas, Aquila and Priscilla, and Clement of Rome. There are both resemblances and dissimilarities to the theology and style of Paul, but Paul frequently appeals to his own apostolic authority in his letters, while this writer appeals to others who were eyewitnesses of Jesus' ministry (2:3). It is safest to say, as did the theologian Origen in the third century, that only God knows who wrote Hebrews.*

Readership   *Three questions are involved in determining the readership of this letter. (1) What was the racial background of these readers? Although some have held that they were Gentiles, all evidence points to their Jewish background—the title of the book, "to the Hebrews," the references to the prophets and angels ministering to Israel, and the citations concerning the Levitical worship. (2) Where did they live? Palestine or Italy have been the answers most often given. The preference seems to be Italy, for these readers were not poor (and the saints in Palestine were, 6:10; 10:34; Rom. 15:26); the Septuagint is used exclusively for quotations from the Old Testament (one would not expect this if the readers were Palestinian); and "those from Italy greet you" (13:24) sounds as though Italians outside of Italy are sending greetings back home. (3) What was their spiritual condition? Most were believers (3:1), though, as in every church group, there were doubtless some who merely professed Christianity. The author calls this letter a "word of exhortation" (13:22) necessitated by the fact that some were in danger of abandoning their faith in Christ and reverting to Judaism. The readers were being persecuted, though not to the point of being martyrs (10:32-34; 12:4), and in the face of this, some were running the risk of becoming apostate. The letter is a stirring apologetic for the superiority of Christ and Christianity over Judaism in terms of priesthood and sacrifice.*

Date   *Various dates have been suggested for the writing of Hebrews, from the 60's to the 90's. However, its use in the book of 1 Clement, which was written in 95, requires a date some time before that. The lack in the book of any reference to the destruction of the temple in Jerusalem as the divine proof that the Old Testament sacrificial system was finished argues strongly for a date before 70. In addition, the mention of Timothy's recent release (13:23), if it was in connection with his ministry to Paul in Rome, requires a date in the late 60's.*

Style   *The author displays outstanding literary and rhetorical skill. His style is a model of Hellenistic prose. Both the author and his readers are very familiar with the Old Testament in the Greek translation (the Septuagint). There are 29 direct quotations from the Old Testament plus 53 clear allusions to various other passages. These are used to demonstrate both the finality of the Christian revelation and its superiority to the old covenant.*

Contents   *The theme of the book is the superiority of Christ and thus of Christianity. The words "better," "perfect," and "heavenly" appear frequently. The outline shows how the theme is developed by proving that Christ is superior both in His person and His priesthood. Favorite passages include 2:3 (so great a salvation), 4:12 (the living Word of God), 4:16 (the throne of grace), 7:25 (the intercession of Christ), 11:1 (the description of faith), 11:4-40 (the heroes of faith), 12:1-2 (the Christian race), and 13:20-21 (a great benediction).*

OUTLINE OF HEBREWS

I. The Superiority of the Person of Christ, 1:1-4:16
A. Christ Is Superior to the Prophets, 1:1-4
B. Christ Is Superior to the Angels, 1:5-2:18
  1. In His divine person, 1:5-14
  2. In His saving proclamation, 2:1-4
  3. In His delivering purpose, 2:5-18
C. Christ Is Superior to Moses, 3:1-6
D. Christ Is the Supreme Object of Faith, 3:7-4:16

  1. The catastrophe of unbelief, 3:7-19
  2. The consequences of unbelief, 4:1-10
  3. The cure for unbelief, 4:11-16
II. The Superiority of the Priesthood of Christ, 5:1-10:39
A. Christ Is Superior in His Qualifications, 5:1-10
B. Parenthetical Warning: Don't Degenerate from Christ, 5:11-6:20

THE LETTER TO THE HEBREWS

I THE SUPERIORITY OF THE PERSON OF CHRIST, 1:1–4:16

A Christ Is Superior to the Prophets, 1:1–4

★ 1-4
★1 aJohn 9:29; 16:13
bActs 2:30; 3:21 cNum. 12:6, 8
★ 2 aMatt. 13:39 bJohn 9:29; 12:25
cJohn 5:26
dPs. 2:8
eJohn 1:3
f1 Cor. 2:7

1 God, after He aspoke long ago to the fathers in bthe prophets in many portions and cin many ways,

2 ain these last days bhas spoken to us in cHis Son, whom He appointed dheir of all things, ethrough whom also He made the fworld.

3 And He is the radiance of His glory and the exact arepresentation of His nature, and bupholds all things by the word of His power. When He had made cpurification of sins, He dsat down at the right hand of the eMajesty on high;

★ 3 a2 Cor. 4:4 bCol. 1:17 cTitus 2:14; Heb. 9:14 dMark 16:19 e2 Pet. 1:17

4 having become as much better than the angels, as He has inherited a more excellent aname than they.

4 aEph. 1:21; Phil. 2:9

B Christ Is Superior to the Angels, 1:5–2:18

1 In His divine person, 1:5–14

5 For to which of the angels did He ever say,

★ 5 aPs. 2:7; Acts 13:33; Heb. 5:5 b2 Sam. 7:14

1:1–4 These verses comprise one majestic sentence in the Greek text and read like the opening of a formal Greek oration rather than the customary "greetings" of a letter.

1:1 *fathers.* I.e., forefathers. *in many portions and in many ways.* I.e., through laws, institutions, ceremonies, kings, judges, prophets.

1:2 *in these last days.* The *last days* here means the entire gospel dispensation extending from the first to the second advent of Christ. *the world.* Lit., the ages, including time, space, and the material world.

1:3 *radiance* = effulgence or flood of resplendent light. The word means an outshining, not a reflection. *the exact representation* of God's essence or *nature.* These expressions in v. 3 are strong assertions of the deity of Christ. *sat down at the right hand of the Majesty on high.* The picture of Christ being seated indicates the finished character of His once-for-all sacrifice for sin (10:10, 12), and the right hand indicates the place of honor which He occupies.

1:5 *the angels.* The word "angel" means messenger. It usually refers to an order of spirit beings, rarely to human beings (as in Luke 7:24; Jas. 2:25). All angels were originally created in a holy state but some followed Satan in his revolt against God and became the demons. Some demons are loose and some are confined (see notes on Matt. 7:22; 2 Pet. 2:4; Jude 6). Angels are created beings who must ultimately answer to their Creator (Col. 1:16). Since they are spirit beings, they are not bound by some of the restrictions that limit human beings (cf. Heb. 1:14; Acts 12:5–10). They are organized and ranked (Isa. 6:1–3; Dan. 10:13; Eph. 3:10; Jude 9). Angels ministered to Christ often during His first advent and will accompany Him at His return (Matt. 2:13; 4:11; 26:53; 28:2, 5; Luke 22:43; 2 Thess. 1:7–8). They serve believers (Heb. 1:14) and observe them (1 Cor. 4:9; 11:10). Michael is the only one designated an archangel (Dan. 10:13, 21; Jude 9), though Gabriel also has an important position (Luke 1:19, 26). *did He . . . say.* Quoting 2 Sam. 7:14 and Ps. 2:7. Never to an angel did God say that he was a son, only to and of Christ. 2 Sam. 7:14 was addressed to Solomon and Ps. 2:7 may have been sung to a monarch on the day of his coronation. Christ, explains the writer of Hebrews, is the ultimate fulfillment of these words.

"ᵃThou art My Son,
Today I have begotten
Thee"?
And again,
"ᵇI will be a Father to Him,
And He shall be a Son to
Me"?

★ 6 ᵃHeb.
10:5 ᵇMatt.
24:14 ᶜDeut.
32:43 [Sep-
tuagint]; Ps.
97:7

6 And when He again ᵃbrings the first-born into ᵇthe world, He says,

"ᶜAnd let all the angels of
God worship Him."

★ 7 ᵃPs.
104:4

7 And of the angels He says,

"ᵃWho makes His angels
winds,
And His ministers a flame
of fire,"

★ 8-9
8 ᵃPs.
45:6 ᵇDeut.
33:27; Ps.
71:3; 90:1;
91:2, 9

8 But of the Son He says,

"ᵃThy ᵇthrone, O God, is
forever and ever,
And the righteous scepter
is the scepter of His
kingdom.

9 ᵃPs. 45:7
ᵇJohn 10:17;
Phil. 2:9;
Heb. 2:9 ᶜIs.
61:1, 3

9 "ᵃThou hast loved righteousness and hated law-
lessness;
ᵇTherefore God, Thy God,
hath ᶜanointed Thee
With the oil of gladness
above Thy companions."

★10-12
10 ᵃPs.
102:25

10 And,

"ᵃThou, Lord, in the beginning didst lay the foun-
dation of the earth,
And the heavens are the
works of Thy hands;

11 ᵃPs.
102:26 ᵇIs.
51:6; Heb.
8:13

11 ᵃThey will perish, but
Thou remainest;
ᵇAnd they all will become
old as a garment,

12 ᵃAnd as a mantle Thou
wilt roll them up;
As a garment they will
also be changed.
But Thou art ᵇthe same,
And Thy years will not
come to an end."

12 ᵃPs.
102:26, 27
ᵇHeb. 13:8

13 But to which of the angels has He ever said,

"ᵃSit at My right hand,
ᵇUntil I make Thine enemies
A footstool for Thy feet"?

13 ᵃPs.
110:1; Matt.
22:44; Heb.
1:3 ᵇJosh
10:24; Heb.
10:13

14 Are they not all ᵃminister-
ing spirits, sent out to render service for the sake of those who will
ᵇinherit ᶜsalvation?

★14 ᵃPs.
103:20f.;
Dan. 7:10
ᵇMatt. 25:34;
Mark 10:17;
Titus 3:7;
Heb. 6:12
ᶜRom.
11:14; 1 Cor.
1:21; Heb.
2:3; 5:9; 9:28
1 ᵃProv.
3:21 [Septua-
gint]

2 In His saving proclamation, 2:1-4

2 For this reason we must pay
much closer attention to what
we have heard, lest ᵃwe drift away
from it.

★ 2 ᵃHeb.
1:1 ᵇActs
7:53 ᶜHeb.
10:28 ᵈHeb.
10:35; 11:26

2 For if the word ᵃspoken
through ᵇangels proved unalter-
able, and ᶜevery transgression
and disobedience received a just
ᵈrecompense,

3 ᵃhow shall we escape if we
neglect so great a ᵇsalvation? After it was at the first ᶜspoken
through the Lord, it was ᵈcon-
firmed to us by those who heard,

3 ᵃHeb.
10:29; 12:25
ᵇRom.
11:14; 1 Cor.
1:21; Heb.
1:14; 5:9;
9:28 ᶜHeb.
1:1 ᵈMark
16:20; Luke
1:2; 1 John
1:1

4 God also bearing witness
with them, both by ᵃsigns and
ᵃwonders and by ᵇvarious miracles and by ᶜgifts of the Holy
Spirit ᵈaccording to His own will.

4 ᵃJohn
4:48 ᵇMark
6:14 ᶜ1 Cor.
12:4, 11;
Eph. 4:7
ᵈEph. 1:5

3 In His delivering purpose, 2:5-18

5 For He did not subject to
angels ᵃthe world to come, concerning which we are speaking.

★ 5 ᵃMatt.
24:14; Heb.
1:6; 6:5

1:6 A combination of Ps. 97:7 with Deut. 32:43 (Septuagint version, the Greek translation of the O.T.).

1:7 *winds.* Quoting Ps. 104:4. Angels are ser-vants (as wind and fire are) and therefore sub-ordinate to the Son.

1:8-9 Historically the psalm quoted (45:6-7) was probably sung at a Hebrew monarch's wed-ding. What was true of the ancient king by virtue of his office, the writer to the Hebrews sees to be wholly true of Christ by virtue of His nature. *Thy companions.* I.e., beyond all others.

1:10-12 Quoting Ps. 102:25-27. Christ is the Creator of all things and the One who, in the midst of change, is unchanging.

1:14 *ministering spirits.* The ministry of angels on behalf of believers continues today. The mention of *salvation* leads the writer into a discussion of this topic (2:1-18).

2:2 *the word spoken through angels.* Refers to the Mosaic law (Ps. 68:17; Acts 7:53). In later Judaism it was held that angels had delivered the law.

2:5 *the world to come.* Lit., the coming inhab-ited earth (as in Luke 2:1). A reference to the

6 *a* 1 Thess.
4:6 *b* Heb.
4:4 *c* Ps. 8:4

6 But one has *a* testified *b* somewhere, saying,

"*c* WHAT IS MAN, THAT THOU
REMEMBEREST HIM?
OR THE SON OF MAN, THAT
THOU ART CONCERNED
ABOUT HIM?

★ **7** *a* Ps.
8:5, 6

7 "*a* THOU HAST MADE HIM FOR
A LITTLE WHILE LOWER
THAN THE ANGELS;
THOU HAST CROWNED HIM
WITH GLORY AND HONOR,
AND HAST APPOINTED HIM
OVER THE WORKS OF THY
HANDS;

★ **8** *a* Ps.
8:6;
1 Cor. 15:27
b 1 Cor.
15:25

8 *a* THOU HAST PUT ALL THINGS
IN SUBJECTION UNDER HIS
FEET."

For in subjecting all things to him,
He left nothing that is not subject
to him. But now *b* we do not yet
see all things subjected to him.

9 *a* Heb. 2:7
b Phil. 2:9;
Heb. 1:9
c Acts 2:33;
3:13; 1 Pet.
1:21 *d* John
3:16 *e* Matt.
16:28; John
8:52 *f* Heb.
6:20; 7:25

9 But we do see Him who
has been *a* made for a little while
lower than the angels, *namely,*
Jesus, *b* because of the suffering of
death *c* crowned with glory and
honor, that *d* by the grace of God
He might *e* taste death *f* for everyone.

★ **10** *a* Luke
24:26 *b* Rom.
11:36 *c* Luke
13:32; Heb.
5:9; 7:28
d Acts 3:15;
5:31
11 *a* Heb.
13:12 *b* Heb.
10:10 *c* Acts
17:28 *d* Matt.
25:40; Mark
3:34f.; John
20:17

10 For *a* it was fitting for Him,
b for whom are all things, and
b through whom are all things, to
bringing many sons to glory, to
c perfect the *d* author of their salvation through sufferings.

11 For both He who *a* sanctifies and those who *b* are sanctified
are all *c* from one *Father;* for

which reason He is not ashamed
to call them *d* brethren,

12 saying,

12 *a* Ps.
22:22

"*a* I WILL PROCLAIM THY NAME
TO MY BRETHREN,
IN THE MIDST OF THE CONGRE-
GATION I WILL SING THY
PRAISE."

13 And again,

13 *a* Is. 8:17
b Is. 8:18

"*a* I WILL PUT MY TRUST IN
HIM."

And again,

"*b* BEHOLD, I AND THE CHILDREN
WHOM GOD HAS GIVEN
ME."

★ **14** *a* Matt.
16:17 *b* John
1:14 *c* 1 Cor.
15:54-57;
2 Tim. 1:10
d John 12:31;
1 John 3:8

14 Since then the children
share in *a* flesh and blood, *b* He
Himself likewise also partook of
the same, that *c* through death He
might render powerless *d* him who
had the power of death, that is,
the devil;

15 *a* Rom.
8:15

15 and might deliver those
who through *a* fear of death were
subject to slavery all their lives.

★ **16**

16 For assuredly He does not
give help to angels, but He gives
help to the descendant of Abraham.

★ **17** *a* Phil.
2:7; Heb.
2:14 *b* Heb.
4:15; 5:2
c Heb. 3:1;
4:14f; 5:5,
10; 6:20;
7:26, 28; 8:1,
3; 9:11;
10:21 *d* Rom.
15:17; Heb.
5:1 *e* Dan.
9:24; 1 John
2:2; 4:10

17 Therefore, He had *a* to be
made like His brethren in all
things, that He might *b* become a
merciful and faithful *c* high priest
in *d* things pertaining to God, to
e make propitiation for the sins of
the people.

18 *a* Heb.
4:15

18 For since He Himself was
a tempted in that which He has

---

millennial kingdom on earth, which will not
be ruled by angels but by Christ and the redeemed.
2:7 *for a little while.* This may mean (1) for a
short time, or (2) more likely, as some versions
render it, a little lower in rank. In the order of
creation, man is lower than angels, and in the
incarnation, Christ took this lower place.
2:8 *his feet . . . him . . . him.* This refers to man
(not Christ) who was given dominion over the
creation (Gen. 1:28) but who lost it when he
sinned (Rom. 8:20) and who will regain it in
the future millennial kingdom because of
Christ's death for sin (Heb. 2:10).
2:10 *to perfect.* I.e., the sufferings of Jesus
made Him qualified to be the leader of man's
salvation.

2:14 *flesh and blood* was an O.T. figure for human nature. *partook of the same.* I.e., the
same human nature. *render powerless.* Lit.,
bring to nought or make inoperative or useless, but not annihilate, for the devil will exist
in torment in the lake of fire forever (Rev.
20:10). This verse states the overriding purpose of Christ's accepting "a lower state."
2:16 Christ did not come to save fallen angels,
but to save fallen men.
2:17 *to make propitiation.* Or, expiation. Propitiation refers to God's wrath being satisfied by
the death of Christ (Rom. 3:25; 1 John 2:2).
Expiation emphasizes the removal of sin by
the sacrifice which satisfied God. Sin inter-
rupts normal relations with God; expiation removes sin and restores the relationship.

suffered, He is able to come to the aid of those who are tempted.

C Christ Is Superior to Moses, 3:1-6

3 Therefore, [a]holy brethren, partakers of a [b]heavenly calling, consider Jesus, [c]the Apostle and [d]High Priest of our [e]confession.

2 He was faithful to Him who appointed Him, as [a]Moses also was in all His house.

3 [a]For He has been counted worthy of more glory than Moses, by just so much as the builder of the house has more honor than the house.

4 For every house is built by someone, but the builder of all things is God.

5 Now [a]Moses was faithful in all His house as [b]a servant, [c]for a testimony of those things [d]which were to be spoken later;

6 but Christ *was faithful* as [a]a Son over His house [b]whose house we are, [c]if we hold fast our [d]confidence and the boast of our [e]hope firm until the end.

D Christ Is the Supreme Object of Faith, 3:7-4:16

1 The catastrophe of unbelief, 3:7-19

7 Therefore, just as [a]the Holy Spirit says,

"[b]TODAY IF YOU HEAR HIS VOICE,

8 [a]DO NOT HARDEN YOUR HEARTS AS WHEN THEY PROVOKED ME,

AS IN THE DAY OF TRIAL IN THE WILDERNESS,

9 [a]WHERE YOUR FATHERS TRIED *Me* BY TESTING *Me*, AND SAW MY WORKS FOR [b]FORTY YEARS.

10 "[a]THEREFORE I WAS ANGRY WITH THIS GENERATION, AND SAID, 'THEY ALWAYS GO ASTRAY IN THEIR HEART; AND THEY DID NOT KNOW MY WAYS';

11 [a]AS I SWORE IN MY WRATH, 'THEY SHALL NOT ENTER MY REST.'"

12 [a]Take care, brethren, lest there should be in any one of you an evil, unbelieving heart, in falling away from [b]the living God.

13 But [a]encourage one another day after day, as long as it is *still* called "Today," lest any one of you be hardened by the [b]deceitfulness of sin.

14 For we have become partakers of Christ, [a]if we hold fast the beginning of our [b]assurance firm until the end;

15 while it is said,

"[a]TODAY IF YOU HEAR HIS VOICE, DO NOT HARDEN YOUR HEARTS, AS WHEN THEY PROVOKED ME."

16 For who [a]provoked *Him* when they had heard? Indeed, [b]did not all those who came out of Egypt led by Moses?

17 And with whom was He angry for forty years? Was it not with those who sinned, [a]whose bodies fell in the wilderness?

18 And to whom did He swear [a]that they should not enter His rest, but to those who were [b]disobedient?

19 And *so* we see that they were not able to enter because of [a]unbelief.

---

1 [a]Acts 1:15; Heb. 2:11; 3:12; 10:19; 13:22 [b]Phil. 3:14 [c]John 17:3 [d]Heb. 2:17; 4:14f.; 5:5, 10; 6:20; 7:26, 28; 8:1, 3; 9:11; 10:21 [e]2 Cor. 9:13; Heb. 4:14; 10:23
2 [a]Ex. 40:16; Num. 12:7; Heb. 3:5
★ **3** [a]2 Cor. 3:7-11
5 [a]Ex. 40:16; Num. 12:7; Heb. 3:2 [b]Ex. 14:31; Num. 12:7 [c]Deut. 18:18f. [d]Heb. 1:1
6 [a]Heb. 1:2 [b]1 Cor. 3:16; 1 Tim. 3:15 [c]Rom. 11:22; Heb. 3:14; 4:14 [d]Eph. 3:12; Heb. 4:16; 10:19, 35 [e]Heb. 6:11; 7:19; 10:23; 11:1; 1 Pet. 1:3

★ **7-11**
7 [a]Acts 28:25; Heb. 9:8; 10:15 [b]Ps. 95:7; Heb. 3:15; 4:7
8 [a]Ps. 95:8

9 [a]Ps. 95:9, 10 [b]Acts 7:36
10 [a]Ps. 95:10
11 [a]Ps. 95:11; Heb. 4:3, 5
12 [a]Col. 2:8; Heb. 12:25 [b]Matt. 16:16; Heb. 9:14; 10:31; 12:22
13 [a]Heb. 10:24f. [b]Eph. 4:22
14 [a]Heb. 3:6 [b]Heb. 11:1 [Gr.]
15 [a]Ps. 95:7f.
16 [a]Jer. 32:29; 44:3, 8 [b]Num. 14:2, 11, 30; Deut. 1:35, 36, 38
17 [a]Num. 14:29; 1 Cor. 10:5
18 [a]Num. 14:23; Deut. 1:34f.; Heb. 4:2 [b]Rom. 11:30-32; Heb. 4:6, 11
★**19** [a]John 3:36

3:3 Christ is better than Moses because Christ is the builder of God's house while Moses was but a servant in the house.
3:7-11 See Ps. 95:7-11. The children of Israel challenged God's authority over them by their rebellion in the wilderness (Num. 14-21). Because of this, they failed to enter into the rest of dwelling in Canaan and they perished in the wilderness.
3:19 *because of unbelief.* See Num. 14; 1 Cor. 10:10-11.

2 The consequences of unbelief, 4:1-10

★ 1 *a*Heb. 12:15

4 Therefore, let us fear lest, while a promise remains of entering His rest, any one of you should seem to have *a*come short of it.

2 *a*1 Thess. 2:13

2 For indeed we have had good news preached to us, just as they also; but *a*the word they heard did not profit them, because it was not united by faith in those who heard.

3 *a*Ps. 95:11; Heb. 3:11 *b*Matt. 25:34

3 For we who have believed enter that rest, just as He has said,

"*a*As I swore in My wrath,
They shall not enter My rest,"

although His works were finished *b*from the foundation of the world.

★ 4 *a*Heb. 2:6 *b*Gen. 2:2 *c*Ex. 20:11; 31:17

4 For He has thus said *a*somewhere concerning the seventh *day*, "*b*And God *c*rested on the seventh day from all His works";

★ 5-9
5 *a*Ps. 95:11; Heb. 3:11

5 and again in this *passage*, "*a*They shall not enter My rest."

6 *a*Heb. 3:18; 4:11

6 Since therefore it remains for some to enter it, and those who formerly had good news preached to them failed to enter because of *a*disobedience,

7 *a*Heb. 3:7f. *b*Ps. 95:7f.

7 He again fixes a certain day, "Today," saying through David after so long a time just *a*as has been said before,

"*b*Today if you hear His voice,
Do not harden your hearts."

★ 8 *a*Josh. 22:4 *b*Heb. 1:1

8 For *a*if Joshua had given them rest, He would not have *b*spoken of another day after that.

9 There remains therefore a Sabbath rest for the people of God.

10 *a*Rev. 14:13 *b*Heb. 4:4

10 For the one who has entered His rest has himself also *a*rested from his works, as *b*God did from His.

3 The cure for unbelief, 4:11-16

★11 *a*2 Pet. 2:6 *b*Heb. 3:18; 4:6

11 Let us therefore be diligent to enter that rest, lest anyone fall through *following* the same *a*example of *b*disobedience.

★12 *a*Jer. 23:29; Eph. 5:26; Heb. 6:5; 1 Pet. 1:23 *b*Acts 7:38 *c*1 Thess. 2:13 *d*Eph. 6:17 *e*1 Thess. 5:23 *f*John 12:48; 1 Cor. 14:24f.

12 For *a*the word of God is *b*living and *c*active and sharper than any two-edged *d*sword, and piercing as far as the division of *e*soul and *e*spirit, of both joints and marrow, and *f*able to judge the thoughts and intentions of the heart.

★13 *a*2 Chr. 16:9; Ps. 33:13-15 *b*Job 26:6
14 *a*Heb. 2:17 *b*Eph. 4:10; Heb. 6:20; 8:1; 9:24 *c*Matt. 4:3; Heb. 1:2; 6:6; 7:3; 10:29 *d*Heb. 3:1

13 And *a*there is no creature hidden from His sight, but all things are *b*open and laid bare to the eyes of Him with whom we have to do.

14 Since then we have a great *a*high priest who has *b*passed through the heavens, Jesus *c*the Son of God, let us hold fast our *d*confession.

4:1 Although God has promised believers today that they may enter His rest, some may fail to experience it because of unbelief.

4:4 See Gen. 2:2. After the work of creation was finished, God rested; i.e., He enjoyed the sense of satisfaction and repose that comes with the completion of a task. It is in this sense that *rest* is used in vv. 1 and 3.

4:5-9 The divine promise still holds good: the believer may enter into God's rest through faith. This is true both of salvation and sanctification. Rest in the Christian life comes through complete reliance on God's promises and full surrender to His will (2 Cor. 5:7; Col. 2:6).

4:8 *Joshua* (Moses' successor) could not lead all the people into the rest of dwelling in their promised land because of their unbelief. Like-

wise the believer today cannot enjoy a fully satisfying Christian life unless he believes all the promises of God, and even then he looks forward to that perfect future rest.

4:11 *Let us . . . be diligent.* The same Greek word is used in Eph. 4:3; 2 Tim. 2:15; 2 Pet. 1:10; 3:14.

4:12 *the word of God.* Here meaning His inspired Word, the Scriptures. *living and active.* It has the power to reach to the inmost parts of one's personality and to judge the innermost thoughts.

4:13 *with whom we have to do.* Better, to whom we must give an account—lit., to whom is our word. A play on the Greek term for "word"; i.e., if our lives conform to the *word of God* (v. 12), then our word (account) in the day of judgment will be acceptable to God.

★15 aHeb.
2:17 bHeb.
2:18 c2 Cor.
5:21; Heb.
7:26

15 For we do not have *a high priest who cannot sympathize with our weaknesses, but one who has been *tempted in all things as *we are, yet *without sin.

16 aHeb.
7:19 bHeb.
3:6

16 Let us therefore *draw near with *confidence to the throne of grace, that we may receive mercy and may find grace to help in time of need.

II THE SUPERIORITY OF THE PRIESTHOOD OF CHRIST,
5:1–10:39
A Christ Is Superior in His Qualifications, 5:1–10

★ 1-10
1 aEx. 28:1
bHeb. 2:17
cHeb. 7:27;
8:3f.; 9:9;
10:11
d1 Cor. 15:3;
Heb. 7:27;
10:12
2 aHeb.
2:18; 4:15
bEph. 4:18;
Heb. 9:7
marg.
cJames 5:19;
1 Pet. 2:25
dHeb. 7:28
3 a1 Cor.
15:3; Heb.
7:27; 10:12
bLev. 9:7;
16:6; Heb.
7:27; 9:7
★ 4 aNum.
16:40; 18:7;
2 Chr. 26:18
bEx. 28:1;
1 Chr. 23:13
5 aJohn
8:54 bHeb.
2:17; 5:10
cHeb. 1:1, 5
dPs. 2:7

5 For every high priest *taken from among men is appointed on behalf of men in *things pertaining to God, in order to *offer both gifts and sacrifices *for sins;

2 *he can deal gently with the *ignorant and *misguided, since he himself also is *beset with weakness;

3 and because of it he is obligated to offer *sacrifices *for sins, *as for the people, so also for himself.

4 And *no one takes the honor to himself, but *receives it when he is called by God, even *as Aaron was.

5 So also Christ *did not glorify Himself so as to become a

*high priest, but He who *said to Him,

> "*Thou art My Son,
> Today I have begotten Thee";

6 just as He says also in another *passage,

> "*Thou art a priest forever According to *the order of Melchizedek."

6 aPs.
110:4; Heb.
7:17 bHeb.
5:10; 6:20;
7:11, 17

7 In the days of His flesh, *He offered up both prayers and supplications with *loud crying and tears to the One *able to save Him from death, and He was heard because of His *piety.

8 Although He was *a Son, He learned *obedience from the things which He suffered.

9 And having been made *perfect, He became to all those who obey Him the source of eternal salvation,

10 being designated by God as *a high priest according to *the order of Melchizedek.

★ 7 aMatt.
26:39, 42,
44; Mark
14:36, 39;
Luke 22:41,
44 bMatt.
27:46, 50;
Mark 15:34,
37; Luke
23:46 cMark
14:36 dHeb.
11:7; 12:28
8 aHeb. 1:2
bPhil. 2:8
9 aHeb.
2:10

★10 aHeb.
2:17; 5:5
bHeb. 5:6

B Parenthetical Warning: Don't Degenerate from Christ, 5:11–6:20

11 Concerning him we have much to say, and *it is* hard to explain, since you have become dull of hearing.

4:15 *but one who has been tempted in all things as we are, yet without sin.* Not that Christ experienced every temptation man does, but rather that He was tempted in all areas in which man is tempted (the lust of the flesh, the lust of the eyes, and the pride of life, 1 John 2:16), and with particular temptations specially suited to Him. This testing was possible only because He took the likeness of sinful flesh (Rom. 8:3), for had there not been an incarnation, Jesus could not have been tempted (cf. Jas. 1:13). Yet our Lord was distinct from all other men in that He was *without sin*; i.e., He possessed no sin nature as we do. Because He endured and successfully passed His tests, He can now offer us mercy and grace to help in time of need, for He knows what we are going through.

5:1–10 The qualifications for high priest are stated in these verses, Aaron serving as the model.

5:4 See Ex. 28:1.

5:7 *offered up both prayers and supplications with loud crying and tears.* Refers to occasions like those of John 12:27 and the experience in Gethsemane (Matt. 26:39–44).

5:10 *according to the order of Melchizedek.* Our Lord could never have been a Levitical priest because He was born of the tribe of Judah (7:14) and not the tribe of Levi. Thus He must be associated with another order of priests, that of Melchizedek. Both Christ and Melchizedek were men (Heb. 7:4; 1 Tim. 2:5); both were king-priests (Gen. 14:18; Zech. 6:12–13); both were appointed directly by God (Heb. 7:21); both were called "King of righteousness" and "King of peace" (Isa. 11:5–9; Heb. 7:2).

12 For though by this time you ought to be teachers, you have need again for someone to teach you *the *elementary principles of the *oracles of God, and you have come to need *milk and not solid food.

13 For everyone who partakes *only* of milk is not accustomed to the word of righteousness, for he is a *babe.

14 But solid food is for *the mature, who because of practice have their senses *trained to *discern good and evil.

6 Therefore *leaving *the elementary teaching about the Christ, let us press on to *maturity; not laying again a foundation of repentance from *dead works and of faith toward God,

2 of *instruction about washings, and *laying on of hands, and the *resurrection of the dead, and *eternal judgment.

3 And this we shall do, *if God permits.

4 For in the case of those who have once been *enlightened and have tasted of *the heavenly gift and have been made *partakers of the Holy Spirit,

5 and *have tasted the good *word of God and the powers of *the age to come,

6 and *then* have fallen away, it is *impossible to renew them again to repentance, *since they again crucify to themselves the Son of God, and put Him to open shame.

7 For ground that drinks the rain which often falls upon it and brings forth vegetation useful to those *for whose sake it is also tilled, receives a blessing from God;

8 but if it yields thorns and thistles, it is worthless and *close to being cursed, and it ends up being burned.

9 But, *beloved, we are convinced of better things concerning you, and things that accompany salvation, though we are speaking in this way.

10 For *God is not unjust so as to forget *your work and the love which you have shown toward His name, in having *ministered and in still ministering to the saints.

11 And we desire that each one of you show the same

Marginal references

★**12** *a*Gal.
4:3 *b*Heb.
6:1 *c*Acts
7:38 *d*1 Cor.
3:2; 1 Pet.
2:2

13 *a*1 Cor.
3:1; 14:20;
1 Pet. 2:2

★**14** *a*1 Cor.
2:6; Eph.
4:13; Heb.
6:1 *b*1 Tim.
4:7 *c*Rom.
14:1

★ **1** *a*Phil.
3:13f. *b*Heb.
5:12 *c*Heb.
5:14 *d*John
8:21; Heb.
9:14

★ **2** *a*John
3:25; Acts
19:3f. *b*Acts
6:6 *c*Acts
17:31f.

3 *a*Acts
18:21

★ **4-6**
4 *a*2 Cor.
4:4, 6; Heb.
10:32 *b*John
4:10; Eph.
2:8 *c*Gal.
3:2; Heb. 2:4

5 *a*1 Pet.
2:3 *b*Eph.
6:17 *c*Heb.
2:5

6 *a*Matt.
19:26; Heb.
10:26f.
2 Pet. 2:21;
1 John 5:16
*b*Heb. 10:29

7 *a*2 Tim.
2:6

8 *a*Deut.
29:22ff.

★ **9** *a*1 Cor.
10:14; 2 Cor.
7:1; 12:19;
1 Pet. 2:11;
2 Pet. 3:1;
1 John 2:7;
Jude 3

10 *a*Prov.
19:17; Matt.
10:42; 25:40;
Acts 10:4
*b*1 Thess.
1:3 *c*Rom.
15:25; Heb.
10:32-34

11 *a*Luke
1:1; Heb.
10:22 *b*Heb.
3:6

5:12 *though by this time.* Better, although by now. I.e., in consideration of the time they had been believers. *milk.* I.e., elementary truth (see 1 Cor. 3:1-3).

5:14 *the mature.* Christian maturity involves (1) time (v. 12); (2) growth in the knowledge of the Word of God (v. 13); and (3) experience in the use of the Word in discerning between good and evil (vv. 13-14).

6:1 *elementary teaching.* I.e., the basic teachings about Christ and the Christian religion. *maturity.* The exhortation to these people is for them to go on to Christian maturity and to stop wasting time and opportunities. They knew the first principles, or basics, of Christianity and are being exhorted to go on from there. *dead works.* I.e., sins.

6:2 *instruction about washings.* Or, as in some versions, baptisms. The distinction between various baptisms is a necessary part of basic Christian doctrine (e.g., the baptism of Jewish proselytes, baptism by John the Baptist, Christian baptism).

6:4-6 This much-debated passage has been understood in several ways. (1) Arminians hold that the people described in these verses are Christians who actually lose their salvation. If this be so, notice that the passage also teaches

that it is impossible to be saved a second time. (2) Some hold that the passage refers not to genuine believers but to those who only profess to be believers. Thus the phrases in vv. 4-5 are understood to refer to experiences short of salvation (cf. v. 9). The "falling away" is from the knowledge of the truth, not personal possession of it. (3) Others understand the passage to be a warning to genuine believers to urge them on in Christian growth and maturity. To "fall away" is impossible (since, according to this view, true believers are eternally secure), but the phrase is placed in the sentence to strengthen the warning. It is similar to saying something like this to a class of students: "It is impossible for a student, once enrolled in this course, if he turns the clock back [which cannot be done], to start the course over. Therefore, let all students go on to deeper knowledge." In this view the phrases in vv. 4-5 are understood to refer to the conversion experience. Notice how the words "enlightened" (10:32), "taste" (2:9), and "partakers" (12:8) are used elsewhere in Hebrews.

6:9 An expression of confidence, though the writer speaks severely. *things that accompany salvation.* I.e., fruit in the Christian life.

diligence so as to realize the [a]full assurance of [b]hope until the end,

12 that you may not be sluggish, but [a]imitators of those who through [b]faith and patience [c]inherit the promises.

13 For [a]when God made the promise to Abraham, since He could swear by no one greater, He [b]swore by Himself,

14 saying, "[a]I WILL SURELY BLESS YOU, AND I WILL SURELY MULTIPLY YOU."

15 And thus, [a]having patiently waited, he obtained the promise.

16 [a]For men swear by one greater *than themselves,* and with them [b]an oath *given* as confirmation is an end of every dispute.

17 In the same way God, desiring even more to show to [a]the heirs of the promise [b]the unchangeableness of His purpose, interposed with an oath,

18 in order that by two unchangeable things, in which [a]it is impossible for God to lie, we may have strong encouragement, we who have fled for refuge in laying hold of [b]the hope set before us.

19 This hope we have as an anchor of the soul, a *hope* both sure and steadfast and one which [a]enters within the veil,

20 [a]where Jesus has entered as a forerunner for us, having become a [b]high priest forever according to the order of Melchizedek.

C Christ Is Superior in the Order of His Priesthood, 7:1—8:13

1 The portrait of Melchizedek, 7:1-3

7 For this [a]Melchizedek, king of Salem, priest of the [b]Most High God, who met Abraham as he was returning from the slaughter of the kings and blessed him,

2 to whom also Abraham apportioned a tenth part of all *the spoils,* was first of all, by the translation *of his name,* king of righteousness, and then also king of Salem, which is king of peace.

3 Without father, without mother, [a]without genealogy, having neither beginning of days nor end of life, but made like [b]the Son of God, he abides a priest perpetually.

2 The preeminence of the Melchizedek priesthood, 7:4—8:13

4 Now observe how great this man was to whom Abraham, the [a]patriarch, gave a tenth of the choicest spoils.

5 And those indeed of [a]the sons of Levi who receive the priest's office have commandment in the Law to collect a tenth from the people, that is, from their brethren, although these are descended from Abraham.

6 But the one [a]whose genealogy is not traced from them

12 [a]Heb. 13:7
[b]2 Thess. 1:4; James 1:3; Rev. 13:10 [c]Heb. 1:14
13 [a]Gal. 3:15, 18 [b]Gen. 22:16; Luke 1:73
★14 [a]Gen. 22:16f.
15 [a]Gen. 12:4; 21:5
16 [a]Gal. 3:15 [b]Ex. 22:11
17 [a]Heb. 11:9 [b]Ps. 110:4; Prov. 19:21; Heb. 6:18
★18 [a]Num. 23:19; Titus 1:2 [b]Heb. 3:6; 7:19
★19 [a]Lev. 16:2; Heb. 9:2f.
★20 [a]John 14:2; Heb. 4:14 [b]Heb. 2:17; 5:6
★ 1 [a]Gen. 14:18-20; Heb. 7:6 [b]Mark 5:7
★ 3 [a]Heb. 7:6 [b]Matt. 4:3; Heb. 7:1, 28
★ 4 [a]Acts 2:29
5 [a]Num. 18:21, 26; 2 Chr. 31:4f.
★ 6 [a]Heb. 7:3 [b]Heb. 7:1f. [c]Rom. 4:13

6:14 See Gen. 22:16-17.

6:18 *two unchangeable things.* The promise made to Abraham and the oath which rests on the very being of God.

6:19 *within the veil.* I.e., in the presence of God. Believers have as strong encouragement as Abraham had in his time, because Jesus has already entered into the presence of God and assures us of our entrance into heaven as well.

6:20 *forerunner.* A word used of a scout reconnoitering, or of a herald announcing the coming of a king; both concepts imply that others are to follow.

7:1 *Melchizedek* is clearly a type of Christ. Everything known about him from the O.T. is found in Gen. 14:17-20 and Ps. 110:4. He was a great king-priest, and it is to his order of priesthood that Christ belongs. See note on

5:10.

7:3 *Without father . . .* This does not mean that Melchizedek had no parents or that he was not born or did not die, but only that the Scriptures contain no record of these events so that he might be more perfectly likened to Christ.

7:4 *gave a tenth.* By taking the role of the one who tithed and the one who received the blessing (v. 1), Abraham, to whom God gave the promises, doubly acknowledged his inferiority to Melchizedek.

7:6 The proof that the Melchizedek priesthood (and Christ's) is superior to the Aaronic, or Levitical, priesthood is that Levi's great-grandfather Abraham paid tithes to Melchizedek, and that Levi, though unborn, was involved (v. 9).

[b]collected a tenth from Abraham, and [b]blessed the one who [c]had the promises.

7 But without any dispute the lesser is blessed by the greater.

★ **8** [a]Heb. 5:6; 6:20

8 And in this case mortal men receive tithes, but in that case one *receives them,* [a]of whom it is witnessed that he lives on.

9 And, so to speak, through Abraham even Levi, who received tithes, paid tithes,

10 for he was still in the loins of his father when Melchizedek met him.

★**11** [a]Heb. 7:18f.; 8:7 [b]Heb. 9:6; 10:1 [c]Heb. 5:6; 7:17

11 [a]Now if perfection was through the Levitical priesthood (for on the basis of it [b]the people received the Law), what further need *was there* for another priest to arise [c]according to the order of Melchizedek, and not be designated according to the order of Aaron?

★**12**

12 For when the priesthood is changed, of necessity there takes place a change of law also.

13 [a]Heb. 7:14 [b]Heb. 7:11

13 For [a]the one concerning whom [b]these things are spoken belongs to another tribe, from which no one has officiated at the altar.

14 [a]Num. 24:17; Is. 11:1; Matt. 2:6 [Mic. 5:2]; Rev. 5:5

14 For it is evident that our Lord was [a]descended from Judah, a tribe with reference to which Moses spoke nothing concerning priests.

15 And this is clearer still, if another priest arises according to the likeness of Melchizedek,

16 [a]Heb. 9:10 [b]Heb. 9:14

16 who has become *such* not on the basis of a law of [a]physical requirement, but according to the power of [b]an indestructible life.

17 [a]Ps. 110:4; Heb. 5:6; 7:21

17 For it is witnessed *of Him,*

"[a]THOU ART A PRIEST FOREVER
ACCORDING TO THE ORDER OF
MELCHIZEDEK."

18 For, on the one hand, there is a setting aside of a former commandment [a]because of its weakness and uselessness

18 [a]Rom. 8:3; Gal. 3:21; Heb. 7:11

19 (for [a]the Law made nothing perfect), and on the other hand there is a bringing in of a better [b]hope, through which we [c]draw near to God.

★**19** [a]Acts 13:39; Rom. 3:20; 7:7f.; Gal. 2:16; 3:21; Heb. 9:9; 10:1 [b]Heb. 3:6 [c]Lam. 3:57; Heb. 4:16; 7:25; 10:1, 22; James 4:8

20 And inasmuch as *it was* not without an oath

21 (for they indeed became priests without an oath, but He with an oath through the One who said to Him,

21 [a]Ps. 110:4; Heb. 5:6; 7:17 [b]Num. 23:19; 1 Sam. 15:29; Rom. 11:29 [c]Heb. 7:23f., 28

"[a]THE LORD HAS SWORN
AND [b]WILL NOT CHANGE HIS
MIND,
'THOU ART A PRIEST [c]FOR-
EVER' ");

22 so much the more also Jesus has become the [a]guarantee of [b]a better covenant.

22 [a]Ps. 119:122; Is. 38:14 [b]Heb. 8:6

23 And the *former* priests, on the one hand, existed in greater numbers, because they were prevented by death from continuing,

24 but He, on the other hand, because He abides [a]forever, holds His priesthood permanently.

24 [a]Heb. 7:23f.

25 Hence, also, He is able to [a]save forever those who [b]draw near to God through Him, since He always lives to [c]make intercession for them.

★**25** [a]1 Cor. 1:21 [b]Heb. 7:19 [c]Rom. 8:34; Heb. 9:24

26 For it was fitting that we should have such a [a]high priest, [b]holy, [c]innocent, undefiled, separated from sinners and [d]exalted above the heavens;

26 [a]Heb. 2:17 [b]2 Cor. 5:21; Heb. 4:15 [c]1 Pet. 2:22 [d]Heb. 4:14

27 who does not need daily, like those high priests, to [a]offer up sacrifices, [b]first for His own sins, and then for the *sins* of the people, because this He did [c]once for all when He [d]offered up Himself.

27 [a]Heb. 5:1 [b]Heb. 5:3 [c]Heb. 9:12, 28; 10:10 [d]Eph. 5:2; Heb. 9:14, 28; 10:10, 12

7:8 *in this case.* Refers to the Levitical priests. *in that case.* Refers to Melchizedek and his priesthood.
7:11 Another proof that Christ is superior to the law and its priesthood is that the law could not give the people *perfection,* i.e., complete communion with God. The sacrificial Levitical system never achieved its aim.

7:12 For Paul's different, but nonconflicting, argument on the abrogation of the Mosaic law, see Rom. 7:1-6; 2 Cor. 3:7-11; Gal. 3:19-25.
7:19 A *better hope* for effecting full and final removal of sin has been introduced, along with a new way of access to God.
7:25 *forever.* Christ's priesthood has authority (vv. 20-22) and permanence.

28 For the Law appoints men as high priests [a]who are weak, but the word of the oath, which came after the Law, appoints [b]a Son, [c]made perfect forever.

8 Now the main point in what has been said is this: we have such a [a]high priest, who has taken His seat at [b]the right hand of the throne of the [b]Majesty in the heavens,

2 a [a]minister in the sanctuary, and in the [b]true tabernacle, which the Lord [c]pitched, not man.

3 For every [a]high priest is appointed [b]to offer both gifts and sacrifices; hence it is necessary that this high priest also have something to offer.

4 Now if He were on earth, He would not be a priest at all, since there are those who [a]offer the gifts according to the Law;

5 who serve [a]a copy and [b]shadow of the heavenly things, just as Moses was [c]warned by God when he was about to erect the tabernacle; for, "[d]See," He says, "THAT YOU MAKE ALL THINGS ACCORDING TO THE PATTERN WHICH WAS SHOWN YOU ON THE MOUNTAIN."

6 But now He has obtained a more excellent ministry, by as much as He is also the [a]mediator of [b]a better covenant, which has been enacted on better promises.

7 For [a]if that first covenant had been faultless, there would have been no occasion sought for a second.

8 For finding fault with them, He says,

"[a]BEHOLD, DAYS ARE COMING, SAYS THE LORD, WHEN I WILL EFFECT [b]A NEW COVENANT WITH THE HOUSE OF ISRAEL AND WITH THE HOUSE OF JUDAH;

9 [a]NOT LIKE THE COVENANT WHICH I MADE WITH THEIR FATHERS ON THE DAY WHEN I [b]TOOK THEM BY THE HAND TO LEAD THEM OUT OF THE LAND OF EGYPT; FOR THEY DID NOT CONTINUE IN MY COVENANT, AND I DID NOT CARE FOR THEM, SAYS THE LORD.

10 "[a]FOR [b]THIS IS THE COVENANT THAT I WILL MAKE WITH THE HOUSE OF ISRAEL AFTER THOSE DAYS, SAYS THE LORD: I WILL PUT MY LAWS INTO THEIR MINDS, AND I WILL WRITE THEM [c]UPON THEIR HEARTS. AND I WILL BE THEIR GOD, AND THEY SHALL BE MY PEOPLE.

11 "[a]AND THEY SHALL NOT TEACH EVERYONE HIS FELLOW CITIZEN, AND EVERYONE HIS BROTHER, SAYING, 'KNOW THE LORD,' FOR [b]ALL SHALL KNOW ME, FROM THE LEAST TO THE GREATEST OF THEM.

12 "[a]FOR I WILL BE MERCIFUL TO THEIR INIQUITIES, [b]AND I WILL REMEMBER THEIR SINS NO MORE."

13 When He said, "[a]A new covenant," He has made the first obsolete. [b]But whatever is becoming obsolete and growing old is ready to disappear.

D Christ Is Superior in His Priestly Ministry, 9:1-10:18

1 The earthly priesthood, 9:1-10

9 Now even the first covenant had [a]regulations of divine

8:1 *the main point.* A priest must have something to offer (v. 3) and a sanctuary in which to do it. Christ was disqualified from using the earthly sanctuary because of His descent from the tribe of Judah; therefore, His sphere of service must be heaven.

8:5 *the pattern.* See Ex. 25:40.

8:6 The covenant Christ mediates is a better covenant, since it is enacted on better prom-

ises. In vv. 6-13, the new covenant is contrasted with *that first covenant* (v. 7); i.e., the Mosaic law (Ex. 19:5). Christ's blood is the basis of the new covenant (Matt. 26:28); Christians are ministers of it (2 Cor. 3:6); and it will yet have an aspect of its fulfillment in relation to Israel and Judah in the millennium (as predicted in Jer. 31:31-34).

---

28 [a]Heb. 5:2 [b]Heb. 1:2 [c]Heb. 2:10

★ **1** [a]Heb. 2:17 [b]Heb. 1:3

2 [a]Heb. 10:11 [b]Heb. 9:11, 24 [c]Ex. 33:7

3 [a]Heb. 2:17 [b]Heb. 5:1; 8:4

4 [a]Heb. 5:1; 8:3

★ **5** [a]Heb. 9:23 [b]Col. 2:17; Heb. 10:1 [c]Matt. 2:12; Heb. 11:7; 12:25 [d]Ex. 25:40

★ **6** [a]1 Tim. 2:5 [b]Luke 22:20; Heb. 7:22; 8:8; 9:15; 12:24

7 [a]Heb. 7:11

8 [a]Jer. 31:31 [b]Luke 22:20; 2 Cor. 3:6; Heb. 7:22; 8:6, 13; 9:15; 12:24

9 [a]Jer. 31:32 [b]Ex. 19:5f.; Heb. 2:16 marg.

10 [a]Jer. 31:33 [b]Rom. 11:27; Heb. 10:16 [c]2 Cor. 3:3

11 [a]Jer. 31:34 [b]Is. 54:13; John 6:45; 1 John 2:27

12 [a]Jer. 31:34 [b]Heb. 10:17

13 [a]Luke 22:20; 2 Cor. 3:6; Heb. 7:22; 8:6, 8; 9:15; 12:24 [b]2 Cor. 5:17; Heb. 1:11

1 [a]Heb. 9:10 [b]Ex. 25:8; Heb. 8:2; 9:11, 24

worship and *b*the earthly sanctuary.

2 For there was *a*a tabernacle prepared, the outer one, in which *were* *b*the lampstand and *c*the table and *d*the sacred bread; this is called the holy place.

3 And behind *a*the second veil, there was a tabernacle which is called the *b*Holy of Holies,

4 having a golden *a*altar of incense and *b*the ark of the covenant covered on all sides with gold, in which *was* *c*a golden jar holding the manna, and *d*Aaron's rod which budded, and *e*the tables of the covenant.

5 And above it *were* the *a*cherubim of glory *b*overshadowing the mercy seat; but of these things we cannot now speak in detail.

6 Now when these things have been thus prepared, the priests *a*are continually entering *b*the outer tabernacle, performing the divine worship,

7 but into *a*the second only *b*the high priest *enters,* *c*once a year, *d*not without taking blood, which he *e*offers for himself and for the *f*sins of the people committed in ignorance.

8 *a*The Holy Spirit *is* signifying this, *b*that the way into the holy place has not yet been disclosed, while the outer tabernacle is still standing,

9 which *is* *a*a symbol for the present time. Accordingly both gifts and sacrifices are *b*offered which cannot *c*make the worshiper perfect in conscience,

10 since they *relate* only to *a*food and *b*drink and various *c*washings, *d*regulations for the

body imposed until *e*a time of reformation.

2 *Christ's priesthood,* 9:11-14

11 But when Christ appeared as a *a*high priest of the *b*good things to come, He entered through *c*the greater and more perfect tabernacle, *d*not made with hands, that is to say, *e*not of this creation;

12 and not through *a*the blood of goats and calves, but *b*through His own blood, He *c*entered the holy place *d*once for all, having obtained *e*eternal redemption.

13 For if *a*the blood of goats and bulls and *b*the ashes of a heifer sprinkling those who have been defiled, sanctify for the cleansing of the flesh,

14 how much more will *a*the blood of Christ, who through *b*the eternal Spirit *c*offered Himself without blemish to God, *d*cleanse your conscience from *e*dead works to serve *f*the living God?

3 *Christ's fulfillment of the promise,* 9:15-10:18

15 And for this reason *a*He is the *b*mediator of a *c*new covenant, in order that since a death has taken place for the redemption of the transgressions that were *committed* under the first covenant, those who have been *d*called may *e*receive the promise of *f*the eternal inheritance.

16 For where a covenant is, there must of necessity be the death of the one who made it.

17 For a covenant is valid *only* when men are dead, for it is never

2 *a*Ex. 25:8, 9 *b*Ex. 25:31-39 *c*Ex. 25:23-29 *d*Ex. 25:30; Lev. 24:5ff.; Matt. 12:4
3 *a*Ex. 26:31-33 *b*Ex. 26:33
★ **4** *a*Ex. 30:1-5; 37:25f. *b*Ex. 25:10ff.; 37:1ff. *c*Ex. 16:32f. *d*Num. 17:10 *e*Ex. 31:18; 32:15; Deut. 9:9, 11, 15
5 *a*Ex. 25:18ff. *b*Ex. 25:17, 20
6 *a*Num. 28:3 *b*Ex. 25:8, 9
★ **7-10**
7 *a*Heb. 9:3 *b*Lev. 16:12ff. *c*Ex. 30:10; Lev. 16:34; Heb. 10:3 *d*Lev. 16:11, 14 *e*Heb. 5:3 *f*Num. 15:25; Heb. 5:2
8 *a*Heb. 3:7 *b*John 14:6; Heb. 10:20
9 *a*Heb. 10:1; 11:19 *b*Heb. 5:1 *c*Heb. 7:19
10 *a*Lev. 11:2ff.; Col. 2:16 *b*Num. 6:3 *c*Lev. 11:25; Num. 19:13; Mark 7:4 *d*Heb. 7:16 *e*Heb. 7:12
11 *a*Heb. 2:17 *b*Heb. 10:1 *c*Heb. 8:2; 9:24 *d*Mark 14:58; 2 Cor. 5:1 *e*2 Cor. 4:18; Heb. 12:27; 13:14
12 *a*Lev. 4:3; 16:6, 15; Heb. 9:19 *b*Heb. 9:14; 13:12 *c*Heb. 9:24 *d*Heb. 7:27 *e*Heb. 5:9; 9:15
13 *a*Heb. 9:19; 10:4 *b*Num. 19:9, 17f.
14 *a*Heb. 9:12; 13:12 *b*1 Cor. 15:45; 1 Pet. 3:18 *c*Eph. 5:2; Heb. 7:27; 10:10, 12 *d*Acts 15:9; Titus 2:14; Heb. 1:3; 10:2, 22 *e*Heb. 6:1 *f*Matt. 16:16; Heb. 3:12
15 *a*Rom. 3:24 *b*1 Tim. 2:5; Heb. 8:6; 12:24 *c*Heb. 8:8 *d*Matt. 22:3ff.; Rom. 8:28f.; Heb. 3:1 *e*Heb. 6:15; 10:36; 11:39 *f*Acts 20:32
★**16**

9:4 *a golden altar.* Though the altar stood before the veil in the Holy Place, its ritual use was connected with the *Holy of Holies* (v. 3), especially on the Day of Atonement which is being described in these verses (see Lev. 16:12-13).

9:7-10 The fact that only the high priest could go into the Holy of Holies and that he had to go each year signified that no final offering for sin was made in O.T. times and that the offerings that were made could not cleanse the

conscience. *reformation.* I.e., the change brought about by the completed sacrifice of Christ and His entering into heaven (vv. 11-12).

9:16 *the one who made it,* I.e., who made the covenant or will. This is strong proof that it is the death of Christ, not His life, which put into effect the new covenant with all its blessings. His sinless life qualified Him to be the suitable sacrifice for sin, but it was His death that made the payment for sin.

in force while the one who made it lives.

18 Therefore even the first *covenant* was not inaugurated without blood.

19 For when every commandment had been ᵃspoken by Moses to all the people according to the Law, ᵇhe took the ᶜblood of the calves and the goats, with ᵈwater and scarlet wool and hyssop, and sprinkled both ᵉthe book itself and all the people,

20 saying, "ᵃTHIS IS THE BLOOD OF THE COVENANT WHICH GOD COMMANDED YOU."

21 And in the same way he sprinkled both the ᵃtabernacle and all the vessels of the ministry with the blood.

22 And according to the Law, *one may* ᵃ*almost say*, all things are cleansed with blood, and ᵇwithout shedding of blood there is no forgiveness.

23 Therefore it was necessary for the ᵃcopies of the things in the heavens to be cleansed with these, but ᵃthe heavenly things themselves with better sacrifices than these.

24 For Christ ᵃdid not enter a holy place made with hands, a *mere* copy of ᵇthe true one, but into ᶜheaven itself, now ᵈto appear in the presence of God for us;

25 nor was it that He should offer Himself often, as ᵃthe high priest enters ᵇthe holy place ᵃyear by year with blood not his own.

26 Otherwise, He would have needed to suffer often since ᵃthe foundation of the world; but now ᵇonce at ᶜthe consummation of the ages He has been ᵈmanifested

to put away sin ᵉby the sacrifice of Himself.

27 And inasmuch as ᵃit is appointed for men to die once and after this ᵇcomes judgment,

28 so Christ also, having been ᵃoffered once to ᵇbear the sins of many, shall appear ᶜa second time for ʳsalvation ᵈwithout *reference to* sin, to those who ᵉeagerly await Him.

10 For the Law, since it has only ᵃa shadow of ᵇthe good things to come *and* not the very form of things, can ᶜnever by the same sacrifices year by year, which they offer continually, ᵈmake perfect those who draw near.

2 Otherwise, would they not have ceased to be offered, because the worshipers, having once been cleansed, would no longer have had ᵃconsciousness of sins?

3 But ᵃin those *sacrifices* there is a reminder of sins year by year.

4 For it is ᵃimpossible for the ᵇblood of bulls and goats to take away sins.

5 Therefore, ᵃwhen He comes into the world, He says,

"ᵇSACRIFICE AND OFFERING
   THOU HAST NOT DESIRED,
BUT ᶜA BODY THOU HAST PREPARED FOR ME;

6 ᵃIN WHOLE BURNT OFFERINGS
   AND *sacrifices* FOR SIN
   THOU HAST TAKEN NO
   PLEASURE.

7 "ᵃTHEN I SAID, 'BEHOLD, I
   HAVE COME
(IN ᵇTHE ROLL OF THE BOOK IT
   IS WRITTEN OF ME)
TO DO THY WILL, O GOD.'"

Cross references (left column):

19 ᵃHeb. 1:1; ᵇEx. 24:6ff.; ᶜHeb. 9:12; ᵈLev. 14:4, 7; Num. 19:6, 18 ᵉEx. 24:7

20 ᵃEx. 24:8; Matt. 26:28

21 ᵃEx. 24:6; 40:9; Lev. 8:15, 19; 16:14-16

★**22** ᵃLev. 5:11f. ᵇLev. 17:11

23 ᵃHeb. 8:5

24 ᵃHeb. 4:14; 9:12 ᵇHeb. 8:2 ᶜHeb. 9:12 ᵈMatt. 18:10; Heb. 7:25

25 ᵃHeb. 9:7 ᵇHeb. 9:2; 10:19

★**26** ᵃMatt. 25:34; Heb. 4:3 ᵇHeb. 7:27; 9:12 ᶜMatt. 13:39; Heb. 1:2 ᵈ1 John 3:5, 8 ᵉHeb. 9:12, 14

Cross references (right column):

27 ᵃGen. 3:19 ᵇ2 Cor. 5:10; 1 John 4:17

★**28** ᵃHeb. 7:27 ᵇ1 Pet. 2:24 ᶜActs 1:11 ᵈHeb. 4:15 ᵉ1 Cor. 1:7; Titus 2:13 ʳHeb. 5:9

★ **1-39**
1 ᵃHeb. 8:5 ᵇHeb. 9:11 ᶜRom. 8:3; Heb. 9:9; 10:4, 11 ᵈHeb. 7:19

2 ᵃ1 Pet. 2:19

3 ᵃHeb. 9:7

4 ᵃHeb. 10:1, 11 ᵇHeb. 9:12f.

★ **5** ᵃHeb. 1:6 ᵇPs. 40:6 ᶜHeb. 2:14; 5:7; 1 Pet. 2:24

6 ᵃPs. 40:6

7 ᵃPs. 40:7, 8 ᵇEzra 6:2 4septuagint]; Jer. 36:2; Ezek. 2:9; 3:1f.

9:22 *almost.* For exceptions to the requirement of blood for cleansing permitted by the law see Lev. 5:11-13; Num. 16:46; 31:50.

9:26 *once* = once for all. *at the consummation of the ages.* The first coming of Christ. (cf. 1 Pet. 1:20).

9:28 *to bear the sins of many.* Quoted from Isa. 53:12. Isaiah was a significant source of early Christian interpretation of Christ. *without reference to sin.* I.e., apart from the sin question. In His first coming Christ dealt with sin

once for all; in His second coming He will take redeemed sinners to Himself in the consummation of their salvation.

10:1-39 In this chapter the author emphasizes the finality of Christ's sacrifice by contrasting it with the lack of finality of the O.T. system of law and sacrifices. Christ's redemption needs no repetition and no supplementation. Therefore, a rejection of His sacrifice is final and unforgivable.

10:5 *He comes* . I.e., Christ.

8 aPs. 40:6;
Heb. 10:5f.
bMark 12:33
cRom. 8:3

9 aPs. 40:7,
8; Heb. 10:7

★10 aJohn
17:19; Eph.
5:26; Heb.
2:11; 10:14,
29; 13:12
bJohn 6:51;
Eph. 5:2;
Heb. 7:27;
9:14, 28;
10:12 cHeb.
2:14; 5:7;
1 Pet. 2:24
dHeb. 7:27
11 aHeb. 5:1
bMic. 6:6-8;
Heb. 10:1, 4
12 aHeb. 5:1
bHeb. 10:14
cHeb. 1:3

13 aPs.
110:1; Heb.
1:13

14 aHeb.
10:1 bHeb.
10:12

15 aHeb. 3:7

★16-17
16 aJer.
31:33; Heb.
8:10

17 aJer.
31:34; Heb.
8:12

8 After saying above, "ᵃSAC-RIFICES AND OFFERINGS AND ᵇWHOLE BURNT OFFERINGS AND *sacrifices* ᶜFOR SIN THOU HAST NOT DESIRED, NOR HAST THOU TAKEN PLEASURE *in them*" (which are offered according to the Law),

9 then He said, "ᵃBEHOLD, I HAVE COME TO DO THY WILL." He takes away the first in order to establish the second.

10 By this will we have been ᵃsanctified through ᵇthe offering of ᶜthe body of Jesus Christ ᵈonce for all.

11 And every priest stands daily ministering and ᵃoffering time after time the same sacrifices, which ᵇcan never take away sins;

12 but He, having offered one sacrifice ᵃfor sins ᵇfor all time, ᶜSAT DOWN AT THE RIGHT HAND OF GOD,

13 waiting from that time onward ᵃUNTIL HIS ENEMIES BE MADE A FOOTSTOOL FOR HIS FEET.

14 For by one offering He has ᵃperfected ᵇfor all time those who are sanctified.

15 And ᵃthe Holy Spirit also bears witness to us; for after saying,

16 "ᵃTHIS IS THE COVENANT THAT
I WILL MAKE WITH THEM
AFTER THOSE DAYS, SAYS THE
LORD:
I WILL PUT MY LAWS UPON
THEIR HEART,
AND UPON THEIR MIND I WILL
WRITE THEM,"

He then says,

17 "ᵃAND THEIR SINS AND THEIR
LAWLESS DEEDS
I WILL REMEMBER NO MORE."

18 Now where there is forgiveness of these things, there is no longer *any* offering for sin.

E Parenthetical Warning: Don't Despise Christ, 10:19-39

19 Since therefore, brethren, we ᵃhave confidence to ᵇenter the holy place by the blood of Jesus,

20 by ᵃa new and living way which He inaugurated for us through ᵇthe veil, that is, His flesh,

21 and since *we have* ᵃa great priest ᵇover the house of God,

22 let us ᵃdraw near with a sincere heart in ᵇfull assurance of faith, having our hearts ᶜsprinkled *clean* from an evil conscience and our bodies ᵈwashed with pure water.

23 Let us hold fast the ᵃconfession of our ᵇhope without wavering, for ᶜHe who promised is faithful;

24 and let us consider how ᵃto stimulate one another to love and ᵇgood deeds,

25 not forsaking our own ᵃassembling together, as is the habit of some, but ᵇencouraging *one another*; and all the more, as you see ᶜthe day drawing near.

26 For if we go on ᵃsinning willfully after receiving ᵇthe knowledge of the truth, there no longer remains a sacrifice for sins,

27 but a certain terrifying expectation of ᵃjudgment, and THE ᵇFURY OF A FIRE WHICH WILL CONSUME THE ADVERSARIES.

28 ᵃAnyone who has set aside the Law of Moses dies without

19 aHeb.
3:6; 10:35
bHeb. 9:25

★20 aHeb.
9:8 bHeb.
6:19; 9:3

21 aHeb.
2:17 b1 Tim.
3:15; Heb.
3:6
22 aHeb.
7:19; 10:1
bHeb. 6:11
cEzek.
36:25; Heb.
9:19; 12:24;
1 Pet. 1:2
dActs 22:16;
1 Cor. 6:11;
Eph. 5:26; Ti-
tus 3:5;
1 Pet. 3:21
23 aHeb. 3:1
bHeb. 3:6
c1 Cor. 1:9;
10:13; Heb.
11:11
★24 aHeb.
13:1 bTitus
3:8
★25 aActs
2:42 bHeb.
3:13 c1 Cor.
3:13

★26 aNum.
15:30; Heb.
5:2; 6:4-8;
2 Pet. 2:20f.
b1 Tim. 2:4

27 aJohn
5:29; Heb.
9:27 bIs.
26:11;
2 Thess. 1:7
28 aDeut.
17:2-6; Matt.
18:16; Heb.
2:2

10:10 *By this will.* I.e., by Christ's doing the will of God in becoming the sacrifice for sin.
10:16-17 See Jer. 31:33-34, quoted earlier in Heb. 8:10-12.
10:20 *a new and living way.* Christ is that way (cf. John 14:6; Heb. 4:14; 6:20; 7:24-25).
10:24 *to stimulate.* I.e., to stir up to an incitement or paroxysm of love and good works. To understand how strong this Greek word is, see its use in Acts 15:39 (sharp disagreement); 17:16 (being provoked); 1 Cor. 13:5 (pro-

voked); Eph. 6:4 (provoke).
10:25 *our own assembling together.* I.e., the gathering of Christians for worship and edification. *the day.* I.e., of Christ's coming (also v. 37; 1 Cor. 3:13; Phil. 1:10).
10:26 *there no longer remains a sacrifice for sins.* If a person rejects the truth of Christ's death for sin, there is no other sacrifice for sin available and no other way to come to God. Only judgment remains (v. 27).

mercy on *the testimony of* two or three witnesses.

29 ^aHow much severer punishment do you think he will deserve ^bwho has trampled under foot the Son of God, and has regarded as unclean ^cthe blood of the covenant ^dby which he was sanctified, and has ^einsulted the Spirit of grace?

30 For we know Him who said, "^aVengeance is Mine, I will repay." And again, "^bThe Lord will judge His people."

31 It is a ^aterrifying thing to fall into the hands of the ^bliving God.

32 But remember ^athe former days, when, after being ^benlightened, you endured a great ^cconflict of sufferings,

33 partly, by being ^amade a public spectacle through reproaches and tribulations, and partly by becoming ^bsharers with those who were so treated.

34 For you ^ashowed sympathy to the prisoners, and accepted ^bjoyfully the seizure of your property, knowing that you have for yourselves ^ca better possession and an abiding one.

35 Therefore, do not throw away your ^aconfidence, which has a great ^breward.

36 For you have need of ^aendurance, so that when you have done the will of God, you may ^breceive what was promised.

37 ^aFor yet in a very little while,

^bHe who is coming will come, and will not delay.

38 ^aBut My righteous one shall live by faith;

And if he shrinks back, My soul has no pleasure in him.

39 But we are not of those who shrink back to destruction, but of those who have faith to the preserving of the soul.

III THE SUPERIORITY OF THE POWER OF CHRIST, 11:1–13:19

A The Power of Faith in Christ, 11:1–40

1 *The description of faith,* 11:1

11 Now faith is the ^aassurance of *things* ^bhoped for, the conviction of ^cthings not seen.

2 *The examples of faith,* 11:2–40

2 For by it the ^amen of old ^bgained approval.

3 By faith we understand that the ^aworlds were prepared ^bby the ^cword of God, so that what is seen ^dwas not made out of things which are visible.

4 By faith ^aAbel offered to God a better sacrifice than Cain,

---

Marginal references (left column):

★**29** ^aHeb. 2:3; ^bHeb. 6:6 ^cMatt. 26:28; Heb. 13:20 ^dEph. 5:26; Heb. 9:13f.; Rev. 1:5 ^e1 Cor. 6:11; Eph. 4:30; Heb. 6:4

30 ^aDeut. 32:35; Rom. 12:19 ^bDeut. 32:36

31 ^a2 Cor. 5:11 ^bMatt. 16:16; Heb. 3:12

★**32** ^aHeb. 5:12 ^bHeb. 6:4 ^cPhil. 1:30

33 ^a1 Cor. 4:9; Heb. 12:4 ^bPhil. 4:14 [Gr.]; 1 Thess. 2:14

★**34** ^aHeb. 13:3 ^bMatt. 5:12 ^cHeb. 9:15; 11:16; 13:14; 1 Pet. 1:4f.

35 ^aHeb. 10:19 ^bHeb. 2:2

★**36** ^aLuke 21:19; Heb. 12:1 ^bHeb. 9:15

Marginal references (right column):

★**37** ^aHab. 2:3; Heb. 10:25; Rev. 22:20 ^bMatt. 11:3

★**38** ^aHab. 2:4; Rom. 1:17; Gal. 3:11

★　**1** ^aHeb. 3:14 [Gr.] ^bHeb. 3:6 ^cRom. 8:24; 2 Cor. 4:18; 5:7; Heb. 11:7, 27

★　**2** ^aHeb. 1:1 ^bHeb. 11:4, 39

★　**3** ^aHeb. 1:2 ^bGen. 1; Heb. 1:2 ^cHeb. 6:5; 2 Pet. 3:5 ^dRom. 4:17

★　**4** ^aGen. 4:4; Matt. 23:35; 1 John 3:12 ^bHeb. 11:2 ^cHeb. 5:1 ^dGen. 4:8-10; Heb. 12:24

10:29 The three indictments specified in this verse describe the enormity of the sin of unbelief.

10:32 *conflict of sufferings* = struggle with sufferings.

10:34 *to the prisoners.* Some Christians apparently had been imprisoned for their faith while others had experienced the *seizure* of their possessions.

10:36 *endurance* = patience.

10:37 See Hab. 2:3.

10:38 This quotation from Hab. 2:4 is used here to teach that the person who has been made righteous by God lives (and survives the coming ordeal) by faith. The believer trusts God in everything. Hab. 2:4 is also quoted in Rom. 1:17 and Gal. 3:11, where Paul uses it to teach that the one who is righteous by faith (rather than by works) shall live. Paul's emphasis is

on salvation by faith; this writer's is on living by faith.

11:1 Faith is described in this great verse as the *assurance* (or reality, the same word translated "nature" in 1:3) *of things hoped for, the conviction* (as in John 16:8) *of things not seen.* Faith gives reality and proof of things unseen, treating them as if they were already objects of sight rather than of hope.

11:2 *men of old.* I.e., the O.T. patriarchs and heroes.

11:3 *the worlds were prepared.* Lit., the ages have been prepared (cf. 1:2). This means the preparation of all that the successive periods of time would contain.

11:4 *Abel.* Actually nothing is said here or in Gen. 4:3–5 as to why Abel's sacrifice was more acceptable, though the fact that it involved blood sacrifice is significant (see Heb. 12:24).

through which he [b]obtained the testimony that he was righteous, God testifying about his [c]gifts, and through faith, though [d]he is dead, he still speaks.

5 By faith [a]Enoch was taken up so that he should not [b]see death; AND HE WAS NOT FOUND BE-CAUSE GOD TOOK HIM UP; for he obtained the witness that before his being taken up he was pleasing to God.

6 And without faith it is impossible to please *Him*, for he who [a]comes to God must believe that He is, and *that* He is a rewarder of those who seek Him.

7 By faith [a]Noah, being [b]warned *by God* about [c]things not yet seen, [d]in reverence [e]prepared an ark for the salvation of his household, by which he condemned the world, and became an heir of [f]the righteousness which is according to faith.

8 By faith [a]Abraham, when he was called, obeyed by going out to a place which he was to [b]receive for an inheritance; and he went out, not knowing where he was going.

9 By faith he lived as an alien in [a]the land of promise, as in a foreign *land*, [b]dwelling in tents with Isaac and Jacob, [c]fellow heirs of the same promise;

10 for he was looking for [a]the city which has [b]foundations, [c]whose architect and builder is God.

11 By faith even [a]Sarah herself received ability to conceive, even beyond the proper time of life, since she considered Him [b]faithful who had promised;

12 therefore, also, there was born of one man, and [a]him as good as dead at that, *as many de-*scendants [b]AS THE STARS OF HEAVEN IN NUMBER, AND INNUMERABLE AS THE SAND WHICH IS BY THE SEASHORE.

13 [a]All these died in faith, [b]without receiving the promises, but [c]having seen them and having welcomed them from a distance, and [d]having confessed that they were strangers and exiles on the earth.

14 For those who say such things make it clear that they are seeking a country of their own.

15 And indeed if they had been thinking of that *country* from which they went out, [a]they would have had opportunity to return.

16 But as it is, they desire a better *country*, that is a [a]heavenly one. Therefore [b]God is not ashamed to be [c]called their God; for [d]He has prepared a city for them.

17 By faith [a]Abraham, when he was tested, offered up Isaac; and he who had [b]received the promises was offering up his only begotten *son*;

18 *it was he* to whom it was said, "[a]IN ISAAC YOUR DESCENDANTS SHALL BE CALLED."

19 He considered that [a]God is able to raise *men* even from the dead; from which he also received him back as a [b]type.

20 By faith [a]Isaac blessed Jacob and Esau, even regarding things to come.

21 By faith [a]Jacob, as he was dying, blessed each of the sons of Joseph, and [b]worshiped, *leaning* on the top of his staff.

22 By faith [a]Joseph, when he was dying, made mention of the exodus of the sons of Israel, and gave orders concerning his bones.

★ 5 [a]Gen. 5:21-24; [b]Luke 2:26; John 8:51; Heb. 2:9

6 [a]Heb. 7:19

★ 7 [a]Gen. 6:13-22; [b]Heb. 8:5; [c]Heb. 11:1; [d]Heb. 5:7; [e]1 Pet. 3:20; [f]Gen. 6:9; Ezek. 14:14, 20; Rom. 4:13; 9:30

★ 8 [a]Gen. 12:1-4; Acts 7:2-4 [b]Gen. 12:7

9 [a]Acts 7:5; [b]Gen. 12:8; 13:3, 18; 18:1, 9; [c]Heb. 6:17

10 [a]Heb. 12:22; 13:14; [b]Rev. 21:14ff.; [c]Heb. 11:16

★11 [a]Gen. 17:19; 18:11-14; 21:2; [b]Heb. 10:23

12 [a]Rom. 4:19 [b]Gen. 15:5; 22:17; 32:12

13 [a]Matt. 13:17 [b]Heb. 11:39 [c]John 8:56; Heb. 11:27 [d]Gen. 23:4; 47:9; Ps. 39:12; Eph. 2:19; 1 Pet. 1:1; 2:11

15 [a]Gen. 24:6-8

16 [a]2 Tim. 4:18 [b]Mark 8:38; Heb. 2:11 [c]Gen. 26:24; 28:13; Ex. 3:6, 15; 4:5 [d]Heb. 11:10; Rev. 21:2

★17 [a]Gen. 22:1-10; James 2:21 [b]Heb. 11:13

18 [a]Gen. 21:12; Rom. 9:7

19 [a]Rom. 4:21 [b]Heb. 9:9

★20 [a]Gen. 27:27-29, 39f.

★21 [a]Gen. 48:1, 5, 16, 20 [b]Gen. 47:31 [Septuagint]; 1 Kin. 1:47

★22 [a]Gen. 50:24f.; Ex. 13:19

11:5 *Enoch.* Enoch was saved from death by being *taken up* (Gen. 5:22-24).

11:7 *Noah.* His *reverence* was fear of God, or piety (Gen. 6:13-22).

11:8 *Abraham.* See Gen. 12:1-4.

11:11 *Sarah.* See Gen. 21:1-5.

11:17 *offered up Isaac.* See Gen. 22:1; Jas. 2:21. This was a severe test, for only through Isaac could Abraham have received the promises of the Lord.

11:20 *Isaac blessed Jacob and Esau.* See Gen. 27:26-40.

11:21 *Jacob . . . blessed each of the sons of Joseph.* See Gen. 48:1-22.

11:22 *Joseph.* See Gen. 50:24-25. Joseph showed his faith in God's promise to Abraham by requesting that his bones be buried in the Land of Promise.

★23 *a*Ex. 2:2 [Septuagint] *b*Ex. 1:16, 22

23 By faith *a*Moses, when he was born, was hidden for three months by his parents, because they saw he was a beautiful child; and they were not afraid of the *b*king's edict.

24 *a*Ex. 2:10, 11ff.

24 By faith Moses, *a*when he had grown up, refused to be called the son of Pharaoh's daughter;

25 *a*Heb. 11:37

25 choosing rather to *a*endure ill-treatment with the people of God, than to enjoy the passing pleasures of sin;

26 *a*Luke 14:33; Phil. 3:7f. *b*Heb. 2:2

26 *a*considering the reproach of Christ greater riches than the treasures of Egypt; for he was looking to the *b*reward.

27 *a*Ex. 2:15; 12:50f.; 13:17f. *b*Ex. 2:14; 10:28f. *c*Col. 1:15; Heb. 11:1, 13

27 By faith he *a*left Egypt, not *b*fearing the wrath of the king; for he endured, as *c*seeing Him who is unseen.

★28 *a*Ex. 12:21ff. *b*Ex. 12:23, 29f.; 1 Cor. 10:10

28 By faith he *a*kept the Passover and the sprinkling of the blood, so that *b*he who destroyed the first-born might not touch them.

★29 *a*Ex. 14:22-29
★30 *b*Josh. 6:20
★31 *a*Josh. 2:9ff.; 6:23; James 2:25
★32 *a*Judg. 6-8 *b*Judg. 4-5 *c*Judg. 13-16
*d*Judg. 11-12 *e*1 Sam. 16:1, 13 *f*1 Sam. 1:20
★33 *a*Judg. 4, 7, 11, 14; 2 Sam. 5:17; 8:2; 10:12 *b*1 Sam. 12:4; 2 Sam. 8:15 *c*2 Sam. 7:11f. *d*Judg. 14:6; 1 Sam. 17:34; Dan. 6:22

29 By faith they *a*passed through the Red Sea as though *they were passing* through dry land; and the Egyptians, when they attempted it, were drowned.

30 By faith *a*the walls of Jericho fell down, *b*after they had been encircled for seven days.

31 By faith *a*Rahab the harlot did not perish along with those who were disobedient, after she had welcomed the spies in peace.

32 And what more shall I say? For time will fail me if I tell of *a*Gideon, *b*Barak, *c*Samson, *d*Jephthah, of *e*David and *f*Samuel and the prophets,

33 who by faith *a*conquered

kingdoms, *b*performed *acts of righteousness*, *c*obtained promises, *d*shut the mouths of lions,

34 *a*quenched the power of fire, *b*escaped the edge of the sword, from weakness were made strong, *c*became mighty in war, *e*put foreign armies to flight.

35 *a*Women received *back* their dead by resurrection; and others were tortured, not accepting their release, in order that they might obtain a better resurrection;

36 and others experienced mockings and scourgings, yes, also *a*chains and imprisonment.

37 They were *a*stoned, they were *b*sawn in two, they were tempted, they were *c*put to death with the sword; they went about *d*in sheepskins, in goatskins, being destitute, afflicted, *e*ill-treated

38 (*men* of whom the world was not worthy), *a*wandering in deserts and mountains and caves and holes in the ground.

39 And all these, having *a*gained approval through their faith, *b*did not receive what was promised,

40 because God had provided *a*something better for us, so that *b*apart from us they should not be made perfect.

★34 *a*Dan. 3:23ff. *b*Ex. 18:4; 1 Sam. 18:11; 19:10; 1 Kin. 19; 2 Kin. 6; Ps. 144:10 *c*Judg. 7:21; 15:8, 15f.; 1 Sam. 17:51f.; 2 Sam. 8:1-6; 10:15ff.
★35-38
★35 *a*1 Kin. 17:23; 2 Kin. 4:36f.

36 *a*Gen. 39:20; Jer. 20:2; 37:15

37 *a*1 Kin. 21:13; 2 Chr. 24:21 *b*2 Sam. 12:31; 1 Chr. 20:3 *c*1 Kin. 19:10; Jer. 26:23 *d*1 Kin. 19:13, 19; 2 Kin. 2:8, 13f.; Zech. 13:4 *e*Heb. 11:25; 13:3

38 *a*1 Kin. 18:4, 13; 19:9

★39 *a*Heb. 11:2 *b*Heb. 10:36; 11:13

40 *a*Heb. 11:16 *b*Rev. 6:11

B The Power of Hope in Christ, 12:1-29

1 *The debatable things of life,* 12:1-2

★1 *a*Heb. 10:39 *b*Rom. 13:12; Eph. 4:22 [Gr.] *c*1 Cor. 9:24; Gal. 2:2 *d*Heb. 10:36

12 Therefore, since we have so great a cloud of wit-

11:23 *Moses.* See Ex. 2:1-15.
11:28 *the Passover.* See Ex. 12:1-28.
11:29 *they passed through the Red Sea.* See Ex. 14:13-31.
11:30 *the walls of Jericho fell down.* See Josh. 6.
11:31 *Rahab.* See Josh. 2:1-21; 6:22-25; Jas. 2:25.
11:32 *Gideon* (Judg. 6:11; 8:32); *Barak* (Judg. 4:6-5:31); *Samson* (Judg. 13:24-16:31); *Jephthah* (Judg. 11:1-12:7); *David* (1 Sam. 16-17); *Samuel* (1 Sam. 7-10).
11:33 *shut the mouths of lions.* See Dan. 6 (Daniel); Judg. 14:5 (Samson); 1 Sam. 17:34

(David).
11:34 *quenched the power of fire.* See Dan. 3:23-28.
11:35-38 The background for much of what is in these verses is likely from the apocryphal book of 2 Maccabees (6:18-7:42).
11:35 *Women received back their dead by resurrection.* See 1 Kings 17:22-23 (the widow of Zarephath's son); 2 Kings 4:35-36 (the Shunammite's son).
11:39 *what was promised.* I.e., all that was included in the actual coming of the Messiah.
12:1 *a cloud of witnesses.* I.e., the heroes of

nesses surrounding us, let [a]us also [b]lay aside every encumbrance, and the sin which so easily entangles us, and let us [c]run with [d]endurance the race that is set before us,

2　fixing our eyes on Jesus, the [a]author and perfecter of faith, who for the joy set before Him [b]endured the cross, [c]despising the shame, and has [d]sat down at the right hand of the throne of God.

2　The disciplines of life,
12:3-11

3　For [a]consider Him who has endured such hostility by sinners against Himself, so that you may not grow weary [b]and lose heart. 4　[a]You have not yet resisted [b]to the point of shedding blood in your striving against sin; 5　and you have forgotten the exhortation which is addressed to you as sons,

"[a]MY SON, DO NOT REGARD
LIGHTLY THE DISCIPLINE OF
THE LORD,
NOR [b]FAINT WHEN YOU ARE
REPROVED BY HIM;
6　[a]FOR THOSE [b]WHOM THE
LORD LOVES HE DISCI-
PLINES,
AND HE SCOURGES EVERY SON
WHOM HE RECEIVES."

7　It is for discipline that you endure; [a]God deals with you as with sons; for what son is there whom his father does not discipline? 8　But if you are without discipline, [a]of which all have become

partakers, then you are illegitimate children and not sons. 9　Furthermore, we had earthly fathers to discipline us, and we [a]respected them; shall we not much rather be subject to [b]the Father of spirits, and [c]live? 10　For they disciplined us for a short time as seemed best to them, but He disciplines us for our good, [a]that we may share His holiness. 11　All discipline [a]for the moment seems not to be joyful, but sorrowful; yet to those who have been trained by it, afterwards it yields the [b]peaceful fruit of righteousness.

3　The direction of life,
12:12-17

12　Therefore, [a]strengthen the hands that are weak and the knees that are feeble, 13　and [a]make straight paths for your feet, so that the limb which is lame may not be put out of joint, but rather [b]be healed. 14　[a]Pursue peace with all men, and the [b]sanctification without which no one will [c]see the Lord. 15　See to it that no one [a]comes short of the grace of God; that no [b]root of bitterness springing up causes trouble, and by it many be [c]defiled; 16　that there be no [a]immoral or [b]godless person like Esau, [c]who sold his own birthright for a single meal. 17　For you know that even afterwards, [a]when he desired to inherit the blessing, he was rejected, for he found no place for

Cross references (left margin)
2 [a]Heb. 2:10 [b]Phil. 2:8f.; Heb. 2:9 [c]1 Cor. 1:18, 23; Heb. 13:13 [d]Heb. 1:3

★ 3 [a]Matt. 10:24; Rev. 2:3 [b]Gal. 6:9; Heb. 12:5

★ 4 [a]Heb. 10:32ff.; 13:13 [b]Phil. 2:8

★ 5-11
5 [a]Prov. 3:11 [b]Heb. 12:3

6 [a]Prov. 3:12 [b]Ps. 119:75; Rev. 3:19

7 [a]Deut. 8:5; 2 Sam. 7:14; Prov. 13:24; 19:18; 23:13f.

8 [a]1 Pet. 5:9

Cross references (right margin)
9 [a]Luke 18:2 [b]Num. 16:22; 27:16; Rev. 22:6 [c]Is. 38:16

10 [a]2 Pet. 1:4

11 [a]1 Pet. 1:6 [b]Is. 32:17; 2 Tim. 4:8; James 3:17f.

12 [a]Is. 35:3

13 [a]Prov. 4:26; Gal. 2:14 [b]Gal. 6:1; James 5:16
14 [a]Rom. 14:19 [b]Rom. 6:22; Heb. 12:10 [c]Matt. 5:8; Heb. 9:28

15 [a]2 Cor. 6:1; Gal. 5:4; Heb. 4:1 [b]Deut. 29:18 [c]Titus 1:15

★16 [a]Heb. 13:4 [b]1 Tim. 1:9 [c]Gen. 25:33f.

17 [a]Gen. 27:30-40

---

faith mentioned in chapter 11 and others. *every encumbrance*. That which hinders the believer from being a winner. *the sin which so easily entangles us.* I.e., unbelief.
12:3 *Him.* Jesus.
12:4 *You have not yet resisted to the point of shedding blood.* None of the readers of this book had yet been martyred.
12:5-11 In these verses the writer discusses why Christians are disciplined. (1) It is part of the educational process by which a believer is fitted to share God's holiness (v. 10). (2) It is

proof of a genuine love relationship between the heavenly Father and His children (vv. 6, 8). (3) It helps train them to be obedient (v. 9). (4) It produces the fruit of righteousness in their lives (v. 11). For additional teaching on this subject see the book of Job; Rom. 8:18; 2 Cor. 1:3-4; 4:16-17; 12:7-9; Phil. 1:29; 2 Tim. 3:12.
12:16 *Esau.* See Gen. 25:33. Though he may not have been *immoral* in the physical sense, Esau was immoral in the spiritual sense, being worldly and materialistic.

repentance, though he sought for it with tears.

4 The drive of life, 12:18-24

★18-24
18 a2 Cor.
3:7-13; Heb.
12:18ff. bEx.
19:12, 16ff.;
20:18; Deut.
4:11; 5:22
19 aEx.
19:16, 19;
20:18; Matt.
24:31 bEx.
19:19; Deut.
4:12 cEx.
20:19; Deut.
5:25; 18:16
20 aEx.
19:12f.

18 *a*For you have not come to *b*a mountain that may be touched and to a blazing fire, and to darkness and gloom and whirlwind, **19** and to the *a*blast of a trumpet and the *b*sound of words which *sound was such that* those who heard *c*begged that no further word should be spoken to them. **20** For they could not bear the command, "*a*IF EVEN A BEAST TOUCHES THE MOUNTAIN, IT WILL BE STONED."

21 aDeut.
9:19

21 And so terrible was the sight, *that* Moses said, "*a*I AM FULL OF FEAR and trembling."

22 aRev.
14:1 bEph.
2:19; Phil.
3:20; Heb.
11:10; Rev.
21:2 cHeb.
3:12 dGal.
4:26; Heb.
11:16 eRev.
5:11
★23 aEx.
4:22; Heb.
2:12 marg.
bLuke 10:20
cGen. 18:25;
Ps. 50:6;
94:2 dHeb.
11:40; Rev.
6:9, 11
24 a1 Tim.
2:5; Heb.
8:6; 9:15
bHeb. 9:19;
10:22; 1 Pet.
1:2 cHeb.
11:4

22 But *a*you have come to Mount Zion and to *b*the city of *c*the living God, *d*the heavenly Jerusalem, and to *e*myriads of angels, **23** to the general assembly and *a*church of the first-born who *b*are enrolled in heaven, and to God, *c*the Judge of all, and to the *d*spirits of righteous men made perfect, **24** and to Jesus, the *a*mediator of a new covenant, and to the *b*sprinkled blood, which speaks better than *c*the blood of Abel.

5 The duty of life, 12:25-29

25 aHeb.
3:12 bHeb.
1:1 cHeb.
2:2f.; 10:28f.
dHeb. 12:19
[Gr.] eHeb.
8:5; 11:7

25 *a*See to it that you do not refuse Him who is *b*speaking. For *c*if those did not escape when they *d*refused him who *e*warned them on earth, much less shall we

escape who turn away from Him who *e*warns from heaven.

26 And *a*His voice shook the earth then, but now He has promised, saying, "*b*YET ONCE MORE I WILL SHAKE NOT ONLY THE EARTH, BUT ALSO THE HEAVEN."

26 aEx.
19:18; Judg.
5:4f. bHag.
2:6

27 And this *expression*, "Yet once more," denotes *a*the removing of those things which can be shaken, as of created things, in order that those things which cannot be shaken may remain.

★27 aIs.
34:4; 54:10;
65:17; Rom.
8:19, 21;
1 Cor. 7:31;
Heb. 1:10ff.

28 Therefore, since we receive a *a*kingdom which cannot be shaken, let us show gratitude, by which we may *b*offer to God an acceptable service with reverence and awe;

28 aDan.
2:44 bHeb.
13:15, 21

29 for *a*our God is a consuming fire.

29 aDeut.
4:24; 9:3; Is.
33:14;
2 Thess. 1:7;
Heb. 10:27,
31

C The Power of the Love of Christ, 13:1-19
1 In relation to social duties, 13:1-6

13 Let *a*love of the brethren continue. **2** Do not neglect to *a*show hospitality to strangers, for by this some have *b*entertained angels without knowing it. **3** *a*Remember *b*the prisoners, as though in prison with them, and those who are ill-treated, since you yourselves also are in the body. **4** *a*Let marriage *be* held in honor among all, and let the *marriage* bed *be* undefiled; *b*for fornicators and adulterers God will judge. **5** Let your character be *a*free from the love of money, *b*being

1 aRom.
12:10;
1 Thess. 4:9;
1 Pet. 1:22
★ 2 aMatt.
25:35; Rom.
12:13; 1 Pet.
4:9 bGen.
18:3; 19:2
3 aCol.
4:18 bMatt.
25:36; Heb.
10:34

4 a1 Cor.
7:38; 1 Tim.
4:3 b1 Cor.
6:9; Gal
5:19, 21;
1 Thess. 4:6
★ 5 aEph.
5:3; Col. 3:5;
1 Tim. 3:3
bPhil. 4:11
cDeut. 31:6;
Josh. 1:5

12:18-24 The old covenant (the law) and the new covenant (the gospel) are contrasted by comparing Mt. Sinai, where the law was given, with Mt. Zion, the spiritual city, eternal in the heavens and symbolic of the gospel of grace.
12:23 *church of the first-born.* Lit., church of first-born ones. N.T. believers who belong to the church, the body of Christ. *spirits of righteous men made perfect.* Believers of O.T. times.
12:27 *those things which cannot be shaken.* I.e., the eternal kingdom to which Christians

belong (v. 28).
13:2 *some have entertained angels without knowing it.* The word "angel" may refer to superhuman beings (see Gen. 18:1-8 for an example of such entertaining) or it may refer to a human being who is a messenger from God (see Jas. 2:25 for an example of such entertaining).
13:5 *He Himself has said.* See Deut. 31:6. The idea is: Christians need not be anxious (cf. Matt. 6:24-34).

content with what you have; for He Himself has said, "ᶜI WILL NEVER DESERT YOU, NOR WILL I EVER FORSAKE YOU,"

6 so that we confidently say,

"ᵃTHE LORD IS MY HELPER, I
WILL NOT BE AFRAID.
WHAT SHALL MAN DO TO
ME?"

2 In relation to spiritual duties, 13:7-19

7 Remember ᵃthose who led you, who spoke ᵇthe word of God to you; and considering the result of their conduct, ᶜimitate their faith.

8 ᵃJesus Christ *is* the same yesterday and today, *yes* and forever.

9 ᵃDo not be carried away by varied and strange teachings; for it is good for the heart to ᵇbe strengthened by grace, not by ᶜfoods, ᵈthrough which those who were thus occupied were not benefited.

10 We have an altar, ᵃfrom which those ᵇwho serve the tabernacle have no right to eat.

11 For ᵃthe bodies of those animals whose blood is brought into the holy place by the high priest *as an offering* for sin, are burned outside the camp.

12 Therefore Jesus also, ᵃthat He might sanctify the people ᵇthrough His own blood, suffered ᶜoutside the gate.

13 Hence, let us go out to Him outside the camp, ᵃbearing His reproach.

14 For here ᵃwe do not have a lasting city, but we are seeking ᵇthe city which is to come.

15 ᵃThrough Him then, let us continually offer up a ᵇsacrifice of praise to God, that is, ᶜthe fruit of lips that give thanks to His name.

16 And do not neglect doing good and ᵃsharing; for ᵇwith such sacrifices God is pleased.

17 ᵃObey your leaders, and submit *to them*; for ᵇthey keep watch over your souls, as those who will give an account. Let them do this with joy and not with grief, for this would be unprofitable for you.

18 ᵃPray for us, for we are sure that we have a ᵇgood conscience, desiring to conduct ourselves honorably in all things.

19 And I urge *you* all the more to do this, ᵃthat I may be restored to you the sooner.

IV CONCLUDING BENEDICTIONS, 13:20-25

20 Now ᵃthe God of peace, who ᵇbrought up from the dead the ᶜgreat Shepherd of the sheep through ᵈthe blood of the ᵉeternal covenant, *even* Jesus our Lord,

21 ᵃequip you in every good thing to do His will, ᵇworking in us that ᶜwhich is pleasing in His sight, through Jesus Christ, ᵈto whom *be* the glory forever and ever. Amen.

22 But ᵃI urge you, ᵇbrethren, bear with this ᵇword of exhortation, for ᶜI have written to you briefly.

23 Take notice that ᵃour brother Timothy has been released, with whom, if he comes soon, I shall see you.

24 Greet ᵃall of your leaders and all the ᵇsaints. Those from ᶜItaly greet you.

25 ᵃGrace be with you all.

Margin references

6 ᵃPs. 118:6

7 ᵃHeb. 13:17, 24 ᵇLuke 5:1 ᶜHeb. 6:12

8 ᵃ2 Cor. 1:19; Heb. 1:12

9 ᵃEph. 4:14; Jude 12 ᵇ2 Cor. 1:21; Col. 2:7 ᶜCol. 2:16 ᵈHeb. 9:10

10 ᵃ1 Cor. 10:18 ᵇHeb. 8:5

★11 ᵃEx. 29:14; Lev. 4:12, 21; 9:11; 16:27; Num. 19:3, 7 ★12 ᵃEph. 5:26; Heb. 2:11 ᵇHeb. 9:12 ᶜJohn 19:17 13 ᵃLuke 9:23; Heb. 11:26; 12:2 14 ᵃHeb. 10:34; 12:27 ᵇEph. 2:19; Heb. 2:5; 11:10, 16; 12:22 15 ᵃ1 Pet. 2:5 ᵇLev. 7:12 ᶜls. 57:19; Hos. 14:2

★16 ᵃRom. 12:13 ᵇPhil. 4:18

★17 ᵃ1 Cor. 16:16; Heb. 13:7, 24 ᵇls. 62:6; Ezek. 3:17; Acts 20:28

18 ᵃ1 Thess. 5:25 ᵇActs 24:16; 1 Tim. 1:5

19 ᵃPhilem. 22

20 ᵃRom. 15:33 ᵇActs 2:24; Rom. 10:7 ᶜls. 63:11; John 10:11; 1 Pet. 2:25 ᵈZech. 9:11; Heb. 10:29 ᵉls. 55:3; Jer. 32:40; Ezek. 37:26

★21 ᵃ1 Pet. 5:10 ᵇPhil. 2:13 ᶜHeb. 12:28; 1 John 3:22 ᵈRom. 11:36

★22 ᵃActs 13:15; Heb. 3:13; 10:25; 12:5; 13:19 ᵇHeb. 3:1 ᶜ1 Pet. 5:12

★23 ᵃActs 16:1; Col. 1:1

★24 ᵃ1 Cor. 16:16; Heb. 13:7, 17 ᵇActs 9:13 ᶜActs 18:2

25 ᵃCol. 4:18

13:11 *outside the camp.* See Lev. 4:21; 16:27.
13:12 *Jesus . . . suffered outside the gate.* See John 19:17-20.
13:16 *sharing* what you have (Phil. 4:18).
13:17 *your leaders.* Church leaders, as also in v. 7. *unprofitable for you* = not to your advantage.
13:21 *equip.* Or, fully provide, adjust, make ready. Some other occurrences of the Greek word are in Matt. 4:21; Gal. 6:1; 1 Thess. 3:10.
13:22 *bear* = be patient with. *briefly.* Perhaps also outspokenly.
13:23 *Timothy.* Apparently he had been imprisoned (see Acts 16:1; Rom. 16:21).
13:24 *saints* = believers.

INTRODUCTION TO
THE LETTER OF JAMES

AUTHOR: James   DATE: 45-50

The General Epistles *James, 1 and 2 Peter, 1, 2, and 3 John, and Jude were called by the early church the "General," "Universal," or "Catholic" epistles because their addresses (with the exceptions of 2 and 3 John) were not limited to a single locality. James, for example, is addressed "to the twelve tribes who are dispersed abroad" (1:1)—a designation for believers everywhere (likely all Jewish Christians at that early date).*

Authorship *Of the four men bearing the name James in the New Testament, only two have been proposed as the author of this letter—James the son of Zebedee (and brother of John) and James the half brother of Jesus. It is unlikely that the son of Zebedee was the author, for he was martyred in A.D. 44 (Acts 12:2). The authoritative tone of the letter not only rules out the two lesser known Jameses of the New Testament ("James the less" and the James of Luke 6:16) but points to the half brother of Jesus who became the recognized leader of the Jerusalem church (Acts 12:17; 15:13; 21:18). This conclusion is supported by the resemblances in the Greek between this epistle and the speech of James at the Council of Jerusalem (1:1 and Acts 15:23; 1:27 and Acts 15:14; 2:5 and Acts 15:13).*

Date *Some, denying the authorship by James because of the excellent Greek used, place the writing of the book at the very end of the first century. However, Galileans knew and used Greek well, along with Aramaic and Hebrew. Further, an early date is indicated by the lack of reference to the Jerusalem Council (A.D. 49), by the use of the word "synagogue" (assembly) for the church in 2:2, and by the strong expectation of the Lord's soon return (5:7-9).*

Canonicity *The canonical status of this letter was questioned until the church realized that its author was almost surely the half brother of Jesus. Luther did not question the genuineness of James, only its usefulness in comparison with Paul's epistles, because it says little about justification by faith, while elevating works.*

Contents *The book is concerned with the practical aspects of Christian conduct; it tells how faith works in everyday life. James's purpose was to provide concrete ethical instruction. Compared to Paul, James shows much less interest in formal theology, though the letter is not without theological statements (1:12; 2:1, 10-12, 19; 3:9; 5:7-9, 12, 14). Many subjects are discussed in this book, making it like a series of brief sayings arranged in the form of a letter. While there is little formal structure to the book, its many instructions explain how to be doers of the Word (1:22). In the 108 verses of the epistle there are references or allusions from 22 books of the Old Testament and at least 15 allusions to the teachings of Christ as embodied in the Sermon on the Mount. Among the key subjects discussed are faith and works (2:14-26), the use of the tongue (3:1-12), and prayer for the sick (5:13-16).*

OUTLINE OF JAMES

THE LETTER OF JAMES

I GREETING, 1:1

★ 1 aActs
12:2, 17 bTi-
tus 1:1
cRom. 1:1
dLuke 22:30
eJohn 7:35
fActs 15:23

1 aJames, a bbond-servant of God and cof the Lord Jesus Christ, to dthe twelve tribes who are edispersed abroad, fgreetings.

II TRIALS, 1:2-18
A The Purpose of Trials, 1:2-12

2 aMatt.
5:12; James
1:12; 5:11
b1 Pet. 1:6

2 aConsider it all joy, my brethren, when you encounter bvarious trials,

3 a1 Pet.
1:7 bHeb.
6:12 cLuke
21:19

3 knowing that athe testing of your bfaith produces cendurance.

4 aLuke
21:19 bMatt.
5:48; Col.
4:12;
1 Thess.
5:23; James
3:2

4 And let aendurance have its perfect result, that you may be bperfect and complete, lacking in nothing.

5 a1 Kin.
3:9f.; Prov.
2:3-6; James
3:17 bMatt.
7:7

5 But if any of you alacks wisdom, let him ask of God, who gives to all men generously and without reproach, and bit will be given to him.

★ 6 aMatt.
21:21 bMark
11:23; Acts
10:20 cEph.
4:14 Matt.
14:28-31

6 But let him aask in faith bwithout any doubting, for the one who doubts is like the surf of the sea cdriven and tossed by the wind.

7 For let not that man expect that he will receive anything from the Lord,

★ 8 aJames
4:8 b2 Pet.
2:14
9 aLuke
14:11

8 being a adouble-minded man, bunstable in all his ways.

9 aBut let the brother of humble circumstances glory in his high position;

10 and let the rich man glory in his humiliation, because alike flowering grass he will pass away.

★10 a1 Cor.
7:31; 1 Pet.
1:24

11 For the sun rises with aa scorching wind, and bwithers the grass; and its flower falls off, and the beauty of its appearance is destroyed; so too the rich man in the midst of his pursuits will fade away.

11 aMatt.
20:12 bPs.
102:4, 11; Is.
40:7f.

12 aBlessed is a man who perseveres under trial; for once he has been approved, he will receive bthe crown of life, which the Lord chas promised to those who dlove Him.

★12 aLuke
6:22; James
5:11; 1 Pet.
3:14; 4:14
b1 Cor. 9:25
cEx. 20:6;
James 2:5
d1 Cor. 2:9;
8:3

B The Pedigree of Trials, 1:13-16

13 Let no one say when he is tempted, "aI am being tempted by God"; for God cannot be tempted by evil, and He Himself does not tempt anyone.

★13 aGen.
22:1

14 But each one is tempted when he is carried away and enticed by his own lust.

★14

15 Then awhen lust has conceived, it gives birth to sin; and when bsin is accomplished, it brings forth death.

15 aJob
15:35; Ps.
7:14; Is. 59:4
bRom. 5:12;
6:23

16 aDo not be deceived, bmy beloved brethren.

★16 a1 Cor.
6:9 bActs
1:15; James
1:2, 19; 2:1,
5, 14; 3:1,
10; 4:11;
5:12, 19

1:1 *to the twelve tribes who are dispersed abroad.* The letter is addressed to Jewish Christians (cf. 2:1; 5:7) scattered throughout the world.

1:6 *doubting.* I.e., going back and forth between belief and unbelief (cf. Rom. 4:20).

1:8 *a double-minded man.* I.e., a man of divided allegiance.

1:10 *his humiliation.* Either by losing his money or by being brought through some circumstance in order to realize that money means little and is at best transitory.

1:12 *once he has been approved.* After having stood the test. *crown of life.* One of the rewards or prizes for the Christian, kingly glory and life. See note on 1 Cor. 3:14.

1:13 *tempted.* To tempt is to test, try, prove, or solicit to evil. In vv. 2 and 12, the same Greek word is used to mean those trials which are designed to prove the quality of one's character. In this verse the word means "a solicitation to evil," and this, James says, is not from God but from man's own inner lust (v. 14). Any attempt at self-excuse is based on ignorance both of God and of the nature of temptation.

1:14 *carried away . . . enticed.* The picture behind these words is that of the hunter or fisherman luring his prey from its safe retreat.

1:16 *Do not be deceived.* Used also in 1 Cor. 6:9; 15:33; and Gal. 6:7.

C The Purpose of God, 1:17–18

★17 aJohn
3:3; James
3:15, 17
bPs. 136:7;
1 John 1:5
cMal. 3:6

17 Every good thing bestowed and every perfect gift is ^afrom above, coming down from ^bthe Father of lights, ^cwith whom there is no variation, or shifting shadow.

★18 aJohn
1:13 bJames
1:15; 1 Pet.
1:3, 23
c2 Cor. 6:7;
Eph. 1:13;
2 Tim. 2:15
dJer. 2:3;
Rev. 14:4

18 In the exercise of ^aHis will He ^bbrought us forth by ^cthe word of truth, so that we might be, as it were, the ^dfirst fruits among His creatures.

III THE WORD, 1:19–27

19 a1 John
2:21 bActs
1:15; James
1:2, 16; 2:1,
5, 14; 3:1,
10; 4:11;
5:12, 19
cProv. 10:19;
17:27 dProv.
16:32; Ec-
cles. 7:9
20 aMatt.
5:22; Eph.
4:26
★21 aEph.
4:22; 1 Pet.
2:1 bEph.
1:13; 1 Pet.
1:22f.
22 aMatt.
7:24-27;
Luke 6:46-
49; Rom.
2:13; James
1:22-25;
2:14-20
★23 a1 Cor.
13:12

19 This ^ayou know, ^bmy beloved brethren. But let everyone be quick to hear, ^cslow to speak and ^dslow to anger;

20 for ^athe anger of man does not achieve the righteousness of God.

21 Therefore ^aputting aside all filthiness and *all* that remains of wickedness, in humility receive ^bthe word implanted, which is able to save your souls.

22 ^aBut prove yourselves doers of the word, and not merely hearers who delude themselves.

23 For if anyone is a hearer of the word and not a doer, he is like a man who looks at his natural face ^ain a mirror;

24 for *once* he has looked at himself and gone away, he has immediately forgotten what kind of person he was.

25 But one who looks intently at the perfect law, ^athe *law* of liberty, and abides by it, not having become a forgetful hearer but an effectual doer, this man shall be ^bblessed in what he does.

★25 aJohn
8:32; Rom.
8:2; Gal. 2:4;
6:2; James
2:12; 1 Pet.
2:16 bJohn
13:17

26 If anyone thinks himself to be religious, and yet does not ^abridle his tongue but deceives his *own* heart, this man's religion is worthless.

26 aPs. 39:1;
141:3; James
3:2-12

27 This is pure and undefiled religion ^ain the sight of *our* God and Father, to ^bvisit ^corphans and widows in their distress, *and* to keep oneself unstained by ^dthe world.

27 aRom.
2:13; Gal.
3:11 bMatt.
25:36 cDeut.
14:29; Job
31:16, 17,
21; Ps.
146:9; Is.
1:17, 23
dMatt. 12:32;
Eph. 2:2; Ti-
tus 2:12;
James 4:4;
2 Pet. 1:4;
2:20; 1 John
2:15-17

IV PARTIALITY, 2:1–13
A The Command, 2:1

2 ^aMy brethren, ^bdo not hold your faith in our ^cglorious Lord Jesus Christ with *an attitude* of ^dpersonal favoritism.

★ 1 aJames
1:16 bHeb.
12:2 cActs
7:2; 1 Cor.
2:8 dActs
10:34; James
2:9

B The Conduct, 2:2–3

2 For if a man comes into your assembly with a gold ring and dressed in ^afine clothes, and there also comes in a poor man in ^bdirty clothes,

★ 2 aLuke
23:11; James
2:3 bZech.
3:3f

3 and you pay special attention to the one who is wearing the

★ 3 aLuke
23:11; James
2:3

1:17 *Every good thing bestowed.* Both the gift and the act of giving. The point is that all these good things come from above. This statement may have come from an early Christian hymn. *Father of lights.* God is the source of all light—physical, intellectual, moral, and spiritual—and He does not change.

1:18 *His will.* God's will or purpose is the cause of our regeneration *(He brought us forth)* by means of the gospel message. *first fruits.* These first believers, largely Jewish in background, were the guarantee of a fuller harvest of believers to come.

1:21 *word implanted.* I.e., the gospel received as it was given (v. 18), as the word of truth.

1:23 *his natural face.* Lit., the face of his birth, his physical features. The contrast in vv. 23-25 is a simple one: the careless man looks in a mirror and forgets what he sees. The earnest man looks into the Word of God and acts upon what he sees there. *like a man.* The word

for *man* is "male" and indicates that men, in contrast to women, who are more sensitive by nature, need this exhortation to careful observance of what they see in the Word.

1:25 *the perfect law, the law of liberty.* The Bible itself, though at the time this letter was written, only the O.T. and the teachings of Christ had scriptural authority. The Word of God is the means of regeneration (1:18), a mirror reflecting man's defects (1:23), the ethical guide for Christian living (1:25; 2:8), and the standard for judgment (2:12).

2:1 *personal favoritism.* I.e., show no partiality, especially in regard to people of position or wealth in the congregation.

2:2 *gold ring.* It was not uncommon for several to be worn as a mark of wealth and social distinction (Luke 15:22).

2:3 *by my footstool.* I.e., in a lowly place, on the floor.

ᵃfine clothes, and say, "You sit here in a good place," and you say to the poor man, "You stand over there, or sit down by my footstool,"

C The Consequences, 2:4–13

★ 4 ᵃLuke 18:6; John 7:24

4 have you not made distinctions among yourselves, and become judges ᵃwith evil motives?

5 ᵃJames 1:16 ᵇJob 34:19; 1 Cor. 1:27f. ᶜLuke 12:21; Rev. 2:9 ᵈMatt. 5:3; 25:34 ᵉJames 1:12

5 Listen, ᵃmy beloved brethren: did not ᵇGod choose the poor of this world to be ᶜrich in faith and ᵈheirs of the kingdom which He ᵉpromised to those who love Him?

6 ᵃActs 8:3; 16:19

6 But you have dishonored the poor man. Is it not the rich who oppress you and personally ᵃdrag you into court?

7 ᵃActs 11:26; 1 Pet. 4:16

7 ᵃDo they not blaspheme the fair name by which you have been called?

8 ᵃMatt. 7:12 ᵇLev. 19:18

8 If, however, you ᵃare fulfilling the royal law, according to the Scripture, "ᵇYOU SHALL LOVE YOUR NEIGHBOR AS YOURSELF," you are doing well.

9 ᵃActs 10:34; James 2:1 ᵇDeut. 1:17

9 But if you ᵃshow partiality, you are committing sin and are ᵇconvicted by the law as transgressors.

★10 ᵃJames 3:2; 2 Pet. 1:10; Jude 24 ᵇMatt. 5:19; Gal. 5:3

10 For whoever keeps the whole law and yet ᵃstumbles in one point, he has become ᵇguilty of all.

11 ᵃEx. 20:14; Deut. 5:18 ᵇEx. 20:13; Deut. 5:17

11 For He who said, "ᵃDO NOT COMMIT ADULTERY," also said, "ᵇDO NOT COMMIT MURDER." Now if you do not commit adultery, but do commit murder, you have become a transgressor of the law.

12 So speak and so act, as those who are to be judged by ᵃthe law of liberty.

12 ᵃJames 1:25

13 For ᵃjudgment will be merciless to one who has shown no mercy; mercy triumphs over judgment.

13 ᵃProv. 21:13; Matt. 5:7; 18:32-35; Luke 6:37f.

V FAITH AND WORKS, 2:14–26
A The Inquiry, 2:14

14 ᵃWhat use is it, ᵇmy brethren, if a man says he has faith, but he has no works? Can that faith save him?

★14 ᵃJames 1:22ff. ᵇJames 1:16

B The Illustration, 2:15–17

15 ᵃMatt. 25:35f.; Luke 3:11

15 ᵃIf a brother or sister is without clothing and in need of daily food,

16 ᵃ1 John 3:17f.

16 and one of you says to them, "ᵃGo in peace, be warmed and be filled," and yet you do not give them what is necessary for their body, what use is that?

17 Even so ᵃfaith, if it has no works, is dead, being by itself.

17 ᵃGal. 5:6; James 2:20, 26

C The Indoctrination, 2:18–26

18 ᵃRom. 9:19 ᵇRom. 3:28; 4:6; Heb. 11:33 ᶜJames 3:13 ᵈMatt. 7:16f.; Gal. 5:6

18 ᵃBut someone may well say, "You have faith, and I have works; show me your ᵇfaith without the works, and I will ᶜshow you my faith ᵈby my works."

★19 ᵃDeut. 6:4; Mark 12:29 ᵇJames 2:8 ᶜMatt. 8:29; Mark 1:24; 5:7; Luke 4:34; Acts 19:15

19 You believe that ᵃGod is one. ᵇYou do well; ᶜthe demons also believe, and shudder.

20 ᵃRom. 9:20; 1 Cor. 15:36 ᵇGal. 5:6; James 2:17, 26

20 But are you willing to recognize, ᵃyou foolish fellow, that ᵇfaith without works is useless?

2:4 judges with evil motives. To show favoritism to the rich is wrong in a number of ways. It shows one's value system to be false (v.3); it fails to honor the poor whom God honors (v. 5); it favors those who oppress you (v. 6); it is sin (v. 9).

2:10 has become guilty of all. One sin, small or great, makes a man a sinner and brings him under condemnation.

2:14 Can that faith save him? I.e., can a nonworking, dead, spurious faith save a person? James is not saying that we are saved by works, but that a faith that does not produce good works is a dead faith. James was not refuting the Pauline doctrine of justification by true faith, but a perversion of it. Both Paul and James define faith as a living, productive trust in Christ. Genuine faith cannot be "dead" to morality or barren to works. An illustration of spurious faith is given in vv. 15–16.

2:19 God is one. The unity of God was a fundamental belief in Judaism, but if that belief did not produce good deeds it was no better than the "monotheism" of the demons.

★21 ᵃGen.
22:9, 10, 12,
16-18

22 ᵃJohn
6:29; Heb.
11:17
ᵇ1 Thess.
1:3

★23 ᵃGen.
15:6; Rom.
4:3 ᵇ2 Chr.
20:7; Is. 41:8

★24

★25 ᵃHeb.
11:31 ᵇJosh.
2:4, 6, 15

26 ᵃGal. 5:6;
James 2:17,
20

★ 1 ᵃMatt.
23:8; Rom.
2:20f.; 1 Tim.
1:7 ᵇJames
1:16; 3:10

★ 2 ᵃJames
2:10 ᵇMatt.
12:34-37;
James 3:2-12
ᶜJames 1:4
ᵈJames 1:26

3 ᵃPs. 32:9

21 ᵃWas not Abraham our father justified by works, when he offered up Isaac his son on the altar? 22 You see that ᵃfaith was working with his works, and as a result of the ᵇworks, faith was perfected; 23 and the Scripture was fulfilled which says, "ᵃAND ABRAHAM BELIEVED GOD, AND IT WAS RECKONED TO HIM AS RIGHTEOUSNESS," and he was called ᵇthe friend of God. 24 You see that a man is justified by works, and not by faith alone. 25 And in the same way was not ᵃRahab the harlot also justified by works, ᵇwhen she received the messengers and sent them out by another way? 26 For just as the body without the spirit is dead, so also ᵃfaith without works is dead.

VI SINS OF THE TONGUE, 3:1-12
A Its Bridling, 3:1-4

3 ᵃLet not many of you become teachers, ᵇmy brethren, knowing that as such we shall incur a stricter judgment. 2 For we all ᵃstumble in many ways. ᵇIf anyone does not stumble in what he says, he is a ᶜperfect man, able to ᵈbridle the whole body as well. 3 Now ᵃif we put the bits into the horses' mouths so that they may obey us, we direct their entire body as well.

4 Behold, the ships also, though they are so great and are driven by strong winds, are still directed by a very small rudder, wherever the inclination of the pilot desires.

B Its Boasting, 3:5-12

5 ᵃPs.
12:3f.; 73:8f.
ᵇProv.
26:20f.

★ 6 ᵃPs.
120:3, 4;
Prov. 16:27
ᵇMatt.
12:36f.;
15:11, 18f.
ᶜMatt. 5:22

8 ᵃPs.
140:3; Ec-
cles. 10:11;
Rom. 3:13

★ 9 ᵃJames
1:27 ᵇ1 Cor.
11:7

5 So also the tongue is a small part of the body, and yet it ᵃboasts of great things. ᵇBehold, how great a forest is set aflame by such a small fire! 6 And ᵃthe tongue is a fire, the very world of iniquity; the tongue is set among our members as that which ᵇdefiles the entire body, and sets on fire the course of our life, and is set on fire by ᶜhell. 7 For every species of beasts and birds, of reptiles and creatures of the sea, is tamed, and has been tamed by the human race. 8 But no one can tame the tongue; it is a restless evil and full of ᵃdeadly poison. 9 With it we bless ᵃ our Lord and Father; and with it we curse men, ᵇwho have been made in the likeness of God; 10 from the same mouth come both blessing and cursing. My brethren, these things ought not to be this way. 11 Does a fountain send out from the same opening both fresh and bitter water?

2:21 justified by works. In Paul's writings, "justification" means to declare a sinner righteous in the sight of God; here in James it means "to vindicate" or "show to be righteous" before God and men. Abraham's justification in Paul's sense is recorded in Gen. 15:6; Abraham's justification in James' sense took place 30 or more years later in the patriarch's crowning act of obedience in offering Isaac (Gen. 22). By this act he proved the reality of his Gen. 15 faith.
2:23 friend of God. This title comes from 2 Chron. 20:7 and Isa. 41:8.
2:24 This verse is the reply to the question of v. 14. Unproductive faith cannot save, because it is not genuine faith. Faith and works are like a two-coupon ticket to heaven. The coupon of works is not good for passage, and the coupon

of faith is not valid if detached from works.
2:25 Rahab. Her story is told in Josh. 2:1-21.
3:1 teachers. Since teachers use their tongues (to instruct others) more, they will be judged more strictly.
3:2 The theme of vv. 1-12 is found in the second clause, If anyone . . . he is a perfect man. "Perfect" means mature, of full moral and spiritual growth.
3:6 the course of our life. I.e., the whole course of human existence. The tremendous destructive power of the tongue comes from hell (lit., Gehenna; see note on Matt. 5:22).
3:9 in the likeness of God. The divine image has been marred by sin, but not totally obliterated. Man's being made in the image of God is the basis for not cursing our fellow man.

12 ^aCan a fig tree, my brethren, produce olives, or a vine produce figs? Neither *can* salt water produce fresh.

VII TRUE WISDOM, 3:13-18

13 Who among you is wise and understanding? ^aLet him show by his ^bgood behavior his deeds in the gentleness of wisdom.

14 But if you have bitter ^ajealousy and selfish ambition in your heart, do not be arrogant and *so* lie against ^bthe truth.

15 This wisdom is not that which comes down ^afrom above, but is ^bearthly, ^cnatural, ^ddemonic.

16 For where ^ajealousy and selfish ambition exist, there is disorder and every evil thing.

17 But the wisdom ^afrom above is first ^bpure, then ^cpeaceable, ^dgentle, reasonable, ^efull of mercy and good fruits, ^funwavering, without ^ghypocrisy.

18 And the ^aseed whose fruit is righteousness is sown in peace by those who make peace.

VIII WORLDLINESS, 4:1-17
A Its Cause, 4:1-2

4 What is the source of quarrels and ^aconflicts among you? Is not the source your pleasures that wage ^bwar in your members?

2 You lust and do not have; *so* you ^acommit murder. And you are envious and cannot obtain; *so*

you fight and quarrel. You do not have because you do not ask.

B Its Consequences, 4:3-6

3 You ask and ^ado not receive, because you ask with wrong motives, so that you may spend *it* on your pleasures.

4 You ^aadulteresses, do you not know that friendship with ^bthe world is ^chostility toward God? ^dTherefore whoever wishes to be a friend of the world makes himself an enemy of God.

5 Or do you think that the Scripture ^aspeaks to no purpose: "He jealously desires ^bthe Spirit which He has made to dwell in us"?

6 But ^aHe gives a greater grace. Therefore *it* says, "^bGOD IS OPPOSED TO THE PROUD, BUT GIVES GRACE TO THE HUMBLE."

C Its Cure, 4:7-10

7 ^aSubmit therefore to God. ^bResist the devil and he will flee from you.

8 ^aDraw near to God and He will draw near to you. ^bCleanse your hands, you sinners; and ^cpurify your hearts, you ^ddouble-minded.

9 ^aBe miserable and mourn and weep; let your laughter be turned into mourning, and your joy to gloom.

10 ^aHumble yourselves in the presence of the Lord, and He will exalt you.

Cross references (margin):

12 ^aMatt. 7:16

★13 ^aJames 2:18 ^b1 Pet. 2:12
14 ^aRom. 2:8; 2 Cor. 12:20; James 3:16 ^b1 Tim. 2:4; James 1:18; 5:19
15 ^aJames 1:17 ^b1 Cor. 2:6; 3:19 ^c2 Cor. 1:12 ^d2 Thess. 2:9f.; 1 Tim. 4:1; Rev. 2:24
16 ^aRom. 2:8; 2 Cor. 12:20; James 3:14
17 ^aJames 1:17 ^b2 Cor. 7:11; James 4:8 ^cMatt. 5:9; Heb. 12:11 ^dPhil. 4:5; Titus 3:2 ^eLuke 6:36 ^fJames 2:4 [Gr.] ^gRom. 12:9; 2 Cor. 6:6
★18 ^aProv. 11:18; Is. 32:17

1 ^aTitus 3:9 ^bRom. 7:23

★ 2 ^aJames 5:6; 1 John 3:15

3 ^a1 John 3:22; 5:14

★ 4 ^aIs. 54:5; Jer. 2:2; Ezek. 16:32; Matt. 12:39 ^bJames 1:27 ^cRom. 8:7; 1 John 2:15 ^dMatt. 6:24; John 15:19
★ 5 ^aNum. 23:19 ^b1 Cor. 6:19; 2 Cor. 6:16

6 ^aIs. 54:7f.; Matt. 13:12 ^bPs. 138:6; Prov. 3:34; Matt. 23:12; 1 Pet. 5:5

★ 7-10
7 ^a1 Pet. 5:6 ^bEph. 4:27; 6:11f.; 1 Pet. 5:8f.
★ 8 ^a2 Chr. 15:2; Zech. 1:3; Mal. 3:7; Heb. 7:19 ^bJob 17:9; Is. 1:16; 1 Tim. 2:8 ^cJer. 4:14; James 3:17; 1 Pet. 1:22; 1 John 3:3 ^dJames 1:8
★ 9 ^aNeh. 8:9; Prov. 14:13; Luke 6:25
10 ^aJob 5:11; Ezek. 21:26; Luke 1:52; James 4:6

3:13 The question which opens this verse sets the theme for vv. 13-18. The answer is: The person who remembers his moral responsibilities.

3:18 *whose fruit is righteousness*. In contrast to 1:20.

4:2 *commit murder*. The logical, but not necessarily usual, outcome of lust. See Matt. 5:21-22.

4:4 *adulteresses*. Symbolic language for unfaithful creatures, as often in the O.T.

4:5 The thought may also be expressed as, Do

you imagine there is no meaning to the Scripture that says, "The Spirit that dwells in us longs jealously over us"?

4:7-10 There are 10 verbs, all commands, in these verses, in a tense which indicates the need for a decisive and urgent break with the old life.

4:8 *double-minded*. See note on 1:8. Worldliness is basically divided allegiance.

4:9 *laughter*. Laughter is sometimes desirable (cf. Ps. 126:2), but not when it reflects worldly frivolity.

D   Its Characteristics, 4:11-17

★11-12
11 ᵃ2 Cor.
12:20; James
5:9; 1 Pet.
2:1 ᵇJames
1:16; 5:7, 9,
10 ᶜMatt.
7:1; Rom.
14:4 ᵈJames
2:8 ᵉJames
1:22

11 ᵃDo not speak against one another, ᵇbrethren. He who speaks against a brother, or ᶜjudges his brother, speaks against ᵈthe law, and judges the law; but if you judge the law, you are not ᵉa doer of the law, but a judge of it.

12 ᵃIs.
33:22; James
5:9 ᵇMatt.
10:28 ᶜRom.
14:4

12 There is *only* one ᵃLawgiver and Judge, the One who is ᵇable to save and to destroy; but ᶜwho are you who judge your neighbor?

★13-17
13 ᵃJames
5:1 ᵇProv.
27:1; Luke
12:18-20

13 ᵃCome now, you who say, "ᵇToday or tomorrow, we shall go to such and such a city, and spend a year there and engage in business and make a profit."

14 ᵃJob 7:7;
Ps. 39:5;
102:3; 144:4

14 Yet you do not know what your life will be like tomorrow. ᵃYou are *just* a vapor that appears for a little while and then vanishes away.

15 ᵃActs
18:21

15 Instead, *you ought* to say, "ᵃIf the Lord wills, we shall live and also do this or that."

16 ᵃ1 Cor.
5:6

16 But as it is, you boast in your arrogance; ᵃall such boasting is evil.

17 ᵃLuke
12:47; John
9:41; 2 Pet.
2:21

17 Therefore, ᵃto one who knows *the* right thing to do, and does not do it, to him it is sin.

IX   RICHES, PATIENCE, AND SWEARING, 5:1-12

1 ᵃJames
4:13 ᵇLuke
6:24; 1 Tim.
6:9 ᶜIs. 13:6;
15:3; Ezek.
30:2

5 ᵃCome now, ᵇyou rich, ᶜweep and howl for your miseries which are coming upon you.

2 ᵃJob
13:28; Is.
50:9; Matt.
6:19f.

2 ᵃYour riches have rotted and your garments have become moth-eaten.

★ 3 ᵃJames
5:7, 8

3 Your gold and your silver have rusted; and their rust will be a witness against you and will consume your flesh like fire. It is ᵃin the last days that you have stored up your treasure!

★ 4 ᵃLev.
19:13; Job
24:10f.; Jer.
22:13; Mal.
3:5 ᵇEx.
2:23; Deut.
24:15; Job
31:38f.
ᶜRom. 9:29

4 Behold, ᵃthe pay of the laborers who mowed your fields, *and* which has been withheld by you, cries out *against you;* and ᵇthe outcry of those who did the harvesting has reached the ears of ᶜthe Lord of Sabaoth.

5 ᵃEzek.
16:49; Luke
16:19; 1 Tim.
5:6; 2 Pet.
2:13 ᵇJer.
12:3; 25:34

5 You have ᵃlived luxuriously on the earth and led a life of wanton pleasure; you have fattened your hearts in ᵇa day of slaughter.

★ 6 ᵃJames
4:2 ᵇHeb.
10:38; 1 Pet.
4:18

6 You have condemned and ᵃput to death ᵇthe righteous *man;* he does not resist you.

★ 7 ᵃJames
4:11; 5:9, 10
ᵇJohn 21:22;
1 Thess. 2:19
ᶜGal. 6:9
ᵈDeut.
11:14; Jer.
5:24; Joel
2:23

7 Be patient, therefore, ᵃbrethren, ᵇuntil the coming of the Lord. ᶜBehold, the farmer waits for the precious produce of the soil, being patient about it, until it gets ᵈthe early and late rains.

8 ᵃLuke
21:19
ᵇ1 Thess.
3:13 ᶜJohn
21:22;
1 Thess. 2:19
ᵈRom.
13:11, 12;
1 Pet. 4:7

8 ᵃYou too be patient; ᵇstrengthen your hearts, for ᶜthe coming of the Lord is ᵈat hand.

9 ᵃJames
4:11 ᵇJames
5:7, 10
ᶜ1 Cor. 4:5;
Heb. 10:25;
James 4:12;
1 Pet. 4:5
ᵈMatt. 24:33;
Mark 13:29

9 ᵃDo not complain, ᵇbrethren, against one another, that you yourselves may not be judged; behold, ᶜthe Judge is standing ᵈright at the door.

10 ᵃJames
4:11; 5:7, 9
ᵇMatt. 5:12

10 As an example, ᵃbrethren, of suffering and patience, take ᵇthe prophets who spoke in the name of the Lord.

★11 ᵃMatt.
5:10; 1 Pet.
3:14 ᵇJob
1:21f., 2:10
ᶜJob 42:10,
12 ᵈEx.
34:6; Ps.
103:8

11 Behold, we count those ᵃblessed who endured. You have heard of ᵇthe endurance of Job and have seen ᶜthe outcome of the Lord's dealings, that ᵈthe Lord

---

4:11-12 The person who judges his brother disobeys the law, thus putting himself above it and treating it with contempt.

4:13-17 The folly of forgetting God in business is another manifestation of worldliness. The itinerant merchants addressed here were Jews who carried on a lucrative trade throughout the world.

5:3 *have rusted.* The rich did not realize that *the last days* were already present (cf. 2 Tim. 3:1).

5:4 *Lord of Sabaoth* = Lord of Hosts (a familiar O.T. title). The Lord Almighty, the omnipotent sovereign, who is not oblivious to injustice.

5:6 *put to death the righteous.* This probably refers to the practice of the rich taking the poor ("the righteous") to court to take away what little they might have, thus "murdering" them.

5:7 *the early* (Oct.-Nov.) *and late* (Apr.-May) *rains.* Palestine has two rainy seasons annually.

5:11 *the endurance of Job.* Job was steadfast in

is full of compassion and *is* merciful.

12 But above all, *a*my brethren, *b*do not swear, either by heaven or by earth or with any other oath; but let your yes be yes, and your no, no; so that you may not fall under judgment.

X PRAYER, 5:13–18

13 Is anyone among you *a*suffering? *b*Let him pray. Is anyone cheerful? Let him *c*sing praises.

14 Is anyone among you sick? Let him call for *a*the elders of the church, and let them pray over him, *b*anointing him with oil in the name of the Lord;

15 and the *a*prayer offered in faith will *b*restore the one who is sick, and the Lord will *c*raise him up, and if he has committed sins, they will be forgiven him.

16 Therefore, *a*confess your sins to one another, and pray for one another, so that you may be *b*healed. *c*The effective prayer of a righteous man can accomplish much.

17 Elijah was *a*a man with a nature like ours, and *b*he prayed earnestly that it might not rain; and it did not rain on the earth for *c*three years and six months.

18 And he *a*prayed again, and *b*the sky poured rain, and the earth produced its fruit.

XI THE CONVERSION OF THE ERRING, 5:19–20

19 My brethren, *a*if any among you strays from *b*the truth, and one turns him back,

20 let him know that he who turns a sinner from the error of his way will *a*save his soul from death, and will *b*cover a multitude of sins.

★12 *a*James 1:16 *b*Matt. 5:34-37

13 *a*James 5:10 *b*Ps. 50:15 *c*1 Cor. 14:15
★14-15
★14 *a*Acts 11:30 *b*Mark 6:13; 16:18
15 *a*James 1:6 *b*1 Cor. 1:21; James 5:20 *c*John 6:39; 2 Cor. 4:14
16 *a*Matt. 3:6; Mark 1:5; Acts 19:18 *b*Heb. 12:13; 1 Pet. 2:24 *c*Gen. 18:23-32

17 *a*Acts 14:15 *b*1 Kin. 17:1; 18:1 *c*Luke 4:25

18 *a*1 Kin. 18:42 *b*1 Kin. 18:45

★19-20
19 *a*Matt. 18:15; Gal. 6:1 *b*James 3:14
20 *a*Rom. 11:14; 1 Cor. 1:21; James 1:21 *b*1 Pet. 4:8

---

his moral integrity. See Job. 1:21; 2:10; 13:15; 16:19; 19:25.

5:12 *do not swear.* Not all oaths are forbidden by this verse, only flippant, profane, or blasphemous ones. Oaths in the sense of solemn affirmations were enjoined in the law (Ex. 22:11) and were practiced by Christ (Matt. 26:63-64) and Paul (Rom. 1:9).

5:14-15 God may heal directly, through medicine, or in answer to prayer, as here. The oil is a symbol of the presence of God (cf. Ps. 23:5); it may also have been considered medicinal in James's day (cf. Luke 10:34), though hardly as being effective for all diseases. Prayers of faith are answered not simply because they are prayed in faith but only if they are prayed in the will of God (1 John 5:14). God does not always think it best to heal (cf. 2 Cor. 12:8). Here the healing is dependent on confession of sin. Historically, the Roman Catholic sacrament of extreme unction developed out of this practice, but the significance is entirely changed, for the Roman Catholic rite has death in view, not recovery.

5:14 *the elders of the church.* Elders are first mentioned in Acts 11:30 as recognized leaders of the churches. Their mention here and in Acts 14:23 relates to about the same period in the early church, in which they were the first leaders, before deacons, and long before bishops.

5:19-20 *any among you.* The reference is evidently to Christians, and the *death* is physical death which sin may cause (1 Cor. 11:30).

INTRODUCTION TO
THE FIRST EPISTLE OF PETER

AUTHOR: Peter   DATE: 63

Readership   *This letter is addressed to "aliens, scattered" or, literally, the "sojourners of the dispersion" (1:1). These were Christians who, like Israel of old, were scattered throughout the world, though the readers of this epistle were predominantly of Gentile rather than Jewish background (1:14; 2:9-10; 4:3-4). Their situation was one of suffering and trial (4:12), but not because of the empire-wide ban on Christianity, since that came later. The sufferings referred to are those which often come to Christians as they live faithfully in a pagan and hostile society. Persecution took the forms of slander, riots, local police action, and social ostracism. The readers are encouraged to rejoice and live above such reproach.*

Circumstances of Writing   *That the apostle Peter was the writer (as stated in 1:1) is confirmed by the many similarities between this letter and Peter's sermons recorded in Acts (1:20 and Acts 2:23; 4:5 and Acts 10:42). The same Silvanus (also called Silas) who accompanied Paul on the second missionary journey was his amanuensis, or secretary (5:12; Acts 15:40).*

The place of writing was "Babylon" (5:13), a symbolic name for Rome much used by writers who wished to avoid trouble with the Roman authorities. Peter was in Rome during the last decade of his life and wrote this epistle about A.D. 63, just before the outbreak of Nero's persecution in 64. Peter was martyred about 67.

Contents   *Peter himself states the theme of the letter in 5:12, "the true grace of God" in the life of a believer.*

OUTLINE OF 1 PETER

I. **Salutation, 1:1-2**
II. **Grace Means Security, 1:3-12**
  A. Doxology, 1:3-9
  B. The Prophets and the Gospel, 1:10-12
III. **Grace Means Sobriety, 1:13-2:10**
  A. In Holiness, 1:13-16
  B. In Fear, 1:17-21
  C. In Love, 1:22-25
  D. In Growth, 2:1-10
IV. **Grace Means Submission, 2:11-3:12**

  A. To Governments, 2:11-17
  B. To Masters, 2:18-25
  C. To Husbands, 3:1-7
  D. Recapitulation, 3:8-12
V. **Grace Means Suffering, 3:13-4:19**
  A. Reasons for Suffering, 3:13-4:6
  B. Reactions in Suffering, 4:7-19
VI. **Grace Means Service, 5:1-11**
VII. **Concluding Remarks, 5:12-14**

THE FIRST LETTER OF PETER

I SALUTATION, 1:1-2

★ 1 a2 Pet.
1:1 b1 Pet.
2:11 cJames
1:1 dActs
2:9 eActs
16:6 fActs
16:7 gMatt.
24:22
★ 2 aRom.
8:29
b2 Thess.
2:13 cRom.
1:5; 6:16;
16:19; 1 Pet.
1:14, 22
dHeb. 10:22;
12:24 e2 Pet.
1:2

1 aPeter, an apostle of Jesus Christ, to those who reside as baliens, cscattered throughout dPontus, eGalatia, dCappadocia, dAsia, and fBithynia, gwho are chosen

2 according to the aforeknowledge of God the Father, bby the sanctifying work of the Spirit, that you may cobey Jesus Christ and be dsprinkled with His blood: eMay grace and peace be yours in fullest measure.

II GRACE MEANS SECURITY, 1:3-12
A Doxology, 1:3-9

★ 3 a2 Cor.
1:3 bGal.
6:16; Titus
3:5 cJames
1:18
d2 Thess.
2:16 e1 Cor.
15:20
★ 4 aActs
20:32; Rom.
8:17; Col.
3:24 b1 Pet.
5:4 c2 Tim.
4:8
5 aJohn
10:28; Phil
4:7 bEph.
2:8 c1 Cor.
1:21 dRom.
8:18
6 aRom.
5:2 b1 Pet.
5:10 c1 Pet.
3:17 dJames
1:2

3 aBlessed be the God and Father of our Lord Jesus Christ, who baccording to His great mercy chas caused us to be born again to da living hope through the eresurrection of Jesus Christ from the dead,

4 to obtain an ainheritance which is imperishable and undefiled and bwill not fade away, creserved in heaven for you,

5 who are aprotected by the power of God bthrough faith for ca salvation ready dto be revealed in the last time.

6 aIn this you greatly rejoice, even though now bfor a little while, cif necessary, you have been distressed by dvarious trials,

7 that the aproof of your faith, being more precious than gold which is perishable, beven though tested by fire, cmay be found to result in praise and glory and honor at dthe revelation of Jesus Christ;

8 and athough you have not seen Him, you blove Him, and though you do not see Him now, but believe in Him, you greatly rejoice with joy inexpressible and full of glory,

9 obtaining as athe outcome of your faith the salvation of your souls.

7 aJames
1:3 bJob
23:10; Ps.
66:10; Prov.
17:3; Is.
48:10; Zech.
13:9; Mal.
3:3; 1 Cor.
3:13 cRom.
2:7, 10;
2 Cor. 4:17;
Heb. 12:11
dLuke 17:30;
1 Pet. 1:13;
8 aJohn
20:29 bEph.
3:19
9 aRom.
6:22

B The Prophets and the Gospel, 1:10-12

10 aAs to this salvation, the prophets who bprophesied of the cgrace that would come to you made careful search and inquiry,

11 seeking to know what person or time athe Spirit of Christ within them was indicating as He bpredicted the sufferings of Christ and the glories to follow.

12 It was revealed to them that they were not serving themselves, but you, in these things which now have been announced to you through those who

★10-12
10 aMatt.
13:17; Luke
10:24; 1 Pet.
1:10-12
bMatt. 26:24;
Luke 24:27,
44 cCol. 3:4;
1 Pet. 1:13
11 aRom.
8:9; 2 Pet.
1:21 bMatt.
26:24; Luke
24:27, 44
★12 a1 Pet.
1:25; 4:6
bActs 2:2-4
cLuke 2:13;
Eph. 3:10;
1 Tim. 3:16

1:1 aliens = sojourners, exiles, foreign residents. The word is applied to those who settled in a town or region without making it their permanent place of residence. The readers, whose true citizenship was in heaven, are viewed as temporary residents of the provinces of Asia Minor named in this verse.

1:2 The idea expressed in this verse is that God in His wisdom has chosen us to salvation through the work of the Holy Spirit, applying in us the worth of the death of Christ so that we might be obedient to Him. foreknowledge. God's prior knowledge of all things, based on His causative relation to them, is the basis of our election. Foreknowledge involves God's active consciousness of all that is to come to pass (see 1:20; Rom. 8:29; 11:2 for the same word and concept; and see note on Eph. 1:5).

Father . . . Spirit . . . Christ. An early formulation of the doctrine of the Trinity. sprinkled with His blood signifies the personal application of the sacrifice of Christ.

1:3 Here begins Peter's recital of the blessings of God's redeemed children, concluding at 2:10.

1:4 undefiled = unstained by evil. will not fade away. I.e., unimpaired by time.

1:10-12 Though the O.T. prophets spoke of grace being given to Gentiles, they did not understand all that was involved in God's saving Gentiles through a suffering Messiah (see Col. 1:26-27). The O.T. prophets did predict both the suffering (Isa. 53) and glory (Isa. 11) of the Messiah, without distinguishing that the former would be fulfilled at His first coming and the latter at His second.

1:12 angels. See note on Eph. 3:10.

[a]preached the gospel to you by [b]the Holy Spirit sent from heaven—things into which [c]angels long to look.

III GRACE MEANS SOBRIETY, 1:13–2:10
A In Holiness, 1:13–16

13 Therefore, [a]gird your minds for action, [b]keep sober *in spirit,* fix your [c]hope completely on the [d]grace to be brought to you at [e]the revelation of Jesus Christ.

14 As [a]obedient children, do not [b]be conformed to the former lusts *which were yours* in your [c]ignorance,

15 but [a]like the Holy One who called you, [b]be holy yourselves also [c]in all *your* behavior;

16 because it is written, "[a]YOU SHALL BE HOLY, FOR I AM HOLY."

B In Fear, 1:17–21

17 And if you [a]address as Father the One who [b]impartially [c]judges according to each man's work, conduct yourselves [d]in fear during the time of your [e]stay *upon earth;*

18 knowing that you were not [a]redeemed with perishable things like silver or gold from your [b]futile way of life inherited from your forefathers,

19 but with precious [a]blood, as of a [b]lamb unblemished and spotless, *the blood* of Christ.

20 For He was [a]foreknown before [b]the foundation of the world, but has [c]appeared in these last times [d]for the sake of you

21 who through Him are [a]believers in God, who raised Him from the dead and [b]gave Him glory, so that your faith and [c]hope are in God.

C In Love, 1:22–25

22 Since you have [a]in obedience to the truth [b]purified your souls for a [c]sincere love of the brethren, fervently love one another from the heart,

23 for you have been [a]born again [b]not of seed which is perishable but imperishable, *that is,* through the living and abiding [c]word of God.

24 For,

"[a]ALL FLESH IS LIKE GRASS,
AND ALL ITS GLORY LIKE THE FLOWER OF GRASS.
THE GRASS WITHERS,
AND THE FLOWER FALLS OFF,

25 [a]BUT THE WORD OF THE LORD ABIDES FOREVER."

And this is [b]the word which was preached to you.

D In Growth, 2:1–10

2 Therefore, [a]putting aside all malice and all guile and hypocrisy and envy and all [b]slander,

2 [a]like newborn babes, long for the [b]pure milk of the word, that by it you may [c]grow in respect to salvation,

3 if you have [a]tasted [b]the kindness of the Lord.

4 And coming to Him as to a living stone, [a]rejected by men, but choice and precious in the sight of God,

5 [a]you also, as living stones, are being built up as a [b]spiritual

★13 [a]Eph. 6:14 [b]Rom. 12:3; 1 Thess. 5:6, 8; 2 Tim. 4:5; Titus 2:6; 1 Pet. 4:7; 5:8 [c]1 Pet. 1:3 [d]Col. 3:4; 1 Pet. 1:10 [e]Luke 17:30; 1 Pet. 1:7; 4:13
★14 [a]1 Pet. 1:2 [b]Rom. 12:2; 1 Pet. 4:2f. [c]Eph. 4:18
15 [a]1 Thess. 4:7; 1 John 3:3 [b]2 Cor. 7:1 [c]James 3:13
★16 [a]Lev. 11:44f.; 19:2; 20:7
★17 [a]Ps. 89:26; Jer. 3:19; Mal. 1:6; Matt. 6:9 [b]Acts 10:34 [c]Matt. 16:27 [d]2 Cor. 7:1; Heb. 12:28; 1 Pet. 3:15 [e]Eph. 2:19; 1 Pet. 2:11
18 [a]Is. 52:3; Matt. 20:28; 1 Cor. 6:20; Titus 2:14; Heb. 9:12; 2 Pet. 2:1 [b]Eph. 4:17
★19 [a]Acts 20:28; 1 Pet. 1:2 [b]John 1:29; Heb. 9:14
20 [a]Acts 2:23; 1 Pet. 1:4; 1 Pet. 1:2; Rev. 13:8 [b]Matt. 25:34 [c]Heb. 9:26 [d]Heb. 2:14
21 [a]Rom. 4:24; 10:9 [b]John 17:5, 24; 1 Tim. 3:16; Heb. 2:9 [c]1 Pet. 1:3
★22 [a]1 Pet. 1:2 [b]James 4:8 [c]John 13:34; Rom. 12:10; Heb. 13:1; 1 Pet. 2:17; 3:8
23 [a]John 3:3; 1 Pet. 1:3 [b]John 1:13 [c]Heb. 4:12
★24-25
24 [a]Is. 40:6ff.; James 1:10f.
25 [a]Is. 40:8 [b]Heb. 6:5
1 [a]Eph. 4:22, 25, 31; James 1:21 [b]James 4:11
2 [a]Matt. 18:3; 19:14; Mark 10:15; Luke 18:17; 1 Cor. 14:20 [b]1 Cor. 3:2 [c]Eph. 4:15f.
3 [a]Heb. 6:5 [b]Ps. 34:8; Titus 3:4
★4-8
4 [a]1 Pet. 2:7
5 [a]1 Cor. 3:9 [b]Gal. 6:10; 1 Tim. 3:15 [c]Is. 61:6; 66:21; 1 Pet. 2:9; Rev. 1:6 [d]Rom. 15:16; Heb. 13:15

1:13 *gird your minds for action.* = be disciplined in your thinking. A figure of speech (lit., gird up the loins of your mind) based on the gathering and fastening up of the long Eastern garments so that they would not interfere with the individual's activity.
1:14 *do not be conformed.* The only other occurrence of this term is in Rom. 12:2.
1:16 *You shall be holy.* See Lev. 11:44-45.

1:17 *in fear.* I.e., reverently.
1:19 *unblemished and spotless.* Refers to the sinlessness of Christ (see Lev. 22:19-25).
1:22 *fervently* = earnestly.
1:24-25 See Isa. 40:6-8.
2:4-8 Christ is the living stone (v. 4), the cornerstone (v. 6), the rejected stone (v. 7), and the stumbling-stone (v. 8).

house for a holy ᶜpriesthood, to ᵈoffer up spiritual sacrifices acceptable to God through Jesus Christ.

6 For *this* is contained in Scripture:

> "ᵃBEHOLD I LAY IN ZION A
> CHOICE STONE, A ᵇPRECIOUS
> CORNER *stone*,
> AND HE WHO BELIEVES IN HIM
> SHALL NOT BE DISAP-
> POINTED."

7 ᵃThis precious value, then, is for you who believe. But for those who disbelieve,

> "ᵇTHE STONE WHICH THE
> BUILDERS ᶜREJECTED,
> THIS BECAME THE VERY COR-
> NER *stone*,"

8 and,

> "ᵃA STONE OF STUMBLING AND
> A ROCK OF OFFENSE";

ᵇfor they stumble because they are disobedient to the word, ᶜand to this *doom* they were also appointed.

9 But you are ᵃA CHOSEN RACE, A royal ᵇPRIESTHOOD, A ᶜHOLY NA-TION, ᵈA PEOPLE FOR *God's* OWN POS-SESSION, that you may proclaim the excellencies of Him who has called you ᵉout of darkness into His marvelous light;

10 ᵃfor you once were NOT A PEOPLE, but now you are THE PEOPLE OF GOD; you had NOT RECEIVED MER-CY, but now you have RECEIVED MERCY.

IV GRACE MEANS SUBMISSION, 2:11–3:12

A To Governments, 2:11-17

11 ᵃBeloved, ᵇI urge you as ᶜaliens and strangers to abstain from ᵈfleshly lusts, which wage ᵉwar against the soul.

12 ᵃKeep your behavior excellent among the Gentiles, so that in the thing in which they ᵇslander you as evildoers, they may on account of your good deeds, as they observe *them*, ᶜglorify God ᵈin the day of visitation.

13 ᵃSubmit yourselves for the Lord's sake to every human institution, whether to a king as the one in authority,

14 or to governors as sent by him ᵃfor the punishment of evildoers and the ᵇpraise of those who do right.

15 For ᵃsuch is the will of God that by doing right you may ᵇsilence the ignorance of foolish men.

16 *Act* as ᵃfree men, and do not use your freedom as a covering for evil, but *use it* as ᵇbondslaves of God.

17 ᵃHonor all men; ᵇlove the brotherhood, ᶜfear God, ᵈhonor the king.

B To Masters, 2:18-25

18 ᵃServants, be submissive to your masters with all respect, not only to those who are good and ᵇgentle, but also to those who are unreasonable.

19 For this *finds* favor, if for the sake of ᵃconscience toward God a man bears up under sorrows when suffering unjustly.

20 For what credit is there if, when you sin and are harshly treated, you endure it with patience? But if ᵃwhen you do what is right and suffer *for it* you patiently endure it, this *finds* favor with God.

21 For ᵃyou have been called

Cross references (margin):

6 ᵃIs. 28:16; Rom. 9:32, 33; 10:11; 1 Pet. 2:6, 8 ᵇEph. 2:20

7 ᵃ2 Cor. 2:16; 1 Pet. 2:7, 8 ᵇPs. 118:22; Matt. 21:42; Luke 2:34 ᶜ1 Pet. 2:4

★ 8 ᵃIs. 8:14 ᵇ1 Cor. 1:23; Gal. 5:11 ᶜRom. 9:22

★ 9 ᵃDeut. 10:15; Is. 43:20f. ᵇIs. 61:6; 66:21; 1 Pet. 2:5; Rev. 1:6 ᶜEx. 19:6; Deut. 7:6 ᵈTitus 2:14 ᵉIs. 42:16; Acts 26:18; 2 Cor. 4:6

10 ᵃHos. 1:10; 2:23; Rom. 9:25; 10:19

★11 ᵃHeb. 6:9; 1 Pet. 4:12 ᵇRom. 12:1 ᶜLev. 25:23 ᵈRom. 13:14; ᵉJames 4:1

12 ᵃ2 Cor. 8:21; Phil. 2:15; Titus 2:8; 1 Pet. 2:15; 3:16 ᵇActs 28:22 ᶜMatt. 5:16; 9:8; John 13:31; 1 Pet. 4:11, 16 ᵈIs. 10:3; Luke 19:44 ★13–17 13 ᵃRom. 13:1

14 ᵃRom. 13:4 ᵇRom. 13:3

★15 ᵃ1 Pet. 3:17 ᵇ1 Pet. 2:12

16 ᵃJohn 8:32; James 1:25 ᵇRom. 6:22; 1 Cor. 7:22

17 ᵃRom. 12:10; 13:7 ᵇ1 Pet. 1:22 ᶜProv. 24:21 ᵈProv. 24:21; Matt. 22:21; 1 Pet. 2:13

18 ᵃEph. 6:5 ᵇJames 3:17

19 ᵃRom. 13:5; 1 Pet. 3:14, 17

20 ᵃ1 Pet. 3:17

21 ᵃActs 14:22; 1 Pet. 3:9 ᵇ1 Pet. 3:18; 4:1, 13 ᶜMatt. 11:29; 16:24

2:8 *appointed.* The same divine purpose which has chosen some has ordained others (those who are disobedient) to the only alternative.

2:9 *a people for God's own possession.* I.e., God's own people.

2:11 Beginning here, and ending at 4:11, Peter sets forth the duties of Christians in the world.

2:13-17 Christians are to be law-abiding citizens. If the law of one's government violates the revealed will of God, then, of course, the believer must obey God, though he may have to suffer the penalties of that government's laws. See Rom. 13:1-7 and Titus 3:1-2.

2:15 *foolish men.* I.e., the slanderers mentioned in v. 12.

for this purpose, *b*since Christ also suffered for you, leaving you *c*an example for you to follow in His steps,

22 WHO *a*COMMITTED NO SIN, NOR WAS ANY DECEIT FOUND IN HIS MOUTH;

23 and while being *a*reviled, He did not revile in return; while suffering, He uttered no threats, but kept entrusting *Himself* to Him who judges righteously;

24 and He Himself *a*bore our sins in His body on the *b*cross, that we *c*might die to sin and live to righteousness; for *d*by His wounds you were *e*healed.

25 For you were *a*continually straying like sheep, but now you have returned to the *b*Shepherd and Guardian of your souls.

C To Husbands, 3:1-7

3 *a*In the same way, you wives, *b*be submissive to your own husbands so that even if any *of them* are disobedient to the word, they may be *c*won without a word by the behavior of their wives,

2 as they observe your chaste and respectful behavior.

3 *a*And let not your adornment be *merely* external—braiding the hair, and wearing gold jewelry, or putting on dresses;

4 but *let it be* *a*the hidden person of the heart, with the imperishable quality of a gentle and quiet spirit, which is precious in the sight of God.

5 For in this way in former times the holy women also, *a*who hoped in God, used to adorn themselves, being submissive to their own husbands.

6 Thus Sarah obeyed Abraham, *a*calling him lord, and you have become her children if you

do what is right *b*without being frightened by any fear.

7 *a*You husbands likewise, live with your wives in an understanding way, as with a weaker *b*vessel, since she is a woman; and grant her honor as a fellow heir of the grace of life, so that your prayers may not be hindered.

D Recapitulation, 3:8-12

8 To sum up, *a*let all be harmonious, sympathetic, *b*brotherly, *c*kindhearted, and *d*humble in spirit;

9 *a*not returning evil for evil, or *b*insult for insult, but giving a *c*blessing instead; for *d*you were called for the very purpose that you might *e*inherit a blessing.

10 For,

"*a*LET HIM WHO MEANS TO LOVE
LIFE AND SEE GOOD DAYS
REFRAIN HIS TONGUE FROM
EVIL AND HIS LIPS FROM
SPEAKING GUILE.

11 "*a*AND LET HIM TURN AWAY
FROM EVIL AND DO GOOD;
LET HIM SEEK PEACE AND PURSUE IT.

12 "*a*FOR THE EYES OF THE LORD
ARE UPON THE RIGHTEOUS,
AND HIS EARS ATTEND TO
THEIR PRAYER,
BUT THE FACE OF THE LORD IS
AGAINST THOSE WHO DO
EVIL."

V GRACE MEANS SUFFERING, 3:13-4:19

A Reasons for Suffering, 3:13-4:6

13 And *a*who is there to harm you if you prove zealous for what is good?

Cross references (left margin):

★22-24
22 *a*Is. 53:9;
2 Cor. 5:21

23 *a*Is. 53:7;
Heb. 12:3;
1 Pet. 3:9

24 *a*Is. 53:4, 11; 1 Cor. 15:3; Heb. 9:28 *b*Acts 5:30 *c*Rom. 6:2, 13 *d*Is. 53:5 *e*Heb. 12:13; James 5:16
25 *a*Is. 53:6 *b*John 10:11; 1 Pet. 5:4

★ 1 *a*1 Pet. 2:18; 3:7 *b*Eph. 5:22 *c*1 Cor. 9:19

★ 3 *a*Is. 3:18ff.; 1 Tim. 2:9

★ 4 *a*Rom. 7:22

5 *a*1 Tim. 5:5; 1 Pet. 1:3

6 *a*Gen. 18:12 *b*1 Pet. 3:14

Cross references (right margin):

★ 7 *a*Eph. 5:25; Col. 3:19 *b*1 Thess. 4:4

8 *a*Rom. 12:16 *b*1 Pet. 1:22 *c*Eph. 4:32 *d*Eph. 4:2; Phil. 2:3; 1 Pet. 5:5
★ 9 *a*Rom. 12:17; 1 Thess. 5:15 *b*1 Cor. 4:12; 1 Pet. 2:23 *c*Luke 6:28; Rom. 12:14; 1 Cor. 4:12 *d*1 Pet. 2:21 *e*Gal. 3:14; Heb. 6:14; 12:17
10 *a*Ps. 34:12, 13

11 *a*Ps. 34:14

12 *a*Ps. 34:15, 16

13 *a*Prov. 16:7

2:22-24 *who committed no sin . . . bore our sins.* The sinless Jesus was the perfect substitute, in His death, for the sins of mankind.

3:1 *without a word.* I.e., an unsaved husband can better be won to Christianity by seeing it work in his wife's godly life than by always hearing about it from her lips.

3:3 This verse does not prohibit all jewelry; if it did, it would also prohibit all clothing! It con-

demns ostentation and enjoins modesty and meekness.

3:4 *hidden person* See Eph. 3:16.

3:7 *that your prayers may not be hindered.* The man who fails to give his wife due consideration can hardly pray with her.

3:9 This verse is an echo of Christ's words (Luke 6:27-28).

14 a1 Pet.
2:19ff.; 4:15f.
bJames 5:11
cIs. 8:12f.;
1 Pet. 3:6

14 But even if you should a suffer for the sake of righteousness, b you are blessed. c AND DO NOT FEAR THEIR INTIMIDATION, AND DO NOT BE TROUBLED,

★15 a1 Pet.
1:3 bCol. 4:6
c1 Pet. 1:3
d2 Tim. 2:25
e1 Pet. 1:17

15 but sanctify a Christ as Lord in your hearts, always *being* ready b to make a defense to everyone who asks you to give an account for the c hope that is in you, yet d with gentleness and e reverence;

16 a1 Tim.
1:5; Heb.
13:18; 1 Pet.
3:21 b1 Pet.
2:12, 15

16 and keep a a good conscience so that in the thing in which b you are slandered, those who revile your good behavior in Christ may be put to shame.

17 a1 Pet.
2:20; 4:15f.
bActs 18:21;
1 Pet. 1:6;
2:15; 4:19

17 For a it is better, b if God should will it so, that you suffer for doing what is right rather than for doing what is wrong.

18 a1 Pet.
2:21 bHeb.
9:26, 28;
10:10 cRom.
5:2; Eph.
3:12 dCol.
1:22; 1 Pet.
4:1 e1 Pet.
4:6
★19 a1 Pet.
4:6

18 For a Christ also died for sins b once for all, *the* just for *the* unjust, in order that He might c bring us to God, having been put to death d in the flesh, but made alive e in the spirit;

19 in which also He went and a made proclamation to the spirits *now* in prison,

20 aRom.
2:4 bGen.
6:3, 5, 13f.
cHeb. 11:7
dGen. 8:18;
2 Pet. 2:5
eActs 2:41;
1 Pet. 1:9,
22; 2:25;
4:19
★21 aActs
16:33; Titus
3:5 bHeb.
9:14; 10:22
c1 Tim. 1:5;
Heb. 13:18;
1 Pet. 3:16
d1 Pet. 1:3

20 who once were disobedient, when the a patience of God b kept waiting in the days of Noah, during the construction of c the ark, in which a few, that is, d eight e persons, were brought safely through *the* water.

21 a And corresponding to that, baptism now saves you— b not the removal of dirt from the flesh, but an appeal to God for a c good conscience—through d the resurrection of Jesus Christ,

22 aMark
16:19 bHeb.
4:14; 6:20
cRom.
8:38f.; Heb.
1:6

22 a who is at the right hand of God, b having gone into heaven, c after angels and authorities and powers had been subjected to Him.

4 Therefore, since a Christ has suffered in the flesh, b arm yourselves also with the same purpose, because c he who has suffered in the flesh has ceased from sin,

★ 1 a1 Pet.
2:21 bEph.
6:13 cRom.
6:7

2 a so as to live b the rest of the time in the flesh no longer for the lusts of men, but for the will of God.

2 aRom.
6:2; Col. 3:3
b1 Pet. 1:14

3 For a the time already past is sufficient *for you* to have carried out the desire of the Gentiles, b having pursued a course of sensuality, lusts, drunkenness, carousals, drinking parties and abominable idolatries.

3 a1 Cor.
12:2 bRom.
13:13; Eph.
2:2; 4:17ff.

4 And in *all* this, they are surprised that you do not run with *them* into the same excess of a dissipation, and they b malign *you*;

4 aEph.
5:18 b1 Pet.
3:16

5 but they shall give account to Him who is ready to judge a the living and the dead.

★ 5 aActs
10:42; Rom.
14:9; 2 Tim.
4:1

6 For a the gospel has for this purpose been preached even to those who are dead, that though they are judged in the flesh as men, they may live in the spirit according to *the will of* God.

★ 6 a1 Pet.
1:12; 3:19

3:15 *sanctify Christ* = reverence Christ.

3:19 *made proclamation to the spirits now in prison.* Some understand this to mean that Christ, between His death and resurrection, descended into Hades and offered to those who lived before Noah (v. 20) a second chance for salvation, a doctrine that is without scriptural support. Others say that it was simply an announcement of His victory over sin to those in Hades without offering a second chance. Most likely this is a reference to the preincarnate Christ preaching through Noah to those who, because they rejected that message, are now spirits in prison.

3:21 *baptism.* Though water itself cannot save, baptism with water is the vivid symbol of the changed life of one who has a conscience at peace with God through faith in Christ.

4:1 The thought is: Christ suffered in the flesh. He is your example. So, arm yourselves by taking the same view of suffering as Christ took, which is to accept it in the will of God. Thereby the dominion of sin is broken in practical experience.

4:5 *the living and the dead.* I.e., all generations.

4:6 *those who are dead.* I.e., deceased Christians. The gospel was preached to those martyrs now dead. They were judged in the flesh and condemned to martydom according to human standards, but they are alive in the spirit after death. Another interpretation relates this preaching to that of 3:19.

B Reactions in Suffering,
4:7-19

7 aRom.
13:11; Heb.
9:26; James
5:8; 1 John
2:18 b1 Pet.
1:13
8 a1 Pet.
1:22 bProv.
10:12; 1 Cor.
13:4ff.;
James 5:20

9 a1 Tim.
3:2; Heb.
13:2 bPhil.
2:14
★10 aRom.
12:6f.
b1 Cor. 4:1

★11
a1 Thess.
2:4; Titus
2:1, 15; Heb.
13:7 bActs
7:38 cEph.
1:19; 6:10
d1 Cor.
10:31; 1 Pet.
2:12 eRom.
11:36; 1 Pet.
5:11; Rev.
1:6; 5:13

★12 a1 Pet.
2:11 b1 Pet.
1:6f.

13 aRom.
8:17; 2 Cor.
1:5; 4:10;
Phil. 3:10
b1 Pet. 1:7;
5:1 c2 Tim.
2:12
14 aJohn
15:21; Heb.
11:26; 1 Pet.
4:16 bMatt.
5:11; Luke
6:22; Acts
5:41 c2 Cor.
4:10f., 16
15 a1 Pet.
2:19f.; 3:17
b1 Thess.
4:11;
2 Thess.
3:11; 1 Tim.
5:13

7 aThe end of all things is at hand; therefore, bbe of sound judgment and sober *spirit* for the purpose of prayer.

8 Above all, akeep fervent in your love for one another, because blove covers a multitude of sins.

9 aBe hospitable to one another without bcomplaint.

10 aAs each one has received a *special* gift, employ it in serving one another, as good bstewards of the manifold grace of God.

11 aWhoever speaks, *let him speak*, as it were, the butterances of God; whoever serves, *let him do so* as cby the strength which God supplies; so that din all things God may be glorified through Jesus Christ, eto whom belongs the glory and dominion forever and ever. Amen.

12 aBeloved, do not be surprised at the bfiery ordeal among you, which comes upon you for your testing, as though some strange thing were happening to you;

13 but to the degree that you ashare the sufferings of Christ, keep on rejoicing; so that also at the brevelation of His glory, cyou may rejoice with exultation.

14 If you are reviled afor the name of Christ, byou are blessed, cbecause the Spirit of glory and of God rests upon you.

15 By no means alet any of you suffer as a murderer, or thief, or evildoer, or a btroublesome meddler;

16 but if *anyone suffers* as a aChristian, let him not feel ashamed, but in that name let him bglorify God.

17 For *it is* time for judgment ato begin with bthe household of God; and if *it* cbegins with us first, what *will be* the outcome for those dwho do not obey the egospel of God?

18 aAND IF IT IS WITH DIFFICULTY THAT THE RIGHTEOUS IS SAVED, WHAT WILL BECOME OF THE bGODLESS MAN AND THE SINNER?

19 Therefore, let those also who suffer according to athe will of God entrust their souls to a faithful Creator in doing what is right.

★16 aActs
5:41; 28:22;
James 2:7
b1 Pet. 4:11

★17 aJer.
25:29; Ezek.
9:6; Amos
3:2 b1 Tim.
3:15; Heb.
3:6; 1 Pet.
2:5 cRom.
2:9
d2 Thess.
1:8 eRom.
1:1
18 aProv.
11:31; Luke
23:31
b1 Tim. 1:9
19 a1 Pet.
3:17

VI GRACE MEANS SERVICE, 5:1-11

5 aTherefore, I exhort the elders among you, as *your* bfellow elder and cwitness of the sufferings of Christ, and a dpartaker also of the glory that is to be revealed,

2 shepherd athe flock of God among you, exercising oversight bnot under compulsion, but voluntarily, according to *the will of* God; and cnot for sordid gain, but with eagerness;

3 nor yet as alording it over those allotted to your charge, but proving to be bexamples to the flock.

4 And when the Chief aShepherd appears, you will receive the bunfading ccrown of glory.

5 aYou younger men, likewise, bbe subject to your elders; and all of you, clothe yourselves

★ 1 aActs
11:30
b2 John 1;
3 John 1
cLuke 24:48;
Heb. 12:1
d1 Pet. 1:5,
7; 4:13; Rev.
1:9
2 aJohn
21:16; Acts
20:28 [Gr.]
bPhilem. 14
c1 Tim. 3:8

3 aEzek.
34:4; Matt.
20:25f.
bJohn 13:15;
Phil. 3:17;
1 Thess. 1:7
★ 4 a1 Pet.
2:25 b1 Pet.
1:4 c1 Cor.
9:25
★ 5 aLuke
22:26; 1 Tim.
5:1 bEph.
5:21 c1 Pet.
3:8 dProv.
3:34; James
4:6

4:10 *a special gift.* I.e., a spiritual gift. See note on 1 Cor. 1:7. This is the only occurrence of the word in the N.T. outside the writings of Paul.

4:11 *utterances of God.* One who speaks should preach God's words.

4:12 *do not be surprised.* Peter now turns to the trials of Christians in the world, concluding at 5:11.

4:16 *Christian.* See note on Acts 11:26.

4:17 The idea is this: If even Christians must be judged (by purging), what fate must await unbelievers who will be punished for their sins?

5:1 *elders.* See note on 1 Tim. 3:1. Elders are to feed, lead (but not lord it over), and be an example to their people.

5:4 *crown of glory.* Faithful church leaders, who are often dishonored on earth, will receive glory in heaven from Christ, the chief Shepherd. Victorious athletes were awarded floral crowns, which quickly faded away. See note on 1 Cor. 3:14.

5:5 *humility.* Christianity made humility a major virtue. It is an attitude of mind that realizes that one is without any reason for distinction in God's sight.

with ^chumility toward one another, for ^dGOD IS OPPOSED TO THE PROUD, BUT GIVES GRACE TO THE HUMBLE.

6   ^aHumble yourselves, therefore, under the mighty hand of God, that He may exalt you at the proper time,

7 casting all your ^aanxiety upon Him, because He cares for you.

8   ^aBe of sober *spirit,* ^bbe on the alert. Your adversary, ^cthe devil, prowls about like a roaring ^dlion, seeking someone to devour.

9   ^aBut resist him, ^bfirm in your faith, knowing that ^cthe same experiences of suffering are being accomplished by your brethren who are in the world.

10 And after you have suffered ^afor a little while, the ^bGod of all grace, who ^ccalled you to His ^deternal glory in Christ, will

Himself ^eperfect, ^fconfirm, strengthen *and* establish you.

11   ^aTo Him *be* dominion forever and ever. Amen.

VII   CONCLUDING REMARKS, 5:12–14

12 Through ^aSilvanus, our faithful brother (for so I regard *him*), ^bI have written to you briefly, exhorting and testifying that this is ^cthe true grace of God. ^dStand firm in it!

13 She who is in Babylon, chosen together with you, sends you greetings, and so *does* my son, ^aMark.

14   ^aGreet one another with a kiss of love.

^bPeace be to you all who are in Christ.

5:7 *He cares for you.* Lit., it matters to Him concerning you.

5:13 *my son, Mark.* John Mark, the writer of the Gospel, who was not Peter's natural son but his son in the faith.

5:14 *kiss of love.* The "holy kiss" (Paul's term, Rom. 16:16) was an expression of Christian love and was apparently restricted to one's own sex.

6 ^aJames 4:10

★ **7** ^aMatt. 6:25

8 ^a1 Pet. 1:13 ^bMatt. 24:42 ^cJames 4:7 ^d2 Tim. 4:17

9 ^aJames 4:7 ^bCol. 2:5 ^cActs 14:22; Heb. 12:8

10 ^a1 Pet. 1:6 ^b1 Pet. 4:10 ^c1 Cor. 1:9; 1 Thess. 2:12 ^d2 Cor. 4:17; 2 Tim. 2:10 ^e1 Cor. 1:10; Heb. 13:21 ^fRom. 16:25; 2 Thess. 2:17; 3:3

11 ^aRom. 11:36; 1 Pet. 4:11

12 ^a2 Cor. 1:19 ^bHeb. 13:22 ^cActs 11:23; 4:10 ^d1 Cor. 15:1

★ **13** ^aActs 12:12

★ **14** ^aRom. 16:16 ^bEph. 6:23

INTRODUCTION TO
THE SECOND LETTER OF PETER

AUTHOR: Peter   DATE: 66

Authorship *Many have suggested that someone other than Peter wrote this letter after A.D. 80 because of (1) differences in style, (2) its supposed dependence on Jude, and (3) the mention of Paul's letters having been collected (3:16). However, using a different scribe or no scribe would also have resulted in stylistic changes; there is no reason why Peter should not have borrowed from Jude, though it is more likely that Jude was written later than 2 Peter; and 3:16 does not necessarily refer to all of Paul's letters but only those written up to that time. Furthermore, similarities between 1 and 2 Peter point to the same author, and its acceptance in the canon demands apostolic authority behind it. Assuming Petrine authorship, the letter was written just before his martyrdom in 67 and most likely from Rome.*

Contents *The letter is a reminder (1:12; 3:1) of the truth of Christianity as opposed to the heresies of false teachers. Important passages include those concerning the transfiguration (1:16-18), the inspiration of Scripture (1:21), and the certainty of the second coming of Christ (3:4-10).*

OUTLINE OF 2 PETER

I. **Greetings, 1:1-2**
II. **The Development of Faith, 1:3-21**
  A. The Growth of Faith, 1:3-11
  B. The Ground of Faith, 1:12-21
III. **The Denouncing of False Teachers, 2:1-22**
  A. Their Conduct, 2:1-3
  B. Their Condemnation, 2:4-9

  C. Their Characteristics, 2:10-22
IV. **The Design of the Future, 3:1-18**
  A. Derision, 3:1-7
  B. Delay, 3:8-9
  C. Dissolution, 3:10-13
  D. Diligence, 3:14-18

THE SECOND LETTER OF PETER

I GREETINGS, 1:1-2

★ **1** aRom.
1:1; Phil. 1:1;
James 1:1;
Jude 1
b1 Pet. 1:1
cRom. 1:12;
2 Cor. 4:13;
Titus 1:4
dRom. 3:21-
26 eTitus
2:13
★ **2** aRom.
1:7; 1 Pet.
1:2 bJohn
17:3; Phil.
3:8

1 Simon Peter, a abond-servant and bapostle of Jesus Christ, to those who have received ca faith of the same kind as ours, by dthe righteousness of eour God and Savior, Jesus Christ:

2 aGrace and peace be multiplied to you in bthe knowledge of God and of Jesus our Lord;

II THE DEVELOPMENT OF FAITH, 1:3-21
A The Growth of Faith, 1:3-11

3 a1 Pet.
1:5 bJohn
17:3; Phil.
3:8; 2 Pet.
1:2, 8; 2:20;
3:18
c1 Thess.
2:12;
2 Thess.
2:14; 1 Pet.
5:10
★ **4** a2 Pet.
3:9, 13
bEph. 4:13,
24; Heb.
12:10;
1 John 3:2
c2 Pet. 2:18,
20 d2 Pet.
2:19 eJames
1:27
5 a2 Pet.
1:11 b2 Pet.
1:3 cCol.
2:3; 2 Pet.
1:2
★ **6** aActs
24:25 bLuke
21:19 c2 Pet.
1:3
7 aRom.
12:10; 1 Pet.
1:22

3 seeing that His adivine power has granted to us everything pertaining to life and godliness, through the true bknowledge of Him who ccalled us by His own glory and excellence.

4 For by these He has granted to us His precious and magnificent apromises, in order that by them you might become bpartakers of the divine nature, having cescaped the dcorruption that is in ethe world by lust.

5 Now for this very reason also, applying all diligence, in your faith asupply bmoral excellence, and in your moral excellence, cknowledge;

6 and in your knowledge, aself-control, and in your self-control, bperseverance, and in your perseverance, cgodliness;

7 and in your godliness,

abrotherly kindness, and in your brotherly kindness, love.

8 For if these qualities are yours and are increasing, they render you neither useless nor aunfruitful in the true bknowledge of our Lord Jesus Christ.

9 For he who lacks these qualities is ablind or shortsighted, having forgotten his bpurification from his former sins.

10 Therefore, brethren, be all the more diligent to make certain about His acalling and bchoosing you; for as long as you practice these things, you will never cstumble;

11 for in this way the entrance into athe eternal kingdom of our bLord and Savior Jesus Christ will be cabundantly dsupplied to you.

8 aCol.
1:10 bJohn
17:3; Phil.
3:8; 2 Pet.
1:2, 3; 2:20;
3:18
★ **9** a1 John
2:11 bEph.
5:26; Titus
2:14
★**10** aMatt.
22:14; Rom.
11:29; 2 Pet.
1:3
b1 Thess.
1:4 cJames
2:10; 2 Pet.
3:17; Jude
24
★**11** a2 Tim.
4:18 b2 Pet.
2:20; 3:18
cRom. 2:4;
1 Tim. 6:17
d2 Pet. 1:5

B The Ground of Faith, 1:12-21

12 aPhil. 3:1;
1 John 2:21;
Jude 5 bCol.
1:5f.; 2 John
2
★**13** aPhil.
1:7 b2 Cor.
5:1, 4; 2 Pet.
1:14 c2 Pet.
3:1
★**14** a2 Cor.
5:1; 2 Tim.
4:6 bJohn
13:36; 21:19
15 aLuke
9:31

12 Therefore, aI shall always be ready to remind you of these things, even though you already know them, and have been established in bthe truth which is present with you.

13 And I consider it aright, as long as I am in bthis earthly dwelling, to cstir you up by way of reminder,

14 knowing that athe laying aside of my earthly dwelling is imminent, bas also our Lord Jesus Christ has made clear to me.

15 And I will also be diligent that at any time after my

1:1 *to those who have received a faith of the same kind as ours.* The thought is this: I write to those who have obtained a faith of equal standing with ours (i.e., the apostles') by reason of the impartiality of Christ's blessings.
1:2 *knowledge.* Lit., full or true knowledge (also in v. 3).
1:4 *by these.* I.e., by the glory and excellence (v. 3). *partakers of the divine nature.* The believer shares in the life of God by means of Christ and the Spirit living in him (Rom. 8:9; Gal. 2:20).
1:6 *self-control.* As in Gal. 5:23. *godliness.* The

attitude and conduct of a person who is God-fearing.
1:9 *former sins.* Sins committed prior to conversion.
1:10 *make certain about His calling.* I.e., confirm one's profession of faith by godly living.
1:11 *abundantly.* A Christian life that can be rewarded will provide that abundant entrance into heaven.
1:13 *earthly dwelling.* I.e., Peter's human body.
1:14 *the laying aside of my earthly dwelling.* Because of Christ's prediction (John 21:18), Peter knew that he would soon die.

[cross-references margin: ★16 a1 Tim. 1:4; 2 Pet. 2:3 bMark 13:26; 14:62; 1 Thess. 2:19 cMatt. 17:1ff.; Mark 9:2ff.; Luke 9:28ff.]

ᵃdeparture you may be able to call these things to mind.

16 For we did not follow cleverly devised ᵃtales when we made known to you the ᵇpower and coming of our Lord Jesus Christ, but we were ᶜeyewitnesses of His majesty.

[margin: 17 aMatt. 17:5; Mark 9:7; Luke 9:35 bHeb. 1:3]

17 For when He received honor and glory from God the Father, such an ᵃutterance as this was made to Him by the ᵇMajestic Glory, "This is My beloved Son with whom I am well-pleased"—

[margin: 18 aEx. 3:5; Josh. 5:15]

18 and we ourselves heard this utterance made from heaven when we were with Him on the ᵃholy mountain.

[margin: ★19 a1 Pet. 1:10f. bHeb. 2:2 cPs. 119:105 dLuke 1:78 eRev. 22:16 f2 Cor. 4:6]

19 And so we have ᵃthe prophetic word made more ᵇsure, to which you do well to pay attention as to ᶜa lamp shining in a dark place, until the ᵈday dawns and the ᵉmorning star arises ᶠin your hearts.

[margin: ★20 a2 Pet. 3:3 bRom. 12:6]

20 But ᵃknow this first of all, that ᵇno prophecy of Scripture is a matter of one's own interpretation,

[margin: ★21 aJer. 23:26; 2 Tim. 3:16 b2 Sam. 23:2; Luke 1:70; Acts 1:16; 3:18; 1 Pet. 1:11]

21 for ᵃno prophecy was ever made by an act of human will, but men ᵇmoved by the Holy Spirit spoke from God.

III THE DENOUNCING OF FALSE TEACHERS, 2:1-22

A Their Conduct, 2:1-3

[margin: ★1 aDeut. 13:1ff.; Jer. 6:13 b2 Cor. 11:13 cMatt. 7:15; 1 Tim. 4:1]

2 But ᵃfalse prophets also arose among the people, just as there will also be ᵇfalse teachers ᶜamong you, who will ᵈsecretly introduce ᵉdestructive heresies, even ᶠdenying the ᵍMaster who ʰbought them, bringing swift destruction upon themselves.

[margin: dGal. 2:4; Jude 4 e1 Cor. 11:19; Gal. 5:20 fJude 4 gRev. 6:10 h1 Cor. 6:20]

2 And many will follow their ᵃsensuality, and because of them ᵇthe way of the truth will be ᶜmaligned;

[margin: 2 aGen. 19:5ff.; 2 Pet. 2:7, 18; Jude 4 bActs 16:17; 22:4; 24:14 c[Gr.] Rom. 2:24; 1 Tim. 6:1]

3 and in their ᵃgreed they will ᵇexploit you with ᶜfalse words; ᵈtheir judgment from long ago is not idle, and their destruction is not asleep.

[margin: 3 a1 Tim. 6:5; 2 Pet. 2:14; Jude 16 b2 Cor. 2:17 marg.; 1 Thess. 2:5 cRom. 16:18; 2 Pet. 1:16 dDeut. 32:35]

B Their Condemnation, 2:4-9

[margin: ★4 aGen. 6; Jude 6 bRev. 20:1f.]

4 For ᵃif God did not spare angels when they sinned, but cast them into hell and ᵇcommitted them to pits of darkness, reserved for judgment;

[margin: ★5 aEzek. 26:20; 2 Pet. 3:6 b1 Pet. 3:20 c2 Pet. 3:6]

5 and did not spare ᵃthe ancient world, but preserved ᵇNoah, a preacher of righteousness, with seven others, when He brought a ᶜflood upon the world of the ungodly;

[margin: ★6 aGen. 19:24; Jude 7 bMatt. 10:15; 11:23; Rom. 9:29 [Is. 1:9]; Jude 7 cJude 15]

6 and if He ᵃcondemned the cities of Sodom and Gomorrah to destruction by reducing them to ashes, having made them an ᵇexample to those who would ᶜlive ungodly thereafter;

[margin: ★7 aGen. 19:16, 29 bGen. 19:5ff.; 2 Pet. 2:2, 18; Jude 4 c2 Pet. 3:17]

7 and if He ᵃrescued righteous Lot, oppressed by the ᵇsensual conduct of ᶜunprincipled men

---

1:16 *eyewitnesses of His majesty.* Peter is referring here to his witnessing the transfiguration of Christ (Matt. 17:1-8). This event confirmed the truth of the O.T. prophecies and made them even more sure from a human viewpoint (2 Pet. 1:19).

1:19 *until the day dawns.* Possibly a reference to the second coming of Christ.

1:20 *one's own interpretation.* Several meanings are possible: (1) Prophecies must be interpreted in the light of other Scriptures; (2) prophecies are often capable of several fulfillments; (3) prophecies must be interpreted only with God's help, since they were given only as the prophets were moved by God, and not by any impulse of man.

1:21 *moved.* Lit. borne along. This shows the dual authorship of God's Word—the Holy Spirit guiding and guarding the men involved in the actual writing. See note on 2 Tim. 3:16.

2:1 *denying the Master who bought them.* The price for the sins of all men (including these false teachers) was paid by the death of Christ, though no man can have benefit of this forgiveness except through faith in the Savior. See 1 Cor. 6:20; 1 Pet. 1:18-19.

2:4 *angels when they sinned.* These are the fallen angels who sinned grievously by cohabiting with women, as described in Gen. 6:1-4. See Jude 6. The logic is that if God so punishes angels, surely He will not spare these false teachers.

2:5 *with seven others.* Noah was the eighth, along with the seven other members of his family (his wife and his three sons and their wives).

2:6 *Sodom and Gomorrah.* See Gen. 19:15-29.

2:7 *righteous Lot.* He was a righteous man in

8 *a*Heb.
11:4

8 (for by what he saw and heard that *a*righteous man, while living among them, felt *his* righteous soul tormented day after day with *their* lawless deeds),

9 *a*1 Cor.
10:13; Rev.
3:10 *b*Matt.
10:15; Jude
6

9 *a*then the Lord knows how to rescue the godly from temptation, and to keep the unrighteous under punishment for the *b*day of judgment,

C　Their Characteristics,
2:10-22

★**10** *a*2 Pet.
3:3; Jude 16,
18 *b*Ex.
22:28; Jude
8 *c*Titus 1:7

10 and especially those who *a*indulge the flesh in *its* corrupt desires and *b*despise authority. Daring, *c*self-willed, they do not tremble when they *b*revile angelic majesties,

★**11** *a*Jude 9

11 *a*whereas angels who are greater in might and power do not bring a reviling judgment against them before the Lord.

12 *a*Jude 10
*b*Jer. 12:3;
Col. 2:22

12 But *a*these, like unreasoning animals, *b*born as creatures of instinct to be captured and killed, reviling where they have no knowledge, will in the destruction of those creatures also be destroyed,

★**13** *a*2 Pet.
2:15 *b*Rom.
13:13
*c*1 Thess.
5:7 *d*1 Cor.
11:21; Jude
12

13 suffering wrong as *a*the wages of doing wrong. They count it a pleasure to *b*revel in the *c*daytime. They are stains and blemishes, *b*reveling in their deceptions, as they *d*carouse with you,

14 having eyes full of adultery and that never cease from sin, *a*enticing *b*unstable souls, having a heart trained in *c*greed, *d*accursed children;

15 forsaking *a*the right way they have gone astray, having followed *b*the way of Balaam, the *son* of Beor, who loved *c*the wages of unrighteousness,

16 but he received a rebuke for his own transgression; *a*for a dumb donkey, speaking with a voice of a man, restrained the madness of the prophet.

17 These are *a*springs without water, and mists driven by a storm, *b*for whom the black darkness has been reserved.

18 For speaking out *a*arrogant *words* of *b*vanity they *c*entice by fleshly desires, by *d*sensuality, those who barely *e*escape from the ones who live in error,

19 promising them freedom while they themselves are slaves of corruption; for *a*by what a man is overcome, by this he is enslaved.

20 For if after they have *a*escaped the defilements of the world by *b*the knowledge of the *c*Lord and Savior Jesus Christ, they are again *d*entangled in them and are overcome, *e*the last state has become worse for them than the first.

21 *a*For it would be better for them not to have known the way of righteousness, than having

★**14** *a*2 Pet.
2:18 *b*James
1:8; 2 Pet.
3:16 *c*2 Pet.
2:3 *d*Eph.
2:3

★**15** *a*Acts
13:10 *b*Num.
22:5, 7; Deut.
23:4; Neh.
13:2; Jude
11; Rev. 2:14
*c*2 Pet. 2:13

16 *a*Num.
22:21, 23,
28, 30f.

★**17** *a*Jude
12 *b*Jude 13

★**18** *a*Jude
16 *b*Eph.
4:17 *c*2 Pet.
2:14, *d*2 Pet.
2:2 *e*2 Pet.
1:4; 2:20

19 *a*John
8:34; Rom.
6:16

★**20** *a*2 Pet.
2:18 *b*2 Pet.
1:2 *c*2 Pet.
1:11; 3:18
*d*2 Tim. 2:4
*e*Matt. 12:45;
Luke 11:26

21 *a*Ezek.
18:24; Heb.
6:4ff.;
10:26f.;
James 4:17
*b*Gal. 6:2;
1 Tim. 6:14;
2 Pet. 3:2
*c*Jude 3

---

that he believed God and was vexed at the licentiousness of the wicked people about him, though his life was lived for himself.

2:10 *despise authority.* I.e., especially God's. False teachers speak rashly in disbelief of the power and authority of angels.

2:11 *against them.* Probably a reference to the false teachers. In other words, even though the false teachers speak evil of angels, angels do not denounce them but leave all judgment to God.

2:13 *reveling in their deceptions.* The false teachers turned Christian fellowship meals into riotous drinking parties.

2:14 *accursed children.* A phrase which simply means that the false teachers themselves, not their children, are accursed.

2:15 *the way of Balaam.* The covetousness of one who hires himself to do religious work for

personal gain (see Num. 22:7, 17 and note on Jude 11). This "way" is contrasted with "the right way" (2 Pet. 2:15).

2:17 *springs without water.* The barrenness of the false teachers mocks the thirsty soul who sincerely wants to learn God's way from them. *mists driven by a storm.* These mists, like the false teachers, seem to promise refreshment, but in reality do no good. *the black darkness.* I.e., eternal torment (cf. Matt. 8:12).

2:18 *sensuality* = sexual excesses.

2:20 *escaped the defilements of the world.* These teachers had apparently made some sort of profession of the truth without possessing the new life of Christ. They then rejected what they professed, becoming slaves of corruption (v. 19) and showing their true, natural, unchanged condition (v. 22).

known it, to turn away from [b]the holy commandment [c]delivered to them.

22 It has happened to them according to the true proverb, "[a]A DOG RETURNS TO ITS OWN VOMIT," and, "A sow, after washing, *returns* to wallowing in the mire."

IV THE DESIGN OF THE FUTURE, 3:1–18

A Derision, 3:1–7

3 This is now, [a]beloved, the second letter I am writing to you in which I am [b]stirring up your sincere mind by way of reminder,

2 that you should [a]remember the words spoken beforehand by [b]the holy prophets and [c]the commandment of the Lord and Savior *spoken* by your apostles.

3 [a]Know this first of all, that [b]in the last days [c]mockers will come with *their* mocking, [d]following after their own lusts,

4 and saying, "[a]Where is the promise of His [b]coming? For *ever* since the fathers [c]fell asleep, all continues just as it was [d]from the beginning of creation."

5 For when they maintain this, it escapes their notice that [a]by the word of God *the* heavens existed long ago and *the* earth was [b]formed out of water and by water,

6 through which [a]the world at that time was [b]destroyed, being flooded with water.

7 But [a]the present heavens and earth by His word are being reserved for [b]fire, kept for [c]the day of judgment and destruction of ungodly men.

B Delay, 3:8–9

8 But do not let this one *fact* escape your notice, [a]beloved, that with the Lord one day is as a thousand years, and [b]a thousand years as one day.

9 [a]The Lord is not slow about His promise, as some count slowness, but [b]is patient toward you, [c]not wishing for any to perish but for all to come to repentance.

C Dissolution, 3:10–13

10 But [a]the day of the Lord [b]will come like a thief, in which [c]the heavens [d]will pass away with a roar and the [e]elements will be destroyed with intense heat, [f]the earth and its works will be burned up.

11 Since all these things are to be destroyed in this way, what sort of people ought you to be in holy conduct and godliness,

12 [a]looking for and hastening the coming of the day of God, on account of which [b]the heavens will be destroyed by burning, and the [c]elements will melt with intense heat!

13 But according to His [a]promise we are looking for [b]new heavens and a new earth, [c]in which righteousness dwells.

D Diligence, 3:14–18

14 [a]Therefore, [b]beloved, since you look for these things, be diligent to be [c]found by Him in peace, [d]spotless and blameless,

22 [a]Prov. 26:11

1 [a]1 Pet. 2:11; 2 Pet. 3:8, 14, 17 [b]2 Pet. 1:13

2 [a]Jude 17 [b]Luke 1:70; Acts 3:21; Eph. 3:5 [c]Gal. 6:2; 1 Tim. 6:14; 2 Pet. 2:21

3 [a]2 Pet. 1:20 [b]1 Tim. 4:1; Heb. 1:2 [c]Jude 18 [d]2 Pet. 2:10

4 [a]Is. 5:19; Jer. 17:15; Ezek. 11:3; 12:22, 27; Mal. 2:17; Matt. 24:48 [b]1 Thess. 2:19; 2 Pet. 3:12 [c]Acts 7:60 [d]Mark 10:6

★ **5** [a]Gen. 1:6, 9; Heb. 11:3 [b]Ps. 24:2; 136:6; Col. 1:17 [Gr.]

★ **6** [a]2 Pet. 2:5 [b]Gen. 7:21f.

7 [a]2 Pet. 3:10, 12 [b]Is. 66:15; Dan. 7:9f.; 2 Thess. 1:7; Heb. 12:29 [c]Matt. 10:15; 1 Cor. 3:13; Jude 7

★ **8-9** [a]2 Pet. 3:1 [b]Ps. 90:4

9 [a]Hab. 2:3; Rom. 13:11; Heb. 10:37 [b]Rom. 2:4; Rev. 2:21 [c]1 Tim. 2:4; Rev. 2:21

★**10** [a]1 Cor. 1:8 [b]Matt. 24:43; 1 Thess. 5:2; Rev. 3:3; 16:15 [c]2 Pet. 3:7, 12 [d]Matt. 24:35; Rev. 21:1 [e]Is. 24:19; 34:4; Mic. 1:4; Gal. 4:3 [f]2 Pet. 3:7

★**12** [a]1 Cor. 1:7 [b]2 Pet. 3:7, 10 [c]Is. 24:19; 34:4; Mic. 1:4; Gal. 4:3

13 [a]Is. 65:17; 66:22 [b]Rom. 8:21; Rev. 21:1 [c]Is. 60:21; 65:25; Rev. 21:27

14 [a]1 Cor. 15:58; 2 Pet. 1:10 [b]2 Pet. 3:1 [c]1 Pet. 1:7 [d]Phil. 2:15; 1 Thess. 5:23; 1 Tim. 6:14; James 1:27

3:5 *it escapes their notice.* Or, they willfully ignore. Peter begins his attack on those who doubt the truth of Christ's return by referring to the dependability of God's word as demonstrated in Creation.

3:6 *flooded with water.* The judgment of the flood in the days of Noah also demonstrates the truthfulness of God's word.

3:8–9 To believers, Peter now says that the seeming delay of Christ's return is for the purpose of allowing more people to repent.

3:10 *the day of the Lord.* See note on 1 Thess. 5:2.

3:12 *on account of which.* I.e., after the dissolution of the present heavens, the day of God, which is eternity (Rev. 21:1), will come. The certainty of this dissolution makes doubly urgent a life of godliness now.

15 and regard the ᵃpatience of our Lord *to be* salvation; just as also ᵇour beloved brother Paul, ᶜaccording to the wisdom given him, wrote to you,

16 as also in all *his* letters, speaking in them of ᵃthese things, ᵇin which are some things hard to understand, which the untaught and ᶜunstable distort, as *they do* also ᵈthe rest of the Scriptures, to their own destruction.

17 You therefore, ᵃbeloved, knowing this beforehand, ᵇbe on your guard lest, being carried away by ᶜthe error of ᵈunprincipled men, you ᵉfall from your own steadfastness,

18 but grow in the grace and ᵃknowledge of our ᵇLord and Savior Jesus Christ. ᶜTo Him *be* the glory, both now and to the day of eternity. Amen.

★15 ᵃ2 Pet. 3:9 ᵇActs 9:17; 15:25; 2 Pet. 3:2 ᶜ1 Cor. 3:10; Eph. 3:3

★16 ᵃ2 Pet. 3:14 ᵇHeb. 5:11 ᶜ2 Pet. 2:14 ᵈlls. 28:13; 2 Pet. 3:2

17 ᵃ2 Pet. 3:1 ᵇ1 Cor. 10:12 ᶜ2 Pet. 2:18 ᵈ2 Pet. 2:7 ᵉRev. 2:5

18 ᵃ2 Pet. 1:2 ᵇ2 Pet. 1:11; 2:20 ᶜRom. 11:36; 2 Tim. 4:18; Rev. 1:6

3:15 *regard . . . to be salvation.* I.e., understand that the delay of the return of the Lord is intended as an opportunity for men to be saved (see v. 9).

3:16 Paul's epistles are here put on a par with *the rest of the Scriptures.*

INTRODUCTION TO
THE FIRST LETTER OF JOHN

AUTHOR: John   DATE: 90

Authorship   *Though it is generally agreed that the same person wrote the Gospel of John and these three epistles, some feel that they were not written (as traditionally held) by John the apostle, the son of Zebedee, but by another John (the elder or presbyter, 2 John 1; 3 John 1). It is argued that (1) an uneducated man (Acts 4:13) could not have written something so profound as this Gospel; (2) a fisherman's son would not have known the high priest as did John the apostle; and (3) an apostle would not have called himself an elder. But "uneducated" did not mean illiterate, but only without formal training in the rabbinic schools; some fishermen were well-to-do (cf. Mark 1:20); and Peter, though an apostle, called himself an elder (1 Pet. 5:1). Further, if John the elder is the "beloved disciple" and the author of the Gospel, why did he not mention John the son of Zebedee, an important figure in the life of Christ, in that Gospel? Every evidence points to John the elder being the same as John the apostle and the author of this letter.*

Date and Place of Writing   *Strong tradition says that John spent his old age in Ephesus. Lack of personal references in this letter indicates that it was written in sermonic style to Christians all over Asia Minor (much like Ephesians). It was probably written after the Gospel and before the persecution under Domitian in 95, which places its writing in the late 80's or early 90's.*

Gnosticism   *The heresy of Gnosticism had begun to make inroads among churches in John's day. Among its teachings were: (1) knowledge is superior to virtue; (2) the nonliteral sense of Scripture is correct and can be understood only by a select few; (3) evil in the world precludes God's being the only Creator; (4) the incarnation is incredible because deity cannot unite itself with anything material such as a body (Docetism); and (5) there is no resurrection of the flesh. The ethical standards of many Gnostics were low, so John emphasized the reality of the incarnation and the high ethical standard of the earthly life of Christ.*

Contents   *The letter shows John's obvious affection for his "little children" and concern for their spiritual welfare. The book is filled with contrasts—light and darkness (1:6-7; 2:8-11); love of world and love of God (2:15-17); children of God and children of the devil (3:4-10); the Spirit of God and the spirit of Antichrist (4:1-3); love and hate (4:7-12, 16-21).*

OUTLINE OF 1 JOHN

I. **Introduction: The Purpose of the Epistle,**
   1:1–4
II. **Conditions for Fellowship, 1:5–2:2**
   A. Conformity to a Standard, 1:5–7
   B. Confession of Sin, 1:8–2:2
III. **Conduct in Fellowship, 2:3–27**
   A. The Character of our Conduct—Imitation,
      2:3–11
   B. The Commandment for our Conduct—
      Separation, 2:12–17
   C. The Creed for our Conduct—Affirmation,
      2:18–27
IV. **Characteristics of Fellowship, 2:28–3:24**
   A. In Relation to our Prospect: Purity,
      2:28–3:3

B. In Relation to our Position: Righteousness
   and Brotherly Love, 3:4–18
C. In Relation to our Prayers: Answers,
   3:19–24
V. **Cautions of Fellowship, 4:1–21**
   A. Concerning False, Lying Spirits, 4:1–6
   B. Concerning a True, Loving Spirit, 4:7–21
      1. The ground of brotherly love, 4:7–10
      2. The glories of love, 4:11–21
VI. **Consequences of Fellowship, 5:1–21**
   A. Love for the Brethren, 5:1–3
   B. Victory over the World, 5:4–5
   C. Verification of Christ's Credentials, 5:6–12
   D. Assurance of Eternal Life, 5:13
   E. Guidance in Prayer, 5:14–17
   F. Freedom from Habitual Sin, 5:18–21

THE FIRST LETTER OF JOHN

I INTRODUCTION: THE PURPOSE OF THE EPISTLE, 1:1-4

★ **1** *a*John 1:1f.; 1 John 2:13, 14
*b*Acts 4:20
*c*John 19:35; 2 Pet. 1:16; 1 John 1:2
*d*John 1:14; 1 John 4:14
*e*Luke 24:39; John 20:27
*f*John 1:1, 4

2 *a*John 1:4; Rom. 16:26 *b*John 19:35; 1 John 1:1
*c*John 15:27
*d*John 10:28
*e*John 1:1

3 *a*John 19:35; 2 Pet. 1:16; 1 John 1:1 *b*Acts 4:20; 1 John 1:1 *c*John 17:3, 21

4 *a*1 John 2:1 *b*John 3:29

1 What was *a*from the beginning, what we have *b*heard, what we have *c*seen with our eyes, what we *d*beheld and our hands *e*handled, concerning the *f*Word of Life—

2 and *a*the life was manifested, and we have *b*seen and *c*bear witness and proclaim to you *d*the eternal life, which was *e*with the Father and was *a*manifested to us—

3 what we have *a*seen and *b*heard we proclaim to you also, that you also may have fellowship with us; and indeed our *c*fellowship is with the Father, and with His Son Jesus Christ.

4 And *a*these things we write, so that our *b*joy may be made complete.

II CONDITIONS FOR FELLOWSHIP, 1:5-2:2

A Conformity to a Standard, 1:5-7

★ **5** *a*John 1:19; 1 John 3:11 *b*1 Tim. 6:16; James 1:17

6 *a*John 8:12; 2 Cor. 6:14; Eph. 5:8; 1 John 2:11 *b*John 8:55; 1 John 2:4; 4:20
*c*John 3:21

5 And *a*this is the message we have heard from Him and announce to you, that *b*God is light, and in Him there is no darkness at all.

6 *a*If we say that we have fellowship with Him and *yet* walk in the darkness, we *b*lie and *c*do not practice the truth;

7 but if we *a*walk in the light as *b*He Himself is in the light, we have fellowship with one another, and *c*the blood of Jesus His Son cleanses us from all sin.

B Confession of Sin, 1:8-2:2

8 *a*If we say that we have no sin, we are deceiving ourselves, and the *b*truth is not in us.

9 *a*If we confess our sins, He is faithful and righteous to forgive us our sins and *b*to cleanse us from all unrighteousness.

10 *a*If we say that we have not sinned, we *b*make Him a liar, and *c*His word is not in us.

2 *a*My little children, I am writing *b*these things to you that you may not sin. And if anyone sins, *c*we have an *d*Advocate with the Father, Jesus Christ the righteous;

2 and He Himself is *a*the propitiation for our sins; and not for ours only, but also *b*for *those of* the whole world.

★ **7** *a*Is. 2:5 *b*1 Tim. 6:16 *c*Titus 2:14; Heb. 9:14; Rev. 7:14
★ **8** *a*Job 15:14; Prov. 20:9; Rom. 3:10ff.; James 3:2 *b*John 8:44; 1 John 2:4
★ **9** *a*Ps. 32:5; Prov. 28:13 *b*Titus 2:14; Heb. 9:14; Rev. 7:14
★**10** *a*Job 15:14; Prov. 20:9; Rom. 3:10ff.; James 3:2 *b*John 3:33; 1 John 5:10 *c*1 John 2:14
★ **1** *a*John 13:33; Gal. 4:19; 1 John 2:12, 28; 3:7, 18; 4:4; 5:21 *b*1 John 1:4 *c*Rom. 8:34; 1 Tim. 2:5; Heb. 7:25; 9:24 *d*John 14:16
★ **2** *a*Rom. 3:25; Heb. 2:17; 1 John 4:10 *b*John 4:42; 11:51f.; 1 John 4:14

III CONDUCT IN FELLOWSHIP, 2:3-27

A The Character of our Conduct—Imitation, 2:3-11

3 And *a*by this we know that we have come to *b*know Him, if we *c*keep His commandments.

★ **3-5**
3 *a*1 John 2:5; 3:24; 4:13; 5:2 *b*1 John 2:4; 3:6; 4:7f. *c*John 14:15; 1 John 3:22, 24; 5:3

1:1 *was.* The verb means "was already in existence," not "came into existence." I.e., at creation, *the beginning. handled.* The same Greek word is used in one of Christ's post-resurrection appearances ("touch," Luke 24:39).

1:5 *from Him.* I.e., from Christ. *God is light.* I.e., God is holy and pure. This symbol was much used by John (John 1:4; 3:19-21; 8:12). Notice also the other "God is . . ." phrases in John 4:24 and 1 John 4:8.

1:7 *but if we walk in the light.* To walk in the light is to live in obedience to God's commandments. The contrast of light and darkness characterizes the section 1:5-2:17.

1:8 *have no sin.* A reference to the indwelling

principle of sin rather than to acts of sin.

1:9 *confess* means to say the same thing about sin that God does.

1:10 *we have not sinned.* I.e., have not committed sin. Even believers sin; if we deny past sin and present guilt, we are deceiving ourselves, mocking God, and not walking in the light.

2:1 *Advocate.* Lit., one summoned alongside, a helper or patron in a lawsuit. Used only by John in the N.T. and translated "Helper" in John 14:16, 26; 15:26; 16:7.

2:2 *propitiation* = satisfaction. Christ is the only offering that satisfied God concerning sin (cf. Rom. 3:25). See note on Heb. 2:17.

2:3-5 Obedience to Christ's commandments is the down-to-earth test of our faith.

★ **4** aTitus
1:10
b1 John 3:6;
4:7f. c1 John
1:6 d1 John
1:8
★ **5** aJohn
14:23
b1 John 4:12
c1 John 2:3;
3:24; 4:13;
5:2
6 aJohn
15:4 bJohn
13:15; 15:10;
1 Pet. 2:21

7 aHeb.
6:9; 1 John
3:2, 21; 4:1,
7, 11
b1 John
3:11, 23;
4:21; 2 John
5 c1 John
2:24; 3:11;
2 John 5, 6
★ **8** aJohn
13:34 bRom.
13:12; Eph.
5:8; 1 Thess.
5:4f. cJohn
1:9

9 a1 John
2:11; 3:15;
4:20 bActs
1:15; 1 John
3:10, 16;
4:20f.
★**10** aJohn
11:9; 1 John
2:10, 11

11 a1 John
2:9; 3:15;
4:20 bJohn
12:35;
1 John 1:6
c2 Cor. 4:4;
2 Pet. 1:9

4 The one who says, "aI have come to bknow Him," and does not keep His commandments, is a cliar, and dthe truth is not in him;

5 but whoever akeeps His word, in him the blove of God has truly been perfected. cBy this we know that we are in Him:

6 the one who says he aabides in Him bought himself to walk in the same manner as He walked.

7 aBeloved, I am bnot writing a new commandment to you, but an old commandment which you have had cfrom the beginning; the old commandment is the word which you have heard.

8 On the other hand, I am writing aa new commandment to you, which is true in Him and in you, because bthe darkness is passing away, and cthe true light is already shining.

9 The one who says he is in the light and yet ahates his bbrother is in the darkness until now.

10 aThe one who loves his brother abides in the light and there is no cause for stumbling in him.

11 But the one who ahates his brother is in the darkness and bwalks in the darkness, and does not know where he is going because the darkness has cblinded his eyes.

B The Commandment for our Conduct—Separation, 2:12-17

12 a1 John
2:1 bActs
13:38; 1 Cor.
6:11

12 I am writing to you, alittle children, because byour sins are forgiven you for His name's sake.

13 I am writing to you, fathers, because you know Him awho has been from the beginning. I am writing to you, young men, because byou have overcome cthe evil one. I have written to you, children, because dyou know the Father.

14 I have written to you, fathers, because you know Him awho has been from the beginning. I have written to you, young men, because you are bstrong, and the cword of God abides in you, and dyou have overcome the evil one.

15 Do not love athe world, nor the things in the world. bIf anyone loves the world, the love of the Father is not in him.

16 For all that is in the world, athe lust of the flesh and bthe lust of the eyes and cthe boastful pride of life, is not from the Father, but is from the world.

17 And athe world is passing away, and also its lusts; but the one who does the will of God abides forever.

C The Creed for our Conduct— Affirmation, 2:18-27

18 Children, ait is the last hour; and just as you heard that bantichrist is coming, ceven now many antichrists have arisen; from this we know that it is the last hour.

19 aThey went out from us, but they were not really of us; for if they had been of us, they would have remained with us; but they

★**13** a1 John
1:1 bJohn
16:33;
1 John 2:14;
4:4; 5:4f.;
Rev. 2:7
cMatt. 5:37;
1 John 2:14;
3:12; 5:18f.
dJohn 14:7;
1 John 2:3

14 a1 John
1:1 bEph.
6:10 cJohn
5:38; 8:37;
1 John 1:10
d1 John 2:13

★**15** aRom.
12:2; James
1:27 bJames
4:4

★**16** aRom.
13:14; Eph.
2:3; 1 Pet.
2:11 bProv.
27:20
cJames 4:16

17 a1 Cor.
7:31

★**18-27**
★**18** aRom.
13:11; 1 Tim.
4:1; 1 Pet.
4:7 bMatt.
24:5, 24;
1 John 2:22;
4:3; 2 John 7
cMark 13:22;
1 John 4:1, 3

19 aActs
20:30
b1 Cor.
11:19

2:4 *truth.* Not merely correct knowledge, but the demonstration of the reality of God's love.
2:5 *perfected.* I.e., realized in practice.
2:8 *the true light.* I.e., the revelation of God in Christ.
2:10 *there is no cause for stumbling in him.* I.e., there is nothing in him that would cause others to stumble.
2:13 *the evil one.* I.e., the devil.
2:15 *the world.* The world (Greek, *cosmos*) is that organized system headed by Satan which leaves God out and is a rival to Him. Though

God loves the world of men (John 3:16), believers are not to love at all that which organizes them against God. See 1 John 5:19; John 3:19; Jas. 1:27; 4:4.
2:16 *pride of life.* Vainglory, display, or boasting about one's possessions.
2:18-27 The author now contrasts truth and falsehood.
2:18 *antichrist.* John speaks about (1) the spirit of antichrist (4:3) which refers to demonic forces behind antichristian teaching and activity; (2) the great coming Antichrist (Rev.

went out, bin order that it might be shown that they all are not of us.

20 But you have an ªanointing from bthe Holy One, and cyou all know.

21 I have not written to you because you do not know the truth, but ªbecause you do know it, and because no lie is bof the truth.

22 Who is the liar but ªthe one who denies that Jesus is the Christ? This is bthe antichrist, the one who denies the Father and the Son.

23 ªWhoever denies the Son does not have the Father; the one who confesses the Son has the Father also.

24 As for you, let that abide in you which you heard ªfrom the beginning. If what you heard from the beginning abides in you, you also bwill abide in the Son and in the Father.

25 And ªthis is the promise which He Himself made to us: eternal life.

26 These things I have written to you concerning those who are trying to ªdeceive you.

27 And as for you, the ªanointing which you received from Him abides in you, and you have no need for anyone to teach you; but as His anointing bteaches you about all things, and is ctrue and is not a lie, and just as it has taught you, you abide in Him.

IV CHARACTERISTICS OF FELLOWSHIP, 2:28-3:24
A In Relation to our Prospect: Purity, 2:28-3:3

28 And now, ªlittle children, abide in Him, so that when He bappears, we may have cconfidence and dnot shrink away from Him in shame at His ecoming.

29 If you know that ªHe is righteous, you know that everyone also who practices righteousness bis born of Him.

3 See ªhow great a love the Father has bestowed upon us, that we should be called bchildren of God; and *such* we are. For this reason the world does not know us, because cit did not know Him.

2 ªBeloved, now we are bchildren of God, and cit has not appeared as yet what we shall be. We know that, when He dappears, we shall be elike Him, because we shall fsee Him just as He is.

3 And everyone who has this ªhope *fixed* on Him bpurifies himself, just as He is pure.

B In Relation to our Position: Righteousness and Brotherly Love, 3:4-18

4 Everyone who practices sin also practices lawlessness; and ªsin is lawlessness.

*20 ª2 Cor. 1:21; 1 John 2:27 bMark 1:24; Acts 10:38 cProv. 28:5; Matt. 13:11; John 14:26; 1 Cor. 2:15f.; 1 John 2:27
21 ªJames 1:19; 2 Pet. 1:12; Jude 5 bJohn 8:44; 18:37; 1 John 3:19
*22 ª1 John 4:3; 2 John 7 bMatt. 24:5, 24; 1 John 2:18; 4:3; 2 John 7
23 ªJohn 8:19; 16:3; 17:3; 1 John 4:15; 5:1; 2 John 9
24 ª1 John 2:7 bJohn 14:23; 1 John 1:3; 2 John 9
25 ªJohn 3:15; 6:40; 1 John 1:2
26 ª1 John 3:7; 2 John 7
*27 ªJohn 14:16; 1 John 2:20 bJohn 14:26; 1 Cor. 2:12; 1 Thess. 4:9 cJohn 14:17

*2:28-3:24
28 ª1 John 2:1 bLuke 17:30; Col. 3:4; 1 John 3:2 cEph. 3:12; 1 John 3:21; 4:17; 5:14 dMark 8:38 e1 Thess. 2:19
29 ªJohn 7:18; 1 John 3:7 bJohn 4:7; 5:1, 4, 18 [3 John 11]
* 1 ªJohn 3:16; 1 John 1:12; 11:52; Rom. 8:16; 1 John 3:2, 10 cJohn 15:18, 21; 16:3
2 ª1 John 2:7 bJohn 1:12; 11:52; Rom. 8:16; 1 John 3:1, 10 cRom. 8:19, 23f. dLuke 17:30; Col. 3:4; 1 John 2:28 eRom. 8:29; 2 Pet. 1:4 fJohn 17:24; 2 Cor. 3:18
3 ªRom. 15:12; 1 Pet. 1:3 bJohn 17:19; 2 Cor. 7:1; 2 Pet. 3:13f.; 1 John 2:6
* 4 ªRom. 4:15; 1 John 5:17

13:1-10); and (3) many antichrists present and active in his time and throughout church history. The ones of whom John is here speaking belonged to the visible church but were not believers (v. 19). They denied the reality of the incarnation of Christ and His relationship to the Father (vv. 21-23; cf. 2 John 7).
2:20 *you have an anointing from the Holy One.* I.e., you have been anointed by the Holy Spirit, and thus can discern between truth and error. See also note on 2:27.
2:22 *the liar.* The supreme liar is the one who denies that Jesus Christ came in the flesh, i.e., that He was both man and God. The separation of the human and the divine was an early (Docetic) heresy.

2:27 *you have no need for anyone to teach you.* The Spirit whom they had received would teach them how to distinguish truth from error (John 16:13). The Spirit may use human teachers to accomplish this (Eph. 4:11-14).
2:28-3:24 John's third great contrast is between life and death. (Cf. notes on 1:7 and 2:18.)
3:1 *children of God.* Born ones of God, as in John 1:12. We can, even now, know Him as a child knows its father; the future relationship no words can describe.
3:4 *sin is lawlessness.* Lawlessness is used here in its broadest sense, defection from any of God's standards.

5 a1 John
1:2; 3:8
b John 1:29;
1 Pet. 1:18-
20; 1 John
2:2 c2 Cor.
5:21; 1 John
2:29
6 a1 John
3:9 b1 John
2:3; 3 John
11
7 a1 John
2:1 b1 John
2:26 c1 John
2:29
★ **8** a Matt.
13:38; John
8:44; 1 John
3:10 b Matt.
4:3 c1 John
3:5 d John
12:31; 16:11
★ **9** a John
1:13; 3:3;
1 John 2:29;
4:7; 5:1, 4,
18 [3 John
11] b James
1:18
10 a John
1:12; 11:52;
Rom. 8:16;
1 John 3:1, 2
b Matt. 13:38;
John 8:44;
1 John 3:8
c Rom.
13:8ff.; Col.
3:14; 1 Tim.
1:5; 1 John
4:8 d1 John
2:9
11 a1 John
1:5 b1 John
2:7 c John
13:34f.
★ **12** a Gen.
4:8 b Matt.
5:37; 1 John
2:13f. c Ps.
38:20; Prov.
29:10; John
8:40, 41
13 a John
15:18; 17:14
14 a John
5:24 b John
13:35;
1 John 2:10
★ **15** a Matt.
5:21f.; John
8:44 b Gal.
5:20f.

5 And you know that He ^aappeared in order to ^btake away sins; and ^cin Him there is no sin.

6 No one who abides in Him ^asins; no one who sins has seen Him or ^bknows Him.

7 ^aLittle children, let no one ^bdeceive you; ^cthe one who practices righteousness is righteous, just as He is righteous;

8 the one who practices sin is ^aof the devil; for the devil has sinned from the beginning. ^bThe Son of God ^cappeared for this purpose, ^dthat He might destroy the works of the devil.

9 No one who is ^aborn of God ^bpractices sin, because His seed abides in him; and he cannot sin, because he is born of God.

10 By this the ^achildren of God and the ^bchildren of the devil are obvious: anyone who does not practice righteousness is not of God, nor the one who ^cdoes not love his ^dbrother.

11 ^aFor this is the message ^bwhich you have heard from the beginning, ^cthat we should love one another;

12 not as ^aCain, *who* was of ^bthe evil one, and slew his brother. And for what reason did he slay him? Because ^chis deeds were evil, and his brother's were righteous.

13 Do not marvel, brethren, if ^athe world hates you.

14 We know that we have ^apassed out of death into life, ^bbecause we love the brethren. He who does not love abides in death.

15 Everyone who ^ahates his brother is a murderer; and you know that ^bno murderer has eternal life abiding in him.

16 We know love by this, that ^aHe laid down His life for us; and ^bwe ought to lay down our lives for the ^cbrethren.

17 But ^awhoever has the world's goods, and beholds his brother in need and ^bcloses his heart against him, ^chow does the love of God abide in him?

18 ^aLittle children, let us not love with word or with tongue, but in deed and ^btruth.

C In Relation to our Prayers: Answers, 3:19–24

19 We shall know by this that we are ^aof the truth, and shall assure our heart before Him,

20 in whatever our heart condemns us; for God is greater than our heart, and knows all things.

21 ^aBeloved, if our heart does not condemn us, we have ^bconfidence before God;

22 and ^awhatever we ask we receive from Him, because we ^bkeep His commandments and do ^cthe things that are pleasing in His sight.

23 And this is His commandment, that we ^abelieve in ^bthe name of His Son Jesus Christ, and love one another, just as ^cHe commanded us.

24 And the one who ^akeeps His commandments ^babides in Him, and He in him. And ^cwe know by this that ^dHe abides in us, by the Spirit whom He has given us.

★**16-17**
16 a John
10:11; 15:13
b Phil. 2:17;
1 Thess. 2:8
c1 John 2:9
17 a James
2:15f. b Deut.
15:7 c1 John
4:20

18 a1 John
2:1; 3:7
b2 John 1;
3 John 1

19 a1 John
2:21

★**20**

21 a1 John
2:7 b1 John
2:28; 5:14
22 a Job
22:26f.; Matt.
7:7; 21:22;
John 9:31
b1 John 2:3
c John 8:29;
Heb. 13:21
23 a John
6:29 b John
1:12; 2:23;
3:18 c John
13:34; 15:12;
1 John 2:8
★**24** a1 John
2:3 b John
6:56; 10:38;
1 John 2:6,
24; 4:15
c John 14:17;
Rom. 8:9, 14,
16; 1 Thess.
4:8; 1 John
4:13 d1 John
2:5

3:8 *practices* = continually practices. I.e., sins as a regular way of life.

3:9 *No one . . . practices sin . . . he cannot sin.* I.e., habitually (see note on v. 8). Habitual actions indicate one's character. *seed.* I.e., the divine nature given the one born of God (cf. John 1:13; 2 Pet. 1:4). This nature prevents the Christian from habitually sinning.

3:12 *Cain.* See Gen. 4:8.

3:15 *a murderer.* The heart that is full of hate is potentially capable of murder (cf. Matt. 5:21–22).

3:16-17 Self-sacrificing love is required of the believer. Though not many are called on to sacrifice their lives, all can give sacrificially of their substance. *world's goods* = the material necessities of life.

3:20 *God is greater than our heart.* We may be either too strict or too lenient in examining our lives; therefore, John's word of comfort is: God the all-knowing is also the all-loving.

3:24 *abides.* The same word as in John 15:1-10. To abide in Christ requires keeping His commandments.

V CAUTIONS OF FELLOWSHIP,
4:1-21

A Concerning False, Lying Spirits, 4:1-6

★ 1 a 1 John
2:7 b Jer.
29:8; 1 Cor.
12:10;
1 Thess.
5:20f.;
2 Thess. 2:2
c Jer. 14:14;
2 Pet. 2:1;
1 John 2:18

2 a 1 Cor.
12:3 b 1 John
2:23 c John
1:14; 1 John
1:2

★ 3 a 1 John
2:22; 2 John
7 b 1 John
2:18, 22
c 2 Thess.
2:3-7; 1 John
2:18

★ 4 a 1 John
2:1 b 1 John
2:13 c 2 Kin.
2:16; Rom.
8:31; 1 John
3:20 d John
12:31

5 a John
15:19; 17:14,
16

6 a John
8:23; 1 John
4:4 b John
8:47; 10:3ff.;
18:37
c 1 Cor.
14:37 d John
14:17
e 1 Tim. 4:1

4 a Beloved, do not believe every b spirit, but test the spirits to see whether they are from God; because c many false prophets have gone out into the world.

2 By this you know the Spirit of God: a every spirit that b confesses that c Jesus Christ has come in the flesh is from God;

3 and every spirit that a does not confess Jesus is not from God; and this is the *spirit* of the b antichrist, of which you have heard that it is coming, and c now it is already in the world.

4 You are from God, a little children, and b have overcome them; because c greater is He who is in you than d he who is in the world.

5 a They are from the world; therefore they speak *as* from the world, and the world listens to them.

6 a We are from God; b he who knows God listens to us; c he who is not from God does not listen to us. By this we know d the spirit of truth and e the spirit of error.

B Concerning a True, Loving Spirit, 4:7-21

1 *The ground of brotherly love,* 4:7-10

★ 7-12
7 a 1 John
2:7 b 1 John
3:11 c 1 John
5:1 d 1 John
2:29 e 1 Cor.
8:3; 1 John
2:3

7 a Beloved, let us b love one another, for love is from God; and c every one who loves is d born of God and e knows God.

8 a 1 John
4:7, 16

8 The one who does not love does not know God, for a God is love.

9 a John
9:3; 1 John
4:16 b John
3:16f.;
1 John 4:10;
5:11

9 By this the love of God was manifested a in us, that b God has sent His only begotten Son into the world so that we might live through Him.

10 a Rom.
5:8, 10;
1 John 4:19
b John 3:16f.;
1 John 4:9;
5:11 c 1 John
2:2

10 In this is love, a not that we loved God, but that b He loved us and sent His Son *to be* c the propitiation for our sins.

2 *The glories of love,* 4:11-21

11 a 1 John
2:7 b 1 John
4:7

11 a Beloved, if God so loved us, b we also ought to love one another.

12 a John
1:18; 1 Tim.
6:16; 1 John.
4:20 b 1 John
2:5; 4:17f.

12 a No one has beheld God at any time; if we love one another, God abides in us, and His b love is perfected in us.

13 a Rom.
8:9; 1 John
3:24

13 a By this we know that we abide in Him and He in us, because He has given us of His Spirit.

14 a John
15:27;
1 John 1:2
b John 3:17;
4:42; 1 John
2:2

14 And we have beheld and a bear witness that the Father has b sent the Son *to be* the Savior of the world.

15 a 1 John
2:23 b Rom.
10:9; 1 John
3:23; 4:2;
5:1, 5
c 1 John
2:24; 3:24

15 a Whoever confesses that b Jesus is the Son of God, God c abides in him, and He in God.

★16 a John
6:69 b John
9:3; 1 John
4:9 c 1 John
4:7, 8
d 1 John
4:12f.

16 And a we have come to know and have believed the love which God has b for us. c God is love, and the one who d abides in love abides in God, and God abides in him.

★17 a 1 John
2:5; 4:12
b 1 John 2:28
c Matt. 10:15
d John 17:22;
1 John 2:6;
3:1, 7, 16

17 By this, a love is perfected with us, that we may have b confidence in c the day of judgment; because d as He is, so also are we in this world.

18 a Rom.
8:15; Gal.
4:30f.
b 1 John 4:12

18 There is no fear in love; but a perfect love casts out fear,

---

4:1 *do not believe every spirit.* Apparently some of John's readers were being led astray by Gnosticism (see Introduction to 1 John).

4:3 *spirit of the antichrist.* The false prophets were influenced by demonic spirits.

4:4 *He who is in you.* I.e., the Holy Spirit (cf. 3:24). *he who is in the world.* I.e., Satan (cf. John 12:31).

4:7-12 This is one of John's greatest passages. *God is love.* Love is His supreme quality. God can be known only by those who live in love. Yet we could not know how, nor be able, to love Him if He had not first loved us. If we love one another, God abides in us and His love is perfected or matured in us (v. 12).

4:16 To live a love-filled life is to be God-filled.

4:17 *confidence in the day of judgment.* The believer who has practiced love during his earthly life will be able to approach the judgment seat of Christ without any shame. Such assurance is not presumption, because *as He is, so also are we in this world;* i.e., we are like Him in love.

because fear involves punishment, and the one who fears is not [b]perfected in love.

19 [a]We love, because He first loved us.

20 [a]If someone says, "I love God," and [b]hates his brother, he is a [c]liar; for [d]the one who does not love his brother whom he has seen, [e]cannot love God whom he has not seen.

21 And [a]this commandment we have from Him, that the one who loves God [b]should love his brother also.

19 [a]1 John 4:10

20 [a]1 John 1:6, 8, 10; 2:4 [b]1 John 2:9, 11 [c]1 John 1:6 [d]1 John 3:17 [e]1 Pet. 1:8; 1 John 4:12

21 [a]Lev. 19:18; Matt. 5:43f.; 22:37ff.; John 13:34 [b]1 John 3:11

VI   CONSEQUENCES OF FELLOWSHIP, 5:1-21

A   Love for the Brethren, 5:1-3

5 [a]Whoever believes that Jesus is the Christ is [b]born of God; and whoever loves the Father [c]loves the *child* born of Him.

2 [a]By this we know that [b]we love the children of God, when we love God and observe His commandments.

3 For [a]this is the love of God, that we [b]keep His commandments; and [c]His commandments are not burdensome.

1 [a]1 John 2:22f.; 4:2, 15 [b]John 1:3; 3:3 marg.; 1 John 2:29; 5:4, 18 [c]John 8:42

2 [a]1 John 2:5 [b]1 John 3:14

3 [a]John 14:15; 2 John 6 [b]1 John 2:3 [c]Matt. 11:30; 23:4

B   Victory over the World, 5:4-5

4 For whatever is [a]born of God [b]overcomes the world; and this is the victory that has overcome the world—our faith.

5 And who is the one who overcomes the world, but he who [a]believes that Jesus is the Son of God?

4 [a]John 1:13; 3:3 marg.; 1 John 2:29; 5:1, 18 [b]1 John 2:13; 4:4

5 [a]1 John 4:15; 5:1

C   Verification of Christ's Credentials, 5:6-12

★ 6 This is the one who came [a]by water and blood, Jesus Christ;

★ 6 [a]John 19:34

not with the water only, but with the water and with the blood.

7 And it is [a]the Spirit who bears witness, because the Spirit is the truth.

8 For there are [a]three that bear witness, the Spirit and the water and the blood; and the three are in agreement.

9 [a]If we receive the witness of men, the witness of God is greater; for the witness of God is this, that [b]He has borne witness concerning His Son.

10 The one who believes in the Son of God [a]has the witness in himself; the one who does not believe God has [b]made Him a liar, because he has not believed in the witness that God has borne concerning His Son.

11 And the witness is this, that God has given us [a]eternal life, and [b]this life is in His Son.

12 [a]He who has the Son has the life; he who does not have the Son of God does not have the life.

7 [a]John 15:26; 16:13-15 [Matt. 3:16f.]

8 [a]Matt. 18:16

9 [a]John 5:34, 37; 8:18 [b]Matt. 3:17; John 5:32, 37

10 [a]Rom. 8:16; Gal. 4:6; Rev. 12:17 [b]John 3:18, 33; 1 John 1:10

11 [a]1 John 1:2; 2:25; 4:9; 5:13, 20 [b]John 1:4

12 [a]John 3:15f., 36

D   Assurance of Eternal Life, 5:13

13 [a]These things I have written to you who [b]believe in the name of the Son of God, in order that you may know that you have [c]eternal life.

13 [a]John 20:31 [b]1 John 3:23 [c]1 John 1:2; 2:25; 4:9; 5:11, 20

E   Guidance in Prayer, 5:14-17

14 And this is [a]the confidence which we have before Him, that, [b]if we ask anything according to His will, He hears us.

15 And if we know that He hears us *in* whatever we ask, [a]we know that we have the requests which we have asked from Him.

★14 [a]1 John 2:28; 3:21f. [b]Matt. 7:7; John 14:13; 1 John 3:22

15 [a]1 John 5:18, 19, 20

5:6 *by water and blood.* The water refers to the inauguration of Christ's earthly ministry at His baptism by John (Mark 1:9-11); the blood refers to the close of His earthly life at His crucifixion. Jesus proved Himself to be the Christ (Messiah) at His baptism and by pouring out His soul to death.

5:14 *according to His will.* A gracious limitation, because God's will is always best for His children.

★16 *a*James 5:15 *b*Num. 15:30; Heb. 6:4-6; 10:26 *c*Jer. 7:16; 14:11

16 If anyone sees his brother committing a sin not *leading* to death, *a*he shall ask and *God* will for him give life to those who commit sin not *leading* to death. *b*There is a sin *leading* to death; *c*I do not say that he should make request for this.

17 *a*1 John 3:4 *b*1 John 2:1f., 5:16

17 *a*All unrighteousness is sin, and *b*there is a sin not *leading* to death.

18 *a*1 John 5:15, 19, 20 *b*1 John 3:9 *c*James 1:27; Jude 21 *d*1 John 2:13 *e*John 14:30

F   Freedom from Habitual Sin, 5:18-21

18 *a*We know that *b*no one who is born of God sins; but He who was born of God *c*keeps him and *d*the evil one does not *e*touch him.

19 *a*We know that *b*we are of God, and *c*the whole world lies in *the power of* the evil one.

20 And *a*we know that *b*the Son of God has come, and has *c*given us understanding, in order that we might know *d*Him who is true, and we *e*are in Him who is true, in His Son Jesus Christ. *f*This is the true God and *g*eternal life.

21 *a*Little children, guard yourselves from *b*idols.

19 *a*1 John 5:15, 18, 20 *b*1 John 4:6 *c*John 12:31; 17:15; Gal. 1:4
20 *a*1 John 5:15, 18, 19 *b*John 8:42; 1 John 5:5 *c*Luke 24:45 *d*John 17:3; Rev. 3:7 *e*John 1:18; 14:9; 1 John 2:23; Rev. 3:7 *f*1 John 1:2 *g*1 John 5:11
★21 *a*1 John 2:1 *b*1 Cor. 10:7, 14; 1 Thess. 1:9

5:16 *sin not leading to death.* Believers can sin to the point where physical death results as the judgment of God (cf. 1 Cor. 11:30). The Greek reads *sin,* not *a sin,* in vv. 16 and 17.

5:21 *idols.* An idol is anything that substitutes for God.

INTRODUCTION TO
THE SECOND LETTER OF JOHN

AUTHOR: John   DATE: 90

Destination   *The destination of this second letter is enigmatic. Some believe that the "chosen lady" is a figurative way of designating a particular church ("chosen sister," v. 13, would then mean a different church). Others hold that the letter was addressed to an individual Christian and her family (in which case the "sister" would be her natural sister).*

Date   *The circumstances and subjects of this letter indicate that it was written about the same time as the other letters of John and from the same place, Ephesus. See the Introduction to 1 John.*

Contents   *The main teaching of 2 John is walking in Christ's commandments.*

OUTLINE OF 2 JOHN

I. Introduction and Greeting, 1-3
II. Commendation for Walking in Truth, 4
III. Commandment to Love One Another, 5-6

IV. Cautions Concerning False Teachers, 7-11
V. Concluding Remarks and Greetings, 12-13

THE SECOND LETTER OF JOHN

I INTRODUCTION AND GREETING, 1-3

★ **1** *a*Acts 11:30; 3 John 1; 1 Pet. 5:1
*b*Rom. 16:13 [Gr.]; 1 Pet. 5:13; 2 John 13 *c*2 John 5 *d*1 John 3:18; 2 John 3; 3 John 1 *e*John 8:32; 1 Tim. 2:4
2 *a*2 Pet. 1:12 *b*1 John 1:8 *c*John 14:16
3 *a*Rom. 1:7; 1 Tim. 1:2

1 *a*The elder to the *b*chosen *c*lady and her children, whom I *d*love in truth; and not only I, but also all who *e*know the truth, 2 for *a*the sake of the truth which abides *b*in us and will be *c*with us forever: 3 *a*Grace, mercy *and* peace will be with us, from God the Father and from Jesus Christ, the Son of the Father, in truth and love.

II COMMENDATION FOR WALKING IN TRUTH, 4

★ **4** *a*3 John 3f.

4 *a*I was very glad to find *some* of your children walking in truth, just as we have received commandment *to do* from the Father.

III COMMANDMENT TO LOVE ONE ANOTHER, 5-6

5 And now I ask you, lady, *a*not as writing to you a new commandment, but the one which we have had *a*from the beginning, that we *b*love one another. 6 And *a*this is love, that we walk according to His commandments. This is the commandment, *b*just as you have heard *c*from the beginning, that you should walk in it.

5 *a*1 John 2:7 *b*1 John 3:11

★ **6** *a*1 John 2:5; 5:3 *b*1 John 2:24 *c*1 John 2:7

---

1 *her children.* Either the congregation (if the *chosen lady* was a local church) or her natural offspring (if she was an individual Christian). *the truth.* I.e., the gospel message; also in v. 2.

4 *walking in truth.* Ordering one's life by the Word of God.
6 *love* is defined as obeying His commandments.

IV CAUTIONS CONCERNING FALSE TEACHERS, 7-11

★ 7 a1 John
2:26 b1 John
2:19; 4:1
c1 John 4:2;
d1 John 2:18

7 For ªmany deceivers have ᵇgone out into the world, those who ᶜdo not acknowledge Jesus Christ *as* coming in the flesh. This is ªthe deceiver and the ᵈanti-christ.

★ 8 aMark
13:9 b1 Cor.
3:8; Heb.
10:35

8 ªWatch yourselves, ᵇthat you might not lose what we have accomplished, but that you may receive a full reward.

9 aJohn
7:16; 8:31;
1 John 2:23

9 Anyone who goes too far and ªdoes not abide in the teaching of Christ, does not have God; the one who abides in the teaching, he has both the Father and the Son.

★10 a1 Kin.
13:16f.; Rom.
16:17

10 If anyone comes to you and does not bring this teaching, ªdo not receive him into *your* house, and do not give him a greeting;

★11 a1 Tim.
5:22; Jude
23

11 for the one who gives him a greeting ªparticipates in his evil deeds.

V CONCLUDING REMARKS AND GREETINGS, 12-13

★12 a3 John
13, 14 bJohn
3:29; 1 John
1:4

12 ªHaving many things to write to you, I do not want to do so with paper and ink; but I hope to come to you and speak face to face, that your ᵇjoy may be made full.

13 a2 John 1

13 The children of your ªchosen sister greet you.

---

7 *coming.* This present tense participle seems to include the past coming of Christ in flesh at the incarnation, the present continuance of His risen humanity, as well as His future coming to earth. By contrast, the perfect tense participle in 1 John 4:2 emphasizes only His incarnation. *antichrist.* See note on 1 John 2:18.

8 *we.* Better manuscripts read "you" (plural).

10 *do not receive him into your house.* I.e., do not give a false teacher hospitality.

11 *participates.* Lit., fellowships. He who gives such a person a greeting actually fellowships in the work of Antichrist.

12 *paper and ink.* The pith from papyrus reeds was cut into strips, which were laid across each other at right angles, pressed, and pasted together to form sheets of writing material. The word *ink* simply means black, for ink in ancient times was compounded of charcoal, gum, and water.

INTRODUCTION TO
THE THIRD EPISTLE OF JOHN

AUTHOR: John   DATE: 90

Characteristics of the Letter *This is a very personal letter, addressed to Gaius, which focuses on an ecclesiastical problem regarding traveling teachers. Gaius had given them hospitality, while Diotrephes, a self-assertive leader in one of the churches, had refused to receive them. John exhibits his apostolic authority in his rebuke of Diotrephes (v. 10). Demetrius, who himself may have been a traveling teacher, probably delivered the letter to Gaius.*

OUTLINE OF 3 JOHN

I. **Opening Greetings, 1**
II. **The Influence of Gaius, 2-8**
  A. His Godly Life, 2-4
  B. His Generous Treatment of Traveling
      Ministers, 5-8
III. **The Indictment of Diotrephes, 9-11**

  A. His Selfish Ambition, 9
  B. His Selfish Activities, 10-11
IV. **The Introduction of Demetrius, 12**
V. **Concluding Remarks and Benediction,**
      13-14

THE THIRD LETTER OF JOHN

I OPENING GREETINGS, 1

★ 1 ᵃ2 John
1 ᵇ1 John
3:18;
2 John 1

1 ᵃThe elder to the beloved Gaius, whom I ᵇlove in truth.

II THE INFLUENCE OF GAIUS, 2-8
A His Godly Life, 2-4

★2
3 ᵃ2 John 4
ᵇActs 1:15;
Gal. 6:10;
3 John 5, 10
★ 4 ᵃ1 Cor.
4:14f.; 2 Cor.
6:13; Gal.
4:19;
1 Thess.
2:11; 1 Tim.
1:2; 2 Tim.
1:2; Philem.
10; 1 John
2:1
ᵇ2 John 3

2 Beloved, I pray that in all respects you may prosper and be in good health, just as your soul prospers.
3 For I ᵃwas very glad when ᵇbrethren came and bore witness to your truth, *that is,* how you ᵃare walking in truth.
4 I have no greater joy than this, to hear of ᵃmy children ᵇwalking in the truth.

B His Generous Treatment of
Traveling Ministers, 5-8

★ 5 ᵃActs
1:15; Gal.
6:10; 3 John
3, 10 ᵇRom.
12:13; Heb.
13:2
★ 6 ᵃActs
15:3; Titus
3:13 ᵇCol.
1:10;
1 Thess. 2:12

★ 7 ᵃJohn
15:21; Acts
5:41; Phil.
2:9 ᵇActs
20:33, 35

5 Beloved, you are acting faithfully in whatever you accomplish for the ᵃbrethren, and especially *when they are* ᵇstrangers;
6 and they bear witness to your love before the church; and you will do well to ᵃsend them on their way in a manner ᵇworthy of God.
7 For they went out for the sake of ᵃthe Name, ᵇaccepting nothing from the Gentiles.

---

1 *elder.* See note on 1 Tim. 3:1.
2 *be in good health.* I.e., physical health. Perhaps Gaius had been ill.
4 *my children.* I.e., beneficiaries of John's ministry, whom he had probably led to Christ.
5 *for the brethren, and . . . strangers.* Gaius had aided both "brethren" and "strangers," the latter being the more difficult and therefore the more praiseworthy form of hospitality (cf. Heb. 13:2). Traveling evangelists and teachers

were dependent on men like Gaius for shelter and sustenance.
6 *send them on their way.* I.e., to help them on their journey with food, money, arrangements for companions, means of travel, etc.
7 *accepting nothing from the Gentiles.* These traveling missionaries declined to receive help from those who were not converted, lest they should appear to be selling the gospel.

8 Therefore we ought to support such men, that we may be fellow workers with the truth.

what is evil, but what is good. [b]The one who does good is of God; [c]the one who does evil has not seen God.

III THE INDICTMENT OF DIOTREPHES, 9–11
A His Selfish Ambition, 9

9 [a]2 John 9 marg.

9 I wrote something to the church; but Diotrephes, who loves to [a]be first among them, does not accept what we say.

IV THE INTRODUCTION OF DEMETRIUS, 12

12 Demetrius [a]has received a good testimony from everyone, and from the truth itself; and we also bear witness, and [b]you know that our witness is true.

12 [a]Acts 6:3; 1 Tim. 3:7 [b]John 19:35; 21:24

B His Selfish Activities, 10–11

★10 [a]2 John 12 [b]2 John 10; 3 John 5 [c]Acts 1:15; Gal. 6:10; 3 John 3, 5 [d]John 9:34

11 [a]Ps. 34:14; 37:27 [b]1 John 2:29; 3:10 [c]1 John 3:6

10 For this reason, [a]if I come, I will call attention to his deeds which he does, unjustly accusing us with wicked words; and not satisfied with this, neither does he himself [b]receive the [c]brethren, and he forbids those who desire to do so, and [d]puts them out of the church.

11 Beloved, [a]do not imitate

V CONCLUDING REMARKS AND BENEDICTION, 13–14

13 [a]I had many things to write to you, but I am not willing to write them to you with pen and ink;

14 but I hope to see you shortly, and we shall speak face to face. [a]Peace be to you. The friends greet you. Greet the friends [b]by name.

★13 [a]2 John 12

★14 [a]John 20:19, 21, 26; Eph. 6:23; 1 Pet. 5:14 [b]John 10:3

---

10 puts them out of the church. Some sort of exclusion, whether formal excommunication or not.

13 pen. This pen was a reed pointed at the end.
14 Peace be to you. In some texts and translations this phrase begins a new verse (15).

INTRODUCTION TO
THE LETTER OF JUDE

AUTHOR: Jude   DATE: 70–80

Authorship *Jude identifies himself as the brother of James (v. 1), the leader of the Jerusalem church (Acts 15), and the half brother of the Lord Jesus. Jude is listed among Christ's half brothers in Matthew 13:55 and Mark 6:3. Although, by his own statement, he intended to write a treatise on salvation, pressing circumstances required him to deal instead with the false teachers (v. 3).*

Purpose *This letter was written to defend the apostolic faith against false teachings which were arising in the churches. Alarming advances were being made by an incipient form of Gnosticism— not ascetic, like that attacked by Paul in Colossians, but antinomian. The Gnostics viewed everything material as evil and everything spiritual as good. They therefore cultivated their "spiritual" lives and allowed their flesh to do anything it liked, with the result that they were guilty of all kinds of lawlessness. (See "Gnosticism" in the Introduction to 1 John.)*

Extrabiblical Quotations *In verses 14 and 15, Jude quotes the pseudepigraphal apocalypse of 1 Enoch and in verse 9 alludes to a reference in another pseudepigraphal book, The Assumption of Moses. This does not mean that he considered these books to be inspired as the canonical Scriptures were. Paul quoted from heathen poets without implying their inspiration (Acts 17:28; 1 Cor. 15:33; Titus 1:12).*

Readership *The readers are not identified, but we know that they were beset by false teachers who were immoral, covetous, proud, and divisive.*

Contents *Condemning the heretics in no uncertain terms, Jude exhorts his readers to "contend earnestly for the faith" (v. 3).*

OUTLINE OF JUDE

THE LETTER OF JUDE

I THE SALUTATION AND PURPOSE, 1-4

★ 1 ᵃMatt.
13:55; Mark
6:3; [Luke
6:16; John
14:22; Acts
1:13?]
ᵇRom. 1:1
ᶜRom. 1:6f.
ᵈJohn
17:11f.;
1 Pet. 1:5;
Jude 21
2 ᵃGal.
6:16; 1 Tim.
1:2 ᵇ1 Pet.
1:2; 2 Pet.
1:2
★ 3 ᵃHeb.
6:9; Jude 1,
17, 20 ᵇTitus
1:4 ᶜ1 Tim.
6:12 ᵈActs
6:7; Jude 20
ᵉ2 Pet. 2:21
ᶠActs 9:13
★ 4 ᵃGal.
2:4; 2 Tim.
3:6 ᵇ1 Pet.
2:8 ᶜActs
11:23
ᵈ2 Pet. 2:7
ᵉ2 Tim. 2:12;
Titus 1:16;
2 Pet. 2:1;
1 John 2:22

1 ᵃJude, a ᵇbond-servant of Jesus Christ, and brother of James, to ᶜthose who are the called, beloved in God the Father, and ᵈkept for Jesus Christ:

2 ᵃMay mercy and peace and love ᵇbe multiplied to you.

3 ᵃBeloved, while I was making every effort to write you about our ᵇcommon salvation, I felt the necessity to write to you appealing that you ᶜcontend earnestly for ᵈthe faith which was once for all ᵉdelivered to ᶠthe saints.

4 For certain persons have ᵃcrept in unnoticed, those who were long beforehand ᵇmarked out for this condemnation, ungodly persons who turn ᶜthe grace of our God into ᵈlicentiousness and ᵉdeny our only Master and Lord, Jesus Christ.

II EXPOSURE OF THE FALSE TEACHERS, 5-16
A Their Doom, 5-7

★ 5 ᵃ2 Pet.
1:12f.; 3:1f.
ᵇ1 John 2:20
ᶜ1 Cor. 10:5-
10; Heb.
3:16f.

5 Now I desire to ᵃremind you, though ᵇyou know all things once for all, that the Lord, ᶜafter saving a people out of the land of Egypt, subsequently destroyed those who did not believe.

6 And ᵃangels who did not keep their own domain, but abandoned their proper abode, He has ᵇkept in eternal bonds under darkness for the judgment of the great day.

7 Just as ᵃSodom and Gomorrah and the ᵇcities around them, since they in the same way as these indulged in gross immorality and ᶜwent after strange flesh, are exhibited as an ᵈexample, in undergoing the ᵉpunishment of eternal fire.

★ 6 ᵃ2 Pet.
2:4 ᵇ2 Pet.
2:9

7 ᵃ2 Pet.
2:6 ᵇDeut.
29:23; Hos.
11:8 ᶜ2 Pet.
2:2 ᵈ2 Pet.
2:6 ᵉMatt.
25:41;
2 Thess.
1:8f.; 2 Pet.
3:7

B Their Denunciation, 8-10

8 Yet in the same manner these men, also by dreaming, ᵃdefile the flesh, and ᵃreject authority, and ᵃrevile angelic majesties.

9 But ᵃMichael ᵇthe archangel, when he disputed with the devil and argued about ᶜthe body of Moses, did not dare pronounce against him a railing judgment, but said, "ᵈTHE LORD REBUKE YOU."

10 But ᵃthese men revile the things which they do not understand; and ᵇthe things which know by instinct, ᵃlike unreasoning animals, by these things they are destroyed.

★ 8 ᵃ2 Pet.
2:10

9 ᵃDan.
10:13, 21;
12:1; Rev.
12:7
ᵇ1 Thess.
4:16; 2 Pet.
2:11 ᶜDeut.
34:6 ᵈZech.
3:2
10 ᵃ2 Pet.
2:12 ᵇPhil.
3:19

---

1 Jude addresses the *called;* i.e., all Christians who have been called to a knowledge of God through Christ. They are *beloved in God* and *kept for Jesus Christ* at His second coming.

3 *contend earnestly for the faith which was once for all delivered.* I.e., stand for the body of truth once for all given, not to be added to or subtracted from (cf. Gal. 1:23).

4 *deny our only Master and Lord, Jesus Christ.* The Greek word here for "Master" may be translated "despot" (cf. Acts 4:24, 1 Tim. 6:1), and is applied here to Jesus. To deny Jesus as Lord was to disbelieve the most basic Christian tenet.

5 *destroyed those who did not believe.* The possibility of lapsing is illustrated by the disbelieving Israelites who were saved out of Egypt but subsequently destroyed.

6 *angels who did not keep their own domain.* A reference to that group of fallen angels whom Satan persuaded to cohabit with women (Gen. 6:1-4) and who were confined immediately because of the gross nature of that sin. The apocryphal book of Enoch describes their dramatic end. See note on 2 Pet. 2:4.

8 *angelic majesties.* Refers to angels (cf. 2 Pet. 2:10), though it may include leaders of the church as well.

C　Their Description, 11–16

*11 aGen.
4:3-8, Heb.
11:4; 1 John
3:12 bNum.
31:16; 2 Pet.
2:15; Rev.
2:14 cNum.
16:1-3, 31-35

11　Woe to them! For they have gone ᵃthe way of Cain, and for pay they have rushed headlong into ᵇthe error of Balaam, and ᶜperished in the rebellion of Korah.

*12 a1 Cor.
11:20ff.;
2 Pet. 2:13
and marg.
bEzek. 34:2,
8, 10 cProv.
25:14; 2 Pet.
2:17 dEph.
4:14 eMatt.
15:13

12　These men are those who are hidden reefs ᵃin your love feasts when they feast with you ᵇwithout fear, caring for themselves; ᶜclouds without water, ᵈcarried along by winds; autumn trees without fruit, doubly dead, ᵉuprooted;

13 aIs. 57:20
bPhil. 3:19
c2 Pet. 2:17;
Jude 6

13　ᵃwild waves of the sea, casting up ᵇtheir own shame like foam; wandering stars, ᶜfor whom the black darkness has been reserved forever.

*14 aGen.
5:18, 21ff.
bDeut. 33:2;
Dan. 7:10;
Matt. 16:27;
Heb. 12:22

14　And about these also ᵃEnoch, in the seventh generation from Adam, prophesied, saying, "ᵇBehold, the Lord came with many thousands of His holy ones,

15 a2 Pet.
2:6ff. b1 Tim.
1:9

15　ᵃto execute judgment upon all, and to convict all the ungodly of all their ungodly deeds which they have done in an ungodly way, and of all the harsh things which ᵇungodly sinners have spoken against Him."

16 aNum.
16:11, 41;
1 Cor. 10:10
b2 Pet. 2:10;
Jude 18
c2 Pet. 2:18
d2 Pet. 2:3

16　These are ᵃgrumblers, finding fault, ᵇfollowing after their own lusts; they speak ᶜarrogantly, flattering people ᵈfor the sake of gaining an advantage.

III　EXHORTATIONS TO BELIEVERS, 17–23

17 aJude 3
b2 Pet. 3:2
cHeb. 2:3

17　But you, ᵃbeloved, ᵇought to remember the words that were spoken beforehand by ᶜthe apostles of our Lord Jesus Christ,

18 aActs
20:29; 1 Tim.
4:1; 2 Tim.
3:1f.; 4:3;
2 Pet. 3:3
bJude 4, 16

18　that they were saying to you, "ᵃIn the last time there shall be mockers, ᵇfollowing after their own ungodly lusts."

*19 a1 Cor.
2:14f.; James
3:15

19　These are the ones who cause divisions, ᵃworldly-minded, devoid of the Spirit.

20 aJude 3
bCol. 2:7;
1 Thess. 5:11
cEph. 6:18

20　But you, ᵃbeloved, ᵇbuilding yourselves up on your most holy ᵃfaith; ᶜpraying in the Holy Spirit;

21 aTitus
2:13; Heb.
9:28; 2 Pet.
3:12

21　keep yourselves in the love of God, ᵃwaiting anxiously for the mercy of our Lord Jesus Christ to eternal life.

22　And have mercy on some, who are doubting;

*22

23 aAmos
4:11; Zech.
3:2; 1 Cor.
3:15 bZech.
3:3f.; Rev.
3:4

23　save others, ᵃsnatching them out of the fire; and on some have mercy with fear, ᵇhating even the garment polluted by the flesh.

IV　THE BENEDICTION, 24–25

*24-25
24 aRom.
16:25
b2 Cor. 4:14
c1 Pet. 4:13

24　ᵃNow to Him who is able to keep you from stumbling, and to ᵇmake you stand in the presence of His glory blameless with ᶜgreat joy,

25 aJohn
5:44; 1 Tim.
1:17 bLuke
1:47 cRom.
11:36 dHeb.
13:8

25　to the ᵃonly ᵇGod our Savior, through Jesus Christ our Lord, ᶜbe glory, majesty, dominion and authority, ᵈbefore all time and now and forever. Amen.

---

11 the way of Cain. I.e., his rejection of God's provision for acceptance with Himself (Gen. 4:1–12). Today, it is the rejection of God's offer of forgiveness through Christ. the error of Balaam. Balaam hired himself out as a prophet and epitomizes deceit and covetousness (cf. Num. 22–24; 2 Pet. 2:15; Rev. 2:14). the rebellion of Korah. The sin of Korah was rebellion against duly constituted authority (Num. 16).

12 love feasts. These fellowship meals were eaten in connection with the Lord's Supper (see note on 1 Cor. 11:20). Pride, greed, and rebellion summarize the iniquities of the ungodly men (v. 4) who corrupted these love-feasts.

14 Enoch. Though this prophecy is found in the noncanonical book of Enoch (1:9), the original prophecy was uttered by the Enoch of the Bible (Gen. 5:19-24; cf. Heb. 11:5-6) and was later expanded and incorporated in the book of Enoch.

19 ones who cause divisions. I.e., heretical groups, who are worldly-minded or, as they are called in 1 Cor. 2:14, "natural." Jude declares that these false teachers were not truly redeemed (cf. Rom. 8:9).

22 have mercy on. Some manuscripts read "convince." who are doubting. Thus the verse says, "Have mercy on, or convince, those who are doubting."

24-25 One of the great benedictions of the N.T. Savior. God is the Savior of the O.T. and in the N.T. that title survives, occurring seven times.

INTRODUCTION TO
THE REVELATION TO JOHN

AUTHOR: John   DATE: 90's

Authorship *According to the book itself the author's name was John (1:4, 9, 22:8), a prophet (22:9). Traditionally this John has been identified as John the apostle, the son of Zebedee (see the Introduction to 1 John). That the style of the Revelation is different from that of the Gospel and the three epistles of John does not prove that the Revelation was written by a different John. The nature of apocalyptic literature, the fact that this revelation was given in a vision, and the circumstances of John's being a prisoner could easily account for the differences in style.*

Date *Clearly the Revelation was written in a period when Christians were threatened by Rome, undoubtedly by pressure to make them recant their faith and accept the cult of emperor worship. Some maintain that the book was written during Nero's persecution of Christians after the burning of Rome in A.D. 64. However, the more probable date is during the harsh reign of that warped personality Domitian (A.D. 81-96). This later date for the book was held by the church father Irenaeus and other early Christian writers, and it agrees better with the picture of complacency and defection of the churches in chapters 2 and 3. This dating is widely accepted by modern scholars.*

Interpretation *There are four principal viewpoints concerning the interpretation of this book: (1) the preterist, which views the prophecies of the book as having been fulfilled in the early history of the Church; (2) the historical, which understands the book as portraying a panorama of the history of the Church from the days of John to the end of time; (3) the idealist, which considers the book a pictorial unfolding of great principles in constant conflict, without reference to actual events; and (4) the futurist, which views most of the book (chaps. 4-22) as prophecy yet to be fulfilled. The futurist is the viewpoint taken in these notes, based on the principle of interpreting the text plainly.*
    The book is a revelation, or apocalypse (1:1), and as such is expected to be understood. Much of it is frighteningly clear. Some symbols are explained (1:20; 17:1, 15), others are not. It is always important to notice carefully the words "like," "as," and "as it were" (6:1; 9:7), for these words indicate a comparison, not an identification.

Contents *This is the revelation of Jesus Christ, and He is the center of the entire book (1:1). In His risen glory (chap. 1) He directs His churches on earth (chaps. 2-3). He is the slain and risen Lamb to whom all worship is directed (chaps. 4-5). The judgments of the coming seven-year period of tribulation on this earth are the display of the wrath of the Lamb (chaps. 6-19; see especially 6:16-17), and the return of Christ to this earth is described in 19:11-21. The millennial reign of Christ is described in chapter 20, and the new heavens and new earth in chapters 21 and 22.*
    The outline of the book is indicated in 1:19. The things which John had seen include the vision of the risen Christ in chapter 1. The "things which are" comprise the letters to the seven churches of Asia Minor in chapters 2 and 3. The "things which shall take place after these things" are the prophecies of chapters 4-22.

OUTLINE OF REVELATION

I. The Prologue, 1:1-8
  A. The Superscription, 1:1-3
  B. The Salutation, 1:4-8
II. "The Things Which You Have Seen,"
    1:9-20
  A. Circumstances of the Vision, 1:9-11
  B. Content of the Vision, 1:12-16
  C. Consequences of the Vision, 1:17-20
III. "The Things Which Are," 2:1-3:22
  A. The Message to Ephesus, 2:1-7
  B. The Message to Smyrna, 2:8-11
  C. The Message to Pergamum, 2:12-17
  D. The Message to Thyatira, 2:18-29

  E. The Message to Sardis, 3:1-6
  F. The Message to Philadelphia, 3:7-13
  G. The Message to Laodicea, 3:14-22
IV. "The Things Which Shall Take Place
    After These Things," 4:1-22:5
  A. The Tribulation Period, 4:1-19:21
    1. The throne in heaven, 4:1-11
      a. The throne, 4:1-3
      b. The throng, 4:4-8
      c. The theme, 4:9-11
    2. The scroll in heaven, 5:1-14
      a. The scroll, 5:1
      b. The search, 5:2-5

THE REVELATION TO JOHN

I THE PROLOGUE, 1:1-8

A The Superscription, 1:1-3

★ **1** *a*John 17:8; Rev. 5:7 *b*Rev. 22:6 *c*Dan. 2:28f.; Rev. 1:19 *d*Rev. 17:1; 19:9f.; 21:9; 22:16 *e*Rev. 1:4, 9; 22:8

1 The Revelation of Jesus Christ, which *a*God gave Him to *b*show to His bond-servants, *c*the things which must shortly take place; and He sent and communicated *it* *d*by His angel to His bond-servant *e*John,

2 *a*1 Cor. 1:6; Rev. 1:9; 6:9; 12:17; 20:4 *b*Rev. 12:17

2 who bore witness to *a*the word of God and to *b*the testimony of Jesus Christ, *even* to all that he saw.

★ **3** *a*Luke 11:28; Rev. 22:7 *b*Rom. 13:11; Rev. 3:11; 22:7, 10, 12

3 *a*Blessed is he who reads and those who hear the words of the prophecy, and heed the things which are written in it; *b*for the time is near.

B The Salutation, 1:4-8

★ **4** *a*Rev. 1:1, 9; 22:8 *b*Rev. 1:11, 20 *c*Acts 2:9 *d*Rom. 1:7 *e*Ex. 3:14; Is. 41:4; Heb. 13:8; Rev. 1:8, 17; 4:8; 16:5 *f*Is. 11:2; Rev. 3:1; 4:5; 5:6; 8:2

4 *a*John to *b*the seven churches that are in *c*Asia: *d*Grace to you and peace, from *e*Him who is and who was and who is to come; and from *f*the seven Spirits who are before His throne;

★ **5** *a*John 8:14; 18:37; 1 Tim. 6:13; Rev. 3:14; 19:11 *b*1 Cor. 15:20; Col. 1:18 *c*Dan. 2:47; 1 Tim. 6:15; Rev. 17:14; 19:16 *d*Rom. 8:37

5 and from Jesus Christ, *a*the faithful witness, the *b*first-born of the dead, and the *c*ruler of the kings of the earth. To Him who *d*loves us, and released us from our sins by His blood,

6 and He has made us *to be* a *a*kingdom, *a*priests to *b*His God and Father; *c*to Him *be* the glory and the dominion forever and ever. Amen.

6 *a*Ex. 19:6 *b*Rom. 15:6 *c*Rom. 11:36

7 *a*BEHOLD, HE IS COMING WITH THE CLOUDS, and *b*every eye will see Him, even those who pierced Him; and all the tribes of the earth will *c*mourn over Him. Even so. Amen.

★ **7** *a*Dan. 7:13; Matt. 16:27f. *b*Zech. 12:10; John 19:37 *c*Luke 23:28

8 "I am *a*the Alpha and the Omega," says the *b*Lord God, "*c*who is and who was and who is to come, the Almighty."

★ **8** *a*Is. 41:4; Rev. 21:6; 22:13 *b*Rev. 4:8; 11:17; 15:3

II "THE THINGS WHICH YOU HAVE SEEN," 1:9-20

A Circumstances of the Vision, 1:9-11

★ **9** *a*Rev. 1:1 *b*Acts 1:15 *c*Matt. 20:23; Acts 14:22; 2 Cor. 1:7; Phil. 4:14 *d*2 Tim. 2:12 *e*2 Thess. 3:5 *f*Rev. 1:2

9 *a*I, John, your *b*brother and *c*fellow partaker in the tribulation and *d*kingdom and *e*perseverance which are in Jesus, was on the island called Patmos, *f*because of the word of God and the testimony of Jesus.

★ **10** *a*Matt. 22:43 *b*Acts 20:7 *c*Rev. 4:1

10 I was *a*in the Spirit on *b*the Lord's day, and I heard behind me a loud voice *c*like *the sound* of a trumpet,

11 *a*Rev. 1:2, 19 *b*Rev. 1:4, 20 *c*Rev. 2:1 *d*Rev. 2:8 *e*Rev. 2:12 *f*Acts 16:14 *g*Rev. 3:1, 4 *h*Rev. 3:7 *i*Col. 2:1; Rev. 3:14

11 saying, "*a*Write in a book what you see, and send *it* to the

---

1:1 *of Jesus Christ* = from Jesus Christ. Jesus Christ gave this revelation from God, by means of an angel, to John. *shortly.* This word does not indicate that the events described in this book will necessarily occur soon, but that when they do begin to happen they will come to pass swiftly (the same Greek word is translated "speedily" in Luke 18:8).

1:3 *Blessed.* There are 7 beatitudes in Revelation. This is the first; the others are found at 14:13; 16:15; 19:9; 20:6; 22:7, 14. John wanted the book read at once, and preferably aloud, in the churches.

1:4 *seven.* The number 7, occurring 54 times in the book, appears more frequently than any other number. In the Bible it is associated with completion, fulfillment, and perfection (cf. Gen. 2:2; Ex. 20:10; Lev. 14:7; Acts 6:3). In the Revelation there are 7 churches and 7 spirits (1:4), 7 lampstands (1:12), 7 stars (1:16), 7 seals on the scroll (5:1), 7 horns and 7 eyes of the Lamb (5:6), 7 angels and 7 trumpets (8:2), 7

thunders (10:3), 7 heads of the dragon (12:3), 7 heads of the beast (13:1), 7 golden bowls (15:7), and 7 kings (17:10). *the seven Spirits.* Many understand this to refer to the Holy Spirit in His perfect fullness (see Isa. 11:2; Rev. 4:5), though some take this as a reference to 7 angels who are before God's throne.

1:5 *first-born of the dead.* I.e., Christ was the first to receive a resurrection body which is immortal. See Col. 1:15 where He is designated the firstborn of every creature (cf. Ps. 89:27).

1:7 See Matt. 24:29-30.

1:8 *the Alpha and the Omega.* The first and last letters of the Greek alphabet, indicating that the Lord God is the beginning and end of all things.

1:9 *Patmos.* A small island in the Aegean Sea, SW. of Ephesus.

1:10 *in the Spirit.* I.e., in a state of spiritual ecstasy.

[b]seven churches: to [c]Ephesus and to [d]Smyrna and to [e]Pergamum and to [f]Thyatira and to [g]Sardis and to [h]Philadelphia and to [i]Laodicea."

B   Content of the Vision,
1:12–16

★12 [a]Ex. 25:37; 37:23; Zech. 4:2; Rev. 1:20; 2:1

12 And I turned to see the voice that was speaking with me. And having turned I saw [a]seven golden lampstands;

★13 [a]Rev. 2:1 [b]Ezek. 1:26; Dan. 7:13; 10:16; Rev. 14:14 [c]Dan. 10:5 [d]Rev. 15:6

13 and [a]in the middle of the lampstands one [b]like a son of man, [c]clothed in a robe reaching to the feet, and [d]girded across His breast with a golden girdle.

★14 [a]Dan. 7:9 [b]Dan. 7:9; 10:6; Rev. 2:18; 19:12

14 And His head and His [a]hair were white like white wool, like snow; and [b]His eyes were like a flame of fire;

15 [a]Ezek. 1:7; Dan. 10:6; Rev. 2:18 [b]Ezek. 43:2; Rev. 14:2; 19:6

15 and His [a]feet were like burnished bronze, when it has been caused to glow in a furnace, and His [b]voice was like the sound of many waters.

★16 [a]Rev. 1:20; 2:1; 3:1 [b]Is. 49:2; Heb. 4:12; Rev. 2:12, 16; 19:15 [c]Matt. 17:2; Rev. 10:1 [d]Judg. 5:31

16 And in His right hand He held [a]seven stars; and out of His mouth came a [b]sharp two-edged sword; and His [c]face was like [d]the sun shining in its strength.

C   Consequences of the Vision,
1:17–20

17 And when I saw Him, I [a]fell at His feet as a dead man. And He [b]laid His right hand upon me, saying, "[c]Do not be afraid; [d]I am the first and the last,

18 and the [a]living One; and I [b]was dead, and behold, I am alive forevermore, and I have [c]the keys of death and of Hades.

19 "[a]Write therefore [b]the things which you have seen, and the things which are, and the things which shall take place [c]after these things.

20 "As for the [a]mystery of the [b]seven stars which you saw in My right hand, and the [c]seven golden lampstands: the [b]seven stars are the angels of [d]the seven churches, and the seven [e]lampstands are the seven churches.

★17 [a]Dan. 8:17; 10:9, 10, 15 [b]Dan. 8:18; 10:10, 12 [c]Matt. 14:27; 17:7 [d]Is. 41:4; 44:6; 48:12; Rev. 2:8; 22:13
★18 [a]Luke 24:5; Rev. 4:9f [b]Rom. 6:9; Rev. 2:8; 10:6; 15:7 [c]Job 38:17; Matt. 11:23; 16:19; Rev. 9:1; 20:1
★19 [a]Rev. 1:11 [b]Rev. 1:12-16 [c]Rev. 4:1
20 [a]Rom. 11:25 [b]Rev. 1:16; 2:1; 3:1 [c]Ex. 25:37; 37:23; Zech. 4:2; Rev. 1:12; 2:1 [d]Rev. 1:4, 11 [e]Matt. 5:14f.

III   "THE THINGS WHICH ARE,"
2:1–3:22

A   The Message to Ephesus,
2:1–7

★ 1 [a]Rev. 1:11 [b]Rev. 1:16 [c]Rev. 1:12f.

2 "To the angel of the church in [a]Ephesus write:

1:12 *lampstands.* These represent the 7 churches mentioned in v. 11 (see also v. 20).

1:13 Christ's clothing designates Him as priest and judge. Notice the description of the Ancient of Days in Dan. 7:9.

1:14 *His eyes were like a flame of fire.* Compare the figure used in 1 Cor. 3:13 in relation to judgment.

1:16 *in His right hand He held seven stars.* The right hand is the place of honor (cf. Eph. 1:20). The stars are the "angels of the seven churches" (v. 20). The word "angel" may mean a superhuman being, implying that each church has a special guardian angel or, more likely here, it refers to the human leader of each local church (see Luke 9:52 and Jas. 2:25 where the word "angel," translated "messenger," is used of human beings). *sword.* A symbol both of the truth and of the severity of the Word of God (Heb. 4:12).

1:17 *I am the first and the last.* In v. 8 God is called the Alpha and Omega. Here Christ gives Himself a similar title.

1:18 *the keys of death and of Hades.* The keys denote the authority of Christ over physical death and Hades, the place which temporarily holds the immaterial part of the unbeliever

between death and the ultimate casting into the lake of fire (see Rev. 20:14).

1:19 This verse gives the basic outline of the book: (1) *things which you* (John) *have seen,* as recorded in chapter 1; (2) *things which are;* i.e., the present state of the churches (chaps. 2–3); and (3) *things which shall take place after these things.* The third section clearly begins with 4:1, since the same phrase is used there.

2:1 The 7 churches addressed in chapters 2 and 3 were actual churches of John's day. But they also represent types of churches in all generations. This idea is supported by the fact that only seven were selected out of the many that existed and flourished in John's time, and by the statement at the close of each letter that the Spirit was speaking to the churches (vv. 7, 11, etc.). *Ephesus.* Under Caesar Augustus, Ephesus became the capital of the Roman province called Asia, which today is the western portion of Turkey (Pergamum had been the capital earlier). It was the residence of the apostle John before and after his exile on Patmos, and it was the site of the great temple of Artemis (Latin, Diana) (see the Introduction to Ephesians).

The One who holds *b*the seven stars in His right hand, the One who walks *c*among the seven golden lampstands, says this:

2 '*a*I know your deeds and your toil and perseverance, and that you cannot endure evil men, and you *b*put to the test those who call themselves *c*apostles, and they are not, and you found them *to be* false;

3 and you have perseverance and have endured *a*for My name's sake, and have not grown weary.

4 'But I have *this* against you, that you have *a*left your first love.

5 'Remember therefore from where you have fallen, and *a*repent and *b*do the deeds you did at first; or else I am coming to you, and will remove your *c*lampstand out of its place—unless you repent.

6 'Yet this you do have, that you hate the deeds of the *a*Nicolaitans, which I also hate.

7 '*a*He who has an ear, let him hear what the Spirit says to the churches. *b*To him who overcomes, I will grant to eat of *c*the tree of life, which is in the *d*Paradise of God.'

B The Message to Smyrna, 2:8-11

8 "And to the angel of the church in *a*Smyrna write:

*b*The first and the last, who *c*was dead, and has come to life, says this:

9 'I know your *a*tribulation and your *b*poverty (but you are *b*rich), and the blasphemy by those who *c*say they are Jews and are not, but are a synagogue of *d*Satan.

10 'Do not fear what you are about to suffer. Behold, the devil is about to cast some of you into prison, that you may be *a*tested, and you will have tribulation *b*ten days. Be *c*faithful until death, and I will give you *d*the crown of life.

11 '*a*He who has an ear, let him hear what the Spirit says to the churches. *b*He who overcomes shall not be hurt by the *c*second death.'

C The Message to Pergamum, 2:12-17

12 "And to the angel of the church in *a*Pergamum write:

The One who has *b*the sharp two-edged sword says this:

13 'I know where you dwell, where *a*Satan's throne is; and you hold fast My name, and did not deny *b*My faith, even in the days of Antipas, My *c*witness, My *d*faithful one, who was killed among you, *e*where Satan dwells.

14 'But *a*I have a few things against you, because you have

---

2 *a*Rev. 2:19; 3:1, 8, 15 *b*John 6:6; 1 John 4:1 *c*2 Cor. 11:13

★ **3** *a*John 15:21

★ **4** *a*Jer. 2:2; Matt. 24:12
★ **5** *a*Rev. 2:16, 22; 3:3, 19 *b*Heb. 10:32; Rev. 2:2 *c*Matt. 5:14ff.; Phil. 2:15; Rev. 1:20

★ **6** *a*Rev. 2:15

★ **7** *a*Matt. 11:15; Rev. 2:17; 3:6, 13, 22; 13:9 *b*Rev. 2:11, 17, 26; 3:5, 12, 21; 21:7 *c*Gen. 2:9; 3:22; Prov. 3:18; 11:30; 13:12; 15:4; Rev. 22:2, 14 *d*Ezek. 31:8 [Septuagint]; Luke 23:43
★ **8** *a*Rev. 1:11 *b*Rev. 1:17 *c*Rev. 1:18

9 *a*Rev. 1:9 *b*2 Cor. 6:10; 8:9; James 2:5 *c*Rev. 3:9 *d*Matt. 4:10; Rev. 2:13, 24

★**10** *a*Rev. 3:10; 13:14ff. *b*Dan. 1:12, 14 *c*Rev. 2:13; 12:11; 17:14 *d*1 Cor. 9:25; Rev. 3:11

★**11** *a*Matt. 11:15; Rev. 2:7, 17, 29; 3:6, 13, 22; 13:9 *b*Rev. 2:7, 17, 26; 3:5, 12, 21; 21:7 *c*Rev. 20:6, 14; 21:8

★**12** *a*Rev. 1:11 *b*Rev. 1:16; 2:16
★**13** *a*Matt. 4:10; Rev. 2:13, 24 *b*1 Tim. 5:8; Rev. 14:12 *c*Acts 22:20; Rev. 1:5; 11:3; 17:6 *d*Rev. 2:10; 12:11; 17:14 *e*Rev. 2:9
★**14** *a*Rev. 2:20 *b*2 Pet. 2:15 *c*Acts 15:29; 1 Cor. 10:20; Rev. 2:20

2:3 *not grown weary.* I.e., have not given up.
2:4 *you have left your first love.* "Left" implies an intentional, not accidental, act. More than 30 years before, this church had been commended for its love (Eph. 1:15-16).
2:5 *remove your lampstand.* I.e., remove the usefulness of that local church.
2:6 *the Nicolaitans.* Followers of Nicolas (see Acts 6:5), according to early church fathers. These were apparently a sect which advocated license in matters of Christian conduct, including free love, though some understand from the meaning of the name ("conquering of the people") that they were a group which promoted a clerical hierarchy (see Rev. 2:15 also).
2:7 *To him who overcomes.* Not a reference to an especially spiritual group among the believers, but to all true Christians (cf. 1 John 5:5).
2:8 *Smyrna.* A seaport city about 35 miles N. of Ephesus (called Izmir today). It was a center of the imperial cult of Rome.

2:10 *you will have tribulation ten days.* This may refer to a ten-day period of intense persecution to come, or it may indicate ten periods of persecution from Nero to Diocletian. *crown of life.* The reward of one who is faithful under trial or unto death (see Jas. 1:12 and note on 1 Cor. 3:14).
2:11 *the second death.* I.e., eternal separation from God in the lake of fire (see 20:14; also note on Rom. 6:2).
2:12 *Pergamum.* About 45 miles N. of Smyrna, it boasted one of the finest libraries of antiquity and was the place where parchment was first used. It had once been the capital of the Roman province of Asia.
2:13 *where Satan dwells.* Lit., where Satan's throne is—a reference to Pergamum's worship either of the Roman emperor or of Zeus at his altar on the local acropolis (or both).
2:14 *the teaching of Balaam.* See notes on 2 Pet. 2:15 and Jude 11.

there some who hold the [b]teaching of Balaam, who kept teaching Balak to put a stumbling block before the sons of Israel, [c]to eat things sacrificed to idols, and to commit *acts of* immorality.

15 aRev. 2:6

15 'Thus you also have some who in the same way hold the teaching of the [a]Nicolaitans.

16 aRev. 2:5
bRev. 22:7,
20 c2 Thess.
2:8; Rev.
1:16

16 '[a]Repent therefore; or else [b]I am coming to you quickly, and I will make war against them with [c]the sword of My mouth.

★17 aRev.
2:7 bJohn
6:49f; cIs.
56:5; 62:2,
65:15; dRev.
14:3; 19:12

17 '[a]He who has an ear, let him hear what the Spirit says to the churches. [a]To him who overcomes, to him I will give *some* of the hidden [b]manna, and I will give him a white stone, and a [c]new name written on the stone [d]which no one knows but he who receives it.'

D   The Message to Thyatira, 2:18–29

★18 aRev.
1:11; 2:24
bMatt. 4:3
cRev. 1:14f

18 "And to the angel of the church in [a]Thyatira write:

[b]The Son of God, [c]who has eyes like a flame of fire, and His feet are like burnished bronze, says this:

19 aRev. 2:2

19 '[a]I know your deeds, and your love and faith and service and perseverance, and that your deeds of late are greater than at first.

★20 aRev.
2:14 b1 Kin.
16:31; 21:25,
2 Kin. 9:7
cActs 15:29;
1 Cor. 10:20;
Rev. 2:14

20 'But [a]I have *this* against you, that you tolerate the woman [b]Jezebel, who calls herself a

prophetess, and she teaches and leads My bond-servants astray, so that they [c]commit *acts of* immorality and eat things sacrificed to idols.

21 aRom.
2:4; 2 Pet.
3:9 bRom.
2:5; Rev.
9:20f; 16:9,
11

21 'And [a]I gave her time to repent; and she [b]does not want to repent of her immorality.

22 aRev.
17:2; 18:9

22 'Behold, I will cast her upon a bed *of sickness,* and those who [a]commit adultery with her into great tribulation, unless they repent of her deeds.

23 aPs. 7:9,
26:2, 139:1;
Jer. 11:20;
17:10; Matt.
16:27; Luke
16:15; Acts
1:24; Rom.
8:27

23 'And I will kill her children with pestilence; and all the churches will know that I am He who [a]searches the minds and hearts; and I will give to each one of you according to your deeds.

★24 aRev.
2:18 b1 Cor.
2:10 cActs
15:28

24 'But I say to you, the rest who are in [a]Thyatira, who do not hold this teaching, who have not known the [b]deep things of Satan, as they call them—I [c]place no other burden on you.

25 aRev.
3:11 bJohn
21:22

25 'Nevertheless [a]what you have, hold fast [b]until I come.

26 aRev. 2:7
bMatt. 10:22;
Heb. 3:6
cPs. 2:8;
Rev. 3:21;
20:4

26 'And [a]he who overcomes, and he who keeps My deeds [b]until the end, [c]TO HIM I WILL GIVE AUTHORITY OVER THE NATIONS;

★27 aRev.
12:5; 19:15
bIs. 30:14;
Jer. 19:11

27 AND HE SHALL [a]RULE THEM WITH A ROD OF IRON, [b]AS THE VESSELS OF THE POTTER ARE BROKEN TO PIECES, as I also have received *authority* from My Father;

★28 a1 John
3:2; Rev.
22:16

28 and I will give him [a]the morning star.

29 aRev. 2:7

29 '[a]He who has an ear, let him hear what the Spirit says to the churches.'

2:17 *hidden manna.* Refers to the sufficiency of Christ for the believer's needs, as manna was for the Hebrews' during the wilderness wanderings. The *white stone* may refer to the custom of voting for the acquittal of an accused person by using a white stone (indicating that the believer can be assured of his acquittal before God, cf. Rom. 8:1); or it may refer to the sufficiency of Christ (from the custom of wearing amulets around the neck).

2:18 *Thyatira.* A city noted for its numerous trade guilds and for its wool and dyeing industry (see Acts 16:14). It was about 35 miles SE. of Pergamum.

2:20 *Jezebel.* This false prophetess may actually have been named Jezebel; more probably,

however, she was a well-known woman whose actions made her a contemporary counterpart of the notorious Jezebel of 1 Kings 16 and 2 Kings 9.

2:24 *the deep things of Satan.* To those of you (John says) who have not been seduced by these false doctrines, these deep things of Satan, I say only . . .

2:27 *he shall rule them with a rod of iron.* A reference to Christ's reign on earth. See 12:5; 19:15; Ps. 2:9.

2:28 *the morning star.* Probably a reference to Christ Himself (cf. 22:16; 2 Pet. 1:19) or, perhaps, the immortal life that one will receive from Christ.

E   The Message to Sardis, 3:1-6

★ 1 aRev
1:11 bRev
1:4 cRev
1:16 dRev
2:2; 3:8; 15
e1 Tim 5:6

3 "And to the angle of the church in aSardis write:

He who has bthe seven Spirits of God, and cthe seven stars, says this: 'dI know your deeds, that you have a name that you are alive, but you are edead.

2 'Wake up, and strengthen the things that remain, which were about to die; for I have not found your deeds completed in the sight of My God.

3 aRev 2:5
bRev 2:5
c1 Thess.
5:2; 2 Pet
3:10; Rev.
16:15 dMatt.
24:43

3 'aRemember therefore what you have received and heard; and keep it, and arepent. If therefore you will not wake up, bI will come clike a thief, and you will not know at dwhat hour I will come upon you.

★ 4 aActs
1:15 marg.
Rev. 11:13
marg. bRev.
1:11 cJude
23 dEccles.
9:8; Rev. 3:5,
18; 4:4; 6:11;
7:9, 13f.;
19:8, 14
5 aRev. 2:7
bRev. 3:4
cLuke 10:20;
Rev. 13:8;
17:8; 20:12,
15; 21:27
dMatt. 10:32;
Luke 12:8
6 aRev. 2:7

4 'But you have a few apeople in bSardis who have not csoiled their garments; and they will walk with Me din white; for they are worthy.

5 'aHe who overcomes shall thus be clothed in bwhite garments; and I will not cerase his name from the book of life, and dI will confess his name before My Father, and before His angels.

6 'aHe who has an ear, let him hear what the Spirit says to the churches.'

F   The Message to Philadelphia, 3:7-13

★ 7 aRev.
1:11 bRev.
6:10 c1 John
5:20; Rev.
3:14; 19:11
dJob 12:14;
Is. 22:22;
Matt. 16:19;
Rev. 1:18

7 "And to the angel of the church in aPhiladelphia write:

bHe who is holy, cwho is true, who has dthe key of David, who opens and no one will shut, and who shuts and no one opens, says this:

8 aRev. 3:1
bActs 14:27
cRev. 2:13

8 'aI know your deeds. Behold, I have put before you ban open door which no one can shut, because you have a little power, and have kept My word, and chave not denied My name.

9 aRev. 2:9
bIs. 45:14;
49:23; 60:14
cIs. 43:4;
John 17:23

9 'Behold, I will cause those of athe synagogue of Satan, who say that they are Jews, and are not, but lie—behold, I will make them to bcome and bow down at your feet, and to know that cI have loved you.

10 'Because you have akept the word of bMy perseverance, cI also will keep you from the hour of dtesting, that hour which is about to come upon the whole eworld, to test fthose who dwell upon the earth.

★10 aJohn
17:6; Rev.
3:8 bRev
1:9 c2 Tim.
2:12; 2 Pet.
2:9 dRev.
2:10 eMatt.
24:14; Rev.
16:14 fRev.
6:10; 8:13;
11:10; 13:8,
14; 17:8

11 'aI am coming quickly; bhold fast what you have, in order that no one take your ccrown.

11 aRev. 1:3;
22:7, 12, 20
bRev. 2:25
cRev. 2:10

12 'aHe who overcomes, I will make him a bpillar in the temple of My God, and he will not go out from it anymore; and I will write upon him the cname of My God, and dthe name of the city of My God, ethe new Jerusalem, which comes down out of heaven from My God, and My fnew name.

★12 aRev.
3:5 b1 Kin.
7:21; Jer.
1:18; Gal.
2:9 cRev.
14:1; 22:4
dEzek.
48:35; Rev.
21:2 eGal.
4:26; Heb.
13:14; Rev.
21:2, 10
fRev. 2:17

13 'aHe who has an ear, let him hear what the Spirit says to the churches.'

13 aRev. 3:6

3:1 *Sardis.* The capital of ancient Lydia, situated about 30 miles S. of Thyatira. The imperial cult was strong there. *you are dead.* I.e., devoid of spiritual life and power.

3:4 *who have not soiled their garments.* I.e., persons who had remained faithful to Christ.

3:7 *Philadelphia.* The word means brotherly love. A lesser city than the others addressed, it was located about 38 miles SE. of Sardis. Its chief deity was Dionysus, the god of wine. *the key of David.* A quotation from Isa. 22:22, where it is a symbol of authority. Compare the

"keys of death and of Hades" (1:18) and the "keys of the kingdom" (Matt. 16:19).

3:10 *I also will keep you from the hour of testing.* A promise that believers will be delivered from the tribulation period which will come upon the entire earth (Matt. 24:14-21; see note on 1 Thess. 4:17).

3:12 *a pillar in the temple of My God.* A promise that believers will be honored in the New Jerusalem, referring to the custom of honoring a magistrate by placing a pillar, in his name, in one of the temples in Philadelphia.

G The Message to Laodicea,
3:14–22

*14 aRev.
1:11 b2 Cor.
1:20 cRev.
1:5; 3:7
dGen. 49:3;
Deut. 21:17;
Prov. 8:22;
John 1:3;
Col. 1:18;
Rev. 21:6;
22:13
15 aRev. 3:1
bRom. 12:11
*16

14 "And to the angel of the church in aLaodicea write:

bThe Amen, cthe faithful and true Witness, dthe Beginning of the creation of God, says this:

15 'aI know your deeds, that you are neither cold nor hot; bI would that you were cold or hot.

16 'So because you are lukewarm, and neither hot nor cold, I will spit you out of My mouth.

17 aHos.
12:8; Zech.
11:5; Matt.
5:3; 1 Cor.
4:8

17 'Because you say, "aI am rich, and have become wealthy, and have need of nothing," and you do not know that you are wretched and miserable and poor and blind and naked,

*18 aIs.
55:1; Matt.
13:44
b1 Pet. 1:7
cRev. 3:4
dRev. 16:15

18 I advise you to abuy from Me bgold refined by fire, that you may become rich, and cwhite garments, that you may clothe yourself, and that dthe shame of your nakedness may not be revealed; and eyesalve to anoint your eyes, that you may see.

19 a1 Cor.
11:32; Heb.
12:6 bRev.
2:5

19 'aThose whom I love, I reprove and discipline; be zealous therefore, and brepent.

*20 aMatt.
24:33; James
5:9 bLuke
12:36; John
10:3 cJohn
14:23

20 'Behold, I stand aat the door and bknock; if anyone hears My voice and opens the door, cI will come in to him, and will dine with him, and he with Me.

21 aRev. 2:7
bMatt. 19:28;
2 Tim. 2:12;
Rev. 2:26;
20:4 cJohn
16:33; Rev.
5:5; 6:2;
17:14
22 aRev. 2:7

21 'aHe who overcomes, I will grant to him bto sit down with Me on My throne, as cI also overcame and sat down with My Father on His throne.

22 'aHe who has an ear, let him hear what the Spirit says to the churches.' "

IV "THE THINGS WHICH SHALL TAKE PLACE AFTER THESE THINGS," 4:1–22:5

A The Tribulation Period,
4:1–19:21

1 The throne in heaven, 4:1–11

a The throne, 4:1–3

4 After athese things I looked, and behold, ba door *standing* open in heaven, and the first voice which I had heard, clike *the sound* of a trumpet speaking with me, said, "dCome up here, and I will eshow you what must take place after these things."

1 aRev.
1:12ff.; 19
bEzek. 1:1;
Rev. 19:11
cRev. 1:10
dRev. 11:12
eRev. 1:19;
22:6

2 Immediately I was ain the Spirit; and behold, ba throne was standing in heaven, and cOne sitting on the throne.

3 And He who was sitting *was* like a ajasper stone and a bsardius in appearance; and *there was* a crainbow around the throne, like an demerald in appearance.

★ 2 aRev.
1:10 b1 Kin.
22:19; Is.
6:1; Ezek.
1:26; Dan.
7:9; Rev.
4:9f. cRev.
4:9

★ 3 aRev.
21:11 bRev.
21:20 cEzek.
1:28; Rev.
10:1 dRev.
21:19

b The throng, 4:4–8

4 And aaround the throne were btwenty-four thrones; and upon the thrones I saw ctwenty-four elders dsitting, clothed in ewhite garments, and fgolden crowns on their heads.

5 And from the throne proceed aflashes of lightning and sounds and peals of thunder. And

★ 4 aRev.
4:6; 5:11;
7:11 bRev.
11:16 cRev.
4:10; 5:6, 8,
14; 19:4
dMatt. 19:28;
2 Tim. 2:12;
Rev. 2:26;
20:4 eRev.
3:18 fRev.
4:10

★ 5 aEx.
19:16; Rev.
8:5; 11:19;
16:18 bEx.
25:37; Zech.
4:2 cRev. 1:4

3:14 *Laodicea.* A city about 90 miles due E. of Ephesus and 45 miles SE. of Philadelphia. Under Roman rule it was a wealthy city.

3:16 *I will spit you out of My mouth.* Lit., I will vomit. . . .

3:18 *gold . . . white garments . . . eyesalve.* These perhaps refer to the city's three main sources of wealth—banking, production of wool cloth, and medicines. Laodicea was a center for making medicines, including a tablet that was powdered, mixed with water, and smeared on the eyes.

3:20 *I stand at the door and knock.* How incredible that Christ should be kept outside His own church! How gracious that He should still seek entrance!

4:2 *I was in the Spirit.* As in 1:10.

4:3 *jasper.* Clear as crystal (cf. 21:11). *sardius.* Blood red. *emerald.* Light green.

4:4 *twenty-four elders.* Some understand these to be angelic beings, though it is likely that the 24 elders represent redeemed men who are glorified, crowned, and enthroned.

4:5 *seven Spirits of God.* See note on 1:4.

there were [b]seven lamps of fire burning before the throne, which are [c]the seven Spirits of God;

6 and before the throne there was, as it were, a [a]sea of glass like crystal; and in the center and [b]around the throne, [c]four living creatures [d]full of eyes in front and behind.

7 [a]And the first creature was like a lion, and the second creature like a calf, and the third creature had a face like that of a man, and the fourth creature was like a flying eagle.

8 And the [a]four living creatures, each one of them having [b]six wings, are [c]full of eyes around and within; and [d]day and night they do not cease to say,

"[e]HOLY, HOLY, HOLY, is THE [f]LORD GOD, THE ALMIGHTY, [g]who was and who is and who is to come."

c   The theme, 4:9-11

9 And when the living creatures give glory and honor and thanks to Him who [a]sits on the throne, to [b]Him who lives forever and ever,

10 the [a]twenty-four elders will [b]fall down before Him who [c]sits on the throne, and will worship [d]Him who lives forever and ever, and will cast their [e]crowns before the throne, saying,

11 "[a]Worthy art Thou, our Lord and our God, to receive glory and honor and power; for Thou [b]didst create all things, and be-

cause of Thy will they existed, and were created."

2   The scroll in heaven, 5:1-14

a   The scroll, 5:1

5 And I saw in the right hand of Him who [a]sat on the throne a [b]book written inside and on the back, [c]sealed up with seven seals.

b   The search, 5:2-5

2 And I saw a [a]strong angel proclaiming with a loud voice, "Who is worthy to open the book and to break its seals?"

3 And no one [a]in heaven, or on the earth, or under the earth, was able to open the book, or to look into it.

4 And I began to weep greatly, because no one was found worthy to open the book, or to look into it;

5 and one of the elders *said to me, "Stop weeping; behold, the [a]Lion that is [b]from the tribe of Judah, the [c]Root of David, has overcome so as to open the book and its seven seals."

c   The Savior-Sovereign, 5:6-7

6 And I saw between the throne (with the four living creatures) and [a]the elders a [b]Lamb standing, as if [c]slain, having seven [d]horns and [e]seven eyes, which are [f]the seven Spirits of God, sent out into all the earth.

★ 6 aEzek. 1:22; Rev. 15:2; 21:18, 21 bRev. 4:4 cEzek. 1:5; Rev. 4:8f.; 5:6; 6:1, 6; 7:11; 14:3; 15:7; 19:4 dEzek. 1:18; 10:12
★ 7 aEzek. 1:10; 10:14

8 aEzek. 1:5; Rev. 4:6, 9; 5:6; 6:1, 6; 7:11; 14:3; 15:7; 19:4 bIs. 6:2 cEzek. 1:18; 10:12 dRev. 14:11 eIs. 6:3 fRev. 1:8 gRev. 1:4

9 aPs. 47:8; Is. 6:1; Rev. 4:2 bDeut. 32:40; Dan. 4:34; 12:7; Rev. 10:6; 15:7

10 aRev. 4:4 bRev. 5:8, 14; 7:11; 11:16; 19:4 cPs. 47:8; Is. 6:1; Rev. 4:2 dDeut. 32:40; Dan. 4:34; 12:7 eRev. 4:4; 10:6; 15:7

11 aRev. 1:6; 5:12 bActs 14:15; Rev. 10:6; 14:7

★ 1 aRev. 4:9; 5:7, 13 bEzek. 2:9, 10 cIs. 29:11; Dan. 12:4

2 aRev. 10:1; 18:21

3 aPhil. 2:10; Rev. 5:13

★ 5 aGen. 49:9 bHeb. 7:14 cIs. 11:1, 10; Rom. 15:12; Rev. 22:16

★ 6 aRev. 4:4; 5:8, 14 bJohn 1:29; Rev. 5:8, 12f.; 13:8 cRev. 5:9, 12; 13:8 dDan. 8:3f. eZech. 3:9; 4:10 fRev. 1:4

4:6 *four living creatures.* Or, living ones. These may be angels, probably cherubim (cf. Ezek. 10:15-20), or they may be representations of the attributes of God Himself (since they are said to be in the center of the throne).

4:7 Many see a similarity between the four living ones and the fourfold manner in which Christ is portrayed in the Gospels. In Matthew He appears as the Lion of the tribe of Judah; in Mark, as the Servant who became the sacrifice for sin (the calf was a sacrificial animal, Heb. 9:12, 19); Luke's emphasis is on the Son of Man; and *a flying eagle* links Him with heaven, as does John's Gospel.

5:1 *a book.* Lit., a scroll. This may be called the "Book of Redemption," as it contains the story of man's fall through sin and rise through Christ (Heb. 2:5-9).

5:5 *the Lion that is from the tribe of Judah* (cf. Gen. 49:9), *the Root of David* (cf. Isa. 11:1, 10). The Messiah, John is assured, is competent and worthy to break the seven seals and open the scroll to release the plagues.

5:6 *as if slain.* Christ, the Lamb, bears the marks of His death (see Luke 24:40; John 20:20, 27) even in His glorified state. *horns* are a symbol of strength (cf. 1 Kings 22:11; Zech. 1:18).

7 aRev. 5:1

7 And He came, and He took ait out of the right hand of Him who asat on the throne.

d   The song, 5:8-14

★ **8** aRev. 4:6; 5:6, 11, 14 bRev. 4:4; 5:6, 14 cRev. 4:10 dJohn 1:29; Rev. 5:6, 12f.; 13:8 eRev. 14:2; 15:2 fRev. 15:7 gPs. 141:2; Rev. 8:3f.

8 And when He had taken the book, the afour living creatures and the btwenty-four elders cfell down before the dLamb, having each one a eharp, and fgolden bowls full of incense, which are the gprayers of the saints.

9 And they *sang a anew song, saying,

9 aPs. 40:3; 98:1; 149:1; Is. 42:10; Rev. 14:3; 15:3 bRev. 4:11 cRev. 5:6, 12; 13:8 d1 Cor. 6:20; Rev. 14:3f. eDan. 3:4; 5:19; Rev. 7:9; 10:11; 11:9; 13:7; 14:6; 17:15

"bWorthy art Thou to take the book, and to break its seals; for Thou wast cslain, and didst dpurchase for God with Thy blood *men* from every tribe and tongue and people and nation.

10 aRev. 1:6 bRev. 3:21; 20:4

10 "And Thou hast made them *to be* a akingdom and apriests to our God; and they will breign upon the earth."

11 aRev. 4:4 bRev. 4:6; 5:6, 8, 14 cRev. 4:4; 5:6, 14 dDan. 7:10; Heb. 12:22; Jude 14; Rev. 9:16

11 And I looked, and I heard the voice of many angels aaround the throne and the bliving creatures and the celders; and the number of them was dmyriads of myriads, and thousands of thousands,

12 aRev. 1:6; 4:11; 5:9 bJohn 1:29; Rev. 5:6, 13; 13:8

12 saying with a loud voice, "aWorthy is the bLamb that was bslain to receive power and riches and wisdom and might and honor and glory and blessing."

13 aPhil. 2:10; Rev. 5:3 bRev. 5:1 cJohn 1:29; Rev. 5:6, 12f.; 13:8 dRom. 11:36; Rev. 1:6

13 And aevery created thing which is in heaven and on the earth and under the earth and on the sea, and all things in them, I heard saying,

"To Him who bsits on the throne, and to the cLamb, dbe blessing and honor and glory and dominion forever and ever."

---

14 And the afour living creatures kept saying, "bAmen." And the celders dfell down and worshiped.

14 aRev. 4:6; 5:6, 8, 11 b1 Cor. 14:16; Rev. 7:12; 19:4 cRev. 4:4; 5:6, 8 dRev. 4:10

3   The seal judgments, 6:1-17

a   First seal: cold war, 6:1-2

6 And I saw when the aLamb broke one of the bseven seals, and I heard one of the cfour living creatures saying as with a dvoice of thunder, "Come."

1 aJohn 1:29; Rev. 5:6, 12f.; 13:8 bRev. 5:1 cRev. 4:6; 5:6, 8, 11, 14 dRev. 14:2; 19:6

★ 2 aZech. 1:8; 6:3f.; Rev. 19:11 bZech. 6:11; Rev. 9:7; 14:14; 19:12 cRev. 3:21

2 And I looked, and behold, a awhite horse, and he who sat on it had a bow; and ba crown was given to him; and he went out cconquering, and to conquer.

b   Second seal: open war, 6:3-4

3 And when He broke the second seal, I heard the asecond living creature saying, "Come."

3 aRev. 4:7

4 And another, aa red horse, went out; and to him who sat on it, it was granted to btake peace from the earth, and that *men* should slay one another; and a great sword was given to him.

4 aZech. 1:8; 6:2 bMatt. 10:34

c   Third seal: famine, 6:5-6

5 And when He broke the third seal, I heard the athird living creature saying, "Come." And I looked, and behold, a bblack horse; and he who sat on it had a cpair of scales in his hand.

5 aRev. 4:7 bZech. 6:2 cEzek. 4:16

6 And I heard as it were a voice in the center of the afour living creatures saying, "A quart of wheat for a denarius, and three quarts of barley for a denarius; and bdo not harm the oil and the wine."

★ 6 aRev. 4:6f. bRev. 7:3; 9:4

d   Fourth seal: death, 6:7-8

7 And when He broke the fourth seal, I heard the voice of

7 aRev. 4:7

5:8 *bowls.* Like saucers.
6:2 *he who sat on it.* Probably a reference to Antichrist (see note on 1 John 2:18). His method of conquest does not seem to include open warfare, since peace is not removed from the earth until the second seal is opened (v. 3).

This corresponds to the description of delusion in 1 Thess. 5:3.
6:6 *denarius.* A Roman silver coin which had a normal purchasing power of 8 quarts of wheat or 24 of barley. A severe shortage of food is indicated. See note for Matt. 18:28.

the ^afourth living creature saying, "Come."

8 And I looked, and behold, an ^aashen horse; and he who sat on it had the name ^bDeath; and ^bHades was following with him. And authority was given to them over a fourth of the earth, ^cto kill with sword and with famine and with pestilence and by the wild beasts of the earth.

e Fifth seal: martyrdom, 6:9–11

9 And when He broke the fifth seal, I saw ^aunderneath the ^baltar the ^csouls of those who had been slain ^dbecause of the word of God, and because of the ^etestimony which they had maintained;

10 and they cried out with a loud voice, saying, "^aHow long, O ^bLord, ^choly and true, wilt Thou refrain from ^djudging and avenging our blood on ^ethose who dwell on the earth?"

11 And ^athere was given to each of them a white robe; and they were told that they should ^brest for a little while longer, ^cuntil *the number of* their fellow servants and their brethren who were to be killed even as they had been, should be ^dcompleted also.

f Sixth seal: physical
disturbances,
6:12–17

12 And I looked when He broke the sixth seal, and there was a great ^aearthquake; and the ^bsun became black as ^csackcloth *made* of hair, and the whole moon became like blood;

13 and ^athe stars of the sky

fell to the earth, ^bas a fig tree casts its unripe figs when shaken by a great wind.

14 And ^athe sky was split apart like a scroll when it is rolled up; and ^bevery mountain and island were moved out of their places.

15 And ^athe kings of the earth and the great men and the commanders and the rich and the strong and every slave and free man, hid themselves in the caves and among the rocks of the mountains;

16 and they *^asaid to the mountains and to the rocks, "Fall on us and hide us from the presence of Him ^bwho sits on the throne, and from the ^cwrath of the Lamb;

17 for ^athe great day of their wrath has come; and ^bwho is able to stand?"

4 Interlude: the redeemed of
the tribulation, 7:1–17

a The 144,000 Jews, 7:1–8

7 After this I saw ^afour angels standing at the ^bfour corners of the earth, holding back ^cthe four winds of the earth, ^dso that no wind should blow on the earth or on the sea or on any tree.

2 And I saw another angel ascending ^afrom the rising of the sun, having the ^bseal of ^cthe living God; and he cried out with a loud voice to the ^dfour angels to whom it was granted to harm the earth and the sea,

3 saying, "^aDo not harm the earth or the sea or the trees, until we have ^bsealed the bondservants of our God on their ^cforeheads."

★ **8** ^aZech. 6:3 ^bProv. 5:5; Hos. 13:14; Matt. 11:23; Rev. 1:18; 20:13f. ^cJer. 15:2f.; 24:10; 29:17f.; Ezek. 5:12, 17; 14:21

★ **9** ^aEx. 29:12; Lev. 4:7; John 16:2 ^bRev. 14:18; 16:7 ^cRev. 20:4 ^dRev. 1:2, 9 ^eRev. 12:17

10 ^aZech. 1:12 ^bLuke 2:29; 2 Pet. 2:1 ^cRev. 3:7 ^dDeut. 32:43; Ps. 79:10; Luke 18:7; Rev. 19:2 ^eRev. 3:10

★**11** ^aRev. 3:4, 5; 7:9 ^b2 Thess. 1:7; Heb. 4:10; Rev. 14:13 ^cHeb. 11:40 ^dActs 20:24; 2 Tim. 4:7

★**12** ^aMatt. 24:7; Rev. 8:5; 11:13; 16:18 ^bMatt. 24:29 ^cIs. 50:3; Matt. 11:21

13 ^aMatt. 24:29; Rev. 8:10; 9:1 ^bIs. 34:4

14 ^aIs. 34:4; 2 Pet. 3:10; Rev. 20:11; 21:1 ^bIs. 54:10; Jer. 4:24; Ezek. 38:20; Nah. 1:5; Rev. 16:20

15 ^aIs. 2:10f., 19, 21; 24:21; Rev. 19:18

★**16** ^aLuke 23:30; Rev. 9:6 ^bRev. 4:9; 5:1 ^cMark 3:5

17 ^aIs. 63:4; Jer. 30:7; Joel 1:15; 2:11., 11, 31; Zeph. 1:14f.; Rev. 16:14 ^bPs. 76:7; Nah. 1:6; Mal. 3:2; Luke 21:36

1 ^aRev. 9:14 ^bIs. 11:12; Ezek. 7:2; Rev. 20:8 ^cJer. 49:36; Zech. 6:5; Matt. 24:31 ^dRev. 7:3; 8:7; 9:4

2 ^aIs. 41:2; Rev. 16:12 ^bRev. 7:3; 9:4 ^cMatt. 16:16 ^dRev. 9:14

3 ^aRev. 6:6 ^bJohn 3:33; Rev. 7:3-8 ^cEzek. 9:4, 6; Rev. 13:16; 14:1, 9; 20:4; 22:4

6:8 *ashen* = a sickly, yellowish-green. *Death.* Probably representing the inevitable result of disease which accompanies war and famine.
6:9 *the souls of those who had been slain.* Evidently the martyrs of the first months of the tribulation period.
6:11 *rest for a little while longer.* I.e., wait a little while. It is difficult for these martyrs to understand why God would allow their mur-

derers to live; yet God asks these saints to trust Him.
6:12 These cosmic disturbances are predicted elsewhere in Scripture (Isa. 34:4; Joel 2:30-31; Matt. 24:29).
6:16 When the tribulation comes, men will act as if they believe the end of the world is at hand.

★ 4 *a*Rev.
9:16 *b*Rev.
14:1, 3

4 And I heard the *a*number of those who were sealed, *b*one hundred and forty-four thousand sealed from every tribe of the sons of Israel:

5 from the tribe of Judah, twelve thousand *were* sealed, from the tribe of Reuben twelve thousand, from the tribe of Gad twelve thousand,

6 from the tribe of Asher twelve thousand, from the tribe of Naphtali twelve thousand, from the tribe of Manasseh twelve thousand,

7 from the tribe of Simeon twelve thousand, from the tribe of Levi twelve thousand, from the tribe of Issachar twelve thousand,

8 from the tribe of Zebulun twelve thousand, from the tribe of Joseph twelve thousand, from the tribe of Benjamin, twelve thousand *were* sealed.

b   The multitude of Gentiles, 7:9-17

★ 9 *a*Rev.
5:9 *b*Rev.
7:15 *c*Rev.
22:3 *d*Rev.
6:11; 7:14
*e*Lev. 23:40

9 After these things I looked, and behold, a great multitude, which no one could count, from *a*every nation and *all* tribes and peoples and tongues, standing *b*before the throne and *c*before the Lamb, clothed in *d*white robes, and *e*palm branches *were* in their hands;

10 *a*Ps. 3:8;
Rev. 12:10;
19:1 *b*Rev.
22:3

10 and they cry out with a loud voice, saying, "*a*Salvation to our God *b*who sits on the throne, and to the Lamb."

11 *a*Rev. 4:4
*b*Rev. 4:6
*c*Rev. 4:10

11 And all the angels were standing *a*around the throne and around *a*the elders and the *b*four living creatures; and they *c*fell on their faces before the throne and worshiped God,

12 saying,
"*a*Amen, *b*blessing and glory and wisdom and thanksgiving and honor and power and might, *be* to our God forever and ever. *a*Amen."

12 *a*Rev.
5:14 *b*Rev.
5:12

13 And one of the elders *a*answered, saying to me, "These who are clothed in the *b*white robes, who are they, and from where have they come?"

13 *a*Acts
3:12 *b*Rev.
7:9

14 And I said to him, "My lord, you know." And he said to me, "These are the ones who come out of the *a*great tribulation, and they have *b*washed their robes and made them *c*white in the *d*blood of the Lamb.

14 *a*Matt.
24:21
*b*Zech. 3:3-
5; Rev. 22:14
*c*Rev. 6:11;
7:9 *d*Heb.
9:14; 1 John
1:7

15 "For this reason, they are *a*before the throne of God; and they *b*serve Him day and night in His *c*temple; and *d*He who sits on the throne shall spread His *e*tabernacle over them.

15 *a*Rev. 7:9
*b*Rev. 4:8;
22:3 *c*Rev.
11:19; 21:22
*d*Rev. 4:9
*e*Lev. 26:11;
Ezek. 37:27;
John 1:14;
Rev. 21:3

16 "*a*They shall hunger no more, neither thirst anymore; neither shall the sun beat down on them, nor any heat;

16 *a*Ps.
121:5f.; Is.
49:10

17 for the Lamb in the center of the throne shall be their *a*shepherd, and shall guide them to springs of the *b*water of life; and *c*God shall wipe every tear from their eyes."

17 *a*Ps.
23:11.; Matt.
2:6; John
10:11 *b*John
4:14; Rev.
21:6; 22:1
*c*Is. 25:8;
Matt. 5:4;
Rev. 21:4

5   The six trumpet judgments, 8:1-9:21

a   The seventh seal opened, 8:1-6

8 And when He broke the *a*seventh seal, there was *b*silence in heaven for about half an hour.

★ 1 *a*Rev.
5:1; 6:1, 3, 5,
7, 9, 12
*b*Rev. 5:9
2 *a*Matt.
18:10; Rev.
1:4; 8:6-13;
9:1, 13;
11:15
*b*1 Cor.
15:52;
1 Thess. 4:16

2 And I saw *a*the seven angels who stand before God; and seven *b*trumpets were given to them.

7:4 *one hundred and forty-four thousand sealed.* These are Jews from the 12 tribes (12,000 each) who are protected in order to perform some service for God during these days. Perhaps they are evangelists. The omission of the tribe of Dan may be because Dan was guilty of idolatry on many occasions (Lev. 24:11; Judg. 18; 1 Kings 12:28, 29).

7:9 *a great multitude.* This multitude is composed of many racial and geographic groups who will be redeemed during the tribulation period (v. 14). In these difficult days, many will find Christ as Savior.

8:1 *broke the seventh seal.* With the breaking of the seventh seal comes the second series of judgments—the seven trumpets. Apparently the judgments announced by the trumpets follow chronologically those of the other seals.

3   And [a]another angel came and stood at the [b]altar, holding a [c]golden censer; and much [d]incense was given to him, that he might add it to the [d]prayers of all the saints upon the [e]golden altar which was before the throne.

4   And [a]the smoke of the incense, with the prayers of the saints, went up before God out of the angel's hand.

5   And the angel took the censer; and he [a]filled it with the fire of the altar and [b]threw it to the earth; and there followed [c]peals of thunder and sounds and flashes of lightning and an [d]earthquake.

6   [a]And the seven angels who had the seven trumpets prepared themselves to sound them.

b   First trumpet: the earth smitten, 8:7

7   And the first sounded, and there came [a]hail and fire, mixed with blood, and they were thrown to the earth; and [b]a third of the earth was burned up, and [b]a third of the [c]trees were burned up, and all the green [c]grass was burned up.

c   Second trumpet: the sea smitten, 8:8–9

8   And the second angel sounded, and *something* like a great [a]mountain burning with fire was thrown into the sea; and [b]a third of the [c]sea became blood;

9   and [a]a third of the creatures, which were in the sea and had life, died; and a third of the [b]ships were destroyed.

d   Third trumpet: the waters smitten, 8:10–11

10   And the third angel sounded, and a great star [a]fell from heaven, burning like a torch, and it fell on a [b]third of the rivers and on the [c]springs of waters;

11   and the name of the star is called Wormwood; and a [a]third of the waters became [b]wormwood; and many men died from the waters, because they were made bitter.

e   Fourth trumpet: the heavens smitten, 8:12–13

12   And the fourth angel sounded, and a [a]third of the [b]sun and a third of the [b]moon and a [a]third of the [b]stars were smitten, so that a [a]third of them might be darkened and the day might not shine for a [a]third of it, and the night in the same way.

13   And I looked, and I heard an eagle flying in [a]midheaven, saying with a loud voice, "[b]Woe, woe, woe, to [c]those who dwell on the earth, because of the remaining blasts of the trumpet of the [d]three angels who are about to sound!"

f   Fifth trumpet: men smitten, 9:1–12

9   And the [a]fifth angel sounded, and I saw a [b]star from heaven which had fallen to the earth; and the [c]key of the [d]bottomless pit was given to him.

2   And he opened the

Cross-references (margin):

3 [a]Rev. 7:2
[b]Amos 9:1;
Rev. 6:9
[c]Heb. 9:4
[d]Rev. 5:8
[e]Ex. 30:1, 3;
Num. 4:11;
Rev. 8:5;
9:13

4 [a]Ps. 141:2

5 [a]Lev. 16:12 [b]Ezek. 10:2 [c]Rev. 4:5 [d]Rev. 6:12

6 [a]Rev. 8:2

★7 [a]Is. 28:2; Ezek. 38:22; Joel 2:30 [b]Zech. 13:8, 9; Rev. 8:7-12; 9:15, 18; 12:4 [c]Rev. 9:4

8 [a]Jer. 51:25 [b]Zech. 13:8, 9; Rev. 8:7-12; 9:15, 18; 12:4 [c]Ex. 7:17ff.; Rev. 11:6; 16:3

9 [a]Zech. 13:8, 9; Rev. 8:7-12; 9:15, 18; 12:4 [b]Is. 2:16

10 [a]Is. 14:12; Rev. 6:13; 9:1 [b]Zech. 13:8, 9; Rev. 8:7-12; 9:15, 18; 12:4 [c]Rev. 14:7; 16:4

★11 [a]Zech. 13:8, 9; Rev. 8:7-12; 9:15, 18; 12:4 [b]Jer. 9:15; 23:15

★12 [a]Zech. 13:8, 9; Rev. 8:7-12; 9:15, 18; 12:4 [b]Ex. 10:21ff.; Rev. 6:12f.

13 [a]Rev. 14:6; 19:17 [b]Rev. 9:12; 11:14; 12:12 [c]Rev. 3:10 [d]Rev. 8:2

★1 [a]Rev. 8:2 [b]Rev. 8:10 [c]Rev. 1:18 [d]Luke 8:31; Rev. 9:2, 11 2 [a]Gen. 19:28; Ex. 19:18 [b]Joel 2:2, 10

8:7 Though the implications are staggering, there is no reason not to understand this and the other judgments plainly.

8:11 *Wormwood.* Many species of wormwood grow in Palestine, and all have a strong, bitter (but not poisonous) taste, which causes the plant to be used as a symbol of bitterness, sorrow, and calamity. This plague will make a third part of the fresh water supply of the earth unfit for human consumption.

8:12 Compare Luke 21:25.

9:1 *a star.* Represents an intelligent creature, apparently the angel of the bottomless pit (v. 11). Note the "he" in v. 2. *the bottomless pit.* Lit., the shaft of the abyss (for other uses of this phrase see Luke 8:31; Rom. 10:7; Rev. 9:11; 11:7; 17:8; 20:1, 3). Luke 8:31 indicates that this is the abode of the demons.

bottomless pit; and [a]smoke went up out of the pit, like the smoke of a great furnace; and [b]the sun and the air were darkened by the smoke of the pit.

★ 3 [a]Ex. 10:12-15; Rev. 9:7; Ex. [b]2 Chr. 10:11, 14; Ezek. 2:6; Rev. 9:5, 10

3 And out of the smoke came forth [a]locusts upon the earth; and power was given them, as the [b]scorpions of the earth have power.

★ 4-5 **4** [a]Rev. 6:6 [b]Rev. 8:7 [c]Rev. 7:2, 3

4 And they were told that they should not [a]hurt the [b]grass of the earth, nor any green thing, nor any tree, but only the men who do not have the [c]seal of God on their foreheads.

5 [a]Rev. 9:10 [b]2 Chr. 10:11, 14; Ezek. 2:6; Rev. 9:3, 10

5 And they were not permitted to kill anyone, but to torment for [a]five months; and their torment was like the torment of a [b]scorpion when it stings a man.

6 [a]Job 3:21; 7:15; Jer. 8:3; Rev. 6:16

6 And in those days [a]men will seek death and will not find it; and they will long to die and death flees from them.

7 [a]Joel 2:4

7 And the [a]appearance of the locusts was like horses prepared for battle; and on their heads, as it were, crowns like gold, and their faces were like the faces of men.

8 [a]Joel 1:6

8 And they had hair like the hair of women, and their [a]teeth were like *the teeth* of lions.

9 [a]Jer. 47:3; Joel 2:5

9 And they had breastplates like breastplates of iron; and the [a]sound of their wings was like the sound of chariots, of many horses rushing to battle.

10 [a]2 Chr. 10:11, 14; Ezek. 2:6; Rev. 8:3, 5 [b]Rev. 9:19 [c]Rev. 9:5
★11 [a]Luke 8:31; Rev. 9:1, 2 [b]John 5:2; Rev. 16:16 [c]Job 26:6; 28:22; 31:12; Ps. 88:11 marg.; Prov. 15:11

10 And they have tails like [a]scorpions, and stings; and in their [b]tails is their power to hurt men for [c]five months.

11 They have as king over them, the angel of the [a]abyss; his name in [b]Hebrew is [c]Abaddon, and in the Greek he has the name Apollyon.

12 [a]The first woe is past; behold, two woes are still coming after these things.

12 [a]Rev. 8:13; 11:14

g Sixth trumpet: men killed, 9:13-21

13 And the sixth angel sounded, and I heard a voice from the four [a]horns of the [b]golden altar which is before God,

13 [a]Ex. 30:2f., 10 [b]Rev. 8:3

14 one saying to the sixth angel who had the trumpet, "Release the [a]four angels who are bound at the [b]great river Euphrates."

14 [a]Rev. 7:1 [b]Gen. 15:18; Deut. 1:7; Josh. 1:4; Rev. 16:12

15 And the four angels, who had been prepared for the hour and day and month and year, were [a]released, so that they might kill a [b]third of mankind.

★15 [a]Rev. 20:7 [b]Rev. 8:7; 9:18

16 And the number of the armies of the horsemen was [a]two hundred million; [b]I heard the number of them.

★16 [a]Rev. 5:11 [b]Rev. 7:4

17 And this is how I saw [a]in the vision the horses and those who sat on them: *the riders* had breastplates *the color* of fire and of hyacinth and of [b]brimstone; and the heads of the horses are like the heads of lions; and [c]out of their mouths proceed fire and smoke and [b]brimstone.

17 [a]Dan. 8:2; 9:21 [b]Rev. 9:18; 14:10; 19:20; 20:10; 21:8 [c]Rev. 11:5

18 A [a]third of mankind was killed by these three plagues, by the [b]fire and the smoke and the brimstone, which proceeded out of their mouths.

★18 [a]Rev. 8:7; 9:15 [b]Rev. 9:17

19 For the power of the horses is in their mouths and in their tails; for their tails are like serpents and have heads; and with them they do harm.

20 And the rest of mankind, who were not killed by these plagues, [a]did not repent of [b]the works of their hands, so as not to

★20 [a]Rev. 2:21 [b]Deut. 4:28; Jer. 1:16; Mic. 5:13; Acts 7:41 [c]1 Cor. 10:20 [d]Ps. 115:4-7; 135:15-17; Dan. 5:23

9:3 *locusts.* The facts that these creatures come from the abyss and their unusual description in vv. 7-11 indicate that they are demonic.

9:4-5 The limitations which God places upon the activities of these creatures show that He is still in full control of these events.

9:11 *Abaddon . . . Apollyon.* Both words mean destruction.

9:15 *the hour.* Lit., this particular hour.

9:16 *the armies.* The 200,000,000 creatures who compose this supernatural cavalry may be human beings or demons or demon-possessed humans. For other supernatural armies, see 2 Kings 2:11; 6:14-17; Rev. 19:14).

9:18 *by these three plagues.* I.e., by the fire, smoke, and brimstone.

9:20 The religion of many will involve demon and idol worship.

*worship demons, and ᵈthe idols of gold and of silver and of brass and of stone and of wood, which can neither see nor hear nor walk;

21 and they ᵃdid not repent of their murders nor of their ᵇsorceries nor of their ᶜimmorality nor of their thefts.

6 The little scroll, 10:1–11

10 And I saw another ᵃstrong angel ᵇcoming down out of heaven, clothed with a cloud; and the ᶜrainbow was upon his head, and ᵈhis face was like the sun, and his ᵉfeet like pillars of fire;

2 and he had in his hand a ᵃlittle book which was open. And he placed ᵇhis right foot on the sea and his left on the land;

3 and he cried out with a loud voice, ᵃas when a lion roars; and when he had cried out, the ᵇseven peals of thunder uttered their voices.

4 And when the seven peals of thunder had spoken, ᵃI was about to write; and I ᵇheard a voice from heaven saying, "ᶜSeal up the things which the seven peals of thunder have spoken, and do not write them."

5 And the angel whom I saw standing on the sea and on the land ᵃlifted up his right hand to heaven,

6 and swore by ᵃHim who lives forever and ever, WHO ᵇCREATED HEAVEN AND THE THINGS IN IT, AND THE EARTH AND THE THINGS IN IT, AND THE SEA AND THE THINGS IN IT,

that ᶜthere shall be delay no longer,

7 but in the days of the voice of the ᵃseventh angel, when he is about to sound, then ᵇthe mystery of God is finished, as He preached to His servants the prophets.

8 And ᵃthe voice which I heard from heaven, *I heard* again speaking with me, and saying, "Go, take ᵇthe book which is open in the hand of the angel who ᵇstands on the sea and on the land."

9 And I went to the angel, telling him to give me the little book. And he *said to me, "ᵃTake it, and eat it; and it will make your stomach bitter, but in your mouth it will be sweet as honey."

10 And I took the little book out of the angel's hand and ate it, and it was in my mouth sweet as honey; and when I had eaten it, my stomach was made bitter.

11 And ᵃthey *said to me, "You must ᵇprophesy again concerning ᶜmany peoples and nations and tongues and ᵈkings."

7 The two witnesses, 11:1–19
a Temple, 11:1–2

11 And there was given me a ᵃmeasuring rod like a staff; and ᵇsomeone said, "Rise and measure the temple of God, and the altar, and those who worship in it.

2 "And leave out the ᵃcourt which is outside the temple, and do not measure it, for ᵇit has been

---

Cross-references (side margins)

★**21** ᵃRev. 9:20 ᵇIs. 47:9, 12; Rev. 18:23 ᶜRev. 17:2, 5

1 ᵃRev. 5:2 ᵇRev. 18:1; 20:1 ᶜRev. 4:3 ᵈMatt. 17:2; Rev. 1:16 ᵉRev. 1:15

2 ᵃRev. 5:1; 10:8-10 ᵇRev. 10:5, 8

3 ᵃIs. 31:4; Hos. 11:10 ᵇPs. 29:3-9; Rev. 4:5

4 ᵃRev. 1:11, 19 ᵇRev. 10:8 ᶜDan. 8:26; 12:4, 9; Rev. 22:10

5 ᵃGen. 14:22; Ex. 6:8; Num. 14:30; Deut. 32:40; Ezek. 20:5; Dan 12:7

★**6** ᵃRev. 4:9 ᵇRev. 4:11 ᶜRev. 6:11; 12:12; 16:17; 21:6

★**7** ᵃRev. 11:15 ᵇAmos 3:7; Rom. 16:25

8 ᵃRev. 10:4 ᵇRev. 10:2

★**9** ᵃJer. 15:16; Ezek. 2:8; 3:1-3

11 ᵃRev. 11:1 ᵇEzek. 37:4, 9 ᶜRev. 5:9 ᵈRev. 17:10, 12

★**1** ᵃEzek. 40:3-42:20; Zech. 2:1; Rev. 21:15f. ᵇRev. 10:11

★**2** ᵃEzek. 40:17, 20 ᵇLuke 21:24 ᶜIs. 52:1; Matt. 4:5; 27:53; Rev. 21:2, 10; 22:19 ᵈDan. 7:25; 12:7; Rev. 12:6; 13:5

9:21 *sorceries.* I.e., magical arts, potions, and poisons (see Gal. 5:20; Rev. 18:23; 21:8; 22:15). From the Greek word, we derive the English word "pharmacies."

10:6 *there shall be delay no longer.* I.e., when the seventh angel sounds his trumpet (11:15), the bowl judgments will be poured out (16:1-21) and the tribulation will come to an end with the return of Christ.

10:7 *the mystery of God.* Truth concerning God Himself which will not be revealed until His kingdom is established on earth.

10:9 The eating of the little scroll was to remind John that although these truths from God may be pleasant to his taste, they were bitter when

digested, because they spoke of judgment. The revelation of God's judgment, on careful reflection, should always bring heaviness of heart to the child of God. Compare Ezek. 2:8-3:3.

11:1 *the temple of God.* Apparently the temple which will be built during the tribulation days, in which Jewish worship will be carried on during the first part of that period and in which, at the mid-point of the seven-year period, the man of sin will exalt himself to be worshiped (2 Thess. 2:4).

11:2 *forty-two months.* This equals three and one-half years and probably refers to the last half of the tribulation period.

given to the nations; and they will [b]tread under foot [c]the holy city for [d]forty-two months.

b Time, 11:3

3 "And I will grant *authority* to my two [a]witnesses, and they will prophesy for [b]twelve hundred and sixty days, clothed in [c]sackcloth."

c Traits, 11:4-6

4 These are the [a]two olive trees and the two lampstands that stand before the Lord of the earth.

5 And if anyone desires to harm them, [a]fire proceeds out of their mouth and devours their enemies; and if anyone would desire to harm them, [b]in this manner he must be killed.

6 These have the power to [a]shut up the sky, in order that rain may not fall during [b]the days of their prophesying; and they have power over the waters to [c]turn them into blood, and to smite the earth with every plague, as often as they desire.

d Termination, 11:7-10

7 And when they have finished their testimony, [a]the beast that comes up out of the [b]abyss will [c]make war with them, and overcome them and kill them.

8 And their dead bodies *will lie* in the street of the [a]great city which mystically is called [b]Sodom and [c]Egypt, where also their Lord was crucified.

9 And those from [a]the peoples and tribes and tongues and nations *will* look at their dead bodies for three and a half days, and [b]will not permit their dead bodies to be laid in a tomb.

10 And [a]those who dwell on the earth *will* rejoice over them and make merry; and they will [b]send gifts to one another, because these two prophets tormented [a]those who dwell on the earth.

e Translation, 11:11-14

11 And after the three and a half days [a]the breath of life from God came into them, and they stood on their feet; and great fear fell upon those who were beholding them.

12 And they heard a loud voice from heaven saying to them, "[a]Come up here." And they [b]went up into heaven in the cloud, and their enemies beheld them.

13 And in that hour there was a great [a]earthquake, and a tenth of the city fell; and seven thousand people were killed in the earthquake, and the rest were terrified and [b]gave glory to the [c]God of heaven.

14 The second [a]woe is past; behold, the third woe is coming quickly.

f Seventh trumpet, 11:15-19

15 And the [a]seventh angel sounded; and there arose [b]loud voices in heaven, saying,
"[c]The kingdom of the world has become *the kingdom* of our

★3 [a]Rev. 1:5; 2:13 [b]Dan. 7:25; 12:7; Rev. 12:6; 13:5 [c]Gen. 37:34; 2 Sam. 3:31; 1 Kin. 21:27; 2 Kin. 19:1f.; Neh. 9:1; Esth. 4:1; Ps. 69:11; Joel 1:13; Jon. 3:5f., 8
★4 [a]Ps. 52:8; Jer. 11:16; Zech. 4:3, 11, 14
★5-6
5 [a]2 Kin. 1:10-12; Jer. 5:14; Rev. 9:17f. [b]Num. 16:29, 35
6 [a]Luke 4:25 [b]Rev. 11:3 [c]Rev. 8:8
★7 [a]Rev. 13:1ff. [b]Rev. 9:1 [c]Dan. 7:21; Rev. 13:7
★8 [a]Rev. 14:8; 16:19; 17:18; 18:2, 10, 16, 18, 19, 21 [b]Is. 1:9, 10; 3:9; Jer. 23:14; Ezek. 16:46, 49 [c]Ezek. 23:3, 8, 19, 27
9 [a]Rev. 5:9; 10:11 [b]1 Kin. 13:22; Ps. 79:2f.
10 [a]Rev. 3:10 [b]Neh. 8:10, 12; Esth. 9:19, 22
★11 [a]Ezek. 37:5, 9, 10, 14
12 [a]Rev. 4:1 [b]2 Kin. 2:11; Acts 1:9
★13 [a]Rev. 6:12; 8:5; 11:19; 16:18 [b]John 9:24; Rev. 14:7; 16:9; 19:7 [c]Rev. 16:11
14 [a]Rev. 8:13; 9:12
15 [a]Rev. 8:2; 10:7 [b]Rev. 16:17; 19:1 [c]Rev. 12:10 [d]Acts 4:26 [Ps. 2:2] [e]Dan. 2:44; 7:14, 27; Luke 1:33

11:3 *twelve hundred and sixty days.* This also equals three and one-half years and refers to the period of the ministry of the two witnesses.

11:4 *two olive trees.* For the symbolism see Zech. 4:3, 14. *two lampstands* that give out a witness (v. 3).

11:5-6 The miraculous powers of the two witnesses are reminiscent of those of Elijah and Moses (cf. Ex. 7:20; 8:1-12:29; 1 Kings 17:1; 18:41-45; 2 Kings 1:10-12).

11:7 *the beast.* The Antichrist (see note on 1

John 2:18), also called the man of lawlessness (2 Thess. 2:3). The same person is mentioned in Rev. 6:2; 13:1; 14:9, 11; 15:2; 16:2; 17:3, 13; 19:20; 20:10. He cannot kill these two witnesses until God allows him to.

11:8 *the great city.* I.e., Jerusalem.

11:11 *and they stood on their feet.* Imagine the effect the resurrection of these two men will have on those who, only the moment before, were viewing their corpses in the street!

11:13 *the rest.* Those who were not killed by the earthquake.

Lord, and of ^dHis Christ; and ^eHe will reign forever and ever."

16 And the twenty-four elders, who ^asit on their thrones before God, ^bfell on their faces and worshiped God,

17 saying,

"We give Thee thanks, ^aO Lord God, the Almighty, who art and who wast, because Thou hast taken Thy great power and hast begun to ^breign.

18 "And ^athe nations were enraged, and Thy wrath came, and ^bthe time came for the dead to be judged, and the time to give their reward to Thy ^cbond-servants and to the saints and to those who fear Thy name, ^dthe small and the great, and to destroy those who destroy the earth."

19 And ^athe temple of God which is in heaven was opened; and ^bthe ark of His covenant appeared in His temple, and there were flashes of ^clightning and sounds and peals of thunder and an earthquake and a ^dgreat hailstorm.

8　War, 12:1–17

a　War on earth: phase I, 12:1–6

12 And a great ^asign appeared ^bin heaven: ^ca woman ^dclothed with the sun, and the moon under her feet, and on her head a crown of twelve stars;

2 and she was with child; and she *^acried out, being in labor and in pain to give birth.

3 And ^aanother sign appeared in heaven: and behold, a great red ^bdragon having ^cseven heads and ^dten horns, and on his heads *were* ^eseven diadems.

4 And his tail *swept away a ^athird of the stars of heaven, and ^bthrew them to the earth. And the ^cdragon stood before the woman who was about to give birth, so that when she gave birth ^dhe might devour her child.

5 And she gave birth to a son, a male *child*, who is to ^arule all the nations with a rod of iron; and her child was ^bcaught up to God and to His throne.

6 And the woman fled into the wilderness where she *had a place prepared by God, so that there she might be nourished for ^aone thousand two hundred and sixty days.

b　War in heaven, 12:7–12

7 And there was war in heaven, ^aMichael and his angels waging war with the ^bdragon. And the dragon and ^chis angels waged war,

8 and they were not strong enough, and there was no longer a place found for them in heaven.

9 And the great ^adragon was thrown down, the ^bserpent of old who is called the devil and ^cSatan, who ^ddeceives the whole world; he was ^ethrown down to the earth, and his angels were thrown down with him.

10 And I heard ^aa loud voice in heaven, saying,

Cross references (left margin):

16 ^aMatt. 19:28; Rev. 4:4 ^bRev. 4:10

17 ^aRev. 1:8 ^bRev. 19:6

18 ^aPs. 2:1 ^bDan. 7:10; Rev. 20:12 ^cRev. 10:7; 16:6 ^dPs. 115:13; Rev. 13:16; 19:5

19 ^aRev. 4:1; 15:5 ^bHeb. 9:4 ^cRev. 4:5 ^dRev. 16:21

★ **1** ^aMatt. 24:30; Rev. 12:3 ^bRev. 11:19 ^cGal. 4:26 ^dPs. 104:2; Song of Sol. 6:10

2 ^aIs. 26:17; 66:6-9; Mic. 4:9, 10

Cross references (right margin):

★ **3** ^aRev. 12:1; 15:1 ^bIs. 27:1; Rev. 12:4, 7, 9, 13, 16f.; 13:2, 4, 11; 16:13; 20:2 ^cRev. 13:1; 17:3, 7, 9ff. ^dDan 7:7, 20, 24; Rev. 13:1; 17:12, 16 ^eRev. 13:1; 19:12

★ **4** ^aRev. 8:7, 12 ^bDan. 8:10 ^cIs. 27:1; Rev. 12:3, 7, 9, 13, 16f.; 13:2, 4, 11; 16:13; 20:2 ^dMatt. 2:16

★ **5** ^aRev. 2:27 ^b2 Cor. 12:2

★ **6** ^aRev. 11:3; 13:5

★ **7** ^aJude 9 ^bRev. 12:3 ^cMatt. 25:41

★ **9–11**
9 ^aRev. 12:3 ^bGen. 3:1; 2 Cor. 11:3; Rev. 12:15; 20:2 ^cMatt. 4:10; 25:41 ^dRev. 13:14; 20:3, 8, 10 ^eLuke 10:18; John 12:31

10 ^aRev. 11:15 ^bRev. 7:10 ^cJob 1:11; 2:5; Zech. 3:1; Luke 22:31; 1 Pet. 5:8

12:1 *a woman.* She represents Israel, who gave Christ to the world (v. 5) and who will be persecuted severely during the tribulation (v. 13).

12:3 *a great red dragon.* Satan (v. 9).

12:4 *a third of the stars of heaven.* This may refer to Satan's past rebellion against God (Ezek. 28:15); if so, it suggests that a third of the angels joined Satan and were cast out of heaven with him. Or the reference may be to a meteor-shower judgment on the earth.

12:5 *her child was caught up to God.* A reference to the ascension of Christ.

12:6 *one thousand two hundred and sixty days.* The last three and one-half years of the tribulation period will see intense persecution of Israel. Details are given in vv. 13–17. No men-

tion is made of the many hundreds of years between the ascension (v. 5) and the future tribulation (v. 6). See Dan. 9:27; Matt. 24:14, 21; 1 Thess. 4:17.

12:7 *Michael . . . the dragon.* This likely will occur at the mid-point of the tribulation. Michael is the only angel designated an archangel in the Bible (Jude 9).

12:9–11 Notice two of Satan's activities in these verses: to deceive the world and to accuse the brethren. The believer's defense against Satan is (1) to bank on the merits of the death of Christ, (2) to be active in witnessing, and (3) to be willing to make any sacrifice, including death (v. 11).

"Now the ᵇsalvation, and the power, and the ᵃkingdom of our God and the authority of His Christ have come, for the ᶜaccuser of our brethren has been thrown down, who accuses them before our God day and night.

11 "And they ᵃovercame him because of ᵇthe blood of the Lamb and because of ᶜthe word of their testimony, and they ᵈdid not love their life even to death.

12 "For this reason, ᵃrejoice, O heavens and ᵇyou who dwell in them. ᶜWoe to the earth and the sea, because ᵈthe devil has come down to you, having great wrath, knowing that he has *only* ᵉa short time."

c War on earth: phase II, 12:13–17

13 And when the ᵃdragon saw that he was thrown down to the earth, he persecuted ᵇthe woman who gave birth to the male *child*.

14 And the ᵃtwo wings of the great eagle were given to the woman, in order that she might fly ᵇinto the wilderness to her place, where she *was nourished for ᶜa time and times and half a time, from the presence of the serpent.

15 And the ᵃserpent poured water ᵇlike a river out of his mouth after the woman, so that he might cause her to be swept away with the flood.

16 And the earth helped the woman, and the earth opened its mouth and drank up the river which the dragon poured out of his mouth.

17 And the dragon was enraged with the woman, and went off to ᵃmake war with the rest of her ᵇoffspring, who ᶜkeep the commandments of God and ᵈhold to the testimony of Jesus.

9 The beast and his prophet, 13:1–18

a The beast, 13:1–10

13 And he stood on the sand of the seashore.

And I saw a ᵃbeast coming up out of the sea, having ᵇten horns and ᵇseven heads, and on his horns *were* ᶜten diadems, and on his heads *were* ᵈblasphemous names.

2 And the beast which I saw was ᵃlike a leopard, and his feet were *like those* of ᵇa bear, and his mouth like the mouth of ᶜa lion. And the ᵈdragon gave him his power and his ᵉthrone and great authority.

3 And *I saw* one of his heads as if it had been slain, and his ᵃfatal wound was healed. And the whole earth ᵇwas amazed *and followed* after the beast;

4 and they worshiped the ᵃdragon, because he ᵃgave his authority to the beast; and they worshiped the beast, saying, "ᵇWho is like the beast, and who is able to wage war with him?"

5 And there was given to him a mouth ᵃspeaking arrogant words and blasphemies; and authority to act for ᵇforty-two months was given to him.

6 And he opened his mouth in blasphemies against God, to blaspheme His name and His tabernacle, *that is,* ᵃthose who dwell in heaven.

7 And it was given to him to ᵃmake war with the saints and to

---

13:1 *And he stood.* I.e., the dragon. *a beast.* The Antichrist. See note on 11:7. Many emperors of Rome deified themselves but Antichrist will far outstrip all his predecessors in his blasphemous ways. *ten horns.* The ten kings that will give their power and authority to the Antichrist (17:12-13).
13:2 *the dragon gave him his power.* Satan gives Antichrist his power.

13:3 *his fatal wound was healed.* Apparently Satan will miraculously restore Antichrist to life in imitation of the resurrection of Christ. No wonder the world will acclaim Antichrist.
13:5 *forty-two months.* Apparently the last three and one-half years of the tribulation period during which Antichrist's power is practically unrestrained.

11 ᵃJohn 16:33; 1 John 2:13; Rev. 15:2 ᵇRev. 7:14 ᶜRev. 6:9 ᵈLuke 14:26; Rev. 2:10
12 ᵃPs. 96:11; Is. 44:23; Rev. 18:20 ᵇRev. 13:6 ᶜRev. 8:13 ᵈRev. 12:9 ᵉRev. 10:6

13 ᵃRev. 12:3 ᵇRev. 12:5
14 ᵃEx. 19:4; Deut. 32:11; Is. 40:31 ᵇRev. 12:6 ᶜDan. 7:25; 12:7
15 ᵃGen. 3:1; 2 Cor. 11:3; Rev. 12:9; 20:2 ᵇIs. 59:19; Hos. 5:10

17 ᵃRev. 11:7; 13:7 ᵇGen. 3:15 ᶜ1 John 2:3; Rev. 14:12 ᵈRev. 1:2; 6:9; [14:12]; 19:10

★ **1** ᵃDan. 7:3; Rev. 11:7; 13:14, 15; 15:2; 16:13; 17:8 ᵇRev. 12:3 ᶜRev. 12:3; 17:12 ᵈDan. 7:8, 11:36; Rev. 17:3
★ **2** ᵃDan. 7:6; Hos. 13:7f. ᵇDan. 7:5 ᶜDan. 7:4 ᵈRev. 12:3; 13:4, 12 ᵉRev. 2:13; 16:10
★ **3** ᵃRev. 13:12, 14 ᵇRev. 17:8
4 ᵃRev. 12:3; 13:2, 12 ᵇEx. 15:11; Is. 46:5; Rev. 18:18
★ **5** ᵃDan. 7:8, 11, 20, 25; 11:36; 2 Thess. 2:3f. ᵇRev. 11:2
6 ᵃRev. 7:15; 12:12
7 ᵃRev. 11:7 ᵇRev. 5:9

overcome them; and authority over [b]every tribe and people and tongue and nation was given to him.

8 And all who [a]dwell on the earth will worship him, *everyone* [b]whose name has not been written [c]from the foundation of the world in the book of life of [d]the Lamb who has been slain.

9 [a]If anyone has an ear, let him hear.

10 [a]If anyone *is destined* for captivity, to captivity he goes; [b]if anyone kills with the sword, with the sword he must be killed. Here is [c]the perseverance and the faith of the saints.

b The false prophet, 13:11–18

11 And [a]I saw another beast coming up out of the earth; and he had [b]two horns like a lamb, and he spoke as a [c]dragon.

12 And he [a]exercises all the authority of the first beast [b]in his presence. And he makes [c]the earth and those who dwell in it to [d]worship the first beast, whose [e]fatal wound was healed.

13 And he [a]performs great signs, so that he even makes [b]fire come down out of heaven to the earth in the presence of men.

14 And he [a]deceives [b]those who dwell on the earth because of [c]the signs which it was given him to perform [d]in the presence of the beast, telling those who dwell on the earth to make an image to the beast who *had the [e]wound of the sword and has come to life.

15 And there was given to him to give breath to the image of the beast, that the image of the beast might even speak and cause [a]as many as do not [b]worship the image of the beast to be killed.

16 And he causes all, [a]the small and the great, and the rich and the poor, and the free men and the slaves, to be given a [b]mark on their right hand, or on their forehead,

17 and *he provides* that no one should be able to buy or to sell, except the one who has the [a]mark, *either* [b]the name of the beast or [c]the number of his name.

18 [a]Here is wisdom. Let him who has understanding calculate the number of the beast, for the number is that [b]of a man; and his number is six hundred and sixty-six.

10 Various announcements, 14:1–20

a Concerning the 144,000, 14:1–5

14 And I looked, and behold, [a]the Lamb *was* standing on [b]Mount Zion, and with Him [c]one hundred and forty-four thousand, having [d]His name and the [d]name of His Father written [e]on their foreheads.

2 And I heard a voice from heaven, like [a]the sound of many waters and like the [b]sound of loud thunder, and the voice which I heard *was* like *the sound of* [c]harpists playing on their harps.

3 And they *sang [a]a new song before the throne and before the [b]four living creatures and the [c]elders; and [d]no one could learn the song except the [e]one hundred and forty-four thousand who had been [a]purchased from the earth.

Marginal references:

8 [a]Rev. 3:10; 13:12, 14 [b]Rev. 3:5 [c]Matt. 25:34; Rev. 17:8 [d]Rev. 5:6

9 [a]Rev. 2:7

★10 [a]Is. 33:1; Jer. 15:2; 43:11 [b]Gen. 9:6; Matt. 26:52; Rev. 11:18 [c]Heb. 6:12; Rev. 14:12

★11 [a]Rev. 13:1, 14; 16:13 [b]Dan. 8:3 [c]Rev. 13:4

12 [a]Rev. 13:4 [b]Rev. 13:14; 19:20 [c]Rev. 13:8 [d]Rev. 13:15; 14:9, 11; 16:2; 19:20; 20:4 [e]Rev. 13:3

13 [a]Matt. 24:24; Rev. 16:14; 19:20 [b]1 Kin. 18:38; Luke 9:54; Rev. 11:5; 20:9

14 [a]Rev. 12:9 [b]Rev. 13:8 [c]2 Thess. 2:9f. [d]Rev. 13:12; 19:20 [e]Rev. 13:3

15 [a]Dan. 3:3ff. [b]Rev. 13:12; 14:9, 11; 16:2; 19:20; 20:4

16 [a]Rev. 11:18; 19:5, 18 [b]Gal. 6:17; Rev. 7:3; 14:9; 20:4

17 [a]Gal. 6:17; Rev. 7:3; 14:9; 20:4 [b]Rev. 14:11 [c]Rev. 15:2

★18 [a]Rev. 17:9 [b]Rev. 21:17

★ 1 [a]Rev. 5:6 [b]Ps. 2:6; Heb. 12:22 [c]Rev. 7:4; 14:3 [d]Rev. 3:12 [e]Rev. 7:3

2 [a]Rev. 1:15 [b]Rev. 6:1 [c]Rev. 5:8

3 [a]Rev. 5:9 [b]Rev. 4:6 [c]Rev. 4:4 [d]Rev. 2:17 [e]Rev. 7:4; 14:1

13:10 Assurance that God will punish evildoers sustains the faith of those who are persecuted during these days. See also note on 14:12.

13:11 *another beast.* This man is Antichrist's lieutenant, who will enforce the worship of Antichrist by performing miracles (v. 13), by making and animating an image of Antichrist (vv. 14–15), by sentencing to death those who disobey (v. 15), and by requiring a mark on the hand or forehead in order that men may buy and sell (vv. 16–17).

13:18 *his number is six hundred and sixty-six.* Somehow, unknown to us, this number will play an important part in the identification of the Antichrist in a future day.

14:1 *the Lamb.* I.e., Christ. *one hundred and forty-four thousand.* Evidently the same group introduced in 7:4, though now their work on earth is finished and they are in heaven.

★ 4 aMatt.
19:12; 2 Cor.
11:2; Eph.
5:27; Rev.
3:4 bRev.
3:4; 7:17;
17:14 cRev.
5:9 dHeb.
12:23; James
1:18

4 aThese are the ones who have not been defiled with women, for they have kept themselves chaste. These are the ones who bfollow the Lamb wherever He goes. These have been cpurchased from among men das first fruits to God and to the Lamb.

5 aPs. 32:2;
Zeph. 3:13;
Mal. 2:6;
John 1:47;
1 Pet. 2:22
bHeb. 9:14;
1 Pet. 1:19;
Jude 24

5 And no lie was found ain their mouth; they are bblameless.

b *Concerning the everlasting gospel, 14:6–8*

★ 6 aRev.
8:13 b1 Pet.
1:25; Rev.
10:7 cRev.
3:10 dRev.
5:9

6 And I saw another angel flying in amidheaven, having ban eternal gospel to preach to cthose who live on the earth, and to devery nation and tribe and tongue and people;

7 aRev.
15:4 bRev.
11:13 cRev.
4:11 dRev.
8:10

7 and he said with a loud voice, "aFear God, and bgive Him glory, because the hour of His judgment has come; and worship Him who cmade the heaven and the earth and sea and dsprings of waters."

★ 8 aIs.
21:9; Jer.
51:8; Rev.
18:2 bDan.
4:30; Rev.
16:19; 17:5;
18:10 cJer.
51:7 dRev.
17:2, 4; 18:3

8 And another angel, a second one, followed, saying, "aFallen, fallen is bBabylon the great, she who has cmade all the nations drink of the dwine of the passion of her immorality."

c *Concerning beast worshipers, 14:9–13*

9 aRev.
13:12; 14:11
bRev.
13:14f.;
14:11 cRev.
13:16
10 aIs.
51:17; Jer.
25:15f., 27;
Rev. 16:19;
19:15 bPs.
75:8; Rev.
18:6 cEzek.
38:22;
2 Thess. 1:7;
Rev. 19:20;
20:10, 14f.;
21:8 dMark
8:38

9 And another angel, a third one, followed them, saying with a loud voice, "If anyone aworships the beast and his bimage, and receives a cmark on his forehead or upon his hand,

10 he also will drink of the awine of the wrath of God, which is mixed in full strength bin the cup of His anger; and he will be tormented with cfire and brim-

stone in the presence of the dholy angels and in the presence of the Lamb.

11 "And the asmoke of their torment goes up forever and ever; and bthey have no rest day and night, those who cworship the beast and his cimage, and whoever receives the dmark of his name."

11 aIs. 34:8-
10; Rev.
18:9, 18;
19:3 bRev.
4:8 cRev.
13:12; 14:9
dRev. 13:17

12 Here is athe perseverance of the saints who bkeep the commandments of God and ctheir faith in Jesus.

★12 aRev.
13:10 bRev.
12:17 cRev.
2:13

13 And I heard a voice from heaven, saying, "Write, 'aBlessed are the dead who bdie in the Lord cfrom now on!' " "Yes," dsays the Spirit, "that they may erest from their labors, for their fdeeds follow with them."

13 aRev.
20:6 b1 Cor.
15:18;
1 Thess. 4:16
cRev. 11:18
dRev. 2:7;
22:17 eHeb.
4:9f.; Rev.
6:11 f1 Tim.
5:25

d *Concerning the harvesting of the earth, 14:14–20*

14 And I looked, and behold, a awhite cloud, and sitting on the cloud was one blike a son of man, having a golden ccrown on His head, and a sharp sickle in His hand.

14 aMatt.
17:5 bRev.
1:13 cPs.
21:3; Rev.
6:2

15 And another angel acame out of the temple, crying out with a loud voice to Him who sat on the cloud, "bPut in your sickle and reap, because the hour to reap has come, because the char vest of the earth is ripe."

15 aRev.
11:19; 14:17
15:6; 16:17
bJoel 3:13;
Mark 4:29;
Rev. 14:18
cJer. 51:33;
Matt. 13:39-
41

16 And He who sat on the cloud swung His sickle over the earth; and the earth was reaped.

17 And another angel acame out of the temple which is in heaven, and he also had a sharp sickle.

17 aRev.
11:19; 14:15;
15:6; 16:17
18 aRev.
16:8 bRev.
6:9; 8:3
cJoel 3:13;
Mark 4:29;
Rev. 14:15
dJoel 3:13

18 And another angel, athe one who has power over fire, came out from bthe altar; and he

---

14:4 *not . . . defiled with women.* This may simply mean that the 144,000 were unmarried, or it may indicate their purposeful celibate state of separation unto God (cf. 2 Cor. 11:2). *first fruits.* The salvation of the 144,000 will forerun the salvation of a larger group of Israelites, who will turn to the Lord at the end of the tribulation (cf. Isa. 2:3; Rom. 11:15).

14:6 *an eternal gospel to preach.* God's last call

of grace to the world before the return of Christ in judgment.

14:8 *fallen is Babylon.* This fall is described in detail in chapters 17-18. For *Babylon,* see note on 17:5.

14:12 Saints will be able to endure, knowing that God will punish their enemies (vv. 9–11). See also note on 13:10.

called with a loud voice to him who had the sharp sickle, saying, "ᶜPut in your sharp sickle, and gather the clusters from the vine of the earth, ᵈbecause her grapes are ripe."

19 And the angel swung his sickle to the earth, and gathered *the clusters from* the vine of the earth, and threw them into ᵃthe great wine press of the wrath of God.

20 And the wine press was trodden ᵃoutside the city, and ᵇblood came out from the wine press, up to the horses' bridles, for a distance of two hundred miles.

11 Prelude to the bowl judgments, 15:1-8

15 And I saw ᵃanother sign in heaven, great and marvelous, ᵇseven angels who had ᶜseven plagues, *which are* ᵈthe last, because in them the wrath of God is finished.

2 And I saw, as it were, a ᵃsea of glass mixed with fire, and those who had ᵇcome off victorious from the ᶜbeast and from ᵈhis image and from the ᵉnumber of his name, standing on the ᵃsea of glass, holding ᶠharps of God.

3 And they *sang the ᵃsong of Moses ᵇthe bond-servant of God and the ᶜsong of the Lamb, saying,

"ᵈGreat and marvelous are
    Thy works,
ᵉO Lord God, the Al-
    mighty;
Righteous and true are
    Thy ways,
Thou ᶠKing of the nations.

4 "ᵃWho will not fear, O
    Lord, and glorify Thy
    name?
For Thou alone art holy;

For ᵇALL THE NATIONS WILL
    COME AND WORSHIP BEFORE
    THEE,
For Thy ᶜrighteous acts
    have been revealed."

5 After these things I looked, and ᵃthe temple of the ᵇtabernacle of testimony in heaven was opened,

6 and the ᵃseven angels who had the seven plagues ᵇcame out of the temple, clothed ᶜin linen, clean *and* bright, and ᵈgirded around their breasts with golden girdles.

7 And one of the ᵃfour living creatures gave to the ᵇseven angels seven ᶜgolden bowls full of the ᵈwrath of God, who ᵉlives forever and ever.

8 And the temple was filled with ᵃsmoke from the glory of God and from His power; and no one was able to enter the temple until the seven plagues of the seven angels were finished.

12 The bowl judgments, 16:1-21

a First bowl: grievous sores, 16:1-2

16 And I heard a loud voice from ᵃthe temple, saying to the ᵇseven angels, "Go and ᶜpour out the ᵈseven bowls of the wrath of God into the earth."

2 And the first *angel* went and poured out his bowl ᵃinto the earth; and it became a loathsome and malignant ᵇsore upon the men ᶜwho had the mark of the beast and who worshiped his image.

b Second bowl: seas smitten, 16:3

3 And the second *angel* poured out his bowl ᵃinto the sea,

---

19 ᵃIs. 63:2f.; Rev. 19:15

★**20** ᵃHeb. 13:12; Rev. 11:8 ᵇGen. 49:11; Deut. 32:14

1 ᵃRev. 12:1, 3 ᵇRev. 15:6-8; 16:1; 17:1; 21:9 ᶜLev. 26:21 ᵈRev. 9:20

2 ᵃRev. 4:6 ᵇRev. 12:11 ᶜRev. 13:1 ᵈRev. 13:14f. ᵉRev. 13:17 ᶠRev. 5:8

3 ᵃEx. 15:1ff. ᵇJosh. 22:5; Heb. 3:5 ᶜRev. 5:9f., 12f. ᵈDeut. 32:3f.; Ps. 111:2; 139:14; Hos. 14:9 ᵉRev. 1:8 ᶠ1 Tim. 1:17 marg.

4 ᵃJer. 10:7; Rev. 14:7 ᵇPs. 86:9; Is. 66:23 ᶜRev. 19:8

★**5** ᵃRev. 11:19 ᵇEx. 38:21; Num. 1:50; Heb. 8:5; Rev. 13:6

6 ᵃRev. 15:1 ᵇRev. 14:15 ᶜEzek. 28:13 ᵈRev. 1:13

7 ᵃRev. 4:6 ᵇRev. 15:1 ᶜRev. 5:8 ᵈRev. 14:10; 15:1 ᵉRev. 4:9

8 ᵃEx. 19:18; 40:34f.; Lev. 16:2; 1 Kin. 8:10f.; 2 Chr. 5:13f.; Is. 6:4

1 ᵃRev. 11:19 ᵇRev. 15:1 ᶜPs. 79:6; Jer. 10:25; Ezek. 22:31; Zeph. 3:8; Rev. 16:2ff. ᵈRev. 5:8

★**2** ᵃRev. 8:7 ᵇEx. 9:9-11; Deut. 28:35; Rev. 16:11 ᶜRev. 13:15-17; 14:9

★**3** ᵃEx. 7:17-21; Rev. 8:8f.; 11:6

14:20 Apparently a reference to Armageddon (16:16; cf. 19:17-19), when the blood from the slaughter will flow 200 miles, to the depth of about 4½ feet (14:20).

15:5 *the temple of the tabernacle of testimony.* I.e., the Holy of Holies.

16:2 *a loathsome and malignant sore.* Lit., foul and evil sore. Probably a plague of ulcers. The brief descriptions of these last seven judgments (vv. 2-12, 17-21) may suggest they occur in rapid succession.

16:3 *every living thing in the sea died.* See 8:9. Imagine the stench and disease that will accompany this.

and it became blood like *that* of a dead man; and every living thing in the sea died.

c Third bowl: rivers smitten, 16:4-7

4 And the third *angel* poured out his bowl into the *a*rivers and the springs of waters; and they *b*became blood.

5 And I heard the angel of the waters saying, "*a*Righteous art Thou, *b*who art and who wast, O *c*Holy One, because Thou didst *d*judge these things;

6 for they poured out *a*the blood of saints and prophets, and Thou hast given them *b*blood to drink. They deserve it."

7 And I heard *a*the altar saying, "Yes, O *b*Lord God, the Almighty, *c*true and righteous are Thy judgments."

d Fourth bowl: scorching, 16:8-9

8 And the fourth *angel* poured out his bowl upon *a*the sun; *b*and it was given to it to scorch men with fire.

9 And men were scorched with fierce heat; and they *a*blasphemed the name of God who has the power over these plagues; and they *b*did not repent, so as to *c*give Him glory.

e Fifth bowl: darkness, 16:10-11

10 And the fifth *angel* poured out his bowl upon the *a*throne of the beast; and his kingdom became *b*darkened; and they gnawed their tongues because of pain,

11 and they *a*blasphemed the *b*God of heaven because of their pains and their *c*sores; and they *d*did not repent of their deeds.

f Sixth bowl: Euphrates dried, 16:12-16

12 And the sixth *angel* poured out his bowl upon the *a*great river, the Euphrates; and *b*its water was dried up, that *c*the way might be prepared for the kings *d*from the east.

13 And I saw *coming* out of the mouth of the *a*dragon and out of the mouth of the *b*beast and out of the mouth of the *c*false prophet, three *d*unclean spirits like *e*frogs;

14 for they are *a*spirits of demons, *b*performing signs, which go out to the kings of the *c*whole world, to *d*gather them together for the war of the *e*great day of God, the Almighty.

15 ("Behold, *a*I am coming like a thief. *b*Blessed is the one who stays awake and keeps his garments, *c*lest he walk about naked and men see his shame.")

16 And they *a*gathered them together to the place which *b*in Hebrew is called Har-*c*Magedon.

g Seventh bowl: widespread destruction, 16:17-21

17 And the seventh *angel* poured out his bowl upon *a*the air; and a *b*loud voice came out of

---

Marginal references:

4 *a*Rev. 8:10 *b*Ex. 7:17-20; Rev. 11:6

5 *a*John 17:25 *b*Rev. 11:17 *c*Rev. 15:4 *d*Rev. 6:10

★ 6 *a*Rev. 17:6; 18:24 *b*Is. 49:26; Luke 11:49-51

7 *a*Rev. 6:9; 14:18 *b*Rev. 1:8 *c*Rev. 15:3; 19:2

8 *a*Rev. 6:12 *b*Rev. 14:18

★ 9 *a*Rev. 16:11, 21 *b*Rev. 2:21 *c*Rev. 11:13

10 *a*Rev. 13:2 *b*Ex. 10:21f.; Is. 8:22; Rev. 8:12; 9:2

★11 *a*Rev. 16:9, 21 *b*Rev. 11:13 *c*Rev. 16:2 *d*Rev. 2:21

★12 *a*Rev. 9:14 *b*Is. 11:15f.; 44:27; Jer. 51:32, 36 *c*Is. 41:2, 25; 46:11 *d*Rev. 7:2

★13 *a*Rev. 12:3 *b*Rev. 13:1 *c*Rev. 13:11, 14; 19:20; 20:10 *d*Rev. 18:2 *e*Ex. 8:6

★14 *a*1 Tim. 4:1 *b*Rev. 13:13 *c*Rev. 3:10 *d*1 Kin. 22:21-23; Rev. 17:14; 19:19; 20:8 *e*Rev. 6:17

15 *a*Rev. 3:3, 11 *b*Luke 12:37 *c*Rev. 3:18

★16 *a*Rev. 19:19 *b*Rev. 9:11 *c*Judg. 5:19; 2 Kin. 23:29f.; 2 Chr. 35:22; Zech. 12:11

17 *a*Eph. 2:2 *b*Rev. 11:15 *c*Rev. 14:15 *d*Rev. 10:6; 21:6

16:6 *They deserve it.* I.e., they deserve to drink blood because they shed the blood of saints and prophets.

16:9 *they did not repent.* See v. 11 and 9:21.

16:11 *their sores.* I.e., those referred to in v. 2.

16:12 *the kings from the east.* Lit., the kings from the rising of the sun. The armies of the nations of the Orient will be aided in their march toward Armageddon by the supernatural drying up of the Euphrates River.

16:13 *the dragon.* Satan. *the beast.* Antichrist (13:1-10). *the false prophet.* The lieutenant (13:11-18).

16:14 *the war of the great day of God, the Almighty.* The war will consist of several battles, beginning with Antichrist's campaign into Egypt (Dan. 11:40-45) and including a siege of Jerusalem (Zech. 14:2) as well as the final battle at Armageddon (Rev. 16:16).

16:16 *Har-Magedon (or Armageddon).* Lit., Mount of Megiddo, near the city of Megiddo at the head of the plain of Esdraelon. This area was the scene of many O.T. battles, notably those of Barak with the Canaanites (Judg. 4) and of Gideon with the Midianites (Judg. 7).

the ᶜtemple from the throne, saying, "ᵈIt is done."

18 And there were flashes of ᵃlightning and sounds and peals of thunder; and there was ᵇa great earthquake, ᶜsuch as there had not been since man came to be upon the earth, so great an earthquake *was it, and* so mighty.

19 And ᵃthe great city was split into three parts, and the cities of the nations fell. And ᵇBabylon the great was ᶜremembered before God, to give her ᵈthe cup of the wine of His fierce wrath.

20 And ᵃevery island fled away, and the mountains were not found.

21 And ᵃhuge hailstones, about one hundred pounds each, *came down from heaven upon men; and men ᵇblasphemed God because of the ᶜplague of the hail, because its plague *was extremely severe.

13 Religious Babylon, 17:1-18

a The description, 17:1-7

17 ᵃAnd one of the ᵇseven angels who had the ᶜseven bowls came and spoke with me, saying, "Come here, I shall show you ᵈthe judgment of the ᵉgreat harlot who ᶠsits on many waters,

2 with whom ᵃthe kings of the earth committed *acts of* immorality, and ᵇthose who dwell on the earth were ᶜmade drunk with the wine of her immorality."

3 And ᵃhe carried me away ᵇin the Spirit ᶜinto a wilderness; and I saw a woman sitting on a

ᵈscarlet beast, full of ᵉblasphemous names, having ᶠseven heads and ten horns.

4 And the woman ᵃwas clothed in purple and scarlet, and adorned with gold and precious stones and pearls, having in her hand ᵇa gold cup full of abominations and of the unclean things of her immorality,

5 and upon her forehead a name *was* written, a ᵃmystery, "ᵇBABYLON THE GREAT, THE MOTHER OF HARLOTS AND OF ᶜTHE ABOMINATIONS OF THE EARTH."

6 And I saw the woman drunk with the ᵃblood of the saints, and with the blood of the witnesses of Jesus. And when I saw her, I wondered greatly.

7 And the angel said to me, "Why do you wonder? I shall tell you the ᵃmystery of the woman and of the beast that carries her, which has the ᵇseven heads and the ten horns.

b The interpretation, 17:8-18

8 "The beast that you saw ᵃwas and is not, and is about to ᵇcome up out of the ᶜabyss and to ᵈgo to destruction. And ᵉthose who dwell on the earth will ᶠwonder, ᵍwhose name has not been written in the book of life ʰfrom the foundation of the world, when they see the beast, that ᵃhe was and is not and will come.

9 "ᵃHere is the mind which has wisdom. The ᵇseven heads are seven mountains on which the woman sits,

10 and they are seven ᵃkings; five have fallen, one is, the other

---

18 ᵃRev. 4:5 ᵇRev. 6:12 ᶜDan. 12:1; Matt. 24:21

★19 ᵃRev. 11:8; 17:18; 18:10, 18f. 21 ᵇRev. 14:8 ᶜRev. 18:5 ᵈRev. 14:10

20 ᵃRev. 6:14; 20:11

21 ᵃRev. 8:7; 11:19 ᵇRev. 16:9, 11 ᶜEx. 9:18-25

1 ᵃRev. 1:1; 21:9 ᵇRev. 15:1 ᶜRev. 15:7 ᵈRev. 16:19 ᵉIs. 1:21; Jer. 2:20; Nah. 3:4; Rev. 17:5, 15f. 19:2 ᶠJer. 51:13; Rev. 17:15 **2** ᵃRev. 2:22; 18:3, 9 ᵇRev. 3:10; 17:8 ᶜRev. 14:8 **3** ᵃRev. 21:10 ᵇRev. 1:10 ᶜRev. 12:6, 14; 21:10 ᵈMatt. 27:28; Rev. 18:12, 16 ᵉRev. 13:1 ᶠRev. 12:3; 17:7, 9, 12, 16

4 ᵃEzek. 28:13; Rev. 18:12, 16 ᵇJer. 51:7; Rev. 18:6

★ 5 ᵃ2 Thess. 2:7; Rev. 1:20; 17:7 ᵇRev. 14:8; 16:19 ᶜRev. 17:2

6 ᵃRev. 16:6

7 ᵃ2 Thess. 2:7; Rev. 1:20; 17:5 ᵇRev. 17:3

★ 8 ᵃRev. 13:3, 12, 14; 17:11 ᵇRev. 11:7; 13:1 ᶜRev. 9:1; 13:1 ᵈRev. 13:10; 17:11 ᵉRev. 3:10 ᶠRev. 13:3 ᵍRev. 3:5 ʰMatt. 25:34; Rev. 13:8

9 ᵃRev. 13:18 ᵇRev. 17:3

10 ᵃRev. 10:11

16:19 *the great city.* Either Jerusalem (11:8; cf. Zech. 14:4) or Babylon (Rev. 18:2).

17:5 *Babylon the Great.* Though the famous city of Babylon was on the Euphrates River, the name here seems to be a symbolic reference to Rome (see v. 9 and 1 Pet. 5:13). In chapter 17 Babylon represents the false religious system that will center in Rome during the tribulation period. In chapter 18 it represents more the political and commercial aspect of the revived Roman Empire headed by Anti-

christ. Thus the term stands both for a city and for a system (religious and commercial) related to the city (much like "Wall Street," which is both a place and a system). For other references to Babylon see Gen. 10:10; 11:9 ("Babel"); Isa. 13:19-20; Jer. 50-51. *mother of harlots.* The false religious system is unfaithful to the Lord and thus is described as a harlot (vv. 1, 15-16).

17:8 *is about to come up out of the abyss.* See 11:7. *and to go to destruction.* See 19:20.

has not yet come; and when he comes, he must remain a little while.

11 "And the beast which [a]was and is not, is himself also an eighth, and is *one* of the seven, and he [b]goes to destruction.

12 "And the [a]ten horns which you saw are ten kings, who have not yet received a kingdom, but they receive authority as kings with the beast [b]for one hour.

13 "These have [a]one purpose and they give their power and authority to the beast.

14 "These will wage [a]war against the Lamb, and the Lamb will [b]overcome them, because He is [c]Lord of lords and [c]King of kings, and [d]those who are with Him *are the* [e]called and chosen and faithful."

15 And he *said to me, "The [a]waters which you saw where the harlot sits, are [b]peoples and multitudes and nations and tongues.

16 "And the [a]ten horns which you saw, and the beast, these will hate the harlot and will make her [b]desolate and [c]naked, and will [d]eat her flesh and will [e]burn her up with fire.

17 "For [a]God has put it in their hearts to execute His purpose by [b]having a common purpose, and by giving their kingdom to the beast, until the [c]words of God should be fulfilled.

18 "And the woman whom you saw is [a]the great city, which reigns over the kings of the earth."

14 Commercial Babylon, 18:1-24

a Announcement, 18:1-3

18 After these things I saw [a]another angel [b]coming down from heaven, having great authority, and the earth was [c]illumined with his glory.

2 And he cried out with a mighty voice, saying, "[a]Fallen, fallen is Babylon the great! And she [b]has become a dwelling place of demons and a prison of every [c]unclean spirit, and a prison of every unclean and hateful bird.

3 "For all the nations have drunk of the [a]wine of the passion of her immorality, and [b]the kings of the earth have committed *acts of* immorality with her, and the [c]merchants of the earth have become rich by the wealth of her [d]sensuality."

b Appeal, 18:4-8

4 And I heard another voice from heaven, saying, "[a]Come out of her, my people, that you may not participate in her sins and that you may not receive of her plagues;

5 for her sins have [a]piled up as high as heaven, and God has [b]remembered her iniquities.

6 "[a]Pay her back even as she has paid, and give back *to her* double according to her deeds; in the [b]cup which she has mixed, mix twice as much for her.

7 "[a]To the degree that she glorified herself and [b]lived sensuously, to the same degree give her torment and mourning; for she says in her heart, '[c]I SIT *as* A QUEEN AND I AM NOT A WIDOW, and will never see mourning.'

8 "For this reason [a]in one day her plagues will come, pestilence and mourning and famine, and she will be [b]burned up with fire; for the Lord God who judges her [c]is strong.

Marginal references

11 [a]Rev. 13:3, 12, 14; 17:8 [b]Rev. 13:10; 17:8

★12 [a]Rev. 12:3; 13:1; 17:16 [b]Rev. 18:10, 17, 19

13 [a]Rev. 17:17

14 [a]Rev. 16:14 [b]Rev. 3:21 [c]1 Tim. 6:15; Rev. 19:16 [d]Rev. 2:10f. [e]Matt. 22:14

★15 [a]Is. 8:7; Jer. 47:2; Rev. 17:1 [b]Rev. 5:9

★16 [a]Rev. 17:12 [b]Rev. 18:17, 19 [c]Ezek. 16:37, 39 [d]Rev. 19:18 [e]Rev. 18:8

17 [a]2 Cor. 8:16 [b]Rev. 17:13 [c]Rev. 10:7

18 [a]Rev. 11:8; 16:19

1 [a]Rev. 17:1, 7 [b]Rev. 10:1 [c]Ezek. 43:2

2 [a]Rev. 14:8 [b]Is. 13:21f.; 34:11, 13-15; Jer. 50:39; 51:37; Zeph. 2:14f. [c]Rev. 16:13

3 [a]Rev. 14:8 [b]Rev. 17:2; 18:9 [c]Ezek. 27:9-25; Rev. 18:11, 15, 19, 23 [d]1 Tim. 5:11; Rev. 18:7, 9

★4 [a]Is. 52:11; Jer 50:8; 51:6, 9, 45; 2 Cor. 6:17

5 [a]Jer. 51:9 [b]Rev. 16:19

6 [a]Ps. 137:8; Jer. 50:15, 29 [b]Rev. 17:4

7 [a]Ezek. 28:2-8 [b]1 Tim. 5:11; Rev. 18:3, 9 [c]Is. 47:7f.; Zeph. 2:15

★8 [a]Is. 47:9; Jer. 50:31f.; Rev. 18:10 [b]Rev. 17:16 [c]Jer. 50:34; Rev. 11:17f.

17:12 *ten kings.* The 10-nation federation which will form in the west and will be headed by Antichrist (see Dan. 7:23-24 and note on Rev. 13:1). *one hour.* I.e., for one purpose (as in Luke 22:53).

17:15 The apostate church will be ecumenical, or world-wide.

17:16 *these will hate the harlot.* The political power headed by Antichrist will overthrow the false church organization (probably at the mid-point of the tribulation).

18:4 *my people.* God's people are to separate themselves from the Babylonian system (cf. 2 Cor. 6:14-17; 1 John 2:15-17).

18:8 *in one day.* The judgment will be consummated in a single day, as happened once before to Babylon, when it was taken by Darius (Dan. 5:1, 3-5, 30).

c Anguish, 18:9-19

9 "And ᵃthe kings of the earth, who committed *acts of* immorality and ᵇlived sensuously with her, will ᶜweep and lament over her when they ᵈsee the smoke of her burning,

10 ᵃstanding at a distance because of the fear of her torment, saying, 'ᵇWoe, woe, ᶜthe great city, Babylon, the strong city! For in ᵈone hour your judgment has come.'

11 "And the ᵃmerchants of the earth ᵇweep and mourn over her, because no one buys their cargoes any more;

12 cargoes of ᵃgold and silver and precious stones and pearls and fine linen and purple and silk and scarlet, and every *kind of* citron wood and every article of ivory and every article *made* from very costly wood and bronze and iron and marble,

13 and cinnamon and spice and incense and perfume and frankincense and wine and olive oil and fine flour and wheat and cattle and sheep, and *cargoes* of horses and chariots and slaves and ᵃhuman lives.

14 "And the fruit you long for has gone from you, and all things that were luxurious and splendid have passed away from you and *men* will no longer find them.

15 "The ᵃmerchants of ᵇthese things, who became rich from her, will ᶜstand at a distance because of the fear of her torment, weeping and mourning,

16 saying, 'ᵃWoe, woe, ᵇthe great city, she who ᶜwas clothed in fine linen and purple and scarlet, and adorned with gold and precious stones and pearls;

17 for in ᵃone hour such great wealth has been laid ᵇwaste!' And ᶜevery shipmaster and every passenger and sailor, and as many as make their living by the sea, ᵃstood at a distance,

18 and were ᵃcrying out as they ᵇsaw the smoke of her burning, saying, 'ᶜWhat *city* is like ᵈthe great city?'

19 "And they threw ᵃdust on their heads and were crying out, weeping and mourning, saying, 'ᵇWoe, woe, the great city, in which all who had ships at sea ᶜbecame rich by her wealth, for in ᵇone hour she has been laid ᵈwaste!'

d Acclaim, 18:20-24

20 "ᵃRejoice over her, O heaven, and you saints and ᵇapostles and prophets, because ᶜGod has pronounced judgment for you against her."

21 And a ᵃstrong angel ᵇtook up a stone like a great millstone and threw it into the sea, saying, "Thus will Babylon, ᶜthe great city, be thrown down with violence, and will not be found any longer.

22 "And ᵃthe sound of harpists and musicians and flute-players and trumpeters will not be heard in you any longer; and no craftsman of any craft will be found in you any longer; and the ᵇsound of a mill will not be heard in you any longer;

23 and the light of a lamp will not shine in you any longer; and the ᵃvoice of the bridegroom and bride will not be heard in you any longer; for your ᵇmerchants were the great men of the earth, because all the nations were deceived ᶜby your sorcery.

24 "And in her was found the ᵃblood of prophets and of saints and of ᵇall who have been slain on the earth."

18:12 *citron wood.* A dark, hard, and fragrant wood, valued by the Greeks and Romans for use in cabinet making.

18:20 *God has pronounced judgment for you against her.* I.e., God has judged her for her treatment of you. Heaven and the martyrs may now rejoice.

18:22-23 No music, no worker, no machinery, no light, no happiness shall be found in Babylon any more.

Cross references (margin):

9 ᵃRev. 17:2; 18:3 ᵇ1 Tim. 5:11; Rev. 18:3, 7 ᶜEzek. 26:16f.; 27:35 ᵈRev. 14:11; 18:18; 19:3

10 ᵃRev. 18:15, 17 ᵇRev. 18:16, 19 ᶜRev. 11:8; 16:19; 18:16, 18, 19, 21 ᵈRev. 17:12; 18:8, 17, 19

11 ᵃEzek. 27:9-25; Rev. 18:3, 15, 19, 23 ᵇEzek. 27:27-34

★12 ᵃEzek. 27:12-22; Rev. 17:4

13 ᵃEzek. 27:13; 1 Chr. 5:21 marg.; 1 Tim. 1:10

15 ᵃRev. 18:3 ᵇRev. 18:12, 13 ᶜRev. 18:10

16 ᵃRev. 18:10, 19 ᵇRev. 18:10, 18, 19, 21 ᶜRev. 17:4

17 ᵃRev. 18:10 ᵇRev. 17:16; 18:19 ᶜEzek. 27:28f.

18 ᵃEzek. 27:30 ᵇRev. 18:9 ᶜEzek. 27:32; Rev. 13:4 ᵈRev. 18:10

19 ᵃJosh. 7:6; Job 2:12; Lam. 2:10 ᵇRev. 18:10 ᶜRev. 18:3, 15 ᵈRev. 17:16; 18:17

★20 ᵃJer. 51:48; Rev. 12:12 ᵇLuke 11:49f. ᶜRev. 6:10; 18:6ff.; 19:2

21 ᵃRev. 5:2; 10:1 ᵇJer. 51:63f. ᶜRev. 18:10

★22-23
22 ᵃIs. 24:8; Ezek. 26:13; Matt. 9:23 ᵇEccles. 12:4; Jer. 25:10

23 ᵃJer. 7:34; 16:9 ᵇIs. 23:8; Rev. 6:15; 18:3 ᶜNah. 3:4; Rev. 9:21

24 ᵃRev. 16:6; 17:6 ᵇMatt. 23:35

15 The second coming of Christ, 19:1-21

a Announcements, 19:1-10

19 After these things I heard, as it were, a ᵃloud voice of a great multitude in heaven, saying,

"ᵇHallelujah! ᶜSalvation and ᵈglory and power belong to our God;

2 ᵃBECAUSE HIS ᵇJUDGMENTS ARE ᶜTRUE AND RIGHTEOUS; for He has judged the ᵈgreat harlot who was corrupting the earth with her immorality, and HE HAS ᵉAVENGED THE BLOOD OF HIS BOND-SERVANTS ON HER."

3 And a second time they said, "ᵃHallelujah! HER ᵇSMOKE RISES UP FOREVER AND EVER."

4 And the ᵃtwenty-four elders and the ᵇfour living creatures ᶜfell down and worshiped God who sits on the throne saying, "ᵈAmen. ᵉHallelujah!"

5 And a voice came from the throne, saying,

"ᵃGive praise to our God, all you His bond-servants, ᵇyou who fear Him, the small and the great."

6 And I heard, as it were, ᵃthe voice of a great multitude and as ᵇthe sound of many waters and as the ᶜsound of mighty peals of thunder, saying,

"ᵃHallelujah! For the ᵈLord our God, the Almighty, reigns.

7 "Let us rejoice and be glad and ᵃgive the glory to Him, for ᵇthe marriage of the Lamb has come and His ᶜbride has made herself ready."

8 And it was given to her to clothe herself in ᵃfine linen, bright and clean; for the fine linen is the ᵇrighteous acts of the saints.

9 And ᵃhe *said to me, "ᵇWrite, 'ᶜBlessed are those who are invited to the marriage supper of the Lamb.'" And he *said to me, "ᵈThese are true words of God."

10 And ᵃI fell at his feet to worship him. ᵇAnd he *said to me, "Do not do that; I am a ᶜfellow servant of yours and your brethren who ᵈhold the testimony of Jesus; worship God. For the testimony of Jesus is the spirit of prophecy."

b Advent of Christ, 19:11-16

11 And I saw ᵃheaven opened; and behold, a ᵇwhite horse, and He who sat upon it is called ᶜFaithful and True; and in ᵈrighteousness He judges and wages war.

12 And His ᵃeyes are a flame of fire, and upon His head are many ᵇdiadems; and He has a ᶜname written upon Him which no one knows except Himself.

13 And He is clothed with a ᵃrobe dipped in blood; and His name is called ᵇThe Word of God.

14 And the armies which are in heaven, clothed in ᵃfine linen, ᵇwhite and clean, were following Him on white horses.

15 And ᵃfrom His mouth comes a sharp sword, so that

Marginal references

★ 1 ᵃJer. 51:48; Rev. 11:15; 19:6 ᵇPs. 104:35 marg.; Rev. 19:3, 4, 6 ᶜRev. 7:10 ᵈRev. 4:11

2 ᵃPs. 19:9 ᵇRev. 6:10 ᶜRev. 16:7 ᵈRev. 17:1 ᵉDeut. 32:43; 2 Kin. 9:7; Rev. 16:6; 18:20

3 ᵃPs. 104:35; Is. 34:10; Rev. 19:1, 4, 6 ᵇRev. 14:11 4 ᵃRev. 4:4, 10 ᵇRev. 4:6 ᶜRev. 4:10 ᵈPs. 106:48; Rev. 5:14 ᵉPs. 104:35; Rev. 19:3, 6 5 ᵃPs. 115:13; 134:1; 135:1 ᵇRev. 11:18

6 ᵃJer. 51:48; Rev. 11:15; 19:1 ᵇRev. 1:15 ᶜRev. 6:1 ᵈRev. 1:8 7 ᵃRev. 11:13 ᵇMatt. 22:2; 25:10; Luke 12:36; John 3:29; Eph. 5:23, 32; Rev. 19:9 ᶜMatt. 1:20; Rev. 21:2, 9

★ 8 ᵃRev. 15:6; 19:14 ᵇRev. 15:4

9 ᵃRev. 17:1; 19:10 ᵇRev. 1:19 ᶜLuke 14:15; 22:16 ᵈRev. 17:17; 21:5; 22:6

★10 ᵃRev. 22:8 ᵇActs 10:26; Rev. 22:9 ᶜRev. 1:11; ᵈRev. 12:17

★11 ᵃJohn 1:51; Rev. 4:1 ᵇRev. 6:2; 19:19, 21 ᶜRev. 3:14 ᵈIs. 11:4

★12 ᵃRev. 1:14 ᵇRev. 6:2; 12:3 ᶜRev. 2:17; 19:16

★13 ᵃIs. 63:3 ᵇJohn 1:1 14 ᵃRev. 19:8 ᵇRev. 3:4; 19:8 ★15 ᵃRev. 1:16; 19:21 ᵇIs. 11:4; 2 Thess. 2:8 ᶜRev. 2:27 ᵈRev. 14:19, 20

Footnotes

19:1 Hallelujah = praise the Lord. The word occurs only in this chapter in the entire N.T. It does appear as a brief doxology in several Psalms, e.g., 150:1, 6.

19:8 the righteous acts of the saints. The good works of believers will constitute the wedding garment when the congregation of the faithful are joined to Him in marriage (cf. 2 Cor. 11:2; Eph. 5:26-27).

19:10 Do not do that. Men are not to worship angels, only God. For the testimony of Jesus is the spirit of prophecy. Prophecy is designed to unfold the loveliness of Jesus.

19:11 heaven opened. This is the second coming of Christ to the earth—during the war of Armageddon, in which He will be the Victor and in which all who oppose Him will be slain (vv. 19, 21). See notes on 14:20; 16:14, 16. Faithful and True. These terms have been used previously of Christ (1:5; 3:7).

19:12 His eyes are a flame of fire. See 1:14; 2:18. a name written . . . which no one knows. This is perhaps the same name He will write on the overcomer (2:17; 3:12).

19:13 The Word. This name, applied here to Christ, is found only in the writings of John (cf. John 1:1, 14; 1 John 1:1).

19:15 wine press. It consisted of two receptacles, or vats, placed at different levels, in the upper one of which the grapes were trodden, while the lower one received the juice (cf. 14:20).

16 aRev.
2:17; 19:12
bRev. 17:14

bwith it He may smite the nations; and He will crule them with a rod of iron; and dHe treads the wine press of the fierce wrath of God, the Almighty.

16　And on His robe and on His thigh He has aa name written, "bKING OF KINGS, AND LORD OF LORDS."

c　Armageddon, 19:17-21

★17-18
17 aRev.
19:21 bRev.
8:13 c1 Sam.
17:44; Jer.
12:9; Ezek.
39:17 dIs.
34:6; Jer.
46:10
18 aEzek.
39:18-20
bRev. 6:15
cRev. 11:18;
13:16; 19:5

17　And I saw an angel standing in the sun; and he cried out with a loud voice, saying to aall the birds which fly in bmidheaven, "cCome, assemble for the dgreat supper of God;

18　in order that you may aeat the flesh of kings and the flesh of commanders and the flesh of mighty men and the flesh of horses and of those who sit on them and the flesh of all men, bboth free men and slaves, and csmall and great."

19 aRev.
11:7; 13:1
bRev. 16:14,
16 cRev.
19:11, 21

19　And I saw athe beast and bthe kings of the earth and their armies, assembled to make war against Him who csat upon the horse, and against His army.

20 aRev.
16:13 bRev.
13:13 cRev.
13:12 dRev.
13:14 eRev.
13:16f. fRev.
13:15 [12]
gRev. 20:10,
14f.; 21:8
hIs. 30:33;
Dan. 7:11;
Rev. 14:10

20　And the beast was seized, and with him the afalse prophet who bperformed the signs cin his presence, by which he ddeceived those who had received the emark of the beast and those who fworshiped his image; these two were thrown alive into the glake of hfire which burns with brimstone.

21 aRev.
19:15 bRev.
19:11, 19
cRev. 19:17

21　And the rest were killed with the sword which acame from the mouth of Him who bsat upon

the horse, and call the birds were filled with their flesh.

B　The Millennium, 20:1-15
1　Satan bound, 20:1-3

20　And I saw aan angel coming down from heaven, having the bkey of the abyss and a great chain in his hand.

1 aRev.
10:1 bRev.
1:18; 9:1

2　And he laid hold of the adragon, the serpent of old, who is the devil and Satan, and bbound him for a thousand years,

★ 2 aRev.
12:9 bIs.
24:22; 2 Pet.
2:4; Jude 6

3　and threw him into the aabyss, and shut it and bsealed it over him, so that he should cnot deceive the nations any longer, until the thousand years were completed; after these things he must be released for a short time.

3 aRev.
20:1 bDan.
6:17; Matt.
27:66 cRev.
12:9; 20:8,
10

2　Saints resurrected, 20:4-6

4　And I saw athrones, and bthey sat upon them, and cjudgment was given to them. And I saw dthe souls of those who had been dbeheaded because of the etestimony of Jesus and because of the word of God, and those who had not fworshiped the beast or his image, and had not received the gmark upon their forehead and upon their hand; and they hcame to life and ireigned with Christ for a thousand years.

★ 4 aDan.
7:9 bMatt.
19:28; Rev.
3:21 cDan.
7:22; 1 Cor.
6:2 dRev.
6:9 eRev. 1:9
fRev. 13:15
[12] gRev.
13:16f. hIs.
26:14; John
14:19 iRev.
3:21; 5:10;
20:6; 22:5

5　The rest of the dead did not come to life until the thousand years were completed. aThis is the first resurrection.

6　aBlessed and holy is the one who has a part in the first

★ 5 aLuke
14:14; Phil.
3:11;
1 Thess. 4:16
6 aRev.
14:13 bRev.
2:11; 20:14
cRev. 1:6
dRev. 3:21;
5:10; 20:4;
22:5

19:17-18 So great will be the slaughter in the war of Armageddon that an angel will call together the fowls of heaven to eat the flesh of those who fall in battle.

20:2 *a thousand years.* Since the Latin equivalent for these words is "millennium," this period of time is called the millennium. It is the time when Christ shall reign on this earth (Isa. 2:3; Dan. 7:14; Zech. 14:9). Satan will not be free to work (Rev. 20:2), righteousness will flourish (Isa. 11:3-5), peace will be universal (Isa. 2:4), and the productivity of the earth will be greatly increased (Isa. 35:1-2). At the conclusion of the time Satan will be loosed to

make one final attempt to overthrow Christ, but without success (Rev. 20:7-9).

20:4 *the souls of those who had been beheaded because of the testimony of Jesus.* These are the martyrs of the tribulation days who will share the joys of the millennial kingdom.

20:5 *The rest of the dead.* The wicked dead will be raised and judged after the millennium. *the first resurrection.* Refers back to the end of v. 4. This resurrection includes all the righteous (the resurrection of life, John 5:29, and the resurrection of the righteous, Luke 14:14), who will be raised before the millennium begins.

resurrection; over these the [b]second death has no power, but they will be [c]priests of God and of Christ and will [d]reign with Him for a thousand years.

3　Sinners rebelling, 20:7-9

7 [a]Rev. 20:2

7　And when the thousand years are completed, Satan will be [a]released from his prison,

★ 8 [a]Rev. 12:9; 20:3, 10 [b]Rev. 7:1 [c]Ezek. 38:2; 39:1, 6 [d]Rev. 16:14 [e]Heb. 11:12

8　and will come out to [a]deceive the nations which are in the [b]four corners of the earth, [c]Gog and Magog, to [d]gather them together for the war; the number of them is like the [e]sand of the seashore.

9 [a]Ezek. 38:9, 16; Hab. 1:6 [b]Deut. 23:14 [c]Ps. 87:2 [d]Ezek. 38:22; 39:6; Rev. 13:13

9　And they [a]came up on the broad plain of the earth and surrounded the [b]camp of the saints and the [c]beloved city, and [d]fire came down from heaven and devoured them.

4　Satan doomed, 20:10

10 [a]Rev. 20:2f. [b]Rev. 19:20; 20:14, 15 [c]Rev. 16:13 [d]Rev. 14:10f.

10　And [a]the devil who [a]deceived them was thrown into the [b]lake of fire and brimstone, where the [c]beast and the [c]false prophet are also; and they will be [d]tormented day and night forever and ever.

★11-15
11 [a]Rev. 4:2 [b]Rev. 6:14; 21:1 [c]Dan. 2:35; Rev. 12:8
★12 [a]Rev. 11:18 [b]Jer. 17:1, 10; Dan. 7:10 [c]Rev. 3:5; 20:15 [d]Rev. 11:18 [e]Matt. 16:27; Rev. 2:23; 20:13

5　Sinners judged, 20:11-15

11　And I saw a great white [a]throne and Him who sat upon it, from whose presence [b]earth and heaven fled away, and [c]no place was found for them.
12　And I saw the dead, the [a]great and the small, standing before the throne, and [b]books were opened; and another book was opened, which is [c]the book of life; and the dead [d]were judged from the things which were written in the books, [e]according to their deeds.

13 [a]1 Cor. 15:26; Rev. 1:18; 6:8; 21:4 [b]Is. 26:19 [c]Matt. 16:27; Rev. 2:23; 20:12

13　And the sea gave up the dead which were in it, and [a]death and Hades [b]gave up the dead which were in them; and they were judged, every one of them [c]according to their deeds.

14 [a]1 Cor. 15:26; Rev. 1:18; 6:8; 21:4 [b]Rev. 19:20; 20:10, 15 [c]Rev. 20:6

14　And [a]death and Hades were thrown into [b]the lake of fire. This is the [c]second death, the lake of fire.

15 [a]Rev. 20:12; 3:5

15　And if anyone's name was not found written in [a]the book of life, he was thrown into the lake of fire.

C　The Eternal State, 21:1—22:5
1　Descent of New Jerusalem, 21:1-8

★ 1 [a]Is. 65:17; 66:22; 2 Pet. 3:13 [b]2 Pet. 3:10; Rev. 20:11

21 And I saw [a]a new heaven and a new earth; for [b]the first heaven and the first earth passed away, and there is no longer any sea.

★ 2 [a]Rev. 11:2; 21:10; 22:19 [b]Rev. 3:12; 21:10 [c]Heb. 11:10; 16; Rev. 21:10 [d]Is. 61:10; Rev. 19:7; 21:9; 22:17

2　And I saw [a]the holy city, [b]new Jerusalem, [c]coming down out of heaven from God, [d]made ready as a bride adorned for her husband.

3 [a]Lev. 26:11f.; Ezek. 37:27; 48:35; Heb. 8:2; Rev. 7:15 [b]John 14:23; 2 Cor. 6:16

3　And I heard a loud voice from the throne, saying, "Behold, [a]the tabernacle of God is among men, and He shall [b]dwell among them, and they shall be His people, and God Himself shall be among them,

---

20:8 *Gog and Magog.* Symbolic names for the worldwide enemies of Christ.

20:11-15 Here is pictured the judgment of the unbelieving dead. It occurs at the close of the millennium; it is based on works, in order to show that the punishment is deserved (v. 12, though of course these unsaved people are first of all in this judgment because they rejected Christ as Savior during their lifetimes); and it results in everyone in this judgment being cast into the lake of fire. This is the resurrection of judgment (John 5:29).

20:12 *before the throne.* Upon which Christ sits as Judge (see v. 11; John 5:22, 27).

21:1 *a new heaven and a new earth.* The present creation will be destroyed so that it may be cleansed from all the effects of sin (2 Pet. 3:7, 10, 12).

21:2 *new Jerusalem.* This heavenly city will be the abode of all the saints (Heb. 12:22-24), the bride of Christ (Rev. 21:9-10), and the place Christ is preparing for His people (John 14:2). During the millennium the new Jerusalem (described in detail in Rev. 21:9-22:5) apparently will be suspended over the earth, and it will be the dwelling place of all believers during eternity (as is emphasized in 21:1-8).

4 aRev.
7:17 b1 Cor.
15:26; Rev.
20:14 cIs.
25:8; 35:10;
51:11; 65:19
d2 Cor. 5:17;
Heb. 12:27

4 and He shall ªwipe away every tear from their eyes; and ᵇthere shall no longer be *any* death; ᶜthere shall no longer be *any* mourning, or crying, or pain; ᵈthe first things have passed away."

5 aRev. 4:9;
20:11
b2 Cor. 5:17;
Heb. 12:27
cRev. 19:9;
22:6

5 And ªHe who sits on the throne said, "Behold, I am ᵇmaking all things new." And He *said, "Write, for ᶜthese words are faithful and true."

6 aRev.
10:6; 16:17
bRev. 1:8;
22:13 cIs.
55:1; John
4:10; Rev.
7:17; 22:17
dRev. 7:17

6 And He said to me, "ªIt is done. I am the ᵇAlpha and the Omega, the beginning and the end. ᶜI will give to the one who thirsts from the spring of the ᵈwater of life without cost.

7 aRev. 2:7
b2 Sam.
7:14; 2 Cor.
6:16, 18;
Rev. 21:3
★ 8 a1 Cor.
6:9; Gal.
5:19-21; Rev.
9:21; 21:27;
22:15 bRev.
19:20 cRev.
2:11

7 "ªHe who overcomes shall inherit these things, and ᵇI will be his God and he will be My son.

8 "ᵈBut for the cowardly and unbelieving and abominable and murderers and immoral persons and sorcerers and idolaters and all liars, their part *will be* in ᵇthe lake that burns with fire and brimstone, which is the ᶜsecond death."

2 Description of the New Jerusalem, 21:9-27

9 aRev.
17:1 bRev.
15:7 cRev.
15:1 dRev.
17:1 eRev.
19:7; 21:2

9 ªAnd one of the seven angels who had the ᵇseven bowls full of the ᶜseven last plagues, came and spoke with me, saying, "ᵈCome here, I shall show you the ᵉbride, the wife of the Lamb."

10 aEzek.
40:2; Rev.
17:3 bRev.
1:10 cRev.
21:2

10 And ªhe carried me away ᵇin the Spirit to a great and high mountain, and showed me ᶜthe holy city, Jerusalem, coming down out of heaven from God,

★11 aIs.
60:1f.; Ezek.
43:2; Rev.
15:8; 21:23;
22:5 bRev.
4:3; 21:18,
19 cRev. 4:6
12 aEzek.
48:31-34
bRev. 21:15,
21, 25; 22:14

11 having ªthe glory of God. Her brilliance was like a very costly stone, as a ᵇstone of ᶜcrystal-clear jasper.

12 It had a great and high wall, ªwith twelve ᵇgates, and at the gates twelve angels; and names *were* written on them,

which are *those* of the twelve tribes of the sons of Israel.

13 *There were* three gates on the east and three gates on the north and three gates on the south and three gates on the west.

14 And the wall of the city had ªtwelve foundation stones, and on them *were* the twelve names of the ᵇtwelve apostles of the Lamb.

14 aEph.
2:20; Heb.
11:10 bActs
1:26

15 And the one who spoke with me had a gold measuring ªrod to measure the city, and its ᵇgates and its wall.

15 aRev.
11:1 bRev.
21:12, 21, 25

16 And the city is laid out as a square, and its length is as great as the width; and he measured the city with the rod, fifteen hundred miles; its length and width and height are equal.

17 And he measured its wall, seventy-two yards, *according to* ªhuman measurements, which are *also* ᵇangelic *measurements.*

17 aDeut.
3:11; Rev.
13:18 bRev.
21:9

18 And the material of the wall was ªjasper; and the city was ᵇpure gold, like clear ᶜglass.

18 aRev.
21:11 bRev.
21:21 cRev.
4:6

19 ªThe foundation stones of the city wall were adorned with every kind of precious stone. The first foundation stone was ᵇjasper; the second, sapphire; the third, chalcedony; the fourth, ᶜemerald;

★19-20
19 aEx.
28:17-20; Is.
54:11f.;
Ezek. 28:13;
Rev. 21:19.

20 the fifth, sardonyx; the sixth, ªsardius; the seventh, chrysolite; the eighth, beryl; the ninth, topaz; the tenth, chrysoprase; the eleventh, jacinth; the twelfth, amethyst.

20 aRev. 4:3

21 And the twelve ªgates were twelve ᵇpearls; each one of the gates was a single pearl. And the street of the city was ᶜpure gold, like transparent ᵈglass.

21 aRev.
21:12, 15, 25
bIs. 54:12;
Rev. 17:4
cRev. 21:18
dRev. 4:6
22 aMatt.
24:2; John
4:21 bRev.
1:8 cRev.
5:6; 7:17;
14:4
23 aIs.
24:23; 60:19,
20; Rev.
21:25; 22:5
bRev. 21:11
cRev. 5:6;
7:17; 14:4

22 And I saw ªno temple in it, for the ᵇLord God, the Almighty, and the ᶜLamb, are its temple.

23 And the city ªhas no need of the sun or of the moon to shine upon it, for ᵇthe glory of God has

---

21:8 *brimstone* = sulphur.
21:11 *jasper.* See note on 4:3.
21:19-20 *chalcedony.* Probably a greenish-blue agate stone. (The exact composition and color of all these precious stones is not known.) *sar-* donyx. Red and white stone. *sardius.* Bright red. *chrysolite.* Golden in color. *beryl.* Sea green. *topaz.* Yellow-green. *chrysoprase.* Apple-green. *jacinth.* Blue. *amethyst.* Purple.

illumined it, and its lamp *is* the ^cLamb.

24 And ^athe nations shall walk by its light, and the ^bkings of the earth shall bring their glory into it.

25 And in the daytime (for ^athere shall be no night there) ^bits gates ^cshall never be closed;

26 and ^athey shall bring the glory and the honor of the nations into it;

27 and nothing unclean and no one who practices abomination and lying, ^ashall ever come into it, but only those whose names are ^bwritten in the Lamb's book of life.

3 Delights of the New Jerusalem, 22:1-5

22 And ^ahe showed me a ^briver of the ^cwater of life, clear ^das crystal, coming from the throne of God and of the Lamb,

2 in the middle of ^aits street. And ^bon either side of the river was ^cthe tree of life, bearing twelve *kinds of* fruit, yielding its fruit every month; and the ^bleaves of the tree were for the healing of the nations.

3 And ^athere shall no longer be any curse; and ^bthe throne of God and of the Lamb shall be in it, and His bond-servants shall ^cserve Him;

4 and they shall ^asee His face, and His ^bname *shall be* on their ^cforeheads.

5 And ^athere shall no longer be *any* night; and they shall not have need ^bof the light of a lamp nor the light of the sun, because the Lord God shall illumine them; and they shall ^creign forever and ever.

V EPILOGUE, 22:6-21
A Words of Comfort, 22:6-17

6 And ^ahe said to me, "^bThese words are faithful and true"; and the Lord, the ^cGod of the spirits of the prophets, ^dsent His angel to show to His bond-servants the things which must shortly take place.

7 "And behold, ^aI am coming quickly. ^bBlessed is he who heeds ^cthe words of the prophecy of this book."

8 And ^aI, John, am the one who heard and saw these things. And when I heard and saw, ^bI fell down to worship at the feet of the angel who showed me these things.

9 And ^ahe *said to me, "Do not do that; I am a ^bfellow servant of yours and of your brethren the prophets and of those who heed the words of ^cthis book; worship God."

10 And he *said to me, "^aDo not seal up ^bthe words of the prophecy of this book, ^cfor the time is near.

11 "^aLet the one who does wrong, still do wrong; and let the one who is filthy, still be filthy; and let the one who is righteous, still practice righteousness; and let the one who is holy, still keep himself holy."

12 "Behold, ^aI am coming quickly, and My ^breward *is* with Me, ^cto render to every man according to what he has done.

13 "I am the ^aAlpha and the Omega, ^bthe first and the last, ^cthe beginning and the end."

14 Blessed are those who ^awash their robes, that they may have the right to ^bthe tree of life, and may ^center by the ^dgates into the city.

★24 ^aIs. 60:3, 5; Rev. 22:2 ^bPs. 72:10f.; Is. 49:23; 60:16; Rev. 21:26

25 ^aZech. 14:7; Rev. 21:23; 22:5 ^bRev. 21:12, 15 ^cIs. 60:11

26 ^aPs. 72:10f.; Is. 49:23; 60:16

27 ^aIs. 52:1; Ezek. 44:9; Zech. 14:21; Rev. 22:14f. ^bRev. 3:5

★ 1-2
1 ^aRev. 1:1; 21:9; 22:6 ^bPs. 46:4; Ezek. 47:1 ^cRev. 7:17; 22:17 ^dRev. 4:6

2 ^aRev. 21:21 ^bEzek. 47:12 ^cRev. 2:7; 22:14, 19

3 ^aZech. 14:11 ^bRev. 21:3, 23 ^cRev. 7:15

4 ^aPs. 17:15; 42:2; Matt. 5:8 ^bRev. 14:1 ^cRev. 7:3

5 ^aZech. 14:7; Rev. 21:25 ^bRev. 21:23 ^cDan. 7:18, 27; Matt. 19:28; Rom. 5:17; Rev. 20:4

6 ^aRev. 1:1; 21:9 ^bRev. 19:9; 21:5 ^c1 Cor. 14:32; Heb. 12:9 ^dRev. 1:1; 22:16

7 ^aRev. 1:3; 3:3, 11; 16:15; 22:12, 20 ^bRev. 1:3; 16:15 ^cRev. 1:11; 22:9, 10, 18f.

★ 8-9
8 ^aRev. 1:1 ^bRev. 19:10

9 ^aRev. 19:10 ^bRev. 1:1 ^cRev. 1:11; 22:10, 18f.

10 ^aDan. 8:26; Rev. 10:4 ^bRev. 1:11; 22:9, 18f. ^cRev. 1:3

★11 ^aEzek. 3:27; Dan. 12:10

12 ^aRev. 22:7 ^bIs. 40:10; 62:11 ^cJer. 17:10; Matt. 16:27; Rev. 2:23

13 ^aRev. 1:8 ^bRev. 1:17 ^cRev. 21:6

★14 ^aRev. 7:14 ^bRev. 22:2 ^cRev. 21:27 ^dRev. 21:12

21:24 *the nations.* The nations that exist on earth during the millennium.

22:1-2 These descriptive phrases indicate fullness of life and continuous blessing in the new Jerusalem.

22:8-9 Again John is commanded not to worship angels (see 19:10).

22:11 When Christ comes there will be no more opportunity for a man to change his destiny. What he is then he will be forever.

22:14 *Blessed are those who wash their robes.* I.e., believers.

★15 *a*Matt.
8:12; 1 Cor.
6:9f.; Gal.
5:19ff.; Rev.
21:8 *b*Deut.
23:18; Matt.
7:6; Phil. 3:2

16 *a*Rev. 1:1
*b*Rev. 1:1;
22:6 *c*Rev.
1:4, 11; 3:22
*d*Rev. 5:5
*e*Matt. 1:1
*f*Matt. 2:2;
Rev. 2:28

17 *a*Rev. 2:7;
14:13 *b*Rev.
21:2, 9 *c*Rev.
21:6 *d*Rev.
7:17; 22:1

★18 *a*Rev.
22:7 *b*Deut.
4:2; 12:32;
Prov. 30:6
*c*Rev. 15:6-
16, 21 *d*Rev.
22:7

19 *a*Deut.
4:2; 12:32;
Prov. 30:6
*b*Rev. 22:7
*c*Rev. 22:2
*d*Rev. 21:10-
22:5

★20 *a*Rev.
1:2 *b*Rev.
22:7 *c*1 Cor.
16:22 marg.

21 *a*Rom.
16:20

15 *a*Outside are the *b*dogs and the sorcerers and the immoral persons and the murderers and the idolaters, and everyone who loves and practices lying.

16 "*a*I, Jesus, have sent *b*My angel to testify to you these things *c*for the churches. I am *d*the root and the *e*offspring of David, the bright *f*morning star."

17 And the *a*Spirit and the *b*bride say, "Come." And let the one who hears say, "Come." And *c*let the one who is thirsty come; let the one who wishes take the *d*water of life without cost.

B Words of Warning, 22:18-19

18 I testify to everyone who hears *a*the words of the prophecy of this book: if anyone *b*adds to them, God shall add to him *c*the plagues which are written in *d*this book;

19 and if anyone *a*takes away from the *b*words of the book of this prophecy, God shall take away his part from *c*the tree of life and from the holy city, *d*which are written in this book.

C Closing Benediction, 22:20-21

20 He who *a*testifies to these things says, "Yes, *b*I am coming quickly." Amen. *c*Come, Lord Jesus.

21 *a*The grace of the Lord Jesus be with all. Amen.

22:15 *dogs.* Not animals, but people of low character (cf. Phil. 3:2).

22:18 For similar O.T. warnings against additions or omissions see Deut. 4:2; 12:32; Prov. 30:6.

22:20 *Yes, I am coming quickly.* The third occurrence of this promise (see vv. 7, 12). The believer's reaction is, "Do come, quickly, Lord Jesus!"

HARMONY OF THE GOSPELS*

Contents.	Matt.	Mark	Luke	John
Incidents of the Birth and Boyhood of Jesus Christ Till He was Twelve Years of Age.				
1. Introduction, ...			1: 1-4	1: 1-14
2. The genealogies—Matthew the legal, Luke the natural descent, ...	1: 1-17		3: 23-38	
3. Birth of John announced to Zacharias, ...			1: 5-25	
4. Birth of Jesus announced to Mary at Nazareth six months later, ...			1: 26-38	
5. Mary's visit to Elizabeth, and her hymn, ...			1: 39-56	
6. John the Baptist's birth, and Zacharias' hymn,			1: 57-80	
7. The angel appears to Joseph, ...	1: 18-25			
8. Birth of Jesus at Bethlehem, ...			2: 1-7	
9. Angelic announcement to the shepherds. (In spring flocks are watched by night.), ...			2: 8-20	
10. Circumcision of Jesus, and presentation in the temple, where He is welcomed by Simeon and Anna, 41 days after nativity (Lev. 12:3, 4)			2: 21-38	
11. Visit of the Magi, in the house—no longer in manger; epiphany to Gentiles, ...	2: 1-12			
12. Flight into Egypt, ...	2: 13-15			
13. Herod's murder of the innocents, ...	2: 16-18			
14. Return to Nazareth, fearing Archelaus' cruelty, shown from the first, ...	2: 19-23		2: 39, 40	
15. Jesus, at the age of twelve, goes up to the Passover, and is found with the doctors in the temple; then follows His 18 silent years . . .			2: 41-52	
Inauguration of Christ's Public Ministry.				
16. Preparatory preaching of John the Baptist, . . .	3: 1-12	1: 1-8	3: 1-18	
17. Christ's baptism in river Jordan at Perean Bethany, ...	3: 13-17	1: 9-11	3: 21-23	
18. The Spirit leads Him to desert of Judea, where Satan tempts Him, ...	4: 1-11	1: 12, 13	4: 1-13	
19. The Baptist's witness to Jesus, ...				1: 15-34
20. Two of John's disciples follow Jesus; Andrew brings his brother Simon, ...				1: 35-42
21. Christ returns to Galilee; finds Philip, who in turn finds Nathanael, ...				1: 43-51
22. First miracle at Cana, and visit to Capernaum,				2: 1-12
Public Ministry of Christ from the First Passover to the Second.				
23. Christ goes up to Jerusalem for the Passover, and, with a scourge, expels the sellers and money-changers from the temple; works miracles, convincing many, ...				2: 13-25
24. Nicodemus is convinced; has a night interview with Jesus, ...				3: 1-21
25. Christ leaves Jerusalem, stays eight months in N. E. Judea, and His disciples baptize.				3: 22, 4: 2
26. John, baptizing in Ænon, again witnesses to the Christ, ...				3: 23-36
27. Imprisonment of John, ...			3: 19, 20	

*Based on the harmony of A. R. Fausset.

From His Second to His Third Passover.

The Last Passover Week, Ending with the Crucifixion.

First Day of the Week.

Second Day.

Third Day.

Seventh Day.

Christ's Resurrection, His Appearances during Forty Days, and Ascension.

First Day—Easter Sunday.

Contents.	Matt.	Mark	Luke	John

A SYNOPSIS OF BIBLE DOCTRINE

by Charles C. Ryrie

DOCTRINE OF THE SCRIPTURES

I. INTRODUCTION
A. Terminology.　1. **Bible.** Derived from *biblion*, "roll" or "book" (Luke 4:17).
2. **Scripture.** Used in N.T. of the sacred books of O.T. which were regarded as inspired (2 Tim. 3:16; Rom. 3:2). Also used in N.T. of other parts of N.T. (2 Peter 3:16).　3. **Word of God.** Used of both O.T. and N.T. in written form (Matt. 15:6; John 10:35; Heb. 4:12).
B. Attitudes Toward the Bible.　1. **Rationalism.**　a. Extreme form denies the possibility of any supernatural revelation.　b. Moderate form admits possibility of divine revelation, but human mind is final judge of revelation.　2. **Romanism.** Bible is the product of the church, therefore the Bible is not the sole or final authority.　3. **Mysticism.** Experience is authoritative along with the Bible.　4. **Neoorthodoxy.** The Bible is a fallible witness to the revelation of God in the Word, Christ.　5. **Cults.** The Bible and the writings of the particular cult's leader are equally authoritative.　6. **Orthodoxy.** The Bible alone is the ground of authority.
C. The Wonders of the Bible.　1. **Its formation.** 1500 years.　2. **Its unity.** About 40 different authors, yet one book.　3. **Its preservation.**　4. **Its subject matter.**　5. **Its influence.**

II. REVELATION
A. Definition. "A disclosure; especially God's communicating His message to man."
B. Means of Revelation.　1. Through nature (Rom. 1:18-21; Ps. 19).　2. Through providential dealings (Rom. 8:28).　3. Through preservation of the universe (Col. 1:17).
4. Through miracles (John 2:11).　5. Through direct communication (Acts 22:17-21).
6. Through Christ (John 1:14).　7. Through the Bible (1 John 5:9-12).

III. INSPIRATION
A. Definition. Inspiration is God's superintending of human authors so that, using their own individual personalities, they composed and recorded without error in the words of the original autographs His revelation to man.
B. Theories of Inspiration.　1. **Natural**—no supernatural element involved. Bible was written by men of great genius.　2. **Mystical or illumination.** Writers of Scripture were Spirit-filled just as Christians today can be.　3. **Dictation or mechanical.** Writers of Scripture were passive instruments in God's hand, like typewriters on which He wrote. Admittedly, parts of the Bible were dictated (e.g., Ten Commandments).　4. **Partial.** Only the unknowable parts of the Bible were inspired (e.g., creation, spiritual concepts).
5. **Conceptual.** Concepts but not words were inspired.　6. **Degree.** Writers were more inspired than ordinary men.　7. **Neoorthodox.** Human writers could only produce a record with errors.　8. **Verbal, plenary.** This is the true doctrine and means that the very words (verbal) and all of them (plenary) were inspired in the sense of the definition above.
9. **Fallible inspiration.** An increasingly popular theory that the Bible is inspired but is not without error.

C. Distinctives of Verbal, Plenary Inspiration. 1. The true doctrine concerns the original manuscripts. 2. It extends to the actual words. 3. It views God as superintending, not dictating. 4. It includes inerrancy.

D. Proof of Verbal, Plenary Inspiration. 1. 2 Timothy 3:16. *Theopneustos*, God-breathed. Affirms that God is author of Scripture and that Scripture is the product of His creative breath. 2. 2 Peter 1:21. The "how" of inspiration—men "borne along" by the Spirit. 3. Specific commands to write the word of the Lord (Exodus 17:14; Jer. 30:2). 4. The use of quotation (Matt. 15:4; Acts 28:25). 5. Jesus' use of Scripture (Matt. 5:17; John 10:35). 6. N.T. asserts that other parts of the N.T. are Scripture (1 Tim. 5:18; 2 Peter 3:16). 7. Writers were conscious of writing God's word (1 Cor. 2:13; 1 Peter 1:11–12).

E. Proofs of Inerrancy. 1. The trustworthiness of God's character (John 17:3; Rom. 3:4). 2. The teaching of Christ (Matt. 5:17; John 10:35). 3. Arguments based on a word or form of a word (Gal. 3:16, "seed"; Matt. 22:31-32, "am").

IV. CANONICITY

A. Fundamental Considerations. 1. The Bible is self-authenticating and church councils have only recognized the authority inherent in the books themselves. 2. God guided the councils so that the canon was recognized.

B. The Canon of the O.T. 1. Some assert that all books of the O.T. canon were collected and recognized by Ezra (5th cent. B.C.). 2. The N.T. refers to the O.T. as Scripture (Matt. 23:35, the equivalent of saying, "From Genesis to Malachi"; cf. Matt. 21:42; 22:29). 3. The Synod of Jamnia (A.D. 90). A teaching house of rabbis who recognized the books of the O.T., though some questioned Esther, Ecclesiastes, Song of Solomon.

C. The Principles of the Canonicity of N.T. Books. 1. **Apostolicity.** Was the book written or backed by an apostle? 2. **Content.** Was it of sufficient spiritual character? 3. **Universality.** Was it widely accepted? 4. **Inspiration.** Did it give internal evidence of inspiration?

D. The Formation of the N.T. Canon. 1. The period of the apostles. They claimed authority for their writings (1 Thess. 5:27; Col. 4:16). 2. The postapostolic period. All recognized except Hebrews, 2 Peter, 2 and 3 John. 3. The Council of Carthage, 397, listed the 27 canonical N.T. books.

V. ILLUMINATION

A. In Relation to the Unsaved. 1. The need for (1 Cor. 2:14; 2 Cor. 4:4). 2. The Spirit's convicting ministry (John 16:7–11).

B. In Relation to the Christian. 1. The need for (1 Cor. 2:10–12; 3:2). 2. The Spirit's teaching ministry (John 16:13–15).

VI. INTERPRETATION

A. Principles of Interpretation. 1. Interpret grammatically and historically. 2. Interpret according to the immediate and wider contexts. 3. Interpret in harmony with the whole Bible by comparing scripture with scripture.

B. General Divisions of the Bible. 1. O.T. a. Historical books—Genesis to Esther. b. Poetical books—Job to Song of Solomon. c. Prophetic books—Isaiah to Malachi. 2. **N.T.** a. Gospels—Matthew to John. b. History—Acts. c. Epistles—Romans to Jude. d. Prophecy—Revelation.

C. Biblical Covenants. 1. **Noahic** covenant (Gen. 8:20-22). 2. **Abrahamic** covenant (Gen. 12:1-3). 3. **Mosaic** covenant (Exodus 19:3—40:38). 4. **Palestinian** covenant (Deut. 30). 5. **Davidic** covenant (2 Sam. 7:5-17). 6. **New** covenant (Jer. 31:31-34; Matt. 26:28).

THE DOCTRINE OF GOD

I. THE EXISTENCE OF GOD

A. Naturalistic Arguments for Existence. 1. **Cosmological** (*cosmos,* "world"). The universe is an effect which requires an adequate cause, and the only sufficient cause is God (Ps. 19:1). 2. **Teleological** (*telos,* "end"). The universe not only proves a maker but also a designer (Rom. 1:18-20). There is observable purpose in the universe which argues for the existence of God as its designer. 3. **Anthropological** (*anthropos,* "man"). Since man is a moral and intellectual being, he must have had a maker who is also a moral and intelligent being (Acts 17:29). Man's moral nature, religious instincts, conscience, and emotional nature argue for existence of God. 4. **Ontological** (*on,* "being"). Man has the idea of the Most Perfect Being. This idea includes the idea of existence, since a being, otherwise perfect, who did not exist would not be as perfect as a perfect being who did exist. Therefore, since the idea of existence is contained in the idea of the Most Perfect Being, the Most Perfect Being must exist.

B. Biblical Arguments for Existence. Biblical writers both assume and argue for the existence of God.

II. THE ATTRIBUTES OF GOD

A. Definition. An attribute is a property intrinsic to its subject and by which the subject is distinguished or identified.

B. Classifications. Most systems of classifying the attributes are based on the fact that some attributes belong to God alone (e.g., infinity) and some are found in a limited and relative sense in man (e.g., love); thus, incommunicable and communicable; absolute and relative; immanent and transitive; constitutional and those pertaining to personality.

C. Description. (Absolute, incommunicable, or constitutional attributes Nos. 1-9.) 1. **Simplicity.** a. Meaning. God is uncompounded, incomplex, indivisible. b. Scripture. John 4:24. c. Problem. Does simplicity invalidate doctrine of the Trinity? No, because simplicity has to do with God's essence, and Trinity with His subsistence. 2. **Unity.** a. Meaning. God is one. b. Scripture. Deuteronomy 6:4. 3. **Infinity.** a. Meaning. Without termination and finitude. b. Scripture. 1 Kings 8:27; Acts 17:28. 4. **Eternity.** a. Meaning. Free from succession of time. b. Scripture. Genesis 21:33; Psalm 90:2. c. Problem. Is time unreal to God? No, He recognizes successiveness of events, but all past, present, and future events are equally vivid to Him. 5. **Immutability.** a. Meaning. God is unchanging and unchangeable. b. Scripture. James 1:17. c. Problem. Does God change His mind or repent (Gen. 6:6), as seems apparent from our viewpoint; or is this an expression of God's permissive decree? 6. **Omnipresence.** a. Meaning. God is everywhere (not in everything; that is pantheism). b. Scripture. Psalm 139:7-12. 7. **Sovereignty.** a. Meaning. God is the supreme ruler. b. Scripture. Ephesians 1. 8. **Omniscience.** a. Meaning. God knows all actual and possible things. b. Scripture. Matt. 11:21. 9. **Omnipotence.** a. Meaning. All power. b. Scripture. Revelation 19:6. (Relative, communicable, or personality attributes Nos. 10-14.) 10. **Justice.** a. Meaning. Moral equity, "no respect of persons." b. Scripture. Acts 17:31. 11. **Love.** a. Meaning. God seeking the highest good of displaying His own will. b. Scripture. Ephesians 2:4-5. 12. **Truth.** a. Meaning. Agreement to and consistency with all that is represented by God Himself. b. Scripture. John 14:6. 13. **Freedom.** a. Meaning. Independence from His creatures. b. Scripture. Isaiah 40:13-14. 14. **Holiness.** a. Meaning. Righteous. b. Scripture. 1 John 1:5.

III. THE NAMES OF GOD

A. Primary O.T. Names. 1. **Jehovah** (YHWH). a. Meaning. Self-existent One (from Exodus 3:14, "I AM THAT I AM"). b. Characteristics. It is a name of relationship between the true God and His people and, when used, emphasizes God's holiness, hatred of sin,

and love of sinners. 2. **Elohim.** a. Meaning. Strong one. b. Characteristics. Used of the true God and heathen gods. It is a plural word and is the plural of majesty. The plural does allow for the subsequent revelation of the Trinity in the N.T. but does not teach the Trinity per se. 3. **Adonai.** a. Meaning. Lord. b. Characteristics. Used of men and of God and indicates the master-servant relationship.
B. Compound O.T. Names. 1. **With El.** a. *El Elyon,* translated the Most High (lit., the strongest strong one, Isa. 14:13-14). b. *El Roi,* the Strong One who sees (Gen. 16:13). c. *El Shaddai,* Almighty God (Gen. 17:1-20). d. *El Olam,* Everlasting God (Isa. 40:28). 2. **With Jehovah.** a. *Jehovah Jireh,* the Lord will provide (Gen. 22:13-14). b. *Jehovah Nissi,* the Lord my banner (Exodus 17:15). c. *Jehovah Shalom,* the Lord is peace (Judges 6:24). d. *Jehovah Sabbaoth,* the Lord of hosts (1 Sam. 1:3). e. *Jehovah Maccaddeshcem,* the Lord thy Sanctifier (Exodus 31:13). f. *Jehovah Raah,* the Lord is my Shepherd (Ps. 23:1). g. *Jehovah Tsidkenu,* the Lord our righteousness (Jer. 23:6). h. *Jehovah El Gmolah,* the Lord God of recompense (Jer. 51:56). i. *Jehovah Nakeh,* the Lord that smiteth (Ezek. 7:9). j. *Jehovah Shammah,* the Lord who is present (Ezek. 48:35).

IV. THE DECREE OF GOD
A. Definition. "The decree of God is His eternal purpose, according to the counsel of His own will, whereby, for His own glory, He hath foreordained whatsoever comes to pass."
B. Terms Involved. 1. **Omniscience.** Knowledge of all things, actual and possible. 2. **Foreknowledge.** Prior knowledge of all things included in the actual course of events. 3. **Predestination.** The predetermining of the destiny of the elect. 4. **Retribution.** Deserved punishment. 5. **Election.** God's choosing a people for Himself. 6. **Preterition.** Passing by of the nonelect.
C. Nature of the Decree. 1. There is only one decree involving everything, though in the outworking of events there is successiveness. There is also a convenient distinction between directive and permissive decrees. 2. The decree is all-inclusive (Eph. 1:11), although God does not sustain the same relationship to each thing in the decree. 3. All the desires of God are not necessarily incorporated into His plan. 4. What God has decreed is ultimately for His own glory. 5. Wrong is never made right simply because sin was included as part of God's purpose.
D. Objections to the Decree. 1. It is inconsistent with human freedom. (But all means like prayer and witnessing are part of His plan.) 2. The decree makes God the author of sin. (Although God has included sin in His plan, He is never responsible for the committing of sin.) 3. The doctrine of decree is the same as fatalism. (Fatalism emphasizes only ends, and makes chance, not God, the governing power.)

V. THE TRINITY
A. Definition. There is only one God, but in the unity of the Godhead there are three eternal and coequal Persons, the same in substance but distinct in subsistence.
B. Proof. 1. **O.T. intimations.** The O.T. does not reveal the Trinity but it allows for the later revelation of it. a. Passages which use the plural word *Elohim* and plural pronouns referring to God (Gen. 1:1, 26; Isa. 6:8). b. Passages which speak of the Angel of Jehovah (Gen. 22:11, 15-16). 2. **N.T. confirmation.** In the N.T. there is clear revelation that Father, Son, and Spirit are God; thus a Triunity or Trinity (neither is a biblical word). a. The Father is God (John 6:27; Eph. 4:6). b. Jesus Christ is God (Heb. 1:8). c. The Spirit is God (Acts 5:3-4). d. The three Persons are associated equally and as one (Matt. 28:19, "name"; 2 Cor. 13:14).

VI. THE FATHER
A. The Relationships of the Father. 1. Father over all creation (Acts 17:29). 2. Father of the nation Israel (Exodus 4:22). 3. Father of the Lord Jesus Christ (Matt. 3:17). 4. Father of believers in Christ (Gal. 3:26).

B. The Particular Works of the Father. 1. Author of the decree (Ps. 2:7-9). 2. Author of election (Eph. 1:3-6). 3. Begetter and sender of Christ (John 3:16). 4. Disciplinarian of His children (Heb. 12:9).

THE DOCTRINE OF CHRIST

I. HIS PREEXISTENCE
A. Proved by the O.T. (Micah 5:2; Isa. 9:6, "Father of eternity").
B. Proved by the N.T. 1. John 1:1 in comparison with verse 14. 2. John 8:58, "Before Abraham came into being I was already in existence."
C. Proved by Works ascribed to Christ which require preexistence (e.g., creation, Col. 1:16).
D. Proved by the Appearance of the Angel of Jehovah (Exodus 3:2, 4).
E. Proved by His Names. 1. **Logos.** 2. **Son of God.** 3. **Jehovah.**

II. HIS INCARNATION
A. Meaning. In flesh.
B. Means. The virgin birth. 1. **Predicted** (Isa. 7:14). 2. **Proved.** Feminine relative pronoun used in Matthew 1:16, which declares that the birth of Jesus was of Mary only and not of Joseph.
C. Reasons. 1. To reveal God to men (John 1:18). 2. To provide an example for living (1 Peter 2:21). 3. To provide the sacrifice for sin (Heb. 10:1-10). 4. To destroy the works of the devil (1 John 3:8). 5. To be a merciful High Priest (Heb. 5:1-2). 6. To fulfill the Davidic covenant (Luke 1:31-33). 7. To be highly exalted (Phil. 2:9).
D. The Person. The Person of the incarnate Christ included: 1. Undiminished deity. 2. Perfect humanity. 3. United in one Person forever.

III. HIS HUMANITY
A. He Had a Human Body. 1. Born of a woman (Gal. 4:4). 2. Subject to growth (Luke 2:52). 3. Seen and handled by men (1 John 1:1; Matt. 26:12). 4. Sinless (Heb. 4:15).
B. He Had a Human Soul and Spirit (Matt. 26:38; Luke 23:46).
C. He Was Subject to the Limitations of Humanity. 1. He hungered (Matt. 4:2). 2. He was thirsty (John 19:28). 3. He grew tired (John 4:6). 4. He wept (John 11:35). 5. He was tested (Heb. 4:15).
D. He Had Human Names. 1. Son of Man (Luke 19:10). 2. Jesus (Matt. 1:21). 3. Son of David (Mark 10:47). 4. Man (Isa. 53:3; 1 Tim. 2:5).
E. He Was Able to Die.

IV. HIS DEITY
A. Proved by His Names. 1. God (Heb. 1:8). 2. Son of God (Matt. 16:16; 26:61-64a). 3. Lord (Matt. 22:43-45). 4. King of kings and Lord of lords (Rev. 19:16).
B. Proved by His Characteristics. 1. Omnipotence (Matt. 28:18). 2. Omniscience (John 1:48). 3. Omnipresence (Matt. 18:20). 4. Life (John 1:4). 5. Truth (John 14:6). 6. Immutability (Heb. 13:8).
C. Proved by His Works. 1. Creates (John 1:3). 2. Sustains (Col. 1:17). 3. Forgives sin (Luke 7:48). 4. Raises the dead (John 5:25). 5. Judges (John 5:27). 6. Sends the Holy Spirit (John 15:26).
D. Proved by Worship that Is Given Him. 1. By angels (Heb. 1:6). 2. By men (Matt. 14:33). 3. By all (Phil. 2:10).
E. Proved by Equality in the Trinity. 1. With the Father (John 14:23; 10:30). 2. With the Father and the Spirit (Matt. 28:19; 2 Cor. 13:14).

V. HIS EARTHLY LIFE
A. His Preparation. 1. Birth. 2. Infancy, childhood, and growth to maturity. 3. Baptism. 4. Temptation.
B. His Preaching. 1. Early ministry in Judea (John 2:13—4:3). 2. Ministry in Galilee (Mark 1:14—9:50). 3. Perean ministry (Luke 9:51—19:28).
C. His Passion. 1. The last week in Jerusalem (Luke 19:29—22:46). 2. Betrayal and arrest (John 18:2-13). 3. Trial before Annas (John 18:12-24). 4. Trial before Caiaphas (Mark 14:53—15:1). 5. Trial before Pilate (Mark 15:1-5). 6. Trial before Herod (Luke 23:8-12). 7. Second trial before Pilate (Mark 15:6-15). 8. Crucifixion. 9. Burial. 10. Resurrection.
D. His Postresurrection Ministry and Ascension.

VI. THE KENOSIS
A. Meaning. Literally, emptying; i.e., What were the limitations of the incarnate Christ on earth?
B. Scripture. Philippians 2:7, "made himself of no reputation."
C. True Doctrine of Kenosis. It involves: 1. The veiling of His preincarnate glory. 2. His condescension in taking the likeness of sinful flesh in the incarnation. 3. The voluntary nonuse of certain attributes during His earthly life.
D. False Theory of Kenosis. Christ gave up certain attributes during His earthly life. If so, then He ceased to be God during that time.

VII. HIS IMPECCABILITY
A. Meaning. Christ was not able to sin. It does not mean merely that Christ was able not to sin.
B. Objection. If Christ was unable to sin, He could not have been tempted genuinely and therefore could not be a sympathetic High Priest (Heb. 4:15).
C. Answer. The reality of testing does not lie in the moral nature of the one tested, and the possibility of sympathizing does not depend on one-to-one correspondence in the problems faced.
D. Results. 1. Testing proved sinlessness of Christ. 2. Testing made Him a sympathizing High Priest.

VIII. HIS DEATH (See also Doctrine of Salvation)
A. Its Prominence. 1. In O.T. it is the scarlet thread of which Christ Himself spoke (Luke 24:27, 44). 2. In N.T. it is mentioned at least 175 times. 3. In relation to the incarnation it is its purpose (Matt. 20:28; Heb. 2:14). 4. In relation to the gospel it is its heart (1 Cor. 15:1-3).
B. Its Description. 1. **A ransom.** The death of Christ paid the price of the penalty for sin (Matt. 20:28; 1 Tim. 2:6). 2. **A reconciliation.** The position of the world was changed by Christ's death so that all men are able now to be saved (2 Cor. 5:18-19). 3. **A propitiation.** God is satisfied with that which Christ's death accomplished (1 John 2:2). 4. **A substitution.** Christ died in the place of the sinner (2 Cor. 5:21). 5. **A proof** of the love of God (Rom. 5:8).
C. False Theories of Christ's Death. Almost all false theories can be classified into three categories. 1. **Moral influence or example theory.** Christ's death was only for the purpose of exerting a good influence on us. 2. **Governmental.** God's government necessitated His making an example of Christ to show His displeasure toward sin. 3. **Neoorthodox view.** Christ's death was a revelation of the love of God and the sinfulness of man but not a substitution for man's sin. 4. **The ransom to Satan view,** which held that Christ's death was a ransom to Satan.

IX. HIS RESURRECTION

A. The Fact of the Resurrection. 1. The empty tomb. 2. The appearances. a. To Mary Magdalene (John 20:11-17). b. To the other women (Matt. 28:9-10). c. To Peter (1 Cor. 15:5). d. To disciples on road to Emmaus (Luke 24:13-35). e. To the ten disciples (Luke 24:36-43). f. To the eleven disciples (John 20:26-29). g. To seven disciples by Galilee (John 21:1-23). h. To more than 500 (1 Cor. 15:6). i. To the eleven at the ascension (Matt. 28:16-20). 3. The existence of the Christian Church. 4. The change in the disciples. 5. The day of Pentecost. 6. The change of the day of worship to Sunday.
B. The Nature of His Resurrection Body. 1. It was a real body (John 20:20). 2. It was identified as the same one laid in the tomb (John 20:25-29). 3. It was changed so as never again to be subject to death and limitations.
C. The Significance of the Resurrection. 1. **To Christ.** a. It proved Him to be the Son of God (Rom. 1:4). b. It confirmed the truth of all He said (Matt. 28:6). 2. **To all men.** a. It makes certain the resurrection of all (1 Cor. 15:20-22). b. It makes certain the coming judgment (Acts 17:31). 3. **To believers.** a. It gives assurance of acceptance with God (Rom. 4:25). b. It guarantees power for service (Eph. 1:19-22). c. It guarantees the believer's resurrection (2 Cor. 4:14). d. It designates Christ as Head of the Church (Eph. 1:19-22). e. It means a sympathetic High Priest in heaven (Heb. 4:14-16).

X. HIS ASCENSION

A. Characteristics (Acts 1:9-11).
B. Significance. 1. End of period of limitation. 2. Exaltation (Eph. 1:20-23). 3. Forerunner (Heb. 6:20). 4. High priestly ministry (Heb. 4:14-16). 5. Preparing a place (John 14:2). 6. Headship over the Church (Col. 1:18).

XI. HIS PRESENT MINISTRY

Christ's present ministry in heaven is all directly or indirectly related to His mediatorship and is revealed under seven figures.
A. Last Adam and New Creation (1 Cor. 15:45; 2 Cor. 5:17). Meaning: to give life.
B. Head and Body of Christ (Col. 1:18, 24). Meaning: direction, nurture, giving of gifts.
C. Shepherd and Sheep (John 10). Meaning: leading, caring.
D. Vine and Branches (John 15). Meaning: fruit.
E. Chief Cornerstone and Stones of the Building (1 Cor. 3:11; 1 Peter 2:4-8). Meaning: life, security.
F. High Priest and Royal Priesthood (1 Peter 2:5-9). Meaning: sacrifice, intercession.
G. Bridegroom and Bride (Eph. 5:25-27). Meaning: preparedness.

XII. HIS RETURN   (See Doctrine of Future Things)

THE DOCTRINE OF THE HOLY SPIRIT

I. THE PERSONALITY OF THE SPIRIT

A. Proved by His Characteristics. 1. He is intelligent (1 Cor. 2:10-11). 2. He has feelings (Eph. 4:30). 3. He has will (1 Cor. 12:11).
B. Proved by His Works. 1. He teaches (John 14:26). 2. He guides (Rom. 8:14). 3. He commissions (Acts 13:4). 4. He commands men (Acts 8:29). 5. He restrains (Gen. 6:3). 6. He intercedes (Rom. 8:26). 7. He speaks (John 15:26; 2 Peter 1:21).
C. Proved by What Is Ascribed to Him. 1. He can be obeyed (Acts 10:19-21). 2. He can be lied to (Acts 5:3). 3. He can be resisted (Acts 7:51). 4. He can be reverenced (Ps. 51:11). 5. He can be blasphemed (Matt. 12:31). 6. He can be grieved (Eph. 4:30). 7. He can be outraged (Heb. 10:29).
D. Proved by Unusual Grammar. In spite of the fact that the Greek word for Spirit is neuter in gender, several times masculine pronouns are used to replace the neuter noun,

contradicting all normal rules of grammar but indicating the personality of the Spirit (John 16:13-14; 15:26; 16:7-8).

II. THE DEITY OF THE SPIRIT

A. Proved by His Names. 1. Names which relate the Spirit equally to other Persons of the Trinity (1 Cor. 6:11). 2. Names which show Him doing works which only God can do (Rom. 8:15; John 14:16).

B. Proved by His Characteristics. The Spirit possesses divine attributes. 1. Omniscience (1 Cor. 2:10-11). 2. Omnipresence (Ps. 139:7). 3. Omnipotence (Gen. 1:2). 4. Truth (1 John 5:6). 5. Holiness (Luke 11:13). 6. Life (Rom. 8:2). 7. Wisdom (Isa. 40:13).

C. Proved by His Works. Works which only God can do are said to be done by the Spirit. 1. Creating (Gen. 1:2). 2. Inspiring (2 Peter 1:21). 3. Begetting Christ (Luke 1:35). 4. Convincing men (John 16:8). 5. Regenerating (John 3:5-6). 6. Comforting (John 14:16). 7. Interceding (Rom. 8:26-27). 8. Sanctifying (2 Thess. 2:13).

D. Proved by His Being Equally Associated with other Persons of the Trinity (Acts 5:3-4; Matt. 28:19; 2 Cor. 13:14).

III. THE PROCESSION OF THE SPIRIT

A. Definition. Procession is an attempt to describe the eternal relationship between the Spirit and the other two Persons of the Trinity. He proceeded from them eternally and without any dividing of or change in God's nature.

B. History. This concept was formulated in the Constantinopolitan Creed in 381. In 589 the Synod of Toledo added the famous "filioque" clause, which stated that the Spirit proceeded from the Father *and* the Son.

C. Scripture. John 15:26 expressly says the Spirit proceeds from the Father, while the idea of His proceeding from the Son also comes from such verses as Galatians 4:6, Romans 8:9, and John 16:7.

IV. TYPES AND ILLUSTRATIONS OF THE SPIRIT

A. Clothing (Luke 24:49, NASB).
B. Dove (Matt. 3:16; Mark 1:10; Luke 3:22; John 1:32).
C. Earnest (2 Cor. 1:22; 5:5; Eph. 1:14).
D. Fire (Acts 2:3).
E. Oil (Luke 4:18; Acts 10:38; 2 Cor. 1:21; 1 John 2:20).
F. Seal (2 Cor. 1:22; Eph. 1:13; 4:30).
G. Servant (Gen. 24).
H. Water (John 4:14; 7:38-39).
I. Wind (John 3:8; Acts 2:1-2).

V. THE WORK OF THE SPIRIT IN THE O.T.

A. In Creation. The Spirit gave to the creation: 1. Life (Ps. 104:30; Job 33:4). 2. Order (Isa. 40:12; Job 26:13). 3. Adornment (Ps. 33:6; Job 26:13). 4. Preservation (Ps. 104:30).

B. In Man. 1. Selective indwelling. a. The Spirit was *in* certain people in O.T. times (Gen. 41:38; Num. 27:18; Dan. 4:8; 5:11-14; 6:3). b. The Spirit came *upon* many (Judges 3:10; 6:34; 11:29; 13:25; 1 Sam. 10:9-10; 16:13). c. The Spirit *filled* some (Exodus 31:3; 35:31). Thus His personal relationship to men in the O.T. was limited, for not all experienced His work nor was it necessarily permanent in each case (Ps. 51:11). 2. Enablement for service (especially in the construction of the tabernacle, Exodus 31:3, but also in other instances, Judges 14:6). 3. General restraint of sin (Gen. 6:3).

VI. THE WORK OF THE SPIRIT IN REVELATION AND INSPIRATION

A. Definitions. 1. Revelation means the disclosure of that which was previously unknown. Revelation concerns the material (i.e., what). 2. Inspiration is God's superintending of human authors so that, using their own individual personalities, they composed and recorded without error His revelation to man in the words of the original autographs. Inspiration concerns the manner (i.e., how).

B. The Author of Revelation Is the Holy Spirit (2 Peter 1:21; cf. 2 Sam. 23:2; Ezek. 2:2; Micah 3:8; Matt. 22:43; Acts 1:16; 4:25).

C. The Means of Revelation. The Spirit used: 1. Spoken word (Exodus 19:9). 2. Dreams (Gen. 20; 31). 3. Visions (Isa. 6:1). 4. Written Word (John 14:26; 1 Cor. 2:13). 5. Christ.

D. The Author of Inspiration Is the Spirit. 1. Of the O.T. (2 Sam. 23:2-3; 2 Tim. 3:16; Mark 12:36; Acts 1:16; 28:25; Heb. 3:7; 10:15-16). 2. Of the N.T. a. N.T. inspiration was preauthenticated by Christ (John 14:26). b. It is asserted by the writers of the N.T. (1 Cor. 14:37; Gal. 1:7-8; 1 Thess. 4:2, 15; 2 Thess. 3:6, 12, 14). c. It is attested to by the apostles of each other's writings (1 Tim. 5:18; 2 Peter 3:16).

VII. THE WORK OF THE SPIRIT IN THE LIFE OF CHRIST

A. In His Virgin Birth. The Spirit caused Christ's conception in Mary's womb (Luke 1:35).

B. In His Life. 1. Christ was anointed by the Spirit (Luke 4:18; Acts 10:38). It occurred at His baptism but was not the same as baptism (John 1:32). Anointing meant empowering for service. 2. Christ was filled with the Spirit (Luke 4:1). 3. Christ was sealed with the Spirit (John 6:27). 4. Christ was led by the Spirit (Luke 4:1). 5. Christ was empowered by the Spirit (Matt. 12:28).

C. In His Death (Heb. 9:14, and some use Rom. 1:4).

D. In His Resurrection (1 Peter 3:18 possibly).

VIII. THE WORK OF THE SPIRIT IN SALVATION

A. Convicting (John 16:8-11). 1. **Definition.** To convict (John 16:8) means to place the truth of the Gospel in a clear light before the unsaved so that it is acknowledged as truth whether or not Christ is received as Saviour. 2. **Detail.** a. Of sin. Man's state of sin is because of his unbelief. b. Of righteousness. Man is convinced of Christ's righteousness because He ascended to the Father. c. Of judgment. The Spirit convicts of coming judgment because Satan (the greatest enemy) has already been judged.

B. Regenerating (Titus 3:5). 1. **Definition.** The act of begetting by God, which imparts eternal life. 2. **Means.** It is a work of God, particularly of the Spirit (John 3:3-7; Titus 3:5). Faith is the human requirement which enables the Spirit to regenerate, and the Word of God provides the content for faith. 3. **Characteristics.** a. It is instantaneous, not a process (though its antecedents and consequences may be processes). b. It is nonexperiential (not derived from or based on experience, though the experiences of the Christian life will follow). 4. **Consequences.** a. A new nature (2 Cor. 5:17). b. A new life (1 John 2:29).

C. Indwelling (1 Cor. 6:19). 1. **The persons indwelt.** All true believers because: a. Sinning Christians are said to be indwelt (1 Cor. 6:19). b. The Spirit is a gift (Rom. 5:5). c. The absence of the Spirit is a proof of being unsaved (Rom. 8:9b). 2. **The permanence of indwelling.** Believers may lose the filling but not the indwelling (John 14:16). 3. **Some problems in indwelling.** a. Is obedience a condition (Acts 5:32)? Yes, but it is obedience to the faith (Acts 6:7; Rom. 1:5). b. Were not some only temporarily indwelt? Yes, but not since Pentecost (1 Sam. 16:14). c. What is the relation of anointing to indwelling? They occur at the same time but for different purposes: indwelling to bring the presence of God into the Christian's life, and anointing to enable the Christian to be taught (1 John 2:20, 27).

D. Baptizing (1 Cor. 12:13). 1. **Characteristics of baptizing.** a. It occurs only in the Church Age (it was still future in Acts 1:5). b. It involves all believers (1 Cor. 12:13; Eph. 4:5). c. It happens only once (aorist tense in 1 Cor. 12:13). 2. **Consequences of baptiz-**

ing. a. It makes believers members of the Body of Christ. b. It unites them with Christ in His death with respect to the sin nature (Rom. 6:1-10).

E. Sealing. 1. **The agent**—the Father (2 Cor. 1:22; Eph. 1:13; 4:30). 2. **The means**—the Spirit is the seal. 3. **The extent**—for all believers. 4. **The time**—at the time of conversion. 5. **The purpose.** Sealing means the certainty of being possessed by God and preserved until the day of redemption. It is a guarantee of the Christian's security.

IX. THE GIFTS OF THE SPIRIT

A. Definition. A spiritual gift is a God-given ability for service. It is not a place of service nor a ministry to an age group nor a procedure.

B. Distribution. 1. **Source**—the Spirit (1 Cor. 12:11). 2. **Extent.** Every believer has some but not all gifts (1 Peter 4:10). 3. **Time.** Every generation may or may not have all the gifts. Some gifts were for the founding of the church (Eph. 2:20) and would not be expected to be given after the foundation had been laid. Certain spectacular gifts were given to the first generation of Christians but not to the second (Heb. 2:3-4).

C. Development. Abilities can and must be developed by the one to whom given; e.g., the gift of teaching needs development by study.

D. Description. Lists of gifts are found in Romans 12:6-8; 1 Corinthians 12:8-10, 28-30; Ephesians 4:11.

X. THE FILLING OF THE SPIRIT

A. Definition. Being filled means being controlled by the Spirit (Eph. 5:18).

B. Characteristics. 1. Filling is commanded (Eph. 5:18, the verb is imperative). 2. Filling is repeated (Acts 2:4; 4:31). 3. Filling produces Christlikeness (Gal. 5:22-23).

C. Conditions for Being Filled. 1. **A dedicated life.** Yielding to the Spirit's control, while commanded, is voluntary and necessitates an act of dedication. This includes two aspects: initial dedication (Rom. 12:1-2) and continual dedication of one's life (Rom. 8:14). 2. **An undefeated life.** Victory over sin in daily experience is necessary in being controlled by the Spirit (Eph. 4:30). This means responding to the light of the Word as it is continually revealed (1 John 1:7). 3. **A dependent life** (Gal. 5:16).

D. Consequences. Being filled or controlled by the Spirit means: 1. A Christlike character (Gal. 5:22-23). 2. Worship and praise (Eph. 5:18-20). 3. Submissiveness (Eph. 5:21). 4. Service (John 7:37-39).

XI. OTHER MINISTRIES OF THE SPIRIT

A. Teaching (John 16:12-15).
B. Guiding (Rom. 8:14).
C. Assuring (Rom. 8:16).
D. Praying (Rom. 8:26; Eph. 6:18).

XII. THE WORK OF THE SPIRIT IN THE FUTURE

A. In the Tribulation. The Spirit will work in salvation and filling (Zech. 12:10; Joel 2:28-32).
B. In the Kingdom. 1. The Spirit will be upon the King (Isa. 11:2-3). 2. The Spirit will be in God's people (Jer. 31:33).

THE DOCTRINE OF ANGELS

I. THE EXISTENCE OF ANGELS

A. The Teaching of Scripture. Existence taught in at least 34 books of Bible. The word angel occurs about 275 times.
B. The Teaching of Christ. Christ knew of and taught the existence of angels (Matt. 18:10; 26:53).

II. THE CREATION OF ANGELS
A. **Fact** of their creation is shown in Colossians 1:16.
B. **Time.** Before the creation of the world (Job 38:6-7).
C. **State** of their creation was in holiness (Jude 6).

III. THE PERSONALITY OF ANGELS
A. **Intellect** (1 Peter 1:12).
B. **Emotion** (Luke 2:13).
C. **Will** (Jude 6).

IV. THE NATURE OF ANGELS
A. **They Are Spirit Beings** (Heb. 1:14).
B. **They Are Without Power to Reproduce** after their kind (Mark 12:25). Angels are designated by masculine gender in Scripture (Gen. 18:1-2; cf. Zech. 5:9 for possible exception).
C. **They Do Not Die** (Luke 20:36).
D. **They Are Distinct from Human Beings** (Ps. 8:4-5).
E. **They Have Great Power** (2 Peter 2:11).

V. NUMBER OF THE ANGELS. Innumerable (Heb. 12:22).

VI. ORGANIZATION OF THE ANGELS
A. **One Archangel Is Named, Michael** (Jude 9).
B. **Chief Princes** (Dan. 10:13).
C. **Ruling Angels** (Eph. 3:10).
D. **Guardian Angels** (for all, Heb. 1:14; for children, Matt. 18:10).
E. **Seraphim** (Isa. 6:1-3). Have to do with worship of God.
F. **Cherubim** (Gen. 3:22-24). Guarding holiness of God.
G. **Elect Angels** (1 Tim. 5:21).

VII. THE MINISTRIES OF ANGELS
A. **To Christ.** 1. Predicted His birth (Luke 1:26-33). 2. Announced His birth (Luke 2:13). 3. Protected the Baby (Matt. 2:13). 4. Strengthened Christ after temptation (Matt. 4:11). 5. Prepared to defend Him (Matt. 26:53). 6. Strengthened Him in Gethsemane (Luke 22:43). 7. Rolled away stone from tomb (Matt. 28:2). 8. Announced the resurrection (Matt. 28:6).
B. **To Believers.** 1. General ministry of aiding (Heb. 1:14). 2. Involved in answering prayer (Acts 12:7). 3. Observe Christians' experiences (1 Cor. 4:9; 1 Tim. 5:21). 4. Encourage in time of danger (Acts 27:23-24). 5. Interested in evangelistic effort of Christians (Luke 15:10; Acts 8:26). 6. Care for righteous at death (Luke 16:22; Jude 9).
C. **To the Nations.** 1. Michael seems to have a special relationship to Israel (Dan. 12:1). 2. Angels are God's agents in the execution of His providence (Dan. 10:21). 3. Angels will be involved in the judgments of the Tribulation (Rev. 8, 9, 16).
D. **To Unbelievers.** 1. Announce impending judgments (Gen. 19:13; Rev. 14:6-7). 2. Inflict punishment (Acts 12:23). 3. Act as reapers in separation at end of the age (Matt. 13:39).

THE DOCTRINE OF SATAN

I. THE EXISTENCE OF SATAN
A. **The Teaching of Scripture.** The existence of Satan is taught in seven O.T. books and by every N.T. writer.
B. **The Teaching of Christ.** He acknowledged and taught the existence of Satan (Matt. 13:39; Luke 10:18; 11:18).

II. THE PERSONALITY OF SATAN
A. He Possesses Intellect (2 Cor. 11:3).
B. He Has Emotions (Rev. 12:17).
C. He Has a Will (2 Tim. 2:26).
D. He Is Treated as a Morally Responsible Person (Matt. 25:41).
E. Personal Pronouns Are Used of Him (Job 1).

III. THE DESIGNATIONS OF SATAN
A. Names. 1. **Satan** (adversary). 2. **Devil** (slanderer). 3. **Lucifer** (son of the morning). 4. **Beelzebub** (Matt. 12:24). 5. **Belial** (2 Cor. 6:15).
B. Titles. 1. **Evil one** (1 John 5:19, ASV). 2. **Tempter** (1 Thess. 3:5). 3. **Prince of this world** (John 12:31). 4. **God of this age** (2 Cor. 4:4). 5. **Prince of the power of the air** (Eph. 2:2). 6. **Accuser of the brethren** (Rev. 12:10).
C. Representations. 1. **Serpent** (Rev. 12:9). 2. **Dragon** (Rev. 12:3). 3. **Angel of light** (2 Cor. 11:14).

IV. THE NATURE OF SATAN
A. His Character. 1. He is a creature (Ezek. 28:14). 2. He is a spirit being (Eph. 6:11-12). 3. He is of the order of angels called cherubim (Ezek. 28:14). 4. He was the highest of all angelic creatures (Ezek. 28:12).
B. His Personality Traits. 1. He is a murderer (John 8:44). 2. He is a liar (John 8:44). 3. He is a confirmed sinner (1 John 3:8). 4. He is an accuser (Rev. 12:10). 5. He is an adversary (1 Peter 5:8).
C. His Limitations. 1. He is a creature and therefore not omniscient or infinite. 2. He can be resisted by the Christian (James 4:7). 3. God places limitations on him (Job 1:12).

V. THE ORIGINAL STATE AND FALL OF SATAN
A. Satan's Privileges (Ezek. 28:11-15).
B. Satan's Sin (Isa. 14:12-20). 1. **The Person** (vv. 12, 15-20). a. His name (v. 12). b. His power (vv. 15-20). 2. **The Sin** (vv. 13-14). a. "I will ascend into heaven." b. "I will exalt my throne above the stars of God." (Either actual stars or other angels.) c. "I will sit on the mount of the assembly in the far north." (Either assembly of angels or of Israel under Messianic rule.) d. "I will ascend above the heights of the clouds [usurp the glory of God]." e. "I will be like the most High." (Satan wanted to be the possessor of heaven and earth.) His sin is called pride in 1 Timothy 3:6, and it may be characterized as counterfeiting God (like the Most High).
C. Satan's Punishment (Ezek. 28:16-19).

VI. SATAN'S JUDGMENTS
A. Cast Out of His Original Position in Heaven (Ezek. 28:16).
B. Judgment Pronounced in Eden (Gen. 3:14-15).
C. Judged at the Cross (John 12:31).
D. Cast Out in the Midst of the Tribulation Period (Rev. 12:13).
E. Confined in the Abyss at the Beginning of the Millennium (Rev. 20:2).
F. Cast into the Lake of Fire at the End of the Millennium (Rev. 20:10).

VII. THE WORK OF SATAN
A. In Relation to the Redemptive Work of Christ. 1. Prediction of conflict (Gen. 3:15). 2. Temptation of Christ (Matt. 4:1-11). 3. Satan used various people to attempt to thwart the work of Christ (Matt. 2:16; John 8:44; Matt. 16:23). 4. He possessed Judas' body for the betrayal (John 13:27).
B. In Relation to the Nations. 1. He deceives them now (Rev. 20:3). 2. He will gather them to the battle of Armageddon (Rev. 16:13-14).

C. In Relation to Unbelievers. 1. He blinds their minds (2 Cor. 4:4). 2. He snatches the Word from their hearts (Luke 8:12). 3. He uses men to oppose God's work (Rev. 2:13).

D. In Relation to the Christian. 1. He tempts him to lie (Acts 5:3). 2. He accuses and slanders him (Rev. 12:10). 3. He hinders his work (1 Thess. 2:18). 4. He employs demons to attempt to defeat him (Eph. 6:11-12). 5. He tempts to immorality (1 Cor. 7:5). 6. He sows tares among believers (Matt. 13:38-39). 7. He incites persecutions against them (Rev. 2:10).

VIII. THE DEFENSE OF THE BELIEVER AGAINST SATAN

A. The Present Intercessory Work of Christ (John 17:15).

B. The Purpose of God May Include Using Satan for Beneficial Purposes in the Life of the Christian (2 Cor. 12:7).

C. The Christian Should Never Speak of Satan Contemptuously (Jude 8-9).

D. The Believer Should Be on Guard (1 Peter 5:8).

E. The Believer Should Take a Stand Against Satan (James 4:7).

F. The Believer Should Use His Armor (Eph. 6:11-18).

DOCTRINE OF DEMONS

I. ORIGIN OF DEMONS

A. Souls of Departed Evil People. A heathen Greek view.

B. Disembodied Spirits of a Pre-Adamic Race. The Bible nowhere speaks of such a race.

C. The Offspring of Angels and Antediluvian Women (Gen. 6:1-4).

D. Fallen Angels. Satan is an angel, and is called prince of the demons (Matt. 12:24) indicating that the demons are angels, not a pre-Adamic race. Furthermore, Satan has well-organized ranks of angels (Eph. 6:11-12), and it is reasonable to suppose that these are the demons. Some demons are confined already (2 Peter 2:4; Jude 6) and some are loose to do Satan's work. It is thought by some that the reason certain demons are presently confined is that they participated in the sin of Genesis 6:1-4.

II. CHARACTERISTICS OF DEMONS

A. Their Nature. They are spirit beings. Note that the demon in Matthew 17:18 is called an unclean spirit in the parallel account in Mark 9:25. See also Ephesians 6:12.

B. Their Intellect. They know Jesus (Mark 1:24), their own doom (Matt. 8:29), the plan of salvation (James 2:19). They have a well-developed system of doctrine of their own (1 Tim. 4:1-3).

C. Their Morality. They are called unclean spirits, and their doctrine leads to immoral conduct (1 Tim. 4:1-2).

III. ACTIVITY OF DEMONS

A. In General. 1. Demons attempt to thwart the purpose of God (Dan. 10:10-14; Rev. 16:13-16). 2. Demons extend the authority of Satan by doing his bidding (Eph. 6:11-12). 3. Demons may be used by God in the carrying out of His purposes (1 Sam. 16:14; 2 Cor. 12:7).

B. In Particular. 1. Demons can inflict diseases (Matt. 9:33; Luke 13:11, 16). 2. Demons can possess men (Matt. 4:24). 3. Demons can possess animals (Mark 5:13). 4. Demons oppose the spiritual growth of God's children (Eph. 6:12). 5. Demons disseminate false doctrine (1 Tim. 4:1).

1945

IV. DEMON POSSESSION

A. Definition of Demon Possession. Demon possession means a demon residing in a person, exerting direct control and influence over that person, with certain derangement of mind and/or body. Demon possession is to be distinguished from demon influence or demon activity in relation to a person. The work of the demon in the latter is from the outside; in demon possession it is from within. By this definition a Christian cannot be possessed by a demon since he is indwelt by the Holy Spirit. However, a believer can be the target of demonic activity to such an extent that he may give the appearance of demon possession.

B. Effects of Demon Possession. 1. Sometimes physical disease (Matt. 9:32-33), but physical disease and demon possession are distinguished in Scripture (Acts 5:16). 2. Sometimes mental derangement is due to demon possession (Matt. 17:15) but not always (Dan. 4).

C. Extent of Demon Possession. 1. **As to persons.** Only unbelievers may be possessed. In the time of Christ, most instances of demon possession were among non-Israelites. 2. **As to time.** Usually there is an outbreak of demon activity when truth and light are the strongest (e.g., time of Christ).

V. DESTINATION OF DEMONS

A. Temporary Destiny. 1. Some free ones were cast into the abyss (Luke 8:31; cf. Rev. 9:11). 2. Some confined ones will be loosed in the Tribulation (Rev. 9:1-11; 16:13-14). **B. Permanent Destiny.** Eventually all demons will be cast with Satan into the lake of fire (Matt. 25:41).

THE DOCTRINE OF MAN

I. THE ORIGIN OF MAN

A. Types of Evolutionary Theories. 1. Atheistic evolution sees spontaneous generation as the original cause. 2. Theistic evolution sees a Divine Power as the original cause and guiding force. Both may include accidental variation, natural selection, and inheritability of acquired characteristics.

B. Creationism. 1. **The evidence of biblical revelation.** a. Extent of evidence. Although the Bible is not a textbook of science, whenever it relates a scientific fact it records it without error. b. Authority of evidence. Whatever is said as truth is authoritative. 2. **The facts in the evidence.** a. *Bara'* is used in Genesis 1:1, 21, 27. b. The word **day** is used of what we now calibrate in 24 hours, and it is used also of a longer period of time. c. Creation is regarded as historical fact in many places in Scripture (Exodus 20; Ps. 8; Matt. 19; Heb. 4). d. The beginning of the first day is at Genesis 1:3. A long period of time may be involved in verse 2. e. The geological ages may be due to a catastrophe (related or not to the fall of Satan) after the original creation, or they may have been caused by the Flood.

II. THE MATERIAL PART OF MAN (BODY)

A. Its Creation (Gen. 2:7; 3:19).
B. Its Designations. 1. Body (Matt. 6:22). 2. **Flesh** (Gal. 2:20, where it is a synonym for **body**). Flesh sometimes stands for the whole person (1 Peter 1:24) and sometimes for the sin nature (Rom. 7:18). 3. **Body of humiliation** (Phil. 3:21). 4. **Earthen vessel** (2 Cor. 4:7). 5. **Temple of the Holy Spirit** (1 Cor. 6:19).
C. Its Future. All men will be raised from the dead (John 5:28-29). The unredeemed will be resurrected to eternal existence in the lake of fire (Rev. 20:12, 15) and the redeemed to heaven.

III. THE IMMATERIAL PART OF MAN (SOUL AND SPIRIT)

A. Its Origin (Gen. 2:7).

B. Its Characteristic—"image and likeness of God." Adam's original state was one of unconfirmed creaturely holiness. He lost this by the Fall, but man still retains vestiges of God's image and likeness (1 Cor. 11:7; James 3:9).

C. The Transmission of the Immaterial Part of Man. 1. **Preexistent theory.** The souls of all men were created at the beginning and are confined in physical bodies. 2. **Creationism.** The soul of man is created by God when the body is born. 3. **Traducianism.** The soul is transmitted by natural generation just as the body is.

D. The Facets of the Immaterial Part of Man. 1. **Soul.** Soul stands for the personal life or for the individual. It has emotion (Jer. 31:25) and wars against the lusts of the flesh (1 Peter 2:11). 2. **Spirit.** Spirit is related to higher aspects of man (Rom. 8:16). All men have a spirit (1 Cor. 2:11). It may also be corrupted (2 Cor. 7:1). Although there is distinction between soul and spirit, they both are facets of man's immaterial nature of man. 3. **Heart.** Heart is the largest concept of all the facets of man's immaterial nature. It is the seat of intellectual, emotional, volitional, and spiritual life of man (Heb. 4:12; Matt. 22:37; Heb. 4:7). 4. **Conscience.** Conscience is a witness within that has been affected by the Fall but which nevertheless can be a safe guide at times (1 Peter 2:19; Heb. 10:22). 5. **Mind.** The mind is the facet of man's immaterial nature in which understanding is centered. The mind was affected by the Fall but is able to be renewed in Christ (Rom. 12:2). 6. **Flesh.** When flesh means the sin nature, then this too is an aspect of man's immaterial nature. It is completely corrupt and cannot be renewed but will be eradicated at death.

IV. THE FALL OF MAN

A. Attitudes Toward Genesis 3. 1. **The liberal view**—a legend, a general picture of religion and morals in the light of a later period. 2. **The neoorthodox view**—myth, primal history, or "true myth." Barthians consider the account as not being historical but as expressing truths; i.e., truth without fact (if that is possible).

B. The Test. The prohibition not to eat of the fruit of the tree of the knowledge of good and evil ultimately was a test of obedience to the revealed will of God. It was certainly not merely a matter of proper diet!

C. The Fall. First, Satan attempted to get Eve to doubt the goodness of God because He had held back one tree from them (Gen. 3:1, "every"). **Second,** Satan offered Eve his substitute plan which would allow eating without the penalty (vv. 4–5). **Third,** Eve prejustified her eating (v. 6). **Fourth,** Eve ate and Adam followed.

D. The Penalties. 1. **On the serpent** (Gen. 3:14). 2. **On Satan** (v. 15). a. Enmity between hosts of evil and seed of the woman. b. Satan would be allowed to give Christ a painful but not deadly wound ("heel"). c. Satan would be given a fatal wound ("head"). 3. **On Eve and women** (v. 16). a. Pain in childbirth. b. Submission to husband. 4. **On Adam and man** (vv. 17-19). a. Cursing of the ground. b. Hard labor. 5. **On the race** (vv. 20-24). a. Broken fellowship with God. b. Physical death. c. Expulsion from Eden.

THE DOCTRINE OF SIN

I. THE ORIGIN OF SIN

A. In Relation to God. God cannot sin, and yet God's plan must have included the allowing of sin to enter the world because it included a Saviour from before the foundation of the world.

B. In Relation to Satan. Sin was found in Satan (Ezek. 28:15). This is the closest the Bible comes to stating definitely the origin of sin.

C. In Relation to the Angels. Some followed Satan in his sin.

D. In Relation to Man. Sin originated in Eden.

II. THE DEFINITION OF SIN

A. Sin Is an Illusion. This idea has taken a variety of forms of expression; e.g., our lack of knowledge is the reason we have the illusion of sin; or when evolution has had time to help us progress further, sin will disappear.

B. Sin Is that Eternal Principle of Dualism, Outside of God and Independent of Him.

C. Sin Is Selfishness. This is the most frequently heard definition of sin. It is scriptural but inadequate.

D. Sin Is a Violation of the Law. This too is scriptural but inadequate, unless the concept of law is expanded to include the character of God Himself.

E. Sin Is Anything Contrary to the Character of God.

III. PERSONAL SIN

A. Meaning. Sins committed by individuals. They may be willful or in ignorance. Missing the mark also involves hitting the wrong mark.

B. Penalty. Loss of fellowship.

C. Remedy. 1. **Forgiveness**—takes away the guilt of sin. 2. **Justification**—the declaration of the addition of Christ's righteousness to the believing sinner.

IV. THE SIN NATURE

A. Meaning. The sin nature is the capacity and inclination to do those things that can in no way commend us to God.

B. Scriptures (2 Corinthians 4:4; Ephesians 4:18; Romans 1:18—3:20).

C. Results of the Sin Nature. 1. Total depravity (unmeritoriousness of man in the sight of God). 2. Spiritual death.

D. Transmission of the Sin Nature—from parents to children (Ps. 51:5).

E. Remedy. 1. Redemption, which brings a new nature or new capacity to serve Christ. 2. The power of the indwelling Holy Spirit to give victory over the judged sin nature.

V. IMPUTED SIN

A. Meaning. That which resulted from man's participation in Adam's first sin.

B. Scripture (Romans 5:12). All mankind was in Adam participating in his sin and bearing the resultant guilt.

C. Transmission of Imputed Sin. Transmitted directly from Adam to each individual member of the race.

D. Penalty—physical death.

E. Remedy—imputed righteousness of Christ (2 Cor. 5:21).

VI. SIN IN THE CHRISTIAN'S LIFE

A. The Fact of the Believer's Sinning (1 John 1:8–10).

B. The Standard for the Christian—"Walk in the light" (1 John 1:7).

C. The Preventives for Sin in the Christian's Life. 1. The Word of God (Ps. 119:11). 2. The intercession of Christ (John 17:15). 3. The indwelling Holy Spirit (John 7:37–39).

D. The Penalties for Sin in the Christian's Life. 1. Loss of fellowship (1 John 1:6). 2. Church excommunication (1 Cor. 5:4-5). 3. Chastisement (Heb. 12:6). 4. Sometimes physical death (1 Cor. 11:30).

E. The Remedy for Sin in the Christian's Life—confession (1 John 1:9).

THE DOCTRINE OF SALVATION

I. THE DOCTRINE OF ELECTION

A. Proof of the Election. 1. From nature. Selectivity is obvious in God's creative activity everywhere. 2. From Scripture (Rom. 9; Eph. 1; Acts 13:48; Rom. 8:27-30).

B. Meaning of Election. God's unconditioned and pretemporal choice of those individuals whom He would save.

II. THE DEATH OF CHRIST

A. The Accomplishments of the Death of Christ. **1. Substitution.** a. Meaning. Christ died in the place of sinners. b. Words involved. (1) *Anti* is a Greek preposition which clearly means "in the place of" (Matt. 20:28). (2) *Huper* is a Greek preposition which sometimes means "for the benefit of" and sometimes "in the place of" (as in a nonatonement passage like Philemon 13 and in atonement passages like 2 Cor. 5:21 and 1 Peter 3:18). c. Results. (1) Sins are removed by substitution. (2) The righteousness of Christ is added. **2. Redemption.** a. Meaning. (1) To pay the ransom price (2 Peter 2:1). (2) To remove from the marketplace (slave market, Greek of Gal. 3:13). (3) To effect a full release (Matt. 20:28). b. Benefits. Sin paid for and the sinner released from all the consequences of sin. **3. Reconciliation.** a. Meaning. Man's state of alienation from God is changed so that he is able to be saved (2 Cor. 5:19). b. Need for reconciliation—man's enmity (Rom. 5:10). **4. Propitiation.** a. Need—wrath of God (Rom. 1:18). b. Meaning. God is satisfied with the death of Christ for sin. c. Scripture (1 John 2:2). d. Means—blood of Christ (Rom. 3:25). **5. Judgment of the sin nature.** a. Meaning. The death of Christ made inoperative the reigning power of the sin nature (Rom. 6:1-10). b. Results. Possibility of holy living through the reigning power of the Spirit. **6. End of the Mosaic Law** (Rom. 10:4; Col. 2:14; 2 Cor. 3:7-11). **7. Ground for the Christian's cleansing from sin** (1 John 1:7-9). **8. Basis for removal of precross sins** (Rom. 3:25). **9. Basis for the judgment of Satan and his hosts** (Col. 2:15; John 12:31). **B. The Types of the Death of Christ.** **1.** Offering of Isaac (Gen. 22). **2.** The Passover (Exodus 12). **3.** The Levitical offerings (Lev. 1—5). **4.** The red heifer (Num. 19). **5.** The Day of Atonement (Lev. 16). **6.** The tabernacle. **C. The Theories of the Death of Christ.** **1. Ransom to Satan.** The death of Christ constituted a ransom paid to Satan for sin. **2. Recapitulation theory.** Christ recapitulated in Himself all the stages of human life and by His life reversed the course started by Adam. His obedience compensated for the disobedience of Adam. **3. Satisfaction theory of Anselm.** Satisfaction made to the honor of God which was offended by man's sin. **4. Moral influence theory.** Christ's death manifested the love of God, and this should influence man to do good. Taught by Abelard. **5. Example theory of Socinus.** Christ was a martyr who is our example. **6. Governmental theory.** The death of Christ was required to show God's displeasure over sin. The setup of God's government required Christ's death. Held by Grotius, Dale, Cave, Miley. **7. Mystical theory.** Similar to the moral influence, though the influence in the mystical theory occurs in a more mystical way. **D. The Extent of the Death of Christ.** Limited or unlimited atonement? Did Christ die for the elect or for all men? **1. The meaning of redemption, reconciliation, and propitiation.** a. Redemption extends to all men as far as paying the price for sin is concerned (2 Peter 2:1). b. The whole world was reconciled to God (2 Cor. 5:19). c. Propitiation concerns the sins of the whole world, not simply of the elect (1 John 2:2). **2. The relevance of the universal Gospel offer.** Does limited atonement vitiate the whosoever Gospel invitations? **3. The testimony of Scripture** (1 Tim. 4:10; 1 John 2:2). **4. The necessity of faith.** Christ is not defeated in having died for all even though all are not ultimately saved, because personal faith is as necessary for salvation as the death of Christ. Summary: The death of Christ is unlimited in its value—it was for all men; but the death of Christ is effective only for the elect—it is applied only to those who believe.

III. THE WORK OF THE HOLY SPIRIT

A. The Need for the Spirit's Ministry. Man's depravity (Rom. 3:10-18; 1 Cor. 2:14; 2 Cor. 4:3-4; Eph. 2:1-3).
B. The Nature of the Spirit's Ministry. **1.** The Spirit convicts (John 16:7-11). See Doctrine of the Holy Spirit. **2.** The Spirit regenerates (Titus 3:5).

IV. THE BLESSINGS OF SALVATION

A. The Blessing of Acceptance. This is expressed by such terms as: 1. Redeemed (Rom. 3:24). 2. Reconciled (2 Cor. 5:19-21). 3. Forgiven (Rom. 3:25). 4. Delivered (Col. 1:13). 5. Accepted (Eph. 1:6). 6. Justified (Rom. 3:24). 7. Glorified (Rom. 8:30).

B. The Blessing of Position. The Christian's position is: 1. Citizen of heaven (Phil. 3:20). 2. Member of a holy and royal priesthood (1 Peter 2:5, 9). 3. Member of the family of God (Eph. 2:19). 4. Adopted (Gal. 4:5). 5. Member of a peculiar people (1 Peter 2:9).

C. The Blessing of an Inheritance. The child of God: 1. Is complete in Christ (Col. 2:9-10). 2. Possesses every spiritual blessing (Eph. 1:3). 3. Is an heir of heaven (1 Peter 1:4).

D. The Blessing of Enablement. Enablement is assured because the believer is: 1. Under grace (Rom. 6:14). 2. Freed from the law (2 Cor. 3:6-13). 3. Indwelt by the Persons of the Godhead (Gal. 2:20; 1 Cor. 6:19).

V. THE SECURITY OF THE BELIEVER

A. The Issue. Can a true believer ever lose his salvation by sinning, ceasing to believe, or in any other way?

B. The Proof of Security. The doctrine of eternal security rests on a proper concept of what God actually does when He saves a soul. 1. He loves to the uttermost (John 13:1). 2. He purposes to keep in spite of everything (John 10:28-30). 3. He intends to present us faultless before Himself (Jude 24). 4. His Son ever lives to make intercession to keep us saved (Heb. 7:25; 1 John 2:1). 5. His Spirit has placed us into the Body of Christ (1 Cor. 12:13). 6. His Spirit has sealed us until the day of redemption (Eph. 4:30). 7. His Word guarantees that nothing (including ourselves) can separate us from Christ (Rom. 8:28-39). In order to lose one's salvation all of these works of God would have to be undone, and the Bible nowhere even hints that this is possible.

C. The Problem Passages. 1. Hebrews 6:4-6. If this teaches that one can lose his salvation, it also teaches that one can never be saved a second time. 2. John 15:6. Probably refers to the judgment seat of Christ. 3. James 2:14-26. Nonworking faith is not a faith that saves in the first place. 4. 2 Peter 2 and Jude are referring to false teachers, who in Jude's estimation were not true believers (Jude 19; cf. Rom. 8:9). 5. Matthew 24:13. End of what? (The Great Tribulation.)

VI. THE CONDITION FOR SALVATION

A. The Condition. Salvation is conditioned solely on faith in Jesus Christ. Nearly 200 times faith, or belief, is stated as the single condition in the N.T. (John 1:12; Acts 16:31). That faith must be placed in Christ as one's substitute for and Saviour from sin. It is not easy to believe someone whom you have never seen about the most important matter of eternal destiny, but this and only this is the way to be saved.

B. The False Additions to Faith. Through the ages other requirements in addition to faith have been wrongly added. Some of these are: 1. **Surrender** to the lordship of Christ. Christ must be Lord in the sense of Jehovah in order to be a qualified Saviour (Rom. 10:9), but Christ's personal lordship over the individual's life is not a condition for salvation. It should be a consequence of salvation and is a condition for dedication in full discipleship. 2. **Baptism.** Baptism is the visible testimony to one's salvation, but not a condition for it. Acts 2:38 should be translated, "Repent and be baptized on the basis of the remission of sins." Acts 22:16 teaches that baptism followed the arising, just as forgiveness followed the calling on the name of the Lord. The two parts of the verse should be kept distinct. Mark 16:16 is probably not a genuine part of Mark's Gospel. 3. **Repentance.** This is a valid condition for salvation when understood as a synonym for faith. It is a false addition to faith when understood as a prerequisite, requiring the cleansing of the life in order to be saved. 4. **Confession.** Confession is a normal result of being saved, though it may also accompany the initial act of believing. Nowhere is public confession required. In this connection, prayer may be helpful in clinching a decision, but it is not in itself a requirement for salvation.

THE DOCTRINE OF THE CHURCH

I. THE MEANING OF THE CONCEPT OF THE CHURCH
A. Negative Considerations. 1. **The Church is not Judaism** continued and enlarged. Although there is a continuity between the redeemed of all ages, the Church is a "new man" (Eph. 2:15). 2. **The Church is not the kingdom.** The kingdom is God's rule; the Church is Christ's Bride.
B. The Meaning and Uses of the Word. 1. **Literally,** "called-out group or assembly." 2. **By usage** the word *church* may refer to: a. The assembly of the Jewish people (Acts 7:38). b. A heathen assembly (Acts 19:32, 39, 41). c. The Body of Christ (Col. 1:18). d. The local assembly (1 Cor. 1:2).
C. The Meaning of the Body of Christ. It is that spiritual organism of which Christ is the Head, and is composed of all regenerated people from Pentecost to the rapture.
D. The Meaning of Church in the Local Sense. A local church is a group of professing believers in Christ who have been baptized and who have organized themselves for the purpose of doing God's will.

II. THE LOCAL CHURCH
A. Its Organization (Heb. 13:7, 17). 1. **Elders.** a. Meaning and distinctions. *Elder* emphasizes the office as leader in the church. *Bishop* emphasizes the function as overseer. *Pastor* is the gift of shepherding (Acts 20:28). b. Number. Every city had plurality of elders (Acts 14:23), but each house-church may have had only one or more (1 Tim. 3:1-7). c. Duties. To oversee (1 Tim. 3:1), to rule (1 Tim. 5:17), to guard right doctrine (Titus 1:9). d. Qualifications (1 Tim. 3:1-6; Titus 1:7-9). e. Ordination (1 Tim. 4:14; Titus 1:5). 2. **Deacons.** a. Meaning. Servant. b. Qualifications (1 Tim. 3:8-10, 12-13). c. Duties. Deacons were the servants of the elders (Acts 6:1-6) and an officially recognized group in the church (Phil. 1:1). 3. **Deaconesses.** Some justify the order of deaconess from Romans 16:1 and 1 Timothy 3:11.
B. Its Ordinances. 1. **Definition.** An outward rite prescribed by Christ to be performed by His Church. The word **sacrament** adds the idea of directly conveying grace through the ordinance. 2. **The Lord's Supper.** a. The order (1 Cor. 11:23-26). b. The meaning. (1) True view—it is a memorial. (2) Consubstantiation (Lutheran view). Body and blood of Christ are present and combined with the elements. (3) Transubstantiation (Roman Catholic view). Elements are changed into body and blood of Christ. (4) Spiritual presence (Calvin). c. Frequency. "As oft," though the early church seemed to observe once a week (Acts 20:7). 3. **Baptism.** a. Meaning. Baptism means identification or association with a message and/or a group. b. Arguments for nonimmersion. (1) The Greek word *baptizo* is used in a secondary sense, "to bring under the influence," and affusion best pictures this. (2) Affusion pictures the Spirit's coming upon the believer. (3) Immersion was impossible or improbable in Acts 2:41; 8:38; 10:47; 16:33. (4) In Hebrews 9:10 the word "baptize" is used to include O.T. rituals of sprinkling. (5) Three-fourths of the Church does not immerse. c. Arguments for immersion. (1) This is the primary meaning of the Greek word *baptizo*. (2) The normal understanding of "into" and "out of" the water indicates immersion. (3) Jewish proselyte baptism was a total immersion, which points to John's and Christian baptism being the same. (4) The practice of the early Church was immersion. (5) Every case allows for it. (6) The Greek language has words for "sprinkle" and "pour" but these are never used of baptism. (7) Immersion best pictures what the baptizing work of the Spirit accomplishes according to Romans 6. 4. **Infant baptism.** a. Arguments for.

(1) Baptism in the new covenant is analogous to circumcision in the old, which was done to infants. (2) Household baptisms in the N.T. must have included infants (Acts 16:33). (3) Household promises allow for infant baptism (1 Cor. 7:14). b. Arguments against. (1) The meaning of baptism restricts it to those who can consciously exercise faith. (2) Household baptisms do not specify infants though children may have been included. **C. Its Government.** Types of church government. 1. **National church** (Lutheran in Scandinavia). 2. **Hierarchical church** (Roman Catholic). 3. **Federal government** (Presbyterian with congregation vesting powers in ruling board of elders and deacons). 4. **Congregational** (such as Baptists, with congregation itself deciding most questions). **D. Its Purpose.** 1. To glorify God. 2. To evangelize. 3. To produce holy Christians. 4. To care for its own (1 Tim. 5). 5. To do good in the world (Gal. 6:10).

III. THE UNIVERSAL CHURCH
A. The Fact of Its Existence (Matt. 16:18; Col. 1:18; Eph. 3:10).
B. The Founding of It. 1. Christ was the Founder in the sense that He was its Teacher, Builder, and the Sender of the Spirit who actually formed the Body of Christ. 2. Pentecost was the beginning since the Body of Christ is formed by the baptizing work of the Spirit (1 Cor. 12:13) and this was first performed on Pentecost (Acts 1:5; 11:15).
C. The Foundation of It—Christ (Matt. 16:18; 1 Peter 2:4-8).
D. The Figures of It. 1. The Shepherd and the sheep (John 10). 2. The Vine and the branches (John 15). 3. The Cornerstone and the stones of the building (Eph. 2:19-21). 4. The High Priest and a kingdom of priests (1 Peter 2). 5. The Head and the Body (1 Cor. 12). 6. The Last Adam and the new creation (Rom. 5). 7. The Bridegroom and the Bride (Eph. 5).
E. The End of the Church Age—at the rapture (2 Thess. 2; Rev. 3:10-11; 1 Thess. 1:10).

THE DOCTRINE OF FUTURE THINGS

I. THE SECOND COMING OF CHRIST
A. Postmillennial View. 1. **Meaning.** The second coming of Christ is after the Millennium. 2. **Order of events.** The latter part of the Church Age (that is, the last 1,000 years of it) is the Millennium, which will be an era of peace and abundance brought about through the efforts of the church. After this, Christ will come. Then will follow general resurrection and judgment and eternity. 3. **Method of interpretation.** Postmillennial interpretation is largely spiritualized with regard to prophecy. However, Revelation 20 will be fulfilled in the earthly kingdom that is brought in through the church's efforts.
B. Amillennial View. 1. **Meaning.** The second coming of Christ is at the end of the Church Age and there is no earthly Millennium. Strictly, amillenarians believe that the present state of the righteous in heaven is the Millennium, but there is no earthly Millennium. 2. **Order of events.** The Church Age will end in a time of trouble, Christ will come, there will be general resurrection and judgment, then eternity. 3. **Method of interpretation.** Amillennial interpretation spiritualizes the promises made to Israel as a nation and says they are fulfilled in the Church. According to this view, Revelation 20 describes the scene of souls in heaven during the time between the first and second comings of Christ.
C. Premillennial View. 1. **Meaning.** The second coming of Christ will occur before the Millennium. 2. **Order of events.** The Church Age ends in the time of Tribulation, Christ returns to the earth, He sets up and rules His kingdom for 1,000 years, the resurrection and judgment of the unsaved occur, then eternity. 3. **Method of interpretation.** Premillennialism follows the plain, normal, literal, historical, and grammatical method of interpretation. Revelation 20 is understood literally. 4. **The question of the rapture.** Among premillennialists there is no agreement as to the time of the rapture (see next section).

II. THE RAPTURE OF THE CHURCH

A. The Time of the Rapture. Postmillennialists and amillennialists both see the rapture of the Church at the close of this age and concurrent with the second coming of Christ. Among premillennialists there are several views. 1. **Pretribulation rapture.** a. Meaning. The rapture of the Church (i.e., the coming of the Lord in the air for His saints) will take place before the seven-year period of the Tribulation begins. Therefore, the Church will not go through any of the Tribulation period according to this view. b. Proof cited. (1) The promise to be kept out of the hour of trouble (Rev. 3:10). (2) The removal of the residence aspect of the indwelling Spirit's work in believers requires the removal of believers too (2 Thess. 2). (3) The Tribulation is a time of the outpouring of the wrath of God and the Church is exempt from wrath (Rev. 6:17; cf. 1 Thess. 1:10; 5:9). (4) The rapture can be imminent only if it is pretribulational (1 Thess. 5:6). 2. **Midtribulation rapture.** a. Meaning. The rapture will occur after three and a half years of the Tribulation have passed. b. Proof cited. (1) The last trump of 1 Corinthians 15:52 is the same as the seventh trumpet of Revelation 11:15 and that is sounded at the middle of the Tribulation. (2) The Great Tribulation is only the last half of Daniel's 70th week and the Church is promised deliverance only from that (Rev. 11:2; 12:6). (3) The resurrection of the two witnesses pictures the rapture of the Church, and their resurrection occurs at the middle of the period (Rev. 11). 3. **Posttribulation rapture.** a. Meaning. The rapture will occur at the end of the Tribulation. The Church will be on earth during the entire Tribulation. The rapture is distinct from the second coming though separated by only a very short interval of time. b. Proof cited. (1) The rapture and the second coming are described by the same words. (2) Preservation from the wrath means supernatural protection while living in that time, not deliverance from the period (as Israel was protected from the plagues while living in Egypt). (3) Saints are seen on the earth during the Tribulation (Matt. 24:22). 4. **Partial rapture.** a. Meaning. Only saints who are worthy will be raptured before the wrath of God is poured out; those who have not been faithful will remain on the earth to endure the Tribulation. b. Proof cited—verses like Hebrews 9:28, which require preparedness.

B. The Description of the Rapture. 1. **The Scripture.** 1 Thessalonians 4:13–18; 1 Corinthians 15:51–57; John 14:1–3. 2. **The events.** a. The descent of Christ. b. The resurrection of the dead in Christ. c. The change from mortal to immortal bodies for Christians living at the time. d. The meeting with Christ in the air to ascend to heaven.

III. THE TRIBULATION

A. Its Duration. It is the 70th week of Daniel and is therefore of seven years' duration (Dan. 9:27). Half the period is said to be 42 months or 1,260 days (Rev. 11:2–3).

B. Its Distinctiveness (Matt. 24:21; Rev. 6:15–17).

C. Its Description. 1. Judgment upon the world. The three series of judgments describe these judgments (seals, Rev. 6; trumpets, Rev. 8–9; bowls, Rev. 16). 2. Persecution of Israel (Matt. 24:9, 22; Rev. 12:17). 3. Salvation of multitudes (Rev. 7). 4. Rise and dominion of Antichrist (2 Thess. 2; Rev. 13).

D. Its End. The Tribulation ends in the gathering of the nations to the battle of Armageddon and the return of Christ to the earth (Rev. 19).

IV. THE MILLENNIUM

A. Definition. The Millennium is the 1,000-year period of the earthly reign of Christ in fulfillment of the Abrahamic, Davidic, and new covenants.

B. Its Designations. The Millennium is called the kingdom of heaven (Matt. 6:10), the kingdom of God (Luke 19:11), the kingdom of Christ (Rev. 11:15), the regeneration (Matt. 19:28), the times of refreshing (Acts 3:19), and the world to come (Heb. 2:5).

C. Its Government. 1. Its Head will be Christ (Rev. 19:16). 2. Its character. A spiritual reign which will bring in peace, equity, justice, prosperity, and glory (Isa. 11:2-5). 3. Its capital will be Jerusalem (Isa. 2:3).

D. Its Relation to Satan. During this period Satan will be bound until the very end, when he will be loosed in order to deceive the nations and lead one final revolt against Christ (Rev. 20). Satan will be defeated and cast into the lake of fire forever.

V. THE FUTURE JUDGMENTS

A. Judgment of Believers' Works.   1. Time. After the Church is raptured.   2. Place. In heaven.   3. Judge. Christ.   4. Subjects judged. All in the Body of Christ.   5. Basis. Works done since time of salvation.   6. Result. Rewards or loss of rewards.   7. Scripture. 1 Corinthians 3:11-15; 2 Corinthians 5:10.

B. Judgment of the Gentiles (or Nations).   1. Time. At the second coming of Christ. 2. Place. Valley of Jehoshaphat.   3. Judge. Christ.   4. Subjects judged. Gentiles living when Christ comes.   5. Basis. Treatment of Christ's "brethren," i.e., Israel.   6. Result. Saved to enter the kingdom, or lost and cast into lake of fire.   7. Scripture. Matthew 25:31-46; Joel 3:2.

C. Judgment of Israel.   1. Time. At the second coming of Christ.   2. Place. On the earth.   3. Judge. Christ.   4. Subjects judged. Jews who are living when Christ comes. 5. Basis. Acceptance of Messiah.   6. Result. Saved to enter the kingdom, or lost. 7. Scripture. Ezekiel 20:37-38.

D. Judgment of Fallen Angels.   1. Time. Probably after the Millennium.   2. Place. Unspecified.   3. Judges. Christ and believers.   4. Subjects judged. Fallen angels. 5. Basis. Disobedience to God in following Satan in his revolt.   6. Result. Cast into the lake of fire.   7. Scripture. Jude 6; 1 Corinthians 6:3.

E. Judgment of the Unsaved Dead.   1. Time. After the Millennium.   2. Place. Before the Great White Throne.   3. Judge. Christ.   4. Subjects judged. All unsaved men who have died from the beginning to this time.   5. Basis. Rejection of the Saviour places them in this judgment, but they are shown on the basis of their own works that they deserve eternal punishment.   6. Result. Lake of fire.   7. Scripture. Revelation 20:11-15.

VI. THE RESURRECTIONS

A. The Resurrection of the Just (Luke 14:14; John 5:28-29).   1. Includes the dead in Christ, who are raised at the rapture of the Church (1 Thess. 4:16).   2. Includes those saved during the Tribulation period (Rev. 20:4).   3. Includes O.T. saints (Dan. 12:2— some believe they will be raised at the rapture; others, at the second coming). All these are included in the first resurrection.

B. The Resurrection of the Unjust. All unsaved people will be raised after the Millennium to stand before the Great White Throne in judgment (Rev. 20:11-15). This second resurrection results in the second death for all involved.

THE INSPIRATION OF THE BIBLE

Every man has a basis of authority on which he thinks and acts. For the Christian this is the Bible, claimed to be a book that is different from all others. Let's examine this claim.

The English word *Bible* is derived from the Greek word which means "roll" or "book"—actually a roll of papyrus (Luke 4:17; Dan. 9:2). The term *scripture* is used in the New Testament of the sacred books of the Old Testament which were regarded as inspired (2 Tim. 3:16; and Rom. 3:2) and also of other parts of the New Testament (2 Peter 3:16). The phrase, "Word of God," is used in the New Testament of both Old and New Testaments in written form (Matt. 15:6, ASV; John 10:35; Heb. 4:12). Each of these terms refers to the Book *par excellence*, the unique and recognized record of God's revelation to man.

By some very obvious tests the Bible is a unique book. It was written over a period of 1,500 years by about 40 different authors, and yet it is one book without contradictions in what it says. And what it says is remarkable, for it speaks with equal ease and authority of the known and unknowable, of the pleasant and unpleasant, of man's accomplishments and failures, of the past and the future. Few books ever attempt such scope; none is completely accurate except the Bible.

The Meaning and Means of Revelation

The word *revelation* simply means "unveiling." It is often defined in relation to the Bible as God making known to men what otherwise would be unknown. However, this is really not a good definition because there are many things in the Bible which were known simply because men were eyewitnesses to the events. But there are also many things that we would never know except for divine revelation. The word is also used in 1 Corinthians 2:10 in the sense of the illuminating work of the Spirit. Thus revelation can be through natural means or supernatural means; it can relate to persons or propositions; it can refer to particular parts of the Bible ("God revealed the future to the prophets") or to the entire Bible, and it can refer to the content of the Bible or to the interpretation of that content (illumination).

The means of revelation have generally been divided into the two categories: general and special revelation. General revelation includes all means apart from Christ and the Bible; that is, God's revelation through nature (Rom. 1:18-21), through His providential dealings with man (Rom. 8:28), and through His preservation of the universe (Col. 1:17), and man's moral nature (Gen. 1:26; Acts 17:29). Special revelation is that which has come through Christ (John 1:18) and through the Bible (1 John 5:9-12). General revelation is sufficient to alert a man to his need of God and to condemn him if he rejects what he can learn through nature, but only faith in Christ is sufficient to save (Acts 4:12). If this does not seem fair, look at it this way: Suppose you knew of a student who needed $400 to pay his school bill, and you gave him $3 to help pay that debt (the $3 being more than you could really afford). If he returned it to you, asking sarcastically what good that little bit would do toward a $400 debt, would you feel any obligation at all to give him $100 the next day if you received a large gift in the mail? Undoubtedly not. But if he gratefully took the $3 you offered, you would be anxious to help him further as soon as you were able. Just so, God's general revelation if rejected brings just condemnation; but if accepted, then He will bring the further necessary message of the gospel in order that that man might be saved (Acts 10:3-6).

From *A Survey of Bible Doctrine*, by Charles C. Ryrie (Moody Press). © 1972 by The Moody Bible Institute of Chicago.

What Is Meant by "Inspiration"?

Revelation concerns the material or content by which God is disclosed, and inspiration concerns the record of that content, the Bible. Strictly speaking, *inspiration* means to fill or breathe into. In 2 Timothy 3:16 the word usually translated "inspiration" is more accurately "spiration," that is, "God-breathed." In other words, the verse simply says that Scripture is God-produced and it does not actually indicate any of the means that God may have used in producing it.

A Definition

My own definition of biblical inspiration is that it is God's superintendence of the human authors so that, using their own individual personalities, they composed and recorded without error His revelation to man in the words of the original autographs. Several features of the definition are worth emphasizing: (1) God superintended but did not dictate the material. (2) He used human authors and their own individual styles. (3) Nevertheless, the product was, in its original manuscripts, without error.

Views of Inspiration

Not all agree with the above definition and its implications.

(1) Some hold that the writers of the Bible were men of great genius, but that their writings were inspired no more than those of other geniuses throughout history. This has been called the view of *natural inspiration,* for there is no supernatural dimension to it.

(2) A step up is the view which may be labeled the *mystical* or *illumination* view of inspiration, which sees the writers of the Bible as Spirit-filled and guided believers just as any believer may be even today. Logically, one might conclude that any Spirit-filled Christian could write Scripture today. Similar to this is the idea that the biblical writers were inspired to a greater *degree* than others.

(3) The usual caricature of verbal inspiration is that it means *dictation;* that is, the writers were completely passive and God simply dictated to them what was to be recorded. Of course it is true that some parts of the Bible were dictated (like the Ten Commandments and the rest of the law), but the definition proposed above incorporates the idea that God allowed the writers varying degrees of self-expression as they wrote.

(4) *Partial inspiration* views certain parts of the Bible as supernaturally inspired, namely, portions which would otherwise have been unknowable (accounts of creation, prophecy, etc.).

(5) A very popular concept of inspiration is that only the *concepts* but not the very words were inspired. This seems to allow for a measure of authority without the necessity of the words being completely accurate.

(6) The *neoorthodox* or Barthian view of inspiration is that the Bible is a witness to the Word of God, though a Barthian would not be adverse to saying also that the Bible is the Word of God. But this is true only in a secondary sense (Christ being primarily the Word), and his Bible is full of errors because it is merely the product of fallible writers. The Barthian accepts the teachings of liberalism concerning the Bible and then tries to give it a measure of authority on the ground that in a fallible way it does point to Christ.

(7) Among many conservatives today a view is held that might be labeled the *inspired purpose* view of the Bible. This simply means that while the Bible contains factual errors and insoluble discrepancies in its content, it does have "doctrinal integrity" and thus accomplishes perfectly God's purpose for it. Those who hold this idea can and do use the words *infallible* and *inerrant,* but it is important to notice that they carefully limit the Bible's infallibility to the main purpose or principal emphasis of the Bible and do not extend it to include the accuracy of all its historical facts and parallel accounts. One recent writer put it this way: "I confess the infallibility and inerrancy of the Scriptures in accomplishing God's purpose for them—to give man the revelation of God in His redemptive

love through Jesus Christ." In other words, the principal revelation of God—salvation—has been transmitted infallibly by means of the records which, nevertheless, are quite fallible. In contrast to Barthians, those who hold this concept of inspiration would hold a more conservative view toward matters like authorship and dates of the books of the Bible and would in general consider the Bible as a whole more trustworthy. But it is still fallible and errant; and if that be so in historical matters, who can be sure it is not also fallible in doctrinal matters? Besides, how can one separate doctrine and history? Try to in relation to the great events of Christ's life. Those doctrines depend on the accuracy of the historical facts.

The Biblical Testimony

Just to illustrate how times have changed, not many years ago all one had to say to affirm his belief in the full inspiration of the Bible was that he believed it was "the Word of God." Then it became necessary to add "the inspired Word of God." Later he had to include "the verbally, inspired Word of God." Then to mean the same thing he had to say "the plenary (fully), verbally, inspired Word of God." Then came the necessity to say "the plenary, verbally, infallible, inspired Word of God." Today one has to say "the plenary, verbally, infallible, inspired, and inerrant-in-the original-manuscripts Word of God." And even then, he may not communicate clearly!

What does the Bible claim for itself?

(1) It claims that all Scripture is God-breathed (2 Tim. 3:16). This means that God, who is true (Rom. 3:4), breathed out truth.

(2) But did man corrupt that truth in the process of recording it? No, for the Bible also testifies that the men who wrote were "carried along by the Holy Spirit" (2 Peter 1:21, TEV). The Spirit, thus, became a Coauthor with each human writer of the Bible. Notice a number of places in the New Testament where portions of the Old Testament which were written by various men are assigned to the Holy Spirit as the Author. The only way to account for this phenomenon is to recognize a dual authorship (see Mark 12:36, where the Spirit is said to be the Author of what David wrote in Ps. 110; Acts 1:16 and 4:24-25, where Ps. 41 and Ps. 2 are ascribed to the Holy Spirit; and Heb. 3:7; 10:15-16).

(3) But sometimes the record quite obviously reflects the styles and expressions of the human authors. This is to be expected in a book of dual authorship, and does not mean at all that in employing their own styles the authors recorded error (see Rom. 9:1-3 for one such example).

(4) Indeed, the Bible claims inerrancy for itself. How else is it possible to explain the Lord's claim for the abiding character of the letters which spell the words of Scripture: "For verily I say unto you, Till heaven and earth pass, one jot or one tittle shall in no wise pass from the law, till all be fulfilled" (Matt. 5:18)? The jot is the Hebrew letter *yod*, the smallest one in that alphabet. The tittle is the minor stroke that distinguishes certain Hebrew letters from others (like a *dalet* from a *res*). In a normal font of type it would not be more than 1/32 of an inch. In other words, the Lord was saying that every letter or every word is important, and the Old Testament would be fulfilled exactly as spelled out letter by letter and word by word.

The Lord also insisted on the importance of a present tense in Matthew 22:32. In order to reinforce the truth of resurrection, He reminded the Sadducees that God *is* the God of the living because He identified Himself to Moses by saying "I *am*" the God of Abraham, Isaac and Jacob though they had died hundreds of years before. If resurrection were not a fact He should have said, "I *was*" their God. The Lord also based a crucial argument concerning His own deity on the word *Lord* (Matt. 22:41-46) as quoted from Psalm 110:1. If He did not consider the words of Scripture to be inerrant, the argument would have been meaningless. On another occasion He vindicated Himself from the charge of blasphemy by focusing on a single word in Psalm 82:6 (John 10:34). Then He enforced His argument by reminding His accusers that the Scripture cannot be broken. Paul, too, insisted on the importance of a singular in contrast to a plural in his argument in Galatians 3:16. Such an argument would be invalid unless the difference between singulars and plurals can be trusted. All of these examples force us to admit that the Bible claims inerrancy for itself.

(5) No one who holds to inerrancy denies that the Bible uses ordinary figures of speech (like "corners of the earth," Rev. 7:1), but they are accurately used.

(6) Nor do we deny that authors sometimes researched their facts before writing (Luke 1:1-4). But the product, we believe, was kept from error by this superintending work of the Spirit.

(7) Neither do we deny that there are problems in the text that we presently have. But problems are quite different from errors. Indeed, in the face of the claims that the Bible apparently makes for itself about inspiration and inerrancy, it would seem more reasonable when confronted with problems to place one's faith in the Scriptures which have been proved to be true again and again than in any fallible human opinion. Man's knowledge of these problems is limited and has in some instances been proved to be wrong. Time will undoubtedly continue to bring to light facts which will help solve the yet unsolved problems in the Bible.

UNDERSTANDING THE BIBLE

A proper understanding of the Bible depends on two things: (1) the illuminating work of the Holy Spirit, and (2) the interpreting work of the reader.

Illumination

Although the word *illumination* has been applied to several aspects of doctrine (like the general enlightenment that the coming of Christ brought to all men, John 1:9, and the illumination theory of inspiration), it is generally thought of in connection with the ministry of the Holy Spirit which makes clear the truth of the written revelation in the Bible. In reference to the Bible, *revelation* relates to its content or material, *inspiration* to the method of recording that material, and *illumination* to the meaning of the record. The unsaved man cannot experience the illuminating ministry of the Spirit since he is blinded to the truth of God (1 Cor. 2:14). This does not mean he cannot learn anything of the facts of the Bible, but he considers what he knows as foolishness.

On the other hand, the Christian has been promised this illumination of the text (John 16:12-15; 1 Cor. 2:9—3:2). Taking these two passages together, several facts emerge:

(1)   The most obvious is that the Spirit Himself is the Teacher, and His presence in the life of the believer is the guarantee of the effectiveness of this ministry.

(2)   The content of His teaching encompasses "all the truth" (the definite article is present in John 16:13). It specifically includes an understanding of prophecy ("things to come").

(3)   The purpose of the Spirit's illumination is to glorify Christ, not Himself.

(4)   Carnality in the believer can hinder and even nullify this ministry of the Spirit (1 Cor. 3:1-2).

Interpretation

Illumination, though assured, does not always guarantee automatic understanding. As indicated above, the believer must be in fellowship with the Lord in order to experience this ministry. But also he must study, using the teachers God has given to the church (Rom. 12:7) and the abilities and means at his own disposal.

The basic principle of interpretation is to interpret plainly. The word *literal* is avoided here because it creates connotations which have to be corrected. Plain, straight-forward interpretation includes at least the following concepts:

(1)   To interpret plainly one must first of all understand what each word means in its normal grammatical historical sense.

(2)   Plain interpretation does not exclude the use of figures of speech. Indeed, a figure of speech may communicate more clearly, but what it communicates is plain. In other words, behind every figure of speech is a plain meaning, and that is what the interpreter seeks.

(3)   Always read with understanding the context in which a verse or passage appears, for this will throw light on its meaning. Beware, for instance, of the speaker who says, "Now you don't need to turn to this verse." He may be taking it out of its context and giving it another meaning. It is not only always safe but prudent to read what precedes and what follows.

(4)   Recognize the progress of revelation. Remember that the Bible was not handed down all at once as a complete book but that it came from God through many different

From *A Survey of Bible Doctrine*, by Charles C. Ryrie.

writers over a period of about 1,600 years. This means that in the progress of revealing His message to man, God may add or even change in one era what He had given in another. The New Testament adds much that was not revealed in the Old. Furthermore, what God revealed as binding in one period may be rescinded in another (as the prohibition of eating pork, once binding on God's people, has been lifted today, 1 Tim. 4:3). This is most important; otherwise, the Bible would contain apparently unresolvable contradictions (as Matt. 10:5-7 compared with 28:18-20).

(5) Expect the Bible to use what is technically called phenomenal language. This simply means that it often describes things as they appear to be rather than in precise scientific terms. Speaking of the sun rising or setting (neither of which it does) is an example of this (Matt. 5:45; Mark 1:32), but this is a plain and normal way to communicate.

(6) Recognize the important divisions of the Bible when interpreting it. The most basic is the difference between the Old and New Testaments. But there are also different kinds of writings—historical, poetic, prophetic—which must be recognized as different if they are to be interpreted correctly. Other landmarks in the Bible which affect proper interpretation are things like the great covenant made with Abraham (Gen. 12:1-3) and the one with David (2 Sam. 7), the mystery of the church as the body of Christ (Eph. 3:6), and the difference between law and grace (John 1:17; Rom. 6:14).

These suggestions are simply facets of the basic concept of plain interpretation. And that is the way God intended His inspired Bible to be understood.

HOW WE GOT OUR BIBLE

The question of which books belong in the Bible is called the question of the canon. The word *canon* means rule or measuring rod, and in relation to the Bible it refers to the collection of books which passed a test of authenticity and authority; it also means that those books are our rule of life. How was the collection made?

The Tests for Canonicity

First of all it is important to remember that certain books were canonical even before any tests were put to them. That's like saying some students are intelligent before any tests are given to them. The tests only prove what is already intrinsically there. In the same way, neither the church nor councils made any book canonical or authentic; either the book was authentic or it was not when it was written. The church or its councils recognized and verified certain books as the Word of God, and in time those so recognized were collected together in what we now call the Bible.

What tests did the church apply?

(1) There was the test of the authority of the writer. In relation to the Old Testament, this meant the authority of the lawgiver or the prophet or the leader in Israel. In relation to the New Testament, a book had to be written or backed by an apostle in order to be recognized. In other words, it had to have an apostolic signature or apostolic authorization. Peter, for instance, was the backer of Mark, and Paul of Luke.

(2) The books themselves should give some internal evidences of their unique character, as inspired and authoritative. The content should commend itself to the reader as being different from an ordinary book in communicating the revelation of God.

(3) The verdict of the churches as to the canonical nature of the books was important. There was in reality surprising unanimity among the early churches as to which books belonged in the inspired number. Although it is true that a few books were temporarily doubted by a minority, no book whose authenticity was doubted by any large number of churches was later accepted.

The Formation of the Canon

The canon of Scripture was, of course, being formed as each book was written, and it was complete when the last book was finished. When we speak of the "formation" of the canon we actually mean the recognition of the canonical books by the church. This took time. Some assert that all the books of the Old Testament canon were collected and recognized by Ezra in the fifth century B.C. References by Josephus (A.D. 95) and in 2 Esdras 14 (A.D. 100) indicate the extent of the Old Testament canon as the thirty-nine books we know. The discussions by the teaching-house at Jamnia (A.D. 70-100) seemed to assume this existing canon. Our Lord delimited the extent of the canonical books of the Old Testament when He accused the scribes of being guilty of slaying all the prophets God had sent Israel from Abel to Zechariah (Luke 11:51). The account of Abel's death is, of course, in Genesis; that of Zechariah is in 2 Chronicles 24:20-21, which is the last book in the order of the books in the Hebrew Bible (not Malachi as in our English Bibles). Therefore, it is as if the Lord had said, "Your guilt is recorded all through the Bible—from Genesis to Malachi." And He did not include any of the apocryphal books which were in existence at that time and which contained the accounts of other martyrs.

The first church council to list all twenty-seven books of the New Testament was the Council of Carthage in A.D. 397. Individual books of the New Testament were acknowledged as Scripture before this time (2 Peter 3:16; 1 Tim. 5:17) and most were accepted in the era just after the apostles (Hebrews, James, 2 Peter, 2 and 3 John and Jude were

From *A Survey of Bible Doctrine*, by Charles C. Ryrie.

debated for some time). The selection of the canon was a process that went on until each book proved its own worth by passing the tests of canonicity.

The twelve books of the Apocrypha were never accepted by the Jews or by our Lord on a par with the books of the Old Testament. They were revered but were not considered Scripture. The Septuagint (the Greek translation of the Old Testament done in the third century B.C.) included the Apocrypha with the Old Testament canonical books. Jerome (c. A.D. 340-420) in translating the Vulgate distinguished the canonical books from the ecclesiastical books (the Apocrypha), which had the effect of according them a secondary status. The Council of Trent (1548) recognized them as canonical, though the Reformers rejected this decree. In our English Bibles the Apocrypha was set apart in the Coverdale, Geneva, and King James versions. The first English Bible to exclude it entirely as a matter of policy was an Amsterdam edition of the Geneva Bible published in 1640, and the first English Bible printed in America (the Aitken Bible, 1782) omitted it.

Is Our Present Text Reliable?

The original copies of the Old Testament were written on leather or papyrus from the time of Moses (c. 1450 B.C.) to the time of Malachi (400 B.C.). Until the sensational discovery of the Dead Sea Scrolls in 1947 we did not possess copies of the Old Testament earlier than A.D. 895. The reason for this is simply that the Jews had an almost superstitious veneration for the text which impelled them to bury copies that had become too old for use. Indeed, the Masoretes (traditionalists), who between A.D. 600 and 950 added accents and vowel points and in general standardized the Hebrew text, devised complicated safeguards for the making of copies. They checked each copy carefully by counting the middle letter of pages, books and sections. Someone has said that everything countable was counted. When the Dead Sea Scrolls were discovered, they gave us a Hebrew text from the second to first century B.C. of all but one of the books (Esther) of the Old Testament. This was of the greatest importance, for it provided a much earlier check on the accuracy of the Masoretic text, which has now proved to be extremely accurate.

Other early checks on the Hebrew text include the Septuagint translation (middle of third century B.C.), the Aramaic Targums (paraphrases and quotes of the Old Testament), quotations in early Christian writers, and the Latin translation of Jerome (A.D. 400) which was made directly from the Hebrew text of his day. All of these give us the data for being assured of having an accurate text of the Old Testament.

More than 5,000 manuscripts of the New Testament exist today, which makes the New Testament the best-attested document in all ancient writings. The contrast is quite startling.

Not only are there so many copies of the New Testament in existence, but many of them are early. The approximately seventy-five papyri fragments date from A.D. 135 to the eighth century and cover parts of twenty-five of the twenty-seven books and about 40 percent of the text. The many hundreds of parchment copies include the great Codex Sinaiticus (4th century), the Codex Vaticanus (also 4th century), and the Codex Alexandrinus (5th century). In addition, there are 2,000 lectionaries (church service books containing many Scripture portions), more than 86,000 quotations of the New Testament in the church Fathers, old Latin, Syriac and Egyptian translations dating from the third century, and Jerome's Latin translation. All of this data plus all of the scholarly work that has been done with it assure us that we possess today an accurate and reliable text of the New Testament.

THE MEANING AND BLESSINGS OF SALVATION

The doctrine of salvation is both simple and complex. On the one hand, most of us can quote at least a part of John 3:16 or of Paul's response to the Philippian jailor's question about how to be saved (Acts 16:31). On the other hand, who can explain how a holy God-man could become sin and die for the sake of sinful and rebellious men?

Salvation is extremely important to understand correctly. An anathema (curse) is placed on anyone (including angels or preachers) who presumes to teach a different gospel of salvation from what is taught in Scripture (Gal. 1:8). What then is true salvation? How is it provided? How is it gained? What are its benefits and blessings?

True salvation is that which is provided by God Himself through the sacrificial death of His Son Jesus Christ. There is no other way that a man can be saved from eternal condemnation and to eternal life (Acts 4:12).

Some Accomplishments of Christ's Death

It Was a Substitution for Sin

There are many facets to the meaning of Christ's death, but the central one—without which the others have no eternal meaning—is substitution. This simply means that Christ died in the place of sinners. The use of the Greek preposition *anti* clearly teaches this because it means "in the place of." It is used, for instance, with this meaning in a passage that has nothing to do with the death of Christ (Luke 11:11). But more significantly, it is used in a passage which gives our Lord's own interpretation of the meaning of His death (Matt. 20:28; Mark 10:45). His death, He said, was to be a payment in the place of many.

However, another preposition, *huper*, is also used in the New Testament, and it has two meanings: sometimes it means "for the benefit of" and sometimes "in the place of." Of course the death of Christ was *both* in our place and for our benefit, and there is no reason why *huper* when it is used in relation to His death does not include both ideas. See, for instance, 2 Corinthians 5:21 and 1 Peter 3:18.

It Provided Redemption from Sin

The doctrine of redemption is built on three words in the New Testament. The first is a simple word which means "to buy or purchase or pay a price for something." It is used, for instance, with this ordinary, everyday meaning in the parable of the treasure hid in a field which motivated the man to buy (redeem) the field (Matt. 13:44). In relation to our salvation, the word means to pay the price which our sin demanded so that we could be redeemed.

The second word is the same basic word indicated above, prefixed with a preposition which has the force of intensifying the meaning. This can be easily expressed in English because the preposition means "out of," thus making the second word mean "to purchase out of the market." Thus the idea in this second word is that Christ's death not only paid the price for sin but also removed us from the marketplace of sin in order to give us full assurance that we will never be returned to the bondage and penalties of sin.

The third word for redemption is an entirely different one. Its basic meaning is "to loose" and thus it signifies that the purchased person is also released and set free in the fullest sense. The means of this release is through the substitution Christ made (see 1 Tim. 2:6 where the prepositional prefix to this third word is *anti*); the basis is the blood of Christ (Heb. 9:12); and the intended result is to purify a people zealous of good works (Titus 2:14). Thus, the doctrine of redemption means that because of the shedding of the blood of Christ, believers have been purchased, removed from bondage, and liberated. From *A Survey of Bible Doctrine*, by Charles C. Ryrie.

It Effected Reconciliation

To reconcile means to change. Reconciliation by the death of Christ means that man's state of alienation from God is changed so that he is now able to be saved (2 Cor. 5:19). When a man believes, then his former state of alienation from God is changed into one of being a member of His family.

It Provides Propitiation

To propitiate means to appease or to satisfy a god. This naturally brings to mind the question, Why does the deity need to be appeased? The biblical answer to that question is simply that the true God is angry with mankind because of their sin. The theme of the wrath of God appears throughout the Bible, including the teachings of Christ (Mark 3:29; 14:21). Wrath is not merely the impersonal and inevitable working out of the law of cause and effect, but it is a personal intervention of God in the affairs of mankind (Rom. 1:18; Eph. 5:6).

The death of Christ propitiated God, averting His wrath and enabling Him to receive into His family those who place their faith in the one who satisfied Him. The extent of the propitiatory work of Christ is to be whole world (1 John 2:2), and the basis of propitiation is His shed blood (Rom. 3:25).

Because Christ has died, God is satisfied. Therefore, we should not ask anyone to try to do anything to satisfy Him. This would mean trying to appease someone who is already appeased, which is totally unnecessary. Before the cross a person could not be certain that God was satisfied with whatever he brought to Him. That is why the publican prayed (literally) "God be propitiated toward me a sinner" (Luke 18:13). Today such a prayer would be a waste of breath, for God is propitiated by the death of Christ. Therefore, our message to men today should not suggest in any way that they can please God by doing something, but only that they be satisfied with the sacrifice of Christ which completely satisfied the wrath of God.

It Judged the Sin Nature

The death of Christ had an important benefit for us in making inoperative the reigning power of our sin nature (Rom. 6:1-10). Though this is not an easy concept to understand, Paul says that our union with Christ by baptism involves sharing His death so that we are dead to sin. The baptism must be that of the Holy Spirit, for no water, in whatever amount, could accomplish what is said to have been accomplished in this passage. The idea of death, so prominent in this passage, does not mean either extinction or cessation, but, as always, separation.

The crucifixion of the Christian with Christ means separation from the domination of sin over his life. The question "Shall we continue in sin?" is answered by an emphatic no on the basis of our dying with Christ (Rom. 6:1). This "destroyed" the body of sin. That word "destroy" does not mean to annihilate, for if it did, then the sin nature would be eradicated, a fact which our experience scarcely confirms! It means to make the sin nature ineffective.

The believer is therefore now free to live a life pleasing to God. Although it is still possible to listen to and follow the promptings of sin, it will never be possible for sin to regain the domination and control it had before conversion.

It Brought the End of the Law

The fact that the death of Christ brought an end to the Mosaic law is quite clearly stated in the New Testament (Rom. 10:4; Col. 2:14). The importance of this fact is related to (1) justification and (2) sanctification, the former being much easier to see than the latter. The reason is simply that the law could not justify a sinner (Acts 13:39; Rom. 3:20); therefore, if men are to be justified, another way must be provided. The law can show man his need but it cannot provide the answer to that need (Gal. 3:23-25). Thus the death of Christ provided the way for justification by faith in Him alone.

But the relation of the end of the law to sanctification is more difficult to comprehend simply because portions of the Mosaic law are repeated in the New Testament in relation to the believer's sanctification. Furthermore, those specifics which are repeated are not from just one section of the law (like the Ten Commandments). As a matter of fact, nine of the Ten Commandments are repeated, and other parts of the law are too (Rom. 13:9). This makes it impossible to say that the law is done away with except for the Ten Commandments.

Furthermore, 2 Corinthians 3:7-11 states quite clearly that the Ten Comandments ("that which was written and engraven in stones") were done away with. How do you put all these facts together? Is the Christian under the Mosaic law in relation to sanctification or not?

The only realistic solution that has ever appealed to the present author is that which distinguishes a code and the commandments contained in that code. The Mosaic law was one of several codes which God has given throughout history, and as a code it is finished. The code under which the believer lives today is called the law of Christ (Gal. 6:2) or the law of the Spirit of life (Rom. 8:2).

As one code ends and another is instituted, not all of the commands in the new one will themselves be new and different. The permission to eat meat in the law of Christ (1 Tim. 4:3) was also part of the code under which Noah lived after the Flood (Gen. 9:3). Likewise, some of the specifics which were part of the Mosaic code have been incorporated into the law of Christ and some have not. But the entire code, as a code, has been done away with.

It is the Ground for the Believer's Cleansing From Sin

The blood (death) of Christ is the basis of our constant cleansing from sin (1 John 1:7). This does not mean that there is a recrucifixion or a dipping into blood with which to touch the erring Christian, but that the once-for-all death of our Lord provides constant cleansing when we sin as believers. Our family relationship is kept right by His death; our family fellowship is restored by our confession.

Some Benefits of Christ's Death

Among the almost innumerable blessings of salvation are many which are obvious to believers because they can be experienced, for example, prayer. But there are also many benefits which in themselves are not experienced (though their results are) and which are often not so well understood. And yet these are the vital bases for a normal Christian life.

Justification

That Christ's death makes us acceptable before God is expressed in such doctrines as redemption (Rom. 3:24), reconciliation (2 Cor. 5:19-21), forgiveness (Rom. 3:25), deliverance (Col. 1:13), acceptance in the Beloved (Eph. 1:6), assured future glorification (Rom. 8:30), and justification (Rom. 3:24).

To justify is to declare righteous. It is a judicial term indicating that a verdict of acquittal has been announced, excluding all possibility of condemnation. Indeed, in Scripture, justification is invariably set over against condemnation (Deut. 25:1; Rom. 5:16; 8:33-34). The claims of God's law against the sinner have been fully satisfied. Justification is not because of any overlooking, suspending or altering of God's righteous demands, but because in Christ all of His demands have been fulfilled. Christ's perfect life of obedience to the law and His atoning death which paid its penalty are the bases for our justification (Rom. 5:9). Justification could never be based on our good works, for God requires perfect obedience, which is impossible for man.

The *means* of justification is faith (Rom. 3:22, 25, 28, 30). Faith is never the ground of justification; it is the means or channel through which God's grace can impute to the believing sinner the righteousness of Christ. When we believe, all that Christ is, God puts to our account; thus we stand acquitted. Then God can justly announce that, acquittal, and that pronouncement is justification.

Adoption

Adoption is a particularly wonderful benefit of Christ's death for the believer. The doctrine is taught explicitly only by Paul. Every time you read "son" in relation to a believer (not of Christ) in John's writings, for instance, you should translate it "child," for John does not write of the sonship of the believer. Only Paul reveals that we are adopted as sons. It is true that we are children of God by the new birth, but it is also true that we are adopted into God's family at the same time. In the act of adoption a child is taken by a man from a family not his own, introduced into a new family, and regarded as a true son with all the privileges and responsibilities that belong to this new relationship. The imagery in the idea of a child of God is one of birth, growth, development into maturity; the idea in sonship is that of full-fledged privileges in the new family of God. Adoption bestows a new status on the one who receives Christ.

The results of adoption are deliverance from slavery, from guardians, and from the flesh (Gal. 4:1-5; Rom. 8:14-17), and it is the Holy Spirit who enables us to enjoy the privileges of our position.

Sanctification

The word *sanctify* means to set apart (it has the same root as the words *saint* and *holy*). For the Christian, sanctification has three aspects. First, the believer has been set apart by his position in the family of God. This is usually called positional sanctification. It means being set apart as a member of the household of God. It is true of every believer regardless of his spiritual condition, for this concerns his spiritual state. Read 1 Corinthians 6:11 and remember the carnal condition of these believers. That this positional sanctification is based on the death of Christ is clear from Hebrews 10:10.

Of course, there is also the experiential aspect of sanctification. Because we have been set apart we are to be increasingly set apart in our daily lives (1 Peter 1:16). In the positional sense no one is more sanctified than another, but in the experiential aspect it is quite correct to speak of one believer as being more sanctified than another. All the exhortations of the New Testament concerning spiritual growth are pertinent to this progressive and experiential facet of sanctification.

There is also a sense in which we will not be fully set apart to God until our position and practice are brought into perfect accord, and this will occur only when we see Christ and become as He is (1 John 3:1-3). This is our ultimate or future sanctification, which awaits our complete glorification with resurrection bodies (Eph. 5:26-27; Jude 24-25).

BETWEEN THE TESTAMENTS

Political Developments

The term, "silent years," frequently employed to describe the period between the Old Testament and the New Testament writings, is a misnomer. Although no inspired prophet arose in Israel during these centuries, and the Old Testament was regarded as complete, events took place which gave to later Judaism its distinctive ideology and providentially prepared the way for the coming of Christ and the proclamation of His Gospel.

Persian Supremacy

For about a century after Nehemiah's time, the Persian Empire exercised control over Judea. The period was relatively uneventful, for the Jews were permitted to observe their religious institutions without molestation. Judea was ruled by high priests, who were responsible to the Persian government, a fact which both insured the Jews a large measure of autonomy and degraded the priesthood into a political office. Jealousy, intrigue, and even murder played their part in the contests for the distinction of being high priest. Johanan, son of Joiada (Neh. 12:22), is reported to have slain his brother Joshua in the Temple itself.

Persia and Egypt were engaged in constant struggles during this period, and Judea, situated between the two nations, could not escape involvement. During the reign of Artaxerxes III (Ochus) many Jews were implicated in a revolt against Persia. They were deported to Babylonia and the shores of the Caspian Sea.

Alexander the Great

Following the defeat of Persian armies in Asia Minor (333 B.C.), Alexander marched into Syria and Palestine. After stubborn resistance, Tyre was taken, and Alexander moved southward toward Egypt. Legend states that as Alexander neared Jerusalem, he was met by Jaddua, the Jewish high priest, who told him of Daniel's prophecies that the Greek army would be victorious (Dan. 8). The story is not taken seriously by historians, but it is true that Alexander dealt kindly with the Jews. He permitted them to observe their laws; he granted them exemption from tribute during Sabbatical years; and when he built Alexandria in Egypt (331 B.C.), he encouraged the Jews to settle there and gave them privileges comparable to those of his Greek subjects.

Judea Under the Ptolemies

After the death of Alexander (323 B.C.), Judea was first subject for a time to Antigonus, one of Alexander's generals who controlled part of Asia Minor. It subsequently fell to another general, Ptolemy I (by now master of Egypt), surnamed Soter, or *Deliverer*, who seized Jerusalem on a Sabbath day in 320 B.C. Ptolemy dealt kindly with the Jews. Many of them settled in Alexandria, which continued as an important center of Jewish thinking for many centuries. Under Ptolemy II (Philadelphus), the Jews of Alexandria translated their Law, i.e., the Pentateuch, into Greek. This translation was subsequently known as the Septuagint, from the legend that its seventy (more correctly 72—six from each of the twelve tribes) translators were supernaturally inspired to produce an infallible translation. In later years the entire Old Testament was included in the Septuagint.

Adapted from "From Malachi to Matthew," by Charles F. Pfeiffer. ©1962 by The Moody Bible Institute of Chicago.

Judea Under the Seleucids

After about a century, during which time the Jews were subjected to the Ptolemies, Antiochus III (the Great) of Syria wrested Syria and Palestine from Egyptian control (198 B.C.). The Syrian rulers are known as Seleucids because of the fact that their kingdom, built on the ruins of Alexander's empire, was founded by Seleucus I (Nicator).

During the early years of Syrian rule, the Seleucids allowed the high priest to continue to govern the Jews in accord with their law. Strife broke out, however, between the Hellenistic party and the orthodox Jews. Antiochus IV (Epiphanes) allied himself with the Hellenizing group and appointed to the priesthood a man who had changed his name from Joshua to Jason and who encouraged the worship of the Tyrian Hercules. Jason was displaced in two years, however, by another Hellenist, a rebel named Menahem (Greek, *Menelaus*). When the partisans of Jason contended with those of Menelaus, Antiochus marched on Jerusalem, plundered the Temple, and killed many of the Jews (170 B.C.). Civil and religious liberties were suspended, the daily sacrifices prohibited, and an altar to Jupiter was erected on the old altar of burnt offering. Copies of the Scriptures were burned, and the Jews were forced to eat swine's flesh contrary to their law. A sow was offered on the altar of burnt offering in contempt for the Jewish religious conscience.

The Maccabees

The oppressed Jews were not long in finding a champion. When the emissaries of Antiochus arrived at the small town of Modin, about fifteen miles west of Jerusalem, they expected the aged priest, Mattathias, to set a good example to his people by offering a pagan sacrifice. He not only refused, but he also killed an apostate Jew at the heathen altar, along with the Syrian officer who was presiding at the ceremony. Mattathias fled to the Judean highlands and, with his sons, waged guerrilla warfare on the Syrians. Although the aged priest did not live to see his people freed from the Syrian yoke, he commissioned his sons to complete the task. Judas, surnamed "the Maccabee," took the leadership at the death of his father. By 164 B.C. Judas had gained possession of Jerusalem. He purified the Temple and reinstituted the daily offerings. Soon after the victories of Judas, Antiochus died in Persia. However, struggles continued between the Maccabees and the Seleucid rulers for about twenty years.

Aristobolus I was the first of the Maccabean rulers to take the title, "King of the Jews." After a short reign he was succeeded by the tyrannical Alexander Jannaeus, who, in turn, left the kingdom to his mother, Alexandra. Alexandra's reign was a relatively quiet one. At Alexandra's death a younger son, Aristobolus (II), dispossessed his brother. Thereupon, the governor of Idumaea, Antipater, espoused the cause of Hyrcanus, and civil war threatened. Consequently Pompey marched into Judea with his Roman legions to settle matters and further the aims of Rome. Aristobolus sought to defend Jerusalem against Pompey, but the Romans took the city and penetrated to the Holy of Holies in the Temple. Pompey did not, however, touch the Temple treasures.

Rome

Mark Anthony supported the cause of Hyrcanus. After the murder of Julius Caesar, and of Antipater (father of Herod), who for twenty years had been virtual ruler of Judea, Antigonus, the second son of Aristobolus, sought the throne. For a time he actually ruled in Jerusalem, but Herod, the son of Antipater, returned from Rome and became king of the Jews with Roman support. His marriage to Mariamne, granddaughter of Hyrcanus, provided a link with the Maccabean rulers.

Herod was one of the cruelest rulers of all time. He murdered the venerable Hyrcanus (31 B.C.), and put to death his own wife Mariamne and their two sons. From his deathbed Herod ordered the execution of Antipater, a son by another wife. In Scripture Herod is known as the king who ordered the death of the innocents of Bethlehem because he feared as a rival One who was born to be King of the Jews.

Jewish Religious Groups

When, following Alexander's conquest, Hellenism challenged the thinking of the Near East, some Jews clung more tenaciously than ever to the faith of their fathers, while others were willing to adapt their thinking to the newer ideas emanating from Greece. Ultimately the clash between Hellenism and Judaism gave rise to a number of Jewish sects.

Pharisees

The Pharisees were the spiritual descendants of the pious Jews who had fought the Hellenizers in the days of the earlier Maccabees. The name *Pharisee*, "separatist," was probably given them by their enemies to indicate that they were nonconformists. It may, however, have been used in scorn because their strictness separated them from their fellow Jews as well as from the heathen. Loyalty to truth sometimes produces pride and even hypocrisy, and it is this perversion of the earlier Pharisaic ideal that is denounced by Jesus. Paul reckoned himself a member of this orthodox group within the Judaism of his day (Phil. 3:5).

Sadducees

The Sadducean party, probably named for Zadok, the high priest appointed by Solomon (1 Kings 2:35), denied the authority of tradition and looked with suspicion on all revelation later than the Mosaic law. They denied the doctrine of resurrection, and they did not believe in the existence of angels or spirits (Acts 23:3). They were largely people of wealth and position, and they cooperated gladly with the Hellenism of the day. In New Testament times they controlled the priesthood and the Temple ritual. The synagogue, on the other hand, was the stronghold of the Pharisees.

Essenes

Essenism was an ascetic reaction from the externalism of the Pharisees and the worldliness of the Sadducees. The Essenes withdrew from society and lived lives of asceticism and celibacy. They gave attention to the reading and study of Scripture, prayer, and ceremonial cleansings. They held their possessions in common and were known for their industry and piety. Both war and slavery were contrary to their principles.

The monastery at Qumran, near the caves in which the Dead Sea Scrolls were found, is thought by most scholars to have been an Essene center in the Judean wilderness. The scrolls indicate that members of the community had left the corrupt influences of the Judean towns to prepare, in the wilderness, "the way of the Lord." They had faith in the coming Messiah and thought of themselves as the true Israel to whom He would come.

Scribes

The Scribes were not, strictly speaking, a sect but rather members of a profession. They were, in the first instance, copyists of the Law. They came to be regarded as the authorities on the Scriptures, hence exercised a teaching function. Their thoughts were usually akin to those of the Pharisees, with whom they are frequently associated in the New Testament.

Herodians

Herodians believed that the best interests of Judaism lay in cooperation with the Romans. Their name was taken from Herod the Great, who sought to Romanize the Palestine of his day. The Herodians were more of a political party than a religious sect.

Roman political oppression, symbolized by Herod, and the religious reactions expressed in the sectarian reactions within pre-Christian Judaism, provided the historical framework into which Jesus came. Frustrations and conflicts prepared Israel for the advent of God's Messiah, who appeared "when the fulness of the time was come" (Gal. 4:4).

ARCHAEOLOGY AND THE BIBLE

Nature and Purpose of Biblical Archaeology

The word "archaeology" comes from two Greek words, *archaios* and *logos,* which mean literally "a study of ancient things." But the term now usually applies to a study of excavated materials belonging to a former era. Bible archaeology may be defined as an examination of ancient things which have been lost and found again, as those recovered objects relate to the study of Scripture and the portrayal of life in Bible times.

Archaeology is basically a science. Knowledge in the field is acquired by systematic observation or study, and facts discovered are evaluated and classified into an organized body of information. Archaeology is a composite science because it seeks assistance from many other sciences, such as chemistry, anthropology, and zoology.

Of course, some subjects of archaeological investigation (such as obelisks and temples of Egypt and the Parthenon at Athens) have never been "lost" at all, but perhaps some knowledge of their original form and purpose and the meaning of inscriptions on them have been lost.

Functions of Biblical Archaeology

Archaeology helps us understand the Bible. It reveals what life was like in biblical times, what obscure passages of Scripture really mean, and how the historical narratives and contexts of the Bible are to be understood.

Archaeology also helps confirm the accuracy of biblical texts and contents. It has shown the falsity of some theories of biblical interpretation. It has helped to establish the accuracy of the Greek and Hebrew originals and to show that the biblical text has been transmitted with a remarkable degree of accuracy. And it has confirmed the accuracy of many passages of Scripture, e.g., statements concerning numerous kings and the whole patriarchal narrative.

One should not be dogmatic in his statements concerning confirmation, however. Archaeology has also created numerous problems for the Bible student. For instance, recovered Babylonian and Sumerian accounts of the creation and the Flood, having striking parallels to the Old Testament, puzzle the Bible scholar. There is also the problem of interpreting the relationship between the Ras Shamra texts and the Mosaic code. But one can confidently believe that answers to the problems will be forthcoming. To date there has not been an instance of archaeology conclusively demonstrating the Bible to be in error!

Why Ancient Cities and Civilizations Disappeared

We know that many ancient civilizations and cities disappeared because of the direct judgment of God. Scripture is full of such indications. But some natural explanations should also be briefly noted.

Cities were usually built on easily defensible sites possessing a good water supply and located near important trade routes. Such sites were at a premium in the ancient Near East. So, if some catastrophe brought about the destruction of a town, the tendency was to rebuild on the same location. A town might be largely destroyed by earthquake or invasion. Famine or pestilence might depopulate a city or territory. In the latter instance, the inhabitants might conclude that the gods had leveled a curse on them and they might fear to return. Uninhabited sites would quickly fall into ruins. And when former inhabitants

Adapted from "Archaeology," by Howard F. Vos, *Wycliffe Bible Encyclopedia,* ©1975 by The Moody Bible Institute of Chicago.

returned or when new settlers came into the area, they usually simply smoothed out the rubble and built a new city. Thus mounds, or tells, rose up with many superimposed layers of habitation. Sometimes the water supply dried up, rivers changed their courses, trade arteries were rerouted or political fortunes changed—resulting in permanent abandonment of a site.

Excavating a Mound

The biblical archaeologist may undertake excavation of a mound for many reasons. If the mound he is studying is known to cover a biblical site, he probably seeks to uncover the layer or layers of occupation having relevance for the biblical narrative. He may be looking for a city which is known to have existed but has not yet been identified. Perhaps he seeks to resolve doubts concerning proposed identification of a site. Possibly he is searching for information concerning Bible characters or events that will help illuminate the Scripture narrative.

Once the excavator has chosen a site to dig and has made proper arrangements (including permits, finances, equipment and staff), he is ready to begin operations. A careful surface exploration is usually carried out first to learn all that is possible from pottery or other artifacts on the surface, to discover whether a configuration of ground houses the remains of a building, or to figure out something of the history of the mound. Then a contour map of the mound is drawn and a sector or sectors chosen where digging is to be carried on during a season of excavation. These sectors are then usually subdivided into one meter squares to facilitate labeling of finds.

Archaeology and the Text of the Bible

While most people think of huge monuments and museum pieces and exploits of kings when biblical archaeology is referred to, they have become increasingly aware that inscriptions and manuscripts also have an important contribution to make to biblical study. Although most archaeological work used to center on biblical history, today it is increasingly concerned with the text of the Bible.

Intensive study of the more than 3,000 New Testament Greek manuscripts dating from the 2nd century A.D. and following has shown that the New Testament text has been remarkably preserved in transmission from the 3rd century to the present. Not one doctrine has been perverted. Westcott and Hort concluded that only about one word in a thousand of the Greek original has serious question upon it.

It is one thing to demonstrate that the New Testament text has been remarkably preserved from the 2nd century to the present: it is quite another to show that the Gospels, for instance, did not gradually evolve into their present form during the early centuries of the Christian era or that Christ was not gradually deified by Christian legend. At the turn of the 20th century a new science was born that would help to show that neither the Gospels nor the Christian view of Christ evolved into their present form. B. P. Grenfell and A. S. Hunt excavated in the Fayum district of Egypt (1896–1906), finding large quantities of papyri and launching the science of papyrology.

The papyri, written on a kind of paper made from the papyrus reed of Egypt, include a wide variety of topics presented in several languages. The number of fragmentary papyrus manuscripts containing portions of the New Testament now stands at 77. These fragments help to confirm the general text found in the longer vellum manuscripts dating to the 4th and following centuries, and to bridge more of the gap between the later manuscripts and the originals.

The impact of papyrology upon biblical study has been phenomenal. Many of the papyri date to the first three centuries after Christ. Thus it is possible to establish the development in the grammar of that period, and on the basis of the argument from historical grammar, to date the composition of New Testament books to the 1st century A.D. In fact, one fragment of the Gospel of John found in Egypt can be dated on the basis of paleography to about A.D. 125. Allowing time for the book to get into circulation, a date toward the end of the 1st century must be assigned to the fourth Gospel—and that is what Christian tradition has always assigned to it. No one doubts that the other three Gospels date to a period somewhat earlier than John. If the New Testament books were written during the 1st century, they were written close to the events they record and there was no time for an evolutionary development to occur.

But the contributions of the mass of papyri of all types do not stop here. They have shown that New Testament Greek is not some form of language invented by New Testament writers, as formerly thought. Instead it was generally the language of the people of the first centuries of the Christian era. Fewer than 50 words in the New Testament were coined by the apostles. Moreover, the papyri have shown that New Testament grammar was good grammar, judged by 1st century standards rather than those of the classical period. Furthermore, the nonbiblical Greek papyri have helped to clear up the meaning of uncertainly understood New Testament words and to throw new light on others fairly well understood.

The story of Old Testament textual criticism can hardly be told here. Suffice it to say that Old Testament manuscripts are not as close to their originals in time as those of the New Testament, but they were copied with even greater care and have fewer variations.

Until recently, the oldest known Hebrew manuscript of any length did not date earlier than the first part of the 10th century after Christ, and the oldest complete Hebrew Bible dates about a century later. Then, in the spring of 1948, the religious and academic worlds were rocked with the announcement that an ancient Isaiah manuscript had been found in a cave near the NW corner of the Dead Sea. Since that time a total of 11 caves in that area have disgorged their treasures of scrolls and fragments. Tens of thousands of leather fragments and some of papyrus have been recovered. While most of the materials are nonbiblical, fragments representing over a hundred manuscripts contain Scripture portions. So far, all Old Testament books except Esther are represented in the finds. As might be expected, fragments of Old Testament books quoted most in the New Testament (Deuteronomy, Isaiah, Psalms) are most numerous there also. The longest and most nearly intact biblical scrolls include two of Isaiah, one of Psalms and one of Leviticus.

The significance of the Dead Sea Scrolls is tremendous. They have pushed the history of the Old Testament text back 1,000 years (after much controversy the date has been assigned to the first centuries B.C. and A.D.). They have provided an abundance of critical material for research on the Old Testament comparable to what has been available to New Testament scholars for many years. Third, the Dead Sea Scrolls have provided a more adequate context for the New Testament, demonstrating, for instance, the essential Jewish background of the Gospel of John—rather than a Greek background as scholars have frequently asserted. Fourth, they help to establish the accuracy of the Old Testament text. The Septuagint (Greek Old Testament) has been shown by studies in the scrolls to be more accurate than often thought. Fifth, the scrolls provide new material to help establish the meaning of Hebrew words.

THE MIRACLES OF JESUS

The Gospels record 35 separate miracles performed by Christ. Matthew mentions 20 of them; Mark, 18; Luke, 20; and John, 7. These, however, are not all of the miracles of our Lord. Matthew, for instance, alludes to 12 occasions when Jesus performed a number of wonderful works (4:23-24; 8:16; 9:35; 10:1, 8; 11:4-5; 11:20-24; 12:15; 14:14; 14:36; 15:30; 19:2; 21:14). The Gospel writers selected according to their purpose from the large number which the Lord performed. There are many ways of arranging the individual miracles noted in the Gospels, depending on the purpose of the commentator. Following is the order of their occurrence, as nearly as that order can be determined.

1. Turning water into wine (John 2:1-11)
2. Healing a nobleman's son at Cana (John 4:46-54)
3. Healing a lame man at the pool of Bethesda (John 5:1-9)
4. First miraculous catch of fish (Luke 5:1-11)
5. Delivering a synagogue demoniac (Mark 1:23-28; Luke 4:31-36)
6. Healing Peter's mother-in-law (Matt. 8:14-15; Mark 1:29-31; Luke 4:38-39)
7. Cleansing a leper (Matt. 8:2-4; Mark 1:40-45; Luke 5:12-16)
8. Healing a paralytic (Matt. 9:2-8; Mark 2:3-12; Luke 5:18-26)
9. Healing a man with a withered hand (Matt. 12:9-13; Mark 3:1-5; Luke 6:6-10)
10. Healing a centurion's servant (Matt. 8:5-13; Luke 7:1-10)
11. Raising a widow's son (Luke 7:11-15)
12. Healing a blind and dumb demoniac (Matt. 12:22; Luke 11:14)
13. Stilling a storm (Matt. 8:18, 23-27; Mark 4:35-41; Luke 8:22-25)
14. Delivering the Gadarene demoniacs (Matt. 8:28-34; Mark 5:1-20; Luke 8:26-39)
15. Healing a woman with an issue of blood (Matt. 9:20-22; Mark 5:25-34; Luke 8:43-48)
16. Raising Jairus' daughter (Matt. 9:18-19, 23-26; Mark 5:22-24, 35-43; Luke 8:41-42, 49-56)
17. Healing two blind men (Matt. 9:27-31)
18. Delivering a dumb demoniac (Matt. 9:32-33)
19. Feeding the 5,000 (Matt. 14:14-21; Mark 6:34-44; Luke 9:12-17; John 6:5-13)
20. Walking on the water (Matt. 14:24-33; Mark 6:45-52; John 6:16-21)
21. Delivering a Syrophoenician's daughter (Matt. 15:21-28; Mark 7:24-30)
22. Healing a deaf mute in Decapolis (Mark 7:31-37)
23. Feeding 4,000 (Matt. 15:32-39; Mark 8:1-9)
24. Healing a blind man at Bethsaida (Mark 8:22-26)
25. Delivering a demon-possessed boy (Matt. 17:14-18; Mark 9:14-29; Luke 9:38-42)
26. Finding the tribute money (Matt. 17:24-27)
27. Healing a man born blind (John 9:1-7)
28. Healing a crippled woman on the Sabbath (Luke 13:10-17)
29. Healing a man with dropsy (Luke 14:1-6)
30. Raising of Lazarus (John 11:17-44)
31. Cleansing ten lepers (Luke 17:11-19)
32. Healing blind Bartimaeus (Matt. 20:29-34; Mark 10:46-52; Luke 18:35-43)
33. Cursing the fig tree (Matt. 21:18-19; Mark 11:12-14)
34. Restoring Malchus' ear (Luke 22:49-51; John 18:10)
35. Second miraculous catch of fish (John 21:1-11)

THE PARABLES OF JESUS

1. The Sower	Sermon on the seashore	Matt. 13:5-8; Mark 4:3-8; Luke 8:5-8.
2. The Tares	Sermon on the seashore	Matt. 13:24-30.
3. The Mustard Seed	Sermon on the seashore	Matt. 13:31, 32; Mark 4:31, 32; Luke 13:19.
4. The Leaven	Sermon on the seashore	Matt. 13:33; Luke 13:21.
5. The Hid Treasure	To the disciples alone	Matt. 13:44.
6. The Pearl of Great Price	To the disciples alone	Matt. 13:45, 46.
7. The Drag Net	To the disciples alone	Matt. 13:47-50.
8. The Unmerciful Servant	In answer to Peter's question, How oft shall I forgive, etc.?	Matt. 18:23-35.
9. The Laborers in the Vineyard	Teaching the self-righteous	Matt. 20:1-16.
10. The Two Sons	The chief priests demand his authority	Matt. 21:28-32.
11. The Wicked Husbandman	The chief priests demand his authority	Matt. 21:33-46; Mark 12:1-12; Luke 20:9-19.
12. Marriage of the King's Son	In answer to remark of a self-righteous guest	Matt. 22:1-14.
13. The Ten Virgins	In prophesying the Second Advent	Matt. 25:1-13.
14. The Talents	At the house of Zaccheus	Matt. 25:14-30.
15. The Seed Growing Secretly	Sermon on the seashore	Mark 4:26-29.
16. The Two Debtors	At Simon the Pharisee's self-righteous reflection	Luke 7:41-43.
17. The Good Samaritan	The lawyer's question, Who is my neighbor?	Luke 10:25-37.
18. The Friend at Midnight	Disciples ask a lesson in prayer	Luke 11:5-8.
19. The Rich Fool	Brothers ask him to divide an inheritance	Luke 12:16-21.
20. The Barren Fig Tree	Informed of the execution of the Galileans	Luke 13:6-9.
21. The Great Supper	In answer to one dining with him	Luke 14:16-24.
22. The Lost Sheep	Answer to Pharisees' and scribes' murmuring	Matt. 18:12-14; Luke 15:4-7.
23. The Lost Piece of Money	Answer to Pharisees' and scribes' murmuring	Luke 15:8-10.
24. The Prodigal Son	Answer to Pharisees' and scribes' murmuring	Luke 15:11-32.
25. The Unjust Steward	To the disciples	Luke 16:1-9.
26. The Rich Man and Lazarus	Rebuking the covetousness of Pharisees	Luke 16:19-31.
27. The Unprofitable Servants	Teaching self-righteous ones	Luke 17:7-10.
28. The Unjust Judge	Teaching the disciples	Luke 18:1-8.
29. The Pharisee and the Publican	Teaching the self-righteous	Luke 18:10-14.
30. The Pounds	At the house of Zaccheus	Luke 19:12-27.

TABLES OF WEIGHTS, MEASURES, AND COINS

Weights

Terms Heb. or Gr.	KJV	Ratio	Approximate Metric	Equivalent U.S.
In the OT				
Kikkar	talent	3,000 *shekels*	34.2 kg.	75 lb.
Maneh, mina	pound	50 *shekels*	.57 kg.	1.25 lb.
Shekel				
(official,				
625 B.C.)			11.4 gm.	0.4 oz.
Pim		2/3 *shekel*	7.6 gm.	0.27 oz.
Bekah		1/2 *shekel*	5.7 gm.	0.20 oz.
Gerah		1/20 *shekel*	0.57 gm.	0.02 oz.
In the NT				
Litra	pound		0.34 kg.	12 oz.
Talanton	talent			58–80 lb.

Dry and Liquid Measures

Terms Heb. or Gr.	KJV	Ratio	Approximate Metric	Equivalent U.S.
In the OT				
Homer—kor		10 *ephahs* or	220 liters	6.25 bu.
		10 *baths*		58 gal.
Letek		1/2 *homer*	110 lit.	3.12 bu.
Ephah—bath			22 lit.	0.625 bu.
				5.8 gal.
Seah		1/3 *ephah*	7.33 lit.	6.67 dry qt.
Hin		1/6 *bath*	3.67 lit.	1 gal.
Omer—				
'issarón		1/10 *ephah*	2.2 lit.	2 dry qt.
Qab (cab)		1/18 *ephah*	1.3 lit.	2.3 pt.
Log		1/72 *bath*	0.31 lit.	0.64 pt.
In the NT				
Koros	measure			11–17 bu.
Batos	measure	72 *sextarii*	39.6 lit.	10.4 gal.
Metretes	firkin		35 lit.	9 gal.
Saton	measure	24 *sextarii*	13.2 lit.	12 dry qt.
Modios	bushel	16 *sextarii*	8.8 lit.	1 peck
Choinix	measure	2 *sextarii*	1.1 lit.	1 qt.
Xestes	pot	1 *sextarius*	0.55 lit.	1 pt.

Linear Measures

Terms Heb. or Gr.	KJV	Ratio	Approximate Metric	Equivalent U.S.
In the OT				
qaneh	Reed	6 cubits	2.67 m.	8 ft. 9 in.
	Reed (Ezek)	6 cubits	3.12 m.	10 ft. 3 in.
ammá	Cubit (6 handbreadths)		44.45 cm.	17.5 in.
	Cubit (Ezek) (7 handbreadths)		52 cm.	20.5 in.
zeret	Span	1/2 cubit	22.2 cm.	9 in.
tepah	Hand-breadth	1/6 cubit	7.4 cm.	3 in.
'esba'	Finger	1/24 cubit	1.85 cm.	3/4 in.
In the NT				
milion	Mile	Roman mile	1.48 km.	4,854 ft.
stadion	Furlong	(1000 paces)		
orguia	Fathom	1/8 Roman mile	185 m.	607 ft.
pechys	Cubit	4 cubits	1.85 m.	6 ft.
			46.25 cm.	18 in.

Coins

Jewish	Greek	Roman	Approximate U.S. Equivalent
Lepton ("mite")			
		1/2 *quadrans*	1/8 cent
		quadrans ("farthing")	1/4 cent
		assarius ("farthing")	1 cent
	drachma	*denarius* ("penny")	16 cents
	didrachma	2 *denarii*	32 cents
	stater	4 *denarii*	64 cents
	25 *drachma*	*aureus*	4 dollars
	mina ("pound")	100 *denarii*	16 dollars
	talent	240 *aurei*	960 dollars

THROUGH THE BIBLE IN A YEAR

JANUARY

Date	Morning		Evening
1 GEN.	1,2	MATT.	1
2 GEN.	3,4,5	MATT.	2
3 GEN.	6,7,8	MATT.	3
4 GEN.	9,10,11	MATT.	4
5 GEN.	12,13,14	MATT.	5:1–26
6 GEN.	15,16,17	MATT.	5:27–48
7 GEN.	18,19	MATT.	6
8 GEN.	20,21,22	MATT.	7
9 GEN.	23,24	MATT.	8
10 GEN.	25,26	MATT.	9:1–17
11 GEN.	27,28	MATT.	9:18–38
12 GEN.	29,30	MATT.	10:1–23
13 GEN.	31,32	MATT.	10:24–42
14 GEN.	33,34,35	MATT.	11
15 GEN.	36,37	MATT.	12:1–21
16 GEN.	38,39,40	MATT.	12:22–50
17 GEN.	41	MATT.	13:1–32
18 GEN.	42,43	MATT.	13:33–58
19 GEN.	44,45	MATT.	14:1–21
20 GEN.	46,47,48	MATT.	14:22–36
21 GEN.	49,50	MATT.	15:1–20
22 EXOD.	1,2,3	MATT.	15:21–39
23 EXOD.	4,5,6	MATT.	16
24 EXOD.	7,8	MATT.	17
25 EXOD.	9,10	MATT.	18:1–20
26 EXOD.	11,12	MATT.	18:21–35
27 EXOD.	13,14,15	MATT.	19:1–15
28 EXOD.	16,17,18	MATT.	19:16–30
29 EXOD.	19,20,21	MATT.	20:1–16
30 EXOD.	22,23,24	MATT.	20:17–34
31 EXOD.	25,26	MATT.	21:1–22

FEBRUARY

Date	Morning		Evening
1 EXOD.	27,28	MATT.	21:23–46
2 EXOD.	29,30	MATT.	22:1–22
3 EXOD.	31,32,33	MATT.	22:23–46
4 EXOD.	34,35,36	MATT.	23:1–22
5 EXOD.	37,38	MATT.	23:23–39
6 EXOD.	39,40	MATT.	24:1–22
7 LEV.	1,2,3	MATT.	24:23–51
8 LEV.	4,5,6	MATT.	25:1–30
9 LEV.	7,8,9	MATT.	25:31–46
10 LEV.	10,11,12	MATT.	26:1–19
11 LEV.	13	MATT.	26:20–54
12 LEV.	14	MATT.	26:55–75
13 LEV.	15,16,17	MATT.	27:1–31
14 LEV.	18,19	MATT.	27:32–66
15 LEV.	20,21	MATT.	28:1–20
16 LEV.	22,23	MARK	1:1–22
17 LEV.	24,25	MARK	1:23–45
18 LEV.	26,27	MARK	2
19 NUM.	1,2	MARK	3:1–21
20 NUM.	3,4	MARK	3:22–35
21 NUM.	5,6	MARK	4:1–20
22 NUM.	7	MARK	4:21–41
23 NUM.	8,9,10	MARK	5:1–20
24 NUM.	11,12,13	MARK	5:21–43
25 NUM.	14,15	MARK	6:1–32
26 NUM.	16,17	MARK	6:33–56
27 NUM.	18,19,20	MARK	7:1–13
28 NUM.	21,22	MARK	7:14–37
29 NUM.	23,24,25	MARK	8:1–21

Divide chapters for Feb. 29 and read
them Feb. 28 and Mar. 1 when
February has only 28 days.

MARCH

Date	Morning		Evening
1 NUM.	26,27	MARK	8:22–38
2 NUM.	28,29	MARK	9:1–29
3 NUM.	30,31	MARK	9:30–50
4 NUM.	32,33	MARK	10:1–31
5 NUM.	34,35,36	MARK	10:32–52
6 DEUT.	1,2	MARK	11:1–19
7 DEUT.	3,4	MARK	11:20–33
8 DEUT.	5,6,7	MARK	12:1–27
9 DEUT.	8,9,10	MARK	12:28–44
10 DEUT.	11,12,13	MARK	13:1–13
11 DEUT.	14,15,16	MARK	13:14–37
12 DEUT.	17,18,19	MARK	14:1–25
13 DEUT.	20,21,22	MARK	14:26–50
14 DEUT.	23,24,25	MARK	14:51–72
15 DEUT.	26,27	MARK	15:1–26
16 DEUT.	28	MARK	15:27–47
17 DEUT.	29,30	MARK	16
18 DEUT.	31,32	LUKE	1:1–23
19 DEUT.	33,34	LUKE	1:24–56
20 JOSH.	1,2,3	LUKE	1:57–80
21 JOSH.	4,5,6	LUKE	2:1–24
22 JOSH.	7,8	LUKE	2:25–52
23 JOSH.	9,10	LUKE	3
24 JOSH.	11,12,13	LUKE	4:1–32
25 JOSH.	14,15	LUKE	4:33–44
26 JOSH.	16,17,18	LUKE	5:1–16
27 JOSH.	19,20	LUKE	5:17–39
28 JOSH.	21,22	LUKE	6:1–26
29 JOSH.	23,24	LUKE	6:27–49
30 JUDG.	1,2	LUKE	7:1–30
31 JUDG.	3,4,5	LUKE	7:31–50

APRIL

Date	Morning		Evening
1 JUDG.	6,7	LUKE	8:1–21
2 JUDG.	8,9	LUKE	8:22–56
3 JUDG.	10,11	LUKE	9:1–36
4 JUDG.	12,13,14	LUKE	9:37–62
5 JUDG.	15,16,17	LUKE	10:1–24
6 JUDG.	18,19	LUKE	10:25–42
7 JUDG.	20,21	LUKE	11:1–28
8 RUTH	1,2,3,4	LUKE	11:29–54
9 I SAM.	1,2,3	LUKE	12:1–34
10 I SAM.	4,5,6	LUKE	12:35–59
11 I SAM.	7,8,9	LUKE	13:1–21
12 I SAM.	10,11,12	LUKE	13:22–35
13 I SAM.	13,14	LUKE	14:1–24
14 I SAM.	15,16	LUKE	14:25–35
15 I SAM.	17,18	LUKE	15:1–10
16 I SAM.	19,20,21	LUKE	15:11–32
17 I SAM.	22,23,24	LUKE	16:1–18
18 I SAM.	25,26	LUKE	16:19–31
19 I SAM.	27,28,29	LUKE	17:1–19
20 I SAM.	30,31	LUKE	17:20–37
21 II SAM.	1,2,3	LUKE	18:1–17
22 II SAM.	4,5,6	LUKE	18:18–43
23 II SAM.	7,8,9	LUKE	19:1–28
24 II SAM.	10,11,12	LUKE	19:29–48
25 II SAM.	13,14	LUKE	20:1–26
26 II SAM.	15,16	LUKE	20:27–47
27 II SAM.	17,18	LUKE	21:1–19
28 II SAM.	19,20	LUKE	21:20–38
29 II SAM.	21,22	LUKE	22:1–30
30 II SAM.	23,24	LUKE	22:31–53

MAY

Date	Morning		Evening
1 I KINGS	1,2	LUKE	22:54–71
2 I KINGS	3,4,5	LUKE	23:1–26
3 I KINGS	6,7	LUKE	23:27–38
4 I KINGS	8,9	LUKE	23:39–56
5 I KINGS	10,11	LUKE	24:1–35
6 I KINGS	12,13	LUKE	24:36–53
7 I KINGS	14,15	JOHN	1:1–28
8 KI.	16,17,18	JOHN	1:29–51
9 I KINGS	19,20	JOHN	2
10 I KINGS	21,22	JOHN	3:1–21
11 II KINGS	1,2,3	JOHN	3:22–36
12 II KINGS	4,5	JOHN	4:1–30
13 II KINGS	6,7,8	JOHN	4:31–54
14 II KI.	9,10,11	JOHN	5:1–24
15 II KI.	12,13,14	JOHN	5:25–47
16 II KI.	15,16,17	JOHN	6:1–21
17 II KINGS	18,19	JOHN	6:22–44
18 II KI.	20,21,22	JOHN	6:45–71
19 II KI.	23,24,25	JOHN	7:1–31
20 I CHRON.	1,2	JOHN	7:32–53
21 I CHRON.	3,4,5	JOHN	8:1–20
22 I CHRON.	6,7	JOHN	8:21–36
23 I CHR.	8,9,10	JOHN	8:37–59
24 I CHR.	11,12,13	JOHN	9:1–23
25 I CHR.	14,15,16	JOHN	9:24–41
26 I CHR.	17,18,19	JOHN	10:1–21
27 I CHR.	20,21,22	JOHN	10:22–42
28 I CHR.	23,24,25	JOHN	11:1–17
29 I CHR.	26,27	JOHN	11:18–46
30 I CHR.	28,29	JOHN	11:47–57
31 II CHR.	1,2,3	JOHN	12:1–19

JUNE

Date	Morning		Evening
1 II CHR.	4,5,6	JOHN	12:20–50
2 II CH.	7,8,9	JOHN	13:1–17
3 II CH.	10,11,12	JOHN	13:18–38
4 II CHR.	13–16	JOHN	14
5 II CH.	17,18,19	JOHN	15
6 II CH.	20,21,22	JOHN	16:1–15
7 II CH.	23,24,25	JOHN	16:16–33
8 II CH.	26,27,28	JOHN	17
9 II CH.	29,30,31	JOHN	18:1–23
10 II CH.	32,33	JOHN	18:24–40
11 II CH.	34,35,36	JOHN	19:1–22
12 EZRA	1,2	JOHN	19:23–42
13 EZRA	3,4,5	JOHN	20
14 EZRA	6,7,8	JOHN	21
15 EZRA	9,10	ACTS	1
16 NEH.	1,2,3	ACTS	2:1–13
17 NEH.	4,5,6	ACTS	2:14–47
18 NEH.	7,8	ACTS	3
19 NEH.	9,10,11	ACTS	4:1–22
20 NEH.	12,13	ACTS	4:23–37
21 ESTHER	1,2,3	ACTS	5:1–16
22 ESTHER	4,5,6	ACTS	5:17–42
23 ESTHER	7–10	ACTS	6
24 JOB	1,2,3	ACTS	7:1–19
25 JOB	4,5,6	ACTS	7:20–43
26 JOB	7,8,9	ACTS	7:44–60
27 JOB	10,11,12	ACTS	8:1–25
28 JOB	13,14,15	ACTS	8:26–40
29 JOB	16,17,18	ACTS	9:1–22
30 JOB	19,20	ACTS	9:23–43

JULY

Date	Morning		Evening
1	JOB	21,22	ACTS 10:1-23
2	JOB	23,24,25	ACTS 10:24-48
3	JOB	26,27,28	ACTS 11
4	JOB	29,30	ACTS 12
5	JOB	31,32	ACTS 13:1-23
6	JOB	33,34	ACTS 13:24-52
7	JOB	35,36,37	ACTS 14
8	JOB	38,39	ACTS 15:1-21
9	JOB	40,41,42	ACTS 15:22-41
10	PS.	1,2,3	ACTS 16:1-15
11	PS.	4,5,6	ACTS 16:16-40
12	PS.	7,8,9	ACTS 17:1-15
13	PS.	10,11,12	ACTS 17:16-34
14	PS.	13-16	ACTS 18
15	PS.	17,18	ACTS 19:1-20
16	PS.	19,20,21	ACTS 19:21-41
17	PS.	22,23,24	ACTS 20:1-16
18	PS.	25,26,27	ACTS 20:17-38
19	PS.	28,29,30	ACTS 21:1-14
20	PS.	31,32,33	ACTS 21:15-40
21	PS.	34,35	ACTS 22
22	PS.	36,37	ACTS 23:1-11
23	PS.	38,39,40	ACTS 23:12-35
24	PS.	41,42,43	ACTS 24
25	PS.	44,45,46	ACTS 25
26	PS.	47,48,49	ACTS 26
27	PS.	50,51,52	ACTS 27:1-25
28	PS.	53,54,55	ACTS 27:26-44
29	PS.	56,57,58	ACTS 28:1-15
30	PS.	59,60,61	ACTS 28:16-31
31	PS.	62,63,64	ROM. 1

AUGUST

Date	Morning		Evening
1	PS.	65,66,67	ROM. 2
2	PS.	68,69	ROM. 3
3	PS.	70,71,72	ROM. 4
4	PS.	73,74	ROM. 5
5	PS.	75,76,77	ROM. 6
6	PS.	78	ROM. 7
7	PS.	79,80,81	ROM. 8:1-18
8	PS.	82,83,84	ROM. 8:19-39
9	PS.	85,86,87	ROM. 9
10	PS.	88,89	ROM. 10
11	PS.	90,91,92	ROM. 11:1-21
12	PS.	93,94,95	ROM. 11:22-36
13	PS.	96,97,98	ROM. 12
14	PS.	99-102	ROM. 13
15	PS.	103,104	ROM. 14
16	PS.	105,106	ROM. 15:1-20
17	PS.	107,108	ROM. 15:21-33
18	PS.	109,110,111	ROM. 16
19	PS.	112-115	I COR. 1
20	PS.	116-118	I COR. 2
21	PS.	119:1-48	I COR. 3
22	PS.	119:49-104	I COR. 4
23	PS.	119:105-176	I COR. 5
24	PS.	120-123	I COR. 6
25	PS.	124-127	I COR. 7:1-24
26	PS.	128-131	I COR. 7:25-40
27	PS.	132-135	I COR. 8
28	PS.	136-138	I COR. 9
29	PS.	139-141	I COR. 10:1-13
30	PS.	142-144	I COR. 10:14-33
31	PS.	145-147	I COR. 11:1-15

SEPTEMBER

Date	Morning		Evening
1	PS.	148-150	I CR. 11:16-34
2	PROV.	1,2	I COR. 12
3	PROV.	3,4	I COR. 13
4	PROV.	5,6	I COR. 14:1-20
5	PROV.	7,8	I CR. 14:21-40
6	PROV.	9,10	I COR. 15:1-32
7	PROV.	11,12	I CR. 15:33-58
8	PROV.	13,14	I COR. 16
9	PROV.	15,16	II COR. 1
10	PROV.	17,18	II COR. 2
11	PROV.	19,20	II COR. 3
12	PROV.	21,22	II COR. 4
13	PROV.	23,24	II COR. 5
14	PROV.	25,26,27	II COR. 6
15	PROV.	28,29	II COR. 7
16	PROV.	30,31	II COR. 8
17	ECCLES.	1,2,3	II COR. 9
18	ECCLES.	4,5,6	II COR. 10
19	ECCLES.	7,8,9	II CR. 11:1-15
20	ECC.	10,11,12	II CR. 11:16-33
21	SOL.	1,2,3	II COR. 12
22	SOL.	4,5	II COR. 13
23	SOL.	6,7,8	GAL. 1
24	ISA.	1,2,3	GAL. 2
25	ISA.	4,5,6	GAL. 3
26	ISA.	7,8,9	GAL. 4
27	ISA.	10,11,12	GAL. 5
28	ISA.	13,14,15	GAL. 6
29	ISA.	16,17,18	EPH. 1
30	ISA.	19,20,21	EPH. 2

OCTOBER

Date	Morning		Evening
1	ISA.	22,23	EPH. 3
2	ISA.	24,25,26	EPH. 4
3	ISA.	27,28	EPH. 5
4	ISA.	29,30	EPH. 6
5	ISA.	31,32,33	PHIL. 1
6	ISA.	34,35,36	PHIL. 2
7	ISA.	37,38	PHIL. 3
8	ISA.	39,40	PHIL. 4
9	ISA.	41,42	COL. 1
10	ISA.	43,44	COL. 2
11	ISA.	45,46,47	COL. 3
12	ISA.	48,49	COL. 4
13	ISA.	50,51,52	I THESS. 1
14	ISA.	53,54,55	I THESS. 2
15	ISA.	56,57,58	I THESS. 3
16	ISA.	59,60,61	I THESS. 4
17	ISA.	62,63,64	I THESS. 5
18	ISA.	65,66	II THESS. 1
19	JER.	1,2	II THESS. 2
20	JER.	3,4	II THESS. 3
21	JER.	5,6	I TIM. 1
22	JER.	7,8	I TIM. 2
23	JER.	9,10	I TIM. 3
24	JER.	11,12,13	I TIM. 4
25	JER.	14,15,16	I TIM. 5
26	JER.	17,18,19	I TIM. 6
27	JER.	20,21,22	II TIM. 1
28	JER.	23,24	II TIM. 2
29	JER.	25,26	II TIM. 3
30	JER.	27,28	II TIM. 4
31	JER.	29,30	TITUS 1

NOVEMBER

Date	Morning		Evening
1	JER.	31,32	TITUS 2
2	JER.	33,34,35	TITUS 3
3	JER.	36,37	PHILEM.
4	JER.	38,39	HEB. 1
5	JER.	40,41,42	HEB. 2
6	JER.	43,44,45	HEB. 3
7	JER.	46,47,48	HEB. 4
8	JER.	49,50	HEB. 5
9	JER.	51,52	HEB. 6
10	LAM.	1,2	HEB. 7
11	LAM.	3,4,5	HEB. 8
12	EZEK.	1,2,3	HEB. 9
13	EZEK.	4,5,6	HEB. 10:1-23
14	EZEK.	7,8,9	HEB. 10:24-39
15	EZEK.	10,11,12	HEB. 11:1-19
16	EZEK.	13,14,15	HEB. 11:20-40
17	EZEK.	16	HEB. 12
18	EZEK.	17,18,19	HEB. 13
19	EZEK.	20,21	JAS. 1
20	EZEK.	22,23	JAS. 2
21	EZEK.	24,25,26	JAS. 3
22	EZEK.	27,28	JAS. 4
23	EZEK.	29,30,31	JAS. 5
24	EZEK.	32,33	I PET. 1
25	EZEK.	34,35	I PET. 2
26	EZEK.	36,37	I PET. 3
27	EZEK.	38,39	I PET. 4
28	EZEK.	40	I PET. 5
29	EZEK.	41,42	II PET. 1
30	EZEK.	43,44	II PET. 2

DECEMBER

Date	Morning		Evening
1	EZEK.	45,46	II PET. 3
2	EZEK.	47,48	I JOHN 1
3	DAN.	1,2	I JOHN 2
4	DAN.	3,4	I JOHN 3
5	DAN.	5,6	I JOHN 4
6	DAN.	7,8	I JOHN 5
7	DAN.	9,10	II JOHN
8	DAN.	11,12	III JOHN
9	HOS.	1-4	JUDE
10	HOS.	5-8	REV. 1
11	HOS.	9,10,11	REV. 2
12	HOS.	12,13,14	REV. 3
13	JOEL	1,2,3	REV. 4
14	AMOS	1,2,3	REV. 5
15	AMOS	4,5,6	REV. 6
16	AMOS	7,8,9	REV. 7
17	OBAD.		REV. 8
18	JONAH		REV. 9
19	MIC.	1,2,3	REV. 10
20	MIC.	4,5	REV. 11
21	MIC.	6,7	REV. 12
22	NAH.		REV. 13
23	HAB.		REV. 14
24	ZEPH.		REV. 15
25	HAG.		REV. 16
26	ZECH.	1-3	REV. 17
27	ZECH.	4,5,6	REV. 18
28	ZECH.	7,8,9	REV. 19
29	ZECH.	10,11,12	REV. 20
30	ZECH.	13,14	REV. 21
31	MAL.		REV. 22

TOPICAL INDEX OF SCRIPTURE

ANGER

Prov. 14:17. A quick-tempered man acts foolishly, and a man of evil devices is hated. 29. He who is slow to anger has great understanding, but he who is quick-tempered exalts folly.

Prov. 15:1. A gentle answer turns away wrath, but a harsh word stirs up anger. 18. A hot-tempered man stirs up strife, but the slow to anger pacifies contention.

Jas. 1:19. *This* you know, my beloved brethren. But let every one be quick to hear, slow to speak *and* slow to anger; 20. for the anger of man does not achieve the righteousness of God.

Gen. 49:7; Prov. 12:16; 19:11; 22:24, 25; 25:28; Eph. 4:26, 31; Col. 3:8; 1 Tim. 2:8.

ASSURANCE

Eph. 3:12. In whom we have boldness and confident access through faith in Him.

2 Tim. 1:12. For this reason I also suffer these things, but I am not ashamed; for I know whom I have believed and I am convinced that He is able to guard what I have entrusted to Him until that day.

1 John 3:14. We know that we have passed out of death into life, because we love the brethren. He who does not love abides in death. 19. We shall know by this that we are of the truth, and shall assure our heart before Him.

Job 19:25, 26; Ps. 4:3; Isa. 12:2; Rom. 8:16, 38, 39; Phil. 3:21; Col. 2:2; 1 Thess. 1:5; Heb. 6:11, 19; 12:28; 1 John 4:18; 5:13.

BACKSLIDING

Deut. 4:9. "Only give heed to yourself and keep your soul diligently, lest you forget the things which your eyes have seen, and lest they depart from your heart all the days of your life; but make them known to your sons and your grandsons."

Matt. 24:12. "And because lawlessness is increased, most people's love will grow cold."

Mark 8:38. "For whoever is ashamed of Me and My words in this adulterous and sinful generation, the Son of Man will also be ashamed of him when He comes in the glory of His Father with the holy angels."

Luke 9:62. But Jesus said to him, "No one, after putting his hand to the plow and looking back, is fit for the kingdom of God."

John 15:6. "If anyone does not abide in Me, he is thrown away as a branch, and dries up; and they gather them, and cast them into the fire, and they are burned."

Gal. 1:6. I am amazed that you are so quickly deserting Him who called you by the grace of Christ, for a different gospel.

Deut. 8:11-14; Hos. 11:7; 1 Tim. 6:10; 2 Tim. 2:12; 4:10; Heb. 6:4-6; 10:26-27, 38; 12:15; 2 Peter 2:20-21.

BLESSING

Ps. 55:22. Cast your burden upon the LORD, and He will sustain you; He will never allow the righteous to be shaken.

Acts 20:32. "And now I commend you to God and to the word of His grace, which is able to build you up and to give you the inheritance among all those who are sanctified."

1 Cor. 2:9. but just as it is written, "THINGS WHICH EYE HAS NOT SEEN AND EAR HAS NOT HEARD, AND *which* HAVE NOT ENTERED THE HEART OF MAN, ALL THAT GOD HAS PREPARED FOR THOSE WHO LOVE HIM."

2 Cor. 9:8. And God is able to make all grace abound to you, that always having all sufficiency in everything, you may have an abundance for every good deed.

Eph. 3:20. Now to Him who is able to do exceeding abundantly beyond all that we ask or think, according to the power that works within us.

Phil. 4:7. And the peace of God, which surpasses all comprehension, shall guard your hearts and your minds in Christ Jesus. 19. And my God shall supply all your needs according to His riches in glory in Christ Jesus.

Jas. 1:17. Every good thing bestowed and every perfect gift is from above, coming down from the Father of lights, with whom there is no variation, or shifting shadow.

Ps. 103:2. Bless the LORD, O my soul, and forget none of His benefits; 3. who pardons all your iniquities; who heals all your diseases; 4. who redeems your life from the pit; who crowns you with loving-kindness and compassion; 5. who satisfies your years with good things, *so that* your youth is renewed like the eagle.

Rev. 2:10. " 'Do not fear what you are about to suffer. Behold, the devil is about to cast some of you into prison, that you may be tested, and you will have tribulation ten days. Be faithful until death, and I will give you the crown of life.' "

Ex. 19:5; Deut. 11:26; Ps. 145:15; Prov. 3:1; 16:7; Mal. 3:10; 4:2; Phil. 1:6; 2:13; Col. 1:11; 1 John 1:9.

CHILDREN

Ps. 127:3. Behold, children are a gift of the LORD; the fruit of the womb is a reward.

Prov. 17:6. Grandchildren are the crown of old men, and the glory of sons is their fathers.

Prov. 22:6. Train up a child in the way he should go, even when he is old he will not depart from it.

Isa. 54:13. "And all your sons will be taught of the LORD; and the well-being of your sons will be great."

Matt. 19:14. But Jesus said, "Let the children alone, and do not hinder them from coming to Me; for the kingdom of heaven belongs to such as these." 15. And after laying His hands on them, He departed from there.

Eph. 6:1. Children, obey your parents in the Lord, for this is right. 2. HONOR YOUR FATHER AND MOTHER (which is the first commandment with a promise).

Ex. 20:12; Deut. 5:16; 6:6–7; Ps. 103:17–18; 119:9; Prov. 1:8–9; 20:20; 29:3, 15–17; Eccl. 12:1; Joel 1:3; Matt. 18:4–5, 10; Mark 9:36–37; 10:16; Acts 2:39; Eph. 6:4; Col. 3:21; 2 Tim. 2:22.

CHURCH

Acts 20:28. "Be on guard for yourselves and for all the flock, among which the Holy Spirit has made you overseers, to shepherd the church of God which He purchased with His own blood."

1 Cor. 12:5. And there are varieties of ministries, and the same Lord. 28. And God has appointed in the church, first apostles, second prophets, third teachers, then miracles, then gifts of healings, helps, administrations, various kinds of tongues.

Col. 3:11. —a renewal in which there is no distinction between Greek and Jew, circumcised and uncircumcised, barbarian, Scythian, slave and freeman, but Christ is all, and in all. 15. And let the peace of Christ rule in your hearts, to which indeed you were called in one body; and be thankful.

Ps. 111:1; Acts 2:41; 6:2–6; 7:38; 14:23; 15:2–20; 1 Cor. 3:11; 7:17; Eph. 2:20–22; 4:11–12; Col. 2:10, 19; 1 Thess. 5:12; 1 Tim. 3:1–13; 5:17; Heb. 13:17; Jas. 5:14–15.

CONSCIENCE

Matt. 6:22. "The lamp of the body is the eye; if therefore your eye is clear, your whole body will be full of light. 23. But if your eye is bad, your whole body will be full of darkness. If therefore the light that is in you is darkness, how great is the darkness!"

Acts 24:16. "In view of this, I also do my best to maintain always a blameless conscience both before God and before men."

Rom. 2:14. For when Gentiles who do not have the Law do instinctively the things of the Law, these, not having the Law, are a law to themselves, 15. in that they show the work of the Law written in their hearts, their conscience bearing witness, and their thoughts alternately accusing or else defending them.

Rom. 9:1. I am telling the truth in Christ, I am not lying, my conscience bearing me witness in the Holy Spirit.

1 Cor. 10:27. If one of the unbelievers invites you, and you wish to go, eat anything that is set before you, without asking questions for conscience' sake. 28. But if anyone should say to you, "This is meat sacrificed to idols," do not eat it, for the sake of the one who informed you, and for conscience' sake; 29. I mean not your own conscience, but the other man's; for why is my freedom judged by another's conscience?

Titus 1:15. To the pure, all things are pure; but to those who are defiled and unbelieving, nothing is pure, but both their mind and their conscience are defiled.

Job 27:6; Ps. 51:3; Prov. 28:1; John 8:9; Rom. 7:15; 14:22; 1 Cor. 8:7; 1 Tim. 4:2; Heb. 10:22; 1 John 3:20.

CONTENTMENT

Ps. 37:7. Rest in the LORD and wait patiently for Him; fret not yourself because of him who prospers in his way, because of the man who carries out wicked schemes. 16. Better is the little of the righteous than the abundance of many wicked.

1 Cor. 7:17. Only, as the Lord has assigned to each one, as God has called each, in this manner let him walk. And thus I direct in all the churches.

1 Tim. 6:6. But godliness actually is a means of great gain, when accompanied by contentment.

Heb. 13:5. Let your character be free from the love of money, being content with what you have; for He Himself has said, "I WILL NEVER DESERT YOU, NOR WILL I EVER FORSAKE YOU."

Ps. 16:6; Prov. 16:8; 17:1, 22; Eccl. 5:12; 6:9; Gal. 5:26.

COURAGE

Prov. 28:1. The wicked flee when no one is pursuing, but the righteous are bold as a lion.

1 Cor. 16:13. Be on the alert, stand firm in the faith, act like men, be strong.

2 Tim. 1:7. For God has not given us a spirit of timidity, but of power and love and discipline.

COVETOUSNESS

Ex. 20:17. "You shall not covet your neighbor's house; you shall not covet your neighbor's wife or his male servant or his female servant or his ox or his donkey or anything that belongs to your neighbor."

Ps. 119:36. Incline my heart to Thy testimonies, and not to dishonest gain.

Eccl. 5:10. He who loves money will not be satisfied with money, nor he who loves abundance with its income. This too is vanity. 11. When good things increase, those who consume them increase. So what is the advantage to their owners except to look on?

Deut. 5:21; Prov. 11:24–26; 22:16; Isa. 5:8; 56:11; Matt. 16:26.

DEATH

Ps. 49:15. But God will redeem my soul from the power of Sheol; for He will receive me.

Ps. 116:15. Precious in the sight of the LORD is the death of His godly ones.

Dan. 12:2. "And many of those who sleep in the dust of the ground will awake, these to everlasting life, but the others to disgrace and everlasting contempt."

John 11:25. Jesus said to her, "I am the resurrection and the life; he who believes in Me shall live even if he dies, 26. and everyone who lives and believes in Me shall never die."

Rom. 5:12. Therefore, just as through one man sin entered into the world, and death through sin, and so death spread to all men, because all sinned— 14. Nevertheless death reigned from Adam until Moses, even over those who had not sinned in the likeness of Adam's offense, who is a type of Him who was to come.

1 Cor. 15:21. For since by a man came death, by a man also came the resurrection of the dead. 22. For as in Adam all die, so also in Christ all shall be made alive. 26. The last enemy that will be abolished is death. 55. "O DEATH, WHERE IS YOUR VICTORY? O DEATH, WHERE IS YOUR STING?" 56. The sting of death is sin, and the power of sin is the law; 57. but thanks be to God, who gives us the victory through our Lord Jesus Christ.

Rev. 21:4. "And He shall wipe away every tear from their eyes; and there shall no longer be any death; there shall no longer be any mourning, or crying, or pain; the first things have passed away."

Job 34:20; Ps. 23:4; 39:4, 13; 73:24; Prov. 14:2, 32; Eccl. 7:1; Luke 12:20; John 11:26; Rev. 20:14.

DESPONDENCY

Ps. 31:22. As for me, I said in my alarm, "I am cut off from before Thine eyes"; nevertheless Thou didst hear the voice of my supplications when I cried to Thee.

Ps. 77:7. Will the Lord reject forever? And will He never be favorable again? 8. Has His lovingkindness ceased forever? Has His promise come to an end forever? 9. Has God forgotten to be gracious? Or has He in anger withdrawn His compassion?

Prov. 13:12. Hope deferred makes the heart sick, but desire fulfilled is a tree of life.

Num. 17:12-13; Job 3:1-3; Jer. 8:20; Lam. 3:1-11.

DISCIPLESHIP

Matt. 10:32. "Every one therefore who shall confess Me before men, I will also confess him before My Father who is in heaven. 33. "But whoever shall deny Me before men, I will also deny him before My Father who is in heaven. 34. "Do not think that I came to bring peace on the earth; I did not come to bring peace, but a sword. 35. "For I came to SET A MAN AGAINST HIS FATHER, AND A DAUGHTER AGAINST HER MOTHER, AND A DAUGHTER-IN-LAW AGAINST HER MOTHER-IN-LAW; 36. and A MAN'S ENEMIES WILL BE THE MEMBERS OF HIS HOUSEHOLD. 37. "He who loves father or mother more than Me is not worthy of Me; and he who loves

son or daughter more than Me is not worthy of Me. 38. "And he who does not take his cross and follow after Me is not worthy of Me. 39. "He who has found his life shall lose it, and he who has lost his life for My sake shall find it."

Luke 14:27. "Whoever does not carry his own cross and come after Me cannot be My disciple. 28. "For which one of you, when he wants to build a tower, does not first sit down and calculate the cost, to see if he has enough to complete it? 31. "Or what king, when he sets out to meet another king in battle, will not first sit down and take counsel whether he is strong enough with ten thousand men to encounter the one coming against him with twenty thousand? 33. "So therefore, no one of you can be My disciple who does not give up all his own possessions. 34. "Therefore, salt is good; but if even salt has become tasteless, with what will it be seasoned? 35. "It is useless either for the soil or for the manure pile; it is thrown out. He who has ears to hear, let him hear."

John 21:15. So when they had finished breakfast, Jesus said to Simon Peter, "Simon, son of John, do you love Me more than these?" He said to Him, "Yes, Lord; You know that I love You." He said to him, "Tend My lambs." 16. He said to him again a second time, "Simon, son of John, do you love Me?" He said to Him, "Yes, Lord; You know that I love You." He said to him, "Shepherd My sheep." 17. He said to him the third time, "Simon, son of John, do you love Me?" Peter was grieved because He said to him the third time, "Do you love Me?" And he said to Him, "Lord, You know all things; You know that I love You." Jesus said to him, "Tend My sheep."

DISCIPLINE

Matt. 18:15. "And if your brother sins, go and reprove him in private; if he listens to you, you have won your brother. 16. "But if he does not listen to you, take one or two more with you, so that BY THE MOUTH OF TWO OR THREE WITNESSES EVERY FACT MAY BE CONFIRMED. 17. "And if he refuses to listen to them, tell it to the church; and if he refuses to listen even to the church, let him be to you as a Gentile and a tax-gatherer."

Rom. 16:17. Now I urge you, brethren, keep your eye on those who cause dissensions and hindrances contrary to the teaching which you learned, and turn away from them.

1 Cor. 4:19. But I will come to you soon, if the Lord wills, and I shall find out, not the words of those who are arrogant, but their power.

1 Cor. 5:1. It is actually reported that there is immorality among you, and immorality of such a kind as does not exist even among the Gentiles, that someone has his father's wife. 2. And you have become arrogant, and have not mourned instead, in order that the one who had done this deed might be removed from your midst. 3. For I, on my part, though absent in body but present in spirit, have already judged him who has so committed this, as though I were present. 4. In

the name of our Lord Jesus, when you are assembled, and I with you in spirit, with the power of our Lord Jesus, 5. *I have decided* to deliver such a one to Satan for the destruction of his flesh, that his spirit may be saved in the day of the Lord Jesus.

2 Cor. 2:6. Sufficient for such a one is this punishment which was *inflicted by* the majority, 7. so that on the contrary you should rather forgive and comfort *him,* lest somehow such a one be overwhelmed by excessive sorrow. 8. Wherefore I urge you to reaffirm *your* love for him.

Job 5:17; Ps. 94:12; Prov. 3:11–12; 17:3, 22; John 15:2; Rom. 5:3; Gal. 6:1; 1 Thess. 5:14; 2 Thess. 3:6, 14–15; 1 Tim. 5:1–2, 19–20; 6:3–5; Titus 3:10–11.

DIVORCE

Mal. 2:14. "Yet you say, 'For what reason?' Because the LORD has been a witness between you and the wife of your youth, against whom you have dealt treacherously, though she is your companion and your wife by covenant. 15. "But not one has done *so* who has a remnant of the Spirit. And what did *that* one *do* while he was seeking a godly offspring? Take heed then, to your spirit, and let no one deal treacherously against the wife of your youth. 16. "For I hate divorce," says the LORD, the God of Israel, "and him who covers his garment with wrong," says the LORD of hosts. "So take heed to your spirit, that you do not deal treacherously."

Matt. 5:31. "And it was said, 'WHOEVER DIVORCES HIS WIFE, LET HIM GIVE HER A CERTIFICATE OF DISMISSAL'; 32. but I say to you that every one who divorces his wife, except for *the* cause of unchastity, makes her commit adultery; and whoever marries a divorced woman commits adultery."

Matt. 19:3–9; Luke 16:18; 1 Cor. 7:10–17.

DOUBT

Ps. 42:5. Why are you in despair, O my soul? And *why* have you become disturbed within me? Hope in God, for I shall again praise Him *for* the help of His presence.

Matt. 8:26. And he said to them, "Why are you timid, you men of little faith?" Then He arose, and rebuked the winds and the sea; and it became perfectly calm.

John 20:25. The other disciples therefore were saying to him, "We have seen the Lord!" But he said to them, "Unless I shall see in His hands the imprint of the nails, and put my finger into the place of the nails, and put my hand into His side, I will not believe." 27. Then He said to Thomas, "Reach here your finger, and see My hands; and reach here your hand, and put it into My side; and be not unbelieving, but believing."

Isa. 49:14–15; Matt. 14:29–31; 17:14–21.

ENVY

Ps. 37:1. Fret not yourself because of evildoers, be not envious toward wrongdoers. 7. Rest in the LORD and wait patiently for Him; fret not yourself because of him who prospers in his way, because of the man who carries out wicked schemes.

Jas. 3:14. But if you have bitter jealousy and selfish ambition in your heart, do not be arrogant and *so* lie against the truth. 16. For where jealousy and selfish ambition exist, there is disorder and every evil thing.

Ps. 49:16; 73:3; Prov. 23:17; 27:4; Song 8:6; Rom. 13:13; 1 Cor. 13:4; 1 Peter 2:1.

FAITH

Ps. 118:8. It is better to take refuge in the LORD than to trust in man.

Prov. 3:5. Trust in the LORD with all your heart, and do not lean on your own understanding.

Isa. 26:3. "The steadfast of mind Thou wilt keep in perfect peace, because he trusts in Thee."

Mark 11:22. And Jesus answered saying to them, "Have faith in God."

John 3:16. "For God so loved the world, that He gave His only begotten Son, that whoever believes in Him should not perish, but have eternal life. 17. "For God did not send the Son into the world to judge the world; but that the world should be saved through Him."

Rom. 5:1. Therefore having been justified by faith, we have peace with God through our Lord Jesus Christ, 2. through whom also we have obtained our introduction by faith into this grace in which we stand; and we exult in hope of the glory of God.

Gal. 2:16. Nevertheless knowing that a man is not justified by the works of the Law but through faith in Christ Jesus, even we have believed in Christ Jesus, that we may be justified by faith in Christ, and not by the works of the Law; since by the works of the Law shall no flesh be justified.

Eph. 2:8. For by grace you have been saved through faith; and that not of yourselves, *it is* the gift of God.

Ps. 5:11; 32:10; 62:8; Nah. 1:7; Mark 9:23; 16:16; Luke 17:6; John 1:7; 6:35; 7:38; 8:24; 13:19; 20:31; Rom. 3:26; 4:3–5; 10:1–17; Eph. 3:12; 6:16; 1 Thess. 4:14; 5:8; 1 Tim. 4:10; 2 Tim. 4:7–8; Heb. 11:1–40; Jas. 1:3; 2:14–20; 1 Peter 1:7; 1 John 3:23.

FAITHFULNESS

Ex. 34:6. Then the LORD passed by in front of him and proclaimed, "The LORD, the LORD God, compassionate and gracious, slow to anger, and abounding in lovingkindness and truth."

Ps. 92:1. It is good to give thanks to the LORD, and to sing praises to Thy name, O Most High; 2. to declare Thy lovingkindness in the morning, and Thy faithfulness by night.

Ps. 103:17. But the lovingkindness of the LORD is from everlasting to everlasting on those who fear Him, and His righteousness to children's children.

1 Cor. 10:13. No temptation has overtaken you but such as is common to man; and God is faith-

ful, who will not allow you to be tempted beyond what you are able, but with the temptation will provide the way of escape also, that you may be able to endure it.

FAMILY

Deut. 11:19. "And you shall teach them to your sons, talking of them when you sit in your house and when you walk along the road and when you lie down and when you rise up. 20. "And you shall write them on the doorposts of your house and on your gates."

Isa. 54:13. "And all your sons will be taught of the LORD; and the well-being of your sons will be great."

Gen. 2:23-24; 18:19; Josh. 24:15; Eph. 5:22-24; 1 Tim. 3:2-5.

FELLOWSHIP

Gen. 5:24. And Enoch walked with God; and he was not, for God took him.

Ps. 55:14. We who had sweet fellowship together, walked in the house of God in the throng.

Ps. 119:63. I am a companion of all those who fear Thee, and of those who keep Thy precepts.

John 13:34. "A new commandment I give to you, that you love one another, even as I have loved you, that you also love one another."

Gen. 6:9; Ex. 33:14-15; Lev. 26:12; Amos 3:3; Zech. 2:10; Mal. 3:16; Matt. 18:20; Mark 9:37; John 15:4-7; 17:21; Rom. 8:9; 1 Cor. 1:9-10; 3:16; 12:27; Gal. 6:2, 10; 1 Thess. 5:11; Heb. 10:24; 13:1; Jas. 5:16; 1 Peter 2:17; 1 John 1:3.

FORGIVENESS

Ex. 23:4. "If you meet your enemy's ox or his donkey wandering away, you shall surely return it to him. 5. If you see the donkey of one who hates you lying *helpless* under its load, you shall refrain from leaving it to him, you shall surely release *it* with him."

Prov. 24:17. Do not rejoice when your enemy falls, and do not let your heart be glad when he stumbles. 29. Do not say, "Thus I shall do to him as he has done to me; I will render to the man according to his work."

Matt. 18:21. Then Peter came and said to Him, "Lord, how often shall my brother sin against me and I forgive him? Up to seven times?" 22. Jesus said to him, "I do not say to you, up to seven times, but up to seventy times seven."

Prov. 19:11; 25:21-22 (Rom. 12:20); Matt. 5:7; Mark 11:25; Luke 6:35; Rom. 12:14-21; 1 Cor. 4:12-13; Eph. 4:32; 1 Peter 3:9.

FRIENDSHIP

Prov. 17:9. He who covers a transgression seeks love, but he who repeats a matter separates intimate friends. 17. A friend loves at all times, and a brother is born for adversity.

Prov. 18:24. A man of *many* friends *comes* to ruin, but there is a friend who sticks closer than a brother.

Amos 3:3. Do two men walk together unless they have made an appointment?

GOD, access to

Ps. 145:18. The LORD is near to all who call upon Him, to all who call upon Him in truth.

John 14:6. Jesus said to him, "I am the way, and the truth, and the life; no one comes to the Father, but through Me."

Heb. 4:16. Let us therefore draw near with confidence to the throne of grace, that we may receive mercy and may find grace to help in time of need.

Jas. 4:8. Draw near to God and He will draw near to you. Cleanse your hands, you sinners; and purify your hearts, you double-minded.

GOD, Creator

Gen. 1:1. In the beginning God created the heavens and the earth. 26. Then God said, "Let Us make man in Our image, according to Our likeness; and let them rule over the fish of the sea and over the birds of the sky and over the cattle and over all the earth, and over every creeping thing that creeps on the earth." 27. And God created man in His own image, in the image of God He created him; male and female He created them.

Neh. 9:6. "Thou alone art the LORD. Thou hast made the heavens, the heaven of heavens with all their host, the earth and all that is on it, the seas and all that is in them. Thou dost give life to all of them and the heavenly host bows down before Thee."

Ps. 24:1. The earth is the LORD's, and all it contains, the world, and those who dwell in it. 2. For He has founded it upon the seas, and established it upon the rivers.

Ex. 20:11; 1 Sam. 2:8; Ps. 8:3; 33:6; 146:6; Isa. 40:12; Jer. 51:15; Acts 14:15; Eph. 3:9.

GOD, grace

Rom. 3:24. Being justified as a gift by His grace through the redemption which is in Christ Jesus.

Rom. 11:5. In the same way then, there has also come to be at the present time a remnant according to *God's* gracious choice. 6. But if it is by grace, it is no longer on the basis of works, otherwise grace is no longer grace.

Eph. 2:8. For by grace you have been saved through faith; and that not of yourselves, *it is* the gift of God.

2 Peter 3:18. But grow in the grace and knowledge of our Lord and Savior Jesus Christ. To Him *be* the glory, both now and to the day of eternity. Amen.

Gen. 6:8; Ps. 51:1; John 1:16; Rom. 5:2; 2 Cor. 12:9; Heb. 4:16.

GOD, holiness of

Ex. 15:11. "Who is like Thee among the gods, O LORD? Who is like Thee, majestic in holiness, awesome in praises, working wonders?"

Lev. 19:2. "Speak to all the congregation of the sons of Israel and say to them, 'You shall be holy, for I the LORD your God am holy.'"

Hab. 1:13. *Thine* eyes are too pure to approve evil, and Thou canst not look on wickedness *with favor.* Why dost Thou look with favor on those who deal treacherously? Why art Thou silent when the wicked swallowed up those more righteous than they?

Rev. 4:8. And the four living creatures, each one of them having six wings, are full of eyes around and within; and day and night they do not cease to say, "Holy, holy, holy, *is* the Lord God, the Almighty, who was and who is and who is to come."

GOD, love of

Isa. 54:10. "For the mountains may be removed and the hills may shake, but My lovingkindness will not be removed from you, and My covenant of peace will not be shaken," says the Lord who has compassion on you.

John 3:16. "For God so loved the world, that He gave His only begotten Son, that whoever believes in Him should not perish, but have eternal life."

John 17:23. "I in them, and Thou in Me, that they may be perfected in unity, that the world may know that Thou didst send Me, and didst love them, even as Thou didst love Me. 26. And I have made Thy name known to them, and will make it known; that the love wherewith Thou didst love Me may be in them, and I in them."

Rom. 8:31. What then shall we say to these things? If God *is* for us, who *is* against us? 32. He who did not spare His own Son, but delivered Him up for us all, how will He not also with Him freely give us all things? 38. For I am convinced that neither death, nor life, nor angels, nor principalities, nor things present, nor things to come, nor powers, 39. nor height, nor depth, nor any other created thing, shall be able to separate us from the love of God, which is in Christ Jesus our Lord.

GOD, sovereignty of

Ex. 18:11. "Now I know that the Lord is greater than all the gods; indeed, it was proven when they dealt proudly against the people."

Ps. 93:1. The Lord reigns, He is clothed with majesty; the Lord has clothed and girded Himself with strength; indeed, the world is firmly established, it will not be moved. 2. Thy throne is established from of old; Thou art from everlasting.

Ps. 95:3. For the Lord is a great God, and a great King above all gods, 4. in whose hand are the depths of the earth; the peaks of the mountains are His also. 5. The sea is His, for it was He who made it; and His hands formed the dry land.

Matt. 6:10. " 'Thy kingdom come. Thy will be done, on earth as it is in heaven. 13. 'And do not lead us into temptation, but deliver us from evil. [For Thine is the kingdom, and the power, and the glory, forever. Amen].' "

Rom. 14:11. For it is written, "As I live, says the Lord, every knee shall bow to Me, and every tongue shall give praise to God."

Ex. 15:18; Deut. 4:39; Josh. 2:11; 1 Chron. 29:11; Ps. 24:1; 96:10; Dan. 6:26; Matt. 11:25; Acts 17:24; 1 Tim. 6:15; Rev. 19:6.

HAPPINESS

Job 5:17. "Behold, how happy is the man whom God reproves, so do not despise the discipline of the Almighty."

Prov. 16:20. He who gives attention to the word shall find good, and blessed is he who trusts in the Lord.

1 Peter 3:14. But even if you should suffer for the sake of righteousness, *you are* blessed. And do not fear their intimidation, and do not be troubled.

Job 20:5; Ps. 40:8; 144:15; 146:5; Prov. 14:21; Isa. 12:2–3; 1 Peter 4:12–13.

HEAVEN

2 Chron. 2:6. "But who is able to build a house for Him, for the heavens and the highest heavens cannot contain Him? So who am I, that I should build a house for Him, except to burn *incense* before Him?"

Isa. 66:1. Thus says the Lord, "Heaven is My throne, and the earth is My footstool. Where then is a house you could build for Me? And where is a place that I may rest?"

Mark 16:19. So then, when the Lord Jesus had spoken to them, He was received up into heaven, and sat down at the right hand of God.

John 14:2. "In My Father's house are many dwelling places; if it were not so, I would have told you; for I go to prepare a place for you. 3. "And if I go and prepare a place for you, I will come again, and receive you to Myself; that where I am, *there* you may be also."

2 Peter 3:13. But according to His promise we are looking for new heavens and a new earth, in which righteousness dwells.

Deut. 26:15; 1 Kings 8:30; Job 3:17; Ps. 2:4; 16:11; 17:15; 23:6; 73:24; Isa. 33:17; Dan. 12:3; Mal. 3:17; Matt. 3:17; 5:3; 6:9, 20; Luke 12:32; 16:22; 23:43; 2 Cor. 12:4; 1 Thess. 4:17; Rev. 7:9; 8:1; 21:1, 25–27.

HELL

Ps. 9:17. The wicked will return to Sheol, *even* all the nations who forget God.

Isa. 33:14. Sinners in Zion are terrified; trembling has seized the godless. "Who among us can live with the consuming fire? Who among us can live with continual burning?"

Mark 9:43. "And if your hand causes you to stumble, cut it off; it is better for you to enter life crippled, than having your two hands, to go into hell, into the unquenchable fire," 44. [where their worm does not die, and the fire is not quenched].

Luke 16:23. "And in Hades he lifted up his eyes, being in torment, and saw Abraham far away, and Lazarus in his bosom. 24. "And he cried out and said, 'Father Abraham, have mercy on me, and send Lazarus, that he may dip the tip of his finger in water and cool off my tongue; for I am in agony in this flame.' "

Prov. 9:17-18; 23:13-14; Matt. 3:12; 7:13; 8:12; 16:18; 2 Thess. 1:9; Rev. 19:20; 21:8.

HOLINESS

Lev. 11:44a. " 'For I am the LORD your God. Consecrate yourselves therefore, and be holy; for I am holy.' "

Ps. 119:1. How blessed are those whose way is blameless, who walk in the law of the LORD. 2. How blessed are those who observe His testimonies, who seek Him with all *their* heart. 3. They also do no unrighteousness; they walk in His ways.

Rom. 6:12. Therefore do not let sin reign in your mortal body that you should obey its lusts, 13. and do not go on presenting the members of your body to sin *as* instruments of unrighteousness; but present yourselves to God as those alive from the dead, and your members *as* instruments of righteousness to God. 14. For sin shall not be master over you, for you are not under law, but under grace.

Phil. 2:15. That you may prove yourselves to be blameless and innocent, children of God above reproach in the midst of a crooked and perverse generation, among whom you appear as lights in the world.

Gen. 17:1; Ex. 19:6; Lev. 20:7; Ps. 32:2; Isa. 35:8; John 17:23; Acts 24:16; Rom. 11:16; 12:1; 1 Cor. 3:16-17; 5:7; Phil. 4:8; 2 Tim. 2:19-22; 3:17; Heb. 12:1; 2 Peter 1:5-8.

HOLY SPIRIT

Isa. 61:1. The Spirit of the Lord GOD is upon me, because the LORD has anointed me to bring good news to the afflicted; He has sent me to bind up the brokenhearted, to proclaim liberty to captives, and freedom to prisoners.

Zech. 4:6. Then he answered and said to me, "This is the word of the LORD to Zerubbabel saying, 'Not by might nor by power, but by My Spirit,' says the LORD of hosts."

John 15:26. "When the Helper comes, whom I will send to you from the Father, *that is* the Spirit of truth, who proceeds from the Father, He will bear witness of Me."

Gen. 1:2; 6:3; 41:38; Isa. 42:1; Ezek. 36:27; Matt. 1:18; 3:11, 16-17; 10:20; John 14:16-17, 26; 16:7-8; 20:22; Acts 1:5-8; 2:2-4; 4:8, 31; 9:31; 13:2-4; Rom. 5:5; 8:26; 1 Cor. 3:16; Gal. 4:6; Eph. 4:30; 1 Thess. 5:19.

HONESTY

Prov. 11:1. A false balance is an abomination to the LORD, but a just weight is His delight.

Luke 6:31. "And just as you want men to treat you, treat them in the same way."

2 Cor. 8:21. For we have regard for what is honorable, not only in the sight of the Lord, but also in the sight of men.

1 Thess. 4: 11. And to make it your ambition to lead a quiet life and attend to your own business and work with your hands, just as we commanded you; 12. so that you may behave properly toward outsiders and not be in any need.

Lev. 19:35-36; Deut. 25:13-16; Ps. 24:4; Acts 24:16; Heb. 13:18.

HOPE

Ps. 31:24. Be strong, and let your heart take courage, all you who hope in the LORD.

Ps. 71:5. For Thou art my hope; O Lord GOD, *Thou art* my confidence from my youth. 14. But as for me, I will hope continually, and will praise Thee yet more and more.

Col. 1:5. Because of the hope laid up for you in heaven, of which you previously heard in the word of truth, the gospel.

Ps. 33:18; 39:7; 43:5; Rom. 12:12; 1 Cor. 15:19; Heb. 11:1; 1 Peter 3:15.

HUMILITY

Prov. 15:33. The fear of the LORD is the instruction for wisdom, and before honor *comes* humility.

Prov. 27:2. Let another praise you, and not your own mouth; a stranger, and not your own lips.

Rom. 12:3. For through the grace given to me I say to every man among you not to think more highly of himself than he ought to think; but to think so as to have sound judgment, as God has allotted to each a measure of faith.

Gen. 32:10; Ps. 9:12; 86:1; 147:6; Prov. 22:4; Isa. 51:1; 1 Cor. 10:12; 15:10; Gal. 5:26; Jas. 4:6, 10.

JESUS CHRIST, divinity

Matt. 3:17. And behold, a voice out of the heavens, saying, "This is My beloved Son, in whom I am well-pleased."

John 1:1. In the beginning was the Word, and the Word was with God, and the Word was God. 2. He was in the beginning with God.

John 5:17. But He answered them, "My Father is working until now, and I Myself am working. 22. For not even the Father judges any one, but He has given all judgment to the Son, 23. in order that all may honor the Son, even as they honor the Father. He who does not honor the Son does not honor the Father who sent Him."

Matt. 1:23; 8:29; John 10:30; 20:28; Phil. 2:6; Heb. 1:8; 13:8; Rev. 1:8.

JESUS CHRIST, Savior

Matt. 1:21. "And she will bear a Son; and you shall call His name Jesus, for it is He who will save His people from their sins."

Luke 2:11. "For today in the city of David there has been born for you a Savior, who is Christ the Lord." 30. "For my eyes have seen Thy salvation, 31. which Thou hast prepared in the presence of all peoples, 32. A LIGHT OF REVELATION TO THE GENTILES, and the glory of Thy people Israel."

Acts 16:31. And they said, "Believe in the Lord Jesus, and you shall be saved, you and your household."

Rom. 6:23. For the wages of sin is death, but the free gift of God is eternal life in Christ Jesus our Lord.

Zech. 9:9; Mal. 4:2; Luke 1:68; 19:10; Acts 5:31; 15:11; Rom. 4:25.

JESUS CHRIST, Lord

Luke 2:11. For today in the city of David there has been born for you a Savior, who is Christ the Lord.

John 13:13. "You call Me Teacher and Lord; and you are right; for so I am."

Phil. 2:11. That every tongue should confess that Jesus Christ is Lord, to the glory of God the Father.

Luke 1:46; 6:46; Rom. 14:8-9; 1 Cor. 1:31; 7:32; 12:3; Eph. 4:5; 6:7; 1 Tim. 6:15; 2 Tim. 4:8; Jude 14; Rev. 4:11; 17:14.

JUDGMENT

Ps. 9:7. But the Lord abides forever; He has established His throne for judgment.

Eccl. 12:14. Because God will bring every act to judgment, everything which is hidden, whether it is good or evil.

Matt. 12:36. "And I say to you, that every careless word that men shall speak, they shall render account for it in the day of judgment."

1 Chron. 16:33; Ezek. 18:20; Dan. 7:9-10; Jer. 17:10; Matt. 12:36-37; 25:41; John 5:22; 12:48; Acts 10:42; Rom. 2:5-16; 14:10; 1 Cor. 3:13; 4:5; 2 Cor. 5:10; 2 Tim. 4:1, 8; 2 Peter 2:4, 9; 3:7-12; Rev. 6:15-17; 22:12.

KINDNESS

Lev. 19:34. " 'The stranger who resides with you shall be to you as the native among you, and you shall love him as yourself; for you were aliens in the land of Egypt: I am the Lord your God.' "

Matt. 5:42. "Give to him who asks of you, and do not turn away from him who wants to borrow from you."

Eph. 4:32. And be kind to one another, tenderhearted, forgiving each other, just as God in Christ also has forgiven you.

Deut. 22:1; Matt. 5:7; 25:34-36; Acts 20:35; Rom. 15:1-5; Heb. 5:2; 13:2; 1 Peter 4:8.

LAW

Ps. 1:1. How blessed is the man who does not walk in the counsel of the wicked, nor stand in the path of sinners, nor sit in the seat of scoffers! 2. But his delight is in the law of the Lord, and in His law he meditates day and night.

Matt. 5:17. "Do not think that I came to abolish the Law or the Prophets; I did not come to abolish, but to fulfill. 18. "For truly I say to you, until heaven and earth pass away, not the smallest letter or stroke shall pass away from the Law, until all is accomplished."

1 John 5:3. For this is the love of God, that we keep His commandments; and His commandments are not burdensome.

Ps. 19:7-8; 119:1-2; Prov. 28:4; Matt. 5:18-19; John 1:17; Rom. 8:3; Col. 2:14; Heb. 10:1.

LIFE, physical

Ps. 39:4. "Lord, make me to know my end, and what is the extent of my days, let me know how transient I am."

Ps. 103:14. For He Himself knows our frame; He is mindful that we are but dust. 15. As for man, his days are like grass; as a flower of the field, so he flourishes. 16. When the wind has passed over it, it is no more; and its place acknowledges it no longer.

1 Sam. 20:3; 2 Sam. 14:14; 1 Chron. 29:15; Job 8:9; Ps. 90:9-10; Luke 12:20.

LIFE, spiritual, eternal

Ps. 121:8. The Lord will guard your going out and your coming in from this time forth and forever.

John 5:24. "Truly, truly, I say to you, he who hears My word, and believes Him who sent Me, has eternal life, and does not come into judgment, but has passed out of death into life."

Rev. 22:17. And the Spirit and the bride say, "Come." And let the one who hears say, "Come." And let the one who is thirsty come; let the one who wishes take the water of life without cost.

Isa. 25:8; Dan. 12:2; John 1:4; 3:3; 11:25; 20:31; 1 John 2:25; 5:20; Rev. 22:1-5.

LOVE, by God

Deut. 7:7. "The Lord did not set His love on you nor choose you because you were more in number than any of the peoples, for you were the fewest of all peoples, 8. but because the Lord loved you and kept the oath which He swore to your forefathers, the Lord brought you out by a mighty hand, and redeemed you from the house of slavery, from the hand of Pharaoh king of Egypt."

Prov. 8:17. "I love those who love me; and those who diligently seek me will find me."

John 3:16. "For God so loved the world, that He gave His only begotten Son, that whoever believes in Him should not perish, but have eternal life."

Eph. 2:4. But God, being rich in mercy, because of His great love with which He loved us, 5. even when we were dead in our transgressions, made us alive together with Christ (by grace you have been saved).

1 John 3:1. See how great a love the Father has bestowed upon us, that we should be called children of God; and such we are. For this reason the world does not know us, because it did not know Him.

Deut. 10:15-18; 23:5; 33:3, 12; Ps. 42:8; 63:3; Jer. 31:3; John 14:21-23; 16:27; 17:10, 23, 26; Rom. 1:7; 5:8; 2 Thess. 2:16; Titus 3:4-5; Heb. 12:6; 1 John 4:8-19; Jude 21.

LOVE, for God

Deut. 6:5. "And you shall love the Lord your God with all your heart and with all your soul and with all your might."

Ps. 31:23. O love the Lord, all you His godly ones! The Lord preserves the faithful, and fully recompenses the proud doer.

1 Cor. 8:3. But if any one loves God, he is known by Him.

Ex. 20:6; Deut. 7:9; 10:12; Josh. 22:5; Ps. 18:1; 73:25-26; 91:14; Jer. 2:2; Mark 12:29-33; Luke 11:42; John 16:27; Rom. 5:5; 8:28; 1 Cor. 16:22; 2 Thess. 3:5; 2 Tim. 1:7; 1 John 3:17-18; 4:12, 16-21; 5:1-3; Jude 21.

LOVE, for others

Lev. 19:18. " 'You shall not take vengeance, nor bear any grudge against the sons of your people, but you shall love your neighbor as yourself; I am the Lord.' "

John 15:12. "This is My commandment, that you love one another, just as I have loved you."

Eph. 5:2. And walk in love, just as Christ also loved you, and gave Himself up for us, an offering and a sacrifice to God as a fragrant aroma.

Deut. 10:19; Ps. 133:1-3; Prov. 10:12; 15:17; 17:9, 17; John 13:14; Rom. 12:9-10; 13:8-10; Gal. 5:14; 1 Thess. 4:9; Heb. 13:1-2; 1 Peter 1:22; 2:17.

MARRIAGE

Gen. 2:24. For this cause a man shall leave his father and his mother, and shall cleave to his wife; and they shall become one flesh.

Mark 10:9. "What therefore God has joined together, let no man separate."

1 Cor. 7:1-40; 11:11; 1 Tim. 3:2; Heb. 13:4.

MORALITY

Ps. 24:3. Who may ascend into the hill of the Lord? And who may stand in His holy place? 4. He who has clean hands and a pure heart, who has not lifted up his soul to falsehood, and has not sworn deceitfully. 5. He shall receive a blessing from the Lord and righteousness from the God of his salvation.

Matt. 5:8. "Blessed are the pure in heart, for they shall see God."

2 Tim. 2:21. Therefore, if a man cleanses himself from these things, he will be a vessel for honor, sanctified, useful to the Master, prepared for every good work. 22. Now flee from youthful lusts, and pursue righteousness, faith, love and peace, with those who call on the Lord from a pure heart.

Ps. 19:8; 51:7; Prov. 20:9; 30:12; Isa. 1:18; Dan. 12:10; Phil. 4:8; 1 Tim. 1:5; 3:9; Jas. 4:8; 1 John 3:3.

OLD AGE

Gen. 15:15. "And as for you, you shall go to your fathers in peace; you shall be buried at a good old age."

1 Chron. 29:28. Then he died in a ripe old age, full of days, riches and honor; and his son Solomon reigned in his place.

Ps. 71:9. Do not cast me off in the time of old age; do not forsake me when my strength fails. 18. And even when I am old and gray, O God, do not forsake me, until I declare Thy strength to this generation, Thy power to all who are to come.

Isa. 46:4. Even to your old age, I shall be the same, and even to your graying years I shall bear

you! I have done it, and I shall carry you; and I shall bear you, and I shall deliver you.

Titus 2:2. Older men are to be temperate, dignified, sensible, sound in faith, in love, in perseverance. 3. Older women likewise are to be reverent in their behavior, not malicious gossips, nor enslaved to much wine, teaching what is good.

Gen. 47:9; Deut. 34:7; 2 Sam. 19:34-37; Job 11:17; 12:12; 32:4-9; Ps. 90:10; 92:14; 148:12; Prov. 16:31; Eccl. 6:3, 6; 12:1-7; Luke 2:37; Philem. 9.

PATIENCE

Ps. 37:7. Rest in the Lord and wait patiently for Him; fret not yourself because of him who prospers in his way, because of the man who carries out wicked schemes. 8. Cease from anger, and forsake wrath; fret not yourself, it leads only to evildoing.

Eccl. 7:8. The end of a matter is better than its beginning; patience of spirit is better than haughtiness of spirit. 9. Do not be eager in your heart to be angry, for anger resides in the bosom of fools.

Rom. 5:3. And not only this, but we also exult in our tribulations, knowing that tribulation brings about perseverance.

Heb. 10:36. For you have need of endurance, so that when you have done the will of God, you may receive what was promised.

Jas. 5:7. Be patient, therefore, brethren, until the coming of the Lord. Behold, the farmer waits for the precious produce of the soil, being patient about it, until it gets the early and late rains. 8. You too be patient; strengthen your hearts, for the coming of the Lord is at hand.

Prov. 15:8; Lam. 3:26-27; 21:19; Rom. 8:25; 12:12; 15:4; 1 Cor. 13:4; 2 Cor. 6:4-6; 12:12; Gal. 6:9; Eph. 4:1-2; Col. 1:10-11; 3:12-13; 1 Thess. 1:3; 2 Thess. 3:5; 1 Tim. 3:2-3; 6:11; 2 Tim. 2:24-25; Titus 2:1-2; Heb. 6:12, 15; 12:1; Jas. 1:3; 1 Peter 2:19-23; 2 Peter 1:5-6; Rev. 14:12.

PRAISE

Ps. 34:1. I will bless the Lord at all times; His praise shall continually be in my mouth.

Ps. 100:4. Enter His gates with thanksgiving, and His courts with praise. Give thanks to Him; bless His name.

2 Sam. 22:4; 1 Chron. 23:30; Job 36:24; Ps. 9:11; 28:7; 34:1-3; 43:3-4; 92:1; 95:1-7; 107:8; 148:2-4; Isa. 43:21; Luke 2:13-14; Rev. 4:8.

PRAYER

2 Chron. 7:14. If . . . My people who are called by My name humble themselves and pray, and seek My face and turn from their wicked ways, then I will hear from heaven, will forgive their sin, and will heal their land.

Ps. 145:18. The Lord is near to all who call upon Him, to all who call upon Him in truth.

1 Tim. 2:8. Therefore I want the men in every place to pray, lifting up holy hands, without wrath and dissension.

Deut. 4:7; Ps. 32:6; 34:15-17; 37:4; 91:15; Isa. 55:6; 65:24; Jer. 33:3; Matt. 6:6; 7:7-8; 21:22; John 14:13-14; 15:7; Rom. 8:26; Eph. 3:20; Heb. 4:16; 11:6; Jas. 5:17-18.

PRIDE

Ps. 101:5. Whoever secretly slanders his neighbor, him I will destroy; no one who has a haughty look and an arrogant heart will I endure.

1 Cor. 10:12. Therefore let him who thinks he stands take heed lest he fall.

Jas. 4:6. But He gives a greater grace. Therefore it says, "GOD IS OPPOSED TO THE PROUD, BUT GIVES GRACE TO THE HUMBLE."

1 Sam. 2:3-5; Ps. 10:2-11; 12:3-4; 57:7; 73:6-9; Prov. 8:13; 11:2; Jer. 9:23-24; Mal. 4:1; Matt. 23:6-12; Mark 12:38-39; Luke 1:51-52; Rom. 12:3, 16; 1 Cor. 1:29; 3:18; 4:6-10; 2 Cor. 10:5, 12, 18; Gal. 6:3; 1 Tim. 2:9; 2 Tim. 3:2; Rev. 3:17-18.

REPENTANCE

2 Chron. 7:14. If . . . My people who are called by My name humble themselves and pray, and seek My face and turn from their wicked ways, then I will hear from heaven, will forgive their sin, and will heal their land.

Prov. 28:13. He who conceals his transgressions will not prosper, but he who confesses and forsakes them will find compassion.

1 John 1:9. If we confess our sins, He is faithful and righteous to forgive us our sins and to cleanse us from all unrighteousness.

Neh. 1:9; Job 33:26-28; 34:31-32; Ps. 34:14, 18; 51:17; Isa. 55:6-7; Luke 5:32; 15:7; 24:47; Acts 3:19.

RESURRECTION

Job 19:25. "And as for me, I know that my Redeemer lives, and at the last He will take His stand on the earth. 26. "Even after my skin is destroyed, yet from my flesh I shall see God; 27. whom I myself shall behold, and whom my eyes shall see and not another. My heart faints within me."

Ps. 49:15. But God will redeem my soul from the power of Sheol; for He will receive me.

Luke 14:14. "And you will be blessed, since they do not have the means to repay you; for you will be repaid at the resurrection of the righteous."

John 11:23. Jesus said to her, "Your brother shall rise again." 24. Martha said to Him, "I know that he will rise again in the resurrection on the last day." 25. Jesus said to her, "I am the resurrection and the life; he who believes in Me shall live even if he dies."

1 Cor. 15:12. Now if Christ is preached, that He has been raised from the dead, how do some among you say that there is no resurrection of the dead? 13. But if there is no resurrection of the dead, not even Christ has been raised; 14. and if Christ has not been raised, then our preaching is vain, your faith also is vain.

2 Cor. 4:14. Knowing that He who raised the Lord Jesus will raise us also with Jesus and will present us with you.

Job 14:12-15; Ps. 16:9-10; Isa. 26:19; Ezek. 37:1-14; Dan. 12:2-3, 13; Hos. 13:14; Matt. 22:23-32; 24:31; 27:52; Luke 20:35-38; John 5:21-29; 6:39-40, 44, 54; 14:19; Acts 2:26-31; 4:1; 17:18, 32; 23:6-8; 24:14-15; Rom. 4:16-21; 8:10-23; 1 Cor. 6:14; 15:12-57; Phil. 3:10-11, 21; 1 Thess. 4:14-16; 2 Tim. 1:10; 2:18; Heb. 6:2; 11:19, 35; Rev. 1:18; 20:4-13.

REWARDS

Isa. 3:10. Say to the righteous that it will go well with them, for they will eat the fruit of their actions.

Rom. 2:10. But glory and honor and peace to every man who does good, to the Jew first and also to the Greek.

Rev. 22:12. "Behold, I am coming quickly, and My reward is with Me, to render to every man according to what he has done."

Ex. 20:12; Lev. 25:18-19; Deut. 4:40; Isa. 40:10; Matt. 10:32; Rev. 2:10.

RIGHTEOUSNESS

Gen. 15:6. Then he believed in the LORD; and He reckoned it to him as righteousness.

2 Chron. 16:9. "For the eyes of the LORD move to and fro throughout the earth that He may strongly support those whose heart is completely His. You have acted foolishly in this. Indeed, from now on you will surely have wars."

Matt. 5:6. "Blessed are those who hunger and thirst for righteousness, for they shall be satisfied."

Ps. 1:1-3; 24:3-5; Prov. 4:18; 2 Cor. 5:17; Eph. 3:17-19; Col. 1:12-13; 2 Tim. 2:22; 4:8.

SALVATION

Ex. 15:2. "The LORD is my strength and song, and He has become my salvation; this is my God, and I will praise Him; my father's God, and I will extol Him."

Acts 4:12. "And there is salvation in no one else; for there is no other name under heaven that has been given among men, by which we must be saved."

Eph. 2:8. For by grace you have been saved through faith; and that not of yourselves, it is the gift of God.

Ps. 46:4; Isa. 1:18; Matt. 18:3; Luke 19:10; John 3:14-17; 5:24; 6:44, 47; Rom. 5:1-2; 11:6; 1 Cor. 1:21; Eph. 2:1-9; Col. 1:19-20.

SATAN

John 8:44. "You are of your father the devil, and you want to do the desires of your father. He was a murderer from the beginning, and does not stand in the truth, because there is no truth in him. Whenever he speaks a lie, he speaks from his own nature; for he is a liar, and the father of lies."

Eph. 6:11. Put on the full armor of God, that you may be able to stand firm against the schemes of the devil. 12. For our struggle is not against flesh and blood, but against the rulers, against the powers, against the world forces of this darkness, against the spiritual *forces* of wickedness in the heavenly *places.*

Gen. 3:1-5; 1 Chron. 21:1; Job 1:6-7ff.; Isa. 14:12; Ezek. 28:12-15; Zech. 3:1-2; Matt. 12:24; 13:19, 38; John 12:31; 14:30; 16:11; Rom. 16:20; 2 Cor. 4:4; Eph. 2:2; 4:27; 1 Thess. 3:5; 1 Peter 5:8; Rev. 9:11; 12:10.

SELFISHNESS

Prov. 28:27. He who gives to the poor will never want, but he who shuts his eyes will have many curses.

1 Cor. 10:24. Let no one seek his own *good,* but that of his neighbor.

Phil. 2:4. Do not *merely* look out for your own personal interests, but also for the interests of others. 20. For I have no one *else* of kindred spirit who will genuinely be concerned for your welfare. 21. For they all seek after their own interests, not those of Christ Jesus.

1 John 3:17. But whoever has the world's goods, and beholds his brother in need and closes his heart against him, how does the love of God abide in him?

Prov. 11:26; 18:17; 24:11-12; Ezek. 34:18; Mic. 3:11; Hag. 1:4-10; Mal. 1:10; Matt. 19:21-22; Rom. 14:15; 15:1-2; 2 Cor. 5:15; Gal. 6:2; 2 Tim. 3:2-4; Jas. 2:15-16.

SEX

Gen. 2:24. For this cause a man shall leave his father and his mother, and shall cleave to his wife; and they shall become one flesh. 25. And the man and his wife were both naked and were not ashamed.

Matt. 5:27. "You have heard that it was said, 'YOU SHALL NOT COMMIT ADULTERY'; 28. but I say to you, that every one who looks on a woman to lust for her has committed adultery with her already in his heart."

1 Cor. 7:2. But because of immoralities, let each man have his own wife, and let each woman have her own husband. 3. Let the husband fulfill his duty to his wife, and likewise also the wife to her husband. 4. The wife does not have authority over her own body, but the husband *does;* and likewise also the husband does not have authority over his own body, but the wife *does.* 5. Stop depriving one another, except by agreement for a time that you may devote yourselves to prayer, and come together again lest Satan tempt you because of your lack of self-control.

Prov. 2:16-19; 6:25-33; Mark 7:21; John 8:10-11; Rom. 13:13; 1 Cor. 7:1-36; 9:27; Heb. 13:4.

SIN

Ps. 51:2. Wash me thoroughly from my iniquity, and cleanse me from my sin. 3. For I know my transgressions, and my sin is ever before me. 4. Against Thee, Thee only, I have sinned, and done what is evil in Thy sight, so that Thou art justified when Thou dost speak, and blameless when Thou dost judge.

Isa. 1:18. "Come now, and let us reason together," says the LORD, "though your sins are as scarlet, they will be as white as snow; though they are red like crimson, they will be like wool."

Rom. 5:12. Therefore, just as through one man sin entered into the world, and death through sin, and so death spread to all men, because all sinned—

Job 9:20; Ps. 38:3-4; 40:11; 103:12; Isa. 6:5; 59:1; Jer. 17:9; Matt. 1:21; 26:28; Gal. 6:7-8; Heb. 9:22; 1 John 2:1-12.

SUFFERING

Ps. 34:19. Many are the afflictions of the righteous; but the LORD delivers him out of them all.

Eccl. 7:14. In the day of prosperity be happy, but in the day of adversity consider—God has made the one as well as the other so that man may not discover anything *that will be* after him.

Phil. 1:29. For to you it has been granted for Christ's sake, not only to believe in Him, but also to suffer for His sake.

Gen. 35:3; 1 Kings 1:29; Job 5:7; Ps. 9:9; 27:5; 46:1; John 14:1, 27; Rom. 8:17, 35; 1 Cor. 12:26; 2 Cor. 1:7; 4:8; 6:4; Phil. 3:8-10; Heb. 5:8; 11:25; Jas. 5:13; 1 Peter 2:21; 3:14; 5:10; Rev. 2:10.

TEMPTATION

Prov. 1:10. My son, if sinners entice you, do not consent.

1 Cor. 10:13. No temptation has overtaken you but such as is common to man; and God is faithful, who will not allow you to be tempted beyond what you are able, but with the temptation will provide the way of escape also, that you may be able to endure it.

2 Peter 2:9. The Lord knows how to rescue the godly from temptation, and to keep the unrighteous under punishment for the day of judgment.

Gen. 3:1-6; Matt. 6:13; 26:41; Luke 8:13; Gal. 4:14; 1 Tim. 6:9; Jas. 1:2, 12; 1 Peter 1:6; 5:8-9; Rev. 3:10.

TRUTH

Ps. 51:6. Behold, Thou dost desire truth in the innermost being, and in the hidden part Thou wilt make me know wisdom.

John 14:6. Jesus said to him, "I am the way, and the truth, and the life; no one comes to the Father, but through Me."

John 16:13. "But when He, the Spirit of truth, comes, He will guide you into all the truth; for He will not speak on His own initiative, but whatever He hears, He will speak; and He will disclose to you what is to come."

1 Kings 17:24; Ps. 25:5; 43:3; 100:5; 119:30; John 1:17; 8:44; 14:17; 17:17; 2 Cor. 6:7; Eph. 4:15; 6:14; 2 Tim. 2:15; 1 John 3:19; 3 John 4, 8.

WORD OF GOD

Ps. 33:4. For the word of the LORD is upright; and all His work is *done* in faithfulness. 6. By the word of the LORD the heavens were made, and by the breath of His mouth all their host.

Jer. 22:29. "O land, land, land, hear the word of the Lord!"

John 1:14. And the Word became flesh, and dwelt among us, and we beheld His glory, glory as of the only begotten from the Father, full of grace and truth.

Deut. 30:11-14; Josh. 1:8; Ps. 19:7; 107:20; Dan. 10:21; Matt. 22:29; Luke 1:37; 11:28; 24:45; John 2:22; 10:35; Rom. 1:2; 1 Cor. 15:3-4; Gal. 3:8; Col. 3:16; 2 Tim. 3:15-16; 1 Peter 2:2-3; 2 Peter 1:20; 3:16; Rev. 22:18-19.

WORLDLINESS

John 12:43. For they loved the approval of men rather than the approval of God.

Rom. 12:2. And do not be conformed to this world, but be transformed by the renewing of your mind, that you may prove what the will of God is, that which is good and acceptable and perfect.

1 John 2:15. Do not love the world, nor the things in the world. If any one loves the world, the love of the Father is not in him.

1 Sam. 8:19-20; Job 21:11-15; Prov. 14:12; Matt. 10:39; 16:26; Luke 12:19; John 5:44; 15:19; Col. 3:2; 1 Tim. 5:6; Jas. 4:4; 1 Peter 2:11; 1 John 2:15-17.

WORSHIP

Ps. 29:2. Ascribe to the Lord the glory due to His name; worship the Lord in holy array.

Ps. 95:6. Come, let us worship and bow down; let us kneel before the Lord our Maker.

Phil. 2:10. That at the name of Jesus every knee should bow, of those who are in heaven, and on earth, and under the earth, 11. and that every tongue should confess that Jesus Christ is Lord, to the glory of God the Father.

Ex. 20:3; Deut. 16:11, 14; 2 Kings 17:36; 1 Chron. 16:29; Ps. 22:22; 24:3-6; 66:4, 13-14; Isa. 12:5-6; 49:13; Matt. 18:20; Luke 4:8; 24:52; John 4:23-24; 1 Tim. 2:8; Heb. 10:25; 1 Peter 2:5; Rev. 4:11; 14:6-7; 15:4.

INDEX TO PRINCIPAL SUBJECTS IN THE NOTES

High places, 1 Sam. 9:12; 1 Kings 3:2; Hos. 10:8
Hillel, Matt. 19:3
Hinnom, Jer. 7:31; 31:40
Hiram, 1 Kings 5:1; 9:10-14
Hittites, Gen. 23:3; Judg. 1:26; Ezek. 16:3
Hivites, Josh. 9:7
Holy, Ps. 99:3
Holy Spirit, Gen. 6:3; Judg. 3:10; 1 Sam. 16:14;
    Ps. 51:11; Ezek. 37:11-14; Matt. 12:31; Luke
    3:16; 11:13; John 3:5; 7:39; 14:16; 15:26;
    16:8-11, 15; 20:22; Acts 1:5; 4:31; 10:44;
    19:2; Rom. 8:26; 2 Cor. 3:17; Gal. 4:6; Eph.
    1:13; 5:18; 2 Thess. 2:7, 13; Tit. 3:5; 1 John
    2:20; Rev. 1:4
Homosexuality, Lev. 18:22; Deut. 23:17-18
Horeb, Exod. 3:1
Horn, 1 Sam. 2:1; Ps. 132:11-18
Hosanna, Matt. 21:9
Hosea, Introduction to Hosea
Humility, Matt. 18:4
Hymenaeus, 1 Tim. 1:20; 2 Tim. 2:17
Hyssop, Exod. 12:22

Ichabod, 1 Sam. 4:21
Idolatry, Isa. 1:29; 17:8; 30:33; Jer. 10:1-16
Idumea, Mark 3:8
Illyricum, Rom. 15:19
Image of God, Gen. 1:26; 5:3; 9:5-6; Jas. 3:9
Images, Gen. 31:19
Imprecatory Psalms, Introduction to Psalms
Infant salvation, 2 Sam. 12:23
Isaac, Gen. 17:19; 21:9
Isaiah, 2 Kings 21:16; Introduction to Isaiah
Ishmael, Gen. 16:11; 25:9

Jacob, Gen. 25:26; 49:1
James, Matt. 4:21; see also Matt. 26:37; Mark
    6:3; Acts 12:2; 15:13
Jannes and Jambres, 2 Tim. 3:8
Jason, Acts 17:9
Jeconiah, Jer. 22:30; Matt. 1:11
Jehoiachin, 2 Kings 25:27-30
Jehoiakim, 2 Kings 23:35; Dan. 1:1
Jehoshaphat, 1 Kings 22:41-50
    valley of, Joel 3:2-3, 14
Jehu, 2 Kings 10:1-11
Jeremiah, Introduction to Jeremiah, Matt. 16:14;
    27:9
Jericho, see various notes on Josh. 6; Luke 10:30
Jeroboam I, 1 Kings 12:29; 14:11-13
Jeroboam II, Hos. 1:1; Introduction to Amos,
    Introduction to Jonah
Jerusalem, Josh. 15:63; Judg. 1:8; 19:10; 1 Sam.
    17:54; 2 Sam. 5:7; Isa. 29:1; Heb. 12:18-24;
    Rev. 21:2
Jesus Christ, see Christ
Jethro, Exod. 2:18
Jezebel, 1 Kings 16:29-31; 21:10; Rev. 2:20
Jezreel, Hos. 1:4, 10-11; 2:22-23
Joash of Israel, 2 Kings 13:10-13
    of Judah, 2 Kings 11:2; 12:20
Job, Job 1:1; 2:7; Jas. 5:11
Joel, Introduction to Joel
John, Matt. 26:37; Mark 1:21; John 13:23; 18:15
John the Baptist, Matt. 11:11; 17:11-12; Luke
    7:24-25; John 1:6

Jonah, Introduction to Jonah, Matt. 12:39; Luke
    11:30
Joseph, Gen. 37:3; 45:5-8
Joseph, Matt. 1:19; Luke 3:23
Joshua (Moses' successor), Num. 13:16;
    Introduction to Joshua; Heb. 4:8
Joshua (the High Priest), Introduction to
    Haggai; Introduction to Zechariah
Josiah, 2 Kings 23:16
Jot and tittle, Matt. 5:18
Jotham, Isa. 1:1; Introduction to Micah
Jubilee, year of, Lev. 25:8-12
Judges, Judg. 2:16
Judgment, Eccl. 3:19-22; 12:14; John 3:16;
    5:21-27; 12:31; Heb. 4:13
    of angels, 1 Cor. 6:2
    of Christians, 1 Cor. 3:15; 9:27; 2 Cor. 5:10;
        1 John 4:17
    of Gentiles, Matt. 25:32
    of Israel, Ezek. 20:33-44
    of unbelievers, Rev. 20:11-15
Judicial procedures, Deut. 17:6-7; 19:15-21
Justification, Rom. 3:24; 4:25; Gal. 2:16; Jas. 2:21

Kadesh-barnea, Num. 14:22
Kenites, Judg. 1:16; 1 Sam. 15:6
Keturah, Gen. 25:1
Keys of the kingdom, Matt. 16:19
Kidron, John 18:1
King, of Israel, Luke 23:2; John 1:49; 6:15
    of the North, Joel 2:1-11
    requirements for, Deut. 17:15-20; 1 Sam.
        8:10-18, 22; Eccl. 8:6-8
Kingdom, Matt. 16:28; Mark 11:10; Acts 1:6;
    Col. 1:13
    gospel of, Matt. 4:23; 24:14
    of God, Mark 1:15; 10:14
    of heaven, Matt. 3:2
Kinsman-redeemer, Ruth 3:9
Kiss, holy, 1 Pet. 5:14
Kohathites, 1 Chron. 6:33
Korah, Num. 16:1-3

Lamb, Exod. 12:11; John 1:29
Land of Israel, Ezek. 47:13-20
Latter days, Deut. 4:27-31; Dan. 10:14
Laver, 1 Kings 7:23-26
Law, Deut. 4:8; 2 Kings 22:8; Matt. 15:2; John
    10:34; Rom. 3:31; 7:9; 1 Cor. 9:20; 2 Cor.
    3:6; Gal. 3:11; Col. 2:14; 1 Tim. 1:8;
    Heb. 2:2; 7:11
Lawyer, Matt. 22:35
Laying on of hands, Lev. 1:4; Acts 6:6
Leaven, Exod. 23:18-19; Matt. 13:33; Mark 8:15;
    1 Cor. 5:7
Legions, Matt. 26:53
Leprosy, Lev. 13:2; 2 Kings 7:3-4; Matt. 8:2;
    Luke 5:12
Levi, Luke 5:27
Leviathan, Job 3:8; 41:1; Ps. 104:26
Levites, Num. 3:12; 4:3; 18:2-7; 35:2; Josh. 21:2;
    Ezek. 44:20; 48:31-34; Mal. 2:8-9
Lex talionis, Lev. 24:20; Matt. 5:38
Libya, Ezek. 38:5-6
Light, John 8:12
Loans, Exod. 22:25-27

The New American Standard

CONCORDANCE

to the

Old and New Testaments

A collection of the principal common words with their most widely used examples in text and lesser usages in reference. Related words, or synonyms follow the key word. The key word is abbreviated in the text to its first letter, e.g., "abide" is "a". Variants add suffixes or prefixes, e.g., "abiding" appears as "a-ing".

A

ABANDON—*leave* Judg. 6:13, LORD has **a-ed** us
1 Sam. 12:22; Ps. 94:14, LORD ... **a** His people
2 Kin. 21:14, I will **a** the remnant
Ps. 27:9, Do not **a** me nor forsake me
Jer. 23:33, I shall **a** you
Acts 2:27, Thou wilt not **a** my soul to
   27:20, hope of our being saved ... **a-ed**
Ps. 16:10; Prov. 17:14; Is. 2:6; Jer. 12:7;
   Ezek. 29:5
ABASE—*humble* Ezek. 21:26; Mal. 2:9
ABATE—*decrease* Gen. 8:8,11, water was **a-d**
Deut. 34:7, his vigor **a-d**
ABBA Mark 14:36, saying, **A!** Father
Rom. 8:15, by which we cry out, **A!** Father
Gal. 4:6, crying, **A!** Father
ABHOR—*despise, detest, loathe*
Rom. 12:9, **A** what is evil
Deut. 7:26; Job 19:19; Ps. 78:59; Prov. 24:24;
   Is. 49:7
ABIDE—*remain, stay* Ps. 9:7, the LORD **a-s**
   forever
Ps. 15:1, who may **a** in Thy tent
   91:1, Will **a** in the shadow
   102:12, LORD, dost **a** forever
John 3:36, wrath of God **a-s** on him
   5:38, His word **a-ing** in you
   8:31, you **a** in My word
   14:25, while **a-ing** with you
   15:4, **A** in Me ... it **a-s** in the vine ... you **a** in
    Me
   15:6, If anyone does not **a** in Me
   15:7, **a** in Me, and My words **a** in you
   15:9, **a** in My love
   15:10, you will **a** in My love ... **a** in His love
1 Cor. 13:13, But now **a** faith, hope, love
Heb. 10:34, a better possession and an **a-ing**
   one
1 Pet. 1:23, living and **a-ing** word of God
   1:25, BUT THE WORD OF THE LORD **A-S** FOREVER
1 John 3:17, how does the love of God **a** in him
   4:12, God **a-s** in us
ABILITY—*strength* Ezra 2:69, according to ... **a**
Dan. 1:4, who had **a** for serving
Matt. 25:15, according to his own **a**
ABLE—*adequate* 1 Sam. 6:20, Who is **a** to stand
Matt. 3:9, God is **a** from these stones
   9:28, believe that I am **a** to do this
   10:28, fear Him who is **a** to destroy
   20:22, Are you **a** to drink the cup
John 10:29, no one is **a** to snatch them
Acts 6:10, they were **un-a** to cope with the
   wisdom

Rom. 8:39, shall be **a** to separate us
1 Cor. 10:13, tempted beyond what you are **a**
Eph. 3:18, may be **a** to comprehend
2 Tim. 2:2, who will be **a** to teach
James 4:12, the One who is **a** to save
Jude 24, Now to Him who is **a** to keep
1 Kin. 3:9; 2 Chr. 2:6; Rev. 5:3; 6:17
ABOARD Acts 21:2, went **a** and set sail
ABODE—*habitation* Jer. 31:23; Jude 6
John 14:23, and make Our **a** with him
ABOLISH—*destroy* Matt. 5:17, I did not come
   to **a**
Eph. 2:15, by **a-ing** in His flesh
2 Tim. 1:10, Christ Jesus, who **a-ed** death
ABOMINABLE—*detestable, rejected*
Jer. 44:4, do not do this **a** thing
Ezek. 16:25, made your beauty **a**
1 Pet. 4:3, drinking parties and **a** idolatries
Ps. 14:1; 53:1; Rev. 21:8
ABOMINATION—*detestable thing*
Ex. 8:26, an **a** to the Egyptians
Prov. 3:32, an **a** to the LORD
   8:7, an **a** to my lips
Ezek. 33:29, because of all their **a-s**
Dan. 12:11, the **a** of desolation
Rev. 17:5, the **a-s** of the earth
Lev. 18:26; Deut. 7:26; 29:17
ABOUND—*excel, multiply*
Ex. 34:6, **a-ing** in lovingkindness and truth
Prov. 28:20, a faithful man will **a** with blessings
Dan. 4:1, May your peace **a**
Rom. 15:13, that you may **a** in hope
1 Cor. 15:58, always **a-ing** in the work of the
1 Cor. 14:12; 2 Cor. 7:15; 9:8
ABOVE—*over* Ex. 20:4, what is in heaven **a** or on
Ps. 8:1, Thy splendor **a** the heavens
Matt. 10:24, A disciple is not **a** his teacher
John 3:31, He who comes from **a** is **a** all
   8:23, I am from **a**
Phil. 2:9, the name which is **a** every name
Col. 3:1; 2 Thess. 2:4; James 1:17
ABSENT Gen. 31:49, we are **a** one from the other
1 Cor. 5:3, though **a** in body, but present
2 Cor. 5:6, we are **a** from the Lord
   5:8, **a** from the body and to be
   10:1, but bold toward you when **a**
ABSTAIN—*depart, separate* Num. 6:3
Acts 15:20, that they **a** from things
1 Thess. 5:22, **a** from every form of evil
1 Tim. 4:3, **a-ing** from foods, which
2 Tim. 2:19, who names ... the Lord **a** from
   wickedness
1 Pet. 2:11, strangers to **a** from fleshly lusts

ABUNDANCE—*surplus, plenty, full, plenteous*
  Gen. 41:34, seven years of **a**
  Ps. 52:7, the **a** of his riches
    72:7, And **a** of peace till
  Is. 55:2, delight yourself in **a**
  Matt. 13:12, and he shall have an **a**
  Luke 12:15, when one has an **a** does his life
  Rom. 5:17, receive the **a** of grace
  Phil. 4:18, everything in full, and have an **a**
  Gen. 41:29; Deut. 28:47; Neh. 9:25; Ps. 36:8;
    72:16; 73:10; Prov. 24:6; Eccles. 5:10;
    Phil. 4:12
ABUNDANT—*plenteous* Job 36:28; Ezek. 16:49
  Gen. 41:47, land brought forth **a-ly**
  Ps. 86:5, **a** in lovingkindness to all
  2 Cor. 1:5, our comfort is **a** through Christ
ABUSE Judg. 19:25, **a-d** her all night
  1 Chr. 10:4, lest these ... come and **a** me
  Matt. 27:39, passing by were hurling **a** at Him
ABUSIVE—*filthy* Col. 3:8, **a** speech from your
  mouth
ABYSS—*deep, depth* Rom. 10:7, DESCEND INTO
  THE **A**
  Rev. 20:3, threw him into the **a**
  Luke 8:31; Rev. 11:7; 17:8; 20:1
ACCEPT—*receive* Deut. 33:11, And **a** the work
  Job 2:10, **a** good from God and not **a** adversity
  Jer. 2:30, They **a-ed** no chastening
  Mark 4:20, hear the word and **a** it
  Rom. 15:7, **a** one another
  1 Tim. 1:15, statement, deserving full **a-ance**
ACCEPTABLE—*favorable, pleasing* Ps. 69:13, at
  an **a** time
  Rom. 15:31, may prove **a** to the saints
  2 Cor. 6:2, At the **a** time ... the **a** time
  Phil. 4:18, an **a** sacrifice
  1 Tim. 2:3, good and **a** in the sight
ACCESS Eph. 2:18, have our **a** in one Spirit
  Eph. 3:12, confident **a** through faith in Him
ACCOMPLISH—*perform* 1 Kin. 5:9, you shall **a**
  my desire
  Ps. 57:2, God who **a-es** *all things*
  John 4:34, and to **a** His work
  James 5:16, prayer of a righteous man can **a**
ACCOMPLISHED—*realized, wrought*
  Neh. 6:16, work had been **a** ... God
  Luke 1:1, things **a** among us
  John 17:4, having **a** the work
  Rom. 15:18, what Christ has **a** through me
  James 1:15, when sin is **a**
  Luke 12:50; John 19:28; 1 Pet. 5:9
ACCORD—*unite* Josh. 9:2; Acts 5:12
  Acts 4:24, voices to God with one **a**
    8:6, the multitudes with one **a**
    12:20, one **a** they came to him
    18:12, one **a** rose up against Paul
    19:29, rushed with one **a** into the
  2 Cor. 8:17, gone to you of his own **a**
ACCORDING Gen. 30:34, be **a** to your word
  Matt. 16:27; Rom. 2:6, **a** to his deeds
  Rom. 8:28, **a** to *His* purpose
  Gal. 3:29, heirs **a** to promise
  Rev. 22:12, render to every man **a**
  Job 34:11; Jer. 17:10; John 7:24; 18:31;
    Rom. 12:6; 16:25; 2 Cor. 8:12
ACCOUNT—*declaration, sake, tell*
  Gen. 2:4, is the **a** of the heavens and the earth
    8:21, curse the ground on **a** of man
  Esth. 10:2, full **a** of the greatness of Mordecai
  1 Sam. 12:22, on **a** of His great name
  Matt. 5:11, evil ... falsely on **a** of Me
  Luke 1:1, compile an **a** of the things
    accomplished
  Rom. 3:19, become **a-able** to God
  Num. 12:11; Judg. 7:15
ACCUMULATE—*heap* 2 Tim. 4:3, **a** for
  themselves teachers
ACCURATE Job 31:6; Acts 18:25
ACCURSED Is. 65:20; Matt. 25:41
  Josh. 6:18, make the camp of Israel **a**

Rom. 9:3, wish that I myself were **a**
1 Cor. 12:3, no one ... says, Jesus is **a**
Gal. 1:8, let him be **a**
ACCUSATION—*charge* Ezra 4:6, wrote an **a**
  against
  Dan. 6:4, find no ground of **a** or
  John 18:29, What **a** do you bring against
  Acts 28:19, had any **a** against my nation
  1 Tim. 5:19, Do not receive an **a** against
ACCUSE—*testify* Matt. 27:12, while He was
  being **a-d**
  John 5:45, I will **a** you before the Father
  Acts 22:30, why he had been **a-d** by the Jews
  Deut. 19:18; Titus 1:6
ACKNOWLEDGE—*confess* Ps. 32:5, I **a-d** my sin
  Prov. 3:6, In all your ways **a** Him
  Acts 23:8, Pharisees **a** them all
  Rom. 1:28, see fit to **a** God
ACQUAINT Ps. 139:3, **a-ed** with all my ways
  Is. 53:3, **a-ed** with grief
ACQUAINTANCE Ps. 88:8, removed my **a-s** far
  from me
  Luke 23:49, all His **a-s** and the women
  Job 19:13; Ps. 31:11; 88:18; Luke 2:44
ACQUIRE—*get, purchase* Ruth 4:10; Prov. 1:5;
  18:15
  Prov. 4:5, **A** wisdom! **A** understanding
    4:7, with all your **a-ing**, get understanding
  Matt. 10:9, Do not **a** gold, or silver
ACQUIT—*cleanse* Job 10:14; Ps. 19:12
ACT—*behave* Ps. 103:7, made known His ... **a** to
  the
  1 Cor. 16:13, **a** like men, be strong
  John 8:4; 1 Cor. 13:5
  A-s of Solomon, 1 Kin. 11:41

Jeroboam,	14:19
Rehoboam,	14:29
Abijam,	15:7
Asa,	15:23
Nadab,	15:31
Baasha,	16:5
Elah,	16:14
Zimri,	16:20
Omri,	16:27
Ahab,	22:39
Jehoshaphat,	22:45
Ahaziah, 2 Kin.	1:18
Joram,	8:23
Jehu,	10:34
Joash,	12:19
Jehoahaz,	13:8
Joash,	13:12
Jehoash,	14:15
Amaziah,	14:18
Jeroboam,	14:28
Azariah,	15:6
Zechariah,	15:11
Shallum,	15:15
Menahem,	15:21
Pekahiah,	15:26
Pekah,	15:31
Jotham,	15:36
Ahaz,	16:19
Hezekiah,	20:20
Manasseh,	21:17
Amon,	21:25
Josiah,	23:28
Jehoiakim,	24:5
David, 1 Chr.	29:29
Uzziah, 2 Chr.	26:22

ACTION—*deed, work* Acts 5:38, plan or **a** should
  be of men
  1 Sam. 2:3; Dan. 11:28,32; Luke 23:51
ACTIVITY Eccles. 11:5, you do not know the **a** of
  God
  2 Thess. 2:9, accord with the **a** of Satan
ADDER—*serpent, viper* Is. 59:5, They hatch **a-s**

ADJURE—*implore* 1 Kin. 22:16, many times
    must I **a**
  Matt. 26:63, I **a** You by the living God
  Acts 19:13, I **a** you by Jesus
ADMINISTRATION 1 Cor. 12:28, **a-s** ... kinds of
    tongues
  2 Cor. 8:20, in our **a** of this
  Eph. 1:10, an **a** suitable to the fulness of the
    times
    3:9, **a** of the mystery
ADMONISH—*warn* Acts 20:31, cease to **a** each
    one
  Acts 27:9, Paul *began* to **a** them
  Rom. 15:14, able also to **a** one another
  1 Cor. 4:14, to **a** you as my ... children
  Col. 1:28, **a-ing** every man
    3:16, **a-ing** one another with psalms
  1 Thess. 5:14, **a** the unruly
  2 Thess. 3:15, **a** him as a brother
ADOPTION Rom. 8:15, spirit of **a** as sons
  Rom. 8:23, waiting eagerly for *our* **a** as sons
    9:4, to whom belong the **a**
  Gal. 4:5, receive the **a** as sons
  Eph. 1:5, predestined us to **a**
ADORN—*clothe, array* 1 Tim. 2:9, women to **a**
    themselves
  1 Pet. 3:3, let not your **a-ment**
  Rev. 21:2, as a bride **a-ed** for her husband
  Job 40:10; Is. 61:10; Ezek. 16:11; Matt. 23:29;
    Luke 21:5; Rev. 17:4; 18:16; 21:19
ADULTERATING 2 Cor. 4:2, not ... **a** the word of
    God
ADULTERER Lev. 20:10; Ps. 50:18; Heb. 13:4
ADULTERESS—*strange woman* Prov. 22:14,
    mouth of an **a**
ADULTERY Ex. 20:14; Deut. 5:18; Matt. 5:27, 28;
    Luke 18:20; James 2:11; 2 Pet. 2:14
ADVANCE Gen. 24:1; Luke 1:7
ADVANTAGE—*profit* Prov. 21:5; 2 Cor. 2:11
  Eccles. 1:3, What **a** does man have in all his
    work
    7:12, the **a** of knowledge
  John 16:7, to your **a** that I go away
  2 Cor. 12:17, I have not taken **a** of you
ADVERSARY—*opponent, foe*
  1 Cor. 16:9, and there are many **a-es**
  Heb. 10:27, which will consume the **a-es**
  1 Pet. 5:8, Your **a**, the devil
  Ex. 23:22; 1 Kin. 11:14; Ps. 27:2; 89:23
ADVERSITY—*distress, privation* Deut. 30:15;
    Job 2:10
  Ps. 10:6, I shall not be in **a**
    94:13, relief from the days of **a**
  Prov. 17:17, is born for **a**
ADVISE—*inform, counsel* Num. 24:14; Rev. 3:18
ADVOCATE—*witness* Job 16:19, my **a** is on high
  1 John 2:1, we have an **A** with the Father
AFFAIRS 1 Chr. 26:32, all the **a** of God and ... the
    king
  2 Tim. 2:4, entangles himself in the **a**
AFFECTION—*devotion, passion*
  2 Cor. 6:12, restrained in your own **a-s**
    7:15, his **a** abounds
  Deut. 10:15; Phil. 1:8; 2:1; 1 Thess. 2:8
AFFLICT—*oppress, distress, trouble*
  Deut. 26:6, Egyptians ... **a-ed** us
  Judg. 16:5, we may bind him to **a** him
  Ps. 82:3, justice to the **a-ed** and destitute
    147:6, LORD supports the **a-ed**
  Is. 61:1, bring good news to the **a-ed**
    63:9, He was **a-ed**
  Lam. 3:33, does not **a** willingly
  2 Cor. 4:8, *we are* **a-ed** in every way
  Ex. 1:11,12; 22:22,23; Num. 24:24; 2 Sam. 7:10;
    1 Kin. 11:39; 2 Kin. 17:20; Ps. 105:18;
    Prov. 15:15; Nah. 1:12
AFFLICTION—*misery, oppression*
  Deut. 16:3, the bread of **a**
  Job 36:15, delivers the afflicted in their **a**
  Ps. 25:18, Look upon my **a**
  Mark 4:17, when **a** or persecution arises
    5:29, she was healed of her **a**

2 Cor. 2:4, out of much **a** and anguish
    8:2, in a great ordeal of **a**
  2 Thess. 1:6, **a** those who afflict you
  Gen. 29:32; 31:42; 41:52; Job 5:6; 30:16; Eccles.
    6:2; Acts 20:23
AFRAID—*dread, fear* Ex. 3:6, **a** to look at God
  Deut. 20:8, Who is the man that is **a**
  Ps. 56:4, not be **a**. What can *mere* man
    91:5, **a** of the terror by night
  Is. 51:12, are **a** of man who dies
  Matt. 14:27, do not be **a**
    21:46, they became **a** of the multitudes
  Luke 9:34, they were **a** as they entered
    12:4, **a** of those who kill the body
  Gen. 3:10; Ex. 20:20; Josh. 11:6; Judg. 7:3;
    Job 3:25; 19:29; Prov. 31:21; Eccles. 9:2;
    Matt. 1:20; Mark 4:41; 5:36; 9:32; 11:18;
    11:32; Luke 12:32; 19:21; John 9:22; 2 Cor.
    11:3; 12:20; Heb. 13:6
AFTER Acts 13:22, a man **a** My heart
  Acts 24:17, **a** several years I came
  Gal. 2:1, **a** an interval
  Gen. 7:4; Judg. 16:22; Dan. 2:39
AFTERWARD—*later, after* Gen. 38:30, And **a** his
    brother came
  Matt. 21:30, he **a** regretted *it*
  Mark 16:14, And **a** He appeared
AGAINST Gen. 16:12, hand *will be* **a** everyone
  Lev. 20:3, set My face **a** that man
  Matt. 12:30, not with Me is **a** Me
  Gal. 5:23, **a** such things there is no law
  Rev. 2:4, have *this* **a** you
  Gen. 4:8; Job 16:4; Luke 4:11; Acts 19:38;
    1 Pet. 3:12
AGE—*world, generations, elder*
  1 Chr. 23:1, Now when David reached old **a**
  Job 12:12, Wisdom is with **a-d** men
  Matt. 12:32, this **a**, or in the **a** to come
  Luke 16:8, sons of this **a** are more shrewd
  John 9:21, he is of **a**, he shall speak
  Eph. 2:7, that in the **a-s** to come
  Col. 1:26, hidden from the *past* **a-s**
  Heb. 6:5, powers of the **a** to come
  Job 15:10; 32:7; Jer. 6:11; John 9:23; Philem. 9
AGITATION Ps. 38:8, the **a** of my heart
AGONY Luke 22:44, being in **a** He was praying
  Acts 2:24, putting an end to the **a** of death
AGREE—*consent* Matt. 18:19, if two of you **a** on
    earth
  John 9:22, Jews had already **a-d**
  Acts 5:9, Why is it that you have **a-d** together
    15:15, words of the Prophets **a**
    28:25, when they did not **a** with one another
  Matt. 20:13; Acts 23:20; 1 Tim. 6:3
AGREEMENT Acts 8:1, Saul was in hearty **a**
  2 Cor. 6:16, what **a** has the temple
  1 John 5:8, the three are in **a**
AILMENT—*infirmity* 1 Tim. 5:23, and your
    frequent **a-s**
AIR 1 Cor. 9:26, not beating the **a**
  Eph. 2:2, prince of the power of the **a**
  1 Thess. 4:17, meet the Lord in the **a**
  Job 41:16; 1 Cor. 14:9
ALARM Jer. 4:19, The **a** of war
  Num. 10:5,6,7,9; Ps. 31:22; 116:11; Joel 2:1
ALAS—*woe* 2 Kin. 6:5, A, my master! For it was
  Judg. 6:22; 11:35; Amos 5:16
ALERT—*watch* Matt. 24:42; Acts 20:31, be on
    the **a**
  1 Cor. 16:13, Be on the **a**, stand firm
  1 Thess. 5:6, let us be **a** and sober
ALIEN—*stranger, foreigner*
  Deut. 10:19, show your love for the **a**
    14:21, **a** who is in your town
  Acts 7:6, A-S IN A FOREIGN LAND
  Eph. 2:19, no longer strangers and **a-s**
  2 Sam. 1:13; Ps. 69:8; Lam. 5:2
ALIENATED Col. 1:21, you were formerly **a**
ALIVE Num. 16:33; 2 Kin. 5:7; Ps. 55:15
  Gen. 43:7; 45:3, Is your father still **a**

ALIVE (Continued)
Acts 1:3, presented Himself **a**
Rom. 6:13, those **a** from the dead
1 Cor. 15:22, Christ ... made **a**
Eph. 2:5, made us **a** together with Christ
1 Pet. 3:18, made **a** in the spirit
Rev. 1:18, I am **a** forevermore
ALL—*whatever* Jer. 1:7, And **a** that I command you
Matt. 6:32, **a** these things the Gentiles
Mark 16:15, Go into **a** the world and preach
Luke 2:10, great joy which shall be for **a** the people
3:6, A FLESH SHALL SEE THE SALVATION OF GOD
4:6, I will give you **a** this domain
Acts 2:1, **a** together in one place
1 Cor. 10:26, LORD'S, AND **A** IT CONTAINS
ALLEGORY Gal. 4:24, This contains an **a**
ALLIANCE 1 Kin. 3:1, Solomon ... marriage **a** with Pharaoh
ALLIED 2 Chr. 18:1; Ps. 94:20
ALLOT Job 7:3, I **a**-ed months of vanity
Rom. 12:3, as God has **a**-ed to each a measure of faith
ALLOW Ex. 12:23, **a** the destroyer to come
Ps. 16:10, **a** Thy Holy One to see the pit
Acts 2:27, **A** THY HOLY ONE TO UNDERGO
22:22, not be **a**-ed to live
1 Cor. 10:13, not **a** you to be tempted
1 Tim. 2:12, do not **a** a woman to teach
ALLOWANCE 2 Kin. 25:30, for his **a**, a regular **a** was given
Jer. 52:34, a regular **a** was given him
ALLY Gen. 14:13, these were **a**-es with Abram
ALMIGHTY Gen. 17:1, I am God **A**
Ps. 91:1, shadow of the **A**
Rev. 4:8, *is* THE LORD GOD, THE **A**
11:17, the **A**, who art and who wast
Ex. 6:3; Job 11:7; 29:5; 37:23
ALMS—*charity* Matt. 6:2, therefore you give **a**
Matt. 6:4, your **a** may be in secret
Acts 10:2; 24:17
ALONE Gen. 2:18, not good for the man to be **a**
Matt. 4:4, MAN SHALL NOT LIVE ON BREAD **A**
Luke 9:18, He was praying **a**
John 8:16, I am not **a**
Job 7:16; Mark 14:6
ALREADY—*utterly* Eccles. 1:10, **A** it has existed for ages
Matt. 5:28, committed adultery with her **a**
John 3:18, who does not believe ... judged **a**
9:27, He answered them, I told you **a**
11:17, had **a** been in the tomb four days
1 Cor. 5:3, I ... have **a** judged him who
6:7, it is **a** a defeat for you
2 Thess. 2:7, mystery of lawlessness is **a** at work
ALTAR Ps. 43:4, I will go to the **a**
Ezek. 6:4, your **a**-s will become desolate
Matt. 5:23, your offering at the **a**
Rev. 9:13, four horns of the golden **a**
Gen. 8:20; Ex. 17:15; Lev. 6:9; Judg. 6:24; Matt. 23:19
ALWAYS—*forever, ever* Matt. 28:20, lo, I am with you **a**
Mark 14:7, you do not have Me
Phil. 4:4, Rejoice in the Lord **a**
1 Thess. 4:17, thus we shall **a** be with the Lord
Deut. 14:23; 2 Tim. 3:7; Heb. 7:25
AM Ex. 3:14, I **A** WHO I **A**
Matt. 18:20, there I **a** in their midst
1 Cor. 15:10, grace of God I **a** what I **a**
Gal. 4:12, brethren, become as I **a**
AMASS—*heap* Ps. 39:6, He **a**-es *riches*
AMAZE—*astonish, astound*
Matt. 7:28, were **a**-d at His teaching
Luke 9:43, **a**-d at the greatness of God
Rev. 13:3, the whole earth was **a**-d
Mark 2:12; Luke 24:22; John 9:30
AMAZEMENT—*astonishment* Acts 3:10, with wonder and **a**

AMBITION 1 Thess. 4:11, make it your **a** to lead
James 3:14,16, bitter jealousy and selfish **a**
AMBUSH—*wait* Josh. 8:2, Set an **a** for the city
Josh. 8:4,7,12,14,19,21; Jer. 51:12
AMEN Num. 5:22, the woman shall say, **A. A**
Ps. 41:13; 72:19; 89:52, **A** and **A**
Matt. 6:13, *the glory, forever.* **A**
Rev. 3:14, The **A**, the faithful and true Witness
ANALYZE—*discern* Luke 12:56, **a** this present time
ANCIENT—*aged, everlasting, old*
Deut. 33:15, of the **a** mountains
1 Chr. 4:22, the records are **a**
Ps. 24:7, be lifted up, O **a** doors
Dan. 7:9,13,22, **A** of Days
Matt. 5:21, the **a**-s were told
ANGEL Matt. 4:6, GIVE HIS **A**-S CHARGE
Luke 20:36, for they are like **a**-s
22:43, an **a** from heaven appeared
John 20:12, beheld two **a**-s in white
2 Cor. 11:14, as an **a** of light
Col. 2:18, worship of the **a**-s
Gen. 24:7; Ps. 78:25; Is. 63:9; Matt. 1:20,24; 2:13; Acts 6:15; 23:8; Heb. 13:2; 2 Pet. 2:4; Rev. 2:1,8,12; 9:11
ANGER—*exasperation, wrath, indignation*
Ex. 32:19, Moses' **a** burned
Deut. 13:17, from His burning **a**
Job 5:2, And **a** kills the simple
Ps. 30:5, His **a** is but for a moment
Prov. 15:18, the slow to **a**
22:24, a man given to **a**
Eph. 4:26, sun go down on your **a**
James 1:19, slow to speak *and* slow to **a**
Gen. 39:19; 49:7; Ex. 22:24; Neh. 9:17; Job 9:13; Ps. 37:8; 38:1; Prov. 14:29; Eccles. 5:17; Is. 5:25; 51:17; 54:8; Gal. 5:20
ANGRY—*indignant, enraged*
Prov. 29:22, An **a** man stirs up strife
Is. 64:9, Do not be **a** beyond measure
Eph. 4:26, BE **A** ... DO NOT SIN
Gen. 4:6; 18:30; Esth. 1:12; Jon. 4:4; Matt. 5:22; Heb. 3:10
ANGUISH—*distress, pain* Ps. 55:4; Is. 30:6; Jer. 6:24
ANIMAL—*beast, creature, cattle*
Gen. 6:7, from man to **a**-s to creeping things
7:8, Of clean **a**-s and **a**-s that are not
8:20, took of every clean **a** and
Acts 10:12, four-footed **a**-s and crawling creatures
2 Pet. 2:12, like unreasoning **a**-s
Ex. 22:19; Ps. 104:25; Jer. 27:6
ANNOUNCE—*proclaim* Is. 52:7, **a**-s peace ... **a**-s salvation
ANNUAL 1 Sam. 7:16, used to go **a**-ly on circuit
ANOINT Matt. 6:17, fast, **a** your head
Mark 14:8, she has **a**-ed My body
16:1, they might come and **a**
Ex. 28:41; Ps. 23:5; 105:15; Luke 7:46; Acts 10:38; 2 Cor. 1:21; Rev. 3:18
ANSWER—*respond* Ps. 65:5, Thou dost **a** us
Prov. 15:1, **a** turns away wrath
Eccles. 10:19, money is the **a** to everything
Mic. 3:7, there is no **a** from God
Luke 2:47, amazed at ... His **a**-s
Deut. 27:15; Prov. 55:19; Prov. 24:26; 26:4,5; Matt. 26:62; Mark 14:60; John 19:9; Acts 12:13
ANT Prov. 6:6, Go to the **a**, O sluggard
Prov. 30:25, The **a**-s are not a strong folk
ANTICHRIST 1 John 2:18, **a** is coming
2 John 7, the deceiver and the **a**
1 John 2:22; 4:3
ANXIETY—*sorrow* Ps. 38:18, full of **a** because of my sin
Jer. 49:23, There is **a** by the sea
ANXIOUS—*worry, concern, thought* Jer. 17:8
Matt. 6:25, do not be **a** for your life
6:27; Luke 12:25, being **a** can add a single
6:31, Do not be **a** then, saying

6:34, be a for tomorrow
10:19, a about how or what you will speak
Mark 13:11, do not be a beforehand about what
Luke 12:26, why are you a about other
Phil. 4:6, Be a for nothing
APART—*separate, without* Matt. 10:29, a from
 your Father
John 1:3, a from Him nothing came into being
Acts 13:2, Set a for Me Barnabas and
Rom. 3:28, justified by faith a from works
APOSTASY—*backsliding, faithlessness*
Hos. 14:4, I will heal their a
2 Thess. 2:3, *not come* unless the a comes first
Jer. 2:19; 5:6; 8:5; 14:7
APOSTLE Matt. 10:2, names of the twelve **a-s**
Rom. 1:1, called *as* an a
 11:13, a of the Gentiles
Eph. 4:11, He gave some as **a-s**
Luke 11:49; 1 Cor. 15:9; 2 Cor. 12:11; Gal. 1:19;
 1 Tim. 2:7; 2 Tim. 1:11
APPALL—*astound, amaze, astonish*
Job 17:8, upright shall be **a-ed**
Ps. 40:15, Let those be **a-ed** because of their
 shame
 143:4, My heart is **a-ed** within me
Lev. 26:32; Jer. 2:12; Ezek. 4:17; Dan. 4:19
APPAREL—*garment* 2 Sam. 1:24, gold on your a
Is. 63:1, is majestic in His a
Luke 24:4, two men ... in dazzling a
Acts 12:21, put on his royal a
APPEAL—*ask, beg, entreat* Acts 25:11, I a to
 Caesar
Acts 28:19, I was forced to a to Caesar
1 Tim. 5:1, a to him as a father
Philem. 9, for love's sake I rather a to you
Acts 25:12,21,25; 26:32
APPEAR—*be seen* Gen. 12:7, LORD **a-ed** to
 Abram
Ex. 3:2, **a-ed** to him in a blazing
Mal. 3:2, who can stand when He **a-s**
Acts 2:3, **a-ed** to them tongues as of
 16:9, a vision **a-ed** to Paul in the
 27:20, sun nor stars **a-ed** for many days
2 Cor. 5:10, we must all a before
Heb. 9:24, now to a in ... of God for us
 9:28, shall a a second time
1 Pet. 5:4, Chief Shepherd **a-s**
1 John 3:2, it has not **a-ed** ... if He should a
Gen. 19:14; Num. 14:10; 2 Sam. 22:11;
 Matt. 1:20; 2:13; 27:53; Mark 16:9
APPEARANCE—*brightness, radiance, sight*
1 Sam. 16:7, man looks at the *outward* a
Matt. 6:16, for they neglect their a
 28:3, his a was like lightning
Phil. 2:8, found in a as a man
2 Thess. 2:8, a of His coming
Num. 11:7; 1 Sam. 16:12; 2 Sam. 11:2; 14:27;
 Dan. 1:15; Nah. 2:4; Luke 9:29; Rev. 4:3
APPETITE—*stomach, desire* Prov. 23:2, man of
 great a
Phil. 3:19, whose god is *their* a
Num. 11:6; Job 38:39; Eccles. 6:7; Hab. 2:5;
 Rom. 16:18
APPLE Ps. 17:8, a of the eye
Prov. 25:11; Song 2:3,5
APPOINT—*name* Num. 3:10, you shall a Aaron
1 Chr. 17:9, I will a a place for My people
Jon. 1:17, **a-ed** a great fish to swallow
Mark 3:14, He **a-ed** twelve, that they
Heb. 9:27, **a-ed** for men to die
Gen. 4:15; Job 36:23; Jer. 49:19; John 15:16;
 1 Tim. 2:7
APPORTION—*distribute* Josh. 13:7, a this land
 for an
Job 21:17, Does God a destruction
2 Cor. 10:13, sphere which God **a-ed** to us
APPRAISE—*discern*
1 Cor. 2:14, they are spiritually **a-d**
APPROACH Matt. 21:34, the harvest time **a-ed**
Luke 24:15, Jesus Himself **a-ed**
Lev. 18:14,19; Judg. 19:25

APPROPRIATE Eccles. 3:11, everything a in its
 time
Ezek. 36:5, **a-d** My land for themselves
APPROVAL Heb. 11:2, men of old gained a
Heb. 11:39, having gained a through
APPROVE—*attest* Rom. 14:18, and **a-d** by men
Rom. 16:10, **a-d** in Christ
2 Tim. 2:15, present yourself **a-d** to God
APRON Acts 19:12, handkerchiefs or **a-s**
ARCHANGEL 1 Thess. 4:16; Jude 9
ARGUE—*dispute, question* Mark 8:11
Prov. 25:8, out hastily to a *your case*
 25:9, A your case with your neighbor
Mark 9:14, *some* scribes **a-ing** with them
Acts 9:29, talking and **a-ing** with Hellenistic
 Jews
ARGUMENT Job 23:4, fill my mouth with **a-s**
Ps. 38:14, whose mouth are no **a-s**
ARISE—*rise, stand* Gen. 31:13, a, leave this land
Job 31:14, do when God **a-s**
Ps. 27:3, war a against me
Dan. 11:2, three more kings are going to a
Matt. 11:11, has not **a-n** *anyone* greater
 24:11, false prophets will a
Acts 10:13, A, Peter, kill and eat
Eph. 5:14, AND A FROM THE DEAD
2 Pet. 1:19, morning star **a-s** in your hearts
Deut. 9:12; Ps. 3:7; Song 2:13; Matt. 2:13,20;
 Acts 22:16
ARK Gen. 6:14, an a of gopher wood
Heb. 9:4, a of the covenant
Ex. 37:1; Matt. 24:38; Rev. 11:19
ARM (n.)—*hand, side* Deut. 33:27, the
 everlasting **a-s**
Ps. 37:17, **a-s** of the wicked ... broken
Mark 10:16, took them in His **a-s**
Ex. 6:6; Job 26:2; Ps. 98:1; Song 8:6; Is. 60:4;
 Zech. 13:6
ARM (v.) Num. 31:3, A men from among you
Luke 11:21, a strong *man* fully **a-ed**
1 Pet. 4:1, a yourselves also
ARMOR—*weapon, harness* 1 Kin. 20:11; 22:34;
 Luke 11:22
Rom. 13:12, put on the a of light
Eph. 6:11,13, full a of God
ARMY—*host, war* Deut. 24:5; 1 Chr. 12:22;
 2 Chr. 26:11
AROMA Gen. 8:21, LORD smelled the soothing a
2 Cor. 2:16, a from death ... a from life
AROUSE—*raise, stir* Is. 42:13, He will a His zeal
 like
Acts 13:50, Jews **a-d** the devout women
Job 14:12; Is. 41:25; 45:13; Jer. 51:11
ARRAY—*adorn, clothe* Matt. 6:30, God so **a-s**
 the grass
Judg. 20:20; Luke 12:28
ARROGANCE—*pride* Prov. 8:13, Pride and a and
 the evil way
Is. 13:11, a of the proud
 16:6, *Even* of his a, pride, and
Jer. 48:29, his a and his self-exaltation
 49:16, a of your heart has deceived you
ARROGANT—*proud* Jer. 48:26, become a
 toward the LORD
Rom. 1:30, insolent, a, boastful
Jude 16, they speak **a-ly**
Rev. 13:5, a words and blasphemies
Jer. 50:32; Dan. 5:20; 2 Pet. 2:18
ARROW—*dart, missile* 1 Sam. 20:36, he shot an
 a past him
Job 6:4, **a-s** of the Almighty
Jer. 9:8, Their tongue is a deadly a
Job 41:28; Ps. 45:5; Prov. 7:23; Lam. 3:12
ART 2 Chr. 16:14, blended by the perfumers' a
Acts 17:29, image formed by the a
ASCEND Ps. 24:3, may a into the hill of
Ps. 139:8, If I a to heaven
John 3:13, no one has **a-ed**
 6:62, behold the Son of Man **a-ing**
 20:17, I a to My Father
Rom. 10:6, WHO WILL A INTO HEAVEN

ASH Gen. 18:27, am *but* dust and **a-es**
   Job 13:12, sayings are proverbs of **a-es**
     42:6, repent in dust and **a-es**
   Ps. 102:9, eat **a-es** like bread
   Is. 61:3, a garland instead of **a-es**
   Matt. 11:21, repented … sackcloth and **a-es**
   Luke 10:13, sitting in sackcloth and **a-es**
   Lev. 6:11; Num. 19:17; 1 Sam. 2:8; 2 Sam. 13:19;
     1 Kin. 13:3,5; Esth. 4:1; Job 2:8; 30:19;
     Ps. 147:16; Is. 44:20; 58:5; Jer. 6:26; Mal.
     4:3; Heb. 9:13
ASHAMED—*confused* Ps. 71:1, me never be **a**
   Mark 8:38, the Son of Man … **a** of him
   Rom. 1:16, not **a** of the gospel
   Heb. 11:16, not **a** to be called their God
   Gen. 2:25; Ps. 25:2; Is. 24:23; 2 Tim. 1:8;
     1 Pet. 4:16
ASHERAH, ASHERIM (pl.)
   1 Kin. 15:13, made a … image as an **A**
   Ex. 34:13; 2 Kin. 17:10; 2 Chr. 19:3; 33:19;
     Mic. 5:14
ASIDE 1 Sam. 8:3, turned **a** after dishonest gain
   1 Pet. 2:1, putting **a** all malice
ASK—*appeal, beg, inquire* 1 Kin. 3:5, **A** what *you*
   wish
   Ps. 27:4, One thing I have **a-ed** from the LORD
   Prov. 30:7, Two things I **a-ed** of Thee
   Jer. 6:16, **a** for the ancient paths
   Matt. 5:42, Give to him who **a-s** of
     7:7, **A**, and it shall be given to you
   Mark 10:38, not know … **a-ing** for
   John 4:40, they were **a-ing** Him to stay
     14:16, I will **a** the Father
   James 1:5, let him **a** of God
   Ruth 3:11; Job 42:4; Ps. 2:8; Is. 7:11; Zech. 10:1;
     Matt. 21:22; Mark 10:35; 11:24; Luke 11:11;
     1 Cor. 1:22; 10:25; Eph. 3:13; 1 John 5:15
ASLEEP Matt. 9:24, not dead, but **a**
   Mark 4:38, was in the stern, **a**
     13:36, come suddenly and find you **a**
   John 11:11, Our friend Lazarus has fallen **a**
   Acts 7:60, having said this, he fell **a**
   1 Cor. 15:6, some have fallen **a**
   1 Thess. 4:14, those who have fallen **a** in Jesus
     5:10, whether … awake or **a**
   Judg. 4:21; 1 Thess. 4:13,15
ASSEMBLE—*gather* 1 Chr. 13:5; 15:3, David **a-d**
   all Israel
   Lev. 8:3; Num. 8:9; 20:8; Deut. 4:10; 31:12;
     Is. 43:9; Jer. 4:5; 8:14; Ezek. 11:17; Hos.
     7:14; Amos 3:9
ASSEMBLY—*band, congregation, convocation*
   Ps. 1:5, in the **a** of the righteous
   Joel 1:14; 2:15, Proclaim a solemn **a**
   Heb. 12:23, to the general **a** and church
   Ex. 12:16; Lev. 23:36; Num. 20:10,12; Job 11:10;
     Ps. 26:5; 111:1; Acts 19:39
ASSERT Acts 25:19, whom Paul **a-ed** to be alive
   1 Tim. 1:7, they make confident **a-ions**
ASSIGN—*distribute* 1 Cor. 7:17, Lord has **a-ed** to
   each
ASSOCIATE Rom. 12:16, but **a** with the lowly
   Job 19:19; Ps. 50:18; Zech. 13:7; 2 Thess. 3:14
ASSURANCE—*confidence* Job 24:22, no one has
   a of life
   Col. 2:2, full **a** of understanding
   Heb. 6:11, full **a** of hope
     10:22, full **a** of faith
     11:1, faith … **a** of things hoped for
ASTONISH—*amaze, astound*
   Matt. 13:54, so that they became **a-ed**
     22:33, they were **a-ed** at His teaching
   Mark 6:2, many listeners were **a-ed**
     7:37, they were utterly **a-ed**
     10:26, they were even more **a-ed**
     11:18, all the multitude were **a-ed**
   Job 21:5; Matt. 19:25; Luke 1:63
ASTOUND—*amaze, astonish* Jer. 4:9, prophets
   will be **a-ed**
   Dan. 8:27, **a-ed** at the vision
   Mark 5:42; 10:26

ASTRAY—*err* Ps. 119:176, gone **a** like a lost
   sheep
   Is. 53:6, sheep have gone **a**
   1 Tim. 6:21, gone **a** from the faith
   Ps. 119:110; Prov. 10:17; Is. 3:12; 9:16;
     Matt. 18:13; Heb. 3:10
ATE—*eat* Jer. 15:16, words were found and I **a**
   them
   1 Cor. 10:3, all **a** the same spiritual food
   Luke 13:26; 24:43; Acts 9:9
ATONEMENT—*reconciliation* Lev. 23:27; 25:9,
   the day of **a**
   Ex. 30:15; 2 Sam. 21:3
ATTAIN—*acquire* Rom. 9:30, **a-ed** righteousness
   Phil. 3:11, **a** to the resurrection
ATTENTION—*heed, regard* Prov. 4:1, give **a** …
   gain understanding
   16:20, who gives **a** to the word
   Is. 5:12, not pay **a** to the deeds
   Heb. 2:1, we must pay closer **a**
   Ex. 5:9; Job 33:31; Prov. 29:12; 1 Tim. 1:4; 4:13
ATTEST Acts 2:22, a man **a-ed** to you by God
AUTHOR—*source* Heb. 12:2, the **a** and perfecter
   of faith
AUTHORITY Eccles. 8:8, **a** over the day of death
   Matt. 7:29, teaching them as one having **a**
     8:9, For I too am a man under **a**
     9:6, **a** on earth to forgive
     10:1, **a** over unclean spirits
     21:23, By what **a** are You doing these things
     28:18, **a** has been given to Me
   Luke 5:24, Son of Man has **a** on earth to forgive
     9:1, gave them power and **a**
     19:17, be in **a** over ten cities
     20:8, by what **a** I am doing these things
   John 5:27, **a** to execute judgment
     10:18, **a** to lay it down … **a** to take it up
     17:2, Thou gavest Him **a** over all mankind
   Acts 8:19, Give this **a** to me as well, so
   Rom. 13:1, no **a** except from God
   1 Cor. 15:24, all rule and all **a**
   1 Tim. 2:12, to teach or exercise **a**
   Titus 2:15, reprove with all **a**
   2 Pet. 2:10, and despise **a**
   Jude 25, majesty, dominion and **a**
   Rev. 2:26, GIVE **A** OVER THE NATIONS
   Num. 27:20; Is. 22:21; Hab. 1:7; Luke 10:19; 12:5
AVAIL—*profit* Jer. 7:8, deceptive words to no **a**
AVENGE—*vengeance, revenge* 1 Sam. 24:12
   Jer. 5:9,29, Shall I not **a** Myself
   2 Cor. 7:11, what zeal, what **a-ing** of wrong
AVOID—*refuse* Prov. 4:15, **A** it, do not pass by it
   1 Tim. 6:20, **a-ing** worldly *and* empty chatter
   2 Tim. 3:5, **a** such men as these
AWAIT—*wait* 1 Cor. 1:7, **a-ing** eagerly the
   revelation
AWAKE—*watch* Ps. 139:18, when I **a**, I am still
   with Thee
   Eph. 5:14, **A**, SLEEPER
   Rev. 16:15, Blessed is the one who stays **a**
   Judg. 5:12; Ps. 17:15; Is. 51:9; John 11:11;
     Rom. 13:11
AWARE Luke 8:46, I was **a** that power had gone
AWE—*fear* Ps. 33:8, inhabitants … in **a** of Him
   Ps. 119:161, stands in **a** of Thy words
   Heb. 12:28, with reverence and **a**
AWESOME—*fearful* Gen. 28:17, How **a** is this
   place
   Ex. 15:11, **A** in praises
   Judg. 13:6, angel of God, very **a**
   Neh. 1:5, the great and **a** God
   Job 37:22, Around God is **a** majesty
   Ps. 89:7, **a** above all those … around Him
   Song 6:4, **a** as an army with banners
   Joel 2:31, great and **a** day of the LORD
AXE—*hatchet* 2 Kin. 6:5, **a** head fell into the
   water
   Matt. 3:10, **a** is already laid at the root
   Luke 3:9, the **a** … root of the trees
   1 Sam. 13:20; 1 Kin. 6:7

B

BABBLER Acts 17:18, this idle **b**
BABE—*immature* Matt. 11:25, reveal ... to **b-s**
  1 Cor. 3:1, to **b-s** in Christ
  Heb. 5:13, for he is a **b**
  1 Pet. 2:2, like newborn **b-s**
  Ps. 8:2; 17:14; Matt. 21:16; Luke 10:21
BABY—*babe, immature* Luke 2:12; 2:16
BACK—*backward* Is. 38:17, sins behind Thy **b**
  Num. 24:11; 1 Sam. 10:9; Neh. 9:26; Ezek. 2:10;
    Mark 13:16
BACKBITING—*slanders* Prov. 25:23, a **b** tongue
BACKSLIDE—*apostasy, faithless*
  Prov. 14:14, **b-r** in heart will have his fill
  Jer. 49:4, O **b-ing** daughter Who trusts
BACKWARD 2 Kin. 20:10, shadow turn **b** ten
  steps
  Gen. 9:23; 49:17; Job 23:8; Jer. 7:24
BAD—*evil, wrong* Gen. 24:50; 31:24,29;
  Lev. 27:12,14,33; Num. 13:19; 24:13; 2 Sam.
    13:22; 2 Cor. 5:10, good or **b**
  Lev. 27:10, good for a **b**, or a **b** for a good
  Matt. 7:18, good tree cannot produce **b** fruit
  Gen. 43:6; Is. 3:11; Jer. 24:2,3; Matt. 13:48
BAG—*purse* Deut. 25:13; 1 Sam. 17:40
  Job 14:17, My transgression is sealed up in a **b**
  Matt. 10:10, or a **b** for *your* journey
  2 Kin. 5:23; Prov. 7:20; 16:11; Mic. 6:11
BAGGAGE 1 Sam. 17:22, David left his **b**
BAKE Gen. 19:3; 40:17; Ex. 12:39; 16:23; Lev. 2:4;
  24:5; 26:26; Num. 11:8; 1 Sam. 28:24; Is. 44:15
BAKER Gen. 40:1, **b** of the king of Egypt
  Gen. 41:10; 1 Sam. 8:13; Jer. 37:21; Hos. 7:4
BALANCE—*scale* Lev. 19:36, shall have just **b-s**
  Prov. 11:1, A false **b** is an abomination to the
    LORD
    16:11, A just **b** and scales belong to the LORD
  Job 6:2; Ps. 62:9; Is. 40:12; Ezek. 45:10;
  Hos. 12:7
BALD—*baldhead* Lev. 13:41, head becomes **b**
  Jer. 48:37; Ezek. 29:18
BALDHEAD—*bald* 2 Kin. 2:23, Go up, you **b**
BALDNESS Mic. 1:16, **b** like an eagle
  Lev. 21:5; Ezek. 7:18; Amos 8:10
BALM Jer. 8:22, no **b** in Gilead
  Gen. 37:25; 43:11; Jer. 46:11; 51:8; Ezek. 27:17
BAND—*bond, chain, fetter* Ex. 27:10; 28:8; 38:10;
  Judg. 8:26; Ps. 107:14; Is. 58:6
BANISH 2 Sam. 14:13,14; Ezra 7:26
BANK—*mound* Gen. 41:17, **b** of the Nile
  Matt. 25:27, put my money in the **b**
  Gen. 41:3; Ex. 2:3; 7:15; Ezek. 47:7; Luke 19:23
BANNER—*standard* Ps. 20:5; 60:4
  Song 2:4, his **b** over me is love
  6:4, awesome as an army with **b-s**
BANQUET—*feast, supper*
  Song 2:4; Dan. 5:10; Amos 6:7
  Esth. 5:4, the **b** that I have prepared for him
  Matt. 23:6; Mark 12:39; Luke 20:46, place of
    honor at **b-s**
  Mark 6:21, Herod on his birthday gave a **b**
BAPTISM—*washing*
  Matt. 3:7; Mark 10:38; 1 Pet. 3:21
  Matt. 21:25; Mark 11:30; Luke 7:29, **b** of John
  Luke 20:4; Acts 1:22; 18:25; 19:3, **b** of John
  Mark 1:4; Luke 3:3; Acts 13:24; 19:4, **b** of
    repentance
  Luke 12:50, I have a **b** to undergo
  Rom. 6:4, buried with Him through **b**
  Col. 2:12, buried with Him in **b**
  Eph. 4:5, one Lord, one faith, one **b**
BAPTIZE Matt. 3:11, I **b** you in water
  Matt. 3:14, I have need to be **b-d** by You
    28:19, **b-ing** them in the name of the Father
  Mark 1:8; Luke 3:16, **b** you with the Holy Sp.
  John 3:22, He was ... with them and **b-ing**
  Acts 1:5, John **b-d** with water
    2:41, those ... were **b-d**
    8:16, **b-d** in the name of the Lord Jesus
    9:18, Saul ... arose and was **b-d**
    19:4, John **b-d** with the baptism

  Rom. 6:3, **b-d** into Christ Jesus ... **b-d** into His
    death
  1 Cor. 1:13, were you **b-d** in the name of Paul
    12:13, by one Spirit we were all **b-d**
  Mark 16:16; Luke 3:7,12,21; 7:29; John 1:25,33;
    4:1; Acts 2:38; 8:12,36; 10:47; 16:15,33; 18:8;
    22:16; 1 Cor. 10:2; 15:29
BARBARIAN Rom. 1:14; 1 Cor. 14:11
BARBER Ezek. 5:1, use it as a **b-'s** razor
BARE—*naked* Is. 52:10; 1 Cor. 15:37; Heb. 4:13
BARK Ex. 11:7; Is. 56:10
BARLEY Ex. 9:31; Deut. 8:8; Ruth 1:22; John 6:9
BARN Matt. 6:26, nor gather into **b-s**
  Luke 12:18, I will tear down my **b-s**
  Joel 1:17; Hag. 2:19; Matt. 3:12; 13:30;
    Luke 12:24
BARRACKS Acts 21:34; 22:24
BARREN—*unfruitful* Gen. 11:30; 29:31; Ex.
  23:26; Job 24:21; Is. 54:1; Luke 1:7,36; 23:29
BARS 1 Sam. 23:7; Ps. 107:16; Is. 45:2;
  Ezek. 38:11
BASE 1 Cor. 1:28, the **b** things of the world
BASIN Ex. 12:22; 1 Chr. 28:17; Jer. 52:19;
  John 13:5
BASKET Ex. 2:3; 29:23; Judg. 6:19; Jer. 24:2;
  Amos 8:1; Matt. 14:20; 15:37; 16:9; Mark 6:43;
  8:8; 8:19; Luke 9:17; John 6:13
BAT Lev. 11:19; Deut. 14:18; Is. 2:20
BATH—*measure* 1 Kin. 7:26; 2 Chr. 2:10; Ezra
  7:22; Is. 5:10
BATHE—*wash* Song 5:12, eyes ... **b-d** in milk
  Lev. 15:5,22; 17:16; Num. 19:7; 2 Sam. 11:2
BATTER—*bruise, crush*
  Matt. 12:20, B-ED REED ... NOT BREAK
BATTLE—*war* 1 Sam. 17:47, **b** is the LORD'S
  2 Chr. 20:15, the **b** is not yours
  1 Sam. 17:20; 1 Chr. 5:20; Job 39:25; 41:8;
    Ps. 18:39; 55:18; 140:7; 144:1; Eccles. 9:11;
    Is. 21:15; Jer. 50:22; Luke 14:31
BEACH Matt. 13:2; John 21:4; Acts 21:5
BEAM—*log* 2 Kin. 6:2; Ps. 104:3
BEAR (n.) 1 Sam. 17:34; 2 Sam. 17:8; Prov. 17:12;
  Is. 11:7; 59:11; Hos. 13:8; Amos 5:19
BEAR (v.)—*carry, sustain* Gen. 43:9; 44:32
  Gen. 4:13, punishment is too great to **b**
  Ex. 20:16, You shall not **b** false witness
  Ps. 91:12, They will **b** you up
  Matt. 1:23, VIRGIN ... SHALL B A SON
    27:32, to **b** His cross
  Mark 15:21, that he might **b** His cross
  John 1:7, **b** witness of the light
    16:12, you cannot **b** *them* now
  Rom. 8:16, Spirit Himself **b-s** witness
  1 Cor. 13:7, **b-s** all things
    15:49, **b** the image of the heavenly
  Gal. 6:2, B one another's burdens
    6:5, each one shall **b** his own load
    6:17, I **b** on my body
  1 John 1:2, we have seen and **b** witness
  Ex. 28:12; Lev. 24:15; Deut. 1:9; Prov. 18:14;
    Lam. 3:27; Ezek. 23:49; Matt. 1:21; Luke
    11:46; John 5:31; 8:18; 15:27; Rom. 13:4;
    15:1; Heb 9:28
BEARD Lev. 13:29; 1 Sam. 21:13; 2 Sam. 10:4;
  20:9; 1 Chr. 19:5; Ps. 133:2; Ezek. 5:1
BEARING—*carrying* Rom. 2:15; Gal. 4:24
  John 19:17, **b** His own cross
  Col. 3:13, **b** with one another
  Heb. 13:13, **b** His reproach
BEAST—*animal, creature* Lev. 26:22; Job 12:7;
  18:3
  Ps. 50:10, every **b** of the forest is Mine
  147:9, He gives to the **b** its food
  Eccles. 3:19, no advantage for man over **b**
  1 Cor. 15:32, I fought with wild **b-s**
  Ps. 49:12; 73:22; Prov. 12:10; James 3:7
BEAT—*flog, hammer* Judg. 6:11; Matt. 26:67
  Prov. 23:14, **b** him with the rod
  Joel 3:10, B your plowshares into swords
  Luke 18:13, was **b-ing** his breast

BEAT (Continued)
  1 Cor. 9:26, as not **b**-ing the air
  2 Cor. 11:23, **b**-en times without number
BEAUTIFUL—*appropriate, lovely* Lev. 23:40
  Gen. 6:2, daughters of men were **b**
    12:11, you are a **b** woman
  Is. 4:2, the Branch of the LORD will be **b**
    64:11, Our holy and **b** house
  Matt. 23:27, tombs which on the outside
    appear **b**
  Acts 3:2, gate of the temple which is called **B**
  Rom. 10:15, How B ARE THE FEET
  Judg. 15:2; Ps. 48:2; Song 1:8; 6:4; Is. 52:1; Jer.
    11:16; 13:20
BEAUTY 2 Sam. 1:19; Prov. 31:30; Is. 3:18;
  Zech. 9:17
  Ps. 27:4, To behold the **b** of the LORD
    50:2, Out of Zion, the perfection of **b**
BECAME Gen. 26:13, and the man **b** rich
  Heb. 11:34, **b** mighty in war
BECOME Ps. 33:1, Praise is **b**-ing to the upright
  Luke 2:40, Child . . . to grow and **b** strong
BED—*pallet* Ps. 63:6, remember Thee on my **b**
  Matt. 9:6, Rise, take up your **b**
  2 Kin. 4:10; Job 7:13; 33:15; Is. 28:20;
    Ezek. 17:10; Mark 4:21; Luke 8:16
BEES Deut. 1:44; Judg. 14:8; Ps. 118:12; Is. 7:18
BEFALL—*happen* Gen. 42:4; 49:1; Deut. 31:29
  Gen. 44:29, harm **b**-s him
  Ps. 91:10, No evil will **b** you
BEFIT—*proper, worthy* Ps. 93:5, Holiness **b**-s
  1 Tim. 2:10, as **b**-s women making a claim to
    godliness
BEG—*appeal, ask* Ps. 37:25, his descendants
  b-ing bread
  Luke 16:3, I am ashamed to **b**
    18:35, blind man by the road, **b**-ing
  John 9:8, the one who used to sit and **b**
  Ps. 109:10; Prov. 20:4; Luke 9:38
BEGINNING 1 Sam. 3:12; Prov. 8:22,23
  Gen. 1:1, In the **b** God created the heavens
  Job 8:7, your **b** was insignificant
  Ps. 111:10, **b** of wisdom
  Prov. 1:7, **b** of knowledge
  Eccles. 7:8, end . . . better than its **b**
  Luke 24:47, **b** from Jerusalem
  John 1:1, In the **b** was the Word
  Rev. 21:6, the **b** and the end
  Matt. 19:8; John 2:11; 2 Cor. 3:1; 8:6; Col. 1:18;
    Heb. 3:14; Rev. 22:13
BEGOTTEN—*born* Ps. 2:7, Today I have **b** Thee
  Job 38:28; Acts 13:33; Philem. 10; Heb. 1:5; 5:5
BEHALF—*place, sake* Job 36:2, more . . . said in
  God's **b**
  2 Cor. 1:11, thanks may be given . . . on our **b**
    5:20, we beg you on **b** of Christ
BEHAVE—*act* 1 Sam. 18:30, David **b**-d himself
  more wisely
  1 Thess. 2:10, how devoutly . . . we **b**-d
BEHAVIOR—*conduct* James 3:13, his good **b**
  1 Pet. 1:15, holy . . . in all *your* **b**
    2:12, keep your **b** excellent
BEHEAD Luke 9:9; Rev. 20:4
  Matt. 14:10, had John **b**-ed in prison
  Mark 6:16, John whom I **b**-ed
BEHOLD—*look* Num. 24:17; Ps. 37:37
  Matt. 18:10, angels . . . **b** the face of My Father
  John 17:24, that they may **b** My glory
  2 Cor. 3:18, **b**-ing as in a mirror
BEING Gen. 2:7, man became a living **b**
  Matt. 7:11, **b** evil, know how to give
    12:34, **b** evil, speak . . . good
  John 4:9, **b** a Jew, ask me
  1 Cor. 8:7, conscience **b** weak
    9:21, **b** without the law
  Eph. 2:20, **b** the chief cornerstone
BELIEVE—*faith, trust* Ex. 4:5; Matt. 8:13; 9:28
  Num. 14:11, how long will they not **b** in Me
  Ps. 78:22, Because they did not **b** in God
  Prov. 14:15, The naive **b**-s everything
  Matt. 21:22, everything you ask . . . **b**-ing you
  Mark 5:36, Do not be afraid . . . only **b**
    9:23, All things are possible to him who **b**-s

  Luke 8:13, they **b** for a while
    24:25, slow of heart to **b**
  John 2:22, they **b**-d the Scripture
    7:5, not even His brothers were **b**-ing in Him
    8:24, unless you **b** that I am He
    10:38, though you do not **b** Me, **b** the works
    11:26, everyone who . . . **b**-s in Me shall never
      die
    11:27, Yes, Lord; I have **b**-d
    11:48, all men will **b** in Him
    17:21, that the world may **b** that Thou didst
      send Me
    20:25, Unless I shall see . . . I will not **b**
    20:29, Blessed *are* they who . . . yet **b**-d
  Rom. 4:11, the father of all who **b**
  Heb. 11:6, he who comes to God must **b** that
  James 2:19, You **b** that God is one . . . the
  1 Pet. 2:6, HE WHO **B**-S IN HIM SHALL NOT BE
  Matt. 21:25; 27:42; Mark 11:24,31; 16:13;
    Luke 8:50; 24:41; John 1:7; 3:12; 5:44,47;
    6:36; 7:48; 10:37; 11:15; 12:36; Acts 4:32;
    9:26; 13:39,48; 16:34; Rom. 4:18; 9:33;
    10:14; 2 Cor. 4:13; Gal. 3:22; 2 Thess. 1:10
BELLY—*stomach* Gen. 3:14, On your **b** shall you
  go
BELONG Luke 23:7, He **b**-ed to Herod's
  1 Cor. 3:21, all things **b** to you
    3:23, **b** to Christ . . . **b**-s to God
BELOVED—*chosen* Ps. 127:2, He gives to His **b**
  Matt. 3:17; 17:5, This is My **b** Son
  Eph. 1:6, bestowed on us in the **B**
    5:1, be imitators of God, as **b** children
  Col. 1:13, kingdom of His **b** Son
  2 Tim. 1:2, to Timothy, my **b** son
  Philem. 16, more than a slave, a **b** brother
  Jude 1, **b** in God the Father
  Deut. 33:12; Jer. 12:7; Mark 1:11; 9:7; Luke 3:22;
    Rom. 11:28; 12:19; 16:9; 1 Cor. 10:14;
    2 Cor. 7:1; 12:19; Phil. 4:1; Col. 4:9; 1 Pet.
    2:11; 2 Pet. 1:17
BELOW—*beneath* Gen. 1:9; Deut. 4:39; Prov.
  15:24; Jer. 31:37; John 8:23
BELT—*girdle* Mark 1:6, John . . . a leather **b**
  Acts 21:11, took Paul's **b** and bound his own
    feet
  1 Sam. 18:4; 2 Sam. 18:11; 20:8; Ps. 109:19;
    Prov. 31:24; Is. 3:24; 5:27; 11:5; Ezek. 23:15;
    Matt. 3:4
BEND—*bow* Ps. 11:2, the wicked **b** the bow
BENEFACTOR Luke 22:25, those . . . called **B**-s
BENEFIT—*profit, blessing* Ps. 103:2, forget none
  of His **b**-s
  Ps. 116:12, For all His **b**-s toward me
  1 Tim. 6:2, those who partake of the **b**
  2 Chr. 32:25; Is. 65:8; Rom. 3:1; 1 Tim. 6:2
BEREAVE—*deprive* Gen. 27:45; 42:36; Lev.
  26:22; Jer. 15:7; Ezek. 5:17; 36:12
BESIDE Ps. 23:2, He leads me **b** quiet waters
  Is. 43:11, there is no saviour **b**-s Me
    44:6, there is no God **b**-s Me
  Matt. 13:4, *seeds* fell **b** the road
  2 Cor. 5:13, if we are **b** ourselves, it is for God
  Deut. 11:30; Ruth 2:14; 2 Kin. 21:16; Is. 32:20
BESIEGE Deut. 20:19; 2 Sam. 11:1; 1 Kin. 16:17;
  Is. 1:8; Ezek. 4:3; 6:12
BEST Ps. 39:5, man at his **b** is a mere breath
  Luke 15:22, bring out the **b** robe
  Gen. 43:11; 1 Sam. 9:9,15; 2 Sam. 18:4
BESTOW—*grant* Ex. 32:29, He may **b** a blessing
  upon you
  1 Chr. 29:25, **b**-ed on him royal majesty
  1 Cor. 12:23, we **b** more abundant honor
  1 John 3:1, love the Father has **b**-ed on us
BETRAY Matt. 27:4, I have sinned by **b**-ing
  Mark 14:11, he *began* seeking how to **b** Him
  Luke 22:21, the hand of the one **b**-ing Me
  1 Cor. 11:23, the night . . . He was **b**-ed
  Is. 16:3; Matt. 24:10; 26:16; Mark 14:18;
    Luke 22:22; John 6:64; 21:20
BETROTH Hos. 2:19,20, I will **b** you to Me
  Jer. 2:2; Matt. 1:18; 2 Cor. 11:2

BETTER 1 Sam. 15:22, to obey is **b** than sacrifice
Ps. 63:3, Thy lovingkindness is **b** than life
Heb. 11:16, they desire a **b** country
2 Pet. 2:21, **b** for them not to have known the
way
1 Kin. 19:4; Eccles. 2:24; 4:9; 7:10; Song 1:2;
Heb. 1:4
BEWARE Deut. 8:11, **B**, lest you forget the LORD
Deut. 15:9, **B**, lest there is a base thought
Matt. 6:1, **B** of practicing your righteousness
10:17, But **b** of men
16:6, **b** of the leaven of the Pharisees
Mark 12:38, **B** of the scribes
Luke 12:15, **B**, and be on your guard against . . .
greed
Ex. 19:12; Job 36:18; Mark 8:15; Luke 12:1;
20:46; Phil. 3:2
BEWITCHED Gal. 3:1, You foolish Galatians,
who has **b**
BEYOND 2 Cor. 8:3, **b** their ability
Gal. 1:13, persecute the church of God **b**
measure
Gen. 35:21; Deut. 3:20; John 3:26; Acts 7:43
BIER 2 Sam. 3:31, David walked behind the **b**
BILLOWS—*waves* Jon. 2:3, **b** passed over me
BIND—*wrap* Num. 30:2, an oath to **b** himself
Prov. 6:21, **B** them continually on your heart
Is. 61:1, **b** up the brokenhearted
Matt. 16:19, **b** on earth shall be bound in
heaven
Job 38:31; Matt. 12:29; 18:18; Mark 3:27
BIRD—*fowl, swallow* Lev. 20:25, unclean **b**
Ps. 84:3, **b** also has found a house
124:7, Our soul has escaped as a **b**
Matt. 6:26, Look at the **b-s** of the air
8:20, **b-s** of the air *have* nests
Gen. 1:20; 6:7; 2 Sam. 21:10; Ps. 8:8; 11:1;
Prov. 1:17; Eccles. 10:20; Jer. 9:10; 12:9;
Hos. 9:8; Luke 9:58; Rev. 19:17
BIRTH Eccles. 7:1, better than the day of **b**
Matt. 1:18, **b** of Jesus Christ was
John 9:1, a man blind from **b**
Gen. 38:27; Is. 66:9; Luke 1:14
BIRTHRIGHT Gen. 25:31, First sell me your **b**
Gen. 27:36, Jacob . . . took away my **b**
Heb. 12:16, sold his own **b** for a single meal
BIT (n.) Ps. 32:9; James 3:3
BITE Prov. 23:32; Eccles. 10:8; Amos 5:19; 9:3;
Mic. 3:5; Gal. 5:15
BITTER Ex. 1:14, **b** with hard labor
Ex. 12:8, unleavened bread and **b** herbs
15:23, waters of Marah . . . were **b**
2 Kin. 14:26, affliction of Israel . . . was very **b**
Is. 24:9, Strong drink is **b** to those who drink
Matt. 26:75, went out and wept **b-ly**
Job 21:25; Is. 5:20; Luke 22:62
BITTERNESS—*gall* Job 10:1, **b** of my soul
Prov. 14:10; 17:25, heart knows its own **b**
Eph. 4:31, Let all **b** and wrath . . . be put away
Heb. 12:15, no root of **b**
1 Sam. 15:32; Is. 38:15; Lam. 3:19; Rom. 3:14
BLACK Matt. 5:36, make one hair **b** or white
Jude 13, for whom the **b** darkness has been
reserved
Rev. 6:5, behold a **b** horse
BLADE Judg. 3:22, fat closed over the **b**
Mark 4:28, first the **b**, then the head
BLAMELESS Ps. 119:80, May my heart be **b**
Prov. 11:20, **b** in their walk are His delight
Acts 24:16, maintain always a **b** conscience
1 Cor. 1:8, **b** in the day of our Lord Jesus Christ
Eph. 1:4, holy and **b** before Him
2 Sam. 22:26; Ps. 119:1; Phil. 1:10; 2:15; 3:6;
Jude 24; Rev. 14:5
BLASPHEME—*spoke* Is. 52:5, My name is
continually **b-d**
Matt. 9:3, This *fellow* **b-s**
26:65, He has **b-d**
Mark 3:29, **b-s** against the Holy Spirit

2 Sam. 12:14; Acts 26:11; Rom. 2:24;
1 Tim. 1:20; James 2:7
BLASPHEMY Matt. 12:31, **b** against the Spirit
Matt. 26:65, you have now heard the **b**
Mark 3:28, whatever **b-es** they utter
Rev. 2:9, the **b** by those who say they are Jews
13:5, arrogant words and **b-es**
Mark 14:64; Luke 5:21; John 10:33
BLEMISH—*spot* Heb. 9:14, offered Himself
without **b**
Num. 19:2; Song 4:7; Ezek. 43:22; 45:18; 46:4
BLEND 2 Chr. 16:14, **b-ed** by the perfumers' art
BLESS—*happy* Josh. 17:14, LORD has . . . **b-ed**
Ps. 144:15, **b-ed** are the people whose God is
the LORD
Prov. 3:13, **b-ed** is the man who finds wisdom
10:7, memory of the righteous is **b-ed**
Luke 6:28, **b** those who curse you
Acts 20:35, more **b-ed** to give than to receive
Titus 2:13, looking for **b-ed** hope
James 3:9, we **b** *our* Lord and Father
Rev. 14:13, Write, **B-ed** are the dead
Gen. 22:17; Deut. 28:3-6; 33:29; Judg. 5:2;
1 Chr. 4:10; Ps. 127:5; Prov. 28:14; Is. 32:20;
65:16; Hag. 2:19; Mal. 3:15; John 13:17;
Rom. 12:14; 2 Cor. 11:31; Titus 2:13;
James 5:11; 1 Pet. 3:14; 4:14
BLESSING—*benefit* Gen. 39:5, LORD's **b** was
upon all
Prov. 10:22, **b** of the LORD that makes rich
28:20, faithful man will abound with **b-s**
Mal. 3:10, pour out for you a **b**
Rom. 15:29, the fulness of the **b** of Christ
1 Cor. 10:16, Is not the cup of **b**
Gen. 27:35; Deut. 11:26; 23:5; Neh. 13:2;
Job 29:13; Mal. 2:2; 2 Cor. 1:15; James 3:10;
Rev. 5:12
BLIND Ex. 23:8, bribe **b-s** the clear-sighted
Matt. 11:5, *the* **B** RECEIVE SIGHT
2 Cor. 4:4, **b-ed** the minds of the unbelieving
1 John 2:11, darkness has **b-ed** his eyes
Deut. 16:19; 1 Sam. 12:3
BLINDNESS Deut. 28:28; 2 Kin. 6:18; Zech. 12:4
BLOOD Gen. 9:6, Whoever sheds man's **b**, By
man his **b**
Ps. 72:14, their **b** will be precious in his sight
Ezek. 9:9, the land is filled with **b**
Matt. 16:17, because flesh and **b** did not reveal
27:4, by betraying innocent **b**
Luke 22:20, new covenant in My **b**
22:44, His sweat became like drops of **b**
Acts 20:28, He purchased with His own **b**
21:25, abstain from meat . . . and from **b**
Rom. 3:25, a propitiation in His **b**
5:9, justified by His **b**
1 Cor. 10:16, sharing in the **b** of Christ
11:27, guilty of the body . . . **b** of the Lord
15:50, flesh and **b** cannot inherit the kingdom
Eph. 1:7, redemption through His **b**
Heb. 9:22, shedding of **b** there is no forgiveness
1 Pet. 1:19, the **b** of Christ
Rev. 12:11, the **b** of the Lamb
Gen. 9:4; Ex. 12:22; Lev. 3:17; Josh. 2:19;
1 Kin. 2:32; Is. 9:5; Ezek. 18:13; Matt. 27:25;
Mark 14:24; John 1:13; 6:54,55,56;
Acts 15:20; 1 Cor. 11:25; Heb. 10:29;
Rev. 7:14
BLOSSOM Gen. 40:10; Eccles. 12:5; Is. 17:11;
27:6; 35:1; Hos. 14:5; Hab. 3:17
BLOT—*erase* Ex. 32:32, please **b** me from Thy
book
Deut. 9:14, **b** out their name from heaven
Ps. 51:1, Thy compassion **b** out my
transgressions
51:9, **b** out all my iniquities
69:28, May they be **b-ed** out of the book of
life
Deut. 25:19; 29:20; 2 Kin. 14:27; Neh. 4:5;
Ps. 109:13,14; Prov. 6:33; Jer. 18:23
BLOWS Prov. 19:29, **b** for the back of fools

BOAST—*glory, rejoice, talk* Ps. 34:2, soul . . .
  make its **b**
  Ps. 49:6, **b** in the abundance of their riches
  Prov. 27:1, do not **b** about tomorrow
  Rom. 2:23, You who **b** in the Law
  James 4:16, all such **b-ing** is evil
  1 Sam. 2:3; 1 Kin. 20:11; 2 Chr. 25:19; Ps. 5:5;
    75:4; Prov. 20:14; Rom. 2:17; 3:27;
    1 Cor. 5:6; 2 Cor. 11:16; Gal. 5:26; Eph. 2:9;
    James 3:5; 4:16
BOAT Is. 33:21; John 6:22; Acts 27:16; 27:30
BODILY Luke 3:22, Holy Spirit descended . . . in **b**
  form
  Col. 2:9, fulness of Deity dwells in **b** form
  1 Tim. 4:8, **b** discipline is only little profit
BODY—*corpse, flesh* Matt. 6:22, whole **b** . . . full
  of light
  Mark 5:29, she felt in her **b** that she was healed
    6:29, his **b** and laid it in a tomb
  Luke 12:22, do not be anxious . . . for your **b**
  Acts 19:12, carried from his **b** to the sick
  Rom. 6:6, that our **b** of sin might be done away
    12:1, present your **b-es** a living . . . sacrifice
    12:4, many members in one **b**
    12:5, we . . . are one **b** in Christ
  1 Cor. 9:27, but I buffet my **b**
    13:3, if I deliver my **b** to be burned
  2 Cor. 5:8, prefer to be absent from the **b**
  Gal. 6:17, I bear on my **b** the brand-marks of
    Jesus
  1 Pet. 2:24, bore our sins in His **b**
  Gen. 47:18; Eccles. 12:12; Matt. 5:29; 6:23;
    Luke 11:34; 17:37; John 2:21; Rom. 7:24;
    1 Cor. 12:14; 2 Cor. 12:2; Phil. 3:21
BODYGUARD—*guard* Gen. 40:4; Jer. 39:9
BOISTEROUS—*clamor*
  Prov. 9:13, woman of folly is **b**
BOLD Prov. 28:1, righteous are **b** as a lion
  Acts 13:46, Paul and Barnabas spoke out **b-ly**
  Ex. 14:8; Num. 33:3; Rom. 10:20; 2 Cor. 10:2;
    10:12
BOLDNESS—*confidence* Acts 4:31, speak . . .
  with **b**
  Eph. 3:12, we have **b** and confident access
  Phil. 1:20, with all **b**, Christ . . . be exalted
BOND—*cord* Hos. 11:4, with **b-s** of love
  Eph. 4:3, in the **b** of peace
  Col. 3:14, perfect **b** of unity
  Ezek. 20:37; Luke 13:16; Jude 6
BOND-SERVANT—*servant* Luke 2:29, let Thy **b**
  depart
  Rom. 1:1, Paul, a **b** of Christ Jesus
  Phil. 1:1, Paul and Timothy, **b-s** of Christ
  Titus 1:1; James 1:1; 2 Pet. 1:1
BONE Ezek. 37:7, **b-s** came together, **b** to its **b**
  Luke 24:39, spirit does not have flesh and **b-s**
  John 19:36, NOT A **B** OF HIM SHALL BE BROKEN
  Gen. 2:23; Ex. 12:46; Job 20:11; Ps. 51:8;
    Prov. 12:4; Matt. 23:27
BOOK Is. 34:16, Seek from the **b** of the LORD
  Mal. 3:16, **b** of remembrance
  John 21:25, world itself would not contain
    the **b-s**
  Phil. 4:3, names are in the **b** of life
  Ex. 17:14; Ezra 4:15; Job 19:23; Luke 4:17;
    Acts 19:19; 1 Tim. 4:13; Rev. 3:5; 13:8; 17:8;
    20:12; 21:27; 22:19
BOOTHS Gen. 33:17; Lev. 23:42,43; Neh. 8:14
BOOTY—*plunder* Num. 31:32; Is. 53:12; Jer. 38:2;
  49:32
BORDER Gen. 47:21, one end of Egypt's **b** to the
  other
  Ex. 34:24, drive out nations . . . . . . **b-s**
  Jer. 15:13, . . . within all your **b-s**
    50:26, Come to her from the farthest **b**
  Gen. 23:17; Num. 21:13; 34:3; 35:26; Deut. 3:17;
    Josh. 12:5; 2 Kin. 3:21; 1 Chr. 4:10;
    Ps. 147:14; Is. 19:19; 60:18; Ezek. 11:10
BORE—*bear, carry, pierce, yield*
  Ex. 19:4, how I **b** you on eagles' wings
  Is. 53:4, our griefs He Himself **b**
    53:12, He Himself **b** the sin of many

  1 Pet. 2:24, He Himself **b** our sins
  Num. 17:8; 2 Kin. 12:9; Jer. 31:19
BORN—*begotten, forth* Job 5:7, man is **b** for
  trouble
  Job 14:1, Man, who is **b** of woman
  Is. 9:6, For a child will be **b** to us
    66:8, Can a land be **b** in one day
  John 1:13, who were **b** not of blood
    3:3, unless one is **b** again
    3:6,8, **b** of the Spirit
  1 Cor. 15:8, one untimely **b**
  1 Pet. 1:3, **b** again to a living hope
  1 John 4:7, every one who loves is **b** of God
    5:4, whatever is **b** of God overcomes the
    world
  Job 3:3; 15:14; 25:4; Ps. 87:4; 90:2; Prov. 17:17;
    Matt. 11:11; 1 Pet. 1:23; 1 John 5:1
BORNE Is. 46:3, been **b** by Me from birth
  Job 34:31; Lam. 5:7; Matt. 20:12
BORROW Deut. 28:12, you shall not **b**
  Prov. 22:7, **b-er** *becomes* the lender's slave
  Ex. 22:14; Deut. 15:6; 2 Kin. 4:3; Ps. 37:21;
    Matt. 5:42
BOSOM—*breast* Prov. 6:27, fire in his **b**
  Is. 40:11, carry *them* in His **b**
  Luke 16:22, carried . . . to Abraham's **b**
  John 1:18, in the **b** of the Father
  Ex. 4:6; Job 31:33; Ps. 35:13
BOTHER—*trouble* Matt. 26:10, do you **b** the
  woman
BOTTLE—*jug, wineskin* Judg. 4:19; Ps. 56:8
BOUGH—*branch* Ps. 80:10, cedars of God with
  its **b-s**
  Gen. 49:22; Lev. 23:40; Deut. 24:20; Ps. 80:10;
    Is. 17:6; Ezek. 31:6
BOUGHT Luke 14:18, I have **b** a piece of land
  1 Cor. 6:20, been **b** with a price
    7:23, You were **b** with a price
  2 Pet. 2:1, denying the Master who **b** them
BOUND—*gird, yoke* Prov. 22:15, Foolishness is **b**
  up in
  Matt. 16:19, **b** in heaven
  Acts 20:22, **b** in spirit, I am on my way to
    Jerusalem
  1 Cor. 7:27, Are you **b** to a wife
  2 Cor. 6:14, Do not be **b** together
  Gen. 44:30; Mark 5:4
BOUNDARY Prov. 8:29, He set for the sea its **b**
BOUNTIFUL—*generous*
  Ps. 13:6, He has dealt **b-ly** with me
    116:7, the LORD has dealt **b-ly** with you
  2 Cor. 9:6, he who sows **b-ly** . . . reap **b-ly**
  Ps. 119:17; 2 Cor. 9:5
BOUNTY 1 Kin. 10:13, according to his royal **b**
BOW—*bend, worship* Is. 66:23, to **b** down
  1 Sam. 2:36; Ps. 10:10; Is. 60:14
BOWL—*dish, pitcher* Eccles. 12:6, golden **b** is
  crushed
  Matt. 26:23, who dipped his hand in the **b**
  Num. 7:25; 1 Kin. 17:12; Amos 6:6; Zech. 4:2;
    Mark 14:20
BOY—*child* Is. 11:6, a little **b** will lead them
  Joel 3:3, Traded a **b** for a harlot
  Gen. 25:27; Zech. 8:5
BRACELET Gen. 24:22; 24:30; 24:47; Ex. 35:22;
  Num. 31:50; 2 Sam. 1:10; Is. 3:19; Ezek. 16:11;
  23:42
BRAMBLE—*briar* Judg. 9:14, trees said to the **b**
  Judg. 9:15, fire come out from the **b**
BRANCH—*bough* Jer. 23:5, raise up for David a
  righteous **B**
  Matt. 13:32, THE BIRDS . . . NEST IN ITS **B-ES**
    21:8, others were cutting **b-es**
  John 15:2, every **b** that bears fruit
    15:4, **b** cannot bear fruit of itself
    15:5, I am the vine, you are the **b-es**
  Judg. 9:48; Ezek. 31:3; Mark 11:8; Luke 13:19;
    John 12:13; 15:6; Rom. 11:16
BRAND—*torch* Zech. 3:2; 1 Tim. 4:2

BRAY Job 6:5, wild donkey **b** over *his* grass
BREACH Judg. 21:15, LORD had made a **b** in . . . Israel
  Job 16:14, breaks through me with **b** after **b**
  Gen. 38:29; Ex. 22:9; 1 Kin. 11:27; Neh. 4:7; 6:1;
    Ps. 60:2; 106:23; Is. 22:9; 30:13; 58:12;
    Amos 4:3; 9:11
BREAD—*food* Ex. 16:4, I will rain **b** from heaven
  Deut. 8:3, man does not live by **b** alone
  Job 22:7, you have withheld **b**
  Ps. 132:15, satisfy her needy with **b**
  Prov. 31:27, does not eat the **b** of idleness
  Eccles. 11:1, Cast your **b** on the surface of the waters
  Is. 55:2, spend money for what is not **b**
    55:10, seed to the sower and **b** to the eater
  Matt. 4:3, command these stones become **b**
    6:11, Give us this day our daily **b**
  Mark 7:27, take the children's **b**
  Acts 2:42, the breaking of **b**
    20:7, gathered together to break **b**
  Ex. 23:25; Josh. 9:5; Judg. 7:13; 1 Kin. 17:6;
    Job 33:20; Prov. 9:17; 12:11; Matt. 4:4;
    Luke 4:3,4; 24:35; Acts 27:35; 2 Thess. 3:8
BREAK—*broke, profane* 2 Chr. 32:1, to **b** into them
  Is. 42:3, reed He will not **b**
  Luke 5:6, their nets began to **b**
    24:30, He took the bread . . . and **b-ing** it
  1 Cor. 10:16, bread which we **b** a sharing in . . . Christ
  Job 19:10; Jer. 4:3; Hos. 10:12; Matt. 12:5,20;
    14:19; Acts 21:13
BREASTPIECE Ex. 25:7; 28:4,15,22,23; 35:9,27;
  39:8; Lev. 8:8
BREASTPLATE Is. 59:17, put on righteousness like a **b**
  Eph. 6:14, PUT ON THE **B** OF RIGHTEOUSNESS
  1 Thess. 5:8, put on the **b** of faith and love
  Neh. 4:16; Rev. 9:9,17
BREATH—*spirit, wind* Gen. 2:7, **b** of life
  Job 7:16, my days are *but* a **b**
    12:10, the **b** of all mankind
    27:3, **b** of God is in my nostrils
  Ps. 150:6, Let everything that has **b** praise the LORD
  Acts 17:25, He Himself gives to all life and **b**
  Gen. 6:17; 7:15; Eccles. 3:21; Is. 2:22;
    Ezek. 37:5,10
BREATHE Gen. 2:7, **b-d** into his nostrils the breath
  Ezek. 37:9, **b** on these slain
  Acts 9:1, **b-ing** threats and murder
  Deut. 20:16; Josh. 10:40; 11:11,14; Ps. 27:12;
    John 20:23
BRETHREN—*brother* Ps. 22:22, tell of Thy name to my **b**
  Is. 66:20, all your **b** from all the nations
  1 Cor. 14:39, my **b**, desire earnestly to prophesy
  2 Cor. 11:26, dangers among false **b**
  Gal. 1:2, all the **b** who are with me
    2:4, because of false **b**
  Eph. 6:23, Peace be to the **b**
  Col. 1:2, saints and faithful **b** in Christ
  1 Thess. 4:9, love of the **b**
  1 Pet. 1:22, sincere love of the **b**
  1 John 3:14, because we love the **b**
  Mic. 5:3; Rom. 1:13; 7:1; 8:12; Heb. 13:1
BRIAR—*thistle* Luke 6:44, nor . . . pick grapes from a **b**
BRIBE Ex. 23:8, not take a **b**, for a **b** blinds
  Is. 1:23, Every one loves a **b**
    5:23, justify the wicked for a **b**
  Deut. 10:17; 27:25; 1 Sam. 8:3; 12:3; Ps. 26:10;
    Is. 33:15; Mic. 7:3
BRICK Gen. 11:3; Ex. 1:14; 5:7; Is. 9:10; 65:3
BRIDE Rev. 21:2, as a **b** adorned for her husband
  21:9, the **b**, the wife of the Lamb
  22:17, the Spirit and the **b** say, Come
  Is. 49:18; 61:10; 62:5; Jer. 2:32; 7:34; 16:9; 25:10;
    33:11; Joel 2:16; John 3:29; Rev. 18:23

BRIDEGROOM Jer. 7:34; 16:9; 25:10; 33:11
  Matt. 25:1, virgins . . . went out to meet the **b**
  John 3:29, He who has the bride is the **b**
  Rev. 18:23, voice of the **b**
  Ex. 4:25; Ps. 19:5; Is. 61:10; 62:5; Joel 2:16;
    Matt. 9:15; Mark 2:19; John 2:9
BRIDLE—*guard* James 1:26, not **b** his tongue
  2 Kin. 19:28; Prov. 26:3; Is. 37:29
BRIGHT Rev. 22:16, **b** morning star
  Lev. 13:2; Job 37:21; Matt. 17:5
BRIGHTNESS—*radiance* Is. 60:3, kings to the **b** of your
  Is. 62:1, righteousness goes forth like **b**
BRIMSTONE Gen. 19:24; Is. 30:33; Rev. 9:17;
  14:10; 19:20
BRISTLE Job 4:15, hair . . . **b-d** up
BROAD—*wide* Ps. 119:96, commandment is exceedingly **b**
  Matt. 7:13, way is **b** that leads to destruction
  1 Chr. 4:40; Ps. 104:25; Matt. 23:5
BROILED Luke 24:42, gave Him a piece of **b** fish
BROKE—*break* John 19:32, **b** the legs of the first man
  Eph. 2:14, **b** down the barrier
  1 Sam. 4:18; 2 Kin. 23:14; 2 Chr. 34:4;
    Matt. 15:36; 26:26; Mark 6:41
BROKEN—*loose, void* Job 17:1, My spirit is **b**
  Ps. 51:17, a **b** spirit; A **b** and a contrite heart
    69:20, Reproach has **b** my heart
    119:126, have **b** Thy law
  Eccles. 12:6, the silver cord is **b**
  Jer. 2:13, **B** cisterns
  John 10:35, Scripture cannot be **b**
    19:36, NOT A BONE OF HIM SHALL BE **B**
BROKENHEARTED
  Ps. 34:18, Lord is near to the **b**
BRONZE Deut. 28:23; 2 Sam. 22:35; Ezra 8:27;
  Jer. 15:12
BROOD Matt. 3:7, You **b** of vipers, who warned you
  Luke 13:34, a hen *gathers* her **b**
BROOK 1 Sam. 17:40; Ps. 110:7
  Ps. 42:1, deer pants for the water **b-s**
BROTHER—*brethren* Gen. 4:9, Am I my **b-'s** keeper
  Prov. 18:24, friend who sticks closer than a **b**
  Matt. 10:21, **b** will deliver up **b** to death
    23:8, you are all **b-s**
  Luke 18:29, no one who has left . . . **b-s**
  John 7:5, not even His **b-s** were
  1 Cor. 6:6, **b** goes to law with **b**
  Gen. 42:8; Prov. 17:17; 18:9,19; 19:7; Eccles. 4:8;
    Matt. 5:23; Mark 3:35; 10:29; 2 Thess. 3:15
BROTHERHOOD Amos 1:9, covenant of **b**
BROTHERLY Rom. 12:10, in **b** love
  2 Pet. 1:7, *your* **b** kindness
BROUGHT—*escape* Matt. 10:18, shall . . . be **b** before governors
BROW Luke 4:29, led Him to the **b** of the hill
BRUISE—*batter, crush* Gen. 3:15, shall **b** you
  Is. 1:6, **b-s**, welts, and raw wounds
    42:3, A **b-d** reed He will not break
BRUTAL—*senseless, stupid, fierce* Ezek. 21:31;
  2 Tim. 3:3
BUCKET Num. 24:7, flow from his **b-s**
  Is. 40:15, nations are like a drop from a **b**
BUD—*sprout* Num. 17:8; Is. 18:5
BUFFET—*beat* 2 Cor. 12:7, to **b** me
BUGLE—*trumpet* 1 Cor. 14:8, **b** produces an . . . sound
BUILD 1 Chr. 17:12, He shall **b** for Me a house
  Ps. 127:1, Unless the LORD **b-s** the house
  Eccles. 3:3, a time to **b** up
  1 Cor. 3:12, if any man **b-s** upon the foundation
  2 Chr. 6:9; Luke 14:30; Acts 20:32; Rom. 15:20
BUILDER—*maker* Ps. 118:22, the **b-s** rejected
  Heb. 11:10, whose architect and **b** is God
  1 Pet. 2:7, STONE WHICH THE **B-S** REJECTED
  1 Kin. 5:18; Ezra 3:10; Matt. 21:42; Mark 12:10;
    Luke 20:17; Acts 4:11

BUILDING 1 Cor. 3:9, you are ... God's **b**
  2 Cor. 5:1, we have a **b** from God
  Eph. 2:21, **b**, being fitted together
BUILT Eccles. 2:4, I **b** houses for myself
  Matt. 7:24, **b** his house upon the rock
  Eph. 2:22, **b** together into a dwelling of God
BULL Lev. 4:3, a **b** without defect
BULRUSHES Is. 19:7, **b** by the Nile
BUNDLE Gen. 42:35; Acts 28:3
  1 Sam. 25:29, bound in the **b** of living
  Matt. 13:30, bind them in **b-s** to burn
BURDEN—*load* Ps. 55:22, Cast your **b** upon the
  LORD
  Matt. 20:12, borne the **b** and ... heat of the day
  Luke 11:46, weigh men down with **b-s** hard to
   bear
  Gal. 6:2, Bear one another's **b-s**
  Acts 15:28; 2 Cor. 11:9; 12:16; 1 Thess. 2:9
BURIAL John 19:40, **b** custom of the Jews
  Gen. 23:4; Eccles. 6:3; Jer. 22:19; Matt. 26:12
BURN—*kindle* Ex. 3:2, bush was **b-ing** with fire
  Ps. 39:3, While I was musing the fire **b-ed**
  Prov. 26:23, **b-ing** lips and a wicked heart
  Is. 9:18, wickedness **b-s** like a fire
   42:3, dimly **b-ing** wick He will not
  Luke 3:17, He will **b** up the chaff
   24:32, our hearts **b-ing** within us
  John 5:35, He was the lamp that was **b-ing**
  1 Cor. 13:3, deliver my body to be **b-ed**
  Rev. 18:8, she will be **b-ed** up with fire
  Gen. 30:2; Ex. 32:12,19; Ps. 11:6; Is. 33:14;
   Mal. 4:1; Matt. 13:30; Rom. 12:20; Heb. 6:8;
   Rev. 4:5; 19:20
BURNT OFFERING Gen. 22:7; Lev. 1:4; 6:9;
  Is. 61:8
  Ps. 40:6, **B** and sin offering Thou hast not
   required
  Jer. 6:20, **b-s** are not acceptable
  Hos. 6:6, knowledge of God rather than **b-s**
  Mark 12:33, more than all **b-s** and sacrifices
BURST—*break* Job 32:19; Matt. 9:17; Mark 2:22;
  Luke 5:37
BURY Rom. 6:4, **b-ed** with Him through baptism
  1 Cor. 15:4, and that he was **b-ed**
  Gen. 23:4; 47:29; Matt. 8:21,22; 14:12;
   Luke 9:59,60; Acts 8:2; Col. 2:12
BUSHEL—*ephah* Amos 8:5, To make the **b** smaller
BUSINESS—*matter* Ps. 107:23, Who do **b** on
  great waters
  1 Thess. 4:11, attend to your own **b**
  James 4:13, engage in **b** and make a profit
  Gen. 24:33; Josh. 2:14; Matt. 22:5; Acts 19:25
BUSYBODIES—*meddler* 2 Thess. 3:11, acting
  like **b**
  1 Tim. 5:13, also gossips and **b**
BUTTER—*curds* Job 29:6; Prov. 30:33
  Ps. 55:21, His speech was smoother than **b**
BUY Is. 55:1, **b** and eat ... **b** wine and milk
  Matt. 13:44, sells all that he has and **b-s** that
   field
  Rev. 3:18, **b** from Me gold refined by fire
   13:17, no one should be able to **b** or to sell
  Gen. 42:2; 47:19; Lev. 22:11; Ruth 4:4;
   Prov. 23:23; Matt. 25:9; John 4:8; Rev. 18:11
BUYER Is. 24:2; Ezek. 7:12
  Prov. 20:14, Bad, bad, says the **b**
BYWORD—*taunt* Job 30:9
  1 Kin. 9:7, Israel will become ... a **b** among all
   peoples
  2 Chr. 7:20, a **b** among all peoples
  Job 17:6, a **b** of the people
  Ps. 44:14, **b** among the nations

C

CAGE Jer. 5:27, a **c** full of birds
CAKE Gen. 18:6; 1 Kin. 17:13; 2 Kin. 20:7
CALAMITY—*destruction* Job 31:23, **c** from God
  is a terror
  Prov. 1:27, **c** comes on like a whirlwind
  2 Sam. 22:19; 24:16; 1 Chr. 21:15; Job 6:30;
   21:17; 31:3; Ps. 18:18; Prov. 24:16; 27:10;
   Jon. 3:10; 4:2

CALCULATE—*count* Is. 40:12, **c-d** the dust of
  the earth
  Luke 14:28, sit down and **c** the cost
CALF Luke 15:23, bring the fattened **c**
  Heb. 9:12, blood of goats and **c-ves**
  Gen. 18:7; Is. 11:6; Rev. 4:7
CALL—*address* Gen. 4:26, to **c** upon the name
  Ps. 4:1, Answer me when I **c**
  Is. 7:14, **c** His name Immanuel
  Matt. 9:13, not come to **c** the righteous
  Luke 6:46, why do you **c** Me, Lord, Lord
  John 13:13, **c** Me Teacher, and Lord
  1 Cor. 1:26, consider your **c**, brethren
  1 Thess. 4:7, God has not **c-ed** us for ...
   impurity
  Deut. 4:26; Ruth 1:20; Ps. 18:3; Prov. 8:1;
   Is. 5:20; Jer. 3:19
CALLING—*summoning* Is. 1:13, the **c** of
  assemblies
  Rom. 11:29, gifts and the **c** of God
  2 Tim. 1:9, called us with a holy **c**
  Heb. 3:1, partakers of a heavenly **c**
CALM—*still* Is. 7:4, be **c**, have no fear
  Jon. 1:11, the sea may become **c**
  Matt. 8:26, it became perfectly **c**
  Acts 19:36, you ought to keep **c** ... do nothing
   rash
CAMEL Gen. 24:64; Mark 1:6
  Matt. 3:4, John ... a garment of **c-'s** hair
   19:24, easier for a **c** ... eye of a needle
   23:24, out a gnat and swallow a **c**
CAMP—*settle* Ex. 14:19, before the **c**
  Deut. 23:14, God walks ... your **c**
  Gen. 32:2; Num. 31:19; Ps. 69:25; Is. 29:3;
   Zech. 9:8; Rev. 20:9
CANCEL—*blot, erase* Is. 28:18; Col. 2:14
CAPTIVE Luke 4:18, RELEASE TO THE **C-S**
  Eph. 4:8, LED **C** A HOST OF **C-S**
  Ps. 68:18; Jer. 13:17; Col. 2:8
CAPTIVITY Is. 46:2, have themselves gone into **c**
CAPTURE Job 5:13, **c-s** the wise
CARCASS—*corpse* Gen. 15:11; Judg. 14:8
CARE—*concern, worry*
  Gen. 50:24, God ... take **c** of you
  Ps. 142:4, No one **c-s** for my soul
  Ezek. 34:12, I will **c** for My sheep
  Luke 10:34, to an inn, and took **c** of him
  1 Tim. 3:5, take **c** of the church
  1 Pet. 5:7, because He **c-s** for you
  Ps. 8:4; Mark 4:38; 1 Cor. 12:25
CAREFUL—*guard, diligent* Luke 15:8
  Prov. 23:1, Consider **c-ly** what is before you
  Eph. 5:15, be **c** how you walk
CARELESS—*idle* Matt. 12:36, every **c** word
CARGO—*merchandise* Rev. 18:12, **c-es** of gold
CAROUSE Rom. 13:13, not in **c-ing** and
  drunkenness
CARPENTER—*craftsmen* 2 Sam. 5:11;
  2 Kin. 22:6; Matt. 13:55; Mark 6:3
CARRIED—*wrought* Is. 53:4, our sorrows He **c**
  Matt. 8:17, **c** away our diseases
  Luke 16:22, was **c** away by the angels
  Heb. 13:9, not be **c** away by ... teachings
  1 Pet. 4:3, **c** out the desire of the Gentiles
CARRY—*bear, wear* Luke 10:4, **c** no purse, no
  bag
  23:26, placed on him the cross to **c**
  2 Cor. 4:10, **c-ing** about in the body the dying of
   Jesus
  Ex. 23:1; Num. 10:17; 11:14; Deut. 1:31;
   1 Sam. 2:28; Ps. 126:6; Is. 40:11; 52:11; 63:9;
   Mark 14:13
CART 1 Sam. 6:8, ark of the LORD ... on the **c**
  1 Sam. 6:7,14; Is. 5:18; 28:28
CASE—*matter* Job 19:28; 37:19
  Deut. 17:8, any **c** is too difficult for you
  Mic. 6:2, the LORD has a **c** against His people
CASSIA Ex. 30:24; Ps. 45:8; Ezek. 27:19

CAST—*drive, throw, thrust*
Ps. 51:11, Do not **c** me away
Eccles. 11:1, **C** your bread on the ... waters
Luke 4:29, **c** Him out of the city
   12:49, **c** fire upon the earth
John 6:37, will certainly not **c** out
1 Pet. 5:7, **c-ing** all your anxiety upon Him
Josh. 18:10; Job 6:27; Mark 15:32
CATCH—*trap* Ps. 10:9; Prov. 6:25; Song 2:15;
   Luke 5:10
CATTLE—*herd* Ps. 50:10, **c** on a thousand hills
Ex. 12:29; 20:10; Lev. 22:19; Num. 31:28;
   Ps. 104:14; Hab. 3:17
CAUGHT—*seized* 2 Cor. 12:4, was **c** up into
   Paradise
Gal. 6:1, if a man is **c** in any trespass
Gen. 22:13; Ex. 22:7; Judg. 15:4; John 21:3
CAUSE—*purpose* Gen. 2:24, For this **c** a man
   shall leave
Ps. 67:1, **c** His face to shine upon us
Prov. 3:30, Do not contend ... without **c**
Matt. 19:5, THIS C A MAN SHALL LEAVE
John 15:25, HATED ME WITHOUT A C
Ps. 112:5; Is. 45:7; Rom. 16:17; 1 Cor. 3:6
CAVE—*shelter* 1 Kin. 18:4; Zeph. 2:6; John 11:38;
   Heb. 11:38
CEASE Ex. 23:12, day you shall **c** *from labor*
Ps. 46:9, He makes wars to **c**
Luke 7:45, not **c-d** to kiss My feet
1 Cor. 13:8, *are* tongues, they will **c**
1 Thess. 5:17, pray without **c-ing**
Gen. 8:22; Deut. 15:11; Ps. 37:8; Prov. 23:4
CEDAR—*fir* 1 Kin. 5:6; 6:15; Job 40:17; Ps. 92:12
CENSER Ezek. 8:11; Rev. 8:3,5
CENSUS—*tax* Luke 2:1, a **c** ... of all the
   inhabited earth
Acts 5:37, rose up in the days of the **c**
CENT Matt. 5:26, paid up the last **c**
Matt. 10:29, sparrows sold for a **c**
Mark 12:42, two small copper coins ... a **c**
CERTAIN—*sure* 2 Pet. 1:10, make **c** about His
   calling
CERTIFICATE Matt. 5:31, A C OF DISMISSAL
CHAFF Ps. 1:4; Matt. 3:12
CHAIN—*band* Acts 12:7, **c-s** fell off his hands
Heb. 11:36, also **c-s** and imprisonment
Judg. 16:21; 1 Kin. 6:21; Eccles. 7:26; Mark 5:3;
   Luke 8:29; Rev. 20:1
CHALCEDONY Rev. 21:19, the third, **c**
CHAMBER—*room* Gen. 43:30; Judg. 3:20,24;
   2 Kin. 4:10; Ps. 19:5; Joel 2:16
CHAMPION 1 Sam. 17:4,23
CHANCE—*happen* Eccles. 9:11, for time and **c**
   overtake
Luke 10:31, by **c** a certain priest
CHANGE—*transform* Ps. 46:2, earth should **c**
Jer. 13:23, the Ethiopian **c** his skin
Mal. 3:6, I, the LORD, do not **c**
1 Cor. 15:51, we shall all be **c-d**
Gen. 35:2; Job 14:14; Prov. 24:21; Dan. 2:21
CHANNEL Job 28:10, hews out **c-s**
CHARCOAL—*coal, soot* John 18:18; 21:9
CHARGE—*accusation, crime* Lev. 8:35, **c** of the
   LORD
2 Chr. 23:6, keep the **c** of the LORD
Ps. 91:11, give His angels **c** concerning
Matt. 24:45, master put in **c** of his household
Ex. 23:7; Matt. 4:6; 27:37; Acts 25:27;
   1 Cor. 9:18; 1 Tim. 5:21; 1 Pet. 5:3
CHARIOT Ps. 20:7, Some boast in **c-s**
Ps. 104:3, makes the clouds his **c**
Acts 8:28, sitting in his **c** ... reading
Gen. 46:29; 2 Kin. 2:11; Ps. 46:9
CHARITY—*alms* Luke 12:33, sell ... give to **c**
CHARM—*favor* Prov. 31:30, **C** is deceitful
CHARMER—*babbler* Ps. 58:5; Eccles. 10:11
CHASE—*drive* Lev. 26:7,8; Deut. 32:30; Job 20:8
CHASTE—*pure* 1 Pet. 3:2, **c** and respectful
   behavior
CHASTEN—*discipline* Is. 53:5, **c-ing** for our
   well-being
Ps. 38:1; 94:12

CHATTER—*babbling* 1 Tim. 6:20; 2 Tim. 2:16
CHEAT—*deceive, mislead*
Gen. 31:7, father has **c-ed** me
CHEEK Job 16:10; Is. 50:6; Matt. 5:39
CHEER—*merry* Judg. 9:13; 1 Sam. 15:32;
   Prov. 15:13
Prov. 15:15, **c-ful** heart *has* a continual feast
2 Cor. 9:7, God loves a **c-ful** giver
James 5:13, Is anyone **c-ful**
CHEESE 1 Sam. 17:18; 2 Sam. 17:29; Job 10:10
CHICK Matt. 23:37, way a hen gathers her **c-s**
CHILD Prov. 22:6, Train up a **c** ... should go
Prov. 23:13, hold back discipline from the **c**
Is. 9:6, a **c** will be born to us
Matt. 1:18, Mary ... with **c** by the Holy Spirit
   2:8, make careful search for the **C**
   2:9, stood over where the **C** was
   2:13,20, take the **C** and His mother
1 Cor. 13:11, When I was a **c**
Gen. 21:8; Jer. 31:20; Matt. 18:2; Mark 5:39;
   Luke 8:54
CHILDBIRTH Ps. 48:6; Rom. 8:22
CHILDHOOD Eccles. 11:9, during your **c**
2 Tim. 3:15, from **c** you have known
CHILDREN—*babes, immature* Gen. 3:16; 1 Sam.
   16:11
Ps. 103:13, father has compassion on *his* **c**
Prov. 31:28, **c** rise up and bless her
Jer. 31:15, Rachel is weeping for her **c**
Ezek. 18:2, **c-'s** teeth are set on edge
Matt. 2:16, slew all the male **c**
   2:18, RACHEL WEEPING FOR HER C
   10:21, C WILL RISE UP AGAINST PARENTS
   18:3, and become like **c**
Is. 3:4; 49:21; Matt. 3:9; 11:16; 19:14; 1 John 2:1;
   Rev. 2:23
CHOICE—*pleasant* 1 Sam. 9:2, **c** and handsome
   man
Rom. 9:11, God's purpose according to *His* **c**
1 Thess. 1:4, knowing ... His **c** of you
Gen. 23:6; 2 Sam. 10:9; Song 4:16; Acts 15:7;
   Rom. 11:5,28
CHOKE Matt. 13:22, riches **c** the word
Mark 4:19, **c** the word
Luke 8:14, **c-d** with worries
CHOOSE—*take* Heb. 11:25, **c-ing** ... endure ill
   treatment
2 Pet. 1:10, calling and **c-ing** you
Ex. 17:9; Deut. 1:13; Josh. 24:15; Is. 7:15
CHOSEN—*elect, beloved, esteemed, loved,*
   choose
Is. 65:9, My **c** ones shall inherit
Luke 9:35, This is My son, *My* **C** One
Col. 3:12, who have been **c** of God
2 Tim. 2:10, endure all things ... who are **c**
1 Pet. 2:9, you are A C RACE
Deut. 7:6; Ps. 119:30; Is. 42:1; 45:4; Matt. 12:18;
   Rom. 11:7; 1 Tim. 5:21; 1 Pet. 1:1; 2 John 1
CHRIST—*Messiah, Lord* 2 Thess. 3:5; 2 John 9
Matt. 16:16, Thou art the **C**, the Son
Luke 24:46, the **C** should suffer
Acts 2:36, made Him both Lord and **C**
1 Cor. 1:23, we preach **C** crucified
Phil. 1:21, to live is **C**
Col. 3:4, **C**, who is our life
1 Thess. 4:16, the dead in **C** shall rise
CHRISTIAN Acts 11:26, first called **C-s** in
   Antioch
Acts 26:28, persuade me to become a **C**
1 Pet. 4:16, if *anyone suffers* as a **C**
CHURCH Matt. 16:18, rock I will build My **c**
Matt. 18:17, tell it to the **c**; refuses to listen ... **c**
Acts 15:4, received by the **c**
1 Cor. 11:18, come together as a **c**
   14:35, for a woman to speak in **c**
2 Cor. 11:8, robbed other **c-es**
Eph. 5:23, Christ ... head of the **c**
1 Tim. 3:5, how will he take care of the **c**
Heb. 12:23, general assembly and **c**
CIRCULATE 1 Sam. 2:24, LORD's people **c-ing**

CIRCUMCISE Phil. 3:5, **c-d** the eighth day
  Col. 2:11, in Him you were also **c-d**
  Gen. 17:10; Deut. 30:6; Luke 1:59
CIRCUMSTANCE—*degree*
  James 1:9, humble **c-s**
CISTERN—*dungeon* Eccles. 12:6, wheel at the **c**
  is crushed
  Jer. 2:13, hew for themselves **c-s**, Broken **c-s**
  Prov. 5:15; Jer. 38:6
CITIZEN—*free* Eph. 2:19, fellow-**c-s** with the
  saints
  Luke 15:15; Acts 21:39; 22:28
CITY Num. 35:6; Josh. 15:59, **c** of refuge
  Ps. 46:4, make glad the **c** of God
    107:4, an inhabited **c**
    127:1, Unless the Lord guards the **c**
  Zech. 8:3, the **C** of Truth
  Matt. 2:23, resided in a **c** called Nazareth
    4:5, took Him into the holy **c**
    5:14, a **c** set on a hill
    10:11, whatever **c** or village you enter
    21:10, all the **c** was stirred
  Acts 8:8, much rejoicing in that **c**
  Heb. 11:10, a **c** which has foundations
    12:22, the **c** of the living God
  Rev. 21:2, I saw the holy **c**
  Gen. 4:17; 11:4; 2 Sam. 19:37; Eccles. 9:14;
    Is. 1:26; 19:18; 33:20; Matt. 10:14; 21:10;
    Luke 9:5; 24:49; Acts 7:58
CLAMOR—*boisterous* Eph. 4:31, anger and **c**
CLAN—*thousand* Is. 60:22, become a **c**
CLAP Ps. 47:1, O **c** your hands, all peoples
  Is. 55:12, trees of the field will **c**
  2 Kin. 11:12; Job 27:23; 34:37; Ps. 98:8;
    Lam. 2:15; Ezek. 25:6
CLASS—*reckon* Luke 22:37, He was **c-ed**
CLAW—*hoof* Dan. 4:33, nails like birds' **c-s**
CLAY Job 4:19, who dwell in houses of **c**
  Job 33:6, formed out of **c**
  Jer. 18:6, **c** in the potter's hand
  1 Kin. 7:46; Is. 64:8; Dan. 2:33; John 9:6;
    Rom. 9:21
CLEAN—*cleanse, acquit, purify*
  Ps. 19:9, fear of the Lord is **c**
    24:4, who has **c** hands
    51:10, Create in me a **c** heart
  Matt. 3:12, thoroughly **c** His threshing floor
  Matt. 8:2; Mark 1:40; Luke 5:12, Thou canst
    make me **c**
  John 15:3, **c** because of the word
  1 Cor. 5:7, **C** out the old leaven
  2 Kin. 5:12; Job 14:4; Is. 1:16; 52:11; Matt. 23:26;
    Luke 11:39,41; John 13:10
CLEANSE—*clean, purify, wash*
  Matt. 8:3; 10:8; 11:5, I am willing; be **c-d**
  Mark 7:4, not eat unless they **c** themselves
  Acts 10:15; 11:9, What God has **c-d**
    15:9, **c-ing** their hearts by faith
  James 4:8, **C** your hands, you sinners
  1 John 1:7, blood . . . **c-s** us from all sin
  Prov. 20:9; Luke 4:27; 7:22; 17:17; 2 Cor. 7:1
CLEAR—*pure, plain* Is. 40:3, **C** the way for the
  Lord
  Matt. 7:5, you will see **c-ly** *enough*
  Rom. 1:20, have been **c-ly** seen
  Rev. 22:1, water of life, **c** as crystal
  Gen. 20:16; Num. 14:18; Job 26:13; Is. 32:4
CLEAVE—*cling* Gen. 2:24, shall **c** to his wife
  Hab. 3:9, **c** the earth with rivers
  Matt. 19:5; Eph. 5:31
CLEFT Song 2:14; Is. 2:21; Jer. 49:16
CLEVER—*skillful, wise* 1 Cor. 1:17, not in **c-ness**
  1 Cor. 1:19, **c-ness** of the **c** I will set aside
  2 Pet. 1:16, not follow **c-ly** devised tales
CLIMB 1 Sam. 14:13; Jer. 48:44; Luke 19:4;
  John 10:1
CLING Josh. 23:8, **c** to the Lord your God
  Ps. 63:8, My soul **c-s** to Thee
    102:5, My bones **c** to my flesh
  John 20:17, Stop **c-ing** to Me
CLOAK—*mantle, coat* Ruth 3:15, Give me the
  c . . . on you
  Is. 3:7; Matt. 9:20; Acts 12:8; 2 Tim. 4:13

CLOD—*crust* Job 21:33, **c-s** of the valley
CLOSE (adj.)—*intimate, near*
  Prov. 18:24, a friend who sticks **c-r** than
  Judg. 20:34; Ps. 41:9
CLOSE (v.)—*shut, stop* Gen. 7:16; 8:2, Lord **c-d** it
  behind
  Num. 16:33, the earth **c-d** over them
  Acts 28:27, they have c-d their eyes
  Rom. 3:19, every mouth may be **c-d**
  1 John 3:17, **c-s** his heart against him
  Rev. 21:25, its gates shall never be **c-d**
  Judg. 19:9
CLOTH 1 Sam. 21:9; Matt. 9:16; Luke 2:7;
  John 11:44
CLOTHE—*array, adorn, wrap* Job 10:11, **C** me
  with skin
  Matt. 6:29, Solomon . . . not **c-d** like
    25:36, naked, and you **c-d** Me
  1 Pet. 5:5, **c** yourselves with humility
  Rev. 7:13, are **c-d** in the white robes
  1 Kin. 11:29; Job 40:10; Ps. 65:13; 93:1; Is. 52:1;
    Luke 24:49; Rev. 3:5
CLOTHES—*dress, garment* Matt. 22:11, not . . . in
  wedding **c**
  James 2:3, one who is wearing the fine **c**
  Deut. 29:5; Josh. 9:5; 1 Sam. 19:13;
    2 Sam. 12:20; Mark 14:63; James 2:2
CLOTHING—*clothes, dress, raiment*
  Matt. 6:25, food, and the body than **c**
    7:15, come to you in sheep's **c**
  1 Tim. 2:9, with proper **c**
  Deut. 8:4; Job 24:10; Jer. 10:9
CLOUD—*darkness* Gen. 9:13, My bow in the **c**
  Ex. 13:21, a pillar of **c** by day
    20:21, Moses approached the thick **c**
    24:15, **c** covered the mountain
  Matt. 24:30, Son of Man coming on the **c-s**
  Mark 9:7, a **c** formed . . . voice came out of the **c**
  Luke 12:54, see a **c** rising in the west
    21:27, in a **c** with power and great glory
  Acts 1:9, a **c** received Him out of their sight
  1 Thess. 4:17, caught up . . . in the **c-s**
  Rev. 1:7, He is coming with the **c-s**
  Ex. 14:24; 33:9; 1 Kin. 8:12; 2 Chr. 6:1; Ps. 99:7;
    105:39; Ezek. 30:3; Jude 12
CLUSTER Is. 65:8, new wine is found in the **c**
  Num. 13:23; Mic. 7:1; Rev. 14:18
COAL—*soot, charcoal* Prov. 6:28; Is. 6:6
  Prov. 25:22, heap burning **c-s** on his head
  Rom. 12:20, heap . . . c-s upon his head
COAST Acts 27:2, the regions along the **c**
COAT—*cloak* Matt. 5:40, let him have your **c** also
COBRA Job 20:16, He sucks the poison of **c-s**
  Ps. 58:4, Like a deaf **c**
    91:13, tread upon the lion and **c**
COCK Matt. 26:34,75, before a **c** crows
  Mark 13:35, at **c**-crowing, or in the morning
COFFIN—*bier* Gen. 50:26; Luke 7:14
COIN—*money* Matt. 22:19, Show Me the **c** *used
  for*
  Luke 15:8, woman . . . loses **c**
COLD Prov. 25:25, Like **c** water to a weary soul
  Matt. 10:42, a cup of **c** water
    24:12, love will grow **c**
  Rev. 3:15, that you were **c** or hot
  Gen. 8:22; Job 24:7; 37:9; Prov. 25:13;
    John 18:18; 2 Cor. 11:27
COLLAPSED—*fell* Luke 6:49, immediately it **c**
COLLECT—*exact* Luke 3:13, **C** no more
  Luke 19:23, would have **c-ed** it with interest
COLLECTION 1 Cor. 16:1, the **c** for the saints
COLOR Ezek. 16:16, high places of various **c-s**
COLT—*foal* Zech. 9:9, a **c**, the foal of a donkey
  Matt. 21:2, a donkey tied *there* and a **c** with her
  John 12:15, king comes . . . on a donkey's **c**
COMBINE 1 Cor. 2:13, **c-ing** spiritual *thoughts . . .
  words*
COME—*enter, return* Ps. 95:6, **C**, let us worship
  Zech. 9:9, your king is **c-ing** to you
  Matt. 6:10, Thy kingdom **c**
    11:28, **C** to Me, all who are weary

Mark 10:14, children to **c** to Me
Luke 21:27, Son of Man **c-ing**
John 17:1, Father, the hour has **c**
Rev. 22:20, I am **c-ing** quickly
Mark 14:38; Luke 19:23; 2 Thess. 2:2

COMFORT—*consolation, rest*
Ps. 23:4, Thy rod ... they **c** me
Is. 61:2, To **c** all who mourn
Matt. 5:4, who mourn, for they shall be **c-ed**
Acts 9:31, in the **c** of the Holy Spirit
2 Cor. 1:3, God of all **c**
  1:6, for your **c** and salvation
1 Thess. 4:18, **c** one another
2 Thess. 2:17, **c** and strengthen your hearts
Job 29:25; Ps. 77:2; Prov. 29:17; Eccles. 4:1; Is.
  54:11; Lam. 1:21; Matt. 2:18; Luke 6:24;
  16:25; 2 Cor. 7:4,13; 2 Thess. 2:16

COMFORTER—*helper* Job 16:2, Sorry **c-s** are
  you all
Ps. 69:20, looked for ... **c-s**, but I found none
Nah. 3:7, Where will I seek **c-s** for you

COMING 2 Sam. 3:25, your going out and **c** in
Mal. 3:2, endure the day of His **c**
Matt. 11:3, Are You the **C** One
  24:30, Son of Man **c**
  26:64, **c** on the clouds of heaven
John 5:25, an hour is **c** and now is
James 5:8, **c** of the Lord is at hand
2 Pet. 3:4, promise of His **c**

COMMAND—*declare, spoke* Gen. 18:19;
Lev. 24:12; Deut. 2:37
Ps. 33:9, He **c-ed**, and it stood fast
Jon. 2:10, Lord **c-ed** the fish
Matt. 1:24, angel of the Lord **c-ed** him
  4:3, Son of God, **c** that these stones
  20:21, **C** that ... these two sons of mine
Luke 8:25, He **c-s** even the winds
  9:54, **c** fire to come down from heaven
John 15:14, do what I **c** you

COMMANDER—*general* Judg. 5:9; 1 Chr. 27:34;
Is. 55:4

COMMANDMENT—*instruction, duty*
Ex. 20:6, keep My **c-s**
  34:28, tablets ... the Ten **C-s**
Ps. 19:8, **C** of the Lord is pure
Matt. 5:19, one of the least of these **c-s**
  22:36, which is the great **c**
John 14:15, If you love Me ... keep My **c-s**
Prov. 6:20; Eccles. 12:13; Matt. 22:40;
  John 15:10

COMMEND—*praise* Eccles. 8:15, So I **c-ed**
  pleasure
Acts 20:32, I **c** you to God
1 Cor. 8:8; 2 Cor. 3:1

COMMISSION Acts 26:12, authority and **c** of ...
  priests

COMMIT—*entrust, practice, wrought*
Ex. 20:14, You shall not **c** adultery
Ps. 31:5, into Thy hand I **c** my spirit
  37:5, **C** your way to the Lord
Luke 23:46, into Thy hands I **c** My spirit
John 8:34, every one who **c-s** sin
Ex. 32:30; Lev. 20:12; Prov. 16:3; Luke 18:20;
  1 Pet. 2:22

COMMON—*prevalent* Lev. 4:27; Jer. 26:23
Acts 2:44, had all things in **c**
Titus 1:4, in a **c** faith
Jude 3, write you about our **c** salvation

COMMOTION—*disturbance* Jer. 10:22, great **c**
  out of ... land

COMPANION—*fellow* Prov. 13:20, **c** of fools will
  suffer
Heb. 1:9, oil of gladness above Thy **c-s**
Ex. 2:13; Job 30:29; Eccles. 4:10

COMPANY—*congregation*
Job 15:34, the **c** of the godless

COMPARE Prov. 3:15, nothing ... **c-s** with her
Matt. 11:16, to what shall I **c** this generation
Rom. 8:18, not worthy ... **c-d** with the glory

COMPARISON Judg. 8:2; Hag. 2:3

COMPASSION—*lovingkindness, p*
Ex. 33:19, **c** on whom I will show
Ps. 25:6, Remember ... Thy **c**
  72:13, **c** on the poor and needy
  103:13, father has **c** on *his* childr
  111:4, Lord is gracious and **c-ate**
Col. 3:12, put on a heart of **c**
Matt. 9:36; 15:32; Luke 15:20; Rom.

COMPEL—*force, press* Luke 14:23, **c** t
  come in

COMPETE—*strive* 1 Cor. 9:25, everyon
2 Tim. 2:5, **c-s** as an athlete

COMPLACENCY Prov. 1:32, **c** of fools s
  destroy them

COMPLAIN James 5:9, Do not **c** ... again
  another
Job 7:11; Ps. 55:17

COMPLAINING—*babbling*
Prov. 23:29, Who has **c**
1 Pet. 4:9 without **c**

COMPLAINT—*grudge* 1 Pet. 4:9 without **c**

COMPLETE—*fulfill, full, utterly*
Is. 2:18, idols will **c-ly** vanish
Col. 2:10, in Him ... made **c**
James 1:4, that you may be perfect and **c**
1 John 1:4, our joy may be **c**
Rev. 20:3, thousand years were **c-d**
Gen. 2:1; 29:27; Ex. 5:13; Num. 15:31; Esth. 1:5,
  1 Cor. 1:10; Rev. 20:7

COMPOSE Job 16:4, I could **c** words against you

COMPOSURE Eccles. 10:4, **c** allays great
  offenses

COMPREHEND—*calculate*
Job 37:5, things ... cannot **c**
John 1:5, darkness did not **c** it

COMPREHENSION—*understanding*
Phil. 4:7, peace ... surpasses all **c**

COMPULSION—*constrain*
1 Pet. 5:2, not under **c**, but

CONCEAL—*cover, hide* Prov. 12:23; Is. 3:9;
  Jer. 50:2
Ps. 40:10, have not **c-ed** thy lovingkindness
Prov. 27:5, love that is **c-ed**

CONCEIT—*pride*
Phil. 2:3, nothing ... selfishness or empty **c**
1 Tim. 6:4, is **c-ed** *and* understands nothing

CONCEIVE Num. 11:12; Job 15:35; Ps. 51:5;
  Matt. 1:20; Acts 5:4; James 1:15

CONCERN—*care* Col. 4:13, he has a deep **c** for
  you
1 Sam. 1:16; Matt. 4:6; John 12:6; Rom. 1:3;
  1 Cor. 7:32; 9:9; 12:1

CONCILIATE—*entreat*
1 Cor. 4:13, slandered, we try to **c**

CONCLUSION
Eccles. 12:13, The **c** when all has been heard

CONDEMN—*discredit, judge*
Is. 50:9, Who ... **c-s** Me
Mark 16:16, who has disbelieved shall be **c-ed**
Gal. 2:11, because he stood **c-ed**
1 John 3:20, in whatever our heart **c-s** us
Job 9:20; Prov. 12:2; Mark 10:33; Luke 6:37;
  Rom. 2:1; 14:23

CONDEMNATION—*judgment* Rom. 3:8, Their **c**
  is just
Rom. 8:1, no **c** for those who are in
Matt. 23:14; Mark 12:40; Luke 20:47; 23:40;
  Rom. 13:2

CONDUCT—*bring, behavior* Job 33:17; Ezek.
  7:27; Acts 17:15
Col. 4:5, **C** yourselves with wisdom
2 Pet. 2:7, sensual **c** of unprincipled men

CONDUIT 2 Kin. 18:17; 20:20; Is. 7:3; 36:2

CONFER—*consult* Acts 4:15; 25:12

CONFESS—*acknowledge* Matt. 3:6, they **c-ed**
  their sins
Matt. 10:32, **c** Me before men ... **c** him before
  My Father
Mark 1:5, baptized ... **c-ing** their sins
Rom. 10:9, **c** with your mouth
James 5:16, **c** your sins to one another
1 John 1:9, If we **c** our sins, He is
Ps. 32:5; John 1:20; Rom. 10:10

Confe...

CON...ON 2 Cor. 9:13, your **c** of the gospel of

CON...13; Heb. 10:23

...**NCE**—*boldness, trust* Prov. 3:26;
    . 3:6
    1:24, have put my **c** in gold
    2:17, quietness and **c** forever
    or. 1:12, For our proud **c** is this
    il. 1:26, your proud **c** in me
    3:3, and put no **c** in the flesh
    Ieb. 4:16, draw near with **c** to the throne of grace
    1 John 4:17, we may have **c** in the day of judgment

CONFIDENT Eph. 3:12, **c** access through faith in Him

CONFIRM—*establish* Ps. 90:17, **c** the work of our hands
    Rom. 15:8, to **c** the promises *given* to the fathers
    1 Cor. 1:8, also **c** you to the end
    Matt. 18:16; Mark 16:20

CONFIRMATION Phil. 1:7, defense and **c** of the gospel
    Heb. 6:16, an oath *given* as **c** is an end

CONFORM Rom. 8:29, *to become* **c-ed** to the image
    Rom. 12:2, do not be **c-ed** to this world
    Phil. 3:10, being **c-ed** to His death

CONFOUND Josh. 10:10; Is. 19:3

CONFUSE Gen. 11:7, **c** their language

CONFUSION—*disorder*
    1 Sam. 14:20, *was* very great **c**
    1 Cor. 14:33, not *a God* of **c**

CONGREGATION—*company, assembly*
    Ex. 12:3, Speak to all the **c**
    Ps. 82:1, His stand in His own **c**
    149:1, **c** of the godly ones

CONQUER Rom. 8:37, **c** through Him
    Rev. 6:2, went out **c-ing**, and to **c**

CONSCIENCE Acts 23:1, lived ... good **c** before God
    Rom. 13:5, also for **c** sake
    1 Cor. 8:7, their **c** being weak
    1 Tim. 3:9, faith with a clear **c**
    4:2, **c** as with a branding iron
    1 Pet. 3:16, keep a good **c**
    Acts 24:16; Rom. 2:15; Heb. 9:14; 10:22

CONSECRATE—*sanctify*
    Lev. 11:44, **C** yourselves
    1 Sam. 21:4, there is **c-d** bread
    Matt. 12:4, They ate **c-d** bread
    Ex. 28:38,41; 29:1,21,29,35; 40:9; Lev. 12:4;
      16:19; 25:10; Num. 6:11; 1 Sam. 21:6;
      1 Kin. 8:64; 9:3,7; 2 Chr. 7:7

CONSENT—*agree* Prov. 1:10; Is. 1:19; Luke 23:51

CONSIDER—*notice, observe*
    Ps. 41:1, blessed is he who **c-s** the helpless
    Eccles. 7:14, in the day of adversity **c**
    Luke 12:24, **C** the ravens, for they
    Heb. 10:24, let us **c** ... one another
    11:26, **c-ing** the reproach of Christ
    2 Sam. 19:19; Ps. 44:22; 48:13; 77:5

CONSIDERATION
    Acts 27:3, Julius treated Paul with **c**

CONSIST Luke 12:15, his life **c** of his possessions

CONSOLATION—*comfort* Job 15:11, Are the **c-s** of God ... small
    Phil. 2:1, if there is any **c** of love

CONSPIRACY—*plot* 2 Sam. 15:12, the **c** was strong

CONSTRAIN—*persuade, urge* Job 32:18

CONSULT—*confer, counsel* 1 Kin. 12:6,8
    Gal. 1:16, I did not ... **c** with flesh and blood

CONSUME—*eat, devour*
    Ex. 3:2, yet the bush was not **c-d**
    Ex. 24:17; Is. 29:6; 30:27,30; 33:14, **c-ing** fire
    Deut. 4:24, God is a **c-ing** fire
    Ezek. 15:7, yet the fire will **c** them

Lev. 10:2; Deut. 5:25; 32:24; Ps. 39:11; 49:14;
    69:9; 90:7; Eccles. 4:5; Luke 9:54; John 2:17;
    Gal. 5:15; James 5:3

CONSUMMATION—*end* Heb. 9:26, at the **c**

CONSUMPTION Lev. 26:16; Deut. 28:22

CONTAIN 1 Kin. 8:27; 1 Pet. 2:6

CONTAINER Luke 8:16, covers it over with a **c**

CONTEMPT Rom. 14:10, regard your brother with **c**
    2 Cor. 10:10, his speech **c-ible**
    Job 12:21; Prov. 18:3; Dan. 12:2

CONTEND—*strive* Is. 50:8, Who will **c** with Me
    Is. 57:16, I will not **c** forever
    Jude 3, **c** earnestly for the faith
    Judg. 8:1; Job 40:2; Prov. 3:30; Is. 49:25; Jer. 2:9

CONTENT—*satisfy* Luke 3:14, be **c** with your wages
    Phil. 4:11, I have learned to be **c**
    1 Tim. 6:6, accompanied by **c-ment**
    2 Cor. 12:10; Heb. 13:5

CONTENTIOUS Prov. 21:19; 25:24; 1 Cor. 11:16

CONTINUAL—*unceasing, constant* Num. 4:16;
    28:24
    Prov. 15:15, cheerful heart *has* a **c** feast

CONTINUALLY—*perpetual*
    1 Chr. 16:11, Seek His face **c**
    Ps. 34:1, praise shall **c** be in my mouth
    Prov. 6:21; Luke 18:5

CONTINUE—*persevere*
    Acts 13:43, **c** in the grace of God
    Heb. 13:1, Let love of the brethren **c**

CONTRARY—*hostile*
    Matt. 14:24, for the wind was **c**
    Rom. 11:24, grafted **c** to nature
    16:17, **c** to the teaching
    2 Cor. 2:7, on the **c** ... rather forgive
    Gal. 2:7, on the **c**, seeing that I
    1 Tim. 1:10, **c** to sound teaching

CONTRIBUTE Rom. 12:13, **c-ing** to the needs of the saints

CONTRIBUTION Rom. 15:26, make a **c** for the poor

CONTRITE—*crush* Ps. 51:17, broken and a **c** heart
    Is. 66:2, humble and **c** of spirit

CONTROL—*rule* Prov. 25:28, no **c** over his spirit
    2 Cor. 5:14, love of Christ **c-s** us

CONTROVERSY—*dispute*
    Jer. 25:31, **c** with the nations

CONVERSE—*discuss*
    Luke 24:15, while they were **c-ing**
    Acts 17:18, philosophers were **c-ing** with him

CONVERSION Acts 15:3, **c** of the Gentiles

CONVERT—*restore*
    Matt. 18:3, unless you are **c-ed**

CONVICT—*reprove*
    John 8:46, Which one of you **c-s** Me
    16:8, **c** the world concerning sin
    Heb. 11:1, the **c-ion** of things not seen

CONVINCE—*persuade* Rom. 14:14, am **c-d** in the Lord Jesus
    Heb. 6:9, **c-d** of better things

COOK 1 Sam. 8:13; 9:23,24

COOL Gen. 3:8; Luke 16:24

COPE Acts 6:10, unable to **c** with the wisdom

COPPER Deut. 8:9, you can dig **c**
    Matt. 10:9, Do not acquire gold ... or **c**

COPPERSMITH 2 Tim. 4:14, Alexander the **c**

COPY—*transcribe* Deut. 17:18; Josh. 8:32;
    Heb. 9:24

CORBAN Mark 7:11, have been helped by is **C**

CORD—*band, chain*
    Ps. 18:4, **c-s** of death encompassed me
    Prov. 5:22, held with the **c-s** of his sin
    Eccles. 12:6, the silver **c** is broken
    John 2:15, made a scourge of **c-s**
    2 Sam. 22:6; Job 36:8; 38:31; 41:1; Is. 5:18

CORNER Prov. 7:12, lurks by every **c**
    Matt. 6:5, synagogues and on the street **c-s**
    Acts 10:11, lowered by four **c-s** to the ground
    Rev. 7:1, at the four **c-s** of the earth

CORNERSTONE—*corner* Ps. 118:22, the chief **c**
 Matt. 21:42, BECAME THE CHIEF **C**
 Eph. 2:20, Christ ... being the **c**
 Job 38:6; Is. 28:16
CORPSE—*body* Is. 14:19; Nah. 3:3; Matt. 24:28
CORRECT—*reprove*
 Prov. 29:17, **C** your son, and he will
 Jer. 10:24, **C** me ... but with justice
 2 Tim. 3:16, profitable ... for **c-ion**
CORRUPT—*depraved, rotten*
 Gen. 6:11, the earth was **c**
 Ps. 14:1, They are **c**, they have committed
 1 Cor. 15:33, Bad company **c-s** good morals
 Job 15:16; Is. 1:4; Jer. 6:28; 2 Cor. 7:2; Eph. 4:22
CORRUPTIBLE—*perish*
 Rom. 1:23, in the form of **c** man
CORRUPTION—*decay* Lev. 22:25; Rom. 8:21;
 2 Pet. 2:19
 Gal. 6:8, shall from the flesh reap **c**
 2 Pet. 1:4, the **c** that is in the world
COST—*wealth, price*
 Ps. 49:8, redemption ... soul is **c-ly**
 Is. 55:1, Without money and without **c**
 Matt. 26:7, vial of very **c-ly** perfume
 2 Sam. 24:24; 1 Kin. 5:17; Ezra 6:4,8; John 12:3;
 1 Tim. 2:9
COUCH—*pallet* Gen. 49:4,9
 Ps. 6:6, dissolve my **c** with my tears
COUNCIL Mark 15:43; Luke 23:50
 Jer. 23:18, stood in the **c** of the LORD
 Acts 5:27, stood them before the **C**
 6:12, brought Stephen before the **C**
COUNSEL—*advice, opinion*
 Ps. 1:1, not walk in the **c**
 33:11, **C** of the LORD stands
 73:24, With Thy **c** ... guide me
 Prov. 13:10, those who receive **c**
 19:20, Listen to **c** and accept
 Is. 28:29, made *His* **c** wonderful
 John 12:10, chief priests took **c**
 Eph. 1:11, after the **c** of His will
 Ex. 18:19; Judg. 19:30; 1 Kin. 12:6; 2 Chr. 10:9;
 Ezra 4:5; Ps. 32:8; 62:4; Matt. 22:15;
 Luke 14:31
COUNSELOR
 Is. 9:6, will be called Wonderful **C**
 Rom. 11:34, WHO BECAME HIS **C**
 Job 12:17; Prov. 11:14; Mic. 4:9
COUNT—*consider, number* 2 Cor. 5:19;
 James 5:11
 Gen. 15:5, **c** the stars, if you are able
 Prov. 17:28, closes his lips ... **c-ed** prudent
 1 Cor. 4:15, have **c-less** tutors in Christ
 Phil. 3:8, I **c** all things to be loss
 2 Pet. 3:9, as some **c** slowness
COUNTENANCE Gen. 4:6, why has your **c** fallen
 Num. 6:26, The LORD lift up His **c**
 Ps. 4:6; 89:15, light of Thy **c**
COUNTRY—*region*
 John 4:44, no honor in his own **c**
 Gen. 12:1; Matt. 2:12; Luke 15:13
COURAGE—*cheer* 2 Chr. 15:7, strong and do not
 lose **c**
 Ps. 27:14, let your heart take **c**
 John 16:33, take **c**; I have overcome
 Matt. 9:2,22; 14:27; Acts 23:11
COURAGEOUS Deut. 31:6; Josh. 1:7
COURSE Ps. 19:5, strong man to run his **c**
 2 Tim. 4:7, have finished the **c**
 James 3:6, sets on fire the **c** of our life
 Judg. 5:20; Acts 20:24
COURT—*council* Ps. 84:10, a day in Thy **c-s**
 Ex. 27:9; Ps. 135:2; Matt. 10:17
COURTEOUS Acts 28:7, entertained us **c-ly** three
 days
COVENANT Job 31:1; Acts 3:25; Gal. 4:24
 Gen. 6:18, I will establish My **c**
 Num. 10:33, ark of the **c** of the LORD
 2 Kin. 23:2, book of the **c**
 Ps. 25:10; 103:18, To those who keep His **c**
 Matt. 26:28, My blood of the **c**
 Luke 22:20, This cup ... is the new **c**

2 Cor. 3:6, servants of a new **c**
 3:14, reading of the old **c**
 Heb. 7:22, Jesus ... guarantee of a better **c**
 8:6, mediator of a better **c**
 13:20, blood of the eternal **c**
 Rev. 11:19, the ark of His **c**
COVER—*hide* Ps. 32:1, Whose sin is **c-ed**
 Ps. 91:4, **c** you with His pinions
 Prov. 10:12, love **c-s** all transgressions
 Matt. 10:26, nothing **c-ed** that will not be
 revealed
 James 5:20, will **c** a multitude of sins
 1 Pet. 4:8, love **c-s** a multitude of sins
 Gen. 37:26; Ex. 2:3; Job 36:32; Is. 6:2; 50:6;
 Luke 23:30
COVERING—*raiment*
 Ps. 105:39, spread a cloud for a **c**
 1 Cor. 11:15, her hair is given ... for a **c**
 Gen. 3:7; 2 Sam. 17:19; Is. 50:3; 1 Tim. 6:8
COVET—*crave, desire* Mic. 2:2; Rom. 13:9
 Ex. 20:17, You shall not **c**
 Mark 7:22, deeds of **c-ing** *and* wickedness
 Acts 20:33, have **c-ed** no one's silver
 Rom. 7:8, produced in me **c-ing** of every kind
COW—*ox* Is. 11:7, the **c** and the bear will graze
 Lev. 22:28; Job 21:10
COWARDLY—*fearful* Rev. 21:8, for the **c** and
 unbelieving
CRAFT—*deceit* Job 15:5, language of the **c-y**
 Ex. 21:14; Is. 2:16; 2 Cor. 12:16
CRAFTINESS—*shrewd* 2 Cor. 4:2, walking in **c**
CRAFTSMEN 2 Kin. 24:14; Hos. 13:2; Zech. 1:20;
 Acts 19:24
CRANE—*thrush* Is. 38:14
CRASH Zeph. 1:10, a loud **c** from the hills
CRAVE—*desire, covet* Mic. 7:1
 Prov. 13:4, soul of the sluggard **c-s** and gets
 nothing
 21:26, All day long he is **c-ing**
CRAWL—*creep* Acts 10:12, **c-ing** creatures of
 the earth
CREATE—*form* Gen. 1:1, **c-d** the heavens and
 the earth
 Ps. 51:10, **C** in me a clean heart
 Is. 45:12, made the earth, and **c-d** man
 Mal. 2:10, Has not one God **c-d** us
 Eph. 2:10, **c-d** in Christ Jesus
 4:24, God ... **c-d** in righteousness
 Col. 1:16, in Him all things were **c-d**
 Is. 57:19; 65:17; Mark 13:19; Eph. 3:9;
 1 Tim. 2:13
CREATION Mark 10:6, beginning of **c**, *God* MADE
 THEM
 Mark 13:19, **c** which God created
 16:15, preach the gospel to all **c**
 Rom. 1:20, since the **c** of the world
 8:22, whole **c** groans
 2 Pet. 3:4, from the beginning of **c**
CREATOR Eccles. 12:1, Remember also your **C**
 Is. 40:28, **c** of the ends of the earth
 Rom. 1:25, the creature rather than the **C**
 1 Pet. 4:19, to a faithful **C**
CREATURE—*animal, beast* Gen. 1:21, every
 living **c**
 Lev. 11:47, the edible **c** and the **c** ... not to be
 eaten
 2 Cor. 5:17, *he is* a new **c**; the old things
 Rom. 1:23; James 1:18
CREDIT—*thanks* Luke 6:32, what **c** *is that* to you
CREDITOR Ps. 109:11; Is. 50:1
 Deut. 15:2, every **c** shall release what ... loaned
CREEP Gen. 1:26; Ps. 148:10
CRESCENT Is. 3:18, will take away ... **c**
 ornaments
CRIME Job 31:11; Ezek. 7:23
CRIMINAL 2 Tim. 2:9, suffer hardship ... as a **c**
CRIMSON 2 Chr. 2:7, in purple, **c** and violet
 Is. 1:18, like **c**, They will be like wool
CRIPPLE Matt. 18:8, better ... to enter life **c-d**
 Luke 14:21, bring in **c-d** and blind

CRITICIZE Is. 29:24, those who **c** ... accept instruction
CROCUS Is. 35:1, blossom; Like the **c**
CROOKED—*perverse* Deut. 32:5; Prov. 21:8; Phil. 2:15
   Ps. 125:5, turn aside to their **c** ways
   Eccles. 1:15, **c** cannot be straightened
   Luke 3:5, THE **C** SHALL BECOME STRAIGHT
CROP Lev. 1:16, take away its **c**
CROSS—*tree* Matt. 10:38, take his **c**
   Matt. 27:40, come down from the **c**
   John 19:17, went out, bearing His own **c**
   19:25, standing by the **c** of Jesus
   Acts 5:30, hanging Him on a **c**
   1 Cor. 1:17, that the **c** of Christ should not
   Gal. 6:14, except in the **c** of our Lord
   Phil. 2:8, even death on a **c**
   3:18, enemies of the **c** of Christ
   Heb. 12:2, endured the **c**, despising
   1 Kin. 1:6; 1 Cor. 1:18; Eph. 2:16; Col. 1:20
CROUCH—*bow* Job 38:40; Ps. 10:10
CROW Matt. 26:74, immediately a cock **c-ed**
   Mark 14:72; Luke 22:34; 22:60
CROWD—*press*
   Mark 2:4, unable to get to Him ... **c**
   5:27, in the **c** behind *Him*, and touched
CROWN—*wreath* Ps. 8:5, **c** him with glory
   Ps. 103:4, **c-s** you with lovingkindness
   Prov. 12:4, excellent wife is the **c** of
   14:18, are **c-ed** with knowledge
   14:24, **c** of the wise is their
   16:31, gray head is a **c** of glory
   17:6, grandchildren are the **c** of old men
   Heb. 2:9, Jesus ... **c-ed** with glory and honor
   Gen. 49:26; Ps. 21:3; 65:11
CRUCIFIXION Matt. 26:2, delivered up for **c**
CRUCIFY Matt. 27:22, Let Him be **c-ed**
   Matt. 28:5, Jesus who has been **c-ed**
   Mark 15:13, shouted back, **C** Him
   1 Cor. 1:23, we preach Christ **c-ed**
   Gal. 2:20, I have been **c-ed** with Christ
   6:14, world has been **c-ed** to me
   Heb. 6:6, **c** to themselves the Son of God
   Matt. 20:19; 27:35; 1 Cor. 1:13; 2 Cor. 13:4
CRUEL—*fierce* Prov. 11:17; Matt. 15:22
CRUMBS Matt. 15:27; Mark 7:28
CRUSH—*batter* Ps. 34:18, saves those ... **c-ed** in spirit
   Is. 53:5, **c-ed** for our iniquities
   53:10, Lord was pleased to **c** Him
   Amos 4:1, who **c** the needy
   Rom. 16:20, **c** Satan under your feet
   2 Cor. 4:8, but not **c-ed**
   Lev. 22:24; 2 Kin. 18:21; Job 39:15; Jer. 17:18
CRUST Job 7:5, flesh is clothed ... a **c** of dirt
CRY—*outcry*
   Gen. 4:10, your brother's blood is **c-ing**
   Ps. 9:12, the **c** of the afflicted
   130:1, Out of the depths I have **c-ed**
   Matt. 3:3, ONE **C-ING** IN THE WILDERNESS
   Rev. 21:4, no ... mourning, or **c-ing**
   Ex. 2:6; 32:18; Lev. 13:45; Ps. 17:1; 27:7; Is. 42:2; Mark 15:37
CRYSTAL Ezek. 1:22; Rev. 4:6; 21:11
CUB 2 Sam. 17:8; Jer. 51:38; Nah. 2:11
CUBIT Gen. 6:15, length of the ark 300 **c-s**
   Esth. 5:14, a gallows fifty **c-s** high
   Matt. 6:27, add a single **c** to his life's span
   Deut. 3:11; Ezek. 43:13
CUCUMBER Num. 11:5; Is. 1:8
CUD Lev. 11:3; Deut. 14:6
CULTIVATE—*till* Gen. 2:5, no man to **c** the ground
   Ps. 37:3, Dwell in the land and **c** faithfulness
   Gen. 2:15; Deut. 28:39; 2 Sam. 9:10; Ezek. 36:9
CUMMIN Matt. 23:23, and dill and **c**
CUP Ps. 23:5, My **c** overflows
   Matt. 10:42, a **c** of cold water
   20:22, able to drink the **c**
   23:25, outside of the **c**
   26:27, took a **c** and gave thanks
   26:39, let this **c** pass from Me

   Luke 22:20, **c** ... is the new covenant
   John 18:11, the **c** which the Father has given
   1 Cor. 10:16, the **c** of blessing
   Ps. 116:13; Prov. 23:31; Mark 7:4; 1 Cor. 10:21
CUPBEARER Gen. 40:1; 41:9; 1 Kin. 10:5; 2 Chr. 9:4; Neh. 1:11
CURDLE Job 10:10, and **c** me like cheese
CURDS—*butter* Judg. 5:25; Is. 7:15,22
CURE Luke 7:21, At that very time He **c-d** many
   Luke 13:32, perform **c-s** today and tomorrow
CURSE—*oath* Ex. 22:28, You shall not **c** God
   Mal. 4:6, smite the land with a **c**
   Luke 6:28, bless those who **c** you
   Rom. 3:14, WHOSE MOUTH IS FULL OF **C-ING**
   Gal. 3:13, redeemed us from the **c**
   Gen. 3:14; 12:3; 27:12; Lev. 19:14; 1 Sam. 3:13; Jer. 42:18; 44:12; Mic. 6:10; Zech. 14:11; Mark 14:71; Rom. 12:14; James 3:9
CURTAIN Ex. 26:1; Song 1:5; Is. 40:22
CUSHION Mark 4:38, asleep on the **c**
CUSTODY—*prison* Esth. 2:3,8,14; Matt. 4:12
CUSTOM—*manner* Luke 4:16, as was His **c**
   Acts 16:21, **c-s** which are not lawful
   Judg. 11:39; Ezra 4:13; John 18:39; 19:40; Acts 28:17; Rom. 13:7
CUT Matt. 3:10, not bear good fruit is **c** down
   Matt. 21:8, others were **c-ing** branches
   26:51, and **c** off his ear
   Acts 7:54, they were **c** to the quick
   Rom. 11:22, you also will be **c** off
   Ex. 9:15; Judg. 1:6; Ps. 12:3; Prov. 10:31; Is. 45:2; Jer. 7:29; Matt. 5:30; 24:51
CYMBAL 2 Sam. 6:5; 1 Chr. 15:16; 16:5; Ps. 150:5; 1 Cor. 13:1

D

DAILY—*continual* Ps. 68:19, who **d** bears our burden
   Prov. 8:30, I was **d** His delight
   Matt. 6:11; Luke 11:3, Give us ... our **d** bread
   Luke 9:23, take up his cross **d**
   Acts 16:5, churches ... increasing in number **d**
   17:11, examining the Scriptures **d**
   1 Cor. 15:31, I die **d**
   Dan. 1:5; Acts 6:1; James 2:15
DAINTY Gen. 49:20; Jer. 6:2
DAMAGE—*loss* Ezra 4:13,22; Acts 27:10
DANCE—*skip* 2 Sam. 6:14, David was **d-ing** before the Lord
   Ps. 30:11, turned ... mourning into **d-ing**
   149:3, praise His name with **d-ing**
   150:4, Praise Him with timbrel and **d-ing**
   Eccles. 3:4, a time to **d**
   Matt. 11:17, We played ... you did not **d**
   14:6, daughter of Herodias **d-d**
   Ex. 32:19; Judg. 21:23; 1 Sam. 18:6; Jer. 31:13; Lam. 5:15; Mark 6:22; Luke 7:32
DANGER Acts 19:27; 27:9
DARE—*presume*
   Acts 5:13, none ... **d-d** to associate
   Rom. 5:7, someone would **d** even to die
   1 Cor. 6:1, **d** to go to law before the unrighteous
   Job 41:10; Jude 9
DARK—*dim, shadow* Num. 12:8, not in **d** sayings
   Joel 2:10, sun and the moon grow **d**
   Luke 12:3, whatever you have said in the **d**
   Gen. 15:17; Job 24:16; Is. 9:2; Lam. 4:1
DARKEN—*obscure*
   Job 38:2, Who is this that **d-s** counsel
   Eccles. 12:2, stars are **d-ed**
   Matt. 24:29, THE SUN WILL BE **D-ED**
   Rom. 1:21, their foolish heart was **d-ed**
   11:10, LET THEIR EYES BE **D-ED** TO SEE NOT
   Eph. 4:18, being **d-ed** in their understanding
   Ex. 10:15; Mark 13:24; Rev. 16:10
DARKNESS—*cloud, gloom* Gen. 1:2, **d** was over the surface
   Ex. 10:21, **d** over the land of Egypt ... **d** which
   2 Sam. 22:29, the Lord illumines my **d**

Ps. 91:6, pestilence that stalks in **d**
107:10, those who dwelt in **d**
112:4, Light arises in the **d**
Eccles. 2:13, as light excels **d**
2:14, the fool walks in **d**
Matt. 6:23, full of **d**, how great is the **d**
10:27, What I tell you in **d**, speak
22:13, cast him into the outer **d**
Luke 1:79, SHINE UPON THOSE WHO SIT IN D
John 1:5, light shines in the **d**
3:19, men loved the **d** rather than the light
12:35, **d** may not overtake
Acts 26:18, they may turn from **d** to light
Rom. 2:19, a light to those who are in **d**
2 Cor. 6:14, what fellowship has light with **d**
Eph. 5:11, unfruitful deeds of **d**
6:12, world forces of this **d**
1 Pet. 2:9, out of **d** into His marvelous light
1 John 1:5, in Him there is no **d** at all
2:9, hates his brother is in the **d**
Deut. 28:29; 1 Sam. 2:9; 2 Sam. 22:10; Job 3:5;
10:22; 12:25; 30:26; Ps. 18:9,28; 88:12; 97:2;
139:12; Prov. 20:20; Is. 58:10; Matt. 25:30;
Luke 22:53; 23:44; Rom. 13:12; 1 Cor. 4:5;
2 Cor. 4:6; Col. 1:13; Heb. 12:18; 2 Pet. 2:4;
1 John 1:6
DART—*arrow, missile* Job 41:26, the **d** or the
DASH—*shatter* Is. 13:16, **d-ed** to pieces
Nah. 2:4, **d** to and fro like lightning
2 Kin. 8:12; Ps. 137:9; Jer. 13:14; Hos. 13:16
DATE—*time* Gal. 4:2, the **d** set by the father
DAUGHTER—Gen. 6:1, **d-s** were born to them
Num. 27:8, transfer his inheritance to his **d**
Prov. 31:29, Many **d-s** have done nobly
Eccles. 12:4, **d-s** of song will sing softly
Is. 22:4, destruction of the **d** of my people
Mic. 7:6, **D** rises up against her mother
Heb. 11:24, son of Pharaoh's **d**
Gen. 24:23,47; 27:46; Ex. 21:7; Deut. 28:53;
Judg. 11:34; 2 Sam. 1:20; 12:3; Ps. 45:9;
144:12; Prov. 30:15; Jer. 8:21; 9:1; Lam.
2:11; 3:48; Matt. 10:35; Luke 8:42; 12:53;
13:16
DAWN—*light, morning* Deut. 33:2; Josh. 6:15;
Judg. 19:26
Ps. 119:147, I rise before **d** and cry for help
139:9, take the wings of the **d**
2 Pet. 1:19, until the day **d-s**
Job 7:4; 38:12; Joel 2:2
DAY—*age, time* Gen. 1:5, God called the light **d**
1 Chr. 29:15, our **d-s** on the earth are like a
shadow
Ps. 19:2, **D** to **d** pours forth speech
41:1, deliver him in a **d** of trouble
84:10, a **d** in Thy courts is better
118:24, This is the **d** which the LORD has
made
Prov. 3:2, For length of **d-s** and years of life
27:1, you do not know what a **d** may bring
Eccles. 7:1, **d** of *one's* death is better than
12:1, **d-s** of your youth, before the evil **d-s**
Is. 2:12, LORD of hosts will have a **d** of
reckoning
13:6, **d** of the LORD is near
58:5, an acceptable **d** to the LORD
Joel 2:11, **d** of the LORD is indeed great
Zech. 4:10, who has despised the **d** of small
things
Mal. 3:2, who can endure the **d** of His coming
Matt. 6:11, this **d** our daily bread
24:36, But of that **d** and hour no one knows
John 6:39, raise it up on the last **d**
8:56, Your father Abraham rejoiced to see
My **d**
9:4, We must work . . . as long as it is **d**
Rom. 14:5, One man regards one **d** above
another
1 Cor. 3:13, the **d** will show it
2 Cor. 6:2, ON THE **D** OF SALVATION
Phil. 1:6, will perfect it until the **d** of Christ
1 Thess. 5:5, all sons of light and sons of **d**

2 Pet. 3:8, one **d** is as a thousand years
Gen. 27:2; Deut. 4:32; 1 Sam. 25:8; 2 Kin. 7:9;
Neh. 4:2; Job 1:4; 7:1; 8:9; 14:6; 21:30;
Ps. 77:5; Prov. 4:18; Is. 2:2; 10:3; 13:9; 27:3;
65:20; Joel 1:15; 2:1; Mic. 4:1; Zeph. 1:7,14;
Zech. 14:1; Mal. 4:5; Matt. 7:22; 24:50;
25:13; Mark 13:32; Luke 12:46; 21:34; John
11:24; 12:48; Acts 2:17,20; 17:31; Rom. 2:5;
1 Thess. 5:2; 2 Tim. 3:1; Heb. 1:2; James
5:3; 2 Pet. 3:3,10; Rev. 6:17; 16:14; 20:10
DAZZLE—*shine* Song 5:10, My beloved is **d**-ing
Luke 24:4, men . . . in **d-ing** apparel
DEAD 1 Sam. 24:14; 2 Sam. 9:8; 16:9, **d** dog
Ps. 31:12, I am forgotten as a **d** man
Eccles. 9:4, a live dog is better than a **d** lion
Is. 26:19, Your **d** will live
Matt. 11:5, and *the* **d** are raised up
22:32, God is not *the God* of the **d**
23:27, full of **d** men's bones
John 5:25, **d** shall hear the voice of the Son of
God
Acts 10:42, Judge of the living and the **d**
26:23, *His* resurrection from the **d**
Rom. 6:11, consider yourselves to be **d** to sin
14:9, Lord both of the **d** and of the living
1 Cor. 15:15, if in fact the **d** are not raised
2 Cor. 1:9, God who raises the **d**
Eph. 2:1, you were **d** in your trespasses and sins
1 Tim. 5:6, **d** even while she lives
Heb. 6:1, repentance from **d** works
James 2:17, faith, if it has no works, is **d**
2:26, body without the spirit is **d**
Rev. 1:18, I was **d**, and behold, I am alive
3:1, name that you are alive, and you are **d**
14:13, Blessed are the **d** who die in the Lord
Gen. 23:3; Ex. 12:30; Lev. 19:28; Ruth 1:8;
Ps. 115:17; Prov. 9:18; Eccles. 4:2; 9:5; 10:1;
Jer. 22:10; Matt. 2:19,20; 8:22; 9:24; 10:8;
Mark 9:10,26; Luke 7:22; 15:24,32; 16:31;
Rom. 7:4; 1 Cor. 15:35; Eph. 5:14; Col. 1:18;
2:13; 1 Thess. 4:16; 2 Tim. 4:1; Heb. 11:4;
13:20; 1 Pet. 4:6; Jude 12; Rev. 1:5;
20:5,12,13
DEADLY 1 Sam. 5:11; Ps. 17:9; Mark 16:18;
James 3:8
DEAF Matt. 11:5, lepers are cleansed and *the* **d**
hear
Ex. 4:11; Lev. 19:14; Ps. 58:4; Is. 29:18; 42:18;
43:8; Mark 7:37; 9:25; Luke 7:22
DEAL—*allot, treat* Prov. 12:22, those who **d**
faithfully are
Ex. 1:10; Lev. 19:11; Ps. 25:3; Is. 21:2; 24:16;
26:10; Jer. 6:13; Hos. 5:7
DEALINGS Judg. 18:7, had no **d** with anyone
John 4:9, Jews have no **d** with Samaritans
DEAR—*beloved* Jer. 31:20, Is Ephraim My **d** son
Acts 20:24, I do not consider my life . . . as **d**
1 Thess. 2:8, you had become very **d** to us
DEATH—*grave* Num. 23:10; Judg. 16:16; 2 Sam.
22:5
Judg. 16:30, whom he killed at his **d** were more
Ruth 1:17, if *anything but* **d** parts you and me
1 Sam. 15:32, Surely the bitterness of **d** is past
2 Sam. 1:23, in their **d** they were not parted
Ps. 23:4, valley of the shadow of **d**
89:48, what man can live and not see **d**
107:10, darkness and in the shadow of **d**
116:15, Precious . . . Is the **d** of His godly ones
Song 8:6, love is as strong as **d**
Is. 25:8, He will swallow up **d** for all time
Ezek. 33:11, no pleasure in the **d** of the wicked
Matt. 2:15, there until the **d** of Herod
16:28; Mark 9:1; Luke 9:27, shall not taste **d**
26:38; Mark 14:34, to the point of **d**
John 5:24, has passed out of **d** into life
8:51, never see **d**
Acts 10:39, **d** by hanging Him on a cross
Rom. 6:23, the wages of sin is **d**
8:2, free from the law of sin and **d**
8:36, WE ARE BEING PUT TO **D** ALL DAY LONG

DEATH (Continued)
1 Cor. 11:26, proclaim the Lord's **d** until He comes
15:21, by a man *came* **d**
15:56, the sting of **d** is sin
2 Cor. 4:12, **d** works in us
Phil. 2:8, obedient to the point of **d**, even **d** on
Heb. 2:9, suffering of **d** ... He might taste **d**
2:15, through fear of **d** were subject to slavery
James 1:15, sin ... brings forth **d**
5:20, will save his soul from **d**
Rev. 1:18, I have the keys of **d** and of Hades
2:10, Be faithful until **d**
6:8, he who sat on it had the name **D**
9:6, men will seek **d** ... and **d** flees from them
21:4, there shall no longer be *any* **d**
2 Chr. 25:4; Job 3:21; 7:15; 30:23; Ps. 6:5; 13:3; 18:4; 22:15; 49:14; 68:20; 102:20; 116:3; Prov. 7:27; 8:36; 14:12; 16:25; Is. 38:18; Jer. 8:3; Ezek. 18:32; Hos. 13:14; Jon. 4:3,8; Matt. 10:21; 15:4; Mark 7:10; Luke 2:26; 22:33; John 11:4; 12:33; 18:31,32; 21:19; Acts 2:24; Rom. 1:32; 5:10,14,17; 6:5,21; 1 Cor. 3:22; 15:55; 2 Cor. 1:9; 11:23; James 5:6; 1 John 3:14; 5:16; Rev. 2:11; 20:6

DEBATE—*dispute* Acts 15:2,7; 1 Cor. 1:20
DEBT Matt. 6:12, forgive us our **d-s**
1 Sam. 22:2; 2 Kin. 4:7; Neh. 10:31; Prov. 22:26; Matt. 18:27
DEBTOR—*obligation*
Ezek. 18:7, restores to the **d**
Matt. 6:12, as we also have forgiven our **d-s**
Luke 7:41, a certain money-lender had two **d-s**
16:5, summoned each of his master's **d-s**
DECAY—*corruption* Job 21:20, own eyes see his **d**
Acts 2:27, HOLY ONE TO UNDERGO **D**
DECEIT—*falsehood, deception* Ps. 32:2; 36:3; 50:19
Ps. 10:7, mouth full of curses and **d** and oppression
34:13, your lips from speaking **d**
55:23, Men of bloodshed and **d** will not live
Prov. 12:5, counsels of the wicked are **d-ful**
31:30, Charm is **d-ful** and beauty is vain
Jer. 17:9, heart is more **d-ful** than all else
2 Cor. 11:13, false apostles, **d-ful** workers
1 Pet. 2:22, NOR WAS ANY **D** FOUND
Prov. 27:6; Is. 57:4; Jer. 5:27; 48:10; Dan. 8:25; Hos. 11:12; Zeph. 1:9; Mark 7:22; 2 Cor. 12:16; Eph. 4:14,22
DECEITFUL—*false* Ps. 120:3, You **d** tongue
Ps. 17:1; 26:4
DECEITFULNESS—*deception*
Matt. 13:22; Mark 4:19, **d** of riches
DECEIVE—*cheat, mislead, steal* Gen. 31:20,27; Num. 25:18
Gen. 29:25, Why then have you **d-d** me
Jer. 42:20, you have *only* **d-d** yourselves
Matt. 27:63, we remember that ... that **d-r** said
Rom. 3:13, THEY KEEP **D-ING**
2 Cor. 6:8, *regarded* as **d-rs** and yet true
Eph. 5:6, 1 John 3:7, Let no one **d** you
1 John 1:8, If we say ... no sin, we are **d-ing**
2 John 7, many **d-rs** ... This is the **d-r** and the antichrist
Rev. 12:9, Satan, who **d-s** the whole world
Deut. 11:16; Josh. 7:11; 9:22; 1 Kin. 22:22; 2 Kin. 19:10; Is. 37:10; 44:20; Jer. 20:7; 37:9; Obad. 3; 1 Cor. 6:9; 15:33; Gal. 6:7; 2 Thess. 2:3; 1 Tim. 2:14; 2 Tim. 3:13; James 1:16; Rev. 19:20
DECEPTION—*deceit*
Jer. 3:10, return to Me ... in **d**
Matt. 27:64, last **d** will be worse than the first
Col. 2:8, philosophy and empty **d**
DECEPTIVE Mic. 6:11, a bag of **d** weights
DECIDE—*determine* 1 Sam. 20:7, he has **d-d** on evil
2 Chr. 2:1, Solomon **d-d** to build a house
Ex. 21:22; Acts 3:13; 1 Cor. 7:37

DECISION—*rebuke* Prov. 16:33, every **d** is from the LORD
Joel 3:14, day ... is near in the valley of **d**
Mic. 4:3; Zeph. 3:8
DECK Is. 61:10, As a bridegroom **d-s** himself
DECLARATION—*account*
Job 13:17, let my **d** fill your ears
DECLARE—*explain, relate* Ps. 75:9, I will **d** it forever
Ps. 92:2, To **d** Thy lovingkindness
145:4, shall **d** Thy mighty acts
Is. 43:21, Will **d** My praise
45:19, **D-ing** things that are upright
46:10, **D-ing** the end from the beginning
John 4:25, He will **d** all things to us
Acts 20:27, **d-ing** to you the whole purpose of God
Rom. 1:4, **d-d** with power *to be* the Son of God
Deut. 30:18; Job 31:37; Ps. 9:11; 30:9; 51:15; Is. 41:26; 45:21; 66:19; Acts 17:30
DECORATE—*deck* Jer. 4:30; 10:4
DECREASE—*abate, subside* Gen. 8:3, the water **d-d**
Ps. 107:38, He does not let their cattle **d**
John 3:30, He must increase, but I must **d**
DECREE—*decide, determine* Job 22:28; Ps. 94:20; 148:6
Dan. 11:36, that which is **d-d** will be done
Prov. 8:15; Dan. 2:9; 9:24; Acts 16:4; 17:7
DEDICATE—*devote*
Ex. 32:29, **D** yourselves today to the
1 Kin. 7:51, Solomon brought things **d-d**
8:63, sons of Israel **d-d** the house of the LORD
Deut. 20:5; Judg. 17:3; 1 Kin. 15:15; 1 Chr. 18:11; 26:27
DEED—*action, practice, work* Gen. 44:15; 2 Sam. 12:14
Ps. 9:1, committed abominable **d-s**
28:4, according to the **d-s** of their hands
Is. 1:16, Remove the evil of your **d-s**
59:18; Jer. 25:4, according to their **d-s**
Luke 24:19, prophet mighty in **d** and word
John 3:19, their **d-s** were evil
Acts 7:22, man of power in words and **d-s**
Gal. 5:19, **d-s** of the flesh are evident
Col. 3:17, whatever you do in word or **d**
Titus 3:1, ready for every good **d**
1 John 3:18, not love with word ... but in **d** and truth
Rev. 2:2, I know your **d-s** and your toil
14:13, for their **d-s** follow with them
Ezra 9:13; Neh. 13:14; Ps. 66:5; Prov. 20:11; Jer. 32:10,44; Luke 11:48; 23:41; John 8:41; Rom. 2:6
DEEP—*abyss, depth*
Gen. 7:11, fountains of the great **d**
Job 28:14, the **d** says, It is not with me
Ps. 36:6, Thy judgments are *like* a great **d**
42:7, **D** calls to **d**
Prov. 19:15, Laziness casts into a **d** sleep
Matt. 26:38; Mark 14:34, soul is **d-ly** grieved
Luke 5:4, Put out into **d** water
Rom. 8:26, groanings too **d** for words
Gen. 8:2; Deut. 33:13; Job 4:13; 38:30; Ps. 33:7; 77:16; 106:9; 107:24; Prov. 22:14; 23:27; Is. 7:11; Luke 6:48; John 4:11
DEER Ps. 42:1, **d** pants for the water brooks
Is. 35:6, lame will leap like a **d**
Deut. 12:15; 14:5; 1 Kin. 4:23
DEFEAT 1 Chr. 18:1, David **d-ed** the Philistines
Jer. 37:10, had **d-ed** the entire army
Gen. 14:15; 36:35; Num. 22:6; Josh. 10:33; 12:1,7; 1 Chr. 1:46; 14:11; 18:3; Jer. 46:2
DEFECT—*spot* Lev. 21:17; Deut. 15:21; 2 Sam. 14:25; Job 11:15; Dan. 1:4
DEFEND—*protect*
Zech. 9:15, LORD of hosts will **d** them
Acts 7:24; Rom. 2:15; 2 Cor. 12:19
DEFENSE Acts 19:33; 22:1
Phil. 1:7, in the **d** ... of the gospel
DEFICIENT—*want* Dan. 5:27, and found **d**

DEFILE—*pollute, profane* Lev. 21:4; Is. 59:3;
    Jer. 2:7
    2 Kin. 23:13, high places . . . the king **d-d**
    Neh. 13:29, they have **d-d** the priesthood
    Ps. 74:7, **d-d** the dwelling place of Thy name
      79:1, **d-d** Thy holy temple
    Matt. 15:11,18,20; Mark 7:15,20,23, **d** the man
    Titus 1:15, to those who are **d-d** . . . nothing is
      pure
    Heb. 12:15, by it many are **d-d**
    James 3:6, that which **d-s** the entire body
    Jude 8, these men also by dreaming **d** the flesh
    Ezek. 23:38; 36:17; Dan. 1:8; John 18:28;
      1 Cor. 8:7
DEFILEMENT—*filth* 2 Cor. 7:1, from all **d**
DEFRAUD—*deprive, wrong*
    1 Cor. 6:7,8; 1 Thess. 4:6, transgress and **d**
    1 Sam. 12:3; Lam. 3:36; Mark 10:19
DEGENERATE Jer. 2:21, **d** shoots of a foreign
    vine
DEGRADE Rom. 1:26, gave them over to **d-ing**
    passions
DEGREE—*standing* 1 Chr. 17:17; Ps. 62:9
DEITY Col. 2:9, fulness of **D** . . . bodily form
DELAY—*hinder, linger*
    Ex. 32:1, the people saw that Moses **d-ed**
    Deut. 23:21, shall not **d** to pay it
    1 Tim. 3:15, in case I am **d-ed**
    Rev. 10:6, there shall be **d** no longer
    Gen. 24:56; Ex. 22:29; Acts 9:38; 25:17
DELEGATION—*messenger*
    Luke 19:14, sent a **d** after him
DELICACY—*dainty, delicate* Ps. 141:4; Prov.
    23:3; Lam. 4:5
DELICATE—*dainty* Deut. 28:54,56; Is. 47:1
DELIGHT (n.)—*affection, luxury, observe,*
    pleasure
    2 Sam. 15:26, I have no **d** in you
    Ps. 1:2, his **d** is in the law of the LORD
    Prov. 8:31, *having* my **d** in the sons of men
      11:1, a just weight is His **d**
      12:22, those who deal faithfully are His **d**
    Job 27:10; Ps. 16:3; 119:24,77,92,143,174;
      Prov. 8:30; 15:8; 16:13; Song 2:3; Is. 58:13;
      62:4
DELIGHT (v.)—*desire*
    Job 22:26, you will **d** in the Almighty
    Ps. 37:4, **D** yourself in the LORD
      37:11, **d** themselves in abundant prosperity
      51:16, Thou dost not **d** in sacrifice
    Eccles. 5:4, He takes no **d** in fools
    Is. 42:1, My chosen one *in whom* My soul **d-s**
      55:2, **d** yourself in abundance
    Mic. 7:18, He **d-s** in unchanging love
    1 Sam. 15:22; Neh. 1:11; Ps. 94:19; Prov. 1:22;
      2:14; 18:2; 23:26; Is. 11:3; Hos. 6:6; Mal. 3:1
DELIGHTFUL Mal. 3:12, you shall be a **d** land
DELIVER—*rescue, save* Ex. 3:8; Num. 35:25;
    Deut. 32:39
    Job 5:19, From six troubles He will **d** you
    Ps. 56:13, **d-ed** my soul from death
    Is. 43:13, none who can **d** out of My hand
      50:2, have I no power to **d**
    Matt. 6:13, **d** us from evil
      10:17, they will **d** you up to *the* courts
      10:21, brother will **d** up brother
    Acts 2:23, **d-ed** up by the predetermined plan
    Rom. 4:25, who was **d-ed** up because of our
      transgressions
    2 Cor. 1:10, **d-ed** us from so great a *peril of*
      death
    Gal. 1:4, He might **d** us out of this present evil
      age
    Jude 3, faith which was . . . **d-ed** to the saints
    Judg. 7:2; 1 Sam. 10:27; 2 Chr. 20:9; 32:13;
      Ps. 33:17; Prov. 24:11; Eccles. 9:15; Jer. 1:8;
      39:17; Dan. 3:17; 6:14; Joel 2:32; Matt.
      26:15; Acts 7:34; 2 Cor. 4:11; 2 Tim. 4:18
DELIVERANCE—*victory, salvation* Gen. 45:7,
    by a great **d**
    Ps. 32:7, surround me with songs of **d**
    68:20, God is . . . a God of **d-s**

DELUDE 2 Thess. 2:11, God will send . . . a **d-ing**
    influence
DEMON—*satyr* Matt. 8:31, **d-s** *began* to entreat
    Him
    Mark 3:15, authority to cast out the **d-s**
    James 2:19, **d-s** also believe and shudder
      3:15, is earthly, natural, **d-ic**
    Lev. 17:7; Deut. 32:17; Ps. 106:37; Matt. 10:8;
      1 Cor. 10:20; Rev. 9:20
DEMONSTRATE—*show* Rom. 5:8, God **d-s** His
    own love
    Rom. 9:22, willing to **d** His wrath
DEMONSTRATION 1 Cor. 2:4, in **d** of the Spirit
    and of power
DEN Jer. 7:11, Has this house . . . become a **d** of
    robbers
    Dan. 6:7, shall be cast into the lions' **d**
    Judg. 6:2; Job 37:8; Is. 11:8; Amos 3:4; Matt.
      21:13; Mark 11:17
DENOUNCE—*slander* Jer. 20:10, **D** *him*; yes, let
    us **d** him
DENY—*conceal* Matt. 10:33, whoever shall **d** Me
    before men
    1 Tim. 5:8, he has **d-ed** the faith
    2 Tim. 2:13, for He cannot **d** Himself
      3:5, they have **d-ed** its power
    Titus 2:12, instructing us to **d** ungodliness
    Josh. 24:27; Job 6:10; Prov. 30:9; Titus 1:16
DEPART Job 21:14, they say to God, **D** from us
    Job 28:28, to **d** from evil is understanding
    Ps. 6:8, **D** from me, all you who do iniquity
    Prov. 22:6, when he is old he will not **d** from it
      27:22, his folly will not **d** from him
    Is. 26:14, **d-ed** spirits will not rise
    John 13:1, hour had come that He should **d**
    2 Cor. 12:8, entreated . . . that it might **d**
    Phil. 1:23, desire to **d** and be with Christ
    Gen. 49:10; Job 22:17; Ps. 18:21; 34:14; 37:27;
      105:38; Matt. 2:13,22; 7:23; 25:41;
      Luke 2:29; 4:13; 13:27; 21:21; Acts 7:3
DEPARTURE—*death* Luke 9:13, His **d**
    2 Tim. 4:6, the time of my **d** has come
    2 Pet. 1:15, at any time after my **d**
DEPEND—*hang* Matt. 22:40, two
    commandments **d** . . . Law
DEPOSE Dan. 5:20, he was **d-d** from his royal
    throne
DEPRAVE Rom. 1:28, gave them over to a **d-d**
    mind
    2 Tim. 3:8, men of **d-d** mind
DEPRIVE Is. 38:10, **d-d** of the rest of my years
    1 Cor. 7:5, Stop **d-ing** one another
    1 Tim. 6:5, **d-d** of the truth
DEPTH—*abyss, deep*
    Ps. 95:4, In whose hand are the **d-s** of the earth
      107:26, they went down to the **d-s**
    Prov. 25:3, heavens for height . . . for **d**
    Mic. 7:19, cast all their sins Into the **d-s** of the
      sea
    Matt. 13:5, they had no **d** of soil
      18:6, better . . . be drowned in the **d** of the sea
    Mark 4:5, it sprang up because it had no **d** of
      soil
    Rom. 8:39, nor height, nor **d** . . . separate us
      11:33, **d** of the riches
    1 Cor. 2:10, searches all things, even the **d-s** of
      God
    Job 41:31, Ps. 86:13; Prov. 8:24; Is. 63:13
DEPUTY—*proconsul* 1 Kin. 22:47, a **d** was king
DERIDE—*mock, scoff, sneer* Ps. 119:51, utterly **d**
    me
DERISION—*laughingstock, shame* Ex. 32:25;
    Ps. 79:4
    Ps. 44:13, a **d** to those around us
    Jer. 20:8; Ezek. 23:32; 36:4; Hos. 7:16
DESCEND Gen. 28:12, angels of God . . . **d-ing**
    Matt. 7:25,27, rain **d-ed**, and the floods came
    Mark 1:10, Spirit like a dove **d-ing** upon Him
    Rom. 10:7, WHO WILL **D** INTO THE ABYSS

DESCEND *(Continued)*
Ps. 49:17; Prov. 30:4; Matt. 11:23; John 1:32,33;
Eph. 4:10
DESCENDANT—*seed* Ps. 37:28, **d-s** of the
wicked will be
Rom. 4:18, So SHALL YOUR **D-S** BE
DESCENT Luke 19:37, near the **d** of the Mount
DESCRIPTION Josh. 18:4, write a **d** of it
according to
DESERT—*wild* Ps. 78:40, grieved Him in the **d**
Is. 35:1, the **d** will be glad
40:3, in the **d** a highway for our God
43:19, Rivers in the **d**
51:3, her **d** like the garden of the LORD
Prov. 21:19; Jer. 17:6; 25:24; 50:39; Luke 1:80
DESERT—*leave, forsake* 2 Kin. 25:11, the **d-ers**
who had
2 Tim. 4:16, but all **d-ed** me
Heb. 13:5, I WILL NEVER **D** YOU
DESERVE—*due, worthy*
Matt. 26:66, He is **d-ing** of death
Luke 23:41, receiving what we **d** for our deeds
1 Tim. 1:15, statement, **d-ing** full acceptance
Judg. 9:16; Ezra 9:13
DESIGN—*device, devise* Ex. 31:4; 35:32,35;
2 Chr. 2:14
DESIRABLE Ps. 19:10, more **d** than gold
Prov. 19:22, What is **d** in a man is his kindness
Ezek. 23:6,12,23, **d** young men
Gen. 3:6; Prov. 8:11
DESIRE (n.)—*appetite* Job 31:16; Ps. 10:3; 140:8;
Prov. 13:12
Gen. 3:16, your **d** shall be for your husband
Ps. 21:2, given him his heart's **d**
37:4, He will give you the **d-s** of your heart
112:10, **d** of the wicked will perish
145:16, satisfy the **d** of every living thing
Prov. 10:24; 11:23, the **d** of the righteous
Mic. 7:3, great man speaks the **d** of his soul
Rom. 10:1, my heart's **d** . . . is for *their* salvation
Eph. 2:3, **d-s** of the flesh and of the mind
Phil. 1:23, having the **d** to depart
Prov. 21:25; Ezek. 24:16,21,25; Mark 4:19;
Col. 3:5
DESIRE (v.)—*want, wish, crave* Deut. 14:26;
1 Sam. 2:16
Ps. 34:12, Who is the man who **d-s** life
51:6, Thou dost **d** truth
73:25, besides Thee, I **d** nothing on earth
Luke 22:15, earnestly **d-d** to eat this Passover
1 Cor. 12:31, earnestly **d** the greater gifts
14:1, yet **d** earnestly spiritual *gifts*
Gal. 6:12, who **d** to make a good showing in the
flesh
Heb. 11:16, they **d** a better *country*
Job 13:3; Ps. 40:6; 45:11; 107:30; Prov. 3:15,
23:3; Eccles. 2:10; Matt. 13:17; Gal. 4:9;
1 Tim. 3:1
DESOLATE—*lonely, waste* Lev. 26:31; Is. 54:1;
62:4
Matt. 23:38, your house is being left to you **d**
Jer. 2:12; 12:10; Ezek. 6:6; Joel 2:3; Zech. 7:14;
Luke 13:35; Acts 1:20; Gal. 4:27
DESOLATION—*ruins, waste*
Jer. 25:9; Ezek. 35:9, an everlasting **d**
32:43, a **d** without man or beast
Dan. 9:26, there will be war; **d-s** are determined
11:31; 12:11, abomination of **d**
Zeph. 1:15, day of destruction and **d**
2 Kin. 22:19; Josh. 8:28; Ps. 46:8; Is. 61:4;
Luke 21:20
DESPAIR—*faint, sorrow* 1 Sam. 27:1; Job 6:26;
Eccles. 2:20
Deut. 28:65, failing of eyes, and **d** of soul
2 Cor. 4:8, perplexed, but not **d-ing**
DESPERATE Jer. 17:9, The heart . . . is **d-ly** sick
DESPISE—*reject, scorn, spurn* Gen. 16:4;
Num. 15:31
Gen. 25:34, Esau **d-d** his birthright
Job 5:17, do not **d** the discipline of the
Almighty
36:5, God is mighty but does not **d** *any*

Ps. 51:17, a contrite heart . . . Thou wilt not **d**
Prov. 1:7, Fools **d** wisdom and instruction
15:32, He who neglects discipline **d-s** himself
Eccles. 9:16, wisdom of the poor man is **d-d**
Zech. 4:10, who has **d-d** the day of small things
Matt. 6:24; Luke 16:13, hold to one and **d** the
other
18:10, do not **d** one of these little ones
1 Cor. 1:28, base things . . . and the **d-d**
Heb. 12:2, endured the cross, **d-ing** the shame
1 Sam. 2:30; 2 Sam. 6:16; Neh. 4:4; Job 19:18;
Ps. 73:20; 102:17; 119:163; Prov. 6:30; 13:13;
15:20; Is. 5:24; 49:7; Jer. 49:15; Ezek. 21:10;
22:8; Mal. 1:6; 1 Cor. 11:22; 16:11;
1 Thess. 5:20
DESPONDENCY—*anguish, distress*
Ex. 6:9, on account of *their* **d**
DESTINE—*appoint, name*
1 Thess. 5:9, God has not **d-d** us for wrath
DESTITUTE—*deprive* Ezek. 32:15
Ps. 102:17, regarded the prayer of the **d**
Heb. 11:37, being **d**, afflicted, ill-treated
DESTROY—*defile, pollute, abolish, ruin, waste*
2 Sam. 1:14, **d** the LORD's anointed
Ps. 40:14, seek my life to **d** it
Prov. 1:32, complacency of fools shall **d** them
Is. 23:14, your stronghold is **d-ed**
Matt. 2:13, search . . . to **d** Him
6:19, where moth and rust **d**
10:28, fear Him who is able to **d**
12:14; Mark 3:6, they might **d** Him
Mark 14:58, I will **d** this temple
Luke 6:9, is it lawful . . . to save a life or **d** it
17:27, flood came and **d-ed** them all
1 Cor. 3:17, If any man **d-s** the temple
Gal. 1:13, church of God . . . tried to **d** it
1:23, the faith which he once tried to **d**
2:18, if I rebuild what I *once* **d-ed**
2 Pet. 3:12, heavens will be **d-ed** by burning
1 John 3:8, **d** the works of the devil
Gen. 6:17; Ex. 22:20; Deut. 9:14; 1 Sam. 15:6;
Job 10:8; Ps. 63:9; 145:20; Prov. 28:24; 31:3;
Eccles. 9:18; Is. 10:7; 11:9; Jer. 13:14; 23:1;
Ezek. 9:1; 22:27; Dan. 8:24; Matt. 22:7;
Mark 1:24; 11:18; 12:9; 15:29; Luke 4:34;
20:16; John 2:19; Rom. 14:15; James 4:12;
2 Pet. 2:12; 3:11; Jude 5
DESTROYER—*robber* Judg. 16:24, Even the **d** of
our country
Job 12:6; 15:21; Is. 49:17; Jer. 22:7
DESTRUCTION—*calamity, ruin* Ps. 35:8, Let **d**
come upon him
Ps. 52:2, Your tongue devises **d**
91:6, **d** that lays waste at noon
Prov. 16:18, Pride goes before **d**
Is. 19:18, called the City of **D**
59:7, Devastation and **d** are in their highways
Lam. 2:11; 3:48; 4:10, **d** of the daughter of my
people
Matt. 7:13, way is broad that leads to **d**
Rom. 9:22, vessels of wrath prepared for **d**
Phil. 3:19, whose end is **d**
1 Thess. 5:3, **d** will come upon them suddenly
1 Tim. 6:9, desires plunge to ruin and **d**
2 Chr. 22:4; Esth. 8:6; Job 21:17; Ps. 5:9; 57:1;
73:18; Prov. 17:19; 19:13; Is. 10:22; 14:23;
28:2; Jer. 17:18; 50:22; Hos. 13:9; Rom. 3:16;
2 Thess. 1:9; 2 Pet. 2:1,3; 3:16; Rev. 17:8
DESTRUCTIVE—*false* Prov. 17:4, a **d** tongue
2 Pet. 2:1, secretly introduce **d** heresies
DETAIN Judg. 13:15,16; 1 Sam. 21:7
DETERMINE—*decide* Job 14:5, his days are **d-d**
Luke 22:22, Son . . . as it has been **d-d**
Acts 17:26, having **d-d** *their* appointed times
1 Cor. 2:2, I **d-d** to know nothing
DETEST—*despise, loathe* Deut. 7:26; Jer. 4:1;
Amos 6:8
DETESTABLE—*abominable*
Deut. 14:3, eat any **d** thing
Is. 66:17, swine's flesh, **d** things
Luke 16:15, is **d** in the sight of God

Job 15:16; Jer. 16:18; Ezek. 5:11; 7:20; 11:18; 37:23

DEVASTATE—*waste* Nah. 2:2; 3:7

DEVASTATION—*oppression*
Ps. 12:5, the **d** of the afflicted

DEVICE—*design, plan, scheme*
Prov. 1:31, satiated ... own **d-s**

DEVIOUS—*perverse* Prov. 4:24, put **d** lips far from you

DEVISE—*design, plan, scheme, fashion*
Prov. 3:29, Do not **d** harm against your neighbor
6:14, **d-s** evil continually
14:22, will they not go astray who **d** evil
2 Pet. 1:16, cleverly **d-d** tales
Esth. 9:25; Ps. 2:1; 10:2; 21:11; 35:4; 41:7; 94:20; Prov. 6:18; 12:2; Is. 32:7,8; Zech. 7:10; Acts 4:25

DEVOTE—*dedicate* Rom. 12:10, Be **d-d** to one another
Col. 4:2, **D** yourselves to prayer
Num. 18:14; Ezek. 44:29

DEVOTION Eccles. 12:12, excessive **d** *to books* is wearying

DEVOUR—*consume, swallow*
2 Sam. 2:26, Shall the sword **d** forever
11:25, the sword **d-s** one as well as another
Zeph. 1:18; 3:8, all the earth will be **d-ed**
Matt. 13:4, birds came and **d-ed** them
23:14, you **d** widows' houses
Luke 15:30, son of yours ... has **d-ed** your wealth
Gal. 5:15, if you bite and **d** one another
Gen. 37:20; 2 Sam. 18:8; 22:9; Job 18:13; Ps. 18:8; 50:3; 52:4; Prov. 30:14; Is. 1:7,20; Jer. 2:30; 30:16; Amos 4:9; Mal. 3:11; Mark 12:40; Luke 8:5; 2 Cor. 11:20

DEVOUT—*God-fearing*
Luke 2:25, Simeon ... righteous and **d**
Acts 2:5; 8:2, **d** men
Acts 10:2; 13:50; 22:12

DEW Gen. 27:28, God give you of the **d** of heaven
Judg. 6:37, If there is **d** on the fleece only
2 Sam. 17:12, we will fall on him as the **d** falls
Prov. 3:20, the skies drip with **d**
Is. 18:4, Like a cloud of **d** in the heat of harvest
Dan. 4:15,23,25,33, drenched with the **d** of heaven
Ex. 16:13; Num. 11:9; Deut. 32:2; 33:13; 2 Sam. 1:21; 1 Kin. 17:1; Job 29:19; 38:28; Ps. 110:3; 133:3; Prov. 19:12; Is. 26:19; Hos. 6:4; 13:3; 14:5; Hag. 1:10

DIADEM—*turban* Is. 28:5; 62:3

DIAMOND Ex. 28:18; 39:11; Jer. 17:1; Ezek. 28:13

DID—*put* Gen. 6:22; Job 1:5
2 Chr. 18:23, How **d** the Spirit ... pass
Matt. 13:58, He **d** not do many miracles
John 9:26, What **d** He do to you
15:24, works which no one else **d**
1 Cor. 13:11, **d** away with childish things

DIE—*depart* Gen. 2:17; 20:7; 1 Sam. 14:44; 22:16; 1 Kin. 2:37,42; Ezek. 3:18; 33:8, you shall surely **d**
Deut. 14:21, not eat anything which **d-s** of itself
Ruth 1:17, Where you **d**, I will **d**
1 Sam. 26:16, *all* of you must surely **d**
Job 2:9, his wife said ... Curse God and **d**
3:11, Why did I not **d** at birth
14:14, If a man **d-s**, will he live *again*
21:23, One **d-s** in his full strength
Ps. 49:10, *even* wise men **d**
49:17, when he **d-s** he will carry nothing away
Prov. 10:21, fools **d** for lack of understanding
Eccles. 2:16, wise man and fool alike **d**
Ezek. 18:4, soul who sins will **d**
18:32, no pleasure in ... who **d-s**
Matt. 26:35, Even if I must **d** with you
Luke 8:52, she has not **d-d**, but is asleep
16:22, poor man **d-d** ... rich man also **d-d**

John 6:49, ate the manna ... and they **d-d**
11:25, who believes ... live even if he **d-s**
11:51, that Jesus was going to **d** for the nation
12:24, a grain of wheat falls ... and **d-s**
Rom. 5:6, Christ **d-d** for the ungodly
5:7, one will hardly **d** for a righteous man
6:2, How shall we who **d-d** to sin
14:9, Christ **d-d** and lived *again*
14:15, him for whom Christ **d-d**
1 Cor. 15:31, I **d** daily
2 Cor. 5:14, one **d-d** for all, therefore all **d-d**
Phil. 1:21, to **d** is gain
Col. 2:20, If you have **d-d** with Christ
1 Thess. 4:14, we believe that Jesus **d-d** and rose
5:10, who **d-d** for us, that ... we may live
Heb. 9:27, appointed for men to **d** once
11:13, All these **d-d** in faith
Gen. 3:3; 25:8; 27:4; 45:28; Lev. 10:6; Num. 18:32; Prov. 14:32; 30:7; Jer. 26:8; 27:13; Ezek. 18:20,31; 33:11,14; Matt. 22:25; Mark 5:39; John 11:44; 19:7; Acts 9:37; 21:13; Rom. 6:10; 7:9; 8:34; 14:7; 1 Cor. 8:11; 15:3,22; Gal. 2:19; 2 Tim. 2:11; 1 Pet. 2:24; Rev. 9:6; 14:13

DIFFER Rom. 12:6, we have gifts that **d**
1 Cor. 15:41, star **d-s** from star in glory
Deut. 25:13; Gal. 4:1

DIFFERENCE—*distinction* Ezek. 44:23

DIFFICULT—*hard* Jer. 32:27; Ezek. 3:5
Gen. 18:14, Is anything too **d** for the LORD
1 Kin. 10:1; 2 Chr. 9:1, test Solomon with **d** questions
Jer. 32:17, Nothing is too **d** for Thee
John 6:60, This is a **d** statement

DIG Ex. 21:33; Deut. 6:11; 8:9; Job 3:21; 24:16; Ezek. 12:5; Luke 13:8; 16:3

DIGNITY—*majesty* Gen. 49:3; Esth. 6:3; 1 Tim. 2:2

DILIGENCE—*effort, speed* Ezra 6:12, carried out with all **d**
Prov. 4:23, Watch over your heart with all **d**
Rom. 12:11, not lagging behind in **d**

DILIGENT—*careful, eager, thorough* Prov. 1:28; Heb. 4:11
Prov. 11:27, **d-ly** seeks good seeks favor
Eph. 4:3, **d** to preserve the unity
2 Tim. 2:15, Be **d** to present yourself approved
2 Pet. 1:15, I will also be **d**

DILL Is. 28:25,27

DILUTE—*mix* Is. 1:22, drink **d-d** with water

DIM—*dark* Job 17:7, My eye has also grown **d**
1 Cor. 13:12, see in a mirror **d-ly**
Gen. 27:1; 48:10; Deut. 34:7; 1 Sam. 3:2; Ps. 69:23; Eccles. 12:3

DIMINISH—*dwindle, reduce* Lev. 25:16; Ezek. 16:27

DINE—*eat* Gen. 43:16; Prov. 23:1

DINNER—*lunch, supper* Matt. 22:4; Luke 14:12
Luke 14:16, certain man was giving a big **d**

DIP 2 Kin. 5:14, **d-ed** *himself* seven times in the Jordan
Matt. 26:23, **d-ed** his hand with Me in the bowl
Luke 16:24, **d** the tip of his finger in water and
Rev. 19:13, clothed with a robe **d-ed** in blood
Gen. 37:31; Lev. 4:6; 9:9; Josh. 3:15; Ruth 2:14; 1 Sam. 14:27; Mark 14:20; John 13:26

DIRECT—*arrange, order* Is. 40:13; Jer. 10:23; 1 Thess. 3:11
Prov. 16:9, the LORD **d-s** his steps
23:19, **d** your heart in the way
2 Thess. 3:5, **d** your hearts into the love of God

DIRGE Matt. 11:17, we sang a **d**

DIRTY James 2:2, a poor man in **d** clothes

DISAPPOINT—*frustrate* Ps. 22:5, they trusted ... not **d-ed**
1 Pet. 2:6, SHALL NOT BE **D-ED**

DISASTER—*evil* Jer. 17:17; Ezek. 7:5

DISCERN—*appraise, analyze, recognize*
1 Kin. 3:9, **d** between good and evil
Matt. 16:3, **d** the appearance of the sky

DISCERN *(Continued)*
Heb. 5:14, senses trained to **d** good and evil
Gen. 41:33; Deut. 32:29; 2 Sam. 14:17; Job 4:16;
  6:30; Prov. 7:7; 8:5
DISCERNING—*understanding*
Deut. 1:13, Choose wise and **d**
1 Kin. 3:12, a wise and **d** heart
Prov. 16:21, wise in heart will be called **d**
DISCERNMENT—*judgment*
Ps. 119:66, Teach me good **d**
Is. 27:11, not a people of **d**
1 Sam. 25:33; 1 Kin. 3:11
DISCIPLE—*pupil* Matt. 10:24, A **d** is not above
his teacher
Matt. 12:2, Your **d-s** do what is not lawful
  26:56, all the **d-s** left Him and fled
  28:7, tell His **d-s** that He has risen
  28:19, make **d-s** of all nations
Mark 14:14; Luke 22:11, Passover with My **d-s**
Luke 6:13, He called His **d-s** to Him
  11:1, just as John also taught his **d-s**
  14:26,27, cannot be My **d**
  19:37, **d-s** began to praise God joyfully
  19:39, Teacher, rebuke Your **d-s**
John 2:11, His **d-s** believed in Him
  6:66, many of His **d-s** withdrew
  13:5, began to wash the **d-s'** feet
  13:35, all men will know you are My **d-s**
  19:26, **d** whom He loved standing nearby
Acts 9:26, associate with the **d-s**
  11:26, **d-s** were first called Christians
Is. 8:16; Matt. 10:1,42; 11:1; 15:2; 17:16; 19:13;
  20:17; 22:16; 26:18,35; 28:13; Mark 2:18;
  4:34; 7:2,5; 10:13; Luke 5:30,33; 6:20; 14:33;
  John 4:2; 6:22; 7:3; 8:31; 9:27,28; 15:8;
  18:1,15,16,17,25; 19:38; 20:2,18,26;
  21:7,20,23,24; Acts 9:1; 20:30; 21:16
DISCIPLINE—*chasten, exercise*
Job 5:17; Prov. 3:11, not despise **d** of the
  Almighty
Prov. 16:22, **d** of fools is folly
  19:18, **D** your son while there is hope
1 Cor. 11:32, we are **d-d** by the Lord
1 Tim. 4:7, **d** yourself for the purpose of
  godliness
Heb. 12:6, THE LORD LOVES He **D-S**
Deut. 4:36; 8:5; 1 Kin. 12:11; Heb. 12:8
DISCONTENTED 1 Sam. 22:2, everyone ... **d**
DISCOURAGE—*dishearten* Num. 32:7,9
DISCOVER—*reveal, find* Job 11:7, **d** the depths
of God
DISCREDIT—*condemn*
2 Cor. 6:3, the ministry be not **d-ed**
  8:20, no one should **d** us
DISCRETION—*understanding, wisdom*
1 Chr. 22:12, LORD give you **d**
Prov. 11:22, beautiful woman who lacks **d**
DISCUSS—*converse, reason* Matt. 16:7; Mark
  9:33; Luke 6:11; 24:15
DISDAIN 1 Sam. 17:42, he **d-ed** him (David)
Job 30:1, whose fathers I **d-ed**
DISEASE—*affliction* Ps. 103:3, heals all your **d-s**
Matt. 4:23, healing every kind of **d**
Luke 9:1, gave them power ... to heal **d-s**
Ex. 15:26; Deut. 7:15; 28:60; 2 Chr. 16:12;
  Ezek. 34:4; Matt. 4:24; Acts 28:9
DISGRACE—*shame, reproach* Gen. 34:7; Lev.
  20:17; Job 10:15; Prov. 6:33; 14:34; Jer. 14:21;
  1 Cor. 11:4,5,6
DISGUISE—*pretend* 1 Sam. 21:13, David **d-d** his
  sanity
1 Sam. 28:8, Saul **d-d** himself
1 Kin. 22:30; 2 Chr. 18:29, king of Israel **d-d**
  himself
1 Kin. 14:2; 20:38; 2 Chr. 35:22; Job 24:15
DISGUST—*exclude, alienate* Ezek. 23:17,
  became **d-ed** with
DISH—*bowl* Gen. 27:4; 2 Kin. 21:13
DISHEARTEN Is. 42:4, will not be **d-ed** or
  crushed
DISHONEST Amos 8:5, cheat with **d** scales

DISHONOR—*disgrace, shame* Ezra 4:14; Ps.
  35:26; 71:13
John 8:49, I honor My Father, and you **d** Me
1 Cor. 15:43, it is sown in **d**
2 Cor. 6:8, by glory and **d**
2 Tim. 2:20, some to honor and some to **d**
Ps. 83:16; Prov. 12:16; Rom. 1:24; 2:23;
  James 2:6
DISLOCATE—*joint*
Gen. 32:25, Jacob's thigh was **d-d**
DISMAY—*astound, discourage*
Deut. 1:21, Do not fear or be **d-ed**
Deut. 31:8; Josh. 1:9; 8:1; 10:25; 1 Sam. 17:11;
  1 Chr. 22:13; 28:20; 2 Chr. 20:15,17; 32:7;
  Job 41:22; Jer. 1:17; 8:9,21; 17:18; 30:10;
  46:27; Ezek. 2:6; 3:9; Obad. 9
DISMISS 2 Chr. 23:8; Acts 19:41
DISOBEDIENCE Rom. 5:19, one man's **d**
Eph. 2:2, spirit ... working in the sons of **d**
  5:6 wrath of God comes upon the sons of **d**
Heb. 2:2, **d** received a just recompense
DISOBEDIENT—*rebellious* Neh. 9:26; Luke 1:17;
  Titus 3:3
Acts 26:19, did not prove **d** to the heavenly
  vision
Rom. 1:30; 2 Tim. 3:2, **d** to parents
  10:21, A **D** AND OBSTINATE PEOPLE
1 Pet. 3:20, spirits who once were **d**
DISOBEY 1 Kin. 13:26, **d-ed** the command of the
  LORD
DISORDER—*confusion* James 3:16, **d** and every
  evil thing
DISPERSE—*spread* Esth. 3:8; Is. 11:12; Ezek.
  20:23; 36:19; Zeph. 3:10
DISPERSION Jer. 25:34; John 7:35
DISPLAY—*declare* Esth. 1:11; Ps. 60:4; Is. 3:9
Ps. 8:1, Who hast **d-ed** Thy splendor above
John 9:3, works of God might be **d-ed**
DISPLEASE Gen. 48:17; Num. 22:34;
  1 Sam. 8:6; 18:8; Prov. 24:18; Is. 59:15;
  Jon. 4:1
DISPLEASURE—*anger, fury*
Deut. 9:19, anger and hot **d**
DISPOSSESS Num. 14:12; Deut. 7:17
DISPUTE—*contend, controversy, debate* Deut.
  25:1; Heb. 7:7
Phil. 2:14, Do all things without ... **d-ing**
Jude 9, when he **d-d** with the devil
DISREGARD—*despise* Titus 2:15, Let no one **d**
  you
DISSENSION—*division* Acts 23:7
Acts 15:2, Paul and Barnabas had great **d**
Rom. 16:17, keep your eye on those who
  cause **d-s**
1 Tim. 2:8, without wrath and **d**
DISSIPATION Eph. 5:18, wine, for that is **d**
Titus 1:6, accused of **d** or rebellion
DISSOLVE—*melt* Ps. 6:6, I **d** my couch with my
  tears
Job 30:22; Nah. 2:6
DISTAFF Prov. 31:19, her hands to the **d**
DISTANCE Gen. 22:4; Matt. 26:58
DISTANT—*far* Luke 15:13, into a **d** country
DISTILL—*drip* Deut. 32:2, My speech **d** as the
  dew
DISTINCTION—*difference* Ex. 11:7; Lev. 11:47;
  20:25
Lev. 10:10, **d** between the holy and the profane
Rom. 3:22; 10:12; for there is no **d**
Ezek. 22:26; Acts 15:9; 1 Cor. 14:7
DISTINCTLY—*plain*
Deut. 27:8, all the words ... **d**
DISTINGUISH—*discern* Ezra 3:13; 1 Cor. 12:10
2 Sam. 19:35, Can I **d** between good and bad
Mal. 3:18, **d** between the righteous and the
  wicked
DISTORT—*pervert* Gal. 1:7, **d** the gospel of
  Christ
DISTRACTED Luke 10:40, Martha was **d** with
DISTRESS—*adversity, privation* Gen. 35:3; Deut.
  4:30
2 Chr. 20:9, cry to Thee in our **d**

Ps. 25:17, Bring me out of my **d-es**
Prov. 1:27, when **d** *and* anguish come on you
Mark 14:33, began to be very **d-ed**
1 Thess. 3:7, in all our **d** and affliction
James 1:27, orphans and widows in their **d**
Deut. 28:53; 1 Sam. 26:24; 2 Sam. 4:9; 24:14;
  2 Kin. 19:3; 2 Chr. 33:12; Prov. 24:10;
  Is. 25:4; 29:2; 33:2; Jer. 16:19; Lam. 1:20;
  Zeph. 1:17; Luke 21:23; Rom. 2:9;
  1 Cor. 7:26; Phil. 1:17; 1 Tim. 5:10
DISTRIBUTE—*apportion*
Luke 18:22, **d** it to the poor
John 6:11, He **d-d** to those who were seated
DISTURBANCES
Luke 21:9, when you hear of war and **d**
DISTURBED 1 Sam. 28:15, Why have you **d** me
  by bringing
Ps. 42:5; 43:5, Why have you become **d** within
  me
DIVIDE—*apportion* 1 Kin. 3:25, **D** the living
  child in two
Ps. 22:18, **d** my garments among them
Prov. 16:19, **d** the spoil with the proud
Luke 11:17, Any kingdom **d-d** against itself
Eph. 2:14, broke down the barrier of the **d-ing**
  wall
Is. 53:12; Dan. 2:41; Matt. 27:35; Luke 15:12
DIVINATION Acts 16:16, having a spirit of **d**
Num. 22:7; Jer. 14:14; Ezek. 13:6,9
DIVINE Heb. 9:1, regulations of worship
2 Pet. 1:4, partakers of *the* **d** nature
Gen. 30:27; Mic. 3:11; Zech. 10:2
DIVISION—*dissension* Ex. 8:23, put a **d** between
  My people
1 Chr. 23:6, divided them into **d-s**
John 7:43, arose a **d** in the multitude
1 Cor. 1:10, and there be no **d-s** among you
DIVORCE Lev. 21:14, widow, or a **d-d** woman
Deut. 24:1,3, a certificate of **d**
Jer. 3:8, given her a writ of **d**
Matt. 5:31, Whoever d-s his wife
DO—*practice, work* Gen. 11:6; 30:31; 1 Kin. 2:6
Ex. 20:9, Six days . . . labor and **d** all your work
Ps. 1:3, in whatever he **d-es**, he prospers
  34:14, Depart from evil and **d** good
Eccles. 3:14, everything God **d-es** will remain
  forever
Matt. 12:50, whoever shall **d** the will of My
  Father
John 7:17, If any man is willing to **d** His will
  15:5, apart from Me you can **d** nothing
Acts 16:30, what must I **d** to be saved
Rom. 13:3, **D** what is good
1 Cor. 9:23, I **d** all things for the sake of the
  gospel
  11:24, **d** this in remembrance of Me
Gal. 6:10, let us **d** good to all men
2 Tim. 4:5, **d** the work of an evangelist
Heb. 10:7, Behold, I have come . . . to d Thy
  will
1 Pet. 3:11, turn away from evil and d good
Prov. 12:24; 24:29; Matt. 23:3; John 2:5; 5:30
DOCTRINE—*teaching*
Eph. 4:14, every wind of **d**
1 Tim. 4:6, of the faith and of the sound **d**
Titus 1:9, able both to exhort in sound **d**
DOER—*workmen* Rom. 2:13, the **d-s** of the Law
  will be justified
James 1:22, prove yourselves **d-s** of the word
  4:11, you are not a **d** of the law
DOG Eccles. 9:4, a live **d** is better than a dead lion
1 Sam. 17:43; 2 Sam. 3:8; Ps. 22:16; 59:6;
  Is. 56:10; Luke 16:21; Phil. 3:2; Rev. 22:15
DOING—*deeds*
Acts 10:38, He went about **d** good
Rom. 2:7, perseverance in **d** good
Gal. 6:9, let us not lose heart in **d** good
Eph. 6:6, **d** the will of God from the heart
2 Thess. 3:13, do not grow weary of **d** good
2 Cor. 8:11; 1 Pet. 2:15; 3:17

DOMAIN—*estate* Jude 6, angels who did not
  keep their own **d**
Luke 4:6; Col. 1:13
DOMINION—*kingdom, rule*
Ps. 103:22, in all places of His **d**
Zech. 9:10, His **d** will be from sea to sea
Col. 1:16, thrones or **d-s** or rulers
1 Pet. 4:11, belongs the glory and **d** forever
1 Chr. 29:11; Job 25:2; Eph. 1:21; Rev. 1:6
DONE—*wrought* Matt. 6:10, Thy will be **d**
Matt. 18:19, shall be **d** for them by My Father
Mark 14:6, has **d** a good deed to Me
Gen. 20:9; Ex. 31:15; Eccles. 2:11
DONKEY Zech. 9:9, mounted on a **d**
Matt. 21:2, you will find a **d** tied *there*
Num. 22:30; Prov. 26:3; Jer. 22:19; Matt. 21:5;
  2 Pet. 2:16
DOOMED—*silenced* Ps. 79:11, those who are **d** to
  die
Jer. 8:14, God has **d** us
DOOR—*entrance*
Gen. 4:7, sin is crouching at the **d**
Ex. 12:7, put it on the two **d-posts**
Ps. 141:3, Keep watch over the **d** of my lips
Matt. 6:6, when you have shut your d, pray
John 10:9, I am the **d**
1 Cor. 16:9, a wide **d** for effective *service*
James 5:9, Judge is standing right at the **d**
Rev. 3:8, put before you an open **d**
Gen. 6:16; 18:1; Judg. 4:20; 2 Sam. 11:9;
  2 Chr. 12:10; Job 31:9; Prov. 26:14;
  Ezek. 40:38; Matt. 25:10; John 18:16;
  Rev. 4:1
DOUBLE—*twice* Gen. 43:12; Ps. 12:2; 1 Tim. 5:17
2 Kin. 2:9, **d** portion of your spirit be upon me
Is. 40:2, **D** for all her sins
James 1:8, *being* a **d-minded** man
Jude 12, without fruit, **d-ly** dead
DOUBT—*misgiving* Matt. 14:31, you of little
  faith, why did you **d**
Matt. 21:21, if you have faith and do not **d**
  28:17, but some were **d-ful**
Luke 24:38, why do **d-s** arise in your hearts
Rom. 14:23, he who **d-s** is condemned if he eats
DOUGH—*flour* 2 Sam. 13:8, Tamar took a,
  kneaded *it*
DOVE Ps. 55:6, O that I had wings like a **d**
Matt. 3:16, Spirit of God descending as a **d**
  10:16, shrewd as serpents . . . innocent as **d-s**
Gen. 8:8; Song 1:15; Is. 38:14; John 1:32
DOWN Ps. 23:2, makes me lie **d** in green pastures
Matt. 4:6, Son of God throw Yourself **d**
  8:32, whole herd rushed **d** the steep bank
Gen. 12:10; 2 Sam. 3:35; Eccles. 3:21; John 8:6
DRAG—*draw* James 2:6, the rich who . . . **d** you
  into court
Jer. 12:3; 15:3; Acts 8:3
DRAGON Is. 51:9; Rev. 20:2
DRANK—*drink* 1 Cor. 10:4, all **d** the same
  spiritual drink
Gen. 9:21; Dan. 1:5; Mark 14:23; John 4:12
DRAW Ps. 69:18, **d** near to my soul
Is. 12:3, **d** water from the springs of salvation
Jer. 31:3, I have **d-n** you with lovingkindness
Luke 21:28, your redemption is **d-ing** near
John 4:11, You have nothing to **d** with
  12:32, if I be lifted up . . . will **d** all men to
  Myself
Heb. 10:22, let us **d** near with a sincere heart
James 4:8, **D** near to God . . . He will **d** near to
  you
Gen. 24:13; Judg. 3:22; 19:9; Prov. 20:5;
  Zeph. 3:2; Acts 11:10
DREAD—*fear* Ps. 27:1, Whom shall I **d**
Prov. 1:27, **d** comes like a storm
Deut. 28:66; Job 3:25; Ps. 14:5; Is. 7:16; 8:13
DREAM Gen. 28:12, he had a **d**, and behold, a
  ladder
Gen. 37:19, Here comes this **d-er**
Dan. 1:17, Daniel understood all . . . **d-s**
Joel 2:28, Your old men will **d** dreams

DREAM *(Continued)*
Matt. 2:12, warned *by God* in a **d**
2:13, appeared to Joseph in a **d**
Jude 8, these men also by **d-ing** defile the flesh
Gen. 20:3; Judg. 7:13; Job 20:8; Ps. 73:20; 126:1;
Is. 29:7; Matt. 1:20; 2:19; 27:19; Acts 2:17
DRENCHED—*wet* Dan. 4:15, **d** with the dew of
heaven
DRESS—*array, clothe* Mark 15:17; Luke 7:25;
1 Pet. 3:3
Matt. 11:8, A man **d-ed** in soft *clothing*
DREW Gen. 47:29; Matt. 26:51; Acts 5:37
Ex. 2:10, I **d** him out of the water
Acts 1:26, they **d** lots for them
DRIED—*parched, withered* Job 18:16; Jer. 23:10
Gen. 8:7, water was **d** up from the earth
Ps. 22:15, My strength is **d** up
DRIES Joel 1:12, rejoicing **d** up
DRINK—*libation* Lev. 10:9, Do not **d** wine or
strong **d**
Job 21:20, **d** the wrath of the Almighty
Ps. 80:5, made them to **d** tears
Prov. 20:1, strong **d** a brawler
Is. 22:13, Let us eat and **d**, for tomorrow
Matt. 11:18, neither eating nor **d-ing**
25:35, I was thirsty and you gave Me **d**
26:27, **D** from it, all of you
26:29, day when I **d** it new with you
27:34, GAVE HIM WINE TO **D** MINGLED WITH
GALL
1 Cor. 10:4, all drank the same spiritual **d**
10:21, You cannot **d** the cup of the Lord
11:25, as often as you **d** *it*
Num. 6:3; 1 Kin. 17:6; Prov. 5:15; 7:18;
Eccles. 9:7; Is. 24:9; Joel 1:5; Luke 5:39;
17:27; John 6:55; 18:11; Rom. 12:20;
Heb. 6:7
DRIP Prov. 27:15, constant **d-ing** on a day of
steady rain
Job 36:28; Ps. 65:11; Song 4:11; Is. 45:8
DRIVE—*chase* Ps. 1:4, chaff which the wind **d-s**
away
Gen. 4:14; 21:10; Judg. 11:7; 2 Kin. 9:20;
Ps. 35:5; Is. 58:3
DROP—*leak, drip* Deut. 32:2; Job 36:27
Is. 40:15, nations are like a **d** from a bucket
Luke 22:44, His sweat became like **d-s** of blood
DROUGHT—*famine* Jer. 14:1, in regard to the **d**
DROVE John 2:15; Acts 13:50
DROWNED Ex. 15:4, his officers are **d** in the Red
Sea
Matt. 18:6, **d** in the depth of the sea
DROWSY Matt. 25:5, got **d** and *began* to sleep
DRUNK—*drink* Eph. 5:18, do not get **d** with wine
Lev. 11:34; Deut. 32:42; Is. 29:9; 63:6; John 2:10;
1 Thess. 5:7
DRUNKARD Deut. 21:20; Ps. 69:12; Joel 1:5;
1 Cor. 5:11
DRUNKENNESS
Luke 21:34, weighted down with . . . **d**
Rom. 13:13, not in carousing and **d**
Gal. 5:21, envyings, **d**, carousings and things
DRY—*parch, scorch, wither*
Ezek. 37:4, O **d** bones, hear the word
Gen. 1:9; Ps. 63:1; Prov. 17:1; Ezek. 17:24;
Luke 23:31
DUE—*deserve, owe* Gal. 6:9, in **d** time we shall
reap
Lev. 10:13; Ps. 104:27
DUG Ps. 7:15; 57:6; Is. 51:1; Ezek. 8:8; Matt.
21:33; 25:18; Luke 6:48
DULL—*red* Gen. 49:12, eyes are **d** from wine
DUMB—*silent* Mark 7:37, deaf to hear, and **d** to
speak
Ps. 31:18, Let the lying lips be **d**
Ex. 4:11; Ps. 39:2; Matt. 9:32; 1 Cor. 12:2;
2 Pet. 2:16
DUNGEON—*pit* Gen. 41:14, out of the **d**
DUST Gen. 2:7, LORD God formed man of **d**
Gen. 3:19, you are **d**, And to you shall return
Ps. 103:14, He is mindful we are *but* **d**
Matt. 10:14, shake off the **d** of your feet

Gen. 3:14; 13:16; 1 Sam. 2:8; 2 Sam. 22:43;
Job 30:19; 34:15; 42:6; Ps. 18:42; 30:9; 72:9;
Is. 26:19; 40:15; 65:25; Dan. 12:2; Luke
10:11; Acts 22:23; Rev. 18:19
DWELL—*abide, remain, live*
Ps. 5:4, No evil **d-s** with Thee
15:1, Who may **d** on Thy holy hill
23:6, will **d** in the house of the LORD
24:1, world, and those who **d** in it
91:1, **d-s** in the shelter of the Most High
Prov. 3:33, He blesses the **d-ing** of the righteous
Luke 16:9, receive you into the eternal **d-ings**
2 Cor. 5:2, our **d-ing** from heaven
Eph. 2:22, **d-ing** of God in the Spirit
3:17, Christ may **d** in your hearts
Phil. 4:8, mind **d** on these things
Col. 1:19, for all the fulness to **d** in Him
1 Tim. 6:16, **d-s** in unapproachable light
2 Pet. 1:14, laying aside . . . *earthly* **d-ing**
Gen. 4:20; Deut. 12:11; 1 Chr. 17:1; Ezra 7:15;
Ps. 33:14; Prov. 15:31; Is. 57:15; Luke 21:35
DWELT—*sat* Ps. 107:10, those who **d** in darkness
DWINDLE—*diminish*
Prov. 13:11, wealth . . . by fraud **d-s**

E

EACH Acts 17:27, not far from **e** one of us
Rom. 14:12, **e** one of us shall give account
Phil. 2:3, let **e** of you regard one another
2 Thess. 1:3, the love of **e** one of you
Ex. 18:7; Ps. 85:10; Is. 57:2; Ezek. 4:6; Acts 2:3
EAGER—*hasty* Ps. 17:12; Eccles. 7:9
EAGERLY—*fervently*
Rom. 8:19, creation waits **e** for
Gal. 4:17, They **e** seek you
2 Tim. 1:17, in Rome, he **e** searched for me
EAGLE Ps. 103:5, youth is renewed like the **e**
Is. 40:31, with wings like **e-s**
Ex. 19:4; Deut. 28:49; 2 Sam. 1:23; Job 9:26;
39:27; Ezek. 1:10; 17:3; Dan. 4:33; Obad. 4;
Rev. 4:7; 12:14
EAR Prov. 20:12, The hearing **e** and the seeing
eye
Prov. 25:12, a wise reprover to a listening **e**
Is. 55:3, Incline your **e** and come to Me
1 Cor. 2:9, EYE HAS NOT SEEN AND **E** HAS NOT
HEARD
Rev. 2:7, He who has an **e**, let him hear
Neh. 1:6; Job 12:11; 29:11; 42:5; Ps. 45:10; 58:4;
78:1; 94:9; Prov. 15:31; 18:15; 22:17;
Eccles. 1:8; Is. 48:8; 50:4; 59:1; Jer. 9:20;
Amos 3:12; Matt. 11:15; 1 Cor. 12:16
EARLY Gen. 26:31; Song 7:12; Hos. 6:4; Mark
16:2; Luke 24:22; John 20:1; James 5:7
EARNEST—*pledge* 2 Cor. 8:8; Phil. 1:20
EARNESTLY—*diligently, fervently*
Ps. 63:1, seek Thee **e**
1 Cor. 12:31, But **e** desire the greater gifts
Col. 4:12, always laboring **e** for you
James 5:17, he prayed **e** that it might not rain
Jude 3, contend **e** for the faith
EARNS Hag. 1:6, he who **e**, **e** wages to put into a
purse
EARS—*hearing* 2 Sam. 7:22, heard with our **e**
Job 15:21, Sounds of terror are in his **e**
28:22, With our **e** we have heard
Ps. 34:15, His **e** are open to their cry
115:6, They have **e**, but they cannot hear
Prov. 21:13, shuts his **e** to the cry of the poor
26:17, *Like* one who takes a dog by the **e**
Mark 8:18, HAVING **E**, DO YOU NOT HEAR
2 Tim. 4:3, wanting to have their **e** tickled
James 5:4, reached the **e** of the Lord
1 Pet. 3:12, HIS **E** ATTEND TO THEIR PRAYER
Ps. 135:17; Is. 6:10; Matt. 10:27; 11:15; 13:15,16;
26:51; 28:14; Mark 4:9; 7:33; 14:47;
Acts 7:51; 17:20
EARTH—*ground, land, soil*
Gen. 18:25, Shall not the judge of all the **e** deal
Ex. 9:29, the **e** is the LORD's

Num. 14:21, all the **e** will be filled with the glory
Josh. 3:11; Zech. 6:5, Lord of all the **e**
Job 26:7, hangs the **e** on nothing
Ps. 8:1, Thy name in all **e**
   24:1, The **e** is the LORD's
   33:5, **e** is full of the lovingkindness of the LORD
   46:6, raised His voice, the **e** melted
   97:1, LORD reigns; let the **e** rejoice
   104:5, He established the **e**
   104:24, The **e** is full of Thy possessions
Eccles. 1:4, the **e** remains forever
Is. 11:9, **e** will be full of the knowledge
   51:6, the **e** will wear out like a garment
   66:1, the **e** is My footstool
Jer. 51:15, made the **e** by His power
Mic. 1:2, Listen, O **e** and all it contains
Hab. 2:14, **e** will be filled with the knowledge
   3:3, the **e** is full of His praise
Zech. 4:10, eyes of the LORD ... the **e**
Matt. 5:5, gentle, for they shall inherit the **e**
   6:10, on **e** as it is in heaven
   6:19, treasures upon **e**
   16:19; 18:18, shall bind on **e**
Luke 2:14, on **e** peace
John 12:32, lifted up from the **e**
   17:4, I glorified Thee on the **e**
1 Cor. 15:47, first man is from the **e**, **e-y**
   15:48, As is the **e-y**, so also ... who are **e-y**
Col. 3:2, not on the things that are on **e**
2 Pet. 3:13, new heavens and a new **e**
Rev. 20:11, from whose presence **e** and heaven fled
   21:1, a new **e**
Gen. 1:1,11; 7:10; 8:22; 10:25; Deut. 32:1;
   Josh. 23:14; 1 Kin. 8:27; 2 Kin. 5:17;
   2 Chr. 6:18; Job 9:24; 12:8; 19:25; 38:4;
   41:33; Ps. 2:8; 16:3; 34:16; 41:2; 46:2,8,10;
   47:9; 50:4; 57:5; 58:11; 63:9; 65:8,9; 67:6;
   68:8; 71:20; 72:6,16; 73:25; 75:3; 83:18; 90:2;
   97:9; 99:1; 102:25; 104:13; 108:5; 112:2;
   115:16; 119:19,64,90; 146:4; 147:8; 148:13;
   Prov. 3:19; 8:23,26; 11:31; 25:3;
   30:14,16,21,24; Eccles. 3:21; 12:7; Is. 4:2;
   13:13; 14:16; 24:1,19; 26:9,21; 34:1; 40:22,28;
   44:24; 45:22; 48:13; 49:13; 65:16; Jer. 31:22;
   Ezek. 34:27; 43:2; Hos. 2:22; Amos 8:9;
   Jon. 2:6; Mic. 6:2; 7:17; Nah. 1:5; Zeph. 3:8;
   Hag. 1:10; Matt. 5:35; 10:34; 23:9;
   Mark 4:28; 9:3; John 3:31; Acts 1:8; 22:22;
   Rom. 10:18; 1 Cor. 15:49; Heb. 8:4; 11:13;
   12:25,26; James 3:15; 5:5,18; 2 Pet. 3:7,10;
   Rev. 5:10; 7:3; 18:1; 20:9
EARTHEN Jer. 19:1; Lam. 4:2
   2 Cor. 4:7, have this treasure in **e** vessels
EARTHLY John 3:12, If I told you **e** things
   2 Cor. 5:1, **e** tent which is our house
   Phil. 3:19, set their minds on **e** things
   James 3:15, wisdom ... is **e**, natural, demonic
EARTHQUAKE 1 Kin. 19:11; Is. 29:6; Amos 1:1;
   Zech. 14:5; Matt. 24:7; 27:54; Acts 16:26; Rev.
   6:12; 8:5; 11:13; 16:18
EASE—*rest, prosperity* Job 12:5, He who is at **e**
   Amos 6:1, Woe to those who are at **e**
   Zech. 1:15, nations who are at **e**
   Matt. 19:24; Mark 10:25; Luke 18:25, **e-ier** for a camel
   Luke 12:19, take your **e**
   Heb. 12:1, sin which so **e-ily** entangles us
   Ex. 18:22; Job 21:23; Is. 32:9,11
EAST Judg. 6:3; 7:12, 1 Kin. 4:30, sons of the **e**
   Ps. 103:12, As far as the **e**
   Matt. 2:1, magi from the **e**
   2:2, His star in the **e**
   Gen. 28:14; Ex. 10:13; Job 1:3; Ps. 48:7; 75:6;
   Is. 27:8; 43:5; Ezek. 8:16; 17:10; Hos. 12:1;
   Joel 2:20; Jon. 4:5; Zech. 8:7; 14:4;
   Matt. 8:11; 24:27; Luke 13:29; Rev. 16:12;
   21:13
EASY Prov. 14:6, knowledge is **e** to him
   Matt. 11:30, My yoke is **e**

EAT—*consume, dine, feast* Prov. 31:27, not **e** the bread
Is. 55:1, come, buy and **e**
Ezek. 3:1, **e** this scroll
Dan. 4:33, began **e-ing** grass like cattle
Matt. 6:25; Luke 12:22, what you shall **e**
   11:19, Son of Man came **e-ing** and drinking
   15:20, **e** with unwashed hands
   26:26, Take, **e**; this is My body
Mark 2:16, He was **e-ing** with the sinners
Luke 12:19, **e**, drink *and* be merry
   15:2, receives sinners and **e-s** with them
   22:30, may **e** and drink at My table
John 4:32, food to **e** that you do not know about
Acts 12:23, **e-en** by worms and died
Rom. 14:17, kingdom of God is not **e-ing**
1 Cor. 11:29, **e-s** and drinks judgment to himself
2 Thess. 3:10, not work, neither let him **e**
Heb. 13:10, have no right to **e**
Rev. 2:7, **e** of the tree of life
Gen. 2:16; 3:17; 9:4; Lev. 19:26; Deut. 6:11; 8:10;
   12:16; Josh. 5:12; 1 Kin. 19:5; 2 Kin. 6:28;
   Neh. 5:2; 8:10; Ps. 22:26; 80:13; Prov. 1:31;
   24:13; 25:27; Eccles. 5:12; Is. 1:19; 3:10; 4:1;
   7:15; 11:7; 65:13, 25; Jer. 24:2; 29:17; 31:29;
   Ezek. 18:2; Hos. 4:10; 10:13; Mic. 6:14;
   Hag. 1:6; Matt. 9:11; 12:1; 14:16;
   Mark 6:31,37; 11:14; Luke 9:13; 10:8; 15:23;
   John 6:53; Acts 10:13; Rom. 14:2;
   1 Cor. 8:13; 9:4; 10:27,31; Rev. 10:10; 19:18
EDGE—*bank* Josh. 3:8; Eccles. 10:10; Jer. 31:30
   Prov. 5:4, sharp as a **two-e-d** sword
EDICT—*word* Ezra 6:11, violates this **e**
EDIFICATION Rom. 15:2, please his neighbor ... to his **e**
   1 Cor. 14:3, speaks to men for **e**
   14:26, all things be done for **e**
EDIFY—*encourage* 1 Cor. 8:1, but love **e-es**
   1 Cor. 10:23, lawful, but not all things **e**
   14:5, church may receive **e-ing**
EDUCATE Acts 22:3, **e-d** under Gamaliel
EFFECT—*wise* Acts 7:6, God spoke to this **e**
EFFECTIVE 1 Cor. 16:9, door for **e** *service*
   James 5:16, The **e** prayer
EFFEMINATE 1 Cor. 6:9, Do not be deceived ... nor **e**
EFFORT—*diligence* 2 Tim. 4:9; Jude 3
EGG Job 6:6; 39:14; Is. 59:5; Jer. 17:11
   Luke 11:12, asked for an **e** ... give him a scorpion
ELDERS—*older, aged* 1 Sam. 15:30; Job 12:20;
   32:9
   Matt. 15:2; Mark 7:3, tradition of the **e**
   Acts 14:23, appointed **e** for them in every church
   1 Tim. 5:17, Let the **e** who rule
   James 5:14, call for the **e**
   Prov. 31:23; Titus 1:5; 1 Pet. 5:1; Rev. 4:4; 7:13
ELECT—*chosen* Matt. 24:22; Mark 13:20, sake of the **e**
   Matt. 24:24, mislead, if possible, even the **e**
   Mark 13:22, to lead the **e** astray
   Luke 18:7, God bring about justice for His **e**
   Rom. 8:33, charge against God's **e**
ELEMENT Gal. 4:3, **e-al** things
   2 Pet. 3:10, **e-s** will be destroyed
ELOQUENT—*skillful* Ex. 4:10, never been **e**
   Acts 18:24, Jew named Apollos ... an **e** man
ELUDE—*escape* John 10:39, He **e-d** their grasp
EMBITTERED Acts 14:2, **e** them against
EMBRACE 2 Kin. 4:16, Prov. 5:20; Song 2:6
   Gen. 33:4, Esau ran ... and **e-d** him
   48:10, Joseph ... and **e-d**
   Eccles. 3:5, a time to **e** ... to shun **e-ing**
   Luke 15:20, ran and **e-d** him
EMBROIDER—*weave* Ex. 35:35; Ezek. 16:10,13;
   27:7,16,24
EMERALD Ex. 28:17; Ezek. 28:13; Rev. 4:3; 21:19
EMINENT—*foremost* 2 Cor. 11:5, inferior ... **e** apostles

EMPTINESS—*vanity* Is. 34:11, plumb line of **e**
Jer. 2:5, And walked after **e**
EMPTY—*vain, void* 2 Kin. 18:20, *they are* only **e**
words
Is. 55:11, not return to Me **e**
Eph. 5:6, deceive you with **e** words
1 Tim. 6:20, worldly and **e** chatter
Gen. 31:42; Ex. 3:21; 23:15; Deut. 15:13;
Judg. 7:16; Ruth 1:21; 2 Sam. 1:22;
2 Kin. 4:3; Job 22:9; 26:7; Mark 12:3;
Luke 1:53; 20:10
ENCAMP Ps. 27:3; 34:7; 53:5; Jer. 50:29
ENCIRCLE Ps. 22:12, bulls of Bashan have **e-d**
me
ENCLOSE Job 38:8; Ps. 139:5
ENCOUNTER James 1:2, when you **e** various
trials
ENCOURAGE—*strengthen* 2 Chr. 35:2; Is. 41:7
Deut. 1:38; 3:28; 2 Sam. 11:25, **e** him
1 Sam. 23:16, **e-d** him in God
Ezra 6:22, to **e** them in the work
1 Thess. 5:11, Therefore **e** one another
Heb. 3:13, **e** one another
10:25, but **e-ing** *one another*
ENCOURAGEMENT—*consolation*
Acts 4:36, Son of **E**
Rom. 15:5, God who gives perseverance and **e**
Phil. 2:1, if . . . any **e** in Christ
Heb. 6:18, may have strong **e**
ENCUMBRANCE—*weight*
Heb. 12:1, also lay aside every **e**
END—*goal, outcome* Gen. 6:13, **e** of all flesh
Job 6:11, what is my **e**
Ps. 2:8, *very* **e-s** of the earth
7:9, wicked come to an **e**
39:4, LORD, make me to know my **e**
Prov. 14:12, **e** is the way of death
Eccles. 4:8, no **e** to all his labor
Is. 9:7, no **e** to the increase of *His* government
Jer. 8:20, Harvest is past, summer is **e-ed**
Ezek. 21:25; 35:5, punishment of the **e**
Matt. 10:22; Mark 13:13, endured to the **e**
13:39, harvest is the **e** of the age
28:20, with you always, even to the **e**
Luke 1:33, His kingdom will have no **e**
21:9, the **e** *does* not *follow* immediately
John 13:1, He loved them to the **e**
Rom. 10:4, Christ is the **e** of the law
Heb. 7:3, beginning of days, nor **e** of life
Rev. 21:6; 22:13, the beginning and the **e**
Num. 23:10; Ps. 9:6; 19:6; 73:17; 102:27; 107:27;
Eccles. 7:8; Jer. 5:31; Lam 4:18; Ezek. 7:2;
Dan. 11:45; 12:13; Matt. 24:6,13; Mark 13:7;
Heb. 6:8
ENDLESS Eccles. 12:12, writing . . . books is **e**
1 Tim. 1:4, attention to myths and genealogies
ENDOW—*clothe* Gen. 30:20; 2 Chr. 2:13
ENDURANCE—*patience*
James 1:4, let **e** have *its* perfect
5:11, **e** of Job
ENDURE—*persevere* Ps. 104:31, LORD **e** forever
Ps. 111:3; 112:3, His righteousness **e-s** forever
Mal. 3:2, who can **e** the day of His coming
Matt. 10:22, one who has **e-d** to the end
24:13, **e-s** to the end
1 Cor. 9:12, but we **e** all things
13:7, **e-s** all things
2 Tim. 2:12, if we **e**, we shall also reign
4:3, not **e** sound doctrine
James 5:11, count those blessed who **e-d**
Ex. 18:23; Esth. 8:6; Job 6:11; Ps. 72:5,17;
Prov. 27:24; Is. 66:22; Ezek. 22:14;
Joel 2:11; Mark 13:13; Heb. 12:7
ENEMY—*foe* Ps. 23:5, in the presence of my **e-es**
Ps. 61:3, tower of strength against the **e**
72:9, his **e-es** lick the dust
Prov. 24:17, Do not rejoice when your **e** falls
25:21, **e** is hungry, give him food to eat
Matt. 5:44; Luke 6:27,35, love your **e-es**
10:36, A MAN'S E-ES . . . HIS HOUSEHOLD
Acts 2:35, I MAKE THINE E-ES A FOOTSTOOL

Rom. 5:10, while we were **e-es**, we were
reconciled
James 4:4, friend of the world . . . **e** of God
Ex. 23:22; Deut. 32:31; Judg. 5:31; 1 Kin. 21:20;
Job 13:24; Ps. 8:2; 119:98; 127:5; Prov. 16:7;
27:6; Is. 63:10; Mic. 7:6; Rom. 12:20;
Gal. 4:16
ENGAGE 1 Chr. 9:33; Luke 1:27
ENGINE 2 Chr. 26:15, he made **e-s** of *war*
ENGRAVE—*graven* Ex. 28:11; 32:16; 35:35;
38:23; 39:14; Zech. 3:9; 2 Cor. 3:7
ENGULF Ps. 78:53, the sea **e-ed** their enemies
ENJOY Lev. 26:34, land will **e** its sabbaths
2 Chr. 36:21, land had **e-ed** its sabbaths
Eccles. 2:1, **e** yourself
5:18, **e** oneself in all one's labor
1 Tim. 6:17, supplies us with all things to **e**
Heb. 11:25, **e** the passing pleasures of sin
ENLARGE—*extend* Gen. 9:27; Is. 5:14
Ps. 25:17, troubles of my heart are **e-d**
119:32, Thou wilt **e** my heart
ENLIGHTEN—*illumine*
Ps. 19:8, pure, **e-ing** the eyes
Eph. 1:18, eyes of your heart may be **e-d**
Heb. 6:4, those who have once been **e-ed**
ENMITY—*hostile* Gen. 3:15; Luke 23:12; Eph.
2:15,16
ENOUGH—*plenty, much* Num. 16:9, **e** . . . that
the God of Israel
Matt. 6:34, *Each* day has **e** trouble
Mark 14:41, It is **e**; the hour has come
Luke 15:17, hired men have more than **e** bread
Gen. 45:28; Ex. 36:5; Num. 16:3; 2 Sam. 24:16;
1 Kin. 19:4; 1 Chr. 21:15; Prov. 30:15;
Hos. 4:10; Hag. 1:6; Matt. 10:25; 25:9;
Luke 22:38
ENRAGE—*angry* Prov. 6:34, jealousy **e-s** man
Matt. 2:16, Herod . . . became very **e-d**
ENRICH 1 Sam. 17:25; Ps. 65:9; Ezek. 27:33
1 Cor. 1:5, in everything you were **e-ed**
2 Cor. 9:11, be **e-ed** in everything
ENSLAVED Titus 3:3, **e** to various lusts and
pleasures
ENTANGLE—*trap* 2 Tim. 2:4, No soldier . . . **e-s**
himself
Heb. 12:1, sin which so easily **e-s** us
ENTER—*come* Ps. 100:4, E His gates with
thanksgiving
Ps. 118:20, righteous will **e** through it
Is. 57:2, He **e-s** into peace
Ezek. 44:16, They shall **e** My sanctuary
Matt. 5:20, you shall not **e** the kingdom
7:13, E by the narrow gate
10:5; do not **e** . . . city of the Samaritans
10:11, village you **e**, inquire
10:12, **e** the house, give it your greeting
18:8; Mark 9:43, better . . . **e** life crippled
19:17, if you wish to **e** into life, keep
25:21, **e** into the joy of your master
Luke 9:34, afraid as they **e-ed** the cloud
22:46, that you may not **e** into temptation
John 10:1, does not **e** by the door
10:9, if anyone **e-s** through Me
Rom. 5:12, sin **e-ed** into the world
1 Cor. 2:9, *which* HAVE NOT E-ED THE HEART
Gen. 6:18; Job 22:4; 38:16; Is. 2:10; 26:2,20;
Ezek. 2:2; Hab. 3:16; Luke 13:24; John 3:5;
2 Tim. 3:6; Heb. 3:11,18; 4:10; 6:20
ENTICE—*deceive, seduce* Judg. 14:15; 16:5;
2 Chr. 18:19
Prov. 1:10, if sinners **e** you
James 1:14, **e-d** by his own lust
2 Pet. 2:14, **e-ing** unstable souls
2:18, they **e** by fleshly desires
ENTRANCE—*door* Ezek. 8:5, jealousy at the **e**
Matt. 27:60, rolled a large stone against the **e**
2 Pet. 1:11, **e** into the eternal kingdom
ENTREAT—*appeal, ask, beg* Ex. 8:8; 32:11;
2 Sam. 24:25
Matt. 8:34, they **e-ed** Him to depart from their
region

Mark 5:10, he *began* to **e** Him earnestly
2 Cor. 5:20, as though God were **e-ing** through us
Eph. 4:1, I therefore ... **e** you to walk
1 Tim. 2:1, I urge that **e-es** *and* prayers
1 Kin. 13:6; 2 Chr. 33:12; Job 21:15; Prov. 19:6;
     Jer. 26:19; Matt. 8:5,31; Luke 8:31; 15:28;
     2 Cor. 12:8
ENTRUST—*commit*
Luke 12:48, whom they **e-ed** much
ENVIOUS Ps. 37:1; 73:3
Prov. 24:1, Do not be **e** of evil men
     24:19, Or be **e** of the wicked
ENVY (n.)—*jealousy* Matt. 27:18; Mark 15:10
Rom. 1:29, full of **e**, murder
Phil. 1:15, preaching Christ even from **e**
1 Tim. 6:4, out of which arise **e**
Titus 3:3, spending life in malice and **e**
1 Pet. 2:1, putting aside all malice ... and **e**
ENVY (v.) Gen. 26:14, Philistines **e-ed** him
Prov. 3:31, Do not **e** a man of violence
     23:17, Do not let your heart **e** sinners
Gal. 5:26, **e-ing** one another
EPHAH—*bushel* Ex. 16:36; 29:40; Lev. 19:36;
     Ezek. 45:10; Zech. 5:8
EPHOD Ex. 28:4; 39:2; Judg. 8:27; 17:5;
     1 Sam. 2:18; 23:9; Hos. 3:4
EPOCH—*season*
Dan. 2:21, changes times and **e-s**
Acts 1:7, to know times or **e-s**
EQUAL—*equity, right* John 5:18, Himself **e** with God
2 Cor. 8:14, that there may be **e-ity**
Phil. 2:6, not regard **e-ity** with God
Job 28:17,19; Ps. 55:13; Is. 40:25; 46:5;
     Matt. 20:12
EQUIP—*furnish*
2 Tim. 3:17, **e-ed** for every good work
Heb. 13:21, **e** you in every good thing
EQUITY—*equal, uprightness, straight* Ps. 17:2;
     98:9
Prov. 1:3, Righteousness, justice, and **e**
     2:9, discern righteousness ... and **e**
ERASE—*blot* Rev. 3:5, I will not **e** his name
ERECT—*upright*
Gen. 33:20, Then he **e-ed** there an altar
     37:7, sheaf rose ... stood **e**
ERR—*stray, mistake* Ps. 95:10, people who **e**
ERROR—*mistake, sin* Is. 32:6; 2 Pet. 3:17;
     Jude 11
Ps. 19:12, Who can discern *his* **e-s**
Eccles. 10:5, evil I have seen ... like an **e**
James 5:20, from the **e** of his way
1 John 4:6, we know ... the spirit of **e**
ESCAPE—*deliverance, refuge, elude*
Prov. 19:5, he who tells lies wll not **e**
Eccles. 7:26, who is pleasing to God will **e**
Is. 20:6; Heb. 2:3, how shall we **e**
1 Cor. 10:13, provide the way of **e**
Heb. 11:34, **e-d** the edge of the sword
2 Pet. 1:4, **e-d** the corruption that is in the world
Gen. 19:17; Deut. 23:15; 1 Kin. 18:40;
     2 Kin. 9:15; Esth. 4:13; Job 11:20; 19:20;
     Ps. 124:7; Obad. 17; Matt. 23:33;
     Mark 14:52; Luke 21:36; Heb. 11:34
ESSENTIAL—*excellent*
Rom. 2:18, approve ... that are **e**
ESTABLISH—*confirm, direct, plant, strengthen*
Ps. 119:5, that my ways may be **e-ed**
     119:38, **E** Thy word to Thy servant
Prov. 16:12, throne is **e-ed** on righteousness
Is. 16:5, A throne ... **e-ed** in lovingkindness
Rom. 16:25, able to **e** you according to
1 Thess. 3:13, He may **e** your hearts
2 Pet. 1:12, been **e-ed** in the truth
Gen. 17:19; Job 37:15; Ps. 65:6; Prov. 3:19; Is.
     51:16; Jer. 10:12; 51:15; Rom. 3:31; 10:3
ESTATE—*domain, standard* Ps. 136:23, low **e**
Luke 15:13, squandered his **e** with loose living
ESTEEM—*regard, consider*
Ps. 119:128, I **e** right ... precepts
1 Thess. 5:13, I **e** them very highly in love

ESTEEMED—*beloved, chosen, loved* 1 Sam.
     18:23; Dan. 9:23
1 Sam. 2:30, despise Me will be lightly **e**
Is. 53:4, we ourselves **e** Him stricken
Luke 16:15, highly **e** among men
ESTIMATION—*imagination*
Rom. 11:25, wise in your own **e**
ESTRANGE Job 19:13; Ps. 58:3; Ezek. 14:5
ETERNAL—*everlasting* Deut. 33:27; Matt. 18:8
Is. 9:6, name will be called ... **E** Father
Matt. 19:16, I may obtain **e** life
     19:29, shall inherit **e** life
     25:46, righteous into **e** life
Mark 10:17; Luke 10:25, what ... to inherit **e** life
     10:30, in the world to come, **e** life
John 3:15, may in Him have **e** life
     3:16, whoever believes ... have **e** life
     3:36, who believes in the Son has **e** life
     5:39, search the Scriptures ... have **e** life
     6:68, You have words of **e** life
     10:28, I give **e** life to them
     12:25, hates his life ... keep it to life **e**
     17:3, **e** life, that they may know Thee
Rom. 2:7, seek for glory and honor ... **e** life
     5:21, righteousness to **e**
     6:23, free gift of God is **e** life
2 Cor. 4:17, an **e** weight of glory
     4:18, things which are not seen are **e**
     5:1, house ... **e** in the heavens
Gal. 6:8, from the Spirit reap **e** life
Eph. 3:11, in accordance with the **e** purpose
1 Tim. 1:17, Now to the King **e**, immortal
     6:12, take hold of the **e** life
Titus 1:2, in the hope of **e** life
Heb. 5:9, source of **e** salvation
     9:14, through the **e** Spirit
1 Pet. 5:10, called you to His **e** glory in Christ
1 John 2:25, promise ... made to us, **e** life
     5:11, God has given us **e** life
Rev. 14:6, having an **e** gospel to preach
Matt. 25:41,46; Mark 3:29; Luke 16:9; 18:18;
     John 4:14,36; 6:54; 12:50; 17:2;
     Acts 13:46,48; Rom. 6:22; 16:26;
     2 Thess. 1:9; 2:16; Heb. 6:2; 9:12,15;
     1 John 1:2; 3:15; 5:20; Jude 6,7
ETERNITY—*world*
Eccles. 3:11, set **e** in their heart
Mic. 5:2, goings forth ... from the days of **e**
EUNUCH—*chamberlain, official* Esth. 1:10; Is.
     56:3; Matt. 19:12; Acts 8:27
EVANGELIST Acts 21:8, Philip the **e**
Eph. 4:11, He gave some ... *as* **e-s**
2 Tim. 4:5, do the work of an **e**
EVAPORATE—*fail, gone* Ex. 16:14; Job 14:11
EVENING—*close* Ps. 104:23, to his labor until **e**
Jer. 6:4, shadows of the **e** lengthen
Zech. 14:7, at **e** time there will be light
Luke 24:29, for it is *getting* toward **e**
Judg. 20:23; 1 Sam. 14:24; 1 Kin. 17:6; Ps. 55:17;
     90:6; 141:2; Eccles. 11:6; Matt. 8:16; 14:23;
     Mark 1:32
EVER—*forever* Ps. 52:8; Matt. 21:19; Mark 11:14;
     Rev. 14:11
Ps. 48:14, Our God forever and **e**
     51:3, my sin is **e** before me
Rev. 11:15, He will reign forever and **e**
     22:5, they shall reign forever and **e**
EVERLASTING—*endure, eternal, ancient, perpetual*
Gen. 21:33; Is. 40:28, the **E** God
Deut. 33:27, underneath are the **e** arms
Ps. 90:2, from **e** to **e**, Thou art God
     106:1; 107:1; 136:1, lovingkindness is **e**
     139:24, lead me in the **e** way
Is. 26:4, in God ... *have* an **e** Rock
     35:10; 51:11; 61:7, **e** joy
Jer. 31:3, loved you with an **e** love
Gen. 9:16; Ps. 103:17; 119:142; 138:8; Prov. 8:23;
     10:25; Is. 45:17; 54:8; 55:13; 56:5; 60:19,20;
     63:12; Dan. 4:34; 7:14

EVERMORE—*ever, forever* Ps. 92:7; John 6:34
EVERY Gen. 6:5, e intent . . . of his heart was only
   evil
   Ps. 119:101, restrained my feet from e evil way
      119:104, I hate e false way
   Prov. 30:5, E word of God is tested
   Eccles. 3:1, a time for e event under heaven
   Is. 45:23, e knee will bow
      55:1, Ho! E one who thirsts
   Jer. 25:5, Turn now e one from his evil way
   Matt. 4:4, ON E WORD THAT PROCEEDS
      7:8, For e one who asks receives
   John 3:8, so is e one who is born of the Spirit
   2 Cor. 10:5, taking e thought captive
   Eph. 1:21, far above all rule . . . e name
   2 Tim. 2:21, prepared for e good work
   Heb. 12:1, lay aside e encumbrance
   James 1:17, E good thing . . . e perfect gift
   1 John 4:1, do not believe e spirit
   Rev. 20:13, e one of them according to their
      deeds
      22:12, e man according to what he has done
   Deut. 4:4; Prov. 2:9; 7:12; John 18:37;
      Rom. 14:11; 1 Tim. 2:8; 2 Tim. 2:19
EVERYONE Ps. 32:6, e who is godly pray
   Eccles. 10:3, demonstrates to e *that* he is a fool
   Luke 11:10, For e who asks receives
      19:26, to e who has shall *more* be given
EVERYTHING Prov. 14:15, The naive believes e
   1 Tim. 4:4, e created by God is good
EVERYWHERE Mark 1:45; 16:20; Acts 17:30
EVIDENCE—*mouth* Deut. 17:6, the e of two
   witnesses
EVIDENT—*see* Gal. 3:11; Heb. 7:14
EVIL—*bad, wicked, reproach*
   Gen. 38:7, e in the sight of the LORD
   Deut. 23:9, keep yourself from every e
   1 Kin. 21:25, sold himself to do e
   Ps. 15:3, Nor does e to his neighbor
      23:4, I fear no e
      34:14; 37:27, Depart from e, and do good
      91:10, No e will befall you
      97:10, Hate e, you who love the LORD
   Jer. 7:26, did e more than their fathers
   Matt. 5:11, all kinds of e against you falsely
      6:13, deliver us from e
      7:11; Luke 11:13, If you then, being e
      12:45, this e generation
      27:23; Mark 15:14, what e has He done
   Mark 9:39, speak e of Me
   Luke 6:45, e *man* out of the e *treasure*
   John 3:20, does e hates the light
   Rom. 12:17, Never pay back e for e to anyone
      12:21, overcome e with good
   Eph. 5:16, because the days are e
   1 Thess. 5:22, abstain from every form of e
   1 Tim. 6:10, love of money is a root of all e
   James 3:8, tongue; *it is* a restless e
   1 John 2:13, overcome the e one
      5:19, world lies . . . power of the e one
   Gen. 6:5; 8:21; 50:20; Deut. 31:29; 2 Sam. 14:17;
      1 Kin. 3:9; Ezra 4:12; Job 30:26; Ps. 35:12;
      40:12; 109:5; Prov. 3:7; 6:18; 14:19; 15:3;
      17:13; Is. 5:20; 7:15,16; 57:1; Jer. 2:13,19;
      Hab. 1:13; Matt. 9:4; 22:10; Luke 6:22,35;
      Acts 23:5; Rom. 7:19; 1 Thess. 5:15;
      3 John 11
EVILDOERS Ps. 37:1, Fret not . . . because of e
   Ps. 37:9, e will be cut off
   Ps. 119:115; Is. 1:4; 9:17; Luke 13:27; 1 Pet. 4:15
EWE Num. 6:14; 2 Sam. 12:3; Ps. 78:71
EXACT—*lend, collect* Deut. 15:2, he shall not e it
   Heb. 1:3, e representation of His nature
EXALT—*extol, lift, raise* Ps. 34:3, let us e His
   name
   Ps. 46:10, I will be e-ed in the earth
      108:5, Be e-ed, O God, above the heavens
   Prov. 4:8, Prize her, and she will e you
      14:34, Righteousness e-s a nation
   Matt. 11:23; Luke 10:15, e-ed to heaven
      23:12; Luke 14:11; 18:14, e-s himself

Luke 1:46, My soul e-s the Lord
Acts 5:31, He is the one whom God e-ed
Phil. 1:20, Christ shall . . . be e-ed in my body
   2:9, God highly e-ed Him
Ex. 15:1; 1 Sam. 2:10; 1 Chr. 29:11; Job 37:23;
   Ps. 89:16; 92:10; 97:9; Prov. 11:11; Is. 52:13;
   Ezek. 21:26; Dan. 4:37; 2 Cor. 12:7;
   2 Thess. 2:4; James 4:10; 1 Pet. 5:6
EXAMINE—*investigate, search* Job 7:18; Acts
   22:24
   Ps. 26:2, E me, O LORD
   Acts 17:11, e-ing the Scriptures daily
   1 Cor. 11:28, let a man e himself
   2 Cor. 13:5, e yourselves
EXAMPLE—*model, pattern* James 5:10;
   2 Pet. 2:6; Jude 7
   John 13:15; I gave you an e
   1 Cor. 10:6, these things happened as e-s
      10:11, to them as an e
   1 Tim. 4:12, an e of those who believe
   Heb. 4:11, same e of disobedience
   1 Pet. 2:21, Christ also . . . leaving you an e
      5:3, proving to be e-s to the flock
EXASPERATE—*anger*
   Col. 3:21, do not e your children
EXCEED—*great, surpass, utterly*
   Ps. 43:4, God my e-ing joy
      119:96, Thy commandment is e-ingly broad
   Prov. 30:24, Four things . . . are e-ingly wise
   Jon. 3:3, Nineveh was an e-ingly great city
   Mark 9:3, His garments became . . . e-ingly
      white
   Eph. 3:20, able to do e-ing abundantly
   Gen. 27:34; Num. 14:7; 1 Kin. 10:7; Matt. 2:10
EXCEL Prov. 31:29, you e them all
   Eccles. 2:13, wisdom e-s folly
   1 Thess. 4:1, that you may e still more
EXCELLENCE—*great, preeminent*
   Ex. 15:7, of Thine e
   Ruth 3:11, are a woman of e
   Phil. 4:8, if there is any e
   2 Pet. 1:5, supply moral e . . . knowledge
EXCELLENT—*noble* Prov. 12:4, e wife is the
   crown
   1 Cor. 12:31, a still more e way
   Phil. 1:10, approve the things that are e
   Heb. 1:4, a more e name
   Prov. 17:7; 22:20; Is. 12:5
EXCEPT—*save* Gen. 14:24; Ps. 18:31
   Matt. 11:27, knows the Son, e the Father
   Luke 18:19, No one is good e God alone
   Acts 26:29, e for these chains
   Rom. 9:29, E THE LORD . . . HAD LEFT TO US A
      POSTERITY
EXCESS Is. 16:6; 1 Pet. 4:4
EXCHANGE Matt. 16:26; Mark 8:37, give in e for
   his soul
   Luke 24:17, these words that you are e-ing
   Rom. 1:25, they e-d the truth of God
EXCLUDE—*alienated*
   Eph. 4:18, e-d from the life of God
EXCUSE Luke 14:18, began to make e-s
   Rom. 1:20, they are without e
EXECUTE—*perform* Deut. 33:21; Ps. 149:7
   Ps. 9:16, He has e-d judgment
   John 5:27, Him authority to e judgment
   Rom. 9:28, LORD WILL E HIS WORD
   Jude 15, to e judgment
EXEMPT Matt. 17:26, the sons are e
EXERCISE Jer. 9:24, the LORD who e-s
   lovingkindness
   Matt. 20:25; Mark 10:42, e authority over them
EXHAUST Judg. 4:21; 1 Kin. 17:14
EXHORT Acts 2:40, many other words . . . e-ing
   them
   2 Tim. 4:2, e, with great patience
   Titus 1:9, able both to e in sound doctrine
      2:15, e and reprove
   1 Pet. 5:12, e-ing and testifying
EXHORTATION Luke 3:18; Acts 20:2; Rom. 12:8;
   Heb. 13:22

EXILE 2 Sam. 15:19; Is. 51:14
EXORCISTS Acts 19:13, some of the Jewish **e**
EXPANSE—*firmament* Gen. 1:6; Ezek. 1:25
EXPECT Gen. 48:11; Job 30:26; Luke 6:35;
   Acts 3:5
EXPECTATION Prov. 10:28; 11:7,23
   Phil. 1:20, my earnest **e** and hope
   Heb. 10:27, terrifying **e** of judgment
EXPEDIENT—*advantageous*
   John 11:50, **e** for you that one
EXPERT Jer. 50:9; Acts 26:3
EXPLAIN Luke 24:27, **e-ed** to them
   Luke 24:32, He was **e-ing** the Scriptures
   John 1:18, He has **e-ed** *Him*
   Acts 18:26, **e-ed** to him the way of God
     28:23, **e-ing** to them ... about the kingdom of
     God
EXPLICIT 1 Tim. 4:1, Spirit **e-ly** says
EXPLORE Eccles. 2:3, I **e-d** with my mind
EXPOSE—*reprove*
   Eph. 5:11, instead even **e** them
EXPRESS
   Ezek. 1:3, word of the LORD came **e-ly**
EXTEND Is. 44:13, he **e-s** a measuring line
   Deut. 12:20; Ezra 7:28; Ps. 109:12; Is. 66:12
EXTOL—*exalt* Ex. 15:2, will **e** Him
   Ps. 30:1; 145:1, I will **e** Thee
EXTORTIONER Is. 16:4, **e** has come to an end
EXTRAORDINARY Dan. 5:12; 6:3
EXULT—*rejoicing*
   1 Thess. 2:19, or joy or crown of **e-ation**
EYE—*look* Gen. 3:7; 27:1; 49:12; Num. 10:31;
   24:3,15
   Ex. 21:24; Lev. 24:20; Deut. 19:21; Matt. 5:38, **e**
     for **e**
   Deut. 12:8; Judg. 17:6; 21:25, right in his **e-s**
     16:19, bribe blinds the **e-s** of the wise
     32:10, as the pupil of His **e**
   2 Chr. 16:9, **e-s** of the LORD move
   Job 19:27, whom my **e-s** shall see
   Ps. 11:4, **e-s** ... test the sons of men
     19:8, enlightening the **e-s**
     34:15, **e-s** of the LORD are toward the
     righteous
     36:1, no fear of God before his **e-s**
     69:3; 119:82; Lam. 2:11, My **e-s** fail
   Prov. 6:17, Haughty **e-s**, a lying tongue
     27:20, Nor are the **e-s** of man ever satisfied
   Is. 33:17, **e-s** will see the King
     40:26; Jer. 13:20, Lift up your **e-s**
   Jer. 5:21, Who have **e-s**, but see not
     16:17, My **e-s** are on all their ways
   Zech. 4:10, **e-s** of the LORD which range
   Matt. 6:22, lamp of the body is the **e**
     13:16, blessed are your **e-s**
     18:9, **e** causes you to stumble, pluck it out
   Mark 8:18, HAVING **E-S**, DO YOU NOT SEE
   Luke 4:20, **e-s** ... were fixed upon Him
     24:16, their **e-s** were prevented from
     recognizing
   John 9:6, applied clay to his **e-s**
   Heb. 4:13, laid bare to the **e-s** of Him
   1 John 2:16, the lust of the **e-s**
   Deut. 3:27; 4:19; 34:7; 1 Kin. 1:20; 8:29,52; 20:6;
     2 Kin. 6:17; 2 Chr. 6:20,40; 34:28; Job 10:18;
     29:11,15; Ps. 15:4; 33:18; 94:9; 119:18; 132:4;
     145:15; Prov. 10:26; 20:12; 23:29; 30:17;
     Eccles. 1:8; 2:14; 6:9; 11:7; Is. 1:15; 22:4;
     29:10; 32:3; 42:7; 52:8; 64:4; Jer. 9:1; 13:17;
     14:17; 24:6; Ezek. 12:2; 24:16,25; Hab. 1:13;
     Matt. 5:29; Luke 11:34; John 11:37;
     1 Cor. 2:9; Gal. 3:1; 4:15; Eph. 1:18;
     1 Pet. 3:12; 2 Pet. 2:14
EYESALVE Rev. 3:18, **e** to anoint your eyes
EYESERVICE Eph. 6:6, not by way of **e**
EYEWITNESSES Luke 1:2, **e** and servants of the
   Word
   2 Pet. 1:16, we were **e** of His majesty

F

FABLES—*myths* 1 Tim. 4:7, worldly **f** fit only for
   old women
FACE—*countenance*
   Gen. 3:19, By the sweat of your **f**
   Num. 6:25, Lord make His **f** shine on you
   Ps. 34:16, the **f** of the Lord is against evildoers
     67:1, cause His **f** to shine upon us
     84:9, look upon the **f** of Thine anointed
   Is. 25:8, wipe tears away from all **f-s**
   Matt. 6:17, when you fast ... wash your **f**
   Luke 24:5, bowed their **f-s** to the ground
   John 11:44, his **f** was wrapped around with a
     cloth
   2 Cor. 3:18, with unveiled **f** beholding
   1 Pet. 3:12, THE **F** OF THE LORD IS AGAINST
   Rev. 1:16, His **f** was like the sun shining
   Gen. 17:3; Ex. 33:11; 33:23; 2 Kin. 14:8; Ezra 9:6;
     Job 33:26; Ps. 13:1; 24:6; 83:16; Prov. 15:13;
     27:19; Eccles. 8:1; Is. 50:6; Jer. 5:3;
     Matt. 6:16; 26:67
FADE—*wither*
   James 1:11, rich man ... will **f** away
   1 Pet. 1:4, an inheritance ... will not **f** away
   Ps. 90:6; Is. 28:1
FAIL—*spent, lack* Deut. 31:6, He will not **f** you or
   Luke 22:32, that your faith may not **f**
   1 Cor. 13:8, Love never **f-s**
   Deut. 4:31; 1 Sam. 3:19; 17:32; Neh. 4:10;
     Job 11:20; 19:14; Ps. 38:10; Is. 44:12,25;
     Hab. 3:17
FAILURE Rom. 11:12, their **f** be riches for the
   Gentiles
FAINT—*languish* Job 23:16, has made my heart **f**
   Ps. 61:2, when my heart is **f**
   Luke 21:26, men **f-ing** from fear
   Is. 1:5; Jon. 2:7; Matt. 15:32
FAIR Ps. 45:2; Is. 11:4; Matt. 16:2; Acts 27:8;
   Col. 4:1
FAITH—*believe, trust* Matt. 9:2; 15:28; Mark 4:40
   Hab. 2:4, the righteous will live by his **f**
   Matt. 6:30, O men of little **f**
     17:20, **f** as a mustard seed
   Mark 11:22, Have **f** in God
   Luke 7:50, Your **f** has saved you
     17:5, Increase our **f**
     18:8, will He find **f** on earth
     22:32, that your **f** may not fail
   Acts 14:27, door of **f** to the Gentiles
     15:9, cleansing their hearts by **f**
   Rom. 5:1, having been justified by **f**
     10:17, **f** comes from hearing
   1 Cor. 15:14, your **f** also is vain
     16:13, stand firm in the **f**
   2 Cor. 13:5, if you are in the **f**
   Gal. 2:16, through **f** in Christ Jesus
   Eph. 2:8, by grace ... through **f**
     4:5, one Lord, one **f**, one baptism
     6:16, taking up the shield of **f**
   Col. 2:5, stability of your **f** in Christ
   1 Thess. 5:8, breastplate of **f** and love
   2 Thess. 1:3, your **f** is greatly enlarged
   1 Tim. 4:1, some will fall away from the **f**
   2 Tim. 4:7, I have kept the **f**
   Heb. 10:22, in full assurance of **f**
     12:2, author and perfecter of **f**
   James 1:3, testing of your **f** produces
     endurance
   1 Pet. 1:5, power of God through **f**
   Jude 20, building ... on your most holy **f**
   Rev. 2:13, did not deny My **f**
   Luke 8:25; Acts 6:5; 20:21; Rom. 4:14;
     1 Cor. 13:2; Gal. 5:5; Phil. 1:25; 1 Thess. 1:3;
     1 Tim. 1:2; 3:9; Titus 1:13; 2:2,10;
     Heb. 10:39; 11:1; James 2:1; 2 Pet. 1:5
FAITHFUL—*trustworthy*
   Ps. 31:23, The Lord preserves the **f**
   Prov. 12:22, who deal **f-ly** are His
     27:6, **F** are the wounds of a friend
   1 Cor. 1:9, God is **f**, through whom you were

FAITHFUL (Continued)
Eph. 1:1, who are f in Christ Jesus
1 Thess. 5:24, F is He who calls you
1 Tim. 1:12, He considered me f
2 Tim. 2:2, these entrust to f men
Heb. 10:23, He who promised is f
Rev. 2:10, Be f until death
Num. 12:7; Deut. 7:9; 1 Sam. 2:35; 2 Kin. 12:15;
	Neh. 9:8; Ps. 101:6; 119:86; Prov. 13:17;
	14:5; Is. 1:21; Matt. 24:45; 25:23; 1 Pet. 4:19;
	Rev. 1:5; 19:11
FAITHFULNESS—truth Deut. 32:4, A God of f
	and without
Ps. 143:1, Answer me in Thy f
Rom. 3:3, nullify the f of God
Gal. 5:22, Kindness, goodness, f
Deut. 32:20; Ps. 89:1; Is. 11:5; Matt. 23:23
FAITHLESS Jer. 3:6,8,11,12,22; 31:22
FALL Ps. 16:6, The lines have f-en ... in pleasant
	places
Matt. 7:25, house; and yet it did not f
	7:27, and great was its f
	10:29, not one ... will f to the ground
	15:14, both will f into a pit
Mark 14:27, You will all f away
Luke 8:13, in time of temptation f away
1 Cor. 10:12, take heed lest he f
	15:6,18, have f-en asleep
Gal. 5:4, you have f-en from grace
1 Tim. 3:6, f into the condemnation
	6:9, rich f into temptation
Heb. 6:6, and then have f-en away
	10:31, f into the hands of the living God
Judg. 18:25; Job 4:13; Ps. 5:10; 37:24; 38:17;
	Prov. 24:16; Eccles. 4:10; 11:3; Dan. 3:5;
	11:26; Mic. 7:8; Matt. 12:11; Luke 2:34;
	Rom. 14:4; Heb. 4:11; 2 Pet. 3:17
FALSE—deceitful, vain
Ex. 5:9, pay no attention to f words
	20:16, you shall not bear f witness
	23:1, shall not carry a f rumor
Ps. 33:17, horse is a f hope for victory
	119:104,128, I hate every f way
Prov. 6:19; 12:17; 14:5; 19:5, f witness
Matt. 24:24, f Christs and f prophets
Ex. 23:7; Lam. 2:14; Zech. 10:2; Matt. 19:18;
	Mark 13:22; 2 Thess. 2:9
FALSEHOOD—deceitfulness Ps. 144:8; Jer.
	13:25; Mic. 2:11
Ps. 24:4, lifted up his soul to f
	119:163, I hate and despise f
Prov. 20:17, Bread obtained by f is sweet
Jer. 14:14, prophesying f in My name
Eph. 4:25, laying aside f
FALSELY Jer. 5:31, The prophets prophesy f
Matt. 5:11, say ... evil against you f
Luke 3:14, accuse anyone f
1 Tim. 6:20, what is f called knowledge
Gen. 21:23; Lev. 6:3; Deut. 19:18; Hos. 7:1
FAME 1 Kin. 10:1, the f of Solomon
Is. 66:19, heard My f
2 Cor. 8:18, whose f in the things of
Num. 14:15; Josh. 6:27
FAMILY Gen. 12:3, all the f-es of the earth
Eph. 3:15, every f in heaven
Gen. 10:5; Deut. 29:18; Judg. 6:15; Job 31:34;
	Ps. 107:41; Jer. 3:14; 31:1
FAMINE—drought Gen. 12:10; 41:27,54; 42:19
Matt. 24:7, there will be f-s and earthquakes
Mark 13:8, will also be f-s
Luke 15:14, a severe f occurred in that country
Rom. 8:35, or f, or nakedness, or peril
2 Kin. 4:38; 1 Chr. 21:12; 2 Chr. 6:28; Neh. 5:3;
	Job 5:20; Ps. 33:19; Is. 14:30; Jer. 14:12;
	Amos 8:11; Acts 7:11; 11:28
FAMISH—hunger Gen. 41:55, Egypt was f-ed
FAMOUS 1 Chr. 5:24, men of valor, f men
FANG Joel 1:6, the f-s of a lioness
FAR—distant Ps. 22:11, Be not f from me
Ps. 103:12, As f as the east is from the west
	119:155, Salvation is f from the wicked
Prov. 15:29, LORD is f from the wicked

Jer. 23:23, a God f off
Matt. 15:8, THEIR HEART IS F AWAY FROM ME
Mark 12:34, are not f from the kingdom
Acts 17:27, though He is not f from
2 Cor. 4:17, glory f beyond all comparison
Eph. 1:21, f above all rule
Gen. 18:25; Ex. 23:7; Deut. 13:7; Josh. 9:6;
	2 Sam. 20:20; Ps. 97:9; Prov. 4:24; 27:10;
	Is. 60:4; Ezek. 11:15; John 21:8; Eph. 2:17
FARE Jon. 1:3, Tarshish, paid the f
FAREWELL Acts 15:29, you will do well. F
FARTHEST—utmost Mark 13:27, F END of the
	earth
FASHION—appearance Job 10:8, Thy hands f-ed
Ps. 33:15, He who f-s the hearts
1 Kin. 7:15; Job 31:15; Is. 44:12; Jer. 18:11
FAST Matt. 4:2, after He had f-ed forty days
Matt. 6:16, whenever you f, do not ... as the
	6:17, when you f, anoint your head
Acts 13:3, when they had f-ed and prayed
Is. 58:3,4,5,6; Joel 1:14; Zech. 7:5; Mark 2:18,19;
	Luke 18:12
FASTING—hungry Ps. 109:24, weak from f
Matt. 6:16,18, seen f by men
Luke 2:37, serving ... with f-s and prayers
Acts 14:23, having prayed with f
Esth. 4:3; Ps. 35:13; Joel 2:12; Mark 2:18
FAT Prov. 13:4, soul of the diligent is made f
Prov. 15:30, Good news puts f on the bones
Luke 15:23, bring the f-ned calf
James 5:5, you have f-ned your hearts
Gen. 45:18; Judg. 3:17; Neh. 8:10; 9:25; Ps. 73:4;
	119:70
FATE Eccles. 2:14; 9:2,3
FATHER Gen. 2:24, leave his f and his mother
Gen. 9:23, covered the nakedness of their f
	17:4, f of a multitude of nations
Ex. 20:12, Honor your f and your mother
Job 29:16, I was a f to the needy
Ps. 22:4, In Thee our f-s trusted
	103:13, as a f has compassion on his
Prov. 10:1, A wise son makes a f glad
	17:6, glory of sons is their f-s
Is. 9:6, Eternal F, Prince of Peace
	63:16, Thou art our F
Matt. 3:9, We have Abraham for our f
	5:16, glorify your F who is in heaven
	6:1, your F who is in heaven
	6:4,6,18, your F who sees in secret
	6:9, Our F who art in heaven
	7:21, he who does the will of My F
	10:35, SET A MAN AGAINST HIS F
	11:25, I praise Thee O F, Lord of
	11:27, knows the Son, except the F
	28:19, baptizing ... name of the F
Mark 8:38, comes in the glory of His F
Luke 2:49, be in My F-'s house
	11:2, F, hallowed be Thy name
	23:34, Jesus was saying, F forgive them
	23:46, F ... HANDS I COMMIT
John 2:16, stop making My F-'s house a
	5:17, My F is working until now and
	10:15, F knows me and I know the F
	14:2, In My F-'s house are many
	17:1, F, the hour has come; glorify
2 Cor. 1:3, F of mercies and God of all
Eph. 3:14, I bow my knees before the F
	6:4, f-s, do not provoke your children
Phil. 2:11, to the glory of God the F
Heb. 1:5, I will be a F to Him
1 Pet. 1:3, Blessed be the God and F
2 Pet. 1:17, honor ... from God the F
Jude 1, are the called, beloved in God the F
Rev. 1:6, priests to His God and F
Gen. 4:20; 43:7; 48:17; Ex. 21:15; Deut. 5:9;
	1 Sam. 17:34; 2 Sam. 7:12; Job 17:14; 38:28;
	Ps. 68:5; 89:26; Prov. 1:8; 6:20; Jer. 3:19;
	Mal. 2:10; Matt. 11:26; 26:29; Mark 14:36;
	Luke 10:21; 15:18; 24:49; 1 Cor. 4:15;
	Heb. 3:9; 1 John 2:13; 2 John 4
FATHERLESS—orphan
Prov. 23:10, the fields of the f

FATNESS—*abundance*
Ps. 65:11, Thy paths drip *with* f
Gen. 27:28; Judg. 9:9; Ps. 63:5; 73:7
FAULT—*offense* 1 Sam. 29:3; Ps. 19:12; Rom.
    9:19
FAULTLESS—*blameless*
Heb. 8:7, *covenant* had been f
FAVOR—*beauty, charm, grace, pleasure,*
    supplication
Ps. 90:17, let the f of the Lord our God
Prov. 8:35; 12:2; 18:22, obtains f from the LORD
    13:15, Good understanding produces f
Luke 2:52, increasing … in f with God and men
Acts 2:47, having f with all the people
Gen. 6:8; 39:21; Ex. 3:21; 33:12; Deut. 33:23;
    1 Sam. 13:12; Esth. 2:17; Ps. 5:12; 30:5;
    51:18; 85:1; Prov. 14:35; 19:12; Eccles. 9:11;
    Dan. 1:9; Zech. 11:7
FAVORABLE—*acceptable*
Ps. 77:7, will He never be f again
Is. 61:2, proclaim the f year of the LORD
FEAR (n.)—*dread, awe, terror* Gen. 9:2; 20:11;
    Deut. 2:25
Ps. 19:9, the f of the LORD is clean
    53:5, in great f *where* no f had been
    111:10; Prov. 9:10, f … is the beginning of
    wisdom
Prov. 1:7, f … is the beginning of knowledge
    10:27, f of the LORD prolongs life
    14:26, f of the LORD there is strong
    confidence
    14:27, f of the LORD is a fountain of life
    15:16, better is a little with the f of the LORD
    19:23, the f of the LORD *leads* to life
    29:25, the f of man brings a snare
Luke 21:26, men fainting from f
John 7:13; 19:38; 20:19, for f of the Jews
Rom. 13:3, not a cause of f for good behavior
1 Cor. 2:3, in weakness and in f
2 Cor. 5:11, knowing the f of the Lord
    7:5, conflicts without, f-s within
    7:11, what f, what longing, what zeal
Eph. 6:5; Phil. 2:12, with f and trembling
Deut. 11:25; 1 Chr. 14:17; Job 4:6; 39:22;
    Ps. 34:11; 36:1; Prov. 3:25; Is. 8:12;
    Jer. 32:40; Matt. 14:26; Rom. 3:18;
    Heb. 2:15; Jude 12,23
FEAR (v.)—*be afraid, revere* Gen. 22:12; 42:18
1 Kin. 18:12, I … have f-ed the LORD from my
    youth
Job 1:9, Job f God for nothing
Ps. 27:1, Whom shall I f
    118:6, will not f; what can man do
Prov. 31:30, woman who f-s the LORD, she shall
    be praised
Eccles. 12:13, f God and keep His
    commandments
Matt. 10:26, Therefore do not f them
    10:28, do not f those who kill the body
    10:31, do not f; you are of … value
Luke 23:40, Do you not even f God
Ex. 1:21; 14:13; 18:21; Deut. 4:10; 5:29; 28:58;
    Neh. 7:2; Job 11:15; Ps. 27:3; 31:19; 34:9;
    66:16; 76:7; 86:11; 112:7; 115:11; 119:74;
    Prov. 3:7; 24:21; 28:14; Eccles. 3:14; 5:7;
    Is. 8:12; 35:4; 41:10; 43:5; Jer. 5:24; 10:7;
    33:9; Dan. 6:26; Mal. 3:16; Matt. 14:5; 21:26;
    Mark 5:33; Luke 12:5; 18:2; 20:19;
    Acts 10:35; 13:26; Rom. 8:15; 11:20;
    Gal. 4:11; Col. 3:22; Heb. 4:1; 1 John 4:18
FEARFUL Ps. 139:14, I am f-ly and wonderfully
    made
1 Tim. 5:20, that the rest also may be f
FEAST—*banquet* Judg. 14:10; Esth. 9:17
Prov. 15:15, heart *has* a continual f
John 7:37, the great *day* of the f
Job 1:4; Ps. 35:16; Eccles. 7:2; 10:16; Is. 1:14;
    Jer. 16:8; Mal. 2:3; Luke 2:42; John 7:8,14;
    13:29; 1 Cor. 5:8; Jude 12
FEATHERS—*plumage, wings*
Dan. 4:33, hair … like eagles' f

FED Deut. 8:3, humbled you and f you with
    manna
Ezek. 34:8, shepherds f themselves and did not
    feed
Luke 16:21, longing to be f with the *crumbs*
FEEBLE Job 4:4, you have strengthened f knees
Is. 35:3, strengthen the f
Heb. 12:12, strengthen … the knees that are f
Gen. 30:42; Neh. 4:2
FEED—*tend* 1 Kin. 22:27; Ps. 81:16; Prov. 30:8
Prov. 15:14, the mouth of fools f-s on folly
Matt. 6:26, your heavenly Father f-s them
    25:37, see You hungry and f you
Luke 12:24, *yet* God f-s them
Rom. 12:20, ENEMY IS HUNGRY, F HIM
Is. 44:20; Jer. 3:15; Hos. 12:1; Matt. 15:27;
    Mark 7:28
FEEL Gen. 27:12, Perhaps my father will f me
Judge. 16:26, Let me f the pillars
Ps. 115:7, have hands, but they cannot f
1 Tim. 5:11, f sensual desires in disregard of
FEET—*footstool* Ps. 8:6, all things under his f
Ps. 22:16, pierced my hands and my f
    31:8, set my f in a large place
    40:2, set my f upon a rock
    56:13; 116:8, my f from stumbling
    66:9, does not allow our f to slip
    119:105, word is a lamp to my f
    122:2, f are standing within your gates
Prov. 1:16; 6:18; Is. 59:7, their f run to evil
    5:5, Her f go down to death
Is. 49:23; Matt. 10:14; Mark 6:11; Luke 9:5, dust
    of your f
    52:7, lovely on the mountains Are the f
Dan. 2:33, f partly of iron and partly of clay
    10:6, f … of polished bronze
Nah. 1:3, clouds are the dust beneath His f
    1:15, the f of him who brings good news
Zech. 14:4, His f will stand on the Mount of
    Olives
Luke 1:79, guide our f into the way of peace
    8:35, sitting down at the f of Jesus
    24:39, See My hands and My f
John 12:3, anointed the f of Jesus
    13:5, began to wash the disciples' f
Acts 4:35,37; 5:2, laid … at the apostles' f
Rom. 3:15, THEIR F ARE SWIFT TO SHED BLOOD
    10:15, How BEAUTIFUL ARE THE F OF THOSE
    WHO
    16:20, crush Satan under your f
Eph. 6:15, shod your f with the preparation
Rev. 1:15, 2:18, f like burnished bronze
    1:17, I fell at his f as a dead man
    19:10, I fell at his f to worship
    22:8, I fell down to worship at the f of
Gen. 49:10; Josh. 3:15; Ruth 3:14; 1 Sam. 2:9;
    2 Sam. 4:4; 22:37; 2 Kin. 6:32; 9:35; 13:21;
    Neh. 9:21; Job 29:15; Ps. 73:2; 115:7;
    Prov. 4:26; 6:13,28; 7:11; 19:2; Song 5:3; 7:1;
    Is. 3:16; 6:2; 23:7; 26:6; 60:13; Lam. 3:34;
    Ezek. 2:1,2; 3:24; 24:17,23; 25:6; 32:2;
    34:18,19; Matt. 7:6; 18:8; 28:9; Mark 12:36;
    Luke 7:38; 10:39; John 11:2; 12:3; 20:12;
    Acts 3:7; 21:11; 1 Cor. 12:21; 1 Tim. 5:10;
    Rev. 13:2
FELL—*came, collapsed* Gen. 4:5; Josh. 6:20;
    1 Kin. 18:38
Matt. 13:4, some seeds f beside the road
Luke 8:23, Jesus f asleep
    10:30, he f among robbers
    13:4, on whom the tower in Siloam f
Acts 1:26, the lot f to Matthias
    10:44, the Holy Spirit f upon all those
    19:35, *image* which f down from heaven
    20:9, Eutychus … f down from the third floor
2 Kin. 6:5; Jon. 1:7; Luke 10:36; Acts 13:36;
    2 Pet. 3:4; Rev. 16:19
FELLOW Ps. 45:7, oil of joy above Thy f-s
Acts 24:5, pest and a f who stirs up
Rom. 8:17, and f-heirs with Christ

FELLOW (Continued)
Eph. 2:19, **f-citizens** with the saints
  3:6, Gentiles are **f-heirs**
2 Kin. 9:11; Matt. 24:49; Acts 22:22; Heb. 8:11
FELLOWSHIP—share Ps. 55:14, had sweet **f**
  together
2 Cor. 6:14, What **f** has light with darkness
  13:14, **f** of the Holy Spirit
Gal. 2:9, right hand of **f**
1 John 1:3, our **f** is with the Father
  1:7, **f** with one another
FELLOW-WORKER—helper
Rom. 16:3, Prisca and Aquila my **f-s**
Phil. 2:25, my brother and **f**
  4:3, **f-s**, whose names are in the book
1 Thess. 3:2, **f** in the gospel of Christ
Philem. 24, as do . . . my **f-s**
3 John 8, **f-s** with the truth
FELT Gen. 27:22, he **f** him and said, The voice
Matt. 9:36, He **f** compassion for them
Ex. 10:21; Mark 5:29
FEMALE Gen. 1:27, male and **f** He created them
Gen. 6:19; Lev. 3:1; 5:6; Num. 5:3; Deut. 4:16;
  Matt. 19:4; Mark 10:6; Gal. 3:28
FERTILE—fruit Is. 5:1, vineyard on a **f** hill
FERTILIZER Luke 13:8, dig around it and . . . **f**
FERVENT Acts 18:25, being **f** in spirit
Rom. 12:11, **f** in spirit, serving
1 Pet. 4:8, keep **f** in your love
FERVENTLY Luke 22:44, in agony He was
  praying very **f**
FESTIVAL—feast Amos 5:21; 8:10; Matt. 26:5;
  Mark 14:2
FETTER—band, chain 2 Sam. 3:34; Job 36:8; Ps.
  2:3; 105:18; Prov. 7:22; Luke 8:29
FEVER Matt. 8:14, mother-in-law . . . sick in bed
  with a **f**
Luke 4:38, suffering from a high **f**
John 4:52, seventh hour the **f** left him
Deut. 28:22; Matt. 8:15; Acts 28:8
FEW Gen. 47:9, **f** and unpleasant . . . years
Matt. 9:37, but the workers are **f**
  22:14, many are called, but **f** are chosen
  25:21, faithful with a **f** things
Mark 8:7, had a **f** small fish
1 Pet. 3:20, a **f**, that is, eight persons
Rev. 2:14, I have a **f** things against you
Gen. 24:55; 29:20; 34:30; Lev. 25:52;
  Num. 13:18; Deut. 4:27; 33:6; Josh. 7:3;
  1 Sam. 14:6; 1 Chr. 16:19; 2 Chr. 29:34;
  Neh. 2:12; Job 10:20; Ps. 105:12; 109:8;
  Eccles. 5:2; 9:14; Ezek. 12:16; Luke 12:48;
  13:23
FIELD—garden Prov. 31:16, She considers a **f**
Matt. 6:28, how the lilies of the **f** grow
  13:38, the **f** is the world
  27:10, GAVE THEM FOR THE POTTER'S F
Luke 2:8, shepherds staying out in the **f-s**
  15:15, sent him into his **f-s**
  17:36, Two men will be in the **f**
John 4:35, **f-s** . . . white for harvest
Acts 1:18, acquired a **f** with the price
  1:19, that is, F of Blood
Gen. 2:5,20; 23:20; 25:29; Ex. 9:19,22; 10:15;
  23:11; Lev. 19:9,19; Num. 23:14;
  Deut. 11:15; 20:19; Judg. 9:43; Ruth 2:3,8;
  1 Sam. 20:24; 30:11; 2 Sam. 14:6;
  1 Kin. 11:29; Job 5:23; Ps. 96:12;
  Prov. 24:30; Is. 1:8; 5:8; Jer. 4:17; 26:18;
  32:44; Lam. 4:9; Dan. 4:15; Hos. 2:12;
  Joel 1:20; James 5:4
FIERCE Rev. 19:15, **f** wrath of God the Almighty
Gen. 49:7; Num. 25:4; Job 41:10; Prov. 27:4;
  Is. 33:19
FIERY Num. 21:6; Deut. 28:22; Ps. 21:9;
  1 Pet. 4:12
FIFTEEN Gen. 5:10; Judg. 8:10; Hos. 3:2;
  Gal. 1:18
FIFTH Gen. 1:23; Lev. 5:16; Neh. 6:5; Jer. 1:3;
  Rev. 6:9

FIFTY Lev. 25:10, consecrate the **f-eth** year
Gen. 6:15; Ex. 18:21; 26:5; Lev. 23:16;
  Esth. 5:14; Luke 9:14; John 8:57; Acts 13:19
FIG Gen. 3:7, they sewed **f** leaves together
Matt. 21:19, the **f** tree withered
Mark 13:28, the parable from the **f** tree
Luke 6:44, men do not gather **f-s** from thorns
James 3:12, Can a **f** tree . . . produce olives
Rev. 6:13, as a **f** tree casts its unripe **f-s**
Deut. 8:8; Judg. 9:11; Jer. 29:17; Matt. 7:16;
  Mark 11:13; John 1:48
FIGHT Ex. 14:14, The LORD will **f** for you
1 Tim. 1:18, you may **f** the good **f**
  6:12, F the good **f** of faith
James 4:2, so you **f** and quarrel
Josh. 9:2; 1 Sam. 8:20; Neh. 4:20; Ps. 35:1
FIGURATIVE 1 Cor. 4:6, I have **f-ly** applied to
  myself
FIGURE—graven Lev. 26:1; Deut. 4:16
FILL Gen. 42:25, gave orders to **f** their bags
Jer. 23:24, **f** the heavens and the earth
Gen. 1:22; Job 41:7; Ps. 83:16; Prov. 7:18; Is. 8:8;
  65:11; Mic. 3:8; Matt. 22:10
FILTH—uncleanness
Is. 4:4, LORD has washed away the **f**
  64:6, deeds are like a **f-y** garment
James 1:21, putting aside all **f-iness**
Is. 28:8; Nah. 3:6
FIND—discover Gen. 18:26, If I **f** in Sodom fifty
Num. 32:23, be sure your sin will **f** you out
Deut. 4:29, you will **f** Him if you search
Prov. 8:35, he who **f-s** Me **f-s** life
  18:22, he who **f-s** a wife **f-s** a good thing
Is. 35:10, They will **f** gladness and joy
Matt. 7:7, Seek, and you shall **f**
  10:39, lost his life . . . shall **f** it
  11:29, YOU SHALL F REST FOR YOUR SOULS
Mark 13:36, **f** you asleep
Luke 2:12, you will **f** a baby wrapped
  15:8, search . . . until she **f-s** it
  23:4, I **f** no guilt in this man
John 10:9, go in and out, and **f** pasture
Acts 7:46, **f** a dwelling place for the God of
Gen. 32:5; Ruth 1:9; 2 Sam. 15:25; 20:6;
  Prov. 1:13; 3:4; Song 3:1; 5:8; Matt. 21:2;
  Mark 11:2; Luke 11:9; John 18:38;
  Acts 23:9; 2 Cor. 9:4; Rev. 18:14
FINE—good Ps. 19:10, than much **f** gold; Sweeter
Matt. 13:45, merchant seeking **f** pearls
Luke 16:19, in purple and **f** linen
Rev. 19:14, clothed in **f** linen, white
Gen. 41:42; Ex. 16:14; 25:4; Ps. 81:16
FINGER John 8:6, Jesus . . . with His **f** wrote on
  the ground
John 20:25, put my **f** into the place of the nails
  20:27, Reach here your **f**
Ex. 8:19; Lev. 4:6; Deut. 9:10; 2 Sam. 21:20;
  1 Kin. 12:10; 1 Chr. 20:6; Prov. 6:13;
  Jer. 52:21; Mark 7:33; Luke 11:20; 16:24
FINISH—end, spend 2 Chr. 7:11, Solomon **f-ed**
  the house
John 19:30, said, It is **f-ed**
Acts 20:24, that I may **f** my course
Ex. 40:33; Ps. 90:9; Mark 3:26; 2 Cor. 8:11
FIR—cedar 2 Sam. 6:5; Ps. 104:17; Ezek. 27:5
FIRE—flame, burn Ex. 13:21, pillar of **f** by night
Num. 3:4, offered strange **f** before the LORD
1 Kin. 18:38, Then **f** of the LORD fell
Neh. 9:12, with a pillar of **f** by night
Ps. 105:39, **f** to illumine by night
Is. 66:15, the LORD will come in **f**
Dan. 3:25, walking about in the midst of the **f**
Matt. 3:11, baptize you . . . Holy Spirit and **f**
Mark 9:43, into the unquenchable **f**
Acts 2:3, tongues as of **f**
1 Cor. 3:13, to be revealed with **f**
Rev. 3:18, gold refined by **f**
  21:8, lake that burns with **f** and brimstone
Gen. 19:24; 22:6; Ex. 3:2; 9:24; Lev. 6:13; Deut.
  9:3; Job 18:5; Ps. 46:9; Jer. 23:29;
  Matt. 3:10,12; Luke 3:17; 12:49; Jude 7
FIREPAN Lev. 16:12, take a **f** full of coals

FIRM—*hard, steadfast* Josh. 3:17, LORD stood **f** on dry
Is. 22:23, *like* a peg in a **f** place
1 Cor. 7:37, stands **f** in his heart
2 Tim. 2:19, the **f** foundation of God stands
Heb. 3:6, hope **f** until the end
1 Pet. 5:9, resist him, **f** in *your* faith

FIRMAMENT—*expanse* Ps. 19:1, **f** is declaring the work of

FIRST—*leader, eminent, foremost* Gen. 38:28
Matt. 6:33, seek **f** His kingdom
7:5, **f** take the log out of
19:30, many *who are* **f** will be last
20:27, be **f** among you
28:1, the **f** *day* of the week
1 John 4:19, because He **f** loved us
Rev. 1:17, I am the **f** and the last
2:4, you have left your **f** love
21:4, the **f** things have passed away
22:13, Omega, the **f** and the last
Deut. 26:10; Prov. 3:9; 18:17; Hos. 2:7; Mark 3:27; 10:44; Acts 1:1

FIRST-BORN Luke 2:7, she gave birth to her **f** son
Heb. 12:23, church of the **f**
Gen. 10:15; 19:37; 27:19; Ex. 11:5

FIRST FRUITS Ex. 23:16, the **f** of your labors
Rom. 8:23, the **f** of the Spirit
James 1:18, the **f** among His creatures
Rev. 14:4, **f** to God and to the Lamb

FISH Matt. 14:17, five loaves and two **f**
Luke 5:6, a great quantity of **f**
11:11, asked by his son for a **f**
Gen. 1:26; Num. 11:5; 2 Chr. 33:14; Is. 50:2; Jon. 1:17; John 21:10

FISHERMEN Is. 19:8; Jer. 16:16

FISHERS—*fishermen* Matt. 4:19, I will make you **f** of men
Mark 1:17, I will make you become **f** of men

FIT—*ready, prepare, worthy*
Matt. 3:11, not . . . **f** to remove His sandals
Luke 9:62, **f** for the kingdom of God
Eph. 2:21, whole building, being **f-ed** together
4:16, whole body, being **f-ed** and held together

FITTING—*opportune* Matt. 3:15, it is **f** for us to fulfill
Eph. 5:4, jesting, which are not **f**
Col. 3:18, as is **f** in the Lord

FIVE 1 Sam. 17:40, **f** smooth stones from the brook
Matt. 14:17, **f** loaves and two fish
25:2, **f** of them were foolish . . . **f**
25:20, who had received the **f** talents
Gen. 5:6; Ex. 22:1; Lev. 26:8; 2 Chr. 4:2; 2 Cor. 11:24; Rev. 17:10

FIXED Luke 16:26, there is a great chasm **f**

FLAG 1 Sam. 30:17, a **f** on a mountain top

FLAME—*fire* Is. 4:5, of a **f-ing** fire by night
Rev. 19:12, eyes *are* a **f** of fire
Gen. 3:24; Judg. 13:20; Ps. 106:18; Song 8:6; Is. 5:24; 10:17; Ezek. 20:47; Dan. 7:9; 10:6; Joel 2:5; Acts 7:30; 2 Thess. 1:7

FLASH Job 15:12, why do your eyes **f**
Acts 22:6, bright light suddenly **f-ed** from heaven
Deut. 32:41; Ezek. 1:13; 21:10; Nah. 3:3

FLASK—*vessel* Matt. 25:4, took oil in **f-s**

FLAT Josh. 6:5,20, wall fell down **f**

FLATTER Job 32:21, Nor **f** *any* man
Ps. 5:9, They **f** with their tongue
Prov. 7:21, **f-ing** lips she seduces him
1 Thess. 2:5, we never came with **f-ing** speech

FLAX Ex. 9:31; Judg. 15:14; Ezek. 40:3

FLEA 1 Sam. 24:14; 26:20

FLED—*escape* Matt. 26:56, left Him and **f**
Mark 16:8, **f** from the tomb
Rev. 20:11, whose presence earth and heaven **f**
Gen. 14:10; 31:21; 39:18; Is. 22:3

FLEE—*wander* Lev. 26:17, **f** when no one is pursuing

Ps. 11:1, **F** *as* a bird to your mountain
139:7, I **f** from Thy presence
Prov. 28:1, wicked **f** when no one
Is. 16:2, like **f-ing** birds
Matt. 3:7, **f** from the wrath to come
1 Tim. 6:11, But **f** from these things, you man
2 Tim. 2:22, **f** from youthful lusts
Gen. 16:8; Is. 30:16; Matt. 2:13; Rev. 9:6

FLEECE—*shear* Judg. 6:37; Job 31:20

FLESH—*body, meat, life*
Gen. 2:24, they shall become one **f**
Ps. 84:2, **f** sing for joy to the living God
136:25, Who gives food to all **f**
Is. 40:6, All **f** is grass
Matt. 16:17, because **f** and blood did not reveal
26:41, but the **f** is weak
Luke 24:39, spirit does not have **f** and bones
John 1:14, the Word became **f**
3:6, which is born of the **f** is **f**
Rom. 8:6, mind set on the **f** is death
2 Cor. 1:17, according to the **f** . . . should be
10:4, weapons . . . not of the **f**
Gal. 6:8, **f** shall from the **f** reap
Eph. 2:3, indulging the desires of the **f**
5:31, TWO SHALL BECOME ONE **F**
6:12, struggle is not against **f**
1 Pet. 2:11, abstain from **f-ly** lusts
Gen. 2:23; 7:21; 37:27; Num. 16:22; Job 19:26; 41:23; Ps. 16:9; Rom. 9:8; Jude 23; Rev. 19:21

FLIES—*fly* Job 20:8; Ps. 78:45; Prov. 23:5; Eccles. 10:1

FLIGHT Amos 2:14, **F** will perish from the swift
Matt. 24:20, your **f** may not be in the winter
Heb. 11:34, put foreign armies to **f**

FLINT—*stone* Zech. 7:12, hearts like **f** so
Ex. 4:25; Deut. 8:15; 32:13; Ps. 114:8; Is. 5:28; Ezek. 3:9

FLOCK—*fold, sheep* Gen. 4:2,4; 29:2; 30:31,38
Is. 40:11, Like a shepherd He will tend His **f**
Jer. 23:2, scattered My **f** and driven
Matt. 26:31, SHEEP OF THE **F** SHALL BE SCATTERED
Luke 2:8, keeping watch over their **f** by night
12:32, Do not be afraid, little **f**
John 10:16, become one **f** *with* one Shepherd
1 Pet. 5:2, the **f** of God among you
Ex. 2:16; 10:9; Judg. 5:16; 1 Sam. 16:19; 17:34; 2 Chr. 32:28; Ps. 77:20; Prov. 27:23; Is. 13:20; Ezek. 45:15; Amos 6:4; Hab. 3:17

FLOG Mark 13:9, you will be **f-ed**

FLOOD Gen. 7:17, **f** came upon the earth
Gen. 9:15, never . . . the water become a **f**
Matt. 7:25, **f-s** came, and the winds blew
Luke 17:27, **f** came and destroyed them all
Gen. 6:17; Dan. 9:26

FLOODGATES Gen. 7:11, **f** of the sky were opened

FLOOR Gen. 50:11; Ruth 3:3; 1 Kin. 6:30; 7:7; Joel 2:24; Matt. 3:12

FLOUR—*dough* Ex. 29:2; Lev. 2:1; Ezek. 16:13; Rev. 18:13

FLOURISH—*blossom, green*
Ps. 72:7, may the righteous **f**
92:7, all who did iniquity **f-ed**
103:15, a flower . . . so he **f-es**
Prov. 11:28, will **f** like the *green* leaf
Ezek. 17:24, make the dry tree **f**

FLOW—*gush* Ex. 3:8, land **f-ing** with milk and honey
John 7:38, shall **f** rivers of living water
Job 20:28; Ps. 147:18; Jer. 9:18; Joel 3:18; Mark 5:29

FLOWER Ps. 103:15, As a **f** of the field, so he
1 Pet. 1:24, AND THE **F** FALLS OFF
Job 14:2; Song 2:12; Is. 28:1

FLUENTLY—*well* Ex. 4:14, he speaks **f**

FLUSH Job 16:16, My face is **f-ed** from weeping

FLUTE 1 Sam. 10:5; 1 Kin. 1:40; 1 Cor. 14:7; Rev. 18:22

FLY Job 5:7, As sparks **f** upward
Gen. 1:20; Is. 14:29; Rev. 8:13; 12:14; 19:17

FOAL—*colt* Job 11:12; Zech. 9:9
FOE—*enemy*
  1 Chr. 21:12, swept away before your **f-s**
FOLD—*flock* Eccles. 4:5, The fool **f-s** his hands
  John 10:16, sheep, which are not of this **f**
  Num. 32:24; Ps. 50:9; Prov. 6:10
FOLLOW—*cling, imitate, pursue* Gen. 24:5; 44:4;
    Ex. 11:8
  Ruth 1:16, turn back from **f-ing** you
  Ps. 23:6, goodness and lovingkindness will **f** me
  Matt. 4:19, He said to them, **F** Me
    4:20, left the nets, and **f-ed** Him
    8:19, **f** You wherever You go
    12:15, And many **f-ed** Him
    16:24, take up his cross, and **f** Me
    19:21, and come, **f** Me
  Luke 22:39, disciples also **f-ed** Him
  John 10:27, I know them, and they **f** Me
  Jude 16, **f-ing** after their *own* lusts
  Rev. 14:4, the ones who **f** the Lamb
  Num. 15:39; 1 Sam. 12:14; Ps. 119:150; Jer. 48:2;
    Mark 5:37; 14:54; Luke 22:10; John 18:15;
    Acts 5:36; Rev. 14:13
FOLLY—*foolishness*
  Prov. 14:18, The naive inherit **f**
    15:2, mouth of fools spouts **f**
    24:9, devising of **f** is sin
  Judg. 19:23; Prov. 15:21
FOND—*greedy* 1 Tim. 3:8, or **f** of sordid gain
FONDLE Is. 66:12, **f-d** on the knees
FOOD—*bread, meat* Ps. 69:21, gall for my **f**
  Ps. 136:25, Who gives **f** to all flesh
  Matt. 6:25, Is not life more than **f**
  John 4:34, My **f** is to do the will of Him
    6:55, My flesh is true **f**
  1 Cor. 6:13, **F** is for the stomach
  James 2:15, in need of daily **f**
  Gen. 1:29; 2:9; 3:6; 43:2; Lev. 3:11; Deut. 10:18;
    Ruth 1:6; Job 38:41; Ps. 78:25; 145:15;
    Prov. 6:8; 20:13; 23:3; 28:19; 30:8; Is. 65:25;
    Matt. 3:4; 1 Tim. 6:8
FOOL—*foolish, unwise* Ps. 14:1, The **f** has said in
  his
  Prov. 1:7, **F-s** despise wisdom and instruction
    15:5, A **f** rejects his father's discipline
    26:3, a rod for the back of **f-s**
    29:11, A **f** always loses his temper
  Eccles. 10:14, the **f** multiplies words
  Rom. 1:22, wise, they became **f-s**
  1 Cor. 4:10, We are **f-s** for Christ's sake
  1 Sam. 26:21; 2 Sam. 3:33; Prov. 24:7; Hos. 9:7;
    Matt. 5:22; 23:17
FOOLISH—*fool, boastful, folly, unwise*
  Prov. 14:17, quick-tempered man acts **f-ly**
  Luke 24:25, O **f** men and slow of heart
  Rom. 1:14, the wise and to the **f**
  1 Cor. 3:18, let him become **f**
  Eph. 5:17, then do not be **f**
  Gen. 31:28; Deut. 32:6; Job 5:3; Lam. 2:14;
    Matt. 25:8; 1 Pet. 2:15
FOOLISHNESS—*folly* Prov. 14:24; Is. 9:17;
  2 Cor. 11:21
FOOT Prov. 25:17, **f** rarely be in your neighbor's
  house
  Matt. 4:6, Lest You strike Your **f**
  Luke 4:11, strike Your **f** against a stone
  Rev. 10:2, placed his right **f** on the sea
  Gen. 8:9; 41:44; Deut. 2:28; 33:24; Num. 11:21;
    Josh. 14:9; 2 Sam. 8:4; 21:20; 1 Chr. 20:6;
    Ps. 26:12; 91:12; 121:3; Prov. 3:23; 25:19;
    Jer. 12:5; Matt. 22:13
FOOTSTOOL—*feet* 1 Chr. 28:2, for the **f** of our
  God
  Ps. 99:5, And worship at His **f**
    110:1, Thine enemies a **f**
    132:7, Let us worship at His **f**
  Is. 66:1, the earth is My **f**
  James 2:3, or sit down by my **f**
FORBEARANCE Eph. 4:2, showing **f** to one
  another
  Prov. 25:15; Rom. 3:25

FORBID—*hinder* 1 Cor. 14:39, do not **f** to speak
  in tongues
  1 Tim. 4:3, *men* who **f** marriage *and*
  Num. 30:5,8,11; Luke 23:2
FORCE—*compel* Matt. 5:41, **f** you to go one mile
  Luke 3:14, Do not take money ... by **f**
  Gen. 31:31; 1 Sam. 2:16; Job 30:18; 36:19;
    Dan. 11:10; Matt. 11:12; Heb. 9:17
FOREHEAD 1 Sam. 17:49, stone sank into his **f**
  Rev. 9:4, seal of God on their **f-s**
    17:5, upon her **f** a name *was* written
  Ex. 28:38; Lev. 13:42; Is. 48:4; Jer. 3:3;
    Ezek. 3:8; 9:4
FOREIGN—*strange* Gen. 35:2, Put away the **f**
  gods
  Ex. 2:22, a sojourner in a **f** land
  1 Kin. 11:1, Solomon loved many **f** women
  Ezra 10:2, have married **f** women
  Ps. 137:4, Lord's song in a **f** land
  Heb. 11:34, put **f** armies to flight
FOREIGNER—*alien, sojourner*
  Ruth 2:10, since I am a **f**
  Prov. 5:20, embrace the bosom of a **f**
  Deut. 14:21; 15:3; Job 19:15; Obad. 11
FOREMOST—*first*
  Matt. 22:38, great and **f** commandment
  Mark 12:28, commandment is the **f** of all
  1 Tim. 1:15, among whom I am **f** *of all*
FOREST—*wood* Ps. 50:10, every beast of the **f** is
  Mine
  James 3:5, how great a **f** is set aflame
  1 Sam. 22:5; 2 Sam. 18:8; 1 Kin. 7:2;
    1 Chr. 16:33; Ps. 83:14; Is. 10:18; 44:14;
    56:9; Jer. 5:6; 21:14; Ezek. 15:2; Amos 3:4
FOREVER—*always, evermore, utmost* Gen. 3:22;
  6:3
  1 Chr. 17:14, throne shall be established **f**
  Ps. 9:7, the Lord abides **f**
    16:11, there are pleasures **f**
    23:6, in the house of the Lord **f**
    29:10, the Lord sits as King **f**
    33:11, counsel of the Lord stands **f**
    86:12, will glorify Thy name **f**
    89:52, Blessed be the Lord **f**
    92:8, O Lord, art on high **f**
    102:12, Thou, O Lord, dost abide **f**
    119:89, **F**, O Lord, Thy word is settled
    121:8, Lord will guard your going out ... **f**
    133:3, the blessing ... life **f**
  Prov. 27:24, riches are not **f**
  Eccles. 3:14, everything God does ... **f**
  Is. 40:8, word of our God stands **f**
    57:15, exalted One Who lives **f**
    57:16, For I will not contend **f**
  John 6:51, eats of this bread, he shall live **f**
    12:34, the Christ is to remain **f**
    14:16, Helper, that he may be with you **f**
  Rom. 9:5, God blessed **f**
  2 Cor. 11:31, Lord Jesus, He who is blessed **f**
  Eph. 3:21, all generations **f** and ever
  Heb. 7:25, He is able to save **f**
    7:28, a Son, made perfect **f**
    13:8, today, *yes* and **f**
  Ex. 14:13; Deut. 5:29; 12:28; 32:40; Ps. 12:7;
    23:6; 61:4; 73:26; 77:8; 113:2; 115:18; 132:14;
    146:6; Prov. 21:28; Is. 26:4; 34:10; Lam. 3:31
FOREVERMORE Rev. 1:18, I am alive **f**
FORFEIT Dan 1:10, make me **f** my head to the
  king
FORGAVE Ps. 78:38, **f** their iniquity, and
  Matt. 18:27, and **f** him the debt
  Luke 7:42, he graciously **f** them both
    7:43, the one whom he **f** more
FORGET—*neglect, forsake*
  Deut. 6:12, lest you **f** the Lord
  Ps. 9:17, all the nations who **f** God
    13:1, Wilt Thou **f** me forever
    74:23, Do not **f** the voice of Thine
    88:12, in the land of **f-fulness**
    119:176, I do not **f** Thy commandments

Prov. 3:1, My son, do not **f** my teaching
Heb. 6:10, **f** your work and the love
Gen. 27:45; 41:51; Deut. 4:9; Prov. 4:5; 31:5;
  Is. 54:4; Jer. 2:32; 23:27
FORGIVE—*forgave, pardon*
Ps. 86:5, good, and ready to **f**
  99:8, a **f-ing** God to them
Matt. 6:12, **f** us our debts, as we
  6:14, if you **f** men for
  6:15, if you do not **f** men
  9:5, Your sins are **f-n**
  9:6, on earth to **f** sins
Mark 2:7, who can **f** sins but God alone
  11:26, if you do not **f**
Luke 7:47, sins … many, have been **f-n**
  23:34, Father **f** them
2 Cor. 2:10, whom you **f** anything, I **f** also
Eph. 4:32, **f-ing** each other
Col. 2:13, **f-n** us all our transgressions
1 John 1:9, righteous to **f** us our sins
Gen. 50:17; Ex. 32:32; Num. 30:5; Ps. 25:18;
  79:9; Jer. 18:23
FORGIVENESS—*pardon*
Neh. 9:17, art a God of **f**
Ps. 130:4, there is **f** with Thee
Matt. 26:28, for **f** of sins
Mark 1:4; Luke 24:47, repentance for the **f** of
  sins
  3:29, Holy Spirit never has **f**
Acts 10:43, has received **f** of sins
  13:38, through Him **f** of sins is proclaimed
  26:18, they may receive **f** of sins
Eph. 1:7, the **f** of our trespasses
Col. 1:14, redemption, the **f** of sins
Heb. 9:22, shedding of blood … no **f**
FORGOT Deut. 32:18, **f** the God who gave you
  birth
FORGOTTEN—*neglect* Job 19:14, friends have **f**
  me
Ps. 9:18, needy will not always be **f**
Ezek. 23:35, Because you have **f** Me
Matt. 16:5, had **f** to take bread
Luke 12:6, is **f** before God
James 1:24, **f** what kind of person
Gen. 41:30; Job 28:4; Ps. 31:12; 77:9; Jer. 2:32;
  Lam. 2:6
FORK 1 Sam. 2:13; Matt. 3:12
FORM—*fashion* Ps. 95:5, His hands **f-ed** the dry
  land
Is. 53:2, no *stately* **f** or majesty
Mark 4:32, **f-s** large branches
  16:12, He appeared in a different **f**
1 Cor. 7:31, the **f** of this world is passing
Gal. 4:19, until Christ is **f-ed** in you
2 Pet. 3:5, earth was **f-ed** out of water
Gen. 1:2; 2:7; Job 4:16; 33:6; Song 2:14; Is. 43:1;
  44:13; 45:7; Amos 4:13; 7:1; Acts 17:29
FORMER—*past* 1 Pet. 1:14, conformed to the **f**
  lusts
Gen. 40:13; Deut. 4:32; 24:4; Ruth 4:7; Is. 42:9;
  46:9; 65:16; Ezek. 16:55
FORNICATION—*immorality* Matt. 15:19; John
  8:41
FORSAKE—*fail, leave, reject* Job 6:14; Ps. 27:9;
  38:21
Josh. 1:5, not fail you or **f** you
2 Chr. 15:2, **f** Him, He will **f** you
Ezra 9:9, our God has not **f-n** us
Ps. 22:1, God, why hast Thou **f-n** me
  27:10, father and my mother have **f-n** me
Prov. 1:8, do not **f** your mother's teaching
  9:6, **F** *your* folly and live
Is. 53:3, despised and **f-n** of men
  55:7, Let the wicked **f** his way
Matt. 27:46, GOD, WHY HAST THOU **F-N** ME
2 Cor. 4:9, persecuted, but not **f**
Heb. 13:5, NOR WILL I EVER **F** YOU
Jer. 5:7; Ezek. 9:9; 20:8; Mark 15:34; 2 Pet. 2:15
FORSOOK—*left, deserted* Deut. 32:15; 1 Kin.
  12:8; 2 Chr. 12:1
FORTIFICATION—*stronghold*
Is. 25:12, unassailable **f-s** of

FORTIFY—*strengthen* Num. 32:17; Deut. 3:5;
  Josh. 10:20; 1 Sam. 6:18; 2 Kin. 3:19; Is. 34:13;
  Jer. 5:17; 51:53
FORTRESS—*stronghold, power*
2 Sam. 22:2, my rock and my **f**
Ps. 91:2, My refuge and my **f**
2 Sam. 22:33; Ps. 18:2; Dan. 11:19
FORTY Gen. 7:4, the earth **f** days and **f** nights
Ex. 16:35, Israel ate the manna **f** years
Matt. 4:2, fasted **f** days and **f** nights
Gen. 7:17; Ex. 34:28; Num. 33:38; Ps. 95:10;
  Mark 1:13
FORWARD—*further*
2 Kin. 20:9, shadow go **f** ten steps
Job 23:8; Is. 41:21; Jer. 7:24; Ezek. 1:9;
  Acts 19:33
FOUGHT—*waged war* Num. 21:1, then he **f**
  against Israel
Judg. 5:20, stars **f** from heaven
2 Chr. 20:29, the LORD had **f** against
1 Cor. 15:32, I **f** with wild beasts
2 Tim. 4:7, I have **f** the good fight
FOUL Ezek. 32:2; 34:19
FOUND—*caught, proved*
Judg. 14:18, not have **f** out my riddle
Jer. 15:16, Thy words were **f** and I
Dan. 5:27, weighed on the scales and **f** deficient
Matt. 8:10, not **f** such great faith
  10:39, He who has **f** his life shall
Mark 14:37, **f** them sleeping
Luke 2:46, they **f** Him in the temple
  15:6, I have **f** my sheep
  24:2, **f** the stone rolled away
John 1:41, We have **f** the Messiah
Acts 13:22, I have **f** David the son of
1 Cor. 15:15, we are even **f** *to be* false witnesses
Phil. 2:8, being **f** in appearance
Gen. 2:20; 6:8; Lev. 6:3; Deut. 17:2;
  Ruth 2:10,13; Job 28:12; Ps. 84:3;
  Prov. 25:16; Eccles. 7:29; Is. 51:3; Dan. 6:11;
  Mal. 2:6; Matt. 27:32; Mark 11:4; 14:40;
  Rev. 18:24
FOUNDATION—*habitation, founded* 2 Sam.
  22:8; Job 4:19
Ps. 89:14; 97:2, Right and justice are the **f**
Matt. 13:35, SINCE THE **F** OF THE WORLD
Luke 6:48, laid a **f** upon the rock
Rom. 15:20, upon another man's **f**
2 Tim. 2:19, the firm **f** of God stands
Heb. 1:10, DIDST LAY THE **F** OF THE EARTH
  6:1, a **f** of repentance
Ps. 87:1; 104:5; Prov. 10:25; Is. 28:16
FOUNDED Ps. 24:2, He has **f** it upon the seas
Prov. 3:19, by wisdom the earth
Matt. 7:25, **f** upon the rock
Ex. 9:18; Amos 9:6
FOUNTAIN—*spring, well* Gen. 7:11, **f-s** of the
  great deep
Ps. 36:9, with Thee is the **f** of life
Prov. 14:27, fear of the LORD is a **f** of life
FOUR Mark 13:27, FROM THE **F** WINDS
Luke 19:8, give back **f** times as much
Gen. 2:10; Ex. 25:12; 2 Kin. 7:3; Is. 11:12;
  Matt. 15:38; John 11:39
FOURTEEN Gen. 31:41; 2 Chr. 13:21; 30:15;
  Is. 36:1; Matt. 1:17; Acts 27:27; 2 Cor. 12:2
FOURTH Gen. 1:19; Ex. 20:5; Judg. 19:5; Matt.
  14:25; Rev. 6:7
FOWL—*bird* 1 Kin. 4:23; Ps. 148:10
FOX Judg. 15:4; Neh. 4:3; Song 2:15; Ezek. 13:4;
  Matt. 8:20; Luke 13:32
FRAGMENT—*piece*
John 6:12, Gather up the left-over **f-s**
FRAGRANCE 2 Cor. 2:15, we are a **f** of Christ
Song 1:3; 2:13
FRANKINCENSE Ex. 30:34; 1 Chr. 9:29; Song
  4:6; Matt. 2:11
FRAUD—*mischief*
Acts 13:10, full of all deceit and **f**

FREE Matt. 10:8, **f-ly** you received, **f-ly** give
  John 8:32, the truth shall make you **f**
  Rom. 6:7, he who has died is **f-d**
    6:22, now having been **f-d** from sin
    8:2, **f** from the law
  Gal. 5:1, that Christ set us **f**
  Gen. 2:16; Deut. 15:8; Josh. 2:20; Ps. 110:3;
    Is. 58:6; Eph. 6:8; Rev. 19:18
FREEDOM—*liberty* 1 Pet. 2:16, use your **f** as a
  Rom. 8:21; Gal. 5:13
FREEWILL Lev. 22:18; Ezra 7:16; Ps. 119:108
FREQUENT 1 Tim. 5:23, your **f** ailments
FRESH Prov. 5:15, **f** water from your own well
  James 3:11, *both* **f** and bitter water
  Job 33:25; Ps. 92:10; James 3:12
FRET Prov. 24:19, Do not **f** yourself because of
FRICTION—*dispute*
  1 Tim. 6:5, constant **f** between men
FRIEND Prov. 17:17, A **f** loves at all times
  Prov. 18:24, a **f** who sticks closer
  Matt. 11:19, a **f** of tax-gatherers and sinners
  John 15:13, lay down his life for his **f-s**
  Gen. 38:12; Ex. 33:11; Judg. 14:20; Job 16:20;
    Ps. 38:11; Mic. 7:5; Matt. 20:13
FRIENDSHIP James 4:4, do you not know that **f**
FROGS Ex. 8:2; Ps. 78:45; 105:30; Rev. 16:13
FRONT Ex. 28:27, ephod, on the **f** of it
FROST—*ice* Gen. 31:40; Ex. 16:14; Ps. 78:47;
  Jer. 36:30
FRUIT—*labor, produce* Ps. 1:3, yields its **f** in its
  season
  Prov. 11:30, **f** of the righteous
  Matt. 3:8, Therefore bring forth **f**
    7:16, know them by their **f-s**
  John 4:36, **f** for life eternal
  Rom. 7:4, bear **f** for God
  Col. 1:10, bearing **f** in every good work
  James 3:17, full of mercy and good **f-s**
  Gen. 1:11; 3:6; Lev. 27:30; Ps. 92:14; 128:2;
    Song 4:16; Jer. 2:7; 6:19
FRUSTRATE Ezra 4:5; Job 5:12; Prov. 15:22; Is.
  14:27
FUEL Is. 9:5,19; Ezek. 15:4; 21:32
FUGITIVE Judg. 12:4; Is. 15:5; 52:12
FULFILL—*complete*
  Matt. 2:15, prophet might be **f-ed**
    2:17, prophet was **f-ed** saying
    3:15, fitting for us to **f** all righteousness
    5:17, not come to abolish, but to **f**
  Luke 22:16, it is **f-ed** in the kingdom
  1 Cor. 7:3, husband **f** his duty to his wife
  Gal. 6:2, **f** the law of Christ
  2 Tim. 4:5, **f** your ministry
  1 Chr. 17:11; 2 Chr. 36:21; Ps. 20:5; 148:8;
    Matt. 1:22
FULL—*complete, whole* 1 Chr. 21:24; Ps. 92:14;
  Prov. 4:18
  Ps. 33:5, earth is **f** of the lovingkindness
  Is. 11:9, will be **f** of knowledge
  Matt. 6:2,5,16, have their reward in **f**
    14:20, twelve **f** baskets
    23:27, **f** of dead men's bones
  Luke 4:1, **f** of the Holy Spirit
    11:34, body also is **f** of light
  John 1:14, **f** of grace and truth
  Eph. 6:11, the **f** armor of God
  James 5:11, the Lord is **f** of compassion
  Acts 2:13; 1 Cor. 7:36; Col. 1:25
FULLER—*launderer* 2 Kin. 18:17; Mal. 3:2
FUNCTION Rom. 12:4, members do not have the
  same **f**
FURIOUS 2 Kin. 9:20; Dan. 2:12
FURNACE—*oven* Ps. 12:6; Is. 31:9; Dan. 3:6,15;
  Matt. 13:42; Rev. 1:15
FURNISH Deut. 15:14; Mark 14:15
FURNITURE Ex. 31:7, all the **f** of the tent
FURROWS Job 31:38; Ps. 65:10; 129:3
FURTHER Ex. 21:22; Num. 22:26; 1 Sam. 10:3;
  Matt. 26:65; Acts 24:4; Heb. 12:9
FURY—*displeasure* Gen. 27:44; Ps. 2:5; Ezek.
  19:12; Heb. 10:27

FUTILE—*vain* 1 Sam. 12:21, **f** things ... because
  they are **f**
  Acts 4:25, PEOPLES DEVISE **F** THINGS
  Rom. 1:21, **f** in their speculations
FUTILITY—*vanity*
  Rom. 8:20, creation was subjected to **f**
  Eph. 4:17, walk, in the **f** of their mind
FUTURE—*end, reward*
  Prov. 24:20, no **f** for the evil man
  Deut. 32:29; Jer. 31:17

G

GAIN—*price, profit* Prov. 10:2, Ill-gotten **g-s** do
  not
  Matt. 16:26; Luke 9:25, if he **g-s** the whole
    world
  Phil. 3:8, that I may **g** Christ
  1 Tim. 6:5, godliness ... means of **g**
  1 Pet. 5:2, not for sordid **g**
  1 Sam. 8:3; Prov. 3:14; Is. 33:15; Ezek. 22:12,27
GALE Mark 4:37, arose a fierce **g** of wind
GALL Ps. 69:21, Matt. 27:34; Acts 8:23
GALLERY Ezek. 41:15; 42:3
GALLOWS Esth. 5:14; 7:10; 9:25
GANGRENE 2 Tim. 2:17, will spread like **g**
GARDEN—*field* Gen. 3:8, God walking in the **g**
  John 18:1, where there was a **g**
    19:41, in the **g** a new tomb
  Gen. 2:8; 3:10; Deut. 11:10; Lam. 2:6; Joel 2:3;
    John 18:26; 20:15
GARMENT—*clothing, dress* Gen. 41:42, in **g-s** ...
  linen
  Ex. 28:2, make holy **g-s** for Aaron
  Ps. 22:18, divide my **g-s** among them
    102:26, wear out like a **g**
  Matt. 27:35, DIVIDED UP HIS **G-S-** ... CASTING
    28:3, his **g** as white as snow
  Luke 23:34, DIVIDING UP HIS **G-S**
  Heb. 1:11, BECOME OLD AS A **G**
  Gen. 3:21; 25:25; 38:14; 39:12; Ex. 19:10;
    Esth. 8:15; Is. 59:17; 63:1; Ezek. 27:24;
    Joel 2:13; Matt. 3:4; Mark 5:28; John 21:7;
    Acts 10:30
GARNER—*barn* Ps. 144:13, *Let our* **g-s** *be full*
GARRISON—*pillars* 1 Sam. 10:5; 14:12;
  1 Chr. 18:13
GASH—*cut* Mark 5:5, **g-ing** himself
GATE Gen. 28:17, this is the **g** of heaven
  Ps. 24:7, Lift your heads, O **g-s**
    100:4, Enter His **g-s** with
  Matt. 7:13, Enter by the narrow **g**
    16:18, **g-s** of Hades shall not
  Gen. 22:17; Judg. 16:3; Is. 38:10; Acts 12:14
GATHER—*assemble* Is. 40:11, His arm ... **g** the
  lambs
  John 4:36, **g-ing** fruit for life
    6:12, G up the ... fragments
  Gen. 1:10; 31:46; 37:7; 41:35; Ps. 33:7; Is. 66:18;
    Matt. 26:3; Acts 19:40; Rev. 14:19
GAVE—*provide* Gen. 2:20, Adam **g** names to all
  Gen. 3:12, Thou **g-st** to *be* with me
  Ps. 69:21, they **g** me vinegar to drink
  Eccles. 12:7, return to God who **g** it
  Mark 8:6, He **g** thanks and broke them
  John 3:16, He **g** His only begotten Son
    13:26, morsel ... He ... **g** it to Judas
    19:30, bowed ... **g** up His spirit
  Rom. 1:28, **g** them over to a depraved mind
  1 Tim. 2:6, who **g** Himself as a ransom
  Is. 50:6; Matt. 10:1; 26:48; Luke 7:44; Eph. 1:22
GAZE Ex. 19:21; Job 31:1
GENEALOGY—*descent* Heb. 7:3,6
GENERAL Heb. 12:23, to the **g** assembly and
  church
GENERATION—*ages* Deut. 1:35; Luke 21:32;
  Eph. 3:5
  Ps. 90:1, dwelling place in all **g-s**
    100:5, His faithfulness to all **g-s**
  Matt. 1:17, to David are fourteen **g-s**
    24:34, this **g** will not pass away

Luke 1:48, all **g-s** will count me blessed
Eph. 3:21, all **g-s** forever and ever
Phil. 2:15, a crooked and perverse **g**
GENEROUS—*bountiful* Prov. 22:9; Is. 32:5
GENTILE—*nations* Matt. 6:7, as the **G-s** do
Luke 2:32, LIGHT OF REVELATION TO THE **G-S**
Acts 4:25, WHY DID THE **G-S** RAGE
14:2, stirred the minds of the **G-s**
Rom. 11:11, salvation *has* come to the **G-s**
Gal. 1:16, I might preach Him among the **G-s**
GENTLE—*compassionate*
1 Kin. 19:12, sound of a **g** blowing
Prov. 15:1, **g** answer turns away wrath
Matt. 5:5, Blessed are the **g**
1 Cor. 4:21, with love and a spirit of **g-ness**
2 Cor. 10:1, **g-ness** of Christ
Gal. 5:23, **g-ness**, self-control
Eph. 4:2, with all humility and **g-ness**
1 Thess. 2:7, we proved to be **g** among you
1 Tim. 6:11, love, perseverance *and* **g-ness**
Titus 3:2, to be uncontentious, **g**
1 Pet. 3:4, a **g** and quiet spirit
Ps. 18:35; Matt. 21:5; 1 Tim. 3:3; Heb. 5:2;
1 Pet. 2:18
GESTURE—*motion*
John 13:24, Simon Peter therefore **g-d**
GET—*acquire, take* Gen. 34:4; Judg. 11:5; 14:2
Prov. 4:7, with all your acquiring, **g**
understanding
Matt. 16:23, **G** behind Me, Satan
Luke 18:12, tithes of all that I **g**
1 Kin. 17:10; Job 9:18; Is. 30:11; 56:12; Jer. 36:21
GIANT—*Rephaim* 1 Chr. 20:6, he ... was
descended from **g-s**
GIFT Gen. 25:6, Abraham gave **g-s** while he was
Ps. 68:18, hast received **g-s** among men
127:3, children are a **g** of the LORD
Prov. 18:16, A man's **g** makes room for him
21:14, A **g** in secret subdues anger
Matt. 2:11, presented to Him **g-s**
John 4:10, you knew the **g** of God
Acts 2:38, the **g** of the Holy Spirit
Rom. 6:23, **g** of God is eternal life
James 1:17, every perfect **g** is from above
GIRD—*bound* Ex. 29:5; Job 38:3; Ps. 45:3; John
13:5
John 21:18, when you were younger ... **g** ...
will **g** you
Eph. 6:14, **G-ED** YOUR LOINS WITH TRUTH
Rev. 1:13, **g-ed** across His breast with a golden
GIRDLE—*belt, waistband* 2 Kin. 1:8; Rev. 1:13;
15:6, golden **g**
Job 12:18, binds their loins with a **g**
GIRL—*maiden, woman* Gen. 24:55; 34:4; Joel 3:3;
Zech. 8:5; Matt. 14:11; 26:69; Mark 6:28; John
18:17; Acts 12:13; 16:16
GIVE Num. 6:26, on you, And **g** you peace
Ps. 21:4, He asked life ... Thou didst **g** it
Prov. 26:16, seven men ... **g** a ... answer
Is. 9:6, a son will be **g-n** to us
Matt. 6:11, **G** us this day our daily
10:8, freely **g**
15:36, **g-ing** thanks, He broke them
16:19, **g** you the keys
26:9, **g-n** to the poor
28:18, All authority has been **g-n** to Me
Luke 6:38, **G**, and it will be **g-n** to you
11:9, ask, and it shall be **g-n** to you
22:19, My body which is **g-n** for you
John 5:22, has **g-n** all judgment
6:11, and having **g-n** thanks
14:27, My peace I **g** to you
Acts 3:6, what I do have I **g** to you
12:23, he did not **g** God the glory
20:35, more blessed to **g** than to
Rom. 12:20, IF HE IS THIRSTY, **G** HIM A DRINK
14:6, he **g-s** thanks to God
1 Cor. 3:10, grace of God which was **g-n**
2 Cor. 12:7, was **g-n** me a thorn in
Eph. 4:27, do not **g** the devil an opportunity
5:20, always **g-ing** thanks

James 4:6, But He **g-s** a greater grace ... **G-s**
GRACE
1 John 5:11, has **g-n** us eternal life
Gen. 1:29; Ex. 20:12; Ps. 29:11; 68:11; 80:1;
145:15; Luke 1:77; 19:8; Rev. 19:8
GLAD Ps. 32:11, Be **g** in the LORD
Ps. 100:2, Serve the LORD with **g-ness**
122:1, I was **g** when they said to me
Prov. 10:1, wise son makes a father **g**
Matt. 5:12, Rejoice and be **g**
Luke 1:14, you will have joy and **g-ness**
6:23, Be **g** in that day, and leap
12:32, Father has chosen **g-ly** to give
Acts 2:46, **g-ness** and sincerity of heart
2 Cor. 11:19, bear with the foolish **g-ly**
Ex. 4:14; Num. 10:10; Deut. 28:47; 1 Chr. 16:31;
Ps. 16:9; Is. 16:10
GLASS—*crystal* Job 28:17; Rev. 4:6
GLEAMING—*glitter*
Nah. 3:3, Swords flashing, spears **g**
GLEAN Lev. 19:10; Ruth 2:8,15,17; Is. 17:6; Jer.
49:9
GLISTEN Ps. 104:15, make his face **g** with oil
GLOOM Deut. 5:22; Job 3:5
Matt. 6:16, **g-y** face as the hypocrites *do*
Heb. 12:18, darkness and **g** and whirlwind
GLORIFY—*honor* Ps. 86:12, will **g** Thy name
forever
Is. 66:5, Let the LORD be **g-ed**
Matt. 5:16, **g** your Father who is in heaven
John 12:28, Father **g** Thy name
13:31, is the Son of Man **g-ed**
16:14, He shall **g** Me
17:1, **g** Thy Son ... **g** Thee
Acts 13:48, **g-ing** the word of the Lord
1 Cor. 6:20, **g** God in your body
Heb. 5:5, Christ did not **g** Himself
GLORIOUS—*exalt, glory, honor*
Neh. 9:5, Thy **g** name
Ps. 87:3, **G** things are spoken of you
1 Tim. 1:11, the **g** gospel of the blessed God
GLORY—*honor, splendor* Ex. 16:7, see ... **g** of
the Lord
Ps. 24:7, the King of **g** may come in
Prov. 16:31, gray head is a crown of **g**
Is. 6:3, earth is full of His **g**
66:19, heard ... nor seen My **g** ... **g** among
the nations
Matt. 6:13, power, and the **g**
6:29, Solomon in all his **g** did not clothe
Luke 2:9, **g** of the Lord shone around
2:14, **G** to God in the highest
17:18, turned back to give **g** to God
John 5:44, you receive **g** from one another
9:24, Give **g** to God
Rom. 2:7, in doing good seek for **g** and honor
3:23, fall short of the **g** of God
2 Cor. 4:4, gospel of the **g** of Christ
Phil. 3:21, with the body of His **g**
Heb. 2:7, THOU HAST CROWNED HIM WITH **G** AND
HONOR
Jude 25, through Jesus Christ ... *be* **g**
Ex. 33:18; 1 Chr. 16:24; 29:11; Job 29:20;
Ps. 105:3; Is. 35:2; Jer. 13:16; Ezek. 10:4;
Hos. 4:7; John 8:50; James 1:9
GLUTTON Prov. 23:20; Matt. 11:19
GNASH—*grind* Ps. 35:16; 37:12; 112:10; Lam.
2:16; Matt. 8:12
GNAT Matt. 23:24, who strain out a **g**
GNAWED Rev. 16:10, they **g** their tongues
GO Ex. 14:15, Tell the sons of Israel to **g** forward
Ex. 23:23, My angel will **g** before you
33:14, My presence shall **g** with you
Ruth 1:16, where you **g**, I will **g**
Ps. 139:7, Where can I **g** from
Matt. 5:41, force you to **g** one mile, **g** ... two
6:6, when you pray, **G** INTO YOUR INNER ROOM
Luke 10:37, **G** and do the same
John 14:12, I **g** to the Father

GO (Continued)
Gen. 12:1; 32:26; Deut. 17:8; 23:23; Job 23:8;
Ps. 42:4; Prov. 22:6; Hos. 2:7; Mic. 2:11;
Matt. 21:29
GOAD Judg. 3:31; 1 Sam. 13:20,21
Eccles. 12:11, words of wise men are like **g-s**
GOAL Phil. 3:14, press on toward the **g**
1 Tim. 1:5, **g** of our instruction is love
GOAT Ex. 26:7; Lev. 3:12; Num. 15:27;
1 Sam. 19:13; Dan. 8:5; Matt. 25:32; Heb. 9:13
GODDESS 1 Kin. 11:5; Acts 19:27,37
GOD-FEARING Acts 10:22, Cornelius . . . a
righteous and **G** man
Acts 17:17, reasoning . . . with the Jews and **G**
Gentiles
GODLESS Job 8:13, hope of the **g** will perish
Job 15:34, company of the **g** is barren
Is. 9:17, every one is **g**
Acts 2:23, hands of **g** men and put Him to death
GODLINESS 1 Tim. 2:2, in all **g** and dignity
1 Tim. 3:16, great is the mystery of **g**
4:8, but **g** is profitable
6:6, **g** actually is a means . . . contentment
2 Tim. 3:5, holding to a form of **g**
2 Pet. 1:7, **g**, brotherly kindness
GODLY 1 Sam. 2:9, keeps the feet of His **g** ones
Ps. 12:1, for the **g** man ceaseth
37:28, not forsake His **g** ones
2 Cor. 1:12, in holiness and **g** sincerity
2 Pet. 2:9, rescue the **g** from temptation
GODS Ex. 20:3, have no other **g** before Me
Judg. 5:8, New **g** were chosen
Is. 37:12, **g** of those nations . . . deliver
Jer. 22:9, bowed down to other **g**
Dan. 2:47, your God is a God of **g**
Gal. 4:8, by nature are no **g**
GOING Ps. 121:8, guard your **g** out
Is. 20:2, **g** naked and barefoot
Matt. 25:8, our lamps are **g** out
Mark 1:16, He was **g** along by the sea of Galilee
10:32, road, **g** up to Jerusalem
John 14:5, not know where You are **g**
Gen. 15:12; Mic. 5:2; Matt. 26:46
GOLD Job 22:25, The Almighty will be your **g**
Ps. 19:10, more desirable than **g** . . . much fine **g**
Prov. 8:19, **g**, even pure **g**
Matt. 2:11, to Him gifts of **g**
Acts 3:6, Peter said . . . not possess silver and **g**
20:33, coveted no one's silver or **g**
1 Pet. 1:7, more precious than **g**
Rev. 3:18, buy from Me **g** refined
Gen. 2:12; 24:22; Ex. 3:22; Job 31:24; Ps. 72:15;
Prov. 16:16; 25:11; Lam. 4:1; Zech. 9:3;
Matt. 10:9; James 2:2; Rev. 21:15
GOLDEN Job 37:22, Out of the north comes **g**
splendor
Lev. 8:9; 1 Sam. 6:18; Dan. 3:5; Rev. 1:12
GOLDSMITH Neh. 3:31,32; Is. 40:19; 46:6
GONE Judg. 19:11, the day was almost **g**
Ps. 19:4, line has **g** out through
Prov. 7:19, **g** on a long journey
Hos. 4:18, Their liquor is **g**
Mark 5:30, power . . . had **g** forth
Rom. 13:12, The night is almost **g**
2 Pet. 2:15, they have **g** astray
Gen. 31:30; Song 2:11; Lam. 1:3
GOOD Gen. 1:4, that the light was **g**
Gen. 50:20, God meant it for **g**
2 Chr. 6:41, godly ones rejoice in what is **g**
Esth. 10:3, sought the **g** of his people
Ps. 106:1; 136:1, give thanks . . . for He is **g**
Prov. 22:1, A **g** name . . . more desired
Is. 1:17, Learn to do **g**
Jer. 33:11, For the LORD is **g**, For His
lovingkindness
Jon. 4:4, Do you have **g** reason
Matt. 3:10, does not bear **g** fruit
19:16, what **g** thing shall I do
Mark 9:50, Salt is **g**, but if the salt
Luke 1:19, to bring you this **g** news
6:27, do **g** to those who hate you
10:42; Mary has chosen the **g** part
John 10:14, I am the **g** shepherd

Acts 23:1, lived my life . . . **g** conscience
Rom. 2:7, perseverance in doing **g**
2:10, every man who does **g**
12:21, overcome evil with **g**
Gal. 6:10, do **g** to all men
Phil. 4:8, whatever is of **g** repute
1 Tim. 6:12, Fight the **g** fight of faith
1 Pet. 3:11, TURN . . . FROM EVIL AND DO **G**
Gen. 15:15; Lev. 27:10; Job 7:7; Prov. 25:25;
Is. 39:8; Jer. 24:3; Amos 5:14; Matt. 25:23;
Luke 18:19; Acts 6:3; Gal. 6:12;
2 Thess. 2:16; James 1:17
GOODNESS Ex. 33:19; 2 Sam. 2:6; Ps. 25:7
Ps. 23:6, Surely **g** and lovingkindness will
follow
31:19, How great is Thy **g**
Gal. 5:22, kindness, **g**, faithfulness
2 Thess. 1:11, fulfill every desire for **g**
GOODS—possessions Gen. 14:21; Ezek. 38:12;
Luke 12:19
GORGEOUS Luke 23:11, dressed Him in a **g** robe
GOSPEL Matt. 4:23, the **g** of the kingdom
Matt. 11:5, HAVE THE **G** PREACHED
Mark 16:15, preach the **g** to all
Luke 4:18, PREACH THE **G** TO THE POOR
Rom. 1:16, I am not ashamed of the **g**
2 Cor. 10:14, in the **g** of Christ
11:4, or a different **g**
Gal. 1:7, distort the **g** of Christ
Eph. 1:13, **g** of your salvation
6:15, **G** OF PEACE
Phil. 1:5, participation in the **g**
Col. 1:23, from the hope of the **g**
Rev. 14:6, an eternal **g**
GOSSIP Rom. 1:29, malice; they are **g-s**
2 Cor. 12:20, **g**, arrogance, disturbances
GOVERN—rule Gen. 1:16, to **g** the day . . . **g** the
night
GOVERNMENT—authority Is. 9:6, **g** will rest on
His
GOVERNOR—commander
Matt. 27:11; Acts 7:10
GRACE—favor Ps. 45:2; 2 Thess. 2:16
Luke 2:40, the **g** of God was upon Him
John 1:16, received, and **g** upon **g**
Rom. 1:5, through whom we have received **g**
5:2, this **g** in which we stand
16:20, The **g** of our Lord Jesus be with you
2 Cor. 9:8, make all **g** abound
12:9, My **g** is sufficient
1 Thess. 1:1, **G** to you and peace
Philem. 25, **g** of the Lord Jesus Christ
Heb. 4:16, the throne of **g** . . . may find **g**
James 4:6, GIVES **G** TO THE HUMBLE
2 Pet. 3:18, grow in the **g**
GRACIOUS—kind Neh. 9:31, art a **g** and
compassionate God
Ps. 6:2, Be **g** to me, O LORD
111:4, LORD is **g** and compassionate
Luke 4:22, wondering at the **g** words
Gen. 43:29; Ex. 33:19; Ps. 77:9; 112:4; 119:29;
Prov. 19:17, 26:25; Amos 5:15
GRAFT Rom. 11:23, God is able to **g** them in
Rom. 11:24, **g-ed** contrary to nature . . .
branches be **g-ed**
GRAIN—kernel John 12:24, unless a **g** of wheat
falls
1 Cor. 15:37, a bare **g**, perhaps of wheat
Gen. 41:5; Lev. 2:14; 2 Sam. 17:19; 2 Kin. 4:42;
Jer. 23:28; Amos 9:9; Matt. 12:1; Mark 4:28
GRANDCHILDREN Prov. 17:6, **G** . . . crown of
old men
GRANDMOTHER 2 Tim. 1:5, in your **g** Lois
GRANT—give, provide
Job 10:12, Thou hast **g-ed** me life
Ps. 85:7, **g** us Thy salvation
Prov. 10:24, of the righteous will be **g-ed**
Mark 10:37, **G** that we may sit
Rev. 3:21, He who overcomes, I will **g** . . . to sit
Is. 63:7; Luke 22:29

GRAPE Num. 6:3; Deut. 32:14; Jer. 49:9;
  Matt. 7:16; Luke 6:44
GRASS—*vegetation*
  Ps. 103:15, man, his days are like g
  Is. 40:6, All flesh is g
    40:7, the g withers, the flower
  Matt. 6:30, if God so arrays the g of the field
  1 Pet. 1:24, ALL FLESH IS LIKE G
  Num. 22:4; 2 Sam. 23:4; 2 Kin. 19:26; Ps. 102:11;
    Prov. 27:25; Is. 5:24; 15:6; 37:27; Dan. 5:21
GRASSHOPPER—*caterpillar*
  Num. 13:33, we became like g-s
  Lev. 11:22; 2 Chr. 6:28; Is. 40:22
GRATITUDE 1 Tim. 4:4, is received with g
GRAVE—*tomb* Gen. 35:20; 2 Sam. 3:32; Ps. 5:9;
  Ezek. 37:12; Nah. 1:14
GRAY Gen. 42:38, bring my g hair down ... in
  sorrow
  1 Sam. 12:2, I am old and g
  Deut. 32:25; Job 15:10; Ps. 71:18; Hos. 7:9
GRAZE—*feed* Is. 5:17; 11:7; 27:10; 65:25
GREAT—*excellent, big* Gen. 12:2; 15:1; Ex. 18:11;
  32:30
  Gen. 1:16, two g lights; the **g-er** light
  Ps. 48:1, G is the LORD
  Mal. 4:5, the g and terrible day
  Matt. 2:10, rejoiced exceedingly, with g joy
    4:16, DARKNESS SAW A G LIGHT
    5:12, your reward in heaven is g
    7:27, g was its fall
    11:11, he who is least ... is **g-er** than he
  Luke 2:10, good news of a g joy
    6:23, your reward is g in heaven
  John 5:20, **g-er** works than these
    15:13, G-er love has no one
  1 Cor. 13:13, **g-est** of these is love
  1 Tim. 6:6, godliness ... a means of g gain
  Jude 24, stand in the presence ... g joy
  Rev. 8:10, a g star fell from heaven
    15:3, G AND MARVELOUS ARE THY WORKS
  Deut. 1:17; 2 Sam. 5:10; 19:32; 1 Chr. 16:25;
    Neh. 9:27; Job 31:25; Ps. 57:10; Prov. 15:16;
    Jer. 9:19; Dan. 4:22; Zeph. 1:14;
    Matt. 15:28; Luke 5:6; Acts 11:5; 2 Cor. 3:12
GREATLY—*utterly*
  Gen. 20:8, men were g frightened
  John 3:29, rejoices g because of the
  Phil. 4:10, I rejoiced in the Lord g
  Gen. 3:16; Num. 14:39; 1 Sam. 28:5; Ps. 89:7;
    Zech. 9:9; Mark 12:27
GREATNESS—*magnitude* Ps. 51:1, g of Thy
  compassion
  Luke 9:43, the g of God
  2 Cor. 4:7, the surpassing g of the power
  Eph. 1:19, surpassing g of His power toward us
  1 Chr. 29:11; Neh. 13:22; Ps. 150:2; Is. 63:1
GREED Is. 56:11, the dogs are **g-y**
  Luke 12:15, Beware ... every form of g
  1 Thess. 2:5, a pretext for g
GREEK Acts 16:1; 21:37; Rom. 2:9; 1 Cor. 12:13;
  Gal. 3:28; Rev. 9:11
GREEN—*luxuriant*
  Ps. 23:2, lie down in g pastures
  Gen. 1:30; Ps. 92:14; Jer. 17:2; Ezek. 17:24;
    Luke 23:31
GREET Matt. 10:12, house, give it your **g-ing**
  1 Cor. 16:20, All the brethren g you. G one
    another
  1 Pet. 5:14, G one another with a kiss
  Matt. 23:7; 2 Tim. 4:21
GREW Gen. 21:8; 1 Sam. 2:21
  Ex. 16:21, when the sun g hot
  Mark 4:7, thorns g up and choked it
GRIEF—*sorrow* Ps. 77:10, It is my g
  Prov. 17:25, A foolish son is a g to his
  Is. 53:4, our **g-s** He Himself bore
  Heb. 13:17, with joy and not with g
GRIEVE Is. 63:10, And **g-d** His Holy Spirit
  Matt. 26:38, My soul is deeply **g-d**
  Mark 3:5, **g-d** at their hardness of heart
  John 21:17, Peter was **g-d** because He

Eph. 4:30, do not g the Holy Spirit of God
  Gen. 6:6; 45:5; Neh. 8:10; Ps. 78:40; Amos 6:6;
    Nah. 3:7
GRIND Is. 3:15, **g-ing** the face of the poor
  Matt. 24:41, women ... **g-ing** at the mill
  Judg. 16:21; Eccles. 12:3,4; Is. 47:2; Mark 9:18
GROAN Ex. 2:24, God heard their **g-ing**
  Acts 7:34, HAVE HEARD THEIR G-S
  Rom. 8:22, whole creation **g-s** and suffers
    8:26, **g-ings** too deep for words
  2 Cor. 5:2, in this *house* we g
  Job 24:12; Is. 42:14; Ezek. 30:24; Joel 1:18
GROPE Deut. 28:29; Job 12:25; Is. 59:10; Acts
  17:27
GROUND—*earth, land, soil*
  Gen. 3:17, Cursed is the g
    4:2, a tiller of the g
  Matt. 25:25, hid your talent in the g
  Luke 19:44, will level you to the g
  John 8:6, His finger wrote on the g
    9:6, He spat on the g
  Acts 7:33, ARE STANDING IS HOLY G
    9:8, Saul got up from the g
  Eph. 3:17, rooted and **g-ed** in love
  Gen. 2:5,7,9; 8:21; Num. 16:30; Deut. 28:56;
    Josh. 3:17; 2 Sam. 14:22; Job 5:6; Ps. 89:44;
    Is. 3:26; 29:4; Jer. 4:3; 14:4; Lam. 2:21;
    Hos. 10:12; Amos 3:5; 9:9; Matt. 25:18;
    Mark 4:31; Acts 9:4; 26:14; Heb. 6:7
GROUP Mark 6:39, recline by **g-s** ... grass
GROVE Judg. 15:5, with the vineyards and **g-s**
GROW 1 Sam. 3:2, eyesight had begun to g dim
  Matt. 6:28, lilies of the field g
    24:12, people's love will g cold
  Luke 2:40, And the Child continued to g
  Acts 12:24, word of the Lord continued to g
    19:20, word of the Lord was **g-ing** mightily
  1 Cor. 3:6, but God was causing the **g-th**
  2 Cor. 10:15, as your faith **g-s**
  Eph. 4:15, we are to g up ... into Him
  1 Pet. 2:2, you may g in respect
  2 Pet. 3:18, g in the grace and knowledge
  Gen. 26:13; 48:16; Judg. 16:22; 2 Sam. 10:5;
    2 Kin. 19:29; Ps. 147:8
GROWL Is. 59:11, All of us g like bears
GROWN Ezek. 7:11, Violence has g into a rod
  Ex. 2:11; Lev. 13:37; Deut. 32:15; 2 Kin. 4:18;
    Prov. 24:31
GRUDGE Lev. 19:18; 2 Cor. 9:7
GRUMBLE Phil. 2:14, Do all things without **g-ing**
  Ex. 17:3; Luke 15:2; John 6:43
GUARANTOR Job 17:3, Who ... will be my g
GUARD—*keep, watch* Ps. 39:1, I will g my ways
  Mark 14:44, lead Him away under g
  Phil. 4:7, g your hearts and minds
  1 Tim. 6:20, g what has been entrusted to you
  1 John 5:21, children, g yourselves from idols
  Ex. 23:13; 1 Chr. 11:25; Job 7:12; Prov. 2:11;
    Ezek. 38:7; Acts 5:23; 28:16
GUARDIAN—*overseer*
  1 Pet. 2:25, Shepherd and G ... souls
GUEST 1 Kin. 1:41; Prov. 9:18; Matt. 22:10
GUIDANCE—*counsel*
  Prov. 11:14, Where there is no g
    20:18, war by wise g
GUIDE—*direct, lead* Ps. 48:14, He will g us until
  death
  Prov. 12:26, righteous is a g to his neighbor
  Is. 58:11, And the LORD will ... g you
  Matt. 15:14, if a blind man **g-s** a blind man
  Luke 1:79, g our feet ... way of peace
  Rom. 2:19, are a g to the blind
  Deut. 32:12; Job 38:32; Matt. 23:16; Acts 8:31
GUILE—*deceit* John 1:47, in whom is no g
  1 Pet. 2:1, all malice and all g
    3:10, LIPS FROM SPEAKING G
GUILT Luke 23:22, found in Him no g *demanding*
  death
  1 Cor. 11:27, **g-y** of the body and the blood
  James 2:10, one *point*, he has become **g-y** of all

GUILT (Continued)
Gen. 42:21; Lev. 6:4; Num. 5:31; 35:31;
Deut. 25:2; 2 Sam. 3:8; 14:13; Ezra 9:6;
Jer. 51:5; Ezek. 22:4; Hos. 10:2; Hab. 1:11;
Luke 23:4; John 18:38; 19:4,6
GUSH—*flow* Ps. 78:20; Is. 48:21; Acts 1:18

H

HABITATION—*abode, camp* Is. 32:18; 33:20;
Acts 17:26
Ps. 26:8, I love the h of Thy house
71:3, Be Thou to me a rock of h
132:13, He has desired it for His **h**
Is. 63:15, Thy holy and glorious **h**
HADES Matt. 16:18; Luke 16:23; Acts 2:31; Rev.
1:18
HAIL Matt. 26:49, **H**, Rabbi
Matt. 27:29, **H**, King of the Jews
Rev. 16:21, **h-stones** ... came down from
heaven upon men
Ex. 9:23; Job 38:22; Ps. 148:8; Is. 28:17; 32:19;
Mark 15:18; Luke 1:28; John 19:3
HAIR 1 Kin. 1:52, not one of his **h-s** will fall
Matt. 3:4, garment of camel's **h**
5:36, cannot make one **h** white
10:30; Luke 12:7, **h-s** of your head ...
numbered
Luke 7:38, wiping them with the **h** of her head
John 11:2, Mary ... wiped His feet with her **h**
1 Cor. 11:14, if a man has long **h**
1 Tim. 2:9, not with braided **h**
Rev. 1:14, His **h** were white like white wool
Gen. 42:38; 44:29; Judg. 20:16; Neh. 13:25;
Job 4:15; Mark 1:6; 1 Pet. 3:3
HAIRY—*rough* Zech. 13:4, **h** robe in order to
deceive
Gen. 25:25; 27:11; 2 Kin. 1:8; Ps. 68:21
HALLELUJAH Rev. 19:1,3,4,6, saying **h**
HALLOWED—*consecrated, sanctified*
Matt. 6:9; Luke 11:2, **H** be Thy name
HAMMER—*beat* Is. 2:4, **h** their swords into
plowshares
Judg. 4:21; 1 Kin. 6:7; Is. 41:7; Jer. 23:29; Mic.
4:3
HAND—*power* Ps. 16:11, In Thy right **h** there are
pleasures
Ps. 24:4, has clean **h-s** and a pure heart
31:5; Luke 23:46, Into Thy **h** I commit my
spirit
90:17, confirm the work of our **h-s**
137:5, my right **h** forget her *skill*
Eccles. 9:10, Whatever your **h** finds to do
Is. 28:4, it is in his **h**
40:12, in the hollow of His **h**
Jer. 18:6, like the clay in the potter's **h**
Lam. 2:4, His right **h** like an adversary
Matt. 3:2; 4:17; 10:7, kingdom ... is at **h**
4:6, ON THEIR **H-S** THEY WILL BEAR
11:27, **h-ed** over to Me by My Father
26:18, My time is at **h**
Mark 14:62, SITTING AT THE RIGHT **H** OF POWER
16:19, SAT DOWN AT THE RIGHT **H** OF GOD
John 10:28, snatch them out of My **h**
2 Cor. 5:1, a house not made with **h-s**
Heb. 10:31, fall into the **h-s** of the living God
James 4:8, Cleanse your **h-s**
1 Pet. 4:7, end of all things is at **h**
1 John 1:1, our **h-s** handled
Gen. 3:22; 16:12; 24:2; 47:29; Ex. 21:24; 33:22;
Deut. 8:17; 19:21; 33:3; 1 Sam. 5:11; 12:3;
26:18; 2 Sam. 24:14; 1 Kin. 18:44;
2 Kin. 5:11; 1 Chr. 21:13; 29:14; Ezra 7:9;
Neh. 2:8,18; Job 12:10; 19:21; 40:14;
Ps. 68:31; 80:17; 139:10; Prov. 3:16; 10:4;
12:24; 19:24; 26:15; Eccles. 2:24; Is. 5:25;
9:12; 10:4; 14:27; 53:10; 56:2; Ezek. 7:17;
21:7; Dan. 4:35; Mic. 7:3; Hab. 2:9;
Zeph. 3:16; Matt. 3:12; 6:3; 18:8; Mark 9:43;
14:41; Luke 3:17; 9:44; John 20:27;
1 Cor. 12:15; Col. 2:11; 1 Thess. 4:11;
1 Tim. 2:8

HANDBREADTH Ex. 25:25; 1 Kin. 7:26;
2 Chr. 4:5; Ezek. 40:5
Ps. 39:5, Thou hast made my days *as* **h-s**
HANDFUL—*hand* Lev. 2:2; 5:12; 1 Kin. 20:10
1 Kin. 17:12, only a **h** of flour in the bowl
HANDKERCHIEF Acts 19:12, **h-s** ... carried
from his body
HANDLE—*touch* Song 5:5; Jer. 2:8; Ezek. 27:29
2 Tim. 2:15, **h-ing** accurately the word of truth
1 John 1:1, our hands **h-d**, concerning the Word
of Life
HANDMAID—*servant, slave* Ps. 86:16; 116:16
HANDSOME—*becoming* 1 Sam. 16:18, and a **h**
man
HANG Deut. 21:23, who is **h-ed** is accursed of
God
Job 26:7, He ... **h-s** the earth on nothing
Matt. 27:5, Judas went away and **h-ed** himself
Gal. 3:13, CURSED IS EVERY ONE WHO **H-S**
HAPPEN—*befall* Lev. 10:19; Deut. 22:6; Judg.
6:13; Dan. 10:14
HAPPINESS—*joy* Deut. 24:5, shall give **h** to his
wife
Eccles. 9:7, eat your bread in **h**
HAPPY—*bless* Job 5:17, **h** is the man whom God
reproves
Prov. 14:21, **h** is he who is gracious to the poor
Rom. 14:22, **H** is he who does not condemn
himself
HARASS Deut. 2:9, Do not **h** Moab
HARBOR—*haven* Acts 27:12, **h** was not suitable
HARD—*difficult, firm* Ex. 1:14; Num. 11:11;
Deut. 1:17
Matt. 19:23, is **h** for a rich man to enter ...
heaven
25:24, I knew you to be a **h** man
Mark 10:24, **h** it is to enter the Kingdom of God
Acts 26:14, **h** for you to kick against the goads
2 Tim. 2:3, Suffer **h-ship** ... as a good soldier
Deut. 15:18; 2 Kin. 2:10; Job 38:30; 41:24;
Prov. 13:15; 18:19; Is. 8:21; Mark 10:23;
Luke 18:24
HARDEN—*hardness* Job 38:38; Prov. 29:1
John 12:40, HE **H-ED** THEIR HEART
Rom. 9:18, He **h-s** whom He desires
Heb. 3:13, **h-ed** by deceitfulness of sin
3:15; 4:7, DO NOT **H** YOUR HEARTS
HARDNESS—*stubborn* Matt. 19:8; Mark 10:5, **h**
of heart
Mark 3:5, grieved at their **h** of heart
16:14, He reproached ... **h** of heart
HARLOT Matt. 21:31, **h-s** will get into the
kingdom
Luke 15:30, devoured your wealth with **h-s**
Josh. 6:17; Prov. 7:10; 29:3; Is. 1:21; 23:17;
Jer. 2:20; Ezek. 16:15; Joel 3:3; Rev. 17:5
HARM—*evil, hurt* Lev. 19:27; Judg. 15:3;
2 Kin. 4:41
1 Chr. 16:22; Ps. 105:15, do my prophets no **h**
Prov. 12:21, No **h** befalls the righteous
1 Pet. 3:13, who is there to **h** you
Prov. 3:30; Jer. 25:6; Acts 16:28; 28:5; Rev. 6:6
HARMONY 2 Cor. 6:15, what **h** has Christ with
HARNESS—*armor* Jer. 46:4, **H** the horses
HARP—*lyre, instrument* 1 Sam. 16:16; Ps. 33:2;
49:4; 57:8
Job 30:31, my **h** is turned to mourning
Ps. 137:2, Upon the willows ... hung our **h-s**
Is. 5:12; 24:8; Amos 6:5; 1 Cor. 14:7; Rev. 5:8;
14:2
HARROW—*instrument* Job 39:10, will he **h** the
valleys
HARRY Job 18:11, terrors ... **h** him at every step
HARSH 1 Sam. 20:10, father answers you **h-ly**
Gen. 16:6; 1 Sam. 25:3; Prov. 15:1
HARVEST—*reap, ripe*
Gen. 8:22, Seedtime and **h** ... cease
Job 4:8, who sow trouble **h** it
Jer. 8:20, **h** is past, summer is ended
Joel 3:13, the **h** is ripe

Matt. 9:37, **h** is plentiful
9:38; Luke 10:2, the Lord of the **h**
13:30, both to grow together until the **h**
13:39, **h** is the end of the age
Mark 4:29, puts in the sickle . . . **h** has come
John 4:35, fields, that they are white for **h**
Rev. 14:15, the **h** of the earth is ripe
Ex. 22:29; 23:16; 34:22; Lev. 19:9; Deut. 24:19;
1 Sam. 12:17; Job 5:5; Prov. 6:8; 10:5; 25:13;
26:1; Is. 9:3; 16:9; 18:4; Jer. 5:17; 51:33
HASTE—*hurry, urgent*
Prov. 7:23, As a bird **h-ns** . . . snare
Prov. 28:22, evil eye **h-ns** after wealth
2 Pet. 3:12, **h-ning** the coming of the day of God
Ex. 12:11; Ps. 22:19; Eccles. 1:5; Is. 52:12;
Mark 6:25
HASTILY—*hurried* Prov. 25:8, Do not go out **h** to
argue
1 Tim. 5:22, lay hands upon any one *too* **h**
HASTY—*impetuous* Prov. 29:20, a man who is **h**
Eccles. 5:2, Do not be **h** in word
HATCH Jer. 17:11, As a partridge that **h-es** eggs
HATCHET—*axe, war-club* Ps. 74:6, smash with
h and hammers
HATE Ps. 81:15, Those who **h** the LORD
Ps. 97:10, **H** evil, you who love the LORD
Prov. 6:16, six things which the LORD **h-s**
8:13, fear of the LORD is to **h** evil
13:24, who spares his rod **h-s** his son
15:10, He who **h-s** reproof will die
Eccles. 3:8, A time to love, and a time to **h**
Matt. 6:24, he will **h** the one and love the other
10:22, Mark 13:13; Luke 21:17, will be **h-d**
Luke 6:22, Blessed are you when men **h** you
6:27, do good to those who **h** you
14:26, not **h** his own father and mother
John 3:20, does evil **h-s** the light
12:25, he who **h-s** his life
15:18; 1 John 3:13, If the world **h-s** you
15:23, He who **h-s** Me **h-s** My Father also
Rom. 1:30, slanderers, **h-rs** of God
7:15, I am doing the very thing I **h**
Eph. 5:29, no one ever **h-d** his own flesh
Titus 3:3, hateful, **h-ing** one another
1 John 2:9; 3:15; 4:20, **h-s** his brother
Gen. 24:60; Lev. 19:17; 26:17; 1 Kin. 22:8;
2 Chr. 18:7; 19:2; Ps. 34:21; 36:2; 139:21;
Prov. 1:22; Is. 1:14; 61:8; Ezek. 23:29;
Amos 5:15; Mic. 3:2; Zech. 8:17; Mal. 1:3;
John 7:7; Rom. 9:13
HAUGHTY—*proud, lofty, high*
Ps. 131:1, nor my eyes **h**
Prov. 16:18, **h** spirit before stumbling
Rom. 12:16, do not be **h** in mind
2 Sam. 22:28; Prov. 6:17; 21:24; Zeph. 3:11
HAUNT—*habitation* Is. 34:13, also be a **h** of
jackals
HAVEN—*harbor* Gen. 49:13; Ps. 107:30
HAWK Lev. 11:16; Deut. 14:15; Job 39:26
HEAD—*chief* 2 Kin. 6:5, axe **h** fell into the water
Ps. 24:7, Lift up your **h-s**, O gates
Prov. 25:22, burning coals on his **h**
Eccles. 2:14, wise man's eyes are in his **h**
Matt. 14:8, Give me . . . **h** of John the Baptist
27:39, WAGGING THEIR **H-S**
Luke 21:18, not a hair of your **h** will perish
21:28, straighten up and lift up your **h-s**
John 13:9, also my hands and my **h**
1 Cor. 11:3, Christ is the **h** of every man
Eph. 1:22, Him as **h** over all things
5:23, Christ also is the **h** of the church
Col. 2:19, not holding fast to the **H**
Rev. 1:14, His **h** and His hair were white
Gen. 3:15; 1 Sam. 1:11; 9:22; 2 Kin. 4:19;
Ps. 66:12; Is. 3:16; 59:17; Jer. 18:16;
Dan. 2:38; 7:6; Matt. 5:36; 6:17; Acts 21:24
HEAL 2 Chr. 7:14, and will **h** their land
Ps. 147:3, He **h-s** the broken-hearted
Prov. 3:8, will be **h-ing** to your body
Is. 53:5, by His scourging we are **h-ed**
Jer. 3:22, I will **h** your faithlessness
Hos. 14:4, I will **h** their apostasy

Matt. 10:8, **H** *the* sick, raise *the* dead
Mark 3:2, He would **h** him on the Sabbath
Luke 4:23, Physician, **h** yourself
9:2, kingdom of God, and to perform **h-ing**
9:11, those who had need of **h-ing**
Acts 9:34, Jesus Christ **h-s** you
1 Cor. 12:9, gifts of **h-ing** by the one Spirit
James 5:16, pray . . . that you may be **h-ed**
Rev. 22:2, the **h-ing** of the nations
Ex. 15:26; Num. 12:13; Deut. 32:39; Job 5:18;
Ps. 6:2; Prov. 13:17; Jer. 17:14; 30:13;
Matt. 4:23
HEALTH Jer. 30:17, will restore you to **h**
3 John 2, prosper and be in good **h**
HEAP—*store* Prov. 25:22, **h** burning coals on his
head
Is. 25:2, made a city into a **h**
Gen. 31:46; Ex. 15:8; Deut. 32:23; Josh. 3:13;
Ps. 33:7; Ezek. 24:10; Hab. 1:10
HEAR Job 27:9, Will God **h** his cry
Ps. 4:1, O God . . . **h** my prayer
135:17, have ears, but they do not **h**
Is. 28:14, **h** the word of the LORD
Ezek. 37:4, dry bones, **h** the word of the LORD
Matt. 11:15, ears to **h**, let him **h**
13:13, while **h-ing** they do not **h**
15:10, **H** and understand
17:5, I am well pleased; **h** Him
Mark 7:37, He makes even the deaf to **h**
John 5:24, he who **h-s** My word
10:3, the sheep **h** his voice
12:47, if any one **h-s** My sayings
Acts 17:32, We shall **h** you again
James 1:19, let every one be quick to **h**
Rev. 3:20, if any one **h-s** My voice
Lev. 5:1; Deut. 6:4; 1 Sam. 15:14; 1 Kin. 8:30;
Job 15:8; 26:14; Ps. 38:13; 65:2; Is. 1:2;
Matt. 10:27; Rom. 11:8
HEARD Matt. 2:18, A VOICE WAS **H** IN RAMAH
Acts 4:4, who had **h** the message believed
19:10, lived in Asia **h** the word
1 Cor. 2:9, EYE HAS NOT SEEN AND EAR HAS
NOT **H**
2 Cor. 12:4, **h** inexpressible words
Phil. 4:9, learned and received and **h**
Rev. 10:4, I **h** a voice from heaven
Gen. 3:10; Ps. 10:17; Eccles. 12:13; Song 2:12;
Is. 65:19; Jer. 31:15; Ezek. 1:24; Matt. 6:7;
Luke 1:13
HEARING—*ears* Prov. 20:12, The **h** ear
Prov. 23:9, Do not speak in the **h** of a fool
Matt. 24:6, you will be **h** of wars
Rom. 10:17, So faith *comes* from **h**
Heb. 5:11, since you have become dull of **h**
HEART—*desire, mind*
Gen. 8:21, intent of man's **h** is evil
1 Sam. 16:7, LORD looks at the **h**
1 Kin. 3:9, an understanding **h**
15:3, his **h** was not wholly devoted
1 Chr. 28:9, serve Him with a whole **h**
Ps. 19:14, the meditation of my **h**
44:21, He knows the secrets of the **h**
51:10, Create in me a clean **h**
51:17, broken and contrite **h**
119:11, Thy word I have treasured in my **h**
Prov. 4:23, Watch . . . **h** with all diligence
17:22, joyful **h** is good medicine
25:20, sings songs to a troubled **h**
Jer. 17:9, **h** is more deceitful than all else
17:10, I, the LORD search the **h**
Matt. 5:8, Blessed are the pure in **h**
5:28, committed adultery . . . in his **h**
6:21, treasure is, there will your **h** be
11:29, I am gentle and humble in **h**
15:8, THEIR **H** IS FAR AWAY FROM ME
19:8, Because of your hardness of **h**
Mark 12:30, LOVE THE LORD . . . YOUR **H**
Luke 2:19, pondering them in her **h**
2:51, treasured all *these* things in her **h**
24:25, slow of **h** to believe
John 14:1, Let not your **h** be troubled

HEART *(Continued)*
Acts 2:37, they were pierced to the **h**
Rom. 8:27, He who searches the **h-s** knows
  10:10, for with the **h** man believes
Eph. 3:17, Christ may dwell in your **h-s**
  5:19, making melody with your **h**
  6:5, in the sincerity of your **h**
Phil. 4:7, guard your **h-s** and your minds
Col. 3:22, but with sincerity of **h**
2 Thess. 3:5, Lord direct your **h-s** into
Heb. 4:12, thoughts and intentions of the **h**
  10:22, draw near with a sincere **h**
James 1:26, deceives his *own* **h**
2 Pet. 1:19, morning star arises in your **h-s**
Ex. 4:21; 31:6; Num. 15:39; Deut. 28:65;
  Josh. 5:1; Judg. 5:16; 1 Sam. 10:9; 13:14;
  2 Sam. 6:16; 2 Chr. 15:15; Job 23:16; 29:13;
  41:24; Ps. 4:7; 9:1; 12:2; 15:2; 17:3; 22:14;
  27:3; 38:10; 111:1; Prov. 12:20; 16:5; 23:7,26;
  Eccles. 8:5; 11:9; Song 8:6; Is. 35:4; 47:10;
  Jer. 11:20; 24:7; Ezek. 11:19; 18:31; 21:7;
  44:7,9; Joel 2:13; Mal. 4:6; Matt. 12:34;
  2 Cor. 3:3; 6:11; 9:7
HEAT—*outburst* Gen. 8:22; 18:1; Job 24:19; Is.
  25:4
2 Pet. 3:10, be destroyed with intense **h**
Rev. 16:9, men were scorched with fierce **h**
Jer. 2:24; Hos. 7:4; Matt. 20:12
HEAVEN—*sky* Gen. 1:1, God created the **h-s**
Gen. 1:8, God called the expanse **h**
  28:17, this is the gate of **h**
Ps. 19:1, **h-s** are telling . . . glory of God
  103:11, high as the **h-s** are above the earth
Is. 65:17, new **h-s** and a new earth
Mal. 3:10, open for you the windows of **h**
Matt. 3:2, Repent . . . kingdom of **h** is
  3:17, behold, a voice out of the **h-s**
  5:3, Blessed . . . theirs is the kingdom of **h**
  5:12, your reward in **h** is great
  6:9, Our Father who art in **h**
  6:10, On earth as it is in **h**
  6:14, your **h-ly** Father will also forgive
  10:7, kingdom of **h** is at hand
  16:19, keys of the kingdom of **h**
Mark 13:31, **H** and earth will pass away
Luke 10:20, your names are recorded in **h**
  15:18, have sinned against **h**
John 3:13, from **h**, *even* the Son of Man
1 Cor. 15:40, are also **h-ly** bodies
  15:47, second man is from **h**
2 Cor. 5:1, eternal in the **h-s**
  12:2, was caught up to the third **h**
Gal. 1:8, or an angel from **h**, should preach
Eph. 6:9, their Master and yours is in **h**
Phil. 3:20, our citizenship is in **h**
Heb. 11:12, AS THE STARS OF **H**
  12:23, who are enrolled in **h**
James 5:12, do not swear, either by **h**
Rev. 4:1, a door *standing* open in **h**
  21:1, I saw a new **h**
Ex. 20:22; Deut. 33:13; 1 Sam. 2:10; 1 Kin. 8:27;
  2 Kin. 7:2; Job 11:8; 22:12,14; Eccles. 5:2;
  Is. 14:12; Jer. 7:18; 23:24; Ezek. 32:8;
  John 3:12; 1 Cor. 15:48
HEAVY Matt. 11:28, who are weary and **h** laden
Matt. 26:43, their eyes were **h**
Ex. 17:12; 2 Chr. 10:10,11; Ps. 38:4; Prov. 27:3;
  Zech. 12:3; Matt. 23:4
HEDGE Luke 14:23, highways and along the **h-s**
Job 1:10; Prov. 15:19; Mic. 7:4
HEED Ps. 17:1; 55:2; Jer. 2:31
HEEL Gen. 3:15; 25:26; 49:17; Ps. 41:9
HEIGHT Rom. 8:39, nor **h**, nor depth
Job 22:12; Prov. 25:3; Rev. 21:16
HEIR Rom. 8:17, **h-s** also, **h-s** of God
Gal. 4:7, an **h** through God
James 2:5, **h-s** of the kingdom
Gen. 15:3; Jer. 49:1; Matt. 21:38
HELD Ezek. 31:15, and **h** back its rivers
HELL Mark 9:47, to be cast into **h**
James 3:6, tongue . . . is set on fire by **h**
2 Pet. 2:4, angels . . . cast them into **h**
Matt. 5:22; 10:28; 23:15

HELMET 1 Sam. 17:5, had a bronze **h** on his head
Is. 59:17, **h** of salvation on His head
Eph. 6:17, take the **h** of salvation
HELP 1 Sam. 7:12, the LORD has **h-ed** us
Ps. 33:20, He is our **h** and our shield
  42:11, The **h** of my countenance
  46:1, very present **h** in trouble
  121:1, whence shall my **h** come
Matt. 15:25, Lord, **h** me
Mark 9:24, **h** me *in* my unbelief
2 Cor. 1:11, **h-ing** us through your prayers
Heb. 4:16, grace to **h** in time of need
Job 5:16; 6:13; Is. 41:6,13; Mark 7:11
HELPER—*comforter*
Gen. 2:18, I will make him a **h**
Ps. 10:14, **h** of the orphan
  30:10, O LORD, be Thou my **h**
  54:4, Behold, God is my **h**
John 14:16, will give you another **H**
Heb. 13:6, THE LORD IS MY **H**
HEMORRHAGE—*blood* Matt. 9:20; Mark 5:25;
  Luke 8:43
HEMORRHOIDS Deut. 28:27; 1 Sam. 5:6; 6:4
HERB Luke 11:42, tithe . . . every garden **h**
2 Kin. 4:39; 19:26; Ps. 37:2; Prov. 27:25; Is. 37:27
HERD—*cattle* Gen. 13:5; Jon. 3:7; Matt. 8:30
HERITAGE—*gift, possession* Ps. 16:6, my **h** is
  beautiful
Job 20:29; Ps. 135:12; 136:21,22; Is. 49:8
HESITATE 1 Kin. 18:21, How long *will* you **h**
HID—*cover, secret* Gen. 3:8, man and his wife **h**
  themselves
Matt. 10:26, and **h-en** that will not be known
  13:44, treasure **h-en** in the field
  25:25, **h** your talent in the ground
Mark 4:22, For nothing is **h-en**
1 Cor. 2:7, **h-en** wisdom, which God
  predestined
Col. 3:3, your life is **h-en** with Christ
Deut. 33:19; Josh. 2:4; 1 Sam. 20:24;
  2 Sam. 17:9; Job 40:13; Ps. 19:6,12; 69:5;
  Is. 45:3; Dan. 2:22; Luke 8:17; John 8:59;
  Heb. 11:23
HIDE—*conceal, cover* Gen. 18:17; Job 14:13;
  20:12; Ps. 27:5,9; Is. 2:10; Jer. 38:14
HIGH—*rank* Ps. 103:11, **h** as the heavens are
  above . . . earth
Matt. 4:8, devil took Him to a very **h** mountain
Mark 5:7, Jesus, Son of the Most **H** God
  11:10, HOSANNA in the **h-est**
Luke 2:14, Glory to God in the **h-est**
John 19:31, for that Sabbath was a **h** *day*
Heb. 3:1, Jesus, the Apostle and **H** Priest
Gen. 29:7; Job 11:8; 22:12; Ps. 49:2; 91:14;
  Prov. 24:7; Is. 32:15; Luke 1:78
HIGHWAY—*way*
Num. 20:17, go along the king's **h**
Is. 35:8, **h** . . . called the **h** of holiness
  40:3, a **h** for our God
  59:7, Devastation and . . . in their **h-s**
Deut. 2:27; Prov. 15:19; Is. 11:16; 19:23; 49:11;
  62:10; Matt. 22:9; Luke 14:23
HILL—*mountains*
Ps. 24:3, Who may ascend into the **h**
  50:10, cattle on a thousand **h-s**
Matt. 5:14, city set on a **h** cannot be hidden
Luke 4:29, led Him to the brow of the **h**
Gen. 49:26; Deut. 11:11; Ps. 15:1; Is. 5:1;
  Luke 23:30
HINDER—*delay, forbid, restrain*
Matt. 19:14, do not **h** them from coming to Me
Mark 9:39, But Jesus said, Do not **h** him
Gal. 5:7, who **h-ed** you from obeying
1 Pet. 3:7, your prayers may not be **h-ed**
Mark 9:38; Luke 11:52; 18:16
HINDRANCE 1 Cor. 9:12, cause no **h** to the
  gospel
HIRE Is. 7:20, shave with a razor, **h-d**
Matt. 20:1, went out early . . . to **h** laborers
  20:7, Because no one **h-d** us
Luke 15:19, as one of your **h-d** men

HIT 2 Cor. 11:20, if he **h-s** you in the face
HOARD—*store* Amos 3:10, **h** up violence and
   devastation
HOLD—*keep, retain*
  Prov. 4:13, Take **h** of instruction
  Is. 4:1, seven women ... **h** of one man
  Matt. 6:24, he will **h** to one
  Mark 7:8, **h** to the tradition of men
  Luke 8:15, heard the word, and **h** it fast
  Phil. 2:16, **h-ing** fast the word of life
  1 Thess. 5:21, **h** fast to that which is good
  Titus 1:9, **h-ing** fast the faithful word
  Job 2:9; 27:6; Ps. 64:5; Prov. 4:4; Is. 33:15;
    Jer. 20:9; Acts 7:60; Phil. 2:29
HOLE—*opening* Matt. 8:20, foxes have **h-s**
  2 Kin. 12:9; Is. 11:8; Ezek. 8:7; Hag. 1:6
HOLINESS—*holy, sanctity* Ex. 15:11
  Ps. 93:5, **H** befits Thy house
  Is. 35:8, be called the highway of **h**
  2 Cor. 7:1, perfecting **h** in the fear of God
  1 Thess. 3:13, hearts unblameable in **h**
  Heb. 12:10, we may share His **h**
HOLY—*holiness, sacred, sanctify* Ex. 3:5; 28:36
  Ex. 20:8, sabbath day, to keep it **h**
  Deut. 5:12, Observe the sabbath ... keep it **h**
  7:6, you are a **h** people
  1 Chr. 16:10, Glory in His **h** name
  Ps. 11:4, LORD is in His **h** temple
  16:10, allow Thy **H** One to see the pit
  145:21, bless His **h** name forever
  Is. 6:3, **H, H, H,** is the LORD of hosts
  Hab. 2:20, LORD is in His **h** temple
  Matt. 7:6, not give what is **h** to dogs
  Luke 1:49, **h** is His name
  4:34, the **H** One of God
  John 17:11, **H** Father, keep them in Thy name
  Acts 2:27, THY **H** ONE
  Rom. 12:1, your bodies a living and **h** sacrifice
  1 Cor. 3:17, the temple of God is **h**
  7:34, **h** both in body and spirit
  Eph. 1:4, be **h** and blameless before Him
  Col. 1:22, **h** and blameless
  1 Tim. 2:8, lifting up **h** hands
  2 Tim. 1:9, called us with a **h** calling
  Lev. 20:7; Deut. 33:2; 1 Sam. 2:2; 2 Kin. 4:9;
    1 Chr. 16:29; Job 15:15; Ps. 47:8; 89:5; 99:9;
    Jer. 17:22,24,27; 31:23; Mark 6:20;
    Rom. 16:16
HOLY SPIRIT—*spirit*
  Matt. 1:20, in her is of the **H**
  Matt. 3:11, baptize you with the **H**
  Luke 3:22, **H** descended upon Him in bodily
  4:1, Jesus, full of the **H**
  11:13, give the **H** to those
  12:12, **H** will teach you
  John 14:26, Helper, the **H**
  20:22, Receive the **H**
  Acts 2:4, all filled with the **H**
  2:38, receive the gift of the **H**
  7:51, always resisting the **H**
  10:38, the **H** and with power
  19:2, Did you receive the **H**
  Rom. 9:1, witness in the **H**
  Eph. 1:13, with the **H** of promise
  4:30, do not grieve the **H** of God
  1 Thess. 4:8, God who gives His **H** to you
HOME Eccles. 12:5, man goes to his eternal **h**
  2 Cor. 5:6, are at **h** in the body
  Titus 2:5, sensible, pure, workers at **h**
  Lev. 18:9; Deut. 24:5; 1 Kin. 13:15; 2 Chr. 25:19;
    Prov. 7:19; Mark 5:19; 1 Cor. 11:34; 14:35
HOMESTEAD—*habitation* Luke 11:21; Acts 1:20
HONEST—*good, true* Gen. 42:11, we are **h** men
  Luke 8:15, an **h** and good heart
HONOR—*splendor* Ex. 20:12, **H** your father and
  your mother
  Lev. 19:32, **h** the aged
  Prov. 15:33, before **h** *comes* humility
  Matt. 6:2, that they may be **h-ed** by men
  13:57, A prophet is not without **h**
  15:8, **h-s** ME WITH THEIR LIPS
  John 5:23, all may **h** the Son

Rom. 2:10, glory and **h** and peace
1 Tim. 6:16, To Him *be* **h** and eternal dominion
Heb. 13:4, *Let* marriage *be held* in **h**
1 Pet. 2:17, **H** all men ... **h** the king
  3:7, grant her **h** as a fellow-heir
Rev. 5:13, *be* blessing and **h** and glory
1 Sam. 2:30; 9:6; 1 Kin. 3:13; 1 Chr. 29:28;
  Job 19:9; Ps. 50:23; Eccles. 6:2; Is. 49:5;
  Matt. 15:4; Rom. 12:10; 13:7; 1 Tim. 5:17
HONORABLE—*noble* Is. 9:15; Nah. 3:10
  Rom. 9:21, one vessel for **h** use ... another for
   common
  Phil. 4:8, brethren ... whatever is **h**
  Heb. 13:18, conduct ourselves **h-y** in all things
HOOF—*claw* Lev. 11:3,4,5,6,7,26, whatever
  divides a **h**
  Deut. 14:6,7,8; Ps. 69:31; Is. 5:28; Jer. 47:3;
    Ezek. 32:13; Zech. 11:16
HOOK 2 Kin. 19:28; Is. 37:29, put My **h** in your
  nose
  Job 41:2, pierce his jaw with a **h**
  Ezek. 29:4; 38:4; Amos 4:2
HOPE—*comfort, expectation, confidence, trust*
  Job 13:15, I will **h** in Him
  Ps. 39:7, My **h** is in Thee
  62:5, my **h** is from Him
  Prov. 13:12, **H** deferred *makes* the heart sick
  19:18, Discipline your son while there is **h**
  Acts 2:26, MY FLESH ALSO WILL ABIDE IN **H**
  23:6, **h** and resurrection of the dead
  28:20, for the sake of the **h** of Israel
  Rom. 4:18, **h** against **h** he believed
  5:5, **h** does not disappoint
  8:24, **h** that is seen is not **h**
  12:12, rejoicing in **h**
  15:4, Scriptures we might have **h**
  1 Cor. 13:7, **h-s** all things
  13:13, now abide faith, **h**, love
  2 Cor. 3:12, Having therefore such a **h**
  Gal. 5:5, waiting for the **h** of righteousness
  Eph. 4:4, you were called in one **h**
  Col. 1:23, away from the **h** of the gospel
  1:27, Christ in you, the **h** of glory
  1 Thess. 5:8, as a helmet, the **h** of salvation
  1 Tim. 4:10, our **h** on the living God
  Titus 3:7, *the* **h** of eternal life
  Heb. 6:19, **h** we have as an anchor
  11:1, assurance of *things* **h-d** for
  1 Pet. 1:3, born again to a living **h**
  Ruth 1:12; Job 7:6; Ps. 9:18; 71:5; Prov. 26:12;
    Eccles. 9:4; Is. 20:5; 57:10; Jer. 29:11;
    1 Cor. 9:10; 2 Cor. 1:7; 2 Thess. 2:16
HORN—*trumpet* Gen. 22:13; Lev. 25:9; Josh. 6:5;
  2 Sam. 22:3; 1 Chr. 15:28; Dan. 3:5; 7:7;
  Rev. 5:6
HORRIBLE Jer. 5:30; 23:14; Hos. 6:10
HORROR Ps. 55:5; Jer. 25:18
HORSE Ps. 33:17, A **h** is a false hope
  Gen. 49:17; 1 Kin. 10:29; Job 39:19; Ps. 32:9;
    Prov. 26:3; Jer. 4:13; 46:4; Hos. 14:3
HOSPITABLE 1 Tim. 3:2, must be above
  reproach ... **h**
  Titus 1:8, but **h**, loving what is good
  1 Pet. 4:9, Be **h** to one another
HOSPITALITY Rom. 12:13, practicing **h**
HOST—*army, camp, innkeeper*
  Ps. 24:10, LORD of **h-s**, He is the King
  Luke 2:13, multitude of the heavenly **h**
  Deut. 4:19; Josh. 5:15; Ps. 27:3; Is. 48:2;
    Rom. 16:23
HOSTILE—*enmity, contrary* Lev. 26:21, you act
  with **h-ity**
  Rom. 8:7, mind set on the flesh is **h**
  1 Thess. 2:15, but **h** to all men
  Heb. 12:3, endured such **h-ity** by sinners
  James 4:4, friendship with the world is **h-ity**
HOT—*branding* Ps. 39:3, My heart was **h** within
  me
  Rev. 3:15, are neither cold nor **h**
  Ex. 16:21; Deut. 9:19; Job 6:17; Prov. 6:28
HOT-TEMPERED Prov. 29:22, a **h** man abounds

HOUR—*time* Matt. 20:12, men have worked *only* one **h**
  Matt. 24:36, day and **h** no one knows
    26:40, watch with Me for one **h**
  Mark 15:34, ninth **h** Jesus cried out
  Luke 22:59, about an **h** had passed
  John 5:25, an **h** is coming and now is
    12:27, Father, save Me from this **h**
    17:1, Father, the **h** has come
  Matt. 8:13; Mark 13:32; Luke 12:39; John 11:9; Acts 3:1; Rom. 13:11; Rev. 3:10
HOUSE—*temple* Ps. 23:6, dwell in the **h** of the LORD
  Ps. 127:1, Unless the LORD builds the **h**
  Prov. 9:1, Wisdom has built her **h**
  Matt. 2:11, they came into the **h** and saw
    7:25, winds blew, and burst against that **h**
    10:12, enter the **h**, give it your greeting
    12:25, city or **h** divided against itself
    21:13, MY **H** SHALL BE CALLED A **H**
  Luke 11:17, a **h** divided against itself falls
  John 14:2, Father's **h** are many dwelling places
  Acts 2:46, breaking bread from **h** to **h**
    7:48, does not dwell in **h-s** ... human hands
    7:49, WHAT KIND OF **H** WILL YOU BUILD
  Rom. 16:5, church that is in their **h**
  2 Cor. 5:1, **h** not made with hands
  1 Tim. 5:13, go around from **h** to **h**
  1 Pet. 2:5, built up as a spiritual **h**
  Gen. 15:3; Ex. 20:2,17; Deut. 8:12; 22:8; 2 Kin. 20:1; Neh. 13:8; Job 27:18; 30:23; Ps. 55:14; 84:3; 93:5; 102:7; Prov. 24:3; Eccles. 7:2; Is. 5:8; Matt. 23:38; Mark 12:40; Luke 10:7
HOUSEHOLD—*home* Prov. 31:27, ways of her **h**
  Gal. 6:10, who are of the **h** of the faith
  Eph. 2:19, and are of God's **h**
  1 Tim. 3:4, manages his own **h** well
    3:15, conduct himself in the **h** of God
  Gen. 18:19; 26:14; Ex. 1:1; Matt. 10:36; 13:52; John 19:27; 2 Tim. 3:6
HUMBLE—*abase, gentle* Mic. 6:8, walk **h-ly** with your God
  Matt. 11:29, I am gentle and **h** in heart
    23:12, exalts ... shall be **h-d**; and ... **h-s** himself
  Phil. 3:21, body of our **h** state
    4:12, get along with **h** means
  James 4:6, BUT GIVES GRACE TO THE **H**
  1 Pet. 5:6, **H** yourselves under the mighty hand
  Ex. 10:3; Num. 12:3; Deut. 8:2; 2 Chr. 34:27; Job 40:12; Ps. 35:13; 37:11; Prov. 6:3; 11:2; Dan. 4:37; Zech. 9:9
HUMILIATE 2 Cor. 12:21, my God may **h** me before you
HUMILIATION—*confusion* Is. 45:16; Jer. 3:25
  Acts 8:33, in **h** His judgment was taken
HUMILITY—*humble, self-abasement*
  Prov. 15:33, before honor comes **h**
    18:12, **h** goes before honor
    22:4, The reward of **h**
  Phil. 2:3, with **h** of mind
  Col. 3:12, put on a heart of ... **h**
  1 Pet. 5:5, clothe yourselves with **h**
HUNG Ps. 137:2, Upon the willows ... we **h** our harps
  Matt. 18:6; Mark 9:4; Luke 17:2, better ... millstone be **h** around his neck
HUNGER Ps. 34:10, lions do lack and suffer **h**
  Prov. 10:3, not allow the righteous to **h**
    19:15, an idle man will suffer **h**
  Is. 49:10, They will not **h** or thirst
  Matt. 5:6; Luke 6:21, Blessed are those who **h**
  John 6:35, comes to Me shall not **h**
  Deut. 28:48; Luke 6:25; 15:17
HUNGRY Ps. 146:7, Who gives food to the **h**
  Prov. 25:21, If your enemy is **h**
  Matt. 4:2, He then became **h**
    12:1, His disciples became **h**
    12:3, David did, when he became **h**
    15:32, do not wish to send them away **h**
    25:35, For I was **h**

Rom. 12:20, BUT IF YOUR ENEMY IS **H**
  1 Cor. 11:34, If anyone is **h**
  Deut. 8:3; 2 Sam. 17:29; Job 22:7; Ps. 50:12; Is. 29:8; Ezek. 18:7; 1 Cor. 11:21; Phil. 4:12
HUNT Gen. 10:9, a mighty **h-er** before the LORD
  Gen. 27:5; 1 Sam. 26:20; Ps. 140:11; Ezek. 13:18; Mic. 7:2
HURRIED Prov. 20:21, inheritance gained **h-ly**
HURRY—*speed* 1 Sam. 20:38, H, be quick, do not stay
HURT—*harm* Ps. 15:4, He swears to his own **h**
  Is. 11:9; Mark 16:18
HUSBAND—*bridegroom*
  Prov. 12:4, wife is a crown of her **h**
  John 4:16, Go, call your **h**
  Rom. 7:2,3, if her **h** dies
  1 Cor. 7:3, **h** fulfill his duty to his wife
  Eph. 5:23, **h** is the head of the wife
    5:25, **H-s**, love your wives
  Rev. 21:2, bride adorned for her **h**
  Gen. 3:16; 29:32; 30:20; Is. 54:5; Hos. 3:1; Mark 10:12; 1 Cor. 7:2; 2 Cor. 11:2
HUSH—*silence* Acts 21:40, there was a great **h**
HYMN Matt. 26:30, singing a **h**, they went out
  Eph. 5:19, in psalms and **h-s** and spiritual songs
HYPOCRISY Matt. 23:28, you are full of **h**
  Rom. 12:9, Let love be without **h**
  1 Tim. 4:2, means of the **h** of liars
  James 3:17, wisdom from above ... without **h**
HYPOCRITE—*godless* Matt. 6:2, as the **h-s** do ... synagogues
  Matt. 6:5, not to be as the **h-s**
    6:16, gloomy face as the **h-s** do
    7:5, You **h**, first take the log
    22:18, Why are you testing Me, you **h-s**
    23:13, scribes and Pharisees, **h-s**
  Luke 12:56, You **h-s**! You know how to analyze

I

ICE—*frost* Job 37:10, breath of God **i** is made
IDLE Prov. 19:15, an **i** man will suffer hunger
  Prov. 31:27, not eat the bread of **i-ness**
  Matt. 20:6, Why have you been standing ... **i**
  1 Tim. 5:13, not merely **i**, but also gossips
IDOL—*image* Ex. 20:4, make for yourself an **i**
  Acts 15:20, abstain from ... **i-s**
  1 Cor. 10:7, do not be **i-aters**
  1 John 5:21, guard yourselves from **i-s**
  Lev. 19:4; 26:1; Is. 66:3; Jer. 50:38
IGNORANCE—*unintentionally*
  Acts 17:23, What ... worship in **i**
    17:30, overlooked the times of **i**
  Eph. 4:18, because of the **i** that is in them
  1 Pet. 2:15, silence the **i** of foolish men
IGNORANT 2 Cor. 2:11, not **i** of his schemes
  2 Tim. 2:23, refuse foolish and **i** speculations
ILLEGITIMATE Deut. 23:2; Heb. 12:8
ILLNESS—*infirmity* Gal. 4:13, a bodily **i**
ILLUMINE Ps. 18:28, God **i-s** my darkness
IMAGE—*likeness* Gen. 1:26, make man in Our **i**
  Gen. 9:6, **i** of God He made man
  1 Cor. 11:7, **i** and glory of God
  Col. 1:15, **i** of the invisible God
IMAGINATION—*estimation*
  Prov. 18:11, wall in his own **i**
IMITATE—*follow* 3 John 11, do not **i** what is evil
IMITATORS—*followers* Eph. 5:1, be **i** of God
  1 Thess. 2:14, become **i** of the churches of God
IMMATURE—*babes, children*
  Rom. 2:20, teacher of the **i**
IMMEDIATELY Matt. 3:16, went up **i** from the water
  Matt. 4:20, **i** left the nets
    21:2, you will find a donkey tied
    26:74, And **i** a cock crowed
  Mark 4:15, **i** Satan comes
  Luke 12:54, **i** you say, A shower is coming
    14:5, **i** pull him out ... Sabbath
    21:9, the end does not *follow* **i**

John 5:9, i the man became well
19:34, i there came out blood and water
Acts 9:18, i there fell from his eyes
9:20, i he began to proclaim Jesus
21:30, i the doors were shut
Rev. 4:2, i I was in the Spirit
Matt. 13:21; 26:49; Mark 6:25; Luke 17:7;
Acts 13:11

IMMORALITY—*fornication* Matt. 19:9, except
for i
1 Cor. 6:18, Flee i
1 Thess. 4:3, abstain from sexual i
Rev. 2:20, they commit *acts of* i
17:2, the wine of her i

IMMORTALITY 1 Cor. 15:53, mortal ... put on i
1 Tim. 6:16, who alone possesses i
2 Tim. 1:10, brought life and i

IMPATIENT Num. 21:4, people became i

IMPEL—*drive* Mark 1:12, the Spirit **i-ed** Him

IMPERISHABLE 1 Cor. 9:25, perishable ... an i
1 Cor. 15:52, the dead will be raised i
1 Pet. 1:4, *obtain* an inheritance *which is* i

IMPETUOUS Hab. 1:6, Chaldeans, That fierce
and i people

IMPLORE—*adjure* Job 8:5, i the compassion of
the Almighty
Mark 5:7, I i you by God

IMPOSSIBLE Matt. 19:26, With men this is i
Luke 1:37, nothing will be i with God
Heb. 6:18, it is i for God to lie
11:6, without faith it is i to

IMPROPER 1 Cor. 14:35, i for a woman to speak

IMPROVISE Amos 6:5, Who i to the sound of the
harp

IMPUTE—*reckon* Rom. 5:13, sin is not **i-d** when
there is

INAUGURATED—*dedicated*
Heb. 9:18, first covenant ... not i
10:20, way which He i for us

INCITE Luke 23:14, one who **i-s** the people

INCLINE Josh. 24:23, i your hearts to the LORD
Ps. 119:36, I my heart to Thy
Is. 37:17, I Thine ear, O LORD

INCREASE—*multiply, produce* Job 31:12; Prov.
28:8
Ps. 62:10, riches i, do not set *your* heart
Eccles. 1:18, **i-ing** knowledge results in **i-ing**
pain
Luke 2:52, **i-ing** in wisdom and stature
11:29, the crowds were **i-ing**
Col. 1:10, **i-ing** in the knowledge of God

INDEBTED Rom. 15:27, they are i

INDEED—*surely, truly* Gen. 3:1, I, has God said,
You shall
Ex. 4:25, i a bridegroom of blood
Num. 14:21, but i, as I live
1 Kin. 8:27, God i dwell on the earth
2 Chr. 6:18, will God i dwell with mankind
John 8:36, you shall be free i
Rom. 14:20, All things i are clean
1 Tim. 5:5, she who is a widow, i

INDEPENDENT 1 Cor. 11:11, woman i of man ...
man i ... woman

INDESTRUCTIBLE—*endless*
Heb. 7:16, power of an i life

INDIGNANT Matt. 20:24; Luke 13:14

INDIGNATION—*anger* Jer. 15:17; Nah. 1:6
Ps. 7:11, God who has i every day
69:24, Pour out Thine i on them
Is. 30:27, lips are filled with i

INEXPERIENCED—*tender*
1 Chr. 22:5, My son ... young and i

INFECTION—*plague*
Lev. 13:2, becomes an i of leprosy

INFERIOR—*base* Is. 3:5, And the i against the
honorable

INFIRMITIES—*sickness, weakness*
Matt. 8:17, HIMSELF TOOK OUR I

INFLICT Job 5:18, He **i-s** pain, and gives relief

INFORM—*speak* Ruth 4:4; 2 Sam. 15:28; Ezra
4:16
Job 17:5, who **i-s** against friends

INHABITANTS Gen. 34:30; Num. 13:32; Ps. 49:1;
Joel 2:1

INHABITED—*habitation* Ps. 107:7,36, an i city

INHERIT—*possess, possession* Ex. 32:13, they
shall i *it*
Ps. 37:11, humble will i the land
Prov. 3:35, The wise will i honor
14:18, The naive i folly
Matt. 5:5, gentle ... i the earth
19:29, shall i eternal life
25:34, i the kingdom prepared
Luke 10:25, do to i eternal life
1 Cor. 6:9, shall not i the kingdom
15:50, perishable i the imperishable
Rev. 21:7, who overcomes shall i these things

INHERITANCE—*possession* Judg. 11:2; Ps. 28:9
Ps. 2:8, give the nations as Thine i
94:14, Nor will He forsake His i
Jer. 3:19, most beautiful i of the nations
Mark 12:7, the i will be ours
Acts 7:5, He gave him no i
Eph. 1:11, also we have obtained an i
1 Pet. 1:4, an i which is imperishable
Prov. 13:22; Eccles. 7:11; Jer. 12:7,8,9,15;
Joel 2:17; Mic. 2:2; Mal. 1:3

INIQUITY—*injustice* Lev. 16:22; Job 4:8; 13:26
Deut. 5:9, visiting the i of the fathers
Ps. 25:11, Pardon my i, for it is great
51:9, blot out all my **i-es**
Is. 53:5, He was crushed for our **i-es**
James 3:6, tongue is ... world of i
Ps. 32:5; 51:5; 79:8; Prov. 22:8; Is. 1:4; 31:2;
Jer. 31:30; Ezek. 18:30; 33:8

INJUNCTION—*decree* Dan. 6:7,8

INJURE—*wrong* Acts 7:26, why do you i one

INJUSTICE—*iniquity* Lev. 19:15, do no i
Deut. 32:4, A God of faithfulness without i

INNER—*inward* Matt. 6:6, GO INTO YOUR I ROOM
2 Cor. 4:16, i man is being renewed day by day

INNERMOST—*inward*
Job 38:36, wisdom in the i being

INNKEEPER—*host* Luke 10:35, denarii ... gave
them to the i

INNOCENT—*blameless, righteous* Ex. 23:7
Is. 59:7, hasten to shed i blood
Matt. 27:4, have sinned by betraying i blood
27:24, I am i of this Man's blood
Luke 23:47, this man was i
Phil. 2:15, blameless and i, children of God
Heb. 7:26, holy, i, undefiled
2 Sam. 3:28; Job 4:7; 22:19; Prov. 6:17; Matt.
10:16; 12:5,7

INQUIRE—*ask* Judg. 18:5, I of God
Matt. 2:4, i of them where the Christ

INSANE—*mad* 1 Sam. 21:13, acted **i-ly** in their
hands
John 10:20, has a demon, and is i

INSCRIBE Hab. 2:2, And i *it* on tablets

INSCRIPTION Dan. 5:8, could not read the i

INSECTS Ex. 8:21, I will send swarms of i on you

INSENSITIVE Is. 6:10, Render ... this people i

INSIDE—*within* Gen. 9:21, uncovered himself i
his tent
Matt. 23:26, Pharisee ... clean the i of the cup
Acts 5:23, we found no one i
Rev. 5:1, throne a book written i

INSIGNIFICANT—*mean, small* 2 Sam. 7:19, i in
Thine eyes
Job 8:7, your beginning was i
40:4, Behold, I am i; what can
Acts 21:39, citizen of no i city

INSOLENCE—*pride* 1 Sam. 17:28, I know your i

INSPIRE—*spiritual* Hos. 9:7, **i-d** man is
demented

INSTANT—*moment* Num. 16:21, consume **i-ly**

INSTITUTION 1 Pet. 2:13, Submit ... to every
human i

INSTRUCT—*discipline*
Neh. 9:20, Thy good Spirit to i
Ps. 32:8, I will i you and teach you

INSTRUCT (*Continued*)
Matt. 10:5, twelve Jesus sent ... **i-ing** them
Rom. 2:18, being **i-ed** out of the Law
INSTRUCTION—*admonition*
Job 36:10, He opens ... ear to **i**
Matt. 11:1, **i-s** to His twelve disciples
Rom. 15:4, was written for our **i**
1 Cor. 7:10, **i-s**, not I, but the Lord
10:11, written for our **i**
Eph. 6:4, discipline and **i** of the Lord
1 Tim. 1:5, goal of our **i** is love
Heb. 6:2, of **i** about washing and laying on of
hands
INSTRUMENT—*object, vessel*
Acts 9:15, he is a chosen **i**
Rom. 6:13, as **i-s** of unrighteousness
2 Sam. 12:31; 1 Chr. 20:3; Ps. 150:4; Ezek. 33:32
INSULT—*reproach*
Job 19:3, ten times you have **i-ed** me
Luke 6:22, heap **i-s** upon you
INTEGRITY—*upright* Gen. 20:5; Job 2:3; Prov.
19:1
Ps. 15:2, He who walks with **i**
26:1, have walked in my **i**
Prov. 10:9, who walks in **i** walks securely
20:7, righteous man who walks in his **i**
INTELLIGENT—*prudent*
Matt. 11:25, hide ... wise and **i**
Mark 12:34, Jesus saw that he had ... **i-ly**
INTENSE 2 Pet. 3:10, destroyed with **i** heat
INTENT Gen. 8:21, **i** of man's heart is evil
Deut. 31:21, for I know their **i**
Acts 1:10, gazing **i-ly** into the sky
INTERCEDE 1 Sam. 2:25, who can **i**
Is. 53:12, **i-d** for the transgressors
Rom. 8:26, the Spirit Himself **i-s** for *us*
INTERCESSION—*petition*
Heb. 7:25, always lives to make **i**
INTEREST—*usury* Ex. 22:25, not charge him **i**
Deut. 23:20, You may charge **i** to a foreigner
Ps. 15:5, not put out his money at **i**
Matt. 25:27, my *money* back with **i**
Luke 19:23, collected it with **i**
INTERMARRY Ezra 9:14, and **i** with the peoples
INTERPRET—*understand*
Gen. 41:8, dreams ... no one who could **i** them
1 Cor. 12:10, the **i-ation** of tongues
14:27, and let one **i**
2 Pet. 1:20, *a matter* of one's own **i-ation**
INTIMATE—*close* Job 19:14, my **i** friends have
forgotten
Prov. 17:9, matter separates **i** friends
INTRODUCTION Rom. 5:2, obtained our **i** by
faith
INVALIDATE Matt. 15:6, you **i-d** the word of
God
Mark 7:13, *thus* **i-ing** the word of God
INVESTIGATE—*examine*
Ezra 10:16, convened ... to **i**
INVESTIGATION Acts 25:26, after the **i** has
taken place
INVOLVE—*exercise* Ps. 131:1, Nor do I **i** myself
INWARD—*within* Matt. 7:15, **i-ly** are wolves
IRON 2 Kin. 6:6, and made the **i** float
Job 19:24, with an **i** stylus and lead
Ps. 2:9, break them with a rod of **i**
1 Tim. 4:2, seared ... as with a branding **i**
Gen. 4:22; Deut. 3:11; 8:9; 33:25; Judg. 1:19;
Job 40:18; Prov. 27:17; Jer. 11:4
IRREVERENCE
2 Sam. 6:7, struck him down ... for his **i**
IRRITATE—*fret* 1 Sam. 1:6, provoke ... to **i** her
IVORY 1 Kin. 10:18; Song 7:4; Amos 6:4

J

JACKAL Job 30:29, a brother to **j-s**
Jer. 9:11, Jerusalem ... haunt of **j-s**
JAR—*jug, pitcher, vessel* 1 Kin. 17:10, water in **j**
John 19:29, A **j** full of sour wine
Gen. 24:14; 1 Kin. 14:3; 19:6; 2 Kin. 2:20
JAVELIN—*spear* Josh. 8:18, Stretch out the **j**
Job 41:29, at the rattling of the **j**

JEALOUS—*envy, zealous*
Ex. 20:5, Lord your God, am a **j** God
1 Cor. 13:4, love is kind, *and* is not **j**
Gen. 30:1; 37:11; Ex. 34:14; Num. 11:29; 25:11;
Josh. 24:19; Is. 11:13; Ezek. 31:9; Nah. 1:2;
Acts 7:9; 17:5; Rom. 10:19; 2 Cor. 11:2
JEALOUSY—*envy, jealous* Num. 5:14; Prov. 6:34
Rom. 13:13, not in strife and **j**
1 Cor. 3:3, since there is **j** ... among you
2 Cor. 12:20, *there may be* strife, **j**
James 3:14, if you have bitter **j**
3:16, where **j** and selfish ambition exist
Prov. 27:4; Song 8:6; Acts 13:45; Rom. 11:14;
Gal. 5:20
JEOPARDIZE Ruth 4:6, **j** my own inheritance
JEWEL—*pearl* Prov. 3:15, more precious than **j-s**
Prov. 31:10, her worth is far above **j-s**
JOIN—*couple* Ex. 23:1; 26:6; Is. 5:8
Matt. 19:6, What ... God has **j-ed** together
1 Cor. 6:17, one who **j-s** himself to the Lord
JOINT—*dislocate* Ps. 22:14, bones are out of **j**
JOURNEY—*walk, way*
Ezra 8:21, seek from Him a safe **j**
Mark 13:34, like a man, away on a **j**
Luke 9:3, Take nothing for your **j**
13:33, must **j** on today and tomorrow
15:13, a **j** into a distant country
Acts 9:3, **j-ed**, he was approaching Damascus
2 Cor. 11:26, I have been on frequent **j-s**
Gen. 33:12; Josh. 9:11; Neh. 2:6; Matt. 10:10;
Acts 1:12
JOY Prov. 17:21, father of a fool has no **j**
Matt. 2:10, with great **j**
25:21, enter into the **j** of your master
Luke 15:7, **j** in heaven over one sinner
John 15:11, My **j** may be in you
Rom. 14:17, and **j** in the Holy Spirit
Gal. 5:22, fruit of the Spirit is love, **j**
Phil. 2:2, make my **j** complete
James 1:2, Consider it all **j** ... encounter ...
1 John 1:4, our **j** may be made complete
1 Chr. 15:16; Ezra 3:12; Job 29:13; 33:26
JOYFUL—*merry* Ps. 21:6; 66:1; Is. 52:9
Ps. 126:5, sow in tears ... reap with **j** shouting
Prov. 17:22, **j** heart is good medicine
JUDGE Gen. 18:25, the **J** of all the earth
Matt. 7:1, not **j** lest you be **j-d**
John 3:17, God did not send the Son ... to **j**
7:24, but **j** with righteous judgment
7:51, Our Law does not **j** a man
12:47, not come to **j** the world
Acts 10:42, **J** of the living and the dead
2 Thess. 2:12, all may be **j-d** who did not believe
Heb. 4:12, word of God ... able to **j** the
thoughts
12:23, God the **J** of all
13:4, adulterers God will **j**
Gen. 16:5; Matt. 7:2
JUDGMENT—*justice, sentence*
Ps. 1:5, wicked will not stand in the **j**
19:9, **j-s** of the Lord are true
Matt. 10:15, Gomorrah in the day of **j**
11:24, Sodom in *the* day of **j**
27:19, he was sitting on the **j**-seat
John 3:19, this is the **j**, that the light is
5:29, resurrection of **j**
5:30, judge; and My **j** is just
1 Cor. 11:29, eats and drinks **j** to himself
Heb. 9:27, after this *comes* **j**
10:27, terrifying expectation of **j**
James 3:1, shall incur a stricter **j**
5:12, may not fall under **j**
2 Pet. 3:7, kept for the day of **j**
1 John 4:17, confidence in the day of **j**
Jude 15, to execute **j** upon all
Rev. 18:20, God has pronounced **j** for you
19:2, His **j-s are true and righteous**
Ex. 12:12; Lev. 18:4; Deut. 1:17; Ezra 7:26; Ps.
112:5; 2 Pet. 2:11; Jude 9

JUG—*bottle, wineskin* 1 Sam. 1:24; 10:3; 16:20; 25:18; 26:16; 2 Sam. 16:1
JUST—*right* Job 25:4, can a man be **j** with God
John 5:30, My judgment is **j**
Heb. 2:2, received a **j** recompense
1 Pet. 3:18, Christ also died . . . the **j** for the **un-j**
Lev. 19:36; Ps. 17:1; Luke 23:41
JUSTICE—*right, righteousness*
Job 8:3, Does God pervert **j**
Ps. 89:14, Righteousness and **j** are the
Prov. 28:5, Evil men do not understand **j**
Amos 5:24, let **j** roll down like waters
Mic. 6:8, to do **j**, to love kindness
Gen. 18:19; Deut. 16:19; Job 8:3; 36:6; Prov. 21:3; Is. 59:14; Jer. 10:24
JUSTIFY—*clear, vindicate* Gen. 44:16; Ps. 51:4
Luke 10:29, wishing to **j** himself
Rom. 8:33, God is the one who **j-es**

K

KEEP—*hold, guide, preserve* Gen. 18:19
Ex. 20:6, love Me and **k** My commandments
20:8, sabbath day, to **k** it holy
Num. 6:24, Lord bless you, and **k** you
Ps. 17:8, **K** me as the apple of the eye
34:13, **K** your tongue from evil
Matt. 19:17, enter into life, **k** the commandments
Luke 3:8, fruits in **k-ing** with your repentance
John 8:51, if anyone **k-s** My word
12:25, shall **k** it to life eternal
14:23, If anyone loves Me, he will **k** My word
17:15, **k** them from the evil *one*
1 Tim. 1:19, **k-ing** faith and a good conscience
5:14, bear children, **k** house
5:22, **k** yourself free from sin
James 1:27, **k** oneself unstained by the world
Jude 21, **k** yourselves in the love of God
Lev. 23:32; Prov. 1:15; Eccles. 3:6; Matt. 26:18; 1 Cor. 14:28; 1 Tim. 6:12
KEEPER—*guard* Gen. 4:9, Am I my brother's **k**
Ps. 121:5, The LORD is your **k**
KEPT—*observed* Gen. 37:11, his father **k** the saying
Mark 10:20, Teacher I have **k** all these things
Jude 6, He has **k** in eternal bonds
KERNEL—*grain* Amos 9:9, not a **k** will fall to the ground
KEY Matt. 16:19, **k-s** of the kingdom of heaven
Luke 11:52, taken away the **k** of knowledge
Rev. 1:18, I have the **k-s** of death and of Hades
9:1, **k** of the bottomless pit
KIDNAP—*steal* Deut. 24:7, man is caught **k-ing**
KIDNEY Job 16:13, splits my **k-s** open
KILL 1 Sam. 17:50, Philistine and **k-ed** him
Matt. 10:28, **k** the body . . . unable to **k** the soul
Luke 9:22, **k-ed**, and be raised up . . . third day
15:23, bring the fattened calf, **k** it
John 5:18, Jews were seeking . . . to **k** Him
7:19, Why do you seek to **k** Me
10:10, comes only to steal, and **k**
Acts 11:7, Arise, Peter; **k** and eat
2 Cor. 3:6, the letter **k-s** . . . Spirit gives life
Gen. 4:8,14,23; Ex. 13:15; 21:14; Num. 31:8; 2 Kin. 5:7; Job 5:2; Ps. 10:8; Acts 10:13; 1 Tim. 1:9
KIND—*gentle, gracious* Matt. 5:11, say all **k-s** of evil
1 Cor. 13:4, Love is patient, love is **k**
Eph. 4:32, be **k** to one another
2 Tim. 2:24, but be **k** to all
Gen. 1:11; 6:19; 2 Chr. 10:7
KINDLE—*burn* Ex. 35:3; Prov. 26:21; Is. 50:11
KINDNESS—*goodness, loyalty*
Ruth 3:10, your last **k** to be
Prov. 31:26, teaching of **k** is on her tongue
Acts 24:4, grant us, by your **k**
Rom. 11:22, **k** and severity of God
2 Cor. 6:6, in patience, in **k**, in the Holy Spirit
Col. 3:12, put on a heart of compassion, **k**

1 Pet. 2:3, tasted the **k** of the Lord
2 Pet. 1:7, *your* godliness, brotherly **k**
KING 1 Sam. 8:5, appoint a **k** for us to judge us
1 Sam. 10:24, Long live the **k**
Ps. 5:2, my **K** and my God
24:8, Who is the **K** of glory
Jer. 10:7, fear Thee, O **K** of the nations
Matt. 2:2, who has been born **K** of the Jews
2:9, having heard the **k**
10:18, brought before governors and **k-s** for My sake
21:5, BEHOLD YOUR **K** IS COMING TO YOU
27:11, Are You the **K** of the Jews
Luke 23:2, that He Himself is Christ, a **K**
John 12:15, YOUR **K** COMES SITTING ON A . . . COLT
1 Tim. 6:15, **K** of kings and Lord of lords
1 Pet. 2:17, fear God, honor the **k**
Judg. 9:8; 17:6; Job 18:14; Prov. 8:15; 22:29; Eccles. 10:20; Is. 43:15
KINGDOM—*dominion* Ps. 22:28, For the **k** is the LORD'S
Ps. 145:13, Thy **k** is an everlasting **k**
Matt. 3:2, the **k** of heaven is at hand
4:23, the gospel of the **k**
6:10, Thy **k** come, Thy will be done
13:38, these are the sons of the **k**
16:19, give you the keys of the **k**
19:14, **k** of heaven belongs to such as these
26:29, in My Father's **k**
Mark 10:24, hard it is to enter the **k** of God
12:34, not far from the **k** of God
Luke 6:20, for yours is the **k** of God
12:32, to give you the **k**
22:29, as My Father has granted me a **k**
John 3:3, he cannot see the **k** of God
18:36, My **k** is not of this world
Rom. 14:17, the **k** of God is not eating and drinking
Col. 1:13, to the **k** of His beloved Son
2 Tim. 4:18, bring me safely to His heavenly **k**
James 2:5, heirs of the **k** which He promised
Ex. 19:6; Esth. 1:20; Obad. 21
KISS Matt. 26:48, Whomever I shall **k**
Luke 7:45, has not ceased to **k** My feet
15:20, embraced him and **k-ed** him
22:48, betraying the Son of Man with a **k**
Rom. 16:16, Greet one another with a holy **k**
1 Pet. 5:14, Greet one another with a **k** of love
Gen. 29:11; 2 Sam. 20:9; Song 1:2
KNEE Gen. 41:43, Bow the **k**
Rom. 14:11, EVERY **K** SHALL BOW TO ME
Phil. 2:10, at the name of Jesus every **k** should bow
Heb. 12:12, strengthen . . . the **k-s** that are feeble
KNEEL Gen. 24:11, made the camels **k** down
Ps. 95:6, Let us **k** before the LORD
Matt. 27:29, they **k-ed** down before Him
Luke 22:41, He **k-t** down and *began* to pray
KNEW Jer. 1:5, Before I formed you . . . I **k** you
Matt. 7:23, I will declare . . . I never **k** you
Luke 6:8, But He **k** what they were thinking
John 4:10, If you **k** the gift of God
2 Cor. 5:21, made Him who **k** no sin *to be* sin
KNIFE—*sword* Prov. 30:14, jaw teeth like **k-s**
KNOCK—*smite* Nah. 2:10, knees **k-ing**
Matt. 7:7, **k** and it shall be opened
Luke 13:25, stand outside and **k** on the door
Acts 12:13, when he **k-ed** at the door
Rev. 3:20, I stand at the door and **k**
KNOW—*discern, recognize, understand*
Ex. 1:8, new king . . . who did not **k** Joseph
Deut. 4:9, **k-n** to your sons and your grandsons
Job 19:25, I **k** that my Redeemer lives
Ps. 1:6, the LORD **k-s** the way of the righteous
46:10, **k** that I am God
56:9, This I **k**, that God is for me
Prov. 27:1, do not **k** what a day may bring
Eccles. 8:5, wise heart **k-s** the proper time
Is. 59:8, They do not **k** the way of peace

KNOW (Continued)
Matt. 6:3, left hand **k** what your right hand
7:11, **k** how to give good gifts
7:20, you will **k** them by their fruits
25:12, I do not **k** you
Luke 10:22, no one **k-s** who the Son is
19:42, If you had **k-n** in this day
22:57, Woman, I do not **k** Him
John 8:32, you shall **k** the truth
10:14, I **k** My own, and My own **k** Me
14:7, If you had **k-n** Me . . . **k-n** My Father
21:17, You **k** all things; You **k** that I love You
Acts 1:7, not for you to **k** the times
1 Cor. 1:21, did not *come to* **k** God
13:2, and **k** all mysteries
13:9, we **k** in part and we prophesy
13:12, **k** in part, but then I shall **k** fully
2 Cor. 12:2, **k** a man in Christ . . . caught up
Eph. 3:19, to **k** the love of Christ
2 Tim. 3:15, **k-n** the sacred writings
1 John 3:2, We **k** that, if He should appear
3 John 12, you **k** that our witness is true
Rev. 2:2, I **k** your deeds
19:12, name written . . . no one **k-s** except
Himself
Gen. 3:22; 28:16; Deut. 29:4; 1 Sam. 3:7;
Job 13:18; Ps. 81:5; Eccles. 9:5; Is. 7:15;
Hos. 6:3; Jon. 4:11; Matt. 9:30; 12:33;
Mark 1:24; 13:33; Acts 19:15
KNOWLEDGE Gen. 2:9, tree of the **k** of good and
evil
Ps. 19:2, night to night reveals **k**
139:6, *Such* **k** is too wonderful for me
Prov. 1:7, fear of the LORD the beginning of **k**
10:14, Wise men store up **k**
17:27, who restrains his words has **k**
Is. 11:9, full of the **k** of the LORD
Acts 24:22, more exact **k** about the Way
Rom. 10:2, but not in accordance with **k**
11:33, wisdom and **k** of God
1 Cor. 8:1, **K** makes arrogant, but love edifies
13:8, if *there is* **k**, it will be done away
15:34, some have no **k** of God
Eph. 3:19, love of Christ which surpasses **k**
Col. 2:3, treasures of wisdom and **k**
1 Tim. 2:4, come to the **k** of the truth
2 Pet. 1:5, in *your* moral excellence, **k**
1:6, in *your* **k**, self-control
3:18, grow in the grace and **k** of our LORD
Deut. 1:39; 1 Sam. 2:3; 2 Chr. 1:10; Job 10:7;
21:22; Eccles. 1:18; Is. 28:9; Hos. 4:6;
Luke 11:52

L

LABOR—*fruit, toil, tribute, weary*
Ex. 20:9, Six days you shall **l**
Ps. 127:1, They **l** in vain who build it
Prov. 14:23, In all **l** there is profit
Eccles. 2:22, what does a man get in all his **l**
Is. 42:14, like a woman in **l** I will groan
1 Cor. 15:10, I **l-ed** even more than all of them
Gal. 4:11, perhaps I **l-ed** over you in vain
4:19, again in **l** until Christ
Eph. 4:28, rather let him **l**, performing
Phil. 1:22, this *will mean* fruitful **l**
1 Thess. 1:3, work of faith and **l** of love
2 Thess. 3:8, with **l** and hardship we *kept*
Rev. 12:2, cried out, being in **l** and in pain
Gen. 49:15; Job 7:1; Ps. 78:46; Prov. 12:24;
Eccles. 4:9; 2 Cor. 11:27
LABORER 1 Kin. 9:21, Solomon . . . forced **l-s**
LACK—*need, void, want* Deut. 28:48, in the **l** of
all things
Deut. 32:28, a nation **l-ing** in counsel
Judg. 18:10, place where there is no **l**
Prov. 7:7, young man **l-ing** sense
10:21, fools die for **l** of understanding
Is. 34:16, None will **l** its mate
Matt. 19:20, what am I still **l-ing**
Mark 10:21, One thing you **l**
James 1:4, **l-ing** in nothing
1:5, if any of you **l-s** wisdom
Deut. 8:9; 1 Kin. 8:25; Prov. 6:32; Eccles. 10:3

LADY 2 John 1, to the chosen **l**
LAGGING Rom. 12:11, not **l** behind in diligence
LAID Mark 6:5, He **l** His hands upon a few sick
Luke 12:19, many goods **l** up for many years
John 11:34, Where have you **l** him
2 Tim. 4:8, **l** up for me the crown of
righteousness
1 John 3:16, He **l** down His life for us
1 Kin. 17:19; Job 6:2; 38:6
LAIR Job 38:40, lie in wait in *their* **l**
LAMB Gen. 22:8, God will provide . . . the **l**
Is. 40:11, In His arm He will gather the **l-s**
53:7, Like a **l** that is led to slaughter
65:25, wolf and the **l** shall graze together
Hos. 4:16, Like a **l** in a large field
Luke 10:3, send you out as **l-s**
John 1:29, Behold the **L** of God
21:15, Tend My **l-s**
Acts 8:32, AS A **L** BEFORE ITS SHEARER IS SILENT
1 Pet. 1:19, a **l** unblemished and spotless
LAME Job 29:15, feet to the **l**
Matt. 11:5, and *the* **l** walk
Mark 9:45, better for you to enter life **l**
2 Sam. 9:13; Zeph. 3:19; Matt. 15:31; Acts 14:8
LAMENT—*mourn* Luke 8:52; 23:27; Rev. 18:9
LAMP—*light* Ps. 18:28, Thou dost light my **l**
Ps. 119:105, Thy word is a **l** to my feet
Matt. 5:15, light a **l**, and put it under
6:22, **l** of the body is the eye
25:8, our **l-s** are going out
Rev. 22:5, light of **l** nor . . . of sun
1 Sam. 3:3; 2 Sam. 22:29; Job 18:6; Prov. 20:27;
Zeph. 1:12; Rev. 4:5
LAMPSTAND Ex. 25:31; 1 Kin. 7:49; 2 Kin. 4:10;
Luke 8:16
LAND—*country, earth, ground*
Gen. 1:9, let the dry **l** appear
Deut. 6:3, **l** flowing with milk and honey
Ps. 37:29, righteous will inherit the **l**
88:12, in the **l** of forgetfulness
Is. 66:8, Can a **l** be born in one day
Jer. 22:29, O **l**, **l**, **l**, Hear the word of the LORD
Matt. 2:6, AND YOU, BETHLEHEM, **L** OF JUDAH
27:45, darkness fell upon all the **l**
Luke 14:18, have bought a piece of **l**
23:44, darkness fell over the whole **l**
Heb. 11:29, Red Sea as . . . through dry **l**
Gen. 15:18; Ex. 1:7; Deut. 8:8; 1 Sam. 6:5;
Job 28:13; Ps. 25:13; 37:9,11,22; 60:2;
Prov. 25:25; Eccles. 5:9; Is. 2:7; Jer. 15:10;
Ezek. 9:9; Mic. 7:2; Mal. 4:6; Acts 4:37
LANGUAGE—*word, voice*
Gen. 10:5, one according to his **l**
11:1, whole earth used the same **l**
Ezek. 3:5,6, unintelligible speech or difficult **l**
Acts 2:6, hearing them speak in his own **l**
1 Cor. 14:10, many kinds of **l-s**
LANGUISH—*faint* Ps. 119:81, My soul **l-es** for
Thy salvation
LAPIS LAZULI—*sapphire* Ezek. 28:13, The **l**, the
turquoise
LARGE—*vast* Ps. 31:8; Matt. 28:12; Luke 22:12;
Gal. 6:11
LASHES Luke 12:47, shall receive many **l**
LAST—*utmost* Ps. 30:5, weeping may **l** for the
night
Is. 44:6, I am the first and I am the **l**
Matt. 5:26, have paid up the **l** cent
12:45, the **l** state of that man
19:30, first will be **l**; and *the* **l**, first
John 6:39, raise it up on the **l** day
1 Cor. 15:45, The **l** Adam *became* a life-giving
spirit
15:52, at the **l** trumpet
1 Pet. 1:5, revealed in the **l** time
Rev. 1:17, I am the first and the **l**
Is. 7:9; Luke 11:26
LATER—*afterward* John 13:36, you shall follow **l**
LATTICE—*window*
Is. 60:8, like the doves to their **l-s**

LAUGH—*mock* Gen. 18:13, Why did Sarah l
  Job 8:21, fill your mouth with **l-ter**
  Prov. 14:13, Even in **l-ter** the heart . . . in pain
  Eccles. 3:4, time to weep, and a time to l
  Matt. 9:24, they were **l-ing** at Him
  Luke 6:25, Woe *to you* who l now
  James 4:9, let your **l-ter** be turned
LAUGHINGSTOCK—*derision*
  Jer. 20:7, a l all day long
LAUNDERER—*fuller* Mark 9:3, no l . . . can
    whiten them
LAW—*teaching* Ps. 19:7, l of the LORD is perfect
  Prov. 29:18, happy is he who keeps the l
  Matt. 5:17, came to abolish the **L**
  7:12, this is the **L** and the Prophets
  12:2, disciples do what is not **l-ful**
  12:4, bread . . . not **l-ful** for him to eat
  John 7:51, Our **L** does not judge a man
  Rom. 13:10, love . . . fulfillment of *the* l
  Gal. 3:24, **L** has become our tutor
  5:23, against such things there is no l
  6:2, thus fulfill the l of Christ
  Heb. 7:19, **L** made nothing perfect
  James 1:25, the perfect l, the *l* of liberty
  Ex. 12:49; Josh. 1:8; 2 Kin. 22:8; Prov. 28:7;
    John 19:7; Rom. 2:14; 4:15; 1 Cor. 6:2,7;
    Titus 3:9
LAWLESS—*wicked* 2 Thess. 2:8, l one will be
    revealed
LAWLESSNESS—*iniquity*
  Matt. 24:12, because l is increased
  2 Cor. 6:14, righteousness and l
  1 John 3:4, and sin is l
LAY Ps. 3:5, I l down and slept
  Matt. 6:19, Do not l up for yourselves treasures
  John 10:11, good shepherd **l-s** down His life
  10:15, I l down My life for the sheep
  Rom. 13:12, l aside the deeds of darkness
LAZY—*idle, slothful* Ex. 5:8,17
  Matt. 25:26, You wicked, l slave
  Titus 1:12, evil beasts, l gluttons
LEAD—*guide* 2 Chr. 23:13; Ps. 25:9; 27:11;
    Is. 40:11
  Ex. 13:21, cloud by day to l them on the way
  Ps. 23:2, He **l-s** me beside quiet waters
  25:5, **L** me in Thy truth
  Is. 11:6, a little boy will l them
  Matt. 6:13, do not l us into temptation
  John 10:3, calls his own sheep . . . **l-s** them out
  1 Tim. 2:2, may l a tranquil and quiet life
LEADER—*first, head* Num. 16:2; Luke 22:26
  Matt. 2:6, AMONG THE **L-S** OF JUDAH
LEAK—*drop* Eccles. 10:18, the house **l-s**
LEARN—*instruction* Deut. 31:13; Is. 1:17
  Prov. 1:5, wise man will . . . increase in **l-ing**
  Is. 2:4, never again will they l war
  Matt. 11:29, l from Me
  Acts 26:24, great **l-ing** is driving you mad
  Eph. 4:20, you did not l Christ
  2 Tim. 3:7, always **l-ing**
  Heb. 5:8, He **l-ed** obedience
LEAST—*young* 2 Kin. 18:24, l of my master's
    servants
  Matt. 2:6, NO MEANS **L** AMONG THE LEADERS
  5:19, called l in the kingdom of heaven
  11:11, he who is l . . . is greater
  1 Cor. 15:9, I am the l of the apostles
  Eph. 3:8, To me, the very l of all saints
LEATHER—*skin* Matt. 3:4, John . . . l belt about
    his waist
  Mark 1:6, *wore* a l belt around his waist
LEAVE—*abandon, desert, forsake* Ex. 20:7; Job
    9:27
  Gen. 2:24, man shall l his father . . . mother
  Ruth 1:16, Do not urge me to l you
  Ps. 49:10, l their wealth to others
  Matt. 18:12, does he not l the ninety-nine
  19:5, MAN SHALL **L** HIS FATHER AND MOTHER
  John 14:27, Peace I l with you
  16:28, I am **l-ing** the world again
  Prov. 2:17; 3:3

LEAVEN Ex. 12:19; Lev. 6:17
  Matt. 13:33, kingdom of heaven is like l
  16:6, beware of the l of the Pharisees
  Luke 13:21, It is like l
  1 Cor. 5:6, a little l **l-s** the whole lump
  5:7, Clean out the old l
LEFT—*remain* Matt. 19:27, l everything and
    followed You
  Matt. 26:56, disciples l Him and fled
  Mark 1:18, l the nets and followed Him
  Luke 5:11, l everything and followed Him
  Heb. 11:27, By faith he l Egypt
  Gen. 7:23; Matt. 14:20
LEND—*loan* Deut. 15:6; Neh. 5:10; Luke 11:5
  Prov. 22:7, borrower *becomes* the **l-er's** slave
  Luke 6:34, Even sinners l to sinners
LENGTH—*long* Prov. 3:2; Ezek. 31:7; Eph. 3:18
LENGTHEN Matt. 23:5, l the tassels of *their*
    garments
LEOPARD Jer. 13:23, Or the l his spots
  Rev. 13:2, beast . . . was like a l
  Is. 11:6; Hos. 13:7
LEPER Matt. 10:8, cleanse *the* **l-s**
  Matt. 11:5, *the* **l-s** are cleansed
  Lev. 13:51; 2 Chr. 26:21; Matt. 8:2; Mark 14:3
LEPROUS Lev. 13:51, the mark is a l malignancy
LESS Gen. 1:16, **l-er** light to govern the night
  Is. 40:17, regarded by Him as l than nothing
  2 Cor. 12:15, am I to be loved the l
LET—*suffer* Matt. 19:14, **L** the children alone,
    and
LETTER 2 Cor. 3:2, You are our l
  2 Cor. 3:3, you are a l of Christ
  2 Pet. 3:16, as also in all *his* **l-s**
  2 Chr. 2:11; Acts 15:30; Rom. 16:22; 2 Cor. 7:8;
    Col. 4:16; 2 Thess. 2:15; 3:14
LEVEL—*plain* Ps. 27:11, lead me in a l path
  Luke 19:44, will l you to the ground
LEVY—*collection* 2 Chr. 24:6, the l *fixed by*
    Moses
LIAR Job 24:25; John 8:55
  Rom. 3:4, every man . . . a l
  1 Tim. 4:2, by means of the hypocrisy of **l-s**
  1 John 5:10, God has made Him a l
LIBATION—*drink* Gen. 35:14, poured out a l
LIBERTY Ps. 119:45, I will walk at l
  Is. 61:1, proclaim l to the captives
  2 Cor. 3:17, where the Spirit . . . is, *there* is l
  Gal. 2:4, to spy out our l
  James 1:25, perfect law, the *law of* l
LICK 1 Kin. 21:19; Ps. 72:9; Luke 16:21
LIE—*guile, lay, sleep, vain* Deut. 19:11; 31:16
  Ps. 4:8, In peace I will both l down
  23:2, makes me l down in green pastures
  Rom. 1:25, exchanged the truth of God for a l
  Col. 3:9, Do not l to one another
  Heb. 6:18, impossible for God to l
  Rev. 14:5, no l was found in their mouth
  Job 7:21; 34:6; 40:21; Ps. 119:69; Eccles. 4:11;
    Song 1:7; Jer. 8:8; Acts 5:3
LIFE—*flesh, living, soul* Ex. 21:23; Deut. 30:19
  Gen. 2:7, into his nostrils the breath of l
  Ps. 16:11, make known to me the path of l
  36:9, with Thee is the fountain of l
  89:47, Remember what my span of l is
  133:3, LORD commanded . . . l forever
  Prov. 3:16, Long ! is in her right hand
  8:35, he who finds me finds l
  Matt. 6:25, do not be anxious for your l
  6:27, cubit to his **l-'s** span
  10:39, who has lost his l for My sake
  16:25, whoever wishes to save his l
  19:16, that I may obtain eternal l
  20:28, give His l a ransom for many
  Mark 8:35, wishes to save his l shall lose it
  10:17, shall I do to inherit eternal l
  13:20, no l would have been saved
  Luke 12:23, l is more than food
  18:30, in the age to come, eternal l
  John 4:36, gathering fruit for l eternal
  5:21, Son also gives l to whom He wishes

LIFE (Continued)
  5:24, passed out of death into l
  6:35, I am the bread of l
  10:11, shepherd lays down His l
  11:25, I am the resurrection and the l
  12:25, who loves his l loses it
  14:6, the way, the truth, and the l
  15:13, lay down his l for his friends
  17:3, this is eternal l
  20:31, you may have l in His name
Acts 3:15, put to death the Prince of l
Rom. 6:4, walk in newness of l
  6:23, gift of God is eternal l
  8:11, give l to your mortal bodies
2 Cor. 3:6, but the Spirit gives l
Gal. 6:8, from the Spirit reap eternal l
Phil. 2:16, holding fast the word of l
  4:3, names are in the book of l
Col. 3:4, Christ, who is our l
1 Tim. 2:2, a tranquil and quiet l
Titus 3:7, hope of eternal l
James 1:12, receive the crown of l
1 John 1:1, concerning the Word of L
  5:12, who has the Son has l
Rev. 2:10, give you the crown of l
  13:8, not been written ... book of l of the
    Lamb
Deut. 32:39; Josh. 2:14; 1 Sam. 25:29; Job 10:1;
  Ps. 22:20; 35:17; Prov. 4:13,23; Jer. 21:8;
  31:12; 38:16; Ezek. 18:27; Dan. 12:2;
  Luke 12:15; 15:24; Titus 3:3; Rev. 7:17
LIFT—exalt, set, take Num. 6:26, LORD l up ...
  countenance
Ps. 3:3, the One who l-s my head
  24:7, L up your heads, O gates
  116:13, l up the cup of salvation
  121:1, l up my eyes to the mountains
Is. 2:4, Nation will not l up sword
John 3:14, Moses l-ed up the serpent
Acts 1:9, He was l-ed up
Gen. 13:14; Ex. 14:16; Job 38:34; Ps. 134:2;
  Is. 5:26; 11:12; 13:2; 40:4; Luke 18:13
LIGHT—dawn, lamp Ex. 10:23; Job 18:5; 38:19
Gen. 1:3, Let there be l; and there was l
Ps. 4:6, l of Thy countenance upon us
  27:1, my l and my salvation
  119:105, a l to my path
Is. 2:5, let us walk in the l of the LORD
  60:1, Arise, shine; for your l has come
Matt. 5:14, You are the l of the world
  5:15, Nor do men l a lamp
  6:22, whole body will be full of l
  11:30, My load is l
Luke 2:32, L OF REVELATION TO THE GENTILES
  16:8, more shrewd ... than the sons of l
John 1:7, bear witness of the l
  1:9, There was the true l
  8:12, I am the l of the world
  12:35, Walk while you have the l
1 Cor. 4:5, bring to l the things hidden
2 Cor. 4:4, l of the gospel of glory
Eph. 5:8, walk as the children of l
1 John 1:7, if we walk in the l as He
Prov. 4:18; Eccles. 11:7; Is. 5:20; Jer. 31:35;
  Mic. 7:9; Matt. 10:27
LIKE—desire Luke 20:36,46
LIKENESS—image Ex. 20:4; Deut. 4:16; Matt.
  22:20
Gen. 1:26, in Our image, according to Our l
Rom. 8:3, in the l of sinful flesh
Phil. 2:7, made in the l of men
LILY Song 2:1, l of the valleys
Hos. 14:5, He will blossom like the l
Matt. 6:28, Observe how the l-es of the field
LIMIT—short Num. 11:23, LORD's power l-ed
Job 15:8, l wisdom to yourself
LINE Joel 2:7, they each march in l
LINEN Gen. 41:42; Prov. 31:24; Jer. 13:1;
  Mark 15:46; John 20:5; Rev. 19:14
LINGER 2 Sam. 1:9; Prov. 23:30
LINTEL Ex. 12:7, on the l of the houses

LION
1 Pet. 5:8, devil, prowls about like a roaring l
Gen. 49:9; 1 Sam. 17:34; 1 Chr. 11:22; Job 10:16;
  Ps. 7:2; 57:4; Prov. 28:1; Eccles. 9:4;
  Rev. 9:8
LISTEN—hear Mark 4:3, L to this ... sower
Mark 4:24, Take care what you l to
John 6:60, who can l to it
Eph. 1:13, l-ing to the message of truth
Gen. 4:23; Ex. 18:19; 20:19; Deut. 4:30; 11:27;
  Job 13:17; 35:13; 37:14; Prov. 23:22; 25:12;
  Eccles. 5:1; Dan. 9:19; Amos 5:23
LIT—enlighten Ps. 97:4, His lightnings l up the
  world
LITTLE—small Ps. 8:5, a l lower than God
Ps. 37:16, Better is the l of the righteous
Prov. 6:10, l sleep, a l slumber, A l folding
  15:16, a l with the fear of the LORD
  16:8, Better is a l with righteousness
Is. 11:6, a l boy will lead them
Matt. 6:30, O men of l faith
Luke 7:47, he who is forgiven l, loves l
  12:32, Do not be afraid, l flock
John 7:33, For a l while longer I am with you
1 Cor. 5:6, a l leaven leavens the whole lump
Heb. 2:7, FOR A L WHILE LOWER THAN THE
Gen. 18:4; Judg. 4:19; 1 Sam. 2:19; Eccles. 5:12;
  Song 2:15; Is. 28:10
LIVE—abide, reside, stay Gen. 3:22; 42:18; Deut.
  4:26
Deut. 8:3, man does not l by bread alone
Job 19:25, my Redeemer l-s
Prov. 21:9, better to l in a corner of a roof
Hab. 2:4, righteous will l by his faith
Matt. 4:4, MAN SHALL NOT L ON BREAD ALONE
Mark 12:44, put in ... all she had to l on
Luke 10:28, DO THIS, AND YOU WILL L
  20:38, for all l to Him
John 11:25, who believes in Me shall l even if he
  dies
Rom. 1:17, RIGHTEOUS man SHALL L BY FAITH
  8:12, to l according to the flesh
  14:8, if we l, we l for the Lord
  14:9, Christ died and l-d again
2 Cor. 5:15, no longer l for themselves
Gal. 2:20, no longer I who l, but Christ l-s in me
Phil. 1:21, to me, to l is Christ
James 4:15, If the Lord wills, we shall l
Job 7:16; Ps. 119:175; Is. 55:3; Jer. 49:18;
  Ezek. 5:11; Matt. 12:45
LIVING Gen. 2:7, man became a l being
1 Kin. 3:25, Divide the l child in two
Matt. 16:16, Son of the l God
John 4:10, He would have given you l water
  6:51, I am the l bread
  7:38, rivers of l water
Acts 10:42, Judge of the l and the dead
Rom. 12:1, your bodies a l ... sacrifice
1 Cor. 15:45, Adam, BECAME A L SOUL
2 Cor. 6:16, temple of the l God
Heb. 4:12, word of God is l
Num. 16:48; Deut. 5:26; Job 28:13; Eccles. 7:2;
  Dan. 6:26; 2 Pet. 2:8
LOAD—burden Matt. 11:30, My l is light
Matt. 23:4, they tie up heavy l-s
LOAN—lend
Deut. 23:19, or anything that may be l-ed
LOATHE Ps. 95:10; Amos 6:8
LOATHSOME Gen. 46:34, every shepherd is l
  to ... Egyptians
Job 6:7, are like l food to me
LOAVES 1 Sam. 10:3, carrying three l of bread
Matt. 14:17, five l and two fish
Mark 6:52, the incident of the l
LOBE Ex. 29:13; Lev. 3:4,10,15
LOCK—shut Deut. 33:25; Judg. 16:13; Ezek.
  44:20
Acts 5:23, prison-house l-ed quite securely
LOCUST—grasshopper Ex. 10:13; Lev. 11:22;
  Judg. 6:5; 1 Kin. 8:37; Job 39:20; Prov. 30:27;
  Joel 2:25; Nah. 3:17; Matt. 3:4

LODGE Job 19:4; 41:22
  Ruth 1:16, where you l, I will l
LOFTY Is. 10:33, l will be abased
LOG—*beam* Eccles. 10:9; Luke 6:42
  Matt. 7:5, first take the l out of your own eye
LOINS—*waist* Ex. 12:11; 2 Kin. 4:29
  Eph. 6:14, GIRDED YOUR L WITH TRUTH
LONELY Ps. 25:16, be gracious ... For I am l
LONG—*length* Ex. 2:3; 2 Sam. 3:1; Prov. 3:16
  Matt. 23:14, for a pretense you make l prayers
  1 Cor. 11:14, if a man has l hair
  Eph. 6:3, LIVE L ON THE EARTH
  Rev. 6:10, How l, O Lord
LONG (v.)—*desire* Job 3:21; Ps. 84:2
  Luke 16:21, **l-ing** to be fed with the *crumbs*
  Rom. 8:19, anxious **l-ing** of the creation
  2 Cor. 5:2, **l-ing** to be clothed with our dwelling
  1 Tim. 6:10, by **l-ing** for it have wandered away
  1 Pet. 1:12, things into which angels l to look
  2:2, like newborn babes, l for the pure milk
LOOK—*see* Ex. 3:6, he was afraid to l at God
  Ps. 84:9, l upon the face of Thine anointed
  Matt. 11:3, shall we l for someone else
  14:19, and **l-ing** up toward heaven
  Luke 2:38, **l-ing** for the redemption of
    Jerusalem
  2:44, began **l-ing** for Him among their
  9:62, hand to the plow and **l-ing** back
  John 4:35, l on the fields
  Acts 3:4, Peter ... said, L at us
  10:21, I am the one you are **l-ing** for
  Gal. 6:1, **l-ing** to yourself, lest you
  Phil. 2:4, do not ... l out for your ... interests
  2 Pet. 3:13, **l-ing** for new heavens
  Rev. 14:1, I **l-ed**, and behold, the Lamb
  Gen. 19:17; Ex. 3:2; Job 35:5; Ps. 91:8; 114:3;
    Prov. 23:31; Eccles. 12:3; Is. 17:7; Luke
    17:23
LOOM Judg. 16:14, pulled out the pin of the l
LOOSE—*release* Job 38:31, l the cords of Orion
  Ps. 116:16, Thou hast **l-d** my bonds
  Matt. 16:19, l on earth ... **l-d** in heaven
  Luke 15:13, his estate with l living
LORD 2 Cor. 1:24, Not that we l it over your faith
  2 Thess. 2:2, day of the L has come
LOSE Joel 2:10, stars l their brightness
  Matt. 10:39, who has found his life shall l it
  16:25, save his life shall l it
  Mark 9:41, he shall not l his reward
LOSS—*damage* Dan. 6:2; Acts 27:10
  2 Cor. 7:9, you might not suffer l
LOST—*perish* Lev. 6:3; Ps. 119:176
  Matt. 10:6, go to the l sheep of ... Israel
  18:11, come to save that which was l
  Luke 15:24, he was l and has been found
  John 6:12, fragments that nothing may be l
LOT—*portion* Lev. 16:8; Num. 26:55
  Ps. 22:18, for my clothing they cast **l-s**
  Prov. 1:14, Throw in your l with us
  Jon. 1:7, cast **l-s** and the l fell on Jonah
  John 19:24, Let us not tear it, but cast **l-s** for it
  Acts 1:26, the l fell to Matthias
LOUD—*great* Rev. 21:3, I heard a l voice from
    the throne
LOVE (v.) Ex. 20:6; Neh. 13:26; Ps. 31:23;
    Zech. 8:17
  Lev. 19:18, you shall l your neighbor as yourself
  Deut. 6:5, l the LORD your God with all
  Prov. 3:12, whom the LORD **l-s** He reproves
  8:17, I l those who l me
  12:1, whoever **l-s** discipline **l-s** knowledge
  17:17, friend **l-s** at all times
  20:13, Do not l sleep
  Eccles. 3:8, time to l, and a time to hate
  Amos 5:15, Hate evil, l good
  Matt. 5:44, l your enemies
  6:5, for they l to stand
  6:24, hate the one and l the other
  22:39, L YOUR NEIGHBOR AS YOURSELF
  Luke 6:27, l your enemies
  John 3:16, God so **l-d** the world

2 Cor. 9:7, God **l-s** a cheerful giver
  Eph. 5:2, walk in l, just as Christ **l-d** you
  Col. 3:19, Husbands, l your wives
  Titus 2:4, l their husbands, to l their children
  James 2:8, L YOUR NEIGHBOR AS YOURSELF
  1 John 4:7, let us l one another ... every one
    who **l-s**
LOVE (n.) Prov. 10:12, l covers all transgressions
  Matt. 24:12, most people's l will grow cold
  John 13:35, if you have l for one another
  15:13, Greater l has no one than this
  Rom. 12:9, Let l be without hypocrisy
  1 Cor. 13:1, do not have l
  14:1, Pursue l
  Gal. 5:13, through l serve one another
  Col. 3:14, beyond ... *put on* l
  1 Tim. 1:5, our instruction is l
  6:10, l of money is a root of ... evil
  2 Tim. 2:22, righteousness, faith, l
  Heb. 13:1, Let l of the brethren continue
  1 Pet. 4:8, l covers a multitude of sins
  2 Pet. 1:7, brotherly kindness, Christian l
  1 John 4:7, l is from God
  3 John 6, your l before the church
  Jude 21, keep yourselves in the l of God
  Rev. 2:4, you have left your first l
  Gen. 29:20; 2 Sam. 1:26
LOVELY—*beautiful* Song 1:5, I am black but l
  Is. 52:7, How l on the mountains
LOVINGKINDNESS—*compassion, mercy*
  Ezra 3:11, His l is upon Israel forever
  Ps. 86:15, a God ... abundant in l
  89:1, I will sing of the l of the LORD
  117:2, His l is great toward us
LOW 1 Sam. 2:7, He brings l, He also exalts
  Ps. 8:5, hast made him a little **l-er** than God
  Jer. 9:10, **l-ing** of the cattle
LOWLIEST Dan. 4:17, And sets it over the l of
    men
LOWLY Job 5:11; Ps. 138:6
  Rom. 12:16, associate with the l
LOYALTY 2 Sam. 16:17; Prov. 20:6
LUMP—*cake* Rom. 11:16, *dough* be holy, the l is
    also
  1 Cor. 5:6, leavens the whole l of *dough*
  5:7, that you may be a new l
LUNCH—*dinner* Luke 11:37, Pharisee asked Him
    to have l
LURK Prov. 7:12, And **l-s** by every corner
LUST—*desire* Matt. 5:28, looks on a woman to l
    for her
  Rom. 13:14, no provision ... regard to *its* **l-s**
  James 4:2, You l and do not have
  1 John 2:16, l of the flesh ... l of the eyes
  Jude 16, following after their own **l-s**
LUXURIANT Ps. 37:35; Hos. 10:1
LUXURIOUS James 5:5, lived **l-ly** on the earth
LUXURY Prov. 19:10, L is not fitting for a fool
  Luke 7:25, live in l are *found* in royal palaces
LYING Prov. 6:17, Haughty eyes, a l tongue
  Prov. 12:22, L lips are an abomination
LYRE—*harp* Gen. 4:21; Ps. 57:8; Is. 5:12

M

MAD—*insane* Eccles. 2:2, It is **m-ness**
  Acts 26:24, learning is driving you m
MADE Gen. 1:7, God m the expanse
  Ps. 8:5, m him a little lower than God
  119:73, Thy hands m me
  Eccles. 7:29, that God m men upright
  Matt. 9:22, your faith has m you well
  2 Cor. 5:21, m Him who knew no sin *to be* sin
  Eph. 3:7, of which I was m a minister
  Heb. 6:4, m partakers of the Holy Spirit
  Ex. 4:11; Job 4:14; 17:6
MAGI—*wise* Matt. 2:1, m from the east arrived
  Matt. 2:7, Herod secretly called the m
  2:16, been tricked by the m
MAGIC Acts 19:19, those who practiced m

MAGNIFICENT—*gorgeous*
Ezek. 23:12, **m-ly** dressed, horsemen
MAGNIFY Ps. 34:3, O **m** the LORD with me
Acts 19:17, name ... Jesus was being **m-ed**
Rom. 11:13, I **m** my ministry
2 Sam. 7:26; Job 7:17; Eccles. 1:16
MAGNITUDE—*greatness*
Jer. 13:22, the **m** of your iniquity
MAID Prov. 30:19, way of a man with a **m**
Gen. 16:6; Ruth 2:8; 3:9
MAIDEN Judg. 5:30; Job 41:5; Ps. 68:25
MAINTAIN Rom. 3:28, we **m** that a man is
justified
MAJESTIC—*excellent* Ps. 8:1, Lord, How **m** is
Thy name
Ps. 16:3; 2 Pet. 1:17
MAJESTY—*dignity, excellence*
Ps. 93:1, He is clothed with **m**
Is. 53:2, no *stately* form or **m**
Heb. 1:3, right hand of the **M** on high
Jude 25, glory, **m**, dominion and authority
Job 37:22; Is. 35:2; 2 Pet. 2:10; Jude 8
MAKE Gen. 1:26, Let Us **m** man in Our image
Gen. 2:18, **m** him a helper suitable for him
Ps. 25:4, **M** me know Thy ways, O LORD
Jer. 18:3, he was, **m-ing** something on the
wheel
Matt. 3:3, **M** READY THE WAY OF THE LORD
4:19, I will **m** you fishers of men
5:34, **m** no oath at all
John 1:23, **M** STRAIGHT THE WAY OF THE LORD
James 4:13, engage in business and **m** a profit
2 Pet. 1:10, **m** certain about His calling and
Ex. 20:4,25; Deut. 8:18; Job 17:12; Luke 12:33;
Rom. 10:19
MAKER Job 4:17; 35:10; Is. 17:7; 54:5; Jer. 10:16
MALE Gen. 5:2, He created them **m** and female
Matt. 2:16, slew all the **m** children
19:4, MADE THEM **M** AND FEMALE
Gen. 34:25; Deut. 4:16; Gal. 3:28
MALICE—*wickedness*
Matt. 22:18, Jesus perceived their **m**
1 Pet. 2:1, putting aside all **m**
1 Cor. 5:8; Eph. 4:31; Col. 3:8
MALICIOUS—*false* Ex. 23:1, to be a **m** witness
2 Tim. 3:3, **m** gossips, without
MALIGN—*speak* Titus 3:2, to **m** no one
MAN—*fellow, person, self* Gen. 1:26; 4:23
Gen. 3:22, the **m** has become like one of Us
Job 5:7, For **m** is born for trouble
Ps. 1:1, blessed is the **m** who does not walk in
the
Matt. 4:4, **M** SHALL NOT LIVE ON BREAD ALONE
8:20, Son of **M** has nowhere to lay
26:61, This **m** stated, I am able to destroy
26:71, This **m** was with Jesus
Mark 2:27, not **m** for the Sabbath
10:25, for a rich **m** to enter
Luke 6:45, The good **m** ... the evil **m**
9:22, The Son of **M** must suffer
22:59, this **m** also was with Him
23:2, found this **m** misleading our nation
John 1:6, a **m**, sent from God
3:4, How can a **m** be born when
19:5, Behold, the **M**
1 Cor. 13:11, when I became a **m**
15:21, by a **m** *came* death
Eph. 4:13, to a mature **m**
James 1:8, a double-minded **m**, unstable in
Lev. 16:21; Num. 12:3; 1 Sam. 16:17; 1 Kin. 2:2;
2 Kin. 5:8; Job 14:1; 25:6; 33:12; Ps. 19:5;
37:37; Prov. 3:4; Eccles. 4:8; Is. 2:22; Matt.
26:2; John 7:12; 9:29; 2 Cor. 12:2
MANAGE—*rule* 1 Tim. 3:5, how to **m** his own
household
MANGER Job 39:9; Prov. 14:4; Is. 1:3
MANIFEST—*reveal* John 17:6; Rom. 10:20;
Col. 1:26
MANIFOLD—*various* Eph. 3:10, the **m** wisdom
of God
1 Pet. 4:10, the **m** grace of God

MANKIND 2 Chr. 6:18; Job 4:17
MANNER Gen. 31:35, **m** of women is upon me
MANTLE—*garment* Heb. 1:12, AS A **M** THOU WILT
ROLL THEM UP
1 Kin. 19:19; Is. 59:17
MANURE—*refuse*
Luke 14:35, for the soil or for the **m** pile
MANY—*multitude* Ps. 104:24, how **m** are Thy
works
Song 8:7, **M** waters cannot quench love
Jer. 14:7, our apostasies have been **m**
Matt. 7:22, **M** will say to Me on that day
22:14, **m** are called, but few
Luke 7:47, her sins, which are **m**
21:8, **m** will come in My name
John 14:2, house are **m** dwelling places
Acts 2:43, **m** wonders and signs
Rom. 12:4, **m** members in one body
1 Cor. 11:30, **m** ... are weak ... a number sleep
James 3:1, **m** *of you* become teachers
Jude 14, **m** thousands of His holy ones
Rev. 1:15, sound of **m** waters
Gen. 16:10; 1 Kin. 11:1; Job 13:23; Ps. 71:7;
Prov. 14:20
MARCH—*walk* Joel 2:8, **m** every one in his path
Nah. 2:5, stumble in their **m**
MARK Ps. 37:37, **M** the blameless
2 Thess. 3:17, a distinguishing **m** in every letter
Rev. 14:9, receives a **m** on his forehead
19:20, **m** of the beast
MARKET PLACES
Matt. 11:16, like children sitting in the **m**
Mark 6:56, laying the sick in the **m**
MARRIAGE Matt. 22:30, marry, are given in **m**
Heb. 13:4, Let **m** *be held* in honor
Rev. 19:7, **m** of the Lamb has come
MARRY Matt. 5:32, whoever **m-es** a divorced
woman
Matt. 19:9, **m-es** another commits adultery
19:10, it is better not to **m**
Mark 12:25, they neither **m**, nor
Luke 20:34, sons of this age **m**
1 Cor. 7:9, better to **m** than to burn
1 Tim. 5:11, widows ... want to get **m-ed**
MARVEL—*wonder* Ps. 71:7, I have become a **m**
to many
Matt. 8:10, when Jesus heard *this*, He **m-ed**
15:31, the multitude **m-ed**
Mark 5:20, and everyone **m-ed**
John 3:7, Do not **m** that I said to you
1 Pet. 2:9, out of darkness into His **m-ous** light
Rev. 15:3, GREAT AND **M-OUS** ARE THY WORKS
MASSAH—*temptation* Ps. 95:8, in the day of **M**
MASTER—*dominion, teacher* Job 3:19; Eph. 6:5
Matt. 6:24, No one can serve two **m-s**
10:24, nor a slave above his **m**
Rom. 6:9, death no longer is **m** over Him
1 Cor. 3:10, as a wise **m-builder** I laid
MATERIAL Deut. 22:11, not wear a **m** mixed ...
together
1 Cor. 9:11, we should reap **m** things
MATTER Gen. 21:17; 30:15; 1 Sam. 11:5; 21:8
MEAN—*thought* Gen. 50:20, **m-t** evil against me
Ex. 34:7, by no **m-s** leave *the guilty* unpunished
Matt. 9:13, go and learn what this **m-s**
Acts 17:20, know ... what these things **m**
1 Cor. 14:11, do not know the **m-ing** of the
language
Gal. 5:6, neither circumcision ... **m-s** anything
MEANINGLESS—*vain*
Matt. 6:7, do not use **m** repetition
MEASURE Eph. 4:7, according to the **m** of
Christ's gift
Rev. 21:16, **m-d** the city with the rod
Gen. 18:6; Deut. 25:15; 2 Kin. 7:1; Ps. 80:5;
Matt. 7:2
MEAT—*flesh* Ex. 16:3; Deut. 12:20
MEDDLER—*busybody*
1 Pet. 4:15, troublesome **m**
MEDIATOR Gal. 3:19, by the agency of a **m**
Gal. 3:20, a **m** is not for one *party*

1 Tim. 2:5, one **m** also between God and men
Heb. 8:6, **m** of a better covenant
  12:24, to Jesus the **m** of a new covenant
MEDITATE Gen. 24:63, Isaac went out to **m**
  Ps. 1:2, in His law he **m-s** day and night
  19:14, **m-ion** of my heart
MEDIUM Lev. 19:31; 1 Sam. 28:7
MEETING—*congregation* Acts 13:43, **m** of the
  synagogue had
MELODY Is. 51:3, sound of a **m**
  Eph. 5:19, making **m** with your heart
MELT—*dissolve* Josh. 2:11; Ps. 46:6; 75:3; 97:5;
  Is. 14:31
MEMBER Matt. 10:25, how much more the
  m-s . . . household
  1 Cor. 6:15, your bodies are **m-s** of Christ
  12:12, the body . . . has many **m-s**
  12:14, body is not one **m**, but many
MEMORIAL Ex. 3:15; 17:14; Josh. 4:7; Acts 10:4
MEMORY Prov. 10:7, **m** of the righteous is
  blessed
  Matt. 26:13, spoken of in **m** of her
  Job 18:17; Ps. 9:6; 109:15
MEN Ps. 116:11, All **m** are liars
  Mark 1:17, I will make you . . . fishers of **m**
  Luke 20:4, from heaven or from **m**
  1 Thess. 2:4, not as pleasing **m** but God
  Gen. 4:9; 1 Sam 4:9; Job 11:3; Ps. 26:4; 82:7;
    Matt. 10:17; Mark 6:21; Acts 17:5
MENTION Ps. 71:16; Is. 63:7; Rom. 1:9,10
MERCHANDISE John 2:16, My Father's house a
  house of **m**
MERCHANT 1 Kin. 10:28; Hos. 12:7; Rev. 18:3
MERCY—*compassion*
  2 Sam. 24:14, for His **m-es** are great
  Matt. 5:7, for they shall receive **m**
  · 18:33, I had **m** on you
  Rom. 9:15, M ON WHOM I HAVE M
  12:1, by the **m-es** of God
  1 Cor. 7:25, as one who by the **m** of the LORD
  Eph. 2:4, God, being rich in **m**
  James 5:11, full of compassion and *is* **m-ful**
MERRY—*joyful* Eccles. 8:15, drink and be **m**
  Luke 12:19, eat, drink *and* be **m**
  15:29, might be **m** with my friends
MESSAGE—*tidings, word, report, speech*
  Luke 4:32, His **m** was with authority
  Acts 20:7, his **m** until midnight
  Judg. 3:19,20; Jer. 49:14; Is. 53:1; Luke 4:36
MESSENGER Matt. 11:10, MY M BEFORE YOUR
  FACE
  2 Cor. 12:7, a **m** of Satan
  2 Kin. 6:32; Hag. 1:13
MESSIAH—*Lord, Christ* John 1:41, found the **M**
MIDDLE Josh. 12:2; Ruth 3:8; Prov. 30:19
MIDNIGHT Ps. 119:6; Matt. 25:6; Acts 16:25; 20:7
MIDST—*middle, within*
  Matt. 10:16, sheep in the **m** of
  18:20, there I am in their **m**
  Luke 17:21, kingdom of God is in your **m**
  24:36, He Himself stood in their **m**
  John 20:26, Jesus . . . stood in their **m**
MIGHT Job 39:19, give the horse *his* **m**
  Zech. 4:6, Not by **m** or by power
  Acts 19:20, word . . . was growing **m-ily**
  Eph. 1:19, working of the strength of His **m**
  Col. 1:29, which **m-ily** works within me
  Gen. 49:3; Deut. 6:5; Judg. 5:31; 2 Sam. 6:14;
    Eccles. 9:10; Jer. 9:23
MIGHTY 2 Sam. 1:19, How have the **m** fallen
  Ps. 24:8, strong and **m** . . . **m** in battle
  89:13, Thy hand is **m**
  Jer. 48:17, How has the **m** scepter been broken
  Joel 3:10, weak say, I am a **m** man
  Mic. 4:3, decisions for **m**, distant nations
  Luke 24:19, prophet **m** in deed and word
  Acts 2:11, the **m** deeds of God
  18:24, **m** in the Scriptures
  2 Cor. 13:3, but **m** in you
  1 Pet. 5:6, the **m** hand of God

Gen. 6:4; 10:9; Deut. 10:17; Is. 19:4; 63:1;
  Jer. 32:18
MILE Luke 24:13; John 11:18; Rev. 14:20
MILK Ex. 3:8, land flowing with **m** and honey
  1 Cor. 3:2, I gave you **m** to drink
  Heb. 5:12, you have come to need **m**
  1 Pet. 2:2, pure **m** of the word
  Gen. 49:12; Judg. 4:19; Job 10:10; Prov. 30:33
MIND—*heart* Ps. 7:9, tries the hearts and **m-s**
  Mark 5:15, and in his right **m**
  Acts 28:6, changed their **m-s**
  Rom. 1:28, over to a depraved **m**
  8:7, **m** set on the flesh is hostile
  1 Cor. 1:10, complete in the same **m**
  2 Cor. 13:11, be **like-m-ed**, live in peace
  Phil. 2:2, being of the same **m**
  2:3, with humility of **m** let each
  Col. 3:2, Set your **m** on
  James 1:8, a **double-m-ed** man
  1 Pet. 1:13, gird your **m-s** for action
  Gen. 40:14; Ps. 31:12; Is. 46:8; Jer. 17:10; Dan.
    4:16; Rom. 14:5; 1 Tim. 6:5; 2 Pet. 1:15
MINISTER Is. 61:6; Eph. 3:7
MINISTRY—*service* 1 Cor. 12:5; 2 Cor. 9:12
  Acts 6:4, to the **m** of the word
  2 Cor. 5:18, **m** of reconciliation
  Col. 4:17, Take heed to the **m**
  2 Tim. 4:5, fulfill your **m**
  Heb. 8:6, obtained a more excellent **m**
MIRACLE—*marvel, sign, mighty*
  Matt. 11:21, if the **m-s** had occurred in Tyre
  Ex. 34:10; Mark 6:5; 1 Cor. 12:10
MIRROR 1 Cor. 13:12, we see in a **m** dimly
  James 1:23, his natural face in a **m**
  Ex. 38:8; Job 37:18; Is. 3:23
MISCARRIAGE Ex. 21:22, so that she has a **m**
MISCARRY—*young* Ex. 23:26, no one **m-ing**
MISCHIEF Job 15:35, They conceive **m**
MISERY Job 10:15; Rom. 3:16
MISGIVING Acts 10:20, accompany them
  without **m-s**
MISGUIDE Heb. 5:2, deal gently with the
  ignorant and **m-d**
MISLEAD Deut. 27:18, **m-s** a blind person
  Job 12:16, misled and the **m-er** belong to Him
  Matt. 24:24, so as to **m** . . . even the elect
MISSILE Eph. 6:16, flaming **m-s** of the evil one
MISTAKE Eccles. 5:6; Matt. 22:29; Mark 12:24
MISTREAT—*wrong* Jer. 22:3, do not **m** *or* do
  violence
  Matt. 22:6; Luke 18:32; Acts 7:19
MIX Deut. 22:11; Prov. 23:30; Dan. 2:41; Rev. 18:6
MOCK Prov. 14:9, Fools **m** at sin
  Prov. 20:1, Wine is a **m-er**
  Gal. 6:7, God is not **m-ed**
  2 Kin. 2:23; Job 21:3; 30:1; Hab. 1:10;
    Matt. 27:29
MODE Judg. 13:12, shall be the boy's **m** of life
MODEL 2 Thess. 3:9, offer ourselves as a **m**
MOMENT—*instant* Ps. 30:5, His anger is for a **m**
  Job 34:20, In a **m** they die
  1 Cor. 15:52, in a **m**, in the twinkling of an
MONEY—*gain* Gen. 43:12; Deut. 21:14
  Eccles. 5:10, who loves **m** will not be satisfied
  10:19, **m** is the answer to everything
  Matt. 21:12, tables of the **m-changers**
  Mark 6:8, no **m** in their belt
  Luke 19:23, why . . . not put the **m** . . . bank
  1 Tim. 3:3, free from the love of **m**
  6:10, love of **m** is a root . . . of evil
  2 Kin. 5:26; Eccles. 7:12; Jer. 32:25; Amos 2:6
MONEYLENDER—*creditor*
  Luke 7:41, certain **m** had two
MONGREL Zech. 9:6, a **m** race
MONSTER Gen. 1:21, created the great sea **m-s**
  Job 7:12, sea, or the sea **m**
  Ezek. 32:2, **m** in the seas
MOON—*crescent* Matt. 24:29, M WILL NOT GIVE
  ITS LIGHT
  Luke 21:25, signs in the sun and **m**

MOON (Continued)
　Gen. 37:9; Josh. 10:12; 1 Sam. 20:5; Job 31:26;
　　Ps. 136:9; Song 6:10; Is. 1:13; Joel 2:31;
　　Acts 2:20
MORALS 1 Cor. 15:33, Bad company corrupts
　good **m**
MORNING—early Job 38:7, **m** stars sang
　together
　2 Pet. 1:19, the **m** star arises in your hearts
　Rev. 22:16, the bright **m** star
　Gen. 19:15; Ex. 8:20; Deut. 28:67; Ps. 55:17;
　　Eccles. 11:6
MORSEL—piece Job 31:17; Prov 17:1
MORTAL Rom. 6:12, sin reign in your **m** body
　Rom. 8:11, give life to your **m** bodies
　1 Cor. 15:53, **m** . . . put on immortality
　2 Cor. 4:11, manifested in our **m** flesh
MOST—many, very Matt. 24:12, **m** people's love
　will grow
　2 Cor. 11:5, least inferior to the **m** eminent
MOTHER Gen. 2:24, leave his father . . . **m**
　Ex. 20:12, Honor your father and your **m**
　Matt. 1:18, When His **m** Mary . . . betrothed
　　2:11, Child with Mary His **m**
　　2:13, **m** and flee to Egypt
　　19:19, HONOR YOUR FATHER AND **M**
　John 19:27, the disciple, Behold, your **m**
　Heb. 7:3, Without father, without **m**
　Gen. 2:30; Ex. 22:30; Lev. 22:27; Deut. 22:6; Job
　　17:14; Ezek. 16:44; Hos. 2:2; Matt. 12:48
MOTION Ex. 15:16; Acts 12:17
MOTIVES—thought 1 Cor. 4:5, **m** of men's hearts
　James 2:4, judges with evil **m**
MOUND—bank 2 Sam. 20:15, a **m** against the
　city
MOUNTAINS Ps. 121:1, will lift up my eyes to
　the **m**
　Is. 5:25; Mic. 1:4
MOUNTED Zech. 9:9, **m** on a donkey
　Matt. 21:5, GENTLE, AND **M** UPON A DONKEY
MOURN—weep, wail
　Is. 61:2, To comfort all who **m**
　Matt. 2:18, WEEPING AND GREAT **M**-ING
　　5:4, Blessed are those who **m**
　Luke 6:25, for you shall **m** and weep
　James 4:9, laughter be turned into **m**-ing
　Rev. 1:7, TRIBES . . . **M** OVER HIM
　Gen. 37:35; Deut. 21:13; Jer. 9:17; 15:5;
　　2 Cor. 12:21
MOUTH—speech Ps. 19:14, the words of my **m**
　Ps. 39:1, guard my **m** as with a muzzle
　Prov. 13:3, who guards his **m** preserves
　Song 4:3, your **m** is lovely
　Matt. 4:4, PROCEEDS OUT OF THE **M** OF GOD
　　13:35, OPEN MY **M** IN PARABLES
　Acts 3:21, **m** of His holy prophets
　James 3:3, put the bits . . . horses' **m**-s
　Ex. 4:11; Judg. 7:6; Job 8:21; 15:6; Ps. 8:2; 71:15;
　　Prov. 4:24
MOVE 2 Chr. 16:9, eyes of the LORD **m**
　Mark 1:41, **m**-d with compassion, He stretched
　Acts 17:28, in Him we live and **m**
　2 Pet. 1:21, **m**-d by the Holy Spirit
　Gen. 1:2; Deut. 19:14; 1 Sam. 1:13; Jer. 4:24
MUCH Prov. 25:27, not good to eat **m** honey
　Prov. 29:1, hardens his neck after **m** reproof
　Eccles. 1:18, in **m** wisdom there is **m** grief
　Luke 7:47, for she loved **m**
　　16:10, faithful also in **m**
MULTIPLY Gen. 1:22; Ex. 32:13; Deut. 6:3
MULTITUDE Matt. 14:15, send the **m**-s away
　Luke 23:27, following Him a great **m**
　James 5:20, cover a **m** of sins
　1 Pet. 4:8, love covers a **m** of sins
　Gen. 17:4; Ex. 23:2; Deut. 1:10
MURDER Ex. 20:13, You shall not **m**
　Rom. 1:29, full of envy, **m**, strife
　Matt. 5:21; 19:18
MURDERER Num. 35:16; John 8:44; Acts 28:4;
　1 John 3:15
MURMUR Ps. 55:17, I will complain and **m**
MUSIC 1 Sam. 18:6; Luke 15:25

MUST—ought Acts 5:29, We **m** obey God
MUZZLE Deut. 25:4, not **m** the ox while
　1 Cor. 9:9, 1 Tim. 5:18, NOT **M** THE OX WHILE
MYRRH Matt. 2:11, frankincense and **m**
　John 19:39, mixture of **m** and aloes
　Gen. 43:11; Ps. 45:8; Song 5:13
MYSTERY—secret Dan. 4:9, no **m** baffles you
　Matt. 13:11, **m**-es of the kingdom
　1 Cor. 2:7, God's wisdom in a **m**
　　4:1, stewards of the **m**-es
　　13:2, know all **m**-es . . . knowledge
　Eph. 3:9, administration of the **m**
　　6:19, the **m** of the gospel
　1 Tim. 3:9, the **m** of the faith
MYTHS—fables 1 Tim. 1:4, pay attention to **m**
　Titus 1:14, paying attention to Jewish **m**

N

NAILS John 20:25, in His hands the imprint of **n**
　Deut. 21:12; Dan. 4:33
NAIVE—simple Prov. 14:15, **n** believes
　everything
NAKED—bare Gen. 2:25; Job 1:21; 26:6;
　Matt. 25:36
NAME—appoint Job 1:21, Blessed be the **n** of the
　LORD
　Ps. 8:1, How majestic is Thy **n**
　　18:49, sing praises to Thy **n**
　　72:17, his **n** endure forever . . . **n** increase
　　102:15, nations will fear the **n** of the LORD
　　111:9, Holy and awesome is His **n**
　Prov. 22:1, good **n** is to be more desired
　Matt. 6:9, Hallowed be Thy **n**
　　10:2, **n**-s of the twelve apostles are
　　18:5, one such child in My **n**
　Mark 5:9, My **n** is Legion; for we are many
　Luke 21:8, many will come in My **n**
　John 15:16, you ask of the Father in My **n**
　Acts 3:16, on the basis of faith in His **n**
　　4:12, no other **n** under heaven
　Phil. 2:9, **n** which is above every **n**
　　4:3, whose **n**-s are in the book of life
　Gen. 3:20; 30:28; Ex. 20:7; Deut. 29:20; Neh.
　　9:10; Prov. 30:9; Is. 42:8; 48:2; 57:15; Matt.
　　10:22; Eph. 1:21; 3 John 14
NARROW—strait Matt. 7:13, Enter by the **n** gate
NATION—generation, Gentile
　Ps. 33:12, Blessed is the **n** whose God
　Prov. 14:34, Righteousness exalts a **n**
　Is. 2:4, **N** will not lift up sword against **n**
　Matt. 24:7, **n** will rise against **n**
　　28:19, Go . . . make disciples of all the **n**-s
　Acts 2:5, devout men, from every **n**
　Gal. 3:8, ALL THE **N**-S SHALL BE BLESSED
　Rev. 5:9, and tongue and people and **n**
　Gen. 12:2; 20:4; Ex. 19:6; Lev. 26:33; Ps. 2:1;
　　102:15; Is. 18:2; 52:15; 66:19; Jer. 51:58;
　　John 11:50; Rev. 11:2
NATIVE Acts 28:2,4
NATURAL Rom. 1:26, exchanged the **n** function
　1 Cor. 15:44, it is sown a **n** body
NATURE 1 Cor. 11:14, Does not even **n** itself
　teach
　2 Pet. 1:4, partakers of the divine **n**
NEAR—close Ps. 34:18, **n** to the brokenhearted
　Ps. 145:18, **n** to all who call upon Him
　Mark 13:28, you know that the summer is **n**
　Eph. 2:13, brought **n** by the blood of Christ
　Phil. 4:5, The Lord is **n**
　Heb. 10:22, draw **n** with a sincere heart
　James 4:8, Draw **n** to God and He will draw **n**
　Ex. 19:22; Deut. 4:7; Ps. 22:11; Prov. 27:10;
　　Joel 3:14
NECESSARY—need
　Luke 10:42, only a few things are **n**
　　24:26, Was it not **n** for the Christ to suffer
NECK Gen. 27:16; Ex. 13:13; Deut. 28:48; Prov.
　3:3; Matt. 18:6
NEED—want Prov. 25:16, Eat only what you **n**
　Matt. 6:8, your Father knows what you **n**
　　9:12, not . . . healthy who **n** a physician
　　21:3, The Lord has **n** of them

Luke 15:14, he began to be in **n**
Phil. 4:19, God shall supply all your **n-s**
Heb. 4:16, help in time of **n**
1 John 3:17, beholds his brother in **n**
Rev. 3:17, have **n** of nothing
1 Cor. 12:21; 1 Thess. 4:12
NEEDLESS Gal. 2:21, then Christ died **n-ly**
NEEDY Ps. 9:18, **n** will not always be forgotten
Ps. 72:13, compassion on the poor and **n**
Is. 14:30, **n** will lie down in security
Ex. 23:6; Deut. 15:11; Job 29:16; Ps. 40:17; 69:33
NEGLECT—*forget*
Matt. 6:16, they **n** their appearance
Luke 15:29, I have never **n-ed** a command
Heb. 13:2,16
NEGLIGENCE—*error* Dan. 6:4, no **n** or
corruption was *to be*
NEGLIGENT Prov. 10:4, works with a **n** hand
NEIGHBOR—*fellow-citizen*
Lev. 19:18, you shall love your **n**
Prov. 3:29, Do not devise harm against your **n**
27:10, Better is a **n** who is near
Hab. 2:15, who make your **n-s** drink
Matt. 5:43, YOU SHALL LOVE YOUR **N**
Luke 10:29, who is my **n**
NEST—*lodge* Matt. 8:20, birds have **n-s**
Luke 13:19, birds ... **n-ed** in its branches
Num. 24:21; Deut. 32:11; Jer. 49:16; Obad. 4
NET Job 19:6; Ps. 57:6; Is. 51:20; Matt. 13:47
NEVER Matt. 7:23, I **n** knew you
John 4:14, of the water ... shall **n** thirst
7:46, N did a man speak the way
8:51, he shall **n** see death
Heb. 13:5, I WILL N DESERT YOU
Deut. 15:11; Job 3:16; Ps. 31:1
NEW Lev. 23:14, roasted grain nor **n** growth
Ps. 33:3, Sing to Him a **n** song
Eccles. 1:9, nothing **n** under the sun
Is. 65:17, create **n** heavens and a **n** earth
Ezek. 11:19, put a **n** spirit within them
John 13:34, A **n** commandment I give to you
2 Cor. 5:17, a **n** creature ... **n** things have come
Eph. 4:24, put on the **n** self
Rev. 21:1, a **n** heaven and a **n** earth
NEWS—*tidings* Gen. 29:13, heard the **n** of Jacob
2 Kin. 7:9, day is a day of good **n**
Is. 52:7, feet of him who brings good **n**
Luke 2:10, good **n** of a great joy
1 Thess. 3:6, good **n** of your faith
Prov. 15:30; Matt. 14:1; Mark 1:28,45
NIGHT Ex. 13:21, a pillar of fire by **n**
Ps. 19:2, **n** to **n** reveals knowledge
91:5, not be afraid of the terror by **n**
Is. 21:11, Watchman, how far gone is the **n**
Luke 2:8, watch over their flock by **n**
John 9:4, **n** is coming, when no man can work
Rom. 13:12, **n** is almost gone
2 Cor. 11:27, through many sleepless **n-s**
1 Thess. 5:2, like a thief in the **n**
Gen. 1:5; Josh. 1:8; Job 17:12
NOBLE Ps. 45:9; Prov. 8:6
NOISE—*sound* Is. 22:2, You who were full of **n**
Jer. 50:22, **n** of the battle is in the land
Acts 2:2, came from heaven a **n**
1 Cor. 13:1, have become a **n-y** gong
NONSENSE Luke 24:11, words appeared ... as **n**
NOSTRIL Ezek. 16:12, put a ring in your **n**
NOTHING Job 26:7, hangs the earth on **n**
Ps. 49:17, he will carry **n** away
Prov. 13:7, pretends to be rich, but has **n**
John 15:5, apart from Me you can do **n**
1 Cor. 4:4, conscious of **n** against myself
Gal. 6:3, thinks he is something when he is **n**
Phil. 4:6, Be anxious for **n**
1 Tim. 4:7, have **n** to do with worldly fables
James 1:4, perfect and complete, lacking in **n**
Ex. 21:11; Lam. 1:12; Luke 6:35
NOTICE—*visit* Jer. 15:15, Remember me, take **n**
of me

Matt. 6:1, righteousness ... to be **n-d** by them
Matt. 7:3; Luke 6:41
NOURISH 1 Tim. 4:6, **n-ed** on the words of the
faith
NULLIFY Rom. 3:3; 4:14; Gal. 2:21; 3:17
NUMBER—*measure, count* Num. 1:3; Job 14:16;
Ps. 139:18; Matt. 10:30; 2 Cor. 11:23
NURSE Gen. 35:8; Ex. 2:7; Num. 11:12;
1 Thess. 2:7

O

OAK 2 Sam. 18:10; Is. 1:30; Amos 2:9
OATH—*vow* Gen. 26:3; Josh. 2:20; Acts 23:12
OBEDIENCE Rom. 16:26, to **o** of faith
2 Cor. 10:5, to the **o** of Christ
Heb. 5:8, He learned **o** from the things
OBEDIENT 2 Cor. 2:9, whether you are **o** in all
things
Phil. 2:8, **o** to the point of death
1 Pet. 1:14, As **o** children
OBEY—*follow* Ps. 103:20, **O-ing** the voice of His
word
Matt. 8:27, the winds and the sea **o** Him
Acts 5:29, **o** God rather than men
Eph. 6:1, Children, **o** your parents
Heb. 11:8, By faith Abraham ... **o-ed**
13:17, **O** your leaders
1 Pet. 1:2, that you may **o** Jesus Christ
Ex. 19:5; Josh. 1:17; 1 Sam. 15:22; Is. 1:19
OBLIGATE Matt. 23:16, whoever swears by the
gold ... **o-d**
OBLIGATION Num. 32:22, be free of **o** toward
the LORD
Rom. 1:14, I am under **o** both to Greeks
8:12, we are under **o**, not to the flesh
Gal. 5:3, he is under **o** to keep the whole Law
OBSCURE Prov. 22:29; Luke 23:45
OBSERVE—*keep* Deut. 5:15, to **o** the sabbath
day
Prov. 6:6, **O** her ways and be wise
Matt. 6:28, **O** how the lilies of the field
28:20, teaching them to **o** all that I
commanded
Luke 11:28, hear the word of God, and **o** it
Rom. 14:6, He who **o-s** the day, **o-s** it for the
Lord
Prov. 5:2; 6:20; Jer. 2:10; Gal. 4:10
OBSOLETE Heb. 8:13, He has made the first **o**
OBSTACLE Rom. 14:13, not to put an **o** ... in a
brother's
OBTAIN—*purchase* Prov. 8:35, **o-s** favor from
the LORD
1 Thess. 5:9, for **o-ing** salvation through our
Lord
Heb. 11:35, that they might **o** a better
resurrection
Gen. 16:2; Acts 8:20
OCCASION 1 Tim. 5:14, give the enemy no **o** for
reproach
ODIOUS Ex. 5:21; 1 Sam. 13:4
OFFEND Ex. 2:13, he said to the **o-er**
Job 34:31, I will not **o** *any more*
OFFENSE—*strange* Job 19:17, breath is **o-ive** to
my wife
1 Cor. 10:32, Give no **o**
1 Pet. 2:8, AND A ROCK OF **O**
Gen. 41:9; Eccles. 10:4; Jer. 23:13
OFFER—*present* Ps. 50:14, **O** to God a sacrifice
Mal. 1:8, Why not **o** it to your governor
Matt. 5:23, presenting your **o-ing** at the altar
5:24, come and present your **o-ing**
Luke 6:29, **o** him the other also
Heb. 9:14, **o-ed** Himself without blemish
OFFICE Judg. 5:14; Ps. 109:8; 1 Tim. 3:1; Heb. 7:5
OFFICER—*governor*
Jer. 20:1, chief **o** in the house ... LORD
OFFICIAL 2 Kin. 20:18; 23:11; Is. 39:7; Dan. 1:9;
Matt. 9:18
OFFSPRING Deut. 28:53; Is. 65:9
OFTEN Luke 13:34, How **o** I wanted to gather
1 Cor. 11:26, as **o** as you eat this bread

OIL Matt. 25:8, Give us some of your o
  Luke 10:34, pouring o and wine on them
  Rev. 6:6, harm the o and the wine
  Ex. 25:6; Job 29:6; Ps. 23:5; 45:7; 55:21; 104:15;
    133:2; Prov. 5:3; Luke 7:46
OINTMENT Job 41:31; John 12:5
OLD Matt. 9:17, new wine into o wineskins
  John 3:4, man be born when he is o
  Rom. 6:6, our o self was crucified
  1 Cor. 5:7, Clean out the o leaven
  2 Cor. 3:14, reading of the o covenant
    5:17, the o things passed away
  Col. 3:9, laid aside the o self
  Rev. 12:9, serpent of o who is called the devil
  Gen. 15:15; 44:20; Ruth 1:12; 1 Sam. 12:2; Job
    42:17; Prov. 20:29; Matt. 9:16; Heb. 11:2
OLDER—*aged*
  Job 32:4, waited ... because they were ... o
  Titus 2:2,3, O men are to be temperate
ONCE—*soon* 1 Sam. 9:13, you will find him at o
  Matt. 15:28, daughter was healed at o
    21:20, did the fig tree wither at o
  Rom. 6:10, died to sin, o for all
  Heb. 9:28, offered o to bear the sins
  Gen. 18:32; Is. 66:8
ONE Matt. 6:24, No o can serve two masters
  Matt. 19:5, TWO SHALL BECOME O FLESH
  John 10:30, I and the Father are O
    17:21, that they may all be o
  Gal. 6:4, let each o examine his own work
  Eph. 4:4, o body and o Spirit ... o hope
  1 Tim. 2:5, o God, *and* o mediator
  James 4:12, only o Lawgiver and Judge
  Gen. 1:5; Deut. 6:4; 1 Sam. 21:15; 2 Sam. 6:20;
    Job 33:23; Mark 8:30; John 19:41
ONLY Gen. 6:5, thoughts of his heart ... o evil
  Ps. 62:2, He o is my rock ... salvation
  Luke 24:18, You the o one visiting
  Rom. 16:27, o wise God ... glory forever
  Heb. 11:17, his o begotten *son*
  Jude 25, o God ... our Lord, *be* glory
OPEN—*explain, wide*
  Matt. 7:7, knock and it shall be o-ed
    20:33, we want our eyes to be o-ed
  John 1:51, you shall see the heavens o-ed
  Rev. 4:1, a door *standing* o-ed
    5:2, Who is worthy to o the book
  Gen. 3:5; Job 29:23; Ps. 5:9; 51:15; Prov. 27:5; Is.
    26:2; 42:7; Ezek. 16:63; Luke 13:25
OPENING Prov. 8:3; Song 5:4
OPINION—*counsel* 2 Cor. 8:10, give my o in this
  matter
OPPONENT—*adversary* Matt. 5:25; Luke 18:3;
  Phil. 1:28
OPPORTUNE Mark 14:11, betray Him at an o
  time
OPPORTUNITY—*occasion*
  Gal. 5:13, turn your freedom ... o
  Eph. 4:27, do not give the devil an o
OPPOSE—*resist* Ezra 10:15, Jahzeiah ... o-d this
  Rom. 13:2, he who resists authority has o-d
  James 4:6, GOD IS O-D TO THE PROUD
OPPOSITION Num. 14:34; Gal. 5:17
OPPRESS—*afflict*
  Acts 10:38, healing all who were o-ed
  James 2:6, Is it not the rich who o you
  Gen. 15:13; Lev. 19:13; 1 Sam. 1:15; Job 5:4;
    Hos. 12:7
OPPRESSION—*affliction*
  Ps. 62:10, Do not trust in o
  Eccles. 7:7, o makes a wise man mad
  Is. 30:20; Ezek. 22:12
ORCHARD—*garden* Song 6:11, down to the o of
  nut trees
ORDAIN Ex. 29:29,35; Ps. 8:3; Acts 7:53
ORDER 2 Kin. 20:1; Ps. 5:3; Mark 5:43; Luke 5:14;
  Titus 1:5; Philem. 8; Heb. 5:6
ORDINANCE—*statute* Job 38:33; Rom. 13:2;
  Eph. 2:15
ORPHAN—*fatherless*
  Ex. 22:22, not afflict any widow or o

  James 1:27, visit o-s and widows
  Deut. 10:18; 14:29; 24:17; Job 31:17; Ps. 10:14;
    Is. 1:23; 10:2; Jer. 49:11; Hos. 14:3; Mal. 3:5
OTHER Ex. 22:20; Mark 16:13
OUGHT John 4:20, place where men o to worship
  Heb. 5:12, you o to be teachers
  James 3:10, these things o not to be
OUT Ex. 3:10, bring My people ... o of Egypt
  Ex. 7:5, when I stretch o My hand
  Num. 32:23, your sin will find you o
  Prov. 31:20, she stretches o her hands to
  Matt. 12:13, Stretch o your hand
    12:34, o of that which fills the heart
    13:3, the sower went o to sow
  Mark 1:41, He stretched o His hand and
    touched
    7:26, cast the demon o of her daughter
  2 Tim. 4:2, in season *and* o of season
  Gen. 8:7,8,18; 19:10; 24:45; Ex. 3:11; Judg.
    20:25; 1 Sam. 30:21; 2 Sam. 19:7; Is. 37:36;
    Jer. 32:21
OUTBURST—*heat*
  Deut. 29:24, Why this great o of anger
OUTCOME—*end* Rom. 6:21, the o of those things
  is death
  Rom. 6:22, the o, eternal life
  Heb. 13:7, the o of their way of life
  James 5:11, seen the o of the Lord's dealings
  1 Pet. 1:9, obtaining as the o of your faith
    4:17, what will be the o
OUTCRY Gen. 18:21; Ps. 144:14
OUTER—*outward*
  2 Cor. 4:16, o man is decaying
OUTSIDE—*without* Deut. 32:25, O the sword
  Rev. 22:15, O are the dogs
OUTWARD Rom. 2:28, o in the flesh
OVEN Gen. 15:17, smoking o and a flaming torch
OVER—*spent* Luke 24:29, day is now nearly o
  Eph. 4:6, who is o all
OVERCOME Luke 9:32, companions had been o
  with sleep
  John 16:33, I have o the world
  Rom. 12:21, Do not be o by evil
  1 John 2:13, you have o the evil one
  Jer. 20:7; 23:9
OVEREXTENDING—*stretching*
  2 Cor. 10:14, we are not o
OVERFLOW 2 Cor. 7:4, I am o-ing with joy
  Ps. 23:5; Prov. 3:10; Song 8:7
OVERLAID 2 Chr. 3:5, he o the main room with
  cypress
OVERPOWER—*prevail*
  Matt. 16:18, gates of Hades shall not o it
OVERSEER Phil. 1:1, including the o-s and
  deacons
  1 Tim. 3:1, aspires to the office of o
  Titus 1:7, o must be above reproach
OVERTAKE Amos 9:10; 1 Thess. 5:4
OVERTHROW Ex. 23:24; Acts 5:39
OVERWHELM Ex. 17:13, Joshua o-ed Amalek
OWE—*due* Matt. 18:28, Pay back what you o
  18:34, repay all that was o-d him
  Rom. 13:8, O nothing to anyone
  Philem. 19, you o to me even your own self
OWN Prov. 14:10, heart knows its o bitterness
  John 1:11, came to His o ... o did not receive
    10:3, calls his o sheep by name
  Acts 2:6, speak in his o language
  1 Tim. 5:8, does not provide for his o
  2 Pet. 3:3, following after their o lusts
OX—*cow* Prov. 7:22, as an o goes to the slaughter
  1 Tim. 5:18, MUZZLE THE O WHILE HE IS
    THRESHING
  Lev. 22:28; Job 6:5; Prov. 15:17

P

PACT Is. 28:15, we have made a p
PAIN—*sorrow, torment, grief* Gen. 3:16, multiply
  Your p

1 Chr. 4:9, Because I bore *him* with **p**
Job 6:10, I rejoice in unsparing **p**
Ps. 127:2, eat the bread of **p-ful** labors
Eccles. 1:18, knowledge results in increasing **p**
Is. 14:3, gives you rest from your **p**
Jer. 30:15, Your **p** is incurable
Lam. 1:12, any **p** like my **p**
Matt. 8:6, home, suffering great **p**
Job 2:13; 15:20; Ps. 73:4; Lam. 3:51; Rev. 21:4
PAIR Judg. 19:3; Is. 21:7
PALATE—*mouth*
Job 29:10, their tongue stuck to their **p**
PALLET Mark 2:9, take up your **p** and walk
John 5:11; Acts 5:15
PALPITATING Is. 35:4, to those with **p** heart fear not
PANEL Jer. 22:14; Hag. 1:4
PANGS—*sorrow* Mark 13:8, beginning birth **p**
PANIC—*trouble* Is. 22:5, has a day of **p**
PANT Job 7:2, a slave who **p-s** for the shade
PAPYRUS Is. 18:2, in **p** vessels
PARAPET Deut. 22:8, a **p** for your roof
PARCH—*dried* Ps. 69:3; Is. 53:2
PARDON Is. 55:7 He will abundantly **p**
Luke 6:37, **p**, and you will be **p-ed**
Ex. 23:21; 2 Chr. 30:18; Ps. 25:11
PARENTS Matt. 10:21, CHILDREN WILL RISE UP
    AGAINST **P**
Luke 2:41, His **p** used to go to Jerusalem
    18:29, left house ... or **p**
John 9:2, who sinned, this man, or his **p**
Rom. 1:30, disobedient to **p**
2 Cor. 12:14, for *their* **p**, but **p** for *their* children
Eph. 6:1, Children obey your **p**
2 Tim. 3:2, disobedient to **p**, ungrateful
PART Num. 18:20, nor own any **p** among them
Matt. 5:29, one of the **p-s** of your body perish
Luke 10:42, Mary has chosen the good **p**
John 13:8, you have no **p** with Me
Acts 8:21, You have no **p** or portion
1 Cor. 13:9, we know in **p**
PARTAKERS—*partners* Eph. 5:7, do not be **p**
    with them
Heb. 3:1, **p** of a heavenly calling
    3:14, **p** of Christ
    6:4, **p** of the Holy Spirit
2 Pet. 1:4, **p** of *the* divine nature
PARTIAL Prov. 28:21, To show **p-ity** is not good
Matt. 22:16, for You are not **p** to any
Acts 10:34, God is not one to show **p-ity**
Rom. 2:11, no **p-ity** with God
Lev. 19:15; Deut. 1:17
PARTICIPATE Eph. 5:11, do not **p** in the
    unfruitful deeds
PARTNERS Matt. 23:30, not have been **p** with
    them
PASS Matt. 26:39, let this cup **p** from Me
John 5:24, **p-ed** out of death into life
2 Cor. 5:17, old things **p-ed** away
Heb. 11:25, enjoy the **p-ing** pleasures of sin
Rev. 21:1, first earth **p-ed** away
Gen. 15:17; Ps. 109:23; Prov. 4:15; Is. 16:8;
    Acts 7:30
PASSION Prov. 14:30, But **p** is rottenness to the
    bone
Rom. 1:26, gave them over to degrading **p-s**
Col. 3:5, as dead to ... **p**
1 Thess. 4:5, not in lustful **p**
PASSOVER Ex. 12:11, it is the LORD's **P**
Matt. 26:17, prepare for You to eat the **P**
Luke 22:15, desired to eat this **P**
John 18:39, release someone for you at the **P**
Acts 12:4, intending after the **P**
1 Cor. 5:7, Christ our **P** also has been sacrificed
PAST Song 2:11, the winter is **p**, The rain
Jer. 8:20, Harvest is **p**, summer is ended
PASTOR—*shepherd* Eph. 4:11, some *as* **p-s** and
    teachers
PASTURE—*feed* Song 1:7; Is. 61:5; Jer. 6:3;
    Zech. 11:4

PATCH—*piece* Matt. 9:16, puts a **p** of unshrunk
    cloth
PATH—*way* Job 12:24, makes them wander in a
    p-less waste
Ps. 16:11, make known to me the **p** of life
    119:105, a light to my **p**
Prov. 4:18, **p** of the righteous is like the light
Eccles. 11:5, the **p** of the wind
Matt. 3:3, MAKE HIS **P-S** STRAIGHT
Rom. 3:17, **P** OF PEACE ... NOT KNOWN
Gen. 49:17; Job 28:7; Ps. 27:11
PATIENCE Matt. 18:26, Have **p** with me
2 Cor. 6:6, in **p**, in kindness
Col. 1:11, steadfastness and **p**
2 Tim. 4:2, with great **p** and instruction
PATIENT—*gentle* 1 Cor. 13:4, Love is **p**, love is
    kind
James 5:8, You too be **p**
2 Pet. 3:9, is **p** toward you
PATTERN—*example* Phil. 3:17, according to **p**
PAY Matt. 18:28, **P** back what you owe
Gen. 50:15; Ex. 22:7; Deut. 23:21; Job 22:27;
    Mark 12:15
PEACE Num. 6:26, give you **p**
Ps. 34:14, Seek **p**, and pursue it
    37:37, man of **p** will have a posterity
    119:165, who love Thy law have great **p**
Eccles. 3:8, time for war, and a time for **p**
Is. 9:6, Eternal Father, Prince of **P**
Matt. 10:13, let your *greeting of* **p**
    10:34, I did not come to bring **p**
Mark 9:50, be at **p** with one another
Luke 1:79, guide our feet ... way of **p**
    2:14, on earth **p** among men
John 14:27, **P** I leave you; My **p**
    20:19, **P** be with you
Acts 24:2, we have through you attained **p**
Rom. 15:33, the God of **p** be with you
1 Cor. 7:15, God has called us to **p**
Gal. 5:22, fruit of the Spirit is ... **p**
Eph. 2:14, He Himself is our **p**
Phil. 4:7, **p** of God, which surpasses all
1 Thess. 5:13, Live in **p** with one another
    5:23, may the God of **P** ... sanctify
2 Thess. 3:16, Lord of **p** ... grant you **p**
Heb. 12:14, Pursue **p** with all men
James 2:16, Go in **p**
1 Pet. 5:14, **P** be to you all
Gen. 15:15; Lev. 26:6; 2 Kin. 9:17; Job 15:21;
    Ps. 4:8; 147:14; Prov. 3:17; 16:7; Is. 36:16;
    52:7; 57:19; Jer. 6:14
PEARLS—*jewel*
Job 28:18, acquisition of wisdom ... **p**
PECK Matt. 13:33, hid in three **p-s** of meal
PECK-MEASURE Matt. 5:15; Mark 4:21
PEG—*nail* Judg. 4:21; Is. 22:23
PENALTY 2 Thess. 1:9, pay the **p** of eternal
    destruction
PEOPLE Ps. 100:3, *We are* His **p** and the sheep
Prov. 11:14, no guidance, the **p** fall
    29:18, no vision, the **p** are unrestrained
Matt. 1:21, save His **p** from their sins
Mark 7:6, **P** HONORS ME WITH THEIR LIPS
John 11:50, man should die for the **p**
Jude 16, flattering **p** for ... advantage
Ex. 6:7; Ruth 1:16; Ps. 2:1; Mark 6:5; Acts 5:16
PERCEIVING Mark 2:8, Jesus, **p** in His spirit
PERDITION John 17:12, the son of **p**
PERFECT Deut. 32:4, The Rock! His work is **p**
Ps. 19:7, law of the LORD is **p**
Matt. 5:48, Therefore you are to be **p**
1 Cor. 13:10, but when the **p** comes
2 Cor. 12:9, power is **p-ed** in weakness
Phil. 1:6, **p** it until the day of Christ Jesus
James 1:4, endurance have *its* **p** result
    1:25, **p** law, the *law* of liberty
1 John 4:17, love is **p-ed** with us
PERFECTER Heb. 12:2, author and **p** of faith
PERFORM—*wrought* Is. 26:12, **p-ed** for us all our
    works
Ps. 103:6; Luke 1:8; Rom. 4:21

PERFUME Is. 3:24, instead of sweet **p**
   Matt. 26:7; Luke 7:46
PERFUMERS 1 Sam. 8:13, daughters for **p**
PERHAPS Mark 11:13; Acts 17:27; 1 Cor. 15:37
PERISH—*fail* Ps. 1:6, way of the wicked will **p**
   Matt. 8:25, Save us, Lord; we are **p-ing**
   18:14, one of these little ones **p**
   John 6:27, work for the food which **p-s**
   1 Cor. 9:25, *do it* to receive a **p-able** wreath
   15:42, It is sown a **p-able** body
   15:53, this **p-able** must put on
   2 Cor. 4:3, veiled to those who are **p-ing**
   1 Pet. 1:23, not of seed which is **p-able**
   2 Pet. 3:9, not wishing for any to **p**
   Num. 17:12; 2 Sam. 1:27; Job 34:15; Prov. 22:8;
     Ezek. 37:11
PERJURY Zech. 8:17, do not love **p**
PERMISSION Mark 5:13, And He gave them **p**
PERMIT—*suffer* Matt. 3:15, **P** it at this time
PERPETUAL Ex. 40:15; Num. 25:13, a **p**
   priesthood
   Heb. 7:3, abides a priest **p-ly**
   Ex. 31:16; Ps. 9:6; Jer. 15:18; 51:39; Hab. 3:6
PERSECUTE Matt. 5:11, when *men* revile you,
   and **p** you
   5:44, pray for those who **p** you
   10:23, they **p** you in this city, flee
   John 15:20, If they **p-d** Me, they will also **p**
   Acts 9:4, Saul, why are you **p-ing** Me
   1 Cor. 4:12, when we are **p-d**, we endure
   2 Cor. 4:9, **p-d**, but not forsaken
   Job 19:22; Ps. 143:3
PERSEVERANCE Luke 21:19, By your **p** you will
   win
   Rom. 2:7, by **p** in doing good
   5:3, tribulation brings about **p**
   15:4, **p** and the encouragement of the
     Scriptures
   2 Thess. 1:4, for your **p** and faith
PERSEVERE Rom. 12:12, hope, **p-ing** in
   tribulation
   James 1:12, Blessed is a man who **p-s** under
     trial
PERSON—*soul* Lev. 4:2, If a **p** sins
   unintentionally
   Eccles. 12:13, this *applies to* every **p**
   Is. 32:6, keep the hungry **p** unsatisfied
   Rom. 13:1, Let every **p** be in subjection
   Jude 4, certain **p-s** have crept in unnoticed
PERSUADE 2 Kin. 4:8, she **p-d** him to eat food
   Prov. 25:15, a ruler may be **p-d**
   Acts 26:28, you will **p** me
PERSUASIVE 1 Cor. 2:4, were not in **p** words
   Col. 2:4, delude you with **p** argument
PERVERSE Acts 20:30, speaking **p** things
   Phil. 2:15, a crooked and **p** generation
   Deut. 32:5,20; Ps. 101:4; Prov. 23:33
PERVERSION Lev. 18:23, it is a **p**
PERVERT Deut. 16:19; 2 Sam. 22:27; Job 8:3;
   Prov. 10:31
PETITION Ps. 20:5, the LORD fulfill all your **p-s**
   1 Tim. 2:1, prayers, **p-s** and thanksgivings
   1 Sam. 1:17; Dan. 6:7,13
PHYSICIAN Jer. 8:22, Is there no **p** there
   Matt. 9:12, not . . . healthy who need a **p**
   Luke 4:23, **P**, heal yourself
   Col. 4:14, Luke, the beloved **p**
PICK Mark 16:18, they will **p** up serpents
   Gen. 8:11; Mark 2:23
PIECE Matt. 14:20, left over of the broken **p-s**
   Mark 6:43, twelve full baskets of broken **p-s**
   Gen. 18:5; Ruth 2:14; 1 Sam. 2:36; Luke 24:42
PIERCE—*wound* Judg. 5:26, shattered and **p-d**
   his temple
   Ps. 22:16, They **p-d** my hands . . . feet
   Is. 53:5, **p-d** through for our transgressions
   Zech. 12:10, on Me whom they have **p-d**
   Luke 2:35, **p** even your own soul
   John 19:34, soldiers **p-d** His side

PIETY 1 Tim. 5:4, practice **p** in regard
PILES Job 27:16, he **p** up silver like dust
PILLAGE Nah. 3:1, city, . . . full of lies *and* **p**
PILLAR Gen. 19:26, she became a **p** of salt
   Job 26:11, The **p-s** of heaven tremble
   Gal. 2:9, John, who were reputed to be **p-s**
   1 Tim. 3:15, **p** and support of the truth
   Prov. 9:1; Ezek. 26:11
PILOT James 3:4, inclination of the **p** desires
PIT—*destruction, dungeon*
   Gen. 14:10, Siddim . . . tar **p-s**
   37:20, throw him into one of the **p-s**
   Ex. 21:33, a man opens a **p**, or digs a **p**
   Job 17:14, I call to the **p**, You are my father
   33:18, his soul from the **p**
   Ps. 16:10, Holy One to see the **p**
   103:4, redeems your life from the **p**
   Prov. 23:27, a harlot is a deep **p**
   Lam. 3:53, they have silenced me in the **p**
   Matt. 15:14, both will fall into a **p**
PITCH Gen. 6:14, cover it . . . with **p**
   Gen. 33:19, where he had **p-ed** his tent
   Ex. 2:3, covered it over with tar and **p**
PITCHER—*bowl, jar*
   Judg. 7:16, put trumpets and empty **p-s**
   1 Kin. 18:33, fill four **p-s**
   Eccles. 12:6, the **p** by the well is shattered
   Mark 14:13, man . . . carrying a **p** of water
PITY—*compassion* Ex. 2:6; Deut. 7:16; Job 19:21
PLACE—*room* Deut. 33:27, eternal God is a
   dwelling **p**
   Ps. 31:8, set my feet in a large **p**
   Prov. 15:3, eyes . . . LORD . . . in every **p**
   Matt. 23:6, love the **p** of honor at banquets
   24:51, **p** with the hypocrites
   26:36, a **p** called Gethsemane
   27:33, a **p** called Golgotha . . . **P** of a Skull
   28:6, **p** where He was lying
   Luke 4:17, **p** where it was written
   14:8, do not take the **p** of honor
   John 14:2, go to prepare a **p** for you
   Acts 13:47, I HAVE **P-D** YOU AS A LIGHT FOR
   1 Cor. 14:16, fills the **p** of the ungifted
   2 Pet. 1:19, lamp shining in a dark **p**
   Rev. 20:11, no **p** was found for them
   Gen. 1:9; 30:2; Ex. 3:5; 21:13; Num. 32:14;
     Deut. 2:23; 34:6; Judg. 18:10; Job 9:6; 16:4;
     Ps. 24:3; Is. 49:20; Jer. 51:51; Dan. 8:14;
     Hab. 3:11; Luke 14:9; John 18:2
PLAGUE Gen. 12:17; Rev. 16:21; 21:9
PLAIN—*distinct, clear* Is. 40:4; Mark 7:35; John
   16:25
PLAN—*devise* Ps. 36:4, He **p-s** wickedness upon
   his bed
   Prov. 16:9, mind of a man **p-s** his way
   19:21, Many are the **p-s** in a man's heart
   2 Sam. 14:14; Prov. 15:22; Jer. 18:12
PLANT Gen. 3:18, you shall eat the **p-s** of the
   field
   Ps. 1:3, tree . . . **p-ed** by streams
   Eccles. 3:2, A time to **p**, and a time to
   Matt. 13:32; Mark 4:32, larger than . . . the
     garden **p-s**
   15:13, **p** . . . Father did not **p**
   Mark 12:1, A man **P-ED** A VINEYARD
   Luke 17:6, be **p-ed** in the sea
   1 Cor. 3:6, I **p-ed**, Apollos watered
   Gen. 1:29,30; 2:5,8; 9:3; Ex. 9:22,25; 10:12,15;
     Deut. 6:11; 2 Kin. 19:29; Job 14:9; Ps. 92:13
PLASTER Ezek. 13:10, **p** it over with whitewash
PLAY Gen. 4:21; Ex. 32:6; 1 Sam. 16:17;
   1 Kin. 1:40; Job 41:5; Ps. 33:3; Is. 11:8;
   Matt. 11:17; 1 Cor. 14:7
PLEAD Gen. 42:21; Deut. 3:23; 1 Sam. 12:7;
   Ps. 43:1; Is. 1:17
PLEASANT—*smooth, sweet*
   Ps. 16:6, lines have fallen . . . **p**
   133:1, how good and how **p** it is
   Eccles. 5:12, sleep of the working man is **p**
   2 Sam. 1:23; Prov. 9:17; 16:24; Is. 30:10

PLEASE Matt. 3:17, Son, in whom I am well **p-d**
Rom. 15:1, not *just* **p** ourselves
  15:3, Christ did not **p** Himself
1 Cor. 7:33, how he may **p** his wife
  7:34, how she may **p** her husband
  10:5, God was not well **p-d**
Heb. 13:16, sacrifices God is **p-d**
PLEASING—*acceptable*
Prov. 16:7, man's ways ... **p** ... Lord
Matt. 11:26, it was **well-p** in Thy sight
John 8:29, things that are **p** to Him
2 Cor. 5:9, to be **p** to Him
Eph. 5:10, what is **p** to the Lord
Gen. 2:9; 1 Kin. 3:10
PLEASURE Ps. 16:11, there are **p-s** forever
Ps. 149:4, Lord takes **p** in His people
Luke 8:14, worries and riches and **p-s**
Phil. 2:13, to work for *His* good **p**
Heb. 11:25, the passing **p-s** of sin
Gen. 18:12; Job 36:11; Prov. 21:17; Is. 53:10
PLEDGE Prov. 22:26, among those who give **p-s**
2 Cor. 1:22, the Spirit in our hearts as a **p**
  5:5, gave to us the Spirit as a **p**
Eph. 1:14, given as a **p** of our inheritance
1 Tim. 5:12, set aside their previous **p**
PLENTEOUS Is. 30:23, it will be rich and **p**
PLENTIFUL Ps. 68:9, didst shed abroad a **p** rain
Matt. 9:37, harvest is **p**
PLENTY Gen. 33:9; Prov. 3:10; 12:11; Joel 2:26
PLOT Prov. 30:32, if you have **p-ed** evil
Matt. 26:4; Acts 9:23; 23:13
PLOW Is. 2:4, their swords into **p-shares**
Joel 3:10, **p-shares** into swords
Luke 9:62, putting his hand to the **p**
1 Cor. 9:10, to **p** in hope
Deut. 22:10; Job 4:8; Prov. 20:4
PLUCK Ps. 25:15; Ezek. 17:22
PLUMAGE Job 39:13, pinion and **p** of love
PLUNDER (n.)—*booty* Judg. 5:19; Hab. 2:7;
  Zeph. 1:13
PLUNDER (v.)—*spoil* Matt. 12:29, he will **p** his
  house
Ex. 3:22; Ps. 76:5; Is. 42:22
PLUNGE 1 Tim. 6:9, desires which **p** men into
  ruin
POINT Jer. 17:1; Mark 5:23; James 2:10
POISON Ps. 140:3; Jer. 8:14; Amos 6:12;
  Mark 16:18
POLE—*staff* Num. 13:23, carried it on a **p**
  between two
POLLUTE—*spot* Num. 35:33; Jer. 16:18; Jude 23
POMP Is. 14:11, Your **p** *and* the music
PONDER Prov. 5:6, **p** the path of life
Luke 2:19, **p-ing** them in her heart
POOR Prov. 13:7, *Another* pretends to be **p**
Prov. 20:13, lest you become **p**
Amos 5:11, impose heavy rent upon the **p**
Matt. 5:3, Blessed are the **p** in
  11:5, *the* **p** have the gospel preached
  26:11, **p** you have with you always
Mark 10:21, and give *it* to the **p**
  12:42, And a **p** widow came
Luke 4:18, preach the gospel to the **p**
  19:8, my possessions I will give to the **p**
2 Cor. 8:9, for your sake He became **p**
James 2:5, God choose the **p** of this
1 Sam. 2:8; 2 Sam. 12:4; Prov. 22:22; Is. 3:15;
  1 Cor. 13:3
PORPOISE SKINS Ex. 25:5; 26:14
PORTION Deut. 32:9, Lord's **p** is His people
2 Kin. 2:9, double **p** of your spirit
Ps. 119:57, The Lord is my **p**
Gen. 31:14; 2 Chr. 10:16; Eccles. 11:2; Acts 8:21
POSSESS Gen. 15:7; 24:60; Ps. 44:3; Is. 54:3;
  2 Cor. 6:10
POSSESSION—*property, treasure* Gen. 17:8
Matt. 24:47, in charge of all his **p-s**
Luke 19:8, half of my **p-s** I will give to the
Ex. 6:8; 19:5; 21:16; 34:9; Deut. 4:20; Ps. 104:24;
  Acts 2:45

POSSIBLE Matt. 19:26, with God all things **p**
Matt. 26:39, **p**, let this cup pass
Luke 18:27, are **p** with God
Rom. 12:18, If **p**, so far as it depends
POT Ex. 16:3; 2 Kin. 4:40; Job 41:31; Jer. 1:13
POUR Eccles. 11:3, clouds are full, they **p** out rain
Joel 2:28, **p** out My Spirit on all mankind
Matt. 26:7, **p-ed** it upon His head
Luke 22:20, cup which is **p-ed** ... covenant in
  My blood
John 2:15, **p-ed** out the coins
Acts 10:45, gift of the Holy Spirit ... **p-ed** out
Rom. 5:5, love of God **p-ed** out within our
  hearts
Phil. 2:17, if I am being **p-ed** out as
Rev. 16:2, **p-ed** out his bowl
1 Sam. 1:15; Job 10:10; 29:6; Is. 44:3; Matt. 9:17
POVERTY Prov. 23:21, glutton will come to **p**
Prov. 30:8, neither **p** nor riches
2 Cor. 8:9, through His **p**
POWER—*authority, strength*
Deut. 8:18, you **p** to make wealth
1 Chr. 29:11, the **p** and the glory
Is. 40:29, *who* lacks might He increases **p**
Matt. 6:13, kingdom, and the **p**, and
Mark 5:30, **p** ... from Him had gone forth
  9:1, kingdom of God ... come with **p**
  13:26, in clouds with great **p**
  14:62, at the right hand of **P**
Luke 1:35, **p** of the Most High will overshadow
  4:14, in the **p** of the Spirit
  22:69, right hand of the **p** of God
Acts 1:8, you shall receive **p** when
  8:10, called the Great **P** of God
Rom. 1:4, with **p** to be the Son of God
  1:16, the **p** of God for salvation
1 Cor. 1:24, Christ the **p** of God
  15:56, the **p** of sin is the law
2 Cor. 12:9, **p** is perfected in weakness
Eph. 1:21, authority and **p** and dominion
  2:2, prince of the **p** of the air
Phil. 3:21, exertion of the **p**
Heb. 1:3, by the word of His **p**
  11:34, quenched the **p** of fire
Ex. 15:6; Judg. 7:2; Job 40:16; Ps. 49:15;
  Prov. 3:27; Jer. 18:21; 1 Cor. 5:4; 1 Pet. 3:22
PRACTICE Ps. 28:4, evil of their **p-s**
Matt. 6:1, Beware of **p-ing** your righteousness
Acts 19:18, disclosing their **p-s**
1 Cor. 11:16, we have no other **p**
Col. 3:9, laid aside the old self with its *evil* **p-s**
1 Tim. 5:4, **p** piety in regard to their own family
1 John 1:6, we lie and do not **p** the truth
  3:8, the one who **p-s** sin is of the
PRAETORIUM Matt. 27:27, soldiers ... took
  Jesus into the **P**
Mark 15:16, took Him ... into the palace (that
  is, the **P**)
John 18:28, led Jesus ... into the **P**
  18:33, Pilate ... entered ... into the **P**
PRAISE—*bless, commend*
Ex. 15:11, Awesome in **p-s**
Ps. 89:5, heavens will **p** Thy wonders
Prov. 27:21, man *is tested* by the **p**
Matt. 11:25, I **p** Thee, O Father
Luke 16:8, his master **p-d** the unrighteous
  steward
Rom. 2:29, his **p** is not from men
Phil. 4:8, if anything worthy of **p**
James 5:13, Let him sing **p**
Deut. 10:21; 1 Chr. 16:9; Neh. 12:46; Ps. 22:25;
  Prov. 12:8; Is. 38:18
PRAY—*ask* Is. 45:20, And **p** to a go , who cannot
  save
Matt. 5:44, **p** for those who persecute
  6:5, And when you **p**
  6:6, **p** to your Father ... in secret
  6:7, **p-ing**, do not use meaningless
  14:23, mountain by Himself to **p**
  26:41, Keep watching and **p-ing**, that
Mark 11:24, you **p** and ask, believe
Luke 11:1, Lord, teach us to **p** just
  18:1, they ought to **p** and not
  22:40, **P** that you may not ... temptation

PRAY (Continued)
1 Cor. 11:13, for a woman to **p** to God
  14:14, if I **p** in a tongue
Col. 1:9, not ceased to **p** for you
1 Thess. 5:17, **p** without ceasing
James 5:13, suffering? Let him **p**
  5:16, and **p** for one another
Gen. 20:7; Ex. 33:18; 1 Sam. 7:5; 12:23; Jon. 1:14
PRAYER Ps. 55:1, Give ear to my **p**, O God
Is. 56:7, called a house of **p**
Matt. 17:21, out except by **p** and fasting
  21:22, everything . . . in **p**, believing
Luke 6:12, whole night in **p**
  19:46, A HOUSE OF **P**
Acts 3:1, the hour of **p**
Rom. 1:10, in my **p**-s making request
  12:12, devoted to **p**
1 Cor. 7:5; Col. 4:2, devote yourselves to **p**
1 Pet. 3:7, your **p**-s may not be hindered
1 Kin. 8:45; Neh. 11:17; Ps. 4:1
PREACH—*declare, exhort, proclaim*
Matt. 4:17, that time Jesus began to **p**
  10:7, go, **p**, saying . . . kingdom . . . is at hand
  11:1, and **p** in their cities
  11:5, POOR . . . GOSPEL **P-ED** to them
Mark 13:10, gospel . . . **p-ed** to all the nations
  16:15, **p** the gospel to all
Luke 4:43, **p** the kingdom of God
Acts 13:32, we **p** to you the good news of the
  promise
1 Cor. 1:17, not . . . to baptize, but to **p**
  1:23, we **p** Christ crucified
2 Cor. 4:5, we do not **p** ourselves
1 Tim. 6:2, Teach and **p** these *principles*
2 Tim. 4:2, **p** the word, be ready
PREACHER Eccles. 1:1, words of the **P**
Rom. 10:14, how shall they hear without a **p**
1 Tim. 2:7, I was appointed a **p**
2 Pet. 2:5, Noah, a **p** of righteousness
PREACHING—*talk, word* Matt. 3:1, John . . . **p**
Mark 1:4, **p** a baptism of repentance
  1:39, **p** and casting out the demons
Acts 5:42, teaching and **p** Jesus
  8:4, scattered went about **p** the word
Rom. 16:25, **p** of Jesus Christ
1 Cor. 15:14, then our **p** is vain
PRECEDE 1 Thess. 4:15, **p** those who have fallen
  asleep
PRECEPT—*statute* Ps. 19:8, **p**-s of the LORD are
  right
PRECIOUS—*excellent* Ps. 36:7, How **p** is Thy
  lovingkindness
Ps. 116:15, **P** in the sight of the LORD
Prov. 3:15, more **p** than jewels
Is. 44:9, their **p** things are of no profit
1 Pet. 1:7, more **p** than gold which
  1:19, but with **p** blood . . . of Christ
PREDETERMINE Acts 2:23, **p-d** plan and
  foreknowledge of God
PREEMINENT—*excellence*
Gen. 49:3, **P** in dignity and **p** in
PREPARATION—*serve*
Luke 10:40, distracted with all her **p**-s
PREPARE—*fashion, furnish, ready* Gen. 18:6
Ps. 23:5, dost **p** a table before me
  78:19, God **p** a table in the
Matt. 11:10, WHO WILL **P** YOUR WAY
  25:34, the kingdom **p-d** for you
John 14:2, I go to **p** a place for you
1 Cor. 2:9, **P-D** FOR THOSE WHO LOVE HIM
Heb. 11:3, worlds were **p-d** by the word
Lev. 7:9; Job 12:5; Ps. 57:6; Rom. 9:22
PRESCRIBE—*command*
1 Tim. 4:11, **P** and teach these things
PRESENCE Ex. 33:14, My **p** shall go *with you*
Ps. 23:5, **p** of my enemies
  44:3, light of Thy **p**
  95:2, before His **p** with thanksgiving
Is. 64:2, nations may tremble at Thy **p**
Luke 13:26, ate and drank in Your **p**

Jude 24, **p** of His glory blameless
Rev. 14:10, in the **p** of the Lamb
PRESENT—*offer, yield*
Gen. 43:11, to the man as a **p**
Ps. 46:1, A very **p** help in trouble
Mal. 1:8, **p** the blind . . . **p** the lame and
Luke 2:22, to **p** Him to the Lord
Rom. 6:13, **p**-ing the members of your body to
  sin
  12:1, **p** your bodies a living sacrifice
1 Cor. 5:3, but **p** in spirit
Col. 1:22, **p** you before Him holy and blameless
2 Tim. 2:15, **p** yourself approved to God
  4:10, loved this **p** world
PRESERVATION—*health*
Acts 27:34, food . . . for your **p**
PRESERVE—*guard, keep*
2 Sam. 18:18, no son to **p** my name
Ps. 16:1, **P** me, O God, for I take refuge
  86:2, **p** my soul, for I am a godly man
Prov. 14:3, lips of the wise will **p** them
Luke 17:33, loses *his life* shall **p** it
Eph. 4:3, diligent to **p** the unity of the Spirit
1 Thess. 5:23, soul and body be **p-d** complete
PRESS Matt. 27:32, they **p**-ed . . . to bear His cross
Luke 6:38, good measure **p**-ed down
Phil. 3:14, I **p** on toward the goal
PRESUME—*dare* Rom. 15:18, I will not **p** to
  speak
PRESUMPTION Prov. 13:10, Through **p** comes
  nothing
PRETEND—*disguise* 2 Sam. 14:2, **p** to be a
  mourner
1 Kin. 14:5,6, **p** to be another woman
Luke 20:20, sent spies who **p**-ed to be righteous
PRETTY Jer. 46:20, Egypt is a **p** heifer
PREVAIL Gen. 7:20, water **p**-ed fifteen cubits
  higher
1 Sam. 2:9, not by might shall a man **p**
Ps. 65:3; Jer. 20:7
PREVALENT Eccles. 6:1, an evil . . . it is **p**
PREVENT Matt. 3:14, John tried to **p** Him,
PREY Ps. 76:4; Ezek. 22:25
PRICE Acts 1:18, field with the **p** of his
  wickedness
  5:2, kept back *some* of the **p**
1 Cor. 6:20, you have been bought with a **p**
Lev. 25:16; Dan. 11:39; Mic. 3:11
PRIDE Prov. 16:18, **P** goes before destruction
Mark 7:22, slander, **p** and foolishness
1 John 2:16, the boastful **p** of life
Prov. 8:13; Is. 13:19; 60:15; Ezek. 32:12
PRIEST Gen. 14:18, **p** of God Most High
Ex. 19:6, shall be to Me a kingdom of **p**-s
1 Sam. 2:35, raise up for Myself a faithful **p**
Ps. 110:4, **p** forever . . . order of Melchizedek
Ezek. 44:21, Nor shall any of the **p**-s drink wine
Matt. 2:4, together all the chief **p**-s
  8:4, SHOW YOURSELF TO THE **P**
Heb. 2:17, faithful high **p**
  3:1, High **P** of our confession
  5:6, **P** FOREVER . . . ORDER OF MELCHIZEDEK
2 Chr. 15:3; Is. 24:2
PRIME—*flower* 1 Sam. 2:33, will die in the **p** of
  life
PRINCE—*ruler* Ex. 2:14, Who made you a **p** or a
  judge
2 Sam. 3:38, **p** and a great man has fallen
Is. 9:6, **P** of Peace
Acts 3:15, put to death the **P** of life
  5:31, as a **P** and a Saviour
Eph. 2:2, **p** of the power of the air
PRINCESS—*lady* Judg. 5:29, Her wise **p**-es
  would answer
PRINCIPALITY Rom. 8:38, nor **p**-es . . . nor
  powers
PRISON Judg. 16:21, he was a grinder in the **p**
Ps. 142:7, Bring my soul out of **p**
Matt. 14:10, had John beheaded in the **p**
Acts 5:19, Lord . . . opened the gates of the **p**
  16:27, jailer . . . had seen the **p** doors opened
1 Kin. 22:27; Rev. 18:2

PRISONER Ps. 102:20, groaning of the **p**
Ps. 146:7, the LORD sets the **p-s** free
Matt. 27:15, release for the multitude *any* one **p**
Rom. 7:23, making me a **p** of the law
Eph. 3:1, Paul, the **p** of Christ Jesus
2 Tim. 1:8, ashamed . . . or of me His **p**

PRIVATION—*adversity, distress*
Is. 30:20, given you bread of **p**

PRIZE Col. 2:18, defrauding you of your **p**

PROCEED Deut. 8:3, everything that **p-s** out of
     the mouth
Jer. 9:3, **p** from evil to evil
Matt. 4:4, WORD THAT **P-S** OUT OF THE MOUTH
Mark 7:21, heart of men, **p** the evil thoughts
John 15:26, who **p-s** from the Father
2 Tim. 3:13, imposters will **p** . . . to worse

PROCLAIM—*declare, tell*
Ex. 33:19; Deut. 32:3, **p** the name of the LORD
Is. 61:1, **p** liberty to the captives
     61:2, **p** the favorable year of the LORD
Jer. 34:15, **p-ing** release to his neighbor
Matt. 10:27; Luke 12:3, **p-ed** upon the
     housetops
Acts 17:3, Jesus whom I am **p-ing** to you
     17:23, you worship in ignorance, this I **p** to
     26:23, **p** light both to the *Jewish* and
1 Pet. 3:19, made **p-ation** to the spirits
1 John 1:3, what we have seen and heard we **p**

PROCONSUL—*deputy* Acts 13:7; 18:12; 19:38

PRODUCE—*yield* Deut. 14:22, tithe all the **p**
Ps. 67:6, the earth has yielded its **p**
2 Tim. 2:23, knowing that they **p** quarrels
James 3:12, Neither can salt water **p** fresh
Lev. 25:19; Hos. 10:1

PRODUCTIVE Luke 12:16, land . . . was **p**

PROFANE—*defile, pollute* Lev. 21:7,23;
     Ezek. 22:8
Ex. 31:14, Everyone who **p-s** it . . . put to death
Lev. 20:3, to **p** My holy name
Ezek. 23:38, have **p-d** My sabbaths
1 Tim. 1:9, law . . . for the unholy and **p**

PROFESS—*confession* Rom. 1:22, **P-ing** to be
     wise
Titus 1:16, They **p** to know God

PROFIT Job 15:3, words which are not **p-able**
Prov. 14:23, In all labor there is **p**
     15:27, who **p-s** illicitly troubles his own
Matt. 16:26; Luke 9:25, will a man be **p-ed**
John 6:63, the flesh **p-s** nothing
Acts 16:19; hope of **p** was gone
1 Cor. 6:12; 10:23, not all things are **p-able**
     13:3, not have love, it **p-s** me nothing
1 Tim. 4:8, bodily discipline is only of little **p**
2 Tim. 3:16, Scripture . . . **p-able** for teaching
James 4:13, engage in business and make a **p**
Gen. 37:26; Prov. 3:14; Is. 48:17; Jer. 16:19

PROGRESS Phil. 1:12, greater **p** of the gospel

PROLONG Prov. 10:27, fear of the Lord **p-s** life

PROMINENCE Acts 13:50, devout women of **p**

PROMINENT Mark 15:43, Joseph . . . **p** member

PROMISCUITY Rom. 13:13, not in sexual **p** and
     sensuality

PROMISE Acts 2:33, **p** of the Holy Spirit
Acts 26:6, hope of the **p** made by God
Rom. 4:14, **p** is nullified
     9:8, children of the **p**
Gal. 3:14, might receive the **p** of the Spirit
Eph. 6:2, first commandment with a **p**
2 Tim. 1:1, **p** of life in Christ Jesus
Titus 1:2, **p-d** long ages ago
Heb. 10:23, for He who **p-d** is faithful
2 Pet. 1:4, His precious and magnificent **p-s**

PROMOTE Esth. 5:11; Ps. 140:8

PRONOUNCE—*utter* Jer. 1:16, I will **p** My
     judgments
Luke 23:24, Pilate **p-d** sentence

PROOF Acts 17:31, furnished **p** to all men
2 Cor. 8:24, show them the **p** of your love
13:3, **p** of the Christ who speaks in me

PROPER Rom. 13:13, Let us behave **p-ly** as in the
     day
1 Cor. 11:13, is it **p** for a woman to pray
     14:40, let all things be done **p-ly**
Eph. 5:3, as is **p** among saints
1 Thess. 4:12, you may behave **p-ly** toward
     outsiders
1 Tim. 2:6, testimony *borne* at the **p** time

PROPERTY—*goods*
Gen. 34:10, and acquire **p** in it
Matt. 12:29, carry off his **p**
     19:22, one who owned much **p**
Acts 2:45, selling their **p** and possessions

PROPHECY Dan. 9:24, seal up vision and **p**
1 Cor. 13:2, if I have the gift of **p**
2 Pet. 1:21, no **p** was ever made by . . . human
     will
Rev. 19:10, testimony . . . is the spirit of **p**

PROPHESY 1 Sam. 10:11, he **p-ed** now with the
     prophets
Is. 30:10, not **p** to us what is right
Matt. 7:22, did we not **p** in Your name
     26:68, **P** to us, You Christ
1 Cor. 13:9, know in part, and we **p** in part
1 Chr. 25:3; Jer. 14:14; Ezek. 37:4; Joel 2:28

PROPHET Matt. 1:22, spoken . . . through the **p**
Matt. 2:5, it had been written by the **p**
     2:15, through the **p** might be fulfilled
     2:17, Jeremiah the **p**
     5:12, so they persecuted the **p-s**
     10:41, **p** shall receive a **p-'s** reward
     11:9, one who is more than a **p**
     11:13, all the **p-s** and the Law
     13:57, **p** is not without honor
     21:11, the **p** Jesus, from Nazareth
Luke 4:24, no **p** is welcome in his home town
     6:23, their fathers used to treat the **p-s**
John 1:21, Are you the **P**
     4:19, perceive that You are a **p**
     7:52, see that no **p** arises out of Galilee
Acts 13:15, reading of the Law and the **P-s**
1 Cor. 14:37, If anyone thinks he is a **p**
Eph. 4:11, some *as* apostles, and some *as* **p-s**
Heb. 1:1, to the fathers in the **p-s**
Gen. 20:7; Deut. 13:1; 18:18; Judg. 4:4;
     1 Sam. 9:9; 1 Kin. 20:35; Is. 9:15; Jer. 23:11;
     Ezek. 13:3; Hos. 12:10; Amos 7:14; Acts
     13:6

PROPHETIC 1 Thess. 5:20, do not despise **p**
     utterances
2 Pet. 1:19, the **p** word made more sure

PROSELYTE Matt. 23:15, make one **p**
Acts 2:10, both Jews and **p-s**
     13:43, God-fearing **p-s** followed Paul

PROSPER 1 Sam. 18:14, David was **p-ing**
Ps. 10:5, His ways **p** at all times
Prov. 28:13, his transgressions will not **p**
1 Cor. 16:2, save, as he may **p**
Gen. 39:3; 1 Sam. 18:5

PROSPERITY—*wealth*
Ezra 9:12, never seek . . . their **p**
Job 21:13, spend their days in **p**
Ps. 25:13, His soul will abide in **p**
     73:3, saw the **p** of the wicked
Acts 19:25, our **p** depends upon this business

PROSPEROUS
Prov. 11:25, generous man will be **p**

PROSTITUTES
Hos. 4:14, offer sacrifices with temple **p**

PROSTRATE 2 Sam. 9:6, fell on his face and **p-d**
     himself
Job 14:10, man dies and lies **p**

PROTECT Is. 31:5, He will **p** and deliver it

PROTECTION Num. 14:9, Their **p** has been
     removed
Eccles. 7:12, wisdom is **p** *just as* money is **p**

PROUD—*arrogant, conceited*
Ps. 94:2, recompense to the **p**
Luke 1:51, **p** in the thoughts of their heart
James 4:6, GOD IS OPPOSED TO THE **P**
Is. 3:16; 13:11

PROVE—*test* Prov. 30:6; 2 Cor. 8:8
  Acts 9:22, **p**-ing that this *Jesus* is the Christ
  Rom. 12:2, **p** what the will of God is
PROVERB 1 Kin. 4:32, He also spoke 3,000 **p-s**
  1 Kin. 9:7, Israel will become a **p** and a byword
  Deut. 28:37; Jer. 24:9; 2 Pet. 2:22
PROVIDE—*gave* Gen. 22:8, God will **p** for
  Himself the Lamb
  Neh. 9:15, didst **p** bread from heaven
  1 Tim. 5:8, if any one does not **p** for his own
  Lev. 25:24; 1 Sam. 16:17
PROVISION Josh. 9:5, bread of their **p** was dry
  Ps. 132:15, abundantly bless her **p**
  Rom. 13:14, make no **p** for the flesh
PROVOKE Prov. 20:2, who **p-s** him to anger
  1 Cor. 13:5, is not **p-d**
  Eph. 6:4, do not **p** your children to anger
  2 Chr. 25:19; Job 12:6
PROW Acts 27:41, the **p** stuck fast and remained
PROWL—*walk* Ps. 104:20, beast of the forest **p**
  1 Pet. 5:8, devil, **p-s** about like a roaring lion
PRUDENT Prov. 12:16, **p** man conceals dishonor
  Prov. 19:14, a **p** wife is from the LORD
  Jer. 49:7, good counsel been lost to the **p**
PSALMS Ps. 95:2, shout joyfully to Him with **p**
  Luke 20:42, David ... says in the book of **P**
  24:44, the **P** must be fulfilled
  Eph. 5:19, speaking to one another in **p**
PUGNACIOUS 1 Tim. 3:3, addicted to wine or **p**
PULL Ps. 31:4, **p** me out of the net
  Luke 14:5, **p** him out on a Sabbath day
PULVERIZE Mic. 4:13, That you may **p** many
  peoples
PUNISH—*visit* Lev. 26:18,28, will **p** you seven
  times
  Is. 13:11, **p** the world for its evil
  Lam. 4:22, He will **p** your iniquity
  2 Cor. 10:6, to **p** all disobedience
  Prov. 22:3; Luke 23:16; Acts 26:11
PUNISHMENT Gen. 4:13, **p** is too great to bear
  Job 19:29, the **p** of the sword
  Matt. 25:46, go away into eternal **p**
  2 Cor. 2:6, Sufficient ... is this **p**
  1 John 4:18, because fear involves **p**
  Jude 7, the **p** of eternal fire
PUPIL Deut. 32:10, **p** of His eye
  Luke 6:40, a **p** is not above his teacher
PURCHASE Gen. 49:32, field ... **p-d** from
  Acts 20:28, He **p-d** with His own blood
  Rev. 5:9, **p** for God with Thy blood
PURE Ps. 12:6, words of the LORD are **p** words
  Ps. 19:8, commandment of the LORD is **p**
  24:4, clean hands and a **p** heart
  Matt. 5:8, Blessed are the **p** in heart
  2 Cor. 11:2, present you *as* a **p** virgin
  Phil. 4:8, whatever is **p**
  1 Tim. 1:5, love from a **p** heart
  Titus 1:15, To the **p**, all things are **p**
  2:5, *be* sensible, **p**
  James 1:27, **p** and undefiled religion
  2 Sam. 22:27; Job 4:17; 11:4; 15:15; Song 6:10;
  Dan. 7:9
PURGE Dan. 12:10, Many will be **p-d**, purified,
  refined
PURIFY Ps. 51:7, **P** me with hyssop
  1 Pet. 1:22, obedience ... **p-ed** your souls
  2 Pet. 1:9, **p-cation** from his former sins
  2 Kin. 2:21; Dan. 12:10
PURPOSE—*cause, devise, reason*
  Jer. 49:20, **p-s** which He has **p-d**
  Lam. 2:17, The LORD has done what He **p-d**
  Ezek. 22:9, **p** of shedding blood
  Luke 7:30, rejected God's **p**
  Acts 26:16, for this **p** I have appeared to you
  Rom. 8:28, called according to His **p**
  Eph. 3:11, in accordance with the eternal **p**
  6:22, for this very **p**
  Heb. 6:17, unchangeableness of His **p**
  1 Pet. 4:6, has for this **p** been preached
PURSE Is. 46:6; Hag. 1:6; Luke 12:33

PURSUE—*follow, persecute, sought* Gen. 31:36
  Ps. 34:14, Seek peace, and **p** it
  Prov. 21:21, who **p-s** righteousness and loyalty
  Heb. 12:14, **P** peace with all men
  1 Pet. 3:11, SEEK PEACE AND **P** IT
  Lev. 26:17; Judg. 3:28; 2 Sam. 1:6; Job 30:15; Ps.
  7:1; Is. 5:11
PUSH—*thrust* Ps. 118:13, **p-ed** me violently
PUT Gen. 3:15, I will **p** enmity Between you and
  Ex. 9:15, now I had **p** forth My hand
  Ps. 40:3, **p** a new song in my mouth
  Matt. 1:19, desired to **p** her away secretly
  12:18, I WILL **P** MY SPIRIT UPON HIM
  26:52, **P** your sword back into its place
  Mark 12:42, widow came ... **p** in two
  Luke 9:62, **p-ing** his hand to the plow
  John 19:2, crown of thorns ... **p** it on His head
  20:27, hand, and **p** it into My side
  Rom. 13:14, **p** on the Lord Jesus Christ
  1 Cor. 15:53, **p** on the imperishable, **p** on
  immortality
  Eph. 4:24, **p** on the new self
  6:11, **P** on the full armor of God
  1 Pet. 2:1, **p-ing** aside all malice
  Rev. 14:15, **P** in your sickle
  Josh. 1:18; 2 Chr. 18:22; Job 31:24; 38:36;
  Song 8:6; Mark 4:21; John 21:7

Q

QUAKE—*tremble, shake*
  Judg. 5:4, The earth **q-d**, the heavens
  Judg. 5:5; Ps. 68:8
QUARREL—*contend, war*
  Ex. 21:18, if men have a **q**
  James 4:1, source of **q-s** and conflicts
  Ex. 17:2; Prov. 20:3; 1 Cor. 1:11
QUEEN 1 Kin. 10:1, the **q** of Sheba
  Is. 47:5, the **q** of kingdoms
  Matt. 12:42, **Q** of *the* South shall rise
  Esth. 1:9; Is. 47:7; Jer. 7:18; Acts 8:27
QUENCH 1 Thess. 5:19, Do not **q** the Spirit
  Ps. 104:11; Song 8:7
QUESTION 1 Kin. 10:1, test with difficult **q-s**
  Mark 11:29, I will ask you one **q**
  22:35, a lawyer, asked Him a **q**
  Acts 18:15, **q-s** about words and names
  1 Cor. 10:25, without asking **q-s** for conscience'
  sake
  1 Tim. 6:4, **q-s** and disputes about words
QUICK—*swift, soon* Acts 7:54, cut to the **q**
  Titus 1:7, not **q-tempered**, not addicted to
  James 1:19, every one be **q** to hear
  Judg. 2:23; John 11:31
QUICKLY—*shortly, suddenly*
  Matt. 5:25, Make friends **q** with your opponent
  John 13:27, what you do, do **q**
  Rom. 9:28, EXECUTE HIS WORD ... **Q**
  Rev. 3:11; 22:20, I am coming **q**
  Gen. 18:6; Deut. 7:4; Ps. 31:2; Eccles. 4:12;
  2 Thess. 2:2
QUICK-TEMPERED Prov. 14:17; 14:29; Titus 1:7
QUIET Job 20:20, he knew no **q** within him
  Ps. 23:2, beside **q** waters
  1 Thess. 4:11, your ambition to lead a **q** life
  1 Tim. 2:2, lead a tranquil and **q** life
  Prov. 17:1; Eccles. 9:17; Amos 6:10
QUILT 1 Sam. 19:13, put a **q** of goats' *hair*
QUOTA Ex. 5:18, deliver the **q** of bricks

R

RABBI Matt. 26:25; Mark 9:5
RABBIT Lev. 11:6; Deut. 14:7
RACE Eccles. 9:11, **r** is not to the swift
  Nah. 2:4, chariots **r** madly in the streets
  1 Cor. 9:24, those who run in a **r** all run
  1 Pet. 2:9, A CHOSEN **R**, A ROYAL
RADIANCE Heb. 1:3, **r** of His glory
RADIANT Jer. 31:12, **r** over the bounty of the
  LORD
RAFTER Hab. 2:11, the **r** will answer it
RAGES—*frets* Prov. 19:3, his heart **r** against

RAID Gen. 49:19, raiders shall **r** him . . . **r** at their heels
RAIMENT—*clothing* Is. 63:3, I stained all My **r**
RAIN Gen. 7:12, **r** fell upon the earth for forty days
  Ex. 16:4, will **r** bread from heaven for you
  Matt. 5:45, **r** on *the* righteous . . . unrighteous
    7:25, and the **r** descended
  Heb. 6:7, ground that drinks the **r**
  Lev. 26:4; Deut. 32:2; Job 24:8; Prov. 25:14; 25:23; Song 2:11
RAISE Matt. 20:19, third day He . . . **r-d** up
  John 2:19, in three days I will **r** it up
    6:39, **r** it up on the last day
  1 Cor. 15:13, not even Christ . . . **r-d**
    15:35, How are the dead **r-d**
    15:42, it is **r-d**
    15:44, **r-d** a spiritual body
  Eph. 2:6, **r-d** us up with Him
  Col. 3:1, If . . . been **r-d** up with Christ
  Heb. 11:19, God is able to **r** *men* from
  Deut. 18:18; Judg. 2:16; Is. 2:2; Dan. 12:7; Hos. 6:2; Mic. 4:1; Luke 3:8
RAISIN 2 Sam. 6:19; Song 2:5; Hos. 3:1
RAMPARTS—*siege works* Ps. 48:13; Is. 26:1
RAN—*fled* Luke 8:34, they **r** away and reported
RANK—*high* Ps. 62:9, men of **r** are a lie
RANSOM Matt. 20:28, give His life a **r** for many
  1 Tim. 2:6, gave Himself as a **r** for all
  Ex. 30:12; Prov. 6:35
RAPID—*swift* Prov. 6:18, Feet that run **r-ly** to evil
RARE—*precious*
  1 Sam. 3:1, word from the Lord was **r**
RASH Job 6:3, my words have been **r**
RATION—*provision* Dan. 1:5; Luke 12:42
RAVAGE Gen. 41:30; 1 Sam. 6:5; Acts 8:3
RAVINE—*valley* Luke 3:5, Every R shall be
RAYS Hab. 3:4, He has **r** *flashing* from His hand
READ Hab. 2:2, one who **r-s** it may run
  Luke 4:16, stood up to **r**
  Acts 8:28, was **r-ing** the prophet Isaiah
  2 Cor. 3:14, at the **r-ing** of the old covenant
  1 Tim. 4:13, give attention to the public **r-ing**
  Rev. 1:3, Blessed is he who **r-s**
  Ex. 24:7; Is. 34:16; Dan. 5:8
READINESS 2 Cor. 8:12, if the **r** is present
READY 1 Chr. 7:11; Ps. 86:5; Prov. 24:27
REALIZED Prov. 13:19, Desire **r** is sweet
REALLY—*indeed* Luke 24:34, The Lord has **r** risen
REAP—*harvest* Hos. 8:7, they **r** the whirlwind
  Matt. 6:26, neither do they **r**, nor
    25:26, **r** where I did not sow
  Luke 12:24, ravens . . . neither sow nor **r**
  2 Cor. 9:6, shall also **r** sparingly
  Gal. 6:7, this he will also **r**
    6:8, flesh **r** corruption
    6:9, in due time we shall **r**
  Lev. 19:9; Ps. 126:5; Prov. 22:8; Rev. 14:16
REASON—*thought*
  Job 23:7, the upright would **r** with Him
  Is. 1:18, let us **r** together
  Luke 5:22, Why are you **r-ing** in your hearts
  Acts 17:17, he was **r-ing** in the synagogue
  1 Cor. 3:20, knows the **r-ings** of the wise
  1 Tim. 1:16, for this **r** I found mercy
  James 3:17, gentle, **r-able**, full of mercy
REBEL Ps. 107:11, **r-ed** against the words of God
  Is. 63:10, **r-ed** . . . grieved His Holy Spirit
  Num. 14:9; 1 Sam. 12:15; Ezek. 20:21
REBELLION—*transgression* 1 Sam. 24:11; Job 13:23
REBELLIOUS—*disobedient*
  1 Tim. 1:9, those who are lawless and **r**
  Ex. 23:21; Deut. 9:7; Ps. 66:7; 78:8; Jer. 5:23
REBUILD Is. 58:12, **r** the ancient ruins
REBUKE—*reprove, reproof*
  Matt. 8:26, **r-d** the winds and
    17:18, Jesus **r-d** him, and the demon
  Mark 9:25, **r-d** the unclean spirit

  Luke 4:39, He **r-d** the fever, and it left
  1 Tim. 5:1, not sharply **r** an older man
  Job 26:11; Ps. 38:1; Prov. 27:5; Zech. 3:2
RECEIVE—*accept* Prov. 1:3, **r** instruction in wise
  Matt. 10:8, freely you **r-d**, freely give
    10:14, whoever does not **r** you
    10:40, who **r-s** you **r-s** Me
    10:41, who **r-s** a prophet in *the* name of
    11:5, blind R sight
    18:5, **r-s** one such child
    25:27, **r-d** my money back with interest
  Mark 16:19, **r-d** up into heaven
  Luke 15:2, This man **r-s** sinners
    20:47, **r** greater condemnation
  John 1:11, His own did not **r** Him
    5:44, **r** glory from one another
    14:3, **r** you to Myself
    20:22, R the Holy Spirit
  Acts 20:35, blessed to give than to **r**
  Rom. 5:17, the abundance of grace
    8:15, **r-d** a spirit of adoption
  1 Cor. 3:8, will **r** his own reward
    9:24, one **r-s** the prize
  Gal. 4:5, **r** the adoption as sons
  1 Thess. 1:6, **r-d** the word in much
  2 Thess. 2:10, did not **r** the love of the
  Heb. 2:2, **r-d** a just recompense
  James 1:12, **r** the crown of life
  Job 3:12; Is. 40:2
RECEPTION—*feast* Luke 14:13, you give a **r**
RECKLESS 2 Tim. 3:4, treacherous, **r** . . . lovers of pleasure
RECKON—*impute* Rom. 4:4, his wage is not **r-ed**
  Rom. 4:6, God **r-s** righteousness
RECLINE—*sat* Matt. 9:10; 26:20, He was **r-ing**
RECOGNIZE—*know* Acts 19:15, I **r** Jesus
  Gen. 27:23; 1 Cor. 14:38
RECOMPENSE—*reward*
  Ps. 94:2, Render **r** to the proud
  Heb. 2:2, received a just **r**
  Ps. 28:4; Jer. 51:6
RECONCILE Matt. 5:24, be **r-d** to your brother
  1 Cor. 7:11, be **r-d** to her husband
  2 Cor. 5:20, be **r-d** to God
  Col. 1:20, **r** all things to Himself
RECONCILIATION
  Rom. 5:11, we have now received the **r**
RECORD—*write* Hab. 2:2, R the vision
RECOVERY—*health* Is. 58:8, your **r** will speedily spring
RED—*dull* Gen. 25:25, first came forth **r**, all over
  Ex. 10:19, drove them into the R Sea
  Prov. 23:31, on the wine when it is **r**
  Is. 1:18, they are **r** like crimson
  Zech. 1:8, man was riding on a **r** horse
  Matt. 16:2, fair weather . . . sky is **r**
  Rev. 6:4, another, a **r** horse, went out
REDEEM—*purchase*
  Ex. 6:6, **r** you with an outstretched arm
  Ps. 26:11, R me, and be gracious
    49:15, God will **r** my soul
  Gal. 3:13, **r-ed** us from the curse
  Titus 2:14, R us from every . . . deed
  Ruth 4:4; 2 Sam. 4:9
REDEEMER Job 19:25, know that my R lives
  Ps. 19:14, my rock and my **r**
  Is. 63:16, our Father, Our R
  Jer. 50:34, Their R is strong
REDEMPTION Ps. 130:7, with Him is abundant **r**
  Luke 21:28, your **r** is drawing near
  Rom. 3:24, **r** which is in Christ Jesus
  Eph. 1:7, **r** through His blood
    4:30, sealed for the day of **r**
REDUCE—*diminish* Ex. 5:8, you are not to **r** any of it
REED—*bulrushes, rod*
  Ex. 2:3, set it among the **r-s** by
  Is. 42:3, bruised **r** He will not break
  Matt. 27:30, **r** and *began* to beat Him
    27:48, wine, and put it on a **r**
  Is. 36:6; Matt. 11:7

REEF Jude 12, hidden **r-s** in your love-feasts

REEL Is. 28:7, these also **r** with wine

REFINE—*purify, try* Ps. 12:6, silver ... **r-d** seven times
    Rev. 3:18, gold **r-d** by fire

REFORM Acts 24:2, **r-s** are being carried out

REFRAIN 1 Pet. 3:10, R HIS TONGUE FROM EVIL
    Ex. 23:5; Job 30:10; 1 Cor. 9:6; 2 Cor. 12:6

REFRESH—*comfort* 1 Cor. 16:18, **r-ed** my spirit and yours
    Gen. 18:5; Ex. 23:12; 31:17; Song 2:5

REFUGE—*defense, strength, trust*
    2 Sam. 22:3, God, my rock, in whom I take **r**
    Ps. 46:1, God is our **r** and strength
    Is. 17:10, remembered the rock of your **r**
    33:16, His **r** will be the impregnable rock
    Judg. 9:15; Ps. 55:8; Is. 28:17; Jer. 16:19

REFUSE (n.) Ex. 29:14; Judg. 3:22; Is. 57:20

REFUSE (v.) Gen. 23:6, none ... will **r** you his grave
    Prov. 21:25, his hands **r** to work
    Matt. 2:18, SHE R-D TO BE COMFORTED
    Acts 10:47, no one can **r** the water for these
    2 Tim. 2:23, **r** foolish and ignorant speculations
    Jer. 13:10; Heb. 12:25

REFUTE Job 32:12; Titus 1:9

REGARD Rom. 14:5, **r-s** one day above another
    Phil. 2:3, you **r** one another as more important
    Gen. 4:4; Job 18:3; 41:27; Prov. 15:5; Is. 17:7; Lam. 4:2; Luke 7:2

REGION Matt. 2:22, he departed for the **r-s** of Galilee
    Mark 5:17; Luke 2:8; Acts 27:2

REGISTER—*number, written* Num. 11:26; 2 Sam. 24:4

REGRET 1 Sam. 15:35, the LORD **r-ed** that
    2 Cor. 7:10, produces a repentance without **r**

REGULAR Dan. 8:11; 11:31; 12:11, **r** sacrifice

REIGN—*rule* Ex. 15:18, LORD shall **r** forever and
    Luke 19:14, not want this man to **r** over
    1 Cor. 15:25, must **r** until He has put
    2 Tim. 2:12, we shall also **r** with Him
    Rev. 20:6, **r** with Him for a thousand years
    Gen. 37:8; Judg. 9:8; Prov. 8:15; Is. 32:1

REJECT Prov. 3:11, do not **r** the discipline of the LORD
    Prov. 15:5, A fool **r-s** his father's discipline
    Matt. 21:42, STONE ... BUILDERS R-ED
    Luke 10:16, the one who **r-s** you **r-s** Me
    17:25, **r-ed** by this generation
    John 12:48, He who **r-s** Me
    1 Thess. 4:8, who **r-s** *this* is not **r-ing** man but God
    2 Tim. 3:8, **r-ed** as regards the faith
    1 Pet. 2:4, **r-ed** by men
    2:7; Ps. 118:22, STONE ... BUILDERS R-ED
    Num. 11:20; Ps. 53:5; Is. 14:19; 30:12; 33:15; Jer. 6:30; Ezek. 20:13,16; Hos. 4:6; Amos 2:4

REJOICE Prov. 5:18, **r** in the wife of your youth
    Matt. 2:10, they **r-d** exceedingly
    5:12, **R**, and be glad
    John 14:28, loved Me, you would have **r-d**
    Rom. 12:15, **R** with those who **r**
    1 Cor. 13:6, not **r** in unrighteousness
    Phil. 3:1, brethren, **r** in the Lord
    4:4, **R** in the Lord always
    1 Thess. 5:16, **R** always
    1 Pet. 1:8, **r** with joy inexpressible
    Job 21:12; Eccles. 11:9; Is. 60:5; Luke 10:21; 1 Thess. 3:9

REJOICING Ps. 19:8, LORD are right, **r** the heart
    Ps. 65:12, hills gird themselves with **r**
    Joel 1:12, **r** dries up
    Acts 5:41, **r** ... been considered worthy
    8:39, went on his way **r**
    Rom. 12:12, **r** in hope, persevering
    2 Cor. 6:10, sorrowful yet always **r**

RELATE Acts 8:33, WHO SHALL R HIS GENERATION

RELATIONSHIP
    Matt. 19:10, **r** of the man with his wife

RELATIVE Luke 1:36,58

RELEASE—*deliverance, liberty*
    Lev. 25:10, proclaim a **r** through the land
    Matt. 27:26, Then he **r-d** Barabbas
    Mark 15:9, **r** for you the King ... Jews
    Luke 4:18, PROCLAIM R TO THE CAPTIVES
    23:20, Pilate, wanting to **r** Jesus
    John 19:12, Pilate made efforts to **r** Him
    Rom. 7:6, we have been **r-d** from the Law
    1 Cor. 7:27, Are you **r-d** from a wife
    Heb. 11:35, not accepting their **r**
    Rev. 1:5, **r-d** us from our sins

RELIEF Job 32:20, speak that I may get **r**

RELIEVED Ps. 4:1, Thou hast **r** me in my distress

REMAIN—*abide, live, reside*
    Gen. 8:22, While the earth **r-s**
    Eccles. 1:4, But the earth **r-s** forever
    Matt. 2:13, **r** there until I tell
    11:23, **r-ed** to this day
    26:38, **r** here and keep watch
    John 1:32, He **r-ed** upon Him
    19:31, not **r** on the cross
    21:22, want him to **r** until I come
    1 Cor. 3:14, If any man's work ... **r-s**
    7:8, they **r** even as I
    7:11, let her **r** unmarried
    Gal. 2:5, gospel might **r** with you
    1 Thess. 4:15, **r** until the coming of
    Titus 1:5, set in order what **r-s**
    Rev. 3:2, strengthen the things that **r**
    Ex. 16:29; Deut. 9:9; 1 Sam. 5:7; 16:11; Job 14:2; 21:34; John 8:35

REMARKABLE—*strange*
    Luke 5:26, seen **r** things today

REMEMBER Gen. 9:15, I will **r** My covenant
    Ex. 20:8, **R** the sabbath day
    Job 7:7, **R** that my life is *but* breath
    11:16, As waters ... passed by ... **r** *it*
    Ps. 25:7, not **r** the sins of my youth
    Eccles. 12:1, **R** also your Creator
    Jer. 31:34, their sin I will **r** no more
    Matt. 26:75, Peter **r-ed** the word which Jesus
    27:63, **r** ... that deceiver said
    Luke 17:32, **R** Lot's wife
    23:42, **r** me when You come in
    John 15:20, **R** the word that I said
    Acts 20:35, **r** the words of the Lord
    Gal. 2:10, us to **r** the poor
    Heb. 13:7, **R** those who led you
    Rev. 2:5, **R** ... from where you have fallen
    Deut. 5:15; 32:7; 1 Chr. 16:12; Ps. 63:6; 105:42; Is. 46:8; Jer. 15:15; Lam. 3:20; Ezek. 21:32; Acts 10:31; Heb. 13:3

REMEMBRANCE Mal. 3:16, a book of **r** was written
    Luke 22:19, do this in **r** of Me
    1 Cor. 11:25, drink *it*, in **r** of Me
    Eccles. 1:11; Is. 26:14; 43:26

REMNANT Rom. 11:5, **r** according to *God's* gracious choice
    Deut. 3:11; Jer. 6:9; 23:3; Mal. 2:15

REMOTE—*utmost* Neh. 1:9, most **r** part of the heavens

REMOVE Gen. 8:13, Noah **r-d** the covering of the ark
    Ex. 3:5, **r** your sandals from your feet
    1 Kin. 15:12, **r-d** all the idols
    2 Kin. 17:23, LORD **r-d** Israel from His sight
    Ps. 103:12, **r-d** our transgressions
    Is. 29:13, **r** their hearts far from
    Ezek. 36:26, **r** the heart of stone
    Matt. 3:11, not *even* fit to **r** His sandals
    Luke 22:42, **r** this cup from Me
    John 11:39, **R** the stone
    1 Cor. 13:2, so as to **r** mountains
    Ruth 4:8; 2 Kin. 18:4; Job 24:2

REND 1 Kin. 19:11; Is. 64:1; Joel 2:13

RENDER—*repay* Matt. 22:21, **r** to Caesar the things that
    Rom. 13:7, **R** to all ... due them
    Deut. 32:41; Ps. 94:2; Prov. 24:12

RENEW Ps. 51:10, r a steadfast spirit within
Ps. 103:5, youth is **r-ed** like the
Lam. 5:21, **R** our days as of old
Rom. 12:2, **r-ing** of your mind
2 Cor. 4:16, inner man is being **r-ed** day by day
Col. 3:10, **r-ed** to a true knowledge
Titus 3:5, **r-ing** by the Holy Spirit
REPAY—*recompense* Gen. 44:4, **r-d** evil for good
Matt. 6:4,6,18, in secret will **r** you
Luke 10:35, return, I will **r** you
Rom. 12:19, I WILL **R**, SAYS THE LORD
1 Thess. 5:15, no one **r-s** ... evil for evil
Philem. 19, own hand, I will **r** it
Heb. 10:30, VENGEANCE IS MINE, I WILL **R**
Deut. 7:10; 32:6; 2 Sam. 3:39; Jer. 18:20; 51:56;
　　Luke 14:14
REPENT Job 42:6, r in dust and ashes
Matt. 3:2, **R**, for the kingdom of
　11:21, **r-ed** long ago in sackcloth
Mark 1:15, r and believe in the gospel
　6:12, preached that *men* should **r**
Luke 13:3, unless you r, you will all
　15:7, one sinner who **r-s**
Acts 2:38, **R**, and ... be baptized
　3:19, **R** therefore and return
　26:20, r and turn to God
Num. 23:19; Ezek. 18:30
REPENTANCE Matt. 3:8, fruit ... with *your* **r**
Matt. 3:11, in water for **r**
Mark 1:4, a baptism of **r**
Luke 24:47, r for forgiveness of sins
Acts 26:20, performing deeds ... to **r**
2 Cor. 7:10, God produces a r without regret
Heb. 6:1, laying ... foundation of **r**
2 Pet. 3:9, all to come to **r**
REPHAIM—*giant*
Deut. 3:13, it is called the land of **R**
REPORT Matt. 2:8, have found *Him*, r to me
Matt. 11:4, Go and r to John the things
Luke 7:17, this r concerning Him
John 12:38, WHO HAS BELIEVED OUR **R**
REPROACH Jer. 29:18, a hissing and a **r**
Ezek. 5:14, a r among the nations
Matt. 11:20, He began to r the cities
1 Tim. 3:7, fall into r and the snare of
Titus 2:8, speech which is beyond **r**
Heb. 11:26, considering the r of Christ
Gen. 30:23; Job 27:6; Ps. 4:2; 44:13; 119:39;
　Is. 51:7; Jer. 24:9; Hos. 12:14; Rom. 15:3
REPROBATE Ps. 15:4, a r is despised
REPROOF Prov. 15:10, who hates r will die
2 Tim. 3:16, for teaching, for r, for correction
Prov. 1:30; 10:17; 15:5; 29:1,15
REPROVE—*correct*
Job 5:17, the man whom God **r-s**
Prov. 3:12, whom the LORD loves He **r-s**
Matt. 18:15, r him in private
2 Tim. 4:2, r, rebuke, exhort, with ... patience
Rev. 3:19, I love, I r and discipline
Lev. 19:17; Job 13:10; 40:2; Prov. 9:8; Jer. 2:19
REPUTATION—*report*
Acts 6:3, seven men of good **r**
1 Tim. 5:10, having a r for good works
REPUTE—*report* Phil. 4:8, whatever is of good **r**
REQUEST—*desire*
Rom. 1:10, in my prayers making **r**
Phil. 4:6, let your **r-s** be made known
Judg. 8:24; 1 Kin. 2:16; Neh. 2:4; Job 6:8;
　Mark 15:6
REQUIRE Mic. 6:8, what does the Lord r of you
Luke 12:20, night your soul is **r-d** of you
1 Cor. 4:2, it is **r-d** of stewards
Gen. 9:5; Deut. 10:12; Ezra 3:4; Ps. 10:13;
　Is. 1:12
RESCUE Ps. 144:10; 2 Pet. 2:7
RESERVED 1 Pet. 1:4, r in heaven for you
2 Pet. 3:7, are being r for fire
Gen. 27:36; Job 21:30
RESIDE Matt. 2:23, **r-d** in a city called Nazareth
Lev. 19:34; Eccles. 7:9; Jer. 49:18

RESIST Matt. 5:39, do not r him who is evil
Luke 21:15, opponents will be able to r or
Acts 7:51, are always **r-ing** the Holy Spirit
Rom. 13:2, he who **r-s** authority has opposed
Heb. 12:4, not yet **r-ed** to the point of shedding
James 4:7, **R** the devil, and he
RESOLUTELY—*steadfastly*
1 Chr. 28:7, r performs My
Luke 9:51, He r set His face to go
RESPECT Matt. 21:37, They will r my son
Luke 18:2, and did not r man
Eph. 5:33, let the wife ... r her husband
1 Pet. 3:2, chaste and **r-ful** behavior
Gen. 34:19; Mal. 1:6; 1 Pet. 2:18
RESPOND Is. 19:22, LORD, and He will r to them
Col. 4:6, how you should r to each person
RESPONSE 2 Kin. 4:31, was neither sound nor **r**
REST—*stand* Josh. 1:13, God gives you **r**
Josh. 14:15, the land had r from war
Ps. 37:7, **R** in the LORD and wait
　116:7, Return to your r, O my soul
Prov. 14:33, Wisdom **r-s** in the heart
Is. 11:2, Spirit of the LORD will r upon Him
　11:10, His **r-ing** place will be glorious
Jer. 6:16, find r for your souls
Matt. 11:28, and I will give you **r**
　11:29, **R** FOR YOUR SOULS
Luke 11:24, waterless places seeking **r**
1 Cor. 2:5, r on the wisdom of men
2 Cor. 2:13, I had no r for my spirit
Heb. 3:11, THEY SHALL NOT ENTER MY **R**
1 Pet. 4:2, live the r of the time in
Gen. 5:29; 8:9; 49:15; Ex. 10:5; Deut. 28:65; Ruth
　1:9; 2 Sam. 4:5; Job 3:17; 11:18; Prov. 19:20;
　Eccles. 4:6; Is. 14:3; 38:10; 57:2; Lam. 5:5;
　Matt. 22:6; Rev. 19:21
RESTED Gen. 2:2, and He r on the seventh day
Ex. 24:16, glory of the LORD **r**
Acts 2:3, tongues of fire ... r on each one
RESTITUTION Lev. 6:5; 2 Sam. 12:6
RESTORE—*turn* Ps. 19:7, perfect **r-ing** the soul
Ps. 23:3, He **r-s** my soul; He guides
Matt. 17:11, is coming, and will r all things
Mark 3:5, his hand was **r-d**
James 5:15, prayer ... will r the one who is sick
Gen. 20:7; Neh. 3:8; 4:2; Ps. 80:3; Jer. 30:17
RESTRAIN Prov. 10:19, who **r-s** his lips is wise
Acts 14:18, they with difficulty **r-ed** the crowds
2 Cor. 6:12, You are not **r-ed** by us, but
Gen. 8:2; Job 7:11; 11:10; Jer. 31:16; 2 Pet. 2:16
RESTRICT Jer. 36:5, I am **r-ed**; I cannot go
RESULT—*work* Eph. 4:14, As a r ... no longer
James 1:4, endurance have *its* perfect **r**
RESURRECTION Matt. 22:23, say there is no **r**
Matt. 22:30, r they neither marry, nor
Luke 14:14, at the r of the righteous
　20:27, who say that there is no **r**
　20:36, being sons of the **r**
John 5:29, r of life ... r of judgment
　11:25, the r, and the life
Acts 24:15, r of both the righteous and the
　24:21, For the r of the dead
1 Cor. 15:13, if there is no **r**
Phil. 3:11, attain to the **r**
Heb. 11:35, might obtain a better **r**
1 Pet. 1:3, living hope through the **r**
Rev. 20:5, This is the first **r**
RETAIN John 20:23, r the sins of any ... **r-ed**
RETIRE Ps. 127:2, To r late
RETRIBUTION Hos. 9:7, days of r have come
Rom. 11:9, STUMBLING BLOCK ... A **R**
RETURN—*turn back*
Gen. 43:18, money ... **r-ed** in our sacks
Deut. 30:2, r to the LORD your God
Eccles. 4:9, a good r for their labor
Mal. 3:7, **R** to Me, and I will r to you
Matt. 10:13, let your ... peace r to you
Luke 2:39, they **r-ed** to Galilee
　4:14, **r-ed** ... in the power of the Spirit
　10:17, the seventy **r-ed** with joy
　24:9, **r-ed** from the tomb

RETURN (Continued)
Acts 3:19, Repent therefore and **r**
1 Tim. 5:4, make some **r** to their parents
1 Pet. 2:25, now you have **r-ed** to the
3:9, not **r-ing** evil for evil
Gen. 3:19; 32:9; Ex. 14:28; Ruth 1:12;
1 Sam. 7:3; 25:21; 2 Sam. 1:22; 1 Kin. 22:17;
Job 1:21; 10:21; 33:25; Eccles. 12:2,7; Is.
10:22; 55:11; Jer. 3:22; 4:1; Ezek. 16:55;
Dan. 4:36; Matt. 12:44; Acts 13:34

REVEAL—*manifest* Job 20:27, will **r** his iniquity
Is. 40:5, glory of the LORD will be **r-ed**
53:1, arm of the LORD been **r-ed**
Matt. 11:25, didst **r** them to babes
16:17, blood did not **r** this to you
Luke 17:30, the Son of Man is **r-ed**
Rom. 8:18, glory that is to be **r-ed** to us
8:19, **r-ing** of the sons of God
1 Cor. 3:13, it is to be **r-ed** with fire
Gal. 1:16, to **r** His Son in me
Eph. 3:5, **r-ed** to His holy apostles
2 Thess. 2:3, man of lawlessness is **r-ed**
2:8, lawless one will be **r-ed**
1 Pet. 1:5, be **r-ed** in the last time
1 Sam. 14:8,11; Job 12:22; Prov. 11:13; 25:9; Is.
26:21; Dan. 2:47

REVEL 2 Pet. 2:13, to **r** in the daytime

REVELATION Rom. 16:25, the **r** of the mystery
1 Cor. 1:7, awaiting eagerly the **r**
14:6, speak ... by way of **r**
Gal. 1:12, through a **r** of Jesus Christ
2:2, because of a **r** that I went up
Eph. 1:17, spirit of wisdom and **r**
Rev. 1:1, The **R** of Jesus Christ

REVENGE Jer. 20:10, take our **r** on him
Rom. 12:19, Never take your own **r**

REVERE Lev. 19:30; Zeph. 3:7

REVERENCE—*fear*
Ps. 2:11, Worship the LORD with **r**
5:7, bow in **r** for Thee
Heb. 11:7, in **r** prepared an ark
12:28, service with **r** and awe
Job 15:4; Is. 29:13

REVILE Ps. 74:10, long, will the adversary **r**
Matt. 5:11, when *men* **r** you
Acts 23:4, Do you **r** God's high priest
1 Cor. 4:12, when we are **r-d**, we bless
1 Pet. 2:23, being **r-d**, He did not **r**
4:14, **r-d** for the name of Christ

REVIVE Ps. 119:88, **R** me ... Thy lovingkindness

REWARD—*recompense*
Job 15:31, emptiness will be his **r**
Ps. 58:11, a **r** for the righteous
Prov. 11:18, righteousness gets a true **r**
Is. 62:11, His **r** is with Him
Matt. 5:12, your **r** in heaven is great
6:1, no **r** with your Father who
6:2,5,16, have their **r** in full
10:42, shall not lose his **r**
1 Cor. 3:8, will receive his own **r**
Heb. 11:26, he was looking to the **r**
2 John 8, that you may receive a full **r**
Rev. 22:12, My **r** is with Me
Gen. 15:1; Ruth 2:12; Prov. 11:31; Is. 1:23; 45:13

RICH Gen. 13:2, Abram was very **r** in livestock
Jer. 9:23, **r** man boast of his riches
Matt. 19:23, hard for a **r** man to enter
Luke 1:53, sent away the **r** empty-handed
6:24, woe to you who are **r**
16:1, There was a certain **r** man
16:21, *crumbs* ... falling from the **r** man's table
18:23, for he was extremely **r**
1 Cor. 4:8, filled, you have already become **r**
Eph. 2:4, God, being **r** in mercy
Col. 3:16, word of Christ **r-ly** dwell within
1 Tim. 6:18, to be **r** in good works
James 1:11, **r** man ... will fade away
2:6, Is it not the **r** who oppress you
Rev. 13:16, **r** and the poor, and the free
Gen. 49:20; Ex. 30:15; 1 Sam. 2:7; Ps. 49:2;
Prov. 10:4; 18:23; Eccles. 10:20

RICHES—*possessions* Prov. 11:4, **R** do not profit in the day
Prov. 22:1, more desired than great **r**
30:8, neither poverty nor **r**
Matt. 13:22, deceitfulness of **r**
Luke 8:14, choked with worries and **r**
Rom. 10:12, abounding in **r** for all who call
Eph. 1:7, **r** of His grace
3:8, unfathomable **r** of Christ
1 Tim. 6:17, hope on the uncertainty of **r**
James 5:2, Your **r** are rotted
1 Kin. 3:11; Job 20:15; 36:19; Ps. 62:10;
Prov. 3:16; Jer. 9:23

RIDE 1 Kin. 1:33; Is. 19:1; Ezek. 23:12

RIGHT—*justice, just*
Judg. 17:6, man did what was **r**
Ps. 19:8, precepts of the LORD are **r**
Prov. 14:12, a way which seems **r**
Hos. 14:9, ways of the LORD are **r**
Matt. 5:29, **r** eye makes you stumble
22:44, SIT AT MY **R** HAND
26:64, AT THE **R** HAND OF POWER
Mark 5:15, and in his **r** mind
16:19, SAT DOWN AT THE **R** HAND OF GOD
Luke 22:50, cut off his **r** ear
John 1:12, the **r** to become children of God
Acts 8:21, your heart is not **r**
Rom. 9:21, potter have a **r** over the clay
12:17, **r** in the sight of all men
1 Cor. 9:18, full use of my **r** in the
2 Cor. 13:7, you may do what is **r**
Gal. 2:9, **r** hand of fellowship
Phil. 4:8, whatever is **r**
2 Pet. 2:15, forsaking the **r** way
Rev. 22:14, **r** to the tree of life
Gen. 24:48; Ex. 21:10; Deut. 12:25; 21:17;
2 Kin. 10:15; Job 9:2; 34:6; Prov. 24:26; Is.
41:13; Jer. 40:4; Ezek. 18:25,29; 33:17,20

RIGHTEOUS Gen. 6:9, Noah was a **r** man
Ps. 7:9, establish the **r**
Prov. 10:30, **r** will never be shaken
11:28, **r** will flourish
Jer. 23:5, David a **r** Branch
Hab. 2:4, the **r** will live by his faith
Matt. 5:45, rain on the **r** and the unrighteous
9:13, not come to call the **r**
10:41, a **r** man's reward
13:43, **R** WILL SHINE FORTH
25:46, **r** into eternal life
Luke 15:7, ninety-nine **r** persons
23:50, Joseph ... a good and **r** man
John 7:24, with **r** judgment
Acts 7:52, the coming of the **R** One
Rom. 1:17, THE **R** man SHALL LIVE BY FAITH
3:10, NONE **R**, NOT EVEN
1 Tim. 1:9, Law ... for a **r** man
James 5:16, prayer of a **r** man can
1 Pet. 4:18, THAT THE **R** IS SAVED
1 John 1:9, **r** to forgive us our sins
2:1, Jesus Christ the **r**
Gen. 18:23; Ex. 9:27; 23:7; 1 Sam. 24:17;
Job 9:20; Ps. 1:5; 11:5; 33:1; 37:16; 55:22;
119:75,137; Prov. 2:20; 3:33; 4:18; 13:5;
16:13; 24:16; 28:1; Eccles. 3:17; 7:16; Is.
26:7; 32:1; 53:11; Jer. 33:15; Ezek. 13:22;
Dan. 9:14; Amos 2:6

RIGHTEOUSNESS—*judgment, justice*
Ps. 23:3, in the paths of **r**
96:13, judge the world in **r**
97:6, heavens declare His **r**
111:3, His **r** endures forever
Prov. 14:34, **R** exalts a nation
16:8, Better is a little with **r**
Jer. 22:13, builds his house without **r**
23:6, The LORD our **r**
Dan. 12:3, lead the many to **r**
Matt. 3:15, fitting for us to fulfill all **r**
5:6, hunger and thirst for **r**
5:10, persecuted ... sake of **r**
5:20, your **r** surpasses that
6:1, your **r** before men
6:33, seek first ... and His **r**

Luke 1:75, holiness and r before Him
Rom. 4:3,22; Gal. 3:6, RECKONED TO HIM AS R
  5:18, through one act of r
  8:10, spirit is alive . . . r
2 Cor. 6:14, what partnership have r and
Gal. 2:21, if r *comes* through Law
Eph. 4:24, created in r
  6:14, BREASTPLATE OF R
1 Tim. 6:11, pursue r
2 Tim. 4:8, the crown of r
Heb. 7:2, king of r
  12:11, peaceful fruit of r
James 1:20, anger . . . not achieve the r
1 Pet. 3:14, for the sake of r
1 John 3:10, does not practice r is not
Gen. 15:6; 18:19; 1 Sam. 26:23; Job 27:6; 29:14;
  36:3; Ps. 17:15; 48:10; Prov. 10:2; 11:19;
  Is. 45:8; 48:18; 51:5; 59:17; 60:17; Jer. 31:23;
  Ezek. 18:5; 33:13; Hos. 10:12; Mal. 4:2; Acts
  13:10
RIPE Gen. 40:10; Jer. 24:2; Joel 3:13; Rev.
  14:15,18
RISE Prov. 31:15, She r-s also while
  Matt. 24:7, nation . . . r against nation
  27:63, I *am* to r again
  Mark 12:25, when they r from the dead
  13:12, children will r up against parents
  16:6, He has r-n, He is not here
  Luke 5:23, R and walk
  11:31, Queen of the South shall r
  12:54, cloud r-ing in the west
  22:46, R and pray that
  24:34, Lord has really r-n
1 Thess. 4:16, dead in Christ shall r
Gen. 19:2; Lev. 19:32; Num. 24:17; Josh. 12:1;
  Ps. 35:11; 86:14; 113:3; Is. 32:9; 60:1; Jer.
  47:2; Matt. 14:2; Luke 16:31
RIVER—*water* Ps. 46:4, a r whose streams make
  glad
Eccles. 1:7, All the r-s flow into the sea
Mark 1:5, baptized by him in the Jordan R
John 7:38, shall flow r-s of living water
2 Cor. 11:26, in dangers from r-s
Rev. 22:1, a r of the water of life
Gen. 2:10; Josh. 1:4; 24:2; Job 40:23; Ps. 24:2;
  66:6; 137:1; Is. 11:15; Lam. 2:18; Ezek. 47:5
ROAD—*way* Luke 19:36, garments in the r
Acts 9:27, seen the Lord on the r
ROAM Job 1:7, From r-ing about on the earth
ROAR 1 Pet. 5:8, devil prowls about like a r-ing
  lion
2 Pet. 3:10, heavens pass away with a r
1 Chr. 16:32; Job 4:10; 37:4; Ps. 96:11; Jer. 25:30
ROAST Lev. 2:14, grain r-ed in the fire
ROB Prov. 22:22, Do not r the poor
Mal. 3:8, Will a man r God
2 Cor. 11:8, I r-ed other churches
Judg. 9:25; Prov. 17:12; 28:24; Is. 10:2
ROBBER Jer. 7:11, become a den of r-s
Matt. 21:13, making it a r-s' den
Mark 15:27, crucified two r-s with Him
Luke 10:30, he fell among r-s
  22:52, come out . . . as against a r
John 10:1, he is a thief and a r
  18:40, Now Barabbas was a r
Acts 19:37, neither r-s of temples
ROBBERY Ps. 62:10, do not vainly hope in r
Matt. 23:25, full of r and self-indulgence
Luke 11:39, full of r and wickedness
ROBE—*garment* Is. 61:10, with a r of
  righteousness
Matt. 27:28, put a scarlet r on Him
Mark 12:38, walk around in long r-s
  16:5, young man . . . wearing a white r
Luke 15:22, bring out the best r
  20:46, like to walk around in long r-s
John 19:2, arrayed Him in a purple r
Rev. 1:13, a r reaching to the feet
  7:14, have washed their r-s
  19:16, on His r and on His thigh
1 Sam. 24:4; Job 1:20; 29:14

ROCK—*stone, strength* Num. 20:11, struck the r
  twice
Ps. 19:14, LORD, my r and my redeemer
  31:3, Thou art my r and my fortress
Matt. 7:24, built his house upon the r
  13:5, fell upon the r-y places
  16:18, upon this r I will build My church
Mark 15:46, tomb . . . hewn out in the r
Luke 8:6, other seed fell on r-y *soil*
Rom. 9:33, A R OF OFFENSE
1 Cor. 10:4, were drinking from a spiritual r
Ex. 17:6; 33:22; Deut. 32:4,13; 1 Sam. 2:2;
  2 Sam. 22:2; Job 19:24; 28:2; 29:6; Ps. 18:2;
  27:5; Prov. 30:19; Is. 8:14; 26:4; 51:1; Jer.
  5:3
ROD Ps. 2:9, break them with a r of iron
Ps. 23:4, Thy r and Thy staff, they comfort
Prov. 13:24, spares his r hates his son
2 Cor. 11:25, Three times . . . beaten with r-s
Heb. 9:4, Aaron's r which budded
Rev. 19:15, rule them with a r of iron
Gen. 30:37; Num. 17:8; 2 Sam. 7:14; Prov. 26:3;
  Is. 10:5; Ezek. 20:37; 40:5; 41:8
ROGUE Is. 32:5, r be spoken of *as* generous
ROLL Is. 34:4, sky will be r-ed up
Matt. 27:60, he r-ed a large stone against
  28:2, came and r-ed away the stone
Is. 22:18; Mark 16:3; Heb. 1:12
ROOF Gen. 19:8; Josh. 2:6; 2 Sam. 11:2; Matt. 8:8;
  Mark 2:4
ROOM Jer. 22:14, build myself a r-y house
Matt. 6:6, GO INTO YOUR INNER R
Mark 14:15, large upper r furnished
Luke 2:7, no r for them in the inn
Acts 1:13, went up to the upper r
Gen. 6:14; Judg. 3:24; Prov. 18:16; Matt. 24:26;
  Rom. 12:19
ROOT Matt. 3:10, axe . . . laid at the r of the trees
Mark 4:6, it had no r, it withered
Rom. 11:16, if the r be holy
Eph. 3:17, being r-ed and grounded in love
1 Tim. 6:10, money is a r of all sorts of evil
Deut. 29:18; Job 5:3; Ps. 80:9; Is. 5:24; 53:2;
  Jer. 12:2
ROPE Is. 3:24, Instead of a belt, a r
ROSE (n.) Song 2:1, I am the r of Sharon
ROSE (v.) Josh. 3:16, waters . . . r up in one heap
ROT—*wither* Is. 19:6, reeds and rushes will r
Zech. 14:12, tongue will r in their mouth
James 5:2, Your riches have r-ed
ROTTEN Matt. 7:17, r tree bears bad fruit
ROUND Lev. 19:27, not r off the side-growth
ROUGH Prov. 18:23; Is. 40:4
ROUT Judg. 4:15; 8:12; 2 Sam. 22:15; Ps. 18:14
RUBBISH Phil. 3:8, count them but r
RUIN—*destruction*
  Ex. 9:31, flax . . . barley were r-ed
  Prov. 10:15, r of the poor is their poverty
  18:7, fool's mouth is his r
  26:28, flattering mouth works r
Song 2:15, foxes that are r-ing the vineyards
Luke 6:49, r of that house was great
Acts 15:16, WILL REBUILD ITS R-S
Job 2:3; Ps. 74:3; Prov. 10:14,29; 14:28; Is. 23:13;
  61:4; Lam. 2:13
RULE Judg. 8:22, R over us
  Job 34:30, godless men should not r
  Rom. 15:12, TO R OVER THE GENTILES
  Gal. 6:16, will walk by this r
  Eph. 1:21, far above all r and authority
  Col. 3:15, peace of Christ r in your hearts
  Rev. 2:27, R THEM WITH A ROD OF IRON
  Gen. 1:26; Ps. 8:6; 49:14; Prov. 8:16; 16:32;
  Is. 3:12; 26:13
RULER Ex. 22:28, nor curse a r of your people
  Matt. 2:6, SHALL COME FORTH A R, WHO WILL
  SHEPHERD
  9:34, r of the demons
Mark 10:42, r-s of the Gentiles
John 3:1, Nicodemus, a r of the Jews
  12:31, r of this world shall be cast out

RULER (Continued)
Acts 7:27, WHO MADE YOU A R AND JUDGE
Eph. 6:12, struggle is ... against the **r-s**
Titus 3:1, Remind them to be subject to **r-s**
Gen. 42:6; Ps. 2:2; Prov. 6:7; 29:12; Is. 22:3
RUMOR Matt. 24:6, wars and **r-s** of wars
Ex. 23:1; Ezek. 7:26
RUN Prov. 1:16, their feet **r** to evil
Is. 40:31, **r** and not get tired
1 Cor. 9:24, those who **r** in a race all **r**
Gal. 5:7, You were **r-ing** well
Heb. 12:1, let us **r** with endurance the race
Gen. 49:22; Lev. 15:13; 2 Kin. 4:22; Ps. 18:29;
19:5; Prov. 6:18; Ezek. 32:14; Gal. 2:2
RUSH Matt. 8:32, herd **r-ed** down the steep
Rev. 9:9, many horses **r-ing** to battle
RUSHES—reeds Job 8:11; Is. 19:6
RUST Matt. 6:19, moth and **r** destroy
James 5:3, Your gold and your silver have **r-ed**
RUTHLESS—terrible
Ezek. 28:7, most **r** of the nations

S

SABBATH Ex. 20:8, Remember the **s** day
Lev. 25:8, count off seven **s-s** of years
Matt. 12:8, is Lord of the **S**
28:1, Now late on the **S**
Mark 2:27, **S** was made for man
3:4, on the **S** to do good
John 19:31, that **S** was a high day
Acts 1:12, a **S** day's journey away
Ex. 16:26; 20:11; 31:15; 35:3; Lev. 26:2;
Num. 15:32; Deut. 5:12; 2 Kin. 4:23
SACKCLOTH Matt. 11:21, repented ... in **s**
Rev. 6:12, sun became black as **s** made of hair
Esth. 4:1; Job 16:15; Dan. 9:3
SACRED 2 Kin. 12:18, Joash ... took all the **s**
things
2 Tim. 3:15, have known the **s** writings
SACRIFICE Ps. 51:17, **s-s** of God are a broken
Matt. 9:13, COMPASSION, AND NOT **S**
Rom. 12:1, bodies a living and holy **s**
1 Cor. 8:1, things **s-d** to idols
10:20, they **s** to demons
Phil. 4:18, an acceptable **s**, well pleasing
Heb. 9:26, put away sin by the **s** of
11:4, a better **s** than Cain
13:16, such **s-s** God is pleased
Gen. 31:54; Ex. 12:27; Prov. 15:8; Is. 43:23;
Dan. 11:31; Hos. 6:6; Acts 7:41
SAD—sore Prov. 15:13, when the heart is **s**
Is. 59:11, And moan **s-ly** like doves
Neh. 2:2; Luke 24:17
SADDLE Gen. 31:34, the camel's **s**
SAFE Job 21:9, houses are **s** from fear
Luke 15:27, received him back **s** and sound
Acts 27:43, centurion ... bring Paul **s-ly**
Phil. 3:1, it is a **s-guard** for you
SAFETY Ezek. 39:6, inhabit the coastlands in **s**
SAIL Acts 28:13, from there we **s-ed** around
SAINT Matt. 27:52, bodies of the **s-s** ... were
raised
Acts 26:10, lock up ... **s-s** in prisons
Rom. 1:7, called as **s-s**
8:27, He intercedes for the **s-s**
1 Cor. 6:2, **s-s** will judge the world
Eph. 2:19, fellow-citizens with the **s-s**
Phil. 1:1, all the **s-s** in Christ Jesus
1 Thess. 3:13, Lord Jesus with all His **s-s**
Rev. 14:12, perseverance of the **s-s**
20:9, the camp of the **s-s**
SAKE Ps. 23:3, For His name's **s**
Ps. 44:22, for Thy **s** we are killed
Is. 42:21, for His righteousness' **s**
Matt. 16:25, loses his life for My **s**
Mark 13:20, for the **s** of the elect
Luke 6:22, the **s** of the Son of Man
18:29, for the **s** of the kingdom of God
Rom. 8:36, THY **S** WE ARE ... PUT TO DEATH
13:5, for conscience' **s**

1 Cor. 9:23, for the **s** of the gospel
2 Cor. 8:9, for your **s** He became poor
Phil. 1:29, for Christ's **s** ... suffer for his **s**
1 Tim. 5:23, wine for the **s** of your stomach
Titus 1:11, for the **s** of sordid gain
2 John 2, for the **s** of the truth
SALT Gen. 19:26, became a pillar of **s**
Matt. 5:13, You are the **s** of the earth
Mark 9:50, **S** is good
Col. 4:6, seasoned, as it were, with **s**
James 3:12, can **s** water produce fresh
Judg. 9:45; Job 6:6
SALVATION Ps. 3:8, **S** belongs to the LORD
Ps. 27:1, LORD is my light and my **s**
62:1, From Him is my **s**
85:9, **s** is near to those who fear Him
98:3, seen the **s** of our God
Is. 59:17, helmet of **s** on His head
Luke 1:71, **S** FROM OUR ENEMIES
2:30, mine eyes have seen Thy **s**
3:6, FLESH SHALL SEE THE **S** OF GOD
19:9, **s** has come to this house
Acts 4:12, is **s** in no one else
13:26, word of this **s** is sent out
16:17, proclaiming to you the way of **s**
Rom. 1:16, power of God for **s**
11:11, **s** has come to the Gentiles
2 Cor. 6:2, ON THE DAY OF **S**
7:10, repentance ... leading to **s**
Eph. 6:17, take the helmet of **s**
Phil. 2:12, work out your **s** with fear
1 Thess. 5:9, obtaining **s** through our Lord
2 Tim. 3:15, wisdom that leads to **s**
Titus 2:11, grace of God ... bringing **s**
Heb. 1:14, who will inherit **s**
2:3, if we neglect so great a **s**
9:28, not to bear sin ... for **s**
1 Pet. 1:5, through faith for a **s**
2 Pet. 3:15, patience of our Lord to be **s**
Rev. 7:10, **S** to our God who sits
12:10, Now the **s**, and the power
Gen. 49:18; Ex. 15:2; Deut. 32:15; Job 13:16; Ps.
116:13; 119:155; Is. 12:3; 33:2; 49:6; 51:6;
52:7; 56:1; Jon. 2:9; Zech. 9:9
SAME Ps. 102:27, But Thou art the **s**
Matt. 5:46, even the tax gatherers do the **s**
Luke 2:8, in the **s** region ... shepherds
23:40, under the **s** sentence of
Rom. 10:12, **s** Lord is Lord of all
1 Cor. 12:4, of gifts, the **s** Spirit
Heb. 13:8, Christ ... **s** yesterday and today
SANCTIFY Lev. 22:32, I am the LORD who **s-es**
John 10:36, whom the Father **s-ed**
17:17, **S** them in the truth
Rom. 15:16, **s-ed** by the Holy Spirit
1 Cor. 6:11, washed, but you were **s-ed**
7:14, wife is **s-ed** ... believing husband
1 Thess. 5:23, God of peace ... **s** you entirely
Heb. 2:11, who **s-es** and those who are **s-ed**
Gen. 2:3; Ex. 13:2; Is. 29:23; Ezek. 20:20; 44:24
SANCTITY 1 Tim. 2:15, faith and love and **s**
SANCTUARY Ps. 150:1, Praise God in His **s**
Is. 60:13, beautify the place of My **s**
Heb. 8:2, a minister in the **s**
Ex. 25:8; Lev. 19:30; Ps. 73:17; Amos 7:13
SAND Gen. 32:12, descendants as the **s** of the sea
Matt. 7:26, built his house upon the **s**
Heb. 11:12, **s** ... BY THE SEASHORE
Deut. 33:19; Job 29:18; Prov. 27:3
SANDAL Matt. 3:11, fit to remove His **s-s**
Matt. 10:10, tunics, or **s-s**, or
Ex. 12:11; Deut. 29:5; Amos 2:6; Mark 1:7;
Acts 7:33
SANK Gen. 42:28, their hearts **s**
SAPPHIRE—lapis lazuli Ex. 28:18; Song 5:14;
Rev. 21:19
SASH Ex. 28:40; 29:9
SAT Mark 16:19, **S** DOWN AT THE RIGHT HAND OF
GOD
Luke 7:15, the dead man **s** up
Ex. 2:15; 16:3; Jon. 4:5; Mark 11:2

SATAN Matt. 4:10, Begone, **S**
  Matt. 12:26, **S** casts out **S**
    16:23, Get behind Me, **S**
  Mark 1:13, forty days being tempted by **S**
  Luke 10:18, watching **S** fall from heaven
    22:3, **S** entered into Judas
  Acts 5:3, why has **S** filled your heart
  Rom. 16:20, crush **S** under your feet
  2 Cor. 2:11, no advantage . . . of us by **S**
  1 Thess. 2:18, yet **S** thwarted us
  1 Tim. 1:20, I have delivered over to **S**
  Rev. 3:9, *those* of the synagogue of **S**
    12:9, called the Devil and **S**
    20:7, **S** . . . released from his prison
  Job 1:6; Zech. 3:2
SATIATE Is. 34:5, My sword is **s-d**
SATISFY Ps. 22:26, afflicted shall eat and be **s-ed**
  Ps. 91:16, with long life I will **s** him
  Mark 8:4, **s** these men with bread
  Gen. 25:8; Lev. 26:26; Esth. 5:13; Job 21:23;
    27: 4; 38:27; Ps. 78:30; Prov. 6:30; 27:20; Is.
    29:8; Joel 2:26; Mark 15:15
SATYR—*demon* 2 Chr. 11:15, he set up priests . . .
  for the **s-s**
SAVE—*deliver, escape, except*
  Ps. 6:4, **S** me because of Thy lovingkindness
    86:2, **s** Thy servant who trusts in Thee
  Is. 35:4, God will come . . . He will **s** you
    45:22, Turn to Me, and be **s-d**
    63:1, mighty to **s**
  Jer. 8:20, summer is ended . . . we are not **s-d**
  Matt. 1:21, **s** His people from their sins
    10:22, who has endured . . . will be **s-d**
    16:25, **s** his life shall lose it
    18:11, come to **s** that which is lost
    19:25, Then who can be **s-d**
  Mark 3:4, to **s** a life or to kill
    13:13, one who has endured . . . will be **s-d**
    16:16, been baptized shall be **s-d**
  Luke 7:50, Your faith has **s-d** you; go in peace
    23:35, let Him **s** Himself if . . . the Christ
  John 3:17, world should be **s-d** through Him
    10:9, enters through Me, he shall be **s-d**
    12:27, Father, **s** Me from this hour
  Acts 4:12, by which we must be **s-d**
    16:30, what must I do to be **s-d**
  Rom. 5:10, we shall be **s-d** by His life
    8:24, in hope we have been **s-d**
  1 Cor. 7:16, **s** your husband . . . **s** your wife
    16:2, each . . . put aside and **s**
  Eph. 2:5, by grace you have been **s-d**
  1 Tim. 1:15, into the world to **s** sinners
  2 Tim. 1:9, who has **s-d** us, and called us
  James 1:21, able to **s** your souls
    4:12, able to **s** and to destroy
  1 Pet. 4:18, WITH DIFFICULTY . . . RIGHTEOUS **S-D**
  Deut. 28:29; 33:29; 1 Sam. 14:6; Job 22:29; Ps.
    28:9; 44:7; 60:5; Prov. 20:22; Jer. 30:10;
    42:11; Ezek. 18:27; Amos 2:14; Acts 28:4
SAVIOR 2 Sam. 22:3, My **s**, Thou dost save me
  Ps. 106:21, forgot God their **S**
  Is. 19:20, He will send them a **S**
    43:11, there is no **s** besides Me
    45:21, a righteous God and a **S**
    49:26, know that I, the LORD, am your **S**
  Luke 2:11, a **S**, who is Christ the Lord
  John 4:42, One is indeed the **S** of the world
  Acts 5:31, as a Prince and a **S**
  Eph. 5:23, He Himself *being* the **S** of the body
  1 Tim. 4:10, God, who is the **S** of all men
  2 Tim. 1:10, appearing of our **S** Christ Jesus
  Titus 2:13, God and **S**, Christ Jesus
  2 Pet. 1:11, our Lord and **S** Jesus Christ
  1 John 4:14, sent the Son *to be* the **S**
SAW Gen. 1:4, God **s** that the light was good
  Matt. 2:2, **s** His star in the east
    2:11, **s** the Child with Mary
  Mark 1:10, **s** the heavens opening
  John 1:48, under the fig tree, I **s** you
  Num. 22:23; Job 29:11; Eccles. 2:13; Is. 59:16;
    Dan. 4:5

SAY—*speak* Ps. 106:48, let all the people **s**,
  Matt. 7:22, Many will **s** to Me on that day
    16:13, Who do people **s** . . . Son of Man is
  Luke 7:40, Simon, I have something to **s** to you
    17:21, nor will they **s**, Look, here *it is*
  1 John 1:8, If we **s** that we have no sin
  Rev. 22:17, Spirit and the bride **s**, Come
  Gen. 20:13; Ex. 3:13; Deut. 9:4; Job 33:32; 37:19;
    Prov. 3:28; 30:15; Is.58:9
SAYING Gen. 37:11; Ps. 78:2; Luke 18:34
SCALE Prov. 20:23, a false **s** is not good
  Is. 40:15, as a speck of dust on the **s-s**
  Amos 8:5, to cheat with dishonest **s-s**
  Mic. 6:11, Can I justify wicked **s-s**
  Rev. 6:5, a pair of **s-s** in his hand
  Job 31:6; Is. 40:12; 46:6; Jer. 32:10
SCALE-ARMOR Jer. 46:4; 51:3
SCARCE—*want*
  Ezek. 4:17, bread and water will be **s**
  Is. 13:12; Luke 9:39
SCARLET Is. 1:18, Though your sins are as **s**
  Matt. 27:28, put a **s** robe on Him
  Rev. 17:3, woman sitting on a **s** beast
  Gen. 38:28; Ex. 25:4; Josh. 2:18; Song 4:3;
    Jer. 4:30; Nah. 2:3
SCATTER
  Ps. 92:9, All who do iniquity will be **s-ed**
  Matt. 21:44, it will **s** him like dust
    26:31, the flock shall be **s-ed**
  Lev. 26:33; Job 18:15; 38:24; Ps. 141:7; Prov.
    11:24; Is. 41:16; Jer. 23:1
SCENT Job 39:25, he **s-s** the battle from afar
SCHEME Esth. 8:3; Job 5:5; Ps. 37:7;
  Dan. 11:24,25; Mic. 2:1; 2 Cor. 2:11
SCOFF Ps. 2:4, The Lord **s-s** at them
  Luke 16:14, the Pharisees . . . were **s-ing** at Him
SCOFFER Acts 13:41, BEHOLD, YOU **S-S**, AND
  MARVEL
SCORCH Jer. 4:11, A **s-ing** wind from the bare
  heights
SCORN Deut. 32:15; Prov. 30:17; Ezek. 25:6,15;
  36:5
SCOURGE Job 5:21, hidden from the **s** of the
  tongue
  Matt. 10:17, **s** you in their synagogues
    20:19, mock and **s** and crucify Him
    27:26, but Jesus he **s-d**
  John 2:15, He made a **s** of cords
  Heb. 12:6, **s-s** EVERY SON WHOM HE RECEIVES
SCRIBE Matt. 2:4, chief priests and **s-s** of the
  people
  Matt. 23:13, Woe to you, **s-s** and Pharisees
  Mark 1:22, authority, and not as **s-s**
    12:38, Beware of the **s-s**
  1 Cor. 1:20, Where is the **s**
  Neh. 8:4; Jer. 8:8
SCRIPTURE(S), *writing*
  Matt. 21:42, Did you never read in the **S-s**
    22:29, not understanding the **S-s**
  Mark 14:49, that the **S-s** might be fulfilled
  Luke 4:21, Today this **S** has been fulfilled
    24:32, He was explaining the **S-s** to us
  John 5:39, You search the **S-s**
    10:35, the **S** cannot be broken
    20:9, they did not understand the **S**
  Acts 18:24, he was mighty in the **S-s**
  Rom. 4:3, For what does the **S** say
    15:4, encouragement of the **S-s**
  2 Tim. 3:16, All **S** is inspired by God
SCROLL—*roll* Jer. 36:2, Take a **s** and write
  Ezek. 3:1, eat this **s**, and go
  Zech. 5:1, behold, *there was* a flying **s**
SEA Gen. 1:10, He called **s-s**
  Gen. 1:26, rule over the fish of the **s**
  Ex. 10:19, drove them into the Red **S**
  Ps. 24:2, founded it upon the **s-s**
    107:23, down to the **s** in ships
    146:6, The **s** and all that is in them
  Is. 57:20, wicked are like the tossing **s**
  Matt. 8:26, rebuked the winds and the **s**
    14:26, saw Him walking on the **s**

SEA (*Continued*)
Rev. 4:6, **s** of glass like crystal
  21:1, There is no longer *any* **s**
2 Sam. 17:11; Job 7:12; 38:8; Ps. 65:5; Is. 11:9;
  Jer. 25:22; Nah. 1:4; 2 Cor. 11:26
SEAL—*shut* Dan. 12:4, **s** up the book … end of
  time
Rom. 4:11, **s** of the righteousness of the faith
2 Cor. 1:22, who also **s-ed** us
Eph. 1:13, **s-ed** in Him with the Holy Spirit
Rev. 5:1, **s-ed** up with seven **s-s**
  9:4, **s** of God on their foreheads
1 Kin. 21:8; Job 14:17; Song 4:12; 8:6; Is. 29:11;
  Jer. 32:10; Dan. 9:24; 12:4
SEA MONSTER Ps. 148:7; Matt. 12:40
SEARCH 1 Chr. 28:9, LORD **s-es** all hearts
Job 28:3, to the farthest limit he **s-es** out
Ps. 139:23, **S** me … know my heart
Prov. 20:27, **S-ing** all the innermost parts
Jer. 17:10, I, the LORD, **s** the heart
Matt. 2:8, make careful **s** for the Child
  2:13, Herod is going to **s**
John 5:39, You **s** the Scriptures, because
  7:52, **S**, and see that no prophet arises
2 Tim. 1:17, he eagerly **s-ed** for me
Judg. 5:16; 1 Sam. 26:20; 1 Kin. 1:3
SEASON—*times* Ps. 1:3, yields its fruit in its **s**
Ps. 104:27, their food in due **s**
Luke 14:34, with what will it be **s-ed**
Gal. 4:10, observe days … **s-s** and years
Col. 4:6, with grace, **s-ed**, *as it were*, with salt
2 Tim. 4:2, ready in **s** *and* out of **s**
Gen. 1:14; Lev. 26:4; Job 5:26
SEAT—*sat* Ps. 1:1, Nor sit in the **s** of the scoffers
Matt. 23:6, chief **s-s** in the synagogues
  27:19, sitting on the judgment **s**
Luke 10:39, Mary … **s-ed** at His feet
Rom. 14:10, the judgment **s** of God
Ex. 25:17; 1 Sam. 4:18; Ezek. 28:2
SECOND Matt. 22:39, And a **s** is like it
1 Cor. 15:47, the **s** man is from heaven
Rev. 2:11, not be hurt by the **s** death
Gen. 1:8; Ezek. 10:14
SECRET Ps. 44:21, knows the **s-s** of the heart
Prov. 9:17, bread *eaten* in **s** is pleasant
  21:14, gift in **s** subdues anger
Matt. 6:4, your alms may be in **s**
  6:6,18, your Father who is in **s**
Rom. 2:16, God will judge the **s-s**
  16:25, kept **s** for long ages past
Deut. 27:15; Job 11:6; 15:8; Song 2:14;
  Is. 45:3,19; Hab. 3:14
SECRETLY Josh. 2:1, two men as spies **s**
Judg. 4:21, went **s** to him
Matt. 1:19, Joseph … put her away **s**
  2:7, Then Herod **s** called the
John 11:28, called Mary her sister, saying **s**
Deut. 13:6; Job 13:10; 31:27
SECURE—*sure* Prov. 3:23, walk in your way **s-ly**
Matt. 27:66, made the grave **s**
Acts 16:23, the jailer to guard them **s-ly**
Lev. 26:5; Ezek. 34:27
SECURITY Judg. 18:7, living in **s**
SEDUCES—*entice* Ex. 22:16, if a man **s** a virgin
SEE—*perceive* Ex. 33:20, no man can **s** Me and
  live
Job 19:26, without my flesh I shall **s** God
Ps. 16:10, allow Thy Holy One to **s** the pit
  34:8, **s** that the LORD is good
  66:5, Come and **s** the works of God
  115:5, eyes, but they cannot **s**
Is. 35:2, **s** the glory of the LORD
  62:2, nations will **s** your righteousness
Joel 2:28, young men will **s** visions
Matt. 5:16, may **s** your good works
  11:8, what did you go out to **s**
  16:28, **s** the Son of Man coming
Luke 2:26, would not **s** death before
  8:10, **S-ING THEY MAY NOT S**
John 4:29, **s** a man who told me
  7:52, Search, and **s** that no prophet
  12:19, **s** that you are not doing any good
  16:16, little while, and you will **s** Me

1 Cor. 13:12, now we **s** in a mirror dimly
Heb. 12:14, no one will **s** the Lord
1 John 3:2, we shall **s** Him just as He is
Ex. 10:23; Num 14:23; 24:17; Job 6:28; 9:11;
  24:15; 34:32; Ps. 36:9; 49:19; Eccles. 6:9;
  Song 7:12; Is. 29:18; Ezek. 12:2
SEED—*descendant, offspring*
Gen. 8:22, **S-time** and harvest
Matt. 13:22, **s** was sown among the thorns
  13:31, heaven is like a mustard **s**
Luke 8:5, sower went out to sow his **s**
  8:11, the **s** is the word of God
1 Pet. 1:23, not of **s** which is perishable
Gen. 1:11; Lev. 19:19; 26:16; Eccles. 11:6;
  Is. 55:10; Hag. 2:19
SEEK—*desire, search* 2 Chr. 7:14, pray, and **s** My
  face
Ps. 24:6, generation of those who **s** Him
  34:14, **S** peace and pursue it
  63:1, I shall **s** Thee earnestly
  119:2, **s** Him with all *their* heart
Prov. 8:17, who diligently **s** me will find me
Is. 55:6, **S** the LORD while He may be found
Jer. 29:13, you will **s** Me and find *Me*
Amos 5:4, **S** Me that you may live
Matt. 6:33, **s** first His kingdom
  7:7, **s**, and you shall find
  12:46, His brothers were … **s-ing** to speak
Mark 8:12, this generation **s** for a sign
Luke 11:10, he who **s-s** finds
John 1:38, What do you **s**
  5:30, I do not **s** My own will
  8:50, One who **s-s** and judges
1 Cor. 10:24, Let no one **s** his own *good*
  13:5, it does not **s** its own
Phil. 4:17, Not that I **s** the gift … I **s** for the
  profit
Col. 3:1, keep **s-ing** the things above
Deut. 4:29; 2 Chr. 16:12; Job 7:21; Eccles. 7:25;
  Is. 34:16; Ezek. 7:25; 34:16; Dan. 9:3; Hos.
  10:12; Amos 5:14; Gal. 1:10
SEEM—*appear* Gen. 29:20; Prov. 14:12
SEEN—*appeared* Gen. 9:14, bow shall be **s** in the
  cloud
Is. 6:5, my eyes have **s** the King
Luke 2:30, eyes have **s** Thy salvation
John 1:18, no man has **s** God at any time
Rom. 8:24, hope that is not **s** is not hope
1 Cor. 2:9, EYE HAS NOT **S**
Heb. 11:1, conviction of things not **s**
Gen. 32:30; Job 5:3; 38:22
SEIZE—*take* John 7:30, seeking … to **s** Him
Jer. 50:24; Mic. 2:2
SELECT Acts 6:3, **s** from among you … seven
  men
SELF Rom. 6:6, our old **s** was crucified
Col. 3:9, laid aside the old **s**
SELF-ABASEMENT Col. 2:18, delighting in **s**
Col. 2:23, wisdom in self-made religion and **s**
SELF-CONTROL Acts 24:25, righteousness, **s**,
  and the judgment
Gal. 5:23, gentleness, **s**
SELFISH Phil. 2:3, do nothing from **s-ness**
James 3:14,16, jealousy and **s** ambition
SELL Prov. 23:23, Buy truth, and do not **s** *it*
Matt. 19:21, go *and* **s** your possessions
Gen. 25:31; Lev. 25:29; Deut. 2:28; 2 Kin. 4:7
SEND—*cast* Is. 6:8, Whom shall I **s** … Here
Matt. 5:45, **s-s** rain on *the* righteous
  9:38, **s** out workers into His harvest
1 Cor. 7:13, let her not **s** her husband away
  16:11, **s** him on his way in peace
2 Thess. 2:11, **s** … a deluding influence
Gen. 7:4; 24:7; Num. 13:2; Job 5:10; 38:35
SENSELESS—*stupid* Ps. 49:10, stupid and the **s**
  alike perish
Ps. 92:6, **s** man has no knowledge
SENSIBLE Tit. 2:5, *to be* **s**, pure, workers at home
SENSUAL Ezek. 33:32, like a **s** song
SENSUALITY Eph. 4:19, given … over to **s**
Rev. 18:3, rich by the wealth of her **s**

SENSUOUS Rev. 18:7, she ... lived **s-ly**
SENT Is. 61:1, He has **s** me to bind up the broken-
  hearted
  Matt. 10:5, These twelve Jesus **s** out after
  Luke 4:18, He has **s** Me to proclaim release
  Acts 13:4, So, being **s** out by the Holy Spirit
  Gal. 4:4, God **s** forth His Son
  1 Pet. 1:12, Holy Spirit **s** from heaven
  1 John 4:9, that God has **s** His only begotten
  Gen. 8:7,8; Is. 48:16
SENTENCE—*condemnation*
  Matt. 23:33, escape the **s** of hell
SEPARATE—*divide* Gen. 1:4, God **s-d** the light
  Prov. 16:28, a slanderer **s-s** intimate friends
  Matt. 19:6, let no man **s**
    25:32, He will **s** them from one another
  Rom. 8:35, Who shall **s** us from the love
  Gen. 13:9; Lev. 20:24; Job 41:17; Ps. 22:7
SERIOUS Acts 25:7, **s** charges against him
SERPENT Gen. 3:1, Now the **s** was more crafty
  Num. 21:9, Moses made a bronze **s**
  Ps. 58:4, venom of a **s**
  Matt. 10:16, be shrewd as **s-s**
  Mark 16:18, they will pick up **s-s**
  John 3:14, Moses lifted up the **s** in the
    wilderness
  2 Cor. 11:3, lest as the **s** deceived Eve
  Rev. 12:9, the **s** of old who is called the devil
  Gen. 49:17; Ex. 7:12; Deut. 32:33; Ps. 91:13;
    Prov. 23:32; Is. 30:6; Jer. 8:17
SERVANT—*minister* Job 1:8, have you
    considered My **s** Job
  Ps. 31:16, face to shine upon Thy **s**
  Matt. 20:26, shall be your **s**
  Luke 1:2, and **s-s** of the Word
  2 Cor. 3:6, **s-s** of a new covenant
    11:23, Are they **s-s** of Christ
  1 Tim. 4:6, be a good **s** of Christ Jesus
  Gen. 9:25; Ex. 14:31; Ruth 2:9; 1 Sam. 3:9;
    Ezra 7:24; Job 4:18; Prov. 11:29; Joel 2:29
SERVE—*worship, minister*
  Ps. 100:2, **S** the LORD with gladness
  Matt. 4:10, GOD, AND **s** HIM ONLY
    6:24, No one can **s** two masters
    20:28, not come to be **s-d**, but to **s**
  John 12:26, If any one **s-s** Me, let him
  Acts 24:14, I do **s** the God of our fathers
  Rom. 7:6, so that we **s** in newness of the Spirit
    12:11, fervent in spirit, **s-ing** the Lord
  Gal. 5:13, through love **s** one another
  1 Tim. 3:10, let them **s** as deacons
  Josh. 22:5; 1 Chr. 6:10; 24:2; Jer. 5:19
SERVICE—*ministry*
  Rom. 12:1, *which* is your spiritual **s**
  Eph. 4:12, for the work of **s**
  Phil. 2:30, was deficient in your **s** to me
  Heb. 12:28, offer to God an acceptable **s**
  Is. 32:17; Jer. 22:13
SET Gen. 9:13, I **s** my bow in the cloud
  Ex. 2:3, she ... **s** it among the reeds
  Deut. 30:19, I have **s** before you life and death
  Ps. 40:2, He **s** my feet upon a rock
  Matt. 5:14, A city **s** on a hill cannot
  Col. 3:2, **S** your mind on the things above
  James 3:6, and is **s** on fire by hell
  Lev. 17:10; Prov. 9:2; Eccles. 10:6; Is. 3:24; 38:1;
    Jer. 5:26; Ezek. 2:2
SETTING Prov. 25:11, apples of gold in **s-s** of
    silver
SETTLE—*reckon* Matt. 25:19, came and **s-d**
    accounts with them
  Deut. 21:5; Nah. 3:17
SEVEN Gen. 29:20, Jacob served **s** years for
    Rachel
  Ps. 119:164, **S** times a day I praise Thee
  Is. 4:1, For **s** women will take hold of one man
  Matt. 12:45, along with it **s** other spirits
    18:21, forgive him? Up to **s** times
  Acts 6:3, **s** men of good reputation

Rev. 1:4, John to the **s** churches
    1:12, I saw **s** golden lampstands
    3:1, He who has the **s** Spirits of God
    15:1, **s** angels who had **s** plagues
  Gen. 21:29; Prov. 9:1; Eccles. 11:2; Dan. 9:25;
    Zech. 4:2
SEVERE—*great* Matt. 28:2, a **s** earthquake
  Song 8:6; Ezek. 34:4
SHACK Is. 24:20, it totters like a **s**
SHACKLES Mark 5:4, the **s** broken in pieces
SHADOW 2 Kin. 20:11, **s** on the stairway back
    ten steps
  Ps. 17:8, Hide me in the **s** of Thy wings
    23:4, valley of the **s** of death
    91:1, abide in the **s** of the Almighty
  Col. 2:17, a *mere* **s** of what is to come
  Heb. 8:5, copy and **s** of the heavenly things
  James 1:17, no variation, or shifting **s**
  1 Chr. 29:15; Song 2:17
SHAKE—*tremble*
  Prov. 10:30, righteous ... never be **s-n**
  Is. 13:13, earth ... **s-n** from its place
  Matt. 10:14, **s** off the dust of your feet
    11:7, A reed **s-n** by the wind
  Luke 6:38, pressed down, **s-n** together
  Job 4:14; 16:4; Ps. 109:23
SHAME Acts 5:41, worthy to suffer **s**
  2 Cor. 4:2, things hidden because of **s**
  Phil. 3:19, glory is in their **s**
  1 John 2:28, not shrink ... Him in **s**
  Prov. 19:26; Is. 54:4; Zeph. 3:5
SHARE—*portion* Luke 15:12, **s** of the estate
  1 Cor. 10:16, a **s-ing** in the blood of Christ
    10:20, to become **s-rs** in demons
  Gal. 6:6, **s** ... with him who teaches
  1 Tim. 6:18, ready to **s**
  Heb. 13:16, doing good and **s-ing**
SHARP Deut. 32:41, **s-en** My flashing sword
  Ps. 57:4, tongue a **s** sword
    64:3, **s-ened** their tongue
  Prov. 5:4, **S** as a two-edged sword
    27:17, Iron **s-ens** iron
  Eccles. 10:10, does not **s-en** *its* edge
  Heb. 4:12, **s-er** than any two-edged sword
SHATTER Ex. 15:6; Ps. 2:9
SHAVE Gen. 41:14; Judg. 16:19; 2 Sam. 10:4;
    Is. 7:20; 1 Cor. 11:6
SHEAR Deut. 18:4, first **s-ing** of your sheep
SHED—*pour* Matt. 26:28, My blood ... **s** on
    behalf of many
  Rom. 3:15, feet are swift to **s** blood
  Gen. 9:6; Prov. 1:16
SHEEP—*flock* Ps. 44:22, a **s** to be slaughtered
  Ps. 100:3, the **s** of his pasture
    119:176, astray like a lost **s**
  Is. 53:6, All of us like **s** have gone astray
    53:7, **s** ... silent before its shearers
  Matt. 9:36, **s** without a shepherd
    10:16, I send you out as **s**
    15:24, lost **s** of the house of Israel
    25:32, separates the **s** from the goats
    26:31, **s** of the flock ... scattered
  Luke 15:6, found my **s** which was lost
  John 10:3, calls his own **s** by name
    10:7, I am the door of the **s**
    10:27, My **s** hear My voice
    21:16, Shepherd My **s**
  Heb. 13:20, great Shepherd of the **s**
  1 Pet. 2:25, straying like **s**
  Gen. 29:9; Num. 27:17; 1 Sam. 15:14; Job 31:20;
    Jer. 12:3; 50:6
SHEKELS—*piece* Gen. 23:16; Zech. 11:12
SHELTER Ps. 5:11, mayest Thou **s** them
  Ps. 61:4, refuge in the **s** of Thy wings
  Gen. 19:8; Is. 1:8; 4:6; 32:2; Jon. 4:5
SHEOL Deut. 32:22, burns to the lowest ... of **S**
  Job 17:13, look for **S** as my home
    26:6, Naked is **S** before Him
  Ps. 16:10, not abandon my soul to **S**
    30:3, brought up my soul from **S**
    49:15, redeem ... from the power of **S**
    86:13, my soul from the depths of **S**
    139:8, If I make my bed in **S**

SHEOL (Continued)
Prov. 5:5, Her steps lay hold of **S**
Ezek. 32:21, speak ... from the midst of **S**
Amos 9:2, Though they dig into **S**
Jon. 2:2, help from the depth of **S**
2 Sam. 22:6; Prov. 27:20; Song 8:6; Hab. 2:5
SHEPHERD (n.)—*pastor*
Ps. 23:1, The Lord is my **s**
28:9, Be their **s** also
Is. 40:11, Like a **s** He will tend His flock
Jer. 3:15, I will give you **s-s**
23:1, **s-s** who are destroying ... the sheep
Zech. 11:16, I am going to raise up a **s**
Matt. 9:36, like sheep without a **s**
26:31, I will strike down the **s**
Luke 2:8, **s-s** staying out in the fields
John 10:11, I am the good **s**
Heb. 13:20, the great **S** of the sheep
1 Pet. 2:25, returned to the **S** and Guardian
5:4, when the Chief **S** appears
Rev. 7:17, the Lamb ... shall be their **s**
Gen. 46:34; 48:15; Num. 27:17; 1 Sam. 17:40;
Jer. 10:21; Ezek. 34:5; 37:24; Zeph. 2:6
SHEPHERD (v.)—*fed* Ps. 78:72, David **s-ed**
Matt. 2:6, who will **s** My people
John 21:16, **S** My sheep
Acts 20:28, to **s** the church of God
1 Pet. 5:2, **s** the flock of God
SHIELD Ps. 18:2, My **s** and the horn of my
salvation
Ps. 28:7, my strength and my **s**
91:4, His faithfulness is a **s**
Eph. 6:16, taking up the **s** of faith
Gen. 15:1; 2 Sam. 22:3,31; Ps. 7:10; 89:18;
Prov. 2:7
SHINE Num. 6:25, make His face **s** on you
Job 9:7, sun not to **s**
41:32, Behind him ... a wake to **s**
Prov. 4:18, **s-s** brighter and brighter
Is. 60:1, Arise, **s**; for your light has come
Matt. 5:16, Let your light **s** before men
13:43, righteous will **s** forth
John 1:5, light **s-s** in the darkness
2 Pet. 1:19, a lamp **s-ing** in a dark place
1 John 2:8, true light is already **s-ing**
SHOCK Deut. 1:29, Do not be **s-ed**, nor fear them
SHONE Luke 2:9, glory of the Lord **s** around
Ex. 34:29; 2 Kin. 3:22
SHOOK Neh. 5:13, also **s** out ... my garment
Acts 28:5, he **s** the creature off
Heb. 12:26, His voice **s** the earth
SHOOT Is. 11:1, a **s** will spring from ... Jesse
Is. 53:2, grew up ... like a tender **s**
1 Sam. 20:20; Ps. 11:2; 64:4
SHORT Rom. 3:23, fall **s** of the glory of God
1 Cor. 7:29, time has been **s-ened**
SHOT 1 Sam. 20:20, as though I **s** at a target
SHOULD Matt. 23:23, these ... things you **s** have
done
SHOUT Josh. 6:16, Joshua said ... **S**
Ps. 47:5, God has ascended with a **s**
66:1, **S** joyfully to God
Matt. 25:6, at midnight ... a **s**
1 Thess. 4:16, descend from heaven with a **s**
SHOW—*demonstrate*
Matt. 22:19, **S** Me the coin
John 14:8, Lord, **s** us the Father
1 Cor. 3:13, for the day will **s** it
Gal. 6:12, make a good **s-ing** in the flesh
Gen. 12:1; Ex. 33:18; Deut. 5:10; 2 Sam. 10:12;
1 Chr. 19:13; Job 11:6
SHOWER 1 Kin. 18:41; Ps. 65:10; Jer. 14:22;
Luke 12:54
SHREWD—*wise*
Job 5:13, wise by their own **s-ness**
Matt. 10:16, be **s** as serpents
SHRINE Ezek. 16:24,31,39
SHRINK—*draw* Heb. 10:38, if he **s-s** back, My
soul has no pleasure
SHUDDER Jer. 2:12, and **s**, be very desolate
James 2:19, demons also believe, and **s**

SHUN—*refrain* Eccles. 3:5, time to **s** embracing
SHUT—*close* Matt. 6:6, when you have **s** your
door
Matt. 23:13, **s** off the kingdom of heaven
Gal. 3:23, being **s** up to the faith
Job 5:16; Prov. 21:13; Dan. 6:22
SICK Prov. 13:12, Hope ... *makes* the heart **s**
Matt. 10:8, Heal *the* **s**, raise
25:36, I was **s**, and you visited Me
Mark 1:30, Simon's mother-in-law ... lying **s**
2:17, physician, but those who are **s**
Luke 7:2, and **s** and about to die
John 11:2, brother Lazarus was **s**
James 5:14, Is anyone among you **s**
5:15, prayer ... restore the one who is **s**
Ps. 41:3; Song 2:5
SICKLE Deut. 16:9, put the **s** to the standing
grain
Joel 3:13, Put in the **s** ... harvest is ripe
Rev. 14:15, Put in your **s** and reap
SICKLINESS Is. 17:11, a day of **s** and incurable
pain
SICKNESS Matt. 4:23, healing every kind of **s**
Matt. 10:1, authority ... to heal ... **s**
Luke 13:12, are freed from your **s**
John 5:5, thirty-eight years in his **s**
11:4, This **s** is not unto death
Deut. 7:15; 2 Kin. 1:2; 8:8,9
SIDE Ezek. 36:3, crushed you from every **s**
John 19:34, pierced His **s** with a spear
20:20, showed ... His hands and His **s**
SIEGEWORKS Deut. 20:20; Eccles. 9:14
SIGHT Ps. 19:14, acceptable in Thy **s**
Ps. 90:4, thousand years in Thy **s**
Matt. 11:5, blind receive **s**
20:34, they received their **s**
Luke 4:18, recovery of **s** to the blind
Acts 9:9, three days without **s**
22:13, Saul, receive your **s**
2 Cor. 5:7, walk by faith, not by **s**
Gen. 2:9; 18:3; Ruth 2:13; Job 19:15
SIGN—*signal, witness, wonder*
Gen. 9:12, the **s** of the covenant
Ex. 3:12, this shall be a **s** to you
12:13, blood shall be a **s** ... on the houses
Ps. 86:17, Show me a **s** for good
Matt. 12:38, we want a **s** from You
16:3, cannot *discern* the **s** of the times
24:3, *will be* the **s** of Your coming
Mark 13:22, show **s-s** and wonders
16:20, confirmed the word by the **s-s**
Luke 1:22, he kept making **s-s** to them
21:25, will be **s-s** in sun
23:8, hoping to see some **s** performed
John 2:11, beginning of *His* **s-s** Jesus did
10:41, John performed no **s**
11:47, this man is performing many **s-s**
Acts 5:12, many **s-s** and wonders were taking
place
1 Cor. 1:22, Jews ask for **s-s**
Phil. 1:28, a **s** of destruction
2 Thess. 2:9, all power and **s-s**
Rev. 12:1, a great **s** appeared in heaven
15:1, saw another **s** in heaven
Gen. 4:15; Ex. 31:13; Is. 7:11,14; 55:13;
Ezek. 14:8
SIGNAL Mark 14:44, had given them a **s**
Is. 11:10; 30:17
SILENCE Ps. 62:1, My soul *waits* in **s** for God
Titus 1:11, who must be **s-d**
Rev. 8:1, there was in heaven
SILENT Eccles. 3:7, A time to be **s**
Matt. 26:63, But Jesus kept **s**
Luke 1:20, you shall be **s** and unable to speak
9:36, they kept **s**, and reported to no one
Acts 18:9, go on speaking ... not be **s**
1 Cor. 14:28, keep **s** in the church
14:34, Let the women keep **s**
Judg. 18:19; Esth. 7:4; Job 6:24; 13:13
SILVER Matt. 10:9, Do not acquire gold, or **s**
Matt. 26:15, thirty pieces of **s**

Acts 3:6, I do not possess **s** and gold
  8:20, May your **s** perish with you
  20:33, coveted no one's **s**
James 5:3, gold and **s** have rusted
Gen. 13:2; Job 27:16; Prov. 16:16; 25:11; Is. 1:22;
  39:2; Jer. 6:30; Zech. 11:12
SIMPLE—*naive* Ps. 19:7, making wise the **s**
  Ps. 116:6, LORD preserves the **s**
SIN—*transgression* Ps. 25:7, remember the **s-s**
  Ps. 51:3, my **s** is ever before me
  Prov. 14:9, Fools mock at **s**
  Is. 1:18, your **s-s** are as scarlet
  Matt. 1:21, save His people from their **s-s**
    3:6, as they confessed their **s-s**
    12:31, **s** and blasphemy ... forgiven men
    18:15, if your brother **s-s**
    18:21, brother **s** against me
    26:28, for forgiveness of **s-s**
  Mark 2:7, forgive **s-s** but God alone
  Luke 11:4, forgive us our **s-s**
  John 1:29, Lamb ... takes away **s** of the world
    8:7, He who is without **s**
    8:11, go your way ... **s** no more
    15:22, they have no excuse for their **s**
    16:8, convict the world concerning **s**
  Acts 22:16, wash away your **s-s**
    26:18, receive forgiveness of **s-s**
  Rom. 5:12, **s** entered into the world
    6:23, wages of **s** is death
    14:23, whatever is not from faith is **s**
  1 Cor. 15:3, Christ died for our **s-s**
    15:56, sting of death is **s**
  2 Cor. 5:21, Him who knew no **s** *to be* **s** on our
    behalf
  Heb. 9:7, for the **s-s** of the people
    11:25, enjoy the ... pleasures of **s**
  James 5:16, confess your **s-s** to one another
    5:20, cover a multitude of **s-s**
  1 Pet. 2:22, WHO COMMITTED NO **S**
  1 John 1:8, If we say we have no **s**
    1:9, If we confess our **s-s**
    2:1, If anyone **s-s**, we have an Advocate
    3:4, **s** is lawlessness
    5:16, there is a **s** leading to death
    5:17, All unrighteousness is **s**
  Rev. 1:5, released us from our **s-s**
  Gen. 4:7; 18:20; Ex. 10:17; 32:30; Job 1:22; 2:10;
    Ps. 51:2; 79:9; Is. 30:1; Mic. 6:7
SINCE Matt. 18:25, **s** he did not have *the means*
  to repay
  1 Cor. 11:7, **s** he is the image and glory
  Heb. 2:14, **S** then the children share
  Gen. 41:39; Deut. 12:12
SINFUL Mark 8:38, **s** generation
  Luke 5:8, I am a **s** man, O Lord
  Rom. 8:3, the likeness of **s** flesh
  Num. 32:14; Is. 1:4
SING—*shout, utter* Ps. 5:11, Let them ever **s** for
  joy
  Ps. 33:3, **S** to Him a new song
    100:2, Come before Him with joyful **s-ing**
  1 Cor. 14:15, I shall **s** with the spirit
  Col. 3:16, **s-ing** with thankfulness
  James 5:13, cheerful? Let him **s** praises
  Ex. 15:1; Judg. 5:12; 2 Sam. 22:50; 1 Chr. 16:23;
    2 Chr. 23:13; Job 29:13; Prov. 29:6; Is. 5:1;
    Rev. 5:9
SINK Prov. 2:18, her house **s-s** down to death
SINNED Ps. 41:4, I have **s** against Thee
  Ps. 51:4, Thee only, I have **s**
  Luke 15:18, **s** against heaven
  Rom. 3:23, **s**, and fall short of the glory
    5:12, spread to all men, because all **s**
  1 John 1:10, If we say that we have not **s**
  Lev. 5:16; Deut. 1:41; Dan. 9:15
SINNER Ps. 1:1, stand in the path of **s-s**
  Matt. 9:10, tax-gatherers and **s-s**
    9:13, call *the* righteous, but **s-s**
    11:19, a friend of ... **s-s**
  Mark 2:17, to call *the* righteous, but **s-s**
    14:41, into the hands of **s-s**

Luke 6:34, Even **s-s** lend to **s-s**
  15:7, *more* joy in heaven over one **s**
  18:13, be merciful to me, the **s**
John 9:31, God does not hear **s-s**
Rom. 5:8, while we were yet **s-s**
1 Tim. 1:15, Jesus came ... to save **s-s**
James 4:8, Cleanse your hands, you **s-s**
Prov. 1:10; 13:21; 23:17; Eccles. 9:18
SISTER Job 17:14, my mother, and my **s**
  Matt. 12:50, is My brother and **s**
  Luke 10:39, had a **s** called Mary
  Gen. 12:13; Prov. 7:4; Song 8:8; Rom. 16:1
SIT Ps. 1:1, **S** in the seat of scoffers
  Ps. 26:4, not **s** with deceitful men
  110:1, **S** at My right hand
  Matt. 4:16, WERE **S-ING** IN DARKNESS
    9:9, Matthew, **s-ing** in the tax office
    26:36, **S** here while I go
    27:61, Mary, **s-ing** opposite the grave
  Luke 2:46, temple, **s-ing** ... midst of the
    teachers
    8:35, **s-ing** down at the feet of Jesus
  John 12:15, **S-ING** ON A DONKEY'S COLT
  Acts 8:28, **s-ing** in his chariot
  Gen. 18:1; 1 Kin. 22:19; Job 2:8; Ezek. 28:2
SITUATE Ps. 144:15, people who are so **s-d**
SIZE—*stature* Num. 13:32, are men of *great* **s**
SKILL Ps. 137:5, my right hand forget her **s**
SKILLFUL Gen. 25:27; Ex. 28:8; 1 Sam. 16:16;
  Ps. 139:15; Is. 3:3
SKIN Ex. 34:29, the **s** of his face shone
  Job 2:4, **S** for **s**
    10:11, Clothe me with **s** and flesh
  Jer. 13:23, Ethiopian change his **s**
  Job 19:20; 30:30
SKIP Job 21:11, children **s** about
SKULL Judg. 9:53, Abimelech's head, crushing
  his **s**
  Matt. 27:33, which means Place of a **S**
SKY Ps. 36:5, faithfulness *reaches* to the **s-s**
  Matt. 16:2,3, for the **s** is red
  Luke 12:56, analyze the appearance ... the **s**
  Gen. 1:26,28; Deut. 4:17; 2 Sam. 21:10; Job
    37:18; Prov. 30:19; James 5:18
SLACK Prov. 18:9, who is **s** in his work
SLAIN 1 Sam. 18:7; 29:5, Saul has **s** his thousands
  Rev. 5:12, Worthy ... Lamb that was **s**
SLANDER Ps. 15:3, He does not **s**
  Prov. 30:10, Do not **s** a slave to his master
  1 Cor. 4:13, when we are **s-ed**, we try to
    conciliate
  2 Cor. 12:20, disputes, **s-s**, gossip
  Eph. 4:31, and **s** be put away from you
SLANDERER—*whisperer*
  Prov. 16:28, **s** separates ... friends
  Rom. 1:30, **s-s**, haters of God
SLAP Job 16:10, **s-ed** me on the cheek
  Matt. 5:39, **s-s** you on your right cheek
SLAUGHTER—*sacrifice*
  Ps. 44:22, as sheep to be **s-ed**
  Is. 53:7, lamb that is led to **s**
  Rom. 8:36, AS SHEEP TO BE **S-ED**
  James 5:5, in a day of **s**
  Prov. 7:22; Jer. 46:10
SLAVE Prov. 22:7, borrower becomes the
  lender's **s**
  Matt. 25:21, Well done ... faithful **s**
  1 Cor. 7:21, Were you called while a **s**
    9:27, body and make it my **s**
  Gal. 4:7, no longer a **s**, but a son
  Ex. 23:12; Lev. 19:20; 25:39,44; Deut. 15:15;
    16:12; 24:18; Col. 3:22
SLAVERY—*bondage* Rom. 8:15, a spirit of **s**
  Gal. 5:1, subject again to a yoke of **s**
  Heb. 2:15, subject to **s** all their lives
SLAY—*destroy* Job 5:2, vexation **s-s** the foolish
  man
  Job 13:15, Though He **s** me, I will hope
  Ps. 34:21, Evil shall **s** the wicked
  2 Thess. 2:8, the Lord will **s** with the breath of
SLEDGE Is. 41:15, a new, sharp threshing **s**

SLEEP Gen. 2:21, deep **s** to fall upon the man
Ps. 13:3, **s** the *sleep of* death
Prov. 6:10, A little **s**, a little slumber
Eccles. 5:12, **s** of the working man
Matt. 1:24, Joseph arose from his **s**
  26:40,43, found them **s-ing**
  26:45, Are you still **s-ing** and taking
Acts 20:9, sinking into a deep **s**
1 Cor. 15:51, we shall not all **s**
1 Thess. 5:7, those who **s** do their **s-ing** at night
Ps. 76:6; Prov. 3:24; 20:13; Jer. 31:26; Mark
  14:40
SLEW Matt. 2:16, **s** all the male children
SLING 1 Sam. 17:40, his **s** was in his hand
Judg. 20:16; 1 Sam. 25:29
SLOTHFUL Prov. 12:27, **s** man does not roast
SLOW Ex. 4:10, **s** of speech and **s** of tongue
Ps. 103:8, **S** to anger and abounding
Prov. 16:32, He who is **s** to anger
Luke 24:25, foolish men and **s** of heart
James 1:19, **s** to speak *and* **s** to anger
2 Pet. 3:9, The Lord is not **s**
SLUGGISH Heb. 6:12, that you may not be **s**
SLUMBER Ps. 121:3, who keeps you will not **s**
Prov. 6:10, A little sleep, a little **s**
Job 33:15; Ps. 132:4; Is. 5:27; 56:10
SMALL—*little* Prov. 30:24, Four things are **s** on
  the earth
Mark 8:7, They also had a few **s** fish
James 3:4, directed by a very **s** rudder
  3:5, tongue is a **s** part of the body
Num. 26:56; 35:8; Deut. 25:13; Is. 10:19
SMEAR Ezek. 22:28, prophets have **s-ed**
  whitewash
SMELL Gen. 27:27; Deut. 4:28; Ps. 115:6
SMELT Is. 1:25, **s** away your dross with lye
SMOKE Gen. 15:17; Job 41:20; Ps. 102:3; Prov.
  10:26; Is. 6:4
SMOLDERING Matt. 12:20, **s** WICK HE WILL
SMOOTH Ps. 55:21, speech was **s-er** than butter
Prov. 5:3, **s-er** than oil is her speech
Is. 45:13, I will make all his ways **s**
Luke 3:5, THE ROUGH ROADS **s**
Gen. 27:11,16; 1 Sam. 17:40; Prov. 6:24; 11:5;
  Is. 40:3
SNAKE Matt. 7:10, he will not ... a **s**, will he
SNARE—*web* Prov. 7:23, bird hastens to the **s**
Rom. 11:9, THEIR TABLE BECOME A **S**
2 Tim. 2:26, *escape* from the **s** of the devil
Ex. 10:7; Job 34:30; Ps. 91:3; Eccles. 7:26
SNATCH—*pluck* John 10:12, the wolf **s-es** them
John 10:28, **s** them out of My hand
Jude 23, **s-ing** them out of the fire
SNEER—*scoff* Luke 23:35, the rulers were **s-ing**
SNOW Ps. 51:7, I shall be whiter than **s**
Prov. 26:1, Like **s** in summer
Is. 1:18, scarlet ... be as white as **s**
Matt. 28:3, his garment as white as **s**
Rev. 1:14, white like white wool, like **s**
Num. 12:10; Job 9:30; 38:22; Prov. 25:13
SOBER—*watch* Acts 26:25, utter words of **s** truth
1 Thess. 5:6, let us be alert and **s**
2 Tim. 4:5, be **s** in all things
1 Pet. 4:7, **s** *spirit* ... purpose of prayer
  5:8, Be of **s** *spirit*
SOFT Matt. 11:8, who wear **s** *clothing* are in
Ps. 65:10; Prov. 25:15
SOIL—*earth, ground*
Ezek. 17:5, planted it in fertile **s**
Matt. 13:5; Mark 4:5, did not have much **s**
  13:8, others fell on the good **s**
James 5:7, the precious produce of the **s**
Rev. 3:4, few ... who have not **s-ed** their
  garments
SOJOURN Gen. 26:3; Ex. 12:48
SOJOURNER—*foreigner, alien* Ex. 2:22; 12:45;
  18:3; 20:10
SOLD Gen. 25:33, **s** his birthright
Gen. 45:4, brother Joseph, whom you **s** into
Matt. 10:29, two sparrows **s** for a cent
  13:46, went and **s** all that he had

Acts 5:1, his wife Sapphira, **s** a piece of
Rom. 7:14, of flesh, **s** into bondage to sin
Lev. 25:23; 1 Kin. 21:20; Joel 3:3
SOLDIER Mark 15:16, the **s-s** took Him away
Luke 23:36, the **s-s** also mocked Him
John 19:23, four parts, a part to every **s**
Acts 28:16, with the **s** who was guarding
2 Tim. 2:3, as a good **s** of Christ Jesus
SOLVE—*dissolve*
Dan. 5:12, **s-ing** of difficult problems
  5:16, give interpretations and **s** difficult
SOMEBODY Acts 5:36, Theudas rose up,
  claiming to be **s**
SOMEONE Luke 8:46, **S** did touch Me
SOMETHING—*this* 1 Kin. 2:14, have **s** *to say* to
  you
Hab. 1:5, *I* am doing **s** in your days
Luke 7:40, I have **s** to say to you
Acts 25:26, I may have **s** to write
SON 2 Sam. 13:37, *David* mourned for his **s**
Ps. 2:7, Thou art My **S**
  8:4, **s** of man, that Thou dost care
Prov. 10:1, A wise **s** makes a father glad
  17:25, A foolish **s** is a grief
Is. 7:14, a virgin will ... bear a **s**
  14:12, O star of the morning ... **s** of
  60:4, Your **s-s** will come from afar
Dan. 7:13, One like a **S** of Man
Hos. 11:1, out of Egypt I called My **s**
Matt. 1:25, virgin until she gave birth to a **S**
  2:15, OUT OF EGYPT ... CALL MY **S**
  3:17, This is My beloved **S**
  11:27, No one knows the **S**
  13:55, Is not this the carpenter's **s**
  16:16, the **S** of the living God
  22:42, Christ, whose **s** is He
  26:63, are the Christ, the **S** of God
  27:43, I am the **S** of God
Mark 5:7, Jesus, **S** of the Most High God
  12:6, one more *to send*, a ... **s**
  14:61, the **S** of the Blessed *One*
Luke 1:31, bear a **s**, and you shall name
  2:7, birth to her first-born **s**
  4:22, Is this not Joseph's **s**
  15:11, A certain man had two **s-s**
  15:24, this **s** of mine was dead
John 4:50, Go your way, your **s** lives
  5:21, the **S** also gives life
  6:42, this Jesus, the **s** of Joseph
  12:36, may become **s-s** of light
  14:13, may be glorified in the **S**
  19:26, Woman, behold, your **s**
Acts 4:36, translated ... **S** of Encouragement
Rom. 8:32, did not spare His own **S**
Gal. 4:7, but a **s**; and if a **s**
2 Thess. 2:3, revealed, the **s** of destruction
Heb. 6:6, crucify ... the **S** of God
1 John 2:22, denies the Father and the **S**
Rev. 21:7, be his God ... will be My **s**
Gen. 6:2; 22:2; 37:33; Ex. 20:10; Deut. 8:5; 2 Kin.
  2:3; Job 5:4; Eccles. 4:8; Is. 30:9; Ezek. 2:1;
  Mal. 3:17
SONG—*music, taunt*
Ex. 15:2, LORD is my strength and **s**
Judg. 5:12, Awake, awake, sing a **s**
Job 35:10, gives **s-s** in the night
Ps. 33:3, Sing to Him a new **s**
  137:4, How ... sing the LORD'S **s**
Prov. 25:20, Sings **s-s** to a troubled heart
Eccles. 12:4, the daughters of **s**
Song 1:1, The **S** of **S-s**
Eph. 5:19, hymns and spiritual **s-s**
Is. 5:1; 23:16; 24:9; Ezek. 33:32
SOON—*shortly* Ex. 2:18, you come back so **s**
Job 32:22, Maker would **s** take me away
Heb. 13:23, if he comes **s**
SOOT Lam. 4:8, appearance is blacker than **s**
SOOTHE Gen. 8:21, LORD smelled a **s-ing** aroma
SORDID Titus 1:11, for the sake of **s** gain
SORE Luke 16:21, dogs ... licking his **s-s**

SORROW Gen. 42:38, bring ... down ... in s
Ps. 31:10, my life is spent with s
Eccles. 7:3, **S** is better than laughter
Is. 35:10, s and sighing will flee away
   53:3, A man of s-s
Jer. 8:18, My s is beyond healing
John 16:20, be s-ful, but your s
2 Cor. 2:2, For if I cause you s
   2:5, he has caused s not to me
   2:7, overwhelmed by excessive s
   7:9, made s-ful according to *the will* of God
   7:10, s ... produces a repentance
Jer. 45:3; Luke 22:45
SORRY Gen. 6:6, the LORD was s ... made man
Jer. 13:14, I will not show pity nor be s
SOUGHT—*seek, visit* Is. 26:16, they s Thee in
   distress
Matt. 2:20, who s the Child's life
   21:46, they s to seize Him
Gal. 4:18, to be eagerly s
Ex. 33:7; Eccles. 7:29
SOUL—*life, person*
Deut. 4:29, with all your heart ... s
1 Sam. 1:26, As your s lives
Job 33:30, bring back his s from the pit
Ps. 16:10, not abandon my s to Sheol
   19:7, LORD is perfect, restoring the s
   23:3, He restores my s
   24:4, not lifted up his s to falsehood
   42:1, So my s pants for Thee
   62:1, My s *waits* in silence for God
   63:1, My s thirsts for Thee
   103:1, Bless the LORD, O my s
   107:9, satisfied the thirsty s
Prov. 24:12, who keeps your s
   25:25, cold water to a weary s
Ezek. 18:4, s who sins will die
Matt. 10:28, unable to kill the s
   11:29, FIND REST FOR YOUR S-S
   16:26, world, and forfeits his s
   26:38, My s is deeply grieved
Luke 1:46, My s exalts the Lord
   12:19, say to my s, **S** you have many
John 12:27, My s has become troubled
Acts 4:32, were of one heart and s
1 Thess. 5:23, your spirit and s and body
Heb. 4:12, division of s and spirit
   6:19, as an anchor of the s
   10:39, to the preserving of the s
James 1:21, is able to save your s-s
   5:20, save his s from death
1 Pet. 2:11, which wage war against the s
2 Pet. 2:14, enticing unstable s-s
Deut. 4:9; Judg. 16:16; 1 Sam. 18:1; Job 3:20;
   10:1
SOUND—*roar, shout, voice* Ex. 32:17; Lev. 26:36
Gen. 3:8, heard the s of the LORD God
Prov. 3:21, Keep s wisdom
Luke 15:27, received him back safe and s
1 Tim. 1:10, contrary to s teaching
2 Tim. 1:13, Retain ... standard of s words
Titus 1:13, may be in the faith
Rev. 1:15, s of many waters
   8:7, And the first s-ed
Judg. 4:21; 1 Kin. 18:41; 19:12; Job 15:21; 33:15;
   Prov. 2:7; Eccles. 12:4; Jer. 25:10; Joel 2:1
SOUR Jer. 31:29, fathers have eaten s grapes
SOURCE Heb. 5:9, the s of eternal salvation
SOUTH Matt. 12:42, Queen of *the* **S**
Luke 12:55, see a s wind blowing
Acts 27:13, when a moderate s wind came up
Job 37:9,17; Eccles. 11:3
SOW Job 4:8, those who s trouble harvest it
Ps. 126:5, s in tears shall reap
Prov. 22:8, who s-s iniquity ... reap vanity
Is. 55:10, furnishing seed to the s-er
Matt. 6:26, birds ... they do not s
   13:3, s-er went out to s
Luke 12:24, neither s nor reap
   19:21, reap what you did not s
John 4:36, he who s-s and he who reaps

1 Cor. 9:11, s-ed spiritual things in you
   15:42, s-n a perishable body
   15:44, s-n a natural body
2 Cor. 9:6, he who s-s sparingly
Gal. 6:7, whatever a man s-s
James 3:18, is s-n in peace
Gen. 47:23; Lev. 26:16; Deut. 22:9; Job 31:8;
   Eccles. 11:4,6; Is. 32:20; Jer. 4:3; Hos. 8:7
SPACE—*time* Lev. 25:30, the s of a full year
SPACIOUS—*large* Ex. 3:8, to a good and s land
SPARE Ps. 78:50, s their soul from death
Prov. 13:24, s-s his rod hates his son
Acts 20:29, not s-ing the flock
Rom. 8:32, did not s His own Son
   11:21, not s the natural branches
2 Cor. 9:6, who sows s-ingly
   13:2, I come again, I will not s
2 Pet. 2:4, God did not s angels
Is. 9:19; Jer. 50:14; Mal. 3:17
SPARKLE Prov. 23:31, When it s-s in the cup
SPEAK—*tell, utter* Ps. 135:16, but they do not s
Prov. 23:9, Do not s ... hearing of a fool
Eccles. 3:7, silent, and a time to s
Is. 32:4, stammerers will hasten to s clearly
Matt. 10:19, how or what you will s
   10:20, Spirit of your Father who s-s
Mark 16:17, will s with new tongues
Luke 1:20, silent and unable to s
   6:26, all men s well of you
John 3:11, we s that which we know
   7:46, Never did a man s ... this man s-s
   8:45, because I s the truth
   16:13, not s on His own initiative
Acts 2:4, began to s with other tongues
   18:9, not be afraid ... but go on s-ing
   19:6, they began s-ing with tongues
Rom. 3:5, I am s-ing in human terms
1 Cor. 2:7, we s God's wisdom
   13:1, I s with the tongues of men
   13:11, I used to s as a child
2 Cor. 12:4, a man is not permitted to s
Eph. 5:19, s-ing to one another
   6:20, s boldly, as I ought to s
Titus 3:8, I want you to s confidently
James 1:19, slow to s *and* slow to anger
   2:12, so s and so act
   4:11, not s against one another
1 Pet. 4:11, Whoever s-s, *let him* s
2 Pet. 2:18, s-ing out arrogant *words*
Gen. 18:32; Ex. 4:14; Lev. 1:2; Num. 22:35;
   Deut. 5:24; 1 Kin. 12:7; Job 2:13; 11:5;
   33:14; 34:3; Ps. 28:3; 41:5; 101:7; Is. 29:4;
   40:2; Mark 13:11; John 12:49; 2 Cor. 12:6
SPEAR 1 Sam. 26:7, his s stuck in the ground
2 Sam. 1:6, Saul was leaning on his s
Ps. 46:9, cuts the s in two
Is. 2:4, their s-s into pruning hooks
Joel 3:10, pruning hooks into s-s
John 19:34, pierced His side with a s
SPECIFICALLY 1 Sam. 20:21, If I s say to the lad
SPECULATIONS—*question*
Rom. 1:21, futile in their s
2 Cor. 10:5, *We are* destroying s
2 Tim. 2:23, foolish and ignorant s
SPED—*fly* Ps. 18:10, He s upon the wings of the
   wind
SPEECH—*message, word* Ex. 4:10, slow of s
Rom. 16:18, by their smooth and flattering s
1 Cor. 1:17, not in cleverness of s
2 Cor. 11:6, even if I am unskilled in s
Col. 4:6, s always be with grace
Deut. 32:2; Job 13:17; Prov. 17:7; Is. 33:19;
   Ezek. 3:5
SPEED—*quickly* Is. 5:19, Let Him make s
Luke 18:8, bring about justice ... s-ily
SPELT Ezek. 4:9, beans, lentils, millet and s
SPEND Is. 55:2, Why do you s money
2 Cor. 12:15, I will most gladly s and
Gen. 19:2; Num. 22:8; Job 21:13
SPENT Gen. 47:15, money was all s
Ps. 31:10, my life is s with sorrow
Mark 5:26, s all that she had

SPICE Ex. 35:28; Song 8:2; Ezek. 24:10;
John 19:40
SPIES Gen. 42:9, You are s
Josh. 6:23, young men who were s
Luke 20:20, sent s who pretended
Heb. 11:31, she had welcomed the s
SPIRIT Gen. 1:2, the S of God was moving
Ps. 31:5, Into Thy hand I commit my s
51:10, renew a steadfast s within me
Eccles. 12:7, the s will return to God
Is. 11:2, s of wisdom . . . understanding
32:15, Until the S is poured
61:1, S of the Lord GOD is upon
Joel 2:28, pour out My S on all mankind
Matt. 1:18, with child by the Holy S
3:16, S of God descending
5:3, Blessed are the poor in s
10:1, authority over unclean s-s
10:20, S of your Father who speaks
12:18, PUT MY S UPON HIM
12:31, blasphemy against the S
12:45, seven other s-s more
27:50, cried . . . yielded up *His* s
28:19, Son and the Holy S
Mark 1:8, baptize you with the Holy S
1:10, S like a dove descending
14:38, s is willing, but
Luke 1:15, be filled with the Holy S
4:18, S OF THE LORD IS UPON ME
11:13, give the Holy S to those
24:37, thought . . . seeing a s
24:39, s does not have flesh
John 3:5, is born of water . . . s
4:24, God is s
14:17, *that is* the S of truth
Acts 2:4, all filled with the Holy S
18:25, being fervent in s
Rom. 2:29, by the S, not by
8:6, mind set on the S is life
15:19, in the power of the S
1 Cor. 2:10, the S searches all things
2:13, taught by the S
3:16, S of God dwells in you
5:3, absent . . . present in s
12:4, gifts, but the same S
14:15, I shall pray with the s
2 Cor. 3:6, of the letter, but of the S
13:14, fellowship of the Holy S
Gal. 4:6, sent forth the S of His Son
5:16, walk by the S
5:22, fruit of the S is love
Eph. 1:13, with the Holy S of promise
2:18, access in one S to
4:4, body and one S
4:30, not grieve the Holy S of
Phil. 1:27, standing firm in one s
1 Thess. 5:19, Do not quench the S
Heb. 4:12, division of soul and s
James 2:26, body without *the* s is dead
1 Pet. 4:6, in the s according . . . *will of* God
1 John 4:1, not believe every s
5:7, S who bears witness
5:8, the S and the water . . . blood
Rev. 1:10, in the S on the Lord's
14:13, Yes, says the S
22:17, S and the bride say
Ex. 31:3; Judg. 9:23; 2 Kin. 2:9; Eccles. 7:8; Is.
42:1; 57:15; Ezek. 11:19; Acts 2:17
SPIRITIST Lev. 20:27; 2 Kin. 23:24
SPIRITUAL Rom. 15:27, shared in their s things
1 Cor. 10:3, ate the same s food
14:1, desire . . . s *gifts*
15:44, raised a s body
Eph. 1:3, blessed us . . . every s blessing
5:19, hymns and s songs
1 Pet. 2:5, built up as a s house
SPIT Job 30:10, refrain from s-ing . . . face
Matt. 26:67, they s in His face
27:30, they s on Him
Mark 8:23, after s-ing on his eyes
14:65, some began to s at Him
John 9:6, made clay of the s-tle

SPLENDID—*gorgeous* Luke 7:25, who are **s-ly**
clothed
SPLENDOR—*glory, honor*
Ps. 8:1, hast displayed Thy s
96:6, S and majesty are before Him
SPLIT Lev. 11:3,7,26
SPOIL—*plunder* Gen. 49:27; Prov. 16:19; Is. 10:2;
Ezek. 25:7
SPOKE—*declared, told* Gen. 8:15, God s to Noah
Ps. 33:9, He s, and it was done
40:10, I have **s-n** of Thy faithfulness
62:11, Once God has **s-n**
78:19, they s against God
87:3, Glorious things are **s-n** of you
Prov. 25:11, word **s-n** in right circumstances
Matt. 13:34, Jesus s . . . in parables
Mark 14:9, be **s-n** of in memory
Rom. 14:16, thing be **s-n** of as evil
1 Cor. 14:5, that you all s in tongues
Heb. 1:2, last days has **s-n** to us
2 Pet. 1:21, men . . . s from God
Mal. 3:16; Mark 7:32
SPOT—*blemish, defect*
Gen. 30:32, speckled and **s-ed** sheep
Jer. 13:23, Or the leopard his **s-s**
Eph. 5:27, having no s or wrinkle
1 Pet. 1:19, lamb unblemished and **s-less**
SPREAD—*disperse*
Prov. 15:7, lips . . . wise s knowledge
Matt. 21:8, multitude s their garments
Ex. 1:12; 9:29; Job 29:19; 37:18; Prov. 7:16; 29:5;
Is. 19:8; 33:23; Ezek. 12:15; 16:8; Joel 2:2;
Luke 19:36
SPRING—*well* Ps. 85:11, Truth **s-s** from the earth
Is. 45:8, righteousness s up with it
58:11, like a s of water
John 4:14, well of water **s-ing** up
Heb. 12:15, root of bitterness **s-ing**
Rev. 7:17, **s-s** of the water of life
21:6, thirsts from the s of the water
Gen. 16:7; 2 Kin. 3:19; Prov. 5:16; 25:26;
Song 4:12; Is. 11:1
SPROUT—*grow* Gen. 1:11; Ex. 10:5; Ps. 90:5;
92:7; Is. 61:11
SPURNED—*despised* Ps. 10:13; 107:11; Prov.
1:30; 5:12
SPY Judg. 1:23, house of Joseph **s-ed** out Bethel
SQUANDERED—*wasted* Luke 15:13, s his estate
SQUARE Gen. 19:2; Ex. 27:1; Judg. 19:20;
Rev. 21:16
STABILITY Col. 2:5, s of your faith
STAFF Gen. 38:18, your s that is in your hand
Ex. 7:12, Aaron's s swallowed up
Ps. 23:4, Thy rod and Thy s
Matt. 10:10, sandals, or a s
Ex. 4:4; Judg. 6:21; 2 Kin. 4:29; Is. 14:5;
Ezek. 4:16; Zech. 11:10; Mark 6:8
STAIN 1 Tim. 6:14, commandment without s
2 Pet. 2:13, They are **s-s** and blemishes
STAIRWAY
2 Kin. 20:11, brought the shadow on the s back
Is. 38:8, shadow on the s . . . sun on the s of
STAND—*arise, form, rest, stood* Gen. 18:2
Ps. 1:5, will not s in the judgment
130:3, O Lord, who could s
Is. 40:8, word of our God **s-s** forever
Matt. 6:5, love to s and pray
12:25, house divided . . . shall not s
20:3, **s-ing** idle in the market place
Mark 11:25, whenever you s praying forgive
John 1:26, among you **s-s** One
19:25, were **s-ing** by the cross
20:11, Mary was **s-ing** outside
Acts 1:11, why do you s looking into
7:33, PLACE ON WHICH YOU ARE **S-ING** IS HOLY
21:40, Paul, **s-ing** on the stairs
Rom. 5:2, this grace in which we s
14:4, Lord is able to make him s
1 Cor. 16:13, s firm in the faith
2 Cor. 1:24, in your faith you are **s-ing** firm

Eph. 6:14, **S** firm ... HAVING GIRDED YOUR LOINS
1 Tim. 3:13, obtain ... a high **s-ing**
2 Tim. 2:19, foundation of God **s-s**
Rev. 3:20, Behold I **s** at the door
   5:6, Lamb **s-ing**, as if slain
   20:12, dead **s-ing** before the throne
Ex. 14:13; Num. 22:22; Josh. 10:12; Job 8:15;
   Prov. 22:29; 27:4; Is. 50:8; Jer. 6:16; 35:19;
   Ezek. 2:1; 13:5; Amos 7:7; Nah. 1:6

STANDARD—*banner*
Ps. 74:4, set up their own **s-s** for signs
Is. 13:2, Lift up a **s**
1 Chr. 17:17; Is. 5:26; 18:3; 31:9

STAR Gen. 1:16, *He made* the **s-s** also
Num. 24:17, A **s** shall come forth ... Jacob
Job 38:7, morning **s-s** sang together
Ps. 147:4, counts the number of the **s-s**
Matt. 2:2, saw His **s** in the east
   2:7, ascertained ... time the **s** appeared
   2:10, when they saw the **s**
   24:29, **s-s** WILL FALL from the sky
1 Cor. 15:41, for **s** differs from **s**
2 Pet. 1:19, **s** arises in your hearts
Jude 13, wandering **s-s**, for whom
Rev. 1:16, right hand He held seven **s-s**
   8:10, great **s** fell from heaven
   8:11, **s** is called Wormwood
   22:16, the bright morning **s**
Job 22:12; Ps. 136:9; Jer. 31:35

STARE Song 1:6, Do not **s** at me
STARVE Zeph. 2:11, He will **s** all the gods
STATE—*declare* Josh. 20:4; Luke 1:48
STATEMENT Matt. 5:37, your **s** be, Yes, yes
John 6:60, This is a difficult **s**
1 Tim. 1:15, It is a trustworthy **s**
STATURE—*size* 1 Sam. 16:7, the height of his **s**
Luke 2:52, increasing in wisdom and **s**
   19:3, he was small in **s**
STATUTE—*precept*
Ps. 119:12, Teach me Thy **s-s**
Mal. 3:7, turned aside from My **s-s**
Gen. 26:5; Ex. 29:9; Lev. 18:5; Num. 35:29;
   Is. 10:1; Ezek. 5:7
STAY—*lodge, remain* Luke 2:8, shepherds **s-ing**
Luke 19:5, today I must **s** at your house
   24:29, **S** with us ... over. And ... **s** with them
John 1:38, Rabbi ... where are you **s-ing**
   2:12, there they **s-ed** a few days
Acts 10:6, **s-ing** with a ... tanner *named* Simon
1 Pet. 1:17, time of your **s** *upon earth*
Gen. 19:17; Ruth 2:8; 1 Sam. 20:38; 22:23;
   Ps. 18:18; Hos. 3:3; Luke 1:56; John 1:39;
   Acts 18:3
STEADFAST—*resolute*
Job 11:15, you would be **s**
Ps. 51:10, renew a **s** spirit within me
   57:7, My heart is **s**, O God, my
   112:7, His heart is **s**, trusting
1 Cor. 15:58, brethren, be **s**
Col. 1:11, all **s-ness** and patience
2 Thess. 3:5, into the **s-ness** of Christ
STEAL—*deceive* Matt. 6:19, break in and **s**
Matt. 19:18, YOU SHALL NOT **S**
Ex. 20:15; Lev. 19:11; Deut. 5:19; 2 Sam. 19:3;
   Prov. 30:9; Mark 10:19; Eph. 4:28
STEALTH—*craft* Mark 14:1, to seize Him by **s**
STEED 1 Kin. 4:28; Esth. 8:10
STEP Job 18:8, he **s-s** on the webbing
Rom. 4:12, follow in the **s-s** of the faith
1 Pet. 2:21, you to follow in His **s-s**
1 Kin. 10:19; Job 14:16; 29:6; Prov. 5:5
STERN Eccles. 8:1, causes his **s** face to beam
STEWARD Gen. 43:19, near to Joseph's house **s**
Luke 12:42, faithful and sensible **s**
1 Cor. 4:1, **s-s** of the mysteries of God
   4:2, it is required of **s-s**
STEWARDSHIP Luke 16:2, an account of your **s**
1 Cor. 9:17, I have a **s** entrusted to me
Eph. 3:2, the **s** of God's grace
Col. 1:25, according to the **s** from God

STICK Prov. 18:24, friend who **s-s**
Num. 22:27; 2 Kin. 6:6; Job 33:21; 38:38;
   Ezek. 37:16,19
STILL Lev. 5:17, **s** he is guilty
Judg. 7:4, people are **s** too many
Dan. 11:35, **s** *to come* ... appointed time
Matt. 19:20, what am I **s** lacking
Luke 24:44, while I was **s** with you
Rom. 5:6, while we were **s** helpless
Josh. 10:12; Ps. 65:7; 107:29; Jer. 8:14;
   Mark 4:39
STING 1 Cor. 15:55, O DEATH ... YOUR **S**
1 Cor. 15:56, **s** of death is sin
Prov. 23:32; Rev. 9:10
STINKWEED Job 31:40, And **s** instead of barley
STIR Deut. 32:11, eagle that **s-s** up its nest
Ps. 35:23, **S** up Thyself, and awake
Prov. 10:12, Hatred **s-s** up strife
   15:1, harsh word **s-s** up anger
   28:25, arrogant man **s-s** up strife
   29:22, angry man **s-s** up strife
Acts 14:2, Jews who disbelieved **s-ed** up
2 Pet. 3:1, I am **s-ing** up your
STOCKS Job 13:27; Acts 16:24
STOLE Gen. 31:19; 2 Sam. 15:6; Prov. 9:17
STOMACH Mark 7:19, but into his **s**
STONE Ex. 34:1, Cut out ... two **s** tablets
Deut. 9:9, the tablets of **s**
1 Sam. 17:49, from it a **s** and slung
Ps. 118:22, **s** which the builders rejected
Ezek. 20:32, serving wood and **s**
Dan. 2:34, a **s** was cut out without
Matt. 3:9, God is able from these **s-s**
   4:3, command ... **s-s** become bread
   4:6, YOUR FOOT AGAINST A **S**
   7:9, will give him a **s**
   21:42, **S** WHICH THE BUILDERS REJECTED
   27:60, large **s** against the entrance
   28:2, rolled away the **s** and sat
Luke 19:44, one **s** upon another
John 2:6, six **s** waterpots
   8:7, first to throw a **s** at her
   11:39, Jesus said, Remove the **s**
Acts 7:59, went on **s-ing** Stephen
2 Cor. 3:3, not on tablets of **s**
1 Pet. 2:5, also, as living **s-s**
   2:8, **S** OF STUMBLING
Gen. 11:3; 29:3; Ex. 15:16; 20:25; Lev. 20:2;
   Num. 15:35; Deut. 8:9; 2 Sam. 17:13;
   1 Kin. 6:18; 2 Kin. 12:12; 2 Chr. 34:11; Job
   14:19; 41:24; Ps. 18:12; 91:12; Prov. 26:27;
   27:3; Is. 28:16; 54:11; 57:6; Ezek. 11:19;
   Amos 5:11; Hab. 2:11; Luke 22:41;
   Rev. 2:17
STOOD Deut. 31:15, pillar of cloud **s** at
Josh. 10:13, So the sun **s** still
Matt. 2:9, came and **s** over where
   4:5, devil ... **s** Him on the pinnacle
Luke 4:16, and **s** up to read
   24:36, He Himself **s** in their midst
John 21:4, Jesus **s** on the beach
Rev. 13:1, he **s** on the sand
STOP 1 Kin. 18:44; Ps. 63:11; 2 Cor. 11:10
STORE Prov. 10:14, Wise men **s** up knowledge
Luke 12:17, I have no place to **s** my crops
1 Tim. 6:19, **s-ing** up treasure
James 5:3, have **s-d** up your treasure
STOREHOUSE—*treasure* Deut. 28:12; Job 38:22
STORM—*tempest, whirlwind* Jon. 1:4, a great **s**
Jon. 1:12, this great **s** *has come* upon you
Matt. 16:3, *There will be* a **s** today
Acts 27:18, we were being violently **s-tossed**
2 Pet. 2:17, mists driven by a **s**
Job 21:18; 37:9; Ps. 55:8; 107:25; Is. 25:4;
   Ezek. 38:9
STRAIGHT—*equity* Matt. 3:3, MAKE PATHS **S**
Luke 3:5, CROOKED SHALL BECOME **S**
John 1:23, MAKE **S** THE WAY OF THE LORD
Acts 9:11, street called **S**
Heb. 12:13, make **s** paths for your feet
1 Sam. 6:12, Ps. 5:8; Eccles. 1:15; Mic. 3:9

STRAIGHTFORWARD Gal. 2:14, not **s** about the truth
STRAIT—*narrow* 1 Sam. 13:6; they were in a **s**
STRANGE Heb. 13:9, varied and **s** teachings
1 Pet. 4:12, some **s** thing were happening
Jude 7, went after **s** flesh
STRANGER—*alien, sojourner*
Gen. 23:4, I am a **s** and
Matt. 25:35, I was a **s**, and you invited
27:7, Potter's Field ... for **s-s**
John 10:5, do not know the voice of **s-s**
Eph. 2:19, you are no longer **s-s** and aliens
Heb. 13:2, show hospitality to **s-s**
Gen. 15:13; Ex. 22:21; Is. 1:7; Jer. 22:3
STRATEGIC Mark 6:21, a **s** day came when Herod
STRAW Gen. 24:25; Ex. 5:7; 1 Kin. 4:28; Job 41:27; Is. 11:7
STRAY Prov. 7:25, not **s** into her paths
James 5:19, any among you **s-s** from the truth
1 Pet. 2:25, **s-ing** like sheep
STREAM—*river* Ps. 1:3, planted by the **s-s** of water
Is. 32:2, **s-s** of water in a dry country
STREET—*square*
Prov. 1:20, Wisdom shouts in the **s**
Is. 59:14, truth has stumbled in the **s**
Matt. 6:2, **s-s**, that they may be honored
6:5, pray ... on the **s** corners
Acts 9:11, **s** called Straight
Rev. 21:21, **s** of the city was pure gold
2 Sam. 1:20; 22:43; Jer. 37:21; Nah. 2:4
STRENGTH Ex. 15:2, the LORD is my **s** and song
Ps. 28:7, LORD is my **s** and my shield
46:1, God is our refuge and **s**
Prov. 20:29, glory of young men ... **s**
Is. 40:29, He gives **s** to the weary
Mark 12:30, MIND, AND WITH ALL YOUR **S**
1 Pet. 4:11, by the **s** which God supplies
Rev. 1:16, sun shining in its **s**
Gen. 4:12; Judg. 6:14; 8:21; 16:6; 1 Sam. 28:20; Job 6:12; 21:23; Ps. 84:7; Prov. 31:3; Eccles. 9:16; Is. 41:1; Hab. 3:19
STRENGTHEN—*fortify* 1 Sam. 30:6, David **s-ed**
Is. 35:3, **s** the feeble
Luke 22:32, **s** your brothers
Col. 1:11, **s-ed** with all power
2 Thess. 2:17, **s** your hearts in every
1 Tim. 1:12, who has **s-ed** me
Heb. 13:9, heart to be **s-ed** by grace
James 5:8, **s** your hearts, for the coming
1 Pet. 5:10, confirm, **s** *and* establish you
Deut. 3:28; Judg. 16:28; 2 Chr. 11:11; Job 4:3; Is. 35:3; Ezek. 34:16; Nah. 3:14
STRETCH Ps. 68:31, **s** out her hands to God
Ps. 104:2, **s-ing** out heaven like
Is. 28:20, too short ... to **s** out
Job 30:24; 38:5; Jer. 10:12
STRETCHER
Luke 5:19, let him down ... with his **s**
STRICKEN Is. 53:4, we ... esteemed Him **s**
Is. 1:5; Jer. 14:19
STRICT Acts 26:5, the **s-est** sect of our religion
STRIFE—*quarrel*
Prov. 16:28, perverse man spreads **s**
18:6, fool's lips bring **s**
Rom. 13:13, not in **s** and jealousy
1 Cor. 3:3, jealousy and **s** among you
Gal. 5:20, enmities, **s**, jealousy
Titus 3:9, foolish controversies ... and **s**
Gen. 13:7; Prov. 6:14,19; 10:12; 13:10; 20:3; Is. 58:4
STRIKE Ex. 7:17, I will **s** the water
Ex. 12:12, **s** down all the first-born
Ps. 91:12; Matt. 4:6; Luke 4:11, **s** your foot
Matt. 26:31, I WILL **S** DOWN THE SHEPHERD
Acts 23:3, God is going to **s** you
Gen. 4:23; Prov. 17:26; 19:25; Is. 49:10; Jer. 18:18
STRING Ps. 11:2; 33:2; Hab. 3:19
STRIP Ps. 29:9, **s-s** the forests bare

STRIPES Deut. 25:3, beat him with **s**
STRIVE Gen. 6:3, Spirit shall not **s** with man
Ps. 103:9, not always is *with us*
Luke 13:24, **S** to enter by the narrow door
STRONG—*courage* 2 Sam. 22:33, God is my **s** fortress
Ps. 24:8, the LORD **s** and mighty
Prov. 20:1, **s** drink a brawler
Jer. 50:34, Their Redeemer is **s**
Luke 2:40, Child ... grow and become **s**
1 Cor. 4:10, we are weak, but you are **s**
2 Cor. 12:10, when I am weak, then I am **s**
Eph. 6:10, be **s** in the Lord
Heb. 11:34, from weakness were made **s**
James 3:4, ships ... driven by **s** winds
Gen. 49:14; Ex. 10:19; 14:21; Lev. 10:9; Deut. 31:6; Judg. 14:18; Job 17:9; Ps. 19:5; Prov. 31:6; Song 8:6; Is. 5:11; 41:6; Ezek. 30:21; Luke 14:31
STRONGHOLD—*fortress, refuge*
Ps. 9:9, **s** in times of trouble
59:9,17, For God is my **s**
94:22, the LORD has been my **s**
2 Sam. 5:9; 22:3; 1 Chr. 11:5,7; Ps. 62:2; Prov. 10:29; Ezek. 33:27
STRUCK—*touched*
Job 19:21, hand of God has **s** me
Ex. 7:20; Num. 20:11; 22:23; Acts 12:23
STRUGGLE Col. 2:1, how great a **s** I have
STUBBORN Rom. 2:5, **s-ness** and unrepentant heart
Jer. 3:17; Hos. 4:16
STUMBLE—*fall*
Matt. 5:29, right eye makes you **s**
11:6, blessed ... keeps from **s-ing** over
Luke 17:2, cause one of these ... to **s**
James 3:2, For we all **s** in many *ways*
1 Pet. 2:8, **s** because they are disobedient
2 Pet. 1:10, you will never **s**
Prov. 3:23; Is. 8:14; 40:30; Jer. 50:32; Dan. 11:19
STUMBLING BLOCK—*ruin*
Ezek. 18:30, not become a **s**
Matt. 16:23, Satan! You are a **s** to Me
18:7, Woe ... because of its **s-s**
Gal. 5:11, the **s** of the cross
STUPID—*senseless* Ps. 49:10; Prov. 30:2; Jer. 10:8,21
STUPOR Rom. 11:8, gave them a spirit of **s**
SUBJECT Luke 2:51, He continued in **s-ion** to them
Rom. 8:20, was **s-ed** to futility
Eph. 5:24, church is **s** to Christ
Titus 2:5, **s** to their own husbands
Heb. 2:8, PUT ALL THINGS IN **S-ION** UNDER
12:9, **s** to the Father
1 Pet. 3:22, and powers had been **s-ed** to Him
5:5, be **s** to your elders
SUBMISSIVE 1 Tim. 2:11, instruction with ... **s-ness**
1 Pet. 2:18, be **s** to your masters
3:1, be **s** to your own husbands
SUBSIDED Judg. 8:3, their anger ... **s**
SUBSTANCE Deut. 33:11, O LORD, bless his **s**
SUCCESS Gen. 24:12, grant me **s** today
SUDDENLY Mark 13:36, come **s** and find
Luke 21:34, come on you **s** like a trap
Acts 2:2, **s** there came from heaven
Job 21:13; Is. 29:5
SUFFER Job 3:20, light given to him who **s-s**
Ps. 34:10, lions do lack and **s** hunger
Mark 8:31, Son of Man must **s** many
Luke 24:46, Christ should **s** and rise again
Acts 28:5, into the fire and **s-ed** no harm
2 Tim. 2:3, **S** hardship with *me*
James 5:13, Is anyone among you **s-ing**
1 Pet. 2:21, Christ also **s-ed** for you
4:13, you share the **s-ings** of Christ
SUFFICIENT Ex. 36:7, material they had was **s**
Lev. 25:47, means of a stranger ... becomes **s**
John 6:7, denarii worth of bread is not **s**
2 Cor. 12:9, My grace is **s** for you

SUIT Gen. 2:18; 2 Sam. 15:2
SULLEN 1 Kin. 21:5, your spirit is so s
SUM 1 Pet. 3:8, To s up, let all be harmonious
SUMMER Jer. 8:20, past, s is ended
  Matt. 24:32, you know that s is near
  Gen. 8:22; Ps. 74:17; Prov. 26:1; Zech. 14:8
SUMMON—*call* Num. 10:2, use them for **s-ing**
  Job 9:19, who can s Him
SUN Eccles. 1:9, nothing new under the s
  Is. 38:8 s-'s shadow went back ten steps
  Matt. 5:45, causes His s to rise
    13:43, RIGHTEOUS . . . SHINE FORTH AS THE S
  Luke 21:25, will be signs in s
  1 Cor. 15:41, There is one glory of the s
  Eph. 4:26, s go down on your anger
  Rev. 12:1, woman clothed with the s
    22:5, nor the light of the s
  Gen. 15:12; Ex. 16:21; Lev. 22:7; Josh. 10:12; Ps.
    72:5; 84:11; 104:19; 121:6; Song. 6:10;
    Is. 60:19; Ezek. 32:7; Amos 8:9
SUNK Ps. 38:2, Thine arrows have s deep
SUNRISE Luke 1:78, the S from on high shall
  visit us
SUNSHINE 2 Sam. 23:4, Through s after rain
SUPERIORITY 1 Cor. 2:1, not come with s of
  speech
SUPPER John 13:4, rose from s and laid aside
  1 Cor. 11:20, not to eat the Lord's S
  Rev. 19:9, marriage s of the Lamb
SUPPLANTS Prov. 30:23, maidservant . . . s her
  mistress
SUPPLICATION Ex. 9:28, Make s to the LORD
  Ps. 28:2, Hear the voice of my s-s
  Dan. 9:3, seek *Him* by prayer and s-s
SUPPLY Is. 3:1, s of bread . . . s of water
SUPPORT Matt. 10:10, worker is worthy of his s
  Ex. 17:12; 2 Tim. 4:16
SURE—*trust* Num. 32:23, be s your sin will find
  you out
  Ps. 19:7, testimony of the LORD is s
  Heb. 13:18, s that we have a good conscience
  2 Pet. 1:19, prophetic word made more s
SURELY Gen. 2:17, eat from it you shall s die
  Gen. 28:16, S the LORD is in this place
  Deut. 14:22, s tithe all the produce
  Ps. 23:6, S goodness and lovingkindness
  Is. 53:4, S our griefs He . . . bore
  Mark 14:70 S you are *one* of them
  Heb. 6:14, s BLESS YOU . . . s MULTIPLY YOU
  Ex. 31:13; 2 Sam. 17:11; Job 35:13; Jer. 23:39
SURFACE Gen. 1:2; 7:18; Job 38:30
SURMISE Acts 27:27, sailors *began* to s
SURPASS 2 Chr. 9:6, You s the report I heard
  Eph. 1:19, the **s-ing** greatness of His power
    2:7, the **s-ing** riches of His grace
SURPLUS Mark 12:44, put in out of their s
SURPRISE 1 Pet. 4:12, do not be **s-d** . . . fiery
  ordeal
SURROUND Ps. 18:5, cords of Sheol **s-ed** me
  Luke 19:43, your enemies . . . and s you
SUSTAIN Gen. 13:6; 36:7; Song 2:5
SWALLOW Matt. 23:24, gnat and s a camel
  1 Cor. 15:54, DEATH IS S-ED UP IN VICTORY
  Gen. 41:7,24; Num. 16:34; Job 20:15; Is. 25:8;
    Jon. 1:17; Hab. 1:13
SWEAR Gen. 50:5; Lev. 19:12; Is. 45:23;
  Zech. 5:3; Matt. 23:18; 26:74; Mark 14:71;
  James 5:12
SWEET 2 Sam. 23:1, the s psalmist of Israel
  Ps. 55:14, had s fellowship together
  Prov. 3:24, your sleep will be s
    9:17, Stolen water is s
  Is. 5:20; 43:24; Jer. 6:20
SWELL—*bulge* Num. 5:21,22; Deut. 8:4
SWIFT Job 7:6, My days are **s-er** than
  Eccles. 9:11, race is not to the s
  Rom. 3:15, FEET ARE S TO SHED BLOOD
SWINDLER Luke 18:11, 1 Cor. 5:11, 6:10
SWINE Prov. 11:22, ring of gold in a s-'s snout
  Matt. 7:6, throw your pearls before s
  Mark 5:11, big herd of s feeding there
  Luke 15:15, into his fields to feed s

SWOOP Job 9:26, eagle that **s-s** on its prey
SWORD Gen. 3:24, flaming s which turned
  Gen. 27:40, by your s you shall live
  Ps. 57:4, their tongue a sharp s
    64:3, sharpened their tongue like a s
  Prov. 5:4, Sharp as a two-edged s
  Is. 2:4; Mic. 4:3, hammer their **s-s** into
    plowshares
  Hos. 2:18, abolish the bow, the s, and war
  Matt. 10:34, not . . . peace, but a s
    26:51, drew out his s and struck the slave
    26:52, take up the s shall perish by the s
  Eph. 6:17, s of the Spirit
  Rev. 1:16, mouth became a sharp . . . s
  Ex. 5:3; Deut. 32:25; Judg. 3:16,21,22;
    2 Sam. 2:26; Is. 2:4; Jer. 15:2; Hos. 1:7
SYNAGOGUE Matt. 6:2, the **s-s** and in the streets
  Matt. 6:5, pray in the **s-s** and on
    12:9, He went into their s
    13:54, teaching them in their s
  John 16:2, make you outcasts from the s
    18:20, I always taught in **s-s**
  Acts 9:20, proclaim Jesus in the **s-s**
  Rev. 2:9, but are a s of Satan

T

TABERNACLE Ex. 26:1, t with ten curtains
  Matt. 17:4, make three **t-s** here
  Rev. 21:3, t of God is among men
TABLE Is. 21:5, They set the t
  Matt. 21:12, **t-s** of the money-changers
  Mark 7:28, dogs under the t feed
  John 2:15, overturned their **t-s**
  Acts 6:2, word of God . . . to serve **t-s**
  1 Cor. 10:21, partake of the t of the Lord
  Lev. 24:6; Judg. 1:7; 2 Kin. 4:10; Ps. 23:5
TABLET Ex. 24:12, give you the stone **t-s**
  Ex. 31:18, two **t-s** of the testimony
  Luke 1:63, asked for a t
  2 Cor. 3:3, on **t-s** of human hearts
  Is. 8:1; Jer. 17:1
TAKE Ex. 20:7, not t the name of the LORD
  Ex. 34:9, t us as Thine own possession
  Prov. 4:13, T hold of instruction
  Is. 4:1, seven women will t hold of
  Matt. 5:40, t your shirt
    7:5, first t the log out . . . eye
    11:29, T My yoke upon you
    26:26, T, eat; this is My body
  Mark 2:9, Arise, and t up your pallet
    13:33, T heed, keep on the alert
  Luke 9:3, T nothing for your journey
  John 1:29, **t-s** away the sin of the world
    20:2, have **t-n** away the Lord
  Acts 1:20, HIS OFFICE LET ANOTHER MAN T
  Eph. 6:16, **t-ing** up the shield of faith
  Rev. 10:9, T it, and eat it
  Gen. 3:22; 12:19; 22:2; Num. 30:2; Judg. 21:22;
    1 Sam. 4:3; Ezek. 18:17; 37:19; Hos. 1:2;
    Mic. 2:4; Matt. 21:21; 1 Cor. 13:5
TALE 2 Pet. 1:16, cleverly devised **t-s**
TALK Acts 20:9, as Paul kept on **t-ing**
  Eph. 5:4, *no* filthiness and silly t
  Titus 1:10, empty **t-ers** and deceivers
  Job 11:2; 15:3; Prov. 24:2; Luke 1:65
TARGET—*mark* 1 Sam. 20:20; Lam. 3:12
TASK Eccles. 2:26, sinner He has given the t
TASTE Ex. 16:31, t was like wafers
  Ps. 34:8, t and see that the LORD is good
  Matt. 16:28, shall not t death
  Acts 23:14, t nothing until we have killed Paul
  Heb. 2:9, t death for every one
    6:4, **t-d** of the heavenly gift
  Job 6:6; 34:3; Prov. 24:13; Dan. 10:3
TAUGHT Ps. 71:17, hast t me from my youth
  Is. 54:13, sons will be t of the LORD
  John 8:28, I speak . . . as the Father t Me
  Gal. 1:12, nor was I t it
  1 Thess. 4:9, t by God to love one another

TAUNT Deut. 28:37; Job 30:9
TAX—*tribute* Num. 31:28, levy a t for the LORD
Matt. 17:24, teacher not pay the ... t
22:19, coin *used* for the **poll-t**
Luke 20:22, pay **t-es** to Caesar
Rom. 13:7, t to whom t is *due*
2 Kin. 23:35; Matt. 9:9
TAX-GATHERER Matt. 5:46, even the **t-s** do the same
Matt. 10:3, Matthew the t
Luke 18:13, t, standing some distance away
TEACH Ps. 25:4, T me Thy paths
Ps. 27:11, T me Thy way, O LORD
143:10, T me to do Thy will
Prov. 1:8, do not forsake your mother's **t-ing**
Matt. 7:29, **t-ing** them as *one* having authority
11:1, t and preach in their cities
15:9, **T-ING AS THEIR DOCTRINES**
Mark 1:22, they were amazed at His **t-ing**
4:2, **t-ing** them ... in parables
Luke 11:1, Lord, t us to pray
19:47, **t-ing** daily in the temple
John 7:16, My **t-ing** is not Mine, but His
14:26, He will t you all things
Acts 1:1, Jesus began to do and t
2:42, devoting ... to the apostles' **t-ing**
15:35, **t-ing** and preaching
Rom. 2:21, t another, do you not t yourself
16:17, contrary to the **t-ing** which you learned
1 Cor. 11:14, nature itself t you
Col. 2:22, commandments and **t-ings** of men
3:16, **t-ing** and admonishing
1 Tim. 1:3, not to t strange doctrines
2:12, do not allow a woman to t
2 Tim. 3:10, you followed my **t-ing**
Titus 2:3, **t-ing** what is good
Heb. 8:11, NOT T EVERY ONE HIS FELLOW
Rev. 2:20, **t-es** and leads my bond-servants
2:24, the rest ... who do not hold this **t-ing**
Ex. 4:12; Deut. 32:2; 1 Kin. 8:36; Job 11:4; 15:5;
21:22; 37:19; Prov. 4:2; Is. 28:9
TEACHER Matt. 8:19, T, I will follow You
Matt. 10:24, disciple is not above his t
17:24, Does your t not pay
23:8, for One is your T
Mark 5:35, why trouble the T any more
Luke 2:46, in the midst of the **t-s**
5:17, Pharisees and **t-s** of the law
John 3:2, come from God *as* a t
3:10, Are you the t of Israel
13:13, You call Me T and Lord
Acts 5:34, Gamaliel, a t of the Law
Rom. 2:20, a t of the immature
1 Cor. 12:29, All are not **t-s**
Eph. 4:11, some *as* pastors and **t-s**
1 Tim. 2:7, t of the Gentiles in faith
2 Tim. 4:3, accumulate for themselves **t-s**
James 3:1, Let not many of *you* become **t-s**
2 Pet. 2:1, be false **t-s** among you
1 Chr. 25:8; Prov. 5:13
TEAR—*rend* Eccles. 3:7, time to t apart
Matt. 5:29, makes you stumble, t it out
7:6, turn and t you to pieces
Luke 12:18, I will t down my barns
John 19:24, Let us not t it, but cast
Lev. 10:6; Job 18:4; Ps. 7:2; Prov. 14:1;
Ezek. 13:20
TEAR—*weep* Ps. 80:5, fed them ... bread of **t-s**
Ps. 126:5, sow in **t-s** shall reap with joyful shouting
Is. 25:8, God will wipe **t-s** away
Luke 7:38, wet His feet with her **t-s**
2 Tim. 1:4, even as I recall your **t-s**
Rev. 7:17, God shall wipe away every t
21:4, He shall wipe away every t
2 Kin. 20:5; Ps. 56:8; Eccles. 4:1; Is. 16:9;
Jer. 9:1; Lam. 1:2; 2:18
TEETH Gen. 49:12; Job 13:14; 19:20; 41:14;
Ps. 57:4; Prov. 10:26; Jer. 31:29; Amos 4:6;
Matt. 8:12

TELL 1 Chr. 16:24; Ps. 96:3, T of His glory among
Ps. 19:1, heavens are **t-ing** of the glory of God
66:16, I will t of what He has done for my soul
118:17, t of the works of the LORD
Matt. 8:4, See that you t no one
26:63, t us whether You are the Christ
Luke 13:32, Go and t that fox
John 18:34, did others t you about Me
Ex. 19:3; Lev. 5:1; Judg. 14:14; Ps. 2:7;
Eccles. 10:14; Dan. 2:2,36; Joel 1:3; Zeph.
3:13
TEMPER Prov. 29:11, A fool ... loses his t
TEMPERATE Titus 2:2, Older men are to be t
TEMPEST Job 9:17; Ps. 55:8; Is. 28:2; Amos 1:14
TEMPLE—*house* 2 Sam. 22:7, from His t He heard my voice
Ps. 11:4, LORD is in His holy t
Is. 6:4, t was filling with smoke
Jer. 7:4, t of the LORD, the t of the LORD
Matt. 4:5, pinnacle of the t
12:6, something greater than the t
Mark 14:58, destroy this t made with hands
Luke 23:45, veil of the t was torn
John 2:19, Destroy this t ... I will raise it
2:21, speaking of the t of His body
1 Cor. 3:17, t of God is holy ... what you are
2 Cor. 6:16, we are the t of the living God
2 Thess. 2:4, takes his seat in the t of God
Rev. 21:22, God ... and the Lamb are its t
1 Sam. 1:9; 1 Chr. 29:1; Neh. 6:11
TEMPT—*test* Matt. 4:1, Jesus ... t-ed by the devil
Matt. 4:3, **t-er** came and said to Him
Luke 4:2, forty days while **t-ed** by the devil
1 Cor. 10:13, not allow you to be **t-ed**
1 Thess. 3:5, tempter might have **t-ed** you
Heb. 4:15, **t-ed** in all things as *we are*
James 1:13, God cannot be **t-ed** by evil
TEMPTATION—*trial*
Matt. 6:13, do not lead us into t
26:41, you may not enter into t
Luke 8:13, time of t fall away
1 Cor. 10:13, No t has overtaken you
2 Pet. 2:9, rescue the godly from t
TEN Deut. 10:4, the T Commandments
Ps. 91:7, t thousand at your right hand
Matt. 25:1, comparable to t virgins
Luke 15:8, if she has t silver coins
17:17, Were there not t cleansed
Gen. 31:7; Num. 14:22; Job 19:3; Ps. 33:2;
Song 5:10; Is. 38:8; Ezek. 45:14; Dan. 1:14;
7:7
TEND John 21:15,17
TENDER Is. 53:2, He grew up ... like a t shoot
Matt. 24:32, branch has already become t
Luke 1:78, t mercy of our God
Eph. 4:32, **t-hearted**, forgiving each other
Gen. 18:7; 2 Sam. 23:4; 2 Kin. 22:19
TENT—*tabernacle* 1 Kin. 12:16, To your **t-s**, O Israel
Ps. 15:1, who may abide in Thy t
61:4, dwell in Thy t forever
84:10, in the **t-s** of wickedness
Is. 38:12, Like a shepherd's t
Gen. 4:20; 18:1; 24:67; 25:27; Num. 24:5;
Job 12:6; Song 1:8; Jer. 10:20
TENTH—*tithe* Gen. 14:20, he gave him a t of all
Heb. 7:2, Abraham apportioned a t part
7:5, to collect a t from the people
Rev. 11:13, a t of the city fell
TERMS Gal. 3:15, Speak in t of human relations
TERRIBLE—*dread*
Deut. 8:15, great and t wilderness
Mal. 4:5, the great and t day of the LORD
Mark 9:26, throwing him into t convulsions
TERRIFYING Is. 21:1, wilderness, from a t land
Heb. 10:27, t expectation of judgment
10:31, t thing to fall into the hands of
TERROR—*fear, dread* Ps. 91:5, afraid of the t by night
Luke 21:11, **t-s** and great signs

Lev. 26:16; Deut. 32:25; Job 15:21; 24:17; 41:14;
  Ps. 116:3; Eccles. 12:5; Is. 33:18
TEST—*try* Gen. 22:1, God **t-ed** Abraham
  Ex. 17:2, Why do you **t** the LORD
  Deut. 6:16, shall not put the LORD ... to the **t**
  2 Sam. 22:31, word of the LORD is **t-ed**
  Job 12:11, Does not the ear **t** words
  Ps. 26:2, **T** my mind and my heart
  Prov. 30:5, Every word of God is **t-ed**
  Is. 28:16, a **t-ed** stone ... costly
  Matt. 22:18, Why are you **t-ing** Me
  Acts 5:9, put the Spirit ... to the **t**
  1 Cor. 3:13, fire itself will **t** ... man's work
  2 Cor. 13:5, **T** yourselves *to see* if you are
  James 1:3, **t-ing** of your faith
  1 Pet. 1:7, even though **t-ed** by fire
    4:12, fiery ordeal ... for your **t-ing**
  1 John 4:1, **t** the spirits to see
  Ex. 20:20; 1 Kin. 10:1
TESTIFY
  Acts 2:40, many other words he ... **t-ed**
    20:24, to **t** solemnly of the gospel
    26:22, **t-ing** both to small and great
  Gal. 5:3, **t** again to every man
  1 Pet. 5:12, **t-ing** that this is the true
  Ex. 23:2; 2 Sam. 1:16; 1 Kin. 21:10; Job 15:6;
    Is. 59:12
TESTIMONY—*witness* Ps. 19:7, **t** of the LORD is
  sure
  Ps. 119:46, speak of Thy **t-s** before kings
  Matt. 8:4, the offering ... for a **t**
  Luke 22:71, need do we have of **t**
  John 8:17, the **t** of two men is true
  1 Cor. 1:6, concerning Christ was confirmed
  2 Tim. 1:8, ashamed of the **t** of our Lord
  Titus 1:13, This **t** is true
  Rev. 19:10, **t** of Jesus is the spirit
  Ex. 16:34; 25:16; 31:18; Lev. 16:13; Num. 35:30;
    Is. 8:16
THANK 1 Chr. 16:7, to give **t-s** to the LORD
  1 Chr. 16:34, O give **t-s** to the LORD
  Ps. 92:1, good to give **t-s** to the LORD
    100:4, Give **t-s** to Him
  Matt. 15:36, giving **t-s**, He broke *them*
    26:27, took a cup and gave **t-s**
  Luke 18:11, God, I **t** Thee that I am not
    22:19, when He had given **t-s**, He broke
  Rom. 6:17, But **t-s** be to God
    14:6, he gives **t-s** to God
  1 Cor. 14:16, Amen at your giving of **t-s**
    15:57, but **t-s** be to God
  Eph. 1:16, do not cease giving **t-s** for you
    5:20, always giving **t-s** for all things
  1 Thess. 3:9, what **t-s** can we render to God
    5:18, in everything give **t-s**
  2 Thess. 1:3, always to give **t-s** to God
THANKSGIVING—*gratitude*
  Ps. 26:7, with the voice of **t**
    95:2, before His presence with **t**
    100:4, Enter His gates with **t**
  Phil. 4:6, supplication with **t**
  Rev. 7:12, and **t** and honor and power
  Lev. 7:12; Neh. 11:17
THEIR Gen. 15:13, a land that is not **t-s**
  Matt. 5:3, **t-s** is the kingdom of heaven
  1 Cor. 1:2, Christ, **t** Lord and ours
THEN—*therefore* Gen. 4:26, **T** men began to call
  Ex. 15:1, **T** Moses ... sang this song
  Matt. 6:9, Pray, **t**, in this way
    24:14, **t** the end shall come
  Mark 4:28, first the blade, **t** the head
    13:26, T THEY SHALL SEE THE SON
  Luke 20:25, **T** render to Caesar
  Rom. 3:9, What **t**? Are we better
  1 Cor. 13:12, but **t** face to face
  2 Cor. 12:10, **t** I am strong
THERE Gen. 1:3, Let **t** be light; and **t** was
  Lev. 7:7, **t** is one law for them
  Matt. 2:13, remain **t** until I tell you
    24:23, Behold, here is Christ or **t** *He is*
  Luke 8:32, **t** was a herd of many swine
  Rev. 21:25, **t** shall be no night **t**

THEREFORE 1 Pet. 4:1, **T**, since Christ has
  suffered
  1 Pet. 4:7, **t**, be of sound judgment
THICK Ex. 10:22; Deut. 32:15; Joel 2:2
THIEF Matt. 6:19, **t-s** break in and steal
  John 10:10, **t** comes only to steal
  1 Cor. 6:10, nor **t-s**, nor covetous
  1 Thess. 5:2, just like a **t** in the night
  Deut. 24:7; Job 24:14; Ps. 50:18; Prov. 29:24;
    Is. 1:23; Joel 2:9
THINE Luke 22:42, not My will, but **T** be done
  John 17:10, Mine are **T**, and **T** are Mine
THING Ps. 8:6, put all **t-s** under his feet
  Eccles. 3:1, appointed time for every-**t**
  Matt. 19:20, All these **t-s** I have kept
    19:26, with God all **t-s** are possible
    21:24, I will ask you one **t**
  Mark 9:23, All **t-s** are possible to him
    10:21, One **t** you lack
  Luke 2:19, Mary treasured ... these **t-s**
    10:42, *only* a few **t-s** are necessary
  John 14:14, ask Me any-**t** in My name
  Acts 2:44, had all **t-s** in common
  Phil. 3:13, but one **t** *I do*
    4:8, let your mind dwell on these **t-s**
  1 Tim. 4:15, Take pains with these **t-s**
  James 3:10, **t-s** ought not to be this way
  Rev. 16:3, every living **t** in the sea died
  Gen. 7:23; 15:1; Ex. 20:17; Job 42:2; Ps. 2:1;
    Eccles. 9:5; Is. 7:13; 12:5; Ezek. 8:17
THINK—*esteem, thought* Prov. 23:7, as he **t-s**
  Matt. 5:17, not **t** that I came to abolish
    22:42, do you **t** about the Christ
  John 5:39, you **t** that in them ... life
  Rom. 12:3, but to **t** so as ... sound
    14:14, to him who **t-s** anything to be unclean
  1 Cor. 13:11, child, I **t** as a child
    14:20, do not be children in your **t-ing**
  2 Cor. 11:16, no one **t** me foolish
  Gal. 6:3, anyone **t-s** he is something
  James 1:26, **t-s** himself to be religious
THIRD Ex. 20:5, **t** and fourth *generations*
  Matt. 16:21, raised up on the **t** day
  Luke 24:21, is the **t** day since
  John 21:17, said to him the **t** time
  1 Cor. 15:4, raised on the **t** day
  2 Cor. 12:2, caught up to the **t** heaven
THIRST Ps. 42:2, My soul **t-s** for God
  Matt. 5:6, **t** for righteousness
    25:35, I was **t-y**, and you gave
  John 4:13, drinks of this water shall **t**
    6:35, believes ... shall never **t**
    19:28, said, I am **t-y**
  Rom. 12:20, IF HE IS **T-Y**, GIVE HIM
  2 Cor. 11:27, in hunger and **t**
  Ex. 17:3; Judg. 15:18; Job 24:11; Ps. 69:21;
    104:11; Is. 29:8; 41:17; 49:10; 65:13; Lam.
    4:4
THIRTY Matt. 26:15, to him **t** pieces of silver
  Ex. 21:32; Num. 20:29; Judg. 10:4; 12:9; 14:12;
    Zech. 11:12; Luke 3:23
THIRTY-NINE
  2 Cor. 11:24, received ... **t** *lashes*
THIS—*something* Rev. 2:4, I have **t** against you
THISTLE Is. 34:13, Nettles and **t** in its fortified
  cities
THORN—*hook* Prov. 15:19, as a hedge of **t-s**
  Prov. 26:9, *Like* a **t** ... into the hand of
  Is. 55:13, Instead of the **t** bush the cypress
  Jer. 4:3, not sow among **t-s**
    12:13, sown wheat ... reaped **t-s**
  Matt. 7:16, Grapes ... from **t** bushes
    13:7, others fell among the **t-s**
    27:29, weaving a crown of **t-s**
  John 19:5, wearing the crown of **t-s**
  2 Cor. 12:7, a **t** in the flesh
  Gen. 3:18; Num. 33:55; Judg. 8:7; Eccles. 7:6;
    Song 2:2
THOROUGH—*diligent*
  Deut. 19:18, judges shall investigate **t-ly**

THOUGHT—*reason, motive, plot*
Gen. 6:5, t-s of his heart
1 Chr. 28:9, every intent of the t-s
Job 21:27, I know your t-s
Ps. 94:11, know the t-s of man
Is. 55:8, My t-s are not your t-s
Matt. 9:4, Jesus knowing their t-s
15:19, heart come evil t-s
THOUSAND—*countless, clan*
1 Sam. 18:7, slain his t-s . . . David his ten t-s
Job 9:3, answer Him . . . a t *times*
Ps. 84:10, a day in Thy . . . better than . . . t
91:7, t may fall . . . ten t at your right
Eccles. 7:28, found one man among a t
Mark 6:44, five t men who ate
8:9, about four t were *there*
1 Cor. 14:19, ten t words in a tongue
2 Pet. 3:8, t years as one day
Jude 14, came with many t-s of His
Lev. 26:8; Eccles. 6:6
Song 4:4; Is. 30:17; Jer. 32:18; Dan. 7:10;
Rev. 5:11
THRASH Judg. 8:7, t your bodies with the thorns
THREE Job 2:11, Job's t friends heard
Prov. 30:15, t things . . . not be satisfied
30:18, t things . . . too wonderful
30:21, t things . . . earth quakes
30:29, t things . . . are stately
Dan. 6:10, knees t times a day
Jon. 1:17, fish t days and t nights
Matt. 12:40, JONAH WAS T DAYS AND T NIGHTS
17:4, make t tabernacles here
18:20, two or t have gathered
26:34, deny Me t times
27:63, After t days I *am*
Luke 2:46, after t days they found Him
10:36, Which of these t . . . a neighbor
John 2:19, in t days I will raise it
Acts 2:41, about t thousand souls
9:9, t days without sight
1 Cor. 13:13, faith, hope, love, these t
Gen. 6:10; Ex. 34:23; Eccles. 4:12; Luke 12:52;
2 Cor. 11:25; 12:8
THRESH—*tread, beat, trample*
Deut. 25:4; 2 Sam. 24:21; 1 Chr. 21:20; Is. 21:10;
1 Tim. 5:18
THRESHING FLOOR
Matt. 3:12, thoroughly clean His t
THRESHOLD—*door* Ps. 84:10, stand at the t of
the house
THREW—*toss, put*
2 Sam. 16:13, cast stones and t dust
2 Kin. 9:33, So they t her down
Luke 9:42, t him . . . convulsion
19:35, they t their garments on the colt
THRIVE Job 8:16, He t-s before the sun
THROAT Ps. 69:3, crying; my t is parched
Rom. 3:13, T IS AN OPEN GRAVE
Ps. 5:9; 115:7; Prov. 23:2
THRONE Ps. 11:4, LORD's t is in heaven
Ps. 93:2, t is established from of old
Is. 66:1, Heaven is My t
Matt. 5:34, for it is THE T OF GOD
19:28, sit upon twelve t-s
Acts 7:49, HEAVEN IS MY T
Heb. 1:8, THY T . . . IS FOREVER AND EVER
4:16, with confidence to the t of grace
Rev. 4:2; t was standing in heaven
20:11, I saw a great white t
Gen. 41:40; Ex. 11:5; 1 Kin. 22:19
THRONG Ps. 55:14, in the house of God in the t
THROUGH Is. 43:2, the waters . . . t the fire
Matt. 19:24, camel . . . t the eye of a needle
Luke 6:1, passing t *some* grainfields
John 3:17, world should be saved t Him
Acts 10:43, bear witness that t His name
Rom. 1:8, thank my God t Jesus Christ
Gal. 4:7, then an heir t God
Eph. 2:8, you have been saved t faith
Phil. 4:13, do all things t Him
1 John 4:9, we might live t Him
Gen. 12:6; Ex. 14:16; Eccles. 10:18; Is. 62:10

THROW Gen. 37:20, t him into one of the pits
Eccles. 3:6, time to keep . . . time to t away
Luke 9:39, t-s him into a convulsion
THRUSH Jer. 8:7, the swift and the t
THRUST—*cast, push* Josh. 23:5; Prov. 12:18; 18:5
THUNDER Mark 3:17, Boanerges . . . Sons of T
John 12:29, multitude . . . saying that it had t-ed
Rev. 14:2, voice . . . like the sound of loud t
Ex. 9:23; 1 Sam. 2:10; 2 Sam. 22:14; Job 26:14;
Ps. 81:7; Is. 29:6
THWART 2 Sam. 15:34; 17:14; 1 Thess. 2:18
TIDINGS—*message, news*
Ps. 112:7, He will not fear evil t
Rom. 10:15, BRING GLAD T OF GOOD THINGS
TILL—*cultivate* Jer. 27:11; Heb. 6:7
TIMBER—*wood*
2 Chr. 2:16, cut whatever t you need
TIME—*season, day, hour* Gen. 4:3; Judg. 15:1;
Prov. 25:13
Job 22:16, snatched away before their t
Eccles. 3:1–8, appointed t for everything
9:12, man does not know his t
Is. 25:8, will swallow up death for all t
Dan. 12:7, for a t, t-s, and half a t
Hos. 10:12, it is t to seek the LORD
Matt. 2:7, ascertained from them the t
24:45, give them their food . . . proper t
26:18, My t is at hand
John 7:6, My t is not yet at hand
1 Cor. 7:29, the t has been shortened
Gal. 6:9, in due t we shall reap
1 Tim. 2:6, testimony *borne* at the proper t
Jude 18, In the last t there shall be mockers
Rev. 1:3, for the t is near
2:21, I gave her t to repent
Eccles. 7:17; Song 2:12; Amos 5:13; Hag. 1:2;
Zech. 14:7; Matt. 13:30; 24:43; Acts 5:34
TIMELY Prov. 15:23, how delightful is a t word
TIMES—*season*
1 Chr. 12:32, men who understood the t
Job 24:1, t not stored up by the Almighty
Ps. 9:9, stronghold in t of trouble
31:15, My t are in Thy hand
Dan. 2:21, changes the t and epochs
Matt. 16:3, *discern* the signs of the t
Acts 1:7, not for you to know t
Rev. 12:14, time and t and half a time
TIMID—*fearful* Matt. 8:26; Mark 4:40
TINGLE 1 Sam. 3:11; 2 Kin. 21:12; Jer. 19:3
TIP Job 38:37, Or t the water jars of the heavens
TIRED Gen. 27:46, I am t of living
TITHE—*tenth* Lev. 27:30, all the t of the land
Num. 18:26, take from . . . Israel the t
18:28, offering to the LORD from your t-s
Deut. 12:17, the t of your grain
14:22, t all the produce
Matt. 23:23, you t mint and dill
Luke 18:12, pay t-s of all that I get
Heb. 7:8, mortal men receive t-s
TODAY—*age, day, life* Gen. 41:9, mention t of
my own offenses
Ps. 2:7, T I have begotten Thee
Luke 23:43, t you shall be with Me in Paradise
Acts 13:33; Heb. 1:5, T I HAVE BEGOTTEN THEE
Heb. 13:8, Jesus Christ *is* the same . . . t
TOIL—*labor, work, trouble*
Gen. 5:29, the t of our hands
31:42, and the t of my hands
Job 9:29, Why then should I t in vain
Matt. 6:28, do not t nor do they spin
1 Cor. 15:58, knowing that your t is not *in* vain
TOLD Matt. 24:25, I have t you in advance
Mark 3:9, He t His disciples
Luke 2:18, t them by the shepherds
John 4:39, t me all the things that I *have* done
14:2, not so, I would have t you
TOMB—*grave, place*
Is. 22:16, you have hewn a t for
Matt. 23:27, like whitewashed t-s
27:52, the t-s were opened

John 11:17, been in the **t** four days
　12:17, Lazarus out of the **t**
　19:41, in the garden a new **t**, in which
　20:11, standing outside the **t** weeping
　Rev. 11:9, bodies to be laid in a **t**
TOMORROW Prov. 27:1, Do not boast about **t**
　Is. 22:13, drink, for **t** we may die
　Matt. 6:34, do not be anxious for **t**
　James 4:14, not know ... life will be like **t**
TONE—*voice* Gal. 4:20, and to change my **t**
TONGUE—*language*
　Ex. 4:10, speech and slow of **t**
　Job 5:21, hidden from the scourge of the **t**
　Ps. 5:9, They flatter with their **t**
　　34:13, keep your **t** from evil
　　57:4, their **t** a sharp sword
　　64:3, sharpened their **t** like a sword
　　140:3, sharpen their **t-s** as a serpent
　Prov. 12:18, **t** of the wise brings healing
　　15:4, soothing **t** is a tree of life
　　25:15, soft **t** breaks the bone
　Is. 30:27, His **t** is like a consuming fire
　Mark 7:35, impediment of his **t** was removed
　　16:17, they will speak with new **t-s**
　Luke 16:24, in water and cool off my **t**
　Acts 2:4, began to speak with other **t-s**
　Rom. 14:11, EVERY **t** SHALL GIVE PRAISE
　1 Cor. 13:1, with the **t-s** of men and of
　　14:4, who speaks in a **t** edifies himself
　　14:5, that you all spoke in **t-s**
　　14:14, if I pray in a **t**
　　14:39, do not forbid to speak in **t-s**
　Phil. 2:11, every **t** should confess ... Jesus
　James 3:5, **t** is a small part
　　3:8, no one can tame the **t**
　1 Pet. 3:10, REFRAIN HIS **t** FROM EVIL
　Rev. 5:9, *men* from every tribe and **t**
　Job 6:30; 20:12; 29:10; Prov. 6:17; Is. 50:4;
　　Jer. 9:8
TOOK Gen. 8:9, **t** her, and brought her into the
　ark
　Ex. 4:7, **t** it out of his bosom
TOOTH Ex. 21:24; Lev. 24:20
　Deut. 19:21, eye, **t** for **t**
　Prov. 25:19, like a bad **t**
　Matt. 5:38, EYE FOR AN EYE, AND A **t** FOR A **t**
TOP Gen. 28:12, **t** reaching to heaven
　Ex. 19:20, to the **t** of the mountain
　2 Kin. 19:26, as grass on the house **t-s**
　Matt. 27:51, veil ... torn ... from **t** to bottom
　Heb. 11:21, leaning on the **t** of his staff
TORCH Gen. 15:17, a flaming **t** which passed
　Judg. 15:5, set fire to the **t-es**
　Dan. 10:6, his eyes were like flaming **t-es**
TORE Matt. 26:65, high priest **t** his robes
　2 Sam. 13:19; 1 Kin. 11:30; Job 1:20
TORMENT Job 19:2, How long will you **t** me
　Luke 8:28, do not **t** me
　　16:23, Hades ... being in **t**
　　16:28, to this place of **t**
　2 Pet. 2:8, felt *his* righteous soul **t-ed**
　Rev. 9:5, **t** was like the **t** of a scorpion
TORN Gen. 37:33, Joseph ... been **t** to pieces
　Josh. 9:4, wineskins, worn-out and **t**
　Job 18:14, is **t** from the security
　Matt. 27:51, veil of the temple was **t**
TOSS—*shake* Job 7:4, I am continually **t-ing**
　Is. 54:11, **storm-t-ed**, and not comforted
　Acts 22:23, **t-ing** dust into the air
　Eph. 4:14, **t-ed** here and there by waves
　James 1:6, driven and **t-ed** by the wind
TOTTER Is. 24:20; 28:7
TOUCH—*handle* Gen. 3:3, not eat from it or **t** it
　Ps. 105:15, Do not **t** My anointed ones
　Matt. 9:21, If I only **t** His garment
　Mark 5:30, Who **t-ed** My garments
　Luke 24:39, it is I Myself; **t** Me and see
　1 Cor. 7:1, not to **t** a woman
　Col. 2:21, do not taste, do not **t**
　Ex. 19:12; Lev. 5:2; Job 5:19
TOWARD—*against* Rom. 8:7, is hostile **t** God

TOWER—*stronghold*
　Prov. 18:10, name ... is a strong **t**
　Matt. 21:33, AND BUILT A **t**
　Gen. 11:4; Ps. 48:12; Mic. 4:8
TRADE—*craft* Acts 18:3, he was of the same **t**
　Acts 19:25, with the workmen of similar **t-s**
TRADER 2 Chr. 9:14, the **t-s** and merchants
TRAIN—*fit, instruct* 1 Chr. 12:8, men **t-ed** for
　war
　2 Tim. 3:16, for **t-ing** in righteousness
　Heb. 5:14, senses **t-ed** to discern good and evil
　　12:11, to those who have been **t-ed**
TRAMPLE Job 9:8, **t-s** down the waves
　Prov. 25:26, *Like* a **t-d** spring
　Hab. 3:12, didst **t** the nations
TRANSCRIBE
　Prov. 25:1, proverbs ... king of Judah, **t-d**
TRANSFORM—*change*
　Rom. 12:2, **t-ed** by the renewing of
　Phil. 3:21, who will **t** the body
TRANSGRESS Num. 14:41; Josh. 7:11; Jer. 2:8
TRANSGRESSION—*trespass, sin*
　Job 14:17, My **t** is sealed up
　　33:9, pure without **t**
　Ps. 32:1, he whose **t** is forgiven
　　39:8, Deliver me from all my **t-s**
　　51:3, I know my **t-s**
　　103:12, removed our **t-s** from us
　Matt. 6:14, forgive men for their **t-s**
　Col. 2:13, forgiven us all our **t-s**
　Gen. 31:36; Ex. 34:7; Num. 14:18; Josh. 24:19;
　　Prov. 10:12; 29:6; Is. 53:5; Ezek. 18:30;
　　Matt. 6:15
TRANSGRESSOR
　Ps. 37:38, **t-s** will be ... destroyed
　　51:13, I will teach **t-s** Thy ways
　Is. 53:12, numbered with the **t-s**
　Mark 15:28, reckoned with **t-s**
　James 2:11, become a **t** of the law
TRANSLATE Ezra 4:18, has been **t-d** and read
　John 1:42, which **t-d** means Peter
TRAP—*entangle*
　Matt. 22:15, how they might **t**
　Mark 12:13, to **t** Him in a statement
TREACHEROUS
　Prov. 2:22, the **t** will be uprooted
　　13:15, way of the **t** is hard
　2 Sam. 18:13; Prov. 22:12; Is. 21:2; 24:16;
　　Jer. 3:20; Lam. 1:2; Hos. 5:7; Mal. 2:10
TREAD—*trample* Luke 10:19, **t** upon serpents
　Rev. 19:15, **t-s** the wine press
　Job 24:11; Is. 16:10; 41:25; Jer. 25:30
TREASURE—*possession, gain*
　Gen. 43:23, given you **t** in your
　Is. 33:6, fear of the LORD is his **t**
　Matt. 2:11, opening their **t-s** they presented
　　6:21, where your **t** is, there will
　　12:35, out of his good **t** brings
　　13:44, **t** hidden in the field
　　19:21, you shall have **t** in heaven
　Col. 2:3, hidden all the **t-s** of wisdom
　James 5:3, stored up your **t**
　Deut. 33:19; Job 3:21; 23:12; Prov. 21:20
TREAT Mark 12:4, **t-ed** him shamefully
　Luke 2:48, why have You **t-ed** us this way
TREE—*grove, cross* Gen. 1:11, fruit **t-s** bearing
　Gen. 2:9, **t** of life ... knowledge
　　3:8, God among the **t-s**
　Ps. 1:3, firmly planted by streams
　　37:35, like a luxuriant **t**
　　104:16, **t-s** of the LORD drink their fill
　Prov. 3:18, She is a **t** of life
　Is. 55:12, **t-s** ... will clap *their* hands
　Matt. 3:10, every **t** ... not bear good fruit
　　7:17, good **t** bears good fruit
　　12:33, **t** is known by its fruit
　Mark 8:24, see men ... like **t-s**
　Luke 19:4, climbed up into a sycamore **t**
　John 1:50, saw you under the fig **t**
　Jude 12, autumn **t-s** without fruit
　Rev. 2:7, eat of the **t** of life

TREE (Continued)
Gen. 18:4; 21:33; Deut. 20:19; 21:22; Judg. 9:8;
Prov. 27:18; Song 8:5; Is. 40:20; Mic. 4:4
TREMBLE—*fear*
1 Chr. 16:30; Ps. 96:9, T before Him ... earth
Job 26:11, pillars of heaven **t**
Ps. 4:4, T, and do not sin
Is. 13:13, make the heavens **t**, and the earth
Mark 5:33, woman fearing and **t-ing**
Phil. 2:12, with fear and **t-ing**
2 Pet. 2:10, do not **t** when they revile
Lev. 26:6; Deut. 20:3; Ps. 2:11
TRENCH 2 Kin. 3:16, valley full of **t-es**
TRESPASS—*fault*
Gal. 6:1, if a man is caught in any **t**
Eph. 2:1, dead in your **t-s** and sins
TRIAL Deut. 7:19, great **t-s** which your eyes saw
Acts 4:9, if we are on **t** today
Gal. 4:14, a **t** to you in my bodily condition
James 1:12, a man who perseveres under **t**
TRIBE Gen. 49:28, these are the twelve **t-s**
Num. 1:4, a man of each **t**
Ps. 122:4, even the **t-s** of the LORD
Matt. 24:30, all the **t-s** of the earth
Luke 22:30, judging the twelve **t-s**
TRIBULATION—*affliction*
Matt. 24:21, will be a great **t**
John 16:33, world you have **t**
Rom. 5:3, **t** brings about perseverance
12:12, persevering in **t**
Eph. 3:13, not to lose heart at my **t-s**
TRIBUNAL—*judgment*
Acts 25:10, standing before Caesar's **t**
TRIBUTE—*tax* Ezra 7:24, impose tax, **t** or toll
TRICK—*craftiness* Matt. 2:16, Herod ... **t-ed** by
the magi
Luke 20:23, He detected their **t-ery**
TRIED Ex. 2:15, Pharaoh ... **t** to kill Moses
Ps. 12:6, As silver **t** in a furnace
TRIM Ex. 30:7, when he **t-s** the lamps
TRIUMPH Ex. 32:18, sound of the cry of **t**
TROUBLE—*distress, affliction, pain*
1 Kin. 20:7, see how this man is looking for **t**
Job 4:8, plow iniquity ... who sow **t** harvest it
5:6, does **t** sprout from the ground
5:7, man is born for **t**
Ps. 9:9, A stronghold in times of **t**
25:18, my affliction and my **t**
27:5, day of **t** He will conceal
41:1, deliver him in a day of **t**
Prov. 10:10, who winks the eye causes **t**
25:20, sings songs to a **t-d** heart
31:7, remember his **t** no more
Eccles. 8:6, a man's **t** is heavy
Matt. 2:3, Herod ... heard it, he was **t-d**
Luke 6:18, **t-d** with unclean spirits
24:38, Why are you **t-d**
John 12:27, My soul has become **t-d**
Acts 20:10, Do not be **t-d**
1 Pet. 3:14, DO NOT BE **T-D**
Gen. 41:51; Ps. 77:4; 138:7; Is. 65:16; Ezek. 32:9
TRUE—*sure*
Prov. 11:18, sows righteousness ... **t** reward
Luke 16:11, entrust the **t** riches
John 1:9, There was the **t** light
6:32, gives you the **t** bread
6:55, My flesh is **t** food ... is **t** drink
7:28, He who sent Me is **t**
8:17, testimony of two men is **t**
Rom. 3:4, let God be found **t**
Phil. 4:8, whatever is **t**
Titus 1:13, This testimony is **t**
1 Pet. 5:12, the **t** grace of God
Rev. 3:14, faithful and **t** Witness
TRULY—*indeed* Josh. 7:20, T, I have sinned
Is. 45:15, T, Thou art a God who
Matt. 5:18, For I **t** say to you
John 1:51, T, **t**, I say to you
Gen. 24:49; 2 Sam. 14:5
TRUMPET—*horn* Is. 27:13, great **t** will be blown
Matt. 6:2, alms, do not sound a **t**
Ex. 19:16; Judg. 7:16

TRUST—*faith, confidence*
2 Chr. 20:20, **t** in the LORD ... **t**
Job 8:14, whose **t** a spider's web
Ps. 4:5, And **t** in the LORD
118:8, Than to **t** in man
Prov. 11:28, **t-s** in his riches will fall
31:11, husband **t-s** in her
Is. 26:4, T in the LORD forever
Jer. 7:4, Do not **t** in deceptive words
20:10, All my **t-ed** friends
Mic. 7:5, Do not **t** in a neighbor
2 Cor. 1:9, should not **t** in ourselves
Heb. 2:13, I WILL PUT MY **T** IN HIM
TRUSTWORTHY—*true*
Prov. 20:6, who can find a **t** man
1 Tim. 3:1; 4:9, It is a **t** statement
TRUTH 1 Kin. 2:4, walk before Me in **t**
Ps. 15:2, speaks **t** in his heart
119:160, Thy word is **t**
Prov. 3:3, not let kindness and **t** leave you
23:23, Buy **t**, and do not sell *it*
Matt. 22:16, we know that You are **t-ful**
Luke 4:25, But I say to you in **t**
John 1:14, full of grace and **t**
8:32, **t** shall make you free
14:6, way, and the **t**, and the life
Rom. 1:25, **t** of God for a lie
Gal. 2:5, **t** of the gospel might remain
Phil. 1:18, in pretense or in **t**
1 Tim. 3:15, pillar and support of the **t**
2 Tim. 2:15, handling ... the word of **t**
1 John 1:8, the **t** is not in us
Gen. 42:16; 1 Kin. 22:16; Is. 39:8; Zech. 8:16
TRY—*prove* Luke 14:19, oxen ... going to **t** them
Luke 19:3, **t-ing** to see who Jesus was
Deut. 4:34; Is. 22:4; Acts 9:26
TUNIC—*garment, coat* Gen. 37:3; Lev. 16:4;
Matt. 10:10; Luke 9:3
TURBAN—*diadem* Job 29:14; Ezek. 21:26
TURMOIL—*trouble* Prov. 15:16; Jer. 50:34
TURN 2 Kin. 20:10, shadow **t** backward ten steps
2 Chr. 34:2, did not **t** aside to the right or to the
left
Job 23:11, kept His way and not **t-ed** aside
Ps. 119:157, I do not **t** aside from Thy
Prov. 7:25, Do not let your heart **t** aside
Is. 45:22, T to Me, and be saved
53:6, Each ... has **t-ed** to his own way
Jer. 26:3, everyone will **t** from his evil way
Hos. 11:7, My people are bent on **t-ing** from Me
Joel 2:31, sun will be **t-ed** into darkness
Matt. 5:39, cheek, **t** to him the other
Acts 1:25, from which Judas **t-ed** aside
1 Tim. 5:15, **t-ed** aside to follow Satan
James 5:20, who **t-s** a sinner from the error
1 Pet. 3:11, T AWAY FROM EVIL
Ex. 23:2; Deut. 17:11; Ruth 1:16; 1 Kin. 20:26;
2 Kin. 17:13; Job 1:1; 2:3; 23:13; 36:21; Ps.
80:14; 119:51; Prov. 4:5; Is. 1:4; Jer. 23:20;
Joel 2:14
TUTOR—*instruct* 1 Cor. 4:15, have countless **t-s**
in Christ
TWELVE Gen. 17:20, become the father of **t**
princes
Gen. 35:22, there were **t** sons of Jacob
Matt. 10:1, summoned His **t** disciples
Mark 3:14, He appointed **t**
Luke 2:42, when He became **t**
John 11:9, **t** hours in the day
Rev. 12:1, a crown of **t** stars
TWICE—*doubly*
Gen. 41:32, repeating ... dream to Pharaoh **t**
Num. 20:11, struck the rock **t**
1 Sam. 18:11, David escaped ... **t**
Mark 14:30, before a cock crows **t**
Luke 18:12, I fast **t** a week
TWITTER Is. 38:14, *like* a crane, so I **t**
TWO—*both* Gen. 1:16, God made the **t** great
lights
Ex. 31:18, **t** tablets of the testimony

Matt. 2:16, children ... **t** years old
 5:41, one mile, go with him **t**
 6:24, No one can serve **t** masters
 18:19, **t** of you agree on earth
 19:5, **T** SHALL BECOME ONE FLESH
Luke 17:35, **t** women grinding
1 Cor. 6:16, **T** WILL BECOME ONE FLESH
Gal. 4:24, these *women* are **t** covenants
Eph. 2:15, make the **t** into one new man
Lev. 8:2; Eccles. 4:9

U

UGLY—*bad* Gen. 41:3, **u** and gaunt
UMPIRE Job 9:33, There is no **u** between us
UNAPPROACHABLE
 1 Tim. 6:16, dwells in **u** light
UNAPPROVED
 2 Cor. 13:7, though we ... appear **u**
UNAWARE Rom. 1:13, do not want you to be **u**
UNBELIEF Mark 9:24, help *me in* my **u**
 Rom. 11:23, continue in their **u**
 Heb. 3:12, an evil, **u-ing** heart
UNBELIEVERS Luke 12:46, a place with the **u**
 1 Cor. 14:23, ungifted men or **u**
 2 Cor. 6:14, bound together with **u**
UNBLEMISHED 1 Pet. 1:19, **u** and spotless
UNCEASING Rom. 9:2, sorrow and **u** grief
UNCLEAN Lev. 5:2, person touches any **u** thing
 2 Chr. 29:5, **u-ness** out from the holy place
 Job 14:4, make the clean out of the **u**
 Ps. 106:39, became **u** in their practices
 Is. 6:5, man of **u** lips
 Ezek. 4:13, eat their bread **u**
 Matt. 10:1, authority over **u** spirits
 Mark 5:13, **u** spirits entered the swine
 9:25, He rebuked the **u** spirit
 Luke 9:42, Jesus rebuked the **u** spirit
 Acts 10:14, eaten anything unholy and **u**
 Rom. 14:14, nothing is **u** in itself
 Rev. 16:13, three **u** spirits like frogs
 18:2, prison of every **u** spirit
 21:27, nothing **u** ... shall ever come into it
UNCOVER Ezek. 21:24; Hos. 7:1
UNDEFILED Heb. 7:26, holy, innocent, **u**
 Heb. 13:4, *marriage* bed *be* **u**
 James 1:27, pure and **u** religion
UNDER Ex. 23:5, lying *helpless* **u** its load
 Matt. 5:15, put it **u** the peck-measure
 John 1:50, saw you **u** the fig tree
 Rom. 3:9, Jews and Greeks are all **u** sin
 Eph. 1:22, all things ... **u** His feet
 1 Pet. 5:6, **u** the mighty hand of God
UNDERGARMENTS Lev. 6:10; 16:4; Ezek. 44:18
UNDERSTAND—*know, perceive* 1 Chr. 28:19
 Gen. 11:7, not **u** one another's speech
 Jer. 17:9, the heart ... Who can **u** it
 Matt. 15:17, Do you not **u**
 Luke 24:45, opened ... to **u** the Scriptures
 John 8:43, Why do you not **u** what I am saying
 Acts 10:34, **u** *now* that God is not one
 2 Pet. 3:16, some things hard to **u**
 Prov. 1:6; Is. 6:9; Dan. 8:17; Matt. 15:10
UNDERSTANDING—*comprehending*
 Prov. 2:2, Incline your heart to **u**
 Jer. 10:12, by His **u** He has stretched
 Matt. 15:16, Are you also still without **u**
 Eph. 4:18, being darkened in their **u**
 2 Tim. 2:7, Lord will give you **u**
 Ex. 36:1; Job 17:4; Ps. 32:9
UNDISCIPLINED 2 Thess. 3:7, not act in an **u**
 manner
 2 Thess. 3:11, leading an **u** life
UNDISTURBED Judg. 8:28, land was **u** for forty
 years
 2 Chr. 14:1, land was **u** for ten years
UNEDUCATED Acts 4:13, that they were **u** and
 untrained
UNFAITHFUL Ezra 10:2, **u** to our God
UNFATHOMABLE Rom. 11:33, How ... **u** His
 ways
UNFEELING Ps. 17:10, closed their **u** heart

UNFOLDING Ps. 119:130, **u** of Thy words gives
 light
UNFRUITFUL—*barren*
 2 Kin. 2:19, water is bad, and the land is **u**
 Matt. 13:22; Mark 4:19, and it becomes **u**
 1 Cor. 14:14, my mind is **u**
 Eph. 5:11, **u** deeds of darkness
 2 Pet. 1:8, neither useless nor **u** in the true
 knowledge
UNGIFTED—*uneducated*
 1 Cor. 14:16, the **u** say the Amen
UNGODLY—*wicked, worthless*
 Rom. 5:6, Christ died for the **u**
 Titus 2:12, to deny **u-ness**
 Jude 18, after their own **u** lusts
UNHOLY—*common*
 Acts 10:15, no *longer* consider **u**
UNIMPRESSIVE—*weak*
 2 Cor. 10:10, personal presence is **u**
UNINTENTIONALLY Lev. 4:2; 5:15; Num. 15:27
UNITE Phil. 2:2, same love, **u-d** in spirit
 Heb. 4:2, not **u-d** by faith
UNJUST—*unrighteous*
 Prov. 29:27, **u** man is abominable
 Jer. 17:11, makes a fortune, but **u-ly**
 Heb. 6:10, God is not **u** so as to forget
 1 Pet. 3:18, *the* just for *the* **u**
UNKNOWN Acts 17:23, TO AN **U** GOD
 2 Cor. 6:9, as **u** yet well-known
 Gal. 1:22, I was still **u** by sight
UNLESS—*except* Gen. 32:26, **u** you bless me
 Ps. 127:1, **U** the LORD builds the house
 Matt. 5:20, **u** your righteousness surpasses
 18:3, **u** you are converted
 24:22, **u** those days had been cut short
 Mark 13:20, **u** the Lord had shortened *those*
 days
 Luke 13:3, **u** you repent, you will ... perish
 John 3:2, **u** God is with him
 3:3, **u** one is born again
 4:48, **U** you *people* see signs
 6:53, **u** you eat the flesh
 20:25, **U** I shall see ... imprint of the nails
 Rom. 10:15, shall they preach **u** they are sent
 1 Cor. 15:36, does not come to life **u** it dies
 2 Tim. 2:5, **u** he competes according to the rules
 Deut. 32:30; Is. 1:9; Amos 3:3
UNLOVING Rom. 1:31, untrustworthy, **u**
 2 Tim. 3:3, **u**, irreconcilable
UNOCCUPIED Matt. 12:44, finds it **u**
UNPLEASANT—*evil*
 Gen. 47:9, few and **u** have been the years
UNPROFITABLE Titus 3:9, they are **u** and
 worthless
 Heb. 13:17, this would be **u** for you
UNPUNISHED Ex. 21:19; 1 Kin. 2:9
 Ex. 20:7, LORD will not leave him **u**
UNQUENCHABLE
 Matt. 3:12, burn ... chaff with **u** fire
 Mark 9:43, into the **u** fire
UNREASONING 2 Pet. 2:12, like **u** animals
UNRESTRAIN
 Prov. 29:18, no vision, people are **u-ed**
UNRIGHTEOUS—*unjust*
 Is. 55:7, the **u** man his thoughts
 Matt. 5:45, rain on *the* righteous and *the* **u**
 Luke 16:10, **u** in ... little thing is **u** also in much
 16:11, faithful in the *use of* **u** Mammon
 Rom. 3:5, God who inflicts wrath is not **u**
 1 Cor. 6:9, **u** shall not inherit the kingdom
 2 Pet. 2:9, keep the **u** under punishment
UNRIGHTEOUSNESS
 1 Cor. 13:6, not rejoice in **u**
 1 John 5:17, All **u** is sin
UNRULY 1 Thess. 5:14, admonish the **u**
 2 Thess. 3:6, who leads an **u** life
UNSETTLING Acts 15:24, **u** your souls
UNSTEADY Prov. 25:19, and an **u** foot
UNSUSPECTING Rom. 16:18, hearts of the **u**
UNTAUGHT—*uneducated*
 2 Pet. 3:16, **u** and unstable distort

UNTIE Luke 19:30, a colt ... **u** it and bring it
UNTIL John 5:17, My Father is working **u** now
UNTIMELY 1 Cor. 15:8, to one **u** born
UNTRAINED Acts 4:13, uneducated and **u** men
UNWISE Deut. 32:6, O foolish and **u** people
    Eph. 5:15, walk, not as **u** men
UNWORTHY
    Gen. 32:10, **u** of all the lovingkindness
    Luke 17:10, We are **u** slaves
UP Ex. 15:8, flowing waters stood **u** like a heap
UPHOLD Ps. 119:117, U me that I may be safe
    Is. 41:13, God, who **u-s** your right hand
UPPER 2 Sam. 11:21, woman throw an **u**
    millstone
    Luke 22:12, large, furnished, **u** room
    Acts 1:13, they went up to the **u** room
    19:1, Paul ... passed through the **u** country
UPRIGHT Deut. 32:4, Righteous and **u** is He
    Prov. 4:11, led you in **u** paths
    Eccles. 7:29, God made men **u**
    Mic. 7:2, is no **u** person among men
    Acts 14:10, Stand **u** on your feet
    1 Thess. 2:10, devoutly and **u-ly** and
        blamelessly
    Num. 23:10; Job 1:8; 4:7
UPRIGHTNESS Prov. 17:26; Is. 59:14; Mal. 2:6
UPROAR 1 Kin. 1:41, city making such an **u**
    Ps. 2:1, Why are the nations in an **u**
UPROOT   Job 19:10, has **u-ed** my hope
    Luke 17:6, Be **u-ed** and be planted
UPSET—*turn* 2 Sam. 6:6, oxen nearly **u** *it*
    Acts 17:6, men ... **u** the world have come here
    2 Tim. 2:18, **u** the faith of some
    Titus 1:11, **u-ing** whole families
UPWARD Phil. 3:14, prize of the **u** call
URGE—*constrain* Ruth 1:16, Do not **u** me to
    leave you
    Prov. 16:26, his hunger **u-s** him *on*
    Luke 24:29, And they **u-d** Him, saying
    Rom. 12:1, I **u** you therefore, brethren
URGENT 1 Sam. 21:8, king's matter was **u**
USE Gen. 21:15; Deut. 32:23
    1 Chr. 12:2, **u-ing** both the right hand and
    2 Cor. 3:12, **u** great boldness in *our* speech
    1 Tim. 5:23, **u** a little wine for the sake
USELESS Lev. 26:16, sow your seed **u-ly**
    Rom. 3:12, TOGETHER THEY HAVE BECOME U
USURIOUS Lev. 25:36, not take **u** interest from
    him
USURY—*interest* Neh. 5:10, leave off this **u**
    Prov. 28:8, increases his wealth by ... **u**
UTENSILS Ex. 31:8, the table also and its **u**
UTMOST—*remote*
    1 Thess. 2:16, wrath has come ... to the **u**
UTTER—*speak* Ps. 119:171, Let my lips **u** praise
    Acts 26:25, I **u** words of sober truth
    1 Cor. 14:9, **u** by the tongue speech
UTTERANCE Luke 21:15, give you **u** and wisdom
    Acts 2:4, Spirit was giving them **u**
    2 Cor. 8:7, in faith and **u** and knowledge
    Eph. 6:19, **u** may be given to me
UTTERLY—*greatly* Is. 42:17, be **u** put to shame
    Rom. 7:13, sin might become **u** sinful

V

VAGRANT Gen. 4:12, a **v** and a wanderer
VAIN—*empty, futile* Ps. 2:1, peoples devising a **v**
    thing
    Prov. 12:11, he who pursues **v** *things*
    1 Cor. 15:14, then our preaching is **v**
VALLEY—*ravine*
    Ps. 23:4, through the **v** of the shadow
    Song 2:1, The lily of the **v-s**
    Jer. 31:40, the whole **v** of the dead bodies
    Ezek. 37:1, **v**; and it was full of bones
    Joel 3:14, the **v** of decision
    Gen. 14:17; 19:17; Josh. 10:12; 2 Sam. 18:18;
        1 Kin. 20:28; 2 Kin. 3:16
VALUATION Lev. 5:15, according to your **v** in
    silver
    Lev. 27:25, Every **v** of yours
    Num. 18:16, redeem them, by your **v**

VALUE—*price* Matt. 10:31, you are of more **v**
    than
    Matt. 12:12, how much more **v** is a man than a
        sheep
    13:46, one pearl of great **v**
VANITY—*breath, emptiness, futility*
    Prov. 22:8, sows iniquity will reap **v**
    Eccles. 1:2, V of **v-es**! All is **v**
    2 Pet. 2:18, arrogant *words* of **v**
VARICOLORED—*colored*
    Gen. 37:3, made him a **v** tunic
    Gen. 37:23,32
VARIETY 1 Cor. 12:4, there are **v-es** of gifts
VARIOUS—*manifold*
    Matt. 4:24, taken with **v** diseases
    24:7, in **v** places there will be famines
    2 Tim. 3:6, led on by **v** impulses
    James 1:2, when you encounter **v** trials
    1 Pet. 1:6, distressed by **v** trials
VAST—*large* Is. 22:18, To be cast into a **v**
VAULT Job 22:14, walks on the **v** of heaven
VEGETABLES Deut. 11:10; 1 Kin. 21:2
    Prov. 15:17, better is a dish of **v** where love is
    Rom. 14:2, he who is weak eats **v** *only*
VEGETATION—*grass* Gen. 1:11, earth sprout **v**
    Ps. 104:14, **v** for the labor of man
    Gen. 1:12; Ps. 105:35; Is. 42:15; Jer. 12:4
VEIL Is. 25:7, **v** ... stretched over all nations
    Matt. 27:51, **v** of the temple was torn
    2 Cor. 3:13, put a **v** over his face
    Heb. 6:19, which enters within the **v**
    9:3, behind the second **v**
    Gen. 24:65; Ex. 34:33; Lev. 4:6; Song 4:1;
        Is. 47:2
VENGEANCE—*revenge*
    Lev. 19:18, You shall not take **v**
    Deut. 32:35, V is Mine
    Ps. 94:1, O LORD, God of **v**
    Is. 34:8, the LORD has a day of **v**
    Heb. 10:30, V IS MINE
    Gen. 4:15; 2 Sam. 22:48; Ps. 18:47; Jer. 15:15;
        Nah. 1:2
VENOM—*poison*
    Deut. 32:24, **v** of crawling things
    32:33, wine is the **v** of serpents
    Job 20:14, the **v** of cobras
VENTURE Job 4:2, one **v-s** a word with you
VERY Gen. 1:31, behold, it was **v** good
    Num. 12:3, Moses was **v** humble
    Judg. 3:17, Eglon was a **v** fat man
    1 Sam. 5:11, hand of God was **v** heavy
    Ps. 46:1, A **v** present help in trouble
    Matt. 17:15, an epileptic, and is **v** ill
    Mark 16:2, **v** early on the first day
    Luke 12:7, the **v** hairs of your head
    Ex. 14:10; Mark 6:26
VESSEL Num. 5:17, holy water in ... **v**
    Ps. 31:12, I am like a broken **v**
    Rom. 9:22, **v-s** of wrath
    2 Cor. 4:7, treasure in earthen **v-s**
    2 Tim. 2:21, will be a **v** for honor
    1 Pet. 3:7, as with a weaker **v**
    Rev. 2:27, AS THE **V-S** OF THE POTTER
    Ex. 7:19; 2 Kin. 4:3; Is. 22:24; Jer. 48:11
VEXATION—*wrath* Prov. 12:16, fool's **v** is
    known
VICTORIOUS Rev. 15:2, come off **v** from the
    beast
VICTORY—*deliverance*
    2 Sam. 23:10, LORD brought ... great **v**
    2 Kin. 5:1, had given **v** to Syria
    1 Chr. 11:14, the LORD saved them by a great **v**
    29:11, the glory and the **v**
    Ps. 98:1, holy arm have gained the **v**
    Matt. 12:20, HE LEADS JUSTICE TO **V**
    1 Cor. 15:54, DEATH IS SWALLOWED UP IN V
    15:55, DEATH, WHERE IS YOUR V
    1 John 5:4, **v** that has overcome the world
VIGOR Deut. 34:7, Moses ... nor his **v** abated

VINDICATE Ps. 82:3, V the weak and fatherless
  Matt. 11:19, wisdom is **v-d** by her deeds
VINE Matt. 26:29, drink . . . fruit of the **v**
  John 15:1, I am the true **v**
  Gen. 40:9; Judg. 9:12; 1 Kin. 4:25; Ps. 128:3;
    Song 2:13; Is. 36:16; Jer. 2:21; Ezek. 19:10;
    Joel 1:12; Mal. 3:11
VINEGAR Ruth 2:14; Ps. 69:21; Prov. 10:26
VINEYARD 1 Cor. 9:7, Who plants a **v**, and does
  not eat
  Gen. 9:20; Lev. 19:10; 1 Kin. 21:1; Song 1:6;
    2:15; Is. 1:8; Jer. 12:10; Matt. 20:4
VIOLATE 2 Sam. 13:12, do not **v** me
  Rom. 4:15, law, neither is there **v-ion**
VIOLENCE Gen. 6:11, earth was filled with **v**
  Ps. 55:9, **v** and strife in the city
  Prov. 4:17, drink the wine of **v**
    16:29, man of **v** entices his neighbor
  Is. 53:9, He had done no **v**
  Matt. 11:12, kingdom of heaven suffers **v**
  Gen. 49:5; Job 5:21; Ps. 27:12; Prov. 26:6;
    Is. 60:18; Jer. 22:3
VIOLENT Ps. 18:48, rescue me from the **v** man
  Ps. 37:35, seen a **v**, wicked man
  Prov. 11:16, **v** men attain riches
  Matt. 8:28, so exceedingly **v** that no one
VIPER—*adder, serpent* Job 20:16, **v-'s** tongue
  Matt. 3:7, You brood of **v-s**
  Acts 28:3, a **v** came out because of the heat
  Is. 11:8; 14:29; 30:6
VIRGIN—*maid, maiden*
  Matt. 1:23, V SHALL BE WITH CHILD
    1:25, kept her a **v**
    25:1, comparable to ten **v-s**
  Luke 1:27, **v-'s** name was Mary
  1 Cor. 7:28, if a **v** should marry
  2 Cor. 11:2, to Christ . . . a pure **v**
  Gen. 24:16; Ex. 22:16,17; Judg. 19:24; Job 31:1;
    Ps. 148:12; Jer. 2:32; 31:13
VISIBLE Eph. 5:13, **v** when . . . exposed by the
  light
VISION Prov. 29:18, Where there is no **v**
  Is. 22:1, concerning the valley of **v**
  Joel 2:28, young men will see **v-s**
  Hab. 2:2, Record the **v** And inscribe *it*
  Matt. 17:9, Tell the **v** to no one
  Acts 2:17, YOUNG MEN SHALL SEE V-S
  2 Cor. 12:1, to **v-s** and revelations
  Gen. 15:1; 1 Sam. 3:1; Job 20:8; Lam. 2:9;
    Dan. 2:19
VISIT Ex. 20:5, **v-ing** the iniquity of
  Matt. 25:36, sick, and you **v-ed** Me
  Luke 1:68, **v-ed** us . . . redemption for His
  people
  James 1:27, **v** orphans and widows
VOICE—*sound* Ps. 19:3, Their **v** is not heard
  Prov. 5:13, the **v** of my teachers
  Eccles. 5:3, the **v** of a fool
  Song 2:12, **v** of the turtledove
  Is. 28:23, Give ear and hear my **v**
  Matt. 2:18, V WAS HEARD IN RAMAH
    3:3, V OF ONE CRYING
    3:17, behold, a **v** out of the heavens
  Mark 9:7, **v** came out of the cloud
  Luke 3:4, **v** of one crying . . . wilderness
  John 5:25, **v** of the Son of God
  Acts 10:13, **v** came to him, Arise, Peter
  Rom. 10:18, V HAS GONE OUT INTO ALL
  1 Thess. 4:16, **v** of *the* archangel
  Heb. 12:26, His **v** shook the earth
  2 Pet. 2:16, dumb donkey . . . **v** of a man
  Rev. 3:20, if any one hears My **v**
    5:11, heard the **v** of many angels
  Deut. 4:30; Josh. 6:10; 2 Sam. 19:35; Job 4:10;
    Is. 40:3; Jer. 7:34; Dan. 4:31; Rev. 6:1
VOID—*empty*
  Gen. 1:2, earth was formless and **v**
  Jer. 19:7, make **v** the counsel
  Rom. 4:14, faith is made **v**
VOLUNTARILY—*willing* 1 Cor. 9:17, I do this **v**
VOLUNTEER Judg. 5:2, That the people **v-ed**

VOMIT Job 20:15, will **v** them up
  Prov. 26:11, dog that returns to its **v**
  Is. 19:14, staggers in his **v**
  Jon. 2:10, fish . . . **v-ed** Jonah up
  2 Pet. 2:22, DOG RETURNS TO ITS OWN V
VOTIVE—*vow* Lev. 7:16, his offering is a **v**
VOW—*oath, votive* Gen. 28:20, Jacob made a **v**
  Deut. 23:22, if you refrain from **v-ing**
  Judg. 11:30, Jephthah made a **v**
  2 Sam. 15:7, let me go and pay my **v**
  Ps. 22:25, I shall pay my **v-s**
  Eccles. 5:5, not **v** . . . **v** and not pay
  Matt. 5:33, MAKE FALSE V-S . . . FULFILL YOUR V-S
  Acts 18:18, he was keeping a **v**
VULTURES Matt. 24:28, the **v** will gather
  Luke 17:37, will the **v** be gathered

W

WAGED—*fought*
  Rev. 12:7, dragon and his angels **w** war
WAGES—*hire* Gen. 30:18, God has given me **w**
  Deut. 23:18, the **w** of a dog
  Job 7:2, hired man . . . waits for his **w**
  Luke 3:14, be content with your **w**
    10:7; 1 Tim. 5:18, laborer is worthy . . . **w**
  John 4:36, who reaps is receiving **w**
  2 Pet. 2:13, **w** of doing wrong
    2:15, **w** of unrighteousness
  Gen. 29:15; Ex. 2:9; Lev. 19:13; Deut. 24:15;
    Prov. 11:18; Jer. 22:13; Hag. 1:6; Zech. 8:10;
    11:12; Mal. 3:5
WAIL—*mourn, weep* Jer. 9:19, voice of **w-ing** is
  heard
  Mark 5:38, loudly weeping and **w-ing**
  Esth. 4:3; Mic. 1:8
WAIST Matt. 3:4, leather belt about his **w**
WAISTBAND Jer. 13:1, Go and buy . . . a linen **w**
WAIT Gen. 49:18, For Thy salvation I **w**
  Ps. 25:5, For Thee I **w** all day
    27:14; 37:34, W for the LORD
    119:81, I **w** for Thy word
  Prov. 1:18, **w** for their own blood
  Is. 26:8, have **w-ed** for Thee eagerly
    30:18, He **w-s** on high
  Mark 15:43, **w-ing** for the kingdom
  Luke 12:36, men who are **w-ing**
  Rom. 8:23, **w-ing** eagerly for *our* adoption
  Gal. 5:5, **w-ing** for the hope of
  Phil. 3:20, we . . . **w** for a Savior
  Ruth 3:18; 2 Kin. 5:2; Job 14:14; Lam. 3:10; Dan.
    12:12; Hos. 6:9; Mic. 7:2; Hab. 2:3; 3:16
WALK—*follow, journey* Gen. 3:8, God **w-ing** in
  the garden
  Gen. 5:24, Enoch **w-ed** with God
  Ex. 14:29, Israel **w-ed** on dry land
  Lev. 26:3, If you **w** in My statutes
  Josh. 18:8, Go and **w** through the land
  1 Sam. 2:30, **w** before Me forever
  Job 22:14, **w-s** on the vault of
  Ps. 1:1, not **w** in the counsel of
    15:2, He who **w-s** with integrity
    23:4, **w** through the valley of
    26:3, have **w-ed** in Thy truth
    39:6, man **w-s** about as a phantom
  Prov. 10:9, **w-s** in integrity **w-s** securely
  Eccles. 2:14, fool **w-s** in darkness
  Is. 2:3, we may **w** in His paths
    2:5, **w** in the light of the LORD
    3:16, **w** with heads held high
    9:2, people who **w** in darkness
  Amos 3:3, Do two men **w** together unless
  Mic. 6:8, **w** humbly with your God
  Matt. 9:5, Rise, and **w**
    14:29, Peter . . . **w-ed** on the water
  John 6:19, Jesus **w-ing** on the sea
  Acts 3:6, name of Jesus . . . **w**
    14:8, lame . . . who had never **w-ed**
  Rom. 6:4, **w** in newness of life
  1 Cor. 3:3, fleshly . . . not **w-ing** like mere men
  2 Cor. 4:2, not **w-ing** in craftiness
    5:7, **w** by faith, not by sight

WALK (Continued)
Gal. 5:16, **w** by the Spirit
6:16, **w** by this rule
Eph. 4:1, **w** in a manner worthy of
5:2, **w** in love, just as Christ also
5:8, **w** as children of light
Col. 2:6, so **w** in Him
1 Thess. 2:12, **w** in a manner worthy
1 John 2:6, **w** in the same manner as He **w-ed**
Rev. 3:4, will **w** with Me in white
21:24, nations shall **w** by its light
Deut. 33:25; 1 Kin. 2:4; Job 1:7; Eccles. 10:7;
Jer. 2:5; 9:14; Ezek. 36:12; Hos. 11:10;
Zeph. 1:17; Mal. 2:6; John 7:1
WALL Ex. 14:22, waters *were like* a **w**
Josh. 2:15, she was living on the **w**
2 Kin. 20:2, turned his face to the **w**
Neh. 4:6, So we built the **w**
Acts 9:25, **w**, lowering him in a basket
23:3, strike you, you white-washed **w**
Eph. 2:14, barrier of the dividing **w**
Heb. 11:30, **w-s** of Jericho fell
Rev. 21:12, had a great and high **w**
Gen. 49:22; 1 Kin. 20:30; Job 24:11; Ps. 18:29;
Prov. 18:11; Is. 25:4; Jer. 52:4; Ezek. 4:2;
8:7; 12:5; Joel 2:9; Amos 7:7; Hab. 2:11
WANDER—*flee* Gen. 21:14, **w-ed** about in the wilderness
Ps. 55:7, I would **w** far away
119:21, Who **w** from Thy commandments
Prov. 27:8, bird ... **w-s** from her nest
1 Tim. 6:10, **w-ed** away from the faith
Jude 13, **w-ing** stars, for whom
Job 15:23; Is. 35:8; Lam. 4:14; Hos. 9:17
WANT—*lack, need*
Job 30:3, From **w** and famine they are
Ps. 23:1, shepherd, I shall not **w**
Prov. 28:27, who gives to the poor never **w**
Mark 9:35, If any one **w-s** to be first
Luke 23:8, Herod ... had **w-ed** to see Him
Gal. 4:21, you who **w** to be under law
WAR—*fight, quarrel, battle* Gen. 14:2; Ex. 13:17
Josh. 11:23, the land had rest from **w**
Ps. 46:9, makes **w-s** to cease
55:21, his heart was **w**
76:3, weapons of **w**
Eccles. 3:8, A time for **w**
Is. 2:4, never ... will they learn **w**
Dan. 9:26, to the end there will be **w**
Matt. 24:6, hearing of **w-s** and rumors of **w-s**
Rom. 7:23, waging **w** against the law of my
2 Cor. 10:3, do not **w** according to the flesh
James 4:1, wage **w** in your members
1 Pet. 2:11, which wage **w** against the soul
Rev. 12:7, there was **w** in heaven
19:11, He judges and wages **w**
Num. 21:14; Prov. 20:18; Mic. 2:8; Rev. 2:16
WAR-CLUB Jer. 51:20, You are My **w**
WARD Dan. 4:35, no one can **w** off His hand
WARFARE 2 Sam. 17:8, father is an expert in **w**
2 Cor. 10:4, weapons of our **w** are not
WARM Eccles. 4:11, two lie down ... keep **w**
Mark 14:54, **w-ing** himself at the fire
John 18:25, Peter was standing and **w-ing** himself
James 2:16, be **w-ed** and be filled
1 Kin. 1:1; 2 Kin. 4:34; Job 31:20; Is. 47:14;
Hag. 1:6
WARN Ezek. 33:8, speak to **w** the wicked
Matt. 2:12, having been **w-ed** *by God*
2:22, **w-ed** *by God* in a dream
3:7, vipers, who **w** you to flee
Titus 3:10, after a first and second **w-ing**
Heb. 8:5, Moses was **w-ed** *by God*
11:7, being **w-ed** *by God*
2 Kin. 6:10; Eccles. 12:12
WARRIOR Job 16:14; Eccles. 9:11
WASH—*bathe, cleanse* 2 Kin. 5:10, Go ... **w** in the Jordan
Ps. 26:6, **w** my hands in innocence
51:2, **W** me ... from my iniquity

Is. 1:16, **W** yourselves, make yourselves clean
Matt. 6:17, **w** your face
15:2, not **w** their hands when
Luke 11:38, first ... **w-ed** before the meal
John 9:7, Go, **w** in the pool of Siloam
Acts 22:16, **w** away your sins
1 Cor. 6:11, you were **w-ed** ... sanctified
1 Tim. 5:10, she has **w-ed** the saints' feet
Heb. 6:2, instruction about **w-ings**
9:10, drink and various **w-ings**
10:22; bodies **w-ed** with pure water
Gen. 18:4; Ex. 19:10; 1 Kin. 22:38; Job 9:30; Jer.
4:14; Ezek. 16:9
WASTE Prov. 23:8, And **w** your compliments
Matt. 12:25; Luke 11:17, kingdom ... laid **w**
26:8, What is the point of this **w**
Rev. 18:19, in one hour she has been laid **w**
Lev. 26:31; Ps. 79:7; Is. 5:6; 45:18; Jer. 33:12;
Ezek. 6:6; Joel 1:7
WATCH—*observe, guard* Gen. 31:49, Lord **w**
Ps. 63:6, in the night **w-es**
Prov. 4:23, **W** over your heart with all diligence
8:34, **W-ing** daily at my gates
Eccles. 11:4, He who **w-es** the wind will not sow
Matt. 26:40, could not keep **w** with Me
Luke 2:8, keeping **w** over their flock
Heb. 13:17, they keep **w** over your souls
Ex. 14:24; 2 Kin. 11:5; Job 7:20; Prov. 4:26;
Zech. 11:11
WATCHMAN Is. 21:11, **W**, how far gone is the night
2 Kin. 9:17; Song 3:3; Hos. 9:8
WATER Gen. 1:2, over the surface of the **w-s**
Ex. 2:10, drew him out of the **w**
15:8, The flowing **w-s** stood up
2 Sam. 14:14, like **w** spilled on the ground
Job 14:19, **W** wears away stones
Ps. 1:3, planted by streams of **w**
23:2, beside quiet **w-s**
106:32, wrath at the **w-s** of Meribah
Prov. 9:17, Stolen **w** is sweet
Eccles. 11:1, your bread on the ... **w-s**
Is. 1:30, garden that has no **w**
11:9, As the **w-s** cover the sea
Jer. 2:13, fountain of living **w-s**
Matt. 3:11, baptize you in **w**
10:42, little ones even a cup of cold **w**
Mark 14:13, man ... carrying a pitcher of **w-s**
Luke 7:44, gave Me no **w** for My feet
John 3:5, unless one is born of **w**
4:10, given you living **w**
Acts 1:5, John baptized with **w**
8:36, Look! **W**! What prevents
1 Cor. 3:6, I planted, Apollos **w-ed**
Eph. 5:26, washing of **w** with the word
1 Tim. 5:23, No longer drink **w** *exclusively*
James 3:11, fresh and bitter **w**
1 Pet. 3:20, eight persons ... through *the* **w**
1 John 5:6, who came by **w** and blood
Rev. 22:17, take the **w** of life without cost
Gen. 24:43; Ex. 20:4; Deut. 8:7; Josh. 7:5;
Judg. 5:4; 6:38; 1 Kin. 13:22; 2 Kin. 3:11;
Neh. 9:11; Job 8:11; 11:16; Ps. 22:14; 46:3;
Prov. 5:15; 20:5; Song 5:12; Is. 19:5; 32:2;
Jer. 8:14; Lam. 1:16; Ezek. 4:11; 7:17; Dan.
1:12; 2 Pet. 3:5
WATERLESS Matt. 12:43, unclean spirit ...
passes through **w**
WAVE Ps. 42:7, Thy **w-s** have rolled over me
Is. 48:18, righteousness like the **w-s**
Matt. 8:24, covered with the **w-s**
Mark 4:37, **w-s** were breaking over the boat
Jude 13, wild **w-s** of the sea
2 Sam. 22:5; Job 9:8; Zech. 2:9
WAX Ps. 22:14, My heart is like **w**
WAY—*journey, manner, path, road*
Gen. 3:24, **w** to the tree of life
Josh. 23:14, the **w** of all the earth
Job 3:23, a man whose **w** is hidden

Ps. 1:6, the **w** of the righteous
  18:30, His **w** is blameless
  25:8, instructs sinners in the **w**
Is. 30:21, This is the **w**, walk in it
Jer. 12:1, **w** of the wicked prospered
Ezek. 3:18, wicked from his wicked **w**
Matt. 2:12, departed . . . by another **w**
  3:3, READY THE **W** OF THE LORD
  6:9, Pray, then, in this **w**
  7:13, the **w** is broad
  15:32, lest they faint on the **w**
Mark 1:3, MAKE READY THE **W** OF THE LORD
  9:33, What were you discussing on the **w**
Luke 1:79, into the **w** of peace
John 1:23, STRAIGHT THE **W** OF THE LORD
  14:6, I am the **w**, and the truth, and
Acts 9:2, found any belonging to the **W**
1 Cor. 12:31, a still more excellent **w**
2 Cor. 4:8, afflicted in every **w**
Heb. 10:20, by a new and living **w**
James 5:20, from the error of his **w**
2 Pet. 2:2, **w** of the truth will be maligned
  2:15, forsaking the right **w**
Jude 11, gone the **w** of Cain
1 Sam. 12:23; 2 Sam. 22:33; Neh. 9:19; Ps. 50:23;
  Prov. 7:27; 12:15; Is. 26:7; 40:3; Jer. 2:36;
  6:16; Nah. 1:3; Mal. 3:1
WAYS Deut. 8:6, to walk in His **w**
2 Kin. 17:13, Turn from your evil **w**
Prov. 6:6, ant . . . Observe her **w**
Is. 2:3, teach us concerning His **w**
Hab. 3:6, His **w** are everlasting
Rom. 11:33, unfathomable His **w**
1 Cor. 4:17, **w** which are in Christ
James 1:8, unstable in all his **w**
Judg. 5:6; Prov. 3:17; Lam. 3:40; Ezek. 7:3
WEAK—*unimpressive*
Matt. 26:41; Mark 14:38, but the flesh is **w**
Acts 20:35, you must help the **w**
Rom. 4:19, without becoming **w** in faith
1 Cor. 1:27, **w** things of the world
  4:10, we are **w**, but you are strong
1 Thess. 5:14, help the **w**
Num. 13:18; Judg. 16:17; Is. 14:10; Joel 3:10
WEAKNESS—*infirmity*
Rom. 15:1, bear the **w-es** of those
1 Cor. 1:25, **w** of God is stronger than
  2:3, with you in **w** and in fear
  15:43, it is sown in **w**
2 Cor. 12:9, power is perfected in **w**
  13:4, crucified because of **w**
Heb. 4:15, sympathize with our **w-es**
  11:34, from **w** were made strong
WEALTH—*substance, prosperity* Gen. 31:1
Deut. 8:18, giving you power to make **w**
2 Chr. 1:11, not ask for riches, **w**
Job 5:5, schemer is eager for their **w**
Ps. 49:6, those who trust in their **w**
Prov. 3:9, Honor the LORD from your **w**
  13:7, poor, but has great **w**
  13:11, **W** *obtained* by fraud
Eccles. 5:19, given riches and **w**
Is. 45:3, hidden **w** of secret places
Hag. 2:7, come with the **w** of all nations
2 Cor. 8:2, **w** of their liberality
Rev. 3:17, rich, and have become **w-y**
  18:19, became rich by her **w**
Ruth 2:1; Job 20:10; Prov. 23:4; Is. 5:17
WEAPONS—*armor*
Eccles. 9:18, Wisdom is better than **w**
Jer. 21:4, turn back the **w** of war
Ezek. 32:27, down to Sheol with their **w**
2 Cor. 6:7, **w** of righteousness
  10:4, **w** of our warfare
Deut. 1:41; 1 Sam. 31:9; 2 Chr. 23:10; Neh. 4:17;
  Job 20:24
WEAR Deut. 22:5, woman shall not **w** man's
  clothing
Job 14:19, Water **w-s** away stones
John 19:5, Jesus . . . **w-ing** the crown of
James 2:3, who is **w-ing** the fine clothes
1 Pet. 3:3, and **w-ing** gold jewelry

Ex. 18:18; Deut. 8:4; Is. 50:9; Dan. 7:25;
  Matt. 11:8
WEARY—*faint, exhaust*
Job 3:17, there the **w** are at rest
Prov. 23:4, Do not **w** yourself to gain riches
  25:25, cold water to a **w** soul
Eccles. 12:12, **w-ing** to the body
Is. 5:27, No one in it is **w** or stumbles
  40:29, strength to the **w**
  40:31, They will walk and not become **w**
  50:4, sustain the **w** one with a word
Hab. 2:13, nations grow **w** for nothing
Matt. 11:28, Come to Me, all who are **w**
John 4:6, **w-ed** from His journey
Gal. 6:9, if we do not grow **w**
2 Sam. 17:2; Ps. 69:3; Prov. 25:17; Jer. 6:11
WEATHER—*day* Matt. 16:2, *will be* fair **w**
WEAVE—*embroider* Ex. 28:39; 38:23
WEB Job 18:8, he steps on the **w-ing**
WEDDING—*marriage* Song 3:11, day of his **w**
John 2:1, there was a **w** in Cana
WEEK Gen. 29:27, Complete the bridal **w**
Ex. 34:22, celebrate the Feast of **W-s**
Dan. 9:24, Seventy **w-s** have been decreed
Matt. 28:1, first *day* of the **w**
Luke 18:12, I fast twice a **w**
WEEP 1 Sam. 1:8, Hannah, why do you **w**
Neh. 8:9, do not mourn or **w**
Job 16:16, face is flushed from **w-ing**
  16:20, My eye **w-s** to God
Eccles. 3:4, A time to **w**, and a time to laugh
Matt. 2:18, RACHEL **W-ING** FOR HER
  13:42, **w-ing** and gnashing of
Mark 5:39, Why make a commotion and **w**
Luke 6:21, Blessed *are* you who **w** now
  7:32, you did not **w**
John 11:31, to the tomb to **w** there
Acts 9:39, widows stood beside him **w-ing**
Rom. 12:15, who rejoice, and **w** with
James 4:9, miserable and mourn and **w**
Rev. 5:4, I *began* to **w** greatly
  5:5, Stop **w-ing**; behold, the Lion
Gen. 43:30; Num. 11:13; Deut. 34:8; Judg. 11:37;
  Ps. 6:8; Is. 22:4; Jer. 9:1; Joel 1:5
WEIGH Prov. 16:2, the LORD **w-s** the motives
Dan. 5:27, you have been **w-ed** on the scales
Gen. 23:16; 24:22; 1 Sam. 2:3; Job 6:2; Ps. 58:2
WEIGHT Lev. 19:36, just balances, just **w-s**
Prov. 11:1, a just **w** is His delight
Ezek. 4:16, will eat bread by **w**
2 Cor. 4:17, eternal **w** of glory
Deut. 25:15; Job 28:25; Mic. 6:11
WELFARE 1 Sam. 17:18, the **w** of your brothers
WELL—*health, whole* Gen. 43:28, father is **w**
Deut. 4:40, that it may go **w** with you
1 Sam. 9:10, **W** said; come
2 Sam. 18:29, Is it **w** with the young man
Eccles. 12:6, pitcher by the **w** is shattered
Matt. 3:17, whom I am **w** pleased
Mark 7:37, has done all things **w**
Luke 5:31, not . . . **w** who need a physician
  6:26, men speak **w** of you
John 4:6, Jacob's **w** was there
  5:6, Do you wish to get **w**
Gal. 5:7, You were running **w**
1 Tim. 3:4, his own household **w**
Gen. 4:7; Lev. 24:16; 2 Sam. 17:21; 20:9; 1 Chr.
  11:17; Prov. 5:15; Eccles. 8:13; Song 4:15;
  Acts 15:29
WENT Is. 38:8, sun's *shadow* **w** back ten steps
Mark 1:28, news about Him **w** out
Jude 7, **w** after strange flesh
WEPT—*weep* Gen. 50:17, Joseph **w** when they
Matt. 26:75, went out and **w** bitterly
Luke 19:41, city and **w** over it
John 11:35, Jesus **w**
WEST Gen. 12:8, with Bethel on the **w**
Ex. 10:19, a very strong **w** wind
Ps. 107:3, east and from the **w**
Dan. 8:4, saw the ram butting **w-ward**

WET—*drench* Job 24:8, **w** with the mountain rains
  Luke 7:44, **w** My feet with her tears
WHATEVER—*all* Ps. 1:3, in **w** he does, he prospers
  Eccles. 9:10, **W** your hand finds to do
  Matt. 7:12, **w** you want others to do for you
  Luke 12:3, **w** you have said in the dark
  John 11:22, **w** You ask of God
  Rom. 14:23, **w** is not from faith is sin
  1 Cor. 10:31, eat or drink or **w** you do
  Gal. 6:7, for **w** a man sows
  Eph. 6:8, **w** good things each one does
  Phil. 4:8, **w** is true, **w** is honorable
  Col. 3:17, **w** you do in word or deed
  Gen. 31:16; Job 37:12
WHEAT—*kernel* Matt. 3:12, gather His **w** into the barn
  Luke 22:31, to sift you like **w**
  John 12:24, unless a grain of **w** falls
  Rev. 6:6, quart of **w** for a denarius
  Gen. 30:14; Ex. 34:22; Deut. 8:8; Judg. 6:11;
    1 Sam. 12:17; Job 31:40
WHEEL—*whirl* Eccles. 12:6, **w** at the cistern is crushed
  Is. 5:28, **w-s** like a whirlwind
  Ezek. 1:16, one **w** were within another
  1 Kin. 7:33; Prov. 20:26; Dan. 7:9; Nah. 3:2
WHELP Gen. 49:9; Deut. 33:22
WHERE Gen. 3:9, **W** are you
  Ruth 1:17, **W** you die, I will die
  Job 28:12, **w** can wisdom be found
  Ps. 42:3, **W** is your God
  139:7, **W** can I go from Thy Spirit
  Prov. 29:18, **W** there is no vision
  Is. 19:12, **w** are your wise men
  Matt. 2:2, **W** is He who has been born
  Luke 8:25, **W** is your faith
  John 8:19, **W** is Your Father
    8:21, **w** I am going, you cannot come
    11:34, **W** have you laid him
  Rom. 4:15, **w** there is no law
  Gen. 28:15; 1 Sam. 27:10; 1 Cor. 1:20
WHILE—*moment* Is. 26:20, Hide for a little **w**
  John 5:35, willing to rejoice for a **w**
WHIP 1 Kin. 12:11, disciplined you with **w-s**
  Prov. 26:3, A **w** is for the horse
  Nah. 3:2, The noise of the **w**
WHIRL Ps. 83:13, God, make them ... **w-ing** dust
WHIRLWIND—*storm, wind*
  2 Kin. 2:1, Elijah by a **w** to
  Ps. 58:9, sweep them away with a **w**
  Prov. 1:27, calamity comes on ... **w**
  Jer. 4:13; Hos. 8:7
WHISPER Ps. 41:7, hate me **w** together
WHITE Gen. 49:12, teeth **w** from milk
  Ps. 51:7, I shall be **w-r** than snow
  Is. 1:18, They will be as **w** as snow
  Matt. 5:36, make one hair **w** or black
  Luke 9:29, clothing *became* **w** *and* gleaming
  John 4:35, they are **w** for harvest
  Acts 23:3, you **w-washed** wall
  Rev. 6:2, and behold, a **w** horse
  Num. 12:10; Job 6:6; Dan. 7:9
WHOLE Gen. 2:6, water the **w** surface
  Matt. 6:22, **w** body will be full of light
  1 Cor. 5:6, leavens the **w** lump
  1 John 2:2, *those of* the **w** world
WICK—*flax* Matt. 12:20, SMOLDERING **W** HE WILL NOT PUT OUT
WICKED—*evil, lawless, ungodly* Ex. 23:1
  Ps. 1:1, not walk in the counsel of the **w**
  Prov. 4:19, way of the **w** is like darkness
    10:30, **w** will not dwell in the land
    11:7, When a **w** man dies
    13:9, lamp of the **w** goes out
  Is. 53:9, His grave ... with **w** men
  Acts 17:5, taking along some **w** men from the
    24:15, both the righteous and the **w**
  Job 8:22; 10:15; 11:20; Ps. 10:13; 12:8; 17:13;
    Eccles. 7:17; Ezek. 3:18; Dan. 12:10

WICKEDNESS—*evil* Gen. 6:5, the **w** of man was great
  Ps. 10:7, Under his tongue is ... **w**
  Prov. 4:17, they eat the bread of **w**
  Is. 9:18, **w** burns like a fire
    32:6, his heart inclines toward **w**
  Acts 8:22, repent of this **w** of yours
  Eph. 6:12, spiritual *forces* of **w** in the heavenly
    Judg. 20:3; Jer. 14:20; Ezek. 3:19;
    Hos. 10:13
WIDE Nah. 3:13, gates of your land are opened **w**
  Matt. 7:13, for the gate is **w**
    28:15, story was **w-ly** spread
WIDOW Matt. 23:14, you devour **w-s** houses
  Mark 12:43, **w** put in more than all
  Luke 18:5, this **w** bothers me
  1 Tim. 5:3, Honor **w-s** who are **w-s** indeed
  Gen. 38:11; Ex. 22:22; Lev. 21:14; 2 Sam. 14:5;
    Job 22:9; Ps. 68:5; Is. 1:17
WIELD Judg. 5:14, those who **w** the staff of office
WIFE Gen. 2:24, shall cleave to his **w**
  Ex. 20:17, not covet your neighbor's **w**
  Prov. 12:4, excellent **w** ... crown of her husband
    18:22, finds a **w** finds a good thing
  Matt. 5:31, WHOEVER DIVORCES HIS **W**
  Luke 17:32, Remember Lot's **w**
  1 Cor. 7:2, each man have his own **w**
  Eph. 5:23, husband ... head of the **w**
  1 Tim. 3:2, husband of one **w**
  Lev. 18:15; Job 31:10; Ps. 128:3
WILD Gen. 37:20,33, **w** beast devoured him
  Mark 1:6, John ... diet was locusts and **w** honey
  Gen. 16:12; Job 11:12; Ps. 104:11
WILDERNESS—*desert*
  Deut. 29:5, forty years in the **w**
  Is. 35:6, waters will break forth in the **w**
    40:3, Clear the way ... LORD in the **w**
    43:19, make a roadway in the **w**
  Matt. 3:1, preaching ... **w** of Judea
    3:3, VOICE ... CRYING IN THE **W**
    4:1, led ... into the **w** to be tempted
    24:26, Behold, He is in the **w**
  Mark 1:13, He was in the **w** forty days
  John 6:31, Our fathers ate manna in the **w**
  1 Cor. 10:5, laid low in the **w**
  Heb. 3:8, DAY OF TRIAL IN THE **W**
  Rev. 12:6, woman fled into the **w**
  Gen. 16:7; Ex. 5:3; 14:11; 19:2; Lev. 7:38; Ps.
    65:12; 102:6; Is. 51:3; Jer. 2:6; 17:6
WILL Ps. 40:8, delight to do Thy **w**
  Matt. 6:10, Thy **w** be done
    7:21, who does the **w** of My Father
  Mark 3:35, whoever does the **w** of God
  Luke 22:42, not My **w**, but Thine be done
  John 1:13, **w** of the flesh ... **w** of man
    4:34, **w** of Him who sent Me
  Acts 21:14, **w** of the Lord be done
  Rom. 12:2, may prove what the **w** of God is
  1 Cor. 4:19, if the Lord **w-s**
  Eph. 5:17, what the **w** of the Lord is
  Phil. 2:13, both to **w** and to work
  Heb. 10:9, HAVE COME TO DO THY **W**
  James 4:15, If the Lord **w-s**, we shall live
WILLING Ps. 51:12, with a **w** spirit
  Matt. 26:41, spirit is **w** ... flesh is weak
  Luke 22:42, Father, if Thou art **w**
  Gen. 24:5; Ex. 35:5; 1 Chr. 28:9
WIN—*gain* Prov. 11:30, he who is wise **w-s** souls
  Matt. 28:14, we will **w** him over and keep
  Luke 21:19, perseverance you will **w** ... souls
  1 Cor. 9:20, that I might **w** the Jews
    9:24, Run in such a way that you may **w**
WIND—*breath, whirlwind*
  Job 16:3, no limit to **w-y** words
  Ps. 1:4, chaff which the **w** drives
  Is. 17:13, like the chaff ... before the **w**
  Matt. 7:25, floods came, and the **w-s** blew
    11:7, reed shaken by the **w**
  Mark 4:41, **w** and the sea obey Him

Luke 8:24, He rebuked the **w**
John 3:8, **w** blows where it wishes
Acts 2:2, noise like a violent, rushing **w**
Eph. 4:14, every **w** of doctrine
Heb. 1:7, MAKES HIS ANGELS **W-S**
James 3:4, are driven by strong **w-s**
Jude 12, carried along by **w-s**
Gen. 8:1; 1 Kin. 19:11; 2 Kin. 3:17; Prov. 11:29;
   Eccles. 5:16; Song 4:16; Is. 7:2; Jer. 22:22;
   Ezek. 37:9; Hos. 8:7; Rev. 6:13
WINDOW Josh. 2:15, by a rope through the **w**
Acts 20:9, sitting on the **w-sill**
2 Cor. 11:33, through a **w** in the wall
Judg. 5:28; 2 Kin. 7:2; Jer. 9:21; Joel 2:9
WINE—*vinegar* Lev. 10:9, Do not drink **w**
Ps. 60:3, Thou hast given us **w** to drink
Jer. 35:6, We will not drink **w**
Matt. 9:17, new **w** into old wineskins
   27:48, sponge, he filled it with sour **w**
Mark 15:23, give Him **w** mixed with myrrh
Luke 10:34, pouring oil and **w** on *them*
John 2:3, when the **w** gave out
   2:9, water which had become **w**
   19:29, A jar full of sour **w**
Acts 2:13, are full of sweet **w**
Eph. 5:18, do not get drunk with **w**
1 Tim. 3:3, not addicted to **w**
 Rev. 6:6, not harm the oil and the **w**
Gen. 9:24; 1 Sam. 1:14; 2 Sam. 13:28; Prov. 3:10;
   Eccles. 9:7; Song 1:2; Is. 5:22
WINESKIN—*jug* Job 32:19, Like new **w-s** it is
Ps. 119:83, like a **w** in the smoke
Matt. 9:17; Mark 2:22, new wine ... fresh **w-s**
Josh. 9:13; Luke 5:37
WINGS—*feathers* Job 39:13, ostriches' **w** flap
Ps. 17:8, in the shadow of Thy **w**
   91:4, under His **w** you may seek refuge
Prov. 23:5, *wealth* certainly makes itself **w**
Mal. 4:2, with healing in its **w**
Matt. 23:37, chicks under her **w**
Luke 13:34, her brood under her **w**
Ex. 19:4; Lev. 1:17; Deut. 32:11; Ruth 2:12;
   2 Sam. 22:11; Is. 6:2; Jer. 48:9; Ezek. 1:6;
   Zech. 5:9
WINK Ps. 35:19; Prov. 6:13
WINNOW Is. 30:24; 41:16; Matt. 3:12
WINTER Gen. 8:22; Song 2:11; 1 Cor. 16:6
WIPE—*blot, erase* Is. 25:8, God will **w** tears
Is. 44:22, **w-d** out your transgressions
John 11:2, **w-d** His feet with her hair
Acts 3:19, Repent ... sins may be **w-ed** away
Rev. 21:4, He shall **w** away every tear
WISDOM Ex. 28:3, endowed with the spirit of **w**
1 Kin. 2:6, act according to your **w**
2 Chr. 1:10, Give me now **w**
Job 12:2, with you **w** will die
Ps. 51:6, make me know **w**
Prov. 1:7, Fools despise **w** and instruction
   4:5, Acquire **w**! Acquire understanding
   24:3, By a **w** a house is built
Eccles. 1:18, in much **w** there is much grief
   7:12, **w** preserves the lives
Jer. 9:23, wise man boast of his **w**
Mic. 6:9, it is sound **w** to fear Thy name
Matt. 11:19, **w** is vindicated by her deeds
Luke 2:52, Jesus kept increasing in **w** and
   stature
   21:15, give you utterance and **w**
2 Cor. 1:12, not in fleshly **w**
2 Tim. 3:15, **w** that leads to salvation
James 1:5, if any of you lacks **w**
Rev. 13:18, Here is **w**
WISE—*shrewd* Gen. 3:6, tree ... to make one **w**
Job 17:10, I do not find a **w** man
Ps. 19:7, making **w** the simple
Prov. 3:7, not be **w** in your own eyes
Luke 10:21, hide these things from *the* **w**
Rom. 1:14, the **w** and to the foolish
1 Cor. 1:19, DESTROY THE WISDOM OF THE **W**
   3:18, that he may become **w**
Eph. 5:15, not as unwise men, but as **w**

James 3:13, Who ... is **w** and understanding
Is. 19:12; Hos. 13:13
WISH—*desire*
Luke 5:39, drinking old *wine* **w-es** for new
Luke 8:20, brothers are ... **w-ing**
   10:24, prophets and kings **w-ed** to see
John 16:19, Jesus knew they **w-ed** to question
1 Cor. 10:27, If one ... invites you, and you **w**
2 Pet. 3:9, not **w-ing** for any to perish
WITHDRAW Josh. 8:26; 1 Sam. 14:19
WITHER Ps. 1:3, leaf does not **w**
Ps. 37:2, **w** quickly like the grass
   102:11, I **w** away like grass
Is. 34:4, As a leaf **w-s** from the vine
   64:6, **w** like a leaf
Jer. 8:13, the leaf shall **w**
Zech. 11:17, His arm will be totally **w-ed**
Matt. 13:6, had no root, they **w-ed**
Mark 3:1, man ... with a **w-ed** hand
   11:20, fig tree **w-ed** from the roots up
James 1:11, **w-s** the grass
WITHHELD Job 22:7, from the hungry you ... **w**
   bread
Hag. 1:10, sky has **w** its dew
WITHHOLD Prov. 11:24,26
WITHIN Ps. 51:10, renew a steadfast spirit **w** me
Jer. 31:33, put My law **w** them
Mark 7:23, evil things proceed from **w**
1 Cor. 5:12, not judge those who are **w** *the*
   church
2 Cor. 7:5, conflicts without, fears **w**
Prov. 22:18; Ezek. 11:19
WITHOUT 2 Chr. 15:3, Israel was **w** the true God
Is. 52:3, redeemed **w** money
Matt. 13:57, prophet is not **w** honor
Mark 14:58, made **w** hands
John 8:7, He who is **w** sin
Rom. 12:9, love be **w** hypocrisy
2 Cor. 7:5, conflicts **w**, fears within
Eph. 2:12, no hope and **w** God in the world
1 Thess. 5:17, pray **w** ceasing
1 Tim. 6:14, commandment **w** stain
Heb. 7:3, **W** father, **w** mother, **w** genealogy
   13:2, entertained angels **w** knowing it
James 2:20, faith **w** works is useless
2 Pet. 2:17, are springs **w** water
Jude 12, **w** fear ... **w** water ... **w** fruit
Job 5:9; 8:11; Hos. 7:11; Col. 2:11
WITNESS—*advocate, testimony*
Ex. 4:8, **w** of the last sign
   20:16, shall not bear false **w**
Judg. 11:10, LORD is **w** between us
Job 21:29, do you not recognize their **w**
Ps. 89:37, **w** in the sky is faithful
Matt. 19:18; Mark 10:19, NOT BEAR FALSE **W**
John 1:7, he might bear **w** of the light
   1:32, John bore **w** saying, I have
   3:11, bear **w** ... do not receive our **w**
   5:39, these that bear **w** of Me
   8:14, **w** of Myself, My **w** is true
   21:24, we know his **w** is true
1 Cor. 15:15, found *to be* false **w-es** of God
2 Cor. 1:23, God as **w** to my soul
Phil. 1:8, For God is my **w**
Heb. 10:15, Holy Spirit also bears **w**
1 John 5:8, three that bear **w**
   5:9, If we receive the **w** of men
Rev. 1:5, Christ, the faithful **w**
Gen. 31:48; Deut. 4:26; Job 16:19; Prov. 6:19;
   Is. 19:20
WIVES Deut. 17:17, Neither shall he multiply **w**
Eph. 5:22, **W** *be subject* to ... husbands
1 Pet. 3:1, you **w**, be submissive
   3:7, husbands, live with your **w**
WOE Prov. 23:29, Who has **w**?
Mark 14:21, **w** to that man by whom
Rev. 8:13, **W**, **w**, **w** ... who dwell on the earth
   18:10,16,19, **W**, **w**, the great city
Num. 21:29; Job 10:15; Ps. 120:5; Is. 6:5;
   Jer. 4:13; 44:11; Matt. 11:21
WOLF Is. 65:25, **w** and the lamb shall graze
Matt. 7:15, inwardly are ravenous **w-s**
   10:16, sheep in the midst of **w-s**
Gen. 49:27; Jer. 5:6

WOMAN Gen. 2:23, She shall be called **W**
Ex. 2:9, **w** took the child
Deut. 22:5, **w** shall not wear man's clothing
Ruth 2:5, Whose young **w** is this
  3:11, you are a **w** of excellence
Job 14:1, Man, who is born of **w**
Prov. 11:16, gracious **w** attains honor
Is. 49:15, **w** forget her nursing child
Matt. 5:28, looks on a **w** to lust for her
  15:28, O **w**, your faith is great
Luke 7:44, said to Simon, Do you see this **w**
  10:38, a **w** named Martha
John 4:7, **w** of Samaria to draw water
  8:4, **w** has been caught in adultery
Acts 9:36, **w** abounding with deeds of kindness
1 Cor. 7:1, a man not to touch a **w**
  7:2, each **w** have her own husband
  14:35, a **w** to speak in church
Gal. 4:4, His Son, born of a **w**
1 Tim. 2:11, Let a **w** quietly receive instruction
Rev. 12:1, **w** clothed with the sun
Judg. 11:2; 1 Sam. 1:15; Eccles. 9:9
WOMB Gen. 25:23, Two nations are in your **w**
Ex. 13:2, first offspring of every **w**
Job 1:21, Naked ... from my mother's **w**
Luke 1:41, baby leaped in her **w**
John 3:4, enter ... into his mother's **w**
Acts 3:2, lame from his mother's **w**
Num. 12:12; Deut. 7:13; Ruth 1:11; Ps. 110:3;
  Prov. 30:16; Is. 44:2
WOMEN 2 Sam. 1:26, Than the love of **w**
1 Kin. 11:1, loved many foreign **w**
Ezra 10:2, have married foreign **w**
Prov. 31:3, not your strength to **w**
Is. 4:1, seven **w** will take hold of one man
Matt. 24:41, Two **w** *will be* grinding
Mark 15:40, *some* **w** looking on from afar
Acts 17:4, and a number of the leading **w**
1 Tim. 2:9, **w** to adorn themselves in proper
  4:7, fables fit only for old **w**
2 Tim. 3:6, weak **w** weighed down with sins
Titus 2:4, young **w** to love their husbands
1 Pet. 3:5, the holy **w** also
Gen. 31:35; Judg. 5:24; Song 1:8; Jer. 50:37
WON Matt. 18:15, you have **w** your brother
WONDER—*marvel, sign*
1 Chr. 16:9, Speak of all His **w-s**
Job 37:14, consider the **w-s** of God
Ps. 9:1, I will tell of all Thy **w-s**
  72:18, Who alone works **w-s**
  78:12, He wrought **w-s** before their fathers
Is. 9:6, name will be called **W-ful** Counselor
Joel 2:30, display **w-s** in the sky
Rom. 15:19, power of signs and **w-s**
2 Thess. 2:9, signs and false **w-s**
Deut. 4:34; Dan. 6:27
WONDROUS—*marvelous* Job 9:10, **w** works
Job 37:5, God thunders ... **w-ly**
Ps. 17:7, **W-ly** show Thy lovingkindness
  71:17, I still declare Thy **w** deeds
Joel 2:26, dealt **w-ly** with you
WOOD Gen. 6:14, an ark of gopher **w**
1 Cor. 3:12, stones, **w**, hay, straw
Rev. 18:12, *made* from very costly **w**
Deut. 19:5; 2 Kin. 2:24; 2 Chr. 27:4; Neh. 8:4;
  Job 41:27; Prov. 26:20; Jer. 7:18; Lam. 5:4;
  Ezek. 24:10
WOOL Ps. 147:16, He gives snow like **w**
Is. 1:18, They will be like **w**
Heb. 9:19, scarlet **w** and hyssop
Rev. 1:14, His hair ... white like white **w**
Deut. 22:11; Judg. 6:37; Ezek. 44:17; Dan. 7:9
WORD—*edict, message, speech* Gen. 15:1
Gen. 11:1, same language ... same **w-s**
Ps. 12:6, **w-s** of the Lord are pure **w-s**
  19:3, There is no speech, nor are there **w-s**
  19:14, Let the **w-s** of my mouth
Prov. 15:1, a harsh **w** stirs up anger
  15:23, how delightful is a timely **w**

Is. 5:24, despised the **w** of the Holy One
  29:11, **w-s** of a sealed book
Matt. 4:4, on every **w** that proceeds
  6:7, for their many **w-s**
  7:24, every one who hears these **w-s**
  8:8, but just say the **w**
  10:14, nor heed your **w-s**
  12:36, every careless **w** that men ... speak
Mark 4:14, The sower sows the **w**
  4:18, ones who have heard the **w**
  7:13, invalidating the **w** of God
Luke 1:2, eyewitnesses and servants of the **W**
John 1:1, the beginning was the **W**
  1:14, the **W** became flesh
  6:68, **w-s** of eternal life
  8:51, if anyone keeps My **w**
Acts 2:41, received his **w** were baptized
  6:7, **w** of God kept on spreading
Rom. 10:8, **W IS NEAR YOU** ... **w** of faith
1 Cor. 1:17, kingdom of God ... in **w-s**
  1:18, the **w** of the cross is to those
2 Cor. 4:2, not ... adulterating the **w** of God
Gal. 5:14, Law is fulfilled in one **w**
Eph. 4:29, Let no unwholesome **w** proceed ...
  mouth
  5:6, deceive you with empty **w-s**
Phil. 2:16, holding fast the **w** of life
Col. 3:16, Let the **w** of Christ ... dwell within
  you
  4:3, open up to us a door for the **w**
1 Thess. 1:5, gospel did not come ... in **w** only
2 Thess. 2:17, in every good work and **w**
1 Tim. 4:5, sanctified by the **w** of God
2 Tim. 2:15, handling accurately the **w** of truth
Titus 1:9, holding fast the faithful **w**
Heb. 2:2, **w** spoken through angels
  4:12, **w** of God is living
James 1:21, receive the **w** implanted
  1:22, prove yourselves doers of the **w**
1 Pet. 1:23, living and abiding **w** of God
2 Pet. 1:19, prophetic **w** *made* more sure
1 John 1:1, concerning the **W** of life
Rev. 19:13, name is called The **W** of God
Gen. 30:34; Ex. 20:1; Lev. 10:7; Num. 30:2;
  Deut. 5:5; Josh. 24:26; Judg. 13:12; 1 Sam.
  3:1; 2 Kin. 9:5; 18:36; 1 Chr. 21:19; 2 Chr.
  6:17; Job 2:13; 6:25; 12:11; Ps. 49:13; 55:21;
  Eccles. 5:2; Jer. 5:13; Mal. 1:1
WORK—*deed, labor, toil*
Gen. 2:2, God completed His **w**
Ex. 20:9, Six days ... do all your **w**
  30:25, the **w** of a perfumer
Lev. 23:3, For six days **w** may be done
1 Sam. 14:45, he has **w-ed** with God this day
Neh. 4:6, the people had a mind to **w**
Ps. 9:1, declaring the **w** of His hands
  62:12, a man according to his **w**
Prov. 16:3, Commit your **w-s** to the LORD
Eccles. 5:12, sleep of the **w-ing** man
  7:13, Consider the **w** of God
  10:12, LORD has completed all His **w**
Matt. 5:16, may see your good **w-s**
  11:2, John ... heard of the **w-s** of Christ
  20:12, last men have **w-ed** *only* one hour
Mark 16:20, the Lord **w-ed** with them
Luke 5:5, we **w-ed** hard all night
  13:14, six days in which **w** should be
John 5:17, **w-ing** until now, and I
  6:27, Do not **w** for the food which
  6:28, may **w** the **w-s** of God
  9:4, **w** the **w-s** of Him who sent Me
Acts 18:3, they were **w-ing**
Rom. 2:15, show the **w** of the Law
  3:20, by the **w-s** of the Law no flesh
  3:28, justified by faith apart from **w-s** of the
  Law
  8:28, all things to **w** together for good
  16:12, who has **w-ed** hard in the Lord
1 Cor. 3:13, man's **w** will become evident
  3:14, If any man's **w** ... remains
  4:12, **w-ing** with our own hands

2 Cor. 6:1, **w-ing** together *with Him*
Gal. 2:8, effectually **w-ed** for Peter
Eph. 2:9, not as a result of **w-s**
   4:12, saints for the **w** of service
Phil. 2:12, **w** out your salvation
   2:13, both to will and to **w**
Col. 1:10, bearing fruit in every good **w**
2 Thess. 3:8, labor and hardship we *kept* **w-ing**
   3:10, If anyone will not **w**
1 Tim. 6:18, be rich in good **w-s**
2 Tim. 4:5, do the **w** of an evangelist
Heb. 6:1, repentance from dead **w-s**
James 2:18, show you my faith by my **w-s**
1 John 3:8, destroy the **w-s** of the devil
Deut. 4:28; 1 Sam. 14:6; 1 Chr. 23:4; 2 Chr. 15:7;
   Is. 5:19; Ezek. 46:1
WORKER Ps. 52:2, O **w** of deceit
Prov. 10:29, **w-s** of iniquity
Matt. 10:10, **w** is worthy of his support
1 Cor. 12:29, are not **w-s** of miracles
Phil. 3:2, beware of the evil **w-s**
Titus 2:5, sensible, pure, **w-s** at home
WORKMAN Eph. 2:10, For we are His **w-ship**
   Ex. 38:23; 2 Kin. 22:5
WORLD—*age* 2 Sam. 22:16, foundations of **w**
2 Chr. 16:30, **w** is firmly established
Job 34:13, laid *on Him* the whole **w**
Ps. 17:14, From men of the **w**
Prov. 8:26, first dust of the **w**
Is. 14:21, fill ... the **w** with cities
Matt. 5:14, You are the light of the **w**
   13:38, the field is the **w**
Mark 10:30, **w** to come, eternal life
John 1:10, **w** was made through Him
   3:16, God so loved the **w**
   4:42, Savior of the **w**
   6:33, gives light to the **w**
   7:7, **w** cannot hate you
   8:12, I am the light of the **w**
Acts 17:6, men who have upset the **w**
Rom. 5:12, sin entered into the **w**
1 Cor. 1:28, base things of the **w**
   2:12, not the spirit of the **w**
2 Cor. 7:10, sorrow of the **w** produces death
1 Tim. 6:17, rich in this present **w**
James 1:27, unstained by the **w**
2 Pet. 2:5, did not spare the ancient **w**
1 John 2:15, Do not love the **w**
   2:17, the **w** is passing away
WORLDLY—*profane* 1 Tim. 4:7, **w** fables fit only
   for old
2 Tim. 2:16, avoid **w** *and* empty chatter
WORM Ex. 16:20, it bred **w-s** and became foul
Job 7:5, My flesh is clothed with **w-s**
Ps. 22:6, But I am a **w**
Is. 14:11, And **w-s** are your covering
Mark 9:48, where THEIR **W** DOES NOT DIE
Acts 12:23, he was eaten by **w-s**
Job 24:20; Jon. 4:7
WORMWOOD
Deut. 29:18, poisonous fruit and **w**
Prov. 5:4, she is bitter as **w**
Jer. 23:15, feed them **w**
Amos 5:7, turn justice into **w**
Rev. 8:11, star is called **W**
WORN—*old* Deut. 29:5, sandal has not **w** out
WORRY Luke 8:14, choked with **w-es** and riches
Luke 10:41, you are **w-ed** and bothered
   12:29, do not keep **w-ing**
WORSE Matt. 9:16, a **w** tear results
John 5:14, nothing **w** may befall you
1 Cor. 11:17, better but for the **w**
2 Tim. 3:13, proceed *from bad* to **w**
WORSHIP—*bow, serve*
Ex. 34:14, shall not **w** any other
Ps. 2:11, **W** the LORD with reverence
   29:2, **W** the LORD in holy array
Matt. 2:2, and have come to **w** Him
   2:8, come and **w** Him
   2:11, fell down and **w-ed** Him
   4:10, SHALL **W** THE LORD YOUR GOD

John 4:20, place where men ought to **w**
   4:22, we **w** that which we know
Phil. 3:3, **w** in the Spirit of God
Heb. 9:6, performing the divine **w**
Rev. 4:10, **w** Him who lives forever
Gen. 22:5; Deut. 6:13; 2 Chr. 29:28
WORTH—*price* Prov. 31:10, her **w** is far above
   jewels
WORTHLESS—*ungodly* Prov. 16:27, A **w** man
Matt. 25:30, cast out the **w** slave
Gal. 4:9, **w** elemental things
Titus 1:16, **w** for any good deed
James 1:26, this man's religion is **w**
Judg. 9:4; Is. 5:2
WORTHY—*befit, deserving, fit*
1 Kin. 1:52, If he will be a **w** man
Matt. 10:10, worker is **w** of his support
   10:11, enter, inquire who is **w** in it
   10:13, if the house is **w**
   10:37, who loves father more ... not **w** of Me
Luke 10:7, laborer is **w** of his wages
Rom. 16:2, a manner **w** of the saints
Phil. 1:27, a manner **w** of the gospel
Eph. 4:1, manner **w** of the calling
1 Thess. 2:12, walk in a manner **w** of God
Heb. 11:38, the world was not **w**
Rev. 5:2, Who is **w** to open the book
WOUND—*bruise, pierce*
Luke 10:34, bandaged up his **w-s**
Acts 19:16, fled ... naked and **w-ed**
1 Pet. 2:24, by His **w-s** you were healed
Gen. 4:23; Ex. 21:25; Deut. 32:39; Job 34:6;
   Ps. 147:3; Prov. 23:29; Jer. 30:12,17;
   Nah. 3:19; Mark 12:4
WRANGLE 2 Tim. 2:14, not to **w** about words
WRAPPED Matt. 27:59, **w** it in a clean linen
Mark 15:46, **w** Him in the linen sheet
Luke 2:7, she **w** Him in cloths
Gen. 38:14; 1 Kin. 19:13; Job 26:8; Is. 59:17;
   Ezek. 16:10; 21:15
WRAPPINGS—*cloth* John 11:44; 20:7
WRATH—*anger, indignation* Deut. 29:28
Ps. 6:1, Nor chasten me in Thy **w**
Matt. 3:7, flee from the **w** to come
John 3:36, **w** of God abides on him
Rom. 2:5, **w** for yourself in the day of **w**
   3:5, God who inflicts **w** is not unrighteous
Eph. 2:3, by nature children of **w**
Col. 3:6, **w** of God will come
1 Thess. 5:9, has not destined us for **w**
Heb. 3:11, I swore in My **w**
Rev. 6:16, from the **w** of the Lamb
Ps. 37:8; 89:38; Is. 27:4; Jer. 4:4; 6:11; 30:23;
   Ezek. 5:13; 23:25; Mic. 5:15; Nah. 1:2
WREATH—*crown*
1 Cor. 9:25, to receive a perishable **w**
WRITE—*record* Ex. 17:14; Is. 8:1
Prov. 3:3, **w** them on the tablet of your heart
Mark 10:4, **w** a certificate of divorce
John 19:21, Do not **w**, The King of the Jews
Rom. 16:22, I, Tertius, who **w** this letter
Heb. 10:16, UPON THEIR MIND I WILL **W** THEM
2 John 12, **w** ... not ... with paper and ink
Rev. 14:13, **W**, Blessed are the dead
WRITING—*inscription, letter*
Eccles. 12:12, the **w** of many books is endless
John 5:47, if you do not believe his **w-s**
1 Tim. 3:14, I am **w** these things to you
2 Tim. 3:15, you have known the sacred **w-s**
Philem. 19, **w** this with my own hand
1 John 2:8, **w** a new commandment
2 John 5, **w** ... a new commandment
Ex. 32:16; 1 Chr. 28:19; Dan. 10:21
WRITTEN Ex. 31:18, **w** by the finger of God
Job 19:23, that my words were **w**
Mal. 3:16, book of remembrance was **w**
Matt. 2:5, been **w** by the prophet
   4:4, It is **w**, MAN SHALL NOT LIVE
   4:6, for it is **w**, HE WILL GIVE
   11:10, one about whom it was **w**
John 19:22, What I have **w** I have **w**

WRITTEN (Continued)
Acts 1:20, **w** in the book of Psalms
Rom. 2:15, Law **w** in their hearts
Rev. 13:8, not been **w** . . . in the book of life
17:5, forehead a name *was* **w**
WRONG—*defraud, wicked* Ex. 22:21, not **w** a stranger
Lev. 25:14, you shall not **w** one another
2 Sam. 24:17, I who have done **w**
Matt. 20:13, Friend, I am doing you no **w**
John 18:23, If I have spoken **w-ly**
Rom. 13:10, Love does no **w**
1 Cor. 6:7, Why not rather be **w-ed**
2 Cor. 7:2, we **w-ed** no one
Rev. 22:11, Let the one who does **w**, still do **w**
Gen. 16:5; 1 Chr. 12:17; Esth. 1:16
WRONGDOER—*unrighteous* Ps. 71:4, the **w** and
WROTE Ex. 24:4, Moses **w** down all the words
Jer. 36:18, **w** them with ink on the
Mark 12:19, Teacher, Moses **w**
Luke 1:63, he asked for a tablet and **w**
John 8:6, finger **w** on the ground
3 John 9, I **w** something to the church
WROUGHT—*accomplished* John 3:21, been **w** in

X, Y, Z

YEAR—*annual* Gen. 1:14, for seasons . . . **y-s**
Ps. 90:4, thousand **y-s** in Thy sight
90:9, finished our **y-s** like a sigh
Prov. 4:10, **y-s** of your life will be many
Is. 61:2, favorable **y** of the LORD
Luke 3:23, was about thirty **y-s** of age
Gal. 4:10, months and season and **y-s**
Rev. 9:15, day and month and **y**
Gen. 7:11; Ex. 13:10; Lev. 16:34; Num. 14:34;
2 Sam. 14:26; 1 Kin. 17:1; 2 Chr. 14:6; Job 10:5; Jer. 11:23; Joel 2:25; Matt. 2:16
YEARN—*faint* Ps. 84:2, longed and even **y-ed**
YESTERDAY Ex. 5:14, **y** or today in making brick
Job 8:9, For we are *only* of **y**
Ps. 90:4, in Thy sight Are like **y**
Acts 7:28, KILLED THE EGYPTIAN **Y**
Heb. 13:8, the same **y** and today
YET—*still* Ps. 37:10, **Y** a little while
John 2:4, My hour has not **y** come
Heb. 11:7, things not **y** seen
1 John 3:2, appeared as **y** what we shall be
Deut. 9:29; Jon. 3:4
YIELD—*bear, produce* Ps. 1:3, Which **y-s** its fruit in
Ps. 67:6, earth has **y-ed** its produce
Heb. 12:11, **y-s** the peaceful fruit
YIELDING—*bearing* Gen. 1:11,29; Mark 4:8
YOKE Matt. 11:29, Take My **y** upon you
Matt. 11:30, For My **y** is easy
Gal. 5:1, to a **y** of slavery

1 Tim. 6:1, under the **y** as slaves
Gen. 27:40; Lev. 26:13; Deut. 28:48; 1 Kin. 12:4;
Is. 9:4; Jer. 27:2; Lam. 1:14
YOUNG Ps. 37:25, been **y**, and now I am old
Prov. 20:29, glory of **y** men is their
Eccles. 11:9, Rejoice, **y** man, during your
Is. 11:7, Their **y** will lie down together
Acts 2:17, **Y** MEN SHALL SEE VISIONS
Titus 2:4, **y** women to love . . . husbands
1 John 2:13, I am writing . . . **y** men
Deut. 32:11; Judg. 6:15; 1 Sam. 8:16; Job 19:18;
Ezek. 17:4
YOUNGER Luke 15:13, **y** son gathered
John 21:18, when you were **y**
1 Tim. 5:11, refuse *to put* **y** widows
1 Pet. 5:5, You **y** men, likewise
Gen. 25:23; Judg. 15:2
YOUR—*Thine* Gen. 22:2, **y** son, **y** only son
Ex. 4:4, Stretch out **y** hand and grasp *it*
2 Chr. 20:15, battle is not **y-s** but God's
Luke 6:20, **y-s** is the kingdom of God
15:31, all that is mine is **y-s**
John 15:20, they will keep **y-s** also
2 Cor. 12:14, I do not seek what is **y-s**
Gen. 45:20; Josh. 2:14; 1 Kin. 20:4; Jer. 5:19
YOURSELVES
Matt. 6:19, Do not lay . . . **y** treasures
Mark 9:50, Have salt in **y**
Luke 12:33, make **y** purses
Rom. 6:13, present **y** to God
2 Cor. 13:5, recognize . . . **y**
1 John 5:21, guard **y** from idols
Jude 21, keep **y** in the love of God
Gen. 18:4; Lev. 11:44; Deut. 4:16; Josh. 24:22;
2 Chr. 29:31; Jer. 37:9
YOUTH—*childhood* Acts 26:4, life from my **y** up
1 Tim. 4:12, look down on your **y-fulness**
2 Tim. 2:22, flee from **y-ful** lusts
Gen. 8:21; Num. 30:16; Judg. 8:20; Job 33:25;
Ps. 25:7; Prov. 5:18; Is. 40:30; Jer. 3:4; 31:19
ZEAL—*concern* 2 Kin. 10:16, see my **z** for the LORD
Ps. 119:139, My **z** has consumed me
John 2:17, **Z** FOR THY HOUSE WILL
Rom. 10:2, have a **z** for God
2 Cor. 7:7, your **z** for me
7:11, what longing, what **z**
Phil. 3:6, as to **z**
2 Sam. 21:2; Eccles. 9:6; Is. 26:11; 59:17
ZEALOUS—*eager* 1 Kin. 19:10, very **z** for the LORD
Acts 21:20, all **z** for the law
1 Cor. 14:12, **z** of spiritual *gifts*
Titus 2:14, **z** for good deeds
Rev. 3:19, be **z** therefore, and repent

MAP INDEX

	MAP	GRID
Abana River	1	E 1
	6	E 1
Abdon	4	C 2
Abel	5	B 3
Abel-beth-maachah	4	D 2
	6	D 2
Abel-meholah	4	D 4
	6	C 4
Abel-shittim	4	D 5
Abila (of Decapolis)	8	D 3
Abila (of Abilene)	8	E 1
Abilene	8	E 1
Accho (see also Ptolemais)	1	C 3
	3	C 1
	4	C 3
	5	B 3
	6	C 3
	8	C 3
	11	F 3
Aceldama	10	C 6
Achaia	11	C 2
Achmetha (see Ecbatana)		
Achshaph	4	C 3
Achzib	4	C 2
Adam	4	D 4
Adoraim	6	C 5
Adramyttium	11	D 2
Adria	11	B 1, 2
Adullam	4	C 5
	6	C 5
Aegean Sea	2	A 2
	7	B 2
	11	C 2
Agrigentum	11	A 2
Agrippa's Wall	10	B 2
Ai	3	C 2
	4	C 5
Aijalon	6	B 5
Ajalon River	1	B 5
	4	B 5
Akkad	2	F 3
Akrabbim, Ascent of	1	C 7
	4	C 7
Alalakh	2	D 3
Alexandria	11	D 3
Alexandrium	8	C 4
Alisar Huyuk (see Kushshar)		
Alush	3	B 3
Amalekites	5	B 4
Amardi	7	E 2
Amardos River	2	G 2
Amasia	11	F 1
Amastris	11	E 1
Amathus	8	D 4
	9	D 4
Amisus	11	F 1
Ammon	1	D, E 5
	3	D 2
	4	E 4
	5	C 4
	6	D, E 4, 5
	8	D, E 5
Ammonium	7	B 3
Amorites	2	D, E 3
	3	C 2
Amphipolis	11	C 1
Amygdalon, Pool of	10	B 4
Anab	4	B 6
Ancyra	7	C 2
	11	E 2
Antioch (Asia)	11	F 2
Antioch (Pisidia)	11	E 2
Anti-Taurus Mountains	2	D 2
Antipatris	8	B 4
Antonia, Fortress of	10	C 3
Anxa	11	B 2
Aphek (of Asher)	4	C 3
Aphek (of Ephraim)	3	C 1
	4	B 4
	6	B 4
Aphek (of Manasseh)	4	D 3
	6	D 3
Apii Forum	11	A 1
Apollonia	7	B 1
	8	B 4
	11	C 2
Aqaba, Gulf of	3	C 3
Ar	3	C 2
	4	D 6
	5	B 4
	6	D 6
Arabah	1	C 7
	3	C 2
	5	B 4
Arabia	7	C 2
	8	D, E 6, 7
	11	E, F 3
Arabian Sea	7	F 4
Arachosia	7	F 2, 3
Arad	4	C 6
Aral Sea	7	E, F 1
Aram	6	D, E 2
Aramaeans (see Syrians)		
Ararat, Mount	2	E 2
Araxes River	2	E, F 2
	7	D 2
Arbela	2	E, F 2, 3
	7	D 2
Archelais	8	C 5
Argob	4	E 3
Aria	7	F 2
Arimathaea	8	B 4
'Arish, Wadi el (see Egypt, River of)		
Armenia	7	C, D 2
Arnon River	1	D 6
	3	C 2
	4	C 6
	6	D 6
	8	D 6
Aroer (of Reuben)	4	D 6
	5	B 4
	6	D 6
Aroer (of Simeon)	4	B 6
Arvad	2	C 3
	5	B 2
	7	C 2
Aryans (see Indo-Iranians)		
Arzawa	2	B 2
Ascalon	8	B 5
Ashdod	3	C 2
	4	B 5
	5	B 4
	6	B 5
Asher	4	C 2, 3
Ashkelon	3	C 2
	4	B 5
	5	B 4
	6	B 5
Ashtaroth	3	D 1
	4	E 3
	5	C 3
	6	D 3
Ashur	2	E 3
Asia	11	D 2
Asia Minor	11	D, F 2
Aspadana	7	E 3
Asphaltitis, Lake (see Dead Sea)		
Assos	11	D 2
Assuwa	2	A 2
Assyria	2	E 2, 3
	7	C, D 2
Asur, Tell	1	C 5
Ataroth (of Ephraim)	4	C 4
Ataroth (of Reuben)	4	D 5
	6	D 5
Athens	7	B 2
	11	C 2
Attalia	11	E 2
Auranitis	8	E 3
Azekah	4	B 5
	6	B 5
Azotus	8	B 5
Azzah (see Gaza)		
Baal-meon	4	D 5
	6	D 5
Baal-zephon	3	B 2
Babylon	2	F 3
	7	D 3
Babylonia	2	F 3
Babylonian Empire, New	7	C, D 2, 3
Babylonian Empire, Old	2	E, F 3
Bactra	7	F 2
Bactria	7	F 2
Bagae	7	F 2
Balikh River	2	D 2, 3
Ballah, Lake	3	B 2
Barca	7	B 2
Baris (see Antonia, Fortress of)		
Bashan	1	D, E 3
	3	C, D 1
	4	D, E 3
	5	B, C 3
	6	E 3
	8	D, E 3
Batanaea	8	D, E 3
Beautiful Gate	10	D 4
Beer-sheba	1	B 6
	2	C 4
	3	C 2
	4	B 6
	5	B 4
	6	B 6
Behistun	7	D 2
Bene-berak	4	B 4
Beneventum	11	A 1
Ben Hasan	2	B 4
Benjamin	4	C 5
Berea	11	C 2
Berothai	5	C 3
Bersabee	8	B 6
Besor River	1	A, B 6
Bethabara	9	B 3
	9	D 3
Bethabara (Bethany Beyond Jordan)	9	D 6
Bethany	8	C 5
	9	C 6
Bethany Beyond Jordan (see Bethabara)		
Bethel	2	C 4
	4	C 5
	6	C 5
	8	C 5
	9	C 5
Beth-emek	4	C 3
Bethennabris	8	D 5
Bethesda, Pool of	10	D 3
Beth-haran (see Julias)		
Beth-hoglah	4	C 5
Beth-horon	4	C 5
	6	C 5
Beth-jeshimoth	4	D 5
Bethlehem	1	C 5
	4	C 5
	6	C 5
	8	C 5
	9	C 6
Beth-nimrah	4	D 5
Beth-palet	4	B 6
Bethsaida	8	D 3
	9	B 1
	9	B 4
	9	D 2
Beth-shan	1	C 3

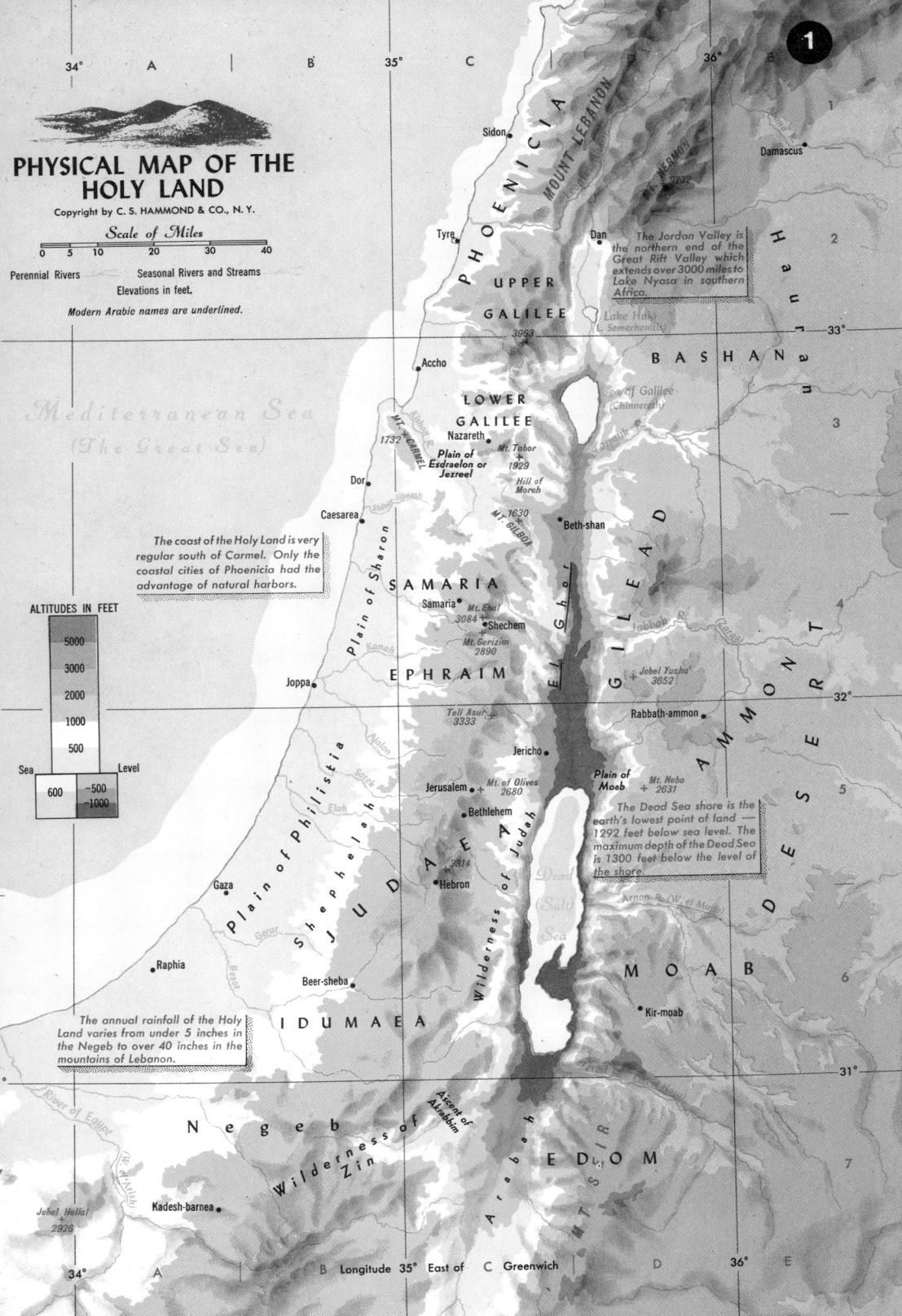

PHYSICAL MAP OF THE HOLY LAND

Copyright by C. S. HAMMOND & CO., N. Y.

Scale of Miles

0 5 10 20 30 40

Perennial Rivers   Seasonal Rivers and Streams
                    Elevations in feet.

Modern Arabic names are underlined.

ALTITUDES IN FEET

5000
3000
2000
1000
500
Sea   Level
600   −500
       −1000

Mediterranean Sea (The Great Sea)

The Jordan Valley is the northern end of the Great Rift Valley which extends over 3000 miles to Lake Nyasa in southern Africa.

The coast of the Holy Land is very regular south of Carmel. Only the coastal cities of Phoenicia had the advantage of natural harbors.

The Dead Sea share is the earth's lowest point of land — 1292 feet below sea level. The maximum depth of the Dead Sea is 1300 feet below the level of the shore.

The annual rainfall of the Holy Land varies from under 5 inches in the Negeb to over 40 inches in the mountains of Lebanon.

PHOENICIA
MOUNT LEBANON
UPPER GALILEE
LOWER GALILEE
Hauran
BASHAN
GILEAD
El Ghor
AMMON
SAMARIA
EPHRAIM
DESERT
JUDAEA
Wilderness of Judah
Plain of Sharon
Plain of Philistia
Shephelah
Plain of Moab
MOAB
IDUMAEA
Negeb
Wilderness of Zin
EDOM
Arabah
MTS. SEIR

Sidon
Damascus
Tyre
Dan
Lake Huleh (L. Semechonitis)
Accho
Sea of Galilee (Chinnereth)
Nazareth
Mt. Tabor 1929
Hill of Moreh
Plain of Esdraelon or Jezreel
Mt. Carmel 1732
Dor
Caesarea
Mt. Gilboa 1630
Beth-shan
Samaria
Mt. Ebal 3084
Shechem
Mt. Gerizim 2890
Jebel Yusha' 3852
Joppa
Tell Asur 3333
Rabbath-ammon
Jericho
Jerusalem
Mt. of Olives 2680
Plain of Moab
Mt. Nebo 2631
Bethlehem
Dead (Salt) Sea
Arnon R. (W. el Mujib)
Gaza
Hebron 3314
Beer-sheba
Kir-moab
Raphia
River of Egypt
Jebel Helal 2926
Kadesh-barnea
Ascent of Akrabbim

3963

34° A B 35° C D 36° E
Longitude 35° East of Greenwich

1 2 3 4 5 6 7

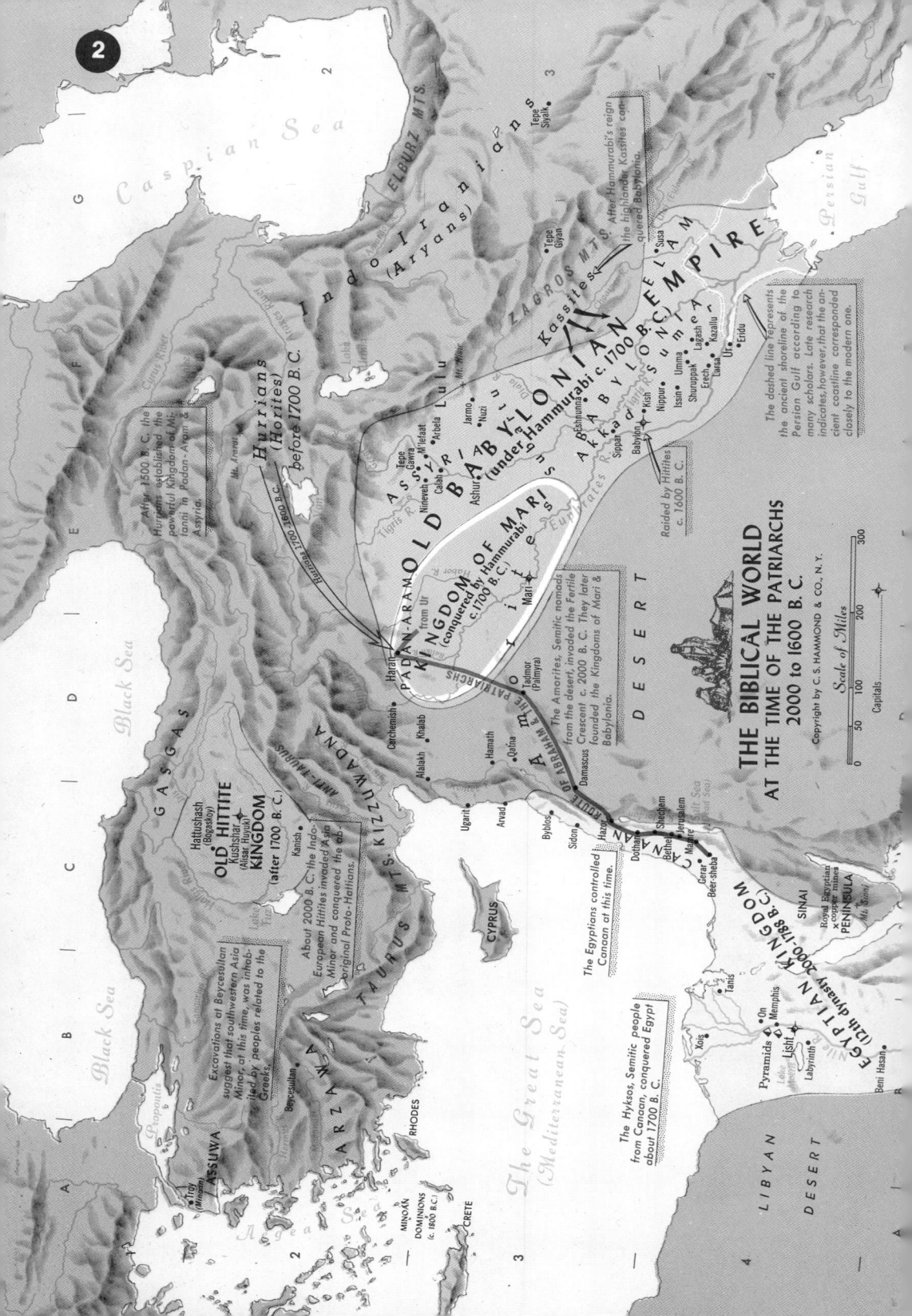

②

THE BIBLICAL WORLD
AT THE TIME OF THE PATRIARCHS
2000 to 1600 B.C.

Copyright by C. S. HAMMOND & CO., N. Y.

Scale of Miles

50   100   200   300

Capitals •

Caspian Sea

Black Sea

The Great Sea
(Mediterranean Sea)

Aegean Sea

Persian Gulf

Indo-Iranians (Aryans)

Hurrians (Horites)
before 1700 B.C.

ELBURZ MTS.

ZAGROS MTS.

Kassites

Lulu

After Hammurabi's reign the highlander Kassites conquered Babylonia.

OLD BABYLONIAN EMPIRE
(under Hammurabi c. 1700 B.C.)

ELAM

SUMER

AKKAD

ASSYRIA

KINGDOM OF MARI
(conquered by Hammurabi c. 1700 B.C.)

PADAN-ARAM

Harran

ROUTE OF ABRAHAM

PATRIARCHS

Amorites

OLD HITTITE KINGDOM
(after 1700 B.C.)

Hattushash
(Boğazköy)

Kushshar
Nesha

Kanish

KIZZUWADNA

KASKA

GASGAS

TAURUS MTS.

ARZAWA

ASSUWA

Troy
(Hissarlik)

RHODES

CYPRUS

CRETE

MINOAN DOMINIONS
(c. 1600 B.C.)

SINAI PENINSULA

Mt. Sinai

Royal Egyptian
× copper mines

EGYPTIAN KINGDOM
(12th dynasty 2000-1788 B.C.)

Memphis
On
Pyramids
Lisht
Labyrinth
Beni Hasan
Tanis
Xois

LIBYAN DESERT

DESERT

Nile R.

Tigris R.

Euphrates R.

Ur
Eridu
Eshnunna
Kish
Babylon
Sippar
Nippur
Isin
Umma
Shuruppak
Erech
Larsa
Lagash
Kazallu
Susa

Ashur
Nineveh
Calah
Arbela
Nuzi
Jarmo
Gawra
Tepe
Arpachiyah
Mt. Ararat

Tepe Siyalk
Tepe Giyan

Carchemish
Khalab
Alalah
Hamath
Qatna
Damascus
Tadmor (Palmyra)
Mari
Ugarit
Arvad
Byblos
Sidon
Tyre
Hazor
Dothan
Shechem
Bethel
Jerusalem
Hebron
Gerar
Beer-sheba
Megiddo
Dead Sea (Salt Sea)

CANAAN

SYRIA

The dashed line represents the ancient shoreline of the Persian Gulf according to many scholars. Late research indicates, however, that the ancient coastline corresponded closely to the modern one.

After 1500 B.C. the Hurrians established the powerful Kingdom of Mitanni in Padan-Aram & Assyria.

Excavations at Beycesultan suggest that southwestern Asia Minor, at this time, was inhabited by peoples related to the Greeks.

About 2000 B.C. the Indo-European Hittites invaded Asia Minor and conquered the original Proto-Hattians.

The Amorites, Semitic nomads from the desert, invaded the Fertile Crescent c. 2000 B.C. They later founded the Kingdoms of Mari & Babylonia.

The Egyptians controlled Canaan at this time.

The Hyksos, Semitic people from Canaan, conquered Egypt about 1700 B.C.

Raided by Hittites c. 1600 B.C.

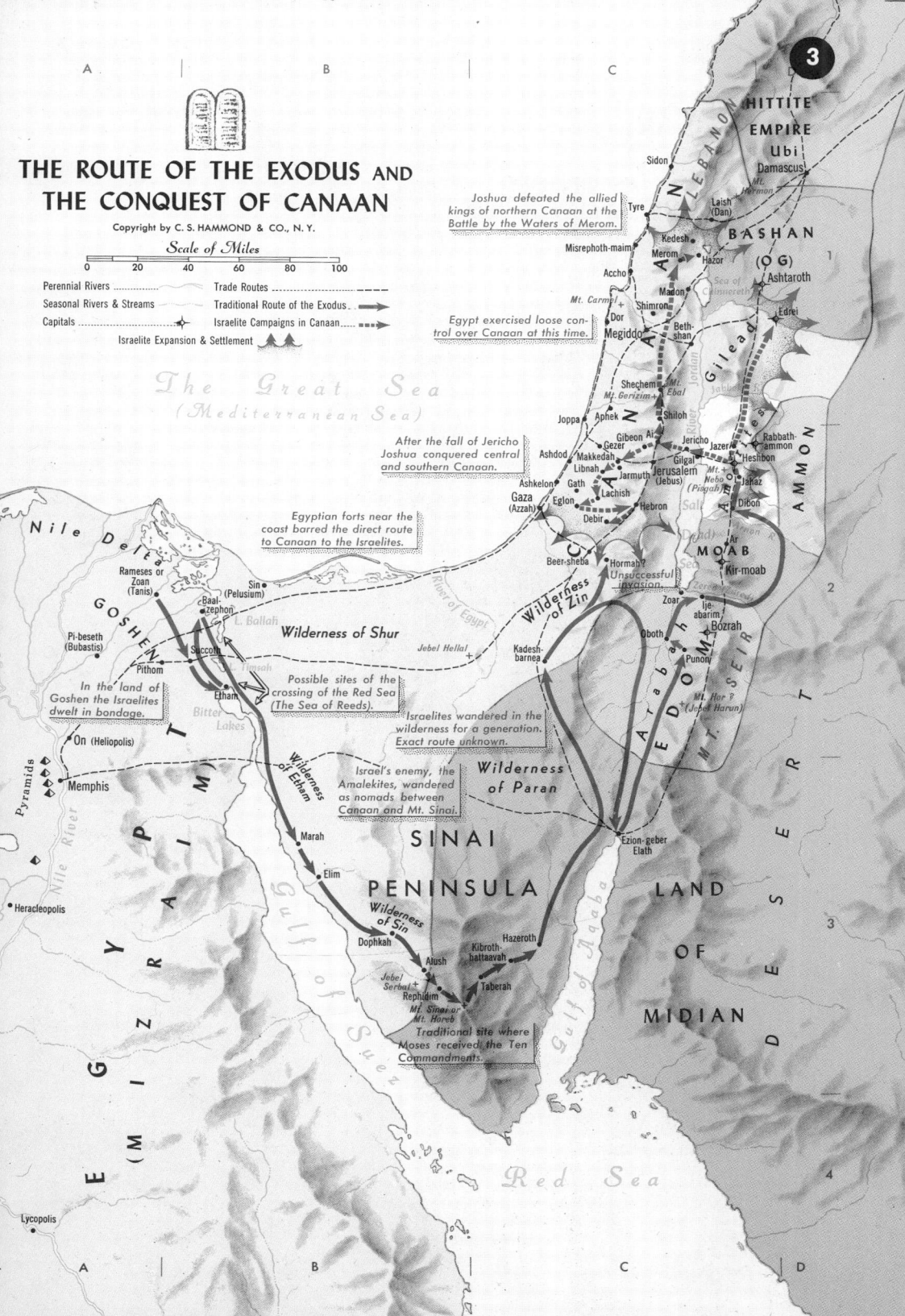

THE ROUTE OF THE EXODUS AND THE CONQUEST OF CANAAN

Copyright by C. S. HAMMOND & CO., N.Y.

Scale of Miles

0   20   40   60   80   100

Perennial Rivers ....
Seasonal Rivers & Streams ——
Capitals ....
Trade Routes --------
Traditional Route of the Exodus ....→
Israelite Campaigns in Canaan ——▶
Israelite Expansion & Settlement

3

Joshua defeated the allied kings of northern Canaan at the Battle by the Waters of Merom.

Egypt exercised loose control over Canaan at this time.

After the fall of Jericho Joshua conquered central and southern Canaan.

Egyptian forts near the coast barred the direct route to Canaan to the Israelites.

In the land of Goshen the Israelites dwelt in bondage.

Possible sites of the crossing of the Red Sea (The Sea of Reeds).

Israelites wandered in the wilderness for a generation. Exact route unknown.

Israel's enemy, the Amalekites, wandered as nomads between Canaan and Mt. Sinai.

Traditional site where Moses received the Ten Commandments.

The Great Sea (Mediterranean Sea)

HITTITE EMPIRE
Ubi
Damascus
BASHAN (OG)
Ashtaroth
Edrei
Gilead
AMMON
Rabbath-ammon
Heshbon
MOAB
Kir-moab
EDOM
MT. SEIR
LAND OF MIDIAN

Sidon
Tyre
Laish (Dan)
Mt. Hermon
Kedesh
Merom
Hazor
Misrephoth-maim
Accho
Madon
Sea of Chinnereth
Mt. Carmel
Shimron
Dor
Bethshan
Megiddo
Shechem
Mt. Gerizim
Mt. Ebal
Shiloh
Joppa
Aphek
Jabbok
Gibeon Ai
Jericho
Jazer
Gezer
Gilgal
Ashdod
Makkedah
Jerusalem (Jebus)
Mt. Nebo (Pisgah)
Jahaz
Libnah
Jarmuth
Ashkelon
Gath
Eglon Lachish
Hebron
Dibon
Gaza (Azzah)
Debir
Salt Dead Sea
Ar
Beer-sheba
Hormah? Unsuccessful invasion
Zoar
Ije-abarim
Bozrah
Wilderness of Zin
Oboth
Kadesh-barnea
Punon
Mt. Hor (Jebel Harun)

Nile Delta

GOSHEN
Rameses or Zoan (Tanis)
Sin (Pelusium)
Baal-zephon
L. Ballah
Pithom
Succoth
Etham
Bitter Lakes
On (Heliopolis)
Pyramids
Memphis
Heracleopolis
Lycopolis

E G Y P T (MIZRAIM)

Nile River

Wilderness of Shur
Jebel Hellal
River of Egypt

Wilderness of Etham

Marah

Elim

Wilderness of Sin

Dophkah
Alush
Jebel Serbal
Rephidim
Mt. Sinai or Mt. Horeb

SINAI PENINSULA

Wilderness of Paran

Kibroth-hattaavah
Hazeroth
Taberah

Ezion-geber Elath

Gulf of Suez

Gulf of Aqaba

Red Sea

D E S E R T

CANAAN AS DIVIDED AMONG THE TWELVE TRIBES
c. 1200-1020 B. C.

Copyright by C. S. HAMMOND & CO., N.Y.

Scale of Miles

0 5 10 20 30 40

Perennial Rivers   Seasonal Rivers & Streams

The tribal divisions marked on this map are only approximate since boundary lists are incomplete.

4

Part of the tribe of Dan, unable to secure its inheritance, migrated north and captured Laish, renaming it Dan.

Although all of Bashan was assigned to the half tribe of Manasseh, it is doubtful that settlement reached beyond the Yarmuk Valley.

The Israelites were unable to capture the fortified towns of the plains during the early period of settlement.

The Israelites were under constant attack from Philistine invaders who occupied the coastal area at about this time.

During the period of Judges, invading Ammonites, Moabites and Midianites were repulsed by the Israelites.

The cities assigned to Simeon were also a part of the inheritance of Judah. Simeon as a tribe was later absorbed by Judah.

The priestly tribe of Levi did not receive a definite territory but instead was allotted 48 cities distributed over the tribal areas.

The Great Sea
(Mediterranean Sea)

Tribes and regions
ASHER · NAPHTALI · DAN · MANASSEH · Bashan · Geshur · Argob · ZEBULUN · ISSACHAR · Havoth-jair · GILEAD · EPHRAIM · MANASSEH · BENJAMIN · AMMON · DAN · JUDAH · Caleb · Kenites · REUBEN · PHILISTINES · Cherethites · SIMEON · MOAB · EDOM · LEVI

Place names
Sidon · Damascus · Zarephath · Tyre · Kanah · Abel-beth-maachah · Laish or Leshem (Dan) · Hammon · En-hazor · Kedesh · Misrephoth-maim · Iron · Hazor · Achzib · Abdon · Beth-emek · Accho · Cabul · Ramah · Hukkok · Chinnereth · Karnaim · Achshaph · Aphek · Rimmon · Madon · Hammath · Gath-hepher · Ashtaroth · Golan · Aphek · Edrei · Hannathon · Shimron · Chesulloth · Mt. Tabor · Jabneel · Ramoth-gilead · Harosheth · Jokneam · Sarid · En-dor · Ophrah · Camon · Dor · Plain of Jezreel · Shunem · Megiddo · Jezreel · Harod · Beth-shan · Pella · Taanach · Mt. Gilboa · Jabesh-gilead · Ibleam · Bezek · Mahanaim · Dothan · Abel-meholah · Tirzah · Thebez · Zaphon · Mt. Ebal · Shechem · Succoth · Pirathon · Mt. Gerizim · Taanath-shiloh · Penuel · Mizpeh · Gath-rimmon · Aphek · Tappuah · Janohah · Adam · Jogbehah · Joppa (Japho) · Bene-berak · Lebonah · Shiloh · Ataroth · Jazer · Betonim · Rabbath-ammon · Ono · Lod · Timnath-serah · Naarath · Beth-nimrah · Jabneel · Ekron · Beth-horon · Gezer · Bethel · Ai · Geba · Jericho · Gilgal · Abel-shittim · Gibbethon · Gibeon · Kirjath-jearim · Beth-hoglah · Elealeh · Ashdod · Eltekeh · Timnah · Zorah · Chesalon · Jerusalem (Jebus) · Mt. Nebo · Heshbon · Makkedah · Azekah · Jarmuth · Etam · Bethlehem · Beth-jeshimoth · Medeba · Ashkelon · Libnah · Adullam · Beth-zur · Tekoa · Baal-meon · Jahaz · Gath · Mareshah · Keilah · Eglon · Lachish · Hebron · Ataroth · Kiriathaim · Dibon · Aroer · Gaza · Debir · Ziph · En-gedi · Gerar · Juttah · Carmel · Maon · Ar · Ziklag · Anab · Eshtemoh · Madmannah · Jattir · Arad · Kir-moab (Kir-haresheth) · Raphia · Sharuhen · Beer-sheba · Moladah · Hormah · Beth-palet · Aroer · Rehoboth · Ascent of Akrabbim · Wilderness of Zin · Salt Sea (Dead Sea) · Sea of Chinnereth · Shihor-libnath · Plain of Sharon · Kanah · Arnon R. · Jabbok R. · Yarmuk R. · Jordan River · Mt. Hermon · Mount Lebanon

Sidonians (Phoenicians)

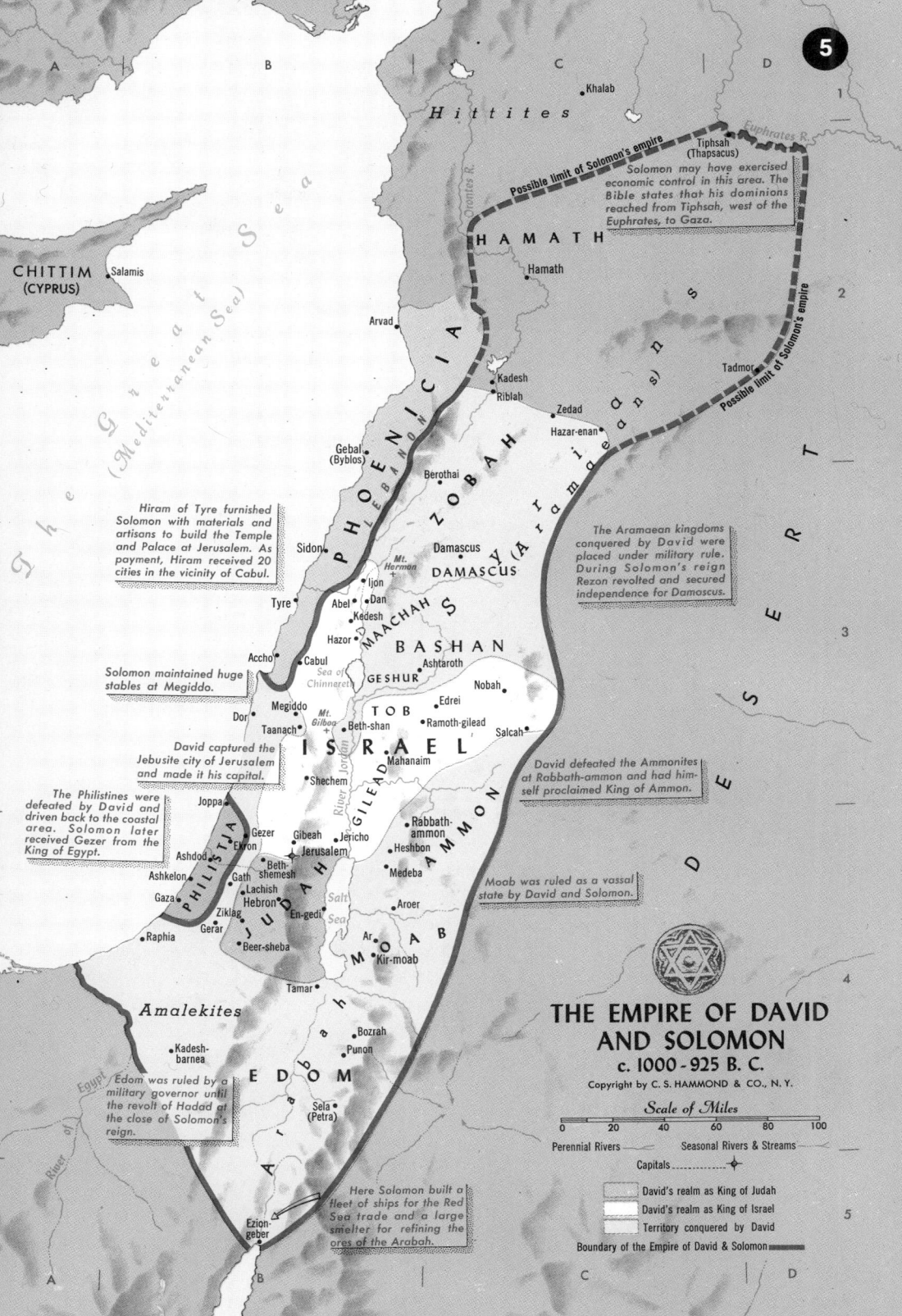

5

THE EMPIRE OF DAVID AND SOLOMON
c. 1000-925 B.C.
Copyright by C. S. HAMMOND & CO., N.Y.

Scale of Miles
0   20   40   60   80   100

Perennial Rivers ——
Seasonal Rivers & Streams ·····
Capitals ·········+

David's realm as King of Judah
David's realm as King of Israel
Territory conquered by David
Boundary of the Empire of David & Solomon ——

Hittites

Hamath — Solomon may have exercised economic control in this area. The Bible states that his dominions reached from Tiphsah, west of the Euphrates, to Gaza.

Possible limit of Solomon's empire

Euphrates R.

Tiphsah (Thapsacus)

Tadmor

Possible limit of Solomon's empire

Khalab

HAMATH

Hamath

CHITTIM (CYPRUS)

Salamis

The Great Sea (Mediterranean Sea)

Arvad

Kadesh
Riblah

Zedad

Hazar-enan

PHOENICIA

Gebal (Byblos)

Berothai

ZOBAH

SYRIA (Aramaeans)

Hiram of Tyre furnished Solomon with materials and artisans to build the Temple and Palace at Jerusalem. As payment, Hiram received 20 cities in the vicinity of Cabul.

The Aramaean kingdoms conquered by David were placed under military rule. During Solomon's reign Rezon revolted and secured independence for Damascus.

Sidon

Damascus

DAMASCUS

Tyre

Mt. Hermon

Ijon
Abel
Dan
Kedesh

MAACHAH

BASHAN

Hazor

Ashtaroth

Accho

Cabul

GESHUR

Nobah

Solomon maintained huge stables at Megiddo.

Sea of Chinnereth

Edrei

Dor

Megiddo

Mt. Gilboa

TOB

Taanach

Beth-shan

Ramoth-gilead

Salcah

ISRAEL

David captured the Jebusite city of Jerusalem and made it his capital.

Mahanaim

GILEAD

Shechem

David defeated the Ammonites at Rabbath-ammon and had himself proclaimed King of Ammon.

Joppa

The Philistines were defeated by David and driven back to the coastal area. Solomon later received Gezer from the King of Egypt.

Gezer

Gibeah

Jericho

Rabbath-ammon

Ekron

Jerusalem

Heshbon

AMMON

Ashdod

Beth-shemesh

Ashkelon

Gath

Lachish

PHILISTIA

Medeba

Gaza

Hebron

En-gedi

Salt Sea

JUDAH

Aroer

Moab was ruled as a vassal state by David and Solomon.

Gerar

Ziklag

MOAB

Raphia

Beer-sheba

Ar

Kir-moab

Tamar

Amalekites

Bozrah

Punon

Kadesh-barnea

EDOM

Edom was ruled by a military governor until the revolt of Hadad at the close of Solomon's reign.

Sela (Petra)

River of Egypt

Arabah

Here Solomon built a fleet of ships for the Red Sea trade and a large smelter for refining the ores of the Arabah.

Ezion-geber

6

THE KINGDOMS OF ISRAEL AND JUDAH
c. 925-842 B.C.

Copyright by C. S. HAMMOND & CO., N.Y.

Scale of Miles

0   5   10   20   30   40

Perennial Rivers ....
Seasonal Rivers & Streams ——

Capitals ....
Egyptian & Syrian Attacks ⟶

Elijah took refuge in Zarephath and brought back to life the widow's son.

In the reign of Baasha the cities of northern Israel were raided by the King of Damascus in league with Asa, King of Judah.

Aram waged almost constant war against Israel. The Syrians were held in check by Ahab until his death in battle at Ramoth-gilead.

The introduction of Phoenician cults following the marriage of Ahab with Jezebel caused violent reactions in Israel that eventually wiped out the house of Omri.

Samaria, fortress capital of Israel was built by Omri c. 870 B.C.

Elijah challenged the prophets of Baal at Mt. Carmel.

Moab was ruled as a vassal kingdom during the Omri dynasty. The Dibon stele commemorates the victory of Mesha, King of Moab, over Israel and the return of Moabite independence.

Shishak (Sheshonk), Egyptian Pharaoh, raided the divided kingdoms, plundering Jerusalem c. 925 B.C.

During the reign of Jehosophat Judah regained control over Edom.

The Great Sea

(Mediterranean Sea)

PHOENICIA

MOUNT LEBANON

MT. HERMON

Damascus

Sidon

Zarephath

Tyre

Ijon

Abel-beth-maachah

Dan

Kedesh

Hazor

Accho

Cabul

Chinnereth

Sea of Chinnereth

GESHUR

Karnaim

Ashtaroth

Aphek

Yarmuk

Bashan

Edrei

Ramoth-gilead

Hammath

Mt. Tabor

Havoth-jair

Dor

Plain of Jezreel

Megiddo

Shunem

Jezreel

Taanach

Beth-shan

Ibleam

Jabesh-gilead

Mahanaim

Tishbe

Dothan

Abel-meholah

Sochoh

Samaria

Tirzah

Mt. Ebal

Shechem

Mt. Gerizim

Penuel

Janohah

Jabbok R.

GILEAD

Joppa

Aphek

Shiloh

Jeshanah

Lod

Zemaraim

Beth-horon

Bethel

Jabneel

Gezer

Mizpeh

Geba

Jericho

Gilgal

Ekron

Gibbethon

Ramah

Cherith

Rabbath-ammon

AMMON

Ashdod

Zorah

Timnah

Elealeh

Heshbon

Ashkelon

Azekah

Beth-shemesh

Jerusalem

Mt. Nebo

Medeba

Baal-meon

Jahaz

Gath

Shoco

Etam

Bethlehem

Libnah

Adullam

Tekoa

Mareshah

Beth-zur

Ataroth

Gaza

Lachish

Hebron

Dibon

Adoraim

Aroer

Debir

Ziph

En-gedi

Arnon R.

Gerar

Wilderness of Judah

MOAB

Ziklag

Ar

Raphia

Beer-sheba

Kir-moab
(Kir-haresheth)

JUDAH

ISRAEL

PHILISTIA

ARAM

Syrians

Salt (Dead Sea) Sea

River Jordan

Kishon

MT. CARMEL

Plain of Sharon

Valley of Salt

EDOM

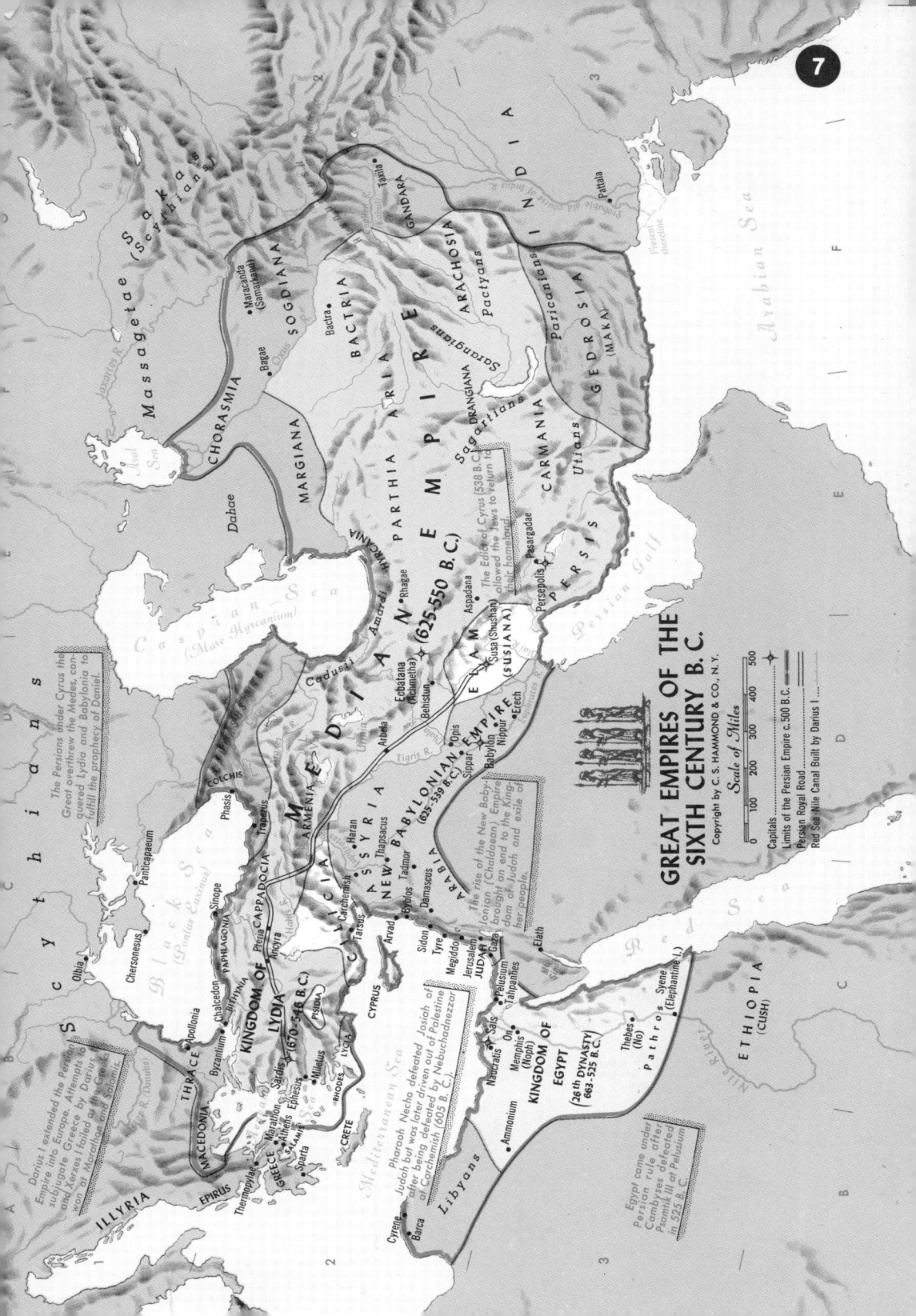

GREAT EMPIRES OF THE SIXTH CENTURY B.C.

Copyright by C. S. HAMMOND & CO., N.Y.

Scale of Miles

0   100   200   300   400   500

Capitals ....
Limits of the Persian Empire c. 500 B.C. ....
Persian Royal Road ....
Red Sea-Nile Canal Built by Darius I ....

7

MASSAGETAE (Scythians)

SAKA

INDIA

GANDARA

Taxila

Kabul R.

Puruṣhapura (near Peshawar)

ARACHOSIA

Pactyans

Paricanians

GEDROSIA (MAKA)

Pattala

(Mouths of the Indus R.)

Arabian Sea

present shoreline

CHORASMIA

SOGDIANA

Maracanda (Samarkand)

Bactra

Bagae

Oxus R.

Jaxartes R.

BACTRIA

ARIA

MARGIANA

Sarangians

DRANGIANA

Sagartians

CARMANIA

Utians

PERSIS

Persian Gulf

Aral Sea

Dahae

Caspian Sea (Mare Hyrcanium)

HYRCANIA

PARTHIA

E M P I R E

The Edict of Cyrus (538 B.C.) allowed the Jews to return to their homeland.

Pasargadae

Persepolis

Aspadana

Rhagae

Amardi R.

Ecbatana (Achmetha)

Behistun

Susa (Shushan) (SUSIANA)

ELAM

M E D I A N   (625-550 B.C.)

Cadusii

Urmia

Arbela

Erech

Opis

NEW BABYLONIAN EMPIRE (625-539 B.C.)

The rise of the New Babylonian (Chaldean) Empire brought an end to the Kingdom of Judah and exile of her people.

Babylon

Nippur

Sippar

Tigris R.

Euphrates R.

Haran

Thapsacus

Tadmor

ASSYRIA

Carchemish

ARMENIA

COLCHIS

Phasis

Trapezus

Panticapaeum

Black Sea (Pontus Euxinus)

Sinope

Ancyra

CAPPADOCIA

Pteria

PAPHLAGONIA

BITHYNIA

Chalcedon

Byzantium

Apollonia

Chersonesus

Olbia

Ister R. (Danube)

THRACE

MACEDONIA

EPIRUS

ILLYRIA

Thermopylae

Marathon

GREECE

Athens

Sparta

SAMOS

CRETE

RHODES

Miletus

Ephesus

PISIDIA

LYCIA

CILICIA

Tarsus

Sardis

KINGDOM OF LYDIA (670-546 B.C.)

Darius I extended the Persian Empire into Europe, subjugating Thrace and Macedonia. Attempts to subjugate Greece were foiled by Darius' defeat at Marathon and Xerxes' failure at Salamis.

Cyprus

Arvad

Byblos

Sidon

Tyre

Damascus

Megiddo

Jerusalem

JUDAH

Gaza

Elath

Pharaoh Necho defeated Josiah of Judah but was later driven out of Palestine after being defeated by Nebuchadnezzar at Carchemish (605 B.C.).

Pelusium

Tahpanhes

Tanis (Zoan)

Sais

Naucratis

On (Heliopolis)

Memphis (Noph)

Ammonium

KINGDOM OF EGYPT (26th DYNASTY 663-525 B.C.)

Egypt came under Persian rule after Cambyses defeated Psamtik III at Pelusium in 525 B.C.

Cyrene

Barca

Libyans

Mediterranean Sea

Red Sea

Thebes (No)

Pathros

Syene (Elephantine I.)

ETHIOPIA (CUSH)

Nile River

ARABIA

The Persians under Cyrus the Great overthrew the Medes, conquered Lydia and Babylonia to fulfill the prophecy of Daniel.

SCYTHIANS

Tanais R. (Don)

8

PALESTINE IN THE TIME OF CHRIST

Copyright by C. S. HAMMOND & CO., N.Y.

Scale of Miles

0   5   10   20   30   40

Perennial Rivers ----------
Seasonal Rivers & Streams ....
Capitals ----------
Roads & Trade Routes ----------

Tetrarchy of Lysanias
Tetrarchy of Philip
Tetrarchy of Herod Antipas
Territory under Roman procurator
Areas tributary to Salome
Decapolis *
Independent *
Roman province of Syria
Cities of the Decapolis □

*The Decapolis and Ascalon retained their independence under the Roman governor of the province of Syria.

The Great Sea

(Mediterranean Sea)

Caesarea
Residence of Roman procurators.

Archelaus, upon Herod's death, became ruler of Judaea, Samaria and northern Idumaea. His reign lasted until 6 A.D. when he was removed and exiled. His territory then was placed under a Roman procurator.

Salome, Herod's sister, was given Jamnia, Azotus, Phasaelis and Archelais. They in turn passed to Livia, wife of Augustus, and then to the emperor Tiberius.

ABILENE
Abila
SYRIA
Sidon
Damascus
Sarepta (Zarephath)
MOUNT LEBANON
MT. HERMON
PHOENICIA
ITURAEA
Tyre
PANIAS
Dan Caesarea Philippi
Cadasa (Kedesh)
ULATHA
Lake Semechonitis
TRACHONITIS
Gischala
Seleucia
GAULANITIS
BATANAEA
Raphana
BASHAN
Ptolemais (Accho)
Chorazin
Bethsaida Julias
Jotapata
Magdala (Dalmanutha)
Capernaum
Tabigha
Gergesa?
Cana
Horns of Hattin
Gamala
GALILEE
Sephoris
Tiberias
Sea of Galilee
Hippos
Dion
AURANITIS
Nazareth
Philoteria
Mt. Tabor
Gadara
Capitolias
Abila
Edrei
Dora
Plain of Esdraelon
Nain
Yarmuk R.
Caesarea
Ginaea
Scythopolis
Salim?
Pella
DECAPOLIS
Plain of Sharon
SAMARIA
Salim
Apollonia
Sebaste (Samaria)
Mt. Ebal
Gerasa
Antipatris
Sychem (Sychar?)
Salim?
Amathus
Mt. Gerizim
Jacob's Well
Jabbok R.
Joppa
Arimathaea
Alexandrium
Lydda (Diospolis)
Gophna
Phasaelis
PERAEA
Bethel
Archelais
Philadelphia (Rabbath-ammon)
Gazara (Gezer)
Ramah
Ephraim
Bethennabris
Jamnia
Emmaus
Mt. of Olives
Jericho
Ekron
Nicopolis (Emmaus)
Julias (Livias, Beth-haran)
Essebon
Azotus
Jerusalem
Bethany
Khirbet Qumrân
Ascalon
Bethlehem
Herodium
Ruins of Essene community found here; also Dead Sea Scrolls in caves nearby.
JUDAEA
Callirhoe
Gaza
Marisa
Bethsura
Hebron
Machaerus
Dibon
Juttah
Ziph
En-gedi
Masada
Raphia
Wilderness of Judaea
Salt or Dead Sea (L. Asphaltitis)
IDUMAEA
MOABITIS
Bersabee
Kir-moab
Elusa
AMMONITIS
ARABIA
NABATAEANS
Brook Zered

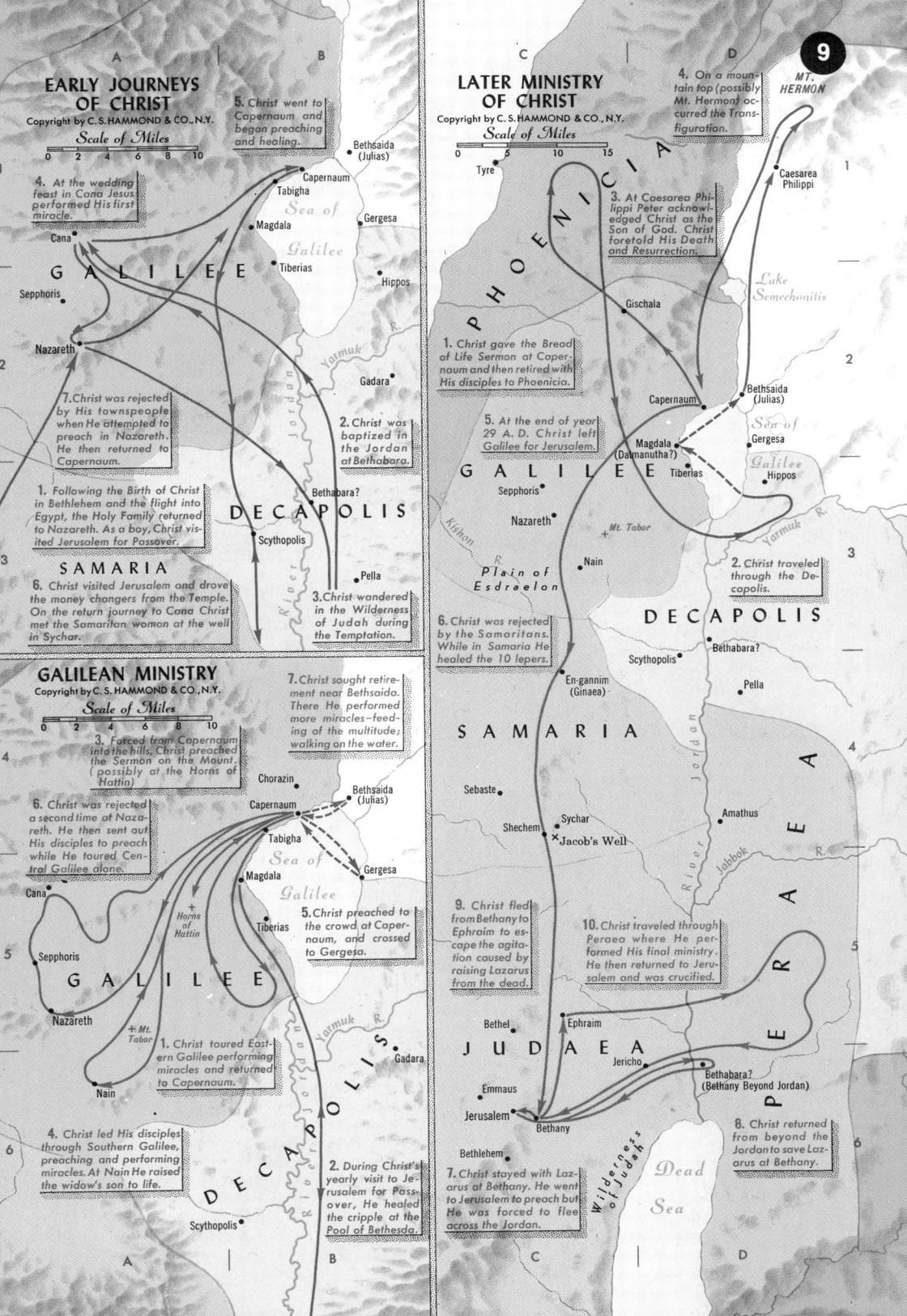

9

EARLY JOURNEYS OF CHRIST
Copyright by C.S.HAMMOND & CO.,N.Y.
Scale of Miles
0 2 4 6 8 10

5. Christ went to Capernaum and began preaching and healing.

4. At the wedding feast in Cana Jesus performed His first miracle.

7. Christ was rejected by His townspeople when He attempted to preach in Nazareth. He then returned to Capernaum.

1. Following the Birth of Christ in Bethlehem and the flight into Egypt, the Holy Family returned to Nazareth. As a boy, Christ visited Jerusalem for Passover.

6. Christ visited Jerusalem and drove the money changers from the Temple. On the return journey to Cana Christ met the Samaritan woman at the well in Sychar.

2. Christ was baptized in the Jordan at Bethabara.

3. Christ wandered in the Wilderness of Judah during the Temptation.

Labels (Early Journeys): Bethsaida (Julias), Capernaum, Tabigha, Sea of Galilee, Magdala, Gergesa, Cana, GALILEE, Tiberias, Hippos, Sepphoris, Nazareth, Gadara, Yarmuk R., Jordan R., DECAPOLIS, Bethabara?, Scythopolis, Pella, SAMARIA

GALILEAN MINISTRY
Copyright by C.S.HAMMOND & CO.,N.Y.
Scale of Miles
0 2 4 6 8 10

3. Forced from Capernaum into the hills, Christ preached the Sermon on the Mount. (possibly at the Horns of Hattin)

7. Christ sought retirement near Bethsaida. There He performed more miracles—feeding of the multitude; walking on the water.

6. Christ was rejected a second time at Nazareth. He then sent out His disciples to preach while He toured Central Galilee alone.

5. Christ preached to the crowd at Capernaum, and crossed to Gergesa.

1. Christ toured Eastern Galilee performing miracles and returned to Capernaum.

4. Christ led His disciples through Southern Galilee, preaching and performing miracles. At Nain He raised the widow's son to life.

2. During Christ's yearly visit to Jerusalem for Passover, He healed the cripple at the Pool of Bethesda.

Labels (Galilean Ministry): Chorazin, Capernaum, Bethsaida (Julias), Tabigha, Sea of Galilee, Magdala, Gergesa, Cana, Horns of Hattin, Tiberias, Sepphoris, GALILEE, Nazareth, Mt. Tabor, Nain, Gadara, Yarmuk R., Jordan R., DECAPOLIS, Scythopolis

LATER MINISTRY OF CHRIST
Copyright by C.S.HAMMOND & CO.,N.Y.
Scale of Miles
0 5 10 15

4. On a mountain top (possibly Mt. Hermon) occurred the Transfiguration.

3. At Caesarea Philippi Peter acknowledged Christ as the Son of God. Christ foretold His Death and Resurrection.

1. Christ gave the Bread of Life Sermon at Capernaum and then retired with His disciples to Phoenicia.

5. At the end of year 29 A.D. Christ left Galilee for Jerusalem.

2. Christ traveled through the Decapolis.

6. Christ was rejected by the Samaritans. While in Samaria He healed the 10 lepers.

9. Christ fled from Bethany to Ephraim to escape the agitation caused by raising Lazarus from the dead.

10. Christ traveled through Peraea where He performed His final ministry. He then returned to Jerusalem and was crucified.

7. Christ stayed with Lazarus at Bethany. He went to Jerusalem to preach but He was forced to flee across the Jordan.

8. Christ returned from beyond the Jordan to save Lazarus at Bethany.

Labels (Later Ministry): MT. HERMON, Caesarea Philippi, Tyre, PHOENICIA, Gischala, Lake Semechonitis, Capernaum, Bethsaida (Julias), Magdala (Dalmanutha?), Sea of Galilee, Gergesa, Tiberias, Galilee, Hippos, GALILEE, Sepphoris, Nazareth, Mt. Tabor, Nain, Yarmuk R., Kishon R., Plain of Esdraelon, DECAPOLIS, En-gannim (Ginaea), Scythopolis, Bethabara?, Pella, SAMARIA, Sebaste, Shechem, Sychar, Jacob's Well, Amathus, River Jordan, River Jabbok, PERAEA, Bethel, Ephraim, Jericho, Bethabara? (Bethany Beyond Jordan), JUDAEA, Emmaus, Jerusalem, Bethany, Bethlehem, Wilderness of Judah, Dead Sea

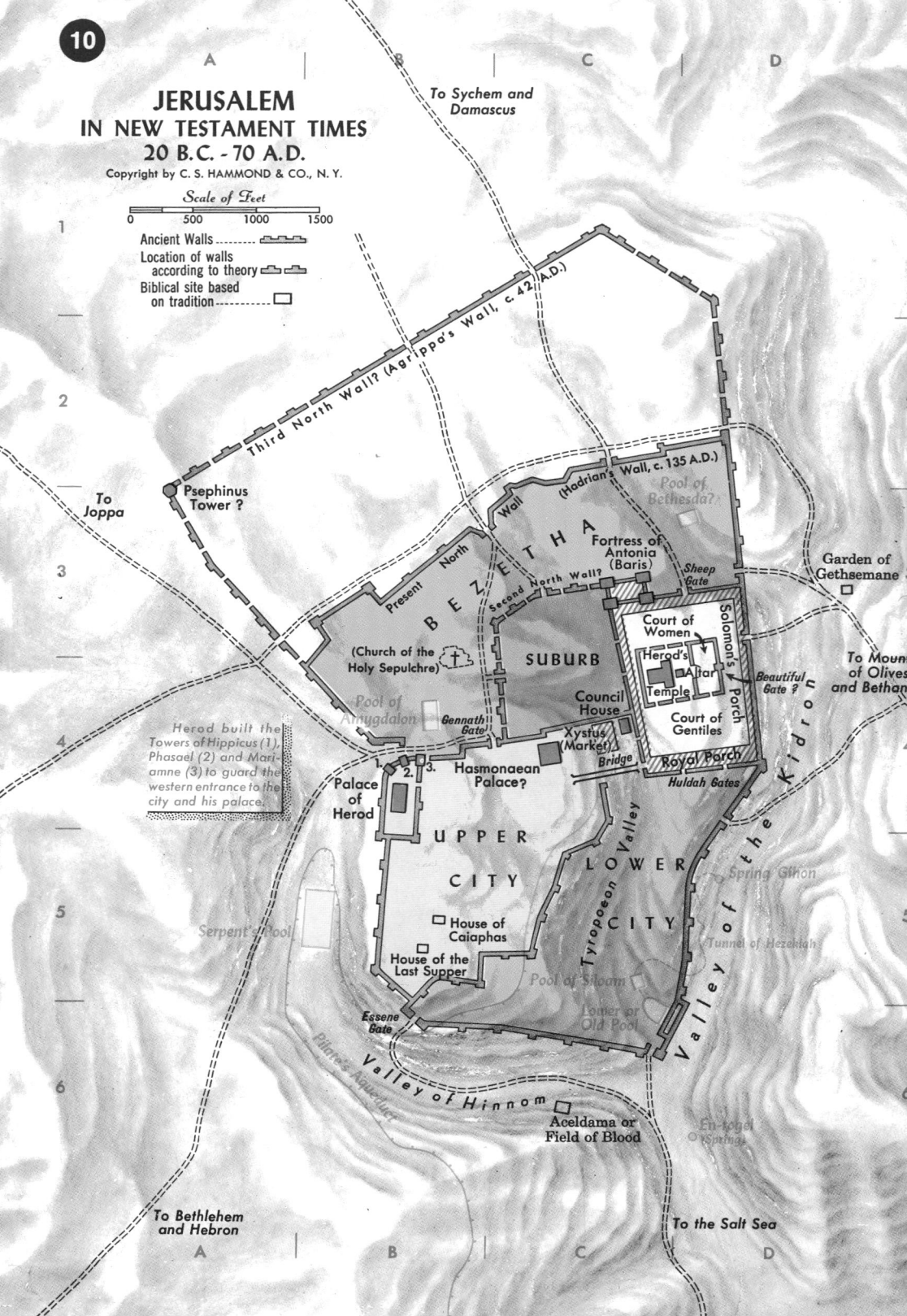

10

JERUSALEM
IN NEW TESTAMENT TIMES
20 B.C. - 70 A.D.

Copyright by C. S. HAMMOND & CO., N. Y.

Scale of Feet

| 0 | 500 | 1000 | 1500 |

Ancient Walls ....
Location of walls
  according to theory .....
Biblical site based
  on tradition ....

To Sychem and
Damascus

Third North Wall? (Agrippa's Wall, c. 42 A.D.)

Psephinus
Tower ?

To
Joppa

(Hadrian's Wall, c. 135 A.D.)

Pool of
Bethesda?

Garden of
Gethsemane

B E Z E T H A

Present North Wall

Second North Wall?

Fortress of
Antonia
(Baris)

Sheep
Gate

(Church of the
Holy Sepulchre) ✝

SUBURB

Court of
Women

Herod's

Temple

Altar

Solomon's
Porch

Beautiful
Gate ?

To Mount
of Olives
and Bethany

Pool of
Amygdalon

Gennath
Gate

Council
House

Court of
Gentiles

Xystus
(Market)

Bridge

Royal Porch

Huldah Gates

Herod built the
Towers of Hippicus (1),
Phasael (2) and Mari-
amne (3) to guard the
western entrance to the
city and his palace.

1. 2. 3.

Palace
of Herod

Hasmonaean
Palace ?

U P P E R

C I T Y

L O W E R

C I T Y

Valley

Spring Gihon

Serpent's Pool

Tyropoeon

Tunnel of Hezekiah

House of
Caiaphas

House of the
Last Supper

Pool of Siloam

Lower or
Old Pool

Essene
Gate

Pilate's Aqueduct

Valley of Hinnom

Aceldama or
Field of Blood

En-rogel
Spring

Valley of the Kidron

To Bethlehem
and Hebron

To the Salt Sea

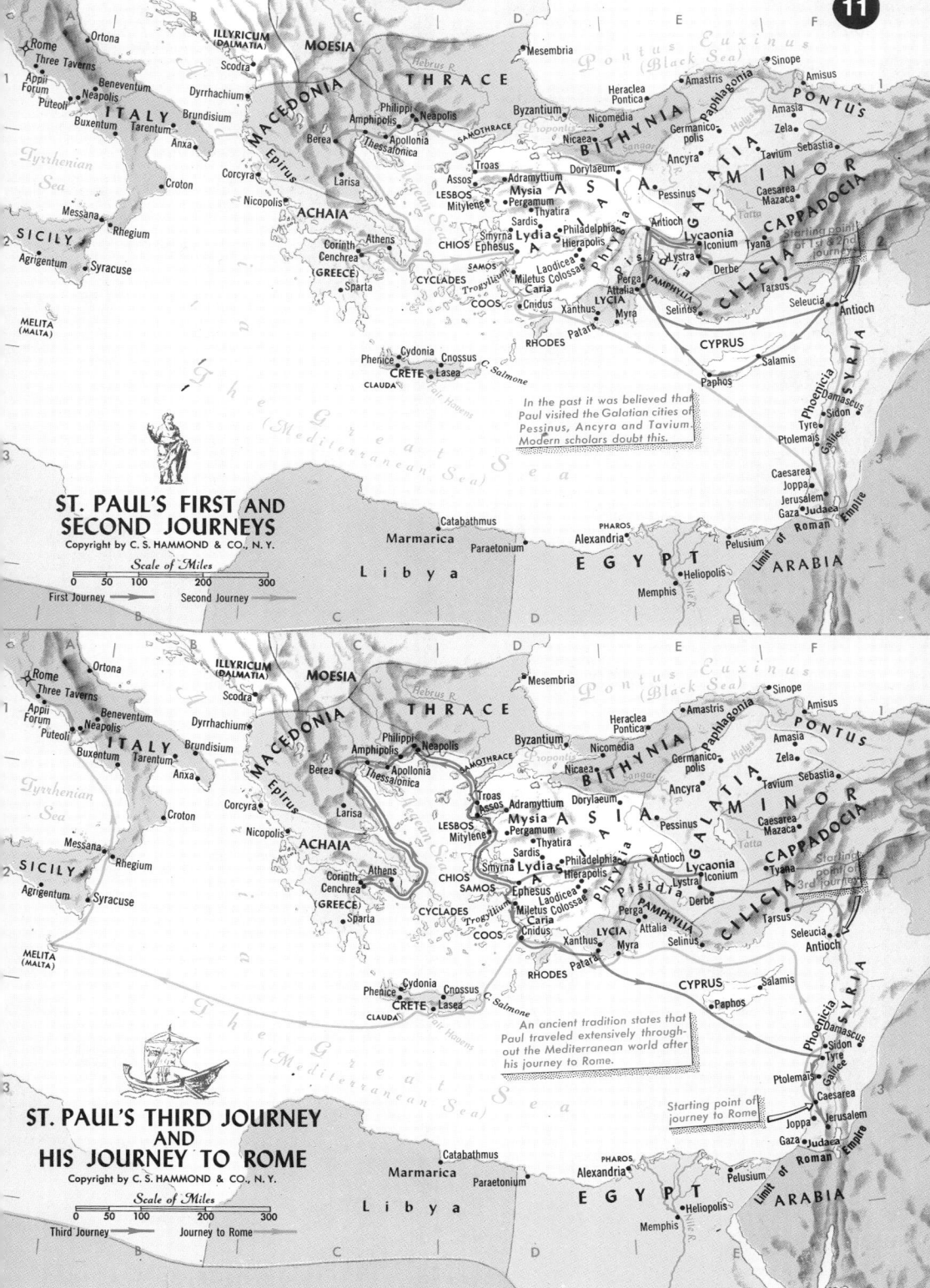

11

ST. PAUL'S FIRST AND SECOND JOURNEYS
Copyright by C. S. HAMMOND & CO., N. Y.

Scale of Miles
0 50 100 200 300

First Journey ▶   Second Journey ▶

In the past it was believed that Paul visited the Galatian cities of Pessinus, Ancyra and Tavium. Modern scholars doubt this.

ST. PAUL'S THIRD JOURNEY AND HIS JOURNEY TO ROME
Copyright by C. S. HAMMOND & CO., N. Y.

Scale of Miles
0 50 100 200 300

Third Journey ▶   Journey to Rome ▶

An ancient tradition states that Paul traveled extensively throughout the Mediterranean world after his journey to Rome.

Starting point of journey to Rome

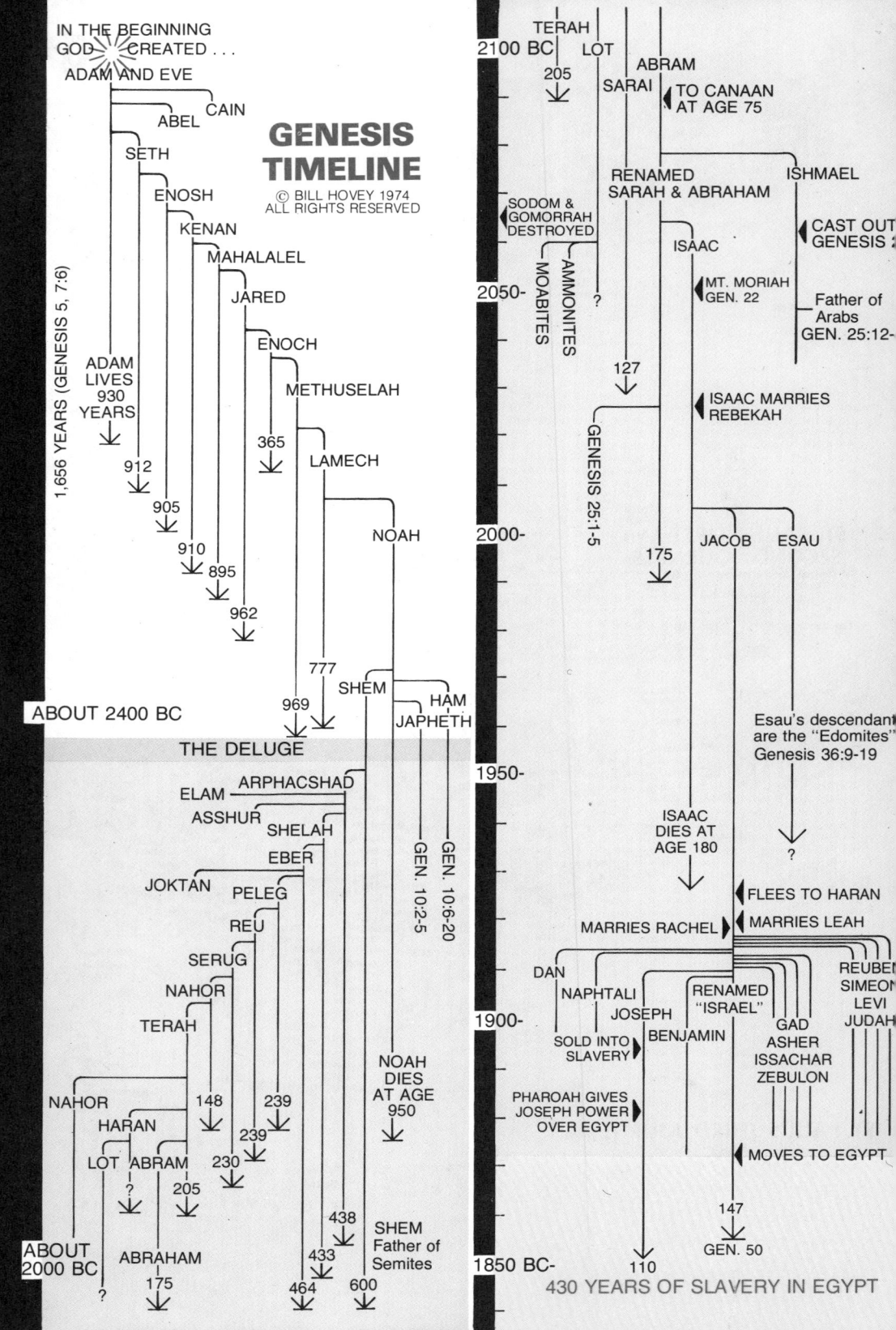

GENESIS
TIMELINE
© BILL HOVEY 1974
ALL RIGHTS RESERVED

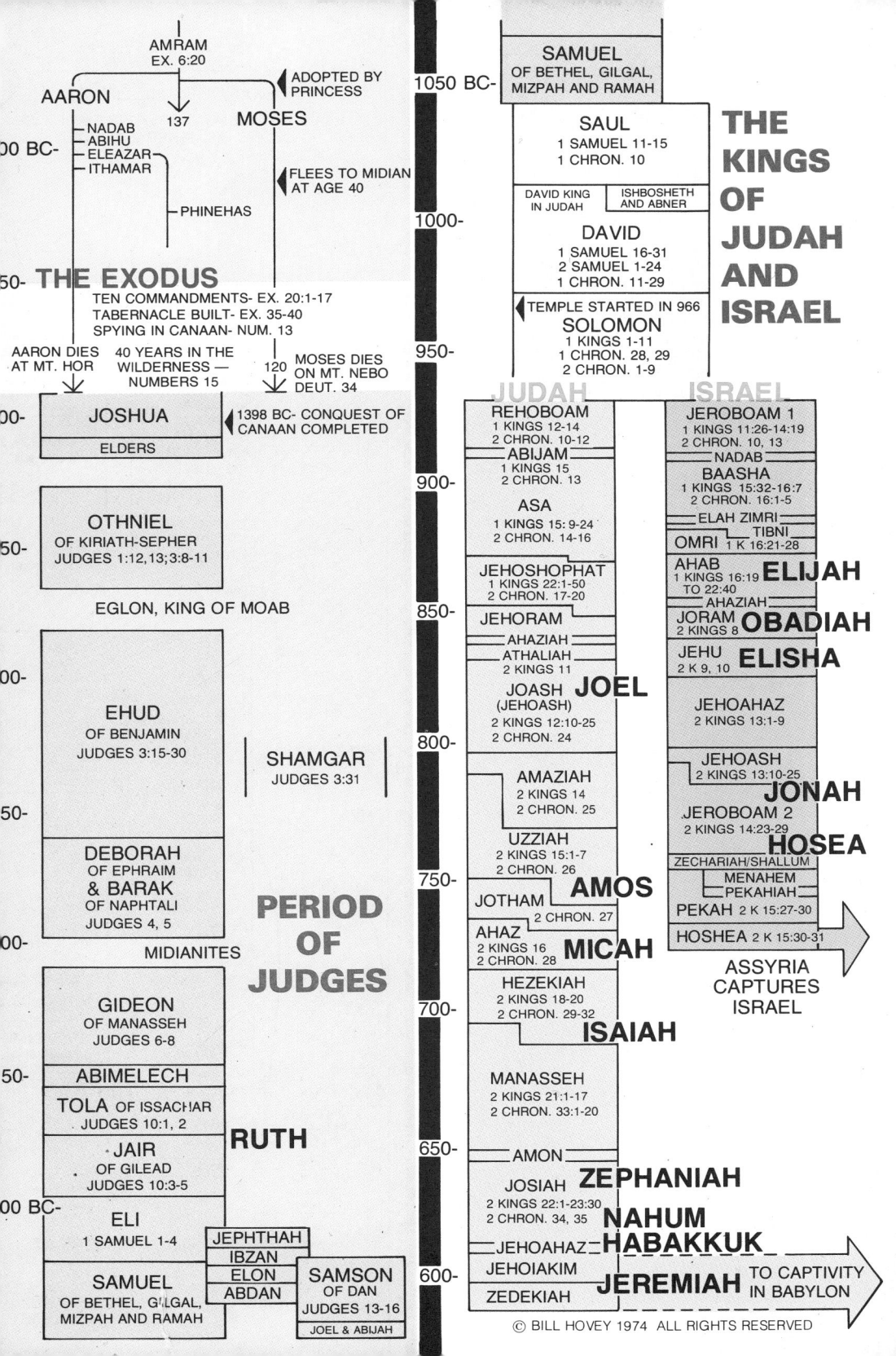

AMRAM
EX. 6:20

ADOPTED BY PRINCESS

AARON
137
MOSES

— NADAB
— ABIHU
— ELEAZAR
— ITHAMAR

FLEES TO MIDIAN
AT AGE 40

— PHINEHAS

THE EXODUS

TEN COMMANDMENTS- EX. 20:1-17
TABERNACLE BUILT- EX. 35-40
SPYING IN CANAAN- NUM. 13

AARON DIES
AT MT. HOR

40 YEARS IN THE
WILDERNESS —
NUMBERS 15

120

MOSES DIES
ON MT. NEBO
DEUT. 34

JOSHUA

1398 BC- CONQUEST OF
CANAAN COMPLETED

ELDERS

OTHNIEL
OF KIRIATH-SEPHER
JUDGES 1:12,13;3:8-11

EGLON, KING OF MOAB

EHUD
OF BENJAMIN
JUDGES 3:15-30

SHAMGAR
JUDGES 3:31

DEBORAH
OF EPHRAIM
& BARAK
OF NAPHTALI
JUDGES 4, 5

PERIOD

MIDIANITES

OF

GIDEON
OF MANASSEH
JUDGES 6-8

JUDGES

ABIMELECH

TOLA OF ISSACHAR
JUDGES 10:1, 2

RUTH

JAIR
OF GILEAD
JUDGES 10:3-5

ELI
1 SAMUEL 1-4

JEPHTHAH
IBZAN
ELON
ABDAN

SAMSON
OF DAN
JUDGES 13-16

SAMUEL
OF BETHEL, GILGAL,
MIZPAH AND RAMAH

JOEL & ABIJAH

1050 BC-

1000-

950-

900-

850-

800-

750-

700-

650-

600-

SAMUEL
OF BETHEL, GILGAL,
MIZPAH AND RAMAH

SAUL
1 SAMUEL 11-15
1 CHRON. 10

THE
KINGS
OF
JUDAH
AND
ISRAEL

DAVID KING
IN JUDAH

ISHBOSHETH
AND ABNER

DAVID
1 SAMUEL 16-31
2 SAMUEL 1-24
1 CHRON. 11-29

TEMPLE STARTED IN 966

SOLOMON
1 KINGS 1-11
1 CHRON. 28, 29
2 CHRON. 1-9

JUDAH   ISRAEL

REHOBOAM
1 KINGS 12-14
2 CHRON. 10-12

JEROBOAM 1
1 KINGS 11:26-14:19
2 CHRON. 10, 13

ABIJAM
1 KINGS 15
2 CHRON. 13

NADAB
BAASHA
1 KINGS 15:32-16:7
2 CHRON. 16:1-5

ASA
1 KINGS 15: 9-24
2 CHRON. 14-16

ELAH ZIMRI
TIBNI
OMRI 1 K 16:21-28

JEHOSHOPHAT
1 KINGS 22:1-50
2 CHRON. 17-20

AHAB
1 KINGS 16:19
TO 22:40

ELIJAH

AHAZIAH

JEHORAM

JORAM
2 KINGS 8

OBADIAH

AHAZIAH
ATHALIAH
2 KINGS 11

JEHU
2 K 9, 10

ELISHA

JOEL

JOASH
(JEHOASH)
2 KINGS 12:10-25
2 CHRON. 24

JEHOAHAZ
2 KINGS 13:1-9

AMAZIAH
2 KINGS 14
2 CHRON. 25

JEHOASH
2 KINGS 13:10-25

JONAH

UZZIAH
2 KINGS 15:1-7
2 CHRON. 26

JEROBOAM 2
2 KINGS 14:23-29

HOSEA

AMOS

ZECHARIAH/SHALLUM

JOTHAM
2 CHRON. 27

MENAHEM
PEKAHIAH

AHAZ
2 KINGS 16
2 CHRON. 28

MICAH

PEKAH 2 K 15:27-30

HOSHEA 2 K 15:30-31

HEZEKIAH
2 KINGS 18-20
2 CHRON. 29-32

ASSYRIA
CAPTURES
ISRAEL

ISAIAH

MANASSEH
2 KINGS 21:1-17
2 CHRON. 33:1-20

AMON

JOSIAH
2 KINGS 22:1-23:30
2 CHRON. 34, 35

ZEPHANIAH

NAHUM
HABAKKUK

JEHOAHAZ

JEHOIAKIM

ZEDEKIAH

JEREMIAH

TO CAPTIVITY
IN BABYLON

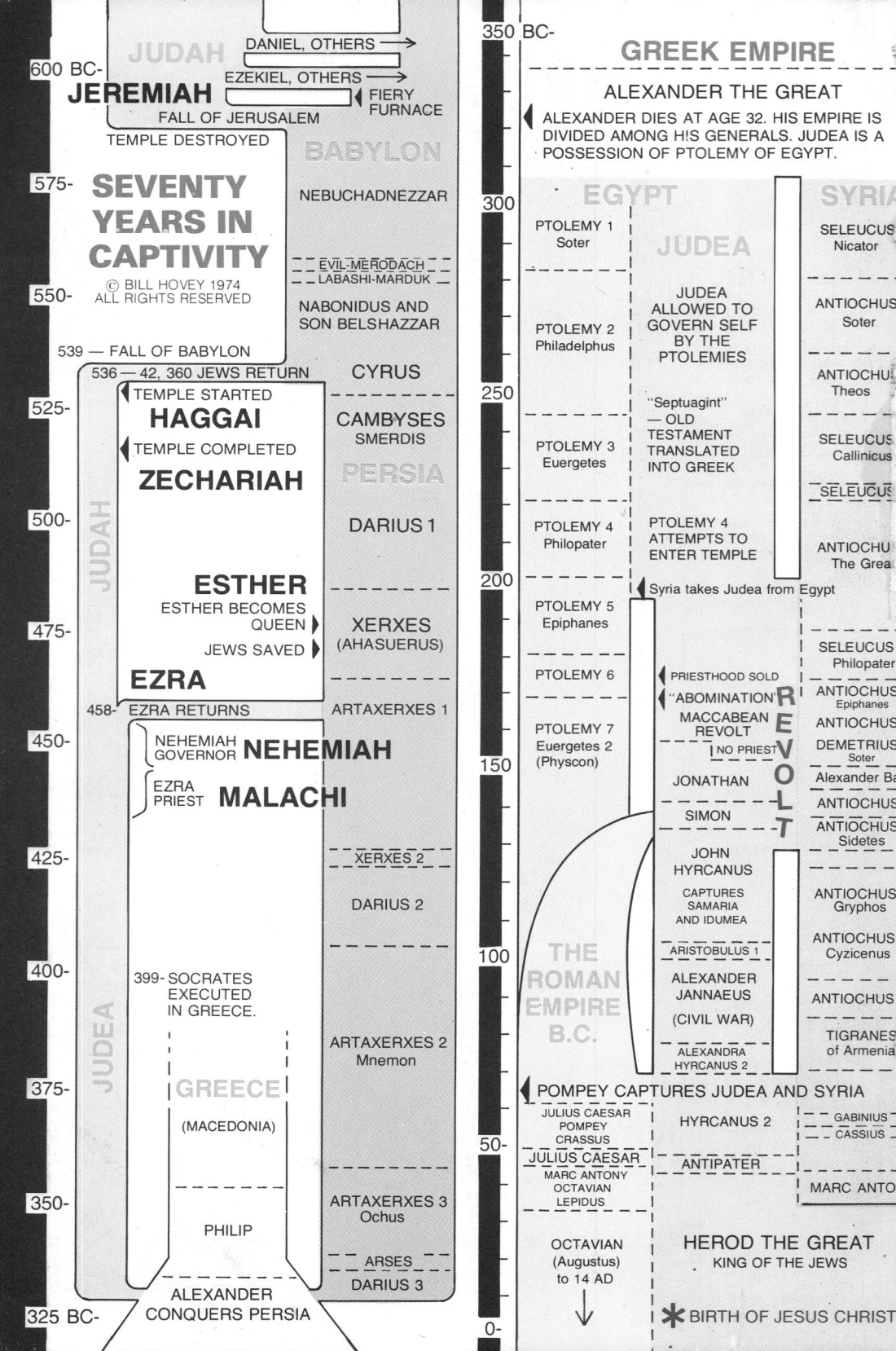

JUDAH

DANIEL, OTHERS →
EZEKIEL, OTHERS →

350 BC-

GREEK EMPIRE

600 BC-
JEREMIAH
◄ FIERY FURNACE
FALL OF JERUSALEM
TEMPLE DESTROYED

ALEXANDER THE GREAT
◄ ALEXANDER DIES AT AGE 32. HIS EMPIRE IS DIVIDED AMONG HIS GENERALS. JUDEA IS A POSSESSION OF PTOLEMY OF EGYPT.

BABYLON

575-
SEVENTY YEARS IN CAPTIVITY
© BILL HOVEY 1974 ALL RIGHTS RESERVED

NEBUCHADNEZZAR

300
EGYPT

SYRIA

PTOLEMY 1 Soter

JUDEA

SELEUCUS Nicator

550-
EVIL-MERODACH
LABASHI-MARDUK
NABONIDUS AND SON BELSHAZZAR

JUDEA ALLOWED TO GOVERN SELF BY THE PTOLEMIES

PTOLEMY 2 Philadelphus

ANTIOCHUS Soter

539 — FALL OF BABYLON

536 — 42, 360 JEWS RETURN
CYRUS

250

ANTIOCHU Theos

525-
▲ TEMPLE STARTED
HAGGAI
CAMBYSES SMERDIS

"Septuagint" — OLD TESTAMENT TRANSLATED INTO GREEK

PTOLEMY 3 Euergetes

SELEUCUS Callinicus

▲ TEMPLE COMPLETED
ZECHARIAH

PERSIA

SELEUCUS

500-
DARIUS 1

PTOLEMY 4 Philopater

PTOLEMY 4 ATTEMPTS TO ENTER TEMPLE

ANTIOCHU The Grea

JUDAH

200
Syria takes Judea from Egypt

ESTHER
ESTHER BECOMES QUEEN ►
JEWS SAVED ►
XERXES (AHASUERUS)

PTOLEMY 5 Epiphanes

SELEUCUS 4 Philopater

475-

PTOLEMY 6

PRIESTHOOD SOLD

ANTIOCHUS Epiphanes

EZRA

"ABOMINATION"
MACCABEAN REVOLT

458-
EZRA RETURNS
ARTAXERXES 1

R

ANTIOCHUS

NEHEMIAH GOVERNOR **NEHEMIAH**

PTOLEMY 7 Euergetes 2 (Physcon)

NO PRIEST

DEMETRIUS Soter

450-

E

Alexander Bal

EZRA PRIEST **MALACHI**

JONATHAN

V

ANTIOCHUS

SIMON

O

ANTIOCHUS Sidetes

425-
XERXES 2

JOHN HYRCANUS

L

T

DARIUS 2

CAPTURES SAMARIA AND IDUMEA

ANTIOCHUS Gryphos

400-

THE ROMAN EMPIRE B.C.

ARISTOBULUS 1

ANTIOCHUS Cyzicenus

399- SOCRATES EXECUTED IN GREECE.

100

ALEXANDER JANNAEUS

JUDEA

ARTAXERXES 2 Mnemon

(CIVIL WAR)

ANTIOCHUS

375-

ALEXANDRA HYRCANUS 2

TIGRANES of Armenia

◄ POMPEY CAPTURES JUDEA AND SYRIA

GREECE
(MACEDONIA)

JULIUS CAESAR POMPEY CRASSUS

HYRCANUS 2

GABINIUS
CASSIUS

50

350-

JULIUS CAESAR
MARC ANTONY OCTAVIAN LEPIDUS

ANTIPATER

ARTAXERXES 3 Ochus

MARC ANTON

PHILIP

ARSES

OCTAVIAN (Augustus) to 14 AD

HEROD THE GREAT
KING OF THE JEWS

DARIUS 3

325 BC-
ALEXANDER CONQUERS PERSIA

0-

↓

✻ BIRTH OF JESUS CHRIST

THE MINISTRY OF JESUS CHRIST

26 A.D.

Spring — Pentecost

BEGINNING OF JOHN THE BAPTIST'S MINISTRY
MT 3:1-6; MK 1:2-6; LK 3:3-6

Summer — Tabernacles

JESUS BAPTIZED—MT 3:13-17; MK 1:9-11; LK 3:21-23

Autumn — Dedication

40 DAYS IN WILDERNESS—THE THREE TEMPTATIONS
MT 4:1-11; MK 1:12, 13; LK 4:1-13

JESUS MEETS FIRST DISCIPLES—JN 1:35-51

FIRST MIRACLE—CANA—JN 2:1-11

Winter — Passover

FIRST CLEANSING OF TEMPLE—JN 2:13-22
NICODEMUS VISITS—JN 2:23—3:21

27 A.D.

Spring — Pentecost

MEETS WOMAN AT WELL IN SAMARIA—JN 4:5-42

"THE GREAT GALILEAN MINISTRY"

Summer

HEALING AT CANA—JN 4:46-54
FIRST REJECTION AT NAZARETH—LK 4:16-31

Autumn — Tabernacles — Dedication

JESUS HEADQUARTERED IN CAPERNAUM-MT 4:13-16
CALLS 4 FISHERS OF MEN—MT 4:18-22; MK 1:16-20; LK 5:1-11
HEALS DEMONIAC ON SABBATH—MK 1:21-28; LK 4:31-37

28 A.D.

Winter

CALLS MATTHEW—MT 9:9-13; MK 2:13-17; LK 5:27-32

Passover

HEALS LAME MAN ON SABBATH—JN 5:1-47

Spring — Pentecost

SABBATH CONTROVERSIES—MT 12:1-14; MK 2:23—3:6; LK 6:1-11
CHOOSES TWELVE APOSTLES—MK 3:13-19; LK 6:12-16
SERMON ON THE MOUNT—MT 5-7; LK 6:20-49

Summer

RAISES WIDOW'S SON AT NAIN—LK 7:11-17

Autumn — Tabernacles — Dedication

"BUSY DAY"—MT 12:22—18:34; MK 3:19—5:20; LK 8:22-39

SECOND REJECTION AT NAZARETH—MT 13:54-58; MK 6:1-6

29 A.D.

Winter — Passover

THE 12 SENT FORTH—MT 10:5-15; MK 6:7-13; LK 9:1-6
JOHN THE BAPTIST BEHEADED—MT 14:1-12; MK 6:14-29; LK 9:7-9
THE 12 RETURN—MK 6:30; LK 9:10

Spring — Pentecost

FEEDS 5,000—MT 14:13-21; MK 6:30-44; LK 9:10-17; JN 6:1-14
REFUSES POPULAR DEMAND TO BE KING—JN 6:14-15, 34-59
WITHDRAWAL TO REGION OF TYRE AND SIDON—MT 15:21; MK 7:24
WITHDRAWAL TO NORTH AND EAST—MT 15:29; MK 7:31
FEEDING OF 4,000—MT 15:30-38; MK 8:1-9
WITHDRAWAL TO BETHSAIDA AND CAESAREA PHILIPPI
THE TRANSFIGURATION—MT 17:1-8; MK 9:2-8; LK 9:28-36

Summer — Tabernacles — Dedication

PHARISEES ATTEMPT TO STONE JESUS—JN 8:21-59
JESUS HEALS A MAN BORN BLIND—JN 9:1-41
THE MISSION OF THE SEVENTY—LK 10:1-24
JESUS DENOUNCES THE PHARISEES—LK 11:37-54

30 A.D.

Winter

MINISTRY IN PEREA

LAZARUS RAISED FROM THE DEAD—JN 11:1-44

Spring — Passover

LAST WEEK—TRIUMPHAL ENTRY—CRUCIFIXION—RESURRECTION
MT 21-28; MK 11-16; LK 19:29—24; JN 12:12—20:35

Pentecost

THE ASCENSION—MK 16:19; LK 24:44-53; ACTS 1:3-12

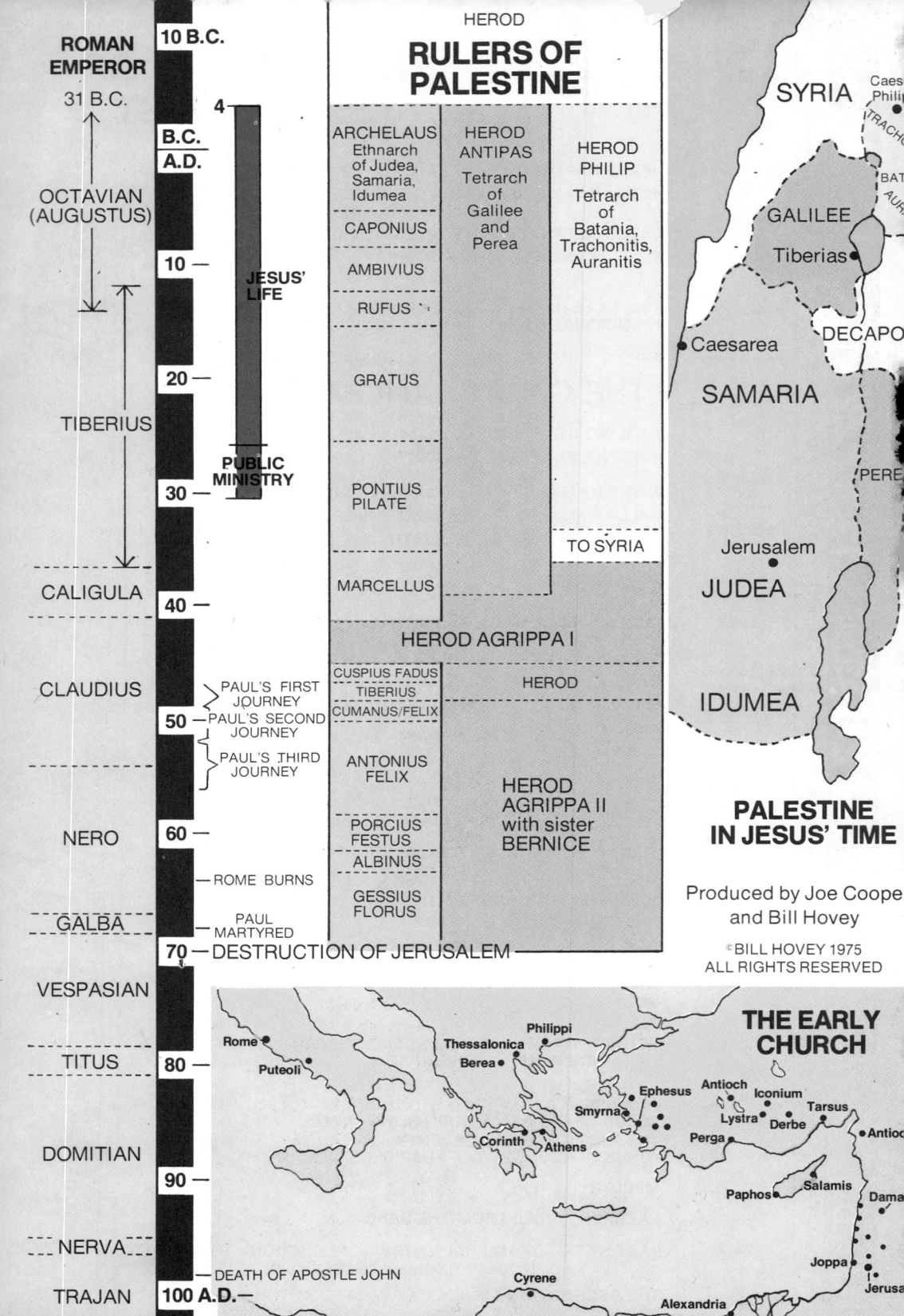

RULERS OF PALESTINE

HEROD

ROMAN EMPEROR		JESUS' LIFE	ARCHELAUS Ethnarch of Judea, Samaria, Idumea	HEROD ANTIPAS Tetrarch of Galilee and Perea	HEROD PHILIP Tetrarch of Batania, Trachonitis, Auranitis

10 B.C.

31 B.C.

4

B.C.
A.D.

OCTAVIAN (AUGUSTUS)

JESUS' LIFE

ARCHELAUS
Ethnarch of Judea, Samaria, Idumea

HEROD ANTIPAS
Tetrarch of Galilee and Perea

HEROD PHILIP
Tetrarch of Batania, Trachonitis, Auranitis

CAPONIUS

10 —

AMBIVIUS

RUFUS

TIBERIUS

20 —

GRATUS

PUBLIC MINISTRY

30 —

PONTIUS PILATE

TO SYRIA

CALIGULA

40 —

MARCELLUS

HEROD AGRIPPA I

CLAUDIUS

PAUL'S FIRST JOURNEY

CUSPIUS FADUS
TIBERIUS

HEROD

50 —

PAUL'S SECOND JOURNEY

CUMANUS/FELIX

PAUL'S THIRD JOURNEY

ANTONIUS FELIX

HEROD AGRIPPA II with sister BERNICE

NERO

60 —

PORCIUS FESTUS

ALBINUS

ROME BURNS

GESSIUS FLORUS

GALBA

PAUL MARTYRED

70 — DESTRUCTION OF JERUSALEM

VESPASIAN

TITUS

80 —

DOMITIAN

90 —

NERVA

DEATH OF APOSTLE JOHN

TRAJAN

100 A.D. —

PALESTINE IN JESUS' TIME

SYRIA
Caes. Phili
TRACHO
BAT
AUR.
GALILEE
Tiberias
Caesarea
DECAPO
SAMARIA
PERE
Jerusalem
JUDEA
IDUMEA

Produced by Joe Coope and Bill Hovey

THE EARLY CHURCH

Rome
Puteoli
Thessalonica
Berea
Philippi
Corinth
Athens
Smyrna
Ephesus
Antioch
Iconium
Lystra
Derbe
Tarsus
Perga
Antioc
Paphos
Salamis
Dama
Cyrene
Joppa
Jerusa
Alexandria